D0450216

THE NEW
Princeton
Encyclopedia
OF
POETRY
AND
POETICS

Edited by Alex Preminger and T.V.F. Brogan

Frank J. Warnke, O.B. Hardison, Jr., and Earl Miner, Associate Editors

Pacific

WITHDRAWN

University

MJF BOOKS
NEW YORK

PACIFIC UNIVERSITY LIBRARY
FOREST GROVE, OREGON

Published by MJF Books
Fine Communications
Two Lincoln Square
60 West 66th Street
New York, NY 10023

Library of Congress Card Catalog # 96-77136
ISBN 1-56731-152-0

Copyright © 1993 by Princeton University Press

Preparation of this volume was made possible in part by generous grants from the National Endowment for the Humanities, an independent federal agency dedicated to furthering the values of humane scholarship and culture in America, and by grants from other major foundations and private donors who wish to remain anonymous. Without their support this book would not have been possible. Publication has been aided by a grant from the Lacy Lockert Fund of Princeton University Press.

All rights reserved. No part of this publication may be reproduced or transmitted in any form or by any means, electronic or mechanical, including photocopy, recording, or any information storage and retrieval system, without the prior written permission of the publisher.

Composed in ITC New Baskerville and custom fonts
Designed and produced by Leximetrics, Inc., South Bend, Indiana

This edition published by arrangement with Princeton University Press

Manufactured in the United States of America on acid-free paper ∞

MJF Books and the MJF colophon are trademarks of Fine Creative Media, Inc.

10   9   8   7   6   5   4   3   2

3 5369 00270 9986

for

Jacqueline Vaught Brogan
Augusta Preminger

and for

R. M. E. De Rycke

PREFACE

This is a book of knowledge, of facts, theories, questions, and informed judgment, about poetry. Its aim is to provide a comprehensive, comparative, reasonably advanced, yet readable reference for all students, teachers, scholars, poets, or general readers who are interested in the history of any poetry in any national literature of the world, or in any aspect of the technique or criticism of poetry. It provides surveys of 106 national poetries; descriptions of poetic forms and genres major and minor, traditional and emergent; detailed explanations of the devices of prosody and rhetoric; and overviews of all major schools of poetry ancient and modern, Western and Eastern. It provides balanced and comprehensive accounts of the major movements and issues in criticism and literary theory, and discussion of the manifold relations of poetry to the other fields of human thought and activity—history, science, politics, religion, philosophy, music, the visual arts.

This third edition follows upon the first edition of 1965, supplemented in 1974, which was well received and which has been consulted, over the years, by countless readers both in America and abroad: indeed, one Burmese scholar wrote us to say "there are relatively few books in our library, and the *Princeton Encyclopedia* is one of the most heavily used of all. We have few good accounts of English poetry available to us here; indeed, we have few reliable accounts of Burmese poetry either. We send our students to the *Encyclopedia* for both."

In late 1984, when the Editors agreed to undertake a third edition, it was obvious to all that what would be required would be almost entirely a new text. The period since 1965 has been a time of extraordinarily vigorous, almost dizzying change in literary studies: both the amount and the variety of work has increased geometrically over that prior to 1965, with the result that issues of interpretation, history, gender, culture, and theory now dominate the critical scene which were largely unknown in 1965. The same can be said for developments in the poetries of Africa, Eastern Europe, Asia, and Latin America: recent political changes in these areas of the world have been swift, extensive, and complex, resulting in burgeoning national literatures. All told, the last 25 years have witnessed enormous changes in both the practice of criticism in the West and also the writing of poetry around the world.

PREFACE

We have sought to produce a work which retains what was most valuable from the last edition, adds extensive coverage of all new poetries and critical theories, provides more extensive bibliographies on every topic for further reading, improves on cross-referencing, and is written in clear prose, yet keeps within the bounds of a single volume. Virtually no former entry has been reprinted without significant changes, and over 90% of the original entries have been extensively revised. Most major entries have been rewritten altogether. We have added 162 entirely new entries. Still, we have not diluted the editorial standards for scope, treatment, accuracy, and clarity of discourse which readers have come to expect from this book. The design of the book, its organizational principles and format, will be familiar to readers of the previous editions.

This edition differs from its predecessors in five respects. First, some of the accounts given in the original edition were the best of their kind available both then and, with moderate revision, now. In these cases, we thought it essential to build the new texts upon what our expert reviewers told us was irreplaceable in the previous editions. We have not sought new treatments simply because they are new. We have not, however, left former treatments unchanged; on the contrary, we have in many cases reduced and combined the treatments given in the original entries so as to make room for discussion of new perspectives on those topics. One of the significant reasons for undertaking a new *Encyclopedia* is not merely so that we can address new topics or approaches but also so that we can survey new work on old topics. We are now able to give much more sophisticated accounts of some traditional subjects (e.g. prosody) than were previously possible.

Second, we have increased dramatically our coverage of emergent and non-Western poetries. It was the present work which first provided American readers with extended surveys of the world's poetries, and we have sought to build upon that foundation. Our foremost concern has been to produce more extensive, more accurate, and more sophisticated accounts of the development of poetry in each language. We now provide coverage of every significant poetic tradition in the world, coverage which has increased, all told, by fully a third over that in the last edition. We have made major expansions of our treatment of African, Middle Eastern, Central American, South American, Caribbean, Pacific, and Asian poetries. Certain traditions have been given greatly increased space. The numerous languages and poetries of the Indian subcontinent are surveyed in an entry on "Indian Poetry" which tripled in size and is flanked by new entries on "Indian Poetics" and "Indian Prosody." African poetry written in both vernacular and foreign languages is now covered in seven entries. Our treatment of the several indigenous languages of the Americas has been expanded.

This effort reflects not an intention to give disproportionate space to one group of traditions over another but rather the dramatic increase in our knowledge of non-Western poetries relative to Western ones over the past 25 years. We have sought to bring a wider perspective into many other kinds of entries as well. In many entries on poetics and theory, e.g. the entry on "Poetics" itself, we have worked to differentiate the discussions of Oriental and Occidental poetics. We have added a comparative dimension to a wide range of entries which treat topics that might be assumed to be chiefly Western, e.g. "Epic," "Narrative Poetry," "Lyric" (now a global survey), "Love Poetry," "Rhyme," "Meter," and "Allegory," and even to smaller entries, e.g. "Rhyme-prose" (which discusses not only Latin but Chinese, Persian, and Arabic) and "Poetic Contests." We have added major new entries on Arabic, Hebrew, Chinese, and Japanese poetics.

Third, we now cover all those movements in recent criticism and literary theory that bear on poetry. We provide entirely new accounts of "Criticism," "Theory," "Poetics," "Romantic and Postromantic Poetics," "Twentieth-century Poetics" (five newly written sections), "Modernism and Postmodernism," "Structuralism," "Semiotics," "Marxist Criticism," "Psychological Criticism," "Feminist Poetics," "Reader-response Criticism," "Cultural Criticism," "Historicism," "Deconstruction," "Ethics and Criticism," "Pluralism," and "Representation." We expanded the entry on "Poetry, Theories of." Several of these new entries are among the longest in the volume. Throughout, we have sought to provide a balanced treatment of critical issues and noncritical ones: many entries are subdivided so as to treat both theory and history, for example.

Still, we must reiterate that this is primarily an encyclopedia of poetry, not an encyclopedia of criticism. We treat those aspects of critical theory that bear on poetry to any significant degree; hence the discussions always return to poetry. When the first edition was compiled, in the early 1960s, the axes of criticism in America were largely aligned with the study of lyric poetry, and New Criticism overwhelmingly dominated pedagogy in American universities. In the intervening 25 years, the axes of criticism have in part shifted away from poetry to the study of criticism itself, and poetry itself is now much less read in America than prose narrative. Yet poetic traditions are flourishing elsewhere in the world, and readers everywhere still want information about the forms and techniques of poetry. Many readers will come to the present work for a clear explanation of hermeneutics or deconstruction, of course, but many others will come for an informative overview of Chinese poetry, and some will come simply wanting an accurate definition of

PREFACE

zeugma. We hope to meet all these needs. In addition, where it has seemed appropriate, we have allowed our coverage to extend a little way past poetry into prose narrative and drama. Theory of narrative is addressed in long entries on "Narrative Poetry" and "Epic," theory of drama, similarly, in "Dramatic Poetry," "Tragedy," and "Comedy." Conversely, some other entries that might be thought merely to concern narrative, e.g. "Fiction" and "Plot," have been conceived more broadly, as is proper.

In the selection of new topics, we have exercised care. Rigorous screening has reduced a much longer list of current critical topics and terms to 162 new entries. We do not provide coverage of critical terms which are minor or narrow or which have had a very short half-life: these can be found in any of the numerous dictionaries and literary handbooks that have appeared in recent years.

Fourth, the Editors have taken a more active role in the building of bibliographies. On virtually every topic, we now provide more extended yet still rigorous finding-lists for further reading. As before, bibliographies are confined to secondary works only; primary texts are normally cited in the text of the entries. Bibliographic items appear in chronological order, all works by one author being listed together; editions cited are the best or most recent ones that are authoritative, not the first, and reprints are ignored. Periodical abbreviations conform to the acronyms in the MLA *International Bibliography* or other standard sources such as *L'Année philologique*.

Fifth, cross-referencing both within entries and by independent blind entries—a practice not fully exploited in previous editions, which were not prepared on computer—has been greatly expanded. Experience with the first two editions showed that the value of cross-references is difficult to overestimate. We have added nearly five hundred new blind entries and literally thousands of cross-references in the text and at the ends of entries. In blind entries, cross-references are often listed in order of significance rather than alphabetically.

The author or authors of each entry are listed by acronym at the ends of their respective contributions. The sequence of initials at the end of an entry does not, therefore, necessarily reflect decreasing order of responsibility for authorship. The relations between old authors and new (i.e. between original texts and revisions) and the proportions of work among multiple authors have been varied and complex; in some cases the author whose initials appear last was the principal author. It has proven impossible to represent all these relations succinctly, and since this entire volume has been very much a collaborative effort, it has seemed to the editors reasonable simply to list authors by initials in chronological se-

PREFACE

quence. Note, too, that sections of longer entries are commonly separately authored, so that one acronym at the end of an entry does not necessarily indicate that it had a sole author. We have tried to give credit to each person who made a significant contribution to an article. The names and affiliations of authors corresponding to their acronyms will be found in the list of Contributors, in a format which we believe to be improved over that used in previous editions. By policy, every manuscript submitted was read by the Editors and refereed by at least one independent expert, often several, then revised by its author in light of these reviews before being accepted for publication.

Some comment should be made about the circumstances in which this volume appears. The original editorial team which began work in 1984 comprised five editors, who divided responsibilities as follows: Professor Preminger handled the national poetry entries; Professor Brogan handled poetics, prosody, rhetoric, and genre; Professor Miner handled Asian poetries; Professor Warnke handled translations; and Professor Hardison handled criticism. But in 1988, Professor Warnke was killed in an accident in Antwerp, and in 1990, Professor Hardison died unexpectedly in Washington, D.C. Finally, Professor Preminger, the major force behind this book since its inception, was forced to withdraw prematurely in 1988 on account of declining health and unsuccessful surgery. Editorial work subsequent to these events fell to the remaining full Editor. For these and, even more directly, other reasons having to do with the state of the professoriate and the conditions of knowledge just now, this has been a difficult time to attempt a work such as the present one.

A reference work must always distance itself from its time while it works to embrace that time. It has not been our aim simply to cover recent trends: an eye for fashion is not one of the requisites of reference works. Our purpose has been to record, assimilate, and appraise new perspectives, not to embody any one of them. In certain respects the shape of the *Encyclopedia* has adapted itself to the changed critical climate which it seeks to embody and describe, while in other respects—and in the long view these are surely the more important—it has sought to place new critical perspectives within the larger philosophical contexts so far developed for discourse in poetics, giving due attention to ways in which the new views may have altered the boundaries of those contexts. In certain respects—on issues of gender, for example—critical work over the past 25 years has altered the nature of our thinking about literature permanently. But some other theories have quickly come and gone, and yet others are still too new to judge very well. We do not bring forth a new edition of this work in the belief that the new modes of thinking of the past two decades have put an end to those of the preceding two millennia; quite the contrary. We have brought forth a new edition because it is now imperative that we take stock, as fully and accurately as is possible within present limitations, of those new modes, and in so doing set them alongside older modes toward the increased understanding of both.

In any event, the standards for discourse have not changed. We support a critical discourse which is pluralist and civil, wherein the same criteria for evidence, persuasion, argument, and proof apply to all who wish to engage critics and readers of poetry. We continue to believe in the necessity of admitting all differing voices as the sole means for ensuring the continuance of that discourse. We reiterate the reality and importance of facts as the indispensable correlates to values. We continue to believe that it is possible to give an account of work on a given topic that is a fair representation of greatly differing perspectives on that topic. We have aimed to present accounts that are not mere summaries of opinions, for in fact some entries in this volume provide more sophisticated theoretical accounts than are presently available anywhere else in print. We see our purpose as one not of putting facts in boxes but of making connections hitherto unmade, of bringing new perspectives to a wider audience, and of bringing all perspectives into constructive conjunction so as to increase the amount and the quality of discourse about poetry.

ACKNOWLEDGMENTS

Among our contributors were three scholars whose assistance extended far beyond work on their own entries. They are Professors Edward R. Weismiller, Jr., Fabian Gudas, and the late W. B. Fleischman. Each made the fruits of his knowledge available to us over a considerable period of time, on an astonishingly wide range of topics, and at some expense to the furthering of his own work. We gratefully acknowledge their sustained generosity and their expert counsel.

Others of our contributors also deserve thanks for generousity with suggestions, information, referrals, and solutions: Roger Allen, Samuel G. Armistead, Beth Bjorklund, Kang-I Sun Chang, Edward Greenstein, James W. Halporn, Diana Der Hovanessian, Daniel Hoffman, Ivar Ivask, Laurence Lerner, Kathleen N. Marsh, Wallace Martin, Julie Meisami, David Lee Rubin, and Tibor Wlassics.

In addition, a large number of other scholars not contributing to the volume nonetheless supported our work, assisting us in their roles of advisers, reviewers, and experts. Among many we must especially thank the following:

Helen C. Agüera, National Endowment for the Humanities; W. Sidney Allen, Cambridge University; James J. Alstrum, Illinois State University; Theodore M. Anderson, Stanford University; The Reverend Harry Aveling, Monash University, Australia; Fr. Nicholas Ayo, University of Notre Dame; Herbert Blau, University of Wisconsin; James Blodgett, Indiana University; Malcolm Bowie, Queen Mary College, University of London; Marianne Burkhard, University of Illinois; William Calin, University of Florida; Matei Calinescu, Indiana University; Dino Cervigni, University of North Carolina; Frederick J. Crosson, University of Notre Dame; Michael Curschmann, Princeton University; Isagani R. Cruz, De La Salle University, The Phillipines; Peter Dronke, University of Cambridge; Hans Eichner, University of Toronto; Roberta Frank, University of Toronto; Stephen Fredman, University of Notre Dame; Ralph Freedman, Princeton University; Henry Louis Gates, Jr., Harvard University; Albert Gérard, University of Liège; Hans Goedicke, Johns Hopkins University; Nili Gold, Columbia University; Mark L. Greenberg, Drexel University; Jean Hagstrum, Northwestern University; Joseph Harris, Harvard University; William Katra, University of Wisconsin at La Crosse; Robert Kellogg, University of Virginia; Anthony Kerrigan, late of the University of Notre Dame; Bernard Knox, University of Michigan; Egbert Krispyn, University of

ACKNOWLEDGMENTS

Georgia; James R. Lawler, University of Chicago; Herbert Lehnert, University of California at Irvine; George Levine, Rutgers University; Barbara K. Lewalski, Harvard University; Herbert Lindenberger, Stanford University; James J. Y. Liu, late of Stanford University; Richard M. Ludwig, Princeton University; George McMurray, Colorado State University; John Matthias, University of Notre Dame; Roland Mortier, Université Libre de Bruxelles; Kenneth E. Nilsen, St. Francis Xavier University; Linda M. Paterson, University of Warwick; Annabel Patterson, Duke University; Derek Pearsall, University of York; Henri Peyre, Yale University; Christopher Prendergast, King's College, Cambridge University; Tilottana Rajan, University of Western Ontario; W. Edson Richmond, Indiana University; Francesca Rochberg-Halton, University of Notre Dame; Margaret Scanlan, Indiana University; Egon Schwarz, Washington University; Eckehard Simon, Harvard University; G. S. Smith, Oxford University; Hans Tischler, Indiana University; Lewis Turco, State University of New York at Oswego; Karl D. Uitti, Princeton University; Helen Vendler, Harvard University; John Welle, University of Notre Dame; René Wellek, Yale University; Ian J. Winter, University of Wisconsin; Anthony C. Yu, University of Chicago; and Theodore Ziolkowski, Princeton University.

We must also thank our editors at Princeton University Press, Loren Hoekzema and Robert Brown, whose patience with this project was extraordinary, as well as our superb editorial assistants, Rose Meisner, Veidre Thomas, and Brenda Bean, whose acumen and dilligence enhanced every entry. Finally, we thank the following authors, publishers, and agents for granting us permission to use brief selections from the copyrighted publications listed below. Great care has been taken to trace all the owners of copyrighted material used in this book. Any inadvertent omissions pointed out to us will be gladly acknowledged in future editions.

Harry Aveling for four lines of his translation of "Nina-bobok" [Lullaby] and seven lines of "Kita adalah pemilik syah republik ini" [The Republic is Ours], two contemporary Indonesian poems, and for four lines of his translations of "Kampung Rakit" [Floating Village] and six lines from "Ini Juga Duniaku" [This Part of My World], two contemporary Malaysian poems.

Charles Bernstein for five lines of "Sentences My Father Used" from *Controlling Interests*, reprinted by permission of Charles Bernstein and ROOF Books.

Robert Bly for two lines of "Snowfall in the Afternoon" and two lines of "Waking from Sleep" from *Silence in the Snowy Fields*, copyright 1962; and four lines of "Six Winter Privacy Poems" from *Sleepers Joining Hands*, all reprinted by permission of Robert Bly.

The University of California Press for five lines of "The Box" from *Collected*

ACKNOWLEDGMENTS

Poems of Robert Creeley, 1945–75, copyright 1983; for two lines of Mounah Khouri and Hamid Algar's translation of "Two Voices" from *An Anthology of Modern Arabic Poetry,* copyright 1974; and for three lines of medieval poetry translated by J. T. Monroe from *Hispano-Arabic Poetry: A Student Anthology,* copyright 1974, all reprinted by permission of The Regents of the University of California.

Cambridge University Press for three lines from *Arabic Poetry* and three lines from *The Poems of al-Mutanabbi,* both translated by A. J. Arberry.

Carcanet Press Ltd. for five lines from "Portrait of a Lady" and eight lines of "The Red Wheel Barrow" from *Collected Poems of William Carlos Williams, 1909–1939,* vol. 1, copyright 1938; and for six lines of "Oread" and five lines of "Storm" from *Collected Poems, 1912–44,* copyright 1982 by the Estate of Hilda Doolittle.

Copper Canyon Press for an excerpt from "A Muse of Water" in *Mermaids in the Basement,* copyright 1984 by Carolyn Kizer.

The Ecco Press for an excerpt from "Meditation at Lagunitas," from *Praise,* copyright 1974, 1979 by Robert Hass.

Faber and Faber, Ltd., for two lines of "For the Time Being" and two lines of "Lullaby" from *Collected Poems* by W. H. Auden; for an excerpt from "September 1, 1939" from *The English Auden: Poems, Essays and Dramatic Writings 1927–1939;* for two lines of *The Waste Land* from *Collected Poems 1909–1962* and five lines of "Little Gidding" from *The Complete Poems and Plays, 1909–1950,* both by T. S. Eliot; for five lines of Canto II and six lines of Canto VII from *The Cantos of Ezra Pound,* copyright 1934 by Ezra Pound; for eight lines of "The Seafarer," two lines of "Homage to Sextus Propertius," four lines of "Translations and Adaptations from Heine," and three lines of "The River-Merchant's Wife" from *Personae,* copyright 1926 by Ezra Pound, reprinted by permission of the publishers.

Farrar, Straus & Giroux for an excerpt from #14 of *The Dream Songs* by John Berryman, copyright 1959, 1969 by John Berryman; for excerpts from "The Fish" and "In the Waiting Room" from *The Complete Poems, 1927–1979* by Elizabeth Bishop, copyright 1940, 1971, renewal copyright 1968 by Elizabeth Bishop, copyright 1979, 1983 by Alice Helen Methfessel; for an excerpt from "Memories of West Street and Lepke" from *Life Studies* by Robert Lowell, copyright 1956, 1959 by Robert Lowell, renewal copyright 1987 by Harriet Lowell; for an excerpt from "The Schooner Flight" from *The Star-Apple Kingdom* by Derek Walcott, copyright 1977, 1978, 1979 by Derek Walcott.

Granada and HarperCollins Publishers for four lines of "Weltende" by Jacob van Hoddes from *Modern German Poetry,* translated by Christopher Middleton; and for eight lines of "Buffalo Bill 's" from *Tulips and Chimneys* by e e cummings, edited

ACKNOWLEDGMENTS

by George James Firmage, copyright 1923, 1925, renewal copyright 1951, 1953 by e e cummings, copyright 1973, 1976 by the Trustees for the E. E. Cummings Trust, copyright 1973, 1976 by George James Firmage.

Harcourt Brace Jovanovich for five lines of "Little Gidding" from *Four Quartets*, copyright 1943 by T. S. Eliot and renewed 1971 by Esme Valerie Eliot; for two lines of *The Waste Land* from *Collected Poems 1909–1962* by T. S. Eliot, copyright 1936 by Harcourt Brace Jovanovich, copyright 1963, 1964 by T. S. Eliot; for five lines from "Praise in Summer" from *The Beautiful Changes and Other Poems*, copyright 1947 and renewed 1975 by Richard Wilbur.

Harper & Row, Publishers, for an excerpt from "Howl" from *Collected Poems 1947–80*, copyright 1955 by Allen Ginsberg.

Henry Holt and Company for two lines from "Nothing Gold Can Stay," eight lines from "Come In," three lines from "Why Wait for Science?" and two lines from "The Gift Outright," from *The Poems of Robert Frost*, ed. Edward Connery Lathem, copyright 1923, 1947, 1969 by Holt, Rinehart and Winston; copyright 1942, 1951 by Robert Frost; copyright 1970, 1975 by Lesley Frost Ballantine.

Indiana University Press for two lines from *Martial: Selected Epigrams*, translated by Rolfe Humphries.

Jonathan Cape, Ltd., for two lines from "Nothing Gold Can Stay," eight lines from "Come In," three lines from "Why Wait for Science?" and two lines from "The Gift Outright," from *The Poems of Robert Frost*, ed. Edward Connery Lathem, copyright 1923, 1947, 1969 by Holt, Rinehart and Winston; copyright 1942, 1951 by Robert Frost; copyright 1970, 1975 by Lesley Frost Ballantine.

Alfred A. Knopf for six lines of "Description Without Place," two lines of "Bantam in Pine Woods," and two lines of "Not Ideas About the Thing but the Thing Itself" from *The Collected Poems of Wallace Stevens*, copyright 1954 by Wallace Stevens.

Liverwright Publishing Corporation, for five lines of "Voyages" and two lines of "Cape Hatteras" from *The Poems of Hart Crane*, edited by Marc Simon, copyright 1986 by Marc Simon; for an excerpt from "Buffalo Bill 's" from *Tulips and Chimneys* by e e cummings, edited by George James Firmage, copyright 1923, 1925, and renewed 1951, 1953 by e e cummings, copyright 1973, 1976 by the Trustees for the E. E. Cummings Trust, copyright 1973, 1976 by George James Firmage.

Macmillan Publishing Company for two lines of "A Coat," two lines of "Leda and the Swan," and two lines of "The Gyres" from *The Collected Poems of W. B. Yeats*, copyright 1928 by Macmillan Publishing Company, renewed 1956 by Bertha Georgie Yeats, copyright 1940 by Georgie Yeats, renewed 1968 by Georgie Yeats,

ACKNOWLEDGMENTS

Michael Bulter Yeats, and Anne Yeats.

New Directions Publishing Corporation for five lines of Canto II and six lines of Canto VII from *The Cantos of Ezra Pound*, copyright 1934 by Ezra Pound; for eight lines of "The Seafarer," two lines of "Homage to Sextus Propertius," four lines of "Translations and Adaptations from Heine," and three lines of "The River-Merchant's Wife" from *Personae*, copyright 1926 by Ezra Pound; for six lines of "Oread" and five lines of "Storm" from *Collected Poems, 1912–44*, copyright 1982 by the Estate of Hilda Doolittle; for five lines of "The Five-Day Rain" from *Collected Earlier Poems 1940–60*, copyright 1958 by Denise Levertov Goodman; for an excerpt from "The Well" from *Poems 1960–67*, copyright 1960 by Denise Levertov Goodman; for five lines from "Portrait of a Lady" and eight lines of "The Red Wheel Barrow" from *Collected Poems of William Carlos Williams, 1909–1939*, vol. 1, copyright 1938 by New Directions Publishing Corporation.

State University of New York Press for four lines of "Lagu Biasa" [An Ordinary Song] and four lines of "Aku" [Me] from *The Complete Poetry and Prose of Chairil Anwar*, edited and translated by Burton Raffel, copyright 1970; for six lines of "Koyan Yang Malang" [Koyan the Unfortunate], by W. S. Rendra, from *An Anthology of Modern Indonesian Poetry*, translated by Burton Raffel, copyright 1968.

The University of North Carolina Press for two excerpts from *The Poems of Phillis Wheatley*, copyright 1989.

Ohio University Press for Epigram no. 68 from *Collected Poems and Epigrams of J. V. Cunningham*, copyright 1971.

Oxford University Press for four lines of *The First Clerihews* by Edmund Clerihew Bentley, copyright 1982 by Mrs. Nicolas Bentley.

Oxford University Press, Kuala Lumpur, for four excerpts from *Modern Malay Verse, 1946–61*, edited by Oliver Rice and Abdullah Majid.

Penguin Books Ltd., for three lines of "Howl" from *Allen Ginsburg: Collected Poems 1947–1980*, copyright 1956 by Allen Ginsberg.

Random House, Inc., for two lines of "For the Time Being" and two lines of "Lullaby" from *Collected Poems* by W. H. Auden, and an excerpt from "September 1, 1939" from *The English Auden: Poems, Essays and Dramatic Writings 1927–1939*, both edited by Edward Mendelson, copyright 1976, 1977 by Edward Mendelson, William Meredith, and Monroe K. Spears, Executors of the Estate of W. H. Auden.

The Royal Irish Academy, for four lines from *Early Irish Metrics* by Gerard Murphy, copyright 1961 by The Royal Irish Academy.

Stanford University Press, for five lines from *Japanese Court Poetry* by Robert H. Brower and Earl Miner, copyright 1961 by the Board of Trustees of the Leland

ACKNOWLEDGMENTS

Stanford Junior University.

Sterling Lord Literistic, Inc., for fourteen lines of "Black Art" from *Black Magic: Collected Poetry 1961–67*, copyright 1990 by Amiri Baraka.

Taylor & Francis, Ltd., for six lines of "Walker Skating" by Brian Morris from *Word & Image*, vol. 2, copyright 1986.

Three Continents Press for "Lazarus 1962," by Khalil Hawi, translated by A. Haydar and M. Beard in *Naked in Exile*, copyright 1984; and *Bayadir al-ju* [The Thrashing Floor of Hunger], by Khalil Hawi, copyright K. Hawi, Beirut, 1965.

Zephyr Press for an excerpt from "The Muse" from *The Complete Poems of Anna Akhmatova*, translated by Judity Hemschemeyer, copyright 1989.

CONTENTS

CONTENTS

CONTENTS

CONTENTS

CONTENTS

CONTENTS

CONTENTS

CONTENTS

CONTENTS

CONTENTS

CONTENTS

CONTENTS

CONTENTS

CONTENTS

CONTENTS

CONTENTS

BIBLIOGRAPHICAL ABBREVIATIONS

Abrams — M. H. Abrams, *The Mirror and the Lamp: Romantic Theory and the Critical Tradition*, 1953.

Analecta hymnica — *Analecta hymnica medii aevi*, ed. G. M. Dreves, C. Blume, and H. M. Bannister, 55 v., 1886–1922.

Auerbach — E. Auerbach, *Mimesis: The Representation of Reality in Western Literature*, tr. W. R. Trask, 1953.

Beare — W. Beare, *Latin Verse and European Song*, 1957.

Bec — P. Bec, *La Lyrique française au moyen âge (XIIe–XIIIe siècles): Contribution à une typologie des genres poétiques médiévaux*, 2 v., 1977–78.

Bowra — C. M. Bowra, *Greek Lyric Poetry from Alcman to Simonides*, 2d ed., 1961.

Brogan — T. V. F. Brogan, *English Versification, 1570–1980: A Reference Guide with a Global Appendix*, 1981.

Brooks — C. Brooks, *The Well Wrought Urn*, 1947.

CBEL — *Cambridge Bibliography of English Literature*, ed. F. W. Bateson, 4 v., 1940; v. 5, *Supplement*, ed. G. Watson, 1957.

CBFL — *A Critical Bibliography of French Literature*, gen. ed. D. C. Cabeen, 1–; 1947–; revisions and supplements, gen. ed. R. A. Brooks, 7 v., 1968–.

Chambers — F. M. Chambers, *An Introduction to Old Provençal Versification*, 1985.

CHCL — *Cambridge History of Classical Literature*, v. 1, *Greek Literature*, ed. P. E. Easterling and B. M. W. Knox, 1985; v. 2, *Latin Literature*, ed. E. J. Kenney, 1982.

CHEL — *Cambridge History of English Literature*, ed. A. W. Ward and A. R. Waller, 14 v., 1907–1916.

CHLC — *Cambridge History of Literary Criticism*, v. 1, *Classical Criticism*, ed. G. A. Kennedy, 1989.

Corbett — E. P. J. Corbett, *Classical Rhetoric for the Modern Student*, 3d ed., 1990.

Crane — *Critics and Criticism, Ancient and Modern*, ed. R. S. Crane, 1952.

Crusius — F. Crusius, *Römische Metrik: Ein Einfürung*, 8th ed., rev. H. Rubenbauer, 1967.

Culler — J. Culler, *Structuralist Poetics: Structuralism, Linguistics, and the Study of Literature*, 1975.

Curtius — E. Curtius, *European Literature and the Latin Middle Ages*, tr. W. R. Trask, 1953.

DAI — *Dissertation Abstracts International.*

Dale — A. M. Dale, *The Lyric Meters of Greek Drama*, 2d ed., 1968.

de Man — P. de Man, *Blindness and Insight: Essays in the Rhetoric of Contemporary Criticism*, 2d ed., 1983.

Derrida — J. Derrida, *Of Grammatology*, tr. 1976.

DHI — *Dictionary of the History of Ideas*, ed. P. P. Wiener, 6 v., 1968–74.

Dronke — P. Dronke, *Medieval Latin and the Rise of European Love Lyric*, 2d ed., 2 v., 1968.

Eliot, Essays — T. S. Eliot, *Selected Essays*, rev ed., 1950.

Elwert — W. T. Elwert, *Französische Metrik*, 4th ed., 1978.

Elwert, Italienische — W. T. Elwert, *Italienische Metrik*, 2d ed., 1984.

Empson — W. Empson, *Seven Types of Ambiguity*, 3d ed., 1953.

Faral — E. Faral, *Les Arts poétiques du XIIe et du XIIIe siècles*, 1924.

Fisher — *The Medieval Literature of Western Europe: A Review of Research, Mainly 1930–1960*, ed. John H. Fisher, 1965.

Fowler — A. Fowler, *Kinds of Literature: An Introduction to the Theory of Genres and Modes*, 1982.

Frye — N. Frye, *Anatomy of Criticism*, 1957.

Gasparov — M. L. Gasparov, *Sovremennyj russkij stix: Metrika i ritmika*, 1974.

GRLMA — *Grundriss der romanischen Literaturen des Mittelalters*, ed. H. R. Jauss and E. Köhler, 9 v., 1968–.

Group Mu — Group Mu (J. Dubois, F. Edeline, J.-M. Klinkenberg, P. Minguet, F. Pire, H. Trinon), *A General Rhetoric*, tr. P. B. Burrell and E. M. Slotkin, 1981.

Halporn et al. — J. W. Halporn, M. Ostwald, and T. G. Rosenmeyer, *The Meters of Greek and Latin Poetry*, 2d ed., 1980.

Hardie — W. R. Hardie, *Res metrica*, 1920.

Hollander — J. Hollander, *Vision and Resonance: Two Senses of Poetic Form*, 2d ed., 1985.

Hollier — *A New History of French Literature*, ed. D. Hollier, 1989.

Jakobson — R. Jakobson, *Selected Writings*, 8 v., 1962–88.

ABBREVIATIONS

Jarman and Hughes
A Guide to Welsh Literature, ed. A. O. H. Jarman and G. R. Hughes, 2 v., 1976–79.

Jeanroy
A. Jeanroy, *La Poésie lyrique des troubadours*, 2 v., 1934.

Jeanroy, Origines
A. Jeanroy, *Les Origines de la poésie lyrique en France au moyen âge*, 4th ed., 1965.

Kastner
L. E. Kastner, *A History of French Versification*, 1903.

Keil
Grammatici latini, ed. H. Keil, 7 v., 1855–80; v. 8, *Anecdota helvetica: Supplementum*, ed. H. Hagen, 1870.

Koster
W. J. W. Koster, *Traité de métrique grecque suivi d'un précis de métrique latine*, 4th ed., 1966.

Lausberg
H. Lausberg, *Handbuch der literarischen Rhetorik*, 2d ed., 2 v., 1973.

Le Gentil
P. Le Gentil, *La Poésie lyrique espagnole et portugaise à la fin du moyen âge*, 2 v., 1949–53.

Lewis
C. S. Lewis, *The Allegory of Love*, 1936.

Lord
A. B. Lord, *The Singer of Tales*, 1960.

Lote
G. Lote, *Histoire du vers français*, 3 v., 1949–56.

Maas
P. Maas, *Greek Metre*, tr. H. Lloyd-Jones, 3d ed., 1962.

Manitius
M. Manitius, *Geschichte der lateinischen Literatur des Mittelalters*, 3 v., 1911–31.

Mazaleyrat
J. Mazaleyrat, *Éléments de métrique française*, 3d ed., 1981.

Meyer
W. Meyer, *Gessamelte Abhandlungen zur mittellateinischen Rhythmik*, 3 v., 1905–36.

MGG
Die Musik in Geschichte und Gegenwart: Allgemeine Enzyklopädie der Musik, ed. F. Blume, 16 v., 1949–79.

MGH
Monumenta germaniae historica.

Michaelides
S. Michaelides, *The Music of Ancient Greece: An Encyclopaedia*, 1978.

Migne, PG
Patrilogiae cursus completus, series graeca, ed. J. P. Migne, 161 v., 1857–66.

Migne, PL
Patrilogiae cursus completus, series latina, ed. J. P. Migne, 221 v., 1844–64.

Miner et al.
E. Miner, H. Odagiri, and R. E. Morrell, *The Princeton Companion to Classical Japanese Literature*, 1986.

Morier
H. Morier, *Dictionnaire de poétique et de rhétorique*, 3d ed., 1981.

Morris-Jones
J. Morris-Jones, *Cerdd Dafod*, 1925, rpt. with Index, 1980.

Murphy
J. J. Murphy, *Rhetoric in the Middle Ages: A History of Rhetorical Theory from St. Augustine to the Renaissance*, 1974.

Navarro
T. Navarro, *Métrica española: Reseña histórica y descriptiva*, 6th ed., 1983.

New CBEL
New Cambridge Bibliography of English Literature, ed. G. Watson and I. R. Willison, 5 v., 1969–77.

New Grove
New Grove Dictionary of Music and Musicians, ed. S. Sadie, 20 v., 1980.

Nienhauser et al.
W. H. Nienhauser, Jr., C. Hartman, Y. W. Ma, and S. H. West, *The Indiana Companion to Traditional Chinese Literature*, 1986.

Norberg
D. Norberg, *Introduction a l'étude de la versification latine médiévale*, 1958.

Norden
E. Norden, *Die antike Kunstprosa*, 9th ed., 2 v., 1983.

OED
Oxford English Dictionary, 1st ed.

Omond
T. S. Omond, *English Metrists*, 1921.

Parry
M. Parry, *The Making of Homeric Verse*, ed. A. Parry, 1971.

Parry, History
T. Parry, *A History of Welsh Literature*, tr. H. I. Bell, 1955.

Patterson
W. F. Patterson, *Three Centuries of French Poetic Theory: A Critical History of The Chief Arts of Poetry in France (1328–1630)*, 2 v., 1935.

Pauly-Wissowa
Paulys Realencyclopädie der classischen Altertumswissenschaft, ed. A. Pauly, G. Wissowa, W. Kroll, and K. Mittelhaus, 24 v. (A-Q), 10 v. (R-Z, Series 2), and 15 v. (Supplements), 1894–1978.

Pearsall
D. Pearsall, *Old English and Middle English Poetry*, 1977.

PLAC
Poetae latini aevi carolini, ed. E. Dümmler (v. 1–2), L. Traube, P. von Winterfeld, and K. Strecker, 5 v., 1881–1937.

Raby, Christian
F. J. E. Raby, *A History of Christian-Latin Poetry From the Beginnings to the Close of the Middle Ages*, 2d ed., 1953.

Raby, Secular
F. J. E. Raby, *A History of Secular Latin Poetry in the Middle Ages*, 2d ed., 2 v., 1957.

Ransom
Selected Essays of John Crowe Ransom, ed. T. D. Young and J. Hindle, 1984.

Reallexikon
Reallexikon der deutschen Literaturgeschichte, 2d ed., ed. W. Kohlschmidt and W. Mohr (v. 1–3), K. Kanzog and A. Masser (v. 4), 4 v., 1958–84.

Reallexikon I
Reallexikon der deutschen Literaturgeschichte, ed. P. Merker and W. Stammler, 1st ed., 4 v., 1925–31.

Richards
I. A. Richards, *Principles of Literary Criticism*, 1925.

ABBREVIATIONS

Saisselin R. G. Saisselin, *The Rule of Reason and the Ruses of the Heart: A Philosophical Dictionary of Classical French Criticism, Critics, and Aesthetic Issues,* 1970.

Sayce O. Sayce, *The Medieval German Lyric, 1150–1300: The Development of Its Themes and Forms in Their European Context,* 1982.

Scherr B. P. Scherr, *Russian Poetry: Meter, Rhythm, and Rhyme,* 1986.

Schipper J. M. Schipper, *Englische Metrik,* 3 v., 1881–1888.

Schipper, History J. M. Schipper, *A History of English Versification,* 1910.

Schmid and Stählin W. Schmid and O. Stählin, *Geschichte der griechischen Literatur,* 7 v., 1920–48.

Scott C. Scott, *French verse-art: A study,* 1980.

Sebeok *Style in Language,* ed. T. Sebeok, 1960.

Sievers E. Sievers, *Altgermanische Metrik,* 1893.

Smith *Elizabethan Critical Essays,* ed. G. G. Smith, 2 v., 1904.

Snell B. Snell, *Griechische Metrik,* 4th ed., 1982.

Spongano R. Spongano, *Nozioni ed esempi di metrica italiana,* 2d. ed., 1974.

Stephens *The Oxford Companion to the Literature of Wales,* ed. M. Stephens, 1986.

Terras *Handbook of Russian Literature,* ed. V. Terras, 1985.

Thieme H. P. Thieme, *Essai sur l'histoire du vers français,* 1916.

Trypanis C. A. Trypanis, *Greek Poetry From Homer to Seferis,* 1981.

Weinberg B. Weinberg, *A History of Literary Criticism in the Italian Renaissance,* 2 v., 1961.

Wellek R. Wellek, *A History of Modern Criticism, 1750–1950,* 8 v., 1955–92.

Wellek and Warren R. Wellek and A. Warren, *Theory of Literature,* 3d ed., 1956.

West M. L. West, *Greek Metre,* 1982.

Wilamowitz U. von Wilamowitz-Moellendorf, *Griechische Verskunst,* 1921.

Wilkins E. H. Wilkins, *A History of Italian Literature,* rev. T. G. Bergin, 1974.

Wimsatt *Versification: Major Language Types,* ed. W. K. Wimsatt, Jr., 1972.

Wimsatt and Brooks W. K. Wimsatt, Jr., and C. Brooks, *Literary Criticism: A Short History,* 1957.

GENERAL ABBREVIATIONS

Two sets of abbreviations are used systematically throughout this volume in order to conserve space. First, general terms (below) are abbreviated both in text and bibliographies. Second, within each entry, the headword or -words of the title of the entry are abbreviated by the first letter of each word, unless the word is a general abbreviation, which takes precedence. Thus in the entry, "Egyptian Poetry," that phrase is regularly abbreviated E. p., while in "English Poetry," the head phrase is abbreviated Eng. p. Both general and headword abbreviations may also show plural forms, e.g. ms. for "metaphors" in the entry "Metaphor" (and "Meter," etc.) and lits. for "literatures" in any entry.

Af.	African	It.	Italian
Am.	American	Jh.	Jahrhundert
anthol.	anthology	jour.	journal
Ar.	Arabic	lang.	language
Assoc.	Association	Lat.	Latin
b.	born	ling.	linguistics
bibl.	bibliography	lit.	literature
c.	century	lit. crit.	literary criticism
ca.	*circa*, about	lit. hist.	literary history
cf.	*confer*, compare	ME	Middle English
ch.	chapter	med.	medieval
Cl.	Classical	MHG	Middle High German
comp.	comparative	mod.	modern
contemp.	contemporary	ms.	manuscript
crit.	criticism	NT	New Testament
d.	died	OE	Old English
devel.	development	OF	Old French
dict.	dictionary	OHG	Old High German
diss.	dissertation	ON	Old Norse
ed.	edition, editor, edited by	OT	Old Testament
e.g.	*exempli gratia*, for example	p., pp.	page, pages
Eng.	English	Port.	Portuguese
enl.	enlarged	Proc.	Proceedings
esp.	especially	pros.	prosody
et al.	*et alii*, and others	Prov.	Provençal, i.e. Occitan
ff.	following	pub.	published
fl.	*floruit*, flourished	q.v.	*quod vide*, which see
Fr.	French	qq.v.	*quae vide*, which see
Ger.	German	Ren.	Renaissance
Gesch.	Geschichte	rev.	revised
Gr.	Greek	Rev.	Review
Heb.	Hebrew	rhet.	rhetoric
hist.	history, histoire	rpt.	reprinted
IE	Indo-European	Rus.	Russian
i.e.	*id est*, that is	Sp.	Spanish
incl.	includes, including	supp.	supplement(ed)
interp.	interpretation	tr.	translation, translated
Intro.	Introduction	trad.	tradition
Ir.	Irish	v.	volume(s)

THE CONTRIBUTORS

A.A.E. Alvin A. Eustis, Professor of French, University of California at Berkeley

A.B. Anna Balakian, Professor of French and Comparative Literature, New York University

A.B.F. Albert B. Friedman, Rosecrans Professor of English, Claremont Graduate School

A.B.L. Albert Bates Lord, late Arthur Kingsley Porter Professor Emeritus of Slavic and Comparative Literature, Harvard University

A.B.M. Arnold B. McMillin, Professor of Russian, University of London

A.BR. Anthony Bradley, Professor of English, University of Vermont

A.C. Albrech Classen, Assistant Professor of German, University of Arizona

A.D.C. A. Dwight Culler, Emily Sanford Professor Emeritus of English, Yale University

A.E.S. Alexandrino E. Severino, Professor of Portuguese, Vanderbilt University

A.F. Angus Fletcher, Distinguished Professor of English and Comparative Literature, City University of New York

A.F.K. Arthur F. Kinney, Thomas W. Copeland Professor of Literary History, University of Massachusetts

A.FO. Alastair Fowler, Regius Professor Emeritus of Rhetoric and English Literature, University of Edinburgh

A.G. Albert Gelpi, Coe Professor of American Literature, Stanford University

A.G.E. Alfred Garvin Engstrom, Alumni Distinguished Professor Emeritus of French, University of North Carolina

A.G.W. Allen G. Wood, Associate Professor of French and Comparative Literature, Purdue University

A.J.M.S. A. J. M. Smith, Professor Emeritus of English, Michigan State University

A.K.R. A. K. Ramanujan, William Colvin Professor of South Asian Languages and Civilizations, University of Chicago

A.L.S. A. Lytton Sells, late Professor of French and Italian, Indiana University

A.M.D. Andrew M. Devine, Professor of Classics, Stanford University

A.O. Ants Oras, late Professor of English, University of Florida

A.P. Anne Paolucci, President, Council on National Literatures

A.PI. Arshi Pipa, Professor of Italian and Albanian, University of Minnesota

A.PR. Alex Preminger, Editor

A.R. Alan Richardson, Assistant Professor of English, Boston College

A.RO. Andrew Ross, Associate Professor of English, Princeton University

A.S. Andras Sandor, Professor of German, Howard University

A.SC. Aldo Scaglione, Professor of Italian, New York University

A.T.C. A. Thomas Cole, Professor of Greek and Latin, Yale University

A.W. Andrew Welsh, Associate Professor of English, Rutgers University

A.W.E. Allen W. Entwistle, Associate Professor of Hindi, University of Washington

A.W.H. Albert W. Halsall, Professor of French, Carleton University

A.W.P. Allen W. Phillips, Professor Emeritus of Spanish, University of California at Santa Barbara

B.A.N. B. Ashton Nichols, Assistant Professor of English, Dickinson College

B.B. Beth Bjorklund, Associate Professor of German, University of Virginia

B.BO. Betsy Bowden, Associate Professor of English, Rutgers University

B.G. Bernard Groom, late Professor of English, McMaster University

B.H.S. Barbara Herrnstein Smith, Braxton Craven Professor of Comparative Literature and English, Duke University

B.J.F. Bernard J. Fridsma, Sr., Professor Emeritus of Germanic Languages, Calvin College

B.N.S. Bernard N. Schilling, Trevor Professor Emeritus of English and Comparative Literature, University of Rochester

B.R. Burton Raffel, Distinguished Professor of English, University of Southwestern Louisiana

B.RO. Beryl Rowland, Distinguished Research Professor, University of Victoria

B.S.M. Barbara Stoler Miller, Samuel R. Milbank Professor of Oriental Studies, Columbia University

C.A. Charles Altieri, Professor of English and Comparative Literature, University of Washington

C.A.K. Charles A. Knudson, late Professor of English, University of Illinois

C.A.M. Charles A. Moser, Professor of Slavic, The George Washington University

C.A.T. C. A. Trypanis, Professor Emeritus of Greek, University of Oxford, and Fellow

CONTRIBUTORS

C.B.   of the Academy of Athens
Cleanth Brooks, Gray Professor Emeritus of Rhetoric, Yale University

C.B.L.   Claudia Brodsky Lacour, Associate Professor of Comparative Literature, Princeton University

C.F.   Carolyn Fowler, Professor of Africana Literature, Clark Atlanta University

C.F.S.   C .F. Swanepoel, Professor of African Languages, University of South Africa

C.H.W.   C. H. Wang, Professor of Chinese and Comparative Literature, University of Washington

C.J.H.   C. John Herington, Talcott Professor of Greek, Yale University

C.K.   Christopher Kleinhenz, Professor and Chairman of the Department of Italian, University of Wisconsin

C.M.E.   Carol M. Eastman, Professor of Anthropology and Adjunct Professor of Linguistics, University of Washington

C.P.   Camille Paglia, Associate Professor of Humanities, Philadelphia College of Performing Arts, University of the Arts

C.P.S.   Charles P. Shepherdson, Henry A. Luce Fellow in Humanities, University of New Hampshire

C.S.   Clive Scott, Lecturer in French, University of East Anglia

C.W.D.   Charles W. Dunn, Margaret Brooks Robinson Professor Emeritus of Celtic Language and Literature, Harvard University

C.W.J.   Charles W. Jones, late Professor of English, University of California at Berkeley

D.-H.N.   Dinh-Hoa Nguyen, Professor of Linguistics and Foreign Languages and Literatures, Southern Illinois University

D.A.   Derek Attridge, Professor of English, Rutgers University

D.B.   David Bromwich, Professor of English, Yale University

D.B.S.J.   D. B .S. Jeyaraj, journalist

D.C.C.   Dorothy Clotelle Clarke, Professor Emerita of Spanish, University of California at Berkeley

D.D.-H.   Diana Der-Hovanessian, poet and translator

D.F.B.   David Frank Beer, author

D.F.D.   David F. Dorsey, Jr., Professor of African Literature and English Linguistics, Clark Atlanta University

D.H.   Dick Higgins, Research Associate, State University of New York at Purchase

D.H.C.   David H. Chisholm, Professor of German, University of Arizona

D.HO.   Daniel Hoffman, Poet in Residence and Felix E. Schelling Professor of English, University of Pennsylvania

D.K.   Donald Kenrick, Romany Institute

D.KI.   Dodonia Kiziria, Associate Professor of Slavic, Indiana University

D.L.   Dov Landau, Professor of Hebrew and Comparative Literature, Bar-Ilan University

D.L.R.   David Lee Rubin, Professor of French, University of Virginia

D.M.L.   D. Myrddin Lloyd, late Keeper of Printed Books, National Library of Scotland

D.M.R.   Douglass M. Rogers, Associate Professor of Spanish, University of Texas

D.P.B.   Daniel P. Biebuyck, H. Rodney Sharp Professor Emeritus of Anthropology and Humanities, Dartmouth College

D.S.   David Semah, Professor of Arabic, University of Haifa

D.S.P.   Douglass S. Parker, Professor of Classics, University of Texas at Austin

D.W.   Donald Wesling, Professor of English Literature, University of California at San DIego

E.A.B.   Edward A. Bloom, Professor of English, Brown University

E.A.H.   Eric A. Huberman, Assistant Professor of Sanskrit and Indic Studies, Columbia University

E.A.P.   Erskine A. Peters, Professor of English, University of Notre Dame

E.B.   Eleanor Berry, author

E.B.J.   Elise Bickford Jorgens, Professor of English, Western Michigan University

E.BO.   Eniko Bollobaś, scholar and diplomat, Hungary

E.C.   Eleanor Cook, Professor of English, Victoria College, University of Toronto

E.D.   Edward Doughtie, Professor of English, Rice University

E.G.   Edwin Gerow, Professor of Religion and Humanities, Reed College

E.H.   Ernst Haüblein, Assistant to the Principal, Alexander-von-Humboldt-Gymnasium

E.H.B.   Ernst H. Behler, Professor of German and Chairman, University of Washington

E.K.   Edmund Keeley, Professor of English and Creative Writing, Princeton University

E.L.G.   Edward L. Greenstein, Professor of Bible, Jewish Theological Seminary of America

E.L.R.   Elias L. Rivers, Professor of Spanish, State University of New York at Stony Brook

E.M.   Earl Miner, Professor of English and Comparative Literature, Princeton University

E.R.   Erica Reiner, John A. Wilson Distinguished Service Professor, University of Chicago

E.R.H.   Edward R. Haymes, Professor of German, Cleveland State University

CONTRIBUTORS

E.R.W.   Edward R. Weismiller, Professor Emeritus of English, George Washington University

E.S.   Elaine Showalter, Professor of English, Princeton University

E.SP.   Ezra Spicehandler, Professor of Hebrew Literature, Hebrew Union College

E.ST.   Edward Stankiewicz, Professor of Slavic and General Linguistics, Yale University

F.A.   Fernando Alegria, Sadie D. Patek Professor Emeritus in the Humanties, Stanford University

F.C.   Fletcher Collins, Jr., Professor Emeritus of Dramatic Arts, Mary Baldwin College

F.F.   Frances Ferguson, Professor of English and the Humanities, Johns Hopkins University

F.G.   Frederick Garber, Professor of Comparative Literature, State University of New York

F.GU.   Fabian Gudas, Professor Emeritus of English, Louisiana State University

F.J.W.   Frank J. Warnke, late Professor of Comparative Literature, University of Georgia

F.L.B.   Frank L. Borchardt, Associate Professor of German, Duke University

F.M.C.   Frank M. Chambers, Professor Emeritus of French, University of Arizona

F.P.W.M.   Frederick P. W. McDowell, Professor Emeritus of English, University of Iowa

F.S.   Francis Sparshott, Professor of Philosophy, University of Toronto

F.SV.   Frantisek Svejkovsky, Professor of Slavic, The University of Chicago

F.T.   Frances Teague, Associate Professor of English, University of Georgia

F.W.   Frederic Will, author

G.A.   Gorka Aulestia, Professor of Literature, University of Nevada

G.C.   Gustavo Costa, Professor of Italian, University of California at Berkeley

G.F.   Graham Furniss, Lecturer in Hausa, University of London

G.F.E.   Gerald F. Else, late Professor of Classical Studies, University of Michigan

G.G.G.   George G. Grabowicz, Dmytro Čyževśkyj Professor of Ukrainian Literature, Harvard University

G.J.J.   Gerald J. Janecek, Professor of Russian, University of Kentucky

G.L.   George Lang, Research Fellow in Comparative Literature, The University of Alberta

G.S.   Guy Sylvestre, Honorary Librarian and Archivist, Royal Society of Canada

G.T.T.   G. Thomas Tanselle, Vice President, John Simon Guggenheim Memorial Foundation

G.T.W.   George T. Wright, Professor of English, University of Minnesota

G.W.   George Woodcock, Professor Emeritus of English, University of British Columbia

H.A.   Hazard Adams, Professor of English and Comparative Literature, University of Washington

H.A.B.   Houston A. Baker Jr., Albert M. Greenfield Professor of Human Relations, University of Pennsylvania

H.B.   Henryk Baran, Associate Professor of Russian, State University of New York at Albany

H.BR.   Huntington Brown, late Professor of English, University of Minnesota

H.B.S.   Harold B. Segel, Professor of Slavic Literatures, Columbia University

H.F.   Harold Fisch, Professor of English, Bar-Ilan University

H.G.   Helena Goscilo, Associate Professor of Slavic, University of Pittsburgh

H.J.B.   Henry J. Baron, Professor of English, Calvin College

H.P.   Henry Paolucci, Professor of Government and Politics, St. John's University

H.PE.   Hla Pe, Emeritus Professor of Burmese, University of London

H.R.E.   Helen Regueiro Elam, Associate Professor of English, State University of New York at Albany

H.S.   Hiroaki Sato, author and translator

H.S.D.   Horst S. Daemmrich, Professor of Germanic and Comparative Literature, University of Pennsylvania

H.T.   Humphrey Tonkin, President, Potsdam College, State University of New York at Potsdam

I.I.   Ivar Ivask, Professor of Modern Languages, University of Oklahoma

I.J.W.   Ian J. Winter, Associate Professor of French, University of Wisconsin at Milwaukee

I.L.   Ilse Lehiste, Professor of Linguistics, Ohio State University

I.S.   Isidore Silver, Rosa May Distinguished University Professor Emeritus in the Humanities, Washington University

J.A.   John Arthos, Distinquished University Professor Emeritus of English, University of Michigan

J.A.W.   James A. Winn, Professor of English, University of Michigan

J.B.   Jeffrey Barnouw, Associate Professor of English and Comparative Literature, University of Texas

J.B.B.   Jess B. Bessinger, Jr., Professor Emeritus of English, New York University

J.B.-N.   Juan Bruce-Novoa, Professor of Mexican and Chicano Literatures, University of California at Irvine

J.B.V.   John B. Vickery, Professor of English and Associate Executive Vice-Chancellor, University of California at Riverside

J.C.   Johnathan Culler, Class of 1916 Profes-

CONTRIBUTORS

sor of English, Cornell University

J.C.K. J. C. Kannemeyer, Senior Research Specialist, Human Sciences Research Council, South Africa

J.C.L.D. J. Craig La Drière, late Professor of Comparative Literature, Harvard University

J.C.S. Joseph C. Sitterson, Jr., Associate Professor of English, Georgetown University

J.E. James Engell, Professor of English and Comparative Literature, Harvard University

J.E.C. J. E. Congleton, Dean Emeritus, School of Humanities and Sciences, University of Findlay

J.E.C.W. John Ellis Cherwyn Williams, Professor Emeritus of Welsh and Celtic Literature, University College of Wales, and Fellow of the British Academy

J.F.A. John F. Andrews, Deputy Director of Educational Programs, National Endowment for the Humanities

J.G.F. Joseph G. Fucilla, late Professor of Romance Languages, Northwestern University

J.H. Janet Hadda, Associate Professor of Yiddish, University of California at Los Angeles

J.H.M. John Henry Marshall, Professor Emeritus of Romance Philology, University of London

J.H.S. Joseph H. Silverman, late Professor of Spanish, University of California at Santa Cruz

J.HO. John Hollander, Professor of English, Yale University

J.J.R. J. J. Ras, Professor of Javanese Language and Literature, State University of Leiden

J.K.N. J. K. Newman, Professor of the Classics, University of Illinois at Urbana-Champaign

J.L. John Lindow, Professor of Scandinavian, University of California

J.L.F. John L. Foster, Professor of English, Roosevelt University

J.L.M. John L. Mahoney, Professor of English, Boston College

J.L.R. James L. Rolleston, Associate Professor of German, Duke University

J.M. John MacInnes, Senior Lecturer, University of Edinburgh

J.M.E. John M. Ellis, Professor of German Literature, University of California at Santa Cruz

J.M.F. John Miles Foley, Professor of English and William H. Byler Distinguished Chair in Humanities, University of Missouri

J.M.P. Jeffrey M. Perl, Professor of Humanities, University of Texas at Dallas

J.N. John Neubauer, Professor of Comparative Literature, Universiteit van Amsterdam

J.O.B. James O. Bailey, Professor of Slavic, University of Wisconsin

J.P.S. Joseph P. Strelka, Professor of German and Comparative Literature, State University of New York at Albany

J.P.W. John P. Welle, Associate Professor of Italian, University of Notre Dame

J.R. Jerome Rothenberg, Professor of Visual Arts and Literature, University of California at San Diego

J.R.B. James Richard Bennett, Professor of English, University of Arkansas

J.R.K. John R. Krueger, Professor of Ural and Altaic Studies, retired, Indiana University

J.S. Juris Silenieks, Professor of French, Carnegie Mellon University

J.S.M. Julie S. Meisami, Lecturer in Persian, University of Oxford

J.V.B. Jaqueline Vaught Brogan, Associate Professor of English, University of Notre Dame

J.W. Joel Weinsheimer, Professor of English, University of Minnesota

J.W.H. James W. Halporn, Professor of Classical Studies and Comparative Literature, Indiana University

J.W.J. James William Johnson, Professor of English, University of Rochester

J.W.JO. John William Johnson, Associate Professor of Folklore, Indiana University

J.WH. Jon Whitman, Senior Lecturer, Hebrew University of Jerusalem

J.W.R. Jarold W. Ramsey, Professor of English, University of Rochester

K.C.F. Kathleen C. Falvey, Associate Professor of English, University of Hawaii at Manoa

K.E. Kathy Eden, Assistant Professor of English and Comparative Literature, Columbia University

K.K.S. Kirsti K. Simonsuuri, Senior Research Fellow, Helsinki University

K.L. Katharine Luomala, Professor Emerita of Anthropology, University of Hawaii

K.N.M. Kathleen N. March, Associate Professor of Spanish, University of Maine

K.R. Kenneth Ramchand, Professor of West Indian Literature, University of the West Indies

K.S.C. Kang-i Sun Chang, Professor of Chinese Literature, Yale University

K.V. Kenneth Varty, Stevenson Professor of French, University of Glasgow

L.A.C.D. L. A. C. Dobrez, Director of Centre for Australian Studies and Professor of Australian, Bond University

L.A.S. Lawrence A. Sharpe, Professor Emeritus of Romance Languages, University of North Carolina

L.B. Lee Bartlett, Professor and Chair, Department of English, University of New

CONTRIBUTORS

L.BI. Lloyd Bishop, Professor of French, Virginia Polytechnic Institute and State University, Mexico

L.B.P. Lucy B. Palache, author

L.C. Leonard Casper, Professor of English, Boston College

L.D.L. Laurence D. Lerner, William R. Kenan Professor of English, Vanderbilt University

L.D.S. Laurence D. Stephens, Professor of Classics, University of North Carolina

L.G. Leon Golden, Director, Program in the Humanities and Chairman, Department of Classics, Florida State University

L.G.W. Lars G. Warme, Associate Professor of Scandinavian Languages and Literature, University of Washington

L.H. Leo Hughes, Professor Emeritus of English, University of Texas

L.H.G. Lewis H. Gordon, Emeritus Professor of Italian and French, Brown University

L.J.Z. Lawrence J. Zillman, Professor Emeritus of English, University of Washington

L.K.C. Lawrence K. Carpenter, Associate Professor of Linguistics and Spanish, University of North Florida

L.L.B. Linton Lomas Barrett, late Professor of Romance Languages, Washington and Lee University

L.M. Lawrence Manley, Associate Professor of English, Yale University

L.ME. Louis Menand, Associate Professor of English, Queens College, City University of New York

L.MET. Lore Metzger, Professor of English, Emory University

L.MO. Luis Monguió, Professor Emeritus of Spanish, University of California at Berkeley

L.N. Leonard Nathan, Professor of Rhetoric, University of California at Berkeley

L.NE. Lowry Nelson, Jr., Professor of Comparative Literature, Yale University

L.P. Laurence Perrine, Frensley Professor Emeritus of English, Southern Methodist University

L.T.M. Louis T. Milic, Professor Emeritus of English, Cleveland State University

L.W. Liliane Wouters, Academie Royale de Langue et de Litterature Française

M.A.C. Mary Ann Caws, Distinguished Professor of English, French, and Comparative Literature, City University of New York

M.B. Michael Beard, Professor of English, University of North Dakota

M.C. Miguel Civil, Professor, Oriental Institute, University of Chicago

M.C.B. Monroe C. Beardsley, late Professor of Philosophy, Temple University

M.CL. Michael Clark, Associate Professor of English and Comparative Literature, University of California at Irvine

M.D. Michael Davidson, Associate Professor of Literature, University of California at San Diego

M.E.B. Merle E. Brown, late Professor of English, University of Iowa

M.E.D. Manuel E. Durán, Professor of Spanish and Catalan Literatures, Yale University

M.G. Michel Grimaud, Associate Professor of French, Wellesley College

M.G.A. Mark G. Altshuller, Associate Professor of Russian Literature, University of Pittsburgh

M.GS. Manfred Gsteiger, Professor of Comparative Literature, University of Lausanne

M.H.A. M. H. Abrams, Class of 1916 Professor Emeritus of English, Cornell University

M.K. Murray Krieger, Professor of English, University of California at Irvine

M.L.R. M. L. Rosenthal, Professor Emeritus of English, New York University

M.M. Michael McCanles, Professor of English, Marquette University

M.MO. Massaud Moisés, Professor of Portuguese, University of São Paulo

M.O'C. Michael Patrick O'Connor, author

M.P. Marjorie Perloff, Professor of English and Comparative Literature, Stanford University

M.P.W. Mabel P. Worthington, late Professor of English, Temple University

M.S. Marianne Shapiro, Visiting Professor of Comparative Literature, Brown University

M.ST. Martin Steinmann, Jr., Professor Emeritus of English, University of Illinois at Chicago

M.STE. Martin Stevens, City University of New York Distinguished Professor of English, City University of New York

M.-T.B. Maria-Teresa Babin, Professor Emerita of Literature, Herbert H. Lehman College, City University of New York

M.T.K. Matthew T. Kapstein, Assistant Professor of the Philosophy of Religion, Columbia University

M.U. Makoto Ueda, Professor of Japanese and Comparative Literature, Stanford University

M.V.F. Michael V. Fox, Professor of Hebrew, University of Wisconsin

M.W. Michael Winkler, Professor of German, Rice University

M.W.B. Morton W. Bloomfield, late Arthur Kingsley Porter Professor of English, Harvard University

N.A.S. Nathan A. Scott, Jr., William R. Kenan Professor of Religious Studies and Professor of English, University of Virginia

N.F. Norman Friedman, Professor of English,

CONTRIBUTORS

Queens College, City University of New York

N.N.H. Norman N. Holland, Milbauer Eminent Scholar, University of Florida

N.S. Norman Simms, Senior Lecturer, University of Waikato

O.B.H. O. B. Hardison, Jr., late University Professor of English, Georgetown University

O.L.S. Olive L. Sayce, Fellow and Tutor, Somerville College, and Faculty Lecturer, University of Oxford

P.D. Phillip Damon, Professor of Comparative Literature and English, University of California at Berkeley

P.DE M. Paul de Man, late Sterling Professor of Comparative Literature, Yale University

P.F. Paul Fussell, Donald T. Regan Professor of English Literature, University of Pennsylvania

P.G.A. Percy G. Adams, Lindsay Young Professor Emeritus of English and Comparative Literature, University of Tennessee

P.H.F. Paul H. Fry, Professor of English, Yale University

P.H.H. Philip H. Highfill, Jr., Professor of English, George Washington University

P.H.L. Peter H. Lee, Professor and Chairman of the Department of East Asian Languages and Cultures, University of California at Los Angeles

P.K.K. Paul K. Kugler, Professor, Senior Training Analyst, and Director of Admissions, Interregional Society of Jungian Analysis

P.M. Pamela McCallum, Associate Professor of English, University of Calgary

P.M.D. Peter M. Daly, Professor of German, McGill University

P.R. Paul Ramsey, Emeritus Poet-in-Residence and Guerry Professor of English, University of Tennessee at Chattanooga

P.RO. Philip Rollinson, Associate Professor of English, University of South Carolina

P.R.S. Penn R. Szittya, Professor of English, Georgetown University

P.S. Peter Sacks, Associate Professor of English, John Hopkins University

P.S.C. Procope S. Costas, late Professor of Classics, Brooklyn College, City University of New York

P.SP. Peter Spycher, Emeritus Professor of German, Oberlin College

P.ST. Peter Steiner, Associate Professor of Slavic Literatures, University of Pennsylvania

P.W. Philip Weller, scholar, Warburg & Courtauld Institute

P.WH. Philip Wheelwright, late Professor of Philosophy, University of California at Riverside

R.A. Robert Alter, Professor of Hebrew and Comparative Literature, University of California at Berkeley

R.A.H. Roger A. Hornsby, Professor Emeritus of Classics, University of Iowa

R.A.S. Roy Arthur Swanson, late Professor of Classics, University of Wisconsin at Milwaukee

R.B. Ross Brann, Assistant Professor of Hebrew Literature, Cornell University

R.BU. Robert Burgoyne, Assistant Professor of English, Wayne State University

R.C. Ruby Cohn, Professor of Comparative Drama, University of California at Davis

R.CO. Robert Cook, Professor of English, University of Iceland

R.D.T. Robert Donald Thornton, Professor Emeritus of English, State University of New York at New Paltz

R.E.P. Richard E. Palmer, Professor of Philosophy and Religion, MacMurray College

R.F. Roger Fowler, Professor of English and Linguistics, University of East-Anglia

R.F.L. René Felix Lissens, Professor Emeritus of Dutch Literature and European Literatures, Universitaire Faculteiten St. Ignatius

R.G. René Galand, Professor of French, Wellesley College

R.G.H. Russell G. Hamilton, Professor of Spanish and Portuguese, Vanderbilt University

R.GR. Roland Greene, Associate Professor of English, Harvard University

R.H.F. Richard Harter Fogle, University Distinguished Professor Emeritus of English, University of North Carolina

R.H.O. Richard H. Osberg, Associate Professor of English, Santa Clara University

R.H.W. Ruth Helen Webb, Frances A. Yates Research Fellow, Warburg & Courtauld Institute

R.J.G. Robert J. Getty, late Paddison Professor of Classics, University of North Carolina

R.J.L. Richard John Lynn, author

R.L. Richard Luxton, Assistant Professor of Anthropology and Sociology, Western New England College

R.L.H. Robert L. Harrison, author

R.L.M. Robert L. Montgomery, Professor of English, University of California at Irvine

R.M. Robert Marsh, late Professor of English, University of Chicago

R.M.A.A. Roger M. A. Allen, Professor of Arabic and Comparative Literature, University of Pennsylvania

R.MCG. Robin McGrath, Professor of English, University of Alberta

R.MI. Rigo Mignani, late Professor of Romance Languages, State University of New York at Binghamton

R.O. Ranjini Obeyesekere, Lecturer, Princeton University

R̥.O.E. Robert O. Evans, Professor Emeritus of English and Comparative Literatue,

CONTRIBUTORS

R.P.A.   University of Kentucky
Robert P. apRoberts, Professor Emeritus of English, California State University at Northridge

R.P.F.   Robert P. Falk, Professor Emeritus of English Literature, University of California at Los Angeles

R.P.S.   Raymond P. Scheindlin, Provost and Professor of Medieval Hebrew Literature, The Jewish Theological Seminary of America

R.S.   Rimvydas Silbajoris, Professor Emeritus of Slavic and East European Languages and Literature, Ohio State University

R.S.C.   R. S. Crane, late Distinguished Service Professor of English, University of Chicago

R.V.H.   Robert von Hallberg, Professor of English, University of Chicago

R.W.   Richard Wendorf, Director, Houghton Library, Harvard University

S.A.   Stuart Atkins, Professor Emeritus of German, University of California at Santa Barbara

S.A.G.   Stephen A. Geller, Visiting Associate Professor of Bible, Brandeis University

S.A.L.   Stephen A. Larrabee, late author

S.B.   Stanislaw Baranczak, Alfred Jurzykowski Professor of Polish Language and Literature, Harvard University

S.BU.   Sidney Burris, Associate Professor of English, University of Arkansas

S.C.   Stephen Cushman, Associate Professor of English, University of Virginia

S.E.H.   Stephen E. Henderson, Professor of Afro-American Studies, Howard University

S.F.   Solomon Fishman, late Professor of English, University of California at Davis

S.F.F.   Stephen F. Fogle, late Professor of English, Adelphi Suffolk College

S.G.   Stephen Gray, Professor of English, Rand Afrikaans University

S.G.A.   Samuel G. Armistead, Professor of Spanish and Comparative Literature, University of California at Davis

S.H.R.   Sven H. Rossel, Professor of Comparative Literature, University of Washington

S.J.K.   Sholom J. Kahn, Professor Emeritus of English, Hebrew University

S.K.C.   Stanley K. Coffman, Professor Emeritus of English, State University of New York at Albany

S.L.   Sarah Lawall, Professor of Comparative Literature, University of Massachusetts at Amherst

S.LY.   Sverre Lyngstad, Distinguished Professor of English, New Jersey Institute of Technology

S.M.G.   Sally M. Gall, author

S.M.N.   Silvia M. Nagy, Assistant Professor of Latin American Literature, Catholic University of America

S.P.R.   Stella P. Revard, Professor of English, Southern Illinois University at Edwardsville

S.R.   Suresh Raval, Professor of English, University of Arizona

S.R.W.   Suzanne R. Westfall, Associate Professor of English, Lafayette College

S.S.L.   Susan S. Lanser, Associate Professor of English, Georgetown University

S.W.   Stephen Wright, late of Addis Ababa University

T.A.K.   Thomas A. Kirby, Professor Emeritus of English, Louisiana State University

T.B.   Timothy Bahti, Associate Professor of Comparative Literature, University of Michigan

T.C.   Thomas Cable, Jane and Roland Blumberg Centennial Professor in English, University of Texas

T.G.   Thomas Gardner, Associate Professor of English, Virginia Polytechnic Institute and State University

T.J.H.   Thomas John Hudak, Associate Professor of Linguistics, Arizona State University

T.J.M.   Timothy J. Materer, Professor of English, University of Missouri

T.J.R.   Timothy J. Reiss, Professor and Chairman of the Department of Comparative Literature, New York University

T.O.S.   Thomas O. Sloane, Professor of Rhetoric, University of California

T.P.R.   Thomas P. Roche, Professor of English, Princeton University

T.R.A.   Timothy R. Austin, Associate Professor of English, Loyola University of Chicago

T.S.H.   Talat S. Halman, author

T.T.   Tulku Thondup Rinpoche, Buddhayana Foundation

T.V.F.B.   T. V. F. Brogan, Indiana University South Bend

T.W.   Tibor Wlassics, William R. Kenan Professor of Italian, University of Virginia

U.K.G.   Ulrich K. Goldsmith, Professor Emeritus of German and Comparative Literature, University of Colorada

U.T.H.   Urban T. Holmes, Jr., late William R. Kenan Professor of Romance Languages, University of North Carolina

U.W.   Uriel Weinreich, late Professor of Yiddish, Columbia University

V.B.L.   Vincent B. Leitch, Professor of English, Purdue University

V.D.   Vinay Dharwadker, Assistant Professor of Commonwealth Literature, University of Georgia

V.D.M.   Vasa D. Mihailovich, Professor of Slavic Literature, University of North Carolina

V.E.   Victor Erlich, Bensinger Professor Emeritus, Russian Literature., Yale University

CONTRIBUTORS

V.H.   Vernon Hall, Jr., Professor Emeritus of Comparative Literature, University of Wisconsin at Madison

V.J.   Vera Javarek, late Lecturer in Serbo-Croatian Language and Literature, University of London

V.P.   Victoria Pedrick, Associate Professor of Classics, Georgetown University

V.P.N.   Virgil P. Nemoianu, Professor of English and Comparative Literature, Catholic University of America

V.W.G.   Vernon W. Gras, Professor of English, George Mason University

W.A.   William Arrowsmith, University Professor and Professor of Classics, Boston University

W.B.   Willard Bohn, Professor of French, Illinois State University

W.B.F.   Wolfgang Bernhard Fleischmann, late Professor of Comparative Literature, Montclair State College

W.B.P.   William Bowman Piper, Professor of English, Rice University

W.C.B.   Wayne C. Booth, Professor of English, University of Chicago

W.D.P.   William D. Paden, Professor of French, Northwestern University

W.E.H.   William E. Harkins, Professor of Slavic Languages, Columbia University

W.F.   Wallace Fowlie, James B. Duke Professor Emeritus of Romance Studies, Duke University

W.H.   Wade Heaton, author

W.H.R.   William H. Race, Associate Professor of Classical Studies, Vanderbilt University

W.H.Y.   William H. Youngren, Professor of English, Boston College

W.J.K.   William J. Kennedy, Professor of Comparative Literature, Cornell University

W.J.T.M.   W. J. T. Mitchell, Professor of English and of Art and Design, University of Chicago

W.L.H.   William L. Hanaway, Professor of Persian, University of Pennsylvania

W.M.   Wallace Martin, Professor of English, University of Toledo

W.P.H.   Wolfhart P. Heinrichs, Professor of Arabic, Harvard University

W.P.L.   Winfred P. Lehmann, Louann and Larry Temple Centennial Professor Emeritus in the Humanities, University of Texas at Austin

W.S.A.   William S. Anderson, Professor of Latin and Comparative Literature, University of California at Berkeley

W.T.   Wesley Trimpi, Professor of English, Stanford University

W.V.O'C.   William Van O'Connor, late Professor of English, University of California at Davis

W.W.   Winthrop Wetherbee, Professor of Classics and English, Cornell University

W.W.P.   Walter Ward Parks, Associate Professor of English, Louisiana State University

THE NEW
PRINCETON
ENCYCLOPEDIA
OF POETRY AND POETICS

A

ABECEDARIUS, Abecedarian (Med. Lat. term for an ABC primer). An alphabetic acrostic (q.v.), a poem in which each line or stanza begins with a successive letter of the alphabet. In modern times the a. has been widely viewed as a mere word game or mnemonic device for children, but in many ancient cultures the form was commonly associated with divinity, being used for prayers, hymns, and oracles. In divine poetry not only the Word but even letters and sounds, given pattern, bear mystical significance and incantatory power—as do numbers (see NUMEROLOGY). The a., only one of several such forms, held even greater significance for being the archetype of the Alpha-Omega trope. But even outside religious contexts the principle held power, since in the a. the master code of the lang. is made the constitutive device of the form. The earliest attested examples are Semitic, and abecedarii held an esp. important place in Heb. religious poetry, to judge from the dozen-odd examples in the OT. The best known of these is Psalm 119, which comprises 22 octave stanzas, one for each letter of the Heb. alphabet, all lines of each octave beginning with the same letter. The more common stanzaic type, however, is that used by Chaucer for his *ABC*, where only the first line of the stanza bears the letter (cf. the ornate initials of illuminated mss.). Psalms 111–12 represent the astrophic type, wherein the initials of each successive line form the alphabet. In the Japanese form, *Iroha mojigusari*, the first line must begin with the first and end with the second letter of the alphabet, the second with the second and third, and so on. A number of abecedarii are extant in Cl. and Alexandrian Gr., but they were also popular in Byzantine Gr. and are copious in Med. Lat.: St. Augustine's well-known abecedarian psalm against the Donatists (Migne, *PL* 43.23 ff.) is the earliest known example of medieval rhythmical verse.—K. Krumbacher, *Gesch. der byzantinischen Lit.*, 2d ed. (1897); C. Daux, *Le Chant abécédaire de St. Augustin* (1905); H. Leclercq, "Abécédaire," *Dictionnaire d'archéologie chrétienne*, ed. F. Cabrol (1907); Meyer, v. 2, ch. 6; F. Dornseiff, *Das Alphabet in Mystik und Magie*, 2d ed. (1925), sect. 14; R. Marcus, "Alphabetic Acrostics in the Hellenistic and Roman Periods," *JNES* 6 (1947); Raby, *Secular.* T.V.F.B.

ABSENCE. See DECONSTRUCTION.

ABSTRACT. See CONCRETE AND ABSTRACT.

ABSTRACT POEM. Edith Sitwell described the poems in her *Façade* (1923) as "abstract poems," that is, "patterns in sound." She may have meant "abstract" as that term is used in painting (i.e. nonrepresentational), or as in music, in the sense in which music is said to be abstract (see ABSTRACT AND CONCRETE). In any event, such a poetry would seem an attempt to continue the program of Fr. *poésie pure* (see PURE POETRY) and perhaps *lettrisme* (q.v.), hence one precursor of later 20th-c. "sound poetry" and "language poetry" (qq.v.).—*A Celebration for E. S.*, ed. J. Garcia Villa (1948); E. Sitwell, "On My Poetry," *Orpheus* 2 (1949); J. Lindsay, Intro. to E. S., *Façade and Other Poems* (1950); Morier, s.v. "Poème abstrait." T.V.F.B.

ACATALECTIC. See CATALEXIS.

ACCENT (Gr. *prosôdia*, Lat. *accentus*, "song added to speech," i.e. the melody of lang.).

   I. TERMINOLOGY
   II. DEGREES AND TYPES
   III. HISTORY

In the general sense, the emphasis or prominence that some syllables in speech bear over others, regardless of how achieved (the intonational means are via pitch, stress, or length); in the specific sense, a synonym for stress, a dimension of speech not reflected in most Western systems of orthography. Technically, "stress" in linguistics denotes intensity of articulatory force, resulting from greater musculatory exertion in forming a sound.

I. TERMINOLOGY. Prominence of a syllable may be produced by stress, but it may also be produced by obtruded (raised or lowered) pitch (fundamental frequency) or increased length (duration) or (most often) by a combination of these factors, which have been found to correlate highly with one another (stressed syllables are often higher in pitch and increased in length as well); together the three phenomena constitute an "intonational contour." Up until the 1950s, it was common to speak of a "pitch a." in tonic (pitch-based) langs. such as Ch., Japanese, and ancient Gr., as opposed to the "stress a." of the mod. Germanic langs., incl. Eng. But subsequent work (e.g. Bolinger), which was in fact in accord with a long line of theorizing by prosodists (e.g. Bright), suggested that pitch was after all the crucial element of "a." even in stress langs. At the same time, Allen has suggested that, contrary to centuries of trad., stress not pitch was the basis of a. in ancient Gr. At present one may say only that the phonetic phenomena concerning a. are still not fully understood. Since stress is not readily isolated from other factors, it is still not clear whether stress is after all a real entity in itself or simply the resultant of perceived prominence caused mainly by pitch and length, but the latter view looks more likely.

Usage of the terms "stress" and "a." consequently shows a welter of variation; Crystal reserves "stress" for word-stress and "a." for prominence at the phrase and sentence levels ("stress belongs to the lexicon, and a. to the utterance"), but many others speak of "sentence stress." Bolinger, emphasizing pitch, distinguishes (word) *stress*, (pitch) *a.* (on stressed syllables), and *intonation* (pitch changes at the sentence level). Liberman and Prince, by contrast, posit stress as a relation between syllables in a hierarchy above the lexical level, rather than assigning it as a feature of the segment (so Jespersen 1901). But these are technical problems in linguistics. In nontechnical usage, the simplest thing to say is that "a." in the sense of emphasis is the more general term, "stress" the more precise, and that "stress" can denote intensity as opposed to pitch or length. Most of the conceptual disputes in metrics over the past two millennia resulted from confusions about the nature of "quantity" vs. "a.," deeply interrelated acoustic phenomena whose subtlety and complexity were not much penetrated until the advent of modern linguistics.

II. DEGREES AND TYPES. Monosyllables and short polysyllables, particularly substantives such as nouns, normally bear a stress; this is "word-stress." In longer polysyllables (which form by compounding shorter words, prefixes, and suffixes), one stress dominates all the others, reducing them to unstressed syllables or to a secondary degree of stress. How many degrees of stress are thus created, and perceived, is a disputed question. The Ren. grammarians, following those in Med. Lat., who in turn followed the ancient Greeks, held that there were three, which they called "acute," "circumflex," and "grave." The structural linguists of the mid 20th c. (i.e. Trager-Smith) claimed there were four (primary, secondary, tertiary, weak, denoted 1-2-3-4, respectively, and based on loudness), as in the noun phrase *elevator operator*, stressed 1-4-3-4 2-4-3-4, though there is some evidence that in ordinary speech auditors do not hear that many degrees. The extra degree added by Trager-Smith is for sentence stress and corresponds to Chomsky and Halle's nucleus; inside a given word there are still only three degrees. As in the formation of polysyllabic words, so in the formation of phrases one stress comes to dominate all the others within its domain. So too at the level of the sentence: this process of dominance, of forming stress hierarchies, is general. All other things being equal, the Nuclear Stress Rule dictates that within any major syntactic constituent, the rightmost major stress will be primary, weakening all others to the left. At the sentence level,

its effect is to make the last major element the strongest.

Word-stress is relatively fixed and is coded into the lexicon (it can be found in the dictionary), being controlled by the phonological and morphological rules of the lang. But phrase- and sentence-stress is more variable, depending in part on syntactic rules but also on context and on the emphases that the speaker wishes to make in that particular context. Word-stress thus controls whether a syllable *can* be stressed, but semantic intent and other factors control whether it *will*. Stress at the phrasal or sentence level was traditionally called "rhetorical a."—so Alexander Gil (1619): "accentus est duplex Grammaticus aut Rhetoricus" (ed. Danielsson and Gabrielson [1972], 124). One result of it is that a speaker can say the same word or sentence several different ways by moving the main a. and mean quite different things. "Prój́ect" is a noun, but "projéct" is a verb. One can say "I never said I loved you," for example, so as to mean (stressing "loved") "I may have said I *liked* you but I never said I *loved* you" or (stressing the second "I") "I said *Jack* loved you" or (stressing "you") "I said I loved *Ann*, not you, Diane."

Such cases as this, where mere shift of stress deeply alters meaning, are instances of the phenomenon known as "contrastive stress," which Shakespeare exploits to effect in Sonnet 130 and which Donne employs frequently (Melton's "arsis-thesis variation"). This is an important device in poetry. If, to take another example, we alter Ben Jonson's line and say, "love me only with thine eyes," which words shall we stress—*love* me with thine eyes (don't give me hateful looks)? love *me* (only me, not anyone else)? only with thine *eyes* (not with any other part of you)? Semantic clues from the wider context of the poem may help us decide. But a more important determinant in metrical poetry is *meter* (q.v.), which is not determined by but must align with and so helps us determine the intended or most probable stressings (meanings) of the line. Meter regulates the placement of stresses in sentences according to a fixed scheme via a process called *modulation*, in which stress values can be demoted or promoted. Knowing the meter will therefore help one to elucidate sense; conversely, grasping the sense of lines in an unfamiliar poem can help one correctly identify its meter. It is one of the great limitations of free verse (q.v.) that it abandons both these hermeneutic instruments.

III. HISTORY. To give a history of a. in the poetries of the West is really to give a history of our progressive understanding, or clarification, of a. in the poetries in the West. In Gr., a. was, according to both the ancient authorities and most modern scholars (though see Allen), determined by pitch. The quantitative meters of Gr. poetry (q.v.), however, were based on syllabic length (see CLASSICAL PROSODY). When Ennius appropriated Gr. meters for Lat. poetry, there may have been an indigenous native trad. of stress-based meters in Italic—the Saturnian (q.v.)—which was thereafter suppressed from Lat. artverse, surviving only in popular verseforms such as soldiers' songs; or it may have served a more important role we do not now well understand (see Beare). In any event, sometime about the 3d–4th cs. A.D., in some massive linguistic transformation still not understood, a. based on pitch was replaced by a. based on intensity or stress in Lat., with the result that a. replaced syllabic length as the basis of verse composition. Subsequent Old Germanic versification is heavily accentual.

With the decline of Rome, understanding of the (artificial) rules of quantity were progressively lost, and Med. Lat. "metrical verse" (based on quantity) begins to be replaced by "rhythmical verse" (based on a.)—first and most importantly in a popular form of poetry, the hymn (q.v.), expressly developed by Augustine, Ambrose, and Hilary for easy singing and memorization by the illiterate masses. Quantitative verse in Lat. continued to be written in quantity at least up to the 12th c., but only as a scholarly exercise.

With the emergence of the European vernaculars, each Romance poetry had to invent a prosody for itself. The general view at present is that the metrical and stanza forms were taken over from Med. Lat., while the rules for accentuation and syllabification varied somewhat in each lang., their prosodies reflecting this fact also (Norberg, Pulgram). Accents do not have the force in Fr. that they do in the Germanic langs. such as Eng. In Eng., word-stress greatly outweighs word-boundary: the stressed syllable is lengthened. But in Fr. the last syllable in the word is characteristically lengthened, while word stress is reduced in favor of phrasal stress. These phrasal stresses at line-end and before the caesura, called *accents toniques*, are bolstered on occasion by *accents d'appui* ("prop" as., made by promotion of weakly stressed syllables) and *accents contre-toniques* (as. on the antepenult of polysyllabic words without mute -e). The Fr. *accent oratoire* corresponds to Eng. "rhetorical a." In sum, Fr. prosody (meter) is phrasal in nature, based on rhythmic groupings in verse identical to those in prose. Eng. prosody, by contrast, developed smaller, nonphrasal groups—feet—each based on one stress. Romance words which came into Eng. (esp. in ME) underwent "recession of a.," by which Eng. speakers shifted left to the beginning of the word the rightward word-stress of the Fr.

In the Ren. reaction against medievalism, the Humanists looked back to Classicism, and esp. the prestigious trad. of Cl. prosody: consequently, quantitative meters were successively attempted in the 16th c. in every vernacular, first It., then Fr., Eng., and Ger. But length is simply not phonemic in the mod. langs., so any metric based on it is doomed to be artificial. Stress, by contrast, is phonemic; and when independent thinking about poetics also emerged in the Ren., many critics and prosodists recognized this fact—though only dimly, and with no accurate terminology with which to describe what they heard and felt when they read poetry. Most of the Eng. Ren. prosodists (collected in Smith) grasped, intuitively, the existence of stress, but they were unable clearly to distinguish stress from pitch (as indeed many still do not), and the terms which they had available—those descended from antiquity—were of little help. The Ren. grammarians often speak of a raising and lowering of the voice; Lily treats a. s.v. "Tonus," and identifies three varieties: grave, circumflex, and acute. An accurate terminology only begins to appear in the 18th c., with its renewed interest in the origin of lang. It is abetted materially by the rise of Philology in the 19th c., esp. in Germany, though here too most of the terminology continues to be explicitly Classical. In Eng. one finds fresh air in the discussions in the London Philological Society in the latter 19th c. (Ellis, Sweet). But it is chiefly in the 20th c. that linguistics, now fully emerged as an autonomous discipline, begins to develop instruments and techniques for analyzing precisely the phenomena of acoustic phonetics. As for integrating stress within a unified theory, structural linguistics described stress patterns by assigning levels or degrees of stress (see above); generative phonology, following upon (and imitating) the transformational grammar of Chomsky, attempted to find rules which would generate correct stressings but exclude all others and which would mesh with the rules of syntax (see Liberman and Prince, Selkirk). "Generative metrics" (q.v.) sought to apply such rules to scansion (see Beaver) but failed to grasp the nature of convention (esp. metrical) in poetry. Modern linguistics has swept away much of the detritus of two millennia of confusion, error, and received opinion. But if concepts such as pitch and stress have become clearer, they also have become far more complex. The state of linguistic theory at present may well suggest that our understanding of these intricate phenomena is still far from complete.

See now ACCENTUAL VERSE; DURATION; FRENCH PROSODY; HOVERING ACCENT; ISOCHRONISM; METER; PITCH; PROSODY; RELATIVE STRESS PRINCIPLE; TIMBRE; VERSIFICATION.

J. Hart, *The Opening of the Unreasonable Writing of Our Inglish Toung* (1551); J. Steele, *Prosodia rationalis*, 2d ed. (1779); A. J. Ellis, *On Early Eng. Pronunciation*, 2 v. (1868–69), "On the Physical Constituents of A. and Emphasis," *TPS* (1873–74); Smith; Schipper, *History*, ch. 8; Thieme, 390—lists Fr. works to 1912; P. Habermann, "Akzent," "Takt," *Reallexikon I*; B. Danielsson, *Studies in the Accentuation of Polysyllabic Loan-Words in Eng.* (1948); G. L. Trager and H. L. Smith, Jr., *An Outline of Eng. Structure* (1951); Beare—still essential; Norberg; P. Habermann and W. Mohr, "Hebung und

Senkung," *Reallexikon* 1.623–29; D. L. Bolinger, *Forms of Eng.* (1965), pt. 1, *Intonation and Its Parts* (1986), ch. 2; S. Chatman, *A Theory of Meter* (1965), chs. 3, 4, App.; J. McAuley, *Versification* (1966); E. J. Dobson, *Eng. Pronunciation 1500–1700*, 2d ed., 2 v. (1968)—historical phonology; P. Garde, *L'A.* (1968); N. Chomsky and M. Halle, *The Sound Pattern of Eng.* (1968)—generative phonology; J. C. Beaver, "Contrastive Stress and Metered Verse," *Lang&S* 2 (1969), "The Rules of Stress in Eng. Verse," *Lang.* 47 (1971); D. Crystal, *Prosodic Systems and Intonation in Eng.* (1969), *Dict. of Linguistics and Phonetics*, 2d ed. (1985); I. Lehiste, *Suprasegmentals* (1970); M. Halle and S. J. Keyser, *Eng. Stress* (1971)—better avoided; W. S. Allen, *A. and Rhythm* (1973), esp. chs. 5, 7, 12, 15, 16—stress in Gr.; E. Pulgram, *Latin-Romance Phonology: Prosodics and Metrics* (1975); S. F. Schmerling, *Aspects of Eng. Sentence-Stress* (1976); M. Liberman and A. S. Prince, "On Stress and Ling. Rhythm," *LingI* 8 (1977)—metrical trees; *Studies in Stress and A.*, ed. L. Hyman (1977); I. Fónagy and P. Léon, *L'A. français contemporain* (1979); D. R. Ladd, *The Structure of Intonational Meaning* (1980); Scott, 24–28, 39–55; Brogan, 54–57, 110–19; Mazaleyrat, ch. 4; Morier, s.v. "A." and "Contre-a.," and also "Consonne," "Voyelle," and "Syllabe," some of the latter very long articles; E. Fudge, *Eng. Word-Stress* (1984); E. O. Selkirk, *Phonology and Syntax* (1984)—grid theory; M. Halle and J.-R. Vergnaud, *An Essay on Stress* (1987); A. C. Gimson, *Intro. to the Pronunciation of Eng.*, 4th ed. (1989); D. Oliver, *Poetry and Narrative in Performance* (1989).   T.V.F.B.

ACCENTUAL VERSE or "stress verse." Verse organized by count of stresses, not by count of syllables. Many prosodists of the 18th, 19th, and early 20th cs. looked upon most medieval verse, a goodly amount of Ren. verse, and all popular verse down to the present as loose, rough, or irregular in number of syllables and in placement of stresses; from this assumption (not demonstration), they concluded that regulated count of stresses was the only criterion of the meter. Schipper for example effectually views most ME and ModE 4-stress verse as descended from OE alliterative verse. But in this he misconceived the nature of OE prosody (see ENGLISH PROSODY); and other prosodists who ought to have known better have lumped together verse of very different metrical textures drawn from widely different social registers and textual contexts, treating all of them under the general rubric of "a. v." But it is not that easy. In other metrical features the several varieties of 4-stress verse vary considerably, as they do also in register and derivation: ballad meter (q.v.), for example, uses only a relatively few rhyme schemes and stanza forms, and 4-stress song lyrics derive from very different sources than early ME accentual verse. These facts suggest that stress-count may not be the only or even the most important characteristic of a. v. as a genus. Isochronism (q.v.) has sometimes been suggested as a criterion, but some metrists hold that this can only be a feature of performance (q.v.), not of meter.

If, consequently, a. v. is to be retained as a distinct metrical category at all, we must isolate the similarities among the species in order to identify the differentia of the class; and then we must show either different features or else gradations in strictness of form which differentiate the species within the class. Though most of that work has not yet been done, several varieties of a. v. have been proposed in the Western langs.: (1) folkverse as opposed to artverse, i.e. the large class of popular (e.g. greeting-card) verse, song, nursery rhymes (q.v.), college cheers and chants, slogans, logos, and jingles—both Malof and Attridge rightly insist on the centrality of the 4-stress line here; (2) ballad and hymn meter, specifically the meter of the Eng. and Scottish popular ballads and of the metrical psalters in the Sternhold-Hopkins line; (3) literary imitations of genuine ballad meter such as the *Christabel* meter (q.v.); (4) popular song (see SONG)—an extremely large class; (5) genuine oral poetry (q.v.), which indeed seems to show a fixed number of stresses per line but in fact is constructed by lexico-metrical formulaic phrases (see FORMULA); (6) simple doggerel (q.v.), i.e. lines that hardly scan at all except for stress count, whether because of authorial ineptitude, scribal misprision, textual corruption, or reader misperception—there are many scraps of late medieval verse which *seem* to be so; (7) literary verse (often stichic) which is less regular than accentual-syllabic principles would demand but clearly not entirely free, e.g. the 4-stress lines which Helen Gardner has pointed out in Eliot's *Four Quartets* (*The Art of T. S. Eliot*, 1949); (8) Ger. *Knittelvers* (q.v.), both in a freer, late-medieval variety subsequently revived for literary and dramatic purposes by Goethe and Brecht, and in a stricter, 16th-c. variety (*Hans-Sachs verse*) in octosyllabic couplets; and (9) Rus. *dol'nik* (q.v.) verse, a 20th-c. meter popularized by Blok, mainly in 3-stress lines: interestingly, this form devolved from literary verse, not folk-, as in Eng. and Ger. In definitions of all the preceding varieties there has been an assumption that a. v. is isoaccentual; if one defines it more broadly (organized only on stresses but not always the same number per line), one would then admit Ger. *freie Rhythmen* and *freie Verse* (qq.v.) and possibly Fr. 19th-c. *vers libéré* (q.v.). But these verge on free verse (q.v.).

Beyond typology, there is evidence to suggest that there is something more distinctive about the metrical organization of a. v. than mere regularity of stress count. When Robert Bridges, the Eng. poet and prosodist, studied a. v. at the turn of the 20th c., he discovered a paradox in claims that a. v. works by counting the natural stresses in the line. For example, despite Coleridge's claims that

Christabel is in a "new" *meter* and that every line in it will be found to have exactly 4 stresses, the poem actually contains a number of problematic lines, like "How drowsily it crew," which cannot by any reasonable standard carry 4 natural accents. Of this line Bridges remarks: "in stress-verse this line can have only two accents . . . but judging from other lines in the poem, it was almost certainly meant to have three, and if so, the second of these is a conventional accent; it does not occur in the speech but in the metre, and has to be imagined because the metre suggests or requires it; and it is plain that *if the stress is to be the rule of the metre, the metre cannot be called on to provide the stress*" (88; italics added). For Bridges, as for everyone else, the definition of true "a. v." is that it operates on only two principles: "THE STRESS GOVERNS THE RHYTHM" and "THE STRESSES MUST ALL BE TRUE SPEECH-STRESSES" (92; caps original). This is not true in accentual-syllabic verse, where it is the function of the meter to establish and preserve in the mind's ear a paradigm, an abstract pattern, such that if the line itself does not supply the *requisite number* of accents *in the requisite places*, the pattern shall supply them mentally. But if we must do this in *Christabel*, either *Christabel* is not a. v. (but rather accentual-syllabic) or else a. v. does not work by simply counting stresses. If the former, and if that proved true of all the other 8 types enumerated above, then a. v. simply does not exist. If the latter, then a. v. is not a *meter*, but rather something else, or less, than metrical. But in effect these amount to the same thing: a. v. is not a meter in the same way that accentual-syllabic verse is meter. Bridges concludes: "Just as quantitative verse has its quantitive prosody, syllabic verse has its syllabic prosody, and a. v. will have its a. prosody. All three are equally dealing with speech-rhythm, and they all approach it differently, and thus obtain different effects. It might be possible, perhaps, as it is certainly conceivable, to base the whole art of versification on speech-rhythm, and differentiate the prosodies secondarily by their various qualities of effect upon the speech. But no one has ever attempted that" (110–11). See now ALLITERATIVE VERSE IN MODERN LANGUAGES; BALLAD METER; EQUIVALENCE; METER; PROSODY; VERSIFICATION; see also NUMBER.

Schipper; R. Bridges, "Appendix on A. V.," *Milton's Prosody* (1901, rev. 1921); G. Saintsbury, *Hist. of Eng. Prosody* (1906–10); W. Kayser, *Kleine deutsche Versschule* (1946); J. Bailey, "The Stress-Meter of Goethe's *Der Erlkönig*," *Lang&S* 2 (1969); J. Malof, *A Manual of Eng. Meters* (1970), chs. 3–4; M. G. Tarlinskaja, "Meter and Rhythm of Pre-Chaucerian Rhymed Verse," *Linguistics* 121 (1974), *Eng. Verse: Theory and Hist.* (1976); Scott; Brogan, 319–37; D. Attridge, *The Rhythms of Eng. Poetry* (1982); Scherr. T.V.F.B.

ACCENTUAL-SYLLABIC VERSE. See METER.

ACCESSUS AD AUCTORES. See MEDIEVAL POETICS.

ACCORD. See NEAR RHYME.

ACEPHALOUS, "headless," said of lines of verse, namely that they are missing an initial syllable (Ger. *fehlende Auftakt*, "suppression of the anacrusis"). Though it is undeniable that in some runs of regular accentual-syllabic verse occasional lines will be found that are simply missing their first syllables, whether from design or defect of textual transmission, the claims that have most often been made about the concept of acephaly have been made on more sweeping grounds, involving metrical phenomena which are, in fact, capable of varying interpretation. It used to be held, for example, that there are some eight or nine a. lines in Chaucer, including—depending on how one treats final -e, hence how one scans—the first line of the *General Prologue* of the *Canterbury Tales*. It was also claimed that a missing first syllable changes rising rhythm to falling (q.v.)—so Schipper. Many temporal and musical theories of meter are congenial to the notion of a. lines as important variants rather than simply defects, but such theories are not now widely accepted. If, however, acephaly, as fore-clipping, is disputed, the converse phenomenon, *catalexis* (q.v.), the cutting off of final syllables, is very well attested; but this may in fact be unrelated. See now ANACRUSIS.—Brogan, K106, K125, K150, K344; Dale, 22 ff.; G. T. Wright, *Shakespeare's Metrical Art* (1988). T.V.F.B.

ACMEISM (Gr. *acme*, "utmost," "a pinnacle of"). A school in modern Rus. poetry. In 1910, A. Akhmatova, S. Gorodetskij, N. Gumilëv, M. Kuzmin, and O. Mandelstam—a group of young Rus. poets gathered about the magazine *Apollon*—set out to chart a new course in Rus. verse writing. The acmeists spurned the esoteric vagueness of symbolism (q.v.), which then dominated the Rus. literary scene, with its vaunted "spirit of music," i.e. the tendency to achieve maximum emotional suggestiveness at the expense of lucidity and sensory vividness. They strove instead for "Apollonian" clarity, for graphic sharpness of outline, and sought to convey the texture of things rather than their inner soul. To the acmeist, the poet was not a seer or a prophet but a craftsman (hence the name of the principal literary association of the acmeists, the "Guild of Poets"). These tenets found expression in the semantically dense and phonically saturated poetry of Osip Mandelstam (1891–1938), which combines classical themes with "modern" compactness of imagery, and in the sparse, intimate verse of Anna Akhmatova (1889–1966), one of modern Russia's finest lyric poets. Nikolay Gumilëv (1886–1921), who, as a leading theorist of the school, preached neoclassicism, often tended in his own poetry toward the flamboyantly exotic and romantic. A. produced much

ACROSTIC

distinguished poetry, but as a literary movement it proved short-lived. Efforts to revive it after the Revolution were hindered by Gumilëv's tragic death in 1921 and by the unhospitable cultural climate, with the official Soviet critics accusing the acmeists of aloofness from social problems and the bulk of the literary avant-garde scorning their alleged aesthetic conservatism. Mandelstam's complex poetic evolution led him well beyond the confines of the initial acmeist poetics of lucidity and precision. Nevertheless, all the surviving members of the acmeist group, with the exception of Gorodetsky, persisted in calling themselves acmeists even as they sought to reinterpret a. as a distinctive moral and cultural stance. See now RUSSIAN POETRY; STRUCTURALISM, *Moscow-Tartu School.*

V. Žirmunskij, "Preodolevshie simvolizm," *Voprosy teorii literatury* (1928); D. S. Mirsky, *A Hist. of Rus. Lit.* (1949); N. Gumilëv, *Sel. Works* (1972); "Toward a Definition of A.," ed. D. Mickiewicz, *RLJ* (Spec. Supp. Iss., 1975); O. Mandelstam, *Complete Critical Prose and Letters* (1979); J. G. Harris, "A.," in Terras.　　　　　　　　　　　　V.E.

ACROSTIC (Gr. "at the tip of the verse"). In an a. the first letter of each line or stanza spells out either the alphabet (an *abecedarius*, q.v.) or a name—usually of the author or the addressee (a patron, the beloved, a saint)—or the title of the work (e.g. Plautus; Ben Jonson's *The Alchemist*). More rarely, the initials spell out a whole sentence—the oldest extant examples, seven Babylonian texts dating from ca. 1000 B.C., are of this sort (they use the first syllable of each ideogram). By far the most common form is that which reveals, while it purports to conceal, the name of the author, as in the a. Cicero says Ennius wrote, or Villon's a. to his mother which spells "Villone." The spelling is usually straightforward but may be in anagram for the sake of concealment. If the medial letter of each line spells out the name, the poem is a *mesostich*, if the final letter, a *telestich*; if both initials and finals are used, the poem is a double a. (two of the Babylonian as. are such), if all three, a triple a. Finals may also read from the bottom up. It is significant that recognition of an a. depends on perceiving not the aural rhythms or the sense of the text but its visual shape.

From the forms just enumerated it is but one step to *carmina quadrata* and the fantastic word-square *intexti* of Hrabanus Maurus—with a modern analogue in Edward Taylor's poem to Elizabeth Fitch—and from there but one step more to *carmina figurata* or true pattern poetry (q.v.), with which as. are commonly found in ancient texts (e.g. the Gr. Anthol.). In the East, as. are found in both Chinese (ring-poems, wherein one can begin reading at any character) and Japanese poetry (*kakushidai* and *mono no na*).

As. are the kind of mannered artifice that will be popular in any Silver Age poetry; they flour-ished in Alexandria and in the Middle Ages, being written by Boniface, Bede, Fortunatus, Boccaccio, Deschamps, and Marot among many. Commodian has a book of 80 as., the *Instructiones*; Aldhelm's *De laudibus virginitatis* is not only a double a. made out of its first line, but the last line is the first line read backwards, making a box. The longest a. in the world is apparently Boccaccio's *Amorosa visione*, which spells out three entire sonnets. In the Ren., Du Bellay excepted the ingenious a. and anagram from his sweeping dismissal of medieval Fr. verseforms. Sir John Davies wrote a posy of 26 as. to Queen Elizabeth (*Hymnes Of Astraea*, 1599). The modern disparagement begins as early as Addison (*Spectator*, 60), but as. were very popular among the Victorians. In Poe's valentine poem to Frances Sargent Osgood, her name is spelled by the first letter of the first line, the second letter of the second line, and so on. Outside verse, this process of elevating initials into a "higher" script produces *acronyms* (snafu, gulag), now very common. In the early Christian church the symbol of the fish is such an acronym: the initials of the five Gr. words in the phrase Jesus-Christ-God's-Son-Saviour spell out the Gr. word for fish, *ichthys*. See also ANAGRAM.

K. Krumbacher, "Die Acrostichis in der griechischen Kirchenpoesie," *Sitzungsberichte der königlich-bayerische Akad. der Wiss., philos.-philol.-hist. Klasse* (1904), 551–691; A. Kopp, "Das Akrostichon als kritische Hilfsmittel," *ZDP* 32 (1900); H. Leclercq, "Acrostiche," *Dictionnaire d'archéologie chrétienne*, ed. F. Cabrol (1907); E. Graf, "Akrostichis," Pauly-Wissowa; Kastner; R. A. Knox, *Book of As.* (1924); F. Dornseiff, *Das Alphabet in Mystik und Magie*, 2d ed. (1925); Lote, 2.305; *Reallexikon*; W. G. Lambert, *Babylonian Wisdom Lit.* (1960), ch. 3; R. F. G. Sweet, "A Pair of Double As. in Akkadian," *Orientalia* 38 (1969); T. Augarde, *Oxford Guide to Word Games* (1984); Miner et al., pt. 4.　　　　　　　　　　　T.V.F.B.

ADNOMINATIO. See PUN.

ADONIC (Adoneus, *versus Adonius*). In Gr. and Lat. poetry, an Aeolic (q.v.) or dactylic clausula which took the form of the last two feet of the dactylic hexameter, i.e. $- \cup \cup - -$, and took its name from the refrain of the song to the god Adonis: *o tŏn Ādōnīn* (Sappho, fr. 168 [Lobel-Page]). According to the Alexandrian grammarians, the A. formed the fourth line of the Sapphic (q.v.) strophe, although often there is no word-end between the third and fourth lines (which suggests the two lines were metrically one), as is true in Lat. also—e.g. Horace *Odes* 1.2.19 ff.: *u/xorius amnis* ($- / - \cup \cup - -$). But Horace seems to have followed the Alexandrians, for usually there is word-end between the Sapphic hendecasyllable (q.v.) and the A., and twice there is hiatus. As. appear together with other aeolic cola in Plautus and Seneca. Columbanus (6th c.) wrote As.;

Boethius combined the hemiepes (q.v.) with the A. (*Cons. phil.* 1.2). The A. verse was also used in stichic poems and in strophes of various lengths in Med. Lat. verse, both in metrical (quantitative) and rhythmical (accentual) meters.—Norberg; C. Questa, *Introduzione alla metrica di Plauto* (1967): Crusius; Halporn et al.   J.W.H.

ADYNATON. The impossibility device: the rhetorical figure for magnifying an event by comparison with something impossible, e.g. "I'd walk a million miles for one of your smiles" (Al Jolson, "My Mammy"); cf. "Hell will freeze over before I will. . . ." Important too is the related figure of the impossibility of finding the right words (*aporia*), i.e. the "inexpressibility topos," e.g. "Words fail me"; "I can't begin to tell you how much. . . ." In Gr. and Lat. lit. the two most common varieties of a. are the "sooner than" type, which claims that the impossible will come true sooner than the event in question will take place, and the "impossible count" type, referring to the number of sands on the shore, stars in the sky, etc. These varieties do not occur in the lit. of the Middle Ages, or are very rare. By contrast, a different brand known as the *fatras* (q.v.) was cultivated by OF writers; this dealt with impossible or ridiculous accomplishments. Occitan poets used an allied form made popular by Petrarch's sonnet "Pace non trovo e non ho da far guerra." The Gr. and Lat. types were, however, abundantly revived by Petrarchists all over Europe, who made use of them either to emphasize the cruelty of the lady or to affirm their love. In *Antony and Cleopatra*, Antony employs a. to dramatize his intent to remain in Egypt despite his Roman responsibilities: "Let Rome in Tiber melt and the wide arch / Of the rang'd empire fall. Here is my space" (1.1.33). A. may also be used negatively to assert a contrary impossibility, as in *Richard II*: "Not all the water in the rough rude sea, / Can wash the balme off from an anointed King" (3.2.54–55). Other famous examples include those found in Marvell's "To his Coy Mistress," Browning's "Up at a Villa—Down in the City," Auden's "As I walked Out one Evening," and, strikingly, in Louis MacKay's "Ill-tempered Lover." In East Asian poetry, varieties of *adynata* are used as a rhetorical device in the poetry of praise. The poems and hymns of blessing and sacrifice in the *Book of Songs*, the oldest extant anthol. of Chinese poetry, use magnificent similes and numbers, and a Middle Korean poem, "Song of the Gong," uses the myth of the impossible ("*when* the roasted chestnut sprouts, *then* . . ."). Lanham's position, that a. is "sometimes a confession that words fail us," would tend to place a. in the category of metalogisms characterized by Group Mu as the suppression of units of expression, i.e. among figures like *litotes, aposiopesis* (qq.v.), *reticentia*, and *silence*. A. thus might also serve the function of promising rather than maintaining silence.—R. H. Coon, "The Reversal of Nature as a Rhetorical

Figure," *Indiana Univ. Studies* 15 (1928); H. V. Canter, "The Figure A. in Gr. and Lat. Poetry," *AJP* 51 (1930); E. Dutoit, *Le Thème de l'a. dans la poésie antique* (1936); Curtius 94–98, 159 ff.; L. C. Porter, *La Fatrasie et le fatras* (1960); R. Lanham, *A Handlist of Rhetorical Terms* (1968); C. Petzsch in *Euphorion* 75 (1981): 303 ff.—on impossibility catalogs; Group Mu.; M. Shapiro, "The A. in Petrarch's Sestinas," *Dante, Petrarch, Boccaccio*, ed. A. S. Bernardo and A. L. Pellegrini (1983).A.W.H.; T.V.F.B.

AEOLIC. The name usually given to a class of ancient Gr. lyric meters, so called because first attested in the poems of Sappho and Alcaeus, which were composed in the A. dialect. What is common to all forms labeled A. is the sequence – ⏑ ⏑ – ⏑ –, which appears occasionally as a colon (q.v.) by itself but much more frequently is preceded and/or followed by a single anceps (syllable either long or short; q.v.), or preceded by the so-called "A. base" (a double anceps in Sappho and Alcaeus, elsewhere either – x , x – , or ⏑ ⏑). Iambic or trochaic may precede or follow within the same colon, and the – ⏑ ⏑ – sequence may be "expanded" into either a dactylic – ⏑ ⏑ – ⏑ ⏑ – (⏑ ⏑ –) or a choriambic – ⏑ ⏑ – – ⏑ ⏑ – (– ⏑ ⏑ –), etc. Typical examples are:

– ⏑ ⏑ – ⏑ – x	aristophaneus
x – ⏑ ⏑ – ⏑ –	telesillean
x x – ⏑ ⏑ – ⏑ –	glyconic
x x – ⏑ ⏑ – – ⏑ ⏑ –	lesser asclepiad
x x – ⏑ ⏑ – ⏑ ⏑ – ⏑ –	Sapphic "fourteener"

The A. sequence – ⏑ ⏑ – ⏑ – may be terminally shortened into – ⏑ ⏑ – x, most notably in the *pherecratean* (x x – ⏑ ⏑ – x) and *reizianum* (x – ⏑ ⏑ – x), as well as replaced by – x – ⏑ ⏑ –, usually in the glyconic equivalent known as the *choriambic dimeter* (see CHORIAMB): x x – x – ⏑ ⏑ –. The latter name is somewhat misleading, however, suggesting as it does a compound out of two independent parts. Genuine dimeters in which the second element is a choriamb do exist, but the first section is either an iamb or another choriamb, and they are much more closely related to pure iambic dimeters (x – ⏑ – x – ⏑ –) or the mixed form – ⏑ ⏑ – x – ⏑ – than they are to A. There also exists a catalectic form of the latter, externally identical with the A. – ⏑ ⏑ – ⏑ – x and called, like it, an *aristophaneus*; but all such dimeters are foreign to the versification of Alcaeus and Sappho. They appear first in Anacreon and have close affinities with the ionic (q.v.) sequences characteristic of him, one of which, ⏑ ⏑ – ⏑ – ⏑ – –, is actually known as the Anacreontic (q.v.). See GREEK POETRY; MELIC POETRY.—D. L. Page, *Sappho and Alcaeus* (1955); Maas, sect. 54; D. S. Raven, *Gr. Metre* (1962); Dale, chs. 9–10; D. Korzeniewski, *Griechische Metrik* (1968); Halporn et al.; Snell; West, 29 ff.; K. Itsumi, "The 'Choriambic Dimeter' in Euripides," *ClassQ* 76 (1982), "The

AESTHETIC DISTANCE

Glyconic in Tragedy," *ClassQ* 78 (1984)—fundamental for the two forms discussed.   A.T.C.

AESTHETIC DISTANCE describes the proper psychological relation of the viewer to the artwork, isolating what is unique to aesthetic, rather than cognitive or affective, experience. The meaning of the term shifts historically and according to genre but should be independent of individual psychology. Thus Aristotle balances pity and fear—the first drawing us toward the protagonist in sympathy, the second drawing us away in terror—so as to establish the catharsis (q.v.) proper to tragic art (*Rhet.* 1382a, 1385b). Similarly, the plot (q.v.) must be sufficiently serious to keep the work tragic rather than spectacular or horrific (*Poetics* 1453b). The audience is thus brought to an understanding that distinguishes aesthetic from simply rational or merely affective experience.

In the Ren., the analogy between aesthetic and religious contemplation allowed a. d. to be understood as a stance governed by neither reason nor appetite. Neoclassical theories, somewhat more normative, differentiated genres not only by structure but also by defining the emotions proper to various forms. Thus, as Aristotle delimits the proper a. d. for tragic emotion, neoclassical theories of comedy require that the object of laughter be a character whose vice or excess is meliorated by a degree of virtue, so that the effect is comic rather than bathetic or ridiculous.

Kant's *Critique of Judgment* defines a. d. as a state of disinterestedness (q.v.). Aesthetic experience is governed by neither ethical nor scientific concepts, on the one hand, nor by mere sensation or appetite, on the other; both conceptual and physical responses are interested. Disinterest thus defines a. d. as a noncognitive relation, but it remains universal and impersonal in that it suspends individual psychology. Accordingly, Kant differentiates the beautiful, which is universally so, from the agreeable, which is only personally pleasing and not properly aesthetic.

The later 19th c. linked a. d. to the concept of organic form (see ORGANICISM): when art is conceived as ordered by internal laws and by the mutual relation of its parts, the proper a. d. must be dictated by the work itself rather than by any extrinsic rules. Aestheticism (q.v.) thus tended to distance aesthetic from all other (cognitive or moral or religious) experience. In 1912, Bullough used the term "psychical distance" to argue along Arnold's lines that aesthetic experience is also knowledge; psychical distance demands a balance between the coldly practical estimate and subjective enthusiasm. But several 20th-c. critics have detached the reception of art from all historical, psychological, ethical and other concerns in order to isolate the aesthetic from other forms of judgment. Daiches, Booth, and many others have argued that different works may set the conditions of their own reception, claiming that diction, nar-

rative voice and other devices provide "an implicit set of directions concerning the distance from the object at which the reader must stand if he is to see it for what it is" (Daiches 63).

But the idea that aesthetic experience can be detached from other influences, and the idea that a. d. can be determined entirely by objective features of the work, have both been disputed recently: New Historicists, Marxists, feminist critics and others have argued that both the production and the reception of art is conditioned by history, class, and gender; other writers following Foucault and Derrida have denied that aesthetic experience can be entirely disengaged from other practices and forms of knowledge, so that the idea of specifically *aesthetic* distance has been brought sharply into question.

E. Bullough, "Psychical Distance as a Factor in Art and an A. Principle," *Brit. Jour. of Psych.* 5 (1912); D. Daiches, *A Study of Lit.* (1948); R. Langbaum, *The Poetry of Experience* (1957), ch. 2; S. Dawson, "Distancing as an A. Principle," *Australasian Jour. of Philosophy* 39 (1961); K. Haidu, *A. D. in Chrétien de Troyes* (1968); G. Dickie, *Art and the A.* (1974), ch. 4–5; W. C. Booth, *The Rhet. of Fiction*, 2d ed. (1983); *Feminist Literary Theory*, ed. M. Eagleton (1986); *Marxism and the Interp. of Culture*, ed. C. Nelson (1988).   C.P.S.

AESTHETICISM. (1) A term signifying that the work of art is self-sufficient and autonomous (see AUTONOMY). In judging the work of art, the critic should reject moral, social, political, religious, and other nonaesthetic standards as irrelevant. (2) Occasional term for the Aesthetic Movement.

The genesis of this view of art can be traced to the writers and philosophers of the Ger. romantic movement—Kant, Schelling, Goethe, and Schiller. Kant stressed the "pure" and disinterested existence of the work of art; Schelling, its fusion of the universal with the particular; Goethe, its life as an independent organism; and Schiller, the all-importance of its form. In England these ideas, at least in part, were diffused by Coleridge and Carlyle; in America, by Emerson and Poe; in France, by Mme. de Stael, Victor Cousin, and Théophile Jouffroy. Cousin made use of the phrase *l'art pour l'art* in his 1818 lecture *Du Vrai, du beau, et du bien* (pub. 1836); and the idea of "art for art" is implicit also in Hugo's Prefaces to *Cromwell* (1827) and *Hernani* (1830).

The first vigorously self-conscious expression of A. in modern lit. is that of Théophile Gautier, who humorously but emphatically denied in the Preface to *Mademoiselle de Maupin* (1835) that art could in any way be useful. From Gautier and from Poe, with his belief that poetry is "the rhythmical creation of Beauty" (*The Poetic Principle*, 1850), Baudelaire derived his aesthetic view of experience and advocated, in writing his crit. and poetry, the sovereignty of the creative imagination and the aspiration to apprehend an ultimate reality

- [10] -

through the perceptions of the senses.

The Fr. symbolist movement (see SYMBOLISM), with Mallarmé and Verlaine as its leaders, assimilated Baudelaire's concept of perception as constituting "a forest of symbols" to which the poet must give order, as well as his theory of the "correspondences" between sense impressions and "spiritual reality" and between one sense and another. The symbolists tried to communicate concentrated feeling by the use of evocative symbols rather than by rational statement, and they also tried (esp. Mallarmé) to refine and purify lang. to obtain intimations of the ineffable and the transcendent. Following Poe, they held that poetry was to approximate the disembodied emotion to be found in music and that an Ideal Beauty (often verging on the abstract) was to be sought beyond the visible world, though paradoxically to be evoked in terms of the visible world—or of symbols. The symbolists were also conscientious craftsmen interested in the complex and subtle relationships among the poem's words and images. In Fr. poetry (q.v.) the line is clear from Baudelaire and Mallarmé to Rimbaud, who emphasized "the derangement of all the senses" to achieve new poetic effects and a sublime freedom for the mind and spirit; to Valéry, who organized his poetry about the vivid image in an effort to achieve a "pure poetry" (q.v.); to Apollinaire, who in his free subjectivity and experimentalism anticipated surrealism (q.v.); to Breton and Eluard, surrealists who in their poetry exploited the unconscious.

A. in England was the product of native and Fr. influence both. In the 1850s, '60s, and '70s the Pre-Raphaelites (see PRERAPHAELITE BROTHERHOOD) appropriated Keats's predominantly aestheticist values, Tennyson's sensuousness, and Ruskin's enthusiastic worship of beauty to foster a decorative conception of art and lit. instead of an ethically oriented one. In the 1870s and later the influence of Walter Pater was paramount. In the Conclusion to *Studies in the Hist. of the Ren.* (1873), A. received an almost official sanction. Pater urged the sensitive individual "to burn always with this hard gemlike flame" and to find the most precious moments in the pursuit of sensations raised to the pitch of "the poetic passion, the desire of beauty, the love of art for art's sake." In the 1880s and '90s the subjectivity (as in Keats and Shelley) and the sometimes exaggerated individualism (as in Byron) of romanticism encouraged the "Aesthetic Movement," as it came to be embodied in the paintings of James McNeill Whistler and in the poetry and life of Oscar Wilde and his coterie. In the 1890s Pater dominated the "aesthetic" (and "decadent") poets—Wilde, Dowson, Lionel Johnson, Arthur Symons, and the early Yeats. Symons and George Moore made the work of the new Fr. writers and painters available in England, while James Huneker performed a similar service for America. Baudelaire's grotesquerie and satanism and Verlaine's insistence that verse

strive for the condition of music influenced the Eng. poets of the 1890s more than did Mallarmé's emphasis upon uncompromising artistry and the work of art conceived as the only indestructible reality. Max Beerbohm in "Enoch Soames" (1919) depicts with humor and subtle irony an aesthetic poet of the 1890s, and his *Zuleika Dobson* (1911) lampoons one of the mythic preoccupations of the time, the fatal woman. W. S. Gilbert's *Patience* (1883) is a delightful satire upon the pretensions and foibles of Eng. A.

Symons in *The Symbolist Movement in Lit.* (1899) introduced the two British and Am. pioneers of modern poetry, Eliot and Pound, to the work of the Fr. symbolists. They incorporated into the Anglo-Am. trad. what was most vital in the A. of Fr. poetry, the concepts of the objective and impersonal existence of the poem and of the artist as rigorous creator. In America the work of H.D., MacLeish, Aiken, Cummings, Moore, Stevens, Crane, Ransom, and Tate owed much to the symbolists' dedication to, and delight in, the exercise of craft and to their refusal to be inhibited by social, moral, and literary conventions. In England the followers of Eliot, Auden, Day Lewis, Spender, and MacNeice absorbed the all-important concept of the autonomy of art, despite their earlier sociological and political orientations. In Germany the earlier verse of Stefan George and Rainer Maria Rilke revealed the influence of Fr. A. For all these authors, the two most valid aspects of A.—a realization that manifestations of the beautiful in the artwork possess an independent importance and that the poet must be technically scrupulous—became prime motivations. See also DECADENCE; GEORGIANISM; SYMBOLISM; ROMANTIC AND POST-ROMANTIC POETICS.

H. Jackson, *The Eighteen Nineties* (1913); J. Farmer, *Le mouvement esthétique et "décadent" en Angleterre* (1931); E. Wilson, *Axel's Castle* (1931); M. Praz, *The Romantic Agony* (1933); P. Martino, *Parnasse et symbolisme, 1850–1900* (1935); A Guerard, *Art for Art's Sake* (1936); M. Raymond, *De Baudelaire au surréalisme*, 2d ed. (1940); G. Matoré, *La Préface de "Mlle. de Maupin"* (1946); G. Michaud, *Le message poétique du symbolisme*, 3 v. (1947); T. S. Eliot, *From Poe to Valéry* (1948), "Arnold and Pater," *Selected Essays* (1950); G. Hough, *The Last Romantics* (1949); J. Buckley, *The Victorian Temper* (1951); R. Z. Temple, *The Critic's Alchemy* (1953); J. Wilcox, "The Beginnings of l'Art pour l'Art," *JAAC* 11 (1953); H. N. Fairchild, *Religious Trends in Eng. Poetry*, v. 4–5 (1957–62); Wimsatt and Brooks; L. Eckhoff, *The Aesthetic Movement in Eng. Lit.* (1959); E. Starkie, *From Gautier to Eliot* (1959); B. Charlesworth, *Dark Passages: The Decadent Consciousness in Victorian Lit.* (1965); Wellek, v. 3–6 (1965–86); L. C. Dowling, *A. and Decadence: A Sel. Annot. Bibl.* (1977); *Decadence and the 1890s*, ed. I. Fletcher and M. Bradbury (1979); *The Aesthetes: A Sourcebook*, ed. I. Small (1979); *Aesthetes and Decadents of the 1890s*, ed. K. Beckson, 2d ed.

(1981); B. Trehearne, *A. and the Canadian Modernists* (1989); J. Loesberg, *A. and Deconstruction* (1991).
F.P.W.M.

AFFECTIVE CRITICISM. See CRITICISM; POETICS; READER-RESPONSE CRITICISM.

AFFECTIVE FALLACY. In an essay called "The A. F.," first published in 1949, W. K. Wimsatt, Jr., and M. C. Beardsley proposed this phrase to designate and condemn a purported type of commentary on poetry which is primarily an account of the emotional, imaginative, or physiological reactions of the critic (or others) to a poem. Wimsatt and Beardsley acknowledge that many theorists from Plato to I. A. Richards have defended a. crit. as appropriate to a conception of the function of poetry as the arousal, cultivation, or communication of feelings or attitudes (see POETRY, THEORIES OF, *Pragmatic Theories*). But they claim that the practical crit. produced by "appreciators" (such as George Saintsbury or Anatole France) is often characterized by vague emotive expression and unhelpful simplifications of the content of a poem. And since the a. reactions of people to poetry are controlled by a multitude of different factors, the a. critic is always in danger of slipping into impressionism and relativism.

In their other works Wimsatt and Beardsley have argued for the desirability of studying poetry from a variety of perspectives, incl. a. response (Beardsley, for example, in his *Aesthetics* and elsewhere gives detailed descriptions of the psychological state evoked by works of art and argues that the aesthetic value of a poem is determined by its capacity to generate a distinctive aesthetic experience). However, both favor an emphasis on the work itself, the characteristic stance of the New Criticism (q.v.). They claim that a. crit. is too often only an excuse for a critic to avoid the difficult problems of making and presenting a detailed analysis of a poem. They advise the critic to regard the poem as an object (a "verbal icon"), study its parts and their intrinsic relations, and temporarily bracket considerations of its relations to external elements such as the psychology of the poet or the effects on the audience. They recommend a "dramatic" view of the poem as the speech act of a fictive speaker directed at a fictive listener which the actual reader is invited, as it were, to overhear. If the critic fulfills her interpretive responsibilities, she can freely express her own enthusiasm for the poem; her explication (q.v.) will have provided the reasons or grounds—an objective correlative (q.v.)—for her emotional reactions and will help the reader to respond similarly to the poem. (In a later work Wimsatt praises Richards' practical crit. as a "rhapsode's explication.")

"The A. F." and the authors' companion piece "The Intentional Fallacy" (see INTENTION) helped to make explicit the theoretical underpinnings of New Critical emphases in practical crit. This posi-tion gradually fell into critical disfavor, challenged in the late 1950s by what Wimsatt called the "New Amateurism" and, more formidably, in the 1970s by the development of various kinds of reader-response crit. (q.v.), which on epistemological, linguistic, and artistic grounds advocated an "a." or "subjective" crit. that makes the relation of poem and reader the focal point of interest.

W. K. Wimsatt, Jr., and M. C. Beardsley, "The A. F.," *SR* 57 (1949); W. K. Wimsatt, *The Verbal Icon* (1954), *Hateful Contraries* (1965), "I. A. Richards: What to Say About a Poem," *I. A. Richards: Essays in His Honor*, ed. R. Brower et al. (1973); Wimsatt and Brooks; M. C. Beardsley, *Aesthetics* (1958), *The Aesthetic Point of View* (1982); D. Bleich, *Subjective Crit.* (1978); S. Fish, *Is There a Text in This Class?* (1980). F.GU.

AFFECTIVE STYLISTICS. See READER-RESPONSE CRITICISM; STYLISTICS.

AFFLATUS. See INSPIRATION.

AFRICAN POETRY.

I. IN THE INDIGENOUS EPIC TRADITION
II. IN EUROPEAN LANGUAGES
    A. *In French*
    B. *In Portuguese*
    C. *In English*

This article provides an overview of the major poetries of the African continent written in both the indigenous langs. and in the three principal European langs. For more detailed surveys, see EGYPTIAN POETRY; ETHIOPIAN POETRY; HAUSA POETRY; SOMALI POETRY; SOUTH AFRICAN POETRY; SWAHILI POETRY. See also AFRO-AMERICAN POETRY; ARABIC POETRY; WEST INDIAN POETRY.

I. IN THE INDIGENOUS EPIC TRADITION. Af. tales, proverbs, and riddles have been profusely collected since the early 19th c. But until the middle of the 20th c., epic poetry remained an unknown, ignored, or neglected topic. Some of the epic fragments which were published early escaped the attention of scholars because the information appeared in obscure journals in unfamiliar langs. (e.g. Flemish), or the data were met with skepticism because some were fragmentary and inadequately explained. Prevailing tendencies in anthropology, linguistics, and folklore focused attention on sociological, historical, or structural matters with little or no interest in Af. oral lit., let alone Af. epic lit. But this situation has changed radically, and the world of oral lit. studies is much richer for it.

The present section of this article does not consider the praise and panegyric lit. richly represented in the heroic recitations of the Ankole of Uganda, the praise poems of Rwanda and of the Luba-Kasaayi (Zaire), or the dynastic praises of the Tswana, Zulu, Sotho, and Xhosa in South Africa (see SOUTH AFRICAN POETRY). This eulogistic lit. exhibits some elements of epic poetry (see EPIC), but in spite of the contentions of some scholars, these praises are not mere preliminaries to the devel. of epic. Nor does the present analysis focus on the cycles of thematically and stylistically converging tales that are constructed about animal protagonists, like Sangba Ture among the Zande (Sudan), or Ananse among the Ashanti (Ghana), or the *enfant terrible* tales of the Dogon, Mande, and San (West Africa). Many of these types of tales are difficult to classify because they are built around a trickster character, like Monimambu of the Kongo, Kabundi of the Luba, or Tiya among the Ngbandi (all in Zaire), where animal and human transformations continuously interplay. Some cycles which developed around a particular heroic character may well be the scattered and incomplete fragments of a sweeping, perhaps defunct, epic trad. Neither does this discussion focus special attention on the numerous historiographic accounts (e.g. those about chief Lubango among the Sanga-Kaonde [Zambia]); such texts are interlaced with the superhuman deeds of chiefs and clan founders, who headed the migrations into a new homeland, and these chiefs' subsequent power struggles and conquests.

The problems of relating these various genres to the major epic trads. remain unsolved; a clear picture has not emerged because of the uneven geographical and cultural coverage of the available texts and the often piecemeal and idiosyncratic approach that characterizes much of the study of Af. oral lit.

The focus here, then, must be on the long oral narratives sung and recited in Af. langs. and built around a historical or mythical or historico-mythical hero and his comitatus, his extraordinary powers and feats set within a framework of marvelous events, strange encounters, tensions, and warfare. Such narratives exhibit a number of thematic and stylistic features that are uncommon or sparse in the other Af. oral genres but are common in epic texts across world cultures.

Af. oral epics have now been recorded in a wide belt of populations ranging from the Gambia and Mali to Nigeria, in West Africa, to the Bantu-speaking peoples of Cameroun and Gabon and culminating among the Bantu-speaking peoples of Zaire. Among the principal epics now well documented are those in West Africa about Kaabu among the Mandinka of The Gambia, Sundyata (also Sunjata or Sonjara) among the Mande, Kambili among the Maninka, Silamaka of the Fulani, and Ozidi of the Ijaw in Nigeria. In West Central and Central Africa, there are the epics of Akoma Mba and Zwe Nguema among the Fang of Cameroun and Gabon. In Zaire the best-known epic narratives revolve around Lianja among the Mongo, Mwindo among the Nyanga, Mubila among the Lega, and Lofokefoke among the Langa-Mbole.

Most of these texts are available in the particular Af. langs. in which they are sung and in Fr., Eng., or Dutch translations (see section II below). They range in length from about 2000 lines (Sonjara) to 10,000 and more (Mubila of the Lega). Some are recorded in different versions recited and sung by several bards over a period of time (Lianja, Mwindo, Sonjara, Kaabu). The societies in which these epic trads. flourish differ widely in their social and political structures: some are politically centralized, others are segmentary lineage organizations or even more fragmented structures; some have sweeping trads. of migration and conquest, others lack such trads. beyond the concept of local movements of groups. However, several cultural features seem to cut across many of the epic-producing groups: hunting trads. are ritually and sociologically prominent (particularly in Zaire epics, hunting and animals play a major role); profound Pygmy influences have molded their past; initiation systems (involving puberty rites and complex cycles of male and female initiations into closed associations) are extremely elaborate; and none of the groups seems to have any developed pantheon of divinities (as distinct from ancestral and nature spirits, or named forces captured from the natural environment and placed in objects by ritual experts). Distinctions frequently made by critics between heroic, historical, shamanistic, and romantic epics cannot be taken literally. In epics where the main character resembles a fictionalized hero, there are nevertheless included many, sometimes subtle, historical details. In fact, as is the case for the Mubila epic of the Lega, the entire unspoken thrust of the narrative points to a time when the unifying bwami association had not yet established itself, i.e. to a time of local migratory movements, intergroup tensions and warfare, and violence in general. In addition, most of the epic heroes rely to some extent on magical devices with which they are born or which they have acquired.

The epic trads. among the various ethnic groups are very old. It is unthinkable, as has been suggested by some scholars, that the emergence of Af. epics was linked with Islamic and European contacts. In Zaire, epics are found among populations that were not affected by Islamic intrusions and where European influences had virtually no ideological impact. Recent work among the Nyanga and Lega leads to the conclusion that Pygmies and other hunters are at the root of the epics (see Biebuyck 1978, 1992).

The epics are traditional, meaning that their original authors are unknown; only the names of the actual singers and some of their predecessors whose trads. they perpetuate have come down to us. There seem to be two categories of singers: in some of the West Af. groups that have centralized and stratified sociopolitical systems, there are professional bards who travel over wide areas at the request of sponsors. In the Bantu-speaking groups, the singers are not professional in the sense that the recitation of the epic is not their primary or sole activity. Bards like Candi Rureke among the Nyanga and Mubila Kambara among the Lega are not members of a caste or an elite group but rather simple hunters and farmers who have developed unique literary, musical, and dramatic skills. Often this is the result of a somewhat unscheduled association with a person of similar skills from whom they learned themes and techniques as companions and assistants, rather than through any formal method. The casualness of the transmission process of the great epics accounts for the fact that, in the second part of the 20th c., as the result of changing social and educational patterns, very few persons could be found who in the minds of Af. listeners still had a full grasp of the intricate trad. In Nyanga society in the mid 1950s, virtually every man and woman could adequately tell tales, but apart from a handful of men who more or less knew the integral trad., there was only one Candi Rureke left. For this reason, our perspective on the distribution and importance of the epic in the past will always be blurred.

As is clear from the limited number of versions of a single epic trad., the singers are highly creative individuals. Although they operate with set characters, themes, plots, and stylistic devices, the singers shape their texts in unique ways by rearranging and recombining elements; reinventing topoi; expanding or reducing motives, plots, themes, and characters; and showing clearcut stylistic preferences. Moreover, even the most humble singers of epics have an unparalleled mastery of their lang., as illustrated in their vast vocabulary, their precision and refinement of word choice, their creative play with names and epithets, their delicate nuancing and shading of verbal conjugations, their handling of elisions and contractions, their inclusion of aphoristic statements and onomatopoeia, and their unusual changes in word order. In a pioneering stylistic analysis of the Mwindo epic, the Nyanga linguist Kahombo Mateene has convincingly shown the importance in the narrative of nine complex style patterns widely found in world epic trads. but only sparsely present in the other Af. genres. C. Seydou has equally emphasized the unique combinations of processes at work in structuring texts for West Af. epics.

The modes of presentation of the epics differ extensively from ethnic group to ethnic group, but there are certain common features. The bard performs for an audience that responds actively with exclamations of approval or disapproval and sings refrains to the songs. The bard, who himself may play a musical instrument, is accompanied by a small group of musicians (e.g. percussionists) and eventually by one or more apprentices, one of whom may act as the most active listener, encouraging the bard through praises and helping him when he has a problem. The text may be sung in its entirety, or sung and recited, or recited with interspersed songs. Some performances include dramatic action during the recitation, the bard enacting, often, some action in which the hero is involved. In most groups, the bard is also dressed, painted, and provided with appropriate paraphernalia for the occasion; for example, he may hold certain objects that suggest the power of the hero's possessions.

The occasions on which epic narratives are traditionally performed are something of a mystery. In areas with professional bards, it is obvious that the performances could be held when the political or ritual authority asks for them or at the bard's initiative; traditionally, the appropriate context might be the coronation or death of a chief or a periodic festival when group values are validated. In other societies with nonprofessional singers, the epic (in its entirety or in installments) can be sung as part of a general rejoicing, e.g. when the inhabitants of adjoining villages celebrate the successful outcome of a big net hunt or a large group of initiates is gathered for initiation rites. It is precisely in the latter context that the present writer heard Kambara Mubila sing the great Lega epic. Among the Mongo, epics are traditionally sung only throughout the night.

Whether the texts of the epics are formulated in rhythmic prose or verse or both, they show consummate mastery of the Af. langs. Hulstaert, who published a vast number of Mongo oral texts, marvels at the extraordinary quality of the verbal skills displayed in the Lianja epic. The bards are interested not merely in the rhythmic flow of the narration following distinctive patterns of line and syllable count, they look for sound effects: alliteration, sound-imitating words, sonorous names. Their constructions are built on recurring technical and stylistic devices: an abundance of names of actors (simple generic ones and descriptive inventions) and epithets; appositives and other descriptive terms for animals, places, and objects; patronymics and group affiliations; kinship and other enumerations; formulas for spatial movements and temporal sequences; repetitions and reduplicatives; lyrical evocations; and inversions of normal word order. The bards manipulate and arrange these devices in original and unexpected ways.

The thematic structures and plots follow a pattern. The hero is born under unusual circumstances (highly variable); the mother has special status (she is a virgin, or she has an unusually long pregnancy or a very short one); the unborn hero speaks in the womb. The hero is born abruptly and in an unusual manner; he is fully ready to confront a hostile world, holding at birth weapons or other objects with magical powers. He possesses certain medicines; he has extraordinary gifts (premonition, the capacity to be reborn, to metamorphosize himself, to travel quickly over great distances, or to hear things far away). He is not necessarily physically strong, but his attributes and certain persons in his entourage or the friendship of beings of the other world make him extremely powerful. The hero has a comitatus, large or small, often comprising powerful and very active women (a mother, a wife, a twin sister, a paternal aunt). His encounters with individuals and groups—humans, animals, monsters, extraterrestrial creatures—lead to challenge, trickery, and violent actions, in the course of which the hero often infringes the basic moral principles and values of his people. In some encounters, the hero may die or succumb, then come back to life through his own will or through some magical device used by a person close to him. Some epics end *in medias res*: the hero is already back in his village, celebrating with his people; in others, the hero disappears mysteriously or dies and is succeeded by a heroic son.

The basic outline of the epics is relatively simple. The Lianja epic among the Mongo (Zaire) starts with the ancestry of the hero, then dwells (in detail) on the hero's parents. The father dies at the hands of his enemies, leaving his wife pregnant. Soon after, she gives birth to insects and other things; the hero Lianja is then born by his own volition through his mother's shin. At birth he is fully prepared for battle, possessing the typical Mongo weapons and magical objects. Right after birth, he goes in search of his father's enemies, whom he defeats. He then begins a series of journeys, accompanied by his sister Nsongo, until he reaches the Zaire River; in the meantime, many groups in his comitatus have split off and settled as separate units in the vast equatorial forest. Having reached his final destination, Lianja, accompanied by his mother and twin sister, climbs a huge palm tree and disappears forever. The concluding parts of the Lianja epic, which differ considerably from version to version, usually deal with Lianja's descendants.

As far as their contents and purposes are concerned, the Af. epics are massive ethnographic documents about institutions, customs, thought patterns, and values. Some are explicit historical documents; in others the historical realities are reduced or latent, sometimes almost nonexistent. However, in some of the Bantu epics, the hero often acts as an anti-hero, somewhat like a much admired villain who continuously infringes on values and institutions until his task is finished and he is back in his village as a wise leader. Consequently, unless the epic contents are analyzed in depth and in a broad cultural context, the real information they provide is lost. The Lega hero Mubila, for example, hears on one of his travels drum messages. He decides to investigate what they are about. When he arrives, he learns that bwami initiations of a lower order are being held and abruptly decides that he too must be initiated. The result is catastrophic: the turmoil leads to violence and death, and the implication is that, in the end, Mubila has not been initiated. For the bard, who himself was an initiate of lower bwami

grade, and for the numerous male and female initiates present at the performance, the hero acts here in total ignorance of, and nonconformity with, the values and sociolegal principles inherent in bwami initiations. He acts as a stranger or as a brute emerging from an earlier period of Lega culture, when bwami did not yet exist or was gradually being introduced. The negative behavior of the hero (who, it turns out later, is not even circumcised—an essential preliminary to initiation) is a powerful warning for the listeners that nobody, not even a hero, can profanate bwami rules and values. The information which the epics are intended to provide the listeners cannot be taken at face value, simply because of the many contradictions in a hero's life and attitude.

E. Boelaert, *Nsong'a Lianja* (1949), *Lianja Verhalen*, I: *Ekofo-Versie* (1957), *Lianja Verhalen*, II: *De Voorouders van Lianja* (1958); J. Jacobs, "Le Récit épique de Lofokefoke," *Aequatoria* 24 (1961); A. de Rop, *Lianja: L'Épopé des Mongo* (1964), *Versions et fragments de l'époépes mongo* (1978); S. Awona, "La Guerre d'Akoma Mba contre Abo Mama," *Abbia* 9–10, 12–13 (1965, 1966); J. Knappert, "The Epic in Africa," *JFI* 4 (1967); D. Biebuyck and K. Mateene, *The Mwindo Epic from the Banyanga* (1969); P. Mufuta, *Le Chant kasala des Luba* (1969); F. Oinas, "Folk Epic," *Folklore and Folklife*, ed. R. Dorson (1972); H. Pepper, *Un Mvet de Zwe Nguema* (1972); C. Seydou, *Silamaka et Poullori: Récit épique peul* (1972), *La Geste de Ham-Bodedio, ou Hama le Rouge* (1976), "A Few Reflections on Narrative Structures of Epic Texts," *Research in Af. Langs.* 14 (1983); G. Innes, *Sunjata: Three Mandinka Versions* (1974); C. Bird et al., *The Songs of Seydou Camara*, I: *Kambili* (1976); J. Clark, *The Ozidi Saga* (1977); E. Belinga, *L'Épopés camerounaise mvet* (1978); D. Biebuyck, "The Af. Heroic Trad.," *Heroic Epic and Saga*, ed. F. Oinas (1978), *Hero and Chief Epic Lit. from the Banyanga* (1978), *The Mubila Epic from the Balega* (1992); I. Okpewho, *The Epic in Africa* (1979); V. Görög et al., *Histoires d'enfants terribles* (1980); V. Görög, *Litt. orale d'Afrique noire: Bibliographie analytique* (1981); A. de Rop and E. Boelaert, *Versioms et fragments de l'épopé mongo* (1983); K. Mateene, "Essai d'analyse stylistique de l'épopé de Mwindo," *Cahiers de litt. orale* 3 (1984); G. Hulstaert, *Het Epos van Lianja* (1985); J. Johnson, *The Epic of Son-Jara* (1986); K. Kesteloot, "The Af. Epic," *Af. Langs. and Cultures* 2 (1989).   D.P.B.

II. IN EUROPEAN LANGUAGES. A. *In French*. The rise of Af. p. in Fr. cannot be understood without reference to the expansion of European imperialism and culture, in particular the slave trade and subsequent colonization of Africa. Nor can the tone of that poetry be appreciated without an awareness of the intense resentment those forces evoke, and the ambiguity that putting them into Fr. might arouse.

Histories of Af. p. in Fr. usually begin in the 1930s with the Négritude movement, but its roots extend further back. The Martinican students who published *Légitime défense* in Paris in 1932 were, after all, challenging the emulation of Western cultural norms and were therefore opposed to certain earlier black writers of poetry in Fr. By the same token, these young proponents of Négritude were themselves pursuing a trad. of soul-searching and revolt exemplified by the Haitians Pierre Faubert (b. 1803) and Oswald Durand (b. 1840), and a culture which took shape in the holds of slave ships and which spoke Af. langs. and creoles before Fr.

That one cites New World writers when defining Af. p. in Fr. is thus no accident. Both Africans and Afro-Americans have had to confront the same racist oppression; they have accordingly made common cause and sought out each other for inspiration and readership, despite real differences. Hence the importance of Harlem Renaissance (q.v.) figures like Langston Hughes and Claude McKay to the founders of Négritude; hence that, among the three poets who two years later established a second journal, *L'Etudiant Noir*, Aimé Césaire (b. 1913) of Martinique, Léon G. Damas (b. 1912) of Fr. Guiana, and Léopold Sédar Senghor (b. 1906), only the last was from Africa itself (Senegal). This tendency towards cross-fertilization with other black lits. has made Af. p. in Fr. intercontinental in scope. Though Césaire and Senghor and later poets repeatedly demonstrate their mastery of Fr. trad., they are drawn both to Third World lits. and to direct contact with Af. lits. This desire to renew traditional oral Af. poetic practice, expressed rhetorically by the theoreticians of Négritude, has become increasingly urgent among recent poets, who are, however, more aware of the difficulties such hybrid literary forms present.

There is no exhaustive definition for the term "Négritude." Coined by Césaire in his 1939 *Cahier d'un retour au pays natal* (Return to My Native Land), it is, in his words, "the simple recognition of the fact that one is black, the acceptance of this fact and of our destiny as blacks, of our history and our culture." But there is nothing simple about this statement; its implications are manifold, and the poetry which sought to express it took many forms, from Damas' explosive *Pigments* (1937) to Césaire's virulent defense of black culture in his *Cahier* and to Senghor's lofty exaltation of Af. values beginning with *Chants d'ombre* (1945). That it is impossible to separate Af. p. from politics is obvious from the positions embraced by the founders of Négritude in the '30s, but also by the fact that the movement was so closely connected to all sides of the anti-colonial movements. It should not be surprising that the literary and political outlines of Fr.-speaking anti-colonialism took shape in postwar Paris and that a third major journal, *Présence Africaine*, was founded there by the Senegalese Alioune Diop: not until actual decolonization were Africans able to shift focus from the former metropolis, but Paris still weighs heavily upon Af. lits. in Fr.

The landmark publication of the postwar period was Senghor's *Anthologie de la nouvelle poésie nègre et malgache de langue française* (1948), with its influential preface by Jean-Paul Sartre, "Orphée noir." In Sartre's view, Négritude was but an antithesis, a second phase of reaction to white racism which, while defending the specificity of black culture, did so only in view of a final synthesis, the transition to a universal (in Sartre's version, proletarian) culture with no oppressors and, ultimately, no specificity. Sartre's perspective was at odds with that of Senghor himself, but it proved to be even more influential and set the grounds for Frantz Fanon's dialectical typology of colonial cultures in *Les Damnés de la terre* (The Wretched of the Earth, 1961), upon which most interps. of post-colonial lit. hist. repose. Indeed, it is common, though sometimes reductive, to apply Fanon's pattern of Af. p. in Fr.—i.e. to conceive of (1) a colonial period of slavish imitation of Western models, (2) a period of revolt, exemplified by Négritude, and (3) a post-colonial period in which Africans have taken control of their own culture.

As for the poets represented in the Senghor *Anthologie*, they are more complex and rewarding than any system might suggest. Though better known as a storyteller, Birago Diop (1906–89) proved himself as a poet. A brilliant talent lost at an early age, David-Mandessi Diop (1927–61) is still revered for his vehemently anti-assimilationist *Coups de pilon*. Evidence that Af. p. in Fr. extended far beyond the founding fathers of Négritude was the inclusion of the Malagasy poets Jean-Joseph Rabéarivélo (1901–37), Jacques Rabemananjara (b. 1913), and Flavien Ranaivo (b. 1914). The first of these, a unique talent who survived in utter isolation from other poets and ideologues, took his own life after producing strikingly original works.

Independence brought a sea change of sensibility to Francophone Africa. It is too simple to claim that the once-external white enemy became internal and black, for neo-colonialism and imperialism have remained major themes since the early 1960s, and condemnation of the West has by no means abated. Still, many writers did turn from the clear commitments of anti-colonialism to more ambiguous and ambitious poetic projects, and this new mood is evident in the 1966 *Présence Africaine* anthology *Nouvelle somme de poésie du monde noire*, not only among the then-younger or lesser-known voices, like Charles Nokan (pseud. Zégoua Konan, b. 1936) and J. M. Bognini (b. 1936) from the Ivory Coast, Annette M. Baye (b. 1926) from Senegal, and Yambo Ouologuem (b. 1940) from Mali, but also among established ones like B. Dadié (b. 1916) from the Ivory Coast, Edouard Maunick (b. 1931) from Mauritius, and Francis Bebey (b. 1929) and René Philombe (b. 1930) from Cameroun. Foremost among them is Tchicaya U Tam'si (1931–88), whose dense and difficult *oeuvre* combines the most contemp. poetic techniques with an anguished concern for the Congo and the ravages of colonialism, esp. in his 1962 *Epitomé*. It is against the dominating figure of Tchicaya that recent Af. Fr.-lang. poets are measured, be they his fellow Congolese Henri Lopès (b. 1937) and J. B. Tati-Loutard (b. 1939), or Cheikh Aliou Ndao (b. 1933) from Senegal. It appears, in fact, that the People's Republic of the Congo has acted in recent decades much as Paris did earlier—as a focal point and a literary clearinghouse for production in Fr. across the continent. Thus the importance of J. B. Tati-Loutard's 1976 *Anthologie de la littérature congolaise d'expression française.*

Though Négritude was a primer, Af. p. in Fr. is now neither limited to nor coterminous with it. Recent poets have been both more universal in scope and more particular. There is now a proliferation of individual national lits. in Fr. Critical studies and anthologies exist for Benin, Cameroun, the Congo, Gabon, the Ivory Coast, Senegal, Togo, and Zaire. It has seemed to some that this parceling up of a continent into national lits. may be too rash, may ignore the common heritage and political realities of the continent, and may thereby serve the interest of the elite in quest of fiefs to rule. Be that as it may, Af. p. in Fr. will doubtless continue to express the vast diversity of Africa and to offer, in doing so, some of the most exciting and moving poetry in that lang.

ANTHOLOGIES: *Poètes d'expression française*, ed. L. Damas (1947); *An Anthol. of Af. and Malagasy Poetry in Fr.*, ed. C. Wake (1965); *Anthologie négro-africaine*, ed. L. Kesteloot (1967); *Anthologie de la litt. gabonaise*, Ministère de l'Education Nationale (1978); *Anthologie de la poésie togolaise*, ed. Y.-E. Dogbe (1980); *Poèmes de demain: Anthologie de la poésie camerounaise de langue française*, ed. P. Dakeyo (1982); *Anthologie de la litt. ivoirienne*, ed. A. Kone et al. (1983).

HISTORY AND CRITICISM: L. Kesteloot, *Les Écrivains noirs de langue fr.*, 3d ed. (1967; Eng. tr. by E. C. Kennedy, 1974); S. Adotevi, *Négritudes et négrologues* (1972); D. Herdeck, *Af. Authors* (1973); R. Cornevin, *Litts. d'Afrique noire de langue française* (1976); A. S. Gérard, *Études de litt. africaine francophone* (1977), ed., *European-Lang. Writing in Sub-Saharan Africa*, 2 v. (1986); R. and A. Chemain, *Panorama critique de la litt. congolais contemporaine* (1979); *Dictionnaire des oeuvres litts. négro-africaines de langue française*, ed. A. Kom (1983); A. Huannou, *La Litt. béninoise de langue française* (1984); J. B. Kubayanda, *The Poet's Africa* (1990).

G.L.

B. *In Portuguese.* Ironically, Af. p. in Port. (also known as Lusophone Af. p.), despite the fact that it appeared first, is lesser known than its counterparts in Eng. and Fr. In 1849, José da Silva Maia Ferreira, an obscure Angolan, probably of Port. heritage, published in Luanda his *Espontaneidades da minha alma* (Outpourings from My Soul), dedicated to "Af. ladies," the first collection of poems

printed in Lusophone Af. and possibly in all of the sub-Saharan region. Both the lesser status of Port. as a world lang. and the closed nature of Lisbon's Af. colonies have contributed to world ignorance of the lits. of Angola, Mozambique, Cape Verde, Guinea-Bissau, and São Tomé e Príncipe. Since the colonies achieved independence (1974–75), however, students of Af. lit. have increasingly turned their attention to these countries' unique poetries, written mainly in Port. but also (as in the case of Cape Verde, Guinea-Bissau, and São Tomé) in local Port.-based creoles.

Precursors such as Ferreira, Joaquim Cordeiro da Matta (1857–94), an early black Angolan poet, and Caetano da Costa Alegre (1864–90) from the Island of São Tomé, wrote verse modeled on European styles and themes, but often from an Af. consciousness. Some wrote verse reflecting their sense of social reformism and dedication to Republican liberalism. Beginning, however, in the 1930s in Cape Verde and in the 1950s in Angola and Mozambique, poems of cultural legitimization and growing social protest, fanned by the winds of nationalism, characterized the literary movements initiated by members of an emerging black and *mestiço* (mixed-race) intelligentsia and their Af.-born or -raised white allies.

On the largely *mestiço* Cape Verde islands in 1936, a trio of poets, Jorge Barbosa (1902–71), Oswaldo Alcântara (pseud. of Baltasar Lopes da Silva, 1907–89), and Manuel Lopes (b. 1907), founded what has come to be known as the Claridade movement, so named for the group's arts and culture journal. Under the influence of Brazilian modernism and Northeast regionalism, Barbosa first codified his islands' creole ethos. He gave artistic expression to the prevailing Cape Verdean themes of solitude, the sea, drought, and emigration with poems like "Momento" (Only a Moment):

This our
refined melancholy
arising from I know not what
a little perhaps
from the solitary hours
wafting over the island
or from the music
of the opposing sea.

In the Angolan cities of Benguela and esp. Luanda, cultural revindication erupted with thinly veiled nationalist fervor (censorship and police repression precluded outspoken militancy) among black, *mestiço*, and not a few white poets, some of whom would form the nucleus of the Movement of the Liberation of Angola (MPLA) founded in 1956. Poets like Agostinho Neto (1922–79), Angola's first president, Viriato da Cruz (1928–73), António Jacinto (b. 1924), Costa Andrade (b. 1936), and M. António (1934–89) produced poems that called for an Af. Angola. Many militant poets, in Mozambique as well as

Angola, took to the bush as guerrilla fighters. Others fled into exile or paid for their militancy with imprisonment.

Throughout the 1960s and until the 1974 coup that toppled the Lisbon government, much Af. p. in Port. went underground. Militants distributed their poems clandestinely or contented themselves with seeing them published abroad. Neto, writing surreptitiously in his Port. prison cell, promised, in his poem "Havemos de voltar," that we shall return "to the sounds of the marimbas and finger pianos / to our carnival." Friends spirited this and other of Neto's poems out of Aljube prison to Kinshasa, Dar-Es-Salaam, Milan, and Belgrade where they were published in bilingual editions. Only after independence did they emerge from secrecy and "return" legitimately to Angola.

In Portugal's former East Af. colony of Mozambique, during the two or so decades prior to national independence, a few Europeans produced poetry, some of it very good, but more a conscious part of Port. lit. than of Mozambique's incipient literary expression. Starting in the 1960s, a few of these Euro-Mozambicans, most notably Rui Knopfli (b. 1933), born and raised in the colonial city of Lourenço Marques (now Maputo), sought to capture the essence of an Af.-European experience. As might be expected, however, a poetry of Af. cultural and racial essentialism, whether by black, mixed-race, or black Mozambicans, coincided with the rise of nationalism in the 1950s and '60s. Thus the *mestiço* poets José Craveirinha (b. 1922) and Noémia de Sousa (b. 1926) wrote a number of memorable poems of cultural revindication. Craveirinha, Mozambique's most celebrated poet, raised his voice with fervor in "Manifesto":

Oh!
My beautiful short kinky hair
and my black eyes
great moons of wonderment on the
    most beautiful night
of the most unforgettably beautiful
    nights of the lands of the Zambeze.

Not altogether surprisingly, true Négritude poetry appeared in Lisbon. And Francisco José Tenreiro (1921–63), a *mestiço* from the island of São Tomé who lived most of his short life in Lisbon, emerged as the greatest writer of Négritude poetry in Port. Under the influence of the Harlem Renaissance (q.v.), Afro-Cuban Negrism, and Francophone poets such as Senghor and Césaire, Tenreiro wrote the poems published posthumously as *Coração em África* (My Heart in Africa, 1964).

Some Angolan writers have proclaimed that their poetry was born in the struggle for liberation, while Négritude was spawned in defeat as a European-based phenomenon that had little to do with Africa. During the decade of anti-colonialist wars in Angola, Mozambique, and Guinea-Bissau,

poetry became increasingly combative and tendentious. Marcelino dos Santos (b. 1929), a high-ranking member of the Mozambique Liberation Movement (FRELIMO), was at the forefront of militant poets who wrote pamphletary verse that during the protracted war served as a didactic instrument as well as a goad to political mobilization.

In the early years after independence (1975), a multiracial array of poets began seeking new forms for new content. In Angola, Manuel Rui (b. 1941) wrote, in "Poesia necessária" (Essential Poetry):

Of new words is a country also made
in this country so made of poems
that production and all else to sow
in another cycle will have to be sung.

The imperative of new discourses for new stories led Rui, along with fellow Angolans such as Arlindo Barbeitos (b. 1941), Rui Duarte de Carvalho (b. 1941), Jofre Rocha (b. 1941), and David Mestre (b. 1948), to form the basis of a new poetry. In Mozambique, Rui Nogar (b. 1933) and Luís Carlos Patraquim (b. 1953); in Cape Verde Corsino Fortes (b. 1933), Oswaldo Osório (b. 1937), and Arménio Vieira (b. 1941); in Guinea-Bissau Helder Proença (b. 1956); and in São Tomé Frederico Augusto dos Anjos (b. 1954) have all attempted, with varying degrees of success, to create such a new poetry. In Angola Carvalho has experimented with an integrated form of Af. oral expression and Brazilian concrete poetry; his compatriot Barbeitos has sought to attain that poetic measure between things and words:

in the forest
of your eyes
one sees only night
in the night
of the leopard
one sees only eyes.

By the close of the 1980s, and in spite of continuing civil war in Angola and Mozambique and of varying degrees of economic woe in all of the former colonies, Af. p. in Port. had achieved both quantity and quality. Since independence, the lang. of this poetry has accelerated its evolution into five variants of a uniquely Af. expression of potentially international appeal. Among the most promising of the cultivators of this lang. are: from Angola, Rui Augusto (b. ca. 1950), Paula Tavares (b. 1952), José Luís Mendonça (b. 1955), and Ana de Santana (b. 1960); from Mozambique, Luís Carlos Patraquim (b. 1953), Hélder Muteia (b. 1960), Armando Artur (b. 1962), and Eduardo White (b. 1964); and from Cape Verde, José L. Hopffer Almada (b. ca. 1958), who organized *Mirabilis*, an anthology of work by some 60 island poets (pub. 1991).

BIBLIOGRAPHY: *Bibliografia das lit. af. de expressão port.*, ed. G. Moser and M. Ferreira (1983).

AFRICAN POETRY

ANTHOLOGIES: *No reino de Caliban: Antologia panorâmica da poesia africana de expressão portuguesa*, ed. M. Ferreira, v. 1: *C. Verde e G.-Bissau* (1975), v. 2: *Angola e S. Tomé e Portugal* (1976), v. 3: *Moç.* (1986); *Antologia temática de poesia af.*, ed. M. de Andrade, v. 1: *Na noite grávida de punhais* (1976), v. 2: *O canto armado* (1979); *Poems from Angola*, tr. M. Wolfers (1979); *A Horse of White Clouds*, tr. D. Burness (1989).

HISTORY AND CRITICISM: G. Moser, *Essays in Port.-Af. Lit.* (1969); R. Hamilton, *Voices from an Empire: A Hist. of Afro.-Port. Lit.* (1975), *Lit. af., lit. necessária*, v. 1: *Angola* (1981), v. 2: *Moç., C. Verde, G.-Bissau, S. Tomé e Portugal* (1983); M. Ferreira, *Lit. af. de expressão port.*, 2 v. (1977).   R.G.H.

C. *In English*. With the end of the colonial period and the concomitant advance of literacy and higher education came a rapid efflorescence of Af. p. written in Eng. This poetry displays the variety to be expected in so diverse a continent, and regional styles have arisen; nevertheless, the most eminent poets have created an international community of poetic values and influences.

In general, Af. p. in Eng. eschews rhyme in favor of alliteration and assonance. Instead of metrical verse, rhythms directly governed by syntax, logic, or rhet. determine line length. Ambiguity is more often syntactic than lexical. The same austerity leads to avoidance of extended conceits unless they are buttressed by hard or sardonic reason or concrete imagery. Oral and other traditional poetry influence recent Af.-Eng. poems primarily in such fundamental elements as the poet's stance as defender of communal values; allusions to the hist., customs, and artifacts of the culture; and the architectonic features adapted from praise song, proverbial tale, epic, and prayer. Experiments in the transmutation of traditional Af. poetic forms into Eng. vary with the culture represented. The internationally published poets, of course, display a mastery of the trads. of mod. Eng. and Am. poetry; one indication of their freedom from these forms, however, is the occurrence of dramas and novels written partly or entirely in verse.

West Africa, particularly Nigeria and Ghana, has the oldest and most influential trad. of sophisticated poetry in Eng. This lyric poetry combines audacious leaps of thought and individualized expression with social responsibility; it privileges the metaphysical, religious, and social concepts of its own society rather than concepts indigenous to European cultural hist. When social protest is overt, it is usually presented with intellectual and artistic complexity rather than simplistic fervor. Exemplary Nigerian poets include Christopher Okigbo (1932–67; *Labyrinths*), John Pepper Clark (b. 1935; *Reed in the Tide; Casualties; A Decade of Tongues; The State of the Union*), and the Nobel Prize winner, Wole Soyinka (b. 1934; *Idanre; Shuttle in the Crypt*), whose plays often include poetry. Less obscure and idiosyncratic in form, allusions, and thought are the poetry of Gabriel Okara (b.

1921; *The Fisherman's Invocation*) and, from Gambia, Lenrie Peters (b. 1932; *Satellites; Katchikali; Selected Poetry*).

Among Ghanaians, experiments in the tr. and adaptation of Af. poetic forms are increasingly common, as in the works of Kofi Awoonor (b. 1935; *Rediscovery: Night of My Blood; Guardians of the Sacred Word; Ride Me, Memory; The House by the Sea*), Kofi Anyidoho (*Elegy for the Revolution; A Harvest of Our Dreams; Oral Poetics*), and Atukwei (John) Okai (b. 1941; *Oath of the Fontomfrom; Lorgorlogi Logarithms*). Closer to Western trads. of sensibility and structure are others such as Kwesi Brew (b. 1924; *The Shadows of Laughter; Af. Panorama*), Albert W. Kayper-Mensah (1923–80; *The Dark Wanderer; The Drummer in Our Time; Sankofa: Adinkra Poems; Proverb Poems; Akwaaba*), Kojo Laing (*Godhorse*), Frank Kobina Parkes (b. 1932; *Songs from the Wilderness*), and Joe de Graft (1924–78; *Beneath the Jazz and Brass*). Among the poets from Sierra Leone we should mention Syl Cheyney-Coker (b. 1945; *Concerto for an Exile; The Graveyard Also Has Teeth*) and Lemuel Johnson (b. 1940; *Highlife for Caliban; Hard on the Navel*).

East Af. p. is dominated by two styles. One originated in Okot p'Bitek's tr. and adaptation of his own Acholi poetry. P'Bitek (1931–82; *Song of Lawino; Song of Ocul; Song of Prisoner; Song of Malaya; Hare and Hornbill*) is probably the most widely read poet of Af. Through long rhetorical monologues usually narrated by a victim of modernization, these poems express social commentary with lucid, graphic imagery, humorous irony, and paradoxical common sense. Another such poet is Okello Oculi (b. 1942; *Orphan; Malak; Kanta Riti; Kookolem*). The other style, more indebted to West Af. p., uses asyndeton, subtler imagery, and more erudite allusions to convey a mordant and individualized vision of mod. life. It includes a wider range of subjects, tones, and frames of reference. Pre-eminent poets include Jared Angira (b. 1947; *Juices; Silent Voices; Soft Corals; Cascades; The Years Go By*), Richard Ntiru (b. 1946; *Tensions*), and Taban lo Liyong (*Meditations in Limbo; Franz Fanon's Uneven Ribs; Eating Chiefs; Another Nigger Dead; 13 Offensives against Our Enemies*).

South Af. p. (q.v.) of necessity is most concerned with subjugation, courage, poverty, prisons, revolt, and the private griefs of public injustice. South Af. poets writing in Eng. before the 1970s were often exiles, whose works therefore also reflected British or Am. experience—e.g. Arthur Nortje (1942–70; *Dead Roots*), Cosmo Pieterse (b. 1930; *Echo and Choruses: "Ballad of the Cells"*), and esp. Dennis Brutus (b. 1924; *Sirens, Knuckles and Boots; Letters to Martha; Poems for Algiers; China Poems; A Simple Lust; Strains; Salutes and Censures; Stubborn Hope*). In this poetry the speaker is often an observer combining passionate concern with reflective distance, and the imagery portrays monstrous abuse in natural and social settings of oblivious serenity.

The experimental adaptation of regional Af. forms to original poetry in the Eng. lang. is best represented by the work of Mazisi Kunene (b. 1930; *Zulu Poems; Anthem of the Decades; Emperor Shaka the Great: A Zulu Epic; The Ancestors and the Sacred Mountain*).

The exile Keroapetse Kgositsile (b. 1938; *Spirits Unchained; For Melba; My Name Is Afrika; The Present Is a Dangerous Place to Live; Herzspuren*) and also Oswald Mbuyiseni Mtshali (b. 1940; *Sounds of a Cowhide Drum; Fireflames*) are forerunners of the dramatic change in and copious output of Af. p. since 1970. Written in South Af. and addressed primarily to fellow South Africans, recent poetry has a more direct militancy which nevertheless meets the dictates of both state censorship and poetic grace. It is more lyrical than hortatory. Rhythms, imagery, narrative events, and sensibility are firmly rooted in quotidian deprivations and defiance. The influence of Afro-Am. musical and poetic forms, esp. jazz, the blues, and the renaissance of the 1960s, looking back to the Harlem Renaissance (q.v.) is often evident (see AFRO-AMERICAN POETRY). Immediacy may be reinforced by including phrases from South Af. langs. or Afrikaans or by directly addressing the reader as a compatriot. Neither reader nor speaker is presented as impartial observer or judge. Because it is the poetry of a people seeking liberation, this poetry is marked by local detail, unromanticized factuality, emphasis on the political consequence of individual choice, and above all by the pervasive assumption that these tragedies will someday yield to victory. Major writers include Mongane Serote (b. 1944; *Yakhal'Inkomo; Tsetlo; No Baby Must Weep; Behold Mama, Flowers; The Night Keeps Winking*), Sipho Sepamla (b. 1932; *Hurry Up to It!; The Blues Is You in Me; The Soweto I Love; The Root Is One; Children of the Earth; Selected Poems*), Mafika Pascal Gwala (b. 1946; *Jol'unkomo; No More Lullabies*), James Matthews (b. 1929; *Cry Rage; Pass Me a Meatball, Jones; Images; No Time for Dreams / Feelings*), Daniel P. Kunene (*A Seed Must Seem to Die; Pirates Have Become Our Kings*), and Wopko Pieter Jensma (b. 1939; *Sing for Our Execution; Where White Is the Colour Where Black Is the Number; I Must Show You My Clippings*).

Politics and economics have denied wide international audience to the poetry of South Africa's Anglophone neighbors. From Malawi, David Rubadiri (b. 1930) and Frank M. Chipasula (b. 1949; *Visions and Reflections; O Earth Wait for Me; Nightwatcher, Nightsong*) have voice only through exile. Jack Mapanje (*Of Chameleons and Gods*) writes from within Malawi. Zambians like Richard A. Chima (b. 1945; *The Loneliness of a Drunkard*) and Patu Simoko (b. 1951; *Africa Is Made of Clay*) speak from within and with greater freedom. Zimbabwe has produced copious poetry reflecting both the price of liberating warfare and the consequences of victory. Pre-eminent poets include Samuel Chimsoro (b. 1949; *Smoke and Flames*),

Charles Mungoshi (b. 1947; *The Milkman Doesn't Only Deliver Milk*), Musaemura Zimunya (b. 1949; *Thought-Tracks; Kingfisher; Jikinya and Other Poems*), Shimmer Chinodya (b. 1957), and Mudereri Kadhani.

With important national and individual differences, the poetry of Southern Africa still has a strikingly identifiable character. It is everywhere premised on an intense affinity for the land, and through that, a close union between the spiritual and physical worlds. Nature is presented as a manifestation of religious forces but is also treated with a more direct, nonsymbolic sensibility than in other Af. p. Poet and personae are more closely identified with their community through a diction which relies on direct address to reader as putative interlocutor, conversational apostrophe, quiet humor, anaphora, irony, and avoidance of strident, vitriolic or erudite effects. Esoteric lyricism and declamation are both rare. The stresses which urban cultures impose upon rural life and upon personal values and identity are common themes, as well as the systemic effects of past and current colonial hegemony. In form and themes, the poetry of this region adapts Eng. to provide sophisticated but unaffected articulation of traditional Af. worldviews in a context of rapid social change.

Despite its immense cultural and individual variety, one can hear a distinctive Af. voice in Af. p. in Eng. It maintains close identification with communal values and experience while conveying personal perceptions. A tone of responsible sincerity is everywhere demanded and achieved through elaborate technique and studied experimentation with the Eng. lang. Shared metaphysical, ethical, and aesthetic visions are sources for its vigor and originality.

BIBLIOGRAPHIES: *Bibl. of Creative Af. Writing*, comp. J. Janheinz et al. (1971); *Black Af. Lit. in Eng.* (1979), and *Supplement to Black Af. Lit. in Eng. 1977–1982* (1985), both ed. B. Lindfors; *New Reader's Guide to Af. Lit.*, ed. H. M. Zell et al., 2d ed. (1983); *Companion to South Af. Eng. Lit.*, comp. D. Adey et al. (1986).

ANTHOLOGIES: *West Af. Verse*, ed. D. Nwoga (1966); *Poems from East Africa*, ed. D. Cook et al. (1971); *The Word Is Here: Poetry from Mod. Africa*, ed. K. Kgositsile (1973); *Poems of Black Africa*, ed. W. Soyinka (1975); *A World of Their Own: South Af. Poets of the Seventies*, ed. S. Gray (1976); *Intro. to East Af. P.*, ed. J. Kariara et al. (1977); *Zimbabwean Poetry in Eng.*, ed. K. Z. Muchemwa (1978); *Af. P. in Eng.*, ed. S. H. Burton et al. (1979); *Summons: Poems from Tanzania*, ed. R. S. Mabala (1980); *Somehow We Survive*, ed. S. Plumpp (1982); *The Return of the Amasi Bird*, ed. T. Couzens et al. (1982); *A New Book of Af. Verse*, ed. J. Reed et al. (1984); *The Heritage of Af. P.*, ed. I. Okpewho (1984); *The Penguin Book of Mod. Af. P.*, ed. G. Moore et al., 3d ed. (1984); *When My Brothers Come Home: Poems from Central and Southern Africa*, ed. F. M. Chipasula (1985); *The Fate of Vultures*, ed. M.

Zimunya et al. (1989).

HISTORY AND CRITICISM: A. Roscoe, *Mother Is Gold: A Study of West Af. Lit.* (1971), *Uhuru's Fire: Af. Lit. East to South* (1977); O. R. Dathorne, *The Black Mind: A Hist. of Af. Lit.* (1974); K. Awoonor, *The Breast of the Earth* (1975); R. N. Egudu, *Four Mod. West Af. Poets* (1977); G. Moore, *Twelve Af. Writers* (1980); K. L. Goodwin, *Understanding Af. P.: A Study of Ten Poets* (1982); T. Olafioye, *Politics in Af. P.* (1984); T. O. McLoughlin et al., *Insights: An Intro. to the Crit. of Zimbabwean and Other Poetry* (1984); A. Z. Davies et al., *How to Teach Poetry: An Af. Perspective* (1984); J. Alvarez-Pereyre, *The Poetry of Commitment in South Africa*, tr. C. Wake (1984); U. Barnett, *A Vision of Order: A Study of Black South Af. Lit. in Eng. (1914–1980)* (1985); R. Fraser, *West Af. P.: A Crit. Hist.* (1986); *European-Lang. Writing in Sub-Saharan Africa*, ed. A. S. Gérard, 2 v. (1986); E. Ngara, *Ideology and Form in Af. Poetry* (1990).

D.F.D.

AFRIKAANS POETRY. See SOUTH AFRICAN POETRY.

AFRO-AMERICAN POETRY. Though it did not begin to enter the established Am. canon until the 1930s, the Afro-Am. trad. in poetry reaches back into the 18th c. and may be said to have had its beginning when Lucy Terry (1728–1821), a slave owned by one Ebenezer Wells of Deerfield, Mass., composed a semiliterate poem ("Bars Fight") of 28 lines describing how Indians attacked Deerfield in August of 1746. And she in turn was followed by Jupiter Hammon (1711–86?), who spent his life as a slave of Henry Lloyd's family in Queen's Village, Long Island, New York. Hammon appears to have been a man of considerable intelligence, and one who attained some measure of prestige among the slaves in his neighborhood for his power as a preacher in their religious services. Indeed, it is the voice of the homilist we hear in the handful of poems he produced, as they echo the Methodist hymnody on which he had been reared.

It is, however, Phillis Wheatley (ca. 1753–84) who is the major figure among Am. Black poets of the 18th c. Though in their silence about her many of the standard literary histories simply erase her from the trad., she was in fact one of the more notable writers of the Colonial period, and after the publication of her *Poems on Various Subjects, Religious and Moral* in London in 1773, she won a more substantial European reputation than any other Am. poet of her time.

Phillis was brought to the Colonies after being kidnapped by slave traders in the region today embracing the African states of Senegal and Gambia, and, as a 7- or 8-year-old child, she was purchased on a Boston dock in 1761 by the wife of a wealthy tailor, John Wheatley, in whose household she was gently and carefully reared. After little more than a year of residence with the Wheatley family, she was reading Eng. so well as to be able easily to make her way through the more difficult passages of the Bible. She began her study of Lat. at the age of 12 and was soon rendering Eng. trs. of Ovid in heroic couplets. But it was Alexander Pope who early became her great poetic model, and much of her work clearly reveals how decisive was his influence. Though hers was a poetry infinitely more sophisticated than Jupiter Hammon's, it too reflects a deep commitment to the Christian faith; her first published poem, "On the Death of the Reverend Mr. George Whitefield" (1770), expresses the hope that the people of her ancestral community will accept the Christian evangel:

> Take him, ye *Africans*, he longs for you;
> *Impartial Saviour* is his title due;
> Wash'd in the fountain of redeeming
> blood,
> You shall be sons, and kings, and
> priests to God.

Her poetry is by no means much given over to racial themes, but, unlike Hammon, Wheatley did not hesitate forthrightly to express at once her devotion to liberty and her abhorrence of slavery; and both find expression in her poem "To the Right Honorable William, Earl of Dartmouth, His Majesty's Principal Secretary of State for North America":

> Should you, my lord, while you peruse
> my song,
> Wonder from whence my love of Free-
> dom sprung,
> Whence flow these wishes for the com-
> mon good,
> By feeling hearts alone best under-
> stood;
> I, young in life, by seeming cruel fate
> Was snatch'd from Afric's fancy'd
> happy seat;
> What pangs excruciating must molest,
> What sorrows labor in my parent's
> breast?
> Steel'd was that soul and by no misery
> mov'd
> That from a father seiz'd his babe be-
> lov'd;
> Such, such my case. And can I then
> but pray
> Others may never feel tyrannic sway?

Given her time and her place, it was, of course, virtually inevitable that her poetic idioms should be wholly derivative from neoclassical norms, and the imitativeness of her work is not to be gainsaid. Yet one feels that Thomas Jefferson's remark, in his *Notes on the State of Virginia*, that her work is "below the dignity of crit.," reflects more than anything else—particularly when considered in relation to its immediate context in the *Notes*— how abysmal was his regular failure of imagination when Blacks were in view. For what is surely the more appropriate response to Wheatley's achievement is marveling astonishment at the swiftness and ease with which this young African's prodigious intelligence so thoroughly took possession of the New England culture of her period as to permit her becoming one unsurpassed as a poet in her moment of Am. history.

Nor was the South unrepresented in this early Afro-Am. trad., for one of its strongest exemplars is George Moses Horton, originally a slave belonging to James Horton, whose plantation was near Chapel Hill, N.C. He is thought to have been born in the year 1797 (d. 1883?), and his first volume of poems, *The Hope of Liberty*, had already been issued by 1829; a second ed. was published in 1837 under the title *Hope of Liberty—Poems by a Slave*. In 1845 his second volume, *The Poetical Works of George M. Horton*, appeared; and his third volume, *Naked Genius*, was published in 1865, the year in which Horton at last won his freedom. How he came to master the arts of reading and writing remains something of a mystery, but the pedagogic method was doubtless self-administered (as would almost certainly have had to be the case, the bestowal of literacy on slaves having been prohibited by law throughout the ante-bellum South). Though his poetry is not without a richly humorous vein and scans a variety of interests and experience, what is particularly remarkable is the passionate candor with which he speaks of the terrible indignities entailed by his servitude. Whereas Wheatley's themes generally touch not at all the human condition as it was known by Black slaves, Horton boldly expresses throughout much of his work an uncowed militancy of spirit in his cries of outrage at the cruel disadvantage suffered by his kind, and his characteristic tone is expressed in the poem "On Liberty and Slavery":

> Alas! and am I born for this,
> To wear this slavish chain?
> Deprived of all created bliss,
> Through hardship, toil and pain.
> . . . .
> Oh, Heaven! and is there no relief
> This side the silent grave—
> To soothe the pain—to quell the grief
> And anguish of a slave?

These early Black poets were followed by a steady succession through the 19th c., incl. such figures as Frances Ellen Watkins Harper (1825–1911), James M. Whitfield (1830–70), and Albery A. Whitman (1851–1902). But it was not until 1896, after Paul Laurence Dunbar's third volume, *Lyrics of Lowly Life*, that a Black poet won a national audience, partly (in Dunbar's case) as a result of the endorsement offered by the novelist and critic William Dean Howells, then widely influential in Am. literary life as the editor of the *Atlantic Monthly*. Though he produced several novels and a sizable body of short stories, Dunbar (1872–1906) is today chiefly thought of as a lyricist in

dialect poetry of Black peasant life. In this there is a certain irony, for his deep affection for the poetry of Keats, Shelley, and Tennyson led him to invest by far his greatest efforts in poems written in standard Eng., these making up more than half of his total poetic production. They reveal him to have been a gifted minor poet who, had his life not been cut short at 33 years of age, might well have grown very considerably in stature. But it was his dialect poems—"When Malindy Sings," "When de Co'n Pone's Hot," "Little Brown Baby," and a vast number of others—which had a great vogue in his lifetime, this so embittering him that in one of his late poems ("The Poet") he is led to say:

> He sang of love when earth was young
> And Love itself was in his lays.
> But ah, the world, it turned to praise
> A jingle in a broken tongue.

With the exception of James Weldon Johnson (1871–1938), for the Black poets after Dunbar who came to the fore in the first quarter of the 20th c.—such figures as William Stanley Braithwaite (1878–1982), Angelina Grimke (1880–1958), Georgia Douglas Johnson (1886–1966), and Claude McKay (1889–1948)—the plantation and minstrel trads. which his dialect poems had mined carried no appeal. Indeed, they felt them to make not only for sentimentality and bathos but also for a general depreciation of the dignity of the human image in Black life. Even Weldon Johnson, though he put to the finest kind of use the rhythms and intonations of Black folk sermons in his splendid volume of 1927, *God's Trombones*, was careful to liberate his material from dialectal idioms, while at the same time retaining the distinctive flavor of the Black pulpit; and he was certain that it was only by way of this kind of transformation that folk material could be made truly to fecundate a sophisticated art.

By the late 1920s an extraordinary efflorescence of talent among Black writers was bursting upon the scene, and since many of the more prominent figures—James Weldon Johnson, Claude McKay, Jean Toomer (1894–1967), Jessie Fauset (1882–1961), Rudolph Fisher (1897–1934), Arna Bontemps (1902–73), Wallace Thurman (1902–34), Nella Larsen (1891–1964), Zora Neale Hurston (1891–1960)—had one or another kind of connection with New York City's Harlem, this whole insurgency has come to be spoken of as the Harlem Renaissance (q.v.). Its literary expressions were largely in the medium of prose fiction, but (apart from Johnson and McKay, who, being older, had won recognition earlier) there were three notable young poets who were a part of the movement—Langston Hughes (1902–67), Countee Cullen (1903–46), and Sterling Brown (1901–88).

Hughes was, of all the poets whom we associate with the Harlem Ren., by far the most productive, his active publishing career stretching from 1926 to 1967, the year of his death; and his *oeuvre* embraces not only 9 volumes of fiction but also 15 volumes of verse. His is a poetry predominantly devoted to the urban scene, and it is often filled with the racy rhythms of the blues (q.v.) and jazz:

> Thump, thump, thump, went his foot
>   on the floor.
> He played a few chords then he sang
>   some more—
> "I got the Weary Blues
> And I can't be satisfied.
> Got the Weary Blues
> And can't be satisfied—
> I ain't happy no mo'
> And I wish that I had died."

Indeed, his work, unmarked by cynicism or by any kind of distortion or special pleading, rehearses Black experience more richly and variously than does perhaps the work of any other Afro-Am. poet. And it is no doubt the depth of its rootedness in all the concrete materialities of Black life that accounts for the immense affection with which it has been regarded by his large and devoted body of readers.

Countee Cullen, on the other hand, was a poet whose style and orientation were very different from Hughes's. He was quite untouched, for example, by such a penchant as Hughes had for risk-taking and innovation in the handling of poetic forms; indeed, he was, as he himself said, "a rank conservative, loving the measured line and the skillful rhyme," and he appears—in such books as *Color, Copper Sun, The Black Christ and Other Poems*, and *On These I Stand*—to have been most responsive to Keats and Shelley and to such Am. traditionalists as Elinor Wylie and Robert Hillyer, finding little or nothing at all quickening in the great avatars of 20th-c. modernism. Nor, despite his plangency about the sufferings enforced upon his people, does he seem ever to have been capable of passionately identifying himself with the Black multitudes; and over and over again he permits himself a kind of self-pity (as in the following lines from "The Shroud of Color") that Hughes's robustness and unfailing sanity would never have allowed:

> "Lord, being dark," I said, "I cannot
>   bear
> The further touch of earth, the
>   scented air;
> Lord, being dark, forewilled to that de-
>   spair
> My color shrouds me in, I am as dirt
> Beneath my brother's heel; there is a
>   hurt
> In all the simple joys which to a child
> Are sweet; they are contaminate, de-
>   filed
> By truths of wrongs the childish vision
>   fails

> To see; too great a cost this birth en-
>   tails.
> I strangle in this yoke drawn tighter
>   than
> The worth of bearing it, just to be man.
> I am not brave enough to pay the price
> In full; I lack the strength to sacrifice."

Then, in 1932, Sterling Brown's *Southern Road* was issued by Harcourt, Brace. Unlike Hughes, Brown, though educated at Williams College and Harvard and a member of the English faculty at Howard University, was imaginatively committed, at least in his first book, not so much to the urban scene of the Black proletariat as to the rural world of Southern Black peasants; *Southern Road* is drenched in this ethos. Also, unlike most of his contemporaries among Black poets who had discarded dialect forms, Brown chose to use the living speech of the Black demos, making it serve, in the highly nuanced uses to which he put it, an artistry which, in its dependence on folk idioms, finds its only analogue in modern poetry in the work of the distinguished Scots poet Hugh MacDiarmid.

It was most principally these three—Hughes, Cullen, and Brown—who, together with Johnson and McKay, provided the enabling examples for the Black poets whose careers began in the 1940s; and among these writers the major figures are Melvin Tolson, Gwendolyn Brooks, and Robert Hayden.

Tolson (1900–66) was the first Black poet deeply to appropriate the work of the classic 20th-c. avant-garde (Apollinaire, Pound, Eliot, Crane, Williams), though this became evident only in his remarkable *Libretto for the Republic of Liberia* (1953), commissioned by the Liberian government in 1947 as the nation's centennial poem. For in his first book, *Rendezvous with America* (1944), he was still much under the influence of such poets as Vachel Lindsay, Carl Sandburg, and Stephen Vincent Benet. And his commitment to the allusive, condensed, ironic lang. of high modernism appears to be even more resolute in his final book, *Harlem Gallery* (1965). His complex, difficult rhetoric has no doubt forfeited him the esteem of many of his Black critics, who feel it to be inapposite to the realities of Black experience, but this he was untroubled by, for though he never deserted those realities, he did not as a poet choose to present himself as merely a special case of ethnic ferment. And, for all the neglect he may as a consequence have suffered, the genuine distinction of his work is not to be gainsaid.

Gwendolyn Brooks (b. 1917) is no less preoccupied with issues of technique and craft than was Tolson, but her work is far more accessible to the general reader. Though born in Topeka, Kansas, she has spent most of her life in Chicago, and her writing is largely devoted to what she has witnessed in the daily round of the Black community there. Her earlier poetry (*A Street in Bronzeville*, 1945; *Annie Allen*, 1949—which won the Pulitzer Prize for poetry in 1950; *The Bean Eaters*, 1960) was "integrationist" in the kind of vision it embraced of how the world ought to be ordered in a multiracial society; but her 1968 book, *In the Mecca*, signalled her having taken a new turning toward the Black nationalism that was then beginning to be fostered by the holocaustal race riots that were sweeping across Am. cities. But, notwithstanding the new sternness that at this point entered her poetry, it has lost neither the shrewd, unsentimental realism nor the relish for humor that were initially a part of its great charm.

Of the poets who emerged in the 1940s—incl., as one should, not only Tolson and Brooks but also Margaret Walker (b. 1915) and Owen Dodson (1914–83)—it is Robert Hayden (1913–80) who is perhaps the most consistently interesting. Though his work searchingly renders the experience of Black Americans with that intimacy of knowledge which is born of love, he insistently refused any designation for himself other than simply that of "Am. poet." Claiming none of the easy exemptions being offered in the 1960s and early '70s by the strategists of the so-called Black Aesthetic, he took the highest kind of advantage of the whole range of expressive resources developed by the modernist movement in poetry; and "A Ballad of Remembrance," "Those Winter Sundays," "Frederick Douglass," "Runagate Runagate," "The Night-Blooming Cereus," "On Lookout Mountain," "El-Hajj Malik El-Shabazz," and a large number of other poems are among the masterpieces of modern Am. poetry. Indeed, his *Collected Poems* (1985) is one of the key poetic texts of its period, and "Middle Passage" (based in part on the 1839 insurrection on the Sp. slaveship the *Amistad*) is one of the great Am. long poems.

The turbulence in the relations between the races on the Am. scene was by the mid 1960s generating in the Black community a new pride in racial heritage so exigent that it often became a radically separatist ethnicism proposing to disengage itself not only from the Am. literary establishment but also from whatever else in the received cultural trad. might be conceived to be indelibly "Eurocentric" and "white." This undertaking found its principal expression in an immense flood of poetry from such writers as Dudley Randall (b. 1914), Margaret Danner (b. 1915), Mari Evans (b. 1923), Sarah Webster Fabio (b. 1928), Conrad Rivers (1933–68), Etheridge Knight (b. 1933), Audre Lorde (b. 1934), Sonia Sanchez (b. 1934), Lucille Clifton (b. 1936), and Nikki Giovanni (b. 1943), to mention but a few. But the immoderateness of his anger and the stringency of his expostulations made the poet and playwright Imamu Amiri Baraka (b. 1934) the presiding genius of the enterprise. The anthology of Afro-Am. p. that he and Larry Neal (b. 1937) published in 1968 (when Baraka's name was still

LeRoi Jones), *Black Fire*, gave to the movement a sense of its identity and effective advertisement. And the collection of his own poetry that appeared in the following year—*Black Magic: Poetry, 1961–1967*—offered what immediately became in effect for his confreres the benchmark of authenticity. Indeed, such a poem as Baraka's "Black Art" very nicely exemplifies the violence of spirit with which the poets of the Black Arts Movement were seeking to quicken in their people a new power of self-affirmation:

> Poems are bullshit unless they are
> teeth or trees or lemons piled
> on a step. . . .
> . . . .
>   We want poems
> Like fists beating niggers out of Jocks
> Or dagger poems in the slimy bellies
> of owner-jews. Black poems to
> smear on girdlemamma mulatto
>   bitches
> whose brains are red jelly stuck
> between 'lizabeth taylor's toes. Stinking
> Whores! We want "poems that kill."
> . . . .
> We want a black poem. And
> a Black World.
> Let the world be a Black Poem.

It may be too soon for many relative discriminations to be risked in relation to those poets who are among the more central figures of the present time, but they can at least be said to represent important achievement and large promise. Rita Dove (b. 1952), whose book *Thomas and Beulah* won the Pulitzer Prize for poetry in 1987, is surely by any reckoning in the vanguard not merely of Afro-Am. p. but of her generation at large in Am. poetry (q.v.); significantly, she, like such figures as Jay Wright (b. 1935) and Michael Harper (b. 1938), quite forswears the sentimentalities attendant upon an obsessive racial particularism and the technical indiscipline represented by the Black Arts Movement. The great charm and grace of her work result in part from an increasingly strict economy of lang. (as in the remarkable performance represented by the poems making up *Grace Notes* [1989]), from the richness of her historical imagination (as in many of the poems in *The Yellow House on the Corner* [1980] and *Museum* [1983]), and from a kind of pure attentiveness to experience that enables her easily to interweave personal and public themes.

Jay Wright's work presents, in relation to Rita Dove's, a poetry equally elegant and commanding. He emphatically asserts his fate to be that of an Afro-Am., but he happens to come out of Albuquerque, New Mexico, and thus he appears to be one who, in being originally poised, as it were, toward South America, found himself committed to a kind of borderland existence which, in his case, has resulted in a radical "de-provincializing" of the normal scene of Afro-Am. p.: the geography of that country of the spirit in which he dwells is not only hemispheric (in its extensions beyond North America to Mexico and Venezuela and Brazil) but also transatlantic, particularly in its embrace of Sp. and Af. cultures. So the explorations that are recorded in such books as *Death as History* (1967), *The Homecoming Singer* (1971), *Dimensions of History* (1976), and *The Double Invention of Komo* (1980) entail enormous complexity; and his *Selected Poems* (1987) confronts us with a lyrical talent whose range and power put us immediately in mind of Whitman and Hart Crane and Derek Walcott.

Nor can one fail to think of Michael Harper when one considers the poets of Afro-Am. descent who have moved to the fore as the century approaches its end. In such books as *Dear John, Dear Coltrane* (1970), *History Is Your Own Heartbeat* (1971), *Song: "I Want a Witness"* (1972), *Nightmare Begins Responsibility* (1975), and *Healing Song for the Inner Ear* (1985), Harper has created a body of work which, though it has won much respect and admiration, deserves to be far more widely known than it is. It is a poetry drenched in pieties, about his wife Shirley ("Shirl") and their children, her forebears and his own, his friends (e.g. Robert Hayden, Sterling Brown), various historical figures (W. E. B. DuBois, Patrice Lumumba), and many jazz musicians (John Coltrane, Miles Davis, Charlie "Bird" Parker, Bud Powell) who have all in deeply nourishing his life disclosed the real meaning of "kinship" as an affair not merely of biological accident but of the essential nature of the human condition. We are, in other words, as St. Paul says, "members one of another," and it is from this fundamental premise that his prophetic judgments of the misshapenness of the modern world spring.

Finally, if one more figure may be brought forward, Audre Lorde (b. 1934) should be spoken of, for she is one who, though originally appearing perhaps to be but yet another voice of the Black Arts Movement of the '60s and early '70s, by far outstretches the range of that moment in Afro-Am. p. She declares herself to be a "Black lesbian feminist warrior poet," but the spluttering fierceness that appears to be invoiced in this title she bestows on herself is belied by the beautiful precision and quiet eloquence of the profoundly moving poetry that we encounter in such books as *Chosen Poems Old and New* (1982) and *Our Dead Behind Us* (1986). She specializes in the contemplative lyric, and hers is a lyricism that has shaped some of the most remarkable love poems that have been written in Eng. since Graves, Roethke, and Auden. But hers is a lyricism so commodious as to be capable of talking also about the stresses and joys of being Black and being a woman, or about any of the circumstances and occasions that belong to the daily round; and the delicacy and passionateness of the lang. she supervises prompt

an increasingly devoted readership to feel that she is indeed, as Adrienne Rich says, "an indispensable poet."

The numerousness of other poets whose work also deserves to be considered here—June Jordan (b. 1936), Sonia Sanchez, Margaret Danner, Ai (Florence Anthony; b. 1947), and many others—does most assuredly indicate that the Afro-Am. presence will be a major factor in Am. literary life over the coming years, and its vitality promises significant future developments that cannot now be foreseen. See also AFRICAN POETRY; AMERICAN POETRY; BLUES; DOZENS; HARLEM RENAISSANCE; SIGNIFYING; SPIRITUALS; TOAST.

ANTHOLOGIES: *The New Negro*, ed. A. Locke (1925); *Caroling Dusk*, ed. C. Cullen (1927); *The Book of Am. Negro Poetry*, ed. J. W. Johnson (1931); *Early Negro Am. Writers*, ed. B. Brawley (1935); *The Negro Caravan*, ed. S. A. Brown et al. (1941); *Am. Negro Poetry*, ed. A. Bontemps (1963); *Kaleidoscope*, ed. R. Hayden (1967); *Black Fire*, ed. L. Jones and L. Neal (1968); *Dark Symphony*, ed. J. A. Emanuel and T. L. Gross (1968); *Black Voices* (1968), *New Black Voices* (1972), both ed. A. Chapman; *The New Black Poetry*, ed. C. Majors (1969); *Black Poetry*, ed. D. Randall (1969); *Early Black Am. Poets*, ed. W. H. Robinson (1969); *Black Am. Lit.*, ed. D. T. Turner (1969); *Black Expression* (1969), *The Black Aesthetic* (1971), both ed. A. Gayle, Jr.; *The Poetry of the Negro*, ed. L. Hughes and A. Bontemps (1970); *Dynamite Voices*, ed. D. L. Lee (1971); *Afro-Am. Lit.*, ed. R. Hayden et al. (1971); *Cavalcade*, ed. A. P. Davis and J. S. Redding (1971); *Black Lit. in Am.*, ed. H. A. Baker (1971); *Black Writers of America*, ed. R. Barksdale and K. Kinnamon (1972); *Mod. and Contemp. Afro-Am.P.*, ed. B. Bell (1972); *Early Negro Writing*, ed. D. Porter (1972); *Understanding the New Black Poetry*, ed. S. Henderson (1973); *The New Negro Ren.*, ed. A. P. Davis and M. W. Peplow (1975); *Chant of Saints*, ed. M. S. Harper and R. B. Stepto (1979); *Afro-Am. Writing*, ed. R. A. Long and E. W. Collier (1985); *Collected Black Women's Poetry*, ed. J. R. Sherman, 4 v. (1988).

HISTORY AND CRITICISM: B. G. Brawley, *The Negro in Lit. and Art* (1910); V. Loggins, *The Negro Author* (1931); S. A. Brown, *Negro Poetry and Drama* (1937); J. S. Redding, *To Make a Poet Black* (1939); M. J. Butcher, *The Negro in Am. Culture* (1956); *The Black American Writer*, v. 2, ed. C. W. E. Bigsby (1969); N. I. Huggins, *Harlem Ren.* (1971); J. Wagner, *Black Poets of the U.S.* (1973); *Mod. Black Poets*, ed. D. Gibson (1973); B. Jackson and L. D. Rubin, Jr., *Black Poetry in America* (1974); A. P. Davis, *From the Dark Tower* (1974); E. B. Redmond, *Drumvoices: The Mission of Afro-Am.P.* (1976); D. Perkins, *A Hist. of Mod. Poetry*, 2 v. (1976, 1987), v. 1, ch. 18, v. 2, ch. 25; N. A. Scott, Jr., "Black Lit.—Since 1945," *Harvard Guide to Contemp. Am. Writing*, ed. D. Hoffman (1979); M. G. Cook, *Afro-Am. Lit. in the 20th C.* (1984); H. A. Baker, Jr., *Blues, Ideology and Afro-Am. Lit.* (1984), *Afro-Am. Poetics* (1988); *Black Am. Poets Between Worlds, 1940–1960*, ed. R.

B. Miller (1986); H. L. Gates, *The Signifying Monkey* (1988); J. R. Sherman, *Invisible Poets: Afro-Americans of the 19th-C.*, 2d ed. (1989); B. Jackson, *A Hist. of Afro-Am. Lit.*, v. 1 (1989).   N.A.S.

AGRARIANS. See FUGITIVES.

AÍ FHREISLIGI (ae freislighe, literally "lying down poetry"). Ir. meter comprising four heptasyllabic lines, the first and third ending in trisyllables, the second and fourth ending in disyllables. There is rhyme between the two trisyllabic words and between the two disyllabic words, e.g.

> A bhean fuair an falachán,
> do-chiú ar fud do chiabh snáithmhín
> ní as a bhfuighthear achmhasán
> d'fholt Absolóin mhic Dháivídh.
>   (Tomás ó Rhathile, *Dánta Grádha*,
>   1926)

("O woman with the snood that I see over your locks of soft threads that would put to shame the hair of Absalom son of David.") There are varieties of a. f.: *aiclech* ("with *aicill*" [q.v.]), *bec* ("small"), *for dechnad* ("modeled on *dechnad*").—K. Meyer, *Primer of Ir. Metrics* (1909); G. Murphy, *Early Ir. Metrics* (1961); E. Knott, *Ir. Syllabic Poetry 1200–1600* (1974).   J.E.C.W.

AICILL. Rhyme in classical (syllabic) Ir. poetry is of three kinds: final (i.e. between words which terminate lines), internal (between a word in the interior of one line of a couplet and a word in the interior of the next), and final-interior (between a word at the end of the first line of a couplet and a word in the interior of the next). The technical term for the final-internal variety is *aicill* and the meter in which it occurs is called *aiclech*. The following verse in rannaighecht mór meter illustrates *aicill* in lines 3 and 4:

> Im-ráidi baís cen bríg mbaí:
>   is súaichnid ní gaís fris-gní.
> An-as-bir-siu bid rád fÁS:
>   bid nessa ar mbÁS 'síu 'ma-rrí.

"Thy mind is set on profitless folly: / clearly it is not wisdom thou pursuest. / What thou sayest will be empty speech: / our death will be nearer before it come to pass" (Murphy, 8–9).
    K. Meyer, *Primer of Ir. Metrics* (1909); G. Murphy, *Early Ir. Metrics* (1961); E. Knott, *Ir. Syllabic Poetry 1200–1600* (1974).   J.E.C.W.

AIR. (1) A melody or tune; that part of a vocal or instrumental composition that has an identity apart from any accompaniment or harmony. In the 16th and 17th cs., the term a. (Eng. *ayre*, Fr. *air de cour*, It. *aria*) usually denoted a song (q.v.) consisting of a text set to accompanied melody, though some instrumental dances were also called airs. In England, airs were often printed so that they could be performed as vocal solos accompa-

nied by the lute or other instruments, or as part songs with a dominant upper voice. This focus on one voice allowed for a clear presentation of the text, which in turn allowed for musical treatment of longer (usually strophic) and more complex poems than feasible in the madrigal (q.v.) or other polyphonic forms. (2) In the writings of some of the late 16th- and 17th-c. Eng. musical theorists such as Morley and Butler, the mode or key of a piece. (3) By extension of the sense of a. as "manner or bearing," the aesthetic quality of the combination of musical elements. Roger North (1651–1734) writes that "Ayre in Musick, is like witt in poetry, not fixt upon any one quality, but being taken all-together gives the recommendation." See also SONG.—T. Morley, *A Plaine and Easie Intro. to Practicall Musicke* (1597); C. Butler, *Principles of Musick* (1636); P. Warlock, *The Eng. Ayre* (1926); *Roger North on Music*, ed. J. Wilson (1959); U. Olshausen, *Das lautenbegleitete Sololied in England um 1600* (1963); *Lyrics from Eng. Airs, 1596–1622*, ed. E. Doughtie (1970); I. Spink, *Eng. Song: Dowland to Purcell* (1974); N. Fortune and D. Greer, "A.," *New Grove*; E. Jorgens, *The Well-Tun'd Word* (1982); L. Schleiner, *The Living Lyre in Eng. Verse* (1984); E. Doughtie, *Eng. Ren. Song* (1986); W. Maynard, *Elizabethan Lyric Poetry and its Music* (1986).   E.D.

AKKADIAN POETRY. See ASSYRO-BABYLONIAN POETRY.

ALBA (Occitan), *aube, aubade* (OF), *Tagelied* (Ger.; q.v.). A dawn song, ordinarily expressing the regret of two lovers that day has come so soon to separate them. Its counterpart, the serenade or evening song (*serena*), is somewhat less common. It has no fixed metrical form, but in Occitan each stanza usually ends with the word *alba*. The earliest examples in Occitan and OF date from the end of the 12th c. The a. probably grew out of the medieval watchman's cry, announcing from his tower the passing of the night hours and the return of day. In one a. it is a watchman who speaks, a friend of the lover's, who has been standing guard. Others are dialogues between lover and beloved, with occasional comments from the author. In Eng. poetry, examples can be found in Chaucer (*Troilus and Criseyde* and the *Reeve's Tale*) and in Browning ("Parting at Morning"); in the 20th c., the form has been attempted by Ezra Pound ("A."), W. H. Auden, William Empson, Louis MacNeice, and Philip Larkin, among others. Indeed, the genre is far from being limited to the Romance or Romance-derived trads.: analogues can be found in a great many lits. (Hatto). See LOVE POETRY.
    R. E. Kaske, "An Aube in the *Reeve's Tale*," *ELH* 26 (1959) and *MLN* 75 (1960); A. T. Hatto, "Das Tagelied in der Weltliteratur," *DVLG* 36 (1962), ed., *Eos* (1965)—major anthol.; J. Saville, *The Med. Erotic A.* (1972); D. Rieger, *Gattungen und Gat-*

ALBANIAN POETRY

tungsbezeichnungen der Trobadorlyrik (1976), and in *GRLMA*, v. 2, pt. 1B; E. W. Poe, "The Three Mo-dalities of the Old Prov. Dawn Song," *RPh* 37 (1984), "New Light on the A.: A Genre Redefined," *Viator* 15 (1984); Chambers; H. U. Seeber, "Intimität und Gesellschaft: Zur Ren. der Aubade in der englischen Lyrik des 20. Jhs.," *Gattungs-probleme in der anglo-amerikanischen Lit.*, ed. R. Borgmeir (1986).   F.M.C.; T.V.F.B.

ALBANIAN POETRY. A. lit. dates from the 16th c., the oldest printed book being a missal by Gjon Buzuku (1555), the first in a long series of Roman Catholic priests and writers. Pjetër Budi, translator of a *Dottrina Christiana* (1618), was the first to add religious poems, about 800 *abab* quatrains in the national A. line, a trochaic octosyllable, often catalectic. The line occurs in two dialectal variants. The older Tosk (Southern) variant ignores stress, the ictus falling indifferently on tonic or atonic syllables, whereas the Gheg (Northern) variant is stressed on the 3rd and the 7th, with a break after the 3rd or the 4th, the metrical ictus and tonic accent usually coinciding. Budi's verse is ictic and also quantitative, a long often being resolved into two shorts. Budi's ictic and quantitative metric (Gheg differentiates between long and short vowels, whereas Tosk does not) yields to an accentual-syllabic metric in Pjetër Bogdani's *Cuneus prophetarum* (1685), a doctrinal work interspersed with *abababcc* octaves of Italianate octosyllables.

The oldest A. poem is a Tosk hendecasyllabic octave of the Sicilian type (see STRAMBOTTO). The *abababab* poem introduces a *Dottrina Christiana* (1592) tr. by Lukë Matranga, a Byzantine Arbëresh (Italo-Albanian) priest of Sicily, where several A. settlements existed at the time. The first collection of A. folksongs, found in the Chieuti Codex (1737), is also in Tosk. The authors, two Byzantine Arbëresh priests, were descendants of Arvanites (Greco-Albanians) who fled Morea when it was invaded by Turks. The Arbëresh verse is ictic like Budi's verse, but unrhymed. The Codex also contains religious poems in Italianate meters. Jul Variboba's *Gjella e Shën Mërisë Virgjër* (Life of St. Mary Virgin, 1762) is written in similar Italianate meters, quatrains of double pentasyllables with internal rhyme, and teems with Italianisms. The author, a Byzantine Calabro-Albanian priest, scoffs at the immaculate conception while lashing at the Church for turning the Virgin into the "Great Queen" of heaven, no longer caring for the wretched of the earth.

A byproduct of either Roman Catholic liturgy or Byzantine Arbëresh culture, A. p. includes, from the 18th c. on, a third, lay Moslem component. These poems, in Arabic script, follow oriental patterns, *aaab* or *abab* stanzas of fluctuating Tosk octosyllables, and *abab* stanzas of basically trochaic Gheg *beyts*. The major poet, Nezim Frakulla (ca. 1760), wrote a *divan* couched in Arabic and Persian nomenclature.

Thus far, A. p. is a discordant agglomeration of poetries, developing separately from different religions. Missing is a national consciousness that would bring them together. The Greek War of Independence, in which the Arvanites played an important part, was the first incentive for the birth of a national romantic poetry. Its pioneer is Girolamo De Rada (1814–1903), a Calabro-Albanian professor whose first work, *Songs of Milosao* (1836), a suite of lyrics in the unrhymed Arbëresh octosyllable, draws generously from folksongs collected by De Rada, which he deftly interweaves into a romantic story combining patriotism and *mal de siècle*. The poem was a model to younger Arbëresh poets. Gabriele Dara, Jr. (1826–85) wrote *Kënga e Sprasme e Balës* (Last Song of Bala) in the same Arbëresh meter. Italianate meters prevail in the exalted lyrics of Giuseppe Serembe (1843–91), who died insane. Antonio Santori (1819–94) wrote the first A. drama. A master of verse, Giuseppe Schirò (1865–1927) even tried Cl. meters.

In A. proper, romantic poetry flourished after the Congress of Prizren (1878–81), marking the A. *Risorgimento*. Tosk poetry resurged with Naim Frashëri (1846–1900), a noble patriot and a mystic belonging to the Shia Bektashi sect. His popular ictic octosyllable appealed to the masses. Andon Chako (Çajupi, 1866–1930), a democratic poet, was to the Orthodox what Frashëri had been to Moslems. First among Tosks, Aleks Drenova (Asdren, 1872–1947) made use of Western metrical forms, incl. the sonnet. Fan Noli's poetic talent was spent mostly in translations—deservedly famous is his tr. of Omar Khayyám's *Ruba'iyat* (1927). Lasgush Poradeci (1899–1988) is admired for the melody of his verse.

Gheg poetry was concentrated in Shkodër. Its main representatives were Gjergj Fishta (1871–1940), a Franciscan friar, and Ndré Mjeda (1866–1937), a Jesuit. Considered by Ghegs a national poet, Fishta wrote lyric, satiric, and epic verse mostly in Western meters. His monumental *Lahuta e Malcís* (The Mountain Lute), based on North A. heroic and epic songs, is written in the popular stressed octosyllable; it recounts the battles between the North Albanians and the South Slavs during the A. *Risorgimento*. Mjeda composed lyrics set in learned meters, his sonnets (*Lissus, Scodra*) being a model of the genre. Filip Shiroka (1859–1935) wrote in exile. Among the younger generation of the Shkodër school, the most influential were Ernest Koliqi (1903–75), better known as a narrative writer, and Millosh Gjergj Nikolla (Migjeni, 1911–38). His *Vargjet e lira* (Free Verse) brought into A. lit. a *souffle nouveau*, that of social revolution. His verse, often imperfect, is nevertheless redeemed by a unique expressive power and by his original metaphors.

Contemp. A. Socialist Realism has not yet produced a poet who can compare with Migjeni. Its preeminent representative, Ismail Kadare, styled some original poems at his debut, then moved to narrative. Dritëro Agolli wrote some genuine proletarian poetry before becoming the regime's official poet. Nor is the situation better in Kosova, the Yugoslav "autonomous province" inhabited overwhelmingly by Albanians. After a promising start, due to a modicum of freedom enjoyed by Yugoslav writers, the Kosovar bark ran aground when the Kosovars, who are all Gheg, adopted for political reasons the so-called "unified literary Albanian," in fact a variant of Tosk. Because of basic phonological differences between the two dialects, their metric systems remain different.

The major living poet, Martin Camaj, is an exile who holds the Munich Albanology chair. He has published several volumes of poetry. Yet his masterpiece, *Dranja* (1981), is a suite of "madrigals" in poetic prose. It tells of the adventures of an "imperfect being," a turtle, with which the poet identifies. Written in emblematic lang., something novel in A. lit., the work succeeds in grafting the author's poetics onto the pagan mythology and ancestral customs of his Gheg highland people—a real *tour de force*, through which the poet transcends trad. while remaining faithful to his origins.

ANTHOLOGIES AND COLLECTIONS: *Rapsodie di un poema albanese*, comp. G. De Rada (1866); *Albanike Melissa—Bëlietta shqypëtare* (The A. Bee), comp. E. Mitko (1878); *Kângë popullore gegnishte* (Gheg Folk Songs), comp. V. Prennushi (1911); *Kângë kreshnikësh dhe legenda* (Heroic Songs and Legends), comp. B. Palaj and D. Kurti (1937); *Poesia popolare albanese*, tr. E. Koliqi (1957); *Chansonnier épique albanais*, tr. K. Luka (1983); *Contemp. A. Poems*, tr. B. Pogoni (1985).

HISTORY AND CRITICISM: F. Cordignano, *La poesia epica di confine nell'Albania del Nord* (1943); S. Skendi, *A. and South Slavic Oral Epic Poetry* (1954); M. Lambertz, *Die Volksepik der Albaner* (1958); G. Schirò, Jr., *Storia della letteratura albanese* (1959); A. Pipa, *A. Lit.: A Social Perspective* (1978), *A. Folk Verse: Structure and Genre* (1978); *Historia e letërsisë shqiptare* (Hist. of A. Lit.), ed. D. Shuteriqi; R. Eslie, *Dict. of A. Lit.* (1986). A.PI.

ALCAIC. An Aeolic (q.v.) strophe named after Alcaeus of Lesbos (fl. early 6th c. B.C.) and which consists of two 11-syllable lines (A. hendecasyllables) having the form x – ◡ – x – ◡ ◡ – ◡ – followed by a third line which is a rhythmic extension of the first two: x – ◡ – x – ◡ x – ◡ ◡ – ◡ ◡ – ◡ – ◡ – (so Snell). The Alexandrian grammarians separated the third line into two parts, after the ninth position, creating a 4-line stanza, the third line of nine syllables (x – ◡ – x – ◡ – –) and the fourth of ten (– ◡ ◡ – ◡ ◡ – ◡ – –). The first two lines, the hendecasyllables, are known as Greater As., the decasyllable (line 4) as a Lesser A. Horace, who used this strophe more than any other in his *Odes* (37 times), seems to have regarded it as a 4-line stanza, allowing hiatus between lines 3 and 4 (e.g. *Odes* 2.14.3–4). Hor-

ace's A. strophe was used by medieval poets: Hilary of Poitiers (4th c. A.D.) in his first hymn created a stanza consisting of a glyconic (q.v.) alternating with either an A. hendecasyllable or an asclepiad (q.v.); Prudentius (late 4th c.) used the A. hendecasyllable for stichic verse; and the hendecasyllable in quatrains, devised by Ennodius (late 5th c.), became the most used A. form of the Middle Ages. It was adapted in It. by Gabriello Chiabrera (1552–1638), Paolo Rolli (1687–1765), and Giovanni Fantoni (1755–1807). Like Chiabrera, Ren. metrists in England and France attempted imitations of As. on both accentual and quantitative principles. In 18th-c. Germany, F. G. Klopstock ("An meine Freunde," "An Fanny") composed 17 A. odes, as did Hölderlin ("An die Parzen," "Der Main"), von Platen, and others in the 19th. Tennyson's A. ode to Milton ("O mighty-mouth'd inventor of harmonies") makes the most serious effort of his age to reproduce the Cl. rules for quantitative scansion without replacing quantity by stress; and the *In Memoriam* stanza (q.v.) Tennyson considered to be related to the A. By contrast, Clough and Swinburne wrote accentual As. Translations of Cl. As. in the 20th c. incl. examples by Richmond Lattimore (*Gr. Lyrics* [1955]) and J. B. Leishman's tr. of Horace (1956). See now CLASSICAL METERS IN MODERN LANGUAGES.

F. V. Graeser, *De stropha alcaica* (1865); E. Brocks, "Die Fortleben der alkäische Strophe," *GRM* 13 (1925); O. Francabandera, *Contribuzioni alla storia dell'alcaica* (1928); Norberg; Bowra; W. Bennett, *Ger. Verse in Cl. Metres* (1963); Koster; N. A. Bonavia-Hunt, *Horace the Minstrel* (1969); R. G. M. Nisbet and M. Hubbard, *A Commentary on Horace: Odes Book I* (1970); E. Schäfer, *Deutscher Horaz* (1976); Halporn et al.; Snell; West; D. Schaller, "Der alkäische Hendekasyllabus im frühen Mittelalter," *MitJ* 19 (1984). R.A.S.; J.W.H.; T.V.F.B.

ALCMANIC VERSE. A final colon in the strophe of the *Partheneion* of the Gr. lyric poet Alcman (7th c. B.C.) which can take two forms, – ◡ ◡ – ◡ ◡ – ◡ – – or – ◡ ◡ – ◡ ◡ – ◡ ◡ – (West). The latter, a dactylic tetrameter brachycatalectic, is the one to which the term usually refers, although some scholars call the full dactylic tetrameter the A. and the catalectic dactylic tetrameter the Archilochian (q.v. [so Klingner]).—*Horatius: Opera*, ed. F. Klingner, 3d ed. (1959); Maas; Halporn et al.; Snell; West. J.W.H.

ALEXANDRIANISM.

I. ALEXANDRIA
II. VARYING CONNOTATIONS OF ALEXANDRIANISM
III. CALLIMACHUS AND EPIC
IV. THE ALEXANDRIAN CODE
V. ALEXANDRIANISM IN ROME: VIRGIL
VI. ALEXANDRIANISM IN MODERN LITERATURE

ALEXANDRIANISM

I. ALEXANDRIA, founded in 331 B.C. by Alexander the Great at the mouth of the Nile, was an immensely wealthy entrepôt ruled over by the dynasty of the Ptolemies (Fraser). Seeking to bolster their position, the Ptolemies drew to the Museum ("shrine of the Muses") and enormous Library adjacent to the Royal Palace scholars and scientists from all over the Gr. world. These tax-exempt, residential scholars had no duties except to conduct research and to edify or amuse their royal patrons.

II. VARYING CONNOTATIONS OF ALEXANDRIANISM. Befitting the inhabitants of a large commercial metropolis, in antiquity "Alexandrian" implied "impudent," "witty" (Quintilian 1.2.7). Nowadays, the term is often used to define an over-refined, precious, bookish literary style limiting itself to the shorter poetic genres. This is what certain ancient critics would have attributed to one particular Alexandrian poet, Callimachus of Cyrene (ca. 305–240 B.C.), and his followers (*Gr. Anthol.* 11.321–22).

III. CALLIMACHUS AND EPIC. But Callimachus himself wrote an epic, the *Hecale*, in reply, we are told, to those who criticized him for not being able to write a "big poem" (Pfeiffer 2.53, v. 106; cf. fr. 378–79); and his elegiac *Aetia* in four books was evidently felt to be ambitious enough to inspire imitation in epic by Apollonius of Rhodes, described by ancient Lives as Callimachus' disciple. (There is no reliable evidence for the old-fashioned view that Apollonius and Callimachus quarreled over epic.) Apollonius' *Argonautica* (also in four books) thus acquires fresh importance as major evidence of Callimachean epic, and its imitation by Virgil in the *Aeneid* (see sect. V below) becomes more intelligible.

Since Homer was pre-empted as the figurehead and patron of the kind of propagandizing, eulogistic epic favored by his literary enemies, whom he nicknames Telchines, Callimachus borrowed another venerable Gr. epic and didactic poet, Hesiod, as his counter figure, notably in the opening scene of the *Aetia*. This enabled the poet to praise the didactic poetry of Aratus of Soli as legitimate because it was in Hesiod's manner (epigram 27). Callimachus was never so foolish as to attack Homer himself—only his uninspired imitators symbolized by Creophylus (epigram 6). The *Hecale* showed how the Homeric legacy could be recovered, not by tub-thumping, univocal parallels between some modern general and heroic Achilles, but by the polyphonic (ironic) echoes awakened when the Homeric Odysseus in Eumaeus' hut is recalled by the scene between young Prince Theseus and motherly old Hecale in her cottage in the woods of Attica (Pfeiffer on frag. 239), or when the gargantuan repasts of conventional epic are "reduced" to the modest salad shared by the Callimachean pair (frags. 248–52). This is more than parody. It is a graceful, regretful evocation of a vanished and innocent time.

In his epic, Callimachus follows "tragic and comic vocabulary everywhere" (Pfeiffer on frag. 233). Had this been understood, a great many subsequent epic poets, incl. Dante, might have been spared the criticisms of their lang. by self-appointed guardians of classical purity (Weinberg).

IV. THE ALEXANDRIAN CODE. By study of all of Callimachus' programmatic statements it is ultimately possible to establish an Alexandrian code or complex of motifs which together or singly indicate the presence of the Alexandrian modification in lit. The most important are allusions to Hesiod, Helicon, Ascra, or pastoral (particularly developed in Theocritus); to the poet as water drinker (a later but natural extension: Pfeiffer, 1.11); to the poet as treading a narrow, difficult, or original path; to the poet's refusal (*recusatio*: see Wimmel) to meet conventional expectations (the "warning Apollo" motif, later modified to the promise to write epic "one day" or to the referral of a patron's request for such epic to another and by implication better poet); to the "crowd" (the insensitive and crude critics) and to its envy of the poet; to the need for brevity; to the poet as poor and his rival as rich; and to irony and play as legitimate poetic ideals, yet paradoxically to poetry itself as hard and ultimately unfinishable work (the Alexandrian poetic *ponos*-ideal: cf. Theocritus 7.51).

V. ALEXANDRIANISM IN ROME: VIRGIL. With the transference of A. to Rome at least as early as Ennius, and marked in Lucilius (Puelma), the Callimachean/Apollonian opening towards epic was magnified. This is already apparent in Catullus (poem 64) and in Lucretius, whose didactic *De rerum natura* is far more than an exercise in turning philosophical prose into verse. In Virgil the conflicting claims of A. and eulogistic epic led to an early abandonment of plans for a history poem and to a reflective excursion into pastoral (the *Eclogues*, 36 B.C.?). The sixth eclogue quotes from the Preface to the *Aetia* of Callimachus (motif of the warning Apollo), though not to reject epic so much as to postpone its challenge. The poetry sketched after this *recusatio* anticipates themes of Ovid's *Metamorphoses*, and both legitimizes that poem within the cl. epic trad. and points to the proper interp. of the *Aeneid* as a tragic series of metamorphoses in which characters blend into one another and into different Homeric counterparts in a technique already described for Callimachus' *Hecale*. The path to epic for Virgil lay through the Hesiodic *Georgics* (2.176; cf. *Eclogues* 6.70). The influence of Apollonius is equally clear (Dido = Hypsipyle/Medea). The *Aeneid* is not a historical, eulogistic epic of the type favored by Callimachus' adversaries, even though symbolically and obliquely it comments on Roman history, and even though it incidentally eulogizes Augustus. In this sense, given the stark ancient alternatives, it is correct to speak of Virgil as having written a Callimachean epic.

VI. ALEXANDRIANISM IN MODERN LITERATURE. "A." is a recurrent phenomenon. In our own age, Fr. practitioners and theorists such as Valéry and Mallarmé show many parallels with ancient ideas (Howald). Am. poets such as Pound and Eliot illustrate both the hostility of the new poetry to traditional epic (in their case, Milton) and the push beyond the small scale notable in Callimachus—even, in Eliot's case, into the drama. A great work of mutual reconciliation between the ancient and modern worlds will be accomplished by the realization of the modernity of the ancient and antiquity of the modern. In this work, the proper study and assessment of the real scope of A. will be essential. See also CLASSICAL POETICS, sect. V; GREEK POETRY, Classical.

TEXTS: Select Papyri III: Lit. Papyri, ed. D. L. Page (1950); Callimachus: Aetia, Iambi, Hecale and other Frags., ed. and tr. C. A. Trypanis (1958); Callimachus, ed. R. Pfeiffer, 2 v. (1965–69).

HISTORY AND CRITICISM: U. von Wilamowitz, Hellenistische Dichtung in der Zeit des Kallimachos, 2 v. (1924); J. U. Powell, Collectanea Alexandrina (1925); W. Allen, Jr. "The Epyllion," TAPA 71 (1940); E. Howald, Der Dichter Kallimachos von Kyrene (1948)—illuminating comparisons with mod. Fr. poetry; M. Puelma Piwonka, Lucilius und Kallimachos (1949); W. Wimmel, Kallimachos in Rom (1960); Weinberg; G. N. Knauer, Die Aeneis und Homer (1964)—exhaustive documentation of Virgil's use of Homeric subtexts; A. Lesky, Hist. of Gr. Lit, tr. Willis and de Heer (1966); J. K. Newman, Augustus and the New Poetry (1967)—appendix on "A. in Mod. Eng. Poetry," The Cl. Epic Trad. (1986)—incl. bibl.; R. Pfeiffer, Hist. of Cl. Scholarship (1968); P. M. Fraser, Ptolemaic Alexandria, 3 v. (1972); R. Häussler, Das historische Epos der Griechen und Römer bis Virgil (1976), Das historische Epos von Lucan bis Silius und seine Theorie (1978); Trypanis; R. D. Brown, "Lucretius and Callimachus," Illinois Cl. Studies 7 (1982); Supplementum Hellenisticum, ed. H. Lloyd-Jones and P. Parsons (1983); N. Hopkinson, A Hellenistic Anthol. (1988); G. O. Hutchinson, Hellenistic Poetry (1988); CHCL.   J.K.N.

ALEXANDRINE. In Fr. prosody (q.v.), a line of 12 syllables. From the 16th c. up to vers libre (q.v.), the a. has been the standard meter of Fr. poetry, in which it has had an importance comparable to that of the (quantitative) hexameter in Gr. and Lat. or the iambic pentameter in Eng.; it has been used esp. in narrative and dramatic forms.

The earliest Fr. as. appear in Le Pèlerinage de Charlemagne, a chanson de geste (q.v.) of the early 12th c. which abandons the traditional decasyllable (q.v.) of the med. Fr. epics for the longer line. But the a. probably takes its name from a slightly later poem, the Roman d'Alexandre (ca. 1170; in couplets) of Lambert le Tort, one of many romances of the late 12th to late 14th c. based on the legendary exploits of Alexander the Great.

The term "a." itself first appears in the anonymous Les Regles de la seconde rhetorique (ca. 1411–32): the name of the hero of the cycles is transferred metonymically to their form (cf. "Sapphic"; "Hudibrastic"). Having fallen into disuse in the later Middle Ages when replaced by prose, the meter was revived in the 16th c. by J. A. de Baïf and was widely used by Ronsard and other members of the Pléiade (q.v.). After being perfected by the great dramatists of the 17th c., esp. Corneille and Racine, it became the principal meter for all serious Fr. poetry. A certain regularity, characteristic of even the earlier a. verse, was intensified and standardized by the theory and practice of the 17th-c. poets, and the cl. form of the a. known as the tétramètre (q.v.) emerged. Most significant for the line's rhythmic structure was the fixed medial caesura, with its accompanying accent on the sixth syllable, which, dividing the line into two hemistichs, made it an apt vehicle for dramatic polarization, paradox, parallelism, and complementarity:

Lui céder, c'est ta gloire, et la vaincre, ta
    honte
(To yield to it is your glory, and to sup-
    press it your shame)
        (Corneille, Cinna)

J'embrasse mon rival, mais c'est pour
    l'étouffer
(I will embrace my rival, but only to suf-
    focate him)
        (Racine, Britannicus)

This medial articulation, its common tetrametric shape, and its syntactic integrity suited the a. for periodic and oratorical utterance in the grand manner, making it ideal for tragedy. But Molière was equally able to exploit the a. for comedy, not only for mock-heroic purposes, but also because it was sufficiently flexible and leisurely to handle lang. at much lower temperatures (the a. familier). After its 17th-c. heyday, the a. became increasingly subject to conventionalized diction and mechanical rhymes and syntax until the advent of the Fr. romantics, who rejuvenated it by generating both a new diction and by increasing the incidence both of enjambment (q.v.) and of the effaced caesura and the tripartite form of the a. known as trimètre (q.v.); thus Hugo:

J'ai disloqué / ce grand niais / d'alexan-
    drin
(I have dislocated this great simpleton,
    the alexandrine)

The evolution toward a line which is more a freely structured sequence of 12 syllables than a rule-governed system of rhythmic segmentation was carried to its conclusion in the vers libéré (q.v.) of Verlaine, Rimbaud, and Mallarmé; the alexandrin libéré with its frequent obliteration of the caesura, deemphasized rhymes, more extreme kinds of enjambment, and masking of rhythmic contours by intensified acoustic activity, brought regular Fr. verse to the brink of *vers libre* (q.v.). Since symbolism, the a. has continued to explore the whole gamut between Malherbian rigidity and liberated evanescence.

The a. has had a great importance in the poetry of several other langs., particularly Dutch, in which it was the most widely used meter from the early 17th c. until around 1880. It is a common meter in 17th-c. Ger. poetry—widely used by the school of Opitz because of the sanction lent it by *Pléiade* practice, and imaginatively exploited by Andreas Gryphius because of its formal appropriateness to his highly antithetic style. From the a. also developed the *cuaderna via* (q.v.), the important 14-syllable Sp. meter, as well as the It. meter analogous to it. The Eng. a. is composed of iambic feet with six stresses rather than the fluid four (occasionally three or two) of the Fr. a. Spenser adopted the a. as the ninth line of the Spenserian stanza (q.v.): the slight increase in length contrasts with the eight preceding pentameter lines, giving emphasis and closure to the stanza. Several longer Eng. poems—Drayton's *Polyolbion*, Browning's *Fifine at the Fair*—are written entirely in as., but in general the Eng. a. never took hold for continuous use; virtually all as. after 1600 are allusively Spenserian. Strictly speaking, the term "a." is appropriate to Fr. syllabic meters, and it may be applied to other metrical systems only where they too espouse syllabism as their principle, introduce phrasal accentuation, or rigorously observe the medial caesura, as in Fr. (e.g. Bridges' *Testament of Beauty*, though Bridges' a. has no fixed caesura).

E. Träger, *Der Französische Alexandriner bis Ronsard* (1889); H. Thieme, *The Technique of the Fr. A.* (1898); T. Rudmose-Brown, *Étude comparée de la versification française et de la versification anglaise* (1905); V. Horak, *Le Vers a. en français* (1911); G. Lote, *L'A. d'après la phonétique expérimentale*, 3 v. (1911–12); A. Rochette, *L'A. chez Victor Hugo* (1911); Thieme, 360 ff., 374 ff.; P. Verrier, *Le Vers français*, 3 v. (1931–32), v.2–3; J. B. Ratermanis, "L'Inversion et la structure de l'a.," *FS* 6 (1952); M. Burger, *Recherches sur la structure et l'origine des vers romans* (1957); Elwert; Mazaleyrat; P. Lusson and J. Roubaud, "Mètre et rythme de l'a. ordinaire," *LF* 23 (1974); J. Roubaud, *La Vieillesse d'Alexandre* (1978); Morier; Scott; B. de Cornulier, *Théorie du vers* (1982); C. Scott, *A Question of Syllables* (1986).　　A.PR.; C.S.; T.V.F.B.

ALLÆOSTROPHA. The Gr. term *alloiostropha* is used by Hephaestion (ed. Consbruch, p. 69) to describe one type of *apolelymena* (literally, "released" or "free" verse—verse which does not exhibit a repeated pattern of any sort). *Apolelymena* too short to constitute what Hephaestion regards as a single strophe are called *astropha* (*astrophic*), those which do not exhibit any single recognizable pattern of division into strophes are *atmeta* ("indi-

visibles"), and those composed of two or more contrasting strophes are *heterostropha* ("composed of strophes of which the one is different from the other") if there are only two such strophes, and *alloiostropha* ("different strophied") if there are more than two. Milton uses the term, spelled *allæostropha* (for reasons unknown), in the preface to *Samson Agonistes* to describe verse in irregular stanzas. Hephaestion was pub. in Turnebus' ed. in 1553, a work that Milton almost surely would have known, it being the only ed. available in the 17th c., and Hephaestion the standard authority for all ancient metrical doctrine. See now HETEROMETRIC; ODE; STANZA; STICHOS; STROPHE.—Maas, sects. 30, 71, 72; West 135–37.　　A.T.C.

ALLEGORY.

    I. WESTERN
        A. *Text and Concept*
        B. *Text and History*
        C. *Text and Structure*
        D. *Text and Consciousness*
    II. NONWESTERN

I. WESTERN. A. (Gr. *allos*, "other," and *agoreuein*, "to speak") is a term that denotes two complementary procedures: a way of composing lit. and a way of interpreting it. To compose allegorically is to construct a work so that its apparent sense refers to an "other" sense. To interpret allegorically ("allegoresis") is to explain a work as if there were an "other" sense to which it referred. Not only do both of these procedures imply each other; the two forms of a. increasingly stimulate one another as they develop into full-scale literary and interpretive movements in their own right.

Because a. is so various in its operations, turning from one sense to another in widely divergent texts and times, it resists any attempt at strict and comprehensive definition. It can be argued, for example, that any composition may have some "other" sense. The question of which kinds of composition are specifically "allegorical" has received diverse responses since ancient definitions of the term in Gr. and Roman rhetorical treatises. By the late 1st c. A.D., the term is applied by Quintilian (*Institutio oratoria* 8.6.44–59) to a brief trope (Virgil's shepherd "Menalcas" signifying Virgil himself), a sustained metaphor (Horace's "ship of state" ode), and an ironic form of discourse, in which a speaker says something other than what he intends (Cicero's mocking praise of a man's "integrity" in order to blame him). At times the term has been associated with even more general tensions attributed to literary lang.—from the aspiration of works to express the "inexpressible" (F. Schlegel, *Gespräch über die Poesie*, 1800) to the liability of narratives to betray conflicts in their own value systems (de Man 1979). Perhaps the dominant attitude in current classifications is that there are degrees of allegorical composition, depending on the extent to which a text displays two divided tendencies. One tendency is for the elements of the text to exhibit a certain fictional autonomy. The other tendency is for these elements to imply another set of actions, circumstances, or principles, whether found in another text or perceived at large. The story of a journey, for example, may develop into an a. of the Exodus by its evocation of a wilderness and a promised land. The extent of such an a. diminishes, however, insofar as the "journey" is either reduced to a short-lived figure of speech or elaborated into an explicit paraphrase of the biblical account itself. Insofar as a composition is allegorical, it tends to signal the ambivalence or allusiveness of its lang. and to prescribe the directions in which a reader should interpret it.

While interpretive a. is implicit in the design of works composed allegorically, it is not limited to works intended to be allegorized. Allegoresis has a momentum of its own. By the time of the Jewish biblical exegete Philo (1st c. B.C.–1st c. A.D.) and the near-contemporary Gr. Homeric commentator Heraclitus the Allegorizer, the term itself appears with reference to both brief passages and sustained narratives in the service of explanations ranging from the spiritual (the planting of a garden in Eden as the planting of virtues in the soul [Philo, *De plantatione*]) to the physical (the angry Apollo sending a plague as the fiery sun provoking disease [Heraclitus, *Homerika problēmata*]). Recent crit. sometimes applies the term to all interp., viewed as the reformulation of a text in other terminology. The normal application of the word, however, does not include many interpretive procedures: philological notes on an ancient text, scholastic "questions" about a biblical expression, historical background for a modern novel. It is arguable whether even pointing the moral of a tale is necessarily to "allegorize" it. To say, for example, that the labors of Hercules display the triumph of fortitude over hardship seems different in degree, if not in kind, from saying that they represent the victory of reason over passion. The latter interp. entails the kind of shift in categories of understanding that is now normally associated with "allegorical" interp. Because such categories themselves change over time, the degree to which an interp. is considered allegorical varies with the degree of difference perceived between the apparent sense of a text and the other-sense assigned to it. Given these changes in perspective, interp. that is considered allegorical does not necessarily offer a less functional reading than do other interpretive attempts to reconstitute a work written in a different place or time. Like them, it needs to be tested against those elements of the work which it excludes. In the end, allegorical interp. may help to preserve a text by applying it to contemporary circumstances or even by creating the terms under which understanding itself can take place.

As allegorical interp. and composition turn into broad movements, their approaches to the relation between one sense and another change in emphasis. Although these approaches overlap in character and time, a number of major relationships may be selected for special consideration.

A. *Text and Concept.* In its earliest systematic forms, interpretive a. tends to treat the other-sense as a conceptual framework that provides the only "true" significance of a text. Developing in the 6th and 5th cs. B.C. with Gr. efforts to interpret Homer and Hesiod according to certain "scientific" or moral categories and to defend the poets against charges of immorality, such strategies intensify in Stoic exegesis of the last centuries B.C. and 1st c. A.D. A story like Homer's battle of the gods (*Iliad*, Bk. 20), for example, turns into the physical interaction of the elements, with Hera as air and Poseidon as water. Interp. of this kind, initially called not a. but *hyponoia*, the "under-sense," coincides with broader movements in antiquity from mythological to "logical" thought. It tends to divide the text, along with the gods, into an apparent form and an underlying significance. By late antiquity, Neoplatonic interpreters are correlating different figures of a narrative with different levels of an orderly universe; to Plotinus in the 3d c. A.D., the Hesiodic succession from Uranus to Cronos to Zeus signifies the cosmic emanation from "One" to "Mind" to "Soul." Such strategies, which continue to be adapted long after antiquity, help to turn the personalities and features of mythological stories into conceptual principles which can be deployed in a philosophical or ethical argument.

Related tendencies develop early in the compositional trad. In ancient Gr. drama, figures like Aeschylus' Themis ("Justice") and Euripides' Lyssa ("Madness") are in one sense daemonic personalities in their own right, in another sense dramatic projections of human concerns. Eventually, writers of epic lit. itself give their divine figures multiple dimensions. Thus, Virgil associates Juno so closely with the physical element of air and the emotional principle of passion that she scarcely appears in the *Aeneid* without stirring up a storm. Already by the era of the ancient Gr. stage, however, a complementary procedure is developing alongside this deployment of dramatic characters as abstract principles: the deployment of abstract principles as dramatic characters. "Personification" (q.v.—Gr. *prosōpopoiia*), which long after this period comes to be considered central to Western a., in fact refers originally to the dramatic practice of "staging" personalities, figures whose masks (Lat. "personae," Gr. *prosōpa*) reveal inner meanings. The practice itself develops well outside drama, from Prodicus' 5th-c. B.C. "Choice of Heracles," in which Virtue and Vice confront a man at a crossroads, to Martianus Capella's 5th-c. A.D. *Marriage of Mercury and Philology*, in which abstract figures interact with the gods in a tale of human ascent through different levels of the cosmos. Allegorical writing, however, operates not just by the compositional process of turning conceptual systems into narrative ones, or by its antique interpretive counterpart, the process of turning narrative systems into conceptual ones. By late antiquity, a. is developing other ways of relating its divided reference points to each other.

B. *Text and History.* One of these ways is to associate both the provisional sense and the projected sense of a text with the progression of actual events over time. In the interpretive trad., this strategy begins to develop systematically with the exegesis of a text treated not as a mythological tale but as a sacred history: the story of Scripture. Tendencies to allegorize aspects of Scripture appear early in Jewish interp., from Rabbinical treatments of certain biblical passages as predictions of later events to Philo's elaborate allegorization of the text according to ethical and philosophical designs. When in the 1st c. A.D., however, the Christian Paul calls the biblical account of two wives of Abraham and their sons an a. (*Gal.* 4:24), he gives this divided relationship a different kind of historical orientation, interpreting it as the relationship between an Old Covenant and a New one. Early Christian exegetes increasingly explain the narrative transition from Old to New Testament as an historical transition from the "types" or "figures" of an early order to their eventual fulfillment in a later one. In Augustine's influential phrase, the a. of Scripture takes place "in facto," in historical events. In late antiquity and the Middle Ages, the exegesis of changing events sometimes turns into a more static form of "typology": the study of recurrent patterns. Such tendencies appear not only in the classification of natural phenomena according to spiritual categories (the lion, for example, as Christ or the Devil), but in the interp. of selected Scriptural passages according to "four senses": (1) "literal" or "historical" facts recorded in the text; (2) their "allegorical" fulfillment in Christ and/or the Church (a specific use of "allegorical"); (3) their moral or "tropological" application to the individual; and (4) their "anagogic" ("leading up") significance in the other world (see INTERPRETATION, FOUR-FOLD METHOD OF). A widespread example of the method occurs in a critical piece once attributed to Dante, the letter to Can Grande, which aligns a Scriptural reference to the Exodus with (1) the departure of the Israelites from Egypt; (2) the redemption of Christ; (3) the conversion of the soul from sin to grace; and (4) the departure of the soul to eternal glory. Yet formal strategies of this kind have counter-implications. By the late Middle Ages and the Ren., exegetes are increasingly adapting mythological stories to the multifaceted order of the Christian cosmos. Thus, to the author of the 14th-c. *Ovide moralisé*, Jupiter's metamorphosis into creatural form suggests the Incarnation of the Christian God; to Boccaccio, poetic "fable" and Scriptural "figure" so broadly overlap that ancient mythology at large becomes

an early form of theology, gradually revealed over time. In this kind of continuum, although mythological tales themselves remain at some remove from hist., they are increasingly correlated with the world "in facto."

Nothing more strikingly displays the influence of the element of time upon the compositional trad. than the first full-scale Western personification a., Prudentius' early Christian *Psychomachia* (5th c. A.D.). The poem has two parts; the author uses the brief preface to recall what he terms the "figura" of Old Dispensation events; he uses the main plot to play out this "figure" in a New Dispensation battle between personified Virtues and Vices. Here the technique of personification has more than a conceptual function, as in the "Choice of Heracles"; now it has a chronological force, turning the a. toward eschatology. Yet attempts to dramatize the movement from figure to fulfillment *after* the time of Scripture have an ambiguous relation to their Scriptural source. As later figurations of the divine story in their own right, these compositions look back to Scripture as a prior hist. that authorizes their own efforts, while they simultaneously look forward to a future hist. that they themselves cannot fully compose. The effort to engage and transfigure this state of suspension, similar in some respects to the suspended typology of "patterns" in certain uses of fourfold exegesis, helps to organize Dante's late medieval *Divine Comedy.* Here even the conceptual dimensions of the other world turn into individual souls forever playing out their particular histories, while the wayfarer himself converts to his divine author by historically recreating the Christian model of descent and ascent. This kind of pressure to pass from the sense of a story to the other-sense of hist. takes more apocalyptic forms near the end of the Middle Ages in Langland's *Piers Plowman*, where Scriptural quotations keep disrupting and reorienting the narrative, as if God himself needed to compose the tale and fulfill it "in facto."

C. *Text and Structure.* The internal strains produced by such shifts between fiction and fact increasingly direct allegorists toward the problems of their own formal designs. Particularly in Ren. and neoclassical approaches to a., the question of how one sense of a text relates to another becomes a formal issue of how the imaginative lang. of a work relates to its controlling structure. Insofar as writers in this period try to establish strict rules of structural decorum, they tend to restrict a., with its divided reference points, to special cases. Thus, 16th-c. It. critics influenced by Aristotle's *Poetics* stress that a story must be "unified" and "credible" to be true; those who reserve a place for a. treat it primarily as a specialized device for giving marvelous tales this kind of plausibility. In the exegesis of sacred lit., Protestants largely reject the "four senses" of Scripture on behalf of its "plain" sense, spiritually illuminated; at the same time, by emphasizing the need to display that illumination in the inner world of the soul, such Reformers bring their own typology of the spirit into biblical interp. In the critique of ancient mythology at large, 17th- and 18th-c. critics such as Vico tend to "rationalize" myth as an early historical phenomenon yet revalue it as a "picturesque" testimony to the primal, imaginative impulses in human development. In such interpretive movements, a. no sooner disappears than it begins to reappear in changed forms.

In the Western compositional trad., allegorists long before the It. Ren. make the formal control of diverse figures a thematic concern. The 12th-c. *Cosmographia* of Bernard Silvestris, for example, elaborately organizes its cosmological *dramatis personae* around their divine source, while the 13th-c. *Romance of the Rose* carefully orchestrates its psychological figures around the human personality. With the expansive works of Ariosto and Tasso, however, the problem of structural coherence takes the form of a general tension between the diversity of marvels and the unity of truth; Tasso himself, assisted by the *Poetics*, self-consciously analyzes the problem in a critique of his own *Jerusalem Delivered*. The part/whole relation often takes less fluid but visually arresting forms in the influential emblem books and emblematic art works of the 16th c., with their allusive characters and objects conspicuously posed as distinct facets of a philosophic design. In lit. of this period a particularly intricate treatment of such tensions is Spenser's *Faerie Queene*, where the narrative sequence and the moral progress both develop as characters interact with diverse allegorical aspects of themselves. Thus, a Spenserian knight scarcely abandons the consolidating figure of Una before he befriends the divisive figure of Duessa, while Una herself is deceived by the arch-image-maker Archimago, disguised as the knight she has lost. With Bunyan's 17th-c. *Pilgrim's Progress*, allegorical romance of this kind develops into more programmatic fiction; diversity of incident is subordinated to the inner reflections and Scriptural prooftexts of the Puritan pilgrim. By the 18th c., the question of reconciling imaginative expression with structural control takes forms ranging from Swift's *Tale of a Tub*, which elaborately parodies certain strategies of Christian exegesis while repeatedly digressing from its own story, to the more stylized lyric, which often reduces allegorical abstractions to picturesque, though animated, expressions of a rational design.

D. *Text and Consciousness.* The effort to give imaginative expression a logic of its own provokes a critique of the very basis of allegorical writing: its differentiation between the apparent sense of a text and some other sense. The critique develops esp. in theorists of the romantic period, who argue that in a., an image can be separated from the abstract concept that it signifies. By contrast, they maintain, in the preferred forms of "symbol" and "myth" (qq.v.), an image inherently participates

in the whole that it reveals. The specific terms and emphases of such theorists vary. For Goethe, "symbolic" objects of experience include a "certain totality"; for Coleridge, a growing plant is a "symbol" of the organic world to which both the plant and the perceiving mind belong (see OR-GANICISM); for Schelling, a mythological god is inseparable from the general principle it embodies. Such challenges to a. are gradually qualified by both practical and theoretical concerns. In practice, the decision about which images are separable from the thoughts and emotions they evoke often proves difficult even for romantic critics to make, esp. in works like the *Divine Comedy* and the *Faerie Queene*. In theory, romantic assumptions about "symbolic" harmonies of mind, nature, and lang. increasingly yield to attitudes more reminiscent of a. Thus, in early 20th-c. psychological and anthropological theories stimulated by Freud, Jung, and Frazer, myths and symbols themselves turn into hidden, explanatory structures underlying disparate strains in human activity at large (see MYTH CRITICISM; PSYCHO-LOGICAL CRITICISM). In aesthetic theory of this period, Walter Benjamin charges that the romantic notion of the "symbol" tends to obscure the disruptive effect of time on any effort to unify an ephemeral object with an eternal idea. By contrast, he argues, a. allows nature to be seen not "in bud and bloom" but in its inevitable "decay," leaving allegorical fragments of a desired whole. In the later 20th-c. poststructuralist crit. of Paul de Man and others (see DECONSTRUCTION), this disparity in hist. is largely treated as a disparity in lang., in which a sign evokes an origin with which it can never coincide. In such crit., the very effort to construct a whole like the "self" or the "world" depends upon, and is undermined by, the differentiation of senses associated with allegorical writing.

The critical theory of a distinction between "symbol" or "myth" and a. has its counterpart in the writing of romantic poetry itself. Here the distinction often takes the form of a tension between the poet's imaginative vision and the analytic framework it implies. In dramatic myths like Blake's *Jerusalem* and Shelley's *Prometheus Unbound*, the plot is partly an a. of the very psychological and social conditions which the poet seeks to transcend with his prophetic vision. In the more reflective lyrics of Wordsworth, Hölderlin, and, later, Baudelaire and other Fr. poets associated with the turn toward symbolist poetry, the visionary is a character who at once invites and resists the possibility that the imaginative landscape which frames him is an a. of his own consciousness. When more than one consciousness is placed in a "symbolic" scene, as in Am. romantic narratives like Hawthorne's *Scarlet Letter* or Melville's *Moby Dick*, enigmatic objects like the letter "A" and the white whale nearly allegorize the conflicting mentalities of the very characters (and readers) who

ALLEGORY

seek to interpret their "significance." In such writing, standards of significance tend to shift from a realm of authoritative, public norms to a realm of limited, private perceptions. The dilemma of orientation implied by such a shift develops in several 20th-c. works where a. is both suggested and deflected, as in Joyce's *Ulysses*, where a day of urban wandering distantly recalls the primal myth of the *Odyssey*, or in Kafka's *The Castle*, where a human personality struggles inconclusively to establish the other-sense of the institutions which impinge upon it.

By definition, allegorical writing is a particularly elusive procedure. No account of selected changes in its operation, including the one presented here, can fully show the interplay of its compositional and interpretive forms. The very elusiveness of a., however, generates a certain equilibrium of its own. For if a. is always criticizing the systems on which it appears to depend, it also keeps creating new systems in turn. In the process, a. not only complicates the strategies of composition and interp., it also helps to coordinate the sense of the one with the sense of the other. See also INTERPRETATION, FOURFOLD METHOD OF; PLATONISM AND POETRY.

Lewis; Auerbach; Curtius; F. Buffière, *Les Mythes d'Homère et la pensée grecque* (1956); E. D. Leyburn, *Satiric A.: Mirror of Man* (1956); Frye; E. Auerbach, "Figura," *Scenes from the Drama of European Lit.* (1959); E. Honig, *Dark Conceit: The Making of A.* (1959); H. de Lubac, *Exégèse médiévale: les quatre sens de l'écriture*, 2 pts. in 4 v. (1959–64); J. Daniélou, *From Shadows to Reality: Studies in the Biblical Typology of the Fathers* (1960); A. C. Hamilton, *The Structure of A. in the Faerie Queene* (1961); D. W. Robertson, Jr., *A Preface to Chaucer* (1962); A. Fletcher, *A.: The Theory of a Symbolic Mode* (1964); O. Seel, "Antike und Frühchristliche Allegorik," *Festschrift für Peter Metz*, ed. U. Schlegel and C. Z. von Manteuffel (1965); R. Tuve, *Allegorical Imagery* (1966); A. C. Charity, *Events and Their Afterlife: The Dialectics of Christian Typology in the Bible and Dante* (1966); R. Hahn, *Die Allegorie in der antiken Rhetorik* (1967); H. R. Jauss and U. Ebel, "Entstehung und Strukturwandel der allegorischen Dichtung," *GRLMA*, v. 6.1 (1968); R. Hollander, *A. in Dante's "Commedia"* (1969); M. Murrin, *The Veil of A.* (1969), *The Allegorical Epic* (1980); D. C. Allen, *Mysteriously Meant* (1970); J. MacQueen, *A.* (1970); M.-R. Jung, *Études sur le poème allégorique en France au moyen âge* (1971); U. Krewitt, *Metapher und tropische Rede in der Auffassung des Mittelalters* (1971); P. Piehler, *The Visionary Landscape* (1971); G. Clifford, *The Transformations of A.* (1974); P. Dronke, *Fabula: Explorations into the Uses of Myth in Med. Platonism* (1974); J. Pépin, *Mythe et allégorie: les origines grecques et les contestations judéo-chrétiennes*, enl. ed. (1976), *La Tradition de l'allégorie de Philon d'Alexandrie à Dante* (1987); J. A. Coulter, *The Literary Microcosm: Theories of Interp. of the Later Neoplatonists* (1976); W.

Benjamin, *The Origin of Ger. Tragic Drama*, tr. J. Osborne (1977); H.-J. Klauck, *Allegorie und Allegorese in synoptischen Gleichnistexten* (1978); S. A. Barney, *As. of Hist., As. of Love* (1979); B. K. Lewalski, *Protestant Poetics and the 17th-C. Religious Lyric* (1979); M. Quilligan, *The Lang. of A.: Defining the Genre* (1979); P. de Man, *As. of Reading* (1979), "The Rhet. of Temporality" in de Man; H. Brinkmann, *Mittelalterliche Hermeneutik* (1980); P. Rollinson, *Cl. Theories of A. and Christian Culture* (1981); *A., Myth, and Symbol*, ed. M. W. Bloomfield (1981); H. Adams, *Philosophy of the Literary Symbolic* (1983); L. Barkan, *The Gods Made Flesh: Metamorphosis and the Pursuit of Paganism* (1986); R. Lamberton, *Homer The Theologian: Neoplatonist Allegorical Reading and the Growth of the Epic Trad.* (1986); *Midrash and Lit.*, ed. G. H. Hartman and S. Budick (1986); J. Whitman, *A.: The Dynamics of an Ancient and Med. Technique* (1987); S. M. Wailes, *Medieval As. of Jesus' Parables* (1987); *Allegoresis: The Craft of A. in Med. Lit.*, ed. J. S. Russell (1988); *Med. Literary Theory and Crit. ca. 1100–ca. 1375: The Commentary Trad.*, ed. A. J. Minnis and A. B. Scott (1988); G. Teskey, "A.," *The Spenser Encyc.*, ed. A. C. Hamilton et al. (1990); D. Stern, *Parables in Midrash* (1991).   J.WH.

II. NONWESTERN. Most of the distinctions that can be drawn about Western a. can be found elsewhere—e.g. that between a. as a compositional procedure and allegoresis as an interpretive procedure, as also the problem of distinguishing between the two. Practice outside the West is not uniform, however. For example, sustained poetic narrative a. is typical almost solely of Sanskrit and other later Indic lits. There, the sacred and profane may be not so much allegorically related as aspects of each other. The boundaries are clearer in the teaching of Buddha, as in the *Lotus Sūtra*, in which there are seven major parables, and as in the concepts of expedients (*upāya*), adaptive means of teaching that gave credit to fictionality in Asia. And these religious, prose sources have their counterparts in mythical and other religious lyricism from the Middle East to East Asia.

In Chinese poetry, a. is often said to make historical and political references ("contextualization") in contrast to medieval Western as., where referents are usually philosophical or religious rather than historical facts. Of course, Daoist and Buddhist poets did write religious as., but they did not determine the main currents of Chinese poetics. As a mode of hermeneutics, allegorical interp. is as old as the Chinese literary trad. itself. The Confucian classics, for example, depict diplomats using tags from poetry in lieu of direct statement. Commentators since the 2d c. B.C. have developed a trad. of reading the *Classic of Poetry* (China's first anthology of poems), and subsequently, poetry in general, as referring obliquely to political situations. This ancient habit has provided the foundation for Chinese allegorical (*jituo*) writing. At the center of Chinese a. is a poetics of implicit imagery or symbolism, the goal of which is to create an impression of distancing while yet guiding readers to the intended meaning. Such imagistic a. flourished esp. during periods of dynastic transition—i.e. in periods of cultural crisis—because it lent itself so readily to expressing, indirectly but effectively, a poet's secret loyalty to the fallen dynasty.

Chinese practice had effect also in Korea and Japan, though chiefly on poetry written in Chinese. In Japan, a. is confined almost solely to lyric, although secular narrative echoes of Buddhist scriptures and allegoresis may be found. A. in lyrics is of two kinds: the incomplete or "open," in which nonallegorical features are also present, and the complete or "closed," in which nothing in the poem itself signals a.; external evidence is required. The incomplete kind is found in poems devoted to love (a very large category) and to congratulations or complaints (as for failure to gain promotion). The complete kind marks many poems on Buddhist topics: commonly the a. would be missed entirely without a headnote to direct interp. In both kinds natural imagery is normally the signifier of other meaning. There is also frequent use of figural imagery, e.g. the moon as a figure of enlightenment or the sky as a figure for the doctrine of Emptiness. In highly allusive poetic passages, e.g. in nō, and in allegoresis, the line between the allegorical and the nonallegorical may be difficult to draw, as in other lits.

In Ar. and Persian lit., a. is both a structural principle and a hermeneutic method. Ar. literary a. developed out of allegorical exegesis of the Koran, which distinguished between the literal (ẓāhir) and inner (bāṭin) meaning of Scripture, and was later extended to encompass other texts, until ultimately all creation was viewed as a system of signs pointing to concealed meanings. But allegorical exegesis was ultimately rejected by the orthodox; in consequence, both it and much literary a. are heterodox and esoteric, and incorporate many Iranian and Hellenizing elements. Mystical a. informs both prose treatises and lyric poems such as those of Ibn al-Fāriḍ (d. 1195?) and Ibn al-ʿArabī (d. 1240), e.g. Tarjumān al-ashwāq (The Interpreter of Desires), to which the poet later added an allegorical commentary. Moral a., which developed independent of exegesis and was influenced by trs. from Middle Persian, is found primarily in animal fables such as the Kalila and Dimna and the "trial of man by the animals" included in the Rasāʾil (Epistles) of the Ikhwān al-Ṣafāʾ.

In Persian lit., a. pervades all literary types, prose and verse, narrative and lyric, and serves a wide range of purposes. The lyric and maṣnavī (q.v.) works of Farīd al Dīn ʿAṭṭār (d. 1220), the ghazals (q.v.) and Maṣnavī maʿnavī (Spiritual Masnavi) of Jalāl al-Dīn Rūmī (d. 1273), the ghazals of ʿIrāqī (d. 1289) and the romances of Jāmī (d. 1492) provide examples of mystical a. Moral a.

informs Sanāʾī's (d. 1135) Sayr al-ʿibād ilā al-maʿād (The Believers' Journey Toward the Eternal Return). Panegyric qaṣīdas (q.v.) often employ topical a.; for example, Manūchihrī (d. 1040–41) uses the extended metaphor of Spring's battle against Winter to allude to contemp. political events. Ḥāfiẓ (d. 1389) combines topical, moral, and philosophical a. in many of his ghazals. Mystical allegoresis was widely employed as a means of legitimizing works whose content was regarded as being of dubious orthodoxy; this is particularly true in the case of Ḥāfiẓ, whose ghazals are interpreted according to a lexical code equating poetic images with mystical concepts. Such reading must be regarded as highly suspect.

R. H. Brower and E. Miner, *Japanese Court Poetry* (1961); P. Nwyia, *Exégèse coranique et langage mystique* (1970); J. W. Clinton, *The Divan of Manūchivī Dāmaghānī* (1972); A. Hamori, *On the Art of Med. Ar. Poetry* (1974); L. Hurvitz, *Scripture of the Lotus Blossom of the Fine Dharma* (1976); A. H. Plaks, *Archetype and A. in the Dream of the Red Chamber* (1976); E. Gerow, *Indian Poetics* (1977); M. Kiyota, *Shingon Buddhism: Theory and Practice* (1978); A. Schimmel, *The Triumphal Sun: A Study of the Works of Jalāl al-Dīn Rūmī* (1978); J. S. Meisami, "Allegorical Techniques in the *Ghazals* of Hāfez," *Edebiyat* 4 (1979), *Med. Persian Court Poetry* (1987); Fowler; K. S. Chang, "Symbolic and Allegorical Meaning in the *Yüeh-fu pu-t'i* Poem Series," *HJAS* 46 (1986); P. Yu, *The Reading of Imagery in the Chinese Poetic Trad.* (1987); L. Zhang, "The Letter or the Spirit: *The Song of Songs*, Allegoresis, and the Book of Poetry," *CL* 39 (1987).

J.WH.; E.M.; K.S.C.; J.S.M.

ALLITERATION. The repetition of the sound of an initial consonant or consonant cluster in stressed syllables close enough to each other for the ear to be affected. The term is sometimes also used for the repetition of an initial consonant in unstressed syllables, as in Poe's "lost Lenore," where the weak second *l* affects the ear less than the long *o* followed by *r*, but this less direct patterning is arguably not of the same class as stress-enhanced a. From Cl. times up to the 20th c., a. as a figure in rhet. meant the repetition of the initial *letter* of words; and in the absence of the relatively recent term *assonance* (q.v.), a. formerly included the echo of initial vowels, even of initial letters in weak syllables—a fact that explains Churchill's 18th-c. attack on those who unsuccessfully "pray'd / For apt alliteration's Artful aid." But it must constantly be borne in mind that since a. is a device of the *sound* stratum of poetry, the vagaries of spelling systems must be discounted: it is sounds not letters that count, as in Dickinson's "The cricket sang / And set the sun," or Dryden's "Thy force, infus'd, the fainting Tyrians prop'd; / And haughty Pharoah found his Fortune stop'd" (*Ab. & Ac.*, 842–43), where the [f] phone begins six stressed syllables, one in a medial syllable, one spelled *Ph.*

In the alliterative meter of OHG and OE poetry, esp. *Beowulf* (see ENGLISH PROSODY, *Old English*), a. usually binds three (at least two) of the four stressed syllables in the line structurally, i.e. by fixed metrical rule, as in "Oft Scyld Scefing sceathena threatum," but the same vowel can also begin the stressed syllables (today called assonance) and any vowel can "alliterate" with any other. In poetry after OE, by contrast, a. is neither linear nor structural; in fact it is often carried through several lines. Today, then, a. is one of the three most significant devices of phonic echo in poetry (see ASSONANCE and CONSONANCE: see also RHYME).

One must remember that unintentional a. will occur less often than unintentional assonance, since in most IE langs. consonants outnumber vowels. Corollary facts are (1) that the semi-vowels *h, y,* and *w* in Eng. are universally said to alliterate rather than to assonate and (2) that each of certain consonant clusters (e.g. *st, sp,* and *sc* [sk]) has traditionally been said to alliterate only with itself—this practice derives from OE. Housman, aware of this trad., lets his poet in "The Grecian Galley" alliterate seven *st* clusters in three lines.

Almost every major poetry in the world except Israeli, Persian, and Arabic seems to have made considerable use of a., which has been more popular and persistent than rhyme. Although there is disagreement about the nature or importance of stress in Gr. and Lat. poetry, it is certain that Cl. poets understood the uses of a. Aeschylus echoed initials to emphasize key words and phrases, to point up a pun, to aid onomatopoeia, or simply to please the ear (Stanford, *Aeschylus*). Lucretius revelled in phonic echoes, incl. a., while Virgil, a quieter poet, wrote many lines like these two, heavy with assonance, in which eight important syllables also bear initial [k] or [l]: "cuncta mihi Alpheum linquens locusque Molorchi / cursibus et crudo decernet Graecia caestu."

More than most others, the Romance langs. have neglected a. in favor of assonance, the reason perhaps being that It., Sp., and Port. poetry have traditionally preferred short lines with vowel (often followed by consonant) echoes in the final two syllables. Even though it is said that Fr. poetry by the 17th c. considered a. "mauvaise" (Thieme), the Fr. cl. alexandrine (q.v.) did make some use of it, as in Boileau's "Des traits d'esprit semés de temps en temps pétillent." But most Fr. poets from Hugo to St.-John Perse have found other devices more appealing to the ear.

Even the Oriental tone langs. have been as fond of a. as of other phonic echoes. Chinese, a monosyllabic lang. with short-line poems based on parallel structure and patterning of rising vs. falling tones, insists on rhyme and plays much with repeated vowels and consonants, as with initial *ch* in the opening lines of "Fu on Ascending a Tower" by Wang Ts'an (ca. A.D. 200 [Frankel]). Also tonal,

but polysyllabic, Japanese poetry has from ancient times employed much a. (Brower).

All of the Celtic langs., but esp. Ir. and Welsh, have been renowned for their elaborate schemes of phonic ornamentation. Early Welsh and Ir. "cadenced" verse was seldom rhymed but used much a. for linking words and lines. By the 6th c. this verse gave way to "rhyming" verse in which each line has stressed word pairs that alliterate or assonate, all to go with the "generic rhyming" that links lines of a stanza (see CELTIC PROSODY). By the 14th c., Welsh bards had evolved the elaborately decorated *cynghanedd* (q.v.) based on exact rhymes in couplets and complex echoes of vowels and consonants, incl. a. (Dunn).

Of the poetry in Germanic langs., modern Ger. has employed a. consistently while Eng. has liked it perhaps even more. Goethe used a. much as Shakespeare did, in conjunction with other phonic devices and normally with restraint. He might, however, open a lyric (e.g. "Hochzeitlied") with heavy a. or help elevate Faust's most important speech to Mephistopheles with "Dann will ich gern zu Grunde gehn!" Heine preferred rhymed short-line verse and needed a. less, but he often tended to heavy ornament (e.g. "Ein Wintermarchen"). Gottfried Benn and Rilke were perhaps more sound-conscious than most other 20th-c. Ger. poets, and while they too preferred assonance, Benn could write dozens of lines like this one in "Untergrundbahn": "Druch all den Frühling kommt die fremde Frau," a line no more ornate than some by Rilke.

Eng. poets continued to use a. widely, if not in such a mannered way, after the 14th-c. revival of alliterative verse in England and Scotland. Spenser makes use of it in the *Shepheardes Calender*, and in *The Faerie Queene* the first 36 lines have 7 trisyllabic alliterations—by some standards very heavy. In *MND* (5.1.147–48) Shakespeare makes fun of a., but he employs it heavily in the early long poems (e.g. *Lucrece*)—less so in the lyrics, sonnets, and plays—though a. is often conspicuous in the plays. Milton, who loved the sound of words even before his blindness, preferred assonance, but he also liked a., e.g. in "L'Allegro" ("And to the stack, or the barn door, / Stoutly struts his Dames before") and in *P.L.* ("Moping melancholy, / And moonstruck madness" [2.424–25]). Eng. poets from 1660 to 1780 worked hard with phonic echoes in order to vary not only their couplets but their blank verse and octosyllables. Dryden, Pope, Gay, and Thomson used a. best to tie adjectives to nouns, to balance nouns or verbs or adjectives, to stress the caesura and end rhyme, to join sound to sense, and to decorate their lines. After 1780, poets used a. less; still, almost every poet from Blake to Hopkins to Housman used it well, sometimes excessively, as with this typical burst in Browning's "The Bishop Orders His Tomb": "And stretch my feet forth straight as stone can point." Tennyson is reported to have said, "When I spout my lines first, they come out so alliteratively that I have sometimes no end of trouble to get rid of the a." (H. Tennyson, *Memoir* [1897]).

In the 20th c., Frost, Pound, and Williams are relatively unornamental, though Frost could sometimes alliterate heavily—"Nature's first green is gold, / Her hardest hue to hold." Others—Stevens, Eliot, Yeats—are less sparing with a., as Eliot is in the Sweeney poems and "Prufrock," though sometimes they indulge sudden excesses, as with Stevens's "Winding across Wide Waters." But there is a larger group of recent poets who, learning from Hopkins and Hardy, have depended very much on phonic echoes, esp. in unrhymed verse. Among these are Owen and Thomas in Britain and Jeffers, Moore, Crane, Roethke, Lowell, and Wilbur in the U.S. Jeffers, typical of this group, echoes not only initial consonants but also important vowels in almost every line—"Sun-silt rippled them / Asunder," "Rail-squatters ranged in nomad raillery." Although Thomas, with his charged lang. and syntax, has much a., it is no heavier than his other phonic echoes and seldom includes more than two syllables. See also SOUND; SOUND EFFECTS IN POETRY.

R. E. Deutsch, *The Patterns of Sound in Lucretius* (1939); W. B. Stanford, *Aeschylus in His Style* (1942), *The Sound of Gr.* (1967); N. I. Hérescu, *La Poésie latine* (1960); L. P. Wilkinson, *Golden Lat. Artistry* (1963); J. D. Allen, *Quantitative Studies in Prosody* (1968); Wimsatt, esp. the essays by Frankel, Brower, Lehmann, and Dunn; J. A. Leavitt, "On the Measurement of A. in Poetry," *CHum* 10 (1976); P. G. Adams, *Graces of Harmony* (1977); J. T. S. Wheelock, "Alliterative Functions in the *Divina Comedia, LeS* 13 (1978); Brogan, esp. items C111–C170, L65, L406 (Jakobson), L150, L474, L564, L686, and pp. 479–585.   P.G.A.

ALLITERATIVE VERSE. See GERMAN PROSODY, *Old Germanic*; ENGLISH PROSODY; METER.

ALLITERATIVE VERSE IN MODERN LANGUAGES. The modern revival of interest in imitations of classical OE alliterative verse (hereafter AV) is due almost entirely to the advent of Anglo-Saxon studies in university curricula. In the 19th c. only Tennyson and Hopkins show any interest in AV; Tennyson's tr. of the *Battle of Brunanburh* (1880) uses alliteration fairly consistently to link half-lines, and Hopkins' sprung rhythm (q.v.) resembles OE meter in its heavy use of alliteration and in its disregard for syllable-count, even though in other respects his metric is radically unlike cl. OE verse.

Modern imitations of true AV fall into two categories: translations from OE and analogues of OE metrical principles in modern meters. The best-known example of the first case, Pound's tr. of the OE *Seafarer* (in *Personae*, 1926) is also the first to recreate OE verse patterns:

Cuckoo calleth with gloomy crying,
He singeth summerward, bodeth sorrow,
The bitter heart's blood. Burgher knows not—
He the prosperous man—what some perform
Where wandering them widest draweth.
So that but now my heart burst from my breastlock,
My mood 'mid the mere-flood,
Over the whale's acre, would wander wide.

Despite occasional infelicities, Pound employs the major features of OE metric: alliteration to bind the heavy stresses in each half-line across a strong medial caesura; enjambment (q.v.), as in line four; and the kenning (q.v.), as in "whale's acre." The stress patterns too are typical of OE meter (see ENGLISH PROSODY, *Old English*): Sievers' Type A, "Cuckoo calleth"; Type A with anacrusis, "He singeth summerward"; Type B, "would wander wide"; Type C, "Over the whale's acre"; and Type D, "Where wandering."

As for the second case, however, major changes in the lang. over the past millennium make it nearly impossible to imitate the verse types of OE prosody consistently (in a modern imitation, as Lehmann has shown, Sievers' Type B is uncharacteristically predominant) or to find equivalents for its more subtle effects. The OE distinction between long and short syllables, for instance, cannot really be reproduced. In short, Modern Eng. is sufficiently unlike OE, OHG, or OS that only a handful of authors have been able to make use successfully of the verse types, rhetorical variation, parallelism, or kennings of cl. AV. Pound makes the effort in his first *Canto*, but the result is mainly stylistic artificiality. In England, J. R. R. Tolkien, C. S. Lewis, W. H. Auden, and Thom Gunn have all tried their hands at accentual AV, of which Lewis's exhibition poem "The Planets" is representative. Auden had studied Anglo-Saxon, and two of his works were strongly influenced by OE poetic practice: *The Age of Anxiety* and "Daniel . . . A Sermon," composed for a production of the med. *Play of Daniel* in January 1958. Am. poets who have imitated OE poetic techniques include Richard Wilbur ("Junk"), James Dickey ("Mary Sheffield"), and Fred Chappell ("My Grandfather's Church Goes Up"). Cf. CLASSICAL METERS IN MODERN LANGUAGES.

J. D. Niles, "The Old AV Form as a Medium for Poetry," *Mosaic* 11 (1978); R. Lehmann, "Contrasting Rhythms of OE and New Eng.," *Ling. and Lit. Studies A. A. Hill*, ed. M. A. Jazayery, v. 4 (1979); R. Oliver, "OE Verse and Mod. Poets," *Allegorica* 5 (1980); J. A. W. Bennett, "Survival and Revivals of Alliterative Modes," *LSE* 14 (1983).   R.H.O.

ALLUSION (Ger. *Anspielung, Zitat*). A poet's deliberate incorporation of identifiable elements from other sources, preceding or contemporaneous, textual or extratextual. A. may be used merely to display knowledge, as in some Alexandrian poems; to appeal to those sharing experience or knowledge with the poet; or to enrich a poem by incorporating further meaning. A. differs from repetition (q.v.) by recalling portions only of the original; from parody and imitation (qq.v.) in not being necessarily systematic (although Rochester's "A. to Horace" is an imitation); from source borrowing because it requires readers' knowledge of the original borrowed from; and from use of topoi (see TOPOS), commonplaces, and proverbs (q.v.) in having, in each instance, a single identifiable source.

A. is also distinguishable from intertextuality (q.v.), from precedented lang., and from plagiarism. It was said in praise of Tu Fu's late poems that every word and phrase was precedented. In Japanese poetry-matches and in poetry written on other formal occasions, some judges held that the lang. should be restricted to that used in the first few royal collections. Intertextuality is involuntary: in some sense, by using any given real lang., one draws on the intertexts from which one has learned the words, and neither the poet nor the reader is aware of the connections. Precedented poetic lang. is somewhat similar, except that the words are in principle traceable to identifiable sources. But without the special meaningfulness of connection required for a., the awareness is solely of a poetic lang. traceable to numerous possible sources. The test for a. is that it is a phenomenon that some reader or readers may fail to observe. Plagiarism is deliberate and text- or words-specific, but the plagiarizer presents what is stolen as personally original, and there is none of the interaction required by a.

Although poetic a. is necessarily manifested in words, what it draws on in another work need not be verbal. The words of the alluding passage may establish a conceptual rather than a verbal connection with the passage or work alluded to. Nonverbal a. was recognized by medieval Japanese critics and poets as belonging to conception rather than to words and verbal phrasing. This was of course thought particularly true of a poem alluding to a nonpoetic source. If a. to another poem was conceived of as working a foundation poem (*honkadori*), a. to a prose predecessor was taken as working a foundation story (*honzetsu*). There is obviously no possibility of verbal connection in a poet's a. to a historical situation or to a work in another art (as Auden's to Breughel's "Icarus" in "Musée des beaux arts"). A. presumes, then, either intentionality or whatever other name a voluntary, deliberate effort goes under (see INTENTION).

A. assumes: (1) prior achievements or events as sources of value; (2) readers sharing knowledge with the poet; (3) incorporation of sufficiently familiar yet distinctive elements; and (4) fusion of the incorporated and incorporating elements. A. is not restricted to poetry, and has analogues in other arts, religious writings, and other possible uses of echo (q.v.). It usually presumes a close relation between poet and audience, a social emphasis, a community of knowledge, and a prizing of tradition (q.v.), even fears of the loss of valued trad. Sometimes it offers coded messages. A. is also a matter of interpretation (q.v.), since readers may disagree as to the deliberateness or intentionality of a poet's incorporation of elements (see INTENTION). Debates turn on whether Jonson's *Cataline* alludes to the Gunpowder Plot; whether Milton alludes to Interregnum or Restoration events in specific passages of *Paradise Lost* and *Paradise Regained*; and whether a Ch. poem on a woman abandoned (e.g. Tu Fu, "Jiaren") alludes to the poet's disfavor under a new regime. Examples of a. in *Paradise Lost* show a variety of effects and issues. The claim to write "Things unattempted yet in Prose or Rhime" (1.16) puts Ariosto, *Orlando Furioso* 1.2, into Eng., but the result is not clear. Milton's "Thick as Autumnal Leaves" simile (1.303–4) is not an a. but a topos, as in Isaiah 34:4, Homer, *Iliad* 6.146, Virgil, *Aeneid* 5.309–10, and Dante, *Inferno* 3.112–15. There is no question but that Milton recalls a famous passage, *Aeneid* 6.126–31 (the descent to Avernus is easy, reascent barred to all but those favored by Jupiter and of bright virtue), for allusive correction of the fallen angels, as in 2.81, but less certainly in 1.633 and 2.432–33.

Kinds: (1) *Topical* a. normally refers to recent events and need not be textual. (2) *Personal* a. involves facts drawn from the poet's life, necessarily apparent or to some degree familiar, as in much of Horace, in the Petrarchan lyric sequence (q.v.), and in Shakespeare and Donne punning on their own names; it should be distinguished from East Asian assumptions of literary nonfictionality and from romantic direct use of personal experience. (3) *Formal* a. is exemplified in Ch. poetry by the use of another poet's rhymes (the use of a common form such as the sestina or sonnet is insufficiently specific without additional evidence, e.g. an acrostic). (4) *Metaphorical* a., found chiefly in periods valuing trad. (e.g. Rome, pre-modern China, Korea, Japan, and 16th- to 20th-c. England), uses the incorporated elements as signifiers to generate signification in the new context (for example, Dryden's a. to *Aeneid* 5–6 in his poem on Oldham expresses, through metaphor, the relation both between himself and Oldham and between Roman and Eng. cultural values). (5) *Imitative* a. varies, whether specific (e.g. Johnson in *London* to Juvenal, *Satire* 3, so sustained as to constitute imitation; this form, the picking up of a specific verbal string, typically a phrase, from an antecedent text of some canonical authority, is perhaps the most common variety), generic (Dryden to epic in *Absalom and Achitophel*), parodic

(Philips to Milton in *The Splendid Shilling*), or synthetic (Pope's *Rape of the Lock*, specific to Milton and others, generic to epic, and parodic). (6) *Structural* a. gives form to a new work by recalling the organization of an older—in this it resembles other kinds, but clearly differs when the a. is to works in other genres or arts (e.g. the *Odyssey* used by Joyce in *Ulysses* and music by Eliot in *Four Quartets*). In spite of Lessing's strictures in *Laok-oön*, many poets have also alluded, sometimes in descriptions, sometimes less visually, to other arts than verbal ones (e.g. Auden in "Musée des Beaux Arts" to Breughel's *Icarus*; see VISUAL ARTS AND POETRY).

Rules governing a. are rare, but in some Japanese crit., verbal a. is thought to require roughly a certain proportion of echoed words, whereas particularly famous poems (e.g. Narihira, "Tsuki ya aranu," *Kokinshū* 15.747) are to be used for conceptual rather than verbal a. Often a. resembles allegory, figuration, imitation, intertextuality, or parody (qq.v.). Another distinction lies in subject matter: thus Ch. a. is unusually given to a. that is historical-political. Religious a. is the prevailing variety in many cultures and in certain periods; Islamic lit., for example, is dominated as no other by its holy book. See also CLASSICISM; ECHO VERSE; IMITATION; INFLUENCE; INTERTEXTUALITY; META-LEPSIS; TEXTUALITY; TRADITION.

Although there are numerous studies of a. in individual authors, no comprehensive study exists. A fully comparative study would be very valuable. R. D. Havens, *The Influence of Milton on Eng. Poetry* (1922); G. Smith, *T. S. Eliot's Poems and Plays: Sources and Meanings* (1956); S. P. Bovie, "Cl. As.," *CW* 52 (1958); R. Brower, *Alexander Pope: The Poetry of A.* (1959); R. H. Brower and E. Miner, *Japanese Court Poetry* (1961); D. P. Harding, *The Club of Hercules* (1962); A. Hamori, *On the Art of Med. Ar. Poetry* (1974); Z. Ben-Porat, "The Poetics of Literary A.," and A. L. Johnson, "A. in Poetry," both in *PTL* 1 (1976); C. Perri et al., "A. Studies: An Internat. Annot. Bibl., 1921–1977," *Style* 13 (1979); J. Hollander, *The Figure of Echo* (1981); Morier; G. B. Conte, *The Rhet. of Imitation*, ed. and tr. C. Segal (1986); P. Yu, *The Reading of Imagery in the Ch. Poetic Trad.* (1987); E. Stein, *Wordsworth's Art of A.* (1988); E. Cook, *Poetry, Word-play, and Word-war in Wallace Stevens* (1988); *Intertextuality, A., and Quotation: An Internat. Bibl. of Crit. Studies*, ed. U. J. Hebel (1989); R. Garner, *From Homer to Tragedy: The Art of A. in Gr. Poetry* (1989).   E.M.

ALTERNATION OF RHYMES. See MASCULINE AND FEMININE.

AMBIGUITY. An utterance is ambiguous if it is open to more than one interp. (q.v.) in the context (linguistic and pragmatic) in which it occurs. Such linguistic a. is obvious even in the ordinary use of a lang., and it has been the subject of sophisticated treatment by logicians, linguists, and rhetoricians since Cl. times. In 20th-c. lit. crit., a. has become a key concept particularly for critics interested in the complex problem of distinguishing the lang. of poetry from the precise, literal, univocal lang. required by scientific and other expository prose. The popularity of a. began in 1930 with the publication of William Empson's *Seven Types of A.* His detailed explications of the as. he found in poems became a model for the methods of "close reading" advocated esp. by the New Criticism (q.v.).

Empson says that in ordinary usage, a. is associated with equivocal, doubtful, or confused meaning; with carelessness, evasiveness, or deceit. But the linguistic mechanisms producing a. can also generate desirable results only some of which have been fully appreciated (e.g. by the punster or the allegorist). Empson proposed to use "a." for "any verbal nuance, however slight, which gives room for alternative reactions to the same piece of lang." For him, "a." becomes an umbrella term for the multiple readings of a passage made possible by the use of polysemous or homonymous words; by double or deviant syntax; by unconventional or omitted punctuation; by sound structure; by incomplete or misleading contexts in which words or sentences appear; by descriptive or affective connotation (q.v.); by the use of vague or very general words; by trope, allusion, paradox, or symbol (qq.v.); by tautology, contradiction, or irrelevance; or by irony, puns (qq.v.), or portmanteau words. The multiple readings may have a variety of relations with each other: they may be of equal relevance and importance, or one may be a mere overtone or innuendo; they may supplement each other, may be fused into a larger unity of meaning, or may be mutually exclusive; they may produce polyphony or dissonance. The subtlety, density, and depth of meaning made possible by the use of these devices demonstrate that "the machinations of a. are among the very roots of poetry."

Empson says that he has arranged his seven types as "stages of advancing logical disorder" generated by a poet's use of one or more of the above mechanisms. He sees these degrees as objective linguistic facts that appear in a poem. But his classification also depends in part on psychological considerations: (1) the degree of perplexity caused in the reader or the degree of effort required to "work out" the latent meanings and their relations; and (2) the degree of tension or conflict in the mind of the author that is reflected by the presence of a. His first few types show how the multiple meanings of an expression tend to support and enrich each other or resolve themselves into a single meaning, while in his later types the multiple meanings diverge, until in his seventh type the variety of meanings reflect contradictions and unresolvable alternatives (best illustrated in his extended analysis of Hopkins' "The Windhover").

Not all critics have been happy with the extension of ordinary usage that Empson had proposed for "a." or with the clarity, logic, or usefulness of his classification of as. Beardsley, Kooij, and Rimmon make a case for restricting the term "a." to utterances whose multiple interpretations are mutually exclusive and thus lead to indecisiveness of meaning. Other terms have been suggested for lang. conveying conjoined multiple meanings: "resourcefulness" (I. A. Richards); "plurisignation" (Wheelwright); "extralocution" (Nowottny). Kaplan and Kris, wishing to retain Empson's insights but to make his theoretical scheme more precise, have suggested "disjunctive a." for as. in which the separate meanings are interpreted as mutually exclusive; "additive a.," "conjunctive a.," and "integrative a." for those kinds in which the separate meanings are conjoined in one way or another; and "projective a." for cases in which the "responses vary altogether with the interpreter"—that is, cases in which different interps. of a text are due not to properties of the text but to the varying subjectivities of reader response (q.v.).

Other critics have debated whether "a." should not be extended even further to cover the linguistic phenomena (anticipated in Empson's seventh type) that deconstructionist critics call "undecidability," "unreadability," "dissemination," or "misreading" (see DECONSTRUCTION). In a century of discord and alienation, human uncertainty and ambivalence, some readers have developed a taste for the opaque and inscrutable, the labyrinth and the abyss. They delight in opportunities for "creative" reading; they study the interplay, or "free play," of possible meanings previously unsuspected, or at least unvalued, in the masterpieces of the past. And some poets, particularly since Rimbaud, are composing "enigma" texts, poems deliberately written to frustrate the expectations of traditional readers for clarity and coherence. Because of the nature of lang. and the complexities and unpredictability of human experience, clarity and coherence, it is said, are illusions. Lit. can provide no answers; at best, it can only raise questions. The relations between a "poetics of a." and a "poetics of indeterminacy" remain to be worked out (see esp. Perloff).

One extension that does seem advisable is to regard a. as a potential problem (or resource) not just of lang. but of the use of a sign in any semiotic context (see SEMIOTICS, POETIC). Signs, linguistic and nonlinguistic, are involved in the interp. of most of the strata of a literary work: the thoughts, attitudes, motivations of the characters represented; the nature of their actions, verbal and nonverbal; the degree of reliability of the narrator; the values and attitudes of the implied or real author toward the characters and their actions; the theme (q.v.) or thesis of the work; and the nature of the organizing principles of the work. If there are gaps or contradictions in the system of signs which the reader must use as clues to arrive at an interp. on any of these levels, the reader may be left with a number of plausible interps. or a sense of bewilderment.

Linguistic a., at least the kind that is caused by polysemy, has also become an important concern in metacriticism (q.v.). In his earliest writings I. A. Richards pointed out the various senses in which certain terms (e.g. "beauty," "meaning," "poetry," "sincerity" [q.v.], "fiction" [q.v.]) were used in aesthetics and lit. crit. In his writings of the 1930s and 1940s he recommended the linguistic discipline of "multiple definition" to help readers get over the "habit of behaving as though if a passage means one thing it cannot at the same time mean another and incompatible thing."

The documentation of the polysemy of many other terms used in poetics has interested other scholars; an excellent example of such a study is Richard McKeon's "Imitation and Poetry" (*Thought, Action, and Passion* [1954]). In this essay McKeon lists a veritable multitude of senses in which "imitation" (q.v.) has been used in poetics. Besides such exercises in historical semantics, efforts have been made to account for this polysemy and explore its consequences. One position is that the polysemy of the key terms of poetics, like that of most words used in humanistic studies, is inevitable. The objects of humanistic concern are extraordinarily complex and, more important, change as the result of new philosophical or political orientations. A theorist can handle only a limited "aspect" of a subject matter, and the terms that she inherits from the past undergo shifts of reference which can lead to confusion and misunderstanding. What can save the theorist is an abandonment of dogmatism and a commitment to pluralism. The concepts of poetics should be considered "open" or "essentially contested" concepts. The various advantages of this position have been pointed out by a number of critics, incl. Richards, Abrams, and Booth. See also MEANING, POETIC; INTERPRETATION.

I. A. Richards and C. K. Ogden, *The Meaning of Meaning* (1923); I. A. Richards, *The Philosophy of Rhet.* (1936), *How to Read a Book* (1942); W. B. Stanford, *A. in Gr. Lit.* (1939); A. Kaplan and E. Kris, "Aesthetic A.," *PPR* 8 (1948); E. Olson, "William Empson," *MP* 47 (1950); W. Empson, *The Structure of Complex Words* (1951), *Seven Types of A.*, 3d ed. (1953); J. D. Hubert, *L'Esthétique des "Fleurs du Mal"* (1953); M. C. Beardsley, *Aesthetics* (1958); W. Nowottny, *The Lang. Poets Use* (1962); T. Tashiro, "A. as Aesthetic Principle," *DHI*; P. Wheelwright, *The Burning Fountain*, 2d ed. (1968); J. G. Kooij, *A. in Natural Lang.* (1971); M. H. Abrams, "What's the Use of Theorizing about the Arts?" *In Search of Literary Theory*, ed. M. W. Bloomfield (1972); J. R. Kincaid, "Coherent Readers, Incoherent Texts," *CritI* 3 (1977); S. Rimmon, *The Concept of A.* (1977); M. Weitz, *The Opening Mind* (1977); W. C. Booth, *Critical Understanding* (1979); M. Perloff, *The Poetics of Indeterminacy* (1981); D. N. Levine, *The Flight from A.* (1985). F.GU.

AMERICAN INDIAN POETRY.

    I. NORTH AMERICAN
    II. CENTRAL AMERICAN
    III. SOUTH AMERICAN

I. NORTH AMERICAN. The lyric impulse in North Am. I. cultures is rich, diverse, and persistent. Since about 1960, new foundations for the understanding of the traditional forms of this impulse have been emerging in the work of linguists, anthropologists, and literary scholars—and corresponding to this renewal of interest in traditional native lyric art, there has been a remarkable flowering of poetry by Native Am. writers. Taken together, the new scholarship and the new writing have spurred a re-examination of the place of I. lit. in the Am. literary canon.

Examples of traditional Native Am. poetry and song have been recorded since Roger Williams' *Key into the Lang. of Am.* (1643), but Anglo understanding and assimilation have been problematic because the native poetries come to us from three removes, each involving severe intertextual difficulties: (1) they must be tr. into Eng. from native langs. about which, in most cases, we have only imperfect knowledge; (2) they must be rendered into texts from their original status as oral traditional songs (generally with musical settings); and (3) they must be transfigured out of the tribal contexts that shaped them into terms intelligible to modern Anglo culture.

Small wonder, then, that the study and tr. of I. lyrics have been on the whole a losing battle against the forces of ignorance and ethnocentricity, and in particular against the temptation to render such works according to Western literary assumptions. In a seminal essay, Dell Hymes has shown how well-known translations by Schoolcraft and others are vitiated by the distortions of Anglo formal and prosodic biases—in favor of regular metrics, for example, and against extensive repetition. Such studies make it clear that only through rigorous application of linguistic and ethnographic knowledge can we hope to repossess the traditional lyrics in anything like their full authenticity and expressive power. To do so is the aim of the movement known as "ethnopoetics" (q.v.). The full ethnopoetic program is handsomely exemplified in Evers and Molina.

In general, Am. I. traditional poetry seems to have existed in three broad functional categories. (1) As independent lyrics, "songs" per se, ranging from lullabies and love-songs to complaints, curses, war-cries, and death-songs. For the most part, such compositions appear to have been communal property, like Anglo folksongs—but in certain tribes, notably the Papago of Arizona, song-making was a prestigious individual endeavor, and songs were identified with their composers. (2) As songs embedded in narratives, performed by raconteurs taking the part of characters who break into song, generally at moments of dramatic ten-

sion—much as Shakespeare's songs figure in his romantic comedies. For example, this mourning song is sung by Mouse at the end of a Coos story about his ill-fated marriage: "My wife! My wife! / You were so pretty, so pretty. / My heart is sad that you died. / My wife! My wife!" (3) As ceremonial poetry—works serving ritual purposes: healing, political consolidation, or propitiation of deities. Such poetry can range in length and scope from a Modoc shaman's brief incantation—"What do I suck out? / The disease I suck out"—to the immense and elaborately structured *Condolence Ritual* of the Iroquois and the *Night Chant* of the Navajo, which implicate the entire ethos of their cultures.

The most radical perception of ethnopoetic research is that *all* performative verbal forms—narrative and oratory as well as sung—is best understood as poetry, and that prose as such did not exist in native traditional verbal art. Working from tape-recorded performances of Zuni story-telling, Tedlock has found evidence of poetic lineation, indicated by regular pauses, pitch and stress changes, and so on, while Hymes' examination of Chinookan narrative texts has revealed that they are measured poetically according to a complex system of syntactic and grammatical markers.

Considered more narrowly as *lyric*, specimens of I. oral poetry share certain formal and expressive features that set them apart from Western verse. Reflecting their anonymous, collective modality, they tend to be personal and immediate without being intimate or autobiographical; the "I" of an I. lyric, rather like the "I" of traditional Eng. lyrics like "Western Wind," is universalized. A famous Pawnee song, for example, is poignant without being confessional: "Let us see, is this real / Let us see, is this real / This life I am living?" Conspicuously lacking in native lyrics is that element of *authorial irony* so pervasive in modern British and Am. poetry. Not that the native poems eschew irony—"I, even I, must die sometime / So what value is anything, I think" (Winnebago)—but it is irony as perceived in experience rather than as cultivated as a stance.

The traditional lyrics are often notable for their brevity and compression; often they seem elliptical, even fragmentary—"In the great night my heart will go out. / Toward me the darkness comes rattling. / In the great night my heart will go out" (Papago). This abrupt quality may be partly, of course, a cross-cultural phenomenon—as a Papago informant said to R. Underhill, "The song is very short because we understand so much." But a native habit of mind, an ingrained imaginative reticence, suggestive of the Oriental bias against direct declaration, is also probably at stake. A general model for such reticence existed in most tribes in the form of a taboo against directly identifying one's spirit-guide—Thunder, Elk, Wolf—as revealed in the course of solitary "power quests." One could, however, *hint* at this great secret in singing and dancing.

In structural terms, native Am. I. p. relies on relatively simple configurations—esp. repetition (with or without variation) and parallelism (q.v.). In this respect, of course, the poetry reflects its oral/performative origins, esp. its association with music and singing. Whole poems were apparently meant to be sung over and over; in other cases there is extensive repetition of lines within the texts, which typically have been reduced or cut out altogether in Anglo trs., thereby obliterating the incantatory effects often achieved in the originals. One might say that if Anglo poetry generally is premised on proliferation of detail, *copia*, native traditional poetry is premised on expressive repetition.

The examples of I. p. already given illustrate its intensely visual, image-centered character: no wonder that early imagist poets and theorists like Mary Austin claimed it as a precedent and source. The ability to embody philosophical abstractions in concrete terms that Bierhorst has identified as a major achievement of Native Am. oral lit. is esp. evident in the poetry. Bound up in physical experience, its lang. is persistently figurative, not so much in formal metaphor and simile as in forms of synecdoche—concrete parts imaging and figuring complex wholes: "Wherever I pause— / the noise of the village" (Haida).

Underlying all such literary features of the traditional poetry is a magical conception of lang.—words uttered "just so" are thought to be capable of a magical instrumentality, invoking and *expressing* power in the human, natural, and supernatural realms. The Inuit word for "song," *anerca*, is also the word for "breath" and "spirit": in the traditional cultures of the Inuits and all other Native Am. peoples, song is the paramount vehicle of spiritual power. Song can make things happen, attracting good, repelling evil, or in the case of curses, drawing calamity upon one's enemies.

This belief in the magical properties of lang., even when the lang. is modern Am. Eng., is one of the main lines of continuity between traditional I. p. and the work of modern I. poets. They, too, are "singers for power," and most would subscribe to the declaration of N. Scott Momaday, in the course of acknowledging his debt to the Kiowa literary trad., that "man has consummate being in lang., and there only. The state of human *being* is an idea, an idea which man has of himself. Only when he is embodied in an idea, and the idea is realized in lang., can man take possession of himself."

The formal and thematic diversity of modern Am. I. p. is remarkable, and expressive of the complexity of modern I. experience, with its polarization of heroic past and deculturated present and its compulsion to find out ethnic continuities. Though many Native Am. poets do not in fact reside in their tribal homelands, most cultivate in their work a distinctive sense of ancestral and personal place, and for many there are strong regional identifications—with the Southwest, pre-eminently, but also with the Pacific Northwest. A pan-I. *feminist* vision is shared by a growing number of Native women writing poetry, notably Paula Gunn Allen (Laguna) and Wendy Rose (Hopi/Miwok).

Stylistically, contemp. Native Am. poetry ranges widely, from the narrative directness of Simon Ortiz (Acoma), Joseph Bruchac (Abenaki), and Maurice Kenny (Mohawk), to the imagistic, often incantatory lyricism of Linda Hogan (Chickasaw) and Joy Harjo (Creek), to the personal density and mythic allusiveness of Duane Niatum (Klallam), Elizabeth Woody, (Wasco) and Ray Young Bear (Mesquaki). Western literary influences range from Yvor Winters and the metaphysical poets (in the work of Momaday) to Whitman, Williams, Ginsberg, and Neruda—most of today's I. writers are well schooled in cl. Western lit. But the chief informing influence on the poets who are contributing to what has been aptly called the Native Am. literary renaissance seems to be their awareness of tribal poetic and narrative trads. What they self-consciously inherit of the old ways of the Native imagination, their individual 20th-c. talents are recreating and reaffirming—as in Duane Niatum's "Runner for the Clouds and Rain":

> I am the fox roaming for your changes.
> I am the salmon dreaming in the waters of the sun.
> I am the mushroom celebrating rains.
> I am the bear dancing for the gentle woman.
> I am the guardian of the infant child.
> I am the carrier of the Elders' song.
> I run for the dead and the rainbow!
> (*Digging Out the Roots*, 1977)

PRIMARY TRADITIONAL TEXTS AND ANTHOLOGIES: W. Matthews, *The Night Chant* (1902); E. Curtis, *The N. Am. I.*, 20 v. (1908–24); J. Swanton, "Haida Texts and Myths," *Smithsonian Inst. Bureau of Am. Ethnology Bull.* 29 (1905); R. Lowie, *Myths and Trads. of the Crow Indians* (1918); F. Densmore, *Am. Indians and Their Music* (1926); R. Underhill, *Singing for Power* (1938); A. G. Day, *The Sky Clears* (1951); M. Astrov, *Am. I. Prose and Poetry* (1962); J. Bierhorst, *On the Trail of the Wind* (1971), *Four Masterworks of Am. I. Lit.* (1974)—Mayan, Iroquois, Navajo texts; D. Tedlock, *Finding the Center* (1972)—Zuni; J. Ramsey, *Coyote Was Going There* (1977)—Northwest; L. Evers, *The South Corner of Time* (1980)—Southwest; L. Evers and F. Molina, *Yaqui Deer Songs* (1986).

HISTORY AND CRITICISM: D. Brinton, *Aboriginal Am. Authors* (1883); E. Sapir, "Song Recitative in Paiute Mythology," *JAF* 23 (1910); M. Austin, *The Am. Rhythm* (1923); T. Waterman and E. Walton, "Am. I. P.," *AA* 27 (1925); E. Carpenter, "Eskimo Poetry," *Explorations* 4 (1958); I. Nicholson, *Firefly in the Night: A Study of Ancient Mexican Poetry and Symbolism* (1959); M. Leon-Portilla, *Pre-Columbian*

Lit. of Mexico (1969); D. Hymes, *"In Vain I Tried to Tell You": Essays in Native Am. Ethnopoetics* (1983)—esp. "Some N. Pacific Poems"; D. Tedlock, *The Spoken Word and the Work of Interp.* (1983); *Smoothing the Ground*, ed. B. Swann (1983)—esp. essays by K. Kroeber; *Studies in Am. I. Lit.*, ed. P. G. Allen (1983)—esp. "The Sacred Hoop"; J. Ramsey, *Reading the Fire: Essays in the Traditional I. Lit. of the Far West* (1984); *Native Am. Discourse: Poetics and Rhet.*, ed. J. Sherzer and A. C. Woodbury (1987); A. L. B. Ruoff, *Am. I. Lits.: Intro., Bibl. Rev., Sel. Bibl.* (1990).

ANTHOLOGIES OF MODERN INDIAN POETRY: *Voices of the Rainbow*, ed. K. Rosen (1975); *Voices from Wa'Kon-Tah*, ed. M. Dodge and J. McCullough (1975); *Carriers of the Dream Wheel*, ed. D. Niatum (1975); *Many Voices*, ed. D. Day and M. Bowering (1976)—Canadian poets; *The Remembered Earth*, ed. G. Hobson (1981)—esp. Momaday, "The Man Made of Words"; *Songs from This Earth on Turtle's Back*, ed. J. Bruchac (1983); *Harper's Anthol. of 20th-C. I. P.*, ed. D. Niatum (1988).

HISTORY AND CRITICISM: A. Keiser, *The I. in Am. Lit.* (1935); K. Roemer, "Bear and Elk: The Nature(s) of Contemp. I. P.," *JES* 5 (1977); L. Hogan, "19th-C. Native Am. Poets," *Wasaja* 13 (1980); J. Ruppert, "The Uses of Oral Trad. in Six Contemp. Native Am. Poets," *AICRJ* 4 (1980); K. Lincoln, *Am. I. Ren.* (1983); A. Wiget, *Native Am. Lit.* (1985); *Survival This Way: Interviews with Am. I. Poets*, ed. J. Bruchac (1988). J.W.R.

II. CENTRAL AMERICAN. The C. Am. area presents us with a cultural and linguistic interface more complex than anywhere else in Indian America. Maya culture (600 B.C. to present day) alone comprises over 20 separate forms, which can be roughly classified into Lowland and Highland. Within the Maya area, which includes the lower half of Mexico, Guatemala, Belize, western Honduras, and parts of El Salvador, there are Nahuatl enclaves, as well as Lencan, Jicaquean, and Payan groupings with Carib-Arawak-Amazonian affiliations. South of the Maya area, the cultural and linguistic picture shades into Macro-Chibchan, a large stock with many subdivisions originating in highland South America.

To the north of the Maya, in highland central Mexico, the Aztecs (A.D. 1325–1519) inherited a long poetic trad. originating with the Toltecs. Within this Aztec trad. we find three major genres: lyric, epic, and dramatic. The lyric trad. concentrates on the major themes of Nahua religion, on war and the heroic, on philosophical speculations on the ontological basis of human life, and, to a lesser degree, on biographical accounts. The main topics of the Aztec epics concern their original pilgrimage to Anahuac, described in five pictographic sources, the *Codex Boturini, The Codex Aubin of 1576*, the *"Mapa de Siguenza"*, the *Codex Azcatitlan*, and *The Codex Mexicanus*. Each of these is quite divergent from the others, although certain features are common. In addition, theme poems about Quetzalcoatl and about the hist. of Tenochtitlan are prevalent. Finally, a few examples of the Aztec dramatic genre have survived, most notably the "Death of Nezahuacoyotl" in the *Cantares Mexicanos*.

The most comprehensive and detailed picture of C. Am. I. lit. is provided by the surviving Maya and Aztec texts in both pre-Columbian hieroglyphic and colonial Roman Script. The Highland Maya texts form a distinctive group; among these, the Quiché Maya Book of Counsel known as the *Popol Vuh*, the dramatic text of the *Rabinal Achi*, and the Cakchiquel Maya *Memorial of Solola* are outstanding examples of a genre of works which are simultaneously land titles, mythological recitations, dramatic enactments, and theological and philosophical elaborations. They were first composed in the 16th c. as native "readings" of earlier hieroglyphic codices now lost. Much of the content of these texts can be traced back to the Cl. Maya era of 350–900 A.D. Passages in the *Popol Vuh*, for example, explain scenes depicted on Cl. Maya pottery.

In the case of the Lowland Yucatec Maya, a series of community texts known as the *Books of Chilam Balam* (the Jaguar Priest) of surviving Maya townships such as Maní, Chumayel, and Tizimin demonstrate that a centralized Yucatec Maya literary trad. survived the Sp. conquest in 1539. These books are markedly different in emphasis from the Highland Maya texts even though they too were first composed and written down in the 16th c. They sustain the continuity of the Cl. Maya calendar into colonial times and center on documenting the social and economic effects of the arrival of the Spaniards in the peninsula and the native response to Christianity. Unlike the surviving Highland texts or the Aztec material, the *Books of Chilam Balam* are explicitly political:

> Thrice the tidings of justice of our Father,
> Descend over the multitudes of the town,
> Then a great war,
> Descends over the "white beans" of the town,
> To comprehend the true severity of everything.

The unifying center of native C. Am. poetry is the shaman's trance, used for communication with the spirit world. It is the belief that invisible spirits can be addressed and petitioned for favors which inspires the variety of poetic forms. This center is enshrined iconographically in the "uinal" cycle of 20 days at the heart of Maya and Aztec lit., in Kuna I. "ikarkana" poetry, and elsewhere.

The I. poet also works his craft to articulate individual experience, to record a vision quest, to mourn the departed, to reflect humor and to entertain, to mark the search for love and attention, to express prowess in hunting and war, to communicate a personal anecdote, to overcome the hardship of physical labor, to pass the long evenings, in short, to communicate a sense of self unbound, a "flowering." It was because poetry and song contained this unbounded self that, on becoming a subject after capture in battle, an I. warrior traditionally surrendered his personal songs as part of the tribute paid (Brotherston).

The poems of the C. Am. Indians can best be understood as special forms of dialogue (q.v.) in which performance is a central characteristic. Dialogue, whether it be with the gods or other men, evokes the original creation. In the opening lines of the Quiché Maya Book of Counsel, the *Popol Vuh*, the gods *Tepeu* and *Gucumatz* create the world by dialogue: "They talked then, discussing and deliberating. They agreed; they united their words and their thoughts." This is in striking contrast to the European biblical heritage with its singular Word and monologue (Burns). It also emphasizes the role that oral recitation plays in native poetic trads., even where a strong scriptural trad. existed.

C. Am. I. p. does not rely on long, detailed descriptions of context, but rather assumes that context will be manifested by other features in performance such as costume, facial expression, voice quality, phrasing, and gesture. Thus, to fully comprehend the content of a poem, an intimate knowledge of the social and spiritual context of the cultural group within which the poem was fashioned is crucial. An ethnopoetic approach that also interprets performance is necessary (see ETHNOPOETICS).

A pervasive use of parallelism (q.v.) and a profound dualism permeate the poetic forms of the C. Am. Indians. Rhetorical questions, prophecies, riddles, allegory, personification (qq.v.), question and answer sessions, insults, metaphorical strings, euphony, and onomatopoeia are also displayed. Poems vary in length from a few words to extended ceremonial presentations that might last for days. The written native texts available to us, notably the Quiché Maya *Popol Vuh*, the Yucatec *Books of Chilam Balam* (The Jaguar Priest), and the Kuna *ikar*, are written entirely in verse and contain extensive scripts for what were dramatic reenactments of the legends of the gods and ancestors.

To the Indian, poetic ability is power. To be able to converse with the spirits in their special lang., to be able to persuade people and find agreement in counsel, and to show linguistic dexterity and a profound knowledge of custom and history are prerequisites for claiming title and rank. Because songs and poems were and are such important instruments of prestige and control, every Indian seeks to a greater or lesser extent to be a practicing poet.

ANTHOLOGIES: *General*: *The Song of Quetzalcoatl*, ed. J. H. Cornyn (1930); *First Fire*, ed. H. Fox (1978); *Image of the New World*, ed. and tr. G. Brotherston (1979). *Costa Rica*: *Leyendas y tradicio-*

nes borucas, ed. E. S. Maroto (1979). *El Salvador*: *Mitologia cuzcatleca*, ed. M. Mendez Efrain (1979). *Honduras*: E. Conzemius, *Los Indios Payas de Honduras*, pts. 1–2, v. 19–20 (1927–28); M. Medardo, *Comizahual* (1981); *Los hijos de la muerte: el universo mitico de los Tolupan-Jicaques*, ed. A. M. Chapman, 2d ed. (1982); *Hijos del copal y la candela. Tomo 1: Ritos agrarios y tradicion oral los lencis de Honduras* (1985). *Maya, Lowland*: *The Book of Chilam Balam of Chumayel* (1933) and *The Ritual of the Bacabs* (1965), both ed. and tr. R. Roys; A. B. Vazquez, *El Codice Perez* (1939); *An Epoch of Miracles*, ed. and tr. A. F. Burns (1983); D. Boremanse, *Contes et Mythologie des Indiens Lacandons* (1986); *Jaguar Prophecy: The Counsel Book of the Yucatec Maya*, tr. R. Luxton and P. Balam (1990)—annotated. *Maya, Highland*: *Annals of the Cakchiquels*, ed. S. G. Morley and A. Recinos (1945); *Popol Vuh*, ed. and tr. D. Tedlock (1985); *Cantares Mexicanos*, tr. J. Bierhorst (1985). *Nahuatl*: *Ancient Nahuatl Poetry*, ed. D. Brinton (1887). *Panama*: F. W. Kramer, *Lit. Among the Cuna Indians* (1970); *Cuna Cosmology: Legends from Panama*, tr. and ed. A. G. McAndrews (1978); J. Sherzer, *Kuna Ways of Speaking* (1986).

HISTORY AND CRITICISM: A. Tozzer, *A Comparative Study of the Mayas and the Lacandones* (1907)—highland Maya; K. A. M. Garibay, *La poesia lirica Azteca*, (1937)—Nahuatl; *Epica Nahuatl* (1945); *The Maya and Their Neighbors*, ed. C. L. Hay et al. (1948); *Handbook of Middle Am. Indians*, v. 5, ed. N. A. McQuown (1964–76); G. H. Gossen, *Chamulas in the World of the Sun* (1974); D. M. Sodi, *La Literatura de los Mayas*, 2d ed. (1978)—lowland Maya; B. N. Colby and L. M. Colby, *The Daykeeper, the Life and Discourse of an Ixil Diviner* (1981); D. Gifford, *Warriors, Gods, and Spirits from Central and South Am. Mythology* (1983); M. Leon Portilla, *Literatura de Mesoamerica* (1984); *The Southeast Maya Periphery*, ed. P. A. Urban and E. M. Schortman (1986); *Recovering the Word: Essays on Native Am. Lit.*, ed. B. Swann and A. Krupat (1987). R.L.

III. SOUTH AMERICAN. The South Am. continent was and continues to be one of the most linguistically and culturally diverse regions of the planet. The range of this exquisite complexity is constantly being expanded as continuing research and investigation yield more detailed information on various lang. groups, their speakers, and their artistic trads. The major division of the native or indigenous groups of South America is between the lowland or Tropical Forest groups and those of the Andean highlands. While focusing primarily on the Andean region due to the high civilizations that developed there and the information currently available, what follows is an attempt to treat both highland and lowland native groups. Although attempts were made in the 16th and early 17th cs. by European and Mestizo chroniclers (Cristobal de Molina, Francisco de Avila, Santa Cruz Pachacuti Yamqui Salcamaygua, Guaman Poma de Ayala) to record and transcribe the poetic trads. of different groups (such as the Nay-lamp legend and the Waru Chiri ms.), one must remember that the conquerors were not invited guests, nor ones who appreciated or understood the nature of the native South Am. trads. Consequently, much of the poetic record of the Conquest and Colonial periods (16th through early 19th cs.) consists of those examples that more closely matched or could be made to conform to the western European ideal. Furthermore, the majority of these examples comes from the great civilizations such as the Inca that were contacted and conquered first. As a result, the information currently available on the South Am. poetic trad. at the time of the Sp. Conquest (1532) comes from a relatively small number of sources and must represent only a small part of the poetic trads. in existence at that time.

Fortunately, since the 1970s the full range, form, and content of native South Am. p. is beginning to be clarified, due in part to more rigorous empirical studies *in situ* and to re-examination of early poetic data in light of the most recent information and methodologies. Studies of lang. in its social context and, more specifically, those dealing with ethnopoetics (the study of the indigenous interp. of native verbal art) help to illustrate not only the form and function of indigenous poetic genres but also the intricate relationship of such genres to other aspects of culture. In order to recognize the poetic nature of this oral lit., one must be aware of the parameters of what constitutes "poetry" within each particular ethnic group and of the subtlety of expression available in the non-IE langs.

The poetic genres of South Am. indigenous oral lit. consist primarily of three types: song lyrics, myths and legends, and the epic trads. of the Incas and the Chilean Mapuche. All three forms were productive and recorded in the 1500s, but only the songs, myths, and legends continue to be productive today. Now as in the early Conquest and Colonial periods (15th and early 17th cs.), much of this poetry is still produced in the Quechua (or Runa Simi "people speech") and Aymara langs.

The majority of poetic texts available today are the lyrics of songs which are still created and performed by both Tropical Forest and Andean ethnic groups. These range from the simple repetitive chants of Chaco groups and upper Amazon shamans to the complex call-and-response song couplets of the various Tupí-Guaraní groups of Brazil. In addition to the range of forms, the uses of such songs are quite varied as well. For example, the Aymara and Jaqaru of the Andean highlands employ work songs in the cleaning of irrigation canals to make the work more enjoyable, reinforce the role of each family group in the communal work, and reassert its beneficial outcome. Among the Tapirapé, the Karajá, Nambicuara, Xingu, and the Javajé of Brazil, recreational and rhythmical work-songs are common. Love songs are used by the Quichua speakers of the upper Amazon to send messages to distant loved ones and call them back to the singer. Among the isolated Huaorani of the Ecuadorian Amazon, recreational songs usually involve spontaneous social singing. Wedding songs among the Otavalo are often spontaneous ribald entertainment and also carry socialization information both for the newlyweds and for those yet unmarried. Common to many of these ethnopoetic forms is the repetition of an underlying structure and treatment that is pan-Amazonian and/or pan-Andean.

Structurally repetitive form, which is also prevalent in myths and legends, can be easily manipulated for effect. Among the Loreto Quichua of the Ecuadorian Amazon, the structures of both the myth and the Quichua lang. allow allusions to other important themes and texts of the culture. In the excerpt below from a creation myth, the interplay of verbal suffixes with the couplet form of the myth is akin to preparing a warp for weaving:

Siluma riska nin chay wawa,
Silupi *yaykuska* ishkaynti.
(Those children went to the sky, they say,
And both of them *entered* the sky.)

Ishkaynti *yaykupi*,
Mama, washa, *katiska* nin silu punku-
    manta.
(When both had *gone in*,
the mother, behind [them], *followed*
    [them] from the sky's door, they
    say.)
Katipika,
chay wawakuna piñaska nin.
(Her having *followed* [them],
The children got mad, they say.)

In addition to the linguistic interplay, the repetition of "they say / one says" and other elements provides an almost hypnotic rhythm (and rhyme) not evident on the printed page. Furthermore, semantic coupling of key words in a couplet allows for an additional "rhyme of meaning" while maintaining the rhythmic integrity of the form.

In addition to songs, myths, and legends, an important epic trad. consisting of official and popular poetry also existed at the time of the Sp. Conquest and into the early Colonial period; from examples such as *Ollántay*, a drama written in verse, it is clear that this is the finest poetic trad. in South America recorded by the early European conquerors and missionaries. Poetic trads. were a vital part of Inca culture and were a repository of prescribed social behavior, mythology, and Inca revisionist history. Often such poems were composed by Inca royalty and performed before large crowds during various seasonal celebrations in the main plazas of Cuzco. As the oral lit. of an empire without a writing system, the various poetic genres were some of the few available means of passing on cultural values from one generation to the next. The early European attempt to impose elements of their own culture by utilizing manipulated versions of these trads. is evidence of the importance of their role in the Inca Empire.

The following example of an Inca hymn of supplication illustrates the religious function of poetry:

> Father Wiracocha
> Wiracocha of the world
> Creator
> Fertile procreator
> In this lower world
> "Let them eat, let them drink,"
> Saying to those you've placed here,
> Making their destinies.

While the epic narrative poems and the long poetic dramas of pre-Colombian times have been for the most part lost, the trads. of song and myth continue to be productive. Even though such ethnopoetic trads. have changed by incorporating European themes and by reflecting current social environment, the various genres available are still seen as an integral part of native culture; their successful use and performance continue to be highly esteemed.

GENERAL: *Handbook of South Am. Indians*, ed. J. Steward, 6 v. (1946–49)—surveys of many ethnic groups, incl. their lits., with excellent bibl.

ARAUCANIAN: T. Guevara Silva, *Historia de la civilización de Araucania* (1898), *Folklore araucano* (1911); F. José de Augusta, *Lecturas araucanas* (1910); B. Köessler-Ilg, *Tradiciones Araucanas* (1962); L. C. Faron, *The Mapuche Indians of Chile* (1968).

INCA AND QUECHUA: G. Poma de Ayala, *Nueva corónica y buen gobierno* (1613); E. Middendorf, *Dramatische und lyrische Dichtungen der Keshua-Sprache* (1891); P. A. Means, *Ancient Civilizations of the Andes* (1931); R. Rojas, *Himnos Quichuas* (1937); J. María Arguedas, *Canto Kechwa* (1938); *Canciones y Cuentos del Pueblo Quechua* (1949); J. Basadre, *Literatura Inca* (1938); J. Rowe, "Inca Culture at the Time of the Sp. Conquest," in Steward (above), v. 2; J. Lara, *La Poesia Quechua* (1947); J. M. B. Farfán, *Colección de Textos Quechuas del Perú* (1952); J. Lira and J. M. B. Farfán, "Himnos Quechuas Católicos Cuzqueños," *Folklore Americano* 3 (1955); L. Cadogan, *La Literatura de Los Guaranies* (1965); G. Taylor, *Rites et trads. de Huarochiri* (1980); G. L. Urioste, *Hijos de Pariya Qaqa: La Tradición Oral de Waru Chiri* (1983); L. K. Carpenter, "Notes from an Ecuadorian Lowland Quechua Myth," *Lat. Am. Indian Lits. Jour.* 1 (1985); C. Itier, "A Propósito de Los Dos Poemas en Quechua de la Crónica de Fray Martín de Murúa," *Revista Andina* 5 (1987).

OTHER GROUPS: G. Reichel-Dolmatoff, *Amazonian Cosmos: The Sexual and Religious Symbolism of the Tukano Indians* (1971); M. de Civrieux, *Watunna: An Orinoco Creation Cycle* (1980).L.K.C.

AMERICAN POETICS. See ROMANTIC AND POST-ROMANTIC POETICS; TWENTIETH-CENTURY POETICS, *American and British*.

AMERICAN POETRY.

I. THE COLONIAL PERIOD
II. NINETEENTH-CENTURY ROMANTICISM
III. MODERNIST POETRY, 1900–1945
IV. THE POSTWAR PERIOD

The often idiosyncratic strength, boldness, and ambition of Am. p. derives from two interrelated factors: its problematic and often marginalized relation to Am. society, and the lack of a defined and established literary class, culture, and audience. As a result, Am. p. developed through a dialectic between a sense of indebtedness to and derivation from British antecedents and, esp. in the best poets, a drive to resist those antecedents by conforming the trad. to peculiarly Am. circumstances or by evolving out of those circumstances the forms and motifs expressive of a distinctive sensibility. There seemed little need for arts and letters in a society of emigrants settling a harsh, alien wilderness and severing ties with the Old World while pressing the frontier ever westward to encompass the whole continent in their self-made, self-promoting prosperity. The rough-and-tumble economic expansion without the refinements of civilization allowed the Eng. commentator Sidney Smith in 1820 to sum up Am. cultural inferiority with rhetorical assurance: "In the four quarters of the globe, who reads an Am. book? or goes to an Am. play? or looks at an Am. painting or statue?"

Many besides Smith were not yet able to grasp the essential paradox of the New World: that Am. materialism and expansiveness were inseparable from a strain of introverted, self-analyzing idealism just as deep. In fact, the decade after Smith's sneer saw the beginnings of a self-conscious cultural expression and of a literary profession in the U.S. which by the early 20th c. would make Am. lit. and arts, as well as technology, recognized and imitated worldwide. Am. p.—marginalized economically but essential to psychological, moral, and religious life—played a powerful part in that act of self-creation and self-expression. Oddly, Am. poets, even those who affiliated themselves with groups and movements, conceived their task in painfully personal and private terms, yet felt their plight, however agonized, to be one connected with national destiny. Their words, however private, expressed the consciousness of their fellow Americans.

I. THE COLONIAL PERIOD. There was no poet of significant ability or accomplishment from the middle Atlantic states until Philip Freneau, nor from the Southern states until Edgar Allan Poe. But given the rigors of life on the 17th-c. frontier, the mere existence of the occasional ode, elegy, or satire is remarkable. In New England the intensities of Calvinist piety prompted a number of well-read Puritans to versify. *The Bay Psalm Book* (1640), probably the first book printed in Eng. in the New World, translated biblical texts into a plain style hammered into fourteeners (q.v.). Michael Wigglesworth's *The Day of Doom* (1662), a graphic rendering of the Last Judgment in thumping quatrains, became almost equally popular. In a more personal vein, Philip Pain's *Daily Meditations* (1668) recorded his afflictions and hopes wrangling with the paradoxes of sin and salvation.

The Puritans also produced two poets of abiding importance. Anne Bradstreet (1612?–72) arrived in the Massachusetts Bay Colony on the *Arbella* in 1630 as wife of a future governor. She almost certainly heard John Winthrop's shipboard address before debarkation envisioning their settlement as a "City upon a Hill" which would illuminate the Old World, but her comment on her new situation mingled candor with humility: "I found a new world and new manners at which my heart rose. But after I was convinced it was the way of God, I submitted to it and joined the church at Boston." Amidst family chores she wrote long, conventional, didactic poems on the four elements, the four seasons, and the four ages of hist., which admiring friends caused to be published in England as *The Tenth Muse Lately Sprung up in America* (1650), the inaugural book of Am. p. But Bradstreet is best known now for her domestic poems—love lyrics to her husband, poems on the birth and death of her children, an elegy for her father, a meditation on mortality after the burning of the family house—published posthumously in 1678. The emotional depth and honesty of these lyrics convert the conceits and meters of Ren. verse into personal statements affirming love in the face of loss, faith in the face of tribulation. Our first poet could be ruefully ironic about her situation as woman in a male world of letters, but the several elegies about her attest to the warm regard she enjoyed as person and as poet.

The 1937 discovery of a 400-page ms. by Edward Taylor (1642?–1729) brought to light the work of this major poet. A Harvard graduate (with one of the largest libraries of his time) and the staunchly orthodox minister to the frontier hamlet of Westfield, Taylor wrote for his own spiritual needs rather than for publication, but preserved the poems sturdily bound in a book. The bulk of the ms. consists of two long sequences: *God's Determinations Touching His Elect*, a part-lyric, part-allegorical presentation of the redemption of the elect, written in various meters and probably completed before 1690; and *Preparatory Meditations Before My Approach to the Lord's Supper. Chiefly upon the Doctrine Preached upon the Day of Administration.* The *Meditations* were written about every two months between 1682 and 1725 for the Sabbaths on which Taylor administered and received communion, and were all composed in the 6-line stanza (quatrain and a closing couplet) which Taylor learned from George Herbert. Using his Sunday sermon's scriptural text as a point of departure, the poems prepare him for the sacrament by exploring the psychology of grace and conversion, wrestling to rest his often explosive emotions, which burst out again in the next meditation. Despite Taylor's indebtedness to the Eng. metaphysical poets, we begin to hear—in the rough rhythmic emphases of his questions and declarations, the burly, clumsy colloquiality and directness of his diction, the nervy quirks and risks of his metaphorical leaps—the idiom and temper of Am. poetic speech separate itself from the more restrained and refined trad. of Eng. verse. Here is a characteristic stanza from the 23rd Meditation:

> I know not how to speak't, it is so good:
>   Shall Mortall, and Immortal marry?
>   nay,
> Man marry God? God be a Match for
>   Mud?
>   The King of Glory Wed a Worm? mere
>   Clay?
>   This is the Case. The Wonder too in
>   Bliss.
> Thy Maker is thy Husband. Hear'st
>   thou this?

Most of the writing in early America, however, was prose—in the 17th c., sermons, spiritual journals, tracts, letters; in the 18th c., a political focus overtaking the religious as the divisions leading to the Revolution quickened. Whatever the political differences with the mother country, the models for 18th-c. poetry were unashamedly Eng.: the neoclassicism of Pope and Swift, the pastoralism of Thomson and Gray, the hymnology of Watts—from the *Poems on Several Occasions* (1744) by Mather Byles (a Bostonian minister but also, by then, a would-be wit and man of letters) to the *Poems on Several Occasions* (1736) by a clever but anonymous "Gentleman of Virginia." The first black to become known as a poet, Phillis Wheatley (1753?–84), brought from Africa as a slave, was educated by her masters; her *Poems on Various Subjects, Religious and Moral* (1773) reflect her Eng. reading more than her African experience: her favorite book besides the Bible was Pope's *Iliad* (see AFRO-AMERICAN POETRY).

The first "school" of Am. poets was the "Connecticut Wits" of Yale and Hartford. Conservative Federalists except for Joel Barlow, they collaborated in Popean couplets on such satiric projects as *The Anarchiad* and *The Echo.* The painter John Trumbull (1750–1831) used the tetrameters of Swift and Butler's *Hudibras* for his caricatures of local types in *The Progress of Dulness* (1772) and *M'Fingal* (1782). Timothy Dwight (1752–1817), who became president of Yale, composed a ponderous epic in couplets called *The Conquest of Canaan* (1785), in which the journey of the Israelites under Joshua to the promised land can be read as the advance of the Americans under Gen. Washington to nationhood. Dwight also wrote

AMERICAN POETRY

Greenfield Hill (1794) in post-Miltonic blank verse (q.v.) to demonstrate that the new republic could yield pastoral poetry of philosophical seriousness worthy of Denham's *Cooper's Hill* and Goldsmith's *Deserted Village*. The poem concludes, as does Joel Barlow's *The Columbiad*, with a visionary prospect of America's future happiness and prosperity; both versions of paradise regained in an industrializing age represent early instances of the recurrent Am. effort to project for the unstoried nation a myth of the future commensurate with its size and ambitions. Barlow (1752–1812) had recognized the inadequacies of the Miltonic diction and heroic couplets of *The Vision of Columbus* (1787) and revised it into *The Columbiad* (1807). But *The Hasty Pudding* (1796), dedicated to Martha Washington, remains vigorous and delightful; its mock-pastoral, mock-epic couplets celebrate cornmeal mush, which New Englanders adopted from the Indians as a dietary staple.

At Princeton, Philip Freneau (1752–1832) wrote "The Power of Fancy" and co-authored "The Rising Glory of America," exhibiting early the combination of preromantic feeling and patriotic fervor which would characterize his work. He enthusiastically supported the Revolution and afterwards edited newspapers attacking the Federalists and advocating Jefferson's republicanism. His war experiences as a blockade runner and prisoner of war fueled the polemics of "The British Prison Ship" (1781). Today his public poems (e.g. "America Independent") sound bombastic; his Deistic poems on the benevolence of nature (e.g. "The Wild Honey Suckle") seem too blandly sweet; his poems about the Am. Indian (e.g. "The Indian Burying Ground") slip into patronizing sentimentality. In the heady excitement of the new republic, Freneau had high hopes for Am. lit. and for himself as the first Am. poet of stature. But despite public acclaim as the "Poet of the Revolution," Freneau spent his last years in relative obscurity and, after dying of exposure in a snowstorm, was buried under a stone inscribed "Poet's Grave."

The poetry of the Colonial period was, understandably, imitative. The question of literary nationalism—i.e., of whether Am. p. was or ought to be original or derivative, part of the European (and particularly the Eng.) trad. or a native devel. with the power of its rudeness—did not become urgent until the professionalization of lit. in the second quarter of the 19th c. Neoclassicism was not strong enough in the U.S. to precipitate a vehement romantic reaction against it. Instead, Puritan Calvinism remained sufficiently strong, both North and South, that by the time the new energies of romanticism reached Boston and New York and Charleston in the 1820s and '30s, they defined themselves not against neoclassical rules and constraints but in terms of the lingering aesthetic and epistemological assumptions of Puritanism. Thus Am. romanticism adapted the transatlantic stimulus from Coleridge and Wordsworth

and Carlyle, Rousseau and Mme. de Stael, Kant and Fichte and Goethe to its own character and emphasis.

The Puritan plain style—in lit. as in architecture, dress, and worship—bespoke a deeply ambivalent suspicion of art as false, deceptive, seductive: an appeal to the carnal and the irrational, a portrayal of a fiction as a truth. In "Of Poetry and Style," Cotton Mather could still inveigh in 1726: "Be not so set upon poetry, as to be always poring on the passionate and measured pages. Let not what should be sauce, rather than food for you, engross all your application. . . . [L]et not the Circean cup intoxicate you. But esp. preserve the chastity of your soul from the dangers you may incur, by a conversation with muses that are no better than harlots." The "food" was the nourishing meat of Scripture and nature, the "sauce" the steamy smothering of style and artifice, meter and metaphor. What the Circe-muse fed you could turn you into a swine. Peter Bulkeley's Preface to a book called *Poetic Meditations* (1725) wondered whether a person could be both an "Accomplish'd Poet" and a "Great Man," since the latter peruses truth and virtue and the former is "misled by Similitude," by an "Affinity to take one thing from another," and by "Wit, . . . or, to speak more plain, an aptness at Metaphor and Allusion."

To preserve the distinction between "food" and "sauce," the Puritans contrasted two modes of perceiving, imaging, or expressing. "Types," a term derived from a method of interpreting Scripture (see ALLEGORY) and extended into reading the "book" of nature, reveal the spiritual truths inherent and made manifest in the phenomenal world by divine constition. "Tropes" are mere figures of speech, similitudes and allusions gestated by the fertile fancy. Thus the great Puritan theologian Jonathan Edwards declared: "The things of this world are ordered [and] designed to shadow forth spiritual things," for "God makes the inferiour in imitation of the superiour, the material of the spiritual, on purpose in order to have a resemblance or shadow of them." Typological resemblance *presents* the God-made symbolism of objective reality, beyond the verbal skill or interpretive powers of the artist; tropological resemblance *represents* or recomposes reality in poet-made metaphors. Types present directly extrinsic truths; tropes represent indirectly imaginative inventions. Puritans used tropes, but warily. In Bradstreet and Taylor, however, typological conviction liberated and propelled their verbal and metaphorical inventiveness.

The Puritan aesthetic set the agenda for Am. p. into the 19th c. and down to the present. The hermeneutical and epistemological assumptions behind the literary distinction between type and trope, the different implications of how things come to mean and how the imagination and lang. function and participate in that process, established the poles for an ongoing dialectic that later

- [49] -

poets would resume and resolve on their own terms.

II. NINETEENTH-CENTURY ROMANTICISM. William Cullen Bryant (1794–1878) brought the first stirrings of romanticism to Am. p. The transition from his grandfather's Federalist Calvinism to his father's Unitarianism to his own career as a nature poet and a liberal reformer sums up the declension of New England intellectual and religious life. Bryant wrote "Thanatopsis," a stoic meditation on human mortality in the round of nature, at the age of 17, and had written many of his best poems by the publication of *Poems* in 1821. His move to New York in 1825 embroiled him in the hurly-burly of journalism, crusading for labor and against slavery. His *Lectures on Poetry* (1825) argued for the possibility of an Am. art and lit. indigenous to Nature's Nation (cf. the admonitory sonnet, "To Cole, the Painter, Departing for Europe"). Despite his public activities he continued to publish poetry, meditating on landscapes from the Berkshires ("Inscription for the Entrance to a Wood," "A Forest Hymn") to the Illinois plains ("The Prairies") with a melancholy optimism. "To a Waterfowl" sets out to read as a type of God's Providence the bird's solitary flight in the twilit sky to its eventual resting place, but the imagery and hesitant rhythms reveal the difficulty of affirmation. Bryant became known as the "Am. Wordsworth," but for him the woods were not so much the manifestation of the Power that rolls through all things as a soothing, healing haven from the stresses of secular, urban living. In the end he was more like the 18th-c. meditative precursors than the visionary poet of "Tintern Abbey."

Ralph Waldo Emerson (1803–82) marks the real watershed of Am. p. After resigning his Unitarian pulpit in Boston because he could no longer adhere to the tenets of Christianity, Emerson immersed himself in Eng. and Ger. romanticism and issued his manifesto *Nature* (1836). The prophet of Transcendentalism drew many disciples, incl. Henry David Thoreau (1817–62), and he spread his message on the lecture circuit around the country, all the way to California. The "Sage of Concord" assimilated Neoplatonism, Ger. idealism, and Oriental mysticism into a Yankee conviction that individuals who trusted their powers of intuitive insight (which he called transcendental Reason) would discover in their own experience, rather than in doctrines or institutions, their harmony with nature and with the Oversoul immanent in nature. He elaborated his philosophy in *Essays* (1841, 1844) and *Representative Man* (1850).

Philosopher as poet, poet as seer ("transparent eyeball," in the phrase from the opening epiphany of *Nature*), seer as sayer: Emerson enunciated an Am. poetics so powerful that both contemporaries and succeeding generations have had to contend with it by affirmation, qualification, or denial. The three axioms laid down in the "Language" chapter of *Nature* postulated an intrinsic correspondence between words, things, and absolute truth: "1. Words are the signs of natural facts. 2. Particular natural facts are symbols of particular spiritual facts. 3. Nature is symbol of Spirit." There is a clear line from Edwards' declaration that "the material and natural world is typical of the moral, spiritual, and intelligent world, or the City of God" to Emerson's axioms. "The Poet," as Emerson expatiates in his essay of that title (1844), is the receptive and expressive medium of the Spirit in Nature, distinguished by the "power to receive and impart" his typological experience. But Emerson's unchurched experience of types rested not on the certitude of Scripture and doctrine but on the instabilities of subjective experience: "the individual is his world," he said in "Self-Reliance." That individualizing and psychologizing of experience, which is the essence of romanticism, and which was itself a result of the general decline of theological and philosophical assurance in the West and of Puritanism in the U.S., served to undermine the distinction between types and tropes; indeed, Emerson tends to use the terms almost interchangeably.

But that ambiguity was the unacknowledged subtext; what people responded to was Emerson's call to believe in "the infinitude of the private man," his affirmation of the power both of imagination (q.v.) to realize its perceptions and of America's natural sublimity as the source of a new poetry capable of idealizing Am. materialism and building a new society. Since realization required the seer to be also a sayer or "Language-maker," Emerson proposed an aesthetic of organicism (q.v.). "Every word was once a poem. Every new relation is a new word." Consequently, organic form is not antecedent to the poem; even though the form and meaning coexist in the completed work, form does not proceed *ab extra*—i.e. from the technique of following out conventional rules and patterns—but from the impulse of the insight: "a thought so passionate and alive that like the spirit of a plant or an animal it has an architecture of its own and adorns nature with a new thing." The shape of the poem ought to be the extension of the generative experience into words.

Emerson versified his Transcendentalism in poems such as "Each and All," "Bacchus," and "Brahma"; his image of the poet in "Merlin" and "Uriel"; and his notion of organic form in "The Snow-Storm." He admitted that the pieces he collected in *Poems* (1847) and *May-Day* (1867) did not adequately exemplify the ideals he proposed, and that much of his best poetry was in his prose. Still, his rhythmic roughness and irregularity (even in metered verse), his verbal directness and freshness, often antipate the revolution in form and expression which Whitman and Dickinson would initiate. "Merlin" contrasts the authentic native poet with the imitative "jingling serenader":

Thy trivial harp will never please

Or fill my craving ear;
Its chords should ring as blows the
breeze,
Free, peremptory, clear.
No jingling serenader's art,
Nor tinkle of piano strings,
Can make the wild blood start
In its mystic springs.

Emerson might have been thinking of Poe (whom he called "the jingle-man") as the negative contrast to the Am. bard here. Edgar Allan Poe (1809–49), though born in Boston of traveling actors, was orphaned by the age of three and reared by the Allan family of Richmond. A Southerner by defiant choice, and a poet by aspiration, Poe struggled to support himself through journalism, writing the famous short stories and the voluminous reviews which make him the first Am. critic of stature.

A Southern strain of Calvinism not only disposed Poe to the Gothic but disabused him of the Transcendentalists' claims. The poem "Israfel" indicates his susceptibility to the idea of the exalted seer-sayer and his disillusionment with it. What can we do if "our flowers are merely—flowers," not types but phenomena in the material flux? In compensation we make flowers into tropes and, with conscious craft and calculated effect, construct from disordered nature an intricately composed artifice. The imagination functions not to discover typological truth but to devise metaphorical connection. By explicating the text of "The Raven" as a rational construction of an irrational narrative, "The Philosophy of Composition" (1846) mounts a withering attack on the supposition of ecstatic inspiration in "the so-called poetry of the so-called transcendentalists."

Emerson's distinction between poetry as the eternal verities "all written before time was" and the poem which can never adequately express those verities allowed him to judge Poe a bad poet who sometimes wrote good poems and Thoreau a poet so possessed of the spirit of poetry that he was impatient with the craft required for good poems. However, Poe's essay on "The Poetic Principle" (1848), dismissing "the heresy of The Didactic" and defining poetry as "The Rhythmical Creation of Beauty," concludes that "there neither exists nor *can* exist any work more thoroughly dignified . . . [than] this poem which is a poem and nothing more—this poem written solely for the poem's sake."

The Raven and Other Poems (1845) collected Poe's verse with an apologetic preface. Their mannered artifice represents the attempt to invent the harmony and beauty life lacks (cf. "The Conqueror Worm," "The Haunted Palace"). The woman doomed to die for her purity and beauty (cf. "Annabel Lee," "Ulalume") is the symbol of nature's failure to match the poet's ideal. "To One in Paradise" illustrates the manner and the theme:

For, alas! alas! with me
The light of Life is o'er!
—No more—no more—no more—
(Such language holds the solemn sea
To the sands upon the shore)
Shall bloom the thunder-blasted tree,
Or the stricken eagle soar!

The prose poem *Eureka* (1848) was a last effort to fend off disaster by imagining a scientific cosmology. Found dying in the streets of Baltimore, Poe is the romantic genius cut down by the height of his aspirations.

Another tormented dissent from Transcendentalism after an initial fascination came from Herman Melville (1819–91). He associated with the Young America Group of literary nationalists in New York in the late 1840s and wrote fictional romances, often drawn from his adventures as a sailor and increasingly charged with philosophical and psychological themes. After abandoning fiction out of disillusion with his audience and resigning himself to obscurity as a customs inspector, Melville turned to poetry. *Battle Pieces and Aspects of the War* (1866), *John Marr and Other Sailors* (1888), and *Timoleon* (1891), the last two privately printed, were derided and forgotten, as was *Clarel* (1876), a verse novel of some 18,000 tetrameter couplets which explores through a journey-quest to the Holy Land the dilemma of Christian faith or Darwinian skepticism.

Walt Whitman (1819–92) took no note of his almost exact contemporary Melville but acknowledged Poe the romantic neurotic as the antithesis of what he wanted to make himself into. A dreamy boy from a large, mentally unstable, working-class Brooklyn family, Whitman as poet sublimated his sexual anxieties into an ideal of a joyous soul in a robust body. He left school at 15 to become a printer and journalist, editing various newspapers in Brooklyn and Manhattan during the 1840s and trying his hand for a popular audience with sentimental fiction and a temperance novel, *Franklin Evans* (1842). But nothing in the biography hints at the emergence of Whitman as poet. Later he would tell a friend about steeping himself in Emerson: "I was simmering, simmering, simmering; Emerson brought me to a boil." The poems that bubbled up were radical in technique and content. Out of Emerson's call for organic form, Whitman distilled, from translations of the Old Testament and Homer and operatic arias and recitativo, a revolution in verse technique that came to be called free verse (q.v.): lines irregular in length and stresses, patterned not by meter or rhyme but by repetition of phrase (see SYNTAX, POETIC) and rhythm (q.v.). Out of Emerson's call for an Am. seer-prophet, Whitman devised the persona (q.v.) whose colloquial, expansive, often exclamatory voice sounded a "different relative attitude towards God, towards the objective universe, and still more (by reflection, confession, assumption) the quite changed attitude of the ego, the one chanting or talking, towards himself and towards his fellow humanity." He was "large" and sought to "contain multitudes"—the city and countryside, the people and places of America. The opening lines of "Song of Myself," his epic of the democratic individual's consciousness struck, that expansive note from the start:

> I celebrate myself, and sing myself,
> And what I shall assume you shall assume,
> For every atom belonging to me as good belongs to you.
>
> I loafe and invite my soul,
> I lean and loafe at my ease observing a spear of summer grass.
>
> My tongue, every atom of my blood, form'd from this soil, this air,
> Born here of parents born from parents the same, and their parents the same,
>
> I, now thirty-seven years old in perfect health begin,
> Hoping to cease not till death.

In July, 1855, *Leaves of Grass* appeared in a large book designed and printed by the poet. His picture as the people's Everyman provided the frontispiece, but he remained anonymous on the title page and up to the middle of the first and longest of 12 untitled poems (later "Song of Myself"), which itself erupted for 43 pages to occupy half of the book. The "Preface" of sprawling, incantatory paragraphs identified the author as the Am. bard Emerson had anticipated. Whitman sought to compensate for the shocked response of reviewers by publishing several adulatory reviews anonymously and by sending complementary copies to literati. When Emerson responded immediately with rhapsodic praise, Whitman's vocation was confirmed. The next year he published a second edition, now 56 poems, incl. "Crossing Brooklyn Ferry," with Emerson's words on the spine as advertisement.

Emerson's enthusiasm cooled, however, with Whitman's continued emphasis on the body as much as the soul and his identification of the life force with the sexual "urge." But the self-reliant Whitman maintained his independence and devoted his life ("that electric self seeking types") to the organic expansion of *Leaves of Grass* through a succession of editions, though he could not find a commercial publisher until the decade before the "Death-Bed Edition" (1891–92). Whitman revised old poems as he added new ones, reordering the sequence and groupings. With the third edition (1860) the sea-dirges "Out of the Cradle Endlessly Rocking" and "As I Ebb'd with the Ocean of Life," written during the late 1850s out of a profound but mysterious distress, explored

the death theme coexistent from the beginning with the celebration of life; and the "Children of Adam" and "Calamus" sections celebrated alternatively love between men and women and love between manly comrades. The edition of 1867 added *Drum Taps*, the Civil War poems, and the Lincoln elegy "When Lilacs Last in the Dooryard Bloom'd."

By then most of Whitman's best poetry was written, but despite failing health he continued to write voluminously in verse and prose with flashes of the old power and compassion. Despite his admirers and disciples, he never received the broad audience and recognition he had hoped for as the Am. bard; but a final Preface, "A Backward Glance O'er Travel'd Roads" (1888), reaffirmed the goals and achievements that he knew had transformed modern poetry.

Though the only comment of Emily Dickinson (1830–86) about Whitman was that she had heard he was "disgraceful," the two represent complementary aspects of the Am. poet stemming from Emerson: the democratic projection of the self into nature and the city, the hermetic absorption of the world into the private self. The religion of the Connecticut River valley where Dickinson grew up as daughter of a prominent Amherst lawyer and public servant was still Congregational, not Unitarian, much less Transcendentalist. But Dickinson, the only family member not to join the local church, committed herself, in part (like Thoreau) under Emerson's inspiration, to another vocation: recording with unwavering attention the interior drama of consciousness.

Adapting the quatrain of the hymnal (and perhaps the sigla of elocution manuals) to her own purposes, Dickinson lines out, not sentence by sentence but word by word, single moments of perception and emotion. Each taut, spare poem expresses with unblinking fidelity the truth of its moment, and the accumulation of poems charts the extremes of her experience: God as present or absent, love as fulfillment or renunciation, nature as harmonious or alien. A poem beginning "The loss of something ever felt I" locates the first act of consciousness as an experience of radical bereavement, after which the individual consciousness seeks completion either through its relation to the other—nature, lover, God—or through focusing on its own integration. Though Dickinson found relation to nature, lover, or God much chancier, less assuredly typological than Emerson, this pair of separate and contrasting quatrains poses the alternatives in typically compact, gnomic terms:

> Circumference thou Bride of Awe
> Possessing thou shalt be
> Possessed by every hallowed Knight
> That dares to covet thee
>
> Lads of Athens, faithful be,
> To Thyself,

And Mystery—
All the rest is Perjury—

A recluse in her father's house by the age of 30, Dickinson maintained the independence her poetry required from the demands made on an unmarried woman in a bourgeois Victorian household. In the late 1850s she began making fair copies of poems and binding them with thread into packets which were found in a dresser drawer after her death. During the early 1860s a crisis, perhaps involving frustrated or thwarted love, precipitated an extraordinarily creative outburst: 681 poems between 1862 and '64, over a third of her 1800-odd poems. The "He" in her love poems seems to be Jesus, or a human lover (the biographical evidence is suggestive rather than conclusive), or the masculine aspect of her self—or overlays of all these. Her word for the ecstatic fulfillment of consciousness in triumphant selfhood was Immortality, sometimes expressed as a marriage, often one deferred to the next life; and despite deprivation and renunciation she experienced momentary intimations of Immortality in the upstairs bedroom which often served as images of her secluded consciousness.

In 1862 Dickinson was sufficiently confident to write to the critic Thomas Wentworth Higginson, sending three poems and asking his advice. His prompt expression of interest, she said, saved her life, but his well-intentioned insensitivity to her oddities of phrasing, rhythm, capitalization, and punctuation, as well as his caution against publication, confirmed Dickinson's sense that she would have to be content with posthumous fame. Though poems and letters began to appear after her death with some of the eccentricities normalized, the unbowdlerized collected *Poems* (1955) and *Letters* (1958) assured her place as the only woman among the great romantic poets.

Frederick Goddard Tuckerman (1821–73) was another Massachusetts recluse (living near Greenfield) whose poetry dissented from Emersonian optimism with a melancholy regret deepened by his wife's death in 1857. Though his verse appeared in magazines and in *Poems* (1860), and though he had Emerson, Tennyson, and Longfellow as admirers, Tuckerman was known during his lifetime as a botanist rather than a poet. The bulk of his work consists of five series of sonnets, notable for experimenting with that tight form and for focusing feeling in a sharply observed image, as when he depicts the soul "shooting the void in silence" like "a bird that shuts his wings for better speed." Yvor Winters called "The Cricket," Tuckerman's long meditation on the individual in nature, "the greatest poem in Eng. of the century." The other great sonneteer of the century was yet another Massachusetts recluse, Jones Very (1813–80), who infused his Puritan spirit with Transcendentalist exaltation. Visiting Very after intense mystical experiences sent him briefly into an asylum, Emerson pronounced him "profoundly sane."

The reputation of the Massachusetts poets popularly known (along with Emerson) as the "Household Poets" has diminished with time. More Victorian than romantic, they run to moralizing sentiment and prefer conventional forms to experimentation. The popularity of Henry Wadsworth Longfellow (1807–82) rivaled Tennyson's on both sides of the Atlantic. As a Harvard professor he helped to introduce Ger. lit. to the U.S., and he translated Dante. His most famous narrative poems are: *Evangeline* (1847), a tragic romance in hexameters about the exodus of Fr. Canadians to Louisiana; *The Song of Hiawatha* (1855, the year of the first ed. of *Leaves of Grass*), an epic rendering of Am. Indian legends into tetrameters imitative of the Finnish *Kalevala*; and *The Courtship of Miles Standish* (1858), a blank verse version of the famous Puritan love triangle. "The Psalm of Life" answers human mortality with a call to the work ethic, and "Excelsior" expresses a Browningesque summons to strive in the face of failure. Longfellow's chief poetic interest now lies in lyrics like "The Jewish Cemetery at Newport" and "The Cross of Snow."

James Russell Lowell (1819–91) succeeded to Longfellow's chair at Harvard and became the first editor of the *Atlantic Monthly* and a powerful liberal voice in Am. journalism. 1848 was Lowell's *annus mirabilis*, during which he published *A Fable for Critics*, a spoof of contemp. Am. writers in Popean couplets and outrageous rhymes; the first series of *The Biglow Papers*, written in a rollicking version of Yankee dialect for a down-home satire on such political issues as slavery and the Mexican War; and *The Vision of Sir Launfal*, a didactic extension of the Grail legend. "The Ode Recited at the Harvard Commemoration" of the Civil War dead (1865), written largely in one night, is perhaps his noblest poem. The literary, as opposed to medical, fame of Oliver Wendel Holmes (1809–94) rests on the several volumes of *Breakfast Table* episodes collected from the *Atlantic* and on such verse favorites of Boston local color as "Old Ironsides," "The Last Leaf," "The Chambered Nautilus," "Dorothy Q.: A Family Portrait," and "The Deacon's Masterpiece: Or, The Wonderful 'One-Hoss Shay.'"

In contrast to these Boston Brahmins, the only yeoman among the Household Poets was John Greenleaf Whittier (1807–92). Inspired by Robert Burns' Scots poetry, Whittier began to versify his Quaker piety and his Abolitionist opposition to slavery. Today "Barbara Fritchie" seems marred by flag-waving patriotism, and "The Barefoot Boy," "Maud Mullen," and "Telling the Bees" by mawkish sentiment. However, *Snow-Bound* (1866) remains a movingly nostalgic idyll of rural New England life.

Dickinson's poetry emerges from—and stands out from—the work of a number of female writers so commercially successful that Hawthorne complained enviously of the "scribbling women." The best known was Lydia Sigourney (1791–1865), the "Sweet Singer of Hartford," whose readership vied with that of the British Mrs. Felicia Hemans. Tearjerking titles such as "Widow at Her Daughter's Funeral," "Death of an Infant in Its Mother's Arms," and "Wife of a Missionary at Her Husband's Grave" evoke the morbidity that account for Mrs. Sigourney's popularity and its decline.

The contrast between Sidney Lanier (1842–81) and Stephen Crane (1871–1900) illustrates the exhaustion of romanticism in Am. p. Born of old Virginia stock, Lanier pursued a career in both music and lit. even after service in the Confederate army and four months as a military prisoner brought on the consumption that made his remaining years a strenuous effort to stave off death. The extreme musicality of his lang. and the lush metaphorical straining for a diffuse effect indicate his admiration for Poe; in *The Science of Eng. Verse* (1880) Lanier used his knowledge of music theory and his experience as a symphony flautist to codify Poe's correlation of music and poetry into strict rules based on the assumption that the metrical foot, like the musical bar, was governed not just by pattern of stress but by syllabic duration. "Corn" and "The Symphony" established his fame in 1875 with a fiercely Southern denunciation of corrupt commerce in favor of a chivalric-agrarian ideal. "The Marshes of Glynn" and "Sunrise," the latter written in a high fever on his deathbed, express the last gasp of romantic typology as they celebrate the dying of the individual back into the sublimity of nature and nature's God. By contrast, the terse, irregular verse in Crane's *The Black Riders* (1895) and *War Is Kind* (1899), written in part in response to the angularity of Dickinson's newly published poems, extends the anti-romantic naturalism of his fiction, but Crane's tough-guy irony before man's fate in a universe of chance does not mask the wistful vulnerability, even sentimentality, of his tender heart.

Some names from the end of the century which warrant mention are: Thomas Bailey Aldrich (1836–1907) and Bayard Taylor (1825–78), genteel New York "bohemians" in search of the Ideal; the Harvard aesthetes George Santayana (1863–1952), Trumbull Stickney (1874–1904), and William Vaughn Moody (1869–1910), the last of whom came up against the brashness of Chicago when he took a post at the university there; James Whitcomb Riley (1849–1916), the "Hoosier Poet" of sentimental dialect poems; Paul Laurence Dunbar (1872–1906), son of Kentucky slaves, who wrote both dialect poems of plantation life and conventional lyrics; Lizette Woodworth Reese (1856–1935), the Baltimore schoolteacher who sang of nature and death in clean, direct lines that marked a departure from Mrs. Sigourney and her sisters; and Joaquin Miller (1841?–1913), who was born in a covered wagon on the way west and whose

Songs of the Sierras (1871) earned him his role as swaggering bard of the Far West. But these are all decidedly minor figures. The romantic ideology which had made for the energy and experimentation of the middle years of the century had played itself out. Am. culture needed the jolt of a new ideology—modernism—to galvanize a generation of poets whose achievement rivals that of the Eng. Ren.

III. MODERNIST POETRY, 1900–1935. Edwin Arlington Robinson (1869–1935), Robert Frost (1874–1963), and John Crowe Ransom (1888–1974) are premodernists. Like their modernist contemporaries, they felt the increasing gravity and precariousness of the human predicament, as the decline of religious belief and metaphysical certitude, the subversion of Enlightenment rationalism and then of romantic intuition left the unprotected individual at risk in an indifferent universe and an increasingly violent social world. But the strongly regional conservatism of these three made them resist breaking the old forms and reject the formal experimentation that impelled modernism internationally. Robinson grew up in Gardiner, Maine, the model for his Tilbury Town. His poetry ran to long Arthurian narratives in strong blank verse: *Merlin* (1917), *Launcelot* (1920), *Tristram* (1927). But his most widely read poems are the tragic vignettes of the people of Tilbury Town—"Miniver Cheevy," "Eros Turannos," "Mr. Flood's Party"—and the ruefully melancholy sonnets about faith and doubt, such as "Maya" and "New England." Frost's tribute to Robinson applies equally to Frost himself: "His theme was unhappiness, but his skill was as happy as it was playful. . . . We mourn, but with the qualification that, after all, his life was a revel in the felicities of lang."

Frost's long career from *North of Boston* (1914) to *In the Clearing* (1962) made him revered in the U.S. and England, where he lived as a young man and learned from the pastoral, regional verse of Thomas Hardy and his friend Edward Thomas. Receiving the Emerson-Thoreau medal in 1958, he said that from Emerson he learned to write sentences crafted so close to the flesh and bone that they would bleed if cut, but he dissented from Emerson's blindness to evil and insisted that an unresolved dualism was the dialectic of nature and man. His New England pastorals—"Home Burial," "For Once, Then, Something," "Design," "West-Running Brook," "Directive"—test out the premises of Puritanism and Transcendentalism and leave the answer open. Aesthetic form provided "a momentary stay against confusion" for those provisional conclusions that allow us to persist in pitting our wits and will against ultimate defeat. Scorning free verse, Frost argued that poetic skill lay in making the dramatic tones and inflections of the speaking voice break through the strict pattern of meter and rhyme. Frost and Ransom the Tennessean admired each other's work and shared a sense of form as necessary control for the voice's ironic modulations. Ransom's "Dead Boy," "Judith of Bethulia," "Janet Waking," "The Equilibrists," and "Persistent Explorer" delineate a fallen world in which death is an omnipresent fact, transcendence a nostalgic idea, and the conflict of head and heart an impasse that paralyzes love. After *Chills and Fever* (1924) and *Two Gentlemen in Bonds* (1927) Ransom devoted himself chiefly to teaching and advocating the New Criticism (discussed below, and q.v.).

These poets' skepticism unsettled the typological sense of Edwards and Emerson and allowed only the double terms of trope: in Frost's words, "play's the thing. All virtue in 'as if.'" But the modernists refused to reside in ironic paradox and pressed heroically on to find the terms and means by which the imagination, even without the epistemological and metaphysical claims of romanticism (q.v.), might still function as the supreme faculty of human cognition, potent enough to meet the psychological, moral, and political crises of the 20th c. Their manifestoes vehemently rejected romantic idealism and optimism. They brought to the point of rupture and release the irony which increasingly threatened to subvert romantic holism in the course of the 19th c., and thereby they reconstituted the key issue of romanticism: the validation of the imagination as the agency of individual coherence, outside systems and structures, in a secular, relativized world.

In contrast to romanticism, modernism assumed a disjunction between art and life: meaning not revealed but made. Construction was itself the cognitive act; mastery of the medium disclosed the form of perception, organic now not to the operations of nature but to the internal relations of its structure. Yet the dialectic between symbolism and imagism (qq.v.)—the two most widely influential and persistent strains within modernist poetry—represent differing inclinations that resume in more complex formulations the distinction between tropes and types which had become cloudier and more problematic during the 19th c. As the romantic synthesis of subject and object through the agency of Spirit became harder to maintain, the destabilized focus of perception veered back and forth. Symbolism, developing out of Poe through Baudelaire and Rimbaud to Mallarmé and Valéry, exemplified the tendency to turn inward on subjective consciousness and absorb impressions of the external world into the expressions of moods and feelings of increasing subtlety. Imagism, initiated by Pound in 1912 as an alternative to symbolism, signaled the countertendency to fix consciousness in its encounter with the phenomenal world. Both symbolism and imagism are modernist rather than romantic because modernism validates subject (symbolism) and object (imagism) in the authority of the artwork rather than of Spirit. But symbolism seeks the multivalent suggestiveness of metaphor and the rich imprecision of music, where imagism seeks a clean-edged delineation of image and a painterly disposition of elements.

Ezra Pound (1885–1972) defined the image as the presentation of "an intellectual and emotional complex in an instant of time" and drew up the imagist axioms: "1. Direct treatment of the 'thing,' whether subjective or objective. 2. To use absolutely no word that does not contribute to the presentation. 3. As regarding rhythm: to compose in the sequence of the musical phrase, not in the sequence of a metronome." Direct presentation opposed romantic reflection and didacticism and mandated a rendering of the experience so that the poem rendered itself as experience. Strict verbal economy militated against emotional diffuseness. Breaking the pentameter allowed a rhythmic variety and precision unique to the particular aesthetic presentation.

In Whitman, Pound recognized the authentic Am. poetic impulse, but he took it as his vocation to educate and civilize their impulse with Old World culture. Pound's early poetry showed the influence of *fin de siècle* decadence, esp. that of early Yeats, and during the London years just before and after World War I, Pound, the energetic polemicist for modern art, apprenticed himself by writing in imitation of Gr., Lat., Provençal, Old Eng., and Chinese poetry, collected in *Personae* (1926). "Hugh Selwyn Mauberley" (1920) marked a turning point; venting his outrage at the war and a dying Eng. culture and exorcising the remnants of a decadent romanticism, he departed for Paris, and thence to Italy, and took up his life-long epic, *The Cantos*.

But how to write a historical epic which was also modern (and romantic) in locating itself in the individual consciousness? The lessons of imagism had to be extended and accommodated to temporal devel. for the longer venture. Pound felt that Amy Lowell (1874–1925) had perverted his movement with a soft-focus romantic impressionism that he dubbed "Amygism." In 1914 he wrote an essay on "Vorticism" (q.v.), the short-lived attempt by artists and writers around Wyndham Lewis to vitalize arts and culture in the London "vortex," and the notion of the image as vortex charged it with energetic movement and power drawn from the analogues of the machine and the whirlpool. But the big conceptual breakthrough came with Pound's absorption during the mid-teens in the notebooks of the Am. philosopher and Orientalist Ernest Fenollosa. Pound edited for publication Fenollosa's essay on "The Chinese Written Character as a Medium for Poetry," and he made Fenollosa's literal transcription of Chinese and Japanese poems into the magnificent Eng. renderings of *Cathay* (1915). Fenollosa reconnected Pound with his romantic roots by presenting ideogrammic lang. as pictographs grounded in the divinely ordained operations of nature and communicating directly without the logical and discursive machinery of parts of speech and syntax (see IDEOGRAM). *The Cantos* began as an extended effort, in its juxtaposition of phrases and images, at an Eng. equivalent of the ideogrammic presentation of ideas as actions.

The Cantos came out in segments throughout Pound's life, and the posthumous collection (1972) ends with Canto 120. His prose volumes include *ABC of Reading* (1934), *Guide to Kulchur* (1938), *Literary Essays* (1954), and *Selected Prose* (1973). Denounced for his anti-Semitism and sympathy with Mussolini before and during World War II, Pound was brought to Washington, D.C., in 1945 to be charged with treason, and spent 13 years in a mental hospital before returning to Italy for his final years. The ideogrammic method, historical scope, mythological references, and erudite sources of *The Cantos* are demanding, but the poem constitutes a heroic effort at resolving polarities: on the psychological level, reason with instinct, Apollonian control with Dionysian energy, archetypal masculine with feminine, sexuality with mysticism; philosophically, Gr. Neoplatonism with Confucianism; economically, individual freedom with governmental regulation of money; and historically, the record of war and violence with the possibility of building a paradisal society on earth. Beneath the modernist collage technique, the underlying romantic premises become more explicit in the course of the poem. Despite the massive egotism of the undertaking, Pound ends up insisting that the individual submit to the *Tao* and find his humble place within the eternal round of nature, that healthy economics extend the *Tao* into social organization, and that art seek to express these (typological) truths. In this ideogram from Canto 2 the union of the nymph Tyro with Poseidon presents a momentary epiphany of the sexual and metaphysical energy irradiating and resolving natural and human activity:

And by the beach-run, Tyro,
  Twisted arms of the sea-god,
Lithe sinews of water gripping her,
  cross-hold,
And the blue-grey glass of the wave
  tents them,
Glare azure of water, cold-welter, close
  cover.

William Carlos Williams (1883–1963) and Pound met at the University of Pennsylvania and remained lifelong if contentious friends. Williams teased that where Pound's word was caviar his was bread; resolutely the naturalist ("no ideas but in things"), Williams steered clear of myths and metaphysics. Critical of Pound's and more esp. Eliot's expatriation, Williams the literary nationalist committed himself as doctor and poet to poor, grimy, industrial Rutherford, next to Paterson, New Jersey ("The local is the universal"). The prose sections of *Spring and All* (1923) hail the imagination as a primal force, decreating and re-creating the world into an aesthetic invention which takes its place as an object in the world. Williams was fascinated by the experiments of Gertrude Stein (1874–1946) with words as things but shied away from her attempt to detach words from referentiality. For Williams, the art-work, though integral to itself, was not disjunct from or opposite to nature but "apposite" to it. His interest in painting and his friendship with precisionist painters like Charles Sheeler and Charles Demuth taught him to make his imagism into a kind of verbal cubism (q.v.), using lineation as an analytical device to work against rather than with the syntactic groupings of words, splicing and rearranging the expected verbal relationships so as to focus maximum attention on the words themselves and the complexities of their relationships, as in:

so much depends
upon

a red wheel
barrow

glazed with rain
water

beside the white
chickens.

The many books of shorter lyrics—incl. such other favorites as "Spring and All," "The Pot of Flowers," "To a Poor Old Woman," "The Yachts," "Flowers by the Sea"—are now edited into a two-volume *Collected Poems* (1986–89). However, by the late 1930s Williams was experimenting with a longer, more complex project (*The Cantos* and Joyce's *Finnegans Wake* were two sources) published as *Paterson* in five books between 1946 and 1958 and in a single volume in 1963. Establishing the identification of the doctor-poet with his city, the poem's fragmented vignettes follow out the city's history and the human lifespan in a self-generating, self-completing open form that finds its way, then circles back on itself.

This engagement with time and history required a different sense of prosody. As Williams' *Autobiography* (1951), *Selected Essays* (1954), and *Selected Letters* (1957) show, he became obsessed in his later years with defining a measure more appropriate to the Am. idiom, and in "The Descent" he felt he discovered the principle of the "variable foot" (q.v.), which conceived poetic lines as musical bars having roughly the same duration but containing varying numbers of syllables and stresses like notes within the bar. He explored the possibilities of the variable foot, the lines stepped gracefully in tercets down the page in such poems—longer, more personal and meditative than the early work—as "To Daphne and Virginia" (his daughters-in-law), "For Eleanor and Bill Monahan" (old friends), "The Sparrow" (dedicated to his father), and "Of Asphodel, That Greeny

Flower" (for his wife of many years).

Hilda Doolittle (1886–1961) met Pound in Philadelphia, was briefly engaged to him, and became part of his London literary circle. He gave her the *nom de plume* "H. D." and coined the term "imagist" to describe early poems of hers such as "Oread":

> Whirl up, sea—
> whirl your pointed pines,
> splash your great pines
> on our rocks,
> hurl your green over us,
> cover us with your pools of fir.

H. D. was drawn to Dickinson's poems as they were published in the 1920s; the two women were akin not in external circumstances but in their extraordinary sensitivity and their unswerving attendance upon recording the life of consciousness. H. D. saw her own destiny played out within the violent sexual and international politics of her time, and her autobiography turned on crucial events: the oedipal conflicts with her father and mother; the love conflicts with Pound, the Eng. poet Richard Aldington, D. H. Lawrence, and later male "initiators"; the breakup of her marriage to Aldington during World War I; the birth of her daughter by another man; the sudden advent of the Eng. novelist Bryher as the woman who rescued her from despair and death at war's end; the moments of cosmic consciousness in which she participated in life's mystery. These traumas brought her to Freud in the mid 1930s for therapy, but throughout her life real relief came from her ability to find in Gr. and Egyptian myths and mystery cults the archetypes for her own experience and then—a more remarkable achievement—to project her life into myth, in the poems of *Sea Garden* (1916), *Hymen* (1921), and *Heliodora* (1924), in the impressionistic fiction of her middle period, and in the memoirs and poetic sequences of her last phase.

The fiction taught H. D. to constellate images in a larger temporal/narrative framework, opening up form and perspective, which made possible *Trilogy* (three poems pub. separately in war-torn London and together in 1973), *Helen in Egypt* (1961), and *Hermetic Definition* (1972). *Helen*, an anti-epic told in lyrics with prose bridges, resumes the matter of Troy, which from Homer to Pound provided the theme of love and war, from the woman's perspective. It is perhaps the most ambitious poem written by a woman in Eng. and fulfills its ambition.

H. D. edited with Bryher the first selection of poems by Marianne Moore (1887–1972), though Moore's chaste modesty and reserve put her at the opposite temperamental pole. In "Poetry" her imagist dislike of metaphorical obfuscation called for "imaginary gardens with real toads in them." And Moore's Presbyterian faith gave her imagism a clear typological purpose; keying her keen eye

to the mind's perceptions, she read flora and fauna as quirky, witty emblems of human virtue and weakness spun out in elaborate, elegant syllabics. The *Complete Poems* (1967) contained such admired pieces as "The Fish," "To a Snail," "In the Days of Prismatic Color," "The Mind Is an Enchanting Thing," "The Wood Weasel," and "He 'Digesteth Harde Yron'" (on the ostrich).

The declaration in 1928 by T. S. Eliot (1888–1965), already a British subject, that he was classicist in lit., royalist in politics, and Anglo-Catholic in religion would seem to sum up his distance from the Am. scene. But Eliot recognized that he combined a "Catholic cast of mind" with "a Calvinist heritage, and a Puritanical temperament" and that his Am. roots, his growing up in St. Louis and New England, were the deepest sources of his personality and poetry. Both in poetic practice and in his criticism, however, Eliot trained himself to mask the autobiographical impulse. Though he admitted that "a poet in a romantic age cannot be a 'classical' poet except in tendency," the early essays set the norms for a modernist "classicism": the need for an "historical sense" in an "impersonal" poet ("Trad. and the Individual Talent"); the "autotelic" character of aesthetic form ("The Function of Crit."); metaphorical image as the "objective correlative" (q.v.) of emotion ("Hamlet and His Problems"); and the crippling "dissociation of sensibility" (q.v.) since the 17th c. which required reintegration ("The Metaphysical Poets").

Eliot dated his poetic maturation from reading Arthur Symons' *The Symbolist Trad. in Lit.* in 1908. "The Love Song of J. Alfred Prufrock," "Preludes," and "Rhapsody on a Windy Night," and others in *Prufrock and Other Observations* (1917), the volume which Pound thought established Eliot as the poet of his generation, echo Laforgue and Baudelaire; and symbolism provided the perspective and techniques for finding in urban life the tropes to objectify the twists and turns of his acute self-consciousness. *Poems* (1920) used extreme verbal compression in tight quatrains to anatomize the conflict between sexual body and paralyzed spirit in modern society. The anxiety of Eliot's unhappy marriage precipitated *The Waste Land* (1922), which Pound helped edit into a brilliant collage of episodes in different voices and styles. So successful was Eliot's dramatization of his disillusionment and his ache for deliverance that *The Waste Land* became the most influential poem of the postwar "Lost Generation."

"The Hollow Men" (1925) was a coda to the early period, but after his conversion to Christianity, Eliot introduced, in the "Ariel" poems of the late '20s and in *Ash Wednesday* (1930), a more personal voice, now echoing Scripture, Dante, and the Book of Common Prayer to meditate on opening the concupiscent heart to redemptive grace. The essay "From Poe to Valéry" (1948) exorcised symbolism as self-enclosing, self-defeating narcissism, and "The Music of Poetry" (1942) indicated the swing from prosodic experimentation to the traditional forms and musical structure of *Four Quartets* (1943). Eliot's Calvinist sense made it difficult for him to read manifestations of the Incarnation in a sinful world, but each quartet uses a five-part structure similar to *The Waste Land* to concentrate on a place of autobiographical importance as a typological "point of intersection of the timeless / With time." "The Dry Salvages," the third Quartet, uses the Mississippi River and the Massachusetts coastline to invoke the Incarnation, while "Little Gidding" moves from the flames of the London Blitz to a fusion of Pentecostal fire and the Dantesque rose of the Paradiso:

> And all shall be well
> And all manner of thing shall be well
> When the tongues of flame are in-
> folded
> Into the crowned knot of fire
> And the fire and the rose are one.

Eliot's verse is contained in the *Collected Poems* (1963) and the *Collected Plays* (1967).

Where Eliot took his inspiration from the symbolism of Laforgue and Baudelaire, Wallace Stevens (1879–1955) took his from the symbolism of Mallarmé and Valéry, and it deepened in the course of a poetic career slowed initially by Stevens' career as an insurance lawyer and executive in Hartford, CT. "Sunday Morning" (1915) expressed in gorgeously textured blank verse a sad affirmation that the death of God obligated the mortal imagination to invest nature with the aura of paradise. Other poems in *Harmonium* (1923) aimed at a symbolist "pure poetry" whose agile wit and exotic effects of sound and color rendered discordant states of sensibility without discursive commentary, as in "Domination of Black," "The Emperor of Ice Cream," or "Bantam in Pine Woods," which begins: "Chieftain Iffucan of Azcan in caftan / Of tan, with henna hackles, halt!"

"The Idea of Order at Key West" (1934) answers the charge of escapist hedonism from Yvor Winters and Marxist critics of the '30s by demonstrating the imagination's power to satisfy the mind's "rage for order" through recomposing experience into a fiction which comprehends the flux yet reflects back on it the notion of a possible pattern. Connections and relations are not prescribed by God or nature but contrived in figures of speech. *Notes toward a Supreme Fiction* (1942) explores the tropological process under the subheadings "It Must Be Abstract," "It Must Change," and "It Must Give Pleasure." The essays in *The Necessary Angel* (1951) complement the later poems by showing how the shifting interaction between reality and the "mundo" of the imagination "help[s] us to live our lives." Here is the moral validation of the symbolist trope from "Description Without Place" (1945):

> It matters, because everything we say
> Of the past is description without
> place, a cast
>
> Of the imagination, made in sound;
> And because what we say of the future
> must portend,
>
> Be alive with its own seemings, seem-
> ing to be
> Like rubies reddened by rubies redden-
> ing.

In the later poems in the *Collected Poems* (1954) and *Opus Posthumous* (1957, 1989)—"A Primitive like an Orb," "Final Soliloquy of the Interior Paramour," "The World As Meditation"—the ironic highjinks of *Harmonium* give way to a sinuous, incantatory harmonizing of abstract lang. and recurrent archetypal figures in slow, stately pentameters. At one point Stevens wanted to call *Collected Poems* "The Whole of Harmonium."

When Hart Crane (1899–1932) gave *White Buildings* (1926) an epigraph from Rimbaud, he signaled his hope of achieving through symbolist means—synaesthesia (q.v.), dense overlays of connotative and metaphorical suggestiveness, oracular apostrophe—the romantic rapture that mortality and flux denied him, as in these lines from the sequence about love and loss called "Voyages":

> Bind us in time, O Seasons clear, and
> awe.
> O minstrel galleons of Carib fire,
> Bequeath us to no earthly shore until
> Is answered in the vortex of our grave
> The seal's wide spindrift gaze toward
> paradise.

The *Letters* (1965) and essays like "Mod. Poetry" explore the efficacy of a symbolist "logic of metaphor" in a machine age. Through association with Waldo Frank's circle of literary nationalists in Manhattan, Crane embarked on an epic with the Brooklyn Bridge as its central symbol: an engineering marvel that yoked opposing shores (and, metaphorically, psychological and moral contradictions) and manifested a technological sublime to match the sublimity of the wilderness. *The Bridge* (1930) sought to elide past and present in the poet's consciousness and thus synthesize a myth or mystique strong enough to defeat *The Waste Land*'s impotent disillusionment by projecting Whitman's prophecy into an industrialized, urban America. Crane's overwrought psyche cracked under the stress of alcoholism, neurosis, and fear that *The Bridge* was a failure. "The Broken Tower" articulates the ecstatic despair that led to his suicide: he never knew whether he was a seer or a fake in seeking to break through rational categories and glimpse godhead in the compressed indirections of metaphor.

Whitman was a touchstone for others besides Crane. The Harlem Renaissance (q.v.) of the

1920s and '30s was the first big movement in the arts for Am. blacks and signaled their growing political and cultural consciousness. In poetry James Weldon Johnson (1871–1938) was a transitional figure; the major voices were Claude McKay (1891–1948), Countee Cullen (1903–46), and—most importantly—Langston Hughes (1902–67), who claimed to be Whitman's "darker brother" in singing his America through spirituals (q.v.), jazz, and the blues (q.v.). The Midwest also had its populist Whitmanesque bards: Carl Sandburg (1878–1967) with *Chicago Poems* (1916), *Smoke and Steel* (1920), and *The People, Yes* (1936); Vachel Lindsay (1879–1931) with "The Congo," "General William Booth Enters into Heaven," and "Abraham Lincoln Walks at Midnight"; and Edgar Lee Masters (1868–1950) with *Spoon River Anthology* (1915).

Other minor poets confirm, even beneath the modernist manner, the lingering romantic tenor of the period. Archibald MacLeish (1891–1982) was an expatriate aesthete in the '20s, echoing experimentalists like Eliot and Pound ("Ars Poetica" [1926], *The Hamlet of A. MacLeish* [1928]), and a social bard during the Depression and war years (*Frescoes for Mr. Rockefeller's City*, 1933); but his best poems show him to be an elegantly skilled lyric poet in the elegiac mode. e e cummings (1894–1962) played the iconoclast with his eccentric punctuation, typography, and spatial arrangement, and he talked tough in order to shock. But, as his *Complete Poems* (1972) show, he is unabashedly romantic, celebrating at once the individual's integrity and his transcendence through union with the beloved and nature. cummings' religious sense of life's sacredness goes back through his Unitarian minister-father to New England Transcendentalism. Conrad Aiken (1889–1973) flirted with imagism but found symbolism and the verbal lushness of fellow-Southerners Poe and Lanier more congenial to his introspective, sometimes psychoanalytic, sometimes philosophical mode. The lyrics of Elinor Wylie (1885–1928) and Edna St. Vincent Millay (1892–1950), dissecting the pain of love, death, and beauty in the woman's heart, are traditional in form and echo the Eng. and Am. romantics.

Another generation reformulated modernism in the '30s. Objectivism (q.v.) tightened further the imagist sense of the poem as constructing an encounter with things into a poem which itself has the integrity of (in Emerson's phrase) "a new thing." The chief objectivists, all proletarian in politics like Williams rather than elitist like Pound, were Louis Zukofsky (1904–78), whose indebtedness to his friend Pound, despite his Judaism and Marxism, is clear from his long autobiographical poem *A* (1979), and George Oppen (1908–84), whose *Discrete Series* (1934) intensified Williams' jagged, angular minimalism (q.v.).

At the more conservative end of the spectrum, the New Criticism (q.v.) translated modernist assumptions into an explicitly *literary* method of textual explication (q.v) separate from biography or psychoanalysis or hist. The New Criticism studied the technical and structural properties of (in Poe's words) "this very poem—this poem *per se*" to show how the interplay of paradox, irony, tension (qq.v.), and sound create (again Poe) the "totality, or unity, of effect" in the (now Eliot) "autotelic" artwork. The phrase "New Criticism" was coined by Ransom to describe the critical inclination of I. A. Richards, William Empson, Eliot, and Winters. His essays in *The World's Body* (1938), *The New Criticism* (1941), and *Beating the Bushes* (1972)—many of which are collected in *Selected Essays* (1984)—called for and illustrated an "ontological crit." Through Ransom's teaching and editing and that of his students and followers, the New Criticism dominated the academic study and crit. of poetry well into the 1960s. Both Allen Tate (1899–1979) and Robert Penn Warren (b. 1905–89) were members of Ransom's Fugitives (q.v.), a group of poets and economic agrarians at Vanderbilt, whose manifesto *I'll Take My Stand* (1930) defended Western humanism against the secular materialism and socialist collectivism that had corrupted the North and was corrupting their Southern homeland. Tate was deeply influenced by Poe, the Fr. symbolists, and, most obviously, Eliot. His metrical and rhyme patterns serve as a vise to contain the explosive compression of lang., metaphor, and sound effects. Like Eliot, Tate longed to shed his symbolist imagination for a genuinely symbolic one like Dante's, and his conversion to Catholicism in 1950 allowed the later poems to postulate love, human and divine, as the release from solipsistic impotence (cf. Tate's *Collected Poems* [1977] and *Essays of Four Decades* [1968]). Tate foresaw Warren's development by addressing him in "To a Romantic," for Warren's early "metaphysical" manner, characterized by New Critical tightness and paradox, gave way to a diffuse emotiveness elegizing the mortal self and the disjunction between ideals and experience (cf. *New & Selected Poems* [1985]).

Two important figures, both Californians, cast themselves as anti-modernists. Yvor Winters (1900–68) began by experimenting with both imagism and symbolism (*Early Poems*, 1966); however, in the late 1920s he concluded that both strains of modernist poetry exhibited a morally dangerous romanticism for which Emerson and Whitman were the Am. prophets and Hart Crane's breakdown and suicide the logical outcome, and he set about writing a formalist verse modeled on the Eng. Ren. as a rationally controlled reflection on morally significant experience (cf. *Collected Poems* [1978]). *In Defense of Reason* (1947) contains his essays articulating the critical norms he taught at Stanford for decades. Winters had only contempt for the poetry of Robinson Jeffers (1887–1962), who ignored both Winters and the modernist experimenters to prophesy an apocalyptic romanticism to a doomed age. The long, loose lines of his free verse, reflecting the scale of the Carmel and Big Sur landscape, identified him as a shadow-bard to Whitman. Narratives such as *Roan Stallion* (1925) and *The Double Axe* (1948) dramatize the tragedy of a human consciousness whose alienation from nature issues in neuroses and psychoses. The shorter lyrics and meditations urge, often ecstatically, the extinction of consciousness in the "brute beauty" of things which constitutes "the beauty of God," and they anticipate in the extinction of the species a return to cosmic harmony (cf. *Collected Poetry*, 1988–).

Both Winters and Jeffers rejected modernist aestheticism and insisted on value and truth extrinsic to art: Winters in a theistic humanism, Jeffers in a pantheistic inhumanism. But beyond their own work, the contradictory terms of their opposition to each other and to modernism illuminate in reverse perspective the dialectic through which imagism and symbolism resumed the old Puritan distinction between type and trope which lay at the heart of romanticism.   A.G.

IV. THE POSTWAR PERIOD. The poets who came of age in the period immediately following World War II found themselves in a difficult relation to their modernist predecessors. On the one hand, the work of Eliot, Pound, Stevens, Frost, Moore, and Crane had provided younger poets with an extraordinary range of formal and thematic resources, yet this same variety also proved a stumbling block to further experimentation. It seemed to Randall Jarrell that modernism, "the most successful and influential body of poetry of this century—is dead." Such an elegiac assessment of the era masked a desire felt by many poets of this generation to have a clean slate. Innovative works such as *Spring and All, The Cantos, Stanzas in Meditation,* or *The Waste Land* had challenged the structure of traditional verse; now it was time for a stock-taking that would seize upon the liberating advantages of Fr. *vers libre* and the derived Anglo-Am. free verse (qq.v.) but curb their excesses.

Writers born in the first two decades of the 20th c.—Theodore Roethke (1908–63), Elizabeth Bishop (1911–79), John Berryman (1914–72), Randall Jarrell (1914–65), Robert Lowell (1917–77), Howard Nemerov (b. 1920), and Richard Wilbur (b. 1921)—turned away from free verse and developed a technically complex, rhetorically difficult poetry modeled on metaphysical poets such as Donne and Herbert as well as the late modernists, John Crowe Ransom, Allen Tate, and Robert Penn Warren. Where poets of the first generation capped their careers by writing long epic or dramatic poems, postwar poets perfected a kind of reflective, ironic lyric that would become the formal model for the two decades following World War II.

T. S. Eliot's lit. crit. provided a major impetus for many of these tendencies, and his cultural crit. introduced a religio-ethical frame within which

poetry could be assessed. Many of the values associated with the New Criticism—the importance of trad., the necessity for authorial detachment, the autonomy of the objective artifact—could be found in Eliot's essay, "Trad. and the Individual Talent," which became a *locus classicus* for the postwar era. Eliot's theories of impersonality were extended by the New Critics into prohibitions against intentionalism and affectivity, qualities that would turn the poem into a vehicle of personal expression rather than the site of endistanced meditation. Hence the characteristic voice in poems written during this period is arch and ironic, cautious of bardic pronouncements yet assured in its mastery of complexity and contradiction. Irony now implies more than saying one thing while meaning another; it signals that the artist is in control, able to moderate feeling by transforming it into rhetoric. In a paradox that seemed quite normal to the age, Richard Wilbur spoke of irony as being the "source . . . of what richness and honesty we may sense in a poem," as illustrated by his own example from *The Beautiful Changes* (1947):

> Does sense so stale that it must needs
>   derange
> The world to know it? To a praiseful eye
> Should it not be enough of fresh and
>   strange
> That trees grow green, and moles can
>   course in clay,
> And sparrows sweep the ceiling of our
>   day?
>   ("Praise in Summer")

This poem, with its careful management of ironic tension, richly embroidered figuration, and steady iambic meters, seems destined less for sensual appreciation than for explication and exegesis. As Jarrell conceded, it was an "age of crit." in which the techniques of close reading and scientific analysis were perfected in ways that ultimately affected how poems were written. The postwar years saw colleges and universities expanding their enrollments with students on the G. I. Bill, and the curriculum needed practical critical methodologies to accommodate this influx. For the first time in history, poets in increasing numbers became teachers, and for the first time "creative writing" became part of the literary curriculum. Whereas for the first generation of modernists, poetry emerged within bohemian enclaves and expatriate communities, it now became a province of the university quarterly and the English Department classroom.

Arguably, the three poets who most typify—but at the same time challenge—the conservative tenor of the times were Robert Lowell, John Berryman, and Elizabeth Bishop. Lowell's first two books, *Land of Unlikeness* (1944) and *Lord Weary's Castle* (1946), exhibit the effects of his close relationship to his New Critical mentors, Ransom and

Tate. In these works Lowell takes the metaphysical mode to an extreme, employing a gnarled, convoluted syntax and alliterative lang. to dramatize issues of incarnation and existential doubt. With *Life Studies* (1959) Lowell shocked his teachers and friends by dropping his metaphysical style and speaking in a more personal voice about his ambivalent relationship to his patrician New England family as well as about his troubled marriages, mental breakdowns, and theological anxieties. Despite Lowell's new personalism, he still maintained the formal diction and iambic cadences of his earlier work:

> These are the tranquilized *Fifties*,
> and I am forty. Ought I to regret my
> seedtime?
> I was a fire-breathing Catholic C. O.,
> and made my manic statement,
> telling off the state and president. . . .
>   ("Memories of West Street and
>   Lepke")

Lowell's rather archaic diction and heavy alliterations temper his confessionalism with a need to contain feeling within definite formal boundaries. In later volumes (*History, For Lizzie and Harriet,* and *The Dolphin* [all 1973]) he returned to a more traditional verse, working extensively in unrhymed, blank-verse sonnets.

John Berryman began by writing in the style of Auden and Yeats, but with "Homage to Mistress Bradstreet" (1956) and even more powerfully in *77 Dream Songs* (1964), he developed an idiosyncratic use of persona that permitted him a wide range of voices to dramatize various sides of his rather volatile personality. In the former poem, he collapses his own voice into that of America's first poet, speaking of his own existential malaise through Anne Bradstreet's confessions of spiritual doubt. His major work, *The Dream Songs* (1969), confronts the poet's own biography in a long sequence of lyrics, each built on three 6-line stanzas, written from 1955 until the time of his death in 1972. Despite its autobiographical content, *The Dream Songs* utilizes a complex series of personae in which mocking accusation merges with ironic self-deprecation:

> Life, friends, is boring. We must not say
> so.
> After all, the sky flashes, the great sea
> yearns,
> we ourselves flash and yearn,
> and moreover my mother told me as a
> boy
> (repeatedly) "Ever to confess you're
> bored
> means you have no
> Inner Resources."
>   ("Dream Song 14")

Elizabeth Bishop, though less rhetorically explosive than either Lowell or Berryman, combined irregular syllabics with microscopically sharp observations to achieve a broken, tense lyricism reminiscent of Marianne Moore. She describes the skin of a fish as

> . . . hung in strips
> like ancient wallpaper,
> and its pattern of darker brown
> . . . like wallpaper: shapes like full-
>   blown roses
> stained and lost through age.
>   ("The Fish")

In such lines, lang. isolates and refines the image until it loses its conventional associations and becomes something exotic and even heroic. Without moralizing commentary, Bishop sees a world of vivid particulars that gain luster by her patient, at times obsessive, enumerations. In Bishop, as in her two poetic peers, formal mastery implies less the creation of seamless edifice than it does a charged linguistic and rhetorical field in which cognitive acts may be tested. Lowell's and Berryman's harsh, crabbed lang. and Bishop's enjambed, condensed lines represent a formalism impatient with its own limits, dramatizing by sheer verbal energy areas of psychological intensity that cannot yet be expressed.

Lowell's post-*Life Studies* poetry made an indelible mark on a number of writers, incl. Sylvia Plath (1932–63), Anne Sexton (1928–75), W. D. Snodgrass (b. 1926), and, to a lesser extent, John Berryman. Despite their emphasis on autobiographical materials—Plath's black comedy of suicide and patricide, Sexton's explorations of biological and psychological trauma, Berryman's brooding, self-mocking lyrics, and Snodgrass's middle-age-crisis poems—these poets reflect a much more carefully modulated response to their personal content. The strength of Plath's vehement attack in "Daddy," to take the most famous example, comes not from its specific address to her actual father, Otto Plath, who died when she was a child, but from its conscious and careful manipulation of conflicting discursive modes (childhood rhymes, holocaust imagery, obsessive repetitions) that form an "objective correlative" (q.v.) to her psychological condition. "Confessionalism," as M. L. Rosenthal pointed out in his inaugural essay on that movement, should be considered not as a prescriptive formula held by any one group but as a general permission felt by most poets of the period to treat personal experience, even in its most intimate and painful aspects.

If Eliot, Auden, and Frost exerted the most pervasive influence on the dominant trad. of the 1950s, Pound and Williams began to exert a like effect on an emerging avant-garde. Pound's *Cantos* had provided new interest in a historical, "open" poetry, and Williams' hard, objectivist lyrics had encouraged a poetics of visual clarity and metrical experimentation. Charles Olson's (1910–70) essay on "Projective Verse" (1950; q.v.) extended their ideas with a special emphasis on the poetic line as a register of physiological and emotional contours. He sought to reinvigorate poetic lang. by what he called "composition by field," in which poetic form extends directly from subject matter and in which the line is a register of momentary attentions. According to Olson, the New Critical, autotelic poem left the poet little room for developing a historical or critical "stance toward reality beyond the poem," a stance he wanted to regain, as he felt Pound had done in *The Cantos*. He explored this stance in his *Maximus Poems* (1950–70), a long poem dwelling on the separation of individual from locale due to the ill effects of entrepreneurial capitalism.

Although Olson's essay had few adherents when it first appeared, it was a harbinger of things to come as poets sought a loosening of poetic forms and an alternative to New Critical strictures. The most public announcement of a change came from Allen Ginsberg (b. 1926), whose long poem "Howl" (1956) revived romanticism in its most vatic form and with Whitmanesque enthusiasm made the poet's specific, personal voice the center of concern:

> I saw the best minds of my generation
> destroyed by madness, starving hys-
> terical naked,
> dragging themselves through the ne-
> gro streets at dawn looking for an
> angry fix,
> angelheaded hipsters burning for the
> ancient heavenly connection to the
> starry dynamo in the machinery of
> night. . . .

Ginsberg's protest against institutional mind-control and McCarthy-era paranoia was made in what he called his "Hebraic-Melvillian bardic breath" and in a lang. as direct and explicit as Wilbur's or Lowell's was oblique. The carefully nuanced ironies of the period were jettisoned in favor of a tone alternately funny, frank, and self-protective. The fact that "Howl" received its first major critical forum in the courtroom of the San Francisco Municipal Court when its publisher went on trial for pornography added new meaning to the poem's social indictment and brought a mass readership to the work of other Beat generation writers. Many of Ginsberg's colleagues—Jack Kerouac (1922–69), Lawrence Ferlinghetti (b. 1920), Gregory Corso (b. 1930), Michael McClure (b. 1932)—provided their own critique of the era, reviving on the one hand a demotic, populist poetics inspired by Whitman and Williams, as well as the romantic, visionary work of Blake and Shelley. Performing their poetry in jazz clubs or coffee houses, occasionally accompanied by jazz, the Beat poets (q.v.) made the poetry reading a primary fact of postwar literary life.

The Beat movement is the most public face of a general romantic revival during the late 1950s and '60s. Whether through Olson's ideas of composition by "field," or through Robert Bly's (b. 1926) ideas of the psychological "deep image," or through Frank O'Hara's (1926–66) "personism," poets began to think of the poem not as a mimesis of experience but as an experience itself, a map of moment-to-moment perceptions whose value is measured by immediacy and sincerity rather than artistic unity. As Robert Duncan (1919–88) said, "the order man may contrive upon the things about him . . . is trivial beside the divine order or natural order he may discover in them." Duncan's remark reinvests Keats's "negative capability" (q.v.) with sacramental implications: the poet relinquishes order that he may discover an order prior to and immanent within experience. The older romantic idea of a synthetic creative imagination (the artist's imperative to order fragmentary reality) gives way to a poetics of "open forms" in which the poem becomes a spontaneous register of phenomenological moments. As with abstract expressionist painting during the same period, the poetics of open form stresses gestural and expressive response over reflective or meditational experience.

In the late 1950s, these general tendencies could be seen in little magazines such as *Origin*, *The Black Mountain Review*, *Yugen*, *The Fifties*, *Evergreen Review*, and, most importantly, in Donald Allen's 1960 anthol., *The New American Poetry*, which first divided the experimental tendencies of Am. p. into five groups. One group consisted of the poets associated with Black Mountain College in North Carolina, incl. Charles Olson, Robert Creeley (b. 1926), Robert Duncan, Denise Levertov (b. 1923), and Edward Dorn (b. 1929). Another group, associated with the New York art world, incl. Frank O'Hara, John Ashbery (b. 1927), Kenneth Koch (b. 1925), and James Schuyler (b. 1923). The "San Francisco Renaissance" was represented by poets such as Jack Spicer (1925–65), Robin Blaser (b. 1925), Brother Antoninus (William Everson; b. 1912), and Philip Lamantia (b. 1927). A fourth category included other West Coast writers such as Gary Snyder (b. 1930), Philip Whalen (b. 1923), and David Meltzer (b. 1937). Along with the Beats, these groups shared less a common aesthetic than a spirit of bohemian exuberance and anti-establishment camaraderie.

In a similar vein but coming from different sources, Robert Bly, James Wright (1927–80), W. S. Merwin (b. 1927), Galway Kinnell (b. 1927), Mark Strand (b. 1934), and others were developing a poetics of the psychological "deep image." Using Sp. (and to a lesser extent Fr.) surrealism as a source, they experimented with associative techniques that would circumvent discursive thought and tap into unconscious realms. Bly called his practice a "leaping poetry" which manifested "a long floating leap around which the work of art in ancient times used to gather itself like steel shavings around the magnet." Among Deep Image poets one can draw a distinction between those who create discontinuous "leaps" within a minimal, denuded landscape and those for whom the "leap" implies access to a world of numinous presence. Strand and Merwin would be examples of the first sort, creating poems in which lang. has been reduced to a bare minimum. In Wright's or Bly's poetry, conversely, the deep image serves to join quotidian, unreflective experience with realms of spiritual or natural value. Taking a walk, mailing a letter, wasting time become initiatory rites of passage into archetypal experiences. In Bly, a snowstorm transforms a barn into a "hulk blown toward us in a storm at sea; / All the sailors on deck have been blind for many years." Waking in the morning "is like a harbor at dawn; / We know that our master has left us for the day." Unlike their imagist precursors, Deep Image poets strive for clarity without relying on the criterion of verisimilitude.

Surrealism provided a common ground for another group which was initially associated with Bly and Wright but which ultimately moved in a very different direction. David Antin (b. 1932), Jackson MacLow (b. 1922), Jerome Rothenberg (b. 1931), and Armand Schwerner (b. 1927) merged a strong interest in European avant-garde movements such as dada and surrealism (qq.v.) with the poetics of Gertrude Stein, the aesthetic theories of Marcel Duchamp and John Cage, and the theatrical "happenings" movement. In a desire to find aesthetic models that exist outside of Western trad. (or marginalized *within* it), many of these poets turned to oral and nonliterate cultures, creating along the way an "ethnopoetics" (q.v.) that stresses cultural and social sources of poetry.

Of course, group designations such as "Black Mountain," "Beat," or "Deep Image" do little to accommodate local variations and individual styles. O'Hara and Snyder are seldom mentioned in the same context, yet the former's desultory chronicles of New York urban life and the latter's descriptions of the natural landscape share a common interest in quotidian movement and surface detail. Poets such as Galway Kinnell or William Stafford (b. 1914) obviously share many "immanentist" or transcendentalist values with Duncan and Levertov, yet they have seldom appeared in the same anthols. or poetry readings. The anthol. "wars" of the 1960s between "open" and "closed," "raw" and "cooked," "Beat" and "square" verse served only to separate poets into warring camps and to provide confused critics with ammunition for dismissive reviews. At the same time, dissension fueled discussion, and the '60s were lively if combative years for Am. p. If there was literary warfare within periodicals, most poets of the period were united in their opposition to Am. adventurism abroad, particularly in the case of the Vietnam War. Furthermore, many of the younger generation identified a poetics of openness and innovation with the social goals of the New Left in which social action, alternate lifestyle, and cultural production were intertwined.

The emergence of political activism among poets, combined with the development of cheap, offset printing technologies, brought new constituencies into the poetry world. Increased activity in Black poetry (see AFRO-AMERICAN POETRY), gay poetry (see LOVE POETRY), Asian poetry, Native-Am. poetry (see AMERICAN INDIAN POETRY), and Chicano poetry (q.v.) coincided with the increased social consciousness among minorities during the '60s. The Black poet and playwright LeRoi Jones (b. 1934) threw off his previous Black Mountain and Beat affiliations and adopted the name Imamu Amiri Baraka to signal his alliance with the Black Nationalist movement. In similar fashion, other Black poets—David Henderson (b. 1942), Audre Lorde (b. 1934), June Jordan (b. 1936), Alice Walker (b. 1944), Michael Harper (b. 1938)—worked to foreground Black cultural experience and lang. Although alternate cultural sources became important allies in this endeavor (the use of jazz rhythms in Black writing, the use of oral chant in Native-Am. p., bilingualism in Chicano poetry), the primary formal imperatives came from the more populist, oral styles of the Beats and other new poetry movements.

Coinciding with the growth of literary communities among ethnic minorities, women writers began to write out of the social and political context of the feminist movement. Presses, reading spaces, distribution services, and anthols. provided a range of new resources for women writers, many of whom—like Adrienne Rich (b. 1931)—began their careers within the predominantly male literary community. Although "women's poetry" defines less a set of stylistic features than a historical fact, most women writers would agree with the necessity for revision as defined by Rich: "the act of looking back, of seeing with fresh eyes, of entering an old text from a new critical direction." Many of Rich's poems are just such revisions of previous texts as she sorts through the "book of myths" ("Diving Into the Wreck") to find moments in which women have been marginalized—or ignored outright. Although she began by writing poems very much in the formalist mode of the 1950s, Rich's style gradually loosened to admit her own changing awareness of women's oppression and to express her anger at patriarchal authority. See FEMINIST POETICS.

The proliferation of poetic styles during the 1970s and '80s has, to some extent, repeated many of the tendencies of the whole modern period, though with obvious refinements. Poets have rejected the more bardic and expressive gestures—what Stanley Plumly calls "experience in capital letters"—of the 1960s in favor of a certain discursiveness, even chattiness, for which the achievement of distinctly personal realms must be accomplished through careful management of tone and diction. The dominant mode of the 1970s and '80s is a reflective lyricism in which technical skill is everywhere evident but nowhere obtrusive. The overtly romantic stance of 1960s poetry, with its emphasis on participation, orality, and energy, has given way to quiet speculation.

Within the major trad. of the 1970s and '80s one can identify three general areas of practice, all of which display a common concern with voice and tone (qq.v.). Among the first group, A. R. Ammons (b. 1926), John Ashbery (b. 1927), Robert Pinsky (b. 1940), Louise Gluck (b. 1943), Sandra McPherson (b. 1943), and Robert Hass (b. 1941) merge the philosophical skepticism of Wallace Stevens with the ethical, cultural concerns of Yvor Winters or Robert Penn Warren. Ashbery's poetry, perhaps the most sophisticated and complex of the group, manifests what he calls "the swarm effect" of lang. vacillating between opposing lures of "leaving out" or "putting in." His long, desultory lyrics such as "The Skaters" (1966), "Self-Portrait in a Convex Mirror" (1975), and the prose trilogy *Three Poems* (1972) record the fluctuating patterns of a disjunct consciousness. Unable to believe either in a supreme fiction or in a self-sufficient ego, Ashbery leaves "the bitter impression of absence" in lines that are often hilariously funny even as they are self-deprecating. Ammons' poetry, while similar to Stevens' treatment of philosophical issues, builds upon Frost's naturalism and his concern for the morality of "place." For Ammons, "small branches can / loosen heavy postures" ("Essay on Poetics"), and he has conducted a quiet campaign for the restorative effects of weather, seasonal change, animal life, and horticulture as they interact with the speculative intellect. Hass's poetry continues Ammons' naturalist concerns (Roethke and Rexroth are important sources as well), but builds upon subtle shifts of voice and tone. Philosophical speculation alternates with epiphanic moments as in "Meditation at Lagunitas":

> All the new thinking is about loss.
> In this it resembles all the old thinking.
> The idea, for example, that each particular erases
> the luminous clarity of a general idea.
> That the clown-
> faced woodpecker probing the dead sculpted trunk
> of that black birch is, by his presence,
> some tragic falling off from a first world
> of undivided light.

A second group, closely aligned with the first but extending more directly out of the "deep image" aesthetic of Bly and Merwin, would incl. poets such as C. K. Williams (b. 1936), Marvin Bell (b. 1937), Philip Levine (b. 1928), Tess Gallagher (b. 1943), Charles Wright (b. 1935), Stanley Plumly (b. 1939), and Carolyn Forché (b. 1950). In their

work surrealist juxtaposition combines with a spare, sometimes minimalist style to expose unconscious or atavistic resonances in everyday events. Less inclined towards the ecstatic "leaps" of Bly and Wright, these poets prefer a more narrative progression and a considerably chastened diction. The use of long lines and prosaic speech creates a leisurely tone often at odds with the poetry's darker subject matter. In C. K. Williams' "Tar," for example, the poet reflects on the grim legacy of nuclear waste, focusing his anger through an image of children using shards of roofer's tar to scribble on sidewalks hieroglyphics of rancor and love, anathematizing the current generation's "surfeits and submissions."

A third variation on the dominant mode is what Robert von Hallberg characterizes as "The Cosmopolitan Style" and which is represented by John Hollander (b. 1929), Richard Howard (b. 1929), James Merrill (b. 1926), and Anthony Hecht (b. 1923), as well as younger poets grouped loosely under the label of "New Formalism" (q.v.). In this work, discursiveness becomes a foil for strategies of self-preservation and effacement. At the same time, a tendency toward conversation conflicts with the use of formal meters and complex internal and terminal rhymes. This tension can be felt in the work of Merrill, whose work often uses its own aesthetic virtuosity to mock aesthetic solutions. His poems are willfully bookish, his tone arch and urbane, derived to some extent from Auden (who appears as one of the spirit guides in *Book of Ephraim*). Merrill's reticence and detachment are calculated frames for viewing a conflicted personal hist., a condition given fullest treatment in his trilogy, *The Changing Light at Sandover* (1982). In this long poem, the poet's personal ardors, his "divine comedies," are subjected to an extraordinary anthology of literary forms, from sonnets and verse dramas to blank verse paragraphs, all subsumed under the pose of having been received during ouija board seances. Like many of his earlier poems, *The Changing Light at Sandover* is a poem about writing, a celebration of the "surprise and pleasure [of] its working-out" which offers an elaborate allegory about erotic and spiritual love in an increasingly secularized society.

Merrill is usually regarded as a principal influence on a more recent movement among younger writers known as the New Formalists and which would include Alfred Corn (b. 1943), Marilyn Hacker (b. 1942), Brad Leithhauser (b. 1953), Katha Pollitt (b. 1949), and Gjertrud Schnackenberg (b. 1953). Their renewed interest in traditional forms (as well as the possibilities of narrative poetry) has been undertaken less as a rear guard attack on debased culture (as it was for many late modernists) but as a recovery of the liberating potential of limits. In their anthology of New-Formalist verse, Philip Dacey and David Jauss stress that writing in traditional forms aims to rebalance scales that had tipped too strongly in the direction of free verse since the 1960s, leading, as a result, to a rather amorphous autobiographical lyricism in which open form became simply an excuse for sloppy practice. But the presence of pattern may be experienced as a kind of liberation, "just as a dancer might praise the limitation of gravity for making dance possible in the first place." The challenge for New Formalists has been to hide or at least diminish pattern through the use of slant rhyme, nonce forms, syllabics and expressive variants on repeated meters. At the same time, poets attempt to combine their use of regular meters and rhyme with diction drawn from contemp. life, using the idiom of urban experience, technology, and advertising to blur the usual association of traditional forms with "high" or nonstandard diction. "Form's what affirms," James Merrill says, suggesting that far from imposing a straightjacket on lang., formalism makes the saying of what is difficult a matter of ethical as well as literary choice.

All of these tendencies, whether loosely or tightly formed, could be linked by their resistance to the more autobiographical and vatic modes of the 1960s. But if the dominant trad. in recent poetry has returned to the subtleties of voice and diction that characterized the work of the 1940s and '50s, a more complex critique of expressivist poetics has come from writers gathered under the rubric "language poetry" (q.v.). The work of Lyn Hejinian (b. 1941), Bruce Andrews (b. 1948), Carla Harryman (b. 1952), Charles Bernstein (b. 1950), Ron Silliman (b. 1946), Clark Coolidge (b. 1939), and Barrett Watten (b. 1948) explores the degree to which the "self" and "experience" are constructs, enmeshed in social discourse. Working within a trad. that stems from Black Mountain and objectivist poetics, these poets attempt to foreground lang. as signifying system within larger social structures. Their strategies of fracturing and fragmentation open up new realms of play and semantic complexity, and their interest in the prose poem (q.v.) and in new forms of prose challenges the generic boundaries of lined verse. That interest can be taken as a marker of a certain *crise de vers* that haunts recent poetry in general. If "a word is a bottomless pit" (Hejinian), it is also the agency by which that pit shall be explored, and postmodern poets have taken this realization as a generative fact. Modernism foregrounded the materiality of lang. by removing it from conventional and contrived usage, making it "new" by making it strange. Late modernists from Ransom to Hecht sought to curb the excesses of linguistic and metrical "defamiliarization" by making formal control of tension and ambiguity the cornerstone of a continuing humanist enterprise. Poets of the 1960s rebelled against the limitations of that enterprise insofar as it removed lang. from voice and personal expression. If the poetry of this era sometimes became grandiose and inflated in its testimentary role, it also re-established a dialogue with the reader. As O'Hara gleefully reported, "the poem is at last between two persons instead of two pages."

It has been for the post-1960s generation to investigate how thoroughly "deep" the word is, esp. when it lacks the epistemological and ontological supports it enjoyed in previous eras. Lacking either Whitman's all-encompassing Self or the authority of Eliot's detached personae, poets have renegotiated the territory of subjectivity as an intersubjective and historical phenomenon. Whether the poet seeks to achieve ever more subtle subjective states or to deconstruct the notion of subjectivity altogether, the task must be done with the full recognition of lang.'s mediate function. What Stevens called our "never-ending meditation" is made of "A few words, an and yet, and yet, and yet—." Between these small words, something like a "post" modernism emerges.

M.D.

See also AFRO-AMERICAN POETRY; BEAT POETS; CUBISM; FREE VERSE; IDEOGRAM; IMAGISM; LANGUAGE POETRY; LYRIC SEQUENCE; MODERN LONG POEM; MODERNISM AND POSTMODERNISM; NEW FORMALISM; OBJECTIVISM; PROJECTIVE VERSE; PROSE POEM; SOUND POETRY; TWENTIETH-CENTURY POETICS, *American and British*; VORTICISM.

BIBLIOGRAPHIES: *Lit. Hist. of the U.S.*, ed. R. E. Spiller et al., 3d ed. rev., v. 2, *Bibl.* (1963); K. Malkoff, *Crowell's Handbook of Contemp. Am. P.* (1973); C. Altieri, *Mod. Poetry* (1979); J. Ruppert and J. R. Leo, *Guide to Am. P. Explication*, 2 v. (1989).

JOURNALS: *AL* (1929–); *AmerP* (1983–); *APR* (1972–); *Boundary 2* (1972–); *ConL* (1960–).

ANTHOLOGIES: *Mid-Century Am. Poets*, ed. J. Ciardi (1950); *A Comprehensive Anthol. of Am. P.*, ed. C. Aiken (1944); *Oxford Book of Am. Verse*, ed. F. O. Matthiessen (1950); *Faber Book of Mod. Am. Verse*, ed. W. H. Auden (1956); *New Poets of England and America*, ed. D. Hall et al. (1957); *The New Am. P.*, ed. D. Allen (1960); *Am. P. and Poetics*, ed. D. Hoffman (1962); *Mod. Am. P.*, ed. L. Untermeyer (1962); *Am. P.*, ed. G. W. Allen et al. (1965); *An Anthol. of Am. Verse*, ed. O. Williams (1966); *Major Am. Poets to 1914*, ed. F. Murphy (1967); *Poems of Our Moment*, ed. J. Hollander (1968); *Naked Poetry, The New Naked Poetry*, both ed. S. Berg and R. Mezey (1969, 1976)—"open form" poetry; *The Poetry of the Negro*, ed. L. Hughes and A. Bontemps (1970); *No More Masks*, ed. F. Howe and E. Bass (1973); *Out of the Vietnam Vortex: A Study of Poets and Poetry Against the War*, ed. J. F. Mersmann (1974); *New Oxford Book of Am. Verse*, ed. R. Ellmann (1976); *Black Sister*, ed. E. Stetson (1981); *Longman Anthol. of Contemp. Am. P. 1950–1980*, ed. S. Friebert and D. Young (1983); *The Generation of 2000*, ed. W. Heyen (1984); *Contemp. Am. P.*, ed. A. Poulin (1985); *The Morrow Anthol. of Younger Am. Poets*, ed. D. Smith and D. Bottoms (1985); *Harvard Book of Contemp. Am. P.*, ed. H. Vendler

(1985); *In the Am. Tree*, ed. R. Silliman (1986); *Lang. Poetries*, ed. D. Messerli (1986); *Strong Measures*, ed. P. Dacey and D. Jauss (1986); *Writing Red: Anthol. of Am. Women Writers, 1930–40*, ed. C. Nekola and P. Rabinowitz (1987); *The Harper Am. Lit.*, ed. D. McQuade et al., 2 v. (1987); *The Norton Anthol. of Am. Lit.*, ed. N. Baym et al., 3d ed., 2 v. (1989); *Shadowed Dreams: Women's Poetry of the Harlem Ren.*, ed. M. Honey (1989); *An Ear to the Ground*, ed. M. Harris and K. Aguero (1989).

HISTORY AND CRITICISM: W. Stevens, *The Necessary Angel* (1951); R. Jarrell, *Poetry and the Age* (1953); W. C. Williams, *Selected Essays* (1954); A. Tate, *The Man of Letters in the Mod. World* (1955); *A Casebook on the Beats*, ed. T. Parkinson (1961); G. Cambon, *Recent Am. P.* (1962); A. Ostroff, *The Contemp. Poet as Artist and Critic* (1964); R. J. Mills, Jr., *Contemp. Am. P.* (1965); R. H. Pearce, *The Continuity of Am. P.*, 2d ed (1965); C. Olson, *Selected Writings* (1966); M. L. Rosenthal, *The New Am. Poets* (1967); H. H. Waggoner, *Am. Poets from the Puritans to the Present* (1968); D. Schwartz, *Selected Essays* (1970); R. Creeley, *A Quick Graph* (1970); R. Howard, *Alone with America* (1970)—Am. poets since mid-century; H. Bloom, *Ringers in the Tower* (1971); H. Kenner, *The Pound Era* (1971); *The Poetics of the New Am. P.*, ed. D. Allen and W. Tallman (1973); E. Fussell, *Lucifer in Harness* (1973); D. Antin, "Modernism and Postmodernism," *Boundary 2* 1 (1972–73); K. Rexroth, *Am. P. in the 20th C.* (1973); D. Levertov, *The Poet in the World* (1973); *Understanding the New Black Poetry*, ed. S. Henderson (1973); *The Craft of Poetry*, ed. W. Packard (1974); R. Mills, *The Cry of the Human* (1974); D. Stauffer, *A Short Hist. of Am. P.* (1974); A. Gelpi, *A Coherent Splendor: The Am. Poetic Ren. 1910–1950* (1987), *The Tenth Muse*, 2d ed. (1991); F. O'Hara, *Standing Still and Walking in New York* (1975); D. Perkins, *A Hist. of Mod. Poetry*, 2 v. (1976, 1987); R. Pinsky, *The Situation of Poetry* (1976); R. Wilbur, *Responses* (1976); E. Watts, *The Poetry of Am. Women from 1632 to 1945* (1977); D. Kalstone, *Five Temperaments* (1977); S. Plumly, "Chapter and Verse," *APR* 7 (Jan.-Feb. and May-June, 1978); B. Duffey, *Poetry in America* (1978); C. Altieri, *Enlarging the Temple* (1979), *Self and Sensibility in Contemp. Am. P.* (1984), *Painterly Abstraction in Modernist Am. P.* (1989); A. Rich, *On Lies, Secrets and Silence* (1979); C. Molesworth, *The Fierce Embrace* (1979); D. Hoffman, *The Harvard Guide to Contemp. Am. Writing* (1979); *A Field Guide to Contemp. Poetry and Poetics*, ed. S. Friebert and D. Young (1980); J. Holden, *The Rhet. of the Contemp. Lyric* (1980); P. A. Bove, *Destructive Poetics: Heidegger and Mod. Am. P.* (1980); H. Vendler, *Part of Nature, Part of Us* (1980), *The Music of What Happens* (1988); M. Perloff, *The Poetics of Indeterminacy* (1981), *The Dance of the Intellect* (1985), *Poetic License: Essays on Modernist and Postmodernist Lyric* (1990); C. Nelson, *Our Last First Poets* (1981), *Repression and Recovery: Mod. Am. P. and the Politics of Cultural Memory* (1990); S. Paul, *The Lost Amer-*

ica of Love (1981); M. L. Rosenthal and S. M. Gall, *The Mod. Poetic Sequence* (1983); A. Ostriker, *Writing Like a Woman* (1983); J. E. B. Breslin, *From Mod. to Contemp.: Am. P. 1945–65* (1984); *The L=A=N=G=U=A=G=E Book*, ed. B. Andrews and C. Bernstein (1984); R. Hass, *20th-C. Pleasures* (1984); R. von Hallberg, *Am. P. and Culture, 1945–1980* (1985); R. Duncan, *Fictive Certainties* (1985); B. Watten, *Total Syntax* (1985); R. B. DuPlessis, *Writing Beyond the Ending* (1985); A. S. Ostriker, *Stealing the Lang.: The Emergence of Women's Poetry in America* (1986); A. Ross, *The Failure of Modernism* (1986); C. Bernstein, *Content's Dream* (1986); L. Keller, *Re-Making It New* (1987); H. A. Baker, Jr., *Modernism and the Harlem Ren.* (1987), *Afro-Am. Poetics* (1988); J. Radway and P. Frank, "Verse and Popular Poetry," *Handbook of Am. Popular Lit.*, ed. M. T. Inge (1988); *Columbia Lit. Hist. of the U.S.*, ed. E. Elliott et al. (1988); A. Shucard, *Am. P.* (1988), et. al., *Mod. Am. P. 1865–1950* (1989); M. Davidson, *The San Francisco Ren.* (1989); W. Kalaidjian, *Langs. of Liberation: The Social Text in Contemp. Am. P.* (1989); J. V. Brogan, *Part of the Climate: Am. Cubist P.* (1991).　　　　A.G.; M.D.

AMERICAN PROSODY. See ENGLISH PROSODY.

AMERICAN STRUCTURALISM. See STRUCTURALISM.

AMERIND. See AMERICAN INDIAN POETRY.

AMHARIC POETRY. See ETHIOPIAN POETRY.

AMOEBEAN VERSES. See PASTORAL.

AMPHIBRACH (Gr. "short at both ends"). In Cl. prosody, a metrical sequence consisting of a long syllable preceded and followed by a short one. The a. is rare in Cl. poetry either as an independent unit or as a continuous meter, and equally a rarity in the accentually based prosodies of the mod. langs., suggesting it may not exist except as an experiment. Amphibrachic word-shapes (a stress flanked by slacks) are easy to finger, esp. polysyllables formed of a monosyllabic prefix + base + suffix (e.g. *inspection*, *romantic*), but the a. as a meter risks monotony and is very rare. Byron tried it ("The black bands came over"); Goethe, Matthisson, and Arndt wrote a number of poems in as. in Ger. In running series with ambiguous ends, amphibrachich lines would be nearly impossible to differentiate from other ternary ones such as dactylic or anapestic (see BINARY AND TERNARY).
　　　　T.V.F.B.

AMPHIMACER. See CRETIC.

AMPLIFICATION. An ambiguous term, perhaps best avoided in lit. crit. which seeks to distinguish rather than to confuse rhetorical taxonomy. In Cl. rhet., a. is one of the "special" topics used in epideictic (q.v.) or ceremonial discourse, usually for praise, but it has been used to refer to both the expansion and the diminution of an idea or argument. Its hist. in rhetorical theory and practice helps to explain how a. came to be regarded, at different periods, as a subset of both *inventio* and *dispositio*. Aristotle in the *Poetics* (19) mentions "maximizing and minimizing" as important elements of thought (i.e. rhet.), but in the *Rhetoric* (2.26.1) he contrasts a. and depreciation, while admitting that both derive from "enthymemes which serve to show how a thing is great or small." It was Cicero (*De oratore* 3.26) who introduced the confusion between a. and attenuation by saying that the "highest distinction of eloquence consists in a. by means of ornament, which can be used to make one's speech not only increase the importance of a subject and raise it to a higher level, but also to diminish and disparage it." Quintilian (*Institutio oratoria* 8.4.3) increased the confusion, presenting a. as a mini-*inventio*, when he spoke of four principal means of a.: augmentation (*incrementum*), comparison, reasoning, and accumulation (*congeries*). Quoting from Cicero, Quintilian (8.4.4) gives as an example of a. the following climax: "It is a sin to bind a Roman citizen, a crime to scourge him, little short of the most unnatural murder to put him to death; what then shall I call his crucifixion?" Murphy has shown how the confusion spread in medieval rhet., which fused *inventio* and *dispositio*, when a., referred to variously as a set of 8 or 10 figures valuable to those writing sermons, speeches, or letters, becomes at the same time a figure and not a figure, a set of figures and an arrangement of figures. Eng. Ren. rhetoricians perpetuated the confusion, supplying different totals for the rhetorical phenomena grouped under the general heading "a.," from 17 (Sherry [1555]), to 64 (Peacham [1577]), to 11 (Hoskins [1599]). More recently, Perelman remarks that ancient writers (e.g. Quintilian 3.8.6.73) tended to see both a. and attenuation as varieties of hyperbole (q.v.). Corbett calls a. "a way of reminding audiences of the importance or cogency or superiority of our points" (313).

A. may be obtained by enumeration and parallelism (q.v.), as in Othello's speech, when he has just realized that Desdemona is innocent: "Whip me, ye devils, / From the possession of this heavenly sight! / Blow me about in winds! Roast me in sulphur! / Wash me in steep-down gulfs of liquid fire! / O Desdemona! Desdemona! dead!" (5.2.276–80). Or, if a. means the devel. of a single principle, idea, or word, a whole poem may be structured by a., e.g. Dylan Thomas's "The Hand that Signed the Paper."

The confusion remains to be sorted out. If kept, the term "a." should be defined precisely and used with care; its limits only become clear when a text signals by some other means (semantic: change of subject; syntactic: end of stanza or poem; pragmatic: change of voice, person, or form of address)

a change of direction. If rhet. and crit. are to regain credibility as offering a precise theory of textuality rather than a confused taxonomy whose classes, subclasses, and individual phenomena constantly commingle, with terms being made now synonymous, now antithetical, then terms like "a." must be disentangled or dropped.—W. Taylor, *A Dict. of the Tudor Figures of Rhet.* (1937); W. G. Crane, *Wit and Rhet. in the Ren.* (1937); C. Perelman et al, *The New Rhet.* (tr. 1969); Murphy; Lausberg; Corbett.
A.W.H.; T.V.F.B.

ANACLASIS (Gr. "bending back"). Transposition of short and long positions within a metron or colon (qq.v.). The best known anaclast is the Anacreontic (q.v.), which is an ionic (q.v.) dimeter with a transposition of the fourth and fifth positions (∪ ∪ – – ∪ ∪ – – becomes ∪ ∪ – ∪ – ∪ – –). West regards this as something like modern musical syncopation, in which maintaining the time-values is sufficient for keeping the same rhythm.—Maas; Koster; Halporn et al.; West.
J.W.H.

ANACOLUTHON (Gr. "wanting sequence"). A term of grammar designating a change of construction in the middle of a sentence that leaves its beginning uncompleted, ordinarily seen as a fault, as betraying a lazy or confused mind. In rhet., however, a. has been treated as a figure, a natural and perspicuous mode of expression in spoken discourse. Hervey (583) cites Matthew 7:9, which runs, in the Authorized Version, "Or what man is there of you, whom if his son ask bread, will he give him a stone?" Shakespeare sometimes shows depth of feeling in his characters by this means, as at *Henry 5* 4.3.34–36 where the king says: "Rather proclaim it, Westmoreland, through my host, / That he which hath no stomach to this fight, / Let him depart." Lausberg finds the commonest form of a. to be the so-called absolute nominative (as in the Shakespeare above).

Related to a. is the absence of the second of a pair of correlative expressions, which is known as *particula pendens* when it has to do with correlative particles (e.g. "either . . . or," "both . . . and"), otherwise by the related term *anapodoton* (Gr. "wanting the apodosis," i.e. the main clause in a conditional sentence). Ernesti cites the authority of a scholiast on Thucydides 3.3; the passage runs: "If the attempt succeeds," the understood but unexpressed apodosis being, "it will be well"; so also Lausberg.

Group Mu classifies a. among "metataxes" which act upon the form of sentences by focusing on syntax. Like syllepsis, which includes "any rhetorical omission relating to the rules of agreement between morphemes and syntagms, whether it is agreement of gender, number, person, or tense" (75), a. produces through bifurcation a break in sentence-structure. Modern poetry's frequent suppression of punctuation removed a. from the list of taboo figures drawn up by prescriptive rhetoricians. The deletion of punctuation produces rhetorical effects by combining in a single utterance large numbers of agrammatical or potentially incoherent units of discourse. The interior monologues of Leopold and Molly Bloom contain countless examples of a.—C. T. Ernesti, *Lexicon technologiae graecorum rhetoricae* (1795); H. Bahrs, *Die Anacoluthe bei Shakespeare* (1893); Lausberg; G. W. Hervey, *Christian Rhet.* (1973); Morier; L. Edelman, *Transmemberment of Song* (1987).

H.BR.; A.W.H.

ANACREONTIC. In Cl. poetry this is a line-form, but to the moderns it is a strophe, an ode form. Named after the Gr. poet Anacreon of Teos (6th c. B.C.), the regular A. verse (◡ ◡ – ◡ – ◡ – –) is created by transposition of the fourth and fifth positions in the ionic (q.v.) dimeter (◡ ◡ – – ◡ ◡ – –) by anaclasis (q.v.), whence the transference of the name from the meter and author to the genre. There is a run of As. in Euripides' satyr-play *Cyclops* (495–500). Subsequently, A. lines were employed by the authors of the *Anacreontea*, about 60 short lyrics on wine, women, and song, composed in imitation of Anacreon from antiquity into the Byzantine period. As. were also written in Lat. by the Emperor Hadrian (*Scriptores Historiae Augustae: Hadrian* 16.4) and, in combination with iambs or other ionic meters, by Seneca and Claudian among others. Other writers of the late Empire like Martianus Capella (fl. later 4th c. A.D.) used the form, as did Prosper of Aquitaine, Boethius, and several Carolingian poets. In the modern period, as first ed. by Stephanus (Henri Estienne) in 1554, they had a considerable influence on Ren. and later European poets, e.g. on Ronsard and Rémy Belleau in 16th-c. France and, in 16th-, 18th-, and 19th-c. Italy, on Tasso, Parini, Monti, Foscolo, and Leopardi, who translated and imitated many of these poems. A. imitation was even more in vogue in 18th-c. Germany among the so-called *Anakreontiker* (Gleim, Uz, Götz, and their predecessor Hagedorn). In England, Sidney experimented with an A. (*Old Arcadia* 32); Abraham Cowley seems to have first used the term in his *Anacreontiques* (1656), but probably the best known verse tr. is *Odes of Anacreon* (1800) by the Ir. poet Thomas Moore, dubbed by Byron "Anacreon Moore."—L. A. Michelangeli, *Anacreonte e la sua fortuna nei secoli* (1922); E. Merker, "Anakreontik," *Reallexikon I*; Norberg; K. Preisendanz, "Anacreontea," *Der kleine Pauly*, v. 1 (1964); D. Korzeniewski, *Griechische Metrik* (1968); H. Zeman, *Die deutsche anakreontische Dichtung* (1972); M. Baumann, *Die Anakreonteen in englischen Übersetzungen* (1974); Michaelides; B. E. Kochis, "Literary Equivalence in the Rus. 18th-C. A.," *DAI* 40 (1979): 895A; Halporn et al.; Snell; West; D. A. Campbell, *Gr. Lyric*, v. 2 (1988); P. A. Rosenmeyer, *The Poetics of Imitation* (1992).

P.S.C.; J.W.H.; T.V.F.B.

ANACRUSIS (Gr. "the striking up of a tune"; Ger. *Auftakt*, "upbeat"). One or more extrametrical syllables at the beginning of a line, normally unstressed. "Procephalous" would be a more accurate and better attested descriptor. "A." was adopted by the 18th-c. Cl. scholar Richard Bentley in principle and then by Gottfried Hermann in fact, as well as by most of his Ger. successors in the 19th c., who extended the principles they discovered in the quantitative prosodies of Cl. verse to the analysis of the accentual prosodies of the mod. vernaculars without due consideration of the systemic differences between the two systems. In modern times, a. has been posited on the analogy with music, where extra notes can precede the first bar of the melody without objection. Some temporal and musical theories of meter (e.g. Steele, Heusler) treat verse lines as if they were set to music, i.e. as if stresses began bars, so that all unstressed syllables which precede the first stress—e.g. the first syllable in the iambic pentameter line—are instances of a. Outside of such theories, not now generally held, and outside of song meters themselves, a. is rare, though indisputable cases do exist, as in Shakespeare. The old belief that a. could alter rising rhythms to falling, or vice versa, is outmoded. In these two lines from Blake's poem "The Tyger," for example—"When the stars threw down their spears / And watered heaven with their tears"—one might take "And" to be an a., noticing that the seven syllables which follow would then be identical in pattern to the seven in the preceding line. But in fact it is the second line which is regular (an iambic tetrameter); the preceding line is headless (see ACEPHALOUS), and this type of rhythm—called "8s and 7s"—is a distinctive type in modern Eng. verse. Or again, a. may seem to appear in the third line of the following patch:

> Use it up,
> Wear it out,
> Make do with less or
> Do without.

If this be accentual verse (q.v.), there would seem to be two stresses per line, and "Make" is a. But the measures might also be perceived thus:

> Úse it / úp (pause), //
> Wéar it / óut, Make //
> Dó with / léss or //
> Dó with/óut (pause).

Now there it is no a. at all; "Make" is the last member of the fourth measure not the first of the fifth. Since musical theories of meter implicitly treat a. as if it were extrametrical, only the very first syllable would seem to qualify.

OE verse, however, seems to include a. as part of the metrical system—it ia a component of the analyses of Sievers, Pope, and Cable—but OE verse was perhaps recited to the accompaniment of a harp.—Schipper 3.950 (Index); Dale; N. A.

ANAGRAM

Bonavia-Hunt, *Horace the Minstrel* (1954); J. C. Pope, *The Rhythm of* Beowulf, 2d ed. (1966); T. Cable, *The Meter and Melody of* Beowulf (1974), ch. 3; Morier; P. Bethel, "Notes on the Incidence and Type of A. in *Genesis B*: Similarities to and Differences from A. Elsewhere in OE and OS," *Parergon* 2 (1984), "A. in the Psalms of the Paris Psalter," *NM* 89 (1988). R.J.G.; T.V.F.B.

ANADIPLOSIS, also *epanadiplosis* (Gr. "doubled back"). In Cl. rhet., a figure of word repetition that links two phrases, clauses, lines, or stanzas by repeating the word at the end of the first one at the beginning of the second: "The crime was common, common be the pain" (Pope, "Eloisa to Abelard"); "More safe I Sing with mortal voice, unchang'd / To hoarse or mute, though fall'n on evil dayes, / On evil dayes though fall'n, and evil tongues" (Milton, *Paradise Lost* 7.24–26). Sometimes more than one word repeats: "When I give I give myself" (Whitman, "Song of Myself"). As such, a. is the mechanism of concatenation (q.v.) and is the usual vehicle for the rhetorical strategy of climax (q.v.). It can also be used to link speeches in drama, the second character picking up the train of thought of the first from his or her last word:

> Othello: "What dost thou think?"
> Iago: "Think, my lord?"
> Othello: "Think, my lord? By heaven
>   he echoes me."
>   (3.3.105)

Among the Ren. sonneteers, the use of both a. within the sonnet and a. to link sonnets together was common practice—visible in Petrarch, Tasso, Ronsard, Du Bellay, Sidney, Barnes, and many others—Shakespeare showing rather less interest in such effects than most, and certainly than in Daniel. But Shakespeare's sonnet 129 has: "On purpose laid to make the taker mad. / Mad in pursuit and in possession so" (8–9). A. fixed at the level of the line and adapted into prosody as a figure of rhyme was practiced by the *Rhétoriqueurs* (q.v.), who called it *rime annexée* and *rime fratrisée*; see CHAIN RHYME.—Patterson; Sr. M. Joseph, *Shakespeare's Use of the Arts of Lang.* (1947), 82–83; A. Quinn, *Figures of Speech* (1982), 89–90; B. Vickers, *Cl. Rhet. in Eng. Poetry*, 2d ed. (1989); Corbett 440. T.V.F.B.

ANAGOGIC INTERPRETATION. See INTERPRETATION, FOURFOLD METHOD OF.

ANAGRAM. In its original, narrower sense, an a., a rearrangement of the letters (sounds) of a word or phrase to produce another word or phrase, is an explicit, consciously constructed device. It is related to the palindrome (q.v.), in which a textual sequence reads the same way backwards as forwards, and to paronomasia (see PUN). Examples of the a. are found occasionally in ancient writers

and quite frequently in the 17th c., primarily in occasional verse (q.v.): thus each text in Mary Fage's *Fame's Roll* [of British royalty and nobility] (1637) is prefaced by the name of its subject and by an a. of it (THOMAS HOWARD // OH, DRAW MOST, HA!). The a. has also been widely used by authors to create pseudonyms (e.g. Rabelais, John Bunyan, Lewis Carroll) and occasionally used in acrostics (q.v.).

More recently, the a. has come to be conceived by many critics as a substantive component of poetic discourse occurring in a number of poetic trads. This view, which subsumes conscious instances of the a., originates with the partial publication in the 1960s of Ferdinand de Saussure's notebooks (for 1906–9) containing his researches on as. Saussure studied the role of several types of sound structure in texts of various provenience, incl. IE poetry, Lat. poetry (Saturnian [q.v.] verse), such authors as Virgil and Lucretius, and Vedic hymns. These structures range from paired repetitions of sounds, either individually or in groups, to the looser reproduction in the phonic material of the work of elements of a *key-word* (*mot-thème*, later *hypogram*) central to the plot (q.v.) of the text. Frequently this word is the name of the hero or deity to whom the text (such as a hymn) is dedicated.

In the Saussurean model, the functioning of the a. presupposes both a poet capable of sophisticated operations on verbal material (the segmentation of a key-word into elements and their dissemination in the text) and a reader able to recognize the presence of an a. and to reconstitute the hidden whole. To the extent that this conception is valid, it has profound implications for lit. hist. and theory. For a time, Saussure regarded the a. as a fundamental principle of IE poetry; subsequently, however, he came to question both his methodology and conclusions, in part because there is no explicit testimony by ancient authors about such use of the a. But Saussure's ideas have been further developed by both linguists and literary theorists. From linguistics has come added evidence concerning the principle of word-analysis in the IE poetic trad. (e.g., in archaic Ir. verse).

In literary theory, focus on the a. has stimulated a deeper look at the nature of the sound-meaning nexus in poetry; this in turn has led some researchers to emphasize the role of the a. as a semantic category which, under certain conditions, generates added meaning in the poem, semanticizing elements of the lowest levels of the text. Semiotic theory (see SEMIOTICS, POETIC), which has explored the role of trad. as a factor in the autonomous development of sign systems, has provided a framework within which the issue of authorial intention (q.v.) may be removed as a point of contention. New evidence concerning the presence of as. in the work of modern poets has been produced by members of the Moscow-Tartu school (see STRUCTURALISM): Toporov and Ivanov among others have demonstrated numerous as. in Rus. poetry (q.v.) of the early 20th c., where certain poets and schools attached a special ontological significance to the role of names and developed systems of composition resulting in complex, esoteric, and often encrypted messages.

Future research will need to address the problem of the objective verification of as. and also the question of whether the a. operates on a subliminal as opposed to a denotative or connotative level. Resolving these problems will involve finding answers to such questions as: (1) the conditions under which semantic information "overflows" onto the lower levels of the text, increasing the interconnections between formally discrete elements (recent studies have suggested that as. are most likely to appear in the work of poets who use paronymy extensively); and (2) the genres in which as. are most likely to arise.

H. B. Wheatley, *Of As.* (1862); F. de Saussure, *Cours de linguistique generale* (1916); P. Habermann, "A.," *Reallexikon*; A. Liede, *Dichtung als Spiel*, 2 v. (1963); J. Starobinski, *Les Mots sous les mots* (1971, tr. 1979); P. Wunderli, *F. de Saussure und die Anagramme* (1972); M. Meylakh, "À propos des anagrammes," *L'Homme* 16,4 (1976); V. V. Ivanov, "Ob anagrammax F. de Sossjura," in F. de Saussure, *Trudy po jazykoznaniju* (1977); A. L. Johnson, "Anagrammatism in Poetry," *PTL* 2 (1977); S. Baevskij and A. D. Košelev, "Poetika Bloka: anagrammy," *Blokovskij sbornik 3* (1979); D. Shepheard, "Saussure's Vedic As.," *MLR* 77 (1982); S. C. Hunter, *Dict. of As.* (1982); T. Augarde, *Oxford Guide to Word Games* (1984); V. N. Toporov, "K issledovaniju anagrammatičeskix struktur (analizy)," *Issledovanija po strukture teksta*, ed. T. V. Civ'jan (1987); *Očerki istorii jazyka russkoj poezii XX veka. Poetičeskij jazyk i idiostil'. Obščie voprosy. Zvukovaja organizacija teksta*, ed. V. P. Grigor'ev (1990).   H.B.

ANALOGY. See SYMBOL.

ANALYSIS. Richard Robinson in his *Definition* (1950) says that "a." is a "highly ambiguous" word and distinguishes six senses in which it has been used in modern philosophy. In some of these senses "a." and "synthesis" are correlative terms, and both involve concepts of "whole," "part," and "relation." Thus "a." has been defined as the procedure of discriminating elements that belong to a complex whole, and "synthesis" as the procedure of combining elements into a complex which can be apprehended as a whole. Sometimes "a." is used to cover both procedures, particularly when a full and systematic a. of a whole is required. Such an a. must define the nature of the whole, discriminate all of its parts and subparts, describe the properties of those parts, and show their relations to each other and to the whole. The purpose of making an a. is to get a clearer and fuller understanding of the whole being studied. The degree of difficulty in making an a. depends on the degree to which the whole is unfamiliar, obscure, puzzling, or complex, or incorporates structures, relations, and implications that are not immediately obvious.

The procedures for making a systematic a. will differ depending on the kind of whole being analyzed. Thus a whole may be an object, locality, event, process, experience, state of affairs, concept, class, theory, problem, etc. Clearly each of these kinds of wholes will require a different set of categories for distinguishing and characterizing their parts. Differing relationships among these parts (e.g. temporal or spatial juxtaposition, means and ends, similarity and difference, subordination or dominance, opposition, causal interdependence, balance, repetition) and differing synthesizing principles for establishing their relevance, ordering them, and bringing them into some type and degree of coherence and integration will generate wholes of different kinds (e.g. sum, aggregate, mosaic, compound, conglomerate, medley, Gestalt, organic structure, etc.) and influence analytic procedures.

What is the procedure that will produce valid and useful results in the a. of poetry? Traditional poetics has formulated a considerable variety of recommendations for the conduct of a. Perhaps the most important influence determining these recommendations is whether the critic holds that a poem should be regarded as an autonomous whole (see AUTONOMY) or whether the critic says that a poem can be properly read and appreciated only when it is seen as part of some larger whole (see below).

Formalist and objectivist critics assume that it is sensible and desirable to regard a poem as an hypostatized object, a well wrought urn, a microcosm, independent and self-sufficient. Of course, a poem, like other entities, has obvious and nonobvious connections with the real world. But in the study of poetry such external relations should be bracketed as much as possible because they tend to distract a reader from enjoying the poem as poem, its beauty, its intrinsic value. To assist a reader to make an a. of a poem (or a genre of poetry or all poetry), formalist poetics tries to group the distinguishable elements of a poem into an exhaustive set of categories for a. Thus Aristotle categorizes the constituents of tragedy as plot, character, thought, diction, music, and spectacle. Analyzing narrative, Seymour Chatman begins with two major categories—story and discourse—each subdivided into smaller units: story into events and existents, existents into characters and setting, events into actions and happenings, etc. Wellek and Warren and other theorists adapt Roman Ingarden's view that a literary work can be analyzed into a hierarchy of "strata": the sound stratum, semantic stratum, mimetic stratum, thematic stratum, and stratum of aesthetic qualities (the tragic, grotesque, sublime, etc.). Each of these strata can be considered a separable whole, a structure also subject to a. (Categories of a. for some of these strata have been developed with sophistication and minuteness, esp. in the work of prosodists and narratologists.) In addition, the analyst must account for the temporal sequence of the poem and describe the interactions of the various strata with each other, which, in the good poem, will reflect a set of "polyphonic" relationships that synthesize the strata into an organic whole. It should be noted that in this respect, "synthesis" is both a structural and a normative principle.

Opposed to formalist critics are those who recommend treating a poem as a part of some larger whole, or domain, of discourse or experience. These larger wholes are various. Expressionist and biographical critics study the relation between the poem and its author. They see their problem as the a. of a whole which is an historical event—the stages and causes, conscious or unconscious, of the creative act by which the poem came into being. Or the poem becomes a means for gaining an insight into the rich visionary consciousness of the poet or the quality of his or her synthesizing imagination. The larger whole within which rhetorical, communication, or reader-response critics choose to study poetry is the reading process. The principal categories for the a. of this kind of whole are the poem, the reader, and their complex interaction. A version of such crit. has always flourished (see POETRY, THEORIES OF: *Pragmatic Theories*); among the moderns this mode has been practiced by the early Richards, Dewey, Booth, Iser, Fish, Bleich, and Holland. There is no agreement among these critics as to the qualities of the experience generated by poetry, its values, the temporal sequence of its arousal and subsidence, the varying kinds and degrees of control which the poem does (or should) exercise to guide and constrain the experience, the nature of the equipment required by the (ideal) reader (such as certain mental capacities and training, incl. a knowledge, conscious or unconscious, of linguistic and cultural codes and conventions, strategies for interp., and the ability to synthesize parts of an ongoing sequence of events). Finally, poems have been regarded as parts of some nonaesthetic context which, it is claimed, explains their nature and value and within which they function in ways appropriate to or dictated by the whole. Larger contexts for the study of poetry have been found in politics, hist., myth, sociology, psychology, philosophy, and, recently, even all discourse (see INTERTEXTUALITY). The categories of a. used by such critics are usually dictated by the discipline within which poetry is being studied.

Such differences among theorists have led to the development in the past 50 years of metacriticism (q.v.), a critical a. of crit., whose goal is the clarification (and perhaps improvement) of the concepts and logic used in poetics and aesthet-ics. One important contribution to metacriticism is Richard McKeon's "The Philosophic Bases of Art and Crit." (in Crane), which lists many more varieties of analytic procedures than have been enumerated above. Metacritics also try to classify the systems of poetics that have flourished in the past. Some metacritics (e.g. Richards, Crane, Abrams) have argued that these systems are not contradictory but complementary to each other, each representing one perspective on a complex field. A literary theory is, says Richards, a "speculative instrument," which both determines and limits what a viewer will see. Thus the various critical perspectives should be regarded simply as possible emphases in the study of lit. Indeed, few critics dogmatically limit themselves to a single perspective, denigrating all others to the status of fallacies or heresies. Thus Ingarden, after publishing his formalistically oriented *The Literary Work of Art*, produced an equally detailed reader-oriented study, *The Cognition of the Literary Work of Art*. The proposals for an integration of critical methods that appear at the end of Stanley Hyman's *The Armed Vision* (1948), an extensive treatment of the critical procedures of 12 critics, are well known. Kenneth Burke also welcomed a variety of critical procedures and tried to synthesize them within an all-embracing theory of human action. Human actions can be classified into various types—e.g. cognitive, expressive, rhetorical, aesthetic—but the same categories of a. are applicable to all of them: act, scene, agent, means, purpose, and attitude.

But other metacritics have doubted that the study of lit. can be regarded as a single enterprise within which the various modes of a., interp., and evaluation (qq.v.) can be synthesized. To them, metacriticism has demonstrated that the principal terms used in crit. (e.g. "poetry," "tragedy," "whole," "expression") do not have and cannot be expected to have the precise denotations of terms in the natural sciences. The referents of critical terms are "fluid," "essentially contested," "open-textured," or "range" concepts whose variability of application cannot be remedied. The reason is that crit. deals with human products whose creation, interp., and evaluation are guided by conventions that are culturally determined and that change in the course of history. Other determinants of poetic theory (as McKeon points out) are the theorist's philosophical commitments, esp. in epistemology, metaphysics, and methodology. The hist. of crit. seems to indicate that agreement in these areas is not very likely to occur. The influence of these theoretical and pragmatic differences is evident in the antianalytic and antisynthetic positions that some modern theorists have taken.

An early 20th-c. antianalytic position was that of Croce, who centered aesthetics on "intuition" (q.v.), "expression" (q.v.), and "spiritual activity." In artistic creation, expression fuses elements into an organic whole, creating a single indivisible object. In aesthetic response, the mind works on an intuitive rather than a logical or conceptual level, and a. would simply destroy the work. "Intuition" is also a key term in Bergson's philosophy (made available to Eng. critics by T. E. Hulme). The human intellect operates by abstracting elements from experience and dissecting them by analytic procedures. However necessary this cognitive process of abstraction and a. may be for scientific and practical purposes, it distorts and veils the true nature of concrete reality, which is a perpetual flow of elements that are inextricably fused and which exhibits constant change, novelty, creation, evolution. Intuition (q.v.) is the faculty that perceives this reality. "Intuition" is, of course, an old and ambiguous word, and refers not only to the Bergsonian immediate awareness of the "intensive manifolds" of "lived experience," but also to mystical visions of spiritual truth. Most theorists who celebrate intuition downplay the operations of the meddling intellect; an intuition, they say, is unanalyzable. The creation and appreciation of art become functions of intuition, and art becomes a cognitive activity conveying knowledge inexpressible in the vocabulary and syntax of scientific lang.

A different set of philosophical assumptions has generated a recent tendency (which, according to some scholars, can be traced back to the New Critical stress on ambiguity, irony, paradox, tension, and polysemy) to question the possibility and value of a synthetic apprehension of a literary text (at least of the type specified by organicist theory). A deconstructive a. of a text (see DECONSTRUCTION) shows that it has discontinuities, gaps, arbitrary elements, and unresolvable contradictions. These characteristics open the text to multiple (perhaps unlimited) interpretations, and there is no way to decide which is the "correct" one. During the reading process the reader, under the influence of a long-standing literary convention, expects to find structure (q.v.), coherence, and closure (q.v.) in what she reads and, consciously or unconsciously, imposes a synthesis of some kind on the text. But the text is radically indeterminate and, if studied closely, will subvert any synthesis imposed on it. When an old-fashioned reader, expecting that a text should "make sense," contemplates the consequences of the deconstructive discovery of the "unreadability" of a text, she may feel uncomfortable or even despairing. But the reader should be persuaded to accept disunity rather than synthesis as an aesthetic (and ethical) value. Authors should also be encouraged to compose works that provide the reader with ever greater opportunities for a free play among linguistic signs and aesthetic conventions, a free play which is an encouragement to individuation, a breaking away from no longer viable religious, humanist, or political visions of harmonious synthesis.

For additional information about the various procedures for a.-synthesis recommended by traditional and modern schools of crit., see CRITICISM; THEORY; POETRY, THEORIES OF; NEW CRITICISM; CONTEXTUALISM; CHICAGO SCHOOL; GENEVA SCHOOL; MYTH CRITICISM; STRUCTURALISM; READER-RESPONSE CRITICISM; SEMIOTICS; HISTORICISM; DECONSTRUCTION. Other articles treat problems of a. of the various strata of poetic works: see the entries ALLITERATION, PROSODY, RHYME, and SOUND for the sound stratum; see CONNOTATION AND DENOTATION, EXPLICATION, LEXIS, MEANING, POETIC, METAPHOR, SEMANTICS AND POETRY, SEMIOTICS, POETIC, and SYMBOL for the semantic stratum; LINGUISTICS AND POETICS, POETICS, STYLE, and STYLISTICS for both the sound and semantic strata; REPRESENTATION AND MIMESIS and also PLOT for the mimetic stratum; and THEME for the ideational stratum. The problems of synthesis are treated in FORM, ORGANICISM, STRUCTURE, and UNITY. See also SIMPLICITY AND COMPLEXITY and INTERPRETATION.

T. E. Hulme, *Speculations* (1924); Richards; R. Ingarden, *Das literarische Kunstwerk* (1931, tr. 1973), *Vom Erkennen des literarischen Kunstwerks* (1968, tr. 1973); C. Lalo, "The Aesthetic A. of a Work of Art," *JAAC* 7 (1949); W. Shumaker, *Elements of Critical Theory* (1952); R. S. Crane, *The Langs. of Crit. and the Structure of Poetry* (1953); I. A. Richards, *Speculative Instruments* (1955); S. J. Kahn, "Towards an Organic Crit.," *JAAC* 15 (1956); Wellek and Warren; C. L. Stevenson, "On the 'A.' of a Work of Art," *Phil. Rev.* 67 (1958); M. C. Beardsley, *Aesthetics* (1958); *Parts and Wholes*, ed. D. Lerner (1963); M. Krieger, "Literary A. and Evaluation—and the Ambidextrous Critic," *Crit.*, ed. L. S. Dembo (1968); M. H. Abrams, "What's the Use of Theorizing about the Arts?" *In Search of Literary Theory*, ed. M. W. Bloomfield (1972); J. M. Ellis, *The Theory of Lit. Crit.* (1974), ch. 6; M. Weitz, *The Opening Mind* (1977); W. Iser, *The Act of Reading* (1978); S. Chatman, *Story and Discourse* (1978); W. C. Booth, *Critical Understanding* (1979); G. Genette, *Narrative Discourse* (1980); *Reader-Response Crit.*, ed. J. P. Tompkins (1980); A. M. Wright, *The Formal Principle in the Novel* (1982); C. Segre, *Intro. to the A. of the Literary Text* (1988).
F.GU.

ANAPEST, anapaest (Gr.; of uncertain meaning, perhaps "beaten back," i.e. a reversed dactyl). In the quantitative meters of Cl. poetry, a metrical foot of two short syllables followed by one long (ᴗ ᴗ – , e.g. *dĕĭtās*), or, in verse-systems based on accent, two unstressed syllables followed by one stressed (x x ∕, e.g. *interrupt*). In Gr. the a. usually appears as a dipody or metron which takes the form ᴗ ᴗ – ᴗ ᴗ – . The metron shows total equivalence of single longs and double shorts, unique in Gr.; consequently in the dimeter (the commonest form) there is usually diaeresis (q.v.) between metra. As. were used first as a warlike marching rhythm, then later in Gr. drama as a song meter, both purely, as in the choruses of tragedy and comedy, commonly anapestic te-trameter catalectic, and in combination with other meters. Runs of as. are often closed with a catalectic dimeter or paroemiac (q.v.). The single foot replaced the metron as the unit of measure when the rhythm was taken over by the Romans. Plautus made wide use of anapestic verse, esp. in 4-foot units (anapestic quaternarii), and acatalectic and catalectic 8-foot units (anapestic septenarii and octonarii). Seneca, however, uses as. in the Gr. manner (i.e. in metra, not feet) in his tragedies, as anapaestic dimeters, a form used later by Boethius and Prudentius. See CLASSICAL PROSODY.

In the accentual prosodies of the Ren. and after, the a. was used in Eng. mainly for popular verse until the beginning of the 18th c.; it was subsequently employed for serious poetry by Cowper, Scott, Byron, Browning ("How They Brought the Good News"), Morris, and esp. Swinburne, who used it in lines of every possible length ("Dolores"). While the a. is characteristically the foot of hurried motion and excitement, e.g. "The Assyrian came down like a wolf on the fold" (Byron, "The Destruction of Sennacherib"), it can also be slow-moving and effective in conveying mourning or sadness, as, for instance, in Matthew Arnold's "Rugby Chapel." But in fact pure as. are comparatively rare in Eng., and are in any case exceedingly difficult to distinguish in running series from other ternary meters such as dactylic or amphibrachic (see BINARY AND TERNARY). The most common generic usage by far is in the limerick (q.v.).—A. Raabe, De metrorum anapaesticorum apud poetas Graecos usu (1912); J. W. White, The Verse of Gr. Comedy (1912); Hardie, ch. 4; Wilamowitz, pt. 2, ch. 11; Koster, ch. 7; Crusius; C. Questa, Introduzione alle metrica de Plauto (1967); D. Korzeniewski, Griechische Metrik (1968); Dale, ch. 4; Halporn et al.; Snell, 30 ff.; West, passim; J. G. Fitch, Seneca's As.   D.S.P.; J.W.H.; T.V.F.B.

ANAPHORA (Gr. "a carrying up or back"); also epanaphora. The repetition of the same word or words at the beginning of successive phrases, clauses, sentences, or lines. Conversely, epistrophe (also called epiphora, e.g. Shakespeare, Merchant of Venice 3.3.4) repeats words at the ends of clauses, lines, or stanzas; so Tennyson repeats "the days that are no more" at the end of each stanza of "Tears, Idle Tears." Synonyms for epistrophe are epiphora and antistrophe (in the rhetorical sense). Combining both figures is symploce (3 Henry 6 2.5.103–8). Sonnet 62 of Bartholomew Griffin's Fidessa is a Ren. tour de force of symploce, each of the 14 lines beginning "Most true that" and ending "love." Discussions of symploce date from Alexander, the Gr. rhetorician of the 2d c. A.D. (Peri schematon 2; rpt. in C. Walz, Rhetores graeci, 9 v. [1832–36] 8.464–65) and the Rhetorica ad Herennium (4.13). Repetition of the same word at the

beginning and end of each phrase, clause, or line is epanalepsis (King John 2.1.329–30; q.v.). Linking of the end of one member to the beginning of the next is anadiplosis, a form of concatenation (qq.v.). Demetrius (1st c. A.D.; On Style 268) and Longinus (On the Sublime 20.1–2) use the term epanaphora, and virtually all postclassical authorities treat a. as its exact synonym.

A. has been a favored device in the poetry of many cultures, particularly in the form where the repeated words or phrases begin lines: this structure enhances the sense of the line even as it foregrounds the larger enumerative sequence. A. may thus be seen as one form of parallelism (q.v.) which uses the repetitions to bring the metrical and syntactic frames into alignment. It has been used particularly in religious and devotional poetry—where in part, it may be thought, the device echoes the iterations of ecstatic experience—and is common in the Middle Ages; Martianus Capella (5th c.) remarks on the 21 repetitions of sol in a Lat. poem. In the Bible many examples foreground "The Lord" or "He," e.g. Psalms 23 and 29. It is conspicuous too in the lyric, esp. the sonnet (q.v.). Daniel (Delia) uses as. regularly, preferring triple repetitions, Shakespeare more sparingly—only 16 times in the 154 Sonnets, with 6 of these triple—though the 10-line a. of "And" in sonnet 66 is striking; this sort of extended, plurilinear a. is instanced in Petrarch, no. 145; in Ronsard, Amours 1.54; in Spenser Amoretti 9 and 15; and in Hekatompathia 75 and 77. A. is also common in Shakespeare's plays, particularly the early plays, e.g. Richard 2 2.1.40–42 and 4.1.207 ff.; Richard 3 4.4.92–104; and Othello 3.3.345–47. Sidney is enchanted with it—witness more than 40 examples in Astrophil and Stella.

In verse where the bonds of strict meter have loosened or partly disappeared, a. is still very much of value. It is Whitman's most frequent device, serving to give structure to his extended catalogues and syntactically involuted constructions; no poet has exploited the device more than Whitman. In T. S. Eliot most instances are no longer than in most of the Ren. sonneteers, but it dominates section V of The Waste Land. In recent years anaphoric structures have been the subject of considerable research in linguistics. But the definitive historical and theoretical study of a. in poetry still remains to be written.

Sr. M. Joseph, Shakespeare's Use of the Arts of Lang. (1947); C. Schaar, An Elizabethan Sonnet Problem (1960); A. Quinn, Figures of Speech (1982), 83–87; Norden; J. Aoun, A Grammar of A. (1985); B. Vickers, In Defence of Rhet. (1988), Cl. Rhet. in Eng. Poetry, 2d ed. (1989); Corbett.   T.V.F.B.

ANAPODOTON. See ANACOLUTHON.

ANASTROPHE. See HYPERBATON.

ANCEPS (Lat. "indeterminate"). A Neo-Lat. term

widely used to designate three different metrical phenomena. (1) Syllabic or "prosodic" a.—i.e. fluctuation in quantity created by the existence of a variable syllable boundary. The word *agro*, for example, may begin with either a short or a long, depending on whether its initial syllable is open (*a-gro*) or closed (*ag-ro*). For a. in this sense the preferred term is "common" (Gr. *koiné*; Lat. *communis*). (2) "Final a." At the end of a line or stanza, a syllable which may be either long or short, which the ancients referred to as the *syllaba indifferens* (Gr. *adiáphoros*). the pause that ensues at this point allows, or requires, lengthening of the syllable immediately preceding, and since almost all verses and stanzas end at a point where the metrical pattern itself either allows or requires a long, the normal quantity of a syllable becomes metrically "indifferent" when it appears in a final position—that is, it makes no difference whether the poet decides to use a long or a short there. A normally short syllable that has undergone final lengthening in sense (2) may be called final a., but it is more frequently and correctly referred to as *(syllaba) brevis in (elemento) longo*, a phrase coined by Maas. (3) A. positions. Any position in the metrical pattern which permits either a long or a short syllable. This is simply to say that some positions in the meter are not important to perception of the pattern, hence are not regulated strictly. Modern usage of the term a. tends to be restricted to sense (3) and to insist, correctly, that it is not the *syllable* which is a. but the *position* in the metrical pattern it fills. The ancients sometimes regarded long syllables in these positions as "irrational" (Gr. *alogos*)—shorter than normal longs by some indeterminate amount. Double a. at the beginning of the line is referred to as "aeolic base"; see AEOLIC.—Maas; L. E. Rossi, "*A.*: vocale, sillaba, elemento," *RFIC* 91 (1963); A. M. Dale, *Collected Papers* (1969); Snell; M. L. West, "Three Topics in Greek Metre," *ClassQ* 32 (1982). A.T.C.

ANCIENTS AND MODERNS, BATTLE OF. See QUERELLE DES ANCIENS ET DES MODERNES.

ANGLO-SAXON PROSODY. See ENGLISH PROSODY, *Old English.*

ANIMAL EPIC. See BEAST EPIC.

ANTANACLASIS. See POLYPTOTON.

ANTHIMERIA (Gr. "one part for another"). The use of one part of speech for another. Shakespeare, who seems to have coined more than a thousand new words, uses a. as one of his chief strategies; examples include "A mile before his tent fall down and knee / Thy way into his mercy" (*Coriolanus* 5.1.5), "And I come coffin'd home" (*Cor* 2.1.193), and "Lord Angelo dukes it well" (*Measure for Measure* 3.2.100). He esp. develops the use of nouns, pronouns, and adjectives as verbs, securing thereby the greater energy that verb forms convey. But no Eng. poet used this figure more than Milton, many of whose examples suggest Milton found it effective for securing compression of meaning (Havens). In *Paradise Lost* examples include "May serve to better us and worse our foes" (6.440; adj. for verb) and "seamonsters tempest the ocean" (7.412; noun for verb); chaos is described as "the palpable obscure" and "the vast abrupt," while the sky is "Heaven's azure" (adj. for noun). In modern poetry even more audacious transferences have been made by e e cummings, many of whose as. are famous (or infamous), e.g. "he sang his didn't he danced his did" and "anyone lived in a pretty how town." In grammar the gerund, a verb form serving the syntactic function of a noun, is the same kind of word-class transfer.—Sr. M. Joseph, *Shakespeare's Use of the Arts of Lang.* (1947), 62–64; A. Quinn, *Figures of Speech* (1982); Corbett 449. T.V.F.B.

ANTHOLOGY (*Florilegium, Chrestomathie*). Etymologically a "bouquet," from Gr. *anthos* (flower) and *legein* (to gather, pick up). In the hist. of Western lit. the most influential a. is unquestionably the Bible, a heterogeneous collection of Jewish (Heb.) and Christian (Gr.) texts written over more than a millennium. The OT includes historical, genealogical, legal, proverbial, wisdom, and prophetic texts codified in its present form by rabbinical council in 90 A.D. The NT includes epistolary and apocalyptic texts and a hybrid genre related to but not biography (the Gospels) codified about the 4th c. The term "Apocrypha" is used sometimes to refer to the 7 texts accepted by Catholics but rejected by Protestants, but more often for all texts whose canonical status is disputed.

In Gr., the a. was originally a collection of epigrams (q.v.), generally composed in elegiac distichs (q.v.) and treating specific subjects or poets. Compilations were made at least as early as the 4th c. B.C. About 90 B.C., Meleager of Gadara collected a *Garland* of short epigrams in various meters, but chiefly elegiac, and on various subjects; some fifty poets from Archilochus (7th c. B.C.) to his own era (incl. himself) were represented. About A.D. 40, Philippus of Thessalonica collected a *Garland* of exclusively elegiac epigrams by poets since Meleager. Approximately a century later Straton of Sardis put together some hundred epigrams on a single subject (homosexual love). About A.D. 570, the Byzantine anthologist Agathias collected a *Circle* of epigrams in various meters; he included selections, arranged by subject, from both *Garlands* as well as a large selection of contemporary epigrams.

Constantinus Cephalas, a Byzantine Greek of the 10th c., compiled an a. combining and rearranging the collections of Meleager, Philippus, Straton and Agathias. In all, it included 15 divisions: Christian epigrams, descriptions of statuary, temple inscriptions, prefaces (by Meleager, Philippus, and Agathias), erotic poems, dedicatory poems, epitaphs (including Simonides' famous lines on the Spartan dead at Thermopylae), epigrams by St. Gregory of Nazianzus, epideictic (q.v.) epigrams, moral epigrams, social and satirical epigrams, Straton's collection, epigrams in special meters, riddles, and miscellaneous epigrams. This a., or the *Gr. A.*, as it is now called, was edited, revised, and expurgated in 1301 by the monk Maximus Planudes. His was the only available text until 1606, when the great Fr. scholar Claude Saumaise (Salmasius) discovered a single manuscript of Cephalas in the Elector Palatine's library at Heidelberg. Thereafter this latter text came to be known as the *Palatine A.*; it supplanted the *Planudean A.* but retained a Planudean appendix as a 16th division. The first ed. of the *Palatine A.* was published by Friedrich Jacobs in 13 vols. from 1794 through 1814.

The influence of the *Gr. A.* in the modern world dates from Janus Lascaris' Florentine ed. of Planudes in 1494. Trs. of the epigrams into Lat. and later into the vernacular langs. multiplied consistently until about 1800, when enthusiasm for the unpointed Gr. epigram was supplanted by one for the pointed epigram as perfected by Martial (1st c. A.D.). Interest in the *Gr. A.* in the 20th c. is evidenced by a number of eds., selections, and trs., e.g. that by Kenneth Rexroth.

Other important Cl. as. include the 5th-c. Stobaeus' Gr. *Eclogae* (Selections) and *Anthologion* and the *Anthologia latina* (ed. Riese, Bücheler, and Lommatzsch, 1894–1926, and incl. otherwise uncollected Lat. verse and a 6th-c. compilation which contained the *Pervigilium Veneris*). Medieval as. were created and preserved mainly by the clerical orders, and survive in influential ms. collections such as the OE *Proverbs of Alfred* and the Eng. lyric collection called the Harley Ms. (British Museum Ms. Harley 2253; ca. 1330); among other medieval *florilegia*, esp. notable are the *Carmina Cantabrigiensia* ("Cambridge Songs"; 11th c.) and the *Carmina Burana* (collected at the Ger. monastery at Benediktbeuren in Bavaria in the 13th c.; see GOLIARDIC VERSE). Ren. collections of proverbs drew inspiration from Erasmus' *Adagia* (early 16th c.).

As. took on new importance in the Ren. with a vogue inaugurated in England by the collection assembled by Richard Tottel and now called Tottel's Miscellany (originally *Songes and Sonettes, written by the ryght honorable Lorde Henry Haward late Earle of Surrey, and others*, 1557; ed. Rollins, rev. ed., 2 v., 1965). After Tottel the vogue for the "miscellanies," as they were called (accent on the second syllable), grew to a flood in the last quarter of the century, incl. Clement Robinson's *Very Pleasaunt Sonettes and Storyes in Myter* (1566; surviving only as *A Handefull of Pleasant Delites*, 1584; ed. Hyder E. Rollins, 1924); Richard Edwards' *The Paradyse of Daynty Devises* (1576; ed. Rollins, 1927); Thomas

Proctor's *A Gorgious Gallery of Gallant Inventions* (1578; ed. Rollins, 1926); *The Phoenix Nest* (1593; ed. Rollins, 1931); *Englands Helicon* (1600, 1614); Francis Davison's *A Poetical Rapsody* (1602; ed. Rollins, 2 v., 1931); and Nicholas Breton's *Brittons Bowre of Delights* (1591; ed. Rollins, 1933) and *The Arbor of Amorous Devices* (1597; ed. Rollins, 1936).

Other significant European as. are the massive *Flores poetarum* compiled early in the 16th c. by Octavianus Mirandula and used throughout Europe until the 18th c.; Jan Gruter's *Delitiae* (It., Fr., Belgian, and Ger. poems in Lat.; 1608–14); J. W. Zincgref's *Anhang unterschiedlicher aussgesuchter Gedichten* (1624); Thomas Percy's *Reliques of Ancient Eng. Poetry* (1765), an a. of the popular ballads which proved very influential in the 18th-c. revival of antiquarian interest in primitive poetry; Oliver Goldsmith's *The Beauties of Eng. Poetry* (1767); Thomas Campbell's *Specimens of the British Poets* (1891); and Francis Palgrave's *Golden Treasury of the Best Songs and Lyrical Poems in the Eng. Lang.* (1861–; 5th ed. supp. J. Press, 1987), the most important Victorian a. of lyric poetry.

The popularity of as. in the 20th c. has if anything increased, with the expansion of the institutions of higher education, esp. in America. Important as. include the *Oxford Book of Eng. Verse*, successively edited by Sir Arthur Quiller-Couch (1900, 1939) and Helen Gardner (1972); *The New Poetry* (1917) by Harriet Monroe and Alice C. Henderson, which influenced the high modernists; Sir Herbert Grierson's *Metaphysical Lyrics and Poems* (1921), which inaugurated the vogue for metaphysical poetry (q.v.); W. B. Yeats's *Oxford Book of Modern Verse* (1936); Brooks and Warren's *Understanding Poetry* (1938; 4th ed. rev. extensively, 1976), which codified for pedagogy and practical crit. the principles of the New Criticism (q.v.); Donald Hall's *The New Am. Poetry* (1960), which opened up the formalist canon; and the seemingly ubiquitous Norton As. of Lit. in their several manifestations (World, Eng., Am.) and As. of Poetry and of Lit. by Women—which, for all practical purposes, in each successive revision, effectually constitute the canon (q.v.). In the later 1980s these began to be seriously challenged by competitors offering much more radically revisionary as. See now COLLECTIONS, POETIC; EPIGRAM; LYRIC SEQUENCE.

J. O. Halliwell-Phillipps, *Early Eng. Miscellanies* (1855); *An OE Miscellany*, ed. R. Morris (1872); F. Lachère, *Bibliographie des receuils collectifs de poésies publiés de 1597 à 1700* (1901); A. Wifstrand, *Studien zur griechischen Anthologie* (1926); A. E. Case, *A Bibl. of Eng. Poetical Miscellanies, 1521–1750* (1935); J. Hutton, *The Gr. A. in Italy to the Year 1800* (1935), *The Gr. A. in France and in the Writers of the Netherlands to the Year 1800* (1946); *The Harley Lyrics*, ed. G. L. Brook (1948); A. S. F. Gow, *The Gr. A.: Sources and Ascriptions* (1958); *Anthologia graeca*, ed. H. Beckby, 4 v. (1965); R. F. Arnold, *Allgemeine Bücherkunde*, 4th ed. (1966); *Die deutschsprachige Anthologie*, ed. J. Bark and D. Pforte, 2 v. (1969–70); *New CBEL* 2.327 ff.; E. W. Pomeroy, *The Elizabethan Miscellanies, Their Devel. and Conventions* (1973); *The Gr. A.*, sel. and tr. P. Jay (1973); Pearsall 94 ff.; R. McDowell, "The Poetry A.," *HudR* 42 (1990).   T.V.F.B.; R.A.S.

ANTHROPOLOGY AND POETRY. The discipline of man and his works in its relation to poetry brings to mind first of all the names of scholars such as Sir James Frazer, Gilbert Murray, C. G. Jung, and Claude Lévi-Strauss who also wrote about poetry and poetics. The most famous anthropologist since 1950 is Lévi-Strauss, whose originality lies in his power to synthesize, and who established a method for analyzing the phenomena of cultural a. such as kinship, ritual, and myth (q.v.). In his "structural" theory, all levels and forms of human culture rank equally, no one level being the primary determinant (see STRUCTURALISM). Lévi-Strauss also discerned structures in works of poetry which are strikingly analogous to those revealed in his analysis of myth. He began to regard myths not merely as arrangements of concepts but as works of art which, like poems, arouse in those who hear them profound aesthetic emotions. However, critics have found the method itself more interesting than the uses to which it has been put. His analysis of Baudelaire's sonnet "Les Chats" (co-authored with Roman Jakobson), for example, produced rather poor results, and it has not been difficult to show the limitations of the outcome (Riffaterre; Culler).

Still, it would be oversimplifying and incorrect to contrast Frazer, Murray, and Jung as the older school with Lévi-Strauss as representative of the new school. First of all, the three older scholars are quite different from one another: Frazer was an anthropologist, while Murray was a Cl. scholar and Jung a psychologist. Further, there is a gulf between the traditional positivism of Frazer and the idealistic approach of Jung. Besides, Jung is not at all outdated, and the concept of the archetype (q.v.), which is used differently by different theorists (e.g. Northrop Frye), has continued to be influential. It was Frye who claimed rightly that the structural principles of lit. are as closely related to mythology and comparative religion as those of painting are to geometry. In point of fact, the association between cultural a. and poetry is relevant to many disciplines: Jung, perhaps the most fruitful scholar in this respect, and others in other fields study myths, rites, and patterns of "primitive" culture as they are expressed in poetry. These scholars include anthropologists from Karl Kerényi to Joseph Campbell, philosophers from Ernesto Grassi to Philip Wheelwright, orientalists such as Heinrich Zimmer, art historians such as Luc Benoist, and scholars of comparative religion such as Mircea Eliade. Many of these scholars are also indebted to Jungian psychology, which in turn is involved in cultural a. as well (see PSYCHOLOGICAL CRITICISM).

On the one hand, cultural and chronological primitivism (q.v.) in lit. sometimes stimulated the growth of a., while on the other hand, a. has deepened the understanding of poetry by helping Westerners to understand "primitive" societies of the past, enabling a better appreciation of their poetics. A prime case is that of epics such as the Homeric *Iliad* and *Odyssey*, the OE *Beowulf*, the East Indian *Mahabharata*, the Finnish *Kalevala*, and the MHG *Nibelungenlied*. The decisive step of our time was taken by the Cl. scholar Milman Parry, who, having surmised from the Cl. texts that they seemed to take the form he hypothesized as constitutive of traditional oral compositions, started field work in the remote mountains of Yugoslavia in search of similar, indeed parallel, heroic epics under parallel conditions. Parry, who died young, was followed by Albert Lord, who developed a general theory of "oral epic song" (see ORAL POETRY) which holds that the Homeric epics were composed over many generations by illiterate "singers of tales" (see ORAL-FORMULAIC THEORY). Each epic is built of lines of metrical verse composed of formulaic expressions (see FORMULA). According to Lord, these formulas are not "ossified clichés" but capable of change and productive of other new formulas. Other scholars subsequently argued that the OE *Beowulf* was constructed in a similar fashion. In a similar way, the Finnish folk epic *Kalevala* (first pub. 1835) consists of selections of songs from oral trad. dealing with ancient nature myths, heroic tales, and assimilated Christian legends.

Another way in which a. has deepened our comprehension of poetry and poetics is by enabling better understanding of "primitive" societies. One of the most extensive works embracing aspects of primitive man both ancient and modern is Henry and Nora Chadwick's *The Growth of Lit.* (3 v., 1932–40), which describes the development of early oral literary trads. to the beginnings of written lit. Their study covers OE, ON, early Gr., ancient Ir., early Rus., Indian, and Heb. lits. and Yugoslav oral poetry; significantly, they note that oral poetry continues to be a living art down to our time. Unlike Parry, however, the Chadwicks did not do their own field work but relied on older reports from travelers, thus arriving at more limited conclusions.

Given the manner in which it originates and develops via performance, oral poetry is inherently characterized by a fluidity of text (since no single "text" exists) and by parataxis (q.v.). Since each performer is a composer and since each performance is unique, each song, both generic and specific, has multiple authors and texts. The changes from performance to performance do not happen deliberately or by chance but by an insistent, conservative urge for preservation of an essential idea as expressed either in a single theme or group of themes. Despite appearances, multiformity is essentially conservative in traditional lore.

In a subsequent analysis of oral lit. in Africa, Ruth Finnegan argues that simple generalizations about the collective nature of art in preliterate cultures collapse in light of evidence about the creative activity of the individual poet: such evidence reveals a far more complex process of artistic composition. Finnegan also finds less support than expected for the mythopoetic or archetypal interp. of Af. oral lit. She rejects the attempt to explain away this lit. by reference to social or even "symbolic" function, claiming that in fact it survives due to the impact of literate, wealthier, and more "progressive" cultures. While some genres are receding, others—political songs, dance songs, religious lyrics—are increasing in importance. Finnegan asserts that oral lit. continues to play a part in not just traditional but developing Africa as well. See AFRICAN POETRY.

Margot Astrow reached a similar conclusion regarding the oral poetry of the Am. Indians. "The" Indian, she claims, is an abstraction. The diversity of Am. Indian poetry (q.v.), which is tremendous, results from three factors: individual disposition, group configuration, and natural environment. Healing songs and songs of germination and growth outnumber all other songs on account of their magic implications: this kind of poetry aims to change either the singer himself or his fellow beings or nature. Ruth Underhill, commenting on Papago songs, claimed that they make the Indian visualize the eagle with all its peculiarities. Thus the eagle's power is asserted, so that, being the superior of man according to Indian belief, it will then cleanse man from impurities, free him from disease, and even ward off death.

The studies and theories of C. M. Bowra reach especially far. Bowra sought to return to the very beginnings of human song. He limited his inquiries to a select group of societies who live by hunting and gathering because these are the modern counterparts of the lost races of the Paleolithic age. Bowra concluded from archaeological findings and anthropological insights that Paleolithic man had at least some kind of music. Bowra was able to find detailed and reliable information about the oral poetry of the Bushmen, the Pygmies, the Australian aborigines, the Veddas, the Selk'nam and Yamana Indians, the Inuit ("Eskimos"), and the Semang people of Malaya.

One of the major findings of this approach is that the "primitive" imagination works differently from the imagination of the modern Westerner; it is not concerned with what is absent in time or place but with what it believes to be present but invisible. Far from creating its subjects out of nothing and making them live in their own authority, it assumes that they already exist; the singer's task is simply to show what in fact they are. The sphere of the "primitive" imagination is confined to the supernatural. Therefore the songs use images which are not, like most of our own, literary devices to stress one or another aspect of a subject, but a means to make sense of what is otherwise mysterious.

The thinking expressed in primitive songs is also different from our thinking; it moves more by association of symbols and images than by development of ideas. Primitive songs allow societies to express and answer their most basic questions, enable them to pursue action with confidence, and bring them into touch with gods and spirits.

Besides the oral songs of primitive man ancient and modern, a. has had a direct impact on the poetry of more advanced, modern civilizations as well. In some cases the practical results of cultural a. are expressed in poetry. Examples of poets influenced by a. incl. Longfellow, whose "Song of Hiawatha" recounts the adventures of the Algonquin hero Manabozho (attributing them to the Iroquois chieftain Hiawatha); Garcia Lorca, who included gypsy folklore in some of his poems; Robert Graves, whose poem "The White Goddess" celebrates the "Mountain Mother" representing both nature and the primitive trad. of a matriarchal religion; and W. B. Yeats, whose early poetry in particular is rife with Celtic folklore and mythology. In several cases it is even anthropological theory that has influenced poetry. Just as Frazer had an impact on D. H. Lawrence, so the now often-disparaged theories of Harrison, Frazer, and Weston became significant for T. S. Eliot's *The Waste Land*.

Haskell Block was not so much concerned with the content and meaning of anthropological aspects within lit. crit. but rather gave an overview of the different critical methods used in this respect. The Fr. anthropologist Gilbert Durand surveyed the ideas of several Fr. critics in his book on basic structures of imagination, mutually illuminating a number of perspectives. Probably the most important anthropological implication in the literary realm is the basic distinction between poetic lang. and the lang. of everyday and scientific communication. Philip Wheelwright speaks of expressive lang. or depth lang., or the lang. of symbolism, versus literal lang.; and he sets the dimension of myth over against the perspective of logos. Mythos, however, is not self-intelligible: rite and ceremony have engendered it and shaped its final form. Wheelwright uses the example of a Fiji death chant to explain the interrelationships of rite and myth. What the mourners mythopoetically enact in ritual and envision through the chant is the unification of the chanting survivors, the recently deceased, and the ancient ancestral spirits. This strongly felt togetherness during the song is achieved mainly by the strongly marked rhythms, both vocal and ideational, of the chant.

Northrop Frye claimed that we simply cannot study the archetypal aspect of a literary genre without a literary anthropologist. If the latter relates the Hamlet legend to nature-myths, for example, he is not running away from Shakespeare but drawing closer to the archetypal form which Shakespeare recreated. One must not limit oneself to those few authors who consciously use the discoveries of anthropologists and folklorists; one must also hearken to the many writers who live their lore (Rosenberg). Thus when Chaucer retells the common folktale "The Flood," he is not using something alien to him but recreating and transmitting one aspect of his culture.

Andrew Welsh achieved results of significance when he traced the anthropological roots of poetry. He found poetic elements embodied in the riddles, charms, and chants of primitive and folk poetry. Distinguishing three roots of the melopoeia of lyric poetry: song (words sung to the rhythm and melody of music), charm (magic incantations carried on the singsong of a magician at work), and speech (the music we are probably most accustomed to hearing in poetry), he refers to song-melos, charm-melos, and speech-melos. According to Welsh, the rhythmical situation in a lyric poem is more complex than just the syncopation of metrical pattern and speech rhythm: there are also present other rhythms derived from other uses of lang.—old, compelling forces whose purpose was to move and which we know mostly through cultural anthropology. The distinctive rhythm of lyric is therefore a complex interplay of rhythms in lang., a syncopation that crosses the rhythms of speech-melos, charm-melos, and song-melos. Thus modern poets who break the metrical patterns to explore other rhythms are working not to invent something new but to recover something old.

Prospecting in a more theoretical way, Wolfgang Iser has sketched out a possible literary a. which requires a heuristic of its own in order to answer questions such as why we need fiction. He turns away from the text itself to the function and impact of the text and thereby aims at a reader-response a. See also ARCHETYPE; MYTH; MYTH CRITICISM; ORAL POETRY; PRIMITIVISM; READER-RESPONSE CRITICISM; RELIGION AND POETRY.

J. G. Frazer, *The Golden Bough*, 3d ed., 12 v. (1911–15); H. Werner, *Die Ursprünge der Lyrik* (1924)—still very good; H. M. and N. K. Chadwick, *The Growth of Lit.*, 3 v. (1932–40); R. Underhill, *Singing of Power: The Song Magic of the Papago Indians in Southern Arizona* (1938); M. Artrov, *The Winged Serpent* (1946); C. G. Jung, *Aion* (1951); D. Whitelock, *The Audience of Beowulf* (1951); H. M. Block, "Cultural A. and Contemp. Lit. Crit.," *JAAC* 11 (1952); C. J. Geertz, *Religious Belief and Economic Behaviour in a Central Javanese Town* (1955); J. Campbell, *The Hero with a Thousand Faces* (1956); Frye; E. Grassi, *Kunst und Mythos* (1957); M. Eliade, *Rites and Symbols of Initiation* (1958); Lord; C. M. Bowra, *Primitive Song* (1962); R. Jakobson and C. Lévi-Strauss, "*Les Chats* de Charles Baudelaire," *L'Homme* 2 (1962, rpt. in Jakobson, v. 3); M. Riffaterre, "Describing Poetic

Structures: Two Approaches to Baudelaire's *Les Chats*," *YFS* 36–37 (1966); *Die Eröffnung des Zugangs zum Mythos*, ed. K. Kerényi (1967); C. Lévi-Strauss, *Mythologies*, 3 v. (1964–68); P. Wheelwright, *The Burning Fountain*, 2d ed. (1968); G. Durand, *Les Structures anthropologigues de l'imagination* (1969); W. Muschg, *Die dichterische Phantasie* (1969); R. Finnegan, *Oral Lit. in Africa* (1970), *Oral Poetry* (1977); Parry; *Mythology*, ed. P. Miranda (1972); *The Scapegoat*, ed. J. B. Vickery and J. M. Sellery (1972); L. Benois, *Signes, Symbols et Mythes* (1975); Culler, ch. 2; B. A. Rosenberg, "Folklore Methodology and Med. Lit.," *JFI* 13 (1976), "Lit. and Folklore," *Interrelations of Lit.*, ed. J. P. Barricelli and J. Gibaldi (1982); A. Welsh, *Roots of Lyric* (1978); D. E. Bynum, *Serbo-Croatian Heroic Songs*, 14 v. (1979); W. E. Mühlmann, *Pfade in die Weltliteratur* (1984); A. Bewell, *Wordsworth and the Enlightenment* (1989); W. Iser, *Prospecting* (1989); *Modernist A.: From Field Work to Text*, ed. M. Manganaro (1990); *The Cambridge Ritualists Reconsidered*, ed. W. M. Calder III (1991).   J.P.S.

ANTICLIMAX is a term apparently first used by Dr. Johnson, quoting Addison; Johnson defines it as "a sentence in which the last part expresses something lower than the first" (*Dictionary* [1755]). "Lower" in this context concerns the ideas or objects referred to and, as such, restricts the phenomenon to *semantic* a., frequently quoted examples of which include Pope's series of a. from *The Rape of the Lock*: "Or stain her Honor, or her new Brocade," "Or lose her heart, or necklace, at a ball." *Syntactic* a. would include sentences, lines of verse, or propositions which, after a series of elements of increasing length, suddenly introduce in the final position a considerably shorter syntagm, e.g. "Alfred de Musset, charming, likeable, subtle, graceful, delicate, exquisite, small" (Victor Hugo). When used to designate an ineptly expressed idea meant to be superlatively grandiose or pathetic, a. becomes synonymous with the rhetorical figure *bathos* (q.v.). Similarly bathetic is a. used for a deliberately ironic letdown, as in various absurd similes in Henry Fielding's burlesque of Elizabethan and Restoration tragedy (King Arthur is speaking to his queen, Dollalola): "Whence flow those Tears fast down thy blubber'd Cheeks, / Like a swoln Gutter, gushing through the Streets?" (*The Tragedy of Tragedies* [1731] 1.2.6–7); or Lord Grizzle's impassioned address to the Princess Huncamunca: "Oh! Huncamunca, Huncamunca, Oh! / Thy pouting Breasts, like Kettledrums of Brass, / Beat everlasting loud Alarms of Joy" (2.5.1–3). The effect of a. in all forms is almost invariably comic.—C. Perelman and L. Olbrechts-Tyteca, *The New Rhet.* (tr. 1969), s.v. *gradatio*; Group Mu.   H.B.; A.W.H.

ANTIMASQUE. See MASQUE.

ANTIMETABOLE (Gr. "transposition"). A species

of chiasmus (q.v.), or word repetition in reverse. The term is apparently first recorded in Quintilian (*Institutio oratoria* [1st c. A.D.] 9.3.85), who defines it merely as a figure of words "repeated with variation in case or tense" (others would call this *polyptoton* [q.v.]), but illustrates with examples in which two words are later repeated in reverse order, e.g. "non ut edam vivo, sed ut vivam edo" ; it is specifically this symmetrical *abba* pattern of word repetition that the term is most often made to designate by later rhetoricians (e.g. John Smith, *The Mysterie of Rhetorique Unvailed* [1657]). Examples of such specifically verbal chiasmus in Eng. poetry can be seen in the final line of Shakespeare's Sonnet 154, "Love's fire heats water, water cools not love," and in Hamlet's "What's Hecuba to him, or he to Hecuba?" (2.2.559). All in all, it would seem better to use the term "chiasmus" for the genus of reversal figures, whether of sound, syntax, or meaning, without necessarily involving specific word repetition, and restrict *a.* to the narrower meaning of a single reversed word pair.—A. Quinn, *Figures of Speech* (1982); B. Vickers, *In Defence of Rhet.* (1988), *Cl. Rhet. in Eng. Poetry*, 2d ed. (1989); Corbett. T.V.F.B.; A.W.H.

ANTISPAST. The metrical sequence ᴗ – – ᴗ , used by ancient Gr. metrists (Hephestion, *Enchiridion* 10) for the analysis of Aeolic (q.v.) meters and viewed by some moderns (e.g. Koster) as an authentic foot, but largely abandoned by most others except to describe a word shape of that pattern.—P. Shorey, "Choriambic Dimeter and the Rehabilitation of the A.," *TAPA* 38 (1907); West. T.V.F.B.

ANTISTROPHE (Gr. "counterturning"). (1) In Cl. prosody, the second part of the regular ode (q.v.) in Gr. choral dance and poetry. The a. follows the first part, the "strophe" (q.v.), and is in turn followed by the third and concluding section, the "epode" (q.v.). The a. corresponds to the strophe exactly in meter, while the epode does not, giving a double-triple *aab* structure that is replicated in several other major verseforms (see CANZONE). (2) In Cl. rhet., the repetition of words in reversed order, e.g. "the master of the servant and the servant of the master" (cf. CHIASMUS). A. is also occasionally used as a term for repetition of a word at the end of successive phrases or clauses, but the preferable term is *epistrophe* (q.v.). R.A.H.; T.V.F.B.

ANTITHESIS, *antitheton* (Gr. "opposition"; Lat. *contentio*). The juxtaposition of contraries: the contrast of ideas, sharpened or pointed up by the use of words of opposite or conspicuously different meaning in contiguous or parallel phrases or clauses. A. is a form of expression recommended as satisfying by Aristotle "because contraries are easily understood and even more so when placed side by side, and also because a. resembles a syllogism, for it is by putting opposing conclusions side by side that you refute one of them" (*Rhetoric* 3.9.8). The anonymous *Rhetorica ad Alexandrum* (3d. c. B.C., ch. 26) observes that a. may oppose words or ideas or both, and later authorities likewise stress the clarity and force that an a. may impart to an idea (e.g. *Rhetorica ad Herennium* [1st c. B.C.], 4.15.21; Johannes Susenbrotus [1541], s.v. *contentio*).

A. is one of the two or three fundamental strategies of biblical parallelism (q.v.) first defined by Bishop Lowth (1753) and is fairly frequent in OE poetry. In both these trads., as in nearly all others, a. achieves heightened effect when confined to the two halves of a hemistichic line or two lines of a couplet, securing thereby the reinforcement of meter. A. was cultivated by the Cl. poets, and while these poets sometimes contrive a strict balance of form (the figure of *parison* [see ISOCOLON] in cl. rhet.) or a complex opposition of idea, e.g. "He aims to fetch not smoke from a flash, but light from smoke" (Horace, *Ars poetica* 142–43), this kind of ingenuity is even more characteristic of the Eng. and Fr. poets of the 17th and 18th cs., e.g. "I would and would not, I am on fire yet dare not" (Corneille, *Cinna* [1640] 1.2.122). A. Albalat once declared a. to be "the generating principle of half of Fr. lit., from Montaigne to Hugo"; certainly it is the predominant figure in the romantic poetry of Victor Hugo.

In Eng. poetry, Shakespeare uses a. 209 times in the *Sonnets*, i.e. about once per sonnet, both a. of content and of form (syntax); he also experiments with double a. regularly (e.g. 27.12) and at least once with triple (11.5). He particularly exploits a. in series, to develop the (Petrarchan) contrariety of emotional conflict (94, 119, 129, 150): love–hate, truth–falsity, beauty–ugliness, fertility–sterility. But it is the heroic couplet (q.v.), which emerged in the course of the 17th c. to become the preferred meter of the Restoration and 18th-c. poets, that offered nearly the ideal medium for that balanced, concise, antithetical expression, serious and witty alike, which is the major characteristic of neoclassical style. In Dryden and Pope it becomes an inestimable device for the display of satirical wit: "Thus wicked but in will, of means bereft, / He left not faction, but of that was left" (Dryden, *Absalom and Achitophel* ll.567–68); "It is the slaver kills, and not the bite" (Pope, *Epistle to Dr. Arbuthnot* 1.106); "Be not the first by whom the new are tried, / Nor yet the last to lay the old aside" (*Essay on Crit.* 2.335–36). In contemp. writing a. continues to be used to achieve effects, as for example in Eliot: "We are the hollow men / We are the stuffed men" ("The Hollow Men").

The antitheses quoted above are among the many forms of expression that exhibit two or more figures of speech as these were defined in cl. rhet. and may be labelled with one term or another according to the particular feature to be distinguished. Thus the second line of the quotation from Dryden exhibits *chiasmus, epanalepsis,* and *isocolon* (qq.v.). If the contrastive members of the a. are set in adjoining clauses which are not parallel but rather contrastive, syntactically, the figure is termed *syncrisis.* A. combined with chiasmus may be seen in the old definition of the scholar: "one who knows something about everything and everything about something." More recently, Group Mu describes a. as a metalogism of addition, which asserts both "X" and "X is not non-X." Quinn puts this similarly: "rather than saying something and then repeating it in other words, you both deny its contrary and assert it," so that "you have said the thing in two different ways." A. thus offers "the advantage of giving a sense of completeness with only two items" (67). See also EPIGRAM; OXYMORON.

A. Albalat, *La Formation du style par l'assimilation des auteurs* (1921); P. Beyer, "Antithese," *Reallexikon*; Sr. M. Joseph, *Shakespeare's Use of the Arts of Lang.* (1947); A. Kibédi-Varga, *Les Constantes du poème* (1963); G. K. Spring, "An Analysis of A. as a Basis of Epic Rhetorical Patterns," *DAI* 26 (1966): 6030; M. Kallich, "Balance and A. in Pope's *Essay on Crit.*," *TSL* 12 (1967); C. Perelman and L. Olbrechts-Tyteca, *The New Rhet.* (tr. 1969); Lausberg; Sr. M. M. Holloway, "Hopkins' Theory of 'Antithetical Parallelism,'" *HQ* 1 (1974); M. Isnard, "Antithese et oxymoron chez Wordsworth," *Rhétorique et communication* (1979); R. F. Gleckner, "Antithetical Structure in Blake's *Poetical Sketches*," *SIR* 20 (1981); A. Quinn, *Figures of Speech* (1982); Group Mu 141–42; Corbett 429–30.

T.V.F.B.; A.W.H.

ANTITHETICAL CRITICISM. See INFLUENCE.

ANTODE. See PARABASIS.

ANTONOMASIA (Gr. "naming instead"). A figure in which an epithet or appellative or descriptive phrase is substituted for a proper name (e.g. "The Bard" for Shakespeare; "It was visitors' day at the vinegar works / In Tenderloin Town," [W. H. Auden, "For the Time Being"]), or, conversely, in which a proper name is substituted for an individual, a class, or type ("blonde Venus" for a beautiful woman; "the Eng. Diana" for Queen Elizabeth; "Some mute, inglorious Milton here may rest" [Gray, *Elegy Written in a Country Churchyard*]). Similar to the first form above is *periphrasis* (q.v.). Group Mu (101–3), however, identifies the two types, respectively, as "particularizing" and "generalizing" varieties of synecdoche (q.v.).

Quintilian (*Institutio oratoria* 8.6.29) also holds that a., which is very common in poetry but less so in oratory, may be accomplished in two ways—by substitution of epithets for names (such as "Pelides" [that is, son of Peleus] for Achilles) and by substitution of the most striking characteristic of an individual for her or his name ("Divum pater atque hominum rex" [Father of gods and king of men; Virgil, *Aeneid* 1.65]). To these he adds a third type, wherein acts may indicate the individual; this, however, may be a spurious emendation. He too points to the relation of a. to synechdoche. Puttenham (*Arte of Eng. Poesie* [1589]) distinguishes between *epitheton* ("fierce Achilles," "wise Nestor"), where the name and epithet both appear, and a., use of the one for the other.—Morier; Lausberg; Group Mu.

R.O.E.; T.V.F.B.

ANXIETY. See INFLUENCE.

APHAERESIS (Gr. "a taking away"). In prosody the technical term for one form of elision, namely omission of a word-initial syllable, esp. a vowel, e.g. *'gainst* for *against, mid* for *amid, 'neath* for *beneath.* Often the following consonant then clusters with the succeeding word, e.g. *'tis* for *it is, 'twere* for *it were.* An iambic word or phrase thereby becomes a stressed monosyllable. In Gr. poetry, the suppression of an initial short "e" following a word ending in a long vowel or diphthong. The Lat. term for this phenomenon is *prodelision*: when a Lat. word ending in a vowel or a vowel followed only by *m* comes before *es* or *est*, the second vowel is "squeezed out," as in Virgil's "Usque adeone mori miserum est? vos a mihi Manes" (*Aeneid* 12.646). See ELISION; METRICAL TREATMENT OF SYLLABLES.

T.V.F.B.; R.A.H.

APHORISM. See EPIGRAM.

APOCOPE (Gr. "a cutting off"). In prosody the technical term for one form of elision, namely loss of a word-final syllable or vowel, e.g. *eve* or *even* for *evening.* Often the apocopated word then fuses with the one following, e.g. "th'Empyrean" for "the Empyrean," "th'army," etc., thereby avoiding *hiatus* (q.v.). A. is a common linguistic process. See ELISION; METRICAL TREATMENT OF SYLLABLES.— T. Sasaki, "A. in Mod. Eng. Verse." *SEL* (Tokyo) 13 (1933); Sr. M. Joseph, *Shakespeare's Use of the Arts of Lang.* (1947), 52, 294.

T.V.F.B.

APOLLONIAN-DIONYSIAN. An antinomy prefigured in certain writings of Ger. romanticism, esp. by Schlegel, Hölderlin, Schelling, and others, but made prominent and given broader cultural meaning (in the sense of conflicting world views and artistic drives) by Friedrich Nietzsche in *The Birth of Tragedy out of the Spirit of Music* (1871). Nietzsche describes the A. world as that of dreams, poetic inspiration, beautiful illusion, form, individuality, light, and human measurement, and altogether as a joyous experience instilling the desire for continual repetition. The D. world, by contrast, is one of intoxication, of an altogether gruesome and crushing experience of enormous dimensions into which we are nevertheless drawn with instinctive desire. The A. experience is so called after the Delphic god of order, form, and distance, whereas the D. mode takes its name from the Thracian god of wine, sexual proliferation, ecstasy, and all that ecstasy entails: joy and pain. In the arts the A. finds its purest expression in the plastic arts and in epic poetry, whereas music and dithyrambic chorus are the most genuine expressions of D. feeling. In reality, however, the A. and D. elements always fuse in art, and a pure embodiment of the one or the other tends to dissolution and extinction.

From this point of view, the A. constitutes the external structure of a work, the D. its inner motivation. This can be seen in Gr. tragedy, in which dialogue, plot, and characterization are the A. structure, while the chorus and its message in rhythmic, musical expression form the D. counterparts. From the point of view of cultural hist., Nietzsche attempted to level the artistic structure of A. culture in Greece stone by stone until its D. foundations became visible. In this attempt he opposed the dominant interp. of the Gr. world given by Winckelmann, Goethe, and Ger. Classicism as a joyous, serene, and artful world of beautiful forms, and pointed instead to an underlying dark and emotional experience. He maintained that this D. experience was in fact primary and that the A. world of art was created by the Greeks in order to withstand, master, and subdue the destructive D. drive. From here he developed the more general conviction that our experience of the world in general is dominated by D. forces and that existence can be tolerated only if these are sublimated, transformed into aesthetic phenomena.

Nietzsche discovered varying degrees of balance between these two principles in the Gr. tragedians. Aeschylus represented the balance in paradigmatic fashion; in Sophocles, the dialogic elements became dominant; and in Euripides, Gr. drama lost its D. basis and turned more and more into a rhetorical, rational exercise. This change in the devel. of tragedy was accompanied by a more general tendency toward rationalism in Cl. Greece. Socrates appears in Nietzsche's speculations as the originator of a rationalistic style of thinking in the West guided by a belief in the almightyness of reason until Kant through his *Critique of Reason* and Schopenhauer through his *The World as Will and Representation* set a limit to the domination of reason. A new manifestation of the D. principle came forth with the "musical drama" shaped by Richard Wagner's *Gesamtkunstwerk*. From this, Nietzsche expected a renewal of intellectual culture in the West through the renewed influence of the D. Later, however, he became severely critical of these expectations and condemned them as "romantic." More and more, the original interaction of the A. and D. disappears from Nietzsche's later writings for the sake of an emphasis on the D. principle as such, given its most succinct formulation in *Twilight of the Idols*. Nietzsche's A.-D. antinomy was of considerable influence upon subsequent Classical studies as

well as poetics, influencing a great variety of modern poets such as the Fr. and Rus. symbolists, the school of expressionism (q.v.), Rainer Maria Rilke, Stefan George, Thomas Mann, and D. H. Lawrence.

A. H. J. Knight, *"Dionysius" in Some Aspects of the Life and Work of Nietzsche* (1933); O. Klein, *Das Apollinische und Dionysische bei Nietzsche und Schelling* (1935); C. S. Faulk, "The A. and D. Modes in Lyric Poetry and Their Devel. in the Poetry of W. B. Yeats and Dylan Thomas," *DAI* 24 (1964): 4173; G. F. Else, *The Origin and Early Form of Gr. Tragedy* (1965); M. L. Baeumler, "Die zeitgeschichtliche Funktion des dionysischen Topos in der romantischen Dichtung," *Gestaltungsgesch. und Gesellschaftsgesch.*, ed. H. Kreuzer and K. Hamburger (1969), "Zur Psychologie des Dionysischen in der Literaturwissenschaft," *Psychologie in der Literaturwissenschaft*, ed. W. Paulsen (1971), "Das moderne Phänomen des Dionysischen und seine Entdeckung durch Nietzsche," *Nietzsche-Studien* 6 (1977); E. Behler, "Die Auffassung des Dionysischen durch die Brüder Schlegel und Nietzsche," *Nietzsche-Studien* 12 (1983). E.H.B.

APORIA. See DECONSTRUCTION; INFLUENCE.

APOSIOPESIS (Gr. "a becoming silent"). A speaker's abrupt halt midway in a sentence, accountable to his being too excited or distraught to give further articulation to his thought (so Quintilian, *Institutio oratoria* 9.2.54); less commonly, the speaker thinking to impress his addressee the more with the vague hint of an idea too awesome to be put into words (so Demetrius, *On Style* 2.103). These two motives are not always distinguishable in given examples, e.g. Neptune's threat (*Aeneid* 1.133–35) of punishment to the winds: "How dare ye, ye winds, to mingle the heavens and the earth and raise such a tumult without my leave? You I will—but first I must quiet the waves"; or King Lear's threat of vengeance on his wicked daughters: "I will have revenges on you both / That all the world shall—I will do such things—" (2.4.282–83). If at the point of breaking off the speaker actually verbalizes the failure of words to adequately convey the emotion, the figure becomes *adynaton* (q.v.). Related is the figure *paraposiopesis*, interrupting the sentence with an expression of emotion; and to *anacoluthon* (q.v.), ending the sentence with a different construction than that with which it began.

According to the Gr. rhetorician Alexander (*Peri schematon* [2d c. A.D.]), a. is always followed by the speaker's explanation that she is passing over in silence matters either already known to the addressee or too sordid to be mentioned; but Quintilian remarks that it is sometimes used as a merely transitional device, where the speaker wishes to introduce a digression or announce an impromptu change in the planned conduct of her argument, such as the circumstances of the moment might suggest (9.2.55–57).

Pope defined a. as an "excellent figure for the ignorant, as '*What shall I say?*' When one has nothing to say; or '*I can no more*' when one really can do more: expressions which the gentle reader is so good as never to take in earnest" (*Peri bathous* [1727]). Group Mu points out that some as. "have the force of 'etc.,'" while others, "where conjecture is enjoined about the suppressed sequence, may be interpreted as a refusal to proceed"; they "refuse metabole, and precisely for this reason they are metaboles that economize the code . . . as a way of indicating its insufficiencies, of showing that it offers nothing or is, in fact, even a danger" (139). A. should not be confused with *paralipsis*, the device whereby a speaker pretends not to discuss a subject while actually doing so.—Lausberg; Group Mu; A. Quinn, *Figures of Speech* (1982); B. Vickers, *In Defence of Rhet.* (1988).
H.B.; A.W.H.

APOSTROPHE (Gr. "to turn away"). A figure of speech which consists of addressing an absent or dead person, a thing, or an abstract idea as if it were alive or present. Examples include Virgil's "Quid non mortalia pectora cogis, / auri sacra fames!" (*Aeneid* 3.56); Dante's "Ahi, serva Italia, di dolore ostello" (*Purgatorio* 6.76); Shakespeare's "O judgment! thou art fled to brutish beasts" (*Julius Caesar* 3.2.106); Wordsworth's "Milton! thou should'st be living at this hour" ("London, 1802"); and Tennyson's "Ring out, wild bells" (*In Memoriam* 106). The traditional epic invocation of the Muse (q.v.) is an a. A. is particularly useful in sonnet sequences (q.v.) for addresses to the beloved, to other parties, and to abstractions. Fully 134 of Shakespeare's 154 sonnets contain an a., 100 of which are direct addresses (to the lady, the friend); these are almost always to a specific person, and only very rarely to a personified abstraction, e.g. Time (only twice), Love (thrice), or the Muse (twice). The term originally referred to any abrupt "turning away" from the normal audience to address a different or more specific audience, whether present or absent (Quintilian, *Institutio oratoria* 4.1.63–70, 9.3.24). Corbett reminds us that a. is a figure of *pathos*, i.e. "calculated to work directly on the emotions" (460), but other critics have seen it as a metapoetic device by means of which a speaker "addresses" his own utterance. Shelley's "Ode to a Skylark" begins with the conventional kind of a.: "Hail to thee, blithe spirit"; Robert Burns' "Address to the Unco Guid," on the other hand, sarcastically apostrophizes the speaker's moral opponents: "O ye wha are sae guid yoursel, / Sae pious and sae holy" (1–2). The a. in Charles Calverley's "Ballad" parodies the device's artificiality: "O Beer. O Hodgson, Guinness, Allsop, Bass. / Names that should be on every infant's tongue." Ezra Pound uses a. metapoetically in "Coda": "O my songs, / Why do you look so eagerly and so curiously into people's faces, / Will you find

your lost dead among them?" Culler attempts to identify a. "with lyric itself" in order to deconstruct the notion of lyric timelessness, seeing the lyric as *écriture*, though this approach ignores the explicit emphasis on orality in Quintilian and others.—Sr. M. Joseph, *Shakespeare's Use of the Arts of Lang.* (1947), 246–47; C. Perelman and L. Olbrechts-Tyteca, *The New Rhet.* (tr. 1969); M. R. McKay, "Shakespeare's Use of the A.," *DAI* 30 (1970): 4459A; J. T. Braun, *The Apostrophic Gesture* (1971); Lausberg; J. Culler, "A.," *The Pursuit of Signs* (1981), ch. 7; L. M. Findlay, "Culler and Byron on A. and Lyric Time," *SiR* 24 (1985); P. Lang, *The Apostrophic Moment in 19th- and 20th-C. Ger. Lyric Poetry* (1988); Corbett.   L.P.; A.W.H.; T.V.F.B.

ARABIC POETICS.

    I. CLASSICAL
    II. MODERN

I. CLASSICAL. The first Ar. works on poetics were composed at the end of the 9th and beginning of the 10th cs. A.D. Four different groups of scholars were in varying degree instrumental in shaping this new literary genre: the experts on ancient poetry, the poets and critics of modern poetry (for ancient vs. modern, see second following paragraph below), the Koranic scholars, and the (Aristotelian) logicians. Earlier, the pre-Islamic poets very likely had had their professional lang. for technical features of their poetry, and subsequently there are reports about comparative evaluation of poets, but none of this amounts to an explicit *ars poetica*.

In the field of poetry two developments are noteworthy. Ancient, i.e. pre- and early Islamic, poetry became canonized as a corpus of classical texts. This meant, first and foremost, that ancient poetry was considered a repository of correct and authoritative speech. As such, it became the domain of the philologists, who, around the middle of the 8th c., began to collect the extant poetry into *dīwāns* and anthologies; to these they later added interlinear glosses on lexical and grammatical matters. But once the task of editing and writing commentaries had been mostly achieved, we do find one book which may be called a grammarian's poetics: the *Qawāʿid al-shiʿr* (Foundations of Poetry) ascribed to the Kufan grammarian Thaʿlab (d. 291/904 [dates refer to the Muslim and the Christian eras, respectively]). This is a logically arranged collection of technical terms often provided with definitions and always exemplified with a number of *shawāhid* ("evidentiary verses"). Significantly, it starts with an enumeration of four basic types of sentences (command, prohibition, report, question) which are introduced as the "foundations of poetry," and it ends with a verse typology (based on the syntactic independence or interdependence of the two hemistichs of the line) in which the highest aesthetic value is accorded those lines that have two independently meaningful hemistichs. This molecularistic approach to the study and evaluation of poetry prevails in most of the theoretical lit.

The second notable event which had a decisive (indeed greater) effect on the devel. of poetics and literary theory was the rise, around the middle of the 8th c., of a new school of poetry, that of the *muḥdathūn* ("moderns"). By contrasting them with their forebears, the *qudamāʾ* ("ancients"), critics and theorists became aware of some of the basic dichotomies in poetry. It should be noted, however, that the model character of ancient poetry was never seriously challenged, which meant that the innovations of the moderns pushed their poetry toward mannerism, and poetry increasingly revolved around earlier poetry. The critical discussion focused on a phenomenon called *badīʿ*—literally, "new, original, newly invented." The earliest attestations of the word suggest that it was originally used to refer to a special type of metaphor (imaginary ascriptions such as "the *claws* of death") which played an important role in the poetic technique of the moderns, who created some outrageous—and severely criticized—specimens (e.g. "the eyes of religion were cooled," meaning that the Islamic armies were victorious). However, the term soon spread to other figures of speech. The poet Ibn al-Muʿtazz (d. 296/908), who devoted the first monograph to this topic, *Kitāb al-Badīʿ* (The Book of the Novel [Style]), reckoned five figures to be covered by the term—metaphors of the kind just mentioned, paronomasia, antithesis (qq.v.), epanalepsis, and playful dialectics imitating theological jargon—but he does not insist on these, leaving it to the reader to choose. The main goal of his book is to demonstrate that the *badīʿ* phenomena are not new but can be found already in ancient poetry as well as in the Qurʾān (Koran) and in wisdom aphorisms; it is only their exaggerated use that is truly new.

Coming from one of the foremost poets of his time, this line of argument obviously served to legitimize the use of *badīʿ*. Ibn al-Muʿtazz's book became influential in several ways: (a) following the title of his book, the discipline dealing with rhetorical figures was named "the science of *badīʿ*"; (b) the discovery of legitimizing precedent in ancient texts, esp. the Qurʾān, became commonplace, and as a result the system of the rhetorical figures came to be considered an integral and static part of the lang.: their proliferation in later rhetorical works was thus thought to be due to closer analysis rather than new invention; (c) the emphasis on figures of speech as the central concern of literary theory originated here; and (d) the difference between poetry and prose in most respects save the purely formal one was considered unimportant.

The result of factor (d) in particular meant that, although works on literary theory—mostly rhetorical in outlook—continued to be produced, works

on poetics proper tended to become the exception. Two of them were composed by younger contemporaries of Ibn al-Muʿtazz, one by the poet Ibn Ṭabāṭabā (d. 322/934) entitled *ʿIyār al-shiʿr* (The Standard of Poetry), the other by the state scribe and logician Qudāma ibn Jaʿfar (d. after 320/932). Ibn Ṭabāṭabā, though not using the word *badīʿ* in its technical sense, is well aware of the predicament of the moderns, who can no longer simply utter truths, as did the ancients, but have to display their wits in a subtle treatment of well-known motifs. He is also remarkable for giving a step-by-step description of the production of a poem; this is quite rare because works on poetics usually offer theories of poetic criticism rather than *artes poeticae* in the strict sense.

This characterization is esp. true of Qudāma's poetics, which the author describes as the first book on the "science of the good and the bad in poetry" and aptly entitles *Naqd al-shiʿr* (The Assaying of Poetry). His work is at the same time the first representative of the third approach to literary theory (besides the grammatical and the poetic already mentioned), viz., that of the logician in the Aristotelian trad. This characterization refers, however, less to the content than to the structure and presentation of his work: he starts with a definition ("Poetry is metrical, rhymed utterance pointing to a meaning") which yields the four constitutive elements, meter, rhyme, wording, and meaning; he then discusses first the good qualities of these elements and their combinations, followed by the bad. Although Qudāma was much quoted by later authors, his "foreign" method did not find followers.

The controversies about the modern poets' use of *badīʿ*, though reflected in theory, can more accurately be gauged from works of applied crit. such as the books devoted to the controversial "rhetorical" poets Abū Tammām (d. 231/845) and al-Mutanabbī (d. 354/965). The major topics that emerge are the following: (1) The relationship between *ṭabʿ* ("natural talent") and *ṣanʿa* ("artful or artificial crafting"). The latter term came to mean the application of *badīʿ* to the motif at hand. According to taste and predilection, some considered this *takalluf* (constraint, artificiality), while others pointed to the element of *taʿjīb* (causing amazement) which it imparted to well-known motifs. Given the general drift towards mannerism, this was a much sought-after effect. (2) The role of *lafẓ* (wording) vs. *maʿnā* (meaning) in poetry. Already at the end of the 8th c. a consensus had been reached that poetry was to be judged by its wording, since the meaning was nothing but the material to be shaped. Some authorities are said to have given precedence to the meaning, but on closer inspection it appears that they intended the *maʿnā al-ṣanʿa* (the special meaning created by the application of a figure of speech; this comes close to the "conceit" [q.v.] in Western mannerist poetry [see MANNERISM]) and thus did not undermine the priority of the wording. (3) The relationship between poetry and reality, whether *ṣidq* (truth) or *kadhib* (falsehood). Basically poetry is presumed to depict reality mimetically. Obvious "falsehoods" such as imaginary metaphors and hyperboles therefore tended to provoke objections on the part of the critics. Such figures became so predominant in later Abbasid poetry, however, that some theorists (Ibn Fāris, Ibn Ḥazm) posited falsehood as one of the constituent elements of poetry. (4) The question of *sariqa* (plagiarism). Although this word means "theft" and originally denoted flagrant literary larceny, with the increasing tendency toward mannerism in modern poetry, *sariqa* became a way of life, and the disreputable connotation of the term gave way to the more neutral one of "taking over" (an earlier motif); critics even began to talk of "good *sariqas*." Taking over an earlier poet's motif and improving upon it, mostly by the application of *badīʿ*, constituted an *istinqāq* ("better claim" [to that motif]), for which the poet earned high praise.

Ar. p., fostered by the rise of modern poetry, soon experienced something like arrested growth. The work of the Koranic scholar and grammarian al-Rummānī (d. 384/994), *al-Nukat fī iʿjāz al-Qurʾān* (Thoughtful Remarks on the Inimitability of the Qurʾān), in which he undertook to prove this dogma on the basis of the Qurʾān's *balāgha* (eloquence), soon began to influence works on poetics and rhetorical figures. The first major compilation which resulted, the *Kitāb al-Ṣināʿatayn* (Book of the Two Crafts [i.e. Poetry and Prose]) by Abū Hilāl al-ʿAskarī (d. 395/1004), expressly mentions proving the inimitability of the Qurʾān as its main goal and makes extensive use of al-Rummānī's work. The confluence of the two different technical terminologies, "Koranic" and "poetic," at first created a notable confusion which was only gradually eliminated, esp. by the greatest of all Ar. literary theorists, ʿAbd al-Qāhir al-Jurjānī (d. 471/1078). In his *Asrār al-balāgha* (The Mysteries of Eloquence), he tried to establish a clear and unambiguous taxonomy for the theory of imagery (simile, analogy, metaphor based on simile, metaphor based on analogy), and for the first time he finds, designates, and describes the phenomenon of *takhyīl* ("fantastic interpretation," i.e. inventing imaginary causes, effects, and proofs, often on the basis of metaphors taken literally)— which is so characteristic of later Abbasid poetry. Although not a comprehensive work on poetics, the "Mysteries" certainly is the most sustained effort to reach to the core of Ar. poetry.

Al-Jurjānī's books, the one just mentioned and his *Dalāʾil al-iʿjāz* (Signs for the Inimitability), were later reworked into parts of the scholastic *ʿilm al-balāgha* ("science of eloquence") which, from the 13th c. on, dominated the teaching of rhetoric—consisting of stylistics, theory of imagery, and figures of speech—in the institutions of higher

learning. Poetics was thus incorporated into a discipline that served the religious purpose of demonstrating the inimitability of the Qurʾān, whence it ceased to exist in its own right.

Some theoretical and critical works were produced outside the Koranic trad. One of them, *al-ʿUmda* (The Pillar), by the poet Ibn Rashīq (d. 456/1063 or later), deserves to be cited as a comprehensive handbook for poets that contains well-informed accounts of all the major topics in poetics mentioned above.

I. Goldziher, "Alte und neue Poesie im Urtheile der arabischen Kritiker," *Abhandlungen zur arabischen Philologie* 1 (1896, rpt. 1982), ch. 2; G. E. von Grunebaum, "Ar. Lit. Crit. in the 10th C. A.D.," *JAOS* 61 (1941), "The Concept of Plagiarism in Ar. Theory," *JNES* 3 (1944), ed., *A 10th-C. Document of Ar. Literary Theory and Crit.: The Sections on Poetry of al-Bâqillâni's Iʿjâz al-Qurʾân* (1950); A. Trabulsi, *La Critique poétique des arabes jusqu'au Ve siècle de l'Hégire (XIe siècle de J.-C.)* (1955); I. Y. Krachkovsky, "Deux Chapitres inédits de l'oeuvre de Kratchkovsky sur Ibn al-Muʿtazz," *Annales de l'Institut des Études Orientales* (Algiers) 20 (1962); W. Heinrichs, *Arabische Dichtung und griechische Poetik* (1969), "Literary Theory—The Problem of Its Efficiency," *Ar. Poetry—Theory and Devel.*, ed. G. E. Von Grunebaum (1973), *The Hand of the Northwind—Opinions on Metaphor and the Early Meaning of Istiʿâra in Ar. P.* (1977); I. ʿAbbās, *Taʾrīkh al-naqd al-adabī ʿind al-ʿarab* (1971); S. A. Bonebakker, *Materials for the Hist. of Ar. Rhet. from the Hilyat al-muḥa-dara of Ha-timi* (1975); J. E. Bencheikh, *Poétique arabe* (1975); V. Cantarino, *Ar. P. in the Golden Age* (1975)—anthol. in tr., with introductory essays often ignorant of earlier lit.; K. Abu Deeb, *Al-Jurjānī's Theory of Poetic Imagery* (1979); G. J. Van Gelder, *Beyond the Line—Cl. Ar. Literary Critics on the Coherence and Unity of the Poem* (1982); A. Arazi, "Une Épître d'Ibrāhīm ben Hilāl al-Ṣābī sur les genres littéraires," *Studies in Islamic Hist. and Civilization in Honour of David Ayalon*, ed. M. Sharon (1986). W.P.H.

II. MODERN. From the 13th to the 18th c., Ar. p. tended to reflect the priorities of the audience for the lit. of the period: the intellectual elite at the various centers of political authority. Elaborating on earlier developments in poetics, commentators and anthologizers placed primary emphasis on the formalities of rhetoric and the compilation of ever-expanding lists of poetic devices and themes. It was the task of pioneers in the 19th c., such as Ḥusayn al-Marṣafī (d. 1890), to revive interest in the great cl. works of poetics. However, such exercises in neoclassical revival gradually receded into the background, superseded by the increasing domination of Western literary genres and critical approaches.

From the first intimations of what has been termed "preromanticism" with poets such as Khalīl Muṭrān (1872-1949) Ar. poetry and p. has undergone what one critic has termed a series of "rapid chain explosions of European culture." The poetics of romanticism are reflected in works such as *Al-Ghurbāl* by Mīkhāʾīl Nuʿayma (b. 1889) and *Al-Dīwān* by two Egyptian critics, Al-ʿAqqād (d. 1964) and al-Māzinī (d. 1949). The application of Western critical approaches, predominantly Fr. and Eng., to the lit. is also evident in the writings of critics such as Ṭāhā Ḥusayn (d. 1973), Mārūn ʿAbbūd (d. 1962), and Muḥammad Mandūr (d. 1965).

Following the Second World War and the achievement of independence by many Arab nations, lit. of "commitment" (*iltizām*) becomes *de rigeur* and has been much reflected in critical writings. The Lebanese literary periodical *Al-Ādāb*, founded by Suhayl Idrīs in Beirut in 1953, had "commitment" as its major guiding force and continues to serve as a major conduit and catalyst for trends in modern Ar. p. In that role it has been joined by a number of other journals, most prominent among which is *Fuṣūl*, pub. in Cairo. More recently, growing interest in literary theory, linguistics, and folklore has led to significant changes in approach to the Ar. literary trad. as a whole. Numerous Western studies in semiotics, structuralism, and poststructuralism have been read by Arab critics either in the original or in the rapidly increasing library of such works in translation. The emergence of these new disciplines and approaches can be seen in the publication of critical and theoretical studies which not only reconsider the nature and precepts of the Ar. literary canon (e.g. in the realms of popular narrative and prosody), but also address genres from all periods of the trad. in entirely new ways. In a number of works, the major poet-critic Adūnīs (b. 1930) has devoted himself to a detailed investigation of the issue of modernity itself and the reinterpretation of the past. This process, at once highly controversial and stimulating, is having a profound effect on both the poetic trad. itself and on attitudes toward the adoption of various modes of interp.—D. Semah, *Four Mod. Egyptian Critics* (1974); Adūnīs, *Al-Thābit wa-al-mutaṇawwil*, 3 v. (1974–79), *Intro. to Ar. P.* (1985), tr. C. Cobham (1990); S. al-Jayyusi, *Trends and Movements in Mod. Ar. P.* (1977); I. J. Boullata, "Adūnīs: Revolt in Mod. Ar. P.," *Edebiyât* 2 (1977). R.M.A.A.

ARABIC POETRY.

    I. INTRODUCTION
    II. 6TH TO 13TH CENTURIES
    III. 13TH TO 18TH CENTURIES
    IV. 19TH AND 20TH CENTURIES

I. INTRODUCTION. Until relatively recently, poetry has served as the predominant mode of literary expression among those who speak and write in Ar. Poetry was, in the traditional phrase, "*dīwān al-ʿarab*," the register of the Arabs, and poets had and continue to have a particular status in their own community. The Ar. word for "poetry," *shiʿr*,

is derived from the verb denoting a special kind of knowledge which was believed in the earliest times to have magical or mantic properties. While poetry has afforded poets the opportunity for personal expression, it has been more often than not a *public* phenomenon, whether addressed to the tribe of ancient times, the patron during the predominance of the Caliphate and the many dynasties of the med. Islamic world, or the many political causes of the present-day Middle East.

Most histories of Ar. p. have adopted a dynastic approach based primarily on political and social devels., concentrating mainly on the poets, their role in society, and their themes. This approach serves to illustrate the close links between poetry and poetics on the one hand and divisions of the Islamic sciences on the other. However, it should be borne in mind that, while bibliographical sources provide evidence of the richness of the trad. available to us, they also make clear not only that large amounts of poetry are lost to us, but also that much more poetry remains unpublished and unassessed within the critical canon. Further, the hist. of Ar. p. has recently been undergoing a re-evaluation, based on two interlinked phenomena. First, Ar. p. itself has been going through a period of transformation and radical experimentation since the beginning of the 1950s: this process has led some critics to attempt a redefinition of what poetry is (or should be) and therefrom to initiate projects aimed at a reassessment of the corpus of cl. Ar. p. Second, critics have applied new ideas in analysis and theory—e.g. structuralism (q.v.), oral-formulaic and genre theories, and metrics—to the corpus of Ar. p.

II. 6TH TO 13TH CENTURIES. A. *The Beginnings: Oral Tradition.* What have been recorded as the beginnings of Ar. p. are versions of a poetic corpus that is already highly developed in the late 5th c. A.D. The trad. is an oral one, similar to that of the Homeric poems and Serbo-Croatian songs analyzed by Parry and Lord. Thus, each poem, or rather the differing versions of each poem, represent a single, isolated yet privileged point in a long process of devel. and transmission from poet to reciter (*rāwī*). Each poem would have been performed before an audience (perhaps accompanied by music or rhythmic beat) and transmitted through generations from one "singer of tales" to another.

B. *The Poet.* The ability to improvise was (and often still is) part of the craft of Arab poets. Many occasions would arise at which they would extemporize a poem or recite a work from memory. They were important members of the tribe, in effect propagandists, whose role was to extol the tribal virtues—bravery, loyalty, endurance, swiftness of vengeance—and to lampoon the lack of such virtues in the tribe's enemies. The various thematic "genres" used—eulogy, elegy, and satire—all concerned praise or its antithesis. The elegy (*rithāʾ*) provides some of the most moving examples of the poetic voice, as in the poems of al-Khansāʾ (d. ca. 644) for her brother, Ṣakhr, killed in tribal combat:

I was sleepless and I passed the night
　　keeping vigil, as if my eyes had
　　been anointed with pus, . . .
For I had heard—and it was not news
　　to rejoice me—one making a re-
　　port, who had come repeating
　　intelligence,
Saying, "Sakhr is dwelling there in a
　　tomb, struck to the ground beside
　　the grave, between certain stones."
　　　　　　　　　　(tr. A. J. Arberry)

The poet used the different genres to depict companionship, the benefits of tribal solidarity, the beauties of women, the qualities of animals, and the joys of wine. Part of this same environment, but from a totally different social perspective, were a number of vagabond (ṣuʿlūk) poets such as al-Shanfarā (d. ca. 525), his companion Thābit ibn Jābir (known by his nickname, "Taʾabbaṭa Sharran"—he who has put evil under his armpit), and ʿUrwa ibn al-Ward (d. ca. 594). Ostracized from tribal society, they and their peers wrote stirring odes about their ability to withstand prolonged isolation, hunger, and thirst and their feelings of affinity with the wilder animals of the desert, as in this extract from a poem by al-Shanfarā:

To me now, in your default, are com-
　　rades a wolf untired,
A sleek leopard, and a fell hyena with
　　shaggy mane.
True comrades, they ne'er let out the
　　secret in trust with them,
Nor basely forsake their friend because
　　he brought them bane.
　　　　　　　　　　(tr. R. A. Nicholson)

In contrast to this stark vision of life stands that of the courts of the Ghassanids, the tribe which served as a buffer between the Arabs and Byzantium, and the Lakhmids, who fulfilled the same function vis à vis Sasanid Iran from their center at al-Ḥīra (in present-day Iraq). To these courts would come not only tribal poets but also professional bards like Ṭarafa ibn al-ʿAbd (d. ca. 565) and Maymūn al-Aʿshā (d. 629) in search of patronage and reward for their eulogies.

C. *The Structure of the Poem.* The process of oral transmission and the later recording of poetry in written form have not preserved the stages in the early devel. of the Ar. poem. Thus we find examples of both the short, monothematic poem (*qiṭʿa*) and the multi-sectional, polythematic *qaṣīda* (q.v.). Several examples of the latter came to be highly valued, esp. by the early Muslim Caliphs and the ruling Arab aristocracy, which regarded these poems as a source and standard for the study and teaching of the cl. Ar. lang. Seven (and later ten) of the longer odes were gathered into what became the most famous collection of early Ar. p., the *muʿallaqāt*. The *muʿallaqa* of Imruʾ al-Qays (d. ca. 540) is the most famous poem in the collection and indeed probably in all of Ar. lit. Yet each *muʿallaqa* manages to reflect its poet's vision of life in pre-Islamic Arabia: that of Zuhayr ibn Abī Sulmā is placed within the context of settling a tribal dispute, while the ode of Labīd (d. ca. 662), with its elaborate animal imagery and concluding aphorisms, is virtually a hymn to tribal values.

Recent analyses of some examples of the pre-Islamic *qaṣīda* have challenged the received view that its structure is fragmented, a view canonized in part by the conservative critical trad. of ʿamūd al-shiʿr ("the essentials of poetry"). It is now suggested that the choice and ordering of the various segments of these poems reflect the poet's desire to illustrate by conjunction and opposition the glaring contrasts in community life, making these elaborate poems a public event of almost liturgical significance. Thus, the *nasīb* (erotic prelude) of many poems will often be placed within the context of the *aṭlāl*, the section describing the poet's arrival at a deserted encampment. The opening lines of the *muʿallaqa* of Imruʾ al-Qays are esp. famous: "Halt (you two) and let us weep for memory of a beloved and an abode / In the edge of the sand dune between ad-Dakhul and Hawmal." A transitional section describing a departure or desert journey allows the poet to give a description of his riding animal which is often elaborate and lengthy, and provides some of the most memorable lines from this corpus of poetry. From this interweaving of segments the poet will then turn—often by means of aphoristic sentiments—to the purpose of the poem: the bolstering of the community through praise of its virtues, criticism of contraventions of them, and sheer self-aggrandizement as a means of fostering tribal pride and solidarity.

D. *The Advent of Islam.* While the advent of Islam brought about radical changes in beliefs and customs in the society of the Arabian Peninsula, the poetic environment changed relatively little. Muḥammad himself was not averse to poetry, as sections of *Kitāb al-aghānī* make abundantly clear. Indeed, Ḥassān ibn Thābit (d. 673) is known as "the poet of the Prophet." His contemporary, Kaʿb ibn Zuhayr, the son of the famous pre-Islamic bard Zuhayr ibn Abī Sulmā, composed a famous poem addressed to Muḥammad which illustrates the continuation of the poetic trad. into the new social context; the poem is called *al-Burda* ("The Cloak"), since, upon hearing it, Muḥammad is alleged to have placed his cloak around the poet:

I was told that the Messenger of Allah
　　threatened me (with death), but
　　with the Messenger of Allah I have
　　hope of finding pardon.

Gently! mayst thou be guided by Him
who gave thee the gift of the Koran,
wherein are warnings and a plain
setting-out of the matter.
(tr. R. A. Nicholson)

The spirit of defiance in the face of imminent
danger and even death which characterizes much
pre-Islamic poetry is also to be found in the odes
of poets belonging to groups which broke away
from the incipient Muslim community on relig-
ious grounds and fought vigorously for their con-
ception of Islam. The poetry of the supporters of
the Kharijite cause, such as al-Ṭirimmāḥ (d. ca.
723), and of the Shīʿa, such as Al-Kumayt ibn Zayd
(d. 743), is esp. noteworthy in this regard. The
pre-Islamic penchant for satire of rivals and ene-
mies finds fertile ground in the tribal squabbles
which continue well into the period of the
Umayyads (660–750). In a series of increasingly
ribald satires (gathered into a collection known as
Al-Naqāʾiḍ), the poets Jarīr (d. 732) and Al-
Farazdaq (d. ca. 730), joined among others by the
Christian poet Al-Akhṭal (d. 710), followed the
pattern of earlier satirical poetry in both form and
imagery and adopted rhetorical strategies charac-
teristic of verbal dueling in the Arab world.

E. *The Emergence of New Genres.* The oral trans-
mission of poetry continued into the Islamic pe-
riod, insuring that the Arab poet's attachment to
many of the themes and images of the desert
lingered long after such environments were super-
seded by the emerging urban centers of the Mus-
lim community. Thus Dhū al-Rumma (d. 735) was
often referred to as "the last of the poets" because
he continued to use desert motifs in his poems a
century after the advent of Islam. Inevitably, how-
ever, the gradual process of change led to the
emergence of different priorities expressed in dif-
ferent ways. On the political level, the changes
were far-reaching. During the first century or so of
Islam, Muslim armies took the religion to the
borders of India in the East and across North
Africa to Spain in the West. The center of Caliphal
authority moved out of the Arabian Peninsula first
to Damascus under the Umayyads and then to the
newly founded city of Baghdad in 756 under the
Abbasids. Under the impetus of this vast exercise
in cultural assimilation, authors from different
areas of the Islamic world began to adapt the
traditional Ar. literary forms and to introduce new
themes and genres.

Various segments of the *qaṣida* gradually
evolved into distinct genres. The collected works
of poets composed during the first century of
Islam begin to contain separate sections devoted
to specific categories: hunt poems (*ṭardiyyāt*) and
wine poems (*khamriyyāt*)—both of these most no-
tably in the verse of Al-Ḥasan ibn Hāniʾ (d. ca.
810), usually known by his nickname, Abū Nuwās.
His wine poetry is noted not only for its disarming
lasciviousness but also for the way in which he

occasionally parodies the desert imagery of the
earlier poetry:

The lovelorn wretch stopped at a (de-
serted) camping-ground to
question it, and I stopped to inquire
after the local tavern.
May Allah not dry the eyes of him that
wept over stones, and may He not
ease the pain of him that yearns to
a tent-peg.
(tr. R. A. Nicholson)

The blind poet, Bashshār ibn Burd (d. 783),
displayed a similar impatience with Arabian con-
ventions, though in his case it is linked to a desire
to express pride in his own Persian ancestry. An-
other poet of the period, Abū al-Atāhiya (d. 828),
is primarily remembered for his moral and ascetic
poems (*zuhdiyyāt*).

One of the most remarkable devels. along these
lines is that of the love poem (*ghazal*, q.v.). Soon
after the advent of Islam, two distinct trends ap-
pear in the Arabian Peninsula. The first, emerging
from within the tribal poetic trad., placed the
aloof and imperious beloved on a pedestal while
the poet suffered the pangs of love from a dis-
tance, often leading to a love-death. This trad. is
termed ʿUdhrī after the Banū ʿUdhra tribe, noted
for having many such lovers, among whom was
Jamīl (d. 701), one of the most illustrious expo-
nents of ʿUdhrī poetry. Each of these love poets
also carried the name of his beloved: Jamīl, for
example, is Jamīl Buthayna, the beloved of
Buthayna; other poets of this type are Kuthayyir
ʿAzza (d. 723) and, most famous of all, Majnūn
Laylā. The other trad., sensual and self-centered,
developed in the cities of the Ḥijāz; it is usually
associated with its most famous exponent, ʿUmar
ibn Abī Rabīʿa (d. 719). With the gradual devel.
of the genre the two separate strands fused, as can
be seen in the works of poets such as ʿAbbās ibn
al-Aḥnaf (d. ca. 807) in the East and Ibn ʿAbd
Rabbihi (d. 940) in al-Andalus (as Islamic Spain
was known).

F. *The Badīʿ Style: Imagery and Rhetoric.* During
the Caliphate of ʿUthmān (d. 644), a generally
accepted version of the Qurʾān (Koran) was estab-
lished in writing, a process which set in motion
many intellectual currents later to have a pro-
found effect on poetry. Scholars in Kūfa and Baṣra
(both in present-day Iraq) began to prepare the
materials needed for authenticating the transmis-
sion of the Qurʾān, interpreting its text, and codi-
fying the Ar. lang. in which the sacred text pro-
claims itself to have been revealed. Anthols. of
poetry of different genres and from particular
tribes were made, a process which involved the
devel. of basic critical terms for the evaluation of
literary works. A philologist of Baṣra, Al-Khalīl Ibn
Aḥmad (d. 791), analysed the sounds and rhythms
of the earliest poetry and set down his results as a
set of meters which formed part of a definition of

poetry (as "rhymed and metered discourse") which was widely regarded as canonical up to the end of World War II (see ARABIC PROSODY). This philological activity was accompanied by a gradual shift away from the predominantly oral culture of pre-Islamic Arabia toward a society in which verbal art was committed to writing.

Within this environment of compilation, authentification, and analysis, there now emerges in Ar. p. *badīʿ*, a term which literally means "innovative" but which involves a greater awareness of the potential uses of poetic imagery. The poet-Caliph Ibn al-Muʿtazz (d. 908) wrote a famous analysis of the five most significant tropes (incl. simile and metaphor) entitled *Kitāb al-badīʿ*, a work which took many of its examples from early poetry and the text of the Qurʾān. This was to be the first in an increasingly complex series of rhetorical analyses. The discussions which evolved around the subject of *badīʿ* were part of a dynamic period in the devel. of Islamic thought on religious, ethnic, ideological, and cultural issues. They also raised questions of literary taste and provoked fierce debate between proponents of the "new" (*muṇdathūn*) poets and the old. Much critical opprobrium was reserved for the poet Abū Tammām (d. 846), who was widely condemned for carrying the use of *badīʿ* to excessive lengths. At a later date, the great critic ʿAbd al-Qāhir al-Jurjānī (d. 1078) pioneered the analysis of the psychological impact of imagery on the reader and thereby accentuated the *originality* of many of Abū Tammām's ideas, a verdict gaining increasing credence in modern crit.

With the growth of the bureaucracy at the Caliph's court and the expansion of the Islamic dominions—accompanied almost automatically by the emergence of local potentates—plentiful sources of patronage became available to reward poets who would compose occasional poems. During the heyday of cl. Ar. p., many such centers existed: the Umayyads and their successors in al-Andalus; the Hamdanids in Aleppo, Syria; the Ikhshidids in Egypt; and the court in Baghdad. To all these centers poets would come in search of favor and reward. The poet who best exemplifies this patronage system is al-Mutanabbī (d. 965). He composed poems for all kinds of occasions and for a number of rulers and patrons, some of whom are eulogized and later mercilessly lampooned. Developing the use of the *badīʿ* style and combining a superb control of the lang. with an innate sense of the gnomic phrase, he was soon widely regarded as the greatest of the cl. Ar. poets. His *Dīwān* (collected poetry) provides us with many splendid examples of the *qaṣīda* as occasional poem; his examples of eulogy (*madīḥ*) are among the most famous contributions to a genre which was a major form of verbal art in Arab civilization:

> Whither do you intend, great prince?
>   We are the herbs of the hills and
>   you are the clouds;

> We are the ones time has been miserly
>   towards respecting you, and the
>   days cheated of your presence.
> Whether at war or peace, you aim at
>   the heights, whether you tarry or
>   hasten.
>   (tr. A. J. Arberry, 1965)

A great admirer of al-Mutanabbī's poetry was Abū al-ʿAlāʾ al-Maʿarrī (d. 1057). This blind poet and philosopher began by imitating his great predecessor, but his collection of poems entitled *Luzūm mā lā yalzam* (Requirement of the Non-required), the title of which reflects the fact that he imposes strict formal rules on himself, combines consummate skill in the use of poetic lang. with some of the most pessimistic sentiments to be found in the entire Ar. canon:

> Would that a lad had died in the very
>   hour of birth
> And never sucked, as she lay in child-
>   bed, his mother's breast!
> Her babe, it says to her or ever the
>   tongue can speak,
> "Nothing thou get'st of me but sorrow
>   and bitter pain."
>   (tr. R. A. Nicholson)

Three poets of al-Andalus from this same period deserve particular mention: Ibn Shuhayd (d. 1035) and Ibn Ḥazm (d. 1063), both of whom contributed to crit. as well as to poetry; and Ibn Zaydūn (d. 1070), who celebrated his great love, the Umayyad Princess Wallāda, and then rued her loss to a rival at court. The Iberian Peninsula was also to contribute to Ar. p. two strophic genres, the *muwashshaṇa* (see HEBREW PROSODY) and *zajal* (see ZEJEL). The origins and prosodic features of both genres are the subject of continuing and intense debate. The final strophe or refrain known as the *kharja* ("envoi") was originally a popular song in Romance or a mixture of Romance and Hispano-Ar. sung by a girl about her beloved:

> My beloved is sick for love of me.
> How can he not be so?
> Do you not see that he is not allowed
>   near me?
>   (tr. J. T. Monroe)

This refrain provides the rhyme scheme for the other strophes in the poem which are in literary Ar. Interspersed between them are other verses with separate rhymes. In the *zajal* genre the colloquial lang. sometimes encountered in the *kharja* of the *muwashshaṇa* is used in the body of the poem itself. With its illustrious exponent Ibn Quzmān (d. 1159) the fame of the genre spread to the East.

As the corpus of poetics and rhetoric increased

in scope and complexity, poetry itself tended to become more stereotyped and convention-bound, e.g. the poetry of Ibn ʿArabī (d. 1240), one of the major figures in Islamic theology; the mystical poet Ibn al-Fāriḍ (d. 1235); and Bahāʾ al-dīn Zuhayr, whose death in 1258 coincides with the capture of Baghdad by the Mongols, an event generally acknowledged as signaling the end of the cl. period in Islamic culture.

III. 13TH TO 18TH CENTURIES. The period between the 13th and early 19th cs. is often characterized as one of "decadence," a designation which not only reflects the distaste of subsequent critics for poetry in which a penchant for verbal virtuosity and poetic tropes prevailed, but which also serves to conceal a general lack of research. To the initial stages of the period belong such poets as al-Būṣīrī (d. 1294), who wrote a second "Burda" poem (after that of Kaʿb ibn Zuhayr). This poem found a wide audience within the mystical circles of popular Islam much in evidence throughout the period. Concurrently in Spain Ḥāzim al-Qarṭājannī (d. 1285) was not only a major contributor to the trad. of Ar. poetics but a poet in his own right.

During much of this period the Ar.-speaking world was governed by non-Arabs, particularly the 15th–18th cs. when most of the area became part of the Ottoman Empire. The lang. of administration and official communication was Turkish, while that of literary culture, even among the Turks, was often Persian. Among the poets who composed in Ar. during this period and whose names have been preserved are the Iraqi poet Ṣafī al-dīn al-Ḥillī (d. 1349), who in addition to writing his own poetry composed a study of the *muwashshaḥa* and *zajal*, and the Egyptian, al-Idkāwī (d. 1770). Both of these poets were adept at composing verse full of embellishments, e.g. poems in which each word begins with the same letter, or each word starts with the final grapheme of the previous word. This was indeed a period of verbal artifice but also one of compilation (incl. the major Ar. dictionaries) and explication. Ibn Mālik (d. 1274) composed a poem in 1000 verses on Ar. grammar, a text which was still in use in Egyptian religious schools at the turn of the 20th c.

The limited size of the audience for the elite lit. just outlined may account for the considerable vigor of the popular literary trad. during these centuries. This is most evident in the greatest of all narrative collections, *The 1001 Nights*, as well as in other popular tales which contain large amounts of poetry in a variety of styles. And, while the trad. of popular poetry is sparsely documented, some intimations of its liveliness and variety can be gauged from the (albeit bawdy) poetry to be found in the shadow plays of the Egyptian oculist, Ibn Dāniyāl (d. 1311).

IV. 19TH AND 20TH CENTURIES. A. *The Beginnings of the Modern Revival*. The process whereby Ar. p. enters a new phase is termed *al-nahḍa* (re-vival). Two principal factors are involved: what one scholar has termed "the Arab Rediscovery of Europe" on the one hand, and a re-examination of the cl. trad. of Ar. poetry and poetics on the other. Esp. noteworthy figures in this revival are Rifāʿa al-Ṭahṭāwī (d. 1873) in Egypt, and Buṭrus al-Bustānī (d. 1883), Nāṣif al-Yāzijī (d. 1871—who was particularly inspired by the poetry of al-Mutanabbī), and Aḥmad Fāris al-Shidyāq (d. 1887) in Lebanon.

B. *Neoclassicism*. Al-Mutanabbī was also the inspiration of one of the first major figures in the neoclassical movement, the Egyptian Maḥmūd Sāmī al-Bārūdī (d. 1904), who advocated a return to the directness and purity of cl. Ar. p. and composed poetry to illustrate his ideas. Within the chronology of its own modern history, every Arab country fostered neoclassical poets, e.g. the Egyptian Ḥāfiẓ Ibrāhīm (d. 1932), the Iraqis Jamīl Ṣidqī al-Zahāwī (d. 1936) and Maʿrūf al-Ruṣāfī (d. 1945), and somewhat later, the Palestinian Ibrāhīm Ṭūqān (d. 1941). However, critical opinion is virtually unanimous in judging Aḥmad Shawqī (d. 1932) as the greatest poet of the neoclassical school. Whether in his stirring calls to the Egyptian people, his more personal descriptive verse, or his still popular operettas, his superbly cadenced poetry seems destined to secure him a place in the pantheon of great Ar. poets. While recent devels. in Ar. p. have produced many changes, several poets have continued to compose poetry in the traditional manner, esp. Muḥammad al-Jawāhirī, Badawī al-Jabal (pseudonym of Muḥammad Sulaymān al-Aḥmad), and Al-Akhṭal al-Ṣaghīr (pseudonym of Bishāra al-Khūrī, d. 1968).

C. *Romanticism*. Signs of a reaction against the occasional nature of much neoclassical verse can be found in the works of the Lebanese poet Khalīl Muṭrān (d. 1949), although not so much in his own poetry as in his writings about poetry and particularly the introduction to his collected poems (1908). Full-blooded romanticism in Ar. p. comes from the poets of *al-mahjar* (the "emigre school"), as the Arab poets of the Americas are called. While Amīn al-Rīḥānī (d. 1940) was certainly much admired in the Middle East, the undisputed leader of the Northern group was Khalīl Jubrān [Kahlil Gibran] (d. 1931), as famous for his works in Eng. as for those in Ar.:

> Give me the flute and sing! Forget all
>   that you and I have said.
> Talk is but dust in the air, so tell me of
>   your deeds.
>   (tr. Khouri and Algar)

Far removed from their native land, Jubrān and his colleagues, among whom were Mīkhāʾīl Nuʿayma (b. 1889), Īliyyā Abū Māḍī (d. 1957), and Nasīb ʿArīḍa (d. 1946), proceeded to experiment with lang., form, and mood, and in so doing introduced a new voice into Ar. p. Jubrān was also in constant touch with his fellow-countrymen in

South America, among whom Fawzī Maʿlūf (d. 1930) is the most significant figure.

In the Middle East the ideals of Eng. romanticism were vigorously advocated by three Egyptian poets: al-ʿAqqād, Ibrāhīm al-Māzinī (d. 1949), and ʿAbd al-Raḥmān Shukrī (d. 1958). While all three wrote poetry, the primary function of the group was to criticize the neoclassical school in favor of a new, more individual role for the poet. The 1930s and '40s were the heyday of romanticism in Ar. p. In 1932 Aḥmad Zakī Abū Shādī (d. 1955) founded the Apollo Society in Cairo, which pub. a magazine to which several poets, incl. Ibrāhīm Nājī (d. 1953), ʿAlī Maḥmūd Ṭāhā (d. 1949), and the Tunisian Abū al-Qāsim al-Shābbī (d. 1934) made contributions. Among other important figures in the devel. of romantic Ar. p. are ʿUmar Abū Rīsha in Syria, Yūsuf Tījānī al-Bashīr (d. 1937) in the Sudan, and Ṣalāḥ Labakī (d. 1955) and Ilyās Abū Shabaka (d. 1947) in Lebanon. As a critic Labakī also devoted his attention to the devel. of a symbolist school of poetry, much indebted to Fr. poetic theory and associated with the Lebanese poets Yūsuf Ghuṣūb and (esp.) Saʿīd ʿAql.

D. *The Emergence of "New Poetry": The Role of the Poet.* The period following World War II was one of political uncertainty, frequent changes of government, and revolution. The creation of the State of Israel in 1948 served as a major psychological catalyst in the Arab World. In the revolutionary atmosphere during the 1950s, the poetry of the late romantics, and in particular symbolists such as Saʿīd ʿAql, came to be regarded as elitist, ivory-tower lit. Along with the prevalence of such causes as Palestinian rights, nationalism (whether the Pan-Arab or local variety), revolution, and communism came the rallying cry for "commitment" (*iltizām*). Not surprisingly, among the most prominent contributors to poetry of commitment have been a large group of Palestinian poets; particularly noteworthy are Maḥmūd Darwīsh (b. 1942), Fadwā Ṭūqān (b. 1917), and Samīḥ al-Qāsim (b. 1939). The other overriding topic of political poetry has been life among the poorer classes in both the cities and provinces of the Arab World nations: the earlier poetry of Badr Shākir al-Sayyāb (d. 1964), ʿAbd al-Wahhāb al-Bayyātī (b. 1926), and Ṣalāḥ ʿAbd al-Sabūr (d. 1982) shows this concern, as do the works of Aḥmad ʿAbd al-Muʿtī Ḥijāzī (b. 1935) and Muḥammad Miftāḥ al-Faytūrī (b. 1930). The dark visions of Khalīl Ḥāwī (d. 1982) show a more subtle kind of commitment, tinged with bitterness, as in the prescient commentary on the Arab World in the 1960s, "Lazarus 1962":

Deepen the pit, gravedigger,
Deepen it to bottomless depths
beyond the sun's orbit;
night of ashes, remnants of a star
buried in the wheeling abyss.
(tr. Haydar and Beard)

The most widely read poet in the contemp. Middle East is undoubtedly Nizār Qabbānī (b. 1923), who earned enormous popularity for his several volumes of sensuous love poetry. During the 1950s he also wrote poems of social protest, such as his famous "Bread, Hashish and Moonlight"; particularly since the June War of 1967, political and social issues have been constant topics in his poetry.

With Adūnīs (pseudonym of ʿAlī Aḥmad Saʿīd, b. 1930) a different kind of commitment is encountered. After editing with his colleague, the Lebanese Christian poet Yūsuf al-Khāl (d. 1987), the journal *Shiʿr*, which has had immense influence in the devel. of a modern poetics in the Arab World, Adūnīs broke away and in 1968 founded his own journal, *Mawāqif*. He has pub. numerous poetry collections of startling originality:

To a father who died, green as a cloud
with a sail on his face, I bow.
(*JArabL* 2 [1971])

Using his journal and its coterie as a conduit for his ideas, he advocates the need for "innovation," viewing the primary purpose of poetry as the use of words in new ways.

E. *Changes in Form.* Strophic Ar. p. has existed from at least the 10th c. The modern period has also witnessed other experiments, such as blank and free verse (qq.v.). Also noteworthy are metrical experiments within folk poetry, particularly in Lebanon where Rashīd Nakhla (d. ca. 1940) and Michel Ṭrād composed poems in strophic form and with mixed meters. In 1947 two Iraqi poets, Nāzik al-Malāʾika (b. 1923) and al-Sayyāb, initiated a break from the concept of the line as poetic unit and thus paved the way for the emergence of *shiʿr ḥurr* ("free verse"). In fact, al-Malāʾika's attempt to establish a new set of rules based on the single foot (*tafʿīla*) rather than the line (*bayt*) was soon discarded as poets began to experiment with both traditional and new quantitative patterns in their poetry. Other poets have pursued this trend even further by composing prose poetry (*qaṣīdat al-nathr*) in which the sheer conjunction and musicality of words contribute to the poetic moment: alliteration, assonance, and imagery (qq.v.) are combined in the works of poets such as Jabrā Ibrāhīm Jabrā (b. 1919), Muḥammad al-Māghūṭ (b. 1934), and Tawfīq Ṣāyigh (d. 1971).

The Arab poet today continues to be influenced and inspired by the great cl. trad., but the stimuli provided by his own time and world are now international and of considerable variety. Thus the *qaṣīda* lives alongside the prose poem as contemp. Ar. p. draws its inspiration from both its past and present.

GENERAL REFERENCE WORKS: C. Brockelmann, *Gesch. der Arabischen Literatur*, 2 v. (1898–1902), *Supplementbanden*, 3 v. (1937–42); A. Fischer, *Schawahid Indices* (1945); *Encyc. of Islam*, 2d ed. (1954–); J. D. Pearson, *Index Islamicus 1906–1955* (1958), *Supplements* (1956–80); F. Sezgin, *Gesch.*

des Arabischen Schriftums, v. 2 (1975); *The Fihrist of al-Nadim,* tr. B. Dodge, 2 v. (1970); M. Alwan, "A Bibl. of Mod. Ar. P. in Eng. Tr.," *Middle East Jour.* (Summer 1973). ANTHOLOGIES: Ar. P. *for Eng. Readers,* ed. W. A. Clouston (1881); *Ancient Ar. P.,* ed. C. J. Lyall (1885); W. S. Blunt, *Seven Golden Odes of Pagan Arabia* (1903); R. A. Nicholson, *Trs. of Eastern Poetry and Prose* (1922); *Mod. Ar. P.,* ed. and tr. A. J. Arberry (1950); *The Seven Odes,* tr. A. J. Arberry (1957); *Al-Majānī al-ṇadītha ʿan Majānī al-Ab Shaykhū,* ed. F. Afram al-Bustānī, 3 v. (1960–61); *Dīwān al-Shiʿr al-ʿArabī,* ed. Adūnīs (1964–68); *Ar. P.* (1965), *Poems of al-Mutanabbi* (1967), both ed. A. J. Arberry; *Anthologie de la litt. arabe contemporaine: la poésie,* tr. L. Norin and E. Tarabay (1967); *An Anthol. of Mod. Ar. Verse,* ed. M. Badawi (1970); *Hispano-Ar. P.,* ed. and tr. J. T. Monroe (1974); *Mawsūʿat al-Shiʿr al-ʿArabī,* ed. K. Ḥāwī and M. Ṣafadī (1974–); *An Anthol. of Mod. Ar. P.,* tr. M. Khouri and H. Algar (1974); *Mod. Arab Poets 1950–1975,* tr. I. Boullata (1976); *Women of the Fertile Crescent,* ed. K. Boullata (1978); K. Hawi, *Naked in Exile,* tr. A. Haydar and M. Beard (1984); *Majnun et Layla: l'amour fou,* tr. A. Miquel and P. Kemp (1984); *Cl. Ar. P.,* tr. C. Tuetey (1985); *Mod. Ar. P.: An Anthol.,* ed. S. K. Jayyusi (1987).

HISTORY AND CRITICISM: W. Ahlwardt, *Über Poesie und Poetik der Araber* (1856); I. Goldziher, *Short Hist. of Cl. Ar. Lit.* (1908), tr J. Desomogyi (1966); R. A. Nicholson, *Lit. Hist. of the Arabs* (1914), *Studies in Islamic Poetry* (1921), *Studies in Islamic Mysticism* (1921); Ṭ. Ḥusayn, *Al-Shiʿr al-Jāhilī* (1926)—pre-Islamic poetry and its "authenticity"; H. A. R. Gibb, *Ar. Lit.* (1926); U. Farrukh, *Das Bild der Frühislam in der arabischen Dichtung* (1937); N. al-Bahbītī, *Tārīkh al-Shiʿr al-ʿArabī* (1950)—hist. of early Ar. p.; M. al-Nuwayhī, *Al-Shiʿr al-Jāhilī* (n.d.)—critical approaches to pre-Islamic poetry; R. Serjeant, *South Ar. P.* (1951); R. Blachère, *Histoire de la litt. arabe,* 3 v. (1952–66); G. Gomez, *Poesia arabigoandaluza* (1952); G. von Grunebaum, *Kritik und Dichtkunst* (1955); N. al-Asad, *Maṣādir al-Shiʿr al-Jāhilī* (1956)—sources of pre-Islamic poetry; I. ʿAbbās, *Tārīkh al-Adab al-Andalusī* (1959)—hist. of Andalusian lit.; J. al-Rikābī, *Fi al-Adab al-Andalusī* (1960)—hist. of Andalusian lit.; N. al-Malāʾika, *Qaḍāyā al-shiʿr al-muʿāṣir* (1962)—issues in mod. Ar. p.; S. Dayf, *Tārīkh al-Adab al-ʿArabī,* 4 v. (1963–73)—hist. of Ar. lit., *Al-Taṭawwur wa-al-tajdīd fī al-shiʿr al-Umawī* (1974)—innovation in Umayyad poetry; J. Kamāl al-dīn, *Al-Shiʿr al-ʿArabī al-nadūth wa-rūḥ al-ʿaṣr* (1964)—mod. Ar. p.; E. Wagner, *Abu Nuwas* (1965); M. Ullmann, *Untersuchungen zur Ragazpoesie* (1966); I. Ismāʿīl, *Al-Shiʿr al-ʿArabī al-muʿāsir* (1967)—mod. Ar. p.; G. Shukrī, *Shiʿrunā al-nadīth: ilā ayn?* (1968)—mod. Ar. p.; J. Vadet, *L'Esprit courtois en Orient dans les premiers siècles de l'Hégire* (1968); W. Heinrichs, *Arabische Dichtung und griechische Poetik* (1969); M. Bateson, *Structural Continuity in Poetry* (1970); M. al-Nuwayhī,

Qaḍiyyat al-shiʿr al-jadīd (1971)—issues in mod. Ar. p.; R. Jacobi, *Studien zur Poetik der altarabischen Qaside* (1971); J. T. Monroe, "Oral Composition in Pre-Islamic Poetry," *JArabL* 3 (1972); M. Ṣubḥī, *Dirāsāt tanḥīliyya fī al-shiʿr al-ʿArabī al-muʿāsir* (1972)—mod. Ar. p.; *Ar. P.: Theory and Devel.,* ed. G. von Grunebaum (1973); R. Scheindlin, *Form and Structure in the Poetry of Al-Muʿtamid ibn ʿAbbād* (1974); S. M. Stern, *Hispano-Ar. Strophic Poetry* (1974); A. Hamori, *On the Art of Med. Ar. Lit.* (1974); J. ʿAsfūr, *Al-Ṣūra al-fanniyya fī al-turāth al-naqdī wa-al-balāghī* (1974)—imagery in traditional crit. and rhet.; M. Badawi, *A Crit. Intro. to Mod. Ar. P.* (1975); J. Bencheikh, *Poétique arabe* (1975); S. A. Bonebakker, *Materials for the Hist. of Ar. Rhet. from the Hilyat al-muhādara of Hātimī* (1975); J. Stetkevych, "The Ar. Lyrical Phenomenon in Context," *JArabL* 6 (1975); S. Moreh, *Mod. Ar. P. 1800–1970* (1976); L. F. Compton, *Andalusian Lyrical Poetry and Old Sp. Love Songs* (1976); S. K. Jayyusi, *Trends and Movements in Mod. Ar. P.* (1977); R. Hitchcock, *The Kharjas: Research, Bibls., and Checklists* (1977); M. Zwettler, *The Oral Trad. of Cl. Ar. P.* (1978); K. Kheir Beik, *Le Mouvement moderniste de la poésie arabe contemporaine* (1978); Y. al-Yūsuf, *Al-Shiʿr al-ʿArabī al-muʿāṣir* (1980)—mod. Ar. p.; M. Abdul-Hai, *Trad. and Eng. and Am. Influence in Ar. Romantic P.* (1982); G. van Gelder, *Beyond the Line* (1982); *Ar. Lit. to the End of the Umayyad Period,* ed. A. Beeston et al. (1983); M. Ajami, *The Neckveins of Winter* (1984); S. Stetkevych, "The Ṣuʿlūk and His Poem: A Paradigm of Passage Manqué," *JAOS* 104 (1984); S. A. Sowayan, *Nabati Poetry* (1985); Adunis, *Intro. à la poétique arabe* (1985); M. R. Menocal, *The Ar. Role in Med. Lit. Hist.* (1988); S. Sperl, *Mannerism in Ar. P.: A Structural Analysis of Sel. Texts, 9th C.–11th C. A.D.* (1989); C. Bailey, *Bedouin Poetry from Sinai and the Negev* (1991); S. P. Stetkevych, *Abū Tammām and the Poetics of the ʿAbbāsid Age* (1991).

R.M.A.A.

ARABIC PROSODY. The earliest extant examples of Ar. poetry (q.v.), which date to the middle of the 6th c. A.D., already show highly developed metrical organization. Yet an elaborate system describing the meters of this poetry was laid down only two centuries later by al-Khalīl Ibn Aḥmad (d. ca. 791), who is generally regarded as the founder of Ar. pros. He proposed that all Ar. poetry was composed according to a system comprising 15 meters (to which a 16th was later added). He also found that, in terms of rhythms, these 15 meters could be reduced to five groups or circles. Despite signs of disagreement with certain aspects of this analysis from scholars such as al-Jawharī (d. 1003), al-Khalīl's account was generally accepted as the only authoritative prosodic system in Ar. and adhered to by poets from the 9th c. until modern times.

Like Gr. and Lat., Ar. pros. is essentially quantitative; the rhythm is based on temporal duration.

Yet although the Ar. lang. has easily identifiable long and short syllables, the ancient grammarians lacked the concept of syllable. They analyzed words into *sākin* ("quiescent"), i.e. a consonant, and *mutaṇarrik* ("moving"), a consonant followed by a vowel. This shortcoming did not hinder the formulation of a coherent metrical system, however, for Ar. pros. is not solely based on an alternation of "long" and "short."

Al-Khalīl observed that verses of the very same poems seldom conform to an identical sequence of "moving" and "quiescent." Instead, they are governed by determinate collocations of easily distinguishable rhythmic entities of fixed length, which he called "pegs" (*watid*, pl. *awtād*), with elements of variable length, which he called "cords" (*sabab*, pl. *asbāb*). He represented the results of his investigation in the form of eight feet which combine in various ways to make the 15 traditional meters of Ar. pros.

For the sake of precision and clarity, it is preferable to describe the rhythmic entities in terms of their syllables. "Short" syllable denotes an open syllable, like *ba*, composed of consonant and short vowel (CV), and is represented by a breve (◡). "Long" syllable denotes either a closed syllable, like *bal*, made of consonant and short vowel followed by consonant (CVC), or an open syllable with a long vowel, like *bā* (CV̄). Both types of "long" (CVC and CV̄), which are represented by a macron (−), are considered metrically equivalent, hence interchangeable. It may be added that due to case inflections poetry in literary Ar., as opposed to colloquial Ar., does not use an extra-long syllable, like *bāb* (CV̄C), except in ultimate positions in certain meters. Finally, the rules of Ar. pros. require that shorts occurring in pausal positions, namely at the ends of lines (and of first hemistichs when they have internal rhymes), be considered metrically long.

Now we have to describe the abstract rhythmic entities posited by al-Khalīl. The cords are of two types:

(a) *khafīf* ("light"), equal to a long syllable (−), which the poet may at will replace by a short (◡), and

(b) *thaqīl* ("heavy"), equal to two shorts (◡◡), which may be freely replaced by one long (−).

The pegs too are of two types:

(a) *majmūʿ* ("joined"), an iamb composed of one short followed by one long (◡−), and

(b) *mafrūq* ("separated"), a trochee composed of one long followed by one short (−◡).

The pegs, being the strong elements which constitute the rhythmic core of the feet, are also subject to quantitative changes; these are governed by a strict set of metric rules. Some prosodists refer to another element called *fāsila*, consist-

ing of two shorts followed by one long (◡◡−), and reject the "heavy" cord as superfluous. Considering that two shorts never appear unless followed by a long, it seems justifiable to consider the *fāsila* as the anapest of Ar. pros.

It should be noted that the two syllables of the iambic peg are so interlocked as to produce one indivisible unit; this rhythm dominates most of Ar. poetry. As implied by its name ("joined"), its two constituent syllables should never be pronounced separately. The trochaic peg and its rhythm are controversial.

The following table gives the eight metrical feet in their mnemonic words. The pegs, which are the rhythmic nucleus, appear in capitals. It will be seen that each foot has one peg plus one or two cords.

1. ◡ − − FAʿŪlun
   (peg *a* + cord *a*)
2. − ◡ − fāʿILUN
   (cord *a* + peg *a*)
3. ◡ − − − MAFĀʿīlun
   (peg *a* + cord *a* + cord *a*)
4. − − ◡ − mustafʿILUN
   (cord *a* + cord *a* + peg *a*) or
   − − ◡ − musTAFʿIlun
   (cord *a* + peg *b* + cord *a*)
5. − ◡ − − fāʿILĀtun
   (cord *a* + peg *a* + cord *a*) or
   − ◡ − − FĀʿIlātun
   (peg *b* + cord *a* + cord *a*)
6. ◡ − ◡ − MUFĀʿalatun
   (peg *a* + cord *b* + cord *a*)
7. ◡ ◡ − ◡ − mutafāʿILUN
   (cord *b* + cord *a* + peg *a*)
8. − − − ◡ mafʿūLĀTU
   (cord *a* + cord *a* + peg *b*).

These feet are classified according to their rhythmic elements into four groups, in which each foot is derived from the others by cyclical permutation.

However, as Weil has shown, only the three feet with an initial iamb and the foot with a final trochee (1, 3, 6, 8), which can be unambiguously divided, could actually serve as the basis of permutation, because both the position and type of their pegs are self-evident. The others are ambiguous, since they can be divided in two different ways. The ideal meters are made up from either the recurrence of one foot or the combination of two (but no more than two) different feet. Weil has discovered the law governing such a combination: two pegs can never succeed each other, but also must be separated by no more than two cords.

The table on the following page represents the mnemonic words of one hemistich of the 16 meters in their respective circles. Several meters emerge from the same sequence of rhythmic units, when one begins and ends at a different point on a circle by way of cyclical permutation. In order to show this principle at work, the basic patterns of all meters, with the exception of the first meter of each circle, are represented so as to begin and end at the intersecting lines drawn precisely under the corresponding points of the first meters. The circles are numbered according to al-Khalīl, but the order in which they appear in this table is that followed by later prosodists such as Ibn al-Sarrāj (d. 1154) and al-Maḥallī (d. 1275).

It will be seen that all pegs and cords of the meters of each circle totally overlap. With the exception of circle 4, all circles begin with a "leading" meter containing only unambiguous feet. The other meters are composed of ambiguous feet, in which the pegs are recognizable only insofar as they are scanned in relation to the "leading" meters. Circle 4 is anomalous in that it combines iambic and trochaic pegs and has no meter totally composed of unambiguous feet.

From circles 1, 2, and 4 it is possible to derive more meters than are actually used in Ar. poetry; these potential meters are termed *muhmal* ("neglected"). Further, the meters as given in the table below are the ideal patterns; actual lines often deviate from these patterns in the number of their feet as in their rhythms. Ideally, all lines are octameter (circles 1, 5), or hexameter (circles 2, 3, 4). Practically, some appear in shortened forms, either invariably or occasionally. *Rajaz* excepted,

all verses are divided into two hemistichs; traditional lines of *rajaz* are trimeter and thus are not so divided.

Nor is there correspondence between the longs and shorts of the ideal meters and actual lines. In practice, there are two sets of quantitative deviations from the abstract schemes. One consists of optional minor variations called *zihāfāt*, falling on the cords; these involve the free use of "short" instead of "long" and the use of "long" instead of two successive "shorts" (cf. RESOLUTION). The latter, occurring only in *wāfir* and *kāmil*, has a greater effect on the rhythm in that it reduces the number of syllables. The second set consists of much greater variations, traditionally called *ʿilal*, or defects, involving the shortening or deletion of pegs as well as the deletion of cords. With the exception of *mutadārik* (repudiated by al-Khalīl), where a pegless, defective foot (– –) freely appears in non-final positions, the use of *ʿilal* is restricted to the final foot of the hemistich. The resulting catalectic feet generate subdivisions of the respective meters. Once the poet chooses to use a defective foot in the first line, he must make sure that the same foot appears throughout the poem.

Ar. pros. is not syllabic. Traditional Ar. poetry exhibits a regular recurrence of quantitative patterns of long and short syllables or, more accu-

METERS	SCANSION WITH MNEMONIC WORDS			
CIRCLE 5	‿ – –	‿ – –	‿ – –	‿ – –
mutaqārib	FAʿŪ-lun	FAʿŪ-lun	FAʿŪ-lun	FAʿŪ-lun
mutadārik	ʿILUN/fā-	ʿILUN/fā-	ʿILUN/fā-	ʿILUN/fā-
CIRCLE 3	‿ – – –	‿ – – –	‿ – – –	
hazaj	MAFĀ-ʿīlun	MAFĀ-ʿīlun	MAFĀ-ʿīlun	
rajaz	ʿILUN/mustaf-	ʿILUN/mustaf-	ʿILUN/mustaf-	
ramal	ʿILĀ-tun/fā-	ʿILĀ-tun/fā-	ʿILĀ-tun/fā-	
CIRCLE 2	‿ – ‿ ‿ –	‿ – ‿ ‿ –	‿ – ‿ ‿ –	
wāfir	MUFĀ- ʿala tun	MUFĀ- ʿala tun	MUFĀ- ʿala tun	
kāmil	ʿILUN/ mutafā-	ʿILUN/mutafā-	ʿILUN/mutafā-	
CIRCLE 1	‿ – –	‿ – – –	‿ – –	‿ – – –
ṭawīl	FAʿŪ-lun	MAFĀ- ʿīlun	FAʿŪ-lun	MAFĀ- ʿīlun
madīd	ʿILUN/fā-	ʿILĀ-tun fā-	ʿILUN fā-	ʿILĀ-tun fā-
basīṭ	ʿILUN fā-	ʿILUN/mustaf-	ʿILUN fā-	ʿILUN/mustaf-
CIRCLE 4	– – ‿ –	– – ‿ –	– – – ‿	
sarīʿ	mustaf- ʿILUN	mustaf- ʿILUN	mafʿū- LĀTU	
munsariḥ	mustaf- ʿILUN	/mustaf- ʿILUN	mafʿū- LĀTU	
khafif	lun fā- ʿILĀ-	tun/fā- ʿILĀ-	tun mus- TAFʿI-	
muḍāriʿ	lā tun MAFĀ-	ʿī lun/ MAFĀ	ʿī lun FĀʿI-	
muqtaḍab	mustaf-ʿILUN	mustaf-ʿILUN	/mafʿū- LĀTU	
mujtathth	lun fā- ʿILĀ-	lun fā- ʿILĀ-	tun/mus- TAFʿI.	

rately, definite sequences of pegs and cords. Sylla-
ble count is alien to this system; verses having an
equal number of syllables do not necessarily be-
long to the same meter and, conversely, verses of
one and the same poem may have a different
number of syllables (as in *wāfir* and *kāmil*). It is
difficult to determine if accent or stress play any
significant part in traditional Ar. pros. Even most
of the meters of the strophic Hispano-Arabic po-
etry (q.v.), i.e. the twin genres of *muwashshah* and
zajal, may be analyzed as quantitative meters, or
unconventional combinations of quantitative feet.
Nevertheless, there are admittedly scores of such
poems that have abnormal meters; these are
thought to be composed according to syllabic or
accentual-syllabic metrics. The same applies to
medieval poems written in nonclassical langs. as
well as to modern *zajal* written in the colloquial.

A number of leading Orientalists (e.g. Ewald,
Guyard, and Hartmann), as well as some Arab
scholars (e.g. I. Anīs, S. ʿAyyād, and K. Abū Deeb),
have speculated that, in addition to duration, an
ictus or metric stress was also functional in Ar.
pros., but disagree on the question of which sylla-
bles bear it. Weil maintained that this stress falls
regularly on the long syllables of the pegs. For him,
al-Khalīl's circles are "meant to express something
in addition" to length, i.e. to show "which syllables
bear the rhythmic stress as *watid* element." The
dubious meters of circle 4, because they incorpo-
rate two kinds of pegs, have a mixed rhythm of rise
and fall, whereas all the others, which contain only
iambic pegs, have a clear rising rhythm (q.v.).

There is, however, no conclusive evidence that
stress is one of the factors shaping Ar. pros. A clear
rhythm emerges from the marked contrast be-
tween cords and pegs (esp. the iambic) provided
that the latter be pronounced as indivisible units.
It is a peculiarity of Ar. pros., where cords may be
represented both by short and long syllables, that
length is fixed only in syllables corresponding to
the pegs of the feet, whose components are insepa-
rable and whose quantities are invariable. Al-
Khalīl's circles, then, may have been constructed
simply to show the exact type and position of the
pegs and hence which syllables are not subject to
the optional quantitative variation.

Toward the middle of the 20th c., Ar. poetry
witnessed a shift away from traditional metrics.
Instead of the bipartite verse, there appeared a
type of poem, wrongly called "free verse," which
has lines of variable length corresponding to un-
fixed numbers of prosodic feet, and in which
rhyme is almost ignored. This type has gained
such wide currency as to preponderate over the
traditional poem. Less widespread is the "prose
poem," which does not conform to any pre-exist-
ing metric scheme. If this type becomes the poets'
favorite, the traditional meters described above
will be a legacy of the past. See also PERSIAN
POETRY; GHAZAL; QASIDA; HEBREW PROSODY AND
POETICS.

G. W. Freytag, *Darstellung der arabischen Vers-
kunst* (1830); S. Guyard, "Théorie nouvelle de la
métrique arabe," *Jour. Asiatique*, ser. 7, v. 7, 8, 10
(1877); M. Hartmann, *Metrum und Rhythmus*
(1896); J. Vadet, "Contribution a l'histoire de la
métrique arabe," *Arabica* 2 (1955); G. Weil, *Grun-
driss und System der altarabischen Metren* (1958),
"'Arūd,'" *Encyc. of Islam*, 2d ed., v. 1 (1960); Ibn
ʿAbd Rabbihi, *al-ʿIqd al-Farīd*, v. 3 (1305 A.H.); Ibn
al-Sarrāj, *al-Miʿyār fī Awzān al-Ashʿār* (1968); S.
ʿAyyād, *Mūsīqā al-Shiʿr al-ayArabī* (1968); I. Anīs,
Mūsīqā al-Shiʿr, 4th ed. (1972); K. Abū Deeb, *Fī
al-Binya al-ʾĪqāʿiyya li al-Shiʿr al-ʿArabī* (1974); E. G.
Gómez, *Métrica de la moaxaja y métrica española*
(1975); J. M. Maling, "The Theory of Cl. Ar. Met-
rics," *al-Abhāth* 26 (1977); D. Semah, "The Rhyth-
mical Function of the *Watid* and the *Fāsila*," *JSS* 28
(1983), "Quantity and Syllabic Parity in the His-
pano-Arabic *Muwashshah*," *Arabica* 31 (1983).

D.S.

ARAUCANIAN POETRY. See AMERICAN INDIAN
POETRY, *South American*.

ARCHAISM. Deliberate use of old, old-fashioned,
or obsolete words, esp. in poetry, in order to evoke
the mood of an earlier time—i.e. to appropriate
that ethos for a text—or else, alternatively, to
recapture a connotation or denotation (q.v.) not
borne by any modern word. As. appear in both
Virgil and Lucretius; in Fr. poetry of the Ren., as.
were promoted in the doctrines of the *Pléiade*
(q.v.). In Eng. poetry, so trad. held, a. found its
deepest source in Spenser's *Faerie Queene* (1589–
96), in which "strange inkhorn terms" seem to be
used for the sake of their association with the
chivalry and romances of the past. But modern
scholarship contradicts the received view: Strang
for example says that Spenser's as. "are superficial
and limited; the essential character of his poetic
lang. is its modernity." As. are less common in
Spenser than was often thought: in fact there are
only about a hundred archaic words in all of the
Faerie Queene, and half of these are used but once.
But Spenser salts his diction regularly: two-thirds
of the 55 stanzas of Book I, Canto 1, contain at least
one archaic locution. Further, the *effect* of a. may
be achieved by a number of lexical strategies
besides resuscitating words found in an older
author, as Spenser did with Chaucer: these in-
clude the addition of archaic prefixes or suffixes
to ordinary contemporaraneous words, capture of
words still in use but rapidly passing out of fashion,
use of rare and unusual (but not obsolete) words,
use of dialectal words, and the coining of words
that look or sound archaic but in fact never ex-
isted. Syntactic strategies such as hyperbaton
(q.v.)—common in Spenser—also give the effect
of a.

All this suggests that one should proceed with
caution in appraising a., for its strategies are vari-
ous and not easily disentangled from innovation.

Too, many words that today may seem archaic might not in fact have been so, or seemed only slightly so, to Spenser's own contemporaries: it requires great erudition to assess with any accuracy exactly how much—and how—a text from the past evoked, from its audience, its own past. What is essential for the critic is the recognition that the desired effect on the audience is that the archaic words seem "strange but not obscure" (McElderry).

Sometimes a. also serves metrical ends when the older form of a word, having a different number of syllables, more readily fits into the meter than its modern equivalent or descendant. Readers of Eng. poetry are familiar with such words as *loved, wished,* etc., used in poetry as disyllables, namely *lovéd, wishéd.* Yet this should not be thought mere exigency. With older texts, one must exercise some caution in weighing the metrical value of as., since it is often difficult to know precisely when a term went out of contemporaneous usage and became an a.: many words, we know, survived for a considerable time in alternative, syllabically variant forms (now called *doublets*) derived from pronunciation (esp. dialect), e.g. "heaven" as a monosyllable or disyllable (see METRICAL TREATMENT OF SYLLABLES).

When archaic words are preserved in verse but not in prose or common speech, and are adopted by poets beyond the usage of some one poet in whose work as. are very prominent, and in that of his followers, such words come to form a select body of "poetic diction" built up by and as trad., and the diction of poetry then comes to be commonly conceived *as* a. This is true for the "School of Spenser" (q.v.) in the 17th c. and the Spenserian imitators of the 18th, and of Pre-Raphaelites such as William Morris in the 19th. (Conversely, some words, such as *morn* for "morning" and *eve* for "evening," become so common that, in time, they lose much of their sense of a. and are felt to be simply "poetic.") Inexorably such movements provoke reaction, e.g. romanticism (q.v.) to the rigidities of the diction of 18th-c. poetry, and modernism (q.v.) to those of Victorian. However, these reactions are far from simple, as witnessed by the as. common in Coleridge. Nor have archaic words ceased to be used in the 20th c., despite the seeming contravention of Pound's dictum to "Make It New": Pound himself drew heavily upon the diction of the past for his own poetry as well as his translations and imitations, and Eliot in the first movement of *East Coker* deploys as. extensively so as to evoke the "country mirth" of "those long since under earth," making "time past" "time present." Elsewhere Eliot says that "last year's words belong to last year's lang."; and if the poet must find new words for new experience, so too must he or she suscitate old words for a sense of the past. See now AUREATE DICTION; EPITHET; LEXIS.

G. Wagner, *On Spenser's Use of As.* (1879); R. S. Crane, "Imitation of Spenser and Milton in the Early 18th C.," *SP* 15 (1918); T. Quayle, *Poetic Diction* (1924); E. F. Pope, "Ren. Crit. and the Diction of the *Faerie Queene,*" *PMLA* 41 (1926); B. R. McElderry, Jr., "A. and Innovation in Spenser's Poetic Diction," *PMLA* 47 (1932); W. L. Renwick, "The Critical Origins of Spenser's Diction," *MLR* 17 (1922); O. Barfield, *Poetic Diction,* 2d ed. (1952); N. Osselton, "A.," and B. M. H. Strang, "Lang., Gen.," *The Spenser Encyc.,* ed. A. C. Hamilton et al. (1990). T.V.F.B.

ARCHETYPAL CRITICISM. See ARCHETYPE; CRITICISM; MYTH CRITICISM; PSYCHOLOGICAL CRITICISM.

ARCHETYPE.

I. HISTORY
    A. *The Anthropological Influence*
    B. *The Psychological Influence*
    C. *Natural and Universal Symbols*
    D. *Northrop Frye*
II. POWERS AND LIMITATIONS

Generally speaking, an a. is an original pattern from which copies are made, or the most essentially characteristic trait shared by the members of a class of things. Thus, the a. of a table would be "a flat horizontal surface upheld by vertical supports for placing things on," and this is the idea of all tables everywhere, when considered apart from their peculiar differentiae of size, shape, material, and so on.

In poetry, an a. may be any idea, character, action, object, institution, event, or setting containing essential characteristics which are primitive, general, and universal rather than sophisticated, unique, and particular. This generality may be found in any aspect or combination of aspects of a work. Birth, coming of age, love, guilt, redemption, and death are archetypal subjects; the conflict between reason and imagination, free will and destiny, appearance and reality, and the individual and society are archetypal themes; the tension between parents and children, the rivalry between brothers, the problems of incestuous desire, the search for a father, the ambivalence of the male-female relationship, and the young man from the country first arriving in the city are archetypal situations; the braggart, buffoon, hero, devil, rebel, wanderer, enchantress, maiden, and witch are archetypal characters; and certain animals, birds, and natural phenomena and settings are archetypal images. When such elements are treated so as to bring forth their basic, essential, and fundamental attributes, they may form an archetypal pattern or patterns. In order to understand and appreciate the meanings and uses of an archetypal approach to lit., we must first trace its origins and devel., and then examine its powers and limitations.

I. HISTORY. The hist. of the archetypal approach may be seen in terms of four movements which arose in roughly chronological order, with some overlap in both time and focus.

A. *The Anthropological Influence.* Since these studies tend to center on the terms "myth" (q.v.) and "ritual," a few basic definitions are in order. A myth, strictly speaking, is a story about supernatural beings; it may also include humans with special or supernatural powers who interact with these divine beings. A ritual, on the other hand, is a ceremonial re-enactment of a sacred myth, but it has not been definitively established whether the myth was created to explain the ritual or the ritual was invented to dramatize the myth. Either way, the usual anthropological account of ritual is that it provides a way for a culture to express its hopes and fears in those dealings with nature which are basic to its survival.

The chief anthropological influence on the archetypal approach was the so-called Cambridge school of comparative anthropology, led by Sir James Frazer and which included Gilbert Murray, J. E. Harrison, J. L. Weston, S. H. Hooke, Lord Raglan, E. M. Butler, and T. H. Gaster. The method of this group, often based on armchair research, was to collect accounts of myths and rituals from various cultures with a view to tracing their fundamental similarities. In Weston's famous *From Ritual to Romance*, for example, which was to have so decisive an influence on T. S. Eliot's *The Waste Land*, such similarities were also found among literary works: the underlying pattern of the Quest for the Holy Grail basic to medieval romance was traced back to Christian legend, and this in turn was traced back to early Gr. fertility cults, which in turn were traced back to the pre-Hindu thunder-god hymns in the *Rig-Veda*. The general effect of this approach was to create the impression that myth and ritual the world over and throughout history formed certain regular and standard patterns (see ANTHROPOLOGY AND POETRY).

The Am. school of anthropologists, however, represented by such field workers as Margaret Mead, R. Benedict, B. Malinowski, and A. I. Hallowell, took a much more pluralistic stance, pointing out that cultures were fundamentally different from one another and that, if there were "similar" patterns among them, these had differing meanings in their differing contexts. And the unresolved problem of making such comparisons remains to plague the archetypal approach to lit. as well, as we shall see.

B. *The Psychological Influence.* One of the principal reasons why Jung broke with Freud was that he found the Freudian theory of the unconscious too limited. After discovering, ostensibly, that the dreams of his various patients revealed certain similar patterns, and further that these patterns were similar to those found in myth and ritual, Jung came to the concept of the Collective Unconscious, which he then distinguished from the Personal Unconscious. It is the former, he claimed, that contains the potentiality of the psyche to manifest itself in definite and specific archaic forms, which he called "archetypes."

J. S. Jacobi explains that there is a distinction between the a. as such and the archetypal *image*: the former has no material existence but must be clothed by the conscious mind in material from the external world. It is not clear, however, whether the a. as such results from the deposit of innumerable experiences on the evolving human psyche or is an *a priori* condition for human experience itself. It is doubtful, biologically speaking, that the effects of experience can be inherited, or inherited in any simple way, which seems to make the latter hypothesis the more plausible. However this may be, the theory might be summed up as follows: if a myth is the "dream" of the race, dream is the "myth" of the individual. As far as lit. is concerned, Jung says that a poet using archetypes speaks in a voice stronger than her or his own: "he raises the idea he is trying to express above the occasional and the transitory into the sphere of the ever-existing. He transmutes personal destiny into the destiny of mankind. . . . That is the secret of effective art" (*Contributions*).

An approach, therefore, which looks in poetry for echoes and reenactments of ancient and ubiquitous patterns—for, in the words of T. Mann, a "mythical identification, as survival, as a treading in footprints already made"—finds general types implicit in the specific elements of a given poem, and then interprets those types as symbols of human desires, conflicts, and problems. It thus emerges as a kind of symbolic approach. One may trace the image of "The Descent into Hell," for instance, from early myth and ritual to Homer, Virgil, medieval romance, Dante, and up to Hart Crane's subway section of *The Bridge* and T. S. Eliot's *The Hollow Men*, and then interpret it as an a. symbolizing the encounter with one's own repressed guilt.

An archetypal symbology (see SYMBOL) may be constructed, then, based on the parallels which exist between the cycles of human life and those of the natural world, and the patterns which these parallels have caused to appear in myth, ritual, dream, and poetry. "In the solar cycle of the day," says Frye, "the seasonal cycles of the year, and the organic cycle of human life, there is a single pattern of significance out of which myth constructs a central narrative around a figure who is partly the sun, partly vegetative fertility and partly a god or archetypal human being" (1951).

C. *Natural and Universal Symbols.* One may, however, develop an approach to mythological and universal symbols without specifically drawing upon the work of either comparative anthropology or psychology, although there may be some overlap. Here one's concern is primarily epistemological—that is, with the relation between Mind and World, and the various langs. and symbol-systems humanity has devised for bringing them together. Noteworthy in this line is the work of Cassirer, Wheelwright, and Campbell. In following this trend of thought, one may notice the many correspondences between physical forms and the forms of thought—stars for guidance, sun for life, spring for renewal, animals for humanity's physical or emotional side, mountain for struggle and achievement, and so on.

D. *Northrop Frye*. Frye has claimed that it is not important whether there is any relationship between lit. and reality, nor whether lit. embodies the truths of depth psychology. What *is* important is that lit., when taken as a whole, reveals inductively the persistence of certain patterns, with the result that lit. is seen to form a highly organized universe of its own. The job of crit., therefore, is to formulate and interpret those patterns—which Frye proceeded to do in *Anatomy of Criticism* (1957) at some length and with a bewildering set of charts and diagrams. In the process he transcended archetypal crit. itself and developed a fourfold set of approaches, of which the archetypal is only one: (1) Historical Crit.: Theory of Modes (Fictional, Tragic, Comic, Thematic); (2) Ethical Crit.: Theory of Symbols (Literal and Descriptive, Formal, Mythical, Anagogic); (3) Archetypal Crit.: Theory of Myths (Spring: Comedy; Summer: Romance; Autumn: Tragedy; Winter: Irony and Satire); and (4) Rhetorical Crit.: Theory of Genres (Epos, Prose, Drama, Lyric).

II. POWERS AND LIMITATIONS. The chief criticism of the archetypal approach is that it is reductive, making simple that which is highly complex—the individual and particular art work. Thus Frye's system, as a conspicuous example, sees all literary works as belonging to an autonomous and coherent organization of forms, and it interprets any given work in terms of its place in the system. No matter how inclusive and complicated the system may be, however, it is still less complex than any individual work. As Frye himself has said, he likes to step back from the work so he can see its underlying patterns, but the problem is whether he returns to take a closer look and, if he does, what he finds there.

If we treat the archetypal approach as we do any interpretive scheme, then its chief advantages are two. The first is that it provides a useful framework for the interp. of symbols and symbolic patterns in a work. The second and related advantage is that it partakes of the essential nature of the human learning process—to compare the unfamiliar with the familiar, the unknown with the known. Thus, a given work may be seen in terms of its relationship to a larger archetypal pattern, as well as of its similarity to a myth, a tale, a ritual, a dream, or another work. The problem then is to complete the interpretive circle, return to the work itself, and, while analyzing it in terms of these resemblances, which may give it a broader and deeper significance, to analyze the resemblances in terms of the particular structure of and effects in the

work itself, for it is the task of the poet to actualize this potential wholly within the special demands of the individual poem. How the poet does this, and how effectively, are questions to be answered by formal literary analysis and cannot be resolved by archetypal systems of resemblance. See also CRITICISM; MYTH CRITICISM; PSYCHOLOGICAL CRITICISM.

THE ANTHROPOLOGICAL INFLUENCE: Sir J. G. Frazer, *The Golden Bough*, 3d ed., 12 v. (1911–15); J. L. Weston, *From Ritual to Romance* (1920); R. Benedict, *Patterns of Culture* (1934); H. M. Block, "Cultural Anthropology and Contemp. Lit. Crit.," *JAAC* 11 (1952); M. Mead, "Cultural Bases for Understanding Lit.," *PMLA* 68 (1953); M. Eliade, *Images and Symbols* (1969); J. B. Vickery, *The Literary Impact of* The Golden Bough (1973); H. Blumenberg, *Work on Myth* (1985); R. Ackerman, *J. G. Frazer: His Life and Work* (1988); I. Strenski, *Four Theories of Myth in 20th-C. Hist.* (1988); R. Ackerman, *The Myth and Ritual School* (1991).

THE PSYCHOLOGICAL INFLUENCE: C. G. Jung, *Psychology of the Unconscious* (1916), *Psychological Types* (1923), *Contributions to Analytical Psychology* (1928); M. Bodkin, *Archetypal Patterns in Poetry* (1934), *Studies of Type-Images in Poetry, Religion and Philosophy* (1951); J. S. Jacobi, *Complex / A. / Symbol in the Psychology of C. G. Jung* (1959); M. H. Philipson, *Outline of a Jungian Aesthetics* (1963); J. M. Jones, *Jungian Psych. and Literary Analysis* (1979); A. V. Pratt, *Archetypal Patterns in Women's Fiction* (1981); B. L. Knapp, *A Jungian Approach to Lit.* (1984); *Feminist Archetypal Theory*, ed. E. Lauter and C. S. Rupprecht (1985); J. van Meurs and J. Kidd, *Jungian Lit. Crit., 1920–1980* (1988)—annot. bibl.

NATURAL SYMBOLS: E. Cassirer, *Lang. and Myth* (1946), *The Philosophy of Symbolic Forms*, 3 v. (tr. 1953–57); R. Chase, *Quest for Myth* (1949); J. Campbell, *The Hero with a Thousand Faces* (1949); W. H. Auden, *The Enchafed Flood* (1950); P. Wheelwright, *Metaphor and Reality* (1962), *The Burning Fountain*, 2d ed. (1968); Wellek and Warren, ch. 15; Wimsatt and Brooks, ch. 31; B. Seward, *The Symbolic Rose* (1960); E. Sewell, *The Orphic Voice* (1961), *The Human Metaphor* (1964); J. B. Vickery, *Myth and Lit.* (1966), *Myths and Texts* (1983); M. Douglas, *Natural Symbols* (1970); H. Slochower, *Mythopoesis* (1970); E. Zolla, *As.* (1981); H. Birenbaum, *Myth and Mind* (1988).

NORTHROP FRYE: Frye; A. Fletcher, *Allegory* (1964); *N. F. in Mod. Crit.*, ed. M. Krieger (1966); P. Kogan, *N. F.* (1969); R. D. Denham, *N. F. and Crit. Method* (1978); F. Lentricchia, *After the New Crit.* (1980), ch. 1; *Centre and Labyrinth*, ed. E. Cook et al. (1983); H. Adams, *Philosophy of the Literary Symbolic* (1983); D. Cook, *N. F.* (1985); I. Balfour, *N. F.* (1988); A. C. Hamilton, *N. F.: Anatomy of His Crit.* (1990). N.F.

ARCHILOCHIAN. The Gr. lyric poet Archilochus of Paros (fl. mid. 7th c. B.C.) drew on earlier verseforms, esp. dactylic and iambic cola, to create a number of complex systems (*asynarteta* and *epodes* [qq.v.]), i.e. lines in which different metrical cola are combined. Scholars define the A. line variously: (a) xDx + ithyphallic (x – ⏑ ⏑ – ⏑ ⏑ – x | – ⏑ – ⏑ – –), where D = hemiepes (q.v.); (b) dactylic tetrameter + ithyphallic (– ⏑ ⏑ – ⏑ ⏑ – ⏑ ⏑ – ⏑ ⏑ | – ⏑ – ⏑ – –) (so Halporn et al.; = Klingner's *versus Archilochius*); (c) dactylic tetrameter catalectic (– ⏑ ⏑ – ⏑ ⏑ – ⏑ ⏑ – – ; so Klingner). Type (a) is found in Archilochus fr. 170 (West; = 109 Diehl); type (b) in fr. 191.1 (West; = 112.1 Diehl); type (c) as the even lines in the First A. strophe of Horace (*Odes* 1.7, 28; Epode 12). Horace has three epodic (strophic) forms named by metrists after Archilochus: First A.: dactylic hexameter + type (c); Second A.: dactylic hexameter + hemiepes (*Odes* 4.7; Epode 12); and Third A.: type (b) + iambic trimeter catalectic, i.e. – – ⏑ – ⏑ – ⏑ – ⏑ – – (*Odes* 1.4).—*Horatius: Opera*, ed. F. Klingner, 3d ed. (1959); Halporn et al.; Snell; West.   J.W.H.

AREOPAGUS. The name formerly applied by some literary historians to a conjectural literary group or club active in London in the 1580s. The group is identified by Edmund Spenser in the first of two letters to Gabriel Harvey published in 1580 and referred to again by Harvey in the same correspondence and later. The term may be only a fanciful nickname for an informal association of poets; no firm evidence for its existence has ever been presented. Still it is true that a group of Elizabethan poet-critics—Sidney, Spenser, Harvey, Sir Edward Dyer—were interested in reforming Eng. versification by subjecting it to cl. rules (see CLASSICAL METERS IN MODERN LANGUAGES), and their common interests may conceivably have led them to organize into a group analogous to the Fr. *Pléiade* (q.v.). Formally organized or not, the common pursuit of the great poets, Sidney and Spenser, went on to develop Eng. verse on It., Fr., and native models, stabilizing the principles of rhyme and accent in *Astrophil and Stella* and *The Faerie Queene*.   L.B.P.

ARGENTINIAN POETRY. See SPANISH AMERICAN POETRY.

ARGUMENT has several senses in crit. Loosely used, it can mean "plot" (q.v.), i.e. a sequence of events; this meaning is sanctioned by Cl. usage (e.g. Terence, *argumentum fabulae*, the plot of the story) and is common during the Ren. It may also refer to a prologue with a prose paraphrase of the verse to follow. But the most common and most important meaning concerns the structure (q.v.) of a poem: the framework or design which propels and shapes the sequencing of events (see PLOT). Must every poem have an a. in this sense? Has its a. much—or anything—to do with its value? Ren. poetry was certainly written in a trad. which linked

poetry with logic, spoke about the "cause" of a poem, and considered details in relation to their logical function (see RENAISSANCE POETICS). The symbolist view, by contrast, finds the value of poetry in those elements which it does not share with prose: the logical or narrative structure of a poem is dispensable. This seems to be the case in such poems as Mallarmé's *L'Après-midi d'un faune* or Valéry's *La Jeune Parque* (though not in all Valéry): no logical thread links the imagery (q.v.) of these poems. The Ezra Pound of imagism (q.v.), Wallace Stevens, and T. S. Eliot stand at least partly in this trad. A rather different antilogical trad. runs from Rimbaud through vorticism to surrealism (qq.v.) and includes Dylan Thomas: here the brute juxtaposition of imagery is not the result of careful construction but a direct expression of the unconscious.

There seem to be three possible conclusions: that a. is unnecessary; that it is mainly a ploy to attract the reader, relying on the rest of the poem to enable true poetic response; that it is sometimes (always?) part of a poem's true value. It would not be possible to claim that it was the whole of the poem's value without maintaining that the paraphrase was worth as much as the poem. The first view is the symbolist theory. The second is implicit in some romantic crit. and is likely to be held by modern admirers of romantic poetry. The perfect illustration would be a poem like *Kubla Khan*. The third is the traditional view, and in modified form is still found among critics who value structure. Roland Barthes makes the case for modernist subversion of logical a. in *Le Degré zéro de l'écriture* (1953) and in *Le Plaisir du texte* (1973). Jacques Derrida questions the usual distinction between lit. and philosophy by giving centrality not to a. but to metaphors and other linguistic devices. Among common readers, however, the third view is all but universal.—J. Kertzer, *Poetic A.* (1989).   L.D.L.

ARISTOPHANEUS. See AEOLIC.

ARISTOTELIAN INFLUENCE. See CHICAGO SCHOOL; CLASSICAL POETICS; CATHARSIS; FICTION, POETRY AS; POETICS; PLOT.

ARMENIAN POETRY. Descendents of the Urartuans and Hittites, Armenians call themselves *Hai* or *Hye* and their country *Haiastan* after Haik, the legendary great-grandson of Noah. The lang. is Indo-European, and ancient Armenia may have been the cradle of the Indo-European peoples. What is today known as Armenia, one of the Soviet Republics, contains only a fraction of its ancient lands, which are now part of Turkey and Iran. A. frontiers have varied greatly as a result of repeated invasions of this region at the crossroads of East and West.

Armenia provides a perfect laboratory for the study of poetry from ancient inscriptions in cuneiform to modern times. Here one can trace the uses of poetry as incantation, benediction, celebration, and political comment; one can observe how pagan chants to the sun evolve into praises of the light of Christ, then see the same rhythms in paeans to the red dawn of Communism. From the earliest ages to the present, poetry has been a vital part of A. life. The poet, honored early as a religious leader, was expected in periods of oppression to be both conscience and witness of his time.

When Armenia became the first Christian nation in 301 A.D., ancient pagan poetry was destroyed. Only a few poems that had been transmitted orally for millennia were preserved by Movses of Khorene in his 5th-c. history. For centuries, folk poems and variations of the cycle of poems comprising the folk epic *David of Sassoun* were also handed down orally, the latter acquiring Christian characteristics after the 4th c. This is the second oldest epic recorded (pub. 1874), preceded only by the Babylonian epic *Gilgamesh* (pub. 1872). A typical folk poem is the *Groung* (Song of the Crane), written in quatrains called *hyrens* (meaning in the A. style) and sometimes attributed to the medieval troubadour Nahabed Koutchag, who wrote hundreds of *hyrens*:

Where do you come from, crane?
I ache to hear your call,
to know you come from home.
Have you any news at all?

I bless your wings, your eyes.
My heart is torn in two,
the exile's soul all sighs,
waiting for bits of news.

After the 5th c., when a written A. alphabet was developed (to keep the A. church separate from the Byzantine), a strong trad. of ecclesiastical poetry evolved, incl. the work of two 8th-c. women writers, Sahakdougkt Siunetsi and Khosrovidoukht Shirag. The hymns of the church, called *sharagans* ("rows of jewels"), with rhythmic listings and musical parallelism, are best illustrated in the work of Krikor Naregatsi (Gregory of Narek, 951–1003). His cadences, insight, and mystical meditations would have earned him a central place in world lit. had he written in a more accessible lang. In Armenia his poems were put under pillows of the sick and buried with the dead. Also well known in Christian A. p. is Nerses Shnorhali (Nerses the Gracious), who used intricate rhymes, prose poems, and riddles.

The first poems about romantic love were written by Gosdantin Erzengatzi (1250–1336) and Hovhannes Erzengatzi Blouse (1230–93). Hovhannes Telgourantsi (14th c.) should also be mentioned for his love ballads and battle narratives. However, the outstanding med. poet was Frik (Katchadour Ketcharetsi), who lived during Mongol invasions (13th–14th cs.) and wrote about the injustices of the time. He was a master of the forms and techniques common to Persian poetry of the era. Other med. A. p. was produced in monasteries. The lyricism of Frik and Koutchag was a strong influence esp. on Nagash Hovnathan (17th–18th cs.) and Sayat Nova (b. 1712), who wrote songs of sentiment and consolation touched with humor and satire. His songs are A. favorites, and his life has been the subject of modern operas and films such as Sergei Paradjanov's *Color of Pomegranates*.

The Ren. in Europe, stimulated by the fall of Constantinople to the Turks (1453?), which drove Byzantine scholars to Europe, brought only darker ages for the Armenians. They became a subjugated people in their own land. Beginning only in the late 18th c., their literary Ren. was brought about by a population shift into large cities, where the A. people had the support of the church and the presence of a European colony (as opposed to the provinces, where protection against oppression was absent). In the eastern regions too, in territories under Rus. Czarist rule, a similar influx of Armenians into Tiflis, an A. cultural center, brought about a literary rebirth. Soon many A. schools in both regions were using the spoken dialects instead of the old written Krapar, which survives only in church ritual.

In the monasteries of Venice and Vienna, where many A. children were sent to study in the 19th c., the A. Mekhitarist monks were responsible for a rebirth of poetry. Poet and translator Ghevont Alishan (1820–1901) was the most influential of these monks and his students composed the poetry of the A. romantic period. Bedros Tourian (1851–72) was the first to write purely subjective poetry. He read contemp. Fr. poetry and wrote lyrics that won a large audience of admirers. But the most lyrical voice of the time belonged to Missak Medzarents (1886–1908), whose two books, *Nor Dagher* (1907) and *Dsiadsan* (1907), have been compared to Shelley and Verlaine.

His contemporary, Raffi (Hagop Melik-Hagopian, 1837–88), when he observed the suffering in Turkish Armenia, renounced poetry for prose, following the lead of Khatchadour Abovian, called the father of modern A. lit. Another well known poet of the time, Michael Nalbandian (1829–66), died in Russia after being imprisoned for political writing. His poem "To Freedom," sung secretly both in Russia and Turkish Armenia, begins: "God of Freedom, since that day / you made life of inert clay / my first and speechless sound / while struggling to be unbound / was my cry for liberty."

The following generation in Tiflis produced Hovaness Toumanian (1869–1923), called the "poet of all Armenians," famous not only for poems, stories, and crit., but for his generosity to other writers. Also noteworthy, Avedik Issahakian (1875–1957) made wide use of legend and proverb. Vahan Derian (1885–1920) produced some of the most lyrical writing in Armenia; Medzarents and he have been called the most musical of A. poets. The most prominent poets writing at the turn of the century in Istanbul were Siamanto (Adom Yarjanian, 1878–1915), Daniel Varoujan (1884–1915), and Roupen Sevag (1890–1915). All three did much to vitalize the lang. by introducing European symbolism, social and political themes, national pride, pagan images, and, in the work of Varoujan, a new sensualism not present since the Middle Ages (he has been called "one of the most life-filled poets in Western lit."). All three are examples of the poet as leader and hero. Varoujan's "Red Soil" begins:

Here on a plate on my desk is a gift
a handful of soil, a clump from the
    fields
of my fatherland. The giver thought
he gave his heart and did not know
he gave with it the heart of
his forefathers.

Other poets who should be mentioned are Indra (Diran Cherakian, 1875–1921) and his student Matteos Zarifian (1894–1924).

The main influence on modern A. p. is politicosocial oppression, which accounts both for poems of protest and for the absence of writing altogether. Of several periods of such oppression the worst were the Turkish massacres of 1886 and 1915; the latter not only exterminated 200 poets but also decimated the entire reading public, two million people, stopping all lit. for almost a generation.

The father of modern Soviet A. p. is Eghishe Charents (1897–1937), who gained fame at 20 with "Dantesque Legend," one of the strongest anti-violence poems in Western lit. He wrote it after the defense of Van, where he had gone as a 16-year-old soldier after the Turkish massacres had removed most of the population, incl. the nation's top writers, in Istanbul. Charents, often called the A. Majakovskij, became a stronger and more versatile writer than the Russian he admired. He died in prison. His fellow poet Gourgen Mahari (1903–69) was sent to Siberia but survived the purges. Other notable contemporaries incl. Gostan Zarian (1885–1969), another daring innovator; Kegham Sarian (1902–76), who managed to produce lyric poetry when many others succumbed to the prescribed Social Realism; and Nayirie Zarian (1900–69).

In the next generation two outstanding poets were Hovaness Shiraz (1915–85), the most popular poet of his time, and Barouyr Sevag (1924–72), whose work moves on many levels: metaphysical, political, patriotic, celebratory. Today the leading poets are Gevorg Emin (b. 1919), who is widely translated; Vahakn Davtian (b. 1923), whose early work has been compared to Yeats's and whose new poems are rooted in native soil but universal in appeal: and Hamo Sahian (b. 1914), whose work is noted for its musicality. Sylva Gaboudikian, Maro Markarian, Hratchia Hovanessian, and Saghatel Haroutunian are the leaders of the estab-

lishment. Important younger poets incl. Arevshad Avakian, Razmig Davoyan, Ardem Haroutiunian, and Hovhaness Grigorian, who, with their free floating syntax, offer fresh imagery. Yuri Sahakian's poems of social comment investigate choice and commitment, while satirist Aramais Sahagian makes playful jabs at A. life. Armen Mardirossian, Davit Hovanness, Ludvig Touryan, Ahahid Barsamian, Medakse, Henrik Edoyan, and Edward Milidonian are names most often seen in the literary journals. Among the very young and promising are Armen Shekoyan and Hrachia Saruchan.

Although A. p. may be compared to contemp. poetry worldwide, much of the love poetry is addressed to the land or lost lands across the border. Ararat, the sacred mountain of the Armenians, is a common image. Gevorg Emin in one of his Ararat poems says it is "always in sight, always out of reach, like a great love."

For an outsider the startling fact about A. p. today is the reader's involvement. Poetry is quoted in everyday life as a matter of course. Poetry books are published in huge runs and often sell out within days.

In the diaspora things are different. The only major poet to escape the genocide was Vahan Tekeyan (1878–1945), who by chance was not in Istanbul that April. His painstakingly honed sonnets have earned him a reputation as a visionary. His poems search for the affirmation and redemption that should follow tragedy, but ironically his most frequently quoted work is a bitter sonnet, "We Shall Say to God" (1917):

Should it happen we do not endure
this uneven fight and drained
of strength and agonized
we fall on death's ground not to rise
and the great crime ends
with the last Armenian eyes
closing without seeing a victorious day,
let us swear that when we find
God in his paradise offering comfort
to make amends for our pain,
let us swear that we will refuse
saying No, send us to hell again.
We choose hell. You made us know it
    well.
Keep your paradise for the Turk.

Younger poets who survived or were born abroad include Aharon Dadourian and Puzand Topalian, both strongly influenced by the Fr. surrealists; Harout Gosdantian, Nighoghos Sarafian, and novelist-poet Shahan Shhnour also settled in France. Yeghivart (Jerusalem), Mousegh Ishkhan, Andranik Zarougian, and Vahe-Vahian, all orphaned children of the genocide, grew up in Syria and Beirut. Hamasdegh (H. Gelenian, 1895–1966), lived in the U.S. Today one of the leading voices of the diaspora poets belongs to Zahrad (Zareh Yaldiciyan, b. 1923) in Istanbul, who writes wry, whimsical verse. Vahe Oshagan (b. 1923) and other expatriates of Beirut, influenced by Fr. surrealists and European absurdists, now live in France or America. Many third-generation diaspora poets are writing in the lang. of the countries where they were born; hence, even though they keep A. names and themes, they belong to other lits. even while using the imagery of their ancestry. Some are doing trs., bringing the riches of A. p., locked for centuries in a difficult lang., to other cultures.

ANTHOLOGIES: *David of Sassoun*, tr. A. K. Shalian (1964); *Anthol. of A. P.*, (1978), *Sacred Wrath* (1983), both ed. and tr. D. Der-Hovanessian and M. Margossian; *Come Sit Beside Me and Listen to Kouchag* (1985), *For You On New Year's Day* (1987), both tr. D. Der-Hovanessian.

HISTORY AND CRITICISM: V. Brussov, "The P. of Armenia," tr. A. S. Avakian, *The A. Rev.* 1 (1948); H. Thorossian, *Histoire de la litt. armenienne* (1951); S. Der-Nercessian, *The Armenians* (1970); M. J. Arlen, *Passage to Ararat* (1975); D. M. Lang, *Armenia: Cradle of Civilization* (1978); C. Walker, *Armenia, Survival of a Nation* (1980); D. Der-Hovanessian and M. Margossian, "A. Lit," *Encyc. of World Lit. in the 20th C.*, rev. ed., ed. L. S. Klein, v. 1 (1981); T. Gamkrelidze and V. Ivanov, *Origins of the Indo-Europeans* (1986). D.D.-H.

ARSIS AND THESIS (Gr. "raising and lowering"). These terms, and their equivalents, a. and *basis* ("step"), and *to anō* ("the up [time]") and *to katō* ("the down"), designate the two rhythmical divisions of the foot (q.v.) in Cl. Gr. and Lat. prosody. The t. always contains a basic *longum* or its resolved equivalent and is the rhythmically prominent portion of the foot; the a. always contains at least one *breve* or an *anceps* and is the nonprominent portion. However, a. and t. should not be equated with the up-and-down beats of Western music. In simple feet such as the iamb ($\cup -$), trochee ($- \cup$), dactyl ($- \cup \cup$), and anapaest ($\cup \cup -$), the a. is the single or double *breve*; the t. is the *longum*.

LINGUISTIC BASIS. The two primary attributes of rhythm are temporal regularity and prominence differentiation. A. and t. pertain to the latter. When subjects in a psychological experiment were presented with a sequence of evenly spaced, identical sounds, they judged alternate sounds to be stronger, i.e. they assigned an alternating a. and t. structure to an objectively undifferentiated sequence. In the rhythm of speech, the prominence is commonly stress: strong or t. syllables have primary or secondary stress, while weak or a. syllables are unstressed. At least one syllable must be mapped onto t., but sometimes no syllable is assigned to a. In some langs., a sequence of two syllables within the same word can be mapped onto one t.; see RESOLUTION.

The terms originally designated the raising and lowering of the foot in walking (Pseudo-Aristotle, *Problemata* 5.41; cf. *Bacchius* 98) and probably entered the technical terminology of music theory from description of the dance. In the later Roman period, a. sometimes refers to the first part of the foot, t. to the second, but their meanings became reversed in the Lat. trad. (e.g. Terentianus Maurus [see Keil 6.366, vv. 1345–46]), probably when the grammarians came to identify a. and t. with the lowering and raising of the voice rather than of the foot. The confusion aroused by this reversal of meanings was carried into mod. Cl. scholarship by Richard Bentley in the 18th c. and Gottfried Hermann in the 19th. It would be better if both terms were now avoided altogether outside of Gr. metrics. In Old Germanic and OE metrics the equivalent terms are *lift* and *dip*; modern metrists speak indifferently of *positions* or else of *ictus* (q.v.) and *nonictus*. See FOOT; ICTUS; METER.—J. Caesar, *Disputatio de verborum "a." et "t." apud scriptores artis metricae latinos . . . significatione* (1885); E. H. Sturtevant, "The Ictus of Cl. Verse," *AJP* 44 (1923); H. Woodrow, "Time Perception," *Handbook of Exper. Psych.*, ed. S. S. Stevens (1951); R. P. Winnington-Ingram, "Fragments of Unknown Gr. Tragic Texts with Musical Notation, II," *SO* 31 (1955); Beare, ch. 5; Maas, sect. 8; Dale, 210 ff.; W. S. Allen, *Accent and Rhythm* (1973); A. J. Neubecker, *Altgriechische Musik* (1977); Michaelides; West. A.M.D.; L.D.S.

ART FOR ART'S SAKE. See AESTHETICISM; POETRY, THEORIES OF.

ARTE MAYOR. As a general Sp. metric term, a. m. may mean any line of nine or more syllables. However, a. m. almost always refers to a line of a certain pattern (*verso de a. m.*) or to the strophe composed of such lines (*copla de a. m.*). The line developed from the late Med. Lat. double Adonic modified by an increasingly liberal use of anacrusis and catalexis (qq.v.). Late med. poets borrowed the a. m. directly from the Galician-Portuguese of the 13th and 14th c. The form reached the peak of its devel. in 15th-c. Sp. poetry, then gave way to the Italianate hendecasyllable in the 16th, since which time it has occupied only a minor position in Sp. poetry. Juan de Mena (1411–56) is considered its greatest master. A recitative measure, it was the vehicle for most poetry of weighty or serious subject matter of the 15th c. Unlike most learned Sp. verse, the a. m. was not restricted by syllable count, but depended largely on rhythmic beat. The basic pattern was a 12-beat verse divided into two hemistichs of six beats each and having triple rhythm, $\cup - \cup \cup - \cup \mid \cup - \cup \cup - \cup$, with the second syllable in each hemistich receiving secondary stress and the fifth syllable in each primary stress. The primary and secondary stress beats (the latter occasionally lacking) of each hemistich are supplied by accented syllables; the unstressed beats between these two are supplied by two obligatory unaccented syllables; the remaining unstressed beats may each be supplied by one or two unaccented syllables or a rest beat. The pattern was not always strictly followed. The a. m. was normally arranged in groups of eight lines to form a stanza, the *copla de a. m.*, rhyming *abbaacca*, less often *ababbccb* or *abbaacac*. Although the original a. m. enjoyed great rhythmic and syllabic freedom, the line in later centuries became primarily a 12-syllable or a 6-plus-6-syllable verse with marked amphibrachic rhythm.—R. Foulché-Delbosc, "Etude sur le *Laberinto* de Juan de Mena," *Revue hispanique* 9 (1902); J. Saavedra Molina, *El verso de a. m.* (1946); Le Gentil; M. Burger, *Recherches sur la structure et l'origine des vers romans* (1957); D. C. Clarke, *Morphology of 15th-C. Castilian Verse* (1964), "Line Formation in the Galician-Portuguese Poetry of the Cancioneiro Colocci-Brancuti," *RPh* 35 (1981); Navarro.

D.C.C.

ARTE MENOR. Sp. octosyllabic verse (sometimes shorter). The term is used in contrast to *arte mayor* (q.v.), which has longer lines, and is generally applied to the verse characteristic of the *copla de a. m.*, a late medieval stanza having the rhyme scheme of any *copla de arte mayor* or variation thereof. Both line and strophe were probably borrowed from the 13th- and 14th-c. Galician-Portuguese.—D. C. Clarke, "*Redondilla* and *copla de a. m.*," *HR* 9 (1941); Navarro. D.C.C.

ARTIFICIAL INTELLIGENCE. See COMPUTER POETRY.

ARUZ. See PERSIAN POETRY; ARABIC PROSODY; TURKISH POETRY.

ARZAMAS. A Rus. literary discussion circle which met between 1815 and 1818. Its members, partisans of the elegant, Westernized style of Nikolaj Karamzin, included the poets Žukovskij, Batjuškov, Vjazemskij, and, most importantly, the young Alexander Pushkin. The chief business of the group was the reading of parodies of the conservative, Slavonicized style of their opponents, the followers of Admiral Šiškov. The circle was significant for the role it played in fostering the "golden age" of Rus. poetry, which came in the 1820s. See RUSSIAN POETRY.—"*A.*" i "*arzamasskie*" *protokoly*, ed. M. S. Borovkova-Majkova (1933); M. I. Gillel'son, *Molodoj Puškin i arzamasskoe bratstvo* (1974); Terras. W.E.H.

ASCLEPIAD, Asclepiadean. An Aeolic (q.v.) line consisting of a glyconic (x x – ◡ ◡ – ◡ – ; q.v.) internally compounded with a choriamb (q.v.), thus: x x – ◡ ◡ – – ◡ ◡ – ◡ – . Though named by later grammarians after the Gr. epigrammatist Asclepiades of Samos (ca. 300 B.C.), it is already found in Alcaeus (7th c. B.C.), and in fact was used long before for both lyric (monodic and choral) and tragedy. The A. was used extensively both as a stichic verse and in combination with other Ae-

olic forms to form strophes. Horace in his *Odes* used the A. frequently, in five different arrangements which have come to be called First through Fifth As., though modern scholars do not agree on which types go with which names. The A. line form shown at the end of the first sentence above is known as the "Lesser A."; the "Greater A." (there seems to be no ancient evidence for this term) adds a third choriamb: x x – ◡ ◡ – – ◡ ◡ – – ◡ ◡ – ◡ – . The Greater A. was used by both the Aeolic poets and by Horace.

In the Middle Ages, As. (or Alcaic hendecasyllables) alternating with glyconics are found in Hilary of Poitiers (4th c. A.D.), Prudentius (late 4th c. A.D.), and the Carolingian poets; as in Horace, there is usually a break after the sixth position: – – – ◡ ◡ – | – ◡ ◡ – ◡ – . The medieval A. strophe kept itself quietly afloat on the steady stream of popularity of the Cl. ode forms—particularly the Sapphic—a stream given its impetus by the authority of Horatian poetics. There are some 40 examples of the A. in the *Analecta hymnica*. In the Ren., accentual imitations and trs. of Asclepiadeans were tried by Ronsard and the *Pléiade*. Sidney attempts some in the *Old Arcadia* (e.g. no. 37, "O sweet woods"), and Collins' "Ode to Evening" is a Fourth Asclepiadean. The young Milton essayed an imitation "as near as the Language will permit" of Horace's Ode 1.5 (a Third A.), rendering *Quis multa gracilis te puer in rosa* as "What slender youth bedew'd with liquid odours." Ger. examples incl. Klopstock's "Der Zürcher See" and Hölderlin's "Heidelberg."—Wilamowitz; H. Sadej, "De versu Asclepiadeo minore apud Romanos obvio," *Eos* 45 (1951); L. Rotsch, "Zur Form der drei Horaz-Oden im Asclepiadeus maior," *Gymnasium* 64 (1957); A. R. Bellinger, "The Lesser Asclepiadean Line of Horace," *YCS* 15 (1957); Norberg; Maas; W. Bennett, *Ger. Verse in Cl. Metres* (1963), ch. 27; L. P. Wilkinson, *Golden Lat. Artistry* (1963); Koster; N. A. Bonavia-Hunt, *Horace the Minstrel* (1969); Halporn et al.; Snell; West.

J.W.H.; T.V.F.B.

ASSAMESE POETRY. See INDIAN POETRY.

ASSOCIATION. See IMAGINATION; ONOMATOPOEIA; SOUND.

ASSONANCE (Lat. *assonare*, "to answer with the same sound"; Ir. *ammus*). In a trad. stemming from OF and OSp., and until the 20th c. with its more varied versification, a. served the same function as rhyme (q.v.), i.e. formalized closures to lines in the poems of most Romance langs. The OF *Chanson de Roland* (early 12th c.) attempts in each *laisse* (q.v.) to have not only the same vowel in the final stressed syllable of each line but also the same vowel in the following weak syllable (if there is one). A similar system prevailed in Sp. and Port., as can be seen not only in the great epic *Os Lusíadas* by Camões (16th c.) but also in his lyrics, sonnets, and pastorals. In It., the final words in four typical consecutive lines of Dante's *Divina commedia* end *viaggio-vide-selvaggio-gride* (91–94). In all of these, it is the vowel that cannot be parted with, the result being, by increasing constraint, a., rhyme, or identity.

Along with these complex end echoes, however, Romance poets have employed much internal a., partly perhaps because their langs., like Lat., are so rich in vocables. Almost any Lat. or Gr. poet can be shown to have loved vowel play (Wilkinson; Stanford). Dryden quotes this line from the *Aeneid* to demonstrate Virgil's "musical ear"—"Quo fata trahunt retrahuntque, sequamur"—which stresses *a* four times against a background of three unstressed *u* sounds. In modern times, Fr. has far more end rhymes than other Romance langs., but because so many Fr. final consonants are not pronounced, the rhyme is sometimes really a. The cl. alexandrine (q.v.) ends in a vowel (i.e. a.) perhaps 20 percent of the time. Furthermore, internal a. is as marked an acoustic device of the alexandrine as of later Fr. poetry, as in *Phèdre*, which has a number of lines with a. of three syllables, this one (1.3.9) with four—"Tout m'afflige et me nuit et conspire a me nuire." Verlaine with his belief in "musique avant toute chose" is often credited with inspiring poets of his day to employ sonorous sounds ("rime or assonate; otherwise, no verse" [1888]); a. was most important in his own versification.

Far less a subject of traditional interest than alliteration (q.v.) but more noticed than consonance (q.v.), a. has often been thought a mere substitute for rhyme. It is true that the Germanic langs. had an early history of alliterative poetries—e.g. *Beowulf*—and continue to employ alliteration, often heavily. True, too, the Celtic langs., notably Welsh, developed schemes of sound correspondence, esp. *cynghanedd* (q.v.), that have complex alliterative patterns. But it is equally true that in nearly all langs., incl. Ir. and Welsh, poets have continually employed a. internally if not as a substitute for end rhyme. The term "a." was borrowed by the Eng. from Sp. and Fr. to describe the various vocalic substitutes for rhyme in the Romance poetries. But end a. is only a small part of the total phenomenon called "a." Consequently, a. is best defined as the repetition of the sound of a vowel or diphthong in nonrhyming stressed syllables near enough to each other for the echo to be discernible. Note the following facts about this definition:

First and most important, a. is an *aural* device. Because alliteration is normally initial in words, it usually receives aid from the reader's eye. But a., since it is normally medial, can expect little such help. Only the ear can respond to Shakespeare's "Time's scythe," Eliot's "recovers / My guts," or MacLeish's "cough / In waltz-time."

Second, because a. is sonant, and since vowels and diphthongs change their pronunciation, sometimes radically, over time and from region to region, while consonants change relatively little, a reader needs to know how the vowels were pronounced by the poet being read. In Eng., because the Great Vowel Shift was largely completed by Shakespeare's time, the verse of Chaucer and other ME poets sounds different from that of later times. Furthermore, a number of vowels continued to change pronunciation after Shakespeare's day; by the 18th c., Eng. poets were still naturally rhyming *Devil-civil, stem-stream, pull-dull-fool, feast-rest, tea-obey,* and *join-fine.*

Third, because there are more consonants than vowels in the IE langs., those langs. will have more accidental a. than accidental alliteration. The consonants in Eng. number about 24, but Eng. has at least 18 different vocalic sounds that poets can employ for rhyme or a. In addition to simple assonances such as *back-cast, rose-float,* and *feat-seek,* or the echoes of diphthongs such as *fine-bride* and *proud-cowl,* poets assonate *er, ir, ur,* and sometimes *ear* in words like *serve, furred, earn, dirge;* or *beard* with *miracle* and *cheer.* Given so many choices, if one can assume that Pope intended the trisyllabic a. in "silver-quivering rills," that Wilbur intended it in "ladders and hats hurl past," and that Lowell intended it in "mast-lashed master," one is perhaps willing to accept as intended the disyllabic a. in Pope's "a lazy state," in Wilbur's "hollow knocks" and "optative bop," or in Lowell's "gagged Italians" ("Falling Asleep over the *Aeneid*").

Ger. poets seem to have found a. even more appealing than alliteration, from Brentano, who has whole poems with a polysyllabic a. in nearly every line, to Goethe, Heine, and modern poets. Goethe in his lyrics and plays has more a. than other phonic echoes, as in Faust's contract with Mephistopheles, which in its last three lines has a six-syllable a. of [aɪ] as well as other echoes: "Dann bist du d*ei*nes Dienstes fr*ei*, / Die Ühr mag stehn, der Z*ei*ger fallen, / Es s*ei* die Z*ei*t fur mich vorb*ei*!" And Rilke, one of the most sonorous of poets, opens "Wendung" with "L*a*nge err*a*ng ers im Anschauen."

Rus. poets too have employed a. consistently, esp. Pasternak, Blok, and Bryusov, the latter two frequently substituting it for end rhyme (Plank; Donchin).

Finally, the notion that a. is no longer used for end rhyme must be dispelled. Blok replaced rhyme with a. in whole series of poems, as did Rilke; Verlaine used a. instead of rhyme perhaps half the time, and Eng. poets such as Thomas in Britain and Jarrell and Crane in the U.S. have often made such a substitution. It should also be pointed out that poets other than Sp. and It. have dabbled with polysyllabic a., the echoes coming only in the weak final syllables. But in Eng. such echoes are rare, difficult, and relatively ineffective. In fact, just as computers would be of little help in finding a., any reader should hesitate before including obviously weak syllables in a study of vowel repetitions.

R. E. Deutsch, *The Patterns of Sound in Lucretius* (1939); W. B. Stanford, *Aeschylus in His Style* (1942), *The Sound of Gr.* (1967); B. Donchin, *The Influence of Fr. Symbolism on Rus. Poetry* (1958); N. I. Hérescu, *La Poésie latine* (1960); W. Kayser, *Gesch. des deutschen Verses* (1960); P. Delbouille, *Poésie et sonorités*, 2 v. (1961, 1984); D. L. Plank, *Pasternak's Lyrics* (1968); L. P. Wilkinson, *Golden Lat. Artistry* (1970); J. Gluck, "A. in Ancient Heb. Poetry," *De Fructu oris sui: Essays in Honor of Adrianus von Selma*, ed. I. H. Eybers et al. (1971); Wimsatt; P. G. Adams, *Graces of Harmony* (1977); R. P Newton, *Vowel Undersong* (1981); Brogan, esp. items C129-30, C150, C152–53, K2, K116, L233, L322, L406, L518.   P.G.A.

ASSYRO-BABYLONIAN POETRY. Of the two main dialects of Akkadian, a Semitic lang., Babylonian (B.) and not Assyrian (A.) was used for most of the poetry. While some poetic texts survive (on clay tablets, written in cuneiform characters) from the end of the third millennium B.C., the earliest creative period can be dated from about ca. 1800 onward, the OB (Old Babylonian) period. Toward the end of the second millennium, ca. 1200 and later, new poetry is composed. Most of the poetry is known from late copies collected in the royal libraries of Tiglathpileser I (ca. 1100 B.C.) in Assur and of Assurbanipal (668–27 B.C.) in Nineveh.

Most of the texts are anonymous; only the author of the epic of the plague god Irra—who claims to have written it down from the god's dictation—and the author of the Gilgamesh Epic are known by name. Names appearing in colophons are those of the scribe, not of the poet; literary catalogues list beside titles of compositions not only personal names but also names of gods and mythological figures.

With respect to genre, the corpus may be divided into narrative, religious, and didactic poems, i.e. epics, hymns, prayers, and "wisdom lit." Purely secular poetry seems not to have been recorded in writing. Charms—against the scorpion, the toothache, or to invoke a star—are embedded in medical or magical prescriptions and suggest a pattern of folk poetry made up of short lines and often concatenated repetitions, such as

> Anger advances like a wild bull
> Jumps at me like a dog,
> Like a lion, it is formidable in progress
> Like a wolf, it is full of fury.

Verses whose lyricism would suggest love poetry, as well as first lines such as "Away, sleep! I want to embrace my lover" (cited in a literary catalogue), concern divine lovers, as in the OB poem

> the women's quarter moans, the bed-
> chamber weeps

wherein we were wont to celebrate the
> wedding;
> the courtyard sighs, the loft laments
> wherein we were wont to do sweet dalli-
> ance.

In an A. elegy a woman who died in childbirth complains:

> I lived with him who was my lover.
> Death came creeping into my bedroom,
> it drove me from my house,
> it tore me from my husband,
> it set my feet into a land of no return.

The formal characteristic of B., as of all Semitic and also Sumerian poetry (q.v.), syntactic parallelism (q.v.), evidenced in the first two examples above, is frequently combined with chiasmus (q.v.—first example), but enjambment and zeugma (qq.v.) are rarely tolerated. Rhyme (internal or final), alliteration, onomatopoeia, anaphora, and epiphora may be used for special effect. Meter is based on stress; a line contains four measures, rarely three or five, with a syntactic break or caesura in the middle. The verse ending is trochaic (suffixes that would make the word a dactyl are truncated). Two types of acrostics (q.v.), such that the initial syllable of the lines spell out a name or a pious wish, and such that each line of a strophe begins with the same sign, are also known; some of these are also telestichs.

Narrative Poetry. B. epics deal with the exploits of gods or mythological beings and are therefore often dubbed "myths." Many of these date to the OB period, although their first-millennium recensions are more complete and more elaborate—e.g. the *Story of the Bird Anzû*, who stole the Tablet of Office from the supreme god Enlil and was defeated by the god Ninurta; the story of the mythical king *Etana*, who ascended to heaven on the back of an eagle to obtain the herb for childbearing; the story of *Atra-hasis* (Exceedingly Wise), who survived the Flood brought about by the gods after they had created mankind; and the *Epic of Gilgamesh*. To the middle of the second millennium date the *Story of Wise Adapa* and of *Nergal and Ereshkigal*, which tells how Nergal came to rule the nether world together with its queen Ereshkigal. Only first-millennium recensions are known of the *Epic of Creation*, the story of the defeat of the forces of chaos by the god Marduk, who was thereby acknowledged supreme god and who created the cosmos out of the body of the primeval monster; the *Epic of Irra*, which describes the calamities that befell Babylon when the plague god Irra replaced its tutelary god Marduk; and the *Descent of Ishtar to the Nether World*.

The 19th-c. discovery of Tablet XI with its account of the Flood so closely paralleling that in the OT triggered Western interest in the *Epic of Gilgamesh*. It deals with basic human concerns of all times—friendship, and the quest for immortality, attainable only by achieving enduring fame. When Enkidu, a semi-savage created by the gods to become Gilgamesh's friend and companion, dies, Gilgamesh realizes the same fate awaits him and so begins the quest which leads him to the sole survivor of the Flood. Just as the *Odyssey* does not end with the death of Odysseus, the *Epic of Gilgamesh* ends not with the death of its hero, but as it began, with the description of the ramparts of Uruk, his lasting achievement. Some narrative poems have kings as heroes, e.g. a cycle about Sargon and Naram-Sin, who built the Akkadian empire in the late third millennium, composed in OB times and also known from later versions. Some are couched as "autobiographies," with the king narrating his own history. The lesson to be drawn from events of the past is held up to the future ruler being addressed in a sort of *envoi* at the end. The A. king Tukulti Ninurta (1243–07 B.C.) and his victory over the B. king Kashtiliash is celebrated in poems written in Assyria, reflecting A. political ideology though in the literary, i.e. B., dialect.

Religious Poetry. B. hymns address a number of gods and goddesses; they are characterized by an elevated, even *recherché* style and a vocabulary of rare terms, indicators of their learned origin and sophisticated audience. They are often divided into strophes; occasional rulings on the tablet after each distich or every 10th line may not coincide with the strophic divisions. The hymn to Shamash (the sun god and god of justice) has exactly 200 lines, divided by rulings into 100 distichs; the hymns to Ishtar, to the Queen of Nippur, and to Nabu each contain over 200 lines. Some hymns, such as the 200-line hymn to Gula, are styled in the first person, the goddess speaking her own self-praise. Some hymns are in praise of cities.

Prayers also address the deity with praise but stress the supplicant's misery and petition. Their poetic virtue lies in their description of mood and feeling. Their plaintive lyricism, in such phrases as "How wet with my tears is my bread!", "Man's sins are more numerous than the hairs on his head," or "What sin have I committed against my god?" reminds us of the penitential Psalms. Prayers to the gods of divination ask for a favorable answer to the oracle query.

Didactic Poetry comprises philosophical dialogues or monologues questioning the fairness of the fate bestowed by the god, such as the *Theodicy*, an acrostic, and the B. *Job*, consisting of four "books" of 120 lines each. Animal fables and poetic contests (q.v.) in which two rivals—trees, cereals—extol their own merits and belittle their opponents', hark back to a well-attested Sumerian genre.

Only a few humorous poems are known: the *Dialogue between Master and Servant*, also classed with "wisdom lit.," may be one; another is the difficult OB *At the Cleaners*, while the *Tale of the Poor Man of Nippur*, having close affinities with the *Tale of the First Larrikin* of the Arabian Nights, has perennial appeal. The *Tale of the Illiterate Doctor*, similarly situated in the Sumerian city of Nippur, draws its humor from the linguistic effects of Sumerian interspersed in the B. text.

ANTHOLOGIES: *Sumerisch-akkadische Hymnen und Gebete*, ed. and tr. A. Falkenstein and W. von Soden (1953)—good intro. and commentary; *Ancient Near Eastern Texts Relating to the O.T.*, ed. J. B. Pritchard, 3d ed. with Supp. (1969); *Les Religions du Proche Orient asiatique: Textes babyloniens, ougaritiques, hittites*, ed. and tr. R. Labat et al. (1970); *Hymnes et prières aux dieux de Babylonie et d'Assyrie*, ed. and tr. M.-J. Seux (1976).

INDIVIDUAL POEMS: O. R. Gurney, "The Tale of the Poor Man of Nippur," *Anatolian Studies* 6–7 (1956–57); C. J. Gadd, "At the Cleaners," *Iraq* 25 (1963) and A. Livingstone in *Alter Orient und Altes Testament, Sonderreihe*, v. 220 (1988); W. G. Lambert, "The Gula Hymn of Bullutsa-rabi," *Orientalia*, n.s. 36 (1967), "The Hymn to the Queen of Nippur," *Studies Presented to F. R. Kraus* (1983); W. von Soden, "Der grosse Hymnus an Nabu," *ZAVA* 61 (1971); S. A. Picchioni, *Il poemetto di Adapa* (1981); A. Schott, *Das Gilgamesch-Epos*, rev. W. von Soden (1982); J. Gardner and J. Maier, *Gilgamesh* (1984); J. V. Kinnier Wilson, *The Legend of Etana* (1985); A. Livingstone in *AOATS* 220 (1988).

HISTORY AND CRITICISM: J. Nougayrol, "L'Epopée babylonienne," *ANLMSF* (1970); O. R. Gurney, "The Tale of the Poor Man of Nippur and its Folktale Parallels," *Anatolian Studies* 22 (1972); K. Hecker, *Untersuchungen der akkadischen Epik* (1974); A. L. Oppenheim, *Ancient Mesopotamia*, 2d ed. (1977); E. Reiner, *Your Thwarts in Pieces, Your Mooring Rope Cut* (1984)—incl. originals and literary evaluations. E.R.

ASYNARTETON (Gr. "disconnected," "disjunct"). A verse composed out of two or more distinct rhythmical cola, usually in synapheia (q.v.) but separated from each other by word end and not analyzable as continuous portions of the same rhythm. The genre was invented, or first given vogue, by Archilochus; and several of the more common examples are linked to his name (see ARCHILOCHIAN). Archilochus' asynarteta are always dicola, and their components are, with one exception, identical to the segments normally marked off by word end within the most common stichic meters—hexameter, trimeter (full and catalectic), and catalectic tetrameter (iambic and trochaic). The imitations produced by later authors are longer and draw on a more varied repertory of rhythms.—Koster, 190 ff.; D. Korzeniewski, *Griechische Metrik* (1968), 122–26; L. E. Rossi, "Asynarteta from the Archaic to the Alexandrian Poets," *Arethusa* 9 (1976); B. M. P. Palumbo Stracca, *La teoria antica degli asynarteti* (1980); Snell; West. A.T.C.

ASYNDETON (Gr. "unconnected"). The omission of conjunctions between phrases or clauses; the

opposite of polysyndeton (q.v.), which is the addition of conjunctions. Omission of conjunctions between words is technically *brachylogia*—fundamental to all forms of series and catalogues (q.v.)—but many writers now use a. as the cover term for all types of conjunction deletion. In this sense, a. is the genus for several species of deletions which enable the poet to achieve effects of speed, breathlessness, headlong momentum, and vehemence. And it is itself, in turn, one species of all figures of ellipsis (q.v.). Homer uses it, as does Virgil (e.g. *Aeneid* 4.594), but the classic examples are Aristotle's "I have done; you have heard me. The facts are before you; I ask for your judgment" (*Rhetoric*) and Caesar's "Veni, vidi, vici." Horace and Statius are fond of the device, and their example was followed by many Med. Lat. poets. Med. Ger. poets (e.g., Walther von der Vogelweide, Wolfram von Eschenbach) also made much use of a., but the figure was esp. favored by baroque (q.v.) poets in Germany (Andreas Gryphius), Spain, and France. In the Latinist Milton as well one can find numerous examples: "Rocks, Caves, Lakes, Fens, Bogs, Dens, and shades of death" (*Paradise Lost* 2.621); "The first sort by their own suggestion fell, / Self-tempted, self-depraved; man falls, deceived / By the other first: man therefore shall find grace, / The other none" (3.129–32). In Eng., a. has occurred particularly in modern poetry—in the work of the imagists, for example, with their cult of brevity (see IMAGISM)—and in W. H. Auden (e.g. "In Memory of W. B. Yeats"), with his fondness for the pithy and loaded phrase. See also BAROQUE.—H. Pliester, *Die Worthäufung im Barock* (1930); Curtius 285; Lausberg; Group Mu; A. Quinn, *Figures of Speech* (1982); E. Blettner, "The Role of A. in Aristotle's Rhet.," *P&R* 16 (1983); J. P. Houston, *Shakespearean Sentences* (1988); Corbett.
A.PR.; T.V.F.B.; A.W.H.

ATTITUDE. See TONE.

AUBADE. See ALBA.

AUDIENCE. See PERFORMANCE; READER-RESPONSE CRITICISM; RHETORIC AND POETRY.

AUDITION COLORÉE. See SYNAESTHESIA.

AUDITORY IMAGINATION. See SOUND.

AUREATE DICTION. Marked density of Latinate-derived words. Aureation in the more general sense has been characteristic of the high style or epic diction since the Middle Ages, as is conspicuous in Milton. And assimilation of Latinate terms as a process is evident in most of the late-medieval vernaculars, e.g. MHG (where it is called *gebluemte Rede*) as the natural extension of macaronic poetry (q.v.), where Lat. words are juxtaposed to vernacular ones. But in the more restricted and usual

sense, a. d. refers to the characteristically overwrought style of ME and Scottish poetry of the 15th c.—that of William Dunbar, John Lydgate and Stephen Hawes in England and King James I and Robert Henryson in Scotland—as well as of that of the contemporaneous *Rhétoriqueurs* (q.v.) in France. This style is based on coinages from Lat. copious to the point of excess, as in Dunbar's "Haile, sterne superne! Haile, in eterne" (Hail, star on high; hail in eternity), which is followed by the native line "In Godis sicht to shine." The excess has long been derided by literary historians. If today a. d. seems less offensive, that is partly because many terms have since been absorbed into the lang. and so do not today strike us as a. But they were exotic coinages in their day. See SCOTTISH CHAUCERIANS; SCOTTISH POETRY.—J. C. Mendenhall, *A. Terms* (1919); P. H. Nichols, "Lydgate's Influence on the A. Forms of the Scottish Chaucerians," *PMLA* 47 (1932); E. Tilgner, *Die A. Terms bei Lydgate* (1936); C. S. Lewis, *Eng. Lit. in the 16th C.* (1954); J. A. Conley, "Four Studies in A. Terms," Diss., Stanford (1956); S. Lerer, "The Rhet. of Fame," *SSt* 5 (1985).   T.V.F.B.

AUSTRALIAN POETRY. Australians possess not one but two poetic trads., one native (Aboriginal), one imported (European). The poetry of Europeans in the country goes back 200 years and at one time or another has suffered most of the disadvantages of a historically prolonged adolescence. Aboriginal poetry, on the other hand, has something like 40,000 years of continuity behind it. If there must be doubt about its future in an age of mass communication, there is none about its achievement to date. Even the randomly preserved ruins of a native oral trad. testify to its strength, subtlety, and maturity. This in spite of the difficulties involved in judging on the basis of not merely translations but translations into forms quite alien to the originals.
Aboriginal poetry is recited or sung as part of a performance or ritual which includes music, dancing, and theater and whose rationale is sacramental and religious. Though form and content are passed on from generation to generation, there is a great deal of room for improvisation and therefore variation. Clearly the reduction of this oral trad. to written Eng. texts entails considerable loss. Nonetheless, something of the quality of the original comes through in translations like T. G. H. Strehlow's of songs from Central Australia ("The ring-neck-parrots are a cloud of wings; / The shell-parrots are a cloud of wings") and R. Berndt's of the great Arnhem Land cycles associated with the earth mother Kunapipi and the ancestral sisters the Wawalag and the Djanggawul ("Although I leave Bralgu, I am close to it. I, Djanggawul, am paddling . . . "). The Berndt Djanggawul cycle describes in epic dimensions the archetypal sea journey of the parents of the tribes from the mythical Bralgu to Australia. Berndt's

lovesong cycles lyrically reenact other archetypal events, e.g. the Jonah-like death and resurrection of the Wawalags, swallowed then vomited up by the python. In this case the symbolism is both sexual and seasonal, linking fertility with the monsoonal rains.

As a whole, Aboriginal oral poetry is characterized by fundamental identification of humans with the land, expressed through myth (q.v.) with the totemic logic analyzed by Lévi-Strauss. Chiefly it is used for initiatory, mortuary, and ritual increase ceremonies, though there are also songs for everyday purposes, not least for amusement. The impact of Aboriginal culture on white poetry has been fitful and superficial. In the 1930s the Jindyworobak group, led by Rex Ingamells (1913–55), derived inspiration from Black identification with the country. More recently, Les Murray has attempted to imitate Berndt's version of the Wonguri-Mandjigai moon-bone cycle.

From the beginning of European settlement in 1788 to the early 20th c., there was a strong white oral or partly oral trad. consisting of folksongs, ballads, and the like. To begin with, this trad. expressed the sufferings of convicts, many of them Irish, condemned to bitter hardship in an isolated penal colony. Protest songs, often treasonable in nature, were sung in defiance of authority, some of the best-known being "Van Diemen's Land," "Jim Jones at Botany Bay," and "Moreton Bay." The last of these was probably the work of Frank McNamara (b. 1811), also responsible for verses such as the grotesquely and grimly humorous "The Convict's Tour of Hell." Convict ballads elevated the figure of the outlaw and rebel, bushrangers like Bold Jack Donahoe, who scorned "to live in slavery, bound down with iron chains." They led, later in the century, to songs about other celebrated victims of the Law, Ben Hall and Ned Kelly, and to an avatar of Donahoe, "The Wild Colonial Boy."

The Gold Rush of 1851 radically altered A. society. Its songs belonged less to an anonymous folk trad. than to the stage, and by then Am. influence was as strong as that from England or Ireland. Charles Thatcher (1831–78), "The Inimitable," produced songs about the diggings which eventually passed into folklore. There were also, in the second half of the century, ballads about life on the land, focusing on squatters, poor farmers (or "cockies"), and pastoral laborers. These are characteristically stoic and often simultaneously ironic and sentimental. They range from the romantic ("The Banks of the Condamine") to work songs ("Click Go the Shears"), songs celebrating Outback life ("A Thousand Mile Away") or workers' sprees ("Lazy Harry's"), to wry or heartbroken comments on suffering and endurance ("The Old Bullock Dray," "The Cocky Farmer"). Of course the distinction between verses originating in a genuine folk trad. and literary ballads imitating that trad. is a difficult one.

From the later 19th into the early 20th c. a number of poets contributed material which became part of the general store. This included the galloping rhymes of Adam Lindsay Gordon and, after that, the ballads of Barcroft Boake (1866–92), who hanged himself by his own stockwhip, Edward Dyson (1865–1931), E. J. Brady (1869–1952), and Will Ogilvie (1869–1963). Henry Lawson (1867–1922), better known for his short stories, also wrote ballads. The most successful of all literary balladists was A. B. ("Banjo") Paterson (1864–1941), whose verse had a popularity in Australia comparable to that of Kipling in Britain. Best known are "The Man from Snowy River" and "Waltzing Matilda," which has become the unofficial national anthem. These authors published regularly in the nationalistic and radical *Bulletin*, expressing more or less consciously their sense of an A. identity and, frequently, their pride in emergent nationhood. By the time of Federation, i.e. the establishment of centralized self-government in 1901, folk ballads and their literary equivalents no longer sang of exile or revolt, though bush hardship was still a theme. Shortly after, their vogue declined, the last example of this popular genre being the work of C. J. Dennis (1876–1936).

The movement towards adaptation to a difficult new environment evident in the ballad emerges in 19th-c. poetry unconnected with the oral trad. For colonial poets the problem, whether acknowledged or not, was to transform the raw material of Australia, to *poeticize* it, and in so doing build a bridge between new and old world experiences. From the standpoint of the tourist, Barron Field eulogized the kangaroo as a divine mistake, fabulous as sphinx, mermaid, or centaur—or sooty swan and duck-mole (platypus). The persistent notion that everything was "new, new, too new / To foster poesy" was early challenged by Charles Harpur (1813–68), though with ambiguous results. Pondering the antipodean landscape like one of Caspar David Friedrich's alpine travelers, Harpur struggles to transcend the sense of the exotic. His Australia recalls Egypt, Assyria, Babylon in ruins. It is peopled by Miltonic Aborigines and viewed through the lens of the Wordsworthian sublime—tinted with 18th-c. Sensibility. Even so, there is a strength, however awkward, in work like "The Creek of the Four Graves" which is missing in the musical, nature-inspired verse of Henry Kendall (1839–82), whose melancholy warbling owes more to Eng. Victorian poetry than to the great romantics. Here too the attachment to Australia is complicated by contradictions: birds sing in September their song of May. And in the writing of the other significant colonial bard of the wilderness, Adam Lindsay Gordon (1833–70), eucalyptus trunks, like Egyptian obelisks, are carved with indecipherable hieroglyphs, native blossoms are scentless, bright birds songless.

It was not until the end of the century that poetic adaptation to the southern hemisphere became evident in the writing of poets associated with the *Bulletin*. At the same time, not all the writers of the period turned to ballads—or to "diggers, drovers, bush race-courses, / And on all the other pages, horses, horses, horses, horses." Victor Daley (1858–1905), Roderic Quinn (1867–1949), and D. M. Wright (1869–1928) created a celtic twilight Down Under; Bernard O'Dowd (1866–1953) produced a Socialist "poetry militant" inspired in part by Whitman; Christopher Brennan (1870–1932), thoroughly acquainted with European lit. from antiquity to Mallarmé, wrote a dense and sometimes profound *Livre composé*. If *Poems (1913*, with its combination of romantic high-mindedness and *fin de siècle* lassitude, is difficult to appreciate as a whole, its more readable sections, such as the Nietzschean and Arnoldian "The Wanderer" sequence, represent some of the most impressive writing to emerge from Australia. The trad. of philosophical verse was carried on, rather shakily, by "William Baylebridge" (1883–1942). However, after Brennan's, the best verse of the period is that of the radical Mary Gilmore (1864–1962) and of John Shaw Neilson (1872–1942). Uneducated, dogged by poverty, Neilson is Australia's most eccentric poetic talent and, at least in the lightness and lyricism of his work, very nearly its finest.

The Great War prompted some sobering reflections in verse, but the tone of the aftermath was escapist and frivolous, dominated by nationalism gone to seed and by an equally spurious internationalism fostered by the followers of Norman Lindsay and the journal *Vision*. Hugh McCrae (1876–1958) favored satyrs and whimsy and, in his early phase, Kenneth Slessor (1901–71) followed the fashion for pseudo-jollity and the pursuit of Pan on the shores of Sydney Harbor. If the 19th-c. issue for poets had been to reconcile European poetic trads. with antipodean realities, the issue in the 20th c. was—and is—to assimilate modernity. Slessor introduced the rhythms of T. S. Eliot to A. p. in his later and best work, producing in the process what is probably the finest individual A. poem, "Five Bells."

However, even after World War II, modernism remained suspect. The Ern Malley hoax, in which the avant-garde journal *Angry Penguins* was persuaded to publish fake modernist verse, was meant to discredit experimentation and succeeded in inhibiting it for decades. In spite of this, A. p. in the 1940s, following economic depression, worldwide political upheaval, the trauma of near-invasion by the Japanese, and the intellectual shock which accompanied the assimilation of Marx and Freud, could scarcely revert to either the gum-trees-and-sheep identity of the 1890s or the Art Deco idyll of the 1920s. Whether conservative or experimental, it chose the exploration of a problematic and angst-ridden inwardness, an analogue for the previous century's exploration of *terra australis incognita*. For Francis Webb (1925–

73) this search terminated in both schizophrenia and at the same time impressive work in a knotted and difficult style. For Judith Wright (b. 1915) it implied the exploration of her identity as woman, poet, and A., increasingly in relation to the fundamental presence of the land. For James McAuley (1917–76) it led from the horrors of modernity to the dubious haven of the church. For A. D. Hope (b. 1907), with McAuley the major representative of the postwar poetry establishment and the country's best-known poet, a writer less tormented than his contemporaries and at home in a witty, urbane style, it led to a reaffirmation of "classical" values and a gently ironic stance. Other poets played major parts in postwar devel., the chief of these being R. D. FitzGerald (1902–87), equally active between the wars, Douglas Stewart (1913–85), David Campbell (1915–79), J. S. Manifold (1915–85), and Rosemary Dobson (b. 1920).

By the late 1950s and early '60s, though, another poetic generation chafed under the régime of the Slessors and Stewarts. Rodney Hall (b. 1935) and Thomas Shapcott (b. 1935), themselves prolific poets, edited the *New Impulses* anthology, with its Cold War poetic manifesto of caution and doubt. This included many poets who have continued to develop their talents to the present, such as Gwen Harwood (b. 1920), Vincent Buckley (1925–88), Bruce Beaver (b. 1928), Bruce Dawe (b. 1930), Chris Wallace-Crabbe (b. 1934), David Malouf (b. 1934), Les Murray (b. 1938), and Geoffrey Lehmann (b. 1940). In the event, the new impulses of the 1950s no sooner emerged than they were overshadowed by the achievements, sometimes merely showy, sometimes substantial, of the so-called Generation of '68. The 1960s poets were young, insistent, and contemporary—though like all Australians they suffered a time-lag in the assimilation of overseas ideas. They read the Americans, listened to rock, smoked pot, marched against Vietnam, and supported a mass of underground magazines. Their anthologies were *A. P. Now, Applestealers*, and *The New A. P.*; their best poets, Michael Dransfield (1948–73) and Robert Adamson (b. 1943), the one dead of an overdose at 24, the other on the run from the law and his own personality until rescued by a hard muse.

If Dransfield, Adamson, and others like Charles Buckmaster (1951–72)—an early casualty—Richard Tipping (b. 1949), Vicki Viidikas (b. 1948), and Nigel Roberts (b. 1941) represented the romantic, often visionary, pole of a Poetry Now aesthetic, there were also more Hard-Edge practitioners such as John Tranter (b. 1943), John Forbes (b. 1950), Jennifer Maiden (b. 1949), and Martin Johnston (b. 1947). In Melbourne the most influential figure was Kris Hemensley (b. 1946), with the older Ken Taylor (b. 1930) providing guidance in the same way as Beaver did in Sydney. A separate group, incl. Laurie Duggan (b. 1949), John Scott (b. 1948), and Alan Wearne (b. 1948), held readings of their own away from the central Melbourne venue of La Mama. Inevitably a battle of the books ensued in which more conservative poets like Robert Gray (b. 1945) and Lehmann produced their own anthology, *The Younger A. Poets*. This gave prominence to the verse of the ebullient Les Murray and included poets like Roger McDonald (b. 1941) and Geoff Page (b. 1940).

At present the argument about modernity and tradition is no more settled than the older debate about nationalism and internationalism. Since the Generation of '68 and its detractors, the public has witnessed the extravagances of Performance Poets, led by the anarchist public servant, Pi O (b. 1951). Predictably, women's anthologies have appeared, as have publications of "ethnic" poetry, not all in Eng., and also of Aboriginal poetry in Eng. Where women's writing has extended the range of poetic possibilities in the 1980s, "ethnic" and Aboriginal poetry may well be in the process of doing something more fundamental: the creation not merely of new speech rhythms and vocabulary but, conceivably, of a new lang. in the making, and one suited to a multicultural society.

ANTHOLOGIES: *Djanggawul* (1952), *Love Songs of Arnhem Land* (1976), both ed. R. Berndt; *A. Bush Ballads* (1955), *Old Bush Songs and Rhymes of Colonial Times* (1957), both ed. D. Stewart and N. Keesing; *Penguin Book of A. Ballads*, ed. R. Ward (1964); *New Impulses in A. P.*, ed. R. Hall and T. Shapcott (1968); *Bards in the Wilderness: A. Colonial Poetry to 1920*, ed. B. Elliott and A. Mitchell (1970); *The New A. P.*, ed. J. Tranter (1979); *Collins Book of A. P.*, ed. R. Hall (1981); *Penguin Book of Mod. A. Verse*, ed. H. Heseltine (1981); *The Younger A. Poets*, ed. R. Gray and G. Lehmann (1983); *New Oxford Book of A. Verse*, ed. L. Murray (1986); *Penguin Book of A. Women Poets*, ed. S. Hampton and K. Llewellyn (1986).

HISTORY AND CRITICISM: *The Lit. of Australia*, ed. G. Dutton (1964); J. Wright, *Preoccupations in A. P.* (1965); *Oxford Hist. of A. Lit.*, ed. L. Kramer (1981); *Rev. of Nat. Lits.: Australia*, ed. A. Paolucci and L. Dobrez (1982); *A Possible Contemp. P.*, ed. M. Duwell (1982); H. M. Green, *A Hist. of A. Lit.*, rev. D. Green (1984–85); W. Wilde et al., *Oxford Companion to A. Lit.* (1985).   L.A.C.D.

AUSTRIAN POETRY. Although A. p. is linguistically related to Ger. poetry (q.v.), there is sufficient justification for regarding it as a separate entity, since the particular ethnic, historical, and political conditions of the area combined to create a unique cultural milieu. A. ruling dynasties—the Babenbergs (976–1246) and the Hapsburgs (1278–1918)—established a strong sense of continuous trad. Its geographic location in Middle Europe made the Monarchy a meeting place between East and West, and the large Hapsburg Empire constituted a virtual melting pot of ethnic elements—Germanic, Magyar, Slavic, Jewish, and Romance. With strong ties to other Alpine lands, particularly Bavaria, and receptive to influences

from Italy and Spain, the absolute center of the Empire was Vienna. Whereas the cultural trad. was consistently strong in music and theater, the poetic trad. reached a high point first in the Middle Ages and then not again until the end of the 19th c.

Med. lit. flourished in the Danube valley, although it is not entirely correct to speak of a national lit., since feudal society was regional and supranational. Ger. medieval poetry (q.v.) is a major trad., with a primary division between High and Low German; A. lit. represents regional variants within the High Ger. trad. Initially, the centers of culture were the monasteries, which produced religious lit. such as the *Wiener Genesis* (ca. 1060), Frau Ava's *Leben Jesu* (ca. 1125), the *Melker Marienlied* (ca. 1130–60), and Heinrich von Melk's *Memento mori* (ca. 1160). As society became more secular, groups of wandering scholars and minstrels cultivated a popular trad. that was to remain strong for centuries (see GOLIARDIC VERSE). The *Nibelungenlied*, a heroic epic written down around 1200 in Passau but representing the oral trad. of an earlier era, is connected to well-known localities in the Danube region, where it was very popular.

Minnesang (q.v.) was a European phenomenon emanating from Provence, and although its origins are disputed, scholars view the early Danubian lyrics as a somewhat indigenous movement. A well-known example is Der von Kürenberg's falcon song (ca. 1150–70) composed in the *Nibelungenstrophe* (q.v.). The precourtly lyrics of Dietmar von Aist (fl. 1140–70), particularly his *Tagelieder* (q.v.), exhibit a simplicity and sincerity absent in the later, more formalized verse. During the classical period of courtly lit. (ca. 1180–1250), the Viennese court was a center of cultural activity. It attracted the Alsatian Reinmar von Hagenau (1160–1210), whose elegiac verses of unrequited love represent the epitome of formal stylization. The greatest lyric poet of the time, Walther von der Vogelweide (ca. 1170–ca. 1230), also found patronage in Vienna, as well as at other courts. Walther not only perfected the high *Minnesang* but also broke through the conventions to achieve an original expression of more natural experience; he is known for his poetry of *niedere Minne* in praise of reciprocal love; and he is also known for his *Spruchdichtung* (q.v.) on affairs of church and state and on the transitoriness of life. This roving singer was an enlightened advocate of humanity and tolerance, and his wide-ranging oeuvre signals the height of Ger.-lang. poetry for centuries to come. Among the numerous postclassical poets, Neidhard von Reuental (ca. 1180–1246), Ulrich von Lichtenstein (ca. 1200–76?), and particularly Oswald von Wolkenstein (1377–1445) wrote poetry of lasting value.

After the decline of the Middle Ages we listen in vain for a great lyric voice, apart from the widespread folk trad., until the 19th c. Although the Ren. court of Maximilian I was an important literary center, attracting the humanist poet Conrad Celtis (1459–1508), literary developments were cut short by the wars of the Reformation; and the success of the Counter-Reformation in Austria restored the hegemony of the Catholic Church and with it Lat. as the lang. of art and learning. Jesuit drama was strong in the 16th c. until influences began to be felt from the It. *commedia dell'arte* and the Sp. court theater. Whereas the 17th-c. baroque culture produced a rich body of lyric in Protestant North Germany, the only poet of rank in the Catholic Austrian South was Catharina Regina von Greiffenberg (1633–94). Austria celebrated the age in its architecture, erecting lavish churches and palaces; and the spirit of the baroque, as well as the centrality of the Church, has remained a formative factor down to the present day. Although the 18th c. Enlightenment brought a measure of reform to the semifeudal A. society, it was too little and too short-lived to provide literary impetus. At the time when Germany produced the Classicism and romanticism of Goethe, Schiller, and the Schlegels, Austria seemed to pour its energies into music and the opera, bringing forth Haydn, Mozart, and Schubert and attracting other great composers such as Beethoven.

Modern A. lit. began in the 19th c. with Franz Grillparzer (1791–1872), who was primarily a dramatist. The leading poet of the period was the Hungarian-born Nikolaus Lenau (1802–50), whose work is characterized by melancholy, restlessness, a bittersweet lyricism, and *Weltschmerz* (19th-c. pessimism). It was the Metternich era of reactionary politics and Biedermeier (q.v.) society, with poetry expressing resignation and a quiet joy in small things. These traits were infused with an element of social criticism by Marie von Ebner-Eschenbach (1830–1916) and Ferdinand von Saar (1833–1906); the poetry of Anastasius Grün (1806–76) demonstrates overt political engagement. On the whole, however, A. p. was averse to confrontation with materialist culture, labor movements, and the Industrial Revolution; and currents of realism and naturalism (qq.v.) were limited mainly to the dialect works of popular lit.

Fin-de-siècle Vienna was the scene of an unprecedented burst of creative activity, and that not only in lit. but also in music, fine art, philosophy, and psychoanalysis. It was as though latent energies had suddenly been activated precisely and paradoxically on the eve of the Monarchy. Freud is only one of the numerous figures of world renown from this era, many of whom were Jewish. Psychological observation had always been more appealing to Austrians than either philosophical abstraction or sociopolitical activism, and the time was ripe. Partly as a reaction to North German naturalism, a group of writers known as Young Vienna (q.v.) focused on nuances of feeling, sensual impressions, and subconscious drives in an effort to create a new aesthetic. The refined coffeehouse culture has been variously associated with impressionism, neoromanticism, symbolism, aestheticism, Jugendstil, and decadence (qq.v.); but no labels do justice to the supreme achievements of Hugo von Hofmannsthal (1874–1929) and Rainer Maria Rilke (1875–1926).

The precocious Hofmannsthal began publishing poetry and lyric plays at the age of 17; ten years later he stopped, and his seminal "Chandos Letter" (1902) describes a crisis of lang. that made poetry impossible. Poetry had come easily to him, as if by magic or in dream—the images he uses to express the creative power—and his early works were already masterpieces. Well-known poems such as "Terzinen über Vergänglichkeit," "Ballade des äusseren Lebens," and "Lebenslied" represent the culmination of a long trad. and demonstrate cognizance of the burden of the past as well as the transitoriness of the present. Consciousness, however, had itself become problematic, and with the loss of naiveté the self-conscious poet is torn between experience and reflection, between the affirmation and negation of life. Awareness of the social responsibility of art led Hofmannsthal to turn his attention to drama after 1902, and he is also known for his opera libretti in collaboration with Richard Strauss.

Rilke, born in Prague, seems to have lived everywhere in Europe and consequently nowhere. He is truly an international figure in terms of both creation and reception, and since his works are discussed in more detail in the essay on Ger. poetry (q.v.), suffice it here to sketch an outline. Rilke's early collections of poetry, such as *Das Stundenbuch* (written 1899–1903, pub. 1905) and *Das Buch der Bilder* (written 1898–1906, pub. 1902 and 1906), reveal mystical intensity and rich imagery, although they are at times overwrought. From Rodin in Paris Rilke learned "to see," as he said, and this encounter with the visual arts resulted in *Neue Gedichte* (1907–8). In it the poet combines observation and precision with inwardness and a phenomenological sense of meaning to give new definition to the concept of *Dinggedicht* (q.v.). After his prose work *Die Aufzeichnungen des Malte Laurids Brigge* (1910) Rilke wrote very little for over a decade. It was a period of existential crisis, as recorded—and poetically transformed—in his great work, the *Duineser Elegien* (written 1912–22, pub. 1923). The ensuing *Sonette an Orpheus* (1923) celebrate this transformation of the world into song. Rilke's oeuvre is so strong that virtually every subsequent poet has been compelled to deal with it; he has thus exerted great influence on the devel. of modern European poetry.

Georg Trakl (1887–1914) is a major poet whose life was cut short by the Great War. Trakl's poetry is often associated with expressionism (q.v.), but in spirit it is far from the political activism of that Ger. movement or even from the emotional appeal of his countryman, the Prague-born Franz Werfel

(1890–1945). Trakl depicts a world caught up in decay, destruction, and death; and whereas death had been the main theme of much of A. p., Trakl's innovation lies in his radically altered use of lang. The ruptured universe finds its correlate in free rhythms, fractured syntax, and enigmatic metaphors known as *Chiffren*, which establish an absolute relation between the incomparable realms of the referential and the ontological (as explicated among others by Heidegger). In Trakl's works the desperation of guilt and despair is expressed in a highly musical lang. of alliteration and assonance that shows the influence of Rimbaud. In the ever-varying kaleidoscopic configurations of sounds and images, all Trakl texts seem to converge in a single unitary vision.

The period between the demise of the Monarchy in 1918 and the union of Austria with Nazi Germany in 1938 was a troubled time of economic crises and political extremism, leading to World War II. There were many good writers—for whom the name Theodor Kramer (1897–1958) can stand as representative—of this "lost generation" whose lives were stymied by war and in some cases by exile or concentration camps. Despite his problematic ideological stance, Josef Weinheber (1892–1945) is a major poet whose works evince a formal mastery of style and lang., from Gr. ode forms to Viennese dialect verse. His *Adel und Untergang* (1934) thematizes the problem of art and the artist and achieves a classicism reminiscent of his model Hölderlin.

The postwar period has produced a rich body of poetry, and posterity will probably find many of its works of lasting value. The first decade is marked by traditional forms and themes in an effort to re-establish a link with the prefascist past. This traditionalism was nonetheless pluralistic, ranging from the religious mysticism of Christine Lavant (1915–73) to the sociopolitical crit. of Erich Fried (b. 1921), with the experiential humanism of Christine Busta (1915–87) and the critical skepticism of Gerhard Fritsch (1924–69) as intermediate stages. Ingeborg Bachmann (1926–73) transcended national boundaries in two lyric volumes, *Die gestundete Zeit* (1953) and *Anrufung des grossen Bären* (1956), which present spellbinding rhythms and powerful metaphors of the existential themes of time and consciousness. But the most prominent poet is Paul Celan (1920–70), who, like Rilke, is international in residence and in influence. His famous "Todesfuge" stands as a memorial to the victims of Nazi persecution, and Jewish themes recur throughout his ten volumes of poetry. Even more pervasive is the problem of lang. itself, as the poet is dispossessed of belief not only in God and man but also in the efficacy of poetic speaking (see BELIEF, PROBLEM OF). The problematic nature of lang. is evident already in *Sprachgitter* (1959), and Celan's poetry in the six volumes thereafter becomes increasingly hermetic and enigmatic, reducing utterance to near silence.

The question of lang. is important enough to serve as a gauge for tracing the devel. of postwar poetry. Reacting against what they perceived to be an outdated traditionalism, writers and artists in the mid 1950s formed the Vienna Group to proclaim a new type of art, termed "experimental." Techniques were adapted from dada and surrealism (qq.v.); particularly characteristic of experimental lit. are montage and collage, permutation and dislocation, and atomizing constellations and chains of discontinuous associations. Since metaphor was felt to be a mask for phony metaphysics, experimental writers stripped lang. of its mimetic intent in an effort to challenge the epistemology behind the structures. The leading poet is H. C. Artmann (b. 1921), whose wide-ranging oeuvre includes grotesque and fantastic lyrics recalling the baroque; he also introduced a sophisticated form of dialect poetry (q.v.). Associated with the group were Friederike Mayröcker (b. 1924) and Ernst Jandl (b. 1925), who developed various innovative forms. Mayröcker is known for her "poetic phenomenology" that unites dreams, memories, and fantasies in a nonreferential network of associative images; and Jandl has achieved a wide public appeal with his reflectively witty concrete poetry (q.v.) and his visual and speech verse.

The Vienna Group had an important liberating effect on conservative A. society, and it served as a springboard for a broader group of avant-garde writers who in 1960 established a literary center in the provincial capital of Graz. The Graz Group includes, besides the illustrious Peter Handke (b. 1942), a broad spectrum of contemp. authors of varying interests, both linguistic and sociopolitical, united by a common critical stance toward the status quo in art and society. Its literary journal, *manuskripte*, is edited by Alfred Kolleritsch (b. 1931), a strong poet in his own right; his recent volumes contain opaque metaphors that examine the content and conditions of consciousness. Also strong is the Viennese poet Jutta Schutting (b. 1937), who, operating in the Wittgensteinian trad., uses lang. to question itself, as poetry investigates the presuppositions of its own existence. New developments continue to appear from both Vienna and Graz, as well as other regional centers, though in all of these developments it is evident that consciousness of trad. and critique of that trad. continue to be the central issues of postwar A. p.

ANTHOLOGIES: *Lyrik aus Deutschösterreich vom Mittelalter bis zur Gegenwart*, ed. S. Hock (1919); *Österr. Lyrik aus neuen Jhn.*, ed. W. Stratowa (1948); *Zwischenbilanz: Eine Anthol. österr. Gegenwartslit.*, ed. W. Weiss and S. Schmid (1976); *Dichtung aus Österreich*, v. 2, *Lyrik*, ed. E. Thurnher (1976); *Zeit und Ewigkeit. Tausend Jahre österr. Lyrik*, ed. J. Schondorff (1978); *Verlassener Horizont.: Österr. Lyrik aus vier Jahrzehnten*, ed. H. Huppert and R. Links (1980); *Die Wiener Moderne: Lit., Kunst und*

Musik zwischen 1890 und 1910, ed. G. Wunberg (1981); *Austria in P. and Hist.*, ed. F. Ungar (1984); *A. P. Today*, ed. M. Holton and H. Kuhner (1985); *Contemp. A. P.*, ed. B. Bjorklund (1986). HISTORY AND CRITICISM: A. Schmidt, *Dichtung und Dichter Österreichs im 19. und 20. Jh.* (1964); C. Magris, *Der habsburgische Mythos in der österr. Lit.* (1966); *Handbook of A. Lit.*, ed. F. Ungar (1973); *Kindlers Literaturgesch. der Gegenwart: Die zeitgenössische Lit. Österreichs*, ed. H. Spiel (1976); *Das junge Wien: Österr. Lit.- und Kunstkritik 1887–1902*, ed. G. Wunberg (1976); *Gesch. der deutschen Lit. vom 18. Jh. bis zur Gegenwart*, ed. V. Žmegač, 3 v. (1978–84); *Die österr. Lit.: Eine Dokumentation ihrer Literarhist. Entwicklung*, ed. H. Zeman, 4 v. to date (1979–); A. Best and H. Wolfschütz, *Mod. A. Writing* (1980); *Formen der Lyrik in der österr. Gegenwartslit.*, ed. W. Schmidt-Dengler (1981); *Mod. A. Lit.* [journal], 1– (1961–). B.B.

AUTHORITY. See INFLUENCE; INTERTEXTUALITY; HISTORICISM; TEXTUALITY.

AUTO SACRAMENTAL. Along with the *comedia*, the *a. s.* was shaped during the second half of the 16th c. as one of the two major artforms of Sp. cl. drama. (The word *auto*, that is, *acto*, had originally been used to refer to any dramatic act or piece but gradually came to refer primarily to a religious play.) The first influential collection of religious *autos* was that of Diego Sánchez de Badajoz, published posthumously in 1554; in them he drew upon medieval antecedents and was able to present theological problems in a dramatic way, using prefiguration and allegory. The most important playwrights further to develop the genre in the 16th c. were Juan de Timoneda, Lope de Vega, and José de Valdivielso. But the *a. s.* received its definitive form in the 17th c. at the hands of Pedro Calderón de la Barca.

The Calderonian *a. s.* was a paraliturgical, allegorical, one-act play written to celebrate the Eucharist; usually financed by a municipality, it was performed on carts and a special stage constructed in a public square during the feast of Corpus Christi. (In Madrid, from 1649 on, Calderón was the only poet officially commissioned to write *autos*.) Allegory was used to give concrete literary form to the abstract theological mysteries of Christianity, consisting essentially of the Fall and redemption of man; original sin leads to the incarnation of Christ and his crucifixion, commemorated in the Mass, which sums up the whole sequence. The theme, then, was always the same, but many plots were used to retell it allegorically. These plots were taken from a wide range of sources—pagan mythology, the Bible, saints' lives, history, secular plays. Emblem (q.v.) lit. and *conceptista* metaphors (see CULTERANISMO) influenced the structure of these ingenious dramatic texts and their theatrical performances, replete with music and elaborate sets. One of the most

typical *autos* is *El gran teatro del mundo*, based on the *theatrum mundi* metaphor, in which God is the Director of the play of human life, distributing costumes and dividing the performance into three acts (under natural law, until the Flood; under the Heb. Old Testament; and under the New Testament of Grace, ending with Judgment Day); Grace is the prompter. After the show, the Director invites most of the cast to a Eucharistic banquet, excluding only the Rich Man, who is sent to Hell.

One of the few playwrights to compare with Calderón in theological ingenuity and literary brilliance was the Mexican nun Sor Juana Inés de la Cruz, who used both cl. and Aztec mythology for her plots. The Calderonian *a. s.* continued to be popular in the Sp. world until, after radical crit. by the Fr. neoclassical theorists, it was finally prohibited by the Bourbon government in 1765.

M. Bataillon, "Essai d'explication de l'*a. s.*," *Bull. Hispanique* 42 (1940); A. A. Parker, *The Allegorical Drama of Calderón* (1943); E. Frutos Cortés, *La filosofía de Calderón en sus autos sacramentales* (1952); B. W. Wardropper, *Introducción al teatro religioso del Siglo de Oro* (1953); E. M. Wilson and D. Moir, *The Golden Age: Drama 1492–1700* (1971); R. Arias, *The Sp. Sacramental Plays* (1980); B. E. Kurtz, "'No Word without Mystery': Allegories of Sacred Truth in the *Autos Sacramentales* of Calderón de la Barca," *PMLA* 103 (1988). E.L.R.

AUTONOMY, POETIC. The concept of a. is fundamental to poetics because it is frequently invoked to sustain two claims about poetic works of art—that their foregrounding of internal formal relations gives them a mode of being that cannot be adequately explained in historical terms, and that the meaning produced by such structures cannot be accounted for by the interpretive strategies that govern our practical judgments in everyday life. In other words, art shares those modes of self-legislation which led Kant to his distinction between a. and heteronomy. And that distinction warrants assertions that these internal relations allow the works to exist for their own sake and establish unique emotional and semantic sites requiring a distinctive mode of aesthetic contemplation. Such emphases often come under attack because they separate art from social reality, but there remain plausible grounds for arguing instead that it is precisely this attention to the conditions of self-legislation which clarifies the fundamental powers that art can make available for such cultural life.

In Kant, behavior is heteronomous when the external conditions give the law to the will, for example when decisions are based on utilitarian criteria such as measures of happiness or profit. Autonomous action, by contrast, treats the will as "a law to itself independently of any property or object of volition." One chooses not in terms of empirical or pragmatic goods but in terms of the character one can define for oneself—as if one could revive the aristocratic ideal of preferring expressive character to calculation. But for Kant aristocratic roles are also heteronomous since they depend on social mythologies, require the approval of others, and perpetuate divisions among social groups. True a. depends upon proving oneself a rational agent. Rational criteria establish categorical principles enabling the individual at once to choose an identity and to feel that the identity is one all rational agents share, since the criteria define those imperatives which make moral action a sublime demand. The autonomous agent chooses a self whose identity is based on principles that are distinctive to rational beings and thus not subject to the heteronomous external causes characterizing the practical order.

But how can Kant reconcile this ideal rational subject with the empirical agent who chooses in terms of specific historical situations? Kant's answer requires turning to the a. available in aesthetic experience as a symbol of the moral good. Taste, like moral judgments, is not a matter of simple preferences. The subject bases its individual pleasure on a reflective desire to claim the "universal agreement of all men." Yet taste cannot be rationalized in the same way that morality allows categorical imperatives, else it would be a deductive science not responsive to innovation. Its universality is therefore not a matter of deduction but of intuition creating a direct bond between the agent's pleasure in the act of judgment and the communal response which the judgment projects. Rejecting immediate interests is not a matter of duty but of the very condition that allows the subject reflective participation in the work. Significant art has the ontological status of an "aesthetical idea," a presentation characterized by a density of internal relations making it an "inexponible" intuition that occasions much thought without becoming the object of any one thought. Such work is self-legislating because it manifests the productive force of genius giving the rule to nature, as if the object projected a "purposiveness without purpose" that could not be correlated with the categories of the understanding determining our purposes. As we align ourselves with this free play of imagination, we can reflect on our own pleasure as giving a law to itself which also binds it to harmonies with nature and with other agents impossible when we are "subjected to a heteronomy of empirical laws" enforced by the understanding.

Kant's conjunction of the aesthetic and the rational did not survive the cultural dichotomies it was intended to resolve. But it did open speculative domains for others to try a variety of strategies for setting the self-legislating dimension of aesthetic experience in opposition to the culture's increasing inability to distinguish Kantian rationality from the heteronomous understanding. Friedrich Schiller, for example, argued that aesthetic experience was not merely a symbol for the moral good but rather provided in itself the conditions of a. which were the psyche's only reliable foundation for nobility. Where rationality must necessarily subordinate individual legislative activity to fixed universals, the artistic spirit establishes its own expressive forms while demonstrating the harmony of those forms with the fluid life of the senses. Thus such forms free sense impressions from the heteronomous order of perceptions and provide vehicles for defining "pure ideal man within himself."

By separating that ideal from the fabric of Kant's rigorous logic, Schiller prepared the way for the aestheticist versions of a. that would dominate the 19th c. Thus Theophile Gautier: "There is nothing truly beautiful except what is of no use: everything useful is ugly, for it is the expression of some need, and man's needs are ignoble and disgusting, like his poor infirm nature. The most useful spot in a house is the bathroom." A. now resides is separating the useful from the beautiful and making that the basis for psychological distinctions between bourgeois servitude and self-legislating genius who, like Baudelaire's dandy, establishes "a personal form of originality within the external limits of social conventions." So if philosophers were to preserve a sense of art as a symbol for the moral good, the best they could do was to locate a. entirely in aesthetic terms. In Schopenhauer, and, later, in the symbolism (q.v.) of Mallarmé, all wanting gets cast as heteronomous, so that moral ideals must depend on suspending desire and turning instead to the contemplative postures which preserve those ideals from our appropriative interests. Subsequently, this logic would generate versions of modernism emphasizing the capacity of art to construct formal objects that both free us from the distortions imposed by practical desires and actually create new fields of internal relations defining an alternative realm of spirit for our contemplative energies. From Clive Bell on aesthetic emotion, to Theodor Adorno on the transcendental dimension of the aesthetic, to Jean Paul Sartre on the internal self-sufficiency of poetry, to John Crowe Ransom on sacramentalism, poetry establishes freedom by demonstrating form's capacity to realize powers and states that are distorted by the mediation of discursive lang. and the social concerns which it deploys.

Postmodern theory of the 1970s and after has viewed such bids for freedom as self-defeating: in emphasizing formal energies, art risks losing its connection to the social world and thus trivializing itself. Claims for aesthetic a. may be little more than a defensive mechanism for idealizing what had already become art's impotence. To Mikhail Bahktin the ideal of artistic purity becomes a "monological" evasion of the dialogic play of languages that characterizes social life, and to Peter Bürger separating art from the praxis of life risks replicating the most alienating properties of bourgeois culture by seducing artists into reifying their own products. Such criticisms lead contemporary artists to project their alternatives to bourgeois life in terms of avant-garde strategies devoted less to creating new models of a. than simply to disrupting prevailing ideological assumptions. Art can do little more than intensify social heteronomy until it produces conditions ripe for revolutionary politics.

Such critiques, however, may seriously underplay the force of Kantian ideas by relying only on the oversimplifications posited by his aestheticist heirs. It is arguable that many of the writers who idealized a. were working within traditional models of liberal education which enabled them to treat artistic composition as a means for articulating the exemplary powers that Kant attributed to moral character. Thus the most elaborate literary appeals to a. occur in poets like Wilde, Yeats, Pound, and Stevens, who tried to make their formal energies sustain an individualist ethics. And while there is no single strong philosophical defense for those claims, one can show that they are consistent with Jurgen Habermas' arguments that modernism preserves Enlightenment virtues necessary for a fully liberated social life. This route then allows one to bring into the arts those philosophers whose efforts to conserve that Enlightenment heritage have required recasting Kant's rationalist model of a. Where Kant posits a sublime agent bound to an internal sense of duty, E. Anscombe shows that a. can consist simply in accepting responsibility for one's actions. In owning up, one owns one's behavior and in effect legislates for oneself. And where Kant insists on categorical imperatives as the fundamental vehicle for rational a., L. Haworth shows how it suffices to base a. on the degree to which actions can be rationalized within specific interpretive communities. From such models it becomes possible to argue that a work's emphasis on its own internal relations becomes its means of taking overt responsibility for the stance on values that it projects. Such work then offers society exemplary modes of forging attitudes which are fundamental to the ideals of moral identity and moral judgment held by the culture.

I. Kant, *Kritik der Praktischen Vernunft* [Critique of Practical Reason] (1788), tr. L. W. Beck (1956), *Kritik der Urteilskraft* [Critique of Judgment] (1790), tr. J. H. Bernard (1931); F. W. Schiller, *Briefe über die ästhetische Erziehung des Menschen* [On the Aesthetic Education of Man] (1795), tr. R. Snell (1954); G. T. Gautier, "Preface," *Mademoiselle de Maupin* (1835), tr. A. Engstrom (1900); A. Schopenhauer, *Die Welt als Wille und Vorstellung* [The World as Will and Idea], 2d ed., v. 1 (1844), tr. R. S. Haldane and J. Kemp (1964); C. Baudelaire, *Le Peintre de la Vie Moderne* [The Painter of Mod. Life], sect. ix (1863), tr. P. E. Charvet (1964); S. Mallarmé, *Crise de Vers* [Crisis of Poetry] (1886), tr. B. Cook (1956); O. Wilde, *The Soul of Man Under Socialism* (1891); B. Croce, *Estetica come*

scienza dell'espressione e linguista generale (1902, tr. D. Ainslie 1909), *Essays on Lit. and Lit. Crit.*, ed. and tr. M. E. Moss (1990); C. Bell, *Art* (1914); J. C. Ransom, "Poetry: A Note in Ontology" (1934), in Ransom; J. P. Sartre, *Qu'est-ce que la Litt.?* [What Is Lit.?] (1948), ch. 1, tr. B. Frechtman (1949); M. Bahktin, *Voprosy Literatury I Estetiki* (essays written in the 1930s), *The Dialogic Imagination*, tr. C. Emerson and M. Holquist (1981); G. E. M. Anscombe, *Intention* (1957); P. Bürger, *Theorie der Avantgarde* [Theory of the Avant-Garde] (1974), tr. M. Shaw (1984)—important foreword by J. Schulte-Sasse; J. Derrida, "La Loi du Genre" (1980), "The Law of Genre," tr. A. Ronnell, *Glyph* 7 (1980); G. Hermerén, "The A. of Art," *Essays on Aesthetics*, ed. J. Fisher (1983); T. Adorno, *Ästhetische Theorie* [Aesthetic Theory] (1970), tr. C. Lenhardt (1984); L. Haworth, *A.* (1986); J. Habermas, *A. and Solidarity*, ed. P. Dews (1986).   C.A.

AUTOTELIC. From Gr. *auto* ("self") and *telos* ("end"), a. can mean four things: complete or perfected; spontaneous or self-originating; having a purpose or end in itself; and final or absolute. In aesthetics, an a. work is thus a complete unity (q.v., and see ORGANICISM) that has no external cause or practical purpose, and that sets the terms of its own existence and meaning (see AUTONOMY). Although crucial to Aristotle, the term becomes most important in the 19th c., when didactic and descriptive poetry are reoriented by the association between poetry and imaginative creation. In this period, the term is used to characterize the form of art as organic; ethical rules, insofar as humanity is viewed not in terms of utility but as an end in itself; and theories of trad. from Kant to Eliot, wherein history is conceived not as a linear, causal series but as a living whole. Much recent crit., motivated by deconstruction (q.v.) and social theory, has disputed the notion in all three uses by questioning aesthetic and historical unity, denying that an a. or self-enclosed, centered structure exists, and pointing to the influence of external or nonaesthetic elements in works of art.—I. Kant, *Critique of Judgment* (1790); W. Pater, "Conclusion" to *The Ren.* (1873); T. S. Eliot, "Trad. and the Individual Talent" (1917); C. Brooks, *The Well-Wrought Urn* (1947); J. Derrida, "Structure, Sign and Play," *The Structuralist Controversy*, ed. R. Macksey and E. Donato (1972).   C.P.S.

AUXESIS. The rhetorical strategy by which members are arranged in ascending or climactic order, as in Sidney, *Astrophil and Stella* 47, and Shakespeare, Sonnet 65. The opposite of meiosis (q..v.). *Climax* (q.v.) concatenates the members, the last element of each becoming the first of the next; *sorites* is logical sequence.—B. Vickers, *Cl. Rhet. in Eng. Poetry* (1989).   T.V.F.B.

AWDL ("ode," "lay"). The most highly regarded form of Welsh bardic composition. The "chair" of the National Eisteddfod of Wales (see EIST-EDDFOD) is awarded for an *a*. The word, originally a variant of the Celtic term for rhyme, *odl* (q.v.), came to mean, successively, the stave bearing the rhyme, a run of monorhyming lines, a complete poem in monorhyme, a poem entirely in certain specified *a*. meters, and, since the 15th c., a poem of some length in *cynghanedd* (q.v.) and in one or more of the 24 "strict meters" (see WELSH PO-ETRY), incl. at least some portions not in the other two classes of "strict meters," *cywydd* and *englyn* (qq.v.). The staple line of the *a*. is most often a long line divided into sections, the final section bearing the main rhyme and the others rhyming with each other, but often printed in codex as a short-line stanza. Many of the best Welsh poems of the last two centuries, as in the medieval period, are *awdlau*.

A. meters incl.: (a) *rhupunt*, a 12-syllable line of three 4-syllable sections, the first and second sections rhyming, with a consonantal correspondence woven around the main stresses of the second and third sections, and with the twelfth syllable bearing the main rhyme; (b) *long rhupunt*, 16 syllables and 4 sections; (c) *cyhydedd naw ban*, a 9-syllable line often in runs of couplets; (d) *hir a thoddaid* (long and blending), a stanza of 10-syllable lines with its own pattern of rhyme scheme and accentuation, and ending in a *thoddaid* couplet of 10 and 9 syllables; and (e) *a. gywydd*, a 14-syllable line divided into two sections, the second section ending in the main rhyme and the first rhyming with a syllable halfway through the second (cf. Ir. *aicill*).

Morris-Jones; Parry, *History*, ch. 6.5, and *Awdlau Cadeiriol Detholedig 1926–50* (1953); Jarman and Hughes, v. 2; Stephens; *Welsh Verse*, ed. T. Conran, 2d ed. (1986)—long intro. and appendix on meters.   D.M.L.; T.V.F.B.

B

BACCHIUS, also bacchiac. In Cl. prosody, the metrical sequence ∪ – – , most frequently encountered in Gr. lyric (monody) and drama as a clausula to a run of iambs. It may be an instance of syncopation (q.v.), i.e. the iambic metron x – ∪ – with suppression of the third syllable. Bacchii (with cretics [q.v.]) are among the most common meters in Plautine cantica (see CANTICUM AND DIVERBIUM), appearing mostly as 4-foot units (*quaternarii*) or in systems (q.v.). The Romans felt the b. to be esp. suitable for a serious or solemn style. The reverse of a b., i.e. a foot composed of 2 long syllables and 1 short one, is known as a *palimbacchius* (Gr. *palin* "back") or *antibacchius.*—W. M. Lindsay, *Early Lat. Verse* (1922); G. E. Duckworth, *The Nature of Roman Comedy* (1952); Koster; Crusius; Dale; Halporn et al.   J.W.H.

BADīᶜ. See ARABIC POETRY.

BALADA. Occitan dance song with refrain, akin to the *dansa* (q.v.) but differing from it in having, besides repetition of the full refrain after each stanza, the first line of the refrain repeated after the first and (usually) second line of each stanza. It is a relatively infrequent form.—Chambers.
                J.H.M.

BALETE. See DANSA.

BALLAD. The "folk," "popular," or "traditional" b. is a short narrative song preserved and transmitted orally among illiterate or semiliterate people. As one of the if not the most important forms of folk poetry, bs. have been composed, sung, and remembered in every age. But wider use of the term "b." recommends that we draw distinctions between the following three types of bs.: (1) the b. as a species of oral poetry (q.v.), which is orally composed and transmitted, popular in register, and mainly rural in provenience: most of the famous examples are late medieval, but survived as folkverse via oral transmission down to the 19th c., when they were discovered and collected; (2) 16th-c. assimilations and adaptations of the oral b., and particularly its meter (see BALLAD METER), to urban contexts and religious uses: these are the broadside (q.v.) or street b. and the hymns, as in the metrical psalters, esp. Sternhold and Hopkins; and (3) literary imitations of the popular b., beginning in the Ren. but flourishing particularly in the later 18th-c. revival of antiquarianism and folk poetry which culminated in romanticism (q.v.), esp. in Goethe and Wordsworth.

Short narrative songs have been collected in all European countries, and though each national balladry has its distinctive characteristics, three constants seem to hold for all genuine specimens. (1) Bs. focus on a single crucial episode. The b. begins usually at a point where the action is decisively directed toward its catastrophe. Events leading up to this conclusive episode are told in a hurried, summary fashion. Little attention is given to describing settings; indeed, circumstantial detail of every sort is conspicuously absent. (2) Bs. are dramatic. We are not told about things happening; we are shown them happening. Every artistic resource is pointed toward giving an intensity and immediacy to the action and toward heightening the emotional impact of the climax. Protagonists are allowed to speak for themselves, which means that dialogue (q.v.) bulks large. At strategic moments, dialogue erupts into the narrative. Such speeches are sparingly tagged; frequently we must deduce the speaker from what is being said. (3) Bs. are impersonal. The narrator seldom allows his or her own attitude toward the events to intrude. Comments on motives are broad, general, detached. There may be an "I" in a ballad, but the singer does not forget his or her position as the representative of the public voice. Bias there is in bs., of course, but it is the bias of a party, community, or nation, not an individual's subjective point of view.

Stylistically, the b. is a distinctive genre. Like folksong, but unlike all the literary genres, the b. is an oral phenomenon and, as a consequence, preserves traces of the archaic modes of preliterature. Plot (q.v.) is the central element: all other artistic possibilities are subordinated to it. The lang. is plain and often formulaic, a small stock of epithets and adjectives serving as formulas (q.v.) for extensive repetition. There are few arresting figures of speech and no self-conscious straining after novel turns of phrase. And because the emphasis is on a single line of action precipitately developed, there is no time for careful delineation of character or exploration of psychological motivation. The heavy amount of repetition and parallelism (qq.v.) characteristic of the bs. only *seems* to be mere ornamental rhet. Repetition in heightened passages is, as Coleridge explained brilliantly, the singers' effort to discharge emotion that could not be exhausted in one saying. Much repetition is mnemonic: in a story being recited or sung, crucial facts must be firmly planted in the memory since the hearer cannot turn back a page to recover a fact that slipped by in a moment of inattention. Much repetition, too, is cumulative in effect: this device is known as "incremental repetition" (q.v.).

Between the balladries of Western and Eastern Europe there are marked differences. Except for certain Romanian bs., rhyme and assonance (qq.v.) are unusual in the Slavic territories and in the Balkans, incl. Greece. The Ukrainian *dumy*, which assonate, are another exception. Finnish bs. employ alliteration as a binding principle. In Western countries, rhyme or assonance is general. All bs. are essentially short narrative poems with a greater or lesser infusion of lyrical elements, and the strength of the lyrical quality is another discriminant in the classification of balladries. As a general rule, strophic (stanzaic) bs. tend to be more lyrical than nonstrophic. Rhyme, assonance, refrains (q.v.), and short-lined meters further suggest lyricism, as do singability and dance animation. Even the *viser* of Denmark, lengthy heroic bs., are kept lyrically buoyant by rhyme, assonance, stanza breaks, and by a refrain technique which shows these bs. were meant to be performed in ring or chain dances. A leader sang the narrative stanza as the ring moved; the dancers paused to sing the refrain, an exultation irrelevant to the progress of the story. Least lyrical of European bs. are the Serbian men's songs on historical or martial topics, written in a heavy pentameter line, and the Sp. *romances* (q.v.), which seem, like the *viser*, to have been cut down from epic lays, and which, though held together by assonance, are not strophic. Lithuania, Poland, France, Italy, and Scotland possess the most lyrical story-songs. As to metrical schemes, British and Scandinavian bs. use the 4–3–4–3 stress verse of the Common Meter quatrain; an octosyllabic line is the staple of Sp., Bulgarian, Rumanian, and much Ger. b. poetry; France and allied b. territory (Catalonia, Northern Italy, Portugal) take as standard a verse of 12 or 16 syllables broken into hemistichs which rhyme or assonate with one another; the scansion of the Rus. *bylina* (q.v.) is free and highly irregular, the musical phrasing governing the organization of the verse.

The charms of British balladry were first brought to the attention of the lettered and learned world in the 18th c. During the period 1790–1830 many important recordings from oral trad. were made. F. J. Child, a professor at Harvard, made the definitive thesaurus of British popular bs. (1882–98), printing 305 bs., some in as many as 25 versions. In the 20th c., about 125 of Child's bs. have been recovered in the United States and Canada from the descendants of 18th-c. immigrants from the British Isles. *Judas*, the oldest b. in Child's collection, is recorded in a late 13th-c. manuscript; it deals with the betrayal of Christ. There are a few other religious bs., mostly concerned with the miracles of the Virgin, but these are far outnumbered by the pieces dealing with the pagan supernatural, like *Tam Lin, The Wife of Usher's Well*, and *Lady Isabel and the Elf-Knight*. In America the supernatural elements have been deleted or rationalized, as they have also been in recent British trad. The commonest b. theme is tragic love of a sensational and violent turn (*Earl Brand, Barbara Allen, Childe Maurice*). Incest and other domestic crimes are surprisingly common. The troubles on the English-Scottish Border in the 15th and 16th cs. inspired a precious body of sanguine heroic bs. (*Johnny Armstrong, Hobie Noble, Edom O'Gordon*), many of which are partly historical. Most other historical bs. are the work of minstrels (q.v.) and transparently urge the causes of their noble patrons. Propaganda seems to inform the Robin Hood bs., which exalt the virtues of the yeoman class.

The origin of the British popular b. was once hotly argued among b. scholars. A school known as "individualists" (John Meier, Louise Pound) asserted that all bs. are the work of individual poets and are "popular" merely in having been taken up by the folk. "Communalists" (F. B. Gummere, W. M. Hart, G. L. Kittredge) insisted that the prototypical b. was concocted in assemblies of the folk in the exultations of choral dance. Current opinion concedes that the traits of "balladness" may be explained by the communal theory, but holds that all extant bs. are originally the work of individuals. As the individualists failed to understand, however, the work of an individual poet does not become a b. until it is accepted by the folk and remodeled by b. conventions in the course of its tour in oral trad.

Perhaps the liveliest recent issue in b. theory is the question of whether the Eng. and Scottish bs. were composed extemporaneously in the same oral-formulaic way that Milman Parry and Albert B. Lord argue for the oral-formulaic composition of epics (see Jones and Friedman 1961). David Buchan based his structural analysis of b. narration on a wholehearted acceptance of the bs. as oral-formulaic compositions. His arguments were attacked by Friedman (in Porter 1983), but Buchan's analyses have been found valuable even by scholars who reject the theory they subtend (see Andersen et al. 1982).

Native Am. bs., influenced partly by the British traditional bs. but mainly by the broadsides, exist alongside the imported bs. The oldest perhaps is *Springfield Mountain*, the story of a Yankee farmboy fatally bitten by a snake, which may be pre-Revolutionary. Better known are outlaw songs like *Jesse James* and *Sam Bass*, the lumberjack classic *The Jam on Gerry's Rock*, the cowboys' *The Streets of Laredo*, and the popular favorites *Casey Jones, John Henry, Frankie and Albert* (*Frankie and Johnny*), *Tom Dooley*, and *Big John*.

Bs. have had an enormous influence on Eng. and Ger. literary poetry, though Entwistle exaggerates when he claims that "the debt of [romantic] lit. to the b. has been comparable to that of the Ren. to the Gr. and Lat. classics." The early

18th-c. imitations, Thomas Tickell's *Lucy and Colin*, for example, patterned themselves on broadsides and dealt mainly with village tragedies. Wordsworth and Hardy pursued a similar vein in much of their b.-colored poetry. Bishop Percy, the editor of the famous *Reliques* (1765), sentimentalized and prettified the b. style in *The Hermit of Warkworth*, but some of his completions of genuine fragments were reasonably faithful. His reconstruction of *Sir Cauline* lent many touches to Coleridge's *Christabel*. Scott's poetic career began with a translation of Bürger's *Lenore*, a Ger. literary b., and he concocted several counterfeit bs. in his early years, but he eventually came to feel that b. impersonality and the stylization of b. lang. were contrary to the aesthetic of composed poetry. In the b.-like poems of Coleridge, Keats, Rossetti, Meredith, and Swinburne, we see the popular b. style being crossed with borrowings from medieval romances and from minstrel poetry to yield poems of richer texture, more circumstantial and more contrivedly dramatic than are the bs. *La Belle Dame Sans Merci* and *The Ancient Mariner*, perhaps the finest of the literary bs. or b. imitations, could never pass for the genuine article but are greater poems than any b. Yeats's bs. (*Moll Magee, Father Gilligan* etc.) are bs. only in stanza structure and simplicity; they do not employ stock lang. or the rhet. peculiar to traditional song.

Herder's encouragement of folksong collecting resulted in Arnim and Brentano's *Des Knaben Wunderhorn* (1805–8), a collection which exerted an almost tyrannical influence over the Ger. lyric throughout the 19th c. Many of the best shorter poems of Heine, Mörike, Chamisso, Eichendorff, Uhland, and Liliencron purposely resemble *Volkslieder*. The narrative element in these poems is usually so completely overwhelmed by the lyrical that they would hardly be considered bs. by Eng. standards. See also BALLAD METER; BROADSIDE BALLAD; BYLINA; CAROL; FORMULA; NARRATIVE POETRY; ORAL POETRY; ROMANCE (Sp.); SONG; TRADITION. A.B.F.

T. Percy, *Reliques of Ancient Eng. Poetry*, 3 v. (1765); W. Wordsworth, Preface to *Lyrical Bs.*, 3d ed. (1802); W. Scott, *Minstrelsy of the Scottish Border* (1803); F. J. Child, *The Eng. and Scottish Popular Bs*, 10 v. (1882–98); F. B. Gummere, *The Popular B.* (1907)—use with caution; R. Menéndez Pidal, *Poesía popular y poesía tradicional* (1922); G. Grieg, *Last Leaves of Traditional Bs.* (1925)—post-Child Scottish coll.; W. P. Ker, *Form and Style in Poetry* (1928); P. Barry et al., *British Bs. from Maine* (1929); G. H. Gerould, *The B. of Trad.* (1932); J. and A. Lomax, *Am. Bs. and Folk Songs* (1934); L. K. Goetz, *Volkslied und Volksleben der Kroaten und Serben* (1936–37); S. B. Hustvedt, *A Melodic Index of Child's B. Tunes* (1936); W. Kayser, *Gesch. der deutschen Ballade* (1936); W. J. Entwistle, *European Balladry* (1939); M. J. C. Hodgart, *The Bs.* (1950); M. Dean-Smith, *A Guide to Eng. Folk Song Collections* (1954); *The B. Book*, ed. M. Leech (1955);

Viking Book of Folk-Bs., ed. A. B. Friedman (1956); A. B. Friedman, "The Late Med. Ballade and the Origin of Broadside Balladry," *MÆ* 27 (1958), *The B. Revival* (1961); *Traditional Tunes of the Child Bs.*, 4 v. (1959–72), *The Singing Trad. of Child's Popular Bs.* (1976), both ed. B. H. Bronson; D. K. Wilgus, *Anglo-Am. Folksong Scholarship since 1898* (1959); *The Critics and the B.*, ed. M. Leach and T. P. Coffin (1960); J. H. Jones, "Commonplace and Memorization in the Oral Trad. of the Eng. and Scottish Popular Bs.," *JAF* 74 (1961), with foll. reply by Friedman; A. K. Moore, "The Literary Status of the Eng. Popular B.," *ME Survey*, ed. E. Vasta (1965); *Deutsche Balladen*, ed. H. Fromm, 4th ed. (1965); C. M. Simpson, *The British Broadside B. and its Music* (1966); J. B. Toelken, "An Oral Canon for the Child Bs.," *JFI* 4 (1967); L. Vargyas, *Researches into the Med. Hist. of Folk B.* (tr. 1967), *Hungarian Bs. and the European B. Trad.*, 2 v. (tr. 1983); D. C. Fowler, *A Lit. Hist. of the Popular B.* (1968); B. H. Bronson, *The B. as Song* (1969); *Die deutsche Ballade*, 3d ed. (1970), *Moderne deutschen Balladen* (1970), both ed. K. Bräutigam; D. W. Foster, *The Early Sp. B.* (1971); D. Buchan, *The B. and the Folk* (1972); G. M. Laws, Jr., *The British Literary B.* (1972); S. M. Bryant, *The Sp. B. in Eng.* (1973); B. Nettl, *Folk and Traditional Music of the Western Continents* (1973); J. S. Bratton, *The Victorian Popular B.* (1975); *Penguin Book of Bs.*, ed. G. Grigson (1975); J. Reed, *The Border B.* (1975); M. R. Katz, *The Literary B. in Early 19th-C. Rus. Lit.* (1976); *B. Studies*, ed. E. B. Lyle (1976); T. P. Coffin, *The British Traditional B. in America*, 2d ed. (1977); *The European Med. B.*, ed. O. Holzapfel (1978); *Bs. and B. Research*, ed. P. Conroy (1978); B. R. Jonsson et al., *The Types of the Scandinavian Med. B.* (1978); W. Hinck, *Die deutsche Ballade vom Bürger bis Brecht*, 3d ed. (1978); W. Freund, *Die deutsche Ballade* (1978); A. Bold, *The B.* (1979); *Balladenforschung*, ed. W. Müller-Seidel (1980); R. de V. Renwick, *Eng. Folk Poetry: Structure and Meaning* (1980); *The B. as Narrative*, ed. F. Andersen et al. (1982); *The B. Image*, ed. J. Porter (1983); R. Wildbolz, "Kunstballade," and R. W. Brednich, "Volksballade," *Reallexikon* 1.902–9, 4.723–34; C. Freytag, *Ballade* (1986); *Sp. Bs.*, ed. and tr. R. Wright (1987)—anthol.; *The Pepys Bs.*, ed. W. G. Day, 5 v. (1987); P. Cachia, *Popular Narrative Poetry of Mod. Egypt* (1988)—Arabic; *Hispanic Balladry Today*, ed. R. H. Webber (1989); W. E. Richmond, *B. Scholarship: An Annot. Bibl.* (1989); C. Preston, *A Concordance to the Child Bs.* (1990); W. B. McCarthy, *The B. Matrix* (1990); *The B. and Oral Lit.*, ed. J. Harris (1991). T.V.F.B.

BALLAD METER, hymn meter. In Eng. poetry the term "b. m." refers to the meter of the Eng. and Scottish popular ballads (see BALLAD) as collected by F. J. Child in the later 19th c., though probably they date from late medieval times, i.e. the 14th–15th cs., and quite possibly from considerably earlier: the oldest extant ballad, *Judas*, is in a

13th-c. ms. It is essential to bear in mind that though ballads were not transcribed until the 18th c., they were a species of oral poetry (q.v.) transmitted orally for centuries, at times by illiterate singers, at times by professional poets and musicians.

The origin and devel. of b. m. is one of the most interesting problems in the genealogy of Eng. verseforms—Saintsbury called it "the subject . . . of the very greatest importance" for the whole history of Eng. prosody (1.246). The nature of b. m. has been the subject of much dispute. Just to begin, one may say that all its varieties are based on a quatrain of lines each having 4 stresses (or 3) rhyming *abcb* or *abab*. The dispute concerns whether b. m. is accentual verse (q.v.), counting only stresses and isochronous (see ISOCHRONISM), or accentual-syllabic verse, regulating syllable-count and not timed. Many 19th-c. metrists derived b. m. from the Med. Lat. *septenarius* (q.v.) or iambic tetrameter catalectic, a line of 7 stresses and 14 syllables (so Schipper). They argued that a couplet of these long lines was scissored by internal rhyme (q.v.) and broken into hemistichs, perhaps due to the physical exigencies of the codex page, to give a quatrain of short lines. The term was convenient, but the implied derivation—a folk meter confined mainly to oral. trad. and the illiterate derived from Church Lat. hymn verse—came to seem increasingly untenable. A variant theory holds the b. m. quatrain evolved from the native longline couplet called the "fourteener" (q.v.). But the fourteener is distinctively a Ren. form, has an altogether different effect, was stichic not strophic, and was used in differing contexts for narrative verse not song. Another group of scholars (e.g. Gummere), not well acquainted with the sophisticated prosody of OE, derived much ME verse from what they viewed as the rough 4-stress lines of Anglo-Saxon alliterative verse. But OE prosody is an intricate system which takes account of syllabic quantity, formulaic hemistichs, and structural alliteration—all unknown in the ballads—and is stichic not strophic.

Stewart, whose 1922 study broke new ground, is a syllabist. Much influenced by the common alternation of stress and slack in the *later* ballads, Stewart considers all b. m. essentially footverse and treats variations under such rubrics as trisyllabic substitution and monosyllabic feet, though he recognizes metrical pause and dipodism. We may recall that the tendency to find—or make—metrical regularity was of course fostered by Bishop ·Percy himself, and Stewart is acutely aware how tentative must be any judgments about the meter of the earliest (i.e. ME) ballads. The temporalist approach is taken by Hendren, who relies much on music and draws careful conclusions from treating the ballad as song. Malof, an accentualist, devotes much attention to what he calls the "Folk Meters," treating b. m. a "more rigid subtype of stress-verse" (88) on account of its management of

caesura, pause, and dipodism. Treating b. m. as accentual verse is intuitively appealing, for the isochronism (q.v.) of the lines is apparent in a great many cases, as Malof shows, though he is not careful to separate genuine ballads from other definitely isochronous forms such as popular songs that are not ballads. Malof handles the problem of syllabic regularity by classing instances as either "accentual" or "syllabic," though it is not obvious why isochronous meters could not also regulate syllable count. Here as everywhere it is essential to distinguish types, for the street ballads (q.v.) of the 16th c. and, certainly, later literary imitations of the popular ballad regularize the meter.

Another set of terms for b. m. was developed out of the metrical psalter trad. In the 15th and 16th cs., when vernacular hymn-writers such as Sternhold and Hopkins in England sought to appeal to the hearts and minds of the religious laity by setting the Psalms to music, they did so by the natural expedient of casting their new hymns into the meters, and sometimes the melodies as well, of those songs the laity knew best—the ballads. Hence the meters of the popular ballads passed into Protestant hymnals, where they influenced centuries of not only hymn singing but also the writing of literary poetry (e.g. George Herbert, Emily Dickinson; see Freer), and where they in fact survive today, as attested by the presence of a Metrical Index in the back of many hymnals. Though terms vary somewhat, the following are traditional (numbers denote stresses per line): Long Meter (or Measure; abbreviated L. M.): 4-4-4-4; Common Meter (or Measure; C. M.): 4-3-4-3; Short Meter (S. M.): 3-3-4-3; and (rarely) Half Meter (H. M.): 3-3-3-3. It might seem that the latter three patterns are reduced forms of the first, but in fact L. M. is not the most common pattern, C. M. is. Those scholars who accept either the musical or accentual origin of b. m. have ensured the symmetry of the whole typology by inserting a *metrical pause* (see PAUSE) for the missing fourth stresses in the the 3-stress lines of Common, Short, and Half Meter. Common Meter is thus:

X/ X / X / X /
X / X / X / (p)
X / X / X / X /
X / X / X / (p).

The rhythmic pattern of this, once heard, is unforgettable. In Stewart's dipodic account, the second and fourth stresses are only secondary, and "the structure of the verse rests fundamentally upon the four primarily stressed syllables; these cannot well be omitted, whereas omission of secondarily stressed syllables can be compensated by a pause which does not break up the verse" (1925, 940).

The view that the short-line quatrain and longline couplet forms are identical (Malof), so that syllabically regular Common Meter is simply a pair of fourteeners, and Short Meter is really Poulter's

Measure (q.v.), glosses over major issues of social context, verse type, genre, and function. The really careful and thorough study of b. m. still remains to be written, as does the definitive history of the metrical psalters. See now ACCENTUAL VERSE; HYMN; METER; PSALM.

Schipper; F. B. Gummere, *OE Ballads* (1894); G. Saintsbury, *Hist. of Eng. Prosody*, 3 v. (1906–10); G. R. Stewart, Jr., *Mod. Metrical Technique as Illustrated by B. M. (1700–1920)* (1922), extended in *PMLA* 39 (1924), 40 (1925), and in *JEGP* 24 (1925); J. Julian, *A Dict. of Hymnology* (1925); J. W. Hendren, *A Study of B. Rhythm* (1936); H. Smith, "Eng. Metrical Psalms in the 16th C. and Their Literary Significance," *HLQ* 9 (1946); V. M. Lowell, "Eng. Metrical Paraphrases of the Bible, 1549-1696," Diss., University of Illinois, 1947; G. W. Boswell, "Reciprocal Controls Exerted by B. Texts and Tunes," *JAF* 80 (1967), "Stanza Form and Music-Imposed Scansion," *SFQ* 31 (1967); B. Lindberg-Seyersted, *The Voice of the Poet* (1968); B. H. Bronson, *The B. as Song* (1969); J. Malof, *A Manual of Eng. Meters* (1970); C. Freer, *Music for a King* (1972)—hymn meter; G. S. Lovegrove, "Intro. to Hymn Meter and the Devel. of Prosodic Regularity in 16th-C. Poetry," Diss., Harvard University, 1974; R. B. Weir, "Thomas Sternhold and the Beginnings of Eng. Metrical Psalmody," *DAI* 35 (1975): 7275; Brogan 324–30 and sect. N—bibl. to 1981.
T.V.F.B.

BALLADE. The most important of the OF fixed forms and the dominant verseform of OF poetry in the 14th and 15th cs. The most common type comprises 28 lines of octosyllables, i.e. three 8-line stanzas rhyming *ababbcbC* and a 4-line *envoi* (q.v.) rhyming *bcbC*. As the capital letter indicates, the last line of the first stanza serves as the refrain, being repeated as the last line of each stanza and the *envoi*. In the complexity of its rhyme scheme, restriction of its rhyme-sounds, and use of the refrain, the b. is one of the most exacting of the fixed forms. Some variants of the standard b. employ 10-or (less often) 12-line stanzas with, respectively, 5- and 6-line *envois*. The *envoi*, which frequently begins with the address "Prince," derived from the medieval literary competition (*puy*) at which the presiding judge was so addressed, forms the climatic summation of the poem.

Although the b. may have developed from an Occitan form, it was standardized in northern Fr. poetry in the 14th c. by Guillaume de Machaut, Eustache Deschamps, and Jean Froissart. It was carried to perfection in the 15th c. by Christine de Pisan, Charles d'Orléans, and, most of all, François Villon, who made the b. the vehicle for the greatest of early Fr. poetry. Such works as his "B. des pendus" and his "B. des dames du temps jadis" achieved an unequaled intensity in their use of refrain and *envoi*. The b. continued in favor up to the time of Marot (early 16th c.), but the poets of the *Pléiade* (q.v.), followed by their neoclassical

successors in the 17th c.—with the exception of La Fontaine—had little use for the form and regarded it as barbaric. Both Molière and Boileau made contemptuous allusions to the b.

The b. of the vintage Fr. period was imitated in England by Chaucer and Gower, though now in decasyllables. Chaucer uses it for several of his early complaints and takes the single octave (q.v.) from it for the *Monk's Tale* stanza (q.v.). Beyond their practice, it never established itself firmly. In the later 19th c., the so-called Eng. Parnassians (Edmund Gosse, Austin Dobson, Andrew Lang) and poets of the Nineties (W. E. Henley, Richard Le Gallienne, Arthur Symons) revived the form with enthusiasm, inspired by the example of Banville (*Trente-six Bs. joyeuses à la manière de Villon*, 1873), who gave a new impetus to the b. equally among fellow Parnassian and decadent poets in France (François Coppée, Verlaine, Jean Richepin, Maurice Rollinat). But the modern b., with the possible exception of a few pieces by Swinburne and Pound's Villonesque adaptations ("Villonaud for this Yule" and the freely constructed "A Villonaud: Ballad of the Gibbet"), has not aimed at the grandeur and scope of Villon: it has been essentially a vehicle for light verse (q.v.), e.g. by Chesterton, Belloc, and, more recently, Wendy Cope.

The double b. is composed of six 8- or 10-line stanzas; the refrain is maintained, but the *envoi* is optional (e.g. Villon's "Pour ce, amez tant que vouldrez"; Banville's "Pour les bonnes gens" and "Des sottises de Paris"; Swinburne's "A Double Ballad of August" and "A Double Ballad of Good Counsel"). The "b. à double refrain," which has Marot's "Frère Lubin" as its model, introduces a second refrain at the fourth line of each stanza and again at the second line of the *envoi*, producing, most characteristically, a rhyme scheme of *abaBbcbC* for the stanzas and *bBcC* for the *envoi*; Dobson, Lang, and Henley number among the later 19th-c. practitioners of this variant.

J. Gleeson White, *Bs. and Rondeaus* (1887); G. M. Hecq, *La B. et ses derivées* (1891); Kastner; H. L. Cohen, *The B.* (1915), *Lyric Forms from France* (1922); P. Champion, *Histoire poétique du XVe siècle*, 2 v. (1923); G. Reaney, "Concerning the Origins of the Rondeau, Virelai, and B.," *Musica Disciplina* 6 (1952), "The Devel. of the Rondeau, Virelai, and B.," *Festschrift Karl Fellerer* (1962); A. B. Friedman, "The Late Medieval B. and the Origin of Broadside Balladry," *MÆ* 27 (1958); J. Fox, *The Poetry of Villon* (1962); Morier. A.PR.; T.V.F.B.; C.S.

BALLATA. See FROTTOLA AND BARZELLETTA; LAUDA; RITORNELLO.

BARD. The Eng. word is derived from the Ir. *bard* (pl. *baird*) which, like the Welsh *bardd* (pl. *beirdd*) is derived from the Celtic *bardos* (pl. *bardoi*). Classical authors inform us that the continental Celts had *bards* who were employed to sing eulogies and satires to the accompaniment of instrumental music. It is generally assumed that they formed a branch of the druidic order and that unlike the religious or more specifically druidic branch they survived the transition from paganism to Christianity in the religion of the insular Celts and retained their status and function, to praise the ruler of the land and thus increase the prosperity of both, or, if the ruler were guilty of misgovernment, to threaten or actually to satirize him.

In Ireland these poets became known as *filidh* (sing. *fili*; see FILI) and the name *baird* was applied to one class of poets who were regarded as inferior in qualification and status. The Welsh preserved the generic term *bardd*, but in Wales as in Ireland poets were divided into different classes, culminating in that of the *pencerdd* in Wales and the *ollam(h)* in Ireland. In both countries poets formed a kind of guild; poetry was very much a craft to be learned, and as it involved knowledge (e.g. traditional lore), there were (bardic) schools where apprentices were taught by masters who had themselves graduated and had won their mastership in competition with others. The chief poets stood in a special relationship to the rulers, and their eulogy and satires originally had a sacral character. Later, when the poets sang for patrons who were not rulers, their songs were still regarded as conferring fame (or, in exceptional cases, shame) on their recipients. Perhaps the ideas that poetry is a matter of learning "rules" (q.v.) and that it can be judged by the foremost among its practitioners are best kept alive by the Welsh National Eisteddfod (q.v.) and the institutions set up in imitation of it in Ireland and Scotland.

Hence the trad. of learned craft and proven skill behind the term is far removed from the emotionalism connected with it by the 18th-c. Eng. poets, such as Gray and Beattie, who revived it. The Eng. romantics were fascinated by the antiquity of the Celtic poets or bards and endowed them with their own ideas concerning "true" poetry, ironically attributing to them the qualities that they least prized, spontaneity and unbridled emotion. That emotionalism is essentially preserved in the modern Eng. sense of the term, which denotes any poet but often connotes rhapsodic transcendence and is sometimes used as a pejorative; "bardolatry" is the critical term for the idolization of Shakespeare. Cf. SCOP and SKALD; see also AFRICAN POETRY; IRISH POETRY; WELSH POETRY.—H. I. Bell, *The Devel. of Welsh Poetry* (1936); G. Murphy, "Bards and Filidh," *Éigse* 2 (1940); J. J. Parry, "The Court Poets of the Welsh Princes," *PMLA* 67 (1952); J. E. C. Williams, "The Court Poet in Med. Ireland," *PBA* 57 (1971); P. A. Breatnach, "The Chief's Poet," *Proc. of the Royal Irish Academy* 83, C3 (1983). J.E.C.W.; T.V.F.B.

BARDIC VERSE. See CELTIC PROSODY.

BAROQUE.

I. HISTORY OF THE TERM
II. HISTORY OF THE CONCEPT
III. DEVELOPMENT IN MAJOR EUROPEAN LITERATURES
IV. BAROQUE STYLE IN POETRY

B. describes the style that prevailed in European lit. between roughly 1580 and 1680; in the West, that is, from the *Gerusalemme liberata* to the last *autos* of Calderón. In East Europe, manifestations of b. style occur as late as the first half of the 18th c. For those whose concern is to find a period term for the literary style between the decline of the Ren. and the rise of the Enlightenment, no other word is as convenient. Indeed, no other could now be imposed. Although still not universally accepted as the sole designation for the period, resistance to its use has decreased considerably. Partisans of separate national lits. and their traditional terminology, above all in France and England, have been the slowest to abandon their opposition. By now, however, most Fr. scholarship has followed the rest of the Continent, and only the Eng. lags. Since "b." as a period term has been embattled, and perhaps always will be to some extent, it is necessary to deal with its etymological origin and with the hist. of its application to the arts and to lit. Once these questions are settled, it will then be possible to liberate the term from its wayward origins and to proceed to investigate the traits of the style which it designates.

I. HISTORY OF THE TERM. The older derivation of "b." from *barroco* (Portuguese: "irregular pearl") and eventually *verruca* (Lat.: "declivity," "wart") is unsound: the linguistic evidence is untenable and there is practically no textual support. Instead, a good case can be made for deriving the word from the mnemonic hexameters constructed in the 13th c. by William of Shyreswood as a code version of Aristotle's categories of syllogisms. The early hist. of the word can be traced by putting together citations from writers such as St. Bernardine, Vives, Erasmus, Montaigne, Ferrari, Soldani, Saint-Simon, and others. In all these instances the word *baroco* was singled out as representing the absurd or grotesque pedantry of late medieval logic-chopping.

II. HISTORY OF THE CONCEPT. Until the later 19th c., "b." was used mostly as a fancy synonym for "absurd" or "grotesque." On occasion one finds it used in the older way: Baudelaire, for example, addressing the city of Paris, speaks of "Tes petits orateurs, aux enflures baroques, / Prêchant l'amour" ("Projet d'épilogue pour la seconde éd. de *Les Fleurs du mal*"). The art historians J. Burckhardt (1855) and H. Wölfflin (1888) began the rehabilitation of the term, the first giving it historical limits and the second freeing it of pejorative associations. It was quickly accepted in art hist. as a necessary term to designate the period after the High Ren.; and, in the early 20th c., the

BAROQUE

periodization of styles was made more precise by the introduction of the term "mannerism" (q.v.) to distinguish an intermediate style between High Ren. and b. For lit., the first application of the concept was made in 1888 by Wölfflin, who, in his *Ren. und Barock*, sketched a stylistic contrast between Ariosto (Ren.) and Tasso (b.), based on the opening stanzas of *Orlando furioso* and *Gerusalemme liberata*. He further suggested that the same sort of contrast exists between Boiardo's *Orlando innamorato* and Berni's *rifacimento* of it. From Boiardo to Tasso he traces a continuous trend away from clear visual imagination toward mood and atmosphere ("weniger Anschauung, mehr Stimmung"). Though literary historians were long in responding, it is from Wölfflin's contrast that we can date the beginnings of interest in b. as a literary concept.

Because of its nearly universal acceptance, the concept of b. in art hist. has continued to exert strong influence on literary historiography. In 1922, Theophil Spoerri wrote a thorough study (*Ren. und Barock bei Ariosto und Tasso*) which attempted to fill Wölfflin's prescription. By this time Wölfflin had also published his *Kunstgeschichtliche Grundbegriffe* (1915; Eng. tr. as *Principles of Art Hist.*, 1932), which set forth categories such as "closed" vs. "open" form, "linear" vs. "painterly," for distinguishing between Ren. and b. styles in art. Some have been tempted to apply the categories almost directly to lit. (e.g. D. H. Roaten and F. Sánchez y Escribano, *Wölfflin's Principles in Sp. Drama: 1500–1700* [1952]), while others have emulated them at a distance (e.g. I. Buffum, *Agrippa d'Aubigné's Les Tragiques* [1951]). Buffum takes his point of departure from Wölfflin, as well as purely literary devices such as asyndeton, verbal echo, and oxymoron, and arrives at general characteristics like forcefulness, theatricality, and mutability. With his *Four Stages of Ren. Style* (1955), Wylie Sypher increases the indebtedness to Wölfflin by undertaking to incl. both lit. and art in a set of general stylistic categories. By means of these he attempts to distinguish four distinct styles: Ren. (Spenser); mannerism (*Hamlet, Lear*); b. (*Othello, Paradise Lost*); late-b. (Dryden, Racine).

In varying degrees the debtors to Wölfflin show their awareness of the great difficulties in transferring art categories to lit., but in the end the difficulties remain unsolved. More independent attempts to define b. style in lit. based solely on literary aesthetics have yielded better results. Among the first was Fritz Strich, who in 1916 proposed that the use of the rhetorical figure asyndeton (q.v.) was the most characteristic element of b. style, at least in Ger. poetry. In 1929 H. Hatzfeld, in his analysis of the religious lyric in France, derived what he found to be characteristic motifs or themes, such as veiled antithesis (*Schleierantithese*) and solitude (*tout-seul-Formel*). Later (*Lit. Through Art*, 1952), Hatzfeld undertook to establish other motifs common to lit. and

art of the b.: renunciation, resignation, boundlessness, to name a few. Since then scholars have sought to introduce greater precision into b. as a style term by exploring still other categories of literary devices and motifs.

III. DEVELOPMENT IN MAJOR EUROPEAN LITERATURES. (1) *Germany*: The rapid success of the term among Ger. art historians, and the early work of Strich, Viëtor, and others, led to a general acceptance among literary scholars. It is now taken for granted that b. is the proper name for the period embracing, for instance, Grimmelshausen, Gryphius, Lohenstein, and Angelus Silesius. (2) *Spain*: The old term *siglo de oro* is still in use, but b. has gained widespread acceptance, and newer Sp. scholarship exhibits a definite preference for it. Central figures like Cervantes, Lope de Vega, and Quevedo have been analyzed as b. writers. Góngora, whose rehabilitation began in 1927, is now considered the extreme of b. style. *Culteranismo* (q.v.) and *conceptismo* have been subsumed under the rubric of b. style, but some confusion still results from the continued use of the term *barroquismo*, which has perjorative and nontemporal connotations. (3) *France*: Interest in and scholarship on b. on the part of Fr. critics has increased dramatically since the 1950s. Partly this has come about from a revaluation of the traditional concept of *classicisme* and the *grand siècle*, and partly from a reconsideration of the school of so-called *précieux* poets (e.g. Saint-Amant and Théophile de Viau). The work of Thierry Maulnier and M. Raymond have been influential on numerous subsequent essays and anthols., among them Claude Gilbert's 2-vol. *La poésie baroque* (1969). Early pioneering studies incl. Rousset (1954) and Buffum (1957). Since the 1950s the reputation of Jean de Sponde has been re-established and many long forgotten poets (e.g. Chassignet, Du Bois Hus, Sigogne) have been anthologized and studied. (4) *Italy*: Here the b. was a relative decline. In poetry the important figures are few after Tasso, Marino, Tassoni, Chiabrera, and Redi. Most scholarship on Marino and his followers has been concerned with mechanical detail, biography, or influence on Fr., Ger., and Eng. poets of the time. Marino's influence on b. poetry in Poland, Bohemia, Croatia, and Hungary has also been explored. *Marinismo* had been deplored as a disease; indeed Croce found *barocco* almost synonymous with bad taste. As in France, however, the situation has changed considerably since the 1950s. A new interest in b. resulted in several conferences, more objective assessment of Marino and his followers, and investigation into the connections between the b. in Italy and its devel. elsewhere in Europe. Though the traditional *seicento* seems secure, the term "b." has gained some acceptance as the designation for the age (e.g. Dellepiane, 1973). (5) *England*: Eng. critics have proved the most reluctant to adopt the concept of b. A main source of opposition is the happy coincidence between literary movements and royal reigns. The two phases of the Ren. in England roughly correspond to the reigns of Henry VIII and Elizabeth I, and what elsewhere would be called b. corresponds in its origins to the reign of James I. In Eng. lit. we find a special difficulty: the belated flowering of the Ren. comes so close upon the beginning of the b. that the two styles for a time coexist. Nevertheless, a start has been made toward distinguishing the styles in M. W. Croll's early analysis of b. prose style. The almost universal acceptance of b. in art history has led to its use in some studies of Crashaw, Browne, and Milton.

Thus the term b. has taken hold in almost all Western lits. In East Central Europe, where b. lit. is well developed among the Poles, Czechs, Croats, Hungarians, and Romanians, the term b. has enjoyed favor for a long time. Among the East Slavs, much work has been done on Ukrainian b. since World War II, particularly the pioneering studies by the émigré scholar D. Tschiżewskij. Soviet scholars once resisted the application of b. to Rus. literary historiography because of their identification of it with the Counter-Reformation, but this is no longer the case, and serious attempts to distinguish a Rus. literary b. style have been made by I. Golenishchev-Kutuzov, A. Morozov, and D. Likhachev. An impressive attempt at a ranging synthesis of the b. period among the Slavs was undertaken by A. Angyal in 1961.

IV. BAROQUE STYLE IN POETRY. Among the least promising ways of approaching the question are to view b. as an eternal phenomenon recurrent in all ages, or to limit it to the Counter-Reformation, or to depend wholly on the criteria of art hist. Far preferable are independent formulations that begin with single works of lit. and generalize on the basis of their purely literary properties, such as rhetorical figures (metaphor, paradox), the element of time, the dramatic situation of the poem, and the implied world view.

A common way of describing b. poetic style is to say that it abounds in conceits (q.v.; concetti, conceptos), that is, unusual similes or puns. Examples are Donne's image of the compass and Marino's statement that if he cannot enjoy sleep he will at least enjoy the image of death (which is of course sleep). Although such expressions represent habits of thought known in the Middle Ages and Ren. (e.g. Petrarch's "I burn and am as ice."), the evidence for a very strong b. preference for them is overwhelming. L. Unger's Donne's Poetry and Modern Crit. (1950) persuasively counters arguments that Eng. metaphysical poetry (q.v.) is characterized by extended metaphors running through the poem. Still, much of the metaphysical trad. can be legitimately regarded as compatible with b. aesthetics.

Second, if a poem be looked upon as discourse in time, then time itself becomes an important element of structure. It can be shown that Ren. poetry is generally simple in its use of tense and time reference, whereas b. poetry exhibits not only explicit awareness of the nature and passage of time but also a tendency to manipulate time and exploit its paradoxes.

Third, the dramatic situation of a poem can be defined as the interaction between the speaker, the audience, and the reader. In Ren. poetry, generally speaking, an attitude is expressed and then elaborated. In b. poetry, to state the contrast starkly, a tentative attitude is expressed which is then, through interaction of the several dramatis personae, gradually modified until a new attitude is achieved in a surprising way.

A final possible criterion is the so-called b. world view. B. poetry often attempts to span the entire range between religious sentiments and libertinage, beauty and ugliness, egocentricity and impersonality, temporality and eternity. It is not surprising that such issues should arise in b. poetry: whatever their antiquity, they were presented with new immediacy by the political, religious, and scientific events of the 17th c., and by the contributions of such thinkers as Montaigne, Descartes, Browne, Pascal, and Hobbes. We may look to Montaigne for a touchstone: "Je ne peins pas l'être; je peins le passage" ("Du Repentir"). Words like disequilibrium and disillusionment (the Sp. desengaño) are commonly used of the period. Those who adopt them consider them as expressing transitory resolutions of the problem of opposites.

It must be emphasized that a theory of b. style ought to strike a balance between the general and the particular; and that it ought to be able to account for the major works of the time in such a way as to distinguish, significantly, their style from what preceded and what succeeded them.

F. Strich, "Der lyrische Stil des 17. Jh.," Abhandlungen zur deutschen Literaturgesch.: Festschrift für Franz Muncker (1916), "Die Übertragung des Barockbegriffes von der bildenden Kunst auf die Dichtung," Die Kunstformen des Barockzeitalters, ed. R. Stamm (1956); H. Hatzfeld, Don Quixote als Wortkunstwerk (1927), "Der Barockstil der religiösen klassischen Lyrik in Frankreich," Literaturwiss. Jahr. der Görresgesellschaft 4 (1929); K. Viëtor, Probleme der dt. Barocklit. (1928); B. Croce, Storia dell'età barocca in Italia (1929); W. P. Friederich, Spiritualismus und Sensualismus in der eng. Barocklyrik (1932); M. Mincoff, "B. Lit. in England," Annuaire de l'Université de Sofia, Faculté Historico-Phil. 43 (1947); Revue de sciences humaines (numéro spécial), fasc. 55–66 (1949)—incl. articles by the institutors of b. in France, M. Raymond, R. Lebègue, etc.; O. de Mourgues, Metaphysical, B. and Précieux Poetry (1953); L. Nelson, Jr., "Góngora and Milton: Toward a Definition of the B.," CL 6 (1954), B. Lyric Poetry (1961); J. Rousset, La Litt. de l'âge b. en France: Circé et le paon (1954), Anthol. de la poésie b. française, 2 v. (1961), "La Definition du terme 'B.,'" Internat. Comp. Lit. Assoc. Proc. of the Third Congress (1962); I. Buffum, Studies in the B. from Montaigne to Rotrou (1957); A. Cioranescu,

El barroco (1957); M. Praz, *The Flaming Heart* (1958); A. Angyal, *Die slavische Barockwelt* (1961); F. J. Warnke, *European Metaphysical Poetry* (1961, 1974), *Versions of B.* (1972); R. Daniells, *Milton, Mannerism and B.* (1963); R. Wellek, "The Concept of B." and "Postscript 1962," *Concepts of Crit.* (1963), "B. in Lit.," *DHI*; J. M. Cohen, *The B. Lyric* (1963); M. W. Croll, *Style, Rhet. and Rhythm: Essays,* ed. J. M. Patrick et al. (1966); G. Gillespie, *Ger. B. Poetry* (1971); R. Dellepiane, *Cultura e letteratura del barocco* (1973); J. Pederson, *Images et figures dans la poésie française de l'âge b.* (1974); H. B. Segel, *The B. Poem* (1974); F. Hallyn, *Formes metaphoriques dans la poésie lyrique de l'age baroque en France* (1975); J. P. Hill and E. Caracciolo-Trejo, *B. Poetry* (1975); J. Siles, *El barroco en la poesía española* (1975); A. Baïche, *La Naissance du b. français* (1976); E. B. Gilman, *The Curious Perspective: Literary and Pictorial Wit in the 17th C.* (1978); P. N. Skrine, *The B.: Lit. and Culture in 17th-C. Europe* (1978); M. Roston, *Milton and the B.* (1980); W. Emrich, *Deutsche Lit. der Barockzeit* (1981); D. L. Rubin, *The Knot of Artifice* (1981); A. Suárez Miramón, *La renovación poética del Barroco* (1981); E. Raimondi, *Letteratura barocca* (1982); Terras; J. M. Steadman, *Redefining a Period Style* (1990). L.NE.; H.B.S.

BAROQUE POETICS. It could hardly be claimed that the b. age was original and productive in elaborating a theory of poetry. Actually, it inherited, modified, and passed on to the age of neoclassicism the formulations of the Ren.: Castelvetro, Scaliger, Minturno, and others (see RENAISSANCE POETICS) had placed Aristotle in the center of importance, where his tenets went almost unchallenged until the stirrings of the romantic revolution. B. p., therefore, derived its theory ultimately from the precepts of Aristotle, with a varying admixture of Horatian loci and rhetorical dicta: poetry is both useful and pleasing; the poet must possess the faculty of invention; poetry is related to the real world in that it is an imitation of nature; art is in some way distinct from nature and yet it cannot transgress the norms nature imposes; the poet should be good as well as eloquent. Only in matters of emphasis can a few b. theoreticians be called original.

Apart from exposition of theory, treatises of the time often had ulterior motives: to reaffirm the worth and dignity of poetry, to provide a didactic guide or handbook to poetic practice, and to make a case for poetry in the vernacular. Such purposes had also been served by Ren. "defenses" and "arts of poetry"; in fact, there seems little new in most of the many b. treatises of the kind. Martin Opitz's *Buch von der deutschen Poeterey* (1624), for example, is heavily indebted to Ronsard and Heinsius, among others. Similarly, Ben Jonson's *Timber, or Discoveries* (1641) is almost wholly derivative from Cl. and Ren. sources. For the most part their fame as critics is due to their chronological originality within the hypothetically closed system of a national lit. On the other hand, Jonson's opinions, as recorded in his *Conversations* (1619) with Drummond of Hawthornden, are refreshingly pungent and personal. Though they are hardly argued criticism, they surpass in interest, on account of their sharp and imperious phrasing, the many "roll calls" (to use Spingarn's term) from Cervantes' *Viaje del Parnaso* (1614) to Boileau's historical sketch of poetry in his *Art poétique* (1674).

As the 17th c. progressed there was a trend, parallel with the growing influence of Fr. critics, toward ever stricter interpretation of neoclassical doctrine. At the same time, several relatively new concepts were given some prominence—relatively new, that is, because in one form or another they could be found anticipated in the Ren. In general, they had to do with the "ineffable" in art, the phenomena which transcended analysis. First of all, the notion of taste (q.v.; Eng. *gusto*, Fr. *goût*) became a means for justifying the sometimes bewildering differences of opinion among readers and judgments of critics. Its consequences for later criticism are much greater than its prominence in the b. Second, the notion of "wit" or "genius" (qq.v.; *ingegno, ingenio, génie,* or *esprit*) accounted for the faculty of invention (q.v.) corresponding to "fancy" (q.v.) or "fantasy" and to the later " imagination" (q.v.). The obvious problem presented itself: could a poet without "wit" but possessed of skill write satisfactory poetry; and could a poet with "wit" but without skill do the same? One must keep in mind, while following the word "wit" through its many convolutions, that its meanings, ranging from "ingeniousness" to "imagination," ultimately depend upon the Lat. substratum *ingenium* and its customary contrast with *iudicium* or "judgment." A third important concept evolved during the age was the *je ne sais quoi* (q.v.); in the later phrase of Pope, this is the "grace beyond the reach of art." It is a vague recognition that the "rules" (q.v.) did not account for everything. Later in the century it came to be related to the new interest in the "sublime" (q.v.) which brought about the resuscitation of Longinus. Here again, the substratum is the Lat. *nescio quid*; but it is important to observe that the common locution has become almost a technical term. In most instances, however, these relatively new concepts did not receive thorough exposition and analysis until the age of neoclassicism proper.

It is true that there were conservative and liberal interpretations of the rules. There were, in the major European lits., proponents of the strictest observance (e.g. La Mesnardière, el Pinciano) whose appeal to authority was as dogmatic as it was inadequate. On the other hand, there were independent interpreters of the ancients whose "liberalism" has sometimes been given exaggerated importance. Nothing will make up for the obvious lack of original theory in the age, esp. at a time when new modes of lyric poetry and the drama, not to mention the novel, were being created. In England, for instance, Shakespeare, Milton, and Donne had varying receptions at the hands of different critics and fellow poets, but none, despite often recognized excellence, was properly explicated or accounted for by contemporary crit. The less revolutionary Corneille caused a split in orthodoxy; and even Racine was attacked. Lope de Vega felt himself within the bounds of a liberal classicism, and yet his practice in writing the seemingly hybrid form of the Sp. *comedia* was censured by the strict. In general, it may be said that the critics, as so often happens, were unprepared for novelty: their ready-made theories compelled them to reject anything for which they could not cite precedent; "correctness" or mere mechanical conformity often received their highest praise.

It is a custom to view Fr. lit. at times as a long sequence of controversies or "quarrels." Certainly there is one whose importance cannot be denied and whose international consequences are part of the aesthetics of the age: the *querelle* (q.v.) or battle of the ancients and the moderns. The problem of "imitation" (q.v.; in many of the possible meanings of that unfortunate translation of *mimesis*) led illogically to the problem of how and with what fidelity to "imitate" the ancients, which led illogically in turn to the question of whether the ancients were superior to the moderns. Though the most interesting consequences of that quarrel belong to the succeeding age, it must be recognized that the dispute was already implicit in the tenets of Ren. neoclassicism, and that it was the newly expounded notion of "progress" that brought it into prominence.

In the larger context of aesthetics and philosophy one may find plausible reasons for the absence of an original p. and for the prevailing poetic practice of the time. Generally speaking, the rationalist cast of thought in Bacon and Descartes entailed a separation between reason and imagination, thought and feeling. Hence a theoretical "distrust of the imagination" and a "dissociation of sensibility" (q.v.). But Descartes's neglect of aesthetics and Bacon's perfunctory consideration of poetry had no immediate effect on b. p. Whether the anti-Aristotelian reformer, Petrus Ramus, whose works on dialectic (1555, 1556) long remained textbooks, actually influenced poetic practice by making the elements of poetry a part of logic rather than rhet., remains a difficult, perhaps wrongly posed, problem. There is a danger in mistaking mere reshufflings of terms and categories for real innovation, just as there is a danger in assuming that poets wrote their poetry according to prescription (see RULES). Nevertheless, it is obvious that b. poetry is characterized by intricacy and ingeniousness and that the most original p. of the time were influenced by rhet. and dialectic, whether of the Cl.-med. trad. or from the newer systems.

Before surveying the major countries, it is ap-propriate to recall what was in the common heritage, common above all because most of it was in Latin. Horace was of course immediately available; Aristotle's *Poetics* was available in Lat. and commented on and presented by, for instance, Castelvetro; Vida and Scaliger, too, were in the learned lang. They also had in common the rhetorical trad. which, unlike the trad. of p., had been transmitted continuously from antiquity through the Middle Ages. In fact, before Aristotle became ascendant in the middle of the 16th c., the p. were heavily dependent on rhetorical theory. That dependence continued and can be clearly seen in, for example, Jonson, Gracián, and Tesauro.

Within Fr. lit. of the 17th c. it would be possible to make an elaborate and microscopic analysis of the fortune of various parts of the neoclassical canon, from Malherbe to Boileau. There would, predictably, be the liberals and the conservatives, but the basic theory would appear quite static. If one were to conceive of neoclassicism in the most rigid fashion, it would then be easy to cull eccentric opinions and label them anticlassical (or, as Spingarn does, "romantic"); but under this procedure the whole question would have been formulated falsely. As for the relation between poetry and theory, it may be said that only as poets began to conform to the "rules" did a rapprochement come about. B. poetic theory was certainly powerless to deal with D'Aubigné or even Théophile de Viau. Its precepts, however, could be made to fit more conservative poets such as Malherbe and Voiture. Even the doctrines of *préciosité* (q.v.) are more an evidence of neoclassical purism than a defense of novel poetic practice. The triumph of current theory, in a sense its proof after the fact, lay in the great tragedies of Racine.

In England, aside from occasional comments by Jonson or Milton or other poets (Carew's, in his "Elegy upon the Death of Doctor Donne," are the most perceptive), perhaps the greatest interest is to be found in b. p. is the question of epic poetry. It is presented most fully in the exchange between William Davenant and Thomas Hobbes in regard to Davenant's epic *Gondibert* (1650). Davenant makes the conventional remarks about the epic (q.v.) and argues that it is proper for him to write on a Christian subject, esp. for the purpose of "instruction." True, he allows for effects beyond the rules ("shadowings, happy strokes, secret graces"), but we have seen that b. neoclassicism quickly granted such "liberties." A great deal of the treatise is directed toward demonstrating the moral efficacy of poetry; in fact, he comes close to the *reductio ad absurdum* of neoclassical crit., the sugarcoated-pill theory of poetry. Hobbes's answer is hardly more than a perfunctory agreement. One turns in vain to Cowley's "Preface" to *Poems* (1668) for some sketch of a poetics of the "metaphysicals"; unfortunately, the few hints of theory given there are quite traditional. Nor do Henry Peacham's chapter on poetry in *The Com-*

pleat Gentleman (1622) or Henry Reynold's *My-thomystes* (1633?) arouse more than antiquarian interest.

In Italy there is some rapprochement between contemporary practice and theory. From the letters and some poetic passages of Marino (see MARINISM) one can derive a few traits of a primitive theory of poetry. Its purpose is hardly to instruct at all: it tries to please, to play upon the senses, to be an end in itself. The goal of the good poet is to astonish or dazzle his readers by the brilliance and opulence of his descriptions and turns of phrase. The only important treatise is Emanuele Tesauro's *Cannochiale aristotelico* (1654), which is more a handbook of rhet. than a p. It can be seen as representing the old rhetorical trad., yet its emphasis on wit and the conceit (q.v.) is relatively novel. Of similar interest is Matteo Pellegrini's *Delle acutezze* (1639).

In Spain the situation is generally the same as elsewhere: liberals and conservatives manipulate the same counters. There is some novelty and interest in Gracián's treatise *Agudeza y arte de ingenio* (1642, 1648), which can be set in the same trad. as Tesauro's. Essentially it is an elaborate and not always consistent classification of kinds of wit (*ingenio*). With great patience and perseverance it attempts to categorize and exemplify the "ingenious" effects achieved by poets since antiquity, with special pride of place for such contemporaries as the Argensolas and Góngora. In the main, however, its theory is traditional: there is a sort of poetic substance on which the poet attaches his "ornament" (q.v.), and the "ornament" is a local achievement which is almost seen as independent of the total poem. Gracián's work is mostly a commented anthology of "ingenious" poems and passages.

It could not be gainsaid that there are points of particular interest in b. p., such as the devel. of some important concepts (taste, wit, the *je ne sais quoi*) and a new compenetration of p. and rhet. (e.g. Tesauro and Gracián, and the somewhat exaggerated influence of Ramus). But we must conclude that it was unsuccessful in elaborating an original theory of poetry, that it fails to account for the poetic practice of the age, and that its main importance is to transmit the canons of neoclassical crit. from the Ren. to the full flowering of the age of neoclassicism.

See also CLASSICISM; CONCEIT; GONGORISM; JE NE SAIS QUOI; MARINISM; METAPHYSICAL POETRY; NEOCLASSICAL POETICS; PRECIOSITE; QUERELLE DES ANCIENS ET DES MODERNES; RENAISSANCE POETICS; RULES; TASTE; WIT.

M. Menéndez y Pelayo, *Historia de las ideas estéticas en España*, 9 v. (1883–91); J. E. Spingarn, *A Hist. of Lit. Crit. in the Ren.* (1899), *Crit. Essays of the 17th C.*, 3 v. (1909); B. Croce, *Estetica* (1902; best Eng. ed. 1922), "I trattatisti italiani del Concettismo e Baltasar Gracián," *Problemi di estetica* (1909); H. Gillot, *La Querelle des anciens et des modernes en France* (1914); R. Bray, *La Formation de la doctrine classique en France* (1931); G. Marzot, *L'Ingegno e il genio del seicento* (1944); H. T. Swedenberg, *The Theory of the Epic in England, 1650–1800* (1944); Curtius, ch. 15 and excursuses 22 and 23; R. Tuve, *Elizabethan and Metaphysical Imagery* (1947); E. B. O. Borgerhoff, *The Freedom of Fr. Classicism* (1950); A. Vilanova, "Preceptistas de los siglos XVI y XVII," *Historia general de las literaturas hispánicas*, ed. G. Diaz-Plaja, v. 3 (1953); M. Raymond, *B. et Ren. poétique* (1955); W. S. Howell, *Logic and Rhet. in England, 1500–1700* (1956); A. J. Smith, "An Examination of Some Claims for Ramism," *RES* 7 (1956); Wimsatt and Brooks; S. L. Bethell, "The Nature of Metaphysical Wit," *Discussions of John Donne*, ed. F. Kermode (1962); B. Hathaway, *The Age of Crit.: The Late Ren. in Italy* (1962); R. Wellek, "The Concept of B." and "Postscript 1962," *Concepts of Crit.* (1963); J. V. Mirollo, *The Poet of the Marvelous* (1963); R. L. Colie, *Paradoxia epidemica* (1966); M. W. Croll, *Style, Rhet, and Rhythm: Essays*, ed. J. M. Patrick et al. (1966); W. T. Elwert, *La poesia lirica italiana del seicento* (1967); B. Hathaway, *Marvels and Commonplaces* (1968); L. Fischer, *Gebundene Rede* (1968); K. K. Ruthven, *The Conceit* (1969); G. Conte, *La Metafora barocca* (1972); F. Hallym, *Formes metaphoriques dans la poésie lyrique de l'age b. en France* (1975); D. L. Rubin, *The Knot of Artifice* (1981).   L.NE.

BARZELLETTA. See FROTTOLA AND BARZELLETTA.

BASQUE POETRY. There is a widespread idea that the B. lang. has no lit., but the facts prove otherwise. In the last 25 years, a number of histories have been devoted to the subject; one of them, when completed, will comprise seven volumes.

B. oral lit. is extremely ancient and, moreover, very original. Within it two separate genres may be noted: the *pastorales*, a remnant of what must have been the old drama, and *bertsolarism*, B. troubadour poetry, an improvised form sung before an audience. Written lit., which began considerably later, was essentially religious until the 20th c.; praise of the B. lang. is another main theme. These texts were composed in four dialects spoken in the B. areas of France and Spain.

Linguae vasconum primitiae, the earliest book of B. p., was written in 1545 by the priest B. Detxepare. Consisting of 16 poems on religious and amorous themes, together with praise of the B. lang., it reveals the influence of the Counterreformation. Notable is its realistic diction, esp. in the dialogues between lovers. The dominant metrical form is the medieval *cuaderna via* (q.v.), although the work was written in the Ren.

Oihenart (1592–1667), the first B. poet from the laity, was the outstanding poet of the 17th c. His *Atsotitzak eta Neurititzak* (Proverbs and Refrains, 1657) includes love poems as well as proverbs and refrains. The 18th c. produced no signifi-

BATHOS

cant figure in written poetry, although oral poetry continued to be vigorous, esp. in the northern B. provinces.

The legendary poet and *bertsolari* P. Topet, "Etxahun" (1786–1862), flourished in the province of Zuberoa. One of the most original popular poets in B. lit., he wrote poems laden with highly emotional romantic emphases, in addition to violent personal satires. In the Sp. provinces of the B. country, the loss of the second Carlist War (1872–76) and the consequent loss of the old liberties were a cause of distress. This distress, however, served as a stimulus to the literary revival of the earlier 20th c., a revival anticipated in the work of F. Arrese y Beitia (1841–1906).

The earlier 20th c. saw the creation of the Academy of the B. Lang. (1918), the *Lorejaiak* (Floral Games) and poetry competitions, and the *txapelketak* or championship competitions for troubadours. N. Ormaetxea, "Orixe" (1888–1961), J. M. Aguirre, "Lizardi" (1896–1933), and E. Urkiaga, "Lauaxeta" (1905–37) were the leading poets of the time. Orixe wrote lyrical-mystical poems as well as an epic *Euskaldunak* (*The Basques*); Lizardi is considered by some to be the greatest B. lyric poet; Lauaxeta, the most modern of the group, shows in his work the influence of Fr. symbolism.

The B. lit. Ren. was cut short by the Sp. Civil War (1936–39). Lauaxeta was shot by Franco's troops, and other B. writers were imprisoned or forced into exile. For ten years after the war, publication in the B. lang. was prohibited in the Sp. area of the B. country. Among exile publications may be mentioned *Urrundik* (*From Far Away*, 1945) and *Gudarien Eginak* (The Deeds of Basque Soldiers, 1947), both by T. Monzon (1904–81).

S. Mitxelena (1918–65), in *Arantzazu* (You on the Thorn, 1949) and other works, proved to be the best interpreter of the anguish of the post-Civil War years. Other significant poets were N. Etxaniz (1899–1982) and J. I. Goikoetxea, "Gaztelu" (1908–83), who introduced modern elements into B. poetry. X. Diharce, "Iratzeder" (b. 1920) is an outstanding religious poet.

After 1950, in the B. country as elsewhere in the West, a total break from tradition manifested itself. E. T. A., the B. independence movement, appeared, and, in addition, existentialist, Marxist, and Freudian ideas began to make themselves felt. The "rupturist" poets, chief among them J. Mirande (1925–72) and G. Aresti (1933–75), broke conspicuously with the past. Mirande—antidemocratic, anti-Marxist, anti-Semitic, hostile to B. moderate nationalism—advocated violence and paganism. Against God and Church, he caused sensation by treating such themes as agnosticism, pederasty, Lesbianism, and masturbation. Aresti carried on in the southern B. area the revolution that Mirande had initiated in the northern area.

From the 1960s on, a variety of tendencies became apparent in the work of J. A. Arce,

"Harzabal" (b. 1939, "spatial poetry"), M. Lasa (b. 1938), J. Azurmendi (b. 1941), and L. M. Muxika (b. 1939). B. Gandiaga (b. 1928) moved from religious to nationalistic themes, and J. M. Lekuona (b. 1927) exhibited surrealistic techniques, while X. Lete (b. 1944) denounced social and political injustice.

After the death of Franco, aesthetic rather than social elements reasserted themselves, particularly in the work of José Irazu, "B. Atxaga" (b. 1951) and J. Sarrionaindia (b. 1958). Three significant women poets—A. Urretavizcaja (b. 1947), A. Lasa (b. 1948), and T. Irastorza (b. 1961)— have addressed themselves to feminist themes.

ANTHOLOGIES: E. Zabala, *Euskal Alfabetatzeko Literatura* (1979); K. Etxenagusia et al., *Euskal Idazleak Bizkaieraz* (1980); K. Etxenagusia, *Iparraldeko Euskal Idazleak* (1981); S. Onaindia, *Gaurko Olerkarien Euskal Lan Aukeratuak* (1981); J. Amenabar, *Euskal Poesia Kultoaren Bilduma. I: 1880–1963* and *II: 1963–1982* (1983).

HISTORY AND CRITICISM: P. Lafitte, *Le Basque et la littérature d'expression basque en Labourd, Basse-Navarre et Soule* (1941); L. Michelena, *Historia de la literatura vasca* (1960); L. Villasante, *Historia de la literatura vasca* (1961); J. Torrealday, *Euskal Idazleak Gaur. Historia Social de la Lengua y Literatura Vascas* (1977); X. Amuriza, *Bertsolaritza*, 2 v. (1981).   G.A.

BATHOS (Gr. "depth"). An evaluative term, usually equivalent to the purely descriptive term "anticlimax" (q.v.). (1) Though Longinus made b. a synonym of *hypsos* (the sublime) in *On the Sublime* 2.1, Pope, who can hardly be supposed ignorant of Longinus' meaning, took a new departure and made it an antonym in his parody of Longinus' treatise, *Peri Bathous: or, Martinus Scriblerus His Treatise of the Art of Sinking in Poetry* (1727). The most common meaning of the word ever since has been that of Pope, namely, an attempt at elevated expression which misfires and so has the (unintentional) effect of sudden transport from the sublime to the ridiculous. In the 18th c., what was intended was an expression of pathos (q.v.) in its wide Aristotelian sense, i.e. passion, the emotions; later, of pathos in its more modern, narrower sense of the sad or pitiable. The semantic shift is obviously accountable in no small measure to the accidental similarity of the two Gr. words *pathos* and *b.* Pope illustrates b. with "Ye Gods! annihilate both Space and Time, / And make two Lovers happy." Elizabeth Barrett Browning ardently recalls "Our Euripides, the human— / With his droppings of warm tears" ("Wine of Cyprus" 89–90); and Tennyson misfires with "He suddenly dropt dead of heart-disease" (" Sea Dreams" 64). B. is thus very often the stuff of parody (q.v.). (2) Also common, though less so, is the use of the word for a deliberately contrived effect of pathos *manqué* or any kind of deliberate anticlimax, whether ironic, gay, or serious. This usage is now

perhaps best avoided in evaluative crit., where its evident subjectivity makes it vulnerable to attack.
H.BR.

BATTLE OF THE ANCIENTS AND MODERNS. See QUERELLE DES ANCIENS ET DES MODERNES.

BAYT. See ARABIC POETRY.

BEAST EPIC (Ger. *Tierdichtung*). At first fed by animal fables (see FABLE IN VERSE), often parodying serious epics, romances, and other genres and their conventions, and often, too, mingling realistic observation, comic fantasy, and didactic purpose, b. es. range in tone from the vulgarly comic to the viciously satirical. The first b. e. is *Ysengrimus*, treating a wolf of that name, composed in Lat. ca. 1150 by Nivardus, who lived in what is now northern Belgium. Its 6500 lines tell chiefly of the conflict between Ysengrimus the wolf and the fox Reinardus. Several episodes have had an illustrious history, esp. those in which the cock Sprotinus (later Chanticleer) spars with Reinardus (later Renart), and that in which the fox has an affair with the wolf's wife.

The *Ysengrimus* was the primary source for the Fr. *Roman de Renart* begun in the 1170s. The earliest branches in the lineage of the form are ascribed to Pierre de St. Cloud. Renart's adultery with and subsequent rape of the wolf's wife inspired many other branches, mostly anonymous, dated 1178–1250 and running to some 27,000 octosyllabic lines. The most important is *Le Jugement*, telling of Renart's trial. Their popularity fed other Fr. didactic and allegorical epics, incl. the *Couronnement de Renart, Renart le Nouvel* (13th c.), and *Renart le Contrefait* (14th c.); the vogue continued into the 15th c. Meanwhile the earliest Renart branches had inspired the Alsatian Heinrich der Glichezare's *Reinhart Fuchs* (ca. 1200), while the *Jugement* was chief model for the Dutch *Van den Vos Reynaerde* (13th c.) and the prose *Reynaert's Historie* (14th c.). These Dutch epics enjoyed immense favor and gave rise to most others, chiefly in Ger., Danish, Swedish, and Eng. in both prose and verse, incl. Caxton's 1481 prose text which led to some verse versions, e.g. Shurley's, 1681; the Lübeck Low Ger. poem, 1498 (facsimile, T. Sodmann, 1976; mod. Low Ger. by J. Mähl, 1878, rpt. with Weber's illustrations, 1986); Goethe's *Reineke Fuchs*, 1793 (often rpt. with Kaulbach's 1846 illustrations); and Rodange's Luxemburgish *Renert*, 1871. Chaucer's mini-epic the *Nun's Priest's Tale* was chiefly Fr.-inspired.

Long narrative poems (often allegorical) dominated by animals other than Reynard the fox were also known in Europe. There was the *Ecbasis captivi*, sometimes said to be the first European b. e., though here the animals do not have proper names; this is in 1225 Lat. hexameters by an unknown Ger. monk of Lorraine, ca. 940 A.D. The *Speculum stultorum* in over 3000 Lat. elegaics by

Nigel of Longchamps, a Canterbury monk, was composed ca. 1180, and the *Roman de Fauvel*, in 3280 Fr. octosyllables by Gervais de Bus, ca. 1312. These last two feature asses; the first features a calf and a wolf. One could also mention mini-epics such as *The Owl and the Nightingale* (ca. 1190) and Chaucer's *Parlement of Foules* (ca. 1382), typical "bird debate" poems (see POETIC CONTESTS).

Outside Europe there are numerous other trads. of animal fables and epics, esp. in the Indian subcontinent and China, but the most famous of these are in prose. There is the jackal-dominated *Panchatantra* in Sanskrit, the fountainhead of an Oriental fable trad.; and the monkey-dominated Chinese *Hsi Yu Chi* by Wu Ch'eng-en, ca. 1580. There is a rich animal fable and epic trad. in Africa, largely oral and prose, about which surprisingly little has been written. J. Chandler Harris's *Uncle Remus* stories (1880) are fed by Af. sources, and there are links between Jamaican Annsi stories, West Af. tales, and the *Roman de Renart*. See also BESTIARY; FABLE; FABLIAU; NARRATIVE POETRY.—L. Foulet, *Le Roman de Renart* (1914); H. R. Jauss, *Untersuchungen zur mittelalterlichen Tierdichtung* (1959); J. Flinn, *Le Roman de Renart dans la litt. française et dans les litts. étrangères* (1963); F. P. Knapp, *Das lateinische Tierepos* (1979); T. W. Best, *Reynard the Fox* (1983); *Ysengrimus*, ed. J. Mann (1987); *Reinardus*, Yearbook of the Internat. Reynard Society, 1– (1988–).
K.V.

BEAST FABLE. See FABLE; BEAST EPIC.

BEAT POETS. "B." or "B. Generation" refers to a group of Am. writers who came into prominence in the mid 1950s and whose work was a reaction to the dominant academic formalism of the age, best represented by Brooks and Warren's influential anthology, *Understanding Poetry* (1st ed., 1938). Poet, essayist, and radical social thinker Kenneth Rexroth spearheaded the loosely defined "movement" as a presiding figure (see his "San Francisco Letter" in *Evergreen Rev.* 1 [1957]), drawing together poets from both coasts. Emerging from the East Coast were poets Allen Ginsberg (b. 1926; *Howl*, 1956) and Gregory Corso (b. 1930), poet/playwright LeRoi Jones (later Amiri Baraka), and novelists Jack Kerouac (b. 1922; *On the Road*), John Clellon Holmes, and, peripherally, William Burroughs; from the West Coast, poets Brother Antoninus (later William Everson, b. 1912; *The Rose of Solitude*, 1967), Lawrence Ferlinghetti (b. 1919), Gary Snyder (b. 1930; *Riprap*, 1959), Philip Lamantia, Philip Whalen, and Lew Welch, along with poet/playwright Michael McClure. Important literary journals featuring B. writers included *Beatitude, Big Table*, and *Evergreen Review*; primary book publishers included City Lights, Grove Press, and New Directions.

"B.," John Clellon Holmes wrote in his "This is the B. Generation" article for the *New York Times* (1952), "implies a feeling of having been used, of being raw. It involves a sort of nakedness of mind, and, ultimately, of soul; a feeling of being reduced to the bedrock of consciousness." It connoted, therefore, exhaustion uncovering primal forces. B. writers responded to their sense of alienation in various ways—by exploring alternative religious trads. (Zen and Tantric Buddhism, Hinduism, erotic mysticism) and political responses (anarchism, Marxism, internationalism), as well as by developing an interest in the visionary possibilities of hallucinogenic drugs such as psilocybin, peyote, and LSD. Though these writers formed no programmatic "school," many of their aesthetic strategies and preoccupations overlapped—a sense of form as "open" or "organic," an interest in collage and surrealism (q.v.), direct use of the autobiographical, and an interest in performance (q.v.) and the literary work's relationship to music, esp. jazz. Literary forebears include the Eng. romantics, Rimbaud, Baudelaire, Whitman, D. H. Lawrence, Thomas Wolfe, and Henry Miller. For discussion of the movements which followed B. poetry see SOUND POETRY and LANGUAGE POETRY; see also AMERICAN POETRY; PERFORMANCE.—L. Lipton, *The Holy Barbarians* (1959); *A Casebook on the Bs.*, ed. T. Parkinson (1961); J. Tytell, *Naked Angels* (1976); A. Saroyan, *Genesis Angels* (1979); D. McNally, *Desolate Angel* (1979); L. Bartlett, *The Bs.* (1981); M. McClure, *Scratching the B. Surface* (1982); A. Charters, *The Beats* (1983); M. Davidson, *The San Francisco Ren.* (1989); L. Bartlett, *The Sun Is But a Morning Star* (1989).   L.B.

BEGINNING RHYME. See ALLITERATION; ANAPHORA; RHYME.

BELGIAN POETRY.

    I. IN DUTCH
    II. IN FRENCH

I. IN DUTCH (For Flemish poetry before 1585, see DUTCH POETRY). After the division of the Netherlands (fall of Antwerp to the Spanish, 1585), the southern provinces (now known as Flanders, or Flemish Belgium) lost their economic, cultural, and literary predominance. Nevertheless, although the Ren. poetry of the Netherlands was to reach its high point in the northern provinces, the renewal itself originated in the south. In the circles of the *rederijkers* (q.v.) one finds an interest in humanism, a gradually growing understanding of the spirit of antiquity, and a sensitivity to new moral and aesthetic ideas. Transitional figures are Lucas de Heere (1534–84) and Carel van Mander (1548–1606), in whose work one encounters new poetic forms side by side with conventional *rederijker* verse. De Heere, an admirer of Marot, introduced the sonnet into the poetry of the Netherlands and wrote odes and epigrams. Van Mander wrote sonnets in alexandrines and translated Virgil's *Bucolics* and *Georgics* into iambic verse (1597). But the spirit and form of poetry were decisively

rejuvenated by Jan van der Noot (ca. 1540–95/1600), nobleman, humanist, and man of letters. Under the influence of Petrarch and the *Pléiade* (q.v.), especially Ronsard, he wrote sonnets in the Fr. manner, odes, and an epic; he favored the iambic pentameter and the alexandrine; and he purified the language—all this not in a narrowly formalistic manner but with the inspiration of a true poet (*Het theatre*, 1568; *Het bosken*, 1570[?]; *Cort begrijp der XII boeken olympiados*, 1579).

In the first half of the 17th c., the Ren. found further echoes among the *rederijkers* and even, formally, in religious songbooks. Ren. elements appear in J. D. Heemssen, J. Ysermans, and the most prominent poet of the time, Justus de Harduyn (1582–1636). In his youth he celebrated the beauty and grace of his beloved in a cycle of songs, odes, elegies, and sonnets (*De weerliicke liefden tot Roose-mond*, 1613). Later, as a priest, he wrote sacred love lyrics (*Goddelicke lofsanghen*, 1620) in a more personal, less literary tone which in some songs echoes the religious lyrics of the Middle Ages.

Under the influence of the Counter-Reformation, secular poetry of all sorts was obliged more and more to yield to moral-didactic and popular poetry of religious inspiration. Its most distinguished representative was the Jesuit Adriaan Poirters (1605–74), who practiced c., in *Het masker vande wereldt afgetrocken* (The World's Mask Removed, 1645), the successful genre of the spiritual emblem book: in form, an alternation of illustrations, long poems, and prose pieces, interspersed with short rhymes and verse narratives; in content, narrative, didactic, satirical, and polemic; in spirit, religious and moralistic. Elements of baroque elevation are also to be found in his work as in that of Michiel de Swaen (1654–1707), who closes the 17th c. His religious contemplative poetry suited the spiritual climate, but was distinguished from the popular-didactic poetasting of Poirters' disciples by its more individual tone and its exalted literary aims. Vondel, Cats, and the Fr. classics were his models.

The 18th c. was a period of decadence. Poetry was generally devoid of personal accents, and there were no poets capable of achieving real distinction in the kind of art prescribed by the then-dominant Fr. classical poetics (Boileau's *Art poétique*, tr. 1721). The classical ideal of regularity may be noted in the recommendations of such theorists as J. P. van Male and J. B. Bouvaert, the latter of whom also defended blank verse.

New emphases on personal feeling, national pride, and devotion to nature made themselves felt increasingly at the beginning of the 19th c. (P. J. de Borchgrave), and led to the breakthrough of romanticism, which occasioned the rebirth of Flemish lit. Karel Lodewijk Ledeganck (1805–47) and Prudens van Duyse (1804–59) directed poetry away from the classical style; it became free and spontaneous in the popular rhymes of Th. van

Rijswijck (1811–49) and found an interpreter of *Weltschmerz* in J. A. de Laet (1815–91). But individuality was lacking in the climate of moderate realism which, from the 1850s on, expressed itself in scenes from the life of ordinary people (J. van Beers), songs and airs dealing with the joys and sorrows of domestic life, political and social verses, cantatas and oratorios, and epic tableaux. Strange but not very convincing are the formal-technical experiments undertaken by the so-called "taalvirtuozen" (lang. virtuosos)—Fr. de Cort and J. van Droogenbroeck—on the model of Platen and Rückert (see GERMAN POETRY). Nevertheless, some of J. M. Dautzenberg's work in this vein belongs among the best poetry brought forth in this period, along with the simple anecdotal poems of Rosalie and Virginie Loveling (*Gedichten*, 1870).

One of the most extraordinary assertions of individuality in the modern lyric is to be found in the poetry of Guido Gezelle (1830–99), a humble and learned priest remarkable for his sensuous empathy and his insights into nature as the manifestation of a divine world-order embracing man as well as the flowers, the stars, and the ants. His religious life may have brought him close to the mystical experience. Gezelle remained for a long time on the periphery of recognized poetry but is now widely acknowledged as a poet of international stature, based on his *Dichtoefeningen* (Poetical Exercises), 1858; *Kleengedichtjes* (Little Poems), 1860; *Gedichten, gezangen en gebeden* (Poems, Songs, and Prayers), 1862; *Tijdkrans* (A Wreath of Time), 1893; and *Rijmsnoer* (A Garland of Rhyme), 1897.

The young titan Albrecht Rodenbach (1856–80) wrote, in traditional meters and with neo-romantic inspiration, militant songs, epic verses, and reflective poetry. The impressionistic formalist Pol de Mont (1857–1931) fought for "art for art's sake," and Prosper van Langendonck (1862–1920) interpreted the anguish of the *poète maudit* (q.v.). They anticipated the *fin de siècle* poetry of Karel van de Woestijne (1878–1929). Hypersensitive and hyperintellectual, he explored sensuous experience and the relationship between man and woman in his first volumes—*Het vader-huis* (The Paternal House), 1903; *De boom-gaard der vogelen en der vruchten* (The Orchard of Birds and Fruits), 1905; *De gulden schaduw* (The Golden Shadow), 1910. He clothes his emotions in baroque images, symbols, word-garlands, and slow rhythms. In his later, more sober verses—*De modderen man* (The Man of Mud), 1920; *God aan zee* (God at the Sea), 1926; *Het bergmeer* (The Mountain Lake), 1928—human insufficiency is a source of distress, a concern with God and eternity appears, and the poet reaches a state of renunciation and purification. Contemporary with van de Woestijne were the visionary Cyriel Verschaeve (1874–1949), the mannered Karel van den Oever (1879–1926), and the amiably stoic Jan van Nijlen (1884–1965).

In the early years of the 1920s, expressionism (q.v.) broke radically with the aesthetically oriented poetry of impressionism and symbolism (qq.v.) as well as with traditional verse construction. Under the influence of Verhaeren, Whitman, Tagore, the Fr. *Unanimistes*, and, above all, the Ger. expressionists, a coming world of goodness and brotherhood was proclaimed in emotional free verse with spasmodic imagery (as in van Ostaijen, W. Moens, A. Mussche), or in moral anecdotes (M. Gijsen). Van Ostaijen (1896–1928), who stood at the beginning of this humanitarian expressionism with his volume *Het sienjaal* (The Signal, 1918), came rapidly under the spell of dada (q.v.) as evidenced by his *Bezette stad*, (Occupied City), 1921, and was also influenced by Apollinaire, Cocteau, and especially August Stramm's experiments with the "concentrated word." In incisive essays (e.g. *Gebruiksaanwyzing der lyriek* [Directions for the Use of the Lyric]) he formulated a theory of pure poetry (q.v.) based on the isolated word and on association. He realized his insights in a few late poems published in his posthumous volume, *Het eerste boek van Schmoll* (The First Book of Schmoll), 1928. V. J. Brunclair and G. Burssens took part in van Ostaijen's poetic adventure, and it had a fertilizing effect on M. Gilliams and P. G. Buckinx. Nevertheless, after the early death of Van Ostaijen the dominant force in B. p. remained traditional for a couple of decades (U. van de Voorde, R. Minne, P. Herreman, B. Decorte, K. Jonckheere).

Immediately after World War II, older conceptions of poetry as a statement of human inadequacy in an altered world were reiterated chiefly by A. van Wilderode, H. van Herreweghen, J. de Haes, Reninca (pseud. Renée Lauwers), and Chr. D'haen. The traditional line was continued, with differing accents and with the integration of new techniques, in the next generation by W. Spillebeen, W. Haesaert, G. Mandelinck, and A. van Assche. Around 1950, however, "experimental poetry" broke with the past in a spectacular manner. Its first exponents, the "Vijftigers" (Fiftiers), were grouped around the journal *Tijd en Mens* (1949–55); led by J. Walravens (*Phenomenologie van de poëzie*, 1951), these poets (H. Claus, A. Bontridder, B. Cami, M. Wauters) tried to translate a Sartrean view of life, a feeling of absurdity, chaos, *Angst*, and rebellion into an idiom related to Fr. surrealism (q.v.) and the lyric work of Van Ostaijen. The new idiom also was practiced by two older poets, E. van Ruysbeek and P. Le Roy, who added esoteric and mystical elements. A second wave of experimentalists, the "Fifty-fivers," published mainly in the journals *De tafelronde* (P. de Vree, A. de Roover, J. van den Hoeven) and *Gard sivik* (G. Gils, H. Pernath, P. Snoek). This movement dismissed ethical-social imperatives and metaphysical concerns in favor of a greater, sometimes exclusive, autonomy of word and image.

The most talented virtuoso of lang. and form

was Hugo Claus (b. 1929), who realized and summed up the tendencies of the whole era. He built upon Antonin Artaud, practiced the erudite mannerism of Eliot and Pound, with an abundance of myths, symbols, allusions, and quotations. Claus wrote, and continues to write, pop-style and par-lando-style poems as well as *Knittelverse (q.v.)*, satires, novels, plays, and melodramas, asserting his radical individualism in a notably varied manner.

In the Sixties, experimentation with word and sign was markedly advanced by the group around *Labris* (1962–75), by the concrete poetry (q.v.) of M. Insingel and Paul de Vree (1909–82), this latter a prominent author of sound poetry (q.v.) but more particularly of "poesia visiva," a visual poetry (q.v.) consisting of leftist-oriented montages of photographs, letters, and drawings (*Zimprovaties*, 1968; *Poëzien*, 1971; *Poesia visiva*, 1975). Mannerists such as N. van Bruggen and P. Conrad turned away from experimentation, as did also, in the Seventies, an entirely different movement, "neo-realism," represented by R. Jooris and H. de Coninck. Influenced by pop art and *nouveau realisme* in the visual arts, this movement showed once again an interest in undecorated reality. A counter-movement of "neo-experimentalism," placing a stronger emphasis on language and on the exploratory nature of the poem, was represented by but not limited to such foci as the journals *Morgen* (1967–72) and *Impuls* (1969–79). Among its exponents are R. de Neef, D. Christiaens, A. Reniers, L. Nolens, and H. Speliers.

The most recent trend is "neo-romanticism." As one would expect, this movement returns to inwardness, flees reality (via dream, sometimes via drugs), and cherishes tenderness, sorrow, and the unattainable. The short-lived drug addict Jottie T'Hooft (1956–77)—obsessed by a quest for absolute purity and a desire for death—opened the way for other young, if less dramatically tortured, poets like L. Gruwez.

ANTHOLOGIES: *Onze dichters*, ed. Th. Coopman and V. dela Montagne·(1880); *Vlaamsche oogst*, ed. Ad. Herckenrath (1904); *De Vlaamsche jongeren van gisteren en heden,1910–1927*, ed. Aug. van Cauwelaert (1927); *Vlaamsche lyriek 1830–1890*, ed. M. Gilliams (1937); *De Vlaamsche poëzie sinds 1918*, v. 2: *Bloemlezing*, ed. A. Demedts, 2d ed. (1945); *Breviarum der Vlaamse lyriek*, ed. M. Gijsen, 4th ed. (1953); *Vlaamse dichtkunst van deze tijd*, ed. P. de Ryck, 2d ed. (1959); *Le più belle pagine delle Letterature del Belgio*, ed. A. Mor and J. Weisgerber (1965); *Anthologie de la poésie Néérlandaise: Belgique, 1830–1966*, ed. M. Careme (1967); *Dutch Interior: Post-war Poetry of the Netherlands and Flanders*, ed. J. S. Holmes and W. J. Smith (1984).

HISTORY AND CRITICISM: E. Rombauts, "Humanisme en Ren. in de Zuidelijke Nederlanden" and "De letterkunde der Nederlanden," *Geschiedenis van de letterkunde der Nederlanden*, ed Fr. Baur et al., v. 3, 5 (1945, 1952); A Demedts, *De Vlaamsche poëzie sinds 1918*, v. l, *Studie*, 2d ed.

1945); M. Rutten, *Nederlandse dichtkunst van Kloos tot Claus* (1957), *Nederlandse dichtkunst Achterberg en Burssens voorbij* (1967); J. Weisgerber and A. Mor, *Storia delle letterature del Belgio* (1958); T. Weevers, *Poetry of the Netherlands in its European Context* (1960); R. F. Lissens, *De Vlaamse letterkunde van 1780 tot heden*, 4th ed. (1967); P. de Vree, *Onder experimenteel vuur* (1968); R. P. Meijer, *Lit. of the Low Countries* (1978); R. van de Perre, *Er is nog olie in de lamp der taal. Een overzicht van de hedendaagse poëzie in Vlaanderen (1945–1981)* (1982). R.F.L.; tr. F.J.W.

II. IN FRENCH. Around 1880, 50 years after B. independence, an original Francophone poetry arose. Until then only conventional voices inspired by pompous romanticism or strident nationalism were heard; this earlier poetry does not deserve further attention.

The tempestuous 1880s saw the rise of numerous reviews: *Le Jeune Belgique* (1881), which championed "art for art's sake" without the restrictions of a school, and *La Wallonie* (1886), the favorite mouthpiece of the symbolists. At the same time appeared the first publications of what we now consider classics, among which the work of Emile Verhaeren (1855–1916) comes first. Poet of Flanders, exorcist of personal torments, brawny visionary of the industrial world, he found a sentimental tone to express love. Using a wide range related to that of the symbolists and expressionists, but esp. affirming the genius of his own lang., Verhaeren is, with Maeterlinck and Elskamp, one of the three undeniably great B. poets of his time, and of these, assuredly the most powerful.

In 1889, with a collection of poetry, *Les Serres chaudes* (Hothouses), and a play, *La Princesse Maleine*, a newcomer, Maurice Maeterlinck (1862–1949) rose immediately to pre-eminence in symbolism (q.v.). He represented its quintessence. An unprolific poet who wrote only one other collection, *Les Quinze Chansons* (Fifteen Songs), Maeterlinck created a theater which won him the Nobel Prize in 1911 and thereby thrust him onto the international scene. But his dramatic universe is closely linked to his poetry, and both have a crystalline transparency.

Max Elskamp (1862–1931), obscure during his lifetime, gained an audience only after World War II. Removed from theories and literary groups, he published numerous collections which reveal a profoundly original style, simple yet erudite, even archaic like a litany. He conjured up the drama of his own life. Georges Rodenbach (1855–98), associated for a long time with the symbolists, is instead an elegist in the trad. of Musset. He still moves us by his nostalgic evocations in half-tones, silences, twilights, and morbid regrets. Another elegist and symbolist, Charles Van Lerberghe (1861–1907), undertook *La Chanson d'Eve* (Eve's Song), a sequence with overtones of Mallarmé and Valéry, and the most coherent poetic work of this generation. Finally, Albert Mockel (1866–1945), founder of *La Wallonie*, exemplifies decadent symbolism. His affectations often make him unreadable, but many pages of *Clartés* (Gleams) are miraculously free of his musical theories. Some lesser figures today appear affected or *kitschy*, and need not interest us. But Jean de Boschère wrote virulent pages, Franz Hellens romantic rapture, and Paul Desmeth a constantly reworked text. Marie Nizet deserves attention as a fine poet of unrequited love, and Paul Gérardy retains a wonderful freshness.

If the hist. of Fr. poetry in Belgium covers only a century, the number of poets is nonetheless astonishing. Of the generation born around 1900, some of whose poets are still alive, the only obvious characteristic, aside from marks of dada and surrealism, is their refusal to have a poetics in common. The violent flashes of René Verboom, the discreet interrogation of Robert Vivier, the passionate vehemence of Charles Plisnier, the cosmopolitan breadth of Robert Goffin, the ironic density of René Purnoel, the musical limpidity of Maurice Carême, the delicious fantasy of Paul Neuhuys, the surrealist visions of Ernst Moerman, the militant sincerity of Albert Ayguesparse, and the futurist cadences of Georges Linze could fill an anthology, not to mention Pierre Nothomb, Robert Melot du Dy, Hélène du Bois, Robert Guiette, Eric de Haulleville, and Armand Bernier.

Four major figures emerge from this particularly brilliant constellation: Marcel Thiry (1897–1977), great sculptor of words, whose merit lies in having integrated the technology of modern life with a scholarly, even precious, vocabulary; Norge (b. 1898), also an artisan of lang., but more direct, more fleshy, uniting gravity with irony, managing adeptly both short verse and long; Henri Michaux (1899–1984), a poet with an international audience, a global explorer who charted the human abyss in *Belge en rupture* (Belgian Breaking Apart) and a linguistic man-without-a-country; and finally, Odilon-Jean Périer (1901–28), who in his short career left a perfect work with a fascinating purity.

Dada influenced several poets, but only one figure stands out clearly, Clément Pansaers (1885–1922). His writing signals the appearance of a *Belgique sauvage* (Savage Belgium) from which emerged a large part of surrealism, the entire Phantomas movement, and other avant-garde groups. As for surrealism, it was the painter Magritte who remarked, as a witticism, "There are no B. surrealists except for Delvaux and myself." In hindsight, the B. surrealists finally occupy the place they deserve, having as much dissention but more autonomy than their Fr. counterparts. They had their own humor, ferociously vitriolic, and an exemplary lucidity which came more from experience than automatic writing. The appearance of poetic collections did not constitute the essential element of their immense activity. It is impossible to name all the periodicals, brochures, tracts, or manifestoes coming from the surrealist group in Brussels connected with the review *Correspondance* (founded 1924), which included Louis Scutenaire, Paul Colinet, and Marcel Mariën, and the surrealist group of Hainaut, born of the review *Rupture* (1934), founded by the fine poet Achille Chavée.

Having left surrealism, Christian Dotremont founded in 1948 the movement Cobra (working on painting, writing, objects, the environment) and began in 1962 to experiment with logograms. At first kept underground, his approach later had an enormous influence on the "After-May '68" poets.

If there is a quality specific to Franco-B. lit., it is a corrosive humor raised to its highest point by the surrealists. It is also the attribute of *Phantomas*, a literary and pictorial review emphasizing the ludic and enlivened by the "Sept types en or" (Seven Golden Guys): Paul Bourgoignie, François Jacqmin, Joseph Noiret, Pierre Puttemans, Theodore Koenig, and Marcel and Gabriel Piqueray. *Phantomas* is perhaps the best illustration of this *Belgique sauvage*, which contrasts a little too easily with the official Belgium. It would be overly simplistic to divide B. writers into two categories: those who care about modernity and those who do not. A split nonetheless exists, which has widened since World War II and the return to traditional forms.

It is unclear if one can speak of a neoclassicism, incl. perhaps a Norge or a Thiry; in fixed forms, both poets were innovative. One may wonder if this is the case with certain conformists who present themselves as avant-garde. Trad. does not mean sclerosis, not when it is transcended by a formal rigor (Charles Bertin), an innovative metrics (Gérard Prévot), a sumptuous imagery (Ernest Delève), a blinding virtuosity (Lucienne Desnoues), a permanent metaphysical interrogation (Jean Tordeur), a jubilant registering (Jean Mogin), or a torn humanism (Roger Bodart).

The generation of 1900 is characterized by diversity. The next offers an even less coherent, indeed chaotic, range. Their work extends from the most traditional forms to forms constantly called into question, and it is difficult to situate these poets who lack a common ground. One could stress the soaring flight of feminine poetry (Andrée Sodenkamp, Jeanine Moulin, Anne-Marie Kegels); highlight a cautious approach to world harmony (Philippe Jones, Fernand Verhesen); welcome poets with an extensive register (Georges Thinès, David Scheinert), the new baroques (Gaston Compère, Hubert Juin) or fine lyric poets (Philippe Kammans, Roger Goossens); or even unite in one category unrelated writers who are concerned with serious inquiry: into forms of lang. (André Miguel), the integration of modern myths (Pierre Della Faille), or the psychoanalytical and the sacred (Henri Bauchau).

It was in the 1960s that the literary movements of the first quarter of the century fell away. Writing broke up, chose blank spaces, and rejected the facile phrase, traditional literary genres, and the aesthetics of discourse. To this general questioning appropriate to the period was added a specific malaise, the outbreak of "la Belgique de Papa" (Papa's Belgium). There resulted a stronger feeling of belonging to the Francophone world, incl. (but not limited to) France, and a greater consciousness of an identity baptized as "Belgitude."

There was an abundance of initiatives and activities. The works begun or pursued in this context remain, however, unrelated. B. poets seem to blossom in individualism. On the one hand, we see an increase in the refusal of eloquence: the concise verse of André Schmitz becomes even more concentrated in Christian Hubin, turns elliptical in Jacques Izoard, stammers with Jacques Sojcher, is sketchy with Claude Bauwens, lapidary with Marc Quaghebeur. On the other hand, Jacques Crickillon and Eugène Savitzkaya espouse fullness, while Werner Lambersy moves from minimalist poetry to vast biblical verse. Guy Goffette transcends successfully the simplicity of the everyday. Alone in his mastery of rhyme, William Cliff wrings the neck of the alexandrine (q.v.), while Jean-Pierre Verheggen joyfully parodies literary stereotypes. Attentive to exactness and concision, Lilian Wouters also expresses personal truth without concessions, going as far as cruelty in the poems of *L'aloès* (Aloe, 1983). Philosophy and psychoanalysis profoundly influenced these poets. Manifest in most of them, notably Gaspard Hons, Frans De Haes, and Marc Rombaut, both disciplines are evident throughout the work of Claire Lejeune and Françoise Delcarte.

We have always known that art renews itself in cycles. Without naming the poets who have just begun in the 1980s, we can see the start of a new lyricism. One century after the rise of "La Jeune Belgique," its continuity seems assured.

ANTHOLOGIES: *Poètes française de Belgique de Verhaeren au surréalisme*, ed. R. Guiette (1948); *Lyra Belgica*, tr. C. and F. Stillman, 2 v. (1950–51); *Anthologie du surréalisme en Belgique*, ed. C. Bussy (1972); *Panorama de la poésie française de Belgique*, ed. L. Wouters and J. Antoine (1976); *La poésie francophone de Belgique*, ed. L. Wouters and A. Bosquet, 4 v. (1985–).

GENERAL WORKS: G. Charlier and J. Hanse, *Histoire illustrée des lettres françaises de Belgique* (1958); R. Frickx and R. Burniaux, *La Littérature belge d'expression française* (1980); *Alphabet des lettres belges de langue française* (1982); R. Frickx and R. Trousson, *Lettres françaises de Belgique: Dictionnaire des oeuvres*, v. 2: *La Poésie* (1988); A.-M. Beckers, *Lire les écrivains belges*, 3 v. (1985–); *Bibliographie des écrivains de Belgique* (forthcoming).
L.W.; tr. A.G.W.

BELIEF AND POETRY. As formulated in Cl. aesthetics, the question of belief in poetry, like the question of meaning (q.v.), concerns the relation of the reader to the poem and of the poem to the external world or to the realm of truth, against which its claims can be measured. Plato, for example, considered poetry dangerous not only because it was the mere copy of a copy and so twice removed from the truth, but also for its capacity to make readers believe that what they see before them is truth instead of a shadowy imitation.

After Plato, the concept of mimesis or imitation (qq.v.) evolved quickly beyond this simple notion of copying. Aristotle noted the importance of credibility to the effect of drama on the audience, but he claimed that the formal coherence of the work took precedence over any correspondence between the work and the world it "imitated." Roman rhetoricians such as Cicero, Horace, and Quintilian treated b. mainly as an issue of ethos (q.v.) and technique, a result of convention and decorum (qq.v.) through which the audience's expectations were satisfied (see RHETORIC AND POETRY).

In contrast to this classical subordination of b. to taste and technique, early Christian writers such as Augustine made b. central to the interp. of metaphorical lang. In *De doctrina christiana*, for example, Augustine makes the proper use of signs a test of faith, and he characterizes the use of a sign as a mere "thing" as tantamount to the death of the soul and the denial of Christ. For the Scholastic theologians of the later Middle Ages, b. became the motivating principle behind the fourtiered scheme of exegesis through which metaphorical passages of Scripture were interpreted as doctrinal truths (see INTERPRETATION, FOURFOLD METHOD OF). Thus in the *Summa theologica* Aquinas defends the use of material imagery in the Bible as an illustration of doctrine for "the minds of those to whom the revelation has been made" and as a means of hiding divine truths from nonbelievers.

B. had little to do with the poetics of the most influential secular theorists of the Ren., whose interests in the allegorical connection between truth and poetry were more mimetic than exegetical. Scaliger observed that the poet "imitates the truth by fiction" (*Poetics*, 1561; see FICTION), but for him the link between truth and fiction was established by "persuasion" rather than b. Persuasion was an effect derived from the pleasing aspects of the fiction rather than any immediate appeal to the truth that the fiction revealed. In the work of critics such as Sidney in England and Castelvetro and Mazzoni in Italy, this emphasis on the persuasive power of fictional forms at times obscured their ultimate subordination to the ends of truth or virtuous action; the poem was treated as an obviously artificial or purely fantastic image, with no pretense of soliciting any b. in its truth. Poets never lie, Sidney said, but only because they never affirm what they say to be true. "What child is there," Sidney asked, "coming to a play, and seeing *Thebes* written in great letters upon an old door, doth believe that it is Thebes?" (*Apology for*

Poetry, 1595). To be sure, poetic images must move us to act according to the idealized types of human virtue, but for Sidney the persuasive power of the image is distinct from its veracity: a "feigned Cyrus" may well be more persuasive than the "true" Cyrus and for that reason more appropriate for artistic representation (see VERISIMILITUDE).

Ren. critics thus introduced the possibility of a persuasive effect in poetry distinct from the end to which the reader was persuaded. Nevertheless, unless a critic were willing to reduce the affective power of poetry to sheer delight in the medium itself, it was difficult to explain how an audience could be moved by what it did not believe to be true. Much of 17th-c. aesthetics is occupied with this question, and it remained a central problem in neoclassical poetics (q.v.), which continued to distinguish between the moral and universal truths a poem was to represent and the fictional forms of the representation. In the preface to his edition of Shakespeare (1765), for example, Dr. Johnson described Shakespeare's work as a "mirror of life" but ridiculed the idea that the spectator ever mistakes the representation for reality. How, then, Johnson asks, does the drama move, "if it is not credited?" "It is credited," he replies, "with all the credit due to a drama."

Johnson's deliberate paradox underscores the obvious shortcomings of an affective aesthetics based on b. But a better explanation had to await Coleridge, who suggested in the *Biographia Literaria* (1817) that artworks must induce in the reader a "willing suspension of disbelief," a state that would somehow inspire the emotive power of b. without a corollary degree of conviction as to truth. As Coleridge's powerful phrase suggests, the romantics considered b. an affective condition entirely divorced from truth. In part this separation was a response to the increasingly positivistic character of philosophical and scientific truth in the West, and too, it reflected, more directly, the romantic interest in intuition and imagination (qq.v.) over empirical perception and rational analysis. Poetry was no longer responsible for telling us the truths apprehensible by other forms of thought, or even for persuading us of their importance; rather, poetry was to grant us access to a transcendent world of spirit beyond the realm of ordinary truth and knowledge.

This romantic distinction between b. and truth in poetry resembled the traditional religious distinction between faith and knowledge (it was Augustine who said that men must "believe in order to understand"), and later critics such as Matthew Arnold were to argue that poetry could satisfy the needs that religion had once addressed without competing with science for empirical verification. In both his poetry and prose, Arnold frequently pines for the lost medieval unity of thought and b. Unfortunately, for him this unity had the advantage of being everything but right. What is needed, Arnold seems to suggest ("Lit.

and Science," 1882; "The Study of Poetry," 1880), is a poetry that can offer the emotional satisfaction of b. without demanding rational commitment.

To do that, the statements made in poetry would have to resemble the propositional truth-claims of science and philosophy without actually making those claims. In I. A. Richards' terms, statements made by the poem are "pseudo-statements" (q.v.) that function as part of the "emotive" discourse of poetry, as opposed to the "referential" discourse of science. Distinguishing between what he called " intellectual b." and "emotional b." (*Practical Crit.*, 1929), Richards argued that the emotional conviction a good poem can inspire in the reader need not meet the same kinds of tests that validate a scientific treatise. Whereas intellectual b. requires strict logical consistency among the various ideas we have of the world, and cannot tolerate incompatible claims about that world, emotional b. satisfies particular human needs that can, indeed often do, contradict other needs.

Rather than asking us to suspend disbelief, Richards says, a successful poem will never raise the question of b. at all, at least in the intellectual sense Coleridge's dictum implies. Instead, it will evoke emotional bs. that will be juxtaposed and held in balance with other emotional bs. in terms of the poem rather than tested and resolved in the external world. The shaping influence of that experience as a whole on our minds has an importance far greater than any degree of intellectual assent we may or may not grant to any one of its assertions. Richards defines "sincerity" as the pursuit of this internal mental coherence in the face of temptations to reduce its complexity to the single vision demanded by intellectual b.

Richards' psychologistic concept of b. in poetry contrasts sharply with T. S. Eliot's more orthodox notion of b., but together Richards and Eliot characterize an attitude toward b. that dominated much subsequent crit. of the 20th c. According to Eliot, the poet borrows his bs. from his environment and in the poem deals with how it feels for one to hold them. A poet need neither create his bs. nor defend them, since his concern is not with the bs. themselves—the poet's mere raw materials—but with their "emotional equivalents" as expressed in the poem through their "objective correlatives" (q.v.). If the bs. are puerile or offensive they may block our efforts to respond to the poem, but generally the only function of b. in poetry is to stay out of the way of the emotive aims of the poem.

Together, Eliot and Richards turned poetics away from the question of b. and toward the formalist concerns that occupied Am. crit. over the next four decades. New Critics such as Allen Tate and Cleanth Brooks, viewing the poem as an autonomous object, argued that poetic statements of b. existed only as dramatic utterances that functioned solely in the context of the poem (see NEW CRITICISM; CONTEXTUALISM). Brooks flatly denied that statements of any sort, pseudo- or otherwise, could be understood apart from the imagery and rhythms of the poem's formal elements. This radical fusion of content and form in Am. formalist poetics obviated the possibility of identifying any aspect of the poem—whether universal, emotive, or "objective"—with what previous critics had identified as the experience of b. in poetry. As Brooks argued, a poem should so accurately dramatize a situation that "it is no longer a question of our bs., but of our participation in the poetic experience."

After the New Criticism, b. simply ceased to be an issue for most literary theorists. It was either consigned to the world outside the poem and so treated as irrelevant to poetics, or incorporated into the poem as a purely poetic gesture and treated like any other element in the poem's formal system. Following the 1960s, however, the question of b. surfaced again, but this time in the negative form of ideology. Inspired by the work of Michel Foucault and new varieties of Marxism that focused on the symbolic categories of human experience (see HISTORICISM; MARXIST CRITICISM), literary critics took renewed interest in the tendency of poetic works to inspire a b. in the world represented in their words, even—and esp.—if those words refused to make truth claims about that world.

That tendency was attributed most often to what Foucault called the "discursive apparatus" of society, which governed not only the overtly ideological discourses of politics but also such ostensibly neutral or autonomous discourses as those of religion and poetry. Losing the independence it had assumed since Kant, poetry once again was measured against discourses that directly called for a commitment on the part of their subjects, and its pretensions to freedom from b. were denounced all the more strongly as mystifications of its ultimately ideological functions. The aim of crit. thus became the " demystification" of such pretensions, either as the ideological analysis of discursive continuities between the poem and the social forces of power and constraint, or as a deconstructive analysis of the text's own resistance to the metaphorical projections of the truth and coherence produced by traditional readings (Jameson).

This profound skepticism toward the role of b. in literary experience typifies the more sweeping critique of metaphysical foundations characteristic of poststructuralism. Some recent critics have argued, however, that such a rejection of all "foundational" thought ignores a fundamental dimension of human experience that is preserved in literary works, and they have sought to restore a highly qualified form of "b." to poetics. While few would invoke any sort of transcendental insight for the poetic vision, some do insist that the symbolic categories of poetic discourse provide at least an intuitive sense of an immanent ontological ground that underlies lang. and governs the otherwise free play of symbolic forms (Scott).

For Harold Bloom, too, both poetry and b. elude the discursive limits of truth and meaning. But Bloom conceives of b. not in terms of the subject's attitude toward a world beyond the self or lang. but as the stake in the poet's struggle for selfhood within the lang. of his poem. What makes a great poet great, Bloom says, is the extent to which the poet is willing to "ruin the sacred truths to fable and old song," to *dis*believe in those truths and so make possible a b. in himself as "a sect of one," an original voice and the origin of the poetic self. Poetry and b. must finally be at odds with one another, then. Yet despite their antithetical relation, both are intimately associated by Bloom with a form of subjectivity that transcends the discursive constraints of poststructural poetics and confounds distinctions between literary meaning and religious truth. See now RELIGION AND POETRY.

I. A. Richards, "Poetry and Bs.," *Science and Poetry* (1926), *Practical Crit.* (1929); T. S. Eliot, "Dante," *Selected Essays* (1932), *The Use of Poetry and the Use of Crit.* (1933); C. Brooks, "The Heresy of Paraphrase" and "The Problem of B. and the Problem of Cognition," in Brooks; W. J. Rooney, *The Problem of Poetry and B. in Contemp. Crit.* (1949); *Lit. and B.*, ed. M. H. Abrams (1958); M. Foucault, *The Archaeology of Knowledge* (1969); M. H. Abrams, *Natural Supernaturalism* (1971); R. C. Murfin, *Swinburne, Hardy, Lawrence, and the Burden of B.* (1978); F. Jameson, *The Political Unconscious* (1981); N. Scott, Jr., *The Poetics of B.* (1985); Wellek, v. 5, ch. 6, 7; H. Bloom, *Ruin the Sacred Truths* (1989); J. P. Russo, *I. A. Richards* (1989), ch. 15; J. M. Hill, *Chaucerian B.* (1991). M.K.; M.CL.

BENGALI POETRY. See INDIAN POETRY.

BERGERETTE. See VIRELAI.

BESTIARY. A medieval compilation of stories in verse or prose in which the supposed characteristics of real and imaginary animals (or plants or stones) are allegorized for the purpose of moral or religious instruction. Derived from a lost Gr. work probably written in Alexandria in the 2d or 3d c., it was originally named after its compiler, Physiologus, one who interpreted the natural world allegorically and mystically. The material came from 'fables in ancient mythology, from accounts of Aristotle, Pliny, and other natural historians, and from oral trad. The *Physiologus* was widely imitated and translated; versions exist not only in Fr., Eng., Ger., It., and Sp., but also in Arabic, Armenian, Ethiopian, ON, and Old Syriac. It was subsequently augmented by pseudo-etymologies attributed to Isidore, Archbishop of Seville (ca. 623), to become the b., containing over 100 chapters. As such, it was one of the most popular and influential books of the Middle Ages. Extant in OE is a fragment in the *Exeter Book* on the panther, the whale, and the partridge, and in ME a poem of 800 short lines tr. from the Lat. version of Theobaldus, abbot of Monte Cassino. Philippe de Thaon's *Bestiaire* (ca. 1130), written in 6-syllable couplets, is the earliest poetical b. in the Fr. vernacular. The *Bestiaire d'amour* (ca. 1250) of Richard de Fournival adroitly secularizes the moral lesson into a lover's pleas for his lady's favor, whereas the *Bestiaire divin* of Guillaume le Clerc embellishes traditional material with personal declarations on the importance of faith and good works.

Almost all the Fr. and many of the Lat. bs. are profusely illustrated. While the intention was simply to inculcate the lesson in the text, the result of these striking illustrations was to perpetuate the lore of the b. in lit., art, and daily life for many centuries. The illustrated emblem books early in the Ren. used the moral lessons, and Elizabethan and Jacobean poets and dramatists (Shakespeare, John Webster) found the b. a fruitful source for imagery. Even today animal fables popularized by the b. (e.g. the phoenix rising from its ashes) remain part of our culture. See also BEAST EPIC.—
Fr. Lauchert, *Gesch. des* Physiologus (1889); M. R. James, *The B.* (1928); M. Wellman, "Der *Physiologus,*" *Philologus*, supp. 21 (1930); F. Sbordone, *Richerche sulle fonti e sulla composizione del Physiologus greco* (1936); F. McCulloch, *Med. Lat. and Fr. Bs.*, rev. ed. (1962); B. Rowland, *Animals With Human Faces* (1974); N. Henkel, *Studien zum* Physiologus *im Mittelalter* (1976); M. Curley, *Physiologus* (1979); X. Muratova, *I manoscritti miniati del bestiario medievale* (1985); *Birds and Beasts of the Middle Ages*, ed. W. B. Clark and M. T. McMunn (1989).   B.RO.

BHAKTI POETRY. See INDIAN POETRY.

BIBLICAL POETRY. See HEBREW POETRY; HEBREW PROSODY AND POETICS; HYMN; PSALM.

BIEDERMEIER. A term first used around 1855 to refer ironically to the smug, cozy, philistine, and petty-bourgeois mentality and writing style frequently encountered in South Germany and Austria in the period 1815–48. Soon after 1900, B. began to be used descriptively as a period term referring to the style of furniture and fashions of dress prevalent in Central Europe and Scandinavia during the first half of the 19th c.; the painting of Spitzweg and Weldmüller was considered typical of this stylistic mode, as well as the poetic realism and idyllic nostalgia of Ger.-lang. writers such as Mörike and Stifter, Raimund and Nestroy, and Grillparzer and Annette von Droste-Hülshoff. See GERMAN POETRY.

Historical observation shows that features such as resignation and contentedness, idyllic intimacy and domestic peace, conservatism, morality and lack of passion, innocent drollery, and a mixture of dreamy idealism and realistic devotion to detail are certainly characteristic of many writers of the B. period. However, this poetry is also placed in multiple and complex dialectical relationships with that of writers who emphasized the dynamics of political and social progress, irony, and revolution. Together and in contrast, Mörike and Heine express and define a common sociocultural situation. Additionally, the B. surface of coziness and satisfaction often overlays doubt, oneiric demonism, uncertainty, and ambiguity, which also have to be considered integral parts of B. writing. Ultimately romanticism (q.v.), the Fr. Revolution, and the social upheavals of the Napoleonic age, along with the age of compromise and constriction that succeeded them, created a state of affairs in which a sense of loss, a search for security, individualism, an ironic or tragicomic worldview, and national, political, and social reform could emerge and interact. These features referred back to a common absent center—the idealized heroic age of romanticism and Revolution—with the result that B. writers feel marked by the problematic and the epigonal, a situation to which they respond in a variety of ways, from realistic action to amused or melancholy contemplation.

The B. itself as a cultural phenomenon is perhaps limited to Central Europe, but its complex intermeshing with a given intellectual, cultural, and historical situation finds close analogues in the France of Hugo, Musset, Lamartine, and Vigny; in the Eastern Europe of Mickiewicz, Słowacki, and Pushkin; in the England of the pre-Victorian writers of the 1820s and 1830s; and in North America.

B. provides a useful if somewhat vague explanatory framework for discussions of poetry in the early 19th c. At the same time, it relates in an interesting way to romanticism, as rococo does to baroque, or postmodernism does to modernism.—
M. Greiner, *Zwischen B. und Bourgeoisie* (1953); G. Böhmer, *Die Welt des B.* (1968); *Zur Literatur der Restaurationsepoche*, ed. J. Hermand and M. Windfuhl (1970); F. Sengle, *Biedermeierzeit*, 3 v. (1971–80); *Begriffsbestimmung des literarischen B.*, ed. E. Neubuhr (1974); C. Herin, "B.," *Gesch. der deutschen Lyrik*, ed. W. Hinderer (1983); V. Nemoianu, *The Taming of Romanticism* (1984).   V.P.N.

BINARY AND TERNARY are the modern terms for what used to be called, with considerable inconsistency of usage, "duple" (or "double") and "triple" meter(s). B. meters have two members per foot, as in iambic and trochaic (also pyrrhic and spondaic if one recognizes these as admissible meters—see FOOT), t. meters three, as in anapestic and dactylic (or amphibrachic or cretic). The distinction between two-membered feet and three- is ancient, despite the facts that the basis of Cl. Gr. metrics (quantity) is different from that of the modern langs. (stress) and that, despite the retention of Cl. names for modern feet, the generic registers of b. and t. meters from ancient times to modern have almost exactly reversed: in Gr., anapestic meter was used for serious and lofty subjects (the epic), and the iambic for lighter subjects; but in the modern poetries the opposite is true: iambic is the meter of heroic verse.

In the quantitative theory of Cl. prosody, the members of the intralinear metrical units (feet) have definite durational relations to each other: a long is by convention equivalent to two shorts. Similarly, in modern "Musical" theories of meter (Lanier, Croll, Hendren; see Brogan), stresses are claimed to be double the temporal value of their opposites, and intervals are made isochronous, hence the iambic foot has three "times" (equal to three shorts) and so is said to be in "triple time," and triple meters are in "duple time" (their three members adding up to four "times," a compound of two). Omond, however, for whom time is the basis of meter but speech syllables are too variable to have definite durations as in music, holds that iambic and trochaic are "duple meters" and in "duple time," i.e. the time required for two average syllables (he lets pauses fill gaps), and t. feet are "triple meters" in "triple time." But this contrariety of terms between musical and nonmusical Temporal theories of meter seems pointless to most modern metrists, who are not Timers: for them it is only the number of members (syllables) in the foot that matters.

The usefulness if not the necessity of the distinction between b. and t. arises from the widely acknowledged fact that the distribution of the one class of meters differs from that of the other, even beyond the fact that the former is far more prevalent than the latter: t. meters are often said to have a different felt cadence, or rhythm, than b., hence to be suitable for a different range of subjects— often light-hearted, humorous, rollicking, satirical. What this means is that, in modern verse, generic constraints are differentially assigned in part by metrical class, and hence that this distinction is one valid plane of cleavage in metrical theory.

Further, it is disputed whether the meters within each class are in fact distinct meters: iambic and trochaic are said by some to be interchangeable, or at least interrelated via rhythms established by wordshapes: particularly interesting is the case of iambo-trochaic tetrameters known as "8s and 7s" (see RISING AND FALLING). In Eng., though b. meters appear in early ME, definite t. meters only appear in the Ren., and even then only sporadically—Ker relates them to "tumbling verse" (q.v.), as in Tusser, and remarks that they are "almost always" the product of a musical tune—effectively, they are not common at all until the latter 18th c. (Gray's "Amatory Lines," Gay, Goldsmith), and by far the majority of examples are 19th-c. ("Saul," Swinburne). Further, t. meters are notoriously difficult to differentiate in running series, esp. when line ends are irregular and unpredictable: the sequence x/xx/xx/xx/ may be felt as anapestic tetrameter with a missing first syllable, but it can also be amphibrachic with a missing final syllable. Schipper indicates the syllabic ambiguities in t. meters by treating them as "iambic-trochaic" and "trochaic-dactylic," remarking that "the rising and falling rhythms are not strictly separated but frequently intermingle and even supplement one another." Finally, it appears that there may be intermediate stages between these classes, via the admission of extra (unelidable) syllables into b. meters. But this question, which entails the concept of accentual verse (q.v.), is too complex to be undertaken here (see Weismiller). See now DURATION; METER.

Schipper, v. 2, sect. 224–41, and History, ch. 14; T. S. Omond, A Study of Metre (1903), esp. 49, 52; G. Saintsbury, Hist. of Eng. Pros., 3 v. (1906–10), v. 3, App. 3; W. P. Ker, Form and Style in Poetry (1928); K. Taranovski, Ruski dvodelni ritmovi [Rus. B. Meters] (1953); A. T. Breen, "A Survey of the Devel. of Poetry Written in Trisyllic Metres to 1830," Diss., Nat. Univ. of Ireland (1965); E. R. Weismiller, "Studies of Verse Form in the Minor Eng. Poems," A Variorum Commentary on the Poems of John Milton., ed. M. Y. Hughes, v. 2 (1972), "Triple Threats to Duple Mcter," Rhythm and Meter, ed. P. Kiparsky and G. Youmans (1989); D. L. Hascall, "Triple Meters in Eng. Verse," Poetics 12 (1974); M. L. Gasparov, Sovremennyj russkij stix (1974), Očerk istorii russskogo stixa (1984); Morier, s.v. "Binaire"; Brogan; Scherr; M. G. Tarlinskaja, "Meter and Lang.: B. and T. Meters in Eng. and Rus.," Style 21 (1987).   T.V.F.B.

BIOGRAPHICAL CRITICISM. See CRITICISM.

BLACK MOUNTAIN SCHOOL. See PROJECTIVE VERSE.

BLACK POETRY. See AFRO-AMERICAN POETRY; AFRICAN POETRY.

BLANK VERSE.

    I. IN ITALIAN AND ENGLISH
    II. IN OTHER LANGUAGES

I. IN ITALIAN AND ENGLISH. B. v. first appeared in It. poetry of the Ren. as an unrhymed variant of the endecasillabo (see ITALIAN PROSODY), then was transplanted to England as the unrhymed decasyllable or iambic pentameter. Though these lines are thought to have derived metrically from the Cl. iambic trimeter, they were designed to produce, in the vernaculars, equivalents in tone and weight of the Cl. "heroic" line, the line of epic, the hexameter (q.v.). The unrhymed endecasillabo, while popular and important, never became a major It. meter; in England, however, b. v. became, under the influence of Shakespeare and Milton, the staple meter of Eng. dramatic verse and a major meter of nondramatic verse as well. Fr. poet-critics noted the work of the It. poets and made experiments of their own, but these never took hold in a lang. where word-accent was weak; hence Fr. poetry never developed a significant b.-v.

trad. The Ger., Scandinavian, and Slavic trads. are discussed in section II below.

In *England*, b. v. was invented by Henry Howard, Earl of Surrey (1517–47), who sometime between 1539 and 1546 translated two books of the *Aeneid* (2 and 4) into this "straunge meter." Surrey knew Gavin Douglas's Scottish tr. (written, in rhymed couplets, ca. 1513; pub. 1553); as much as 40% of Surrey's diction is taken directly from Douglas. But the lexical borrowing is localized; in general, Douglas is prolix, Surrey laconic—even more so than Virgil. More significantly, Surrey develops— in part, perhaps, to offset absent rhyme—an extensive network of sound patterning.

Surrey also surely knew Luigi Alamanni's *Rime toscane* (pub. 1532) and other famous It. works in *versi sciolti* (i.e. *versi sciolti da rima* "verse freed from rhyme"; see VERSI SCIOLTI) such as Trissino's tragedy *Sophonisba* (1515) and epic *Italia liberata dai Goti* (pub. 1547), or Liburnio's 1534 tr. of Virgil or the 1539 tr. by the de'Medici circle. But the It. *versi* "freed" from rhyme are hendecasyllables (q.v.), technically of 11 syllables but permissibly also of 9 or 10, and with only one required stress in each hemistich, whereas Surrey clearly intended to produce, in Eng., an alternating (iambic) rhythm in a strict 10-syllable line. Behind Surrey of course stand Chaucer and Wyatt: Chaucer had mastered the Eng. decasyllable over a century earlier, but the rhythm of his verse was lost to Eng. ears in the 15th c. by virtue of phonological changes. From Wyatt's sonnets and sonnet trs. Surrey could have learned a great deal, but there is much irregularity in Wyatt, and all of his verse is rhymed. The precise nature of Surrey's metrical accomplishment is still not entirely understood, and the two features of the b.-v. line— the metrical structure and the forgoing of rhyme— are quite different issues. If Surrey sought to appropriate features of It. verseform to Eng., they would of course be naturalized in Eng. rhythms. It remains to be shown precisely how the rhythms in Surrey's lines derived from ones native to the It. *endecasillabo*.

As b. v. developed in Eng., generic considerations also became important. Clearly verse without rhyme is esp. suited to long works, permitting an idea to be expressed at whatever length is appropriate, not imposing on the lang. a repeated structure of couplet or stanza which would tend to produce conformity in syntactic structures as well. The omission of rhyme promoted continuity, sustained articulation, enjambment, and relatively natural word order. It permitted, on the other hand, the deliberate use of syntactic inversion, an effect comparable to the hyperbaton (q.v.) of Cl. verse. Relatively natural word order made b. v. a fitting vehicle for drama; inversion, suspension, and related stylistic devices suited it to epic.

"Blank" as used of verse (the earliest *OED* citation is by Nashe in 1589) suggests a mere absence (of rhyme), not that liberation from a restrictive requirement implied in the It. term. Eng. defenders of b. v. repeatedly asserted that rhyme acts on poets as a "constraint to express many things otherwise, and for the most part worse than else they would have exprest them" (Milton). That rhyme (q.v.) has its virtues and beauties needs no argument here. That it blocks off more avenues of thought than it opens, for the skilled poet, is doubtful. Rhyme does, however, tend to delimit— even to define—metrical structures; it has its clearest effect when the syllables it connects occur at the ends also of syntactic structures, so that meter and syntax reinforce one another. One associates rhyme with symmetries and closures. Omission of rhyme, by contrast, encourages the use of syntactic structures greater and more various than could be contained strictly within the line, and so makes possible an amplitude of discourse, a natural-seeming multiformity, not easily available to rhymed verse.

Though b. v. appeared in Eng. first in (translated) epic, attempts at Eng. heroic verse after Surrey use, as Hardison remarks, "almost every form *but* b. v." The form achieved its first great flowering in drama. After Surrey the dramatic and nondramatic varieties have significantly different histories, suggesting that they differ in nature more than critics once thought (see Wright; Hardison).

In nondramatic verse, the influence of Petrarchism (q.v.), manifested in the vogue for sonneteering (see SONNET SEQUENCE), ensured that rhyme held sway in Eng. nondramatic verse up to Milton. The heavy editorial regularization by the editor of Tottel's Miscellany (1557) set the trend up to Sidney, who showed that metrical correctness and natural expressiveness were not mutually exclusive (see Thompson), a demonstration extended even further by Donne—but again, in rhyme.

The first Eng. dramatic b. v., Thomas Norton's in the first three acts of *Gorboduc* (1561), is smooth but heavily end-stopped, giving the impression of contrivance, of a diction shaped—and often padded out—to fit the meter. Sackville's verse in the last two acts of the play is more alive, more like the verse of Surrey's *Aeneid*. But the artificial regularity of Norton's verse came to characterize Eng. dramatic poetry until Marlowe came fully into his powers. Marlowe showed what rhetorical and tonal effects b. v. was capable of; his early play *Dido* echoes lines from Surrey's *Aeneid*, and Shakespeare's early works show what he learned from Marlowe. T.V.F.B.; E.R.W.

Shakespeare. Shakespeare's b. v., the major verseform of his plays throughout his career, is marked by several features, some of them shared with or derived from earlier Eng. poets (e.g. Lydgate, Sidney, and Marlowe) but developed with unprecedented coherence. (1) B. v. is always mixed with other metrical modes (e.g. rhymed verse, songs) and (except for *Richard II* and *King John*) with prose; two plays offer more rhymed verse than b. (*Love's Labour's Lost* and *A Midsummer*

Night's Dream), and seven plays (two histories and five middle-period comedies) are largely or predominantly written in prose. Shifts within a scene from one mode to another are often subtle, gradual, and hard to hear; reserving different metrical registers for different social classes, however, can be heard, and helps to identify sets of characters—as in *MND*. (2) Resourceful use of common Elizabethan conventions of metrical patterning and esp. of metrical variation gives many individual lines great flexibility, variety, melody, and speechlike force. (3) Frequent use of lines deviant in length or pattern (short, long, headless, brokenbacked, and epic-caesural) extends the potentialities of expressive variation beyond what was commonly available to Ren. writers of stanzaic verse. (4) Shrewdly deployed syllabic ambiguity, esp. by devices of compression (see METRICAL TREATMENT OF SYLLABLES; ELISION), makes many lines seem packed. (5) Lines become increasingly enjambed: sentences run from midline to midline, and even a speech or a scene may end in midline. Conversely, metrically regular lines may comprise several short phrases or sentences and may be shared by characters ("split lines," q.v.). In the theater, consistently enjambed b. v., unlike Marlowe's endstopped "mighty" line, sounds more like speech but also tests the audience's awareness of the meter. Esp. in the later, more troubled plays, the audience, like the characters it is scrutinizing, follows an uncertain path between comprehension and bafflement.

Deploying all these means in speeches, scenes, and plays that differently approach, complicate, and resolve a varied array of characters and issues, the b. v. Shakespeare uses to negotiate the sometimes tempestuous marriage of phrase and line is fully equal in suppleness and energy to the plays' expressive syntax, imagery, and wordplay. Besides carrying the characters' emotional utterances and conveying (with appropriate intensity) their complex states of mind, this b. v. may figure, through its rich dialectic of pattern and departure-from-pattern, a continuing tension between authority and event, model and story, the measured structures of cosmic order and the wayward motions of erratic individual characters.   G.T.W.

After Shakespeare, and esp. after Donne's (rhymed) *Satyres,* the dramatic b. v. line grew looser in form. Feminine endings (see MASCULINE AND FEMININE), infrequent in all early b. v., became common; in Fletcher they often carry verbal stress. Later, true feminine endings become common even in nondramatic rhymed verse. Milton uses feminine endings in *Paradise Lost* and *Paradise Regained* only with great restraint. They occur rather seldom in the early books of *PL*, but much more frequently after Eve's and Adam's fall, and are thereby appropriated to the speech of fallen mortals.

In dramatic b. v., extrametrical syllables begin to appear within the line—first, nearly always following a strong stress and at the end of a phrase or clause at the caesura; later, elsewhere within the line. In some late Jacobean and Caroline drama, the line has become so flexible that at times the five points of stress seem to become phrase centers, each capable of carrying with it unstressed syllables required by the sense rather than by the metrical count of syllables. But such lines were to call down the wrath of later critics; and the closing of the theaters in 1642 saw also the end of a brilliant—if almost too daring—period of experimentation with the structure of the dramatic b. v. line. When verse drama was written again, after the Restoration, and under the impetus of the newly popular Fr. model, the line was once again a strict pentameter, but now, and for the next century, rhymed. In any event, after the closing of the theaters, b. v. was never to be of major importance in the drama again. The attempt to renew verse drama (incl. b.-v.) in the 20th c.—as in Eliot and Yeats—never won either popular or critical acclaim.

It was *Milton* who returned b. v. to its earliest use as a vehicle of epic, and to strict, though complex, metrical order; his influence was so powerful that the form bore his impress up to the 20th c. He did, of course, write b.-v. drama—*A Mask* (*Comus*) and *Samson Agonistes,* the first much influenced by Shakespeare. In both, b. v., though it is unquestionably the central form, is intermingled with other forms—lyric in *A Mask,* choric in *SA*—to such effect that we think of both works as being in mixed meters. In *SA* Milton is trying to produce the effect of Gr. tragedy (though with a biblical subject); but the b. v. is similar enough to Milton's nondramatic b. v. that discussion of the two may be merged.

We know that Milton was profoundly familiar with the *Aeneid* in Lat., perhaps in It. tr., and in some Eng. versions; he was equally familiar with It. epic and romance. As a theorist of form he wanted to make of b. v. in Eng. the instrument which the Humanist poets had been attempting to forge since Trissino. For his subject in *PL* he needed a dense, packed line, as various as possible in movement within the limits set by broadly understood but absolute metricality; at the same time he needed a syntax complex and elaborate enough to overflow line form, to subordinate it to larger forms of thought, appropriately varied in the scope of their articulation. He needed "the sense variously drawn out from one line into another." The idea was not new, yet no one had managed enjambment in Eng. as skillfully as Milton learned to manage it. Before him—except in Shakespeare's later plays—the congruence of syntax with line form had been too nearly predictable.

Even more than Shakespeare's, Milton's b. v. line differs from his rhymed pentameter—not in basic meter, but in management of rhythm, and not only through enjambment, but also through constant variation of the placement of pause within the line. In the course of enjambing lines, Milton writes long periodic sentences, making liberal use of inversion, parenthesis, and other delaying and complicating devices. Whether or not Milton knew Surrey's *Aeneid*, there are real similarities between the two men's work. Like Surrey, Milton at times uses Italianate stress sequences that disturb the duple rhythm and in some instances all but break the meter. Also important, given his refusal of rhyme, is a more extensive (if irregular) deployment of the varied resources of sound patterning. Numerous forms of internal rhyme occur, as well as final assonance and half-rhyme; and whole passages woven together by patterns of alliteration, assonance, and half-rhyme.

Milton's influence on subsequent nondramatic b. v. in Eng. was, as Havens showed, enormous. Yet it is a fact that all b. v. after Milton became essentially a romantic form—no longer epic, and no longer dramatic, but the vehicle of rumination and recollection. The line of descent leads through Wordsworth (*Michael*; *The Prelude*; *The Excursion*) to Tennyson (*Ulysses*; *Tithonus*; *Idylls of the King*) and Browning (*The Ring and the Book*). By the mid 18th c., the forces of metrical regularity had begun to weaken, and for the first time genuine extra syllables begin to appear in the nondramatic line which cannot be removed by elision, producing triple rhythm. The Eng. pentameter both dramatic and nondramatic between 1540 and 1780 all but disallowed triple rhythms; strict count of syllables was deemed central to line structure. Real, irreducible triple rhythms prior to 1780 were associated with music; they occur fairly commonly in song lyrics and ballads, but not in accentual-syllabic meter. After 1780, however, triple rhythms gradually invade poems in duple rhythm. In part this is because the romantics were devoted to the work of their 16th- and 17th-c. predecessors, and often used the diction of Spenser, Shakespeare, and Milton, though without entirely understanding earlier metrical conventions. There was also a revival of interest in the ballads, which varied the basic duple rhythms with irreducible triple rhythms, a practice soon evident in Blake's *Songs* and even occasionally in Wordsworth.

The rhythmic and syntactic flexibility of the line once called "heroic" had come undeniably closer to that of speech. Conservative trends would still appear: Tennyson uses many fewer triple rhythms than Browning, and most of those he does use seem relaxations of traditional metrical compressions; his choices of rhythm and diction together give an impression of formality, of dignity. Browning, on the other hand, in his dramatic monologues (see MONOLOGUE) achieves an astonishing range of effects, each suited to the persona (q.v.) of the character he is presenting. In the 20th c., comparable shadings of metrical effect can be found in the b. v. of Robinson, Frost, Eliot, Stevens, Jeffers, and Lowell. Lines of b. v. may still be used

to resolve deliberately inchoate materials into form; and they may still arise naturally and as though involuntarily among lines of differing rhythm. But the advent of free verse sounded the death-knell of this meter which was once and for long a powerful, flexible, and subtle form, the most prestigious and successful modern rival to the greatest meter of antiquity.   E.R.W.; T.V.F.B.

See also BINARY AND TERNARY; CLASSICAL METERS IN MODERN LANGUAGES; DRAMATIC POETRY; ENJAMBMENT; EPIC; HEROIC COUPLET; HEROIC VERSE; METER.

S. Johnson, *Rambler*, nos. 86–96 (1751); Schipper; J. B. Mayor, *Chapters on Eng. Metre*, 2d ed. (1901); R. Bridges, *Milton's Pros.* (1921); R. D. Havens, *The Influence of Milton on Eng. Poetry* (1922); A. Oras, *B. V. and Chronology in Milton* (1966); R. Beum, "So Much Gravity and Ease," *Lang. and Style in Milton*, ed. R. D. Emma and J. T. Shawcross (1967); R. Fowler, "Three B. V. Textures," *The Langs. of Lit.* (1971); E. R. Weismiller, "B. V.," "Versif.," and J. T. Shawcross, "Controversy over B. V.," *A Milton Encyc.*, ed. W. B. Hunter, Jr., 8 v. (1978–80); Brogan, 356 ff.; H. Suhamy, *Le Vers de Shakespeare* (1984); M. Tarlinskaja, *Shakespeare's Verse* (1987); G. T. Wright, *Shakespeare's Metrical Art* (1988); J. Thompson, *The Founding of Eng. Metre*, 2d ed. (1989); O. B. Hardison, Jr., *Pros. and Purpose in the Eng. Ren.* (1989).

E.R.W.; T.V.F.B.; G.T.W.

II. IN OTHER LANGUAGES. A. *German*. Outside of England, whence it derived, b. v. celebrated its greatest triumph in Germany. Although 17th-c. Ger. poets knew Shakespeare and Milton, their early attempts at b. v. were inconsequential. After the dominance of the alexandrine (q.v.) and its rhyme had passed, however, b. v. was reprised in the second half of the 18th c. with much greater success. Wieland's tragedy *Lady Johanna Gray* (1758) is the first instance, but Lessing's *Nathan der Weise* (1779) established the most influential precedent. Goethe followed suit by rewriting his earlier prose version of *Iphigenie auf Tauris* (1787) and *Torquato Tasso* (1790) in b. v. Similarly, Schiller rewrote *Don Carlos* (1787), and Kleist used b. v. exclusively for his dramas. A. W. Schlegel's tr. of Shakespeare (1797–1810), continued by Tieck, did much to solidify the convention, which had gained prestige by its association with Weimar Classicism. Throughout the 19th c., b. v. remained the standard meter for Ger. verse drama, as exemplified by the works of Grillparzer, Grabbe, Hebbel, and even Hauptmann (in contrast to his naturalist prose dramas); and b. v. appeared with a final flourish in the lyric dramas of Hofmannsthal.

This broad spectrum points up the main advantage of b. v., its adaptability to diverse styles. At one pole stands Goethe, who labored to perfect a lyrical form of b. v. with end-stopped lines, balanced caesuras, and smooth rhythmic phrasing; at the opposite pole stands Lessing, whose heavily enjambed lines are often divided into short phrases and shared by different speakers, making the verse speechlike. Kleist too overrides the line end; his strong contrasts and rapid shifts impel the verse with a driving thrust. Schiller at first assumes an intermediate position, later developing in the direction of Goethe. But the great flexibility of b. v. has also been seen as a disadvantage, for the form itself lacks a distinctive profile and has been thought monotonous at times. The elder Goethe maintained that b. v. "reduced poetry to prose," which recalls Dr. Johnson on Milton, a sentiment echoed after Goethe by other poets and critics such as Heusler. But b. v. can accommodate many expressive possibilities, much depending on precisely how the metrical pattern is realized.

The relative lack of contour to b. v. in Ger. may explain why it was not common in traditional Ger. lyric (though Schiller's *Das verschleierte Bild zu Sais* is a notable exception). Still, b. v. was picked up by the early modern poets, such as Meyer, George, Hofmannsthal, and Rilke, who gave it a distinctly formal tone, thus distancing themselves from the rhymed folk poetry of the 19th c. Two of the 10 elegies in Rilke's *Duineser Elegien* are in b. v. In contrast to the liberties allowed in the dramatic form, b. v. in the lyric is very strict, similar to its counterpart, rhymed iambic pentameter, which like the sonnet form derived from the It. *endecasillabo*, was more common than b. v. throughout the lyric trad. In the 20th c., Ger. lyric b. v. was largely supplanted by *freie Rhythmen* and free verse (qq.v.), as dramatic b. v. was by prose, though a ghostly form of traditional meter often remains in the background—just behind the arras, as T. S. Eliot said. B.B.

B. *Scandinavian*. The Scandinavian countries received b. v. from Italy, England, and Germany, the chief models being the dramatic verse of Goethe and Schiller. With *Balders Død* (1773), Johannes Ewald introduced hendecasyllabic b. v. in Denmark, evidently of It. extraction. Preferring the decasyllable with masculine endings, Oehlenschläger created a medium capable of a wider range of dramatic effects; his treatment of b. v. in his numerous historical tragedies is much like that of the later Schiller. Oehlenschläger's followers in the drama, Ingemann and Hauch, naturally adhered to the verseform of their master; more individual is the b. v. used later by Paludan-Müller (in his dramatic poems on mythological subjects) and by Rørdam. In Swedish poetry, b. v. was introduced with Kellgren's narrative fragment *Sigvarth och Hilma* (1788) in the It. form acquired from Ewald. Excellent Eng. b. v. appeared as early as 1796 in a few scenes of a projected historical play by the Finn Franzén; but not until 1862 did Wecksell, another Finn, produce the only significant b.-v. drama in Swedish, *Daniel Hjort*. Unlike the situation in Denmark and Norway, where b. v. appears infrequently in narrative, didactic, satirical, and reflective poetry, in Sweden b. v. has a long and still living trad. in these genres, with contribu-

tions by such poets as Tegnér, Stagnelius, Sjöberg, Malmberg, Edfelt, and Ekelöf. The form of Swedish b. v. is generally conservative, not unlike that of Goethe. Norwegian poets started using b. v. about the same time, but the first significant works are several farces and dramas beginning in 1827 by Wergeland, whose metrical usage, modeled on Shakespeare, is very free. Neither Andreas Munch's imitations of Oehlenschläger (beginning in 1837) nor Ibsen's *Catilina* (1850) displays a distinctive form of b. v. The rhymed verse intermittently used in *Catilina* is far superior to the b. v., which may explain Ibsen's subsequent preference for rhyme. Bjørnson, on the other hand, composed excellent b. v. in his saga dramas in a free form which points to Shakespeare and Schiller as the chief models.

C. *Slavic*. In Russia, b. v. appeared with Žukovskij's tr. of Schiller's *Die Jungfrau von Orleans* (1817–21). It was subsequently used by Puškin in *Boris Godunov* (1825; pub. 1831) and his "Little Tragedies," and by Mey, Ostrovsky, and A. K. Tolstoy in their historical dramas. Tolstoy's *Czar Fyodor Ioannovich* (1868) has been a popular success up to recent years. B. v. also appears in narrative and reflective poetry. In Russia, as elsewhere, b. v. varies within a certain range, from the conservative line-structured form with constant caesura of *Boris Godunov* to the more loosely articulated verse of "little tragedies" like *Mozart and Salieri* and *The Covetous Knight*. In Poland, the hendecasyllabic b. v. of It. origin used by Kochanowski in his tragedy *Odprawa posłów greckich* (The Dismissal of the Gr. Envoys, 1578) failed to inaugurate a trad. Rhymed verse became standard for Polish drama, and neither J. Korzeniowski's many b.-v. plays (beginning in 1820) nor his persistent theoretical advocacy of the medium greatly modified the situation. Among individual works in b. v. may be mentioned *Lilla Weneda* (1840), one of Słowacki's best tragedies, Norwid's comedy *Miłość* (Chaste Love at the Bathing Beach), and J. Kraszewski's epic trilogy *Anafielas* (1840). S.LY.

F. Zarncke, *Über den fünffüssigen Jambus... durch Lessing, Schiller, und Goethe* (1865); A. Sauer, *Über den fünffüssigen Jambus vor Lessings Nathan* (1878); L. Hettich, *Der fünffüssigen Jambus in den Dramen Goethes* (1913); O. Sylwan, *Den svenska versen från 1600-talets början*, 3 v. (1925–34), *Svensk verskonst från Wivallius till Karlfeldt* (1934); A. Heusler, *Deutsche Versgesch.* (1925–29), v. 3; K. Taranovski, *Ruski dvodelni ritmoci*, 2 v. (1953); B. Unbegaun, *Rus. Versif.* (1956); R. Haller, "Studie über den deutschen Blankvers," *DVLG* 31 (1957); P. Habermann, "Blankvers," *Reallexikon*; R. Bräuer, *Tonbewegung und Erscheinungsformen des sprachlichen Rhythmus; Profile des deutschen Blankverses* (1964); L. Schädle, *Der frühe deutsche Blankvers* (1972); B. Bjorklund, *A Study in Comp. Pros.* (1978); Brogan; Scherr. B.B.; S.LY.

BLASON. According to Thomas Sebillet, *Art poétique françoys* (ed. F. Gaiffe, 1932), the b. is a poetic genre devoted to the praise or blame of something. V.-L. Saulnier, however, indentifies two types of b.: the *b. satirique* and the *b. médaillon*. The purpose of the former is satiric; that of the latter is to describe briefly a single object. The genre had its origin in 1536 with Clément Marot's *B. du beau tétin*. Sebillet is inclined to think (incorrectly) that the b. represented an effort to do in poetry what heraldic art did with armorial bearings. In reality, the satiric b. is a distant descendant of Lat. satire (q.v.), while the descriptive b. traces its beginnings to the Gr. epigram (q.v.) and to the "effictio" trope of Cl. rhet. The good b., says Sebillet, will be brief, will be set in octo- or decasyllabic verses, and will have a sharp (i.e. epigrammatic) conclusion. Most bs., like the one by Marot that initiated the genre, celebrated some part of the female body, and by 1536 it was possible to gather many of them into an anthol. entitled *Blaisons anatomiques du corps feminin*. From the perspective of feminist poetics (q.v.), the b. may be seen as a male inventory of the female body. See also CATALOGUE; PETRARCHISM.—J. Vianey, *Le Pétrarquisme en France au XVIe siècle* (1909); R. E. Pike, "The *Bs.* in Fr. Lit. of the 16th C.," *RR* 27 (1936); V. L. Saulnier, *Maurice Scève*, 2 v. (1948–49); H. Weber, *La Création poétique au XVIe siècle*, 2 v. (1956); K. Kazimierz, "Des Recherches sur l'évolution du b. au XVIe siècle," *ZRL* (1967); D. B. Wilson, *Descriptive Poetry in France from B. to Baroque* (1967); A. and E. Tomarken, "The Rise and Fall of the 16th-c. Fr. B.," *Symposium* 29 (1975); A Saunders, "16th-c. Collected Eds. of *Blaisons anatomiques*," *Library* 31 (1976). 						I.S.; T.V.F.B.

BLUES are more than sad songs about lost love and loneliness. They exist as instrumental and vocal music, as psychological state, as lifestyle, and as philosophical stance. As folk or popular poetry, b. lyrics are distinguished by graphic imagery and themes drawn from a wide range of group and personal experiences. Thematically, they address suffering, struggle, and sexuality. They confront life head-on, with an indomitable will expressed in sarcasm, wit, and "signifying" (q.v.) humor, and they move on an expressive spectrum ranging from the grim and the bawdy to the tragic. These features and concerns are rooted in the Black Am. oral trad.—in secular rhymes and "toasts" (q.v.), in ritual verbal combat (the "dozens," q.v.) and ironic teasing in tales and jokes. Their dynamic pattern of "confrontation, improvisation, affirmation, and celebration" (Murray) evokes the history and texture of the Black Am. presence.

B. must be seen then in their dynamic contextuality with Black oral trad. and Am. popular culture, which they adopt and transform through critique and improvisation. Thus there are b. versions of ballads like "John Henry," as well as allusions to standard hymns, spirituals, popular songs, and topical events. In effect, around the turn of the 20th c. the b. emerged out of the work songs and field hollers as a durable, elastic artform that could efficiently digest and render the contradictory elements in Am. life. In the classic b. form, the first line makes a statement which is repeated with a variation in the second. The third line provides an ironic contrast or extension. Thus all kinds of combinations are possible, incl. call and response patterns between the voice and the accompanying instrument (guitar, harmonica) or band.

Early b. may be classified as city or country, with the former being recorded first. They may also be called classic or rural. Of the first great classic singers the best known were Gertrude "Ma" Rainey and Bessie Smith. Among the rural singers were Charley Patton, Ed "Son" House, and the legendary Robert Johnson.

Formally, there are many different kinds of b., but they may be usefully discussed within the country/city framework. Both forms share features like the three-line song lyric and the so-called blue notes, in which the third and seventh notes of the scale are flattened. These intervals give rise to haunting melodies and harmonies and add a distinctive coloration to any song regardless of its verbal content. Thematically, the classic b. were written for entertainment but retain strong connections with earlier rural styles. The personal lyrical voice from which the form arose remained a feature of the classic style. In fact, the two styles developed simultaneously during the first two decades of this century, nourishing and strengthening one another. In contrast to the classic style with its emphasis on conflict and sexuality, the country b. responded to everything, and often retains elements of other songforms like the ballad and popular song.

Although, taken as a whole, the b. are tragicomic in both a thematic and structural sense, they often sustain a tragic tone, as in Robert Johnson's "Hellhound on My Trail," with its image of a man driven by fate stumbling through a b. storm; in this depiction of Native Son as Orestes, Johnson reveals himself as one of the most poetic of b. singers.

The b. entered the literary canon as "folk poetry" in anthologies such as *The Negro Caravan*, and as "literary poetry" or poems in the folk manner in collections such as Langston Hughes' *The Weary Blues*, where the title poem is not, strictly speaking, b. at all but a lyric framework with narrative elements. The poem dramatizes the b. experience as performance, as social ritual, and as existential experience. Explicit in the poem is the relationship of performer to audience, to his art, and to his experience of the b. Questions of this sort were raised fairly early by b. commentators such as Hughes, Sterling A. Brown, and others. Recent scholarship demonstrates the usefulness of the b. in understanding the unique qualities of Am., esp. Black Am., life and art. Thus the b. are relevant to presentations and analyses of dance, fiction, cinema, dress, and other modes—from Ellison's *Invisible Man* to the paintings of Romare Bearden and Jacob Lawrence to the novels of Gayle Jones and Alice Walker. Indeed, Houston A. Baker has projected a challenging theory of Black lit. based on his understanding of the b., while elsewhere discussions of the Black Aesthetic are being subsumed in the B. Aesthetic—P. Oliver, *The Meaning of the B.* (1963); A. Murray, *Stomping the B.* (1976); J. T. Titon, *Early Downhome B.* (1977); M. Taft, *B. Lyric Poetry*, 2 v. (1983, 1988)—anthol. and concordance; H. A. Baker, Jr., *B., Ideology and Afro-Am. Lit.* (1984); M. L. Hart et al., *The B.: A Bibl. Guide* (1989).   S.E.H.

BOB AND WHEEL. A distinct form of heterometric (q.v.) or tailed stanza in ME and Middle Scots poetry, the best example of which is *Sir Gawain and the Green Knight*; Stanley lists about 40 known examples. Since Guest the phrase has denoted a short line, often of only two syllables, at the end of a stanza (the bob), followed by two to four slightly longer lines which rhyme internally (the "wheel"). Their metrical structure and derivation is disputed; Borroff treats the wheel lines as syllabic and footed despite the alliterative meter of the stanza. Bobs also appear separately as refrain- and tag-lines; Saintsbury calls them, aptly, "short-line pivots."—E. Guest, *Hist. of Eng. Rhythms* (1838); Schipper, s.v. in the Index, 3.955; M. Borroff, *Sir Gawain and the Green Knight: A Stylistic and Metrical Study* (1962); E. G. Stanley, "The Use of Bob-Lines in *Sir Thopas*," *NM* 73 (1972); T. Turville-Petre in *RES* 25 (1974); H. Kirkpatrick, "The Bob-Wheel and Allied Stanzas in ME and Middle Scots Poetry," *DAI* 37 (1976), 3608.   T.V.F.B.

BOOK. See INTERTEXTUALITY.

BOUTS-RIMÉS. A sequence of words rhyming in accordance with a predetermined rhyme scheme (often that of the sonnet) and used as the basis of a versemaking game; also (by metonymy) the game itself. The object of the game, which is said to have been invented by Gilles Ménage (1613–92) and was popular in *précieux* circles of 17th-c. Paris, is to write a poem incorporating the given rhyme-words so as to achieve effects as witty as they are seemingly uncontrived. Accordingly, the sequence of rhymes is made as bizarre and incongruous as possible. From the first, b.-r. tried the ingenuity of even the most considerable poets (Corneille, Boileau), and the diversion spread to England and Scotland and survived as a source of 19th-c. *vers de société* (q.v.). But any school of poets which regards rhyme as the generative principle of verse composition will favor a method of working essentially by b.-r., as did the Parnassians (q.v.), for example, guided by Banville's axiom that "an imaginative gift for rhyme is, of all qualities, the one which makes the poet." Mallarmé's enigmatic "ptyx" nonce-sonnet may be a b.-r. The rhyming dictionary itself will, when the combinations it offers are severely limited, act as a purveyor of b.-r. (see the octave of Baudelaire's *Sed non satiata*). In terms of the metaphysics of writing, b.-r. are like the cryptic fragments of an oracular utterance which only the priest-poet has the power to reconstitute or construe; the poet is the paleographer of the invisible. See POETIC CONTESTS.—Kastner; T. Augarde, *Oxford Guide to Word Games* (1984).   C.S.

BRACHYCATALECTIC. See CATALEXIS.

BRACHYLOGIA. See ASYNDETON.

BRAZILIAN POETRY. B. lit., like the Portuguese lit. from which it springs and derives its main trends, at least up to the 19th c., is characterized to an unusual degree by poetic activity. The first manifestations of poetry in Brazil appear in the middle of the 16th c. with the arrival of the Jesuits, esp. José de Anchieta, (1534–97). In 1601, the publication of *Prosopopéia*, a poem of only 94 stanzas with epic intentions, inspired by Camões' *Os Lusiadas* (The Lusiads, 1572), heralds the appearance of the first B. poet, Bento Teixeira (1561–1600). In spite of its mediocrity, the poem announces the onset of the baroque school of B. p. from which arises the strong poetic personality of Gregório de Matos (1633–96). Depicting in verse the defects of colonial society, he reflects not only preoccupation with the landscape, as in his lyrics, but also concern with the human scene in his satiric poems.

During the mid 18th-c. gold rush in Minas Gerais, those who were to form the *mineira* school were born. Educated in Portugal, with some becoming members of the literary "academies" proliferating at the time, these youths wrote poetry in the academic-Arcadian fashion and, once back at home, conspired in the ill-timed, ill-fated *Inconfidência Mineira*, the earliest attempt at revolt against Portugal. Their artistic leader, Tomás Antônio Gonzaga (1744–1810), is regarded as one of Brazil's greatest lyric poets and is the author of the most popular collection of love poems in the lang., *Marilia de Dirceu* (1792). Three other names complete the quartet of the great *mineiro* lyric poets: Cláudio Manuel da Costa (1729–89), Alvarenga Peixoto (1744–93), and Silva Alvarenga (1749–1814).

Still other *mineiros* wrote epics in Brazil. The more original and sensitive epic, a major precursor of romantic Indianism, is *O Uraguai* (1764) by Basílio da Gama (1741–95). It recounts the war waged by Portugal, with Spain's aid, against the Indians of the Mission towns who rebelled at transfer from Jesuit to Portuguese rule. More truly B. in subject, but less original and less imbued with poetic genius, is *Camaruru* (1781) by Santa Rita Durão (1722–84). It is the story of Diogo Álvares, the shipwrecked sailor who discovered Bahia and

- [143] -

became chieftain among the Indians there under the name of Caramuru (Moray). In these poems, nature varies from the bucolic, pantheistic nature of Arcady to the majestic, indigenous nature as seen through baroque, gongoristic eyes: nature stylized, not as it really is.

The *mineiros*, influenced by theories absorbed from Rousseau and other Encyclopedists, have been called preromantics. But it is only later, with political independence, that romanticism first asserts itself, firmly based, after its early steps, upon the idealized aborigine. The movement, however blurred the lines, falls into three phases:

1. The first phase, which still reflects much of the preceding Ren. and Arcadian periods, begins with *Suspiros Poéticos e Saudades* (Poetic Signs and Yearnings) by Gonçalves de Magalhães (1811–82). The best poetic talent of this first phase was Gonçalves Dias (1823–64), however. He dominates all romantic poetry through his sense of sobriety and harmony. All is balanced: love and religion, feeling for nature, patriotism, sympathy for the Indian. He, better than most, infused life into the Indian theme. One of his most famous poems is "Canção do Exílio" (Song of Exile), a delicate, poignant expression of *saudade* (yearning) for Brazil. Casimiro de Abreu (1839–60), the author of characteristically ingenuous poems, is the other good poet of the period. He died in his early twenties, shortly after the publication of *Primaveras* (Springs).

2. The second, romantic phase begins with the publication of *Obras Poéticas* (1853) by Álvares de Azevedo (1831–52) and is characterized by individualism, subjectivism, and pessimism. Least B. of all, these poets cultivated the worst habits and practices of the European decadents, and most died young. Along with de Azevedo should be mentioned Junqueira Freire (1832–55). We may add to this group of Byronic, ultra-romantic poets the name of Fagundes Varela (1841–75), whose poetry wavers between patriotism and elegiac themes with epic overtones.

3. The *Condoreira* (from the condor, symbolic of grandeur of flight) school of social poetry (1870–ca. 1880) was linked with abolitionism and the Paraguayan War (1865–70). Now the movement bound itself more closely to B. reality while yet remaining romantic and lyrical. The great "condor" poet, Castro Alves (1847–71), developed a social conscience, turning away from native Indianism to nativist antislavery themes, so felicitously expressing contemporary sentiment that he became one of the most popular poets in Brazil. His verses exude the physical and spiritual anguish of the Negro slave, as do they also the desire of the most progressive elements in Brazil for the abolition of the Empire. His *Os Escravos* (The Slaves, 1883) contains the two poems in which he reaches supreme heights of inspiration: *Vozes de África* (Voices of Africa) and *Navio Negreiro* (Slave Ship). Chronologically, but not thematically, there is an-

other poet of great epic inspiration whose work may be placed within this period. He is Sousândrade (1833–1902), perhaps the best of the romantics, author of *Guesa* (1888), his masterpiece.

Sated with such grandiloquent flights of lang. and with the wild subjectivism of the ultra-romantics, poets welcomed Parnassianism (see PARNASSIANS) as a kind of panacea. Although essentially identical with the Fr. original, the movement shows some tropical modification in Brazil. Alberto de Oliveira (1857–1937), most rigidly Parnassian of the major trio, even so reflects better than the other two the lure of B. nature. Raimundo Correia (1859–1911) is more subtle, musical, pessimistic, of graver and more intense emotion. Olavo Bilac (1865–1918) shows a more facile sensibility, an evident virtuosity, and a fluent, brilliant grace of lang. Parnassianism having entered the country, symbolism (q.v.) inevitably followed and found many disciples, among whom Cruz e Sousa (1863–98) was the major poet reacting to the narrow materialism of the naturalists and the chill polish of the Parnassians. Even though short-lived as an organized literary movement, symbolism persists throughout the first decades of the 20th c. as a seminal influence. The mystic poet par excellence of B. symbolism is Alphonsus de Guimaraens (1870–1921), who found inspiration in the themes of his Catholic faith.

The turn of the century saw a complex of influences in B. lit.: skepticism, the sarcasm of an Oscar Wilde, the defeatist satire of an Eça de Queirós, the "barbaric" meters of a Carducci or a d'Annunzio, the ironic agnosticism of an Anatole France. Poetry was no coherent genre, had no common aim. The best poet from this period is Augusto dos Anjos (1884–1914), a poet from the Baudelairian school whose book of poems, *Eu*, has undergone innumerable editions since its publication in 1912. Constructive action came only in 1922, when a group of young poets in São Paulo organized a *Semana de Arte Moderna* (Modern Art Week) consisting of a series of concerts, lectures, and exposition of the plastic arts, the whole inaugurated with an address by the celebrated novelist Graça Aranha, who lent his support to the new movement. So began B. modernism, not to be confused with other "modernisms."

These poets, at first destructive (first phase, 1922–30) in order to be constructive later, broke with the past, stripped away Parnassian eloquence and symbolist mistiness, cast off logic together with the syntax and vocabulary of Portugal, ignored meter and rhyme in favor of absolutely free verse, extended the scope of poetry to include the most prosaic details of life, and took on a markedly national tone, reinterpreting their country's past and present by stressing the Negro elements in its formation. Among the pioneers of modernism, the principal name is Mário de Andrade (1893–1945), who in 1922 published his *Paulicéia Desvairada* (Hallucinated City), a volume of modern poems that became the bible of B. modernism, as its author came to be called the "Pope of the new creed," a role thrust upon him. Not only a poet, he was a master of modernism in music and the visual art, as well as in aesthetics and crit. Some of the first generation, like Menotti del Picchia (1892–1988) and Guilherme de Almeida (1890–1969), were converts from earlier movements; some, like Ronald de Carvalho (1893–1936), Sérgio Buarque de Hollanda (1902–82), and, greatest of these, Manuel Bandeira (1886–1968), became literary historians and critics also. Bandeira, called "the Saint John the Baptist of the new poetry" for elements in his work prior to 1922, is an independent spirit even though he shared in the establishment of modernism. He warns that the poet must first look to genuine inspiration, and only then to technique. His lang. is simple, but his concepts are not. Besides his verse, his importance lies in his rare ability to interpret B. p. to the public. The world of his poetry is the commonplace daily world, apparently unpoetic yet transmuted by his genius to lyricism.

The first generation São Paulo poets were the most radical, their liveliest leader Oswald de Andrade (1890–1954; no relation to Mário). The cult of nationalism and regionalism permeated the group, united for a time in the magazine *Klaxon* (synonym of "horn"). The ebullient Oswald de Andrade advocated what he termed "primitivism." A restless soul, he later formed the group that published the magazine *Antropofagia* (Cannibalism), a name inspired by Montaigne's famous essay. Opposing such Fr. influence, and indeed all alien "isms," Menotti del Picchia, along with Cassiano Ricardo (1895–1974), who reached the fullness of his powers only much later, Plínio Salgado (1901–75), and others, founded the *verde-amarelo* (green-yellow) group; nationalistic on an Amerindian basis, their magazine was *Anta* (Tapir), an animal which they said symbolized the barbaric original power of the land.

Modernist groups in Rio were less eager to shock the bourgeoisie and tended to be more conservative in general. A representative example would be the group of symbolist inspiration that published *Festa* (Party), to which many modernists contributed. The highest feminine poetic genius of Brazil, Cecília Meireles (1901–64), was a member. Their manifesto included four points: *velocidade* (velocity of expression, not physical speed), *totalidade* (total view of reality in all its aspects), *brasilidade* (B. nationality and reality), and *universalidade* (universality).

The next generation of modernists is nationwide in distribution, but in general their works possess similar characteristics, both philosophical and religious—or, more accurately, sociopolitical and religiomystical. Carlos Drummond de Andrade (1901–87) represents the sociopolitical trend. A master of irony, his *Brejo das Almas* (Fens of Souls, 1934) was one of the most important books of the

decade. Lately this great poet has lost some of his earlier illusions about politics (e.g. belief in socialism or communism as the ideal society) but none of his reverence for poetry. Murilo Mendes (1901–75), Augusto Frederico Schmidt (1906–65), and Cecília Meireles are the finest examples of the religiomystical current. Mendes has written surrealistic poetry, metaphysical in tone; Schmidt has combined biblical inspiration and Whitmanesque rhythms; Meireles has turned to nature and Brazil's heroic past, as well as to medieval Europe, for her material. Vinicius de Morais (1913–80) and Jorge de Lima (1895–1953) must be mentioned. Despite his youth, relative to the first generation, Morais's poetic evolution has brought him closer to those older poets, although his first two books show a sustained gravity of tone in their universal themes, religion and death. Jorge de Lima, who wished to "restore poetry in Christ" and wrote the mystical *A Túnica Inconsútil* (The Seamless Robe, 1938), compellingly presents the Negro theme in *Poemas Negros* (1946). His work is profoundly Christian and wholly B., grave in tone, deliberate in rhythm, and expressed in long lines. His later works, e.g. *Livro de Sonetos* (Book of Sonnets, 1949) and *Invenção de Orfeu* (Invention of Orpheus, 1952), remain constant in feeling if they lack the proselyting force of his earlier poems. Contemporary with the oldest generation, Jorge de Lima showed himself highly versatile as he underwent successive spiritual experiences, ending with a phase of symbolic verse of personal anguish.

The poets who have appeared since 1942 can be categorized only arbitrarily. Some call themselves the "Generation of 1945," although all came on the scene either before or after that year. Amoroso Lima (pseud. Tristão de Ataíde) calls this period *Neomodernismo*, saying that modernism died in 1945. Lêdo Ivo (b. 1924), Domingos Carvalho da Silva (b. 1915), Péricles Eugênio da Silva Ramos (b. 1919), João Cabral de Melo Neto (b. 1920), and Geir Campos (b. 1924) are the principal names among these poets. Meanwhile, the older poets still living continue their creative work, although most have evolved beyond their early phases. Generally there is now a sense of discipline in the construction and polishing of the poem.

In the early Fifties, Concretism (see CONCRETE POETRY) appears on the B. poetic scene, a movement based on the idea that "a poem is a graphic object." Augusto de Campos, Haroldo de Campos, and Décio Pignatari are not only the leaders of the B. concrete movement but also its best poets. With the appearance of concrete poetry a "neo-avant-garde" begins, its main trends being: (1) *poesia-experiência* (poetry as experience), whose main advocate was Mário Faustino (1930–62); (2) *instauração-praxis* (instauration-praxis), proposed by Mário Chamie (b. 1933) in 1962; and (3) *poema-processo* (poem-process), brought forth by Wlademir Dias-Pino (b. 1927). These are the most important poets, but there are others, such as Pedro Xisto,

José Lino Grünewald, and Edgard Braga in the field of Concretism, and Armando Freitas Filho, O. C. Louzada Filho, and Antônio Carlos Cabral, who were interested in praxis experimentation. In the early Sixties, a group of young poets of São Paulo, incl. Álvaro Alves de Faria, Carlos Felipe Moisés, Cláudio Willer, Eduardo Alves da Costa, and Roberto Piva, published *Antologia dos Novíssimos* (Anthology of the Newest, 1962), where is notorious the influence of Fernando Pessoa, Carlos Drummond de Andrade, Murilo Mendes, and Jorge de Lima. Lindolf Bell, an inspired poet of the state of Santa Catarina, was also linked with the group. In the same year appeared in Rio de Janeiro *Violão de Rua* (Guitar of the Street) gathering poets of socialist temper, such as Ferreira Gullar, Moacir Félix, Geir Campos, José Paulo Paes, Félix de Ataíde, and Afonso Romano de Sant'Anna. During the 1970s and early '80s, the neo-avant-garde movement reduced in force considerably; a new trend began to make itself felt, political poetry, whose principal voice is Ferreira-Gullar (b. 1930), a "concrete" poet turned political. A similar evolution is evident in the poetry of Afonso Romano de Sant'Anna. José Paulo Paes has had a phase of concrete experimentation which did not, however, interrupt his deep and remarkable inclination for irony and the epigram.

Other poets who have been creating their poems independently of the tensions produced by the avant-garde and the political situation, or who can be considered latecomers, can be mentioned: Joaquim Cardozo, a poet of symbolist accent with modernist and formalist inflection; Dante Milano, a poet of classic modulation; Sosígenes Costa, author of sonnets of plastic reverberations; Carlos Nejar, a lyric poet with epic accent; Mário Quintana, an older poet in the symbolist trad.; Henriqueta Lisboa and Alphonsus de Guimarãens Filho, both also of symbolist accent; Paulo Bonfim, an heir of Guilherme de Almeida and a modernist poet of the lyrical trad. and the "Generation of '45"; Gerardo de Melo Mourão, Tiago de Melo, Geraldo Pinto Rodrigues, Alberto da Costa e Silva, and João Paulo Moreira da Fonseca, followers of the "Generation of '45" but not always obeying its rules with strictness; Armindo Trevisan and Adélia Prado, who have cultivated a lyricism of mystic inflection; and Walmir Ayala, Gilberto Mendonça Teles, Hilda Hilst, Olga Savary, Renata Pallotini, and Marly de Oliveira, whose work revives the line and the poem after years of the iconoclasm of the avant-garde. See also GAUCHO POETRY; PORTUGUESE POETRY; SPANISH AMERICAN POETRY.

ANTHOLOGIES: F. A. de Varnhagen, *Florilégio da Poesia Brasileira*, 3 v. (1850–63)—v. 1 is a historical sketch of B. letters and a pioneer work of great probity; *Antol. dos Poetas Bras. da Fase Romântica*, 2d ed. (1940), *Antol. dos Poetas Bras. da Fase Parnasiana*, 2d ed. (1940), *Apresentação da Poesia Bras.*, 2d ed. (1954), all ed. M. Bandeira—excellent intros., with crit. essay, to B. p.; *Panorama do Movimento Simbolista Bras.*, ed. A. Muricy, 3 v. (1951–52)—anthol. of B. symbolist verse with bio. and bibl. notes; *Panorama da Poesia Bras.*, ed. M. da Silva Brito, 6 v. (1959); *Mod. B. P.*, ed. and tr. J. Nist (1962)—brief but informed intro.; *Poesia do Ouro* (1964), *Poesia Romântica* (1965), *Poesia Simbolista* (1965), *Poesia Barroca*, (1967), *Poesia Moderna* (1967), *Poesia Parnasiana* (1967), all ed. P. E. da Silva Ramos; *Anthol. of 20th-C. B. P.*, ed. E. Bishop (1972); *B. P., 1950–1980*, ed. E. Brasil and W. J. Smith (1983).

HISTORY AND CRITICISM: S. Romero, *História da Lit. Bras.*, 5th enl. ed., 5 v. (1888; 1953–54)—sociological attitude causes bias, but still fundamental, though should be reevaluated in light of subsequent crit.; I. Goldberg, *Studies in B. Lit.* (1922)—a pioneer work in Eng.; A. A. Lima, *Estudos*, 6 v. (1927–33)—crit. essays on many subjects, incl. poetry, *Contribuição à Hist. do Modernismo, I: O. Pré-Modernismo* (1939), *Poesia Bras. Contemporânea* (1942); A. Grieco, *Evolução da Poesia Bras.* (1932); R. de Carvalho, *Pequena Hist. da Lit. Bras.*, 7th ed. (1944)—valuable for crit. opinions, his attitude a synthesis of Romero and Veríssimo; S. Putnam, *Marvelous Journey* (1948)—comprehensive, very readable intro. in Eng.; José Veríssimo, *Hist. da Lit. Bras.*, 3d ed. (1954)—coldly objective on art as such, with scant attention to artist or society, but still basic; M. Bandeira, *Brief Hist. of B. Lit.* tr. R. E. Dimmick (1958)—valuable despite its brevity for the insight of an active participant in B. p.; A. Bosi, *História Concisa da Lit. Bras.* (1970)—useful handbook with sharp analysis of B. poets from a sociological point of view; M. Moisés, *História da Lit. Bras.*, 3 v. (1982–85); *A Lit. no Brasil*, ed. A. Coutinho, 3d ed., 6 v. (1986)—the most ambitious attempt yet at a collaborative lit. hist. of Brazil on aesthetic principles.

L.L.B.; M.MO.

BRETON POETRY. The lang. of Lower Brittany in France (*Breizh Izel*) belongs, like Welsh and Cornish, to the Brythonic or "P"-Celtic Group, and is derived from the speech of settlers from southwest Britain who left their homeland from the 5th to the 7th c. when the Saxons were encroaching from the east. There is evidence, from Marie de France and others, that med. B. poets sang of heroes and romance, and that these lost compositions were the source of Marie's own form, the *lai* (q.v.); but the earliest B. p. to survive dates from the 14th c. and consists of only a few scraps of verse. Fewer than 20 lines are all that remain of a body of popular verse in an indigenous metrical system related to that of early Welsh. The main feature is the occurrence in each line of a form of internal rhyme very similar to the *cynghanedd lusg* (q.v.): "An hegu*en* am lou*enas* / An hegar*at* en lac*at* glas" (Her smile gladdened me, / The blue-eyed love). The native prosody survived to the 17th c., when it was superseded by the Fr. system of syllable-counting and end rhyme.

BRETON POETRY

After the Treaty of Union between Brittany and France (1532), dialectal fragmentation set in, and four main dialects emerged: those of Léon, Tréguier, Cornouailles, and Vannes. Following the lead of the grammarian Le Gonidec (1775–1838), however, B. writers have endeavored to establish a cultivated literary norm, so that most works published nowadays are accessible to all contemporary readers.

Most of the verse from the 15th to the beginning of the 19th c. consists of works of religious edification, hymns, carols, a Book of Hours, and the long and dreary *Mirouer de la mort* (1519). One poem stands out: *Buhez Mabden*, a powerful meditation on death printed in 1530 but probably written a century earlier. The prophetic *Dialog etre Arzur Roe d'an Bretoned ha Gwynglaff* dates back to 1450. There are also numerous plays in verse. A few popular plays, such as the *Pevar Mab Emon* are based on chivalric romances, but most derive from the Bible and saints' lives. The influence of Fr. models is evident, with a few notable exceptions, mainly mystery plays which recount the lives of Celtic saints.

New stirrings begin with the two mock-epic poems of Al Lae (close of the 18th c.), but the real impetus comes with the rise of 19th-c. romanticism. The great event is the appearance in 1839 of La Villemarqué's *Barzaz Breiz* (Poetry of Brittany), whose contents have been shown by recent scholarship to be more ancient and more authentic than was hitherto believed. The effect was profound. A romantic vision of the B. past was created which stirred the imagination of many and led to new literary enthusiasm. Luzel was impelled to collect B. folk p., of which there were two main kinds: the *gwerzioù*, usually dramatic in form, simple and direct in style, and concerned with local events and folklore; and the *sonioù*, more lyrical verse, including love songs and satires.

Prosper Proux recounted his escapades with rough humor in his native Cornouailles dialect in 1839, though by 1866 he had acquired a more "literary" (and less vigorous) expression. The Vannetais dialect was used mostly by priests who found inspiration in their faith and in their love for their native land. Esp. popular were Msgr. Joubiouz' *Doue ha mem bro* (1844) and Joakim Gwilhom's imitation of Virgil's *Georgics, Livr el labourer* (1849). From the 1850s to the 80s, only minor talents emerged. Living uprooted from the B. countryside, these poets expressed in artificial diction their love of the simple life, of the homeland, and of their inheritance which was no longer secure. This nostalgic trad. was maintained and reinvigorated in the '90s by the rich lyricism of Taldir and the more artistic Erwan Berthou, but the outstanding poet of their generation was Yann Ber Kalloc'h, killed in action in 1917. His poems, written in Vannetais and published posthumously, express strong religious and patriotic convictions enhanced by a rich and powerful imagery.

The 20th c. has seen the vigorous growth of B. literary periodicals, each with its coterie. Vannetais writers found expression in *Dihunamb*, edited by the poet-peasant Loeiz Herrieu. The *Gwalarn* group, under the leadership of Roparz Hémon, proved by far the most talented and creative. Maodez Glanndour and Roparz Hémon stand out from the group, although nearly all were gifted poets. *Gwalarn* did not survive the "Libération," but patriotic young writers launched new publications. Most did not last. The single exception was *Al Liamm*: under the guidance of Ronan Huon, it became the leading B. literary journal. In their poetry, Huon and his contemporaries Youenn Olier, Per Denez, and Per Diolier, later joined by Youenn Gwernig and Reun ar C'halan, have respected the literary standards set by *Gwalarn*. Women have also played a significant role in the survival of B. p., esp. Anjela Duval, Vefa de Bellaing, Benead, Naïg Rozmor, Tereza, and, more recently, Maï Jamin and Annaïg Renault. The journal *Brud* (now *Brud Nevez*), founded in 1957, counted one of the best contemporary poets, Per Jakez Hélias, among its first contributors. The 1960s witnessed a strong resurgence of B. nationalism. The *Union Démocratique Bretonne*, created in 1964, attracted several young militant poets: Paol Keineg, Yann Ber Piriou, Erwan Evenou, and Sten Kidna. Other poets have since come to the fore: Abanna, Alan Botrel, Yann-Baol an Noalleg, Koulizh Kedez, Padrig an Habask, Gwendal and Herle Denez, Tudual Huon, Bernez Tangi, to name but a few. Since 1974, the journal *Skrid* has welcomed new writers.

Finally, songs have always been an important part of the B. poetic heritage. This trad. has been maintained by a number of popular singers: Glenmor, Youenn Gwernig, Jili Servat, Jef Philippe, Louis Bodénès, and the internationally famous Alan Stivell. B. may be a threatened lang., but B. p. remains very much alive.

ANTHOLOGIES: *Barzaz Breiz*, ed. H. de la Villemarqué (1839); *Gwerzioù Breiz Izel*, ed. F. M. Luzel, 2 v. (1868–74); *Sonioù Breiz Izel*, ed. F. M. Luzel and A. le Braz, 2 v. (1890); *Barzhaz: kant barzhoneg berr, 1350–1953*, ed. P. Denez (1953); *Défense de cracher par terre et de parler breton*, ed. Y. B. Piriou (1971); *Le Livre d'Or de la Bretagne*, ed. P. Durand (1975); *Du a Gwyn*, ed. D. M. Jones and M. Madeg (1982); *Barzhonegoù*, ed. Skrid (1986).

SURVEYS: F. Gourvil, *Langue et Littérature bretonnes* (1952); *Istor Lennegezh Vrezhonek an Amzer-Vremañ*, ed. Abeozen [i.e. Y. F. M. Eliès] (1957); Y. Olier, *Istor hol lennegezh "Skol Walarn,"* 2 v. (1974–75); Y. Bouëssel du Bourg and Y. Brekilien, "La littérature bretonne," *La Bretagne*, ed. Y. Brekilien (1982); J. Gohier and R. Huon, *Dictionnaire des écrivains d'aujourd'hui en Bretagne* (1984).

PROSODY: E. Ernault, *L'Ancien Vers Breton* (1912); F. Kervella, *Diazezoù ar sevel gwerzioù* (1965).
D.M.L.; R.G.

BREVE

BREVE. See QUANTITY; SCANSION.

BREVIS BREVIANS. See IAMBIC SHORTENING.

BREVIS IN LONGO. See ANCEPS.

BRIDGE (Gr. *zeugma*). In metrics, bs. are constraints on word end at certain locations within the line. In Cl. prosody (q.v.), the most important bs. in (1) the iambic trimeter (see TRIMETER) are the following: (a) Knox's trochee b.: in the iambographers (Archilochus, Semonides, Solon, Hipponax), a trochaic wordshape may not end in third *anceps* (q.v.), and is still somewhat constrained in tragedy. (b) Porson's b.: after long third *anceps* outside of comedy, no full word boundary may occur. (c) There is also evidence for a general, if weak, constraint on word end after short third *anceps*. (d) Knox's iamb b.: an iambic wordshape may not end in fifth *longum* in the iambographers. (e) Wilamowitz' b.: a spondaic wordshape may not end in fifth *longum* in the iambographers. (f) Word boundary should not split a resolution or substitution (qq.v.) or divide them from the following syllable. Each of the foregoing bs. has its counterpart in the trochaic tetrameter (q.v.).

The most important bs. in (2) the dactylic hexameter (see HEXAMETER) are: (a) Iterated trochaic division of the first and second feet before a feminine caesura is avoided in all styles. A line beginning

$$- \cup \quad \cup - \cup \quad \cup - \cup$$

autis epeita pedonde
(*Odyssey* 11.598)

is rare and probably more constrained when all three words are lexical. (b) Meyer's b.: trochaic division of the second foot is not permitted before a masculine caesura in Callimachus unless either the word before the division or the word after it is nonlexical. (c) Hermann's b.: trochaic division of the fourth foot is strongly avoided. (d) Bulloch's b.: in Callimachus, if a word ends with the third foot, the verse must have a regular caesura and a bucolic diaeresis, and the syntactic boundary at either or both of the latter positions must be of higher rank than the boundary at the end of the third foot. Callimachus would not permit a line such as

$$- - \quad - \quad - - \quad \quad \cup \cup \quad - - - \quad \cup \cup - x$$

ede gar deron chronon allelon apechonta
(*Iliad* 14.206)

(e) Spondee zeugma: word end after contraction (– for $\cup \cup$) is avoided in the fourth foot, rare in the second, and practically excluded in the fifth. In Callimachus, the zeugma is stricter.

There are also constraints on nonfinal heavy syllables in arsis (q.v.) which are clearly related to some bs. For example, type (1e) above cannot be subsumed along with (1d) under a generalized constraint on disyllables, so that the initial heavy syllable of spondee-shaped words is independently constrained. Furthermore, in the iambographers, words of the shape $- - \cup$ x are strongly avoided beginning in third *anceps*. In the hexameter, words of the shape $- -$ x are strongly avoided beginning in the arsis of the fifth foot. These constraints unite with the bs. to form a finely structured hierarchy of strictness according to genre and style.

The definition of a b. as a point in the verse line where word end is forbidden is adequate for certain descriptive and philological purposes like identifying corrupt lines, but in offering no explanation it obscures more than it reveals. Some bs., such as Knox's bs. (1a, 1d), are apparently simple constraints on patterned iteration of word end. Others, like Bulloch's b. (2d), are constraints against potential phrase boundary. A third group of bs. (incl. Porson's b. [1b], which is often regarded as prototypical, and the constraints against "split" resolution [1f]) are not, properly speaking, sensitive to word end at all. What is constrained by these latter is how the syllables of the word are mapped onto arsis and thesis (q.v.). Word end is simply the right edge of the domain within which syllables are rhythmically organized for speech. Apparent exceptions to b. rules generally involve function words (e.g. articles, pronouns, prepositions), which coalesce with their head word into a single domain, or fixed phrases. Some styles of verse allow function words at bs. with great freedom, others much less so: this variation reflects the degree to which a verse style allows itself access to fluent speech.

R. Porson, *Euripidis Hecuba*, 2d ed. (1802); G. Hermann, *Orphica* (1805); J. Hilberg, *Das Prinzip der Silbenwaegung und die daraus entspringenden Gesetze der Endsilben in der griechischen Poesie* (1879); W. Meyer, "Zur Gesch. des griechischen und lateinischen Hexameters," *SBAW* (1884); L. Havet, *Cours élémentaire de métrique grecque et latine* (1896); Wilamowitz; A. D. Knox, "The Early Iambus," *Philologus* 87 (1932); Maas; A. W. Bulloch, "A Callimachean Refinement of the Gr. Hexameter," *CQ* 20 (1970); W. S. Allen, *Accent and Rhythm* (1973); A. M. Devine and L. D. Stephens, "Bs. in the Iambographers," *GRBS* 22 (1981), *Lang. and Metre* (1984); Snell; West.　　A.M.D.; L.D.S.

BRIGADE. See PLEIADE.

BROADSIDE BALLAD, street ballad. A song printed on a single sheet and hawked about the streets, esp. in British towns and country fairs during the period 1500–1920 and in Germany. The broadsheet was usually decorated with a crude woodcut or border and recommended that the song be sung to a popular tune, though musical notation was seldom given. Their authors were often maligned as "pot poets," a reference to the alehouse. Although the bs. were mainly doggerel (q.v.) verse, and their subjects most often topical songs, political satire, love lyrics, violent crimes, and executions, literary poetry was occasionally vended on broadsheets. Gascoigne says that their form was usually *ababcc* sixains in 8s and 6s, or sometimes decasyllables, but ballad meter (q.v.) must have been equally common. Their popularity is attested by the frequency of attacks on them in the Ren. (Falstaff threatens Prince Hal with them in *1 Henry 4*) and by a Parliamentary ban in 1649. Several of the Ren. miscellanies contain them, particularly *A Handful of Pleasant Delights* (1584). Many b. bs. were remade by rural trad. into folksong; reciprocally, folksongs were sometimes printed as bs. In America the three of four decades after the Civil War were the heyday of b. balladry, whose last stronghold is to be found in Afro-Am. communities before World War I.

In Germany the *Bänkelsang* or *Moritat* was a similar kind of ballad sung at fairs and markets from the 17th to the 20th c., also sensational and didactic in content; but characteristically the *Bänkelsänger* stood on a platform (*Bank*) and depicted scenes from the story on a poster (*Schild*) while the texts were hawked. In the 19th c. these songs were assimilated to the literary ballad and political parody, esp. after the 1848 Revolution, and, with Wedekind and Holz, to the cabaret. Brecht ("Die Moritat von Mackie Messer," 1928) and other 20th-c. poets have continued to write them.

F. Rebiczek, *Der Wiener Volks- und Bänkelsang 1800–1848* (1913); H. E. Rollins, "The Black-Letter B. B.," *PMLA* 34 (1919); *Bänkelsang und Singspiel vor Goethe*, ed. F. Brüggemann (1937); *The Common Muse*, ed. V. de Sola Pinto and A. E. Rodway (1957); E. Janda and F. Nötzhold, *Die Moritat vom Bänkelsang oder Lied von der Strasse* (1959); L. Shepard, *The B. B.* (1962); K. V. Riedel, *Der Bänkelsang* (1963); K. Riha, *Song, Bänkelsang: Gesch. der modernen Ballade* (1965); C. M. Simpson, *The British B. B. and Its Music* (1966); *Later Eng. B. Bs.*, ed. J. Holloway and J. Black (1975); E. Seemann, "Bänkelsänger," *Reallexikon* 1.128–29; N. Würzbach, *The Rise of the Eng. Street Ballad 1550–1650* (tr. 1990). T.V.F.B.; A.B.F.

BROKEN RHYME (Ger. *gebrochener Reim*, Fr. *rime enjambée*), sometimes "rhyme-breaking," is the Eng. term for the division (hyphenation) of a word at the end of a line in order to produce a rhyme with the word ending the next line: e.g. "for *get-* / *ful . . . debt*" (Pope); "*tu-*tor *. . . U-* / niversity (George Canning). In Eng., poets from Shakespeare to Ogden Nash have used b. r. for comic and satiric effects; it is one of the innumerable rhyme tricks up Byron's sleeve. Gerard Manley Hopkins uses it as a resource for serious poetry, e.g. in "The Windhover" and "To what serves Mortal Beauty?" even going so far as to pick up isolated sounds from the beginning of the following line to make the r. ("at the door / Drowned" rhymes with "reward"); this he called the "rove over" rhyme. B. rs. have also been used by Donne (*Satyres* 3 and 4)

and e e cummings, but while it is a novelty in Eng., it has been used in modern Fr. poetry by Aragon and was developed extensively in Rus. poetry, particularly in the work of the 20th-c. poets Velimir Xlebnikov and Joseph Brodsky.

Breaking is however a a more general phenomenon of verse-structure which results from the manipulation of morphology; unrhymed verse can also be broken at line-end by enjambment (q.v.), which should be seen as the counterpart of b. r. in rhymed verse. Note too that the effect relies partly on visual form, and that, for all the "breaking," the binding of the syllables within the broken word is in fact stronger than the line-end—hence the tension. But the prosodic terminology is unstable: Ger. *Reimbrechung* denotes, rather, systematic rhyme-breaking against syntax in rhymed couplets by ending sentences at the ends of the first lines of the couplets, which the Eng. call "open couplets"; and while Eng. usage sometimes distinguishes b. r. from mosaic r. (q.v.), Ger. (*Spaltreim*, "split r.") does not. Cf. CHAIN RHYME. T.V.F.B.

BUCOLIC is the ancient term for that type of poetry which would now generally be called pastoral (q.v.). Virgil's ten pastoral poems, to which he refers as "pastorem carmen" in the fourth georgic (q.v.) and to which the term "eclogue" (q.v.) is now generally applied, were called "bs." by the Lat. grammarians. During the Ren. and 17th c., there was a critical tendency to reserve the term "b." for Virgil's *Eclogues* and imitations of them: the critics argued that in primitive times wealthy men were the keepers of cattle, not of sheep or goats, and since pastorals in the Virgilian trad. portray people of culture and refinement, it would be more accurate to use the term "b." to refer to poems of this type. See ECLOGUE; GEORGIC; IDYLL; PASTORAL.—G. Knaack, "Bukolik," in Pauly-Wissowa, 3.998 ff.; J. Hubaux, *Les Thèmes bucoliques dans la poésie latine* (1930); A. S. F. Gow, *Theocritus* (1950); *Europäische Bukolik und Georgic*, ed. K. Garber (1976); C. Segal, *Poetry and Myth in Ancient P.* (1981); D. M. Halperin, *Before P.: Theocritus and the Ancient Trad. of B. Poetry* (1983); K. Krautter, *Die Ren. der Bukolik in der lateinischen Literatur des XIV Jhs.* (1983); *Theokrit und die griechische Bukolik*, ed. B. Effe (1986); E. A. Schmidt, *Bukolische Leidenschaft* (1987); B. Effe and G. Binder, *Die antike Bukolik: Eine Einfuhrung* (1989). J.E.C.; T.V.F.B.

BUCOLIC DIAERESIS. See DIAERESIS; HEXAMETER.

BULGARIAN POETRY. Though B. culture is very ancient, modern B. lit.—incl. B. p.—came into its own only in the decades immediately preceding the country's political liberation in the Russo-Turkish War of 1877–78. Poetry, and esp. lyric poetry, has, however, claimed a prominent place in B. lit. in the 20th c.

Pre-liberation poets like Petko Slavejkov (1827–95) were not very prolific; moreover, they limited themselves largely to nationalistic themes. The one great poet of that epoch, Xristo Botev (1848–76), killed in the April Uprising of 1876 against the Turks, left a small group of superb lyrics in which he voiced his homeland's aspirations for freedom and other socially radical ideas.

Botev did not live to see an independent Bulgaria, but his contemporary Ivan Vazov (1850–1921) did. Vazov, who eventually achieved the status of the B. national writer, celebrated in his lyric poetry the beauties of his native land and the virtues of his people, and, in such works as the narrative poems comprising *The Epic of the Forgotten* (early 1880s), immortalized the heroes of the B. liberation. Poetry was a major component of Vazov's body of work.

By the turn of the century, the national pride expressed in Vazov's writing over the previous two decades was yielding to internationalism, forms of symbolism and modernism, and variants on individualism. Petko's son Penčo Slavejkov (1866–1912) reverted to the liberation as the subject of his ambitious but unfinished narrative *Song of Blood*. Designed as an epic of European rather than merely B. scope, the work did not measure up to its author's hopes.

Slavejkov was not a born poet, but others of his generation were, esp. Pejo Javorov (1877–1914), one of Bulgaria's finest lyric poets but a victim of metaphysical despair whose career ended in suicide, and Dimčo Debeljanov (1887–1916), the most prominent B. writer killed in World War I. Toward the end of his short life, Debeljanov's verse reflected the influence of symbolism, which took root in B. lit. quite late.

After World War I, the paths of those who had crowded the symbolist highroad before the war diverged. One group of poets brought B. symbolism to its zenith during the 1920s, when the movement had faded elsewhere. A poet's poet among this group was Nikolaj Liliev (1885–1960), who achieved great formal perfection in but a small number of poems on a narrow range of subjects. But the chief theoretician and practitioner of B. symbolism (though he had begun to publish well before 1914) was Teodor Trajanov (1882–1945). He led the battle in favor of symbolist doctrine during the 1920s through the journal *Hyperion*, which he edited; he published his best-known collection of symbolist poetry in 1929.

The other group of symbolists and modernists at war's end deserted their previous allegiances to embrace Marxism and social radicalism. This group included Ljudmil Stojanov (1888–1973), who after 1944 became a major literary power in communist Bulgaria. But most radical writers of the 1920s did not survive nearly so long as Stojanov: poets like Xristo Jasenov (1889–1925) and Geo Milev (1895–1925) perished in the wave of political repressions which swept over the country in 1923–25. Indeed, Milev was arrested for publishing a narrative poem, *September*, celebrating the anti-government uprisings of 1923 which engendered the repressions. Milev's earlier modernism left a considerable imprint on his radical poetry, which was also influenced by that of Vladimir Majakovskij. Other lyric poets of radical persuasion included Xristo Smirnenski (1898–1923), author of verse both gentle and satirical, who died very early of tuberculosis; and Nikola Vapcarov (1909–42), whose work called his countrymen to the bright future of communism and who was executed by the government for resistance activities during World War II.

Over the complicated but very interesting period between the two World Wars, a number of fine poets who were neither symbolists nor communists gathered around the leading literary journal of the day, *Zlatorog*, edited by the critic Vladimir Vasilev (1883–1963). In its pages appeared the leading B. woman poet of this century, Elisaveta Bagrjana (b. 1893), whose lyrics spoke of the modern age of machinery, steel, and concrete, but also of individual liberation from social obligations. Bagrjana wandered freely through the world; in time she also acknowledged the bonds created by love and human closeness.

Asen Razcvetnikov (1897–1951) and Nikola Furnadžiev (1903–68) joined the *Zlatorog* group in the mid 1920s after breaking with the communist movement, but their poetry of the late 1920s and early 1930s expressed a cosmic nihilism which can be traced back to poets of an earlier generation such as Stojan Mixajlovski (1856–1927), who set forth pessimistic and aristocratic views in his narrative and lyric poetry. Another characteristic poet of the period, one whose verse displayed religious overtones, was Emanuil Popdimitrov (1887–1943).

Bulgaria between the wars was an overwhelmingly peasant country which boasted a powerful Agrarian political movement. That movement, however, found little literary expression. Rural Bulgaria found its finest voice in the work of Nikola Rakitin (1885–1934), who took no interest in politics and was determined to remain close to the land. In contrast, the communist transformation of B. society after 1944 had profound repercussions in lit., esp. in the years before Stalin's death, when even Ivan Vazov was regarded with suspicion. At such a time only dedicated communist bureaucrats like Xristo Radevski (b. 1903) could flourish (he presided over the Union of B. Writers, (1949–58), whereas an idealistic communist poet like Penjo Penev (1930–59) ended by taking his own life.

The guardian of poetic integrity during the high Stalinist period was Atanas Dalčev (1904–78), whose lyric output beginning in the 1920s was very limited but of exquisite quality. During the literary repressions after 1944 Dalčev fell silent in principled protest; and thus when, in the early 1960s, it became possible to write more freely, an entire generation of technically skilled younger poets looked to him with admiration. Some among them, like Konstantin Pavlov (b. 1933), went much further than he to become genuine poetic dissidents, and therefore became very popular with young audiences. Others, like Valeri Petrov (b. 1920), specialized in poetic satire with a bite. Still others, like Blaga Dimitrova (b. 1922) or Krastjo Stanišev (b. 1933), confined themselves firmly to personal themes, or else historical topics, incl. medieval ones, which have always had a strong appeal to the B. mind, but esp. so in recent years, as B. culture has sought to recover a sense of its past. B. p. has also survived among the postwar political emigration, as in the work of Christo Ognjanoff (b. 1911), now a resident of West Germany. Poetry has always occupied a place of honor in B. letters. In the hands of the very capable contemporary generation of B. poets, it seems certain to maintain that footing into the future. For discussion of B. prosody, see SLAVIC PROSODY.

ANTHOLOGIES: *Under the Eaves of a Forgotten Village: Sixty Poems from Contemp. Bulgaria*, ed. J. R. Colombo and N. Roussanoff (1975); *Mod. B. P.*, ed. B. Bojilov, tr. R. Macgregor-Hastie (1976); *Südwinde: Neuere bulgarische Lyrik*, ed. C. Ognjanoff (1978); *Anthol. of B. P.*, tr. P. Tempest (1980); *Poets of Bulgaria*, ed. W. Meredith, tr. J. Balaban (1985).

HISTORY AND CRITICISM: D. Markov, *Bolgarskaja poezija pervoj četverti XX veka* (1959); R. Likova, *Za njakoi osobenosti na balgarskata poezija 1923–1944* (1962); *B. Poets of Our Day: Lit. Sketches*, tr. E. Mladenova and B. Tonchev (1971); C. Moser, *A Hist. of B. Lit. 865–1944* (1972).   C.A.M.

BURDEN, *burthen* (OE *byrthen*; OHG *burdin*—constantly confused with *bourdon, burdoun*, from Fr. *bourdon*, S *bordin*—there is little or no separation of the two words from the earliest citations in the OED): (a) in the Eng. Bible (cf. *onus* in the Vulgate), tr. from Heb. *massa*, a raising of the voice, utterance, oracle; (b) the bass or undersong, accompaniment (the same as *bourdon*): "For burden-wise I'll hum on Tarquin still"—Shakespeare, *Lucrece* 1133—cf. Chaucer's obscene pun about the Summoner, *Gen. Prol.* 673; (c) the chief theme, the leading sentiment or matter of a song or poem: "The burden or leading idea of every couplet was the same"—L. Hunt, *Men, Women, & Books* 1.11.199; (d) the refrain or chorus of a song: "Foot it featly here and there; And, sweet sprites, the burden bear. Hark, hark! *Burden dispersedly.* Bow-wow."—Shakespeare, *Tempest* 1.2.381; in particular, the refrain line in the carol (q.v.). Cf. RITORNELLO.—R. H. Robbins, "The B. in Carols," *MLN* 57 (1942); R. L. Greene, *The Early Eng. Carols*, 2d ed. (1977).   R.O.E.; T.V.F.B.

BURLESQUE. A b. is a literary work that mocks serious lit. by marrying a well-known form to an incongruous content; it uses nonsense, satire, or vulgarity to underline the incongruity, crucial for the effect, which may range from amusing to savage. Lewis Carroll's nonsense poem is a b. of the nursery rhyme:

> Twinkle, twinkle, little bat!
> How I wonder what you're at!
> Up above the world you fly,
> Like a teatray in the sky.

This one parodies Joyce Kilmer: "I think that I shall never hear / A poem lovely as a beer." The earliest extant bs. are Cl. Gr., esp. the mock-epic *Batrachomyomachia* (Battle of the Frogs and the Mice) and passages in the plays of Aristophanes that mock Euripides. The importance of dramatic bs. and travesties has continued unabated throughout Western theatrical trad. (Jacobs and Johnson; Clinton-Baddeley). One well-known branch of b. is the mock heroic (see MOCK EPIC): we laugh to hear a chicken declaiming like a hero from a medieval romance (Chaucer's *Nun's Priest's Tale*). An important related form is the travesty, a good example of which is Paul Scarron's *Virgile travestie* (1648–52), one of many that enjoyed a vogue in 17th-c. France. Another branch of b. is Hudibrastic verse (q.v.), which takes its name from Samuel Butler's *Hudibras* (1663–64), a poem that jeers at the Presbyter Hudibras by recounting his adventures as if he were a noble knight in jogging octosyllables with unexpected rhymes for satirical purposes.

One problem in defining b. is the difficulty of specifying precise boundaries or distinctions among the forms of b., parody, travesty, and pastiche. There is no clear critical agreement on which of these forms is a subclass of the other. As early as 1811, John Poole wrote that "the terms *b.* and *travesty* are properly distinct, b. being more *general* in its application, travesty more *particular*: the former is leveled against blemishes and defects, which its object is to expose and ridicule, and pleases by *comparison*; the latter is constructed upon the various excellencies of any *particular* work, and derives its effect solely from the force of *contrast*" (Jacobs and Johnson 10); but how these terms are related to parody in Poole's mind is less clear. Karrer reviews the terminology but does not offer suggestions for making it more precise, concluding that "the classifications reveal their inadequacies all too clearly." Bond and Broich both regard b. as the dominant form, a choice with which Karrer concurs, although he disagrees with their definition and arrangement of subclasses. Weisstein places parody (q.v.) above b. and regards mock-heroic as a form separate from b.; Markiewicz regards parody, travesty, and b. as roughly equal forms. Karrer himself subdivides b. into forms that depend on incongruity (parody and travesty) and those which are more mechanical (pastiches).

Agonizing over such schemes might in itself seem to b. the critical process were it not for the fact that, in practice, critical discussions of specific works show a dismaying lack of agreement in terminology. Following Addison, Bond discusses *Don Quixote* as an example of b., and Jump agrees with him, while Rose identifies it as parody; to round things out, Bond quotes Pope's identification of *Don Quixote* as a mock-epic and notes Voltaire's claim that it is Menippean satire. In the face of such a diversity of usages, rigid and absolute distinctions seem impossible. But in practice at least some distinctions would seem useful. Pastiche and parody both imitate a work's form and content, although in pastiche imitation is an end in itself, while in parody the imitation is a means to mockery. B. retains the form of a work and mocks the content, while travesty retains the content and mocks the form. It is also important to recognize what is shared by all these forms: all are essentially conservative, all depend on imitation (q.v.), all make their greatest appeal to an audience familiar with their source works. In other words, these comedies of imitation assume that a canon (q.v.) of lit. exists, that it can be mocked by irreverent imitation, and that its readers will recognize and welcome such mockery. A b. may implicitly criticize its target, but it also thereby reasserts, implicitly, the target's importance. See also FARCE.

K. F. Flögel, *Geschichten des Burlesken* (1794); E. Gosse, "B.," *Selected Essays* (1928); G. Kitchin, *A Survey of B. and Parody in Eng.* (1931); R. P. Bond, *Eng. B. Poetry, 1700–1750* (1932); V. C. Clinton-Baddeley, *The B. Trad. in the Eng. Theatre after 1660* (1952); I. Jack, *Augustan Satire* (1952); F. Bar, *Le Genre b. en France au 17th siècle* (1960); U. Weisstein, "Parody, Travesty, and B.," *Proc. 4th Congress of the ICLA* (1966); H. Markiewicz, "On the Def. of Literary Parody," *To Honor Roman Jakobson* (1967); U. Broich, *Studien zum Komischen Epos* (1968); J. D. Jump, *B.* (1972); H. Jacobs and C. Johnson, *Annot. Bibl. of Shakespearean B., Parody, and Travesty* (1973); W. Karrer, *Parodie, Travestie, Pastiche* (1977); M. Rose, *Parody // Meta-Fiction* (1979); P. Bec, *B. et obscenite chez les troubadours* (1984); A. L. Martin, *Cervantes and the B. Sonnet* (1991).   F.T.

BURMESE POETRY. Many B. poems have been discovered in stone inscriptions dating from A.D. 1310 onward. The passages describing the glory and achievements of kings and princes, and the noble lineage of queens and princesses, are usually in verse, as are also prayers for the donor and his friends and curses on those who damage his benefaction. These stone poems were clearly designed to be permanent records.

Side by side with these there existed another kind of poetry, less formal and more emotional in character. This was scratched with stylus on palm-leaves; the best known of the older specimens is dated A.D. 1455. From the 15th to the last quarter of the 19th c., under the patronage of Buddhist monarchs, poems of varied lengths and on varied subjects were composed by monks (Shin Thi-la-wun-tha, Shin Ra-hta-tha-ra), courtiers (Na-wa-de the First and Nat-shin-naung), or royal ladies (Mi Hpyu and the Hlaing Princess). Their poems were not addressed to posterity but to royal patrons or loved ones.

There are altogether more than 50 different kinds of poems and songs, among which the most important are: (1) *E-gyin*, historical ballads, some of which were sung as cradle songs, while others informed young princes or princesses of the achievements of their ancestors; (2) *Maw-gun*, panegyric odes, perhaps the oldest type of poem—their subjects range from the arrival at the Court of a white elephant to the conquest of Siam, and from the completion of a canal to an essay on cosmography; (3) *Pyo*, metrical versions of Buddhist and non-Buddhist stories, in narrative or expository form, transferred to a B. setting and made more vivid by small imaginative details, and homilies in verse; (4) *Lin-ga*, (Sanskrit *alaṁkāra*, ornamentation), a variety of *Pyo* but generally shorter, often used as a generic term for all kinds of verse; (5) *Ya-du*, (Sanskrit *ritú*, season), the shortest type, usually of three or fewer stanzas, dealing generally with romantic subjects such as the emotions called forth by the changing seasons, the mood of longing, and memories of loved ones.

The popular generic term for poetry in B. is *kabya lin-ga*, derived from two Sanskrit words, *kāvya*, poetry, and *alaṁkāra*, an ornamentation of sound or sense.

The primary device used to achieve verbal melody in early B. p., in which the basic number of words or syllables in the line is four, is rhyme. Vowel length and stress play virtually no part in its structure. B. is a tonal lang.; syllables are differentiated from one another not only by the consonantal and vocalic elements of which they are composed, but also by pitch and voice quality; and the lang. is largely monosyllabic—that is, broadly speaking, each syllable has a meaning and can be used as a word.

These two features—the rhyme and the number of syllables in a group—are disposed in many arrangements, but the basic scheme is to have a rhyme in the fourth syllable of one line, the third syllable of the second line and the second of the third line, while the fourth syllable of the third line will be the rhyme for the following two lines, and so on. To give an example of this "climbing" rhyme:

> za-tí pon-*nyá*
> gon ma-*ná* -hpyín
> than-*pá* hòn-*sòn*
> hpet-mé *kyòn*-thà
> à-*thòn* htaung-htà.

To have this 4/3/2 scheme throughout the stanza would be monotonous, however, so B. poets introduced six other schemes: 4/3/1, 4/3, 4/2, 4/1,

3/2, and 3/1. The last line of a stanza usually has 5, 7, 9, or 11 syllables.

In other forms of verse which appeared later, the lines may consist of 3, 4, 5, or more syllables. A rhyme may be confined to two lines. And though the climbing principle persists, the rhyme schemes are less rigid and sometimes more elaborate, esp. in drama, which made its debut later than the other genres, in the "mixed style" of prose and poetry. These forms, however, are variations of the basic scheme. Embellishments of the sense are chiefly similes, metaphors, tropes, hyperboles, allusions, synonyms, and verbal gymnastics.

The last century has witnessed the advent of the printing press, the cessation of royal patronage in 1885, the intro. of Eng. education, the founding of the University of Rangoon in 1920, and the creation of the Union of Burma in 1948. During this eventful period B. p. underwent significant changes. In the 1930's an influential literary movement called *Khitsan* ("Experiment for a new age") was formed, which stressed simplicity, directness, and purity of lang. Commoners have assumed the role of poets and have to cater to a larger public with a more catholic taste. Short poems have replaced the traditional long epic.

After 1948 there was an upsurge of national pride and aspiration as well as the emergence of new political, social, and cultural environments. All these provided fertile material for B. poets. Their poems may be grouped under four categories: those (1) having the eternal themes—love and nature tinted with Buddhism—by romantic poets; (2) deprecating some malaise of society such as war, social evils, or economic exploitation—by angry poets; (3) tackling moral and spiritual problems in life—by didactic poets; and (4) advocating the need for amity among the peoples of Burma—by patriotic poets. Of the contemporary poets, two may be singled out: Nú Yin (b. 1916), distinguished by her subtle approach and sensuous lang., and Daùng Nwe Hswei (1931-85), angry, innovative, and evocative. As with the Cl. and Khitsan poets, the modern writers seldom limit themselves to one form of p. And though a few poets are attempting to popularize free verse, B. p. still retains its distinctive characteristics.

IN ENGLISH AND FRENCH: *Jour. of the Burma Research Society*, Rangoon (1910), esp.: (a) Ba Han, "Seindakyawthu, Man and Poet," v. 8; (b) Po Byu and B. H., "Shin Uttamagyaw and his Tawla, a Nature Poem," v.7–10; (c) G. H. Luce, "Prayers and Curses," v. 26; (d) Hla Pe, "B. p. (1300-1971)," v. 54—incl. (1) birth, devel., scope, and nature, and (2) content and form; *BSOAS* (London), v. 12 and esp. v. 13 (art. on *Maw-gun* by Hla Pe); Maung Htin Aung, *B. Drama* (1937); Hla Pe, *Konmara Pya Zat* (1952)—pt. 1, intro. and tr., contains various rhyme schemes and forms of B. prosody; U On Pe, "Mod. B. Lit.: Its Background in the Independence Movement," *Atlantic Monthly* 201 (1958); *Minthuwun*, Eng. tr. G. H. Luce (1961)—a selection of Minthuwun's poems and prose; *Littératures contemporaines de l'Asie du Sudest*, ed. Lafont and Lombard (1974); *Lit. and Society in Southeast Asia*, ed. Tham Seong Chee (1981).

IN BURMESE: *Anthol. of B. Lit.*, ed. U. Kyaw Dun, 4 v. (1926–31); U Tin, *Kabyabandhathara Kyan* (1929)—B. prosody; Pe Maung Tin, *Hist. of B. Lit.* (1947); Ba Thaung, *Sa-hso-daw-may Athokpat-ti* [Biog. of B. Authors] (1962); Hti-la Sit-Thu, *Hna-hse-ya-zú myan-ma sa-hso myan-ma kabya* [20th-c. Poets and Poems] (1985). H.PE.

BURNS STANZA, also called "Scottish stanza" and "standard Habbie." One variety of tail rhyme (q.v.), the B. s. is a 6-line stanza rhyming *aaabab*, the *a*-lines being tetrameter and the *b*-lines dimeter. It takes its name from the use made of it by Robert Burns in many of his Scottish dialect poems. The stanza, however, may be found as early as the 11th c. in the poems of the Occitan troubadour William of Poitiers. Other close variants of tail-rhyme stanzas are also popular in the Middle Ages. Despite its intricacy, the form is an effective one: following the crescendo of the initial tercet, the short lines lend themselves well to effects of pointing, irony, and closure:

> Ye ugly, creepin, blastit wonner,
> Detested, shunn'd by saunt an' sinner,
> How daur ye set your fit upon her,
> Sae fine a lady!
> Gae somewhere else, and seek your dinner
> On some poor body.
> ("To a Louse")

The meter was also used by Wordsworth, appropriately, for his "At the Grave of Burns."—A. H. MacLaine, "New Light on the Genesis of the B. S.," *N&Q* 198 (1953); H. Damico, "Sources of Stanza Forms Used by Burns," *SSL* 12 (1975). T.V.F.B.

BYELORUSSIAN POETRY expresses the spiritual richness and resilience of a small East Slav country set between Poland and Russia, formerly the westernmost republic of the USSR. The earliest examples of verse in B. belong to Frančisk Skaryna (ca. 1485–ca. 1540), the Bible translator, publisher, and engraver, but he had no successors as a poet, and the panegyric genre of armorial epigrams which flourished at the end of the 16th c., particularly in the hands of Andrej Rymša, was a separate devel. More public panegyrics or "declamations" characterize the main surviving works of Simiaon Połacki (1629–80), better known for his contribution to Rus. lit., but the outstanding example of 17th-c. B. p. is the recently rediscovered *Lament* on the death of Abbot Laoncij Karpovič (1620). Although the B. lang. had enjoyed official status during the period of the Grand Duchy of Lithuania, after Union with Poland the upper classes became Polonized, leaving preservation of the vernacular to the peasantry.

Thus, the birth of modern B. p. after the B. lands had been brought into the Rus. Empire was an almost total re-birth without trad. or continuity. Paŭluk Bahrym (1813–91) is acclaimed as the first B. peasant poet, though only one poem survives. An *Aeneid* travesty, based on those of Osipov and Kotlyarevśky, enjoyed great popularity, as did another anonymous comic poem, *Taras on Parnassus* (possibly by the same author), satirizing serfdom and the Rus. and Polish literary worlds. The first half of the 19th c. is characterized by ethnographic and didactic poetry, as liberal B. landowners like Jan Čačot (1796–1847) and Vikienci Dunin-Marcinkievič (1807–84) helped to create a poetry and through it a literary lang. and concomitant national awareness. Official hostility hindered the devel. of poetry throughout the century, and in the 1890s the illegal work of Adam Hurynovič (1864–94), Ivan Łučyna (1851–97), and esp. Frańcišak Bahuševič (1840–1900) displayed anguished and often bitter sociopolitical concerns, expressed in short forms reflecting clearly the influence of folk poetry. Bahuševič, sometimes called the father of B. p., proclaimed in the intro. to his verse collection *The B. Pipe* (Krakow, 1891) the sovereign worth of the B. lang., thus inaugurating an important patriotic theme that continues to the present day.

A major boost to B. national awareness was the Vilna-based newspaper *Naša niva* (Our Field), which provided a forum for the exchange of ideas and an outlet for literary endeavor. In the cultural efflorescence associated with this publication emerged many of the greatest B. poets, whose achievement remains unsurpassed to this day, making them national classics. Particularly treasured are the highly musical lyrics of Janka Kupała (Ivan Łucievič, 1882–1942), who first appealed eloquently for the B. peasant "to be called human." In narrative and dramatic poems such as *The Eternal Song* (1908), *Dream on a Gravemound* (1910), and *Bandaroŭna* (1913), Kupała broadened the scope of B. p., drawing on Eastern and Western European models, esp. the example of Shevchenko. After the Revolution of 1917, he continued to be a national figure symbolic of the B. Ren., but most of his later work lacks élan and freshness, while a number of suppressed poems like "Before the Future" (1922) show clearly his difficulties in adapting to the country's new circumstances. His contemporary Jakub Kołas (Kanstancin Mickievič, 1882–1956) adapted more successfully, producing fine nature lyrics as well as sociopolitical poetry and some talented prose works. It is, however, in two magnificent narrative poems that Kołas's genius finds its fullest expression: *The New Land* (1911–23), an epic panorama of B. life centered on a peasant family's quest, and *Symon the Musician* (1911–25), which describes with metrical virtuosity, musical lyricism, and great psychological subtlety a musician's search for recognition and self-expression; the contrast

between these masterpieces emphasizes the breadth of Kołas's achievement.

Three other poets of the *Naša niva* period deserve individual mention: Žmitrok Biadula (Samuił Płaŭnik, 1886–1941), Maksim Bahdanovič (1891–1917), and Aleś Harun (Alaksandr Prušynski, 1887–1920). Biadula wrote quirkily poignant verses, but this Jewish writer's fervent "Oath of Allegiance" (1919) is an exceptionally stirring example of B. patriotic poetry. With Bahdanovič's exiguous but highly sophisticated poetic heritage (mostly collected in *A Garland*, 1913) B. lit. made a quantum leap. Having omitted such traditional stages as Classicism, romanticism, and symbolism in its compressed literary devel., B. p. was freed from over-reliance on folk models by Bahdanovič's finely chiseled short lyrics, which introduced such hitherto-unknown forms as sonnets, octaves, and triolets. Like Bahdanovič, Harun lived many years of his life far from Byelorussia, sending his highly subjective verses to *Naša niva* from Siberian exile. His sole volume, *A Mother's Gift*, appeared during Byelorussia's brief period of national independence in 1918, but until recently suffered political suppression.

Among the many poems welcoming the postrevolutionary new life, the work of two poets stands out, both for technical quality and nihilistic vigor. Bombastic extravaganzas like "Barefoot on the Embers" (1921) and "Dance on the Gravestones" (1922) by Michaś Čarot (Michaś Kudzielka, 1896–1936) and "Assault on Form" (1922) and "In Seven-league Boots" (1923) by Michajła Hramyka (1885–1969) welcome a brash new future purged of all reminders of the past. Other poets were less extravagant, but it is only with the anti-national repression of the 1920s and late 30s that paeans to the new order automatically need to be suspected of time-serving insincerity. In the earlier years a hymn to industrialization and construction like "The Tenth Foundation" (1927) by Paŭluk Trus (1904–29) could still ring a note of genuine enthusiasm.

However, subversive strains are to be heard in the work of many poets, particularly after the suppression of the B. National Republic and the partitioning of the country into Western Byelorussia under Polish rule and Soviet Byelorussia in the East. Two of the major poets of the 1920s, Uładzimir Duboŭka (1900–76) and Jazep Pušča (Jazep Płaščynski, 1902–64), both protested against the subjugation of Byelorussia in subtly ambiguous poems depicting the lot of the B. intelligentsia; works such as Duboŭka's lyric cycle *Circles* (1925–26) and Pušča's *Letters to a Dog* (1927) and *And Purple Sails Unfurled* (1929) have not been reprinted since their first appearance.

Conditions in Western Byelorussia were equally unfavorable; many poets first began writing in prison. Kazimir Svajak (Fr. Kanstancin Stapovič, 1890–1926) published a fine book of spiritual verse, *My Lyre* (1924) (the other main religious poet was Andrej Ziaziula [Fr. Aleksandr Astramovič, 1878–1921]); and Uładzimir Žyłka (1900–33), a disciple of Bahdanovič and Harun, in addition to romantic nature lyrics, produced a convincing reply to Čačot in his major work, *Conception* (1922), which traced the various stages of the national movement. Communist poets imprisoned for their beliefs included Valancin Taŭłaj (1914–47) and Pilip Piestrak (1903–78), but by far the most outstanding was Maksim Tank (Jaŭhien Skurko, b. 1912), who combined thematic breadth with technical virtuosity and strikingly imaginative imagery in *Staging Posts* (1936), *Cranberry Blossom* (1938), and *Under the Mast* (1938); in such narrative poems as the highly symbolic *Lake Narač* (1937), *Kalinoŭski* (1938) on the 19th-c. nationalist leader; and in a brilliantly stylized folk legend, *The Tale of Vial* (1937). Tank continued to write good poetry after the reunification and represents the older generation of poets at their best. Many who came to prominence under Stalin and contributed to the revival of the panegyric genre in the late 1930s and 40s are destined for swift oblivion, but the satirical fables of Kandrat Krapiva (Kandrat Atrachovič, b. 1906) and the wide-ranging romantic lyrics of Arkadź Kulašoŭ (1914–78) retain their value, as do the brightly colored, supple nature lyrics of Natalla Arsieńnieva (b. 1903), whose West B. work was never really matched by what she wrote in the BSSR and, later still, in the USA. She was the only major poet of the B. emigration.

Although poetry has not flourished to the same degree as prose in Byelorussia, it continues to play a large part in national culture. A process of increasing sophistication continues, despite strong conservative tendencies in form, meter, lexis, and, indeed, theme, with folk influence still perceptible in the work of many poets; prosodically, the devel. has been from syllabic to syllabotonic and, most commonly, tonic verse. In the 1960s, however, much modernist experimentation appeared in the poetry of, among others, Piatruś Makal (b. 1932), Janka Sipakoŭ (b. 1936), and Ryhor Siemaškievič (1945–82), in Makal's case often used effectively in conjunction with vigorous anti-Stalinist sentiments. Other major poets in the postwar period include Danuta Bičel-Zahnietava (b. 1938), Ryhor Baradulin (b. 1935), Nił Hilevič (b. 1931), and Uładzimir Karatkievič (1930–84). A valuable publishing venture has been the "Poet's First Book" series begun in 1968. A major twin theme in the 1960s which continues today is that of Byelorussia and the B. lang., expressed most movingly in Baradulin's poem "My Language" (1963). The latter is, indeed, under constant threat of erosion, and its best chances for survival would seem to lie with B. p., for, as Harun expressed it in the first poem of *A Mother's Gift*, "the very nation is a bard." See also SLAVIC PROSODY.

ANTHOLOGIES: *Chrestam. novaj b. lit.*, ed. I. Dvarčanin (1927); *Antaloh. b. paezii*, ed. P. U. Broüka (1961); *Like Water, Like Fire*, tr. V. Rich (1971);

The Images Swarm Free, tr. V. Rich, ed. A. B. McMillin (1982); *Weissrussische Anth.*, ed. F. Neureiter (1983). HISTORY AND CRITICISM: M. Harecki, *Hist. b. lit.* (1920); A. Adamovich, *Opposition to Sovietization in B. Lit. (1917–1957)* (1958); *Hist. b. dakastryč. lit.*, ed. V. Barysienka (1968–69); I. Ralko, *B. vierš* (1969); M. Hrynčyk, *Šlachi b. vieršaskładannia* (1973); S. Akiner, "Contemp. Young B. Poets (1967–1975)," *JBStud* 3 (1976), "Contemp. B. Lit. in Poland," *MLR* 78 (1983); A. B. McMillin, *A Hist. of B. Lit. from Its Origins to the Present Day* (1977); *Ist. b.-soviet lit.*, ed. I. Naumenko (1977). A.B.M.

BYLINA (pl. *byliny*). Scholars use the word b. for the Rus. oral epic, but singers employ *starina* or *starinka*, terms denoting a past or old event. Most likely the b. originated in Kievan Russia from the 10th through the 12th c. and reflects struggles with nomadic groups in the steppe. After the Tartar conquest around 1240, adversaries in the byliny were changed to Tartars. The earliest collection is attributed to Kirsha Danilov, who probably took down the songs in Western Siberia in the mid 18th c. Most subsequent recordings were made from peasant singers in northern regions around Lake Onega and the White Sea; the trad. died out in the 1950s. Byliny can be divided into Novgorod cycles and Kiev or Vladimir cycles. Prince Vladimir, similar to King Arthur, rules in Kiev, and the epic heroes (*bogatyr*) gather around him. The b. comprises several subgenres: heroic epics, novelistic epics or romances, magic tales, ballads, historical songs, religious verses, satirical songs of the minstrels (*skomorok*). Ordinarily byliny contain 300 to 500 lines, are performed by one male or female singer, are unaccompanied (although texts refer to the *gusli*), are without rhyme or stanza form, and are each devoted to one episode; long composite songs combining several episodes did not develop. Byliny display typical epic subjects, are concerned with the distant past, possess special linguistic and poetic devices, and are impersonal in tone. Members of the Rus. historical school advanced a theory about the aristocratic origin of the b. in the princes' retinues, but Soviet folklorists have rejected this interpretation.—A. Skaftymov, *Poetika i genezis bylin* (1924); N. Chadwick, *Rus. Heroic Poetry* (1932); A. Astaxova, *Russkij bylinnyj èpos na Severe* (1948), *Byliny: Itogi i problemy izučenija* (1966); M. Pliseckij, *Istorizm russkix bylin* (1962); Y. Sokolov, *Rus. Folklore* (1970); A. E. Alexander, *B. and Fairy Tale* (1973); J. O. Bailey, "The Metrical Typology of Rus. Narrative Folk Meters," *Am. Contribs. to the 8th Internat. Congress of Slavists*, v. 1 (1978); M. L. Gasparov, "Russkij bylinnyj stix." *Issledovanija po teorii stixa*, ed. V. M. Žirmunskij et al. (1978); F. J. Oinas, "Rus. Byliny," *Heroic Epic and Saga* (1978); B. P. Scherr, "Tonic Versification," in Terras; *Byliny*, ed. B. Putilov (1986). J.O.B.

BYZANTINE POETRY.

The majority of B. literary works labor under the Cl. Gr. linguistic and literary traditions, which smothered much of their originality. Only in religious poetry did B. lit. break fresh ground and approach greatness, and only from the 13th c. onward did it use a lang. approximating that spoken by contemporary Greeks.

The first three cs. of the Eastern Roman Empire were a period of transition from pagan Roman and Hellenistic Gr. to a Christian B. culture. This is reflected in the poetry of the time. Christian fervor appears side by side with an orgiastic love of life; hymns are composed in a Christian and pagan spirit, and grandiose *ekphraseis* (descriptions of works of art; see EKPHRASIS) celebrate Christian and pagan masterpieces. Of these the description of the Church of Sancta Sophia by Paul the Silentiary (fl. 563) is undoubtedly the most significant, extolling the twin grandeur of church and state around which B. life was to revolve.

I. RELIGIOUS POETRY. Originally B. religious p. used a number of Cl. Gr. meters—the hexameter, elegiac, iambic, anacreontic, and anapaestic (qq.v.)—as can be seen from the writing of Methodius, Synesius, and Gregory of Nazianzus (4th–5th cs.). But very soon the new rhythmic meters prevailed, whose effect relied on the number of syllables and the place of the accents within a line. These, together with admiration for the martyrs and devotion to the mysteries of the new religion, gave B. religious p. a power and freshness which remained unequaled in subsequent Med. Gr. writings.

The rhythmic B. hymns fall into three periods, the first (4th–5th cs.) characterized by short hymns, the *Troparia*; the second (6th–7th cs.) by long and elaborate metrical sermons, the *Kontakia*; and the third (7th–9th cs.) by a form of hymn-cycle called *Kanon*. The second is the great period of Gr. hymnography. In its early part lived Romanos (6th c.), the most celebrated B. religious poet. Some 85 of his works have been preserved, all metrical sermons for various feasts of the Orthodox Church. They were accompanied by music, which is now lost, and were apparently rendered in a kind of recitative resembling oratorios. Romanos, being a conscientious Christian, treated his subjects exactly as the church ordained. Occasionally, however, he gives rein to his fancy, and at such times becomes grandiloquent in the style of epideictic oratory. His lang. on the whole is pure; he is rich in metaphor and imagery, and often interweaves in his narrative whole passages from Holy Scripture. His main fault is an oriental love of size, unpalatable to the modern reader.

Andrew, Bishop of Crete (ca. 660–740), initiates the third period of B. religious p. with his *Major Kanon*, a composition of huge size, in which elaboration of form results in a decline of power and feeling. The two most important representatives of this period are St. John Damascene (7th–8th cs.) and his foster brother Kosmas of Maiouma. As a hymnographer, Damascene was greatly renowned. He returned to the use of quantitative verse, even endeavoring to combine it with modern meters.

The storm of the iconoclastic controversy, which broke out in the lifetime of Damascene, brought in its wake a reaction which resulted in a new florescence of hymnography. Works (mostly anonymous) of writers of this period finally found their way into the liturgy of the Eastern Church and replaced the older hymns and metrical sermons of the days of Romanos. Of the posticonoclast poets, Symeon the Mystic (949–1022) certainly ranks highest. In B. p. he is the most important figure after Romanos, although his fervent mystical poems tend to be formless and often obscure. Moreover, he is the first person known to have used the 15-syllable line (*politikos stichos*; see POLITICAL VERSE) in personal poetry, the verse which in later years was to become supreme in the poetry of the Gr. world.

B. religious p. was to accomplish a great historical mission. It not only kept alive Gr. national and Christian feeling in the face of numerous barbarian invasions, but it also scattered to East, West, and North the seeds that later blossomed into the literatures and cultures of other peoples—the Russians, the Southern Slavs, the Romanians, the Syrians, the Copts, and the Armenians.

II. EPIC POETRY. The historical court epics of the late Hellenistic era survived in the early B. centuries. If we are to judge by their scanty remains, they had limited artistic merit. The greatest representative of the historical epic, or rather the epic encomium, and one of the most distinguished B. poets was George Pisides (7th c.). Some of his most important verse is in praise of his patron, Emperor Heraclius, whose victory over the Persians he celebrated. In the hands of Pisides new B. meters begin to take shape, in particular the B. 12-syllable iambic verse, which was to become the principal meter of subsequent Med. Gr. artverse. But the most important B. epic cycle apparently originated in the provinces of the East in the course of the 10th c. It centered on the heroic figure of Digenes (who symbolized the ideal of Med. Gr. manhood) and spread from the deserts of Syria to the Rus. steppes, even reaching the remote Gr. colonies of Southern Italy. Of this we possess today only a small number of isolated folk songs (the *Akritic Ballads*), some of great power and beauty, and half a dozen versions, ranging from the 12th to the 17th c., of a long poem now lost, the so-called *Epic of Basil Digenes Akritas*.

They all differ in lang. and style and even in the sequence of the narrative. In this epic we find Gr. and Hellenistic motifs blended with Eastern elements, as well as a number of baffling historical facts anything but contemporary.

III. LYRIC POETRY. The epigram (q.v.) in the Hellenistic sense of the term (the short occasional poem) was the type of lyric poetry most cultivated in Byzantium. At first it followed the late Hellenistic patterns, as the works of Agathias (6th c.), Paul the Silentiary, and others show. But from the 7th c. the new religious spirit permeates it, expressed in a predilection for churches, monastic life, and holy relics as subjects. Theodore Studites (759–826) is the most important representative in this trend. Cassia, often and unjustly called the Sappho of Byzantium, followed him in the 9th c. But the heyday of the B. epigram spans the 10th–11th cs. For it was then that John Geometres (Kyriotes), Christophoros of Mitylene, and John Mavropous flourished. They reverted to the older Hellenistic influences, and their verse displays both feeling and refined wit. The only other type of B. high lyric p. worth mentioning is the *lament*. This often takes the form of an address to the poet's soul, or of a dirge or complaint, full of the ascetic spirit of the time. It was influenced by the long and insipid autobiographical poetry of Gregory of Nazianzus, yet many important B. poets indulged in it, and it continued in the form of "a moral admonition" or "the prayer of a sinner" until the end of the B. era.

Medieval erudite poetry, permeated as it was by the ascetic spirit, did not draw on profane love for inspiration, one of the greatest sources of lyricism of all centuries. Such B. love p. as has survived is written in a more or less demotic tongue and is to be found in the love letters (the *Pittakia*) of the verse romances (see below) or in certain modern Gr. folksongs whose origins can be traced back to the Middle Ages.

IV. VERSE ROMANCES. After the fall of Constantinople to the Fourth Crusade (1204), Frankish chivalrous poetry was translated into Gr. and, influenced by this, a new type of Gr. chivalrous poetry arose. It used a more supple and lively lang. and broke away from the sterile trad. of the highbrow B. verse romances of Niketas Eugenianos (12th c.) and Theodoros Prodromos (12th c.), which blindly followed the patterns of the late Hellenistic romances of Heliodorus and Achilles Tatius. Such are *Callimachos and Chrysorrhoe*, *Belthandros and Chrysantza*, *Imperios and Margarona*, and *Florios and Platsiaflora*, all the works of unknown poets. The essence of these tales is boundless romanticism. Arduous love and the amazing fortitude of their heroes color the narrative. Yet in the hands of the B. poets Western elements are blended with Eastern, so that an oriental atmosphere of magic suffuses certain episodes, lending them a charm and a character of their own. Closely connected to these are two long biographical verse romances, *The Poem of Alexander the Great*

and *The Story of the Famous Belissarios*. The first follows the pseudo-Callisthenes' life of Alexander; the second has as its subject the deeds of Belissarios, the famous general of the Emperor Justinian. To this group one should perhaps add the *Achilleis*, which treats of the life and deeds of Achilles, presenting him, however, as a medieval Western knight.

V. SATIRICAL VERSE. In the 12th c. certain satirical didactic poems appeared, permeated by a mordant B. humor, not always refined. These are generally grouped under the title of *Prodromic Poems* and are traditionally attributed to the beggar and scholar Theodoros Prodromos. Their chief interest lies in the picture of social and monastic life they give and in the type of lang. they use, in which demotic (spoken) forms abound.

VI. DIDACTIC POETRY AND DRAMA. If we exclude the epigram, perhaps no other poetic form was so assiduously and continuously practiced in Byzantium as didactic poetry (q.v.). But these endless prose-in-verse creations on birds, fish, stones, vegetables, etc., are certainly not poetry in the real sense of the word, and it is very doubtful if their authors ever sought original artistic effect; information was all they wished to convey. Moreover, drama proper remained unknown in Byzantium. Such lit. as exists in dramatic form (of which the 11th-c. cento *Christus Patiens* is the most important example) was always meant to be read and not acted. The dramatic instinct of the Greeks revealed itself in the long dialogues of the *Kontakia* and in the Acclamations to the Emperors, and found ample nourishment in the pageantry of the palace ceremonies and the liturgies of the Gr. Orthodox Church. See also GREEK POETRY; POLITICAL VERSE.

ANTHOLOGIES: *Anthologia graeca carminum christianorum*, ed. W. Christ and M. Paranikas (1872); *Byzantinische Dichtung*, ed. G. Soyter (1930); *Poeti byzantini*, ed. R. Cantarella, 2 v. (1948); *Med. and Mod. Gr. Poetry*, ed. C. A. Trypanis (1951)—bibls. for all important B. poets in the notes; *Kontakia of Romanos, B. Melodist*, ed. and tr. M. Carpenter, 2 v. (1970–72); C. A. Trypanis, *Penquin Book of Gr. Verse*, 3d ed. (1984); *An Anthol. of B. P.*, ed. B. Baldwin (1985).

HISTORY AND CRITICISM: K. Krumbacher, *Gesch. der byzantinischen Literatur*, 2d ed. (1897)—still the standard work; P. Maas, "Das Kontakion," *Byzantinische Zeitschrift* 19 (1910); Schmid and Stählin; F. Dölger, *Die byzantinische Dichtung in der Reinsprache* (1948); F. H. Marshall, "B. Lit.," in N. H. Baynes and H. St. L. B. Moss, *Byzantium* (1948); N. B. Tomadakis, *Eisagoge eis ten Byzantinen Philologian* (1952); H.-G. Beck, *Gesch. der byzantinischen Volksliterataur* (1971); H. Hunger, *Die hochsprachliche Profane Literatur*, 2 v. (1978); Trypanis; R. Jakobson, "The Slavic Response to B. P.," in Jakobson, v. 6; *Oxford Dict. of Byzantium*, ed. A. P. Kazhdan (1991).   C.A.T.

C

CACCIA. An It. verseform first used in the early 14th c. by Magister Piero, Giovanni da Cascia, and Jacopo da Bologna. Three early c. were cast in the form of the madrigal (q.v.). The highly developed c. consisted of a random number of 11-, 7-, or 5-syllable lines of verse. As in the madrigal, a refrain might occur as the final section. Other features incl. onomatopoeia, elliptical syntax, and exclamatory remarks. As the name indicates, the c. originated as a hunting song (It. *cacciare*, to hunt); Boccaccio's *C. di Diana* (1336), in *terza rima* (q.v.), is the first. Niccolò Soldanieri (d. 1385) created the best examples; later poets such as Giannozzo and Franco Sacchetti, Ghirardello da Firenze, and Francesco Landini extended the motive and also included battle scenes, fishing scenes, dancing, etc. Musically the c. consists of a canon in two parts for upper voices, which "hunt" each other, normally accompanied by an instrumental tenor. In 1332 Antonio da Tempo wrote the first extensive theoretical treatise of the c., the *Summa artis rithmici* (ed. R. Andrews, 1977). The c. was particularly popular between 1360 and 1380; after 1400 only a few examples are extant. Forms of the c. existed in most European countries, such as the Fr. *chace* (*chasse*), the Eng. *chase*, the Sp. *caça*, and the Ger. *Jagdlied* (Oswald von Wolkenstein). Since the 16th c., the term has generally been applied to hunting songs of various types, e.g. the songs by J. Gombert or C. Janequin, or the *catch* in England. Haydn (Symphony no. 73) and E. N. Méhul (overture of his opera *Le jeune Henri*, 1795) applied the term *Chasse* to their works.—*14th-c. It. Cacce*, ed. W. T. Marrocco (1942); N. Pirrotta, "Per l'origine e la storia della c. e del madrigale trecentesca," *RMI* 48–49 (1946–47); F. Ghisl, "C.," *MGG*; F. A. Gallo, "C.," *Handwörterbuch der musikal. Terminologie* (1979); K. von Fischer, "C.," *New Grove*; A. Classen, "Onomatopoesie in der Lyrik von Jehan Vaillant, Oswald von Wolkenstein und Niccolò Soldaniere," *ZDP* (1989); *Diana's Hunt*, ed. and tr. A. K. Cassell and V. Kirkham (1991). A.C.

CACOPHONY. The use of harsh-sounding words; the quality or fact of being dissonant; the opposite of euphony (q.v.). Though poets ordinarily avoid c., on occasion they may use it deliberately to reinforce meaning. C. may result from a variety of causes: frequent jumps, in short succession, from front to back vowels or from open to close vowels (Musset: "Sur le frelon nacré qu'elle *en*ivre *en* m*our*ant"), such jumps requiring more muscular effort than a succession of cognate sounds; hiatus (*La Chanson de Roland*: "*Jo i* ferrai de Durendal

m'espée"); a high concentration of unvoiced plosives (*p, t, k*) (Browning: "Ir*ks* *c*are the *c*ro*p*-full bird? Fre*ts* doub*t* the maw-*c*rammed beas*t*?"); a high frequency of *s* or *sh* sounds (Tennyson described his attempts to rid his verse of sibilants as "kicking the geese out of the boat"). Several ancient poets attempted to write *s*-less poems. When a Fr. writer such as Racine indulges in such *sigmatism* ("Pour qui sont ces serpents qui sifflent sur vos têtes?"), it is immediately felt by a native ear as deliberate (here, onomatopoeic). See also DISSONANCE; ONOMATOPOEIA; SOUND; SOUND EFFECTS IN POETRY.—L. P. Wilkinson, *Golden Lat. Artistry* (1963); P. Honan, "Mathew Arnold and C.," *VP* 1 (1963), "The Iron String in the Victorian Lyre," *Browning's Mind and Art*, ed. C. Tracy (1968); Brogan; Morier. L.BI.

CADENCE. (1) Technically, the fixed patterning of quantities in the clausula, i.e. the last few syllables of a phrase or clause, in Med. Lat. artprose (see CURSUS); also, by extension, such pre-final patterning in metrical verse, such as IE. "It is a fairly common principle of structure," says Hardie, "that the primary rhythm should become apparent at the close" (50). (2) More generally, the general rhythmic pattern or intonational contour of a sentence or line, referring to its accentual pattern, the timing of its delivery, its pitch contour, or any combination of these. (3) A term formerly often used to describe the rhythmical flow of such nonmetrical prosodies as Biblical poetry, Whitman, free verse of several stripes, and prose poetry. Drawn from music, the term used in this last sense implies a looser concept of poetic rhythm than that applied to metrical poetry, and mainly refers to phrasing, which is foreign to foot-based scansion. Most of the poets experimenting in the avantgarde prosodies of the later 19th and early 20th cs. subscribed to some version of Pound's or William Carlos Williams's injunctions to compose in loose cadences. Pound exhorted poets to "compose in the sequence of the musical phrase, not in sequence of a metronome" (*Make It New*, 1934); Williams developed the notorious "variable foot" (q.v.). See also COLON; PERIOD; PROSE RHYTHM; PUNCTUATION.—Hardie; M. M. Morgan, "A Treatise in C.," *MLR* 47 (1952); W. Mohr, "Kadenz," *Reallexikon*, 1.803–6; Lausberg, 479 ff.; Morier, s.v. "Clausule"; Scott 187 ff.; Norden 2.909 ff.

T.V.F.B.

CAESURA, cesura (Gr. *tome*; Fr. *césure*, Ger. *Zäsur*). In Cl. prosody (q.v.) the term "c." has, since the time of Boeckh (1811), been used to refer to a word-boundary falling within a metrical foot (it was not so used by the ancients; see West). The modern sense of the term, however, refers to a break or joint in the continuity of the metrical structure of the line (where word-boundary is all but universal) and so concerns the division of lines into distinguishable cola. It is *diaeresis* (q.v.) in Cl. prosody (coincidence of foot-end and word-end) which comes closest to the modern sense of c., though in fact these two terms denote but two of a variety of phenomena concerning word-boundaries that have been closely studied in Cl. poetry but virtually ignored in modern. The semantic shift may perhaps be isolated in Ronsard, who uses the term in two senses in the *L'Abrégé de l'art poétique* (1565). In the Ren., the concept of the c. first surfaces in the prosody manuals of the *Séconde Rhétorique* of early 16th-c. France; and a rule forbidding an extra syllable before the c. (the so-called "epic c.," a term coincd only in the 19th c.; see below) is set forth in the *Pleine rhétorique* of Pierre Fabri (1521) and in the *Art poétique* (1555) of Jacques Peletier du Mans, who seems to have been the first to use the term *césure* in Fr.

C. vs. Pause. In every sentence of any length there will be a syntactic juncture or pause between phrases or clauses, usually signaled by punctuation (q.v.) but sometimes not. C. is the metrical phenomenon which corresponds to this break in the syntax of the line. Often the relevant terms are not carefully distinguished in prosody and lit. crit.: thus critics often use "pause," "rest," and "c." almost interchangeably. But in most meters c. is subject to metrical rule as to where words may end—such rules being related to their opposites, prohibitions on word boundary in certain positions (see BRIDGE)—while syntactic junctures are not, being controlled by semantic intent. Other paralinguistic or performative ("rhetorical") pauses, incl. breath-points, pauses for rhetorical emphasis, and the slight pauses subject to variance of speech tempo, are matters of performance (q.v.) and have nothing to do with metrical design. Nor do so-called "metrical pauses" (see PAUSE)— missing syllables in accentual verse (q.v.) and other verse systems whose time is filled by a rest— have to do with c. In various verse-systems, a line may have one c., or more than one, or none; and such a line may have any number of syntactic junctures or performative, rhetorical, or breath pauses: these must be kept separate. The only relation assumed is that a c. will be realized in performance by a pause. Some prosodists have even claimed that, strictly speaking, c. is not a part of meter at all (Malof), or is only realized in performance (Chatman in Sebeok 166), but these are minority views. Chatman's identification of c. with line-end pause, however, is implicitly accepted by many.

Position. Regulation of caesural position (and number) varies from one verse-system to another.

In Cl. prosody, cs. or caesurae are regulated more as to position than as to number, and technical terms have been developed to designate the most common placements in the hexameter (q.v.), "penthemimeral" (c. after the first long syllable of the third foot, i.e. after the fifth half-foot) and "hephthemimeral" (after the seventh half-foot). Caesural division of the hexameter into two equal halves was avoided by the ancients. Fixed c.-placement is a major criterion in the Romance prosodies, esp. Fr. prosody (q.v.), where c. holds higher status than the measure-boundary or *coupe* (q.v.). Indeed, Victor Hugo's moving of the c. in the Fr. alexandrine to create the *trimètre* (q.v.) was one of the most revolutionary moments in Fr. romanticism. In OE verse, lines are divided into hemistichs bound together by structural alliteration: here the break is a c. which, as in Gr. (so West), divides the line into independent but related cola—as witnesses the fact that the hemistichs were once printed as couplets.

In modern Eng. verse of the artverse trad., c. placement varies considerably according to metrical subgenre (dramatic verse vs. narrative and lyric; rhymed couplets vs. blank verse), a fact that has forced some prosodists to make a virtue of necessity. It was Schipper who did most to promote the doctrines that the c. is essential to the structure of the iambic pentameter (fully half of the 50 pages devoted to Chaucerian meter in *Englische Metrik* treat c.; see esp. 1.449) and that variation in c. placement is a deliberate strategy to combat monotony. A century later, "varied and expressive c. placement" is still said to be a "subtle prosodic device" (Fussell).

Extra Syllables. The terminology for line-endings is sometimes still applied to cs.; thus a c. which follows a stressed syllable is called masculine, and one which follows an unstressed syllable feminine (see MASCULINE AND FEMININE). Romance philologists and prosodists of the later 19th c. (Diez, Rochat, Tobler, Stengel) developed the terms "epic" and "lyric" to refer to two types of feminine cs. which followed, respectively, a weak syllable that is not counted as part of the metrical pattern and a weak syllable that is, based on their belief that these features were characteristic of, respectively, the OF epics and the lyric verse of the troubadours and trouvères. (In OF and Occitan the extra weak syllable is the unelided atonic vowel or mute -*e*.) In 1903, however, Kastner showed that the notion of "epic c." was "not justified by facts" and "based on texts printed for the most part from only a single manuscript" (119–20); his own inventory of 5000 lines by six trouvères and seven troubadours revealed incidences of epic c. of less than half of one percent. Unfortunately, however, these terms were taken up by Ten Brink and Schipper (*Metrik* 1.438; *History* 210) to describe caesural variation in Chaucer, with the implication that Eng. patterns of syllabic variation around the c. "strictly correspond to their

Fr. models" (*History* 133). But evidence for the latter is weak. Schipper found extra syllables around the c. in only 16% of the lines in a Chaucer sample and a distribution too various to be obviously Romance: 60% after the 4th syllable, 17% after the 5th, 18% after the 6th, and 6% after the 7th (*Metrik* I.481–83; *History* 213n). Bischoff found 4,433 instances of "epic" c. in Chaucer, or 12% over the canon, but 3000 of these qualified only via final -*e*. Wright, drawing on Chambers' data, concluded that extra syllables appear at the c. more than 1600 times in Shakespeare's dramas—once every 38 lines—but not at all in the poems. New and systematic data for Eng. is greatly wanted, but in general, one can say that c. placement in Eng. verse—esp. Chaucer and Shakespeare—does not seem strictly regulated. In some subgenres, such as the heroic couplet (q.v.), it might be said that c. after the fourth syllable is by far the most common, but this is only a generalization. By definition a c. is a joint in a metrical line, and the essence of the concept of a joint is both a gap and a bridging of that gap, so that movement across it is smooth (cf. Maas on "dovetailing").

Schipper; O. Bischoff, "Über zweisilbige Senkung und epische Caesur bei Chaucer," *Englische Studien* 24–25 (1898–99); L. E. Kastner, "The Epic C. in the Poetry of the Trouvères and Troubadours," *MLQ* 6 (1903): H. Reger, *Die epische Cäsur in der Chaucerschule* (1910); Schipper, *History*; Thieme, 365; A. L. F. Snell, *Pause* (1918); C. C. Spiker, *The Historical Devel. of the C. in the Fr. Decasyllable* (1922); E. H. Sturtevant, "The Doctrine of the C., a Philological Ghost," *AJP* 45 (1924); P. Habermann, "Zäsur," *Reallexikon I* 3.509–11; A. W. de Groot, *Wesen und Gesetze der Caesur* (1935); Patterson; H. Drexler, "Caesur und Diaerese," *Aevum* 24 (1950); A. Oras, *Pause Patterns in Elizabethan and Jacobean Drama* (1960); Sebeok; Maas; J. Malof, *A Manual of Eng. Meters* (1970); W. S. Allen, *Accent and Rhythm* (1973) 114 ff.; J. P. Poe, *C. in the Hexameter Line of Lat. Elegiac Verse* (1974); R. Tsur, *A Perception-Oriented Theory of Metre* (1977), ch. 2; Scott; Brogan; Morier; G. B. Killough, "Punctuation and C. in Chaucer," *SAC* 4 (1982); Chambers—for Occitan; Scherr—for Rus.; G. T. Wright, *Shakespeare's Metrical Art* (1988); West; M. L. West, "Three Topics in Gr. Metre," *ClassQ* 32 (1982).   T.V.F.B.

CALLIGRAMME. The c. derives its name from Guillaume Apollinaire's *Calligrammes* (1918) and represents one type of visual poetry (q.v.). Its antecedents incl. the ancient forms of pattern poetry (q.v.), Gr. *technopaigneia* and Lat. *carmina figurata*, as well as medieval religious verse, Ren. emblems (q.v.), and, latterly, Mallarmé's *Un Coup de dés*. It thus occupies an intermediary position between the older forms of pattern poetry and the more recent concrete poetry (q.v.). In the context of the early 20th century, the c. reflects the influence of cubist painting (see CUBISM), It. futurism (q.v.),

and the ideogram (q.v.; the first examples were called *idéogrammes lyriques*) and thus inaugurates a period of radical experimentation by fusing art and poetry (see VISUAL ARTS AND POETRY) to form a complex interdisciplinary genre or intermedium.

Like other forms which dissolve the traditional barriers between visual and verbal, the c. mediates between the two fundamental modes of human perception, sight and sound. Whereas the futurists preferred abstract visual poetry, Apollinaire's compositions are largely figurative, portraying objects such as hearts, fountains, mandolins, and the Eiffel Tower, as well as animals, plants, and people. Still, a significant number are abstract, making generalization difficult, though on the whole the abstract cs. are later works. Of the 133 works arranged in realistic shapes, the visual image duplicates a verbal image in about half the cases. Some of the poems are autonomous, but most are grouped together to form still-lifes, landscapes, and portraits, an important innovation in the visual poetry trad. which complicates the play of visual and verbal signs. As Apollinaire himself remarks, "the relations between the juxtaposed figures in one of my poems are just as expressive as the words that compose it." Although some of the cs. are solid compositions, most feature an outlined form that emphasizes the genre's connection with drawing. Unlike most of his predecessors, however, Apollinaire weds visual poetry to lyric theme. Some of the cs. are in verse, but many others are in prose. One group, composed in 1917, continues Apollinaire's earlier experiments with *poésie critique* and functions as art crit. Although its critical reception has been mixed, the c. was widely imitated in France, Italy, Spain (esp. Catalonia), Mexico, the United States, and elsewhere. See also LETTRISME.

A.-M. Bassy, "Les Schématogrammes d'Apollinaire," *Scolies* 3–4 (1974–75); G. Apollinaire, *Cs.*, ed. and tr. A. H. Greet and S. I. Lockerbie (1980); C. Debon, *Guillaume Apollinaire après Alcools, I* (1981); *Que Vlo-Ve?*, 1st ser., 29–30 (1981)—an important colloquium; D. Seaman, *Concrete Poetry in France* (1981); J. G. Lapacherie, "Écriture et lecture du c.," *Poétique* 50 (1982); G. H. F. Longrée, *L'Expérience idéo-calligrammatique d'Apollinaire* (1984); W. Bohn, *The Aesthetics of Visual Poetry, 1914–1928* (1986); Hollier, 842 ff.   W.B.

CANADIAN POETRY.

   I. IN ENGLISH
   II. IN FRENCH

I. IN ENGLISH. The first poet to write in what later became Canada was that engagingly smug Jacobean, Robert Hayman (1575–1629), a friend of Ben Jonson who in 1621 became governor of the colony of Harbour Grace in Newfoundland. He wrote of Newfoundland from a viewpoint that seemed to combine the attitudes of an early publicity agent and a slightly utopian admirer of *The Tempest*, which had been produced only shortly beforehand:

> The Aire in Newfound-land is whole-
> some, good;
> The Fire, as sweet as any made of wood;
> The Waters, very rich, both salt and
> fresh;
> The Earth more rich, we know it is no
> lesse.
> Where all are good, *Fire, Water, Earth
> and Aire,*
> What man made of these foure would
> not live there?

But Hayman's efforts were isolated; he had no immediate successors. The real Eng. C. poetic trad. began nearly two centuries later with Loyalists who fled the Am. revolution and settled in New Brunswick and Upper Canada, and with immigrants from Britain who began to arrive in large numbers after the Napoleonic wars. They were largely unwilling exiles who brought their preconceptions about life and poetry with them. Some, like the younger Oliver Goldsmith (1781–1861) in *The Rising Village,* tried to present the New World as materially kinder if culturally cruder than the Old, but more often they resembled Standish O'Grady (ca. 1793–1841) in his bitter invocations of the land:

> Thou barren waste; unprofitable strand,
> Where hemlocks brood on unproduc-
> tive land,
> Whose frozen air in one bleak winter's
> night
> Can metamorphose *dark brown hares
> into white!*

The tendency to alternate between the elegiac (regretting a forsaken past) and the satiric (scorning an inadequate present), which characterized these poets has persisted in C. verse. But as the 19th c. continued and native-born poets appeared beside the immigrants, other strands also emerged, most notably the concept of a poetic trad. The earliest idea of the way to establish a local trad. was to turn back to previous periods in Eng. poetry, which explains the powerfully anachronistic neo-Jacobean dramas (*Saul* and *Count Filippo*) that Charles Heavysege (1816–76) wrote in his spare time as a woodcarver in Montreal, and the detached landscape poems of Charles Sangster (1822–93), which make one think of a late Augustan tinged with romanticism taking the measure of a new land. An echo of Chartist radicalism emerged in the poetry of emigrant poverty which Alexander McLachlan (1818–96) wrote, as did the first flickerings of C. nationalism in the descriptive poems in which Charles Mair (1838–1927) celebrated the western prairies.

There is a sense of something new entering C. p. with Isabella Valancy Crawford (1850–87). The diction, imagery, and metrical form of her poems are not greatly different from those of the Eng. late romantics, and if Keats had not written, and Landseer not painted, Crawford would not be quite the poet she became. What is novel in her is the way she gives herself to her poetry. Her poems grip the imagination because they are moved by frustrated passion, by the power of an inner vision that has little to do with the objective world. The bizarre hidden personality of this woman of obscure life emerges most strikingly in the way she uses conventional imagery to serve her fantasy:

> They hung the slaughter'd fish like
> swords
> On saplings slender—like scimitars
> Bright, and ruddied from new-dead
> wars,
> Blaz'd in the light—the scaly hordes.

Crawford inhabits a private world of the poetic persona. It is the so-called Confederation poets—Wilfred Campbell (1858–1919), Charles G. D. Roberts (1860–1944), Bliss Carman (1861–1927), Archibald Lampman (1861–99), and Duncan Campbell Scott (1862–1947)—who first begin to describe a recognizable Canada and in whose work the first intimations of a truly C. poetic voice can be heard. By the late Victorian era, at least in eastern and central Canada, the pioneer age had ended. Ties with the mother countries were weakening and, for the new generation, a love for the place of childhood experience was understandably more real than nostalgia for a land never seen. In giving voice to this transference of emotional allegiance, the Confederation poets at their best not only celebrated C. scenes, which Sangster and Mair had already done; they also reported with accuracy the life they harbored. Realism inevitably entered the process, as it always does when writers have to recognize the nature of the world they inhabit before they can apply to it the transfiguring processes of the imagination.

And so, in Roberts and Lampman, in Scott and at times in Carman, we see not only a strange luminous factualism in evoking the landscape, but also a new use of imagery, of lang., eventually of poetic form. It emerges in lines and stanzas more memorable, because more original, than any used before in Canada. There is that magically unprecedented line from Roberts' sonnet, "The Mowing": "The crying knives glide on; the green swath lies." And there is that final stanza of "Low Tide at Grand Pré," which has given Bliss Carman a lasting niche among C. poets:

> The night has fallen and the tide . . .
> Now and again comes drifting home
> Across these aching barrens wide,
> A sigh like driven wind or foam:
> In grief the flood is bursting home.

Modern critics find Duncan Campbell Scott the most interesting of this group because, like

Roberts to an extent, but unlike the metrically conservative Lampman and Carman, he felt uneasily that a new approach to the C. land required new formal expression, and in the end went very near free verse. Already by 1905, poems like "The Forsaken," about an old Indian woman left to die in the barren land, have a broken-line pattern which shows how eager Scott was to seek in unconventional metrical forms a way of giving expression to the strange things he had seen in the C. north.

This gradual liberation of the verse of Scott and Roberts is perhaps the chief thread of continuity in C. p. in the early 20th c., for after the almost simultaneous appearance of these poets and of Carman and Lampman during the 1880s, no poet of major significance emerged until E. J. Pratt (1882–1964) published *Newfoundland Verse* in 1923. And Pratt has always seemed an anomalous figure, ushering in modernity by turning to the past. He chose epic and mock-epic forms for his major works (*Brébeuf and His Brethren, The Titanic*), and he went back to 17th-c. Hudibrastic meters to write his often heavy-handed satires, but he did explore the use of C. vernacular in verse and early recognized the importance of C. history and geography as basic subject matter.

A very different figure was W. W. E. Ross (1894–1966), who published his first book, *Laconics*, in 1930. The very title was revealing: Ross brought to C. p. a new simplicity of expression and an emphasis on imagistic clarity. His influence on his contemporaries was considerable; "Rocky Bay" is almost a model of the modern C. landscape poem:

> The iron rocks
> slope sharply down
> into the gleaming
> of northern water
> and there is a shining
> to northern water
> reflecting the sky
> on a keen cold morning.

Certainly one of the ingredients of C. modernism as it appeared in the 1930s was an imagist way of looking which, by stressing the visual, enabled poets to perceive their environment and translate their perceptions into words with an appropriateness their predecessors had never attained. Poems of this period, such as "The Lonely Land" by A. J. M. Smith (1902–80), show this process at work in a clear relationship to Ross's sharper imagism:

> This is a beauty
> of dissonance,
> this resonance
> of stony strand,
> this smoky cry
> curled over a black pine
> like a broken
> and wind-battered branch
> when the wind
> bends the tops of the pines

and curdles the sky
from the north.

But the poets working together in Montreal in the late 1920s and 1930s—notably Smith, F. R. Scott (1899–1985), and A. M. Klein (1909–72)—were much too polymorphous in attitude to confine themselves to imagism in their search for alternatives to the outworn 19th-c. modes most C. poets still followed. They found affinities with the Eng. poets of the 1930s and with earlier masters such as Pound and Eliot.

The C. modernist poets of this time formed interlocking groups like that centered on the *McGill Fortnightly Review* in the late 1920s (Smith, Scott, and others) and the later Montreal groups associated in the 1940s with *Preview* (P. K. Page, Patrick Anderson, Scott, Klein) and *First Statement* (Irving Layton, Louis Dudek, Raymond Souster). These groups were partly associations of convenience among poets who found it hard to get their work published in ordinary periodicals; each in his or her own way was rebelling against conventional poetics and seeking a way of expression that suited a personal vision. A vague cultural nationalism was also at large among them, but the desire to find their own voices was primary, and the movement to create a distinctive C. p. largely derived from the poets' realization that they could be fully themselves only by living in their own place and time and giving expression to the experience they knew. But paradoxically the model for giving that expression they often had to find elsewhere; for rough convenience, C. poets of this period can be divided into Anglophiles and Americanophiles.

Not only Smith and Scott were influenced by Eng. poetry of the time. Patrick Anderson (1915–79), the leading spirit of *Preview*, was a temporarily transplanted Eng. poet. Dorothy Livesay (b. 1909) dates her poetic awakening from her discovery of Auden and Spender, who showed that lyricism and a social conscience were compatible, though in the later years of her long career it is not her Marxism of the 1930s but her intense feminism that has emerged most strongly, a feminism less concerned with politics than with the intensities and ambiguities of a passionate life:

> I walk beside you
> trace
> a shadow's shade
> skating on silver
> hear
> another voice
> singing under ice.
> ("The Uninvited").

Earle Birney (b. 1904), who also began to write in the 1930s, first found a new way of talking about Canada through his study of OE poetry, whose density and power, and even diction, are strongly present in his early poems. Since then, in decades of restless experimentation, he has developed a conversational, loping rhythm that serves to convey sharp visual images and hint at their philosophic implications, as in his vivid travel poem, "Bear on the Delhi Road":

> They are peaceful both   these spare
> men of Kashmir   and the bear
> alive in their living   too
> If   far on the Delhi way
> around him galvanic they dance
> it is merely to wear   wear
> from his shaggy body the tranced
> wish forever to stay
> only an ambling bear
> four-footed in berries.

P. K. Page (b. 1916), whose intermittent career also dates from the 1940s, clearly began writing under the influence of the socially conscious British poets of the 1930s, but has moved into an extraordinarily individualized combination of verbal economy and visionary intensity; as Margaret Atwood once said, she is "both a dazzling technician and a tranced observer who verges on mysticism"; she sees indeed the technique as part of the trance.

If the *Preview* poets looked to British models for inspiration, the rival *First Statement* group initiated another recent C. trend by upholding New World poets; for them any Old World, even an Old World in revolt, was anathema. This marks the beginning of Ezra Pound's powerful if intermittent influence in Canada. Of course neither Louis Dudek (b. 1918) nor Raymond Souster (b. 1921)—much less Irving Layton (b. 1912)—appears as a mere imitator of Pound; indeed, the difference between their styles shows how each took one aspect of Pound and adapted it to his own poetic ends. Dudek is more the philosophic poet, concerned with historical issues on a global scale, and so it is the Pound of the *Cantos* whose echo we sometimes catch in a long meditative poem like *Atlantis*. An earlier, imagist Pound stands behind Souster, who adapted and refined imagism into a remarkable instrument for bringing the visible world clearly alive, while giving it a transparency through which we see the poet's mind ironically reflecting, with the thought always a consequence of the experience. Souster has written so eloquently of Toronto and its life that he has become that rare phenomenon, an urban regional poet. By contrast, Irving Layton's attachment to Pound, later to William Carlos Williams, was tenuous at most. His Dionysian attitude (one can hardly call it a philosophy), derives partly form Nietzsche and partly from Lawrence. Essentially he is a hyper-romantic, reaching a poetic extravagance and density of imagery far from anything Pound would have accepted, and at times, with luck, he can be very good. His "Tall Man Executes a Jig" is certainly one of the best poems written in Canada.

As the situation changes, up through the 1950s to the explosive 1960s, with the public attitude to poetry improving and poets becoming more self-assured, it becomes difficult to think in terms of movements. Some poets, like the austerely yet luminously religious Margaret Avison (b. 1918), were always too uncompromisingly themselves to be grouped in any meaningful way with other writers. Others, like Al Purdy (b. 1918), show in their work so broad a grasp of what it means to write poetry about Canada that they seem to epitomize a generation's experience. Yet Purdy stands, in his idiosyncratic way, quite outside categorization. He writes directly from experience; his poems often read like fragments of an autobiography. Yet there is a haunting, disillusioned love of the land in them that is more telling than any stridently nationalist verse:

> This is the country of our defeat
>   and yet
> during the fall plowing a man
> might stop and stand in a brown valley
>   of the furrows
>   and shade his eyes to watch for the
>   same
>   red patch mixed with gold
>   that appears in the same
>   spot in the hills
>   year after year
>   and grow old
> plowing and plowing a ten-acre field
>   until
> the convolutions run parallel to his
>   own brain.

Purdy's recent *Collected Poems* (1986) shows him a major C. poet by any standards. His melding of the sense of history in a new country suddenly grown old in its feelings with an awareness of place as a visual reality has enlightened younger poets, so that a kind of geohistorical trad. has come into being, represented by writers like John Newlove (b. 1938), Sid Marty (b. 1944), Andrew Suknazki (b. 1942), and, perhaps most notably, that fine rural poet of the Maritimes, Alden Nowlan (1933–83). The Western writer Patrick Lane (b. 1939) shows a remarkable evolution from a tough working poet to a philosophic poet who has movingly recorded the alienation of modern man, with compassion its only antidote.

Another strain running through recent C. p. is more concerned with the artifice of versecraft and directed to the inner landscape of memory and myth, of dream and feeling. Notable in this line have been James Reaney (b. 1926), Jay Macpherson (b. 1931), and Eli Mandel (b. 1922), poets who were once somewhat hastily classed together as a "Mythopoeic" school. Most versatile among these poets has been Margaret Atwood (b. 1939), who has also gained high reputation as a novelist and a critic, and whose work in all genres shows an extraordinary combination of mental toughness and elliptic economy. As she says in *Power Politics*:

Beyond truth,
tenacity: of those
dwarf trees & mosses,
hooked into straight rock
believing the sun's lies & thus
refuting / gravity.

& of this cactus, gathering
itself together
against the sand, yes tough
rind & spikes but doing
the best it can

Among other poets who have in their special ways demonstrated the extraordinary variegation and enrichment of C. p. during recent decades are Leonard Cohen (b. 1934) and Gwendolyn MacEwen (b. 1941), George Bowering (b. 1935) and Michael Ondaatje (b. 1943), and perhaps most deserving of mention because her clear, spare gravity went so long unrecognized, Phyllis Webb (b. 1927), whose long verse address, "To Friends Who Have Also Considered Suicide," is a poem in intent both serious and satirical, in tone at once grave and strangely gay. It contains a whole philosophy, a whole critique of our views of existence.

Some people swim lakes, others climb
flagpoles,
some join monasteries, but we, my
friends,
who have considered suicide take our
daily walk
with death and are not lonely.
In the end it brings more honesty and
care
than all the democratic parliaments of
tricks.
It is the "sickness unto death"; it is
death;
it is not death; it is the sand from the
beaches
of a hundred civilizations, the sand in
the teeth
of death and barnacles our singing
tongue:
and this is "life" and we owe at least
this much
contemplation to our western fact; to
Rise,
Decline, Fall, to futility and larks,
to the bright crustaceans of the oversky.

Younger Canadian poets—those born in the late 1940s and the 1950s—are now emerging into prominence, notable among them Dale Zieroth (b. 1946), Marilyn Bowering (b. 1949), and Roo Borson (b. 1952). Perhaps the most striking recent phenomenon is that of poets with strongly ethnic links and attitudes who write in Eng. In the past in Canada there were strong minor trads. in such langs. as Icelandic and Ukrainian, but now the children of immigrants tend to write in English even though they may continue to think in their parents' lang. Thus, particularly among those of It. descent—like Pier Giorgio di Cicco (b. 1949) and Mary di Michele (b. 1949)—we have notable poets who use the same lang. as their contemporaries, but continue to project their distinctive trads., filtered through the lens of C. experience.

ANTHOLOGIES: *The Book of C. P.*, 3d rev. ed. (1957), *Oxford Book of C. Verse* (Eng. and Fr.; 1960), *Mod. C. Verse* (Eng. and Fr.; 1967)—all ed. by A. J. M. Smith; *The Penguin Book of C. Verse*, ed. R. Gustafson (1959); *The New Oxford Book of C. Verse in Eng.*, ed. M. Atwood (1982); *The New C. Poets*, ed. D. Lee (1986).

HISTORY AND CRITICISM: W. E. Collin, *The White Savannahs* (1936); E. K. Brown, *On C. P.*, rev. ed. (1944); D. Pacey, *Creative Writing in Canada*, rev. ed. (1961); *Lit. Hist. of Canada*, ed. C. F. Klinck and W. H. New, 4 v. (1965–90); D. G. Jones, *Butterfly on Rock* (1970); N. Frye, *The Bush Garden* (1971); *Oxford Companion to C. Lit.*, ed. W. Toye (1983); G. Woodcock, *Northern Spring: The Flowering of C. Lit.* (1987); C. Bayard, *The New Poetics in Canada and Quebec* (1989); *Studies on C. Lit.*, ed. A. E. Davidson (1990).   G.W.

II. IN FRENCH. Very few pieces of verse have reached us from the early Fr. colonial period, but it may be worthy of mention that one of the first Fr. explorers, Marc Lescarbot (1570?–1630?) is probably the author of the first poems written in and about North America (*Les Muses de la Nouvelle-France*, 1609). Much later, following the British conquest (1763), newspapermen, politicians, and clergymen resorted to verse to comment on current events; many of these pieces were collected by James Huston in his *Répertoire national* (4 v., 1848–50). They are invariably bad poetry, but they throw much light on the attitudes of the first generations of Fr. Canadians who lived under British rule. The best of the genre is Michel Bibaud's *Epîtres, satires, chansons et autres pièces de vers* (1830), the first book of verse published by an author born in Canada. More important for later poetry, though not poetry itself, is the *Histoire du Canada* (4 v., 1845–52) by historian François-Xavier Garneau, a book which played a vital role in the emergence of a Fr. C. lit., incl. poetry, by providing local writers with challenging historical subjects and patriotic themes. Without him, it is virtually certain that Fr. Can. lit. would have developed differently and somewhat later.

The later poets, Crémazie, Fréchette, and Chapman, owe much to Garneau. The earliest Fr. C. poet to achieve a certain level of excellence was Octave Crémazie (1827–79), whose poetry is generally made up of narratives inspired by historical events described by Garneau. This is largely true also of the prolific Louis-Honoré Fréchette (1839–1908), the leading Fr. C. poet of the 19th c., who, however, in addition wrote about C. nature and rural life. His major work, *La Légende d'un peuple*

(1887), a series of short epics, glorifies the most popular Fr. C. heroes and historical events. Both his inspiration and style owe much to Victor Hugo: his manner is more oratorical than lyrical. The same can be said of his rival William Chapman (1850–1917), whose works are, however, less ambitious and forceful. But the overwhelming prevalence of historical themes naturally led to a reaction, as did the pervasive influence of the Fr. romantic school.

The earlier poets who turned their backs on historical subjects were (paradoxically) the historian's son, Alfred Garneau (1836–1904), a gifted minor poet who wrote mainly about nature, friendship, and death. The simple life and secular trads. of the still predominantly rural Fr. C. population are the main themes of such poets as the prolific Pamphile Lemay (1837–1918) and the delicate Nérée Beauchemin (1850–1931). It was obvious that local poets had discovered and been influenced by recent Fr. poetry, esp. the Fr. Parnassians and the symbolist school. The romantic trad. was to be maintained well into the 20th c., but new themes, trends, and techniques were introduced toward the end of the 19th c., esp. by the members of the Ecole littéraire de Montréal and some other independent poets. It is significant that at the end of the 19th c. Montréal replaced Québec City as the main center of Fr. C. lit., a fact which goes a long way in explaining how Fr. C. p. evolved from one concerned mainly with traditional values to one influenced more by the solitary and frequently disquieting life in a modern industrial metropolis. Fr. C. p. gradually became more personal and more lyrical, concerned less with historical or current events and more with inner life, with personal emotions, aspirations, sorrows, and dreams. At the same time, it also became more diversified in inspiration and more accomplished in craftsmanship.

Although the influence of such Fr. poets as Baudelaire, Verlaine, Rimbaud, and others is still visible in the works of the following generation, esp. in the poetry of the most outstanding poet of the Ecole littéraire de Montréal, Emile Nelligan (1879–1941), there is no denying that much of the new Fr. C. p. started to break away from literary colonialism. There began to be heard a distinct new voice expressing the soul of a new people. Before going out of his mind in his early twenties, Nelligan authored some of the best verse written in Canada. There is also a good deal of melancholy in the poems of the sentimental Albert Lozeau (1878–1924), but the inspiration of their contemporary Charles Gill (1871–1918) is mainly epic in his colored descriptions of the country and its legends. Lesser poets of the Ecole littéraire were Jean Charbonneau, Alphonse Beauregard, Albert Dreux (a master of free verse), Lionel Léveillé, Gonzalve Desaulniers, and Albert Ferland. The Ecole did not aim at imposing any common aims or rules; it was a forum where the most diverse

poets, from the philosophical Charbonneau to the rustic Desaulniers or Ferland, could engage in dialogue. At the edge of the Ecole, one find also independent poets like Louis Dantin, Jean-Aubert Loranger, and the ultimate craftsman, Paul Morin, who drew his subjects from the most exotic themes from Italy, Spain, and the Arab world (*Le Paon d'émail*, 1911).

Between the two World Wars, most Fr. C. p. remained rather conservative, or traditional, in both form and content, much of it written in regular verse and dealing with C. themes: winter, solitude, nature, or more universal themes like love (or its absence), friendship, soul searching. There is still a great deal of romanticism in the poetry of Robert Choquette (*À travers les vents*, 1925; *Suite marine*, 1953), Simone Routier (*L'Immortel Adolescent*, 1928), Jovette Bernier (*Les masques déchirés*, 132) or Medjé Vézina (*Chaque heure a son visage*, 1934). Love is the main theme of these neo-romantic poets. The leading poet of that generation, however, Alfred Desrochers depicted with force and emotion the rude life of pioneers in a new world still largely undeveloped (*À l'ombre de l'Orford*, 1930), and a younger poet of the same vein, Clément Marchand (*Les Soirs rouges*, 1947) introduced in Fr. C. p. proletarian themes in depicting the hard times endured by city-dwellers.

Yet between the Wars there also emerged new themes and, even more so, a new style, a much freer prosody or no prosody at all, as *vers libre* gave way to poetic prose. Here the leading representatives were Hector de Saint-Denys-Garneau, Alain Grandbois, Anne Hébert, and Rina Lasnier. Although highly personal in style and substance, the work of these poets shares common features: all four express, more or less esoterically, spiritual experiences rooted in the simultaneous realizations that the beauty of the world is constantly threatened by death, that all things are in a state of flux, and that human aspirations toward eternal bliss are mixed with the recurring misfortunes of life. There is something metaphysical about this poetry, from Garneau's *Regards et jeux dans l'espace* (1937) and Grandbois' *Iles de la nuit* (1944) to Anne Hébert's *Le Tombeau des rois* (1953) and Rina Lasnier's *Présence de l'absence* (1956). The key words of these titles are themselves very revealing of the new dimensions of this poetry: space, night, tomb, presence, absence. This is a poetry of the mind and of the soul, even if the outside world is ever-present, frequently as an enemy. These works mark the end of parochial as well as academic poetry. Henceforth, Fr. C. p. would remain modern in inspiration and style. Soon it would also proclaim the rejection of traditional values and of society itself, as an increasing number of poets would be adepts of Marxism or even anarchists (esp. at the time when Québec separatism was at its peak).

These themes have been pursued and renewed

by more recent poets such as Gilles Hénault, Pierre Trottier, Paul-Marie Lapointe, Roland Giguère, Fernand Ouellette, Michèle Lalonde, Gaston Miron, and Gatien Lalointe. Although several younger poets are dealing with political and social themes and use poetry as a tool for transforming society, most recent Fr. C. p. deals with the more universal themes of love and despair, friendship and the quest for happiness. It is decidedly contemporary in matter and form.

ANTHOLOGIES: *La Poésie canadienne*, ed. A. Bosquet (1962); *Anthologie de la poésie québéçoise*, ed. G. Sylvestre, 7th ed. (1974); *La Poésie québéçoise: Anthologie*, ed. L. Mailhot and P. Nepveu (1986).

HISTORY AND CRITICISM: L. Dantin, *Poètes de l'Amérique française*, 2 v. (1928, 1934); G. Marcotte, *Une Littérature qui se fait* (1962), *Le Temps des poètes* (1969); *Mod. C. Verse in Eng. and Fr.*, ed. A. J. M. Smith (1967); *The P. of Fr. Canada in translation*, ed. J. Glassco (1970); J. Blais, *De l'ordre et de l'aventure: La Poésie au Québec de 1934 à 1944* (1975); R. Hamel, J. Hare, and P. Wyczynski, *Dictionnaire pratique des auteurs québéçois* (1976). G.S.

CANCIÓN. The term is now loosely applied to any Sp. isostrophic poem in Italianate lines (11 and 7 syllables) and in which the poet invents a first strophe and then models all subsequent strophes on it exactly, in responsion. *Canciones* of a few lines are often called *liras, canciones aliradas, canciones clásicas,* and *odas.* Many variations have been developed since the Italinate *c.* (cf. CANZONE) was introduced by Boscán and Garcilaso near the middle of the 16th c. The *c. petrarquista* (also called *c. a la italiana, c. extensa,* and *estancias)* is generally considered the purest form of the Italianate type.

In the 15th and early 16th c., before the use of the Italianate form, an entirely different type of *c.*—an octosyllabic form of *cantiga* (cf. DECIR)— was widely employed. Although some variety in pattern was allowed in the early period, by the end of the 15th c. the form was usually restricted to either a quatrain (*abab* or *abba*) followed by a *copla de arte menor* (eight lines only), whose last four rhymes are identical with those of the initial quatrain though the order of the rhymes may be changed, or a *quintilla* (two rhymes only, no set order) followed by a *copla real* or a *copla de arte menor* of nine or ten lines, whose last five rhymes are identical with and follow the same sequence as those of the initial *quintilla.* Variation in the first type, then, may occur only in the order of rhymes, and in the second type only in the length of the second strophe. F. Vendrell de Millás (ed. *El Cancionero de Palacio,* 1945, pp. 95–100) lists other variations. This *c.* may be distinguished from the closely related *villancico* (q.v.), according to Le Gentil (2.263 ff.), by its longer refrain (four or five lines having *redondilla, serventesio,* or *quintilla* rhyme); its *vuelta,* which parallels exactly the initial theme; its shorter length, which rarely exceeds one stanza; and its courtly nature and love theme.—Le Gentil. D.C.C.

CANCIONEIROS. See CANTIGA.

CANON (Ger. *kanon,* "rule" or "standard"; also "list" or "catalog" [see Childs 24–25]). The two etymological senses of the term c. are conflated in its most common use: an authoritative list of books forming the Judeo-Christian Bible—authoritative here meaning inspired by God or legitimized by the believing community. In secular lit. crit., c. has three senses: (a) rules of crit.; (b) a list of works by a single author; and (c) a list of texts believed to be culturally central or "classic" (see CLASSICISM). Whatever the practical difficulties in determining specific rules or authorship, usage in the first two senses is clear, e.g. "the cs. of taste" or "the c. of Shakespeare's works." The third sense—the subject of the remainder of this entry—is more problematic, since it supposes that secular texts can be authoritative in a manner analogous to sacred texts. Authority here is located not in a single text or author but in a particular group of texts whose formulators see that group as esp. valuable to its culture (see EVALUATION). Although the word c. is not used in the Bible itself, the formation and continuing existence of the various biblical cs. are instructive for studying secular cs. since there the issue of authority is necessarily foregrounded.

The word c. was first applied to the Bible in the 4th c. A.D. The first early medieval non-biblical c. was patristic, followed by the medieval *auctores,* lists for school study of authors both Christian and pagan (Hardison). Except for the inevitable Christian-pagan tension—often alleviated by allegorical accommodation of pagan to Christian (see ALLEGORY)—this Lat. c. remained relatively uncontroversial until the rise of the vernacular langs. in the Ren., beginning in Italy, motivated c. change (Curtius, Auerbach, Weinberg). Subsequent 17th- and 18th-century c. formulations (see NEOCLASSICAL POETICS) from national and comparative perspectives alike usually linked cs. with cultural values explicitly (Dryden, S. Johnson), as did Matthew Arnold and T. S. Eliot in late 19th- and early 20th-c. England (see also Sainte-Beuve).

If we exclude accident (e.g. the fact that the destruction of the Alexandrian Library in effect helped canonize works in the surviving mss.), the central factors in c. formation are ideological, religious, and aesthetic values in particular and complex combinations (Kermode 1985, Mitchell, van Hallberg). These factors may be intertwined but are not always consciously or explicitly acknowledged to be so. As a modern example, much New Critical emphasis on the "tradition" (q.v.) seeks to ground it in exclusively aesthetic value. Brooks is "concerned with the poems as poems"; poems "in the main stream of the trad.," and aesthetically most valuable, "giv[e] us an insight which preserves the unity of experience and which . . . triumphs over the apparently contradictory and conflicting elements of experience by unifying them into a new pattern" (Brooks 215, 214, 192). But "unity of experience" is more than an aesthetic value.

Biblical and secular canonical crit. alike study not only c. formation but the subsequent life of a c. already formed. Secular crit. that takes for granted a c. practices, whether self-consciously or not, a hermeneutics of accommodation, mediating between the classic text and the modern reader (Kermode 1975). And late 20th-c. crit., despite its theoretical self-consciousness, often takes cs. for granted. Marxist crit. (q.v.) mostly reads canonical texts, as does deconstruction (q.v.), although the latter draws from more diverse psychoanalytic, philosophical, and critical cs. (e.g. Freud, Nietzsche, Derrida, de Man) as often as literary ones—thus opening the c. horizontally, to include nonliterary texts, but not vertically. Reader-response crit. (q.v.) is most often interested in educated readers responding to canonical texts (cf. Sammons). Implicit challenges to Western literary cs. have come from structuralism and semiotics (qq.v.), disciplines which consider any literary text—if not any cultural product at all—appropriate for study. But the most explicit challenges to Western literary cs. have come from Fr. and Am. feminist crit. (q.v.), curricular crit. (Graff), working-class writing in England, and third-world writing, which often view existing cs. as ideologically oppressive in effect if not always in motive (Eagleton).

There have probably always been cs. (cf. Barr), formalized or not, and they have always had—or been capable of being given, which is not the same—ideological relevance. Such relevance however is not easily predictable. How and in what contexts a c. is read, taught, or learned may or may not reinforce a particular ideological rationale for constituting that c. For example, the belief that classics ultimately express harmony rather than discord, and thus serve or at least complement empire (e.g. Roman, British), does not explain why other texts expressing harmony are not canonized, or why such classics cannot also be read as undermining "unity of experience" and expressing discord rather than harmony (W. Johnson). Likewise, the relation of ideology to life cannot be taken for granted (Abercrombie). No generalization about these relationships has been adequate to cover all instances of c. formation and effect. See also HISTORICISM.

J. Dryden, Preface to *Fables Ancient and Modern* (1700); S. Johnson, *Lives of the Poets* (1781); C. Sainte-Beuve, "What is a Classic?" (1850), "On the Literary Trad." (1858); M. Arnold, *Essays in Crit.* (1865, 1888); C. Brooks, *Mod. Poetry and the Trad.* (1939); Brooks; Eliot, *Essays,* and *On Poetry and Poets* (1956); Curtius, 247–72; E. Auerbach, *Liter-ary Lang. and Its Public in Late Lat. Antiquity and in the Middle Ages* (1958; tr. 1965); Weinberg; W. Johnson, "The Problem of the Counter-classical Sensibility and Its Critics," *Calif. Studies in Cl. Antiquity* 3 (1970); *Med. Lit. Crit.,* ed. O. B. Hardison, Jr., et al. (1974); F. Kermode, *The Classic* (1975), *Forms of Attention* (1985); J. Sammons, *Literary Sociology and Practical Crit.* (1977); N. Abercrombie et al., *The Dominant Ideology Thesis* (1980); Fowler; J. Barr, *Holy Scripture* (1983); T. Eagleton, *Literary Theory* (1983); *The Politics of Interp.,* ed. W. J. T. Mitchell (1983); B. Childs, *The New Testament as C.* (1984); *Cs.,* ed. R. von Hallberg (1984); J. Weber, *Kanon und Methode* (1986); G. Graff, *Professing Lit.* (1987); J. Guillory, "C.," *Critical Terms for Literary Study,* ed. F. Lentricchia and T. McLaughlin (1990); W. V. Harris, "Canonicity," *PMLA* 106 (1991); C. Kaplan and E. C. Rose, *The C. and the Common Reader* (1991); C. Altieri, *Cs. and Consequences* (1991); P. Lauter, *Cs. and Context* (1991). J.C.S.

CANSO, *chanso, chanson.* A love song, the literary genre *par excellence* among the troubadours (q.v.). Its distinguishing characteristics are precisely the two great contributions of the troubadours to all subsequent European lit.—a new conception of love involving the exaltation of the lady (see COURTLY LOVE; LOVE POETRY), and a constant striving for perfection and originality of form. It is impossible to draw a sharp line between the c. and the older *vers* (q.v.); but by the time the name c. came into common use (toward the end of the 12th c.), the ideals of courtly love had become generally accepted and the technique of composition more polished, so that the c. is apt to be more artistic, but also more conventional and artificial, than the *vers.*

The typical c. has five or six stanzas of identical structure, plus a *tornada* (Occitan) or *envoi* (Fr.; qq.v.). Far from following any set metrical pattern, every c. was expected to have a stanzaic structure and a tune that were completely original. This proved too high a hurdle for many poets, but the metrical diversity of the extant *chansos* is still very impressive. Unfortunately, the same cannot always be said for their contents, which often ring the changes on a few well-worn themes and situations. The poet's lady love is almost never named, and she is described in such vague generalities that identification is ordinarily out of the question. The proper names used in a c. (commonly secret names, or *senhals,* in the *tornada*) are for the most part those of friends or patrons to whom the poem is dedicated. See also CANZONE; SONG.

R. Dragonetti, *La Technique poétique des trouvères dans la chanson courtoise* (1960); M. Lazar, *Amour courtois et fin'amors* (1964); H. van der Werf, *The Chansons of the Troubadours and Trouvères* (1972); L. T. Topsfield, *Troubadours and Love* (1975); Elwert, sect. 194; Sayce; *Chanter m'estuet,* ed. S. N. Rosenberg and H. Tischler (1981); *A Med. Song-*

book, ed. F. Collins, Jr. (1982); M. L. Switten, *The "Cs." of Raimon de Miraval* (1985); Chambers.

F.M.C.

CANTAR. Throughout Sp. lit. the term c. has been used loosely to mean words for a song. In the 15th c., it was probably the equivalent of *cantiga* (q.v.). In modern times it has come to mean specifically an octosyllabic quatrain having assonance (occasionally true rhyme) in the even-numbered lines and, preferably, unrhymed oxytones in the odd-numbered: "Algún día me verás / cuando no tenga remedio; / me verás y te veré, / pero no nos hablaremos." The composition, also called *copla*, is usually confined to one strophe. The *seguidilla gitana* (see SEGUIDILLA) is sometimes called c. The c. is sometimes defined as an octosyllabic 5-line monostrophic poem assonating *ababa*. The *c. de soledad*, also known as *soledad, soleá, terceto*, and *triada gallega*, is an octosyllabic c. reduced to three lines. The first and third lines rhyme in either assonance or true rhyme and the second is left unrhymed. The form is of popular origin. Dance songs, such as the *jota* and the *malagueña*, are also termed "c." The *c. de gesta*, also called simply c., is usually a med. epic poem. The lines vary in length but are long and divided into hemistichs. The poem is divided into *laisses* (q.v.) of unequal length, each *laisse* being monorhymed in assonance. The anonymous *C. de Mio Cid* (ca. 1140) is the most famous example.—N. Alonso Cortés, *Elementos de preceptiva literaria*, 6th ed. (1919); S. G. Morley, "Recent Theories about the Meter of the 'Cid,'" *PMLA* 48 (1933); Navarro; C. Smith, *The making of the Poema de mio Cid* (1983). D.C.C.

CANTE JONDO. A type of primitive Andalusian popular song or lament which persists to this day in poetry, music, and dance (*baile flamenco*). The origins of the c. j. have never been completely explained, but it undoubtedly has roots in Christian and Muslim religious chants, which in turn were fused with traditional gypsy music and folkloric elements in Southern Spain. A Jewish heritage has been claimed on the basis of the chanting nature of c. j., which is then taken to mean "deep song"; those favoring a Hebrew source say it derives from *Jom Tov*, "feast day."

The most familiar forms of the c. j. are the *sequiriya* or *seguidilla* (according to García Lorca, the most genuine—[q.v.]), the *soleá*, the *saeta*, the *petenera*, the *polo*, and the *martinete*. Among its celebrated interpreters are Pastora Pavón (*La Niña de los Peines*), Juan Breva, Manuel Torres, and Silverio Franconetti. In addition to Sp. musicians such as Manuel de Falla (*El Amor Brujo*) and Albéniz (*Iberia*), composers of other nationalities, including Debussy and Glinka, have been influenced by these songs of incantatory rhythm and plaintive tremulos. The classification of the various types of c. j. is highly complex, but all have in common the expression of deep, dramatic passion and suffering and anguish. The singer uses enharmonism and often slides his or her voice from note to note with minute changes—features thought to be of Byzantine-Oriental origin. Full of pathos and lament, c. j.'s principal themes are love and death, often linked to telluric forces, expressed in solemn ritual. Lorca and Rafael Alberti were especially successful at integrating these popular motifs into their sophisticated verse, an achievement which gave rise to the trend of neopopularism. The former published his *Poema del c. j.* in 1931. Twenty years earlier Manuel Machado had edited *Cante hondo: Cantares, canciones y coplas, compuestas al estilo popular de Andalucía*. In June of 1922 the *Fiesta del C.J.*, organized by de Falla and Lorca, was held in Granada.—I. Brown, *Deep Song: Adventures with Gypsy Songs and Singers in Andalusia and Other Lands* (1929); K. Schindler, *Folk Music of Spain and Portugal* (1941); M. de Falla, *Escritos sobre música y músicos* (1950); G. Chase, *The Music of Spain*, 2d ed. (1959); L. F. Compton, *Andalusian Lyrical Poetry and Old Sp. Love Songs* (1976). A.W.P.; K.N.M.

CANTICUM AND DIVERBIUM. In Roman drama, the *c.* is the part of the play that was declaimed or sung to musical accompaniment, as opposed to the *d.* or spoken dialogue. The *cantica* of Plautus are very numerous, constituting approximately two-thirds of each play, while those of Terence are few. *Cantica* are chiefly monodies or duets sung or declaimed by an actor or actors, and appear in a great variety of meters. The *cantica* of Seneca are choral songs written in meters which derive primarily from the metrical system of Horace. The *diverbia* were written, as a rule, in iambic senarii. In some mss. of Plautus the *d.* is indicated by the marginal notation DV and the *c.* by C.—Crusius; H. Drexler, *Einführung in die römische Metrik* (1967); C. Questa, *Introduzione alla metrica di Plauto* (1967); L. Braun, *Die Cantica des Plautus* (1970); A. S. Gratwick, "Drama," *CHCL*, v. 2.

P.S.C.; J.W.H.

CANTIGA. A species of literary and folk songs of the Iberian Peninsula; more particularly, a body of around 2000 Galician-Portuguese lyrics written between the late 12th and 14th cs. and contained chiefly in three *cancioneiros* (Port., "songbooks") of the 14th and 15th cs. According to subject, the four main categories are: *cs. de amigo*, sung by a woman to or about her lover; *cs. de amor*, addressed by a man to his lady; *cs. de escarnio* or *de mal dizer*, songs of vilification, sometimes obscene; and religious songs, dealing principally with miracles of the Virgin, as in Alfonso X's *Cs. de Santa María*. The *c. de amigo* is the Galician-Portuguese genre *par excellence*; it contains a mixture of lyrical, dramatic and narrative elements. The best are characterized by *saudade*, or melancholy longing, in simple, haunting, rhythmic structures, with parallelism of form and idea, refrains, and systematic synonymy. The vocabulary tends to be limited, while rhythm and musicality are essential. Rodrigues Lapa sees it as exploration of female eroticism and psyche, for like a dialogue, it is the answer to the sentiments expressed by the poet in the *c. de amor.* The latter type reveals the impossibility of requited love, although the description of the anguish or *coita* reveals no physical details, being more concentrated on moral beauty and platonic experience. The *Cs. de Santa María* represent an important cultural effort to achieve European creative levels, as well as to combat St. James' power through the Marian cult. Galician-Portuguese cs. concern the individual rather than society; contrary to those of Occitan, the *escarnio* forms are nonmoralizing. It is sometimes said that the *c. de escarnio* is a covert satire, whereas that of *mal dizer* is a direct attack upon its subject. Occitan inspiration is obvious in *pastorelas* (shepherd songs), *albas* (dawn songs), and *bailadas* (dances). See GALICIAN POETRY; PORTUGUESE POETRY.

TEXTS OF CANCIONEIROS: *Il canzoniere portoghese della Biblioteca Vaticana*, ed. E. Monaci (1875); *Cancioneiro da Ajuda*, ed. C. Michaëlis de Vasconcellos, 2 v. (1904); diplomatic ed. by H. H. Carter (1941); *Cancioneiro da Biblioteca Nacional, antigo Colocci-Brancuti*, ed. E. Pacheco Machado and J. Pedro Machado, 7 v. (1949–60); *Cantigas de Santa María*, ed. Marques de Valmar (1889), ed. W. Mettman (1981).

ANTHOLOGIES: *Cantigas d'amigo dos trovadores galego-portugueses*, 3 v. (1926–8), *Cantigas d'amor dos trovadores galego-portugueses* (1932)—both ed. J. J. Nunes; *Escolma da poesía galega*, v. 1, ed. X. M. Álvarez Blázquez (1952); *An Anthol. of Med. Lyrics*, ed. and tr. A. Flores (1962).

HISTORY AND CRITICISM: A. F. G. Bell et al., *La poesía med. portuguesa*, 2d ed. (1947); Le Gentil, v. 2; J. M. D'Heur, *Troubadors d'oc et troubadors galiciens-portugais* (1973); C. Alvar, *La poesía trovadoresca en España y Portugal* (1977); G. Tavani, "La poesia lirica gallego-portoghese," *GRLMA*, v. 2.1.6 (1980); M. Rodrigues Lapa, *Lições de literatura portuguesa: Época med.*, 10th ed. (1981); X. R. Pena, *Literatura Galega Med.*, v. 1 (1986).
L.A.S.; K.N.M.

CANTO. A longer subsection of an epic or narrative poem, as distinguished from shorter subsections such as stanzas, and corresponding roughly to chapters in a novel (a series of cantos may form a Book in a poem such as *The Faerie Queene*). The term is of It. origin and is synonymous with such designations as "movement" or "fit" in other lits.; it has been used in works by Dante, Ariosto, Tasso, Ercilla, Voltaire, Pope, Byron, and Pound, among others. In the case of Pound, *Canto* was from the beginning only a working title for the long poem he envisioned, witness the fact that the titles of the first three installments all began "A Draft of. . . ." But his own life took unexpected turns, and the extent to which the published *Cantos* reveal any integrative architecture is uncertain. Pound

clearly meant his 800-page "tale of the tribe" to be read as a modern verse epic, based to some degree on Homeric, Ovidian, and Dantean models, while at the same time, such a title, in foregrounding the poem's units of construction rather than subject matter, emphasized that the poet was still working toward an as yet unseen vision of order which would unify the poem's component parts.—R. Sale, "C.," *The Spenser Encyc.*, ed. A. C. Hamilton et al. (1990).
T.V.F.B.; T.G.

CANZONE. In *De vulgari eloquentia* Dante defines the *c.* as the most excellent It. verseform, the one which is the worthy vehicle for those "tragic" compositions which treat the three noblest subjects: martial valor, love, and moral virtue. Noting the intimate link between poetry and music (the term *canzone* comes from *cantio*, a song), Dante remarks that "although all that we put in verse is a 'song' (*cantio*), only *canzoni* have been given this name" (2.3.4). As a result, the term *c.* has come to be applied to quite a number of verseforms with differing metrical patterns. Among the better known types is the *c. epico-lirica*, whose center of diffusion was originally the Gallo-It. dialect area: it belongs to the Celtic substratum and is akin to compositions of the same genre in France and Catalonia. More indigenous to the It. soil is the *c. a ballo* or *ballata* and other popular compositions such as the *frottola* and *barzelletta* (q.v.), the *canto carnascialesco*, and the *lauda sacra* (see LAUDA). At various times these types have been used by the *poeti d'arte*, but the type exclusively employed for refined artistic expression is the so-called *c. petrarchesca*, which bears strong traces of Occitan influence. The It. *strambotto* and *ballata* (qq.v.) and Ger. Minnesang (q.v.) are also said to have conditioned its architectonic structure.

In Italy the first forms of the *c.* are found among the poets of the Sicilian School (q.v.). It is employed extensively by Guittone d'Arezzo and his followers and by the poets of the *dolce stil nuovo* (q.v.), but acquires fixed patterns and perfection in Petrarch's *Canzoniere*, hence the qualifying adjective *petrarchesca*. Its greatest vogue in Italy occurred during the age of Petrarchism (q.v.), which lasted until the death of Torquato Tasso (1595). While the Petrarchan *c.* was employed in England by William Drummond of Hawthornden and in Germany by A. W. von Schlegel and other Ger. romantic poets, Spain and Portugal were really the only countries outside Italy where it was used to a considerable extent.

One structural feature of the *c.* proved to be of lasting importance for the subsequent devel. of a number of lyric genres in the European vernaculars, esp. Occitan, OF, and MHG. This is the organization of the poem into a structure that is simultaneously tripartite and bipartite. In the terminology Dante gives in *De vulgari eloquentia* (2.10), the poem is divided into a *fronte* (Lat. *frons*) and a *sirma* (Lat. *cauda*)—head and tail—but the *frons* itself is further subdivided into two *piedi* (*pedes*, feet) which are metrically and musically identical, making the essential structure AA/B. Subsequent Ger. terms for these partitions are the *Aufgesang* divided into *Stollen* and the *Abgesang*. This structure appears in analogues as late Chaucerian *rhyme royal* (q.v.), the Venus and Adonis stanza (q.v.), and the Shakespearean sonnet, where the octave, unlike the sestet, neatly divides into quatrains. (In some cases the *sirma* may be divided into two identical parts called *volte* [Lat. *versus*].) In the It. c. there is, further, usually a single *commiato* at the close of the poem serving as a valediction. Stanzaic length is indeterminate, varying from a minimum of 7 to a maximum of 20 verses. The lines are normally hendecasyllables with some admixture of heptasyllables (qq.v.), and this mix of 11s and 7s became distinctive of the form. After Tasso, under the strong influence of the Fr. *Pléiade* (q.v.), this type was supplanted by new forms labeled *canzoni*—the Pindaric and Anacreontic (q.v.) odes, whence the inexact use of *ode* (q.v.) as a translation for *c.* Chiabrera played a leading role in their diffusion. He also revived the *canzonetta* originally employed by the poets of the Sicilian School. This became the favorite type used by Metastasio and the Arcadian school. Toward the close of the 17th c., Alessandro Guidi acclimated the *c. libera*, which reached its highest devel. at the hands of Leopardi. See also ITALIAN PROSODY.

P. E. Guarnerio, *Manuale di versificazione italiana* (1893); O. Floeck, *Die Kanzone in der deutschen Dichtung* (1910); F. Flamini, *Notizia storica dei versi e metri italiani* (1919); R. Murari, *Ritmica e metrica razionale ital.* (1927); V. Pernicone, "Storia e svolgimento della metrica," *Problemi ed orientamenti critici di lingua e di letteratura italiana*, ed. A. Momigliano, v. 2 (1948); E. Segura Covarsí, *La canción petrarquista en la lírica española del Siglo de Oro* (1949); E. H. Wilkins, "The C. and the Minnesong," *The Invention of the Sonnet* (1959); I. L. Mumford, "The *C.* in 16th-C. Eng. Verse," *EM* 11 (1960); L. Galdi, "Les origines provencales de la métrique des canzoni de Petrarque," *Actes romanes* 74 (1966); M. Pazzaglia, *Il verso e l'arte della C. nel "De vulgari eloquentia"* (1967), *Teoria e analisi metrica* (1974); E. Köhler, "'Vers' und Kanzone," *GRLMA*, v. 2.1.3; Spongano; Wilkins; M. Fubini, *Metrica e poesia*, 3d ed. (1975); D. Rieger, *Gattungen und Gattungsbezeichungen der Trobadorlyrik* (1976); J. A. Barber, "Rhyme Scheme Patterns in Petrarch's *Canzoniere*," *MLN* 92 (1977); C. Hunt, "*Lycidas*" and the It. Critics (1979); G. Gonfroy, "Le reflet de la canso dans *De vulgari eloquentia* et dans les *Leys d'amors*," *CCM* 25 (1982); F. P. Memmo, *Dizionario de metrica italiana* (1983), s.v. "C." et seq.; Elwert, *Italienische*, sect. 79.   J.G.F.; C.K.

CAPITOLO (It. "chapter"). Petrarch's term for the subdivisions of his *Trionfi* (Triumphs, ca. 1340–74). The c. is an It. verseform based on and identical in structure to Dante's *terza rima* (q.v.), i.e. tercets linked by concatenation (*c. ternario—aba bcb*, etc.). Through the 15th c. it was used for didactic subjects—an alternative form, the *c. quadernario*, derives from the Occitan *sirventes* (q.v.). The *petrarchisti* of the 16th c. employed the c. for ethical meditations, often solemnly allegorized. Ariosto in his *Satire* adopted the form to versified memoirs; F. Berni transformed it into a vehicle for parody (*c. bernesco*). After Ariosto the form survived into the 18th and 19th cs., to Alfieri, Leopardi, and Carducci, as the chief form for It. verse satire and for quotidian topics treated in a light vein.—Spongano; M. Pazzaglia, *Teoria e analisi metrica* (1974); *La metrica*, ed. R. Cremante and M. Pazzaglia, 2d ed. (1976); Elwert, *Italienische*, sect. 93.2.   T.W.; C.K.

CARIBBEAN POETRY. See PUERTO RICAN POETRY; WEST INDIAN POETRY.

CARMEN. This Lat. term usually meant "song" or "lyric," e.g. Catullus' *Carmina*; occasionally it had the broader meaning of "poetry," incl. epic, drama, and lampoon. Its broadest usage covered prophecies, oracular responses, incantations, triumphant hymns, epitaphs, charms, and even legal formulas. The word seems to connote divine inspiration, the song of the poet as the agent of a god or muse (q.v.), as in Horace's usage in the *Odes*.—D. Norberg, "C. oder Rhythmus?" *MitJ* 19 (1984).   R.A.H.

CARMINA FIGURATA. See PATTERN POETRY.

CAROL. The medieval carol was a lyric of distinct verseform which derived from and for long preserved a close connection with the dance. The Fr. form, the *carole*, was a dance-song similar in structure and movement to the early Eng. carol and probably its ancestor. But by 1550, dancing at religious festivals had fallen into desuetude, leaving the element of song. Hence, since the 16th c., the word has come to mean any festive religious song, whatever its metrical or stanzaic form, sung to a tune which in pace and melody follows secular musical traditions rather than those of hymnody. In America the carol is now almost invariably associated with Christmas; this is less true in England, where Easter carols are also widely sung. The Fr. *noël* (from Lat. *natalis*), a joyous song of the Nativity, is the counterpart of the Christmas carol; it has been an established song type since the 15th c.

Medieval carols are composed of uniform stanzas which are preceded by an initial refrain, the *burden* (q.v.), usually a rhymed couplet, which is then repeated after every stanza. Often the stanza is a quatrain of three 4-stress lines in monorhyme followed by a shorter tag line rhyming with the burden. The following slightly modernized example is from a 15th.-c. carol of moral advice:

Man, beware, beware, beware,
And keep thee that thou have no care.

Thy tongue is made of flesh and blood;
Evil to speak it is not good;
By Christ, that died upon the rood,
So give us grace our tongues to spare.

More commonly the stanza rhymes *abab*; it may also be extended to 5, 6, or 8 lines and bound together by a variety of rhyme schemes. The burdens, too, are sometimes extended by one or two lines. Perhaps the single most notable variation from the norm is having the tag line identical with a refrain line, an integration that is common when a dance-song ceases to be danced.

In the round dances at which carols were originally performed, the stanza was probably sung by the leader of the dance and the burden by the chorus as they executed an accompanying dance figure. Modern children's games like "Now We Go 'Round the Mulberry Bush" and "A Tisket, A Tasket" represent corrupt descendants of the medieval round dances—then an adult pastime. From the violent denunciations of caroling that fulminated from medieval clerics, it is clear that caroling was regarded as a wicked pagan survival, though perhaps it was more than the songs that the clerics were concerned about: many of the older specimens are highly erotic and some very explicit. Doubtless the reason why caroling waxed strongest at Christmas and Easter was that these Christian festivals supplanted earlier winter and spring fertility revels. Of some 500 medieval carols extant in ms., about 200 deal directly or indirectly with Advent and the Nativity. But political, moral, and satirical carols are also abundant.

Carols were popular not only among the folk but in courtly circles as well; most of those extant show learned influences such as Lat. tags. Differing ms. versions of the same carol do not exhibit the kinds of variation that one would expect if carols had been orally transmitted in the manner of folksong.

With the Reformation, the medieval carol began to die out, mainly due to the more sober fashion of celebrating Christmas and other religious holidays. The formal carol was thus gradually replaced by festive songs learned from broadsides, chapbooks, and devotional songbooks. Some carols of this new kind, like *The Seven Joys of Mary, I Saw Three Ships, God Rest You Merry, Gentlemen*, and *The Virgin Unspotted*, are regularly described as "traditional," a term which means only that such pieces were long popular and are anonymous, not necessarily that they are folksongs or oral-formulaic.

The carols which supplanted the medieval carols were themselves beginning to wither in popularity when musical antiquaries like Gilbert Davies (*Some Ancient Christmas Carols*, 1822) and William Sandys (*Christmas Carols, Ancient and Mod.*, 1833) collected and revived them. J. M. Neale and Thomas Helmore in 1852 introduced the practice, since followed in most British and Am. carol books, of plundering Fr., Basque, Dutch, Sp., It., Ger., and Scandinavian collections for tunes to which Eng. words could be adapted. After 1870 the rural counties of England were scoured for folk carols, and the collectors' discoveries have been impressive. By being made available in excellent arrangements by Cecil J. Sharp, Vaughan Williams, and other folk-music experts, the folk carols have been artificially revitalized among educated people. In America, folk carols are comparatively rare; the only ones widely reported in this century, *The Seven Joys of Mary, Jesus Born in Bethlehem*, and *The Twelve Days of Christmas*, are all British imports.

A. E. Gillington, *Old Christmas Carols of the Southern Counties* (1910); C. J. Sharp, *Eng. Folk Carols* (1911); R. V. Williams, *Eight Traditional Carols* (1919); *Oxford Book of Carols*, ed. P. Dearmer (1928); P. Verrier, *Le Vers français*, v. 1 (1931), "La Plus Vieille Citation de carole," *Romania* 58 (1932); Sir R. R. Terry, *Two Hundred Folk Carols* (1933); *F. C. Brown Coll. of North Carolina Folklore*, v. 2 (1952), 199–212—abundant references to other sources on Am. folk carols; R. H. Robbins, "ME Carols as Processional Hymns," *SP* 56 (1959), "Greene's Revised Carols," *Review* 1 (1979); E. Routley, *The Eng. Carol* (1959); R. L. Greene, "Carols in Tudor Drama," *Chaucer and ME Studies*, ed. B. Rowland (1971), *The Early Eng. Carols*, 2d ed. (1977)—the definitive collection of medieval carols, with superb and lengthy critical intro.; F. McKay, "The Survival of the Carol in the 17th C.," *Anglia* 100 (1982).　　　　A.B.F.; T.V.F.B.

CARPE DIEM (Lat. "pluck [enjoy] the day"). A phrase from Horace, *Odes* 1.11, that enjoins full utilization of the present time. The hedonistic form of the motif ("eat, drink, and be merry . . .") is already fully developed in the Egyptian "Song of the Harper" and in the advice of Siduri to Gilgamesh (Pritchard). Typically, the c. d. injunction is pronounced amid warnings about the transience of life, the uncertainty of the future, and the inevitability and finality of death (". . . for tomorrow we die"). The motif occurs in many genres of Gr. poetry: lyric (Alcaeus, fr. 38a; *Anacreontea* 32), elegiac (Theognis 973-78), drama (Aeschylus, *Persians* 840-42; Euripides, *Alcestis* 780-802), and epigrams (*Anthologia Palatina* 5.79, 5.118, 11.38). The advice to enjoy the present can range from eating (*Iliad* 24.618-19) and drinking (Alcaeus, fr. 38a) to love (Catullus, *Carmina* 5: "Let us live, my Lesbia, and let us love"). The Roman master of the motif was Horace, many of whose poems urge a refined, Epicurean enjoyment of the day (e.g. *Odes* 1.4, 1.9, 1.11, 2.14, 3.29, 4.7). In order to stress the urgency of enjoying the present in the face of fleeting time, the speaker often draws analogies from nature; consequently, the subgenre is full of references to rising and setting suns, seasonal changes, and flowers.

The late Lat. poem *De rosis nascentibus* attributed to Ausonius (ca. 400 A.D.), which describes roses blooming at Paestum and concludes with the advice "Gather, maiden, roses, while the bloom is fresh and youth is fresh," established the rose as one of the emblems of the c. d. poem (e.g. Ronsard, "Mignonne, allons voir si la rose"; Spenser, *FQ* 2.12.74-75; Herrick, "Gather ye rosebuds while ye may"; and Waller, "Go, lovely rose"). In Ren. poetry the c. d. theme often serves as the basis of "persuasions" to seduce coy young women, as in Daniel (Sonnet 31), Carew ("To A. L. Perswasions to love") and Milton (*Comus* 736-54), but the best known example is Marvell's "To His Coy Mistress," which prominently exhibits the syllogistic form implicit in many c. d. poems. In the 19th c. FitzGerald's versions of *The Rubáiyát of Omar Khayyám* popularized the hedonistic c. d. theme. Recent examples include A. E. Housman's "Loveliest of Trees, the Cherry Now" and John Crowe Ransom's "Blue Girls."—F. Bruser, "Comus and the Rose Song," *SP* 44 (1947); H. Weber, *La Création poétique au XVIe siècle en France* (1956); J. B. Pritchard, *Ancient Near Eastern Texts* (1969); R. G. M. Nisbet and M. Hubbard, *A Commentary on Horace*, Odes Book I (1970).　　　　　W.H.R.

CATACHRESIS (Gr. "misuse"). The misapplication of a word, esp. to produce a strained or mixed metaphor. Most often it is not a ridiculous misapplication, as in doggerel verse, but rather a deliberate wresting of a term from its proper signification for effect. Sometimes it is deliberately humorous. Quintilian calls it a necessary misuse (*abusio*) of words and cites *Aeneid* 2.15–16: "equum divina Palladis arte / ædificant" (They build a horse by Pallas' divine art). Since *aedificant* literally means "they build a house," it is a c. when applied to a horse. A disapproving view of c. might call it a mixed metaphor, which is a fault, but many examples, e.g. "the sword shall devour," make sense and are striking. Two celebrated examples are found in Shakespeare—"To take arms against a sea of troubles" (*Hamlet* 3.1.60)—and in Milton—"Blind mouths! that scarce themselves know how to hold a sheep-hook" (*Lycidas* 119–20). A very effective c. is Shakespeare's "'Tis deepest winter in Lord Timon's purse" (*Timon of Athens* 3.4.15), which suggests comparison with some of the strained metaphors and conceits (qq.v.) of metaphysical poetry (q.v.) and modern poetry, e.g. "The sun roars at the prayer's end" (Dylan Thomas, *Visions and Prayer*). In any event, the semantic transference produced by c. generates new meaning insofar as it is accepted as a successful effect; Joseph (146) says Shakespeare uses it to achieve "sudden concentrations of meaning," together with "compression, energy, and intensity." See FIGURE, SCHEME, TROPE.—Sr. M. Joseph, *Shakespeare's Use of the Arts of Lang.* (1947); Lausberg; Morier; A. Quinn, *Figures of Speech* (1982), 94–96; S. R. Levin, "C.: Vico and Joyce," *P&R* 20 (1987).　　　　　M.T.H.; T.V.F.B.

CATALAN POETRY. (This article treats poetry in Catalan, the lang. of the eastern region of the Iberian peninsula; for the poetries of the western and central langs., see GALICIAN POETRY and SPANISH POETRY.)

It has been the peculiar fate of the poetry of the Catalans that during a number of centuries it was written by them mainly in langs. that were not their own: Occitan in the Middle Ages, Castilian during the age of Sp. ascendancy. It is only since romanticism that a poetry in their own vernacular has continuously flourished in Catalonia and the C.-speaking Valencia and Balearics.

In the Middle Ages, the geographic, linguistic, and political propinquity of Catalonia and Provence, and the European prestige of Occitan poetry (q.v.), caused the Catalans to write theirs in the literary lang. of Provence, borrowing also the patterns—courtly love (q.v.), satire, moralization—with the poetics of the troubadours (q.v.). Most C. poets held to this practice from the 12th c. to the 15th. Guillem de Berguedà (1140–ca. 1200) and Cerverí de Girona (fl. 1250–80) are among the best of the early C. troubadours and Jaume March (1335–1410?) and Pere March (1338?–1413) among the late ones.

Relics have been found, however, of a poetry written in Catalonia in the same centuries, not in literary Occitan, but in C.: a popular, religious poetry (mainly Marian, and usually addressed to the Virgin of Montserrat), of a type still common in C. lit. Ramon Llull (1232?–1316) wrote more formal poetry in C., reaching lyric heights in his *Desconhort* (Distress) and the *Cant de Ramon* (Ramon's Song). His greatest lyric is the *Llibre d'Amic e Amat* (The Book of the Friend and his Beloved), a prose poem somewhat influenced by the Arab mystics and celebrating the ascension of Man's soul through Love toward God.

In the 14th and 15th cs. narrative poetry appeared in Catalonia, usually written in octosyllabic couplets. One might include in this type the *Spill* (Mirror) or *Llibre de les dones* (A Book about Women) by Jaume Roig (d. 1478), a book on the wiles and vices of women, written in 4-syllable couplets.

The close political ties of the Crown of Aragon with Sicily, Naples, and Italy in general soon added to the Occitan influence the influence of the It. *dolce stil nuovo* (q.v.). A slight Petrarchan tinge has been noticed in the verse of Jordi de Sant Jordi (ca. 1400–24), although he was still very much a writer in the Occitan trad. Ausiàs March (1397–1459) is the heir to both troubadour and It. lyricism. Within these trads., March reveals a profound psychological insight that can transform medieval or Italianate topics into expressions of universal human emotions. His work is usually divided into songs of love, songs of death, moral songs, and spiritual songs, in all of which—as he himself said—there is no fiction, but rather truth, trouble, and solitude. Completing the trilogy of great C. poets of the 15th c. is Joan Roïc de Corella (ca. 1430–ca. 1490), a poet first of sensual love, then of pure love and finally of divine love. He was a writer of great visual and imagistic power, and also the first to introduce into C. poetics the It. hendecasyllable (q.v.).

Just as it seemed that C. p. had established itself in the work of Ausiàs March and Roïc de Corella and the minor poets that followed them, a decadence set in which vitiated C. p. almost completely. In fact, from the beginning of the 16th c. to the beginning of the 19th, most C. poets abandoned C. to write in Castilian, and although the C. lang. remained the tongue of the people of Catalonia, it was used in poetry only by minor writers. The only poetic genres in C. that remained truly alive during the period were the ballad and the popular religious song, both transmitted orally by a people more attached to trad. than were the literate upper classes.

In the 19th c., with the spread of the romantic ideals of individualism and nationalism, a revival or rebirth—la Renaixença—of C. lit. took place. Romanticism (q.v.) naturally tended to foster a return to the native tongue as the means of expressing the sentiments of the people of a C. nation that was finding again its ancient pride and soul. The ode to La Pàtria (1833) by Bonaventura Carles Aribau (1798–1862) has often been cited as the symbolic beginning of this rebirth. Then the work of a number of poet-scholars like Joaquim Rubió i Ors (1818–99) and Manuel Milà i Fontanals (1818–84) gave it leadership and momentum. The revival in 1859 of the annual "Jocs Florals" (poetry contests) inspired a number of writers consistently to exercise their faculties in the vernacular. The instrument was finally ready and all previous efforts were crowned with the work of Jacint Verdaguer (1845–1902), a peasant priest.

After Verdaguer, no C. poet has had to apologize for the literary use of his native tongue. Verdaguer's poetry ranges from the epic in L'Atlàntida (Atlantis, 1877) and in Canigó (1886), to religious poetry, nature poetry, and the most subjective and intimate lyricism.

After Verdaguer, modern C. p., having come of age, shed its Romantico-Renaixença character. Joan Maragall (1860–1911) brought to it a new sense of freedom by using free verse as well as traditional forms. Maragall's poetry expresses his enjoyment of beauty, his love of life, of nature, strength, work, and creation: what is now called the "Maragallian optimism." Perhaps his best-loved books are Pirenenques (Pyreneean Poems), Vistes al mar (Views of the Sea), and Cants (Songs). He was the poet whose "measure was human" and could say:

If the world is already so beautiful,
   Lord,
when one looks at it with your Peace
   within one's eye,

what more can You give us in another
   life?

While Maragall observed or broke the classical rules, the Balearic poets of C., Miquel Costa i Llobera (1854–1922), the author of Horacianes (Horatian Poems, 1906), and Joan Alcover (1854–1926), the author of Cap al tard (Toward the Evening, 1909) and Poemes bíblics (Biblical Poems, 1918), reasserted the love of measure and of wisdom, the classical Mediterranean inheritance of C. culture.

The following generation of poets was heir to both the classicism of Costa i Llobera and Alcover and the vitalism of Maragall. Joan Salvat Papasseit (1894–1924) expressed the restiveness of the avant-garde. Josep Carner (1884–1969), sensuous, refined, ironic, appealed both to the critics and general readers. Carles Riba (1893–1959) brought the symbolist style (see SYMBOLISM) to its utmost refinement in his Elegies de Bierville (Bierville Elegies, 1943). Both Carner and Riba went into exile after the Sp. Civil War (1936–39). Other major poets chose to stay. Among them are Josep Maria de Sagarra (1894–1961), folksy yet subtle and occasionally powerful, and Josep-Vicenc Foix (1894–1986), a great craftsman of sonnets and also a visionary poet in the surrealist line whose poems remind us of the landscapes painted by his friends Salvador Dalí and Juan Miró.

The post-Civil War generation managed to keep alive C. p. in spite of the cruel persecution of C. lang. and culture under Franco's dictatorship. Salvador Espriu (1913–82) is one of the most influential voices of the postwar period. Elegy, satire, and social crit. are fused in his work to convey dark humor and existentialist anguish. Cementiri de Sinera (Sinera's Churchyard, 1946) has been compared favorably with Dylan Thomas's Under Milk Wood. Agustí Bartra (1899–1984) spent long years in exile, where he published L'Arbre de Foc (Tree of Fire, 1946) and Odisseu (Odysseus, 1953). A poet of imagination and epic grandeur, he managed to fuse surrealism and the Cl. myths in a powerful poetic lang. During the 1960s and '70s, esp. after Franco's death and the rebirth of democracy, the image of the phoenix rising from its ashes aptly portrays the rebirth of C. p. An explosion of works by young poets dominates the literary scene. Among the outstanding new voices are Joan Brossa (b. 1919), Marta Pessarrodona (b. 1941), Narcís Comadira (b. 1942), Francesc Parcerisas (b. 1944), and Pere Gimferrer (b. 1945).

BIBLIOGRAPHIES: A. Elías de Molins, Diccionario biográfico y bibliográfico de escritores y artistas catalanes del siglo XIX (1889–95); J. Massó i Torrents, "Bibliografia dels antics poetes catalans," Anuari de l'institut d'estudis catalans (1913–14), Repertori de l'antiga literatura catalana, v. 1, La poesia (1932); J. Molas and J. Massot i Muntaner, Diccionari de la literatura catalana (1979).

ANTHOLOGIES: *Anthol. of C. Lyric P.*, ed. J. Triadú and J. Gili (1953); *Ocho siglos de poesía catalana: antología bilingüe*, ed. J. M. Castellet, 2d ed. (1976); *Antología general de la poesia catalana*, ed. J. M. Castellet and J. Molas (1979); *Mod. C. P.: An Anthol.*, and *Postwar C. P.*, both ed. and tr. D. H. Rosenthal (1979, 1991).

HISTORY AND CRITICISM: L. Nicolau D'Olwer, *Resum de literatura catalana* (1927); M. de Riquer, *Resumen de literatura catalana* (1947); J. Ruiz i Calonja, *Història de la literatura catalana* (1954); G. Díaz Plaja, *De literatura catalana* (1956); J. Fuster, *La poesia catalana*, 2 v. (1956), *Contra el noucentisme* (1978); J. Ruiz i Calonja and J. Roca i Pons, "Med. C. Lit." in Fisher; J. Bofill i Ferro and A. Comas, *Un segle de poesía catalana*, 2d ed. (1981); A. Terry, *C. Lit.* (1972), *Sobre poesía catalana contemporània* (1985). L.MO.; M.E.D.

CATALEXIS (Gr. "coming to an abrupt end"). The process by which a metrical colon or line is shortened on the end. The adjectival form, "catalectic," describes omission of one syllable, the final one; the older, technical term for double catalectic forms is "brachycatalectic." The normal form, where no syllable is lacking, is sometimes called "acatalectic"; and when extra syllables appear at the end, the colon or line is said to be hypermetric (q.v.). C. applies only to ends; shortening at the beginning is normally treated separately, since the metrical environment differs (see ACEPHALOUS).

C. is evident in both Cl. Gr. and Sanskrit prosody and seems to have derived in part from Indo-European prosody (q.v.), though it would have appeared indigenously as a normal linguistic process. In Cl. Gr., all the most common metrical cola (dactylic, anapestic, iambic, trochaic, aeolic) have catalectic forms in which the last two syllables are shortened to one *longum*. But the precise mechanism of c. in Cl. prosody (q.v.) is complex and varies from meter to meter. More importantly, the c. often appears at the end of a metrical period or stanza—esp. in dactylic, trochaic, and anapestic verse—so that the principle of shortening or blunting has double effect, as it were.

In the modern poetries, c. is not common at all in iambic verse but is frequent in trochaic and ternary meters (see BINARY AND TERNARY), where the unexpectedly sudden and forceful close (on a stress) gives bite. In Eng., the trochaic tetrameter of 8 syllables is often found together with a catalectic line of 7, both forms meshing smoothly together. Why c. should operate well in some meters but not others still awaits definitive explanation; temporal metrists would say that in accentual verse (q.v.) and other meters which retain a close association with music and song, the missing weak syllable at the end is filled by a rest. In any event, it is manifest that c. is one of the fundamental principles of rhythm (q.v.), and provision must be made for it in any theory of meter.—L. P. E. Parker, "C.," *ClassQ* 26 (1976); Morier; M. L. West, "Three Topics in Gr. Metre," *ClassQ* 32 (1982). T.V.F.B.

CATALOG, catalog verse. A list of persons, places, things, or ideas in poetry which have some common denominator such as heroism, beauty, or death; it is also extended as the structure and meaning of entire poems, called c. v. The c. device is of ancient origin and found in almost all lits. of the world. In antiquity the c. often had a didactic or mnemonic function, as may be seen in the genealogical lists commonly found in ancient lits., e.g. in the Bible (Genesis 10) and in Old Germanic verse. In some Polynesian and Abyssinian verses, lists of places seem intended to furnish geographical information (see DIDACTIC POETRY). But frequently c. v. has a more clearly aesthetic function, such as indicating the vastness of a war or battle or the power of a prince or king. This is the primary purpose of the c. of heroes in epic lit., for example the heroes of the Trojan war found in *Iliad* 2, the Argonauts in Apollonius Rhodius' *Argonautica* 1, the heroes in *Aeneid* 7, and the list of fallen angels in Milton's *Paradise Lost*, Book 2. Closely allied is the treatment of God's power in the "Benedicite omnia opera domini" in the *Book of Common Prayer*.

In medieval and Ren. poetry, the c. device is often used for itemizing topics such as the beauty of women (see BLASON). Such usage seems to follow from ancient example, e.g. Ovid's c. of trees in *Metamorphoses*, and can even be found in modern song writing, e.g. Cole Porter's "They couldn't compare with you." At other times catalogs seem used for the sake of play, or because the poet enjoyed the sound of particular words, e.g. the list of jewels in Wolfram von Eschenbach's *Parzifal*. In 19th- and 20th-c. European and Am. poetry, other functions of the c. have emerged. Whitman, for example, employs long lists to demonstrate the essential unity of the universe amid its seemingly endless multeity. Modern poets such as Rilke and George as well as Auden and Werfel have in varying degrees followed Whitman in this use.

A particularly important type is the c. of women, which in the West derives from Hesiod and Homer, and is practiced thereafter by Virgil, Ovid, Juvenal, Plutarch, Boccaccio, and Chaucer. McLeod argues that the c. of the "good woman" type (e.g. Boccaccio, Chaucer) helped preserve gender stereotypes.

T. W. Allen, "The Homeric C.," *JoHS* 30 (1910); D. W. Schumann, "Enumerative Style and its Significance in Whitman, Rilke, Werfel," *MLQ* 3 (1942), "Observations on Enumerative Style in Mod. Ger. Poetry," *PMLA* 59 (1944); S. K. Coffman, "'Crossing Brooklyn Ferry': A Note on the C. Technique of Whitman's Poetry," *MP* 51 (1954); L. Spitzer, "La enumeración caótica en la poesía moderna," *Linguística e historia literaria* (1955); H. E. Wedeck, "The C. in Lat. and Med. Lat. Poetry," *M&H* 13 (1960); S. A. Barney, "Chaucer's Lists," *The Wisdom of Poetry*, ed. L. D. Benson and S.

CATHARSIS

Wenzel (1982); M. L. West, *The Hesiodic C. of Women* (1985); N. Howe, *The OE C. Poems* (1985); C. Goodblatt, "Whitman's Cs. as Literary Gestalt," *Style* 24 (1990); G. McLeod, *Virtue and Venom: Cs. of Women from Antiquity to the Ren.* (1991).
R.A.H.; T.V.F.B.

CATCH. See CACCIA.

CATHARSIS. The use of the word c. ("purgation," "purification," or "clarification") in connection with the theory of lit. originates in Aristotle's celebrated definition of tragedy in the 6th chapter of the *Poetics*. Unfortunately, Aristotle merely uses the term without defining it (though he may have defined it in a putative second book of the *Poetics*), and the question of what he actually meant is a *cause célèbre* in the history of lit. crit. Insofar as there is still no universal agreement, all definitions, including this one, must be regarded as interpretations only. The discussion which follows is given fuller context in CLASSICAL POETICS.

The essential function of tragedy, according to Aristotle's definition, is a representation (*mimesis*, q.v.) of an action that is serious or noble, complete, and of appropriate magnitude: and when such representation is effectively carried out it will succeed "in arousing pity and fear in such a way as to accomplish a *catharsis* [in one of its fundamental senses] of such emotions." The definition was doubtless framed as an answer to Plato's charge that poetic drama encourages anarchy in the soul by feeding and watering the passions instead of starving them. Aristotle held, to the contrary, that anarchy in the soul is most effectively prevented not by starving and repressing the emotions but by giving them expression in a wisely regulated manner. Tragedy he regarded as a chief instrument of such regulation, for it works in a twofold way, first exciting the emotions of pity and fear and then allaying them through the cathartic process.

Aristotle's somewhat technical conception of c. acquires its particular character from a linguistic heritage that is part medical, part religious, and part intellectual. Out of this matrix come several possible meanings of c. as the key aesthetic term in the *Poetics*. As a medical term, c. finds early expression in the Hippocratic School of Medicine to describe the process of purging the body of humors and impurities which are the cause of disease (Laín Entralgo). The medical view of c., influentially advocated by Bernays, suggests that pity and fear can build up into pathological states that require a therapeutic *purgation* that is provided by the emotional stimuli of tragedy and which results in pleasurable relief and cure (Lucas). C. as a religious term is closely associated with the concept of *purification* as it applies to rites required for the entry into a holy place, the purification required of believers by certain sects, or the cleansing of guilt by someone who has committed a crime (Laín Entralgo). In the *Phaedo*

Plato uses the term in this religious sense (as well as in an intellectual one) to describe the separation of body from soul, an act that is prerequisite for casting off the illusory world of imitations and shadows and approaching the world of true reality. The interpretation of c. as "purification" has been extended to mean purification of any excess or deficiency of pity and fear so that the proper mean of these emotions is achieved (Lessing, Janko) and to indicate the purification of the tragic deed of the hero from moral pollution so that the audience is able to experience the emotions of pity and fear (Else). The interpretation of c. as "intellectual clarification" is based on the use of the term by Plato and others in this sense (Golden, Nussbaum), the internal argument of the *Poetics* (Golden, von Fritz), and the actual practice of Gr. medicine (Laín Entralgo). Two significant variations on "intellectual clarification" have also been suggested: "emotional" (as well as intellectual) clarification (Nussbaum) and "ethical" clarification (Wagner).

When Aristotle's definition is reconsidered in light of all three of these strands, an important corollary stands forth. Since the new blending which is attained in the cathartic process is psychic, and not merely physical, it must involve a new emotional perspective and even, arising from that, a new intellectual vision. A wisdom is distilled from tragic suffering: man is *pathei mathos*, "taught by suffering," as the chorus in the *Agamemnon* sings. The tragic c. and the ensuing emotional calm have produced in the spectator a new insight into what the plot of the drama, its action—which is to say, its meaning in motion—most essentially represents. Such insight is what justifies Aristotle's assertions (ch. 4) that the essential goal and pleasure of artistic mimesis is "learning and inference" (*manthanein kai syllogizesthai*) and (ch. 9) that "poetry is something more philosophical and more significant than history, for poetry tends to express universals, history particulars" (see HISTORY AND POETRY).

On the whole, subsequent critics have been more inclined to accept than to reject the doctrine of c., although their acceptance has usually involved some degree of reinterpretation. In the Ren., Aristotle's definition was revived by such writers as Minturno (*De poeta*, 1563) and Castelvetro (*Poetica d'Aristotele vulgarizzata e sposta*, 1570; abridged tr. A. Bongiorno, *Castelvetro on the Art of Poetry*, 1984), although in the former the emphasis is shifted to the "delight and profit" which result to the spectator from his cathartic experience. In France a century later both Corneille and Racine accept the principle of c. in the fairly plain moral sense of regarding the spectator as purified by the tragedy and thus as deterred from performing such evil acts as he has been witnessing. Corneille assumes in addition that either pity or fear may operate separately.

In Germany, Lessing in his influential *Laokoön*

(1766) opposed the latter view of Corneille, insisting that the special effect of tragedy must come from the union of the two emotions, from which there emerges the cosmically oriented emotion of *awe*, as the spectator recognizes through the tragedy the sword of destiny that is suspended above us all. Lessing also emphasizes (*Hamburger Dramaturgie*, 1768) the applicability of Aristotle's ethical standard of "due measure" to the principle of c.: tragedy, if it is to transform our pity and fear into virtue, "must be capable of purifying us from both extremes"—from "too little" by its emotional contagion, and from "too much" by the restraint which its formal pattern imposes. Schiller in his essay "On Tragic Art" (1792) reaffirms the importance of measure, and in "On the Sublime" (1801) he draws two corollaries: that the most perfect tragedy is one which produces its cathartic effect not by its subject matter but by its tragic form; and that it has aesthetic worth only insofar as it is "sublime" (q.v.)—that is, as it represents the indifference of the universe to moral ends and so produces in the soul of the spectator an "inoculation against unavoidable fate." Goethe, in his *Nachlass zu Aristoteles Poetik* (1827), sees the main importance of the purgatorial or cathartic situation not in reference to the spectator, whose condition is incidental and variable, but in the reconciliation and expiation of the characters in the play. Among later Ger. writers on aesthetics we may note Schopenhauer (*The World as Will and Idea*, 1819), who equates the cathartic principle of tragedy with an idealized and universal experience of fellow-suffering wholly disproportionate to moral deserts; and Nietzsche (*The Birth of Tragedy*, 1872), who interprets the matter through the complementary symbols of Dionysus and Apollo, the unresisting plunge into whatever sufferings and joys life may offer and the calm vision that results from this self-surrender (see APOLLONIAN-DIONYSIAN).

Of Eng.-speaking writers, Milton in the Preface to *Samson Agonistes* (1671) interprets Aristotle to mean that tragic c. operates on the homeopathic principle; he draws an analogy from medicine, wherein "things of melancholic hue and quality are used against melancholy, sour against sour, salt to remove salt humours." Wordsworth, shifting the reference from dramatic to lyric poetry, offers a humanitarian interpretation: that readers are to be "humbled and humanized," and to be purged of the prejudices and blindnesses arising from false sophistication and snobbery "in order that they may be purified and exalted." ("Essay, Supplementary to the Preface," 1815). I. A. Richards (*Principles of Lit. Crit.*, 1925) interprets the cathartic process as a reconciliation and reëquilibration of "Pity, the impulse to approach, and Terror, the impulse to retreat," along with various other groups of discordant impulses, and he affirms the importance of tragedy on the ground that "there is no other way in which such impulses, once awakened, can be set at rest without suppression."

Subsequently, Northrop Frye (*Anatomy of Crit.*, 1957) described c. as "not the raising of an actual emotion, but the raising and casting out of an actual emotion on a wave of something else." He identifies that "something else" as "exhilaration or exuberance," an experience "as much intellectual as it is emotional." While c. has long been interpreted as some form of purgation or purification, there has been increasing momentum in this century toward recognizing the important cognitive dimensions of this major aesthetic concept (Abdulla).

TRANSLATIONS AND COMMENTARIES: I. Bywater (1909); L. Cooper (1913); S. H. Butcher (1917); P. Wheelwright (1951); G. F. Else (1957), with later defense and revision of his original views in *Plato and Aristotle on Poetry* (1986); L. Golden and O. B. Hardison, Jr. (1968); D. W. Lucas (1968); R. Janko, *Aristotle on Comedy* (1984), *Poetics* (1987); S. Halliwell (1986).

SECONDARY WORKS: M. T. Herrick, *The Poetics of Aristotle in England* (1903); H. House, *Aristotle's Poetics* (1956); B. Hathaway, *The Age of Crit.* (1962); T. Brunius, "C.," *DHI*; P. Laín Entralgo, *The Therapy of the Word in Cl. Antiquity* (1970), ch. 5; D. Keesey, "On Some Recent Interps. of C.," *Cl. World* (1978–79); T. J. Scheff, *C. in Healing, Ritual, and Drama* (1979); F. Sparshott, "The Riddle of Katharsis," *Centre and Labyrinth*, ed. E. Cook et al. (1983); C. Wagner, "'Katharsis' in der aristotelischen Tragödiendefinition," *Grazer Beiträge* (1984); A. K. Abdulla, *C. in Lit.* (1985); M. C. Nussbaum *The Fragility of Goodness* (1986).   P.W.; L.G.

CAUDA, coda (Lat. "tail"). A short line, or tail, which in a stanza of longer lines usually rhymes with another, similar line, making the stanza heterometric (q.v.). Dante in *De vulgari eloquentia* divides the *canzone* (q.v.) into two parts, *frons* and *c.*, subdividing the *frons* further into two *pedes*. The form *aabccb* and its derivatives, with *b*-line caudae rhyming, which developed in Med. Lat. and was popular in Fr. and ME metrical romances, is known as tail rhyme (q.v.). The Sapphic (q.v.) is another caudate form. The caudate sonnet (q.v.) has a longer, plurilinear tail; cf. the bob and wheel (q.v.).   T.V.F.B.

CAUDATE SONNET. A sonnet (q.v.) augmented by coda or tail (Lat. *cauda*). Usually the coda following the 14 lines is introduced by a half-line and followed by a couplet in pentameters; it may also be followed by additional tails. Established in It. by Francesco Berni (1497–1536), the c. s. has usually been employed for satire, as in Milton's "On the New Forcers of Conscience Under the Long Parliament," the coda of which is as follows:

> That so the Parliament
> May with their wholesome and preven-
> tive shears

Clip your phylacteries, though baulk
 your ears,
  And succour our just fears,
When they shall read this clearly in
 your charge,—
New *Presbyter* is but old *Priest* writ large.

Other c. ss. have been written by Gerard Manley Hopkins in Eng. ("That Nature is a Heraclitean Fire," *abbaabbacdcdcd*, the 3 codas *deecfffggg*), by Albert Samain in Fr., and by Rainer Maria Rilke in Ger. The bob and wheel (q.v.), though in shorter lines, is analogous. Tailing is a common form of stanzaic variation (see TAIL RHYME). Contrast the shortened form, Hopkins' "curtal sonnet" (q.v.)—J. S. Smart, *The Sonnets of Milton* (1921), 127; J. Dubu, "Le Sonetto caudato de Michel-Ange à Milton," *Le Sonnet à la Ren.*, ed. Y. Bellenger (1988).
T.V.F.B.

CAVALIER POETS, Cavalier lyrists. The modern term for a group of Eng. poets in the time of Charles I (1625–49), characterized by the lightness, grace, and polish of their verse and by the wit and gallantry of their attitudes (several were soldiers and courtiers first and poets second). The C. poets were influenced by the precept and example of Ben Jonson (1572–1637), hence the older terms for the group, "Tribe of Ben" and "Sons of Ben." Most of them imbibed Jonsonian wit and Classicism in highly informal meetings at various London taverns frequented by their master. The greatest of the group was Robert Herrick (1591–1674), who praised his master in *An Ode for Ben Jonson* (1637). Others include Henry Carew and Sir John Suckling (both of whom also show the influence of Donne), as well as Lovelace, Randolph, Cartwright, and Godolphin.

In their lyrics, the C. poets cultivated a tight and chiseled form (modeled on the lyrics of the *Greek Anthology*), a shorter line, more precise diction, and a tighter logical structure than was usual in Ren. verse. And, like Jonson, the Cavaliers abandoned the sonnet almost entirely; their preference for the genres of epigram and satire (qq.v.) also indicates their Cl. orientation. In all of this the Jonsonian "school" represents one form of 17th-c. revolt from the Italianate and moralistic emphases of the "school of Spenser" (q.v.), the other being represented by "metaphysical poetry" (q.v.), best exemplified by Donne.

Love was the favorite theme of the C. poets, and their treatments of the subject ranged from the conventional Petrarchism (q.v.) of Lovelace to the cynicism of Suckling and the pagan sensuality of Carew. Poems of courtly compliment, *jeux d'esprit*, and expressions of loyalty to the king are also typical. Perhaps the best known of their poems are Suckling's "Why so pale and wan, fond lover?," Lovelace's "To Althea, from Prison" and "To Lucasta, on Going to the Wars," Herrick's "Delight in Disorder," and Carew's "Ask me no more where

Jove bestows." Browning's *Cavalier Tunes*, written in imitation of these 17th-c. poets, illustrate their attitudes and evoke the spirit of their time. See ENGLISH POETRY.—K. A. McEuen, *Cl. Influence upon the Tribe of Ben* (1939); G. Walton, "The C. Poets," *From Donne to Marvell*, ed. B. Ford (1956); H. M. Richmond, *The School of Love* (1964); R. Skelton, *C. Poets* (1970); J. H. Summers, *The Heirs of Donne and Jonson* (1970); E. Miner, *The Cavalier Mode from Jonson to Cotton* (1971); G. Braden, *The Classics and Eng. Ren. Poetry* (1978); *Classic and Cavalier: Essays on Jonson and the Sons of Ben*, ed. C. J. Summers and T.-L. Pebworth (1982); G. Hammond, *Fleeting Things: Eng. Poets and Poems, 1616–1660* (1989).
F.J.W.

CELTIC PROSODY. The Celts emerged as a distinct linguistic group of Indo-European (IE) tribes in central Europe around the 8th c. B.C., but even the earliest examples of C. poetry can be dated to only the 6th c. A.D. In Gaul, according to Caesar (*Gallic Wars* [ca. 51 B.C.]), the Celts maintained schools where candidates who wished to become druids would spend as much as 20 years learning "verses." Their esoteric lore was designed for oral transmission not for written record, however; and by the 6th c. A.D., successive invasions first from Rome and later from the Germanic north almost extinguished the use of the C. lang. in Gaul and elsewhere on the Continent.

Meanwhile, long before this extinction, C.-speaking peoples had spread to Britain and Ireland and had become divided into two distinct linguistic subgroups—Brittonic and Goidelic. The Brittonic group is still today represented by Welsh in Wales, Cornish in Cornwall, and Breton in Brittany; the Goidelic by Irish (Gaelic) in Ireland, Manx in the Isle of Man, and Scottish Gaelic in the Scottish Highlands and Islands. These native cultures have produced a diverse body of C. poetry (see BRETON POETRY; CORNISH POETRY; IRISH POETRY; SCOTTISH GAELIC POETRY; WELSH POETRY); and the earliest extant vernacular manuals of prosody in Europe are Ir., dating back to the end of the 8th c. (Thurneysen [1912], 78–89).

The C. prosodic trad. is remarkable in three respects: the early poets or bards (q.v.) exercised an authoritative function in society as members of a professional class; the earliest recorded C. poetry perpetuated an archaic form of Indo-European prosody (q.v.); and later C. poets developed extraordinarily complex prosodic systems. As Watkins has shown, the most archaic form of versification employed in Old Ir. seems to be a reflex of the IE cadenced verseform that appears in Gr., Sanskrit, and Slavic, if due allowance is made for the fact that IE prosodic patterns were determined by alternation of long and short syllables, whereas Goidelic had adopted alternation of stressed and unstressed syllables as a patterning feature.

The Old Ir. cadenced verseform occurs in genealogies, legal tracts, and in some of the poems and "rhetorics" preserved within mythological and legendary prose narratives. Its features are three: a fixed number of syllables per line, free stress in the initial portion, and, at a fixed point in the line, a word-boundary followed by a fixed end-line cadence or clausula. This was presumably the dominant type in C. poetry from IE times down to at least the 6th c. A.D.

At the earliest recorded stage, however (late 6th c. A.D.), poets had already begun to superimpose verse decoration upon this IE survival. Thus in most extant Old Ir. examples, alliteration (q.v.) is used as an optional decoration linking stressed words both within the line and also between the line-end and subsequent line-beginning.

After the archaic phase, Goidelic and Brittonic poets developed highly stylized patterns in which decoration became paramount. The new patterns variously demanded strict employment of consonance, assonance, dissonance, rhyme, internal rhyme, masculine-feminine rhyme, generic rhyme, and linkage or *cynghanedd* (qq.v.). At some unidentified time there emerged a trad. of composing lines of measured syllabic length that were tied together by generic rhyme rather than full rhyme and were, esp. in Goidelic, measured off in stanzas. The theory that C. poets adopted the use of rhyme and stanzaic form from the example of the Med. Lat. hymns, composed from the 3d–4th cs. by Ambrose, Augustine, and Hilary of Poitiers, is now regarded as dubious. But some relationship is undeniable, and is substantiated by the sudden emergence of such strict forms as Ir. quatrains of octosyllables.

Of major importance in this process was the devel. of canons for generic rhyme (q.v.), which appear from the 6th c. A.D. In Welsh poetry, final consonants were allowed to rhyme within four phonetic classes. In Ir. and Scottish Gaelic verse, however, six rhyming groups were distinguished. Out of this divergence, Goidelic and Brittonic poets developed differing verse systems, each distinguished by an intricacy almost unparalleled in European poetry. The complexity of Goidelic prosody is paralleled only by that of skaldic poetry (see OLD NORSE POETRY), and in the latter the influence of traveling Ir. bards seems evident. Typical of the Ir. form of complexity is the following stanza in a late medieval praise-poem describing the decorations on a goblet owned by a ruler of Connaught:

Eoin bas n-dearg 's a n-druim r' a
 thaoibh,
mar do chuim an ceard go cōir
lucht 'gar chasmhail cleasa ceoil—
eoin 's a sleasa d' asnaibh ōir.
 (McKenna, *Aithdioghluim Dána*, no.
 9).

[Birds crimson-clawed are backed around its rim, so deftly crafted by the artist that they seem about to sing—birds whose shapes are ribbed with gold.]

Here the prosody depends on cadence, syllabic count, generic rhyme, consonance, dissonance, and alliteration. This particular meter, known as *rannaigheacht mhōr* (the Great Versification), requires a stanza of 4 lines, each of which must contain 7 syllables and end in a stressed monosyllable. The last syllables in lines 2 and 4 must show generic rhyme with one another (*coir* : *oir*). The last syllables in lines 1 and 3 must provide vocalic dissonance (*aoi, oi; eoi, oi*) and generic consonance (*bh, r; l, r*) with the last syllables in lines 2 and 4.

Each of the nonfinal stressed words in line 2 must show generic rhyme with a stressed word in line 1 (*chuim* : *druim; ceard* : *dearq*); and each of the nonfinal stressed words in line 4 must show generic rhyme with a stressed word in line 3 (*eoin* : *ceoil; sleasa* : *cleasa; asnaibh* : *chasmhail*). In a disyllabic rhyme such as the latter, both syllables must provide generic rhyme.

Each line must show at least one alliteration between adjacent stressed words, and in the last line this alliteration must be between the last two stressed words: (1) *dearq, druim*; (2) *chuim, ceard, coir*; (3) *chasmhail, cleasa, ceoil*; (4) *asnaibh, oir*. A consonant alliterates either with itself or with the corresponding initial form produced by grammatical mutation; a vowel alliterates with itself or any other. Frequently also in such a poem (though not in this one), the first stressed word in the first line of the first stanza is echoed as a closure (*dunad*) by the last stressed word in the last line of the last stanza (see RING COMPOSITION).

The Welsh poets superimposed decorative complexity on cadenced verse in an entirely different manner. Dafydd ap Gwilym's address to a seagull (14th c. A.D.) is typical:

Yr wylan deg ar lanw | dioer,
Unlliw ag eiry neu | wenlloer,
Dilwch yw dy degwch | di,
Darn fel haul, dyrnfol | heli.

[Fair sea gull on the certain tide, of color like snow or the bright moon, spotless is your beauty, a patch like sunlight, gauntlet of the sea.]

As in the tradition of archaic C. cadenced verse, each line contains a fixed number of syllables per line (7), allows free stresses in the initial portion, and at a fixed point in the line contains a word-boundary that is followed by a fixed cadence at the end of the line. Rhyme must be full rather than generic; here, it is alternating masculine/feminine. Additionally, each line must be decorated by any one of four different forms of *cynghanedd*. Thus the complete sequence of consonants D R N F L L in the first half of line 4 is echoed in the second half (DaRN FeL HauL : DyRNF oL HeLi). Furthermore, the linked consonants, as in Irish dissonance, must be associated with dissonant vowels (yR/aR, etc.).

Generally speaking, the C. bards, rather like the Ir. illuminators of the *Book of Kells*, chose to fill minute spaces decoratively. At their best, as in the Ir. and Welsh examples just quoted, they were capable of providing not only an intricate phonetic texture but also a brilliant network of imagery that illuminated their poems in a manner that is still perceptible even in translation.

With the decline of the bardic orders in the C. countries, new and simpler meters emerged. In part these are the products of amateur versification, in part they may represent the legitimization of popular and perhaps ancient song-meters hitherto unrecorded, and in part they certainly represent the adaptation of foreign meters. When the secret of generic rhyme was lost, the most appealing device for Ir. and Scottish Gaelic poets seems to have been assonance (q.v.). Typical is an Ir. song composed by Geoffrey Keating (17th c.), which is in the new Ir. stressed verse known as *abhrān* and begins:

> Om sgeol ar ard-mhagh Fail ni chod-
> laim oidhche.

The last stressed vowel of the five stressed syllables in the first line assonates with each of the last stressed syllables in all of the following lines of the stanza, as in the OF *laisse* (q.v.). But, additionally, each of the other four stressed vowels in the first line assonates with its counterparts in all of the following lines, so that the melody of the stanza consists of a sequence of five stressed vowels (here o-a-a-o-i).

In the 16th c., Welsh popular poets correspondingly avoided the complexities of *cynghanedd* and turned to what they called "free metre," for which they adopted a new complexity in place of the old. Typically, in a four-line stanza the second and fourth lines must contain final rhyme, while the first and third lines must provide final/internal rhyme with the second and fourth lines:

> Gwrandewch feddwl dyn o'r byd,
> A roes i fryd un ystig,
> I folliannu y mab rhad,
> A gad ar ddiw Nadolig.

In the 20th c., Ir. scholars such as Osborn Bergin have composed strict bardic verse, and some of the Welsh bards who compete at the National Eisteddfod (q.v.) still use the intricate traditional measures, but in general C. poets have adopted much less restricted verseforms, including *vers libre* (q.v.). At the same time, the intricacies of C. p. have gained international recognition. Gerard Manley Hopkins, Wilfred Owen, and Rolfe Humphries, among others, have introduced C. prosodic features into Eng. versification—as Vaughan had done in the 17th c. Such undertakings face problems similar to those that are connected with vernacular imitations of classical meters. For instance, given a feature-for-feature tr. of Dafydd ap Gwilym, can an Eng.-speaking listener recognize the echo of the consonantal sequence D-R-N-F-L-L (cited above) in the second half of a 7-syllable line? The full appreciation of such a poet requires an acute ear and a dedicated attention to the technical details of C. p., for a good poem written in the strict C. meters derives much of its force from the subtleties of its workmanship.

See also AWDL; CYNGHANEDD; CYWYDD; HEN BENILLION; MASCULINE AND FEMININE; ODL; PRYDDEST.

GENERAL: J. E. C. Williams, "The Court Poet in Medieval Ireland," *PBA* 57 (1971); C. W. Dunn, "C.," in Wimsatt; Brogan, 611 ff.; M. W. Bloomfield and C. W. Dunn, *The Role of the Poet in Early Societies* (1989).

IRISH: R. Thurneysen, "Zur irischen Accent-und Verslehre," *Révue Celtique* 6 (1883–85), 309–47, "Mittelirische Verslehren," in *Irische Texte*, ed. W. Stokes and E. Windisch, v. 3 (1891), esp. 138–66, "Zu den mittelirischen Verslehren," *Abh. der königl. Akad. der Wiss. zu Gött., philol.-hist. Klasse*, v. 14, no. 2 (1912), 59–90; K. Meyer, *A Primer of Ir. Metrics* (1909, but cf. *Eriu* 8 [1916]), "Über die älteste irische Dichtung," *Abh. der königl. Preussische Akad. der Wiss., philos.-hist. Klasse*, nos. 6, 10 (1914); O. Bergin, "The Principles of Alliteration," *Eriu* 9 (1921–23); *Tadhg Dall O Huiginn*, ed. and tr. E. Knott (1922–26)—good intro. to bardic verse; W. Meyer, "Die Verskunst der Iren in rhythmischen lateinischen Gedichten," in Meyer, v. 3; *Aithdioghluim Dána*, ed. and tr. L. McKenna (1939–40)—wide variety of bardic meters succinctly classified; E. Knott, *An Intro. to Ir. Syllabic Poetry of the Period 1200–1600*, 2d ed. (1957), *Ir. Cl. Poetry* (1957); G. Murphy, *Early Ir. Metrics* (1961), but see rev. in *Éigse* 10 (1962–63), 238–41; C. Watkins, "Indo-European Metrics and Archaic Ir. Verse," *Celtica* 6 (1963); P. MacCana, "On the Use of the Term *Retoric*," *Celtica* 7 (1966); *Ir. Bardic Poetry*, ed. and tr. O. Bergin (1970); J. Travis, *Early C. Versecraft* (1973); E. Campanille, "Indogermanische Metrik und altirische Metrik," *ZCP* 37 (1979); *Early Ir. Verse*, ed. and tr. R. P. M. Lehmann (1982).

WELSH: J. Loth, *La métrique galloise*, 2 v. (1900–2), but see the rev. by Morris-Jones in *ZCP* 4 (1903), 106–42; Morris-Jones—still valuable, and indexed in the rpt. (1980); D. Bell, "The Problem of Tr.," *Dafydd ap Gwilym: Fifty Poems*, tr. H. I. Bell and D. Bell (1942); Parry, *History*; Jarman and Hughes, esp. E. Rowlands, "*Cynghanedd*, Metre, Prosody"; R. M. Jones, "Mesurau'r canu rhydd cynnar," *BBCS* 28 (1979); A. T. E. Matonis, "The Welsh Bardic Grammars and the Western Grammatical Trad.," *MP* 79 (1981); Stephens; *Welsh Verse*, ed. T. Conran, 2d ed. (1986)—long intro. and useful appendices; R. Bromwich, *Aspects of the Poetry of Dafydd ap Gwilym* (1986).

SCOTTISH GAELIC: W. J. Watson, *Bardachd Ghaidhlig*, 2d ed. (1932)—important though insufficient.   C.W.D.; T.V.F.B.

CELTIC REVIVAL. See IRISH POETRY.

CENTO (Lat. "patchwork"). A verse composition made up of lines selected from the work or works of some great poet(s) of the past. Homer largely served this purpose in Gr. lit., ranging from the adaptations by Trygaeus of various lines in the *Iliad* and *Odyssey* reported by Aristophanes (*Peace* 1090–94) to the *Homerokentrones* of the Byzantine period. Similarly, Virgil was the most popular source for centos in later Roman times. The oldest of those extant is the tragedy *Medea* by Hosidius Geta (2d c. A.D.), while the *C. nuptialis* of Ausonius and the *C. Vergilianus* of Proba (4th c. A.D.) are among others drawn from his work. Ren. and later works of this kind included the It. *Petrarca spirituale* (1536) and the Eng. *Cicero princeps* (1608), which was a treatise on government compiled from Cicero. Centos are still occasionally published, e.g. in the first issue of *The Formalist* (1990), and are now almost invariably humorous, the humor arising from both the clever juxtaposition of famous lines into a new semantic matrix and also recognition of the diversity of their sources.—J. O. Delepierre, *Tableau de la litt. du centon chez les anciens et chez les modernes*, 2 v. (1874–75); R. Lamacchia, "Dall'arte allusiva al centone," *Atene e Roma* n.s. 3 (1958); "C.," *Oxford Cl. Dict.*, 2d ed. (1972); T. Augarde, *Oxford Guide to Word Games* (1984).   R.J.G.; T.V.F.B.

CHAIN RHYME, interlocking r., interlace r. (Ger. *Kettenreim, äusserer Reim, verschränkter Reim*). Any r. scheme in which a r. in one line or stanza is used as a link to the next line or stanza. Terza rima (q.v.) is one form: here the medial r. in each tercet becomes the proximal ones of the next, *aba bcb cdc*, etc. Frost extends this scheme to the quatrain in "Stopping by Woods on a Snowy Evening." But the term is normally reserved for linking of one line to the next by last word to first word: in Fr. prosody, the *Grands Rhétoriqueurs* (see RHÉTORIQUEURS) of the late 15th and early 16th cs. developed the terms *rime fratrisée, entrelacée, enchaînée,* and *annexée* for a r. sound or syllable at line-end repeated at the beginning of the next line. The repeated syllable must, however, carry a different meaning. Clément Marot has:

Dieu gard ma Maistresse et regente
Gente de corps et de façon.
Son cueur tient le mien en sa tente
Tant et plus d'un ardant frisson.

Occasional examples of c. r. may be found in Eng.: Gerard Manley Hopkins has " . . . to despair / Despair . . . " and " . . . Spare! / There . . . " ("The Leaden Echo and the Golden Echo"). C. r. extended into full identity of syllables beconmes one form of repetition, the rhetorical figure of *anadiplosis* (q.v.), a type of concatenation (q.v.), which is the genus.—Patterson.   T.V.F.B.

CHANGGA. See KOREAN POETRY.

CHANSO, CHANSON. See CANSO.

CHANSON DE TOILE. See FRENCH POETRY.

CHANSONS DE GESTE is the term by which the OF epic poems relating the deeds of Charlemagne and his barons, or other feudal lords of the Carolingian era, were known in their own time, principally the 12th and 13th cs. "Geste" has, aside from the original sense of "deeds," additional senses of "history" and "historical document," and by further extension it comes to mean "family, lineage." About 120 poems survive, in whole or in part, in existing mss., some of them in several redactions. They celebrate heroic actions, historical or pseudo-historical, and the chivalric ideals of a Christian, monarchical, and feudal France. There is no critical consensus as to whether the ideological preoccupations are primarily those of Carolingian times or of the period of the Crusades and 12th-c. France. The history is at best considerably overlaid with legend, and many of the epics are largely or wholly fictitious, reworking themes made popular by earlier works from oral tradition. This is particularly true where the taste for the romantic and the fantastic nurtured by the medieval romance (q.v.) and by folklore was carried over into the invention of plots for the epics: this hybrid type is best illustrated by poems like *Huon de Bordeaux, Renaud de Montauban,* and *Le Chevalier au Cygne.*

I. CYCLES. Several more or less well-defined groups of poems may be distinguished. The most cohesive of these (24 poems) is the cycle of Guillaume d'Orange, to be identified with the historical Count Guillaume de Toulouse, contemporary of Charlemagne, and in which are recounted his deeds and those of his six brothers, his nephews, particularly Vivien and Bertrand, his father Aymeri de Narbonne, and others of his line. The principal poems of this cycle are *Le Couronnement de Louis, Le Charroi de Nîmes, La Prise d'Orange, Le Couvenant Vivien, La Chanson de Guillaume, Aliscans, Le Moniage Guillaume,* and *Aymeri de Narbonne.*

The so-called cycle of Charlemagne is less extensive and less unified. To it are assigned the poems treating of Charlemagne's wars (*La Chanson de Roland, Aspremont, Les Saxons*) or youth (*Mainet*), or earlier royal heroes such as the son of Clovis the Merovingian (*Floövant*). One of these is the partly comic *Pélerinage de Charlemagne,* which includes the description of a highly fanciful visit to the court of the Emperor of Constantinople.

The third main group has as its common element the theme of a feudal lord's revolt, usually provoked by an act of injustice, against his *seigneur,* who is in several cases Charlemagne, as in *Girart de Roussillon* (the only *c. de g.* surviving in a dialect of the *langue d'oc*), *La Chevalerie Ogier de Danemarche, Renaud de Montauban,* known also as *Les Quatre fils Aymon,* and *Huon de Bordeaux.* In the oldest poem of this group, the 11th-c. *Gormont et*

Isembart, surviving only in a fragment, the renegade Isembart fights against his lord King Louis III. *Raoul de Cambrai* relates the sombre violence of feudal warfare following a forcible dispossession. The unforgiving bitterness of struggle between two great families is the subject of a minor cycle, *Les Lorrains,* of which the principal poems are *Garin le Lorrain* and *Hervis de Metz.*

II. LA CHANSON DE ROLAND is the masterpiece of the genre and the earliest surviving example, composed around 1100, transcribed probably around 1150 in continental France, and preserved in an Anglo-Norman manuscript of the mid-12th c. (Oxford version). Later versions lengthen the poem and insert additional episodes. The historical event on which the poem is based is the annihilation of Charlemagne's rear guard under Count Roland while recrossing the Pyrenees after an expedition against Saragossa in 778. In the poem the attackers are referred to as Saracens, whereas they were in all probability Basques, and a succession of councils is related, leading to the decision to leave Spain. A traitor Ganelon is introduced, as Roland's stepfather, who urges the Saracens to attack the rear guard in revenge for Roland's having designated him for the perilous embassy to the enemy camp. The disaster is assured when Roland overconfidently refuses to call back Charlemagne by sounding his horn when attacked, in spite of the urgings of his companion Oliver. After the defeat at Roncevaux, the poem ends with another battle in which Charlemagne is victorious, and with the trial and execution of Ganelon. The *Chanson de Roland* is as remarkable for the ideals it exalts—unstinting devotion to God and to feudal lord, and to the fatherland, "douce France"—as for its vigorous and incisive portrayals of great characters, closely knit structure, elevation of tone, and firm, concise lang.

III. FORM, VERSIFICATION, STYLE. The usual line is a decasyllable (q.v.) with caesura after the fourth syllable; unstressed syllables (mute -e) after the accented fourth or tenth syllables, when they appear, are not counted (see FRENCH PROSODY). In the earlier epics, octosyllables or alexandrines (qq.v.) are sometimes used (*Gormont et Isembart, Pélerinage de Charlemagne*). The strophic form is that of the *laisse* (q.v.), a variable number of lines bound together by assonance in the earlier poems, by rhyme in the later ones. In the *Chanson de Roland,* the *laisses* average 14 lines in length; in later poems they tend to be much longer. In length, the *c. de g.* range from about a thousand lines (*Pélerinage de Charlemagne*) to over 35,000; the *Chanson de Roland* has four thousand in the Oxford version. As their name would indicate, the *c. de g.* were sung, and musical notation has been preserved for some.

In coherence of composition, the epics vary greatly, from well-knit poems like the *Chanson de Roland* or the *Pélerinage de Charlemagne* to rambling and even self-contradictory successions of episodes. The style is vigorous in the best poems but diffuse and filled with clichés and formulaic diction in the poorer ones. The formulaic diction provides some evidence for the view that the epics were improvised orally by *jongleurs* (q.v.), itinerant minstrel-performers of the later Middle Ages. It is certain that the epics contain genuine elements of oral poetry (q.v.) as defined in the terms of the oral-formulaic theory (q.v.) of Parry and Lord, but the issues are complicated by the presence of later, literary elements in the written texts.

IV. ORIGINS. The debate over the origins and the prehistory of the *c. de g.* was for nearly a century the outstanding controversy in Fr. medieval lit. hist. In the 19th c., it was customary to consider the surviving *c. de g.* as deriving ultimately from poems inspired by contemporary historical events, composed anonymously, and altered and expanded constantly in the course of oral transmission, over two, three, or even four centuries. At the beginning of the 20th c., however, Bédier denied the continuity-of-transmission theory, arguing instead that the historical content of the poems amounted only to such information as could have been discovered by jongleur-poets in sanctuaries along the pilgrimage routes in the 11th and 12th cs. (incl. learned and written sources), that the poems were composed relatively late, and that the composers were specific individuals little interested in "tradition."

But Bédier's "individualism," as it has been called, has increasingly been attacked by scholars who have revived the older view and buttressed it with new arguments. It is principally around the *Chanson de Roland* that controversy wages, according to the degree of originality the critic is willing to ascribe to the author of the Oxford version. Traditionalists see him as a mere arranger of a poem with a long prehistory of collective elaboration; an intermediate group finds his sources in Med. Lat. hagiography or epic; and "individualists" minimize his debt to hypothetical predecessors and credit him with the largest possible measure of creativeness.

V. DIFFUSION. The *c. de g.* quickly became popular outside northern France and Norman England, being translated notably into MHG (see GERMAN POETRY) and Old Norse and Icelandic (see OLD NORSE POETRY; ICELANDIC POETRY). In Italy they were made accessible in an Italianized Fr. before serving as the models for wholly It. poems. They were known in Spain, where, however, national heroes were preferred for epic (the *Cid*). In France, the 15th and 16th cs. knew the epic legends through prose adaptations before these in turn were forgotten through two and a half centuries of Classicism. See also EPIC; FRENCH POETRY; LAISSE; NARRATIVE POETRY.

L. Gautier, *Épopées françaises,* 2d ed., 4 v. (1878–92), supp. by his *Bibliographie des c. de g.* (1897)—still valuable despite the obsolescence of many of its views; J. Bédier, *Légendes épiques,* 4 v. (1908–13);

CBFL, v. 1; Lote; I. Siciliano, *Les Origines des c. de g.*, 2d. rev. ed. (1951), *Les C. de g. et lépopée* (1968); J. Horrent, *La Chanson de Roland dans les litts. française et espagnole au moyen âge* (1951); R. Bossuat, *Manuel bibliographique de la litt. française du moyen âge* (1951, supp. 1955, 1961); M. Delbouille, *Sur la genèse de la* Chanson de Roland (1954); P. Le Gentil, *Chanson de Roland* (1955); J. Rychner, *La C. de g.: Essai sur l'art épique des jongleurs* (1955)—oral transmission with improvisation; A. Junker, "Stand der Forschung zum Rolandslied," *GRM* (1956); M. de Riquer, *Les C. de g. françaises*, 2d ed. (tr. 1957); *La Technique littéraire des c. de g.* (1959); R. Menéndez Pidal, *La Chanson de Roland et la trad. épique des Francs*, 2d. rev. ed. (1960)—the neotraditionalist view; Lord; W. B. Calin, *The Epic Quest: Studies in Four OF C. de G.* (1966), *A Muse for Heroes: Nine Cs. of the Epic in France* (1983); Parry; J. Duggan, *The Song of Roland: Formulaic Style and Poetic Craft* (1973); G. J. Brault, "The Fr. C. de G.," *Heroic Epic and Saga*, ed. F. J. Oinas (1978), ed., *The Song of Roland* (1979); N. Daniel, *Heroes and Saracens* (1984); *Au carrefour des routes d'Europe: La C. de g.: Xe Congres international de la Société Rencesvals pour l'étude des épopées romanes* (1985); B. Guidot, *Recherches sur la c. de g. au XIIIe siècle* (1986); R. F. Cook, *The Sense of the* Song of Roland (1987); H.-E. Keller, *Autour de Roland* (1989); Hollier.

C.A.K.; T.V.F.B.

CHANT (OF *chanter*, Lat. *cantare*, "to sing"). Less a definite form than a mode of verbal performance somewhere between speech and song (q.v.). Presumably any verbal text can be chanted. The Lat. texts of the Roman Catholic liturgy have been sung since the early Middle Ages in monodic, unaccompanied, and metrically flexible Gregorian c., or "plainsong." More strictly, c. is oral poetry (q.v.) organized rhythmically by both the internal rhythms of lang. and the external rhythms of music. The rhythm may range from relatively loose recitative to a steady drum-beat. Many forms of oral poetry are specifically composed as cs., and these are distinguished by various strong patterns of repetition (q.v.): phonetic repetition (e.g. stress, alliteration, nonsense syllables), lexical and phrasal repetition (key words or stock formulas, anaphora, refrains), and grammatical and semantic parallelism (q.v.) and contrast (catalogues, stichic or hemistichic structures, recurring names, images, or allusions). Such devices may be reinforced with percussive instruments (tapping-sticks, drums, rattles, hand-claps, foot-stamps) and by dance steps. Speech forms tend to be distorted in c. as the lang. is bent to the rhythmical pattern.

Cs. are performed by both individuals and groups, but even individual cs. frequently invoke a social context—e.g. the praise-songs and dirges of traditional African societies, the former streetcries of London hawkers, the chanted sermons of black Am. preachers. A communally performed c., by bringing individuals together into a single body of chanters or dancers, can in effect create a society, at least temporarily, through the c.-rhythm. This important social function appears in numerous forms of communal chanting: the dance-songs of Eskimo villages; the great mythological cs. of aboriginal Australian, Polynesian, and southwest Am. Indian ritual; communal prayer, such as the temple-chanting of Buddhist monks and the litanies of Christian congregations; work-songs of various kinds (for hoeing and threshing fields, digging in mines, laying rails, or hauling up anchors); the game-songs of children (jump-rope rhymes, counting-out verses, taunts).

In written lit., cs. appear as far back as the Vedas of India and the Psalms of the Heb. Bible. The oral form has been imitated in various ways by literate poets such as Christopher Smart, William Blake, Walt Whitman, W. B. Yeats, Vachel Lindsay, and Allen Ginsberg—usually in an attempt to draw upon the c.'s communal associations and thus create a voice larger than the individual. Modern experimental drama has also incorporated cs., hearkening back to the drama of traditional rituals in which cs. were an important element. See also INCANTATION.—M. S. Edmonson, *Lore* (1971), ch. 4; R. Finnegan, *Oral Poetry* (1977), ch. 4 and bibl.; A. Welsh, *Roots of Lyric* (1978), ch. 7. A.W.

CHANT ROYAL. One of the most complex and difficult of the OF verseforms, a 60-line poem. Related to the *ballade* (q.v.), the c. r. in its most common form (as described in the 14th c. by Eustache Deschamps) consists of five stanzas of 11 lines each rhyming *ababccddedE* (the capital denotes a refrain), followed by a five-line *envoi* (q.v.) rhyming *ddedE*. It is further distinguished by the use of the refrain at the end of each stanza and the *envoi*, and by the fact that, except in the *envoi*, no rhyme words may be used twice. Thus, 60 lines must be rhymed on five rhyme sounds—a formidable technical task. Its most common theme is love, spiritual or human love embodied in the beautiful courtly lady. The name probably derives from its popularity in literary contests in the bourgeois poet-guilds of northern France (*puys royaux*). The term first appears in Nicole de Margival's "Dit de la panthère d'amours" (late 13th c.), but the form, not yet fixed, was used by troubadours and trouvères in the 12th c. Through Machaut, Froissart, and Deschamps in the 14th c., the c. r. found wide recognition, but by the 15th c. its popularity waned. Clément Marot composed four *chant royaux*, mainly on religious themes. The *Pléiade* banned the form, but in the 19th and 20th cs., attempts were made to revive it by Théodore de Banville and others. Some of these, like Deschamps, used it for satirical commentary as well as for elevated themes; others, e.g. Richard Le Gallienne, reduced it to *vers de société*. Valéry remarked that, by comparison, the sonnet is child's play.—Kastner; Patterson; L. Stewart, "The C. R., a Study of the Evolution of a Genre," *Romania* 96

(1975); Morier, s.v. "Ballade."   A.PR.; B.RO.

CHANTE-FABLE. A medieval Fr. dramatic recitation composed, as the name implies, of sections of verse and prose, the former intended to be sung, the latter spoken, perhaps by two jongleurs alternately. The verseform is unusual: a 7-syllable line in assonance, each lyric ending in a 4-syllable line without assonance. Alternating verse and prose is not a rare practice in Med. Lat. (see PROSIMETRUM), Arabic, Celtic, ON, and Occitan writers. But only the anonymous 13th-c. author of *Aucassin et Nicolette* terms his work a "c.-f." *A. et N.* is a beautifully constructed, well unified love story, with distinct dramatic elements, rich in humor and irony; and it skillfully parodies contemporary epic and romance. But it survives in only a single ms., and the extent to which it represents a vogue is disputed (Holmes). Interestingly, in China some 10th-c. *Pien-wen* (narratives) are in a c.-f. form.—J. R. Reinhard, "The Literary Background of the *C.-F.*," *Speculum* 1 (1926); *CBFL*, v. 1, nos. 2127-35; *MGG* 2.1082–84; U. T. Holmes, *Hist. of OF Lit.* (1962); L. Ch'en, "*Pien-wen* Chantefable and *A. et N.*," *CL* 23 (1971); *Aucassin et Nicolette*, ed. J. Dufournet (1973); J. Trotin, "Vers et prose dans *A. et N.*," *Rom* 97 (1976); P. Menard, "La Composition de *A. et N.*," *Mélanges J. Wathelet* (1978); W. Godzich and J. Kittay, *The Emergence of Prose* (1987), ch. 5.

I.S.; B.RO.

CHARACTER (THEOPHRASTAN). See ETHOS.

CHARM (Lat. *carmen*, "song" or "lyric poetry"; also "magic formula" or "incantation" [q.v.]). Now both a physical amulet worn for magical purposes and a verbal formula used for magical effects. In practice, verbal cs. accompany ritual actions and are themselves treated as physical actions or "verbal missiles" (Malinowski)—thus can be turned back by a stronger magician. Cs. are used worldwide in traditional cultures for healing (medicinal cs., fertility cs.), success (hunting cs., weather cs., love cs.), and attack and defense (curses, protection cs.). They are usually fixed, traditional texts, partly in a "special lang." of power marked by thick, irregular patterns of repetition (sounds, words, phrases) and often involving archaic vocabulary, unusual phonological and grammatical forms, esoteric names and allusions, or other elements of obscure meaning. A dozen metrical cs. survive in OE, accompanied by directions in prose for ritual actions, and the power of several (e.g. "For Infertile Land," "Against a Sudden Stitch") can still be felt.

Magical cs. have been directly imitated in Eng. lit. from *Beowulf* (the curse laid on the gold, 3069–75) through Shakespeare (the witches' c. in *Macbeth* 4.1.1–38) to Ezra Pound ("The Alchemist"). On a deeper level, the principle of cs. lies beneath both love poems (words used to attract a beloved) and satire (words used to wound an enemy). Even deeper connections exist in the belief that power resides in sound (q.v.): poetry strongly influenced by thick sound-patterns of alliteration, assonance, internal rhyme, and word-repetition (e.g. Spenser, Poe, Hopkins) resembles and partakes somewhat of the ethos of lang. selected for magical purposes and is primarily concerned with evoking and transmitting power.—H. M. and N. K. Chadwick, *The Growth of Lit.*, v. 1 (1932), ch. 15; A. Huxley, "Magic," *Texts and Pretexts* (1933); B. Malinowski, *Coral Gardens and Their Magic*, 2 v. (1935)—texts and theory of Trobriand cs.; *The Anglo-Saxon Minor Poems*, ed. E. V. K. Dobbie (1942)—texts of OE metrical cs.; Frye; R. C. Elliott, *The Power of Satire* (1960); H. D. Chickering, Jr., "The Literary Magic of 'Wið Færstice,'" *Viator* 2 (1971)—on OE; N. Frye, "Cs. and Riddles," *Spiritus Mundi* (1976); A. Welsh, *Roots of Lyric* (1978).   A.W.

CHASTUSHKA. The miniature Rus. lyric folksong genre called c. ("fast song") emerged in the 1860s and has since become the most productive form in Rus. folklore. The c. originates in both city and village; mixes literary and folk elements; ranges from "true" folk poetry to political slogans; may be sung, recited, accompanied by a musical instrument, or danced to; is highly improvisational and topical; and concerns mainly young people. The most common type consists of four lines, which are usually rhymed. A female lead singer and chorus may perform such "ditties" in long thematically related strings. Jarxo connects the c. with similar songs in Ger. and Sp.—B. Jarxo, "Organische Struktur des russischen Schnaderhüpfles (Častuška)," *Germanoslavica* 3 (1935); S. Lazutin, *Russkaja častuška* (1960); V. Bokov and V. Baxtin, *Častuška* (1966); B. Stephan, *Studien zur russischen Častuška und ihrer Entwicklung* (1969); Y. Sokolov, *Rus. Folklore* (1970); Terras.   J.O.B.

CHIASMUS (Gr. "a placing crosswise," from the name of the Gr. letter X, "chi"; but the term is first attested only in 1871, in Eng., not appearing as a Lat. term until 1903). Any structure in which elements are repeated in reverse, so giving the pattern *ABBA*. Usually the repeated elements are specific words, and the syntactic frames holding them (phrases, clauses) are parallel in construction, but may not necessarily be so. The c. may be manifested on any level of the text or (often) on multiple levels at once: phonological (sound-patterning), lexical or morphological (word repetition; see ANTIMETABOLE), syntactic (phrase- or clause-construction), or semantic/thematic. The fourth of these requires one of the preceding three, and the second usually entails the third. C. of sound will be found in the first sentence of Coleridge's "Kubla Khan"; of word repetition (the commonest form) in Shakespeare's *Julius Caesar.* "Remember March, the ides of March remember" (4.3.18); of syntax, Milton's "That all this good of evil shall produce, / And evil turn to good" (*PL*

12.470–71); of sense or theme, Coleridge's "Frost at Midnight," which sets up the thematic sequence frost–secret ministry–lull–birdsong–birdsong–lull–secret ministry–frost (Nänny). Other poems for which chiastic structures have been claimed are Chaucer's *Parlement of Foules* and Tennyson's *In Memoriam*. C. is thus but another term for an envelope (q.v.) pattern, and will be seen too as one form of inversion within repetition (q.v.). In cl. rhet., c. is the pattern of a sentence consisting of two main clauses, each modified by a subordinate clause, in which sentence each of the subordinate clauses could apply to each of the main clauses, so that the order of these four members could be altered in several ways without change in the meaning of the whole (Hermogenes [2d c. A.D.], *Peri heureseōn* 4.3, in Walz 3.157).

Lausberg defines c., usefully, as the criss-cross placing of sentence members that correspond in either syntax or meaning, with or without exact verbal repetition. Group Mu classifies c. among "metataxes," i.e. figures which "focus attention on syntax," and describes it as a syntactic device which effects a "complete" suppression and addition of semes and taxemes. They add that such crossed symmetry "emphasizes both meaning and grammar." Mahood shows how a simple inverted parallelism in c. can achieve economically a relatively complex effect. In *Richard II*, Bolingbroke receives the following answer when he asks the King if he is content to abdicate: "Ay, no; no, Ay: for I must nothing bee: / Therefore no, no, for I resign to thee" (4.1.202–3). Mahood comments that Richard's reply, "besides suggesting in one meaning (Ay, no; no, Ay) his tormenting indecision, and in another (Ay—no; no I) the overwrought mind that finds an outlet in punning, also represents in the meaning 'I know no I' Richard's pathetic play-acting, his attempt to conjure with a magic he no longer believes. Can he exist if he no longer bears his right name of King?" (87). A less complex modern example which nonetheless shows c. affecting both semantics and syntax is Hopkins' "This seeing the sick endears them to us, us too it endears" ("Felix Randal," 9–10), which concludes with an ellipsis (q.v.) of the grammatical object. And Adrienne Rich uses the fully parallel, repetitive potentiality of c. in "Planetarium": "A woman in the shape of a monster / a monster in the shape of a woman" (1–2). Quinn defines c. by comparing it to other repetitive figures like *epanodos* (amplification or expansion of a series), *antimetabole*, and *palindrome* (q.v.), a sentence which spells the same words forwards or backwards. These figures all manifest rhetoric's multilevelled and synchronous functions in the text.—
C. Walz, *Rhetores graeci*, 9 v. (1832–36); Sr. M. Joseph, *Shakespeare's Use of the Arts of Lang.* (1947); M. M. Mahood, *Shakespeare's Wordplay* (1957); Lausberg; A. Di Marco, "Der C. in der Bibel," *Linguistica Biblica* 37–39 (1976); *C. in Antiquity: Structures, Analyses, Exegesis*, ed. W. Welch (1981);

Group Mu, 45, 80, 124–25; A. Quinn, *Figures of Speech* (1982), 93–95; H. Horvei, *The Chev'ril Glove* (1984); R. Norrman, *Samuel Butler and the Meaning of C.* (1986); M. Nänny, "C. in Lit.: Ornament or Function?" *W&I* 4 (1988); Corbett.
T.V.F.B.; A.W.H.

CHICAGO SCHOOL. Originally the "Chicago critics" were the authors of *Critics and Crit.: Ancient and Modern* (1952), and were so called because of their association with the University of Chicago; the label has since been extended to some of their pupils and to others who have acknowledged indebtedness to them. The present account summarizes the the features of their approach to crit. which distinguish the group most clearly from other 20th-c. critical schools. These may be summed up under two heads: (1) what they have called their "pluralism" (q.v.) and (2) what has been called by others their "Neo-Aristotelianism," the two terms referring, respectively, to their concern, as theorists and historians of crit., with investigating the logical grounds of variation among critical positions, and to their interest, as students of lit., in exploring the possibilities of a particular approach to the analysis and evaluation (q.v.) of literary works which has seemed to them too much neglected.

(1). The most explicit statements of their pluralism are contained in McKeon's "The Philosophic Bases of Art and Crit.," Olson's "An Outline of Poetic Theory," and Crane's *The Langs. of Crit. and the Structure of Poetry*. The basis of the view is the recognition that what any critic says on a literary subject, general or particular, is determined only in part by direct experience with literary works; it is conditioned no less importantly by the tacit assumptions concerning the nature of lit. and the most appropriate method of studying it which are brought to the immediate task: the critic will say different things about a given poem, for example, or at least mean different things, according to she or he conceives of poetry as a species of artistic making or as a mental faculty or as a special kind of knowledge; and the results will likewise differ widely according to whether the critic's reasoning about it rests primarily on literal definitions and distinctions within the subject matter or primarily on analogies between it and other things; and so on through a good many other possible variations in principle and method.

The C. critics thought that much of the notorious diversity in doctrine and interp. observable in the crit. of all ages can be accounted for in these terms; and they took this possibility as a working hypothesis in their writings on critics and critical movements from Plato and Aristotle to the present. They sought to judge the achievements of critics not by any universal criterion of what lit. or poetry "truly" is or of what crit. "ought" to be, but by the relative standard of what these critics have given us, within the limits of their widely variant principles and methods, in the way of verifiable and usable solutions to the different problems they set out to solve. In short, they have proceeded on the assumption that though some modes of crit. are more restricted in scope than others, there are and have been many valid critical approaches to lit., each of which exhibits the literary object in a different light and each of which has its characteristic powers and limitations, so that the only rational ground for adhering to any one of them over any of the others is its superior capacity to give us the special kind of understanding and evaluation of lit. we want to get, at least for the time being.

(2). The so-called Neo-Aristotelianism of the C. S. represents a choice of this pragmatic sort. The special interest in the *Poetics* which appears in their earlier work had its origin in their concern, as teachers of lit., with developing a kind of practical crit. of literary texts that (1) would emphasize the specifically *artistic* principles and reasons governing their construction, as distinct from their verbal meanings, their historical and biographical backgrounds, or their general qualitative characteristics, and that (2) would attach more importance to the principles peculiar to different kinds of texts and to individual texts within a given kind than to those common to lit. in general. Questions to be asked of a text in this sort of crit. would concern problems of organization, presentation, and expression imposed on its writer by the particular end she or he was trying to achieve in composing it, the nature of the means employed in solving them, and the reasons governing the choice of these means rather than others. They would be questions, in short, the correct answers to which, since they pertain to a unique work of human art, can never be predicted in advance or deduced from any *a priori* critical theory, but have to be arrived at by considering which one among various conceivable answers best accounts for what is in the text. But if general presuppositions about what any given literary work must be can only serve to impede the critic's inquiry into what its writer was actually attempting to do, and why, that critic is almost certain, on the other hand, to become more accurate and discriminating in her judgments the more she knows of what it might be—of the range of possible things that writers may do in different kinds of works and of their reasons for doing them, insofar as these can be induced from their productions.

The appeal of Aristotle to the C. S. lay in the fact that he, more than any other critic they knew, had conceived of literary theory in this *a posteriori* and differential way and had not only formulated some of its necessary distinctions and principles, in his brief discussions of ancient tragedy and epic, but pointed the way to further inquiries of the same sort in other literary arts still unrealized at the time he wrote, particularly the lyric, the drama, and the novel.

The C. S. bequeathed to its students and followers not just its pluralism and Neo-Aristotelianism but a general interest in the history of crit. By contrast, an intense interest in lang. was more characteristic of the New Criticism (q.v.) and later poststructuralism (see DECONSTRUCTION). Still, the influence of the C. S. can be seen particularly in recent narrative theory and in continued recourse to issues surrounding the Cl. concepts of imitation (q.v.). See also TWENTIETH-CENTURY POETICS, *American and British*.

PRIMARY SOURCES: R. McKeon, "The Philosophic Bases of Art and Crit.," *MP* 41 (1943–44); *Critics and Crit.: Ancient and Mod.*, ed. R. S. Crane (1952), abridged ed. with new intro. and list of other related writings (1957); R. S. Crane, *The Langs. of Crit. and the Structure of Poetry* (1953), *The Idea of the Humanities* (1967); W. J. Hipple, Jr., *The Beautiful, the Sublime, and the Picturesque in 18th-C. Brit. Aesthetic Theory* (1957); R. Marsh, "The 'Fallacy' of Universal Intention," *MP* 55 (1958); N. Friedman and C. A. McLaughlin, *Poetry: An Intro. to Its Form and Art* (1961); E. Olson, *Tragedy and the Theory of Drama* (1961), *The Theory of Comedy* (1968), *On Value Judgment in the Arts* (1976); W. C. Booth, *Critical Understanding* (1979), *The Rhet. of Fiction*, 2d ed. (1983).

CRITICAL DISCUSSIONS: W. K. Wimsatt, Jr., "The C. Critics," *The Verbal Icon* (1954); M. Krieger, *The New Apologists for Poetry* (1956); H. P. Teesing, "The C. S.," *OL*, supp. 2 (1958); J. Holloway, "The New and the Newer Critics," *The Charted Vision* (1960); W. Sutton, *Mod. Am. Crit.* (1963); *Aristotle's Poetics and Eng. Lit.*, ed. E. Olson (1965); Wellek, v. 6; V. B. Leitch, *Am. Lit. Crit. from the Thirties to the Eighties* (1988), ch. 3. R.S.C.; H.A.

CHICANO (MEXICAN AMERICAN) POETRY.

New Spain's northern provinces, now the U.S. Southwest, were the scene and inspiration of Sp. poetry before the Eng. colonized the Atlantic coast (see SPANISH AMERICAN POETRY). The Oñate expedition (1598) not only founded some of this country's oldest cities, it performed dramas in verse and brought Gaspar Pérez de Villagrá to chronicle the voyage in his epic poem, *Historia de la Nueva México* (1610). Among the colonizing adventures, Villagrá recorded the battle of Acoma, the first poetic rendering within the present U.S. territory of the racial and cultural conflicts that have plagued the country since the European arrival and which contemp. C. p. continues to document. Popular poetry flourished, as evidenced by the rich trad. of romances still found in New Mexico and by the *corrido*, an evolved form of romance chronicling events of communal interest, popular esp. along the Mexican-U.S. border. These traditional forms provided folkloric context and historic memory for C. poets. Cultured forms were used to a lesser extent, often by recent arrivals from Mexico or members of the educated class.

After U.S. annexation of Mexico's northern

states in 1848, the Mexicans remaining in the territory continued to produce poetry, with a notable increase of written material appearing in newly founded local newspapers. Romanticism's influence was marked, as was a tendency to use verse for didactic or satirical purposes. Into the 20th c., Sp. dominated both written and oral production, and alongside poems of a personal nature there appeared poetry on themes of cultural defense and affirmation. Already in the 1850s newspapers featured poems protesting matters perennially pertinent: broken promises by U.S. politicians; discriminatory law enforcement, courts, and schools; the imposition of Eng., and socioeconomic divisions along ethnic or racial lines. Affirmation took the forms of praising Hispanic culture and, ironically, proclaiming the Mexican Am. community's loyalty to the U.S., as proven by participation in the Sp. Am. War and, later, in World War I.

In the 20th c., Eng. appeared more frequently in written poetry produced by Mexican-Americans, though community newspapers still published in Sp. poems by leading Lat.-Am. writers. During the Mexican Revolution and its aftermath (1910–36), a number of Mexican intellectuals immigrated to the U.S. and worked on newspapers; the best of Lat.-Am. *Modernista* poetry was belatedly introduced to Mexican-Am. readers during this period. The Sp. oral trad. was also bolstered by massive immigration. Yet public schooling was almost exclusively conducted in Eng., affecting both linguistic capabilities and the knowledge of a formal poetic trad. in Sp.; it is this fact which, coupled with the pro-Eng. bias of the print media, explains the increase in poetry written in Eng. by Mexican-Americans in the first half of the 20th c. Fray Angélico Chávez's *Clothed with the Son* (1939) and *Eleven Lady-Lyrics and Other Poems* (1945) were acclaimed by critics. This trend continued after World War II, a period which saw the demise of many Sp.-lang. newspapers. By the mid-1960s, when the Chicano Movement for civil rights arose, the majority of Chicanos spoke and wrote in Eng., and poetic expression was as likely to be in one as the other. Many writers attempted to mix the two (bilingualism or "code switching"), some thereby reflecting their normal speech pattern, others as a calculated political statement.

Most Chicano Movement poetry was committed to the communal struggle of the minority culture, a position reflected in its predominant themes: an identification with Mexico, esp. the pre-Columbian and revolutionary periods; a revision of U.S. history; the glorification of heroic figures; the exaltation of communal cohesion in the *barrio* (neighborhood), the family, and *carnalismo* (brotherhood); and the channeling of solidarity into political action. Its imagery spotlighted distinctively Chicano subjects, although the underlying experiences mirror those of other U.S. immigrant groups. The most significant works reveal a common structure: (1) U.S. society threatens cultural survival; (2) cultural characteristics are invested in a representative figure under direct attack; (3) that figure's images are catalogued to rescue them from destruction; (4) the poem substitutes for the threatened figure, becoming a new centering force for readers which in effect can turn individuals into a community through the shared act of reading.

Rodolfo Gonzales' manifesto, *I Am Joaquín/Yo Soy Joaquín: An Epic Poem* (1967), demanded Chicanos withdraw from U.S. social oppression into their communal traditions to rediscover their identity as survivors and warriors. Abelardo Delgado's "Stupid america" (1969) proclaimed the nation's future greatness if Chicanos were allowed to fulfill their creative potential, and the self-destruction that was the alternative. Alurista's *Floricanto en Aztlán* (Flowersong in Aztlán, 1971) proposed a hybrid of pre-Columbian philosophy and the Third-World anticapitalism as a survival strategy amid U.S. racism and class exploitation. Ricardo Sánchez' *Canto y grito mi liberación* (I Sing and Shout My Liberation, 1971) railed against U.S. life as an alienating prison. In *Perros y antiperros* (Dogs and Anti-dogs, 1972) Sergio Elizondo toured the history and geography of the Southwest to denounce Anglo-Am. encroachment and the dehumanizing character of U.S. society, positing a refuge in the C. community's love and humanity. And while Tino Villanueva's *Hay Otra Voz Poems* (There is Another Voice Poems, 1972) prefigured the introspective turn and the heightened awareness of lyric craft and tropes to come in the mid 1970s, it culminated in a declaration of the poet's dedication to communal political struggle in an interlingual lang. that is itself a metaphor of the ideological message.

This poetry's most distinctive stylistic features were (1) the predominance of narrative and mimetic over lyrical and tropical modes of expression, and (2) interlingualism, a combination of Sp., Eng., and sub-dialects. Prime exponents of the latter were José Montoya and Alurista:

> Hoy enterraron al Louie
>   (Today they buried El Louie)
> And San Pedro o sanpinche
>   (St. Peter or saintdamned)
> are in for it. And those
> times of the forties
> and the early fifties
> lost un vato de atolle
>   (a real great guy)
>   (Montoya, "El Louie").

> mis ojos hinchados
>   (my swollen eyes)
> flooded with lágrimas
>   (tears)
> de bronze
>   (of bronze)
> melting on the cheek bones

CHINESE POETICS

of my concern
    (Alurista, "Mis ojos hinchados").
Interlingualism makes comprehension impossible for monolingual readers, while dialectal usages, like Montoya's slang, can perturb even bilinguals. Although interlingual poets of the '60s and early '70s insisted that they were simply using the community's native speech patterns, the result was poetry for initiates, unfortunately inaccessible to those Chicanos not sharing the specific linguistic context. At a simpler level, many texts were published with facing translations, e.g. *I Am Joaquín/Yo Soy Joaquín* or *Perros y antiperros*, which opened C. p. to a wider readership.

The mid 1970s brought changes. The national decline in political activism was mirrored in a poetry less ideologically or communally oriented and more personal and individualistic. Coinciding with this change, women's poetry emerged, some with a feminist perspective. Notable was an increased concern with craft. Some of the principle figures were university trained writers, exemplified by the Fresno School of C. p. groomed by Philip Levine at Fresno State University (Gary Soto, Leonard Adame, Robert Vásquez). While the use of tropes increased, narrative tendencies still predominated, reflecting their popularity in mainstream poetry.

Interlingualism has also decreased, although it still flourishes among authors who direct their work at the C. community. Blatant political statements have waned, as has the need to stress the writing's ethnic character. C. content has become more subtle, with less attempt to create uniquely C. images. More universal qualities are freely displayed. Luis Omar Salinas, known as a '60s Movement poet for his "Aztec Angel" poem, has few C. references in *Darkness Under the Tress / Walking Behind the Spanish* (1982), but his status among C. poets has, if anything, increased. Bernice Zamora's *Restless Serpents* (1976), Gary Soto's *Black Hair* (1985), and Lorna Dee Cervantes's *Emplumada* (1981) are C. texts, yet readers could easily place them within a broader framework of the U.S. experience. Many of their poems contain no Chicano references or else contextualize them to function without need of ethnic knowledge. Rafael Jesús González' "Ars poetica" (1977) ends with just such a cultural juxtaposition of universals:

the sky-eagle
devouring the earth-serpent
as a sign.
The Aztec ball player
losing the game lost his heart
to keep alive the gods.
    The wells claim it:
    Li Po
    would die
    needing it
    for the moon.

               ("Coin, Ars poetica")

The Oriental reference is more esoteric than the Aztec ones, which are sufficiently clear for general understanding. Other poets are more subtle, as is Bernice Zamora in her parodies of Shakespeare, Robinson Jeffers, or Roethke; or Lucha Corpi, who ends her tribute to Emily Dickinson with:

We are . . . migrant
workers in search of
floating gardens as yet
unsown, as yet, unharvested.

These are specific images, yet they allude to Chicano themes of migrant work and the Aztec's founding of a promised city which probably would have received more blatant treatment a decade before.

Yet C. p. has not fully assimilated. At the community level, the 1960s-style political rhetoric still resounds, with perhaps a more profound sense of social disparity after the relatively meager progress made by the C. community since the 1970s. Some poets have infiltrated the small literary magazine network, and fewer still have published with major publishers—without the threat of Affirmative Action that prompted some houses to issue a few titles around 1970—and some poets— Gary Soto, Lorna Dee Cervantes, Luis Omar Salinas, Alberto Ríos—have been awarded significant prizes by mainstream institutions. Recognition and acceptance, however, are evidenced better, if on a limited scale, in the fact that C. p. begins to appear in major academic anthologies of Am. lit.

ANTHOLOGIES: *El ombligo de Aztlán*, ed. Alurista (1972); ENTRANCE: *Four C. Poets* (1975); *El Quetzal emplumece*, ed. C. Montalvo (1976); *Siete poetas* (1978); *Fiesta in Aztlán*, ed. T. Empringham (1981); *Contemp. C. P.*, ed. W. Binder (1986).

HISTORY AND CRITICISM: J. Bruce-Novoa, *C. Authors, Inquiry By Interview* (1980); *C. P., A Response to Chaos*; M. Sanchez, *Contemp. C. P., A Critical Approach to an Emerging Lit.* (1985); C. Candelaria, *C. P.: A Critical Intro.* (1986); W. Binder, *Partial Autobiographies: Interviews With 20 C. Poets* (1986); J. E. Limón, *Mexican Ballads, C. Poems* (1991).
                                   J.B.-N.

CHILEAN POETRY. See SPANISH AMERICAN POETRY.

CHINESE POETICS. The Ch. have had much to say about the nature and function of poetry throughout their history. The earliest remarks that have bearing on poetics are found in the philosophical writings of pre-Confucian, Confucian, and other early thinkers—notably Daoist [Taoist]—from the 6th c. B.C. to the 2d c. A.D. Later came a number of separate treatises on lit. that are devoted in large part to poetics: Cao Pi (187–226), *Discourse on Lit.* (*Lunwen*); Lu Ji (261–303), *Exposition on Lit.* (*Wenfu*); Zhong Hong (ca.

- [187] -

469–518), *Classes of Poetry* (*Shipin*); and Liu Xie (ca. 465–ca. 520), *Elaborations on the Literary Mind* (*Wenxin diaolong*). These works—which both amplified concepts borrowed from the earlier philosophical texts and also developed new ideas—are concerned with the nature and function of various elements in poetry: emotion and individual personality, human nature, the vital or life force (*qi*), language, perception, reason, mind, talent or genius, learning and practice, artistry or craft (formal or technical stylistics), and pragmatic or moral qualities.

Such issues were also debated during the following Tang era (618–907), the so-called "Golden Age" of Ch. poetry, but another great upsurge of critical thinking and writing began with the Song period (960–1279), stimulated both by attempts to come to terms with and understand the great Tang poets of the previous era and by contemporary developments in intellectual thought: principally (1) the spread throughout secular literary culture of Buddhist—chiefly Chan (Japanese Zen)—ideas concerning mind, consciousness, perception, and spontaneity, and (2) the continuing Neo-Confucian synthesis of classical Confucian ethics and its philosophy of human nature with Daoist and Buddhist thought. Important Song-era critics include Su Shi (1037–1101), Huang Tingjian (1045–1105), Yang Wanli (1127–1206), Yan Yu (ca. 1195–ca. 1245), and the contemporary northern Jin dynasty poet-critic Yuan Haowen (1190–1257). Some of the chief issues they discuss involve the tension between talent and learning, the advantages and disadvantages of emulating past masters, the definition of a correct or "orthodox" canon of poetry (and the criteria for such orthodoxy), the means for creating a poetry of the "spontaneous and natural" (i.e. poetic "enlightenment"), and the paradox of poetic lang. (how a limited medium can and should communicate infinite meaning).

Crit. during the rest of the traditional era is marked by continuing discussion of the above issues as well as new developments: (1) the emergence of a full-fledged archaist (*fugu*, "return to antiquity") movement in poetic theory and practice during the Ming dynasty (1368–1644)—championed by such figures as Li Mengyang (1475–1529) and Ho Jingming (1483–1521)—which advocated emulating Tang-era masters and, in some cases, promoted poetry as a mode of Neo-Confucian self-cultivation (as did Xie Zhen [1495–1575]); (2) a persistent, anti-archaist, individualist-expressionist countercurrent, exemplified, for instance, by Yang Weizhen (1296–1370), Tu Mu (1459–1525), and Yuan Hungdao (1568–1610); and (3) the appearance during the Qing dynasty (1644–1911) of coherent "schools" (*pai*) which emphasized particular types or aspects of poetry. Of these there were chiefly four: the "Spirit [Intuition] and [Personal] Tone" (*shenyun*) School led by Wang Shizhen (1634–1711) (intui-

tive cognition, intuitive control over the poetic medium, and an oblique, tenuous expressionism), the "Stylistics and Euphony" (*gediao*) School led by Ye Xie (1627–1703) and Shen Deqian (1673–1769) (the particularity and concreteness of poetic lang., its euphony, and the interdependence of poetic form and personal and moral expression; Shen was an esp. strong advocate of moral didacticism in poetry), the "Native Sensibilities" (*xingling*) School led by Yuan Mei (1716–1798) (straightforward expression of emotions and individual personality), and the "Sensuous Texture" (*jili*) School led by Weng Fanggang (1733–1818) (rules governing the formal textures of poetic lang.).

A major problem facing the modern student of Ch. p. is that of how to develop a scheme of analysis that can induce the various theories of poetry that lie inherent in the critical trad., for this trad. is diverse and complex—there is not one "Ch. p." but a number of different theories of poetry, some complementary and some diametrically opposed. The most successful attempts to develop such a scheme have used the "coordinates of art crit." (universe, work, artist, audience) in Abrams as their point of departure and have tried, with varying degrees of adjustment and amplification, to describe Ch. theories in terms similar to Abrams' categories: mimetic (the relation of work to universe), pragmatic (work to audience), expressive (work to writer), and objective (work as object). (See Abrams' *The Mirror and the Lamp* [1953] or, for the same taxonomy, POETRY, THEORIES OF.) The most extensive such analysis to date is given by Liu (*Ch. Theories of Lit.*), who divides Ch. theories into six categories: metaphysical (focusing on the interaction between universe and writer), deterministic (also an interaction between universe and writer), expressive (interaction between writer and work), technical (work as object), aesthetic (also work as object), and pragmatic (interaction between work and audience).

Mimesis—"art as essentially an imitation of aspects of the universe" (Abrams)—seems an inappropriate term to designate the relation of work to universe as it is treated in Ch. theories of poetry, primarily because of the range of meaning it has in the thought of Plato and Aristotle and in subsequent Neoplatonic and neo-Aristotelian systems of crit. in the West: since no counterparts to either Plato's transcendent Ideal forms or Aristotle's Universals ever developed in Ch. thought (which generally conceived of Reality in monistic and immanent terms), there was neither the incentive nor the rationale for Ch. poetry—in either theory or praxis—to concern itself with the imitation or representation of such ideals or standardized universal types. Unlike Aristotle and his heirs, who largely regarded poetry as a process of "making," the Ch. trad. seems to have regarded it instead as a process which involves "knowing" and "action," and poems thus become not objects that imitate some aspect of reality but records of experience that articulate the encounter of the poet with reality; as such, an element of subjectivity seems always present, for it is not just aspects of reality that are articulated in poems but those aspects as they are filtered through, fused with, or otherwise permeated by elements of the poet's consciousness—albeit at times de-personalized or de-individualized and thus enlightened and "universal." It is, in fact, theories which advocate such de-personalized and enlightened poetry that Liu calls "metaphysical," a rubric which subsumes "theories that are based on the concept of lit. as a manifestation of the principle of the universe . . . generally referred to as the Tao [Dao] (literally, "Way") . . . the unitary principle of all things and the totality of all being." The way the poet apprehends the Dao is through intuitive knowledge, cognition, or apprehension—a faculty that is "suprarational" and transcends sense perceptions (Liu 1975).

However, as much as theories that focus on the relationship of work to universe sometimes advocate the exercise and articulation of the mystic union with Reality as Macrocosm, more often they prescribe a quiet and intimate visionary approach to experience—the exploration of microcosms and the capturing of "essences." It may be that "metaphysical" is too weighty a term to designate these theories as a whole and that "intuitionalist" (which Liu had used in 1962) or "phenomenological" might be more appropriate, given certain apparent similarities with Western phenomenological crit.—for instance, interests in the "solidarity of the subject and object," the intuitive grasp of "the essence of things," and the "rediscovery of the prereflective and preconceptual state of consciousness" (Liu). Another term, "cognitive" (conceptually and culturally more neutral), has also been used to describe such theories which deal with the poet's intuitive apprehension or awareness of reality (Lynn).

As for deterministic theories of poetry, they "expound the concept of lit. as an unconscious and inevitable reflection or revelation of contemporary political and social realities" (Liu), and these too, according to Liu, focus on the interaction between universe and writer, but here the "universe" is not the cosmic Dao of Nature but rather human society. However, it is arguable that what Liu calls "deterministic" theories are not actually theories of poetry—since they are only descriptive and have no prescriptive dimension—but rather a kind of literary hermeneutics: poets can and often do unconsciously reflect political and social realities, facts which both the casual reader and the serious critic should be aware of in making interpretations, but it would be nonsense for a theory of poetry to *prescribe* that poets should *unconsciously* reflect things. (In "metaphysical" or "cognitive" theories the mind is often regarded as passive and spontaneous, i.e. free of deliberation

or intentionality, but is never thought to be "unconscious" as such.) Statements in the Ch. critical trad. dealing with determinism are always concerned with the way works should be read, never with the way they should be written. Moreover, even in terms of hermeneutics, determinism is not simply a factor in interpreting the way writers interact with the universe but also something that can elucidate how the poet's subjective feelings—the expressive qualities of his work—can be affected by social and political conditions (writer–work relationship), and how the tastes and expectations of literary audiences (audience–work relationship) and the development and sustenance of formal poetic style (work as object) can be shaped by such extra-literary forces.

The relationships between work and audience and work and writer are characterized in both Abrams' and Liu's systems as "pragmatic" and "expressive," respectively. As in the West, Ch. pragmatic theories of poetry emphasize the way poetry should achieve various political, social, moral, or religious ends. The pragmatic concept (which might also be called "didactic" or "moralistic") was probably the most widespread view of poetry in premodern China, primarily because it was sanctioned by Confucianism but also because the other main intellectual and religious trads.— Daoism in both its philosophical and popular religious versions and Buddhism in its various forms—often regarded poetry as an effective educational or proselytizing tool. Also prevalent throughout Ch. hist. was the tendency to define the nature of poetry in terms of self-expression— the revelation of the poet's inner world, sometimes emphasizing his thoughts, feelings, and emotions, sometimes personal character, individuality, or nature (whether in a "natural" or "cultivated" state). At times the emphasis is on less tangible and more subtle feelings—mood, tone, atmosphere—and in such cases there is a convergence with theories that focus on the interaction between universe and writer, so that it is sometimes difficult to determine whether the fusing or filtering process of the poet's consciousness in its interaction with the external world should be regarded as cognition or expression. In fact, some critics seem to advocate a merger of the two processes—in effect, formulating "cognitive-expressionist" theories (Wang Shihzhen). Moreover, some expressionist theories are concerned with these personal qualities as they are expressed by unique individuals, and others regard them either as manifestations of representative personality types common to all ages or as responses typical of poets in general but limited to particular kinds of historical (social, economic, and political) circumstances—the expressive counterpart, in effect, of the concept of "period style" found in some technical theories of poetry which recognize the role of deterministic extra-literary forces in the development of formal style.

Orientations that view the work primarily as a

formal artifact involve either "technical" or "aesthetic" theories. The term "objective" seems inappropriate to describe such Ch. theories because they never seem to have gone so far as to develop the concept that a poem is "a heterocosm, a world of its own, independent of the world into which we are born, whose end is not to instruct or please but simply to exist" (Abrams). Instead, such theories tend to concentrate on the nature of writing as a craft or technique—"technical" from the writer's point of view—or as a complex of aesthetic effects—"aesthetic" from the reader's point of view. (A similar distinction is made by McKeon, whose "formal" and "technical" modes of crit. correspond respectively to Liu's "technical" and "aesthetic" theories.) Although the role of the poet in these theories was often likened to that of the "Creator" (*Chuangzaozhe*)—a metaphor for the processes of "Great Nature" (*Daziran*)—and the "perfect poem" often said to be "a natural object," the product of a "natural event" that has transcended the limits of mere mortal craft, it is control over the poetic medium that is of paramount concern in Ch. p. and not the idea that the poem can and should be some kind of new, separate reality that goes beyond nature itself. The Ch. trad., after all, seems to have regarded the divine, spiritual, or noumenous as immanent in nature rather than transcendent to it, and so it is to be expected that the "divine" powers of the poet result not in heterocosms or "objects" which embody a separate, second nature created *ex nihilo* but in perfectly "natural" poetic "creations"—in perfect communion with nature. Instead of resembling what Abrams calls "objective theories," Ch. technical/aesthetic theories seem to have more in common with Western rhetorical approaches to poetry, with an additional emphasis on spontaneous, intuitive, or "natural" control over the poetic medium.

A. Fang, "Rhymeprose on Lit. [*Wenfu*]," *HJAS* 14 (1951), rpt. in *Studies in Ch. Lit*, ed. J. Bishop (1965); R. McKeon, "The Philosophical Bases of Art and Crit.," in Crane; Abrams; Liu Xie, *The Literary Mind and the Carving of Dragons [Wenxin diaolong]*, tr. V. Y. C. Shih (1959); J. J. Y. Liu, *The Art of Ch. Poetry* (1962), *Ch. Theories of Lit.* (1975), *Lang.—Paradox—Poetics: A Ch. Perspective*, ed. R. J. Lynn (1988); D. E. Pollard, *A Ch. Look at Lit.: The Literary Values of Chou Tso-jen in Relation to the Trad.* (1973); R. J. Lynn, "Orthodoxy and Enlightenment: Wang Shih-chen's Theory of Poetry and Its Antecedents," *The Unfolding of Neo-Confucianism*, ed. W. T. de Bary (1975), "The Talent-Learning Polarity in Ch. Poetry: Yan Yu and the Later Trad.," *CLEAR* 5 (1983), "Chu Hsi as Literary Theorist and Critic," *Chu Hsi and Neo-Confucianism*, ed. W. T. Chan (1986), "The Sudden and the Gradual as Concepts in Ch. Poetry Crit.: An Examination of the Ch'an-Poetry Analogy," *The Sudden-Gradual Polarity: A Recurrent Theme in Ch. Thought*, ed. P. Gregory (1987), "Sung Dynasty Theories of Poetry," *Sung Dynasty Sources of Neo-Confucianism*, ed. I. Bloom (1989); A. A. Rickett, *[Wang Kuo-wei's] Jen-chien Tz'u-hua: A Study in Ch. Lit. Crit.* (1977); *Ch. Approaches to Lit. from Confucius to Liang Ch'i-ch'ao*, ed. A. A. Rickett (1978); P. Yu, "Ch. and Symbolist Poetic Theories," *CL* 30 (1978), *The Reading of Imagery in the Ch. Poetic Trad.* (1987); *Studies in Ch. Poetry and Poetics*, ed. R. C. Miao (1978); T. T. Chow, "Ancient Ch. Views on Lit., the *Tao*, and Their Relationship," *CLEAR* 1 (1979); J. T. Wixted, *Poems on Poetry: Literary Crit. by Yuan Hao-Wen* (1982), "The *Kokinshu* Prefaces: Another Perspective," *HJAS* 43 (1983)—important bibliographical references; S. K. Wong, *Early Ch. Lit. Crit.* (1983); *Theories of the Arts in China*, ed. S. Bush and C. Murck (1983); Nienhauser et al.—10 survey articles on poetry, prose, rhetoric, and lit. crit., *inter alia*, and entries on Ch. critics and works of criticism. R.J.L.

CHINESE POETRY.

I. CLASSICAL
II. MODERN

I. CLASSICAL. Poetry was uniquely important in traditional China as a means of expression. From cl. antiquity (722–481 B.C.), it has been assumed that what is felt inwardly will find natural expression in words (*shi yan zhi*), an idea appearing in a chronicle in 546 B.C. This longstanding conception of poetry, which later also came to influence Japanese poetic theory (see JAPANESE POETICS), may be attributed to the Ch. consciousness of the power of writing, the notion that human configurations (*wen*) and natural patterns (*wen*) are parallel manifestations of the *Dao* or cosmic principle. From this derives the general belief that poetry, if powerfully imbued with human feeling, can bear upon political, social, and cosmic order. A standard presentation of this expressive-affective view of poetry is the "Great Preface" prefixed to China's first anthol. of poetry, the *Shi jing* (Classic of Poetry). It is in reference to this collection that the generic term for the chief form of poetry, *shi*, first appears.

Comprising 305 songs, the *Shi jing* was probably compiled sometime after 600 B.C., though its oldest parts may date as early as the 11th c. B.C. Whether or not Confucius (551–479 B.C.) himself selected the 305 poems from an earlier compilation of 3000, as alleged by the historian Sima Qian (ca. 145–85 B.C.), it is true that Confucius gave the anthol. an important place in his curriculum and that it subsequently became the fundamental text of Confucian education. The *Classic* includes folk, courtier, and dynastic songs and ceremonial hymns. All of these were originally sung and chanted. The songs cover a wide variety of subjects that reflect the daily activities of early Ch. society (before the 6th c. B.C.)—courtship, farming, hunting, feasting, war, sacrifices. These poems already evince several expressive devices basic to later Ch. p. and Ch. poetics (q.v.): abundant rhyme, strong auditory effects, formal compactness, and the use of nature imagery.

The basic rhythmic unit of a Ch. poem is the single character (*zi*), and since every character is pronounced as one syllable, the number of characters in each line determines the meter. Songs in the *Classic of Poetry* are predominantly written in 4-character lines, with occasional longer or shorter lines. Rhyme schemes are fairly complex and varied at times, but the usual pattern is *abcb*. Most poems consist of short stanzas that are nearly identical in metrical structure, i.e. isometrical. The following verse, entitled "Guan ju," is the first and the best-known of the songs (every line in the original contains four characters):

> "*Guan quan*," the ospreys cry
> On the islet in the river:
> A beautiful young girl
> Is a fine match for the gentleman.
>
> Water plants of varied length,
> Left and right (we) trail them:
> That beautiful young girl—
> Awake, asleep, (he) longs for her.
>
> (He) longs for her but to no avail,
> Awake, asleep, (he) thinks of her.
> Yearningly, yearningly,
> (He) turns, tossing from side to side.
>
> Water plants of varied length,
> Left and right (we) pick them:
> That beautiful young girl,
> Zithers and lutes welcome her.
>
> Water plants of varied length,
> Left and right (we) sort them:
> That beautiful young girl,
> Bells and drums delight her.

Reduplicated sounds, such as the onomatopoetic *quan quan* in the opening line of this poem, appear frequently in the songs. Other recurrent auditory devices include alliteration and rhyming compounds, such as *cen ci* ("of varied length") and *yao tiao* ("beautiful and young"). The basic device of parallelism, based on the principle of repetition with variation, prefigures the more formalized systems of parallelism (q.v.) to be developed several centuries later.

Compared to Western poems, these songs are remarkably terse and compressed, esp. if read in the original, where pronouns often disappear and grammatical connections are kept to a minimum. This quality of compactness may be due to the particular nature of the Ch. lang., but more importantly, it reflects a basic aesthetic attitude typical of *shi* poetry, wherein suggestion is prized over exposition, "less" over "more." Closely related is the effect of economy and reticence achieved by an imagistic device called *xing* ("stimulus" or "metaphorical allusion"), which is used in the opening lines of most of the *Classic*'s lyric poems

to connect metaphorically the natural world with the human situation. The element of *xing*, such as the brief description of the osprey in "Guan ju," intensifies the associative and allusive power of natural imagery. Because the metaphorical connection between *xing* and the human context is left unspecified, readers are provoked to infer something more, or other, as the true meaning of the poem. Thus, in Confucius' time, *xing* were alluded to by diplomats as a means of indirect reference to sensitive political situations. This explains why traditional commentators since the Han dynasty (206 B.C.–A.D. 220), instead of reading "Guan ju" as a simple love song, have developed a trad. of reading that poem, and in fact the entire *Classic* and subsequently poetry in general, as bearing moral and political significance. That is, later poets, under the influence of this long-lasting exegetical trad., would sometimes write poems to the same allegorical patterns they read in (or read into) the works of others. Recently, perhaps inspired by the revaluation of allegory (q.v.) in Western crit., sinologists have devoted much attention to the problem of "allegorization" or "contextualization" (P. Yu's term) in Ch. p., often citing Western treatments of Solomon's *Song of Songs* for comparison.

Whereas the *Classic of Poetry* represents the Northern roots of Ch. culture, China's second anthol., *Chu ci* (the Songs of Chu), reflects life in the Southern "colonies" around the Yangzi basin in the Warring States period (403–221 B.C.)—though recent scholarship has demonstrated that the North-South distinction should not be taken too literally. What we can be sure of is that songs in the Chu collection—which include the "Nine Songs," "Nine Changes," "Nine Pieces" ("nine" being not the number but perhaps a musical term meaning simply "many"), and a long personal lament called *Li sao* (On Encountering Trouble)—are all, in one way or another, founded on Shamanism, a religion that initially flourished in the Northern dynasty of Shang (ca. 18th–12th c. B.C.) but subsequently fell from favor there and found its permanent home in the Chu region. In terms of style and content, the Chu songs are markedly different from those of the *Classic of Poetry*: they are exuberant and colorful in imagery, inclined to erotic pursuit of water goddesses and imaginary airborne flights inspired by the practice of Shamanism. In contrast to the predominant 4-character rhythm in the *Classic*, these songs are written in a new meter, with a caesura marked by the exclamation-syllable *xi* in the middle. The two basic patterns are: (1) tum tum tum *xi* tum tum tum, and (2) tum tum tum ti tum tum *xi* tum tum ti tum tum (*tum* representing full words, and *ti* particles). The second pattern is known as the "Sao style," because *Li sao*, the longest poem in the anthol. and believed to have been written by the first Ch. poet recorded by name, Qu Yuan (d. 315 B.C.?), is the earliest example of it.

Qu Yuan's genius enabled him to invent not only the "Sao style" of poetry but also a striking intensity of lyricism reinforced by a symbolism of fragrant plants and flowers. He was China's Pindar, the first person to have developed a distinct individual voice in Ch. p. Poems in the "Nine Changes" and "Nine Pieces," perhaps written by later authors, are obviously influenced by *Li sao* both in form and content. But without discrediting its originality and power, one may say that *Li sao* has become famous in Ch. lit. mainly because its author represents a model of Confucian virtue for later literati to emulate. Qu Yuan was a loyal minister of Chu who drowned himself after scheming officials slandered him to the king of Chu, causing him to be rejected by his sovereign. Trad. has it that before his suicide Qu Yuan composed *Li sao* to defend his loyalty: the poem describes the poet's long fantastic journey to mythical realms and his persistent, though unsuccessful search for the "fair ladies." Its rich and varied implications have not prevented *Li sao* from being read almost exclusively as a political allegory. Perhaps this is because scholars have found it necessary to view the work as reflecting political reality in order to place it within the Confucian exegetical trad., a trad. long established by commentators of the *Classic*. Other arguments can be adduced: surely, Qu Yuan, an educated member of the Chu royal house, would have learned the conventional method of allegorical reading and might indeed have purposely composed the work as a political allegory.

The poetic genre known as *fu* (rhapsodies), which became the typical court poetry of the Han dynasty, may be regarded as deriving from *sao* poetry. The *fu* generally opens with a short introduction in prose, and the main body in verse employs a variety of line lengths (3-, 4-, 6-, or 7-character lines), end rhymes, onomatopoeia, dazzling images, occasional verbal and syntactic parallelism, lengthy enumeration of fantastic objects and place names, etc. Like *sao*, the early *fu* tends to take a panoramic, cosmological approach, focusing on imaginary celestial journeys with an aim to impress and enrapture the reader. Song Yu, supposedly a disciple of Qu Yuan, was the earliest putative author of this form. But it was Sima Xiangru (179–117 B.C.), the greatest poet of the Han dynasty, who first developed the *fu* into a major literary genre. His long *fu* on the Shang-lin Park is the symbol of a splendid age: its elaborate, if imaginary, account of rivers, hills, animals, and exotic fruits and trees in the hunting park conveys a powerful image of the Han empire during the rule of Emperor Wu. This exuberant style also characterizes, to a large extent, the numerous *fu* on capitals by later authors. Besides the panoramic *fu*, there was another type, "*fu* on objects" (*yongwu fu*), which also achieved popularity. The *yongwu fu* focuses on the description of such small objects as flowers, birds, and musical instruments, and some of the works extant today are quite brief. It is impossible to know whether these short pieces in the *yougwu* mode were parts of longer *fu* or originally intended to stand alone. After the Han there emerged gradually a particular type of "lyrical" *fu*. A case in point is Tao Qian's (365–427) "*Fu* on Calming the Passions," a poem strongly marked by personal emotion.

In addition to *fu*, a genre called *yuefu* became important in the Han. Originally the name of the Music Bureau established by Emperor Wu to collect folksongs, *yuefu*, has been broadly applied to both ritual hymns and popular ballads, and also to literary imitations of the genre. It is said that when new music was first imported from Central Asia, many *yuefu* songs were composed for the new melodies; hence the use of irregular meters ranging from 3 to 7 characters in a line. Like folksongs everywhere, *yuefu* ballads employ devices of direct speech, dialogue, formulaic expressions, hyperbole, repetition with variations, etc. They usually present dramatic situations that have direct bearing on contemp. social realities: beautiful women resisting the advances of powerful officials, the hardships of the orphan, the abandoned wife, the old soldier. Indeed, the *yuefu* served as an appropriate genre for many authors to air social criticism anonymously. The longest of the extant *yuefu*, "Southeast Fly the Peacocks," tells of the tragic fate of a loving young couple who are forced by the man's mother to separate and who eventually take their own lives, reportedly a true story that occurred in the Later Han (A.D. 25–220). With the appearance of this long ballad, written in a 5-character rhythm, the *yuefu* became increasingly standardized in structure (though some earlier, shorter works in this genre were already composed according to the same meter). A few decades later, numerous anonymous southern *yuefu* were written in the 5-character line in quatrains. Subsequent literary imitations of this genre further developed new formal, rhetorical, and imagistic devices.

Perhaps under the influence of the *yuefu* ballads, a new verseform, the 5-character line *shi*, rose to prominence around the 2d c. A.D., largely replacing the 4-character *shi* meter dominant from the age of the *Classic of Poetry*. This 5-character line form created an overwhelming preference for fluid poetic rhythms based on an odd, rather than even, number of characters—a tendency that was to last for centuries. Among the most important features of this new form are: (1) the regularized use of a caesura after the second character, and a secondary caesura either after the third or the fourth; (2) couplets serving as independent metrical units, with the rhyme falling on the end of the second line of the couplet; and (3) independence from musical rhythms. The sudden flowering of the 5-character line *shi* inspired poets to use it as a vehicle for deep reflection and introspection. The earliest extant, though anonymous, *shi* poems written in this form, known collectively as the "Nineteen Old Poems," are dominated by subjectivity and emotion, focusing primarily on the problems of death and separation. The general tendency for *shi* poems to adopt paratactic lines and brief images gives these 19 poems the quality of restraint, thus inciting generations of commentators to view them as embodying the virtue of "gentleness and sincerity" so potently celebrated by the trad. of the *Classic of Poetry*. But it is precisely this poetics of suggestiveness that most attracted later poets. The use of the 5-character line *shi* by literati was first promoted by the poetically talented members of the Cao family (later founders of the Wei dynasty), esp. during the Jian-an period (196–220) when many first-rate poets, the Caos among them, wrote some of the finest works in the lang. The supreme value of poetry, the Jian-an literati believed, lies primarily in the individual's creative vigor (*qi*), a kind of operative energy that gives lit. immortality. Their concern with the intrinsic power of poetry led poets to become preoccupied with self-expression during the Wei-Jin era (220–316), as is eminently demonstrated by Ruan Ji's (210–63) series of 82 poems entitled "Singing of My Thoughts."

The times of the Eastern Jin (317–420) and the Southern Dynasties (420–581) were plagued by constant wars and intrigues: the Ch. government moved south in 317 after foreign invaders had taken over the north, and a constant struggle for power between great families in the south lasted nearly 300 years. But it was during this period of political disunity that Ch. poets discovered the true power of nature's beauty. Tao Qian (365–427), now customarily described as one of China's two or three greatest poets but largely overlooked during his lifetime, explores in his poetry the rustic quietude of the "farmland" (*tianyuan*). His trust in the workings of nature comes essentially from his belief that everything moves in a cyclical order and that life and death are necessary phases of nature's creation. A recluse who describes himself as living in a noisy human world yet with a detached heart, Tao Qian is deservedly the first poet to awaken in poetry the full potentiality of Daoism. The extraordinary way in which he mingles personal feelings and natural images has led later critics to use the term *qingjing jiaorong* ("fusion of feeling and scene") to describe the special quality of his poetry. But, perhaps, a more typical poet of the period was Xie Lingyun (385–433), known as the champion poet of "mountains and water" (*shanshui*) poetry. An aristocrat endowed with a strong love of landscape and travel, Xie develops a poetic style that is more visually descriptive and sensory than ever before. One senses that his elaborate use of parallelism (q.v.), as if intended to capture the complementary relationship of mountains and rivers, reflects not only the Ch. ideas of the principles of the universe but also a profound influence of the earlier panoramic *fu*. But compared to earlier models in *fu*, which often

detail mythical animals and fictitious objects, Xie's landscape poetry is distinguished by a descriptive realism, a desire to capture a "formal likeness" of nature. Indeed, it was the notion of verisimilitude (q.v.; *xingsi*) that dominated aesthetic taste in the Southern Dynasties. The basic tenet in lit. crit. was that poetry should be characterized primarily by skillful and detailed descriptions of the natural world. In the beginning, this approach took the form of landscape poetry, as may be demonstrated by the works of Xie Lingyun and a younger poet, Bao Zhao (412?–466?). But toward the end of the 5th c., it gradually developed into a poetry focused on small objects (*yongwu shi*)—musical instruments, curtains, lamps, candles, etc.—a reflection of the literary salons of the Southern Dynasties with their intimate aestheticism and high-bred preciosity. In the 6th c., the *yongwu shi* ideal of verisimilitude was further realized in Palace Style poetry, where palace women became the main "objects" of description. An aesthetic attitude, a belief that beauty itself embodies its own *raison d'etre*, distinguishes these poems from the works of previous ages. Perhaps it is on account of this self-sufficient aestheticism, independent of moral and political considerations, that traditional critics have judged Palace Style poetry frivolous.

Parallel to the descriptive orientation was a poetic formalism that also came onto the literary horizon during the Southern Dynasties. Poets, knowing the privileged character of their poetry, began to define the boundaries of the genre: that which employs rhyme is *wen* (pure lit.); that without it is *bi* (plain writing). The main purpose of this distinction was to narrow the meaning of the classical term *wen* (patterns), which originally had a broad denotation covering both *wenxue* (lit.) and *wenzhang* (composition in general). A formal criterion such as rhyme seemed best for defining the normative boundary of this new concept of *wen*. The extent of controversy provoked by this formal revisionism was something similar to, if not greater than, the European Ren. debate over poesy. These Southern Dynasties poets also went further to experiment with tonal variations and other prosodic schemes, some of which were to evolve into important rules in Tang poetry. Shen Yue (441–513) is credited with having devised the "four tone" system, with the four tones (i.e. pitches) referring to the "level" and the three "oblique" tones ("rising," "departing," "entering"). The "level" tone corresponds to the first and second tones of today's standard Mandarin, while the "rising" and "falling" tones are distributed into the present third and fourth tones. The "entering" tone no longer exists in modern Mandarin, as it has long been redistributed among the other tones. The true significance of Shen Yue's "four tone" prosody lies in the correlation, and hence the opposition, of the "level" (O) and the "oblique" (X) tones within the individual lines—e.g. O O O X X. Ch. may have been a tonal lang. from its beginnings, but some historical linguists place the introduction of tones in the Han dynasty or later, and argue that Shen Yue's "discovery" of the four tones was in fact the observation of a new phenomenon in Ch. lang. as it called on tones (i.e. pitch) to compensate for the loss of some other phonemically distinctive features. If the tonal revolution led by Shen Yue represented a definitive break from traditional prosody, it was the talented Xie Tiao (464–499) who exhibited the true merits of this new scheme in his "New Style poetry" (*xin ti shi*), so that even hundreds of years later poets looked back to Xie Tiao as an ideal model in *shi* composition. As the successor to these early promoters of tonality, Yu Xin (512–580) combined tonal refinement and powerful lyricism in his poetry in such a way as to influence contemp. *fu* poetics, giving the *fu* genre a new formalistic outlook. This new cross-generic phenomenon is best demonstrated by the *fu*, *Lament for the South*, which he wrote after the fall of his dynasty, the Liang dynasty (502–57).

During the Tang dynasty (618–907), generally acknowledged as the golden age of Ch. p., the gradual codification of Regulated Verse (*lushi*)—based on the original conception of the Southern Dynasties' "New Style poetry"—brought to the Ch. trad. a whole new spectrum of poetic experience. First, the earlier "open-ended" format becomes a prescribed 8-line structure, with a level-tone rhyme falling at the end of each couplet. (Rhyme is also permissible at the end of the first line of the first couplet.) Second, the 4-couplet verse has a specific rule concerning the distribution of parallelism: the second and the third couplets are made up of parallel lines, while the last couplet is not and the first couplet usually not as well. Third, parallelism develops into an enclosed system based on symmetry, with each component in the first line matched by a grammatically similar and semantically related, yet tonally antithetical, component in the corresponding position of the second line, thus forming a perfect mirror effect. Fourth, the coherence of the poem's phonic pattern is governed by the cumulative effect of contrast (*dui*) and connection (*nian*), as in the following example:

```
X X O O X
O O X X O
O O O X X
X X X O O
X X O O X
O O X X O
O O O X X
X X X O O.
```

With its insistence, in 5-character or 7-character line forms, on a rigid tonal system and a structure of parallelism, Regulated Verse was believed to represent the perfect form of poetry. In this period the long-established quatrain form (now called *jueju*), which constituted a major portion of the popular *yuefu* ballads during the Southern Dynas-

ties, also began to be written in a similar manner. An extended form of Regulated Verse was *pailu*, verse of unprescribed length (often several hundred lines) which observed the basic tonal patterns but was allowed to change the rhyme several times in the middle of the poem. Generally, the term "Regulated Verse" came to refer to the "new" poetry as opposed to the "Ancient Style poetry" (*gushi*) which was meant to include both old poems produced before the Tang and new poems written in the old style.

The compact and highly schematized form of Regulated Verse helped to consolidate a new aesthetics that was to become the trademark of Tang poetry: the integrity of the lyric moment. In the two middle, parallel couplets, the focus of perception is inevitably a lyric moment in which superficially referential data have been turned into static, qualitative images. Thus, the sense of subjective reality brought forth by the opening couplet is bound to be swept away by this heightened, deliberately timeless vision. Only after this momentary world of poetic reverie is over do statements of personal judgment begin to appear in the final couplet. The lyric moment is an effective poetic device for uniting the expressive and descriptive elements in poetry, and certainly a good counterweight for the prevailing objective mode so confidently celebrated by Palace Style poetry for nearly two centuries. During the 7th c., the "Four Talents" of the Early Tang were already conscious of developing a penetrating, expressive voice suited to the compactness of the new format. But it was not until the High Tang (8th c.), when Regulated Verse was hailed as an ideal form, that poets began to create a heightened lyrical vision, fully internalizing their perceptions of the natural world. Wang Wei (701–61) in particular looked up to Tao Qian as a model poet, in an attempt to convey through the new verse the effortless mingling of self and nature. One of his best-known couplets captures the completeness of a lyric moment, casual but lasting: "Walking to where the water ends, / Sitting, watching the clouds rising."

Two other High Tang poets, Li Bo (701–62) and Du Fu (712–70), have traditionally been paired together as two literary giants whose poetic styles are in sharp contrast with each other, and the evaluation of their relative merits has been a major preoccupation of critics since the Song dynasty. Li Bo is customarily viewed as a spontaneous genius, Daoist mystic, and carefree romantic, Du Fu as a meticulous craftsman, Confucian "sage of poetry," and responsible spokesman for suffering mankind. Though somewhat exaggerated, these stereotypes are not groundless: they owe much to the poets themselves, who sought to cultivate such images of self in their poetry. Their differences are clearly revealed in their respective preferences for different kinds of verse: Li Bo favored the open-ended format of Ancient Style and *yuefu* verse, with their freedom from prescribed tonal and verbal parallelism, while Du Fu, though skilled in all forms, took up Regulated Verse with particular enthusiasm, tackling great technical difficulties while pursuing formal perfection. Esp. noteworthy is Du Fu's contribution to 7-character line form of Regulated Verse in his late years, after years of living through misery and warfare, and of wandering. His typical works in this period, chief among them "Autumn Sentiments," are distinguished by an imagistic density and a complexity of symbolism which fuse personal feelings with historical allusions, thus invoking wider cultural associations and a new aesthetic sensibility.

The hist. of Ch. p. is a story of constant revival and revision. During the Middle Tang (ca. 765–835), one of the most important forms of poetry is "New *Yuefu*," an imitation of the ancient *yuefu*, written in a simple style and with an eye to expressing social criticism. The most popular poet writing in this form is Bo Juyi (772–846), even though posterity has retained as his most famous poem the "Song of Everlasting Sorrow," a romantic ballad which narrates, without overt moralization, the love story of the Emperor Minghuang and his consort Yang Guifei. In the late Tang (ca. 835–907) poets reverted to the style of complexity and density inaugurated by Du Fu's 7-character line Regulated Verse. The highly allusive and sensuous imagery of Li Shangyin's (813?–58) love poetry, which fuses reality with imagination, stands out as an effective means of expressing degrees of emotional sensitivity not previously attained in the Ch. poetic trad.

Toward the end of the Tang, a new genre, *ci* (lyric), emerged in response to the popularity of foreign musical tunes newly imported from Central Asia. At first, *ci* was regarded as a continuation of *yuefu*, but it gradually became a special trad. of composition. In contrast to the titles of *yuefu* poems, which do not refer to fixed metric patterns, *ci* titles always point to particular *ci pai* (tune patterns) for which the poems are composed. These *ci pai*, totaling about 825 if the numerous variant forms are excluded, came to be viewed as definite verse patterns. Even today, poets still write to these tune patterns, though without knowing the original melodies. This unique practice of *ci* composition is called "filling in words" (*tian ci*). *Ci* poetry is characterized often by lines of unequal length, in sharp contrast to Regulated Verse. The difference of this genre lies in its retaining—as well as refining—the major aspects of tonal metrics advanced by Regulated Verse, while varying the line lengths. The result of this crucial change is a radically new way of scansion, thus allowing also for new flexibility of expressiveness. Among some of the distinctive qualities of *ci* are: its striking intensity of emotional content, esp. that of romantic love; its mood of melancholy; and its preference for refined and delicate images. Long before Tang poets began to view *ci* as a serious poetic genre, it already flourished as a "popular song form." Songs

preserved in a ms. found in a cave in Dunhuang attest to this fact. "Popular" *ci* songs were vital to the devel. of the *ci* of the literati, and, in fact, the evolution of the *ci* genre may be seen as a hist. of the intermingling of the two styles. Although authors such as Bo Juyi had already experimented with occasional *ci*, the late Tang poet Wen Tingyun (ca. 812–ca. 870) has been regarded as the pioneer poet of the genre. His style of refined subtlety and parataxis, obviously influenced by late Tang Regulated Verse, became typical of early *ci*. The only poet during this period to break away from the overwhelming influence of Wen was Wei Zhuang (ca. 836–910). Wei's poetic voice was deliberately more direct, and thus represented a style contrary to Wen's. A few decades later Li Yu (837–978), known as one of the greatest poets in traditional China, went a step further and synthesized these two stylistic modes. The last monarch of the Southern Tang (937–75) who became a political prisoner in the Song capital from 976 until his death, Li Yu produced *ci* poems that are intensely lyrical, viewing his own personal suffering in the light of the destiny of all mankind.

Ci, however, are generally associated with the Song dynasty (960–1279), for the genre reached the height of its literary status during this period. Liu Yong (978–1053), the poet-musician, changed the direction of *ci* by boldly mixing the "popular" song style with the literati style in such a manner that it was difficult for critics to place his work in a particular stylistic category. It was Liu Yong who first borrowed the longer *manci* mode from the "popular" song trad. and transformed it into a vehicle that allowed for more complex lyrical expression. During the early Song dynasty, only Su Shi's (1037–1101) achievement in extending the poetic scope of *ci* paralleled Liu Yong's formal contributions. In Su Shi's hands, *ci* finally entered the inner circle of Song dynasty poetics and became a genre through which a poet could express the full range of his ideas and feelings. It was under his influence that *ci* began to free itself from music and became primarily a literary creation. During the Southern Song (1127–1279), poets began to explore new metaphorical complexities that tended toward symbolism, as demonstrated by the numerous *yongwu ci* (*ci* on objects), where personal feelings are expressed through small natural objects. Jiang Kui (ca. 1155–ca. 1221), Wu Wenying (ca. 1200–60), Wang Yisun (ca. 1232–ca. 1291), Zhang Yan (1248–1320), and Zhou Mi (1232–98) were representative poets in this new mode. The rise of poetry clubs during this time also served as a stimulus to the popularity of *yongwu ci*, esp. because the *yongwu* mode in poetry had always been closely connected with social gatherings. Meanwhile, during the dynastic transition from the Song to the Yuan—in what appeared to be a period of personal and cultural crisis—the *yongwu ci*, which favored implicit voice and somewhat disparate images, eventually became the perfect symbolic and allegorical medium for poets wishing to express their unwavering loyalty to the Song court and their resentment toward the Mongols. Perhaps the best examples are the 37 poems in the series of "New Subjects for Lyric Songs" (*yuefu buti*) written by 14 Southern Song loyalist poets in 1279. These poems, through the use of symbolism invoked by such objects as lotus and cicada, are believed to be allegorically related to the desecration of Song imperial tombs in 1278 by a Tibetan lama who was acting on orders from the Mongols.

A striking exchange of generic roles was noticeable during the Song: while *ci* poetry became as perfect a form for pure lyricism as Regulated Verse had been in the Tang dynasty, *shi* poetry began to slowly venture out of the pure lyrical domain. Unlike *shi* poetry in the Tang, Song dynasty *shi* had a tendency to dwell on philosophical issues and intellectual arguments. Mei Yaochen (1002–60) coined the term *pingdan* to refer to the special quality of "plainness" and "calmness" that characterizes works of his own and his contemporaries. The serene and joyful tone of Song dynasty verse, as in Ouyang Xiu's (1007–72) 800 poems, may be directly influenced by the idea of self-cultivation central to Neo-Confucian thought. Generally, *shi* poetry of this period (e.g. Su Shi; Yang Wanli, 1124–1206) is distinguished by the use of plain lang. and simple description of the details of everyday life.

During the Yuan dynasty (1280–1368), a new song form called *sanqu* emerged to become the major form of lyricism. The *sanqu* is characterized by lines of unequal length, a set of prescribed tones and tunes, and an extensive use of colloquial lang. The structure of a *sanqu* is more flexible than that of a *ci* because the poet, while composing a *sanqu* to a tune, is allowed to add "padding words" (*chenzi*) to considerably extend the length of a line. But other technical requirements of this genre are highly complex and varied, often further complicated by the use of the "suite" style (*taoshu*), a device which it shares with lyric drama (*qu*). A suite is a series of songs set to the same mode, arranged according to a special sequence prescribed by the mode. The "suite" style allows a poet to compose a string of arias on a particular theme which could form part of a lyric play. But the best known *sanqu* are short ones written in the form of a single stanza, like the much admired pieces by Ma Zhiyuan (1260?–1324?).

The *shi* poetry of the Yuan, the Ming (1368–1644), and the Qing (1644–1911) Dynasties has so far been largely ignored by modern scholarship, partly because of an inappropriate, though understandable, notion of generic evolution prevailing among Ch. scholars—that the Tang dynasty was the golden age of *shi*, the Song dynasty of *ci*, the Yuan of *qu* and drama, and the Ming and Qing of vernacular fiction. While such a scheme has the advantage of viewing the hist. of Ch. lit. as a sequence of genre innovations, with each newly vital genre naturally succeeding a former period's, it nevertheless seriously distorts the real nature of generic devel. in traditional China. For, in effect, genres such as *shi* and *ci*, once created, rarely became obsolete; they continued to be used and to develop.

One considerable accomplishment of the Yuan, Ming, and Qing periods was the increasing connection of the *shi* genre with painting and calligraphy. In the Yuan, many painter-poets began to inscribe poems to their paintings with the same brush, as the crucial final step toward completing a creative process. During the Ming and the Qing, we find the same practice continuing and growing, with an unusually high percentage of poets who were also painters and calligraphers (Shen Zhou, 1427; Tang Yin, 1470–1523; Wen Zhengming, 1470–1559; Wu Weiye, 1609–72; Zhu Da, 1626–ca. 1705). The painter-calligrapher-poet trad. is the culmination of an old ideal and occasional practice existing since the Tang: the Tang poet Wang Wei is said to have produced "poems which are like paintings, and paintings like poems" (see UT PICTURA POESIS). And the Song dynasty poet Su Shi was an accomplished painter and calligrapher.

Another phenomenon which distinguishes Ming and Qing poets from earlier authors was their enormously ardent concern for past models and for criticism. This tendency grows out of the basic Ch. belief that the past, having accumulated so much of the civilization's wisdom, should be regarded as an enduring authority from which individual creativity must necessarily draw inspiration. To the Ming poets, who saw themselves as restoring the glories of Ch. culture after the foreign rule of the Mongols, the question was: what literary models from the past should be used in order to renew the vitality of poetry in the present? The result was the emergence of an ever-increasing number of schools and a poetry that was repeatedly redefining itself along theoretical lines (though to a much lesser degree this tendency already existed during the Song dynasty). The various schools of Ming and Qing poetry were extremely diverse in their approaches, but they can be roughly grouped into two camps: (1) those who took the High Tang poets as models, and (2) those who preferred the style of Song poetry. This Tang-Song opposition obviously seems simplistic, esp. when applied to individual authors whose stylistic preferences changed from one period of their lives to another. But most poets, given their own temperament and literary associations, seemed to have regarded themselves, or were judged by others, as belonging to one of these two camps. Thus, the Former Seven and Latter Seven Masters during the 16th c. belonged to the Tang School; so did Chen Zilong (1608–47), Wu Weiye (1609–71), Wang Shizhen (1634–1711), and Shen Deqian (1673–1769). On the other hand, Qian Qianyi (1582–1664), Zha Shenxing (1650–1727), and Li E (1692–1752) were known for their pro-

CHINESE POETRY

motion of "Song dynasty style" poetry. But individualist poets such as Yuan Hongdao (1568–1610) and Yuan Mei (1716–97) stood outside these two groupings, simply preaching the importance of self-expression. In general, for poets in this period poetry had become not just a form of expression but an object of speculation and contemplation. Poetry is judged not so much according to its content as according to its handling and effect.

The 17th c. saw a renaissance of *ci* poetry which was to last until the beginning of this century. This renaissance was due largely to the efforts of the late Ming poet Chen Zilong (1608–1647), who organized the "Yunjian School of *ci*" to call attention to the unfortunate "fall" of Ming *ci* from a golden age which he located in the Southern Tang. A slightly later poet, Zhu Yizun (1629–1709), advocated the importance of elegance in *ci* writing and modeled his own work after the polished and elegant style of the Southern Song. Chen Weisong (1626–82), however, promoted the Northern Song style. Throughout the Qing many schools of *ci* arose, all searching for particular modes as models for emulation and basis for devel. The constant competition among various schools eventually made *ci* poetry a subject of serious scholarly pursuit and theoretical debate—a devel. unprecedented in the hist. of *ci*. Aside from a few individualist poets such as Nalan Xingde (1655–85) and Xiang Hongzuo (1798–1835), *ci* poets in the Qing were primarily scholars. The one critical approach that is essential to these scholar-poets is allegoresis (see ALLEGORY),reading *ci* as political allegories in the manner of the Han Confucian exegesis in the *Classic of Poetry*, though now with fresh urgency—a phenomenon which obviously reflects the wide consciousness of political pressure under the rule of the foreign-born Manchus, who were always quick to root out political subversion. Thereafter, by a process we have outlined above, allegorical reading became the basis for allegorical writing. While the Qing poets advocated the use of allegory in *ci*, they eschewed an over-explicit presentation. They esp. recommended Southern Song poets as models for imitation, since these earlier authors had, in their view, mastered the poetics of implicit, imagistic association in the "*ci* on objects," by at once creating the impression of distancing and guiding readers to their intended meaning. Judged by the standards of Western poetry, their allegorical devices may seem to be only pseudo-allegorical strategies. The images are not usually connected in a goal-oriented narrative progression, nor do they refer to some philosophical or religious truth. But they are nonetheless allegories—imagistic allegories that point to historical and political truths by means of the associative power of symbolism.

Varied and diversified as it is, the Ch. poetic trad. is characterized by certain recurrent traits: (1) the use of understated but powerful imagery, whose significance lies in the implicit meaning, (2) an emphasis on the harmony of man and nature, (3) the assumption that poetry is based on personal, daily experience, (4) the feeling that individual talent is inseparable from past models, (5) an emphasis on the individual's "creative" expression, which is not to be confused with a cult of originality *per se*, and (6) the poet's faith in being recognized by posterity. By and large, Ch. poets hope to intervene meaningfully in the life of their times, and almost always nurture a sense of cultural responsibility for the future. But the concept of "the poet" as a specialized professional of verse was absent in traditional China, where every educated Ch. was expected to have mastered the art of poetic composition. In a general sense, every educated man was a "poet," though he might not be a distinguished one. For the Ch., writing poetry was a self-inspired, self-expressive activity, not a career closed to all but poetic geniuses.

ANTHOLOGIES: *The Jade Mountain*, tr. W. Bynner and K. Kiang (1929); *The Book of Songs* (1937; 1987 ed. contains forward by S. Owen), *Ch. Poems* (1946), both ed. and tr. A. Waley; *The Book of Odes*, tr. B. Karlgren (1950)—contains Ch. text and authoritative, literal tr. of *Shi Jing*; *Poems of the Late T'ang*, tr. A. Graham (1965); *Anthol. of Ch. Lit.*, ed. C. Birch, 2 v. (1965, 1972); *Anthol. of Ch. Verse*, tr. J. Frodsham and C. Hsi (1967); *Ch. Rhyme-Prose* (1971), *Columbia Book of Ch. P.* (1984), both ed. and tr. B. Watson; *Sunflower Splendor*, ed. W. Liu and I. Lo (1975); *Among the Flowers*, tr. L. Fusek (1982); *New Songs from a Jade Terrace*, tr. A. Birrel (1982); *Wen Xuan*, tr. D. Knechtges, v. 1 (1982), v. 2 (1987); *The Songs of the South*, tr. D. Hawkes, 2d ed. (1985)—valuable background information; *Columbia Book of Later Ch. P.*, tr. J. Chaves (1986); *Waiting for the Unicorn: Poems and Lyrics of China's Last Dynasty*, ed. I. Y. Lo and W. Schultz (1986).

HISTORY AND CRITICISM: *P. and Career of Li Po* (1950); J. Hightower, *Topics of Ch. Lit.*, rev. ed. (1953); *The Poetry of T'ao Ch'ien* (1970); W. Hung, *Tu Fu* (1952); G. W. Baxter, *Index to the Imperial Register of Tz'u Pros.*, rev. ed. (1956)—with bibl. note; A. Waley, *Yüan Mei (1956); J. J. Y. Liu*, The Art of Ch. P. *(1962)*, Major Lyricists of the Northern Sung *(1974)*, Ch. Theories of Lit. *(1975)*, Lang.—Paradox—Poetics, *ed. R. J. Lynn (1988); F. Mote*, The Poet Kao Ch'i *(1962); B. Watson*, Early Ch. Lit. *(1962)*, Ch. Lyricism *(1971); J. Diény*, Les Dix-neuf Poemes Anciens *(1963); K. Yoshikawa, An Intro. to Sung Poetry, tr. B. Watson (1967)*, Five Hundred Years of C.P., 1150–1650 *tr. J. T. Wixted (1989), with W. S. Atwell's important "Afterword"; Y. Kao and T. Mei, "Syntax, Diction, and Imagery in T'ang Poetry," HJAS 31 (1970), "Meaning, Metaphor, and Allusion in T'ang Poetry," HJAS 38 (1978); W. Schlepp*, San-ch'u *(1970); H. Frankel, "Cl. Ch. [Versification]," in Wimsatt, and* The Flowering Plum and the Palace Lady *(1976); Studies in Ch. Lit. Genres, ed. C. Birch (1974); A. Cooper*, Li Po and Tu Fu *(1974); C. H. Wang*, The Bell and the Drum

(1974), From Ritual to Allegory *(1988); J. Chaves,* Mei Yao-ch'en and the Devel. of Early Sung Poetry *(1976)*, *"Moral Action in the Poetry of Wu Chia-chi (1618–84),"* HJAS *46 (1986), "The Yellow Mountain Poems of Ch'ien Ch'ien-i (1582–1664),"* HJAS *48 (1988); D. Holzman,* Poetry and Politics *(1976); D. Knechtges,* The Han Rhapsody *(1976); H. Stimson,* Fifty-five T'ang Poems *(1976); W. Yip,* Ch. P.: Major Modes and Genres *(1976); D. Bryant, "Selected Ming Poems,"* Renditions *8 (1977),* Lyric Poets of the Southern T'ang *(1982); H. C. Chang,* Ch. Lit., *v. 2,* Nature Poetry *(1977); F. Cheng,* L'Écriture poétique Chinoise *(1977; Eng. ed. 1982); S. Owen,* The Poetry of the Early T'ang *(1977),* The Great Age of Ch. P.: The High T'ang *(1981),* Traditional Ch. P. and Poetics *(1985),* Remembrances: The Experience of the Past in Cl. Ch. Lit. *(1986); S. Lin,* The Transformation of the Ch. Lyrical Trad. *(1978); Approach to Lit. from Confucius to Liang Ch'i-Ch'ao,* ed. A. Rickett *(1978); K. S. Chang,* The Evolution of Ch. Tz'u Poetry *(1980),* Six Dynasties Poetry *(1986),* "Symbolic and Allegorical Meanings in the *Yüeh-fu pu-t'i* Series," HJAS *46 (1986), "The Idea of the Mask in Wu Wei-yeh (1609–1671),"* HJAS *48 (1988),* The Late-Ming Poet Ch'en Tzu-lung *(1991);* Ling. Analysis of Ch. P., spec. iss. of JCL *8 (1980)—8 articles on metrics,* The Late Ming Poet Ch'en Tzu-lung *(1991); P. Yu,* The Poetry of Wang Wei *(1980),* The Reading of Imagery in the Ch. Poetic Trad. *(1987); P. Kroll,* Meng Hao-Jan *(1981); A. Davis,* T'ao Yuan-ming, *2 v. (1983); Liu Hsieh,* The Literary Mind and the Carving of Dragons, *tr. V. Shih, 2d ed. (1983); S. Leys,* La Forêt en feu *(1983; enl. Eng. ed., 1985)—good discussion of poetry and painting; R. Egan,* The Literary Works of Ou-Yang Hsiu *(1984); S. Chou, "Allusion and Periphrasis as Modes of Poetry in Tu Fu's 'Eight Laments,'"* HJAS *45 (1985); C. Hartman, "Poetry," in Nienhauser et al.;* The Vitality of the Lyric Voice, *ed. S. Lin and S. Owen (1986)—contains Y. Kao's important article on Regulated Verse; G. Fong,* Wu Wenying and the Art of Southern Song Ci Poetry *(1987); L. Zhang, "The Letter or the Spirit: The* Song of Songs, *Allegoresis, and the* Book of Poetry," CL *39 (1987); R. Mather,* The Poet Shen Yüeh *(1988); D. Levy,* Ch. Narrative P. *(1988); M. Fuller,* The Road to East Slope *(1990); D. R. McCraw,* Ch. Lyricists of the 17th C. *(1990).* K.S.C.

II. MODERN. Ch. p. entered a new period in 1917. Hu Shi, who had published an article entitled "Suggestions for a Reform of Lit." earlier that year, returned from America in the summer and actively began writing new poetry according to the principles he set forth. Some of his colleagues at Beijing University, notably Liu Fu, Shen Yinmo, and Zhou Zuoren, joined in the effort. While they differed from one another in goals and styles, these young intellectuals shared one conviction: new poetry should be written freely in vernacular as opposed to cl. lang. In 1920, when Hu Shi published his first collection of poems, *Changshi ji* (Experiments), he claimed that they were "verse in vernacular lang."

During the next five years (1921–26), more than 30 books of vernacular Ch. p. appeared. Many young poets were either returned students or still studying abroad, either in Japan (Guo Moro), America (Kang Baiqing, Xu Dishan, Xie Bingxin, Wen Yido, Zhu Xiang), or Europe (Liang Zongdai, Xu Zhimo, Li Jinfa, Wang Duqing, Dai Wangshu), while some distinguished literati specializing in cl. scholarship, such as Yu Pingbo and Zhu Ziqing, also made remarkable contributions. A critic of the *Experiments* predicted that poetry written in vernacular lang. would corrupt itself presently, but few poets writing new poetry chose cl. lang. as their medium. The new poetry appeared to be emancipated completely from traditional prosody, and many formal, syntactic, and rhetorical features therein remind one of Western poetry in the hands of Goethe, Wordsworth, or Whitman. At times, even traces of such exotic forms as the Sanskrit gatha, Gr. epigram, Japanese haiku, and (esp.) the prose poems of Tagore were detectable. The most serious attempts at a new prosody were made by Wen Yido, Xu Zhimo, and Zhu Xiang, principally on the model of Eng. Victorian verse.

Major themes which concerned the poets of the early 1920s were conventionally centered on love and nature. However, some poets did treat such relatively new topics as revolt, mysticism, legends, exoticism, hallucination, and children. They proved that a different form could give new life to an old poetry, in a new cadence effective for expressing the moods of a nation continually caught up in political and cultural crises. Poets and writers organized clubs to promote ideas in response to social events. Led by Guo Moro, a group of students formed a society called "Creation" (1921) and published several magazines. Others would associate themselves with the editorial board of a journal or a literary supplement in a newspaper. A typical journal was the *Xinyue* (Crescent, 1928), initially edited by Wen Yido and Xu Zhimo, which published political comments, stories, book reviews, and lit. crit. as well as poems.

New Ch. p. experienced steady devel. over the next ten years (1927–37), until the war broke out. Amid the problems created internally by rival military forces and externally by Japanese aggression, China witnessed strong poetic creativity. The most phenomenal figure of this period was Xu Zhimo. Back from England in 1922, Xu was very active in the promotion of romanticism not only in his poetry but also in his style of living. His audacious expressions of idealism, sympathy for the poor, and contempt for hypocrisy won him loud applause across the land. Academic critics, on the other hand, praised him for his tireless pursuit of creative lang., original metaphor and imagery, and effective stanza forms. When he died in an airplane crash in 1931, he left the readers of Ch. p. an indelible image of the passionate, rebellious romantic poet. Western influence on Ch. lit. was conspicuous during this period. In poetry, there was Ger. influence on Feng Zhi; Fr. on Liang Zong-dai, Li Jinfa, and Dai Wangshu; and Eng. on Xu Zhimo, Bian Zhilin, and Sun Dayu. These poets also wrote some of the most enduring, thoughtful poems of 20th-c. China. It was during the 1930s, too, that some poets began practicing a kind of free verse in excessively sweeping style, politically oriented, and often on grandiose subjects in a resounding mixture of extollment and lamentation. Ai Qing and Zang Kejia represented this tendency. Though their legitimate predecessors could include Guo Moro, who was sometimes described as "Whitmanian," they probably owed their spirited mannerism more to Yesnin and Majakovskij.

One of the most important books of poetry published before the war was *Hanyuan ji* (Han Garden, 1936), a collection of lyrical poems by Li Guangtian, He Qifang, and Bian Zhilin. This book, along with Hu Shi's *Experiments*, Guo Moro's *Nushen* (Goddess, 1921), Xu Zhimo's *Feilengcui zhi yi ye* (A Night in Florence, 1927), Wen Yido's *Si shui* (Dead Water, 1928), and Dai Wangshu's *Wo de jiyi* (My Memories, 1929), established the major types of new Ch. p. Together they formed the essence of a new trad. to be elaborated over the next two decades; they inspired the modernist movement on Taiwan during 1958–68 and set a model for young poets to restart their experimental poetry in China after 1978. These books were the six most influential sources of new Ch. p., published before the Second World War. As to the reason why Li, He, and Bian should redirect their literary styles and themes thereafter, the cause was obviously political ideology, which, though historically significant, perhaps, proved fatal to lyricism.

With the outbreak of war in July 1937 and the advance of Japanese troops across eastern China, a consensus arose among the poets to serve their country by writing propaganda into their poetry. The disputes over what Lu Xun advocated as the "Proletarian Lit. of a National Revolutionary War" and the so-called "Lit. of the United Front in Resistance to the Japanese Aggression" (1936) led to an extravagant emphasis on the political purposes of poetry at the expense of artistic quality. Instantly a great number of magazines and pamphlets were born which published pieces on the consequences of the war—separation, fear, blood, hunger, death—described in vivid emotional tones charged with sorrow and anger. These poems were called *langsong shi* (verses for oral delivery), which obviously required immediate responses from the audience in the marketplaces, temple squares, and military campgrounds where they were delivered to ensure success. Considering the fact that the majority of people at that time were illiterate, it would be rash to underestimate the contribution *langsong shi* made toward mobilizing the people against the enemy. Their simple, crude, and sentimental quali-

ties made these verses useful on many occasions in that era and, for the same reason, made them unmemorable today.

Under such circumstances, most poets in the early 1940s neglected artistic pursuit, which was once their urgent concern during the decade 1927–37. Neither form nor thematic content was a problem any more. Then, after Mao Zedong unfolded his mandate through the "Talks at the Yan'an Forum on Lit. and the Arts" (1942), even some distinguished poets, who had been devoted to the artistic perfection of their work, changed their attitude to conform to the prescribed topics. Fortunately, there were two groups of poets who seemed able to resist the fashion: the young talents in colleges (esp. the Southwestern Associate University in Kunming), such as Mu Dan and Zheng Min; and the poets in Japanese-occupied regions, such as Feiming, Dai Wangshu, and Xin Di. Relatively unaffected by ideological pressures, they continued to merge traditional lyricism and contemporary sensibility. Enriched by their reading of Western lit., they created a style that belonged unmistakably to the 1940s, a style which can be said to identify distinctively China's "premodern" poetry.

With the founding of the People's Republic of China in 1949, many intellectuals fled the Communists to Taiwan. While the Nationalist government in Taipei, like its antagonist in Beijing, ceaselessly encouraged the writing of occasional verses for political use—a strained continuation of the partisan interference with art—the poets on Taiwan seemed freer in their literary experiments than their peers across the straits. A large number of little magazines appeared on Taiwan beginning in the early 1950s. In 1956 China launched the authoritative *Shi Kan*, a poetry journal sanctioned by the Party and graced in its inaugural issue by a group of Mao's poems in classical style. In that year, too, a "Modernist School" was formed on Taiwan without political influence from anywhere. Ji Xian, an ardent poet and editor of the magazine *Xiandai shi* (Modern Poetry), collected more than 100 poets, both Taiwanese and mainlanders, to sign a manifesto which stressed that modern Ch. p. would have to be a poetry "horizontally transplanted" from Europe but not "vertically inherited" from classical China. Amid the lasting debates that ensued, many young men and women published excellent works which not only defied political ideologies current in the civil war but also initiated a maturing modern poetry to ratify the "premodern" style of a decade earlier as the mainstream of 20th-c. Ch. lit. The controversy over "transplanting" or "inheriting" was resolved in the late 1960s as the poets came to believe that what they wrote was both *modern* and *Chinese*.

Since 1949, new poetry in China has followed a double-tracked course. Official journals publish discreet pieces which proffer political guidance and rally around the Party, while some uncomfortable voices have formed, during the last quarter of the 20th-c., a new Ch. p., sometimes called "menglong shi" (poetry in veils). The "menglong shi," which claims to have originated in the early 1970s, became known to the world only after the Cultural Revolution (1966–76), with the publication of an underground magazine *Jintian* (1978–81). The experimental nature of this poetry, which in its surrealistic and quasi-existentialist tendencies resembles the Taiwanese poetry written during 1958–68, has won many readers' confidence in the creativity of China's new literary generation. Ambiguity is the common quality of poetry in times of turmoil, as Ch. history attests, when it seeks to grow independently of political control. China is in the process of rapid social change, which poetry will certainly reflect sensitively and comment on thoughtfully, in the way it always has over the last three millennia.

ANTHOLOGIES: *Zhong-guo xin wen-xue da-xi*, v. 8, ed. Zhu Ziqing (1935); *Mod. Ch. P.*, ed. and tr. H. Acton and S. H. Chen (1936); *Contemp. Ch. P.*, ed. R. Payne (1947); *La poesie chinoise contemporaine*, ed. and tr. P. Guillermaz (1962); *20th-C. Ch. P.*, ed. and tr. K. Y. Hsu (1963); *Xien-dai zhong-guo shi xuan*, ed. M. M. Y. Fung et al. (1974); *An Anthol. of Contemp. Ch. Lit.*, v. l, ed. P. Y. Chi et al. (1975); *Lit. of the People's Republic of China*, ed. K. Y. Hsu (1980); *Columbia Book of Later Ch. P.*, tr. J. Chaves (1986); *The Isle Full of Noises*, ed. and tr. D. Cheung (1987); *Xien-dai zhong-guo shi xuan*, ed. Y. Mu and Z. Shusen (1989).

HISTORY AND CRITICISM: K. Y. Hsu, "The Life and Poetry of Wen I-to," *HJAS* 21 (1958); C. Birch, "Eng. and Ch. Meters in Hsu Chih-mo's Poetry," *Asia Major* 7 (1959); T. T. Chow, *The May Fourth Movement* (1960); S. H. Chen, "Metaphor and the Conscious in Ch. P. under Communism," *ChinaQ* 13 (1963); M. Stolzova, "The Foundation of Mod. Ch. Poetics," *ArOr* 36 (1968); B. S. McDougall, *Paths in Dreams* (1976); D. Cheung, *Feng Chih* (1979); *Trees on the Mountain*, ed. S. C. Soong and J. Minford (1984); M. Yeh, *Mod. Ch. P.: Theory and Practice Since 1917* (1991). C.H.W.

CHINESE PROSODY. See CHINESE POETRY.

CHŌKA. See JAPANESE POETRY.

CHOLIAMBUS or *scazon* (Gr. "lame iambic," "limping"). Hipponax of Ephesus (ca. 540 B.C.) employed this meter for invective (q.v.). Its "limping" effect was suggested by the substitution of a long for a short in the penultimate position of the normal iambic trimeter, thus: ∪–∪– | ∪–∪– | ∪ ––x. When the first position in the third metron was also long, the verse was called *ischiorrhogic* ("with broken hips") and was ascribed to Ananius (also 6th c. B.C.). The c. was used in the Alexandrian period by Herodas for his *mimiambi* and by Callimachus. In Lat. poetry, Catullus uses this meter for eight of his poems (8, 22, 31, 37, 39, 44, 59, 60), all but one of them invectives; the line has

a hardened ending that suits a hardened tone. Catullus and his successors apparently imitated Callimachus in altering only the final two syllables. The form is clearly meant as mimetic, a deformed meter for the subject of depravity. Modern imitations of limping iambics have mainly tried the analogous structure of reversing the fifth foot in the iambic pentameter from an iamb to a trochee: the effect is very distinctive, since the fifth foot is the most highly constrained (least variable) of all in this meter. Examples of choliambic lines or poems include Tennyson's "Lucretius" 186, Stevens' line "Elations when the forest blooms; gusty / Emotions on wet roads on autumn nights" ("Sunday Morning" 2.11), Auden's "Down There" (in *About the House*), and John Fredrick Nims' "Love Poem."—Koster; Halporn et al.; West. T.V.F.B.; R.J.G.

CHORAL LYRIC. See GREEK POETRY; MELIC POETRY.

CHOREE. See TROCHAIC.

CHORIAMB (Gr. "consisting of a choree [i.e. a trochee] and an iamb"). A metron of the structure – ∪ ∪ – , frequently found in Gr. lyric verse—it is used often by Sappho and Alcaeus—and dramatic choruses, and, in Lat. poetry, by Horace. It is very often found in combination with other cola, esp. glyconics and asclepiads (see AEOLIC) but sometimes purely, as in Sophocles, *Oedipus Tyrannus* 484.

"Choriambic dimeter" (c. d.) is a term coined by Wilamowitz to cover a variety of related 7- and 8-syllable cola ending in – ∪ ∪ – ; modern usage generally restricts it to the colon o o – x – ∪ ∪ – (where x represents anceps and oo the aeolic base (see AEOLIC): one of the two must be long). Maas, who treats it as an anaclastic glyconic, uses the honorific but awkward term "wilamowitzianus." The term "c. d." is doubly a misnomer, since the sequence is not a dimeter at all but a single indivisible sequence or colon, or at best the sequence – x – ∪ ∪ – preceded by an aeolic base, and the sequence – ∪ ∪ – – ∪ ∪ – is actually quite distinct. C. ds. appear in the "eupolidean" meter of the parabasis (q.v.) in Old Comedy, but they are most conspicuous in tragedy. Sophocles uses them occasionally, but they are a favorite of Euripides', being varied more widely later in his career. They are closely related to—and presumably derived from—glyconics (q.v.), with which they mix and respond.

Accentual imitations of the c. are very rare in the modern vernaculars, and usually appear in poems expressly meant as Cl. imitations, as in Klopstock's "Siona," in Goethe's *Pandora* (c. ds.), and in Platen. In Eng., such usage as exists ranges from single lines such as Marvell's "Lilies without, roses within" ("The Nymph and her Fawn") to Swinburne's more extended experiments in his

"Choriambics" (*Poems and Ballads, Second Series* [1878]). A few modern metrists have interpreted the sequence / x x / in the first four syllables of the iambic pentameter, as in lines beginning "Roses have thorns" or "Look in thy Glass," not as an "initial trochaic substitution" but as a c., but this misunderstands both the nature of Cl. prosody and the relation of that to the modern system.— Wilamowitz, pt. 2, chs. 3, 7; E. W. Scripture, "The Choriambus in Eng. Verse," *PMLA* 43 (1928)—unsound; Maas; Koster, ch. 10; Dale; K. Itsumi, "The C. D. of Euripides," *ClassQ* 32 (1982); West.

D.S.P.; T.V.F.B.

CHORIAMBIC DIMETER. See CHORIAMB.

CHORUS (Gr. *choreuein*, "to dance"). Presumably, Gr. tragedy somehow arose from, or in conjunction with, the lyric and religious performances of a ch. of masked and singing dancers. But despite the crucial bond between tragedy and its characteristic ch. (no extant 5th-c. tragedy lacks a fully developed ch.), our information is lamentably scant. The following facts, however, deserve mention. (1) The tragic ch., rectangular in formation and often military in movement, is *not* to be confused with the "cyclical" ch. of dithyramb (q.v.). (2) The early number of the ch. is said (on flimsy evidence and by an improbable analogy with the dithyrambic ch.) to have been 50; Aeschylus (cf. *Agamemnon* 1347–1371) used 12, and Sophocles is said to have raised the number to 15. (3) Choral odes (incl. *kommoi*) were *sung* by all or part of the ch., while the lines of the *coryphaeus* (or chorus leader) were *spoken*. (4) The expenses of training the ch. were assigned by the state to a wealthy man (called the *choregus*), and the "giving of a chorus" by the archon constituted the poet's official admission to the tragic contest.

Both tragedy and ch. appear to have been religious in origin. However, whereas tragedy and comedy in the later 5th c. became secularized as they lost touch with their ritual origins, the ch. remained the conservative soul of the play, the articulate spokesman for traditional religion and society, clinging stubbornly to the forms and wisdom and even the style of the worshipping group from which it arose. This conservatism is visible not only in the elaborately figured archaic lyrics, with their "poetic" syntax and heavy load of Doricisms in sharp contrast to more colloquial dialogue, but in the traditionalism of its moral beliefs, its conventional social theodicy, and its commitment to proverbial social wisdom. And so the normal mode of choral utterance is a characteristic group speech, of great power but often limited precision, rising from sheer banality to the apocalyptic gnomic richness of the Aeschylean ch. Dramatists might adapt the ch. to their practical needs by making it serve such simple functions as spectacle, widening emotional range, and so on, but they seem to have found it difficult to alter this communal and traditionalizing role of the ch. There is, however, little tension between the nature of the ch. and the dramatist's needs until the time of Euripides. But as Olympian religion declined and the old social order went under in the convulsions of the late 5th c., the ch. lost the context that gave it life as a convention, and in post-Euripidean tragedy appears to have been degraded to ornament. According to Aristotle, it was in the 4th c. that the practice arose of writing choral odes that had little or nothing to do with the play.

Conservatism was strengthened by function. For the ch. attends the action as a dependent society in miniature, giving the public resonance of individual action. Thus the ch. exults, fears, wonders, mourns, and attempts, out of its store of traditional moralities, to cope with an action whose meaning is both difficult and unfamiliar. By so doing, the ch. generalizes the meaning of the action, and at the same time the action revives and refreshes the choral wisdom. But almost never is the chorus' judgment of events authoritative; if it is an intruded voice, it is normally the voice of trad., not of the dramatist. In Aeschylus perhaps the ch. is least fallible, but in both Aeschylus and Sophocles the ch. tends to lag behind the meaning implicit in the action; that lag is the secret of the chorus' *dramatic* power and the means whereby the tension between the tragic hero and his society is made clear. Euripides, less easy with trad. and hence self-conscious, tends to rely on his ch. more for poetic intensity than dramatic tension (though in no Gr. play is the ch. so fully and ironically exploited against trad. as in the *Bacchae*).

The power of the choral convention explains why the ch. has been so constantly revived in subsequent lit.—in the undramatic virtuoso choruses of Seneca; in Milton's *Samson Agonistes*, formally and dramatically the most perfect Gr. choruses in Eng.; in the quasi-Euripidean ch. of Fr. tragedy; in the cosmic choruses of Shelley and Goethe, and finally in the remarkable ch. of Eliot's *Murder in the Cathedral*, to mention but one of the many modern attempts to resuscitate the choral convention. But with almost all of these revivals, no matter how remarkable the mastery, the choral convention has failed somehow to flourish, or flourished only as a literary and archaic device, deprived of the context and ground that in the Gr. theater gave it a natural rightness. Only Eliot, by placing his ch. within the context of a religious society in the dramatic act of worship, has overcome the difficulties, but the limits imposed by such a context must prove unacceptable to a living and secular theater.

See also GREEK POETRY, *Classical*; PARABASIS; STASIMON.

E. W. Helmrich, *Hist. of the Ch. in the Ger. Drama* (1912); A. W. Pickard-Cambridge, *Dithyramb, Tragedy and Comedy* (1927), *The Dramatic Festivals of Athens*, 2d ed. rev. and corr. (1989); H. Schauer and U. Gauwerky, "Chor," and H. Kolb, "Chorische

Poesie," *Reallexikon* 1.208–12; M. Bieber, *The Hist. of the Gr. and Roman Theater*, 2d ed. (1961); T. B. L. Webster, *The Gr. Ch.* (1970); P. Arnott, *The Ancient Gr. and Roman Theatre* (1971); C. Calame, *Les Choeurs de jeunes filles en Grèce archaïque*, 2 v. (1977); O. Taplin, *Gr. Tragedy in Action* (1978); W. Mullen, *Choreia* (1982).   W.A.

CHRISTABEL METER. Term for the verseform of Coleridge's *Christabel* (1797–1800, pub. 1816). Coleridge thought that it was a species of accentual verse (q.v.), i.e. verse regulated solely by count of stresses not syllables, for he says in the Preface to the poem that "in each line the accents will be found to be only four," that this is a "new principle" in Eng. poetry, and that variations in syllable-count are made intentionally. Up to the turn of the 20th c., Coleridge was generally believed in his claims, and *Christabel* widely viewed as an important example of accentual verse. But all three of Coleridge's claims happen to be false. Robert Bridges showed in 1901 (*Milton's Prosody*, Appendix, rev. 1921: see discussion in ACCENTUAL VERSE) that Coleridge is really writing metrical verse. And Snell showed in 1929 that "four-fifths of the lines of *Christabel* are perfectly regular; that is, they are the conventional four-stress iambic verse" and "the remaining one-fifth of the poem is also not irregular" if occasional light syllables are ignored. The meter is "iambic with monosyllabic and anapestic substitutions" (95–96). In short, the poem is heavily iambic and effectively octosyllabic: of the 655 lines of the poem, 523 (80%) are perfectly regular octosyllables, and 92% vary by only one syllable one way or the other. All of the 35 lines which drop a syllable do so at the onset of the line, leaving the interior rhythm intact. And only 5 lines in the entire poem are clearly ternary (anapestic). Finally, Coleridge's implication, in the Preface, that his use of syllabic variation for metrical expressiveness is also original seems an unreasonable slight to Shakespeare's poetic craft, if not Donne's or Milton's.—A. L. F. Snell, "The Meter of *Christabel*," *Fred Newton Scott Anniv. Papers* (1929); Brogan.
                                                        T.V.F.B.

CHRONICLE PLAY. See HISTORY PLAY.

CHU. See CHINESE POETRY.

CI. See CHINESE POETRY.

CINQUAIN. See QUINTAIN.

CLASSICAL INFLUENCE. See CLASSICISM.

CLASSICAL METERS IN MODERN LANGUAGES. Throughout the hist. of European poetry since the Ren. there have been attempts to introduce into the versification of the vernacular langs. the metrical principles, the specific meters, and the stanza forms of Cl. Gr. and Lat. verse. The most obvious motivation for this endeavor has been the continuing high status of the Cl. langs. and esp. of Cl. poetry, which for many has represented the epitome of Western literary achievement. In addition, many writers in the modern European langs., even when not seeking to emulate the achievement of Cl. verse, have drawn upon Cl. examples to extend the variety of metrical forms in their own literary trads.

These attempts were most frequent in the Ren., esp. in the 15th and 16th cs. Humanism placed a high valuation on Cl. lit. at a time when the modern European langs. were for the most part without a literary trad. of equal stature. The practice of imitation (q.v.) had long been fundamental to literary art, and the project of enriching the vernacular was encouraged by the growing cultural nationalism of the period. The highly organized nature of Cl. prosody (q.v.) also appealed to the Ren. aesthetic sense, which favored the artificial and the complex. These factors were most powerful in the 15th and 16th cs. By the 17th c., the native verse trads. had established themselves more securely, and there was less incentive to look to ancient Greece and Rome for models. The romantic desire to challenge established verseforms produced a resurgence of interest in Cl. meters, esp. in Germany (Klopstock) and England (Coleridge, Southey), and the rise of a more historically informed Classicism in the late 19th and early 20th c. resulted in attempts to devise more exact vernacular equivalents to Gr. and Lat. meters (e.g. Bridges). The experiments of modernism led once more to a free use of Cl. verseforms as a quarry for new poetic directions.

Imitations of Cl. meters can be broadly divided into two types: those that seek to establish a principle of quantity in the vernacular on which to base scansion; and those that retain the indigenous phonological prominence of the lang. in question (usually stress) as the *marker* of the meter but seek to imitate or reproduce the metrical *patterns* of Cl. verse.

I. *Quantitative Imitations*, or "quantitative [hereafter, q.] verse." To appreciate the attempts to write Cl. verse in the vernacular langs. based upon a principle of quantity, it is less important to understand what quantity (q.v.) was in the spoken langs. of ancient Greece and Rome than to understand what the poets of the Ren. and after *believed* it to have been. The terms traditionally used to describe the two types of syllables in quantitative poetry are "long" and "short," and there is a very old claim, inherited from the Gr. *rhythmici* (q.v.), that long syllables take twice the time of short ones in pronunciation. Regardless of whether or not this claim accurately described linguistic reality in antiquity (the evidence suggests that quantity was more a structural difference than a temporal one), it bore little relation to the phonetic facts of Lat. as pronounced during the Ren., and in any event, the claim had long since become a *convention*, accepted without inquiry. This meant that the metrical schemes of Lat. verse were realized only very fitfully in actual reading: the conception of meter that arose was a largely abstract and visual one based on an intellectual classification of syllables according to learned rules.

This accounts for the initially puzzling fact that Ren. Cl. imitations frequently have no perceptible rhythmic patterning—or if they do, it is a pattern of accents which cuts across the quantitative scheme. The scheme is there, however, deducible by the rules of Cl. prosody; and a Ren. reader trained in Lat. prosody as part of the regular grammar school education could perceive and enjoy it. Strictly speaking, this verse should be called "pseudo-q.," since to follow the rules of Lat. quantity in a lang. with a different phonological structure does not produce the same syllabic organization.

The earliest q. verse in a modern vernacular appears to have been written in It. by Leon Battista Alberti and Leonardo Dati in 1441. The extent of the It. q. movement can be gauged from the *Versi, et regole de la nuova poesia toscana* of 1539, collected by Claudio Tolomei, which contained verse written on q. principles by 24 named poets and several anonymous contributors. Numerous other It. poets attempted q. verse in the 15th and 16th cs., many of whom were collected by Carducci in 1881.

The Fr. q. movement seems to have begun in the late 15th c. with the unpub. work (incl. a treatise) of Michel de Boteauville; in the latter part of the 16th c. many of France's best-known poets attempted *vers mesurés à l'antique* (q.v.). The link between q. meter and music arising from the theoretical basis in strict durations was most productive in the compositions of Antoine de Baïf's "Académie de Poésie et de Musique." In Germany, the earliest q. experiments were made by Conrad Gesner in 1555; other Ren. adherents of the new meters were Johann Clajus, Johann Fischart, Johann Kolross, and Andreas Bachmann. The Ren. also saw q. imitations in Dutch and Hungarian and in the Scandinavian and Slavic langs. under the international aegis of humanism.

The q. movement in England had its beginnings in discussions by Roger Ascham, Thomas Watson (later Bishop of Lincoln), and Sir John Cheke at Cambridge, ca. 1540. Two hexameters which survive from these discussions, quoted by Ascham in *The Scholemaster* (1570), will serve as an example of q. imitation:

$$-\ \ \cup\cup\ |\ -\ \ -\ |\ -\ \cup\ \cup\ |\ -\ \ \ -$$
All travellers do gladly report great
$$|\ \ \ -\ \ \ \cup\ \cup\ |\ -\ -$$
prayse of Ulysses,
$$-\ \ \cup\ \ \cup\ |\ -\ \ \cup\cup\ |\ -\ \ -\ |\ -$$
For that he knew many mens maners,
$$-\ |\ -\ \ \cup\ \cup\ |\ -\ -$$
and saw many Cities.

These lines do not attempt to create aural patterns, either of stresses or of longs and shorts. Stresses may fall in short positions (first syllable of "travellers" and "many"); unstressed syllables may be long and may fall in the ictus position at the beginning of the foot (last syllable of "travellers" and "maners"). The ear does not perceive the sequence "-ers and" as two long syllables, and the stress on the first syllable of "many" gives it greater length in pronunciation than the second. But Ascham's admiration of these lines is not, in his own terms, misplaced. The lines observe the two most important Cl. prosodic rules taught in Tudor grammar schools: the penultimate rule (in words of three or more syllables, a stressed penultimate syllable is long and an unstressed one is short) and the rule of "position" (a syllable is long if its vowel is followed by more than one consonant in the same or the following words). "Great" is long both by position and because its vowel is a diphthong. (In fact the rule pertained to digraphs, since like the rule of position it applied not to pronunciation but to *spelling*; one resource available to many q. poets of this period was the variability of orthography.) Where no rules applied, Watson was free to determine quantity himself, provided he was consistent.

Ascham included some q. translations in *Toxophilus* (1545), and James Sandford pub. specimens in 1576, but the major impetus for the movement in England was Sidney's example in writing q. poems for the *Arcadia*, probably between 1577 and 1580, and his discussions with Thomas Drant, Edward Dyer, and Spenser on the question of Cl. imitations (Sidney's q. rules for Eng. have survived—see Ringler). Examples by Spenser and by Gabriel Harvey appear in their correspondence. Numerous poets wrote Eng. q. verse over the next 20 years. One of the strictest, technically speaking, was Richard Stanyhurst, who translated four books of the *Aeneid* (1582); one of the most prolific was Abraham Fraunce, who pub. several q. works between 1587 and 1592; and one of the most skilled was Mary Herbert, Countess of Pembroke, in her trs. of the Psalms in the 1590s. Several treatises were written in at least partial support of q. imitations, notably by William Webbe (1586), George Puttenham (1589), and Thomas Campion (1602). After 1602 the movement virtually came to an end.

The Ren. q. movement died when the changing aesthetic climate caused an intellectual notion of meter to give way to a metrical practice based on the experienced rhythms of the lang.—at least partly under the influence of the drama—and when the native verse trads. demonstrated unequivocally that metrical principles arising from the modern langs. themselves could yield poetry of a grace and power matching that of antiquity. The role of the q. experiments in the devel. of the vernacular metrical trads. was, however, significant: they showed the dangers of interpreting the notion of imitation too literally, and they led to other successful innovations such as the introduction of blank verse (q.v.). Later attempts to devise a strict q. principle for modern langs. (e.g. Robert Bridges) succeeded only in showing that quantity is not a phonological feature which can be transferred from the Cl. langs.

II. *Accentual Imitations.* Although modern scholarship has for the most part held the view that Lat. verse should be read with its normal prose stresses, for a long time there existed an alternative mode of reading in which the ictus of each foot is stressed, thereby converting the Cl. metrical pattern into a kind of accentual verse. This trad. has sometimes encouraged prosodists (e.g. Saintsbury) to use the terminology of Cl. prosody (esp. *longs* and *shorts*) in discussing accentual meter. There is evidence of this mode of reading in Ren. schools, and it was firmly entrenched in 19th-c. Eng. and Ger. pedagogy. As a result, the rhythms of these accentual equivalents of Cl. meters were familiar to many poets, and it is not surprising that a number attempted to use such meters in their own langs. Two Lat. forms in particular produce distinctive rhythmic patterns when converted into accentual verse: the hexameter and the Sapphic (qq.v.); the latter esp. has had a long hist. in European lit. The influence of accentual versions of Cl. meters can be seen in many Ren. imitations, and one of the most significant features of Campion's relatively successful experiments is that they combine a strict pseudo-q. scansion with an accentual one. In Germany, Opitz argued for an equivalence between length and stress in 1624, while in Spain accentual imitations, esp. Sapphics, date from the mid 16th c. However, it was not until the second half of the 18th c. that experiments with accentual imitation became common, and in the 19th c. they are legion. The most influential poet in this movement was F. G. Klopstock, whose accentual hexameters had a profound effect on later Ger. versification (see GERMAN POETRY; GERMAN PROSODY), and whose example was followed by numerous Ger. and Eng. poets. Goethe, Schiller, A. W. Schlegel, and Hölderlin all wrote accentual imitations of Cl. schemes, followed by Eduard Mörike, Christian Morgenstern, R. A. Schroeder, and Rilke, while scholars such as Schlegel, Platen, and J. H. Voss attempted a stricter transfer of Cl. metrical principles.

Imitations based on Klopstock's principles were introduced into Eng. by William Taylor in the late 18th c., followed by Coleridge and Southey. Tennyson made attempts to combine the accentual principle with a q. one, while long poems in accentual hexameters by Longfellow ("Evangeline"), Kingsley, and Clough achieved some success. Swinburne and Meredith also experimented with accentual Cl. imitations, as have many 20th-c. poets, incl. Pound, MacNeice, and Auden. Rus. accentual imitations also date from the latter part of the 18th c.; Trediakovsky's hexameters were particularly influential, and a number of poets, incl.

Pushkin, used the form in the 19th c., esp. for trs. The accentual pattern that is produced is close to that of the *dol'nik* (q.v.), a folk meter which became important in the 20th c. It. imitations present a somewhat different picture, since the lang. and verseforms are less strictly based on stress. The most influential naturalizer of Cl. versification was Carducci, whose *Odi barbare* (Barbarian Odes, 1877–89; 2d ed., 1878, with useful preface by Chiarini) made use of the accentual patterns of Cl. meters (when read with their normal prose stresses) and ignored the q. patterns. He was thus able to bring Cl. imitations close to the native trad. of It. verse, though at the cost of the Cl. metrical schemes themselves. He added a historical study to his own experiments in 1881.

For a different modern attempt to imitate the meters of an ancient poetry, this one Germanic, see ALLITERATIVE METERS IN MODERN LANGUAGES. See also CLASSICAL PROSODY; HEXAMETER; ITALIAN PROSODY; SAPPHIC.

K. Elze, *Die englische Hexameter* (1867); *La poesia barbara nei secoli XV e XVI*, ed. G. Carducci (1881); A. H. Baxter, *The Intro. of Cl. Metres into It. Poetry* (1901); R. B. McKerrow, "The Use of So-called Cl. Metres in Elizabethan Verse," *MLQ* (London) 4–5 (1901); Kastner, ch. 11; G. L. Bickersteth, Intro., *Carducci* (1913); Omond—valuable survey; P. Habermann, "Antike Versmasse und Strophenformen im Deutschen," *Reallexikon*—extensive bibls.; G. D. Willcock, "Passing Pitefull Hexameters," *MLR* 29 (1934); G. L. Hendrickson, "Elizabethan Quantitative Hexameters," *PQ* 28 (1949); A. Burgi, *Hist. of the Rus. Hexameter* (1954); Beare; A. Kabell, *Metrische Studien II: Antiker Form sich nähernd* (1960)—wide-ranging; *The Poems of Sir Philip Sidney*, ed. W. A. Ringler (1962); W. Bennett, *Ger. Verse in Cl. Metres* (1963); Elwert, *Italienische* (1968); B. A. Park, "The Quantitative Experiments of the Ren. and After as a Problem in Comparative Metrics," *DAI* 29 (1968): 905A; Wilkins; D. Attridge, *Well-weighed Syllables* (1974)—Elizabethan imitations; *Die Lehre von der Nachahmung der antike Versmasse im Deutschen*, ed. H.-H. Hellmuth and J. Schröder (1976); H. M. Brown, "Vers mesurés," *New Grove* 19.G80; Brogan; Navarro; Scherr.					D.A.

CLASSICAL POETICS.

I. DEFINITION. Cl. p. can be defined in either of two ways: (1) as the aggregate of opinions and doctrines which were put forward concerning poetry during Cl. antiquity, i.e. roughly between 750 B.C. and A.D. 200; or (2) as that more or less coherent body of critical doctrine which is represented chiefly by the *Poetics* of Aristotle and the so-called *Ars poetica* of Horace, and which gave rise, during the Ren., to the poetic creed called "Classicism" (q.v.). We shall take up the notion of Cl. p. here in the first and broader of the two senses, but with particular attention to the origin and devel. of Classicism.

II. PRE-PLATONIC POETICS AND CRITICISM. So far as the Western world is concerned, the very concept of poetics, in fact of literary crit. in general, is a Gr. invention. Although it is a commonplace that crit. follows rather than precedes the making of lit., in the case of the Greeks the striking thing is not how late the critical impulse was in making its appearance, but how early. Crit. followed close on the heels of poetry, and insisted from the beginning on raising fundamental questions and fundamental issues.

Before summarizing this earliest stage of Gr. crit., we must point to certain tacit presuppositions which it shared with Gr. poetry itself and which underlie the whole later devel. (1) The chief subjects of poetry are the actions and lives of mankind (indeed, the Homeric gods, with their advanced anthropomorphism and their consuming interest in human beings, confirm rather than belie this principle). (2) Poetry is a *serious, public concern*, the cornerstone of education and of civic life, and a source, for good or for evil, of insight and knowledge. (3) It is also a *delightful thing*, endowed with a fascination that borders on enchantment (Walsh). (4) It is not merely terrestrial and utilitarian, but somehow *divine*, being inspired by the gods or the Muses. (5) It is at the same time an *art* (*techne*), a craft or profession, requiring native talent, training, and long practice. (6) The poet, though inspired from on high, is after all not a priest or a prophet but a *secular person*. His work is respected, even revered, but it can be criticized.

Some of these preconceptions can be detected in the Homeric poems themselves, esp. the *Odyssey*; in any case, the poems were later judged by the Greeks in terms of them. Gr. crit. was born and grew to maturity on Homer, assuming implicitly that he was—as indeed he had become—the teacher of his people. The earliest criticisms were not "literary" or aesthetic but moral and philosophical, and the issues they raised were fundamental ones, as to the truth and moral value of poetry. Hesiod (7th c. B.C.; *Theogony* 27–28) and Solon (early 6th c.; fr. 21 [Diehl]) agree that, as the latter puts it, "the bards tell many a lie." Xenophanes (ca. end of the 6th c.) objects to the immoral goings-on of Homer's gods and casts ridicule on the whole concept of anthropomorphism (fr. 11–16 [Diehl]). These are, for us, the opening guns of what Plato (*Republic* 10) calls "the ancient

feud between poetry and philosophy." The objectors grant that poetry, esp. the epic, is a source of delight and the recognized custodian of truth and moral values, but insist that she is an unworthy custodian. This struggle between philosophy and poetry (q.v.) for the position of teacher to the Gr. people is of fundamental importance for the later hist. of Western critical theory.

One way of saving Homer's gods was to take their quarrels as representing conflicts of natural elements (earth, air, fire, water) or of social and political principles. This "allegorical interp.," which was to have a long hist. (see ALLEGORY), originally sprang from a scientific motive and went hand in hand with the rise of cosmology and the natural sciences. Appearing as early as the end of the 6th c. (Theagenes of Rhegium), it was adopted by some of the Sophists and later by the Stoics, though rejected by Plato (*Phaedrus*).

Pindar, the aristocratic Theban poet (518–ca. 445 B.C.), shows an interesting blend of trad. and personal attitudes toward poetry. For him poetry is both an exacting craft and a thing inspired (see particularly his *First Olympian* and *First Pythian*). The poet's wisdom (*sophia*) embraces both technical proficiency and insight into truth; his mission is to glorify great prowess or achievement ("virtue," *arete*) and guide his fellow men. Pindar was conscious of the dubious morality of some of the older tales; his solution was to leave them untold.

In the 5th c., poetry was still, as it had always been, the basis of primary education and an official repository of truth. But two potent new forces came into play at Athens which enhanced and at the same time undercut the honor traditionally paid to poetry. These were the drama and the Sophists. Tragedy and comedy (qq.v), with their vividness of presentation and their semiofficial status, tended to bring every citizen into direct contact with lit., making each a potential critic. Moreover, the Old Comedy arrogated to itself the right to satirize anything, including poetry. The Sophists, in addition to their other activities, were characteristically grammarians, philologists, and expounders of lit., but they were also rationalists, skeptics, and positivists, and the effect of their teaching was to break down trad. standards, in lit. as in other fields. It has been suggested but not proven that Gorgias was the first promulgator of a poetic theory; in any case he had a shrewd and accurate idea of the *effect*, particularly the emotional effect, of poetry on its hearers.

We can gauge the impact of these new tendencies by the reaction they called forth in Aristophanes (ca. 445–ca. 385 B.C.). His brilliant gift for literary satire, esp. parody, was exercised above all on Euripides and other representatives of modernism (intellectualism, skepticism, preciosity) in poetry. His unremitting crusade against Euripides (see particularly the *Acharnians*) and the *Thesmophoriazusae* reaches its climax in the *Frogs* (405 B.C.), the most sparkling exhibit of judicial crit. in antiquity. Aeschylus, champion of old-fashioned moral principles and lofty style, finally wins his bout against the challenger Euripides—logic-chopper, corrupter of morals, and writer of dull prologues—but not before the two combatants have agreed that the poet's duty is to instruct his fellow citizens. But beneath this momentary agreement on the purpose of poetry lies a powerful disagreement which has sparked from antiquity to the present controversy about the role of art in society. Euripides is the advocate of fully instructing mankind about the nature of historical reality, however savage, repellent, or obscene that reality may be. Aeschylus is the proponent of inspiring mankind with illustrious and ennobling ideals that lead to higher levels of achievement and existence.

III. PLATO (427–347 B.C.). With Plato, a born poet and lover of poetry who renounced it for the higher truth of philosophy, the "ancient feud" reaches a major climax and crisis. There is no room in Plato's thought for lit. crit. or theory as a separate intellectual pursuit. Truth is one, and Poetry must appear before that inflexible judge on the same terms as any other human activity. Nevertheless, the great issue of the justification of lit. haunted Plato all his life, and he grapples with it repeatedly in the dialogues—nowhere, however, in truly complete and systematic form. He tends to view poetry from two quite different, perhaps incommensurate, points of view; as "inspiration" (*enthousiasmos*) and as "imitation" (q.v.). Seen inwardly, in its native character as experience, poetry is inspiration (q.v.) or "possession," a form of poetic madness (q.v.) quite beyond the poet's control. The reality of the experience is unquestionable; its source and value remain an enigma. Is it merely irrational, i.e. subrational (*Ion*; cf. the end of the *Meno*), or might there be a suprarational poetic inspiration, winged by Love (Eros), that could attain Truth (*Phaedrus*)? The question is left open. Meanwhile, viewed externally, in its procedures and its product, poetry appears as *mimesis* (see REPRESENTATION AND MIMESIS) or "imitation," and as such falls under the ban of excommunication (*Republic* 3;10) or at least under rigid state control (*Laws* 2;7). Plato's utterances about poetry have a deep ambivalence which has aroused fascinated interest, but also fierce protest, ever since. On the one hand, he expresses deep distrust of that mimetic art which contradicts his conceptions of truth and morality, and he asserts the strong need to censor or ban it; on the other, he makes full use of the mimesis which harmonizes with those very principles of truth and morality. His own dialogues, as Aristotle points out in the *Poetics*, are themselves forms of mimesis; and it is also true, and of great importance, that myths (another powerful form of artistic mimesis) in all their imaginative and evocative splendor form the climax of a number of important arguments in the dialogues (including the *Republic*). This should alert us to the fact that Plato's concept of mimesis is a complex, varied, and profound one (see McKeon, Verdenius).

IV. ARISTOTLE (384–322 B.C.). Aristotle was no poet. His cooler spirit was devoted to poetry in quite another way: as an objective, uniquely valuable presentation of human life in a particular medium. The *Poetics* is not formally or in method a polemical work, but in effect it constitutes an answer to Plato's doubts and objections and thereby a resolution of the ancient feud. Here, conducted in a dispassionate, scientific spirit, is an inquiry into the nature of poetry which restores it to an honorable—not a supreme—place in the scheme of things. The heart of Aristotle's achievement is a new theory of *poetic structure* based on a new concept of "imitation" not as copying of ordinary reality but as a generalized or idealized rendering of character and action (ch. 9). At the climax of this process of imitation arises the most important and serious of human pleasures, the pleasure of learning and making inferences (*manthanein kai syllogizesthai*) which accompanies the insight that is evoked into the nature of the action represented (ch. 4). Thus Aristotle answers some of Plato's deepest misgivings about poetry by asserting the intellectual, indeed philosophical (ch. 9) dimensions of imitative art. In Aristotle's eyes, that which constitutes poetry is not the writing of verses but the building of a poetic "structure of events." This structure is the plot (*mythos*) of the poem; it therefore is by far the most important part of the poet's task (chs. 6, 9). The other constituent elements of the poem, or rather of the art of making a poem (*poiesis*, "making"), viz. (1) character portrayal (*ethos*), (2) "thought" (*dianoia*), i.e. the presentation of ideas or arguments by the characters, (3) poetic language or expression (*lexis*), (4) song composition (*melopoeia*), and (5) spectacle (*opsis*), stand in decreasing order of importance (ch. 6); but none can vie with plot (q.v.). The making of plots is essentially a creative activity. But poetic creativity is not, for Aristotle, a subjective efflorescence. It goes to the bodying forth of reality, the essential truth about human beings and their actions, not the invention of fantasies or private worlds.

A poetic structure should be *beautiful*. This requires (a) unity (the famous "unity of action"; see UNITY), (b) symmetry of the parts with each other and with the whole, and (c) proper length, such that the poem can make a sizable aesthetic impression while yet not so great as to blur or dissipate it. The crux of the matter is the unity of action, and the corollary—duly emphasized by Aristotle himself—is that the events which constitute the action must succeed each other according to the law of necessity or probability, not mere contiguity (see HISTORY AND POETRY).

A tragedy (q.v.) ought to be not only serious and beautiful, but tragic as well; whether this requirement also applies to the epic is a question to which

CLASSICAL POETICS

the *Poetics* gives no clear answer. Plato had said (*Republic* 10) that poetry threatens the moral equilibrium in states and individuals alike by "feeding" the appetitive and emotional side of human nature, esp. its tendencies to pity and fear. Aristotle implicitly sets aside this verdict. But he also calls for something to be done to or with or through pity and fear which he designates by the much debated term "catharsis" (q.v.). Whatever we decide catharsis means, it must stand as an answer to Plato's criticism of poetry. In any event, if pity and fear are desirable effects of tragedy, certain kinds of plot are better fitted to arouse them than others. All tragic actions involve a change or passage from one pole of human fortune—"happiness" or "unhappiness"—to the other (ch. 7, end). In a simple plot the change is direct and linear; in a complex plot it is brought about by a sudden and unexpected reversal (*peripeteia*), or a recognition (*anagnorisis*), or both (ch. 11). Aristotle demands that the hero who undergoes the tragic vicissitude be a good man, but not a perfect one. The change to unhappiness, which is the tragic change *par excellence*, should not be caused by wickedness but by some *hamartia* (ch. 13). Here, as in the case of "catharsis," battles of interpretation have raged (does *hamartia* mean "moral flaw" or "intellectual error"?) without a resolution of the question. It may well be that different nuances of the term are appropriate in different dramatic circumstances. Aristotle further prescribes (ch. 15) that the tragic characters be "appropriate," i.e. true to type; "like," i.e. true to life or human nature in general; and self-consistent.

Aristotle regarded the linguistic side of the poet's activity as needful in order to please and impress the public, but ultimately less important than plot construction and character-drawing. The first virtue of poetic diction, as of language in general, is to be *clear* (ch. 22). But it also should not be "low": that is, it should maintain a certain elevation above the level of ordinary life, through the use of archaic, foreign, or unfamiliar words, ornamental epithets, and figures, esp. metaphor. For further remarks on style, including poetic style, see Book 3 of the *Rhetoric*.

The discussion of the epic (chs. 23–25) forms a kind of appendix to Aristotle's analysis of tragedy. The epic should have a central action, like tragedy, but may "dilute" it generously with episodes. It also has a special license to deal in marvels and the supernatural. In these, as indeed in all respects, Homer is the perfect exemplar. For Aristotle, tragedy is, however, superior to epic because it has everything which can be found in epic as well as attractive characteristics unique to itself, and, moreover, because it accomplishes its mimetic goal and produces its mimetic pleasure much more effectively than epic (ch. 26).

Considerable controversy surrounds the discussion of Aristotle's theory of comedy. Some scholars believe that this discussion was contained in a lost second book of the *Poetics* (see Janko). Whether or not that is the case, Aristotle dealt in some detail with the nature of comedy in the *Poetics* as we now have it (see chs. 1–5). A document of obscure provenience and date known as the *Tractatus Coislinianus* purports to represent Aristotle's theory of comedy, but disagreement has arisen about the validity of this claim because of the unusual, even eccentric assertions made in this work. Some scholars, however, have argued for its possible or probable authenticity as a witness to genuine Aristotelian doctrine (Cooper, Janko). On the other hand, Aristotle's clear identification of comedy as a painless mimesis of the ridiculous (*Poetics* ch. 5) and his identification (*Rhetoric* 1386b8) of *nemesan* ("to feel indignation") as the polar opposite of *eleos* ("pity") have been cited as a fully adequate basis for establishing an Aristotelian theory of comedy (Golden).

The *Poetics* is a work of paramount importance not only historically, as the fountainhead of "Classicism" (q.v.), but in its own right. It does not deal as fully with epic as it does with tragedy, and it ignores lyric. Also, it is uncertain whether the *Poetics* was directly known to anybody in antiquity after Aristotle's death, though many of his ideas were transmitted by his pupils. In any case, the fully developed doctrine of Classicism embraces a number of interests and attitudes which are not Aristotelian, and which still remain to be accounted for.

V. HELLENISTIC POETICS (3d–1st c. B.C.). Both poetry and poetic crit. were carried on in a new environment in the Hellenistic age. The center of gravity in lit., as in other fields, shifted from old Greece, with its civic traditions, to Alexandria, Pergamum, and other royal courts. Alexandria in particular, with its Library and "Museum"—originally sprung from Aristotle's Lyceum—was a hive of literary scholarship (philology, grammar, textual editing, *Literaturgeschichte*) with which crit. now came in close contact. Indeed we owe the terms "critic" and "criticism" to the Hellenistic grammarians, who regarded the judgment of poems, *krisis poiematon*, as the capstone of their art. The typical critic is now a scholar who dabbles in poetry and poetic theory. Unfortunately, of the lively critical squabbles of the time we have only *disjecta membra* such as Callimachus' disparagements of long poems, "I loathe a cyclic poem" and "Big book, big nuisance" (it may be only a coincidence that he was the compiler of the catalogue of the Alexandrian library, in 120 vols.), or Eratosthenes' dictum that "poetry is for delight."

We can, however, discern that two ideas of basic importance for the devel. of Classicism were, if not invented, at least given canonical form in the Hellenistic period: (a) the concept of a "classic" (the word is Roman but the idea is Gr.), and (b) the concept of genre (q.v.). A belief which had been implicit in the *Poetics* was now proclaimed explicitly: the great age of poetry lay in the past

(7th through 5th c.), and it contained all the models of poetic excellence. This backward-looking view was enshrined in official lists (*kanones*), e.g. the Nine Lyric Poets, the Three Tragedians. Further, each poetic "kind" was thought of as an entity more or less to itself, with its special laws of subject matter, arrangement, and style, and its particular supreme model, Homer for epic, Sappho or Alcaeus for love poetry, Archilochus for "iambic" poetry. These ideas needed only to be reinforced by the rhetorically inspired idea of imitation (see sect. VII below) to become the full-fledged doctrine of Classicism (q.v.). Since the genres were defined primarily by their versification and style, a further result was a tendency toward absorption in style at the expense of other interests.

The philosophical schools participated unevenly in the devel. of criticism. The Stoics officially approved of poetry, esp. the Homeric epic, but tended to judge it by moral and utilitarian standards and therefore indulged rather freely in the allegorizing of Homer. Orthodox Epicureanism frowned on poetry as "unnatural" and a bait for the passions, but the Epicurean Philodemus (1st c. B.C.), who was himself a poet and who had influence on Horace and other Roman poets, put forward a theory that recognized multiple forms and aims of poetry and granted wide autonomy to the poet. From polemical remarks of his we can reconstruct a Peripatetic doctrine put forward by one Neoptolemus of Parium in the 3d c. B.C. which some scholars believe underlies Horace's *Ars poetica*. In it the subject was treated under the triple heading of *poiesis* (poetic composition), *poiema* (the poem), and *poietes* (the poet). Actually *poiesis* had to do chiefly with the selection or invention and the arrangement of subject matter (*hypothesis* or *pragmata; res*) and *poiema* chiefly with style (*lexis; elocutio*).

Others, such as the Platonizing Stoic Posidonius (1st c. B.C.), accepted at least parts of this scheme, and it provided a handy framework for discussion of the three cardinal issues that were much agitated in the Hellenistic period: (a) which is more important, subject matter or expression? (b) which is the purpose or function of poetry, instruction or delight? and (c) which is more essential for the poet, native genius (*physis; ingenium*) or art (*techne; ars*)? In these formulations we see Cl. p. taking on the physiognomy which it was to keep down through the Middle Aage to the Ren. The answers were various. We have already quoted Eratosthenes' dictum that the end of poetry is delight; others, esp. the Stoics, argued the claims of (moral) instruction; while the Peripatetic view called for both (Horace: "omne tulit punctum qui miscuit utile dulci"). Similarly with the debate over subject matter and style. It would seem, however, that a considerable amount of tacit agreement underlay the dispute, namely that poetry is a way of discoursing about "things," and that these

things, whether matters of historical or scientific fact (*historia; fama*), myth (*mythos, fabula*), or pure invention (*plasma; res ficta*), were all equally admissible (hence, e.g., didactic poetry [q.v.], which Aristotle had excluded from the realm of poetry altogether) and had essentially the status of facts, i.e. were to be judged by reference to the ordinary laws of reality. Nowhere do we find a reaffirmation of Aristotle's principle that the objects of poetry are universals.

VI. HORACE (65–8 B.C.) We have devoted what may seem a disproportionate amount of space to the Hellenistic period because, although most of its critical production is lost, it played an even more important role than Plato or Aristotle in the rise of Classicism and exerted a decisive influence upon Roman and therefore Ren. thinking about poetry. The most significant transmitter of this influence is Horace. To be sure, neither Horace nor his literary milieu was Gr. He was a thorough Italian, blessed with a consuming interest in people, a sharp eye for their foibles—and his own— and sturdy independence of judgment. He came to lit. crit. by an indirect road, through satire, and to the end his treatment of it remained occasional and essentially unsystematic. Criticism of his own *Satires* led him to a spirited defense of the genre and of his right to pursue it in his own way (*Satires* 1.4 and 10). He admits that satire (q.v.) is not quite true poetry, because it lacks inspiration and sublimity of style (1.4.43); but it performs a useful and honorable social function by exposing vice and folly. Attacked for depreciating his predecessor Lucilius, Horace insists (1.10) on appropriateness of style and above all on elegance and polish, attained by hard work. Again and again (*Satires* 2.1.12 ff.; *Epistles* 2.1.208, 250 ff.; cf. *Odes* 1.6; 4.2) he resists the importunities of friends urging him to write epic or drama; it is essential that the poet choose and stick to the genres for which he is best fitted.

These themes recur in the three major critical letters in verse which constitute the second Book of the *Epistles*, but against a broader background. The *Epistle to Augustus* (2.1) surveys the current literary scene, derides the blind worship of the poetry of the past (the *Roman* past), and deplores the vulgarity of popular taste. The essay, with its blend of urbanity and seriousness, reveals especially well two important aspects of Horace's Classicism: (1) he felt deeply that Rome deserved and was capable of a great lit., to set alongside that of Cl. Greece; but (2) he was convinced that the result could be achieved only by hard work and the emulation of that same Cl. Gr. lit. Thus Classicism was in Horace's eyes a progressive and patriotic creed, the means to a specifically Roman achievement. The paradox has significant parallels in the Ren. in both Italy and France.

The *Epistle to Florus* (2.2) returns to one of Horace's favorite themes, the haste and sleaziness of much of the current scribbling of poetry. But it is in the *Epistle to the Pisos* (2.3), the so-called *Ars poetica* (the name comes from Quintilian), that he gives fullest expression to his view of poetry. Based though it is on the Hellenistic poetics described in sect. V. above, it carefully maintains the easy, discursive air appropriate to its genre: it is after all a verse epistle, not a formal treatise. Still, the tone is a shade more systematic and apodictic than usual. *Poiesis* (sect. V. above) is dealt with summarily in the first 45 lines, with a plea for poetic unity. The rest of the first sect., down to line 294, really treats of Horace's main interests: style and matters connected therewith—i.e. originality and appropriateness (*decorum*; lines 46–98); emotional appeal (99–113); faithfulness either to poetic trad. or to type in character portrayal (114–78). As he progresses, it become clear that Horace, following the Peripatetic doctrine (not contemporary affairs of state in Rome), is assuming drama, and particularly tragedy, to be the major poetic genre. Hence we find a number of detailed prescriptions for the dramatist (179 ff.: no deed of violence on the stage; five acts, no more and no less; three actors; choral odes germane to the plot; etc.); a thumbnail history of the drama, interrupted by a long passage on the satyr-play; and finally (280 ff.), the adjuration—really the most important of all—to polish, polish, polish ("the labor of the file") rather than publish, publish, publish. The last sect. of the poem (295–476) is devoted to the poet: his training (309–332), with emphasis on moral philosophy (Socratic dialogues); his purpose, which may be either to profit or to please or, best of all, to do both (333–46); his faults, venial and otherwise (347–90); his need for *both* ability and training, and for unsparing criticism (419–52). The end-piece (453–76) is an uproarious sketch, in Horace's best satirical vein, of the mad poet.

Our summary may suggest how many of the leading ideas of Classicism are enshrined in the *Ars poetica*. What no summary, and no translation, can convey is the brilliance of the poem as a poem: not in its structure but in its texture, its striking figures, and memorable phrases. "Purpureus pannus" (purple patch), "brevis esse laboro, obscurus fio," "in medias res" (q.v.), "bonus dormitat Homerus," and dozens of others have passed into the common stock. To the It. critics of the Ren., Latinists and stylists all, it was a breviary. Aristotle they might admire; Horace was in their bones. And they learned more from him than rules. He encouraged them in the proud belief that poetry is an honorable and exacting craft, fit to offer serious counsel and occupy a high place in the culture of a nation.

VII. RHETORICAL CRITICISM, GREEK AND ROMAN. The establishment of rhet. as the prevailing mode of higher education, esp. at Rome in the 1st c. B.C. (in Greece proper it goes back to the 4th c.), had major effects on both poetry and poetics. Poetry itself began to show rhet. tendencies, and, more important for our purpose, lit. crit. now tended to become the professional property of the rhetoricians. (Horace is the lone exception among extant critics from this period.) In the rhet. schools poets were read, and to an increasing extent imitated, on the same basis as prose writers. This practice helped to foster the extension of two influential concepts from the rhet. sphere into the poetic: (1) "imitation" (q.v.) in the sense of imitation of authors, and (2) the analysis of style into three (occasionally four) kinds or levels, high (or grand), middle, and low (or plain) (see STYLE; SUBLIME). It also tended to dislodge poetry from its old pre-eminence in the curriculum, in favor of a more catholic view of all "literature" (*grammata*; *litterae*), prose and verse alike, as the basis of a liberal education.

The extant crit. works which represent this trend all belong—not by accident—to the 1st cs. B.C. and A.D. We can mention them here only briefly, without distinction between Greeks and Romans (in any case rhet. study in that period was essentially international). The treatises of "Demetrius" *On Style* (1st c. B.C.?) and of Dionysius of Halicarnassus *On Literary Composition* (actually on the placing of words; perhaps ca. 10 B.C.), though technical and rhet. in nature, deal with prose and poetry impartially. Poets like Sappho, Pindar, Sophocles, Euripides, and above all, Homer, are cited and analyzed, particularly by Dionysius, in illuminating detail. Cicero is a conservative but intelligent and informed critic of poetry ancient and modern, a not contemptible poet himself, and a firm believer (see particularly the speech *For Archias* and the *De oratore*) in the necessity of a liberal (i.e. literary) education for the orator and man of affairs. Tacitus's *Dialogue on Orators* (date uncertain; perhaps a youthful work) canvasses the reasons for the decline of oratory and lit., and presents poetry as a garden of refreshment and delight, a retreat from the hurly-burly of everyday life. Quintilian, Imperial Professor of Rhetoric, incorporated into Book 10 of his major work, the *Institutio oratoria* (The Training of the Orator; after A.D. 88), a complete sketch and appraisal of all the important Gr. and Lat. authors, poets and prose writers, from the point of view of their uses in education and as exemplars of style.

"Longinus" (see SUBLIME) stands apart, a "sport" among the rhetoricians. In his lexicon Homer and Archilochus, Pindar and Sophocles figure equally with Plato and Demosthenes—Homer above the rest—as models of greatness of spirit. It is he who gives us the best definition of a classic, as a work that has had an intense effect, intellectual and emotional, on human beings of all ages, tastes, and situations throughout the centuries. His enthusiasm for great lit. is perennially infectious. With his indifference to poetic structure, and to genre and the rules of genre, he stands outside the trad. of Classicism as it was formulated in antiquity, but he also provides an important supplement to it.

VIII. SURVIVAL AND INFLUENCE. Ancient crit.

was never, at any stage of its hist., a continuous, stable enterprise. Its survival into the modern world was even more precarious. From Cl. Greece only Aristophanes, Plato, and Aristotle outlasted antiquity. Plato, though preserved complete, was not completely known or studied in the West until the Ren., and then seen mainly through Neoplatonic spectacles. The *Poetics* survived perhaps by accident through its inclusion in a miscellany of rhet. works by "Demetrius," Dionysius, and others. A Med. Lat. tr. by William of Moerbeke (1278) came to light in the middle of the 20th c.; otherwise, the treatise was available to the Middle Ages and the early Ren. only in a Lat. tr. of an Arabic paraphrase by Averroes. Horace and the Roman rhetoricians were never lost, though considerable parts of Cicero and Quintilian were not recovered until the Ren. By far it was Horace who had the most extensive and sustained influence on the transmission of crit. through the Middle Ages.

Poetic theory as such could not flourish in the Middle Ages, being assigned, like rhet., to a humble place in the *trivium*, as a part of grammar or logic. Petrarch and his followers, the humanists of the early Ren., began the process of recovery of the ancient heritage, but only gradually and, as it were, backward. The literary ideal of the Quattrocento was the Poeta Orator, and its critical attitudes were mainly Horatian, rhetorical, and based on Lat. lit. To the early It. humanists, whose consuming passions were Lat. style (in prose and verse) and personal glory, Horace, Cicero, and Quintilian spoke a familiar lang. that the Greeks could not rival. Plato, however, was drawn to some extent into the battle over the *defense of poetry*, which gained new point from the reawakened enthusiasm for pagan lit. In this struggle it was natural that he should appear now on the side of the attackers (e.g. Savonarola in the *De divisione ac utilitate omnium scientiarum*, ca. 1492), now on the side of the defense (either for the idea of inspiration or for the notion—actually Neoplatonic in origin—that the artist creates according to a true "Idea").

Systematic theorizing about the *art* of poetry as such, its nature, effects, and species, appears only in the 16th c., in the train of the rediscovery and gradual dissemination of the *Poetics* (Lat. tr. by Giorgio Valla, 1498; *editio princeps* of the Gr. text, Aldus, 1508; Lat. tr. by Paccius [Pazzi], 1536, It. by Segni, 1549; commentaries by Robortelli, 1548, Madius [Maggi], 1550, Victorius [Vettori], 1560, Castelvetro, 1570, and many others). The first treatises on poetics by Vida (1527) and Daniello (1536) were still essentially Lat. and Horatian. It was Minturno's *De poeta* (1559) and Scaliger's *Poetices libri septem* (1561), together with Castelvetro's commentary, *Poetica d'Aristotele vulgarizzata e sposta* (ed. W. Romani, 2 v., 1978; abridged tr. A. Bongiorno, *Castelvetro on the Art of Poetry*, 1984), that established Aristotle's dictatorship over lit.; but even these works are only very imperfectly and

halfheartedly Aristotelian.

In spite of the rage for "Longinus" in the 18th c., and sporadic phenomena like Shelley's literary Platonism in the 19th, the prestige and influence of Cl. p. diminished after Lessing's dethronement (*Hamburgische Dramaturgie*, 1767–69) of the "French"—actually It. —rules (q.v.). A revival, however, of critical and scholarly interest in Aristotle occurred in the second half of the 20th c., led by the critics of the Chicago School (q.v.) and by the attack on long-held orthodox interpretations of key concepts in the *Poetics* in which Gerald Else played a major role. See also APOLLONIAN-DIONYSIAN; CLASSICISM; CRITICISM, bibl.; GENRE; GREEK POETRY, *Classical*; IMITATION; REPRESENTATION AND MIMESIS; RHETORIC AND POETRY; cf. HEBRAISM.

PRIMARY WORKS:
Ancient Lit. Crit., ed. D. A. Russell and M. Winterbottom (1972)—comprehensive anthol. of cl. texts on crit.

(1) *Plato*. Standard tr. of complete works by B. Jowett, 5 v. (1892); *Collected Dialogues*, ed. E. Hamilton and H. Cairns (1961). *Phaedrus, Ion*, etc., tr. L. Cooper (1938). *Phaedrus*, tr. R. Hackforth (1952). *Republic*, tr. F. M. Cornford (1941); tr. A. Bloom (1968); tr. G. M. A. Grube (1974); tr. R. W. Sterling and W. C. Scott (1985).

(2) *Aristotle. Complete Works*, ed. J. Barnes, 2 v. (1984). *Poetics*: See L. Cooper and A. Gudeman, *A Bibl. of the Poetics of Aristotle* (1928), supp. M. T. Herrick, *AJP* 52 (1931), G. F. Else, "A Survey of Work on Aristotle's *Poetics*," *CW* 48 (1954–55). *Gr. text*: ed. R. Kassel (1965). *Eds. with Gr. text and commentary*: I. Bywater (1909); S. H. Butcher, *Aristotle's Theory of Poetry and Fine Art*, 4th ed. (1911); G. F. Else, *Aristotle's* Poetics: *The Argument* (1957); D. W. Lucas (1968); R. Dupont-Roc and J. Lallot, *Aristote: La Poétique* (1980). *Trs. without text*: L. Cooper, 2d ed. (1947); L. J. Potts, *Aristotle on the Art of Fiction* (1953); G. M. A. Grube (1958); L. Golden and O. B. Hardison, Jr. (1968, 1981)—with extensive commentary; R. Janko (1987). "Amplified versions" of the *Poetics*: L. Cooper, *Aristotle on the Art of Poetry* (1921), *An Aristotelian Theory of Comedy* (1922). *Rhetoric*: ed. and tr. with commentary by E. M. Cope and J. E. Sandys, 3 v. (1877).

(3) *Horace*. A. S. Cook, *The Poetical Treatises of Horace, Vida, and Boileau* (1892); *Ars poetica*: ed. H. Fairclough (1929)—text and Eng.

(4) *Rhetorical Critics*. Demetrius, *On Style*, and Dionysius of Halicarnassus, *The Three Literary Letters*, (1902; Loeb. ed. 1927), *On Literary Composition*, all ed. W. Rhys Roberts (1901; 1910). Cicero, *Pro archia, Brutus, Orator*, and *De oratore*, all in the Loeb series. Tacitus, *Dialogue on Oratory*, tr. W. Peterson (1914). Quintilian, *Institutio oratoria*, tr. H. E. Butler, 4 v. (1920–22). Longinus: see SUBLIME.

SECONDARY WORKS:
(1) *General*: G. Saintsbury, *Hist. of Crit. and*

Literary Taste in Europe, 3 v. (1900–4); C. S. Baldwin, Ancient Rhet. and Poetic (1924); E. E. Sikes, The Gr. View of Poetry (1931); S. F. Bonner, The Literary Treatises of Dionysius of Halicarnassus (1939); J. F. D'Alton, Roman Lit. Theory and Crit. (1931); W. C. Greene, "The Gr. Crit. of Poetry," HSCL 20 (1950); R. R. Bolgar, The Cl. Heritage and its Beneficiaries (1954); A. W. Gomme, The Gr. Attitude to Poetry and Hist. (1954); Wimsatt and Brooks; G. M. A. Grube, The Gr. and Roman Critics (1965); K. Borinski, Die Antike in Poetik und Kunsttheorie, 2d ed., 2 v. (1965); M. Fuhrmann, Einführung in die antike Dichtungstheorie (1973); H. Fränkel, Early Gr. Poetry and Philosophy (tr. 1975); J. D. Boyd, The Function of Mimesis and Its Decline, 2d ed. (1980); D. A. Russell, Crit. in Antiquity (1981); W. J. Verdenius, "The Principles of Gr. Lit. Crit.," Mnemosyne 4 (1983); G. B. Walsh, The Varieties of Enchantment (1984); M. Heath, The Poetics of Gr. Tragedy (1987); S. Rosen, The Quarrel Between Philosophy and Poetry (1988); CHLC.

(2) Pre-Aristotelian Criticism: M. Pohlenz, "Die Anfänge der gr. Poetik," Göttinger Nachrichten (1920); G. Finsler, Platon und die Aristotelische Poetik (1900); W. C. Greene, "Plato's View of Poetry," HSCP 29 (1918); R. Harriott, Poetry and Crit. Before Plato (1969); P. Vicaire, Platon critique littéraire (1960); J. A. Elias, Plato's Defence of Poetry (1984); G. F. Else, Plato and Aristotle on Poetry, ed. P. Burian (1986).

(3) Aristotle: J. Vahlen, "Beiträge zu Aristoteles Poetik," SAWW (1865–67); A Rostagni, "Aristotele e aristotelismo nella storia dell' estetica antica," Studi italiani di filologia classica, n.s. 2 (1922); L. Cooper, The Poetics of Aristotle, Its Meaning and Influence (1923); F. L. Lucas, Tragedy in Relation to Aristotle's Poetics (1927); H. House, Aristotle's Poetics (1956); R. Ingarden, "A Marginal Commentary on Aristotle's Poetics," JAAC 20 (1961–62); J. Jones, On Aristotle and Gr. Tragedy (1962); O. B. Hardison, Jr., "Poetics, Ch. 1: The Way of Nature," YCGL 16 (1967); L. Golden, "Aristotle on Comedy," JAAC 42 (1984); R. Janko, Aristotle on Comedy (1984); S. Halliwell, Aristotle's Poetics (1986); S. Kemal, "Arabic Poetics and Aristotle's Poetics," BJA 26 (1986); C. E. Butterworth, Averroes' Middle Commentary on Aristotle's Poetics (1986); Essays on Aristotle's Poetics, ed. A. O. Rorty (1992). See also the editions mentioned above by Butcher, Else, and Golden and Hardison.

(4) Hellenistic: G. M. A. Grube, A Gr. Critic: Demetrius on Style (1961); N. A. Greenberg, "The Use of Poiēma and Poiēsis," HSCP 65 (1961); D. M. Schenkeveld, Studies in Demetrius, On Style (1964).

(5) Horace: J. F. D'Alton, Horace and his Age (1917), ch. 7; G. C. Fiske and M. A. Grant, Cicero's De oratore and Horace's Ars poetica (1929); O. Immisch, "Horazens Epistel über die Dichtkunst," Philologus Supplementband 24,3 (1932); C. O. Brink, Horace on Poetry, 3 v. (1963–82)—cf. the review by G. W. Williams, JRS 54 (1964); P. Grimal, Horace: Art poétique (1966); K. Reckford, Horace (1969); D. A. Russell, "Ars poetica," Horace, ed. C. D. Costa (1973).   G.F.E.; L.G.

CLASSICAL PROSODY.

I. GREEK
   A. Quantity and Musical Performance
   B. Early Lyric and Nonlyric Meters
   C. The Fifth Century
   D. Post-Fifth Century Developments
II. LATIN

I. GREEK. A. Quantity and Musical Performance. Cl., and esp. Cl. Gr., pros. is distinguished by a variety and complexity that has no parallel elsewhere in world lit.—a natural consequence of its fundamentally quantitative character, and of the close association of Gr. poetry (q.v.) with song, dance, and instrumental music throughout the most innovative period in its hist. (ca. 700–400 B.C.). Quantitative pros. (see QUANTITY) is based on a phonemic contrast between long and short (in Allen's terminology, "heavy" and "light") that is determined by the phonetic structure of the individual syllable: syllables ending in a vowel ("open" syllables) are short for metrical purposes if the vowel is short; all others, both those ending in a long vowel or diphthong and those "closed" by a final consonant, are metrically long. Though most ancient verseforms show, in addition, some trace of the operation of two other principles (syllable counting and durational equivalence—see below), this does not alter the fact that the essential rhythmical identity of a piece of Gr. or Lat. poetry is determined by the ordering of its longs and shorts. This long-short contrast is a binary opposition capable of being used in a highly sophisticated way for purely rhythmical ends.

Quantity does not have the further role, which stress, for example, has in an accentual system, of marking basic semantic units (words and phrases normally consisting of single stressed syllables with one or more unstressed syllables attached to them). Nor is it, like stress, the primary means of underlining the relative importance or urgency of what is being said. Regular alternation of stress and nonstress inevitably suggests—as regular alternation of long and short need not—orderly calm, and vice-versa; Lear's "Howl, howl, howl, howl. O you are men of stone" cannot possibly be recited as a regular accentual pentameter, but Philoctetes' even more anguished howl "apappa-pappa pappapappapappapai" is a perfect quantitative trimeter. It is precisely because rhythmical design is an independent variable in Cl. verse that the ancient poet has at his disposal a multiplicity of basic patterns denied to the modern poet. He need not limit himself to patterns simple enough that they can still be perceived in the midst of the contrapuntal variations necessary to keep an accentual pattern from becoming monotonous. Complex designs require steady reiteration if they are to continue to be perceptible, and when accents are substituted for long quantities, this reiteration quickly becomes an insistent, droning beat that absorbs the attention of the hearer to the exclusion of almost everything else. Hence the inevitable failure of modern accentual imitations of Cl. quantitative verse (see CLASSICAL METERS IN MODERN LANGUAGES), as well as of translations "in the original meters," even when produced by accomplished poets.

Complexity carried beyond a certain point, however, involves larger, longer designs, encouraging—and encouraged by—a link with music and the dance. The individual melodies which can be put together out of notes on the lyre, like the movements that can be executed by dancing feet, can go on at greater length than the individual phrases and sentences which the unaccompanied speaking voice can put together out of words; and if a single melodic or choreographic sequence is to be repeated to form a composition of any length, longer sequences will be not only possible but actually sought after as a means of avoiding monotony.

"Strophic" composition in repeated stanzas is thus preferred to "stichic" composition in repeated single lines even in the earliest sung Gr. poetry of which any record has survived (late 7th c. B.C.); and there is a fairly steady tendency, as the devel. of poetry, music, and dance proceed *pari passu*, for the repeated sequence to become longer and more complicated. The maximum number of identical metra or cola (see METRON; COLON) that can be linked together to produce it increases, yielding what ancient metrists called systems (see SYSTEM) rather than lines; and its components may be set off from each other as separate paragraphs or periods (see PERIOD). The latter are sometimes different from each other in their basic rhythmical structure, and sometimes themselves composed of contrasting sub-components. When the component periods are sufficiently long and exhibit an *aab* pattern, it is customary to regard the larger repeated sequence as a triad divided into strophe, antistrophe, and epode (qq.v.). This is esp. true of texts composed to be sung and danced by a chorus (q.v.) rather than for simpler, "monodic" performance by a single singer accompanied on the lyre or flute (see MONODY). (Stesichorus, the traditional name of the 6th-c. inventor of triadic composition, actually means "chorus master.") The tendency toward increasing length and complexity only ends with the Hellenistic period, by which time poetry and music have begun to go their separate ways.

B. *Early Lyric and Nonlyric Meters.* Comparative metrics can give us some idea of the way in which Gr. metric complexity originally came into being out of something plainer and more rudimentary. One influential view is that the most common "aeolic" (q.v.) verseforms, those first attested in the lyrics of Sappho and Alcaeus (ca. 600 B.C.—see MELIC POETRY) are similar enough to those of Vedic Sanskrit (see INDIAN PROSODY) to suggest derivation from a common IE ancestor (see INDO-EUROPEAN PROSODY)—an essentially syllable-counting versification based on 8-, 11-, and 12-syllable lines; preference for certain "cadential" orderings of longs and shorts in the close of each line; and grouping into 2-, 3-, or 4-line stanzas. Line length and grouping into stanzas are much the same in the Gr. derivative, but quantitative principles have largely replaced syllabic ones. The syllable-counting equivalence of long to short is now encountered only in the "anceps" (q.v.) position (denoted in scansion as x) of certain verse types, and in the double anceps (xx) of aeolic (the so-called "aeolic base").

Since the new, quantitative principles involve schematized recurrence of long and short patterns containing 3, 4, 7, or 8 syllables, octosyllables may, and hendecasyllables and dodecasyllables must, now be felt as compound movements subdivided as 4-4, 8-3, 3-8, 4-7, 7-4, 4-4-4, 4-8, or 8-4, rather than as simple aggregations marked as such by a fixed cadence. The octadic pattern most frequently encountered, here and in all subsequent aeolic, is what later came to be called the glyconic (x x – ᴗ ᴗ – ᴗ –); the tetradic and triadic patterns are the familiar iamb (ᴗ – ᴗ –), trochee (– ᴗ – ᴗ), ionic (– – ᴗ ᴗ or ᴗ ᴗ – –), choriamb (– ᴗ ᴗ –), and dactyl (– ᴗ ᴗ ; qq.v.). Heptadic patterns combine with iambic or trochaic to yield the two most famous aeolic forms, the Alcaic and Sapphic (qq.v.) hendecasyllable (respectively x – ᴗ – + x – ᴗ ᴗ – ᴗ – and – ᴗ – x + – ᴗ ᴗ – ᴗ – x). Dactylic and choriambic are inserted rather than prefixed or suffixed to other forms, yielding, for example, the lesser Asclepiad (x x – ᴗ ᴗ – – ᴗ ᴗ – ᴗ –) through combination of choriambic (– ᴗ ᴗ –) with glyconic. Eventually the new feeling of quantitative-syllabic movement created by these patterns becomes strong enough to allow discarding of inherited line and stanza length altogether, as when the lesser Asclepiad is further "choriambicized" into the greater Asclepiad (x x – ᴗ ᴗ – – ᴗ ᴗ – – ᴗ ᴗ – ᴗ –), or the glyconic "dactylized" into the Sapphic "fourteener" (x x – ᴗ ᴗ – ᴗ ᴗ – ᴗ ᴗ – ᴗ –). Alternatively, inherited lines may fuse together to produce a single sequence that is not felt as a series of discrete units but as a continuous fabric (see EPIPLOKE) that defies any single system of segmentation.

No comparable pedigree can be reconstructed, however, for the verseform which offers the clearest contrast to aeolic in the earliest period of Gr. poetry, the (dactylic) hexameter (q.v.) of Cl. epic. Here there is little if any trace of syllable counting, and every foot except the last allows for the operation of a different principle—rigidly excluded from Sappho and Alcaeus—by which two short syllables may via "contraction" (q.v.) by replaced by one long (which is by convention regarded as their durational equivalent). Whether or not, as some have suggested, the hexameter (or the durational rhythmical principle it embodies) has an "Aegean" or "Mediterranean" rather than an IE origin, it and its derivatives tend to remain, at least until the 5th c. B.C., functionally and formally distinct from the trad. represented by aeolic. They are used in narrative or didactic verse that is intended for recitation or chanting rather than singing to musical accompaniment, are composed largely in the Ionic dialect, and are dedicated to themes of historical and cultural significance. Sung verse, on the other hand, whether choral or monodic, is usually composed in Aeolic or Doric and is concerned with occasional subject matter—erotic, convivial, ceremonial, encomiastic.

The main exceptions to this generalization are, first, the iambic or trochaic organizations of inherited octosyllables and dodecasyllables which yield the iambic trimeter (q.v.) and trochaic tetrameter (8 + 8, shortened by one syllable into $- \cup - \times -$ $\cup - \times + - \cup - \times - \cup -$) first attested in the Ionian poet Archilochus (early 7th c.; see ARCHILO-CHIAN). Neither of these meters is as closely associated with song and instrumental accompaniment as are the other descendants of Indo-European forms, and the former of them came to be felt as the spoken—i.e. nonlyric—verse *par excellence* once it was taken over for the dialogue portions of Athenian drama. On the other side, the dactylic movement of the recited hexameter is imported into lyric as the basis for homogeneous passages of varying length—these increase as time goes on—and is combined with iambic and trochaic to produce the so-called dactylo-epitrite (q.v.). Both rhythms are first extensively attested in Stesichorus (early 6th c.) and occur frequently in all subsequent choral poetry.

Elsewhere the main lines of division between song and speech meters are preserved even as the repertory is expanded. Along with tetrameters and trimeters, Archilochus introduces the elegiac distich (q.v.), a combination of hexameter with pentameter, as well as various combinations—best known through their imitation in Horace's *Epodes*—of hexameter and trimeter (see ASYNARTE-TON). Hipponax (ca. 550 B.C.) uses a variant on the trimeter, the so-called choliambus (q.v.) for satire and invective. On the lyric side, the three great masters of late-archaic choral song, Simonides, Pindar, and Bacchylides, produce new variations on dactylo-epitritic as well as new combinations of iambic, trochaic, or dactylic with heptadic and octadic aeolic forms, while the monodist Anacreon concentrates on the possibilities inherent in the tetradic types—iambic, trochaic, ionic, and choriambic.

Three new forms of local origin complete the lyric repertory. Cretics (q.v.) were probably—as the name indicates—an import from Crete, introduced into Greece in the 7th c. The anapest ($\cup$ $\cup - \cup \cup -$), first attested in Spartan soldiers' songs of the 7th c., is—as might be expected in a

meter designed to keep marching feet in time—the most consistent in its use of the durational principle that equates two shorts with one long. Contraction is frequent, as is the reverse phenomenon, the resolution (q.v.) of single long into double short (see METRICAL TREATMENT OF SYLLABLES). The nearest rival of the anapest in this respect is the frequently resolved $\times - - \times -$ of the dochmiac (q.v.), the preferred meter for moments of agony or hysteria in Attic drama, and one that may have been invented with such moments in mind by Aeschylus or an earlier tragedian.

C. *The Fifth Century*. The specific needs of Attic drama account for most of the 5th-c. innovations in prosodic technique. March anapests are taken over to accompany the entrances and exits of the chorus or, in comedy, formalized debate between protagonists. The trimeter develops in the way already indicated, supplemented, where livelier or more stylized exchange between actors is called for, by trochaic and iambic tetrameters. Musical holds and rests (see SYNCOPATION) and, in longer stanzas and periods, a regularized colon structure make possible a heightening of dramatic intensity and emphasis. Most pervasively, repeating stanzaic or triadic composition is abandoned, so that it is easier for the rhythm to become a mimetic accompaniment to the forward movement of the drama. The last devel., which makes lyric composition a series of single poetic sentences or paragraphs, is usually associated with a late 5th-c. innovation, the virtuoso song for a professional soloist, whether in drama or dithyramb (q.v.). But even the earliest drama that survives (Aeschylus' *Persae* [472 B.C.]) has already moved in this direction by limiting itself mainly to single repetitions of a given stanzaic pattern followed, in longer compositions, by further single repetitions of completely different patterns—*aa' bb' cc'*, etc., rather than the *a a' a"* (or, with triads, *aab a'a'b' a"a"b"* of earlier lyric).

D. *Post-Fifth Century Developments*. The prominence of compositions for professional soloists is symptomatic of the way the devel. of music was beginning to outstrip that of poetry, and the resulting separation of the two arts is the main reason for the transformation of Gr. versification that took place in the 4th c. New techniques of vocal and musical embellishment were making the inherited multiplicity of verseforms based on the ordering of long and short syllables irrelevant or even distracting. Poets who wrote for performances by specialists in these techniques tended to confine themselves to a monotonous succession of durationally equivalent metra not unlike the bars of modern Western music. Other poets, forerunners of the Alexandrians, turned to the task of adapting the hexameters, elegiacs, and trimeters of earlier recited verse to the needs of a reading rather than a listening public. All but the simplest stanzas disappear from such compositions for readers, though occasionally an isolated sequence of syllables will be lifted from an earlier stanzaic context and repeated stichically to form a "new" verseform, often named after its supposed inventor: glyconic, asclepiad, phalaecean, sotadean (qq.v.). Pattern poetry (q.v.), written for eye rather than ear, now makes its first appearance. See AL-EXANDRIANISM; DURATION; GREEK POETRY.

II. LATIN. It was this divided trad. that the Romans took over when they began, in the late 3d c. B.C., to replace such native verseforms as they had (the Saturnian [q.v.] and, perhaps, the *versus quadratus* [see below]) with imports from Greece. The aliterary, performance-oriented side of the trad. is probably reflected in the *cantica* of Plautine comedy (see CANTICUM AND DIVERBIUM), though many *cantica* are considerably more complex than anything in the Gr. texts which survive from the period. After Plautus the literary side dominates, as the Romans confine themselves to forms already well established in Gr. Only Horace and Seneca go beyond the Hellenistic repertory—either toward a much closer and more extensive reproduction of stanzas found in Alcaeus and Sappho (Horace), or toward totally new structures produced by excerpting and recombining lines and line sections from those Horatian reproductions (Seneca).

Elsewhere there is, if anything, reduction and simplification rather than expansion, partially as a result of the different prosodic structure of the Lat. lang.: Lat. contains far fewer short syllables than Gr., hence is less comfortable with a rhythmical system based solely on the long/short contrast. Hence, contraction and the use of long syllables in anceps positions become more frequent, in an effort to accommodate extended runs of longs to patterns that call for single or double shorts. In the quantitatively nondescript sequences which result, word accent tends to play an organizing role it would not have had otherwise; and even outside such sequences the operation of the so-called "penult law" (all words whose next-to-last syllable is long must bear their accent on that syllable) means that accented syllables in Lat. are far more often long than short. The result is a system in which stress patterns now reinforce, now supplement or clash with quantitative ones (see HOMODYNE AND HETERODYNE) to such an extent that rhythm cannot avoid having an added dimension, semantic and expressive as well as purely formal. One of its essential ingredients is the tension between harmony and dissonance, i.e. expectation fulfilled and expectation frustrated, which is largely foreign to Gr. but familiar to readers of Ren. and post-Ren. verse in the langs. of modern Europe. Such interplay between constancy in underlying design and fluctuation in particular instances requires that the designs show an equally modern—and very unGreek—simplicity.

Whether clash and tension were ever replaced by an actual substitution of accentual for quantitative principles is the subject of continuing debate among scholars. The verse that went furthest in this direction is Plautus' favorite line, the trochaic septenarius (q.v.). Though it corresponds to the Gr. tetrameter, the septenarius is occasionally referred to by a purely Lat. name, *versus quadratus*, and it has the distinction of being the only important Cl. form that continues to be important—once suitably modified—in the accentual-syllabic versification of Med. Lat. Some metrists are inclined to see here a "substrate" phenomenon: a partially Hellenized native meter bearing witness to a subliterary type of Lat. versification whose accentual basis made it totally different from any considered in this article, and which was ultimately destined to provide the basis for all medieval and modern Western pros. It should be stressed, however, that the *septenarii* which survive from the Cl. period, while often *capable* of being scanned accentually, can always be scanned according to the quantitative system as taken over from Gr. and modified to suit Lat. The fate of the native *versus quadratus*—if such ever existed—is yet another illustration of the truth of Horace's famous dictum on captive Greece as captor, *Graecia capta subegit*. It is only with the radical transformation of both ancient cultures that the captured Muse of the conqueror reasserts her independence. See now LATIN POETRY; see also ACCENT; ARSIS AND THESIS; BRIDGE; COLON; EPIPLOKE; FOOT; METER; METRON; PERIOD; PROSODY; QUANTITY; RESOLUTION; RESPONSION; SUBSTITUTION; SYNAPHEIA; SYSTEM; VERSIFICATION.
.A.T.C.

BIBLIOGRAPHIES: *L'Année philologique* 1–(1927–), s.v. "Métrique, rythmique, prosodie"—annual bibl., coverage beginning 1924; A. M. Dale, "Gr. Metric 1936–57," *Lustrum* 2 (1957); P. W. Harsh, "Early Lat. Meter and Prosody 1935–55," *Lustrum* 3 (1958); R. J. Getty, "Cl. Lat. Metre and Prosody 1935–60," *Lustrum* 8 (1964); L. P. E. Parker, "Gr. Metric 1957–70," *Lustrum* 15 (1970); D. W. Packard and T. Meyers, *A Bibl. of Homeric Scholarship* (1974).

PRONUNCIATION AND LINGUISTICS: W. S. Allen, *Vox latina*, 2d ed. (1978), *Vox graeca*, 3d ed. (1987); F. Householder and G. Nagy, "Gr.," *Current Trends in Linguistics*, ed. T. A. Sebeok, v. 9.2 (1972).

DICTIONARIES: O. Schroeder, *Nomenclator metricus* (1929)—terms in Gr. and text in Ger., but still not superseded; Michaelides—musical and metrical terms.

STUDIES: J. W. White, *The Verse of Gr. Comedy* (1912)—still valuable; Wilamowitz—the fullest modern study, esp. chs. 1–4; W. M. Lindsay, *Early Latin Verse* (1922); A. Meillet, *Les Origines indo-européennes des mètres grecques* (1923); J. D. Denniston, "Metre, Gr.," and J. F. Mountford, "Metre, Lat.," *Oxford Cl. Dict.* (1949); C. G. Cooper, *Intro. to the Lat. Hexameter* (1952); Beare—comparative and still useful; Norberg—for Med. Lat.; R. Heinze, "Die lyrischen Versen des Horaz," *Vom Geist des Römertums* (1960); Maas—excellent but extremely concise; L. P. Wilkinson, *Golden Lat. Art-*

istry (1963)—sound and rhythmic effects; D. S. Raven, *Lat. Metre* (1965); Koster; Crusius; C. Questa, *Introduzione alla metrica di Plauto* (1967); W. B. Stanford, *The Sound of Gr.* (1967); D. Korzeniewski, *Griechische Metrik* (1968)—relations between content and metrical form; A. M. Dale, *The Lyric Metres of Gr. Drama* (1968)—fundamental for dramatic meters, *Collected Papers* (1969)—new theory of basic rhythmic structure; W. F. Wyatt, *Metrical Lengthening in Homer* (1969); L. Braun, *Die Cantica des Plautus* (1970); E. Wahlström, *Accentual Responsion in Gr. Strophic Poetry* (1970); Parry; A. T. Cole, "Cl. Gr. and Lat." in Wimsatt, and *Epiploke* (1988); W. S. Allen, *Accent and Rhythm* (1973)—argues for stress in Cl. Gr. pros.; B. Peabody, *The Winged Word* (1975); E. Pulgram, *Lat.-Romance Phonology: Prosodics and Metrics* (1975); L. E. Rossi, "Verskunst," *Der kleine Pauly*, v. 5 (1975); Halporn et al.; Snell; West, abridged as *Intro. to Gr. Metre* (1987); A. M. Devine and L. D. Stephens, *Lang. and Metre* (1984); J. M. van Ophuijsen, *Hephaestion on Metre* (1987).   T.V.F.B.; A.T.C.

CLASSICISM.

    I. WESTERN
    II. NONWESTERN

I. WESTERN. Seven different senses of "classic," "Classical" (Cl.), and Classicism (C.) may be used as a frame of reference for a general definition of C. within the development of Western poetics: (1) "classic" as implying "great" or "first class." (2) As "What is read in school." (3) As a term used to denote "greatest" or "standard" works of lit. or periods of eminent literary development. C. as (4) the thematic or (5) the formal imitation of Gr. and Roman models. (6) As the antithesis of romanticism. (7) As a period designation in lit. hist.

    A. *"Classic" as Implying "Great" or "First Class."* The concept must be distinguished from the word. The concept is far older. In the *Frogs* (405 B.C.), Aristophanes contrasts good old Aeschylus with new-fangled decadent Euripides in a way that looks suspiciously like "Cl." vs. "romantic." At the end of the 5th c. B.C., Choerilus of Samos bewailed his own latecomer status in epic, a genre in which Homer and Hesiod already enjoyed supreme prestige. In Alexandria (3d c. B.C.), *pinakes* or lists of "accepted" (literally *enkrithentes*, "judged-in") authors were made by the scholars of the Library, and thus later antiquity knew canons (though "canon" [q.v.] in this sense was not used) of nine lyric poets and ten orators. Significantly, the Alexandrian scholars excluded the living from acceptance. In a modification of this trad., Aimeric (11th c. A.D.) drew up lists of Golden and Silver (as well as "Tin" and "Leaden") Lat. authors.

    In Rome, Plautus (2d c. B.C.) distinguishes *oratio vetus et antiqua* ("old-fashioned, high-falutin' style") from *proletarius sermo* ("common talk" [*Mil. Glor.* 751–52]). Cicero (*Acad.* 2.73) describes certain Stoic philosophers as *quintae classis* ("of the

fifth class") by comparison with Democritus. These were terms of Roman social organization. Thus Aulus Gellius, a grammarian of the 2d c. A.D., is treading a beaten path when he cites Cornelius Fronto as distinguishing a *scriptor classicus adsiduusque* from a *scriptor proletarius*, an "upper-class and established" from a "proletarian" writer. The *scriptor classicus* writes in pure lang. for the few; the *proletarius* for the many. This Alexandrian nuance of "classic" and "Cl." survives, for example, in Marxist crit., where "proletarian" designates the opposite of aristocratic or bourgeois lit. But the quite false idea, propagated by more ancient critics than Fronto and Gellius, that a Cl. author must only use refined lang., has bedeviled lit. crit. far more than Marxists.

    In the early 16th c., *classicus* was revived (perhaps first by Beatus Rhenanus, 1512) to denote the ancient authors, with the implication of superiority. Plutarch is described by Melanchthon as a *classicus auctor* (1519), and Fonseca, Archbishop of Toledo, refers to Augustine as an *auctor ex classicis* (1528).

    B. *"Classic" as "What Is Read in School."* Both Greeks and Romans read and imitated standard authors in school. Magnus Felix Ennodius (6th c. A.D.) spoke of a student who attends classes in school as a *classicus*. Modern It. and Fr. meanings of *classicismo* and *classicisme* are still colored by the earlier association of the term with school usage, already found in their lits. in the 16th c.

    C. *"Classic" as a Term Used to Denote "Greatest" or "Standard" Works of Lit. or Periods of Eminent Literary Development.* This still current definition was first developed in the 16th c., and when applied to modern authors showed no small degree of self-confidence. In Thomas Sebillet's *Art Poëtique Françoys* (1548), Alain Chartier and Jean de Meung are "bons et classiques poètes françoys," i.e. "standard or model authors." The *Discorsi Fiorentini* (1581) of Agnolo Segni similarly speak of "autori classichi e toscani." The *OED* notes the use of "classicall" meaning "canonical" or "worthy of imitation" for the years 1599 (George Sandys) and 1608–11 (Bishop Hall). The Ger. term *klassisch* (*classisch*) to denote standard works of literary excellence did not become current until the second half of the 18th c.

    Modern uses of the term "classic" in this sense are (a) the division of lit. hist. into "classic ages," ages of highest poetic achievement rather than of specific literary forms, and (b) the naming of collections incl. works of recognized merit, though of no common literary form, as "classics." Sainte-Beuve, Babbitt, and others have attempted to give formal definitions of what a classic, understood as a work of excellence, should be. T. S. Eliot's definition in *What is a Classic?* (1944) is that such a work must be the product of a mature civilization reflected in a mature mind and must show a "common style" which fully exploits the possibilities of the lang. in which the work is composed. A classic should comprehensively represent the spirit of the nationality to which it belongs and have some claim to universal meaning, to dealing with questions of general philosophical import. F. Kermode (1975) has modified this to suggest that a classic text is one admitting a variety of interps. while still preserving an underlying essence.

D. *C. as the Thematic Imitation of Greek and Roman Models.* The imitation of Cl. themes had already begun in Gr. lit. and was a marked feature of the Alexandrian period. This trend was continued by the Romans. Virgil emulated Homeric themes, Seneca those of Sophocles and Euripides. In modern lit., thematic imitation of Graeco-Roman models began with the Fr. and Ger. courtly romances of the 12th c. (Benoît de Saint Maure's *Le Roman de Troie*, Heinrich von Veldeke's *Eneit*). These inaugurated a still-living trad. of recasting Gr. and Roman stories into the lang. of the day and country. This meaning of C. was largely to merge with the emulation of Gr. and Roman poetic forms (see section 5 below).

In the late 19th and early 20th c., however, many authors have used Graeco-Roman myth and legend to comment on perennial human problems, without paying conscious heed to the literary forms assumed by their stories in Gr. and Roman lit. In lyric poetry, Stéphane Mallarmé's *L'Après midi d'un faune* (1876), Carl Spitteler's *Der Olympische Fruehling* (1900–10), and T. S. Eliot's *The Waste Land* (1922) are notable examples. Since, however, these modern experiments have sometimes led to a better understanding of the form of the ancient classics (e.g. of the musical structure and use of Homeric patterns in the *Aeneid*), the distinction between thematic and formal imitation cannot always be securely maintained. In the 20th c., anthropology (J. G. Frazer), psychiatry (S. Freud), and psychology (C. G. Jung) have also renewed their interest in the thematic imitation in lit. of Graeco-Roman models.

E. *C. as the Formal Imitation of Greek and Roman Models.* Cl. practice had already been misunderstood by critics in antiquity (e.g. the demand for "refined lang.": see section 1 above), and these errors were perpetuated in medieval theory, e.g. "Virgil's Wheel." They persisted even in 16th-c. Italy, when the misconstrued and over-interpreted *Poetics* of Aristotle was used to justify rules (q.v.) that came to exercise a tyranny over European drama from 1560 to 1780. The ideas of poetry as imitation (q.v.—to be interpreted in 17th-c. France as a mode of imitation of nature [q.v.], with Aristotelian regularity understood as nature), the exaltation of epic and tragedy as the "highest" forms of poetry demanding equally high vocabulary, and, above all, the idea of unity of action in tragedy (later extended to unities of place and time [see UNITY]) were the main tenets of the neo-Aristotelian poetics disseminated by It. commentators on Aristotle's *Poetics* like Fr. Robortelli

(1548), P. Vettori (1560), L. Castelvetro (1570), and A. Piccolomini (1575—see RENAISSANCE POETICS). Scaliger's *Poetices libri septem* (1561) and Giangiorgio Trissino's *La poetica* (Books 1–4, 1529; Books 5–6, 1562) used Aristotle's theory as a basis for often appallingly aberrant practical crit. Coincidental with the rise of neo-Aristotelian poetics was a revival of interest in the drama of Seneca. Examples of this "Cl." drama, influential in the 17th and 18th cs., are Trissino's *Sofonisba* (1515), Jodelle's *Cléopâtra captive* (1553), and Sackville and Norton's *Gorboduc* (1561).

Horace's *Art of Poetry* inspired the idea of *decorum* ("propriety") central to imitative C.: the use of the right form to suit the subject, of lang. to suit the character's social and native background, and of action to match the nature of the character. But *decorum* (q.v.) too often became confused with consistency, conformity to expectation, and moral acceptability to the spectator. Horace also urged polished craftsmanship and long labor to achieve a consciously balanced work of art—an ultimately Alexandrian doctrine much stressed in the poetics of this aspect of C., but in its origins indicating how composite an amalgam the so-called "Cl." inheritance was. This doctrine was propagated in Italy by such works as Vida's *De arte poetica* (1527) and Minturno's *De arte poetica* (1563). Robortelli's paraphrase of Horace in his edition of Aristotle's *Poetics* coupled the two critical theories in one volume. By 1598, Angelo Ingegneri in his *Dalla poesia rappresentativa* had assembled all the precepts that would be found in a Fr. theorist of 1675.

In France, Joachim du Bellay's *Défense et illustration de la langue française* (1549), itself influenced by It. ideas, and Pierre de Ronsard's *Abrégé de l'art poétique français* (1565) were poetics allegedly Horatian-Aristotelian in spirit with an almost immediate effect on styles and forms in verse and drama. Yet though the Horatian-Aristotelian doctrine was expounded in Sir Philip Sidney's *Apologie for Poetry* (1595) and Martin Opitz's *Buch von der deutschen Poeterei* (1624), its canon dominated 17th-c. lit. only in France, where it was supremely codified in the *Art poétique* (1674) of Nicolas Boileau-Despréaux (1636–1711).

Paradoxically, however, Boileau was the first translator into Fr. in this same year (1674) of the *Peri Hypsous* ("On the Sublime") long attributed to "Longinus." This in itself may be viewed as a recognition that the "rules" were too stifling. The treatise "gave the generations from Boileau to Edmund Burke (*The Origin of Our Ideas of the Sublime and the Beautiful,* 1757) the sense that they could indulge a natural pride in being bold, lawless, and original without making fools of themselves and on reputable, civilized authority" (Russell). It therefore planted at the heart of Cl. prescriptions a seed, at first not wholly recognized, of freedom in the service of imagination (q.v.) that would eventually grow into romanticism (q.v.).

For Boileau, reason should be the poet's guide

in selecting what he desires to imitate from nature; outstanding Gr. and Roman works are even safer to imitate than nature itself. Indeed they were, in a sense, nature. Pope in the *Essay on Crit.* (1711) echoes this in his lines on Virgil's imitation of Homer (132–35). Of Gr. and Roman genres to be imitated, Boileau stressed the epic, tragedy, comedy, ode, eclogue, elegy, satire, and fable (qq.v.). Forms inaugurated or developed mainly in the vernacular trad.—the sonnet, the ballad (qq.v.), or the novel—were also to observe the same regularity of proportion and the same proprieties as genres imitated from the ancients. Among outstanding Fr. works which were thought to anticipate, parallel, or reflect theories codified in the *Art Poétique* the most important were: the tragedies of Pierre Corneille (1606–84), Jean Racine (1639–99), and Voltaire (1694–1778); the comedies of Molière (1622–73); the fables of Jean de la Fontaine (1621–95); and Boileau's own satires. In England, Boileau's critical precepts (but with due attention to the sublime [q.v.]) were expounded by John Dryden (1631–1700), Thomas Rymer (1641–1713), and Alexander Pope (1688–1744); and best reflected in the works of Dryden and Pope, in tragedies like Thomas Otway's *Titus and Berenice* (1677) and Joseph Addison's *Cato* (1713), and in the satirical style of Jonathan Swift. While Daniel Georg Morhof's *Unterricht von der deutschen Sprache und Poesie* (1682) already upheld Corneille and Molière as dramatic models for the Ger. theater, and while Boileau's verse was imitated during his lifetime by Friedrich von Canitz (1654–99), the Fr. canon of formal Cl. imitation was introduced to Germany by the dramatist Johann Christoph Gottsched (1700–66), whose *Versuch einer kritischen Dichtkunst* (1730) paraphrased Boileau's *Art poétique*. Yet the only Ger. poets of merit to follow Fr. doctrine were Gottsched himself, the fabulist Friedrich von Hagedorn (1708–54), and the dramatic poet Johann Elias Schlegel (1718–49). Later in the 18th c., Ger. lit. was to develop another aspect of formal C. (see below).

In France, England, and Germany, works like Swift's *Battle of the Books* (1704) defending the "ancients" or Charles Perrault's *Parallèles des Anciens et des Modernes* (1688) defending the "moderns" had less real relevance to poetic practice (see QUERELLE DES ANCIENS ET DES MODERNES). The example of Shakespeare alone showed that Cl. theoretical demands must either be modified or dismissed; and so learned a classicist as Johnson defended Shakespeare, following the precedent set by Dryden and Pope, in this sense (*Rambler*, no. 56 [1751]; *Preface to Shakespeare* [1756]). The learned *Poetica* (1737) of Ignacio Luzan significantly had no practical import in Spain. In Italy, the Fr. neoclassical canon was eminently realized only in the 19 tragedies written by Vittorio Alfieri (1749–1803) in the style of Corneille and Racine. But almost every European country had its "Cl." period under Fr. influence. The task of the comparativist is to disentangle what really happened during these periods from what was said to be happening, and the relationship of the latter not to Boileau, but to the writers of Greece and Rome (see NEOCLASSICAL POETICS).

Ger. C. (*Klassizismus, Klassik*) consciously rejected both Fr. neoclassical poetics and Roman works of art as models in favor of a direct imitation of Gr. forms. For Johann Joachim Winckelmann (1717–68), Gr. graphic and plastic forms were models of human perfection. His conception of all Gr. art as the emanation of a harmonious soul was challenged by Gotthold Ephraim Lessing (1729–81) whose *Laokoön* (1766) points to the realism of Gr. lit. and its portrayal of both beautiful and ugly elements in human nature. After this controversy, Gr. letters were seen as both pre-eminent aesthetically and human in their emotional appeal. Lessing's *Hamburgische Dramaturgie* (1767–69) found in Aristotle's *Poetics* an emphasis on the purgation of pity and fear in the spectator of tragedy rather than on formal unities. Lessing rejected the tragedies of Corneille and Racine as true imitations of Aeschylean and Sophoclean tragedy. Among Ger. writers, Johann Wolfgang von Goethe (1749–1832), Friedrich Schiller (1759–1805), and Friedrich Hölderlin (1770–1843) most notably imitated Gr. forms by using them for non-Gr. themes or for the expression of personal feeling. Outstanding examples are Goethe's epic *Hermann und Dorothea* (1797), Schiller's tragedy *Wilhelm Tell* (1804), and the Pindaric hymns of Hölderlin (1801 ff.). Both Friedrich Nietzsche's (1844–1900) preoccupation with the Apollonian-Dionysian (q.v.) components of Gr. tragedy and the use of elegy and hymn in the poetry of Stefan George (1868–1933) and Rainer Maria Rilke (1875–1926) can be seen as further manifestations of the continuing Ger. cult of Gr. form. (For a discussion of imitation of Gr. and Lat. meters and verseforms in the European vernaculars, see CLASSICAL METERS IN MODERN LANGUAGES.)

F. C. as the Antithesis of Romanticism. The antinomy "C. vs. romanticism," first coined by Friedrich von Schlegel (1772–1829), saw C. as an attempt to express infinite ideas and emotion in finite form (*Das Athenaeum* [1798]—see ROMANTIC AND POSTROMANTIC POETICS). Schlegel envisaged a finite (Cl.) poetics coexisting with his own idea of romanticism—a progressive universal poetry in the making of which the poet was a law unto himself. Mme. de Staël (1766–1817), whose *De l'Allemagne* (1813) first brought this antinomy to the attention of Fr. and Eng. critics, radically rejected C. as a sterile and mechanical imitation, by means of predetermined rules, of Graeco-Roman models statically conceived. Whereas Schlegel saw romanticism as antithetical to Goethe's *Klassik*, and with implicit reference to Schiller's antithesis of naive and sentimental (q.v.), Mme. de Staël's polemic rejected the Fr. trad. of Cl. imitation on both aesthetic and political grounds. Accordingly,

De l'Allemagne engendered 19th-c. views of C. vs. romanticism as meaning "conservative" vs. "revolutionary," as well as "bound by sterile rules" vs. "originally creative." Goethe (in a conversation with Eckermann, 1820) originated yet another view of this antinomy by equating C. with health and romanticism with sickness. This idea has retained its currency in the 20th c. (cf. M. Praz, *The Romantic Agony* [1933]). Generally, however, 20th-c. critics have come to see the contrast between C. and romanticism as one of an emphasis on poetic form and conscious craftsmanship opposed to a poetics of personal emotion and logically incommensurable inspiration. It is in this sense that T. S. Eliot (*The Sacred Wood* [1920]) rejected romanticism in letters in favor of C.

G. *C. as a Period Designation in Literary History.* Since C. is essentially a *post-factum* creation, the aesthetic and historical grounds for establishing national or general Cs. in lit. have to be reconstructed from hindsight. The period 1660–1700 is noted by Fr. literary historians as the high point of Fr. C.; the influence of its critical theory and literary works upon the lits. of 18th-c. Europe constitutes an international age of C. However, Ger. literary historians tend to see the Fr. Cl. canon as a *Neo*classical one (with the pejorative connotation of mannerism and second-rate literary production) and place the period of adherence to Boileau's standards in the devel. of Ger. letters (ca. 1725–45) within the neoclassical category. By contrast, the period 1787–1800, when Goethe's and Schiller's emulation of Gr. form reached its high point, is taken to be the epoch of true Ger. C. Because there is no clearcut distinction on aesthetic grounds between that *Klassik* and the chronologically overlapping romantic period, art history has been invoked for plastic concepts to distinguish the restrained style of what is considered Cl. from the "open" forms of romanticism and the irregularities of the baroque (q.v.). Further, the notion of "classic" as "model" tends to enter Ger. notions of C. Since Goethe, Schiller, and Hoelderlin represent the best of Ger. lit., their age is therefore Cl.

The "Augustan Age" of Eng. letters, often defined as the period from 1680–1750, takes its center in the reign of Queen Anne (1702–14), though in fact, emulation and imitation of Graeco-Roman motifs and forms runs from 1550 to the present and was perhaps more intensive among the romantic and Victorian poets of the 19th c. than among the late 17th- and 18th-c. followers of Boileau. Thus Matthew Arnold (1822–88) rejects romantic subjectivism for the authority of the ancients, asserting (1853) "the all-importance of the choice of a subject; the necessity of accurate construction; and the subordinate character of expression." Historians of Eng. letters sometimes therefore speak of Cl. "contexts" and "aspects" related to individual works or groups of writers. A definition of C. in Eng. lit., based on these phe-

nomena, has yet to be formed. Historians of other European lits. usually apply the term "C." to epochs in which their national lit. imitated the Fr. 17th-c. doctrine of formal Cl. imitation. Scholars of comparative, general, or world lit. have either analyzed European C. as a Fr. or Gallic phenomenon or else have attempted to see the poetics of such diverse writers as Boileau, Goethe, and Eliot as aspects of one historical trend. The many and at times contradictory meanings of "C." should certainly lead scholars to apply it with great caution, although increasing awareness of the complexity and polyvalence of the Graeco-Roman aesthetic and its forms makes some associations of the modern with the ancient less implausible than they might once have appeared. Both old and new will profit from the continuance of this dialogue. See also ALLUSION; CLASSICAL POETICS; NEOCLASSICAL POETICS; RULES; cf. HEBRAISM.

A. Spingarn, *A Hist. of Lit. Crit. in the Ren.* (1908); C. H. Wright, *Fr. C.* (1920); E. von Sydow, *Die Kultur der deutschen Klassizismus* (1926); G. Murray, *The Cl. Trad. in Poetry* (1927); R. Bray, *La Formation de la doctrine classique en France* (1931); H. Brown, "The Cl. Trad. In Eng. Lit.," *HSNPL* 18 (1935); E. M. Butler, *The Tyranny of Greece over Germany* (1935); W. Jaeger *Paideia* (1939); H. Peyre, *Le Classicisme français* (1942), *Qu'est-ce-que le classicisme?*, 2d ed. (1942), "Classicisme," *Hist. des litts. occidentales*, ed. R. Queneau (1956); Wellek and Warren; W. J. Bate, *From Classic to Romantic* (1946); M. T. Herrick, *The Fusion of Horatian and Aristotelian Lit. Crit., 1531–1555* (1946); P. Van Tieghem, *Hist. littéraire de l'Europe et de l'Amérique de la ren. à nos jours* (1946); J. A. K. Thompson, *The Cl. Background of Eng. Lit.* (1948), *Cl. Influences on Eng. Poetry* (1951); G. Highet, *The Cl. Trad.* (1949); A. Heussler, *Klassik und Klassizismus in der deutschen Lit.* (1952); H. Wölfflin, *Classic Art*, tr. P. and L. Murray (1952); W. Rehm, *Griechentum und Goethezeit* (1952); T. E. Hulme, "Romanticism and C.," *Mod. Lit. Crit.*, ed. R. B. West (1952); Curtius, ch. 14; R. R. Bolgar, *The Cl. Heritage* (1954); W. P. Friederich, *Outline of Comp. Lit.* (1954); H. Levin, *Contexts of Crit.* (1957); H. Cysarz, "Antikisierende Dichtung," "Klassik," "Klassiker," "Klassizismus," *Reallexikon*; G. Luck, "Scriptor Classicus," *CL* 10 (1958); F. Schultz, *Klassik und Romantik der Deutschen*, 3d ed., 2 v. (1959); Weinberg; F. Strich, *Deutsche Klassik und Romantik*, 5th ed. (1962); R. M. Ogilvie, *Lat. and Gr.: A Hist. of the Influence of the Classics on Eng. Life from 1600–1918* (1964); *Longinus*, On the Sublime, ed. D. A. Russell (1964); W. D. Anderson, *Matthew Arnold and the Cl. Trad.* (1965); K. Borinski, *Die Antike in Poetik und Kunsttheorie*, 2d ed., 2 v. (1965); D. Bush, "The Classics and Imaginative Lit.," *Preface to Ren. Lit.* (1965); *Fr. C.*, ed. J. Brody (1966); R. Pfeiffer, *Hist. of Cl. Scholarship*, 2 v. (1968, 1976); W. Rehm, *Griechentum und Goethezeit*, 4th ed. (1968); J. W. Velz, *Shakespeare and the Cl. Trad.: A Crit. Guide to Commentary,*

CLERIHEW

1660–1960 (1968); R. Wellek, "C. in Lit.," *DHI*, "The Term and Concept of 'C.' in Lit. Hist.," *Discriminations* (1970); *Cl. Influences on European Culture, A.D. 500–1500* (1971), *Cl. Influences on European Culture, A.D. 1500–1700* (1976), *Cl. Influences on Western Thought, A.D. 1650–1870* (1979), all ed. R. Bolgar; D. Secretan, *C.* (1973); F. Kermode, *The Classic* (1975); W. Brandt, *Das Wort Klassiker* (1976); G. Braden, *The Classics and Eng. Ren. Poetry* (1978), *Ren. Tragedy and the Senecan Trad.* (1985); *Cl. Models in Lit.*, ed. Z. Konstantinovic et al. (1981); I. Silver, *Ronsard and the Hellenic Renaissance in France*, 2 v. (1981); C. Kallendorf, *Lat. Influences on Eng. Lit. from the Middle Ages to the 18th C.* (1982); J. Granarolo, "Quand les études classiques trouvent un second souffle dans la litt. comparée," *Actes du groupe de recherches sur l'expression littéraire et les sciences humaines* (1983), 41–49; *The Cl. Temper in Western Europe*, ed. J. Hardy and A. McCredie (1983); H. Lloyd-Jones, *Blood for the Ghosts* (1983); E. Smith, *Dict. of Cl. References in Eng. Poetry* (1984); H. Carlsen, *A Bibl. to the Cl. Trad. in Eng. Lit.* (1985); J. K. Newman, *The Cl. Epic Trad.* (1986); G. deForest Lord, *Cl. Presences in 17th-C. Eng. Poetry* (1987); W. H. Race, *Cl. Genres and Eng. Poetry* (1988); *The Poets on the Classics*, ed. S. Gillespie (1988); D. Stanton, "C. (Re)constructed: Notes on the Mythology of Lit. Hist.," *Continuum* 1 (1989); C. and M. Martindale, *Shakespeare and the Uses of Antiquity* (1990).

W.B.F.; J.K.N.

II. NONWESTERN lits. vary greatly in their positing and describing of a cl. period. The Slavic trad., for example, remains close to the Western, borrowing its terms for "Cl." and "C." from Lat., and employing them in the same range of meanings as do the Western langs. The African version of the Cl., at the opposite extreme, is only of local and specific character, tribal trads. setting the lines of devel. Until recently—in post-Independence, print-centered Africa—the canon has been oral, deeply rooted in tribal history and sacred lore—so deeply, in fact, that tribal, or lang.-group, identity has depended on those roots.

The Oriental and Indian trads. presume cl. assumptions. Chinese literary culture exceeds Western in its preoccupation with former achievements and models. The *Shijing* (Classic of Poetry; ca. 600 B.C.) compiles songs, lyrics, and hymns from before the time of Confucius, and has consistently served as a touchstone (q.v.) of greatness, so that much of later Chinese poetry (q.v.) is a complex web of allusions to that cl. achievement. Later, works from the Han (206 B.C.–A.D. 220) and the Six Dynasties (222–589) were added to the canon of generative literary acts—and so on as later ages widened their senses of what constitutes classic greatness. Craft, simplicity, and pregnancy of implication consistently mark the achievements deemed cl. by later Chinese taste. Japanese literary trad. accommodates more experimentation and change than Chinese, thus proving more vola-

tile in forming a cl. canon. Nevertheless, anthologies like the *Man'yōshū* (compiled ca. 760 A.D.), the *Kokinshū* (ca. 900), and the *Shinkokinshū* (ca. 1206) have until this day been treasured as cl. touchstones of Japanese poetry (q.v.). The nearly two thousand poems of the last collection, for example, have been woven into what is virtually a single poem of ten thousand lines by the linkage technique that led to renga (q.v.), haikai, and some kinds of haiku (q.v.) composition. All the criteria for the Western sense of the cl., except 1 and 4 above, apply to the canon-establishment strategies of the Asian poetries. Indian poetry (q.v.) creates against a background of scriptures, ancient tales, and religious epics a constellation of texts—the *Vedas*, the *Mahābhārata*, the *Rāmāyaṇa*—which still today serve as norms of literary excellence, of moral principle, and of religious inspiration.

What can we conclude, from this brief survey of the nonwestern "classical"? Positing prior models of style and maturity is essential to the devel. of a literary continuity. Having a cl. canon to engage gives any present a finite achievement to follow, to adapt, to learn from, to quarrel with, and to measure itself by. It must be remembered, though, that literary periods establish their cl. counterweights only when they reach a point of critical maturity, self-reflection, and need—as did Western Europe in the Ren., or the Chinese already by the time of Christ. The formation of this critical maturity seems to be based on the existence and esteem of what is precedented. In that sense, what is "classical" is really neoclassical.

F.W.

CLAUSULA. See PROSE RHYTHM.

CLERIHEW. A form of light verse (q.v.) which consists of two couplets that purport to give biographical information about famous people; the lines are of unequal length and the rhymes often eccentric. The c. is named for Edmund Clerihew Bentley, who invented it as a schoolboy (1890) by writing:

> Sir Humphrey Davy
> Detested gravy
> He lived in the odium
> Of having discovered sodium.

The c. enjoyed instant popularity with Bentley's fellow students, among whom was G. K. Chesterton. Later practitioners include W. H. Auden, Clifton Fadiman, and Bentley's son Nicholas. As the example shows, the c. mocks both the famous and the learned by providing a cockeyed look at the great. The c. differs from other light-verse forms by its roughness: while other light verse is polished, the c. is deliberately clumsy, and might be said to burlesque (q.v.) a form such as the limerick.—E. C. Bentley, *Biography for Beginners* (1905), *The Complete Cs.* (rpt. 1981), *The First Cs.* [facsimile of his school notebook] (rpt. 1982); C.

Fadiman, "Cleriheulogy," *Any Number Can Play* (1957); P. Horgan, *Cs. of Paul Horgan* (1985). F.T.

CLIMAX (Gr. "ladder"; Lat. *gradatio*). The figure in rhet. for an ascending series, usually of phrases or clauses concatenated together by *anadiplosis* (q.v.), leading to a summative or cumulative conclusion. The corresponding device in logic is *sorites*, exemplified by Sidney in the first sonnet of *Astrophil and Stella*: "Pleasure might cause her reade, reading might make her know, / Knowledge might pitie winne, and pitie grace obtaine" (1.3–4). Here the linked elements are truncated syllogisms in a chain of argument, the conclusion of each becoming the premise of the next, e.g. "my sonne ruleth my wife; my wife commaundeth me: I the Athenians; the Athenians all Graece: Therefore my sonne ruleth all Graece" (attributed to Themistocles by Abraham Fraunce, *The Lawiers Logike* [1588]). Most examples of c. are also examples of sorites. According to the anonymous *Rhetorica ad Herennium* (Bk. 4), c. is the "figure in which the speaker passes to the following word only after advancing by steps to the preceding one."

Murphy remarks that c. "joins with epanaphora, antistrophe, interlacement and transplacement or antanaclasis (*traductio*) to form a complete theory of repetition" (368). The Tudor rhetorician John Hoskyns described c. as "a kinde of Anadiplosis (q.v.) leadinge by degrees and makynge the last [i.e. preceding] word a stepp to the further meaninge" (*Direccions for Speech and Style* [1599]).

Intensified anadiplosis arranged in syntactic units of equal length (*isocolon*) produces semantic units of increasing importance in the following Shakespearian example, which also includes a mimetic reference to the figure of c. itself: "For your brother and my sister no longer met but they look'd, no sooner look'd but they lov'd, no sooner lov'd but they sigh'd, no sooner sigh'd but they ask'd one another the reason, no sooner knew the reason but they sought the remedy; and in these degrees have they made a pair of stairs to marriage" (*As You Like It* 5.2.31–38).

The meaning currently designated by c. is the point of supreme interest or intensity of any graded series of events or ideas, most commonly the crisis or turning point of a story or play, e.g. the fall of Adam in *Paradise Lost* or the murder of the king in *Macbeth*. In 1863, Gustav Freytag (*Technik des Dramas*), in describing the structure (Freytag's Pyramid) which bears his name and which he discerned in the plot of the typical five-act play, identified c. as its high point. Metaphorically then, the parts of such a play are: introduction, rising action, c., crisis or turning point, falling action, and catastrophe. Cf. AUXESIS.

C. Perelman and L. Olbrechts-Tyteca, *The New Rhet.* (tr. 1969), s. v. *gradatio*; J. J. Murphy, *Rhet. in the Middle Ages* (1974); Group Mu; B. Vickers, *Cl. Rhet. in Eng. Poetry*, 2d ed. (1990); Corbett.
H.B.; A.W.H.; T.V.F.B.

CLOAK AND SWORD. See COMEDIA DE CAPA Y ESPADA.

CLOSE RHYME (Ger. *Schlagreim*, "hammer r."). Two contiguous or close words that rhyme. Common in idioms, proverbs, and formulaic expressions, c. r. is one of only three modes for forming reduplicatives (binomial word-pairs), these modes being identical repetition (e.g. *beep beep*), ablaut change (*zigzag, clip-clop, tick-tock*), and r. (*mumbo jumbo*). Close-rhymed formulae in doublet form are legion: *hobnob, hubbub, humdrum, harum-scarum, hodgepodge, helter-skelter, hurly-burly, ill will, powwow, double trouble, riffraff, true blue, Steel Wheels*. They also come in trinomials—*fair and square, wear and tear, near and dear, high and dry, make or break, slim and trim, turn and burn, only the lonely*. Slightly longer formulae—e.g. *put the pedal to the metal*—almost automatically become metrical (this one a trochaic tetrameter) and thus cross into poetry itself, where such figuration is often treated as one or another form of internal rhyme (q.v.) or else that kind of spaced repetition-with-a-difference treated in Cl. rhet. as *polyptoton* (q.v.). It was Wilhelm Grimm who maintained that poetic (end) r. itself arose from such rhymed formulae as these. C. rhyming in poetry thus may be seen to cover a small range from the tight forms, e.g. Eliot's "Words after speech reach / Into silence" (one of a dozen examples in *Four Quartets*) or Poe's "Thrilled me, filled me" ("The Raven"), to whole lines. Its compacting effect can also be gained by shortening the lengths of the lines, as in the Skeltonic (q.v.) and in much heterometric (q.v.) verse: Donne has "And swear / Nowhere / Lives a woman true, and fair" ("Song"). In Gerard Manley Hopkins the technique is all but universal; the effect is that much weight is redistributed from the line-ends back into the lines, distributing the maximum amount of force through the entire line. C. r. is also extremely common in short-lined popular song lyrics, e.g. Jackson Browne's "The way these days just rip along, / too fast to last, too vast, too strong." Notice how Swinburne uses c. r. to suggest the darting flight of the bird in "Sister, my sister, O *fleet sweet* swallow." It can even be obtained, and concealed, by breaking over line-end, as in Louis MacNeice's "The sunlight on the gardens / Hardens and grows cold." It is the device which actuates echo verse (q.v.). T.V.F.B.

CLOSET DRAMA is drama meant to be read in the study (closet) or recited to a small private audience rather than performed on a public stage in the usual manner. The c. d. has been called a "contingent category" (Cox) because it represents the shifting distance between a dramatist's intentions and theatrical realities: a given work may be intended for stage production but be found unsuitable for the theater of its time or may constitute a dramatic experiment looking forward to a theater of the future. The classic example of a closet dramatist, Seneca, wrote plays for private declamation at a time when the Roman stage was monopolized by mimes and tumblers; his c. ds. are highly rhetorical and are marked (as c. d. often is) by a diminishment of action and an intensification of lang. Seneca's works were performed in the Elizabethan period and influenced the stage dramas of Kyd and Marlowe; during the same period, an academic and mainly aristocratic group produced Senecan plays for reading only, most notably Fulke Greville's *Mustapha*. In c. d. the conventions of a past theater are sometimes revived: Milton adapted cl. Greek dramaturgy in *Samson Agonistes*, a work explicitly intended for reading rather than performance.

The 19th c. saw a number of poets writing dramatic works either for an unreceptive audience or for a theater existing only in the reader's imagination. Byron created what he called a "mental theatre," reviving Alfieri's neoclassical dramaturgy in his historical plays and experimenting in *Manfred* and *Cain* with a "metaphysical drama" intentionally unsuited for stage representation. Shelley wrote both a neo-Elizabethan tragedy, *The Cenci*, and a "lyrical drama," *Prometheus Unbound*, which fuses several genres. Wordsworth, Landor, and Beddoes among many other romantic poets wrote c.ds. Their contemporary, Lamb, argued in his notorious essy "On the Tragedies of Shakespeare," that even Shakespeare's plays were "brought down" by performance and best appreciated in the closet. In France, Hugo turned from the stage to write for an imagined *Théâtre en Liberté*; de Musset wrote "armchair" plays (*Un Spectacle dans un fauteuil*), some of which were eventually staged. Goethe's *Faust* is rarely called a c. d., although *Faust* Part II is virtually unperformable in its entirety. Later examples incl. Browning's *Paracelsus*, Arnold's *Empedocles Upon Etna*, and Hardy's *The Dynasts*. 20th-c. poets such as Yeats, Eliot, and Fry wrote verse dramas for the stage which have been far more often read than performed; a few minor figures such as Lawrence Binyon and W. W. Gibson wrote plays intended solely for reading. See DRAMATIC POETRY.—F. L. Lucas, *Seneca and Elizabethan Tragedy* (1922); D. Donoghue, *The Third Voice* (1959); C. Affron, *A Stage for Poets* (1971); T. Otten, *The Deserted Stage* (1972); J. N. Cox, *In the Shadows of Romance* (1987); A. Richardson, *A Mental Theater* (1988); J. R. Heller, *Coleridge, Lamb, Hazlitt, and the Reader of Drama* (1990). A.R.

CLOSURE refers most broadly to the manner in which texts end or the qualities that characterize their conclusions. More specifically, the term "poetic c." is used to refer to the achievement of an effect of finality, resolution, and stability at the end of a poem. In the latter sense, c. appears to be a generally valued quality, the achievement of which is not confined to the poetry of any particular period or nation. Its modes and the techniques by which it is secured do, however, vary in accord with stylistic, particularly structural, variables.

Closural effects are primarily a function of the reader's perception of a poem's total structure; i.e. they are a matter of his/her experience of the relation of the concluding portion of a poem to the entire composition. The generating principles that constitute a poem's formal and thematic structure characteristically arouse continuously changing sets of expectations, which elicit various "hypotheses" from a reader concerning the poem's immediate direction and ultimate design. Successful c. occurs when, at the end of a poem, the reader is left without residual expectations: his/her developing hypotheses have been confirmed and validated (or, in the case of "surprise" endings, the unexpected turn has been accommodated and justified retrospectively), and s/he is left with a sense of the poem's completeness, which is to say of the integrity of his/her own experience of it and the appropriateness of its cessation at that point.

C. may be strengthened by certain specifically *terminal* features in a poem, i.e. things that happen at the end of it. These include the repetition and balance of formal elements (as in alliteration and parallelism [qq.v.]), explicit allusions to finality and repose, and the terminal return, after a deviation, to a previously established structural "norm" (e.g. a metrical norm). Closural failures (e.g. anticlimax) usually involve factors that, for one reason or another, leave the reader with residual expectations. They may also arise from weak or incompatible structural principles or from a stylistic discrepancy between the structure of the poem and its mode of c. Weak c. may, however, be deliberately cultivated: much modernist poetry shares with modernist works in other genres and artforms a tendency toward apparent "anticlosure," i.e. the rejection of strong closural effects in favor of irresolution, incompleteness and, more generally, a quality of "openness." See also ORGANICISM.—B. H. Smith, *Poetic C.: A Study of How Poems End* (1968); P. Hamon, "Clausules," *Poétique* 24 (1975); *Concepts of C.*, spec. iss. of *YFS* 67 (1984). B.H.S.

COBLA. This is the usual word for "stanza" in Occitan. It is also used, either alone or in the expression *c. esparsa* (isolated stanza), to designate a poem consisting in its entirety of a single stanza. These *coblas* are fairly common from the end of the 12th c. on. In theme they are usually like miniature *sirventes* (q.v.), and in their concision they represent the troubadours' closest approach to the epigram (q.v.). It often happened that a *cobla* would inspire an answering *cobla*, and this might well follow the metrical structure of the first, in which case the resultant combination resembles a short *tenso* (q.v.). See OCCITAN POETRY.—Jeanroy, v. 1; C. Leube in *GRLMA* 2.1B.67 ff. F.M.C.

COCKNEY SCHOOL of poetry. A derisive epithet applied to a group of writers associated with London, incl. Leigh Hunt, Keats, and Hazlitt, in a series of hostile articles in *Blackwood's Magazine* beginning in October 1817. Hunt and Keats were the main targets of the attacks, usually attributed to J. G. Lockhart, which charge the "School" with "vulgar" diction, "loose, nerveless versification," and "Cockney rhymes," e.g. Keats' rhyming of "thorns" with "fawns" in "Sleep and Poetry" and of "Thalia" with "higher" in "To * * * *." The reviewer's hostility is patently motivated both by the group's association with political and social radicalism and by class bias: the humble origins of Keats and Hunt are stressed, while Shelley, though a "Cockney" in politics, is excused for his "genius" and aristocratic birth. The term was adopted by John Wilson Croker in his notorious attack on Keats' *Endymion* in the *Quarterly Review* for April 1818. Cf. LAKE SCHOOL; see also DIALECT POETRY; RHYME.—J. O. Hayden, *The Romantic Reviewers* (1969); W. Keach, "Cockney Couplets," *SiR* 25 (1986).   A.R.

CODE. See STRUCTURALISM; DECONSTRUCTION.

COLLECTIONS, POETIC. Groups of poems possessing a sequential or other holistic form. Virgil's ten *Eclogues* and four *Georgics* have recently been examined in detail for their symmetrical properties, such as pairs of poems within the larger whole and passages on similar topics at similar length in similar places. Such thematic forms have been shown to unify the episodes of Ovid's *Metamorphoses*; and some looser form has long been observed in Martial's *Epigrams* and Statius' *Silvae*. Occasionally a form was provided, as with some Ren. editions of Juvenal dividing his 16 satires into books.

In the Middle Ages and the Ren., narrative and lyric sequences were very common, often employing other devices to impart unity (see LYRIC SEQUENCE). Dante's *Vita nuova* and Petrarch's *Canzoniere* (one of the familiar titles of the *Rerum vulgarium fragmenta*, meaning simply "c. of poems"; the other familiar title, *Rime sparse*, means "scattered poems") give sequences of love poems in which an idealized profane love may lead by stages to divine love. Recent crit. has discovered in these collections certain calendrical or other structures that provide one version of numerological form (see NUMEROLOGY). The sonnet sequences (q.v.) of Edmund Spenser (*Amoretti*), of Sir Philip Sidney (*Astrophil and Stella*), and, less certainly, of Shakespeare incorporate narrative features, along with other symptoms of order in p. cs. Two of the best Eng. examples of p. cs. appeared in the 17th c.: George Herbert's collection of divine poems, *The Temple*, and John Dryden's collection, chiefly of narratives and translations, *Fables Ancient and Modern*. Varieties of linking by echoing of words, devel. of plot, and variations on themes assist Herbert and Dryden, the former in developing ideas of the vicissitudes of the soul in

a eucharistic series; and the latter, versions of the good life. Emblem (q.v.) books frequently showed such a progression, particularly in dealing with the vanity of earthly things or the vicissitudes of the soul. Francis Quarles treats the former topic in the first two books of his *Emblemes* and the latter in the last three. Because discovery of the unifying principles of such collections has come only relatively recently, it seems very likely that further study will reveal numerous other p. cs. in Cl., Ren., and subsequent texts.

The extraordinary features of certain Japanese p. cs. have also recently become known. The first imperial collection, the *Kokinshū* (early 10th c.) contains 1111 poems in 20 books. The most important groups of books are those on the seasons and on love, both of which are ordered temporally, the former on a natural basis and in relation to the *Ceremonies of the Year* (*Nenchū Gyōji*), the latter on the pattern of a courtly love affair. The progressive integration of the *Kokinshū* bore the possibility, partly realized in that collection, of associative linkage in terms of diction, imagery, and topic. The possibility was fully realized by the eighth imperial collection, the *Shinkokinshū* (early 13th c.), in which the 20 books of almost 2000 poems are integrated editorially into a sequence of nearly 10,000 lines. The central feature of such integration is the art of the editors or compilers in bringing together poems written by different poets of different ages into a single whole, with integration rather than authorship or historical chronology determining order. On the model of such imperial collections, various shorter collections employing associative and progressive integration came into being. Some of these involved editorial integration, e.g. *Superior Poems of Our Time* (*Kindai Shūka*), a sequence integrated by the poet Fujiwara Teika. Other such Japanese p. cs. were modeled on the imperial collections and were made up of poems composed by a single poet and editorially ordered by him or her. The most frequent version of such p. cs. was the hundred-poem sequence (*hyakushuuta*), out of which developed later linked forms by poets writing stanzas in alternation. The brevity of the Japanese *tanka* (q.v.) enabled other editorial manipulation into episodes accompanied by prose. See JAPANESE POETRY; RENGA.

In the 19th and 20th cs., somewhat similar groupings of poems will be found in various lits. A few examples incl. Charles Baudelaire's *Fleurs du mal*, Rainer Maria Rilke's *Sonette an Orpheus*, and Edgar Lee Masters' *Spoon River Anthology* In numerous poetics trads., various other methods of bringing two or more poems together have existed; see COMPANION POEMS. See also ANTHOLOGY; LYRIC SEQUENCE; SONNET SEQUENCE.

L. L. Martz, *The Poetry of Meditation* (1954); C. S. Singleton, *An Essay on the Vita nuova* (1958); R. H. Brower and E. Miner, *Japanese Court Poetry* (1961); B. Otis, *Virgil: A Study in Civilized Poetry*

(1963), *Ovid as an Epic Poet* (1966); E. Miner, *Dryden's Poetry* (1967); B. Stirling, *The Shakespeare Sonnet Order: Poems and Groups* (1968); M. J. C. Putnam, *Virgil's Pastoral Art* (1970); T. P. Roche, "Shakespeare and the Sonnet Sequence," *Hist. of Lit. in the Eng. Lang. (1540–1674)*, ed. C. Ricks, v. 2 (1970), and "Calendrical Structure in Petrarch's *Canzoniere*," *SP* 71 (1974); N. Fraistat, *The Poem and the Book* (1985), ed., *Poems in Their Place: The Intertextuality and Order of P. Cs.* (1986); H. Adams, *The Book of Yeats's Poems* (1990); *The Ladder of High Designs*, ed. D. Fenoaltea and D. L. Rubin (1991).
E.M.

COLOMBIAN POETRY. See SPANISH AMERICAN POETRY.

COLON (Gr. "limb, member") as a metrical term may refer to at least three different things: (1) a basic metrical or rhythmical unit, similar to the foot or metron (qq.v.) but longer than either and often found alongside cola of a different character—hence, a means of articulating a larger rhythmical sequence, rather than measuring it into the equivalent subsections called feet or metra; (2) a syntactic or rhetorical phrase, usually marked off by punctuation, which combines with comparable phrases to articulate the meaning of a sentence; and (3) the portion of a rhythmical pattern that intervenes between any two positions at which instances of the pattern show frequent word end. Sense (1) is *metrical* and has to do with the rhythm of verse design; (2) is *rhetorical* and concerns the words of a particular verse instance; and (3) is *verbal-rhythmical* and concerns the relation of a rhythmical design to its verbal instantiations. Sense (1) is usually what a writer has in mind in discussing those forms in which the colon rather than the metron is felt to be the basic rhythmical unit. Sense (3) appears frequently in discussions of the structure of metric forms such as the Gr. trimeter (q.v.), which in the earliest stages of its devel. was clearly conceived as a dicolon, either $x - \cup - x + - \cup - x - \cup -$, or $x - \cup - x - \cup + - x - \cup -$, depending on whether the penthemimeral or hephthemimeral caesura, one or the other of which was obligatory, appears in the particular line under consideration. It is perfectly possible, however, for this "verbal-rhythmical" (3) dicolon to be simultaneously a "rhetorical" (2) tricolon, as in Menander's "O dystyches! O dystyches! O dystyches!" ("Woe! Woe! Woe!" [*Dyskolos* 574]). Here the first verbal-rhythmical colon ends after the second "O," the first rhetorical one after "dystyches." (Compare the structure of the *alexandrin ternaire* [see TETRAMETRE]—which shows a rhetorical 4–4–4 grouping of syllables but usually retains word end after the sixth syllable, as in the bipartite Cl. alexandrine). As the number of attested instances of any given design decreases, it becomes increasingly difficult to distinguish (2) from (3), and when metra are absent both types

tend to merge or become confused with (1) as well. In such situations overall structure is often so irregular that identification of (1) is only possible if one assumes that rhetorical boundaries (2) or recurring verbal boundaries (3) coincide with the boundaries of basic rhythmical units. This assumption, perfectly justified in many instances, has been standard practice ever since Aristophanes of Byzantium (ca. 250–185 B.C.) established his "measuring into cola" (*colometry*) for the lyric poets and the lyric portions of drama, and began the practice of allotting to each colon its separate line of text. It is not valid in all instances, however, and one must reckon with the further possibility, raised by Dale, that the whole notion of the colon as a basic structural unit analogous to the metron is inappropriate in dealing with certain types of rhythm. See now FOOT; METRON; PERIOD; SYSTEM; see also PUNCTUATION.

Wilamowitz, 103, 441 ff., esp. 447 ff.; J. Irigoin, *Recherches sur les mètres de la lyrique chorale grecque* (1953), with rev. by L. P. E. Parker, *BICS* 5 (1958): 13–24; Beare, 76–77; Maas, sects. 52, 61–66; Koster; L. E. Rossi in *RFIC* 94 (1966); G. S. Kirk, "The Structure of the Homeric Hexameter," *YCS* 20 (1966); Dale, chs. 1–2, and *Collected Papers* (1969), ch. 4; L. P. E. Parker in *Lustrum* 15 (1970): 51–53; Halporn et al.,; West 4–6, 198, 200.
A.T.C.

COLONIALISM. See CULTURAL CRITICISM.

COMEDIA DE CAPA Y ESPADA. A play of intrigue, very popular during the Sp. Golden Age, that elaborates upon the life of the lower aristocracy or upper middle class; it takes its name from the cloak (*capa*) and sword (*espada*) that were part of the street costume of these classes. The plot usually centers on the obstacles raised by chance or society to the marriage of one or two couples, obstacles overcome at the end. A comic subplot creates a parallel situation among the servants that also ends happily in marriage. The plot is often complicated by disguises, mistaken identities, and misunderstandings. Although the origin of the *comedia* may be seen in the *Comedia Ymenea* (1517) of Torres Naharro, the great masters of the form are Lope de Vega (1562–1635) and Pedro Calderón de la Barca (1600–81). Like all other plays of the Sp. Golden Age, it is in verse. Lope de Vega (*Arte nuevo de hacer comedias*, 1609) gives advice (which he himself did not always heed) on the type of verse to be used for each dramatic situation: *décimas* (q.v.) for sad scenes, *romance* (q.v.) for narration, *redondillas* (q.v.) for love scenes, and sonnets and tercets for grave and serious matters.—R. Schevill, *The Dramatic Art of Lope de Vega* (1918); M. Menéndez y Pelayo, *Estudios sobre el teatro de Lope de Vega*, 7 v. (1919–27); A. Valbuena-Prat, *Calderón* (1941); B. W. Wardropper, "La comedia española del Siglo de Oro," appendix to E. Olson, *Teoría de la comedia* (1978);

COMEDY

H. Ziomek, *A Hist. of Sp. Golden Age Drama* (1984).
                                                    R.MI.

COMEDY.

I. DEFINITION
II. ANCIENT
III. RENAISSANCE AND MODERN EUROPEAN
IV. RELATION TO TRAGEDY

I. DEFINITION. Like tragedy (q.v.), the Western trad. of comic theater is considered to have begun with the ancient Greeks. Such a claim is however less clear than that made on behalf of tragedy, if only because no known culture appears to lack some form of comic performance. This fact has inspired various speculative theses concerning laughter—like reason and speech—as one of the defining characteristics of humanity. As in the case of tragedy, therefore, we need to distinguish with some care between speculative generalizations about the "comic spirit," and that more precise historical description needed to analyze the function of c. in society. We must also discriminate between such description and attempts to analyze the "psychology" of laughter, because the event of c. and the eruption of mirth are by no means the same. (I should add that although the term "c." has been applied to any literary genre that is humorous, joyful, or expresses good fortune, what follows will concern above all the theater, even if some observations have a broader application.)

The name "c." comes from Comus, a Gr. fertility god. In ancient Greece "c." also named a ritual springtime procession presumed to celebrate cyclical rebirth, resurrection, and perpetual rejuvenation. Modern scholars and critics have thus taken c. to be a universal celebration of life, a joyous outburst of laughter in the face of either an incomprehensible world or a repressive socio-political order. Carnival, festival, folly, and a general freedom of action then indicate either an indifference to and acceptance of the first, or a resistance to the second. But scholars have taken such notions yet further: if tragedy represents the fall from some kind of "sacred irrationality," c. on the contrary becomes the triumphant affirmation of that riotous unreason, marking some ready acceptance of human participation in the chaotic forces needed to produce Life. The comic protagonist's defeat is then the counterpart to the tragic protagonist's failure, both versions of some ritual cleansing by means of a scapegoat—in this case one representing life-threatening forces. Such speculations have been advanced in one form or another by classicists (F. M. Cornford, Jane Harrison, Gilbert Murray), philosophers (Mikhail Bakhtin, Susanne Langer), and literary critics (C. L. Barber, Northrop Frye), not to mention anthropologists and even sociologists.

How much these theories help us understand what *cs.* are is another, and perhaps a different, question. For in the last resort such arguments depend on the assumption that beneath all and any particular c. is some kind of profound universal "carnival," a common denominator of the human in all times and places. Recalling Nietzsche's *Gay Science*, Jean Duvignaud has thus spoken of "laughter that for a fleeting moment pitches humans before an infinite freedom, eluding constraints and rules, drawing them away from the irremediable nature of their condition to discover unforeseeable connections, and suggesting a common existence where the imaginary and real life will be reconciled" (229–30). But theories of this sort depend upon the idea that one can obtain the deepest comprehension of cs. by removing them from their distinct historical moment and social environment. They forget that such carnival and such laughter are themselves the creations of a particular rationality, just as Dante's *Divine Comedy* universalized a particular theology. Even so seemingly fantastic a theater as that of Aristophanes (ca. 445–385 B.C.) is misconstrued by a theory that neglects c.'s essential embedding in the social and political intricacies of its age and place (Athens during the Peloponnesian Wars).

Setting aside these broad metaphysical speculations, then, we must look at accounts of laughter as a human reaction to certain kinds of events. By and large, these may be divided into two theories. The one asserts that laughter is provoked by a sense of superiority (Hobbes' "sudden glory"), the other that it is produced by a sudden sense of the ludicrous, the incongruous, some abrupt dissociation of event and expectation. The theory of superiority is the more modern one, developed mainly by Hobbes, Bergson, and Meredith. It presumes our joy in seeing ourselves more fortunate than others, or in some way more free. Bergson's notion that one of the causes of laughter is an abrupt perception of someone as a kind of automaton or puppet, as though some freedom of action had been lost, is one version of this.

The theory of c. as the ludicrous or as the dissociation of expectation and event has a longer pedigree. It begins with Aristotle and has come down to us via Kant, Schopenhauer, and Freud. In the *Poetics*, Aristotle mentions another work on c., now lost; what remains are a few comments. In *Poetics* 5 Aristotle remarks that c. imitates people "worse than average; worse, however, not as regards any and every sort of fault, but only as regards one particular kind, the Ridiculous, which is a species of the Ugly. The Ridiculous may be defined as a mistake or deformity not productive of pain or harm to others" (tr. Bywater). Similar remarks exist in his *Rhetoric* and in a medieval Gr. ms. known as the *Tractatus Coislinianus*, Aristotelian in argument and possibly even an actual epitome of Aristotle's lost writing on c. (ed. Janko, 1984). Save for suggesting some detail of dissociative word and action, this text adds little to what may be gleaned from extant texts of Aristotle. It does make a parallel between c. and tragedy, however, by saying that catharsis (q.v.) also occurs in c., "through pleasure and laughter achieving the purgation of like emotions." The meaning of such a phrase is not at all clear, although it suggests c. as an almost Stoic device to clean away extremes of hedonism and to root out any carnivalesque temptations.

Although both theories involve the psychology of laughter, the superiority theory seems less particularly applicable to c. than that of incongruity, for the latter seeks both to indicate *devices* specifically provocative of laughter and to explain their *effect* on a spectator. The "Aristotelian" analyses suggest several matters. First, their kind of laughter requires oddness, distortion, folly, or some such "version of the ugly," but without pain. Such laughter thus depends on sympathy. Second, although this theory is kinder than that of superiority, it too has its part of cruelty, just because of the touch of ugliness. Third, theories of superiority and of incongruity both take laughter as *means*, as commentary upon or correction of what we may call the real or even "local" world—unlike metaphysical theories, which make mirth an end in itself and an escape into some "universality." Fourth, both these theories (which supplement rather than oppose one another) require the laugher to be aware of some disfiguring of an accepted norm. C. and laughter imply a habit of normality, a familiarity of custom, from which the comic is a deviation. It may indeed be the case that c., like tragedy, shows the construction of such order, but above all it demonstrates why such order must be conserved.

II. ANCIENT. The fourth theory would at least partly explain why comic competition was instituted at the Athenian Dionysia some 50 years *after* that for tragedy (in 486 B.C.). Aristotle has told us the first competition was won by Chionides, who with Magnes represented the first generation of writers of c. Around 455 a comic victory was won by Cratinus, who with Crates formed a second generation. Many titles have survived and some fragments, but these constitute nearly the sum total of extant facts about Athenian c. until Aristophanes' victory with *Acharnians* in 425. We know that in this competition Cratinus was second with *Kheimazomenoi*, and Eupolis third with *Noumeniai*. These names tell us little, but we may perhaps assume that Aristophanic c. was fairly typical of this so-called Gr. "Old C.": a mixture of dance, poetry, song, and drama, combining fantastic plots with mockery and sharp satire of contemp. people, events, and customs. Most of his plays are only partly comprehensible if we know nothing of current social, political, and literary conditions.

Aristophanes did not hesitate to attack education, the law, tragedians, the situation of women (though it is clearly an error to take him for a "feminist" of any kind), and the very nature of Athenian "democracy." Above all he attacked the demagogue Cleon, the war party he led, and the war itself. This says much about the nature of Athenian freedoms, for Aristophanes wrote during the struggle with Sparta, when no one doubted at all that the very future of Athens was in question. Aristophanes' last surviving play (of 11, 44 being attributed to him) is *Plutus* (388), a play criticizing myth, but whose actual themes are avarice and ambition. Quite different in tone and intent from the preceding openly political plays, *Plutus* is considered the earliest (and only extant) example of Gr. "Middle C."

The situation of c. was, however, quite different from that of tragedy, for another powerful trad. existed. This was centered in Sicilian Syracuse, a Corinthian colony, and claimed the earliest comic writer, Epicharmus, one of the authors at the court of Hieron I in the 470s. We know the titles of some 40 of his plays. Other comic poets writing in this Doric trad. were Phormis and the slightly younger Deinolochus, but the Dorians were supplanted by the Attic writers in the 5th c. and survive only in fragments. The best known composer of literary versions of the otherwise "para-" or "sub-" literary genre of comic mime was another Sicilian, Sophron, who lived during the late 5th c. From the 4th c. we have a series of vase paintings from Sicily and Southern Italy which suggest that c. still throve there. The initiative had largely passed, however, to the Gr. mainland. *Plutus* is an example of that Middle C. whose volume we know to have been huge. Plautus' Lat. *Amphitruo* (ca. 230 B.C.) seems to be a version of another one, and, if so, one characteristic was the attack on myth. (Aristophanes' earlier *Frogs* [405], attacking Euripides and Aeschylus, tried in the underworld, may well be thought a forerunner.)

By the mid 4th c., so-called "New C." held the stage. Among its poets the most celebrated and influential was unquestionably Menander (ca. 342–290 B.C.). His "teacher" was a certain Alexis of Thurii in southern Italy, so we can readily see how the "colonial" influence continued, even though Alexis was based in Athens. He is supposed to have written 245 plays and to have outlived his pupil. We know of Philemon from either Cilicia or Syracuse, of Diphilos from Sinope on the Black Sea, and of Apollodorus from Carystos in Euboea—worth mentioning as illustrating the great spread of c. Until the 1930s, however, only fragments seemed to have survived. Then what can only be considered one of the great literary discoveries turned up a papyrus containing a number of Menander's cs., complete or almost so. These plays deal not with political matters or crit. of myth, but with broadly social matters (sometimes using mythical themes). The situations are domestic, the c. is of manners, the characters are stock.

The widespread familiarity of comic forms helps explain why c. was soon diffused once again over the Gr. and Roman world. By the mid 3rd c., not only had itinerant troupes spread from Greece throughout the Hellenistic world, but already by 240, Livius Andronicus, from Tarentum in southern Italy, had adapted Gr. plays into Lat. for public performance. Like Gnaeus Naevius and later Quintus Ennius, this poet composed both tragedy and c. From the 3rd c. as well dates Atellan farce (named from Atella in Campania), using stock characters and a small number of set scenes, and featuring clowns (called Bucco or Maccus), foolish old men, and greedy buffoons. These farces were partly improvised, on the basis of skeletal scripts, much like the *commedia dell'arte* of almost two millennia later. The influence of Etrurian musical performance, southern It. drama, Gr. mime, New C., and Atellan farce came together in the cs. of Titus Maccius Plautus, who wrote in the late 3rd c. (he is said by Cicero to have died in 184). By him 21 complete or almost complete cs. have survived. A little later Rome was entertained by the much more highbrow Publius Terentius Afer (Terence), by whom six plays remain extant. These two authors provided themes, characters, and style for c. as it was to develop in Europe after the Ren. (though farces, *sotties*, and comic interludes [q.v.] were widely performed in the Middle Ages).

III. RENAISSANCE AND MODERN EUROPEAN. As in the case of tragedy, c. was rediscovered first in Italy. While humanist scholars published and then imitated both Plautus and Terence (see IMITATION), vernacular art developed alongside such efforts. The early 16th c. saw the publication of much school drama in both Lat. and It., while just a little later there developed the *commedia dell'arte*, whose influence was to be enormous. This was a c. of improvisation, using sketchy scripts and a small number of stock characters—Harlequin, Columbine, Pantaloon, the Doctor and others—placing these last in various situations. These plots were as frequently derived from antiquity as they were from folk art. Later on, these two forms of c. tended to feed one another; the popular *Comédie italienne* of late 17th-c. France was one outcome. The *Commedia*'s influence was equally visible in Marivaux (1688–1763) and Goldoni (1707–93), though in the case of the first, the *Italienne* was just as important. The *Commedia* survives vividly in our own time in the theater of the San Francisco Mime Troupe, which has put the old characters to work in the service of powerful political satire.

Spain vied with Italy in its devel. of c., starting with the late 15th-c. *Celestina* of Fernando de Rojas, written in Acts and in dialogue but never really ·intended for performance. By the late 16th c., Spain's theater was second to none in Europe. Lope de Vega (1562–1635), Calderón (1600–81), and a host of others produced a multitude of romantic and realistic c. dealing mainly with love and honor. They provided innumerable plots, themes, and characters for comic writers of France and England. These two countries started rather later than the South, but, like them, benefited from both an indigenous folk trad. and the publication of Lat. c. The influence of It. humanist c. was significant in both nations during the 16th c., and that of Spain particularly in France in the early 17th c.

In France, humanist c. gave way in the late 1620s to a romantic form of c. whose threefold source was the prose romance and novella of Spain, Italy, and France, Sp. c. (esp. that of Lope and Cervantes), and It. dramatic pastoral. The first influential authors in this style were Pierre Corneille (1606–84) and Jean de Rotrou (1609–50). They were followed by many, incl. Cyrano de Bergerac, Thomas Corneille, and the poet whom many consider the greatest writer of c. of all times, Jean-Baptiste Poquelin Molière (1622–73). He wrote an enormous variety, in verse and prose, ranging from slapstick farce to something approaching bourgeois tragic drama. *Comédie ballet*, c. of situation, of manners, of intrigue, and of character all flowed from his pen. He did not hesitate to write on matters that provoked the ire of religious *dévots* or of professional bigots, nor did he shirk the criticism of patriarchy, and many of his plays have political overtones. Having begun his theatrical career as leader of a traveling troupe, Molière made full use of folk trad., of provincial dialect, of *Commedia* and of farce, as well as of Cl. example. Many of his characters have become familiar types in Fr. trad. (e.g. the "misanthrope," "tartuffe," "don juan"); many of his lines have become proverbial. While his plays do contain the now familiar young lovers, old men both helpful and obstructive, wily servants both female and male, sensible wives and mothers (whereas husbands and fathers are almost always foolish, headstrong, cuckolded, or downright obstructive), they bear chiefly upon such matters as avarice, ambition, pride, hypocrisy, misanthropy, and other such extreme traits. What interests Molière is how such excess conflicts directly with the well-regulated and customary process of ordered society.

Having followed a similar trajectory to that of its southern neighbors in the first half of the 16th c., England created a comic trad. unique in variety and longevity. The extraordinarily diverse c. of Shakespeare (1564–1616) and the so-called c. of humors (q.v.) favored by Jonson (1573–1637) seemed about to create two distinct comic trads. Shakespeare wrote in almost every mode imaginable: aristocratic romance, bitter and problematic farce, c. of character, slapstick farce, and the almost tragic *Troilus and Cressida*. If any c. may be analyzed with some "metaphysical" theory it is no doubt Shakespeare's, with its concern for madness and wisdom, birth and death, the seasons' cycles, love and animosity. Yet Shakespeare's c. remained unique, and he had no successor in this style. Jonson's more urbane c. of types and of character, satirizing manners and morals, social humbug and excess of all kinds, and falling more clearly into the forms already seen, was soon followed by the quite remarkable flowering of Restoration c., with a crowd of authors, incl. Dryden, Wycherley, Congreve, Behn, and Centlivre, among many others. They produced a brittle c. of manners and cynical wit whose major impression is one of decay and an almost unbalanced self-interest. They were in turn succeeded by a widely varied 18th-c. c. from the staunch complacency of Steele through the political satire of Gay to the joyous and mocking cynicism of Goldsmith, Inchbald, and Sheridan. This trad. was pursued through the late 19th and early 20th cs. by a series of great Irish dramatists: Shaw, most notably, then Wilde, Yeats, Synge, and O'Casey.

During this period France was equally productive, but with few exceptions failed to attain the quality represented by the names just mentioned. At the turn of the 17th c., Regnard produced serious and significant social satire, as did Lesage (esp. in *Turcaret*, 1706). Marivaux dominated the first half of the 18th c., as Voltaire did the middle and Beaumarchais the end. If any new form appeared it was doubtless the *comédie larmoyante*, a sentimental drama whose main (and stated) purpose was to draw the heartstrings; in a way, it did for c. what the later melodrama did for tragedy. In the 19th c. Musset produced his delicate c. of manners, while Dumas *fils* and others strove to produce a c. dealing with society's ills. This culminated on the one hand in Scribe's "well-made play," on the other in the "realist" drama of Zola and Antoine at the end of the century.

In other European lands, authors tended to be isolated: in late 19th-c. Norway, Ibsen; in early 20th-c. Russia, Chekhov; slightly later in Italy, Pirandello. To mention them so briefly is to be unjust, for they were all major creative figures. In many ways they foreshadowed that breakdown of traditional c. that marks the mid to late 20th c. Laughter tends to become mingled problematically with that sense of discomfort in the world and unease in the self which is perhaps a principal sign of our age. Among representative authors one might mention such as Witkiewicz, Mrozek, and Gombrowicz from Poland; Brecht, Dürrenmatt, and Handke from Germany, Switzerland, and Austria; Adamov, Ionesco, Arrabal, and Beckett in France; Čapek, Fischerova, Havel, and Kohut in Czechoslovakia; Pinter, Arden, Bond, Stoppard, Benton, Hare, and Churchill in England; and Hellman, Albee, Baraka, and Simon in America. All have been writing plays that sport ironically with the political, social, and metaphysical dimensions of the human condition. Usually such issues are no longer held separate, and all are fair game for an ambiguous, perplexed, and uncertain derision. Such theater is now widely distributed, as strong in Lat. America as in Czechoslovakia, in Italy or Spain as in Nigeria. It is almost as though c. had lost a sense of that social norm to which we referred at the outset, as if it were increasingly imbued with an inescapable sense of the tragic.

IV. RELATION TO TRAGEDY. C. had from the start a rather ambiguous relation to tragedy, and it was never difficult to see in Aristophanes' *Thesmophoriazusai* an inversion of Euripides' *Bacchae*, for example. A celebrated passage at the end of Plato's *Symposium* has Socrates obliging Agathon and Aristophanes to agree that c. and tragedy have the same source. Chekhov's *The Cherry Orchard* has been played as both c. and tragedy; so has *The Merchant of Venice*. Even the elements compounding the confrontation may be identical, as in *Macbeth*, Jarry's *Ubu Roi*, or Ionesco's *Macbett*. When the comic protagonist acquires attributes of typicality or of some absolute, then c. may take on overtones of tragedy. A critic of Molière's *Tartuffe* (1667) remarked that whatever "lacks extremely in reason" is ridiculous: anything contrary to a predictable reaction or an expected and habitual situation is absurd. This is of course straight from the Aristotelian trad., but the emphasis on excess is significant. It shows just how close c. always was to tragedy, explaining such cs. as *Dom Juan* or *Le Misanthrope*. Both focus on an idealism either misplaced or preposterous. Dom Juan's ideal self is misplaced because it serves a violent and injurious sexuality; Alceste's self-righteous scorn becomes comic when he refuses even the most innocent concession, and his responses become inappropriate to his urbane surroundings. Yet if he lowered his tone to suit his milieu he would fall short of his ideal: the dilemma is that of dissonance between the ideal and the situation where it is expressed—incongruity again. The excessive ideal in this case contradicts society's needs and fails its norm.

Tragedy appears to require a world view such that a recognized human quantity may be pitted against a known but inhuman one (variously called Fate, the gods, the idea of some Absolute, etc.), permitting the "limits" of human action and knowledge to be defined. C. seems rather to oppose humans to one another, within essentially *social* boundaries. And if, as both the superiority and the incongruity theories hold, c. is essentially a social phenomenon, then wherever humans are will be somehow conducive to it; whereas tragedy seems to signify a moment of passage from one sociocultural environment to another. That *social* nature of c. may be why its characters seem to us so down-to-earth, pragmatic, and familiar. Even where a theater's real (external) social context is very different we can still recognize creatures of a *social* order. That is also why cs. are in league with their audience, obtaining their spectators' sympathy for what are given as the dominant social interests. Volpone menaces that order, as do Shylock, Tartuffe, and Philokleon (Aristophanes, *Wasps*). Volpone and Shylock are defeated in the name of the Venetian Republic, as is Tartuffe in that of the King, and Philokleon in that of a city longing for peace. In Plautus' *Epidicus*, the eponymous slave—archetypal outsider for 3rd-c. Rome—

is absorbed into and becomes a part of the social system. In Pirandello's *Six Characters in Search of an Author*, the actors remain at loose ends because they are unable to situate either themselves *or* a social order. Similarly, Beckett's two tramps remain despairingly expectant at the end of *Waiting for Godot*. C. has always emphasized the conservation of an order it may well have helped construct. When we can no more grasp or even envisage that order, then derisive irony may make us laugh, but it also leaves us painfully disturbed. See also BURLESQUE; DRAMATIC POETRY; FARCE; GENRE; GREEK POETRY, *Classical*; PARODY; TRAGICOMEDY.

G. Meredith, *An Essay on C.* (1877; ed. W. Sypher, 1980); F. Nietzsche, *The Gay Science* (1882); H. L. Bergson, *Laughter* (1912; ed. W. Sypher, 1980); F. M. Cornford, *The Origin of Attic C.* (1914); S. Freud, *Wit and Its Relation to the Unconscious* (1916); L. Cooper, *An Aristotelian Theory of C.* (1922); M. A. Grant, *The Ancient Rhetorical Theories of the Laughable* (1924); J. Harrison, *Themis* (1927); K. M. Lea, *It. Popular C.*, 2 v. (1934); J. Feibleman, *In Praise of C.* (1939); M. T. Herrick, *Comic Theory in the 16th C.* (1950), *It. C. in the Ren.* (1960); G. E. Duckworth, *The Nature of Roman C.* (1952); W. Sypher, *C.* (1956); Frye; S. Langer, *Philosophy in a New Key*, 3d ed. (1957); A. Artaud, *The Theater and Its Double*, tr. M. C. Richards (1958); C. L. Barber, *Shakespeare's Festive C.* (1959); E. Welsford, *The Fool* (1961); J. L. Styan, *The Dark C.* (1962); A. Nicoll, *A Hist. of Eng. Drama, 1660–1900*, 6 v. (1952–59), *The World of Harlequin* (1963); *Theories of C.*, ed. P. Lauter (1964); N. Frye, *A Natural Perspective* (1965); H. B. Charlton, *Shakespearean C.* (1966); W. Kerr, *Tragedy and C.* (1967); M. M. Bakhtin, *Rabelais and His World*, tr. H. Iswolsky (1968); E. Olson, *The Theory of C.* (1968); E. Segal, *Roman Laughter: The C. of Plautus* (1968); L. S. Champion, *The Evolution of Shakespeare's C.* (1970); G. M. Sifakis, *Parabasis and Animal Choruses: A Contribution to the Hist. of Attic C.* (1971); W. M. Merchant, *C.* (1972); K. J. Dover, *Aristophanic C.* (1972); M. C. Bradbrook, *The Growth and Structure of Elizabethan C.*, 2d ed. (1973); R. B. Martin, *The Triumph of Wit: A Study of Victorian Comic Theory* (1974); A. Rodway, *Eng. C.: Its Role and Nature from Chaucer to the Present Day* (1975); M. Gurewitch, *C.: The Irrational Vision* (1975); F. H. Sandbach, *The Comic Theatre of Greece and Rome* (1977); A. Caputi, *Buffo: The Genius of Vulgar C.* (1978); E. Kern, *The Absolute Comic* (1980); R. Nevo, *Comic Transformations in Shakespeare* (1980); R. W. Corrigan, *C.: Meaning and Form*, 2d ed. (1981); Trypanis; Fowler; K. H. Bareis, *Comoedia* (1982); D. Konstan, *Roman C.* (1983); E. L. Galligan, *The Comic Vision in Lit.* (1984); R. Janko, *Aristotle on C.* (1984); J. Duvignaud, *Le Propre de l'homme: histoire du comique et de la dérision* (1985); K. Neuman, *Shakespeare's Rhetoric of Comic Character* (1985); E. W. Handley, "C.," *CHCL*, v. 1; R. L. Hunter, *The New C. of Greece and Rome* (1985); W. E. Gruber, *Comic Theaters* (1986); T. Lang, *Barbarians in Gr. C.* (1986); T. B. Leinward, *The City Staged: Jacobean C., 1603–1613* (1986); E. Burns, *Restoration C.: Crises of Desire and Identity* (1987); H. Levin, *Playboys and Killjoys* (1987); L. Siegel, *Laughing Matters: Comic Trads. in India* (1987). T.J.R.

COMEDY OF HUMORS. A play emphasizing eccentric characters whose peculiarities of personality and action are the result of imbalances in bodily fluids called "humors." The idea that an individual's traits of character and behavior depend on a balance of four bodily fluids or "humors"—blood, phlegm, and black and yellow bile—can be traced to Hippocrates (5th c. B.C.), though it finds its main exponent in Galen (2d c. A.D., the Gr. physician who systematized medical knowledge). In *The Anatomy of Melancholy* (1621), Robert Burton (1577–1640) explored the effects of melancholy, which was caused by an excess of black bile. Phlegm created a phlegmatic character; yellow bile, a choleric character; blood, a sanguine character. Burton and other such Ren. writers as Thomas Linacre, Sir Thomas Elyot, and Thomas Wright adapted and explored these theories and emphasized the connection between physical and psychological balance that led to a well-balanced personality and to decorum.

In 1597 George Chapman dramatized the theory in *A Humourous Day's Mirth*. Following Chapman's lead, Ben Jonson wrote a number of comedies of humor: *Every Man in His Humour* (1598) and *Every Man out of His Humour* (1599) are the clearest examples, but in his introduction to *The Magnetic Lady* (1632) Jonson suggests that all his comedies have been studies of humors. In the "Induction" to *Every Man out of His Humour*, Jonson says that a person suffers from a humor

> when some one peculiar quality
> Doth so possess a man, that it doth draw
> All his affects, his spirits, and his powers,
> In their confluctions, all to run one way,
> This may be truly said to be a humor.

He also derides those who have overused the term h. until it has become jargon and those who affectedly claim a h. when they have a small idiosyncrasy. To Jonson's mind a true h. is a dangerous and corrupting sickness; the comedy takes root in the process of its correction.

Restoration comedy revived and altered humors comedy, with Thomas Shadwell's claim to be Jonson's heir nearly devastated by Dryden in *Mac Flecknoe*. In the comedies of both, and of their successors, humors characters shade into the Witwouds, Horners, Lovewells, and Lady Cockwoods of comedy of manners. From that devel., eccentric characters or characters dominated by single pronounced traits populate novels from Fielding to Dickens.—B. Jonson, *Works*, ed. C. H. Herford and

P. and E. Simpson (1925–54); P. V. Kreider, *Elizabethan Comic Character Conventions* (1935); H. L. Snuggs, "The Comic Hs.: A New Interp.," *PMLA* 62 (1947); J. J. Enck, *Jonson and the Comic Truth* (1957); J. D. Redwine, Jr., "Beyond Psychology," *ELH* 28 (1961); D. H. Brock, *A Ben Jonson Companion* (1983). F.T.

COMMEDIA DELL'ARTE. See COMEDY; FARCE.

COMMON METER, COMMON MEASURE. See BALLAD METER; HYMN.

COMMON RHYTHM. See RUNNING RHYTHM.

COMMONPLACES. See THEME; TOPOS.

COMPANION POEMS. Two poems designed to be read as complements, opposites, or replies. Truly paired poems are not common in Western poetry. Some of Shakespeare's Sonnets are paired, e.g. 44–45 (on the four elements) and 46–47 (eye and heart), but the best known companion poems in Eng. poetry are Milton's *L'Allegro* and *Il Penseroso*, which are truly paired, in the manner of rhetorical essays preferring the rival claims of day and night, youth and age, etc. After Milton, there are Abraham Cowley's "Against Hope" and "For Hope," the former of which was also paired with Richard Crashaw's "For Hope"; and John Oldham's "Satyr against Virtue," with the "Counterpart." Such opposed poems were sometimes printed together in alternating stanzas: so Cowley and Crashaw on hope; the 17th-c. Dutch poet Maria Tesselschade Visscher's "Wilde en Tamme Zangster" (Wild and Tame Singer); Robert Burton's "Author's Abstract of Melancholy"; and Edmund Waller's "In Answer of Sir John Suckling's Verses," interwoven with Suckling's "Against Fruition." Some of the poems paired by one author against those by another are answer poems with parodic elements: Christopher Marlowe's "Come live with me and be my love" excited a number of such replies. Thus Anthony Hecht's "Dover Bitch" may be thought a kind of "answer" to Arnold's "Dover Beach" a century earlier. John Donne's two *Anniversaries—The Anatomy of the World* and *The Progress of the Soul*—are companion poems more by virtue of relation and contrast in theme, tone, and occasion. William Blake's *Songs of Innocence* and *Songs of Experience* include a number of poems set against each other and understandable only by their contrasts. Similarly, Robert Browning's "Meeting at Night" and "Parting at Morning" pair two related experiences (see ECHO).

In Eastern poetry, however, true answer poems, implying social intercourse in verse address, will be found in large numbers in collections of Chinese, Korean, and Japanese poetry. The cl. poetic trads. of those countries assumed that the persons addressed were also poets, and in fact poetry was often exchanged on occasions that today would call for a letter or telephone call. Chinese poets often matched a poem received from a friend by writing another in the same form and using the same rhymes. It sometimes happened that Japanese poems not actually paired were brought together editorially with a headnote describing the (imaginary) situation, leading to a genre known as "tales of poems" (*uta-monogatari*) of which *The Tales of Ise* (*Ise Monogatari*) is the best known example. Another Japanese example that flourished in cl. times was the poetry-match (*utaawase*), in which two or more people competed by writing poems on given topics, with a judgment given by judges (see POETIC CONTESTS).—P. Mahony, "The Structure of Donne's *Anniversaries* as C. Ps.," *Genre* 5 (1972); J. J. Roberts, "The C. Ps. of Robert Browning," *DAI* 33 (1972): 1148A; D. Van, "The Dichotomous Imagination: A Study of Eng. C. Ps., 1596–1630," *DAI* 47 (1986): 1737A. F.J.W.; E.M.

COMPETENCE. See LINGUISTICS AND POETICS.

COMPLAINT (Gr. *schetliasmos*) is an established rhetorical term by the time of Aristotle's *Rhetoric* (1395a9); in later rhetoricians it designates that portion of a lament (q.v.) or farewell speech in which the speaker rails against cruel fate (Menander Rhetor; Cairns). Catullus and the Roman elegists often employ a c. (Lat. *querela*) in their love poetry, directing it against a reluctant mistress, sometimes in the form of a *paraclausithyron*, a lament by the beloved's door (Copley). In the Middle Ages and Ren., three sometimes overlapping strains of c. are evident: (1) satiric poems that expose the evil ways of the world (*contemptus mundi*, e.g. Alain de Lille, *De planctu naturae*, and Spenser's collection, *Cs., Containing sundrie small Poems of the Worlds Vanitie*); (2) didactic, that relate the fall of great persons (e.g. Boccaccio, *De casibus virorum illustrium*; Chaucer, *The Monk's Tale*, and the Ren. collection *The Mirror for Magistrates*); and (3) amatory, incl. both short poems written in the plaintive Petrarchan mode (e.g. by Wyatt and Surrey in Tottel's Miscellany [1557]) and more ambitious monologues (e.g. Daniel, *The C. of Rosamond*, and Shakespeare, *A Lover's C.*). In addition, elegies like Milton's "Lycidas" retain the traditional function of the c. in laments. Other prominent examples of c. incl. Chaucer, "A C. unto Pity" (Chaucer has many early, experimental cs., on the model of Fr. and It., as *ballades* or in *ottava rima*); Cowley, "The C."; and Young's long discursive poem *C., or Night Thoughts*. In Occitan poetry (q.v.) the c. takes the form of the *enueg*, whence Ezra Pound found the model for the 36th of his *Cantos*. See also ELEGY; LAMENT; PETRARCHISM.

H. Stein, *Studies in Spenser's Cs.* (1934); *The Mirror for Magistrates*, ed. L. B. Campbell (1938); F. O. Copley, *Exclusus amator* (1956); J. Peter, *C. and Satire in Early Eng. Lit.* (1956); H. Smith, *Elizabethan Poetry* (1964); F. Cairns, *Generic Composition in Gr. and Roman Poetry* (1972); R. Primeau,

"Daniel and the *Mirror* Trad.," *SEL* 15 (1975); *Menander Rhetor*, ed. D. A. Russell and N. Wilson (1981); W. A. Davenport, *Chaucer: C. and Narrative* (1988).   W.H.R.

COMPLEXITY. See SIMPLICITY AND COMPLEXITY.

COMPOSITION. See VERSIFICATION; ORAL-FORMULAIC THEORY; POET; RHETORIC AND POETRY.

COMPOUND EPITHETS. See EPITHET; LEXIS.

COMPOUND RHYME. See RHYME; TRIPLE RHYME.

COMPUTER POETRY. A computer is a processor that can manipulate numerical or verbal symbols rapidly. Given a lexicon of available words and a set of rules for permissible combinations of them, it can be programmed to generate verbal strings. It becomes an interesting question, then, whether to call these strings poetry. Our current conception of what poetry is might encourage us to treat as poetry any sentence, such as: "What did she put four whistles beside heated rugs for?" which is syntactically well-formed but violates some of the semantic rules which normally govern the combining of words in Eng. For the average reader, any well-formed sentence hard to interpret or whose logic seems obscure is likely to be assumed to be poetic: "The old horse staggers along the road. Newspapers are on sale in Wall Street." Although the average reader of prose would consider this latter sequence incoherent, a reader of modern poetry, conditioned to allusion, will supply the missing relationships and thus create a discourse. In an earlier era, however, the reader of Milton or Pope would not have done so, because the poetry of those eras was governed by the same logic of discourse as prose. Our age demands more logic from prose than from poetry.

Computer poems are of two kinds: formulary and derivative. Formulary poems consist of strings of sentences generated by means of a formula or syntactic rule such as the following: Sentence = Noun + Verb + Adverb. Each word-class in the formula contains a set of words (e.g. Verb = scavenge, misplace, corrupt, vary, yawn). As the program runs, each word in each class is selected and arranged in sequence. If each word-class contains five items, the rule could generate the following sentences: (1) *Craters scavenge nervously*; (2) *Suits misplace wrongly*; (3) *Messiahs corrupt ably*; (4) *Sentiments vary never*; (5) *Graves yawn hungrily*. The resulting sentences are of varying levels of regularity: (3) is well-formed; (2) is ill-formed (*misplace* requires an object); (4) is inverted; (5) is metaphoric (*yawn* requires a mammal as subject); and (1) is well-formed but its violation of semantic rules, unlike (5), produces not metaphor but nonsense. The program might then generate all the permutations of the three sets of words. The following stanzas by Marie Borroff result from a formulary generation:

> The landscape of your clay mitigates
>   me.
> Coldly,
> By your recognizable shape,
> I am wronged.
>
> The perspective of your frog feeds me.
> Dimly,
> By your wet love,
> I am raked.

These stanzas, resulting from two sentence rules and one stanza rule (Sentence 1 = Nominal + Prepositional Phrase + Verb + Personal Pronoun; Sentence 2 = Adverb + Prepositional Phrase + Pronoun + Passive Verb; Stanza = Sentence 1, Sentence 2), display the characteristic unexpectedness of juxtaposition. At the same time, the repetitive structure undermines the effect, implying a mechanical approach to composition. A more sophisticated program, however, can provide both variety of structure and unusual juxtapositions. But to create poetic objects by this process, syntactic and semantic rules of greater complexity must be devised and constraints such as length of line, meter, and rhyme must be added. Metrical constraints require the prior syllabification and stress-marking of each word in the lexicon. To permit rhyming, letters must be recoded into their phonetic equivalents, or the process may be simulated by storing sets of rhyming words.

The second kind of c. p. is derivative. Here the basic principle is to take an existing line or poem and alter it in some systematic way. Hamlet's famous utterance might become "To speak or not to speak, that is the riddle," "To know or not to know, that is the struggle." The following example is based on a stanza from Dylan Thomas's poem "In the beginning" and results from marking all the nouns, verbs, and adjectives in the original, arranging them in alphabetical order, and returning them to the poem. The product is a poem containing only Thomas's own words, yet very evidently not his work. In a number of experiments, college students have usually failed to identify the original:

> In the beginning was the root, the rock
> That from the solid star of the smile
> Set all the substance of the sun;
> And from the secret space of the signa-
>   ture
> The smile spouted up, translating to
>   the stamp
> Three-pointed sign of spark and spark.

Thomas more than most poets strove for the exceptional collocation, even using mechanical means at times to achieve it. That it is difficult to distinguish between his own collocations and the computer's reveals less about c. p. than about his.

Because words have subtle but at times extensive connotative connections with each other, certain collocations are regularly inhibited even for poets, who are freer than the norm in this respect. The complete disregard of these inhibitions in c. p. gives it both its fresh and its outrageous character.

The achievement of c. p. is that it has contributed to a more accurate notion of poetic lang. No important computer poems have been produced, and none seem likely. As for the question of the author of a computer poem, the "poet" is not the computer but the programmer, whose choice of words and rules determines the final product. The poem is both the actual verse object and the program, both the abstract structure of instructions and the data, of which the actual output is only one incidental product.

C. p. probably originated simultaneously in several locations in the 1950s when engineers engaged in tasks such as machine translation began to explore the capacities of the computer for word-play. The earliest examples appear in the pages of technical journals. During the next decade, these devels. came to the attention of poets, critics, and scholars with some access to computer techniques and vocabulary. They took interest both in the possibilities of this new tool and its disturbing implications: its apparently superhuman inventiveness and the reader's inability to distinguish with certainty between machine and human productions. Interest in the production of c. p. soon declined, but the problem of generating well-formed linguistic sequences attracted both linguists as well as those studying artificial intelligence. Programs exist which simulate the surface structure of an existing text; these may eventually lead to the production of well-formed discourse itself. See also OULIPO; VISUAL POETRY.—*Cybernetic Serendipity* (London: Museum for Contemp. Art, 1968); M. Borroff, "C. as Poet," *Yale Alumni Mag.* 34 (1971); L. T. Milic, "The Possible Usefulness of Poetry Generation," *The Computer in Lit. and Ling. Research,* ed. R. A. Wisbey (1971), *Erato* (1971); A. A. Moles, *Kunst und Computer* (1973); R. W. Bailey, "Computer-Assisted Poetry," *CHum* 8 (1974); H. Kenner and J. O'Rourke, "Travesty," *Byte* 9 (1984); M. Newman, "Poetry Processing," *Byte* 11 (1986).   L.T.M.

CONCATENATION (Lat. *concatenatio,* "chaining"). Stanza- or verse-linking by verbal repetition. Linking of the end of one line to the beginning of the next is treated in Cl. rhet. under the rubric of *anadiplosis* (q.v.) and in prosody under the rubric of "chain rhyme" (q.v.); the present entry treats stanza-linking. C., said T. E. Hulme, "is the essence of poetry," for it "refreshes the word by new associations."

In strophic verse, and particularly in long narrative poems which are strophic rather than stichic, some means of linking stanzas enhances continuity through the whole, since rhyme-schemes tend to emphasize the integrity of the stanza. The simplest means to this end is to carry over a rhyme-sound from one stanza to the next, as in terza rima (q.v.); alliteration and other sound-echoes are also sometimes used. But the strategies more of interest involve repetition of an important word or phrase from the last line of one stanza to the beginning (or sometimes end) of the first line of the next. Less often, the entire line may be repeated or else its sense paraphrased or amplified.

Relatively rare in Med. Lat. (where it is called *rime serpentine*), c. was more popular in Occitan (as *copla capfinidas*). But it was a central feature of Celtic prosody during the Middle Ages. The most elaborate example in Eng. is the ME *Pearl,* whose hundred stanzas are divided into 20 groups of five, the stanzas within each group being unified by a refrain and linked by a key word, that word also linking each group to the next. The other ME examples—six alliterative romances, the York mystery plays, and a number of shorter poems—seem to have taken over the device from Welsh. In the Ren., the devel. of lyric and sonnet sequences (qq.v.) raised the issue of how poems might be linked together—whether (only) thematically, or verbally (as the more direct manifestation of the former). Gascoigne is the first Eng. poet to link his sonnets via repetition of an entire line. Spenser's practice in the *Faerie Queene* follows Ariosto closely, though Virgil too is fond of anadiplosis. C. has also been a significant resource in the Eastern poetries, particularly Japanese *renga* (q.v.). See also JAPANESE POETRY; POLYPTOTON.

M. P. Medary, "Stanza-Linking in ME Verse," and A. C. L. Brown, "On the Origin of Stanza-Linking in Eng. Alliterative Verse," *Romanic Rev.* 7 (1916); T. Brooke, "Stanza Connection in the *Faerie Queene,*" *MLN* 37 (1922); J. M. Bullitt, "The Use of Rhyme Links in the Sonnets of Sidney, Drayton, and Spenser," *JEGP* 49 (1950); J. C. McGalliard, "Links, Lang., and Style in *Pearl,*" *Studies in Lang., Lit., and Culture of the Middle Ages* (1969); E. Miner, *Japanese Linked Poetry* (1979); Morier.   T.V.F.B.

CONCEIT. A complex and arresting metaphor, in context usually part of a larger pattern of imagery, which stimulates understanding by combining objects and concepts in unconventional ways; in earlier usage, the imagination or fancy (qq.v.) in general. Derived from the It. *concetto* (concept), the term denotes a rhetorical operation which is specifically intellectual rather than sensuous in origin. Its marked artificiality appeals to the power of reason to perceive likenesses in naturally dissimilar and unrelated phenomena by abstracting from them the qualities (or logical "places") they share.

We may distinguish two types, the Petrarchan and the metaphysical. In the Petrarchan c., physical qualities or experiences are metaphorically described in terms of incommensurate physical objects, e.g. "When I turn to snow before your burning rays . . . (Petrarch, *Canzone* 8). The Petrarchan c. greatly influenced poetics (q.v.) in Italy, France, and England—it was widely used by the Elizabethan sonneteers and by Tasso—before giving way to the more codified styles of Petrarchism (q.v.) and, later, Marinism (q.v.), whose catalogues of incongruous images function less like forms of c. than like mnemonic epithets.

By contrast, distinctly conceptual vehicles of comparison characterize the metaphysical c. (the kind of c. usually intended in critical discussions of the term), for here internal qualities are conveyed by vehicles with which they share no physical features. The "metaphysical poets" were so dubbed by Dr. Johnson because, in his view, their poems "imitated" nothing, "neither . . . nature nor life" (*Life of Cowley*). Ever since Donne, the first and foremost of the metaphysicals, took erotic and, later, religious love for his themes, the ingeniousness of the metaphysical c. has been associated with esp. intense sensual and spiritual experience. Aiming at describing the incomparable nature of that experience by way of figural comparisons, Donne's imagery veered from the concrete toward objects of essentially abstract content (the book, the mind, the tear, the picture) and of cosmological proportions (the sun, the heavens, the sphere), and such rhetorical figures as hyperbole, catachresis, and paradox (qq.v.). The antimimetic logic of the metaphysical c. allowed for extended metaphor sometimes bordering on allegory (q.v.), but usually returning to restate the opening terms of its analogy, as in Donne's famous figure, in *A Valediction: Forbidding Mourning*, of lovers' souls as compass legs:

If they be two, they are two so
As stiff twin compasses are two,
Thy soul the fixed foot, makes no show
To move, but doth, if th'other do.
. . . .
Thy firmness makes my circle just,
And makes me end, where I begun.

In modern poetry and poetics the c. has been associated chiefly with T. S. Eliot, who championed his own interp. of the polyvalent "sensibility" of the metaphysicals. But its chief resurgence after the metaphysicals occurred in Fr. Romantic and Symbolist poetry, as in the combination of metaphor and personification in Baudelaire's "Spleen": "I am a graveyard abhorred by the moon, / Where long worms drag themselves on like remorse / Relentlessly devouring my most cherished dead." The uncommon, often unbecoming, objectifications of Baudelaire's cs. both disturb and please by describing artificially what the mind can imagine and recognize but the imitation of nature cannot express, significant relations found in the least expected of places.

This capacity for forging improbable relations—once called *wit* (q.v.)—is central to the c., for the sense evoked by a c. is not simply surprise or, in Dr. Johnson's terms, wonder at the perversity which created it. Succinct in its immediate effect, while allowing for ever greater amplification and development, the c. imitates the fiction-making capability of metaphor itself.

R. M. Alden, "The Lyrical C. of the Elizabethans," *SP* 14 (1917), "The Lyrical Cs. of the Metaphysical Poets," *SP* 17 (1920); K. M. Lea, "Cs.," *MLR* 20 (1925); G. Williamson, *The Donne Trad.* (1930); C. Brooks, "A Note on Symbol and C.," *Am. Rev.* 3 (1934); M. Praz, *Studies in 17th-C. Imagery* (1939); G. E. Potter, "Protest Against the Term C.," *PQ* 20 (1941); Tuve; T. E. May, "Gracián's Idea of the 'Concepto,'" *HR* 18 (1950); J. A. Mazzeo, "A Critique of Some Mod. Theories of Metaphysical Poetry," *MP* 50 (1952); D. L. Guss, *John Donne, Petrarchist* (1966); K. K. Ruthven, *The C.* (1969); E. Miner, *The Metaphysical Mode from Donne to Cowley* (1970); F. Warnke, *Versions of Baroque* (1972); A. Fowler, *Conceitful Thought* (1975); C. Brodsky, "Donne: The Imaging of the Logical C.," *ELH* 49 (1982); A. A. Parker, "'Concept' and 'C.': An Aspect of Comp. Lit. Hist.," *MLR* 77 (1982). F.J.W.; C.B.L.

CONCEPTISMO. See CULTERANISMO.

CONCRETE AND ABSTRACT. As paired terms, c. and a. represent an old philosophical dichotomy which entered into critical theory with Plato's assault on poetry. Socrates in the *Ion* ridicules the rhapsode's claim that he can explicate the works of Homer but not of other poets. Socrates implicitly defines intelligence as a capacity to deal with a. concepts; hence the rhapsode, who can speak of one poet but not of poetry, must be a mindless vessel of the gods. The *Republic* extends that logic to the evaluation of Homer, whom Socrates views as incapable of reasoning from c. particulars to universal a. forms. In Platonic ontology, abstraction is the ultimate reality; hence poetry, being c., must be among the least real of phenomena. Aristotle's defense is in part to show that poetry, while not a., is still ideal (or "philosophic")—its c. particulars, unlike those of the historian, describe not the thing that *has been* but the kind of thing that *could be*. In *De anima*, Aristotle further holds that the speculative intelligence cannot conceive a. ideas without the aid of "sensible spatial magnitudes," so that a c. poetic image could serve as stimulant to cognition, and a poem affect the intellect, without dealing in abstractions. Supporting both his psychology and his poetics is Aristotle's metaphysics, according to which a universal and a. essence *inheres in* each c. particular of any given category. Critics from Horace to Boileau offered versions of these (almost totemic) doctrines, because with them Aristotle had established a place for poetry in a world that increasingly came to value the abstractions of philosophy and science.

Platonic critics, esp. in the Middle Ages (e.g. Bernardus Silvestris) and 18th c. (Reynolds), instead relied on theories of allegory or, in the case of Dr. Johnson, moral exemplum, both of which explain poetic images as symbolic of a. ideas (see ALLEGORY). Romantic critics (e.g. F. Schlegel, Blake), in rebellion against this dichotomy of text and meaning, less apologized for the c. images of poetry than attacked abstractions as by definition false. Romantic historians of lit., like Coleridge (*Biographia Literaria*, ch. 1), used the terms c. and a. to distinguish between the neoclassical verse they disliked (e.g. Pope: "Hope springs eternal in the human breast: / Man never is, but always to be blest") and the poetry they wrote themselves (Coleridge: "I would build that dome in air, / That sunny dome! those caves of ice!"). The critique of theoretical lang. was developed further by imagists (see IMAGISM) and other modernists who turned the distinction against romanticism, and esp. against Wordsworth, whom Pound and the early Eliot found a. and discursive. The early modernists' contempt for "ideas" and for discursive poetry became in the work of the New Criticism (q.v.) a systematic and a. hermeneutics: Wimsatt and Ransom carried on a belated and ambivalent debate with Kantian idealist philosophy (see CONCRETE UNIVERSAL). But by the 1950s the literary critique of theoretical lang. had entered into the mainstream of philosophy (e.g. Quine) just at the time when crit. itself was becoming increasingly theoretical and a. Postmodern verse, however, may be c. in the extreme, avoiding (as in some "concrete poetry" and in "sound poetry"—qq.v.) the use even of words as too great a concession to abstraction. Many recent poets, in America at least, are indebted to the example of objectivism (q.v.) and of W. C. Williams, whose motto was "no ideas but in things." —F. Nietzsche, "The Question of Socrates," *Twilight of the Idols* (1888); O. Barfield, *Poetic Diction* (1928); J. C. Ransom, *The World's Body* (1938); W. Quine, *From a Logical Point of View* (1953), ch. 2; W. K. Wimsatt, Jr., "The Substantive Level," *The Verbal Icon* (1954); F. Kermode, *Romantic Image* (1957); J. Weinberg, "Abstraction in the Formation of Concepts," *DHI*; R. Rorty, *Consequences of Pragmatism* (1982), chs. 4, 6, 8; J. Milstead, "'C.' and 'A.' as Stylistic Descriptions," *Lang&S* 16 (1983); A. Danto, *The Philosophical Disenfranchisement of Art* (1986); C. Altieri, *Painterly Abstraction in Modernist Am. Poetry* (1989). J.M.P.

CONCRETE POETRY is visual poetry, esp. of the 1950s and 1960s, in which (1) each work defines its own form and is visually and, if possible, structurally original or even unique; (2) the piece is without any major allusion to any previously existing poem; and (3) the visual shape is wherever possible abstract, the words or letters within it behaving as ideograms. This dissociates the prototypical c. poem from the freer-form visual poems of futurism and dada (qq.v.) as well as from the less consciously programmatic visual poetry of the 1920s through the 1940s, epitomized in e e cummings' "l(a." The term "c. p." was adopted in 1955 when the Swiss poet Eugen Gomringer (b. 1924) met Decio Pignatari (b. 1927), who had founded, with his fellow Brazilians Augusto and Haroldo de Campos (b. 1931 and 1929), the Noigandres Group (see SWISS POETRY; BRAZILIAN POETRY). The term was adapted from the Swiss sculptor Max Bill (b. 1908), who called some of his works *konkretionen* and whose secretary Gomringer was at that time; however, it had already been used independently in 1953 by the Swedish poet and artist Öyvind Fahlström to describe his own visual poems, which are unlike those of the later group. The main manifesto of the Noigandres group, "Pilot Plan for C. P." (1958), is reprinted in Solt (1968) and may be taken as describing the early concrete program.

Over the next four years the group expanded to include such Germans as Claus Bremer, Dieter Roth, and Franz Mon, the Swiss Daniel Spoerri, the Austrians Gerhard Rühm and Ernst Jandl, the Scot Ian Hamilton Finlay, and the expatriate Am. Emmett Williams. By the middle 1960s, when the largest-scale anthols. of c. p. appeared, those edited by Williams (1967) and by Mary-Ellen Solt (1969), the movement included several dozen more poets in countries as various as Spain, Italy, Argentina, and Japan. By that point the rigid original definition had been stretched and some degree of textual allusion and visual mimesis was allowed, though with the growing fashion for c. p., not everyone who called himself a "c. poet" was accepted by everyone else. But the influence of the anthols. and the dissemination to a larger audience encouraged many other poets who were by no means avant-garde to experiment with visual poetry (still known as "c." in most cases). This was the case with such Am. poets as May Swenson, M. L. Rosenthal, and John Hollander. Thus c. p. became not the style of a group but a possible form for the mainstream. The most conspicuous result of this popularization was a widespread confusion about the term "c. p." which has persisted to the present day.

From the late 1960s onward, some younger visual poets formed new groups, calling their works "post-c." (Cavan McCarthy), "visuelle Gedichte" (K. P. Dencker) or, ultimately, *poesia visiva* (sometimes attributed to Luciano Ori but actually first used by Eugenio Miccini as early as 1962); because "visual poetry" (q.v.) describes the general field of works which fuse visual and literary art, *poesia visiva* is used untranslated, and has become the commonest term in the Eng.-speaking world to describe the visual poetic forms that have developed since c. p. *Poesia visiva* typically combines photography and graphic techniques with letters, and these do not always make sense semantically, so that with *poesia visiva* one truly enters the world of visual art more than lit. As for the original c. poets, many of them turned to sound poetry (q.v.)

after the 1960s and today combine the media of c. and sound poetry into activities for radio, television, and cinema. See also CALLIGRAMME; LETTRISME; PATTERN POETRY; VISUAL POETRY.

R. H. Fogle, *The Imagery of Keats and Shelley* (1949), ch. 5; R. L. Beloof, "E. E. Cummings: The Prosodic Shape of His Poems," *DAI* 14 (1954); *An Anthol. of C. P.*, ed. E. Williams (1967); *C. P.: A World View*, ed. M.-E. Solt and W. Barnstone (1969); R. P. Draper, "C. P.," *NLH* 2 (1971); "Konkrete Poesie I, II," *Text & Kritik* 25, 30 (1974–75); *Theoretische Positionen zur konkreten Poesie*, ed. T. Kopfermann (1974); A. Marcus, "Intro. to the Visual Syntax of C. P.," *VLang* 8 (1974); H. Hartung, *Experimentelle Literatur und konkrete Poesie* (1975); L. Gumpel, "*C.*" *P. from East and West Germany* (1976)—conflates terms; A. and H. de Campos and D. Pignatari, *Teoria da poesia concreta* (1975); J. L. McHughes, "The Poesis of Space," *QJS* 63 (1977); *Visual Lit. Crit.* (1979), *Am. Writing Today* (1982), both ed. R. Kostelanetz; D. W. Seaman, *C. P. in France* (1981); W. Steiner, "Res poetica," *The Colors of Rhet.* (1982); G. Janecek, *The Look of Rus. Lit.* (1984); *Poetics of the Avant-Garde / C. P.*, Spec. Iss. of *PoT* 3, 3 (1982); *Verbe et image: Poésie visuelle*, ed. D. Higgins and K. Kempton, Spec. Iss. of *Art contemporain* 5 (1983); E. Sacerio-Gari, "El despertar de la forma en la poesía concreta," *RI* 50 (1984); *The Ruth and Marvin Sackner Archive of C. and Visual P. 1984* (1986)—catalog and bibl.; K. McCullough, *C. P.: An Annot. Internat. Bibl.* (1989); C. Bayard, *The New Poetics in Canada and Quebec* (1989). D.H.

CONCRETE UNIVERSAL. In a 1947 essay, W. K. Wimsatt, Jr., proposed "c. u." as a key concept for any poetics that aimed to be "objective and absolute." During the 19th and early 20th c., various idealist philosophers (e.g. J. Royce, B. Bosanquet, F. H. Bradley) had tried to clarify the concept of c. u., which they had inherited from Hegel (*Phenomenology of Spirit*), and to show its relevance to logic and aesthetics. Wimsatt does not provide a hist. of the varying senses in which philosophers have used the concept or of the objections raised to it; rather, he defends his proposal by pointing out that, like philosophers, many literary critics ancient and modern have been preoccupied with an opposition in which one extreme is called "u.," "general," or "abstract," and the other "particular," "individual," or "c." (see CONCRETE AND ABSTRACT). In philosophical terms this is the problem of the nature and reality of universals. Critics have used this opposition to define poetry, to determine its subject matter and structure, and to generate principles for evaluation. It has been incorporated in critical dicta such as the following: poetry "tends to express the universal, hist. the particular" (Aristotle); the poet "coupleth the general notion with the particular example" (Sidney); "the business of a poet is to examine, not the individual, but the species" (Johnson); the object of poetry is "truth, not individual and local, but general, and operative" (Wordsworth); Shakespeare had "the universal, which is potentially in each particular, opened out to him" (Coleridge). The recurrence of this opposition suggests that the concepts of "concrete" and "universal" must both appear in any acceptable theory of the nature and structure of poetry. Wimsatt held that 20th-c. crit., esp. that of Empson, Brooks, Blackmur, and Tate, had finally formulated correctly the doctrine which had been adumbrated in earlier critical writings such as those above.

Wimsatt classified as a c. u. any natural or artificial object which exhibits "organized heterogeneity" of a complexity sufficiently great to make it seem "in the highest degree individual." The criteria for determining whether or not an object is a c. u. are diversity of parts, interrelatedness of parts, completeness, unity, independence, and self-maintenance. Perhaps the chief reason for Wimsatt's preference for "c. u." is that it provides him with a pair of polar terms which suggest the structure of the organic unity of the poem. He regards poetry as discourse which expresses a "meaning," "value," "idea," "concept," or "abstraction" (the u.) by means of the specific details (the c.) which constitute the matter of the poem. Thus the meaning is the form or unifying principle; and the poem is an organic unity if the characters, actions, metrical devices, words, and metaphors combine to body forth this u. Furthermore, the c. is the only possible means for expressing the u., which (in a good poem) is so novel, subtle, and individual that ordinary lang. cannot provide a substantive class name for it.

Thus the u. is not just an everyday generality or even a Platonic idea. It is not an abstract u. (like "yellow" or "horse" or "love") which is usually opposed to the individual. Abstract universals, whether they be concepts of attributes ("blue," "round") or of syntheses of attributes ("dog," "man"), are only mental creations and as such have no "real" existence. Indeed in a good poem the u. is the very principle of individuality, embodied in all the diverse particulars of which the poem is composed. According to Wimsatt, c. u. is applicable not only to the poem as a whole but also to any prominently distinguishable part of it, e.g. a character, metaphoric imagery, or a narrative sequence.

Wimsatt's proposal evoked a critical response from John Crowe Ransom, a lifelong opponent of "Hegelianism" and other versions of holistic aesthetics. Ransom attacked the organicist implications of the concept. His model for the c. u. is a complex machine in which each part has significance and justification only as it works with the other parts to achieve the purpose for which the machine was designed. A natural object is not a c. u. in this sense; it always exhibits characteristics which are "irrelevant" in terms of human conceptions of order and purpose. Poetry arises from the human desire to contemplate and enjoy the confused multitudinous particularity of nature for its own sake. Hence holistic structure in poetry, which would necessarily impose a "rational order" on the objects imitated, would prevent the satisfaction of this desire. An analysis of a good poem will indeed show the presence of a "logical structure" or "argument" (q.v.) that provides a skeletal organization for the poem and may be interesting or valuable in itself; but it will also show the presence of irrelevant "local details" which reflect the particularity of nature and which cannot be fitted into or assimilated by the logical structure. Should analysis show that the local details in a poem are being used only to support, illustrate, or express the argument, the poem may justly be called a c. u., but it then becomes a species of what Ransom has called "Platonic poetry"—discourse "which is really science but masquerades as poetry by affecting a concern for physical objects" (121–22).

See also AUTONOMY; INTUITION; PHILOSOPHY AND POETRY; SIMPLICITY AND COMPLEXITY.

J. C. Ransom, *The World's Body* (1941), "The C. U., I, II," (1954–55), rpt. in Ransom; W. K. Wimsatt, Jr., "The C. U.," *The Verbal Icon* (1954); Wimsatt and Brooks, ch. 15.   F.GU.

CONFESSIONAL POETRY. See AMERICAN POETRY.

CONNECTICUT WITS. See AMERICAN POETRY.

CONNOTATION AND DENOTATION. In theorizing about the nature of poetic meaning and explicating individual poems, 20th-c. critics have used c. and d. to mark distinctions in the semantic values of words. Words are arbitrary signs whose meaning and use are determined by the semantic conventions or rules of a particular speech community. In the case of words that stand for "things" ("things" in the broadest sense—real or imaginary objects, events, qualities, relations, concepts), the most important rule is that which specifies the definitional components of a word—the attributes that a thing must have if it is to be correctly recognized as referred to by that word. This is the d. of a word (its intension), though d. is also used to point to the thing or class of things to which the word refers (its extension). D. as intension is also called the "conceptual," "cognitive," "stated," "descriptive," or "primary" meaning of a word.

In appropriate verbal and pragmatic contexts, a word can also convey "secondary" meanings that are "in addition" to its d. For example, Shelley's greeting to the skylark ("Hail to thee, blithe Spirit! / Bird thou never wert") categorizes the skylark as a spirit and denies that it was ever a bird; but the lines convey much more than this denotative or propositional meaning. Thus certain phonetic, lexical, and syntactic characteristics of these lines are signs that the passage probably belongs to a certain genre of discourse traditionally called poetic and invites strategies of interp. appropriate to such discourse. The lines do not state but only imply Shelley's emotional reaction to first hearing the song of the skylark: exaltation, excitement, joy, reverence. Part of this emotion is encoded in the exclamation "Hail," but more importantly Shelley reveals his emotional state by the intonation of the lines, the use of the emotionally toned "blithe Spirit," and his extravagant denial that the skylark is a bird. The fuller significance of his experience is suggested by the identification of the bird and "Spirit," which the reader can appreciate fully only by recalling the meanings that cultural hist. has associated with these two words. A bird as an icon of the soul and birdsong as an inspirer of joy and reflection are symbols that have appeared in numerous poems. The conceptual and emotional associations of the polysemous word "Spirit," deriving from its long hist. of usage in religion, philosophy, and poetry, are extensive. Of particular importance for determining the symbolic values of the skylark are the values that "Spirit" (or "Soul") has carried in the Platonic trad., to which Shelley had devoted much study.

The term c. has been used by 20th-c. critics to designate one or more of the types of such secondary meanings. These meanings differ in the kind of information conveyed and in the linguistic and psychological mechanisms operative in such conveyance. It is also obvious that a discussion of the cs. of individual words slides inevitably into a consideration of the secondary meanings expressed by larger linguistic units—e.g. the presuppositions and implications of sentences; the inferences required for a full understanding of the world depicted in a poem—a depiction in which gaps almost always appear; the interp. of the ideology latent in a poem or of a "subtext" that undermines its explicit ideology. Such considerations have led some theorists—e.g. E. D. Hirsch and W. K. Wimsatt, Jr.—to recommend abandoning "c.," a concept which they consider imprecise, inadequately analyzed, and subject to a variety of narrow definitions. On the other hand, a strong defense for using "c." in a broad sense appears in Kerbrat-Orecchioni.

The genre, purposes, and intended audience of a discourse determine the effectiveness of the means selected by its author to convey meaning. If clear and easy communication is the aim, the use of words with largely agreed upon ds., ordered by conventional syntax, is indispensable. In such discourses as mathematics, factual reporting, cookbook recipes, and rules of chess, c. is irrelevant and possibly misleading—mere noise in the channel. But to some poets (e.g. the Fr. symbolists and their followers) and to many 20th-c. critics good poetry is discourse in which a substantial part of the meaning is conveyed via suggestion and implication. The poetry of "statement," which, it is claimed, dominated the 18th and 19th centuries, has been demoted to a lower rank; and the values of "fluid" discourse (I. A. Richards), "oblique" poetry (E. M. W. Tillyard), or the poetry of "indirection" (C. Brooks) have been of the greatest interest to critics from the 1930s to the present. Much effort has been expended in describing the effects achievable by connotative means and in enumerating the variety of textual characteristics—phonetic, graphemic, syntactic, as well as semantic—that require a connotative interp. or encourage associative or inferential activity on the part of the reader. On the semantic level, the stress has been on paradox, irony, ambiguity (qq.v.), polysemy, figures of speech (esp. metaphor and metonomy, qq.v.), and symbol (q.v.), all of which devices depend on secondary meaning for their interp.

The values claimed for c. in poetry are various. Many traditional critics, rhetorically oriented, recommended that secondary meaning be used to ornament, reinforce, or exemplify moral or other programmatic truths. Modern critics stress not only the obvious values of c. in enriching texture and economizing means but also the reader's pleasure in exploring seeming irrelevancies, resolving ambiguities, making discoveries, even being a participant in the creation of poetic meaning (see READER-RESPONSE CRITICISM). C. is considered particularly useful when lang. is used for emotive purposes. D. can name feelings, but it cannot express or evoke them with fullness and intensity, esp. when the feeling is a unique moment of rich consciousness. But perhaps the most important values of c. are cognitive. The lang. of indirection, it is claimed, presents types of knowledge not possible to convey through the categorical rigidities and abstractions of rule-bound d. It provides empathic understanding of various kinds of human experience; it gives us a sense of immediate reality, of lived fullness, of the ineffable; it reflects the intricacies of a complex and perhaps confused existential situation, or, conversely, it is the means by which human intuition can break through to transcendental realms of being.

Most critics distinguish between c. and "personal associations." C. belongs to interp. and is subject to the control of the linguistic, literary, and cultural competencies of poet and reader. But conventions change, and even at a particular time rules differ as to the stringency of their application. Thus, compared with d., c. is less stable—more elusive, uncertain, and variable. Its presence in poetry makes the problem of achieving a single correct interp. difficult. Since cs. may be multiple and even contradictory, how can a reader tell which should be exploited and which suppressed? The New Critics tried to solve this problem by postulating an organicism (q.v.) that provides a contextual control for determining which potential meanings of a word are to be actualized. But deconstructionists have argued that the demand for coherence is a convention that is inevitably frustrated. The nature of lang., loaded with secondary meaning, militates against any conception of a "centered" text. The New Critic is accused of operating with a naive epistemology and superficial linguistic principles. Questions are raised about the referential function of words and the possibility of fixed denotative meanings. By this account, in poetry, more than in any other discourse, there is only the "free play" of signifiers in which it becomes impossible to determine what is "primary" and what "secondary." A poem celebrates indeterminacy, duplicity, and open-endedness; there is no closure, only internal contradiction, with intertextuality (q.v.) becoming the prime source for an infinite regress of associative meanings. See also DECONSTRUCTION; INTERPRETATION; MEANING, POETIC; NEW CRITICISM; SEMANTICS AND POETRY; SYMBOL.—J. Sparrow, *Sense and Poetry* (1934); E. M. W. Tillyard, *Poetry Direct and Oblique*, 2d. ed. (1945); Brooks; W. Empson, *The Structure of Complex Words* (1951); Empson; W. K. Wimsatt, Jr., "The Substantive Level," *The Verbal Icon* (1954), "What to Say about a Poem," *Hateful Contraries* (1965); M. C. Beardsley, *Aesthetics* (1958); I. C. Hungerland, *Poetic Discourse* (1958); E. D. Hirsch, Jr., *Validity in Interp.* (1967); R. Barthes, *S/Z* (1970; Eng. tr. 1974); K. Rayan, *Suggestion and Statement in Poetry* (1972), *Text and Sub-Text* (1987); C. Kerbrat-Orecchioni, *La C.* (1977). F.GU.

CONSOLATION. See LAMENT.

CONSONANCE. In addition to its general meaning of harmony (agreement), c. has been used interchangeably in prosody with a wide variety of terms intended to designate certain phonic echoes. In a definition popular for some time, c. was said to require the repetition in stressed syllables of two or more consonant sounds without the intervening vowel echo, as *live-leave*. And indeed a few poets have played with this kind of double echo—Hopkins, Owen, and Thomas, as well as Auden with his "rider to reader" poem—with a precedent in Pulci, who in the *Morgante Maggiori* wrote lines such as "Stille le stelle ch'a tetto era tutta." Other terms sometimes used are "bracket alliteration" and "bracket consonance," though neither is logical since one of the echoes is alliteration (q.v.). Through the centuries, however, and esp. in the 20th c., poets have far more often echoed final consonants in stressed syllables that do not alliterate or rhyme, as *live-move* or Lowell's "iro*nic* rai*n*bow" and "Go*bb*ets of blu*bb*er." The terms "half-rhyme" and "near rhyme" (q.v.) are unsatisfactory for this kind of echo because each can also describe assonance (q.v.), while "slant rhyme" is worse since it confuses the meaning of "rhyme" (q.v.). C. strictly defined, then, is the repetition of the sound of a final consonant or consonant cluster in stressed, unrhymed syllables near enough to each other for the echo to affect the ear, as in Pope's "Ah ne'er so di*re* a Thir*st* of

Glory boa*st*," where *st* or *r* ends every stressed syllable.

Thus defined, c. parallels the repetitions in alliteration (initial consonant) and assonance (medial vowel); it permits us to say that "rider" both alliterates and consonates with "reader"; and, most important, it leads to emphasis not on substitutes for rhyme but on the great majority of examples of c., i.e. those *within* lines of poetry.

Few scholars realize what an extraordinary number of poets have known the aural appeal of consonance. Lucretius has many lines such as "Cernere adorari licet et sentire sonare," with four final *r*'s in stressed syllables. Even in Fr., which so often does not pronounce the final written consonant(s), Boileau could echo final *s* and *r* in "Changer Narcisse en fleur, couvrir Daphné d'écorce." In Eng., esp. from 1500 on, the examples are legion. Shakespeare normally preferred other phonic echoes, but his couplet from *R&J* (2.3.3–4) is far from unique: "And flecked darkness like a drunkard reels / From forth days path and Titan's fiery wheels," where 6 of 10 ictic peaks consonate with *k* or *th*. Spenser, Milton, Pope, Thomson, Collins, Shelley, Byron, Browning, and Tennyson have enough c. to show that they knew its worth, while in America Edward Taylor has more internal c. than any other major poet before Dickinson, and Emerson employed c. often instead of certain end rhymes. Dryden used it for parallelism, often with other echoes ("piercing wi*t* and pregnant though*t*); for joining adjective to noun ("o*d*ious ai*d*," "exte*nd*ed wa*nd*"); and for onomatopoeia ("A buzzing noise of bees his ears alarms," where the *z* of *buzz* ends every stressed syllable).

In the 20th c. dozens of poets not only have made it a frequent substitute for end rhyme but have used it internally even more. The great influence here is perhaps Hopkins, notorious for phonic echoes, who linked alliteration with his internal c. (*fickle-freckled*) and just as often put assonance with it for internal rhymes (*fall-gall*), but occasionally he retreated to mere c. (*Ghostbreast, yellow sallows*). Owen has more c. by itself (*shrill-wailing-call*), as do Roethke and Crane, who lets the c. of *r* dominate a whole stanza of "Voyage II."

K. Burke, "On Musicality in Verse," *The Philosophy of Lit. Form* (1941); A. Oras, "Surrey's Technique of Phonetic Echoes," *JEGP* 50 (1951), "Lyrical Instrumentation in Marlowe," *Studies in Shakespeare*, ed. A. D. Matthews (1953); D. Masson, "Vowel and Consonant Patterns in Poetry" and "Thematic Analyses of Sounds in Poetry," and A. Oras, "Spenser and Milton: Some Parallels and Contrasts in the Handling of Sound," *Essays on the Lang. of Lit.*, ed. S. Chatman and S. R. Levin (1967); P. G. Adams, *Graces of Harmony* (1977).
P.G.A.

CONSTRUCTIVISM as a modern art movement first emerged among Rus. painters around 1913 and included such artists as Vladimir Tatlin and Naum Gabo; the new trend spread to Western Europe in the early 1920s. The constructivists called for the union of art with science and technology. Gradually the movement's ideas spread to lit., and poetry in particular. The initiator of this trend was A. N. Čičerin (1889–1960), who drafted the first manifesto, "Znaem" (We Know, 1923), and was its most radical practitioner, progressing from short, phonetically transcribed poems to more compressed, even wordless visual artifacts in accordance with the principle of maximum expression using a minimum of material. In 1924 a group of Rus. writers organized under the banner of c.; these included the poets Il'ja Selvinskij, Eduard Bagritskij, and Vera Inber, as well as the movement's other theoretician, K. L. Zelinskij. The group called for the absorption of the lexicon of science and technology by lit.; they also emphasized what they called "localization" of word pattern and other literary devices, which meant their subordination to subject matter; thus, a poem on war might employ a marching rhythm. But the group's theories were at best hazy and, with the exception of Selvinskij, little more than lip service was paid to them. The movement broke up after 1930.—K. L. Zelinskij, *Poèzija kak smysl': kniga o konstruktivizme* (1929); H. Ermolaev, *Soviet Literary Theories, 1917–1934* (1963); G. Weber, "C. and Soviet Lit.," *Soviet Union* 3,2 (1976); E. Možejko, "Rus. Literary C.: Towards a Theory of Poetic Lang.," *Canadian Contribs. to the VIII Internat. Congress of Slavists* (1978); R. Grübel, *Russischer Konstruktivismus* (1981), "Russkij literaturnyj konstruktivism," *RusL* 17 (1985), "Kan-Fun: Konstruktivizm-funkcionalizm," *RusL* 21 (1987); Terras.
W.E.H; G.J.J.

CONTE DÉVOT. A type of OF pious tale in prose or verse, popular in the 13th and 14th cs. It is distinct from the saint's legend and the moral tale (see EXEMPLUM). The best known c. d. is the *Tombeor Nostre Dame*, or *Jongleur de Notre Dame*, in which a minstrel (q.v.) whose only talent is in dancing performs before the image of Our Lady, to her approval. Such tales were undoubtedly inspired by the great collections known as the *Vitae patrum* and the *Miracles Nostre Dame*. Many of the c. d. are miracle tales, though not all. In the *Chevalier au barisel*, a knight is instructed by his confessor to fill a small keg with water but proves unable to do so, despite many attempts, until he sheds one tear of true repentance, which fills the keg miraculously. In the *Conte del'hermite et del jongleour*, a holy hermit is told by an angel that his companion in heaven will be a minstrel. In disgust the hermit goes to the town marketplace, where he talks with a poor minstrel and listens to his life story. Realizing the poor man is better than he, the hermit repents, and eventually the two are admitted to heaven together.—O. Schultz-Gora, *Zwei*

CONTESTS, POETIC

altfranzösische Dichtungen, 4th ed. (1919); E. Lommatzsch, *Del Tumbeor Nostre Dame* (1920); F. Lecoy, *Le chevalier au barisel* (1955). U.T.H.

CONTESTS, POETIC. See POETIC CONTESTS.

CONTEXTUALISM. A term used to describe certain doctrines of Am. New Criticism (q.v.) and other formalist or "objectivist" movements, all of which share premises concerning the primacy of the poem as an autonomous object separate in kind from other modes of discourse. Its usage derives from Murray Krieger's *The New Apologists for Poetry* (1956), which explored the concept of poetic "context" proposed by New Critical works such as Cleanth Brooks's *The Well Wrought Urn* (1947). C. claims that the verbal structure of the literary work strips words of their reference to the world and replaces that world with the internal relations of the work itself. The poem thus becomes the autonomous context that generates meanings (see AUTONOMY). C. therefore separates a work's intramural structure from the world outside the work, insists on the independence of the poem from all extrapoetic discourse, and frees the poem from the constraints of immediate social pressures and from historical contingency.

This definition of c. excludes many other kinds of "context" for the work of art. One view (Pepper) holds that a work of art can be interpreted only as an expression of its cultural moment; the context that defines and limits the meaning of a word is cultural. Similarly, biographical critics situate the works they study within the context of an author's personal history or the author's whole corpus considered as a single extended work or verbal context. Myth or archetypal critics describe one or more mythic narratives as the context that supports the literary text (see MYTH CRITICISM). Marxist critics invoke History as the ultimate context in which all texts are written and read (see MARXIST CRITICISM). None of these theories would be considered contextualist in the formalist sense, however, because in each case the context is exterior to the poem and constitutes a ground to which the text is referred.

The theoretical origins of the formalist concept of c. may be traced to Aristotle's privileging of the formal coherence of a work over its mimetic correspondence to the world, for "probable impossibilities" over "improbable possibilities." The modern roots of the term lie in Kant's separation of the "disinterested" aesthetic experience (see DISINTERESTEDNESS) from moral judgment and practical application, and in Coleridge's claim for the "organic" unity of any beautiful object. Most directly, however, the contextualist theory is linguistic; it relies on the work of I. A. Richards for a theory of lang. that could translate Coleridge's romantic organicism into a method of formalist analysis.

In his early works (*Principles of Lit. Crit.*, 1924;

The Philosophy of Rhet., 1936), Richards distinguished poetry from science by employing the opposition between emotive and referential discourse. In science, verbal signs have relatively fixed meanings and point to objects in the external world. In poetry, such reference is blocked by the multiplication of ambiguous and ironic complexities that establish an emotional state rather than producing knowledge: the emotional impulses thus aroused in the reader are linked to each other rather than to the world. Brooks' sense of context owed much to Richards. He transformed Richards's interest in complexity, however, by conceiving of an *objective* poetic context controlled by cross-referential ironies and paradoxes. The reader discovers the interrelations among the features of the work, transformations of recognizable elements of human experience which create a new and sovereign context—the poem itself. This shift from a subjective to an objective ground for poetic meaning (q.v.) changed Richards' dichotomy between referential and emotive discourse into one between referential and contextual discourse. The poem is therefore discontinuous with other forms of discourse, and—this is the fundamental tenet of all varieties of formalism—its meaning is inseparable from the actual verbal configuration of the poem. As a result, Brooks claimed, any attempt to translate the meaning of a poem into ordinary lang. was to commit the "heresy of paraphrase" (q.v.). On the other hand, the poem may be said to enhance our everyday life by expanding the forms in which that life is ordinarily experienced.

C. has been criticized on two fronts. Its insistence on the discontinuity between the work and the world led to charges of aestheticism (Ohmann). Even critics willing to grant c. its formalist limits, however, have been skeptical about the poem's discontinuity with other discourse and the total coherence of the poem's contextual system (Sutton). After 1970, such premises began to appear hopelessly idealist and naive in the light of deconstructive critiques that insisted on (1) the tropological basis of all lang. and (2) the universal tendency of lang. to expose the limits of its own metaphoric claims (see DECONSTRUCTION). Formalism, incl. c., lacked a viable defense against these charges, and the influence of contextualist critics rapidly waned in the face of the more skeptical philosophical rigor of poststructuralist theory.

Nevertheless, Krieger has maintained a strong contemporary defense of contextualist theory by expanding the formalist premises of c. to recognize the phenomenological dimension of literary response. In his *Theory of Crit.: A Trad. and Its System* (1976) and *Poetic Presence and Illusion* (1979), Krieger admits the inevitably incomplete nature of actual poems and their equally inevitable tendency to turn outward to the world rather than inward to their own creations. Rather than cancelling their referential properties, Krieger argues, the metaphoric terms of the poem actually carry within them the seeds of their metonymic association with the world, opening the poem to the vicissitudes of that world even as the poem struggles for independence from it. For Krieger, poetic "autonomy," the perfect, self-sufficient unity of the poem, is not a property of the object "out there" but is produced by the poem as an "intentional" object of human desire, an illusion governed by the formal properties of poetic lang. but situated somewhere between the objective ground of imperfect words and the reader's subjective dream of a perfect world. By calling attention to the metaphoric presence of the poem as a *self-conscious* illusion, Krieger argues that the poem satisfies our human needs for wholeness and meaning without denying the chaotic complexities of the external world. Krieger's dialectical analysis of the interaction between metaphor and metonymy in poetic discourse thus resembles the contextualist distinction between poetic and ordinary discourse, and his defense of the importance of formal closure in human experience resurrects the most fundamental value of c. against the radical philosophical skepticism of deconstruction. See also CRITICISM; TENSION; THEORY.

Richards; S. C. Pepper, *Aesthetic Quality* (1938); Brooks; C. Brooks, "Irony as a Principle of Structure," *Literary Opinion in America*, ed. M. D. Zabel (1951); M. Krieger, *The New Apologists for Poetry* (1956), *Theory of Crit.* (1976), *Poetic Presence and Illusion* (1979); W. Sutton, "Contextualist Theory and Crit. as a Social Act," *JAAC* 19 (1961); G. Graff, *Poetic Statement and Critical Dogma* (1970); L. W. Hyman, "Autonomy and Distance in a Literary Work," *JAAC* 31 (1973); R. Ohmann, *Eng. in America* (1976); Wellek, v. 5, ch. 7, v. 6, ch. 11; *Murray Krieger and Contemp. Critical Theory*, ed. B. Henricksen (1986).　　　　　　　M.K.; M.CL.

CONTRACTION. See ELISION; METRICAL TREATMENT OF SYLLABLES; SUBSTITUTION.

CONTRASTIVE STRESS. See ACCENT.

CONTRE-REJET. See REJET.

CONUNDRUM. See RIDDLE.

CONVENTION. By "c." is meant any rule that by implicit agreement between a writer and some of his or her readers (or of his audience) allows him certain freedoms in, and imposes certain restrictions upon, his or her treatment of style, structure, genre, and theme and enables these readers to interpret his work correctly. Combining social and objective functions, literary cs. are intersubjective; they hold (like linguistic cs.) the normative force which underlies the possibility of communication at all.

Unlike users of linguistic cs., readers who are party to literary cs. may be very few indeed, else a writer could never create a new c. (e.g. free verse or sprung rhythm [qq.v.]), revive an old c. (such as alliterative meters in modern languages [q.v.]), or abandon an old c. (the pastoral elegy). Readers who are ignorant of—or at least out of sympathy with—the c. must to some extent misinterpret a work that exemplifies it, and when the number of such readers becomes large, writers may abandon the c.—though of course works that exemplify it remain to be interpreted. Dr. Johnson in his judgment of *Lycidas* is an instance of a reader who misinterprets a work because he is ignorant of or out of sympathy with its cs. (*Life of Milton*).

Cs. govern the relations of matter to form, means to ends, and parts to wholes. Some examples of cs. of style are the rhyme scheme of the sonnet and the diction of the ballad; of structure, beginning an epic *in medias res* (q.v.) and the strophic structure of the ode; of genre, representing the subject of a pastoral elegy as a shepherd; of theme, attitudes toward love in the Cavalier lyric and toward death in the Elizabethan lyric. The function of any particular c. is determined by its relationship to the other cs. which together form the literary system. At any point in the hist. of its transmission, this system provides for the finite articulation of infinite literary possibilities.

Cs. both liberate and restrict the writer. Because cs. usually form sets and are motivated by traditional acceptance, a writer's decision to use a certain c. obliges him or her to use certain others or risk misleading the reader. The cs. of the epic, for example, allow a writer to achieve effects of scale but compel her or him to forgo the conversational idiom of the metaphysical lyric.

To break with cs. (or "rules," q.v.) is sometimes thought a merit, sometimes a defect; but such a break is never abandonment of all cs.—merely replacement of an old set with a new. Wordsworth condemns 18th-c. poetry for using poetic diction (Preface to the 1800 *Lyrical Ballads*); F. R. Leavis condemns Georgian poetry for adhering to "19th-c. cs. of 'the poetical.'" The institutional character of c. supports theories of literary change based on the dialectic of trad. and innovation. In the New Criticism (q.v.), "conventional 'materials'" are "rendered dramatic and moving" by the individual work (Brooks 98), while in Rus. Formalism (q.v.), dominant cs. change in function as they are displaced by the nascent ones they contain.

The social nature of cs. also distinguishes them from universals. R. S. Crane proposes that the sense of "c." be restricted to denote "any characteristic of the matter or technique of a poem the reason for the presence of which cannot be inferred from the necessities of the form envisaged but must be sought in the historical circumstances of its composition" (198). In other words, those features that all works in a certain genre must by definition share are not (in Crane's sense) cs. He would not count an unhappy ending as a c. of tragedy but does count the chorus of Gr. tragedy as such. Structuralism (q.v.), by contrast, concedes the conventionality of all norms but seeks to identify the universal relational laws by which they are organized. The pervasiveness of c. accounts for poststructuralism for the absorption of subjectivity and authorial intention into *écriture*, the autonomous productivity of writing as an institution— (Barthes, 1953, 17–29) and for the concept of a plural, "writable" text whose meaning is unintelligible in traditional, "readerly" terms and must be written or invented by its readers (1970, 11–12). In the New Historicism (see HISTORICISM), the social basis of literary cs. allows for their resituation in relation to the cs. of nonliterary discourse and of nondiscursive practices and institutions. Because cs. mediate between nature (q.v.) and its representation, as well as between authors and readers, different theories of c. (and different historical periods) will lay stress on their relation to universals or to the poetic system, to the individual or to society.

J. L. Lowes, *C. and Revolt in Poetry* (1922); F. R. Leavis, *New Bearings in Eng. Poetry* (1932); Brooks; R. S. Crane, *The Langs. of Crit. and the Structure of Poetry* (1953); R. Barthes, *Le Degre zero de l'écriture* (1953), *S/Z* (1970); R. M. Browne, *Theories of C. in Contemp. Am. Crit.* (1956); N. Frye, "Nature and Homer," *Fables of Identity* (1963); S. R. Levin, "The Cs. of Poetry," *Literary Style: A Symposium*, ed. S. Chatman (1971); V. Forrest-Thomson, "Levels in Poetic C.," *JES* 2 (1972); J. Culler, *Structuralist Poetics* (1976), "C. and Meaning: Derrida and Austin," *NLH* 13 (1981); L. Manley, *C., 1500–1750* (1980), "Concepts of C. and Models of Critical Discourse," *NLH* 13, 1 (1981)—spec. iss. on c.; M. Steinmann, "Superordinate Genre Cs.," *Poetics* 10 (1981); Fowler; *NLH* 14, 2 (1983)—spec. iss. on c.; C. E. Reeves, "The Langs. of C.," *PoT* 7 (1986), "'Conveniency to Nature': Literary Art and Arbitrariness," *PMLA* 101 (1986).   M.ST.; L.M.

CONVERSATION POEM. A type of informal, colloquial poem whose tone is meant to echo relaxed conversation. The term originates in Coleridge's subtitle for his blank verse meditative lyric, "The Nightingale," and has since been applied to other of his poems, incl. "The Eolian Harp," "This Lime-Tree Bower My Prison," and "Frost at Midnight," as well as to Wordsworth's Tintern Abbey poem ("Lines"). Like the dramatic monologue (q.v.) which it anticipates, the c. p. situates itself between speech and writing, between artifice and spontaneity, and between the subjectivity of the lyric voice and the objectivity of dramatic exchange. Coleridge characterized both "Fears in Solitude" and "Reflections on having left a Place of Retirement" (originally subtitled "A Poem which affects not to be Poetry") as *sermoni propriora*, citing Horace's rubric for his *Epistles and Satires* ("more appropriate for conversation"). While Horace's epistles (and such Eng. imitations as Pope's "Epistle to Dr. Arbuthnot") provided

models for the c. p.'s informal, intimate, yet serious tone, Cowper's *Task* influenced its relaxed, frequently enjambed blank verse, its use of colloquialisms, and its apparent immediacy and spontaneity.

Central to most c. ps. is a "native auditor" (Rajan) who receives the poet's words and helps intensify the sense of immediacy. Wordsworth's *Prelude*, in which Coleridge functions as auditor, can be read as an epic c. p., Coleridge's "To William Wordsworth," in which the auditor replies to the poet, as an inverted c. p. In later 19th- and 20th-c. poetry the dramatic monologue tends to eclipse the c. p., although Robert Pinsky's "An Explanation of America" is a striking recent example of the mode.—G. M. Harper, "Coleridge's C. Ps.," *QR* 484 (1925); R. H. Fogle, "Coleridge's C. Ps.," *TSE* 5 (1955); M. H. Abrams, "Structure and Style in the Greater Romantic Lyric," *From Sensibility to Romanticism*, ed. F. W. Hilles and H. Bloom (1965); A. S. Gérard, *Eng. Romantic Poetry* (1968); T. Rajan, *Dark Interpreter* (1980).   A.R.

COPLA. Since the Sp. term "c." often means simply "stanza," it is necessary to specify the type, such as *c. de arte mayor* (see ARTE MAYOR) or *c. de arte menor* (see ARTE MENOR). The *c. de pie quebrado*, which developed during the 14th and 15th cs., is any variation of the *c. de arte menor* in which one or more lines have been reduced to half-length (four syllables or their equivalent) or half-lines have been added or both. The most famous, though not the most common, has the rhyme scheme ABcABcDEfDEf (capital letters denote full-length lines) and is often called *c.* (or *estrofa*) *de Jorge Manrique*, or *c. manriqueã* after the author of the famous *Coplas por la muerte de su padre*. The *c. real* (also called *décima*, *décima falsa*, *estancia real*, or *quintilla doble*) is an important 15th-c. variation of the *c. de arte menor*. It is a 10-line octosyllabic strophe, the equivalent of two *quintillas*, the two usually having different rhyme schemes. The *c. real* was widely used in the 16th c., but in the 17th gradually gave way in popularity to one of its late 16th-c. variations, the *espinela*. See also CANTAR.— F. Rodríguez Marín, *El alma de Andalucía en sus mejores coplas amorosas* (1929); D. C. Clarke, "The C. Real" and "The 15th-C. C. de Pie Quebrado," *HR* 10 (1942); Navarro.   D.C.C.

COQ-À-L'ÂNE ("cock and bull"). Name derived from an OF proverbial expression, "C'est bien sauté du cocq a l'asne" ("That's a fine spring from cock to ass"), which was, and still is, used to describe an incoherent manner of speaking or writing. The content of the genre is the satiric treatment of the vices, faults, and foibles of individuals, social groups, or even institutions. Clément Marot, who created the form in 1530, was the author of 4 c., all of them generally in the form of octosyllabic verse epistles of varying length. Du Bellay discusses the c. in the *Deffense et illustration de la langue françoyse* (1549).—C. E. Kinch, *La Poésie satirique de Clément Marot* (1940); Patterson; H. Meylan, *Epîtres du c.* (1956); P. Zumthor, "Fatrasie et c.," *Mélanges offerts à R. Guiette* (1961); C. A. Mayer, "C.: Définition–Invention–Attributions," *FS* 16 (1962); I. D. McFarlane, *Ren. France, 1470–1589* (1974). I.S.

CORNISH POETRY. The C. lang., now extinct, belonged to the Brythonic or "P"-Celtic group, but had closer affinities with Breton than with Welsh. It died out in the 18th c. Apart from one long narrative poem and five plays, all on religious topics, the literary remains are meager in the extreme. Although Cornwall must have supplied to medieval romance (q.v.) some of the "Matter of Britain," in the extant C. lit. this rich vein is left unexploited. The earliest verse to survive is a fragment of 41 lines on a charter dated 1340, but the poem may have been copied on it some 60 years later and seems to be part of a lost play. In it a speaker gives advice on marriage (drawn from C. folklore) to a lady. The rhyme scheme is *aabccb*, with lines varying from 4 to 9 syllables. *Pascon agan Arluth* (The Passion of our Lord) is a narrative poem of 259 octaves of 7-syllable trochaic lines, the lines rhyming alternately. The earliest ms. is mid 15th c. The theme is the fasting and temptation of Christ, followed by the story of Holy Week.

The main interest of C. p. lies in the plays. These were composed by men of learning but for a popular audience and were performed in open-air theaters, the "plenys-an-gwary," spaces enclosed by circular banks of earth now known as "rounds," some of which can still be seen, e.g. at St. Just and Perranzabuloe. Three of the plays, called the *Ordinalia*, form a sequence. These are the *Origo mundi* (2846 lines), based on Old Testament history and some incongruent legendary material, the *Passio domini* (3242 lines), recounting the life and death of Christ, and the *Resurrectio domini* (2646 lines), which has a greater accretion of legend, incl. saints' lives and the death of Pilate. The rhythm is basically trochaic but stress regularity is not meticulously observed. Rhymes are often stricter to the eye than to the ear, a sure sign of learned composition. Full lines of 8 or 7 syllables can rhyme alternately, as can shorter lines or half-lines of 4 syllables, and lines of varying or equal length within the same sequence or "stanza" can conform to *aabccb* or *aabaab* rhyme schemes. More intricate patterns also occur, but otherwise such metrical features as alliteration and internal rhyme are random and not woven into a strict pattern as in Welsh *cynghanedd* (q.v.).

Beunans Meriasek (The Life of St. Meriasek, 4568 lines), was discovered by Stokes in a ms. written in 1504. This play has linguistic forms which indicate a later period than the *Ordinalia*, but metrically it is similar. Local references associate it with the cult of Meriasek at Camborne, a 7th-c. saint whose legendary life forms the topic of the play. The latest of the C. plays, at least in its extant form, is *Gwreans an Bys* (The Creation of the World, 2548 lines); the earliest ms. is dated 1611. The play borrows much from *Origo mundi* but has features of its own. Lucifer and his demons revert to Eng. except when they are on their good behavior—then they speak C. The most noticeable metrical innovation is a more frequent disregard of syllable-counting. In all the plays there are passages of touching poignancy and considerable literary merit, but the quality is not sustained.

The few remaining scraps of late C. verse (mostly 17th-c.) indicate a falling away from the more strictly syllabic verse patterns of medieval C. It is uncertain whether this was merely a phase of the decay of the lang. or an increased awareness of stress as a metrical principle. A few enthusiasts in our own day have learned C., and poems in this long-neglected Celtic tongue have been written and published in recent years. A "C. Song Movement" which demanded of its participants that they should compose their own texts as well as sing traditional ones arose in the 1970s. Among the more prominent members were Richard Gendall and Anthony Snell. Other recent C. poets of note incl. the meditative D. Wall, the sensitive Brian Webb, and the ever-resourceful Tim Saunders.— *The Ancient C. Drama*, ed. and tr. E. Norris, 2 v. (1859, rpt. 1963); "Pascon agan Arluth: The Play of the Sacrament," *TPS* (1860–61), "*Gwreans an Bys*," *TPS* (1864), "*Beunans Meriasek*" (1872; tr. M. Harris, 1977), all ed. W. Stokes, *TPS* (1860–61, 1864, 1872); H. Jenner, "The Hist. and Lit. of the Ancient C. Lang.," *Jour. of the Brit. Archaeological Assoc.* 33 (1877), *Handbook of the C. Lang.* (1904); D. C. Fowler, "The Date of the C. *Ordinalia*," *MS* 23 (1961); R. Longsworth, *The C. Ordinalia: Religion and Dramaturgy* (1967); P. B. Ellis, *The C. Lang. and its Lit.* (1974); J. A. Bakere, *The C. Ordinalia: A Crit. Study* (1980); *The Creation of the World*, ed. and tr. P. Neuss (1983). D.M.L.; J.E.C.W.

CORONA. Like the *catena* (chain), the c. ("crown" or "garland") is one of several formal devices in It. poetry for joining a series of sonnets to one another (see SONNET; SONNET SEQUENCE). In the simple c., the last line of each of the first six sonnets is used as the first line of the succeeding sonnet, with the last line of the seventh being a repetition of the opening line of the first; a further restriction prohibits the repetition of any given rhyme sound once it has been used in the series. We find the c. appearing early in the hist. of the It. sonnet with Fazio degli Uberti's series on the seven deadly sins. A more complex c., not unlike the sestina (q.v.), consists of a "sonetto magistrale" preceded by 14 dependent sonnets: the first of these begins with the first line of the master-sonnet and ends with its second line; the second sonnet begins with its second line and ends with its third, and so on, until the 14th sonnet, which begins with the 14th line of the master-sonnet and ends with its first; the master-sonnet then closes the interwoven garland. In Eng. the best-known c. is that which serves as the prologue to John Donne's *Holy Sonnets*; it consists of seven sonnets, one on each mythic stage in the Life of Christ, beginning and ending with this line: "Deigne at my hands this crown of prayer and praise." Written shortly before 1610 (pub. 1633), Donne's c. draws upon both the It. trad. of the *c. di sonnetti* and upon a specific way of reciting the Rosary; he may well have known, too, Annibel Caro's famous c. of 1588 linking 9 sonnets and Chapman's "Coronet for his Mistress Philosophy" of 1595 linking 10. A 20th-c. example is the classical *C. de sonettos* (1953) written in blank verse by the Brazilian poet Geir de Campos. See also CONCATENATION; RING COMPOSITION.—L. L. Martz, *The Poetry of Meditation* (1954); W. Mönch, *Das Sonett* (1955).   E.L.R.; T.V.F.B.

CORONACH. A funeral lament (q.v.) or dirge originating in Ireland and in the Scottish Highlands. The term, which in Gaelic means "wailing together," owes its currency in Eng. literary history to Sir Walter Scott, who refers to the custom in his novels and introduces into his *Lady of the Lake* (3.16) a c. of his own composition beginning: "He is gone on the mountain. / He is lost to the forest, / Like a summer-dried fountain, / When our need was the sorest. . . ." According to Scott's account, the c. was usually sung by women.   A.PR.

CORRELATIVE VERSE (Lat. *versus rapportati*, Fr. *vers rapportés*). A literary style and subgenre in which lines or stanzas exhibit two (or more) series of elements, each element in the first corresponding to one in the same position in the second, respectively. This structuring device is known as correlation. An epigram from the *Greek Anthology* (3.241) provides an example: "You [wine, are] boldness, youth, strength, wealth, country / To the shy, the old, the weak, the poor, the foreigner." Examples of correlation are found in Gr. poetry from the 3d c. B.C. and in Lat. poetry from the 1st c. A.D. Med. Lat. poets were very fond of the device, as were the Occitan troubadours, and early Ren. poets made use of it (Jodelle, "Des Astres"; Du Bellay, *Amours* 17). A special type of c. v., the disseminative-recapitulative type, was used by Petrarch and subsequently spread, together with Petrarchism (q.v.), throughout Italy, France, Spain, and England in the 16th and early 17th cs. Examples include Sidney's

> Vertue, beautie, and speeche, did
>   strike, wound, charme
> My heart, eyes, ears, with wonder, love
>   delight.   (Pal 37)

(see also *Astrophil* nos. 43, 65, 100; *Certain Sonnets* 18; *Old Arcadia* 60), Shakespeare's

> Ho! hearts, tongues, figures, scribes,
>   bards, poets, cannot

> Think, speak, cast, write, sing, num-
>   ber—ho!—
> His love to Antony.
>   (*Antony and Cleopatra* 3.2.16–18),

and Milton's

>   Air, Water, Earth
> By Fowl, Fish, Beast, was flown, was
>   swum, was walkt,
>   (*PL*, 7.502);

others appear in Donne.

C. v. has been found in Sanskrit, Persian, Arabic, and Chinese poetry (Alonso 1944) and thus seems to be one form of structure available to any verse tradition.

D. Alonso, "Versos plurimembros y poemas correlativos," *Revista de la Biblioteca, Archivo y Museo del Ayuntamiento de Madrid* 13 (1944), "Antecedentes griegos y latinos de la poesía correlativa moderna," *Estudios dedicados a Menéndez Pidal*, v. 4 (1953), "Poesía correlativa inglesa en los siglos XVI y XVII," *Filología moderna* 2 (1961), *Pluralità e correlazione in poesia* (1971); D. Alonso and C. Bousoño, *Seis calas en la expresión literaria española* (1951); Curtius 286; J. G. Fucilla, "A Rhetorical Pattern in Ren. and Baroque Poetry," *SRen* 3 (1956); L. P. Wilkinson, *Golden Lat. Artsitry* (1963); N. C. Andreasen, "Donne and the C. Trad.," *DAI* 24 (1964): 3320A; H. Zeman, "Die 'Versus rapportati' in der deutschen Lit. des XVI. und XVII. Jhs.," *Arcadia* 9 (1974).   T.V.F.B.; R.MI.

CORRESPONDENCE. See EQUIVALENCE; RESPONSION.

CORRESPONDENCE RULES. See GENERATIVE METRICS; METER.

COUNTERPOINT. (1) *Meter and Language.* One of the central tenets of modern metrical theory has been the distinction between rhythm and meter, developed most clearly in 20th-c. structural metrics as the interaction between "prose rhythm" and meter (Fowler). This distinction amounts to saying that the intonation (including stressing) that a line of poetry would receive if it were ordinary speech or prose changes when it comes under the influence of meter. Many 20th-c. metrists have tried to describe what happens when we read a line of metrical verse, particularly since such lines often do not fully conform to the abstract pattern of the meter. Such efforts at once raise questions about whether meter is in fact abstract, about what constitutes a performance (q.v.) of a poem, and about how and how far meter alters normal intonation when we read poetry aloud or silently. Some have found attractive the concept of "c.," taken over from music and first applied to poetry by Hegel (*Phenomenology of Mind*, 1807; *Aesthetics*, 1835–38). In music, c. is the result of two melodic lines proceeding, or diverging, simultaneously, so that the ear actually hears two differing lines at once. In metrics, however, the term has been used more loosely to refer to the notion that when we read a line we hear the actual line with our outer ear, while the "mind's ear" plays back simultaneously the ideal metrical pattern to which the line is meant to conform; the recognition of the differences between the two patterns, it is claimed, makes for most of the pleasure or interest in reading metrical verse. C. S. Lewis once called this "double audition."

However, a number of critics have rightly complained that only one line is ever actually heard (Wright 188), and even then in the mind not the ear; some of these critics have preferred to speak of metrical "tension" between the actual line and the ideal pattern "behind" or "underneath" it, while others have preferred to speak of "expectations" created in the mind on the basis of prior experience of metrical verse—expectations which, in the microenvironment of the line during the reading process, are minutely and rapidly fulfilled or thwarted, creating thereby a complex and subtle interplay of cognitive response. The disagreement concerns precision in terms; the essential question is whether in cognition we are aware of the meter and the prose rhythm of the line as two separate entities running together or whether they merge into one thing, the metrical pattern "tilting" (Wimsatt's term) what would otherwise be the normal articulation of the line. Note however that the musical sense, "two or more strains of tune going on together," is what Gerard Manley Hopkins has in mind when he speaks of "counterpoint rhythm" (q.v.). Hollander (5–7) points out that the correct analogy from music would be *syncopation*, the momentary alteration of timing in a run of notes which *gives the impression* of a new time signature, when the listener knows that in fact it is not—the effect is only a temporary illusion. See METER.

(2) *Line and Syntax*. Similarly, critics also sometimes speak of a "c." between the metrical frame that is the line and the syntactic frame that is the sentence. Very little verse is such that every line-end coincides with sentence-end; consequently, segmentation is differentially effected, though in but the one set of words. Line-ends falling elsewhere than at a syntactic (phrasal) boundary create the tensioned phenomenon of enjambment (q.v.), as do syntactic boundaries within lines verse sentences and verse paragraphs (q.v.). Here again, as above, the term is applied by analogy from music and usually is meant to denote the reader's multiple simultaneous awareness of two patterns which do not coincide but do not clash: in the terminology of physics, the interference is constructive.—Hollander; G. T. Wright, *Shakespeare's Metrical Art* (1988).   T.V.F.B.

COUNTERPOINT RHYTHM. C., or syncopation, is a rhythmical effect achieved through metrical variation, that is, through temporary departure from the dominant metrical base, so that two rhythmic patterns begin to be noticed simultaneously, the new one being heard against the ground rhythm of the meter (q.v.). Thus, in these lines from Yeats's "Leda and the Swan" (x denotes weak syllables, / strong ones):

x / x / x x / x / x /
Above the staggering girl, her thighs caressed

x x / / x / / x x /
By the dark webs, her nape caught in his bill,

the dominant iambic is interrupted in the first line by a momentary metrical variation, a third-foot anapest—"stagg'ring" would maintain the meter but lose the aptness of a metrical "stagger"—and in the second by a pyrrhic substitution in the first foot, a spondaic substitution in the second, and by a trochaic substitution in the fourth. The rhythmical figure established in the 4th through 7th syllables of line 1 and 7th through 10th of line 2 will, if repeated again close enough for the echo to be noticed, come to constitute c. Note that c. cannot occur except against the ground of a relatively regular meter, for it is the ground which makes variation possible at all.

But intermittent single-foot substitutions like these are not sufficient to create "c. r." as described by Gerard Manley Hopkins. If an alternative rhythm is to be superimposed on, or heard against, a given metrical base, then (1) it should normally occupy at least two consecutive feet (and particularly, perhaps, what Hopkins calls the "sensitive" second foot), and (2) it should constitute a *reversal* of the dominant meter (e.g. trochaic rhythm mounted on iambic, or dactylic on anapaestic). Criterion (2) is a necessary qualification both because pyrrhic and spondaic feet can only be substitute *feet*, not substitute *rhythms*, and because any counterpointing of, say, a rising rhythm (iambic) by another rising rhythm (anapestic) will produce not c. r., but what Hopkins calls "logaoedic" or mixed rhythm. C. r. occurs in the first two feet of this line from Hopkins' "God's Grandeur":

/ x / x x / x / x /
Generations have trod, have trod, have trod.

Hopkins claims that if the poet counterpoints throughout, so that only the c. r. comes to be heard, then the line will be "sprung" into a new mode, "sprung rhythm" (q.v.). This is not convincing. The consistent superimposition of a c. r. on another meter will only produce the c. r., which would then no longer be counterpointing. Sprung rhythm can only be arrived at by the consistent substitution of a *variety* of c. feet.—G. M. Hopkins, "Author's Preface," *Poetical Works*, ed. N. H. MacKenzie, 5th ed. (1990).   C.S.; T.V.F.B.

COUNTRY-HOUSE POEM. See EKPHRASIS.

COUPE. Cs. are the vertical or oblique bar-lines used to separate measures and so indicate the rhythmic segmentation of the Fr. line (cf. Eng. foot-divisions). Normally they fall immediately after each accented vowel inside the line. In fact, the c. marks the occurrence of accentuation, and although it is usually accompanied by syntactic juncture in varying degree, it has no necessary connection with juncture; in Lamartine's "Ainsi / toujours poussés / vers de nouveaux / rivages," the measures are 2 / 4 / 4 / 2.

The c. is a tool of verse-analysis, a convenience in scansion which has little bearing on the enunciation of the line. It does have some consequences for enunciation, however, where the Fr. *e atone* (or mute *-e*) is concerned. When a tonic syllable is followed by an articulated (unelided) *e atone*, it is customary to place the c. immediately after the accented vowel, so that the *e atone* is counted as the first syllable of the following rhythmic measure. This c., called the *c. enjambante*, produces a seamless and supple continuity in the reading of the line. But there may be syntactic or expressive reasons for marking a juncture after the *e atone*, so that the *e atone* more properly belongs with the accented vowel rather than initiating the measure that follows (*c. lyrique*, sometimes called *c. féminine*). But the *c. lyrique* is fairly exceptional and produces rhythmic disruption, fragmentation, and discontinuity. In Fr. metrics the caesura (q.v.) is both a c. and something more: a fixed metrical articulation which combines measures into larger units (hemistichs), divides the line intonationally, and acts as a fulcrum about which the semantic forces of the line play. See now FOOT.—Morier; Mazaleyrat; Scott; C. Scott, *A Question of Syllables* (1986).   C.S.

COUPLET (Lat. *distich*, Fr. *rime plate* and [obs.] *vers commun*, Ger. *Reimpaar*; from Lat. *copula*; Welsh *cywydd*). Two contiguous lines of verse which function as a metrical unit and are so marked (usually) either by rhyme or syntax or both. Since the advent of rhymed verse in the European vernaculars in the 12th century, the c. has counted as one of the principal units of versification in Western poetry, whether as an independent poem of a gnomic or epigrammatic nature (see EPIGRAM), as a subordinate element in other stanzaic forms— two of the principal stanzaic forms of the later Middle Ages and the Ren., *ottava rima* and rhyme royal [qq.v.], both conclude with a c., as does the Shakespearean sonnet [see SONNET]—or as a stanzaic form for extended verse composition, narrative or philosophical. In each of these modes the tightness of the c. and closeness of its rhyme make it esp. suited for purposes of formal conclusion, summation, or epigrammatic comment. In dramatic verse, the c. occurs in the cl. Fr. drama, the older Ger. and Dutch drama, and the "heroic plays" (q.v.) of Restoration England. It also fills an important function in Elizabethan and Jacobean drama as a variation from the standard blank verse (q.v.), its principal use being to mark for the audience, aurally, the conclusion of a scene or a climax in dramatic action. The c. occupies a unique and interesting position in the typology of verseforms. Standing midway between stichic verse and strophic, it permits the fluidity of the former while also taking advantage of some of the effects of the latter.

In the medieval Fr. epic, the older assonanted *laisse* (q.v.) gives way to rhyme in cs. around the 12th century. The earliest examples, such as the *Cantilene de Sainte Eulalie* and the *Vie de Saint Léger* are in closed couplets (Meyer 7). It is Chrétien de Troyes (fl. after 1150) who seems to have introduced *enjambement* (see ENJAMBMENT), which by the 13th century is common (e.g. Raoul de Houdenc). After the *Chanson de Roland* (ca. 1100), first the decasyllabic then the alexandrine c. is the dominant form of OF narrative and dramatic poetry (see DECASYLLABLE; ALEXANDRINE). In the hands of the masters of Fr. Classicism—Corneille, Moliére, Racine, La Fontaine—this is end-stopped and relatively self-contained, but a freer use of enjambment is found among the romantics. Under Fr. influence, the alexandrine c. became the dominant metrical form of Ger. and Dutch narrative and dramatic verse of the 17th and 18th centuries. Subsequently, a more indigenous Ger. c., the tetrameter c. called *Knittelvers* (q.v.), was revived by Goethe and Schiller. The term "c." is sometimes used in Fr. prosody with the meaning of stanza, as in the *c. carré* (square c.), an octave composed of octosyllables.

In Eng. poetry, though the octosyllabic or iambic tetrameter c. has been used well (see OCTOSYLLABLE), by far the most important c. form has been isometrical and composed of two lines of iambic pentameter. As perfected by Dryden and Pope, the so-called "heroic c." (q.v.) is "closed"— syntax and thought fit perfectly into the envelope of rhyme and meter sealed at the end of the c.—and in this form dominates the poetry of the neoclassical period: "Know then thyself, presume not God to scan," says Pope in the *Essay on Man*, "The proper study of Mankind is Man." When meter and syntax thus conclude together, the c. is said to be "end-stopped" (q.v.).

The c. is "open" when enjambed, i.e. when the syntactic and metrical frames do not close together at the end of the c., the sentence being carried forward into subsequent cs. to any length desired and ending at any point in the line. This form of the c. is historically older and not much less common than the closed form in Eng. poetry as a whole. It was introduced by Chaucer and continued to be produced (e.g. Spenser, *Mother Hubberd's Tale* [1591]; Nicholas Breton, *Machivils Instructions* [1613]) well into the 17th c. during the very time when the closed or "heroical" c. was being established. Puttenham and other Ren. critics labeled this older form "riding rhyme" (origin of this term unknown). It was further explored in the 19th century (e.g. Browning), proving then as ever esp. suited for continuous narrative and didactic verse. Long sentences in enjambed cs. constitute the rhymed equivalent of the "verse paragraph" (q.v.) in blank verse. In a medial form between closed and open, each two-line sentence ends at the end of the *first* line of the c., making for systematic counterpointing of syntax against meter.

Not all Eng. cs. are isometric, however. Poets as diverse as George Herbert and Robert Browning have developed c. forms which rhyme lines of unequal length: " . . . With their triumphs and their glories and the rest. / Love is best!" (Browning, "Love Among the Ruins"). A related heterometric form of c. which developed in Gr. and Lat., a hexameter followed by a pentameter, came to be known for its generic usage as the *elegiac distich* (q.v.). Passed down through the Middle Ages as a semipopular form (e.g. the *Distichs of Cato*), it survived into modern times. See DISTICH; ELEGIAC DISTICH.

Schipper; P. Meyer, "Le C. de deux vers," *Romania* 23 (1894); C. H. G. Helm, *Zur Rhythmik der kurzen Reimpaare des XVI Jahrhunderten* (1895); C. C. Spiker, "The Ten-Syllable Rhyming C.," *West Va. Univ. Philol. Papers* 1 (1929); P. Verrier, *Le Vers français*, 3 v. (1931–32), v. 2; G. Wehowsky, *Schmuckformen und Formbruch in der deutschen Reimpaardichtung des Mittelalters* (1936); E. N. S. Thompson, "The Octosyllabic C.," *PQ* 18 (1939): F. W. Ness, *The Use of Rhyme in Shakespeare's Plays* (1941), esp. ch. 5, App. C; B. H. Smith, *Poetic Closure* (1968), 70 ff.; J. A. Jones, *Pope's C. Art* (1969); W. B. Piper, *The Heroic C.* (1969); Brogan, 389 ff. T.V.F.B.; W.B.P.

COURTLY LOVE.

    I. EUROPEAN
    II. ARABIC AND PERSIAN

I. EUROPEAN C. l. (Fr. *amour courtois*, Occitan *fine amors*; Ger. *Frauendienst*) is a stylized and idealized treatment of love widely employed during the Middle Ages in the amatory poetry and romance writing of Western Europe, esp. France, and continued in much of the lit. of the Ren. both on the Continent and in England. In the 12th c. a marked change in the conception of man's relationship to woman developed in southern France in the poetry of the troubadours (q.v., and see OCCITAN POETRY); this shift, which owes something to Ovid, is perhaps most clearly reflected in the lyrics of the troubadour Bernart de Ventadorn; in northern France it is most evident in the romances of Chrétien de Troyes, esp. the *Cligès*.

There is little doubt about the existence of courts of l. as a form of social diversion in the later Middle Ages, but they did not exist as formal judicial assemblies. The term c. l. itself, however, was not known in medieval times but is derived from *amour courtois*, first used by Gaston Paris in a long essay on Chrétien's *Lancelot* in 1883 (*Romania*). Much of the misunderstanding about c. l. will disappear if it is kept in mind that the term is modern but the concept is not, and that c. l. may be ennobling l. in one poem, adulterous in another, and unrequited l. in a third. In this respect the late 12th-c. treatise on l., the *De amore* of Andreas Capellanus, who is traditionally thought to have been a chaplain at the court of Marie of Champagne, is still helpful as a point of reference. (An alternate title found in some mss., *De arte honeste amandi*, is more aptly descriptive, for the idea of l. as an art is basic to the notion of c. l.). The view that Andreas most probably wrote with tongue in cheek (and that he is often contradictory) does not lessen the value of his treatise for the modern reader. This longish work is divided into three parts: Books One and Two, which constitute an elaborate analysis of l., largely through a series of dialogues, and the much shorter Book Three, "The Rejection of L.," which concludes with a retraction.

C. l. is a noble passion: the courtly lover idealizes his beloved; she, his sovereign lady, occupies an exalted position above him. His feelings for her ennoble him and make him more worthy; her beauty of body and soul makes him long for union with her, not for passion's sake but as a means of achieving the ultimate in moral excellence. It is a striking paradox that l. as presented by a few of the early troubadours in their noble love-songs (*cansos*) is adulterous and illicit and, at at the same time, ennobling and conducive to virtue. After 1150, *cansos* celebrate covert but not explicitly adulterous love.

The product of an essentially aristocratic and chivalric society, c. l. is intrinsically Ovidian in much of its machinery (its imagery of warfare and love-sickness and its codification of a developing relationship), but it also owes much to the feudalism under which it flourished (imagery of the lover as vassal) and to medieval Christianity, esp. the cult of the Virgin (the exaltation of the beloved). Through literary contacts and patronage, notably that of Eleanor of Aquitane and her offspring, the troubadour concept of l. spread to northern France, where it provided the essentials for the l. poetry of the trouvères (q.v.) and became an important element in the medieval romance (q.v.; cf. esp. Chrétien de Troyes' *Cligès* and *Le Chevalier de la Charrette,* the most polished early treatment of the Lancelot and Guinevere story); to England, where it found its fullest early use in Chaucer, particularly his *Troilus and Criseyde;* to Germany, where it enriched the poetry of the Minnesingers (see MINNESANG); to Italy, where it attained its ultimate refinement in the poetry of the *dolce stil nuovo,* (q.v.; e.g. Guinicelli, Cavalcanti) and esp. in Dante's *Vita nuova.* Largely through the influence of Petrarch, the themes and imagery of c. l. were revitalized in the 16th c.

among Eng. poets (notably the sonneteers and Spenser; see PETRARCHISM) as well as the Fr. poets of the *Pléiade* (q.v.; e.g. Ronsard, Du Bellay). Thus any attempt to frame a single brief statement adequately describing the concept as reflected in so many lits. and forms spread over so many centuries is basically impossible. The paradoxically sensual yet idealized *fin amors* of the troubadours' *cansos* is hardly the same as the adulterous l. of Tristan and Isolde or of Lancelot and Guinevere, nor is married l. totally excluded (e.g. *Parzifal* and Chrétien's *Yvain*).

After Gaston Paris probably the most seminal work on c. l. was C. S. Lewis's *The Allegory of L.* (1936), with its tantalizingly cocksure statement: "Everyone has heard of c. l., and everyone knows that it appears quite suddenly at the end of the 11th c. in Languedoc" (2). Lewis defines c. l. as "l. of a highly specialized sort whose characteristics may be enumerated as Humility, Courtesy, Adultery, and the Religion of L." In the half-century since the publication of *The Allegory of L.* innumerable books and articles have appeared further amplifying Lewis' position or controverting it, with no slackening of the pace of their appearance. Roger Boase, for example, in discussing theories of origin, mentions Hispanic-Arabic, Chivalric-Matriarchal, Crypto-Cathar, Neoplatonic, Bernardine-Marianist, Spring Folk Ritual, and Feudal-Sociological; and Peter Dronke would range even more widely: consider his proposal "that 'the new feeling' of *amour courtois* is at least as old as Egypt of the second millenium B.C., and might indeed occur at any time and place" (I.3). At quite the opposite pole stand those who deny the very existence of c. l. and would abandon use of the term completely; D. W. Robertson, Jr., for example, has argued vigorously against the concept and has proposed that it be dropped as a critical term (in Newman 1968; reiterated in Robertson 1980). See, however, the thundering refutation by Frappier. See now LOVE POETRY; MINNESANG.

T. P. Cross and W. A. Nitze, *Lancelot and Guenevere: A Study on the Origins of C. L.* (1930); Lewis; T. A. Kirby, *Chaucer's* Troilus: *A Study in C. L.* (1940); A. Capellanus, *The Art of C. L.*, tr. J. J. Parry (1941); A. J. Denomy, "An Inquiry into the Origins of C. L.," *MS* 6 (1944), *The Heresy of C. L.* (1947), "C. L. and Courtliness," *Speculum* 28 (1953); T. Silverstein, "Andreas, Plato, and the Arabs: Remarks on Some Recent Accounts of C. L.," *MP* 47 (1949); H. J. Weigand, *Three Chapters on C. L. in Arthurian France and Germany* (1956); D. de Rougemont, *L. in the Western World*, tr. M. Belgion, rev. ed. (1957); W. T. H. Jackson, "The *De amore* of Andreas Capellanus and the Practice of L. at Court," *RR* 49 (1958); M. Valency, *In Praise of L.* (1958); F. Schlösser, *Andreas Capellanus, seine Minnelehre und das christliche Weltbild um 1200* (1960); J. F. Benton, "The Court of Champagne as a Literary Center," *Speculum* 36 (1961), "The Evidence for Andreas Capellanus Re-examined Again," *SP* 59 (1962),

"Clio and Venus: An Historical View of Med. L.," in Newman (1968); D. W. Robertson, Jr., *Preface to Chaucer* (1962), *Essays in Med. Culture* (1980); E. T. Donaldson, "The Myth of C. L.," *Ventures* 5 (1965); F. Goldin, *The Mirror of Narcissus in the C. L. Lyric* (1967); *The Meaning of C. L.*, ed. F. X. Newman (1968); Dronke; D. Kelly, "C. L. in Perspective: The Hierarchy of L. in Andreas Capellanus," *Traditio* 24 (1968); J. M. Steadman, "'C. L.' as a Problem of Style," *Chaucer und seine Zeit*, ed. A. Esch (1968); G. de Lorris and J. de Meun, *The Romance of the Rose*, tr. C. Dahlberg (1971); J. Frappier, "Sur un procès fait à l'amour courtois," *Romania* 93 (1972); F. L. Utley, "Must We Abandon the Concept of C. L.?" *M&H* n.s. 3 (1972); P. Wapnewski, *Was ist minne* (1975); L. P. Topsfield, *Troubadours and L.* (1975); *In Pursuit of Perfection: C. L. in Med. Lit.*, ed. J. M. Ferrante and G. D. Economou (1975); H. A. Kelly, *L. and Marriage in the Age of Chaucer* (1975); R. Boase, *The Origin and Meaning of C. L.* (1977); D. Kelly, *Med. Imagination* (1978); J. C. Moore, "C. L. as a Problem of Terminology," *JHI* 40 (1979); J. D. Burnley, "Fine Amor: Its Meaning and Context," *RES* 31 (1980); *The Expansion and Transformation of Courtly Lit.*, ed. N. B. Smith and J. T. Snow (1980); *Andreas Capellanus on L.*, ed. and tr. P. G. Walsh (1982); I. Singer, *The Nature of L.*, 3 v. (1984–87); A. Karnein, "La Réception de *De amore* au XIIIe siècle," *Romania* 102 (1981), *De amore in volkssprachlicher Literatur* (1985); R. Schnell, *Causa amoris* (1985); B. Bowden, "C. L.," *Women's Studies Encyc.*, ed. H. Tierney, v. 2 (1990). T.A.K.

II. ARABIC AND PERSIAN. In Ar. a lit. of c. l. developed in the 7th–10th cs. with the growth of urban court culture and increasing contact with Iranian and Hellenistic sources. While there is no specific Ar. term for c. l., the concept of refined l. seen in this lit., and its relation to notions of chivalry and manly virtue (*futūwa, murūwa*), justify use of the term as a critical concept. In the Ar. poetry of c. l. two main tendencies appear: the "pure" l. of the desert expressed by "'Udhrī" poets (such as Jamīl, d. 710), and the more sophisticated relationships described by court poets such as al-ʿAbbās ibn al-Aḥnaf (d. ca. 808). An extensive prose lit. on l. also developed which included anthologies of l. poetry, works on the nature and effects of l., and codes of practice of the proper conduct of refined l.

The contribution of Iranian poets and writers to the devel. of the Ar. lit. of c. l. was particularly marked. Iranian notions of c. l. may reflect a pre-Islamic trad. as well as the impact of Hellenized learning on Iranian thought. In Islamic Persian lit., c. l. was an even more pervasive theme than in Ar. The l. relationship depicted in the exordium of the panegyric *qaṣīda* (q.v.) often figures the relation between poet and patron. The *ghazal* (q.v.) poet, in his persona of experienced lover, seeks to instruct his courtly audience in the ideals of noble l. Courtly romance often adopts a critical attitude toward the lyric stance, to which it opposes a broader ethico-philosophical concept of l.

The conventions of c. l. in Ar. and Persian are substantially the same as those of the West: the lover, totally dedicated to the service of an often capricious beloved, is ennobled through the practice of refined and selfless l. service. Notable contrasts include the virtual absence of adulterous l. (a major exception is the Persian romance *Vis and Ramin*, based on an earlier Iranian source), the prevalence of homoerotic poetry esp. in Persian, and criticism of the beloved, despite strictures to the contrary, for what might be described as the breach of l.'s contract. Moreover, with the exceptions of 'Udhrī poetry and of mystical poetry which employs the lang. of c. l. to express the concept of divine l., the sensual aspect of l., while not necessarily explicit, is rarely renounced: human l., a necessary step on the ladder to divine l., is to be sought rather than avoided, so long as it is pursued for the sake of virtue and in a spirit of selflessness.—R. Blachère, *Hist. de la litt. arabe*, 3 v. (1956–66); J.-C. Vadet, *L'Esprit courtois en orient dans les cinq premiers siècles de l'Hégire* (1968); L. A. Giffen, *Theory of Profane L. Among the Arabs* (1971); R. Boase (see bibl. to section I); A. K. Blumstein, *Misogyny and Idealization in the C. Romance* (1977); M. R. Menocal, *The Ar. Role in Med. Lit. Hist.* (1987); J. S. Meisami, *Med. Persian Court Poetry* (1987). J.S.M.

COURTLY MAKERS. A group of court poets who, during the reign of Henry VIII, introduced the two most important forms of Ren. poetry, one strophic, one stichic, into England from Italy and France, laying thereby the foundations for the great poetic achievements of their Elizabethan successors Sidney, Spenser, and Shakespeare. One of their number, Sir Thomas Wyatt (1503?–42), wrote the first Eng. sonnets (q.v.), adapted from the Petrarchan model; another, Henry Howard, Earl of Surrey (1517?–47), produced the first Eng. blank verse (q.v.) in his tr. of two books of the *Aeneid* (ca. 1540), the form a meld of Virgil, Trissino, and Gavin Douglas. In hammering a meter and a form into a new lang. Wyatt is often rough, but some of his lyrics have great power; Surrey is smoother, and plainer, not least because he simplifies the form of the sonnet. But when Tottel published the most important anthology of the century, his *Songes and Sonettes* (1557 and many subsequent eds.), the work of Surrey and Wyatt formed the bulk of the volume, though an unknown editor had regularized their meter into a drone.

It is Puttenham who speaks of the "new company of c. m." (*Arte of English Poesie*, 1589). The term *maker*, as a literal tr. of the Gr. *poiein*, from which *poet* is derived, was in common use in 15th- and 16th-c. England and Scotland.—J. Stevens, *Music and Poetry in the Early Tudor Court* (1961); J. Thompson, *The Founding of Eng. Metre* (1961); R.

Southall, *The Courtly Maker* (1964); P. Thomson, *Sir Thomas Wyatt and His Background* (1964); A. Ostriker, "Thomas Wyatt and Henry Surrey: Dissonance and Harmony in Lyric Form," *NLH* 1 (1970). A.PR.; T.V.F.B.

CRASIS. See SYNALOEPHA; ELISION.

CREATIONISM (Sp. *Creacionismo*). An experimental school which broke with the past, c. was founded by the Chilean poet Vicente Huidobro (1893–1948), who strove by daring metaphors to create new realities without merely copying external reality. The rallying cry was to create, not imitate. Huidobro claimed that his c. was a general aesthetic formulated as early as 1912 or 1913 (at this time he was still a modernist poet under the influence of Rubén Darío), but in his most important early manifesto, *Non serviam* (1914), he states that he no longer wants to be a slave to Nature but rather wishes to discover or invent other absolute realities which exist only in the poet's imagination. In transforming reality into his ideal world, Huidobro eliminates anecdote and description, making a poem just as Nature creates a tree. In the poem "Ars poética" he states:

> Why do you sing the rose, O poets?
> Make it flower in the poem.
> Only for you
> Do all things live under the Sun.
> The poet is a small God.

Thus he conceived of the artist as a divine being with special powers to capture (create) absolute reality. Huidobro wished to be original at all costs and believed in the aesthetic effects of surprise.

Much has been written on the question of who deserves the credit for the invention of c.: Huidobro or the Frenchman Pierre Reverdy. Sometimes compared to cubist poetry (such as that of William Carlos Williams, Max Jacob and others—see CUBISM), c. was a movement more or less simultaneous with ultraism (q.v.), with which it shared many avant-garde qualities. There is also a relationship to Gertrude Stein's "A rose is a rose is a rose" and Archibald MacLeish's "A poem should not mean but be." Huidobro, his theories, and his talent as a writer were persuasive, particularly after his visit to Madrid in 1918. He thus had a strong following: his innovative c. wished to add to lit. a new cosmic dimension and transform life into an independent poetic entity. Huidobro wanted to enhance poetic communication, feeling that the image was more vital to expression than the particular lang. in which it was articulated. A much discussed writer, from both positive and negative perspectives, he was certainly the first Sp.-Am. poet to fully incorporate European vanguardism into his writing. The bibl. on c. is vast, particularly that on Huidobro.—G. Diego, "Poesía y creacionismo de Vicente Huidobro," *Cuadernos Hispanoamericanos* (1968); *Vicente Huidobro y el creacionismo*, ed. R. de Costa

(1975); G. Yúdice, *Vicente Huidobro y la motivación del lenguaje* (1978); M. Camurati, *Poesía y poética de Vicente Huidobro* (1980); E. Busto Ogden, *El creacionismo de Vicente Huidobro en sus relaciones con la estética cubista* (1983).   A.W.P.; K.N.M.

CRETIC or amphimacer (Gr. "long at both ends"). In Cl. prosody, the metrical sequence – ◡ – , sometimes felt as a segment of iambo-trochaic and used alongside iambs and trochees or, like iambic and trochaic, in external compounding with aeolic (q.v.) units. On other occasions, as is obvious from resolution of either long syllable, the cretic is really a form of the paeon (q.v.), and cretic-paeonic measures, though rare in the choruses of Gr. tragedy, are not infrequent in comedy. The cretic meter, different from most other Gr. meters, is thought to have been of foreign origin, from a Cretan poet named Thaletas in the 7th c. B.C. Cretics occur in early Roman drama and are also common in the *clausulae* of Cicero. An example in the former is the song of Phaedromus in Plautus, *Curculio* 147–54:

– ◡ –   – ◡ – – ◡ – – ◡ –

pessuli, heus pessuli, vos saluto lubens,

– ◡ – – ◡ – – ◡ –   – ◡ –

vos amo, vos volo, vos peto atque obsecro

the meaning and meter of which G. E. Duckworth reproduces thus: "Bolts and bars, bolts and bars, gladly I greetings bring, / Hear my love, hear my prayer, you I beg and entreat."
    Like most other of the more complex Gr. feet, cretics do not exist in the mod. vernaculars except as experiments, but some Ren. songs are in cretics, and the song "Shall I die? Shall I fly?" attributed in 1985 to Shakespeare is in cretic dimeters. Cretic lines appear in Tennyson's "The Oak." Cretics sometimes appear in proverbs, idioms, and slang: "After while, crocodile." See PAEON.—G. E. Duckworth, *The Nature of Roman Comedy* (1952); Maas; Koster; Crusius; C. Questa, *Introduzione alla metrica di Plauto* (1967); Snell; West; G. T. Wright in *Eidos* 3,2 (1986).   R.J.G.; A.T.C.; T.V.F.B.

CRISIS. See PLOT.

CRITICISM. This article provides an overview of the practice of crit. in the West from ancient times down to the present. For fuller discussion of the theory of lit. crit., see METACRITICISM and THEORY.

    I. EARLY INTERPRETIVE PRACTICES
    II. MIMESIS
    III. GENRE AND TRADITION
    IV. DIDACTICISM, AFFECT, AND TASTE
    V. IMPRESSIONISM AND OBJECTIVISM
    VI. AUTHORIAL GENIUS, IMAGINATION, AND INTUITION
    VII. THE NEW CRITICISM
    VIII. CONTINENTAL STRUCTURALISM
    IX. PHENOMENOLOGY
    X. MYTH CRITICISM
    XI. READER-ORIENTED CRITICISM
    XII. LITERARY HISTORY
    XIII. DECONSTRUCTION
    XIV. NEW HISTORICISM AND CULTURAL STUDIES
    XV. CONCLUSION

    I. EARLY INTERPRETIVE PRACTICES. The practice of lit. crit. has its historical roots in the early readings of Homer and Scripture, which were most often allegorical in method and philosophical in intent, as in Theagenes of Rhegium (6th c. B.C.), the first known scholar to have interpreted Homer allegorically (none of his works survives), and in the surviving Gr. Scholia to Homer. Often the allegorical readings were Neoplatonic, and in a writer like Philo Judaeus (ca. 50 A.D.), Neoplatonic tendencies appeared in allegorization of the Old Testament. The texts were regarded as historical, but history was presumed to present a total pattern of meaning. Frequently, however, myths were treated as decayed history, following the method employed by Euhemerus (4th c. B.C.). This tendency to see myths and legends as historical accounts distorted by linguistic change and oral transmission persisted into the 18th c. (e.g. Samuel Shuckford [1694–1754]), and even had a 20th-c. practitioner in Robert Graves. By contrast, the mode of ethical or moralistic interp., at least in the Neoplatonic trad. that Porphyry (233–305 A.D.) and others followed, was atemporal and didactic, reading myth and legend as allegories of some part of the Neoplatonic concept of the passage into, through, and out of generation, as in Porphyry's own elaborate treatment of the cave of the nymphs scene in the *Odyssey* (see PLATONISM AND POETRY).
    Early Jewish and Christian interps. of Scripture provide a contrast to each other, with some similarities in the Hellenistic period when both were influenced by Neoplatonic allegorizing. However, the Jewish trad. tended to more creative play with texts (see HEBREW PROSODY AND POETICS), while the Christian practice broke into two somewhat antagonistic methods: allegorization and typological reading (see ALLEGORY). The contrast between the Jewish and Christian trads. is that between a mode of reading that treats the text as rife with possibility, building reading on reading, and a mode that presumes a fundamentally imitative or referential conception of lang. that either represents actual events (see REPRESENTATION AND MIMESIS) or by allegorical interp. finds behind the events the spiritual or moral significance that history displays (see INTERPRETATION, FOURFOLD METHOD). Even 20th-c. biblical typologists such as Jean Danielou still feared that strict allegorical interp. would spirit away the historicity of Scripture, reducing it to mere moral philosophy giving inadequate attention to God's plan of creation, history, and apocalypse. Early typologists, of whom

St. John was certainly one, maintained both the historical and prophetic reliability of the Bible, relating the text to the whole sweep of time and refusing to reduce it to some ahistorical idea. The method was to discover the events of the New Testament foreshadowed in the Old. It was to become incorporated into the fourfold mode of interp. developed by John Cassian (d. ca. 448) and later St. Thomas Aquinas, and explicitly secularized in the letter to Can Grande prefixed to the *Paradiso* and once attributed to Dante.

Critical practice, therefore, began with strong connections to moral philosophy and theology, and has never moved far from ethical concerns (see ETHICS AND CRITICISM), though at times morality narrowly conceived has been eschewed in favor of some form of aestheticism (q.v.). Such moments often come to be understood as expressions of an ethic strongly opposed to dogma, as in the work of Oscar Wilde (1854–1900). Still, on the whole, critical practice has tended toward secularization. When relatively free from any specific moral or theological dogma, it admits a variety of practical problems and evolves numerous modes of behavior. When the earliest crit. was not directly concerned with poetry's being true to truth, whether Platonic or prophetic, it was concerned with its being true to life (see REALISM; VERISIMILITUDE).

II. MIMESIS. The early importance of the concept of mimesis or imitation (qq.v.) as an artistic criterion is attested as early as the 7th c. B.C. in a hymn to Apollo; and the connection between poetry and painting, with its emphasis on accuracy of portrayal, was remarked as early as Simonides (6th c. B.C.; see VISUAL ARTS AND POETRY). The earliest extant Gr. poetry, Pindar's for example (522?–443 B.C.), is clearly interested in being faithful to the facts. To this day, much reviewing presumes some form of accurate imitation of the external world or felt life as a criterion of value. The concept is derived from the analogy with painting, where it long seemed to have more practical use, though Aristotle early observed that "not to know that the hind has no horns is a less serious matter than to paint it inartistically" (*Poetics* 25.5). Virtually every Western critical theory possesses at least some trace of mimetic theory, if only by opposition to it.

The first Western theory of imitation was Plato's. His critique of poetry and visual art mounts an attack on imitation based on his ontological and ethical concerns. He was interested in Truth or Being, i.e. Ideas or Forms. Poems and paintings, tied to appearances, always failed adequately to represent the truth of the Idea. For Plato, the poem had no Being, or only very diminished Being, because it was an imitation twice removed from the Idea, where reality and truth were located. Behind this view was the desire to identify the ethical life with purely abstract thought, and immorality with too great attention to material appearances. The old war between philosophy and poetry to which Plato alluded was for him the war of reality with appearance.

Even for Plato, however, poetry had charm. If he advocated, half-ironically through his mouthpiece Socrates, banishment of poets from his Republic, it was precisely on account of their perceived power to enchant and persuade. Here arises the question of the roles of delight and instruction: in *Ion* and *The Republic* Plato's Socrates was suspicious of the delight poets gave and believed they taught that appearance was reality. In addition, they were irrational, even though he considered their irrationality divinely inspired (see POETIC MADNESS). All of these Platonic shortcomings were however turned into virtues by later critics.

Aristotle attempted to rescue the imitative function in three ways. First, for Aristotle, poetic imitation was not of the Platonic Idea. Second, it was not of objects but of human actions. Third, it had a creative aspect, giving it power to shape materials into new wholes. Finally, against Plato's refusal to allow the poem any being, always treating it as an appearance of an appearance, twice removed from the idea of the object it copied, Aristotle provided for the idea of the poem as inherent within itself: he did not consign the idea to abstraction but allowed it to inhere in the object as its principle of being or motion. In the opposition of Aristotle to Plato there was established the long quarrel between an objectifying formalism and an emphasis on separable content, a quarrel that has had a variety of historical incarnations.

Aristotle's idea of formal unity (q.v.) did not, however, live as easily with the theory of imitation in later critics as it did in the fruitful ambiguities of his own *Poetics*, where he clearly tried to acknowledge poetry's claims to both intrinsic order and also truth to the world. In Ren. Italy and France, after the rediscovery of the *Poetics*, unity was rigidly interpreted in terms of the need for a quite literal imitation. Time, place, and action in a play were restricted in ways that answered to the strictest realism. But even as Aristotle's views became hardened into the Classicist prescription of the so-called "unities," Plato was being subjected to critical misreadings that liberalized his views and readmitted the poet to the commonwealth. This had begun as early as Plotinus (204–70 A.D.), whose elaborate Neoplatonist theory of emanations placed the image (q.v.) or appearance on a stairway upward to truth rather than downward to illusion. Ren. defenses of the image were common, though probably none so ingenious as that of Jacopo Mazzoni (1548–98) in his defense of Dante. The idea that the image might be an improvement on nature, the "second nature" of Sir Philip Sidney's *Apology for Poetry* (1583), rescued poetry once again from Plato and also from a theologically based (and Platonizing) fear that poetry bred only licentiousness and untruthful fictiveness (see FICTION)—a view common in the Christian Middle Ages. Boethius (480–524) had written of "seducing murmurs" and "poisonous sweets" in his *Consolation of Philosophy*, but by the time of Boccaccio (1313–75), poetry was defended on the ground that theology was the poetry of God and that poetry held within itself hidden truth, more pleasing because acquired by toil and therefore better retained. This was an argument which had the stamp of St. Thomas Aquinas (1225–74). In the late Ren., the long period of the domination of ontological concerns ended, and the emphasis on imitation began to wane. Aristotle and Plato, through clever misreadings and selective appropriations, had almost been made to change places.

III. GENRE AND TRADITION. There is one other notion of imitation that has also had considerable practical consequence. This can be traced back to pronouncements like that of Horace (65–8 B.C.) that the imitation of great predecessors is important. Pope carried on this idea in his remark that Virgil discovered that to copy Homer was to copy nature (q.v.). The emphasis on poetic genealogy and tradition (q.v.) entailed by this remark is reflected in all critical practice that pays strong attention to the matter of genre (q.v.). Genre crit. has had a long history, in which poets have been either praised or attacked for their relation to or remoteness from trad. In practice, genre crit. has been both classificatory and judgmental. Many critics—e.g. Joseph Addison (1672–1719)—are not comfortable until they can determine what kind of poem they have before them. At that point, classification can generate judgment according to some standard of decorum (q.v.).

The connection of genre to decorum, however, did not survive the 18th c. unscathed, and since that time genre theory has been turned inside out. One sees the demise of its classificatory role prophesied in the comically absurd list of types of drama in *Hamlet*. Rather than considering a work as belonging to a genre, critics now try to imagine genre as an aspect of a work, and works may after all include many generic suggestions. In recent times, both T. S. Eliot and Northrop Frye have claimed that there is really no acceptable or even possible escape from trad.; indeed, Eliot held that real individuality occurs when the poet has set forth a relation to his or her predecessors. Subsequently this idea was given an unexpected twist—with a strong dash of Freudianism—n Harold Bloom's theory of the anxiety of influence (see INFLUENCE), where the relation of the strong poet to the predecessor is one of willful misreading and competition. Bloom's own critical practice has been to chart this Oedipal strife through the work of those poets who make the most of it—who stand up, that is, to their strong predecessors.

IV. DIDACTICISM, AFFECT, AND TASTE. In practice, the concept of imitation has often had to be squared with a presumed didactic function (see DIDACTIC POETRY). Horace had seemed to treat poetry as a speaking picture (*ut pictura poesis* [q.v.]) and had proposed a twofold aim for poetry that has been much repeated—poetry must delight and instruct. This idea, frequently repeated up to the time of Sidney's *Apology* and even beyond, is the predecessor of later concerns with questions of readerly taste (q.v.) and affect that came into prominence when, with the rise of science in the 17th c., the ontological emphasis gave way to the epistemological. Plato, of course, had been deeply concerned about readers, and his attack on Sophistic rhet. embodied his concern that tropes were seductively deceptive and irrational. Aristotle's *Rhetoric* and the work of later Cl. rhetoricians sought to rescue rhet., but on grounds that Plato surely would have rejected (see RHETORIC AND POETRY). Rhet. was judged useful to both persuasion and delight. Pseudo-Longinus (1st c. A.D.) saw rhet. as the vehicle of poetic transport (see SUBLIME). A century before, Horace had seen nothing at all wrong with delighting while teaching, even as he accepted the idea of poetic imitation.

Affective theories in the 18th c. made more subtle what the effect in the reader might (ought to) be. Thereafter, modes of critical discussion eventuated that were predicated on something happening in the reader attributable to specific characteristics of the text. In the 18th c., critical theories were beginning to recognize a choice of location, or at least starting point, on one side or the other of the scientific bifurcation of nature into objective and subjective realms. Those choosing the side of the object had the problem of explaining away the subjective; those choosing the subjective had the problem of escaping pure solipsism and relativism. To some extent, particularly in matters of value but also in questions of interp., this division and these problems continued to plague critical thought into the late 20th c., as for example in reader-response crit. (q.v.).

The issue with respect to taste was nicely put by David Hume in his 1757 essay "Of the Standard of Taste." His recourse was to "certain general principle of approbation or blame, whose influence a careful eye may trace in all operations of the mind." Hume believed that there was an objective standard of taste, but he was too shrewd to attempt transference of this standard into a description of specific characteristics a work of art should have. "Taste" had become a critical catchword by the time Hume wrote. Joseph Addison had earlier defined it in a *Spectator* essay (1712) as "that Faculty of the Soul, which discerns the Beauties of an Author with Pleasure and the Imperfections with Dislike." The observation begs the question. How is the alleged objective beauty of the work to be connected with subjective pleasure? This problem came to be treated as part of aesthetics, a term coined by Alexander Baumgarten in midcentury to mean the science of perception and sensuous knowledge. Hume thought one had to presume that a standard of taste existed somewhere, and cited the persistent high rank of the classics as evidence. He had begun with the aim of demonstrating that a rational discussion of art must begin as a discussion of human response, but ended with the fiction of a standard that can never be directly apprehended or uttered in particulars; only the results of its workings can be seen in the persistence of what we now call the literary canon (q.v.). Hume was by no means a subjectivist, yet he set forth a problem that eventually led to numerous positions of radical subjectivism, not only in judgment but also in interp.

Driven relentlessly to its extreme, subjectivism results in solipsism of response, such as we find in Pater's conclusion to *The Renaissance* (1873), where isolated experience simply for the sake of the experience is praised as the end of life. Under such conditions the opportunity for the triumph of power, i.e. for someone to make arbitrary decisions about value, is virtually assured. Pater perhaps recognized this when he suppressed his conclusion. Part of his response, and later that of Anatole France, was due to his hatred of the materialistic scientific philosophies of the time.

However, subjectivity has no meaning apart from objectivity—these antinomies define each other—and there is therefore a sense in which the subjective impressionists had been captured by the terms of the enemy. Crit. based on analogy with science went to the opposite pole. So the 19th c. produced not only Pater but also Emile Zola (1840–1902), who would treat writing a novel as if it were a medical experiment, and Hippolyte Taine (1828–93), who would devise a "science" of lit. hist. (see SUBJECTIVITY AND OBJECTIVITY).

The philosopher who had early attempted to mediate—albeit starting from the position of the subject—between these oppositions was Immanuel Kant (1724–1804). His *Critique of Judgment* (1790) was a monumental effort to deal with the problems rapidly accruing to words like "taste," "satisfaction,"·"beauty," and "sublime." No modern theory of poetry is entirely untouched by Kant's effort to traverse what William Blake later named a "cloven fiction." Beginning with the simple notions of pleasure and pain, Kant attempted to dissociate the sense of aesthetic value—beauty and the sublime—from pleasure and pain on the ground that the aesthetic sense was "disinterested" while pleasure and pain were not (see DISINTERESTEDNESS). Kant meant that the sense of beauty or sublimity could not be referred to any personally desirable end. The object, as art, had only "purposiveness without purpose" or "internal purposiveness."

Kant was well aware that in making such a declaration he was appearing to attribute qualities to the object which, to be rigorous, had to be located in the reader or auditor; his own position did not admit the possibility of knowledge of the "thing in itself." What we think of as the object is always constituted, in Kant's view, by the mind according to the categories of the understanding. In contrast, the judgment declares the object beautiful according to the principle of taste, which is "the faculty of judgment of an object or a method of representing it by an entirely disinterested satisfaction or dissatisfaction. The object of such satisfaction is called beautiful." This idea was adopted in England by S. T. Coleridge (1772–1834), and ever after, it has been a main element in the attempt to universalize a specifically artistic value. It was because of this attempt that the New Criticism (q.v.), despite its commitment to objectivist practical analysis and to some of I. A. Richards' anti-Kantian psychologism, tended to be friendly to Kantian aesthetics (conspicuous in John Crowe Ransom), while at the same time it was deeply suspicious of readerly orientations (as in W. K. Wimsatt).

Crit. as practiced by Coleridge and some other romantic writers implied the Kantian position that an aesthetic judgment is subjectively universal and assumes the agreement of others (principally because it is detached from purposiveness). Coleridge's analytic implied that there was a difference between the good and the beautiful (or the sublime). He held that texts were discussible by recourse to analysis (q.v.) of their organic form (see ORGANICISM), thereby avoiding the complete relativity later practiced by Pater and France (the latter of whom was to declare that the critic ought to say "Gentlemen, I am going to talk about myself on the subject of Shakespeare").

V. IMPRESSIONISM AND OBJECTIVISM. The impressionistic mode of crit. was popular for a period in the latter 19th c., but its opposite reared up again in the 20th c., with some mediation by the art-for-art's-sake movement of the *fin de siècle*, in which the poetic object was declared not merely able to affect the reader as beautiful without regard to its use, but actually had to be useless (see DECADENCE). This latter view was fairly short lived, though it did exert some influence on the objectivist crit. which developed out of the work of T. S. Eliot and eventuated in the New Criticism.

A parallel but quite different mode of objectification was meanwhile developing on the Continent, first in Rus. Formalism (q.v.), then in a marriage of linguistic theory and crit. known as structuralism (q.v.). But these new movements did not hold sway in America until the 1950s and '60s, when Eng. trs. first became available. Prior to that time, the other version of subjectivist crit. revealed itself—a biographical crit. emphasizing authorial rather than readerly subjectivity. Much crit. written in the 19th c., and indeed still written today, moves from interest in the work to interest in the author. Wordsworth, for example, declared poetry to be the inner made outer and the "spontaneous overflow of powerful emotion." And in reading Coleridge on Shakespeare's genius, it is difficult to determine whether "Shakespeare" refers to the poems and plays or the person or to both indiscriminately.

VI. AUTHORIAL GENIUS, IMAGINATION, AND IN-
TUITION. The presence of the author was given
more philosophical expression in Coleridge's fa-
mous definition of "imagination" (*Biographia liter-
aria*, ch. 13), which became the central term in
this type of theory until Benedetto Croce sought
to replace it with "intuition" (q.v.). In Croce's
Aesthetic (1902), intuition does not exist apart
from expression (q.v.). In his view, there never
have been any mute inglorious Miltons. One does
not have intuitions that are not expressed, though
they may be expressed only to oneself. Artists are
different only in externalizing their intuitions; this
is what art is. Here Croce ran up against one of the
problems fundamental to all modern critical the-
ory, the problem of the relation of form to content.

In claiming that intuition and expression were
indivisible, Croce closed the gap between the two,
a problem since the invention of the idea of imi-
tation. That concept seemed to imply that content
was one thing—the thing imitated or the idea
conveyed—and the means by which conveyance
was achieved another. But Croce reopened the
gap in another place when he introduced his
notion of externalization. For poetry, the form of
externalization was the oral performance or pro-
duction of a written text. To what extent, however,
was lang. indivisible from intuition? Was intuition
possible apart from lang.? Or was lang. constitu-
tive in the Kantian sense? Were other forms also
constitutive—music, painting, sculpture? Croce's
intuitive expressionism raised these problems but
did not solve them. Ernst Cassirer's Neo-Kantian
theory of a multiplicity of constitutive symbolic
forms sought to bring intuition and externaliza-
tion closer together. Of these forms, lang. was one,
but Cassirer (1874–1945) was equivocal about the
status of lang. vis à vis the others—myth, art,
science, history, religion. Was it fundamental to all
or only one form among many?

Emphasis on authorial expression, usually iden-
tified with feeling as opposed to reason, generated
interest as well in literary biography, where the
author's life and works are treated in close rela-
tion. Such a connection is quite in contrast to Dr.
Johnson's earlier *Lives of the Eng. Poets* (1779–81),
where the two subjects were kept separate, or
Izaak Walton's still earlier life of John Donne
(1670), where Donne's poems are not mentioned
at all. In the 20th c., the devel. of psychoanalysis
after Freud provided a specific method for treat-
ing poems as externalizations of inner life, though
some varieties of psychological crit. (q.v.) inter-
ested themselves, rather, in the characters in the
text, and still others concentrated on the reader.

The 20th-c. objectivist reaction to impression-
istic and biographical crit. was lodged against both
authorial and readerly forms of critical practice.
There is a little more implied about authors and
readers in Eliot's crit. than might be expected,
given his claims that writing ought to be an extin-
guishing of the personality and a striving for the
objective correlative (q.v.) of an emotion (q.v.).
But this emotion was detached from both reader
and author and lodged in the work. I. A. Richards
in his influential early books (esp. *Practical Crit.*
[1929]—the title coined the phrase) also avoided
reference to authors and treated harshly the sub-
jective responses of his students. Poems were for
him not the inner made outer but "pieces" of lang.
The New Critical attacks on the so-called inten-
tional and affective "fallacies" (see INTENTION;
AFFECTIVE FALLACY) exemplified further the ten-
dency to consider a poem an object with a particu-
lar technical structure (q.v.).

The same cutting of lines between poem and
author on the one hand and poem and reader on
the other characterized the analytic practices of
Continental structuralism. An important differ-
ence from the New Crit. was that structuralist crit.
arose out of linguistics, while the orientation of
Richards and his followers arose out of semantics
(see SEMANTICS AND POETRY; SEMIOTICS, POETIC).
New Critical practice, arising mostly out of a very
uneasy and sometimes contradictory relationship
between the ideas of Eliot and Richards, and in
reaction also to both impressionism and a positiv-
istic literary historicism, avoided the didactic and
moralistic and identified itself ultimately with as-
pects of Kantian and Coleridgean aesthetics.

VII. THE NEW CRITICISM. The concept of the
poem held by the New Criticism was of an objec-
tive structure with its own internal relations, vari-
ously described as objectified feelings, emotions,
a density of metaphorical relations, a pattern of
irony or paradox or ambiguity (qq.v.), a tension
(q.v.), a structure and a texture (qq.v.), or state-
ments not strictly propositional but rather
"pseudo-statements" (q.v.), in nature dramatic
rather than discursive. Always the lang. of the
poem was treated as fundamentally different from
the discourse of science in terms of both structure
and ends (see SCIENCE AND POETRY). Much prac-
tical analysis came to conclude that poems were
expressions of their own nature, including their
difference from other uses of lang.; sometimes
poems were characterized as producing an en-
tirely separate form of knowledge (see MEANING,
POETIC) outside the usual categories of belief
(q.v.). Much emphasis was put on beginning with
the formal or technical aspects of the poem, incl.
its prosody and tropological structure, before at-
tempting to state the theme (q.v.) of the poem,
though many New Critics held that it was in fact
impossible to articulate what the poem is "about"
(see PARAPHRASE, HERESY OF). Any suggestion of
a split between form and content was assiduously
denied on organicist principles, and the poem
came to be seen as having a unique mode of being.
New Critics continued to employ the terminology
of genre, but the terms no longer denoted strict
categories into which literary works had to fit.

The objectivism of the New Critics was not,
however, a scientific objectivism in which the ob-

ject was stripped of all its nonmeasureable or so-called secondary qualities. Indeed, the New Criticism was violently opposed to any such reduction. The New Critical object was so named because of its alleged independence from reduction of any sort. The movement's enemy was positivism, despite the fact that Richards, one of its forbears, can be said to have employed at least pseudoscientific methods.

VIII. CONTINENTAL STRUCTURALISM. By contrast, the Continental structuralists considered themselves practitioners of a "human science." Neither the philosophy of symbolic logic nor that of poetic logic was the ground for the rise of structuralist attitudes toward lang., which came to dominate the scene on the Continent esp. in the 1960s and 1970s. Structuralism is often, and perhaps too simply, traced back to the posthumously published work of Ferdinand de Saussure, *Course in General Linguistics* (1913), actually a compilation of lecture notes by his students. In making lang. a system of differences to be scientifically studied apart from speaker or auditor (though still claiming it to be speech), Saussure opened the way in literary theory to the dismissal of both the expressive subject and the responding reader. Lang. was only itself. The disappearance of the subject (and the object inasmuch as lang. was a self-containing differential system) was also desired later by a political mode of crit. that identified the subject with bourgeois individualism and the object—at least the literary object—with elitist aestheticism.

The concept of the differential system took many disciplines on the Continent by storm and became virtually the defining characteristic of what came to be known as the "human sciences." Lang., seen as the differential system par excellence, came to be the model even for psychoanalysis when Jacques Lacan dissolved the human subject into lang. or, as he called it, the "symbolic." Michel Foucault (1926–84) in his historical analysis of Western culture declared the disappearance of Man, in the sense that "Man" had meant the epistemological subject and bourgeois individual. This disappearance appealed to and helped to give new life to Marxist crit. (q.v.), which had always been at odds with Neo-Kantian theories that emphasized the autonomy (q.v.) of the text. The disappearance of "man" in this sense was also not inimical to the interests of feminist crit., which would attack the establishment of the literary canon (see FEMINIST POETICS).

For a Marxist, the problem with a purely structuralist argument would be that the concept of a differential structure, where the empty spaces between words were more important than any idea of the substantial nature of words, did not just call into question the human subject; it also raised questions about the material referent of lang. Saussure had proposed the linguistic sign as composed of a signifier (sound image) and a signified (concept), but he had been equivocal about the referent, and later theorists abandoned the referent entirely as having no demonstrable (other than arbitrary) relation to the sign. The disappearance of the referent seemed to spirit material reality away into a lang. that was all system, lacking even the substance it had had under the concept of the elite object.

For the structuralists and their successors, however, the notion of differential structure was for the most part regarded as radically liberating. Its fundamental principles were the following: (1) the arbitrary relation between the sound or written appearance of a word and what it signified; (2) the diacritical nature of the sign, its division into signifier and signified; (3) the view that a sign is such by virtue of its difference not only within itself but also from every other sign in the system, which is a chain of such differences; (4) the positing of two kinds of linguistic investigation, synchronic and diachronic (the structuralists emphasized synchrony against virtually all linguistics that preceded them); and (5) the use of terminology that called the lang. system "langue" and smaller patterns of usage within it "paroles." Structuralist literary theory tended to treat poems as "paroles" (see SEMIOTICS, POETIC) which were to be revealed as differential structures by stylistic analysis (see STYLISTICS), as in Jakobson and Lévi-Strauss's exhaustive (and exhausting) analysis of Baudelaire's "Les Chats" (1962) or Jakobson and Jones's of Shakespeare's Sonnet 129 (1970).

These principles made it possible to call in question—or simply ignore—some of the most fundamental concepts in Western critical theory. In addition to dispensing with both subjects—reader and author—structuralism rejected imitation, or, in its terms, representation. Rather than the referent being seen as present to lang., it was regarded as absent. The old idea of unity was also threatened; rather than a literary work being a confluence of parts, it was a pattern of differences, with its boundaries therefore problematic. But in spite of its wholesale commitment to difference, structuralism was monolithic in rejecting a difference that crit. had, in one way or another, always insisted on: for structuralism there was no fundamental difference between lit. and any other use of lang., i.e. between modes of discourse (see TEXTUALITY). In some quarters, it is true, space was allowed for the poem's transgression of certain linguistic "rules" (see LINGUISTICS AND POETICS; SYNTAX, POETIC), resulting in a concept of "the literary" after all, most conspicuously in the Prague School notion of "literariness." On the whole, however, one rule applied to all (here was another attack on so-called elitism), and therefore the term "text" came to signify any linguistic phenomenon at all, then any phenomenon whatsoever that happened to fall within the structuralist gaze. The methods of linguistic analysis, analogically applied beyond lang., reduced the world itself to a text. Lang. was now not like the world, as in the doctrine of imitation; the world was like lang.

Structuralist poetics tended, therefore, toward the purely descriptive and ground no axe against science, certainly not linguistic science. Indeed, structuralist crit. was never divided from structuralist practice in other fields such as anthropology; and out of this homogeneity there grew a tendency to reject the notion of lit. itself, both on grounds that the notion was politically elitist and that linguistics had once and for all leveled such hierarchical views of lang. Structuralism did not, in short, try to discover in poetry a culture-saving opposition of poetics to science, as the New Criticism had done.

IX. PHENOMENOLOGY. However, the Continental opponent of structuralism, the phenomenological crit. of the Geneva School (q.v.), with its connections to the philosophers Edmund Husserl and Martin Heidegger, certainly did. Phenomenological crit. based its practices on a notion of intersubjectivity, the medium of which was the poem, which connected authorial consciousness to readerly consciousness without a tour through anything that might be described as an object. In one sense this was a return to a kind of romantic expressivism, and in another it foregrounded lang., but lang. now as the harboring mediator of consciousness itself. In practice, phenomenological crit. tended not to close analysis, since there was no object to analyze, but instead made contact with poetic consciousness. The result was frequently a form of critical discourse verging on the poetic and thereby blurring the boundary that the New Criticism and its historicist predecessors had built up between crit. as a secondary and analytic activity (SEE THEORY) and poetry as a primary and creative one. Now, rather than lit. threatening to disappear, as in structuralism, all discourse threatened to become lit.

Continental structuralism and phenomenology proceeded along their opposed paths, for the most part uninterested in and often ignorant of the New Criticism in America and its sporadic outbreaks in England. Likewise, the New Critics knew little of European critical practice; it was not until the 1960s that the two movements appeared in America, quickly followed by their successor, variously called poststructuralism or deconstruction (q.v.). Am. New Criticism never did have its day in Europe, where an academic trad. of *explication de texte* (see EXPLICATION)—though not of the New Critical sort, with its emphasis on irony and paradox and its antipositivism—had been influential. It can perhaps be said that influence from the Eng. lang. on Continental crit. came more through literary artists like James Joyce than through practicing critics, just as it had come to the 19th-c. Fr. symbolist theorists through the poetry of Edgar Allan Poe not the crit. of Emerson.

X. MYTH CRITICISM. Structuralism, phenomenology, and the New Criticism all reflected a profound shift of philosophical and critical concerns from epistemological questions to linguistic ones. The devel. of modern myth crit. (q.v.) bears a more complex relation to the shift toward linguistic interests. Its sources go back to the many syncretic mythographers of the 18th and early 19th cs. and the convergence of mythological research with the linguistic scholarship of the time, perhaps best represented by Wilhelm von Humboldt (1767–1835). A precursor whose importance came to be realized was Giambattista Vico (1668–1744), whose *New Science* (1725) set forth a theory of poetic logic embedded in myth (q.v.). The principal modern theorist of myth, aside from structuralist anthropologists like Lévi-Strauss, was Cassirer, known for his definition of man as the *animal symbolicum* and for his philosophy of symbolic forms.

In the realm of critical practice, the most noteworthy proponent of myth crit. was Northrop Frye (1912–91), particularly in his works on Blake, Shakespeare, Milton, and the Bible, though his *Anatomy of Crit.* (1957), unquestionably one of the most important critical works of the century, regarded myth crit. as but one (though a fundamental one) of four critical modes. Although myth crit. has been criticized for reducing lit. to extrinsic patterns, it can answer that it brought some of what was ignored by strictly intrinsic formalism back into the text. This was true of its use of the concept of archetypal symbols (see ARCHETYPE), and also true of its revival of the idea of genres.

One form of myth crit. extends into the analytic psychology of Carl Jung (1875–1961), though Frye claimed that his own concept of literary archetypes did not require Jung, only an empirical survey of the literary field and attention to poetic conventions (q.v.). This view connects Frye with Eliot's conception of literary trad. and presumes something called "lit." with its own categories and modes. Thus myth or archetypal crit. was always making connections among works—sometimes, it was complained, at the expense of differences. Jungian crit., with its own emphasis on archetypes, is one form of psychological crit., but of course heretical from the point of view of Freudianism. Freudian critical practice emphasizes the psychology of the author, of the characters in the text, and of the reader. A revisionist brand of psychoanalytic theory developed by Jacques Lacan (1901–81) emphasizes the role of lang. on principles derived from structuralism.

XI. READER-ORIENTED CRITICISM. Critical practice emphasizing the reader has not, however, been dominated by psychoanalytic thinking; it has had a number of different facets, some of which go back to 19th-c. hermeneutics (q.v.). Against a neopositivistic form of interpretation that declares the meaning (q.v.) of a text to be that which scholarship can reasonably show to be an intention (q.v.) carried out by the author (so Hirsch), there is the more historically oriented attempt to establish what a reader or community of readers contemporaneous with the author would have been able to understand. This is the version of readerly crit. known as reception theory or reader-response crit. (q.v.). But all such attempts raise the question, which reader? The reader must be a fiction constructed on some set of principles—either some supposedly empirical, historical construct, or else an ideal form (so Iser), a displacement of the older notion of the aesthetic object. In the hermeneutic theory of Hans-Georg Gadamer (*Truth and Method* [tr. 1960]), any such critical act bears with it its own historical position, so that what is read is the historical space between reader and text, all recovery of the past being "thrown" into time.

From Pater onward, all critical practice with a readerly orientation has had to struggle with the problem of subjectivity and the threat of an uncontrollable relativism. If contemp. Am. reader-response crit. has a locatable beginning, it is probably with Louise Rosenblatt's *Lit. as Exploration* (1938); this work was interested principally in pedagogy and began with the situation of a reader. Subsequent, more theoretically oriented readerly crit. is sometimes driven to embrace a thorough skepticism about objectively fixed meaning. Stanley Fish, for example, began his career by examining how a text controls the reader as it proceeds and later came to conclude that the reader, or a community of readers, controls what can be seen in a text. This control is interpretive power, which is often invested by convention in those in Fish's professional position, namely academic critics. The text itself has none of the objectivity or power invested in it by the New Critics.

XII. LITERARY HISTORY. Nevertheless, except where absolute subjectivity reigns, readerly crit. has an inevitable relation to historical scholarship because of a need, in several of its versions, to establish the linguistic and semantic conventions of a given period. Historical literary scholarship is, however, relatively new, being, in the forms recognizable today, a product of the 19th c. (see HISTORICISM). Taine, for example, claimed to treat all lit. in terms of race, milieu, and epoch. V. L. Parrington early in the 20th c. saw Am. lit. through the lens of Jeffersonian values; Arthur Lovejoy brought into play the history of ideas. Subsequent historicist crit. has sought to develop the notion of reading communities. All through the modern period, there have been various forms of Marxist crit. observing lit. and judging it against the backdrop of the history of class struggle. More recently, Marxist crit. has been allied with other positions that claim all judgments to be historically grounded, and in this sense relativist—and political.

XIII. DECONSTRUCTION. The taking of structuralist thought to its logical extreme was one of the acts of the movement which became known as deconstruction. It has played a key role in the age of linguistics similar to that of Berkeleyan idealism in the 18th c. Berkeley, by expanding John Locke's distinction between primary and secondary qualities of experience, called into question the possibility of knowing the privileged primary qualities at all and thus emphasized the dilemma of subjectivism. After 1967, much of Am. crit. was influenced by Jacques Derrida (b. 1930), the leader of the project of deconstruction, who attacked all notions of presence in the sense of referent, calling in question any "origin" or "center" of meaning and thereby seeking to undercut the entire ground of Western metaphysics—i.e. the concept of reference, the relation of words to their referents in the external world.

The New Critics had held that the literary work—or at least the successful literary work—was a formal unity. For the deconstructionist, there were no works, only "texts," and everything from poems to fashions in clothing were texts; the verbal medium was no longer a criterion for textuality (q.v.). The text was now a disseminating disunity of differences. Things did not come together in a text, if it could be said that there were things (there weren't, strictly speaking). The hope of closure (q.v.) slipped ever down the chain of signifiers. Rather than a totality, the text offered only the endlessness of possibility, and one text flowed toward and into another. Derrida's practice was to analyze a variety of texts, usually not fictive or poetic, to demonstrate that what they seemed to profess as a structure of ideas was in fact contradicted by their own behavior, and that these contradictions were not superficial but fundamental—and finally inescapable. Out of deconstructive theory spread a critical practice that dismantled texts down to their purportedly inevitable contradictions, though in some versions, texts were said to deconstruct themselves.

Derrida had pointed out that structuralist theory taken to its logical end required the abandonment not only of the referent but also the signified, since every signifier signified but another signifier, and so on endlessly. There could be no end to the search for an origin or center, which Derrida named the ever-absent "transcendental signified." It could not be known any more than could Locke's primary qualities according to Berkeley; perhaps it did not exist. There was left only play among the signifiers in a search for meaning that could be carried on properly, in Derrida's view, only with the knowledge that it could not be achieved. There was some analogy here to the Paterian championing of experience for experience's sake, but Derrida's position posed an ethic of irony rather than a passion for exquisite moments.

This deconstructive view was not entirely in contrast to that of the New Criticism, but there were very important differences. The New Critics embraced irony, and regarded it a positive principle of literary structure that held the work together; it was not just a principle of critical behavior or attitude. They could imagine a fictive speaker of the text. They attacked the notion of fixed final meaning on the ground that a paraphrase could never contain a meaning coexistent with the poem's formal being, but did not imagine that being itself was endlessly deferred. In practice, the New Critics tended to produce readings that sometimes violated their own strictures, resulting in allegorization. Derrida had been quick to point out that certain structuralists' analyses inevitably implied the presence of the very "transcendental signified" that their concept of structure could not logically allow. When deconstruction came to America, deconstructionists attacked the New Critics on the same grounds. The work of Frye, which had some characteristics close to structuralism, though not the ground in linguistics, was criticized for creating categories that were substantial rather than differential. Yet Derrida himself never tired of observing that it was in the nature of lang. itself to presume existence of the "transcendental signified."

The trick was to keep one's discourse in motion in order to escape as long as possible this fixity. With irony transferred from poetry to the activity of critical theory itself, it began to appear, from this perspective, that deconstructive discourse was no different from the discourse it gazed upon. The result was, on the one hand, either the disappearance of lit. or the declaration that all discourse was literary, depending on how one felt about the elitist aura of the term "lit." At least in France, where these ideas had originated, it was regarded as elitist. On the other hand, there was a turning in on itself of critical theory toward a degree of self-consciousness of utterance and self-examination previously unknown. Hardly a theoretical statement could be made that was not quickly subjected to analysis. The Age of Crit. had given way to the Age of Theory.

In the deconstructive practice of Paul de Man (1919–83), texts were seen to have the inherent instability of lang. itself, by virtue of the fundamental role of tropes (see FIGURE, SCHEME, TROPE), which are at once both subversive and seductive. De Man called his critical practice "rhetorical." Since ancient times, the practice of rhet. in the West has involved the analysis of a text so as to identify and categorize its tropes (see RHETORIC AND POETRY). Rhetorical treatises were generally encyclopedias of tropes with instruction on their appropriate use for purposes of persuasion, instruction, and delight—chiefly to persuade. De Man's revival of the term "rhet.," however, was for another purpose—revelation of the rule of tropes over the intentions of meaning.

Deconstruction has been characterized as both revolutionary and reactionary. Generally, deconstructionists saw themselves as the former, pointing to their project of criticizing all assumptions of centers, origins, and transcendental signifieds. Certainly deconstruction came about in France in an intellectually radical period, and deconstructionists had declared their sympathy for leftist positions during the student uprisings in France.

On the other hand, it has been argued that deconstruction's critique is so far-reaching, its skepticism so thorough, that it seems incapable of commitment to any specific action. Critics who propose certain political or ethical views have sometimes been interested in deconstructive method while at the same time expressing resistance to it on the ground that its endless irony seems paradoxically to be a dead end.

In the wake of deconstruction, and frequently opposed to it while at the same time often influenced by its methods, came a variety of politically oriented movements, most of which had their roots in the political activities of the 1960s (see POLITICS AND POETRY). Feminist crit. brought about an examination of writing by women, past and present, and a critique of masculine or patriarchal attitudes not only in lit. and crit. but also throughout Western culture (see FEMINIST POETICS). In this, feminism in its own way paralleled deconstruction's critique of Western metaphysics. The feminist attack was principally against the so-called canon of great writers, virtually all male, and was one of the forces setting in motion a debate about canonicity in general. This in turn revived debate about literary value, though almost entirely on political grounds, a debate which had been virtually obliterated earlier in this century by intense preoccupation with problems of interp.

XIV. NEW HISTORICISM AND CULTURAL STUDIES. The New Historicism, heavily under the influence of the writings of Michel Foucault, attempted to reconstitute literary history as a study of power relations (see HISTORICISM). This movement was paralleled by "culture studies," particularly concerned with the social (and power) questions of race, class, and gender (see CULTURAL CRITICISM). These gave particular attention to the pressures of socio-historical circumstances on the production of the literary text, though most often the line between literary and other texts was deliberately blurred. Often, too, specifically lit. crit. or literary theory was tacitly rejected in favor of "critical theory" roughly in the sense established by the Frankfurt theorists (Adorno, Horkheimer, et al.) in the 1930s, when social crit. enclosed literary concerns. In these developments the notion of textuality, as first developed in structuralism, lingered on. The notion of "lit." itself was called in question sometimes as conceptually elitist, sometimes as the victim of reductive tendencies in theories of textuality themselves, where differences between literary (or fictive) and other uses of lang., elaborately developed over centuries of theoretical discourse, were explicitly rejected.

XV. CONCLUSION. Critical practices and theories have developed not only out of or parallel with philosophical trends. They have also appeared as responses to or deliberate defenses of challenging literary texts. Sidney and Wordsworth both defended their own practice. Aristotle responded to both the Platonic theory of imitation and Sopho-

CRITICISM

cles; he thereby set in motion, after the recovery of the *Poetics* in the Ren., a trad. of dramatic crit. that has affected Western poetry and fiction even to this day, the lang. of imitation having been revived by the Aristotelians of the Chicago School (q.v.) in the mid 20th c. Critical practice in the first half of the 20th c. was heavily influenced not only by T. S. Eliot's crit., but also by his poem *The Waste Land* (1922). And the challenge of James Joyce's texts continues to affect critical practice over half a century after the publication of *Finnegan's Wake* (1939).

In the latter half of the 20th c., lit. crit., apart from reviewing in the newspapers and certain magazines, was practiced in America almost entirely by the academic professoriate. This fact had interesting causes and consequences. One consequence may have been the tendency for critical theory (see THEORY) to replace practical crit. as a principal activity. Enormous attention was paid to methodologies, arguments about their relative merits, and unveiling of their often hidden assumptions. Virtually absent from this discourse was any discussion by an artist defending or promoting a practice, or by a critic concerned with the special nature of lit., with specifically literary value, or with the particular excellences of a given literary work.　H.A.

For fuller discussion of specific types of crit., see the entries AUTONOMY; IMITATION; REPRESENTATION AND MIMESIS; AESTHETICISM; HISTORICISM; EXPRESSION; RUSSIAN FORMALISM; STRUCTURALISM; PSYCHOLOGICAL CRITICISM; NEW CRITICISM; CHICAGO SCHOOL; ORGANICISM; CONTEXTUALISM; MYTH CRITICISM; LINGUISTICS AND POETICS; GENEVA SCHOOL; INFLUENCE; MARXIST CRITICISM; CULTURAL CRITICISM; READER-RESPONSE CRITICISM; DECONSTRUCTION; FEMINIST POETICS; ETHICS AND CRITICISM; PLURALISM; and THEORY. See also ANALYSIS; EVALUATION; EXPLICATION; HERMENEUTICS; INDETERMINACY; INTENTION; INTERPRETATION; INTERTEXTUALITY; SIMPLICITY AND COMPLEXITY; SUBJECTIVITY AND OBJECTIVITY; TEXTUAL CRITICISM; TEXTUALITY. For a survey of crit. within the larger context of Western poetics, see POETRY, THEORIES OF. The major periods of Western poetics are discussed in greater detail in CLASSICAL POETICS; MEDIEVAL POETICS; RENAISSANCE POETICS; BAROQUE POETICS; NEOCLASSICAL POETICS; ROMANTIC AND POSTROMANTIC POETICS; AND TWENTIETH-CENTURY POETICS. Non-Western traditions in poetics are surveyed in ARABIC POETICS; CHINESE POETICS; HEBREW PROSODY AND POETICS; INDIAN POETICS; and JAPANESE POETICS. For overview of the Western and Eastern trads. in poetics, see POETICS.

BIBLIOGRAPHIES: Garland Bibls. of Mod. Critics & Critical Schools series, gen. ed. W. E. Cain; *New Literary History International Bibl. of Literary Theory and Crit.*, ed. R. Cohen, 1–(1988 for 1984–85); *Research in Critical Theory Since 1965*, ed. L. Orr (1989).

ANTHOLOGIES: *Comprehensive and General: Lit. Crit. Plato to Dryden*, ed. A. H. Gilbert (1940, 1962); *Lit. Crit. Pope to Croce*, ed. G. W. Allen and H. H. Clark (1941); *Crit.: The Major Texts*, ed. W. J. Bate, enl. ed. (1970); *Lit. Crit. Plato to Dryden*, ed. V. Hall (1970); *Crit.: The Major Statements*, ed. C. Kaplan, 2d ed. (1986); *The Theory of Crit.: From Plato to the Present*, ed. R. Selden (1988); *Lit. Crit. and Theory: The Greeks to the Present*, ed. R. C. Davis and L. Finke (1989); *The Critical Trad.*, ed. D. H. Richter (1989); *Critical Theory Since Plato*, ed. H. Adams, 2d ed. (1992).

Classical and Medieval: J. D. Denniston, *Gr. Lit. Crit.* (1924); *Ancient Lit. Crit.: The Principal Texts in New Trs.*, ed. D. A. Russell and M. Winterbottom (1972), redacted as *Cl. Lit. Crit.* (1990); *Cl. and Med. Lit. Crit.: Trs. and Interps.*, ed. A. Preminger et al. (1974; also pub. separately).

Renaissance: Elizabethan Critical Essays, ed. G. G. Smith, 2 v. (1904); *Critical Essays of the 17th C.*, ed. J. E. Spingarn, 3 v. (1908–9); *Critical Prefaces of the Fr. Ren.*, and *Trattati di poetica e retorica del cinquecento*, both ed. B. Weinberg (1950, 1970); E. W. Tayler, *Lit. Crit. of 17th-C. England* (1967); B. Fabian, *Poetiken de Cinquecento*, 25 v. (1967–69); *The Continental Model: Selected Fr. Critical Essays of the 17th C. in Eng. Tr.*, ed. S. Elledge and D. Schier, rev. ed. (1970).

Eighteenth and Nineteenth Centuries: 18th-C. Critical Essays, ed. S. Elledge, 2 v. (1961); *Ger. Aesthetic and Lit. Crit.*, ed. D. Simpson, K. M. Wheeler, and H. B. Nisbet, 3 v. (1984–85)—Kant, Hegel and the romantics.

Twentieth Century: Contemp. Crit., ed. M. Bradbury and D. Palmer (1970); *Critical Theory Since 1965*, ed. H. Adams and L. Searle (1986)—54 selections; *Mod. Crit. and Theory: A Reader*, ed. D. Lodge (1988)—30 selections in 7 categories; *20th-C. Literary Theory*, ed. K. M. Newton (1988)—50 excerpts; *Contemp. Lit. Crit.*, ed. R. C. Davis and R. Schleifer, 2d ed. (1989)—36 selections in 8 categories; *Contemp. Critical Theory*, ed. D. Latimer (1989)—40 selections in 6 categories.

HISTORIES AND SURVEYS: *Comprehensive and General:* G. Saintsbury, *Hist. of Crit. and Literary Taste in Europe*, 3 v., (1900–4), the Eng. sect. rev. as *Hist. of Eng. Crit.* (1911); Abrams (below); R. Wellek, *A Hist. of Mod. Crit., 1750–1950*, 6 v. (1955–86), *Concepts of Crit.* (1963)—esp. chs. 1, 2, and 11–13, *Discriminations* (1970), "Crit., Literary," in *DHI*, v. 3, *Four Critics* (1981), and "Lit. Crit.," *Encyc. of World Lit. in the 20th C.*, rev. ed., ed. L. S. Klein (1983); W. K. Wimsatt, Jr., and C. Brooks, *Lit. Crit.: A Short Hist.* (1957); W. Krauss, *Grundprobleme der Literaturwiss.* (1968); R. H. Stacy, *Rus. Lit. Crit.: A Short Hist.* (1974), "Lit. Crit." in Terras; K. K. Ruthven, *Critical Assumptions* (1979); D. Daiches, *Critical Approaches to Lit.*, 2d ed. (1982); *A Hist. of Ger. Lit. Crit.*, ed. P. U. Hohendahl (tr. 1988); K. Weimar, *Gesch. der deutschen Literaturwiss. bis zum Ende des 19. Jh.* (1989).

Classical: C. S. Baldwin, *Ancient Rhet. and Poetic*

(1924); J. F. D'Alton, *Roman Lit. Theory and Crit.* (1931); J. W. H. Atkins, *Lit. Crit. in Antiquity: A Sketch of Its Devel.*, 2 v. (1934); G. M. A. Grube, *The Gr. and Roman Critics* (1965), *A Gr. Critic: Demetrius on Style* (1961); R. Harriott, *Poetry and Crit. Before Plato* (1969); D. A. Russell, *Crit. in Antiquity* (1981); W. J. Verdenius, "The Principles of Gr. Lit. Crit.," *Mnemosyne* 4 (1983); *Cambridge Hist. of Lit. Crit.*, v. 1, *Cl. Crit.*, ed. G. A. Kennedy (1989).

Medieval: C. S. Baldwin, *Med. Rhet. and Poetic* (1928); J. W. H. Atkins, *Eng. Lit, Crit.: The Medieval Phase* (1943)—one-sided; W. F. Patterson, *Three Centuries of Fr. Poetic Theory*, 3 v. (1935); O. B. Hardison, Jr., *Med. Lit. Crit.: Trs. and Interps.* (1974); *Med. Lit. Theory and Crit., ca. 1100–ca. 1376: The Commentary Trad.*, ed. A. J. Minnis et al. (1988).

Renaissance: F. E. Schelling, *Poetic and Verse Crit. of the Reign of Elizabeth* (1891); J. E. Spingarn, *Hist. of Lit. Crit. in the Ren.*, 2d ed. (1908); C. S. Baldwin, *Ren. Lit. Theory and Practice*, ed. D. L. Clark (1939); M. T. Herrick, *The Fusion of Horatian and Aristotelian Lit. Crit., 1531–1555* (1946); J. W. H. Atkins, *Eng. Lit. Crit.: The Renascence* (1947); V. Hall, Jr., *Ren. Lit. Crit.* (1959); B. Weinberg, *A Hist. of Lit. Crit. in the It. Ren.*, 2 v. (1961); B. Hathaway, *The Age of Crit.* (1962), *Marvels and Commonplaces: Ren. Lit. Crit.* (1968). Wilkins, s.v. "Poetic Theory," "Lit. Crit.," and "Lit. Theory" in Index.

Eighteenth Century: J. W. H. Atkins, *Eng. Lit, Crit.: 17th and 18th Cs.* (1951); E. R. Marks, *The Poetics of Reason* (1968); J. Engell, *Forming the Critical Mind, Dryden to Coleridge* (1989).

Nineteenth Century: A. H. Warren, *Eng. Poetic Theory (1825–1865)* (1950); M. H. Abrams, *The Mirror and the Lamp* (1953).

Twentieth Century: S. E. Hyman, *The Armed Vision*, rev. ed. (1955); M. Krieger, *The New Apologists for Poetry* (1956); H. Spiegelberg, *The Phenomenological Movement* (1960); R. Molho, *La Critique littéraire en France au XIXe siècle* (1963); P. Moreau, *La Critique littéraire en France* (1965); J. H. Boone, *From Symbolism to Structuralism* (1972); D. C. Hoy, *The Critical Circle* (1972); D. Fokkema and E. Ibsch, *Theories of Lit. in the 20th C.* (1978); F. Lentricchia, *After the New Crit.* (1980)—surveys 5 trends and 4 theorists; E. Kurzweil, *The Age of Structuralism* (1980); V. Erlich, *Rus. Formalism: History, Doctrine*, 3d ed. (1981); C. Norris, *Deconstruction: Theory and Practice* (1982); S. Rimmon-Kenan, *Narrative Fiction* (1983); R. Holub, *Reception Theory* (1984); W. Ray, *Literary Meaning* (1984); W. Martin, *Recent Theories of Narrative* (1986); V. B. Leitch, *Am. Lit. Crit. from the Thirties to the Eighties* (1988); R. Selden, *Reader's Guide to Contemp. Lit. Theory*, 2d ed. (1989); P. Smallwood, *Mod. Critics in Practice: Portraits of British Literary Critics* (1990).

REPRESENTATIVE 20TH-C. CRITICAL AND THEORETICAL STUDIES: G. Lukacz, *Soul and Form* (1910), *Theory of the Novel* (1920); I. Babbitt, *The New Laoköon* (1910), *Rousseau and Romanticism* (1919); T. E. Hulme, *Speculations* (1924); I. A.

Richards, *Principles of Lit. Crit.* (1925), *Practical Crit.* (1929); V. Woolf, *A Room of One's Own* (1929); R. Ingarden, *The Literary Work of Art* (1931, tr. 1973); T. S. Eliot, *Selected Essays, 1917–1932* (1932, rev. 1950); W. Empson, *Some Versions of Pastoral* (1935); J. C. Ransom, *The New Crit.* (1941); K. Burke, *The Philosophy of Literary Form* (1941, rev 1957), *Lang. as Symbolic Action* (1966); E. Cassirer, *An Essay on Man* (1944); Brooks; L. Spitzer, *Linguistics and Lit. Hist.* (1948); A. Tate, *On the Limits of Poetry* (1948); J.-P. Sartre, *What Is Lit.?* (1948); S. de Beauvoir, *The Second Sex* (1949); R. P. Blackmur, *Lang. as Gesture* (1952); Crane; Empson; Auerbach; Abrams; R. S. Crane, *The Langs. of Crit. and the Structure of Poetry* (1953); W. K. Wimsatt, Jr., *The Verbal Icon* (1954); G. Poulet, *Studies in Human Time* (1956); Wellek and Warren; Frye; R. Williams, *Culture and Society, 1780–1850* (1958), *Marxism and Lit.* (1977); H.-G. Gadamer, *Truth and Method* (1960, tr. 1975, rev. 1988); R. Barthes, *On Racine* (1963), *S/Z* (1970); E. Vivas, *The Artistic Transaction* (1963); W. Benjamin, *The Origins of Ger. Tragic Drama* (1963, tr. 1977); G. Bachelard, *The Poetics of Space* (1963); *Rus. Formalist Crit.*, ed. L. Lemon and M. Reis (1965); M. Bakhtin, *Rabelais and His World* (1965), *The Dialogic Imagination* (tr. 1981); F. Kermode, *The Sense of an Ending* (1966); R. Scholes and R. Kellogg, *The Nature of Narrative* (1966); F. E. Sparshott, *The Concept of Crit.* (1967); E. D. Hirsch, *Validity in Interp.* (1967); J. Derrida, *Of Grammatology* (tr. 1967), *Writing and Difference* (tr. 1967); N. Holland, *The Dynamics of Literary Response* (1967); P. Wheelwright, *The Burning Fountain*, 2d ed. (1968); H. Adams, *The Interests of Crit.* (1969), *Philosophy of the Literary Symbolic* (1983); *The Langs. of Crit. and the Sciences of Man*, ed. L. Macksey and E. Donato (1970); T. Adorno, *Aesthetic Theory* (1970); G. Hartman, *Beyond Formalism* (1970); N. Frye, *The Critical Path* (1971); M. Heidegger, *On the Way to Lang.*, and *Poetry, Lang., Thought* (both tr. 1971); I. Hassan, *The Dismemberment of Orpheus* (1971); R. Girard, *Violence and the Sacred* (1972); H. Bloom, *The Anxiety of Influence* (1973), *Agon* (1982); J. M. Ellis, *The Theory of Lit. Crit.* (1974), *Against Deconstruction* (1989); E. W. Said, *Beginnings* (1975), *The World, the Text, and the Critic* (1983); M. Krieger, *Theory of Crit.* (1976), *Words About Words About Words* (1988); N. Goodman, *Langs. of Art*, 2d ed. (1976); W. Iser, *The Act of Reading* (tr. 1976); M. Foucault, *Lang., Counter-Memory, Practice* (1977); J. Lotman, *The Structure of the Artistic Text* (tr. 1977); S. Chatman, *Story and Discourse* (1978); W. Davis, *The Act of Interp.* (1978); R. Macherey, *A Theory of Literary Production* (1978); M. Riffaterre, *Semiotics of Poetry* (1978); G. Webster, *The Republic of Letters* (1979); S. Gilbert and S. Gubar, *The Madwoman in the Attic* (1978); W. C. Booth, *Critical Understanding* (1979); S. Fish, *Is There a Text in This Class?* (1980); J. Kristeva, *Desire in Lang.* (1980), *Revolution in Poetic Lang.* (1984); P. D. Juhl, *Interpretation* (1980); J. Culler, *The Pursuit of Signs* (1981); F.

CUADERNA VÍA

Jameson, *The Political Unconscious* (1981); M. Blanchot, *The Gaze of Orpheus* (1981); D. Carroll, *The Subject in Question* (1982); de Man; H. R. Jauss, *Toward an Aesthetic of Reception* (tr. 1982); J. H. Miller, *Fiction and Repetition* (1982); G. Bataille, *Visions of Excess* (tr. 1985); H. Felperin, *Beyond Deconstruction* (1985); T. Moi, *Sexual/Textual Politics* (1985); A. Jardine, *Gynesis* (1985); P. de Man, *Resistance to Theory* (1986); *Midrash and Lit.*, ed. G. H. Hartman and S. Budick (1986); W. J. T. Mitchell, *Iconology* (1986); *Race, Writing, and Difference*, ed. H. L. Gates (1986).

STUDIES OF IMPORTANT CRITICS (in chronological order of critics): R. C. Lodge, *Plato's Theory of Art* (1953); J. A. Elias, *Plato's Defence of Poetry* (1984); L. Golden, *Aristotle's Poetics: A Tr. and Commentary* (1968); G. Else, *Aristotle's Poetics: The Argument* (1963), *Plato and Aristotle on Poetry* (1986); C. O. Brink, *Horace on Poetry*, 3 v. (1963–82); T. R. Henn, *Longinus and Eng. Crit.* (1934); C. G. Osgood, *Boccaccio on Poetry* (1930); H. B. Charlton, *Castelvetro's Theory of Poetry* (1913); F. Robinson, *The Shape of Things Known: Sidney's Apology and its Philosophical Trad.* (1972); Giacopo Mazzoni, *On the Defence of the Comedy of Dante: Intro. and Commentary*, tr. and intro. R. L. Montgomery (1983); A. D. Sellstrom, *Corneille, Tasso, and Modern Poetics* (1986); R. D. Hume, *Dryden's Crit.* (1970); E. Pechter, *Dryden's Cl. Theory of Lit.* (1975); E. L. Tuveson, *Imagination as a Means of Grace: Locke and the Aesthetics of Romanticism* (1960); A. Warren, *Pope as Critic and Humanist* (1929); L. A. Eliosoff, *The Cultural Milieu of Addison's Lit. Crit.* (1963); E. Burke, *A Philosophical Enquiry into the Origin of Our Ideas of the Sublime and the Beautiful*, ed. J. T. Boulton (1958); T. Brunius, *David Hume on Crit.* (1952); W. J. Bate, *The Achievement of Samuel Johnson* (1955); L. Damrosch, *The Uses of Johnson's Crit.* (1976); D. W. Crawford, *Kant's Aesthetic Theory* (1974); M. Eaves, *Wm. Blake's Theory of Art* (1982); L. P. Wassell, *The Philosophical Background of Friedrich Schiller's Aesthetics of Living Form* (1982); J. R. de J. Jackson, *Method and Imagination in Coleridge's Crit.* (1969); O. Barfield, *What Coleridge Thought* (1971); R. H. Fogle, *The Idea of Coleridge's Crit.* (1962); E. J. Schulze, *Shelley's Theory of Poetry* (1966); B. Bennett, *Goethe's Theory of Poetry* (1986); S. Bungay, *Beauty and Truth: A Study of Hegel's Aesthetics* (1984); E. W. Parks, *Edgar Allan Poe as a Literary Critic* (1964); L. Trilling, *Matthew Arnold* (1939); S. J. Kahn, *Science and Judgment: A Study in Taine's Critical Method* (1953); M. Gilman, *Baudelaire the Critic* (1943); W. E. Buckler, *Walter Pater: The Critic as Artist of Ideas* (1987); G. N. G. Orsini, *Benedetto Croce: Philosopher of Art and Literary Critic* (1961); A. Szathmary, *The Aesthetics of Bergson* (1937); J. J. Spector, *The Aesthetics of Freud* (1973); H. F. Brooks, *T. S. Eliot as Literary Critic* (1987); J. P. Schiller, *I. A. Richards' Theory of Lit.* (1969); J. P. Russo, *I. A. Richards* (1989); T. Todorov, *Mikhail Bakhtin: The Dialogical Principle* (1985); J. T. Jones, *Wayward Skeptic* [R. P. Blackmur] (1986); W. Ince, *The Poetic Theory of Paul Valéry* (1961); G. E. Henderson, *Kenneth Burke* (1988); *The Possibilities of Order: Cleanth Brooks and His Work*, ed. L. Simpson (1976); C. Howells, *Sartre's Theory of Lit.* (1979); R. Denhem, *Northrop Frye's Critical Method* (1978); A. C. Hamilton, *Northrop Frye: Anatomy of His Crit.* (1990); Wellek, v. 5–6—appraisals of 20th-c. Am. and Brit. critics; S. Lawall, "René Wellek and Mod. Lit. Crit.," *CL* 40 (1988); C. Norris, *Derrida* (1987); D. Carroll, *Paraesthetics: Foucault, Lyotard, Derrida* (1987); P. De Bolla, *Harold Bloom* (1988); C. Norris, *Paul de Man* (1988).   H.A.; T.V.F.B.

CRITICISM AND ETHICS. See ETHICS AND CRITICISM.

CROATIAN POETRY. See YUGOSLAV POETRY.

CROSS RHYME, envelope r., enclosed r. (Ger. *Kreuzreim, überschlagender Reim*; Fr. *rime brisée, rime croisée*). The r. scheme *abba*. In long-line verse, such as the Med. Lat. hexameter, two lines whose caesural words rhymed together and end-words rhymed together would have the pattern ———a ———b / ———a ———b; and if these are broken by hemistichs into short-lined verse, which is the hallmark of the lyric, cross rhyming appears.   T.V.F.B.

CROWN OF SONNETS. See CORONA.

CUADERNA VÍA. A Sp. meter (also called *alejandrino, mester de clerecía, nueva maestría*) in which syllable counting was used for the first time in Castilian, though the line soon deteriorated or was modified to one of somewhat more flexible length. It was introduced, probably under Fr. influence, in the first part of the 13th c. or earlier by the clergy (hence the name *mester de clerecía* in contrast to the *mester de juglaría*, or minstrel's meter, typical of the popular epic and other narrative poetry). This meter, particularly in the work of its earliest known exponent, Gonzalo de Berceo (late 12th to mid-13th c.), is notable for its rigidity of form: syllables are counted carefully; each line consists of two hemistichs of seven syllables each; the lines are grouped into monorhymed quatrains having true rhyme rather than assonance. According to Fitz-Gerald, hiatus was obligatory, though various forms of elision and metrical contraction were permitted (see METRICAL TREATMENT OF SYLLABLES). An example of the c. v. from the work of Berceo is the following:

> Yo Maestro Gonzalvo de Berceo nom-
>   nado, iendo en romeria, caeci en
>   un prado, verde e bien sencido, de
>   flores bien poblado; logar cobdi-
>   ciaduero pora homne cansado.

The best known works written largely in c. v. are Juan Ruiz's *Libro de buen amor* and López de Ayala's *Rimado de palacio*, both of the 14th c. The c. v. was employed for most of the serious poetry written in the 13th and 14th cs., but it was completely supplanted in the 15th by the *arte mayor* (q.v.).—J. D. Fitz-Gerald, *Versification of the C. V. as Found in Berceo's* Vida de Santo Domingo de Silos (1905); J. Saavedra Molina, "El verso de clerecia," *Boletin de filología* 6 (1950–51); Navarro.   D.C.C.

CUBAN POETRY. See SPANISH AMERICAN POETRY.

CUBISM. A school in the visual arts led by Picasso and Braque in Paris ca. 1907 to 1925 which, in part as a reaction against impressionism, stressed the geometrical forms conceived to be inherent in the objects it represented—hence "les petites cubes," which irritated Matisse but which ironically led to the name of the school. Although three stages have been postulated for this school (Gray), c. is commonly divided into an "analytic" stage, which dissects the inherent geometrical forms of objects, emphasizing them through a limited palette, and a "synthetic" stage, in which fragments of various objects are reintegrated into a new, self-consciously *aesthetic* object. At its most sophisticated, synthetic c. evolved techniques of *collage* and *papier collé*, incorporating fragments of real objects into the composition, including fragments of verbal texts, thereby challenging a naive acceptance of either visual or verbal representation. C. was enthusiastically embraced by the French poet Apollinaire, who praised the cubist aesthetic in his *Les Peintres cubistes* (1913), thus encouraging a critical controversy still waged today as to whether there is such a genre as *cubist lit.* in general or *cubist poetry* in particular. In part because Apollinaire (and later Reverdy and cummings) denied being a cubist poet, and in part because of a theoretical questioning of the validity of transferring a term from one artistic medium to another, several critics have denied the existence of cubist lit. altogether (Decaudin). However, the term *cubist lit.* was accepted as early as 1941 (Lemaître) and has subsequently gained so much acceptance that Joyce, Eliot, Faulkner, Stevens, cummings, Robbe-Grillet, Ford Maddox Ford, Gertrude Stein, and Max Jacob have all been called cubist writers. The diversity of these writers has led some critics to conclude that c. best describes the 20th-c. perspective (Sypher) and critical temperament (Steiner).

Despite its increased acceptance, the term *cubist poetry* has very different meanings in the hands of different critics. Since, in contrast to imagism, vorticism, or futurism (qq.v.), there is no poetic "Cubist Manifesto," it is possible to find cubist poetry defined as a style marked by "new syntax and punctuation, based on typographical dispersion" (Admussen); as a poetic movement between futurism and expressionism (Hadermann); or as a style characterized by an unusual amount of "punning, contradiction, parody, and word play"

in order to create the ambiguity so characteristic of visual c. (Steiner). Cubist poetry is variously confined to the writings concurrent with the cubist school, esp. 1912–19 (Carmody) or to the works typically printed in *Nord-Sud*, a journal edited by Reverdy (Admussen), or it is extended to works marked by visual fragmentation, such as that of Cummings or Zukofsky, works obsessed with perception, such as Stevens' "Thirteen Ways of Looking at a Blackbird," or works constituted by multiple voices and temporal layers, such as Eliot's *The Waste Land*.

It is useful to remember that even within the visual arts, c. proved to be a highly complex and diffuse movement; and it is reasonable to expect that such diversity would be reflected in the poetry as well, as various poets appropriated different facets of c. into their work. Thus, Williams' "The Red Wheel Barrow," with cubelike stanzas that continually change in perspective, and Eliot's *The Wasteland*, with fragments of various langs., disrupted narrative, and multifaceted allusions, constitute relatively simple and complex versions of the "analytic" pole of poetic c. In contrast, Stevens' "Man with the Blue Guitar," which stresses its ambiguous status as a representational *object* by frustrating its own ability to represent, may be described as the poetic embodiment of synthetic c. Some poets such as Pound and Eliot incorporate not only multiple allusions but the found poem (q.v.) as well, thus approaching the montage or collage that some critics find most characteristic of cubist lit.

In a very different way, the attention to visual form inherent in visual c. invites such visual poetry (q.v.) as Apollinaire's "Coeur couronne et miroir" or such concrete poetry (q.v.) as his "Lettre-Océan." The visual impact of the verbal text is further explored in such experimental poetry as Henri Chopin's "il manque toujours l'y" or Eugen Gomringer's "the black mystery is here" (Steiner), both of which stress their status as artistic objects. More radically, the conjunction of visual and verbal texts typical of the later cubist paintings, as well as the tendency toward the fragmentation or "analysis" of form characteristic of all cubist works, may be realized in such complicated pieces as Marius de Zaya's "mental reactions," in which the fragmentation and reassembly of a poem by Agnes Ernst Meyer with visual forms undermines the distinction between the two arts altogether (Bohn). But the most typical visual mark of cubist poetry is the rupture of normal stanza, line, and word boundaries, which creates a visual text even less traditional than that of free verse (q.v.). The most famous practitioner of this strategy is cummings, whose work includes sentence fragments and open parenthetical phrases, embodying disjunctive forms at the syntactic level.

While it is not possible to devise a list of "cubist" characteristics that will be present in every "cubist" poem, it is possible to say that along the spectrum of analytic and synthetic interpretations, cubist poetry is likely to be characterized by a highly self-conscious sense of its own modernism; attention to visual form (which may move toward the composition of very precise, block-like stanzas bearing an affinity to imagism (q.v.) or toward a more radical arrangement of the printed page); a rupturing of traditional poetic and semantic forms; and a thematic preoccupation with mulitple perspectives, leading to a questioning of the representation itself. Finally, the very fragmentation of form that was ironically so characteristic of a movement preoccupied with form encouraged the blurring of genre and media distinctions, giving rise to the prose poem (q.v.) of Max Jacob and others or to such intermedia as Zukofsky's epic-length "A," which evolves from poetic to musical composition.

G. Apollinaire, *Les Peintres cubistes* (1913), ed. L.-C. Breunig and J.-C. Chevalier (1965); G. Lemaître, *From C. to Surrealism in Fr. Lit.* (1941); C. Gray, *Cubist Aesthetic Theories* (1953); F. Carmody, "L'Esthétique de l'esprit nouveau," *Le Flaneur des deux rives* 2 (1955); W. Sypher, *From Rococo to C. in Art and Lit.* (1960); F. Steegmuller, *Apollinaire: Poet among the Painters* (1963); R. Admussen, "*Nord-Sud* and Cubist Poetry," *JAAC* 27 (1968); J. Golding, *C.: A Hist. and an Analysis, 1907–1914* (1968); B. Dijkstra, *The Hieroglyphics of a New Speech* (1969); G. Kamber, *Max Jacob and the Poetics of C.* (1971); E. Frye, *C.* (1978); P. Hadermann, "De Quelques Procédés 'cubistes' en poésie," *Actes du VIIIe Congrès de l'Assoc. Internationale de Littérature Comparée* (1980); F. Igly, *Apollinaire: Poète ami et défenseur des peintres cubistes* (1982); C. et Lit., Special Issue of *Europe: Revue lit. mensuelle*, no. 638-39 (1982), esp. Decaudin; W. Steiner, *The Colors of Rhet.* (1982), incl. bibl.; W. Marling, *William Carlos Williams and the Painters, 1909–1923* (1982); H. Sayre, *The Visual Text of William Carlos Williams* (1983); M. Perloff, *The Dance of the Intellect* (1985); W. Bohn, *The Aesthetics of Visual Poetry 1914–1928* (1986); J. V. Brogan, *Part of the Climate: Am. Cubist Poetry* (1991).　　　　　J.V.B.

CUBO-FUTURISM. See FUTURISM.

CUECA CHILENA. A South Am. popular dance song, also called *chilenita, zamacueca, zamacueca peruana,* which is an 8-line *seguidilla* (q.v.) in which the basic quatrain is separated from the *estribillo* (refrain) by the insertion of a line that is a repetition of the fourth line plus the word *si.*—F. Hanssen, "La seguidilla," *AUC* 125 (1909).　　　　D.C.C.

CULTERANISMO, originally a satirical term implying literary heresy (like *luteranismo*, Lutheranism) and used to attack the new style of poetry of Luis de Góngora y Argote (1561–1627), or gongorism, is best understood in relation to *conceptismo* or conceptism. In Sp. lit. hist., c. traditionally describes a poetic style in which learned words,

Hispanized from Lat. and Gr., are prominent. Conceptismo, on the other hand, is a style in poetry or prose characterized by ingenious or "precious" ideas (see PRECIOSITE). In other words, according to this view, c. concerns poetic vocabulary, while conceptismo concerns the expression of thought. But even in theory this is too simple: it is impossible absolutely to divorce thought from expression. In practice, c. and conceptismo are often found intermingled. If they are kept provisionally separate in the interests of analysis, c. may be found best exemplified in Góngora and his followers, and conceptismo best exemplified in Francisco de Quevedo y Villegas (1580–1645) and Baltasar Gracián (1601–58).

While it is true that Góngora often drew on Lat. in fashioning neologisms, it must be recognized that Lat. has always been the reservoir of Sp. and also that many new creations did become permanently naturalized. Contemp. testimony in the form of satire (e.g. Quevedo's "La Culta Latiniparla") is misleading in that it suggests that Góngora and his school wilfully displaced good Sp. words with Latinisms and various preciosities. More characteristic of Góngora is his strange use of common words: e.g. *peinar* ("to comb") in the sense of "to plow" or "to pass through" (as in "peinar el viento"). The effect is that of a striking and original metaphor, and, in general, of a new linguistic system built right into the old. In the new lang. common objects or qualities take on a multiple existence: grain becomes gold and wool becomes snow; white may be snow or crystal or ivory. In syntax, Góngora tends to compress by following as closely as Sp. inflection allows the freedom of Lat.; hyperbaton (q.v.), dislocated word-order, is the result.

The major literary contest in the Sp. baroque age was carried on by Góngora and Quevedo. If Quevedo refrained from using Latinate words and bending Sp. words to his own esoteric uses, nevertheless he made capital of wordplay, drawing on slang (*germania,*) double meaning, and etymology. He is also fond of syntactic contrast, paradox, and oxymoron. Quevedo's crit. of Góngora may be reduced, without much loss, to his disapproval of Latinizing Sp. Indeed, c. may be restricted to describing this aspect of gongorine style. The true affinities of the two poets are best seen under the light of general baroque (q.v.) poetic style. Their close relation was, in effect, recognized by the chief theorist of the time, Baltasar Gracián, in his highly specialized anthol. and commentary, the *Agudeza y Arte de Ingenio* (1648; earlier version, *El Arte de Ingenio,* 1642). Gracián himself is a master of baroque artifice, and his work, while emulating the older rhetoric, is in part an original analysis of the poetic taste and practice of the time. In it, Góngora and Quevedo, as well as the whole range of ancient and modern poetry, serve side by side as examples of wit and ingeniousness and art. See also SPANISH POETRY, sect. VIII.

B. Croce, "I trattatisti italiani del concettismo e

Baltasar Gracián," *Problemi di estetica* (1905); L. P. Thomas, *Le Lyrisme et la préciosité cultistes en Espagne* (1909); W. Pabst, "Góngoras Schöpfung in seinen Gedichten *Poliferno* und *Soledades*," *Revue Hispanique* 80 (1930); T. E. May, "Gracián's Idea of the 'Concepto,'" *HR* 18 (1950); D. Alonso, *Poesía española*, 2d ed. (1952), *La lengua poética de Góngora*, 3d corr. ed. (1961), *Góngora y el Polifemo*, v. 2 (1961); F. García Lorca, "La imagen poética en don Luis de Góngora," *Obras completas* (1954); F. Monge. "C. y conceptismo a la luz de Gracian," *Homenaje: Estudios de filología e historia literaria lusohispanas e iberoamericanas* (1966); A. Collard, *Nueva poesía: conceptismo, c. en la crítica española* (1967)—excellent discussion.   L.NE.

CULTISM. See CULTERANISMO.

CULTURAL CRITICISM. During its devel. from the 18th c. onward, c. crit. has been preoccupied with the social roles of the arts and intellectuals; the uses of education and literacy; the effects of population increase and the economic transformations stemming from industrialism; the functions of institutions, esp. the state and the media; the relative status and value of popular (low, mass) and canonical ("high") culture; and the possibilities for social change. Given such concerns, it is not surprising that c. critics share interests and methods not only with anthropologists, communications and media specialists, historians, and sociologists, but with a wide array of literary critics, incl. many Marxists, myth critics, hermeneuticists, semioticians, poststructuralists, ethnic critics, and feminists. The task of c. crit. is to analyze and assess the sociohistorical foundations, distribution networks, and ethicopolitical ramifications of communal artifacts, events, practices, and organizations; its methodologies incl. "textual" explication, survey and interview techniques, historical inquiry, and institutional and ideological analysis.

One of the preoccupations of c. crit. is the definition of "culture." In ordinary usage the word displays a wide range of designations: it names intellectual and artistic practices, esp. lit., music, painting, sculpture, theater, philosophy, and crit.; it describes processes of intellectual, spiritual, aesthetic, and moral devel.; it indicates the distinctive way of life of a people or period or of humanity as a whole; it signals refinement of taste, judgment, and intellect; and it includes manners, conventions, myths, institutions, and patterns of thought. Thus "culture" refers simultaneously to products and processes, to material and symbolic production, to specific and general human devel., to quotidian social practices and high arts, to ethics and aesthetics, to subcultures and civilization. Among c. theorists and critics, the polysemy of the word and the continuous contention surrounding the idea reveal less a failure to isolate a discrete object of inquiry than a recurring magnetic pull characteristic of both the concept and the enterprise of studying culture. Tylor's still influential definition succinctly suggests the richness of the term: culture is "that complex whole which includes knowledge, belief, art, morals, law, custom, and any other capabilities and habits acquired by man as a member of society."

Matthew Arnold's formulations on culture in *Culture and Anarchy* (1869) mark a watershed in the history of c. crit. Arnold sums up and transforms a trad. of thought extending from Swift and Vico through Burke and Herder to Cobbett, Coleridge, and Carlyle. Culture is the pursuit of a best self and a general perfection, motivated by passion for pure knowledge and for social and moral right action, effected by reading, observing, and contemplating the voices of human experience in art, science, poetry, philosophy, history, and religion. Culture leads men to see things as they are; to increase of sympathy and intelligence; to make right reason and the will of God prevail; to do away with social classes; to render everywhere current the best that has been thought and known in the world; to practice spontaneous and disinterested play of thought; and to attain complete, harmonious perfection. The enemies of culture incl. confusion, religious zeal, individualism, sectarianism, industrialism, and anarchy. For Arnold, culture engenders dissatisfaction with, and purgation of, the vulgar philistinism typical of industrial capitalism. Promoted through education undertaken by the state (a collective apparatus embodying higher reason), culture serves as a principle of authority to counteract tendencies toward social disintegration. The agents of culture are a saving remnant of intellectuals who come from all classes, raise themselves above class spirit, and work optimistically and nonviolently, but avoid direct political action.

For Arnold and many other c. critics, poetry is one among a number of arts and sciences that document sociohistorical conditions and, more importantly, enlighten the mind and spirit. Poetry serves an ethicopolitical role in society, providing a high ground for social crit.; it is linked to a broad project of social reform undertaken by the educational establishment and the state. Thus poetry is valued not primarily for its textual refinement, nor for its insight into the artist's soul, nor for its power to move or entertain (as given in the formalist, expressive, and affective theories of Western poetics) but rather for the efficacy of its agency in social action (the mimetic and didactic).

In the Arnoldian trad., c. crit. seeks to foster through the free play of consciousness a better social self and a better world. One impulse of c. crit. is not to place lit. in a hierarchy of aesthetic forms, but rather to situate all literary works within a network of other related cultural forms and practices. Yet another impulse is to focus on superior works, on the best that humankind has created, regarding most popular and mass forms, esp. those produced in the era of industrial capitalism, as degraded and inferior. Arnold is usually taken as representative of the elitist strand of thought, which culminates in the early and mid 20th c. with such diverse groups as the Frankfurt school, New Critics, New York intellectuals, and *Scrutiny* circle. For these thinkers, lit. and culture constitute superior achievements of human excellence critical of the poor state of modern civilization. In secularized Western industrial societies, culture comes to serve displaced religious functions, advocating right action, humility, and harmony.

It is against the tendencies to construe culture as a body of superior works, a standard of excellence or repository of ruling-class values, that Raymond Williams argues in *Culture and Society* (1958), the major modern study of the history of British c. crit. For Williams, a culture is "not only a body of intellectual and imaginative works; it is also and essentially a whole way of life." The skilled and creative activities that constitute culture incl. gardening, metalwork, carpentry, and politics as well as theater, music, lit., and art. Culture is and should be common not selective, democratic not dominative. Like traditional c. forms, new modes of c. practice such as photography, television, cinema, broadcasting, and advertising can only be understood and evaluated by reference to the lived experience of everyday life, to the whole way of existence of a people, incl. manners, habits, memories, and institutions. Significantly, the c. productions and processes of subcultures and class factions make it evident that it is struggle and contradiction which primarily characterize culture—phenomena which discredit nostalgic and static views of culture as an harmonious entity. In line with his commitment to forging a common, democratic culture, Williams emphasizes the communal and communicative functions of the arts.

Widely adopted in the 1970s and thereafter, Antonio Gramsci's concept of *hegemony* has made a decisive contribution to c. crit. and theory. Among the many critics indebted to Gramsci are Williams and the members of the University of Birmingham's Centre for Contemp. Culture Studies (CCCS), a group whose best works during the 1970s and '80s mark a high point in the hist. of c. crit. As a Marxist, Gramsci transforms the received view of ideology with the concept of hegemony. Building on Marxist doctrine that culture is a politicized subordinating force used by ruling elites to portray as positive and universal their own ideas and values, Gramsci distinguishes between coercive domination and negotiated leadership. The success of a controlling group's "ideology"—which is relative, temporary, and subject to challenge—depends not only or even primarily on repressive political control through legal, administrative, military, and educational apparatuses, but also on freely given civil consensus molded through the family, church, school, workplace, union, media, and arts. The leadership of the dominant group needs continuous renewal and maintenance in order for its values and interests to shape consciousness and to constitute common sense.

In this context revolution requires much more than seizing the economic means of production or securing the various arms of government; it entails changing the hearts and minds of contending groups and cementing them into a relative unity. In contrast to the Arnoldian view of culture, the Gramscian account highlights group antagonism and social contradiction; represents civil society as part of the state; stresses everyday activities and negotiations; shows social harmony, perfection, and order to be strictly relative (if not fictions); and presents the state not as the embodiment of higher reason but as the agency of dominant group leadership. Where Arnold casts intellectuals as an elite clerisy above class spirit and direct political action, Gramsci portrays intellectuals as a large, active, heterogeneous ensemble of teachers, journalists, clergy, doctors, lawyers, military officers, writers, technicians, managers, and policymakers whose efforts link strata of culture into a consensual historical bloc.

What characterizes the c. theory of the Birmingham CCCS is a complex *rapprochement* of British culturalism as developed by Williams and others and Fr. (post)structuralism as pioneered by Althusser, Barthes, Foucault, and others. The work of Gramsci serves as a partial bridge. Culturalism conceives culture as a whole way of life and struggle capturable through empirical descriptions that unite symbolic forms and material life. Structuralism (q.v.) and poststructuralism (see DECONSTRUCTION) treat c. forms as semiautonomous discourses open to semiological analyses attentive to formative c. codes and ideological effects. Where culturalism examines experience as embodied in, for example, oral histories, working-class fictions, and teen subcultures, (post)structuralism studies signifying practices and structures at work in avant-garde texts and disciplinary discourses. The Gramscian analysis of consensus formation provides an understanding of social determination and change compatible with the projects of both culturalism and (post)structuralism. In addition, both movements share similar dislikes, being hostile to, for instance, the widespread belletristic celebration of canonical culture, the reigning framework of university disciplines, the antihistoricism and apoliticism of many literary scholars, and the traditional conception of the intellectual as disinterested connoisseur and custodian of culture. Yet crucial differences remain between the two, esp. in their accounts of c. production, of the formation of subjectivity (q.v.), of the usefulness of psychoanalysis, of the continuing pertinence of Marxist theory, and of the possibilities for resistance. Finally, the CCCS has come to serve as a model for the creation of the emergent discipline of c. studies in a number of university departments and programs throughout the Anglophone world.

One exemplary modern study in c. crit. is Edward Said's *Orientalism* (1978), a productive fusion of protocols and principles developed by British culturalism, Gramsci, and Foucault. Said construes the long hist. of Franco-British-Am. writing on the Near Eastern Orient as a massive, systematic, disciplinary discourse engaged not merely in depicting but also in structuring and ruling over the Orient in a consistently racist, sexist, and imperialistic manner. Documents scrutinized by Said range from scholarly books, political tracts, and journalistic reports to travel pieces, religious texts, and literary works. The hegemonic consensus about the East produced and continually reproduced by "Orientalism"—the institutionalized Western ideological "science" of the Orient—bears little relation to actual human experience. A key lesson Said draws is that "study, understanding, knowledge, evaluation, masked as blandishments to 'harmony,' are instruments of conquest." Like many c. critics, Said regards knowledge as joined indissolubly to interest and power, all enabled and constrained by interlocking institutions. This view clearly contradicts Arnold's ideas concerning pure knowledge, disinterested thought, and the benign rational state. Moreover, Said explicitly ties the knowledge-interest-power nexus to aggressive nation states, showing the limitations of Arnold's political thought. Nevertheless, the Arnoldian legacy survives in Said's commitment to see things as they are, to respect actual human experience, to advocate social and moral right, to increase understanding and sympathy, and to struggle against religion, esp. in its overzealous forms.

Focused on such issues as gender, class, ethnicity, and postcolonial nationhood, c. critics often pluralize poetics, believing a single universal theory of poetry will not work given the heterogeneity of peoples, trads., forms, and values existing in the world. From such a perspective, even so capacious a "universal" poetics as Frye's in *Anatomy of Crit.* emerges as a limited, Eurocentric, patriarchal model rooted in the Christian Bible as source of archetypes—which ultimately possess little relevance for numerous other lits. and groups. The non-Western poetries, esp. those of oppressed peoples of color and of colonial "natives," frequently derive from divided, deracinated subjects, from heteroglot lang. trads. and cultural intertexts, and from hybrid, conflictual regimes, none of which traditional poetics takes into account (see POETICS). At a time when some conservative c. critics seek to celebrate with redoubled vigor the canonical trad. of Great Books, progressive c. critics aim to devel. modes of theory, analysis, and pedagogy attentive to the complexities and implications of emergent postcolonial and ethnic lits., the realities of the multicultural era to come.

Among literary intellectuals there are several recurring arguments against key premises of c. crit. To begin with, c. critics de-emphasize the creativity of authors and often ignore literary craft and stylistic technique. Moreover, to equate poetry with ordinary discourses such as advertising is to devalue the specificity—the "literariness" and poeticity—of verbal art. Too, c. critics sever the archetypal connection of poetry with sacred mystery and wisdom, separating the text from its affective and spiritual powers. The direct encounter of the reader with the text is hindered by a requirement that cultural history consciously enter into the transaction. Finally, much c. crit. subordinates lit. to politics, esp. liberal and leftist politics. For their part, c. critics regard such charges as elitist mystifications launched in the interests of aesthetic ideology, religious orthodoxy, or disciplinary specialization. They argue that there is no getting around sociohistorical foundations and complex cultural determinations.

See also CRITICISM; ETHICS AND CRITICISM; EXOTICISM; FEMINIST POETICS; MARXIST CRITICISM; PLURALISM; POLITICS AND POETRY; PRIMITIVISM; THEORY.

E. B. Tylor, *Primitive Culture* (1871); A. L. Kroeber and C. Kluckhohn, *Culture: A Critical Review of Concepts and Definitions* (1952); R. Williams, *Culture and Society* (1958), *Problems in Materialism and Culture* (1980), "Culture," *Keywords*, rev. ed. (1983); T. W. Adorno, "C. Crit. and Society," *Prisms*, tr. S. and S. Weber (1967); L. Althusser, *Lenin and Philosophy*, tr. B. Brewster (1971); A. Gramsci, *Selections from the Prison Notebooks*, ed. and tr. Q. Hoare and G. N. Smith (1971); R. Barthes, *Mythologies*, tr. A. Lavers (1972); E. Said, *Orientalism* (1978), *The World, the Text, and the Critic* (1983); M. Foucault, *Discipline and Punish*, tr. A. Sheridan (1977), *Hist. of Sexuality*, v. 1, tr. R. Hurley (1978), *Power/Knowledge*, ed. C. Gordon, tr. C. Gordon et al. (1980); H. White, *Tropics of Discourse* (1978); D. Hebdige, *Subculture* (1979); L. Johnson, *The C. Critics* (1979); Centre for Contemp. C. Studies, *Culture, Media, Lang.* (1980); S. Hall, "C. Studies: Two Paradigms," *Culture, Ideology and Social Process*, ed. T. Bennett et al. (1981); F. Jameson, *The Political Unconscious* (1981); P. Bourdieu, *Distinction: A Social Critique of the Judgement of Taste*, tr. R. Nice (1984); R. Scholes, *Textual Power* (1985); R. Johnson, "What Is C. Studies Anyway?" *Social Text* 16 (1986–87)—landmark conspectus on CCCS methodology; *Marxism and the Interp. of Culture*, ed. C. Nelson and L. Grossberg (1988); *Classics in C. Crit. I*, ed. B.-P. Lange (1990); *Classics in C. Crit. II*, ed. H. Heuermann (1990); G. Turner, *British C. Studies* (1990); V. B. Leitch, *C. Crit., Literary Theory, Poststructuralism* (1992).   V.B.L.

CURSUS. See PROSE RHYTHM.

CURTAL SONNET. Gerard Manley Hopkins in the "Author's Preface" to his *Poems* identifies "Pied Beauty" and "Peace" as "Curtal-Sonnets," namely sonnets curtailed (shortened), though in this case not on the end but according to the usual proportion of octave to sestet, so that 8:6=6:4.5. This gives a sonnet of 10 lines with a halfline tail. Contrast the expanded form of sonnet, called caudate (q.v.). T.V.F.B.

CYCLE. See LYRIC SEQUENCE; SONNET SEQUENCE; COLLECTIONS, POETIC.

CYCLE PLAYS. See LITURGICAL DRAMA; MIRACLE PLAYS.

CYNGHANEDD. In Welsh poetry (q.v.), an elaborate system of sound correspondences involving accentuation, alliteration, and internal rhyme. Gerard Manley Hopkins described them as "chimes" and admitted that they were a main influence on his own formal experiments. *C.* was well developed in Welsh by the 14th c., although not finally codified until the Caerwys Eisteddfod (Bardic Assembly) of 1524. *C.* was, and still is, a main feature of Welsh "strict-meter" poetry, but it has often been practiced, with varying degrees of strictness, in the "free-meters" as well, and in modern times even in *vers libre*. In the detail and complexity of its patterning, *c.* is the most sophisticated system of poetic sound-patterning practiced in any poetry in the world.

C. is of three kinds: consonantal; *sain*, involving both rhyme and alliteration; and *lusg* (dragging), a form of internal rhyme, which was also practiced in Breton poetry (q.v.). Consonantal *c.* is itself of three kinds: "crossing" (*groes*), "leaping" (*draws*), and "interlinked" crossing.

In all examples of the "crossing" type, the alliteration forms a pattern in relation to two stressed vowels—the last before the caesura and the last in the line. There are three kinds of crossing: stressed, unstressed, and "uneven-falling." In the first type, both halflines are oxytonic, i.e. end on a stressed vowel, and all the consonants within the first half-line are repeated in the same order in the second, e.g. "Yr ydwyf í / ar dy fédd," where the pattern repeated is *r-d-f*. In the unstressed and "uneven-falling" types, the sound relations, though similar to the above, are more complex. In the "leaping" types, the correspondences are as for the crossing types except that after the caesura the repetitions are preceded by one or more unrepeated consonants. Where the crossing is "interlinked," the repetitions begin before the caesura.

In *c. sain* the line falls into three sections, each with a main stress, the first section rhyming with the second, and the second related to the third by repeated pattern of consonants, as in consonantal *c.* In *c. lusg*, each line must end with a paroxytone (i.e. have a feminine ending), the unstressed final syllable bearing the main rhyme and the preceding stressed syllable rhyming with one of the earlier syllables in the same line, which may be stressed or post-stressed.

The rules of *c.* stated above are only a broad outline. Much of the skill and delight of *c.* poetry lies in the variation of types in successive lines and in the contrasting of vowel sounds alongside the repetition of consonants. It is an art form capable of a very rich, subtle, melodious, and highly wrought effect which has been extensively exploited by Welsh poets.—Morris-Jones; Parry, *History*, ch. 5 (App.); G. Williams, *Intro. to Welsh Poetry* (1953), App. A; A. Lloyd and D. Evans in *Poetry Wales* 14 (1978); E. Rowlands, "C.," Metre, Prosody," in Jarman and Hughes; Stephens; R. Bromwich, *Aspects of the Poetry of Dafydd ap Gwilym* (1986); *Welsh Verse*, ed. T. Conran, 2d ed. (1986)—long intro. and appendix on meter.
D.M.L.; T.V.F.B.

CYWYDD. Along with *awdl* and *englyn* (q.v.), one of the three classes of the 24 "strict meters" in Welsh poetry (q.v.). There are four varieties of *c.*, but normally the term is used to refer only to *c. deuair hirion* (heptasyllabic lines in couplets with alternating masculine and feminine [q.v.] endings), popularized by Dafydd ap Gwilym in the 14th c. The 14th to the early 16th centuries are known as the *C. Period* in Welsh poetry because *c.* became the staple Welsh meter during this time. It was revived in the 18th c. by Goronwy Owen and Ieuan Fard and is still popular. The earliest known examples are without *cynghanedd* (q.v.). Dafydd, however, embellished most of his lines with *cynghanedd*, and in the 15th c. this became obligatory in every line. The *c.* is very similar to Ir. *debhidhe* except that in *c.* either type of ending may precede the other.—Morris-Jones; T. Parry in *Trans. of the Hon. Soc. of Cymmrodorion* (1939): 203–31; Parry, *History*, ch. 6; E. Rowlands in *Ysgrifau Beirniadol* 2 (1966); Jarman and Hughes; Stephens; R. Bromwich, *Aspects of the Poetry of Dafydd ap Gwilym* (1986); *Welsh Verse*, ed. T. Conran, 2d ed. (1986)—long intro. and appendix on meters.
D.M.L.; T.V.F.B.

CZECH POETRY. The earliest extant verse in the C. vernacular is a hymn dating from the late 12th or early 13th c. addressed to the patron saint of Bohemia, Václav ("Good King Wenceslaus"). But the 14th c. saw a great flowering of C. p., epic, lyric, and dramatic. Outstanding are an epic about Alexander of Macedon and numerous versified saints' lives, in particular a *Life* of St. Catherine of Alexandria noted for the brilliance of its imagery. These works all had Med. Lat. prototypes, but were often quite original in details. The lyric also came to Bohemia, chiefly from France and Italy; worthy of note is a C. variant of the Prov. *aubade* (see ALBA). An indigenous satiric poetry also flourished in the 14th c.; perhaps the most original example is a burlesque disputation, *Podkoní a žák* (The Groom and the Student), wherein each antagonist maintains that his life is the better. Prosodically, much of 14th-c. C. verse employs trochaic octosyllable in couplets, though the syllable count varies at times.

The Hussite period of the early 15th c. severely curtailed poetic expression, though it did produce interesting polemic poetry. Humanism brought new forms of Lat. verse, but poetic expression in the vernacular lagged behind, though the C. humanists made their native prose one of the most expressive of the written langs. of Europe. The Counter-Reformation, however, which followed the loss of C. independence in 1620, inspired the cultivation of a contemplative religious poetry of hymns and prayers remarkable for its ornate imagery and wordplay. The latter 17th and early 18th cs. witnessed the virtual death of C. national lit.; not until the latter half of the 18th c. were systematic attempts begun to revive C. as a literary lang. This movement was nationalistic and patriotic; rejecting the Jesuit baroque heritage, it reached back to the C. Protestant Humanist trad. of the 16th c. The result was that written C. as revived was somewhat archaic, and indeed has remained so until today. But conversely this unbroken bond with an ancient literary trad. has given modern C. a decided advantage over many other Central and East European literary langs. In the early 19th c., Cl. influences were strong, and a period of vacillation between quantitative and accentual systems of versification ensued. Eventually the accentually based verse triumphed, but syllable length continued to play a prosodic role.

Didactic, biblical, laudatory, and idyllic verse predominated at the end of the 18th c. in the work of A. J. Puchmajer (1769–1820). The beginning of the 19th c. brought preromanticism (q.v.) and a poetry dedicated to the national patriotic cause. The kinship of Czechs with the other Slavic peoples was stressed. The Slovak Ján Kollár (1793–1852), who wrote in C., produced a collection of sonnets, *Slávy dcera* (The Daughter of Sláva, 1824 and 1832), a grandiose and sometimes moving attempt to construct a Slavic mythology and foretell a happier future for the Slavic peoples. F. L. Čelakovský (1799–1852) took inspiration from Slavic folksongs for his *Ohlasy* (Echoes) of Rus. and C. folksongs (1829 and 1839, respectively).

Romanticism arrived full-blown with K. H. Mácha (1810–36), probably, in spite of his early death, the greatest C. poet. His solitary masterpiece, the narrative poem *Máj* (May), written in 1836, is Byronic in subject but remarkable for the saturated intensity of its imagery, portraying the poet's favorite romantic antitheses of youth and age, love and death. May is the time of youth and love:

It was late evening, the first of May—
Evening May—the time of love.
The voice of the turtle-dove called to
    love
Where the pine grove wafted its scent.

These are the best known lines in all of C. p. But the time of childhood innocence is fleeting:

The fury of the times bore that season
    far away,
Far off his dream. . . .
The fair childhood age of the dead.

Mácha introduced iambic verse to C.: before him, modern C. verse had been exclusively trochaic (even Kollár's sonnets were in trochees), because C. has a fixed weak stress on the first syllable of each word, so that lines normally open with a stress; occasional iambic lines were considered trochaic with anacrusis. Mácha varied the treatment of the first foot of the line and, emphasizing the iambic character of the other feet, thus shaped a true iambic verse. More conservative than Mácha was his contemporary K. J. Erben (1811–70), who created the C. romantic ballad, inspired by the popular ballad of folk poetry.

The failure of the Revolution of 1848 brought an end to the independence movement and to the first wave of romanticism. Not until the 1860s did a strong new romantic movement emerge. Here once again the national cause was dominant, but now found more practical expression through the creation of popular institutions, incl. a national theater. Writers were concerned with social problems—democracy, the emancipation of women, and the correction of economic injustice, as well as national liberation. The leading poet of the period was Jan Neruda (1834–91), who strove to develop national consciousness, at times indulging in sharply ironic criticism of his too-contented countrymen. During the 1870s and '80s the nationalist tendency continued to dominate, notably in the work of Svatopluk Čech (1846–1908), a follower of the Pan-Slavist poet Kollár. Čech's style, often bombastic, at times attained real rhetorical power. In his lyrics he dealt with the political misfortunes of his people and, like Neruda, was capable of sarcasm at the national complacency.

The technical side of C. verse had suffered during this era, but the 1870s saw it rise to a new brilliance in the work of the Parnassian poet Jaroslav Vrchlický (pseudonym of Emil Frída, 1853–1912). A superb technician, Vrchlický introduced many new poetic themes and forms from abroad; in this he and his followers opposed the more nationally minded poets of the time. Vrchlický even rejected the traditionally canonical use of folk motifs and forms in C. higher poetry. He wrote voluminously, and translated from most of the European as well as the Cl. langs.; his total production exceeds 100 volumes, incl. much narrative and dramatic as well as lyric verse. A follower of Victor Hugo's evolutionary optimism, he was more limited in ideas than in form. Tending towards aestheticism and the cult of Cl. antiquity, he failed, however, to turn the current of C. p. permanently in either direction.

Vrchlický was followed by J. S. Machar (1864–1942), who sought to create a great poetic panorama of world history; like Nietzsche, he believed that history follows a spiral movement, alternately rising and falling. Machar's disciple Petr Bezruč (pseudonym of Vladimír Vašek, 1867–1958) proclaimed the sufferings of his own people, the Silesian miners; like Walt Whitman, he narrates his songs in a collective voice.

Contemporary with these "realists" were the C. symbolist poets, influenced by Fr. and Belgian symbolism (q.v.) and by Whitman. The greatest of these was Otokar Březina (pseudonym of V. I. Jebavý, 1868–1929), who wrote rhapsodic verse celebrating the mystic union of all people with each other and with the cosmos. Themes of decadence (q.v.) appear in the work of such poets as Jiří Karásek ze Lvovic (1871–1951) and Karel Hlaváček (1874–98). Viktor Dyk (1877–1931) wrote sarcastic epigrams against superficial C. patriotism and brought the C. ballad to a pinnacle in sophisticated irony. The C. symbolists, particularly Březina and Antonín Sova (1864–1928), did much to strengthen the musical aspect of C. verse and to cultivate an impressionistic visual imagery.

The achievement of national independence in 1918 was followed by a period of intense creativity. The early 1920s brought a wave of so-called proletarian poetry, expressing a warm if somewhat naive sympathy for the Soviet experiment. The leading poet of this trend was Jiří Wolker (1900–24). The late 1920s saw a sudden and violent shift to "poetism," a school of "pure poetry" (q.v.) which had its roots in dada, futurism (q.v.), and vitalism. The poets sought to create a poetry of the joy of living, of urban life and technology, a poetry inspired by such peripheral arts as film, the circus, and the musical revue. Leading "poetists" were Vítězslav Nezval (1900–58) and Jaroslav Seifert (1901–86). But the early 1930s saw the collapse of poetism as a movement: Nezval went over to surrealism (q.v.), while Seifert turned to a more personal poetry of love and sensual imagery. The interwar period also saw the cultivation of a spiritual and meditative poetry in the work of Josef Hora (1891–1945). But probably the greatest poet of this period is František Halas (1901–49), a complex writer obsessed by themes of age, death, and decay. Most of these poets were leftists in politics, but their poetry remained individualist.

World War II and the subsequent Communist coup destroyed the older poetic trad. In the spring of 1956, demands for greater freedom began to be heard, and Seifert and František Hrubín (1910–71) sharply criticized the official restrictions placed on lit. The principal poet of the 1960s was Vladimír Holan (1905–80), who published a flood of meditative, spiritualist verse, presumably written in the earlier postwar years. Seifert too found his voice again in this period; and his long and varied career was finally crowned, in 1984, by the award of the Nobel Prize for Lit., the first ever given to a C. writer.

The invasion of Czechoslovakia in 1968 by the Soviet Union and its Warsaw Pact allies dealt a new blow to C. lit and culture, a blow from which they have not yet recovered. The older generation of poets, born in the decade 1900–1910, have all died, but it is difficult to point to anyone of the first rank who has taken their place; one reason must undoubtedly be the fact that the older poets, such as Halas and Seifert, have cast a long shadow. To this we must add the fact that poetry no longer enjoys the predominance that it traditionally had in C. lit. Before World War II, poetry had always been the dominant form of C. letters; the poetic culture attained particularly high levels under symbolism, and again in the 1920s and '30s, in spite of the pervasiveness of nationalist and didactic trends and the weakness of aestheticist, Parnassian, and Classicist tendencies in modern C. lit. The native folk lyric has had a strong influence in many periods, as have the folk epics of other Slavic peoples, e.g. the Russians and Serbs. The lyric has had a stronger trad. than the epic; perhaps the lack of a native folk epos is to blame here. But the literary ballad, a mixed epic-lyric form influenced by the C. folk ballad, has been important. Dramatic poetry is on the whole weak, though there are many plays in verse. In prosodic form, binary meters are virtually exclusive in C. verse, since the lang. has a tendency to accent every odd syllable. Mixed trochaic-dactylic forms based on Cl. or native folk models are common, however, particularly under romanticism. See also STRUCTURALISM, PRAGUE SCHOOL.

ANTHOLOGIES: *Česká lyra* (1911), *Česká epika* (1921), both ed. F. S. Procházka; *Mod. C. P.*, ed. P. Selver (1920); *Anthologie de la poésie tchèque*, ed. H. Jelínek (1930); *Lyrika českého obrození*, ed. V. Jirát (1940); *Mod. C. P.*, ed. E. Osers and J. K. Montgomery (1945); *Česká poesie*, pub. by Československý spisovatel (1951); *Nová česká poesie*, pub. by Československý spisovatel (1955); *The Linden Tree*, ed. M. Otruba and Z. Pešat (1963); *C. P.*, ed. A. French (1973).

HISTORY AND CRITICISM: J. Jakubec and A. Novák, *Gesch. der tschechischen Lit.* (1907); H. Jelínek, *Hist. de la littérature tchèque*, 3 v. (1930–35); J. and A. Novák, *Přehledné dějiny literatury české* (1936–39)—the most thorough survey, abridged and supplemented as *Stručné dějiny literatury české* (1946); J. Mukařovský, *Kapitoly z české poetiky*, 3 v. (1948); *Dějiny české literatury*, ed. J. Mukařovský et al., 3 v. (1959–61); J. Hrabák, *Studie o českém verši* (1959); R. Wellek, *Essays in C. Lit.* (1963); A. French, *The Poets of Prague* (1969)—poetry of the 1920s and '30s; R. Jakobson, "O Češskom stixe" and "Old C. Verse" in Jakobson, v. 5, 6; A. Novák, *C. Lit.*, rev. W. E. Harkins, 2d ed. (1986). W.E.H.

CZECH PROSODY. See SLAVIC PROSODY.

D

DACTYL (Gr. "finger"). In Cl. prosody, a metrical foot consisting of one long syllable followed by two short ones. In the modern prosodies based on accent, an accented syllable followed by two unaccented ones (*suddenly, ominous*). D. is the metrical basis of much of Cl. Gr. and Lat. poetry: in narrative verse it is used particularly for the hexameter and elegiac distich (qq.v.), and in lyric it is used alone and with other cola, esp. the epitrite (q.v.), in various combinations known collectively as *dactylo-epitrite* (q.v.). These latter did not survive the Cl. age, though the d. hexameter remained the meter for much Lat. artverse through most of the Middle Ages. In the transition from Lat. to the vernaculars, however, it lost place to iambic—which even in antiquity had been the meter felt to be closest to common (Gr.) speech and had been used for recitation meters such as dialogue in drama—as the staple meter of artverse and epic. Dactylic verse was however revived in Ger. by A. Buchner in his opera *Orpheus* (1638), arousing a brief vogue, evidenced in Simon Dach and Friedrich von Logau.

The d. is usually mentioned in handbooks of Eng. metrics along with the anapest and perhaps amphibrach (qq.v.) as the three modern ternary meters (see BINARY AND TERNARY), but in running series these are almost impossible to differentiate, esp. if the line-ends are ambiguous. If dactylic meter was suited to Gr., it was less suited to Lat., with its stress accent, and even less suited to the modern langs. Hence the status of this metrical foot in modern times is completely the reverse of its Cl. prestige: it is now used only for light verse and humorous subgenres, such as the recent "Double Dactyls" (q.v.).—A. Köster, "Deutsche Daktylen," *ZfdA* 46 (1901); Wilamowitz, pt. 2, ch. 10; Koster, ch. 4; Dale, ch. 3; Halporn et al.; Snell; West.   T.V.F.B.

DACTYLO-EPITRITE. The name given by the 19th-c. metrists Rossbach and Westphal to a compound rhythm in ancient Gr. lyric poetry which is most extensively attested in Pindar; its basic components were felt to be dactylic, – ∪ ∪ – ∪ ∪ – or – ∪ ∪ – ∪ ∪ – – , and the "Second" and "Third" Epitrites, – ∪ – – and – – ∪ – (see EPITRITE). It is now standard practice in Cl. prosody to describe these rhythms, more precisely and economically, with a set of symbols introduced by Maas. The three principal symbols are D for – ∪ ∪ – ∪ ∪ – , e for – ∪ – , and – for x (a single *anceps* [q.v.], usually long in the Pindaric examples of the meter, hence the designation [above] of the sequences – ∪ – – and – – ∪ – as epitritic rather than iambo-trochaic). In any passage of dactylo-epitritic, D and e sequences alternate with each other, usually (but not always) after an intervening – , giving the following principal types:

– e – e D or – e – D	iambelegus
D – e – (e)	elegiambus
D – D	choerilean
D – e – D	platonicum
– e – D – e –	pindaricum

D. is occasionally extended into – ∪ ∪ – ∪ ∪ – ∪ ∪ – or – ∪ ∪ – ∪ ∪ – ∪ ∪ – ∪ ∪ – , and e – occasionally replaced, through a kind of anaclasis, with – ∪ ∪ – . Maas's notation system brings out clearly the interrelations of various d.-e. sequences—different lengths cut, as it were, from the same rhythmical cloth with three possible places at which to begin and end: either before or after any e, D, or – . The lengths attested in Gr. lyric of the 6th and 5th cs. B.C. become progressively longer, but the character of the earliest attested example, two elegiambi by Alcestus in which D and – e – are separated by word end, suggests that the rhythm began as a brief, asynartete (q.v.) combination of the first two and a half feet of a dactylic hexameter with the corresponding portion of an iambic trimeter. Subsequent devels. would, on this theory, have allowed expansion of dactylic D into D – D, etc., on the model of iambo-trochaic (– e – e and e – e – in Maas's notation) as well as the appearance of D and e segments within the same colon. The rhythm is, by lyric standards, a highly regular one, and was associated, perhaps for this reason, with encomium, dirge (qq.v.), and moral reflection. In the Hellenistic period, it seems to have become the preferred metrical vehicle for "educated bourgeois lyric" (West)—most notably in Aristotle's frigidly correct *Hymn to Virtue.*—Wilamowitz, pt. 2, ch. 14; Maas, sect. 55; Koster, ch. 8; Dale, ch. 11, and *Collected Papers* (1969), chs. 4–5; Snell, 51–54; West, 139–41.   A.T.C.

DADA. In Zurich in 1916 two Romanians, Tristan Tzara and Marcel Janco, an Alsatian, Hans (Jean) Arp, and two Germans, Hugo Ball and Richard Huelsenbeck, chose the word DADA to express their need for total rebellion against the arts, bourgeois society, and the human condition itself. D., independent of specific connotations, signified everything and nothing at the same time, renewing civilized man's periodic urge to create a *tabula rasa.*

DADA

The moment of crisis had been triggered by World War I. But the symptoms of the d. syndrome had been manifested before the advent of official d. As Arp remarked: "we were all d. before d." In the U.S. there had been the impudent Armory Show (1913) and the brazen anti-art productions of the magazine *291* (located at the Stieglitz galleries at 291 Fifth Avenue) with the active participation of Marcel Duchamp and Francis Picabia, both in limbo between France and the U.S., and two Americans, Man Ray and Arthur Cravan, photographer/artist and poet/boxer respectively, who were to be prominent in avant-garde activities in Paris right after the war. In Cologne, in the same rebellious mood was Max Ernst, already involved in his *collages* and *frottages*, and in Berlin, Kurt Schwitters, who encapsulated the notion of d. in the word "Merz," derived from the Ger. for "commercial" (used ironically). In Paris the subversive strain was picked up in the work of Rimbaud and Lautréamont and brought up to date by Jarry and Apollinaire.

The most striking visual and verbal expression of d. occurred in Zurich, in a cabaret rented by Hugo Ball and called "Voltaire" in mockery of the archetype of the Age of Reason. Characteristic manifestations of d. included: public demonstrations with speech and gesture verging on exhibitionism, collage in art and lang. consisting of the juxtaposition of unrelated objects or words, invented objects to undermine the art of representation (Duchamp's "ready-mades"), primitive pantomimes and dances, and a series of manifestoes that appeared in short-lived journals and pamphlets such as *Dada* and *391*. D. waged war against the cliché in imagery and gave clear instructions on how to compose a poem: cut up a newspaper piece, shake the words in a bag, and reassemble them in the order they are removed. "Copy conscientiously / the poem will resemble you."

Tzara was the most articulate of the five who all claimed to be the director of d. In his *Manifesto* of 1918, he proclaimed: "there is a big job, destructive and negative, to be accomplished: sweep, sweep clean." In 1920 d. was welcomed to Paris after considerable correspondence among Tzara and André Breton, P. Soupault, L. Aragon, and Georges Ribemont-Dessaignes, as well as the slightly older, so-called cubist painter, Francis Picabia, who declared in *391*: "The dadaists are nothing, nothing, nothing, assuredly they will amount to nothing, nothing, nothing, signed Francis Picabia who knows nothing, nothing, nothing." Espousing the Cartesian philosophy that doubt is the primordial proof of human cognizance, d. carried the posture of consternation against all beliefs to the brink of anarchy. Tzara's poem, *L'Anti-philosophe* and his *Seven Manifestoes* were the signal-lights: "D. doubts everything," said Tzara; "I destroy the drawers of the brain." During his d. years, Breton wrote the classic poem summing up the d. sense of futility:

> Drop everything
> drop dada
> drop your wife
> drop your mistress
> drop your hopes and fears
> sew your children in the corner of the woods
> drop the prey for the shadow, drop if necessary the easy life
> what is presumed to be a life with a promising future
> Get on the road.
> ("Lâchez tout," *Les Perdus Gallimand* [1969], p. 105)

D. is not a literary or art movement. It is a *current* that has prevailed throughout the 20th c. Benjamin Péret, who moved from d. to surrealism (q.v.), did not foresee d.'s resilience when he declared that "d. was not a beginning but an end." Although the negative posture of d. has been matched by post-World War II existentialism, the novel of the absurd, and later deconstruction (q.v.), the d. spirit can be distinguished in works of art that may be otherwise classified under other labels when such nihilistic tendencies maintain a sense of play and face the *absurd* with bravura instead of a self-conscious philosophical disengagement. Humor, surprise, and shock are the redeeming features in d. that attenuate anguish and avoid the demeanor of the martyr. D.'s weakness in rejecting any kind of artistic discipline has ironically been its strength: it has not produced great works of art, but by the same token it has not gone out of date; when its perpetrators, such as Tzara, Ball, and Arp, have created lasting works, they have by the same token ceased to perform under the aegis of d. Instead of theorizing about doing away with style (e.g. Roland Barthes), it has actually left evidences of the "zero degree of lit." It has violated genre barriers without being involuted about it. Because of its direct expressions of ebullience and irreverence, d. has been easier to translate and has, therefore, attained broader recognition.

D. shares with surrealism certain characteristics, but its sources and intentions differ. The purposes of automatic writing and drawing are fun and pleasure rather than epistemological revelation; the juxtaposition of distant realities aims to be provocative and prankish rather than to unravel the secrets of the subconscious. The obscurities in the use of lang. are mainly produced by the fracture of syntax rather than through elliptical, hermetic structures. D. is the staff of those who believe in the art of spontaneity because it does not hold great hope for the survival of the work of art, which it deems *erasable*: words written in sand, drawing done on the blackboard. But its ephemeral character has reappeared through the century in "happenings," in minimalist art (see

MINIMALISM), in the preponderance of dehumanized abstract art, and in the nonphilosophical character of the Theater of the Absurd. Its spirit has invaded postmodernism. See also OULIPO.

D. Almanac, ed. R. Huelsenbeck (1920; tr. 1980); R. Huelsenbeck, En Avant D.: Eine Gesch. des Dadismus (1920); The D. Painters and Poets, ed. R. Motherwell (1951); R. Hausmann, Courrier D. (rpt. 1958); D., Monograph of a Movement, ed. W. Verkauf, 2d ed. (1961); M. Sanouillet, D. à Paris (1965); Cahiers D., no. 1 (rpt. 1966); R. W. Last, Hans Arp, the Poet of Dadaism (1969); M. Grossman, D. (1971); E. Petersen, Tristan Tzara (1971); M. A. Caws, Tristan Tzara (1973); L. Lippard, "D. in Berlin," Art in America (1978); S. Foster and R. Kuenzli, D. Spectrum (1979); H. Béhar, Le Théâtre d. et surréaliste (1979); A. Young, D. and After (1981); R. Huelsenbeck, ed. R. Sheppard (1982); Sinn aus Unsinn: D. International, ed. W. Paulsen and H. Hermann (1982); M. Sanouillet, D. Vol. II: Dossier critique (1983); Les Avant-Gardes littéraires au 20e siècle, ed. J. Weisgerber (1983); J. Erickson, D.: Performance, Poetry, and Art (1984); D./Dimensions, ed. S. Foster (1985); T. Benson, R. Hausmann and Berlin D. (1987). A.B.

DAINA. See LITHUANIAN POETRY; LATVIAN POETRY.

DALMATIAN POETRY. See YUGOSLAV POETRY.

DANISH POETRY. Rune (q.v.) inscriptions evidence the existence of a lost heroic poetry in Denmark, known only from Saxo Grammaticus' Lat. prose and hexameter rendering in Gesta Danorum (ca. 1200). The Lay of Bjarke (Bjarkamál)—whose heroes also appear in the Anglo-Saxon poems Widsith and Beowulf—and The Lay of Ingjald celebrate courage and loyalty, reflecting an aristocratic ethos that epitomizes the ideals of the Viking age.

During the Middle Ages (1100–1500), D. p. follows the European models of courtly and sacred poetry. In the Mariaviser (Songs to Mary) by Per Räff Lille (ca. 1450–1500), troubadour (q.v.) influences blend with imagery from The Song of Songs. The anonymous Den danske Rimkrønike (The D. Rhymed Chronicle), a hist. of the D. kings, is an important work in knittelvers (q.v.). The dominant genre of the Middle Ages, however, is the folk ballad (q.v.), which reached Denmark from France in the early 12th c. In the 16th c., poetry in the vernacular was still medieval in spirit and form, notably subject to a growing Ger. influence in the wake of the Lutheran Reformation.

In the 17th c., as the Ren. reached Denmark, efforts were made to create a national D. p. on Cl. models. Anders Arrebo (1587–1637) produced a religious epic, Hexaëmeron (ca. 1622; pub. 1661), describing the six days of Creation. Based on Du Bartas' La Semaine, it is composed partly in twice-rhymed hexameter, partly in alexandrines. The artificiality of the poem's Cl.-mythological diction is offset by descriptive details from Scandinavian nature and folk life. Following Martin Opitz' Das Buch der Deutschen Poeterey (A Book of Ger. Poetics, 1624), Hans Mikkelsen Ravn (1610–63) in 1649 published a manual of prosody with illustrations, making available to future poets a varied formal repertoire. Anders Bording (1619–77) is noted for his anacreontic verse, but he also single-handedly published a rhymed monthly newspaper, Den Danske Mercurius (The D. Mercury, 1666–77), composed in stately alexandrines. Thomas Kingo (1634–1703), a much greater poet, was able to fully exploit the new formal variety. His principal achievement is his two volumes of church hymns, still sung today, Aandelige Siunge-Koor (Spiritual Choirs, 1674–81). With their thematic counterpoints, sensuous imagery, and often high-strung metaphors, Kingo's hymns are unmistakably baroque (q.v.) in style, the highlights being his Easter hymns.

In the early 18th c., Fr. neoclassicism entered D. lit., mainly due to the activity of the Dano-Norwegian Ludvig Holberg (1684–1754). Best known for his bourgeois prose comedies, Holberg in his verse mock-epic Peder Paars (1719–20), influenced by Boileau's Le Lutrin and Cervantes' Don Quixote, showed himself a brilliant satirist. The rationalism of Holberg, and of the period, is counterbalanced, however, by a sentimental undercurrent, represented by Ambrosius Stub (1705–58) and Hans Adolf Brorson (1694–1764). Stub practiced a wide variety of genres, from religious lyrics to drinking songs. His concise, graceful form and light, melodious rhythms are influenced by the It. operatic aria, and his delicately picturesque style reveals rococo features. Many of the hymns of Brorson, a religious pietist, are also composed in complex meters derived from the elegant rococo aria, with its dialogue and echo effects.

D. neoclassicism was continued by a group of Norwegian authors living in Copenhagen, members of Det norske Selskab (q.v.—The Norwegian Society), while Johannes Ewald (1743–81), a preromantic deeply influenced by the Ger. poet F. G. Klopstock, championed the claims of subjectivity. Ewald's mythological dramas on ON themes are largely forgotten, but his pietistically inspired lyric verse is very much alive. Like Klopstock, he excelled in the religious ode, exemplified by Rungsteds Lyksaligheder (The Joys of Rungsted, 1773), where nature description is a vehicle for the glorification of God. Ewald's pre-eminence is largely due to his ability to reconcile contraries. Extremely sensitive, acutely aware of himself as a poetic genius, and preoccupied with his own subjective experience, he possessed an admirable artistic discipline which enabled him to produce poems of great formal beauty. The only noteworthy poet of the last 20 years of the century was Jens Baggesen (1764–1826), a mercurial spirit who alternated between Cl. and romantic sensibility in accordance with the tenor of his personal experience.

The breakthrough of romanticism in D. p. was the achievement of Adam Oehlenschläger (1779–1850), whose first collection, *Digte* (Poems, 1803), was inspired by the aesthetics of the Jena school of Schelling and the Schlegels as mediated by the Copenhagen lectures of Henrich Steffens (1802). These poems signified a fierce rejection of the rationalist spirit of the 18th c., together with a rediscovery of Nordic hist. and mythology and a glorification of the creative genius who alone is capable of a unified view of nature and hist. The volume concludes with the Shakespeare-inspired *Sanct Hansaften-Spil* (Midsummer Eve Play), a lyrical comedy in *knittelvers* which satirizes the rationalist view of lit. Oehlenschläger increased his range in *Poetiske Skrifter* (Poetic Writings, 1805), which contained prose and poetry, narrative cycles, drama, lyric, and ballads and romances in varying meters. The high point of the collection is *Aladdin* (Eng. tr. 1968), a philosophical fairy-tale play in blank verse which celebrates the power of genius over chaos and evil. After 1806, Oehlenschläger's subjectivism is tempered by a growing influence from Goethe's and Schiller's objective poetry and from the Heidelberg romantic school, re-orienting his work—as well as D. lit. in general—toward national and patriotic themes. *Nordiske Digte* (Nordic Poems, 1807) included several dramas based on ON figures and themes. Worthy of mention is *Hakon Jarl*, a blank-verse tragedy modeled on Schiller's *Wallenstein*. The narrative cycle *Helge* (1814), with its impressive array of metrical forms and styles marking the subtle shifts of moods, rises to Sophoclean heights in the concluding dramatic episode, which gives a mythic perspective to the entire poem. More consistently national in inspiration was the work of another romantic, N. F. S. Grundtvig (1783–1872), who, while more of a cultural leader than a poet, created an enduring literary monument in his hymns. With their union of humanism and Christianity and their pervasive imagery from D. landscape and Nordic mythology, Grundtvig's hymns represent a unique poetic achievement.

Around 1830, D. p. moved toward greater realism and psychological diversity, its focus shifting from an idealized past to a more complex present. Johan Ludvig Heiberg (1791–1860), the theorist of *romantisme*, as this movement has been called, managed to shuttle elegantly between actuality and the dream world in his romantic plays, which dispelled the taste for Oehlenschläger's tragedies. His "apocalyptic comedy" *En Sjæl efter Døden* (A Soul After Death, 1841) is a brilliant satire of bourgeois philistinism. Christian Winther (1796–1876) typically blends lyric and narrative elements in the idyll, as in *Træsnit* (Woodcuts, 1828), which images village life. Winther's formal virtuosity is demonstrated in the romance *Hjortens Flugt* (The Flight of the Hart, 1855), set in medieval times

and employing a modified Nibelungenstrophe (q.v.). The cycle of love poems *Til Een* (To Someone; 1843, 1849), in which Eros is worshiped as a divine force, is notable for its poignant lyricism. The brief lyrics of the Heine-inspired *Erotiske Situationer* (Erotic Situations, 1838) by Emil Aarestrup (1806–56), with their picturesque detail, psychological complexity, and emotional dissonance, express a distinctly modern sensibility—sophisticated and sensual—and represent a high point in D. love poetry. While the early work of Frederik Paludan-Müller (1809–76)—such as the Byron-inspired lyric-narrative poem *Dandserinden* (The Danseuse, 1833) with its felicitous ottava rima and playful irony—is fraught with aestheticism, *Adam Homo* (1841–48; Eng. tr. 1980), a three-volume novel in verse, embodies a rigorous ethical philosophy. Through its portrait of a gifted, opportunistic anti-hero who pays for worldly success with the loss of his soul, the book presents a satirical picture of contemp. D. culture. The ending, with Adam's post-mortem salvation through the Christian love of the woman he abandoned, recalls the *Divine Comedy* and *Faust*.

After naturalism (q.v.) was introduced by the critic Georg Brandes (1842–1927) around 1870, writers turned their attention to political, social, and sexual problems—fitter subjects for prose than poetry. Yet Brandes was important to both Jens Peter Jacobsen (1847–85) and Holger Drachmann (1846–1908), each with a distinctive profile as a poet. The sparse but first-rate lyrical production of Jacobsen, known chiefly as a novelist, was published posthumously as *Digte og Udkast* (Poems and Sketches) in 1886. Unique are his "arabesques," capriciously winding free-verse monologues—the first modernist poetry in Denmark—whose intellectual probing is veiled in a colorful ornamental lang. and evocative moods influenced by Edgar Allan Poe. The youthful *Digte* (Poems, 1872) of Drachmann more directly echoed the radical ideas of Brandes, as in the poem "Engelske Socialister" (Eng. Socialists). But soon Drachmann abandoned ideology for personal lyricism. In *Sange ved Havet* (Songs by the Sea, 1877), his best collection, the sea, whose changing moods he evokes with deep empathy, is perceived as an image of his own protean spirit. With *Sangenes Bog* (Book of Songs, 1889) radicalism reappeared, though now tempered by an awareness of age and mutability which lends a poignant existential resonance to the texts. Through his free rhythms and melodiousness, formal inventiveness, and unprecedented range of moods and attitudes, Drachmann renewed the style of romantic verse and made an extraordinary impact on subsequent D. p.

Both Drachmann and Jacobsen, as well as Baudelaire and Verlaine, influenced the neoromantic movement of the 1890s in D. p., which rejected naturalism in favor of an aesthetic demand for beauty and a mystically colored religiosity. Its program was formulated in *Taarnet* (The

Tower, 1893–94), edited by Johannes Jørgensen (1866–1956), who with *Stemninger* (Moods, 1892) had introduced the dreams and visions of symbolism (q.v.) into D. p. Jørgensen's later poetry is marked by his 1896 conversion to Catholicism. After 1900 he further refined his condensed mode of expression, employing, like Verlaine, simple meters and rhythms to express a fervent religiosity. A more consistent follower of Fr. symbolism, as a metaphysic as well as an aesthetic theory, was Sophus Claussen (1865–1931). This is evident in his erotic poetry, where the surface sexual theme masks an underlying ontology, one of irreducible opposites. A recurrent theme of *Djævlerier* (Diableries, 1904), Eros as a demonic force, reveals Baudelaire as a primary source of inspiration. Claussen was deeply concerned with the nature of the creative process and with the poet's role. In his last major collection, *Heroica* (1925), a highlight of D. p., art and beauty are invoked as the only means of spiritual survival in a materialistic world. Notable is the poem "Atomernes Oprør" (Revolt of the Atoms), a dystopian fantasy in which Claussen shows himself the last great master of the hexameter in D. p. Other major neoromantics were Viggo Stuckenberg (1863–1905), Helge Rode (1870–1937), and Ludvig Holstein (1864–1943). While Stuckenberg's melancholy meditations on love's tragedy are executed with an exquisite sense of style, Rode's ethereal poems, with their Shelleyan affinities, verge on the ecstatic. The best of Holstein's unadorned lyrics, which are quite unaffected by symbolism, derive from his steady pantheistic vision of the unity of man and nature.

D. p. of the 20th c. encompasses diverse currents and styles, determined partly by international vogues, partly by sociopolitical events. The period before World War I replaced the introverted neoromanticism of the 1890s with realism (q.v.). A Jutland regional lit. emerged, dominated by Jeppe Aakjær (1866–1930), whose melodious poetry about the nature and the folk life of his native region has remained very popular. The central poet of the period, and one of the greatest D. writers altogether, was the Nobel Prize winner Johannes V. Jensen (1873–1950). The burden of his first collection, *Digte* (Poems, 1906), a milestone in modern D. p., is a conflict between longing and a zest for life, alternating with *Weltschmerz*. Characteristic are a number of prose poems in which Jensen voices his worship of 20th-c. technology, together with a yearning for distant places and periods rendered in timeless, mythic images. After 1920 he used more traditional meters as well as alliterative ON forms. Jensen's poetry constitutes a unique blend of precise observation, philosophical reflection, and romantic vision. His innovative poetic diction, whose incongruous mixture of crass realism and refined sensuousness, of bold visionary imagery and muted lyricism, seeks to render the inexpressible flux of experience, has

been enormously influential in D. p., as has his free verse influenced by Goethe and Heine.

During and after World War I, a generation of poets emerged who, inspired by Jensen and by expressionism (q.v.) in painting and in Ger. poetry, endeavored to create new forms of beauty. Most sensational was Emil Bønnelycke (1893–1953), whose exuberant zest for life and glorification of technology were expressed in hymnlike prose poems, but Tom Kristensen (1893–1974) was artistically more accomplished. In *Fribytterdrømme* (Buccaneer Dreams, 1920) Kristensen conveyed the restless spirit and explosive primitivism of the Jazz Age in an orgiastic display of color and sound. After a journey to the Far East, in *Paafuglefjeren* (The Peacock Feather, 1922) he adopted a more traditional style, but without overcoming his sense of malaise. In the poem "Reklameskibet" (The Show Boat, 1923), Otto Gelsted (1888–1968) from a Marxist point of view charged expressionist art with pandering to commercialism while neglecting fundamental human concerns. An admirer of Jensen, Gelsted maintained the radical-humanistic trad. in D. p. in the interwar period.

The poetry of Nis Petersen (1897–1943) and Paul la Cour (1902–56), the dominant figures of the 1930s, is also informed with humanist concerns. Petersen's anguished verse, particularly "Brændende Europa" (Europe Aflame) from *En Drift Vers* (A Drove of Verses, 1933), voices concern for the predicament of Western culture. La Cour, whose sensibility was formed by Claussen and modern Fr. poets, stressed the redemptive nature of poetry, both individually and collectively. His main collection from the 1930s, *Dette er vort Liv* (This Is Our Life, 1936), is permeated with guilt about the state of Europe, for which, like Claussen, he saw art as the only remedy. La Cour's best work, however, belongs to the '40s and after. *Fragmenter af en Dagbog* (Fragments of a Diary, 1948), which mingles philosophy, poetic theory, and verse, profoundly influenced the poets who came to maturity during the War. The surrealist Jens August Schade (1903–78) defined his attitude to the times by espousing a Lawrencean primitivism (q.v.). His *Hjertebogen* (The Heart Book, 1930) contains sexually explicit love poems, along with nature impressions transformed by erotic feeling and a cosmic imagination.

Under the pressure of war and Nazi occupation, the 1940s instilled new vigor and urgency into D. p. Two distinct responses to the brutality and destructiveness of World War II were evident: an activation of political consciousness, on the one hand, and an intensive quest for a meaningful, often metaphysical *Weltanschauung*, on the other. Inspirational was the work of Gustaf Munch-Petersen (1912–38), a literary existentialist who foreshadowed postwar Modernism and, through his death in Spain fighting Fascism, became the prototype of the committed writer. Possessed by a vision of total union between conscious and subconscious, dream and reality, and stimulated by the imagism and surrealism (qq.v.) of the Swedish and Swedo-Finnish Modernists, Munch-Petersen created a remarkable poetry that expressed a personal myth of self-making and self-liberation. Another paradigmatic poet was Morten Nielsen (1922–44), whose hard, weighty, unfinished verse oscillates between an existentialist affirmation of self and renunciation and death. Closely related to these two figures is Erik Knudsen (b. 1922), who, torn between beauty and politics—as shown by a title like *Blomsten og sværdet* (The Flower and the Sword, 1949)—increasingly used poetry as the vehicle for a Marxist critique of society.

The central poets of the 1940s, following la Cour, saw poetry as a means of personal and cultural redemption. Striving for a form that would mirror their perception of a fragmented reality, they shaped a richly symbolic style inspired by Eliot and Rilke. The absence of a shared cultural and spiritual heritage, together with messianic longings, was most convincingly expressed by a group of poets whose original forum was the journal *Heretica* (1948–53). Ole Sarvig (1921–81) and Ole Wivel (b. 1921) embody in their poetry, by way of an essentially Christian symbolism, the pattern of rebirth after cultural catastrophe. In a six-volume cycle (1943–52), Sarvig with great visionary power depicts our civilization as a wasteland. The driving force of his first collection, *Grønne Digte* (Green Poems, 1943), written in an imagist lang. related to abstract painting, is the search for a remedy to this crisis. In later volumes the crisis is overcome through an experience of God and love, a theme which reaches its zenith in his last collection, *Salmer . . .* (Hymns, 1981). A similar metaphysical orientation marks *I Fiskens Tegn* (In the Sign of the Fish, 1948) by Ole Wivel. Both Sarvig and Wivel see love and grace as the liberators from chaos. For Thorkild Bjørnvig (b. 1918), it is poetry itself which liberates. In his first, Rilke-inspired collection, *Stjærnen bag Gavlen* (The Star Behind the Gable, 1947), Eros is the predominant theme, treated with classic discipline in stanzas of great musicality and substance. In the 1970s Bjørnvig changed the focus of his poetry to deal with ecological issues.

Others pursued different paths, unaffected by ideology or metaphysical probing. The woman poet Tove Ditlevsen (1918–76) followed trad. and wrote simple rhymed verse in a neoromantic style. Piet Hein (b. 1905) in his 20 volumes of *Gruk* (1940–63; Eng. tr. *Grooks* 1–6, 1966–78) combined scientific insights with a skillful epigrammatic play of words and ideas. And Frank Jæger (1926–77), an elusive successor to Schade noted for his verbal wizardry, cultivated the idyll, though in a broken form with an ominous undertone.

During the 1960s an extroverted poetic experimentalism emerged, directed both against the materialism of the modern welfare state and against prevailing ivory-tower literary attitudes.

This change was largely due to Klaus Rifbjerg (b. 1931), the most versatile D. postwar writer. Phenomenological in orientation, Rifbjerg's verse registers the chaotic plenitude of experience in technological society by means of a fractured syntax and a vast, often technical-scientific vocabulary, producing a self-reflexive polyphony of themes that constitutes its own reality. His procedure varies from one volume to another. Whereas *Konfrontation* (1960) juxtaposes, often jarringly, photographically precise observations, his principal collection, *Camouflage* (1961), draws upon cinematic montage and free association in a surrealist search for origins and an expanded, liberated self; in *Mytologi* (1970), the expansion occurs through the use of assorted masks. *Amagerdigte* (Amager Poems, 1965) and *Byens tvelys* (Twilight of the City, 1987) are written in a style of "new simplicity," matter-of-fact and reportorial. Jess Ørnsbo (b. 1932) employs a technique of startling juxtaposition similar to Rifbjerg's, adding a distinct social perspective, as in *Digte* (Poems, 1960), where a working-class district in Copenhagen forms the setting.

Two other poets, Jørgen Sonne (b. 1925) and Jørgen Gustava Brandt (b. 1929), continue the introspective approach of the 1940s. The poetry of Sonne, who is influenced by Ekelöf and Pound, is marked by intellectual complexity and formal rigor. In *Krese* (Cycles, 1963), a major work of its time, Sonne seeks to regain the pristine quality of childhood, while *Huset* (The House, 1976), more obscure, launches an ambitious mental journey into memory, fantasy, and hist. through a technique which blends observation, reflection, and visions. A similar technique is employed by Brandt, whose *Ateliers* (Studios, 1967) and *Giv dagen dit lys* (Give the Day Your Light, 1986) are characterized by the use of myths and religious symbols to express a longing for epiphany, a mystical illumination of experience.

Around 1965 there emerges a tendency toward linguistic experimentation and concretism, the use of words as building blocks possessing intrinsic value, without reference to any other reality. Already present in *Romerske Bassiner* (Roman Pools, 1963) by the Marxist poet Ivan Malinovski (b. 1926), this structuralist approach has been skillfully applied by Poul Borum (b. 1934), a practitioner of meta-poetry, and elegantly exploited by Benny Andersen (b. 1929) in his witty, thought-provoking verse based on verbal ambiguity. In the esoteric systemic texts of Per Højholt (b. 1928) and Peter Laugesen (b. 1942), lang. is transformed into intellectually challenging signs and closed symbols. The epitome of this trend is reached with *Det* (It, 1969) by Inger Christensen (b. 1935), an intricately patterned work in which the self of the reader can move from chaos to order through lang., a movement mirrored in the text itself. A related technique is employed in *Hjem* (Home, 1985) by Klaus Høeck (b. 1938), where lang. is recast into complex structures in a unique attempt to illustrate the poet's striving to define God.

The 1970s and '80s display a wide spectrum of attitudes, from poetry of commitment to neoromantic trends. The poems of Vita Andersen (b. 1944) revolve around childhood experiences and the workplace, and the collections of Marianne Larsen (b. 1951), from *Billedtekster* (Captions, 1974) to *Direkte* (1984), analyze sexual repression, class struggle, and imperialism from a feminist perspective. Less ideological, Pia Tafdrup (b. 1952) has, since her appearance in 1981, attempted to blend her experience of the erotic and of nature into images of rhythmic, sensuous beauty. More accessible are the poems of Steen Kaalø (b. 1945) and Kristen Bjørnkjær (b. 1943), who represent the same neoromantic trend, also evident in Henrik Nordbrandt (b. 1945), whose favorite settings are Greece and the Near East. Nordbrandt's *Håndens skælven i november* (The Hand's Tremble in November, 1986), with its sensitive philosophical poetry, is considered a major work of the 1980s.

The linguistic experiments of the 1960s have been continued in the '80s. Thus, F. P Jac (b. 1955), a brilliant equilibrist with words, creates a poetic universe around himself as the omniscient center, raiding the resources of the D. poetic trad. along with the repertoire of contemp. slang. A similarly eclectic approach characterizes Niels Frank (b. 1963), Bo Green Jensen (b. 1955), and Pia Juul (b. 1962), talented representatives of a quite popular postmodernism in D. p. These young poets, with their undogmatic views and enthusiasm for experimentation, will insure the continued versatility, wide scope, and high quality of D. p.

ANTHOLOGIES: *Oxford Book of Scandinavian Verse*, ed. E. W. Gosse and W. A. Craigie (1925); *The Jutland Wind*, ed. R. P. Keigwin (1944); *In Denmark I Was Born*, ed. R. P. Keigwin, 2d ed. (1950); *20th-C. Scandinavian P.*, ed. M. S. Allwood (1950); *Mod. D. Poems*, ed. K. K. Mogensen, 2d ed. (1951); *A Harvest of Song*, ed. S. D. Rodholm (1953); *Danske lyriske Digte*, ed. M. Brøndsted and M. Paludan (1954); *Den danske Lyrik 1800–1870*, ed. F. J. B. Jansen, 2 v. (1961); *D. Ballads and Folk Songs*, ed E. Dal (1967); *A Book of D. Ballads*, ed. A. Olrik (1968); *A Second Book of D. Verse*, ed. C. W. Stork (1968); *Anthol. of D. Lit.*, ed. F. J. B. Jansen and P. M. Mitchell (1971); *A Book of D. Verse*, ed. O. Friis (1976); *Contemp. D. P.*, ed. L. Jensen et al. (1977); *17 D. Poets*, ed. N. Ingwersen (1981); *Scandinavian Ballads*, ed. S. H. Rossel (1982).

HISTORY AND CRITICISM: A. Olrik, *The Heroic Legends of Denmark* (1919); C. S. Petersen and V. Andersen, *Illustreret dansk Litteraturhist.*, 4 v. (1924–34)—standard lit. hist.; H. G. Topsøe-Jensen, *Scandinavian Lit. from Brandes to Our Own Day* (1929); E. Bredsdorff et al., *Intro. to Scandinavian Lit.* (1951)—useful brief survey; P. M. Mitchell, *Bibl. Guide to D. Lit.* (1951), *Hist. of D. Lit.*, 2d ed.

(1971)—best survey in Eng.; J. Claudi, *Contemp. D. Authors* (1952); F. J. B. Jansen, "Romantisme européen et romantisme scandinave," *L'âge d'or* (1953), *Danmarks Digtekunst*, 2d ed., 3 v. (1969); *Danske metrikere*, ed. A. Arnoltz et al., 2 v. (1953–54); S. M. Kristensen, *Dansk litt. 1918–1952*, 7th ed. (1965), *Den dobbelte Eros* (1966)—on D. romanticism; *Modernismen i dansk litt.*, ed. J. Vosmar, 2d ed. (1969); S. H. Larsen, *Systemdigtningen* (1971); *Nordens litt.*, ed. M. Brøndsted, 2 v. (1972); *Opgøret med modernismen*, ed. T. Brostrøm (1974); *Dansk litteraturhist.*, ed. P. H. Traustedt, 2d ed., 6 v. (1976–77)—comprehensive lit. hist.; P. Borum, *D. Lit* (1979); *Danske digtere i det 20. århundrede*, ed. T. Brostrøm and M. Winge, 5 v. (1980–82); S. H. Rossel, *Hist. of Scandinavian Lit. 1870–1980* (1982).   S.LY.; S.H.R.

DANSA. Occitan lyric genre, commonly of three stanzas, set to a lively tune of popular cast. An opening *respos* or refrain (A) was perhaps repeated after each stanza, of which the second part matched the form and tune of the *respos*, while the two symmetrical halves of the first part were independent of it: schematically, *A bba(A) bba(A) bba(A)* for a 3-stanza piece. The OF *balete* shows the same structure.—GRLMA 2.1B; Bec; Chambers. J.H.M.

DEAD METAPHOR. An expression that was originally metaphorical but no longer functions as a figure of speech and is now understood literally, e.g. "taillight," "foot of the mountain," "head of state," "arm of the law." Scholars differ as to how and why a metaphor (q.v.) becomes "dead." The common theory holds that the cause is repeated use over time. If the meaning generated by a metaphor is based on the tension it establishes between two things—subject and analogue, or tenor and vehicle (q.v.)—normally perceived to be different, then a d. m. has lost that tension. Thus, while we may refer to the base of a mountain (tenor) as its "foot" (vehicle), we no longer see it as involving a reference to an object in nature in terms of a human body part.

Some have claimed (e.g. Fenollosa) that this fading process should be reversed, and that it is the special duty of the poet, in the effort to reclaim the original energy of lang., to revive the lost metaphorical powers of d. m. Müller and Thomas have claimed, to the contrary, that d. m. springs from the ordinary necessity to use existing words for naming new concepts or things when new words are not yet forthcoming—"spirit" once meant "breath," for example. This sort of figure has been termed "radical" (referring to roots or origins), also "fossil," "faded," and "petrified." A more neutral term would be "conventional." Poetic and conventional metaphors are therefore not the same: the former are based more on *resemblance*, while the latter are based more on *difference*; if we seek tension in the latter, we seek simple clarity of reference in the former. To "revive" a d. m., therefore, could very well confuse the meaning.

M. Müller, *Lectures on the Science of Lang.*, 2d ser. (1864); E. Fenollosa, *The Chinese Written Character as a Medium for Poetry*, ed. E. Pound (1920); O. Barfield, *Poetic Diction*, 2d ed. (1952); W. K. Wimsatt, Jr., *The Verbal Icon* (1954); C. Brooke-Rose, *The Grammar of M.* (1958); O. Thomas, *M. and Related Subjects* (1969); M. C. Beardsley, "The Metaphorical Twist," *Essays on M.*, ed. W. Shibles (1972); D. Davidson, "What Ms. Mean," *On M.*, ed. S. Sacks (1979); R. Bartel, *Ms. and Symbols* (1983); E. R. MacCormac, *A Cognitive Theory of M.* (1985); E. C. Traugott, "'Conventional' and 'D.' Ms. Revisited," *The Ubiquity of M.*, ed. W. Paprotté and R. Dirven (1985); D. E. Cooper, *M.* (1986); R. Claiborne, *Loose Cannons & Red Herrings* (1988). N.F.

DÉBAT, DEBATE. See POETIC CONTESTS.

DECADENCE. A term used ostensibly in reference to periods or works whose qualities are held to mark a "falling away" (Lat. *de-cadere*) from previously recognized conditions or standards of excellence. The term is often applied to the Alexandrian (or Hellenistic) period in Gr. lit. (ca. 300–30 B.C.) and to the period in Lat. lit. after the death of Augustus (14 A.D.). In modern poetry d. has been identified most persistently in the works of the Fr. symbolist-decadent movement of the late 19th c. (coinciding with a sense of national decline after the Franco-Prussian War of 1870), whose influence in the British Isles encouraged native tendencies already nurtured by the ideas of Walter Pater, the poetry of Rossetti and Swinburne, and the general ambience of the Pre-Raphaelite Movement (q.v.). Symbolist influence was widespread also among the poets of *fin-de-siècle* Europe outside France. It did not significantly affect the poetry of the United States until the 20th c., although Poe was himself a progenitor of important ideas and practices of the Fr. symbolists.

In a limited sense, D. may be seen exemplified in the tastes and habits of such fictional characters as Petrus Borel's Passereau l'Ecolier, Poe's Roderick Usher, Huysmans' Des Esseintes, Wilde's Dorian Gray and Lord Henry Wotton, and Villiers de l'Isle-Adam's Axël d'Auersperg; in passages like those on the lang. of decaying civilizations by Baudelaire and by Gautier; in the apostrophe of Mallarmé's Hérodiade to her mirror; in Verlaine's verses beginning "Je suis l'Empire à la fin de la décadence"; in Beardsley's self-described "strange creatures wandering about in Pierrot costumes or modern dress, quite a new world of my own creation"; in Wilde's *Salomé* and Dowson's famous poem to Cynara; in the affectations of Count Robert de Montesquiou-Fezensac and the remarkable production in 1891 of P. N. Roinard's *Cantique des cantiques*; and in the perfumed atmosphere of Paul Fort's Théâtre d'art. D. in this sense was often a mannerism of the sort prevalent in the England of the "Yellow Nineties," with its brilliant and superficial *fin-de-siècle* aesthetic pose that played perhaps a more significant rôle than is generally recognized in opposing the crushing force of the current materialism. But the word *decadence* has come to be used by hostile critics in a larger sense than this.

A basic characteristic of d. has been a failure to recognize objective or timeless values that transcend and give form and direction to individual experience and effort. In these terms the decadent poet is seen living in a state of Heraclitian or Bergsonian flux, with his values confined within narrowly egocentric limits and unlikely to satisfy his desires. Here the poet tends to be concerned not with "the fruit of experience" but with "experience itself" and with private sensations; and his poems are likely to reveal a number of the following "decadent" characteristics: ennui; a search for novelty, with attendant artificiality and interest in the unnatural; excessive self-analysis; feverish hedonism, with poetic interest in corruption and morbidity; abulia, neurosis, and exaggerated erotic sensibility; aestheticism, with stress on "Art for Art's Sake" in the evocation of exquisite sensations and emotions; dandyism; scorn of contemporary society and mores; restless curiosity, perversity, or eccentricity in subject matter; overemphasis on form, with resultant loss of balance between form and content—or interest in lapidary ornamentation, resulting at times in disintegration of artistic unity; bookishness; erudite or exotic vocabulary; frequent employment of synaesthesia (q.v.) or *transpositions d'art*; complex and difficult syntax; experiments in the use of new rhythms, rich in evocative and sensuous effects alien to those of tradition and often departing from the mathematical principles of control in established prosody; substitution of coherence in mood for coherence and synthesis in thought; "postromantic" irony in the manner of Corbière, Laforgue, and the early Eliot; obscurity, arising from remote, private, or complicated imagery; and a pervasive sense of something lost—a nostalgic semi-mysticism without clear direction or spiritual commitment, but with frequent reference to exotic religions and rituals, e.g. to Tarot cards, magic, alchemy, Rosicrucianism, Theosophy, the Kabbala, Satanism, and the like.

From the foregoing summary emerge certain fundamental distinctions between symbolist and decadent, distinctions which derive from the decadent's essential condition, that of an artist whose symbolist aspirations are constantly thwarted by a persistent naturalism (q.v.). For all his efforts to create for himself an existence of infinitely renewed moments, to concentrate life into a sequence of sensations, the decadent is fatally bound to history, and a Darwinian history at that. While the symbolist inhabits a world of seamless and cumulative duration, a world of temporal synthesis, which accounts for his peculiar equanimity in the face of external events, the decadent endures the forces of heredity which characteristically produce an oscillation between febrility and neurasthenia, culminating in psychological exhaustion. Untouched by disorders of the nerves, the symbolist can submerge personality in the play of universal analogy, can "yield the initiative to words" (Mallarmé); the decadent, on the other hand, feels bound to protect and promote personality, to isolate the self, by the exercise of irony and a vigilant self-consciousness. Consequently, the mask of the decadent is not the symbolist's mask of self-transcendence or self-surrender, but the dandy's mask of self-defense, of noncommitment. Paradoxically, then, the decadent needs the very society he rejects, as an audience against which he can measure his superiority; his art is thus more aggressive than the symbolist's, more intent on strategies of outrage and shock. For this reason, perhaps, the decadent's rebellion by blasphemy and sacrilege can only take place within the framework of Catholic orthodoxy, while the symbolist's "religion" is either atheistic or syncretic.

But the decadent's ineradicable naturalism is most evident in a stubborn materialism, both in taste and style. The decadent is a collector and connoisseur of aesthetic objects with which he can fill his spiritual vacuum and dissociate himself from grosser forms of materialism. Unlike the symbolist, therefore, the decadent aims to aestheticize or refine the object, rather than transform it. And his style is equally materialist; it collects words like aesthetic objects, like possessions, whether they be archaisms, neologisms, technical terms, or exotic images, and sets them, like jewels, in a finely wrought syntax designed to show them off. For all his ostensible rejection of Parnassian and naturalist principles (qq.v.), the decadent remains a descriptive rather than transmutative writer; he can only name words or objects which already have an inherent value for him. It is in his falling short of symbolist ideals, in the paradoxes of his existence, in his exasperated failure to break free from naturalism, that the decadent assumes a certain tragic grandeur.

Totally in keeping with this naturalistic coloring, Dr. Emile Laurent (1897) thought he could identify certain characteristics of a *physiognomie décadente*: lack of forehead; prognathous features; oddly shaped heads ("plagiocéphales, oxycéphales, acrocéphales"); deformed noses; glabrous, asymmetrical faces; wide ears; enormous cheek bones, etc., etc. All this was a continuation of the thesis of Max Nordau's *Entartung* (Degeneration, 1892–93), which found that the Fr. symbolists "had in common all the signs of degeneracy and imbecility." G. B. Shaw's "The Sanity of Art" (1895) was an effective reply to this sort of nonsense. See also SYMBOLISM; AESTHETICISM; HERMETICISM; GEORGIANISM.

T. Gautier, "Charles Baudelaire" (1868); A. Nisard, *Études sur les poètes latins de la décadence*, 4th ed. (1878); A. Symons, "The Decadent Movement in Lit.," *Harper's Magazine* 87 (1893); E. Laurent, *La Poésie décadente devant la science psychiatrique* (1897); A. J. Farmer, *Le Mouvement esthétique et décadent en Angleterre (1873–1900)* (1931); W. Binni, *La poetica del decadentismo* (1949); M. Praz, *The Romantic Agony*, 2d ed. (1951); J. M. Smith, "Concepts of D. in 19th-C. Fr. Lit.," *SP* 50 (1953); A. E. Carter, *The Idea of D. in Fr. Lit., 1830–1900* (1958); P. Jullian, *Esthètes et magiciens: L'Art fin de siècle* (1969); P. Stephan, *Paul Verlaine and the D., 1882–90* (1974); M. Calinescu, *Faces of Modernity: Avant-garde, D., Kitsch* (1977); L. C. Dowling, *Aestheticism and D.: A Sel. Annot. Bibl.* (1977), *Lang. and D. in the Victorian fin de siècle* (1986); J. Pierrot, *L'Imaginaire décadent, 1880–1900* (1977); M. Lemaire, *Le Dandysme de Baudelaire à Mallarmé* (1978); *Pascoli, D'Annunzio, Fogazzaro e il decadentismo italiano*, ed. R. Tessari (1978); J. D. Grossman, *Valery Bryusov and the Riddle of Russian D.* (1985); J. R. Reed, *Decadent Style* (1985); Terras—Rus.; G. A. Cevasco, *Three Decadent Poets* (1990)—annot. bibl.   A.G.E.; C.S.

DÉCASYLLABE. See DECASYLLABLE.

DECASYLLABLE. A line of ten syllables; metrical structures built on it vary, but normally the term refers to the Fr. *décasyllabe* and the Eng. iambic pentameter. In Fr. verse, the d. appeared about the middle of the 11th c., in *La Vie de St. Alexis* and *Le Boèce*, with a caesura after the fourth syllable and two fixed accents on the fourth and tenth syllables (so 4//6; 6//4 is the other classic division, though 5//5 is also to be found, particularly among later poets). With the appearance of the *Chanson de Roland* (ca. 1090) the d. became the standard line of Fr. epic and narrative verse, i.e. the *chansons de geste* (q.v.), until the the appearance of the alexandrine (q.v.) at the beginning of the 12th c., which supplanted it. In OF lyric verse it is more common than the octosyllable (q.v.), making it the principal Fr. meter from the 14th c. to the mid 16th c., when the poets of the *Pléiade* restored the alexandrine to the lyric also. (Ronsard's *Franciade*, however, is in ds.). Thereafter, the alexandrine became the standard line for all serious poetry in Fr., though the d. continued to play an important role in the ode and to serve as the rhythmic vehicle for major poems up to the 20th c. (e.g. Valéry, *Le Cimetière marin*). Ironically, it is in *vers libre* (q.v.) that the Fr. d. recovered much of its lost status.

In It. the *endecasillabo* (11 syllables but with a feminine ending—see HENDECASYLLABLE) appeared early in the 12th c. and was used by Dante, Petrarch, and Boccaccio. Chaucer may have discovered the line in their work (the last syllable would have been dropped in Eng. pronunciation) if he had not already become acquainted with the corresponding Fr. meter in Machaut, Deschamps, and Granson. In any case the decasyllabic line in Chaucer's hands took on the five-stress alternating pattern later to be called "iambic," a form which, regardless of whether one counts syllables or stresses or both, and despite the considerable variation if not distortion it incurred in the 15th c. as Chaucer's successors tried to imitate a meter they very imperfectly understood, was secured by the authority of Chaucer's reputation until "rediscovered"—i.e. reconstructed—by Wyatt and Surrey in the early 16th c. In the hands of Sidney, Spenser, and Shakespeare, the Eng. d.—given a Latinate name (see PENTAMETER) by the Classicizing Ren.—became the great staple meter of Eng. poetry and the foundation of blank verse, the heroic couplet, the Spenserian, the sonnet (qq.v.), and many other stanzaic forms; it has been estimated that some 70% of Eng. poetry of the high artverse trad. has been written in the iambic pentameter line.

Metrically speaking, the number of syllables in a regular Fr. or Eng. d. is ten. The actual number varies in accordance with historical changes and fashions in pronunciation, as well as with other prosodic conventions concerning endings (see MASCULINE AND FEMININE). The early Fr. d. frequently has 11 syllables because of the addition of a feminine ending; it may have 12 if a further syllable is added at the so-called "epic caesura." The It. equivalent of the d., the endecasillabo, normally has at least 11 because of its feminine ending (see VERSO PIANO). In Eng., feminine endings are also sometimes employed, in which case they do not count, but the d. may have as few as nine syllables if the initial syllable is dropped (see ACEPHALOUS). Frequently what appear to be additional extrametrical syllables are in fact suppressed by one or another form of elision in pronunciation (see METRICAL TREATMENT OF SYLLABLES).

A. Rochat, "Étude sur le vers décasyllabe," *Jahrbuch für romanische und englische Literatur* 11 (1870); V. Henry, *Contribution à l'étude des origines du décasyllabe roman* (1886); C. M. Lewis, *The Foreign Sources of Mod. Eng. Versification* (1898); B. Ten Brink, *Chaucers Sprache und Verskunst* (1899); W. Thomas, *Le Décasyllabe roman et sa fortune en Europe* (1904); Thieme, 373; R. Bridges, *Milton's Prosody* (1921); P. Verrier, *Le Vers français*, 3 v. (1931–32), v. 2–3; M. Burger, *Recherches sur la structure et l'origine des vers romans* (1957); L. Rarick, "Ten-Syllable Lines in Eng. Poetry," *NM* 75 (1974); Elwert; Morier; Mazaleyrat; G. T. Wright, *Shakespeare's Metrical Art* (1988).   C.S.; T.V.F.B.

DÉCIMA. Sp. metrical term used loosely to denote any 10-line stanza, but now usually used as the equivalent of *espinela* (q.v.), occasionally of *copla real*. The first *décimas* approximating the final form were the 14th- and 15th-c. 10-line variations of the *copla de arte menor*, though 10-line stanzas may be found earlier. The d. *italiana*, probably first used in the 18th c., is an octosyllabic strophe rhyming *ababc:dedec*, the *c* rhymes being oxytones and the colon denoting a pause. Other meters,

particularly the hendecasyllable with heptasyllable, may be used and the rhyme scheme and position of the pause may vary, or lines may be unrhymed provided that the two oxytones rhyme and be found one at the end of the strophe and the other at the pause. This strophe is directly related to the It. 10-line stanza, *decima rima*; see LAUDA.—Navarro.   D.C.C.

DECIR. Most of the Castilian court poetry of the pre-Ren. period (late 14th through early 16th c.) may be divided, according to Le Gentil, into two principal categories: the free-strophe composition intended to be read or recited and the poem of fixed form intended to be sung, generally termed *decir* (or *dezir*) and *cantiga* respectively. Both forms were borrowed from the Galician-Portuguese but show Fr. influence. The d. usually is narrative, satiric, didactic, or allegorical and sometimes attains considerable length. The *copla de arte mayor* (see ARTE MAYOR), rarely used for the *cantiga* type of poem, was considered the appropriate meter for d., though the *copla de arte menor* (see ARTE MENOR) was also employed. The strophes of a given poem have the same pattern. The best known examples of the d. are *D. a las siete virtudes* heretofore generally attributed to Imperial, and Juan de Mena's *Laberinto de Fortuna*, both of the 15th c.—Le Gentil; Navarro.   D.C.C.

DECONSTRUCTION.

  I. AS PHILOSOPHY
  II. AS CRITICISM

A philosophy of lang. which investigates the unreliable mediation of lang. to access any object taken to exist independently of lang. D. also refers to a kind of literary crit. or reading of lit. identified with the practices of the Yale School, whose members were Paul de Man, Geoffrey Hartman, and J. Hillis Miller. Our treatment of d. will take up first philosophy and then criticism.

I. AS PHILOSOPHY. To understand the importance of d. to literary studies, one must first set forth the idea of Jacques Derrida, who published three books, *La Voix et le phénomène, De la grammatologie,* and *L'Écriture et la différence,* in 1967 and singlehandedly changed Fr. structuralism (see STRUCTURALISM) into poststructuralism. Lang. has been the central problem for Derrida as it has been for Anglo-Am. analytical philosophy. In both the Continental and analytic traditions, this linguistic turn has merged epistemological with ontological concerns while simultaneously diverting these concerns from their ahistorical and individualistic past (Descartes' *cogito ergo sum*) into a historical and social orientation (Thomas Kuhn's paradigms). Derrida, following Nietzsche and Heidegger, comes to the same conclusion as do W. V. Quine, W. Sellars, and D. Davidson (following Frege and Bertrand Russell)—that no philosophical system can provide its own foundation or justification. But Derrida links Ger. phenomenology with Saussurean linguistics. While continuing Heidegger's attack on Western metaphysics as well as his later identification of human existence with lang., Derrida substitutes Saussurean linguistics to explain how lang. is to be understood. Rather than use Heidegger's later poetical, quasi-mystical expressions to provide a nonidolatrous principle of continuity with Being, Derrida insists that the problem of reference admits of no solution. Lang. is not the "house of Being" with the potential for leaping the gap between culture and "nature." Lang. will never become a transparent window to the-world-as-it-really-is. The pursuit of this goal by Western philosophy, the effort to erect foundations, to establish a philosophy on some self-evident truth or presence outside of discourse, can never succeed. To continue this pursuit, says Derrida, would be an exercise in nostalgia and futility.

What makes it futile is the working of lang. itself as Ferdinand de Saussure partially described it in his *Cours de linguistique générale* (1916). Saussure affirmed that the relation between word (signifier) and concept (signified) is arbitrary and that "in lang. there are only differences without positive terms." Lang. is not a naming operation with a neat one-to-one relationship between word and concept. It functions diacritically, with the meaning of a word emerging from its relationship to all the other words within the lang. now viewed as system. A phonological example may clarify how words depend on differential sound relationships to communicate. The sound "let" can function as a meaningful word because it differentiates itself from "bet," "lot," and "led." The traces of these other possible sounds within the limited range allowed by Eng. articulate and distinguish the sound "let" so that it can function as a signifier for a signified. The same holds true for signifieds: "rice" is differentiated by the lang. code and not by any inherent, absolute qualities (cf. the ninefold differentiation of words for rice in South Chinese).

This new orientation to linguistics gave Saussure hope that a general science of signs or semiology (see SEMIOTICS, POETIC) could be established. However, the first offspring of this hope, structuralism (q.v.), was quickly dispatched by Derrida's critique of its scientific pretensions. Science, like religion and metaphysics, grounds its system on presence, on a principle of order that exists outside the operation of lang. and justifies its truth claims. Even though Saussure did away with reference—words get their meaning not from reality but from the differential nature of lang. as it exercises itself phonically and conceptually (as signifier and signified)—yet Claude Lévi-Strauss and Jacques Lacan, the fathers of structuralism, turned lang. itself into a universal structuring activity latent in the human mind itself. According to Derrida, this treatment of lang. as a structuring activity not in the control of a conscious subject

but obeying unconscious laws is just the latest in a long line of philosophical attempts to establish a "metaphysics of presence." Ever since Plato, Western philosophy has attempted to come up with some privileged Truth, some "transcendental signified," which exists outside of and uncontaminated by lang., history, and time. The history of this effort may be traced by uncovering a long list of metaphysical "entities" which have held the center of various philosophical systems, e.g. *eidos, arche, telos, logos,* matter, God, *élan vital,* etc.—each finding itself eventually displaced by a newly arrived substitute. The most recent candidate now seductively beckoning to us, says Derrida, is lang. Both Heidegger and Saussure focus our attention on this latest breakthrough; each induces a major shift in our attitude toward lang., and each sinks back into the metaphysical trad. from which he seemed about to free himself and us. It remains then for Derrida to finish the job, to bring this quest for certainty in all its various modes to an end. This is the goal of d. Derrida wishes to "deconstruct" philosophy, take apart its aspirations for a "presence" or "logos" by showing how the inherent functioning of lang. itself forbids any such consummation. In place of Saussure's semiology, Derrida offers us *grammatology.*

Grammatology announces not simply a science of writing, but of a general writing (*archi-écriture*) that includes both speech and ordinary writing within it. This general writing is produced by a *gram, trace,* or *différance* whose conflictual productivity Saussure should have pursued rather than defining the sign via the binary opposition of signifier/signified. The concept or signified can all too easily emerge as a separate entity, subordinating the signifier to mere instrumentality. Saussure, quite evidently, commited this error when he privileged speech over writing. When he made writing dependent on speech (it merely represents speech graphically, as communication once removed), Saussure indicated that speech has a transparency and immediacy to the concept which writing lacks. But in making this discrimination, Saussure based the sign on a sensible/intelligible distinction in which the signifier (vocal or written) seems better or worse as it gives immediate access or "presence" to the concept or thought. In this model, the signifier (sensible) seems to serve an independent signified (intelligible) rather than creating it. The sign so understood is guilty of *logocentrism,* i.e. of seeking to ground itself on something outside the play of lang. Rejecting Saussure's sign, Derrida places it "under erasure" (*sous rature*) by being more rigorous and consequential in applying Saussure's own insights that signs are arbitrary and operate through differences without positive terms.

The structure of the sign is not binary but marked by *différance.* Derrida changes the spelling of the Fr. word for difference (from e to a) to enable the term to carry two distinct meanings.

First, it means to differ, to be separate from, to discriminate. Second, it wishes to defer, delay, or postpone—a temporalizing that puts off until later what at the moment is not possible. When we cannot make present a thing, take hold of it, show it, we use a sign; we signify a deferred presence, something absent. These two senses of *différance*, to def(diff)er, operate together in lang. and give to it a disseminating force. Each element of lang., whether phoneme or grapheme (spoken or written discourse) can function as a sign only by referring to another element which in turn is never simply present. The phonemes or graphemes interweave on the basis of *traces* left within each by all the other elements related to them in the chain or system. This interweaving process goes on ceaselessly, rippling out from the center to the margins, and extending from the past into the future. What linguists refer to as the paradigmatic/syntagmatic or synchronic/diachronic oppositions within lang., Derrida conflates and makes inseparable as an ongoing play of differences. Another variation of this opposition, *langue/parole*, or code and message, structure and event, that makes up the circle of signification, reveals the impossibility of originating lang. in one or the other. *Langue* must pre-exist as a system in order for utterance (*parole*) to have any meaning. Yet the individual speech acts (*parole*) must have instituted the code in the first place. The only way to escape this circularity, says Derrida, is to recognize the prior production of a system of differences from which one can then abstract the linguistics of *langue, synchrony*, and the *paradigmatic* or the linguistics of *parole, diachrony*, and the *syntagmatic*. The former is spatial, passive, and "factual" (constative) while the latter is temporal, active, and persuasive (performative).

Lang. use, however, can never be one or the other. It is always both. These oppositions come together in *différance*, which is both structure and movement, passive and active, being and doing, while not being governed and organized by what these terms signify. *Différance* is not a resolving, overcoming third term in the Hegelian dialectical sense. Derrida wants no synthesis, no reconceptualization on a higher level. His contradictions remain a conflict of forces or energies, an *archi-écriture* or general writing that in its generative multiplicity explodes every semantic closure while producing every (illusory) full sign. Lang., like every semiotic code, is an effect of the movement of *différance*. Lang. is not a function of the speaking subject. As in existential phenomenology, both the subject and object can only be derived as effects from the meaning-giving process. Neither subject nor object exists as more original, before, apart, or outside the movement of *différance*. "Writing" (*archi-écriture*) operates as a conflictual differential force to ceaselessly produce spoken or written lang. out of which we constitute self and world. With no commanding "presence" outside lang. nor

any ultimate "structure" within lang. to restrict its free play, Derrida offers a non-full, non-unitary, open-ended-without-origin-or-goal, never-to-be-at-rest version of lang.

What Derrida has done is push the play of difference beyond how a present sign links with nonpresent signs to show how a present sign is already a bundle of traces which make its presence possible. *Différance* already works within signs as well as between them. Because the structure of the sign is governed by the *trace* or track of that which is never fully present, the word "sign" must be placed "under erasure." It should be the last entity in the logocentric trad. which has revealed itself to be nonidentical to itself. For with the emergence of *trace* or *différance* as constitutive of lang. (sign) comes the destruction of any simple idea of presence, bringing to an end that long quest of hope and nostalgia motivating Western metaphysics since Plato.

Because philosophy is that discourse which continually forgets that it is a kind of "writing," says Derrida, it needs d. The history of philosophy has been a continuous subordination of the movement of *différance* to favor some "presence," some value or meaning, supposedly antecedent to *différance*, some originary source that ultimately governs its free play. Philosophers have been able to impose their systems only by ignoring or suppressing the disruptive force of lang. Derrida's reading (*lecture*) of other philosophers intends to uncover the tropes and rhetorical strategies by which their systems have been erected.

If world and self are precipitates of lang., understood as *différance*, then a corollary which follows is that there is no reality outside an interpreted reality or text. It is lang. which articulates, structures, creates, and eternally recreates the world. Lang., itself, therefore, will undercut the various transcendental signifieds rhetorically organized and offered as a stable foundation, the really real, etc. Deconstructive readings, thus, must always set to work within a text, giving it a close analytical reading to uncover the *aporia* or undecidable moment in the text which always lurks there to unravel any preferred transcendental signified that supposedly exists outside the text—e.g. nature, Being, the unconscious, etc.

Such historical, biographical, or metaphysical referents never escape lang. History and philosophy organize, structure, and restructure what always already exists within lang. and culture. Thus, every writer works in a cultural milieu which his own discourse cannot completely dominate. He must use and also subserve constituted codes which enable his writing but are not in his total control. Because of this discrepancy between what an author declares and what his discourse reveals, invariably a self-engendered paradox develops in a text whose logical insufficiency can be made public. These logical insufficiencies or undecidables go by different names in Derrida's deconstructive readings. They offer historical variety but functional synonymity. The *pharmakon* in Plato, the *supplement* in Rousseau, *bricolage* in Lévi-Strauss, simple *presence* in Husserl, *phonologism* in Saussure, all mark the moment when a priority in a given binary opposition unconsciously reverses or overturns itself. The deconstructive critic must seek out these moments when the text transgresses the laws it has set up for itself, when it goes against the meaning its own argument privileges. Meaning refers to something outside of textuality (q.v.), outside of the differential operation of lang. It is the referent that lies behind the textual surface which the philosopher as well as the literary critic wishes to make fully present to us. Lang. as *différance* makes the fulfillment of this desire for truth and presence impossible. We can only look forward to interminable commentary, continual reinterpretation, and misreading which will never produce any self-authenticating ground to halt the lateral displacement of signifiers *ad infinitum*.

Of course, lang. is a serviceable tool and lends itself to many aims and desires. But wherever any historical system asserts an atemporal breakthrough, a closure of what must remain a constant interweaving, an intertextuality (q.v.), there deconstructive readings must intervene to liberate and disabuse. These interventions must be done intrinsically, from within, using the very terms put into play by the discourse itself. Derrida wishes to avoid any supposed critical mastery of a text which imports into it some ready-made signified (e.g. Marxism, Freudianism) that exists outside the play of *différance*. A deconstructive critique should not wish to master the text. Once the reversal of a system's hierarchy has been accomplished by revealing that the inferior term is the necessary prerequisite to the existence of the dominant (e.g. writing to speech), then the inferior term (writing) is moved to a higher level (changed into "writing," *archi-écriture*) which undoes the limits of the two opposed terms so they can no longer function as pure logical opponents. A logic of supplementarity invades the text which places writing "under erasure" to indicate that it operates both logically and beyond sense, beyond logical limits. By uncovering this supplementary rhetoric, a deconstructive reading (*lecture*) unleashes a disseminating force in the text which simultaneously overturns the previous hierarchy, opens up the text to dissonance and turbulence, and forbids an exhaustive and closed taxonomy of its themes.

II. AS CRITICISM. Derrida's philosophy has had both a direct and indirect influence on lit. crit. Its direct influence has been felt primarily through the critical writings of the Yale Critics and their students. With the breakup of the Yale School following the death of Paul de Man, d. in its purer, more rigorous application to literary studies seems on the wane. Indirectly, however, the adaptation of d. techniques by Marxists, Freudians, and feminists shows continuing use and widening application.

D. changes our traditional understanding of lit., lit. hist. and crit. Lit., for example, no longer has to defend itself against science or philosophy as a nonserious (fictional) use of lang. Instead, philosophy and science must take on the status of lit. in order to escape their logocentric delusions. As Paul de Man stated, "lit. turns out to be the main topic of philosophy and the model for the kind of truth to which it aspires" (*Allegories of Reading* 115). Indeed, the history of philosophy has been one long flight into referentiality and content and away from self-awareness about its rhetorical origins. To the extent that the literary may be identified with the self-deconstructive movement of a text which asserts a meaning while simultaneously undercutting it, lit. comes closest to embodying *différance* or *archi-écriture*. It celebrates the signifying function, the metaphoric, figural, and imaginative free play of signifiers without closure or ultimate synthesis. Of all the various species of writing-in-general, lit. distinguishes itself by spotlighting its rhetoricity. It foregrounds its metaphors, figures, and images to illustrate the oppositions and contradictions that never ultimately reconcile themselves or come to rest. This conception of lit. as an open-ended intertextuality rather than as a self-contained work or book contrasts with the definition of lit. given by New Criticism (q.v.) as a work with "organic unity" (see ORGANICISM). The New Critics defended lit. on the grounds of its ironic and ambiguous use of lang. In lit., no clear statement sufficed without its polar opposite to complicate, deepen, and widen its experiential horizons. But such experiential insights, thematically reconciled out of the contending forces within a literary work, did ultimately refer. Poetic "truth" did subsist in the external world as a transcendental verity.

Under d., however, the privileged position of lit. arises from its status as untruth or fiction (q.v.). Because poetry celebrates its freedom from "literal" reference and is self-conscious about the imaginative basis of its creations, it suffers less from logocentrism. The importance of lit. under d. lies in its power to extend boundaries by destroying conventional frames of reality, revealing thereby their historically transient nature. Great literary texts, with or without the awareness of their authors, always deconstruct their apparent message by introducing an *aporia* (undecidable) which the deconstructive reading must unravel. Lit., more than any other discourse, reveals the lang. process by which man takes hold of his world temporarily, but never completely or finally.

Traditional lit. hist. with its period and source studies which make lit. into a reflection of some nonlinguistic reality is rejected by deconstructive critics. Such lit. histories direct attention away from the differential play of lang. that actually constitutes lit. hist.; they search for causal or determining influences external to lit. which then find their reflection or echo in literary production.

Such period classifications deny the ongoing free play of signification which a deconstructive reading (*lecture*) serves as the correlative of "writing." Every age will reinterpret the past out of which then comes the future. These readings which are always misreadings constitute any genuine lit. hist. (see INFLUENCE). Because d. trivializes referential claims, it can do little with the traditional genres of lit. hist. A case in point is Paul de Man's *Allegories of Reading* (1979), which began as a historical study but ended as a theory of reading. At most, it contributes to a revisionary history of romanticism by championing allegorical or ironical lang. over the unity of the romantic symbol.

Deconstructive crit., like its philosophical parent, focuses on lang. Topics or motifs emerging from Derrida's d. of philosophy are met again. For example, origin, presence, marginality, supplement, indeterminacy, all governed by lang. as *différance*, become critical foci to be illustrated through a deconstructive reading of a literary text. Like structuralism (q.v.), d. is not interested in establishing a text's specific meaning so much as in revealing how that meaning was rhetorically generated, how some particular value hierarchy came to be established. The emphasis of such crit. has been on demystification, on delegitimizing accepted conventions and traditions.

Because all discourses are governed by "writing," crit. is not some prosaic restatement of a superior literary vision into the inner profundities of existence. Both are just variations of the same differential play of lang. feeding off preceding lang. codes and meanings. Within the Yale School, Geoffrey Hartman seizes on this elevation of crit. to "sing along" with the work being interpreted by giving exuberant expression to puns, verbal allusion, and associations of ideas stimulated but not governed by what normally is taken to be the textual message. J. Hillis Miller often features the *mise en abyme*, the universal lack of ground or center which generates an eternal regression from the present into the past or future in the hope of "cure" or foundation. This vertiginous movement is both celebration and suffering, as lit. in search of the supreme fiction undergoes continual lateral displacement. Paul de Man's crit., usually characterized as the purest kind of d., pursues a rigorously close reading of a given text to worry out its underlying *aporia* in order to illustrate again and again how each text undercuts its own affirmation. Every critical insight owes its existence to a blindness to its own rhetorical mode that contradicts the insight.

Of all discourses, lit. is the clearest about the limitations of its referentiality. It is this limitation that deconstructive readings of lit. must uncover and promote. For de Man, this amounts to an act of liberation by which human freedom can be defended from various encroachments or subjugations to bogus superior principles. Man must remain perpetually free to recast self and world by disallowing any and all reconciling closure. Of course, de Man's own position is a totalizing one. The free play of the signifier becomes absolute, while the historical signified becomes the transitory and illusory "presence" in which the free play embodies itself. To repeat deconstructive readings on various texts with always the same outcomes tends to become monotonous after the early subversive thrills have dwindled. This monotony, the result of an exhausted deconstructive model, probably will bring an end to the direct application of d. to lit.

Indirect use of d. continues vigorously, however. Because of Derrida's embargo on referentiality, rational or cognitive claims for lang. are denigrated. Linguistic claims on truth as correspondence to reality undergo a skeptical transformation. In place of the pursuit of knowledge, lang. is now seen as motivated by Freudian desire, Marxist materialism, or Nietzschean will to power. These irrational desires contribute more powerfully to the meaning-giving process than intellectual cognition. Crit., when informed by such irrational premises, utilizes a hermeneutics of suspicion (see HERMENEUTICS). Such crit. moves from surface values of a text to a subtext whose pragmatic interests control the surface or superstructure. D. has been found quite serviceable to these other crits. as a technique whereby literary lang. can be subtly and deftly opened up in order to connect its creative play with strategies of power, with "real" historical forces. Never mind that d. repudiates any such subordination of lang. to outside forces. The Marxian, Freudian, or Nietzschean critic uses deconstructive methods to undercut authority, to destabilize institutions, and to realign social values and hierarchies. Feminists, in particular, have used the negative power of d. to reveal the blatant contradictions within patriarchal discourse, even though d. is indifferent to gender. All indications point to continued appropriation of d. by literary critics who share its demystifying and revolutionary aims but not the credo that "there is nothing outside the text" (*Of Grammatology* 158).

For further discussion of the devaluation of the aural nature of lang. and poetry in d., see SOUND. See also AMBIGUITY; CRITICISM; CULTURAL CRITICISM; INDETERMINACY; INFLUENCE; INTERPRETATION; INTERTEXTUALITY; MEANING, POETIC; ORGANICISM; POETRY, THEORIES OF, *Recent Developments*; STRUCTURALISM; TEXTUALITY; THEORY; TWENTIETH-CENTURY POETICS, *French and German*; VOICE.

PRIMARY WORKS: F. de Saussure, *Cours de linguistique générale*, (1916), 5th ed. (1955), crit. ed., ed. R. Engler (1967–74), tr. R. Harris (1983); J. Derrida, *L'Écriture et la différence* (1967), *De la grammatologie* (1967), *La Voix et la phénomène* (1967), *La Dissémination* (1972), *Marge de la philosophie* (1972), *Positions* (1972), "White Mythology," *NLH* 6 (1974), "Signature Event Context," *Glyph* 1 (1977), *La Vérité en peinture* (1978); J. H. Miller, "Trad. and Différance," *Diacritics* 2 (1972),

DECORUM

"Stevens' Rock and Crit. as Cure," *GaR* 30 (1976), "The Interp. of Otherness," *Jour. of Religion* 62 (1982), *The Ling. Moment* (1985), *The Ethics of Reading* (1987); *D. and Crit.*, ed. G. Hartman (1979); P. de Man, *Allegories of Reading* (1979), *Blindness and Insight*, 2d ed. (1983), *The Rhet. of Romanticism* (1984), *The Resistance to Theory* (1986); G. Hartman, *Crit. in the Wilderness* (1980), *Saving the Text* (1981).

SECONDARY WORKS: J. Riddel, *The Inverted Bell* (1974); G. C. Spivak, "Translator's Preface" to J. Derrida, *Of Grammatology* (1976); J. Searle, "Reiterating the Différances," *Glyph* 1 (1977); S. Felman, *La Folie et la chose littéraire* (1978); R. Rorty, "Philosophy as a Kind of Writing," *NLH* 10 (1978); R. Gasche, "D. as Crit.," *Glyph* 6 (1979); *Textual Strategies*, ed. J. V. Harrari (1979); F. Lentricchia, *After the New Crit.* (1980), ch. 5; B. Johnson, *The Crit. Difference* (1980), *A World of Difference* (1987); *Untying the Text*, ed. R. Young (1981); J. Culler, *On D.* (1982); M. Ryan, *Marxism and D.* (1982); G. D. Atkins, *Reading D., Deconstructive Reading* (1983); *The Yale Critics*, ed. J. Arac (1983); V. Leitch, *Deconstructive Crit.* (1983), *Am. Lit. Crit. from the Thirties to the Eighties* (1988), ch. 10; C. Norris, *The Deconstructive Turn* (1984), *The Contest of Faculties* (1985), *Paul de Man* (1988), *D.: Theory and Practice*, 2d ed. (1991); *Rhet. and Form: D. at Yale*, ed. R. C. Davis and R. Schleifer (1985); J. Llewelyn, *Derrida on the Threshold of Sense* (1986); *D. and Philosophy*, ed. J. Sallis (1987); M. C. Taylor, *Altarity* (1987); J. M. Ellis, *Against D.* (1989); J. C. Evans, *Strategies of D.* (1991); D. Lehman, *Signs of the Times* (1991). V.W.G.

DECORUM. The Cl. term *d.* (Gr. *to prepon*) refers to one of the criteria to be observed in judging those things in our experience whose excellence lends itself more appropriately to qualitative than to quantitative measurement. This definition depends upon the ancient distinction between two types of measure stated by Plato in *The Statesman* (283d–85a) and adopted by Aristotle in his ethical, political, rhetorical, and literary treatises. Excess and deficiency, Plato says, are measurable not only in terms of the quantitative largeness or smallness of objects in relation to each other but also in terms of each object's approximation to a norm of "due measure." All the arts owe the effectiveness and beauty of their products to this norm, *to metron*, whose criteria of what is commensurate (*to metrion*), decorous (*to prepon*), timely (*to kairon*), and needful (*to deon*) all address themselves to the "mean" (*to meson*) rather than to the fixed, arithmetically defined, extremes. This distinction is central to literary d. because lit. shares its subject matter and certain principles of stylistic representation with the disciplines of law, ethics, and rhet., which also are concerned with the qualitative analysis and judgment of human experience.

With respect to subject matter, Aristotle says that poetry treats human actions (*Poetics* 2, 4, 6–9)

by revealing their universal significance in terms of the "kinds of thing a certain kind of person will say or do in accordance with probability or necessity" (Else, 9.4). The kinds of thing said or done will indicate certain moral qualities (*poious*) of character which, in turn, confer certain qualities (*poias*) upon the actions themselves (6.5–6). Extending the terms of Plato's *Statesman* (283d–85b, 294a–97e) to ethics, law, and rhet., Aristotle defines the concept of virtue necessary to evaluate such qualities of character as a balanced "disposition" (*hexis*) of the emotions achieved by the observation of the "mean" (*mesotes*) *relative to each situation* (*EN* 2.6). Likewise in law, equity is a "disposition" achieved through the individual application of a "quantitatively" invariable code of statutes for (amounts of) rewards and penalties to "qualitatively" variable and unpredictable human actions. As the builder of Lesbos bent his leaden ruler to a particular stone, so the judge, in drawing upon the universal law of nature (*to katholou*), might rectify the particular application of civil law by making a special ordinance to fit the individual case (*EN* 5.7, 10). Equity brings these universal considerations to bear by looking to the qualitative questions of the legislator's intentions and of what kind (*poios*) of man the accused has generally or always been in order to mitigate his present act (*Rhet.* 1.13.13–19).

With respect to stylistic representation, all verbal (as opposed to arithmetical) expression is qualitative, and rests content if it can establish a likely similarity (rather than an exact equivalence) between things (Plato, *Crat.* 432ab, *Tim.* 29cd). Diction achieves d. by a proper balance between "distinctive" words, which contribute dignity while avoiding obtrusiveness, and "familiar" words, which, while avoiding meanness, contribute clarity (Aristotle, *Rhet.* 3.2–3, *Poetics* 21–22). Lang. as a whole achieves d. if the style expresses the degree of emotion proper to the importance of the subject and makes the speaker appear to have the kind of character proper to the occasion and audience. The greater the subject, the more powerful the emotions the speaker or writer may decorously solicit. The more shrewdly he estimates the "disposition" which informs the character of his listeners, the more he can achieve the "timely" (*eukairos*) degree of sophistication appropriate to the occasion (*Rhet.* 3.7; cf. Plato, *Phaedrus* 277bc).

Influenced by the Middle Stoicism of Panaetius and Posidonius, Cicero did most to define and transmit the relation of literary d. to ethics and law, suggested by such words as *decor* and *decet*, in his philosophical and rhetorical treatises (*De Off.* 1.14, 93–161; *Orat.* 69–74, 123–5). From his reformulation of Platonic, Aristotelian, and Isocratean attitudes, there flowed an immense variety of literary and artistic applications of the concept by grammarians, poets, rhetoricians, historians, philosophers, theologians, and encyclopedic writers

DESCRIPTIVE POETRY

on specialized disciplines. Most exemplary, perhaps, of the vitality and versatility of this trad. is St. Augustine's adaptation of it to Christian oratory and exegesis in *De doctrina cristiana*, where, while virtually rejecting the Cl. *doctrine* of "levels of style"—to which d. was often reduced—he gave the Cl. *principle* of d. new life and applications (see Auerbach).

Like the "mean" and "disposition" of ethics and equity, d. is an activity rather than a set of specific characteristics of style or content to be discovered, preserved, and reproduced. It is a fluid corrective process which must achieve and maintain, instant by instant, the delicate balance between the formal, cognitive, and judicative intentions of literary discourse. Its constant resistance to imbalance, taking different forms in different periods, never offers a "solution" to be found or expressed by literary "rules" (q.v.) with which later neoclassical theorists often try to identify it. As soon as they reduce it to a doctrine concerning either a given kind of subject or a given kind of style or a fixed relation of the one to the other, d. ceases to exist, because its activity is a continuous negotiation between the two. For the forms that particular reductions or recoveries have taken, the reader must look to those literary controversies endemic to the specific period, genre, or issue of interest.

E. M. Cope and J. E. Sandys, *The Rhet. of Aristotle*, 3 v. (1877); G. L. Hendrickson, "The Peripatetic Mean of Style and the Three Stylistic Characters," *AJP* 25 (1904), "The Origin and Meaning of the Ancient Characters of Style," *AJP* 26 (1905); J. W. H. Atkins, *Lit. Crit. in Antiquity*, 2 v. (1934); W. Jaeger, *Paideia*, 3 v. (1943)—cultural background; E. De Bruyne, *Études d'esthétique médiévale*, 3 v. (1946)—med. background; M. T. Herrick, *The Fusion of Horatian and Aristotelian Lit. Crit. 1531–1555* (1946); Curtius, ch. 10; Norden; F. Quadlbauer, "Die Genera Dicendi bis Plinius d.J.," *WS* 71 (1958), "Die antike Theorie der Genera Dicendi im lateinischen Mittelalter," *Akad. D. Wissens. zu Wien, Sitzungsberichte* 241.2 (1962); H. I. Marrou, *Histoire de l'éducation dans l'antiquité*, 5th ed. (1960)—cultural background; Weinberg; C. O. Brink, *Horace on Poetry*, 3 v. (1963–82); G. F. Else, *Aristotle's Poetics: The Argument* (1963); E. Auerbach, "*Sermo Humilis*," *Literary Lang. and its Public in Late Lat. Antiquity and in the Middle Ages* (tr. 1965), ch. 1; M. Pohlenz, "*To prepon*," *Kleine Schriften*, ed. H. Dorrie (1965); A. Patterson, *Hermogenes and the Ren.* (1970); T. McAlindon, *Shakespeare and D.* (1973); Murphy; W. Edinger, *Samuel Johnson and Poetic Style* (1977)—18th-c. background; S. Shankman, *Pope's Iliad* (1983), ch. 3; W. Trimpi, *Muses of One Mind* (1983)—see index; T. A. Kranidas, *The Fierce Equation* (1965); K. Eden, *Poetic and Legal Fiction in the Aristotelian Trad.* (1986). W.T.

DEEP IMAGE. See AMERICAN POETRY.

DEFINITION. See POEM; POETICS; THEORY.

DELETION. Syntactic: see ELLIPSIS; SYNTAX, POETIC. Metrical: see ELISION; METRICAL TREATMENT OF SYLLABLES.

DELIVERY. See PERFORMANCE.

DENOTATION. See CONNOTATION AND DENOTATION.

DENOUEMENT. See PLOT.

DESCORT. Occitan and OF lyric genre, courtly in substance, heterostrophic in versification. The d., like the lyric *lai* (q.v.), was constructed from stanzas or versicles, each different from the others but each showing two-fold (sometimes three- or fourfold) metrical and musical symmetry. The title ("discord") referred to this irregularity, to the contrast between lively tunes and melancholy words, and, in one exceptional case, to the five different langs. used in the five stanzas.—H. R. Lang, "The D. in Old Portuguese and Sp. Poetry," *Beiträge zur romanischen Philologie: Festschrift Gustav Gröber* (1899); I. Frank, *Répertoire métrique de la poésie des troubadours*, 2 v. (1953–57), 1.183-95, 2.71-72—indexes; J. Maillard, "Problèmes musicaux et littéraires du d.," *Mélanges . . . à la mémoire d'István Frank* (1957), *Évolution et esthétique du lai lyrique* (1963), 119-27; R. Baum, "Le D. ou l'antichanson," *Mélanges de philologie romane . . . Jean Boutière* (1971); E. Köhler in *GRLMA*, v. 2.1B; J. H. Marshall, "The Isostrophic D. in the Poetry of the Troubadours," *RPh* 35 (1981); D. Billy, "Le D. occitan: Réexamen critique du corpus," *RLR* 87 (1983); Chambers. J.H.M.

DESCRIPTIVE POETRY.

    I. CLASSICAL AND LATE ANTIQUITY
   II. THE MODERN PERIOD

I. CLASSICAL AND LATE ANTIQUITY. D. p. in the West concerns the theory and practice of description in versified texts. D. p. is not a genre in itself, but d. portrayal has always played an important role in verse art, in a continuous trad. reaching back to the oldest surviving poetic texts. Its tenacity is epitomized in Horace's well-known phrase *ut pictura poesis* (*Ars poetica* 361; q.v.), which, divorced from its context, became a Ren. dictum encapsulating the aspiration of poetry to portray its subject matter quasi-visually. Ultimately, description should be considered as a strategy and an instancing of the doctrine of imitation (q.v.; see also REPRESENTATION AND MIMESIS). Plato's condemnation (*Republic* 10) of the powerful mimetic arts of epic and tragic poetry as dangerously misleading "copies of copies" was historically superseded by Aristotle's defense of imitation as satisfying a natural instinct for knowledge and instruction, hence an effective means of learning.

DESCRIPTIVE POETRY

It is impossible in this space to give an exhaustive account of the uses of description in poetry throughout the ages; rather, this article aims simply to point out some of the diverse functions of description in Western poetry, recognizing that its presence in Eastern lits. is equally widespread and profound.

In practice, d. technique has been applied mainly: (1) to the female body, as in the biblical Song of Solomon (1.5,10,15; 4.1–7, 10–15; 6.4–7,10; 7.1–9; but at 1.13–14 and 5.10–16 the man's body is eulogized) and the Fr. *blason* (q.v.); (2) to man's surroundings and habitat, whether natural or cultivated landscape or crafted architecture; and (3) to isolated objects, whether utensils or representational works of art.

In antiquity, a theory of description (*ekphrasis* [q.v.], *descriptio*) was elaborated for practical use by Cl. rhetoricians, but it was equally applicable, with certain modifications, to poetry. Gr. and Lat. rhetorical handbooks frequently cited examples from poetry, esp. epic, to illustrate their points. *Ekphrasis,* one of the elementary rhetorical exercises (*progymnasmata*), was intended to train pupils in the art of "bringing a subject before the eyes [of the audience]." Events and actions unfolding in time were as appropriate to *ekphrasis* as static entities such as cities, landscapes, and buildings. The modern distinction between the narrative thread and interpolated d. 'digressions' does not apply in antiquity. Quintilian (8.3.68–70, quoted by Erasmus, *De copia* 2.5) shows how the summary phrase "a sacked city" can be expanded to show in action the unfolding process of its devastation in pictorial detail. This example would apply not only to prose oratory but also to versified poetry, as can be seen from the fact that the quotations in 6.2.32–33 are all from the *Aeneid.*

Vividness or *enargeia* (q.v.) is the effective quality deriving from poetic description. Its use was didactically codified in rhetorical rather than poetic treatises, yet both arts engage the subjective faculties of the performer (poet, actor, or orator) who delivers the text with those of the audience. The stimulation of inward vision in the imagination (q.v.) and the arousal of concomitant feelings are closely linked. The practical aim is to evoke vividly the scene of an action or the situation of an object. Pseudo-Longinus praises passages in tragedy where the poet seems to have been actually present at the scene (*De sublimitate* 15). The immediacy of the effect of subjective representation is more important than the strict truth of its contents. Veracity—as opposed to verisimilitude (q.v.)—must therefore be guaranteed by other means: professional historiographers and forensic lawyer-orators were therefore advised to scrutinize their material with caution; nevertheless, they too were to appeal to the visual imagination and to the emotions of the audiences. In poetry the intended effect was the qualitatively more striking one of *ekplexis*—astonishment, amazement—which per-mitted, even encouraged, the depiction of fantastic, supernatural, and mythological creatures such as the Furies, allegorical personifications (e.g. the figure of Discord in *Iliad* 4.442, which is praised at the expense of the description of Strife in the pseudo-Hesiodic *Shield of Herakles* in *De sublimitate* 9), and powerful events such as the battle of the Titans in the *Gigantomachia.*

Aristotle (*Rhetoric* 1411b–1412a) always uses the adverbial phrase "before the eyes" (*pro ommathon*) as a concrete synonym for the abstract notion of "vivid(ness)." And he goes further in asserting that this quality produces an effect of "actuality": the Gr. term is *energeia*; and lexical confusion with *enargeia* may stem from this source. The aim of such representation remains that of vitality. And Aristotle recommends the use not only of adjectives of visual or tactile qualities but even more of verbs of motion (esp. present participles) and adverbial phrases denoting—representing—active movement. He draws his examples from Euripides and Homer rather than from prose oratory.

Such prescriptive epitomes for powerful description were a didactic codification of practice within a living trad. The Homeric poems were composed long before any extant rhetorical handbook; yet they are full of vividly described events (battles, Odysseus' adventures) and places (the palace and gardens of Alcinous and the cave of the nymphs in *Odyssey* 7, 13). The most famous and most discussed d. passage in Homer is indubitably the ekphrasis of the Shield of Achilles in *Iliad* 18. The account of the object is presented in a narrative form: Homer depicts Hephaestus actually making the object and describes the scenes on the shield as if they were unfolding in time. Poetry thus invests static spatial objects with vitality by transfusing into them its own rhythmic, temporal succession.

Such use of description for vividly heightened narrative and for pictorial set pieces is to be found throughout the history of epic (q.v.) in authors such as Apollonios Rhodios, Nonnos, and Virgil. Virgil adopts Homer's device of the shield (*Aeneid* 8) but takes the finished object as the point of departure for his description. He imbues it with significance by taking each scene portrayed as the occasion for a prophetic excursus on the future glory of Rome. Different kinds of allegorical exegesis were applied to Homer's descriptions by Late Antique interpreters (e.g. Porphyry, *On the Cave of the Nymphs*). Allegorical significance was detected in Virgil's (d.) pastoral (q.v.) poetry by Servius and other commentators.

The highly polished, smaller-scale genres such as the epigram, pastoral, and epyllion (qq.v.) developed in the Hellenistic age also made use of concentrated description, usually of places and scenes, as in Theocritus' *Idylls.* The physical characteristics and attributes of the pastoral context are explicitly described either by the author or in the speech of the characters (see ECLOGUE; IDYLL). Here, descriptions constitute a nostalgic evocation of a state of rustic innocence remote from urban life, mores, and lit. But the bucolic *locus amoenus* might equally stand for quiet leisure, necessary for sophisticated poetic learning, a simple, agreeable metaphor for *otium* (see BUCOLIC; GEORGIC). In Roman poetry, this theme is developed in accounts of the Golden Age such as in Virgil's fourth *Eclogue*, Horace's sixteenth *Epode*, and, with irony, in Catullus 64.

Isolated objects such as a rustic cup (Theocritus, *Idylls* 1.27–56), a ship ("Phaselus ille," Catullus 4; Horace, *Odes* 1.3) or a water droplet caught in a crystal (Claudian, *Epigrams* 4.2.12, a set of nine different descriptions of the same thing) can be found alongside poems addressed to (and evocative of) real places ("O funde noster," Catullus 44; "O Colonia," Catullus 17) or imagined locations, like the Palace of the Sun and the dwellings of Sleep and Fame in Ovid's *Metamorphoses*.

In descriptions of weather, straight meteorological eulogy (e.g. of Spring, Horace, *Odes* 1.4) may be developed as political allegory (e.g. storms as a metaphor for civic turbulence: Horace, *Odes* 1.2), as observations on the social economics of agriculture (*Odes* 2.15), or as a parable of Fortune and her consolations (*Odes* 1.9); this practice is still evident in the 19th c.

The use of description in dramatic action finds its natural function in evoking absent scenes (remote in time and space), and esp. in messenger speeches, which describe a (usually violent) action which has taken place offstage. Where this device includes reported speech, it is related to the *progymnasma* called *prosopopoiia* or *ethopoiia*, which consists of a recreation of the words of an individual in a certain situation (see ETHOS), an exercise which would have trained an author in the composition of pithy, highly characteristic, direct speech. Pseudo-Longinus cites passages from tragedy to illustrate the dramatic effect of description and to underline the need for the poet to use the visual imagination in the composition process (*De sublimitate* 15). In Euripides' *Hecuba* (444–83), the chorus of captive Trojan women contrast the beautiful images of their memories of the sea, the sun, and the winds with the misery of their present plight and surroundings. Talthybius then enters to relate (518–82) the sacrifice—or murder—of Polyxena by Neoptolemos, son of Achilles. His speech is full of vivid d. detail; and his representation of Polyxena's physical beauty, her decorous *pudeur*, and radiant nobility (557–70) evokes pathos (q.v.) by the intensity of its contrast with the barbarity of the act.

The importance of description in intensifying the rhetorical effect and dramatic impact of messenger speeches is attested by Erasmus (*De copia* 2.5; rev. 1532 ed.) as part of his wide-ranging analysis of description as a powerful device of oratory in all manner of prose and verse genres.

Erasmus' treatment includes four divisions: *descriptio rei, personae, loci, temporis*. He cites examples from lyric, dramatic and epic poetry, as well as from prose speeches, historiography, and "natural science." It remains the most comprehensive classicizing Ren. survey. Homer is again proposed as the supremely vivid poet.

Didactic poetry (q.v.) such as Hesiod's *Works and Days*, Lucretius' *De rerum natura*, and Virgil's *Georgics* uses d. passages and personification (q.v.) to invest the subject matter with immediacy and vitality. Such appeals to the visual imagination may also have reinforced the poets' didactic intentions, since ancient memory techniques relied on visualization to store information in the form of images.

In the early centuries A.D., parallel developments can be seen in the use of description in poetry and rhet. Under the Roman Empire, rhet. changed from being a practical instrument used in courtrooms—and thus directly concerned with real human actions—to a highly sophisticated art form, a showcase for the orator's skill and ingenuity. Judicial rhet. is replaced by epideictic. School exercises such as *ekphrasis* became an end in themselves rather than a means. Speeches were often composed for particular occasions to praise objects such as cities, temples, or civic landmarks. Statius' *Silvae*—a collection of poems describing villas, statues, society weddings—illustrates the use of description in poetry for similar ends (see EPIDEICTIC POETRY).

In Byzantium, which continued the trad. of ancient epideictic, versified poetry often replaced prose rhet.: long *ekphraseis* were composed in poetic meter using a literary, quasi-Homeric lang. Paul the Silentiary's verse *ekphrasis* of Hagia Sophia was publicly recited, like an epideictic speech, at the second consecration of the Church in 563. Like prose *ekphraseis*, these metrical works reproduce a viewer's sense impressions of the building (glittering gold, variegated marble) and expound its spiritual significance, and thus translate the inner response to the subject matter or its figural decoration of biblical scenes. These inward reactions are described in a radically subjective manner: they do not normally provide accurate information as to the exact appearance of the object. Nor are they exact in the archeological sense, permitting the detailed and precise reconstruction of an original. This is a legacy of the emotive function of description in rhet., where *vraisemblance* is more important than truth to nature (see VERISIMILITUDE; NATURE).

It is the meshing of images (*phantasiai*) with emotions (*pathe*) which underlies the affective power of description. Ultimately, these literary and psycho-physiological effects all aspire to the mimetic condition, which revivifies static linguistic constructions so that they reproduce subjectively, via artistic means, the vitality and physical immediacy of natural experience.

II. THE MODERN PERIOD. D. technique is crucial to the effect of Ren. epic. In Tasso's *Gerusalemme liberata*, the interpenetration of vivid imagery, pictorial intensity, and psychological discernment powerfully emphasizes the seriousness of Rinaldo's desertion and reconversion. The fantastic, mythic-encyclopedic vision of the "Mediterranean" (Canto 15), the enchanted palace and gardens of Armida (15, 16), and the picturesque review of the Egyptian armies (17) are all resolved into the transfiguration of Rinaldo (Canto 18).

Ancient pastoral was revived in Ren. Neo-Lat. eclogues (Petrarch, Boccaccio) and in long poems such as Sannazzaro's *Arcadia*. In England, Sidney also wrote an *Arcadia*, and Spenser used d. technique in evoking the surroundings of the "Bower of Bliss" episode in *The Faerie Queene*. Milton composed pastoral poems in both Lat. (*Damon*) and Eng. (*Lycidas*) and used the pastoral setting for his depiction of Eden in *Paradise Lost* (4.689 ff.). But the whole epic is permeated by startling d. and visual style: Satan's call-to-arms ("Pandaemonium," 1.283 ff.) of his legions and their terrestrial advance (4.205 ff.), the portrayal of Raphael (5.246 ff.), and Michael's representation to Adam of a vision of the future course of hist. down to the Flood (Bks. 11, 12) are all splendid examples, as is Satan's temptation of Christ in *Paradise Regained* (4.25 ff.).

In the 17th c., Boileau (*Art poétique* 3.258 ff.) recommended a rich and sensuous elegance in description so as to avoid tedium, inertia, and cold melancholy and to relieve the austerity of the severe high style in epic and romance. Here too, description should enliven narrative. Boileau's acknowledged master is Homer, whose poems are "animated by a felicitous warmth of style" derived from his rich stock (3.297) of graceful and pleasing pictures (3.288) of stimulating beauty. The vibrancy of the images must be matched nuance for nuance by the figures of style: in this way the poet can, like Homer, alchemically transmute his imagined visions into poetic gold ("Everything [Homer] touched was turned to gold; / Everything receives in his hands a new grace" [3.298–99]). In the mind, vividness produces animation, which in turn generates vital warmth.

Racine's messenger speeches (*récits*) too are animated through description (Phèdre 5.6.1498–1592; *Andromaque* 5.3.1496–1524; *Iphigénie* 5.6.1734–90). The premonitory dream of Athalia (*Athalie* 2.5.485–540) colors a supernatural vision with enough appropriate, carefully selected physical detail to make the representation lifelike.

Perhaps the finest example, in this period, of description functioning as laudatory rhet. is La Fontaine's long (though incomplete) *Le Songe de Vaux* (1659–61), which describes the architecture and gardens of Fouquet's Château of Vaux-le-Vicomte and the spectacular celebrations prepared there for Louis XIV in 1661. The poem was intended as a monument in verse to Fouquet's worldly glory and munificence. The close relation in antiquity between *ekphrasis/descriptio* and *encomion/laus* is preserved in 17th-c. Fr. Classicism (q.v.). La Fontaine's work is a combination of commissioned panegyric (q.v.) and theatrical, topographical fantasy. Of equal interest is the cycle of odes by Racine, *Le Paysage*, which describes a journey on foot to a Jansenist convent. It is a eulogy of the retired, contemplative religious life, couched in the pastoral terms of the idyll.

In Ger., the most significant text on poetic description to appear is Lessing's *Laoköon* (1766, 1788), which, although it had immediate polemical intent in a dispute with Winckelmann, presents a pivotal analysis of the effects of poetry in comparison with painting and sculpture. Lessing quotes the epigrammatic statement attributed by Plutarch to Simonides, "painting is dumb poetry and poetry speaking painting," to show that, although there may be similarity or even identity of mental and spiritual effect ("vollkommene Ähnlichkeit der Wirkung") between two different arts, their technical systems of construction and expression remain irreducibly different. Lessing exemplifies his theoretical exposition by citing examples from Virgil and Homer, but he draws on a formidable range of Cl. sources, as well as citing Ariosto, Milton, and Pope. The *Laoköon* is arguably the fundamental Western text for any appraisal of poetic description. Lessing's two main topics concern the necessity of matching moral qualities with physical, and of linking, through art, the different motions of time, events, the eye, the mind, and the feelings.

Goethe rarely presents such full description as can be found in *Ilmenau* (which like *Zueignung* continues a moral allegory) or *Ein zärtlich jugendlicher Kunimer*, but *Harzreise im Winter* shows more typically how vivid sense perception, subjective emotion, and moral reflection are everywhere interwoven in the fabric of Goethe's poetry. A couplet from the seventh *Roman Elegy* ("Now the sheen of the brighter ether illumines the stars; Phoebus the god calls forth forms and colours") shows how closely his poetic eye informs the "Theory of Colours" (*Farbenlehre*). And the lighthearted parable *Amor als Landschaftsmaler* puts in a humorous light Goethe's intuitive sense that Eros is the motivating force in Art as well as in Nature.

In the Eng. 18th c., Thomson's *The Seasons* (1727–30) initiated a literary fashion for poems describing the working conditions and settings of agricultural life, the pictorial elements of landscape, anecdotal details of rustic existence, and man's relation to nature. But the specific genre of topographical poetry was not recognized until 1779, when Samuel Johnson characterized it as "local poetry, of which the fundamental subject is some particular landscape . . . with the addition of such embellishments as may be supplied by his-

torical retrospection, or incidental meditation"
(*Life of Denham*); this prescription of landscape as
subject matter restricts the wide historical appli-
cation of the inherent power of vivid description
of all kinds of objects. Hence, the genre needed to
be sustained by strength of style. Dr. Johnson's
observations were made in regard to Sir John
Denham's *Cooper's Hill* (1642); and indeed, he
found Denham's style to possess compact strength
and concision. Denham had made paraphrastic
translations of Virgil in 1636, and some bucolic
fragments of these found their way into *Cooper's
Hill* (Bush 165–69).

Gottfried van Swieten modeled his libretto for
Haydn's *Die Jahreszeiten* on Thomson's poem. The
poetry and music of this oratorio embody the
loftier aspirations of the topographical genre to-
ward an integrated, quasi-anthropological study
of rural life in its confrontation with nature, but
one which did not deny the sophisticated emo-
tional response expected in pastoral. It blends the
Enlightenment strain of sentimental, moralizing
narrative with a noble feeling for the emotional
and ethical grandeur of nature.

In the hands of Wordsworth, the technical limits
and psychological distinctions of sense perception
respected by earlier writers are dissolved. The
early poems *An Evening Walk* and *Descriptive
Sketches* (1793) show an attention to natural detail
close to 18th-c. practice. But the tendency in the
Tintern Abbey poem, the Intimations Ode, and
The Prelude (e.g. the opening of Books 6 and 12) is
to dissolve the separate boundaries of sense and
cognition so as to achieve an utterly subjective
union with an undifferentiated pantheistic Nature.
This aspiration was made explicit by Wordsworth
himself when he claimed to have "completely ex-
tricated the notions of time and space" and to have
made an attempt "to evolve all the five senses; that
is, to deduce them from one sense, and to state
their growth and the causes of their difference,
and in this evolution to solve the process of life and
consciousness" (Renwick 173). This entailed the
breakdown of the differentiated perceptual sys-
tem within which carefully selected details pro-
vided the concrete material of vivid description.
Instead, the emotions, which would otherwise be
aroused by the mental apprehension of the d.
details, are directly expressed in wholly subjective
terms. Only passing references are made to the
material, constituent elements of the natural
world as normally perceived. This utterly inward
response to nature took to an extreme Johnson's
recommendation to include in d. p. the fruits of
"incidental meditation"; and in so doing it spelled
the end of the topographical poem as such.

The directness of Wordsworth's encounter with
nature is obvious: so many of his poems, from the
Descriptive Sketches onwards, were composed in ec-
static response to a physical confrontation with
landscape. His response is rapturous and utterly
involving, but he rarely provides the common

natural details of description for the reader to
absorb and process mentally, and so to translate
into congruent images.

In Germany, Heine's *Die Harzreise* (1824) and
Die Nordsee (1825–26) show that the confrontation
of a traveler on foot with the natural landscape in
the hills or on the coast could still form the basis
for an extended cyclical poem. But the concrete
representation of landscape tends to fragment into
a series of vignettes which cohere only by virtue of
the underlying current of the poet's subjective
response. The telling d. detail used by Hölderlin
and Mörike always serves the ends of emotion or
of metaphysical speculation. Mörike's fantasy is-
land landscape of Orphid and Hölderlin's baffling
Hälfte des Lebens are two instances of d. evocation
utterly dissimilar in approach.

Wordsworth's revitalization of poetic diction
(see LEXIS) and his practical reform of the aims,
techniques, and limits of poetic description are
linked. Similar parallels can be drawn between the
proliferation of 19th- and 20th-c. poetic move-
ments (e.g. symbolism, imagism, surrealism
[qq.v.]) intent on restating the qualitative virtues
of poetic lang. in resistance to the pressures of
quantitative science and expository prose, and the
practice of individual poets who are also critics
(Baudelaire, Mallarmé, Eliot, Seferis, Auden,
Rilke, Bonnefoy). For all of these varied poets, the
d. values of image and metaphor (q.v.) can be seen
as an essential quality in poetic perception. Trace
elements of sensation, drawn from experience and
recombined to form images, are presented so as to
stimulate vivid awareness of the external world or
to express particular, sometimes extreme inner
states. The result is a kind of "psychological de-
scription" (as detected by De Robertis in Leop-
ardi's *Canti*) which portrays an "interior land-
scape," the *Weltinnenraum* of Rilke or the spiritual
pilgrimage towards Bonnefoy's *arrière-pays*. Even
the ekphrastic poems-about-paintings of Bruno
Tolentino ("About the Hunt," "Those Strange
Hunters") contain more of the reflective "embel-
lishments . . . of incidental meditation," i.e. of
imaginative appraisal of the subject matter, than
an accurate verbal reconstitution of their subjects'
physical construction. For Cavafy too, the act of
radically subjective appropriation is the kernel of
vivid poetic narrative: "You won't encounter
[Odysseus' adventures] unless you carry them
within your soul, unless your soul sets them up in
front of you" (*Ithaka*). And Ungaretti's "Choruses
Descriptive of Dido's States of Mind" (*La Terra
promessa*) attempt a direct physiognomy of the soul
rather than of the external symptoms of emotion.

The modern rural descriptions and nature po-
ems of R. S. Thomas, Seamus Heaney, Ted
Hughes, and Charles Tomlinson show neither the
sophisticated pastoral ease of the urbanite at lei-
sure nor the pantheist fervor of an idealizing
imagination such as Wordsworth's, but rather a
grim confrontation with the pitiless harshness,

even brutality, of the natural world they observe. They describe unsentimentally the struggle for survival within the animal kingdom and the dogged, heroic resistance of real farmers to nature's destructive power. Again, the moral question of the fearless recognition of the true existential plight of man in his habitat is more important in influencing the description of his natural surroundings then the creation of aesthetic pleasure.

Altogether, description on a broad canvas, elaborate, explicit, and comprehensive in scope, has probably been less common in 19th- and 20th-c. poetry than concentration on intensity of d. detail in the imagery of lyric. And while the persistence of certain conventional themes, which create the fictional assumption of a travel journal or pilgrimage, or of a poetic monument to a piece of architecture or sculpture, or of a versified record of a geographical or topographical survey, may give the initial impression that there is a specifically d. genre, there is in fact always another governing intention (moralizing, didactic, persuasive, emotive) which is served, rather than conditioned, by the technique of description, which is rather to be considered as a rhetorical-poetic strategy to be applied in genres established on other grounds, as occasion demands.

See also EKPHRASIS; GEORGIC; ICONOLOGY; IMAGE; IMAGERY; NATURE; PASTORAL; SCULPTURE AND POETRY; VISUAL ARTS AND POETRY.

E. W. Manwaring, *It. Landscape in 18th-C. England* (1925); M. Cameron, *L'Influence des 'Saisons' de Thomson sur la poésie d. en France (1759–1810)* (1927); R. A. Aubin, *Topographical Poetry in 18th-C. England* (1936); D. Bush, *Eng. Lit. in the Earlier 17th C.* (1945); G. De Robertis, *Saggio sul Leopardi* (1960); R. L. Renwick, *Eng. Lit. 1789–1815* (1963); J. Arthos, *The Lang. of Description in 18th-C. Poetry* (1966); A. Roper, *Arnold's Poetic Landscapes* (1969); J. W. Foster, "A Redefinition of Topographical Poetry," *JEGP* 69 (1970); P. Hamon, "Qu'est-ce qu'une description?" *Poétique* 2 (1972); G. Genette, *Figures III* (1972); J. B. Spencer, *Heroic Nature: Ideal Landscape in Eng. Poetry from Marvell to Thomson* (1973); H. H. Richmond, *Ren. Landscapes: Eng. Lyrics in a European Trad.* (1973); R. Williams, *The Country and the City* (1973); E. Guitton, *Jacques Delille (1738–1813) et le poème de la nature en France de 1750 à 1820* (1974); J. Gitzon, "British Nature Poetry Now," *MidwestQ* 15 (1974); D. Lodge, "Types of Description," *The Modes of Mod. Writing* (1977); J. G. Turner, *The Politics of Landscape: Rural Scenery and Society in Eng. Poetry, 1630–1660* (1979); "Towards a Theory of Description," ed. J. Kittay, spec. iss. of *YFS* 62 (1981); B. Peucker, "The Poem as Place," *PMLA* 96 (1981)—the lyric; R. Barthes et al., *Littérature et réalité* (1982); A. Reed, *Romantic Weather* (1983); C.G. Dubois, "Itinéraires et impasses dans la vive représentation au XVIe siècle," *Litt. de la ren.* (1984); D. E. Wellerby, *Lessing's Laocöon: Semiotics and Aesthetics in the Age of Reason* (1984); J. A. W.

Heffernan, *The Re-Creation of Landscape* (1984); J. Holden, "Landscape Poems," *DenverQ* 20–21 (1986); J. Applewhite, *Seas and Inland Journeys: Landscape and Consciousness from Wordsworth to Roethke* (1986); E. W. Leach, *The Rhet. of Space: Literary and Artistic Representations of Landscape in Republican and Augustan Rome* (1988).

R.H.W.; P.W.

DETERMINACY. See INDETERMINACY; MEANING, POETIC.

DEVICE. See RUSSIAN FORMALISM.

DEVOTIONAL POETRY. See RELIGION AND POETRY.

DIACHRONY. See STRUCTURALISM.

DIAERESIS. (1) The pronunciation of two successive vowels as separate sounds and not as a diphthong, e.g. Chloë, coöperate. (2) In Cl. prosody (q.v.), the coincidence of word-end with the end of a metrical unit (foot or metron; so Quintilian), and the opposite of caesura (q.v.), which to the ancients meant the ending of a word within a foot. But "caesura" lost this sense in the Ren., as did d. its Cl. sense; now d. commonly refers only to the absence of elision (q.v.), as in (1). If the two vowels are separated by word-juncture, the effect is called hiatus (q.v.). In the hexameter (q.v.), d. after a fourth-foot dactyl was traditionally called "bucolic d.," by virtue of its supposed frequency in pastoral or bucolic (qq.v.) poetry; West however terms this usage "a modern pedantry" (*CQ* 32 (1982): 292). It would be useful to have modern terms for degree of alignment between lexical and metrical units in verse, but so far none has been developed.—Schipper; Halporn et al.; Snell; West.

R.A.H.; T.V.F.B.

DIALECT POETRY. In every culture or nation-state of any size there is normally more than one distinct way of speaking the lang.; these are ds. The line between two ds. of one lang. and two langs. is very difficult to draw in theory, but in practice the differences seem to be either phonological or lexical—i.e. differing pronunciations or words for common objects. Ds. usually come into existence as a result of either geographical or social boundaries, both causing isolation and differentiation. Over time one d. will usually come to dominate the others, becoming thereby the "standard lang.," but strong local, regional, ethnic, or class identities may well preserve the others; and in some cases several or even many ds. may coexist on a relatively equal footing. (In a case such as Swiss, even distinct langs. may coexist closely.) Political changes and wars may also alter a state, leading to either suppression of native ds. and imposition of a foreign lang. (as happened in England after the Conquest: Norman Fr. was the

DIALECT POETRY

official lang. in England until the mid 14th c. and mixed with ME to form Anglo-Norman) or else revival of older native forms of speech amid the newfound nationalism. It is natural that the identities mentioned above will find expression in poetry, and in fact quite a number of the major lits. of the world have produced poems of major importance in ds. other than the standard lang., whether in the lang. of the provinces (esp. verse preserved in oral trad.), or of the urban poor (working-class verse, often songs), or of minorities. Though studies of d. p. exist in several langs., the definitive theoretical and cross-cultural study still remains to be written. Nevertheless, understanding of d. p. is essential to the thorough appreciation of any national poetry, not only as a trad. or as trads. worthy of study but, even more, as trads. which may well be excluded from normal study as part of the approved canon (q.v.) by virtue of their minority or marginalized status. D. theory recognizes and validates linguistic variation by defining terms and describing phenomena neutrally.

In Western poetry, the most important and most influential instance of d. p. is Cl. Gr., which admitted four ds., among them Attic-Ionic (spoken in southeastern Greece, southwestern Turkey, and the Ionian islands) and Aeolic (spoken chiefly in Lesbos); these ds. diverged after the prehistoric Gr. tribes entered the Peloponnesus. The devel. of the major poetic genres (with their respective meters) in Gr. poetry (q.v.) was such that even d. was attached to a particular genre, so that a writer taking it up was obliged to write in the d. of the form as opposed to his or her native d. Thus the epic d. which was chiefly Ionic with some elements of Aeolic, seems to have already become conventionalized by the time of Homer and exerted an enormous influence thereafter on writers of epic into the Middle Ages. Iambic and trochaic poetry is written in Ionic (also the d. of historical and scientific prose), while the tetrameters and trimeters of (Attic) Gr. drama are in Attic. Lyric and melic poetry (qq.v.), by contrast, as by Sappho and Alcaeus, were written in Aeloic. The choral ode is in Doric, as is, with greater sophistication, the pastoral poetry of Theocritus. The political unification of Greece resulted in the absorption of all these ds. into the *koine*, the standard or common Gr. of the New Testament and the foundation of modern spoken Gr.

The dialectal differences of the Cl. langs. are usually concealed from us now by standardized translations; reproducing d. is a problem for translators, who are faced with the choice of either suppressing it in text and explaining it in footnotes or else finding some modern dialectal equivalent—livelier verse to read but harder by far to write. In Aristophanes the Athenians and Spartans speak the idioms of their regions; and d. is commonly used to identify aurally foreigners, country folk, and servants, a function evident from Cl. Gr. through Ren. It. to 18th-c. Eng. This will serve to remind us that d. is much easier to identify and follow in heard speech than in print, where orthography serves it ill.

In the European poetries several ds. are noteworthy. In France, OF and Occitan (Provençal) vied as ds. in the Middle Ages (and pronunciations still differ in the South to this day), the one producing the poetry of the *trouvères* (rq.v.), the other that of the troubadours (q.v.; and see FRENCH POETRY; OCCITAN POETRY). The Germanic ds. produced poetry of greatness in the several dialects of Old Germanic—esp. OE, ON, and OHG. and OS—particularly the *Beowulf* and the *Edda*. In the late 18th c., interest in Ger. d. p. was renewed and given a theoretical impetus by J. G. Herder and the romantics, for whom d. represented the "pure source" of the Ger. nation which they were striving to conceptualize. J. P. Hebel, writing in Alemannic, is the d. poet still read from the romantic era. But even as the "people's songs" were collected in *Des Knaben Wunderhorn* (Youth's Magic Horn, 1808), a normative High Ger. was achieving definitive form with Schiller and Goethe. Thereafter d. p. defined itself increasingly against this norm, as retrospective, "genuine," and self-consciously provincial. In the late 19th c., Klaus Groth, writing in Low Ger. d., developed a serious, idyllic style, at odds with both urban decadence and the dominance of the comic in d. p. Subsequently, however, seriousness did not blend easily with the empty pathos of Nazi lang.; though officially celebrated between 1933 and 1945, d. p. remained provincial and apolitical until well after World War II. In the mid 1950s, d. became central to the theory and practice of concrete poetry (q.v.), but only as lang. material, as a fluid component of "absolute art." In reaction, the activism of the 1960s projected a new, ideological view of d. p. (e.g. Fitzgerald Kusz, writing in Frankish): readers are to "see through" the d. to the "sociolect," the local expression of a manipulated consumer consciousness. But in the 1970s, political goals were increasingly fused with a traditional, regionalist valuation of d.: Manfred Bosch (Alemannic) and André Weckmann (Alsatian) renewed the quest for genuineness on ecological grounds, defending "nature" by expressing in d. p. a local solidarity based on conviviality, memory, and dreams of freedom. Modern Yiddish, a d. of Hebrew made a pidgin by contact with Ger., is also noteworthy (see YIDDISH POETRY).

But more extensive than either of these is It. d. p. A rich but problematic linguistic diversity has been one of the distinguishing features of the It. peninsula throughout its long history. From the fall of the Roman Empire until national unification in the later 19th c., Italy's political fragmentation helped to produce numerous centers of regional culture. During the Ren., with the debate concerning the search for a national literary standard—the famous *questione della lingua*—Tuscan emerged as the national literary lang. while the other vernaculars, which were at one time also written, gradually came to function primarily as local and regional ds. and were spoken by all social classes (Haller). Despite the preeminence of Tuscan, however, many writers chose and have continued to choose the ds. as the preferred medium of literary communcation. Consequently, Italy has developed the strongest and perhaps most prestigious trad. of d. p. in Western Europe, a trad. that has evolved parallel to and in constant interaction with lit. in Standard It. (Haller). Major d. poets of the 19th c. include the Milanese Carlo Porta, the Roman Giuseppe Belli, and the Sicilian Giovanni Meli. The 20th c. has produced a bevy of excellent poets who write in the ds. They include the Genovese Edoardo Fírpo, the Milanese Delio Tessa, the Venetians Virgilio Giotti, Giacomo Noventa, and Biagio Marin, the Romans Cesare Pascarella and Trilussa, the Neapolitans Salvatore Di Giacomo and Eduardo De Filippo. Finally, other writers and poets such as Pier Paolo Pasolini, Carlo Emilio Gadda, Beppe Fenoglio, Elsa Morante, and Andrea Zanzotto, write predominantly in Standard It. but make use of the ds. for particular expressive purposes. While the roots of It. d. p. extend to the 16th c., the second half of the 20th c. has witnessed a renewed interest in the poetic possibilities afforded by the ds. (see ITALIAN POETRY).

England absorbed but never assimilated Scottish poetry (q.v.) and Irish poetry (q.v.), much less the further-flung Englishes of the Empire and Commonwealth, as in West Indian. In Eng. poetry the first known use of d. in poetry seems to be Chaucer's *Reeve's Tale*, which pokes fun at Northumbrian speech, different from Chaucer's own Midlands Eng. Much of the finest ME verse, including Langland's and the work of the "*Pearl* poet*," is in the native ds. Scottish poetry, arguably strongest in the 15th c., retained its dialectal features the most successfully of all d. poetries in Eng., esp. in the work of Robert Henryson and William Dunbar (see SCOTTISH CHAUCERIANS); but it is Robert Burns who achieved the greatest popularity. The consensus is that Burns commanded a greater artistic skill when using his mother tongue, that of Ayrshire, than when writing in the standard idiom of literary London. Shakespeare gives different idioms to the soldiers in *Henry 5* from various sections of Britain; and in *A Midsummer Night's Dream* he achieves a more sophisticated, analogous effect metrically, giving couplets to the nobles, blank verse to the gentry, and prose to the "mechanicals." Many of Thomas Hardy's best poems use Dorset speech, which he studied assiduously under the philologist William Barnes. The Celtic Revival of the late 19th and early 20th cs. developed new interest not only in Celtic lore but also in OIr diction, evidenced amply in Yeats's lyrics and plays. In 20th-c. America Robert Frost, for one example, has written poetry echoing New England d., but arguably the richest

and oldest trad. of d. p. is Afro-Am. poetry (q.v.), insofar as that is written in versions of Black Eng. Verse in other ds. has had to struggle under the hegemony of Standard Eng. in America.

F. Schön, *Gesch. der deutschen Mundartdichtung*, 4 v. (1920–39); B. Croce, "La letteratura dialettale riflessa, la sua origine nel '600 e il suo ufficio storico," *In Uomini e cose della vecchia Italia*, v. 1 (1927); A. Thumb, *Handbuch der griechischen Dialekte*, rev. ed., 2 v. (1932, 1959); *Poesia dialettale del Novecento*, ed. M. Dell'Arco and P. P. Pasolini (1952); B. Martin, "Hochdeutsche Mundartdichtung," and G. Cordes, "Niederdeutsche Mundartdichtung," *Deutsche Philologie im Aufriss*, ed. W. Stammler, v. 2 (1954); C. D. Buck, *The Gr. Ds.*, rev. ed. (1955); K. Wagner et al., "Mundartdichtung," *Reallexikon* 2.442–538; P. P. Pasolini, *Passione e ideologia* (1960); M. Jaeger, *Theorien der Mundartdichtung* (1964); W. T. Elwert, "Letterature nazionali e letterature dialettali nell'Europa occidentale," *Paideia* 25 (1970); Wilkins; *Letteratura e dialetto*, ed. G. L. Beccaria (1975); *Die neue deutsche Mundartdichtung*, ed. F. Hoffmann et al. (1977); G. Bellosi, *L'altra lingua: Letteratura dialettale e folklore orale in Italia* (1980); *Sonnets of Giuseppe Belli*, tr. M. Williams (1981); A. M. Bowie, *The Poetic D. of Sappho and Alcaeus* (1981); J. Berlinger, *Das zeitgenossische deutsche Dialektgedicht: Zu Theorie und Praxis der deutschsprachigen Dialektlyrik 1950–1980* (1983); *Le parole di legno: Poesia in dialetto del '900 italiano*, ed. M. Chiesa and G. Tesio (1984); M. Chiesa, "Per una mappa della poesia contemporanea in dialetto," *GSLI* 161 (1984); L. M. Eichinger, "Mundartlyrik," *Neun Kapitel Lyrik*, ed. G. Kopf (1984); M. L. Samuels, "Langland's D.," *MÆ* 54 (1985); C. Macafee. "D. Vocabulary as a Source of Stylistic Effects in Scottish Lit.," *Lang&S* 19 (1986); *The Hidden Italy: A Bilingual Ed. of It. D. Poetry*, ed. and tr. H. W. Haller (1986); *Poeti dialettali del Novecento italiano*, ed. F. Brevini (1987).   T.V.F.B.; J.P.W.; J.L.R.

DIALOGIC. See DIALOGUE; POLYPHONIC PROSE.

DIALOGUE is a term used primarily in two ways, to refer to an exchange of words between speakers in lit., and to refer to a literary usage that presents the speech of more than one character without specific theatrical intentions. In the first sense, d. certainly lies at the center of all writing for the stage, although there are also important uses of monologue (q.v.) in dramatic writing. Like dramatic d., poetic d. consists of conversation in which characters and readers achieve varying levels of understanding by listening to a verbal exchange between speakers. The mode allows an author to reveal a wider range of ideas, emotions, and perspectives than would be possible with a single voice. Verbal exchanges between characters, whether in drama, fiction, or poetry, produce heightened dramatic tension and constitute d., while collections of monologues, such as Browning's *The Ring and the Book*, do not. Literary d. demands the interaction occasioned by immediate response, though the exchange need not be limited to two speakers. Monologues broken by interruptions and poems in which one speaker introduces another main voice are not legitimate examples of d. The dialogic technique dramatizes all forms in which it appears and captures the rhythms and nuances of spoken lang.

The best known Cl. examples are the Socratic ds. of Plato. Though written in prose, they were apparently based on 5th-c. B.C. dramatic mimes by Sophron and Epicharmus. Cl. authors included verse d. in pastoral, satiric, and philosophical poems. Lucian modeled his prose *Ds. of the Dead* on Plato's works but used the form primarily for satiric and comic purposes. The satires of Horace became models for poetic exchanges between speakers. Virgil's eclogues present short pastoral d. in verse. D. in poetry often remained purely literary, although it also encouraged recitation, as in philosophical debates and musical forms such as the duet and oratorio. Lyric ds. intended to be sung were used widely in antiphonal music, particularly hymns and litanies. The form lends itself to powerful emotional or philosophical exchanges, as in love lyrics and intellectual debates.

Verse d. flourished in the Middle Ages in "debates" and "flyting" (q.v.). The dualistic philosophical and theological temper of the age fostered d., as in *The Owl and the Nightingale*. A typical subject was the debate between the Soul and the Body. Med. romances and allegories used d. in ways that produce confusion as to whether these poems were meant soley for reading or were also meant to be staged. Many Oriental poems fit this description as well. The 13th-c. *Roman de la rose* employed multiple speakers for satiric and dramatic purposes, while the Fr. *débat* was a form of poetic contest (q.v.) that influenced the devel. of the drama. Villon's d. between heart and body is a notable example. Popular ballads often included more than one speaker in order to heighten dramatic tension or suspense, as in "Lord Randall" and "Edward."

The Ren. saw the rise of specifically philosophical d. in verse, related to the devel. of prose ds. by Elyot, Thomas More, and Ascham. Tasso called the d. *imitazione di ragionamento* (imitation of reasoning), claiming that it reconciled drama and dialectic. In the 16th c., John Heywood's *D. of Proverbs* and Margaret Cavendish's d. poems were effective examples of the form. Songs by Shakespeare, Sidney, and Herrick included questions and answers, emphasizing the close connection between d. and the interrogative mode. Spenser made effective use of multiple voices in *The Shepheards Calender*, developing the d. trad. of Virgil's eclogues. Notable Ren. examples of d. poems incl. Samuel Daniel's *Ulysses and the Siren* and Andrew Marvell's *A D. Between the Soul and the Body*. Courtly masques, like those by Jonson and Milton, combined d. with music and lyrics. Allegorical poems like Dryden's *The Hind and the Panther* provide an occasion for d., as do 18th-c. direct-speech poems like Pope's *Satires*. Many dialect poems adopt multiple speakers, as in the Scottish ballads of Robert Burns and the Dorset eclogues of William Barnes.

Although romantic emphasis on subjectivity increased the monologic aspect of lyric poetry during the 19th c., verse d. appears in poems and dramatic experiments by Byron, Shelley, and Keats. Ger. and Scandinavian writers of songs and romantic ballads made widespread use of the form. The Victorians sought to objectify romantic poetry by dramatizing the single-voiced lyric, but Arnold and later Hardy used d. effectively in their poems; Browning and Tennyson both wrote dramas in verse. Revived interest in prose d. appears in Wilde's *The Critic as Artist* and later, in France, in the d. experiments of Valéry.

The role of d. in 20th-c. poetry is often connected with the blurring of generic distinctions. While Yeats's *D. of Self and Soul* is a clear example of a traditional verse d., other works by Yeats, Beckett, Dylan Thomas, and Robert Frost suggest the role of poetic d. in a wider variety of dramatic and nondramatic forms. Implied d. in poems by Geoffrey Hill and Ted Hughes, for example, objectifies the subject and produces heightened dramatic tension in the lyric. Like the Victorian dramatization of the monologue, d. poems de-emphasize the determinate force of lang., stressing the conditional aspects of all utterances. The term "double lyric" has been used to refer to lyrics that contain a suppressed but significant dialogic element. D. thus remains a significant concern in poetry as traditional distinctions between poetry, prose, and drama are questioned and explored.

In recent years, emphasis on the "dialogic" aspect of all lang. has suggested that even the most seemingly monologic utterances are dependent on the interplay of meanings found only in d. This view has arisen largely as a result of increased interest in the work of the Rus. critic M. M. Bakhtin. Although Bakhtin's own writings emphasize the novel, his analysis of the role of the "dialogic" has implications for the understanding of all literary meaning. Bakhtin argues that every utterance is subject to reinterpretation from the perspective of d. On these terms, even apparent monologues always have a conditional dialogic element. Such a view has important consequences for the interp. of lyric and narrative poetry, where the first-person speaker or narrator often tries to achieve authority for a particular description of emotions or version of events. For Bakhtin, the unsaid, the partially said, and the equivocally said are as potentially meaningful as the clearly said. Likewise, all lang. uses are a product of conflicting social forces. On these terms, every verbal utterance contributes dialogically to the shaping of the world, and the interactions between such utterances produce an endless interplay of voices in d. See now ECLOGUE;

PASTORAL; POETIC CONTESTS; POLYPHONIC PROSE; PREGUNTA.

R. Hirzel, *Der Dialog: ein literarischer-historischer Versuch*, 2 v. (1895); E. Merrill, *The D. in Eng. Lit.* (1911); E. R. Purpus, "The D. in Eng. Lit. 1660–1725," *ELH* 17 (1950); R. Wildbolz, *Der philosophisches D. als literarisches Kunstwerk* (1952); J. Andrieu, *Le D. antique: Structure et presentation* (1954); C. Diesch, "Gespräch," and H. Schelle, "Totengespräch," *Reallexikon*; W. J. Ong, *Ramus, Method, and the Decay of D.* (1958); A. Langen, *Dialogisches Spiel* (1966); G. Bauer, *Zur Poetik des Dialogs* (1969); F. M. Keener, *Eng. Ds. of the Dead* (1973); J. Mukařovskij, *The Word and Verbal Art* (tr. 1977), ch. 2; M. E. Brown, *Double Lyric* (1980); D. Marsh, *The Quattrocento D.* (1980); M. M. Bakhtin, *The Dialogic Imagination* (tr. 1981); T. Todorov, *Mikhail Bakhtin: The Dialogical Principle* (1981, tr. 1984); W. G. Müller, "Das Ich im Dialog mit sich selbst," *DVLG* 56 (1982); A. K. Kennedy, *Dramatic D.: The Duologue of Personal Encounter* (1983); *Tasso's Ds.* [incl. his *Discourse on the Art of the D.*], tr. C. Lord and D. A. Trafton (1983); *Le D. au temps de la ren.*, ed. M. T. Jones-Davies (1984); *Bakhtin: Essays and Ds. on His Work*, ed. G. S. Morson (1986); J. R. Snyder, *Writing the Scene of Speaking: Theories of D. in the Late It. Ren.* (1989); *The Interp. of D.*, ed. T. Maranhão (1989); G. S. Morson and C. Emerson, *Mikhail Bakhtin: Creation of a Prosaics* (1990); M. S. Macovski, *D. and Lit.* (1992); D. H. Bialostosky, *Wordsworth, Dialogics, and the Practice of Crit.* (1992). B.A.N.

DIBRACH. See PYRRHIC.

DICHRONOUS. See QUANTITY.

DICTION. See ARCHAISM; AUREATE DICTION; CONCRETE AND ABSTRACT; CONNOTATION AND DENOTATION; EPITHET; KENNING; LEXIS.

DIDACTIC POETRY.

    I. CONCEPT AND HISTORY
    II. ANTIQUITY
    III. MEDIEVAL, RENAISSANCE, AUGUSTAN
    IV. 19TH AND 20TH CENTURIES

I. CONCEPT AND HISTORY. *Didaktikos* in Gr. relates to teaching, and implies its counterpart: learning. "All men by nature desire knowledge" and all experience (embodied in lang., says Croce); hence all lit. (in the broadest sense) can be seen as "instructive."

Given such interacting complexities, our problem becomes one of "historical semantics" (Spitzer): of modulations and transformations (Fowler) of the d. concept, and of attempts to distinguish it from near neighbors such as allegory, archetype, myth, symbol, fable, and satire (qq.v.). The category of unconscious or unintended teaching could lead us astray into infinite mists and abysses. (What do we learn from "Jabberwocky?" That "nonsense" [q.v.] can make an attractive poem.) Aware of such proliferating contexts, we try to focus here chiefly (but not exclusively) on poetry which clearly *intends* "useful teaching," embodying Horace's "instruction *and* delight" in the genre of "d. poems."

Basic categories relate to the contents ("themes"—q.v.) of poems, inseparable from their forms. In *De vulgari eloquentia*, Dante specified the worthiest objects as Safety, Love, and Virtue—his corresponding poetic themes being War, Love, and Salvation (or Morality: "direction of the will"). To these we add knowledge (Science and Philosophy), Beauty (Aesthetics), Efficiency (e.g. "How to" run a farm or write a poem), and Information ("Thirty days hath September"). Modern discussions have tended to emphasize the problematics of Knowledge and Morality. Beardsley treated "the D. Theory of lit." as seeing "a close connection between truth and value" (426–32). He mentions *De rerum natura*, but no one reads Lucretius' poem today for information on materialism and atomic theory; Beardsley wants rather to clarify the relations among "predications," cognition, and how readers submit poems to experiential "testing"— with reference to "philosophical, economic, social, or religious" doctrines. Arnold Isenberg confronted the "strong case" of "the d. poem or essay" in an intricate analysis (265–81).

Another necessary preliminary is Fowler's concept of "mode," illuminating the continuing life of genres. Fowler writes: "modal terms never imply a complete external form" and "tend to be adjectival"—as in "d. essay" or "d. lyric." He finds it remarkable that "several important literary kinds, notably georgic, essay, and novel, are not supposed to have corresponding modes. Can it be that these modal options have never been taken up? By no means" (108). Once we accept modal extensions of didacticism, its presence and power throughout the hist. of poetry become obvious.

II. ANTIQUITY. A product of lang. and hist., poetry also transcends these via archetypes and translations; and d. modes probably preceded the invention of alphabets and writing. Indeed, for oral trads. (religious and secular) rhythm and metaphor have probably always been used to aid memory and enliven ritual; such speculations about prehistoric poetry seem to be confirmed by surviving fragments and modern anthropology. Religious scriptures in all langs. tend to be "poetic," mingling freely epic hist. (narrative), hymn and psalm (qq.v.), and prophetic vision and preaching. In the Judeo-Christian Bible, for example, there are elements of poetic drama, philosophy, practical wisdom (proverbs, q.v.), and parable—in d. modes.

It was the Greeks who first, in Europe, distinguished clearly between poetry of imitation (Homer) and versified science (e.g. the lost poem by Empedocles); within mimetic uses of melodious lang., between "manners" of narration and drama; and within the latter, analyzed the tragic catharsis (q.v.; Aristotle)—with comedy, epic, and other "kinds" in the background. Plato notoriously banished the poets from his ideal Republic because they taught lies about the gods, and aroused and confused men's passions. Two main tendencies of the d. in verse were created by Hesiod (8th c. B.C.): in *Theogony*, knowledge about the gods, their origins and stories, problems of culture—moving towards philosophic abstractions; and in *Works and Days*, "how to" farm and the like—towards practical and specific information. Each kind (details are fragmentary) leaned towards a different style and meter (e.g. Aratus' "Phainomena" used hexameters); and in later Alexandria, the latter emphasis (erudition, technical information) became popular (e.g. Nicander of Colophon).

The Romans derived from the Greeks not only gods and ideas but most of their poetic genres (translating and adapting Empedocles and Aratus, for example). Four major Lat. poets wrote masterpieces which transformed d. poetry creatively: (a) Lucretius' *De rerum natura* became the prototypical "philosophic" poem (Santayana) in the Empedocles and *Theogony* line, invoking the values of sense-experience and materialistic metaphysics. (b) Virgil's *Georgics*, derived from Hesiod, became the popular "how to" poem: running a farm, living with the seasons, keeping bees, and so forth (see GEORGIC). (c) Horace, on his Sabine farm, not only wrote memorable odes, satires, and epistles, but also wrote letters of practical advice to poets (*Epistulae ad Pisones*, i.e. the *Ars poetica*), some of his ideas and phrases becoming proverbial: e.g. "the labor of the file," "in the midst of things," "from the egg," and "make Greece your model." Finally, (d) Ovid's versified advice related chiefly to "sex and society" (*Ars amatoria*), a Lat. primer in matters of love. Manilius wrote a five-book poem on astrology (ed. A. E. Housman); and there were others.

In sum, Lat. poets gave priority to instructing citizens and artists in a variety of subjects. Satire developed beyond light-hearted Horace to bitter Juvenal ("The Vanity of Human Wishes"). And in Asia, esp., poetry was central to Confucian teaching. Hindu philosophy is embodied in Vedic hymns (with the *Upaniṣads*); Buddhism, in epic poems (Mahābhārata and Rāmāyaṇa); and Persian "teaching" is embodied for Westerners in Omar Khayyam's *Rubáiyát* (quatrains) and the *Avesta* of Zoroaster. The bible of Islam, the *Qurʾān*, is quintessential Ar. poetry.

III. MEDIEVAL, RENAISSANCE, AUGUSTAN. Christian lit. in Europe (indeed, all religious poetry) was almost entirely d. Even in mimetic (narrative and dramatic) modes, its central purpose was to impart religious doctrines and values (see Curtius, ch. 3 and passim). For example, Martianus Capella, *On the Marriage of Mercury and Philology* (Menippean satire), *Le Roman de la rose*, and Spenser's *Faerie Queene* (allegory), Dante, Chaucer—d. elements are everywhere. Vagabond scholars mixed orthodox doctrine and symbols with irreverent satire and "pagan" feeling (see GOLIARDIC VERSE). Medieval lit. is dense with rhymed chronicles, encyclopedias, devotional manuals and saints' lives, popularized excerpts from church doctrine, and collections of aphorisms. Early modes of theater in western Europe—mysteries and moralities (see MORALITY PLAY), Passion plays (q.v.)—aimed to combine indoctrination with celebration and entertainment. This is also true of the late masque (q.v.), where the allegorical teaching is increasingly subordinated to spectacle and dance. Milton's *Comus* (1634), for example, ends with a moral: "Love Virtue."

The emerging Ren. and Reformation saw Lat. poetry enriched by the vernacular langs. In Ger., for example, d. works incl. Luther's Bible, *Bescheidenheit* by "Freidank" (1215–16), *Der Renner* by Hugo von Trimberg (ca. 1300), *Narrenschiff* by Sebastian Brant (1494), *Narrensbeschwörung* and *Gauchmatt* by Thomas Murner (1512–14). In Sp., such authors as Francisco Pacheco, Lopé de Vega, and Cervantes in *Don Quixote* and elsewhere wrote didactically at times. In It., literary theory flourished, reaffirming Cl. ideals and finding Virgil a "better teacher" than Cato (but Fracastoro wrote that "Teaching is *in a measure* the concern of the poet, but *not* in his peculiar capacity" [1555; emphases added]). Such satires as those of Parini and Ariosto mingled d. elements with satire and autobiography; and the *Georgics* were imitated. In France, Rabelais and Montaigne virtually created a lit. which excelled in *raison* as well as *esprit*; masterpieces by Racine and Molière shaped the nation's emerging trad. and education; Diderot preferred the *Georgics* to Virgil's other poetry; A. Chenier's enthusiasm for "modern" science parallels that of Goethe and the Eng. romantics; and Jacques de Lille translated Virgil and wrote *Les Jardins*.

But the d. line (and problem) was most clearly developed, perhaps, in England, as in Sir Philip Sidney's *Defense of Poesie* (1583, passim—but, despite Plato, the poet is for Sidney not a liar: "he nothing affirms and therefore never lieth"). Milton's great epic attempt was "to justify the ways of God to man"; and only in England did the Puritans close the theaters and behead a king in order to establish a Godly commonwealth. Though "engaged" tendencies in verse developed esp. in England and France, they were evident throughout much of Europe. Notoriously, the Restoration in England (one of whose classics is Dryden's *Virgil*) and the Neoclassic century which followed was a long period of transitions leading to romanticism (q.v.). Dryden wrote political, historical, satiric, religious, and theological poems, and translated all four of the great Lat. d. poets; Pope wrote *An Essay on Crit.* (1711) and other imitations of Horace, philosophic and "Moral" essays in verse, and *The Dunciad* (1742–43)—a d. and mock-epic-satiric masterpiece ; and it is hardly necessary to insist on the didacticism of Swift and Dr. Johnson.

As Chalker puts it, important poems in the geor-
gic trad. "were often remote from any practical
purpose, although others were d. *in intention*"
(emphasis added).

Not only the Lat. education of gentlemen who
became poets, but the emergence of Newtonian
science (see Nicolson) and The Royal Society
(Cowley's poems) bore poetic fruit. New concepts
of nature (q.v.) and light (optics) mingled with the
descriptive *paysage moralisé* in complex ways, trans-
forming georgic trad. most effectively in James
Thomson's *The Seasons* (1730; see Cohen). We
recall Dr. Johnson's distinction: the poet "does not
number the streaks of the tulip." Grierson and
Smith's history (1944) shows the dominance of d.
and satiric modes, as well as the representative
"timid revolt" of Gray in his Odes—yet few poems
are more blatantly moralistic than Gray's "Elegy."
The scientific (informative and theoretic) tenden-
cies bore strange and influential fruit in Erasmus
Darwin's poems (e.g. *The Botanic Garden*, 1791).
And we recall the variety of d. elements in Crabbe,
Goldsmith, and Burns: the Am. and Fr. Revolu-
tions did make a difference.

IV. 19TH AND 20TH CENTURIES. After 1800, d.
aims and methods underwent radical transforma-
tions. The main shift was one from an Augustan
use of Cl. and Ren. models to a growing variety of
philosophies and ideologies, followed by later
compromises which made "Victorian" almost syn-
onymous with moralizing in prose and verse—as
in Carlyle, Emerson, Tennyson, Ruskin, some of
the pre-Raphaelites, and Arnold. Few poets are
more obviously d. than Blake, for example—but
his mode became one of vision and prophecy, of
what we now see as "myth-making." Wordsworth
and Coleridge wrestled with didacticism, esp. in
odes and poems of meditation ("The Growth of a
Poet's Mind"); and though Coleridge lived to re-
gret it mildly, he did conclude *The Rime of the
Ancient Mariner* with a moral.

In Shelley's *Defense*, Milton's "bold neglect of a
direct moral purpose" (emphasis added) is seen as
proof of that poet's genius; but neither Blake nor
Shelley was unaware that to seek "to justify the
ways of God to man" was to be essentially d. True,
Shelley wrote in the Preface to *Prometheus Unbound*
that "d. poetry is my abhorrence"—meaning po-
etry whose teaching "can be equally well expressed
in prose" (I. A. Richards' "separable content"—im-
plying superficial moralizing); but surely in
Prometheus and elsewhere Shelley was, and under-
stood himself to be, a prophet-teacher, one of the
"unacknowledged legislators" of the world. Thus
Wimsatt and Brooks characterize his critical posi-
tion correctly as a "rhapsodic didacticism" and "a
didacticism of revolution." And it was Keats who saw
Shakespeare as having lived "a life of allegory,"
Keats who wrote that "Beauty is truth, truth beauty."

One may generalize that the opposites of the
Horatian pleasure-use polarity tend to meet; and
that a strong anti-didacticism usually emerges in

opposition to a boringly conservative culture (cf.
Blackmur's "intolerable dogma"). Thus, when
Poe attacked "the heresy of the D." (a position
later adopted by the Fr. symbolists and others), it
was because, like Shelley, he was surrounded by
inept poetasters spouting clichés; and Whitman
(whose didacticism has been compared to that of
Blake and Wordsworth) picked up Poe's (and
Emerson's) idea of working "indirectly" and sym-
bolically. Even the fin-de-siècle proponents of art
for art's sake were themselves moralists in rebel-
lion against Arnold's "Barbarians" and "Philis-
tines." But the older, moralizing trad. of Bryant,
Longfellow, Whittier, and others in America and
England had a strength of its own. In the 20th c.,
the best poets (e.g. Yeats, Auden) have been ar-
dently "engaged" in various social, political, philo-
sophical, and religious controversies.

In sum, modern didacticism assumed protean
forms that could no longer be forced into the
genre classifications of the Augustans. We can
follow this process clearly through Wellek's *Hist.
of Modern Crit.*: thus when A. W. Schlegel discusses
"the d. philosophical poem," he falls into the trap
(for Wellek) of defining all poetry as "esoteric
philosophy"—excusable, however, when one
means, as the romantics did, "a poetic philosophy,
a thinking in symbols as it was practiced by
Schelling or Jakob Böhme." In this, Wellek is dis-
paraging inferior poems "held together *merely* by
logic." Similarly, Wellek remarks that "with the
years Wordsworth's point of view became . . . more
and more *simply* d. and instructive" (emphases
added). Still, Wellek quotes Wordsworth (1808):
"every great poet is a teacher: I wish either to be
understood as a teacher, or as nothing." This de-
bate about the changing nature of didacticism
took a variety of shapes in England, America, and
Europe. Yet what long poem in Eng. had a more
clearly d. intent (i.e. interp. of hist., fate) than *The
Dynasts*—Hardy's *War and Peace*? Since the sub-
stance of such teachings has become increasingly
complex, fragmented, and problematic, we find the
emphasis now falling on conflict, dialectics, quest,
doubt, psychology, existential immediacy, and plu-
ralism (q.v.) rather than on any fixed doctrine.

For instance, in a poem such as Karl Shapiro's
Essay on Rime, and in much of T. S. Eliot, in the
Pound of *The Cantos*, and in Stevens' "medita-
tions," we witness modal transformations of the d.
Robert Frost's inveterate didacticism finds expres-
sion by transformations of Cl. eclogue and pastoral
(e.g. "Build Soil," "The Lesson for Today"; see
Empson; and see ECLOGUE and PASTORAL). Mod-
ern degradations of didacticism, of course, occur
in the use of poetry for propaganda or even adver-
tising. Anglo-Am. poetry is esp. rich in works with
historical, regional, geographic, philosophic, and
political substance. The "how to" motif is still
evident when Pound writes an *ABC of Reading* or
John Hollander a versified textbook on prosody.
One thinks of such old-new genres as utopian (and

DINGGEDICHT

dystopian) narrative and science fiction; and there is a strong d. element in modern satire (R. Campbell, A. M. Klein). A recent study by H. J. Blackham devotes a chapter to "Modern Instances" and concludes with "The Message" (cf. Scholes). One concludes that the d. *mode* is very much alive in modern lit. (possibly more so in prose than in verse); and that many of the traditional d. genres have undergone complex transformations and modulations. We find not only "modern georgics" (Frost, MacNeice), but epigrams (Ogden Nash), parodies without number, parables (Kafka), and other genres aiming at some sort of didacticism. Critical theory, however, has tended either to skirt the issues or to convert the d. mode into related categories. See also BEAST EPIC; BESTIARY; CRITICISM; ETHICS AND CRITICISM; EXEMPLUM; FABLIAU; GEORGIC; SPRUCHDICHTUNG.

S.J.K.

R. Eckart, *Die Lehrdichtung: ihr Wesen und ihre Vertreter*, 2d ed. (1909); G. Santayana, *Three Philosophical Poets* (1910); W. Kroll, "Lehrgedicht," Pauly-Wissowa; I. A. Richards, "Doctrine in Poetry," *Practical Crit.* (1929); H. M. and N. K. Chadwick, *The Growth of Lit.*, 3 v. (1932–40); T. S. Eliot, *The Uses of Poetry and the Uses of Crit.* (1933), *On Poetry and Poets* (1957), esp. "The Social Function of Poetry"; W. Empson, *Some Versions of Pastoral* (1935); G. Solbach, *Beitrag zur Beziehung zwischen deutschen und italienischen Lehrdichtung im Mittelalter* (1937); H. J. C. Grierson and J. C. Smith, *A Critical Hist. of Eng. Poetry* (1944); M. H. Nicolson, *Newton Demands the Muse* (1946); R. A. B. Mynors, "D. P.," *Oxford Cl. Dict.* (1949); Curtius; Wellek; D. Daiches, *Critical Approaches to Lit.* (1956), chs. 3–4; Wimsatt and Brooks; M. C. Beardsley, *Aesthetics* (1958); G. Pellegrini, *La Poesia didascalia inglese nel settecento italiano* (1958); E. Neumann, "Bispêl," W. Richter, "Lehrhafte Dichtung," and H. Zeltner, "Philosophie und Dichtung," *Reallexikon*; B. F. Huppé, *Doctrine and Poetry* (1959); W. G. Lambert, *Babylonian Wisdom Lit.* (1960); R. Cohen, *The Art of Discrimination: Thomson's The Seasons and the Lang. of Crit.* (1964); H. de Boor, *Fabel und Bispêl* (1966); L. L. Albertsen, *Das Lehrgedicht* (1967); L. Lerner, *The Truthtellers* (1967); R. Scholes, *The Fabulators* (1967); J. Chalker, *The Eng. Georgic* (1969)—good bibl.; C. S. Lewis, *Sel. Literary Essays* (1969); B. Sowinski, *Lehrhafte Dichtung im Mittelalter* (1971); A. Isenberg, "Ethical and Aesthetic Crit.," *Aesthetics and the Theory of Crit.* (1973); C. Siegrist, *Das Lehrgedicht der Aufklarung* (1974); B. Boesch, *Lehrhafte Literatur* (1977); B. Effe, *Dichtung und Lehre* (1977)—typology of Cl. d. genres; Hesiod, *Works and Days*, ed. M. L. West (1978), "Prolegomena"—excellent comparative survey; R. L. Montgomery, *The Reader's Eye* (1979); GRLMA, v. 6, *La Littérature didactique, allegorique et satirique; Europäische Lehrdichtung*, ed. H. G. Rötzer and H. Walz (1981); R. Wellek, "Crit. as Evaluation," *The Attack on Lit. and Other Essays* (1982); M. B. Ross, *The Poetics of*

Moral Transformation: Forms of Didacticism in the Poetry of Shelley (1983); "Lit. and/as Moral Philosophy," spec. iss. of *NLH* 15 (1983); K. Muir, *Shakespeare's D. Art* (1984); L. Sternbach, *Subhasida: Gnomic and D. Lit.* (1984)—Indian; H. J. Blackham, *The Fable as Lit.* (1985); W. Spiegelman, *The D. Muse* (1990). T.V.F.B.; S.J.K.

DIFFERENCE. See DECONSTRUCTION; IMITATION; INTERTEXTUALITY.

DIMETER (Gr. "of 2 measures"). A line consisting of two measures. In Cl. prosody (q.v.), the metron (q.v.) in iambic, trochaic, and anapestic verse is a dipody (pair of feet); hence the Cl. iambic d. contains two metra or four feet. But in the modern prosodies the concept of the metron was never established: here "-meter" is synonymous with foot. The Eng. iambic d. therefore consists of two feet, the trimeter of three feet, etc. This terminology applies only to foot-verse, which is regular, however; accentual verse (q.v.)—e.g. a line of two stresses but a variable number of syllables—is not, properly speaking, a d. Short-lined verse in Eng., such as the Skeltonic (q.v.), is not often regular enough to be called d., but there are examples, particularly among 16th- and 17th-c. lyric, e.g. Drayton's "An Amouret Anacreontic" and Herrick's "To a Lark." T.V.F.B.

DIMINISHING METAPHOR. See METAPHOR.

DINGGEDICHT (Ger. "thing-poem"). A type of poetry that seeks to present concrete objects (or a pictorially perceived constellation of things) with factual precision and in symbolic concentration. This descriptive exactitude results from a process of intense observation that yields insights, often epiphanous in their overpowering suddenness, into the essential nature of things. At the same time, this attitude makes possible the detached expression of inner experiences evoked through contemplative contact with the object. Such transcending of surface descriptions aims at capturing a symbolic and emotive content that is an indissoluble part of a material exterior, which shows the D. to be the last intensification of the ideal symbolist poem. Its most successful practitioner was the Austrian poet Rainer Maria Rilke during his Paris years, 1902–08, when he wrote his *Neue Gedichte* (*New Poems*). Their "sachliches Sagen" (objective lang.) renounces an inspirational *poésie du coeur* in favor of singular images and strives to penetrate to the innermost specificity of natural as well as crafted things as they are transformed into objects of art. This artistic practice of raising select items from a random still-life existence into that mode of being which reveals their innate spirituality celebrated art itself as an autonomous and self-referential value devoid of functional purposes (see AUTONOMY). But exclusive concern with the autonomous "Kunstding" isolated the work of art from the demands of the social world and evoked opposition to the hermetic D. during the expressionist phase of Ger. lit.

Historically, the perfection of thing-poetry after 1900 reflects the fact that quotidian life had become inaccessible to poetic sensibilities and that the lyrical self, alienated from the world around it, found its objective "counter-world" only in the aesthetic realm. This required a refined visual perception and an appreciation of sculptural and architectural forms, which Rilke acquired through study of impressionist paintings and by observing Rodin at work. A further influence was Baudelaire's poetry, esp. where it lets facets of the modern world speak for themselves and not as mere occasions for the allegorizing of the poet's personal moods. Similar intent may be found in poems by Eduard Mörike ("Auf eine Lampe," 1846) and C. F. Meyer ("Der römische Brunnen," 1858) that are exceptional in the way they realize the perfect linguistic fusion of an artistically crafted object's transcendent signification with its precisely delineated appearance. Such structural affinities persuaded K. Oppert, who coined the term "D." in 1926, to claim a postromantic continuity for the "poetry of things." More convincing evidence for the modified relevance of his concept may be found in the poetics of imagism (i.e. Pound's definition of "image" as "that which presents an intellectual and emotional complex in an instant of time"), in T. S. Eliot's notion of the "objective correlative" (q.v.), and in the importance that the early poetry of W. C. Williams ("no ideas but in things"), M. Moore, G. Stein, and W. Stevens attached to unprejudiced observation in the search for poetic truth. See OBJECTIVISM.—K. Oppert, "Das D.," *DVLG* 4 (1926); H. Kunisch, *Rainer Maria Rilke und die Dinge* (1946); F. Martini, "D.," *Reallexikon*; J. Steiner, "Das D.," *Rilke: Vorträge und Aufsätze* (1986).   M.W.

DIONYSIAN. See APOLLONIAN-DIONYSIAN.

DIPODISM, DIPODIC VERSE. In the older sense of the term, used in Cl. prosody (q.v.), "d." refers to the fact that metrical feet in Gr. and Lat. are double the length of what they later became in the European vernaculars. Thus the Gr. iambic dimeter consists of two *metra* (see METRON), each of two iambic feet, the line thus totaling eight syllables, whereas the Eng. iambic dimeter has only two feet totaling four. But primarily the term is now used to refer to a distinctive feature of ballad meter (q.v.), namely stress hierarchy. This is the insight first formulated by Coventry Patmore in 1857 that in ballad meter, not only do the stresses and the slacks alternate, but the primary and secondary stresses alternate as well. In George R. Stewart's formulation, the modern 7-stress line has the form (slashes denoting primary stresses, and p a metrical pause):

x / x / x / x / || x / x / x / (p).

In genuine ballad meter, however, "the seven *stresses* of its line tend to be alternately strong [/] and weak [\]":

x / x \ x / x \ || x / x \ x / (p).

"In other words the ballad line consists not of seven simple, but of four complex units. The structure, therefore, can best be termed *dipodic*, and the units *dipods*" (1925, 935; italics added).

"D." is a misleading term insofar as it evokes the double feet of Gr. prosody: the point is not that the feet double up, but rather simply that the principle of alternation—evident in, for example, iambic feet in the alternation of weak and strong—is extended one level higher, to strong and stronger. Indeed, in this respect d. may seem, *au fond*, simply a logical extension of the nature of Eng. phonology itself. After all, unstressed syllables are not negative or nonreified entities; in articulation they are positive physical events, expulsions of air out of the glottis. Above the unstressed syllable we may identify, in phonology, the secondary stress, and above that the stress on lexical items (words), and above that the major stress in each phrase or word group, and above that, rhetorical accent or emphasis—and so on, doubling our alternations into increasingly wider spans. As Taylor puts it, d. "reveals something basic about our meters, namely their ability quickly to build new multiples out of old." D. is a phenomenon almost never found in artverse (such as the pentameter), hence it may serve, along with isochronism (q.v.) and the metrical pause (see PAUSE), as one of the specific differentiae of ballad meter and accentual verse (q.v.).—C. Patmore, "Eng. Metrical Critics," *North Brit. Rev.* 27 (1857); G. R. Stewart, Jr., *Mod. Metrical Technique as Illustrated by Ballad Meter (1700–1920)* (1922), "The Meter of the Popular Ballad," *PMLA* 40 (1925), *The Technique of Eng. Verse* (1930); G. W. De Schweinitz, "D. in Eng. Verse in the 19th and 20th Cs.," *Univ. of Iowa Abstracts of Dissertations* 9 (1949–52): 394–96; Sr. M. A. Roth, *Coventry Patmore's Essay on Eng. Metrical Law: A Critical Ed. with a Commentary* (1961); J. Malof, *A Manual of Eng. Meters* (1970).   T.V.F.B.

DIPODY. See DIPODISM; FOOT.

DIRGE. A song for the dead, sung at the funeral ceremony itself, or at the procession, or afterwards; the ancients made some generic distinctions. The Eng. term derives from the beginning of the antiphon in Lat. of the Office of the Dead ("Dirige, Domine . . .") adapted from Psalms 5.9. As a literary genre, the d. developed out of Gr. funerary songs, particularly the *epicedium* (q.v.), the song sung over the dead, and the *threnos*, sung in memory of the dead. The Gr. d. influenced the Lat. *nenia*, laments sung by hired professional poets, but these never became a literary genre, nor did the *laudatio funebris*, the public funeral oration. Originally a choral ode, the threnody evolved into a monody (q.v.) which was strophic in form and employed various metrical systems; it is common in Gr. poetry after the 6th c. B.C., and the distinction between epicedium and monody was still recognized in the Ren. (Puttenham).

Although in ancient lit. the d. was sometimes influenced by the *consolatio* and closely connected with the elegy (q.v.), its chief aim was to lament the dead, not console survivors—cf. the lament for Hector at *Odyssey* 24.746 ff. But the subject matter included lamentation and eulogy, often with consolatory reflections, apostrophes, invocations, etc. Not only human beings but also animals might be mourned (cf. Catullus 3). In Gr., Simonides, Pindar, and the Alexandrian poets used the genre; in Lat., Calvus and Catullus used it first, and Propertius brought it to its greatest perfection (4.11). The meter in Lat. was the hexameter or the elegiac distich (qq.v.). The medieval writers combined the Lat. form with the church's lamentation for the dead, employing in the process Christian themes. Eng. examples of ds. incl. Henry King's *Exequy* on his young wife, Emerson's "Threnody on His Young Son," and George Meredith's *D. in the Woods*. See also ENDECHA; ELEGY; LAMENT.—R. Leicher, *Die Totenklage in der deutschen Epik vom der ältesten Zeit bis zur Nibelungen-Klage* (1927); G. Herrlinger, *Totenklage um Tiere in der antiken Dichtung* (1930); E. Reimer, *Die rituelle Totenklage der Griechen* (1938); V. B. Richmond, *Ls. for the Dead in Medieval Narrative* (1966); M. Alexiou, *The Ritual Lament in Gr. Trad.* (1974); E. Vermeule, *Aspects of Death in Early Gr. Art and Poetry* (1979); *Poèmes de la mort de Turold a Villon*, ed. and tr. J.-M. Paquette (1979); *Do Not Go Gentle: Poems on Death*, ed. W. Packard (1981); *Japanese Death Poems*, ed. and tr. Y. Hoffmann (1986).   R.A.H.; T.V.F.B.

DISCOURSE. See POETICS; RUSSIAN FORMALISM; STRUCTURALISM; MEANING, POETIC; POETRY; LINGUISTICS AND POETICS; TWENTIETH-CENTURY POETICS; ROMANTIC AND POSTROMANTIC POETICS; INTERPRETATION; PHILOSOPHY AND POETRY.

DISINTERESTEDNESS designates the stance proper for aesthetic judgment, aiming at a balance between excessively personal or "interested" response and excessive detachment or "uninterestedness." Though Plato and Aristotle regard aesthetic experience as a balance of emotion and reason (see AESTHETIC DISTANCE), d. is, properly speaking, a modern concept, one that emerges in the 18th c., when aesthetic judgment is detached from moral and psychological knowledge. D. thus corresponds to the idea of art as an autonomous field, distinct from cognitive and practical ends (see AUTONOMY); thus it is central to discussions of taste (q.v.). For Addison, Shaftesbury, Burke, and others in the British trad., the concept was meant to establish that the feeling for beauty,

while truly aesthetic, had some kinship with the moral sense. Thus the common ground for art and morals was d., a sensibility (q.v.) free from personal bias and mere utility. The beautiful and the good were thereby rooted in feeling, rather than mere cognition. For Kant and Hegel, d. required that aesthetic judgment be dissociated from personal (appetitive), ethical (prescriptive), and scientific (cognitive) claims. In Germany, moreover, disinterested judgment entailed freedom and universality. D. meant freedom from interests and rules; and although art, as a sensuous form, required feeling, detachment secured the universal significance of aesthetic experience.

In *Biographia literaria* (1817), Coleridge associates d. with imagination, demanding the "willing suspension of disbelief . . . that constitutes poetic faith," thereby separating disinterested judgment from the immediate, interested engagement one has with reality (see BELIEF). Matthew Arnold in "The Study of Poetry" (1888) warns that the proper estimate of art, "the only true one, is liable to be superseded" by the "historic" or the "personal," the one insufficiently, the other excessively engaged. D. appears in "The Function of Crit. at the Present Time" (1864), where crit. is the effort "to see the object as it really is." This will lead to the modern view of d. as the basis for immanent crit., which judges the work on intrinsic rather than extrinsic terms. Accordingly, for Schopenhauer, d. means will-less contemplation. Similarly, Eliot, in "Trad. and the Individual Talent" (1917), argues that art "is not an expression of personality but an escape from personality." Consequently, crit. must regard biographical and historical information as external to aesthetic experience.

New Crit. (q.v.) may be said to have advocated d. in crit., in that it regarded as misguided both the excessively personal response of critics following Pater and the excessively objective approach of historical and biographical critics. More recently, the idea of aesthetic autonomy (q.v.) has been seriously questioned, and criticism has disputed the very possibility of d., thereby demanding a total rethinking of the aesthetic: feminists and New Historicists claim that poetry is marked by gender and sociopolitical context; Marxists examine the ideological agenda; psychoanalytic critics explore art's dependence on linguistic and psychic structures; deconstructive readings disclose the manner in which lit. inevitably extends beyond aesthetic terrain and broaches philosophical questions. All these insist upon the interested and socially situated character of both art and critical judgment, suggesting the difficulty or impossibility of d., or purely aesthetic judgment.—J. Stolnitz, "On the Origins of 'Aesthetic D.,'" *JAAC* 20 (1961); P. Guyer "D. and Desire in Kant's Aesthetics," *JAAC* 36 (1978); J. Derrida, "Parergon," *La Verité en peinture* (1978); A. Reed, "The Debt of Disinterest," *MLN* 95 (1980); D. Bromwich, "The Genealogy of D.," *Raritan* 1 (1982); M. Woodmansee, "The Interests of D.," *MLQ* 45 (1984). C.P.S.

DISPOSITIO. See RHETORIC AND POETRY.

DISSEMINATION. See DECONSTRUCTON; INTERTEXTUALITY; INFLUENCE.

DISSOCIATION OF SENSIBILITY. This phrase first appears in T. S. Eliot's "The Metaphysical Poets" (1921), where Eliot suggests that "something . . . happened to the mind of England between the time of Donne or Lord Herbert of Cherbury and the time of Tennyson and Browning. . . . Tennyson and Browning are poets, and they think; but they do not feel their thought as immediately as the odour of a rose. A thought to Donne was an experience; it modified his sensibility." To explain the change, Eliot proposed a "theory": "the poets of the 17th c., the successors of the dramatists of the 16th, possessed a mechanism of sensibility which could devour any kind of experience. . . . In the 17th c. a d. of s. set in, from which we have never recovered; and this d. . . . was aggravated by the influence of the two most powerful poets of the century, Milton and Dryden." The first consequence of the d. was that "while the lang. became more refined, the feeling became more crude"; the second was the "sentimental age," which "began early in the 18th c., and continued. The poets . . . thought and felt by fits, unbalanced; they reflected." In Eliot's terms, for a poet with a unified s., the sensory world is saturated with meaning, while for one with a dissociated s., feeling either is ungrounded, and becomes sentimentality, or is ruminated about—thought is "tacked on." Eliot's concept thus belongs to the line of prescriptive crit. that tries to preserve the distinctive character of poetry from contamination by or confusion with other modes of writing. Good poetry is neither emotional effusion nor philosophical speculation: it is the record of a singular kind of response to experience, the product, as Eliot implies, of a singular mental faculty. What caused the d. of s.? In "Milton II" (1947), Eliot suggested that it had to do with the issues at stake in the Eng. Civil War; the breakup of the Christian European order, with which the d. of s. coincides, was in Eliot's view the central event of European cultural hist., as it was for many of his New Critical followers. Those who have adopted the term have assigned responsibility variously to Hobbes (Brooks), Bacon (Knights), Cartesian dualism (Willey), and the rise of capitalism (Kramer).

Eliot may have adapted the phrase from a sentence in Gourmont's essay on Laforgue, but the "sensuous apprehension of thought" is one of the ideals of romantic poetics. It was used in the 19th c. to praise the poetry of Keats and Tennyson; its application to Donne and other metaphysical poets was a commonplace when Eliot wrote his essay. But Eliot made the prescription underwrite an *alternative* to the romantic trad., one running from the 17th-c. metaphysicals through the 19th-c. Fr. symbolists (whose sensibilities, he argued, resembled the metaphysicals') to the "difficult" poetry of the Anglo-Am. modernists. Eliot soon questioned his genealogy: in 1926 he denounced both Donne and Laforgue for dissociating thought and feeling, and in 1931 he complained that "in Donne, there is a manifest fissure between thought and s." Eliot's understanding of metaphysical poetry (q.v.)—and of the conceit (q.v.) and its implied resemblance to the 19th-c. symbol (q.v.) in particular—has been critiqued by a number of scholars, notably Tuve. Still, Eliot's theory enjoyed a remarkable success. The hypothetical "d." and the identification of two distinct lines in the hist. of poetry inform such literary histories as F. R. Leavis's *Revaluation* (1936) and C. Brooks' *Mod. Poetry and the Trad.* (1939). Eliot's essay helped inspire interest in 17th-c. poets and influenced 20th-c. poetry. The complaint that 19th-c. Eng. poetry suffers from fuzzy emotionalism and makeshift philosophizing was for a time crucial to this century's understanding of the last.

The belief that culture once possessed a unity now fractured holds an appeal for many critics of modernity, and although the d. of s. is no longer thought to name an actual historical transition, the conception it stands for persists as a buried assumption in much crit. of poetry. Many poststructuralist critics, on the other hand, explain the notion of a lost unity—of thought and feeling, of belief—as a nostalgia for origins, for immediacy, for transparency of lang., for a "golden age." In this sort of analysis, the balance of judgment tips the other way: poets in the romantic trad. are admired for their critique, their "deconstruction," of the myth of origins, and modernism is attacked for a misguided attempt to recover a wholeness that never existed. See also SENSIBILITY.—R. de Gourmont, "La Sensibilité de Jules Laforgue," *Promenades littéraires* 1 (1904); T. S. Eliot, "The Metaphysical Poets" (1921, rpt. *Essays*), "Milton II" (1947, rpt. *On Poetry and Poets*, 1957); L. C. Knights, "Bacon and the 17th-C. D. of S.," *Scrutiny* 11 (1943); R. Tuve, *Elizabethan and Metaphysical Imagery* (1947); F. W. Bateson, "D. of S.," *EIC* 1–2 (1951–52); F. Kermode, *Romantic Image* (1957); B. Willey, *The 17th-C. Background* (1958); J. E. Duncan, *The Revival of Metaphysical Poetry* (1959); J. Kramer, "T. S. Eliot's Concept of Trad.," *NGC* 6 (1975); E. Lobb, *T. S. Eliot and the Romantic Critical Trad.* (1981); P. Meisel, *The Myth of the Mod.* (1987).   L.ME.

DISSONANCE. The quality of being harsh or inharmonious in rhythm or sound; akin to cacophony (q.v.). Insofar as the terms may be distinguished, cacophony is that which is harsh-sounding in itself, d. is that which is discordant or inharmonious with what surrounds it. It is d. rather than cacophony that is invoked in discussions of rhythm; and while cacophony is sometimes unintentional, d. usually implies deliberate choice. By extension the term may also refer to other elements in a poem that are discordant in their immediate context: tonality, theme, imagery (catachresis), or syntax (anacoluthon)—qq.v. Just as there is frequent confusion between the euphonious and the musical, so too there is a tendency among critics and readers to identify d. with the unmusical. But as Northrop Frye reminds us, music is concerned not with the beauty but with the organization of sound. A musical discord is not an unpleasant sound but an energetic one. Applying this principle to poetry we can say, with Frye, that when we find harsh, barking accents, crabbed lang., mouthfuls of consonants, and the like, we are likely to be reading a poet influenced by music. Browning ("Not a plenteous cork-crop: scarcely") and Hopkins ("sheer plod makes plough down sillion / Shine") made notable use of d. It is also frequently found in Fr. baroque, Eng. metaphysical, and Sp. mannerist poetry (qq.v.). See also CACOPHONY; EUPHONY; SOUND; SOUND EFFECTS IN POETRY.—J. B. Douds, "Donne's Technique of D.," *PMLA* 52 (1937); A. Stein, "Donne's Harshness and the Elizabethan Trad.," *SP* 41 (1944); N. Frye, "The Rhythm of Recurrence: Epos," in Frye, "Lexis and Melos," *Sound and Poetry*, ed. Frye (1957); A. Ostriker, "Thomas Wyatt and Henry Surrey," *NLH* 1 (1970); M. Gibson, "The Poetry of Struggle: Browning's Style," *VP* 19 (1981); S. F. Walker, "The Wrong Word at the Right Time," *Proc. Xth Congress of the Internat. Comp. Lit. Assoc.*, ed. A. Balakian et al., v. 2 (1982).   L.BI.

DISTICH. A pair of metrical lines, a couplet (q.v.), heterometric in Cl. poetry but usually isometric in modern. In Cl. poetry the most common type is the elegiac d. (q.v.), consisting of a dactylic hexameter followed by a dactylic "pentameter" and often used for epigram. The widely known *Distichs of Cato* carried the form of the d. from Lat. into the Middle Ages, and in fact it is still common in mod. Gr. poetry. But with the emergence of the Romance vernaculars the couplet (most often octosyllabic) was normally isometric and rhymed. Th. Sebillet was the first to use the term *distique* in Fr. prosody, where it retained more currency than in Eng.—G. Soyter, "Das volkstümliche Distichon bei den Neugriechen," *Laographia* 8 (1925); *Disticha catonis*, ed. M. Boas (1952); Koster.   T.V.F.B.

DISTINCTIVE FEATURE ANALYSIS of verse. A system of metrical analysis developed by Karl Magnuson and Frank G. Ryder in the late 1960s which applies the principles of Prague School d. f. a. in phonology to metered verse in order to identify those fs. which are prosodically (metrically) d. In phonology, d. fs. represent minimal differences between sounds expressed as polar extremes of the same category or the presence or absence of a

particular quality. These differences are *phonemic* when they distinguish the meaning of two words (e.g. by long vowel vs. short: *beat/ bit*). In pros. the identification of d. fs. is based on the occurrence or nonoccurrence of different types of two-syllable sequences relative to the underlying meter. If two prosodic word-types (e.g. *holding/ behold*) occur in mutually exclusive environments, they are in complimentary distribution and differ in at least one prosodically d. f. Magnuson and Ryder found that certain fs. occur most often in metrically prominent positions (called *even*), others in nonprominent positions (*odd*). The former support or "affirm" the meter in prominent positions and disrupt it in nonprominent positions, the latter the reverse.

Magnuson and Ryder originally identified four prosodically d. fs. in Ger. verse and applied them to Eng. verse: STRESS (ST) and WORD ONSET (WO) affirm prominent positions in the meter, while PRESTRESS (PS), assigned to all syllables preceding a stressed syllable within the same word, and WEAK (WK) affirm nonprominent positions. The presence or absence of a f. is indicated by a + or - sign:

Batter my heart, three-person'd God; for you

ST	+	-	-	+	+	+	-	+	-	-
WO	+	-	+	+	+	-	-	+	+	+
PS	-	-	-	-	+	-	-	-	-	-
WK	-	+	+	-	-	+	+	-	+	+

Whereas the "weak" f. (later redefined by Chisholm in lexical terms) is redundant for Eng. (all +STRESS syllables are -WEAK and vice versa), it is d. for Ger. On the basis of these fs., Magnuson and Ryder formulated prosodic rules which account for the presence or absence of all two-syllable sequences in Ger. verse.

At the core of the theory is the concept of a *binary* relation between contiguous positions of the meter such that the poet's selection in the second position may be constrained as a result of his selection in the first. This principle of loss and recovery of metrical equilibrium places constraints on filling a metrical position when the f. filling the preceding position disrupts the meter. If, for example, the STRESS f. occurs in a position which disrupts the meter, it must be followed by a f. (such as STRESS) which "affirms" the meter in the immediately following position:

O X   O XOX O X   O X
Thy youth's *proud livery*, so gazed on now
                    (Shakespeare)

O X   O XO X O X O
Die Nacht *schuf tausend* Ungeheuer
                    (Goethe)

Prosodic distinctiveness varies in different langs.: WORD-ONSET is d. for Ger. but not for Eng. verse; PHRASE TERMINAL, which functions in conjunction with stress in Eng., is less significant in Ger. verse.

R. Jakobson, G. Fant, and M. Halle, *Preliminaries to Speech Analysis* (1965); N. S. Trubetzkoy, *Principles of Phonology*, tr. C. A. M. Baltaxe (1969); K. Magnuson and F. G. Ryder, "The Study of Eng. Pros.," *CE* 31 (1970), "Second Thoughts on Eng. Pros.," *CE* 33 (1971); D. Chisholm, "Lexicality and Ger. Derivational Suffixes," *Lang&S* 6 (1973), *Goethe's Knittelvers* (1975), "Generative Pros. and Eng. Verse," *Poetics* 6 (1977); K. Magnuson, "Rules and Observations in Pros.," *Poetics* 12 (1974); R. Wakefield, *Nibelungen Pros.* (1976); B. Bjorklund, *A Study in Comparative Pros.* (1978); J. B. Lord, Sr., "Some Solved and Some Unsolved Problems in Pros.," *Style* 13 (1979); C. Küper, *Sprache und Metrum* (1987). D.H.C.

DIT (OF, from Lat. *dictum*). In the Middle Ages, a poem imparting a message, a short didactic poem. It is distinguished from the *roman* by its brevity and from the *chant* by its lack of musical accompaniment. The inspiration for the dit seems to have come from the Lat. *exemplum* (q.v.) of the 12th c., but by the middle of the 13th c. its use had broadened to include lyrical allegories (*Dit de la panthère d'amour*), moral allegories (*Dit du vrai aniel, Dit de l'unicorne*), dramatic monologues (*Dit de l'herberie*), and love laments (the *Assembly of Ladies*). The *Dit d'Aristote* speaks of the wiles of women; the *Dit des rues de Paris* lists all 310 streets of the city as they were at the close of the 13th c.; the *Dit d'Urbain le Courtois* is a guide to deportment. Guillaume de Machaut in his *Voir Dit* (True Story) describes his amorous exploits, both real and imaginary. The earliest dits were written in octosyllabic couplets, but with the arrival of Jean Bodel and Gautier de Coincy, monorimed quatrains in alexandrines came into fashion. See DIDACTIC POETRY.—H.-R. Jauss in *GRLMA* 5.1 (1968); P. Zumthor, *Essai de poétique médiévale* (1972); D. Poirion, "Traditions et fonctions du *dit poétique* au XIVe et au XVe siècle," and J. Cerquiglini, "Le Clerc et l'écriture," in *Lit. in der Gesellschaft des Spätmittelalters*, ed. H. U. Gumbrecht (1980); Hollier. R.L.H.; T.V.F.B.

DITHYRAMB. A genre of Gr. choral lyric or melic poetry (q.v.) performed in honor of Dionysus. The earliest reference (Archilochus, fr. 77) associates the d. with drunken revelry: "I know how to lead the beautiful d.-song of Lord Dionysus when my mind is thunder-struck with wine." The genre's origins are obscure, but Arion is credited with introducing formal improvements and a circular chorus in Corinth at the beginning of the 6th c. B.C., while at the end of the same century, Lasus of Hermione improved the music and dance and helped establish dithyrambic contests at Athens. Ds. were also performed at Delos during the winter months, when they replaced paeans (q.v.) to Apollo. Judging from extant 5th-c. examples and from the names given by Alexandrian editors (e.g.

Bacchylides, *The Sons of Antenor, The Youths or Theseus*), heroic narratives, often unconnected with Dionysus, later became a prominent feature of the genre. Although Simonides was a leading composer of ds. (credited with 56 victories in contests), not a verse remains. We possess only fragments of Pindar's two books of ds., but have substantial portions of five ds. and the beginning of a sixth by Bacchylides (Jebb, Burnett). In the 4th c. the d. underwent considerable modification—and evident decline—at the hands of Philoxenus and Timotheus, who originated what is sometimes called the "New D." (Smyth) by abolishing the strophic structure and introducing solo singing along with musical and verbal virtuosity (Pickard-Cambridge). Since there is no appreciable difference between the style of Pindar's and Bacchylides' surviving ds. and that of their other poems, the later reputation of the d. for extreme license (cf. Horace, *Odes* 4.2) must stem from its later stages of development. Although hymns to Bacchus continued to be written (e.g. Horace, *Odes* 2.19, 3.25), the genre of d. was moribund by the 2d c. B.C. In modern usage "dithyrambic" characterizes a style that is ecstatic, vehement, or unpredictable; probably the best-known modern example is Dryden's "Alexander's Feast." See GREEK POETRY, *Classical*.—H. W. Smyth, *Gr. Melic Poets* (1900); O. Crusius, "D.," Pauly-Wissowa; R. C. Jebb, *Bacchylides* (1905); H. Färber, *Die Lyrik in der Kunsttheorie der Antike* (1936); A. E. Harvey, "The Classif. of Gr. Lyric Poetry," *ClassQ* 5 (1955); A. W. Pickard-Cambridge, *D., Tragedy and Comedy*, 2d ed. (1962); A. P. Burnett, *The Art of Bacchylides* (1985). W.H.R.

DITTY, dittie, dictie, etc. From *dict*, a saying (Lat. *dictum*). In ME, d. denoted a composition or treatise, and then a piece of verse; by the 16th c., it had come to mean the words of a song. As a verb, d. could mean to sing a song or to set words to music—now obsolete. In Thomas Morley's *Plaine and Easie Introduction to Practical Musicke* (1597), the section on how to fit music to a text is entitled "Rules to be observed in dittying," and Daniel in the *Defence of Ryme* (1603) remarks that feminine rhymes are "fittest for Ditties." But in its modern sense, a song or tune, especially a light or simple one, d. has almost lost its association with words. E.D.

DIVERBIUM. See CANTICUM AND DIVERBIUM.

DĪWĀN. See ARABIC POETRY.

DIZAIN. A Fr. poem of ten octosyllabic or decasyllabic lines which, with Clément Marot, Hugues Salel, and Mellin de Saint-Gelais, had the rhyme scheme *ababbccdcd*. On the same scheme Maurice Scève wrote the 449 related ds. of his *Délie* (1544). When the d. stood alone as a separate composition, it tended to have the characteristics commonly associated with the epigram (q.v.); and Thomas Sebillet in his *Art poétique françoys* of 1548 (ed. F. Gaiffe, 1932) defines the d. as "l'épigramme aujourd'hui estimé premier." Three or five ds., each group with an *envoi* (q.v.), could be brought together to form a *ballade* or a *chant royal* (qq.v.), respectively. As employed later by the *Pléiade* (q.v.), the d. has the rhyme scheme *ababccdeed*, is less often found as a separate poem, and may be composed of verses of different lengths. With this latter scheme, in octosyllables, it was taken over into Rus. versification in the 18th c. by Lomonosov and Deržavin. Sidney has five ds. in the *Old Arcadia*, which do not, however, keep the double internal couplets and mirror-image rhyme scheming around them of the Marot-Scève model.—P. Martinon, *Les Strophes* (1912); Patterson; H. Chamard, *Hist. de la Pléiade*, v. 4 (1941); M. Scève, *Délie*, ed. I. D. McFarlane (1966); I. D. McFarlane, *Ren. France, 1470–1589* (1974).

I.S.; T.V.F.B.

DOCHMIAC or dochmius (Gr. "slanted"). A metrical sequence found almost exclusively in Gr. tragedy, chiefly in passages expressing intense emotion, agitation, or grief. The basic form is x – – ∪ – (the commonest form x ∪ ∪ – ∪ –), but there are about 30 varieties, and they also appear combined with iambs. Some metrists (e.g. Snell) do not acknowledge the existence of ds. outside of Gr. drama; others find them in Pindar and Bacchylides. Lat. metrists sometimes group such structures among bacchiac cola (see BACCHIUS) or catalectic bacchiac dimeters (so Crusius). The anaclastic (see ANACLASIS) form is called the hypodochmiac (– ∪ – ∪ –).—Maas; N. C. Conomis, "The Ds. of Gr. Drama," *Hermes* 92 (1964)—the fundamental collection of material and statistics; Koster, ch. 12; Crusius; Dale, ch. 7; Halporn et al.; Snell, West.

J.W.H.

DOGGEREL (origin unknown). Rough, poorly constructed verse, characterized by either (1) extreme metrical irregularity or (2) easy rhyme and monotonous rhythm, cheap sentiment, and triviality. Saintsbury and others formerly used the term as a pejorative for accentual verse (q.v.). Chaucer refers to his burlesque *Tale of Sir Thopas* as *rym dogerel*, and Dr. Johnson stigmatized its vices with a famous parody:

As with my hat upon my head
I walk'd along the Strand,
I there did meet another man
With his hat in his hand.
(G. Steevens in *Johnsonian Miscellanies*,
ed. G. B. Hill, v. 2 [1897])

Northrop Frye has characterized d. as the result of an unfinished creative process, in which a "prose initiative" never assumes the associative qualities of true poetry, revealing its failure in a desperate attempt to resolve technical difficulties through any means available. There are, however, some works of real poetic value in which features of d. are deliberately used for comic or satiric effect. John Skelton, Samuel Butler, and Jonathan Swift are all masters of artistic d., and much Ger. *Knittelvers* (q.v.) also achieves a brilliant parodic effect. See ACCENTUAL VERSE.—P. Reyher, *Essai sur le d.* (1909); Frye.

L.B.P.

DOINA. See ROMANIAN POETRY.

DOLCE STIL NUOVO. Term commonly used to designate a group of late 13th-c. It. love poets and to describe the special character of their lyric production. The term first appears in Dante's *Purgatorio* (24.57), where the poet Bonagiunta Orbicciani of Lucca uses it to refer to the wide chasm separating Dante's poetic style from that of the Sicilian and Guittonian poets and to define its characteristics as audibly and intellectually pleasing (*dolce*) and new in concept (*nuovo*). Generally speaking, Dante's term has considerable validity: the "sweetness" of his style is attained, analysts have discovered, through a careful selection and ordering of words of pleasurable sound. The "newness" most probably refers to the poet's inventive variations on traditional poetic themes.

The literary background from which the *s. n.* emerged was chiefly Occitan troubadour poetry (see OCCITAN POETRY), a trad. two centuries old and still vital in Italy at the time of Dante's birth. From Occitan poetry the *stilnovisti* learned the conventions of courtly love (q.v.) with its religious overtones, its idealization of women, its emphasis on gentility (*gentilezza*), and its faith that love is an ennobling influence on the lover. A second influence important for the *s. n.* is the Franciscan revival, which stressed sincerity, simplicity, and a feeling for the unity of man with nature. For their poetry which transcends the secular adoration of woman the *stilnovisti* adapted the lang. and imagery employed for the mystical adoration of the Virgin by the Marian cults. Philosophy, too, had an important influence on the *s. n.* From Guido Guinizelli to Guido Cavalcanti and even Petrarch, all of the important *stilnovisti* had contact with the University of Bologna, where Thomistic theology and medicine were taught, both of which were allied to the great 13th-c. revival of Aristotelianism. Avicenna on medicine and Averroes on Aristotle were not without their influence, too. The joint result of these several influences was to deepen the analysis of love found in the poetry of the *s. n.* In fact, it has been suggested that the philosophical and often metaphysical bent of the poetry of the *s. n.* is its most distinctive characteristic (Vossler). Another important influence is that of the Sicilian school (q.v.) of poets, which flourished in the first half of the 13th c. and whose most prominent figure is the Notary Giacomo da Lentini, originator of the sonnet.

The first of the triad of poets in the group is the

jurisconsultant Guido Guinizelli, who composed the important doctrinal *canzone* "Al cor gentil rempaira sempre amore." His emphasis on the poetics and thematics of praise was imitated by Dante, the third member, in many poems, most notably in the first *canzone* of the *Vita nuova*, "Donne ch'avete intelletto d'amore." Guinizelli repeats the troubadour commonplaces but seems to expand on the basis of Platonic doctrine: the eyes (as in Plato's *Republic*, Book 4) are the most beautiful part of the body—the windows of the soul. The *saluto* ranks second (in accordance with Aristotle's teaching on the "smile"). Love and the noble heart are one and the same; love cannot exist anywhere save in a noble heart, and a noble heart cannot exist without love. This nobility is of the spirit, not of heredity through blood; it derives from one's own virtue. In Guido's conception, the beloved activates the lover's inborn disposition toward good and is instrumental in raising the lover's soul to the Highest Good, making for communion with the Absolute and the Eternal. Guinizelli's method is scholastic, but his manner is distinguished by use of scientific observation of natural phenomena in images and similes to objectify the internal sensations of love.

Guido Cavalcanti, Dante's "first friend," is the second member of the triad. He devoted his doctrinal *canzone* "Donna me prega per ch'eo voglio dire" to his Christian, neo-Aristotelian understanding of love. His treatment of Love's origins and nature may show some Averroistic influence, but in the main his work consists of profoundly intimate reveries upon womanly beauty. Amid the agitation and anguish of his state, he is haunted by the phantom of Love and the spectre of Death.

In the *Vita nuova* Dante discloses his personal poetic and amorous *iter* through a combination of poems and prose narratives or glosses which, by recounting his love for Beatrice, summarize in a specific way the general outline of the evolution of the love-lyric trad. The early poems in the *Vita nuova* are pervaded by morbid introspection, anguish, and self-pity which derive from Cavalcantian models. The first *canzone* of the *Vita nuova* ("Donne ch'avete intelletto d'amore") marks the break with these attitudes and embraces Guinizelli's view of love, and from this point the poems of this work begin a series of paeans of "praise." They contain elements of the Platonic outlook, particularly the seeing of the beloved as angelic. The death of the lady in the case of Dante's Beatrice (as well as of Petrarch's Laura) is a supreme milestone in the pilgrim's progress in love. Having died, she becomes an angelic form who, through the light of the eyes and radiance of the smile, leads the lover, as true guide and symbol of virtue, to God in His Goodness, the ideal of perfection. In Dante's *Convivio* (1304–7) we learn (2.15.10; 3.12.2–3; 4.2) that he reserved a special manner of sweetness of expression for rhymes of love and that his conception of *amore* included the

eager pursuit of knowledge. In his Lat. *De vulgari eloquentia*, written about the same period (2.8,12), Dante further elaborates his ideas on style (the tragic being the highest), lang. (the illustrious vernacular being the sweetest), form (the *canzone* [q.v.] being the noblest), and meter (the hendecasyllable [q.v.] being the most excellent). In the same work he names Cavalcanti, Lapo Gianni, himself, and Cino da Pistoia, whom he favors esp. for his subtlety and sweetness, as those poets who composed lyrics in the high style. Dante's remarks have led some critics to believe in the existence of a more or less self-conscious "school" of the *d. s. n.* More likely it was simply a loosely organized group of friends with more or less common poetic interests. Critics have added to the supposed group Gianni Alfani and Dino Frescobaldi. Later poets such as Guido Novello da Polenta (Dante's host in his exile) and Giovanni Quirini imitate the essential traits of the *d. s. n.*

Petrarch throughout his several reworkings of his *Canzoniere* shows much influence of the *d. s. n.* However, he was not altogether successful in his attempt to subjugate his great passion to the Dantean ideal. His awareness of this dilemma is expressed in the crescendo and diminuendo, the ebb and flow, throughout the carefully contrived *Canzoniere*. Later followers of the *stilnovisti* include Matteo Frescobaldi, Franceschino degli Albizzi, Sennuccio del Bene, Boccaccio (the last two, poetic correspondents of Petrarch), Cino Rinuccini, and Giovanni Gherardi da Prato.

Through the influence of Petrarch, the conventions of the *s. n.* were spread throughout Europe, profoundly affecting the devel. of lyric poetry in France, Spain, England, and elsewhere. Lorenzo de' Medici, the reviver of Petrarchism (q.v) for the It. *Quattrocento*, consciously imitated the *s. n.* He also appreciated the minor *stilnovisti*, as evidenced by his letter to Frederico of Aragon accompanying the anthology of early It. poetry he compiled for him.

TEXTS: *Rimatori del d. s. n.*, ed. L. di Benedetto, 2d ed. (1939); Guido Cavalcanti, *Rime*, ed. G. Favati (1957); *Poeti del Duecento*, ed. G. Contini, 2 v. (1960); *Dante's Lyric Poetry*, ed. and tr. K. Foster and P. Boyde, 2 v. (1967); *The Poetry of Guido Cavalcanti*, ed. and tr. L. Nelson, Jr. (1986); *The Poetry of Guido Guinizelli*, ed. and tr. R. Edwards (1987).

CRITICAL STUDIES: K. Vossler, *Die Göttliche Komödie* (1906), tr. as *Med. Culture* (1929); A. Figurelli, *Il D. s. n.* (1933); A. Lipari, *The D. S. N. According to Lorenzo de' Medici* (1936); J. E. Shaw, *Guido Cavalcanti's Theory of Love* (1949); M. Valency, *In Praise of Love* (1958); G. Petrocchi, "Il D. s. n.," *Storia della letteratura italiana*, ed. E. Cecchi and N. Sapegno (1965); Fisher; E. Pasquini and A. E. Quaglio, *Lo Stilnovo e la poesia religiosa* (1971); P. Boyde, *Dante's Style in His Lyric Poetry* (1971); M. Marti, *Storia dello s. n.*, 2. v. (1973), "S. n.," *Enciclopedia dantesca*, v. 5 (1978); R. Russell, *Tre ver-*

santi della poesia stilnovistica (1973); Wilkins; G. Favati, *Inchiesta sul d. s. n.* (1975); F. Suitner, *Petrarca e la tradizione stilnovistica* (1977); V. Moleta, *Guinizzelli in Dante* (1980); A. Solimena, *Repertorio metrico dello s. n.* (1980)—metrical index; I. Bertelli, *La Poesia di Guido Guinizzelli e la poetica del "d. s. n."* (1983).   L.H.G.; C.K.

DOL'NIK (pl. *dol'niki*). Rus. accentual meter. Unlike Rus. syllabotonic (or accentual-syllabic) meters, which have a constant syllabic interval between ictuses, the d. has a variable interval of one or two syllables. From their introduction around 1740 until the 1890s, syllabotonic meters predominated in Rus. poetry; the only exceptions were imitations of Gr. and Lat. meters, poems stylized after folksongs, and translations of Ger. and Eng. poetry. In Ger. and Eng., the equivalent of the d. appeared toward the end of the 18th c. and was based on native folk verse; in Rus., the d. developed from literary verse and was popularized in the first years of the 20th c. by the symbolist poet Alexander Blok. By 1930, the three-stress d. had become one of the staple meters of Rus. poetry.
  Although the d. exists in 3-, 4-, and variable-stress lines; that with three ictuses prevails. The anacrusis, the number of syllables before the first stress, may be fixed or may vary; the line-end is usually rhymed. The line tends to consist of eight syllables (excluding syllables after the last stress); the first ictus coincides with the third syllable, the second ictus with the fifth or sixth, and the third with the eighth, thus: x x x́ x x x́ x x x́ (x x). Some poets use an isosyllabic line in which the second ictus is fixed on the sixth syllable, a variant sometimes called logaoedic verse.—A. Kolmogorov and A. Proxorov, "O dol'nike sovremennoj russkoj poèzii," *VJa* (1963, 1964); J. Bailey, "Some Recent Developments in the Study of Rus. Versif.," *Lang&S* 5 (1972); Gasparov; G. S. Smith, "Logaoedic Metres in the Lyric Poetry of Marina Tsvetayeva," *SEER* 53 (1975); M. Tarlinskaja, *Eng. Verse: Theory and Hist.* (1976); Terras; Scherr.
                                                                    J.O.B.

DOUBLE DACTYL. A recent genre of light verse in two quatrains. The last lines of the first and second quatrains must rhyme and must comprise four syllables, a dactylic foot followed by a stress. The other six lines are all hexasyllables of two dactylic feet, hence the name. The first line of the poem must be a nonsense phrase, usually "Higgledy piggledy"; the second line must be a proper name; and the second line of the second quatrain must be a polysyllable, often scientific or technical, and the more recondite the better:

> Higgledy-piggledy
> Alex S. Preminger
> Wanted poetical
> Terms to be clear;
>
> He and some friends wrote an

> Encyclopedia,
> Offering instances
> Like this one here.

The form is notoriously flippant. P. Pascal and Anthony Hecht invented d. ds. in the early 1950s; in the 1960s Hecht and John Hollander published the first collection. Since then the d. d. has proven popular with admirers of light verse (q.v.).—A. Hecht and J. Hollander, *Jiggery Pokery* (1966); W. Espy, *Almanac of Words at Play* (1980); A. Harrington, *Tersery Versery* (1982).   F.T.

DOUBLE METER. See BINARY AND TERNARY.

DOUBLE RHYME. See MASCULINE AND FEMININE; RHYME.

DOUBLETS. See ELISION; METER.

DOZENS is a game of exchanging, in contest form, ritualized verbal insults, which are usually in rhymed couplets and often profane. The term is probably a literate corruption of the vernacular *doesn'ts*, relating to forbidden lang. activity. The game is practiced now mostly among adolescent Afro-Am. males, though its origin is thought to lie in the verbal insult contests of West Africa. The d. is a subcategory of *signifying* (q.v.). Sometimes referred to as woofing, sounding, cutting, capping, or chopping, the ritual is most often called "playing the d." The subjects of the insults are frequently the relatives of the verbal opponent, esp. his mother; the insults are frequently sexual. A mildly phrased example of the d. technique and style would be: "I don't play the d., the d. ain't my game, / But the way I loved your mama is a crying shame."
  The players of the d. must display great skill with rhyme, analogy, wit, humor, and rhythm to maintain the momentum and vivacity necessary to win the accolades of their audience. The d. is partly an initiation ritual that teaches a player how to hold his equilibrium by learning to master the power of words and humor. The exchange takes place as a verbal duel in which words and humor are chosen to sting, so that the opponent will be goaded to either greater lexical creativity or defeat. But another purpose is to make the opponent aware of his or her intellectual rank within the group. The notion of the d. as only a game is a rule generally adhered to, in that the players are expected not to base their insults upon their opponent's real life, but if this rule is broken, what might have been a game can turn into an outright battle. Langston Hughes draws upon the trad. of the d., particularly in his long poetic work *Ask Your Mama* (1961), as do Richard Wright and Ralph Ellison. See also INVECTIVE; POETIC CONTESTS.—R. D. Abrahams, *Deep Down in the Jungle* (1970); *Rappin' and Stylin' Out*, ed. T. Kochman (1972); L. W. Levine, *Black Culture and Black Consciousness*

(1977); G. Smitherman, *Talkin and Testifyin* (1977); H. L. Gates, Jr., *The Signifying Monkey* (1988). E.A.P.

DRAMATIC IRONY. See IRONY.

DRAMATIC MONOLOGUE. See MONOLOGUE.

DRAMATIC POETRY. In our time of explosion or implosion of literary genres, we should recall that some two millennia of Western poetics repose on a tacit separation of drama from lyric and narrative (q.v.). Traditionally, the lyric expressed personal emotion; the narrative propelled characters through a plot; the dramatic presented an enactment. All three genres have been hospitable to, may have originated in, verse, which is the simplest synonym for poetry. The contemporary verse dramatist Ntozake Shange has proclaimed: "In the beginning was the beat," but the beat is sounded differently in different langs. Moreover, the beat marks the rhythmic foot, but in poetry the verse line is in tension with the grammatical sentence, and in d. p. that tension may be high.

Western critics have interpreted the phrase d. p. in three main ways: (1) lyrics or short poems that imply a scene; (2) plays that are valorized with the adjective "poetic"; and (3) dramas whose dialogue is calculatingly rhythmed—in rhythms that are often regularized into meters and that are usually presented as discreet lines on the page. Avoiding the impressionism of the first two categories, the following overview focuses on d. p. as verse drama, which embraces such icons of our culture as *Oedipus*, *Faust*, and *Hamlet*. And although the survey is limited to published texts, we must also recall that virtually all d. p. was conceived for performance. In Martin Esslin's telling image, "a dramatic text is a blueprint for mimetic action."

Milestone documents of Eng. lit. hist. vary in their terminology for d. p.: although Sidney's *Apologie for Poetrie* (1581) cites only dramas written in verse, he refers to them as comedy, tragedy, or "play matter"; Dryden's very title subsumes his concern—*Essay of Dramatic Poesy* (1668); Shelley's *Defense of Poetry* (1820) also defends poetic drama; in a number of essays at the turn of the 20th c. W. B. Yeats champions "verse-drama"; and T. S. Eliot, probably the major modern champion of d. p., writes interchangeably of d. p., poetic drama, and verse drama. His spokesman A in his "Dialogue on D. P." (1928) makes the astonishing claim that "the craving for poetic drama is permanent in human nature."

The lineage of d. p. in the West extends back to cl. Greece, where d. p. was a chief form of celebration of the god Dionysus in religious and civic festivals. Although Gr. names are still retained for Eng. verse feet—iamb, trochee, dactyl, anapest, spondee—the accentual nature of the Eng. lang. betrays its Gr. source, which counted syllable quantity rather than stress (see CLASSICAL PROSODY; METER). The duration and not the accent of the syllable determines Gr. metrics, which lays down intricate laws of scansion. In both tragedy and comedy (qq.v.), spoken dialogue (q.v.) alternates with choral song; together, they compose the oldest form of d. p. in the Western world. Typically, a Chorus (q.v.) of commoners interacts with and comments upon the heroic characters of Gr. tragedy. The cl. Gr. Chorus is rich in metrical variety, which was in some way expressive of the music, now lost, but the dialogue of the drama is largely confined to the iambic trimeter (q.v.), which modern scholars, following Aristotle, believe to resemble the rhythm of everyday Gr. speech. The comic trimeter is more amenable than the tragic to metrical substitution, but the speech of both genres occasionally runs to trochaic or anapestic tetrameter. It is, however, the cl. Gr. Chorus whose metrical diversity defeats the translator. From Aeschylus to Euripides in tragedy, as from Aristophanes to Menander in comedy, the choral role shrinks, and dialogue usurps most of the drama. At its epitome, however, the Chorus can provide a cosmic context, a reflective interlude, or an emotional association for the episodes involving the actors. The range of resonance is reflected in the wide range of choral meters in any single drama.

For all the embarrassments in modern staging of Choruses, they lie at the heart of the deepest Gr. tragedies, and they are important enough to figure in the titles of Aristophanes' Old Comedy (e.g. *The Clouds*, *The Wasps*, *The Birds*). A half-century separates Aeschylus' *Oresteia* from Euripides' *Bacchae*, but both tragedies achieve dramatic intensity through their respective Choruses of women (played, like all Gr. roles, by men). The fearsome Erinyes of the final play of Aeschylus' trilogy eschew metrical diversity for iambic and trochaic rhythms of great complexity, and Euripides' nonGreek Bacchantes display a panoply of meters in their Dionysian frenzies.

By Roman times the Chorus virtually disappears from comedy, but not from tragedy. Livius Andronicus in the 3rd c. B.C. is credited with establishing the basic meter for both tragedy and comedy—a free iambic trimeter which modern scholars call the iambic senarius (q.v.). In tragedy Seneca is strict yet versatile in his adherence to the trimeter, sometimes distorting syntax to attain regularity, and he builds to dramatic climaxes with line-for-line repartee, called stichomythia (q.v.). Punctuating the declamations of his characters with four reflective choral passages, Seneca also influenced the structural form of European Ren. drama, in its proclivity for five-act structure.

In Roman comedy the iambic senarius is the meter of choice for Terence, but the favorite of free-ringing Plautus is the trochaic septenarius, which he sprinkles with metrically inventive songs, so that scholars compare his farces to modern musical comedy. Medieval mss. of Plautus and

Terence mark scenes as DV (*diverbium*) for spoken verse and C (*canticum*—qq.v.) for all other meters, but scholars disagree on the gradations between recitative and song. Indisputable is Terence's predilection for quiet control, whereas Plautus is more flamboyant. In Ben Jonson's words: "neat Terence, witty Plautus."

Although an occasional dramatic sport appears in prose, verse is basic to two generative influences on Ren. drama—the Roman legacy and Med. Lat. liturgical plays (see LITURGICAL DRAMA). Lat. is the lang. and Lat. meters the verseform of both these strands, but it is very different Lat. Terence served as the basic Cl. Lat. reading text in Ren. schools, whereas Med. Lat. was increasingly undermined by the various vernaculars. Verse nevertheless remained the norm for medieval European drama, both in Lat. and in the new native meters, such as the nine-line stanzas of the Wakefield Master (Stevens) or the octosyllabic couplets of anonymous Fr. farce. The Englishman animated his *Second Shepherd's Play* with strong alliterative stress as well as internal rhymes in short-lined stanzas. The Wakefield Master could distribute his nine lines among several characters, for both the colloquial conversation of the shepherds and the majestic pronouncements of the angel and of Mary, while across the Eng. Channel his near (15th-c.) contemporary, the anonymous author of *Master Pathelin*, one of the most scintillating comedies of the Fr. lang., could etch characters in colloquial Fr. or bend his line into the several dialects with which the astute Master Pathelin evaded his creditors and delighted his audiences—all in impeccable octosyllables (q.v.).

The Ren. witnessed not the rebirth but the birth of sustained prose drama (e.g. Machiavelli's *Mandragola*), and yet verse or d. p. continued to be the dramatic norm. After some fluctuation in the meters of d. p. in the several langs. of Western Europe, each country settled into its own preferred rhythm. In Italy, opera emerged, based on the assumption that the dialogue of Gr. tragedy was sung rather than spoken; but when music dictates the meter of dramatic dialogue, relegating lang. to a secondary function, the work does not fall into the province of d. p. and hence will not be considered here. Nor will such later forms as operetta and musical comedy.

On the Elizabethan stage Marlowe's mighty line towered above its competitors. Bold and reverberant in the mouths of his over-reachers, the pentameter was also whipped by Marlowe into stichomythic exchanges between his Faustus and Mephistopheles. Whether in tirade or duet, Marlowe's blank verse (q.v.) is regular, resonant, and end-stopped. In moments of dramatic stress, however, Marlowe sometimes breaks the basic meter, as in Faustus' anguished question to himself: "And canst thou not be saved?" Although Marlowe follows what was becoming custom in assigning prose to lower-class characters, he has no scruples against mixing prose and verse for the aristocratic onstage audiences of Faustus' paltry stunts. Unlike Shakespeare, who will shift his rhythm to announce creatures of another world, Marlowe limits both Good and Bad Angels to blank verse— in a virtual extension of the hero's inner conflict, to which Shakespeare's soliloquies would rise matchless.

Except for the prose *Merry Wives of Windsor*, all of Shakespeare's plays are grounded in blank verse, in which he achieved greater suppleness than any other dramatic poet, while also showing mastery of rhyme and prose. As G. R. Hibbard wrote: "Perhaps the major artistic problem that confronted Shakespeare . . . was that of bringing his exuberant delight in words and figures of speech into harmony with the dependence of drama on action and character." It is an understatement to say that Shakespeare solved this problem masterfully. He could infuse the pentameter with the questions of Hamlet, the exclamations of Lear, the imprecations of Timon of Athens. He could break the line in play or in passion (Wright); he could run the pentameters into soliloquies of labyrinthine syntax (q.v.). Although Dorothy Sipe has shown that the late plays also follow the pentameter norm, the mature Shakespeare nevertheless departed from ten-syllable strictness at moments of high tension. The most famous pentameter in the Eng. lang. is a hendecasyllable: "To be, or not to be; that is the question"; Lear rages on the heath: "Then kill, kill, kill, kill, kill, kill!"; Macbeth begins and ends his soliloquy of grief with short lines: "She should have died hereafter," "Signifying nothing." The model of later writers of blank verse, Shakespeare is also deft with rhyme (Ness), inventing stanzas for many of the songs in his d. p. Couplets served him traditionally to cue an entrance, close a scene, or announce a change of mood; his rhymes are heard in prologues, epilogues, choruses, parodies, the sonnets of *Love's Labor's Lost*, the octosyllables of *Measure for Measure*, the dirges of *Cymbeline* and *The Tempest*. In Shakespeare's mature plays his rhythmic virtuosity always functions dramatically (Wright).

Despite T. S. Eliot's distaste for *Hamlet*, its rhythms shape the tragedy. In the very first scene the pentameters are distributed among the several soldiers to convey their disquiet (see SPLIT LINES). In the second scene an entirely different rhythm permeates Claudius' lines in the same meter—glib and regular. Hamlet's first extended blank-verse speech (of grief) rises to the emphasis of a concluding couplet. His first soliloquy reveals his torment by exclamations and self-interruptions; the breaks in iambic fluidity predict: "But break, my heart. . . ." Then the mercurial prince shifts to easy familiarity for his greeting to Horatio—still in blank verse. The same meter questions the Ghost but snaps abruptly in the throes of the oath of secrecy. No other Shakespearean hero speaks so often in prose, a signal for the many levels of Hamlet's "antic disposition." Once the king's conscience is caught, Hamlet bursts exultantly into a ballad-rhyme, but he cannot manage the rhyme for a second ballad, as Horatio points out. Nevertheless, Hamlet utters seven blank-verse soliloquies at key dramatic points of the play's first four acts, and in them as nowhere else in d. p., the mind is caught live in "blooded thought." Ophelia in her madness zigzags from prose to bawdy song to elegy, and the clown sings as he digs her grave, offending Hamlet's sense of decorum. Other characters are sharply differentiated through their blank verse—sanctimonious Polonius, troubled Gertrude, duplicitous Claudius. Hamlet's final words—"the rest is silence"—lay to rest not only the prince but the most dramatically varied rhythms (largely in a single meter) in the Eng. lang.

Shakespeare's virtuosity was unique on the Elizabethan stage, but the age produced unparalleled skill in d. p., whether the panoramic comedies of Ben Jonson, the dark tragedies of Webster and Tourneur, the incisive satire of Marston. Yet by the time of the closing of the theaters in 1642, the energy of Eng. blank-verse drama had ebbed; and with the Restoration came prose comedy and heroic tragedy (see HEROIC PLAY), the latter written in rhyming pentameter couplets. It is puzzling that the same audiences apparently responded to these polar forms; perhaps they were attracted to the frankness of each artifice.

Certainly the artifice of the verse was part of the appeal of d. p. in rhyme-rich Sp. drama of the Golden Age (Morley). In these plays, ruled by an ineluctable poetic justice (q.v.), theatrical variety was confined to incident and rhythm. Lope de Vega was both prime theoretician and practitioner. In his *Arte nuevo de hacer comedias* (1609), he specifies the appropriate verse form for the specific dramatic situation: romance for narration, redondilla for dialogue, sonnet for monologue; he himself was reputed to pour forth every conceivable rhyme and meter in his 400-odd plays.

Calderón's noteworthy contribution to the Sleeper Awakened topos, *Life Is a Dream*, is a typical Golden Age drama in its metrical diversity, where no character "owns" any particular meter. Calderón's scenes of ceremony are couched traditionally in long, irregularly rhyming lines (hendecasyllables, q.v.), but far more frequent are shorter lines (octosyllables, q.v.) linked by assonance, which serve both monologue and dialogue (qq.v.), both action and reflection. In quatrains and quintillas (q.v.), these short lines heighten scenes of pathos, and in ten-line stanzas, or decimas (q.v.), they structure the two soliloquies of the protagonist Segismundo, who learns through suffering to accept the dreamlike quality of life. During the course of the tragicomedy, shifts of meter and placement of rhyme reflect the evanescence of events: thus the play opens on Rosaura's distraught *silva* (q.v.), but soon Segismundo yearns

for liberty in a *decima*; the passionate reactions of this protagonist brim with questions, exclamations, and verbless phrases—in shifting meters. Several scenes bristle with *redondillas* (q.v.) rising at climactic moments to the *octava* (eight octosyllabic lines rhyming abababcc). The *romance* (q.v.) accomplishes narrative summary in the play's few quiet moments. Although this bald listing of forms may suggest a ragged effect, the pattern of the whole moves inexorably toward an almost abstract acceptance of fate, wherein the many rhythms and wayward feelings are finally subdued to a destined order.

In Fr. d. p. of the 17th c., conventions impose order. Physical action is banished from the stage, and the often passionate dialogue is largely confined to alexandrine couplets with fixed rules for pauses. The strict five-act form is built with tense and static scenes, which in turn are built with balanced couplets, but the balance varies with the dramatic moment. In what Jacques Scherer has called "the tyranny of the tirade," monologues and messengers' speeches can run on for a hundred lines, with liberal enjambment: the best-known example is Théramène's account of the death of Hippolytus in Racine's *Phèdre*. In comedy, on the other hand, piquancy is gained by dividing the rhymed lines between two characters, and the alexandrine itself (q.v.) can be split between characters, as in the opening scene of Molière's *Misanthrope*. Thus distributed or, more usually, flowing unimpeded, alexandrine couplets ruled the cl. Fr. stage. Corneille's heroes sometimes sound as though they are impatient with these constraints, but Racine's tragedies gain in power from the very rigor of expression of his erotically disposed heroines. Phèdre's complaint: "Tout m'afflige et me nuit, et conspire á me nuire" becomes a quiet scream through the balance of the stressed /i/ sounds. Or in a celebrated alexandrine: "Venus toute entière à sa proie attachée" conveys Phèdre's helplessness within the bonds of her passion, and yet she does not even mention the subjective first person; the variety of vowels before the caesura dissolves abruptly into five merciless /a/ sounds. The contrast, tension, and symmetry of the whole play is reflected in such an alexandrine.

In Molière's character comedies the alexandrine functions to comic point—the catechism of *The School of Wives*, the lubricious hypocrisies of *Tartuffe*, the minatory manners of *The Misanthrope*. In spite of Molière's wit, however, the alexandrine is primarily associated with tragedy, and although it has not translated well into any other lang., it was imitated in several countries of 18th-c. Europe. Geriatric alexandrines continued to dominate Fr. d. p. until the 20th c., but their stranglehold upon the d. p. of other langs. was broken by the advent of bardolatry as a tenet of romanticism.

In Germany, where romanticism ruled deepest and longest, translations of Shakespeare established blank verse for d. p., with Lessing's *Nathan der Weise* (1779) serving as a model, and with Goethe committing his cl. *Iphigenie auf Tauris* to that meter. Perhaps the single most ambitious work of European d. p. is Goethe's *Faust*, whose composition extended over half a century; whose scenes take place in Heaven, Hell, and many domains of the earth, incl. the theater; whose characters are drawn from commoners, aristocrats, mythological figures, and other-worldly spirits; and whose verse performs acrobatic feats of rhyme. Scholars differ as to whether it is a single unified work at all, since various parts have been played both separately and together, requiring actors well attuned to d. p. In the apparently disjunctive scenes of Part I (but not in the cl. five-act structure of Part II) Goethe relies mainly on two free but traditional Ger. verse forms, the iambic madrigal with its free-ranging rhymes, and Knittelvers (q.v.), or four-beat rhyming couplets with wide latitude for unaccented syllables. Deliberately un-Shakespearean in its virtual rejection of blank verse, the vast panorama of *Faust* called forth the poet in Goethe, subsuming the Cl. heritage (in the Helen scenes), the Med. (the famous *Walpurgisnacht*), the Ren. (Faustus' insatiable desire for experience), and the romantic (the Gretchen story). The verseforms reflect that range: in Part II, for example, Faustus addresses Helen in a redondilla, shifting then to blank verse enhanced by anaphora, word play, and parallelism. Helen herself first speaks a Ger. approximation of quantitative verse but soon moves forward to rhyme in a scene which, while lacking the immediacy of Faustus' first view of Gretchen, nevertheless contains its own drama.

Goethe read Marlowe's *Faustus* (in tr.) only after he had published Part I and was well into Part II. Although both poets follow the 16th-c. *Faustbuch* in their dramatization of a sage who acquires power by selling his soul to the devil, Marlowe damns him, whereas Goethe saves him. Moreover, the Marlovian devil's "Why, this is hell, nor am I out of it," is far more orthodox than Goethe's nihilistic spirit ("Ich bin der Geist, der stets verneint"), who is unable to erode Faust's exhilaration in pure romance. Both dramas have thrived in the 20th-c. theater, which is not intimidated by the Herculean roles, the disjunctive story-lines, and—in Goethe's case—the rhythm shifts and myriad rhymes.

Before the posthumous publication of Goethe's *Faust* Part II in 1832, many of the romantic poets of Europe tried to write d. p.—Tieck and Grabbe in Germany; Musset, Hugo, and Dumas in France; Wordsworth, Coleridge, Keats, Byron, Shelley in England, soon to be followed by Tennyson, Browning, Arnold, and Swinburne. The Eng. were particularly vulnerable to Shakepeare's misleadership, and many 19th-c. hacks loaded frail pentameters with unspeakable images. Unfortunately, competent poets produced dull verbiage,

then as now largely relegated to the closet, although Byron, Browning, and Tennyson did show a certain flair for d. p. and were sporadically staged. With the dominance of prose on the 19th-c. stage, the very sound of verse triggered the expectation of a lofty subject and, less automatically, a tragic ending. This association between d. p. and tragedy carries over to the present.

At the turn of the 20th c., two popular versifiers, one on each side of the Eng. Channel, attracted enthusiastic audiences to their respective theaters—Edmond Rostand in France and Stephen Phillips in England. In spite of the rapid decline of Phillips' popularity, the Am. Maxwell Anderson later lingered on the same blank-verse path, and after World War II Christopher Fry in England sowed it with a richer lexicon. Even such skillful Jacobean pastiche as Djuna Barnes' *Antiphon* or Lawrence Durrell's *Irish Faustus* is anachronistic in the 20th c. Analogous to these speleologists of blank verse are Fr. archaeologists of the alexandrine, notably Cocteau, despite his celebrated distinction between poetry in the theater and poetry of the theater (the latter in prose).

Prose gradually displaced d. p. on the 18th-c. stage, but dramatic prose is beyond the scope of this survey, which is limited to the d. p. of Western Europe. Passing mention must nevertheless be made of the importance of d. p. in the very different lits. of Russia and Poland. Poland in particular, the Nowhere of Jarry's *Ubu roi*, declared adherence to the nationalist aspirations of Mickiewicz's *Forefather's Eve* (1832) and Slovacki's *Kordian* (1834). The new century, still sustaining hope for a Polish nation, was ushered in with Wyspianski's *The Wedding* (1901).

Although Rus. drama begins with prose comedy in the 17th c., plays in syllabic verse soon followed. Theater histories celebrate Sumarokov as the first major Rus. playwright, influenced alike by Voltaire and Shakespeare. In the 18th c., Catherine the Great tried her hand at various genres of d. p. in imitation of the Fr., and the neoclassical influence lingered into the 19th c., particularly in comedy, of which the outstanding example is *Woe from Wit* by Griboedov (1824). A year later Russia's greatest romantic poet, Aleksandr Pushkin, completed his neo-Shakespearean history play *Boris Godunov*, followed by the so-called "little tragedies." Verse satire and Shakespearean tragedy continued into the 20th c., as well as short symbolist d. p. by Tsvetaeva and Gumilyov. Although the adjective "poetic" often precedes the name of Chekhov, his plays are confined to prose, as are those of the antirealists Evreinov and Majakovsij, and even the great poet Pasternak.

The Norwegian Ibsen may serve as exemplar of the late 19th-c. shift from historical d. p. to modern realism. After writing his Faustian *Brand* (1866) and *Peer Gynt* (1867) in several forms of rhyming verse (and, like *Goethe's Faust*, these plays were not conceived for the theater), Ibsen shifted to prose for his comparably cosmic *Emperor and the Galilean* (1873), which was intended for the theater. Thereafter Ibsen never looked back to d. p. By the turn of the 20th c., realistic prose dominated the stage throughout Europe and the Americas, and yet reactions against realism followed hard upon its inauguration—mainly in the prose of such dramatists as Villiers de l'isle Adam and Maeterlinck, but also in verse plays. In Austria the young Hugo von Hofmannsthal leaned lightly on Shakespeare as he dabbled in magic, fantasy, and lyrical longing; later his firmer verse would mold libretti for the music of Richard Strauss. Not dissimilar to the earlier work of Hofmannsthal were the early plays of W. B. Yeats, hovering in Irish mist and myth; later his taut lines in freer verse rhythms, sometimes interspersed with prose, would mold *Four Plays for Dancers* on the model of the Japanese Ghost Nō (q.v.).

At the end of the 19th c., Fr. Paul Claudel began a half-century of dramas that flouted Fr. traditional d. p.; his plots sprawled, his characters spanned countries and centuries, and his long verse line heeded neither tonic accent nor syllable count but took its inspiration from the Bible. Called *verset* (q.v.) rather than *vers* in Fr., this flowing line is sometimes anglicized as "versicle"—particularly by critics who deny that verse can be free. As monolithic in their faith as Sp. Ren. dramas, Claudel's plays only slowly reached the stage, but they pointed the way for a few Fr. poets who later ventured into theater—Henri Pichette, Jules Supervielle, and, most recently, Novarina. The Francophone poet of Martinique, Aimé Césaire, mixed prose and verse in his *Tragedy of King Christophe* as in his adaptation of Shakespeare's *Tempest*; like Claudel, Césaire writes long lines that are rhythmed by rhetorical parallelisms. Although Jacques Vauthier resembles Césaire in his attraction to Shakespearean and Jacobean imagery, the Frenchman writes mainly in prose, but his aptly titled *Sang* swells in Claudelian versicles for a tragedy derived from the Jacobean *Revengers Tragedy*.

Ger. writers are as aware as Eng. of Shakespeare's shadow over d. p. Gerhart Hauptmann versifies several plays based on Gr. tragedy or Shakespearean drama. In sharp contrast, blank-verse passages serve Bertolt Brecht mainly as parody in *St. Joan of the Stockyards* and *The Resistible Rise of Arturo Ui*. Brecht wrote only one play entirely in verse—the opera libretto for *Mahagonny*. Into most of his plays, however, Brecht injects lyrics (called "songs" in Ger.) to teach delightfully. His characters often achieve a degree of self-awareness in their songs, from which they are screened in their prose dialogue, and Brecht means his audience to share that awareness. Brecht's "cool" drama was in part a reaction against the emotions of expressionism, and indeed the expressionist Walter Hasenclever often inserts blank-verse scenes of suffering into his basic prose plays. In postwar East Germany several playwrights reverted to blank verse to disengage themselves from Socialist Realism—Volker Braun, Peter Hacks, Harmut Lange, Stefan Schütz.

More consistent and original is the German Heiner Müller, most of whose plays mix prose and verse: "It is really a problem of the impact of history—even of the tempo of historical devel. When there is stagnation, you have prose. When the process has a more violent rhythm, you have verse." Also in Germany, Rolf Hochhuth seeks emotional distance in his documentary dramas by breaking the dialogue into irregular verse lines, with emphasis falling at the end of the line. Peter Weiss introduced Knittelvers for parodic effect, notably in his *Marat/Sade*, but in other plays (*The Investigation*, *Hölderlin*) Weiss breaks speeches into irregular verse lines determined by syntax, possibly to achieve a Brechtian estrangement.

The most consistent contemporary writer of Ger. d. p. is the Austrian Thomas Bernhard. His short unpunctuated lines clarify his syntax, but he spurns such sonic enhancements as rhyme, assonance, alliteration. In both the dialogue and long monologues of Bernhard's dramas, merciless repetition drenches the stage in a fetid atmosphere that warns the audience away from realism. In spite of their nominally contemporary settings, Bernhard's d. p. probes into the unlocalized cruelty of human relationships. Simple in plot but complex in character, these plays thrive on incisive stage images that are etched the more sharply for the mordant verse lines.

It is, however, the Eng. lang., forever haunted by Shakespeare's ghost, that has hosted most 20th-c. efforts at d. p. Each generation seems to sound its own clarion call for a revival of poetic drama: at the turn of the c., Phillips and Yeats; after World War I, James Elroy Flecker, Gordon Bottomley, Lascelles Abercrombie, Laurence Binyon, John Drinkwater, John Masefield, John Middleton Murry, William Archer, T. Sturge Moore, and dozens of authors who managed a single verse play—almost inevitably in blank verse, with subjects wrenched from myth, history, or what passed for peasant life. Masefield conducted a personal crusade for verse drama, not only hazarding other meters than blank verse, but also building a theater for d. p. at his home in Boars Head, Oxford. At that time too appeared the first of T. S. Eliot's essays on d. p.—"Rhet. and Poetic Drama" (1919), "Euripides and Professor Murray" (1920), and "A Dialogue on D. P." (1928). Also in 1928 began the parade of poetic pilgrims to Canterbury—notably Eliot with his *Murder in the Cathedral* (1935). Eliot's verse plays with contemporary settings did not, however, appear till a generation later, and by that time Auden and Isherwood had turned verse to parody in *The Dog Beneath the Skin* (1936); they enfolded passages of various meters into the basic prose of *The Ascent of F6* (1936) and *On the Frontier* (1938). Stephen

DRAMATIC POETRY

Spender resurrected blank verse for *The Trial of a Judge* (1938), and Louis MacNeice hazarded different meters for his radio plays.

After World War II came another Eng. movement toward d. p.—emanating from the commitment of Eliot. In contrast to Yeats, who desired a small, elite audience, Eliot accommodated himself to the commercial theater of his time, and he invented a verse line commensurate with what he took to be the speech of his time. Earlier (1926) he had verbalized jazz rhythms in the Sweeney fragments he never wielded into a whole, but for *Family Reunion* (1939) he conceived a "rhythm close to contemporary speech . . . a line of varying length and varying number of syllables, with a caesura and three stresses." Although Eliot did not know it at the time, *Family Reunion* was to mold the pattern for his subsequent three contemporary verse plays: 3-stress line, underground Gr. plot, foreground drawing-room drama, and character's discovery of religious vocation. It is in the latter two aspects that Eliot influenced Christopher Fry, Anne Ridler, Norman Nicholson, and Ronald Duncan, who were welcomed either at the Canterbury Festival or the Mercury Theatre of London. Free of these pretensions is *Under Milk Wood*, a prose-verse blend by Dylan Thomas, not quite completed at the time of his death in 1953; commissioned for radio, it has played joyously on stage and screen. By the date of Eliot's last, least lyrical play, *The Elder Statesman* (1958), angry prose had invaded the London stage, spurring the critic Kenneth Tynan to write: "Messrs. Eliot and Fry suggest nothing so much as a pair of energetic swimming instructors giving lessons in an empty pool."

Even on the island of London theater, the pool was not quite so dry as Tynan claimed. Not only did Eliot and Fry attract West End audiences to their d. p. (an attraction that has afterwards flared up sporadically), but Anne Ridler embarked on a new career as librettist: "Libretto-writing, as W. H. Auden said, gives the poet his one chance nowadays of using the high style." Ronald Duncan maintained such a "high style" in his several verse modes—satiric couplets, free rhymes, intricate Italianate stanzas. His *Don Juan* and *Death of Satan* played at the Royal Court Theatre in the same year as *Look Back in Anger*—1956—and that was his misfortune; Duncan's modernized myths paled against the heat of Osborn's vitriolic prose. In Duncan's own bitter opinion: "the convention of Shaftesbury Avenue duchesses fiddling with flower vases was replaced by Jimmy Porters picking their noses in public." Less graphically, Christopher Fry asked: "Do you think that when speech in the theatre gets closer to speech in the street we necessarily get closer to the nature of man?"

Of those playwrights who implied an affirmative answer, several nevertheless revived verse for satiric thrusts. Adrian Mitchell came to theater through his witty trs. of Peter Weiss' Knittelvers in Peter Brook's production of *Marat/Sade*. This launched Mitchell into the deft songs by which he structures—if that is the word—his own wayward plays, such as *Tyger* and *Mind Your Head*. Festive in nature, Michell's d. p. loses ebullience on the printed page, and more recently he has adapted himself to television, where associational fantasy dilutes his earlier satiric bite. More faithful to the theater is David Edgar, who deromanticizes *Romeo and Juliet* into prose, but who twirls couplets in his Watergate parody, *Dick Deterr'd* (1974), which shadows Shakespeare's *Richard III*. Edgar experiments seriously with d. p. in his ambitious *O Fair Jerusalem* (1975), a play within a play. The characters of the frame play, set in 1948, speak in undistinguished modern prose, but those (the same actors) in the inner drama, set in 1348, speak mainly in verse of varying meters. Caryl Churchill, another playwright who is, like Edgar, mainly a social realist, has also turned to verse for her less-than-serious *Serious Money* (1987), a parody of the London Stock Exchange. Where Edgar's *Dick* is a comic-book villain, however, Churchill's (pointedly named) Scilla wavers uncertainly between caricature and character. A similar uncertainty of tone afflicts Steven Berkoff's several verse plays, set in modern London, in which obscenities and misquotations sprinkle flaccid pentameters. More purposeful is the trenchant, sometimes savage antiwar satire in Charles Wood's *H* and *Veterans*. With Pirandellian and filmic dissolves of character into role, Wood parodies the mindless posturing, outworn rhet., and simple greed that propel armies to destroy and be destroyed. His verse lines are short and unmetrical; yet cliché, repetition, wrenched syntax, and subtle rhyme endow the dialogue with a military precision which paradoxically undermines war. On the contemp. London stage the most popular mode of d. p. is parody, but the serious and honorable exception is John Arden, who blends from ten to fifty percent verse into his mainly prose plays. Moreover, he deploys verse like a composer of opera for moments of high dramatic tension. Partial to the ballad, Arden also writes long stretches of dialogue in a kind of sprung rhythm, rhyming freely.

In the wide reaches of the British Commonwealth, dramatic poets have plumbed serious d. p. The heroic verse of the Australian poet Douglas Stewart contrasts with the understated colloquial rambles of his countryman Ray Mathew. During the 1940s, Stewart centered several dramas on the failed yet noble dreams of his protagonists, and a decade later Mathew quietly celebrated the humilities of provincial Australian life. In rhythm-rich Africa several playwrights have mined d. p. in the Eng. lang. Recently awarded a Nobel Prize, Wole Soyinka couches most of his dramas in densely imaged prose, but *A Dance of the Forests* (1960) shifts to verse for tense scenes between the gods. Verse is also the medium for Soyinka's adaptation of *The Bacchae* (1973), sounding out in a multi-rhythmed verbal percussion that does honor to Euripides. Soyinka's fellow Nigerian John Pepper Clark sets his (shorter) plays in the village life of his country, rendering native dialogue in short, colloquial, repetitive verse lines. Outside Africa but linked to its culture is the versatile d. p. of the Trinidadian Derek Walcott. From *The Sea at Dauphin*, a Synge-like tragedy of men who live by the sea, to *Pantomime*, a drama that plays pointedly with race relations, and encompassing the metaphysical *Dream on Monkey Mountain*, the adapted *Joker of Seville*, and the satiric *Remembrance*, Walcott tunes his loose and supple verse line to the particular dramatic situation. Walcott's *Joker of Seville* is only one of many accomplished verse trs. of the classics by which today's Anglophone theater has been enriched—Tony Harrison's *Oresteia* and *Mysteries*, Ted Hughes' *Seneca-Oedipus*, Robert David MacDonald's Molière, Adrian Mitchell's Calderón, and a lonely Am. poet—Richard Wilbur's Molière and Racine.

Several Am. poets dabbled in a verse play or two—e e cummings, Richard Eberhart, Archibald MacLeish, Wallace Stevens, William Carlos Williams. Alone among the poets MacLeish contrived a Broadway success in Bible-based *JB*. In view of the subsequent counter-cultural impact of the Becks' Living Theater, it is rarely recalled that they started humbly as a Poets' Theater, producing several plays of William Carlos Williams. The Living also produced the aleatory plays of Jackson MacLow, where compulsive repetition structures near-abstractions. It may be that this divorce from lexical language, which gives extraordinary freedom to the director, was one of the causes of a revival of interest in Gertrude Stein's undramatic short dramas dating from the 1920s and 1930s. In contrast, the decidedly down-to-earth Beat Poets of the 1950s, who read their poems aloud to jazz, were impervious to the interactive dialogue of drama; the single exception is Michael McClure, whose *Beard* hammers at free-verse patterns. More durable are Robert Lowell's verse dramatizations of stories by Hawthorne and Melville into a trilogy that criticizes the United States as *Old Glory*. Kenneth Koch's short-lined plays are more playful demystifications of Am. history.

A very few contemporary Am. dramatists have dipped into d. p. Arthur Miller wrote his first version of *The Crucible* in verse, and Tennessee Williams, who published a volume of poetry, resorted to free-verse lines in his Lorca-like *Purification*, although Lorca himself adhered to prose after his first play. Edward Albee's *Counting the Ways* is a slight verse piece that departs from a sonnet by Christina Rossetti, but David Mamet's *Reunion* gains poignancy through his short verse lines—a rhythm he also introduces into parts of his *Water Engine*. James Merrill has also written d. p.

By the late 20th c., generic divisions have been undermined, and two major poet-playwrights have been instrumental in such subversion—Bertolt Brecht and Samuel Beckett. Although they have published highly dramatic lyrics, their plays are largely prose. Nevertheless, Brecht's songs heighten memorable moments of his drama; passages of Beckett's plays sound like verse, the leaves stanzas of *Godot*, for example; two Beckett plays even break into lines of formal verse—*Come and Go* and *Rockaby*. The rhythms of *Play* are scored as for music, and the three voice-strands of *That Time* are segmented into free-verse stanzas. The adjective "poetic" is affixed more often to Beckett than to any other playwright of the second half-century, but Brecht and Beckett both were aware of the extra-verbal means of achieving highly dramatic moments, and both verbal masters therefore summoned music and lighting to enhance their polyvalent words. Born into a technological era, later playwrights nevertheless have learned from the lyrical intimacies of Beckett as from the choral dialectics of Brecht to enrich their own prose plays—prose by the arbitrary criteria I imposed at the outset of this survey.

I conclude on a dramatic poet who is poised between accomplishment and promise—the black Am. woman Ntozake Shange. Her *for colored girls who have considered suicide / when the rainbow is enuf* began as individual lyrics, but in performance, she says, "I came to understand these twenty-odd poems as a single statement, a choreopoem" which was nurtured by the tragedies of black women. On stage, a slight pause punctuates Shange's syntactic verse-units; on the page, a slash separates the phrases. Popular both on stage and page, all Shange's work has forged a language and a rhythm of her own in this recent, resonant outpost of d. p.

See also BURLESQUE; CATHARSIS; CHORUS; CLOSET DRAMA; COMEDY; COMEDY OF HUMORS; COMEDIA DE CAPA Y ESPADA; DIALOGUE; FARCE; GENRE; HEROIC PLAY; INTERLUDE; LITURGICAL DRAMA; MIME; MONOLOGUE; MORALITY PLAY; PASSION PLAY; PATHOS; TRAGEDY; TRAGICOMEDY.

L. Abercrombie, "The Function of Poetry in the Drama," *Poetry Rev.* 1 (1912); S. G. Morley, *Studies in Sp. Dramatic Versification of the Siglo de Oro* (1918); T. S. Eliot, *The Sacred Wood* (1920), *Selected Essays* (1950), *Poetry and Drama* (1951); N. Díaz de Escovar and F. de P. Lasso de la Vega, *Historia del teatro español*, 2 v. (1924); W. B. Yeats, *Essays* (1924); H. C. Lancaster, *Hist. of Fr. Dramatic Lit. in the 17th C.*, 9 v. (1929–42); C. V. Deane, *Dramatic Theory and the Rhymed Heroic Play* (1931); J. S. Kennard, *It. Theatre*, 2 v. (1932); H. Granville-Barker, *On Poetry in Drama* (1937); F. W. Ness, *The Use of Rhyme in Shakespeare's Plays* (1941); M. E. Prior, *The Lang. of Tragedy* (1947); B. Brecht, *Kleines Organon für das Theater* (1948); J. L. Barrault, *Reflections on the Theatre* (1951); F. Fergusson, *Idea of a Theater* (1953); G. F. Else, *Aristotle's* Poetics: *The Argument (1957)*; S. Atkins, Goethe's *Faust (1958)*; R. Lattimore, Poetry of Gr. Tragedy *(1958)*; D. Donoghue, The Third Voice: Mod. British and Am. Verse Drama *(1959)*; R. Peacock, The Poet in

DREAM VISION

the Theatre, *rev. ed. (1960); M. Bieber,* Hist. of the Gr. and Roman Theater, *2d ed. (1961); C. Fry, "Talking of Henry,"* 20th C. *169 (1961); W. H. Auden, "Notes on Music and Opera,"* The Dyer's Hand *(1962); C. H. Smith,* T. S. Eliot's Dramatic Theory and Practice *(1963); M. C. Bradbrook,* Eng. Dramatic Form: A Hist. of its Devel. *(1965); Dale; J. Scherer,* La Dramaturgie classique en France *(1968); D. Sipe,* Shakespeare's Metrics *(1968); J. Cocteau, "Préface de 1922,"* Les Mariés de la Tour Eiffel *(1969); R. Williams,* Drama from Ibsen to Genet *(1971); R. Duncan, Preface to* Collected Plays *(1971); K. J. Worth,* Revolutions in Mod. Eng. Drama *(1972); H. H. A. Gowda,* D. P. from Med. to Mod. Times *(1972); A. Nicoll,* A Hist. of Eng. Drama, 1660–1900, *6 v. (1952–59),* Eng. Drama 1900–1930 *(1973); K. Tynan, "Prose and the Playwright,"* A View of the Eng. Stage *(1975); A. P. Hinchliffe,* Mod. Verse Drama *(1977); F. H. Sandbach,* The Comic Theatre of Greece and Rome *(1977); H. Müller, "Heinar Müller on Verse,"* New Ger. Critique Supplement *(1979); J. Baxter,* Shakespeare's Poetic Styles *(1980); D. Breuer,* Deutsche Metrik und Versgeschichte *(1981); C. Freer,* The Poetics of Jacobean Drama *(1981); Trypanis, esp. chs. 3,4,6,9—Greek; G. R. Hibbard,* The Making of Shakespeare's D. P. *(1981); O. Mandel, "Poetry and Excessive Poetry in the Theatre,"* CentR *26 (1982); T. Rosenmeyer,* The Art of Aeschylus *(1982); A. Brown,* A New Companion to Gr. Tragedy *(1983); G. Hoffmann, "Das moderne amerikanische Versdrama,"* Das amerikanische Drama, *ed. G. Hoffmann (1984); M. Carlson,* Theories of the Theatre *(1984);* CHCL, *v. 1, chs. 10–12; C. W. Meister,* Dramatic Crit.: A Hist. *(1985); C. J. Herington,* Poetry into Drama *(1985); K. Pickering,* Drama in the Cathedral *(1985); Terras; R. M. Harriott,* Aristophanes: Poet and Dramatist *(1986); M. Esslin,* The Field of Drama *(1987); M. Stevens,* Four ME Mystery Cycles *(1987), ch. 2—on the Wakefield Master; H. Blau,* The Eye of Prey *(1987); G. T. Wright,* Shakespeare's Metrical Art *(1988); A. W. Pickard-Cambridge,* The Dramatic Festivals of Athens, *2d. ed. rev. and corr. (1989).*
R.C.

DRÁPA. A kind of ON skaldic poem, distinguished from a *flokkr* or loose group of stanzas by features creating repetition and dividing the poem into formal sections. The principal of these features is the *stef,* a refrain comprising a fixed phrase inside a stanza and recurring at regular intervals (e.g. every fifth stanza). An elaborate d. might have more than one *stef.* The *stef* marked off sections of the poem, called *stefjumél;* the sections preceding and following the first and last *stef* were felt to be different in nature, although a term has been retained only for the closing section (*slæmr*). Extant ds. range in length from ca. 20 to 100 stanzas, and there is some evidence that poets tended toward a total number of stanzas divisible by ten.

Ds. are known to have been composed throughout the history of ON poetry (q.v.). Virtually all of the earlier ds. are in the meter *dróttkvætt* (q.v.), and the later ds. are mainly in the meter *hrynhent* (q.v.), but other meters were also used. The earlier ds. tended to be occasional, either shield poems or royal encomia (the distinction is not easy to maintain). Christian topics were soon taken up, and the *hrynhent* ds. of the 13th and 14th cs. in particular treat such figures from the past as Icelandic bishops and European saints.—*The Skalds,* ed. and tr. L. M. Hollander (1945); R. Frank, *ON Court Poetry* (1978).
J.L.

DREAM VISION. A literary work which presents a retrospective account of dream(s) experienced by a first-person narrator who also claims to be the poet. The d. v. was popular from the 12th through the early 16th c. in two primary types: the secular love vision, of which the great exemplar is *Le Roman de la rose,* and the religious/philosophical vision, descended either from the biblical visions of Ezekiel, St. Paul, and St. John, or from the philosophical trad. of Cicero, Boethius, and Macrobius. Most d. vs. are allegorical (see ALLEGORY) and multivalent; they revolve around dream encounters in symbolic landscapes with authoritative figures who impart some revelation or doctrine. The frames of most d. vs. indicate the season (often May), the time of day (morning), the location (garden), the environment (singing birds), and the solitude and the psychological state of the dreamer. Typically, the dreamer is troubled by some need or lack that the dream fulfills. He seems not to be in control of his life, and feels socially or intellectually inferior. D. vs. tend to hold in tension two voices that gradually coalesce: that of the naive dreamer, immersed in the vision, and that of the wiser poet who has already learned from the dream and now writes about it. This double perspective, of past and present, of involvement and distance, helps to make the d. v. a particularly self-conscious and reflexive form which calls attention to its status as imaginative fiction and expresses these poets' relatively new awareness of themselves as poets. The more philosophical d. vs. explore fundamental epistemological issues such as the relation between natural and divine knowledge, the relation of matter and spirit, and the power of human reason.

Two seminal works for the hist. of the form are Macrobius' 5th-c. commentary on the dream of Scipio that concludes Cicero's *De re publica,* and the most influential amorous d. v. of the Middle Ages, the 13th-c *Roman de la rose.* The form was first popular in France, both in philosophical poems like Alain de Lille's *De planctu naturae* and in courtly poetry like that of Guillaume de Machaut and Jean Froissart; but it reached its apogee in 14th–15th c. England, above all with Chaucer's *House of Fame, Book of the Duchess, Parlement of Foules,* and the Prologue to the *Legend of Good Women.* In addition there are many alliterative dream poems, esp. *Pearl* and Langland's *Piers Plow-*

man—the best Eng. example in the genre—but also *Winner and Waster, The Parliament of Three Ages,* and *Mum and the Sothsegger.* The d. v. continued to be popular with 15th- and 16th-c. Eng. writers like John Lydgate, John Clanvowe, and John Skelton, and with Scottish poets like Robert Henryson, William Dunbar, Gavin Douglas, and the author of the *Kingis Quair.* Later analogues of the form include, in prose, Bunyan's *Pilgrim's Progress* and Joyce's *Finnegan's Wake* and, in verse, Keats's *Fall of Hyperion.*—Lewis; H. R. Jauss, *La Génèse de la poésie allégorique française au moyen âge* (1962); C. Hieatt, *The Realism of D. Vs.* (1967); E. Kirk, *The D. Thought of* Piers Plowman (1972); J. Winny, *Chaucer's D. Poems* (1973); A. C. Spearing, *Med. D. Poetry* (1976); *Chaucer's D. Poetry: Sources and Analogues,* ed B. A. Windeatt (1982); K. L. Lynch, *The High Med. D. V.* (1988); J. S. Russell, *The Eng. D. V.* (1988); J. Davidoff, *Beginning Well: Framing Fictions in Late ME Poetry* (1988). P.R.S.

DRÓTTKVÆTT (short for *dróttkvæor háttr,* the meter used by the *drótt,* the retainers of the king). The staple meter of skaldic poetry, the ON and Icelandic trad. which produced, from the 9th through the 14th c., the most elaborate and intricate verseforms of the Middle Ages. Each stanza consists of eight lines of six syllables, three of which are accented and three unaccented, with each line regularly ending in a trochee. Every two lines are bound together by alliteration, which must fall on the first stressed syllable of the second line, with two alliterations in the first line as well. This measure is also characterized by internal rhyme, full rhyme in the even lines, and half rhyme (assonance) in the odd lines. Besides the extravagant use of kennings (q.v.) and other specific poetic vocabulary, word-arrangement and sentence structure are highly intricate: "Brunnu beggja kinna / björt ljos a mik drosar."

The d. measure in all its main features is already found in the stanzas of *Ragnarsdrápa* by Bragi the Old (fl. first half of the 9th c.), who may have devised the form. A related ON meter, *hrynhent* (q.v.), has eight syllables per line rather than six. D. is the standard meter in the earlier forms of the ON poems called *drapa* (q.v.); later forms use *hrynhent.* The d. meter has survived in Icelandic poetry down to the present day. See OLD NORSE POETRY; SKALD.—*The Skalds,* tr. and ed. L. M. Hollander (1945); R. Frank, *ON Court Poetry: The D. Stanza* (1978). J.L.

DUMY. See UKRAINIAN POETRY.

DUPLE METERS. See BINARY AND TERNARY.

DURATION. One of the three intonational characteristics of spoken sound, the other two being stress (see ACCENT) and pitch (q.v.). In poetry, d. concerns the timing of syllables, words, and lines, such timing being either *actual* or *conventional*—much more so the latter than the former. *Actual* d. falls under the category of performance (q.v.). Adjustment of the d. of syllables in utterance, i.e. in the reading of the line, is a matter of delivery speed or tempo: this is not a part of the poem itself, i.e. of meter, but of individual choice and style in delivery. Some readers will read more slowly, deliberately, or expressively than others. Still, some linguistic features of the line obviously do affect tempo, the chief among these being morphology. It has long been known to poets that large numbers of monosyllables slow down delivery of the line, while polysyllables, by contrast, speed it up: Pope makes much use of monosyllables in his mimetic lines in the *Essay on Crit.*, particularly: "Though ten low words oft creep in one dull line" (2.347)—to which compare the speed of "A needless Alexandrine ends the song"—and the contrast is pointed up starkly in Shakespeare's "The multitudinous seas incarnardine, / Making the green one red" (*Macbeth* 2.2.59–60). To some degree this is simply a function of the fact that heavily monosyllabic lines contain more junctures (pauses). Due to the limitations of the human vocal apparatus, the maximum delivery rate is about 8 syllables per second (Lehiste). Langs. control d. change for semantic and signaling purposes: one of the most important is final lengthening before terminal juncture. Syllables may be lengthened to signal the end of a syntagm in speech or line in poetry: this phenomenon is well attested in IE and Gr.

But more important than actual ds. in verse are conventional ones, and by far the most important of these is the opposition of *long* and *short*, known as quantity (q.v.). This much-disputed contrast holds perhaps the central position in the history of Western prosody from archaic Gr. down to the 19th c. At least some ancient grammarians held that certain *vowels* were long, others short; the ancient metrists (*metrici*) held that the former were twice the length of the latter; they then devised a set of rules (including other criteria) for classifying *syllables* as "long" vs. "short," and on this basis constructed a quantitative prosody (see CLASSICAL PROSODY). The ancient musical theorists (*rhythmici*), however, held that there were more distinctions than 2:1 and that some syllables were indeterminate. But over time, actual vowel (or even syllable) length quickly lost ground to conventional classification. Length was indeed phonemic in Cl. Gr., but in the subsequent evolution of the Cl. langs., it was lost, so that auditors no longer heard a long-short distinction at all. Nevertheless, the notion that syllables could be grouped into "long" vs. "short" persisted among grammarians and prosodists literally for millennia. Modern linguists distinguish between "tense" and "lax" vowels (so Jakobson-Halle [1962], see now Jakobson, 1.550 ff.; and Chomsky-Halle [1968], 68–69, 324–26).

The time-value of one short syllable was called

a "mora" by some of the ancient grammarians, and has been used by modern prosodists from time to time; for discussion of varieties of Temporal theories of verse-structure, see METER. The temporality or d. of syllables is a phenomenon of interest to performance theory in regard to tempo and the semantic cues tempo changes can deliver; it is of interest to metrical theory in that some verse-systems use length, as others do stress or pitch, as the marker of the meter—but only when that intonational feature is phonemic. See now ACCENT; BINARY AND TERNARY; FOOT; MEASURE; METER; QUANTITY.—P. Barkas, *Critique of Mod. Eng. Pros.* (1934); I. Lehiste, *Suprasegmentals* (1970), ch. 2, "The Many Linguistic Functions of D.," *New Directions in Linguistics and Semiotics*, ed. J. E. Copeland (1984); W. S. Allen *Accent and Rhythm* (1973), exp. ch. 4; Brogan; West; R. P. Newton, *Vowel Undersong* (1981). T.V.F.B.

DUTCH POETRY. (Belgian poetry in Dutch—i.e. Flemish—from the beginning until 1585 is treated concurrently with D. p. below; for an account of Flemish poetry from 1585 to the present, see BELGIAN POETRY, *In Dutch.*)

The earliest monuments of D. p. are the works of Hendrik van Veldeke, a Fleming who lived during the latter part of the 12th c. The absence of any older vernacular lit. may be attributed to the dominance of Lat. in both courtly and ecclesiastical circles, a dominance which persistently complicated the lit. hist. of the Low Countries. Van Veldeke, whose work has been preserved only in a MHG recension, wrote a versified life of St. Servatius and a courtly romance epic, *Eneide*, which shows the influence of Fr. courtly lit. The first great devel. of D. p. occurred in the 13th c., reaching a climax in the religious verse of the Flemish beguine and mystic Hadewych (fl. 1240). A creation of a very different sort is the beast-epic *Van den Vos Reinaerde* (Reynard the Fox), one of the finest of the genre, which may also be assigned to the early 13th c. It is an irreverent treatment of society and of epic conventions, written with wit and charm, from a decidedly nonaristocratic point of view.

These works typify the three main currents of medieval D. p.—the courtly, the religious, and the bourgeois—related at once to different classes of society and to different ways of interpreting experience. All three types of vision were to be of continuing importance in the intellectual and artistic history of the Netherlands. They were ultimately to give rise to a significant dichotomy which shaped that history, for D. p., in its later manifestations, was to tend toward extremes both of bourgeois practicality and conformity and of individualistic aestheticism and revolt. The religious impulse itself was to find a double expression—in didacticism and in unfettered mysticism.

Courtly, religious, and bourgeois elements were all combined in the work of another Fleming,

Jacob van Maerlant (ca. 1235–ca. 1288), who has been called "the father of D. p.," a title he merits for productivity if for no other reason. In his early period he wrote courtly romances on the standard subjects of the aristocratic trad.—the quest for the Grail, the siege of Troy, and the legendary adventures of Alexander. Later, in his *Rijmbibel*, he treated religious themes, and he also wrote compendious works of erudition. His importance is more historical than artistic.

After the 14th c., a period of relatively little poetic activity in the Low Countries, a new poetic period began, manifesting itself first in the *rederijkerskamers* ("Chambers of Rhetoric"—see REDERIJKERS), bourgeois poetic associations organized in Flanders and, later, in Holland. The *rederijkers* were interested primarily in the theater, and they carried the trads. of the morality play into the Ren. *Elckerlyc* (ca. 1490), which is the source of the Eng. *Everyman*, is the most notable product of their art. The *rederijkers* also interested themselves in problems of lang. and metrics, and though it is easy to be amused by their pedantry and their obsession with the technical rules of versification, one should not underestimate their role in laying a foundation for the great literary works of the 17th c.

The influence of the It. Ren. entered D. p. in the early 16th c. in the work of the Flemings van der Noot and van Mander and the Hollanders van Hout and Coornhert. A kind of fusion of *rederijker* trad. and Ren. influence is evident in the poetry of the later *rederijkers* Visscher and Spiegel, both residents of Amsterdam, which began to assume cultural dominance after the fall of Antwerp in 1585. The 17th c., the greatest period in D. lit., was characterized by an emphasis on drama and the lyric, and in both these modes one finds a typical mixture of native trad. with themes and techniques borrowed from the It. and Fr. Ren. Pieter Corneliszoon Hooft (1581–1647) was the founder of the poetic drama in Holland. Though he was a staunch Calvinist, his imagination was fired by the southern Ren., which he had experienced on a youthful trip to Italy. His plays, though written in the rhymed alexandrines of his predecessors, follow the standard Ren. models. *Granida* is a pastoral drama in the manner of Guarini and Tasso, *Gerard van Velsen* is a Senecan tragedy, and *Warenar* is a comedy based on the *Aulularia* of Plautus.

Hooft's brilliant younger contemporary Gerbrand Adriaenszoon Bredero (1585–1618) worked more closely with the native trad. and was inspired primarily by his instinctive realism and his observant eye. *De Spaansche Brabander* (The Spanish Brabanter) is an excellent and robust comedy, but Bredero's distinctive art reaches its peak in his great *kluchten*, or farces, chief of which are *De Klucht van de Koe* (The Farce of the Cow) and *Der Klucht van de Molenaer* (The Farce of the Miller). In these works the alexandrine couplet is treated with freedom and virtuosity: the strictness of the form never seems to conflict with the raucous quality of the action or the detailed realism of the observation.

Joost van den Vondel (1587–1679), the greatest of D. poets, is also the greatest D. dramatist. Master of a poetic style which suggests Milton in its sublimity, Vondel was at the same time more clearly the heir of the writers of the morality plays than were Hooft and Bredero, for his dramatic art is always ultimately ethical and devotional in its impulse; these qualities are evident both in the early *Palamedes*, a political allegory attacking the extreme Calvinists, and in the towering works of his maturity. The dramas of his early and middle years are of many different types. *Gijsbrecht van Aemstel* is an historical and patriotic drama which, through its sympathetic presentation of Catholic ritual (a symptom of Vondel's approaching conversion to that faith), aroused the ire of the more intransigent Amsterdam Protestants. *Maagden* (The Maidens) is a dramatized saint's legend (and an example of the martyr-tragedy so fashionable during the baroque), and *De Leeuwendalers* is an idyllic pastoral drama.

Vondel's mature dramatic powers expressed themselves in a long series of remarkable biblical plays in which the spirit of the old moralities is given Sophoclean form and articulation. Particularly noteworthy are *Lucifer*, probably his masterpiece, *Adam in Ballingschap* (Adam in Banishment), and *Jephta*. The expansiveness and sublimity of *Lucifer*, both in conception and in imagery, contrast with the restrained inevitability of *Jephta*, and the contrast suggests the range of the poet's powers. Noteworthy too is his use of choruses, written in a variety of strikingly lyrical forms. The choruses of *Gijsbrecht van Aemstel* and *Lucifer* are among his finest achievements. Vondel's nondramatic production is immense—elegies, epithalamia, descriptive poetry—expressed in a wide variety of forms, many of them utilizing internal rhyme and a skillful exploitation of the diminutive endings in which the D. lang. abounds. One should also mention his political poems, his satires, his occasional pieces, and his epic, *Johannes de Boetgezandt* (John the Baptist).

Vondel's fellow-Amsterdammers, Hooft and Bredero, are also noted for their lyric poetry, in which we find an illuminating formal contrast. Hooft, the Italianate aristocrat, is a master of metrical variety. He is particularly fond of the contrapuntal interplay of rhyme and line length, as typified in the following passage:

Amaryl, de deken sacht
    Van de nacht,
Met sijn blaewe wolken buijen,
Maeckt de starren sluimerblint
    En de wint
Soeckt de maen in slaep te suijen.

Amaryl, the cover light

Of the night,
With its bluish clouds aheap,
Makes the stars all slumber-blind,
    And the wind
Seeks to lull the moon asleep.

Bredero, on the other hand, adheres more closely to the metrics of the folksong, and at his best he achieves the lyric simplicity of that mode.

In their imagery, these three great Amsterdammers show a common love for the pictorial and the detailed, a kind of imaginative observation of the visible world which allies them to the great D. painters and serves to define one of the continuing characteristics of D. poetic trad. If Vondel has a special kinship to a painter, it is to Rubens, in the lushly baroque magnificence of his conceptions. Bredero, in contrast, has more affinity with the realistic genre painters Jan Steen and Frans Hals.

The poetry of the D. Ren. was not confined to the Amsterdam circle. To the west, around the Hague, two other poets of note were active—Jacob Cats and Constantijn Huygens. Cats is the bourgeois poet *par excellence*. His didactic verse, devoted to the ethics of practicality, codified homely advice on subjects ranging from home economics to sexual intercourse. He became the most widely quoted of D. poets, not only at home but as far afield as Sweden, but his reputation has undergone an inevitable decline. His friend Huygens is a poet of a very different sort. An admirer of John Donne and of Rembrandt, he is one of the "metaphysical poets" of Holland, particularly in his devotional poetry. Also worthy of note are the religious poets Revius, Camphuyzen, Stalpaert, De Decker, and Dullaert, as well as Maria Tesselschade Visscher, much admired by the Amsterdam circle. The last great poet of the Golden Century was Jan Luyken, whose mystical religious poetry is among the finest written in Holland.

Toward the end of the 17th c., a decline in the quality of D. p. initiated a period of relative barrenness which was to last for two centuries. The lyric trad. of Vondel declined in the hands of his disciples, and the drama, already decadent in the sensationalistic work of Jan Vos, was given its deathblow by the derivative neoclassicism preached by the literary society *Nil Volentibus Arduum* (q.v.). D. p. of the 18th c. is characterized by a consistent but futile striving to escape the double bondage of an imported neoclassicism and a moribund native poetic diction. H. C. Poot and Rhijnvis Feith are the most considerable talents of this undistinguished age.

But the most significant poetic figure of Holland between 1700 and 1880 was Willem Bilderdijk (1756–1831), a perplexing figure. The paradox of his nature, at once rationalistic and romantic, Calvinistic and passionate, did not prevent him from being one of the most prolific of D. poets, though it did, probably, prevent him from fulfilling his potential. The deficiencies of his art become vices in much of the work of his disciple Da Costa and of Tollens, remembered perhaps as the most reputable poets of the most sterile age of D. p., the early 19th c. The triumph of bourgeois sensibility was complete in the Holland of the post-Napoleonic period. In such an atmosphere the romanticism which dominated European letters could find no roots, and the two D. poets of the period who may be classified as "romantics"— van Lennep and Beets—are only the palest reflections of their respective models, Scott and Byron.

As the 19th c. progressed, bolder spirits in D. artistic and intellectual circles grew indignant at the low state to which their country's poetry had sunk. With his friend, the critic Bakhuizen van den Brink, E. G. Potgieter founded *De Gids* (The Guide), a review dedicated to the revival of literary and intellectual vitality. As a poet, Potgieter was handicapped by a temperament which was too self-conscious and critical, a style which was too ponderously learned and allusive. But his example simplified the work of his successors.

The decade of the 1880s was one of the most significant in the hist. of Dutch lit., for at that time a group of gifted, iconoclastic, and energetic young poets set about reviving their country's poetry and placing it once more on the level of general European poetry. The important names of the *Beweging van Tachtig* (Movement of the Eighties—see TACHTIGERS) are Willem Kloos (1859–1938), Frederick van Eeden (1860–1932), Albert Verwey (1865–1937), and Herman Gorter (1864–1927). The first three, together with the critic and novelist Lodewijk van Deyssel (1864–1952) founded *De Nieuwe Gids* (The New Guide), a review which in its very name aimed at following newer paths than even the more progressive elements of the immediate past. But the work of the *tachtigers* was not entirely without forerunners: D. p. in the 1870s had received tremendous impetus from the publication of the sonnet sequence *Mathilde* by the precocious and gifted Jacques Perk (1859–81), who had reintroduced into D. p. that important form which had been neglected since the days of Hooft.

Kloos was important both as poet and critic, and his motto, "the most individual expression of the most individual emotion," summed up the aestheticism, realism, and individualism which were the artistic goals of his group. In retrospect, the achievement of Kloos and the other *tachtigers* seems more significant in ideological, cultural, and historical terms than in purely aesthetic. Some single poems, even single passages, retain their validity, and parts of their ambitious long poems—van Eeden's *Lied van Schijn en Wezen* (The Song of Appearance and Reality), for example, and Gorter's long Keatsian epic *Mei* (May)— have a freshness that does not fade. In any case, they cleared the ground and made it possible for D. p. to enter the modern age. A similar function was performed by poets in Dutch-speaking Belgium.

In their advocacy of individualism and realism, the group around *De Nieuwe Gids* had revived two of the constants of D. culture—respect for the individual and delight in accurate visual representation. Their doctrine of "art for art's sake," however, left out of account a third element of D. trad.—concern for the community, for the collective whole—which had given their nation's culture its distinctive bourgeois quality and which was expressing itself politically and economically in the achievements of late 19th-c. D. liberalism. It was on the issues of individualism and art for art's sake that the *Nieuwe Gids* group dissolved around 1890. Kloos, the intransigent individualist, remained loyal to his original ideals, but his influence steadily waned. Verwey, after a period of silence, moved toward a kind of poetry devoted more to the inner life than to external reality. Van Eeden, the most versatile member of the group, began the long spiritual pilgrimage that was to lead him through Utopian socialism to the Roman Catholic Church. Gorter, after *Mei*, devoted himself to the cause of the proletariat, expressing his communism in ultimately unsuccessful proletarian heroic verse. Eng. romanticism remained the strongest influence on the *Beweging van Tachtig*, but it was modified by Fr. and Ger. influences, notably that of Stefan George on Verwey, who was his close friend.

On the foundation laid by the *tachtigers*, the poets of the early 20th c. continued to build. The important poets between the generation of the 1880s and that of the first World War are J. H. Leopold (1865–1925), Henriette Roland Holst (1869–1952), and Pieter Corneliszoon Boutens (1870–1943). Leopold, considered by some to be Holland's greatest lyric poet since Vondel, was influenced to some degree by the *tachtigers*, but his finely organized lyrics show also the mark of his classical training. Boutens resembles Leopold in his classicism and in his introspection, but his Platonic inner vision is modified by a passionate sensitivity to external nature. He is a superb poet of nature, and none of his contemporaries has so well rendered the beauty of that flat, misty and infinitely various land.

D. p. of the 20th c. has taken an increasing share in international artistic and intellectual movements. Rilke, George, Verlaine, and Yeats were important models for such followers of Verwey as Martinus Nijhoff (who had connections with the artistic movement De Stijl) and Adriaan Roland Holst, and influences from China and India also made themselves felt. A vigorous expressionist movement, typified by the journal *Het Getij* and by the poems of Hendrik Marsman (1899–1940) dominated the poetry of the 1920s, but provoked a reaction in the more socially oriented work of the group orbiting around the periodical *Forum*, the most important members of which were the critic Menno ter Braak and the poet and novelist Simon Vestdijk (1898–1971), perhaps the most important writer of 20th-c. Holland.

Pre-eminent in D. lyric poetry of our century is Gerrit Achterberg (1905–62), who, had he written in a more widely known lang., would probably enjoy an international reputation. His achievement rests on a delicate tension among a number of elements: verbal experimentation versus a traditional sense of form, thematic limitation (virtually his sole theme is communication with a dead beloved) versus varied imagery, and colloquial vocabulary versus technical. He may be seen as a modern metaphysical poet. Other significant poets who emerged during World War II include the "moderate Surrealist" Ed. Hoornik and the Catholic Bertus Aafjes.

The 1950s witnessed a poetic revolution comparable in importance to that of the 1880s. The so-called *vijftigers* ("Fiftiers")—Remco Campert, Jan Elburg, Gerrit Kouwenaar, Lucebert (pseudonym of L. J. Swaanswijk), and Bert Schierbeek—distanced themselves from contemporary society and literary trad. alike, seeking above all immediacy, sincerity, and completeness of expression. Anti-formalist, their work is sometimes anti-intellectual. To some extent that work was anticipated by that of the short-lived Hans Lodeizen (1924–50) and the older Leo Vroman. Still, despite their experimentalism, the *vijftigers* did not abandon the concept of the poem as autonomous verbal artifact rather than as unmediated expression of the author's personality. As elsewhere in Western lit., the 1960s and 1970s saw an erosion of this concept of autonomy, as the work of many contemporaries makes clear. Among those contemporaries whose work may prove memorable may be mentioned J. Bernlef, H. van de Waarsenburg, S. Kuyper, and J. Hamelink.

D. p. of the 20th c. has, while ratifying its membership in the international world of art and thought, persistently adhered to those preoccupations which have been the historical heritage of the Dutch—the honest and vivid representation of observed reality and the untiring exploration of the delicate relationship between the individual and the community.

ANTHOLOGIES: *Zeven eeuwen*, ed. K. H. de Raaf and J. J. Griss, 4 v. (1932)—a crit. anthol.; *Coming After*, ed. A. J. Barnouw (1948); *Spiegel van de Nederlandse poëzie door alle eeuwen*, ed. V. E. van Vriesland, 3 v. (1953–55); *Een inleiding tot Vondel*, ed. A. Verwey (n.d.)—a generous selection of Vondel's works, with crit. commentary; *Dutch Interior:*

Postwar Poetry of the Netherlands and Flanders, ed. J. S. Holmes and W. J. Smith (1984).

HISTORY AND CRITICISM: E. Gosse, *Studies in the Lit. of Northern Europe* (1879); H. J. C. Grierson, *The First Half of the 17th C.* (1906)—good chs. on D. p. of that period, *Two D. Poets* (1936)—studies of Hooft and Boutens; G. Kalff, *Studiën over Nederlandsche dichters der 17de eeuw* (1915); H. Robbers, *De Nederl. litt. na 1880* (1922); A. J. Barnouw, *Vondel* (1925)—a biog. in Eng.; J. A. Russell, *D. P. and Eng.* (1939); F. Baur et al., *Geschiedenis van de letterkunde der Nederlanden*, 9 v. (1939–); G. Knuvelder, *Handboek tot de geschiedenis der Nederlandsen letterkunde*, 2d ed., 4 v. (1957); T. Weevers, *Poetry of the Netherlands in its European Context* (1960); P. Brachin, *La Littérature néerlandaise* (1963); J. Snapper, *Post-War D. Lit.: A Harp Full of Nails* (1972); *A Tourist Does Golgotha and Other Poems by Gerrit Achterberg*, ed. and tr. S. Wiersma (1972); R. P. Meijer, *Lit. of the Low Countries* (1978); J. A. van Dorsten, *Op het kritieke moment: zes essays over Nederlandse poëzie van de 17de eeuw* (1981).   F.J.W.

DYFALU. A poetic technique in Welsh poetry (q.v.) which reaches its highest excellence in the work of Dafydd ap Gwilym (14th c.), but which long remained current practice, and after its degeneration was ridiculed by Ellis Wynne in his *Visions of the Sleeping Bard* (1703). The term also means to guess and has affinities with the riddle and the kenning (qq.v.). D. at its best is an animated play of fancy, whereby the object on which the poet's mind dwells—it may be the stars, or mist, or a bird, a girl's yellow hair, or her white arms—is rapidly compared in a concatenation of metaphors of strong visual imagery with other objects in nature. The stars are the sparks of a conflagration lit by the saints, berries belonging to the frozen moon, the reflection of hail on the sun's bright floor. This onrush of metaphors is well suited by its exuberance to convey Dafydd ap Gwilym's exciting vision of the ever-renewed miracle of creation. Other poets, such as Dafydd Nanmor in the 15th c., employ the same device with fine effect, but later it became mechanical and stereotyped.—J. Vendryes, *La Poésie galloise des XIIe–XIIIe siècles dans ses rapports avec la langue* (1930); Parry, *History*, ch. 6; Jarman and Hughes; Stephens; R. Loomis, *Dafydd ap Gwilym: The Poems* (1982); R. Bromwich, *Aspects of the Poetry of Dafydd ap Gwilym* (1986).   D.M.L.

E

ECHO VERSE. A poem in which the final syllables of the lines are repeated, as by an echo, with the effect of making a reply to a question or a comment, often contrastive, punning, or ironic. A critic of 1665 calls it a "kind of Poem imitating the resounding Rocks, wherein the last Syllables of a sentence repeated, give answer to a question in the same, or divers, and sometime a contrary sence." The poem is sometimes set in couplets, the e. words alone forming the even lines. Examples: "Qu'est-ça du monde la chose la plus infame? Femme!" (Gracien du Pont, 1539); "Echo! What shall I do to my Nymph when I go to behold her? Hold her" (Barnabe Barnes, 1593). Post-Classical e. v. is found in Fr. as early as the 13th c. (Kastner) and was known to the troubadours, but was given its name only in the 16th c. by du Pont. The examples in the *Greek Anthology* (see ANTHOLOGY) inspired a vogue for e. poems in Fr., It., and Eng. verse of the 16th and 17th cs., which are also associated with the eclogue (q.v.) on account of stichomythia (q.v.). Well known examples are by Johannes Secundus, Du Bellay, Opitz, Herbert ("Heaven"), Swift ("A Gentle E. on Woman"), A. W. Schlegel ("Waldgespräch"), and Gerard Manley Hopkins ("The Leaden E. and the Golden E."). Found most often in pastoral (q.v.) poetry and drama, e. v. has unrequited love as its commonest subject, but has also been used for religious poetry, political satire, and society verse. In structure, e. v. would seem to be one (particularly effective) species of close rhyme or else rich rhyme (qq.v.). Hollander takes the return of the sound in e. as a trope for the mode of allusion itself (see ALLUSION; IMITATION).—Kastner 62–63; E. Colby, *The E.-Device in Lit.* (1920); J. Bolte, *Die E. in Volksglauben und Dichtung* (1935); A. Langen, *Dialogisches Spiel* (1966); J. Hollander, *The Figure of E.* (1981); T. Augarde, *Oxford Guide to Word Games* (1984). T.V.F.B.; L.P.

ECLOGUE. A short pastoral (q.v.) poem, usually quasi-dramatic, i.e. a dialogue (q.v.) or soliloquy. The setting, the *locus amoenus* ("pleasant place"), is Arcadian (later Edenic)—rural, idyllic, serene— and the highly finished verse smooth and melodious. But its ends are far from primitive or serene: a poet writes an e., says Puttenham, "not of purpose to counterfeit or represent the rusticall manner of loves and communication, but under the vaile of homely persons and in rude speeches to insinuate and glaunce at greater matters." Such matters might include praise of a person, beloved, worthy, or dead, or disquisition on the nature of poetry or the state of contemp. poetry, or criticism of political or religious corruption. Elevation of rustic life implied denigration of urban.

Derived from Gr. *eklegein* ("to choose"), "e." originally denoted a selection, i.e. a notable passage from a work or a choice poem, as in Statius (*Silvae*, Bks 3–4, Pref.). The term *ecloga* was applied by the grammarians to Horace's Epistles 2.1 and *Epodes*, but most importantly to Virgil's bucolic (q.v.) poems, this application possibly by Virgil himself. From this association "e." became a common designation in Carolingian and Ren. usage for a pastoral poem following the traditional technique derived from the idylls (q.v.) of Theocritus. Though there are precedents in both Cl. and Ren. lit. of city and piscatory es., most es. are pastorals. The term, however, signifies nothing more than form. The spelling *aeglogue* (or *eglog*), popularized by Dante, was based on a false etymology which derived the word from *aix* (goat) and *logos* (speech) and was construed to signify, as Spenser's "E. K." argued, "Goteheards tales."

E. was not a major genre in the Middle Ages, the most famous Christian version being the *Ecloga Theoduli* (9th c.?). It was revived perhaps by Dante (*E.* 1 [1319]), then by Petrarch and Boccaccio (both in Lat.), coming into full flower under the culture of the Ren. Humanists of the 15th and 16th cs. Widely studied and of dominating influence were the es. of Baptista Mantuanus Spagnuoli (mentioned with affection by Shakespeare). Barnabe Googe was the first writer to attempt the e. in Eng. (*Es., Epitaphs, and Sonnets* [1563], ed. J. M. Kennedy [1989]), but the finest flower is certainly Spenser's *Shepheardes Calender* (1579). Pope's es., though called *Pastorals*, epitomize the Neoclassical e. and rococo (q.v.) art. Later in the 18th c., new matter was poured into the mold, yielding a variety of es.—urban, exotic, political, war, school, culinary, Quaker—the most celebrated of which is Swift's *A Town Eclogue. 1710. Scene, The Royal Exchange.* For further discussion of the pastoral e. see PASTORAL; see also BUCOLIC; GEORGIC; IDYLL.

M. H. Shackford, "A Definition of the Pastoral Idyll," *PMLA* 19 (1904); W. W. Greg, *Pastoral Poetry and Pastoral Drama* (1906); W. P. Mustard, Intro. to *The Piscatory Es. of Jacopo Sannazaro* (1914), and "Notes on *The Shepheardes Calender*," *MLN* 35 (1920); R. F. Jones, "E. Types in Eng. Poetry of the 18th C.," *JEGP* 34 (1925); M. K. Bragg, *The Formal E. in 18th-C. England* (1926); A. Hulubei, *L'Eglogue en France au XVIe siècle* (1938); D. Lessig, *Ursprung und Entwicklung der spanischen Ekloge* (1962); P. Cullen, "Imitation and Metamorphosis," *PMLA* 84

(1969); G. Otto, *Ode, Eklogue und Elegie im 18. Jh.* (1973); R. Borgmeier, *The Dying Shepherd* (1976)—the 18th-c. Eng. trad.; P. Alpers, *The Singer of the* Es. (1979); Fowler; R. E. Stillman, *Sidney's Poetic Justice* (1986); *Es. and Georgics of Virgil*, tr. D. R. Slavitt (1990). J.E.C.; T.V.F.B.

ECPHRASIS. See EKPHRASIS.

ÉCRITURE. See SOUND; TEXTUALITY.

ECUADORIAN POETRY. See SPANISH AMERICAN POETRY.

EDDIC POETRY. See OLD NORSE POETRY.

EGO-FUTURISM. See FUTURISM.

EGYPTIAN POETRY. The ancient E. written lang. lasted for three and one half millennia, excluding its latest stage, Coptic, the lit. of which is largely distinct. The lit. under consideration here was written from ca. 2400–300 B.C. When the first connected specimens of writing appear (in tomb biographies and Pyramid Texts), the lang. is already highly developed, indicating centuries of prior devel. Major examples of lit. occur from all three Kingdoms (Old, 2755–2260 B.C.; Middle, 2134–1782 B.C.; and New, 1570–1070 B.C.) and from the Late Period (1070–332 B.C.).

The nature of ancient E. lit. has received a great deal of attention over the last quarter-century; major strides have been made in understanding the poetics underlying that lit., though no scholar should claim definitive conclusions. The widest disagreement probably centers on prosody. Though concensus is not yet possible, most scholars would probably agree with the ensuing description of E. literary style.

Ancient E. lit. (considering only those types we would today call lit., i.e. *belles lettres*, and thus excluding most of the material which is primarily liturgical, incantatory, funerary, or biographical) was almost entirely written in verse; only a few of the New Kingdom tales appear to be written in prose. Stylistically, the poetry is constructed upon a vehicle which consists primarily of verse lines occurring in pairs, the "thought couplet" (Foster). The verse line is syntactic and clausal, consisting of either a dependent or an independent clause; and the two lines together constitute a complete verse sentence. The couplets are sometimes interspersed with triplets and occasional quatrains. The couplet is not only a semantic and grammatical but also a rhetorical unit; and all the usual poetic devices of sound repetition, imagery, epithets, and figurative lang. are developed primarily within its structure. Distinct attention is paid to matters of similarity and difference, comparison and contrast (the "parallelism" [q.v.] of other lits.). The prosody of the verse line is still open to question, since the orthography did not reflect

vowels and the pronounciation of words is not known. One scholar (Fecht), in connection with a theory of the accentuation and syllable structure of E. word groups, argues that the line consists of set numbers of *kola*, or groups of syllables, each *kolon* (see COLON) having one stress and based upon grammatical groupings of words. The line has also been described in terms of modern free verse (Foster). The texture of the verse line might be thought of as a combination of the rhetorical flavor of Pope's heroic couplet (lacking the end rhyme) with the cadences (or free-verse rhythms) of Whitman or the Am. modernist poets. The lit. was courtly and sophisticated, not folk; and the poets enjoyed manipulating words to the end of elegant expression.

Ancient E. lit. was also a religious lit. Secularism, agnosticism, and atheism were not options in the culture. This is not to deny various attitudes toward belief; and examples of pessimism occur ("The Man Tired of Life" and the harper's songs). Poets were conscious of genre, adding most poetic embellishment to the lyric and least to the narrative. The three dominant genres were the didactic (wisdom texts or "instructions"), the lyric (hymns and prayers), and the narrative (esp. tales; some myths). Lesser genres included the love song, epistle, lament, harper's song, and some ritual utterances.

The most prestigious genre consisted of the instructions. They have a secular flavor and were meant to convey the wisdom of life gained by a father, usually from a distinguished public career, and gathered into writing in order to pass it on to his son. Most E. lit. is now anonymous; but the instructions usually were attributed. Their authors were the great sages of the tradition: Imhotep, Hordjedef, Ptahhotep, Khety, Kaires, Ptahemdjehuty, Ipuwer, and, later, Ankhsheshonqy, as well as others. Such wisdom writings are preserved from all three Kingdoms and from the Late Period. An example is Ptahhotep's first Maxim (ca. 2330 B.C.):

> Never be arrogant because of your
> knowledge;
> approach the unlettered as well as
> the wise.
> One never can reach the limits of art;
> no craftsman ever masters his craft.
> More hidden than gems is chiselled ex-
> pression,
> yet found among slave girls grind-
> ing the grain.

The lyric genre, consisting primarily of hymns and prayers, has most survivals. All the great gods of Egypt had hymns composed in their honor: Rē, Osiris, Amon, Ptah, Horus, Hapy (the deified Nile), and the Aton, among many others. A shadowy but fundamental presence behind all these (sometimes identified with one or another of them) was the Creator God, most akin to modern conceptions of the single, ultimate god of monotheism and functioning in much the same capacity, attested in Egypt as early as the 21st c. B.C. in the hymn at the conclusion of the "Instruction for Merikarē":

> The generations come and go among
>   mankind,
>   and God, who knows all natures,
>   still lies hidden.
>
> . . . .
>
> Provide for mankind, the flock of God,
>   for He made earth and heaven for
>   their sake;
>
> . . . .
>
> They are His living images, come from
>   His very self.

The later "Hymn to the Sun," attributed to King Akhenaten (ca. 1340 B.C.), exhibits, as well as its monotheism, a love of nature: "How various is the world You have created, / each thing mysterious, sacred to sight, / O sole God, / beside whom is no other!"

The narrative genre is attested by several tales from both the Middle and New Kingdoms and from the Late Period. From the earliest of these come "The Shipwrecked Sailor," the magicians' tales from Papyrus Westcar, and the surviving masterpiece of ancient E. lit., "The Tale of Sinuhe." From the New Kingdom we have "Horus and Seth," "The Two Brothers," "The Doomed Prince," "Truth and Falsehood," and others. And from the Late Period come the stories of Prince Khaemwas. "The Tale of Sinuhe" (ca. 1920 B.C.) is the "autobiography" of a courtier who ran away under threat of a coup; the story consists of his slow recovery of self-respect during long years of exile in the Syria-Palestine of the 20th c. B.C. (the later "Canaan") and his eventual reconciliation with the king. At one point the aging Sinuhe prays to return home:

> And may the King of Egypt be at peace
>   with me
>
> . . . .
>
> Then would my very self grow young
>   again!
>
> . . . .
>
>   For now old age is come,
> And misery, alone it drives me on;
>   my eyelids fall, my arms are heavy,
>   feet fail to follow the exhausted
>   heart.

The unknown author, in narrating a tale of over 600 verse lines, handles technical matters such as characterization, motivation, suspense, pace, and description with such surety and elegance that in this poem we certainly have one of mankind's earliest masterpieces and one of the high points of pre-Homeric lit.

A lesser genre, the love song, is esp. appealing. The poems deal with human—not divine—love and express, sometimes delicately, sometimes passionately, the full range of emotions and situations between man and woman: "My love is one and only, without peer, / lovely above all Egypt's lovely girls."

Texts are still being discovered and reconstructed (like the Middle Kingdom "Instruction of a Man for his Son") from fragments of ostraca and papyri. Though obscurities remain to hamper translation (points of grammar are still under discussion, the nature of prosody is not agreed upon, and there are still unknown words in the lexicon), E. lit. can now be translated with some confidence—it no longer needs to be "deciphered." The tradition of its translation is still very short— one century as opposed to the two millennia for translation of Gr. and Heb. texts. But soon the masterpieces of E. lit.—along with their Sumero-Akkadian counterparts—will take their rightful place at the beginning of anthologies of world poetry.

J. Towers, "Are Ancient E. Texts Metrical?," *Jour. Manchester Univ. E. and Oriental Soc.* (1936); S. Schott, *Altägyptische Liebeslieder* (1950); G. Fecht, *Wortakzent und Silbenstruktur* (1960), "Stilistische Kunst," *Handbuch der Orientalistik*, ed. B. Spuler et al., 1.1.2, *Ägyptologie: Literatur*, 2d rev. ed. (1970); M. Lichtheim, "Have the Principles of Ancient E. Metrics Been Discovered?" *Jour. of the Am. Research Center in Egypt* (1971–72), *Ancient E. Lit.*, 3 v. (1973–80); G. Posener, "Lit.," *The Legacy of Egypt*, ed. J. Harris (1971); J. L. Foster, *Love Songs of the New Kingdom* (1974), "Thought Couplets in Khety's 'Hymn to the Inundation,'" *JNES* 34 (1975), "*Sinuhe*: the Ancient E. Genre of Narrative Verse," *JNES* 39 (1980), "'The Shipwrecked Sailor': Prose or Verse?" *Studien zur altägyptischen Kultur* 15 (1988), ed., *Echoes of E. Voices: An Anthol. of Ancient E. Poetry* (1992); J. Assmann, *Ägyptische Hymnen und Gebete* (1975); W. Helck et al., *Lexicon der Ägyptologie*, 6 v. (1975–86), esp. "Metrik," "Parallelismus membrorum," "Prosodie," "Stilmittel"; W. Simpson, *The Lit. of Ancient Egypt* (1978); E. Blumenthal, *Altägyptische Reiseerzählungen* (1982); G. Burkard, "Der formale Aufbau altägyptischer Literaturwerke," *Studien zur altägyptischen Kultur* 10 (1983); E. Brunner-Traut, *Lebensweisheit der alten Ägypter* (1985); H. Brunner, *Grundzüge einer Gesch. der altägyptischen Literatur* (1986); P. Cachia, *Popular Narrative Ballads of Mod. Egypt* (1989).

J.L.F.

EISTEDDFOD (bardic session or assembly). A main feature of Welsh literary activity which can be traced back with certainty to the 15th c. and perhaps to the bardic festival held by Lord Rhys in 1176 at Cardigan. The early E. was an assembly of the guild or order of bards, convened under the aegis of a distinguished patron, and in the 16th c. even under royal commission. Its chief function was to regulate the affairs of the profession, such as the establishment of metrical rules, and the issuance of licenses to those who had completed the prescribed stages of their apprenticeship. Awards were also granted for outstanding achievements in poetry and music. The most important of these *eisteddfodau* were Carmarthen (ca. 1450) and Caerwys (1523 and 1568). Decay then set in, and the institution degenerated to the tavern *eisteddfodau* of the 18th c. These were meetings of poetasters, announced in almanacs, mere scenes of disputation in very indifferent verse. After a period of decline, the e. was revived during the 19th c. Today the National E. of Wales is a cultural festival of wide range and influence which provides for poetry, prose, drama, massed choirs, and other vocal and instrumental music. It has given much-needed patronage and publicity to poetry and has enabled several important literary critics to impose standards and to mold literary taste. See also WELSH POETRY.—E. J. Evans, *The Hist. of the E.*, Diss., Univ. of Wales (1913); T. Parry, *E. y Cymry: The E. of Wales*, tr. R. T. Jenkins (1943); Stephens.   D.M.L.

EKPHRASIS, ecphrasis (Gr. "description," pl. *ekphraseis*). E. first appears in rhet. writings attributed to Dionysius of Halicarnassus (*Rhetoric* 10.17). Later it becomes a school exercise, where it is defined as "an expository speech which vividly (*enargōs*) brings the subject before our eyes" (Theon, 2d c. A.D.—Spengel). Among the topics listed by Theon are descriptions of people, actions, places, seasons, and festivals. Priscian's Lat. tr. of the *Progymnasmata* ("School Exercises") attributed to Hermogenes (2d c. A.D.) made instructions for writing ekphraseis (*descriptiones*) available to the West. The medieval poetic *Artes* of Matthew of Vendôme and Geoffrey of Vinsauf devote considerable attention to the composing of descriptions (Faral, Arbusow). A tendency to limit e. to descriptions of works of art is discernable in the later *progymnasmata* of Nicolaus Sophistes (5th c. A.D.) and in the prose works of Libanius, the Philostrati, and Callistratus, but only in modern times does it bear that exclusive meaning.

Still, in this limited sense, as a description of a work of art, e. has had a long and complex history. The *locus classicus* in epic is Homer's description of Achilles' shield (*Iliad* 18.483-608), imitated by the more mannered depiction of Heracles' shield in the *Scutum* (139-320) attributed to Hesiod, and rivaled by Virgil's description of Aeneas' shield (*Aeneid* 8.626-731) (Kurman). A late epic example is the e. of Dionysus' shield in Nonnus' *Dionysiaca* (25.384-567).

During the Hellenistic period, notable ekphraseis occur in epic (Jason's cloak in Apollonius Rhodius, *Argonautica* 1.730-67) and in pastoral (the rustic cup in Theocritus, *Idyll* 1.27-56, and Europa's basket in Moschus' *Europa* 43-62). Roman examples indebted to Hellenistic ekphraseis include the description of the bed cover in Catullus 64 and the portrayal of Mars and Venus in

Lucretius, *De rerum natura* (1.33-40), which appears to be a description of a Hellenistic painting. The ekphraseis of the tapestries of Minerva and Arachne in Ovid's *Metamorphoses* (6.70-128) provide an instructive contrast between Cl. and Hellenistic artistic styles (Race). Spenser provides an extended imitation of Arachne's tapestry in *The Faerie Queene* 3.11.29-46 (DuBois), and Shakespeare includes a lengthy e. on the siege of Troy in *The Rape of Lucrece* (1366-1561; Hulse).

Another strain of e. consists of epigrammatic descriptions and interpretations of paintings and statues. Although first composed in the Cl. period as inscriptions for actual statues, they eventually became a minor genre with many representatives in the *Gr. Anthol.* (Friedländer). Ren. examples include Marino's *La Galeria*, Marvell's "Gallery" (Hagstrum), and emblem (q.v.) poetry. An offshoot is the Ren. *blason* (q.v.), a description of the beloved (Wilson) which often follows the prescription of the *progymnasmata* for describing statues by proceeding from the head to the foot, a practice also recommended by Geoffrey of Vinsauf (*Poetria nova* 562-99). In addition, the popular *Tabula of Cebes* encouraged the combination of description with moral allegory, as in Le Moyne's *Peintures morales* (Hagstrum).

Buildings and their surroundings have been popular subjects for ekphraseis, beginning with the description of Alcinous' palace and garden at *Odyssey* 7.84-132. Aeneas describes the murals on the temple of Juno in Carthage and the doors to the temple of Apollo (*Aeneid* 1.446-93, 6.20-30); Ovid describes the palace of the Sun at *Metamorphoses* 2.1-18. In the Byzantine period churches became a popular subject for description, most notably Paul the Silentiary's description of Santa Sophia. A Ren. example is Milton's description of Pandaemonium in Book I of *Paradise Lost*. The Flavian poet Statius wrote descriptions of villas (*Silvae* 1.3 and 2.2) that influenced Ben Jonson's "To Penshurst," the first in a long line of poems in the 17th and 18th cs. (e.g. by Carew, Herrick, Marvell, and Pope) describing estates and country houses (Hibbard).

A related theme is the depiction of a lovely spot ("pleasance"), traceable to Homer's description of the wild area around Calypso's cave at *Odyssey* 5.63-75. It is also found in Gr. lyric (Sappho, fr. 2) and drama (Sophocles, *Oedipus at Colonus* 668-93), and becomes so frequent in Lat. poetry that it has acquired a topical name, *locus amoenus* (Curtius, Arbusow, Schönbeck), with examples in Ren. epic (Spenser's Bower of Bliss and Milton's Eden) and lyric (Marvell's "The Garden").

The most famous romantic e. is Keats' "Ode on a Grecian Urn." In the 20th c., poets have produced many ekphraseis of paintings, particularly of Brueghel's works. W. H. Auden set the fashion with "Musée des Beaux Arts" and was followed by many others, including William Carlos Williams in his sequence, *Pictures from Brueghel* (Fowler).

Auden's "Shield of Achilles" is an ironic adaptation of the Homeric e. See also DESCRIPTIVE POETRY; ENARGEIA; VISUAL ARTS AND POETRY.

L. Spengel, *Rhetores graeci* 3 v. (1853-56); P. Friedländer, *Johannes von Gaza und Paulus Silentiarius* (1912); Faral; C. S. Baldwin, *Med. Rhet. and Poetic* (1928); H. Rosenfeld, *Das deutsche Bildgedicht* (1935); Curtius; G. R. Hibbard, "The Country House Poem of the 17th C.," *JWCI* 19 (1956); J. H. Hagstrum, *The Sister Arts* (1958); G. Downey, "E.," *Reallexikon für Antike und Christentum* (1959); G. Schönbeck, *Der Locus Amoenus von Homer bis Horaz* (1962); L. Arbusow, *Colores rhetorici* (1963); D. B. Wilson, *Descriptive Poetry in France from Blason to Baroque* (1967); *Three Med. Rhet. Arts,* ed. J. J. Murphy (1971); G. Kranz, *Die Bildgedicht in Europa* (1973), ed., *Gedichte auf Bilder* (1975)—anthol.; G. Kurman, "E. in Epic Poetry," *CL* 26 (1974); M. Albrecht-Bott, *Die bildende Kunst in der italienischen Lyrik der Ren. und des Barkok* (1976); S. C. Hulse, "'A Piece of Skilful Painting' in Shakespeare's *Lucrece,*" *ShS* 31 (1978); E. L. Bergmann, *Art Inscribed* (1979)—e. in Sp. Golden Age poetry; P. DuBois, *Hist., Rhet., Description and the Epic* (1982); Fowler; W. H. Race, *Cl. Genres and Eng. Poetry* (1988); M. Krieger, *E.* (1991). W.H.R.

ELEGIAC DISTICH, elegiac couplet (Gr. *elegeion*). In Gr. poetry, a distinctive meter, consisting of a hexameter followed by a pentameter, which developed in the archaic period for a variety of topics but which came to be associated thereafter with only one, i.e. loss or mourning, hence elegy (q.v.) in the modern sense. It first appears in the 7th–6th cs. B.C. in the work of the Gr. "elegiac poets" (meaning only that they wrote in this meter; the name was not applied until the 4th c.)—i.e. Archilochus, Callinus, Tyrtaeus, Theognis, and Mimnermus—who used it for flute songs at banquets and competitions, war songs, dedications, epitaphs and inscriptions, and laments on love or death. It seems to embody reflection, advice, and exhortation—essentially "sharing one's thoughts." Elegiac meter is a species of the epode (q.v., sense 2), and perhaps was originally used in melic poetry (q.v.), but in any event the shorter second line gives the distinctive and satisfying effect of end-shortening or catalexis (q.v.). Threnodies, ritual laments or cries uttered by professional poets at funerals, may also have been related.

Outside of the "elegiac" context, whether on love or death, the e. d. was specifically the meter of epigrams, esp. after the 4th c., when literary imitations of verse inscriptions were cultivated by the Alexandrian poets. It is this fixation of meter to genre which lasted the longest. Ennius introduced it into Lat., and later, the skill of Martial ensured its passage into the Middle Ages. In Lat. the love-elegy emerges as a major genre. The Augustan elegiac poets (Tibullus, Propertius, Ovid) tended to make the sense end with the couplet, whereas in Gr. poetry and Catullus it was often continuous. Among the refinements which in time became regular in the Roman elegists, esp. Ovid, was the restriction of the final word in the pentameter to a disyllable. In the opening d. of the *Amores,* Ovid jokes that though he intended to write of epic things (hence in hexameters), Cupid stole a foot from his second line, making it hypometric (q.v.), whence the form.

In the Middle Ages the e. d. was associated with leonine verse (q.v.), where it acquired rhyme. In the Ren., poets attempted imitations of Gr. quantitative meters, incl. the e. d., such efforts being revived again in the 18th and 19th cs. Examples are found in Eng. by Spenser, Sidney, Coleridge, Clough, Kingsley, and Swinburne; in Ger. by Klopstock, Schiller, Goethe, and Hölderlin; and in It. by D'Annunzio. Coleridge's tr. of Schiller's e. d. is well known: "In the hexameter rises the fountain's silvery column, / In the pentameter aye falling in melody back." But when the e. d. was naturalized into the accentually based prosodies of the vernacular meters, it was imitated as isometric couplets, as, in Eng., in the work of Grimald and in Marlowe's Ovid, whence it exerted influence on the devel. of the heroic couplet (q.v.). Heterometric (iambic) imitations incl. Swinburne's "Hesperia." For further discussion of this form, see ELEGY; see also DISTICH; EPIGRAM; EPITAPH; cf. EPODE.

R. Reitzenstein, "Epigramme," Pauly-Wissowa; K. Strecker, "Leoninische Hexameter und Pentameter im 9. Jahrhundert," *Neues Archiv für ältere deutsche Geschichtskunde* 44 (1922); C. M. Bowra, *Early Gr. Elegists,* 2d ed. (1938); P. Friedländer, *Epigrammata: Gr. Inscriptions in Verse from the Beginnings to the Persian Wars* (1948); Hardie, ch. 3; M. Platnauer, *Lat. E. Verse* (1951); L. P. Wilkinson, *Golden Lat. Artistry* (1963); T. G. Rosenmeyer, "Elegiac and Elegos," *Calif. Studies in Cl. Antiquity* 1 (1968); D. O. Ross, *Style and Trad. in Catullus* (1969); M. L. West, *Studies in Gr. Elegy and Iambus* (1974); West; A. W. H. Atkins, *Poetic Craft in the Early Gr. Elegists* (1984). T.V.F.B.; A.T.C.

ELEGIAC STANZA, elegiac quatrain, heroic quatrain. The iambic pentameter quatrain rhymed *abab.* The term "e. s." was apparently made popular by its use in Thomas Gray's *Elegy Written in a Country Churchyard* (1751), though in fact the association of the quatrain (q.v.) form with elegy (q.v.) in Eng. appears at least as early as James Hammond's *Love Elegies* (1743) and was employed "almost invariably" for elegiac verse for about a century thereafter (Bate)—cf. Wordsworth's "E. Ss. Suggested by Peele Castle." But the form had also been frequently employed without elegiac feeling or intention by other poets, e.g. Shakespeare in his sonnets and Dryden in his *Annus mirabilis;* and even Gray's great precedent failed to establish a quatrain trad., for both Shelley's *Adonais* and Arnold's *Thyrsis* (pastoral elegies—see PASTORAL) are written in more complex stanzas, and Tennyson's *In Memoriam* stanza (q.v.) is in tetrameters.—W. J. Bate *The Stylistic Devel. of Keats* (1945). T.V.F.B.; S.F.F.

ELEGIAMB. See ARCHILOCHIAN; DACTYLO-EPITRITE.

ELEGY (Gr. *elegeia*, "lament").

    I. PASTORAL ELEGY
    II. HISTORY
    III. FUNCTIONS

In the modern sense of the term, the e. is a short poem, usually formal or ceremonious in tone and diction, occasioned by the death of a person. Unlike the dirge (q.v.), threnody, obsequy, and other forms of pure lament or memorial, however, and more expansive than the epitaph (q.v.), the e. frequently includes a movement from expressed sorrow toward consolation. In the larger historical perspective, however, it has been most often a poem of meditation, usually on love or death. Discussion of the origin and devel. of the e. in Western poetry is complicated by major shifts in definition and has been limited in the past by a failure to distinguish between the elegiac as a mode, or motive, and the several species of e. which fall wholly or partly within that mode (Bloomfield).

I. PASTORAL ELEGY. One of the oldest and most influential species of the genre, the pastoral e. has sometimes been thought a subdivision of the pastoral (q.v.). Since its inception in Cl. lit., it has directed itself toward ceremonial mourning for an exemplary figure, originally associated with forces of fertility or (poetic) creativity. From Theocritus' First Idyll to Yeats's "Shepherd and Goatherd," examples of the pastoral e. will be found among the various elegies listed below. Its practitioners incl. Virgil, Petrarch, Sannazaro, Marot, Spenser, Milton, Goethe, Shelley, and Arnold, among others.

While the pastoral e.'s period of postclassical dominance extended from the Ren. through the 17th c., several of its conventions have informed nonpastoral elegies throughout the history of the genre. Such conventions incl. a procession of mourners, extended use of repetition and refrain (qq.v.), antiphony or competition between voices, appeals and questionings of deities and witnesses, outbreaks of anger or criticism, offerings of tribute and rewards, and the use of imagery such as water, vegetation, sources of light, and emblems of sexual power drawn from a natural world depicted as either injured victim or site of renewal.

The pastoral e. is most notably illustrated in Eng. by Spenser's "November" in the *Shephearedes Calender*, Milton's *Lycidas*, a monody [q.v.] on the death of Edward King, Shelley's *Adonais* (1821) on the death of Keats, and Arnold's *Thyrsis* (1867) on the death of Clough. The gap between *Lycidas* and *Adonais* is due to the fact that, while the e. was

continued in the 18th c., the pastoral e. was often derided: examples between Milton and Shelley—Oldham's on Rochester, Dryden's "Amyntas," Pope's "Winter," Thomson's "Damon"—are relatively weak.

II. HISTORY. In Gr. poetry, the term referred not to a genre or subject matter but to a specific verseform, the elegiac distich (q.v.). In Cl. Gr., the terms *elegion* and (pl.) *elegia* simply denote verse in the elegiac meter regardless of content (so Aristotle). However, *elegos*, pl. *elegoi* (Lat. *elegi*), referred to a sad song (such as those of the 6th-c. Peloponessian poet Echembrotos) sung to the accompaniment of a flute, i.e. a sung lament about death (so Euripides and Apollonius Rhodius 2.782) regardless of meter. As West says, "in archaic Greece it was the occasion, not the meter, that conferred the name" on a poetic class—e.g. paean, dithyramb—but by the 5th c., classifying poems by meter was more acceptable (cf. the *Poetics*), and since elegiac poems had no one function or occasion, the name for the meter came to represent the kind of songs usually written in that meter. The pastoral laments, such as those of Theocritus for Daphnis, of Bion for Adonis, or (reputedly) of Moschus for Bion—laments which seem in subject matter to be prototypes of the modern funeral e.—were classed by the Greeks as "bucolic poetry" (see BUCOLIC), later as "idylls" (see IDYLL), and later still, "pastoral"; by the Ren., "pastoral e." (see PASTORAL), while mainly applied to works of lament, could also simply denote a pastoral written in verse. Cl. Gr. e. was virtually extinct by the first quarter of the 4th c. B.C., but was revived again at the beginning of the Alexandrian age, ca. 300 B.C.

In Lat., the erotic or love e., in the hands of Gallus, Catullus, Propertius, Tibullus, Ovid, and their successors, becomes in effect a new genre, although derived from Gr. materials. It is distinguished from other genres by meter (still the distich), theme, and tone (often complaint). In Ovid the meter and the tone are extended across several subgenres, from the *Heroides*, *Ars amatoria*, and *Remedia amoris* to the *Tristia* and *Epistulae ex ponto*. Virgil's Fifth and Tenth Eclogues, which like Theocritus' First Idyll combine the themes of love and death, also served as models, extending the trad. of pastoral lament. Nemesian's First Eclogue follows Virgil, as do the eclogues of Calpurnius; Radbertus' *Egloga* (9th c.) consolidates the use of pastoral e. for Christian and allegorical purposes, reinforcing thereby the Virgilian influence on the later, Neo-Lat. elegies of Petrarch's Second and Eleventh Eclogues (mid 14th c.), Boccaccio's Fourteenth Eclogue, Poliziano's elegy on Albeira di Tomasso, Sannazaro's piscatory eclogues, and Castiglione's "Alcon" (1505). These poems were crucial to the shaping of the vernacular e. in It., Fr., and Eng.

In Italy, Sannazaro's *Arcadia* (1502, 1504) includes vernacular It. elegies in the direct trad. of

Cl. Gr. and Lat. models. Alamanni uses a different Cl. model for each of the four elegies on the death of Cosimo Rucellai (ca. 1518), and Trissino's *Dafne* (1527) continues this vein. By 1588, Tasso's "Il Rogo Amoroso" uses the pastoral conventions, but with a gloomier sense of historical and biographical pressures. Prosodically, one of the forms by which the Cl. quantitative meters were adapted to the vernacular was *terza rima* (q.v.), a popular vehicle for the subject matter of the e. in the hands of such writers as Tasso and Ariosto, the latter of whose *Rime* and *Satire* received the label of elegies only after his death. The elegiac strain of extended lyrics expressing melancholy and tender sentiments was represented in the baroque (q.v.) period by Filicaia and in the 19th c. by Leopardi and Carducci, whose memorial poem for Shelley is written in elegiac distichs. The elegiac meter has been subsequently used by D'Annunzio, one of whose collections is *Elegie romane* (1892). In the 20th c., impressive elegies have been written by Montale and Pasolini.

In Spain, the e. began as an imitation of It. models, as in Garcilaso de la Vega's *First Eclogue* (ca. 1535) on the death of his lady, and in some of his other poems modeled upon the work of Tasso. Lope de Vega (1562–1635) used octaves and other stanzas in imitation of Tasso for his elegiac verse. In the 20th c., the prevailing tone of Juan Ramón Jiménez in his *Arias tristes* and *Elegías* is melancholy and elegiac. The work of Federico García Lorca, in *Elegía a Doña Juana La Loca* and *Llanto por Ignacio Sánchez Mejías* shows a more direct obsession with the presentiments of death.

In France, the first attempt at copying the e. form from the ancients was by imitating the elegiac distich in alexandrine (q.v.) couplets, first by alternating masculine and feminine rhymes (see MASCULINE AND FEMININE), later by alternating decasyllabic with octosyllabic lines, an experiment of Jean Doublet in his *Élégies* (1559). Ronsard in his *Élégies, Mascarades, et Bergeries* (1565) abandoned the attempt to reproduce the Cl. meter and returned to the subject matter of the Cl. elegists, a treatment also adopted by Louise Labé and Malherbe. In so doing, Ronsard followed the initiative of Marot, whose celebrated lament for Louise of Savoy (1531) faithfully employed the conventions of the pastoral e., thereby setting a precedent not only for Fr. elegists but also for Spenser's introduction of the pastoral e. into England. Other 16th-c. Fr. elegies incl. Baïf's Second Eclogue, Scève's "Arion," and Belleau's "Chant pastoral" on the death of Du Bellay.

With the decline of convincing pastoral, the e. broadens its content: Boileau's *Art poétique* insists on themes either of love or death; and in the 18th c. the genre comes to deal with the tender and the melancholy rather than with grief or mourning. The climax of this tendency is reached with André Chénier at the end of the century. After Lamartine's *Méditations* (1820), the elegiac mode in Fr. poetry becomes confused with others, notably *tombeaux* and poems of homage such as those by Baudelaire, Verlaine, and Valéry.

In Germany, the subject matter of the e. has been so little restricted that Sir Edmund Gosse could say that the e. as a poem of lamentation does not exist in the Ger. lang. There had been a number of attempts during the Ren. to write elegies in Lat., but it remained for Opitz, in the early 17th c., to write elegies in the vernacular. His equivalent for the Cl. meter was alexandrine couplets with alternating masculine and feminine rhymes. In the 18th c., Klopstock, with greater metrical freedom, turned to sentimental subjects, general sadness, and the troubles of love, as well as the memorializing of actual death. The influence of Eng. "graveyard poetry" (q.v.), as well as of Young, Goldsmith, Gray, Ossian, and others, was also felt heavily in Germany. The *Römische Elegien* of Goethe, although imitative of the Lat. elegiac distich, should probably be classed as idylls, his chief e. being *Metamorphosen der Pflanzen*. Schiller in his essay, "On Naive and Sentimental Poetry" (see NAIVE-SENTIMENTAL), distinguishes the elegiac from the satiric and idyllic by saying that the elegiac longs for the ideal while the satiric rails against the present situation and the idyllic represents the ideal as actually existent. His notion of the elegiac is illustrated in his own works *Die Götter Griechenlands*, *Die Sehnsucht*, and *Der Pilgrim*. Hölderlin's elegies also deal with the impossibility of attaining an ideal and the longing for the golden days of Hellenism and youth. Mörike and Geibel produced the only Ger. elegies of note in the remainder of the 19th c. In the 20th c., Rainer Maria Rilke's "Requiem" (1909) and ten *Duino Elegien* (1912–1922) constitute an important extension of the genre in its more symbolic and speculative modes and have been widely influential both inside and outside Germany. More recent work by Trakl and Celan bring the genre to new expressiveness; Celan's "Todesfuge" is one of the most powerful elegies ever written for the victims of the Holocaust.

In England, the OE poems *The Wanderer* and *The Seafarer* are elegiac, while *Beowulf* contains a scene of professional mourning for the hero. In ME, *Pearl* and Chaucer's *Book of the Duchess* are closer to elegies proper. In the Ren., except for Surrey's fine memorials to Wyatt and Clere, and apart from some work by the Tudor poets, the Eng. e. remains unimaginative until the pastoral revivals by Spenser and Sidney. Looking back via Marot to Virgil and Theocritus, Spenser's "November" in the *Shepheardes Calender* (1579), together with Sidney's elegies in the *Old Arcadia*, inaugurate the pastoral e. in England and influence an array of subsequent poets. Spenser's "Daphnaida" (1590) looks back to Chaucer, while "Astrophel," written on the death of Sidney, is the keystone in the first anthology of Eng. elegies, prompting numerous others. In the 17th c., crucial contributions are made by Jonson and Donne. Donne brings a newly direct, argumentative manner to his *Anniversaries* for Elizabeth Drury, while the more restrained, neoclassical style of Jonson's stoicism forges a link between the Lat. epitaph and the 18th c.

As for form, after the few Ren. attempts to imitate the Cl. elegiac distich in quantitative verse, the e. was written in iambic couplets, but the e. never developed a fixed form in Eng.: Donne's elegies are in pentameter couplets; Milton's *Lycidas* is in an intricate *canzone*-like schema of irregularly deployed stanzas, rhymes, and short lines (which may echo the choruses of Tasso and Guarini or may simply be the apt vehicle for grief); thereafter, the "elegiac stanza" (q.v.) was used with some frequency up to romanticism, alongside anapestic tetrameters and couplets.

The term *elegie* was used in the 16th and early 17th cs. for poems with a variety of content, including Petrarchan love poetry as well as laments (q.v.), and carries simply the sense "meditation." The Cl. term thus takes over the native trad. of the complaint (q.v.). The connection between death and e. may have been strengthened by Donne, who chose "A Funeral E." to title the last section of his *First Anniversary* (1611), though most of his twenty-odd elegies (in pentameter couplets) are about love. But it remained for Milton in his pastoral e. *Lycidas* (1637) to establish definitively the e. as a separate genre in Eng., the concerns of which are lament for the dead and the search for consolation in the contemplation of some permanent principle.

In the 17th c., within the larger corpus of Eng. meditative and reflective verse, the distinction between "elegiac" verse and the e. proper was sharpened, although the boundary is by no means sharp—many odes, for example, are elegiac in effect. Notable Eng. elegies or poems in the elegiac mode—excepting here the Eng. pastoral elegies mentioned above—incl. Jonson's Cary-Morison ode, Henry King's "An Exequy," Cowley's e. for William Hervey, Denham's e. on Cowley, Marvell's Horatian ode, Dryden's elegies for Oldham and Mrs. Anne Killigrew, works by the Americans Anne Bradstreet and Edward Taylor, Pope's "E. on the Death of an Unfortunate Lady" and pastoral e. "Winter," Gray's *E. Written in a Country Churchyard* (1751), Young's more diffuse *Night Thoughts*, Johnson's "Vanity of Human Wishes" and e. for Dr. Levet, Swift's parodic "Verses on the Death of Dr. Swift," Wordsworth's Lucy poems and elegiac "Immortality Ode," Tennyson's *In Memoriam* (1850); Whitman's "When Lilacs Last in the Dooryard Bloom'd" (for Lincoln), Hopkins' "Wreck of the Deutschland," Swinburne's "Ave atque vale" (for Baudelaire), E. B. Browning's "Bereavement," Hardy's "A Singer Asleep" (1910, for Swinburne) and elegies of 1912–13 for his first wife, Owen's elegies from the First World War, Yeats's "In Memory of Major Robert Gregory," W. H. Auden's "In Memory of W. B. Yeats" (employing three meters)

and "In Memory of Sigmund Freud" (both 1939) as well as others for Toller and Henry James, Dylan Thomas's anti-elegiac e., "A Refusal to Mourn the Death, by Fire, of a Child in London," Geoffrey Hill's book-length elegiac homage to Charles Péguy, and Seamus Heaney's elegies for the victims of violence in Northern Ireland. Among many 20th-c. Am. elegies of note are Tate's "Ode to the Confederate Dead," Stevens' "The Owl in the Sarcophagus," Lowell's "The Quaker Graveyard in Nantucket" and "For the Union Dead," Bishop's e. for Lowell, Sexton's for Plath, and Berryman's for Delmore Schwartz, as well as innovative works such as Ginsberg's *Kaddish*, Bidart's "E." and "Confessional," Clampitt's "Procession at Candlemas," Olds's poems for her father, Grossman's elegies in *Of the Great House*, and Merrill's epic *The Changing Light at Sandover*, a work whose many elegiac moments renovate the most ancient motives and conventions of the genre.

III. FUNCTIONS. Traditionally the functions of the e. were three, to lament, praise, and console. All are responses to the experience of loss: lament, by expressing grief and deprivation; praise, by idealizing the deceased and preserving her or his memory among the living; and consolation, by finding solace in meditation on natural continuances or on moral, metaphysical, and religious values. Often involving questions of initiation and continuity, inheritance and vocation, the e. has been a favored form not only for mourning deceased poets but also for formulating ambitions and shaping poetic genealogies. As such it is a genre deeply implicated in the making of literary history. Closely related are the epitaph, ode, and satire, eulogy and epideictic poetry, and meditative poetry, often serving many of the same functions on related occasions. Milton takes the occasion for virulent denunciation of ecclesiastical or political corruption. Sacks emphasizes how "repetition itself and the submission to codes are crucial elements in the work of mourning" (326). Many elegies of the past century, however, have reflected the modern skepticism about idealization and consolation. Auden adds criticism to his praise of the dead: Yeats was "silly"; Freud "wasn't clever at all" and was "wrong" and sometimes "absurd." Still, if 20th-c. poets have undercut the traditional conventions of e., they have used the "residue of generic strategies" to do so—as well as to achieve what comfort they can—and the number of works in the elegiac mode makes it clear that in poetry the 20th c. has been a "distinctly elegiac age" (Sacks).

See PASTORAL; see also COMPLAINT; DIRGE; ECLOGUE; ELEGIAC DISTICH; EPIDEICTIC POETRY; GRAVEYARD POETRY; idyll; lament; planh.

H. Potez, *L'Élégie en France avant le Romantisme* (1897); M. Lloyd, *Elegies, Ancient and Modern* (1903); J. H. Hanford, "The Pastoral E. and Milton's *Lycidas*," *PMLA* 25 (1910); G. Norlin, "The

Conventions of the Pastoral E.," *AJP* 32 (1911); J. W. Draper, *The Funeral E. and the Rise of Romanticism* (1929); P. Aiken, *The Influence of the Lat. Elegists on Eng. Lyric Poetry 1600–1650* (1932); C. M. Bowra, *Early Gr. Elegists* (1938); R. Wallerstein, *Studies in 17th-C. Poetic* (1950); M. Platnauer, *Lat. Elegiac Verse* (1951); J. Wiegand, "Elegie," *Reallexikon*; G. Luck, *The Lat. Love E.* (1960); O. B. Hardison, Jr., *The Enduring Monument* (1962); F. Beissner, *Gesch. der deutschen Elegie*, 3d ed. (1965); V. B. Richmond, *Laments for the Dead in Medieval Narrative* (1966); *Milton's Lycidas*, ed. S. Elledge (1966); A. F. Potts, *The Elegiac Mode* (1967); C. M. Scollen, *The Birth of the Elegie in France 1500-1550* (1967); G. Otto, *Ode, Ekloge und Elegie im 18. Jh.* (1973); M. L. West, *Studies in Gr. E. and Iambus*, 2 v. (1974); D. C. Mell, Jr., *A Poetics of Augustan E.* (1974); P. Ariès, *Western Attitudes to Death* (1tr. 1974); M. Alexiou, *The Ritual Lament in Gr. Trad.* (1974); J. E. Clark, *Élégie: The Fortunes of a Cl. Genre in 16th-C. France* (1975); K.-W. Kirchmeir, *Romantische Lyrik und neoklassizistische Elegie* (1976); E. Z. Lambert, *Placing Sorrow* (1976)—pastoral e.; R. Borgmeier, *"The Dying Shepherd"* (1976)—the 18th-c. Eng. eclogue trad.; C. Hunt, *Lycidas and the It. Critics* (1979); T. Ziolkowski, *The Cl. Ger. E. 1795-1950* (1980); Trypanis, ch. 7; Fowler; R. J. Ball, *Tibullus the Elegist* (1983); *The OE Elegies: New Essays in Crit.*, ed. M. Green (1983); A. W. H. Adkins, *Poetic Craft in the Early Gr. Elegists* (1985); *Three Elegies of Ch'u*, tr. G. R. Waters (1985); G. W. Pigman, III, *Grief and Eng. Ren. E.* (1985); *CHCL*, v. 1, ch. 5; P. M. Sacks, *The Eng. E.* (1985); M. W. Bloomfield, "The E. and the Elegiac Mode," *Ren. Genres*, ed. B. K. Lewalski (1986); C. M. Schenk, "Feminism and Deconstruction: Re-Constructing the Elegy," *TSWL* 5 (1986), *Mourning and Panegyric* (1988); R. L. Fowler, *The Nature of Early Gr. Lyric* (1987), ch. 3; P. Veyne, *Roman Erotic E.* (tr. 1988); D. Kay, *Melodious Tears* (1990)—Eng. funeral e.; A. L. Klinck, *The OE Es.: A Critical Ed. and Genre Study* (1992). T.V.F.B.; P.S.; S.F.F.

ELISION (Lat. "striking out"; Gr. *synaloepha*). In prosody the general term for several devices of contraction whereby two syllables are reduced to one. The Gr. term *synaloepha* (q.v.) nowadays tends to be restricted to only one form; other terms formerly used for e. in Cl. prosody incl. *crasis* and *synizesis*. The forms of e. are: (1) *aphaeresis*: dropping of a word-initial syllable (vowel); (2) *syncope*: dropping of a word-internal syllable; (3) *apocope*: dropping of a word-final syllable (vowel); (4) *synaeresis*: coalescing of two voowels within a word; and (5) *synaloepha*: coalescing of two vowels across a word boundary, i.e ending one word and beginning the next. (The corresponding terms for addition of a syllable to the beginning, middle, or end of a word are *prosthesis*, *epenthesis*, and *proparalepsis*, respectively.)

Collectively these are sometimes called, on the analogy of rhet., the "metric figures" (so Elwert);

Susenbrotus, for example, gives a taxonomy, calling the types of e. as *metaplasms*, i.e. the class of figures for adding or subtracting a letter or syllable. E. of whole words or phrases is *ellipsis* (q.v.). Probably at least some of the older terminology is confused, and certainly many prosodists over the centuries have failed to grasp that the reductive processses at work here are normal linguistic ones, not "poetical" devices peculiar to metrical verse. The shortening of words and smoothing out of the alternation of vowels and consonants are both common processes in speech. The opposite of e. is *hiatus* (q.v.).

In Gr., e., variable in prose but more regular in poetry, is indicated by an apostrophe (') to mark the disappearance of the elided vowel (generally short *alpha*, *epsilon*, and *omikron* as well as the diphthong *ai* occasionally in Homer and in comedy); but when e. occurs in Gr. compound words, the apostrophe is not used. In Lat. a final vowel or a vowel followed by final *m* was not omitted from the written lang., but as a rule it was ignored metrically when the next word in the same measure began with a vowel, diphthong, or the aspirate *h*. In the modern vernaculars the apostrophe was retained to indicate graphically certain types of elision, but outside these, there is a larger case of words which have syllabically alternate forms in ordinary speech, e.g. "heaven," which some speakers pronounce as a disyllable, some as a monosyllable. This syllabic variance is of course useful to poets who write in syllable-counting meters; thus Sipe shows that in the overwhelming number of cases, Shakespeare chooses the one or other form of such words, which she terms "doublets," so as to conform to the meter.

There is some presumption that the number of syllables in the word which fits the scansion of the line will be (was) the number uttered in performance (reading aloud) of the line. Bridges, however, who has one of the seminal modern discussions, uses the term "e." in a special sense, to denote syllables which should be elided for purposes of scansion *but not* in pronunciation, a theory which divides scansion from performance. Ramsey has termed this "semi-e." in his criticism of Bridges' position. The problem of poets' alteration of the syllabic structure of their lang. for metrical purposes is far more complex than is usually assumed; indeed, the very problem of determining what was ordinary speech practice at various times in the past itself is difficult—see METRICAL TREATMENT OF SYLLABLES. Most of the history of Eng. metrical theory from ca. 1650 to 1925 could be framed in terms of dispute about e., i.e. syllabic regularity.

T. S. Omond and W. Thomas, "Milton and Syllabism," *MLR* 4–5 (1909–10); R. Bridges, *Milton's Prosody* (1921); T. S. Omond, *Eng. Metrists* (1921); W. J. Bate, *The Stylistic Devel. of Keats* (1945); P. Fussell, Jr., "The Theory of Poetic Contractions," *Theory of Prosody in 18th-C. England* (1954); A. C.

Partridge, *Orthography in Shakespeare and Elizabethan Drama* (1964); S. Chatman, *A Theory of Meter* (1965); R. O. Evans, *Milton's Es.* (1966); J. Soubiran, *L'E. dans la poésie latine* (1966); D. L. Sipe, *Shakespeare's Metrics* (1968); W. S. Allen, *Accent and Rhythm* (1973); P. Ramsey, *The Fickle Glass* (1979), App.; West; Elwert, *Italienische.* T.V.F.B.

ELLIPSIS (or eclipsis; Gr. "leaving out," "defect"; Lat. *detractio*). The most common term for the class of figures of syntactic omission (deletion). (Deletion of syllables for metrical purposes is here treated as elision [q.v.]). E. as a genus includes several species: e. of conjunctions between words is *brachylogia*, between clauses, *asyndeton* (q.v.); e. of a verb (in a different sense) is *zeugma* (q.v.); e. of a clause, particularly the main clause (B) after a subordinate (Y) in a constuction such as "If X then A; if Y then B"—e.g. "If you will do it, all will be well; if not . . ."—is *anapodoton* (q.v.). These differ from figures like *aposiopesis*, the dropping of the end of a sentence, leaving it incomplete, in that in e. the thought is complete; it is only that a word or words ordinarily called for in the full construction but not strictly necessary are omitted (since obvious). This obviousness which makes the omission possible is therefore much facilitated by the use of parallelism (q.v.) of syntactic members in the construction, which explains the importance of such parallelism for achieving that effect of compression which is the hallmark of the closed heroic couplet (q.v.). So Pope has "Where wigs [strive] with wigs, [where] with sword-knots sword-knots strive" (*Rape of the Lock* 1.101).

Gr. rhetoricians permitted omission of substantives, pronouns, objects, finite verbs, main clauses, and (more rarely) clauses; poets since the Ren. have allowed omission of almost any member so long as the meaning remains clear (Quintilian, *Institutio oratoria* 9.3.58). Shakespeare has "And he to England shall along with you" (*Hamlet* 3.3.4) and "when he's old, cashiered" (*Othello* 1.1.48). Modern poets (e.g. Pound, Eliot, Auden, W. C. Williams) have found e. esp. of use for conveying the speed and clipped form of modern colloquial speech and for expressing emotion. See also SYNTAX, POETIC.—E. A. Abbott, *A Shakespearean Grammar* (1886), 279–94—extensive lists of examples; Group Mu, 69 ff.; Corbett—prose examples. T.V.F.B.

ELOCUTIO. See RHETORIC AND POETRY.

EMBLEM. A memorable combination of texts and images into a composite picture, the characteristic e. has three parts (see Schöne): a short motto (lemma, *inscriptio*) introduces the theme or subject, which is symbolically bodied forth in the picture itself (icon, *pictura*); the picture is then described and elucidated by an epigram (*subscriptio*) or short prose text. The three parts each contribute in different ways to the dual functions of representation and interp. that particularly characterize the e.

As a genre (see Daly), the e. is related to various exegetical, literary, and iconographic trads. upon which e. writers drew to differing degrees. Illustrated forerunners include broad sheets, dance-of-death sequences, *biblia pauperum*, and illustrated fables. Even more important are the traditions of the *impresa*, heraldry, Ren. hieroglyphics, the *Greek Anthology*, and medieval Bible allegory and symbolism (see Praz; Schöne; Daly).

When in 1531 the Venetian Andrea Alciato (Alciati, Alciatus) published the first collection of es., *Emblematum liber*, he could not have known that his unlikely little book would launch a new genre that would become immensely popular. Alciato became known as "the father and prince of es." The *Emblematum liber* itself has gone through over 170 eds.; Francis Quarles's *Emblemes* (1635) have appeared at least 50 times; Herman Hugo's *Pia desideria* (1624) enjoyed over 42 Lat. eds., to say nothing of the translations; and Otto van Veen's *Moralia horatiana* (1607) runs to at least 34 eds. It was estimated that some 600 authors produced over 1000 books that appeared in more than 2000 eds. However, since we now know that the Jesuits alone account for over 600 titles (in over 1700 eds. and trs.), the corpus must be much larger.

The function of the e. is didactic in the broadest sense: it is intended to convey knowledge or truth in a brief yet compelling form that would persuade the reader and impress itself upon memory.

In origin humanistic and erudite, the form in the vernacular served a variety of audiences with a panoply of interests ranging from love to war, from social comment to alchemistic mysteries, from encyclopedic knowledge to pure entertainment. Es. were widely employed for the presentation of spiritual and moral instruction and political and religious propaganda.

The first e. book published with Eng. texts is a tr.: Jan van der Noot's *A Theater for worldlings* (1569); the first Englishman's publication of a coll. of trs., incl. some original es., is Geffrey Whitney's *A Choice of Emblems* (1586). The most successful Eng. emblem book is Francis Quarles's collection of spiritual *Emblems* (1635), modeled on Jesuit sources. Later, the Victorian period witnessed a revival of interest in the form (see Green and Höltgen). Rosemary Freeman's study, though outdated in conception, remains the only monograph on the Eng. e. Daniel Russell's study of Fr. es. and devices is methodologically sound and will be recognized as a standard work on the subject.

As an art form and a mode of allegorical thinking (see Jöns), the e. was enormously influential during the 16th and 17th cs. It shaped verbal images in poetry and lit., such as Donne's lovers as "stiff twin compasses," Crashaw's image of Christ's bleeding wounds as "thornes . . . proving rose," the Christian vision of salvation in the extended image of metal worked in a furnace in

Southwell's "The Burning Babe," Spenser's "golden bridle" (an e. of temperance), Ben Jonson's allegorical masque (q.v.) figures (e.g. Reason), Chapman's taper (*Bussy D'Ambois*), Shakespeare's red and white roses (*I Henry IV*), Falstaff's cushion used as a crown, and Shylock's whetted knife.

The book is only one medium through which the emblematic combination of text and picture was disseminated. Emblematic designs are found in painting and portraiture, interior decoration, carving, jewelry, tapestry, and embroidery. Es. were also used as theatrical properties in dramas, pageants, and street processions (see Schöne; Daly). Poets, preachers, writers, and dramatists frequently employed es. and e.-like structures in the spoken as well as the written word (see Green; Praz; Schöne; Jöns; Daly). The e. thus helped shape virtually every form of verbal and visual communication of the 16th and 17th cs.

H. Green, *Andrea Alciati and His Books of Es.* (1872); R. Freeman, *Eng. E. Books* (1948); W. Heckscher and K. Wirth, "E., Emblembuch," *Reallexikon zur deutschen Kunstgesch.*, v. 5 (1959); R. Clements, *Picta poesis: Literary and Humanistic Theory in Ren. E. Books* (1960); M. Praz, *Studies in 17th-C. Imagery*, 2d ed. (1964); D. Jöns, *Das "Sinnen-Bild": Studien zur allegorischen Bildlichkeit bei Andreas Gryphius* (1966); A. Schöne, *Emblematik und Drama im Zeitalter des Barock*, 2d ed. (1968); H. Homann, *Studien zur Emblematik des 16. Jahrhunderts* (1971); *Ausserliterarische Wirkungen barocker Emblembücher*, ed. W. Harms and H. Freytag (1975); *Emblemata: Handbuch zur Sinnbildkunst des XVI. und XVII. Jahrhunderts*, ed. A. Henkel and A. Schöne, 2d ed. (1976); K. Höltgen, *Francis Quarles (1592–1644)* (1977), *Aspects of the E.* (1986); P. Daly, *Lit. in the Light of the E.* (1979), *E. Theory* (1979), ed., *Andrea Alciato and the E. Trad.* (1989); et. al., ed., *The Eng. E. Trad.*, v. 1 (1988), *The Eng. E. and the Continental Trad.*, (1988); A. Young, *Henry Peacham* (1979), *The Eng. Tournament Imprese* (1988); D. S. Russell, *The E. and Device in France* (1985); *Andreas Alciatus: The Lat. Es.: Es. in Tr.*, ed. P. Daly et al., 2 v. (1985); J. S. Dees, "Recent Studies in the Eng. E.," *ELR* 16 (1986); H. Diehl, *An Index of Icons in Eng. E. Books* (1986). P.M.D.

EMOTION. A poem involves two people, writer and reader; and a discussion of the place of e. in poetics can be divided accordingly. The division is chronological as well as logical: until the end of the 18th c., emphasis fell on the reader's e.; since romanticism (q.v.), it has shifted to the poet's.

A. *Reader's E.* A good poem moves the reader: this has been a critical truism (perhaps even *the* critical truism) since lit. crit. as we know it began, though nowadays, under the influence of structuralism (q.v.), the reading of a poem as an emotional experience has moved from the center of attention, replaced by reading as interpretive activity. The e. may be aroused for purely aesthetic purposes—for "delight"—or else as an indirect means of inciting to virtue (see DIDACTICISM). This latter is the Horatian view that poetry is both *dulce et utile*—that it "teaches delightfully"—and it is by far the more common in the Ren.: it can be illustrated from almost any 16th-c. poet who discusses his craft:

> O what an honor is it, to restraine
> The lust of lawlesse youth with good advice . . .
> Soone as thou gynst to sette thy notes in frame,
> O, how the rurall routes to thee doe cleave!
> Seemeth thou dost their soule of sence bereave. . . .
> (Spenser, *The Shepheardes Calender*).

Is the emotional effect normative—i.e. can we say that a good poem arouses strong es., and a bad poem doesn't? Aristotle probably thought not: he admits in the *Poetics* that terror and pity can be aroused by the spectacle (this is not of course an inferior poem, but an inferior element of poetry; but we can surely extend the argument by analogy), though it is preferable to raise them by the words; and he does not indicate that the less preferable method arouses a weaker or even a different e. The usual answer, however, has been yes. When Sidney confesses "I never heard the olde song of *Percy* and *Duglas*, that I found not my heart mooved more then with a Trumpet," he clearly assumes that this is a testimony to the poem's excellence. This normative view was carried much further in the 18th c., when it was claimed explicitly and at length (notably by Diderot) that the good poet must be judged by his power to arouse our es. Thus Pope:

> Let me for once presume t'instruct the times,
> To know the Poet from the Man of rhymes:
> 'Tis he, who gives my breast a thousand pains,
> Can make me feel each Passion that he feigns;
> Inrage, compose, with more than magic Art,
> With Pity, and with Terror, tear my heart
> (*To Augustus*).

This is a tenet of neoclassical doctrine that passed unchanged and naturally into romantic poetics (q.v.).

A common objection to using one's emotional reaction as a touchstone (q.v.) is that it is too completely subjective: a poem has many readers, and they cannot compare their private es. (see SUBJECTIVITY AND OBJECTIVITY). One theoretical reply to this is contained in the doctrine of intersubjectivity (as formulated, for example, by Charles Morris), i.e. the use of lang. as a means for comparing purely private experiences. Nonetheless, the objection is useful if taken as a warning to the practical critic to talk about the words of the poem rather than the e. it arouses; for the latter will result either in vagueness, as in most impressionistic or rhapsodic crit., or in such physiological descriptions as Housman's account of his skin bristling, or Emily Dickinson's "If I feel physically as if the top of my head were taken off, I know that is poetry."

A poem, then, arouses in the reader an emotional response which is intersubjective: what is this e. like? The first question here is whether there is such a thing as a purely aesthetic e. The experience of reading, say, a satire of Pope is not the same as being angry; but critics are divided on whether the difference can profitably be described by postulating a specifically poetic or aesthetic e., which has no more to do with anger than with any other feeling.

The Horatian (*dulce et utile*) trad. would tend to answer yes. The e. of reading poetry was usually called, quite simply, pleasure; but it was clearly thought of as a special kind of pleasure, and there was some discussion in the 18th c. of its exact nature (e.g. by Hume in his essay on tragedy). Modern critics who believe in this e. include Clive Bell ("The starting point for all systems of aesthetics must be the personal experience of a particular e. . . . All sensitive people agree that there is a peculiar e. provoked by works of art") and T. E. Hulme ("You could define art as a passionate desire for accuracy, and the essentially aesthetic e. as the excitement which is generated by direct communication"). One can also mention Freud, who believed that there was a "purely formal, that is, aesthetic pleasure" offered by poetry, and who also (not surprisingly) believed it was unimportant: an "increment," a "bribe," to release a greater pleasure arising from deeper sources in the mind. Freud held exactly the opposite view to Hume (and Wordsworth) on this point: for him, the aesthetic pleasure, or fore-pleasure, is a trigger that releases a discharge of e. that provides the true enjoyment of lit.; whereas for Hume the aesthetic pleasure "softens," for Wordsworth it "tempers" the passions.

Up to the 18th c., the two main views of the reader's e. were the Horatian (that it was a pleasure) and the Aristotelian (that it was a catharsis). There is a potential contradiction between these two in that the catharsis view would tend, implicitly, to deny the aesthetic e.: it is real pity and real terror that are to be felt. In modern times, the aesthetic e. is denied by those anxious to repudiate an ivory-tower or esoteric view of lit.: by Marxists; by I. A. Richards (who says curtly that "psychology has no place for such an entity"); and, in effect, by John Dewey, who, though he uses the term "aesthetic e.," complains that those who believe in "an e. that is aboriginally aesthetic . . .

relegate fine art to a realm separated by a gulf from everyday experiences."

In talking of the reader's e., one must mention those critics who deny that e. has any place at all in reader response. This denial can stem from mainly theoretical motives, as in the case of Eliseo Vivas, who wishes to substitute "attention" as the key concept; or as part of a specific literary program, as in the case of T. S. Eliot. Eliot (who, however, is not always consistent) suggested that the emotions provoked by a work of art "are, when valid, perhaps not to be called es. at all." This can be linked with his doctrine of impersonality (he tends to think of an e. as something personal, even self-regarding); sometimes he prefers the term "feeling." Thomas Mann has also expressed the view that "art is a cold sphere." The "calm" or "cold" that these writers find in the poetic response might by others be considered a kind of e., but there is a real cleavage here. What no one (presumably) denies is that even if the poem kills the e., it must deal with a situation that would have aroused e. in the first place.

Our lang. recognizes only a small number of es.—perhaps a dozen in common usage. To classify by naming the e. must therefore lead to a discussion not of individual poems but of genre; and there has always tended to be a connection between genre and the e. or mood produced in the reader—most interesting in the case of tragedy, which produces uplifting es., as opposed to pathos or sentimental drama, which produces a gentler, more self-regarding e. issuing in the warmth of tears. Northrop Frye incorporates this distinction into his theory of modes, claiming that "the root idea of pathos (q.v.) is the exclusion of an individual on our own level from a social group to which he is trying to belong," and that it normally involves "some failure of expression real or simulated." Comedy and satire, too, can be described in terms of the e. they arouse in the reader or audience (since the arousing of e. is more associated with the theater).

Attempts to discuss individual poems in terms of e. will inevitably regard terms like "anger" or "love" as generalizations, and will maintain, with Collingwood, that beyond classifying "the anger which I feel here and now" as anger, one must add that "it is a peculiar anger, not quite like any anger that I ever felt before," and to become fully conscious of it (which in his view is the first step towards its poetic expression) means "becoming conscious of it . . . as this quite peculiar anger." Dewey too maintained that "save nominally, there is no such thing as *the* e. of fear, hate, love. The unique, unduplicated character of experienced events and situations impregnates the e. that is evoked." And the individuality of the work of art, he believes, comes from its faithfulness to this individual e. Eliot has also, on occasion, linked the precision of good poetry to the definiteness of its e. This naturally fits with the New Critical emphasis on the importance of the specific and the individual in a successful poem.

I. A. Richards maintains that a response to poetry is highly complex, and reading a poem a matter of emotional accommodation and adjustment. He prefers however to direct attention away from e., and to speak of the attitudes ("imaginal and incipient activities or tendencies to action") which poetry organizes in the reader "for freedom and fullness of life." This organization is the function of emotive lang., sharply distinguished by Richards from referential lang., which makes statements (see MEANING; PSEUDO-STATEMENT). William Empson, whose view of lang. was influenced by Richards', goes even further in not wishing to discuss the es. aroused by words: "Normally they are dependent on a Sense which is believed to deserve them"; the way to discuss the emotional impact of a poem is to analyze the structure of sense and implication in its key words.

B. *Poet's E.* Most of the remaining problems are best discussed under this heading. The first point to note is that consideration of the e. of the poet must be a descriptive and not a normative inquiry. A poem in itself can never offer conclusive evidence that the poet did not feel a certain e., nor (except on certain rather naive theories) that he did; this external, biographical fact can only be established separately and has no critical relevance. Ruskin tried to classify certain forms of poetry as worse than others according to whether the poet was insincere or—worse still—deliberately, in hardness of heart, weaving intricate metaphors "with chill and studied fancy." Here we have left lit. crit. for moralizing. As a reaction against this sort of thing, some aestheticians (notably Beardsley and Osborne) have tried to make logical mincemeat of the very concept of artistic expression. It is much easier for them to do this when they are considering it as a normative concept than when treating it as part of literary psychology.

As part of such a descriptive inquiry, there is a great deal to say about the poet's e. First of all, does a poet need to feel any? The view that he does not—that Shakespeare's sonnets, say, are literary exercises—repels most readers; however, it is a view that seems to be supported by the pronouncements of some poets, very conscious of the hard work involved in composition. The Horatian-Ren. critical trad., with its manuals of instruction and its advice on decorum (q.v.), has little to say on the poet's feelings but a great deal to say on craft. Even the famous line in the *Ars poetica*, "si vis me flere, dolendum est primum ipsi tibi" (if you wish to make me weep, you must first feel grief yourself), is addressed to characters in a play and refers simply to the need for good writing or good acting. It might be thought that the Platonic doctrine of inspiration (q.v.) runs counter to this trad., but as expressed by Plato (and, generally, by everyone else) this has nothing to do with the poet's es.: inspiration comes to the poet from without and

enables him, with the Muse's help, to solve problems in his craft that would defy his unaided wit—but they remain problems of craft. The doctrine that art is the expression of e. is one we owe to the romantic movement; earlier statements of it are very hard to find.

Is the e. expressed in a poem the same as that originally experienced by the poet? Most of the difficulties here vanish if we reject too naive a view of the temporal priority of this original e. What a poem expresses is clearly not the e. of the poet *before* he began writing it, but it may be his original e. insofar as the writing of the poem helped him to discover, even to feel it: "Expression is the clarification of turbid e.," says Dewey. Samuel Alexander, however, prefers to postulate two es., the material passion ("the passions appropriate to the subject") and the formal passion (the "passion proper to the artist" which guides him "more surely than conscious ideas . . . unifying his choice of words . . . into an expressive whole"). This formal passion is clearly the equivalent for the poet of the aesthetic e. of the reader; Alexander suggests that the material passion need not be present, citing the example of dramatic poetry: "It is not necessary to suppose that Meredith or Shakespeare actually felt the es. of his characters, but only that he understood them." Middleton Murry, however, who advances an extreme version of the expression theory, would prefer to say that the material passion is not the e. of Macbeth but that of Shakespeare about the *Macbeth*-situation, which is expressed by the play as a whole, and which Shakespeare presumably felt as well as understood.

The central difficulty in any view of art as the expression of e. is to find a way of indicating that the poet, though in the grip of an e., is also in control of it: that he is possessed by his e., but also possesses it. A critic's way of resolving this paradox may often show the heart of his doctrine. A typical Victorian answer is that of Ruskin, for whom the second-order poet is in the grip of his feelings (or chooses to write as if he were), whereas the first-order poet has command over himself and can look round calmly. When it comes to applying this distinction to poems, Ruskin shows a naïveté that is almost ludicrous: the great poet's "control of e." consists mainly in avoiding metaphor and factually untrue statements, even in preferring similes to metaphors. A glance at such a view makes it clear how greatly lit. crit. has deepened its powers in the last century.

Since genuine e., in real life, may well be accompanied by complete inarticulateness, we need to distinguish between its expression in a poem and the symptoms in which it issues in actual situations. Croce views expression as either aesthetic or naturalistic: "there is . . . an abyss . . . between the appearance, the cries and contortions of some one grieving at the loss of a dear one, and the words or song with which the same individual portrays his suffering at another time." Dewey makes a distinction between giving way to, and expressing, an impulse: raging is not the same as expressing rage, and he links it with his more general theory that the arresting of the physiologically normal outlet of an impulse is the necessary precondition of its transformation into a higher level of experience. Perhaps the most valuable formulation of the difference is that of Collingwood, who distinguishes between expressing and betraying an e., linking this with his view of art as an enlarging and clarifying of consciousness.

These are philosophical formulations; to the poet and practical critic, what matters is the application of the distinction to the actual lang. of poetry. The classic instance of failure to draw this distinction is Johnson's attack on *Lycidas* on the grounds that "where there is leisure for fiction, there is little grief." The naturalistic discharge of grief may have no such leisure, but its expression has. This element of control in expression was no doubt one of the things Coleridge wished to indicate by attributing to imagination "a more than usual state of e., with more than usual order"; and that Eliot was thinking of when he described poetry as "an escape from e." Eliot's objections to *Hamlet* spring from a feeling that loose e., inadequately expressed, is betrayed in the play, though he shows some uncertainty whether the e. is Shakespeare's, or also Hamlet's.

Wordsworth's account of poetry as originating in "the spontaneous overflow of powerful feelings" looks like a discharge-theory, but he goes on to add that as well as having "more than usual organic sensibility" the poet must be someone who has "thought long and deeply." Wordsworth was in fact usually aware (though he is inconsistent) that the e. as expressed is not the same as that originally felt: in his account of e. recollected in tranquillity, he remarks that the recollected e., that which issues in the poem, is "kindred" to the original one.

Of all modern theorists, the one who perhaps comes closest to a view of art as the mere discharge of e. is Freud. He happens to be talking of the reader's e., but his view (already mentioned) seems relevant here. He recognizes no element of control in the "release of tension" provided by lit., and sometimes indicates a view of art that equates it with indulgence in wish-fulfillment. (At other times he holds what amounts to a cognitive view.) Jung, though his interpretation is different, holds the same view of what the poetic e. is like and describes it with the same metaphors: "the moment when the mythological situation appears is . . . as though forces were unloosed of the existence of which we had never even dreamed; . . . we feel suddenly aware of an extraordinary release."

There can be no doubt that this distinction between expressing and betraying is invaluable in the actual crit. of lit. Collingwood applies it, briefly but brilliantly, to *Tess of the D'Urbervilles* and

to Beethoven; it provides the best terminology for sorting good from bad in writers such as Shelley, Carlyle, and Lawrence.

How does e. work in the creative process? If writing a poem is like driving a car, the e. can be thought of either as the destination or the gasoline—the subject of literary creation or the force that makes it possible. Eliot holds the first view: "What every poet starts from is his own es.," he says, in contrasting Shakespeare with Dante, and suggests that Dante expresses not belief but certain es. of believing. Alexander on the other hand holds the second view: "The artist aims to express the subject which occupies his mind in the means which he uses. His purpose may be dictated by passion but is still a passionate *purpose*." The resolution of this dispute (which seems at least partly terminological) lies outside literary theory, but the dangers and implications of each view are worth noting. If you believe that the poet's es. are the subject of a poem, you are likely to emphasize, even overemphasize, the typicality of poems dealing explicitly with es., such as Shakespeare's sonnets, Coleridge's *Dejection*, and even (as in the case of many romantic critics) lyric poetry in general. If on the other hand you regard e. as merely the fuel, you have to deal with the fact that the writing of philosophy, psychology, even mathematics may often be fueled by e. The romantic doctrine of the presence of the writer's e. as not merely external cause but in some way intrinsic to the product at least had the advantage that it provided a criterion for distinguishing poetry (more generally, imaginative lit.) from other forms of writing.

The decline of romantic theories and the rise of structuralism (q.v.) in recent years has directed critical attention away from the question of e. Structuralist theories, which treat lit. by the methods of linguistics, have tended to assimilate poetry to other forms of lang., and their emphasis on codes leads to a concentration on the activity of the lang. rather than on the resulting experience. Even the influential school of reader-response criticism (q.v.) concentrates on responses that, as Jonathan Culler points out, "are generally cognitive rather than affective: not feeling shivers along the spine, or weeping, but having one's expectations proved false, or struggling with an unresolvable ambiguity."

Theories of the dispersed or decentered subject, deriving from Althusser, Lacan, and Barthes, which eliminate or at least minimize the individual creative act, will naturally also minimize the importance of e.: if there is no autonomous subject, then there is no originating e. There are, however, examples of poststructuralist critics who do talk about e., if in new ways. Julia Kristeva, for example, sees poetic lang. (by which she means the lang. of modernism) as a struggle against oppression by the social order, and an attempt to express the subversiveness of immediate experience, which she calls desire. It is however an impersonal desire, not an individual experience of desiring. Outside of such theories and theorists, e. will continue to be an important concept for those critics who insist that every poem has an author, who draws on personal experience, and a reader, who is moved withal. For discussion of the importance of e. in non-Western trads. of poetics, see esp. INDIAN POETICS; JAPANESE POETICS. See also PATHOS; POETRY, THEORIES OF, *Pragmatic Theories;* RHETORIC AND POETRY.

J. Ruskin, "The Pathetic Fallacy," *Mod. Painters* (1856), 3.4; B. Croce, *Aesthetic,* tr. D. Ainslie (1909); T. S. Eliot, "The Perfect Critic" *The Sacred Wood* (1920), and "Trad. and the Individual Talent," "Shakespeare and the Stoicism of Seneca," and "Dante" in *Essays;* Richards; S. Freud, "The Relation of the Poet to Day-Dreaming," tr. G. Duff, *Collected Papers,* v. 4 (1925); J. Middleton Murry, *The Problem of Style* (1925); C. G. Jung, "On the Relation of Analytical Psychology to Poetic Art," *Contributions to Analytical Psychology,* tr. H. G. and C. F. Baynes (1928); I. A. Richards, *Practical Crit.* (1929); S. Alexander, *Beauty and Other Forms of Value* (1933); J. Dewey, *Art as Experience* (1934); E. Vivas, "A Definition of the Aesthetic Experience," *JP* 34 (1937); R. G. Collingwood, *Principles of Art* (1938); W. Empson, *The Structure of Complex Words* (1951); E. Kris, *Psycho-analytic Explorations in Art* (1952); Empson; H. Osborne, *Aesthetics and Crit.* (1955)—ch. 7 attacks the expression theory, "The Quality of Feeling in Art," *BJA* 3 (1963); Wimsatt and Brooks, ch. 14; S. O. Lesser, *Fiction and the Unconscious* (1957); J. Hillman, *E.: A Comprehensive Phenomenology of Theories and Their Meanings for Therapy* (1960); N. O. Holland, *The Dynamics of Literary Response* (1968), "The 'Unconscious' of Lit.," *Contemp. Crit.,* ed. Bradbury and Palmer (1970); W. W. Fortenbaugh, *Aristotle on E.* (1975); J. Kristeva, *Desire in Lang.,* tr. T. Gora et al. (1980); W. Lyons, *E.* (1980); J. Culler, *On Deconstruction* (1982). L.D.L.

EMPATHY AND SYMPATHY. E. is usually defined as projection of oneself into the other or identification with the other, but the term has in fact referred to many divergent phenomena in both psychology and aesthetics. Coined by E. B. Titchener to translate a technical term, *Einfühlung,* first used by Theodor Lipps in 1897 in a psychological analysis of aesthetic appreciation, e. originally meant a fusing of self with (or loss of self-awareness in) the object of one's attention. The conception (if not the term) was developed by Lotze and Vischer in elaboration of Hegelian aesthetics, which made e. constitutive of beauty. In the social sciences its meaning shifted to the ability to put oneself in the place of another, imaginatively, or to experience what the other's feelings must be like. Freud saw e. as emerging from identification by way of imitation, a third stage in our taking on the attitudes of others. Some theorists of interp. have made e. in a broad sense basic to hermeneu-tic understanding, but not Dilthey, whose *Nacherleben* (mistranslated as e.) is quite different from *Einfühlen.*

Significant contributions to the conception of e. have also been made by Max Scheler and Martin Buber. Buber's characterization of e. allows us to see how the term could be put to use in readings of romantic poetry (Fogle, Bate, Bloom). "E. means, if anything, to glide with one's own feeling into the dynamic structure of an object, a pillar, or a crystal or the branch of a tree, or even of an animal or a man, and as it were to trace it from within, understanding the formation and motoriality of the object with the perceptions of one's own muscles." Though other theorists do not share this emphasis on the visceral, most agree in contrasting e. with sympathy, which is seen as more reflective, comparative, and cognizant of one's own feelings. The cognitive and social functions of e. were nonetheless anticipated in theories of sympathy developed in the Scottish Enlightenment by Hume, Smith, and others.

Fogle saw e. as the source of personification (q.v.) in poetry and the basis for all metaphor (q.v.) that endows the natural world with features of mind or human feeling. As such, he identified it with "what modern critics have termed the mythical view" and thus with "the essential attitude of poetry and art." In a narrower sense e. refers to metaphors which convey the meaning of an object by evoking a physical (kinesthetic) response to it. Keats's lines, "crag jutting forth to crag, and rocks that seem'd / Ever as if *just rising from a sleep,* / *Forehead to forehead held* their monstrous horns," aptly illustrate the empathic interp. of objects by physical suggestion. However, there is a paradox in such usage insofar as it implies projection of features not to be actually found in the object (cf. PATHETIC FALLACY), since e. is otherwise taken as a form of knowledge or insight.

In its projection into or identification with the object (the metaphysical crux of romantic nature poetry), e. is distinguishable from s. by its element of sensation and its more intimate union with its object—s. runs parallel, while e. unites. The importance of .s. to poetics lies in its relation to extrapoetic issues. The sympathetic imagination, for example, makes possible organized social action by awakening us to the kinship of all things. The Ancient Mariner's crime is a failure of s. toward a creature that has already been associated to humanity: "As if it had been a Christian soul, / We hailed it in God's name." See also NEGATIVE CAPABILITY.—H. Lotze, *Microcosmos,* tr. E. Hamilton and E. E. C. Jones (1886); T. Lipps, *Ästhetik* (1903), *Leitfaden der Psychologie* (1906), *Psychologische Untersuchungen* (1907, 1913); M. Scheler, *The Nature of Sympathy* (1913); V. Lee, *The Beautiful* (1913); H. S. Langfeld, *The Aesthetic Attitude* (1920); I. A. Richards et al., *Foundation of Aesthetics* (1925); G. H. Mead, *Mind, Self and Society* (1934); W. J. Bate, *From Classic to Romantic* (1946), ch. 5;

R. H. Fogle, *The Imagery of Keats and Shelley* (1949), ch. 4; R. L. Katz, E., *Its Nature and Uses* (1963); H. Bloom, *Shelley's Mythmaking* (1969); W. Perpeet, "Einfühlungsästhetik," *Historisches Wörterbuch der Philosophie*, ed. J. Ritter (1971–); M. F. Basch, "Empathic Understanding: A Review of the Concept," *Jour. Am. Psychoanalytic Assoc.* 31 (1983); D. Marshall, *The Surprising Effects of S.* (1988).

R.H.F.; J.B.

ENARGEIA (Gr. *arges*, "bright"; Lat. *evidentia, inlustratio, repraesentatio*) or "vividness" is defined in Cl. rhetorical treatises as a quality which appeals to the listener's senses, principally that of sight. In the *Progymnasmata* (school exercises), e. is, with *sapheneia*, or clarity, one of the defining characteristics of *ekphrasis* (q.v.), the description in poetry of pictorial scenes on objects (a shield, a vase). Aristotle mentions e. in the *Rhetoric* (3.1410b36), but it is Quintilian who gives the most detailed treatment of e. in Cl. rhet.: by penetrating the visual imagination of the listener and involving him in the subject of the speech, the orator can persuade more effectively than through logical argument alone (8.3.62). To achieve e., the orator must use his visual imagination (*phantasia*) to conjure up the scene mentally (10.7.15). He then represents this vision in the delivery of the speech, evoking an analogous image, and producing the concomitant feelings, in the minds of the audience (6.2.29–32). One important descriptive technique for vivid portrayal is the selection and disposition of significant detail (8.3.66, 9.2.40). The theory of e. supposes a close reciprocal relation between mental images and the arousal of emotion (see PATHOS), and is thus linked to the notion of *psychagogia*—leading or enchanting the mind.

Outside practical rhet., e. was also felt to be a desirable quality in historiography and, esp., poetry. The Lat. rhetoricians often drew their examples of e. from Virgil, as the Greeks did from Homer. Ancient commentaries on Homer and on Attic tragedy frequently draw attention to vividly pictorial passages and phrases. For Psuedo-Longinus (*De sublimitate* 15), vivid imagery (which he usually refers to as *phantasia*) is one means of attaining the sublime (q.v.). But he makes an important distinction between the use of such imagery by the orator, who must keep within the bounds of credibility, and by the poets, who are free to invent and elaborate fabulous subjects.

The psychological mechanism linking mental imagery and emotion was known to Aristotle (*Rhet.* 1411b–1412a), who used the concrete adverbial phrase "before the eyes" rather than the abstract term "vividness" to signify the effect of such vision. For Aritstotle, mental picturing produces the semblance of vitality and actuality: the Gr. for this is *energeia*, a term which has often been confused with e. See now DESCRIPTIVE POETRY; INSCAPE AND INSTRESS.

J. H. Hagstrum, *The Sister Arts* (1958); T. Cave,

"E.: Erasmus and the Rhet. of Presence in the 16th C.," *L'Esprit créateur* 16 (1976); D. C. Mantz, "From Emblem to E.," *DAI* 32 (1972): 6987A; Lausberg, sects. 811–17; G. Zanker, "E. in the Ancient Crit. of Poetry," *RMP* 124 (1981); L. Galyon, "Puttenham's E. and Energeia: New Twists for Old Terms," *PQ* 60 (1981); S. K. Heninger, Jr., "A World of Figures: Enargeiac Speech in Shakespeare," *Fanned and winnowed opinions: Shakespearean Essays Harold Jenkins*, ed. J. W. Mahon and T. A. Pendelton (1987); R. Meijering, *Literary and Rhetorical Theories in Gr. Scholia* (1987); I. Yasuyoshi, "The Energeia of Hopkins' Poetry," *DAI* 48 (1988): 2639A; Corbett 298.

R.H.W.; P.W.

ENCOMIUM. Strictly, a Gr. choral lyric performed "in the revel" (*kōmos*) to celebrate a person's achievements. More generally, the name is applied to any poem praising a man rather than a god (Plato, *Republic* 607a; Aristotle, *Poetics* 4), and it overlaps other designations such as panegyric and *epinikion* (qq.v.). In the generic categories devised by the Alexandrian librarians to classify Gr. choral lyric, the e. referred to poems that were less formal than *epinikia* and which were probably, like *skolia* (see SCOLION), performed at banquets. Simonides brought the genre to its maturity, but no examples of his encomia are extant; only fragments remain of the encomia of the two most important subsequent authors, Pindar (fr. 118–28) and Bacchylides (fr. 20Aa–g). In its broadest application, e. becomes indistinguishable from praise as a subdivision of epideictic oratory (Aristotle, *Rhetoric* 1358b18 ff.). Both the First Sophistic movement (5th c. B.C.) and the Second (2d c. A.D.) produced prose encomia of frivolous and paradoxical subjects (Pease), forerunners of Erasmus' *Praise of Folly* (*Moriae encomium*).

Although encomiastic passages can be found throughout Graeco-Roman poetry (Burgess), salient examples include Theocritus, *Idylls* 16 and 17; Horace, *Odes* 4.4 and 4.14; [Tibullus] 3.7; and the anonymous *Laus pisonis*. Encomia continue to be written in the Byzantine period (Viljamaa), Middle Ages (Baldwin), and Ren. (Hardison, Garrison).—T. Burgess, *Epideictic Lit.* (1902); Pauly-Wissowa; G. Fraustadt, *Encomiorum in litteris graecis usque ad romanam aetatem historia* (1909); A. S. Pease, "Things Without Honor," *CP* 21 (1926); C. S. Baldwin, *Med. Rhet. and Poetic* (1928); A. E. Harvey, "The Classif. of Gr. Lyric Poetry," *ClassQ* 5 (1955); O. B. Hardison, Jr., *The Enduring Monument* (1962); W. Meinke, *Untersuchungen zu den Enkomiastischen Gedichten Theokrits* (1965); T. Viljamaa, *Studies in Gr. Encomiastic Poetry of the Early Byzantine Period* (1968); J. D. Garrison, *Dryden and the Trad. of Panegyric* (1975).

W.H.R.

ENDECASÍLLABO. See HENDECASYLLABLE; ITALIAN PROSODY.

ENDECHA. A Sp. dirge or lament, usually written

in 5-, 6-, or 7-syllable lines; the even-numbered lines have assonance, though any simple rhyme scheme in true rhyme and any type of verse may be used, since the name refers primarily to subject matter. The strophe employed in the *e. real,* however, introduced in the 16th c., is usually limited to four lines, generally three heptasyllables plus one hendecasyllable, the second and fourth lines assonating and the others left unrhymed. The position of the hendecasyllables may vary, or the strophe may alternate hendecasyllables with heptasyllables. Alternating rhyme (*serventesio*) may also be used. The short-line forms, according to Le Gentil, are found as early as the 15th c., although the typical assonance of the learned poetry is a devel. of the 16th. The e. is sometimes called *romancillo,* A famous example is Lope de Vega's *Pobre barquilla mia.*—Le Gentil; Navarro.

D.C.C.

END RHYME. See RHYME.

ENDINGS. See LINE; MASCULINE AND FEMININE.

END-STOPPED lines are those in which meter, syntax, and sense come to a conclusion at line-end. "Conclusion" is, however, not an unequivocal absolute: syntactically, the end of a phrase is the minimum requirement, but end of clause or sentence is normal: "Hope springs eternal in the human breast;" Pope says (*Essay on Crit.*), "Man never is, but always to be, blest." A single line may be said to be e.-s., but the term normally applies to the couplet (q.v.), and particularly the closed heroic couplet (q.v.) of Eng. 18th-c. poetry; also to the alexandrine (q.v.) of Fr. Classicism. The term "e.-s." is opposed to "run-on" or *enjambé* (see ENJAMBMENT), terms used to describe the free and uninterrupted carry-over of syntax from one line to the other, as in most Eng. blank verse (q.v.) and most romantic poetry. See now LINE.

A.PR.; T.V.F.B.

ENGLISH POETICS. See RENAISSANCE POETICS; BAROQUE POETICS; NEOCLASSICAL POETICS; ROMANTIC AND POSTROMANTIC POETICS; TWENTIETH-CENTURY POETICS.

ENGLISH POETRY.

  I. OLD ENGLISH (650–1066 A.D.)
  II. MIDDLE ENGLISH (1066–1500)
  III. RENAISSANCE TO MODERN (SINCE 1500)
    A. *The Renaissance*
    B. *Dramatic Poetry to 1642*
    C. *The Seventeenth Century*
    D. *The Augustans*
    E. *The Romantics*
    F. *The Victorians*
    G. *Modernism*

  I. OLD ENGLISH (650–1066 A.D.). Arguments for the continuity of Eng. p. from the OE period to the ME period (1066–1500), whether technical (oral formulaism) or thematic (the Eng. "spirit" of the poetry) have elicited little critical concurrence. It is best to regard the pre-Conquest poetry of England as having its own character and identity. The 30,000 extant lines of OE poetry represent the earliest written evidence of an oral West Germanic verse trad. of the 4th–6th cs., based on alliteration and lexical stress, which gave rise to the written trads. of OE, Old Saxon, Old High German, and Old Icelandic poetry. OE poetry survived thanks to the early Christian conversion of Anglo-Saxon (AS) kingdoms and to the literacy associated with monastic culture. Christian Latinity left its impress on OE verse both in subject matter and by introducing Continental Christian and Cl. influences into native secular trads. In the minor OE corpus, runes, gnomes, maxims, proverbs, and riddles are interspersed with the scriptural and liturgical texts of formal Christianity such as renderings of *The Lord's Prayer, The Creed, The Gloria,* and a good part of the *Psalter.* Similarly, *The Descent into Hell* copies in part the apocryphal Gospel of Nicodemus, and the more important *Christ I* is based on the liturgical Advent antiphons. Associated with the Benedictine reform of the 10th c. are texts like *An Exhortation to Christian Living* and *A Summons to Prayer.* As well for heroic saints' lives like *Andreas* and *Guthlac* as for riddles or the AS Physiologus (*The Panther,* etc.), there were Med. Lat. models in such writers as Caesarius of Arles, Felix of Croyland, Avitus, Symphosius, and Lactantius.

With few exceptions, OE poetry is preserved in four great monastic codices of the 11th c. The Vercelli Book, perhaps the earliest, contains 29 pieces, incl. the *Dream of the Rood, Elene,* and *Andreas.* The Exeter Book, presented to the cathedral by Leofric, first bishop of Exeter (d. 1072), contains some of the best known of OE secular verse— *The Wanderer, The Seafarer, Widsith, Christ,* and the riddles. *Beowulf* and *Judith* comprise the larger part of MS Cotton Vitellius A.xv., now in the British Library. The Bodleian MS Junius XI (after one of its owners, Franciscus Junius) contains *Genesis, Exodus, Daniel,* and *Christ and Satan,* the so-called Caedmonian poems.

Caedmon's Hymn itself, however, the earliest OE poem which can be dated (ca. 657), is preserved in 17 mss. of Bede's *Ecclesiastical History.* Composed less than 50 years after Bishop Paulinus' conversion of King Edwin at York, *Caedmon's Hymn* fuses native AS and Christian Lat. trads. A lay brother at Strenaeshalc (now Whitby), Caedmon was unable to take his turn at verse making when the harp passed around the table until inspired by an angel in a dream. Caedmon's angelically inspired song of the creation was accounted a miracle by Bede, who records that Caedmon went on to turn into melodious verse the whole of Genesis, Exodus, and the teachings of the Apostles.

Although the attribution of the OE *Genesis* and

Exodus to Caedmon has been firmly rejected, the Junius ms. poems are still felt to be of an early date (late 7th to early 9th c.). Critical disagreements persist, however, about the dating not only of these poems but of nearly every poem in the OE corpus. Of the biblical poems, *Exodus* augments its Vulgate source the most; *Genesis* is interesting for its inclusion of a late (9th c.) interpolation of the temptation and fall (11.235–851, *Genesis B*) that seems to translate an Old Saxon poem, a fragment of which is preserved in the Vatican Library.

In the Junius-ms. poems, Christian themes of Old Testament heroism overlap the secular AS ethic. Secular, heroic OE verse seems to have enjoyed favor even in the monastery. Nevertheless, only the fragmentary *The Battle of Finnsburh* (another version is extant in *Beowulf*) survives as an unretouched Germanic lay. Narrative materials associated with an older oral trad. persist in OE verse not only in specific allusion (e.g. reference in *Widsith* and *Deor* to Eormanric [d. 375], Ælfwine [d. 573], and Theodoric) but also in celebration of heroic conduct (aspiration to fame and glory, as in *Waldere*, or the bonds of protection and generosity, loyalty, and service between lords and thanes). The sustained vigor of secular heroic values may be seen in *The Battle of Maldon*, recorded in the *Anglo-Saxon Chronicle* entry for 991, which eulogizes Byrhtnoth's heroic defeat in the words of his follower Byrhtwold: "Resolve shall be higher, heart more bold / Spirit shall be stronger, as our strength diminishes."

Struggle is the primary motif in much of this lit.; life is accepted as fleeting. To lament the vanity of all things even while celebrating their splendor is a principal theme, esp. in the Exeter-book poems generally known as the OE elegies, among which *The Ruin, The Wanderer,* and *The Seafarer* are most renowned. In differing degree secular or Christian, the elegies exhibit a dominant pattern of loss and consolation. *The Wanderer*, e.g., uses themes of exile, ruin, and the *ubi sunt* (q.v.) motif to show that the only constancy is God's. More clearly didactic and perhaps even allegorical, *The Seafarer* presents the sea journey as an emblem of this world's exile from the heavenly kingdom.

In both *Widsith* and *Beowulf*, the minstrel (*scop*, q.v.) sings to the harp. The discovery in the Sutton Hoo ship burial of fragments that have been reconstructed as a Ger. round harp suggests that the instrument provided formal accompaniment to poetic recitation, though much critical controversy remains. Stylistically, too, OE verse looks back to the secular AS heritage (see ENGLISH PROSODY, *Old English*), preserving a special vocabulary, particularly certain archaic words used only in poetry. Its diction, an artificial literary *koine* with mainly West-Saxon features, is characterized by chiefly metonymic words, esp. the riddle-like kennings (q.v.), e.g. "hron-rad" (the whale's road). Other devices include paronomasia, litotes, and meiosis (qq.v.). However, the chief stylistic devices of OE poetry are repetition, apposition, and variation, restatements of the same idea but with slightly altered connotations. Some evidence also points to formulaic composition (see ORAL-FORMULAIC THEORY): the beasts of battle (raven and wolf) accompany armies even when no battle occurs (as in *Exodus*), and sea-voyages are often traditionally elaborated, as in *Guthlac II*, where the Lat. original recounts only a journey by rowboat. The OE storm topos survives into ME verse.

The name Cynewulf has been worked, in runic anagrams, into the conclusions of *Juliana* and *Elene* (and also in *Christ II* and *Fates of the Apostles,* but without the "e"). Cynewulf was probably a West-Mercian cleric living in the early 9th c.; the major theme of his poems is the spiritual battle between good and evil. The most skillful of Cynewulf's poems, the epic *Elene*, recounts the *inventio crucis*, the discovery of the true Cross. Until the late 19th c., Cynewulf was also supposed the author of the *Dream of the Rood, Guthlac II, Christ I, Christ III,* and *Andreas.* Of these poems, the *Dream of the Rood,* considered the finest narrative of the Passion in medieval verse, portrays Christ as a young Germanic warrior-hero.

Beowulf, the greatest of OE poems to survive, is preserved with *Judith* in MS Cotton Vitellius A.xv. Demonstrating extensive Cl. and Christian influence, the poem draws on historical figures verified from Lat. and ON works: Gregory of Tours' *Historia francorum,* Saxo Grammaticus's *Gesta danorum,* and *Hrólfs saga Kraka.* Widsith, for instance, provides corroborating information about Hrothgar, king of the Danes. Still, *Beowulf*'s narrative materials are largely folktale (e.g. "The Bear's Son" tale motif; the "Sandhill" episode of the *Grettir Saga*) and Germanic legend, though these are given epic significance against the 6th-c. background of the Danish Scyldings and Geatish Hrethlings.

Retainer to Hygelac the Geat in the first half of the poem and, 50 years later, Geatish king for the remainder, Beowulf battles three great monsters. The first two encounters take place in Denmark where Beowulf frees Hrothgar's hall (Heorot) from the monster Grendel and then hunts down and slays Grendel's mother, who has come to Heorot seeking revenge. In the third battle, Beowulf loses his life but kills the dragon that has terrorized his people. These three battles are woven into a rich background of oration (individual speeches account for 1300 lines—40% of the total), asides, digressions, and envelope structures that contribute to recurrent, interlaced themes. The thematic structure seems to be one of contrasts: Scyld's burial at the outset and Beowulf's at the end; youth and age; heroic action and elegiac mood. If Beowulf's desire to possess the gold of the dragon's hoard is a failure of character, as some think, he yet dies the ideal Germanic prince, "gentlest, kindest to his people, and most eager for fame."

II. MIDDLE ENGLISH (1066–1500). Some OE

alliterative verse continued to be written after the Norman Conquest (1066), e.g. *Durham*, an early 12th-c. *encomium urbis*. However, under the influence of the Fr. poetry brought into England by the Normans, a fresh spirit and new style characterize Early ME poetry like *The Owl and the Nightingale* (late 12th c.), whose *débat* conventions (see POETIC CONTESTS), octosyllabic line, and *courtois* vocabulary mark a clear break with the AS poetic past. Like the Med. Lat. debates (esp. *Winter and Summer*) which are its closest analogues, *The Owl and the Nightingale* generates its dialectic from the character of the contestants—the solemn Owl on her ivy-clad stump and the merry Nightingale on her bough of blossoms—although interpretations of the contest (sorrow vs. joy, duty vs. pleasure, clerk vs. minstrel) vary widely.

New literary forms proliferate in the 12th and 13th cs. A large body of religious works emerges, mostly translations and paraphrases of the Bible (e.g. *Genesis and Exodus*, ca. 1250; the 14th-c. *Rawlinson Strophic Pieces*), saints' legends (e.g. the *South Eng. Legendary*, late 13th c.; the influential *Gospel of Nicodemus*, ca. 1325), and didactic pieces such as the early *Poema morale* (ca. 1170) and the *Ormulum* (ca. 1200), an incomplete 10,000-line collection of homilies.

The earliest extant lyrics (St. Godric's Hymn, ca. 1160–70) are inspired by Lat. models, as was much of the great outpouring of later devotional verse, esp. that influenced by Franciscan spirituality. Early secular lyrics like "Sumer is icumen in" (a *reverdie* [q.v.]), recorded in a Reading Abbey ms. [ca. 1275] with notation for musical performance as a four-part canon accompanied by two voices) are indebted to OF and AN love lyrics, *chanson* and *pastourelle* (qq.v.). Macaronic verse (q.v.), both secular and sacred, commonly uses Lat. and Eng., but poems mixing Fr. and Eng. or all three langs. also occur. The 14th-c. Vernon ms. preserves a fine collection of religious lyrics; secular lyrics showing importantly the influence of Fr. and Med. Lat. verse as well as the Eng. alliterative trad. are preserved in the well-known MS Harley 2253 (compiled ca. 1330). Other short verseforms worthy of note include poems dealing with contemp. conditions (e.g. the poems of Laurence Minot; the political prophecies attributed to Merlin), carols (q.v.), esp. those of the 15th-c. Franciscan James Ryman, and ballads (q.v.), such as those of the Robin Hood cycle preserved in Bishop Percy's Folio.

Verse is the medium for narratives of all kinds, incl. the verse chronicle (e.g. *Cursor mundi*), beast epic (q.v.; *The Fox and the Wolf*), fabliau (q.v.; *Dame Sirith*), parody (q.v.; *The Land of Cokaygne*), natural history (*The Bestiary*), and, importantly, the medieval romance (q.v.). Loosely defined as narrative poems about knightly prowess and adventure, romances were intended mostly for listening. Romances of varying types and quality appear both in AN and ME. Early Eng. romances like *King Horn*

(ca. 1225) and *Havelok the Dane* (ca. 1280–1300) are preceded by AN versions; others like *Bevis of Hampton* (ca. 1300) and *Guy of Warwick* (ca. 1300) translate AN originals. Most Breton *lais* (q.v.) like *Lai le Freine* (early 14th c.) are also indebted to Fr. originals; some, like *Sir Orfeo*, relate adventures of the faery world. Many ME romances employ the tail-rhyme stanza (q.v.), esp. those written in East Anglia in the 14th c. Chaucer's satiric *Tale of Sir Thopas* plays on the weaknesses of this verse: hackneyed phrasing, tag rhymes, ludicrous plot devices, and cardboard characters.

The romances are usually classified according to their subjects—the matter of France, the matter of Rome, and the matter of Britain. The matter of France is not well represented in ME poetry, *Ashmole Sir Firumbras* (ca. 1380) and the late alliterative *Rauf Coilyear* being the best representatives. The matter of Rome includes the popular Alexander romances (e.g. the three alliterative fragments, *Alisaunder*, *Alexander and Dindimus*, and *Wars of Alexander*, or the quite different *Scottish Alexander Buik* [1438] translating an OF original) and narratives of the fall of Troy like the *Gest Historiale of the Destruction of Troy* (ca. 1350–1400) and the minstrel romance the *Seege of Troye* (ca. 1300–25) which were in fact the most popular and prolific of medieval topoi. Both Chaucer and Lydgate try their hands at Troy stories.

The matter of Britain, however, furnishes the best and most popular romances in ME. King Arthur comes into Eng. p. through verse chronicle, but Layamon's *Brut* (ca. 1205), itself a tr. of Wace's AN *Roman de Brut* (the first to mention the Round Table), derives in its turn from Geoffrey of Monmouth's Lat. *Historia regum britanniae* (ca. 1130–38). Antiquarian and epic without the courtly refinement of Wace, Layamon's style mixes alliterative and rhymed verse. Layamon also introduces Celtic elements into Wace's more restrained version, incl. the prophecy of Arthur's return from Avalon. In addition to Layamon, Arthur's history is chronicled in the alliterative *Morte Arthure* and the ballad, the *Legend of King Arthur*. Of Arthur's knights, Gawain receives the most attention—witness the 12 extant ME Gawain romances. *Sir Gawain and the Green Knight*, the most widely celebrated of the Eng. Arthurian romances, links two plot motifs, the beheading game and the exchange of winnings, in a test of Sir Gawain's courtesy, courage, and loyalty.

The small, unprepossessing ms. in which *Sir Gawain* survives, Cotton Nero A.x., contains three other poems, *Cleanness*, *Patience*, and *Pearl*, possibly by the same author. *St. Erkenwald*, long associated with this poet (called either the *Pearl*-poet or the *Gawain*-poet), has recently been shown to have been authored by another. *Patience* and *Purity* are both homilies with biblical *exempla*; the former is an animated paraphrase of the book of Jonah, the latter, more ambitious poem ranges widely over stories of the Flood, the destruction of Sodom, and

Belshazzar's feast. In *Pearl, courtois* lang. characterizes the heavenly court for which the Pearl-maiden (the poet's daughter? his own soul?) speaks. The dreamer-poet, initially anguished at the loss of his Pearl (the *pretiosa margarita* of Matt. 13.45), awakens from his dream consoled, his will reconciled with God's. Variously interpreted as elegy, *consolatio*, allegory, or dream vision, *Pearl* astonishes with its numerological and prosodic complexities: 1212 lines in 101 stanzas in groups of fives linked by refrain, concatenation (q.v.), and iteration. The poem's elaborate artistry and profound emotion find no parallel in ME poetry.

Pearl aside, the Cotton Nero poems, with others whose origin is North West Midlands (e.g. the *Siege of Jerusalem* [ca. 1390]), Northern (e.g. *The Awntyrs of Arthure at the Terne Wathelyne* [ca. 1430–40]), or Scottish (e.g. *The Scottish Prophecies* [ca. 1400–50]), are written in an unrhymed, alliterative long line which is the staple meter of all those poems that have come to be loosely denominated as the Alliterative Revival (AR). Whether the form of the alliterative line was preserved in the 14th c. through an unbroken oral trad. linked to OE practice, or whether 14th c. poets shaped the line from a continuum of alliterative writing remains controversial (see ENGLISH PROSODY, *Middle English*). Several other poems, like *The Pistel of Swete Susan*, combine the alliterative line with rhyme in complex stanzas. The major genres of AR poems include romances and chronicles in epic style (e.g. the *Wars of Alexander*, tr. from a Med. Lat. original), religious poetry, burlesques, satires, and allegories (qq.v.), many imitating Langland's *Piers Plowman*. For the most part, AR poems exhibit the same high conception of the poet's task, the same learned and bookish character, and the same concern for the social fabric as do the major Ricardian poems written in the last half of the 14th c., i.e. those by the Gawain-poet, Gower (1330–1408), Chaucer (ca. 1343/4–1400), and Langland (ca. 1330?–86?).

Of the poets working in the unrhymed alliterative long line, only Langland's name has come down to us, although the autobiographical sketch he provides in the C text of *Piers Plowman* must be regarded as suspect. In the over 50 surviving mss. of *Piers Plowman*, Skeat found evidence for three versions: a short A text, a much revised and expanded B text, and a fully revised C text (a fourth, or Z text, has also been proposed). The poem is rubricated into the *visio*, which recounts the dreaming narrator's allegorical satire of the "field full of folk"—England of the late 14th c.—and the *vita*, which recounts the pilgrimage to St. Truth through Dowell, Dobet, and Dobest.

If Langland wrote for the clerisy, however, Gower wrote for the court; his great Eng. poem, *Confessio amantis*, was commissioned by King Richard II, although later rededicated to Henry IV. Dedicated also to his friend Chaucer, Gower's *Confessio*, like *Pearl* and Chaucer's *Book of the Duchess*, may be read as a poem of consolation, since its matter is the confession by Amans of the seven deadly sins. The work also involves England's desire for justice and the common good, a theme which dominates Gower's earlier Lat. poem, *Vox clamantis*.

The chronology of Chaucer's poetry is unknown, although on the basis of internal evidence scholars have postulated an early Fr. period marked by the influence of Guillaume de Lorris and Jean de Meun (part of whose poem Chaucer translated in the *Romaunt of the Rose*), Froissart, and Machaut (whose influence may be seen in *The Book of the Duchess*). The middle or It. period, consisting of *The House of Fame, The Parliament of Foules, Troilus and Criseyde*, and *The Legend of Good Women*, is heavily indebted to Dante, Boccaccio, and, to a lesser extent, Petrarch. His late, Eng. period encompasses most of *The Canterbury Tales*.

The occasion for the first of Chaucer's major independent poems seems to have been the death (in 1368/69) of Blanche of Lancaster, wife of Chaucer's patron John of Gaunt, although the poem may have been written later in commemoration. Even this early work demonstrates Chaucer's considerable mastery of *courtois* diction and the conventions of courtly love poetry. Like *The Owl and the Nightingale*, Chaucer's *Parliament of Foules* (1380–82) plays (in part) upon the conventions of a *debat* among birds whose characters are revealed through style and idiom, but here expressed in a new verseform, rhyme royal (q.v.; first tried by Chaucer in *Anelida*). Although other of Chaucer's contemporaries—John Gower, Oton de Grandson, John Clanvowe—composed valentine poems, *The Parliament* is probably the earliest, and certainly the best celebration of St. Valentine's day in Eng. lit.

By the mid 1380s, Chaucer was translating Boethius' *Consolatio de philosophia*. *Troilus and Criseyde, The Knight's Tale*, and *The Legend of Good Women* (written, he claims, as penance for his treatment of Criseyde) are marked by a deepening philosophical coloring and a Petrarchan lyricism. For Troilus' musing on fate in Book IV of *Troilus*, Chaucer provided a passage from Boethius (5.1–2) on necessity (a passage omitted by some scribes), and the *canticus Troili* of Book I translates Petrarch's sonnet 88, "S'amor non e." Based on Boccaccio's *Il Filostrato* and a Fr. tr., *Troilus* sets the personal fate of Troilus in love—"fro wo to wele, and after out of joie"—against the public history of Troy, radically transforming the It. story and its characters. In this work, Chaucer abandons the Fr. poets of occasional verse and seeks the company of the three crowns of Florence—Dante, Petrarch, Boccaccio—learned, philosophical poets in pursuit of fame.

When or under what influences Chaucer struck upon the idea for *The Canterbury Tales* (the frame story is a pilgrimage from London to Canterbury during which the pilgrims engage in a tale-telling contest) continue to be matters of speculation. By the late 1380s, he was working on the unfinished collection of ten extant fragments, whose tales are connected by narrative links. *The General Prologue* with which the poem opens describes the 29 (or 31) pilgrims both as satiric types on the model of *estates satire* (e.g. the hunting monk, the false pardoner) and as individuals (the monk's description suggests he has become the fat, roasted swan he so loves to eat). In many tales, the character of the teller and of the tale are carefully paired; in others the relationship seems sketchy; in a few, *The Shipman's Tale*, for instance, teller and tale are mismatched, a result of the poem's unrevised character. There is a wide variety of genres: saint's life and fabliau, allegory and romance, confession, sermon, satire, manual of penitence. Tale-telling begins in high seriousness with the Knight's Theban romance, and returns to it with *The Man of Law's Tale, The Clerk's Tale, The Prioress's Tale*, and others. Frequently, however, it degenerates into bawdy verbal attack and riposte, with the celebrated marriage debate at the center of the roadside drama. But whether engaged in personal animosity (Miller vs. Reeve, Friar vs. Summoner) or continuing debate (Wife of Bath, Clerk, Merchant, and Franklin), or commenting more subtly on recurring themes (Prioress, Canon's Yeoman), all the pilgrims touch on the great issues of the poem: love both secular and divine, justice, the power of lang., the trust necessary for community, the pilgrimage to God. Continually in print from Caxton's first ed. of 1478, Chaucer's poetry marks a significant artistic and intellectual flowering in ME—from it springs the great trad. of Eng. p.

Both in the Prologue to *The Man of Law's Tale* and in the final *Retraction*, Chaucer lists his *oeuvre*, incl. some poems, like *The Book of the Lion*, that have not survived. A number of other works, however, did survive by attaching themselves to the Chaucer canon, and these Chaucerian apocrypha give some idea of the influence Chaucer's verse exerted over the next century. Courtly poetry remains an important genre until the end of the 15th c., esp. allegorical love narratives like the *Flower and the Leaf, The Assembly of Ladies*, or Thomas Hoccleve's *Letter of Cupid*, a warning to women against false lovers and clerks. Hoccleve (ca. 1368–ca. 1430?) is chiefly memorable, however, for his tribute to Chaucer with its accompanying portrait of the poet in *The Regiment of Princes*, a manual of instruction.

Among the more accomplished of Chaucer's imitators are John Lydgate in England and Robert Henryson and William Dunbar in Scotland. Lydgate (ca. 1370–1449), a monk of Bury St. Edmunds and an untiring versifier in the amplificatory style, enjoyed both civic and royal patronage. He translated Laurent's monumental Fr. verson of *The Fall of Princes* (1431–38), for instance, at the commission of Humphrey, Duke of Gloucester. Writing in every important medieval genre, Lyd-gate was esteemed the greatest poet of his age, and his *Fall of Princes* continued to be admired into the Ren., where it provided material for the *Mirror for Magistrates*. Following Lydgate at least in part, Robert Henryson (ca. 1425/35?–1506?) composed *The Morall Fabillis of Esope*, but he is best remembered for his continuation of Chaucer's *Troilus* in *The Testament of Cresseid*. The other great Scottish Chaucerian (q.v.) or Makar is William Dunbar (ca. 1460–1520/22), a poet at the court of King James IV. He wrote occasional poems (e.g. his courtly dream vision, *The Thrissill and the Rois* [1503]), satires, and flytings (q.v.), and the alliterative *Twa Mariit Wemen and the Wedo* (ca. 1508), a bawdy dialogue.

The civic or cycle plays (also called mystery plays because of guild sponsorship, or *Corpus Christi* plays for their performance on that feast date) comprise the largest corpus of ME drama, a product mainly of the 15th c. (see LITURGICAL DRAMA). Cycles are preserved from York, Chester, and Wakefield (also called the Towneley plays), while non-cycle plays are preserved from Norwich, Shrewsbury, and London, among others. A fourth cycle, known as *Ludus coventriae* (or N-Town plays), seems to have been produced at a number of locations. Although the plays are anonymous and probably the product of several revisions, two great playwrights, the York Realist and the Wakefield Master, whose hand may be seen for instance in the First and Second Shepherds' Plays, have been identified on stylistic and metrical grounds. Several morality plays (q.v.), indebted to medieval sermon trads., also survive, most notably *The Castle of Perseverance* and, at the end of the 15th c., the Eng. version of *Everyman*.

Much ME material continues to exert an influence in the 16th c. (Roger Ascham would not have objected to romances if no one was reading them), but humanism and the It. fashion give a new spur to Eng. p. after 1500; John Skelton is traditionally the last Eng. poet of that great age which precedes the Ren.   R.H.O.

BIBLIOGRAPHIES AND INDEXES: *General*: *CBEL*, v. 1, *600–1660*, and v. 5, *Supp. 600–1900*; *New CBEL*, v. 1; *A Literary Hist. of England*, ed. A. C. Baugh, 2d ed. (1967). The literary histories by Pearsall, J. A. W. Bennett, H. S. Bennett, Chambers, Lewis, Greenfield and Calder, and Bolton listed below also contain bibls. *Old English*: *OE Newsletter* 1– (1967–)—annual bibl.; D. D. Short, *Beowulf Scholarship: An Annot. Bibl.* (1980); S. B. Greenfield and F. C. Robinson, *A Bibl. of Publications on OE Lit. to the End of 1972* (1980)—now the standard bibl. *Middle English*: A. H. Billings, *A Guide to the ME Metrical Romances* (1901); C. Brown and R. H. Robbins, *The Index of ME Verse* (1943), and R. H. Robbins and J. Cutler, *Supp.* (1965); W. Renwick and H. Orton, *The Beginnings of Eng. Lit. to Skelton*, 3d ed., rev. M. F. Wakelin (1966); J. B. Severs and A. E. Hartung, *A Manual of the Writings in ME, 1050–1500*, 7 v. (1967–86); W. Matthews, *Old and*

ME Lit. (1968); *Eng. Drama to 1660,* ed. E. Penninger (1976); M. Andrew, *The Gawain-Poet: An Annot. Bibl. 1839–1977* (1979); R. F. Yeager, *John Gower Materials: A Bibl. Through 1979* (1981); V. DiMarco, *Piers Plowman: A Ref. Guide* (1982); J. A. Rice, *ME Romances: An Annot. Bibl. 1955–85* (1987). *Chaucer*: E. P. Hammond, *Chaucer: A Bibliographical Manual* (1908)—still important; D. D. Griffith, *Bibl. of Chaucer 1908–53* (1955); W. R. Crawford, *Bibl. of Chaucer 1954–63* (1967); A. C. Baugh, *Chaucer,* 2d ed. (1977); *Studies in the Age of Chaucer* 1–(1979–)—annual bibl.; L. Baird-Lange and H. Schnuttgen, *A Bibl. of Chaucer 1974–85* (1988).

ANTHOLOGIES: *Eng. Lyrics of the XIIIth C., Religious Lyrics of the XVth C.,* both ed. C. F. Brown (1932, 1939); *Religious Lyrics of the XIVth C.,* ed. C. F. Brown, 2d ed., rev. G. Smithers (1952); *Secular Lyrics of the XIVth and XVth Cs.,* ed. R. H. Robbins, 2d ed. (1955); *Historical Poems of the XIVth and XVth Cs.,* ed. R. H. Robbins (1959); *Early ME Verse and Prose,* ed. J. A. W. Bennett and G. V. Smithers (1968); *Med. Eng. Lit.,* ed. T. Garbaty (1984); *ME Romances,* ed. A. C. Gibbs (1988); *Alliterative Poetry of the Later Middle Ages,* ed. T. Turville-Petre (1989).

HISTORY AND CRITICISM: *General*: CHEL; E. K. Chambers, *The Close of the Middle Ages* (1945); C. S. Lewis, *Eng. Lit. in the 16th C.* (1954); M. Bloomfield, *Piers Plowman as a 14th-C. Apocalypse* (1962); L. D. Benson, *Art and Trad. in* Sir Gawain and the Green Knight (1965); J. A. Burrow, *A Reading of* Sir Gawain and the Green Knight (1965); V. A. Kolve, *The Play Called Corpus Christi* (1966); P. L. Henry, *The Early Eng. and Celtic Lyric* (1966); R. Woolf, *The Eng. Religious Lyric in the Middle Ages* (1968), *The Eng. Mystery Plays* (1972); W. Bolton, *The Middle Ages* (1970); B. F. Huppé, *The Web of Words: Structural Analyses of OE Poems* (1970); D. Gray, *Themes and Images in the Med. Eng. Religious Lyric* (1972); A. A. Lee, *The Guest-Hall of Eden: Four Essays on the Design of OE Poetry* (1972); S. B. Greenfield, *The Interp. of OE Poems* (1972); M. Carruthers, *The Search for St. Truth: A Study of Meaning in* Piers Plowman (1973); J. A. Burrow, *Ricardian Poetry* (1974); Pearsall—the single most useful book; W. A. Davenport, *The Art of the Gawain Poet* (1978); *ME Alliterative Poetry and Its Literary Background,* ed. D. A. Lawton (1982); E. R. Anderson, *Cynewulf: Structure, Style, and Theme in His Poetry* (1983); A. C. Spearing, *Med. to Ren. in Eng. P.* (1984); L. S. Johnson, *The Voice of the Gawain Poet* (1984); J. A. W. Bennett and D. Gray, *ME Lit.* (1986); S. B. Greenfield and D. G. Calder, *A New Critical Hist. of OE Lit.* (1986); M. Swanton, *Eng. Lit. before Chaucer* (1987); L. A. Ebin, *Illuminator, Makar, Vates* (1988); A. Renoir, *A Key to Old Poems* (1988).

Beowulf: J. R. R. Tolkien, "*Beowulf,* the Monsters and the Critics," *PBA* 22 (1936); D. Whitelock, *The Audience of* Beowulf (1951); A. Brodeur, *The Art of Beowulf* (1959); K. Sisam, *The Structure of* Beowulf (1965); E. Irving, *A Reading of* Beowulf (1968); M. Goldsmith, *The Mode and Meaning of* Beowulf (1970); *The Dating of* Beowulf, ed. C. Chase (1981); J. D. Niles, Beowulf: *The Poem and Its Trad.* (1983).

Chaucer: H. S. Bennett, *Chaucer and the 15th C.* (1947); C. Muscatine, *Chaucer and the Fr. Trad.* (1957); D. W. Robertson, *A Preface to Chaucer* (1962); R. O. Payne, *The Key of Remembrance* (1963); B. F. Huppé, *A Reading of the* Canterbury Tales (1964); P. G. Ruggiers, *The Art of the* Canterbury Tales (1965); M. Bowden, *A Commentary on the General Prologue to the* Canterbury Tales, 2d. ed. (1967); R. M. Jordan, *Chaucer and the Shape of Creation* (1967); E. T. Donaldson, *Speaking of Chaucer* (1970); P. M. Kean, *Chaucer and the Making of Eng. P.* (1972); J. Mann, *Chaucer and Med. Estates Satire* (1973); D. R. Howard, *The Idea of the* Canterbury Tales (1976); V. A. Kolve, *Chaucer and the Imagery of Narrative* (1984). R.H.O.; T.V.F.B.

III. RENAISSANCE TO MODERN (since 1500). A. *The Renaissance.* Where should the history of modern (that is, post-medieval) Eng. p. begin? John Skelton (?1460–1529) can be seen either as the first modern or as the last medieval poet in Eng. Certainly the casual structure of his poems, the colloquial and often mischievous tone, have a strong appeal to the 20th-c. reader, and even make him look like a proto-modern in a more drastic sense of the term; but these very qualities can also be seen as belonging to a native Eng., even medieval, trad. in contrast to the more formal and Italianizing poetry of the Ren. Skelton's most popular poem is "Philip Sparrow," in which "Dame Margery" laments the death of her pet sparrow, killed by "Gyp, our cat," and which, without ever departing from the lightness of tone appropriate to the subject, introduces sexual inuendo, natural history, Cl. mythology, and an informal history of Eng. p. The poem, like much of Skelton, is written in colloquial, fast-moving dimeters, and in a tone well described (and captured) by Skelton himself in his "Colin Clout": "He chideth and he chatters, He prayeth and he patters; He clyttreth and he clatters."

With Sir Thomas Wyatt (1503–42), however, we have undoubtedly reached the Ren. Though in his own time his version of the Penitential Psalms received most attention, it is his lyrics that later ages have valued. A generation after his death, Puttenham commended him and Surrey for introducing It. polish into "our rude and homely manner of vulgar poetry," and praised them as "the first reformers of our Eng. metre and style." It. influence meant above all that of Petrarch, whose poems to Laura, filled with religious imagery and praise of the mistress for her spiritual superiority as well as her beauty, look back to earlier It. poetry (q.v.), and beyond that to the "amour de loinh" of the Troubadours (see COURTLY LOVE; OCCITAN POETRY), and also forward, since Petrarch exercised an enormous influence on the 16th c. (see

PETRARCHISM). Wyatt's love poems, like most 16th-c. love poetry, express the laments of the unrequited or deserted lover rather than the joys of mutuality; and his sonnets introduce many of the topoi that became so popular in the Elizabethan sonnet: sexual love as a hunt, the lover as a ship running aground on the rocks. Technically, Wyatt is important for the musical quality of his lyrics: many of them were meant to be sung, and they are often self-consciously musical (e.g. "My lute, awake"). Scholars have long argued—and still disagree—whether the broken, hesitant rhythms of his lyrics result from our ignorance of 16th-c. pronunciation or are a deliberate departure from regularity in the interests of artistic expressiveness.

The name of Henry Howard, Earl of Surrey (1517–47) is regularly coupled with that of Wyatt. He too introduced It. models into Eng., and he wrote similar, but more conventional, love poems, which often seem stiff and imitative compared with Wyatt's freedom and emotional power. But he has the enormous historical importance of having introduced blank verse into Eng. (in his tr. of Books 2 and 4 of *The Aeneid*).

Several poets collaborated in *A Mirror for Magistrates* (1559–63), a long narrative poem in which various princes and other political figures tell their tragic story. It is chiefly interesting today for what it tells us about didactic views of politics in the 16th c.; also as illustrating the medieval concept of tragedy: a poem (not necessarily dramatic) that narrates the fall of a great man. It is widely agreed that the only parts of poetical interest are the *induction* and the *Complaint of Buckingham*, by Thomas Sackville (1536–1608); though rather stiffly melodramatic, these show interesting anticipations of Spenser. Sackville also collaborated with Thomas Norton on *Gorboduc* (1561), a didactic political drama in Senecan style, that could be considered the first real post-medieval Eng. play.

But if we are looking for the moment when Eng. p. most decisively emerged from the Middle Ages to the Ren., the best answer might be the publication of Spenser's *The Shepherd's Calendar* in 1579. For pastoral (q.v.) is an important Ren. genre, announcing an allegiance to It. poetry—the pioneering work is Sannazaro's *Arcadia* (1504)—and behind that to the ancients—the *Idylls* of Theocritus and the *Eclogues* of Virgil. Ren. pastoral idealizes rustic life and celebrates a Golden Age of simplicity and leisure. Spenser's own "aeglogues" (the pseudo-etymological spelling, to derive from goatherd, is his) are divided into plaintive, recreative (about love, often for an idealized Elizabethan), and moral ("mixed with some satirical bitterness"). Most Elizabethan love poetry makes some use of pastoral conventions, above all that of Sir Philip Sidney (1554–86) in his long, mysterious, and powerful fragment addressed to Queen Elizabeth, *The Ocean to Cynthia*, and that of contributors to the pastoral miscellany *England's Helicon* (1600), who include, besides Sidney and Raleigh, Thomas Greene, Thomas Lodge, Robert Peele, Anthony Munday ("Shepherd Toni"), and, above all, Nicholas Breton. The trad. lives on until Marvell, the most poised and gracious of all pastoral poets, and indeed until Pope, whose Pastorals, in the best Ren. trad., were the work of his youth.

Plaintive pastorals, or pastoral elegies (see ELEGY), often on the death of a fellow poet, all owing something to Virgil's fifth *Eclogue*, were common in the Ren. Spenser's *Astrophel* (1586) laments Sidney, on whom Fulke Greville also wrote an elegy which is a direct statement of grief, without pastoral conventions. But the most famous pastoral elegy is Milton's *Lycidas* (1637), and the genre had an afterlife in Shelley's *Adonais* (1821; on Keats), in Arnold's *Thyrsis* (1867; on Clough), and in Yeats' "Shepherd and Goatherd" (1919; on Robert Gregory). Satirical bitterness was never common in the Eng. pastoral, though *Lycidas* does contain a fierce attack on church corruption.

In the 1590s, half a century after Wyatt introduced the sonnet (q.v.) into Eng., there was a craze for sonnet sequences (q.v.). The originator was Sidney, whose *Astrophil and Stella*, witty, self-mocking, psychologically exploratory, and lyrically eloquent on occasion, was published posthumously in 1591; it was followed by the sonnets of Daniel, Spenser, and Drayton—Spenser has the originality of having written his to the woman he then married. The greatest of the sonneteers was of course Shakespeare, some at least of whose sonnets were written by 1598, when Francis Meres mentions his "sugar'd sonnets among his private friends." Shakespeare rehearses many of the great commonplaces of the other sonneteers, but with unsurpassed and unforgettable eloquence: the fading of beauty ("O, how shall summer's honey breath hold out Against the wrackful siege of battering days") or the immortality bestowed by the poet ("Not marble, nor the gilded monuments / Of princes shall outlive this powerful rhyme"). But Shakespeare's sonnets do not simply do better what the other sonneteers also do; they also differ in their programme. They are, in the first place, written to a man, though they use many of the topoi of compliment that other poets used to women; they exhort the young man to marry, they confess emotional dependence on him, and they hint at, without actually narrating, a quarrel between them. Indeed, when the sonnets were published in 1609, probably without Shakespeare's consent, they were by no means all sugared: they contain bitter poems of self-analysis and moral rebuke, some of them to the young man, some of them reflections on human frailty in the trad. of religious satire ("Tired with all these, for restful death I cry"). There is also a series of twenty-odd poems addressed to the misleadingly nicknamed "Dark Lady" ("black woman" is a phrase that would capture the tone better), which anatomize a degrading love with fierce self-reproach. At their most savage these poems use puns, esp. on the words "lie" and "dark," linking word-play to bitterness with an intensity unmatched in Eng. p.; thus a poem on the unhinging of judgment by passion ends with the fierce couplet: "For I have sworn thee fair, and thought thee bright, / Who art as black as hell, as dark as night."

The next major poet to take the sonnet seriously was Milton, who used it for political themes and personal (though not love) poems, and who used the Petrarchan pattern of octave and sestet rather than the three quatrains and couplet that Shakespeare had popularized. Milton's sonnets illustrate a paradox that postromantic theories of poetry as expression have difficulty coming to terms with: they seem at the same time to be poetry at the extreme of formality and conventionality, and yet poetry at its most deeply personal. After Milton the sonnet slept until its revival by the romantics, esp. Wordsworth and Keats.

Edmund Spenser (1552–99) is a central figure in Ren. poetry. His corpus is dominated by the huge, unfinished epic, The Faerie Queene (1589–96), which, however, did not set a fashion in Eng. p., and remains unique. It derives from the It. romantic epic of Ariosto and Tasso, with its elaborate, interweaving stories. The programme which Spenser himself announced (Epistle to Raleigh) of 12 books figuring forth the 12 moral virtues according to Aristotle, does not correspond well to the six books we have, and some critics claim that these should be regarded as a complete poem, rounded off by an epilogue (the Mutability Cantos, which are proffered as a fragment of the seventh book). The Faerie Queene is probably the most complicated narrative poem in the lang., with its innumerable stories of love, pursuit, flight, and betrayal, in which fleeing maidens and pursuing knights constantly disappear down forest paths. The allegory is very complex and perhaps not meant to be completely unraveled. It is best remembered not for its structural qualities but for its famous set pieces like the Bower of Bliss (2.12), the House of Busirane (3.11–12), the Garden of Adonis (4.6), and Calidore's vision on Mount Acidale (6.10).

The Elizabethans recognized as a separate genre the epyllion (q.v.) or little epic, a narrative of several hundred lines with a mythological story, usually taken from Ovid. The most famous of these are Marlowe's Hero and Leander (unfinished at his death; "completed" by Chapman and pub. 1598), a subtle mingling of the celebratory and the ironic, richly sensuous in parts, which has left us one of the most famous lines in Eng. p., "Who ever loved that loved not at first sight?"; and Shakespeare's Venus and Adonis (1593), with a reluctant Adonis who owes as much to Titian as to Ovid. The publication of this poem may represent Shakespeare's attempt to establish himself as a man of letters; its sequel, The Rape of Lucrece, pub. the following year, is less Ovidian and more monotonous. Other epyllia are Scilla's Metamorphosis by Thomas Lodge (1589), which may have inspired the fashion, and Salmacis and Hermaphrodite by Francis Beaumont (1602).

The other poet who compasses much of the variety of Elizabethan poetry, and in a way overlapping very little with Spenser, is John Donne (1572–1631). Donne is often thought of as not being an Elizabethan, since his witty, realistic, outrageously bold love poems have come to be regarded as the great reaction against the mellifluous charm of the Elizabethan lyric. But chronologically, Donne is as Elizabethan as Shakespeare, and his Songs and Sonets, mostly written in the 1590s, are contemporary with the lyrics of Thomas Nashe ("In Time of Plague"), and precede the songs of Thomas Campion, perhaps the finest of Elizabethan songwriters.

Donne shot to his position as one of the great Eng. poets in the early 20th c., with Sir Herbert Grierson's 1921 rediscovery of metaphysical poetry (q.v.), and he is not likely to lose it again. His poetry was seen to offer just what the age demanded: on the one hand a direct and colloquial treatment of sexual love, in which the speaking voice replaces the idealization of the Delias and Julias of Ren. poetic convention, and on the other the famous metaphysical conceit (q.v.), the delight in outrageous wit, learned ingenuity, and philosophical paradox ("She's all kings, and all princes I; nothing else is"). Now that the flush of rediscovery is over, we can see that Donne was a poet of his time. For one thing, his realistic treatment of the love relationship does not extend to the woman herself, who is as shadowy and unparticularized as any of the Delias and Julias; for another, his boldly individual public poetic personality owes a good deal to that favorite poet of the Elizabethans, Ovid. Ovid appears direct in Elizabethan poetry through the lively but clumsy tr. of the Metamorphoses (1565–67) by Arthur Golding, with its preliminary allegorizing epistle, and also through Marlowe's youthful tr. of the Amores into heroic couplets (pub. posthumously, 1597). Donne owes little to the mythological Ovid (he was even praised, in Carew's famous Elegy, for rescuing Eng. p. from the "train of gods and goddesses"), but he captures the sweet and witty Ovid (and the sour Ovid too) in his Elegies, which are closer in spirit to the Amores than is Marlowe's tr.

Donne's brilliant love poems are as varied in attitude as in metrical pattern (not even Hardy and Auden were more fertile in inventing stanza forms than Donne). The view of love varies from playful cynicism ("Go and Catch a falling star") through savage cynicism ("Love's Alchemy"), delight in mutual love ("The Sun Rising," "The Canonisation"), Platonic affection ("Twickenham Gardens," "The Relic"), the conquest of absence (the four Valedictions), grief at the beloved's death—or mock death ("Nocturnal on St. Lucy's Day"), and many more. Donne's verse epistles (q.v.) are less brilliant, yet their often conventional compliments use witty conceits that are sometimes more extravagant than those in the love poems. It is useful to think of Donne's poetry in terms of the commonplace Ren. doctrine of the three styles, high, middle, and low. His love poems move between the high and the middle styles, with occasional shocking descents into (or, more often, hints of) a coarseness in sentiment or vocabulary; his epistles use the straightforward middle style, then considered fitting for this genre; and his satires use the base style, though they are not as coarse as those of the other two satirists of the 1590s, Joseph Hall (*Vergidemiarum*, 1597–98) and John Marston (*The Scourge of Villainy*, 1598). For the Ren. critics, style derived not from the personality of the poet, but above all from decorum (q.v.), that is, appropriateness to the subject: they would therefore consider it natural to associate stylistic coarseness with a genre (satire) rather than with a particular writer (though it must be added that Marston can be pretty coarse in his plays too). Satire (q.v.) as a genre, and coarse vigor as a quality, were neglected, even despised, in the Victorian view of the Elizabethan poets as a nest of singing birds, a view that is not yet dead; but in the 20th c., there is a more lively appreciation of the tough lang. of Donne and Marston: reading "My spirit is not puffed up with fat fume / Of slimy ale, nor Bacchus' heating grape," we might today find Marston vigorous, not just coarse and self-centered.

Donne's poetic career culminated in religious poetry, in which his love of paradox (q.v.) seems less of a personal quirk than a product of his Christian faith. Donne wrote two sets of religious sonnets, a linked series of thoughtful meditations on theological concepts (*La Corona*), and the violently personal "Holy Sonnets," whose emotional intensity has spoken to many modern readers who yet do not share the religious belief.

The third major figure (apart from Shakespeare) in Ren. p. is Ben Jonson (1572–1637), Cl. scholar, dramatist, epigrammatist, lyric poet. His poetry runs through all the styles, from the tender lyricism of his songs ("Still to be neat, still to be dress'd") to the coarseness of the epigrams he imitated from Martial. His greatest work is certainly in his plays, which he published in 1616 as the *Works of Ben Jonson*, thus making a claim for drama as serious lit., and not merely the script of popular entertainment—a claim posterity has endorsed.

B. *Dramatic Poetry to 1642*. We make fun of what we take seriously; so Shakespeare's mockery of pedantic genre classification in *Hamlet* ("the best players in the world either for tragedy, comedy, historical, pastoral, pastoral-comical . . . tragical-comical-historical-pastoral") may well be evidence that these classifications mattered to the Elizabethans, and that two comedies or two pastorals would for them have had more in common than two plays by the same author. Taking genre (q.v.) seriously need not, however, mean that the boundaries between the genres are clear-cut: it may be precisely the overlap that makes generic affiliation rewarding. In approaching Elizabethan drama by genres, therefore, rather than by authors, we may find ourselves tantalized by the existence of comical-pastoral and historical-tragical.

Three main passions provided the material of tragedy (q.v.): revenge, love, and ambition. Revenge tragedy begins with possibly the most renowned of all Elizabethan plays, *The Spanish Tragedy* by Thomas Kyd (1592), which contains what came to be the stock ingredients of the genre: a ghost, several murders, a skillfully planned revenge, and an aesthetic delight in the skill of its execution. Kyd also wrote a version of the Hamlet story (which Shakespeare reworked), which has perished—thus opening the door to even more hundreds of speculations on the *Hamlet* we have. The popularity of revenge as a theme in Elizabethan drama is due, on one level, to the influence of Seneca, of whom the Elizabethans held a remarkably high opinion. The sinfulness of revenge to a Christian is mentioned in only one play, Tourneur's *The Atheist's Tragedy* (1611): "Attend with patience the success of things, / And leave revenge unto the King of Kings." Such a behest, if taken seriously, would destroy the genre, but it can lead us to ask how the Elizabethan audience responded to such plays. Did they leave their Christian scruples behind as they entered the theater, or were moral awareness and dramatic excitement held in a fruitful (if never explicitly mentioned) tension? One naturally inclines to the second hypothesis for the great plays, several of which can be read this way. There is no questioning of the ethic of revenge in *Hamlet*, but revenge is held suspended in continual tension with other themes (above all with Hamlet's own alienation and neurosis, and with his relationship with his mother). Not Hamlet but Laertes is the single-minded avenger. In Middleton and Rowley's *The Changeling* (1608), too, the dedicated avenger is a minor figure; the main theme is the moral degradation of the central character. In *The Revenger's Tragedy* (1607; probably by Tourneur, perhaps by Middleton) Vindice, the hero, takes on the persona of the avenger when he decides to go to court and is trapped by his role; his satiric gloating over the corruption of court, and his murderous gloating over the artistry of his revenge, become indistinguishable, and the resulting poetry has a resonant mingling of the moral and the decadent. In John Webster's *Duchess of Malfi* (1613), revenge emerges as a central theme only in the final act, when all has gone wrong for the heroine, and the Machiavel-figure of Bosola, in a kind of twisted repentance, turns into an avenger. These four plays, probably the finest of the revenge tragedies, are also in their different ways the most ambivalent.

Other examples are Shakespeare's *Titus Andronicus* (1594) and Marston's *Antonio's Revenge* (1602) and *The Malcontent* (1604), which have many points of contact with *Hamlet.*

Since happy love and courtship are the stuff of comedy, the tragedy of love will involve either adultery or the clash between love and social obligation. The pure tragedy of adultery is found in Middleton's *Women Beware Women* (pub. posthumously, 1657) and Beaumont and Fletcher's *Maid's Tragedy* (1619). Shakespeare's three love tragedies are all different thematically. In *Romeo and Juliet* (ca. 1595) love clashes with family loyalty and the lovers are "star-crossed"; the conflict in *Othello* (1604) can be described as love versus marriage, since the blind idealization of Othello, the romantic lover, makes him susceptible to the machinations of the villain and leads him to destroy both his love and his beloved. In *Antony and Cleopatra* (ca. 1607) the lovers' adultery is secondary to the clash between their love and public duty; this play is perhaps Shakespeare's most morally ambiguous and most poetically daring. The dramatist who dealt most single-mindedly in the tragedy of love was John Ford, esp. in *Lover's Melancholy* (1629), *Tis Pity She's a Whore* (1630), a brilliantly melodramatic play about incest, and *The Broken Heart* (1633).

Ambition in its various forms is the most important of all the Elizabethan tragic themes. It is the stuff of all Marlowe's plays (*Tamburlaine, The Jew of Malta, Dr. Faustus, Edward II*; all written 1587–93) and Shakespeare's *Macbeth* (1606) and *Richard III* (1594). The central figure is always an overreacher, whose histrionic self-awareness makes him both dangerous and dramatically exciting—another example of the tension between moral and aesthetic response that is so central to Elizabethan dramatic poetry. Indeed, ambition is in some degree the theme of all history plays, a genre popular in the 1590s. Shakespeare wrote two tetralogies (q.v.) in this genre, the earlier (*Richard III–Henry VI*) dealing with the Wars of the Roses, and the later (*Richard II–Henry V*) dealing with earlier events: this helps to justify the cross-generic indication in the titles (*The Tragical Hist. of Dr. Faustus; The Tragedy of King Richard II*). Ambition is also the theme of Jonson's one great tragedy, the learned but theatrically exciting *Sejanus* (1603), as well as Shakespeare's *Coriolanus* (1608) and the works of many later tragedians, Fletcher (1579–1625), Massinger (1583–1640), and Shirley (1596–1666).

The tragedy of ambition will naturally be political. A monarch does not need to be ambitious, only an aspiring monarch; the term therefore suggests that the tragic figure will be the usurper. If the king is a good one, the usurper will be the villain (*Richard III*); if he is a tyrant, concentration on the usurper will mean that we are concerned with who is to rule (Richard II or Henry IV) rather than how. This will once again lead to ambivalence, the main figure then becoming a villain-hero, and in a sense it will lead us away from politics towards the more personal theme of succession. It is arguable that this happens in most Elizabethan political tragedy, and that Shakespeare is the only one of the dramatists who shows a real interest in the ruled as well as the rulers.

This discussion of tragedy in terms of the ruling passion has tended to direct attention to plot and theme; we can now ask whether the kind of poetry varies according to the theme. The revenge plays are often rich in sardonic and disturbing poetry, and their lang. sometimes abuts that of satire. This is most signally true of *The Revenger's Tragedy*, whose brilliant verbal effects touch on the surrealistic ("Well, if anything be damned / It will be twelve o'clock at night") and on the morally perverted ("Oh, one incestuous kiss picks open Hell"—a line that seems to wallow in its masochism, yet through the image of a scab conveys a disgust that can be seen as implicitly moral). *Hamlet* too contains powerful sardonic writing, often linked to sexual disgust: Hamlet plays the role of the satirist at times, and the lang. responds. The love tragedies, on the other hand, naturally explore many of the topoi of romantic love; *Romeo and Juliet* is filled with conceits on the relation between love and religion, or between sex and death: when Romeo claims that Juliet's body is uncorrupted because Death wants to make love to her ("The lean abhorred monster keeps / Thee here in dark to be his paramour"), the dramatic irony (we known that Juliet is not actually dead) does not detract from the brilliance of the conceit. Written in the 1590s, *Romeo and Juliet* develops conventional conceits with some originality and power; by the time of *Antony and Cleopatra*, a dozen years later, Shakespeare's poetry has grown more daring and unorthodox. The rhythm of this later play has moved far enough from the regular iambic pentameter (see BLANK VERSE) that some of it could be taken for free verse, and the imagery relates sex and death more daringly than anything before, as in Cleopatra's line about the asp: "Dost thou not see the baby at my breast, / That sucks the nurse asleep."

Comedy (q.v.) can be subdivided into romantic and satiric. Romantic comedy has love as its theme, courtship as its action. It begins with lovers meeting and ends with wedding bells, using as its stock conventions love at first sight, opposition of parents, idealization of the beloved, and teasing by the friends of the lover. With love occuring at first sight, the action of the play is left to result from delaying tactics, usually parental opposition, adventure, and separation (with the heroine disguised as a boy, a convenient device, given that Elizabethan acting companies were exclusively male); the other delaying device is courtship itself, the elaborate rituals and speeches of wooing. With variations, all of Shakespeare's romantic comedies from *Two Gentlemen of Verona* (1594) to

Twelfth Night (1601) fit this pattern. Behind Shakespeare lies John Lyly, who wrote elaborately artificial comedies of wooing which Shakespeare both parodied and learned from. The romantic comedies and tragicomedies of Beaumont and Fletcher (e.g. *Philaster*, 1611) derive from and may in turn have influenced Shakespeare, whose late comedies (*Cymbeline, A Winter's Tale, The Tempest*) move toward tragicomedy (q.v.) and shift attention from the young lovers to the older generation.

Satiric comedy deals with human vices and follies, esp. greed, and verges on nondramatic satire. It produced the finest dramatic writing of the age outside Shakespeare and embraces both the city comedies of Middleton and Massinger (*A Chaste Maid in Cheapside*, ca. 1613; *A New Way to Pay Old Debts*, 1622?) as well as the rich output of Jonson, who explores the humor, or dominant passion (see COMEDY OF HUMORS), very self-consciously in the early *Every Man in his Humour* (1598) and *Every Man out of his Humour* (1599), and implicitly in all his work. *Bartholomew Fair* (1614) and *The Devil is an Ass* (1616) mix topical satire with farce (q.v.). His greatest poetry comes in *Volpone* (1605) and *The Alchemist* (1612), both outstanding for the elegance of their plotting and the brilliance of their poetry.

If we look at Ren. drama more narrowly as poetry, concentrating on style, on local verbal effects, and on verbal inventiveness, it is clear that drama produced the finest poetry of the age because of the predominance of Shakespeare. No simple summary can do justice to the variety of Shakespeare's poetic effects or the complexity of his devel., so a few pointers must suffice. His early comedies show ingenious verbal wit in formal and regular metrical patterns: *Love's Labour's Lost*, for instance, is full of lines like "Light, seeking light, does light of light beguile," where the awareness of a complicated web of meanings is immediate, even though it may take some familiarity with the text to sort out what the meanings are; and also of lines that shift suddenly in register, corresponding to the shifts between elaborate courtship rituals and sexual bluntness—so Berowne says of the heroine, "Aye, and by Heaven one that will do the deed, / Though Argus were her eunuch and her guard," allowing himself a Cl. allusion even in the midst of the insult. It is a line that could be spoken either with a cynical leer or with frank delight. If we turn from the beginning to the end of Shakespeare's career, we find a very different use of lang.—poetry that works through ellipses, contorted syntax, and mixed metaphors, sometimes of such complexity that lang. is being strained to its utmost. On occasions there is an almost perverse avoidance of the straightforward: "Sluttery to such neat excellence oppos'd / Should make desire vomit emptiness, / Not so allur'd to feed," says Iachimo, paying a compliment to Imogen's "neat excellence," and leaving her as bewildered as the audience. But this verbal restlessness is the necessary precondition for the wild fertility of lang. that distinguishes the late plays and seems to provide the only possible means of expression for Coriolanus' irascibility, Leontes' jealousy, or Cleopatra's passion. Even inarticulateness itself is expressed in Shakespeare's late poetry, as when Caliban tells how Prospero taught him "how / To name the bigger light, and how the less, / That burn by day and night"; and that inarticulateness is the necessary precondition for the physical immediacy of some of Caliban's lang., his feeling for the sounds and shapes of the magic island—a feeling that Browning responded to and extended brilliantly in "Caliban upon Setebos." For Shakespeare's greatness shows itself not only in what he wrote himself, but in how he taught other poets to go beyond him.

Shakespeare dominates, but there is striking poetic power in some of the other Ren. dramatists. Marlowe introduced into dramatic poetry a histrionic, magnificently self-conscious rhetoric ("Marlowe's mighty line") that manifests itself even in the crudities of his first play, *Tamburlaine*. The hero is a blustering warrior with scant talent save for killing, yet he expresses himself sometimes with lyric grace, other times with lines that seem to become aware of their bluster, as if the poetry both enacts the swagger and smiles at it ("Where'er I come the fatal sisters sweat"). This is an effect that passed from Marlowe to most of his followers but no later dramatist succeeded in imitating the power of Faustus' last speech before damnation, where Cl. allusion mingles with theological abstractions to express personal anguish.

The greatest verbal artist among Eng. dramatists after Shakespeare is, however, Jonson, whose satiric poetry celebrates (as does so much satire) the very qualities it attacks. Volpone's morning address to his gold, for instance, ("Open the shrine, that I may see my saint") is a religious parody of disconcerting eloquence; and the pompous Sir Epicure Mammon in *The Alchemist* disconcerts too by the way his absurd desires occasionally drop into sensuous and exquisite poetry.

The connection of Eng. p. with the stage, so deep and successful before 1642 (the year the theaters were closed), has since that date virtually ceased. Almost all the major 19th-c. poets wrote plays, few of which succeeded in the theater, and none of which has retained permanent interest; in the 20th c. there have been sporadic outbursts of poetic drama (e.g. T. S. Eliot), but on the whole Eng. drama since 1660 has been in prose. See DRAMATIC POETRY.

C. *The Seventeenth Century*. The traditional way for lit. hist. to map the rich variety of nondramatic poetry in the earlier 17th c. has been in terms of the influence of Spenser, Donne, and Jonson. The "School of Spenser" (q.v.) includes the authors of long allegorical poems like *The Purple Island* (1633) by Phineas Fletcher and *Christ's Victory and Triumph* (1610) by his brother Giles, as well as the pastorals of Micheal Drayton (1563–1631) and William Browne (1591–1643), and that enormous piece of patriotic topography, *Poly-Olbion* (Drayton); it can also claim the young Milton, who praised the "Forests and enchantments drear, / Where more is meant than meets the ear." Donne's followers admired his wit, producing in Sir John Suckling (1609–42) charming and cynical love poems resembling the more light-hearted of the Songs and Sonnets, and in Richard Lovelace (1616–58) something more. The most self-conscious of the three groups were the "Sons of Ben," who admired and imitated Jonson's metrical polish, lyric charm, and classicism (see CAVALIER POETS). They include Suckling and Lovelace as well as Thomas Carew (1598–1639), author of some beautiful, polished lyrics of compliment ("Ask me no more where Jove bestows, / When June is past the fading rose"), and Robert Herrick (1591–1674), one of the most loved of Eng. lyrists ("Gather ye rosebuds while ye may," "To Daffodils").

Of course such a classification must oversimplify, and almost all the poets of the age learned from all three influences, as well as from Shakespeare and directly from Lat. poetry. Herrick for instance must owe some of his pastoralism to Spenser, and can be quite as witty as Lovelace; Carew joins Jonson's polish to a subdued version of Donne's wit in a way that anticipates Marvell. The age had a common sensibility and a living poetic trad. that enabled its minor poets to write better than ever before or since.

A rather different classification recognizes a school of metaphysical poets, a term originally pejorative that later became approbatory. Richard Crashaw (1612–49) can be called "metaphysical" because of his love of paradox and his extravagant conceits: sometimes these present the central doctrines of Christianity, sometimes (as in "The Weeper"), they are simply ingenious. Crashaw has strong Continental links, esp. with the It. Marino, whom he translated, and can be considered England's one true baroque (q.v.) poet.

George Herbert (1593–1633) can also be linked with Donne, whom he knew, and whose love of inventing complicated stanzas he shared; his vivid creation of dramatic situations between himself and God may also owe much to Donne's poetry, both secular and sacred. Yet the most important context for Herbert's poetry is not literary but the trad. of scriptural interp. that insisted on several levels of meaning in a biblical text (see ALLEGORY); the view of lang. that this supposes is central to Herbert. He is unusual among 17th-c. poets in that he wrote only religious poetry. His one volume, *The Temple*, was described by him as containing "a picture of the many spiritual conflicts that have passed betwixt God and my soul." This suggests a strong autobiographical element, and many of the poems are indeed highly personal ("The Collar," "The Pearl"); others, however, explore traditional images or scriptural texts ("Lent," "The Bunch of Grapes"). Given the habit of applying the so-called moral meaning of scripture to one's own life, and of seeing one's own experience in a wider scriptural context, each type keeps tending toward the other.

Herbert's own poetic apologia is found in the two Jordan poems, which defend simplicity and the choice of godly subject matter. They are really palinodes; and like all truly profound recantations, they enact what they reject ("quaint words and trim invention"). Modern deconstructive critics can find in Herbert a powerful statement of the position that a text undermines its assertions by its strategies, just as hunters for ambiguity can disintegrate an apparently simple line like "Shepherds are honest people; let them sing" into unfathomable ambiguities: "shepherds" could refer to priests, and the last three words could be variously emphasized (don't stop them singing; let them, not others, sing; let them sing, not quibble). It is not necessary to remove Herbert from his intellectual context in order to see how much he has to offer to modern theories of poetry.

Henry Vaughan (1622–95) has not got Herbert's superb technical skill, but he was so deeply influenced by Herbert that it is easy to confuse their poems. Vaughan's Christianity is diluted with Hermetic and Neoplatonic thought, and some of his most characteristic and striking poems arise from this, as when he contrasts the "steadfastness and state" of the nonhuman world with his own restlessness: "But I am sadly loose, and stray / A giddy blast each way." At such moments the poetry springs directly from the philosophical and theological ideas that so fascinated Vaughan. Vaughan's best-known work is "The Retreat," a charming poem about childhood that anticipates Wordsworth's Immortality Ode; but a more complex and thoughtful poetry is that in "Man," "And do they so?" "The Morning Watch," and "The Timber."

Andrew Marvell is the finest of the "metaphysicals." He mingles the cl. polish of Jonson with the wit of Donne, and the subtlety with which he deploys his knowledge of Lat. poetry embeds his work profoundly in trad. without lessening its originality. Marvell wrote mostly in tetrameter couplets, and his command of this meter is so complete that it yields a complete command over meaning too—or rather, his poems show how intimately the two skills are connected: a slight metrical nuance or semantic ambiguity can turn a very ordinary and traditional line into one of striking profundity. T. S. Eliot's famous phrase, "a tough reasonableness beneath the slight lyric grace," applies better to Marvell than to anyone else. Marvell's "To his Coy Mistress" is certainly the finest *carpe diem* (q.v.) poem in Eng., and his "Horatian Ode on Cromwell's Return from Ireland" is equally the subtlest political poem; while "The Garden" sums up all the ambivalences of the pastoral trad. in its polished couplets. "No white nor red was ever seen / So amorous as this lovely green" both asserts and smiles at the view that retreat from the world gives us the essence of the experiences we are avoiding.

The mid 17th c. is dominated by John Milton (1608–74), whose poetic career falls clearly into two halves. His early poems, collected in 1645, incl. "L'Allegro" and "Il Penseroso," academic exercises on the contrasting themes of mirth and melancholy, memorable for their generalized yet vivid description and their handling of myth and cl. learning. "Lycidas" was originally pub. in a volume of commemorative verses on Edward King (1637), all the rest of which is forgotten. Milton did not know King well, but by turning him into a generalized figure for the dead poet he produced a poem that was both deeply personal and deeply traditional. The longest work in the 1645 volume was the masque (q.v.) known as *Comus*, produced at Ludlow Castle in 1634 in honor of the Earl of Bridgewater. Masques, combining music, poetry, stage design, dancing, allegory, and compliments to members of the audience, were a popular form of entertainment at court and country houses. Jonson was the most celebrated writer of masques, and collaborated with Inigo Jones at the court of James I, but no other masque has achieved the enduring fame of this humble provincial production by a then little-known poet. The theme of *Comus* is temptation and the magical power of chastity, a didactic theme fitting the Earl's children, who took part. The monster Comus, the tempter, is both the villain and also the operative principle of the masque itself, and raises many of the issues about how moral and aesthetic judgments interact that are later raised by the figure of Satan in *Paradise Lost*.

When the Civil War came, Milton forsook poetry for political pamphleteering. When he returned to poetry, his second poetic career produced only three works. *Paradise Lost* (1667) is still the most important single poem in Eng., a Cl. epic (q.v.) devoted to a Christian subject. By making Satan the hero, in the conventional narrative sense, and using many of the traditional epic devices in the depiction of Hell, Milton produced a poem that in some sense refutes itself, and so offers the reader a deeply ambivalent experience. Critics have ever since tried to simplify its ambivalence, either in the direction of the romantic view that claims he was "a true poet of the devil's party without knowing it" (Blake), or in the direction of the moralistic view, that claims we should simply disapprove of Satan. To appreciate the full flavor of Milton's verse, one needs to read extended passages, but a glimpse of its complex music and its mingling of cl. allusion and personal involvement can be gained from any of the four exordia (to Books 1, 3, 7, and 9): thus in that to Book 7, he exhorts the Muse to "drive far off the barbarous dissonance / Of Bacchus and his revellers, the race / Of that wild Rout that tore the Thracian Bard / in Rhodope, where Woods and Rocks had Ears / To rapture." This expresses his lifelong fascination with the story of Orpheus. The verse enacts some of the dissonance it describes without sacrificing the music of the blank verse; it conveys the terror of the murder while also suggesting a magical quality appropriate to an ancient legend; and it inserts the full force of pagan mythology into a poem that insists on an identification of such stories with the devil. All Milton's ambivalences are present in the lines.

Paradise Regained (1671), a "brief epic," is more austere. Its choice of subject (Christ's 40 days in the wilderness) yields little action, and its choice of style yields little of Milton's verbal richness. Probably the most powerful part is the debate between Cl. learning and Christianity in Book 4 that makes explicit a conflict running not only through all Milton's work but through all Ren. culture. *Samson Agonistes* (1671), Milton's last work, pays (like *Paradise Lost*) one kind of allegiance in its subject and another in its form, the former arising from the Old Testament, the latter being that of Gr. tragedy.

D. *The Augustans*. The later 17th c. brought profound changes in Eng. society, and arguably the sharpest break in the whole history of Eng. p.: from 1660 to 1800, the map is much easier to draw. The term "Augustan," based on the claim to be the new Golden Age of the arts, corresponding to the Rome that Augustus found brick and left marble, expresses a boast made by the age itself. The arrival of Augustan poetry is conveniently shown by the shift from Dryden's "Heroic Stanzas on the Death of Cromwell" (1659), which is in quatrains, and contains some extravagant conceits that could be by Cowley or even Donne, to his *Astraea redux*, on the Restoration of Charles II (1660), which is in couplets, and altogether more bland and balanced in style. Dryden never looked back, either metrically or politically. His poetic career is divided between translation, modernization, and original composition. He Englished Virgil, Ovid, and Chaucer; most of his original poetry falls between the satiric and the didactic (*Absalom and Achitophel* [1681], *Religio laici* [1682], *The Hind and the Panther* [1687]); his most delightful poem is probably *Mac Flecknoe*, which satirizes his poetic rival, Thomas Shadwell.

Dryden has often been praised for the vigor and energy of his couplets: Pope wrote that he joined "the varying verse, the full-resounding line, / The long majestic march, and energy divine." The praise is eloquent and no doubt sincere, but is written with a matching of sound to sense that shows Pope to be an even greater master of the heroic couplet (q.v.). When Dryden died in 1700, Alexander Pope (1688–1744) was only 12 years old, but was already writing, if we are to believe his own claim that "he lisped in numbers, for the numbers came"—the line is adapted from Ovid.

Pope too wrote almost entirely in couplets because that was the meter thought suitable for epic, though for both Dryden and Pope the measure could as well be called the satiric couplet. Pope's career is divided in two by his tr. of Homer. Before that, his output was miscellaneous, incl. most notably the *Essay on Crit.* (1711), stating the Augustan aesthetic with clarity and consummate metrical skill, and *The Rape of the Lock* (1712), a very elegant mock-heroic (q.v.) whose witty surface constantly implies serious possibilities.

In the 1720s Pope, in his own words, "stooped to truth and moralized his song": his settings were now contemporary, and his satire almost unbridled. *The Dunciad* (1728–29) lacks the perfection of *The Rape of the Lock*, but it is a far more complex, extravagant, and profound mock-heroic. Its concluding vision of the triumph of the goddess Dullness has long been recognized as sublime, without ceasing to belong in a comic poem; and on a smaller scale, some of its couplets generate a lyric beauty that is both undermined and reinforced by the satiric intent ("To happy convents, bosomed deep in vines, / Where slumber abbots, purple as their vines": the impact of these lines grows even more complex if we remember that Pope was himself a Roman Catholic). The one nonsatiric poem of the later period is the *Essay on Man* (1730), a versification of many of the commonplaces of 18th-c. philosophy. The four Moral Essays, or Epistles to several persons (1731–35), are free-wheeling reflective poems, and the last two, on the use of riches, can be seen as statements of the ideal of Augustan civilization. The *Imitations of Horace* (1733–38) use the Augustan analogy with great subtlety, moving between cl. allusion (see IMITATION) and contemp. lampoon. The Prologue, in the form of an Epistle to Arbuthnot, has become the favorite among Pope's poems for its easy colloquial grace and rhythm and for its brilliantly savage portraits of Atticus and Sporus.

The other principal satirists of the 18th c. are Swift, Gay, and Johnson. Jonathan Swift (1667–1745) wrote a set of verses on his own death, whose light surface ("The Dean is dead. Pray what is trumps?") may conceal bitterness; and some poems of sexual disgust ("A Beautiful Young Nymph Going to Bed," "Strephon and Chloe") that have been read both as expressions of his own scatological obsession and as pleas for sanity—they may of course be both. John Gay (1685–1732) wrote *Trivia*, a lively mock-heroic (q.v.) on the art of walking the streets of London, and the very successful *Beggar's Opera* (1728), written in prose interspersed with songs that look like very conventional lyrics when read in isolation but take on a rich satiric resonance in context. Samuel Johnson (1709–84) based his two great satiric poems, *London* and *The Vanity of Human Wishes*, on Juvenal, adapting the savage indignation of the original to contemp. subject matter. They have little or no irony, and the cumulative impression of their weighty couplets shows that satire can be wholly serious and still impressive as poetry.

Augustan poetic theory, as we find it in, for instance, Pope's *Essay on Crit.* or Johnson's prose, is a consistent affair (see NEOCLASSICAL POETICS). It values the general over the particular, morality over subversion, clarity over subtlety, and explicitness over obliqueness. To the 20th-c. reader this sounds very like an anti-poetics, and we naturally ask ourselves whether poetry for the 18th c. was something quite different from what it is for us, or whether their theory did not do justice to their practice. Part of the answer may be that what we value most in 18th-c. poetry is satire and burlesque—genres that interrogate and subvert the very qualities that, in theory at least, 18th-c. critics valued so highly. Housman was no doubt making a similar point when he observed that the four finest 18th-c. poets (Collins, Smart, Cowper, Blake) had one thing in common: they were all mad.

But not all 18th-c. poetry is satire, and not all is in couplets. The Pindaric ode was a licensed departure from the preference for order and symmetry: it was supposed to be irregular in meter and full of digressions and uplifting sentiments, a kind of equivalent to the sublime in painting. Thomas Gray (1716–71) and William Collins (1721–59) both wrote such odes, though we remember Collins rather for the descriptive carefulness and tender feeling of his "Ode to Evening," and Gray above all for his "Elegy Written in a Country Churchyard," which expresses memorably many of the pastoral and elegiac commonplaces long central to Eng. p.

The half-century between the death of Pope and the arrival of Wordsworth and Coleridge is the least impressive in the history of Eng. p. It encompasses Oliver Goldsmith (1728–74), whose *Deserted Village* (1770) mingles sentimental social commentary with the pastoral trad.; William Cowper (1731–1800), author of a long blank verse reflection, *The Task* (1785), some memorable hymns, and the powerful lyric "The Castaway," which can be read as an allegory of his own mental disturbance; and Robert Burns (1759–96), Scotland's favorite poet, whose songs are still quoted and sung: "Auld Lang Syne" has become almost an unofficial Scots anthem, and "the best laid schemes o' mice and men / Gang oft a-gley" is one of the most familiar quotations in the lang. Of Burns' longer poems, *The Cotter's Saturday Night* is a sententious idealization of rural life, and *Tam o' Shanter* an uninhibited comic narrative.

George Crabbe (1754–1832) survived into the romantic period but remained an Augustan in spirit. He began with the fierce anti-pastoral *The Village* (1783) and went on to realistic, sometimes grimly humorous narratives in couplets, of which the most famous has become "Peter Grimes": the description of Peter in his depression letting his boat drift through mud-banks, along the "lazy tide," is a tour-de-force of the pathetic fallacy (q.v.) that has no parallel in Eng. p.

William Blake (1757–1827) was neglected during his lifetime but is now ranked with the great romantic poets. He began with a volume of graceful neo-Elizabethan lyrics, *Poetical Sketches* (1783), before turning to the deliberate naivete of the *Songs of Innocence* (1789), the complex lyricism of the *Songs of Experience* (1794), and finally the strange mythology of his Prophetic Books. To the unexpert reader, these books seem almost solipsistic in their thinking, but a great deal of scholarly work has now been devoted to them, so that those willing to study *The Four Zoas, Milton,* or *Jerusalem* with the aid of commentaries can now gain access to a coherent philosophical and even political worldview. Because Blake's poetry is obscure and at the same time immediate in its impact, there is an almost inevitable rift between the learned explicators and the readers who respond strongly and attach meanings which Blake almost certainly did not intend. A famous example is the lyric from *Milton* which asks "And was Jerusalem builded here, Amid these dark Satanic mills?" Generations of readers have taken this as a social commentary on the Industrial Revolution, but Blake scholars have arrived at no consensus regarding these mills, except to agree that they are not factories. Perhaps no poet provides better material for the modern critical argument about the relation between intention and meaning (qq.v.), or between meaning and significance.

E. *The Romantics.* The romantic dawn in Eng. p. is conventionally marked by *Lyrical Ballads*, published by Wordsworth and Coleridge in 1798. Most of the poems are ballads dealing with incidents and situations from common life, with simple and rustic protagonists: there is an almost anti-literary quality to them, esp. in their reliance on plain lang., as if rejecting most of the verbal resources of poetry. Wordsworth defended both his lang. and his subjects in the Preface to the second ed. (1800), which has become the most famous manifesto in Eng. p.: it attacks poetic diction (q.v.) and defends "the lang. really used by men," preferring "humble and rustic life" as material "because in that condition the essential passions of the heart find a better soil."

The two most important poems in *Lyrical Ballads*, however, do not seek to intensify the natural, but rather to render the supernatural natural. One is Coleridge's "Rime of the Ancient Mariner," a long sea narrative, deriving from his omnivorous reading in travel lit.: it is in ballad meter (q.v.), and some of its strongest effects have the terseness of the old ballads ("Water, water, everywhere, / Nor any drop to drink"), but its exploration of extreme situations and its fascination with the exotic and the frighteningly beautiful, as in the descriptions of the icebergs and the water-snakes, make it—in the everyday sense of the term—a much more romantic poem than any of Words-

worth's. Coleridge himself described the division of labor between the two of them as one in which he was to deal with "persons and characters supernatural or at least romantic," and by his treatment "to procure for these shadows of imagination that willing suspension of disbelief for the moment which constitutes poetic faith"; and Wordsworth was to choose characters and incidents "such as will be found in every village," and to "give the charm of novelty to the things of every day." The other major poem in *Lyrical Ballads* is the poem that has come to be known as "Tintern Abbey," an account in blank verse of Wordsworth's emotional development. It claims that the maturity which hears "the still sad music of humanity" is more valuable than his passionate early enthusiasm for nature, but the greatest poetic intensity clings to the early, outgrown experiences—a pattern that is widespread in Wordsworth's finest poetry. "Tintern Abbey" is a seminal poem for the romantic movement. It resembles—and no doubt lies behind—Coleridge's series of "Conversation Poems" (the finest is "Frost at Midnight"), and above all, it foreshadows Wordsworth's masterpiece, the long autobiographical poem we know as *The Prelude.*

Wordsworth never published and never even named this poem, but he realized its importance, and tinkered with it throughout his life. It offers not a coherent psychological theory of his devel. but a series of sketches of his "spots of time"—the episodes, outwardly unimportant, that stand out in memory and helped to form him. He describes himself as "fostered alike by beauty and by fear," and far more of these memories show fear than happiness. *The Prelude* deals with memory and childhood in a way that assumes the true subject of poetry to be the self, and for this reason can be seen as a central romantic poem. It was intended as a preface to the long philosophic poem he never completed, though part of it was pub. as *The Excursion* in 1814. The first book of this contains the story of Margaret, a short bare narrative of unrelieved distress, which, for those who value the early and more radical Wordsworth, can be seen as his masterpiece in the bleak simplicity of its pathos. The later books of *The Excursion* moralize the verse and make it clear that Wordsworth is greatest as a philosophical poet when writing closest to his own experience. His true philosophical achievement was, in fact, *The Prelude* itself.

The second generation of Eng. romantics—Byron, Shelley, Keats—all died young, and were outlived by the first. George Gordon Lord Byron (1788–1824) shot to fame with *Childe Harold's Pilgrimage* (1812–18), the Grand Tour of a sensitive, brooding, passionate young man, a distinctly theatrical version of the poet himself. Today Byron's reputation rests more on a handful of polished lyrics and the long, unfinished *Don Juan* (1819–24), a witty, cynical, colloquial narrative of contemp. life.

Percy Bysshe Shelley (1792–1822) is the most Platonic and political of the romantics. His Platonism issues sometimes as a series of abstractions, sometimes as a vision of the transcendent (most famously in the image used in *Adonais*, "Life like a dome of many coloured glass / Stains the white radiance of eternity"). Most of his poems give no hint of his ardent radicalism and his hostility to the tyranny of priest and king, but those which do (*The Masque of Anarchy* [1832], "Song to the Men of England" [1839]), written with the deliberate intent of being popular, made him a people's poet throughout the 19th c. Shelley could also be intensely personal, and lyrics like the "Ode to the West Wind" or "Stanzas Written in Dejection" can be praised for their passionate feeling or condemned for their adolescent mawkishness.

John Keats (1795–1821) developed astonishingly between the lush sensuousness of his first volume, published in 1817 ("the soul is lost in pleasant smotherings"), and the maturity of his great poetry only three years later. "An artist must serve Mammon," he wrote to Shelley, rejecting all didactic views of poetry; he urged Shelley to curb his magnanimity and "load every rift [of your subject] with ore." The rich verbal texture of Keats's poetry is most apparent in his odes ("To a Nightingale," on escapism; "On a Grecian Urn," on art; "To Psyche," on ancient myth; "To Autumn," on sensuous experience of Nature). Probably no poems in the lang. have been more lingered on and more analyzed for the richness of their verbal effects than these odes: the ending of "To Autumn," for instance ("then in a mournful choir the small gnats mourn / And gathering swallows twitter in the skies") blends all the senses and "conspires" (to use Keats's own word) to imitate the bodily experiences of the watcher, while at the same time introducing, with perfect tact, the theme of death that underlies any poem on autumn. As a narrative poet, Keats took his subjects from folklore ("The Eve of St. Agnes"), from his reading ("Lamia"), and esp. from Cl. mythology: *Endymion*, his longest poem, and the two versions of *Hyperion*—the first abandoned because "too full of Miltonic inversions: Eng. must be kept up," the second also abandoned after being reworked as a more personal and homemade myth, a project similar to, but less obscure than, the complicated mythology of Blake.

Of the other romantic poets the most celebrated was Sir Walter Scott (1771–1830), now thought of as a novelist, though he began as a poet; his metrical romances of Scottish history (*The Lay of the Last Minstrel, Marmion, The Lady of the Lake*) were as popular in their day as the more exotic verse tales of Byron; but a more profound contribution to poetry is almost certainly his creative editing of the *Minstrelsy of the Scottish Border* (1802–3) and his powerful, lapidary lyric, "Proud Maisie." Walter Savage Landor (1775–1864) is the author of some exquisite tiny lyrics; and the poetry

of the agricultural laborer John Clare (1793–1864) is genuinely rural, not pastoral: his choice of the title *The Shepherd's Calendar* provides one of the ironies of Eng. p., since instead of the moralizing, the courtly compliments, and the allegorical figures of Spenser, Clare fills his poem with the real awarenesses of shepherds ("the duck Waddling eager through the muck"). Clare spent much of his later life in an asylum, and this produced the most moving of his many lyrics, that beginning "I am. Yet what I am who cares or knows?"

Though the term "romantic" is universally accepted as a label for the early 19th c., there is little agreement among literary scholars about its meaning (see ROMANTICISM; ROMANTIC AND POSTROMANTIC POETICS). Its main meanings can be illustrated by asking which of the Eng. poets is the representative romantic. The case for Wordsworth has already been stated: on the other hand, his belief in general truths and his faith in "that calm existence which is mine when I / Am worthy of myself" makes him very classical. Keats is the archetypal romantic if we emphasize myth and legend as material, and concrete imagery as stylistic device. Byron, who lacks the verbal genius of these two, has always seemed the archetypal romantic to Continental readers; his histrionic self-projection looks back to Goethe's Werther and Rousseau's self-image, and forward to Pushkin, Lermontov, Stendhal and Hugo.

F. *The Victorians.* Coleridge died in 1832; Tennyson published his first volume in 1830, Browning in 1833; and Queen Victoria came to the throne in 1837: so the 1830s can be considered the transition from romantic to Victorian poetry. Yet though the labels are generally used, they make an odd pair: romantic, as we have seen, attempts to describe qualities in the lit. itself (as well as in other arts), whereas "Victorian" is simply borrowed from political history It might be better to regard Tennyson and Browning as the third generation of romantic poets, and Arnold, Meredith, and the Rossettis as the fourth, rather than postulating a new phase in lit. hist. If we see the romantic movement as continuing until the advent of modernism in our own century, it would still not be as long as the neoclassical or Augustan phase. Certainly the continuity between Keats and Tennyson, between Shelley and the young Browning, between Wordsworth and Arnold, is stronger than that between the first two romantic generations. The rise of the novel to centrality in Victorian lit., and the consequent directing of the realistic impulse into that (see REALISM), may have helped to sustain the romanticism of Victorian poetry: George Eliot, for instance, has elements of Wordsworth and even Byron in her poetry that are much less obvious in her fiction.

Alfred Lord Tennyson (1808–92) had an ear for rhythm and an eye for nature as fine as that of any Eng. poet. Elizabeth Gaskell tells a charming story of how a gardener snorted in indignation when he read the line "black as ash-buds in March," until he looked at the ash the following spring; after that he became a devotee of Tennyson. This descriptive genius combines with a personal melancholy that gives his lyrics a characteristic emotional tone: he is both a nature poet and a highly subjective poet, a combination that came to seem natural to 19th-c. taste. His finest short poems include "Mariana," "Ulysses," and the haunting songs from his feminist/anti-feminist narrative *The Princess*. Tennyson's masterpiece is *In Memoriam*, pub. in 1850 but written over the 17 years since the death of his friend Arthur Hallam. The poem's polished quatrains return constantly to a grief so deep we may wonder about the psychology behind it; at the same time, they contain details to delight any gardener, and reflections on religious belief and the effect on it of geological discoveries. Still, Tennyson's fine poetic sensibility went with a commonplace intellect: he thought like a conventional Victorian, but felt and wrote with a rare sensibility. So, since as Poet Laureate he felt driven to write about some of the controversies of the day, his poetry offers a rare insight into the Victorian mind. He labored for many years over the *Idylls of the King*, his retelling of the Arthurian legends. They are often accused of being more Victorian than medieval. Tennyson, who admitted this, did not see it as a fault.

Tennyson and Browning are now seen as the two pillars of Victorian poetry, but recognition came much later to Browning (1812–89), who, when he married Elizabeth Barrett in 1846, was less famous than she. Browning's notorious obscurity (q.v.) hindered popular acceptance and still leaves his early and late work unread. He is above all the master of the dramatic monologue (see MONOLOGUE), some short and brilliant ("My Last Duchess," "Soliloquy of the Sp. Cloister"), some long and absorbing ("Bishop Blougram's Apology," "Mr. Sludge the Medium"). Italophiles both, the Brownings lived in Italy after their marriage, and Browning's fascination with the It. Ren. produced many of his finest works ("Fra Lippo Lippi," "Andrea del Sarto"), as well as his longest and most ambitious work, *The Ring and the Book* (1868–69), in which a sordid 17th-c. murder case is related from nine viewpoints. Among Browning's lyrics, "Two in the Campagna" can perhaps challenge Donne and Marvell for the position of the finest Eng. love poem.

Browning is a clear exception to the generalization that most Victorian poetry is romantic, exotic, and even escapist; and he is by no means the only Victorian poet to use contemp. setting and realistic treatment. Arthur Hugh Clough (1819–61) wrote two relaxed, ironic narratives about sophisticated contemp. life, *Amours de Voyage* and *The Bothie of Tober-na-Vuolich*. They are written in hexameters, scanned as much by length as by stress; as such they are one manifestation of the 19th-c. vogue for imitations of Cl. quantitative meters, and in Clough's hands the hexameter responds very readily to speech rhythm and ironic tone. *Modern Love* (1862), by George Meredith (1828–1900), is a sequence of 16-line "sonnets" about a failing marriage: the story is hinted at rather than told, and the tone varies from ironic sophistication to tragic plangency. *Aurora Leigh* (1856), a verse novel by Elizabeth Barrett Browning (1806–61), for all its occasional sentimentality and melodramatic plot, is one of the subtlest and most probing narrative poems of the age, remarkable for its proto-feminist awareness as well as its sensitive description of the Eng. landscape. Her other major work, *Sonnets from the Portuguese* (1850), is both deeply personal and deeply traditional: it expresses her love for her husband in the conventions that derive from medieval love poetry, ultimately from the troubadours; and the result is a fascinating ambivalence, depending on whether we imagine the speaker to be male or female.

The social and lit. crit. of Matthew Arnold (1822–88) has always seemed to some readers more important than his poems, but it is arguable that his earnestness, his conservatism, and his nostalgia find a more appropriate expression in verse. His reflective poetry deals directly with the spiritual crisis of the age, most movingly in "Dover Beach," indirectly in *Empedocles on Etna*, and both directly and indirectly in *The Scholar Gypsy*.

The Pre-Raphaelite Brotherhood was mainly a movement in painting; how well the term applies to poetry is questionable (see PRE-RAPHAELITE BROTHERHOOD). Its program very clearly defined medievalism. Dante Gabriel Rossetti (1828–82), both painter and poet, was its central figure. He translated a good deal of early It. poetry, and there is a Dantesque religiosity in much of his own. His sonnet sequence *The House of Life*, somewhat more explicitly erotic than most 19th-c. poetry, led to his being denounced, along with Swinburne, as "the fleshly school of poetry" (q.v.). In Algernon Charles Swinburne (1837–1909), sexuality is more open, extravagant, and perverted, rendering him the nearest thing to an Eng. Baudelaire (on whom he wrote an elegy, "Ave atque vale"), but the careful cl. diction of Baudelaire's poems has nothing in common with Swinburne's incantatory lilt and excessive alliteration. Paradoxically, perhaps, the self-indulgent Swinburne is also the leading Hellenist among Victorian poets, drawing many of his subjects from Gr. mythology. Rossetti's sister Christina (1830–94) wrote simple lyrics about love, about religion (she was a devout Anglican), and a few, esp. "Twice," about both. Some feminist critics claim, with some justice, that her strange, sensuous retelling of the folktale "Goblin Market" is an imaginative achievement on a par with Coleridge's "Ancient Mariner," though it has never achieved the same fame, perhaps because of its predominantly feminine themes (virginity, menarche, anorexia). William Morris (1834–96), also a pre-Raphaelite, wrote long narratives on medieval and Norse themes, a few nostalgic lyrics (his radical politics did not lead to any poetic unconventionality), and one powerful and realistic narrative with a medieval setting, "The Haystack in the Floods."

The radical of Victorian poetry was Gerard Manley Hopkins (1844–89), whose poems were not published until 1918. A Jesuit priest, he had abandoned poetry when he entered the order, then at the suggestion of his Superior wrote a poem on the death of five Franciscan nuns in the shipwreck of The Deutschland in 1875. The Rector can hardly have expected the tortured syntax and obscure diction with which Hopkins explored his own religious experience. He then went on to produce a handful of poems, mainly sonnets, whose technical innovation had a profound influence on 20th-c. poetry: some of them celebrate nature and the God of nature ("Hurrahing in Harvest," "Pied Beauty"), while the "Terrible Sonnets" explore religious despair and the dark night of the soul. No Eng. poetry of any age wrenches lang. so violently and powerfully to fit meaning as Hopkins' profound poems of spiritual despair: his defiantly Saxon vocabulary and his sprung rhythm (q.v.) derive from his interest in OE, while his brilliant experimentalism anticipates much in modern poetry. In his letters Hopkins sketched a poetic theory through the concepts of "inscape" and "instress" (q.v.), the unifying quality of a landscape or an experience that a poem aims to capture—concepts that show the influence of Duns Scotus and his idea of *haeccitas*.

Late 19th-c. poetry is filled with the romantic love of the mysterious and the suggestive, with nostalgia, painful love, and religious longing. It is typified by the early poetry of William Butler Yeats (1865–1939), which gives little indication of his subsequent modernism. Two serious religious poems that emerge from, and never quite forsake, this world are Francis Thompson's "Hound of Heaven" (1893) and Oscar Wilde's *Ballad of Reading Gaol* (1898).

Thomas Hardy (1840–1928) is a late Victorian both in spirit and date, but because he turned to poetry after his career as a novelist was over, and then lived to so advanced an age, most of his poetry falls into the 20th c. There is astonishing variety in his shorter poems, both in form and mood, which can be leisurely or terse, colloquial or musical, and use a greater range of stanza forms—many invented by him—than any other poet in the lang. One of his most loved lyrics, a reflection on his own posthumous reputation called "Afterwards," announces its poetic individuality from the very first line in its quirky diction and meditative rhythm ("When the present has latched its postern behind my tremulous stay"). Closest to the novels in spirit are his ballads; the irony for which he is so renowned as a novelist appears in the poems as self-mockery, as cynicism,

and (sometimes) as profound social commentary ("The Ruined Girl"). His finest poems are the sequence he wrote on the death of his first wife, under the general title "Veteris vestigia flammae—Traces of an Old Flame."

G. *Modernism.* A simplified view sees modernism as a reaction against this tail-end of romanticism, but the true picture is more complicated (see MODERNISM AND POSTMODERNISM). There were several competing poetic schools in the early 20th c.: the rousing masculinity of Rudyard Kipling and Henry Newbolt; the Georgian return to the countryside (which saw itself both as a reaction against glib jingoism and as a realistic rejection of effete romanticism); and the poetry of the First World War, which began in the patriotic enthusiasm of Rupert Brooke and ended in the angry pacifism of Wilfred Owen. To many today, the more distanced and oblique response of David Jones in *In Parenthesis* (1937) is the most memorable work of World War I poetry. The Georgian anthologies, appearing from 1911 to 1922, included Walter de la Mare (1873–1956, the best of the late romantics), Robert Graves (1895–1985), and Edward Thomas (1878–1917), modern in awareness if not in technique. See GEORGIANISM.

The Georgians were very conscious of being Eng., and indeed there has always been a strong native trad. in 20th-c. poetry, hearkening back to Hardy and even to the Dorset dialect poet William Barnes (1801–86): John Betjeman, Philip Larkin and Ted Hughes can all be seen as belonging to it. But on the whole, modernism was an international movement, appearing in Germany as expressionism (q.v.), in Russia in the work of Blok and Majakovskij (see RUSSIAN POETRY), and in England as introduced from France. The seminal figures, Pound and Eliot, were both Americans, though Eliot became very thoroughly Anglicized: their poetry contains a great deal of social commentary and awareness of the ugliness of modern life, yet in many ways they derive more from aestheticism (q.v.) than from any trad. of social realism. T. S. Eliot (1888–1965) can be seen as the man who brought Fr. symbolism (q.v.) to England, both the concentrated, intellectual, gnomic poetry of Mallarmé and Valéry and the colloquial, ironic, self-conscious poetry of Corbière and Laforgue. Eliot's modernist programme derived from the claim that the Eng. metaphysicals used lang. in a way very similar to the Fr. symbolists, and issued in the famous assertion that modern poetry must be difficult: "Our civilisation comprehends great variety and complexity, and this variety and complexity, playing upon a refined sensibility, must produce various and complex results."

Eliot's very small output is certainly the most famous body of Eng. p. in the 20th c. *Prufrock and Other Observations* (1917), his first collection, opens with two dramatic monologues that owe more to Laforgue and Henry James than to Browning. Both speakers are self-conscious to the point of neurosis: J. Alfred Prufrock, in his "love-song," sees himself descending the stair "with a bald spot in the middle of my hair," and the speaker of "Portrait of a Lady" says "My smile falls heavily among the bric-a-brac." The analogy with music is central to the symbolist view of poetry, and it appears in the titles of several of Eliot's poems— "Preludes," "Five-finger Exercises," "Rhapsody on a Windy Night," and *Four Quartets*. The debt to Laforgue is most evident in "Conversation Galante," a free translation of "Celle qui doit. . . ." Eliot's early poetry culminated in *The Waste Land* (1922), fragmentary and allusive in technique, deriving (Eliot claimed) from Jessie L. Weston's *From Ritual to Romance*, a Fraserian interp. of the Grail Legend as a fertility myth. Imagery from the grail story is mingled in the poem with glimpses of modern life, so that the waste land is seen not only as the land rendered barren by the curse on the Fisher King, but also as the 20th c. The poem is filled with religious symbols and with religious despair; by the time of *Ash Wednesday* (1930), which, though just as allusive in method, is much more immediately emotional in impact, Eliot had become an Anglican, and his poetry culminated in the four linked meditations of *Four Quartets* (1936–43), in which Christian symbols are introduced into the waste land: without being any less modern, they offer a more positive relation to trad., as can be seen in the sources of the titles— East Coker, the village from which Eliot's ancestors left for the New World, and Little Gidding, the Anglican community set up by Nicholas Ferrar in the 1630s. Eliot, clearly feeling he had written himself out with these poems, then turned to the stage. He wrote *Murder in the Cathedral*—in metrical verse—in 1936, and then produced a series of plays in free verse more or less disguised as prose, and with a modern setting (e.g. *The Cocktail Party*, 1948).

Eliot regarded Ezra Pound (1885–1972) as his immediate master, and dedicated *The Waste Land* to him with the phrase "il miglior fabbro" (the best craftsman). Pound's origin in aestheticism is even clearer than Eliot's, as is his debt to Browning in his early dramatic monologues. He never ceased to be a literary poet, adapting freely from many langs. (Chinese, Lat. Provençal, even OE). Pound and Eliot reintroduced into Eng. p. the Ren. idea of "imitatio," the insertion into a poem of pieces of earlier poems on the same theme, usually adapted somewhat; Pound carried this to its greatest extreme in the *Cantos*, the huge poem to which he devoted his later years.

Pound's leading Eng. follower is Basil Bunting (1900–85). His most important poem is *Briggflatts* (1966), an oblique and elusive autobiography, named after a village in his native Northumbria. "Brag, sweet tenor bull," it begins: announcing both its modernist terseness and Bunting's insistence that poetry "deals in sound."

W. B. Yeats never became a modernist to the same extent as Pound and Eliot, but he moved away from his early romanticism, partly through verbal pruning ("there's more enterprise / In walking naked"), partly through modern subject matter (esp. Ir. politics, as in "Easter 1916" and *Meditations in Time of Civil War*). His finest poems retain a concern with traditional romantic themes: religion, art, history. "A Dialogue of Self and Soul" sums up the dichotomy that runs through all his poetry. "Sailing to Byzantium" is a 20th-c. equivalent to Keats's "Grecian Urn": both poems set forth the paradox that the timelessness of art can capture the flux of living most perfectly because of its very lifelessness. Yeats was interested in a wide range of fringe religions, esoteric science, the occult, and cyclic views of history. He put these ideas into his prose work *A Vision* (1925), and used them as a basis for many of his greatest poems: his work is therefore a prime case for exploring the relation between poetry and ideas. The painstaking system of historical periods, related to the phases of the moon in *A Vision*, is compressed into terse and resonant statements about the chaos of the modern world in such poems as "The Second Coming" and "Lapis Lazuli," or such memorable couplets as "Hector is dead and there's a light in Troy. / We that look on but laugh in tragic joy," where aesthetic delight and social despair ignite each other.

Eng. p. in the 1930s grew more political: the leftwing enthusiasms of the Popular Front and opposition to fascism run through the work of Auden, Day Lewis, Spender, and MacNeice—and, rather differently, are prominent in the Scots of Hugh MacDiarmid. The Sp. Civil War was the focal conflict of the decade; a Marxist version of it is offered in Auden's "Spain 1937." W. H. Auden (1907–73), the most complex and interesting of these poets, soon left his political phase behind, and later made some attempt to suppress it when revising his early work. His three long poems, *New Year Letter* (1941), *For the Time Being* (1945), and *The Age of Anxiety* (1948), show his growing religious concern and his shift to a more psychological and anthropological stance; yet one of his most powerful political poems, "The Shield of Achilles," appeared as late as 1955. Auden's later devel. was seen as irresponsible by those who regarded him as the political conscience of the 1930s, but can equally be seen as showing a constant vitality and intellectual range. A very different view of the '30s is provided by John Betjeman (1906–83), the idol of the middlebrow public, who by the time he became the Poet Laureate in 1972 was regarded with a grudging respect by the critics, responding to his obvious verbal skill and the deep feeling under the quaint humor.

The Second World War produced surprisingly little poetry of lasting importance (though both Eliot and Dylan Thomas wrote movingly about the air raids). Little of the neoromanticism and revived surrealism of the 1940s now seems of lasting interest, except for the work of Dylan Thomas (1914–53), in whom Rimbaud seems to merge with a Welsh bardic strain. His poems, using a variety of formal verseforms, including experiments of great discipline and complexity, are at times impenetrably turgid, at other times—especially when partly autobiographical—very moving in their verbal richness. His most popular poems are the celebratory "Poem in October" and "Fern Hill," which anticipate the even more popular *Under Milk Wood* (1953), a radio play that mingles bawdiness and a nursery-rhyme magic.

The 1950s saw the rise of The Movement, as it is rather uninformatively labeled, a school of poets that valued clarity, wit, and traditional competence, and was suspicious of bardic afflatus and grand gesture. As a movement it was short-lived, and its main figures, Kingsley Amis (b. 1922), John Wain (b. 1925), Donald Davie (b. 1922), Philip Larkin (1922–86), and Thom Gunn (b. 1929), soon went their separate ways. Larkin was England's most admired poet in the 1960s, his wry melancholy and resigned awareness of the drabness of life being presented with wit and a powerful lyric gift: "Church Going" and "The Witsun Weddings," treating religion and ritual from the stance of a wryly bewildered outsider, may be considered the two most representative poems of the postwar generation. Ted Hughes (b. 1930), who became Poet Laureate in 1984, offers a strong contrast to Larkin: whereas Larkin derives from Hardy, Hughes derives from Lawrence. He is prolific, sometimes obscure, his poems crackling with verbal energy, and ceaselessly inventive. His best known volume is *Crow* (1970), which is explicitly violent and blasphemous, but it lacks the richness and subtlety of some of his shorter poems ("Hawk Roosting," "To Paint a Water-lily"), which convey the same disturbing sense of cruelty in a less blustering way.

Of the poets who rose to prominence after 1970, there is no space for a systematic survey. To group them by movements and tendencies is to risk subordinating the poetry itself to journalistic classification, but there is no real alternative if any sense of the poetic scene is to be conveyed. There has been a second "invasion" of Am. influence, esp. through the work of the "confessional" poets, Lowell, Berryman, and Sylvia Plath (who herself settled in England and married an Eng. poet), as well as through the violently modernist techniques applied to urban life—e.g. in the work of Roy Fisher (b. 1930). Adrian Mitchell (b. 1932) is a popular—and populist—poet of strong political commitment. Since the 1960s, a poetic school of astonishing richness and fertility has arisen in Northern Ireland, with the political violence endemic there since 1969 providing much of the subject matter. The leading figure is Seamus Heaney (b. 1939), whose verbal richness moves powerfully between Irish and personal themes; others are John Montague (b. 1929), Michael

Longley (b. 1939), Derek Mahon (b. 1941), and Paul Muldoon (b. 1951). The work of Craig Raine (b. 1944) and Christopher Reid (b. 1949) has become known as "Martian," because of Raine's poem "A Martian sends a postcard home," a manifesto of defamiliarization, inviting us to see common objects with the eye of a Martian or small child. Many of their best poems are riddles (to which they are sometimes careful not to give the answers).

For the first time in Eng. lit. hist., women are now making a contribution to poetry as substantial as they have always made to the novel. Stevie Smith (1902–71) wrote mischievously naive poetry that verges on doggerel, but achieved a few unforgettable short poems: "Not waving but drowning" has become one of the most famous lyrics of the age. Elizabeth Jennings (b. 1926, associated with the Movement) and Sylvia Plath, who committed suicide in 1963 at the age of 32, both handle mental breakdown and inner disturbance with poise and insight; the control is less steady in Plath, who rides the whirlwind precariously, but who also wrote some very tender poems about motherhood and domestic life. More recent names include Elizabeth Bartlett (b. 1924), U. A. Fanthorpe (b. 1929), Anne Stevenson (b. 1933), Jenny Joseph (b. 1932), and Fleur Adcock (b. 1934).

Inevitably, many of the best poets fit no group. Norman MacCaig (b. 1910) combines a keen eye for nature with a brilliant verbal gift and philosophic probing, and seems at times like a blend of Hopkins and Wallace Stevens. The terse, tough religious poems of R. S. Thomas (b. 1913) are the product of a Christianity after the death of God movement. Charles Tomlinson (b. 1927) also began under the influence of Stevens, and has developed into an urbane, controlled, intelligent and at times witty poet. Peter Redgrove (b. 1932), prolific and uneven, writes in a style that is largely surrealist, or, as he would prefer to call it, erotic. Geoffrey Hill (b. 1932) has written complex, resonant poems in traditional meters (*Tenebrae*) and prose-poems (*Mercian Hymns*) that deal hauntingly with religion and hist. Keeping the classics alive is no longer the task of the privileged class in modern Britain: this can be seen in the career of Tony Harrison (b. 1937) who is at the same time defiantly provincial, writing about his working class origins in Leeds in bluntly powerful autobiographical poems, and an accomplished linguist, translating and adapting work for the stage from many langs. Even this rapid sketch of the contemp. scene should serve to show that the Eng. poetic scene is alive, well, and complicated. See also AMERICAN POETRY; DECADENCE; ENGLISH PROSODY; EPIC; GEORGIANISM; IMAGISM; LYRIC; METAPHYSICAL POETRY; MODERN LONG POEM; MODERNISM AND POSTMODERNISM; NARRATIVE POETRY; NEOCLASSICAL POETICS; RENAISSANCE POETRY; ROMANTIC AND POSTROMANTIC POETICS; TWENTIETH-CENTURY POETICS.

ENGLISH POETRY

BIBLIOGRAPHIES: *New CBEL*; A. E. Dyson, *Eng. P.: Select Bibl. Guides* (1971); R. C. Schweik and D. Riesner, *Reference Sources in Eng. and Am. Lit.: An Annot. Bibl.* (1977); J. L. Harner, *Literary Research Guide* (1989), esp. sect. M.

ANTHOLOGIES: *General: Understanding Poetry*, ed. C. Brooks and R. P. Warren (1938–); *Poets of the Eng. Lang.*, ed. W. H. Auden and N. H. Pearson (1953); *New Poets of England and America*, ed. D. Hall et al. (1958); *Norton Anthol. of Poetry*, ed. A. W. Allison et al. (1975). *Oxford anthologies: Oxford Book of Eng. Verse*, ed. A. T. Quiller-Couch (1900); *Romantic Verse*, ed. H. S. Milford (1928); *Mod. Verse*, ed. W. B. Yeats (1936); *19th-C. Eng. Verse*, ed. J. Hayward (1964); *Ballads*, ed. J. Kinsley (1969); *New Oxford Book of Eng. Verse*, ed. H. Gardner (1972); *20th-C. Verse*, ed. P. Larkin (1973); *Contemp. Verse*, ed. D. J. Enright (1980); *Christian Verse*, ed. D. Davie (1982); *Traditional Verse*, ed. F. Woods (1983); *Narrative Verse*, ed. I. and P. Opie (1983); *18th-C. Verse*, ed. R. Lonsdale (1984); *Short Poems*, ed. P.J. Kavanagh and J. Michie (1986); *New Oxford Book of Victorian Verse*, ed. C. Ricks (1987); *Shakespeare*, ed. S. Wells (1987); *18th-C. Women Poets*, ed. R. Lonsdale (1989); *Oxford Anthol. of Eng. P.*, ed. J. Wain, 2 v. (1991); *New Oxford Book of 16th-C. Verse*, ed. E. Jones (1991); *New Oxford Book of 17th-C. Verse*, ed. A. Fowler (1991). *Penguin anthologies: The New Poetry*, ed. A. Alvarez (1962); *Religious Verse*, ed. R. S. Thomas (1963); *Elizabethan Verse*, ed. E. Lucie-Smith (1965); *Metaphysical Poets*, ed. H. Gardner, 2d ed. (1967); *Restoration Verse*, ed. H. Love (1968); *Eng. Romantic Verse*, ed. D. Wright (1968); *Victorian Verse*, ed. G. Macbeth (1969); *First World War Poetry*, ed. J. Silkin (1969); *18th-C. Verse*, ed. D. Davison (1973); *Eng. Pastoral Verse*, ed. J. Barrell and J. Bull (1975); *Contemp. British Poetry*, ed. B. Morrison and A. Motion (1982); *War Poetry*, ed. J. Stallworthy (1984).

ELECTRONIC TEXTS: *The Eng. P. Full-Text Database* (1992–94).

HISTORY AND CRITICISM: T. Warton, *Hist. of Eng. P.* (1774–81); S. Johnson, *Lives of the Eng. Poets* (1781); W. Wordsworth, Prefaces to *Lyrical Ballads* (1800, 1802) and *Poems* (1815); S. T. Coleridge, *Biographia literaria* (1817)—esp. chs. 13–16; W. Hazlitt, *Lectures on the Eng. Poets* (1818); W. J. Courthope, *A Hist. of Eng. P.* (1895–1910); Smith; W. W. Greg, *Pastoral Poetry and Pastoral Drama* (1906); *Critical Essays of the 17th C.*, ed. J. G. Spingarn (1908); R. D. Havens, *The Influence of Milton on Eng. P.* (1922); O. Barfield, *Poetic Diction* (1928); D. Bush, *Mythology and the Ren. Trad. in Eng. P.* (1933), *Mythology and the Romantic Trad. in Eng. P.* (1937), *Eng. Lit. in the Earlier 17th C.* (1945), *Eng. P.* (1952); W. Empson, *Some Versions of Pastoral* (1935), *The Structure of Complex Words* (1951), *Seven Types of Ambiguity*, 3d ed. (1953); F. R. Leavis, *Revaluation* (1936); C. S. Lewis, *The Allegory of Love* (1936), *Eng. Lit. in the 16th C.* (1954), *The Discarded Image* (1964); Y. Winters, *Primitivism and Decadence* (1937), *The Function of*

Crit. (1957); J. C. Ransom, *The World's Body* (1938); W. J. Bate, *The Stylistic Devel. of Keats* (1945); Brooks; R. Tuve, *Elizabethan and Metaphysical Imagery* (1947); J. Sutherland, *A Preface to 18th-C. Poetry* (1948); G. Hough, *The Last Romantics* (1949), *Image and Experience* (1960); J. Miles, *The Continuity of Poetic Lang.* (1951), *Eras and Modes in Eng. P.* (1962); M. H. Abrams, *The Mirror and the Lamp* (1953), *Natural Supernaturalism* (1971); E. R. Wasserman, *The Finer Tone* (1953), *The Subtler Lang.* (1959); P. Cruttwell, *The Shakespearean Moment* (1954); G. Hartmann, *The Unmediated Vision* (1954), *Wordsworth's Poetry, 1787–1814* (1964); W. K. Wimsatt, Jr., *The Verbal Icon* (1954); D. Davie, *Articulate Energy* (1955), *Under Briggflatts: A Hist. of P. in Great Britain, 1960–1988* (1989); J. Press, *The Fire and the Fountain* (1955), *A Map of Mod. Eng. Verse* (1969); N. Frye, *Anatomy of Crit.* (1957), *Fables of Identity* (1963); F. Kermode, *Romantic Image* (1957), *Ren. Essays* (1971); R. Langbaum, *The Poetry of Experience* (1957), *The Mysteries of Identity* (1977); Wimsatt and Brooks; D. Perkins, *The Quest for Permanence* (1959), *Wordsworth and the Poetry of Sincerity* (1964), *A Hist. of Mod. Poetry*, 2 v. (1976, 1987); ; A. Warren, *Rage for Order* (1959); D. Daiches, *Critical Hist. of Eng. Lit.* (1960); J. Hollander, *The Untuning of the Sky* (1961), *Vision and Resonance*, 2d ed. (1985), *Melodious Guile* (1988); W. Nowottny, *The Lang. Poets Use* (1962); *The Poets and their Critics*, ed. H. S. Davies (1962); I. Jack, *Eng. Lit. 1815–1832* (1963); W. L. Renwick, *Eng. Lit. 1789–1815* (1963); C. K. Stead, *The New Poetic* (1964); K. Burke, *Lang. as Symbolic Action* (1966); R. Cohen, "The Augustan Mode in Eng. P.," *ECS* 1 (1967); B. H. Smith, *Poetic Closure* (1968); H. Kenner, *The Pound Era* (1971); R. L. Colie, *The Resources of Kind* (1973); H. Bloom, *The Anxiety of Influence* (1973); L. Lerner, *An Intro. to Eng. P.* (1974); *20th-C. Poetry*, ed. G. Martin and P. N. Furbank (1975); S. Hynes, *The Auden Generation* (1976); V. Forrest-Thomson, *Poetic Artifice* (1978); P. Hobsbaum, *Trad. and Experiment in Eng. P.* (1979); B. Lewalski, *Protestant Poetics and the 17th-C. Religious Lyric* (1979); J. R. de J. Jackson, *Poetry of the Romantic Period* (1980); B. Morrison, *The Movement* (1980); A. D. Nuttall, *Overheard by God* (1980); H. Vendler, *Part of Nature, Part of Us* (1980); G. S. Fraser, *A Short Hist. of Eng. P.* (1981); E. Rothstein, *Restoration and 18th-C. Poetry, 1660–1780* (1981); Fowler; C. Ricks, *The Force of Poetry* (1984); M. A. Doody, *The Daring Muse: Augustan Poetry Reconsidered* (1985); J. H. Miller, *The Linguistic Moment* (1985); *Lyric Poetry: Beyond New Crit.*, ed. C. Hošek and P. Parker (1985); *Poetry Today: A Critical Guide to British P. 1960–1984*, ed. A. Thwaite (1985); D. Wesling, *The New Poetries* (1985); S. Curran, *Poetic Form and British Romanticism* (1986); *Poststructuralist Readings of Eng. P.*, ed. R. Machin and C. Norris (1987); G. Hammond, *Fleeting Things: Eng. Poets and Poems, 1616–1660* (1989); K. Millard, *Edwardian Poetry* (1992). L.D.L.

ENGLISH PROSODY.

I. OLD ENGLISH (ca. 500–ca. 1100 A.D.). Classical OE verse, like that of the other early Germanic dialects (OS, OHG, ON), is composed in hemistichs (q.v.) or *verses* of distinct types linked by structural alliteration into long lines. In the second hemistich, alliteration occurs on the first stressed syllable only, while in the first hemistich alliteration can occur on either one or two syllables. The patterns for the four most heavily stressed syllables in the line can be represented by *a* (alliterating syllable) and *b* (nonalliterating syllable) as follows: (1) $a\,a:a\,b$; (2) $a\,b:a\,b$; (3) $b\,a:a\,b$.
The third pattern, the least common, occurs only when the first stressed syllable is lighter than the second. Variations in the length of the line result from different numbers of unstressed syllables. Despite some technical differences between the strict metrical style of *Beowulf* or *Exodus* and the freer style of the late poem *The Battle of Maldon* (ca. 991), the extant trad. during the four cs. from Cædmon's *Hymn* (ca. 670) until the Norman Conquest (1066) is remarkably homogeneous. The main variation from this normal meter is the infrequent hypermetric verse (Ger. *Schwellvers*). Of the 30,000 lines of OE poetry there are fewer than 950 hypermetric verses, which usually occur in clusters and exceed the normal metrical limit by several heavy syllables.

It has sometimes also been said that OE poetry is in the "strong-stress" trad. along with modern accentual verse (q.v.), since each hemistich contains two main stresses and an indeterminate number of unstressed syllables. However, such a statement entails far-reaching and dubious theoretical assumptions about the nature of the system and its relation to other subsequent verseforms. It is often held that the patterns of stressed and unstressed syllables within each hemistich occur as one of the Five Types (A through E) set forth in the classic taxonomy of verse-types given by Eduard Sievers in the 1880s:

A	/ x / x	gomban gyldan
B	x / x /	þenden wordum wēold
C	x / \ x	ofer hronrāde
D	/ / \ x	cwēn Hrōðgāres
E	/ \ x /	flōdyþum feor.

However, one may question whether Sievers' types

are the cause (the paradigm) or the effect (epiphenomena of a more basic pattern), and in any case whether the types are compatible with the two-stress idea. Types D and E regularly have three stresses (with the lightest falling on a syllable that elsewhere counts as a full ictus), and many Types A and C appear to have only one stress.

Thus, what is uncontroversial about OE poetry may extend just as far as the superficial features that it shares with the prosody of the other Germanic langs. There is a good possibility that prosody developed in England under the influence of the Lat. trad. in ways that make it essentially a unique meter (Kabell).

One feature that sets OE meter apart from the meters of OHG or OS, as well as from analogies proposed in modern oral poetries, is its precision. Far from being primitive, cl. OE meter is in fact complex and sophisticated. The interaction of such technical features as arsis, thesis, syllabic quantity, resolution (q.v.), suspension of resolution, secondary stress, and anacrusis is more clearly and closely regulated in OE than in any of the other Germanic meters (ON verse has a different kind of precision). In OE poetry a single unstressed syllable in the wrong place (e.g. at the end of type E) makes the whole verse unmetrical.

Metrical ictus in OE poetry depends on linguistic prominence, which is realized by various suprasegmentals—esp. stress, time (both syllabic quantity and phrasal rhythm), and pitch—interacting with each other and with the segmental feature of alliteration. One way of classifying the various theories of OE meter is to say that each begins with stress and alliteration (the Five Types) and then organizes one or more of the other features around this base. The stress theories of Sievers, Bliss, and Russom add syllabic quantity to this base (and differ in the units—"feet" and "breath-groups"—into which they divide the verse). The rhythmical theories of Heusler, Pope, Luecke, and Obst add both syllabic quantity and rhythm beyond the syllable (and differ in their units, in their conceptions of rhythm, and in the role they assign to the harp). Cable's melodic contour theory adds syllabic quantity to the stress-alliteration base and also musical pitch as an enhancement of prominence. Hoover takes stress and alliteration alone, giving priority to the latter.

Because so many diverse theories have been able to construct paradigms that are relatively precise and attain such comparable effects, future studies will doubtless contemplate the prospect that a unifying generalization is still being missed. Present formulations such as Sievers' Five Types might eventually be seen as derivative rather than fundamental. Ultimately, the solution to the problem of OE verseform might come from studies that are both more concrete (e.g. a fuller account of what happens between clashing stresses, or between the stress levels of a derivational and an inflectional syllable within a single word) and more abstract (e.g. the often-ignored four-member frame of Sievers' original theory, which could actually be a plausible mnemonic for a poet). The fact that the four abstract positions correlate closely with single syllables or resolved equivalents (except for the multisyllable first dips of types A, B, and C) suggests that even a principle of syllabism may be a part of the most adequate paradigm of OE meter. Simplicity is a measure of descriptive adequacy because the abstract paradigm is the artifice of meter that is easily made explicit, the thing that is conveyed in the transmission of the trad., and the element that would most easily be lost by an external rupture in the trad. such as that caused by the Norman Conquest. See also ALLITERATIVE VERSE IN MODERN LANGUAGES; RESOLUTION; GERMAN PROSODY, *Old Germanic.*

Schipper; Sievers; A. Heusler, *Deutsche Versgesch.*, 3 v. (1925–29, rpt. 1956); J. C. Pope, *The Rhythm of* Beowulf, 2d ed. (1966); A. J. Bliss, *The Metre of* Beowulf, 2d ed. (1967); T. Cable, *The Meter and Melody of* Beowulf (1974); A. Kabell, *Metrische Studien I: Der Alliterationsvers* (1978); J.-M. Luecke, *Measuring OE Rhythm* (1978); Brogan, sect. K; D. L. Hoover, *A New Theory of OE Meter* (1985); G. Russom, *OE Meter and Ling. Theory* (1987); W. Obst, *Der Rhythmus des* Beowulf (1987).   T.C.

II. MIDDLE ENGLISH. ME prosody, a highly controverted field, has achieved little consensus to date as to the exact nature and origin of forms, or even basic terminology. What is beyond dispute is that between the late 10th and late 14th cs., metrical innovation in ME verse flourished, encouraged by complex influences both foreign and native.

A. *Early ME Accentual Verse.* Alliterative verse (AV) of the classical OE type continued to be written at least into the 11th c. (e.g. *The Description of Durham*, ca. 1104–09), but early ME accentual verse (e.g. *The Departing Soul's Address to the Body, The First Worcester Fragment*, Layamon's *Brut*) is generally characterized as "looser" or "freer" than OE AV. Whether it was modernized in lang. and meter from the cl. OE trad., or descended from a "popular" oral trad., or developed from the "rhythmical alliteration" of Wulfstan's and Ælfric's prose, early ME accentual verse does share some features of OE AV. Lines are composed of two half-lines, each generally of two stresses, and many half-lines are linked by alliteration. However, half-lines carry a greater number of unstressed syllables than in OE AV, and the "rising-falling" rhythm (x / x / x) predominates. Rhythmic patterns are irregular and cannot usefully be categorized on the basis of Sievers' Five Types (see section I above). Unlike OE AV, lines and half-lines are usually complete syntactic units with much parataxis (q.v.) and apposition; characteristic OE strong caesura and enjambment are rare in ME. Both alliteration and leonine rhyme (q.v.) are treated as ornaments, but often neither alliteration nor rhyme occurs. Early ME accentual verse

seems to have died out in the early 13th c., though later examples may have been lost.

B. *ME Accentual-Syllabic Verse.* By the early 12th c., rhyme comes into use as a structural principle, borrowed probably from Med. Lat. (e.g. St. Godric's *Hymns*, ca. 1170), but also under the influence of Fr., particularly the Anglo-Norman *vers decasyllabe*. Finally it supplants alliteration altogether. Fusion of the native 4-stress couplet with Anglo-Norman and Fr. models leads to the octosyllabic couplet, a staple of ME verse, as in Gower's *Confessio amantis* and Chaucer's *House of Fame.* Octosyllabic verse in a variety of forms—couplets, the ballade (q.v.) stanza, cross-rhymed quatrains, and octaves—continues through the 15th c. (see OCTOSYLLABLE).

A number of other forms indebted to both Med. Lat. and Anglo-Norman models come into play at the end of the 12th c.: a long line in mixed lengths of 12 and 14 syllables rhyming in couplets, quatrains, or octaves; the Burns stanza (q.v.); and the ballade. It is believed that couplets of the 14-syllable line, by adding internal rhyme and breaking at the half-lines into short-line quatrains, produced "8s and 6s," a form isomorphic to ballad meter (q.v.). This same internal rhyme breaks the alliterative long line into a short alliterative couplet that persists from Layamon through the late tail-rhyme (q.v.) stanzas (e.g. *Sir Degrevaunt*). Tail-rhyme, also derived from Med. Lat. and Anglo-Norman exemplars, becomes the characteristic stanza of the Eng. metrical romances, usually in 6- or 12-line stanzas. The addition of rhyme to the ornamental alliterative line produces a wide range of stanzas, as in the celebrated Harley lyrics. Generally speaking, the addition of rhyme coincides with a shift from accentual verse to accentual-syllabic verse, so that the number of syllables and the number and position of stresses in the line become relatively fixed. ME verse normally imitates the simple binary meters characteristic of Med. Lat. verse, e.g. the *Poema morale* (ca. 1170), which imitates the Lat. *septenarius.*

C. *The Alliterative Long Line.* Alliterative composition in prose and rhymed verse continues throughout the 13th and 14th cs. in a broad continuum of styles derived from both the native trad. and from Lat. and Fr. The Harley lyrics (ms. composed ca. 1330–40) use alliteration of the stressed syllables in complex stanzas of Fr. derivation linked by concatenation (q.v.) and iteration, a style that culminates in *Pearl.*

Ms. Harley 2253 also marks the emergence of the earliest 14th-c. alliterative long-line poems— e.g. *A Satire against the Pride of Ladies, Old Age*, and *Song of the Husbandman*—whose heavily alliterated 4-stress lines (i.e. *aa/aa, aa/bb, aaa/aa*) occur in a variety of rhymed stanzas, sometimes together with accentual-syllabic verse. Stanzaic poems and dramas in alliterative long lines and in bob-and-wheel (q.v.) continue to be composed to the end of the 15th c.

In the so-called "Alliterative Revival" of the mid 14th c. there emerges a substantial corpus of unrhymed ME AV having alliteration as a structural principle, with the pattern *aa/ax* predominant. A number of theories have been advanced to explain the reemergence of an alliterative meter and diction that resemble so strongly OE practice. It is clear that the style of ME AV does not descend directly from Layamon (1250), but neither the theory of uninterrupted oral trad. (Waldron) nor the theory of ME AV's origins in "baronial discontent" (Hulbert) is wholly satisfactory. Some have argued for continuity by pointing to the loss of written texts (Turville-Petre); others have emphasized the role played by an influential writer or monastic trad. (Pearsall); still others have defended self-conscious literary antiquarianism (Moorman). It has also been suggested that poets refined AV from alliterative prose (Salter).

Despite much variation in diction, syntax, and deployment of alliteration, unrhymed alliterative long lines are governed by a few basic metrical principles. The norm for the line is four stresses. First half-lines are normally longer than second, which show more rhythmic regularity. The line is the metrical unit; enjambment is relatively rare. Alliteration (most commonly *aa/ax, xa/ax,* and *aa/xa*) links half-lines across a strong caesura and also links successive lines into groups; some mss. show evidence of 4-line strophic composition.

D. *Chaucer and the 15th C.* The declining fortunes of Anglo-Norman in the mid 14th c. seem to have encouraged a shifting of attention to strict Fr. forms, and Chaucer's indebtedness to native ME prosody has proved increasingly difficult to demonstrate. Schipper thinks the early octosyllabic couplets imitate the Fr. *décasyllabe;* Ten Brink posits the influence of the native 4-stress couplet. Chaucer can certainly use ornamental alliteration, particularly in battle scenes (e.g. *KtT* 2601 ff.), but his clearest adaptation of native ME prosody, in the tail-rhyme and bob lines of *Sir Thopas,* is satiric. In *The Parlement of Foules,* Chaucer abandons the octosyllabic couplet for rhyme royal (q.v.), his staple stanza for formal poems, (*Troilus and Criseyde*), and a form related to the Monk's Tale stanza (q.v.). Chaucer also imitates the Fr. triple ballade (*Complaint of Venus*) and rondel (q.v.) and the It. terza rima (q.v.; *A Complaint to his Lady*); *Anelida and Arcite* contains much prosodic experimentation.

But Chaucer's most significant technical achievement is the heroic or decasyllabic line (see DECASYLLABLE) in couplets, derived perhaps by expanding the octosyllabic couplet, perhaps from the rhyme royal stanza; its origin is disputed, hence the very terms used to refer to it have never been settled. Chaucer is the first to use the 5-stress or iambic pentameter couplet in Eng. (either in the Prologue to the *Legend of Good Women* or in an early version of the *KtT*). Chaucer seems to fuse native 4-stress habits with a predominantly (but not invariably) decasyllabic line; the pressure of rhyme, particularly on polysyllables, and the caesura both tend to promote a fifth syllable to ictus (q.v.). Despite challenges from 4-stress nativists, most prosodists agree that Chaucer's line has a predominantly "iambic" rhythm with variations: line-initial trochaic substitution (occasionally after the caesura), secondary accent on polysyllables, elision, and occasional extra weak syllables or stresses. Chaucer's greatness as a metrical artist lies in his skill at tensing rhetorical and syntactic accent against the basic metrical pattern.

Chaucer's enormous influence after his death in 1400 preserved his verseforms through the 15th c., though it is not at all clear his disciples understood what they imitated. Lydgate's prosody, which influenced nearly every 15th-c. poet, is characterized particularly by the "broken-backed" line, in which only a caesura separates two strong stresses. The 15th c.'s main contribution is the carol (q.v.), though the pentameter couplet and rhyme royal are its staple forms. See also ALLITERATIVE VERSE IN MODERN LANGUAGES.

GENERAL: Schipper, K. Luick, *Englische Metrik* (1893); B. Ten Brink, *The Lang. and Meter of Chaucer* (1920); J. P. Oakden, *Alliterative Poetry in ME,* 2 v. (1930–35); A. McI. Trounce, "The Eng. Tail-Rhyme Romances," *MÆ* 1–3 (1932–34); F. Pyle, "The Place of Anglo-Norman in the Hist. of Eng. Versif.," *Hermathena* 49 (1935); P. F. Baum, *Chaucer's Verse* (1961); M. Borroff, Sir Gawain and the Green Knight: *A Metrical and Stylistic Study* (1962); M. D. Legge, *Anglo-Norman Lit. and Its Background* (1963); A. Gaylord, "Scanning the Prosodists," *ChaucR* 11 (1976); Pearsall; C. Friedlander, "Early ME Accentual Verse," *MP* 76 (1979); Brogan, sect. K; U. Fries, *Einführung in die Sprache Chaucers* (1985); A. V. C. Schmidt, *The Clerkly Maker* (1987).

ALLITERATIVE REVIVAL: J. R. Hulbert, "A Hypothesis Concerning the A. R.," *MP* 28 (1930); R. A. Waldron, "Oral-Formulaic Technique and ME Alliterative Poetry," *Speculum* 32 (1957); E. Salter, "The A. R.," *MP* 64 (1966–67); C. Moorman, "The Origins of the A. R.," *SoQ* 7 (1969); T. Turville-Petre, *The A. R.* (1977); D. Pearsall, "The A. R.," *ME Alliterative Poetry,* ed. D. A. Lawton (1982); H. Duggan, "The Shape of the B-Verse in ME Alliterative Poetry," *Speculum* 61 (1986); T. Cable, *The Eng. Alliterative Trad.* (1991). R.H.O.

III. MODERN (after 1500). Nearly all the metrical forms of modern Eng. verse took definitive form in the Ren. Even the crisis in Eng. pros. represented by 20th-c. free verse, for example, has its roots in metrical tensions that date back to the Ren.

A. *16th and early 17th C.* High Ren. verse grows out of three older traditions. (1) Rejecting med. values and forms, humanist scholars and poets emulated Cl. models, not only by writing Lat. verse itself but also by making Eng. imitations of Gr. and Lat. quantitative verse, both hexameters and Gr. strophic verse (see CLASSICAL METERS IN MODERN

LANGUAGES), though the effort largely failed, because quantity is not distinctive in the Eng. lang. (2) The accentual and alliterative native trad. persisted up to about 1550 in the tumbling verse (q.v.) of popular drama. (3) But it was the decasyllabic line of Chaucer and his successors, its tone and manner deeply transformed by Petrarchan Fr. and It. influences, which becomes the central vehicle for Eng. verse (see DECASYLLABLE). Forgetting quantity, Elizabethan poets and dramatists learned to adapt the *patterns* of Cl. meters (most of all, the iambic) to an accentual verse system in which accent or stress, not length, is the marker of the pattern. Early forms preferred in the first half of the 16th c. include fourteeners and poulter's measure (qq.v.), but the heroic decasyllable or iambic pentameter line proved the most serviceable, expressive, and even popular. From Surrey to Gascoigne, and in courtly verse as well as popular drama, the poetic line to be heard had to be regular, but poets from Sidney on found the length and pattern of the iambic pentameter flexible enough to admit a vast range of Eng. phrases. Specifically, they learned that (1) the midline phrasal break could be variously located, (2) stressed syllables might be unequal in strength (and unstressed ones, too), (3) variations in the placement of stressing in the line could confer grace and energy, and (4) with occasional, even frequent, enjambment, a passage could flow smoothly through unequal grammatical segments and seem as much speech as verse. Lyric poetry, its measures ranging from the song to the sonnet (qq.v.), is equally inventive in structures and subtle in tone.

Exuberant with its new instruments, verse of the 1590s achieves a flexible elegance, preeminently in Spenser and early Shakespeare. But when devices of enjambment and metrical variation are pushed beyond a certain point, the result is strong, eccentric, highly mannered, even mannerist. Donne's radical elisions and accentual displacements give his rhymed Satyres, Elegies, and Letters the urgency of excited speech. To make blank verse (q.v.) in the theater sound even more speechlike, some dramatists (notably the later Shakespeare, Webster, and Middleton) pepper iambic pentameter with short lines and long lines; weak, double, and triple line endings; and headless, broken-backed, and epic-caesural forms characteristic of the Lydgate trad. (Wright). The verse that results from these techniques, and from the less radical but exploratory craft of such poets as Spenser, Jonson, and Herbert, is varied, resilient, and expressive.

B. *Later 17th and 18th C.* The strongest tendency of verse after Donne, however, is toward a highly regulated, "correct" metrical line. The three poets named just above serve as prosodic models for most nondramatic verse (see SCHOOL OF SPENSER; CAVALIER POETS), which follows as well Daniel's conservative view (*A Defence of Ryme*, 1603?) of the functions and effects of rhyme and of the five-foot line (Smith). The closed couplets avoided by Donne and the Jacobean dramatists in the interest of speechlike verse now become a favored form. Donne's lyric successors (see META-PHYSICAL POETRY), and other poets, incl. Milton and Swift, employ the tetrameter couplet as a balanced form within which their strong and often unsettling perceptions can make apt or ironic points. But the most powerful form to develop in this period, the heroic couplet (q.v.), attracts, among others, Jonson, Waller, Denham, Dryden, and eventually Pope by its formidable capacity to deploy antithetical words and phrases, within the line or in line against line, in a seemingly inexhaustible display of verbal balance, polish, ingenuity, and "bite." Odes (q.v.), Pindaric or Horatian, afford the resourceful poet a different variety of challenging formal (and Cl.) structures.

Milton is the last barrier to Augustan verse. Prosodically correct (though in accordance with rules that are apparently his own—see Bridges, Sprott, and Weismiller) and extraordinarily resourceful, his epic verse, audaciously blank, keeps the grand grammatical sentence diverging from yet counterpoised with the equally heroic line. In *Samson Agonistes* the heroic line seems on the verge of becoming free verse. But the couplet effectively blocks this devel. for more than a century.

Augustan prosodists (Bysshe, Bentley, and Pemberton) and critics (Dr. Johnson) theorize Augustan practice and condemn departures from metrical norms. Correctness becomes a major criterion for appraising poetry. Later 18th-c. theorists, however, admit metrical variation (even anapestic) as a means of avoiding monotony and increasing the elements of surprise and spontaneity in verse (Fussell 1954). By the later 18th c., blank verse has returned, this time as a medium esp. appropriate for reflective poetry; the rediscovery of the ballad (q.v.) stimulates the writing of lyric poems in looser forms and encourages other variation in poems with an iambic base—extra syllables begin to appear in the line which cannot be elided away (see METRICAL TREATMENT OF SYLLABLES).

C. *19th C.* Liberated at last from the couplet, romantic poetry explores rich veins of blank and stanzaic verse of various shapes and dimensions (Curran). But the century's poetry soon begins to split into two distinct prosodic kinds which diverge symmetrically from the iambic pentameter line that once held their opposing tendencies in tension. One move is toward accentual verse, with its strong recurrent pattern of regular beats, the other toward free verse and its highlighting of the rhythmic phrase. Poets seek to escape a standard meter that has lost its excitement, that lugs along the baggage of its historical associations rather than using them to invest it with power and purpose. In part, this must be because the semiotic messages carried by a meter differ in different

ENGLYN

periods. Sentence and meter seem to have functioned in the Ren. as emblems of individual and authority, and in the 18th c. as emblems of person and social norm, but in the 19th c. the tension goes slack as verse shifts its ground of significance from what God or society ordains to what a human subject experiences. Poets lean either toward the accentual pole, expressive of organicism (q.v.) or natural rhythms or toward free verse, expressive (as in Whitman) of loosely measured sequences of self-reliant perceptions.

Esp. prominent as the century wears on are triple meters (Poe and Longfellow), anapestic variation in iambic verse (Browning, Swinburne, Hardy), the accentually sprung rhythm (q.v.) of the *Christabel* meter (q.v.) and Hopkins, and dipodic (q.v.) rhythms (Browning, Meredith, Kipling), all of which, as they strengthen both the equality and the isochronism (q.v.) of the beat, diminish the role of expressive variation within the line. Tennyson and Browning still write compelling blank verse but the form withers in the hands of lesser poets and spoils (until century's end) in the Am. climate.

D. *20th C.* Following Whitman, free verse (q.v.) becomes the chief metrical mode of the poets writing in Eng., but traditional forms recur, sometimes brilliantly redeemed (Yeats, Frost, Auden, Wilbur, Larkin, Hollander, and several contemp. Eng. poets) sometimes mixed with a freer prosody, as in Eliot's *The Waste Land*, where blank verse crumbles along with everything else in Western culture. Poets whose work is often cast in traditional meters (e.g. Stevens, Lowell, Berryman) adapt them freely, as if they represented some order of reality, sanity, or conduct only dimly and intermittently descried; the apparently looser poems of Ashbery often distinctly echo older verseforms. Free-verse writers, following such models as Whitman, Pound, Williams, and Lawrence, either sound their barbaric yawps over the roofs of the new world or weigh line and phrase sensitively to find new combinations of perfect congruence, antithetical tension, and casual overflow. Other forms explored by contemporary poets include syllabic verse (q.v.), which, as it resists any conscious measuring on the part of the listener (or even a reader not disposed to count syllables), serves mainly as a heuristic device for securing an air of casualness (esp. in Marianne Moore and in Auden); and concrete verse (q.v.), which, deriving from the shaped figurative poems of the late 16th and early 17th c. (see PATTERN POETRY), sharply increases the visual element in the poem at the expense of the verbal (see Hollander).

Analysis of poetic modes comes generally after the fact, but in every period prosodic crit. has a moralistic flavor. Adherents of quantitative verse in the Ren. contemn the inexpressive native iambic verse, with its meager and invariable two syllables to a foot (Attridge 1974). Theorists of the 18th-c. scourge the intrusion of anapestic or trochaic variation into the steady iambic current as

harbingers of revolutionary anarchy. Many 19th-c. poets (e.g. Keats, Arnold) disdain their Augustan precursors as writers of mere prose. 20th-c. proponents of free-verse are excoriated by defenders of older forms but in turn condemn the rigid pentameter of trad. Among some late-century poets, however, strict forms have come again into vogue (see NEW FORMALISM). See also AMERICAN POETRY; BLANK VERSE; CLASSICAL PROSODY; COUPLET; ENGLISH POETRY; FOURTEENER; FRENCH PROSODY; GERMAN PROSODY; HEROIC COUPLET; HEROIC VERSE; ITALIAN PROSODY; METER; PROSODY; RHYME; RHYTHM; SOUND; SOUND EFFECTS IN POETRY; STANZA; VERSIFICATION.

Schipper; Smith—texts of Ren. prosodists; G. Saintsbury, *Hist. of Eng. Pros.*, 3 v. (1906–10)—eccentric theoretically; Schipper, *History*; R. Bridges, *Milton's Prosody* (1921); Omond; O. Jespersen, "Notes on Metre," rpt. in his *Linguistica* (1933); G. W. Allen, *Am. Prosody* (1934)—dated but not yet replaced; S. E. Sprott, *Milton's Art of Prosody* (1953); P. Fussell, *Theory of Prosody in 18th-C. England* (1954); W. K. Wimsatt, Jr., and M. Beardsley, "The Concept of Meter," *PMLA* 74 (1959); A. Oras, *Pause Patterns in Elizabethan and Jacobean Drama* (1960); J. Thompson, *The Founding of Eng. Metre* (1961); M. Halpern, "On the Two Chief Metrical Modes in Eng.," *PMLA* 77 (1962)—fundamental; H. Gross, *Sound and Form in Mod. Poetry* (1964); S. Chatman, *A Theory of Meter* (1965); K. Shapiro and R. Beum, *A Prosody Handbook* (1965); W. Nowottny, *The Lang. Poets Use* (1965); W. B. Piper, *The Heroic Couplet* (1969); J. Malof, *A Manual of Eng. Meters* (1970); D. Attridge, *Well-Weighed Syllables* (1974); D. Crystal, "Intonation and Metrical Theory," *The Eng. Tone of Voice* (1975); M. Tarlinskaja, *Eng. Verse: Theory and Hist.* (1976), *Shakespeare's Verse* (1987); E. Weismiller, "Blank Verse," *A Milton Encyc.*, ed. W. B. Hunter et al. (1978); *The Structure of Verse*, ed. H. Gross, 2d ed. (1979); C. O. Hartman, *Free Verse* (1980); Brogan—full list of references with annotations; C. Freer, *The Poetics of Jacobean Drama* (1981); Attridge; D. Wesling, *The New Poetries* (1985); Hollander; S. Curran, *Poetic Form and British Romanticism* (1986); G. T. Wright, *Shakespeare's Metrical Art* (1988); D. Taylor, *Hardy's Metres and Victorian Prosody* (1988); O. B. Hardison, Jr., *Prosody and Purpose in the Eng. Ren.* (1989).   G.T.W.

ENGLYN (pl. *englynion*). Along with *awdl* and *cywydd* (q.v.), one of the three classes of the 24 "strict meters" of Welsh poetry (q.v.). The earliest forms are tercets, but after the 12th c. these are replaced by quatrains in monorhyme or consonance. Six of the eight varieties of *englynion* are quatrains, and the most common line length is the heptasyllable, though combinations of 10, 6, and 7 and also common. Since the 12th c., the most popular variety has been the *e. unodl union* (direct monorhyme e.), a quatrain of lines of 10, 6, 7, and 7 syllables. The main rhyme in the first line appears from one to three syllables before the end of the line, i.e. before the *cyrch* or *gair cyrch*; the line-end itself must alliterate or echo with the first few syllables of line two. The *gair cyrch* ("reaching-out word"; cf. Gerard Manley Hopkins' "outriders") which extends from the first main rhyme to the 10th syllable need only be related to what follows by means of light alliteration, whereas strict *cynghanedd* (q.v.) has been observed in all other parts since the 15th c. If the third line is oxytonic the fourth must be paroxytonic, and *vice versa*, a rule preserved since the 13th c. If the second couplet (*esgyll*, "wings") precedes the first two lines (*paladr*, "shaft"), the form is called *e. unodl crwca* ("crooked" e.). See also CELTIC PROSODY; WELSH POETRY.—Morris-Jones; K. Jackson, "Incremental Repetition in the Early Welsh E.," *Speculum* 16 (1942); Parry, *History*; Stephens; *Welsh Verse*, ed. T. Conran, 2d ed. (1986); *Early Welsh Saga Poetry*, ed. J. Rowland (1990).

T.V.F.B.; D.M.L.

ENHOPLIUS, enoplius, *en(h)oplion, en(h)oplian* (Gr. "in arms," "martial"). A metrical term first attested in Aristophanes (*Clouds* 638) where, however, its exact reference is unclear. Later ancient writers use it more or less interchangeably with *prosodion* or *prosodiac* to designate various forms all of which contain the sequence $- \cup \cup - \cup \cup -$ preceded or followed (or both) by some additional element: this is a single syllable, long or short, when it follows; when it precedes, it may also be a double short. One form of e. ($\cup \cup - \cup \cup - \cup \cup - -$) is thus identical with the paroemiac (q.v.), others with common segments in dactylo-epitritic (q.v.). Some mod. metrists have argued for the existence of a free version of the rhythm as well, identical with the paroemiac but allowing some substitution of single for double shorts. Such "single-short" enoplia are more usually and, probably, more correctly analyzed as aeolic (q.v.)—Wilamowitz, pt. 2, ch. 12; Michaelides; West.

A.T.C.

ENJAMBMENT (Fr. *enjambement*; Ger. *Versüberschreitung* or *Brechung*; Sp. *encabalgamiento*). Nonalignment of (end of) metrical frame and syntactic period at line-end: the overflow into the following poetic line of a syntactic phrase (with its intonational contour) begun in the preceding line without a major juncture or pause. The opposite of end-stopped (q.v.).

In reading, the noncoincidence of the frames of syntax and meter in e. has the effect of giving the reader "mixed messages": the closure of the metrical pattern at line-end implies a stop (pause), no matter how infinitesimal, while the obvious incompletion of the syntactic period says, *go on*. The one scissors the other. These conflicting signals, in heightening readerly tension, also thereby heighten awareness, so that in fact one is made more aware of the word at line-end than its prede-

cessors: rhyme itself, by enhancing closure, will diminish this effect, while absence of rhyme, in blank and free verse, increases it—toward the same end.

In lang., the hierarchy of domains in the syntagm is: sound–syllable–word–phrase–clause (sentence). The joints between elements both within each domain and between domains are bridged by a bonding force; as one moves up the chain, the bonding force between domains weakens and cuts are easier to make. Within domains, however, much greater variability obtains, particularly inside phrases: the bond between determiners and following nouns is stronger than between adjectives and nouns, so that enjambing the former is a little more severe than the latter. In *Troilus and Criseyde* Chaucer has " . . . help me from / the deth" (1.535–36) and, later, "have" and "ben youres al" separated by an entire line (3.100–2). Complex verb phrases offer even more prospects. E. below the phrasal level is radical, with submorphemic examples being rare, but famous—as in Hopkins' intrepid e. ending the first line of "The Windhover": "I caught this morning morning's minion, king- / dom of daylight's dauphin." But splitting a word across line-end can also be used to comic effect, as in Byron. No complete taxonomy of effects has yet been given.

It is often assumed that e. is a phenomenon of rhymeless stichic verse and most suitable for dramatic verse or for extended narrative, such as blank verse (q.v.). However, e. and rhymed verse are not at all incompatible. Rhymed stanzaic verse normally shows an overwhelming coincidence of major syntactic boundaries with borders of (some) metrical frames, esp. stanzaic borders, but in many stanza forms a sentence often occupies most or all of a stanza, and the types of syntactic cuts made at line-end vary widely. Even in couplets, where rhyme is tight, the most constrained form, the Eng. closed or "heroic" couplet (q.v.), was a late development: older and more pervasive are the enjambed or "open" couplets, where rhyme-pairing is preserved while syntactic spans often run to length—as in the opening sentence of the *Canterbury Tales*, which is 18 lines long. In rhymeless verse—particularly Milton—the long syntactic period is known as the "verse paragraph" (q.v.). Free verse (q.v.), abandoning rhyme and meter both, finds e. almost compulsory.

Though the Cl. hexameter (q.v.) is mainly stopped (as is Sanskrit verse), Homer uses e. (Kirk). It is the norm in Old Germanic alliterative verse, incl. OE—e.g. *Heliand* and *Beowulf*—where rhyme is unknown and lines are bound together by alliteration used to mark the meter. Prior to the 12th c., e. is rare in OF poetry: it is the *trouvère* Chrétien de Troyes (fl. after 1150) who seems to have been the first poet in the European vernaculars to break his verses systematically. By the 15th c. it is widely used, and even more so in the 16th, esp. by Ronsard (who coined the term) and the

Pléiade (q.v.). In the 17th c. it was impugned by Malherbe and later Boileau. These neoclassical authorities, however, allowed its use in certain circumstances—in decasyllabic poetry and in the less "noble" genres such as comedy and fable. Occasionally e. occurs even in tragedy. Since André Chénier (1762–94), it has been accepted in all genres. The device was exploited to the full by Hugo, whose famous e. at the beginning of *Hernani*—"Serait-ce déjà lui? C'est bien à l'escalier / Dérobé" (Is he already here? It must be by the secret staircase)—had all the force of a manifesto. E. was a fundamental characteristic of the *vers libéré* (q.v.) of the later 19th c. and the *vers libre* (q.v.) which emerged from it.

In Fr. prosody e. has been a subject of controversy: since Fr. rhythms are in essence phrasal, line-terminal accents naturally tend to coincide with significant syntactic junctures. Consequently the terminology for analyzing types of constructions in e. is more developed in Fr. prosody than in Eng.: see REJET. Modern Ger. poets who have valued e. incl. Lessing (*Nathan*), Goethe, and Rilke.

In Eng., e was used widely by the Elizabethans for dramatic and narrative verse. The closed couplet drove e. from the scene in the 18th c., but the example of Milton to Wordsworth revived it for the romantics, who saw it as the metrical emblem for liberation from neoclassical rules. Keats's *Endymion* supplies some strong examples of e., as does Byron's narrative verse. Hopkins' "sprung rhythm" (q.v.) introduces "roving over," that is, metrical as well as syntactic e., so that "the scanning runs on without a break from the beginning . . . of a stanza to the end." But it is Milton who is the great master of e. effects in Eng. poetry: indeed, in justifying his choice of blank verse for *Paradise Lost* in its preface ("The Verse"), Milton points to e., i.e. "sense variously drawn out from one verse into another," as one of the three central features of his verse. Here *variously* is a crucial term for describing the manifold lengths and positionings of the Miltonic sentence for manifold effects, many of them at line-end. Perhaps chief among these are those instances in which the reader arrives at line-end and makes a prediction about how the next line will complete the phrase—only to have that expectation thwarted. The momentary shock of our *error*, we may believe, is the Miltonic exhibition of our postlapsarian nature:

> . . . Now conscience wakes despair
> That slumber'd, wakes the bitter mem-
> ory
> Of what he was, what is, and what must
> be
> Worse; of worse deeds worse sufferings
> must ensue.
> (*PL* 4.23–26)

One had thought the series of parallel phrases complete at the end of line 25. One was wrong.

Most generally, e. is simply the most conspicuous example of that dialectics of closure and flow which is the whole substance of formal imposition in poetry, and its study one of the central avenues by which the devices of prosody lead directly to the phenomenology of reading. See now LINE.

K. Borinski, "Die Überführung des Sinnes über den Versschluss und ihr Verbot in der neueren Zeit," *Studien zur Literaturgeschichte* (1893); Kastner, ch. 5; F. Klee, *Das E. bei Chaucer* (1913); F. Wahnschaffe, *Die syntaktische Bedeutung der mittelhochdeutschen Enjambements* (1919); P. Habermann, "Brechung," "Enjambement," "Hakenvers," *Reallexikon I*; J. Levý, "Rhythmical Ambivalence in the Poetry of T. S. Eliot," *Anglia* 77 (1959); K. Taranovski, "Some Problems of E. in Slavic and West European Verse," *IJSLP* 7 (1963); G. S. Kirk, "Studies in Some Technical Aspects of Homer's Style," *YClS* 20 (1966), 105 ff.; R. Cremante, "Nota sull'e.,'" *LeS* 2 (1967); M. Parry, "The Distinctive Character of E. in Homeric Verse," in Parry; J. Gruber, *Laura und das Trobar car* (1976)—e. in Occitan and It. lyric; Elwert; H. Golomb, *E. in Poetry* (1979); J. G. Lawler, *Celestial Pantomime* (1979); Mazaleyrat; Scott; Morier, s.v. "Enjambement," "Contre-E.," "Contre-rejet"; J. Hollander, "'Sense Variously Drawn Out,'" in Hollander; S. Cushman, *Wm. Carlos Williams and the Meanings of Measure* (1985), ch. 1; D. Godet, "À propos de quelque es. anarchiques," *Versants* 9 (1986); C. Higbie, *Measure and Music: E. and Sentence Structure in the* Iliad (1991). T.V.F.B.; C.S.

ENSALADA. A Sp. poem consisting of lines and strophes of varying lengths and rhyme schemes, generally depending on the music to which the poem is sung. According to Henríquez Ureña, the earliest known e. is one by Fray Ambrosio Montesinos (d. ca. 1512) found in Barbieri's *Cancionero musical de los siglos XV y XVI* (no. 438). The e. apparently was never very popular.—P. Henríquez Ureña, *La versificación irregular en la poesia castellana*, 2d ed. (1933); Le Gentil; Navarro. D.C.C.

ENSENHAMEN. A didactic poem in Occitan, ordinarily composed in a nonlyric meter, such as rhymed couplets, and designed to give advice or instruction to an individual or a class of persons. Some of the poems are like books of etiquette. Others are addressed to the jongleurs (q.v.) who sang the poets' compositions, telling them the things they should know and how they should perform their task. The knowledge expected is doubtless exaggerated, but the poems have a certain interest for what they reveal about contemporary taste in literary and other matters.—G. E. Sansone, *Testi didattico-cortesi di Provenza* (1977); D. A. Monson, *Les "es." occitans* (1981). F.M.C.

ENVELOPE. The e. pattern is that form of repetition (q.v.) in which a rhyme (sound), phrase, line, or stanza recurs so as to enclose other material, giving the structural pattern *abba*; *chiasmus* (q.v.), derived from rhet., is another term for the same structure. Most often, a phrase or line will bracket a stanza or whole poem; a complete stanza may also enclose a poem or section of a poem. The e. has the effect of framing the enclosed material, giving it unity and closure: the reader recognizes the return to the original pattern after movement away in the interim. Related but less specific effects include those of the burden in carols, the refrain, and incremental repetition (qq.v.); in these the reiterated line gains meaning or force from the new material preceding each occurrence of it, but there is no sense of bracketing or framing. The single-line e., as it applies to a stanza, may be seen in James Joyce's "I Would in That Sweet Bosom Be," as it applies to an entire poem, in Frost's subtle "Acquainted With the Night." A stanza used as an e. for an entire poem may be seen in Blake's "The Tyger" and in Keats's "The Mermaid Tavern." E. rhyme (Ger. *umarmender Reim*, Fr. *rime embrassée*) is the rhyme scheme *abba* or any expanded version thereof; a quatrain having such rhyme is sometimes called the e. stanza: the *In Memoriam* stanza (q.v.) is an iambic tetrameter e. stanza. See also RING COMPOSITION.—C. B. Hieatt, "E. Patterns and the Structure of *Beowulf*," *ESC* 1 (1975), "On E. Patterns and Nonce Formulas," *Comp. Research on Oral Trads.*, ed. J. M. Foley (1987). S.F.F.; T.V.F.B.

ENVOI, envoy (Occitan *tornada*; Ger. *Geleit*). A short concluding stanza found in certain Fr. poetic forms such as the *ballade* and the *chant royal* (qq.v.). In the *ballade* the e. normally consists of 4 lines, in the *chant royal* of either 5 or 7, thus repeating the metrical pattern as well as the rhyme scheme of the half-stanza which precedes it. The e. also repeats the refrain which runs through the poem (e.g. Villon's "Mais ou sont les neiges d'antan?"). In its typical use of some form of address, such as "Prince," the e. shows a trace of its original function, which was to serve as a kind of postscript dedicating the poem to a patron or other important person. However, its true function during the great period of the OF fixed forms was to serve as a concise summation of the poem. For this reason the Occitan troubadours called their envoys *tornadas* (returns). Among the Eng. poets, Scott, Southey, and Swinburne employed envoys. Chaucer wrote a number of *ballades* in which he departs from the customary form by closing with an e. which is equal in length to a regular stanza of the poem, usually his favorite rhyme royal (q.v.).—R. Dragonetti, *La Technique poétique des trouvères dans la chanson courtoise* (1960), pt. 1, ch. 4. A.PR.

EPANALEPSIS (Gr. "a taking up again"; Lat. *resumptio*, a resumption).
(1) In Cl. rhet., a figure most often defined as the repetition of a word or words after intervening words, either (a) for emphasis (e.g. "Hell at last / Yawning receiv'd them whole, and on them clos'd,

/ Hell thir fit habitation" [Milton, *Paradise Lost* 6.874–76]); or (b) for clarity, as to resume a construction after a lengthy parenthesis (so Demetrius, *On Style* 196; e.g. "Say first, for Heav'n hides nothing from thy view, / Nor the deep Tract of Hell, say first what cause / Mov'd our Grand Parents" [*Paradise Lost* 1.27–29; cf. *Lycidas* 1.165]).
(2) In Ren. and modern rhet., e. is more specifically defined as ending a clause or sentence or line or stanza with the word at its beginning. Since e. appears almost exclusively in verse, the repeated words most often begin and end a line: so Abraham Fraunce, *The Arcadian Rhetorike* (1588), who cites Virgil's "Multa super Priamo rogitans, super Hectore multa" (*Aeneid* 1.750), and Sidney's "They love indeed who quake to say they love" (*Astrophil and Stella* 54). Cf. Shakespeare's "Blood hath bought blood, and blows have answered blows; / Strength match'd with strength, and power confronted power" (*King John* 2.1.329), and the related "Past cure I am, now reason is past care" (Sonnet 147.9). Donne brackets each stanza with an epanaleptic line in "The Prohibition." Peacham says it is used "to place a word of importance in the beginning of the sentence to be considered, and in the end to be remembered." Various types have been distinguished in Whitman: more than 40 per cent of the lines of *Leaves of Grass* employ e. of one sort or another. Sometimes the device structures an entire passage or poem. Like *anadiplosis* (q.v.), where the repeated word ends one clause (line) and begins the next, e. strikingly marks the limits of signifying syntagms: "Possessing what we still were unpossessed by, / Possessed by what we now no more possessed" (Frost, "The Gift Outright"). It is one of Eliot's most conspicuous and effective devices in *Four Quartets*.—A. N. Wiley, "Reiterative Devices in *Leaves of Grass*," *AL* 1 (1929); R. A. Lanham, *A Handlist of Rhetorical Terms* (1968); A. Quinn, *Figures of Speech* (1982); B. Vickers, *Cl. Rhet. in Eng. Poetry* (1989); Corbett. R.O.E.; T.V.F.B.; A.W.H.

EPIC.

I. HISTORY
   A. *Ancient*
   B. *Roman*
   C. *Middle Ages*
   D. *Renaissance*
   E. *Eighteenth Century*
   F. *Modern*
II. THEORY
   A. *Classical and Alexandrian Greek*
   B. *Classical Latin and Medieval*
   C. *Renaissance to Modern*

I. HISTORY. An e. is a long narrative poem (q.v.) that treats a single heroic figure or a group of such figures and concerns an historical event, such as a war or conquest, or an heroic quest or some other significant mythic or legendary achievement that is central to the traditions and belief of its culture.

E. usually develops in the oral culture of a society at a period when the nation is taking stock of its historical, cultural, and religious heritage (see ORAL POETRY). E. often focuses on a hero, sometimes semi-divine, who performs difficult and virtuous deeds; it frequently involves the interaction between human beings and gods. The events of the poem, however, affect the lives of ordinary human beings and often change the course of the nation. Typically long and elaborate in its narrative design, episodic in sequence, and elevated in lang., the e. usually begins "in the midst of things" (*in medias res* [q.v.]) and employs a range of poetic techniques, often opening with a formal invocation to a muse (q.v.) or some other divine figure, and frequently employing elaborate formulaic figures (see FORMULA), extended similes (usually termed epic or Homeric similes; see SIMILE), and other stylized descriptive devices such as catalogues of warriors, detailed descriptions of arms and armor (see EKPHRASIS), and descriptions of sacrifices and other rituals. Recurrent narrative features include formal combat between warriors, prefaced by an exchange of boasts; accounts of epic games or tournaments; and fabulous adventures, sometimes with supernatural overtones and often involving display of superior strength or cunning. E. incorporates within it not only the methods of narrative poetry (q.v.), but also of lyric and dramatic poetry (qq.v.). It includes and expands upon panegyric and lament (qq.v.). With its extended speeches and its well-crafted scenic structure, it is often dramatic and is perhaps with the choral ode (q.v.) the true ancestor of ancient drama.

A. *Ancient.* The earliest surviving es. are the Babylonian *Gilgamesh* saga, the Sanskrit *Mahābhārata* and *Rāmāyana*, and the Cl. Gr. *Iliad, Odyssey,* and fragments from the E. Cycle. The Gilgamesh e. (ca. 2000 B.C.) is contained on 12 tablets and runs to approximately 3000 lines in its surviving form. Gilgamesh, a hero of almost superhuman strength, like the Gr. Hercules or the Hebraic Samson, rescues the city of Uruk from misfortune and completes other deeds, among them the destruction of a bull sent by the goddess Ishtar. The e. also includes digressive material on the Creation, the Flood, and the story of Paradise similar to that in Babylonian and Hebraic scripture. Gilgamesh is tempted by demons (incl. one disguised as a serpent) and after the death of Eabani enters the underworld to seek (like the Gr. heroes Hercules, Theseus, and Odysseus) knowledge of the fortunes of the dead. His relationship to Eabani is one of the earliest of e. warrior-friendships, and his grief at his friend's death has its counterpart in Achilles' mourning for Patroclus or Roland's for Oliver.

The Sanskrit es., the *Mahābhārata* and the *Rāmāyana*, while dating in written form from between 400 B.C. and 400 A.D., were probably composed orally and revised repeatedly by different poets over a period of centuries, beginning perhaps as early as 2000 B.C. The *Mahābhārata*, divided into from 18 to 24 books and composed of over 110,000 couplets or *slokas* of 16 syllables each, is the longest e. in existence. The *Rāmāyana* is over 24,000 couplets long. Like the *Iliad*, the *Mahābhārata* tells of a dynastic war between rival princes; like the *Odyssey*, the *Rāmāyana* concerns the wanderings of a hero who must rescue his wife and regain his kingdom. The central plot of both es. is embellished by a vast amount of digressive material that includes didactic and doctrinal lore on religion, morals, law, and philosophy, as well as narrative tales, adventures, anecdotes, and fables. Like the Homeric poems among the Hellenic and the Bible among the Hebraic peoples, the Sanskrit es. acquired the status of sacred texts for the Hindi people. The struggle between the Bharatas and the Pandavas in the *Mahābhārata* may be construed allegorically as the war between Hindi gods and demons. Rama, the hero of the *Rāmāyana*, who on one level may be taken as the incarnation of the god Vishnu, achieves an allegorical victory over Ravana that may be similarly taken as India's victory over the drought-demon. Both es., however, include recognizable e. types: the king, the tragically doomed warring princes, the almost superhuman strongman. The immense Bhima of the *Mahābhārata* and Hanumat, Rama's ally in the *Rāmāyana*, fight like Hercules with a club and are, like Ajax and Achilles, violent and impetuous. Although performing deeds on a more massive scale than those of the Homeric heroes, Bhima subscribes to an heroic code in which the making and keeping of vows and the defense of honor are supreme virtues.

Both the *Iliad* and the *Odyssey*, and in the Middle Ages the battle es. of the Germanic, Anglo-Saxon, and Romance cycles, are intimately connected with the heroic codes of their societies. All agree that a violation of honor must be requited and revenge for a slain friend, dishonored spouse, or wronged family member undertaken. Achilles' terrible anger comes upon him in the *Iliad* because Agamemnon has violated his honor or *timé* by wrongfully seizing the girl Briseis; a comparable anger moves him later when he seeks to kill Hector, to avenge the death of his friend Patroclus. Homer tells us, moreover, that the Trojan War came about not merely because Paris had stolen Menelaus' wife, Helen, but because in so doing he had violated the sanctions of guest-friendship. Similarly, in the *Odyssey* Penelope's suitors have violated the laws of hospitality and so Odysseus is fully justified in dispensing justice and killing them all. The Bharatas in the Sanskrit e. pursue the war against their cousins both because they have cheated them in a game and because they have refused to honor their promise and relinquish the kingdom they wrongfully hold.

Both the Sanskrit and the Homeric es. deal with material that is in part based on historical events.

EPIC

Homer, an Asiatic Greek (fl. ca. 750 B.C.), recounts events that involved the great Mycenean society of the Gr. mainland (ca. 1200 B.C.). The excavations of Heinrich Schliemann from 1870 to 1890 confirmed the existence of Troy, actually 9 Troys, one of them (Troy 6) probably that treated by Homer. Composed from material almost certainly handed down orally by rhapsodes (q.v.), the poems were not written down until the 6th c. B.C. nor organized into the 24 books each now contains until the Alexandrian period. They are both composed in dactylic hexameter (q.v.), the meter that became from Homer's example the standard for all Gr. and Lat. e., and both make extensive use of the metrical and verbal formulas that are distinctive of oral poetry (q.v., and see ORAL-FORMULAIC THEORY). The formulas include epithets (such as "swift-footed" for Achilles) and set phrases arranged in half-lines, whole lines, or sets of lines that can be repeated by the poet to fill the metrical shapes required for his material. Formulaic density varies from scene to scene, tending to predominate in battle scenes or scenes of ceremonial action such as the offering of sacrifices or the launching of ships. Homeric verse is also characterized by the use of simile (q.v.), sometimes brief, sometimes extended, a device much imitated by later Gr., Roman, and Continental and Eng. Ren. poets.

Both the *Iliad* and the *Odyssey* open *in medias res* (q.v.—"in the midst of things") and pursue to conclusion the action set in motion at the beginning: in the *Iliad*, the resolution of Achilles' anger, and in the *Odyssey*, Odysseus' resumption of kingship in Ithaca. Much episodic material is included in each. Achilles and Odysseus are fully mortal and fallible even though each is attended by a protecting goddess. Lesser characters in each e. serve as foils to the heroes; the Trojan hero Hector is Achilles' inevitable opponent, and Telemachus, Odysseus' son, matures to become his father's assistant against the suitors. While Achilles and Odysseus are endowed with almost superhuman strength at the height of the action, the former filling the river Xanthus with dead bodies, the latter slaughtering over 100 suitors with his mighty bow, Homeric heroes are not supreme strongmen, like Hercules or Gilgamesh, nor incarnations of gods like the Hindi heroes. They do, however, act out a predetermined fate. As Rama in the *Rāmāyana* is ordained to be victorious in his fight with Ravana, so Achilles in the *Iliad* anticipates early death and Odysseus in the *Odyssey* perseveres, knowing he is fated to return safely.

Contemp. or later es. in Gr. survive only in fragments. The *Cypria*, the *Aethiopis*, the *Sack of Ilium*, the *Little Iliad*, the *Nostoi*, and the *Telegony* tell other parts of the Troy cycle; the *Thebais*, the *Titanomachy*, the *Oedipoedia*, and the *Epigoni* recount stories from other cycles. These es. provided later Gr. and Roman poets with material and alternative models. Hesiod's *Theogony* and *Works and Days* (ca. 700 B.C.), though not strictly es., are composed in hexameters and are in Homeric dialect; moreover both contain material that attaches itself to the e. trad. The *Theogony* not only tells of the generation of the gods, but also of Zeus's battle with the Titans and with Typhoeus; the *Works and Days*, which recounts the generation and ages of man, is the first extant didactic poem and influenced later Roman semi-es.: the *Georgics, De rerum natura*, and the *Metamorphoses*.

Little remains of the Alexandrian e. of the 4th and 3rd cs. B.C. Even the *Hecale* of Callimachus (b. ca. 330 B.C.), Apollonius of Rhodes' teacher, exists only as a set of fragments that tells how Theseus, on his way to fight the bull of Marathon, converses with the old woman Hecale on the eve of battle. The *Argonautica* of Apollonius of Rhodes, written in hexameters in four books comprising 5834 lines, is the only complete e. of the period and the earliest example of written or purely literary e. Although deliberately imitating Homeric lang. and devices, the *Argonautica* marks a decided departure from the ethos of Homeric e. Its hero, Jason, is neither a super-warrior like Achilles nor a man of endurance like Odysseus; he performs his most impressive acts through magic and presides over a crew of heroes whose deeds frequently surpass his own. Apollonius heightens the marvelous that had been a feature of the apologue of the *Odyssey* and creates with Medea, the virgin-witch, a psychological study of a woman in love. He hands down to the Romans an e. that differs markedly from the oral e. of Homer.

B. *Roman.* The historical e. in Rome dates from Naevius' *Bellum punicum*, now lost, and Ennius' *Annales*, a work in 18 books of which only fragments survive. Ennius (239–169 B.C.), reputed father of Roman e., replaced the older Saturnian (q.v.) meter, used by Livius Andronicus in his tr. of the *Odyssey* (3d c. B.C.), with Lat. hexameters on Gr. metrical principles and employed the conventions of Homeric e. for a semilegendary history of Rome from Aeneas' landing in Italy to his own time. He bequeathed to Virgil (70–19 B.C.) and to later Roman poets the notion that hexameter was the only proper verseform and national destiny the only possible theme for the Roman e. Virgil himself limited his account of Roman history to key prophetic sequences in Books 1 and 6 of the *Aeneid* and to various apostrophes and allusions to future Rome throughout the e. Imitating the *Odyssey*, he recounts in the first six books of the *Aeneid* the story of Aeneas' successful voyage to his new homeland in Italy and in the final six books, imitating the *Iliad*, of Aeneas' ascendance over Turnus, an Achilles-type opponent, in the It. wars. In Virgil's hands Aeneas becomes an exemplar of loyalty to family and comrades and of Roman *pietas*, a stoic leader whose endurance conquers adversity and whose determination brings peace to warfaring Italy, just as Augustus, to whom the e. was dedicated, had brought an end to civil war.

Providential destiny replaces the Homeric *moira* or fate, a force to which not only Aeneas but also Dido, Turnus, and the doomed young warriors of the It. wars must bow. Within a tightly controlled frame, episodic material plays a proscribed role. Hence the story of Troy's downfall in Book 2 is contrasted to Rome's eventual rise. The account in Book 4 of Dido, a character who recalls the Homeric Calypso, Circe, and Nausicaa as well as the abandoned Hypsypyle and love-sick Medea of Apollonius' *Argonautica*, must be more than a digressive episode of ill-fated love; it must foreshadow the future enmity of Carthage, the nation Rome had to destroy to secure its position in the ancient world. Portent, oracle, and sign, used by Apollonius as devices to move the Argo on its forward and return journeys, become in Virgilian e. assurances of Rome's future success. Similarly, the archetypal voyage to the underworld, so prominent in ancient oral e., becomes for Virgil the means for Aeneas to look ahead to the future leaders of Rome. Further, while Virgil may imitate, in Venus' fetching of arms for Aeneas, Thetis' rearming of Achilles in the *Iliad*, he places upon Aeneas' shield scenes that lead inexorably to Augustus' triumph at Actium.

Virgil's most accomplished contemporaries—the older Lucretius (ca. 99–ca. 55 B.C.) and the younger Ovid (43 B.C.–17 A.D.)—both of whom create ambitious long poems in hexameters, follow different e. models from Virgil. Like Hesiod, Lucretius in *De rerum natura* (Of the Nature of Things) writes a philosophical and didactic poem dealing with the creation and the composition of the universe and problems of human existence from the vantage of Epicurean philosophy. Ovid, taking his inspiration from Callimachus' *Aetia* and the Theocritean *epyllion* (q.v.), creates in the *Metamorphoses* a series of tales, some drawn from the ancient e. trad., some from Alexandrian romance, that involve transformations and are told briefly with interlocking narrative material. With particular interest in the erotic and in the marvelous, which had been prominent in Alexandrian e. and *epyllia*, Ovid introduces into the e. trad. material that has enormous impact not only on the later writers of mythological e.—Valerius Flaccus in his *Argonautica* (1st c. A.D.) and Claudian in *De raptu proserpina* (late 4th c. A.D.)—but also on Ren. writers from Dante through Milton. With Lucretius, who makes cosmic and philosophical material the province of e., and with Virgil, who reshapes Homeric e., Ovid is the most important influence on e. writers of the Ren.

Virgil's influence on writers in the e. trad. is both immediate and long-lasting. Even for poets such as Lucan (39–65 A.D.), who abandons the mythological machinery of the *Aeneid* and accepts the boundaries of recent history for his 10-book unfinished e., the *Pharsalia* (or Civil War), Virgil is the inevitable model. Echoes of the dynastic struggle between Aeneas and Turnus resonate in the e. duel between a relentless Caesar and a tragic Pompey. To a greater extent, Silius Italicus (26–101 A.D.), whose 17-book *Punica* on the Second Punic war is the longest Roman e., follows Virgil, imitating his mythological framework and battle scenes, projecting an underworld vision for Scipio modeled on Aeneas', and even constructing a shield for Hannibal embossed, like Aeneas', with scenes from hist. Although he chooses a subject from Gr. rather than Roman hist., Statius (45–96 A.D.) in the *Thebais* depends heavily on the machinery of Virgilian e. Employing supernatural messengers, portents, and dreams, he increases the episodic content of e. and the number of set pieces, describing battle scenes, chariot races, and a journey to the Hall of Sleep, embellished with allegorical imagery. The aim of the later Roman e. poet was to sustain a highly crafted lang. of imitation, based on standard features in Virgil. The high reputation as e. poets that Statius and Lucan enjoyed through the Ren. indicates their success.

C. *Middle Ages.* In the Christian era, e. undergoes a dramatic change. The mythological subject still survives in Claudian and in Nonnus' *Dionysiaca* (5th c.), a compendium in hexameters of stories about Dionysus and the other gods that extends to 48 books. While the first Christian es., such as Juvencus' gospel paraphrases, are little more than versified scripture, Marius Victor's *Alethia* and Avitus's *Poemata* adapt to biblical narratives from Genesis and Exodus the Roman epic's methods of treating historical material. Substituting Christian providence for Roman destiny, they tell how God's people attain the goal of salvation rather than the triumph of empire. Es. such as Prudentius' *Psychomachia* (4th c.) and Dracontius' *Carmen de deo* (5th c.) substitute the battle of the soul against evil for traditional e. combat. Saints begin to assume the place of the e. hero, with the hero of faith superseding the heroic warrior. Not only in Lat. but also in the considerable body of vernacular lit., the religious e. begins to dominate. The Anglo-Saxon *Genesis* A and B, following Lat. e., give heroic proportion to stories from Genesis, Satan as an e. hero making his first appearance in the latter. The OE *Christ*, attributed to Cynewulf, is one of the first poems to give heroic treatment to Christ's birth, death and resurrection, and return at Judgment Day, while *Andreas* and *Elene* tell of the saint's devotion to Christ and search for the true cross. The Christian e., begun in the Middle Ages, revives in the Ren. with renewed interest in hexaemera and es. on biblical subjects.

During the Middle Ages, pre-Christian material from the ancient oral and heroic culture also began to find written form, and in the process pagan and Christian often were synthesized. Like the Gr., the Romance and Germanic e. has its genesis in the heroic *lai* (q.v.) and its roots in a feudal society headed by a king who was surrounded by his vassals or *comitatus* bound by oath to support him in battle in return for protection and gifts. Anglo-Saxon e. pictures the center of the society as the hall, where king and warriors meet and where the bard sings of the heroic past. Many e. events are based upon documented historical events, such as the raid of Hygelac in *Beowulf* or the slaughter of the Burgundians at the court of Attila, narrated in the *Nibelungenlied* and in other Germanic es. The OF *Chanson de Roland* and the Sp. *Poema de mio Cid* recount versions of specific episodes in Charlemagne's struggle against the Saracens in the 8th c. and Castile's repulse of the Moors in the 10th c.

Most Germanic poetry, though emerging from a Christian society, is heavily overlaid with pre-Christian elements. A sense of fatality stronger than Christian providence is conspicuous. Although *wyrd* or fate may relent and save an undoomed man if, as the *Beowulf* poet says, his courage is good, the hero usually fights a losing battle, knowing the odds are against him. He is controlled, moreover, by a strict code of honor that requires at all costs loyalty to lord and friends. The earl Byrthnoth in the Anglo-Saxon *Battle of Maldon*, Roland in the *Chanson de Roland*, and Hagen in the *Nibelungenlied*, having made tragic errors in judgment, all prefer honor to life.

Older stories of pre-Christian gods and heroes who fight monsters with superhuman strength survive side-by-side with stories of dynastic strife. Sigurd, the hero of the Icelandic Elder Edda (ca. 900–1300), is the son of a god; he fights a dragon, wins treasure, and rides through a wall of fire to conquer an Amazonian goddess, deeds attributed in the *Nibelungenlied* (13th c.) to Siegfried, a prince of the Netherlands, who behaves more in the chivalric than the supernaturally heroic style. The Irish hero Cuchulain, also a god's son, can singlehandedly withstand an army. Beowulf, the hero of the 8th-c. OE poem, combines supernatural strength with feudal loyalty and Christian faith. Against a background of dynastic intrigue that dooms the court-society in Denmark and Sweden, Beowulf defeats the monster Grendel in his youth and a marauding dragon in old age.

Germanic e. deals mainly with the tragedy that results from conflicting loyalties to family, spouse, feudal lord, and comrades-in-arms. In the Hildebrand saga (ca. 800) a father, come as champion of an enemy army, is challenged by a son ignorant of his identity and is forced by the code of honor to answer the challenge. Walther, hero of the OE fragment *Waldere*, the fragmentary Ger. e. *Walther*, as well as the Lat. *Waltherius*, having been kept hostage with his friend Hagen in the court of Attila, is challenged by Hagen on his return home. In the various versions of the Nibelungen saga, Hagen murders Siegfried to protect the honor of his liege-lord Gunther, then falls victim to the long-plotted revenge of Siegfried's wife and Gunther's sister Kriemhild, who, like Hagen, must exact an honorable retribution. Assuming the role of the avenging male, unlike most women in Germanic poetry, Kriemhild in the *Nibelungenlied*, like Achilles and Aeneas in Cl. e., denies mercy to Hagen when she sees him wearing Siegfried's sword, the fatal token of his victory over Siegfried.

Early Romance e., like Germanic e., was composed orally for a royal society by poets called minstrels or jongleurs (qq.v.), and is formulaic. Anglo-Saxon and Germanic e. employs a heavily alliterative line, often with 4 stresses and marked with a prominent medial caesura. The most common meter for Romance epic, the one used by the anonymous poet of the *Chanson de Roland* is decasyllabic with a regular caesura after the fourth syllable. It is organized into rhyming units called laisses (q.v.), which average about 14 lines but can vary from 5 to 100.

Romance e., like its counterpart the medieval romance (q.v.), is episodic in structure, arranging adventures in panoramic sequence, often juxtaposing farcical and heroic action, and frequently incl. fantastic and supernatural elements. Although it sometimes involves a love affair, Romance e. focuses on the hero's achievements as a warrior rather than as a lover. With its roots in the *chansons de geste* (q.v.), Romance e. was divided into three main cycles: the matter of France, which told of the deeds of Charlemagne and Roland, and includes the most famous Fr. e., the *Chanson de Roland* (ca. 1100); the matter of Britain, which dealt with King Arthur and his knights of the Round Table; and the matter of Rome, which encompassed material from antiquity, esp. stories of the siege of Troy, and includes the *Roman d'Alexandre* (ca. 1160), which used and gave the verse line, the alexandrine (q.v.), its name. Apart from the *Chanson de Roland*, the most important chansons are the *Chanson de Guillaume*, celebrating the exploits of the historical Duke of Orange, and the *Voyage de Charlemagne*.

The Fr. poet of the *Chanson de Roland* reshapes the historical events of Roland's defeat at Roncevaux (ca. 778) into an e. of betrayal and courage. Divided into three parts, the second of which concludes with the death of Roland, the *Chanson* narrates the events that lead to the betrayal of Roland, describing how the warrior-hero and his peers fight off the Saracens. As in the *Iliad*, descriptions of the aristeias of each warrior follow in rapid succession. Roland's loyalty to his liege-lord is only surpassed by that to his friends, whose deaths he inadvertently causes by his reluctance to summon aid. Nevertheless, Oliver, like Patroclus, dies blessing his friend, having sacrificed his life to defend Roland's honor. As a battle e. the *Chanson* has much in common both with ancient and with med. Germanic e. The warriors of the Fr. *geste* follow the traditional pattern of exchanging vows and boasts with their opponents before combat. Special weapons are prized that are closely identified with the hero and which he alone can wield, such as the huge spear that Achilles possesses or the magnificent sword granted Beowulf to kill Grendel's mother. Like Sigurd or Siegfried before him, and the Cid after him, Roland has a named sword, sent from heaven and made of holy relics, that he would rather destroy than hand over to his enemies. Like Achilles and Sigurd, he has a horse who grieves for his death. The trad. of named swords and loyal horses carries on into Ren. chivalric es., where they often assume allegorical significance.

The great Sp. e., the anonymous *Poema de mio Cid* (ca. 1140), tells the adventures of a hero and his comitatus. As the oldest surviving text of the medieval Castilian e. trad., it is remarkable in that it attains literary form less than 100 years after the events its celebrates: the exploits of Don Roderigo of Castile, dubbed by the Moors he conquers El Cid. Written in *mester de juglaria* (irregular heptasyllabic hemistichs) and divided into three sections or cantars, the e. celebrates a vassal exemplary in his loyalty to his king and to his warring allies but, unlike many of the tragic heroes of Germanic e. and the Fr. Roland, both valiant and successful, defeating his enemies and defending insults to his honor, until finally becoming reconciled to his king and, through his daughters' marriages to princes, a future patriarch himself. Though much shorter than the *Aeneid* or the Sanskrit es., like them it is a national e. that concludes with a prince's successful founding of a royal dynasty.

D. *Renaissance.* Ren. e. begins in Italy with an attempt to reconcile Romance e. to the Christian and Cl. trads. From Dante (1265–1321) in the late Middle Ages on, European e. poetry, espousing the literary values of Virgil and his Cl. predecessors, tries to make e. poetry meaningful to the Christian present and to the national interests of the different Eng. and Continental cultures. For Dante this means uniting, in the *Divine Comedy* (written in the vernacular), the Cl. model of the e. journey quest with the Christian model of the allegorical dream vision (q.v.). Making himself an e. pilgrim and journeying soul, he travels down to survey Hell, then up the pseudogeographical mount of Purgatory to the Earthly Paradise, and finally through the spheres of a Ptolemaic universe to Heaven, where he sees the smile of a triune deity. His journey, unlike those of Odysseus or Aeneas, seeks neither homeland nor political ideal but the soul's place with God and a justification of his native Florence's nonpolitical, nonsectarian destiny. The three realms that Dante surveys are inhabited by historical and mythical characters, as well as contemp. It. sinners and saints. Encountering each successive individual or group as he moves through the circles of Hell, Purgatory, and Paradise (to which he devotes 34, 33, and 33 cantos respectively in his 100-canto poem), Dante approaches closer to numerological perfection and to defining what it would mean to dwell in a society of just and sane people. Not unlike the Cl. Lucretius and the medieval

Boethius (whose philosophical poem *The Consolation of Philosophy* [6th c.] had impact on the writers of intellectual e.), Dante investigates the material and intellectual composition of the universe in order to understand its history and man's destiny.

Dante's immediate successors in Italy—Petrarch (1304–74) and Boccaccio (1313–75)—and in England—Chaucer (ca. 1343–1400) and Langland (ca. 1332–1400)—take a different course with e. material. Petrarch, writing in Lat., attempts to revive in *Africa* the Roman historical e. Boccaccio and Chaucer in the *Teseida* and *The Knight's Tale* (from the *Canterbury Tales*), respectively, and also in *Filostrato* and *Troilus and Criseyde*, attempt to unite e. and medieval romance (q.v.). They narrate stories that involve the traditional heroes of the Theban and Trojan War cycles and that climax in traditional events such as e. tournaments and heroic battle. The narrative thrust of these chivalric es., however, involves the winning of a lady's affection, which will remain an important ingredient in the romantic es. of the next two centuries. Boccaccio and Chaucer eschew the terza rima (q.v.) of Dante's *Commedia* and choose longer stanzaic patterns. Boccaccio develops ottava rima (q.v.), which becomes the meter of choice for writers of romance e.—Pulci, Boiardo, Ariosto, Tasso, and Camoëns. From Boccaccio Chaucer develops rhyme royal (q.v.), which in turn becomes the choice of the Scottish Chaucerians (q.v.) in the 15th c. and leads to Spenser's devel. of the Spenserian stanza (q.v.) for *The Faerie Queene*. Except for Ren. e. in Lat., which uses Virgilian hexameters, e. after Boccaccio typically employs one stanzaic pattern or another, until the mid 17th c., when Milton chooses unrhymed iambic pentameter as the meter for *Paradise Lost*. Langland's *Piers Plowman* (late 14th c.), like the *Divine Comedy*, takes the allegorist's way with a dream vision (q.v.) that surveys mankind as a fair field of folk, considers the alternate temptations of Lady Meed and the Seven Deadly Sins, and unravels the instructions of Holy Church. But despite its pronounced influence on future Eng. allegorists such as Spenser, *Piers Plowman* belongs more to the alliterative trad. that finds its final flowering in the 14th c. than to the Ren.

It. poets of the 15th and 16th cs. look back to the *chansons de geste* and the matter of France for a new chivalric e. in which love and marvelous adventures became as important as heroic battle. Taking seriously the trad. that Homer was the author of the so-called comic e., *Margites*, Luigi Pulci (1432–84) determines in *Morgante Maggiore* (1483) to transform the adventures of Orlando into humor by creating as Orlando's associates two comic giants—Morgante and his semi-giant companion to Margutte. Without being able to change the tragic end to the story—Orlando's betrayal by Ganelon and his death at Roncevaux—Pulci lightens the effect by having Rinaldo, accompanied by the comic devil Astarotte, attempt to save Orlando while burlesque devils and angels snatch at the souls of dying Saracens and Christians. *Orlando Innamorato*, the incomplete e. pub. in two installments in 1486 and 1494 by Matteo Boiardo (1441–94), follows soon after. Influenced by the treatment of love in Arthurian chivalric romances, Boiardo reshapes the character and story of Roland, making his love for the princess Angelica of Cathay the principal theme. Pitting Christian against Saracen knights in battle, in tournaments, and in love, Boiardo makes the golden Angelica the object heroes vie for as once they sought glory or the Golden Fleece in the traditional es. of war and quest. Boiardo heightens the element of the marvelous, moreover, with magic lances and rings, enchanted castles and fountains, for Angelica inherits the role of sorceress Medea once had. War is not entirely banished, however, for the pagan enemies of Charlemagne's peers—the Tartar Agricane and the Moor Gradasso—are fictional counterparts of the real threat that the Turk continued to pose for 15th-and 16th-c. Europe. With his sequel to Boiardo's e., *Orlando Furioso*, pub. first in 1516 and in a definitive edition of 46 cantos in 1532, Ludovico Ariosto (1474–1533) resumed the story of Orlando's pursuit of Angelica. Upon her marriage to a humble-born warrior, Angelica departs, mid-way through the e., leaving Orlando, like the maddened Ajax, to wreak havoc until, restored to his senses, he resumes his proper role as Charlemagne's leading warrior. Ariosto takes an ironic view of the world of men and women, undercutting the very heroism his e. purports to praise and cynically demonstrating the folly of the love that in chivalric romances moves men to brave deeds and women to virtue. Not even Ruggiero and Bradamante, characters inherited from Boiardo and the alleged founders of the dynasty of the d'Estes (for whom both Boiardo and Ariosto wrote), escape Ariosto's satire, for Ruggiero must be rescued from the sorceress Alcina by his warrior-fiancée.

After Ariosto, e. assumes a more serious purpose, with the national and Christian e. coming to the fore in Camões, Ronsard, Tasso, and Spenser. In *Os Lusiadas* Luis de Camões (1524–80) attempted to do for Portugal what Virgil in the *Aeneid* had done for Rome—to write an e. celebrating the national character that both told the hist. of the nation and adhered to the design of traditional Cl. e. Like the contemp. Sp. poet Alonso de Ercilla y Zuñiga (1533–94), who told in the *Araucana* of Spain's conquest of the South Am. Indians, the Araucanians, Camões chose for his e. a national adventure from recent history. Recounting in the *Lusiads* the voyage of Vasco da Gama to India to find a new trade route and establish an empire to rival Spain's, Camões created a contemp. quest e. He adopts the mythological machinery of the *Aeneid*: Vasco's voyage to the East proceeds under the protective eye of a semi-Christian Venus, Aeneas' patroness, and overcomes obstacles posed by a malevolent Bacchus, representing the disorderly pagan anarchy of the East. Vasco's voyage is, as Camões demonstrates through Virgilian digressions and prophecies, the outcome of Portugal's own destiny, in which, having repulsed the Moors and defended its freedom against Spain, Portugal can assume its proper role as the leading defender of Christianity. Formally, the *Lusiads* is in 10 cantos of ottava rima, following It. e. rather than Cl.; the ninth canto, the episode of the Island of Loves, indicates in another way the influence of Ariosto and Boiardo. Pierre de Ronsard (1524–85), although he only completed four books of the *Franciade* (pub. 1572), had an aim similar to Camões—to glorify the future hist. of his nation by telling of its founding by the eponymous Trojan ancestor, Francus, and so to produce a latter-day *Aeneid* for the kings of France. The Croatian poets Brno Krnarutić (1520–72) in *The Capture of the City of Sziget*, Juraj Baraković (1548–1628) in *Vita Slovinska*, and Ivan Gundulić (1588–1638) in *Osman* also produced es. inspired by similar national interests.

Torquato Tasso (1544–95), combining Virgilian and chivalric e., produced in *Gerusalemma liberata* (1582) a Christian e. conscious of its Counter-Reformation mission to urge the liberation of Jerusalem from the Turks, as once the heroes of the poem had liberated the city at the end of the First Crusade. Substituting the pious Godfrey of Bologne for the chivalric Charlemagne of older e. and the impetuous Rinaldo for Orlando as the leading warrior, Tasso considers, as Ariosto and Boiardo had before him, the alternate demands of war and love. Rinaldo, a composite of the Cl. and chivalric hero, is, like Achilles, headstrong and quarrelsome and, like Orlando, led by his love for a woman to neglect his duty. Other characters are divided by their love for pagans and their loyalty to Christianity. Angelic messengers take the parts that pagan deities played in the *Aeneid*. Although written, like the es. of Ariosto and Boiardo, for the d'Estes, and like them in ottava rima (and 20 cantos in length), *Gerusalemma liberata* is more nationalistic and Christian in design. As such, it more nearly resembles the *Faerie Queene* (1590, 1596), the allegorical work that Edmund Spenser (ca. 1552–99) designed as the national e. for England to celebrate the virtues of the perfect knight Arthur and to glorify Elizabeth, the greatest princess of Christendom. Although only six Books of the original 24 projected were completed, each of the six celebrates a different virtue. The *Faerie Queene* adapts material from e., romance, and allegorical trad., not only using Virgil, Tasso, Ariosto, Dante, Chaucer, and Langland as direct models, but also paying attention to what his contemporaries Samuel Daniel and Edward Hall were attempting in producing chronicles and poetic histories for England. Hence in Book I, in recounting the adventures of the Red Crosse Knight, Spenser is also recounting allegorically both how

Protestantism triumphed in England after Henry VIII and how the individual Christian pilgrim, like the typical allegorical hero, aspires to overcome sin in the battle each Christian must wage. Spenser's female knight Britomart, whose adventures occupy Books 3–5, is both one of the proposed ancestresses of Elizabeth Tudor (as Ariosto's Bradamante was of the d'Estes) and the personification of Elizabeth's virtue, Chastity.

Unlike Tasso and Spenser, many Christian writers of the 16th and 17th cs. turned directly to the Bible for their plots and characters, adapting Old Testament narrative, as medieval writers had done, taking Christ as the example of the ideal hero, or elaborating extra-biblical material on Satan and his angels. The Croation writer Marko Marulić (1450–1524) wrote a *Judita* (1521–23) in his native Croatian and a Lat. e. on David, *Davidijada*. Later in the 16th c., Gabriello Chiabrera (1552–1638) produced several short biblical es. on David, Judith, the Deluge, and other subjects, using *versi sciolti* (q.v.), perhaps the Continental precursor to Milton's blank verse. The most famous e. of the century, however, was the *Christiad* (1535) by Girolamo Vida (ca. 1490–1566), composed in six Books in Lat. hexameters, closely modeled on Virgil's, and an important influence on Continental and Eng. writers through Milton. Vida in making Christ the hero of his poem looks forward to the Christian es. of the 17th c. The Fr. Huguenot Guillaume Du Bartas, reviving the hexaemeral trad. in his enormously successful Creation e., *La Semaine* (1578), sparked other Creation es. throughout Europe well into the next century, among them Tasso's *Le Sette Giornate del Mondo Creato* and es. by the Ger. Mollerus (1596), the It. Murtola (1608), and the Sp. Acevedo (1615). A different type of religious e. recounted Satan's rebellion and fall, the most notable being Erasmo de Valvasone's *L'Angeleida* (1590) and Odorico Valmarana's *Daemonomachiae* (1623). The Eng. Spenserians, Giles and Phineas Fletcher, produced es. as diverse as Giles' celebration of *Christ's Victory and Triumph* (1610) and Phineas' dual-lang. Lat. and Eng. *The Locusts* (1627), on the Gunpowder Plot, a subject that also moved the young Milton's first attempt at e. Probably the most promising of the Eng. biblical es. before Milton's, however, was the *Davideia* (1656), Abraham Cowley's ambitious but unfinished work in pentameter couplets that tried to give Cl. scope to the history of David.

John Milton (1608–74), opting for a topic popular in Ren. biblical drama over the Arthurian material he originally considered, composed in *Paradise Lost* (1667, 1674) the first Cl.-style e. on Man's fall to include not only the story of the temptation of Adam and Eve but also accounts of Creation, the battle of the angels, and an extended prophetic sequence on biblical hist. Like Dante, Milton turned away from Cl. notions of the heroic, eschewing as supreme virtue both battle courage and desire for empire (qualities he attributes to the anti-hero Satan), and instead lauding the patience and heroic martyrdom that the Son of God willingly espouses as true merit. He makes Adam and Eve his central characters and the central event their tragic yielding to temptation. Looking back on the didactic semi-es. of Hesiod, Lucretius, and the Virgilian *Georgics*, Milton makes instruction a large component of the e. He modifies the basic structure of the Cl. e., retaining, however, its 12 books, beginning *in medias res*, and including narrative digressions; the invocation to the Muse, the extended simile, and mythic allusion he adapts to the purposes of a Christian e. The sequel, *Paradise Regained*, in four books only and often termed a "brief e.," is plainer in style; Milton chooses, like Vida, Jesus as his hero, and using the techniques of Platonic dialogue and Jacobean debate tells the story of Satan's temptation of Jesus in the wilderness.

E. *Eighteenth Century.* Interest in Cl. e. continues strong in the latter 17th c. and into the 18th. Treatises on e., such as R. Le Bossu, *Traité du poème épique* (1675) and *Treatise of the Epick Poem*, tr. "W. J." (1695), appear; major poets, particularly in England, translate Homer and Virgil; and poets continue to imitate Cl. and Romance e. Voltaire produced a *Henriade* (1723) on the Fr. religious wars, and in Russia M. Lomonosov and M. Kheraskov also wrote nationalistic epics, the former on Peter the Great, and the latter on Ivan the Terrible's capture of Kazan, the *Rossiada* (1779). In England, though minor writers such as Richard Blackmore compose e. after e., no writer of talent after Milton wrote a successful Cl. e. Many successful trs. of Homer and Virgil appear, however, the first having been that of Homer by George Chapman (1559–1634). John Dryden (1631–1700) produced a neoclassical tr. of the *Aeneid*, as did Alexander Pope (1688–1744) and William Cowper (1731–1800) of the Homeric poems. Mock e. (q.v.), however, abounded, from Nicholas Boileau's *Le Lutrin* (1673–83) to Dryden's *Absalom and Achitophel* (1681) to Pope's *Rape of the Lock* (1714), a form employed by Neo-Lat. poets in the previous century and given Cl. approval by the existence of the type in such poems as the 6th-c. B.C. *Batrachomyomachia* (Battle of the Frogs and Mice), attributed in the Ren. to Homer. Pope's most ambitious mock-e. poem, *The Dunciad* (1738, 1742), consigned untalented dabblers in heroic verse to an underworld ruled by the Goddess Dulness. Lyric poets use some techniques of e. in long descriptive poems, such as, in England, James Thomson in *The Seasons* (1726–28); on the Continent, Albrecht von Haller in *Die Alpen* (1732), a preromantic panegyric in 490 hexameters on the beauty of mountains; and in Russia, S. Bobrov in *Tavrida* (1798) or *Khersonida* (1804).

The rediscovery and revival of interest in oral e. (both genuine and spurious) also dates from this period, however, as does serious evaluation of the conditions of composition that produced the Homeric poems (see F. A. Wolf, *Prologomena ad Homerum* [1795]). Even though the most famous of these so-called recovered ancient es.—*Fingal, an Ancient E. Poem in Six Books*—was a hoax, attributed to the Celtic bard Ossian but actually written by James Macpherson (1736–96), the interest generated led to the study of ballads and folksongs. Celtic es. and medieval ballad material began to be gathered in Scotland, Wales, and Ireland. The Irish hero Cuchulain emerges from the Celtic e., the *Taín*, which in its reconstructed version is prosimetric. In Finland the poet-scholar Elias Lönnrot (1802–84) recovered for his nation the e. known as the *Kalevala* (1835, 1840), reconstructed from orally transmitted material.

F. *Modern*. After 1800 few poets attempt to revive Cl. e., though the immense cultural prestige of e., lingering, attracted many of them to displaced or related types of long verse compositions. John Keats (1795–1821) leaves his Miltonically-inspired *Hyperion* unfinished. William Wordsworth (1770–1850) in his long seminarrative poem in blank verse, *The Prelude* (1805, 1850), creates an autobiographical account of his devel. as a poet that qualifies in intellectual scope as a philosophical e. Similarly, Elizabeth Barrett Browning (1806–61) in *Aurora Leigh* (1857) could lay claim to have written a novel in verse or a feminist e. George Gordon Lord Byron (1788–1824), having attempted different types of narrative verse in his Oriental tales and in *Childe Harold's Pilgrimage* (1812, 1816–18), turned to comic e. in ottava rima in the style of Pulci and Ariosto in *Don Juan* (1822), which even in its unfinished state still reaches 16 cantos. In Russia, Aleksandr Puškin (1799–1837) followed Byron's lead, particularly in his exotic oriental tale *The Gypsies* (1824). His romantic e. *Ruslan and Lyudmila* (1820) is in the style of Ariosto but incl. folklore elements; the historical es.—*Poltava* (1829) and *The Bronze Horseman* (1833)—follow earlier Rus. models, and finally the new novelistic e., *Evgeny Onegin* (1833), his most accomplished poem. In England both Alfred Lord Tennyson (1809–92) and William Morris (1834–96) turn back to the Romance and Germanic e. of the Middle Ages. Tennyson attempted in *Idylls of the King* (1888) in a series of 12 linked Books to study the rise, decline, and fall of an heroic society, allegorically representing Camelot as his own England in the waning 19th c. Morris devotes himself to retelling Cl. legend in *The Life and Death of Jason* (1867) and Icelandic saga in *Sigurd and Volsung* (1876), using a rhymed couplet rather than the blank verse Tennyson had employed. In America Henry Wadsworth Longfellow turns to the legends of the Am. Indians for *Hiawatha* (1855), which he writes in the meter of the Finnish *Kalevala*. Walt Whitman (1819–92), publishing the first ed. of *Leaves of Grass* in the same year (1855), heralds the new e. Adding to and reorganizing in successive editions the lyric,

semi-narrative poems that make up the sections of *Leaves of Grass*, Whitman tells the story of America by representing himself as the collective ego of its people. He moves from birth through life to death, touching on the triple realms of physical, historical, and spiritual reality, making—as Dante had—his own personality the center of his poem and making the key figures of Am. hist.—Columbus, Washington, and above all Lincoln—heroic foils to his own persona.

On the Continent, those 19th-c. works most e. in character and scope are either dramatic or novelistic in form. Goethe (1749–1832) collaborated with Friedrich Schiller on an essay "Über epische und dramatische Dichtung" (1797), which attempts to differentiate between e. and dramatic action. Although Goethe generally opposes the confusion of these genres, he created in *Faust*, which in form is dramatic, a poem that takes the e. quest as its theme. Reaching back to the medieval tale of the man who sold his soul to the devil, Goethe enacts on both the human and cosmic level the struggle of man for salvation, a theme that Christian e., and the *Divine Comedy* in particular, has made preeminent in the Western world. In his cycle of music dramas, *The Ring of the Nibelung*, Richard Wagner (1813–83), drawing his material, like William Morris, from the Elder Edda, creates a musical e. in dramatic form. His cycle, like Milton's e., encompasses Creation and rebellion, the struggle of the human heroes Siegmund and Siegfried with their divine progenitor Wotan, the tragic death of Siegfried, and the noble sacrifice of Brunhilde to redeem the ring and make possible a new heaven and new earth. *Les Trojens* by Hector Berlioz (1803–1869), based on Virgil's *Aeneid*, could make a similar claim to musical e. Like the e.-drama or the music drama, the novel often possesses not only the narrative sweep of the e., but also its bardic consciousness. Efforts at e. scope in the novel are made by Manzoni in Italy (*I Promessi Sposi*, 1827), Balzac and Flaubert in France; Tolstoy in Russia; Scott, Dickens, Thackeray, and George Eliot in England; and Melville in America.

In the 20th-c., Homeric e. continues to inspire both writers of verse and prose. The modern version of the Odysseus story can be found both in the psychological novel *Ulysses* (1922), by the Irish writer James Joyce (1882–1941), which narrates one day in the life of a Dubliner, and in the modern narrative poem, *The Odyssey, a Modern Sequel* (1938) by the Gr. poet Nikos Kazantzakis (1885–1957), which recounts the further adventures of Odysseus. While historical novelists and directors of so-called "e." films carry on in one way the trad. of e. narration, 20th-c. poets seek for new underpinnings for the long poem, often using the techniques of lyric, prose fiction, or drama to give their poetry the authority and breadth of statement that e. seems to demand. In *Anabasis* (1924), a brief e. in 10 lyric interludes of varying length,

EPIC

St.-John Perse adopts the persona of a princely hero of the past to describe his founding of an ancient city and undertaking of an expedition, the poem celebrating the heroic spirit in man and his thirst for adventure and conquest. At the same time, Boris Pasternak (1890–1960) in *Lieutenant Schmidt* (1927) and *Spektorsky* (1931) revives the novelistic poem made popular by Puškin a century earlier. Both World Wars have had their effect on writers of long poems. H. D. (1886–1961) in *Trilogy* (1944–46), using the lyric voice to record her experiences of wartime London, tackles the universal problem of war. William Carlos Williams (1883– 1963) in *Paterson* (1944–63) deals with the history and inner life of a city and its inhabitants. In these poems, as in Ezra Pound's *Cantos*, the personal voice of the poet is central and shapes the experiences narrated. The *Cantos*, over 100 in number and published over the course of 50 years, are this century's most serious attempt at verse e. Pound (1885–1972) defines e. as a poem containing history, in which one man speaks for a nation. Placing himself at the center of his poem, like Dante and Whitman, as an e. pilgrim or voyager, Pound encompasses time from the mythic past to the present and civilizations as disparate as Homeric Greece, Imperial China and Rome, Med. France, Ren. Italy, and Federalist America. His lang. can be vulgar or exalted; his vision moves from the common to the mystical and paradisical. Focusing often on the violent episodes in history, on the villains and heroes of the past, Pound attempts to draw heroic exemplars—from Odysseus to the 15th-c. It. Sigismundo Malatesta to Confucius to John Adams and Mussolini—to teach man how to live within the world he must inhabit.

As 20th-c. poets such as Pound extend the boundaries of the e. as genre (see MODERN LONG POEM), 20th-c. critics, from C. M. Bowra to E. M. W. Tillyard to C. S. Lewis, search for a classification scheme or typology, contrasting the primary or oral e. with the secondary or written literary product. Investigations of oral e. in the line of those begun in Yugoslavia by Milman Parry and continued by Albert B. Lord extend now to the study of orally transmitted material in Albania, Turkey, Russia, Africa, Polynesia, New Zealand, and the Americas. And the study of the roots of Chinese and Japanese e., which began in the West only in the present century, is flourishing most strongly at present, as is the study of the numerous, emergent, flourishing African e. trads.

See also AFRICAN POETRY; BALLAD; CHANSONS DE GESTE; GENRE; GREEK POETRY, *Classical*; HEROIC VERSE; MEDIEVAL ROMANCE; MODERN LONG POEM; NARRATIVE POETRY; ORAL POETRY; ORAL-FORMULAIC THEORY.

E. W. Hopkins, *The Great E. of India* (1901); W. P. Ker, *E. and Romance*, 2d ed. (1908); W. M. Dixon, *Eng. E. and Heroic Poetry* (1912); R. Heinze, *Virgils epische Technik*, 3d ed. (1915); R. C. Williams, *The Theory of the Heroic E. in It. Crit. of the 16th C.* (1917); C. G. Osgood, *The Trad. of Virgil* (1930); C. M. Bowra, *Trad. and Design in the* Iliad (1930), *From Virgil to Milton* (1945), *Heroic Poetry* (1952); R. Menéndez Pidal, *Historia y epopeya* (1934), *La epopeya castellana a través de la literatura española* (1945); H. Massé, *Les Épopées persanes* (1935); C. S. Lewis, *A Preface to* Paradise Lost (1942); E. Mudrak, *Die nordische Heldensage* (1943); H. T. Swedenberg, *The Theory of the E. in England, 1650– 1800* (1944); G. Highet, *The Cl. Trad.* (1949); D. Knight, *Pope and the Heroic Trad.* (1951); J. Crosland, *The OFE.* (1951); U. Leo, *Torquato Tasso* (1951); Auerbach; Curtius; G. R. Levy, *The Sword from the Rock* (1953); E. M. W. Tillyard, *The Eng. E. and its Background* (1954); K. H. Halbach, "Epik des Mittelalters," and H. Maiworm, "Epos der Neuzeit," *Deutsche Philologie im Aufriss*, ed. W. Stammler, v. 2 (1954); A. Heusler, *Nibelungensage und Nibelungenlied*, 5th ed. (1955); R. A. Sayce, *The Fr. Biblical E.* (1955); Raby, *Secular*; C. Whitman, *Homer and the Homeric Trad.* (1958); Lord; Weinberg; G. S. Kirk, *The Songs of Homer* (1962), *Homer and the Oral Trad.* (1976); D. Bush, *Eng. Lit. in the Earlier 17th C.* 2d ed. (1962), chs. 11–12; D. M. Foerster, *The Fortunes of E. Poetry* (1962); T. M. Greene, *The Descent from Heaven: A Study in E. Continuity* (1963); J. Clark, *A Hist. of E.P.* (1964); P. Hägin, *The E. Hero and the Decline of Heroic Poetry* (1964); B. Wilkie, *Romantic Poets and E. Trad.* (1965); A. Cook, *The Classic Line* (1966); W. Calin, *The E. Quest* (1966), *A Muse for Heroes: Nine Cs. of the E. in France* (1983); G. Williams, *Trad. and Originality in Roman Poetry* (1968); N. K. Chadwick and V. Žirmunskij, *Oral Es. of Central Asia* (1969); R. Finnegan, *Oral Lit. in Africa* (1970); Parry; P. Merchant, *The E.* (1971); M. P. Hagiwara, *Fr. E. Poetry in the 16th C.* (1972); D. Maskell, *The Historical E. in France, 1500–1700* (1973); *Parnassus Revisited: Mod. Crit. Essays on the E. Trad.*, ed. A. C. Yu (1973); *E. and Romance Crit.*, ed. A. Coleman, 2 v. (1973); J. J. Duggan, The Song of Roland: *Formulaic Style and Poetic Craft* (1973); Wilkins; Pearsall; *Heroic E. and Saga*, ed. F. J. Oinas (1978)—surveys 15 cultures; *Europaïsche Heldendichtung*, ed. K. von See (1978)—34 essays on 9 national poetries; I. Okpeuho, *The E. in Africa* (1979); *Das römische Epos*, ed. E. Burck (1979); G. Nagy, *The Best of the Achaeans* (1979); K. Simonsuuri, *Homer's Original Genius* (1979)—18th-c. concepts; F. C. Blessington, Paradise Lost *and the Cl. E.* (1979); J. E. Miller, Jr., *The Am. Quest for a Supreme Fiction* (1979); *Trads. of Heroic and E.P.*, ed. A. T. Hatto (1980); M. A. Bernstein, *The Tale of the Tribe: Ezra Pound and the Mod. Am. Verse E.* (1980); Trypanis; W. T. H. Jackson, *The Hero and the King* (1982); *Les Épopées romanes*, GRLMA v. 3.1–2; Fowler; J. D. Niles, Beowulf: *The Poem and Its Trad.* (1983); *CHCL*, v. 1, chs. 2, 4; J. Opland, "World E.: On Heroic and E. Trad. in Oral and Written Lit.," *Comp Crit* 8 (1986); C. Martindale, *John Milton and the Transformation of Ancient E.* (1986); J. K. Newman, *The Cl. E. Trad.* (1986); *L'Épopée*, ed. J. Victo-rio (1988); J. Walker, *Bardic Ethos and the Am. E. Poem* (1989); J. P. McWilliams, Jr., *The Am. E.: Transforming a Genre, 1770–1860* (1989); J. M. Foley, *Traditional Oral E.* (1991); J. B. Hainsworth, *The Idea of E.* (1991).   S.P.R.

II. THEORY. A. *Classical and Alexandrian Greek*. The rich e. trad. of the Greeks (Homer, Hesiod, Arctinus, Antimachus) was at first criticized more from an ethical than a literary standpoint. Xenophanes (fr. 11, Diels-Kranz), for example, objected to Homer and Hesiod's depiction of gods as thieves, adulterers, and deceivers. In the *Ion* Plato pokes fun at Homer's interpreters for not having a rational understanding of their topics. In the *Republic* he combines the ethical and literary when he attacks Homer for teaching the young morally pernicious ideas by the pernicious method of imitation (q.v.). Here for the first time the notion of art as imitation, basic to Gr. aesthetics and already familiar as a positive concept to Pindar (*Pythian* 12.21), is developed into an argument that the whole poetic enterprise is corrupt for providing not the truth but a copy of a copy of the truth. Since for Plato, Homer is also the founder of tragedy (q.v.), both genres stand condemned. Much later this position would be adopted by Tolstoy (*What is Art?* 1898), with which the Neoplatonic arguments of Iris Murdoch (*The Fire and the Sun*, 1977) may be compared.

In the *Poetics* Aristotle accepts the Platonic theory of imitation but draws a radically different conclusion. Not only is imitation natural to man, but as intensified by tragedy it can produce, by means of pity and fear, a *katharsis tōn pathēmatōn* (see CATHARSIS). The lost second book of the *Poetics* may have claimed some parallel experience for comedy, according to the surviving work called the *Tractatus Coislinianus*. That for Aristotle this puzzling but evidently drastic effect is also valid for e. follows from his acceptance of another Platonic insight, that e. is inherently dramatic. Since, unlike Plato, Aristotle argued that drama is the superior genre, the best e. must be Homer's because it is already "dramatic" (an adjective which Aristotle may have coined). Since Aristotle believes that drama (Gr. "that which is done") is so important, it follows that the action has primacy. Not the soul of the hero but the mythic interaction of personae is the soul of the play. "Hero" is never used by Aristotle in its modern sense of "principal character," and indeed he criticizes es. which assert their unity merely by hanging a collection of disparate adventures onto a well-known name. Aristotle demands organic unity from the e., and also requires that it be *eusynopton* ("easily grasped in its totality") and that it not exceed the length of dramas shown at one sitting, a period of time usually calculated at six or seven thousand lines. Apollonius Rhodius's *Argonautica*, written in Alexandria (3d c. B.C.), exactly fills the bill.

Aristotle objected to the confusion of e. and historical narrative, perhaps because he had a strict notion of the historian's duty to do nothing but record. He ignores the fact that already Thucydides, for example, had used mythical models to interpret events. In disallowing the versification of Herodotus, however, Aristotle is obviously dismissing the (unmentioned) *Persica* of Choerilus of Samos (late 5th c.), and by implication the whole genre of historical, eulogistic e. dedicated to a patron to which Choerilus' work would give rise. By contrast, in allowing for "poetic" or imaginative prose, Aristotle opened the door to the modern e. novel. The definition of e. attributed to his pupil and successor as Head of the Lyceum in Athens, Theophrastus, as "that which embraces divine, heroic, and human affairs" also shifts the emphasis from form to content. Aristotle's modification in the *Rhetoric* of his views on vocabulary is related. The *Poetics* had laid down that e. vocabulary should be clear but elevated, marked by the use of poetic words or "glosses." The later *Rhetoric*, however, under the impulse of Euripides, permits the use of words from the lang. of everyday life. Aristotle saw in Homer more than the pre-tragic. He accepted as Homeric the comic *Margites* ("The Crazy Man": cf. *Orlando Furioso*), now lost, a silly account in mixed meters of a bumpkin who is not even sure how to proceed on his wedding night. Such openness completely contradicts Plato's severity and that of many later "Aristotelians."

The scholia or interpretive comments written in the margins of Homeric mss. prove that a practical crit. was worked out after Aristotle which preserved and extended his insights. Here the *Iliad* and *Odyssey* are regarded as tragedies, though the notion was not lost that Homer was also the founder of comedy. The contrast between e. and history is maintained. The analogy with painting is approved. "Fantasy" is praised (cf. Dante, *Paradiso* 33.142) both as pure imagination and as graphic visualization of detail. Nonlinear presentation of the story may be made and at a variety of linguistic levels.

Already Callimachus in Alexandria (3d c. B.C.) shared Aristotle's objections to the versification of Herodotus. In rejecting the eulogistic e., he worked out, in his own e. *Hecale*, a different kind of Homerimitatio from the straight comparison of the modern champion to a Homeric counterpart of the type apparently sought by Alexander the Great from the poetaster Choerilus of Iasos. Too little of Callimachus' e. *Galateia* now survives to make judgment possible, but his *Deification of Arsinoe* in lyric meter set the precedent for the appeal by a junior deity to a senior for elucidation that would become a topos (q.v.) of the Lat. eulogy (e.g. in Claudian and Sidonius Apollinaris) and even be adapted by Dante in the first canzone of the *Vita nuova*. Since this topos had Homeric precedent (*Iliad* 1.493 ff.), Callimachus was indicating which parts of the Homeric legacy were imitable, and how. In his elegiac *Aetia*, Callimachus advanced

Hesiod as the figurehead of his new approach to e., since Homer was already pre-empted by the theorists and poets of the rival school. He used Hesiod also to defend the e. of his contemporary, Aratus of Soli (epigram 27), assailed by critics because it was didactic. In later lit., Hesiodic or didactic e. will therefore be a clue to Callimachean allegiance.

The *Argonautica* of Callimachus's pupil Apollonius of Rhodes (3d c. B.C.) is a further demonstration of the Alexandrian theory of e. Out of their element in the heroic ambience, the characters collectively and Jason individually are often gripped by *amēkhaniē* ("helplessness"). Unified by verbal echoes of the red-gold icon of the Fleece, the poem underplays the conventionally heroic in showing both the futility of war and the degradation of the hero who, dependent on a witch's Promethean magic, eventually becomes the cowardly murderer of Apsyrtus. Homeric allusions point the lesson, and the reader knows from Euripides that eventually the marriage of Jason and Medea will end not in triumph but in disaster.

B. *Classical Latin and Medieval.* The Callimachean and Apollonian e., i.e. the kind written by scholar-poets, treated the lit. of the past by allusion and reminiscence in a polyphonic way. Catullus, the bitter foe of historical e., also uses this technique in his poem 64. Similarly, in the *Aeneid*, Virgil uses Homer as a sounding board rarely for simple harmony but to secure extra and discordant resonance for his modern symphony. Thus Dido is at once the *Odyssey*'s Calypso, Circe, Nausicaa, Arete, and the *Iliad*'s Helen and Andromache. Aeneas is Odysseus, Ajax, Paris, Agamemnon, Hector, Achilles. There is no end to the sliding identities and exchanges ("metamorphoses") of the characters. The poet who had quoted from Callimachus in *Eclogue* 6 in order to introduce an Ovidian poetic program, and had progressed to e. through the Hesiodic *Georgics*, may therefore be properly regarded as Callimachean. But he is also Aristotelian, both in the dramatic nature of his poem and in its tragic affinities. In Italy, Aeneas gropes toward victory over the bodies of friend and foe alike. Vengeful Dido by the technique of verbal reminiscence and recurrent imagery is never absent from the poem. Although the e. serves therefore in its way to exalt the origins of Rome, "shadows" (*umbrae*) is characteristically its last word.

The first Alexandrians were scholar-poets, and the third Head of the Library, Eratosthenes (276?–196? B.C.), still exemplified this ideal. But the early divergence of the two vocations led to a split between creative and critical sensibilities. Horace's *Ars poetica* (22? B.C.), written by a poet, is the last trustworthy theorizing about e. from antiquity. Described by an ancient commentator as a versification of the prose treatise of the Alexandrian scholar Neoptolemus of Parium, though clearly in its emphasis on the *vates* (391–407)

more than this, it recommends by its form a musicality in which arrangement and correspondence, interlace and arabesque, will replace the pedestrian logic of prose. In content, it both allows for the closeness of tragic and comic lang. and enjoins the *callida iunctura* ("cunning juxtaposition") by which context will redeem commonplace words.

A Roman and an Augustan, Horace moves beyond Callimachus when he urges that the poet, without in any way betraying Gr. refinement, must also be a *vates*, engaged with his society and with the reform of public morals. This is an aspect of Cl. e. subsumed by Dante in his allusion to *Orazio satiro* (*Inferno* 4.89).

Finally, Horace, who spoke of Homer's "listener" (*auditor*), took for granted a feature of ancient e. theory now often overlooked. E. did not cease to be oral with Homer. The power of Virgil's "acting ability" (*hypocrisis*), the "sweetness and marvelous harlotries" of his voice are attested in the *Life* written by Donatus (4th c. A.D.). This Aristotelian closeness to drama again implies polyphonic composition. There cannot be a single, univocal, "right" interp. of the action. Although in the 12th c. Geoffrey of Vinsauf in his theory of *pronuntiatio* seems to preserve some memory of this orality, it was competely ignored by those Ren. "Aristotelians" who, unlike their master but like Plato (who poked fun at dramatic and oral presentation of e., and of whom Callimachus said that he was incapable of judging poetry), set a statically conceived e. at the head of all the genres.

The crit. of the *Aeneid* for its *communia verba* by Agrippa, recorded by Donatus in his *Life* of Virgil (44), shows that there had developed even under Augustus the theory that e., as the sublimest of genres, demanded the sublimest of lang. Petronius' implied criticisms of Lucan (*Satyricon* 118 ff.) prove the persistence of this notion. At the end of Cl. antiquity, the same theory received a fatally deceptive application. *Rhetorica ad Herennium* (early 1st c. B.C.), influential in the Middle Ages, distinguished three styles, high, middle, and low, and conveniently Virgil had written three major poems: obviously the *Eclogues* must exemplify the low style, the *Georgics* the middle, and the *Aeneid* the high. This was the doctrine that eventually found its medieval canonization in the *Rota virgilii* ("Virgil's Wheel") devised by John of Garland. By this, names, weapons, even trees that could be mentioned in the different styles were carefully prescribed. One part of the deadly consequences of this doctrine was that the opening towards comedy in the e. (the *Margites*) was lost. Yet even the late antique commentator Servius had remarked of *Aeneid* 4: *paene comicus stilus est: nec mirum, ubi de amore tractatur* ("the style is almost comic, and no surprise, considering the theme is love").

On the Gr. side, pseudo-Longinus' *De sublimitate* (*On the Sublime*), variously dated between the 1st and 3d cs. A.D. or later, directly attacks Alexandrian theories of e., denying the Callimachean doctrine of purity of style and rejecting Apollonius in favor of Homer. The author supports his theory of grandeur with Homeric quotations which are in two cases conflated from different passages. Homer is indeed "grand," but in its inadequate appreciation of comedy and irony, and preference for magnificent lang. producing *ekplēxis* ("knockout"), the treatise represents a late and misleading simplification of Aristotle's subtle analysis.

Stung by Platonic crit. of Homer's "lying," Gr. Stoic philosophers in particular had developed a method of interpreting the Homeric narrative in symbolic terms intended to rescue its moral and theological credibility. In his efforts to reclaim all the genres for the new religion, the Christian Lat. poet Prudentius (348–post 405) wrote an e. *Psychomachia* in which the contending champions were no longer flesh-and-blood heroes but abstract qualities of the soul. It was only a short step from this to allegorizing Virgil's *Aeneid*, the most important example of this being Fulgentius (late 5th c.). This method seems in fact to rob the poem of its human immediacy, esp. as taken to extremes by Bernardus Silvestris in the 12th c. (*Commentum super sex libros eneidos virgilii*). The *Ovide moralisé* of Pierre Bersuire (d. 1362) is even less redeemable, since Ovid's interest in morality is slight at best. Highly praised allegorical es. have been written, however, of which the most important is probably Spenser's incomplete *Faerie Queene* (1590, 1596; see ALLEGORY).

The critical failure of later antiquity meant in effect that any e. theory that was to make sense had to be recoverable from the practice of major poets. This fact lent even greater significance to the already towering figure of Dante, since it was he who, as the author of an e. *Comedy* in the vernacular, broke decisively with both medieval prescription and practice, as seen at a relatively naive level in the anonymous *Waltharius* (930?) and with more sophistication in the *Alexandreis* of Walter of Châtillon (1180?). By anticipation Dante also rejects the classicizing poetics of the 16th c. His confrontation with academic orthodoxy in his exchange with Giovanni del Virgilio shows that, like Virgil, he used an eclogue to legitimize the claims of ordinary vocabulary and to reject the grand historical e. eulogy. These arguments are bolstered in Letter X to Can Grande, traditionally ascribed to Dante, with a quotation from Horace bordering on a line (97) which we are expressly told by the late commentator Porphyrio was borrowed from Callimachus.

C. *Renaissance to Modern.* The Ren. critics (Marco Girolamo Vida, *De arte poetica* [1527]; F. Robortelli, *In librum aristotelis de arte poetica explicationes* [1548]; Antonio Minturno, *De poeta* [1559], *De arte poetica* [1563]) were too often prescriptive rather than descriptive. Armed with the *Poetics* (tr. into Lat. by Giorgio Valla in 1498, 1536; Gr. text 1508; It. tr. 1549) and eventually with an amalgam of Aristotle and Horace, they advanced to war down the "unclassical" in e., but were largely the unconscious victims of old ideas. J. C. Scaliger, the most gifted scholar among them (*Poetices libri septem* [1561]), uses the evidence of lang. to decry Homer and exalt Virgil: the display by Homer of *humilitas, simplicitas, loquacitas,* and *ruditas* in his style must make him inferior to the Roman. If Virgil echoes Homer's description of Strife in his picture of Fama in Book 4 of the *Aeneid*, that is an excuse for loading Homer with abuse. The Alexandrian notion of the polyphonically echoed model has been replaced by that of annihilation, as it had been already in pseudo-Longinus.

Like their medieval forbears, therefore, these critics demanded sublimity in lang. and seriousness in theme, denoted by lofty character and moral uplift (Tommaso Campanella, *Poetica* [1595?]); and just as ruthlessly as Agrippa with Virgil they set about Dante, Ariosto, and Tasso for their unclassical backsliding. There was much argument over "probability," which for Aristotle was identical with persuasiveness. Now it came to mean what the rationalist critic would regard as probable, and thus could be used to clip the wings of poetic imagination. In fact, the fidelity of It. e. to the Cl. heritage may be observed both positively, in the minuteness with which it echoes the Alexandrian code both in detail (e.g. the *recusatio* or "refusal" topos) and, more largely, in its assumption of the romantic or pastoral element found also in the es. of Apollonius Rhodius and Virgil; and negatively, in the failure of Petrarch's *Africa*, which had sought to resurrect the historical, eulogistic e. in the manner of Ennius. Similarly, Ronsard's *Hymnes* (1555–) in the style of Callimachus were successful, while his e. *Franciade* (1572), which had been preceded by his rather Horatian *Abrégé d'art poétique* (1565), remained unfinished. In the 17th c., Fr. critics adapted and propagated the It. recension of Aristotle's rules, emphasizing the unities, decorum, and verisimilitude (qq.v.), although the first tr. of the *Poetics* into Fr. did not appear until 1671. André Dacier's edition and commentary (*La Poétique d'Aristote contenant les règles les plus exactes pour juger du poème héroique et des pièces de théâtre, la tragédie et la comédie* [1692]) became standard. This and other critical works (René Rapin, *Réflexions sur la poétique d'Aristote* [1674]; René le Bossu, *Traité du poème épique* [1675]) were regarded as normative throughout Europe. The es. they have inspired have however been universally regarded as failures. In Eng., John Milton (*Paradise Lost*, 1667, *Paradise Regained*, 1671) was greatly influenced by both It. example and precept. He knew Mazzoni's *Della Difesa della Commedia di Dante* (1587) and the theoretical work of Tasso (see Weinberg), whose old patron, Count Manso, he had met during his travels in Italy (1637–39). He quotes from Ariosto's *Orlando Furioso* at the beginning of *Para-*

dise Lost (1.16=*O.F.* I.2.2). His *Epitaphium damonis* (1639) toys with the idea of a historical epic on Arthurian legends, and his notebooks still preserved in Cambridge show that he considered a dramatic treatment of the same topics and of the story of Adam. In returning to epic he fixed on this theological theme, to which the closest Cl. parallel would be Hesiod's *Theogony*. It enabled him to set out his profoundest beliefs in the origin of the moral order of the universe, the human condition, and the Christian promise of atonement. His assumption in the poem of a difficult lang., criticized by Dr. Johnson, is part of the struggle to convey truths larger than life. His *Paradise Regained* uses a simpler style to depict Christ's rebuttal of the temptations of Satan. This successful resistance sums up the Christian victory.

Some Ren. treatises on poetics had argued in favor of the apparently unclassical, "romance" e. (Tasso, *Discorsi dell'arte poetica* [1567–70]), while others (Sidney, *Defence of Poesie* [1595]) had allowed modern authors to become "classical" in time. A wider breach in the "rules" (q.v.) seemed to open when, thanks to the study of Shakespeare in England (e.g. by Dr. Johnson) and in Germany (e.g. by the Schlegels), the deficiencies of normative crit. were recognized and replaced, slowly, by the inductive study of how great poetry is related to its national roots. At first the movement affected drama more than e., but the notion of short popular "lays" later assembled by editorial labor into longer e. poems was advanced by F. A. Wolff in his *Prolegomena ad Homerum* (1795). This theory, however, had the unfortunate consequence of breaking up the transmitted text of Homer into many sometimes incongruous layers (Karl Lachmann, *Betrachtungen ueber Homers Ilias* [1837]). Though it received a fresh boost from the investigations of Milman Parry and Albert B. Lord into Serbo-Croatian oral poetry (see Parry; Lord), nowadays it is seen by some Classicists as reducing Homer's aristocratic masterpieces to an uncouth common denominator. The problem of understanding the Cl. e. trad. is to be solved not by denying its literariness but only by sustaining an awareness of how complex that trad. really was.

Since the Ren., potential writers of e., in seeking new ways to deploy the poetic imagination at its fullest, have been confronted by a bewildering variety of choices and advice. If they choose verse for their mode, they accept all the risks of a genre not now organically related to their culture. This dilemma was adumbrated by Schiller in his *Über Naive und sentimentalische Dichtung* (1795–96) and was subsequently developed by Marxist critics like György Lukács. Such writers also run the danger of ignoring Aristotle's insight (*Poetics*, ch. 26) that drama is superior to e., a view which Berthold Brecht (by his theory of e. drama) still illustrates. More traditional poets either find themselves compelled to treat of lofty themes in a way that is bound to be lifeless and unconvincing, because it

mistakes the polyphonic and potentially even comic nature of the genre, or to ignore the decorum of Cl. e. in an extravagant effort to impress. If they turn away from mythical loftiness (Goethe's *Hermann und Dorothea* [1797]; Wordsworth's *Prelude* [1805, 1850]), they run the opposite risk of seeming to have forgotten their commitment to heroic sublimity. An author like St.-John Perse (*Anabase* [1924]) uses Cl. rhet. to produce a musical evocation of history that appealed to T. S. Eliot. Its relation to the historical e. condemned by Aristotle and Callimachus has not yet been explored. N. Kazantzakis (*Odyssey* [1938], *The Last Temptation of Christ* [1960]) treats both Gr. and Christian myths with flamboyant extravagance, in which, however, the Cl. elements seem to have exploded into unrecognizability.

The fragmentation of the Cl. trad. in our time has sometimes therefore led to impatient rejection of its relevance. Each artist responds freshly to new challenges. Even so, a unifying e. theory may seek to accommodate their individual achievements. Aristotle had allowed for imaginative writing in prose; and though Tolstoy was no friend of the Classics, even *War and Peace*, modestly described by him as a companion piece to the *Iliad*, and with its corrosive irony at the expense of the officially great, may be seen as a blow against the eulogistic e. favored by Callimachus's enemies and as a recovery of Homer's tragicomic picture of the human condition. In another vein, Tolstoy's *Anna Karenina*, with its "endless labyrinth of connections that is the essence of art," is a good introduction to the complexities of the narrative technique of the *Aeneid*. But the Cl. amalgam may be broken into its constituent elements (Pound's *Cantos*), given an Aristotelian push towards the drama (Eliot's *Murder in the Cathedral*), expanded to explore the human comedy and the illusions of eros (Proust), or deployed with all the tragic resonance of a Virgil (Thomas Mann's *Doktor Faustus*). Joyce's *Ulysses* and *Finnegans Wake*, with their allusive learning, verbal echoes, musicality, irony, and parody, are more Ovidian essays in the Alexandrian manner. The e. film may represent the most grandiose modern foray into the genre, recreating its own engagement with contemp. society, popular in appeal, yet, for at least one of its modern theorists, S. M. Eisenstein, profoundly traditional.

D. Comparetti, *Vergil in the Middle Ages*, tr. E. F. M. Benecke (1895); Faral; J. E. Spingarn, *Hist. of Lit. Crit. in the Ren.*, 2d ed. (1925); H. Strecker, "Theorie des Epos," *Reallexikon I* 4.28–38; E. Reitzenstein, "Zur Stiltheorie des Kallimachos," *Festschrift Richard Reitzenstein* (1931), 23–69, esp. 41 ff.; Lewis; M.-L. von Franz, *Die aesthetischen Anschauungen der Iliasscholien* (1943); C. M. Bowra, *From Vergil to Milton* (1945), *Heroic Poetry* (1952); M. T. Herrick, *The Fusion of Horatian and Aristotelian Lit. Crit., 1531–1555* (1946); Auerbach; Curtius; Frye, 318 ff.; Lord; Weinberg; D. M. Foerster, *The Fortunes of E. Poetry: A Study in Eng. and Am.*

Crit. 1750–1950 (1962); F.-J. Worstbrock, *Elemente einer Poetik der Aeneis* (1963); G. N. Knauer, *Die Aeneis und Homer* (1964); S. M. Eisenstein, *Nonindifferent Nature* [1964], tr. H. Marshall (1987); A. Lesky, *A Hist. of Gr. Lit.* (tr. 1966); K. Ziegler, *Das hellenistische Epos*, 2d ed. (1966); J. K. Newman, *Augustus and the New Poetry* (1967), *The Cl. E. Trad.* (1986); E. Fränkel, *Noten zu den Argonautika des Apollonios* (1968); S. Koster, *Antike Epostheorien* (1970); Parry; *Cl. and Med. Lit. Crit.*, ed. A. Preminger et al. (1974); *Homer to Brecht: The European E. and Dramatic Trad.*, ed. M. Seidel and E. Mendelson (1976); R. Häussler, *Das historische Epos der Griechen und Römer bis Vergil* (1976), *Das historische Epos von Lucan bis Silius und seine Theorie* (1978); G. S. Kirk, *Homer and the Oral Trad.* (1976); R. O. A. M. Lyne, *Further Voices in Vergil's Aeneid* (1987); D. Shive, *Naming Achilles* (1987).

J.K.N.

EPIC CAESURA. See CAESURA.

EPIC SIMILE. See SIMILE.

EPICEDIUM (Lat. spelling; Gr. *epikedeion*, "funeral song"). A song of mourning in praise of the dead, sung in the presence of the corpse and distinguished from *threnos*, a dirge (q.v.), which was not limited by time or place. The word does not occur before the Alexandrian period, or in Lat. before Statius (1st c. A.D.), although the lamentations over the bodies of Hector and Achilles in Homer are, properly speaking, *epicedia*. The e. became very popular in the Hellenistic period and was widely imitated in Lat. lit. It was accompanied by a solemn dance with music provided by a flute in the Lydian mode. Written originally in a variety of meters, it was confined after the Cl. period wholly to elegiac distichs and hexameters (qq.v.). *Epicedia* also included lamentations in verse for pet animals and birds (e.g. Catullus 3; Ovid, *Amores* 2.6; Statius, *Silvae* 2.4 and 5). See DIRGE; LAMENT.—Pauly-Wissowa; G. Herrlinger, *Totenklage um Tiere in der antiken Dichtung* (1930); W. Kese, *Untersuchungen zu Epikedion wid Consolatio in der römischen Dichtung* (1950); D. C. Allen, "Marvell's 'Nymph,'" *ELH* 23 (1956); *Oxford Cl. Dict.*; H. H. Krummacher, "Deutsche barocke Epikedeion," *Jahrb. der Dt. Schiller-Gesell.* 18 (1974); M. Alexiou, *The Ritual Lament in Gr. Trad.* (1974); Michaelides.

P.S.C.; T.V.F.B.

EPIDEICTIC POETRY. In Aristotle's *Rhetoric*, oratory is divided into three types: (1) deliberative or political, (2) forensic or legal, and (3) demonstrative or "e." The e. category is that based on praise and blame. Later treatises on rhet. preserved this tripartite division of modes of speech and elaborated on the e. category: e. speeches were said to use praise to stimulate hearers and readers to virtue by imitation of the virtues emphasized in the speech, and to use blame to make vice unattractive; e. rhet. thus places strong emphasis on free use of the figures of speech for ornamentation. For this reason, e. speeches tend to be ornate and in this sense "poetic." Subsequently, the types of e. speeches were described and formulas developed for each. The fullest ancient presentation of the formulas is the *Peri epideiktikon* ("On E. Oratory") of Menander (3rd c. B.C.). Among the types are encomium, panegyric, elegy, and epithalamium (qq.v.), but places and objects can be praised as well as human subjects—whence formulas for praise of a city and praise of a landscape.

E. rhet. was applied wholesale to poetry in late antiquity, and many e. forms became forms of occasional verse (q.v.). The *Sylvae* of Statius is essentially a collection (q.v.) of occasional poems drawing on e. formulas. Poems by Claudian (*Epithalamium*), Ausonius (*Mosella*—an example of "praise" of a river), and Aldhelm (*In Praise of Virginity*) illustrate extensions of the type. Later still, e. formulas were used to "explain" major genres. Epic was considered a form of praise and an "example" of such virtues as fortitude and wisdom, and tragedy a negative image of vice. These trads. underlie Sidney's description of the functions of epic and tragedy in the *Defence of Poesie* and Spenser's explanation of the function of the *Faerie Queene* ("Preface"). Other examples of e. poems in the Ren. incl. Spenser's "Epithalamium," Donne's "Anniversaries on the Death of Elizabeth Drury" (funeral elegy), and Ben Jonson's "To Penshurst" (praise of a country house).—T. Burgess, *E. Lit.* (1902)—still essential; Curtius, 154 ff.; V. Buchheit, *Untersuchungen zur Theorie des Genos Epideiktikon* (1960); O. B. Hardison, Jr., *The Enduring Monument* (1962); B. K. Lewalski, *Donne's Anniversaries and the Poetry of Praise* (1973); T. Cain, *Praise in the Faerie Queene* (1978); B. Vickers, "E. and Epic in the Ren.," *NLH* 14 (1983); A. Hardie, *Status and the Sylvae* (1983); C. Kallendorf, *In Praise of Aeneas: Virgil and E. Rhet. in the Early It. Ren.* (1989); M. McCanles, *Jonsonian Discriminations* (1992).

O.B.H.

EPIGRAM. A form of writing which makes a satiric or aphoristic observation with wit, extreme condensation, and, above all, brevity. As a poetic form, the e. generally takes the shape of a couplet or quatrain, but tone defines it better than verseform. The etymology of the term—Gr. *epigramma*, "inscription"—suggests the brevity and pithiness of the form. Pithy poems in the *Gr. Anthol.*—first assembled in 60 B.C. (see ANTHOLOGY) and the major source of es. in the Western trad.—run a gamut of tones from biting to sharp to gentle, and thus introduce the wider sense of the term (a sense which still lets us distinguish the e. from the proverb [q.v.] and apothegm, which are impersonal and gnomic in tone).

Japanese, Chinese, and Af. trads. exhibit their own versions of e., though the term is hard to translate into any non-Western lang. The Japanese, like the Greco-Roman trad., breaks into two strands—*haikai* (see RENGA; HAIKU) and *senryū*—both of which display a loosely comic thrust. Bashō, the renowned 17th-c. *haikai* poet, typifies the skill: "The salted bream / Look cold, even to their gums, / On the fishmonger's shelf" (tr. E. Miner). The more satiric *senryū*, which came into being in the 18th c., runs to the following realism: "If you ask directions / From a man pounding rice / First he wipes his sweat" (tr. E. Miner).

An 18th-c. Chinese epigrammatist, Cheng Hsieh, cuts from the same block:

> With wild hair, you block out your char-
> acters.
> Deep in the mountains, you engrave
> your poems.
> Don't even mention this man's "bone
> and marrow"—
> Who could even imitate his "skin"?

From the vastness of Af. repartee and wit one might pluck—as a different species of e.—John Pepper Clark's "Ibadan" (1965):

> Ibadan,
> running splash of rust
> and gold—flung and scattered
> among seven hills like broken
> china in the sun.

In the *Greek Anthology*, the romantic or elegiac inscription poem is prominent, amidst other occasional and light verse, but in 1st-c. A.D. Rome it yielded place to the more acid *vers de société* of Martial and Catullus:

> Once there was perfume in this little jar.
> Paphylus sniffed; it turned to vinegar.
> (Martial 7.94, tr. R. Humphries)

This sharp-tongued trad. inspired the Ren. e. both in Lat. and in the vernacular, though by the 18th-c. the double mode of the trad. was apparent again. In the 17th c., the fine Ger. epigrammatist Friedrich von Logau wrote *Sinngedichte* (1654), which inspired Lessing. Among the Eng. the e. is practiced by Heywood, Davies, Harington, More, and Jonson, who called his *Es.* (1616) "the ripest of my studies." The form was a favorite of Herrick's: nearly 200 of the 272 poems in his *Noble Numbers* are es., as "Upon a child that died":

> Here she lies a pretty bud,
> Lately made of flesh and blood:
> Who, as soone, fell fast asleep,
> As her little eyes did peep.
> Give her strewings; but not stire
> The earth, that lightly covers her.

While a harder hitting Donne, treating the same loss, wrote: "By childrens' births, and death, I am become / So dry, that I am now mine own sad tombe" ("Niobe").

Goethe's *Zahme Xenien* belong to both streams of the trad.; as do the critical studies of the e. and its history by Lessing and Herder. In France, where the vernacular e. was initiated by Marot and St. Gelais in the early 16th c., the satiric and personal e. reached perfection in Boileau, Voltaire, and Lebrun. By the 19th c., generic purities fade, yet there remain splendid examples of the major e. trads., as well as paths into new forms. Shelley can weep in the form: "Rome has fallen, ye see it lying / Heaped in undistinguished ruin: / Nature is alone undying" ("Fragment: Rome and Nature").

Max Beerbohm can manage the old rapier in his "Epitaph for G. B. Shaw":

> I strove with all, for all were worth my
> strife.
> Nature I loathed, and, next to Nature,
> Art.
> I chilled both feet on the thin ice of
> Life.
> It broke, and I emit one final fart.

Nietzsche's aphorisms suggest what possibilities lay inside the e. as it met a century concerned with both the natural voice and the ancient form, and eager to honor both freshly.

In the 20th c. the stinging e. survives in Yeats, Pound, Roethke, and J. V. Cunningham, and abroad in the work of such Continental poets as Erich Kästner, Christian Morgenstern, and René Char. At the same time, an almost new genus, the "lyrical e.," makes a fresh move back toward the softer grounds of the *Greek Anthology*, as for example in Robert Bly's

> When I woke, new snow had fallen.
> I am alone, yet
> someone else is with me,
> drinking coffee, looking out at the
> snow.
> (*Sleepers Joining Hands*)

or J. V. Cunningham's

> *Arms and the man I sing*, and sing for joy,
> Who was last year all elbows and a boy.
> (*The Exclusions of a Rhyme*)

There seems to be a balance of self-identity with innovation inside the e. trad., a compacting from which fresh energy is constantly extruded. See also ANTHOLOGY; ELEGIAC DISTICH; GNOMIC POETRY; GREEK POETRY, *Classical*; INVECTIVE; LATIN POETRY, *Renaissance*.

COLLECTIONS: *Epigrammata: Gr. Inscriptions in Verse*, ed. P. Friedländer (1948); *The Lat. Es. of Thomas More*, ed. L. Bradner and C. A. Lynch (1953); *Edo Satirical Verse Anthols.*, ed. R. H. Blyth (1961); *Selected Es.*, tr. R. Humphreys (1963)—Martial; *Deutsche Epigramme aus fünf Jahrhunderten*, ed. K. Altmann (1966); *The Gr. Anthol.*, ed. P. Jay (1973); *Russkaya epigramma vtoroi poloviny XVII-nachalo XXV.*, ed. V. E. Vasil'ev et al. (1975); *The Faber Book of Es. and Epitaphs*, ed. G. Grigson

(1977); *Es. of Martial Englished by Divers Hands*, ed. J. P. Sullivan and P. Whigham (1987).

HISTORY AND CRITICISM: Thieme, 369—Fr.; R. Reitzenstein, "Epigramm," Pauly-Wissowa; T. K. Whipple, *Martial and the Eng. E.* (1925); P. Nixon, *Martial and the Mod. E.* (1927); H. H. Hudson, *The E. in the Eng. Ren.* (1947); G. R. Hamilton, *Eng. Verse E.* (1965); *L'Epigramme grecque*, ed. A. Raubitschek (1967); G. Bernt, *Das lateinische Epigramm im Übergang von der Spätantike zum frühen Mittelalter* (1968); *Das Epigramm*, ed. G. Pfohl (1969); G. Highet, "E.," *Oxford Cl. Dict.* (1970); D. H. Garrison, *Mild Frenzy* (1978); P. Erlebach, *Formgesch. des engl. Es.* (1979); *Das dt. Epigramm des 17. Jhs.*, ed. J. Weisz (1979); F. Will, "E. or Lapidary Engraving," *Antioch Rev.* 40 (1982); Fowler; *CHCL*, v. 1, chs. 18, 20; P. Laurens, *L'Abeille dans l'ambre* (1989). F.W.

EPINIKION, also *epinicion, epinician.* A triumphal song, an ode commemorating a victory at one of the four great Gr. national games. It was sung either on the victor's arrival at his native town, during the solemn procession to the temple, or at the banquet held to celebrate his victory. The ordinary e. consisted of a number of groups, each of three stanzas (strophe, antistrophe, epode), and contained an account of the victory of the hero, a myth (the most important part of the poem, relating the victor's deed to the glorious past of his family), and a conclusion, which returned to the praise of the victor and ended with reflective admonitions or even a prayer. The most eminent representatives of this type of composition are Simonides, Pindar, and Bacchylides. One of the latest *epinikia* on record is that composed by Euripides for Alcibiades on the occasion of the latter's victory in three chariot races at Olympia (420 B.C.).—Schmid and Stählin; M. R. Lefkowitz, *The Victory Ode* (1976); Michaelides; *Pindar's Victory Songs*, ed. and tr. F. J. Nisetich (1980); K. Crotty, *Song and Action* (1982); W. Mullen, *Choreia* (1982); A. P. Burnett, *The Art of Bacchylides* (1985); L. Kurke, *The Traffic in Praise* (1991). P.S.C.; T.V.F.B.

EPIPHORA. See ANAPHORA.

EPIPLOKE (Gr. "plaiting" or "weaving together"). A term occasionally applied by ancient metrists to metrical sequences capable of alternative scansion depending on where the colon or metron (qq.v.) boundary is located—e.g. $x - \cup - x - \cup - x$, which will be iambic if a boundary precedes each anceps, and trochaic if it follows. Such sequences were seen as composed of an "interweaving" of the alternative forms involved—iambic with trochaic, ionic ($\cup \cup - -$) with choriambic ($- \cup \cup -$), bacchiac ($\cup - -$) with cretic ($- \cup -$). With the exception of dochmiacs and dipodic anapests, all Gr. rhythmical types are subject to interweavings of this sort, and certain verse structures are better

described as e. than as a succession of discrete cola and metra, division into units of this latter sort only becoming possible, if at all, once the verse design is instantiated in a particular line, strophe, or antistrophe. There is, however, no agreement as to the frequency of such structures or their general importance in the Gr. prosodic system.—Hephaestion, *Enchiridion*, ed. M. Consbruch (1906), 110–11, 120–21, 127; A. M. Dale, *Coll. Papers* (1969); T. Cole, *E.* (1988), ch. 1. A.T.C.

EPIRRHEMA. See PARABASIS.

ÉPISTÈME. See TWENTIETH-CENTURY POETICS.

EPISTLE, VERSE. See VERSE EPISTLE.

EPISTROPHE. See ANAPHORA.

EPITAPH (Gr. "writing on a tomb"). A literary work suitable for placing on the grave of someone or something which indicates the salient facts about or characteristics of the deceased. A shortened form of the elegy (q.v.), the e. may vary in tone from panegyrical to ribald, frequently addressing its message to the passerby, compelling him to read and reflect on the life of the person commemorated and, by implication, on his own life. In the West, the earliest extant es. are Egyptian, written on sarcophagi and coffins. They generally include the name, the person's descent, his office, and a prayer to some deity, e.g. "Royal chosen offering to Anubis, Director of the Balance . . . that he may give a good wrought Coffin in the Consecrated Enclosure . . . for the votary Osiris . . . deceased." Like the Egyptian material, Japanese tomb inscriptions, medieval Eng. brasses, and tombstone carvings in backcountry Am. graveyards—to suggest the cultural breadth of the activity—abound in efforts to draw favorable attention to the deceased.

Gr. and Roman es. in particular distinguish themselves: they are often highly personal and epigrammatic—note the convergence of epigram (q.v.) with e. (see below)—and their literary level is unusually high. They may be written in verse (usually the elegiac distich, q.v.) or in prose. Their details may include the name of the person, his family, certain facts of his life, a prayer to the underworld (esp. in Roman es.), and a warning or imprecation against defilement, though rarely are all these found in a single e. In Cl. es. we also find conventional topoi and motifs such as Fortuna and Fate, the thread of life, the removal from light, the payment of a debt, and a variety of consolations and lamentations.

The major collection of Cl. es. is Book 7 of the *Greek Anthology* The es. in this collection are of high poetic quality and cover the whole range of the form from satiric and comic to intensely serious. (The following, much imitated and here put literally, gives an idea of the range of modes implicit in such poems: "To Hope and to thee, O Fortune, a long farewell! I have found the haven. You and I have no more to do with each other; make sport of those who come after me.") They have influenced subsequent writers of es. from Roman times (Propertius, Horace, Martial, Ausonius) through the Ren. (Pontanus, Erasmus, More, Jonson) into the present (Pound, Yeats [esp. the tercet which concludes "Under Ben Bulben"], Auden, Edgar Lee Masters). Perhaps the single most famous e. from the *Greek Anthology* is that attributed to Simonides about the Spartan dead at Thermopylae: "Go, tell the Lacedaimonians, passerby, / That here obedient to their words we lie."

The Middle Ages used the Lat. e. both in prose and verse, often leonine verse (q.v.). Following the themes and practices laid down by the Greeks and particularly the Romans, the Eng. used the form, developing it to an exceptionally high art in the 15th and 16th cs., e.g. William Browne's on the Countess of Pembroke and Milton's on Shakespeare. Both Dr. Johnson and Wordsworth wrote essays on the e. as an artform.

The e. has not always been used to commemorate the dead, however. It has been put to satirical use against an enemy who is alive, and it has even been aimed at an institution, e.g. Piron's e. on his rejection by the Fr. Academy. Of the relationship of e. to epigram, Puttenham held that the e. was "but a kind of epigram only applied to the report of the dead person's state and degree, or of his other good or bad partes." The Gr. preposition *epi* (upon) shares out to both these genres the quality of being impressed upon something, and of the concision implicit in carving into a hard material. Ancient assumptions about the nature of the act of writing are evident here. See also ELEGY; LAMENT.

S. Tessington, *Es.* (1857); *Carmina latina epigraphica*, ed. F. Bücheler et al., 2 v. (1894–1926)—Lat. epigraphical verse; W. H. Beable, *Es.* (1925); H. W. Wells, *New Poets from Old* (1940); *Epigrammata*, ed. P. Friedlander (1948); Frye; R. W. Ketton-Cremer, "Lapidary Verse," *PBA* 45 (1959); *Griechische Grabgedichte*, ed. W. Peek, (1960)—Gr. funerary inscriptions; R. A. Lattimore, *Themes in Gr. and Lat. Es.* (1962); G. Pfohl, *Gr. Poems on Stones: Es. from the 7th to the 5th Cs.* B.C. (1967), ed., *Das Epigramm* (1969); R. Brown, *A Book of Es.* (1967); E. Bernhardt-Kabisch, "The E. and the Romantic Poets: A Survey," *HLQ* 30 (1967); J. Sparrow, *Visible Words* (1969); G. Grigson, *The Faber Book of Epigrams and Es.* (1977); J. Bakewell and J. Drummond, *A Fine and Private Place: A Coll. of Es. and Inscriptions* (1977); D. D. Devlin, *Wordsworth and the Poetry of Es.* (1980); F. Will, "The Epigram or Lapidary Engraving," *Antioch Rev.* 40 (1982); K. Mills-Courts, *Poetry as E.* (1990); J. K. Scodel, *The Eng. Poetic E.* (1991).

R.A.H.; F.W.

EPITHALAMIUM (Gr. "at the bridal chamber"). A wedding song. Originally the Gr. *epithalamion*

was a song sung outside the bridal chamber on the wedding night, to be distinguished from the *gamelios*, sung at the wedding celebration or banquet, and the *hymenaios*, sung in the processional taking the newlyweds to their new home, as described by Homer in the *Iliad* (18.391–96) and by Hesiod in *Shield of Herakles* (273–80). Sappho is apparently the first to use the e. as a distinct literary form (fr. 91–95). Brief nuptial songs appear in Aristophanes' *Peace* and *Birds*, but Theocritus is the most significant Gr. poet to have used the form (*Idyll* 18 on the marriage of Helen and Menelaus). In Lat., 17 verse epithalamia are extant by such poets as Ovid, Statius (*Sylvae* 1.2), Claudian, Ausonius, and Venantius Fortunatus (some of them centos), but the most important example was that of Catullus (*Carmina* 61, 62, 64), who was influenced by Sappho. Medieval lit. has devotional poems entitled *Epithalamia*, but these have no connection with the Cl. genre. The Ren. revived the form and used it to great advantage, e.g. by Tasso and Marino in Italy; Ronsard, Belleau, and Du Bellay in France; and Spenser, Sidney, Donne, Jonson, Herrick, Crashaw, Marvell, and Dryden in England. The greatest Eng. e. is Spenser's *Epithalamion*, written for his wedding to Elizabeth Boyle (1595) and arranged in an elaborate numerological design: the 23 stanzas embrace the hours and of the wedding-day (for the meter, see Schipper). His *Prothalamion*, a piece of occasional verse (q.v.) for the marriage of the daughters of the Earl of Worcester in 1596, is plain in comparison. Ren. conventions for the form include liberal use of Cl. allusions and *topoi*. Cf. ALBA; FESCENNINE VERSES; HYMN.

Eng. Epithalamies, ed R. H. Chase (1896)—anthol. with intro.; Schipper, *History* 363; E. F. Wilson, "Pastoral and E. in Lat. Lit.," *Speculum* 23 (1948); A. L. Wheeler, *Catullus and the Trads. of Ancient Poetry* (1934); A. Gaertner, *Die englische Epithalamienlit. im 17. Jh. und ihre Vorbilder* (1936); Lewis; A. S. McPeek, *Catullus in Strange and Distant Britain* (1939); T. M. Greene, "Spenser and the Epithalamic Convention," *CL* 9 (1957); A. K. Hieatt, *Short Time's Endless Monument* (1960); V. Tufte, *The Poetry of Marriage* (1970), ed., *High Wedlock Then Be Honoured* (1970)—anthol.; M. West, "Prothalamia in Propertius and Spenser," *CL* 26 (1974); C. Schenck, *Mourning and Panegyric* (1988); H. Dubrow, *A Happier Eden* (1990).

R.A.H.; T.V.F.B.

EPITHET. An adjective or adjectival phrase, typically attached to a proper name, used for distinctive purposes in poetry, these purposes most often having to do with allusion, connotation, repetition, and meter (qq.v.). In Western poetry the most important es. are undoubtedly those in Homer. The conspicuousness of the Homeric e. was recognized for centuries before Milman Parry demonstrated, in the early 20th c., that its utility for Homer is far greater than merely for lexical embellishment. Parry showed conclusively that in fact Homer uses only a small set of es. for each name, and indeed only a single phrase, with a distinct metrical pattern, for each grammatical case—Parry calls it a "formula" (q.v.). Homer uses these prefabricated metrical building-blocks to facilitate rapid composition of long narrative poems in an oral setting (see ORAL POETRY; ORAL-FORMULAIC THEORY).

Es. also form sensation-complexes or *compounds* which enable poets in their most energetic moments to find or create, in Coleridge's phrase, "*one word* to express *one act* of imagination." The Homeric phrase "Pēlion einosiphullon" (Pelion with quivering leafage) and Aeschylus' "anērithmon gelasma" ("multitudinous laughter," i.e. of the sea) are brilliant examples of this: each produces the effect described by Wordsworth in his poem on the daffodils: "Ten thousand saw I at a glance." This is the imaginative power which Coleridge called "esemplastic." The "embracing" or "extensive" e. occurs frequently in both Gr. and Eng. The compound es. in Gr. beginning with *eury-, tele-,* and *poly-* have their Eng. analogues beginning with *wide-, far-,* and *many-*. The *poly-* or "many" group is particularly large. By the side of Gr. es. having the sense of "rich in flowers," "with many furrows," "with many trees," "with many ridges," "poluphloisbos" ("loud-roaring," Homer's e. for the sea), and many more of like character may be placed Milton's "wide-watered" (shore), Keats's "far-foamed" (sands), and Tennyson's "many-fountain'd" (Ida). Such es. are imaginative in their reduction of multiplicity to unity.

OE poetry possessed an elaborate diction which included periphrases or kennings (e.g. *swanrād*, "swan's-road," for "sea"; see KENNING) and compound es. (e.g. *fāmigheals*, "foamy-necked"). Chaucer also employed compound es. such as *golden-tressed* (*Troilus and Criseyde* 5.8) and *laurer-crouned* (*Anelida and Arcite* 43), as well as picturesque metaphorical verbs such as *unneste* ("fly out of the nest" [*Troilus and Criseyde* 4.305]). But the Eng. poet who most cultivated es. as an enrichment of style is Edmund Spenser. Occasionally he fills a whole line with them, as in his description of Britain as a "saluage wildernesse, / Unpeopled, unmanurd, unprou'd, unpraysd" (*Faerie Queene* 2.10.5). His compound es. are more numerous and memorable than Chaucer's, and are of various kinds: the morally serious (e.g. *hart-murdring* love [*F.Q.* 2.5.16]), the picturesque (*firie-footed* teeme [1.12.2]), the classical (*rosy-fingred* Morning [1.2.7]). Spenser's es. were the model and inspiration of much brilliant work in Marlowe, Shakespeare, Chatterton, Keats, Tennyson, and others. See also KENNING; LEXIS.—M. Parry, "The Traditional E. in Homer" (1928), rpt. in Parry; B. Groom, *The Formation and Use of Compound Es. in Eng. Poetry from 1579* (1937), *The Diction of Poetry from Spenser to Bridges* (1955); N. Peltola, *The Compound E. and Its Use in Am. Poetry from Bradstreet through Whitman* (1956); H. J. Rose, "Es., Divine,"

Oxford Cl. Dict., 2d ed. (1970); N. Austin, *Archery at the Dark of the Moon* (1975), ch. 1; P. Vivante, *The Es. in Homer* (1982).   B.G.; T.V.F.B.

EPITRITE, epitritic (Gr. "one-third as much again"). One of the four categories of rhythm, in Gr. prosody, for any foot containing 1 short and 3 long syllables: so described because the ratio of two longs to a long and a short is, in time-units, 4:3. The position of the short syllable determines the description of the e. as first, second, third, or fourth (respectively ∪ − − − , − ∪ − − , − − ∪ − , − − − ∪), but the first and fourth were avoided by Gr. poets as unrhythmical. See DACTYLO-EPITRITE.—Koster; West; J. M. v. Ophuijsen, *Hephaestion on Metre* (1987).   R.J.G.; T.V.F.B.

EPIZEUXIS. See PLOCE.

EPODE (Gr. "after-song"). (1) The lyric odes of the Gr. melic poets—e.g. Pindar and Bacchylides—and the Gr. dramatists consisted of three parts: the strophe and antistrophe (qq.v.), which were metrically identical in form—i.e. in response (q.v.)—and the concluding e., which differed in meter. Ben Jonson called them, usefully, "turn," "counter-turn," and "stand." Collectively they were sometimes called a "triad." The Gr. word *epodos* used in this sense was feminine in gender, i.e. *epodos strophé*. (2) When the word was masculine, however (*epodos stichos*), it also denoted the second and shorter verse of a couplet—notably an iambic dimeter following an iambic trimeter. The lines of such couplets might even be heterometric (in different meters); for example, a dactylic hexameter might be followed by an iambic dimeter, or an iambic trimeter by a dactylic *hemiepes* (q.v.). Archilochus seems to have been the founder of this kind of composition, which was used for invective and satire (qq.v.). The 10 meters that can now be identified in Archilochus' *Es.* are all formed by combining longer metrical cola with shorter. Horace claims to have introduced the form into Lat. poetry in his *Iambi*, which subsequent grammarians called Es.—Crusius; Dale; D. Korzenewski, *Griechische Metrik* (1968); Snell; West.   R.J.G.; J.W.H.

EPYLLION (Gr. "little epic," "scrap of poetry"). This term, in the specific sense of "little epic," is apparently an invention of the 19th c. to describe a short Cl. narrative poem in dactylic hexameters. This so-called genre embraced mythological subjects which often contained a love interest. It was characterized by elaborate and vivid description, learned allusion, lengthy digression, and an interest in psychology. Esp. cultivated in the Hellenistic era its characteristics were brevity and finish of meter: it narrated only a few events in the life of an epic hero, who is humanized by being placed in ordinary situations; there was a conventionalized digression in the middle. Callimachus' lost

Hecale was well known; and the epyllia of Euphorion of Chalcis, Theocritus, and, even more, Moschus' *Europa* show that it survived in Greece nearly to the end of the 2d c. B.C. In Lat. poetry, it was popular from Catullus to Ovid: the best extant examples are Catullus 64; pseudo-Virgil, *Ciris*; Virgil's own "Aristaeus" (*Georgics* Bk. 4); and Ovid's *Metamorphoses*—itself a series of epyllia worked together. The Byzantine period had its "epyllia" which were longer than the Alexandrian and Roman narrative poems and really were in effect brief epics. Later counterparts of the Cl. e. incl. the troubadour songs, the Rus. *byliny*, and the Scandinavian sagas. Such narratives were more extensively cultivated in the Ren., capped by Milton's "brief epic," *Paradise Regained*. Shakespeare's "Lucrece" and Tennyson's "Oenone" are perhaps the best examples of epyllia in Eng. poetry.—F. Skutsch, Pauly-Wissowa 6.1174 ff.; J. Heumann, *De epyllio Alexandrino* (1904); M. M. Crump, *The E. from Theocritus to Ovid* (1931); J. F. Reilly, "Origins of the Word 'E.,'" *CJ* 49 (1953–54); W. Allen, Jr., "The E.," *TAPA* 71 (1940), "The Non-Existent Cl. E.," *SP* 55 (1958); V. d'Agostino, "Considerazioni sull'epillio," *RSCl* 4 (1956); E. S. Donno, "Naso magister erat," *Elizabethan Minor Epics* (1963); W. Keach, *Elizabethan Erotic Narratives* (1977); K. J. Gutzwiller, *Studies in the Hellenistic E.* (1981); C. Hulse, *Metamorphic Verse* (1981); Trypanis, ch. 8.
R.J.G.; T.V.F.B.

EQUIVALENCE. In Cl. prosody (q.v.), e. is sometimes used to denote resolution (q.v.), the metrical principle whereby one *longum* may replace two *brevia* (though not vice versa): so in the epic hexameter spondees may replace certain dactyls, typically in the sixth foot, as Homer does in the first line of the *Odyssey*, or in the sixth and third feet, as in the first line of the *Iliad*. It is the principle or system of metrical e. which justifies such substitution of feet, not any actual temporal ratio of one long equals two shorts, though that belief has persisted since ancient times. The effect of e. thus allows metrical variety in successive lines while yet ensuring identity in their measure (q.v.), i.e. conformity to the meter (q.v.).

In the older Eng. metrists, the sense of the term is less clear: some believed the rule applied to Eng. literally, while others use it only by analogy. This latter is roughly the sense adopted by Saintsbury, who uses it with intentional vagueness simply to account for extra syllables in Eng. verse: the metrical "foot or group-system requires *correspondence* of feet or groups, and this . . . at once enjoins and explains . . . the main charm of English poetry" even though such correspondence is "not mathematically" exact: "the elasticity of the system" ensures "its suitableness to the corresponding elasticity of English verse." The perhaps better terms *correspondence* and *responsion* (q.v.) are often used synonymously.

The mod. sense of the term, wholly different

and far more central to the very conception of a verse-system itself, was given by Roman Jakobson in 1958 in a classic dictum: "the poetic function (q.v.) [of lang.] projects the principle of e. from the axis of selection into the axis of combination." In communication, lang. serves a number of functions, only one of which is aesthetic (i.e. poetic): a message becomes poetic (in function, regardless of whether it is cast in the mode of verse) whenever it focuses on itself, for its own sake, to the extent that e. becomes not merely ornament but "the constitutive device of the sequence." Thus any given sentence, such as "the child sleeps," is arrayed on two principal axes, one lexical, simultaneous, vertical (the paradigm), the other syntactic, sequential, horizontal (the syntagm). A speaker selects "child" from the lexicon's register of equivalent nouns ("infant," "baby"), as she does with the verb "sleeps," then combines them serially in the syntagm to complete the utterance. Items in the paradigm are related by e. (similarity-dissimilarity), items in the syntagm by contiguity; cf. the Factors of Similarity and Proximity in Gestalt psychology. In ordinary speech and prose the principle controlling both the selection and arrangement of words is essentially semantic (referential), but in poetry the constitutive principle is different: poetic lang. heightens its substantiality and memorability by increasing the degree of its *orders*, and it does this by selection and repetition of an element so as to effect a pattern (see REPETITION). The principle of e., which equates the words in the vertical register of speech, can equate other features in poetry and thus become superimposed upon the horizontal sequence as well (see RESPONSION).

E. is esp. prominent in metrical verse, where one phonological feature is deployed (against its opposite) systematically. E., however, is not the meter but the system which *makes the meter possible*: the particular feature the meter will employ (stress, length, pitch) is determined by the lang., and the specific pattern the meter will assume is mainly a convention (q.v.). Meter, then, is a synecdoche for e., but e. is a metonym for parallelism (q.v.); indeed, Jakobson identifies parallelism as "the fundamental problem of poetry." As with the meter, so with all the other formal elements in the text—sound-patterning, rhetorical figures, lexical echo and allusion, syntactic metaplasm: in every case "equation is used to build up a sequence." E. is thus "the indispensable feature inherent in any piece of poetry." And since the syntagmatic axis presents the sequential unfolding of meaning in lang., even as the paradigm represents the axis of simultaneity, e. in poetry serves to embed the atemporal within the temporal: as the lines proceed through their sequent schemes of meaning, e. counterpoises a firm (if subliminal) sense of unchangingness, of the *re*-creation of the now which came before in the now which is now. This substratum of identities becomes, thereby, the very emblem of poeticalness.

In sum, when similarity (e.) processes are superimposed upon contiguity processes, the superimposition compounds the degree of organization—the amount of order—in the text, thereby increasing the amount of information the text carries (without increasing the number of words), raising the amount of readerly attention necessary to understand the text, and marking the text as aesthetic not utilitarian. E. increases semantic density and brings into play all the effects of rhythm (q.v.). See now VERSE AND PROSE.—R. Bridges, *Milton's Prosody* (1901 ed.), App. F; Saintsbury, *Hist. of Eng. Prosody* (1906), v. 1, App. 1; A. W. de Groot, *Algemene Versleer* (1946); R. Jakobson, "Closing Statement: Linguistics and Poetics," in Sebeok; S. R. Levin, *Linguistic Structures in Poetry* (1962).   T.V.F.B.

EQUIVOCAL RHYME. See MOSAIC RHYME; GRAMMATICAL RHYME.

EROTIC POETRY. See LOVE POETRY.

ESEMPLASTIC. See IMAGINATION.

ESKIMO POETRY. See INUIT POETRY.

ESPERANTO POETRY began with the first booklet on the *Internat. Lang. E.*, pub. in Warsaw in 1887 by the Polish scholar L. L. Zamenhof (1859–1917) under the pseudonym "Dr. E." ("one who hopes"). The booklet included three poems—one translated and two original—to demonstrate that this proposed second lang. for internat. use was no lifeless project but a potential living lang. Zamenhof also produced numerous E. trs., incl. *Hamlet* (1894) and the entire Old Testament. The first E. magazine, *La Esperantisto*, which began in Nuremberg in 1889, also published poetry, early poets drawing on their native trads. to establish poetic norms for E. More than 100 regular periodicals now publish tr. and original E. p. E. lit. runs to several thousand volumes, and the E. lang. is presently used or understood by several million speakers in the world. E. is a European pidgin with a simplified grammar (though inflectional endings are retained) and pronunciation but a very large vocabulary of fresh and interesting wordforms and grammatical combinations unknown in European langs., e.g. Michalski's poetic coinage *ĉielenas* (goes upwards to the sky), in which *-as* denotes the present tense, *-n* direction toward, and *-e* the adverbial ending, while *ĉiel-* is the root associated with sky or heaven, *ĉielo*. Thus *ĉiele* = in the sky; *ĉielen* = towards in-the-sky; *ĉielenas* = is towards in-the-sky.

Serious projects for universal langs. began in the 17th c. with George Dalgarno (1661) and John Wilkins (1668) and engaged the attention of Descartes, Leibnitz, and Newton. Apart from E., only Volapük (1880) and Ido ("offspring"; 1908), a modification of E., developed any significant fol-lowing, now dissipated. By 1900 E. had spread beyond Poland, Russia, and Germany to Western Europe. Several collections of poems appeared, incl. three by the Czech Stanislav Schulhof (1864–1919) and the polished and musical *Tra l'silento* (Through the Silence, 1912) of Edmond Privat (1889–1962). Antoni Grabowski (1857–1921), friend of Zamenhof and skilled linguist, published an internat. anthol., *El parnaso de popoloj* (From the Parnassus of the Peoples, 1913) and a brilliant tr. of the *Pan Tadeusz* of Mickiewicz (1918). His audacious linguistic experiments prepared for the flowering of E. p. The Hungarians Kálmán Kálocsay (1891–1976), in *Mondo kaj koro* (World and Heart, 1921), and Gyula Baghy (1891–1967), in *Preter la vivo* (Beyond Life, 1922), led the way. They founded the influential magazine and publishing house *Literatura Mondo* (Literary World) in 1922.

Zamenhof's interest in E. lit. aimed to create an E. literary and cultural trad., to expand and test the lang. by stretching it to its limits, and to demonstrate that it was as capable of expression as any ethnic lang. Unlike some other projects for an internat. lang. (none of which withstood the test of time), E. did not spring fully armed from its creator's head. Zamenhof's 1887 booklet contained only the basis of E.; others expanded its lexicon and discovered its latent syntactic and morphological possibilities. Kálocsay, in numerous trs. and original poetry, esp. *Streĉita kordo* (Tightened String, 1931), sought diversity: his work includes lyrics, free verse, and strict verseforms. The Rus. Eugen Michalski (1897–1937) wrote introspective poems of startling imagery and linguistic experiment. While Privat and Kálocsay demonstrated E.'s affinities with the European trad., Michalski sought originality. But Stalinism claimed Michalski's life and silenced the talented Nikolai Hohlov (1891–1953). The figure of Kálocsay dominated the interwar years as mentor, editor, and publisher. Kálocsay and Waringhien's *Parnasa gvidlibro* (Guidebook to Parnassus, 1932) with its *Arto poetika* and glossary of literary terms and neologisms helped establish an E. trad.; in 1952, *Kvaropo* (Quartet) extended this trad. This work, by four British poets incl. William Auld (b. 1924), began a new era. Auld's *La infana raso* (The Child Rose, 1956), a poem of great variety and technical virtuosity, is widely regarded as the most impressive achievement of E. poetry to date. Auld's mentors include Michalski and the Eng.-lang. poets MacDiarmid, Pound, and Eliot. Among British contributors to E. poetry are Marjorie Boulton (b. 1930), Albert Goodheir (b. 1912), and Victor Sadler (b. 1937), whose *Memkritiko* (1967) displays concise expressiveness and mordant irony. Poets of the generation of Auld and Boulton include the difficult and introspective Icelander Baldur Ragnarsson (b. 1930), the Brazilian Geraldo Mattos (b. 1931), and the Czech Eli Urbanová (b. 1922).

The past thirty years have seen a widening of the geographic and cultural base as increasing numbers of Chinese and Japanese poets have begun publishing. They incl. Miyamoto Masao (b. 1913), Kuroda Masayuki (b. 1909), Ossaka Kenji (1888–1969), and Ueyama Masao (1910–88). In the E. poetic trad., tr. and original work are closely linked. Trs. incl. many of Shakespeare's plays (some by Kálocsay and Auld), his sonnets (tr. Auld), Camões' *Lusiads*, Dante's *Divine Comedy*, the *Kalevala*, the *Quran*, and volumes by Goethe, Baudelaire, Sophocles, Alves, Omar Khaiyam, Tagore, and numerous others.

Because of its conciseness and suitability for linguistic experiment, E. p. has developed faster than the E. novel or drama, though over 50 original novels have appeared. E.'s lexicon has expanded vastly: Zamenhof's initial vocabulary comprised fewer than 1000 roots, from which perhaps 10,000 words could be formed. The largest contemp. dictionaries now contain 20 times that number. The lexicon remains largely European, but E. grammar and syntax resemble isolating langs., like Chinese, and agglutinative langs., like Swahili and Japanese. The future of E. poetry is promising. Younger poets such as the Brazilian Passos Nogueira (b. 1949) and the precociously talented Mauro Nervi (b. 1959) of Italy (*La turoj de l'cefurbo*, The Towers of the Capital, 1978) live in an era of increased scholarly attention to E. E. appears to have established itself as a linguistic and cultural community with its own critical norms and standards.

L. Kökény and V. Bleier, *Enciklopedio de e.* (1933); *Gvidlibro por supera ekzameno*, ed. A. Pechan (1966); M. G. Hagler, "The E. Lang. as a Literary Medium," Diss. Indiana (1971); W. Auld, *The Devel. of Poetic Lang. in E.* (1976), *Enkonduko en la originalan literaturon de E.* (1979); V. Benczik, *Studoj pri la Esperanta literaturo* (1980); P. Ullman, "Schizoschematic Rhyme in E.," *PLL* 16 (1980); *E. in the Mod. World*, ed. R. and V. S. Eichholz (1982); *Esperanta antologio*, ed. W. Auld (1984)—anthol.; H. Tonkin, "One Hundred Years of E.: A Survey," *LPLP* 11 (1987); D. Richardson, *E.: Learning and Using the Internat. Lang.* (1988). H.T.

ESPINELA. An octosyllabic 10-line Sp. stanza form having the rhyme scheme *abba:accddc*. There is a pause after the fourth line as indicated by the colon. The strophe was supposedly invented by Vicente Espinel (1550–1624) and so named after him, though the form is found as early as ca. 1510, in the *Juyzio hallado y trobado*. The e. is occasionally augmented by two lines rhyming *ed*. Also called *décima* or *décima espinela*, the e. has been termed "the little sonnet," and justly so, since some of the most beautiful lines in Sp. poetry (e.g. in Calderón's *La vida es sueño*) have taken this form. Since the late 16th c., the e. has been widely employed.—D. C. Clarke, "Sobre la e.," *RFE* 23 (1936); J. Millé y Giménez, "Sobre la fecha de la invención de la décima o e.," *HR* 5 (1937); "*Es.* in the *Juyzio hallado y trobado* (c. 1510)," *RomN* 13 (1971); J. M. de Cossío, "La décima antes de Espinel," *RFE* 28 (1944); Navarro. D.C.C.

ESTAMPIDA (Occitan), *estampie* (OF). Lyric genre of pseudo-popular type, its music closely related to instrumental dance-tunes. The structure of the latter (schematically az_1az_2 bz_1bz_2 cz_1cz_2, in which z_1 and z_2 are differently cadenced versions of a recurring musical tail-piece) is reflected in the heterostrophic form of most OF examples. In the few Occitan pieces, a similarly structured but shorter tune matched a single stanza of text and was then repeated for subsequent stanzas, giving a regular isostrophic verseform.—F. Gennrich, *Grundriss einer Formenlehre des mittelalterlichen Liedes* (1932); Bec; P. M. Cummins, "Le Problème de la musique et de la poésie dans l'estampie," *Romania* 103 (1982); D. Billy, "Les Empreintes métriques de la musique dans l'estampie lyrique," *Romania* 108 (1987); Sayce, ch. 9; Chambers. J.H.M.

ESTONIAN POETRY. The E. lang., like Finnish, has the word-accent on the first syllable, is highly inflected, and tends toward polysyllabism. Its relatively small number of initial consonants favors alliteration (q.v.), which, however, is unobtrusive because of the unemphatic articulation. Oral folk poetry, alive in some parts of Estonia until fairly recently and recorded in hundreds of thousands of texts, prefers an octosyllabic meter combining quantitative and accentual principles, as that of the Finnish *Kalevala*. The lines, trochaic when sung (though not when spoken), permit initial short syllables of words to be stressed only at the beginning of the verse, e.g.:

> Kõlise, kõlise, keeli,
> Laja vastu, laasi, suuri.
>
> Ring, ring, tongue,
> Resound, great forest.

Parallelism and periphrastic formulae—not unlike *kenningar* (see KENNING)—abound, creating a rich, ornamental style capable of strong lyrical and dramatic effects. Written poetry since the 17th c. almost entirely discarded this form, using instead either accentual-syllabic or purely accentual meters, largely owing to Ger. influence. The numerous polysyllables, with only one clearly audible stress, often count as one long metrical foot; more frequently, however, the slight secondary stresses are exploited metrically, producing iambic or trochaic patterns, Dactylic, amphibrachic, and anapestic patterns are also frequent enough. There is considerable disinclination to use the weakly stressed inflections as rhymes. Near rhymes, permitting a fuller use of the vocabulary and surprise effects, have become more common since the 1920s.

Foreign—Baltic-Ger. and Rus.—social, economic, and political pressure slowed up the intellectual life of the Estonians until the early 19th c., when poetry, along with other cultural pursuits, began to flower. Stimulated by the romantic conception of a national genius, the leading poets of the E. national Ren. drew much of their inspiration from folklore, aided by their study of cl. antiquity, Finnish, Ger., and partly British romantic and preromantic poetry (see PREROMANTICISM; ROMANTICISM). The first notable poet, the short-lived Kristjan Jaak Peterson (1802–22), wrote inspired Pindarics. F. R. Kreutzwald's epic *Kalevipoeg* (The Kalevid, 1857–61), based on runic folk ballads, whose meter it uses, and of decisive importance as a cultural stimulus, owed much to Lönnrot's Finnish *Kalevala*. The powerful patriotic lyrics of Lydia Koidula (1843–86) with great independence developed the romantic *Lied* genre. Later in the century, political and social changes led to a less public, more intimate and more individually differentiated poetry, most impressively exemplified in the profoundly personal, tragic symbolism of the seemingly simple lyrics of Juhan Liiv (1864–1913). Symbolism (q.v.) in its Western form, intellectually searching, with much emphasis on a highly individualized, sophisticated style, characterizes the verse of the Noor-Eesti (Young Estonia) group, above all that of its leader, Gustav Suits (1883–1957), a revolutionary experimentalist and idealist, constantly torn between high flights of emotion and bitter, satirical skepticism. The poignancy, subtlety, formal richness, and exploratory boldness of his verse decisively affected the further course of E. p. The quiet, introspective mysticism of Ernst Enno (1875–1934), the sensitive island landscapes of Villem Grünthal-Ridala (1885–1942), influenced by Carducci, and the archaic ballads of Jaan Lôo (1872–1939) all added new wealth of language, imagery, and versification to a rapidly expanding lit. A discordant but effective note was struck by the gloomy, visionary primitivism of Jaan Oks (1884–1918).

Toward the end of the First World War, shortly before the E. declaration of independence in 1918, a new group, named after a mythological bird, "Siuru," inaugurated an era of lyrical exuberance and extreme individualism in both form and content. Its leaders, Marie Under (1883–1980) and Henrik Visnapuu (1889–1951), soon abandoned subjectivism for strenuous thought, more universal themes, and more firmly crystallized form. Marie Under, the greatest master of lyrical intensity, passed through psychological and metaphysical crises culminating in a poetry of extraordinary translucency and human insight. The eclectic but keenly picturesque aestheticism of Johannes Semper (1892–1970), the intimate dialect verse of Artur Adson (1889–1977) and Hendrik Adamson (1891–1946), and the principally Rus.-inspired experiments in melodic instrumentation of Valmar Adams (1899) preceded a temporary trend towards robust, nonphilosophic realism, which dominated the early Thirties but was followed by a strongly idealistic reaction. The deeply rooted native tendency toward symbolism, in a disciplined new form, reasserted itself in the verse of the "Arbujad" (Magicians) group, including Uku Masing (1909–1985), Bernard Kangro (b. 1910), and, above all, Heiti Talvik (1904–47) and Betti Alver (b. 1906), both intellectually among the subtlest, formally among the most brilliant of E. verse writers. Keenly aware of the great trad. of European poetry and thought, these poets sought "to enclose in slim stanzas the blind rage of the elements" (Talvik), imposing the finality of perfect expression on the emotional turbulence of a world heading toward chaos. This is equally apparent in the extreme, explosive, but fully controlled condensation of Talvik and in the more diverse output of Betti Alver, whose intense inner struggles are expressed with classical poignancy and clarity, her seriousness tempered by self-irony and sometimes also warm humor. Bernard Kangro's sensitive application of legendary and country lore added a special touch to the verse of this group.

From the Second World War up to the 1960s, which led to the Sovietization of Estonia, only the refugees were able to write freely and produce real art. Some of them, esp. Marie Under, Bernard Kangro in some of his works, and Gustav Suits in his last extensive volume of verse, have grown in breadth and depth. Though akin to the "Magicians" of the 1930s, both Arno Vihalemm (b. 1911) and Aleksis Rannit (1914–85) came into their own only in emigration. While Vihalemm has given voice to the grotesque absurdity of human existence, Rannit has chanted its sole salvation through artistic form. Kalju Lepik (b.1920), Ilmar Laaban (b. 1921), and Raimond Kolk (b.1924) comprise the first generation of exile poets. Lepik has adapted the parallelism and associative alliteration of folksong to ironic and dramatic ends; the linguistically inventive Laaban has been called the only true E. surrealist; Kolk's lyrical voice is most convincing in his dialect verse. Later exile poetry shows both the erotically charged virtuoso verse of Ivar Grünthal (b. 1924) and Ivar Ivask's (b. 1927) free-verse contemplations about being a cosmopolitan exile yet irrevocably rooted in nature, our only home. Urve Karuks (b. 1936) and Aarand Roos (b. 1940) have also made definite contributions. The revival of poetry back in Soviet Estonia was spearheaded by Jaan Kross (b. 1920) in his free-verse experiments in political frankness and by Artur Alliksaar's (1923–60) surrealist-absurdist wordplay. Their example was soon followed by the pronounced nationalist stance of Hando Runnel (b. 1938), the ecologically minded prophetism of Jaan Kaplinski (b. 1941), the polyphonic lyricism of Paul-Eerik Rummo (b. 1942), and the ironical personae employed by actor Juhan Viiding (b. 1948). Of the younger poets, Doris Kareva (b. 1958) has gained attention at home and abroad. Thanks to Gorbachev's policy of "openness," books by émigré poets have begun to be reprinted in Estonia and their work critically assessed. *Sõnarine*, a 4-vol. anthol. now in progress, promises to become the most comprehensive ever because it integrates both branches of E. lit.

ESTRIBILLO

ANTHOLOGIES: *An Anthol. of Mod. E.P.*, ed. W. K. Matthews (1953); *Acht E. Dichter*, (1964), *E. Lit. Reader*, (1968), both ed. A. Oras; *Contemp. East European Poetry*, ed. E. George (1985) *Kalevipoeg*, ed. J. Kurman (1982); *Ilomaile: Anthol. of E. Folk Songs*, ed. J. Kurrik (1985); *Sõnarine*, ed. K. Muru (1989–).

HISTORY AND CRITICISM: W. F. Kirby, *The Hero of Estonia*, 2 v. (1895)—on *Kalevipoeg*; M. Kampmaa, *Eesti kirjandusloo peajooned*, 4 v. (1924–36)—hist. of E. lit.; F. R. Kreutzwald, *Kalevipoeg*, 2 v. (1934–36); W. K. Matthews, "The E. Sonnet," *SEER* 25 (1946–47); E. H. Harris, *Lit. in Estonia*, 2d ed. (1953); H. Salu, *Eesti vanem kirjandus* (1953); G. Suits, *Eesti kirjanduslugu*, v. 1 (1953); A. Oras, "E. P.," *BNYPL* 61 (1957) and "Storia della letteratura estone," in *Storia delle letterature Baltiche*, ed. G. Devoto (1957); *For Ants Oras: Studies in E. P. and Lang.*, ed. V. Kõressaar and A. Rannit (1964); E. Nirk, *E. Lit.* (1987).   A.O.; I.I.

ESTRIBILLO. A refrain in Sp. lyrics and ballads which apparently originated in the *zéjel* (q.v.), of Arabic origin. The *zéjel* came through the Galician-Portuguese to the Sp. court lyric in the 14th c., where it developed into the *cantiga*, which in turn produced various types of poems during the pre-Ren. period. In the early period the e. was the introductory stanza—stating the theme and often called *cabeza* or *texto*—of a poem and was repeated at the end of each stanza of the poem— cf. the Eng. burden (q.v.). Later it is sometimes found only at the end of each stanza. See RE-FRAIN.—Le Gentil; Y. Malkiel, "Sp. e. 'refrain': Its Proximal and Distal Etymologies," *Florilegium Hispanicum*, ed. J. S. Geary et al. (1983); Navarro.
D.C.C.

ETHICS AND CRITICISM.

    I. RELOCATIONS
        A. *From Moral Rules to Ethical Qualities*
        B. *From Form vs. Content to Formed Experience*
        C. *From a Scientific to a Rhetorical Model*
    II. PARTICULARS AND GENRES

I. RELOCATIONS. Of all the possible critical responses to poetry, the one with the most sustained written trad. is the question, "Will the experience of knowing this poem be good for me or my society?" (Here the terms "poem" and "poetry" will be broadened to include fiction and drama; Eng. has no accepted term for the large class roughly covered by the Ger. word *Dichtung*.) We cannot know whether those who heard the first poems recited asked this question. Probably they simply relied on that inescapable prior question, "Do I like these poems?" But once Socrates had made the vexing claims that the poems we love most can damage our souls and that we should, for personal or political reasons, carefully select the poetic voices we allow to enter our lives (Plato, *Republic*,

Bks. 2, 10), critics for two millennia judged poems by their likely effect on souls or societies.

About a century ago, however, overt ethical crit. began to disappear from the work of professional literary critics. As philosophers increasingly claimed that all value judgments are merely "subjective," critics increasingly recommended an analytic, ostensibly objective crit. that could provide a knowledge as incontestable as that of science (see ANALYSIS; EVALUATION). It remained true, of course, that in their practice they could never fully expunge their ethical, political, or religious convictions. But in their theoretical writings, more and more critics either ruled out explicitly or simply ignored the task of appraising the moral or ethical value of poetry. (Political and religious crit. fared somewhat better, perhaps because large institutions, such as the Marxist states and various churches, kept it alive—and in some of its forms, destructively powerful.)

Some purifiers went even further in their acts of extradition, banishing not just moral or political judgments but all efforts at a rational evaluation of poems. As Northrop Frye, perhaps the most famous of the opponents of evaluation in crit., put it, "any attempt to align [art] with morality, otherwise called bowdlerizing, is intolerably vulgar." For him, as for increasing numbers of critics through the 20th c., every act of evaluation is simply "one more document in the history of taste" (25; see TASTE).

The reasons for ethical crit.'s original ubiquity and subsequent decline cannot be traced here (see Booth, ch. 2); pursued fully, they might well lead to a complex history of Western thought. It is equally difficult to explain just why, in the last few decades, ethical crit. has again become respectable, indeed widely so, ranging from left to right politically and from traditional to avant-garde aesthetically. It is not yet possible to have a single coherent picture of all the current crit. that attempts to appraise the moral, ethical, or social value of poems—the feminist reconsiderations (see FEMINIST POETICS), the unmaskings of racism and ethnocentrism, the new religious probings, the varieties of "cultural criticism" (q.v.). But a partial understanding of a deeply controversial scene can be found by looking at some current transformations and repudiations—some relocations—of the methods, definitions, and assumptions that marked traditional ethical crit.

A. *From Moral Rules to Ethical Qualities.* The twin notions that artworks ought to teach us right living, and that when they don't they should be banned, no doubt long predate the *Republic*, and they are still active today. This is hardly surprising, since it is an undisputed fact that poems do "teach" (see DIDACTIC POETRY). Regardless of their composers' intent, poems either implant or reinforce moral codes. No doubt a moral crit. that emphasizes such codes will find practitioners in every age, but the ethical crit. that today claims to go beyond mere personal moral preferences addresses the subtler question of the effects of poetry on the ethos (q.v.), the total character or individuality, of its readers. What patterns of desire, what habits of inference about other people, what visions of the self and the "other" are implanted or reinforced by a lyric poem (or novel, play, story, movie, rock lyric, video, or TV drama)? The ethical effects of a poem depend more on the total pattern of desires stimulated than on any particular code mentioned or preached. And those ethical effects need not be pursued into some future consequence, with hard proof that such and such behavior resulted from such and such a poem: they can be addressed as something that occurs during the time of reading (cf. Taylor's shift from "moral obligation" to "ethical quality").

Though this relocation to the qualities of experience and character may risk overly sentimental crit., it has the great advantage of reminding everyone that the one main motive for practicing ethical crit. in the first place is to share the intuition that—taking poems to be like persons—some literary "company" is worth cultivating, some simply a waste of time, and some positively debasing. Though ethical critics cannot be expected to come to full agreement about just which poems are ennobling or degrading (the scales of value differ from critic to critic), they do agree in defending the validity of appraising what poems do to the lives of those who embrace them.

B. *From Form vs. Content to Formed Experience.* From at least the time of Sidney's *Apologie for Poetrie* (1595), Western critics have tended to talk about form (q.v.) and content as separate entities, with form conceived as linguistic wrapping and content as the human meanings that lang. somehow contains. Such a divorce supported, with the rise of various aesthetic doctrines, those formalisms that identified poetic worth with a form that rendered irrelevant whatever content was "put into" the form (see NEW CRITICISM; RUSSIAN FORMALISM). Recent decades have witnessed a widespread revolt against the concept of form as container, with a restoration of something like the Aristotelian notion that a poem's form is what happens to the human stuff in it. Though there are still many formalists and text-bound critics of the former kind at work, other critics are increasingly attending to the form of the reader's or listener's experience, as shaped by responses to the human shapes the poem represents.

In one branch of the latter, "reader-response crit." (q.v.), the important form lies within the reader, not the text; indeed, some critics go so far as to deny that the text has any independent reality whatever. Though theories of ethical crit. have not often been made explicit by reader-response critics, in most cases their goal has been quite explicitly ethical: the invigoration or empowerment of readers, freeing them into creative activity of their own (see Suleiman; for other efforts to reconnect crit. to readers' lives, see Alter, Brooks, and Coles).

C. *From a Scientific to a Rhetorical Model.* Even the most rigorous formalist crit. has never achieved the kind of scientific consensus that some have sought. And when crit. moves to considerations of ethical value, all hope for logical certainties must be abandoned: norms of induction and deduction simply no longer apply. Judgments that take the form, "All poems that exhibit X moral flaw (or virtue) are bad (or good)," are simplistic and can almost always be undermined by an appeal to experience, e.g.: "Yes, I know that anti-Semitism in literary works is by definition bad, but in this work, which is admittedly anti-Semitic, I find so much of this or that valued quality that I can't simply condemn it out of hand." The redeeming qualities may be of many kinds, because ethical goods are of many kinds. They even include the ethical dimension of achieved form itself: the conscientiousness or genius that produces a beautiful form implies, for most readers, an admirable ethos (Booth, ch. 4).

The ethical critic is thus driven from a private quest for demonstrative proof to an embrace of a community of inquirers—the community of all those who care enough about engaging the poem to enter into serious conversation. Appraisals of individual poems, and even of entire genres (see below), must therefore change over time, not only because critical interests change but because serious discussion illuminates judgment. Critics learn from one another—this point would seem painfully banal were it not so often ignored in theory—about plain misreadings, about overlooked ironies and allusions, about unsuspected intentions, about the minutiae of achieved aesthetic design. They learn about their prejudices and blind spots. And they learn how to broaden, deepen, and sharpen their criteria.

Such malleability is sometimes seen as proof that the ethical critic's statements have no cognitive value—that ethical crit. is indeed essentially nonrational. But the fact that "I do not do it alone, we do it together," in a process that never comes to a full stop, does not mean that ethical crit. need be capricious or merely "subjective" (see SUBJECTIVITY AND OBJECTIVITY). It is true that it can never yield a judgment of absolute ranking and is thus always dependent on the range of each would-be expert's previous experience. But theorists of most other disciplines are by now acknowledging similar co-dependencies of all inquirers.

Current ethical critics generally abandon the search for the one right moral code or the one right method for conducting crit. Instead, they embrace plurality on all fronts (see PLURALISM). When adopted by ethical critics, pluralism means that the critic no longer seeks to describe a value that all good poetry should serve. Instead, the critic will welcome a world of many human goods and many good kinds of poetry serving those goods, and many good particular ways of working within those kinds.

II. PARTICULARS AND GENRES. None of this emphasis on particulars means, however, that ethical critics can permanently abandon appraisals of the relative worth of kinds or genres. But when the worth of genres is in debate, the experienced critic will reject jejune debate on such questions as whether some huge bulk, "tragedy," is superior to some equally huge bulk, "comedy" (qq.v). Rather, the discussion will shift to just what distinctive range of ethical goods each genre has served, in its best instances, or might yet serve, and just why a full human perspective needs both tragedy and comedy (and the many other genres that have proved enduring). And along with such inherently limitless discussions, ethical critics will recognize that they can accomplish most by emulating those earlier critics who, like Samuel Johnson, spent their major energies in quite precise efforts to illuminate the ethical force of particular poems.

Still, even if these relocations become widespread, some critics will want to continue ethical crit. of the traditional kinds, defending or attacking huge lumpings of texts under rubrics like "poetry," "free verse," "the novel," "fiction" and so on (see GENRE). The history of such crit. shows that it must be even less systematic than ethical crit. of individual works. Generic crit., while by no means worthless, achieves its worth by stimulating thought about what a given kind threatens, at its worst, or offers, at its best. It is inherently reductive about the dangers and promises of broad ranges of human achievement. Since particular poems of every poetic kind are capable of performing great good or great harm, quarrels about the value of the broad kinds already mentioned, or of "imitation," "poesie," "the classics," or "popular culture," can never get very far.

Many critics (Sidney, Shelley) have attempted to answer Plato's indictment with the claim that poetry is a better educator of the soul than either philosophy or history, and indeed because of the very powers that Plato warned about: poems were for them in fact what make the world go round, or at least what make it tolerable in its turnings. Poems provide the warm motivation for the abstract propositions that philosophies offer us and the unimaginative recordings of real events offered by histories. In Shelley's famous sentence, "poets are the unacknowledged legislators of the world." At present, ethical critics are generally less ambitious and more inclined to grant Plato his point: poems can do great harm as well as good. It is the task of ethical crit. to develop intelligible ways of talking, with as much precision as the subject allows, about such effects.

A critical world in which people defend the ethical worth of poems will not run smoothly. It will be even less visibly "progressive," in the sense of accumulating shared knowledge, than a critical world in which the chief issue is whether a given work is coherent, or derivative, or resides in this or that trad. Consequently, the scientifically minded—those who reject the relocations described above—will be even less respectful of ethical crit. than they have been of the various formalisms. But the losses of confidence and clarity that ethical crit. entails are surely less important than losing the right to dispute the ethical consequences of engaging with poems. See also CRITICISM; DIDACTIC POETRY; EVALUATION; SOCIETY AND POETRY.

M. Arnold, *Essays in Crit.* (1865); Y. Winters, *In Defense of Reason* (1947); W. K. Wimsatt, Jr., "Poetry and Morals," *The Verbal Icon* (1954); Frye; V. Buckley, *Poetry and Morality* (1959); L. Trilling, *Beyond Culture* (1961); F. R. Leavis, *The Great Trad.* (1969); J. Casey, "Art and Morality," *The Lang. of Crit.* (1969); E. Gilman, "Lit. and Moral Values," *EIC* 21 (1971); T. J. Diffey, "Morality and Lit. Crit.," *JAAC* 33 (1974–75); J. Barzun, *The Use and Abuse of Art* (1975); J. Gardner, *On Moral Fiction* (1978); *The Reader in the Text*, ed. S. Suleiman and I. Crosman (1980); "Lit. and/as Moral Philosophy," spec. iss. of *NLH* 15 (1983); P. Brooks, *Reading for the Plot* (1984); R. Alter, *Motives for Fiction* (1984); G. J. Handwerk, *Irony and E. in Narrative* (1985); C. Clausen, *The Moral Imagination* (1986); W. Berthoff, *Lit. and the Continuances of Virtue* (1988); T. Siebers, *The E. of Crit.* (1988); W. C. Booth, *The Company We Keep* (1988); R. Coles, *The Call of Stories* (1989); L. S. Lockridge, *The E. of Romanticism* (1989); J. H. Miller, *Versions of Pygmalion* (1990); J. S. Hans, *The Value(s) of Lit.* (1990); M. Nussbaum, *Love's Knowledge* (1990); C. Taylor, *Sources of the Self* (1990). W.C.B.

ETHIOPIAN POETRY may be divided into four kinds: (1) verse written in Ge'ez (Ethiopic), a lang. which ceased to be spoken (except in the church) some four or five hundred years ago, yet has continued to be used for literary expression; (2) popular verse composed in Amharic (now the official lang. of Ethiopia), Tigrinya, Tigre, Harari, and other regional langs.; (3) modern devotional and secular poetry in Amharic; and (4) poetry written in European langs., mainly Eng.

Rhyme is the principal formal characteristic in all types of E. p. But this rhyme consists of sounds formed by the initial consonant and medial vowel of a syllable (not vowel plus final consonant, as in Eng.). If the last word of a line ends in what is ordinarily a consonant, in poetry a vowel (something between short *e* and *i*) must be sounded after it. The vowel sound alone does not constitute rhyme, however; the preceding consonant is significant, and generally one full rhyme persists for several lines before another, which differs in both consonant and vowel, begins.

Ambiguity or *double entendre* plays a more important part in traditional E. p. than does beauty of sound and rhythm. Characteristic Ge'ez verse, beginning with the classical *qene*, illustrates this quality: rhymed poems up to a dozen lines long contain intricate allusions and nuances. Even today the principles of *qene* composition require several years of study at monastic schools and a profound knowledge of the Bible, sacred legend, or dogma in order to be understood. Other Ge'ez poetry ranges from epigrammatic couplets through 9-line praise poems to long hymns—one favorite form is the *malk'e* (likeness), usually addressed to a saint and consisting of some fifty 5-line stanzas, each of which begins *salam*, and is a salutation to a different physical or moral attribute of the subject.

The earliest Ge'ez religious verse is attributed to Yared (6th c.), but surviving poems mostly date from the 15th c. or after. Patriotic sentiment and Ethiopic hymnology are often combined, as in the Ge'ez poem composed before the Battle of Adowa (1896), in which E. forces led by Emperor Menelik defeated invading Italians:

> Gomorrah and Sodom, lands of retribu-
>   tion, shall
> find pardon in the terrible day of
>   battle.
> But you, base city of Rome,
> That will come upon you which did not
>   come upon Sodom,
> For Menelik, savior of the world,
> Has sent you swathed in blood to visit
>   Dathan and
> Abiram in the grave. . . .

Although the first poet to write in Amharic was probably Gabre Egzi'abeher (b. 1860), popular verse has been composed orally in Amharic and other regional langs. since at least the 14th c. Such verse has often been occasional, but much praise poetry has been composed by professional minstrels to honor the Emperor or to be recited at notable weddings, funerals, and other events. There are also some love songs and a variety of patriotic verse which in the latter part of the 20th c. has often taken on strong national and propagandistic tones. Like Ge'ez poetry, popular Amharic verse has often aimed at *double entendre*; puns and wordplay are more appreciated than beauty of diction. For example:

> Yimallisau inji iraññau bāwwaqa—
> Yammichilau yallam—yās lām ka-zal-
>   laqa.

> He will bring it back, indeed, will the
>   herdsman,
> in (the way) he knows—
> There is none (other) who can—that
>   cow that
> has strayed.

A rustic situation is described in simple language. But it is possible to take *yas lam* not as "that cow" but as *yā-(i)islām*, "those Moslems." The couplet is now transformed: the "herdsman" stands for God; and *zallaqa* can be taken in the sense of "infiltrate." We now have a pointed comment on the infiltra-

tion into Christian Ethiopia of Moslems, whom only God knows how to send away again.

During the 20th c., Amharic has become firmly entrenched as Ethiopia's national lang. and has taken the place of Ge'ez as a respectable literary lang. Much popular Amharic verse now exists, together with more sophisticated poetic expression. The traditional rhyme system is still generally followed, but with a tendency toward shorter series of rhymes. Poems are often lengthy and didactic, with patriotism and morality as common themes. In the late 1950s, Menghistu Lemma took a step towards writing Amharic poetry in Western forms, and Solomon Deressa's 1972 poem "Legennat" (Childhood) signals the appearance of the first significant modern poetry in Amharic.

Since the 1960s, and following a short period of translations from Amharic to Eng., a body of poetry written in Eng. has appeared. Some has followed the trad. of praise poetry, first for the Emperor Haile Sellassie and then for the subsequent regime. Other themes have included social change and uncertainty about Ethiopia's place in the contemporary world. The Eng. poems of Tsegaye Gabre-Medhin are representative in that they reveal love for an ancient and proud past, a "Time-old / Highland of highlands / Ancient / Where all history ends," and yet also a dark recognition that whether it likes it or not, after centuries of isolation Ethiopia has awakened to find itself in a world where

> man swims
> In the asylum of a beatnik-bomb-age
> or hangs on
> In a sino-american wrestle world.

ANTHOLOGIES: *Matshafa qenē, Inē-nnā wedājochē*, both ed. H. Walde-Sellassie (1926, 1935)—the first contains 1100 Ge'ez poems, the second Amharic and Ge'ez poems; *Amāriññā qenē*, ed. Mahtama-Sellassie Walde-Masqal (1955)—over 1150 short Amharic poems; *Malk'a qubā'ē*, ed. T. Gabre-Sellassie (1955)—coll. of Ge'ez hymns called *malk'e*; *Af. Poems and Love Songs*, ed. W. Leslau and C. Leslau (1970)—incl. E. poetry, songs, and lullabies, in Eng. tr.; *Highland Mosaic: A Crit. Anthol. of E. Lit. in Eng.*, ed. P. Huntsberger (1973)—includes previously pub. works, some difficult to obtain.

HISTORY AND CRITICISM: M. Chaîne, "La Poésie chez les Ethiopiens," *Revue de l'orient chrétien*, 3d ser., 2 (1920– 21); J. M. Harden, *An Intro. to Ethiopic Christian Lit.* (1926); W. Leslau, "Chansons Harari," *Rassegna di studi etiopici* (1947); E. Cerulli, *Storia della letteratura etiopica* (1956); M. Lemma, "Intro. to Mod. E. Lit.," Af.-Scandinavian Writers' Conference, Stockholm (1967); A. S. Gérard, *Four Af. Lits.: Xhosa, Sotho, Zulu, Amharic* (1971); T. Kane, *E. Lit. in Amharic* (1975); D. Beer, "The Sources and Content of E. Creative Writing in Eng.," *Research in Af. Lits.* 8 (1977); *Lits. in Af.*

ETHNOPOETICS

Langs., ed. B. W. Andrzejewski (1985).

S.W.; D.F.B.

ETHNOPOETICS. (1) A comparative approach to poetry and related arts, with a characteristic but not exclusive emphasis on stateless, low-technology cultures and on oral and nonliterate forms of verbal expression. (2) The poetry and ideas about poetry in the cultures so observed or studied. (3) A movement or tendency in contemp. poetry, lit., and social science (anthropology in particular) devoted to such interests.

The history of such an e. covers at least the last 200 years, during which time it has functioned as a questioning of the culturally bounded poetics and poetry of "high European culture." While the designation "e." is a much later coinage, the interrogation has been carried forward in sometimes separated, sometimes interlocking discourses among philosophers, scholars, poets, and artists. It is clearly linked with impulses toward primitivism (q.v.) in both romanticism and modernism (qq.v.) and with avant-garde tendencies to explore new and alternative forms of poetry and to subvert normative views of traditional values and the claims of "civilization" to hegemony over other forms of culture. Yet for all its avant-gardism, the principal ethnopoetic concern has been with classical, even hieratic forms, with fully realized, often long preserved trads.

The emergence in the later 20th c. of e. as both a poetry movement and a field of scholarly study was the culmination of projects that arose within modernism itself. In that sense, e. clearly paralleled the ethnoaesthetic concerns in the visual and performative arts with their well-documented influence on the form and content of contemp. art both in the West and in third-world cultures under European domination. In turn, the growing restivenesss of the Western avant-garde allowed a contemp. viewing of culturally distant forms that revealed both those that resembled familiar Western forms and others drawn from previously unrecognized areas of visual and verbal art. The interests of poets—both formal and ideological—were accompanied or bolstered by scholarly investigations of the contexts and linguistic properties of the traditional works, incl. the nature of oral poetics (see ORAL POETRY) and the particularities of translation from oral sources. Like much modern and postmodern poetry and art, these investigations involved a necessarily intermedial point of view, calling conventional genre boundaries into question.

Prefigured by such work as Johann Gottfried Herder's *Volkslieder* (1778), the ethnopoetic focus—influenced by philology and archaeology, later by anthropology—moved from the archaic/pagan European past and its folkloric present, to literate non-European civilizations, to the later 20th-c. concern with oral and tribal cultures. At the center of modernist movements such as cubism, expressionism, dada, and surrealism (qq.v.), poets like Tristan Tzara, Blaise Cendrars, Benjamin Peret, and Antonin Artaud gathered from scholarly sources or themselves explored the oral poetries of Africa, the Pacific, and the Americas, while others like Ezra Pound appropriated and recast the literate poetries of non-Western civilizations such as China.

The term "e." itself came into the discourse late, a product of the ferment in postwar Am. lit. that expressed itself in the "new Am. poetry" (e.g. Black Mountain, Beats, Deep Image; see AMERICAN POETRY; BEAT POETS) and in a proliferation of movements concerned with ethnicity and gender. First introduced by Jerome Rothenberg in the wake of his 1968 anthology, *Technicians of the Sacred*, its initial public outlet was the magazine *Alcheringa* (1971–80), edited by Rothenberg and the anthropologist Dennis Tedlock. The first international symposium on e. was held in 1975; a second symposium held in 1985 attempted to extend the range of poetries and cultures even further. From its inception, the ethnopoetic discourse implicitly involved a questioning of the traditional literary canon (q.v.).

While varying in emphasis between poetry and scholarship, the themes of e. have included the questioning of a primitive-civilized dichotomy (particularly in its post-Platonic, Western manifestations), the idea of a visionary poetry and of the shaman as the paradigmatic proto-poet, the idea of a "great subculture" (Snyder) and of the persistence of an oral poetics in all the "higher" civilizations, the concept of the wilderness and of the role of the poet as a defender of biological and psychic diversity, the issue of cultural imperialism and pluralism, the question of communal and individual expression in traditional societies, and the reemergence of suppressed and rejected forms and images (e.g. the goddess, the trickster, the human universe). By raising such issues under a single term, e. has left its mark on a great range of contemp. poetry and, through its emphasis on performance and ritual, on a number of related performative arts. E. has also found a place in literary and cultural scholarship, though direct collaboration between scholars and practitioners has rarely been attempted since the mid 1970s. See also AMERICAN INDIAN POETRY.

TEXTS AND ANTHOLOGIES: B. Cendrars, *The African Saga: Anthologie nègre* (1927); R. M. Berndt, *Djanggawul: An Aboriginal Religious Cult of North-Eastern Arnhem Land* (1953); R. Callois and J.-C. Lambert, *Trésor de la poésie universelle* (1958); U. Beier, *African Poetry* (1966); W. Trask, *The Unwritten Song* (1967); J. Rothenberg, *Technicians of the Sacred* (1968), *Shaking the Pumpkin* (1972); D. Tedlock, *Finding the Center* (1972)—Zuni Indian; H. Norman, *The Wishing Bone Cycle* (1976)—Cree Indian; R. Finnegan, *A World Treasury of Oral Poetry* (1978); J. Gleason, *Leaf and Bone: African Praise Poems* (1980); A. Estrada, *María Sabina: Her Life*

EUPHONY

and Chants (1981)—Mazatec.

HISTORY AND CRITICISM: E. Pound, *Guide to Kulchur* (1918); R. Graves, *The White Goddess* (1958); M. Eliade, *Shamanism* (1964); C. Olson, *Human Universe* (1967); G. Snyder, *Earth House Hold* (1969); *Alcheringa: E.* (1970–80)—journal; M. León-Portilla, *Pre-Columbian Lits. of Mexico* (1969); Lord; R. Finnegan, *Oral Lit. in Africa* (1970), *Oral Poetry* (1977); S. Diamond, *In Search of the Primitive* (1974); K. Awoonor, *Breast of the Earth* (1975)—Africa; *Teachings from the Am. Earth*, ed. D. and B. Tedlock (1975); D. Hymes, *"In Vain I Tried to Tell You": Essays in Native Am. E.* (1981); D. Tedlock, *The Spoken Word and the Work of Interp.* (1983); *Smoothing the Ground: Essays on Native Am. Oral Lit.*, ed. B. Swann (1983); R. Schechner, *Between Theater and Anthropology* (1985); *Symposium of the Whole: A Range of Discourse Toward an E.*, ed. J. and D. Rothenberg (1985). J.R.

ETHOS (Gr. "custom," "character"). In Cl. rhet., one means of persuasion: an audience's assessment of a speaker's moral character (e.g. honesty, benevolence, intelligence) primarily as reflected in the discourse although at least secondarily dependent upon the speaker's prior reputation. In the *Rhetoric* (Book 1.1356a), Aristotle distinguishes three ways of achieving persuasion: ethical (*e*), emotional (*pathos* [q.v.]), and logical (*logos*), and although Aristotle comes close to affirming e. as the most potent means of persuasion, he gives it the least theoretical devel.; that devel. must for the most part be traced outside rhet., in the works of moral philosophers on virtue. From the standpoint of education, however, e. became historically the most widely addressed principle of rhet., as theorists from the Sophists through the Ren. humanists made the study of ethics a central means of preparing students for civic responsibilities. Along with *pathos*, e. serves to distinguish rhetoric's inclusive concerns from dialectic's more exclusive concentration on formal validity in *logos*. Although e. centers in the speaker, and *pathos* in the audience, the force of e. consists in arousing emotions; and the nature of *pathos*, or what emotions *can* be aroused, depends upon the character of their host. This conceptually close relation between e. and pathos is evident not only in Cl. rhetorical treatises but also in the long trad. of writing "characters." This literary genre, comprised of short disquisitions on personality types and behaviors, originated with Aristotle's pupil Theophrastus and achieved high popularity in the Ren. The devel. of "humoral psychology" and such works as Ben Jonson's *Every Man in His Humor* further reveal the traditionally close union of e. and pathos. From the standpoint of rhet., e. in poetry bears obvious relations to persona (q.v.) and authorial identity: e. is, in sum, the strategic rationale of both, a determinant of the audience's response to the speaker or speakers *in* a text as well as to the artist as speaker *of* a text, investing the latter speaking role with something of the e.-driven quality of *auctoritas*, famously described by Virgil as belonging to that orator who, "influential in piety and deeds," can rule the ignoble mob with words (*Aeneid* 1.148–53). Among modern critics, e. has figured in the discussion of such subjects as the distinction between dramatized and undramatized speakers, or between dramatic monologues and lyric poetry (see MONOLOGUE; LYRIC), as well as in discussions of the morality of impersonal narration and the character of implied authors. See also RHETORIC AND POETRY.—Sr. M. Joseph, *Shakespeare's Use of the Arts of Lang.* (1947), ch. 5, 9; G. Wright, *The Poet in the Poem* (1962); E. Schütrümpf, *Die Bedeutung des Wortes E. in der Poetik des Aristoteles* (1970); Lausberg; Group Mu, ch. 6; S. Greenblatt, *Ren. Self-Fashioning from More to Shakespeare* (1980); W. Booth, *The Rhet. of Fiction*, 2d ed. (1983), *The Company We Keep* (1988); C. Gill, "The E./Pathos Distinction in Rhetorical and Lit. Crit.," *ClassQ* 34 (1984); J. M. May, *Trials of Character: The Eloquence of Ciceronian E.* (1988); Corbett, esp. 80–86. T.O.S.

ETYMOLOGY. See LEXIS.

EULOGY. See ELEGY.

EUPHONY. The quality of having pleasant, easily pronounced, or smooth-flowing sounds, free from harshness; the pleasing effect of such sounds; the opposite of cacophony (q.v.). E. is an elusive subject: critics often sense it without being able to explain it, or admit it to be recognizable by the sensitive "ear," considering it, rather, an unanalyzable quality of poetry. But those researchers who have worked on the problem agree that e. does lend itself to stylistic analysis. Recent researchers make no apology for using quantitative parameters in studying a delicate subject like e. Indeed, it is not dehumanizing e. to evict it finally from the already overpopulated realm of the *certain je ne sais quoi*. Wherever there is e., there are underlying phonological structures that can be objectively analyzed.

In the first place, the *presence* of e. in a literary text can be ascertained objectively by critical consensus. In Fr. poetry, for example, such a consensus exists with regard to the work of Racine, Lamartine, and Verlaine: e. is commonly mentioned in histories of Fr. poetry as one of the most salient features of their style. A similar consensus exists among Hispanists with regard to the e. of the *Cantar de Mio Cid* and much of the poetry of Ruben Darío, José Marti, García Lorca, Juan Ramón Jiménez, and the Afro-Antillian poet Nicolás Guillén. The Ger. symbolist Georg Trakl is considered a euphonious poet "by all acclaim," as one scholar has written.

In the second place, it is obvious that some sounds are more pleasing to the ear than others. At least as early as the Gr. rhetorician Dionysius of Halicarnassus (1st c. B.C.), vowels were considered more euphonious than consonants (to form a consonant requires obstruction of the airstream), with longer vowels also being preferred to shorter. It is fact, not opinion, that vowels have a much higher sonority (i.e. resonance: the intensification of vocal sounds) than consonants, ranging between 9 and 47 microwatts when measured electronically, whereas consonants range only between 0.08 and 2.11. And all vowels, unlike many consonants, are accompanied by voicing (vibration of the vocal chords) and thus gain additional resonance. But consonants, esp. when arranged in discernible patterns, have more than a merely percussive role to play in the "harmony" of the poetic line. Of the consonant sounds, the most euphonious are the liquids, nasals, and semi-vowels, *l, m, n, r, v, w*. Poe, considering long [o] the most sonorous vowel and [r] the most reproducible consonant, chose "Nevermore" as the refrain word for "The Raven." Opinions differ as to the order in which the other consonants follow, but in general those most easily produced are felt to be the most pleasing to the ear.

E. results not only from choice of sounds, however, but also from their arrangement. Sounds may flow easily into each other or may be placed in difficult combinations, demanding more muscular effort. Meter will also play a role, sometimes clogging a line with heavy accents, sometimes spacing them out more agreeably. With regard to euphonic arrangements of sound, there seem to be three principles or "laws": identity, proximity, and progression.

IDENTITY involves the repetition of the same sounds, as in rhyme, refrain, assonance, alliteration, polysyndeton, chiasmus, and anaphora (qq.v.). Repetitions that create sound-patterns are enjoyed because design (order, pattern, structure) has in itself a pleasing effect apart from its constituent elements (Stanford). Whether repetition satisfies a deep-rooted intellectual thirst for unity, or the sheer aesthetic pleasure of recognition itself, or whether it is an outgrowth of the psychological tendency of intense emotions to express themselves in throbbing litanies, we can only surmise. One thing is certain: it works. Repetition is so obvious a device that the perceptive reader can be simultaneously aware of both the pleasurable effect and the probable cause. As one moves further away from repetition, toward proximity and progression, the *sense* of recognition persists; that is, the *pleasure* of e. remains within the threshold of perception. But the reader will not be able to put her finger on what patterns are working except through rather rigorous and systematic re-reading—that is, analysis (q.v.).

PROXIMITY. There is in e. not only the pleasure of recognition but also an articulatory pleasure experienced when one utters or merely *perceives* sounds produced in the same vicinity; Kenneth Burke calls these "cognate sounds." A feeling of ease is experienced in verses requiring relatively few muscular gymnastics, so that "one seems to modulate from one sound to another" (Frohock). Successive vowels can be analyzed from the point of view of aperture (from close to open) and point of articulation (front to back). Consonants too can be analyzed according to point of articulation (from bilabial and labiodental to alveolar and velar), harshness (unvoiced plosives), softness (liquids), and resonance (voiced vs. unvoiced).

PROGRESSION involves the "melodic" flow of vowels and consonants as they succeed each other, not just in an isolated word or expression but throughout an entire poetic line, passage, or poem. The stylistician can look not only for patterns of repetition but also for a high percentage of cognate or proximal vowels and consonants as the line and the passage progress. In euphonious texts the harsher consonants are not closely clustered but rather buffered by softer sounds.

If one were to analyze a line of Fr. poetry often cited for its e., Racine's "Vous mourûtes aux bords où vous fûtes laissée" (*Phèdre*), one would find the following. Vowel aperture: the only jump, from the open [ɔ] to the close [u], comes at the caesura. This is not a maximal leap, and the caesura itself provides buffering. Further buffering is provided by the fact that [ɔ] and [u] are both back vowels. Vowel articulation: there are only two maximal leaps, from front to back, both well spaced, and there is not a single vowel that is not followed or preceded by an identical or proximal vowel. Consonant progression: there are only two harsh consonants in the line, and they are enveloped in softer sounds. Every vowel is preceded or followed by only one consonant, and most of the consonants (75%) are voiced. The phonemic parallelism at the beginning of the hemistichs creates both assonance and internal rhyme. In short, what is happening in Racine's line is an impressively gradual modulation of vowels and a high percentage of proximal, voiced, and "soft" consonants.

The importance of e. to total poetic effect is a matter of dispute, some finding great pleasure in "linkèd sweetness long drawn out," others insisting that "mere sound in itself can have no or little aesthetic effect" (Wellek and Warren). Admiration of sustained e. in poetry seems to be a matter of taste in readers. A value judgment with regard to e. or cacophony will inevitably turn on an idiosyncratic notion of the correct "dosage." Thus research has centered not on the aesthetic *value* of e., nor its *tone-color* (q.v.)—that is, its emotional and incantatory effect on the reader—nor on special stylistic *devices* that might be created (e.g. an ironic contrast between mellifluous sounds and the "harsh" sense of the general context), but on its very existence, and on the devising of methods for detecting or corroborating that existence (i.e. on showing *structures* to correlate to *perceived effects*).

Since too much euphoniousness might give the impression of weakness or effeminateness, some poets (e.g. Browning) have reacted against it. In general, however, e. is a desired characteristic,

and most poetry is more euphonious than prose, even art-prose, or ordinary speech. Nearly all would agree, however, that e. is to be desired chiefly as a means rather than an end, and that the first measure of its success is appropriateness. See also MELOPOEIA, PHANOPOEIA, LOGOPOEIA; SOUND; SOUND EFFECTS IN POETRY.—A. Spire, *Plaisir poétique et plaisir musculaire* (1949); Wellek and Warren, ch. 13; K. Burke, "On Musicality in Verse," *The Philosophy of Lit. Form*, 2d ed. (1957); L. P. Wilkinson, *Golden Lat. Artistry* (1963); W. M. Frohock, "E. in Fr. Lit.," *An Approach through Close Reading* (1964); M. Grammont, *Le Vers français*, 6th ed. (1967); W. B. Stanford, *The Sound of Gr.* (1967); S. P. Scher, *Verbal Music in Ger. Lit.* (1969); M. Gauthier, *Système euphonique et rythmique du vers français* (1974); L. Bishop, "Phonological Correlates of E.," *FR* 49 (1975), "E.," *Lang&S* 18 (1986); Brogan; Morier; R. P. Newton, *Vowel Undersong* (1981); P. Delbouille, *Poésies et sonorités, II* (1984).
L..BI.

EVALUATION.

 I. AXIOLOGY
 II. LITERARY CRITICISM

Most literary critics, ancient and modern, assume that one of their functions (some would say their most important function) is to evaluate literary works—to determine their worth or degree of goodness. These critics' discussions of lit. are full of explicitly appraisive terms (good and bad, great and worthless, classic and dated, beauties and faults, successes and failures) and of other terms which carry appraisive overtones (exciting, suspenseful, vivid, effective, harmonious, moving, profound). The object evaluated may be an individual poem, some part of a poem (a metaphor, a paradox, a figure of speech, the poem's diction or meter, the theme), an author's complete works, the works of all of the authors of a particular period (as in Arnold's condemnation of neoclassical poetry), a genre, or even all poetry (Shelley's *Defence of Poetry*). In any of these categories the e. may involve a comparison of two or more objects or classes of objects to determine which should be ranked as "better" or "best." (Is *In Memoriam* a better elegy than *Lycidas*? Which is Browning's best poem? Is metaphysical poetry better than romantic? Is tragedy or the epic the higher genre? Is Sidney right in ranking poetry above history and philosophy?)

 I. AXIOLOGY. In making es., critics frequently find themselves in disagreement with other critics. In an effort to explain and resolve such disagreements and to improve their own practice, many critics have felt compelled to analyze their evaluative procedures and compare them with those of other critics. For help in making such analyses some critics have turned to disciplines like metacriticism (q.v.) and to modern value theory. Over the past century, philosophers have been developing a general theory of value called *axiology* that would be applicable to normative problems in all areas of human activity. Its aim is not to formulate yet another dogmatic value system—to compete with, say, Christianity or Utilitarianism—but to clarify the major concepts used in all discussion of value, to classify values, and to formulate the "logic" by which value judgments can be justified. The early phases of this development and the striking differences among theorists are summarized by Frankena (1967) and discussed in greater detail by Taylor (1961). Later developments in value theory which stress problems of e. in aesthetics and lit. crit. may be found in Najder (1975), Smith (1988), and Booth (1988).

Most recent value theory is grounded on modern empirical studies of human behavior, which locate value in a "value situation." Here, living is seen as each person's attempt to satisfy instinctive or culturally acquired needs and wants in the natural and social environment. This interaction between each person and the environment creates a situation in which values come into being. A person will value an object or experience which satisfies one or more "interests," gives enjoyment, or solves a problem. When something in the environment frustrates those interests, causes pain, or is inadequate for some desired purpose, the person will devalue the object.

Such immediate positive or negative responses to experience have been called "es." However, e. in another sense requires considerable reflection and special knowledge. The object or experience being evaluated is regarded as a cause that will produce a variety of effects which will satisfy or fail to satisfy multiple interests. Ideally, such an investigation should predict accurately all of these effects, including the value responses of all the persons who may be affected. But such an ideal can seldom be reached. Usually many unknowns are involved. Also, the projected effects may be multiple, vary in degree of desirability, conflict with each other, involve the interests of a great many people, and become causes that produce effects stretching into the indefinite future. In such cases, the evaluative judgment—a summary statement of the kind and amount of value that the object or experience will generate—may be impossible to formulate or must be formulated only very tentatively.

The recognition of these complexities and uncertainties has led some theorists to recommend a more limited evaluative aim: to estimate the capacity or potential of a functional object to generate the kinds and degrees of valuable effects which it was designed to produce in a particular class of individuals. Making a reliable estimate requires considerable expertise, particularly a knowledge of the characteristics that make for effectiveness in the kind of object that is being evaluated. Such characteristics are the standards whose application to a particular object determines the goodness of that object. The procedure

EVALUATION

is empirical, and the resulting evaluative judgment will have truth value.

II. LITERARY CRITICISM. What are the consequences for lit. crit. of the axiological analysis of value and e.? Though much remains unresolved in axiology, the literary critic can certainly profit from seeing some perennial problems of poetics treated in a broader philosophical perspective. But an even greater benefit may be to encourage certain modern tendencies toward pluralism (q.v.) in crit. and to soften the dogmatic tones of critical conversation.

Modern naturalistic value theory recommends that a poem be regarded as a functional object designed by an author to generate effects that may be of value to someone. What are the functions and effects that distinguish poems from other crafted objects? There is no agreement among poets or critics on the answer to this question. This lack of agreement is reflected in the devel. of many different systems of poetics (q.v.), the multiplicity of genres, and the striking differences among things that have been called "poems": Wordsworth's *The Prelude* is autobiography; Pope's *Essay on Man* is philosophy; Tennyson's *In Memoriam* is a personal expression of grief; Keats's "Eve of St. Agnes" is a fictional narrative; Shelley's "England in 1819" is political rhet.; Byron's "Eng. Bards and Scotch Reviewers" is lit. crit.; Browning's "My Last Duchess" is a monologue spoken by a fictional character; Dryden's "Mac Flecknoe" is a satire on Thomas Shadwell; Yeats's "Second Coming" is prophecy; Herbert's "Easter Wings" is a prayer. All of these works have been honored with the name "poetry." Yet on the basis of function, effect, and potential value, they have affinities with a variety of other types of discourse.

One way of ordering these differences would be to use a distinction common in value theory, that between intrinsic (or terminal or immediate) value and extrinsic (or instrumental) value. A poem has intrinsic value when the reading experience is valued for its own sake—is a good in itself; a poem has extrinsic value when the experience it produces is an effective means to some further valuable end.

Commitment to the e. of poetry in terms of its intrinsic value is most apparent in those critics who speak of "aesthetic experience," the "aesthetic attitude," and "aesthetic values"; whose slogan has been "art for art's sake"; or who urge us to treat "poetry as poetry and not another thing." It is claimed that a special class of "aesthetic" experiences can be distinguished from a person's other experiences in life and that these experiences are intrinsically valuable. The desire for the aesthetic seems to be instinctual and appears among people of all cultures and age groups.

There have been numerous attempts to describe the nature of the aesthetic experience and to specify the quality or qualities an object must have to generate this experience. Differences among theorists have been great. In the 18th c., the aesthetic experience was usually associated with aesthetic *qualities* such as beauty or sublimity. For other theorists, "disinterested contemplation" is the key element (see AESTHETIC DISTANCE; DISINTERESTEDNESS). Or the aesthetic object is said to appeal to the "play" instinct in human nature. Other formulations stress unique feelings of various kinds. The aesthetic experience is a sensation of "living through" an experience rather than being told about it; or its essence is empathy (q.v.), vicarious identification; or it is such a complete loss of the sense of self that it must be described in the lang. of mystical ascent and transcendence. Beardsley defines the aesthetic experience as "fixation of attention on some portion of the sensory or phenomenal field, a sense of liberation from distractions and practical concerns, a notable degree of distance or detachment from emotional oppression, the exhilaration of exercising perceptual and cognitive powers to an unusual degree, a sense of integration and wholeness."

Such differences of opinion on aesthetic experience have naturally led to divergences as to which qualities an object must have to generate an aesthetic effect. Actually, a complex object may have hundreds of elements and relationships which in their interactions arouse and guide the aesthetic experience. Thus critics have found it convenient to group these elements under a few general headings which are then regarded as the principal causes for the aesthetic effect. These then become the norms or standards for evaluating an object's potential to create aesthetic experience.

The aesthetic experience is regarded as valuable for its own sake, and the e. of an aesthetic object consists primarily in estimating the quality and "magnitude" of the experience that it is capable of evoking in a qualified perceiver. But aesthetic experience can also produce valuable extrinsic ends such as increased sensitivity and mental health, emotional balance, or relaxation.

Defenders of the "art-as-such" or "poetry-as-such" theory contrast strikingly with those critics who give precedence to the potential extrinsic values of poetry. Their principal objection to the terminalists has been that these critics are fiddling while Rome burns; by exalting the intrinsic values of poetry and denigrating the extrinsic ("poetry," says Auden, elegizing Yeats, "makes nothing happen"), they ignore the important interests it can satisfy in other realms of value. Critics have argued that poetry can be a powerful influence either for good or ill in a large number of other areas of human experience. There is Plato's warning that the seductive attractions of the intrinsic values of poetry, its verbal charms, make readers forget that it feeds and waters the passions, confuses fiction with fact, and teaches moral and theological falsehoods; even canonical works—incl. Homer—are filled with corrupting influences and should be banished from the Republic.

This stress on the moral and social effects of poetry has had a long history and has been widely used as a criterion for distinguishing good poetry from bad. Thus for Shelley the great poets are prophets, trumpeters, and the true legislators of the World. Arnold insisted that poetry, to be worthy of its high destinies as an ethical influence replacing traditional religion, must be a true crit. of life. For Freud, art is wish fulfillment: it provides human beings with a health-giving release of repressed desires. For Jung, art is a means for psychological renewal, enabling the reader to rediscover the eternal archetypes in the collective unconscious. For anyone intensely committed to social change—like modern Marxist, feminist, and Afro-Am. critics—poetry can be a means to the exposure of current wrongs and a more equitable way of life.

Because of the variety of extrinsic values that poetry can generate and because of humanity's lack of agreement on moral, political, philosophical, and religious questions, the formulation of a universal or even a widely accepted set of standards for evaluating poems extrinsically has been impossible. Today there is increasing agreement that lit. inevitably has ethical influence. Booth (1988), who has traced the resurgence of ethical crit. in the latter part of the 20th c., treats fully the consequences for the e. of lit. which must be conducted in an ideologically pluralistic world.

Some critics hold that intrinsic and extrinsic values are inextricably bound together in a literary work, or at least they incorporate both intrinsic and extrinsic values in their e. of poems. Horace spoke of pleasure and instruction as the double aim of good poetry. Sidney added "moving" the audience to an acceptance of a poem's ethical message as an additional value. Even Beardsley, when speaking of the "full" e. of lit., refuses to limit himself to aesthetic value and recognizes the relevance of the cognitive, moral, and social values of lit. for arriving at judgments of its goodness and greatness. Such recommendations recognize that lit. has the potential for creating a great variety of values. The sensible position would seem to be to find as many goods in a poem as it has to offer.

To summarize: a value judgment of a poem (e.g. "Stevens' 'Sunday Morning' is a very good poem") is elliptical. It must be placed in the context of a particular value situation if it is to be meaningfully discussed. Part of this context is the specification of the function that this poem is intended to serve or the function which the reader prefers to ask that it serve. The function will always be the generation of some kind of valuable effect, and the value judgment will be an estimate of the potential of the poem to achieve this effect. But one part of the value situation has not yet been stressed: the reader(s) for whose benefit the e. is being made.

Readers differ in hundreds of ways—age, sex, race, education, intelligence, experience, maturity, interests, ethical ideals, breadth of reading experience, intensity of unconscious drives, etc.

Any one of these factors can influence greatly the kind and amount of value that a particular reader will get from a poem and thus determine the types of poems that she deems good. Of special importance is the degree to which a reader is familiar with literary conventions, esp. generic, prosodic, and rhetorical ones (see CONVENTION). These conventions function to establish expectations, recommend strategies for interpretation (q.v.), and provide standards to be used in e. They also impose constraints, esp. on interpretation; hence not to understand the conventions used to construct the poem will lead to misinterpretation. Almost all poets press against normative linguistic forms—phonological, grammatical, semantic—as a means for conveying meaning; and critics frequently praise poets for originality, individuality, and departures from conformity. Conventions are culturally determined and subject to change, sometimes very rapid change. In reading a poem from the past, a reader has the choice of whether to use (1) the norms supported by the conventions of the author's age, (2) the norms of her own age, or (3) her own ideas of what the form, function, and rewards of poetry should be. Her choice will determine how she interprets the poem and evaluates it.

Modern reader-response studies have added other uncertainties about interpretation (see READER-RESPONSE CRITICISM). Most literary texts are to some extent indeterminate (see INDETERMINACY). The reader is invited (or forced) to read creatively, filling in gaps, exploring implications, and (esp. with lyric poetry) using imagination, inference, or guesswork to construct a fictive situation or context for the utterance that is the poem. Since there may be no way to determine the correctness of what the reader must supply, readings of the poem will differ from reader to reader and will result in variability of e.

The recognition of the multiple variables in the value situation has led some critics to draw the conclusion that it is useless to speak at all of trying to justify a value judgment. Northrop Frye, for example, has recommended excluding value judgments in building a systematic body of knowledge about lit.: "The sense of value is an individual, unpredictable, variable, incommunicable, indemonstrable, and mainly intuitive reaction to knowledge." When a critic is describing or interpreting literary works, she or he is talking about objective realities; but "when he evaluates, he is talking about himself, or, at most, about himself as a representative of his age." (Frye does mention important social functions that the evaluative critic—esp. as reviewer and teacher—can serve in showing the value possibilities of lit., which, he says, "is a limitless reservoir of potential values.")

Barbara Herrnstein Smith has explored the "contingencies of value" in greater detail than any other modern critic. Her conclusion is that all value judgments, though usually stated in unconditional form, must be interpreted as a "speaker's observation and/or estimate of how well that object, compared to others of the same (even though only implicitly defined) type, has performed and/or is likely to perform some particular (even though unstated) desired/able functions for some particular (even though only implicitly defined) subject or set of subjects under some particular (even though not specified) set or range of conditions." She reminds us that in any value situation there are not only contingencies, which make all value judgments relative, but also "constancies," themselves biologically or culturally determined, which make value judgments possible at all—albeit with the limited applicability she specifies. See now ANALYSIS; CRITICISM; ETHICS AND CRITICISM; INTERPRETATION; PLURALISM; THEORY.

Richards; J. Dewey, *Theory of Valuation* (1939); C. L. Stevenson, *Ethics and Lang.* (1944); *Value: A Cooperative Inquiry, The Lang. of Value*, both ed. R. Lepley (1949, 1957); R. B. Perry, *Realms of Value* (1954); Wellek and Warren, ch. 18; M. C. Beardsley, *Aesthetics* (1958), esp. chs. 10–11, *The Possibility of Crit.* (1970), "In Defense of Aesthetic Value," *Proc. and Addresses Am. Philos. Assoc.* 52 (1979), *The Aesthetic Point of View*, ed. M. J. Wreen and D. M. Callen (1982); P. W. Taylor, *Normative Discourse* (1961); M. Weitz, *Hamlet and the Philosophy of Lit. Crit.* (1964); M. L. Scriven, *Primary Philosophy* (1966), *The Logic of E.* (1981); G. Hough, *An Essay on Crit.* (1966); W. K. Frankena, "Value and Valuation," *Encyc. of Philosophy* (1967); R. S. Hartman, *The Structure of Value* (1967); F. E. Sparshott, *The Concept of Crit.* (1967); *Problems of Literary E.*, ed. J. Strelka (1969); N. Frye, "On Value-Judgments," *The Stubborn Structure* (1970); K. Aschenbrenner, *The Concepts of Value* (1971); J. M. Ellis, *The Theory of Lit. Crit.* (1974), ch. 4; Z. Najder, *Values and Es.* (1975); E. Olson, *On Value Judgments in the Arts* (1976); E. D. Hirsch, Jr., *The Aims of Interp.* (1976); J. Reichert, *Making Sense of Lit.* (1977); R. T. Segers, *The E. of Literary Texts* (1978); *Beschreiben, Interpretieren, Werten*, ed. B. Lenz and B. Schulte-Middelich (1982); R. Shusterman, *The Object of Lit. Crit.* (1984); F. R. Leavis, *Valuation in Crit*, ed. G. Singh (1986); W. C. Booth, *The Company We Keep* (1988); B. H. Smith, *Contingencies of Value* (1988); G. Dickie, *Evaluating Art* (1988); T. Pawlowski, *Aesthetic Values* (1989); J. Striedter, *Literary Structure, Evolution, and Value* (1989). F.GU.

EXEGESIS. See EXPLICATION.

EXEMPLUM. A short embedded narrative used to illustrate a moral point. The term is applied chiefly to the stories used in medieval sermons, first in Lat., then in the vernaculars, and derived from both Cl. rhet. and the parables of the NT; the illustrative anecdote is still, perhaps, the commonest feature of public speaking. The most famous source of such stories was the Lat. prose *Gesta romanorum* (late 13th c.), but collections for the use of preachers were also made in verse, e.g. *Handlyng Synne* (begun 1303) by Robert Mannyng of Brunne, a treatise on the Seven Deadly Sins with illustrative stories, adapted from the Fr. *Somme le roy*. A secular use is shown in John Gower's *Confessio amantis* (ca. 1385), where the *exempla* illustrate sins against Venus. Chaucer's *Pardoner's Tale* furnishes the best Eng. example; not only the main story but many lesser narratives too are used as *exempla* of the Pardoner's text. The ME *Alphabet of Tales* (tr. late 15th c.) lists exempla under rubrics such as Abstinence, Adulation, etc. The MHG form is the *Bîspel*. See DIDACTIC POETRY.—J.-T. Welter, *L'E. dans la litt. religieuse et didactique du moyen âge* (1927); Curtius; E. Neumann, "Bîspel," and J. Klapper, "Exempel," *Reallexikon*; G. R. Owst, *Lit. and Pulpit in Med. England*, 2d ed. (1961); H. de Boor, *Fabel und Bîspel* (1966); F. C. Tubach, *Index exemplorum: A Handlist of Med. Religious Tales* (1969); J. D. Lyons, *E.* (1990).   R.P.A.; T.V.F.B.

EXOTICISM. In a narrow sense (sometimes called "pure" e.), the depiction of the distantly foreign or strange for the sake of novelty or picturesque effect, without concern for accuracy or comprehension. More broadly, however, e. describes any extended use of non-Western, esp. "Oriental," settings, motifs, or cultural references whether for merely decorative or more serious purposes.

"Exotic" implies "outside," hence, in Occidental poetry, what is "outside" the Western trad. In Homer, parts of Asia are presented as alien and bizarre; Aeschylus in *The Persians* and Euripides in *The Bacchae* portray Asia as (respectively) despotic and sensual, irrational and effeminate, connotations that persisted throughout later Western lit. hist. With Roman ascendancy, "Orient" emerges as a term for Asia and North Africa, associated by Virgil, Propertius, Juvenal, and other Lat. poets with luxury, barbarous customs, magic, and colorful dress.

In medieval and early modern European poetry the Orient is identified with Islam, appearing as Christendom's political and religious antagonist in the *Chanson de Roland*, the *Poema de Mio Cid*, in Ariosto, in Tasso, and in Camões' Portuguese epic, *Os Lusiadas*. This Orient is at once exotic and familiar, with Islam a parodic distortion of Christianity, and Muslims sometimes chivalrous and sometimes treacherous, colorful, fierce, and inclined to sorcery and sensuality. In Ren. and neoclassical poetic drama, from Marlowe and Shakespeare through Corneille, Davenant and Dryden to Addison and Johnson, Oriental settings—esp. such border areas as Islamic Spain and the Mediterranean—underscore, socially, divided religious and political loyalties and, psychologically, characters' internal conflicts between (Oriental) irrationality and eroticism and (Occidental) rationality and duty.

Several developments foster the prominence of literary Orientalism in the 18th and early 19th cs.:

EXPLICATION

the cult of *chinoiserie* in gardening and the decorative arts; Galland's tr. of the *Thousand and One Nights* (1704–08) and its many imitations; the new interp. of the Bible advanced by Lowth, Eichhorn, and Herder as essentially Oriental; and the rise of Oriental studies with such important trs. as Sir William ("Oriental") Jones's *A Persian Song of Hafiz* (1771) and *Shakuntala* (1789)—all associated with (if not implicated in) the establishment of European hegemony over the East, esp. the British Empire over India. Picturesque e. becomes prominent in such works as William Collins' *Persian Eclogues* (1742) and William Beckford's *Vathek* (1786), a prose Oriental fantasy which influenced Eng. and Fr. romantic poets. At the same time, a measure of cultural relativism, enabled by the new historicism of Vico and Herder, can be seen in Lowth's use of "Oriental" poetry to criticize neoclassical standards of taste (*De sacra poesi hebraeorum*, 1753) and in the fabrication of an Oriental perspective for the social satire of Montesquieu, Goldsmith, and Voltaire, strategies closely related to primitivism (q.v.).

Orientalism in romantic poetry is marked simultaneously by e. and by the more profound cultural interest in Asia exemplified by Friedrich Schlegel's *Über die Sprache und Weisheit der Indier* (1808). In works like Goethe's *West-östlicher Divan* (1819) and Hugo's *Les Orientales* (1829), the Orient provides both a picturesque locale (as in Delacroix and Ingres) and a cultural alternative. Although the Eng. romantics were deeply interested in Asian mythologies, picturesque e. lay behind the popularity of such poems as Landor's *Gebir* (1798), Southey's *Thalaba* (1800), Byron's *Giaour* (1813), and Moore's *Lallah Rookh* (1816). Chateaubriand, Lamartine, and Nerval wrote poetry which reflected their literary pilgrimages to the Near East. Edward Fitzgerald's translation of *The Rubáiyát of Omar Khayyám* (1859), one of the most popular poems of the Victorian period, reflected a renewed British interest in Persian poetry (q.v.), shared by Fitzgerald's friend Tennyson and by Matthew Arnold, whose *Sohrab and Rustum* (1853) is based on the *Shāh-nāma*, the Persian national epic.

Thereafter, as Europe comes to be seen as increasingly dull, colorless, and mechanized, a purer e., emphasizing the new, the strange, and the sensuous, and associated more with China and Japan than with India and the Near East, develops in the poetry of Théophile Gautier and Judith Gautier, whose *Livre de jade* (1867) esp. inspired such poets of the exotic as Heredia, Cros, and Renaud, with a later Ger. analogue in Hans Bethge. Similarly, in America the cultural interest in India evidenced in Emerson and Whitman eventually yields to the e. of the imagist poets John Gould Fletcher and Amy Lowell (see IMAGISM), although Ezra Pound's engagement with Chinese thought and poetics through Ernest Fenollosa runs much deeper. Recent poet-travellers like James Merrill

manifest a relation to the exotic at once nostalgic and ironic, as technological advances in transportation and communications make the distant near and its strangeness familiar. See also CULTURAL CRITICISM; PRIMITIVISM.—W. L. Schwartz, *The Imaginative Interp. of the Far East in Mod. Fr. Lit., 1800–1925* (1927); P. Jourda, *L'Exotisme dans la litt. fr. depuis Chateaubriand* (1938); R. Schwab, *La Ren. orientale* (1950); E. S. Shaffer, *"Kubla Khan" and The Fall of Jerusalem* (1975); C. Le Yaouanc, *L'Orient dans la poésie anglaise de l'époque romantique 1798–1824* (1975); E. Said, *Orientalism* (1978); B. Yu, *The Great Circle* (1983).   A.R.

EXPLICATION is a member of a family of terms which includes "explanation," "analysis" (q.v.), "exegesis," "interpretation" (q.v.), "elucidation," "exposition," and "paraphrase." Unfortunately, critics do not agree on the nature of the critical jobs named by these terms or on the differences and relations among them. However, all of these jobs have *clarification* as one of their major functions: their aim is to help a puzzled reader understand a literary work, on the presumption that such understanding should deepen the reader's response to the work and enable her to make a more intelligent evaluation. Without understanding, evaluation is nugatory.

Critics differ as to how much of this clarifying process they wish to call "e." and how much by other terms. Thus Beardsley distinguishes several "interpretational tasks" and recommends that "e." be used as the name for the critic's effort to disclose implicit meanings at the lexical level of a poem, e.g. the connotations of a word, the implications of complex or ambiguous syntax, or possible meanings of a metaphor or other trope. Other critics prefer a broader definition, sometimes making "e." equivalent to "analysis": Arms suggests, for example, that e. is "the examination of a work of lit. for a knowledge of each part and for the relation of these parts to each other and to the whole." Spitzer says that a complete e. will show how the details of a poem are an implicit expression not only of the "spirit of the text" but also of "the spirit of the genre," "the psyche of the author," or even of a "national profession of faith."

Usually a critic feels that she must adduce reasoning or evidence if not both to support her e.; otherwise, her commentary may be called merely a report of her subjective associations and personal impressions. Proof is particularly desirable when the critic claims to be reporting a discovery of an element implicit in a poem (e.g. the symbolic meaning of an image, the unstated intentions of a speaker, the attitude of the implied author, the principle that unifies the whole poem, the incoherence of the poem after e. has dismantled it). Is a valid "logic of e." possible (and desirable)? What is the nature of this logic? What kind of evidence should the critic use—extrinsic, intrinsic, or both? How are different (esp. incompat-

EXPLICATION DE TEXTE

ible) es. of the same poem to be handled? In what ways must explicatory methods and proofs differ depending on the nature of the explicatory problem? There is no critical consensus on the answers to any of these questions. The recommendations that a particular critic makes are determined by her theory of poetry and her philosophical orientation. Modern crit. is full of disputes between intentionalists (see INTENTION) and contextualists (see CONTEXTUALISM); rhetoricians and expressivists (see EXPRESSION); the New Critics (see NEW CRITICISM) and the Chicago School (q.v.); traditionalists with a belief in unity and coherence and postmodernists with a rage for chaos or the free play of signifiers (see DECONSTRUCTION); dogmatists and perspectivists; philosophical realists and phenomenologists.

Historically, explicatory commentaries on poems are as old as poetry itself. In Plato's *Protagoras* there is a full-blown e. of a difficult poem by Simonides which reflects many modern concerns about method, validity, and the dangers of overingenuity. Few poems are fully explicit or transparent. In every age some poets for one reason or another have preferred to "hide" or "veil" their meaning (e.g. through symbol, allegory, or irony [qq.v.]) or have written poems with enigmatic, complex, ambiguous, or indeterminate meanings (see PLATONISM; HERMETICISM; OBSCURITY). Their puzzled readers will always need a guide. In the 20th c., e. has been promoted particularly by those who have sought to reorient literary studies from an emphasis on biographical crit., philology, and lit. hist. to exclusive concern with the poem itself. "Soumission au texte" (Rudler) and "understanding poetry" (Brooks and Warren) became the slogans of the proponents of *e. de texte* in France, which was practiced in the schools long before being exported to America, and of the methods of close reading recommended by I. A. Richards, the New Critics, and the Chicago School. The journals *The Explicator*, begun in 1942 (with annual checklists of es. after 1945), and *Explicación de textos literarios*, begun in 1972, are still published. See also HERMENEUTICS; INTERPRETATION; TWENTIETH-CENTURY POETICS, *French and German.*

G. Rudler, *L'E. française: Principes et applications* (1902; 6th ed., 1930); M. Roustan, *Précis d'e. française* (1911); W. K. Wimsatt, Jr., "E. as Crit.," *The Verbal Icon* (1954); G. Arms, "Poetry," *Contemp. Lit. Scholarship*, ed. L. Leary (1958); M. C. Beardsley, *Aesthetics* (1958), *The Possibility of Crit.* (1970); L. Spitzer, *Essays on Eng. and Am. Lit.* (1962), *Representative Essays* (1988); E. D. Hirsch, Jr., *Validity in Interp.* (1967); P. N. Nurse, *The Art of Crit.: Essays in Fr. Lit. Analysis* (1969); W. D. Howarth, and C. L. Walton. *Es.: The Technique of Fr. Literary Appreciation* (1971); J. M. Kuntz and N. C. Martinez, *Poetry E.: A Checklist of Interp. since 1925*, 3d ed. (1980); H. Levin, "The Implication of E.," *PoT* 5,1 (1984); J. Ruppert (v. 1) and J. R. Leo (v. 2), *Guide to Am. Poetry E.*, 2 v. (1989). F.GU.

EXPLICATION DE TEXTE. See EXPLICATION; TWENTIETH-CENTURY POETICS, *French and German.*

EXPRESSION. The term *e.* has had different meanings over the hist. of Western lit. For a long time it coincided with rhetorical theory. In Aristotle's *Rhetoric*, for example, e. is considered the equivalent of those means of persuasion which the orator is supposed to invent and exploit. Since persuasion can rely upon *ethos* (q.v.—the speaker's personal qualities), *pathos* (q.v.—the emotions of the audience), and logical proof founded on the arguments of reason, we may infer three corresponding kinds of e.: ethical, emotional, and logical. The Lat. term *expressio*, which appears only in the 4th c. A.D., has no Gr. exemplar, but two Gr. words can be considered more or less equivalent: *ethos*, namely the delineation of character (or *ethopoiía*, namely the power of characterization), and *diatyposis*, namely vivid representation. Both terms are in the treatise *On the Sublime* (9.15; 20.1), a work erroneously attributed to Longinus, which was highly influential in the 17th and 18th cs. Longinus, however, gives but the embryo of a fully developed theory of e.

In Europe, e. continued to have a rhetorical undertone until the Enlightenment, as appears from vol. 6 of the *Encyclopédie* (1756), where entries are dedicated to e. in (1) lit., (2) music, and (3) the plastic arts. (1) From a literary point of view, e. is considered the representation of a thought. Such representation can be achieved in three different ways: through tone of voice, as, for instance, in moaning; through gestures, as in beckoning somebody to approach or to depart; and through spoken or written words. Es. can be simple, vivid, strong, daring, rich, or sublime according to the nature of our thoughts, but the poet or orator who has beautiful ideas and no power of expressing them is doomed to fail. (2) From a musical point of view, e. is the essence of imitation (q.v.). It is the reproduction of human feelings, which is accomplished through songs in music, through words in poetry, and through colors in painting. (3) From the point of view of the plastic arts, e. is linked to imitation. However, e. refers to actions and passions, while imitation proper deals with forms and colors.

Since the theory of signs was also gradually taking shape on the Continent and in England during the 18th c., e. was increasingly viewed as the manner in which a thing is represented by the various signs which constitute a semiotic system. G. B. Vico's *Scienza nuova* (1725 et seq.) offers probably the best example of the doctrine of signs advocated by Locke in the *Essay Concerning Human Understanding* (4.21.4). According to Vico, the creations of imagination (q.v.), which represent the solid foundation of human civilization, are signs of a kind of universal lang. coinciding with the ideal eternal history. Vico's semiotics encompasses every manifestation of human life—gestures, ceremonies, social behavior, aggression, work—all belonging to a communication system which can be analyzed from a linguistic point of view.

Vico's philosophy was partially reflected in the *Enquiry into the Life and Writings of Homer* by T. Blackwell (1735), a landmark in the devel. of the expressive theory of poetry viewed as the projection of the mentality and feelings of the poet. It was further developed during the 18th c. by such British critics as Shaftesbury and Burke, and reached its climax at the beginning of the 19th c. when Wordsworth proclaimed poetry "the spontaneous overflow of powerful feelings" (Preface to *Lyrical Ballads*). E., like spontaneity and subjectivity (qq.v.), is a central tenet of romantic poetics (q.v.) and, insofar as modern theory extends rather than retracts romantic poetics, of modern poetics as well. It is also, and far more extensively, central to the devel. of the lyric (q.v.) genre, which supplanted epic and romance in the Ren.

The It. heritage of Vico can still be seen in the 20th c., albeit in different forms, in the expressionism of Benedetto Croce and the semiotics of Umberto Eco. Croce's aesthetic theory rests, for better or worse, on his theory of e., which has a distinctly romantic ring (see TWENTIETH-CENTURY POETICS, *Italian*). According to Croce, art is essentially lyrical inasmuch as it is the e. of the artist's emotion. Croce distinguishes the aesthetic e. of emotion from the practical, but such a distinction rests on shaky ground, namely Croce's dialectic of the forms of spiritual activity (the aesthetic, the logical, the "economic," and the ethical). While the aesthetic and the logical categories belong to the sphere of knowledge, the "economic" and the ethical constitute the sphere of praxis. In this system, modeled on a pluralistic pattern in contrast to Giovanni Gentile's monistic philosophy, art is considered as pure intuition, different from thought. On this basis, Croce developed a theory of e. that cannot help us understand those masterpieces of Western lit. which have a strong intellectual content (e.g. Dante's *Paradiso*). This anti-intellectual bias, having its roots in the primitivistic trend of the 18th c. (mainly Vico and Herder), prompted Croce to reject the aesthetic relevance of humor, a position quickly attacked by Luigi Pirandello in his essay *On Humor* (1908, 1920; tr. 1974): "Croce has no objection to speaking individually of one humorist or another; but as soon as one tries to speak of humor in general, then his philosophy becomes a formidable, unshakable iron gate.... But what's behind that gate? Nothing—only the equation: intuition = expression."

The foremost critic of the Crocean theory of e. was Ernst Cassirer, who pointed out what is probably the weakest aspect of Croce's aesthetics, i.e. his distinction between e., having a purely intuitional character, and externalization (*estrinsecazione*), viewed as a nonaesthetic, practical fact. Ac-

cording to Cassirer, art cannot be separated from externalization because it can only exist in a specific vehicle, a medium, treated with an appropriate technique. Contrary to Croce, Cassirer proposed a holistic theory of e. not confined to the boundaries of art. He devoted his attention to various expressive forms appearing in religion, art, lang., and science. Such forms are both subjective and objective, spontaneous and premeditated. Cassirer's *Philosophy of Symbolic Forms* (1923–29; tr. 1953–57) had a considerable impact on Am. aesthetics, as evidenced by Susanne K. Langer's *Feeling and Form* (3d ed., 1957; see MYTH). According to Langer, the symbolic forms are cognitive functions that allow us to investigate culture in all its aspects, as an organic whole. Art is a specific kind of symbolic form, an objectified e. of feelings made manifest through modes of nondiscursive symbolism, as distinct from lang., which employs discursive forms of symbolism. Art is cognitive because it reveals the structure of our inner life through *Schein* (semblance), a category derived from Kant and Schiller but that informs even the thought of Marx (Morawski). Whatever reservations we may have about Langer's philosophical approach to art and e. based on the neo-Kantianism of the Marburg school, there is no doubt that she produced a sophisticated theory of e. which was influential in Am. aesthetics just after mid-century.

Almost at the same time, Rudolf Arnheim offered a theory of e. modeled on Gestalt psychology in his *Art and Visual Perception* (1954) and subsequent works. Since Wertheimer had demonstrated that the perception of e. is not a simple product of learning but is immediate and compelling, we must admit a kind of structural isomorphism or kinship not only between body and mind but also between the stimulus and the e. it conveys. Moreover, Arnheim maintains that e. does not necessarily relate to mind; rather, any object or event, because it has an articulate shape, is expressive. This idea leads us to see nonmimetic art as the logical continuation of traditional art: the "abstract" painter adopts a "musical" approach by reducing the outer and inner worlds to a play of forces. Arnheim's views show a certain similarity with those proposed by Alan Tormey in *The Concept of E.* (1971), where he asserts that es. and ideas, both in persons and works of art, are connected only by logical analogy. On this basis, Tormey attempts what A. C. Danto called "the destruction of that hopeless theory that works of art are the exudates of souls." In fact, such an endeavor had already been made by Arnheim and a host of other thinkers. The popular concept according to which a sign is an e. pointing to a content outside itself has always been rejected by the linguistic trad., initiated by Saussure, as well as by its subsequent devel. in semiotics.

In his *Prolegomena to a Theory of Lang.* (1943; tr. 1963), Louis Hjelmslev maintains that the terms

e. and content (or *e. plane* and *content plane*) are "coordinate and equal entities in every respect," inasmuch as they are solidary functives of a sign function. An expressionless content or a content-less e. are both impossible. The Hjelmslevian model was adopted with some qualifications by Umberto Eco in his *Theory of Semiotics* (1976). According to Eco, the sign function is the equivalent of the correspondence between signifier and signified. As far as aesthetic e. is concerned, it belongs to a special kind of communication, founded on a new code, spoken by only one speaker, and understood by a fit audience though few. This code is the *aesthetic idiolect*, the core of artistic e. and the very essence of a work of art. See also CRITICISM; INTENTION; INTUITION; POETRY, THEORIES OF; THEORY; TWENTIETH-CENTURY POETICS.

Abrams, esp. ch. 4; G. N. G. Orsini, *Benedetto Croce, Philosopher of Art and Literary Critic* (1961); "L'E.," spec. iss. of *RIPh* 16, 1 (1962); W. R. Roberts, *Gr. Rhet. and Lit. Crit.* (1963), ch. 2, 3, 6; J. Hospers, *Artistic E.* (1971); A. Tormey, *The Concept of E.* (1971); Murphy; G. Costa, "Thomas Blackwell fra Gravina e Vico," *BCSV* 5 (1975); V. Aldrich, "'Expresses' and 'Expressive,'" *JAAC* 37 (1978); P. Kivy, *The Corded Shell* (1980)—musical e.; S. Morawski, "Art as Semblance," *JP* 81 (1984); G. Cantelli, *Mente corpo linguaggio: Saggio sull'interpretazione vichiana del mito* (1986); M. E. Moss, *B. Croce Reconsidered* (1987), ed. and tr., *B. Croce: Essays on Lit. and Lit. Crit.* (1990).   G.C.

EXPRESSIONISM. The term e. may best be used to describe the style, poetic programs, and worldview of a literary movement that established post-impressionist modernism in Germany after 1910. At the same time, however, the reception of Fr. symbolism (q.v.), begun with Rainer Maria Rilke and, to some degree, Stefan George, continued in the works of several expressionist poets, most notably Georg Trakl and other Austrians. The structure and imagery of expressionist poetry shows strong affinities with new techniques, both concurrent and slightly earlier, in the visual arts (painting, lithography, sculpture), these resemblances often resulting from the multiple talents of its practitioners.

As a critical label, e. was probably adopted from its use by L. Vauxcelles as the title, *Expressionismes*, for a series of paintings by Julien-August Hervé shown in 1901; the term in Ger. first appeared in the catalogue of the 1911 exhibit of secessionist artists in Berlin that included Fauvist pictures, and was first applied to lit. in a newspaper article in July 1911. After 1914 it was almost routinely applied to any unconventional literary work, denoting at first the activist challenge of young poets to impressionist aestheticism. Not all the avant-garde artists before World War I embraced e., and the older poets shunned its pathos, but most writers of the "youngest generation" went through at least a phase of it.

It is legitimate to distinguish an exploratory stage ("Frühzeit," ca. 1910) of aggressive and versatile experimentation by poets such as J. van Hoddis, A. Lichtenstein, E. Stadler, E. Blass, A. Ehrenstein, A. Stramm, and G. Heym from a short period of distinctive accomplishment (the "Hochexpressionismus") by G. Benn, J. R. Becher, F. Werfel, E. Lasker-Schüler, and M. Herrmann-Neisse. But the creative energies of e. began to wane in little more than a decade, esp. when the educated bourgeoisie, its principal supporters, lost their social stability and began to favor less provocative artistic models that would counterbalance the experience of an apocalyptic war and the fear of revolution. An equally important reason is the fact that the two most influential weeklies of e. lost their integrating function when they turned intensely political after 1918. H. Walden's *Der Sturm* propagated a doctrinaire Bolshevism, and F. Pfemfert's *Die Aktion* (1911–32) espoused the radical left. While some of the stylistic and thematic concerns of e. could be adapted and expanded to speak to the early 1920s (and made a brief reappearance after 1945), much expressionist poetry had by then become repetitive. During the mid 1930s, e. was denounced as "degenerate" by the Nazis and as "protofascist" by some Communist critics.

E. in its most concentrated form is a predominantly Ger. phenomenon. But qualities that distinguish its poetry both from the mimetic reproduction and the symbolist stylizations of nature, emotions, and social thought in late 19th-c. writing can be detected in all European lits., esp. in Eng. vorticism and imagism (qq.v.), in the manifestoes of It. futurism (q.v.), and later in the incipient movements of dada and surrealism (qq.v.). This is not necessarily a matter of traceable influences; it is more a sign of contemporaneous similarities among the vanguard of artistic sensibilities in all the advanced industrial societies of Europe. E., in turn, absorbed non-Ger. influences, most notably the provocative irrationalism of Rimbaud, the expansive free-verse lyricism of Walt Whitman, and various forms of folk- and "primitive" poetry. Its strongest source of inspiration, however, was the rhapsodic, imaged intensity of Nietzsche's gospel, *Thus Spake Zarathustra*. Nietzsche and other critics of bourgeois society and imperialist capitalism, among them G. Simmel and later Sigmund Freud, provided insights and arguments to confirm what most expressionist poets sensed was a profound crisis of the "old order." The resultant disorientation brought about recurrent premonitions that Europe, unawares, was on the verge of cataclysm. The poets, nearly all of them deeply alienated from the spirit of optimism and progress of the times and repelled by life in the industrial cities, turned their anxieties and frustrations into an aggressive hostility against the world of their fathers, seeking a release of pent-up energies, if necessary in war as the ultimate heroic adventure; and they longed for spiritual salvation. Most often their disorientation expressed itself in visions of death, destruction, and decay and inclined toward an apocalyptic rhetoric, but an alternative was a messianic utopianism that burst forth in the many rhymed appeals to the spirit of universal brotherhood. But even in its ecstatic and sarcastic extremes, expressionist poetry is suffused with what may be its most pervasive element: a subtly nuanced tone of fearful melancholy, of sad resignation, or at least of elegiac lament that contrasts with the often proclaimed principle of dynamic vitality.

Expressionist poetry was written in many places, but the pathbreaking activities usually originated in the rival literary clubs and cabarets of Berlin, e.g. the *Neue Club* of K. Hiller with its "Neopathetische Cabaret" (1910), his "Cabaret Gnu" (1911), or the *Romanische Café*, called "Café Megalomania." Also central were the many short-lived and erratic journals. K. Wolff, in his series *Der jüngste Tag* (1913–21), which was open to all good new writing, and K. Pinthus, editor of the expressionist anthol. *Menschheitsdämmerung: Symphonie jüngster Dichtung* (1919), were prominent among expressionist publishers. But much expressionist poetry was circulated in pamphlets and very small editions by underground presses and lingered in bohemian obscurity until it was systematically collected in the 1960s.

Recent scholarship has emphasized the stylistic and thematic diversity of expressionist poetry—its wide range of expressive qualities—but also its dependence on conventional patterns and traditional structuring devices. Still, common denominators have become ever more elusive, and most critics have abandoned their search for the ideal expressionist poem in favor of describing the movement's contradictory complexity.

K. L. Schneider, *Der bildhafte Ausdruck in den Dichtungen Georg Heyms, Georg Trakls und Ernst Stadlers* (1954); *Expressionismus: Gestalten einer Bewegung*, ed. H. Friedmann and O. Mann (1956); C. Heselhaus, *Die Lyrik des E.* (1956); W. H. Sokel, *The Writer in Extremis* (1959); R. Brinkmann, *Expressionismus: Forschungsprobleme 1952–1960* (1961), *Expressionismus Internationale Forschung zu einem internationalen Phänomen* (1980); W. Falk, *Leid und Verwandlung: Rilke, Kafka, Trakl* (1961); U. Weisstein, "E. in Lit.," *DHI*, ed., *E. as an International Phenomenon* (1973); *Expressionismus als Lit.*, ed. W. Rothe (1969); J. Willett, *E.* (1970); *Gedichte der* Menschheitsdämmerung: *Interpretationen*, ed. H. Denkler (1971); R. F. Allen, *Ger. Expressionist Poetry* (1971); G. Martens, *Vitalismus und Expressionismus* (1971); R. P. Newton, *Form in the* Menschheitsdämmerung (1971)—prosody; S. Vietta and H.-G. Kemper, *Expressionismus* (1975); *Begriffsbestimmung des lit. Expressionismus*, ed. H. G. Rötzer (1976); T. Anz, *Literatur der Existenz* (1977); H. Lehnert, *Vom Jugendstil zum Expressionismus* (1978); K.-H. Hucke, *Utopie und Ideologie in der e. Lyrik* (1980); *Expressionismus: Manifeste und Dokumente zur deutschen Lit. 1910–1920*, ed. T. Anz

and M. Stark (1982); W. Paulsen, *Deutsche Lit. des Expressionismus* (1983); *Die Autoren und Bücher des lit. Expressionismus: Ein bibliographisches Handbuch*, ed. P. Raabe and I. Hannich-Bode (1985). M.W.

EXPRESSIVENESS. See SOUND.

EYE RHYME, sight r., visual r. Two (or more) words which to the eye seem to rhyme, in that their spelling is nearly identical (both begin differently but end alike), but to the ear (that is, in pronunciation) do not. A modern example would be: *rough/cough/through/though/plough*. E. rs. must be discriminated with care, for, although their existence is undeniable and, in some ages, their quantity greater than is often thought, still they are on the whole a rarity. It is essential to remember that many words which are spelled similarly but do not now seem to rhyme in the aural sense, and so might be thought e. rs., did rhyme in earlier stages of the lang., or do or did so in other dialects than our own; none of these are for us genuine e. rs. and should be set aside as spurious.

Still, it is certain that poets have at all times been conscious to some degree of the visual dimension of poetry (Hollander's "poem in the eye"). This consciousness extends from larger effects—e.g. conceiving of the poem as a purely visual entity, in the several forms of visual poetry (q.v.) such as pattern poetry and concrete poetry (qq.v.)—to smaller—e.g. playing with the visual shapes of words, chiefly in e. r. Though e. rs. certainly exist in Cl. and Med. Lat., interest was augmented greatly by the invention of printing in the West. And in the poetry of the past two centuries in particular, correspondence of visual forms has been seen as an important strategy for expanding the domains and resources of poetry beyond those of traditional prosody, aurally based.

Strictly speaking, e. r. is not a r. at all, but this is to conceive the issues too narrowly. Genuine cases of e. r. raise the issue of the relations of sound to spelling in lang. and poetry—notice, for example, that spelling differences in aural r. are invisible, whereas spelling similarities in e. r. are opaque; they are the marked form. R. is by definition sound-correspondence, but insofar as spelling is meant to denote sound, we must both ignore it and—when necessary—pay attention to it. Hence accurate knowledge not only of historical phonology and dialectology but also of the spelling conventions of the lang. (the idea of a "correct" spelling scarcely exists before the 19th c.) is essential to the correct understanding of r. in both the aural and visual senses. In this, e. r. points up the very question of the aural and (or versus) the visual modes of poetry. See RHYME.—Schipper; H. C. Wyld, *Studies in Eng. Rs. from Surrey to Pope* (1923); A. Menichetti, "Rime per l'occhio e ipometrie nella poesia romanza delle origine," *CN* 26 (1966); Hollander. T.V.F.B.

F

FABLE. A brief verse or prose narrative or description, whose characters may be animals ("The Cicada and the Ant") or inanimate objects ("The Iron Pot and the Clay Pot") acting like humans; or, less frequently, personified abstractions ("Love and Madness") or human types, whether literal ("The Old Man and the Three Young Men") or metaphorical ("The Danube Peasant"). The narrative or description may be preceded, followed, or interrupted by a separate, relatively abstract statement of the f.'s theme or thesis.

I. HISTORY. Despite suggestions that the *Panchatantra* (transcribed ca. 3d c. A.D.) is the fountainhead of the European f., the genre probably arose spontaneously in Greece with Hesiod's poem of the hawk and the nightingale (8th c. B.C.), followed by Archilochus' fragments on the fox and the eagle (7th c. B.C.). The first collection of Gr. fs. is attributed to Æsop (6th c. B.C.) and is known to us through Maximus Planudes' 14th-c. ed. of a prose text transcribed by Demetrius of Phalerum (4th c. B.C.). Phædrus and Babrius were the first to cast the f. into verse; their works attained such popularity that fs. became part of the regular school exercises.

Phaedrus (1st c. A.D.), the first fabulist we may reckon a poet, imitated Æsop in Lat. iambic senarii, but also invented many new fs., recounted contemp. anecdotes, and introduced political allusions. Babrius, writing in Gr. (2d c. A.D.), went further by inventing racy epithets and picturesque expressions while enlarging the formula of the genre in the direction of satire and the bucolic; his *Muthiamboi aisopeioi*, originally in 10 books, is in choliambics, the meter of the lampoon. A famous collection by Nicostratus, also of the 2d c., is now lost. Avianus (4th c. A.D.) paraphrased and expanded Babrian models, which he enriched with Virgilian and Ovidian phraseology for mock-heroic effect. *Romulus*, a 10th-c. prose tr. of Phaedrus and Babrius, was later versified and enjoyed celebrity into the 17th c. But the best medieval fabulist was Marie de France, who composed 102 octosyllabic fs. (ca. 1200), combining Gr. and Lat. themes with insight into feudal society, fresh observation of man and nature, and Gallic irony. The *Ysopets* (13th and 14th c.) were Fr. verse trs. of older Lat. fs.

The European beast epic (q.v.), in particular the *Roman de Renart*, owes much to many fs. as told in antiquity and in their Med. Lat. forms (notably Babrius and Avianus), and to Marie. It in turn influenced many fs., esp. those in the *Ysopets* and in Robert Henryson's late 15th-c. *Moral Fabillis of Esope*—an innovative version in lowland Scots English. Beast epic differs from f. not only in magnitude and in its exclusively animal cast of characters but also in its single, mock-heroic modality. Bestiary (q.v.) differs from f. in its emphasis on the symbolic and allegorical meanings of the features or traits attributed to its subjects, animals both legendary and real.

The *Fs. choisies et mises en vers* of Jean de La Fontaine (1621–95) are both summative and innovative. In the first two collections (1668), the Fr. poet adapted subjects and techniques from trs. of Phaedrus, Babrius, and Avianus, incl. Gilles Corrozet's *Fs. du très ancien esope phrygien* (1542), which anticipated La Fontaine's use, in the same poem, of *vers mêlés* (q.v.). The second collection and subsequent additions (1678–79; 1693) contained materials from Indic sources, incl. *Le Livre des lumières*, a 1644 tr. of fs. based on an 8th-c. Ar. version of the *Panchatantra*. Two features distinguish La Fontaine's *Fs.* from their predecessors: first, they make thematically significant use of pastiche and parody across a wide spectrum of modes and genres; and second, they are systematically philosophical, setting forth, extending, and revising an epicureanism derived from Lucretius and Gassendi.

La Fontaine was widely imitated during the 17th and 18th cs.: in France, by Eustache le Noble (1643–1711) and J.-P.-C. de Florian (1754–94); in England, by John Gay (1685–1732); in Spain, by Tomás de Iriarte (1750–91); and in Germany, by C. F. Gellert (1715–69). G. E. Lessing (1729–81) modeled his fs. on Æsop.

In the first two decades of the 19th c., the Rus. Ivan Adreyevich Krylov (1769–1844) won wide acclaim for his trs. of La Fontaine and his original fs., still read for their satire and realism of matter and lang. The verse f. trad. was carried on in America by Joel Chandler Harris, who drew on Afro-Am. trads. in his Uncle Remus collections (1881–1906).

II. TYPES. All fs. are didactic in purpose but may be subdivided by technique into three categories, the assertional, the dialectical, and the problematic. Assertional fs. plainly and directly expound simple ideas through a harmonious union of precept and example. The Æsopic trad.—ancient and modern—is in the main assertional. Certain versions of the *Panchatantra* and other Indian collections are dialectical. They present assertional fs. in a sequence where each is clarified, nuanced, or even corrected by those that follow. Problematic fs. feature moral dilemmas or enigmatic presentation. Among the devices used to "problematize" a

f. are omission of the thesis statement, unreliable or playful narration, subtle allusion to other literary works, verbal ambiguity, abstruse metaphors, and symbolism. Many fs. by La Fontaine, Bierce, and Thurber are because of one or more of these devices problematic. See also BEAST EPIC; BESTIARY; FABLIAU; NARRATIVE POETRY.

L. Hervieux, *Les Fabulistes latins depuis le siècle d'auguste jusqu'à la fin du moyen-âge*, 2d ed., 5 v. (1893–99); A. Hausrath, "Fabel," Pauly-Wissowa 6.1704–36; *Krylov's Fs.*, tr. B. Pares (1921); F. Edgerton, *The Panchatantra Reconstructed* (1924); M. Stege, *Die Gesch. der deutschen Fabeltheorie* (1929); "Avianus—*Fabulae*," *Minor Lat. Poets*, ed. and tr. J. W. and A. M. Duff (1934); Marie de France, *Fs.*, ed. A. Ewert and R. C. Johnston (1942); C. Filosa, *La favola e la letteratura esopiana in Italia.* . . . (1952); *Fs. of Æsop*, tr. S. A. Handford (1954); M. Guiton, *La Fontaine: Poet and Counter-Poet* (1961); M. Noejgaard, *La F. antique*, 2 v. (1964–67); *Babrius and Phaedrus*, ed. and tr. B. E. Perry (1965)—invaluable intro. and appendices; H. de Boor, *Fabel und Bispel* (1966); T. Noel, *Theories of the F. in the 18th C.* (1975); *La Fontaine: Sel. Fs.*, tr. J. Michie (1979); H. J. Blackham, *The F. as Lit.* (1985); P. Carnes, *F. Scholarship: An Annot. Bibl.* (1985); R. Danner, *Patterns of Irony in La Fontaine's Fs.* (1985); *La Fontaine: Fs.*, ed. M. Fumaroli (1985)—brilliant intros., revolutionary bibl., penetrating commentary; G. Dicke and K. Grubmüller, *Die Fabeln des Mittelalters und der frühen Neuzeit, ein Katalog der deutschen Versionen und ihrer lateinischen Entsprechungen* (1987); M.-O. Sweetser, *La Fontaine* (1987)—up-to-date commentaries and bibl.; C. D. Reverand, *Dryden's Final Poetic Mode: The Fs.* (1988); D. L. Rubin, *A Pact with Silence* (1991); A. Patterson, *Fs. of Power* (1991).
D.L.R.; A.L.S.

FABLIAU. A comic tale in verse which flourished in the 12th and 13th cs., principally in the north of France. Although the name, which means "little fable" in the Picard dialect, suggests a short story, a few fabliaux run over a thousand lines. Most, however, are short and share a common thread of unabashedly bawdy humor, the subjects being mainly sexual or excretory. A few names, such as Rutebeuf, Philippe de Beaumanoir, Jean Bodel, and Gautier Le Leu, have been associated with the f., but most examples remain anonymous. Critical opinion in the past has been divided as to whether the fabliaux were bourgeois or courtly in origin. Modern scholars favor the view that their authors as well as their audiences were not limited to any one social class. On the other hand, the predominance of courtly and lyrical sentiments make it all but anachronistic to speak of the f. as a bourgeois genre, as Bédier did in his classic study (1st ed. 1893).

The characteristic f. style is simple, unsophisticated, and practical—the materialistic view of everyday life. Though the fabliaux have been accused of antifeminist sentiment, it is interesting to note that, in most instances where such a sentiment is expressed, it is appended to a tale which illustrates female ingenuity and superiority, often over a foolish husband. If there is a prevailing theme in the plots of the fabliaux, it is that of "the trickster tricked." The verseform is commonly octosyllabic couplets.

When critics complain of the obscenity of the f.—and historically many have done so—they usually seem to be offended more by the vulgarity of the lang. than by the prurience of the stories. True, in sexual matters the lang. is routinely explicit, yet the social attitudes underlying it are conventional, even conservative, and may indicate a medieval sensibility toward such matters that underlies and antedates both courtly purity and Christian puritanism.

In the 14th c. the vogue of the f. spread to Italy and England, where Chaucer borrowed freely from the genre for eight or nine of his *Canterbury Tales*, esp. the *Miller's Tale* and *Reeve's Tale*. The f. may fairly be said to be the genre of greatest interest to Chaucer in his mature work. Fr. trad. continued in the prose *nouvelle*, but the influence of the older form may be seen centuries later in the poetry of La Fontaine in France, C. F. Gellert in Germany, and I. A. Krylov in Russia. See also FABLE.

W. M. Hart, "The F. and Popular Lit.," *PMLA* 23 (1908), "The Narrative Art of the OF F.," *Kittredge Anniv. Papers* (1913); J. Bédier, *Les Fabliaux*, 5th ed. (1925); J. Rychner, *Contribution à l'étude des fabliaux*, 2 v. (1960); *The Literary Context of Chaucer's Fabliaux*, ed. L. D. Benson and T. M. Andersson (1971); P. Nykrog, *Les Fabliaux*, rpt. with a "Post-scriptum 1973" (1973); P. Dronke, "The Rise of the Med. F.," *RF* 85 (1973); *The Humor of the Fabliaux*, ed. T. D. Cooke and B. L. Honeycutt (1974); *Gallic Salt*, tr. R. L. Harrison (1974); T. Cooke, *The OF and Chaucerian Fabliaux* (1978); *Cuckolds, Clerics, and Countrymen*, tr. J. Duval (1982); R. E. Lewis, "The Eng. F. Trad. and Chaucer's *Miller's Tale*, *MP* 79 (1982); P. Ménard, *Les Fabliaux (1983);* Nouveau recueil complet des fabliaux, ed. W. Noomen and N. van den Boogaard, 10 v. (1983–); R. H. Bloch, *The Scandal of the Fabliaux (1986);* C. Muscatine, The OF Fabliaux (1986).
A.PR.; R.L.H.

FALLING ACTION. See PLOT.

FALLING RHYTHM. See RISING AND FALLING RHYTHM.

FANCY is the short form, common since the Ren., of fantasy (Lat. *phantasia*, transliterated from Gr. *phanos* "image" and later replaced by *imaginatio*). In Western poetics the history, definition, and use of f. in crit. and psychology are inseparably linked to that of *imagination* (q.v.), the two terms being sometimes distinguished but more often used very similarly if not identically. *Phantasia* originally carried suggestions of creativity and free play of mind, a power generating images and combinations of images not previously found in nature or sense experience. Albertus Magnus uses the term this way, with *imaginatio* reserved for the static mental recording of perceived images. However, even in the Middle Ages, distinctions or inversions of the two terms occur. Aquinas simply uses them synonymously; in a later (failed) attempt to fix them, Addison does, too: usage did not stabilize in Eng. until the later 18th c. In Germany a variety of terms (*Phantasie, Einbildungskraft, Dichtungskraft, Perceptionsvermögen*) are employed throughout the 18th and 19th cs. without strict consistency. In Italy, *fantasia* generally retains its "higher" stature as a creative and altering power, while *immaginazione* pertains more to a form of memory, the retention and reproduction of sense impressions. However, even here there is no rule; Vico uses *fantasia* for both recollective and original, productive functions.

In the period 1660–1820, European crit. self-consciously turns to the issue of discriminating f. from imagination. In Eng., despite early confusion, something of a norm is reached by the 1780s and 90s. Hobbes employed f. for the greatest creative range of mind, but rDryden at least once subordinates f. to imagination. Anticipating later developments, Dryden makes f. responsible only for the manipulation and rearrangement or juxtaposition of images already created or experienced; in poetic composition, f. is the power that distributes and arranges the images already invented. Imagination encompasses both powers, as well as their formulation in words and figures of speech. Addison claims no difference between f. and imagination but in practice tends to elevate imagination to a higher creative plane. As early as Shaftesbury's *Characteristics* (1711), imagination is the stronger term, while f. suggests "mental abandon," which Shaftesbury exemplifies by the same passage from Otway's *Venice Preserved* that Coleridge later quotes in the *Biographia* to illustrate f.: "Lutes, lobsters, seas of milk, ships of amber."

In poetry, the elevation of the term imagination at the expense of f. occurs a litter later; until the romantic period, f. is generally used in poetic diction. Keats uses imagination heavily in his letters and in the late *Fall of Hyperion*; elsewhere, f. may be a fickle power of pleasure ("Fancy"), a power of endlessly novel and procreative embellishment ("Ode to Psyche"), or potentially synonymous with imagination ("Ode to a Nightingale"). It is significant that Wordsworth consciously chooses imagination as the key term in *The Prelude*; unlike Coleridge, however, he views f. and imagination as differing in degree, not kind.

For Coleridge, f. "has no other counters to play with, but fixities and definities. The F. is indeed no other than a mode of Memory emancipated from the order of time and space: and blended with, and modified by that empirical phenomenon of the will, which we express by the word *choice*. But equally with the ordinary memory it must receive all its materials ready made from the law of association" (*BL*, ch. 4). His definition has become a touchstone in part because it captures the essence of a set of emergent Eng. and Ger. distinctions. F. operates without a unifying design and does not meld, transform, or newly create images or ideas. Rather, it juxtaposes or connects them in a more mechanical fashion, appealing to novelty of sense impression instead of strength or grandeur of intellectual conception and power. Often described as "aimless" or "sportive," f. suggests a phantasmagoria of passing, fixed images, whose mingling does not mutually transform or resolve or unify them into larger patterns. Ruskin continues to distinguish the two terms in *Modern Painters*.

In Germany, Wolff, Kant, Jean-Paul, Schelling, Hegel, Schiller, J. G. Fichte, I. G. Fichte, Tetens, and Goethe all make distinctions between f. and imagination, some elaborate, others casual. Schelling and at times Kant parallel the Eng. elevation of imagination (*Einbildungskraft*), while others, such as Jean-Paul, echo the It. supremacy of f. (*Phantasie*) as the highest creative power. Croce in the earlier 20th c. retains the It. primacy of *fantasia*, the equivalent of Eng. imagination, while *immaginazione* corresponds roughly to f. as Coleridge defines it. For bibl., see IMAGINATION.

J.E.

FARCE. If, following the suggestion of Dr. Johnson (*Rambler* no. 125), we confine ourselves to purpose and ignore the more accidental feature of means, we should have no difficulty in arriving at an acceptable definition of f. Its object is to provoke the spectator to laughter, not the reflective kind which comedy (q.v.) is intended to elicit but the uncomplicated response of simple enjoyment. Its means are often shared by other comic forms such as burlesque (q.v.), thus giving rise to frequent confusion among them. Once purpose is established, these means are not hard to visualize. F. exploits the surprise of sudden appearance or disclosure, the mechanism suggested by excessively physical action, repetition, gross exaggeration of character, frequent sexual byplay, and so on. Since it does not share with higher comedy the responsibility of commentary on social conduct, it may pursue its laughter into a world of fantasy where the unpredictable, even the impossible, is commonplace.

The origins of f. are hidden in the mists of prehistory, since the propensity to horseplay seems as natural to humanity as the trait of laughter, which is sometimes alleged to separate us from the other animals. The presence of f. in Aristophanes and the Roman comic writers and its popularity in the mimes and early Atellan fs. of the

Romans attests to its early appeal. Something of the crude horseplay common to f. and such kindred forms as burlesque, mime (q.v.), and satyr play may be observed in surviving vase paintings and statues. The first plays of record to bear the name were Fr., for the name was devised in France from Lat. *farcire* "to stuff." The 15th c. reveals Fr. f. at an early peak as it was developed esp. by the "joyous societies" who contrived numerous pieces from the stuff of folklore and fabliau (q.v.).

Usually rendered in lively octosyllabic couplets, these medieval Fr. fs. exploited themes of commercial trickery and sexual infidelity to show a life, both coarse and vibrant, where conventions—particularly the conventional respect for women and the clergy—were flouted. Two examples of many may be cited: *Le Meunier et le gentilhomme* (ca. 1550), which treats a folk motif traceable as far back as the 7th c. and appearing on four continents, and *Maître Pierre Pathelin* (ca. 1465), most famous of all.

Subsequently, f. never quite regained in France the popularity it had attained in the Middle Ages, yet it enjoyed renewed popular esteem even under Fr. Classicism, when Molière as both actor and playwright helped restore it to theatrical recognition. It managed to survive the competition of both *drame bourgeois* in the 18th c. and *mélodrame* and romantic drama in the 19th, though perhaps no name greater than that of Labiche came to its support. Meanwhile Spain and Germany had their writers of f. In the case of Italy, the bulk of f. was supplied by the improvisations of the widely popular and influential *commedia dell'arte* troupes, which flourished from the 16th to the 18th c.

The first Eng. f. writer of note—there are f. episodes in the earlier mystery plays—is John Heywood (16th c.), a somewhat isolated figure in that he chose to borrow from Fr. f. and also developed an independent genre. The common practice, following the triumph of Cl. models just as the professional Eng. theatre was beginning. was to mix farcical episodes in with more serious matter. In Shakespeare's *Comedy of Errors*, for example, or *Merry Wives*, in Jonson's *Silent Woman*, even more in such popular anonymous plays as *Mucedorus*, we find f. scenes mingled with intrigue, romance, and the satirical portraiture of comedy of humors (q.v.). Only in the droll of the Commonwealth period was Eng. f. independent of other forms. With the establishment of the afterpiece at the beginning of the 18th c. and the consequent demand for short pieces in the Eng. repertory, f. came into its own as a distinct genre. For much of the next two centuries it thrived vigorously. As taste declined, f. took its place, with sentimental comedy and melodrama, as one of the staples of theatrical fare. Of the hundreds of fs. written in this period, few appeared worthy of preservation. Only in the 20th c., with Wilde and Pinero, did f. aspire to be literary, an aspiration usually fatal to a dramatic genre. Though it continued to have a

place in the popular theatre of the 20th c., it no longer enjoys quite the vogue it did in the 17th and 18th cs. Even in the cinema, where with Chaplin and other producers of short pieces it had a renewal of life, the more traditional f. with human actors has been displaced by the animated cartoon and short segments for television such as The Three Stooges.

L. Petit de Julleville, *Hist. du thèâtre en France*, 4th ed. (1896); W. S. Jack, *The Early Entremès in Spain* (1923); W. Klemm, *Die englische F. im 19. Jh.* (1946); P. Frassinetti, *Fabula Atellana* (1953); G. Frank, *The Med. Fr. Drama* (1954); L. Hughes, *A Century of Eng. F.* (1956); L. Breitholtz, *Die dorische F. im griechischen Mutterland vor dem 5. Jh.* (1960); M, Bieber, *Hist. of the Gr. and Roman Theater*, 2d ed. (1961); B. C. Bowen, *Les Caractéristiques essentielles de la f. française* (1964); O. Levertin, *Studien zur Gesch. der F.*, 2d ed. (1970); H. Lewicka, *Études sur l'ancienne f. francaise* (1974); A. Tissier, *La F. en France de 1450 à 1550: Recueil de textes*, 2 v. (1976); A. F. Caputi, *Buffo: The Genius of Vulgar Comedy* (1978); J. M. Davis, *F.* (1978); A. Bermel, *F.: A Hist. from Aristophanes to Woody Allen* (1982); B. D. Chesley, *The Faces of Harlequin in 18th-C. Eng. Pantomine* (1986); J. H. Huberman, *Late Victorian F.* (1986); L. Smith, *Mod. British F.* (1988); G. Mack, *Die F.: Studien zur Begriffsbestimmung und Gattungsgesch. in de neueren deutschen Literatur* (1989); Hollier.   L.H.; T.V.F.B.

FATRAS (also called *fatrasie, fratrasie, resverie*). An irrational or obscure piece of verse, which originated in the Middle Ages. It is generally lively and joyous in style, full of word-play, ridiculous associations of ideas, and deliberate nonsense. Langlois defines two forms: the *f. possible,* which offers a coherent text, and the *f. impossible,* which, like the later *coq-à-l'âne* (q.v.), seems to make no sense at all. *Qua* genre, however, it is not the incoherence of content that constitutes the f. but its very special form: a strophe of 11 lines, the first and last of which form a distich placed at the beginning as the theme of the composition. This is known as the *f. simple.* The *f. double* is formed from this by "restating the initial [distich] in reverse order, and adding a second strophe of ten lines ending with an 11th, a restatement of line one of the [distich]." Porter distinguishes between the (13th-c.?) *fratrasie* and the f., a later (14th-c.?) devel. The former is invariably composed of a single strophe of 11 lines, and its content is always irrational; in the f. the opening distich introduces the next 11 lines, serving as their first and last line and imparting a uniform rhythm to the whole poem. See also ADYNATON; COQ-A-LANE; FROTTOLA AND BARZELLETTA; NONSENSE VERSE.—Patterson; A.-M. Schmidt, "La Trésor des f.," *Les Cahiers de la Pléiade* 11–12 (1950–51); P. Zumthor, *Hist. litt. de la France médiévale* (1954), "Fatrasie et coq-a-lane," *Fin du moyen âge et ren.* (1961); L. C. Porter, *La Fatrasie et le f.* (1960); E.-G. Hessing and R. Viglbrief, "Essai d'analyse des procédés fatrasiques," *Romania* 94 (1963); *Fatrasies,* ed. J.-P. Foucher (1964); W. Kellermann, "Über die altfranzösischen Gedichte des uneingeschränkten Unsinns," *Archiv* 205 (1968). I.S.; T.V.F.B.

FEELING. See EMOTION.

FEIGNING. See FICTION, POETRY AS.

FÉLIBRIGE. A Fr. literary association founded in 1854 by seven Occitan poets who called themselves *félibres,* perhaps meaning "nursling," as Frédéric Mistral explained, because they intended to nurse at the bosom of wisdom. Through the annual publication of the *Armana prouvençau* (Provençal Almanac) the group strove to reform Occitan spelling, to renew the lang., to compose great poetry, and to revive Occitan culture. Joseph Roumanille first organized the movement, which triumphed with the publication in 1859 of Mistral's romantic epic *Mirèio* (Mireille), and again in 1860 with Théodore Aubanel's collection of love poems, *La Mióugrano entre-duberto* (The Split Pomegranate). Originally limited in intention to Provence in the narrow sense (east of the Rhône), *f.* was reorganized in 1876 to include all the Occitan dialects and regions. Perhaps its most lasting achievement was the impetus it gave to dialect lit. in France.—*L'Anthologie du f.,* ed. A. Praviel and J.-R. de Brousse (1909); E. Ripert, *Le F.,* 3d ed. (1948); C. Camproux, *Hist. de la littérature occitane* (1953); *Morceaux choisis des auteurs provençaux de la fondation du f. à nos jours,* ed. L. Bayle, 2 v. (1969–71); R. Lafont and C. Anatole, *Nouvelle Hist. de la litt. occitane,* 2 v. (1970). W.D.P.

FEMININE ENDING, RHYME. See MASCULINE AND FEMININE.

FEMINIST CRITICISM. See FEMINIST POETICS.

FEMINIST POETICS. The term f. p. refers here to those aspects of f. crit. which are specifically concerned with poetry. Like poststructuralism and deconstruction (q.v.), f. crit. developed in the late 1960s. Before f. p., the critical treatment of women's poetic creativity had been primarily misogynistic, emphasizing female incapacity for poetic invention (q.v.) or women's inferiority in matters of experience, education, intellect, and imagination (q.v.). The "poetess," whether bluestocking or sentimentalist, had frequently been the target of satire in masculine poetic texts. Since the romantic period, a number of women critics and writers, incl. Madame de Stael, Elizabeth Barrett Browning, and Virginia Woolf, have speculated on the contribution women might make to poetic trad. and commented on the difficulties of a poetic career for women. But only since the Women's Liberation Movement have critics attempted a systematic critique of lit. hist. and the-

ory from a f. perspective. F. p. brings to the study of poetry theories of sexual difference and of male cultural dominance which are grounded in Marxism, psychoanalysis, and cultural anthropology; a commitment to the political and cultural equality of women; and a belief in the importance of gender as a fundamental variable in the creation and interp. of lit. by both women and men. While it would be premature to claim that f. crit. has established a complete poetic theory, important work has been done on the study of women's poetry, on the representation of women in poetry written by both sexes, and on the more general and central issues of gender and poetics.

According to the Eng. critic Jan Montefiore, "defining a f. p. means primarily understanding the significance of women's poetry." Other forms of crit. than f. have assumed that the poet will be a man and therefore have set out, as universal, concepts of poetic vocation, trad., and form that tacitly presume masculine norms. Women's poetry has been neglected, denigrated, and misread because it has been judged by these inappropriate standards. No definitive hist. of women's poetry has yet been written; nonetheless, through anthologies, editions, essays, specialized studies, and critical biographies, the outline of a female poetic hist. from Sappho to the present is well underway. Research has been carried out in every major national lit., but most thoroughly in Eng. and Am.

The comparative study of women's poetry reveals many patterns of similarity in thought, themes, metaphors, and diction. It also reveals profound contradictions between the image of the poet as the "transcendent speaker of a unified culture" (Kaplan 70) and the image of Woman as silenced, dependent, and marginal. Recurring images of spinning, sewing, and writing, of the mother country or *matria,* and of the body, among others, have been cited by scholars. Yet the notion of a separate female poetic trad. is controversial, since women poets cannot isolate themselves from the influence of the dominant male literary trad. and therefore always write a double-voiced discourse. Women poets must also imitate or revise the tropes of the male trad. As the f. critics Sandra Gilbert and Susan Gubar have noted, "female poets both participated in and diverged from the literary conventions and genres established for them by their male contemporaries" (*Norton Anthol. of Lit. by Women* [*NALW*]). Furthermore, internal differences between women of nationality, class, and race preclude a single poetic matrilineage.

The history of women's poetry in Eng. is marked by gaps and absences, and does not always fit the conventional periodization of poetic history, such as "the Ren." or "romanticism." We do not have any OE poetic texts by women, and few by women in the Middle Ages, although scholars argue that anonymous med. *Frauenlieder,* love-songs narrated by women, may have been the work of female poets. Even in the Ren., however, women had neither the humanist education in the classics, rhet., and logic deemed necessary for poetic careers, nor the financial independence and family support that would have enabled them to write poetry. Furthermore, the social climate was hostile to women's poetic self-expression; women were enjoined to be silent, modest, obedient, and chaste. In the f. classic, *A Room of One's Own* (1928), Virginia Woolf speculates that even if Shakespeare's sister had been born with her brother's genius in the Ren., she would have gone mad or killed herself without writing a word.

Nevertheless, there were a small number of women poets in France and Eng. in the 16th c. Most extant texts are by learned ladies or aristocrats who attempt to reconcile the demands of womanly duty with poetic aspiration, as when Catherine Des Roches claims to be writing "with the spindles and the pen together in my hand" ("A ma quenoille" [16th c.]). Despite severe restrictions, Ren. women poets "did not simply accede to the silencing logic of their culture" but used forms of "negotiation and compromise" (Jones 79, 92) in which the active use of the female voice challenged and revised the linguistic, figurative, and thematic conventions of Neoplatonic and Petrarchan love-poetry.

The entrance of women into the literary professions began in the late 17th c. with the appearance of such poets as Aphra Behn, Anne Bradstreet, and Anne Finch. In their verse, these women primarily asserted their right to speak and write, but they also expressed different attitudes towards the poetic role from that of men. Rather than the conventional address to fame or quest for poetic laurels that inspired male poets of the period, they denied ambition as a literary motive. Finch declares a fear of fame that may simply be expedient when she warns her Muse to "be cautious; / For groves of laurel thou we'ert never meant." On the other hand, Behn's frank eroticism and mockery of male pretensions, like Finch and Bradstreet's explorations of female experience, introduce a new voice and subject-matter into poetry. Yet despite their efforts to conciliate male critics, this appearance of women poets on the literary scene was greeted by a spate of vituperative attacks on "Petticoat Authors," attacks which continued with intensified virulence throughout the 18th c. Women writing within the strict rules of neoclassical poetics (q.v.), using the heroic couplet or the Augustan genres of the satire, the ode, or the epistle (qq.v.), had to confront a poetic establishment explicitly masculine in its ideology and aesthetics and often overtly misogynistic in its texts.

The 19th c. is now considered "the golden age of women's lit." (*NALW*), although even by this point women make a much stronger showing in the new genre of the novel than in poetry. Margaret Homans has argued that women experienced a division between femininity and poetic subjectivity in the romantic period that hindered their success. The masculine romantic poetic self makes the feminine the Other which it must master and transcend, identified either as Nature, a women character, or the desired object of a quest. The image of Mother Nature was not helpful as inspiration or muse (qq.v.) for aspiring women poets, who needed to separate themselves from natural, maternal, and muse roles in order to write.

Women began to publish poetry in much greater numbers by the mid 19th c., but while the male pseudonym was widespread among women novelists in Europe and England from the 1840s on, women poets did not write under men's names. Postromantic and Victorian crit. allotted a place for the woman poet in the lyric, which was considered a feminine form—private, emotional, and brief. In retrospect, even male romantic lyric poets, esp. Shelley and Keats, could be criticized as effeminate, a charge often levelled at Tennyson as well. But the feminization of poetry was not empowering to Victorian women poets. The "poetess" was stereotyped as an artless, genteel, and sentimental songbird, while long philosophical or political poems—as well as the position of Poet Laureate—were reserved for important and serious men. Nonetheless, recent work in f. p. has begun to demonstrate the range, originality, and power of such 19th-c. poets as Elizabeth Barrett Browning, Christina Rossetti, and Emily Dickinson.

By the beginning of the 20th c., the feminine lyric poet became the antagonist of a new school of male modernists. In their eyes, poetry "had become a mawkish, womanly affair full of gush and fine feelings. Lang. had gone soft and lost its virility; it needed to be stiffened up again, made hard and stone-like, reconnected to the physical world" (Eagleton). Modernist aesthetics called for impersonality, intellectuality, abstraction, and emotional distance, "opposed to the aesthetic of soft, effusive, personal verse supposedly written by women and romantics" (*Madwoman* 154). What Gertrude Stein called "patriarchal poetry" functioned as a system that silenced women and kept them out of the modernist canon. F. p. is now re-examining the relations between feminism and modernism, showing how the work of such poets as H.D., Gertrude Stein, and Marianne Moore makes use of matriarchal myths and experiments in lang., technique, and form in order "to excavate a specifically female past" (*NALW* 1241) and to create a new female trad.

In the late 20th c., women's poetry has flourished in the critical climate created by f. p. Since the late 1960s, Am. women's poetry has witnessed an explosion of creativity, the wealth of which praxis itself raises the issue of the relation between creativity and gender. Gilbert and Gubar have analyzed the metaphor of the pen as penis in Eng. lit., while other f. critics have traced the metaphor of creativity as childbirth. In *The Anxiety of Influence* (1973), Harold Bloom describes poetic creativity in Freudian terms (see INFLUENCE) as the son's struggle for priority against the father or strong poetic precursor, while the poet's Muse is figured as feminine, the mother-harlot who has "whored with many before him."

How might poetic influence and the relationship to trad. be different if the poet is a woman? Do women have a Muse (q.v.)? One theory is that for postromantic women poets, the father-precursor and the Muse are the same powerful male figure, both enabling and inhibiting poetic creation. Another theory holds that the woman poet also has a female Muse, modeled on the mother-daughter. Women poets' relation to female literary trad. may be less competitive and anxiety-ridden than men's relation to their precursors, since women desire successful models of female creativity.

F. p. also raises questions about gender and genre, or the relationship between sexual identity and poetic form. According to Gilbert and Gubar, "verse genres have been even more thoroughly male than fictional ones" (*Madwoman* 68). Epic (q.v.) encodes masculine values of heroism and conquest; the pastoral elegy has functioned as "a vocational poem" signaling "admittance of a male novice to the sacred company of poets" (Schenk 13, 15). Women poets have revised and transformed such male genres as the sonnet, the lyric, and the elegy (qq.v.). Furthermore, while women have been missing from the pages of traditional lit. hist. as poets, they have figured prominently as subjects in men's poems, represented as angels, whores, or monsters. As poets, they have revised these images as well as male myths describing such female figures as Eve, Medusa, Cassandra, Circe, Demeter and Persephone, Ariadne, Penelope, and Eurydice. Even meter or punctuation may be seen as connected to gender: Finch has described iambic pentameter as a "patriarchal meter" representing religion, public opinion, and status, while Dickinson's hymn stanzas constitute a f. "anti-meter." Other critics see the orthography of Dickinson's poems as efforts to inscribe sexual difference through the use of dashes, both to refuse grammatical hierarchy and subordination and to introduce feminine ambiguities—gaps, wounds, stitches—into the poem.

Some Am. f. critics and poets have discussed the need to reinvent the "oppressor's lang." and to appropriate it for female experience. Adrienne Rich has described this as the quest for a "common lang." or "mother tongue," both an autonomous lang. of women across social, historical, and racial backgrounds and a vernacular feminine communication akin to Wordsworth's famous definition of the poet as "man speaking to men." But other f. critics ask how women can write in a lang. other than that of the patriarchal trad., and whether poetry can ever discard the figurative

properties of lang. in order to represent experience. Within Fr. f. poststructuralist theory, different questions have been raised about the existence of a feminine poetic lang. Julia Kristeva has described a "revolution in poetic lang." that brings a metaphoric "feminine" utterance into the text through rhythm, prosody, word-play, and nonsense. From this perspective, the "feminine" is not exclusive to women poets but represents a linguistic rupture in avant-garde writing such as the work of Mallarmé. F. p. may then analyze the subversive effects of such techniques.

Finally, f. p. investigates the significance of gender, masculinity, and sexuality in the work of male poets from Homer to the present, a vast project that has already begun to change the poetic canon as well as to revolutionize poetics. See also CRITICISM; THEORY.

BIBLIOGRAPHIES: M. Humm, *An Annot. Critical Bibl. of F. Crit.* (1987); W. Frost and M. Valiquette, *F. Lit. Crit.: A Bibl. of Journal Articles, 1975–1981* (1988).

ANTHOLOGIES: *The Am. Female Poets*, ed. C. May (1848); *The Female Poets of America*, ed. R. Griswold (1860); *The Women Poets in England*, ed. A. Stanford (1972); *No More Masks*, ed. F. Howe and E. Bass (1973); *Rising Tides*, ed. S. Barba and L. Chester (1973); *The World Split Open*, ed. L. Bernikow (1974); *The Other Voice*, ed. J. Bankier et al. (1976); *Black Sister*, ed. G. Hull (1981); *Norton Anthol. of Lit. by Women*, ed. S. Gilbert and S. Gubar (1986).

HISTORY AND CRITICISM: S. Juhasz, *Naked and Fiery Forms* (1976); E. S. Watts, *The Poetry of Am. Women* (1977); "Women's Poetry," ed. G. Bowles, spec. iss. of *WS* 5 (1977); J. F. Diehl, "'Come Slowly—Eden': An Exploration of Women Poets and Their Muse," *Signs* 3 (1978), "Rich's *Common Lang.* and the Woman Poet," *FS* 6 (1980); M. Farwell, "F. Crit. and the Concept of the Poetic Persona," *BuckR* 24 (1978); M. Carruthers, "Imagining Women: Notes Toward a F. P.," *MR* 20 (1979); *Shakespeare's Sisters*, ed. S. Gilbert and S. Gubar (1979); S. Gilbert and S. Gubar, *The Madwoman in the Attic* (1979), *No Man's Land*, 2 v. (1988, 1989); M. Homans, *Women Writers and Poetic Identity* (1980); A. Rich, *On Lies, Secrets, and Silence* (1980); C. Walker, *The Nightingale's Burden* (1982); M. Carruthers, "The Re-Vision of the Must," *HR* 36 (1983); L. Lipking, "Aristotle's Sister," *CI* 10 (1983); A. Ostriker, *Writing Like a Woman* (1983), *Stealing the Lang.* (1986); *F. Critics Read Emily Dickinson*, ed. S. Juhasz (1983); W. Martin, *An Am. Triptych* (1984); *Coming to Light*, ed. D. Middlebrook and M. Yalom (1985); T. Eagleton, *Literary Theory* (1985); C. Schenck, "Feminism and Reconstruction: Re-constructing the Elegy," *TSWL* 5 (1986); A. R. C. Finch, "Dickinson and Patriarchal Meter," *PMLA* 102 (1987); C. Christ, "The Feminine Subject in Victorian Poetry," *ELH* 54 (1987); W. Drake, *The First Wave* (1987); J. Montefiore, *Feminism and Poetry* (1987);

J. Todd, *F. Lit. Hist.* (1988).

FEMINIST LITERARY THEORY: *New Fr. Feminisms*, ed. E. Marks and I. de Courtivron (1978); *Writing and Sexual Difference*, ed. E. Abel (1982); *Making a Difference*, ed. C. Kahn and G. Greene (1985); *The New F. Crit.*, ed. E. Showalter (1985); *Feminist Crit. and Social Change*, ed. J. Newton and D. Rosenfelt (1985); C. Kaplan, *Sea Changes* (1986); T. Moi, *Sexual/Textual Politics* (1986); V. B. Leitch, *Am. Lit. Crit. from the Thirties to the Eighties* (1988), ch. 11; *F. Lit. Crit.: Explorations in Theory*, ed. J. Donovan, 2d ed. (1989)—incl. bibl. 1975–1986; *Feminist Crit.: Theory and Practice*, ed. S. Sellers (1991); *Feminisms*, ed. R. R. Warhol and D. P. Herndl (1991). E.S.

FESCENNINE VERSES (*versus Fescennini*). A form of Lat. occasional verse (q.v.), chiefly lascivious wedding songs, of great antiquity, which perhaps originated as ribald or abusive songs sung at harvest festivals: Claudian's f. v. for the wedding of Emperor Honorius are extant, to which cf. Catullus 61.126–55. F. v. were roughly dramatic, taking the form of a dialogue between peasants, and were probably first composed in the Saturnian (q.v.) meter. In antiquity the name was derived either from *fascinum*, a phallic emblem worn as a charm, or, as is more likely, from the town of Fescennium in Etruria. In the period of the Empire, f. v. were so popular for personal invective that they were outlawed. Livy (7.2) implies that f. v. developed into Roman satire and comedy, but this is disputed. Cf. EPITHALAMIUM.—Pauly-Wissowa, s.v. "Fescennini"; G. E. Duckworth, *The Nature of Roman Comedy* (1952); W. Beare, *The Roman Stage*, 2d ed. (1955). R.J.G.

FICTION, POETRY AS. Although the term in both Gr. (*poiēsis*) and Lat. (*fictio*) denotes *a thing made*, opponents of f. ever since Plato have emphasized its status as falsehood, feigning, and lying. Plato himself accuses the poets of lacking the specialized knowledge necessary to make a product that can serve the community as an instrument of instruction (*Republic* 595a–608b). In the *Poetics*, Aristotle responds to this indictment in part by arguing for the peculiar logic of f.

Setting aside meter as an accidental property of *poiēsis* (*Poetics* 9.1, 9.9), Aristotle considers plot or action essential. The structure of fictional discourse differs from historical narrative (which also presents human action) in that the former discloses a causal rather than a merely temporal relation between events (9.11–12, 10.4, 23.2). Whereas the historian relates *what* has happened, the poet or fiction-writer reveals *why* by incorporating the causal elements of character and motivation into the representation of events. Whereas history records only the particularities of an action, f. embraces its universals, which Aristotle elsewhere maintains (*Posterior Analytics* 86a5–10, 88a5) are the more knowable causes of particulars

that in themselves are difficult if not impossible to know. F., in other words, hypothesizes what a certain type of character would probably do in a given set of circumstances (Vaihinger), and it is in this sense that f. is more philosophical than history (*Poetics* 9.3).

After Aristotle, f. is often defined in terms of the characteristics it shares not only with history and philosophy but also with rhet., where it is associated with the qualitative questions (*status qualitatis*) investigated by legal analysis (Trimpi). Moreover, according to many ancient literary theorists, f. mingles truth and falsehood, where truth is either philosophical or historical (e.g. Horace, *Ars poetica* 151; Strabo, *Geography* 1.2.17; Plutarch, *Moralia* 16b–c, 25b–c). The ancient rhetorical trad. also contributes to this devel. by defining f. (*plasma, argumentum, fictio*) as a kind of narration midway between the facts of history (*historia*) and the falsehood of fable (*mythos, fabula*) (cf. Cicero, *De inventione* 1.19.27; *Ad Herennium* 1.8.13; Sextus Empiricus, *Against the Grammarians* 263–64; Hermogenes, *Progymnasmata* 2.17). In this view, f., lacking historical truth, nevertheless differs from fable through its commitment to verisimilitude (q.v.) or "resemblance to the truth." Whereas f.'s link to the truth enables it to instruct—to be *utile*—its link to the fabulous enables it to please—to be *dulce* (e.g. Horace, *Ars poetica* 333–34, 343–44; Plutarch, *Moralia* 15f–16c).

Both of these traditional notions about f. have their origins in Aristotle's literary theory, but neither is Aristotelian strictly speaking. Although Aristotle himself considers the place of verisimilitude in rhet. argument (*Rhetoric* 1.1.11; cf. *Poetics* 25.26–27), he does not confuse this psychological concept aimed at credibility with the logical concept of probability so important to his theory of f. in the *Poetics*. And whereas Aristotle regards delight as one of the causes of learning (*Poetics* 4.4–6; *Rhetoric* 1.11.23–24), he never isolates these two as the complementary ends of poetry (see Eden).

From Antiquity through the 18th c., however, literary theory both preserves f.'s double aim to please and instruct and upholds verisimilitude (often confused with probability) as one of f.'s defining qualities (Boccaccio, *Geneologia deorum gentilium* [ca. 1363], 14.9; Castelvetro, *Poetica d'Aristotele vulgarizzata e sposta* [1570], ch. 1; Corneille, "Discours de l'utilité et des parties du poème dramatique" [1660]). In his "Preface to Shakespeare" (1765), Dr. Johnson maintains that "The mind revolts from evident falsehood, and f. loses its force when it departs from the resemblance of reality." Even while borrowing the particularity and consequent plausibility of history, however, f. also continues to assert its claim on the universality of philosophy or, in Johnson's words, on "general nature."

Since the 18th c., theorists have continued to discuss the fictionality of poetry in the contexts of history, philosophy, and rhet. (qq.v.), but the terms of the discussions vary widely (see POETRY, THEORIES OF; CRITICISM). Didactic theories of f. have steadily lost currency, however. In addition, modern theory has tended to emphasize the differences between f. and poetry, addressing the nature and function of the latter on the one hand (see TWENTIETH-CENTURY POETICS), and indentifying f. with a particular genre (the novel) on the other. More recently, philosophers of lang. have begun to consider the special linguistic properties of f. Here too, however, its peculiar features as a speech act are qualified in some relation to the conditions governing true and false statements (Searle). See also MEANING, POETIC.

H. Vaihinger, *Philosophy of As If* (1920); O. Barfield, "Poetic Diction and Legal F.," *Essays Presented to Charles Williams*, ed. C. S. Lewis (1947); W. Nelson, *Fact or F.* (1973); J. Searle, "The Logical Status of Fictional Discourse," *NLH* 6 (1975); B. H. Smith, *On the Margins of Discourse* (1978); W. Trimpi, *Muses of One Mind* (1983); R. Levao, *Ren. Minds and Their Fs.* (1985); K. Eden, *Poetic and Legal F. in the Aristotelian Trad.* (1986); P. J. McCormick, *Fs., Philosophies, and the Problems of Poetics* (1988); M. Riffaterre, *Fictional Truth* (1989). K.E.

FIGURATION, the transmutation of ideas into images, is the product of the formative power of human cognition and is realized in all the ways in which verbal, mental, perceptual, optical, and graphic images interact. F. punctuates the complexity of time and space with interpretable forms, including all kinds of signs; the very idea of an "idea" is linked to seeing and hence to the *eidolon* or "visible image." Platonic trad. distinguishes between idea and image (q.v.) by conceiving of the former as a suprasensible realm of forms, types, or species and the latter as a sensory impression that provides a mere likeness (*eikon*). Mental imagery or f. has been a central concern of theories of mind since Plato's cave allegory in the *Republic* and Aristotle's *On Interpretation* and continues to be a cornerstone of psychology, as in Gestalt construction of images. And at least since Macrobius' commentary on the Dream of Scipio in Cicero's *Orator*, dreams and esp. visions have been understood as interpretable in various figural senses.

While it is a function of allegory (q.v.) to personify abstractions, f. works in the reverse direction, treating real persons or things in a formulaic way so that they become concrete or living ideas grounded in a shared quality. In medieval literary fiction and interp., when the things treated are historical persons taking part in God's providential structuring of time (as in Dante's Comedy), imbuing them with the power to delineate events, the resulting narrative is called *figura* (Auerbach). Yet *figura* need not treat only Christian events; in the *Aeneid*, for example, the hero arrives at the site of Pallanteum just at the moment when the rites of Hercules are being performed. The day is to be interpreted as significant because this arrival re-

fers back to Hercules' own rescuing mission at the same site, and at the same time prefigures the advent of the emperor Augustus, Virgil's patron, at the same site again, fresh from his triumph over Antony and Cleopatra at Actium. For Dante, in turn, Aeneas' founding of Roman civilization not only facilitates but also prefigures the birth of Christ within the bounds of the Empire and the resulting renovation of humanity. *Figura*, or narrative typology, is thus but one specialized instance of f., which is essential to all interpretive strategies.

In the constitution of literary works, f. is the means whereby a system of beliefs and ideas is rendered palpable. A large quotient of figurative expression accounts for much of the traditional distrust of poetry among philosophers. Literary discourse provides authors with a great deal of latitude, whereas figures (taken in the sense of rhetorical strategies) which become part of ordinary lang. tend to lose their figural status. For example, Lat. *pastor* 'shepherd' was augmented by a Christian figurative meaning, "head of the congregation," an idea which has survived, defiguralized, in modern Eng. In texts, f. retains a strong visual connotation: when Walter Pater uses the term "figure" to represent the It. Ren., the model for the figure is always visual.

The history and theory of f. is, therefore, inextricably bound up with the status of images. Hume follows Locke and Hobbes in the use of pictorial figures to describe the chains of cognition and signification: ideas are "faint images" or "decayed sensations" that eventually become linked by conventional associations with words. The ensuing conception of meaning traces it back to its origin in an impression, with the consequent understanding of lang. as the means of retrieving that original impression. The view of poetry and of lang. in general as a process of pictorial reproduction exemplifies one idea of f. In romantic poetics (q.v.), verbal, mental, and pictorial imagery were assimilated to the process of imagination (q.v.) as redefined in opposition to the mere "recall" of mental pictures. Abrams finds that figures of expression come to replace figures of mimesis (see IMITATION) in the course of the 19th c. Indeed, an abstract figure such as the Coleridgean symbol displaces or subsumes the notion of the figure as a representation of material reality.

A progressive elevation or sublimation of the figure reaches its logical culmination when an entire poem is regarded as a figure, as in the "verbal icon" of Wimsatt, a synchronic structure embodying a complex figure. Poetic iconicity (q.v.) ranges from a literal basis in shaped and concrete poems (see PATTERN POETRY; CONCRETE POETRY; CALLIGRAMME), in which the text is charged with pictorial features, through forms such as the sestina (q.v.), in which f. is implicit, to ekphrastic poetry (see EKPHRASIS), where the text represents a work of visual art, to dialogue (q.v.) forms, which appropriately figure the dialectical method of argumentation.

Formalist crit. programmatically demonstrates the congruence or lack of congruence among a poem's propositional content, its architectonics, and its figurative energies so as to display the many dynamic patterns cohering within the whole. The concept of the entire poem as figure notwithstanding, the main direction of figurative interp. in the modern era has been to proceed from the manifest or surface content to the word conceived as latent meaning, lying beneath the aesthetic surface. Freud's *Interpretation of Dreams* while not a text of lit. crit., articulates a poetics of dreaming which assimilates the psychic material of which dreams are made to the material of visual art. Dream analysis provides strategies for extracting the hidden verbal message from a possibly misleading and certainly inarticulate pictorial surface, namely the four figurative processes of condensation, displacement, identification, and symbolism.

The symbolic connection of dreams to experience is thus one of f., wherein symbols and the things symbolized are integrated in a speculative reality in which they participate mutually. The establishment of such invisible bonds is characteristic of poetic conceptions of the universe, which may, for example, produce descriptions which intertwine physical setting and human emotion where connections of a causal type might otherwise have been invoked. Yet often a setting presented as figurative by a description, without overt justification, does the work of postulating so strong a participation between persons and environment that the smallest occurrence can assume permanent symbolic value. See now FIGURE, SCHEME, TROPE; ICONOLOGY; IMAGE; IMAGERY; INTERPRETATION, FOURFOLD METHOD; METAPHOR; PSYCHOLOGICAL CRITICISM; RHETORIC AND POETRY; SYMBOL.

Abrams; W. K. Wimsatt, Jr., *The Verbal Icon* (1954); S. Freud, *The Interp. of Dreams* (1955); E. Auerbach, "Figura," *Scenes from the Drama of European Lit.* (1959); A. Fletcher, *Allegory* (1964); F. E. Peters, *Gr. Philosophical Terms* (1967); E. Panofsky, *Idea* (1968); R. Jakobson, "Linguistics and Poetics," in Jakobson, v. 3; W. J. T. Mitchell, *Iconology* (1986); M. and M. Shapiro, *F. in Verbal Art* (1988).
M.S.

FIGURE, SCHEME, TROPE. F., s., and t. are parts of what is collectively called rhetorical or "figurative" lang. But the difficulty of distinguishing and relating these terms, or of giving a principled definition of any one of them, is well known, and writers from Quintilian (1st c. A.D.) to Fontanier (19th c.) and Todorov (20th) have customarily begun by discussing the limitations of all previous positions. The present article considers first some of the attempts at defining t. in terms of f., and f. in terms of t., then returns briefly to a consideration of s.

Discussions of f. and t. have traditionally used the philosophical and linguistic (semiotic) distinctions between word, or sign, and meaning to define t. as a delimited form of the more expansively conceived f. T. is defined by Quintilian (*Institutio oratoria*, ed. H. E. Butler, v. 3 [1920]) as "the artificial alteration of a word or phrase from its proper meaning to another," and f. as "a change in meaning or lang. from the ordinary and simple form"; for Fontanier (*Les Fs. du discours*, 2 v. [1827–30]), ts. are "all the fs. of discourse which consist of the *divergent meaning* of words, i.e. of a meaning more or less removed and different from their proper and literal meaning," and fs. are "the characteristics, forms and turns . . . by which discourse, in the expression of ideas, thoughts and feelings, stands more or less apart from what would have been their simple and common expression." Such classic formulations presuppose both a norm of "proper" meanings and "ordinary" usage from which ts. and fs. can then diverge (to which Todorov [1972] objects that, by this definition, "ordinary" lang. only becomes retrospectively—and inaccurately—viewed as lang. as it ought to be, "normal"), and also a qualitative distinction between changes in the meanings of words (ts.), and changes in the words and meanings of larger units of discourse (fs.). It would appear that there are only changes of meaning in the uses of individual words in such ts. as "rose" for a quality of affection or beauty in "My love is a rose" (metaphor), or "the White House" for the U. S. government (metonymy), or "hands" for seamen in "All hands on deck!" (synecdoche). But the words "rose," "the White House," or "hands" could not have any altered meaning as individual words (ts.) without an altered or at least specified context of *words and meanings* (fs.), following Austin's argument that individual words alone can never have any meaning at all without context (1961). T. could thus appear to be a compressed instance of f., and f. to be an expanded t.

With regard to ts. and fs. as nonliteral, altered, or improper uses of lang.'s words and meanings, this is an aspect of how rhetorical lang. itself has always been viewed. The varying characterizations of this "rhetorical" difference in lang.'s employment bring with them different considerations of t. and f. Plato's denigration of rhet. as manipulative and untruthful when measured against his model lang. of philosophy meant that ts. and fs. would primarily be characterized by falsehood (*Phaedrus*). Aristotle maintains Plato's view of rhet. as manipulative and less-than-philosophic but is appreciative of the pragmatic functions it serves; furthermore, he does not distinguish rhet. as "unlike" logic without at the same time noting the respects in which they are comparable or "like" (*homos*); he also characterizes his syllogistic reasoning as one form or f. of speech among others (*Rhetoric*). Shortly after Aristotle, rhetorical lang. receives its standard division into *inventio* (subjects, arguments, commonplaces), *dispositio* (arrangement of larger units of discourse such as exhortation, narration, peroration), and *elocutio* (choice and arrangement of specific words and phrases); fs. and ts. become simply parts of *elocutio*—which, after Ramus, we call "style" (q.v.)—constituting some of the verbal material of rhet.'s efforts at persuasion, incl. those of literary expression. Longinus similarly sees fs. in poetry as means for effecting emotional "elevation" of the audience (*Peri hypsos*). In Cicero (*De orat.*) and the anonymous *Rhetorica ad Herennium*, fs. of speech (*figurae dicendi*) appear to mean "modes of eloquence" and to designate different levels of style (the "grand" or "full," the middle, and the "simple" or "plain"; see STYLE). Dante refers to certain forms of allegory (q.v.), long classified as a f., as "truth hidden beneath a beautiful lie" (*De vulgari eloquentia*), and Fontanier writes of "fs. of expression" (or words; see below)—which include personification, allegory, allusion, paradox, and irony (qq.v.)—as offering "an apparent illusory meaning in order to allow you better to find or grasp the real and true meaning."

This brief survey of some notable conceptions of rhetorical lang. indicates that the alterations of "ordinary" usage in ts. and fs. may be variously analyzed as ones that change the true to the false, that shape or mold the unstylized into the highly embellished and specifically targeted, and ones that turn via the false or artificial to the true. The general insistence upon ts. and fs.'s divergence from a quasi-natural or basic norm is apparently preserved in the terms themselves, t. being from the Gr. *tropein*, "to turn," "to swerve," f. from the Lat. *figura*, "the made," "the shaped," "the formed." But this view reaches a *terminus ad quem* in accounting for one of the briefest and most common of ts., catachresis (q.v), or the forced (Gr. "abusive") attribution of a new meaning to a given word. Catachresis is not divergence from a literal meaning—in the sense of opposition to a word's proper meaning—but rather its and its word's *extension* to a place where there is no other sign (as in "*leg* of a chair" or "*wing* of a building"), which extension then itself becomes a necessary norm. Catachresis can thus be viewed either as the extension of literal lang. toward t., or as the entry of a t. (close to but more "basic" than metaphor) into "literal" lang. (Derrida).

Fs. function not only as extensions of ts. into larger units of discourse, but also as intrusions of rhet. into thought. In Cl. rhet., the traditional distinction between fs. of words and of thought (*figurae verborum* and *sententiarum*) attempts to address this problem. Quintilian claims that fs. of words always involve a changed aspect of lang. if not of thought (repetition, antithesis, asyndeton [qq.v.]), while fs. of thought always involve an artificial or contrived thought and may either leave lang. unchanged or be composed of several fs. of words. Fontanier similarly distinguishes between ts. (altered meanings of individual words), fs. of "expression" or words (in which the form, order, choice, or assortment of words is affected—e.g. allusion, litotes, inversion, apposition, ellipsis, apostrophe [qq.v.]), and fs. of thought (among which he counts prosopopoeia (q.v.), concession, and description). But there could not be a f. of words such as litotes without its intruding upon the *thought*—that, for example, "not unlike" is weaker than or at least different from "like"; and there could not be an apostrophe to something absent or ordinarily incapable of being an object of audible address without this affecting the thought of the expression. (This difficulty is evident in Quintilian categorizing apostrophe as a f. of thought, but Fontanier as a f. of "expression" or words.) Irony may not alter a single word from an ordinary expression in order to be manifest in a context—"I really like that" may ironically mean that one does not like it at all—and thus Quintilian understands it as a f. of thought; but for the very reason that such a f. involves divergence from—indeed, opposition to—a customary meaning of words, Fontanier considers irony to be a f. of "expression." Fs. of thought, then, may simply be extended instances of or views upon fs. of words: in each case, either words change, or meanings change, or both. Modern linguistics as well as ancient rhet. is hard put to find any instance of sheer fs. of words, in which only sounds or arrangements of words are involved (e.g. repetition, opposition, parallelism, alliteration, assonance [qq.v.]) that does not bring with it at least a minimal f.—alteration or artificing—of thought as well.

Ts. and fs. (with the possible exception of catachresis) may be said always to present two senses under the guise of a single verbal formulation: either they say something unexpected by way of a striking expression precisely because the expression or novel sense rebounds against an expected sense or usage which still attaches to the words in question; or they do not "say" it so much as they let it, contextually, be understood beneath (or even in spite of) the actual expression (as in allegory and irony). This effect of *doubling* a single word or expression's appearance or meaning may be construed as alteration of a first meaning by the addition of a second (Genette summarizes Fontanier's t. as "the *change* of meaning of a word") or as "the *substitution* of one expression for another" (Genette on Fontanier's f.). It allows lang.—which is necessarily thought at any given moment to have more or less customary and stable meanings and uses attached to it—to say and mean *more* or *something other* (to allegorize, from Gr. *allos-agoreuein*, "to speak otherwise"). Minimally, this suggests that ts. and fs. always involve at least the *relating* of other words, meanings, and usages to the ones at hand, or the *comparing* of various meanings for words (ts.) or of one arrangement or usage of words for another possible one (f.). In the 20th c., when figurative lang. has most often been studied as a part of poetics or literary stylistics (q.v.), this view has become part of a psychology of literary response, as in I. A. Richards' position that a metaphor allows two or more ideas of different things to be carried by a single word or expression (the "vehicle"), its meaning (the "tenor") resulting from their "interaction" (cf. Empson).

Opposed to these long-standing views of t. and f. as swerves from normal lang. usage, with their concomitant effects understood psychologically as an audience's reaction to such divergence, there have also been treatments of f. and t. as ineluctable discursive structures, fundamental to the organization of verbal experience and consciousness, and to the production of lang. and understanding themselves. Paul de Man considers the fs. of allegory and irony to be constitutive of interrelated treatments of temporality, allegory projecting a consciousness of meaning in relation to time along an axis of past and future—thus constituting narrative—irony doing so along an axis of a present moment divided between empirical and linguistic or "fictional" selves—thus constituting a divided self-consciousness ("The Rhet. of Temporality"). Roman Jakobson uses the structural linguistic (Saussurian) understanding that all lang. displays two axes of selection (similarity, the "paradigmatic" axis) and combination (contiguity, the "syntagmatic" axis) to argue that metaphor is essentially *selective*, metonymy essentially *combinatory*, and that all lang., incl. all lit., orients itself toward one or another of these principles of verbal organization (see METAPHOR; METONYMY)

With ts. (or fs.) such as allegory, irony, metaphor, and metonymy thus being held to generate literary texts and "original" verbal utterances, it is no longer a matter of t. being understood as a species of f., and f. as a special (divergent) kind of lang., but rather one of t. and f. being used to name and analyze lang. in its fundamental structures. A lineage for this view can be found in such diverse writers as Vico, Hamann ("Über den göttlichen und menschlichen Ursprung der Sprache" [On the Divine and Human Origin of Lang.], 1772), Rousseau ("Essai sur l'origine des langues" [Essay on the Origin of Langs.], 1817), and Nietzsche, who variously take the "origin" of lang. in t. or f. such as catachresis or metaphor (see ROMANTIC AND POSTROMANTIC POETICS). When Nietzsche says that one can only speak figuratively about the relations between lang., fs., and their meaning ("Über Wahrheit und Lüge im aussermoralischen Sinn" [1873]), he recalls Vico's effort to analyze historical "stages" of lang.-use with the names and structures of ts. and fs. (*Scienza nuova* [1725]; see also N. Frye, *The Great Code* [1982]) and anticipates de Man's view that attempts at historical understandings of lang., its origins, and its meanings (Rousseau's and Nietzsche's among them) necessarily show themselves to be ts. and fs., e.g. allegory, metonymy, metalepsis (de Man 1979, 1983; see also H. Bloom, *A Map of Misreading*

[1975], on lit. hist. as the tropological turns, displacements, or alterations of an earlier poet's lang. by later ones). Erich Auerbach shows that, for a millennium, the late Cl. and medieval Christian doctrine of figural exegesis extended *figura* from a domain of eloquence narrowly construed into the interrelations of figurative lang. with identifications of historical meaning.

Independent of these problems of a metalanguage of history being addressed to lang., nonhistorical analytic or descriptive lang. about lang. also appears to involve t. and f. Quintilian, defining t. generically as "transfer of expression," uses the technical term for metaphor (Gr. *metapherein*, "to carry over," "to transfer") to describe the set of which metaphor would be a member; and Fontanier concedes that to speak of "fs. of discourse" at all is itself *metaphoric*, using a metaphor (or perhaps a catachresis) from the traits, form, and contours of the body for those of lang. Derrida has analyzed this persistence of f. and t. in philosophy's discussion of the very terms. Jakobson, observing that "similarity in lang. connects the symbols of a metalanguage with the symbols of the lang. referred to" and that "similarity [the metaphoric pole] connects a metaphorical term with the term for which it is substituted," concludes that this dichotomy "appears to be of primal significance and consequence for all verbal behavior and for human behavior in general."

Whether or not all metalanguage is metaphorical—which would mean that all rhetorical (and grammatical and logical) treatises and also all linguistics are figurative—it is undeniable that all commentaries upon fs. and ts. are metalinguistic, i.e. substitutive, and thus, in the view running from Quintilian to Jakobson, tropaic. From the medieval *trivium* to Fontanier and much modern linguistics, understandings of figurative lang. have traditionally subordinated rhet. to grammar and grammar to logic, but this has not diminished the recurrent power of analyses of fs. and ts. to uncover a disruptive questioning of the ostensible "logic" of explanations of f. and t., and of the tropological forces at the basis of both lang. and metalanguage (de Man 1986). The argument that fs. and ts. are constitutive of and coextensive with lang. has as one of its consequences that lit. becomes not merely an occasion for "foregrounding" lang. or bringing it to consciousness—a view found from Hegel (*Vorlesungen über die Ästhetik*, v. 13–15 [1835–38]) to some Rus. Formalists and Czech and Fr. structuralists (e.g. Riffaterre 1971, 1978)—but also a privileged vehicle or avenue for access to the problems lang. poses for understanding, with de Man "calling 'literary,' in the full sense of the term, any text that implicitly or explicitly signifies its own rhetorical mode and prefigures its own misunderstanding as the correlative of its rhetorical nature; that is, of its 'rhetoricity'" (1986).

S., in its relation to f. and t., enters here as a summary instance of the breadth and complexity of figurative lang. and its understanding. S. in antiquity often means fs. of words and of thought (*schémata lexeós* and *dianoia*), and Cicero, the *Ad Herennium*, Quintilian, and later Ren. rhetoricians frequently appear to use the term for fs. of speech or levels of style. But in Cicero's Lat. trs. of Aristotelian and other Gr. uses of s. for outward appearances, semblances, or perceptible forms and shapes, it can also broadly represent thought and lang. in their relations to reality, its true perception and understanding. Thus Aristotle writes of his *schémata syllogismou*, and of the *schéma tés ideas* (*Metaphys.*), and the atomists Democritus and Lucretius consider ss. to emanate from bodies and to be like images (Auerbach). Kant uses s. to name an order of thought and lang. that cannot be known perceptually or empirically, but in relating s. to such fs. as hypotyposis and symbol, he reintroduces its imagistic and figurative ("shaped" or "formed") aspects (*Critique of Pure Reason, Critique of Judgment*). When one asks colloquially after "the s. of things," this trad. of forms and meanings is summarized as one invokes a nonobvious, nonvisual pattern or sense which attaches to things or events, but which nonetheless can be brought to lang. and thought in the form of a verbal image or narrative.

S. is scarcely used any longer to speak of figurative lang. in rhet. or lit. But it is schematization, in the wider sense of the tropaic rendering of appearances and meanings, that is recalled when de Man analyzes the t. of prosopopeia—from Gr. "to make or give a person or face," and once categorized as a f. of thought or a s. (see PUN)—as both materially a textual f. and, in its catachretic projections, a means by which "face" (Fr. *figure*) and voice are inscribed for lang., cognition, and consciousness ("Hypogram and Inscription," "Anthropomorphism and T. in the Lyric"). Prosopopeia and f., s., and t. are not unique or proper to certain forms of the lyric such as the elegy, the ode, or ekphrastic poetry, nor to lit. in general. Rather, poetry and poetics, to the extent that they can be said to be constructed exclusively of lang., are sites among others where f., s., and t. have been deposited as materials of lang. and modes of thought. See also FIGURATION; RHETORIC AND POETRY.

I. A. Richards, *The Philosophy of Rhet.* (1936); K. Burke, "Four Master Ts.," *A Grammar of Motives* (1945); W. Empson, *The Structure of Complex Words* (1951), *Seven Types of Ambiguity*, 3d ed. (1953); E. Auerbach, "Figura," *Scenes from the Drama of European Lit.* (1959); J. L. Austin, "The Meaning of a Word," *Philosophical Papers* (1961); G. Genette, *Fs.*, 3 v. (1966–72), selections tr. as *Fs. of Literary Discourse* (1982); R. Jakobson, "Two Aspects of Lang. and Two Types of Aphasic Disturbances," in Jakobson, v. 2; R. Lanham, *Handlist of Rhetorical Terms* (1968), 101–3; M. Riffaterre, *Essais de stylistique structurale* (1971), *Semiotics of Poetry* (1978); J. Derrida, "La Mythologie blanche," *Marges de la philosophie* (1972); T. Todorov, "Rhétorique et stylis-

tique" and "F.," *Dictionnaire encyclopédique des sciences du langage* (1972); Lausberg; D. Rice and P. Schofer, *Rhetorical Poetics* (1973); M. and M. Shapiro, *Hierarchy and the Structure of Ts.* (1976); Group Mu, 45—schematic taxonomy; *Rhet. Revalued*, ed. B. Vickers (1982); P. de Man, "The Rhet. of Temporality," and "The Rhet. of Blindness," *Blindness and Insight*, 2d ed. (1983), "Anthropomorphism and T. in the Lyric," *The Rhet. of Romanticism* (1984), "Hypogram and Inscription" and "The Resistance to Theory," *The Resistance to Theory* (1986); R. J. Fogelin, *Figuratively Speaking* (1988). T.B.

FIGURES, METRICAL. See METRICAL TREATMENT OF SYLLABLES.

FIGURES, RHETORICAL. See FIGURE, SCHEME, TROPE; FIGURATION; RHETORIC AND POETRY.

FILI (pl. *filid[h]*, Modern Ir. *file*, pl. *filí*) has always been the Ir. word for poet, and it is unfortunate that a considerable body of Ir. poetry, (*filidheacht, filíocht*) is called in Eng. "bardic" poetry, with the misleading suggestion that it is the work of the Ir. bard (pl. *baird*; see BARD). The word *f.* is cognate with the Welsh *gwel(-ed)* ("to see") and originally the *f.* was the "seer," the "diviner"; hence it does not occasion surprise that *f.* and *druí* ("druid") were at one time interchangeable words, and that some of the knowledge of the *f.* was then regarded as knowledge gained by means of occult practices. However, the *f.* gained most of his knowledge by the more usual process of learning at school—there were special schools for *filid*—and the knowledge thus gained was always regarded as an important part of his qualifications. The *f.* in earlier times was not sharply distinguished from the *breithem*, "judge" (literally, the maker of judgments) and the *senchaid*, "historian," "reciter of lore"; indeed, it is possible that at one time he combined their functions with his own, and that their emergence as separate classes is the result of specialization. The *f.* was from the beginning a member of an important and highly organized corporation classed among the *saer-nemed* (privileged classes). There were seven grades of *filid*, the highest being the *ollam filed*, a fully qualified *f.* appointed to the service of a king. A *f.* was usually attached to the household of a chief, his calling was hereditary, and the office of *f.* to the head of a clan was, in later times at any rate, often the prerogative of a particular family. He was at all times distinguished from the *bard*, whose qualifications and status were inferior. The word *bard* is derived from the Celtic *bardos*, who, among the Gauls, was predominantly the "singer of praise." It is sometimes assumed that the *f.* arrogated to himself the function of the *bard* as a singer of praise (as well as a proclaimer of satire) and that this function as such was overshadowed by those which he must have undertaken in part from the druid at the advent of

FINNISH POETRY

Christianity. However that may be, singing the praise of his chief was the foremost function of the *f.* in the Middle Ages.—G. Murphy, "Bards and Filidh," *Éigse* 2 (1940); J. E. C. Williams, "The Court Poet in Med. Ireland," *PBA* 57 (1971); P. A. Breatnach, "The Chief's Poet," *Proc. of the Irish Royal Academy* 83, C, 3 (1983).   J.E.C.W.

FINE ARTS AND POETRY. See MUSIC AND POETRY; SCULPTURE AND POETRY; VISUAL ARTS AND POETRY.

FINIDA. In 14th- to early 16th-c. Sp. poetry the f. is the approximate equivalent of the *remate* (q.v.) of the later *canción petrarquista.* Lang says: "Like the Provençal *tornada,* the f. serves as a conclusion to a poem, and with the *tornada* and kindred forms, such as the *envoi,* the *desfecha,* the *estribote* and others, this stanza was originally, in all probability, a sequence to a musical composition. According to the *Leys d'Amors,* the *tornada* repeats in its rhyme-order the second part of the last stanza in case this has the same number of verses; otherwise it may have one verse more or less than the last half-stanza. In the Portuguese. . . the *f.,* which is regarded as essential to a perfect composition, may have from one to four verses, and must rhyme with the last stanza or, if the poem be a *cantiga de refram,* with the refrain. The practitioners of the *Cancionero de Baena* (ca. 1450) appear to have followed the example of the Provençals and Catalans."—H. R. Lang, "Las formas estróficas y términos métricos del Cancionero de Baena," *Estudios eruditos "in memoriam" de Adolfo Bonilla y San Martin,* v. 1 (1927); Le Gentil; Navarro.   D.C.C.

FINNISH POETRY.

I. THE BEGINNINGS
II. THE RISE OF FINNISH POETIC LANGUAGE
III. THE MODERN PERIOD

F. p. has developed over a long history, though the oldest extant texts written in F. date only from the middle of the 19th c., and though some of its classics were initially written in Swedish. It presents a complex history of cultural and literary influence, but thematically and taken as a whole, it shows a remarkably unified inspiration from early oral trad. to contemp. modernism. F., which is not an Indo-European lang., has developed alongside the Indo-European family of langs. at the periphery of European civilization.

I. THE BEGINNINGS. A rich treasury of oral-traditional songs and tales is extant, incl. ca. 1,270,000 lines and 85,000 variants of the poetry composed in the so-called *Kalevala* meter (trochaic tetrameter in its simplest form). These are traditionally the work of anonymous singers, both men and women, but some of the principal singers are known by name, such as Arhippa Perttunen and Ontrei Malinen, both of whom were important sources for Elias Lönnrot's compilations, the epic

Kalevala (1835, 1849), and the *Kanteletar,* a collection of lyrics and short narrative poems (1840–41). F. folk p. consists of elements dating from different periods and deriving from various cultural strata. There is evidence of the existence of a vital oral poetry before the period of Swedish expansion during the 12th c. which brought Christianity to Finland. Finno-Ugric mythology, based on animistic and shamanistic religion, is an intrinsic part of the early cosmogonic poems, magic songs, and ritual incantations of this trad. Medieval Christianity introduced new elements to F. folk p. Ballads, legends, and lamentations express both religious and secular themes. In an exquisite cycle about the birth of Christ, a F. maiden, Marjatta, a variant of the Virgin Mary, becomes pregnant by eating cranberries (F. *marja*). The religious basis of these poems, which were composed afresh by individual singers according to their poetic skill, derives from a fusion of Catholic and Gr. Orthodox beliefs.

While oral poetry survived among the illiterate and in the agrarian parts of Finland, its importance decreased as other attempts were made to forge the F. lang. into a literary medium. One such attempt is Mikael Agricola's 1548 tr. of the New Testament, an important linguistic landmark as well as one of the first literary monuments of the Protestant era. At the end of the 17th c., Lat. and Swedish-lang. poetry were composed but did not rise much above the level of conventional verse. It was not until the recovery of the oral trads. in the 18th c., inaugurated by the study of F. folk p. (e.g. Henrik Gabriel Porthan's *De poesi fennica* [1766–78]), that F.-lang. p. began to emerge from obscurity. The realization that the F. people had created poetry worthy of comparison with the *Iliad* and the *Odyssey* had an enormous impact in Finland. The following lines by Arhippa Perttunen illustrate what could be discovered on native ground:

My own finding are my words
my own snatching from the road
my grinding from the grass tops
my snapping from the heather.
          (tr. K. Bosley)

II. THE RISE OF FINNISH POETIC LANGUAGE. While Swedish-lang. poetry of European orientation dominated literary production in Finland, and while the relatively scarce examples of early F.-lang. p. belong to the didactic and exhortatory trad. of the Enlightenment, the termination of Swedish rule in 1809 brought about an altogether new situation. A few Swedish-lang. poets, such as Frans Mikael Franzén (1772–1847), whose poetry expressed a strong preromantic conception of nature and of man as divine creation, were also influential in the devel. of F. p. When the Napoleonic wars resulted in a redistribution of the northern territories of Europe, Finland fell under Rus. rule as a virtually autonomous Grand Duchy in 1809. This situation compelled the Finns, incl. the Swed-

FINNISH POETRY

ish Finns, to turn their philosophical and literary attention to questions of F. national identity. Helsinki became the center of F. cultural and literary life. The University was moved there from Turku in 1827, the F. Lit. Society was founded in 1831, and the newspaper *Helsingfors Tidningar* began to appear in 1829. J. L. Runeberg (1804–77) became the foremost Swedish-lang. poet of the time with his *Dikter* (Poems, 1830). Combining a deep feeling for simple country folk with expert knowledge of both Cl. lit. and F. oral trad., Runeberg renewed lyrical lang. with his mastery of technique. His epic poems (in hexameters), e.g. the *Elgskyttarne* (The Elkhunters, 1832), a narrative about love and hunting, demonstrate how Cl. style can be effectively used to describe humble country life. His romanticism, both lyrical and patriotic, may be seen as an important precursor of the F.-lang. p. which emerged in the 1860s.

The poet Runeberg, the philosopher and writer J. W. Snellman (1806–81), Elias Lönnrot (1802–84), and the writer and poet Zachris Topelius (1818–98) all shaped the F. national consciousness and cultural identity, but conditions were not yet ripe for the production of F. p. of merit. Lönnrot showed some genuine poetic talent in assembling the epic *Kalevala* by introducing lyric material into the narratives, adding songs, and replacing missing lines according to his vision. But the pre-eminent figure at the time was Aleksis Kivi (pseud. of Alexis Stenvall, 1834–72), primarily a playwright and novelist whose poetic achievement was not fully recognized until this century. Kivi's contemporaries considered his poetry unfinished: it was more daring and personal than anything written at the time. Many of his poems were lyrical narratives which broke away from rhyming verse and used free rhythms, creating an intensity familiar from the folk lyric.

After Kivi, there were no major poets until the end of the 19th c., though Kaarlo Kramsu (1855–95) and J. H. Erkko (1849–1906) played an important role in forging a F. poetic that could effectively express new social and historical themes. Industrialization, educational reforms, and new scientific thought were reflected in the work of F. novelists and dramatists, who explored the forms of European realism (q.v.) in the 1880s. Swedish-lang. poetry was mainly represented by the verse drama *Daniel Hjort* (1862) by J. J. Wecksell (1832–1907), and by the poetry of Karl August Tavaststjerna (1860–98), who reflects the new sense of alienation felt by the Swedish-speaking writers, whose minority status was becoming increasingly apparent.

National Neoromanticism was the term coined by the poet Eino Leino (1878–1926) to characterize certain currents in F. lit. and the fine arts influenced by European symbolism (q.v.). It combined enthusiasm, determination, and outstanding talent in all fields: the composer Jean Sibelius, the painter Akseli Gallen-Kallela, and the archi-

tect Eliel Saarinen were all representatives of "Young Finland." A prolific poet, Leino developed an innovative technique which radically changed the F. poetic idiom. Leino put the stamp of originality on everything he wrote. While drawing upon traditional sources such as myth and folk poetry for themes and motifs, he was fully versed in European and Scandinavian lit., and translated Dante, Corneille, Racine, Goethe, and Schiller. His *Helkavirsiä* (Whitsongs, 1903, 1916) recreate the most ancient folk trads. in narrative lyrics of visionary character having a symbolic resonance that transcends the national sphere. Leino's lyrical lang. is supple and resourceful: in "Nocturne" (from *Talvi-yö* [Winter Night], 1905), the melodious lines evoke the infinite in a clearly defined space:

> The corncrake's song rings in my ears,
> above the rye a full moon sails;
> this summer night all sorrow clears
> and woodsmoke drifts along the dales.
> (tr. K. Bosley)

The inner dynamics of Leino's poetry spring from a fruitful tension between an ultra-individualistic, egocentric, amoral *übermensch* and a prophet-seer who could capture and articulate the complex spirit of his epoch. Several of his contemporaries added other elements to the vigorously developing F. poetic lang. L. Onerva (1882–1972) lent a free spirit to explorations of femininity in sensual lyric verse, while Otto Manninen (1872–1950) and V. A. Koskenniemi (1885–1964) wrote in the European classic mode. Manninen, a virtuoso poet, wrote clear, concise verse on symbolist themes and translated Homer, Gr. tragedy, and Molière. Koskenniemi, whose work now seems dated, expressed his pessimistic philosophy in tightly controlled verse inspired by ancient poetry. By 1920 F. poetic lang. had attained a variety and depth that guaranteed it a worthy place among European lits. With Finland's independence in 1917, poetry reconfirmed its central role in the expression of both individual and social sentiments.

III. THE MODERN PERIOD. While Leino has a strikingly modern timbre at times, modernism apppeared in F. p. shortly after World War I in the unique work of the Swedo-F. modernists (q.v.), such as Edith Södergran (1892–1923) and Elmer Diktonius (1896–1961). Literary modernism coincided with anti-positivism in philosophy and was a reaction against 19th-c. empiricism and realism. In the 1920s, European movements such as futurism, cubism, constructivism, expressionism, and surrealism (qq.v.) arrived in Finland almost simultaneously. Denying the ability of art to describe reality, the new poets increasingly turned away from mimetic art even as they rejected the past and everything connected with it. This was first seen in lang. experiments, e.g. in *Jääpeili* (Ice Mirror, 1928) by Aaro Hellaakoski's (1896–1952), in the poetry of Katri Vala (1901–44), in the prose of Olavi Paavolainen (1903–64), and in the early work of P. Mustapää (1899–1973). The new generation that brought modernism to Finland formed a group called the "Firebearers," publishing albums and a journal of that name, *Tulenkantajat*. The Firebearers issued a manifesto in 1928, declaring the sacredness of art and life in tones reminiscent of the writings of the Swedo-F. modernists, but with an even greater fervor and passion. Katri Vala and Uuno Kailas (1901–33) expressed these ideals. Kailas was influenced by expressionism, while Vala, the most typical of the Firebearers, later became a politically committed leftist poet. Another literary group, "Kiila" (The Wedge), devoted itself to radical socialism after 1936. Arvo Turtiainen (1904–80), Viljo Kajava (b. 1909), and the novelist Elvi Sinervo (1912–86) were among its most important members, many of whom were imprisoned during World War II. The nation, divided by the Civil War (1918–19) following F. Independence, unified again for the effort of the Winter War, but the schism was not closed until the postwar era, as is described by Väinö Linna (b. 1920) in his epic trilogy *Täällä Pohjantähden alla* (Here under the North Star, 1959–62).

In the 1950s, poetic modernism became more sharply antitraditionalist. While drawing inspiration from both East and West, its lang., characterized by free rhythms and powerful imagery, turned hermetic. Paavo Haavikko (b. 1931), Eeva-Liisa Manner (b. 1921), Helvi Juvonen (1919–59), and Eila Kivikkaho (b. 1921) were among the most important poets, followed by other original talents such as Mirkka Rekola (b. 1931), Tyyne Saastamoinen (b. 1924), Lassi Nummi (b. 1928), and Pentti Holappa (b. 1927). Pentti Saarikoski (1937–83), whose first collection, *Runoja* (Poems), appeared in 1958, is not tied to any movement or decade. Saarikoski, a maverick genius and iconoclast, was one of the most learned of modern F. poets, as well as a translator of Homer, Euripides, Joyce, and others. With his *Mitä tapahtuu todella?* (What Is Going On, Really?, 1962) F. poetic lang. was taken to a new level where everything had to start from point zero in order to go on: the split word, the word mobile, the collage, and the explicit rejection of poetic structure all conveyed a sense of both freedom and despair. Saarikoski's work culminated in a long, free-floating philosophical poem, *Hämärän tanssit* (The Dances of the Obscure, 1983; written during the period when the poet lived in Sweden), that expresses the poet's yearning for beauty and the unification of all living things.

Haavikko and Manner, in their different ways, have been regarded as the leading F. modernists. Haavikko, director of a Helsinki publishing house, uses compelling rhythmic sequences and incantations to express, through a series of negatives, abstractions, and ironies, his skepticism about the relationship of lang. to the external world. It is an original vision, and in 1984 Haavikko received the Neustadt Prize for his achievement. Manner has explored the conflict between magical order and logical disorder, as she calls it, and has brought to F. p., from her breakthrough collection *Tämä matka* (This Journey, 1956) on, a mythical dimension, a lang. suggestive of another reality.

F. p. in the 1980s shows an unprecedented diversity; all directions seem possible. Among the poets writing in contemp. Finland are Sirkka Turkka (b. 1939), Kari Aronpuro (b. 1940), Pentti Saaritsa (b. 1941), Kirsti Simonsuuri (b. 1945), Caj Westerberg (b. 1946), and Arja Tiainen (b. 1947). Both poetry and prose occupy an important place in cultural life. Swedo-F. modernists like Bo Carpelan (b. 1926) and Solveig von Schoulz (b. 1907) have carried on the earlier modernist trad. while adding new elements. In the 1980s, one is justified in speaking of F. p. as including all verse written by Finns, whether in Swedish or F. and whether in- or outside Finland.

ANTHOLOGIES AND TRANSLATIONS: *Moderne Finnische Lyrik*, ed. and tr. M. P. Hein (1962); *Suomen kirjallisuuden antologia I–VIII*, ed. K. Laitinen and M. Suurpää (1963–75); P. Haavikko, *Sel. Poems*, tr. A. Hollo (1974); *F. Folk P.: Epic*, ed. and tr. M. Kuusi et al. (1977); E. Leino, *Whitsongs*, tr. K. Bosley (1978); *Snow in May*, ed. R. Dauenhauer and P. Binham (1978); *Territorial Song: F. P. and Prose*, tr. H. Lomas (1981); P. Saarikoski, *Sel. Poems*, tr. A. Hollo (1983); E. Södergran, *Complete Poems*, tr. D. McDuff (1983), *Love and Solitude*, tr. S. Katchadourian (1985); *Salt of Pleasure: 20th-C. F. P.*, ed. and tr. A. Jarvenpa and K. B. Vähämäki (1983); *Mod. finlandssvensk Lyrik*, ed. C. Andersson and B. Carpelan (1986); B. Carpelan, *Room Without Walls: Sel. Poems*, tr. A. Born (1987); *The Kalevala*, tr. K. Bosley (1989); *Poésie et prose de Finlande*, ed. M. Bargum (1989); *Enchanting Beasts: An Anthol. of Mod. Women Poets in Finland*, ed. and tr. K. Simonsuuri (1990).

HISTORY AND CRITICISM: E. Enäjärvi-Haavio, "On the Performance of F. Folk Runes," *Folkliv* (1951); J. Ahokas, *Hist. of F. Lit.* (1974); *Mod. Nordic Plays: Finland*, ed. E. J. Friis (1974); T. Wretö, *Johan Ludvig Runeberg* (1980); *The Two Lits. of Finland*, spec. iss. of *WLT* 54 (Winter 1980); M. Kuusi and L. Honko, *Sejd och Saga: Den finska forndiktens historia* (1983); T. Warburton, *Åttio år finlandssvensk litteratur* (1984); G. Schoolfield, *Edith Södergran: Modernist Poet in Finland* (1984); K. Simonsuuri, "The Lyrical Space: The Poetry of Paavo Haavikko," *WLT* 58 (1984); *Europe: Littérature de Finlande*, (June–July 1985); K. Laitinen, *Lit. of Finland: An Outline* (1985), *Finlands Litteratur* (1988); P. Leino, *Lang. and Metre: Metrics and the Metrical System of F.*, tr. A. Chesterman (1986).

K.K.S.

FLAMENCA. See SEGUIDILLA.

FLEMISH POETRY. See BELGIAN POETRY, *In Dutch*; DUTCH POETRY.

FLESHLY SCHOOL OF POETRY. The name applied by Robert Buchanan to Rossetti, Swinburne, and Morris in an article in the October 1871 issue of the *Contemp. Rev.* Rossetti's recently pub. *Poems* (1870), esp. "Nuptial Sleep" and "Jenny," provided the chief target. Buchanan's main objections to the "School" were that they treated the human body with undue freedom and preferred form to substance: "The fleshly gentlemen have bound themselves . . . to extol fleshliness as the distinct and supreme end of poetic and pictorial art; to aver that poetic expression is greater than poetic thought, and by inference that the body is greater than the soul, and sound superior to sense." Buchanan's article had been pub. under a pseudonym, and Rossetti, hypersensitive to crit., chose to focus on this aspect of the attack in his reply, "The Stealthy School of Crit." He denied that his poems, taken as a whole, were "fleshly," or that they lacked a large human theme. Buchanan then expanded his article (under his own name) to a general onslaught against "Sensualism," to which Swinburne replied in a savage pamphlet, *Under the Microscope.* The controversy, which had begun with Buchanan's review of Swinburne's *Poems and Ballads* in 1866 and culminated in Buchanan's successful lawsuit against Swinburne's publisher in 1876, had more to do with personalities than with a critical issue. Nonetheless, there was an issue, that of the freedom of the artist to treat sexual themes. Buchanan claimed that he admired the frank sexuality of Chaucer and Rabelais and only objected to the sickly and self-conscious preoccupation with sex of the F. S., but others have found Buchanan's imagination prurient. In the end, Buchanan recanted and apologized, but not before his reputation had been (somewhat unfairly) destroyed.—T". Maitland," "The F. S. of P.: Mr. D. G. Rossetti," *Contemp. Rev.* 18 (1871), expanded and pub. under Buchanan's own name as *The F. S. of P. and Other Phenomena of the Day* (1872); D. G. Rossetti, "The Stealthy School of Crit.," *Athenaeum* (Dec. 16, 1871); A. C. Swinburne, *Under the Microscope* (1872); O. Doughty, *Dante Gabriel Rossetti* (1949); J. H. Buckley, "The Fear of Art," *The Victorian Temper* (1951); J. A. Cassidy, "Robert Buchanan and the F. Controversy," *PMLA* 67 (1952); C. D. Murray, "The F. S. Revisited," *BJRL* 65 (1982–83). A.D.C.

FLYTING, fliting, is an exchange of verbal abuse, sometimes as highly flamboyant and exaggerated invective, sometimes as insult and boast in anticipation of martial combat. The term is primarily associated with Scottish tradition, whose 15th–16th-c. efflorescence produced such fs. as "The F. of Dunbar and Kennedie" and "Polwart and Montgomerie F." and whose influence was probably felt by John Skelton and, in this century, by Hugh M. Diarmid. Akin to Med. Fr. and Occitan forms such as the *tenso* and *sirventes* (qq.v.), while probably drawing most directly on Gaelic sources,

Scottish f. is marked by its vivid lang., hyperbolic slander, and underlying playfulness. Analogues can be found in other cultures (Gr., Arabic, Celtic, It.) as well as in contemporary popular culture; see POETIC CONTESTS.

Contrasting with these essentially ludic encounters are the fs. of heroes in epic and romance, e.g. *The Iliad, Beowulf,* and *Sir Gawain and the Green Knight.* Intended and received seriously, these volleys of boast and insult are exchanged in the expectation of battle or some other heroic exploit to which the participants are publicly committing themselves. See now INVECTIVE.—A. M. Mackenzie, *Hist. Survey of Scottish Lit. to 1714* (1933); J. Huizinga, *Homo Ludens* (1944); *The Poems of William Dunbar,* ed. J. Kinsley (1979); C. Clover, "The Germanic Context of the Unferth Episode," *Speculum* 55 (1980); P. Bawcutt, "The Art of F.," *ScLJ* 10 (1983); W. Parks, *Verbal Dueling in Heroic Narrative* (1989). W.W.P.

FOLÍA. Sp. stanza form. A popular 4-line variation of the *seguidilla* (q.v.) probably related to a Portuguese dance-song form and normally expressing a nonsensical or ridiculous thought. The lines may be octosyllabic or shorter; if the lines are not of equal length, the even-numbered are generally the shorter and very often—some think properly so—oxytonic. Its origin is unknown, but *folias* antedating 1600 are extant. This example is from Cervantes' *Rinconete y Cortadillo*: "Por un sevillano / rufo a lo valón / tengo socarrado / todo el corazón." D.C.C.

FOLK POETRY. See ORAL POETRY.

FOOT.

    I. CLASSICAL
    II. MODERN

I. CLASSICAL. The f. (Gr. *pous,* Lat. *pes,* Sanskrit *mātrā* "measure," Fr. *pied,* Ger. *Takt* or *Versfuss*) was a basic analytical unit for the prosodic analysis of verse in both the metrical and the musical theories of the ancient Greeks and Romans (see METRICI AND RHYTHMICI), consisting, in metrical theory, of syllables, and in musical theory of abstract temporal units (*morae*) measured in terms of the *chronos prōtos* ("primary time"). These fundamental elements, syllables or times, were organized at one higher level into *arsis* and *thesis* (q.v.), the two components—in most ancient accounts—of every metrical f. Thus, combining two definitions given separately in the scholia to Hephaestion (2d. c. A.D.), Marius Victorinus writes, "the f. is a definite measure of syllables, consisting of arsis and thesis, by which we recognize the form of the entire meter" (6.43, in Keil). Ancient theory classified feet according to (1) the ratio of the duration of arsis to thesis (musically, in terms of "primary times"; metrically, in terms of *breve* = 1, *longum* = 2), and (2) the overall duration of the f. The scheme for the simple feet of Gr. verse is as follows:

genos ison (1:1):

| tetrasemic: | anapaest | ($\cup\cup-$) |
| | dactyl | ($-\cup\cup$) |

genos diplasion (2:1, 1:2):

trisemic:	iamb	($\cup-$)
	trochee	($-\cup$)
hexasemic:	ionic *a minore*	
		($\cup\cup--$)
	ionic *a maiore*	
		($--\cup\cup$)

genos hēmiolion (3:2, 2:3):

pentasemic:	first paeon	
		($-\cup\cup\cup$)
	cretic	($-\cup-$)
	bacchiac	($\cup--$).

Other ratios are also found, and an *alogos* (Gr. "irrational") ratio, not expressible in terms of the lower integers, was also asserted by some.

Unfortunately, we do not have extant any complete exposition of ancient theory with illustrative analyses of extended passages of lyric verse; even in antiquity there were various not completely compatible accounts. Attempts in the 19th c. to interpret ancient theory and apply it to lyric verse, particularly to aeolic (q.v.) meters, did not achieve satisfying results (Westphal). In the 20th c., Cl. prosodists have generally rejected both the reality and the descriptive utility of the f. in favor of units defined strictly in terms of response (q.v.) such as the *metron* (double the length of the simple feet in some meters, and indistinguishable in others; see METRON) and the *colon* (a longer metrical sequence having continuity [see SYNAPHEIA; COLON]).

This rejection, however, has impoverished metrical theory and tended to sever it from its linguistic basis. The f. is the principal unit of rhythmic organization in human behavior and perception: its two primary attributes are temporal regularity and internal prominence differentiation. When subjects in experiments are presented with a sequence of identical or different stimuli ranging from roughly 0.5 to 8 times per second, they rapidly (and involuntarily) perceive and learn a rhythmic pattern. The most favored f. structure in such patterns has two differentiated elements. Acoustic stimuli that are differentiated are perceived as strong and weak on the basis of their differences in intensity, duration, and frequency. Trochaic feet are perceived if the strong element is louder, and iambic feet if it is (significantly) longer. Many langs. have stress on alternating syllables, so that one stressed and one unstressed syllable form a binary f.; ternary systems are rare. Linguistic feet also have some degree of temporal regularity; though they are not strictly isochronous (see ISOCHRONISM), they seem so to listeners. Verse achieves greater regularity than speech by constraining the number of permissible feet. See also ARSIS AND THESIS; CLASSICAL PROSODY; METER;

METRON; PERIOD; RHYTHM; SYSTEM.

F. de Saussure, "Une loi rythmique de la langue grecque," *Mélanges Graux* (1884); Wilamowitz, chs. 3–4, esp. 73, 103; Beare, p. 77; Koster, II.3 ff.; Maas; Dale, 210 ff.; E. Pöhlmann, *Denkmäler altgriechischer Musik* (1970); W. S. Allen, *Accent and Rhythm* (1973), 122 ff.; A. J. Neubecker, *Altgriechische Musik* (1977); Michealides, s.v. "Pous"; West, 6, 195; A. M. Devine and L. D. Stephens, *Lang. and Metre* (1984), "Stress in Greek?" *TAPA* 115 (1985).

A.M.D.; L.D.S.

II. MODERN. The Ren. prosodists and critics, in reaction against medievalism, looked back to Cl. antiquity for doctrine on the making of poetry. Many speak of verse being organized only by syllable count "with some regard of the accent" (Sidney), but British schoolchildren from Shakespeare through Coleridge learned to scan and write the forms of the Lat. feet at school, and Donne in "A Litanie" speaks of "rhythmique Feete." In the early Tudor poets one finds lines which are clearly composed by feet: they have bisyllabic segmentation to excess (Wright). But the better poets soon discovered that the verse paradigms they learned at school were susceptible of manipulation at a higher level of sophistication; insensibly, they began to forget writing verse by thinking in feet, foot by foot, and to write lines which evolved into something which could be composed, and understood, without the need for mechanistic rules, yet which could still be scanned—though more complexly—by such rules. Scholarly treatises on prosody continued to teach the doctrine of feet literally for centuries.

Further, from ca. 1550 up to at least 1900, most Western metrical theories derived from Cl. prosody, as that was understood (reinterpreted) in successive eras—particularly in the 19th c., which saw the rise of Cl. Philology in Germany. Common to all these theories was the presumption that in metrical lines, syllables are to be taken together in groups, as intralinear metrical units; such units occupy a position in the theory midway between the metrical position (syllable) and the line. Both the concept of the metrical f. itself and, in addition, the particular names and forms of the feet were taken directly from Gr., all of them being redefined as the accentual equivalents of the identical patterns in the quantitative prosody of Cl. Gr. Thus the Gr. iamb, short + long, was reformulated as nonstress + stress. The Gr. notion of the metron (q.v.) in certain meters was ignored. Many prosodists continued to *talk* of longs and shorts (see ACCENT)—indeed, for centuries—but the basis of most Western meters had in fact been stress since about the 4th c. A.D. Whether or not the f. was an element of poetic composition, or merely of analysis—i.e. scansion (q.v.)—remained an issue of dispute.

How many types of feet were permitted? Even well into the 20th c., Classicizing prosodists were inclined to admit nearly as many feet in Eng.

poetry as in Gr.: Saintsbury lists 21 feet (1.xvii); Fussell as late as 1979 admits 6 but thinks "it does no harm to be acquainted with" 11 others. But by far the majority (even Schipper, otherwise very Classicist) recognized, by the late 19th c., only 4 to 6 meters: the two commonest binary—iambic and trochaic—and ternary—dactylic and anapestic—meters, with the latter two far less common than the former (see BINARY AND TERNARY), and (for some metrists) the spondee and pyrrhic. A very few other meters, such as amphibrachs, are so rare as to constitute experiments. Some structural linguists admitted many more types of feet by making dinstinctions on the basis of linguistic features: thus Chatman has 32 types, based on whether the stresses fall in mono- or polysyllables; he then groups these into two classes of two categories each (total four) based on whether the stresses are natural (*meter-fixing*) or promoted-demoted (*meter-fixed*). Epstein and Hawkes (see Brogan) admit a staggering 6192 types of iambs and 2376 types of trochees by factoring all possible combinations of the acoustic features of syllables. But these schemes overspecify, and in that, fall prey to a fundamental confusion of (conventional) meter with (linguistic) rhythm: this way madness lies. The actual number of f.-types in Eng. poetry is somewhere between two and five, depending on what criteria are applied (see below).

In the general repudiation, after 1920, of the convoluted attempts by Classicizing prosodists such as Schipper and Saintsbury to map the forms and rules of Cl. prosody directly onto Eng., a reaction abetted without doubt by the rising influence of free verse (q.v.) and other footloose prosodies, the concept of the metrical f. was widely discredited. And, given the grounds on which it had been justified, deservedly so. On the other hand, hasty dismissals always smack of the genetic fallacy. Less hastily, there are at least four grounds on which one might yet hold that the f. is a necessary and authentic component of *any* viable theory of meter, hence of Eng. meters in particular, at least of the high artverse (pentameter) trad.:

(1) *The very concept of meter* as "measure" (q.v.), i.e. the measuring-out of the flow of words in the line. Measuring requires a unit by which the measuring is done, like inches on a ruler, whose dividing lines are fictitious—but necessary—as are, too, the bar lines on a musical score.

(2) *Comparative metrics*. There is at least one metrical unit between the levels of syllable and line in every known verse system in the world. These vary in positioning and scope, of course. In the Romance prosodies, such as Fr., the units are formed at the phrasal level, not at the word-, as in the Germanic. And recently the f. theory has even been applied to OE prosody (Russom). From the point of view of comparative metrics, Gr. prosody has no *a priori* authority—despite the fact that elements of several Western verse-systems were subsequently derived from it, directly or indi-

rectly—except insofar as it can be shown to have identified types of structures that are demonstrable in other lits.

(3) *The structure of the lang. itself.* A number of 20th-c. linguists have developed the conept of a "stress group," which several have even called a "f." In Britain, Abercrombie, followed by Halliday, designated the f. as a stress *followed* by one or more optional unstressed syllables, one or more feet then comprising a "tone group," the last of which (usually) bears the sentence accent. In America, Liberman and Prince, followed by Selkirk, developed a similar concept of the f. in phonology, only over a slightly smaller domain: Selkirk also distinguishes a "prosodic word." Indeed much of the terminology of traditional verse-theory was appropriated, in the 1970s and '80s, for the theory of autosegmental or "metrical" phonology (see ACCENT).

(4) *Perceptual psychology and cognitive science.* There is evidence which suggests that segmentation or grouping is a natural process manifested in the perception of any rhythmic series (see RHYTHM). It is one of the central tenets of modern verse theory that verse, like lang. and all information delivery processes, segments the soundstream into units which are set in a relation of correspondence or equivalence (q.v.; see De Groot; Jakobson) with one another and organized into hierarchies. Thus *segmentation* and *repetition* (q.v.) have come to seem fundamental cognitive and aesthetic processes. As Scott remarks, "we must suppose that any sequence of stresses with a degree of repetition in it will encourage segmentation, if only because the unit of repetition needs to be identified" (4). The stream as a continuum is segmented into parts that are both distinct and articulated (jointed in the sense of connected) in order to enhance perception.

On these grounds one can maintain that the concept of intralinear metrical segmentation holds a natural and necesssary position in the hierarchy of forms that constitutes verse-structure. One then wants to know how many types of feet to allow, which is to say, what principle is used to construct any f. (It is assumed that for any unit to be repeated, it must be simple, hence the maxiumum number of members in a f. is about four, but binary and ternary forms predominate.)

What is the principle of f.-structure? Over the past half-century, several arguments have been advanced that a f. must contain at least two elements, and that these must differ from one another. These arguments posit *alternation* as a fundamental feature of rhythm which is operant at every level of the linguistic hierarchy, hence a fundamental process in verse-design operant at several levels of metrical organization (see RHYTHM). As Allen puts it, the "principle of alternation is crucial to the manifestation of prosodic pattern, since without it there is only formless succession" (122; cf. 101). And for Lotman, "the elementary unit of metre (from the point of view of symmetry) is the f., since the constituents of the f. do not themselves form a symmetry." "Alternation" ("opposition" might be a better term) amounts to the same claim as that put forward in 20th-c. markedness theory (Jakobson; Shapiro), which holds that in every binary pair of distinctive phonetic features, such as + voiced or - voiced, one feature is marked (highlighted, preferred), the other not. The two elements of the f. have been variously termed *arsis* and *thesis* (q.v.) in Cl. metrics, *lift* and *dip* in Old Germanic and OE metrics, and *positions* or else *ictus* (q.v.) and *nonictus* in modern metrics, but the terminology is acutely unstable. These positions in the metrical pattern are filled by syllables in the actual line—usually one each, but sometimes more, as specified by the rules of the particular meter.

Around the turn of the 20th c., some metrists proposed the notion of "monosyllabic feet"—i.e. a stress alone without any attached proclitic or enclitic unstressed syllables (or stress plus a hypothesized pause)—to account for irregularities such as extra syllables or displaced stresses in lines. Sequences such as /xx/ in the first four syllables of the Eng. iambic pentameter were accounted for as either (1) a "trochaic substitution" or "inverted f." (so Bridges) followed by an iamb, or (2) a "monosyllabic f." followed by a "trisyllabic substitution" (so Saintsbury). But on the principle of alternation or opposition of heterogeneous members, "monosyllabic feet" are not legitimate feet at all (a point recognized as early as Aristoxenus: "one *chronos* cannot make a f."), but simply a contradiction in terms. Equally inadmissable are all feet with homogeneous members such as the spondee, pyrrhic, molossus, and tribrach. We will pass over (silently) the confused notions that pauses may fill up parts of feet or even make up whole feet: all such conceptions are based on temporal theories of meter not now widely endorsed, though Gerard Manley Hopkins allowed them in "sprung rhythm" (q.v.).

If the principle umderlying the design of all feet is opposition of heterogeneous members, every f. must contain one stress (only) along with its contiguous unstressed syllables: hence of binary and ternary feet there can be only five types: iamb, trochee, dactyl, anapest, amphibrach. But the latter three are very difficult to differentiate in running series, esp. when line ends are irregular and unpredictable: in modern verse the sequence x/xx/xx/xx/ may be felt as "anapestic tetrameter" with a missing first syllable, but it can also be "amphibrachic" with a missing final syllable—that perception depends on wordshapes in (the morphology of) the line. In practice, all ternaries are effectively one meter. The same argument has been made about the two binary meters by some, though Halpern has suggested, persuasively, that iambic differs from all trochaic, ternary, and accentual meters in that these latter do not admit of modulation (see METER). For him there are only two classes of modern meters, iambic and accentual (see ACCENTUAL VERSE).

Are feet real entities which exist in the lines, or merely an artifice of scansion? Hopkins says that "common Eng. rhythm . . . is measured by feet of either two or three syllables . . . never more or less." He distinguishes "Falling Feet and Falling Rhythms," "Rising Feet and Rhythms," and "Rocking Feet and Rhythms," and views these distinctions (between the three types, not the feet vs. the rhythms) as "real and true to nature" ("Author's Preface" to *Poems*, 1918; 5th ed., ed. N. H. MacKenzie, 1990, 115 ff.). It is clear that Hopkins keeps these "real and true" categories separate from scansion because he chooses "for purposes of scanning" to notate only with the first type, since "it is a great convenience to follow the example of music." Hence for him, standard Eng. verse has only two possible feet, trochees and dactyls, and three rhythms, these two plus their logaoedic mixture.

On this account, the f. is thus more than a mere analytic tool, a device for scansion: it is a principle of structure. It is not necessarily an element in poetic composition as any poet actually carries out that activity, and it is almost certainly not an element of performance (q.v.). In scansion, it can be used to describe and analyze verse whose regularities support it, and not verse which does not. The advantages of f.-scansion are consistency and convenience. One disadvantage is that f.-analysis works only on regular verse—Gummere made this crucial point a century ago. If irregularity exceeds a certain threshhold, even a large inventory of f.-types cannot account for the variety, or only at the expense of a wild profusion of types, many of which are curiosities or scholarly inventions. A more serious disadvantage is that this device, so useful in scansion, naturally tends to become reified, so that readers come to believe that poets actually make verse foot by foot, count on their fingers, labor for a molossus. (It was T. S. Eliot who remarked, apropos of his inability to remember the names and kinds of feet, that "a study of anatomy will not teach you how to make a hen lay eggs"). Description would be fine if it didn't always quietly reify itself and then come to replace the thing it set out only to describe. The fact that a verse can be scanned in feet proves that feet are one component of the verse-structure but says nothing about whether the poet composed, or the performer should recite, in feet.

See also BINARY AND TERNARY; COLON; COUPE; ENGLISH PROSODY; EQUIVALENCE; GRAMMETRICS; FRENCH PROSODY; ITALIAN PROSODY; LINE; MEASURE; METER; METRON; PERIOD; PYRRHIC; RELATIVE STRESS PRINCIPLE; RHYTHM; RISING AND FALLING RHYTHM; SCANSION; SPONDEE; VARIABLE FOOT.

Schipper 1.8; G. Saintsbury, *Hist. of Eng. Pros.* (1906–10), v. 1, App. 5, and v. 3, App. 1, and *Historical Manual* (1910), chs. 4–5—eccentric;

Wilamowitz; P. Habermann, "Versfüss," *Reallexikon I*; A. W. De Groot, *Algemene Versleer* [General Prosody] (1946), "The Description of a Poem." *Proc. 9th Intl. Congr. of Linguists*, ed. H. G. Lunt (1964); M. Whiteley, "Verse and Its Feet," *RES* 9 (1958); M. Halpern, "On the Two Chief Metrical Modes in Eng.," *PMLA* 77 (1962); S. Chatman, *A Theory of Meter* (1965), 114–19, 127–41; D. W. Cummings and J. Herum. "Metrical Boundaries and Rhythm-Phrases," *MLQ* 28 (1967); Dale, 211; H. Wode, "Linguistische Grundlagen verslicher Strukturen im Englischen," *FoLi* 4 (1970); C. L. Stevenson, "The Rhythm of Eng. Verse," *JAAC* 28 (1970); R. Tsur, "Articulateness and Requiredness in Iambic Verse," *Style* 6 (1972); W. S. Allen, *Accent and Rhythm* (1973), esp. 101, 122 ff.; M. Shapiro, *Asymmetry* (1976); J. Lotman, *The Structure of the Artistic Text* (tr. 1977), 136–55; H. J. Diller, "The Function of Verse in Byron's *Don Juan*," *Constance Byron Symposium* (1978); R. Jakobson, "Linguistics and Poetics," rpt. in Jakobson, v. 5; Scott 3–7; Morier, s.v. "Pied métrique"; Brogan. sect. E; West; G. Russom, *OE Meter and Linguistic Theory* (1987); G. T. Wright, *Shakespeare's Metrical Art* (1988).

T.V.F.B.

FORM. Few terms in literary study are more widely used than f., but the term is so variable and inclusive that it ends by being one of the most ambiguous that we have. At one level it can refer to the minutiae of the text, at another to the shape of the text in itself, at a third to the characteristics a text may share with others, at still another level to a transcendental or Platonic model from which the text imperfectly derives; and it may have several of these meanings within the work of a single theorist. Such usage can take in a wide variety of conditions that have to do with f.—its nature, or its location, or its relationship to content and to the world content proclaims. Yet that territory is not only broad but the site of issues so fundamental that they have had to be faced from the beginning of literary study. Recent theorizing on the nature of the literary text gives far less attention to f. than to the related concept of genre (q.v.), quite possibly because so much modern study of f. has been associated with varieties of formalism (see RUSSIAN FORMALISM; NEW CRITICISM). Still, some of the most potent contemporary theories of lit. have considerable (if implicit) significance for the study of this ancient issue.

Whatever the specific import given the concept of f., whatever the period in which it becomes part of literary discussion, the question of representation or mimesis (q.v.) always comes into play, if only, as in parts of our century, to reject the desirability and even possibility of such a process. This inevitable relation of f. to representation explains why Plato and Aristotle have been permanent topics in the study of literary f., the recurring dialectic of their differing concepts of f. always a compel-

ling force. The basic Platonic position appears in the discussion of painter, craftsman, bed, and model in Book Ten of *The Republic*. For Plato a f. is an instance of absolute purity which, because it is purity, has to be distanced from the place of emergence of its necessarily imperfect echoes. The Platonic conception of fs. (*eidei*, ideas) has, therefore, two principal components: first the model's unsullied perfection and second the fact that it is external to its material manifestations. That the f. has its origin outside the text or object seems to have as one of its implications the possibility that f. is imposed upon matter, and as another the corollary that f. and content have to be viewed as separate elements brought together in the manifestation.

It is along these lines in particular that the conception of f. in Aristotle's *Poetics* has to be seen as an answer to Plato, as history's major alternative (see CLASSICAL POETICS). F. in Aristotle is not fixed but emergent and dynamic, not external or transcendental but intrinsic and immanent, coexistent with the matter in which it develops towards its fullest realization. F. so conceived cannot be identified with structure (q.v.) but is, instead, the informing principle that works on matter and causes the text or object to become all it is. In Aristotelian terms f. (the "formal cause") is one of the four causes, the others being the material cause (the matter), the efficient cause (the maker), and the final cause (the end in the sense of both conclusion and purpose). This last involves another crucial distinction between the Platonic and Aristotelian modes, for in Plato f. is identified with origin, a place of beginnings against which the result is to be tested, while Aristotelian f. is based on entelechy, an end which brings about the full and complete being of the object (*telos* has to do not only with ending but with a consummation which is completeness). The implications for literary theory are considerable. René Wellek and others have argued that the concept of organic f. (see ORGANICISM), which rejects any separation of f. and content, began with Aristotle but was ignored until the 18th c., a history which may have much to do with the Platonic understanding of literary f. and its attendant implication that f. is originary, separable, and distinct. Aristotle's own practice clearly rejects originary thinking: in the *Poetics, anagnorisis* (recognition) and *peripeteia* (reversal) are elements both in the f. of a tragedy and in its content as well, as is the insistence that all texts should have a beginning, middle, and end. F. and content so conceived are not only inseparable but indistinguishable, and in later critics may be considered as precisely the same aspect taken from different points of view.

The purity of the Aristotelian distinction between f. and what is often called structure has rarely been kept, the result being the plethora of meanings the term always has. At its least encompassing level, f. is used to refer to metrical patterns

FORM

as well as lexical, syntactic, and linear arrangements: for example, the f. of the heroic couplet or the Spenserian stanza. At this level the term has much to do with matters of technique and style (conceived as ways of performing, of putting into f.) as well as the various implications that emerge from those ways: for example, what Pope's heroic couplets show of his sense of the world, what Byron's use of the Spenserian stanza in *Childe Harold's Pilgrimage* states about lit. hist. (These examples show again how f. is always linked to questions of representation, however different the tangents.) A more encompassing view considers f. as structure, put most simply as the overall "mode of arrangement" (Thomas Munro) of the text; that is, the way textual materials are organized so as to create shape. In a classically rhetorical mode, f. in this sense refers to scheme or argument. In a classically New Critical mode, it refers to the ironic patterns of tension (q.v.) within a text, patterns that create the overall shape of the text's unparaphraseable meanings (Brooks; see PARAPHRASE). Put in terms of structure, f. is esp. prone to problems of the separation of f. and content, a point of particular sensitivity to all manner of modern formalists. It is equally prone to that problem when taken at the same level but in a different context, that is, when identified with genre or kind. Clearly dissatisfied with the blurring of concepts that actually touch only rarely, Claudio Guillén has argued that genre is "an invitation to f." Theodore Greene's more involved distinction between specific f. (unique and essentially incomparable) and generic f. (shared and contextual) seems designed not only to establish practical categories but to satisfy Croceans, formalists, and literary historians at once. At this point f. can become an element or principle of classification, a segment of another order, of a more encompassing f.

The need to satisfy such a plurality of views indicates the variety of positions taken on f. since the middle of the 18th c. The concept of "inner f." was developed by Goethe and others, its immediate origins in Shaftesbury and Winckelmann, its ultimate source Neo-Platonic. The principle concern of inner f. is with the internal totality of the work and the correspondence of that wholeness to the external world, what Shaftesbury speaks of as a microcosmic mirroring of experience (in *Characteristics* he refers to "inward f."). That emphasis on wholeness found its most productive routing in A. W. Schlegel's distinction between organic and mechanical f., surely the most influential reading of the term in modern times. Schlegel speaks in his *Dramatic Lectures* of a f. which is essentially additive, imposed from without and therefore quite possibly arbitrary. This is the mode of neoclassical drama. The opposite is organic f., generated from within, coexistent with the material, complete only when the object itself is complete, working its way just as natural fs. do. This is the Shakespearian mode. Schlegel's pairing is re-peated in the first of Coleridge's *Lectures on Shakespeare*, an influence which (carrying along the attendant ideas of variety in unity and the reconciliation of opposites) led to ways of conceiving f. still at work in our own day. Versions of it appear in Croce and others who are not necessarily Crocean, where f. is thought of not only as implying a new unity of all given materials but as ultimately the only means whereby expression becomes possible (see Greene and La Drière). Critics like Wimsatt and Brooks have argued, however, that Croce is actually concerned with lyric moments rather than wholes, a reading which would place him squarely in line with Poe. Far less useful than the concept of f. as expression is the notion of "significant f.," fathered by A. C. Bradley and furthered by Clive Bell and Roger Fry, which gets more attention in histories than it did in thinking about lit. Significant f. has little or nothing to do with representations of "life" but is, instead, concerned only with color, line, space, and those other elements which arouse aesthetic emotion. That Bell and Fry have their sources in decadence and aestheticism (qq.v.) clarifies their limitations. Potentially much more fruitful, though as yet hardly tapped in general speculations on f., are recent explorations of the question of indeterminacy (q.v.) that are likely to become a major legacy of end-of-the-century theorizing. Fostered by a suspicion of total systems and the fs. that mimic them—suspicions that extend, in some cases, to any sort of absolute closure (q.v.)—such speculations are surely the most potent threat yet to two centuries of Schlegelian thinking about the shape of literary f. Whether one argues that this, too, involves questions of representation, or that we can never really know fixities such as closure, these speculations are likely to compel radical readjustments of a basic literary concept that has too long been taken with complacency.

For discussion of the theoretical bases of poetic form in poetics, see VERSE AND PROSE; for discussion of other modes of f. and structure, see ORGANICISM; for discussion of "open f." in Am. poetry, see AMERICAN POETRY and FREE VERSE. See also GENRE; POETICS; SIMPLICITY AND COMPLEXITY.

C. Bell, *Art* (1914); H. Wölfflin, *Kunstgeschichtliche Grundbegriffe* (1915), 7th Ger. ed. tr. M. D. Hottinger, *Principles of Art Hist.* (1976), ch. 3—"open" vs. "closed" f.; W. P. Ker, *F. and Style in Poetry* (1928); R. Schwinger, *Innere F.* (1935); B. Fehr, "The Antagonism of Fs. in the 18th C.," *ES* 18–19 (1936–37); T. H. Greene, *The Arts and the Art of Crit.* (1940); K. Burke, "Container and Thing Contained," *SR* 8 (1945), "Psychology and F." and "Lexicon Rhetoricae," *Counter-Statement*, 2d ed. (1953), *Philosophy of Literary F.* (1957); Brooks; I. A. Richards, "Poetic F.," *Practical Crit.*, 2d ed. (1948); C. La Drière, "F.," *Dict of World Lit.*, ed. J. T. Shipley (1953); S. Langer, *Feeling and F.* (1953); W. S. Johnson, "Some Functions of Poetic F.," *JAAC*

13 (1955); Wellek; Wimsatt and Brooks; W. A. Davis, "Theories of F. in Mod. Crit.," Diss., Univ. of Chicago (1960), *The Act of Interp.* (1978), ch. 1; R. Wellek, "Concepts of F. and Structure in 20th-C. Crit.," *Concepts of Crit.* (1963); J. Levý, "The Meanings of F. and the Fs. of Meaning," *Poetics, Poetyka, Poetika,* ed. R. Jakobson et al. (1966); W. Tatarkiewicz, "F. in the Hist. of Aesthetics," *DHI*; T. Munro, *F. and Style in the Arts* (1970); C. Guillén, *Lit. as System* (1971); A. Fowler, "The Life and Death of Literary Fs.," and S. Chatman, "On Defining F.," *NLH* 2 (1971); T. E. Uehling, Jr., *The Notion of F. in Kant's Critique of Aesthetic Judgment* (1971); G. S. Brown, *Laws of F.* (1972); *Organic F.: The Life of an Idea,* ed. G. S. Rousseau (1972); K. K. Ruthven, *Critical Assumptions* (1979), ch. 2; J. D. Boyd, *The Function of Mimesis and Its Decline,* 2d ed. (1980); M. Perloff, *The Poetics of Indeterminacy* (1981); R. Duncan, "Ideas of the Meaning of F.," *Claims for Poetry,* ed. D. Hall (1982)—and others therein; Fowler; N. E. Emerton, *The Scientific Reinterpretation of F.* (1984); D. Wesling, *The New Poetries* (1985), ch. 2; Hollander.　　　　F.G.

FORMALISM. See AUTONOMY; CONTEXTUALISM; CRITICISM; MODERNISM AND POSTMODERNISM; NEW CRITICISM; NEW FORMALISM; RUSSIAN FORMALISM; TWENTIETH-CENTURY POETICS.

FORMULA, together with the "theme" and "story-pattern," are the istructural units of oral composition delineated by the oral-formulaic theory (q.v.). Originally defined by Milman Parry in 1928 as "a group of words which is regularly employed under the same metrical conditions to express a given essential idea," the f. has since been identified as the "atom" of oral-traditional phraseology in dozens of trads. The f. is to be distinguished from simple repetition on the basis of its consummate usefulness to the composing oral poet, who employs it not for rhetorical effect but because it is part of the traditional poetic idiom bequeathed to him by generations of bards, an idiom that combines the practical and immediate value of ready-made phraseology with the aesthetic advantage of enormous connotative force.

Although earlier scholars, chiefly the Ger. philologists of the 19th c., had referred in general terms to formulaic diction (esp. Sievers' *Formelverzeichnis* [1878] and the linguistic analyses of Düntzer), Parry was the first to describe the existence and morphology of this phraseological element with precision, to demonstrate its tectonic function, and to link the traditional phrase with composition in oral performance. His studies of Homeric epic (1928–32) showed how traditional composition was made possible by the bard's ability to draw on an inherited repertoire of poetic diction consisting of fs. and *formulaic systems,* each system comprising a set of fs. that share a common pattern of phraseology. Thus he was able to illustrate, for example, how proseûda ("addressed")

could combine with 11 different nominal subjects to constitute a metrically correct measure in the hexameter line (selections below):

proseûda +
$- \cup - -$

dia qeawn　　　　(divine of goddesses)
$- \cup \cup - -$

mantis amumwn　　(blameless seer)
$- \cup \cup - -$

dios 'Acilleus　　　(divine Achilles)
$- \cup \cup - -$

dios 'Odusseus　　(divine Odysseus).

Parry understood the poet's task not as a search for original diction but as a fluency in this traditional idiom—that is, as the talent and learned ability to weave together the ready-made diction and, occasionally, new phraseology invented by analogy to existing fs. and systems to produce metrically correct hexameters. One further useful aspect of this special epic lang. he found to be its *thrift,* whereby more than one f. of the same metrical definition for the same character was but seldom allowed. Having concentrated in his 1928 theses principally on the noun-epithet fs. so typical of Homeric style, Parry then broadened his examination in 1930 and 1932 to consider all of Homer's diction. His analysis of the first 25 lines of the *Iliad* and *Odyssey,* which show graphically how Homer depended on fs. and systems to make his poems, remains a *locus classicus* for the interp. of ancient Gr. epic lang.

These deductions were augmented as a result of fieldwork in Yugoslavia carried out by Parry and Albert Lord (see ORAL-FORMULAIC THEORY). Lord demonstrated that the Yugoslav *guslar* (q.v.) employed a similar formulaic idiom in the making of South Slavic epic, using stock phrases like lički Mustajbeže ("Mustajbeg of the Lika" [a place-name]), as well as more flexible formulaic systems, to compose his poem in oral performance. With the benefit of a large corpus of material, including many songs from the same *guslar,* Lord was able to show that virtually every line of South Slavic oral epic could be understood as a f. or member of a formulaic system.

On this foundation other scholars have erected a series of studies of the f., some on ancient, medieval, and other ms. trads., others on recoverable modern trads.—e.g. Webber (1951) on formulaic frequency in the Sp. ballad; Magoun (1953) on the first 25 lines of *Beowulf*; Duggan (1973) on the OF *chansons de geste* (q.v.), postulating a threshold of 20% straight repetition for probable orality; Lord (1986) on comparative studies; Culley (1986) on the Bible; Edwards (1986, 1987) on ancient Gr.; Olsen (1986, 1987) on OE; Parks (1986) on ME; and Zwettler (1978) on Arabic. Foley provides bibl. (1985) and detailed history (1988).

In recent years scholars have focused on the problem of interpreting a formulaic text: whether the idiom is so predetermined and mechanical as to preclude verbal art as we know it, whether the oral poet can select esp. meaningful fs. appropriate to certain narrative situations and thus place his individual stamp on the composition, or whether some other aesthetic must be applicable. Most have emphasized either the traditional and inherited or the spontaneous and individual. More account needs to be taken of the differences as well as similarities among fs., with attention to different trads., genres, and kinds of texts (e.g. mss. and acoustic recordings). Similarly, the referential fields of meaning commanded by fs. need more investigation, since fs. and other structural units convey meaning not by abstract denotation but by metonymic reference to the trad. as a whole.

H. Düntzer, *Homerische Abhandlungen* (1872); E. Sievers, "Formelverzeichnis," in his ed. of *Heliand* (1878); R. Webber, *Formulistic Diction in the Sp. Ballad* (1951); F. P. Magoun, "The Oral-Formulaic Character of Anglo-Saxon Narrative Poetry," *Speculum* 28 (1953); Lord; Parry; J. Duggan, The *Song of Roland: Formulaic Style and Poetic Craft* (1973); M. Nagler, *Spontaneity and Trad.* (1974); M. Zwettler, *The Oral Trad. of Cl. Arabic Poetry* (1978); J. Foley, *Oral-Formulaic Theory and Research* (1985), *The Theory of Oral Composition* (1988), *Comparative Studies in Traditional Oral Epic* (1989); R. Culley, "Oral Trad. and Biblical Studies," *OT* 1 (1986); A. B. Lord, "Perspectives on Recent Work on the Oral Traditional F.," *OT* 1 (1986); W. Parks, "The Oral-Formulaic Theory in ME Studies," *OT* 1 (1986); M. Edwards, "Homer and Oral Trad.: The F.," *OT* 1-2 (1986-87); A. Olsen, "Oral-Formulaic Research in OE Studies," *OT* 1-2 (1986-87). J.M.F.

FORNYRÐISLAG. ON meter. F. appears to derive directly from common Germanic alliterative poetry but is stanzaic: four Germanic long lines make up the eight-line f. stanza, which generally consists of two syntactically independent four-line units. The principal metrical feature is structural alliteration, which links one or both of the stressed syllables in each odd line with (generally) the first of the two stressed syllables in the following even line. Unstressed syllables are metrically insignificant.

Geyr Garmr mjǫk   fyr Gnipahelli,
festr mun slitna,   enn freki renna

(Garmr bays much before Gnipahellr;
   bonds will burst and the wolf run
   free.)

F. is the major narrative meter for Eddic poetry. Medieval and later prosodists distinguish it from *málaháttr* on the basis of the number of unstressed syllables; f. has fewer, m. more. The only Eddic poem to use this meter in its pure form is the *Atlamál en grænlenzku.*

Grimm vartu, Guðrún,   er þú gera svá
   máttir,
barna þinna blóði   at blanda mér
   dryccio
(Fierce you were, Gudrun, when you
   could do such a thing as to mix a
   drink for me with the blood of your
   children.)

A very old skaldic variation appears to be *kviðuháttr*, in which the syllables are counted; odd lines have only one unstressed syllable, even lines two, so that lines of three and four syllables alternate. The earliest poem in which *kviðuháttr* is found is *Ynglingatal* (before 900). In the 10th c. Egill Skallagrímsson used it effectively in his *Arinbjarnarkvioa* and *Sonatorrek*, and it was also used by some of his contemporaries and later skalds:

Hitt vas fyrr   at fold ruðu
sverðberendr   sínum dróttni
(It happened before, that sword-bearers
reddened the earth with their lord.)

See OLD NORSE POETRY.—*The Poetic Edda*, tr. H. A. Bellows (1923) and L. M. Hollander, rev. ed. (1962); W. P. Lehmann, *The Development of Germanic Verse Form* (1956); P. Hallberg, *Old Icelandic Poetry* (1975). J.L.

FOUND POEM. The f. p. or *objet trouvé* is the presentation of something "found" in the environment—a piece of expository prose, a snatch of poetry or dramatic dialogue, a newspaper page, document, map, painting, photograph, etc.—as a lineated text and hence a poem, or the incorporation of a prior text (see ALLUSION) into a larger poetic structure. The f. p. may claim its origin in the parodic bilingual poems of the Ren. (see MACARONIC VERSE), but it does not become prominent until the 20th c. as the verbal equivalent of collage. An early example is Blaise Cendrars' "Mee Too Boogie" (1914), which is a lineated adaptation of a passage from a 19th-c. travel book about the natives of Tonga. Cendrars' earlier "Le Panama ou les aventures de mes sept oncles" incorporates a train schedule from the Union Pacific Railroad and a prospectus for "Denver, the Residence City and Commercial Center."

Both dada and surrealist (qq.v.) poets (e.g. Kurt Schwitters, Francis Picabia, André Breton) exploited the f. p., but the most prominent example for the Eng.-speaking reader is surely that of Ezra Pound's *Cantos*, which incorporate "real" letters by Jefferson and Adams, Papal documents, poems by Cavalcanti, government and bank documents, etc. Pound's strategy was taken over by William Carlos Williams in *Paterson*, by Charles Olson in the *Maximus Poems*, and by Louis Zukofsky in his epic "A." The pure f. p., on the other hand, may be exemplified by David Antin's "Code of Flag Behavior" or John Cage's mesostich texts. Evidently the f. p.'s contemporary appeal depends upon its ability to combine representational reference and formal composition.—H. Richter, *Dada: Art and Anti-Art* (1964); D. Antin, "Modernism and Post-Modernism," *Boundary 2* (1972); H. Behar, "Débris, collage et invention poétique" and J.-P. Goldenstein, "Vers une systematique du poème élastique," both in *Europe*, Blaise Cendrars Issue (1976); J. Bochner, *Blaise Cendrars: Discovery and Re-Creation* (1978); J. Holden, *The Rhet. of the Contemp. Lyric* (1980); M. Perloff, *The Futurist Moment* (1986).   M.P.

FOUR AGES OF POETRY. Thomas Love Peacock's essay of this title (1820) incisively questions the role of poetry in a society that commodifies all art. Wittily combining a cyclic view of the history of culture with a primitivist evolutionary account of cultural origins in the trad. of Vico, Rousseau, and Herder, Peacock traces two parallel cycles of poetry, one ancient and the other modern, each having four phases: (1) an Iron Age, when "rude bards celebrate in rough numbers the exploits of ruder chiefs"; (2) a Golden Age, when poetry reaches perfection unrivaled by hist., philosophy, or science; (3) a Silver Age, dominated by imitative or didactic poetry, moving toward poetry's extinction; and (4) a Brass Age of social and cultural decadence, when poetry regresses into a "second childhood" while professing "to return to nature and revive the age of gold." In retracing the four ages in the modern cycle, Peacock parodies the solipsistic poetics of contemp. "patriarchs of the age of brass": "while the historian and the philosopher are advancing in, and accelerating, the progress of knowledge, the poet is wallowing in the rubbish of departed ignorance, and raking up the ashes of dead savages to find gewgaws and rattles for the grown babies of the age." At a time when other writers and thinkers were exalting the poet as a divine creator second only to God, Peacock questions his fitness for moral leadership in what Carlyle would call "the Mechanical Age." In his rebuttal to Peacock, Shelley (*Defence of Poetry*), significantly, shares his friend's premise of poetry's social function but reclaims the imagination's moral power. Responding to Abrams' claim that the boundaries of Peacock's irony are indeterminable, recent critics have engaged in spirited debate on the question of whether Peacock is a serious spokesman for utilitarian philosophy (Butler) or a Swiftian ironist who fears that once poetry is judged by marketplace values, by the "progress" of chemistry, economics, or politics, it really is doomed (Prickett).—T. L. Peacock, "The Four Ages of Poetry," rpt. in the *Halliford Edition* of his works, ed. H. F. B. Brett-Smith and C. E. Jones, v. 8 (1934); Abrams; C. Dawson, *His Fine Wit* (1970); M. Butler, *Peacock Displayed* (1979); S. Prickett, "Peacock's *Four Ages* Recycled," *BJA* 22 (1982).

                                                L.MET.

FOURTEENER. A metrical line of 14 syllables which since the Middle Ages has taken two distinct forms used for a variety of kinds of poetry and thus exhibiting widely differing characteristics. When two fs. are broken by hemistichs to form a quatrain of lines stressed 4–3–4–3 and rhyming *abab* they become the familiar "eight-and-six" form of ballad meter (q.v.) called Common Meter or Common Measure (q.v.); Coleridge imitated the looser form of this meter in "Kubla Khan," as did many other 19th-c. poets attempting literary imitations of "folk poetry." The eight-and-six pattern was used widely in the 16th c. for hymns; indeed, Sternhold and Hopkins adapted it from contemporary song specifically to take advantage of its popularity and energy for their metrical psalter (2d ed. 1549). It was also used for polished lyrics such as Herrick's "Gather ye rosebuds while ye may." Shakespeare uses it for comic effect in the "Pyramus and Thisbe" play performed by the "rude mechanicals" in *A Midsummer Night's Dream*. Closely related is Poulter's Measure (q.v.), a line of 12 syllables followed by a f., which when broken into a quatrain gives the 3–3–4–3 pattern of Short Meter (q.v.).

But the f. was also used extensively in the 16th c. for the elevated genres, in particular for tr. Lat. tragedy and epic. It is used for trs. of Seneca's tragedies by Jasper Heywood and others pub. by Thomas Newton in the *Tenne Tragedies* (1581) and by Arthur Golding for his tr. of Ovid's *Metamorphoses*. The most famous and impressive use of fs. in Eng. is doubtless George Chapman's tr. of Homer's *Iliad* (1616). The contrast between the effect of fs. in popular and learned genres is striking:

> The king sits in Dumferline town
>   Drinking the blood-red wine;
> "O whare will I get a skeely skipper
>   To sail this new ship of mine?"
>   (*Sir Patrick Spens*)

> Achilles' banefull wrath resound, O
>   Goddesse, that impos'd
> Infinite sorrowes on the Greekes, and
>   many brave soules los'd
> From breasts Heroique—sent them
>   farre, to that invisible cave
> That no light comforts; and their lims
>   to dogs and vultures gave.
>   (Chapman's Homer)

Opinions differ about the origins of the f. Schipper calls it a *septenarius* (q.v.)—more precisely, the trochaic tetrameter brachycatalectic—implying that it was derived from imitation of Med. Lat. poems in that meter. The native influence of ballad meter is also obvious. But another explanation is equally likely: the great Cl. epic meter, the dactylic hexameter, contains on average about 16 "times," and it may be that early Eng. translators thought the f. was the closest vernacular equiva-

FREE VERSE

lent.—Schipper; P. Verrier, *Le Vers français*, 3 v. (1931–32), v. 2–3; J. Thompson, *The Founding of Eng. Metre* (1961); O. B. Hardison, Jr., *Prosody and Purpose in the Eng. Ren.* (1988). O.B.H.; T.V.F.B.

FRAGMENT. See INTERTEXTUALITY.

FRANKFURT SCHOOL. See MARXIST CRITICISM; TWENTIETH-CENTURY POETICS, *French and German.*

FREE METERS. See WELSH POETRY.

FREE VERSE.

I. TYPES
II. ORDERING PRINCIPLES

F. v. is distinguished from meter by the lack of a structuring grid based on counting of linguistic units and/or position of linguistic features. Some of f. v.'s primary features (nonmetrical structuring, heavy reliance on grammatical breaks, absence of regular endrhyme) may be traced back into the roots of lyric, and f. v. is today a frequently used (if extremely various) set of prosodies for contemporary poetry around the world.

I. TYPES. Many of the same analytical terms and methods employed to describe metrical verse can be applied to f. v. Nonetheless, f. v. brings with it different relations of regularity to irregularity and of the auditory to the visual; and different kinds of repetition, equivalence, and voice (qq.v.).

The term, though not always the formal impulse and practice, is a derivative of metrical verse. It is a prosody of avoidance of meter (q.v.), and at the same time it fuses other prosodies. The term itself is a manifesto and a contradiction-interms first used by Fr. poet Gustave Kahn in the late 1880s at the advent of European modernism. The Fr. term *vers libre* (q.v.) has its counterparts in the Eng. f. v., Ger. *freie Rhythmen* (q.v.), and Rus. *svobodnyj stix, volnyj stix.* In Eng., f. v. was a term of derogation before it became a battle cry or, as today, a more neutral descriptor.

F. v. must be described by integrating historical and structural approaches. The types of f. v. are products of different literary-historical conditions. We could argue that f. v. reaches back to the oral roots of poetry, to the period preceding the devel. of regular metricity. Sumerian, Akkadian, Egyptian, Sanskrit, and Heb. poetries (qq.v.) all share one characteristic: in their texts, repetition and parallelism (qq.v.) create prosodic regularity, while meter in any of its types does not yet regulate the verse.

The first type of f. v., the form partly freed from the constraints of traditional meter, has its origins in Fr. *vers libéré* (q.v.) of the 17th c., when La Fontaine and his followers began to loosen the strictly syllabic lines of Fr. poetry by inventing "liberated" metrical forms. Such was the precursor of those prosodic strainings against meter which in the 19th c. became a major trend. Zhuk-ovskij, Sumarokov, Pushkin in Russia; Klopstock, Goethe, Hölderlin in Germany; Batsányi, Kazinczy, Petőfi in Hungary; Rimbaud, Verhaeren, Apollinaire in France—all wrote with radical deviation from the meters common in their respective national poetries. In Eng., this partial liberation of and from meter existed here and there before Whitman (e.g. Smart's catalogue poems, Scott's "Verses in the Style of the Druids," Arnold's "Strayed Reveler"). This type and, if included, the premetrical form described briefly above, appear as f. v. only in retrospect.

The second type, avant-garde f. v., has no direct roots in the metrical trad., at least in the way the verse-line is built up. Meter is what this self-conscious, self-proclaimed f. v. is free of. This type was born when Walt Whitman's proudly nonmetrical *Leaves of Grass* (1855) flouted accent-and-syllable-counting regularity. Whitman brought back into poetry strong stress at unpredictable places, grammatical emphasis and parallelism, anaphora, and long lines. His oral-derived form is expansive, asymmetrical, mixing dialects and modes, and above all, personal. A related subtype, based in Whitman and possibly also in the Fr. verset or verse-paragraph (q.v.), is the long measure of Allen Ginsberg ("Howl") or Robert Bly ("The Teeth-Mother Naked at Last"), where the line is claimed to derive from the rhythms of breathing, and where it is often used in a list-structure that condemns or celebrates (see CATALOG).

Writers of another subtype, notably William Carlos Williams and those in his trad. like Cid Corman, George Oppen, and Robert Creeley, strive for more delicate dynamics, wrenching tighter Whitman's long and sometimes prolix lines. These writers often use lineation out of phase with grammatical and/or visual units. Still others like the early 20th-c. imagist poets (q.v.), Osip Mandelstam in his one poem (1923) in f. v., the early Wallace Stevens, Carl Sandburg, and D. H. Lawrence habitually use lines coincident with grammatical units.

Williams' theory of the variable foot (q.v.) and Charles Olson's theory of projective verse (q.v.) provide critical justifications for avant-garde f.-v. practice—both more polemical than definitive, both failing to account adequately for even these two poets' own practices.

Many poets now write entirely in f. v. measures, or they move easily from meter through liberated forms to f. v., depending on the needs of the given poem. An international list of avant-garde practitioners would include, among many others, Arthur Rimbaud, André Breton, Paul Éluard, Michel Déguy, Aimé Césaire, Anne-Marie Albiach (Fr.); Kuo Mo Jo, Yip Wai-lim (Chinese); Aleksandr Blok, Velemir Xlebnikov, Nikolai Zabolotskij, Olga Berggolts, Evgeny Evtušenko (Rus.); Pablo Neruda (Sp.—from Chile); Lajos Kassák, Milán Füst (Hungarian); and Gael Turnbull and Charles Tomlinson (Eng.).

FREE VERSE

II. SOME ORDERING PRINCIPLES OF AVANT-GARDE FREE VERSE. None of the principles exemplified briefly below is particular to f. v., but each has a specific usage and weight within the f. v. poem. The relations of regularity to irregularity may vary widely over the whole poem, for example. Much f. v. is, however, as regular as much metrical verse; the difference is that in f. v., regularity is based on linguistic or textual features not much noticed by most scholars of versification (e.g. intonation or length in typewriter ems).

Generalizations may not apply to all subtypes of 20th-c. practice. Broadly speaking, in f. v. one-time-only events tend to be as important as repetitive events in the poem's structure. A pleasure for the reader comes from unpredictability, when lang. is thickened by sound and visual effects that will or will not be echoed later on. F. v. enriches texture by grammatical and other means, by equivalence, symmetry, and repetition, though not to the same extent as in syllable-counting verse. The effect of breaking-off is typical of some subtypes (Williams), while the effect of deliberative or headlong continuity is typical of others (Lawrence, Ginsberg). In f.-v. prosodies as in all other kinds, technologies of typesetting and historically new visual media co-exist with, even modify and extend, earlier practices of reading.

A. *Equivalence subsets of line/rhyme/stanza.* Long lines, after Whitman, have in general been avoided by the Anglo-Am. writers of f. v., though notable exceptions would be David Jones (*In Parenthesis*), Robinson Jeffers, and A. R. Ammons. The short line is preferred for speed, or for slowness gained by isolating clots of phrase, as in Creeley, Denise Levertov, and Elizabeth Bishop. Lines, whether long or short, are equivalent by virtue of being lines and may also be phonological or syntactic units of the same type or equal typographically. Lines of short or medium length have been chosen by writers of extended poems in f. v. such as Pound (*Cantos*), Williams (*Paterson*), and Edward Dorn (*Slinger*). A carrying measure for a long poem after Whitman will usually not be oratorical, but will make the line turn more tightly. 20th-c. long poems often employ a variety of kinds of f. v., variously tighter and looser, as well as prose.

Alternation of long and short lines gives a conversational cast either to extended narratives like Charles Reznikoff's *Witness*, or to brief lyrics like e e cummings':

Buffalo Bill's
defunct
    who used to
    ride a watersmooth-silver
                stallion
and break onetwothreefourfive
    pigeonsjustlikethat
                                    Jesus

he was a handsome man. . . .

No line is the same as any other; f. v. does that habitually, whereas meter does it rarely. Rhyme is missing in this passage, but rhyme is one resource of f. v.—used in unpredictable places (e.g. middles of words and lines) and is used as instance rather than as part of overall design:

O Alessandro, chief and thrice warned,
    watcher,
        Eternal watcher of things,
Of things, of men, of passions.
    Eyes floating in dry, dark air,
E biondo, with glass-grey iris, with an
    even side-fall of hair
The stiff, still features.
            [Pound, *Canto* VII].

Here line-end rhyme occurs, but only once, while rhyme-like repetition makes for a profusion of like sounds which contribute to the noble tone of praise. The accentual cadence, which gives the unique Poundian movement, seems regular but is not; with such variety of stress from line to line, it is pointless to speak of spondee or trochee.

In designs larger than the rhyme-mated pair, f. v. uses stanzas in innovative ways, notably in what has been called the "sight-stanza" (Berry) in Williams and others after him (Creeley, Paul Blackburn). Syntax is driven past the end of a tight, boxlike stanza. In f. v., as usually also in metrical verse, there is often higher-level phonological equivalence between lines and narrative equivalence between stanzas and other kinds of line-groups.

B. *Visual devices* (see VISUAL POETRY). Some f. v. uses visual form, such as heavy capitalization in Aleksej Kručonich (Rus.) and in Kenneth Patchen (Am.), as an overlay rhythm to gain articulation and emphasis. The disposition of the poem across the page in representational designs is another variant, as in Mallarmé's page-fold-out in the shape of a bird's feather in *Un Coup de dés* and in Apollinaire's *Calligrammes* (q.v.). In these patterns, as in the less dramatic symmetries and fragmentings of more ordinary f. v., the whitespace on the page may be as important as the black print— as an image of pause, disjunction, the silence that surrounds and spaces the text. But it is well to remember that arrangement of the page may function expressively and rhetorically without its being in the least representational.

C. *The Verse period* (grammar in the poem; see GRAMMETRICS; SYNTAX). Like visual prosody, the mutual scissoring of sentence and line is an explicit feature of the prosody of f. v. that completely ignores the norm of meter. F. v. depends on a tension between grammar and line-length, stanza length. The cognitive act of sentencing is constantly counterpointing the physical-acoustic and visual features of the poem. The counterpointing patterns of meter, verbal rhythm, lineation, and rhyme exist in metrical verse too, of course, but there they are less determining. In avant-garde f.

v., counterpoint becomes the primary principle because this type, esp., relies on the centrality of the line as the meeting ground of grammatical and prosodic processes.

When the line-breaks occur within phrases, cutting off function-words from lexical words, poetic speech may seem discontinuous. While it remains the choice of the performer whether the notated break is read aloud as such, intraphrasal line-breaking, in the most fragmented kind of f. v., de-automatizes our reading—words and groups of words, even lowly prepositions, tend to stand out more as material entities. However, in long-line verse, low-level breaks in the syntax tend to be subsumed in the process.

All poetry restructures direct experience by means of devices of equivalence (q.v.); all poetry has attributes of a naturalizing and an artificializing rhetoric. However, more explicitly than the metrical poetry of the period from Chaucer to Tennyson, from Pushkin to Tsvetaeva, f. v. claims and thematizes a proximity to lived experience. It does this by trying to replicate, project, or represent perceptual, cognitive, emotional, and imaginative processes. Lived experience and replicated process are unreachable goals, but nevertheless this ethos is what continues to draw writers and readers to f. v.

For discussion of "open form" see AMERICAN POETRY; for discussion of other modern poetic forms see LYRIC SEQUENCE; MODERN LONG POEM; PROSE POEM. See also FREIE RHYTHMEN; VERS LIBRE.

T. S. Eliot, "Reflections on *Vers Libre*," *New Statesman* 8 (1917); E. Pound, "A Retrospect," *Pavannes and Divisions* (1918); J. L. Lowes, *Convention and Revolt in Poetry* (1919); H. Monroe, "The F. V. Movement in America," *Eng. Jour.* 3 (1924); B. Hrushovsky, "On Free Rhythms in Mod. Poetry," in Sebeok; R. Duncan, "Ideas of the Meaning of Form," *Kulchur* 4 (1961); J. McNaughton, "Ezra Pound's Metres and Rhythms," *PMLA* 78 (1963); R. Kell, "Note on Versification," *BJA* 3 (1963); O. Brik, "Ritm i sintaksis," tr. in *Two Essays on Poetic Lang.* (1964); H. Gross, *Sound and Form in Mod. Poetry* (1964); D. Levertov, "Notes on Organic Form," *Poetry* 106 (1965); C. Olson, "Projective Verse," *Sel. Writings* (1966); P. Ramsey, "F. V.: Some Steps Toward Definition," *SP* 65 (1968); *Naked Poetry: Recent Am. Poetry in Open Forms*, ed. S. Berg and R. Mezey (1969)—with authors' statements; L. Ern, *Freivers und Metrik* (1970); R. Mitchell, "Toward a System of Grammatical Scansion," *Lang&S* (1970); E. Fussell, *Lucifer in Harness* (1973); J. Kwan-Terry, "The Prosodic Theories of Ezra Pound," *PLL* 9 (1973); J. Roubaud, *La Vieillesse d'Alexandre* (1978); H.-J. Frey, "Verszerfall," *Kritik des freien Verses*, ed. H.-J. Frey and C. Lorenz (1980); C. O. Hartman, *F. V.* (1980)—unreliable; Scott, ch. 7; M. Perloff, *The Poetics of Indeterminacy* (1981), *The Dance of the Intellect* (1985); Brogan; E. Berry, "Williams' Devel. of a New Prosodic Form," *WCWR* 7 (1981), "Syntacti-cal and Metrical Structures in the Poetry of William Carlos Williams" *DAI* 42 (1982): 4449A; H. Meschonnic, *Critique du rhythme* (1982); C. Miller, "The Iambic Pentameter Norm of Whitman's F. V.," *Lang&S* 15 (1982); "F. V.," Spec. Iss. of *OhR* 28 (1982); "Symposium on Postmodern Form," *NER/BLQ* 6 (1983); R. Hass, *20th-C. Pleasures* (1984); D. Justice, "The F. V. Line in Stevens," *Antaeus* 53 (1984); O. Ovčarenko, *Ruskij Svobodny Stix* (1984); R. Cureton, "Rhythm: A Multi-level Analysis," *Style* 17 (1985); J. Hollander, "Observations on the Experimental," in Hollander; D. Wesling, *The New Poetries* (1985), ch. 5; S. Cushman, *W. C. Williams and the Meanings of Measure* (1985); E. Bollobás, *Trad. and Innovation in Am. F. V., Whitman to Duncan* (1986); C. Scott, *A Question of Syllables* (1986), ch. 6; T. Steele, *Missing Measures* (1990).   D.W.; E.BO.

FREIE RHYTHMEN. In Ger. this term refers to unrhymed, metrically irregular, nonstrophic verse lines of varying length. These lines can usually be distinguished from rhythmical prose not only by their visual arrangement on the page, but also by a tendency toward nearly equal intervals between stressed syllables, as well as phonological and rhythmic correspondences between lines. F. R represent the only major formal innovation which Ger. lit. provided to world lit. in the 18th c. Introduced by Friederich Klopstock in the 1750s (e.g. "Dem Allgegenwärtigen," 1758; "Frühlingsfeier," 1759) as a conscious revolt against the restraints imposed on Ger. poetry by Martin Opitz in the 17th c., f. R. are particularly appropriate as a medium for the free, unrestrained expression of feelings typical of the age of sentimentality (*Empfindsamkeit*):

> Nicht in den Ozean der Welten alle
> Will ich mich stürzen! schweben nicht,
> Wo die ersten Erschaffenen, die Jubel-
>   chöre der Söhne des Licht
> Anbeten, tief anbeten und in Ent-
>   zückung vergehn!
>   (Klopstock, "Frühlingsfeier")

They were used in the 1770s by Goethe in his "Great Hymns" ("Wanderers Sturmlied," "Ganymed," "Prometheus," "Mahomets Gesang," etc.) and later by Friedrich Hölderlin ("Hyperions Schicksalslied"), Novalis ("Hymnen an die Nacht"), Heine, Nietzsche, Arno Holz, Rilke, Trakl, Benn, and other Ger. poets. Ger. terminology draws a clear distinction between f. R. and *freie Verse* (q.v.).

A. Closs, *Die f. R. in der deutschen Lyrik* (1947); F. G. Jünger, *Rhythmus und Sprache im deutschen Gedicht* (1952); W. Mohr and A. Closs, "F. R," *Reallexikon*; H. Enders, *Stil und Rhythmus: Studien zu den f. R. bei Goethe* (1962); L. L. Albertsen, *Die f. R.* (1971), *Neuere deutsche Metrik* (1984); C. Wagenknecht, *Deutsche Metrik: Eine historische Einführung* (1981).   D.H.C.

FREIE VERSE (Fr. *vers libre*, q.v.). (1) Rhymed lines in either iambic or trochaic meter throughout, but with a varying number of stressed syllables and therefore varying in line length. They were first used in It. madrigals, then in Fr. fables and comedies, and in Ger. in the 18th c. by Gellert, Hagedorn, Lessing, and Wieland. (2) Later the term was used more loosely to refer to lines of varying length without any metrical constraints, distinguished from *freie Rhythmen* (q.v.) and rhythmical prose only by rhyme, and occasionally by assonance. See also FREE VERSE; VERS LIBRES CLASSIQUES.—R. Kloepfer, "Vers libre—Freie Dichtung," *LiLi* 1 (1971). D.H.C.

FRENCH POETICS. See FRENCH POETRY; FRENCH PROSODY; MEDIEVAL POETICS; SECOND RHETORIQUE; PLEIADE; RENAISSANCE POETICS; BAROQUE POETICS; CLASSICISM; NEOCLASSICAL POETICS; ROMANTIC AND POSTROMANTIC POETICS; TWENTIETH-CENTURY POETICS.

FRENCH POETRY.

 I. MEDIEVAL
 A. *Lyric*
 B. *Narrative*
 C. *Dramatic*
 II. RENAISSANCE
 III. CLASSICISM
 IV. EIGHTEENTH CENTURY
 V. ROMANTICISM TO SYMBOLISM
 VI. TWENTIETH CENTURY

It has been frequently claimed, e.g. by A. E. Housman in a Cambridge conversation with André Gide (1917), that there is in Fr. p. no trad. comparable to that of England or Germany or Italy. Housman stated that between Villon and Baudelaire—for 400 years—Fr. p. was given over to rhymed discourse in which eloquence, wit, vituperation, and pathos were present, but not poetry. Even the romantics with their abundant lyricism have been denied a place among the legitimate poets.

Gide's first answer to this challenge was to acknowledge that perhaps the Fr. as a nation do have a deficiency in lyric sentiment, but that this very deficiency accounts for the elaborate system of Fr. prosody (q.v.) which developed in the course of those 400 years. Strict rules of versification, acting as constraints on the poet's spontaneity, caused poetry to be looked upon in France as a difficult art form which had been more rigorously perfected there than in other countries. In answer to Housman's second question, "After all, what is poetry?" Gide turned to a definition of Baudelaire's in notes for a Preface to *Les Fleurs du mal*. "Rhythm and rhyme," Baudelaire wrote, "answer man's immortal need for monotony, symmetry, and surprise, as opposed to the vanity and danger of inspiration." This theory, whereby poetry is related to music in that its prosody springs from the deepest, most primitive part of nature, illuminates not only the entire history of Fr. p., but also Baudelaire's significant revolution in that history.

I. MEDIEVAL. The earliest extant Fr. poem is the 9th-c. *Séquence de Sainte Eulalie* (ca. 880), a brief narrative in 14 decasyllabic couplets of the saint's life and passion. In the 10th c. appears the *Vie de Saint Léger*, the earliest Fr. poem in octosyllables (q.v.), the chief Fr. meter up to 1550. Three other religious poems of interest to the modern reader include the 11th-c. *Vie de Saint Alexis*, in decasyllables, with a striking episode in which Alexis, only beginning to realize his calling, commends his young bride of one day to Christ and flees the comforts of his aristocratic heritage; the 13th-c. Life by Rutebeuf of *Sainte Marie l'Egyptienne*, who led the life of a prostitute until her repentance; and the *Vers de la mort* by the Cistercian monk Hélinand de Froidmont, hallucinatory in its kaleidoscopic imagery.

A. *Lyric*. Among the earliest secular Fr. *lyric* poems are the *chansons de toile* (12th c.?), short poems probably accompanying needlework and tapestry weaving (see CANSO; LYRIC). In Southern France, a rich school of Occitan poetry (q.v.), that of the troubadours (q.v.), flourished during the 12th and 13th cs. In the North, the poets who followed the earlier troubadours in the 13th c. and adopted many of their forms and themes—in particular, courtly love (q.v.)—were known as trouvères (q.v.). An innovative noncourtly poet of the 13th c. was Rutebeuf, a contemporary of St. Louis. A forerunner of Villon, he spoke directly of himself, his moral and physical sufferings, the falseness of his friends, and his unhappy marriage.

During the 14th c., the forms of the various types of poems became fixed, the most important being the ballade and the rondeau (qq.v.). Guillaume de Machaut (ca. 1300–77), a canon of Rheims, practically founded a school of poetry. Eustache Deschamps (ca. 1346–ca. 1406), of Champagne, was perhaps the century's most fecund poet; he composed 1500 ballades in addition to poems in all the other known genres. Alain Chartier (ca. 1390–ca. 1440) is today most famous for his *Belle Dame sans merci*. Charles d'Orléans (1391–1465) is the first Fr. poet a few of whose poems are well known today, e.g. his rondeau which begins: "The weather has left its mantle / Of wind and cold and rain."

Great poetry was first created in France by François Villon (b. 1431) from the depths of his affliction, poverty, and suffering. In his two *Testaments*, Villon illustrates the principle of Christian metaphysics that man exists by some mystery—he is unable not to exist. For Villon, as for most medieval writers, the world is only an illusion, and the one reality is his own nature. Although Villon himself had no order in his life, his poetic imagination shows that he shared his time's passion for order. This order is the two natures of man, with the supremacy of spiritual nature over temporal nature. Villon was formed not only by the genius of his race, but by the faith of his mother, of his protector, and of his age:

Lady of heaven, queen of earth,
Empress of the infernal swamps,
Receive me, your humble Christian,
That I may have my place among your
  elect.
  (*Dame du ciel*)

Soon after the dawn of Fr. philosophy, the poet knew, above all, the night of the world: war, famine, poverty. He sees himself in many of his characters, esp. in the role of poverty-stricken culprit. "Le pauvre Villon" betrays coquetry and narcissism. He appears neither heroic nor stoical. He is a poor lover, or, more simply, the poor man surrounded by all the legendary heroes. He is not alone because he understands the greatness of the men who lived before him, who live again in him and in his memory, and who will continue living after him. It is esp. this feeling of union with what is above time that makes Villon a poet. All the themes of the 15th c. are in his work: the Virgin, death, fortune, the martyr-lover, "la Dame sans merci," the harlot, the shepherd, the malice of priests, the vanity of this world, the flight of time. All of these themes find their purest expression in his art.

Formerly considered the wasteland of Fr. lyric p., the period of the *Grands Rhétoriqueurs*, lying roughly between Villon and Clément Marot, is now seen in its true perspective, as a time of audacious formal innovations characterized by exuberance of vocabulary, syntax, prosody, and rhet (see SECONDE RHETORIQUE). The *Rhétoriqueurs* (q.v.), esp. the greatest of them, Jean Lemaire de Belges (ca. 1473–ca. 1525), were gifted humanists who created a pre-Renaissance of sorts and who interpreted the events, customs, and ideals of the time in the light of ancient wisdom. Court poets, they were hardly refined, but spoke out vehemently against contemporary abuses, endowing modern Fr. p. thereby with some of its earliest significant satire.

B. *Narrative*. Long epic poems called *chansons de geste* (q.v.) and dating from the 11th and 12th cs. mark the second phase of Fr. lit. Most scholars today still accept, at least in part, Joseph Bédier's thesis (*Les Légendes épiques*) that these poems originated in churches and monasteries where the monks furnished the half-legendary, half-historical narratives glorifying their sanctuaries. The *chansons de geste* celebrating Charlemagne and the other great feudal lords form a cycle of poems, of which *La Chanson de Roland* is the acknowledged masterpiece. A single rear-guard action is sung of as an epic battle. Historical characters are converted into stylized types: Roland the rash young warrior, Charlemagne the emperor and patriarch, Olivier the wise friend and counselor, Turpin the priest-warrior. Christianity, chivalry, and patriotism are exalted. Two other cycles comparable to

the *chansons de geste* deal with Celtic material or Antiquity. *Le Roman d'Alexandre* used a 12-syllable line which in time displaced the octosyllable to become the standard Fr. line, the alexandrine (q.v.). The *lais* (see LAI) of Marie de France are short narrative poems by the first known Fr. woman poet, writing at the end of the 12th c.

The most fertile narrative poet of the 12th c. was Chrétien de Troyes. The principal author of courtly romances (see MEDIEVAL ROMANCE) in Fr., he drew upon the Arthurian legends of the Round Table in his effort to reconcile the earlier warlike ideals of the *chansons de geste* with the new devotion to woman—whence such characters as Merlin, Lancelot, and Queen Guenivere. Those poets who continued Chrétien's work added poems on the Grail Legend and the story of Tristan, narrated principally by Béroul and Thomas. To the same courtly trad. may be added a charming "chantefable" (q.v.), *Aucassin et Nicolette*, half prose and half verse, describing the trials inflicted by destiny on two lovers before their final happiness.

The *fabliaux* (see FABLIAU) were short comic narratives characterized by immorality and coarseness. Their humor and irony had been more fully developed in *Le Roman de Renart*, a long satirical beast epic (q.v.) written in several parts, or "branches," probably by several poets of the 12th and 13th c. A society of animals stands for human society and presents a caricature of feudal aristocracy, clergy, and lit. themes. Renart the fox symbolizes human intelligence using trickery and ruse in order to mock authority. The multiple sources of this work are to be found in the fables of Antiquity and in European folklore.

The outstanding Fr. allegorical work of the Middle Ages is *Le Roman de la Rose*, in two parts, the first written by Guillaume de Lorris in the first half of the 13th c., the second by Jean de Meun in the second half of the same century. Guillaume de Lorris' poem is a manual of courtly love. He was familiar with Ovid's *Art of Love* and the allegories used by the *clercs* to describe the phases of love. In contrast, the second and longer part of the poem is composed in a far different style and spirit, the fictional element being a mere pretext for digressions on cosmology, life, religion, and morals. Encyclopedic and pedantic, this philosophical treatise is quite emancipated from theology. Nature is both the key to man's rights and virtues and the principle of beauty, reason, and the good. Jean de Meung's poem is the genesis of a moral philosophy which was continued, in varying degree, in the writings of Rabelais, Montaigne, Molière, and Voltaire.

C. *Dramatic*. The first form of dramatic poetry in France was the liturgical drama (q.v.), closely connected with church ritual. Originally acted within the church, *drames liturgiques* were then performed outside on an improvised stage. Gradually texts became secularized. *Le Jeu de Saint Nicolas* by Jean Bodel (end of the 12th c.) represents the definitive form of religious theater—a combination of miracle and farce, with many themes and subplots. Miracle plays (*miracles*), dealing with the intercession of the Virgin, flourished esp. in the 14th c.; morality plays, satires (*soties*), and mystery plays (q.v.—*mystères*) flourished in the 15th c. These last, of excessive length and demanding several days for performance, offered a popular treatment of religious history from the Creation to the time of Saint Louis. The more purely secular comic theatre comprised the pastoral play, such as *Le Jeu de Robin et Marion*, and a more complex type, half satiric, half comic, *Le Jeu de la feuillée*, both by Adam de La Halle (13th c.), as well as farces (15th c.). The masterpiece of the medieval comic theater dates from the middle of the 15th c., *La Farce de Maître Pathelin*. In character devel. and plot, it is a full-fledged comedy, a distant ancestor of Molière's art (see FARCE).

II. RENAISSANCE. Late 15th-c. poetry was dominated by the *Grands Rhétoriqueurs*, many of whom were attached to the Court of Burgundy. Elaborate abstractions characterized their long didactic poems; their shorter poems often depended on riddles and puns. Their influence is visible in Clément Marot (1496–1544), son of the *Rhétoriqueur* Jean Marot. Much of Marot's verse was occasional, written to praise a patron. He was a typical Ren. court poet whose gift for satire was stimulated by his contacts with the law students and lawyers of Paris (*La Basoche*), with Marguerite de Navarre, the King's sister who encouraged him, with the It. court of Ferrara (where he could give free expression to his religious and satiric themes), and with the court of Francis I. His satirical tone is varied and subtle rather than vehement. Although he continued medieval forms—the farcical, rambling, and sometimes obscene *coq-à-l'âne* (q.v.), besides *rondeaux* and *ballades*—he also practiced forms that were to be developed esp. in the 17th c.: the *épître*, a long verse letter, and the *épigramme*, a short, concise poem, usually satiric and with a sting in its tail (see EPIGRAM). Finally, Marot was probably the first writer of the sonnet (q.v.) in Fr.

Marguerite de Navarre (1492–1549) was the first important Fr. woman poet. She was not a profound theologian in her religious poetry, *Les Prisons*, but she drew abundantly on Plato and the doctrines of Christian theology. She participated in all the humanistic activities of the Ren., in philosophy, politics, and poetry; however, the sentiments which directed her life were her love of God and her quest for the Absolute.

Poetry flourished in Lyons, esp. during the reign of Francis I, in a movement which came to be called *l'école lyonnaise*. The one subject of the 3 elegies and the 24 sonnets of Louise Labé (1526–66) is love, carnal love. In the 500 lines comprising her poetic output she expresses vibrantly the causes and symptoms of her suffering without psychological subtleties. She had obviously read Petrarch, but never plagiarized his text. Far more complicated is Maurice Scève (1511–64), both in form and sentiment. Scève too wrote against a background of very conscious literary and philosophical enthusiasms. Platonism and Petrarchism (q.v.) had been the two current fashions in Lyons ever since their introduction by the Florentines in the 15th c. and by Marguerite de Navarre in the early 16th c. Plato's influence is even more apparent in Marguerite's religious poetry than in Scève's *Délie*. Platonism, as taught in Italy in the 15th c., esp. by Marsilio Ficino, had taken on in France the amplitude of a movement of ideas when Ficino became one of Marguerite's favorites. Scève was probably presented to her when she stopped in Lyons between April and July 1536. The title of Scève's work, *Délie*, is an anagram of the word "l'idée," but it is also the fictitious name given to the lady whom Scève loved and whom all the 449 *dizains* (q.v.) concern. Since each *dizain* relates one aspect or moment of the same experience, the work possesses an organic structure. Many follow the trad. of describing the particular beauties of Délie's countenance and body (see BLASON). But in the far more striking *dizains* where Scève analyzes the impossibility of being loved as he loves, he describes a progressive self-knowledge and self-torment which give the work its profoundest unity. The end of the long sequence of poems apostrophizes death, not as a union with the beloved but as a liberation from amorous torment. The absence of any religious philosophy gives Scève's psychology a relentless terror and bareness which is not at all characteristic of the Middle Ages and the Ren., but rather adumbrative of the modern period. Today the *dizains* of Scève are admired and studied for their difficult, often obscure symbolism.

The seven poets known as *La Pléiade* (q.v.) represent the most spectacular triumph of Fr. p. in the Ren. Some of their poetry is of a springlike tenderness and hopefulness, despite their awareness of life's uncertainties and the destruction of sentiment and beauty wrought by the passing of time. Their art is a union of mythology and nature—a combination of pedantic constructs and simple, heartfelt popular poetry. Rivers, woods, roses, dew, and nymphs appear everywhere in their verses, forming the natural setting for the serious themes of happiness, love, and death. Pierre de Ronsard (1524–85), the greatest poet of the *Pléiade*, left a long and varied work. His sonnets, *Les Amours*, have immortalized three women: Cassandre, Marie, Hélène. "When you are old, in the evening, by candlelight, / Seated near the fire, unwinding and spinning, / You will say reciting my verses and marvelling at them: / Ronsard sang of me when I was beautiful." His *Odes* and *Hymnes* made him the most celebrated poet in Europe. Ronsard demanded for the poet the highest position, that of *vates* (seer). The earlier poets had had a sense of professional honor; Villon had been a conscientious writer, as was Scève, with a sense of higher worldly position. But Ronsard instituted the doctrine of poetic *gloire*, a gift which the poet can bequeath and sell. In 1549, Joachim du Bellay (1525–60), the second most important member of the *Pléiade*, drew up the new poets' program and beliefs in *La Défense et illustration de la langue française*. Although Du Bellay treated the ancients with almost fanatical respect, his chief purpose was to prove that the Fr. lang. was equal in dignity to Gr. and Lat. He advised a complete break with medieval trad. and, instead, the imitation of Cl. genres: tragedies and comedies, for example, should supplant the *mystères* and *miracles* of the "Gothic" period. Du Bellay was to a certain extent responsible, in *L'Olive* (1549), for the success which the love sonnet was to have in the 16th and 17th cs. and, in *Les Antiquités de Rome* and *Les Regrets* (1558–59), for the satiric sonnet (see SONNET).

Two poets who wrote at the end of the century have been rediscovered in recent years. Jean de Sponde (1557–95), a Protestant who abjured his faith, as did Henri IV, left a brief work—sonnets on death and other religious poems. Because of the abundance of his metaphor and antithesis, de Sponde's name is today associated with "baroque" poetry (q.v.) and the metaphysical poetry (q.v.) of John Donne. The second discovery was of Jean de la Ceppède (1530–1622), a more prolific poet than Sponde, as witnessed by the 500 sonnets of his *Théorèmes sur le sacré mystère de notre rédemption*. The "theorem" was used by 16th-c. Fr. poets to represent the mystery of the Redemption. The symbolism and beauty of La Ceppède's sonnets seem strikingly modern: the title of Pasolini's 1968 film, *Teorema*, was probably taken from La Ceppède.

Agrippa d'Aubigné (1550–1630) was a prophet-poet as well as a soldier and memorialist. His *Tragiques* are as strongly a satiric work as Hugo's *Châtiments*. They testify to his Calvinist faith and demonstrate a close application of Scripture to the accidents of mortal existence, to the predestined significance of events of seeming chance. The seven books composing *Les Tragiques* describe France in a state of civil war. They denounce the Valois princes, the chambers of justice, and the holocausts of the century, and they reflect all the latter's styles and beliefs: Ronsard's sensitive lyricism, to a degree; a humanistic understanding of man, to a stronger degree; a biblical and apocalyptic interpretation of the day, to an overwhelming degree. D'Aubigné made an important contribution to lyric poetry in his first verse, *Le Printemps du Sieur d'Aubigné*, published long after his death. These love sonnets, begun in 1570, were inspired by Diane Salviati, the niece of Ronsard's Cassandre.

III. CLASSICISM. The Fr. classical style as it developed in the 17th c. was at times opposed by tendencies now often called "baroque" (q.v.). This term, more applicable to a style of architecture and sculpture than to lit., suggests a rich, almost extravagant form, with ornate and intricate flourishes. In lit., "baroque" writing has elements of fantasy and irrationality, and forms that translate the anguish of man in elaborate lang. Cl. art was, by contrast, sober, measured, and clear. The baroque taste was its opposite, and was everywhere in evidence during the years when cl. art was coming into its own (see BAROQUE POETICS; NEO-CLASSICAL POETICS).

The 20th c. has witnessed the rehabilitation of the baroque poets who, from Ronsard's decline to Boileau's rise, enriched Fr. p. with themes and forms (largely of It. origin) running counter to the coalescing cl. trad. Jean de Sponde and Aubigné in the 16th c., and Malherbe himself (in a youthful folly, *Les Larmes de Saint-Pierre*), Théophile de Viau, Saint-Amant, and Tristan L'Hermite in the 17th were the chief representatives of a movement that turned one current of Fr. p. into a contest with the indefinable, mingling religious and profane elements, building up tensions, piling up images, torturing syntax. By the unfinished ("open") character of their poems, their deliberate striving for obscure and bizarre effects, and their stretching of one image over several stanzas or an entire poem (Rubin), these solitary geniuses differed from the 17th-c. *précieux* poets, who wrote polished verses filled with the discreet allusions, witty epigrams, and short metaphors suited for an aristocratic audience.

The influence of François de Malherbe (1555–1628) dominated the poetic scene in the first half of the 17th c. His work as grammarian, poet, and critic helped to define the precepts of a Fr. art which was to be called "classical" and which occupies the central place in the history of Fr. culture. In a celebrated passage of his *Art poétique*, Boileau was later to hail the advent of Malherbe's authority in all things poetical: "At last Malherbe appeared." He was the first craftsman in the history of Fr. p. to discuss analytically, even pontifically, the rules of his craft (Abraham). He denounced erudition in poetry and the unrestrained outburst of lyricism. He purified the Fr. lang. by narrowing its range and making it capable of enunciating truths rather than personal passions. Ronsard and the other *Pléiade* poets had insisted on loftiness of theme and diction. Malherbe was the first to claim ordinary speech for poetry.

The tendencies toward bombast (*emphase*) and preciosity which had developed during the 16th and early 17th c., largely from It. and Sp. models, were opposed by Boileau (1636–1711), whose authority was strong under the reign of Louis XIV. He was a bourgeois of Paris, like Molière and Voltaire, and thus interrupted the central trad. of Fr. lit., hitherto largely aristocratic. Boileau, Molière, and Pascal represented, in their critical attitudes, a strong reaction against the *précieux* poetry of the *salons* and *ruelles*. Boileau attacked the pedantry of Chapelain and the Fr. imitation of It. models. Backed by La Fontaine, Racine, and

Molière, he eventually won over to his side the public and the King himself. Imitation of nature is the highest rule for Boileau: "Let nature be our one study." But this imitation (q.v.) must be carried on rationally, and only insofar as nature conforms to itself, only insofar as it is universal. Hence, the law of the three unities (see UNITY) is applicable in tragedy because it is natural and reasonable. Preciosity, which in poetry emphasized overrefined sentiment and periphrastic ornamental lang., should be condemned because it is unnatural to obscure willfully one's thought. An artist as well as a bourgeois, Boileau was also a craftsman and a painstaking theorist.

The critic Faguet claimed that a century of Fr. p. came to a close with Jean de La Fontaine (1621–95). Eclectic in the choice of his masters (he owed allegiance to Villon, Marot, and Voiture, as well as to Boccaccio and Rabelais), he converted his imitations into an art that is very much his own. His care for technical perfection he owes as theory to Malherbe, but the works themselves, *Adonis*, for example, and *Psyché*, long narrative poems, and his *Contes*, are triumphs in poetic grace, melody, and sentiment. La Fontaine recreated the genre of the fable (q.v.), writing what he himself called "the 100-act comedy whose stage set is the universe." Scenes, characterizations, dialogues, all are struck off with remarkable clarity and concentration. Each fable is a dramatization. The moral value of his teaching has often been questioned, but the poems themselves appear as original creations, thanks to La Fontaine's psychological penetration and his subtle, varied use of free verse (see VERS LIBRES CLASSIQUES). The final lines of *Les Deux Pigeons* illustrate this art of nuance and sentiment:

> Lovers, happy lovers, do you want to travel?
> Do not go very far.
> Be for each other a world always beautiful,
> Always different, always new.

Pierre Corneille (1606–84) was the first poet to apply to Fr. tragedy with any lasting success the principle of the three unities. He was a major pioneer in cl. art. His poetry is vigorous but tends toward the bombastic. His lang. seems today somewhat archaic and oratorical, but he did master the alexandrine; his style has clarity and precision and a strong sense of rhythm. The poetry of his best tragedies, *Le Cid, Horace, Cinna, Polyeucte*, is a poetry of action and an intellectual lang. describing the feelings and dilemmas of the characters.

Jean Racine (1639–99) holds a high place among the religious poets of France. His choruses from *Athalie* and *Esther*, as well as his four *Cantiques spirituels*, testify to a remarkable lyric perfection. The achievement of Racine as dramatist is due in part to his theory of tragic action and to his penetration as psychologist, but in part also to his poetic gifts, the elegance of his expression, and

the magic of his style. Racine's particular triumph lies in the fusion of meaning and music, of tragic sentiment and the pure sound of his alexandrine line. Racine was trained in the school of the *Précieux*, and there are elements of preciosity throughout his tragedies. But on the whole he rejected superfluous ornament and excluded unusual words from his vocabulary. When the occasion calls for it, Racine can write lines as vibrantly eloquent as Corneille's. Fr. p. was not to know again such human poignancy and such artistic simplicity and dramatic meaning until the publication of Baudelaire's *Les Fleurs du mal* in the 19th c.

Several of the major comedies of Molière (1622–73) were written in verse: *L'École des Femmes, Le Tartuffe, Le Misanthrope, Amphitryon, Les Femmes savantes*. As Racine did in the case of tragedy, Molière in his treatment of comedy fused lang. with situation and poetry with characterization. Molière's lang. is at all times vigorous, varied, and colorful. He knew the lang. of the people, the bourgeoisie, and the *Précieux*. In the high comedies, composed in alexandrines, one has the impression of listening to conversation and, at the same time, to something more substantial, thanks to the skillful syntactic organization, the lilt of the rhythm, and the resounding rhymes. Molière's style is purely theatrical—dramatic suitability of the poetic expression was his guiding rule.

IV. EIGHTEENTH CENTURY. The richest periods for lyric poetry in France were, first, the 16th c., when a renaissance of spring abundance had favored the delicate, witty songs of Marot, the sadder, more metaphysical verse of Labé and Scève, and the full maturity of the *Pléiade* poets; and, second, the 19th c., with its three so-called schools of poetry: romantic, Parnassian, and symbolist (qq.v.), which are but three aspects of a single devel. in modern art and sensitivity, and which continued in the major poets of the 20th c.

In the two intervening centuries, lyric poetry had been subdued or lost in other forms of writing. During the 17th c., lyric genius was always subordinated to dramatic genius. The drama of Racine's poetry had been prepared for by almost 200 years of lyric poetry, from Villon at the end of the Hundred Years' War to the advent of Louis XIV. The effusiveness and facility of lyric verse, which are its constant dangers, had been chastened and channeled in the tragedies of *Andromaque* and *Phèdre*, as, in the 19th c., the expansiveness of romantic verse would be chastised by the strict form of the Parnassians and by the severe experience of the symbol in Mallarmé's poetry.

During the 18th c., the poetic genius was taken over by the philosophers, and the exploration of self gave way to the explorations of society and of the universe. The form of poetic tragedy perfected by Racine declined rapidly, to become in the 18th c. a conventionalized, weak genre. Voltaire alone showed some competence in his imitation of Racine. The style of *Zäire*, for example, has a cl. clarity but is lacking in strong characterization. Voltaire tried all forms of poetry. His epic *La Henriade* celebrates the religious wars and the advent of Henri IV. His philosophical poems, epistles, and satires are more successful, yet they are lacking in any real sensitivity. His short poems, *Pièces de circonstance*, are perhaps his best in their elegance and wit.

Voltaire was not only the official poet of the century but also the best defender of poetry. There were many versifiers. Jean-Baptiste Rousseau (1671–1741) was called "le grand Rousseau" in order to humiliate Jean-Jacques. His *Ode et Cantates* (1723) was first published in London. Jean-Baptiste-Louis Gresset (1709–77) wrote a lighter kind of poetry in the trad. of Marot. *Vert-Vert* is a poem about a parrot brought up by nuns; as the bird moves from convent to convent it picks up the lang. of sailors. *Les Saisons* (1769), a pastoral poem by Saint-Lambert (1716–1807), was undoubtedly inspired by *The Seasons* of the Eng. poet James Thomson (1700–46). Jacques Delille (1738–1813) became famous for his translations of Virgil (*Géorgiques*), Milton (*Paradis perdu*), and Pope (*Essai sur l'homme*).

In the wake of many versifiers, André Chénier (1762–94) appeared at the end of the 18th c. as its one legitimate poet. Eventually executed by the guillotine, Chénier wrote his poems, *Les Iambes*, in prison, a work which in satiric force and vituperation takes its place beside d'Aubigné's *Tragiques* and Hugo's *Châtiments*. His extensive literary knowledge, esp. of Gr. poetry, reminds one of the Pléiade poets and their eagerness to learn from the poets of Antiquity. Chénier knew the It. poets and the Bible, the *Arabian Nights*, and the Eng. poets: Shakespeare, Young, Thomson, and Ossian. Ronsard, La Fontaine, and Chénier are the three Fr. poets who were inspired and guided by their study of Antiquity, and yet who never imitated the ancient poets in any servile manner.

V. ROMANTICISM TO SYMBOLISM. Paradoxically, the major poetic work of the 18th c. was written in prose. Its author, Jean-Jacques Rousseau, was certainly concerned with ideas, but he felt them as a poet might, and he succeeded in transmitting them to the romantic poets of the 19th c. Passages from all Rousseau's writings, but esp. his last book, *Rêveries d'un promeneur solitaire*, fixed the characteristics of the romantic temperament and gave the first fevers to a malady which was to deepen during the next hundred years. Jean-Jacques preached that man's oneness with nature was a state to be recaptured. The first stage of the new lyricism was one of "rêverie," largely narcissistic. During the first decade of romantic poetry (1820–30), and in part as a result of Chateaubriand's *René* (in poetic prose) at the turn of the century, Rousseauistic rêverie underwent an important modification. Nature continued to be the fountain of Narcissus for the romantic hero, but the traits he saw reflected in it were no longer peaceful. His

dissatisfaction, vague nostalgia, tearfulness, and even sorrow had changed the visage of the self-seeking and self-reflected hero.

Lamartine (1790–1869), in his *Méditations poétiques* of 1820, expressed this new sensibility in his wanderings through nature and in his efforts to recapture moments of the past when he had experienced happiness. For Lamartine the resurrection of his memory was that of happiness and even ecstasy; his belief in the future, although indistinct, was formed in hope and optimism. It was only the terrible present for which he felt no genius. The state of disillusionment reached its most bitter expression in the verse of Alfred de Vigny (1797–1863). To the disappointment which Lamartine felt in the flux of time, Vigny added an attack on the infidelity of woman and nature herself and on the religions of the world as beneficent lies. The early romantic disillusionment thus culminated with him in undisguised pessimism. He was an uneven poet, but a forceful thinker. To his innate pessimism, Vigny opposed stoicism and a philosophy founded on work and intellection. Coldness and aloofness characterized his attitude, as well as a nobility of thought akin to that of the ancients. Although Vigny did not believe in the ultimate salvation of mankind, he did believe in the greatness of effort, the majesty of human suffering, and the achievements of philosophers and scientists. The impertinence and facility of Alfred de Musset's (1810–57) early poems changed after tragic experience with George Sand, and the "enfant terrible" of the early romantics became in his *Nuits* "un enfant du siècle," the type of the suffering poet and the victim of what has been called *pélicanisme*, after the poet's own interpretation of the pelican symbol in *La Nuit de mai*.

The position of Victor Hugo (1802–85) in the devel. of 19th-c. Fr. p. is extraordinarily important. He played a preponderant part in the gradually increasing violence of the romantic malady by the very vigor of his character and his verse. His first volumes (*Odes et ballades* and *Les Orientales*) were roughly contemporary with the first of Lamartine and Vigny, and his last volumes (*La Légende des siècles* and *La Fin de satan*) came at the time of Baudelaire and Mallarmé. During this long career, which encompassed the other more significantly brief careers of Nerval, Baudelaire, Lautréamont, Rimbaud, and Mallarmé, Hugo's philosophy or, more precisely, his cosmology developed into a form of pantheism which is the source of his best poetry. After being a mirror for the narcissistic Rousseau, a site for the anguished wanderings of Chateaubriand and Lamartine, and a distant, unconsoling splendor for Vigny, nature was sometimes raised by Hugo to a level of religious significance:

> I was alone near the waves, during a
> starry night.

Not a cloud in the heaven, on the sea
　　no sail.
My eyes saw farther than the real
　　world.

External nature, of which man is but one ele-
ment, was for him a multiform manifestation of
occult forces and divinity. A peculiar interpreta-
tion of the Old Testament and the Kabbala led
Hugo to believe that the animation of nature,
when it should be realized, would in turn animate
man and solve his problems. Some of Hugo's dra-
mas were written in verse, e.g. *Hernani, Ruy Blas,
Les Burgraves*, but their value lies more in their
lyricism than in their dramatic or psychological
conceptions: there are many bravura passages,
love dialogues, and meditations in which the
dramatist is essentially a poet. (At the end of the
century, in 1897, *Cyrano de Bergerac* by Edmond
Rostand would represent a return to the ideals of
early romantic drama. It had in its poetry many of
the elements of Hugo's plays: heroism, grace,
bombast, wit. The play had a tremendous success
at a time when naturalistic theater was flourish-
ing.)

Théophile Gautier (1811–72) defined in his
poem *L'Art* some of the principal tenets of the
Parnassian (q.v.) school, which grew up in opposi-
tion to the excessive subjectivity of romantic po-
etry. Art, he claims, finds its justification in its own
intrinsic beauty and not in its relevance to morality
or philosophy. Art alone has eternity, and esp. that
art whose form is difficult to achieve. This doc-
trine of "art for art's sake" was also embraced by
Hérédia and Leconte de Lisle (see AESTHETI-
CISM). Traces of the same convictions are visible
in Baudelaire and Mallarmé.

Hugo's pantheism had represented a moment
in the hist. of man's hope and religious illumina-
tion. The prose and poetry of Charles Baudelaire
(1821–67) holds out the hope of magic in nature.
Baudelaire was the greatest poet of the second half
of the 19th c., in the sense that *Les Fleurs du mal*
(1857) was the richest source of creativeness, be-
ing both an achievement in art and a criticism for
art. (In the same way, Rimbaud was to be the
greatest poet for the first forty years of the 20th c.,
in the sense that *Les Illuminations* and *Une Saison
en enfer* are the two guiding psychological docu-
ments of the period.) Baudelaire's significance
lies not solely in his conception of nature as the
source of sensations and the key to the world of
the spirit. It lies even more preeminently in his
despair over inertia and acedia, in his despair at a
lack-of-feeling he felt which prevented him from
willing not to sin. Hope in nature, in the whole
created universe as the reflection of some half-ex-
perienced sense of unity or Divine Love, on the
one hand, and, on the other, the incapacity to feel
deeply enough the infractions against the laws of
man and God in order to cease perpetrating these
infractions, are the two aspects of Baudelaire's art,
which in *Les Fleurs du mal* he calls (reversing the
order) "Spleen et Idéal." This new definition of
man's basic dualism and struggle with the forces
of good and evil springs from the sensitivity of the
19th-c. artist. Baudelairian "idéal" was yet another
expression of romantic exoticism and Hugo's
hope in nature. It was the need to go to the most
distant, and therefore the most purifying, parts of
the world, to scenes different from the familiar,
where the heart of man could be itself, unasham-
edly, in all of its fathomless innocence. Likewise,
Baudelairian "spleen" was still another expression
of romantic introspection and Vigny's pessimism:

November, angry with the whole city,
From its urn pours out a dark cold
Over the pale inhabitants of the
　　nearby cemetery
And mortality over the foggy suburbs.

Spleen was the poet's incapacity to move out
from himself, to disengage his spirit from the
center of his dilemma, from the center of his body
which had been enslaved. It was the poet's velleity
and ennui which, even if they are absences and
negations, may grow to uncontrollable propor-
tions. "Idéal" in Baudelaire is often translated by
the image of a sea-voyage, by *L'Invitation au voyage;*
and "spleen" is often translated by the image of a
closed room or cell, by a closed brain or a closed
body. "Idéal" is the desire to move and to be free.
"Spleen" is the horror of being unable to move and
of being caught in bondage.

The poems of Arthur Rimbaud (1854–91) are
the first representations of his life (*Poètes de sept
ans* and *Mémoire*) and his first visions (*Bateau ivre*).
His prose work, *Une Saison en enfer*, is fairly devoid
of visions. It is almost a retractation, an effort to
understand his past and his revolt against Christi-
anity. It is his confession of failure. The prose
poems, *Les Illuminations*, are best understood as
coming after *Une Saison* in a new movement of
hope and almost mystical belief in himself as poet
and visionary. In the earlier works, the poet had
learned his lang. of *voyant* and something concern-
ing the failure of living as an artist. *Les Illumina-
tions* have behind them an experience comparable
to the mystic's initiation to failure. Rimbaud's
example will remain that of the poet opposing his
civilization, his historical moment, and yet at the
same time revealing its instability and quaking
torment. He is both against his age and of it. By
refusing to take time to live, he lived a century in
a few years, throughout its minute phases, rushing
toward the only thing that mattered to him: the
absolute, the certainty of truth. He came closest
to finding this absolute in his poet's vision. That
was "the place and the formula" he talked of and
was impatient to find, the spiritual hunt that did
not end with the prey seized. Rimbaud's is the
drama of modern man, by reason of its particular
frenzy and precipitation; but it is also the human
drama of all time, the drama of the quest for what

has been lost, the unsatisfied temporal existence burning for total satisfaction and certitude.

As early as Gérard de Nerval (1808–55), who incorporated the speculations of the 18th-c. *illuminés*, poetry had tried to be the means of intuitive communication between man and the powers beyond him. Nerval was the first to point out those regions of extreme temptation and extreme peril which have filled the vision of the major poets who have come after him.

The lesson of Stéphane Mallarmé (1842–98) is the extraordinary penetration of his gaze at objects in the world and the attentive precision with which he created a world of forms and pure relationships between forms. The object in a Mallarmé poem is endowed with a force of radiation that is latent and explosive. The irises, for example, in *Prose pour des esseintes*, have reached a "purity" from which every facile meaning has been eliminated. This purity is their power to provoke the multiple responses of the most exacting readers, those who insist that an image appear in its own beauty, isolated from the rest of the world and independent of all keys and obvious explanations. Mallarmé's celebrated sonnet on the swan caught in the ice of a lake illustrates this power of a metaphor to establish a subtle relationship between two seemingly opposed objects: a swan and a poet. The relationship is not stated in logical or specific terms but is suggested or evoked by the metaphor:

> Will the virginal, strong and handsome today
> Tear for us with a drunken flap of his wing
> This hard forgotten lake which the transparent glacier
> Of flights unflown haunts under the frost!

For the poet's role of magus and prophet, so histrionically played by Victor Hugo, was thus substituted the role of magician, incarnated not solely by Rimbaud (whose *Lettre du voyant* of 1871 seems to be its principal manifesto), but also by Nerval and Baudelaire who preceded him, by his contemporary Mallarmé, and by his leading disciples, the 20th-c. surrealists, 30 years after his death. This concept of the poet as magician dominates most of the poetic transformations and achievements of the last century. The poet, in his subtle relationship with the mystic, rids himself of the traits of the Hugoesque prophet, as well as the vain ivory-tower attitude of a Vigny. Emphasis on the poet as a sorcerer, in search of the unknown and surreal part of his own being, has further caused him to give up the poetry of love, esp. the facile love poetry of a Musset.

Jules Laforgue (1860–87) has been gradually assuming a place of real importance in the history of symbolism. The first constituted group of symbolist poets were active during 1880–85. The word "decadent" has been associated with them (see DECADENCE). As opposed to the symbolists, the decadents allowed in their verse the direct transcription of emotion and phenomena. There is nothing in the later Laforgue of the grand style of romantic poetry. He is concerned with depicting the shifts and variations of feeling in scenes of the modern city. The dominant mood Laforgue expresses is one of emotional starvation and emotional inhibition. The parody of his own sensibility becomes, in Laforgue's *Moralités légendaires*, the parody of some of the great myths of humanity. He recapitulates the stories of the masters—Shakespeare's Hamlet, Wagner's Lohengrin, Mallarmé's Pan, Flaubert's Salomé—and alters them in order to infuse new meanings. No such thing as a pure hero exists for this poet. He sees the so-called heroes as ordinary creatures and gives them the psychological characteristics of his Pierrots—nervousness, anxiety—and an ephemeral existence.

The first edition of Tristan Corbière's one book, *Les Amours jaunes*, appeared in 1873, which was the year of Rimbaud's *Une Saison en enfer* and Verlaine's *Romances sans paroles*. No attention whatever was paid to these three books at the time. Corbière died two years later, at the age of thirty. Not until 1883, in Verlaine's series of essays on *Les Poètes maudits*, was Corbière presented to the Paris public as a poet of importance. This first label of *poète maudit* (q.v.) has remained associated with his name. He refused to write poetry in accordance with traditional forms. He even refused to be a traditional bohemian. "An ocean bohemian," Laforgue once called him, since most of his life was spent in Brittany, in the towns of Morlaix and Roscoff, and since the themes of his personal suffering are mingled with the dominant theme of the sea. In many ways, Corbière was the spiritual descendent of Villon, esp. in his self-disparagement. He looked upon himself as a failure, both as a man and as a poet, and he looked upon his life as a marriage with disaster. There are strong reminiscences of Baudelaire in *Les Amours jaunes* and Baudelairian traits too in Corbière's impenetrability. There are *concetti* and antitheses almost in Góngora's style, and rhythmical innovations and patterns which Verlaine will develop. Corbière's control of his art is less strong than Baudelaire's or Rimbaud's; his revolt against order and convention is less metaphysical than Rimbaud's.

Mallarmé and Rimbaud are the greatest poets of the symbolist period. To a lesser degree, the example of Paul Verlaine (1844–96) counted also in the symbolist movement. *Fêtes galantes* (1869) evokes the delicacy and licentiousness of Watteau's paintings. His *Art poétique*, written in prison in 1873, became a manifesto for the symbolists. It insists on music, imprecision, and shading in the writing of poetry. But his influence on the devel. of Fr. p. has been slight, despite the fact that he exploited brilliantly the resources of the Fr. lang.

VI. TWENTIETH CENTURY. Verlaine's was a poetry of the heart and of pure sentiment, a trad. maintained by Francis Jammes (1868–1938), who belonged to the first generation of 20th-c. poets. Even more isolated from symbolism and the central evolution of Fr. p. stands Charles Péguy (1873–1914), celebrated between the two wars for his deeply religious poetry on Notre-Dame de Chartres and for his *Mystère de la charité de Jeanne d'Arc* (1910), a celebration echoed in turn by Geoffrey Hill in 1984. Péguy's poetry presents no linguistic or metaphorical difficulties. He is remembered as the patron-poet of peasants and as the pilgrim of La Beauce. Not until Albert Béguin's study of *Eve* in 1948 was there a critical effort to understand and explain the poetry. Péguy fashioned an alexandrine that was recognizably his own (there are ten thousand alexandrines in his work). *Eve* is Péguy's literary expression of his return to the Church, a vision of human history (as well as a poetics) which moves from the Incarnation to the Redemption in a long dialogue between the flesh (Incarnation) and the soul (Redemption), between the Fall, associated with Eve, and the Redemption, associated with Christ.

Paul Valéry (1871–1945) had listened in his early twenties to Mallarmé's conversations on poetry. In his celebrated definition of symbolism, Valéry states that the new poetry is simply trying to recapture from music what belongs to it. But in the practice of so-called symbolist poetry, he revived, and adhered to, all the classical rules of prosody. If the music of lang. is to be rediscovered and recreated, a long process of "research" is necessary into the sounds of syllables, the meanings of words, and word phrases and their combinations. The symbol (q.v.) in poetry establishes a relationship between things and ourselves. It is a kind of bond uniting man with the universe. Valéry appropriates some of the oldest symbols (or myths) in the world, e.g. Narcissus and the Fates, which are the titles of two of his greatest poems. Most of the poems in *Charmes* (1922) derive their title from the leading symbol: *L'Abeille* (bee), *Palme, Au platane* (planetree), *La Ceinture* (sash). Valéry is a singer of knowledge, of subterranean knowledge, where thought may be studied at its birth, in the intermediary stage between the subconscious and the conscious. His poems are metaphysical debates, as in the poems on Narcissus, where a veritable self-inquisition takes place:

> A great calm heeds me in which I listen to hope.
> In the secrets of the extinguished fountain.
> In the secrets which I fear learning.
> (*Charmes*)

At the beginning of *La Jeune Parque* (1917), we learn that some kind of metaphysical catastrophe has taken place, of which the poem develops the consequences. Valéry's fame has been built upon

fragments: poems, aphorisms, dialogues, brief essays. He is the supreme example of a writer indifferent to his public, detached from any need to please his public. The dialogue which he instituted with himself and with the few great writers he turned to appears with the passage of time increasingly dramatic. *Eupalinos* as well as *Mon Faust* are comparable to the form of the Socratic dialogue, in which the resources and agility of man's conscience are explored.

Rimbaud's importance, and esp. the spiritual significance of his work, was first revealed by the poet Paul Claudel (1868–1955). Deep within a work which seems to be composed largely of revolt and blasphemy, Claudel discovered traces of a religious drama which spoke directly to him and to which he owed his return to Catholicism. The reading of Rimbaud and the religious experience he underwent at the age of 18 changed Claudel's world. These were revelations whereby he saw the world as the work of God and worthy of the poet's paean of praise. This was the genesis of his great theme of Joy, the one reality for Claudel, the one requirement for the making of an artistic work. By temperament, Claudel belongs to the race of revolutionaries and conquerors, poets like d'Aubigné and Rimbaud; but he is also like Mallarmé in his will to define poetry in its essence. From Mallarmé, Claudel learned esp. about metaphor (q.v.), which is the essential element in his poetics. A metaphor is a relationship between two subjects; it may even be a relationship between God and the world. The poet's role is to apprehend the metaphors which exist in the world. This means naming each object and restoring it to its rightful place in a new ordering of the universe, in a new lexicon of the world. By naming an object, the poet gives it meaning, as God has originally done in creating the world—by naming it. The total Word, or the total poem, is therefore the universe. Each poet bears in himself a picture of the universe, a subjective maze of images which have relationships with one another. Mallarmé had followed an instinctive quest in naming various objects and seeking to understand their metaphorical meaning; Claudel goes further in willing this quest as if it were a religious obligation. Symbolism, under the guidance of Mallarmé, had been a spiritual way of understanding and celebrating the universe; in the art of Paul Claudel, it becomes a more frankly religious way of discovering, in the midst of endless variety, a secret unity. In his *Art poétique* (1903), Claudel states that metaphor is the logic of the new poetry, comparable to the syllogism of the older logic. Things in the world are not only objects to be known; they are means by which man is being constantly reborn. Claudel's plays are the most important poetic dramas in 20th-c. Fr. lit. They are concerned with human passion (*Partage de midi*) and religious themes (*L'Annonce faite à Marie*). Despite their difficult style and highly metaphorical lang., these plays reveal in production a grandeur and solemnity not found in the art of any other Fr. playwright.

It was quite appropriate that Guillaume Apollinaire (1880–1918), coming after the highly self-conscious symbolist school, would, in rebellion against such artifice, seek to return to the most primitive sources of lyricism. But by his lesson of freedom, gratuitousness, and individual morality, Apollinaire prolongs the lessons of Rimbaud and Mallarmé; like them, he considers poetic activity as a secret means of knowledge—self-knowledge and world-knowledge. The miracle of his poetry is the number of word surprises it contains and the abrupt appearances and disappearances of emotions and images. In his verses the great myths crowd close upon purely personal inventions. He calls upon his immediate knowledge of cities and ports, of unscrupulous *voyous* and popular songs, but speaks in the tone of a prophet and discoverer. The contrast between Apollinaire's extraordinary erudition, nourished on pornography, magic, popular lit., and encyclopedias, and his total simplicity as a song writer explains the profound irony pervading most of his poetry. Apollinaire's appearance, at the beginning of the 20th c., coincided with many new aesthetic preoccupations to which he brought his own inventiveness and speculative inquiry. His work joined that of the poet Max Jacob and the painters Picasso, Braque, Derain, and Matisse in a series of artistic fantasies that have gone far in shaping the modern sensibility. A farcical, festive air presided over many of the modes of art of that time, which were given the names of cubism (q.v.), Fauvism, Negro art, cosmopolitanism, or erotology. Apollinaire himself was responsible for the term "surrealism." He literally became a prophet in his support of aesthetic innovations which were to become the accepted forms of the future.

Surrealism (q.v.), thanks to the examples furnished by Rimbaud and Apollinaire, was to recognize that the real domain of the poet is just outside what is called the world of reason. Apollinaire had taught that the poetic act is the creative act in its fullest purity. Whatever the poet names possesses an ineffable quality; his function is precisely to explain *that*, to study what refuses to be cast into explicit lang. In this way, poetry is able to restore to lang. something of its primitive origins and mystery. Poetry like Apollinaire's does not try to fathom the supernatural or the miraculous, but simply to state the incomprehensibility of the ordinary and the commonplace. Every human expression Apollinaire saw became sphinxlike for him, and every word he overheard resembled a sibyl's utterance. His lang. has a baptismal gravity. Nascent lang., it would seem to be, rediscovering its virginity, as the poet, performing his earliest role of demiurge, calls the world to be born again by naming it.

The surrealist poets, Breton, the early Aragon, Eluard, Tzara, and Soupault, prolonged the trad. of the 19th-c. *voyant*. In the wake of Baudelaire, Rimbaud, and Mallarmé, poetry continued to be for them the effort to find a lost lang. The image or the metaphor is the result of a certain kind of alchemy. In symbolism, the alchemy had tried to go beyond the elaborate consciousness of symbolism to the very source of poetic imagination, to the sleep in which the myths of man are preserved. André Breton (1896–1966) and Paul Eluard (1895–1952), especially, have discovered (or rediscovered) the pure love of woman and sung of this love as ecstatically and vibrantly as any Ronsard. Their very intoxication with liberty seems to find an outlet in their love of woman, in their joy over their love. The human spirit's secrets were revealed to the surrealists, one after the other, in spontaneous and involuntary fashion. Their concept of woman seems to spring from the deepest part of their subconscious and to rise up to their consciousness with a primitive, almost sacred insistence. The surrealists have contributed to a rehabilitation in lit. of the role of woman as the bodily and spiritual equal of man. Love is the immediate (Eluard has entitled one of his volumes *La Vie immédiate*). The mystery of passion is a dialectic in which man makes an extraordinary request, but one which is clearly articulated in the most serious part of the surrealist program. In asking for the experience of passion, he asks for the resolution or the dissolving of the antinomy between the subject and the object, between love and death, between man and woman.

The generation of poets writing in Fr. at mid century was more dramatically allied with action—with the war and the Resistance—than the earlier poets of the century. Sartre defined the new lit. as being "engaged" (*la littérature engagée*), a term for the poetry of this generation so directly concerned with actual circumstances and events. The lesson taught by Mallarmé that there is no such thing as immediate poetry is, however, to such a degree the central legacy of modern poetry that the younger poets pass instinctively from the immediate to the eternal myths just beyond the events, the first reactions, and the first sentiments. The greatness of Pierre-Jean Jouve (1887–1976) illustrates this use of the immediate event in poetry. His universe of catastrophe is described in verse of a lofty Christian inspiration.

Existentialism, as a literary movement, did not develop any poets, with the possible exception of Francis Ponge (b. 1899), on whose work Sartre has written a long essay. His first important publication was *Le Parti pris des choses* (1942), a poetic work of great rigor and objectivity, completely lacking in any subjective lyricism.

The poetry of Jules Supervielle (1884–1960) represents a triumph in verbal simplicity in an age when poetry has not been simple. By his 1925 volume *Gravitations*, Supervielle had found his own voice, which did not vary during the next 25 years. He likes best to transcribe an inner world:

thought and emotion at their birth, the speech of the blood in the veins and the beating of the heart, the land explored by the breath before it leaves the body. What he studies is mystery, that of man in the strange duality of his body and soul.

Max Jacob (1876–1944) became a well-known figure in the avant-garde circles of Paris. He incarnated the characteristics of the period: its love of parody and humor, its nonconformity, its manner of considering philosophical and aesthetic problems. After his conversion to Catholicism, his religious spirit penetrated everything. The apparition of Christ on the wall of his room in Montmarte in 1909 never ceased to count in his life (*La Défense de Tartufe*, 1919). Some of Jacob's earliest friends, notably Picasso, who called him the only poet of the period, looked upon his work as the major expression of modern poetry and art. His gouache paintings are as well known as his poems. He died in the concentration camp at Drancy in March 1944.

The cubist painters Picasso, Braque, and Juan Gris, and their friends the "cubist" poets Apollinaire and Pierre Reverdy (1889–1960), were sensitive to the changes taking place in the world (see CUBISM). Reverdy's book *Les Épaves du ciel* was hailed by the surrealists in 1924 as the work of a master. Each of his poems forms a perfectly homogeneous and static world quite comparable to the cubist paintings of Picasso and Gris. During the last 30 years of his life, Reverdy lived as a lay associate in the Benedictine monastery of Solesmes.

Until the age of 21, Henri Michaux (b. 1899) lived principally in Brussels. His friendship with Supervielle in France helped complete the rejuvenation of poetry. He met the surrealist writers in Paris but preferred the companionship of painters: Ernst, Klee, Masson. His drawings, gouaches, and watercolors at first seemed to be contributions to his poems. But today they appear more independent, a separate means of expression. He is one of the truly authentic poetic talents who is taking his place beside those writers who investigate the strange and the unusual. The relationship that Michaux establishes between the natural and the unbelievable has created a surreal world that has become the familiar world of his poetry.

Since the middle of the century, the example and work of three poets in particular have given prestige to Fr. p. in France and abroad. During the 1950s and into the '60s, the name of Saint-John Perse (1887–1975) was revered and the poet looked upon as the worthy successor to Valéry. Throughout the '60s and well into the '70s the poetry of René Char (b. 1907) was studied with great fervor. He was often called the successor to Mallarmé and Rimbaud. In the '70s and '80s Yves Bonnefoy (b. 1923) assumed a place of eminence as the obvious successor to Rimbaud. Elected to the Collège de France in 1984 to occupy the seat vacated by the death of the critic Roland Barthes,

Bonnefoy was the first poet thus honored since Valéry.

The art of Saint-John Perse (Alexis Saint Léger-Léger, or Alexis Léger) provides one of the noblest contemporary lessons on the meaning of poetry and on the role of the poet, both in his own time and in every age. Born in the Fr. West Indies, he was until 1940 a Fr. diplomat and Secretary-General of Foreign Affairs. Perse and the other poets whose trad. he continues (Baudelaire, Mallarmé, Rimbaud, Valéry, Claudel) represent extremes in their role of demiurge and in their traits of passivity to the cosmic forces. They are technicians drawing upon all the known resources of their art, upon the most modern beliefs in ancient poetic wisdom, and upon the most ancient tenets still visible in symbolism and surrealism. From his earliest poems, *Eleges* of 1910 (tr. by Louise Varèse as *Praises*), through *Anabase* of 1924 (tr. by T. S. Eliot in 1930), *Amers* of 1957 (tr. by Wallace Fowlie as *Seamarks*), and *Oiseaux* of 1963 (tr. by Robert Fitzgerald), Perse has continued to describe and analyze the condition of man in our time, the fate of man at this moment in history. His longest poem, *Amers*, is about the sea, about man submitting to the sea and forming with it an alliance. During the course of the poem the sea becomes a part of the inner life of the poet. Just as navigators take a steeple or a cliff on the mainland as a seamark (*un amer*) in their navigation, so the reader of *Amers* learns to take the marine cosmos, which is the personal universe of the poet, as a guide to the understanding of man and his work. Perse was awarded the Nobel Prize in 1960.

René Char was born in Vaucluse; the world of his poetry is rural and Mediterranean. All the familiar elements of Provence are in it: crickets and almond trees, olives, grapes, figs, oranges, branches of mimosa. The frequently used name of Heraclitus helps to fuse the Gr. spirit with the Occitan. His manner of considering the objects of his landscape, of undertaking the hardest tasks and facing the gravest risks, might be explained by the deep sense of fraternity characterizing Char's love of man and of the soil. His is not the more purely linguistic obscurity of a Mallarmé. It is more metaphorical, more surrealist, since it is lang. seeking essentially to transcribe the subconscious. The vigor of this poet's mind puts him into a separate poetic world. We are moved by the vitality of his thought, but esp. by the vitality of his concreteness. The truths of the world as he sees them are constantly demanding his allegiance. He is a poet characterized by the habit of seeing things charged with meaning—an ordered meaning regarding the relationships between nature and men. The Pléiade edition (1983) of his complete work, of one thousand pages, is a record of his achievement through more than half a century of steady writing.

All three poets (Char, Perse, Bonnefoy) are celebrants of poetry. The sacred character of this celebration is clearly visible in Bonnefoy's art, which now appears stronger than ever and in full development. He has recuperated and enriched the earlier forms of Mallarmé and Rimbaud, of Valéry and the surrealists, in his will to perpetuate the ancient lang. of poetry. His first book of poems, *Du Mouvement et de l'immobilité de douve* (1953) was tr. by Galway Kinnell in 1968. Bonnefoy studies poetry in its relationship to painting and art and has written movingly about such figures as Chagall, Balthus, Mondrian, and Giacometti. He has also translated Shakespeare. His *Ars poétique*, appearing in *L'Improbable* (1959), stresses his belief that a poem perpetuates the presence of what is going to die. Yves Bonnefoy by 1986 had become what Mallarmé was in 1896, a spokesman for poetry. For him, it is nothing less than the art of communicating about existence.

Ways of approaching the subject of poetry vary in time and with time. These ways constitute schools and movements. Today's poet in France is best characterized by an absence of any need to justify or explain his art. For a hundred years, beginning with Baudelaire in the middle of the 19th c., poetry was vibrantly justified and explained. Another poetic age began then in which the poet is the recipient of a long period of poetics, of poetic pedagogy, when he is at last free to play a more receptive role. He writes and sings poetry because it is irresistible. At this present moment in Fr. letters, when the work of poets is being examined more minutely than ever before, the poets themselves of the last two decades, Alain Bosquet (b. 1919), Philippe Jaccottet (b. 1925), André du Bouchet (b. 1924), Yves Bonnefoy and others, remain resolutely isolated from one another, each distinctive in his writing, each determined to think the universe for himself.

See also CLASSICISM; CUBISM; DADA; DECADENCE; FRENCH PROSODY; LETTRISME; NEOCLASSICAL POETICS; PARNASSIANS; PLEIADE; POETE MAUDIT; PURE POETRY; RHETORIQUEURS; ROMANTIC AND POSTROMANTIC POETICS; SECONDE RHETORIQUE; SURREALISM; SYMBOLISM; TWENTIETH-CENTURY POETICS; VERS LIBRE.

ANTHOLOGIES, TRANSLATIONS, AND INDEXES: G. Raynaud, *Bibl. des chansonniers français des XIIIe et XIVe siècles*, 2 v. (1884), partially replaced by F. Spanke, *G. Raynauds Bibl. des altfranzösischen Liedes* (1955); *Poètes d'aujourd'hui*, ed. A. van Bever et P. Léautaud, 3 v. (1929); *Petite Anthol. poétique du surréalisme*, ed. G. Hugnet (1934); *Intro. à la poésie fr.*, ed. T. Maulnier (1939); *Anthol. de la poésie fr.*, ed. A. Gide (1945); *Sixty Poems of Scève* (1949), *Complete Works of Rimbaud* (1966), both tr. W. Fowlie; *Anthol. de la poésie fr. depuis le surréalisme*, ed. M. Béalu (1952); *An Anthol. of Mod. Fr. P.*, ed. C. A. Hackett (1952); *Poètes et romanciers du moyen âge*, ed. A. Pauphilet (1952); *The P. of France*, ed. A. M. Boase (1952); *Panorama critique de Rimbaud au surréalisme*, ed. G.-E. Clancier (1953); *Poètes du 16e siècle*, ed. A.-M. Schmidt (1953); *Fr. P. of the Ren.*, ed. B. Weinberg (1954); *Mid-C. Fr. Poets*, ed. W. Fowlie (1955); *Anthol. de la poésie fr.*, ed. M. Arland, 2d ed. (1956); P. Valéry, *Coll. Works in Eng.*, ed. J. Mathews, 15 v. (1956-75), *The Art of P.*, tr. D. Folliot (1958); *Oxford Book of Fr. Verse: 18th C.–20th C.*, ed. P. M. Jones, 2d ed. (1957); *Anthol. de la poésie baroque fr.*, ed. J. Rousset, 2 v. (1961); *Penguin Book of Fr. Verse*, 4 v. (1958–61); *An Anthol. of Fr. P. from Nerval to Valéry*, ed. A. Flores, 2d ed. (1962); *Contemp. Fr. P.*, ed. A. Aspel and D. Justice (1965); *The Poems of François Villon*, tr. G. Kinnell (1965); *An Anthol. of Fr. Surrealist P.*, ed. J. H. Matthews (1966); *Anthol. poétique fr., moyen âge*, ed. A. Mary, 2 v. (1967); *An Anthol. of Mod. Fr. P., from Baudelaire to the Present Day*, ed. C. A. Hackett (1968); *Coll. Poems of St.-John Perse*, tr. W. H. Auden et al. (1971); *Fr. Individualist Poetry 1686–1760*, ed. R. Finch and E. Joliat (1971); *Chanson Verse of the Early Ren.*, ed. B. Jeffrey (1971); *Poems of René Char*, tr. M. A. Caws and J. Griffin (1976); *Anthologie des grands rhétoriqueurs*, ed. P. Zumthor (1978); G. Apollinaire, *Calligrammes*, tr. A. H. Greet (1980); *Chanter m'estuet*, ed. S. N. Rosenberg (1981); *Roof Slates and Other Poems of Pierre Reverdy*, tr. M. A. Caws and P. Terry (1981); C. Baudelaire, *Les Fleurs du mal*, tr. R. Howard (1982); S. Mallarmé, *Sel. Poems and Prose*, ed. M. A. Caws (1982); *Le Roman de Renart* (1983), *The Song of Roland* (1985), both tr. P. Terry; Y. Bonnefoy, *Poems, 1959–75*, tr. R. Pevear (1985); *La Poésie fr. du premier 17e siècle*, ed. D. L. Rubin (1986); R. Bossuat, *Manuel bibliographique de la litt. fr. du moyen âge*, 3d supp., 1960–80 (1986).

HISTORY AND CRITICISM: C. A. Sainte-Beuve, *Tableau de la poésie fr. au 16e siècle*, 2d ed. (1838); G. Paris, *La Poésie du moyen âge*, 2 v. (1885–95); F. Brunetière, *L'Evolution de la poésie lyrique au 19e siècle* (1894); H. Guy, *Hist. de la poésie fr. au 16e siècle*, v. 1, *L'Ecole des rhétoriqueurs* (1910); R. Lalou, *Vers une alchimie lyrique* (1927); E. Faguet, *Hist. de la poésie fr. de la ren. au romantisme* (1929–); Jeanroy; Patterson; M. Raymond, *De Baudelaire au surréalisme*, 2d ed. (1940); A. Beguin, *L'Ame romantique et le rêve* (1946); *CBFL*; Lote; R. Lebègue, *La Poésie fr. de 1560 à 1630*, 2 v. (1951); H. Peyre, *Connaissance de Baudelaire* (1951); J. Chiari, *Contemp. Fr. P.* (1952); W. Fowlie, *Mallarmé* (1953); J. Rousset, *La Litt. de l'âge baroque en France* (1953); R. Winegarten, *Fr. Lyric P. in the Age of Malherbe* (1954); H. Weber, *La Création poétique au XVIe siècle*, 2 v. (1956); G. Brereton, *An Intro. to the Fr. Poets* (1956); L. J. Austin, *L'univers poétique de Baudelaire: symbolisme et symbolique* (1956), *Poetic Principles and Practice* (1987); M. Gilman, *The Idea of P. in France* (1958); A. M. Schmidt, "Litt. de la Ren.," *Hist. des litts.*, ed. R. Queneau, v. 3 (1958); S. Mallarmé, *Correspondance*, 11 v. (1959–85); J. Frappier, *Poésie lyrique en France au 17e et 18e siècles* (1960); R. Dragonetti, *La Technique poétique des trouvères dans la chanson courtoise* (1960); A. Bosquet, *Verbe et vertige* (1961); W. N. Ince, *The Poetic Theory of Paul Valéry* (1961); I. Silver, *Ronsard* and the Hellenic Ren. in France, 2 v. (1961, 1987); C. A. Knudson and J. Misrahi, "Med. Fr. Lit.," in Fisher; Jeanroy, Origines; D. Poirion, Le Poète et le prince (1965); R. Finch, The Sixth Sense: Individualism in Fr. P., 1686–1770 (1966); R. W. Greene, The Poetic Theory of Pierre Reverdy (1967); J.-C. Payen and J.-P. Chauveau, La Poésie des origines à 1715 (1968); GRLMA; J. Lawler, The Lang. of Fr. Symbolism (1969); C. K. Abraham, Enfin Malherbe: The Influence of Malherbe on Fr. Lyric Prosody, 1605–1674 (1971); U. Mölk and F. Wolfzettel, Répertoire métrique de la poésie française des origines à 1350 (1972); M. A. Caws, The P. of Dada and Surrealism (1971), The Inner Theater of Recent Fr. P. (1972), Presence of René Char (1976); S. Brindeau et al., La Poésie contemporaine de la langue fr. depuis 1945 (1973); Order and Adventure in Post-Romantic Fr. P., ed. E. Beaumont et al. (1973); K. Uitti, Story, Myth, and Celebration in OF Narrative Poetry, 1050–1200 (1973); J. J. Duggan, The Song of Roland: Formulaic Style and Poetic Craft (1973); J. Kristeva, Revolution du langage poétique (1974, tr. 1984); F. Hallyn, Formes métaphoriques dans la poésie lyrique de l'âge baroque en France (1975); Sensibility and Creation: Studies in 20th-C. Fr. P., ed. R. Cardinal (1977); F. Ponge, The Sun Placed in the Abyss, and other Texts (1977)—with trs. by S. Gavronsky; M. Riffaterre, Semiotics of P. (1978); P. Zumthor, Le Masque et la lumière (1978); Bec; B. Johnson, Défigurations du langage poétique (1979), A World of Difference (1986); R. Greene, Six Fr. Poets of Our Time (1979); J. P. Houston, Fr. Symbolism and the Modernist Movement (1980); Scott; D. L. Rubin, The Knot of Artifice (1981); J.-P. Richard, Onze Études sur la poésie moderne (1981); W. Calin, A Muse for Heroes: Nine Cs. of the Epic in France (1983), In Defense of Fr. P. (1987); J. T. Naughton, The Poetry and Poetics of Yves Bonnefoy (1984); J. Derrida, Signéponge/Signsponge (1984); R. H. Bloch, The Scandal of the Fabliaux (1986); P. Knight, Flower Poetics in 19th-C. France (1986); C. Scott, A Question of Syllables (1986), The Riches of Rhyme (1988), Vers Libre (1990); C. de D. Rifelj, Word and Figure: The Lang. of 19th-C. Fr. P. (1987); S. J. Huot, From Song to Book (1987); R. G. Cohn, Mallarmé's Prose Poems (1987); G. Chesters, Baudelaire and the Poetics of Craft (1988); Hollier—the most recent full history; 19th-C. Fr. P., ed. C. Prendergast (1990); L. W. Johnson, Poets as Players (1990). W.F.

FRENCH PROSODY. Fr. pros. derived from Med. Lat. pros. by a series of transformations. Cl. Lat. had a quantitative metric based on patterns of syllables combined according to their length (long or short) and to a system of equivalences (one long syllable was said to have double the "time" of two shorts; see CLASSICAL PROSODY; EQUIVALENCE). Combinations of long and short syllables created the metrical units, feet (see FOOT), which in turn were combined in certain patterns to create the various meters (dactylic hexameter, iambic trimeter, etc.). The emphasis on quantity (q.v.) meant that while in most instances a metrical long would coincide with the tonic accent of the word (see ACCENT), this was not always so. Primitive Lat. verse (the Saturnian [q.v.]), on the other hand, based its metric on accent, as, to a considerable extent, did writers involved with "popular" lang. (Plautus, Terence). Lat. verse was rhymeless and heterosyllabic (the system of equivalences allowed variations in number of syllables).

But Cl. Lat. metric was the metric of a cultural elite. From the 4th c. A.D., the quantitative distinction between vowels was inaudible to a large part of the Empire's population, and the dissemination of Church teachings through hymns and psalms necessitated a metric geared to popular auditory perception. In effect, by suppressing the system of syllabic equivalence, these Christian Lat. poets transformed quantitative meter into a meter based on fixed numbers of syllables. At the same time, the Cl. Lat. accent, with its orientation toward pitch (as in Gr.), had developed into an accent oriented toward intensity. The evolution of Fr. p. out of Med. Lat. can be traced from the 29-line Cantilène de Sainte Eulalie (ca. 880), a vernacular tr. of Lat. double Adonic couplets, through the epic chansons de geste (10th–13th cs. [q.v.]) composed of assonating, usually decasyllabic laisses (q.v.) of varying length, also derived from Lat. meter, as in the 11th-c. Chanson de Roland, to 12th- and 13th-c. Occitan poetry (q.v.) by the troubadours, which generated a wealth of subsequent lyric forms. As these sung or chanted forms of the medieval period developed into the recited or read ones of the Ren., so Fr. accent, which was oxytonic (last syllable of the word) or paroxytonic (penultimate syllable of a word ending in an articulated -e atone) weakened; word-accent shifted to phrasal accent where, correspondingly, it fell on the terminal syllable of the group. This process coincided with the muting of the schwa in the spoken lang.

The standard view of cl. (regular) Fr. verse is thus that its metrical foundation is syllabic and, more precisely, isosyllabic: its lines are composed of a fixed and equal number of syllables. Its system of accentuation depends on the arrangement of word-groups, which in turn depends on the syntactic chain and the coincidence of metrical junctures with syntactic junctures. Although the principle of isosyllabism tends to imply that syllables are quantitatively equal (isochronous), this is clearly not so; experimental phonetics, from the beginning of this century (L'Abbé Rousselet, Souza, Landry), has demonstrated the falsity of this assumption (see ISOCHRONISM). However, scientific demonstrations rarely correspond with the psychology of reading, the perceptual mechanisms of regularization; the differences exploited by poets and registered by readers have to do more with modulations in timbre than with modulations in duration.

Syllabic quality is determined by several factors:

FRENCH PROSODY

by whether the feature of interest is phonetic (in the nature of the sound) or articulatory (in the production of the sound), by whether the syllable is open or closed, by what acoustic features are highlighted by the acoustic environment, by the semantic value or grammatical status of the word in which it appears, and so on. These considerations are not strictly metrical, of course; and a generative metrist like Milner (1974) is justified in treating metrical positions in the Fr. line as vocalic rather than syllabic; but any attempt to build a multi-level rhythmic analysis on a *metrical* base must take the syllable (q.v.) into account; a prosodic description is important more for what it can tell us of the expressive resources of a metrical structure than for merely measuring degrees of conformity or deviation.

An important factor in the diversification of syllabic quality in cl. Fr. verse has been the retention of the articulated schwa (*e atone*) long after its disappearance (via elision [q.v.]) in the spoken lang. In regular verse, a line-internal *e atone* is counted and pronounced when it is followed by a consonant or aspirate *h*, and elided before a vowel or mute *h*. At the end of the line, it is treated as extrametrical, serving to indicate the femininity of the rhyme (see MASCULINE AND FEMININE), but it may of course be phonated to a greater or lesser extent. The articulated *e atone*, therefore, though "numerically" counting as a syllable, generally occurs at lower levels of phonation than other vowels, and might seem to have as much a reinforcing or liaisory function as any independent syllabic identity. In the opening lines from Baudelaire's "Je t'adore à l'egal," for instance:

Je t'adore à l'égal de la voûte nocturne,
O vase de tristesse, ô grande taciturne,

the e's of "voûte," "vase," and "grande" not only lengthen the accented syllables preceding them—the 12 syllables of the first line divide into groupings of 3+3+3+3, and those of the second into 2+4+2+4—but by creating *coupes enjambantes* (see COUPE) add flexibility and seamlessness to the lexical and phrasal junctures. These two factors create a third: a tonal and intonational resource. The *e atone* may, by its protraction of the previous vowel and falling cadence, produce effects of regret, compassion, etc.; or these same features may equally, as here, encode ironic hyperbole.

It might be argued that the longevity of the articulated *e atone* in Fr. verse is due in part to a desire to make a strenuous differentiation between verse and prose. Because metrical presence in Fr. verse is apparently minimal (a question of number, and of caesura where appropriate), and because rhythmic measures coincide with syntactic units, Fr. verse can look dangerously like chopped-up prose. There would be nothing poetic in a line like Baudelaire's "Pour entendre un de ces concerts, riches de cuivre" ("Les Petites Vieilles") were it not for the fact that the *e* of

"riches" is counted/pronounced and that this line occurs in the context of other 12-syllable lines (*alexandrines* [q.v.]), which also enables it to rhyme. This would lend support to de Cornulier's assertion (1982) that what is metrical is not a single line of verse, but groups of mutually confirming lines. To say that a metrical Fr. line is not *inherently* metrical, that it is not a composite of units (such as feet) which already have a metrical identity or purpose, is to entail that its rhythmic structure is only metrified by its companions, and hence that Fr. meter is circumstantial, or effectually strophic (translinear) rather than linear (see below). Such a view would invalidate all those discoveries of chance "alexandrines" in prose. It would also imply that scansion of Fr. verse normally operates within too limited a verse environment.

The metricality of Fr. is thus minimal, a number of syllables validated as a metrical determinant by an isosyllabic context. When this number is 9 or more, the line is articulated by a caesura (q.v.); but only in the regular alexandrine is the position of the caesura predetermined, falling medially, after the sixth syllable. In lines of 9 syllables or 10, etc., caesural position is established by the particular poem and becomes a convention for the duration of that poem only (although certain dispositions in the relatively popular decasyllable were standard for certain periods of its devel.: 4+6 or 6+4 for the cl. decasyllable, but 5+5 in the 19th-c.). The presence of the caesura increases the number of fixed accents in the line to two, one on the last syllable of the line and the other on the last syllable before the caesura. Two other accents usually occur in the regular *alexandrin tétramètre* (see TETRAMETRE), one in each hemistich (half-line); but these secondary accents are optional and mobile (i.e. can appear on any of the five unoccupied syllables of the hemistich). Strictly speaking, these secondary accents are therefore not metrical in the way that the accents on syllables 6 and 12 are; they are rhythmic nonce-products of the syntax, whose position may vary from hemistich to hemistich and line to line. However, inasmuch as they explore and catalogue the possible divisions of the six syllables of the hemistich (1+5, 2+4, 3+3, 4+2, 5+1), they are instruments of metrical realization; meter predicts superordinate groups of six syllables, and in so doing predicts the potentialities of rhythmic division of that group.

The nature of the caesura remains highly problematic. It derives from Lat. verse, but there it fell within measures (feet) rather than at natural metrical junctures, and it was neither medial nor fixed. Its fixity, however, increased in Med. Lat. verse, where its function was specifically musical, the first hemistich rising to the dominant, the cadence of the second hemistich coming to rest on the subdominant. This musical origin is often seen as the origin of the "circumflex" intonational curve practiced in the declamation of the alexandrine. The intonational aspect of the caesura combines with a tendency to privilege its accent by increased intensity or duration. In other words, the caesura is not a pause (interruption) properly speaking, but a point of linguistic and structural (semantic) insistence; it is best seen as a feature *of* the sixth syllable rather than as an event which takes place *after* the sixth syllable. In addition, the caesura is a syllabic checkpoint. If, as de Cornulier's findings indicate (1982), the ear is incapable of reliable syllabic perception beyond a limit of eight syllables, then the caesura is a necessary safeguard of the line's syllabic presence and integrity. In one of the first steps taken by Fr. generative metrics (q.v.), Milner (1974) proposed, as a rule, that the boundary between two metrical segments should *at least* coincide with a boundary between words (i.e. position 6 cannot fall within a word). This is to imply (a) that the sixth syllable must be naturally *accentuable*, and (b) that its accent must be ictic (*accent tonique*) rather than expressive (*accent d'intensité, accent oratoire*). Thus in a line like Verlaine's "Et la tigresse épouvantable d'Hyrcanie" ("Dans la grotte"), there is no caesura, even though the sixth syllable coincides with a syllable that could take an *expressive* accent ("éPOUvantable"). It would, in fact, be truer to say that a spectral caesura enforces an expressive accent on "épouvantable," in default of an ictic alternative. This latter solution may seem preferable to that proposed by Verluyten (1989), whereby a set of rules are formulated to keep the medial caesura in place despite all liberties taken with it. The trouble with the inclusive strategy of generative metrics is its dilution of the notion of metrical constraint (in favor of degrees of tension between metrical and prosodic units). While seeming, paradoxically, to maintain the metrical fixity of the caesura, the generative solution throws in doubt the reasons for maintaining its fixity (by undermining its function as a point of metrical, syntactic, structural and intonational articulation) and fails to respond to shifts in metrical perception which justify Mallarmé's call for a free-rhythmic dodecasyllable: "Those still loyal to the alexandrine, our hexameter, loosen the rigid and puerile mechanism of its measure from the inside; the ear, freed from this meretricious counter, experiences a new pleasure in discerning, unaided, all the possible combinations, among themselves, of 12 notes" ("Crise de vers").

If the Fr. caesura owes much to Med. Lat. verse, so does rhyme (q.v.). Absent from Cl. Lat. verse, it became a feature of Church Lat., at least as line-terminal assonance (q.v.), from the 4th c. A.D. Only in the course of the 12th c. did full rhyme gradually supersede assonance. It is often argued that rhyme was treated as indispensable to Fr. until the end of the 19th c. because it had a metrical or near-metrical function; put another way, the heavy metrical loading of the last syllable of the line naturally attracted rhyme, since rhyme is rhyme

as much by its line-terminal position as by its acoustic properties. The positional significance of rhyme is exploited to mark the end of the syllabic string; the acoustic foregrounding that accompanies rhyme intensifies the line-terminal accent, reinforcing the boundary and the intonational cadence of the line.

Some commentators, de Cornulier in particular (1981), are less convinced of rhyme's line-demarcative function than they are of its strophic function. The stanza (q.v.) as a metrical unit has received pitifully meager attention in all prosodies. Its significance is basically twofold: rhyme schemes (q.v.) are rhythms of recurrent acoustic units, patterns of interval, sometimes complicated by syllabic variations in the line (heterometric [q.v.] stanzas); rhyme schemes are also patterns of intonation—the last two lines of an *abab* stanza (*rimes croisées*; see CROSS RHYME) tend to repeat the intonational configuration of the first two at a slightly lower pitch, while an *abba* stanza (*rimes embrassées*; see ENVELOPE) produces an intonational suspension in its third line, with the fourth taking on a more definitive cadence. Paul-Jean Toulet's *contrerimes* (*Les Contrerimes*, 1921) counterpoint *rimes embrassées* with alternating octosyllables and hexasyllables (8a, 6b, 8b, 6a); Vigny's *ababccb* septain (q.v.) is variously a quatrain followed by a tercet, an alternating mode that shifts into an enclosed mode, quatrain + couplet + clinching last line. If Fr. meter is context-derived, then rhyme is metrical not because of its line-demarcative function but because it is the agent by which lines are bound into the metrical context, and by which other metrifying forces are activated (combination, intonation, patterned acousticity). The metrical privileging of rhyme in Fr. is accompanied by expressive privileging: in contrast to Eng. rhyme, Fr. rhyme distinguishes between different degrees of extension or strength (*faible* or *pauvre, suffisante, riche*), and between masculine and feminine, with their attendant "tonalities" (the rule of alternation of masculine and feminine rhyme-pairs); and, coinciding with word-terminal accent, Fr. rhyme semanticizes suffixes and endings.

Am. generative metrics, based on the proposition that Eng. stress is inherently alternating (Chomsky and Halle, 1968), has had its influence on Fr. metrical thinking. Verluyten has argued for a "*subjacent alternating rhythm* between syllables that are relatively prominent and nonprominent in Fr. words" (1989; italics original). In some senses this renewed interest in the accentual structure of Fr. dates back to the beginnings of free verse in France (1886; see VERS LIBRE) and to the shift in rhythmic perception that made free verse (q.v.) possible. Inasmuch as the constraints of Fr. meter were identified as centering on a preoccupation with the syllable, any countervailing force was bound to reaffirm the claims of accentual thinking. The suggestion that Fr. verse might be accent-timed rather than syllable-timed coincided with an undoing of syllabic stability, i.e. doubts about the status of the schwa or the conventions governing synaeresis and diaeresis (qq.v.). Indeed, the "improvised" nature of free verse rests in part on the ambiguities surrounding syllabic quality; free verse intensifies the "élasticité métrico-prosodique" (Bobillot 1986) already apparent in *vers libéré* (q.v.) and in other verse suspended between the regular and the free. At the same time, accent itself was more flexibly perceived; aside from the *accent tonique* (the word-group accent which segments the syntactic chain into rhythmic measures), free-verse theorists drew attention to intraphrasal accents (which often ambiguate tonicity) and to suprasegmental accents (the accents of speech act, stance, and sustaining tone), called variously the *accent d'impulsion* (Kahn) or the *accent oratoire* (Souza, Mockel).

For many *verslibristes*, rhythm (q.v.) is the result of accentual activity of an intense and varied kind, varied in both degree and origin. Accent is no longer bound to, and ensured by, a fixed number of syllables; the demands of accent govern length of measure, or are careless of it. Ironically, therefore, and although for many poets the line continued to be a central rhythmic *point de repère* (Scott 1990), free verse tended to reinforce the view that the real locus of Fr. rhythmic organization was not the line, but the stanza—though with this difference, that the free-verse stanza affirms a rhythmic inimitability which supersedes the line, while in regular verse the stanza affirms metrical conformity and repeatability, which the line contributes to and is endorsed by. C.S.

See also ALEXANDRINE; ASSONANCE; CLASSICAL PROSODY; ENGLISH PROSODY; ITALIAN PROSODY; LATIN POETRY, *Medieval*; METER; OCCITAN POETRY; PROSODY; RHYME; SPANISH PROSODY; STANCE; STANZA; TETRAMETRE; TRIMETRE; VERS; VERS IMPAIR; VERS LIBERE; VERS LIBRE; VERS LIBRES CLASSIQUES; VERS MESURÉS; VERSIFICATION.

BIBLIOGRAPHIES: Thieme—lists Fr. works 1332–1914, still essential, supp. in his *Bibl. de la litt. fr. de 1800 à 1930*, v. 3, *La Civilisation* (1933), 51–71; Y. Le Hir, *Esthétique et structure du vers français* (1956); J. Mazaleyrat, *Pour une étude rythmique du vers français moderne* (1963); Brogan, 646–60—selective bibl. survey to 1980, supp. in *Verseform* (1988).

STANZA INDEXES: P. Martinon, *Les Strophes: Etude historique et critique*, 2d ed. (1912); U. Mölk and F. Wolfzettel, *Répertoire métrique de la poésie française des origines à 1350* (1972).

HISTORICAL AND THEORETICAL STUDIES: E. Stengel, "Lehre von der romanische Sprachkunst: Romanische Verslehre," *Grundriss der romanischen Philologie*, ed. G. Gröber, 4 v. (1888–1902), v. 2, pt. 1, pp. 1–90; R. de Souza, *Le Rythme poétique* (1892); G. Kahn, "Preface sur le vers libre," *Premiers Poémes* (1897); Kastner; H. Chatelain, *Recherches sur le vers français au XVe siècle* (1908); A. Tobler, *Vom altfranzösischen Versbau alter und neuer Zeit*, 5th ed. (1910); E. Landry, *La Théorie du rythme et le rythme du français déclamé* (1911); M. Grammont, *Le Vers français* (1913); P. Verrier *Le Vers français*, 3 v. (1931–32); Patterson; Lote; P. Guiraud, *Langage et versif. d'après l'oeuvre de Paul Valéry* (1953), *Essais de stylistique* (1969), *La Versif.*, 2d ed. (1973); M. Burger, *Recherches sur la structure et l'origine des vers romans* (1957); Beare; A. Mockel, *Esthétique du symbolisme*, ed. M. Otten (1962); J. Cohen, *Structure du langage poétique* (1966); *Le Vers français au 20e siècle*, ed. M. Parent (1967); F. Deloffre, *Le Vers français* (1969); H. Meschonnic, *Pour la poétique*, 5 v. (1970–78), *Critique du rythme* (1982); N. Ruwet, *Langage, musique, poésie* (1972); J. Milner, "Réflexions sur le fonctionnement du vers français," *Cahiers de poétique comparée* 1 (1974); P. Lusson and J. Roubaud, "Mètre et rythme de l'alexandrin ordinaire," *LF* 23 (1974); E. Pulgram, *Lat.-Romance Phonology: Prosodics and Metrics* (1975); A. Kibédi Varga, *Les Constantes du poème* (1977); J. Roubaud, *La Vieillesse d'Alexandre* (1978); Elwert; Scott; Mazaleyrat; Morier; B. de Cornulier, "La Rime n'est pas une marque de fin de vers," *Poétique* 12 (1981), *Théorie du vers* (1982), "Versifier: Le Code et sa règle," *Poétique*. no. 66 (1986); R. Lewis, *On Reading Fr. Verse* (1982); B. Stimpson, *Paul Valéry and Music* (1984); J.-P. Bobillot, "Rimbaud et le 'vers libre,'" *Poétique* 66 (1986), "L'Élasticité métrico-prosodique chez Apollinaire," *Poétique* 84 (1990); C. Scott, *A Question of Syllables* (1986), *The Riches of Rhyme* (1988), *Vers Libre* (1990); G. Chesters, *Baudelaire and the Poetics of Craft* (1988); S. P. Verluyten, "L'Analyse de l'alexandrin: Mètre ou rythme?" *Le Souci des apparences*, ed. M. Dominicy (1989). T.V.F.B.; C.S.

FRENZY. See POETIC MADNESS; INSPIRATION.

FREUDIAN CRITICISM. See PSYCHOLOGICAL CRITICISM.

FRISIAN POETRY. F., the nearest Continental relative of Eng., was once the speech of an independent and extensive maritime nation along the North Sea coast, but is today the lang. of a minority people living partly in the Netherlands and partly in Germany. It exists in three forms: East and North F., spoken in Germany, and West F., spoken in the Netherlands. Only West F., which now has legal status both in the schools and in the public life of Netherlands Friesland, has developed into a full-fledged literary lang. and *Kultursprache*.

As is the case with other Germanic peoples, lit. among the Frisians began with the songs of bards celebrating the great deeds of kings and heroes, though none of those early epics has survived. What has survived is a valuable body of F. law, the earliest dating from the 11th c., in a distinctive form marked by such literary devices as alliteration and parallelism, and often genuinely poetic in thought and feeling.

FRISIAN POETRY

When, about the year 1500, Friesland came under foreign control, F. lost its position as the lang. of law and public life, and F. lit. sank to a low level. No great poetic figure appeared on the scene until Gysbert Japicx (1603–66), an eminent Ren. poet who with his *Rymlerije* (Poetry), published posthumously in 1668, reestablished F. as a literary and cultural lang. The 18th c. saw the rise of many followers and imitators of Japicx; however, no outstanding poetic figure came to the fore. In the 19th c., Eeltsje Halbertsma dominated the scene; much of his work is folk poetry inspired by Ger. romanticism. Another outstanding figure is Harmen Sytstra (1817–62), a romantic inspired by his country's heroic past, whose work reveals a desire to restore the old Germanic verseforms. The latter half of the 19th c. produced many folk poets, the most popular of whom were Waling Dykstra (1821–1914) and Tsjibbe Gearts van der Meulen (1824–1906), but on the whole their work is uninspired, rationalistic, and didactic. Piter Jelles Troelstra (1860–1930), with themes centering on love, nature, and the fatherland, ushered in a second romantic period.

The 20th c. ushered in a new spirit to F. p., perhaps first evident in the simple and pensive verse of J. B. Schepers, but even more clearly in the work of Simke Kloosterman (1876–1938), whose poetic art is both individualistic and aristocratic. In *De wylde Fûgel* (The Wild Bird, 1932), she gives intense and passionate utterance to the longings and disillusionments of love. Rixt (Hendrika A. van Dorssen, 1887–1979) also wrote verse characterized by emotional intensity. A first-rate poet at the beginning of the century was Obe Postma (1868–1963), whose verse has vigor, penetration, and philosophical insight. Much of it is poetry of reminiscence; still more of it is a paean to life and the good earth. Postma was the first to use free verse in F. and to use it well.

The new spirit came to full expression and ushered in a literary renaissance in the Young F. movement, launched in 1915 and led by the daring young nationalist Douwe Kalma (1896–1953). A talented poet and critic, Kalma sharply denounced the mediocrity and provincialism of 19th-c. F. letters. With him and his movement Friesland began to have an independent voice in European culture. Kalma's genius appears at its freshest in his classic *Keningen fan Fryslân* (Kings of Friesland, 2 v., 1949, 1951), a series of historical plays in blank verse featuring the F. kings and depicting the struggle between Christianity and the heathen. Kalma's lyric poetry, collected in *Dage* (Dawn, 1927) and *Sangen* (Songs, 1936) is technically skillful but often nebulous in content. His work—like that of his school—suffers from aestheticism (q.v.) and a poetic jargon laden with neologisms and archaisms.

Among the poets of merit who had their start in the Young F. school are R. P. Sybesma, an excellent sonneteer, and D. H. Kiestra, a poet of the soil with a vigorous talent. For decades, the most popular and widely read poet was Fedde Schurer (1898–1968), a versatile artist who preferred national and religious themes. His early poems show the influence of Young F. aestheticism; those written after 1946 are more direct, unadorned, and modern. His *Simson* (Samson, 1945), a biblical drama in verse, gained him the Gysbert Japicx Literary Prize. In 1946 he helped launch *De Tsjerne* (The Churn), the literary periodical with which most of the important names in F. letters were associated until 1968.

Around 1935 some of the younger poets, such as J. D. de Jong and Ype Poortinga, showed signs of breaking away from the Young F. movement, both in spirit and in poetic diction. Douwe A. Tamminga (b. 1909) in his *Brandaris* (Lighthouse, 1938) created his own poetic idiom, based largely on the lang. of the people which he transfigured and sublimated into pure art.

Since World War II, nearly 300 books of poetry have been pub. in Friesland. Postwar disillusionment and existential despair informed much of the poetry of the late 1940s and '50s, when biting satire and experimental forms openly declared all trads. meaningless. Among the modern voices were Anne Wadman (b. 1919) and Jan Wybenga (b. 1917), whose *Amoeben* (Amoebae) in 1953 led the way in experimental poetry. An experimentalist group led by Hessel Miedema, Steven de Jong, and Jelle de Jong started its own journal, *Quatrebras* (1954–68), and in 1961 published an anthol. that clearly demonstrated a refusal to be restricted by conventional thought or form. Sjoerd Spanninga (Jan Dykstra, b. 1906) introduced exotic imagery from foreign cultures, esp. Oriental, through a wide variety of forms. The verse of Martin Sikkema, Freark Dam, and Klaas Dykstra was more traditional. Other older poets have continued to write: Douwe A. Tamminga's *In Memoriam* (1968), written after his son's untimely death, is a masterpiece of profound thought and feeling cast in disciplined but fluid form, and a volume of his selected works, *Stapstiennen* (Steppingstones), appeared in 1979. Tiny Mulder (b. 1921) is another distinguished poet who frequently effects a remarkable fusion of significant form and content and evinces a penetrating vision that affirms life without evading its horrors and sorrows. *Tinkskrift*, a collection of four previously published volumes, came out in 1986. Several of the younger poets show equal promise, e.g. Daniel Daen (Willem Abma), who has been not only prolific but also consistently impressive in his ability to fuse the concrete and abstract. Frequent contributions to *Trotwaer*, the successor of *De Tsjerne*, incl. Tsjebbe Hettinga, Bartle Laverman, Eppie Dam, Jacobus Quiryn Smink, and Boukje Wytsma.

ANTHOLOGIES: *Bloemlezing uit Oud-, Middel-en Nieuwfriesche Geschriften*, ed. F. B. Hettema (1887); *It Sjongende Fryslan* (1917), *De nije Moarn* (1922), *De Fryske Skriftekennisse fan 1897–1925*, 2 v. (1928–

31), *De Fryske Skriftekennisse fen 1876–1897* (1939), all ed. D. Kalma; *Fiif en tweintich Fryske Dichters*, ed. F. Schurer (1942); *Frieslands Dichters*, ed. A. Wadman (1949)—excellent anthol. of poetry since 1880, with valuable intro. and Dutch tr.; *op fjouwer winen*, ed. A. R. Oostra et al. (1961)—anthol. of young experimentalists; *Country Fair: Poems from Friesland Since 1945*, tr. R. Jellema (1985).

HISTORY AND CRITICISM: C. Borchling, *Poesie und Humor im friesischen Recht* (1908); T. Siebs, "Gesch. der friesischen Lit.," *Grundriss der germanischen Philologie*, ed. H. Paul (1909); D. Kalma, *Gysbert Japiks* (1939); A. Wadman, *Kritysk Konfoai* (1951); E. H. Harris, *Lit. in Friesland* (1956); J. Piebenga, *Koarte Skiednis fen de Fryske Skriftekennisse*, 2d ed. (1957)—valuable hist.; J. Smit, *De Fryske literatuer 1945–1967* (1968); K. Dykstra, *Lyts hanboek fan de Fryske Literatuer* (1977)—valuable survey of F. lit. from its beginnings to the 1970s; survey of F. poetry 1945–84 in *Trotwaer*, no. 3–4 (1985).   B.J.F.; H.J.B.

FRONS. See CANZONE; CAUDA.

FROTTOLA AND BARZELLETTA (It. "nonsense" [poem], corresponding to Ger. *Spass*). Originally a type of medieval It. nonsense verse, jocose, rambling, and written in very irregular meter and rhymes, with analogues in other European poetries (cf. FATRAS), the f. evolved in the 14th c. in the direction of the epigram, hence came to be referred to increasingly as *frottola-barzelletta*, i.e. a joke with didactic content. In the course of the century this became an important medium for serious moral instruction. The b. is a subspecies of the It. 15th-c. carnival song (*canto carnascialesco*), written for musical setting in octosyllables (*ottonari*) and often following the structure of the *ballata grande* (see RITORNELLO) in which the *ripresa* or refrain has the rhyme scheme *abba*. The b. became very popular in the 15th and 16th cs. in the hands of practitioners such as Politian and Lorenzo de' Medici (1449–92); one well-known example is Lorenzo's carnival poem, the "Trionfo di Bacco e Arianna." See also ADYNATON; COQ-A-LANE; ITALIAN PROSODY; NONSENSE VERSE.—V. Pernicone, "Storia e svolgimento della metrica," *Problemi ed orientamenti critici di lingua e di letteratura italiana*, ed. A. Momigliano, v. 2 (1948); Wilkins; Spongano; M. Pazzaglia, *Teoria e analisi metrica* (1974); Elwert, *Italienische*.   T.W.; C.K.

FU. See CHINESE POETRY.

FUGITIVES, The. A group of Southern poets and critics who met at Vanderbilt University and were associated with the literary magazine *The Fugitive* (19 issues, April 1922 to December 1925, pub. in Nashville), incl. Allen Tate, John Crowe Ransom, Donald Davidson, Robert Penn Warren, and Merrill Moore. Devoted to verse (with occasional brief editorials and reviews), the first issue of the journal declared, "*The Fugitive* flees from nothing faster than from the high-caste Brahmins of the Old South," the second issue that its attitude was "neither radical nor reactionary, but quite catholic." While members of the group disagreed over some important issues (Ransom, for example, argued for traditional prosody against Tate's enthusiasm for the symbolists), their work can generally be described as formalist in technique, often regional and ironic in emphasis, and strongly critical (yet anti-scientific) in intelligence. The Fugitives stood for the South, traditionalism, and regionalism, and correspondingly in aesthetics for concreteness and particularity (see CONCRETE UNIVERSAL). They opposed the urban, industrial culture of the North, with its liberal humanitarianism, its doctrine of progress, and its glorification of science. The 1928 publication of the *Fugitive: An Anthol. of Verse* marked the close of the group's formal association, the energies from which later fueled such projects as New Criticism (q.v.) and Agrarianism.—*I'll Take My Stand: The South and the Agrarian Trad. by Twelve Southerners* (1930); J. M. Bradbury, *The Fs.* (1958); D. Davidson, "The Thankless Muse and Her F. Poets," *SR* 66 (1958); L. S. Cowan, *The F. Group* (1959); *Fugitive's Reunion*, ed. R. R. Purdy (1959); J. L. Stewart, *The Burden of Times* (1965); *The F. Poets*, ed. W. Pratt (1965); L. D. Rubin, "The Fs.," *Hist. of Southern Lit.* (1985); P. K. Conkin, *The Southern Agrarians* (1988).   R.H.F.; L.B.

FULL RHYME. See RHYME.

FUROR POETICUS. See POETIC MADNESS.

FUTURISM.

    I. ITALIAN FUTURISM
    II. RUSSIAN FUTURISM
       A. *Cubo-Futurism*
       B. *Ego-Futurism*
    III. OTHER FUTURISMS

F. was the prototypical 20th-c. avant-garde movement in lit. and the arts, militant in its promotion of extreme artistic innovation and experimentation. Its stance was to declare a radical rejection of the past and to focus on the maximally new in art, technology, and politics, often combined with stylistic primitivism. It rejected psychological sensitivity and the effete lyricism of symbolism (q.v.). Dynamism was glorified, as were all forms of rapid or violent movement such as war, airplanes, cars, radios, and electricity. F. sought out conservative social elements, and confronted them in order to provoke a violent negative response. In contrast to symbolism, which was musically oriented, f. showed a preference for the visual arts. Many of the futurist poets were also painters.

I. ITALIAN FUTURISM began with the "Fondazione e Manifesto del Futurismo" (The Founding and Manifesto of F.) first pub. in Fr. in *Le Figaro* in Paris, 20 Feb. 1909; here F. T. Marinetti (1876–1944) declared that a roaring car was more beautiful than the *Victory of Samothrace*, that no work without an aggressive character could be a masterpiece, that war was hygienic, and that museums were graveyards (which should be destroyed or visited rarely). In succeeding manifestoes, Marinetti enunciated the principles of f. in relation to poetry. *Parole in libertà* (words in freedom) denoted lang. free of syntax and logical ordering and thus better able to convey intense emotion rapidly. *Immaginazione senza fili* (wireless imagination) and *analogia disegnata* (pictorialized analogy) involved maximum freedom of imagery and metaphor. This led to the expressive use of typography, with fonts of various sizes and styles being used in the same line or word and free disposition of words on the printed page, sometimes resembling a typographic collage (e.g. Marinetti's "Joffre après la Marne" or "SCRABrrRrraaNNG," both 1919). Expressive typography and syntactic and metaphoric freedom were intended to give the effect of simultaneous sense-impressions and superimposed time frames (*simultaneità*), e.g. Marinetti's famous poem "Bombardamento," which recreates by onomatopoetic and typographic means the 1912 siege of Adrianopoli. This and the other poems of Marinetti's most important book, *Zang Tumb Tuuum* (Milan, 1914), provide successful illustrations of futurist poetics in practice, which also includes pattern poems (q.v.) such as "Pallone Frenato Turco" (Turkish Hot-Air Balloon). There was an active cross-fertilization among the futurists, the cubist painters (see CUBISM), and Apollinaire, with his calligrammes (q.v.).

Marinetti was a brilliant public performer who could make reading a manifesto the high point of a literary evening, or evoke the sounds of a whole battlefield single-handedly. "Futurist Evenings," the first of which occurred on January 12, 1910, were designed to create a scandal and often ended in riots, official protests, and arrests of the participants. Marinetti's skill in creating and exploiting this notoriety made f. a major cultural force in a short period of time. At the same time, his financial independence allowed him to publish his own works and those of his associates in numerous editions through his Milan publishing house, Edizioni Futuriste di "Poesia," which also put out a poetry journal. F. had centers in a number of other It. cities, notably Florence, where the futurist newspaper *Lacerba* was pub. Jan. 1913–May 1915; with Marinetti's transforming participation from February 1913, *Lacerba* became a leading example of innovative typography. The two major collections of futurist poetry assembled by Marinetti are *I poeti futuristi* (1912) and *I nuovi poeti futuristi* (1925).

Most futurist poetry, incl. Marinetti's own early poetry, while futurist in theme, was closer in form to *vers libre* (q.v.) than to *parole in libertà*, e.g. the works of E. Cavacchioli, L. Folgore, and A. Palazzeschi (1885–1965), the latter a poet of the first magnitude, esp. in his later work. Others, however, some of whom were primarily painters, produced significant works in the parolibrist manner, e.g. C. Carrà, G. Balla, F. Cangiullo, C. Govoni, A. Soffici, and G. Severini. It is sometimes difficult to separate f. works into poems and pictures, since the two artforms were so closely intertwined. It. futurists also made innovative contributions to sculpture, architecture, theater, film, photography, and music. One other important element of It. f. was a militaristic nationalism, which caused it to become aligned with Mussolini and Fascism for a time, this in turn producing an international revulsion against the movement which has only recently dissipated.

II. RUSSIAN FUTURISM. Marinetti claimed that Rus. f. was a direct outgrowth of his It. movement. However, the chief Rus. representatives insisted that they had developed their ideas independently and differed significantly from the Italians. But little distinctively futurist except early poems by Xlebnikov can be found in Russia before 1910. Information on It. f. began to appear in Rus. periodicals by March 1909; thus the influence of It. f. on the early stages of Rus. f. is probable. Both can be seen as emerging from symbolist antecedents in similarly traditional, pre-industrial societies. Yet in quality and breadth of poetic practice, and to some extent in poetic theory, Rus. f. clearly overshadows It. f. Without financial resources comparable to Marinetti's, Rus. publications had to be more modest in cost and number, but this was made a virtue by emphasis on a primitive, deliberately anti-elegant look. The Rus. movement has two branches, cubo-f. and ego-f.

A. *Cubo-Futurism*, originally named *Hylaea*, had its first important publication in the manifesto and collection *Poščečina obščestvennomu vkusu* (A Slap at Public Taste, 1913). This manifesto, drafted in Dec. 1912, was co-written and signed by David Burliuk (1882–1967), Aleksej Kručenyx (1886–1968), Vladimir Majakovskij (1893–1930), and Viktor (Velimir) Xlebnikov (1885–1922). Clearly based in style and content on the earlier It. manifestoes, it advocated throwing Pushkin, Dostoevsky, Tolstoy et al. from the "Steamship of Modernity" and attacked the leading members of the current literary establishment. It then called for increasing the vocabulary with arbitrary and derived words, declared a hatred for previously existing language, and proclaimed the "samovitoe" (self-sufficient) word. The collection featured major poems by Xlebnikov, incl. "Bobèobi pelis' guby" (Bobeobi sang the lips, 1908–09), an example of cubism (q.v) in verse in which a portrait is constructed of facial features expressed in abstract sounds. Xlebnikov was recognized as the most brilliant and inventive of the group. His experiments ranged from arcane neologisms to exotic verseforms, e.g. *Razin* (1920), written in palindromes (q.v.). Imagery in his poems reflects pagan and folk sources rather than urbanism. His poems were usually too complex to be popular, but his innovations still serve as an inspiration to present-day poets.

David Burliuk, the self-styled Father of Rus. f., had first recognized Majakovskij's poetic genius and had suggested the idea of sound poetry (q.v.) to Kručenyx. He was also responsible for the publication of a number of important futurist miscellanies. Though primarily a painter, Burliuk was also a prolific poet, with an anti-aesthetic Rimbaudian bent.

Majakovskij was a true urbanist who read his consonant-rich poetry from the stage in a powerful bass voice. A mixture of hyperbolic, egocentric imagery and painful sensitivity, his poems have a direct emotional impact. After the Revolution, Majakovskij willingly turned his poetic talent into a tool for political propaganda, and he was posthumously canonized by Stalin as the Great Poet of the Revolution. His poems were published in massive editions, were memorized by generations of schoolchildren, and were given extensive, though restricted, critical attention by Soviet scholars. His *lesenka* (stepladder line), introduced in 1923, was adopted by many other poets of his time and remains a common device in Rus. poetry even today.

The idea of the "self-sufficient" word developed in the hands of Kručenyx and Xlebnikov into *zaum'* (trans-rational language), which in its most radical form was pure sound poetry. Although earlier experiments by Xlebnikov have certain features of *zaum'*, the first true example is Kručenyx's sound poem "Dyr bul ščyl" (*Pomada*, 1913), which is prefaced by the statement that the words do not have any definite meaning. Other poems by Kručenyx consist entirely of vowels. In the 1920s he produced a series of useful theoretical works on f.

The years 1913–14 were the high point of cubof., with publication of many books and performances of the dramas *Pobeda nad solncem* (Victory over the Sun) by Xlebnikov and Kručenyx and Majakovskij's *Vladimir Majakovskij, Tragedija*. The end of 1913 and beginning of 1914 saw a tour of 17 provincial cities by Burliuk, Majakovskij, and V. Kamensky (1884–1961), the poet-aviator who wrote typographically elaborate "ferroconcrete" poems.

Other important poets briefly associated with this movement were the theoretician B. Livšic, the dramatist Il'ja Zdanevič, the impressionist Elena Guro, and the early Boris Pasternak. The devel. of Rus. Formalist literary theory (see RUSSIAN FORMALISM) is closely related to cubo-futurist practice, Roman Jakobson and Viktor Šklovskij being associates of the futurists. Jakobson's move to Prague in 1921 stimulated the rise of a similar trend there. A number of later Rus. movements are to some extent based on f., e.g. constructivism (q.v.),

LEF, Oberiu, and the Ničevoki (Nothingists). The works of I. Terent'ev and A. Tufanov continued *zaum'* practice and theory.

B. *Ego-Futurism.* Based in Petersburg and claiming as its founder the popular poet-aesthete Igor'-Severjanin (1887–1941), who was the first to use the term *Futurizm* in the Rus. context (1911), Ego-f. emphasized extravagant urban imagery, foreign words, neologisms, egocentricity, and experimentation in rhyme. Its moving force was Ivan Ignat'ev (1882–1914), who wrote a number of manifestoes and ran a publishing venture, *Peterburgskij glašataj* (Petersburg Herald), which produced several miscellanies and books by group members. The most inventive of these was Vasilisk Gnedov (1890–1978), with his famous "Poema konca" (Poem of the End) consisting of a blank page performed with a silent gesture of resignation. Gnedov also wrote poems of one letter, word, or line, sometimes bordering on *zaum'*. A Moscow offshoot of Ego-f., the Mezzanine of Poetry (1913), was led by V. Šeršenevic (1893–1942), a prolific poet and publisher who later led the movement "Imažinizm" (Imaginism).

III. OTHER FUTURISMS. F. took root in a number of other Slavic national lits. In the Ukraine, Myxajl Semenko (1892–1937) proclaimed *Kverofuturizm* (Querofuturism) in 1914, later named Panfuturism, and put out a series of books and a journal, *Nova Generacija* (New Generation, 1927–31). In Poland, futurist-style manifestoes and poems were written by J. Jankowski as early as 1912. The Cracow poets T. Czyżewski, B. Jasieński, and St. Młodożeniec formed a futurist group in 1919, as did the Warsaw poets A. Stern and A. Wat, the two groups coming together in 1921–22 to produce two important collections, *Jednodńuwka futurystuw* (One-time Issue of the futurists) and *Nuż w bž uhu* (Knife in the Stomach). Czech f., called *Poetismus* (Poetism), included among its founding members the poets V. Nezval, J. Seifert, and K. Biebl and the artist/theoretician K. Teige. The Slovenes had A. Podbevšek. Futurist movements flourished for a time (1917–23) in Georgia and Armenia as well.

In Spain, the influence of It. f. was important to the Catalan poets J.-M. Junoy and J. Salvat-Papasseit and others who wrote parolibristic poems with a strong visual dimension, as did members of the Ultraist movement (1919–1923), most notably G. de Torre (see ULTRAISM). Portuguese f. was short-lived, centering on the activities of J. de Almada Negreiros in 1916–17. The Brazilian poet M. de Andrade and a few others also showed the influence of Marinetti. In England, vorticism (q.v.) was futurist in style, and Marinetti considered it a branch of his movement, but its leaders, Ezra Pound and Wyndham Lewis, the publisher of *Blast* (1914–1915), saw themselves as independents. By the early 1920s, other European movements had taken the lead away from f. and had begun to emphasize other qualities: dada (nihilism, the absurd), surrealism (the subconscious), constructivism (functionalism)—qq.v. Some later movements still retained noticeable elements of f., e.g. concrete poetry, *lettrisme*, and sound poetry (qq.v.).

GENERAL: E. Falqui, *Bibliografia e iconografia del Futurismo* (1959); R. Poggioli, *The Theory of the Avant-Garde* (1968); Z. Folejewski, *F. and Its Place in the Devel. of Mod. Poetry* (1980); W. Bohn, *The Aesthetics of Visual Poetry, 1914–1928* (1986); M. Perloff, *The Futurist Moment* (1986); J. J. White, *Literary F.* (1990).

ITALIAN: R. Clough, *F.* (1961); P. Bergman, *"Modernolatria" et "simultaneità"* (1962); *Futurist Manifestoes*, ed. U. Apollonio (1970); F. Marinetti, *Selected Writings*, ed. R. Flint (1972); *Per conoscere Marinetti e il Futurismo*, ed. L. de Maria (1973); C. Tisdall and A. Bozzolla, *F.* (1977); *Contributo a una bibliografia del futurismo italiano*, ed. A. Baldazzi et al. (1977); N. Zurbrugg, "Marinetti, Boccioni and Electroacoustic Poetry," *CCrit* 4 (1982).

RUSSIAN: *Manifesty i programmy russkogo futurizma*, ed. V. Markov (1967); V. Markov, *Rus. F.* (1968); E. Brown, *Mayakovsky, A Poet in the Revolution* (1973); B. Livshits, *The One and a Half-Eyed Archer* (tr. 1977); S. Compton, *The World Backwards* (1978); *Ardis Anthol. of Rus. F.*, ed. E. and C. Proffer (1980); V. Erlich, *Rus. Formalism: Hist.-Doctrine*, 3d ed. (1981); A Lawton, *Vadim Shershenevich: From F. to Imaginism* (1981); G. Janeček, *The Look of Rus. Lit.* (1984); V. Xlebnikov, *The King of Time*, tr. P. Schmidt (1985); Terras, s.v. "Centrifuge," "F.," "Zaum'"; J. R. Stapanian, *Mayakovsky's Cubo-Futurist Vision* (1986); *Rus. F. through Its Manifestoes, 1912–1928*, ed. A. Lawton and H. Eagle (1988).

OTHER: *Polska avangarda poetycka* 1-2, ed. A. Lam (1969); W. Wees, *Vorticism and the Eng. Avant-Garde* (1972); *L'avanguardia a Tiflis*, ed. L. Magarotto et al. (1982); M. Mudrak, *The New Generation and Artistic Modernism in the Ukraine* (1986).
G.J.J.

FYRTIOTALISTERNA ("The Poets of the Forties"). A group of Swedish modernist poets of the 1940s whose work is characterized by anxiety, pessimism, and stylistic complexity. During its most cohesive phase—between 1944 and 1947, when the journal *40-tal* (The Forties) was published—the movement was quite broad, with a remarkable number of talented young poets. Their literary orientation, combining universalism with social commitment, developed in response to World War II, Sweden's wartime neutrality, and the moral nihilism of influential philosopher Axel Hägerström. This nihilism, together with the growing influence of Marx and Freud, led to a sense of intellectual crisis. The poetry which was generated by this crisis abounds in free association, compressed imagery, ambiguity, allusion, mythic structure, and abstraction, derived from psychoanalysis and from poets such as Mallarmé, T. S. Eliot, the Fr. surrealists, and previous Swedish modernists. As image and figure became the dominant vehicles of poetic expression, reference receded in favor of the self-reflexive poem, whose internal tensions of symbol, feeling, and thought required a co-creator—a total imaginative response from the reader—for full realization.

Beyond their shared modernist principles, the two leaders of F., Erik Lindegren (1910–68) and Karl Vennberg (b. 1910), have little in common. The poetic temper of Lindegren, whose *mannen utan väg* (The Man Without a Way, 1942; tr. 1969) came to epitomize the Forties, combines a restless intellect with sensual and spiritual intensity. Modeled on *The Waste Land* and influenced by surrealist painting and film, the poem is held together by an analogue of musical form. Its proliferating images, jarring disharmonies, polyrhythmic effects, and dizzying associative leaps make for extreme difficulty of reading, and in his next collection, *Sviter* (Suites, 1947), Lindegren adopted a more classical form. Vennberg, whose talent was less idiosyncratic, was better suited to be a model for the younger poets. *Halmfackla* (Straw Torch, 1944) and *Tideräkning* (Reckoning of Time, 1945), with their analytic technique à la Eliot, reveal a mind in the grip of a relentless relativism. The Kafkaesque irony is directed as much against the poet himself as against the political and cultural certainties he questions. Later a tendency toward mysticism and the quotidian idyll appears. Of the younger F. may be mentioned Werner Aspenström (b. 1918), Sven Alfons (b. 1918), and Ragnar Thoursie (b. 1919), whose *Skriket och tystnaden* (The Scream and the Silence, 1946), *Sommaren och döden* (Summer and Death, 1943), and *Emalj-ögat* (The Enamel Eye, 1945), respectively, are variant expressions of the same sensibility of crisis. See SWEDISH POETRY.—*Kritiskt 40-tal*, ed. K. Vennberg and W. Aspenström (1948); *Svensk 40-talslyrik*, ed. B. Holmquist (1951); G. Printz-Påhlson, *Solen i spegeln* (1958), "The Canon of Literary Modernism," *CCrit* 1 (1979)—compares Lindegren and Auden; K. Henmark, *En fågel av eld* (1962); E. Lindegren, *Dikter 1940–1954* (1962); R. Ekner, "The Artist as the Eye of a Needle," *SS* 42 (1970); B. Steene, "Erik Lindegren," *Books Abroad* 49 (1975); K. Vennberg, *Du måste värja ditt liv*, ed. S. Lindner (1975); I. Algulin, *Den orfiska reträtten* (1977); P. Hallberg, "Erik Lindegrens *Mannen utan väg*," *Nordisk litteraturhist.*, ed. M. Bekker-Nielsen et al. (1978).
S.LY.

G

GAELIC POETRY. See SCOTTISH GAELIC POETRY.

GAI SABER (*gaia sciensa*). The art of composing love songs. These terms are most often used in connection with the Academy established at Toulouse in the 14th c. to instill a semblance of life into the dying Occitan lyric. See OCCITAN POETRY.—Jeanroy, v. 1.   F.M.C.

GAITA GALLEGA. A 2-hemistich verse having marked ternary movement and a variable number of syllables, usually averaging about 10 or 11. It is primarily a Galician-Port. meter used in Sp. popular (rarely learned) verse. It is thought to be related to the *muiñeira*, a song to be accompanied by the bagpipe. Henríquez Ureña says: "It seems hardly necessary to note that this meter, in spite of its relationship with the 15th-c. *arte mayor* [q.v.], cannot be confused with it, because, even in the most regular forms, it employs the anapestic decasyllable; moreover, the latter becomes characteristic of the new regular form" (239).—P. Henríquez Ureña, *Versificación irregular en la poesía castellana,* 2d ed. (1933).   D.C.C.

GALICIAN (OR GALLEGAN) POETRY.   (This article treats primarily Sp.p. in Galician, the lang. of the western region of the Iberian peninsula; for the poetries of the central and eastern langs., see SPANISH POETRY and CATALAN POETRY.)

Spreading from the pilgrimage center of Santiago de Compostela throughout Galicia and northern Portugal, G.-Port. *cantigas* (q.v.) were among the earliest lyric forms in the Iberian peninsula. Their form was imposed on troubadours from non-G.-speaking regions of Spain. Most of the secular *cantigas* are preserved in the *Cancioneiro* [songbook] *da Ajuda* (mid 14th c.), *Cancioneiro da Vaticana* (end of 15th c.), and the *Cancioneiro Colocci-Brancuti* (now *Cancioneiro da Biblioteca Nacional de Lisboa,* 16th c.). King Alfonso X ("The Wise") is responsible for the religious *Cantigas de Santa Maria* (13th c.). G. poets from 1200–1350, the period of greatest achievements, incl. Martin Codax, Afonso Eanes de Coton, Bernal de Bonaval, Joan (Garcia) de Guilhade, Joan Airas, Pai Gomes Chariño, Airas Nunes, Pero Garcia, and Pedro Amigo de Sevilla, as well as others from Portugal and the rest of the peninsula. The G.-Port. school, although following Occitan models (see OCCITAN POETRY), is best exemplified by the apparently native *cantiga de amigo,* a song of melancholy nostalgia by a maiden for her absent lover. After the death of Portugal's King Diniz (1325),

the old lyric declines; from 1400 Castilian begins to replace G. as the lang. of poetry in the peninsula (see SPANISH POETRY). The bilingual *Cancioneiro de Baena* (1445) still has a few G. poems by Macias "o namorado" (fl. 1360–90), el Arcediano de Toro (fl. 1379–90), and Alfonso Alvarez de Villasandino (1340?–1428). Until the 18th c., little written G. p. has been preserved. Diego A. Cernadas de Castro (1698–1777), "el cura de Fruime," wrote bilingual occasional verse and with Manuel Freire Castrillón (1751–1820) marks the gradual rebirth of G. lit.

Romanticism brought more interest in Galicia's past and its ancient lit., folklore, and other specific features. Among others, Antolín Faraldo (1823–53) defended G. autonomy and with Aurelio Aguirre (1833–58), the "G. Espronceda," promoted literary regionalism. Francisco Añón y Paz (1812–78), "el Patriarca," is remembered for his patriotic odes and humorous compositions. Alberto Camino (1821–61), author of sentimental and elegiac verse, is a forerunner of the *Rexurdimento* (Renaissance) led by Rosalía de Castro (1837–85). The rebirth was signalled by the Floral Games of La Coruña in 1861, the winning poems of which were published in the *Album de Caridad* (1862). In 1863 Castro pub. *Cantares Gallegos* (G. Songs), the first book written in G. in the modern period. In 1880 her *Follas novas* (New Leaves) appeared. She also wrote in Castilian, but her social concerns are most obvious in G. (*Poems,* tr. A.-M. Aldaz et al. [1991]). Moreover, her themes incl. some of the earliest feminist statements in Galicia if not in the peninsula. Two of her important contemporaries were Eduardo Pondal y Abente (1835–1917), who wrote *Queixumes dos pinos* (Complaints of the Pines), and Manuel Curros Enríquez (1851–1908), forced to emigrate to Cuba after writing anticlerical verse. There he composed the nostalgic *Aires da miña terra* (Airs of My Land, 1880). Valentín Lamas Carvajal (1849–1906) sang elegiacally of the peasant life in works such as *Espiñas, follas e frores* (Thorns, Leaves and Flowers, 1875). Other poets of the later 19th c. are José Pérez Ballesteros (1883–1918), known for his 3-vol. *Cancionero popular gallego* (1885–86); Manuel Leiras Pulpeiro (1854–1912); and Manuel Lugrís Freire (1863–1940).

Among contemp. poets the lang. has become more sophisticated. Troubador trads., *saudade,* and G. patriotism are still present, while numerous foreign poetic movements have also been influential. The foremost poets of the early 20th c. are Antonio Noriega Varela (1869–1947), Ramón

- [449] -

Cabanillas (1876–1959), Victoriano Taibo (1885–1966), and Gonzalo López Abente (1878–1963). Noriega's ruralism is close to the previous generation, but Cabanillas and López Abente reflect Sp.(-Am.) *modernismo* (q.v.). Taibo's peasant themes are expression of his social commitment. The best poet of the avant-garde in Galicia was the sailor Manoel Antonio (1900–30), who collaborated with the artist Alvaro Cebreiro in the iconoclastic manifesto "Máis Alá" (Beyond, 1928). During his lifetime he pub. *De catro a catro* (From Four to Four, 1928); posthumously his nearly complete works have appeared, showing him to be a true disciple of Creationism (q.v.) in the manner of Huidobro. Luis Amado Carballo (1901–27) wrote a more pantheistic, vanguard poetry. Ricardo Carballo Calero, Florencio Delgado Gurriarán, Xulio Sigüenza, and Euxenio Montes also wrote avant-garde verse prior to the Sp. Civil War. Fermín Bouza Brey (1901–73), one of the best known G. writers of the postwar period, employed elements of medieval poetry; others are Alvaro Cunqueiro (1911–81), Eduardo Blanco-Amor (1897–1979), Luz Pozo Garza (b. 1922), and María do Carme Kruckenberg (b. 1926).

Since 1976, G. p. has undergone rapid change. The proliferation of texts and critical studies led to the identification of a "Golden Age" of poetry. Some, such as X. L. Méndez Ferrín, have followed the model of Celso Emilio Ferreiro's and Lorenzo Varela's social poetry, while others have maintained Manoel Antonio's avant-garde orientation, adding a tendency to intimism (Claudio Rodríguez Fer). Several collectives have given impetus to poetic production: *Brais Pinto* (1950s), *Rompente, Alén,* and *De amor e desamor.* G. journals—*Nordés, Dorna, Escrita, A nosa terra, Nó*—have provided space for both the established writers and the new. Several anthols have appeared, and there are more women poets, among them Xohana Torres, Helena Villar, Ana Romaní, Pilar Pallarés, Xela Arias, and Helena de Carlos. X. M. Alvarez Cáccamo, M. A. Fernán-Vello, R. Fonte, M. Forcadela, and V. Vaqueiro also belong to the group of younger poets whose work is strengthening the foundation of modern G. p.

ANTHOLOGIES: *Cancionero popular gallego,* ed. J. Pérez Ballesteros, 2 v. (1942; first pub. 1886); *Escolma de poesía galega,* v. 1 (1952) and v. 2 (1959) both ed. X. M. Alvarez Blázquez, v. 3 (1957) and v. 4 (1955) both ed. F. Fernández del Riego; C. Martín Gaite and A. Ruiz Tarazona, *Ocho siglos de poesía gallega* (1972); M. V. Moreno Márquez, *Os novísimos da poesía galega* (1973); L. Rodríguez Gómez, *Desde a palabra, Doce voces* (1986); X. R. Pena, *Literatura galega medieval,* v. 2 (1986); *Festa da Palabra,* ed. K. N. March (1989)—contemp. G. women poets.

HISTORY AND CRITICISM: B. Varela Jácome, *Historia de la literatura gallega* (1951); A. Couceiro Freijomil, *Diccionario bio-bibliográfico de escritores,* 3 v. (1951–54); J. L. Varela, *Poesía y restauración cultural de Galicia en el siglo XIX* (1958); *GRLMA,* v. 2.1.C; P. Vázquez Cuesta, "Literatura gallega," *Historia de las literaturas hispánicas no castellanas,* ed. J. M. Díez Borque (1980); M. Vilanova and X. M. Alvarez Cáccamo, "Panorama de la poesía gallega de posguerra," *Camp de l'arpa* (May 1980); R. Carballo Calero, *Historia da literatura galega contemporánea. 1808–1936,* 3d ed. (1981); X. L. Méndez Ferrín, *De Pondal a Novoneyra* (1984).
L.A.S.; K.N.M.

GALLIAMB(US). In Cl. prosody, a meter which is a catalectic Ionic (q.v.) tetrameter, named after the Galli, the eunuch priests of the Gr. goddess Cybele. There is an anonymous Gr. fragment, sometimes attributed to Callimachus (fr. *incerti auctoris* 761 [Pfeiffer]) cited by the ancient metrist Hephaestion as an example of this meter, which if true would suggest it was developed by the Alexandrian poets, but the most famous example is Lat., Catullus 63. This takes the form of an anaclastic ionic dimeter (◡ ◡ – ◡ – ◡ – –) + a catalectic ionic dimeter (◡ ◡ – – ◡ ◡ –) with or without anaclasis (q.v.), and with numerous resolutions. In the second dimeter, the second longum is almost always resolved. The first verse of the poem is typical: *super alta vectus Attis / celeri rate maria* (◡ ◡ – ◡ – ◡ – – | ◡ ◡ – ◡ ◡ ◡ –). In the 19th c., both Tennyson ("Boadicea") and George Meredith ("Phaethon") experimented with accentual imitations of gs.—G. Allen, "On the Galliambic Metre," *The Attis of Caius Valerius Catullus Tr. into Eng. Verse* (1892); Wilamowitz; Halporn et al.; West. J.W.H.

GAUCHO POETRY. Taken literally, G. p. is the name for poetic compositions, anonymous or otherwise, which deal with the life and adventures of the Argentinean cowboy. It would be a mistake to apply the same denomination to all popular poetry produced in Sp. America.

Popular poetry, which had its origin in the Sp. *Romancero,* flourished at the end of the 18th c. and reached its peak by the middle of the 19th c. In Uruguay and Argentina, learned writers invaded the field of folk poetry and produced a number of literary imitations of the style of early *Payadores,* or singers of popular poetry. The first of these poets was the Uruguayan Bartolomé Hidalgo (1788–1822), whose famous dialogues expressed the sentiments of the G. in regard to the war of independence against Spain. He was followed by the Argentine Hilario Ascasubi (1807–75), who played an active role in the struggle against the dictatorship of Rosas and who published a number of G. ballads dealing with the siege of Montevideo (*Paulino Lucero o los gauchos del Rio de la Plata,* 1839–51). *Santos Vega, o los mellizos de la Flor* (1851, 1872), his greatest achievement in this type of poetry, tells the story of two brothers, one of whom becomes an outlaw. The main value of the poem resides in its colorful and accurate description of country and city life in mid 19th-c. Argentina. Estanislao del Campo (1834–80) followed the example of these writers and employed pure G. dialect in his *Fausto* (1866), a parody of Gounod's opera.

The greatest of the G. poems is *Martín Fierro* (1872, 1879) by the Argentine José Hernández (1834–86). A well-educated man and a writer deeply conscious of his social mission, Hernández set out to prove the moral fortitude of the G. and his right to gain a respectable position in the life of his country. Dealing with the problem of civilization and barbarism in the Am. continent, he criticized the defenders of "civilization" for their irresponsibility in ruthlessly destroying the trads. of native populations, esp. the nomad Gs. He praised the stoicism of the Sp.-Am. peasants, and with true romantic spirit he envisioned the birth of a new way of life from their epic fight in the midst of a wild continent. Encouraged by the success of his poem, Hernández wrote a second part (1879) in which he told of Martín Fierro's return from the Indian country where he had sought refuge from persecution by the city authorities. The tone of this continuation is no longer rebellious but moderately didactic. Hernández' poem owes its immense popularity in Sp. America to its virile exaltation of freedom and courage, to its forceful display of nationalism, popular wisdom, and pride in the virtues of a people who hold fast to the trad. of their homeland. The critics of yesterday and today are unanimous in considering *Martín Fierro* the highest expression of popular poetry in Sp. America.

At present G. p. is in a period of stagnation. The same may be said about popular poetry in general throughout Sp. America. But scholars and students of the subject are organizing and editing the historical texts. See also SPANISH AMERICAN POETRY.

The G. *Martín Fierro*, tr. W. Owen (1935); M. W. Nichols, *The G.: Cattle Hunter, Cavalryman, Ideal of Romance* (1942); *Poesía gauchesca*, ed. J. L. Borges and A. Bioy Casares, 2 v. (1955); *Antología de la poesía gauchesca*, intro. J. Horacio Becco (1972); F. E. Tiscornia, *Poetas gauchescos* (1974); F. Weinberg, *Trayectoria de la poesía gauchesca* (1977); J. B. Rivera, *Poesía gauchesca* (1977).   F.A.

GAY AND LESBIAN POETRY. See LOVE POETRY.

GAYATRI. See INDIAN PROSODY.

GE'EZ POETRY. See ETHIOPIAN POETRY.

GENDER. See FEMINIST POETICS; LOVE POETRY.

GENEALOGY. See INFLUENCE.

GENERATIVE METRICS. This term covers three differing theories of meter advanced from 1966 through 1977, based on transformational gram-

mar and g. phonology. As such, g. m. represents, like structural metrics before it, a conspicuous example of the shortcomings of purely linguistic methods applied to traditional problems in poetics. In g. theories, the abstract pattern of the meter is analogous to the deep structure of lang., while each particular poetic line constitutes the surface realization of that meter; "correspondence rules" are then given to generate all those lines which a reader with "competence" would recognize as metrical while filtering out or excluding all unmetrical lines. The ordering of these rules then creates a tension index or "scale of delicacy" by which *degrees* of metricality are assessed. The primary focus of all three theories has thus fallen on but one aspect of metrics, namely the limen of unmetricality.

In the first and most widely discussed theory, proposed by Halle and Keyser in 1966, the abstract pattern of the Eng. iambic pentameter is defined not as five "feet" (see FOOT) but as a series of ten positions, (W) S W S W S W S (X) (X), i.e. an alternating pattern with unspecified optional elements on both ends. It is a known fact that rhythmic series, of which meters are a prime example, are least determined at their beginnings and most determined at their ends (see CATALEXIS; RHYTHM); here the ends are left variable to avoid infringing the definition of the "Stress Maximum" (any fully stressed syllable falling between two unstressed syllables in the same syntactic constituent), which is the criterion of unmetricality in the H-K theory. Three "Correspondence Rules" are then adduced in order of increasing constraint: either stressed syllables occur in only and in all S positions (violated by weak syllables in S positions), or in only but not in all S positions (violated by stresses in W positions), or Stress Maxima occur in only but not in all S positions. Marking violations of each rule in sequence yields a score which becomes the index of metricality: violations of the first two rules merely indicate metrical "complexity" (cf. "tension" [q.v.] in New Critical and structural metrics), but violations of the third certify a line as unmetrical.

Such a theory departed from traditional Eng. metrics, which had never reached consensus, in that, for the first time, it made an effort to formulate in a rigorous way what a theory should do; it defined the line as a series of positions rather than a series of segmented "feet"; and it tried to formalize the recognition that readers do perceive degrees of acceptability in metrical lines. A number of amendments and modifications were subsequently developed to account for phenomena such as displaced stress (Beaver) and to extend the theory to other meters (Hascall, Dilligan), older stages of Eng. (Keyser, Sapora), and other langs.

Criticism of H-K took a number of tacks. The concept of the "Stress Maximum" was criticized because it was not a constitutive element of metri-

- [451] -

cal structure (as even the foot had been), but rather a negative index: presence of the SM identifies a line as bad, but absence of it tells us nothing at all about the compositional or constitutive principles of the line. As Youmans later remarked, "metrical complexity is presumed to correlate negatively with frequency of [SM] occurrence." Hence "metricality or unmetricality results from the absence of invariant features, while line complexity results from the absence of variant features" (Harvey). Further, in abandoning the foot, H-K redefined the line simply as a linear sequence. But the single most crucial part of Chomsky's theory of g. grammar was his argument that sentences are not simply beads on a string; rather, they have internal hierarchical structure, transformations of which are ordered and directed by identifiable processes.

Halle and Keyser's desire for sharp metrical "rules" which would neatly differentiate all metrical lines from unmetrical ones led to numerous anomalies (admitting bad lines, excluding good ones), raising doubts about the categorical nature of such rules (q.v.) in aesthetic perception. No experimental confirmation was ever provided showing that experienced readers of poetry in fact perceived metricality in such degrees of delicacy and for the particular reasons implied by the H-K correspondence rules. Obviously readers do recognize some lines as more complex than others and some as simply unmetrical, but their implicit criteria for making such recognitions are not immediately referable to the "Stress Maximum," a negative entity which has no analogue in the long history of metrical theory.

The H-K system was also shown not to apply very well to some verse-trads. outside Eng. pentameter, esp. OE and ME. Some critics, esp. Wimsatt, complained that to predicate the meter and the natural-lang. patterns as fixed entities allowed no room for the meter to "tilt" or modulate normal stressings. The H-K stipulation that constraints on Stress Maxima apply only within major syntactic boundaries, a feature which greatly improved the accuracy of the theory, still seemed an anomaly in that the metricality of the line was being determined not across the line as a whole metrical unit (see LINE) but within each syntactic component. In traditional metrics, by contrast, "caesuras" were certainly noticed, but phrase-boundaries, like word-boundaries, played no part in metrical pattern, which usually had to do with which types of feet appeared in which positions. The generativists validated the legitimacy of such phenomena as line-initial inversions by saying that these did not fulfill the conditions of the SM. But here again the claim was that the criterion validates because it does not apply.

The second theory, advanced by Magnuson and Ryder in 1970, construed the line not as a series of weak and strong positions but of even and odd ones, a variation interesting because there is some evidence to suggest that odd positions in the line are as a class constrained differentially (and more heavily) than even ones. M-R also marked the presence or absence of the Distinctive Features (+ or - ; see DISTINCTIVE-FEATURE ANALYSIS) of each syllable on a taxic grid—i.e. Weak, Strong, Pre-Strong, and Word-Onset; by this last, their system took account not only of phonological features (stress) but of morphological ones as well, i.e. word-boundaries. They wrote Base Rules to account for four relations between even and odd positions, finding that the most highly constrained relation is that of even syllables to following odds. But serious shortcomings in the architecture of the theory prevented it from having much generality beyond describing any single line. In the most productive application, Bjorklund mapped out striking differences of compatibility between the linguistic systems of Eng. vs. Ger. and the abstract pattern of the iambic pentameter.

The third theory, broached by Kiparsky in 1975 but revised radically in 1977 based on a seminal theory of phonology by Liberman and Prince also pub. in 1977 (which, ironically, appropriated the terminology of metrics for the description of lang. itself and so was called "metrical phonology"), is very similar in ultimate effect to H-K, though Kiparsky abandons H-K's notion of the "Stress Maximum" in favor of L-P's simpler treatment and returns, astonishingly, to defining the meter of the iambic pentameter line as composed of five *feet*, which are "bracketed." The surface stress-pattern of the line is then derived via tree-diagrams (like those in transformational grammar) which create another bracketing (of lang.) corresponding to that of the meter. In the great majority of lines, there will be some kind of "mismatch" between the brackets of the lang. and those of the meter. Linguistic S's in metrical W's that are lexical (polysyllabic) cause unmetricality; those that are not lexical create "labeling" mismatches (an awkward term). "Bracketing" mismatches occur when the two patterns of W and S agree but the brackets to each pattern are out of sync—as with trochaic words in an iambic line. (These will be seen to be very different phenomena.) Kiparsky notes, however, that the two types of mismatches never occur simultaneously. Lexical S's in W create unmetricality because the linguistic S is controlled by elements to its left, whereas on the metrical level the W goes with the S following it on the right; at the beginning of syntactic phrases, however, "the bracketing that is necessary for unmetricality can never arise" (Kiparsky). His procedure for assessing the metrical complexity of the line is simply to total the sum of mismatches.

Kiparsky's approach is in several respects simpler than H-K's and closer to one's intuitive sense of how words fit themselves into meter. By postulating *feet* in the meter and then writing rules for closeness of fit, however, Kiparsky returns to the view which the generativists first derided so freely;

his treatment of bracketing would have to be revised radically if the feet were removed. And Kiparsky's "Monosyllabic Word Constraint" amounts to a requirement that the main stress in polysyllables fall under metrical ictus—hardly a new idea. Subsequently, Hayes added metrical "grids" for marking relative stress prominence (also taken from Liberman-Prince) in order to reduce some of the arbitrariness of Kiparsky's metrical filters. More significantly, Hayes made explicit assaults on the scope and importance of meter, claiming that virtually all significant distinctions in meter come straight out of processes in the lang., while at the same time proposing a theory that the rhythmic structure of poetic meter is based on rules that are purely rhythmic and temporal in nature, not linguistic.

In retrospect, there seem to have been as many internal differences and reversals in 20 years of g. m. as there were in 2000 years of traditional metrics. By 1989, Youmans would hold that "g. metrical rules" are only "statistically normative principles rather than categorical constraints"—a seeming abandonment of the notion of a constitutive rule—and would admit that "g. m. is moving toward a consensus that is largely consistent with traditional theories" such that "substantive disagreements between g. metrists and [traditional] prosodists appear to be minor." If so, g. m. was not a refutation but merely a rapid recapitulation of traditional metrics. See also FOOT; METER; PROSODY; SCANSION.

M. Halle and S. J. Keyser, "Chaucer and the Study of Pros.," *CE* 28 (1966), "Illustration and Defense," *CE* 33 (1971), *Eng. Stress: Its Form, Its Growth, Its Role in Verse* (1971)—this last better avoided; D. C. Freeman, "On the Primes of Metrical Style," *Lang&S* 1 (1968); J. C. Beaver, "A Grammar of Pros.," *CE* 29 (1968), "Contrastive Stress and Metered Verse," *Lang&S* 2 (1969), "The Rules of Stress in Eng. Verse," *Lang* 47 (1971); D. L. Hascall, "Trochaic Meter," *CE* 33 (1971), "Triple Meter in Eng. Verse," *Poetics* 12 (1974); S. R. Levin in *Lang* 49 (1973); R. W. Sapora, Jr., *A Theory of ME Allit. Meter* (1977); R. Grotjahn, *Ling. und stat. Methoden in Metrik und Textwiss.* (1979).

CRITICISM AND OTHER APPROACHES: W. K. Wimsatt, Jr., "The Rule and The Norm," *CE* 31 (1970); W. Klein, "Crit. Remarks on G. M.," *Poetics* 12 (1974); R. Standop, "Metric Theory Gone Astray," *Lang&S* 8 (1975); A. M. Devine and L. D. Stephens, "The Abstractness of Metrical Patterns," *Poetics* 4 (1975); R. P. Newton, "Trochaic and Iambic," *Lang&S* 8 (1975). K. Magnuson and F. G. Ryder, "The Study of Eng. Pros.," *CE* 31 (1970), rev. as "Second Thoughts," *CE* 33 (1971); J. B. Lord, "Syntax and Phonology in Poetic Style," *Style* 9 (1975); P. Kiparsky, "Stress, Syntax, and Meter," *Lang.* 51 (1975), "The Rhythmic Structure of Eng. Verse," *LingI* 8 (1977); D. Chisholm, "Phonological Patterning in Ger. Verse," *Computers and the Humanities* 10 (1976), "G. Pros. and Eng. Verse," *Poetics* 6 (1977); M. Liberman and A. Prince, "On Stress and Ling. Rhythm," *LingI* 8 (1977); B. Bjorklund, *A Study in Comp. Pros.: Eng. and Ger. Iambic Pentameter* (1978); M. Barnes and H. Esau, "Eng. Pros. Reconsidered," *Lang&S* 11 (1978); M. Harvey, "Reconciliation of Two Current Approaches to Metrics," *Lang&S* 13 (1980); Brogan, 299–318—full survey to 1980; G. Youmans, "Hamlet's Testimony on Kiparsky's Theory of Meter," *Neophil* 66 (1982), Intro. to *Rhythm and Meter*, ed. P. Kiparsky and G. Youmans (1989); B. Hayes, "A Grid-Based Theory of Eng. Meter," *LingI* 14 (1983), "The Phonology of Rhythm in Eng.," *LingI* 15 (1984). T.V.F.B.

GENERIC RHYME is a species of near rhyme (q.v.) in which the rhyming syllables contain identical vowels followed by consonants that are not identical but belong generically to the same phonetic class. Examples of g. r. appear in passages of Welsh poetry (q.v.) that may date from the 6th c. A.D. In these, final consonants following identical vowels rhyme generically in four classes consisting of (1) g-d-b, (2) dd-l-r, (3) gh-f-w, and (4) certain nasal clusters. Among later Welsh poets, g. rhyming never became requisite, and native grammarians came to refer to the device as "Irish." It did, however, become systematized as a requisite prosodic feature of Ir. and Scottish Gaelic poetry (qq.v.), where by the 8th c. A.D., Ir. grammarians had differentiated six permissible rhyming groups: (1) c-t-p, (2) ch-th-f/ph, (3) g-d-b, (4) gh-dh-bh-mh-l-n-r, (5) m-ll-nn-ng-rr, and (6) s. Occasional g. rs. may be found in Eng. nursery rhymes, particularly between the voiceless stops *c*, *t*, and *p* ("... on the tree t*o*p / ... the cradle will r*o*ck") and between the nasal continuants *m* and *n* ("... for my d*a*me / ... lives in the l*a*ne"). See CELTIC PROSODY; RHYME. C.W.D.

GENEVA SCHOOL. The G. S. of lit. crit. brings together a group of phenomenological critics with varying ties to Geneva. Marcel Raymond and Albert Béguin, the earliest G. S. figures, and Raymond's students Jean Starobinski and Jean Rousset, are all directly associated with the University of Geneva; Georges Poulet, born a Belgian, taught in Switzerland for many years and was directly influenced by Raymond; Jean-Pierre Richard, a Frenchman, and J. Hillis Miller, an Am., both recognize Poulet's influence on their work. Not a "school" in the sense of having a common doctrine or manifesto, they are linked by friendship and by a vision of lit. as a network of existential expressions which combine in a work to delineate an individual artistic consciousness or *cogito*. Although their methods have developed in different directions, these critics generally start from the idea of lit. as a uniquely rich order of human expression, a meaningful arrangement of signs that is first grasped through intuition (q.v.).

This G. S. should not be confused with an earlier G. S. of linguistic theory associated with Ferdinand de Saussure, Charles Bally, and Albert Sechehaye. The later G. critics have commented on Saussure's work, but the roots of their lit. crit. lie not in structural linguistics but in existential and phenomenological theory (Husserl, Jaspers, and Bachelard; in the romantic trad., in a certain line of academic historicism (A. O. Lovejoy), and in Henri Bergson's analyses of the perception of time.

Rejecting "objective" views of a work (whether in historically oriented Continental scholarship or in Am. New Crit. [see NEW CRITICISM; POETRY, THEORIES OF, *Objective Theories*]), the G. critics try to define alternative analytic strategies that are still based on the written text. This text must not be analyzed as an object, however, because on a more important level it is the structural record of an individual human consciousness. The critic may not be able to reach the historical author, but he or she can discern a tracery of interlocking terms having to do with perception, and deduce therefrom a pattern which is no less human for being artistically composed. There are many methods for arriving at this pattern of consciousness; words indicating perception of space and time can be extrapolated and juxtaposed; recurrent types of experience can be compared and followed through the text; these perceptions and experiences themselves can be seen from a more subjective point of view or in an object-centered vision that recaptures the sensual logic of the inner landscape itself. Further, since the G. critics believe that lit. articulates an author's attempt to formulate and cope with experience, they often link these patterns of consciousness with larger metaphysical problems: with an awareness of true presence (Poulet), of divinity (Béguin) or an immanent reality (Miller's early work), and of the precarious viability of expressive forms themselves (Starobinski, Miller, Rousset). A basic metaphor is that of an inner mental space, an initial void from which consciousness emerges to plot the characteristic architecture of its experience.

Since the G. critics see lit. as a structure of consciousness, they consider the proper poetic response an act of sympathetic reading. Readers engaged in this essentially hermeneutic process suspend their own presuppositions and await a "signal" from the work that will direct them to enter its structure from a given angle. Nonetheless, the poem surpasses any single attempt to plot its coordinates, so that each reader finds his or her own way into the work and uses each time a slightly different avenue of approach. Finally, since the properly literary act is a meeting of minds, there can be no judgment or evaluation according to exterior criteria, be they aesthetic, psychological, sociological, or political. In practice, however, the G. critics prefer works that imply "authenticity," in which existential questions and patterns of consciousness (however complex and seemingly contradictory) are worked through in a consistent manner.

Since the G. critics try to grasp the *cogito* embodied throughout an author's works, they rarely limit themselves to studying individual texts. Poulet and Richard characteristically draw upon an author's total production; Rousset and Miller also discuss separate works. The critics in general have been criticized for not valuing the separate identities of different works and for going beyond acceptable boundaries of objective linguistic interpretation. Their analysis of the creative imagination is, in fact, easily adapted to other media. Rousset and Starobinski have written on art and architectural form, as well as on opera. Yet Miller, drawing on his Am. New Critical background, has always linked forms of perception with structures of syntax. Clearly G. crit. can apply to linguistic structures; the real distinction lies not in verbal or nonverbal analysis but in their focus on textual representations of individual consciousness. Those who see lit. as an objective pattern of greater or lesser beauty, or as an example of cultural production, will not agree with G. crit.

There is a surprising variety of methods inside the G. S. Marcel Raymond and Albert Béguin retain a traditional historical framework for their analyses of the spiritual careers of Fr. symbolist and Ger. romantic poets. The later Béguin limits his sympathetic readings to a decreasing circle of Catholic authors. Georges Poulet, the first to propose a complete methodological approach and the main figure in the modern G. S., plots with subtlety and encyclopedic knowledge the temporal and spatial coordinates of the developing creative consciousness in an author's work. Poulet envisages histories of artistic and philosophical consciousness in which would be included the works of gifted critics. In contrast to Poulet and more like the philosopher Gaston Bachelard, Jean Pierre Richard stresses patterns of objects as they appear and change inside a text's mental landscape. His work, always coordinated by themes of sensual perception, has moved closer to a psychological thematics in collections of shorter and more narrowly focused analyses.

Jean Starobinski, trained in medicine as well as lit., is a versatile critic who describes processes of the creative imagination in art, lit., music, and mental illness. More than any other G. S. writer, he emphasizes historical contexts, the history of ideas (incl. ideas of lit. crit.), and interdisciplinary crit. His colleague Jean Rousset pursues transformations of style; the structures of consciousness he perceives in a work are more formal and less personal than those of the other European G. critics. Poulet, Starobinski, Rousset, and Miller locate their individual critiques inside the framework of a changing history of consciousness. Of all these critics, J. Hillis Miller, although originally quite influenced by Poulet, has moved farthest away from the G. S.'s attempt to reconstruct patterns of individual consciousness. His works after 1970 take up many of the same poets and novelists as before, but with a new attention to rhetorical or "deconstructive" poetics. Nonetheless, Miller's desire to analyze structures of meaning, to account for a quality of "strangeness" in lit., and to elucidate an "ethics" of reading still shows the stamp of G. S. concerns.

Later devels. in the G. S. point to an increasing awareness of other modes of crit. Unchanging, however, is an attachment to the analysis of patterns of consciousness, to the study of major works of Western culture, and to the concept of lit. as an intersubjective experience fully realized only in the act of reading. For discussion of the intuitivist presuppositions of G.-S. crit., derivig esp. from Kant, see INTUITION. See also CRITICISM; READER-RESPONSE CRITICISM; SUBJECTIVITY AND OBJECTIVITY.

M. Raymond, *De Baudelaire au surréalisme* (1933), *Génies de France* (1942), *Senancour, sensations et révélations* (1966), *Romantisme et rêverie* (1978); A. Béguin, *L'Ame romantique et le rêve* (1937), *Balzac visionnaire* (1946), *Pascal par lui-même* (1952); G. Poulet, *Études sur le temps human I-IV* (1949–68), *L'Espace proustien* (1963), *La Conscience critique* (1971), *Entre moi et moi* (1976), *La Poésie éclatée* (1980), *La Pensée indéterminée* (1985); J. Rousset, *La Litt. de l'âge baroque en France* (1953), *Forme et signification* (1962), *L'Intérieur et l'extérieur* (1968), *Les Yeux se rencontrèrent* (1981); J.-P. Richard, *Poésie et profondeur* (1955), *L'Univers imaginaire de Mallarmé* (1961), *Onze Études sur la poésie moderne* (1964), *Proust et le monde sensible* (1974), *Microlectures I–II* (1979–82); J. H. Miller, *Charles Dickens, The World of His Novels* (1958), *Poets of Reality* (1965), *The Form of Victorian Fiction* (1968), *Thomas Hardy, Distance and Desire* (1970), "The G. S.," *Mod. Fr. Crit.*, ed. J. K. Simon (1972), *Fiction and Repetition* (1982), *The Ethics of Reading* (1987); J. Starobinski, *L'Invention de la liberté* (1964), *L'Oeil vivant I–II*, 2d ed. (1970), *La Relation critique* (1970), *Jean-Jacques Rousseau, la transparence et l'obstacle*, 2d ed. (1971), *Les Mots sous les mots* (1971), *1789: Les Emblèmes de la raison* (1973), *Montaigne en mouvement* (1982); S. N. Lawall, *Critics of Consciousness* (1968); A. Leonard, "Critique et conscience," *ECr* 14 (1974); *Albert Béguin et Marcel Raymond: Colloque de Cartigny*, ed. P. Grotzer (1979); Spec. Iss. of *Swiss-Fr. Studies* 1,2 (1980)— incl. bibl.; "Hommage à Georges Poulet," *MLN* 97 (1982); *Pour un temps / Jean Starobinski* (1985).

S.L.

GENIUS (Lat. "spirit") is the crucial middle term, developed mainly in the 18th c., in the millennial transition from theories which view the sources of poetic originality and creation as external—i.e. concepts of divine inspiration (q.v.) and poetic madness (q.v.)—to theories which posit them as internal—i.e. as processes of imagination (q.v.) or

of the subconscious. Originally "g." meant the distinctive character of a place, thing, or person—e.g. *genius loci*, the spirit of a place—and was probably considered by the Romans as the equivalent of the Gr. *daimon* (demon). Socrates regarded himself as directed by his *daimon* (we still have in common parlance the phrase "evil genius"), and when Christianity became the official religion of the Roman Empire, *daimon* came to be thought of primarily as diabolical; thereafter, the locus of the concept of "g." was transferred from the outer world of spirits to the inner spirit world of the poet. By the Ren., the modern term was represented by Lat. *ingenium*, with the sense of "natural talent or aptitude, proficiency," without any significant distinction between talent and g. Crucial now is the notion that the artist is born with talent; it is not an acquired skill: *poeta nascitur non fit*. Talent is beyond craft, beyond reason, even beyond the rules (q.v.) of art: it is the transcendent operator, the *je ne sais quoi* (q.v.) of Fr. Classicism, Pope's "Grace beyond the Reach of Art."

But the concept of g. is developed most fully in neoclassical poetics and in preromanticism (qq.v.). Now g. becomes the antithesis of mere "talent." By 1775, g. is unequivocably associated with inventiveness, creativity, and fecundity of imagination. G. surpasses talent just as the sublime (q.v.) exceeds the beautiful. The semantic shift is essentially from g. denoting those at the top of the class of mortal intellects to those above the mortal class altogether. James Russell Lowell's later dictum is canonical: "talent is that which is in a man's power; g. is that in whose power a man is." Important forces driving the shift are the 18th-c. tastes for the Gothic, the sublime, primitivism (q.v.), and other manifestations of the sub- and supra-rational; the adulation of Shakespeare as a natural g.; and the final parting of the ways of the concepts of imitation and originality (qq.v.). In the Ren., and even up to Sir Joshua Reynolds, true imitation is a creative and inventive activity. But the doctrines of spontaneity and originality (qq.v.), those quintessential hieroglyphs of romanticism, degraded the idea of talent as skilled performance.

Important documents in the history of the concept include Longinus, chs. 33–36 (first translated into Eng. in 1554 and refracted for the 17th c. through Boileau), Abbé Du Bos, *Réflexions critiques sur la poésie et la peinture* (1719), and Addison's *Spectator* essay no. 160 (3 Sept. 1711). Between 1751 and 1774, 12 publications treat the concept of g., incl. William Sharpe's *Dissertation Upon G.* (1755), William Duff's *Essay on Original G.* (1767), and Alexander Gerard's *Essay on G.* (written 1758, pub. 1774; ed. B. Fabian 1966 with valuable Intro.), the most important being Edward Young's *Conjectures on Original Composition* (1759), which is essentially a romantic manifesto. Young was a primary influence on Ger. *Sturm und Drang* (q.v.), where g. becomes a primary concept, reformulated in the distinction between fancy and imagination, whence Coleridge (*Biographia literaria*, chs. 2, 15). Hazlitt published two essays on "G. and Common Sense" (*Table Talk*) and one on "Whether G. is Conscious of its Power?" (*The Plain Speaker*); Charles Lamb's "The Sanity of True G." (1826) reasserts psychic balance. In the 20th c., Irving Babbitt in his essays *On G.* and *On Being Original* mounted a sweeping indictment of the romantic mythology of originality and g., though most of the romantic ideas which Babbitt attributes to Rousseau and his influence can be found in Young.

O. Schlapp, *Kants Lehre vom Genie* (1901); L. P. Smith, *Four Words* (1924); E. Zilsel, *Die Entstehung des Geniebegriffs* (1926); H. Thüme, *Beiträge zur Gesch. des Geniebegriffs in England* (1927); B. Rosenthal, *Der Geniebegriff des Aufklärungszeitalters* (1933); H. Sudhiemer, *Der Geniebegriff des jungen Goethe* (1935); P. Grappin, *La Théorie du génie dans le préclassicisme allemand* (1952); Abrams; Wellek, v. 2; Saisselin; G. Tonelli, "G., Ren. to 1770," and R. Wittkower, "G., Individualism," pt. 4, *DHI*, v. 2—with bibls.; J. Chance, *The G. Figure in Antiquity and the Middle Ages* (1975); K. Frieden, *G. and Monologue* (1985); J. Schmidt, *Gesch. des Genie-Gedankens in der deutschen Literatur, Philosophie und Politik*, 2 v. (1985); *G.: The Hist. of an Idea*, ed. P. Murray (1989); C. Battersby, *Gender and G.* (1989); R. R. Monroe, *Creative Brainstorms* (1992).
T.V.F.B.

GENRE. The term "g." is often used interchangeably with "type," "kind," and "form." Western theory on the subject of whether works of lit. can be classified into distinct kinds appears at the beginning of literary study and has sustained active controversies in every stage of lit. hist. Alternately extolled and condemned, praised for its potential for order and ignored as, finally, irrelevant, the concept takes its tone, in every age, from the particular theory that surrounds it. Theorists approached it prescriptively until about the end of the 18th c., descriptively thereafter; and it retains its viability (if not always its honor) through the plethora of modern comments about the nature of possibilities of lit. But built into its ways of working are difficulties that have ultimately to do with a version of the hermeneutic circle: how can we choose specific works from which to draw a definition of, say, epic (q.v.) unless we already know what an epic is? Though answered in various ways, the question continues to insinuate itself.

Classical poetics (q.v.) had no systematic theory about the concept of g. What thinking there is at the beginning of Western poetics originates from a distinction made by Plato between two possible modes of reproducing an object or person: (1) by description (i.e. by portraying it by means of words) or (2) by mimicry or impersonation (i.e. by imitating it). Since poetry according to the mimetic theory (see IMITATION; REPRESENTATION AND MIMESIS; POETRY, THEORIES OF) was con-

ceived as such a reproduction of external objects, these two modes became the main divisions of poetry: dramatic poetry (q.v.) or the theatre was direct imitation or miming of persons, and narrative poetry (q.v.) or the epic was the portrayal or description of human actions.

But since this simple division obviously left out too much, a third division was inserted between the two others (*Republic* 3.392–94): the so-called mixed mode, in which narrative alternates with dialogue (q.v.), as is usually the case in epic poetry (which is rarely pure narrative). But no new principle of classification was thereby introduced, so no room was left for the genre of self-expression or the lyric (q.v.), in which the poet expresses directly her or his own thoughts and feelings. The extensive use of Homer as a model gave clear if implicit preference to the epic, a point echoed in *Laws*, which comments effectually mark the beginning of the hierarchy of gs. The classification is as much moral as it is literary; Plato says subsequently that the guardians should imitate only the most suitable characters (395) but that there are impersonators who will imitate anything (397).

Prior to Plato, during the Attic age, we find a wide variety of terms for specific gs.: the epic or recited poetry; the drama or acted poetry, subdivided into tragedy and comedy (qq.v.); then iambic or satirical poetry, so called because written in iambic meter (see IAMBIC; INVECTIVE; CHOLIAMBUS); and elegiac poetry (see ELEGY), also written in a distinctive meter, the elegiac couplet (see ELEGIAC DISTICH), with its offshoots the epitaph and the epigram (qq.v.), all classed together because composed in the same meter. Then there was choral or melic poetry (q.v.), as it was later called, poetry sung by a chorus to the accompaniment of a flute or stringed instrument. Melic poetry comes closest to our concept of the lyric, but it is not divorced from music and it excludes what we consider the essentially lyric gs. of the elegy and epigram. In addition, there was the hymn (q.v.), the dirge (q.v.) or *threnos*, and the dithyramb (q.v.), a composition in honor of Dionysus which could be anything from a hymn to a miniature play. Songs of triumph or of celebration included the paean, the encomium, the epinikion, and the epithalamium (qq.v.). There was certainly plenty of material in Gr. poetry to make up a concept of lyric poetry, but the early Greeks apparently contented themselves with classifying by such criteria as metrical form.

The purely extrinsic scheme used for the nonce by Plato is taken up by Aristotle in *Poetics* ch. 3, where it becomes the foundation of his main classification of poetic gs. Aristotle gives no express recognition of the lyric there, much less in his statement that in the second of these gs. the poet "speaks in his own person": that is merely Aristotle's way of saying that the narrative is the poet's own discourse and not a speech by a fictitious character of drama. So the traditional tripartite division of poetic gs. or kinds into epic, dramatic, and lyric, far from being a "natural" division first discovered by the Gr. genius, is not to be found in either Plato or Aristotle. It was, rather, the result of a long and tedious process of compilation and adjustment, through the repetition with slight variations of certain traditional lists of poetic gs., which did not reach the modern formula of the three divisions until the 16th c.

Nevertheless, Aristotle's classifications of kind in the *Poetics* make him the source and arbiter of g. study (though often at only second or even third hand, and frequently warped) for nearly two millennia. Like Plato, Aristotle argues that poetry is a species of imitation. The medium of imitation concerns the instrumentality through which the various kinds are presented. The object of imitation, men in action, has both contentual and moral aspects, tragedy and comedy dealing with men as better or worse than they are; but the package is not nearly so neat because Cleophon, though a tragic poet, represents a middle way, men as they are—a significant point which shows how Aristotle's examples can complicate the issue appropriately. On the manner of imitation, Aristotle continues the general Platonic divisions according to the status of the speaker.

All of this supports the view that Aristotle is arguably the first formalist, the first exponent of organic unity (see ORGANICISM); for him, mode, object, and manner, working together, not only make for the "character" of the kind but affect (and effect) all that each aspect does and is. Yet he is formalist and a good deal more, for his connection of g. with tone and moral stance led not only to later quarrels about decorum (q.v.) and mixed modes but also, and more profitably, about the ways in which texts seek to conceive and appropriate the world—that is, the difficult business of representation, incl. his implicit debate with Plato over its possibilities and value.

After Aristotle, it was Alexandrian scholarship that undertook the first comprehensive stock-taking of Gr. poetry and began the process of grouping, grading, and classifying gs. Lists or "canons" of the best writers in each kind were made, which led to a sharper awareness of g. The first extant grammarian to mention the lyric as a g. was Dionysius Thrax (2d c. B.C.), in a list which comprises, in all, the following: "Tragedy, Comedy, Elegy, Epos, Lyric, and Threnos," lyric meaning for him, still, poetry sung to the lyre. In Alexandrian lit., other gs. were added to the list, esp. the idyll and pastoral (qq.v.).

The Gr. conceptions of g. were themselves radically generic in the sense of putting the issues in their elemental forms. What followed—adulation, elaboration, correction, rejection—built on those ways of working. Yet it was clear to later Classicism (q.v.) that these treatises needed supplementary detail, their nearly exclusive emphases on epic and tragedy being insufficient to cover the complex topography of g. Further, with the model of the Greeks so potent that there was no thought of undoing their principles, it seemed best not only to elaborate but to clarify and purify, to establish principles of tact which were not only matters of taste (q.v.) but, ultimately, of the appropriate. The Middle Ages, and later, the 17th c., was a time for codification, which could slip easily into rules (q.v.). Quintilian's *Institutio oratoria* argued for such practices, but most important was Horace's *Ars poetica* (a name given by Quintilian to the *Epistula ad Pisones*), a text of extraordinary influence because so many later students read the Greeks through Horace's letter (see CLASSICAL POETICS). The attitudes of Horace were often taken as the classical ways.

Part of the irony is that his letter is not particularly original: its outstanding contribution is the principle of decorum Aristotle had referred to the interrelation of style with theme, but in Horace this combined with the demands of urbanity and propriety to become the principal emphasis. Tragedy does not babble light verses. Plays ought to be in five acts, no more and no less, with all bloodiness offstage. Plunge into epics *in medias res* (q.v.), but echo the categories of the strong predecessors either by telling those events or having them acted out. At this distance, Horace comes through mainly as the exponent of a set of mind, one who surely had much to do with later equations of social and literary decorum. Given his emphasis on "the labor of the file," he is probably best seen as the ultimate craftsman, completer of the Cl. triumvirate on which g. study built for most of the rest of Western lit. hist.

Scholars are generally agreed that the Middle Ages offered little if any commentary of permanent value on the theory of g., and they usually cite Dante's remarks in *De vulgari eloquentia* (ca. 1305) as the major points of interest. In fact though, Dante's account shows a curious transformation of trad., esp. in his insistence that his poem is a comedy because it has a happy ending and is written in a middle style; this sense of "comedy" Dante found in Donatus, *De comoedia*, and Euanthius, *De fabula*. Dante argued for a quasi-Horatian decorum of g. and style. In a sense the *Commedia* culminates medieval mixtures of the grotesque and the sublime (qq.v.), as in the mystery plays (see LITURGICAL DRAMA), but it also suggests, if unwittingly, an undoing of generic norms that was to cause much bitter controversy in subsequent approaches.

As though to counter such implicit subversion, the theorists of the It. Ren. focused intensely on g. (see RENAISSANCE POETICS); the rediscovery of the *Poetics* around 1500 became an impetus to codifications such as had never been conceived even in the most rigorous late Cl. formulations. Part of the intensity came from the wide variety of gs. and mixed modes such as the *prosimetrum* (q.v.)

practiced in the Middle Ages, leading to the blend of medieval romance (q.v.) and epic in figures such as Ariosto and Tasso. If there were 16th-c. defenders of these "mixed" works—among which tragicomedy (q.v.) was surely the most notorious (Guarini argued in his own defense, but the greatest of the kind were written in England)—there were codifiers such as Scaliger and Castelvetro who had considerable influence well into the 18th c.

Out of these theorists came that ultimate codification, the "unities" of time, place, and action (see UNITY), which was finally put to rest only in the 18th c. by critics such as Samuel Johnson (see NEOCLASSICAL POETICS). Though they were claimed to have their sources in Aristotle's categories, in fact these arguments distorted Aristotle and carried Horatian conservatism to reactionary lengths. Fr. Neoclassicism continued the codification, quite brilliantly in Boileau's *Art poétique*, more ambivalently in Corneille's *Discours*, the latter an apologia for his dramatic practice which is, at the same time, an act of support for the unities. Suggestions that Neoclassical generic hierarchies and standards of decorum have sociopolitical and philosophical implications are, for the most part, convincing: the potential analogies among these favorite subjects ensured their mutual support and offer still another instance of the relations of lit. and power. Yet as both lit. and society worked their way into romanticism (q.v.), most of those hierarchies shifted: in lit. the lyric ascended to the top of the hierarchy, signaling the confirmation of the triad of lyric, epic (i.e. narrative), and drama which is set forth by Hegel and still dominates g. theory. Friedrich Schlegel (in his *Dialogue on Poetry* [1800] and essay on Goethe [1828]) argued for the abolition of generic classification, which would in effect eliminate g. Schlegel and others had in mind the example of Cervantes, expanding the concept of the novel to speak of it as a package that could carry all other genres within itself, e.g. ballads and romances within tales, as in Matthew Gregory Lewis's *The Nonk* and, memorably, Poe's *Fall of the House of Usher*. International romanticism explored such issues routinely. But when 19th-c. Darwinian biology found application to lit., it produced a rigidly evolutionary theory of g. in Brunetière and others, a dead-end whose main value was that it annoyed theorists like Croce, who considered gs. mere abstractions, useful in the construction of classifications for practical convenience, but of no value as aesthetic categories. Thereby it stimulated interest in g. theory in the 20th c., one of the great ages of speculation on the subject.

Croce became the case against which theorists tested themselves for much of the early 20th c. (see EXPRESSION). If g. classifications have a certain convenience, they nevertheless conflict with Croce's conception of the individual work of art as the product of a unique intuition (q.v.). G., in this view, has a merely nominalist existence, a position

echoed in varying ways by later theorists as significant and different as Jameson and, in one of his moods, the unclassifiable Frye—though the latter set up an elaborate system of classification which all commentators have taken as another way of talking about g. Todorov's structuralist attack on Frye resulted in a controversial proposal concerning historical and theoretical gs., but Frye remains the most important theorist of the subject since Croce. Scholars like Fowler have argued eloquently for looser, more historically based readings, recognizing the fact of change and the necessity for flexibility, while concepts like intertextuality (q.v.) obviously have much of importance to say about the workings of g. Formalists of various persuasions have worried about g. in terms of form-content relations (see ORGANICISM). Drawing on the work of Karl Viëtor, Claudio Guillén distinguishes persuasively between universal modes of experience (lyric, epic, drama) and genres proper (tragedy or the sonnet). Other recent theorists argue for the institutional nature of g., for its function as a series of codes, and (less convincingly) as an element in a *lanque-parole* relationship, while Fowler and others, working out of Frye, stress the significance of the concept of "mode." Still, Jameson's argument that g. theory has been discredited by modern thinking about lit. seems now largely convincing. Recognition of the embodiment of lit. in the necessarily shifting conditions of culture has led a number of theorists to argue that a g. is whatever a particular text or time claims it to be. Skepticism about universals has clearly taken its toll, as have, in other ways, the arguments of Croce. Such skepticism has appeared among contemporary artists as well, e.g. the performance artist Laurie Anderson and the composer-writer-performer John Cage, who pull down all walls of distinction among gs. and media as well as what has been called "high art" and "low art." (Here as elsewhere sociocultural elements cannot be separated from other facets of the work.) Terms like "multimedia" and "intermedia" can be complemented by others such as "intergeneric," such practices denying, in varying degree, the validity of absolute distinctions, categories, and hierarchies. Theorizing about g. has not been so vigorous since the 16th c. The suggestiveness of the 20th c.'s quite variegated work makes it a period of extraordinary achievement in the history of this stubborn, dubious, always controversial concept. For further discussion of mode and g. see VERSE AND PROSE; see also CANON; CONVENTION; FORM; ORGANICISM; RULES.

JOURNAL: *Genre* 1– (1968–).

STUDIES: F. Brunetière, *L'Evolution des gs.*, 7th ed. (1922); B. Croce, *Aesthetic*, tr. D. Ainslie, 2d ed. (1922); J. Petersen, "Zur Lehre von den Dichtungsgattungen," *Festschrift Aug. Sauer* (1925); K. Viëtor, "Probleme der literarische Gattungsgesch.," *DVLG* 9 (1931), "Die Gesch. der literarischen

Gattungen," *Geist und Form* (1952); R. Bray, *Des Gs. littéraires* (1937); K. Burke, "Poetic Categories," *Attitudes Toward History* (1937); I. Behrens, *Die Lehre von der Einteilung der Dichtkunst* (1940)— best account of devel. of g. classif. in Western lit.; J. J. Donohue, *The Theory of Literary Kinds*, 2 v. (1943–49)—ancient Gr. g. classif.; I. Ehrenpreis, *The "Types Approach" to Lit.* (1945); C. Vincent, *Théorie des gs. littéraires*, 21st ed. (1951); Abrams, chs. 1, 4, 6; E. Olson, "An Outline of Poetic Theory," in Crane; A. E. Harvey, "The Classif. of Gr. Lyric Poetry," *ClassQ* n.s. 5 (1955); Wellek and Warren, ch. 17; Frye; Wimsatt and Brooks; Weinberg, ch. 13; C. F. P. Stutterheim, "Prolegomena to a Theory of Literary Gs.," *ZRL* 6 (1964); B. K. Lewalski, *Milton's Brief Epic* (1966), Paradise Lost *and the Rhet. of Literary Forms* (1985), ed., *Ren. Gs.* (1986); F. Séngle, *Die literarische Formenlehre* (1967); W. V. Ruttkowski, *Die literarischen Gattungen* (1968)—bibl. with trilingual indices, *Bibliographie der Gattungspoetik* (1973); E. Staiger, *Grundbegriffe der Poetik* (1968), tr. J. C. Hudson and L. T. Frank as *Basic Concepts of Poetics* (1991); K. R. Scherpe, *Gattungspoetik im 18 Jh.* (1968); E. Vivas, "Literary Classes: Some Problems," *Genre* 1 (1968); H.-R. Jauss, "Litt. médiévale et théorie des gs.," *Poétique* 1 (1970); T. Todorov, *Intro. à la lit. fantastique* (1970), *Gs. in Discourse* (tr. 1990); M. Fubini, *Entstehung und Gesch. der literarischen Gattungen* (1971); C. Guillén, *Lit. as System* (1971), chs. 4–5; P. Hernadi, *Beyond G.* (1972); F. Cairns, *Generic Composition in Gr. and Roman Poetry* (1972); R. L. Colie, *The Resources of Kind: G. Theory in the Ren.* (1973); K. W. Hempfer, *Gattungstheorie* (1973); R. Cohen, "On the Interrelations of 18th-C. Literary Forms," and R. W. Rader, "The Concept of G. and 18th-C. Studies," *New Approaches to 18th-C. Lit.*, ed. P. Harth (1974); A. Jolles, *Einfache Formen*, 5th ed. (1974); G. W. F. Hegel, *Aesthetics*, tr. T. M. Knox (1975); G. Genette, "Gs.," 'types,' modes," *Poétique* 32 (1977); K. Müller-Dyes, *Literarische Gattungen* (1978); "Theories of Literary G.," ed. J. Strelka, spec. iss. of *YCC* 8 (1978); Spec. Iss. on G., *Glyph* 7 (1980); Spec. Iss. on G. Theory, *Poetics* 10, 2–3 (1981); F. Jameson, *The Political Unconscious* (1981); Fowler—the major mod. study; H. Dubrow, *G.* (1982); W. E. Rogers, *The Three Gs. and the Interp. of Lyric* (1983); B. J. Bond, *Literary Transvaluation from Vergilian Epic to Shakespearean Tragicomedy* (1984); *Canons*, ed. R. von Hallberg (1984); *Discourse and Lit.: New Approaches to the Analysis of Literary Gs.*, ed. T. A. Van Dijk (1984); T. G. Rosenmeyer, "Ancient Literary Gs.: A Mirage?" *YCGL* 34 (1985); *Postmodern Gs.*, ed. M. Perloff (1989).   F.G.; G.N.G.O.; T.V.F.B.

GEORGIAN POETRY. (This entry treats G. p. in Russian; for Eng. poetry of the G. period, see GEORGIANISM.) G. culture is one of the oldest in the region generally known today as Transcaucasia; archaeological findings in the territory date back to the third millennium B.C. During their history Georgians have often had to fight against formidable enemies—Arabs, Turks, Persians, Mongols—who numerous times invaded the country and laid waste its villages, but against all odds the nation has preserved its culture, lang., and religion. Up to the 19th c., the lit. of Georgia ws the oldest and richest of that of any of the Republics in the former Soviet Union.

The trad. of a written lit. starts in Georgia with the beginning of the Christian era (4th c.). The earliest poetic forms are to be found among liturgical psalms and hymns, initially translated from Gr. Later G. clergy developed similar forms independently, and gradually spiritual songs acquired more secular coloring, evolving into lyric poems.

During the following centuries the genre of narrative poetry emerges, influenced by the lit. of neighboring Persia. The genre reached its peak in the 12th c. during the reign of Queen Tamar (1184–1213). Among the three distinguished poets of her court—Chakhrukhadze, Ioane Shavteli, and Shota Rustaveli—the latter is unanimously acknowledged as the greatest master of G. poetic art. His epic poem *Vepkhis Tqaosani* (The Night in the Tiger's Skin) recounts the adventures of a young prince who aids his friend in search of the latter's beloved, captured by devils. Basically Christian in spirit, the narrative is nevertheless saturated with a pantheistic joy of life. The poem praises chivalrous love, heroic deeds, friendship, and loyalty to one's sovereign. Several digressions reflect codified rules of chivalrous courtship, honor, and poetic art. The poem's exceptional richness of vocabulary, powerful images, exquisite alliterations, and complex rhyming are considered to be yet unsurpassed models in G. p. The poem consists of 1576 quatrains written in the meter *shairi*, a 16-syllable verse with a medial caesura. The metrical pattern permits two types of variation in syllable-grouping: *magali* (high) *shairi* [4 / 4 // 4 / 4] and *dabali* (low) *shairi* [5 / 3 // 5 / 3]. These two types of *shairi* alternate quatrain by quatrain throughout the poem, while the rhyming pattern of each quatrain proceeds in simple monorhyme—*aaaa, bbbb, cccc*, etc.

Rustaveli's poem was viewed as a paradigm by the poets of the following four centuries, a period that marks a low ebb in the devel. of G. p. The themes and plots of *The Night in the Tiger's Skin* are borrowed and imitated in lyric and narrative poems alike, while *shairi* remained the basic meter of G. secular verse. In the 16th–17th cs., several G. kings distinguished themselves as fine poets. King Theimuraz I (1588–1662) was strongly influenced by Persian poetry (q.v.). Graceful poetic images and refined vocabulary are the most prominent features of his works. Archil III (1647–1713) is known for several didactic poems in which he contemplates the destiny of his country, religion and morals, and the art of poetry. He objected to the use of Persian poetic models and tried to purify his vocabulary from foreign borrowings. But a far more radical innovator was David Guramishvili (1705–92). Although his major work, "Davitiani" (The Story of David), is written in the traditional *shairi*, in his shorter lyrics he breaks away from the canons of Rustaveli's verse and introduces a great variety of metrical forms and rhyming patterns. He too reformed the poetic vocabulary, bringing it closer to spoken lang. His love poems describe sentiments of an ordinary man rather than of an enamored knight. "Davitiani" consists of a number of short narrative poems in which the author both expresses his religious and political thoughts and recounts his tumultuous and eventful life.

The next prominent figure of G. p. is Bessarion Gabashvili (1740–91), better known as Besiki, a court poet of King Heraclius II. Love is the major theme of his remarkably elegant and sonorous lyrics. His refined images are at times too ornate, but his vocabulary is rich and innovative. Besiki frequently used an original meter later known as *besikuri* (i.e. Besikian), a 14-syllable verse of the distinct pattern 2 / 3 / 4 / 2 / 3.

At the very beginning of the 19th c., Georgia was annexed by the Russian Empire. G. nobility and intellectuals became acquainted with the lit. trads. of Russia and western Europe. Consequently, G. p. of the following decades displays the noticeable influence of romanticism. The movement is best represented by Alexandre Chavchavadze (1786–1846), Grigol Orbeliani (1804–83), and Nikoloz Baratashvili (1817–45). The poems of Chavchavadze and Orbeliani are often contemplative but never metaphysical. The poets express their pride for Georgia's heroic past or meditate remorsefully on the country's lost glory. Majestic images of nature often serve as a dramatic background for their soliloquies, permeated with pessimism and sadness. Another group of their poems, marked with vibrant sensuality, praise the earthly joys of love, friendship, and feasting. Their poetic virtuosity is best displayed in the genre of *mukhambazi*. These are predominantly love poems consisting of several 5-line stanzas of 14- or 15-syllable verses in monorhyme. Baratashvili is the epitome of G. romanticism. His poetic persona is that of a passionate rhetor and rebel challenging his destiny. In his only narrative poem, "Bedi Kartlisa" (The Fate of Georgia), he depicts with exceptional force the last devastating battle (1795) of Iraklius II against the Persian invaders. Baratashvili also significantly reformed G. versification, introducing new metrical forms and integrating into his poems new motifs and vocabulary from folksongs.

The second half of the 19th c. is marked by an awakening of the national consciousness and increasing dissatisfaction with the oppressive policy of the czarist government. G. poets of this period adjust romantic conventions to their social and political concerns and add a good dose of satirical venom to their verses. The most prominent figure

is Ilia Chavchavadze (1837–1907), the founder of a G.-lang. literary magazine, *Iveria*. An outspoken critic of the policy of Russification, he writes lyrical as well as narrative poems of patriotic appeal. Rhetorical style and strong didactic overtones emphasize the poet's civil convictions. His contemporary Akaki Tsereteli (1840–1915) enjoyed far greater popularity among the general public. The clarity of his images and the simplicity and sonority of his vocabulary make the satirical and political references of his poem less overbearing. Many of his love poems, often written in the genre of *mukhambazi*, have become popular songs. Another outstanding poet of the period, Vazha Pshavela (1861–1915), wrote poems in the vernacular of his native Pshavi that gave unique expressive force to his images. The tragic clash between society's moral values and pragmatic concerns is the major theme of several of his narrative poems that portray action and character of mythic and legendary grandeur.

The first decades of the 20th c. witnessed a new surge of Western influence in a proliferation of poetic schools. In 1916 a group of poets, Titsian Tabidze, Paolo Iashvili, Georgy Leonidze, Nikoloz Mitsishvili, and Valerian Gaprindashvili, published their literary magazine *Tsisperi Qantsebi* (The Blue Drinking Horns), which raised the banner of the symbolist movement in G. p. These poets experimented boldly with vocabulary and versification and adjusted Western genres to the traditional forms of G. p. They praised the intuitive and mystical sources of poetic inspiration and cultivated sensuality and intentional obscurity. Another noteworthy group known as modernists included Konstantine Gamsakhurdia, Ioseb Grishashvili, and Kote Makashvili; they published their highly refined poems in the short-lived periodical *Ilioni* (1922). G. futurists—Nikoloz Shengelaia, Simon Chikovani, Zhango Gogoberidze, and others—hastened to voice their militant aesthetic credos in their literary organ with the endemic title H_2SO_4 (1924). True to their declaration that poetry is but "a vessel of linguistic tricks," they strained the potentialities of the lang. to the breaking point, reflecting the same preoccupation with poetic means and forms as their European and Rus. counterparts (see FUTURISM).

A number of remarkable poets, Grigol Robakidze, Terenti Graneli, and Galaktion Tabidze among them, did not belong to any literary group, but their works attracted keen interest. Tabidze (1891–1959), whose images display spiritual kinship with the symbolists, is considered the most brilliant poet of the century. An acute sense of loneliness and nostalgia find poignant expression in his sonorous verse, whose graceful and subtle images are permeated with innate pessimism.

After the Socialist revolution of 1917, Georgia enjoyed a brief period of political independence (1918–21), but in February of 1921 the Red Army installed the Bolshevik government and the country was forced to enter the alliance of the Soviet Socialist Republics. Initially these cataclysmic events enhanced the creative energy of Georgian intellectuals, and various poetic groups flourished almost until 1930. But soon the ever-tightening control of censorhip forced G. poets to serve the government's demands. Some poets, mostly those of the older generation, managed to maintain high poetic standards in their rare publications, but the majority, even talented Grigol and Irakly Abashidze, produced poems distinguished only by their quasi-optimistic rhetoric and adulation of approved social causes.

By the end of the 1950s, after the official denunciation of Stalin's regime, a new generation of G. poets emerged. These poets, Anna Kalandadze, Mukhran Machavariani, Tamaz and Otar Chiladze, Archil Sulakauri, Shota Nishnianidze, Murman Lebanidze, and Tariel Chanturia, emancipated from harsh ideological restraints, expressed more freely their sentiments. They renewed experiments with metrical forms and enlarged their vocabulary, further urbanizing the themes and styles of G. p.

Since the late 1960s, some G. poets, like Lia Sturua, Besik Kharanauli and a few others, have displayed a distinct preference for *vers libre*. Sturua, an exceptionally gifted poet, is the primary force of the movement. Many young poets, however, such as Manana Chitishvili, represent a more moderate wing that continues the best trads. of G. p. with remarkable vigor, imagination, and technical artistry.

Shot'ha Rust'haveli, *The Man in the Panther's Skin*, tr. M. S. Wardrop (1912); C. Beridze, "G. P.," *Asiatic Review* (1930–31); R. P. Blake, "G. Secular Lit.: Epic, Romance and Lyric (1100–1800)," *Harvard Studies and Notes on Phil. and Lit.* 15 (1933); J. Karst, *Littérature georgienne chrétienne* (1934); *Hist. of G. Lit.* [in Georgian], ed. A. Baramidze, 6 v. (1962–78); *Georgische Poesie aus acht Jahrhunderten*, ed. A. Endler (1971); *L'avangardia a Tiflis*, ed. L. Magarotto (1982); *The Lit. and Art of Soviet Georgia*, ed. S. Dangulov (1987). D.KI.

GEORGIANISM. A poetic movement of the early 20th c. in England, named by its founders for the reigning monarch (George V) and to suggest "that we are the beginning of another 'Georgian period' which may take rank . . . with several great poetic ages of the past." Thus Edward Marsh prefaced *Georgian Poetry 1911–1912* (1912), the first of five anthols. he edited that presented work by poets associated with the movement. Members of the Georgian group included Lascelles Abercrombie, Rupert Brooke, W. H. Davies, John Drinkwater, James Elroy Flecker, W. W. Gibson, Ralph Hodgson, Harold Munro, J. C. Squire, and W. J. Turner; others who occasionally published in *Georgian Poetry* were Robert Graves, D. H. Lawrence, and James Stephens.

Although after the supersession of their movement the Georgians were regarded as timid pastoralists, they were in fact rebelling against the poetic modes influential in Britain since the 1890s—the withdrawal from life of the Aesthetes (Ernest Dowson, Lionel Johnson—see AESTHETICISM) and the Tory imperialism of the public poets (Rudyard Kipling, Sir Henry Newbolt). The Georgians proposed to record actual personal experience in lang. close to common speech (anticipating a similar rejection of public rhet. after the Second World War by The Movement poets in Robert Conquest's anthol. *New Lines*, 1956). As an avant-garde movement, however, the Georgians were quickly outdistanced by the modernists Pound and Eliot and their acolytes, who published their first work during the same decade, 1910–20, and came to prominence in the 1920s. The other factor that made Georgian poetry seem old fashioned was the brutal experience of trench warfare in World War I, which brought to the poetry of Wilfred Owen, Siegfried Sassoon, and, in the 1920s, Robert Graves a harsh realism absent from the Georgians' bucolic reminiscences. Their verse, traditional in technique, was untouched by the modernists' experimentalism or flouting of conventional decorum. Rival publications from the modernist camp were Pound's *Des Imagistes* (1914) and *Wheels* (1916–21), established by Edith, Osbert, and Sacheverill Sitwell.

Although the Georgians' moment in the sun was brief, the influence of the movement outlasted its popularity. Graves, Lawrence, and other British poets were aided in the devel. of their personal styles by the Georgian emphasis upon honesty in place of public rhet.; by the common life as poetic subject rather than a retreat into aestheticism; and by the lang. of actual speech, not false poeticism. These admirable qualities became diluted in the later Georgian collections, however. When Marsh, in his intro. to the last of his anthols. (1922), wrote, "Much admired modern work seems to me, in its lack of inspiration and its disregard of form, like gravy imitating lava," the opponents of G. could dismiss the movement as passé. Its virtues were being more aggressively promoted by Pound and other modernists in the context of bolder treatments of subject, structure, and diction. So the Georgians faded away. Still, at their best, they helped to reform and redeem Eng. poetry from being either too private or too public to express the truth of feeling. See also CUBISM; IMAGISM; VORTICISM; FREE VERSE.—F. Swinnerton, *The Georgian Literary Scene, 1910–35*, 3d ed. (1950); D. Perkins, *Hist. of Mod. Poetry*, v. 1 (1976), ch. 10; C. K. Stead, *The New Poetic: Yeats to Eliot* (1964), ch. 4; R. H. Ross, *The Georgian Revolt* (1966); M. Simon, *The Georgian Poetic* (1978). D.HO.

GEORGIC. A didactic poem primarily intended to give directions concerning some skill, art, or science (see DIDACTIC POETRY). In his "Essay on the G." (1697), which is the most important modern discussion of the genre, Addison specifically distinguished this kind of poetry from the pastoral (q.v.) and crystallized the definition of the g. by pointing out that this "class of Poetry . . . consists in giving plain and direct instructions." The central theme of the g. is the glorification of labor and praise of simple country life. Though this didactic intention is primary, the g. is often filled with descriptions of nature and digressions on myths, lore, or philosophical reflections suggested by the subject matter.

The g. begins as early as Hesiod's *Works and Days* (ca. 750 B.C.) and was used by many of the great ancients—Lucretius, Ovid, Oppian, Nemesianus, Columella. Some of the better known poems in the trad. are Poliziano's *Rusticus* (1483), Vida's *De bombyce* (1527), Alamanni's *La coltivazione* (1546), Tusser's *Five Hundred Points of Good Husbandry* (1573), Rapin's *Horti* (1665), and Jammes' *Géorgiques chrétiennes* (1912). Nevertheless, the finest specimens of the type remain the *Gs.* of Virgil. Virgil's purpose is to celebrate the virtue and dignity of honest toil by the small landowner. The *Gs.* thus differ from pastoral in that work is emphasized instead of leisure, and from epic in planting over killing. It is these virtues—hard work, cultivation—that made the poems appeal to Augustus, newly consolidating the Roman state as empire.

The *Gs.* cast a long shadow over the poetry of the late 17th and 18th cs.: Dryden called the *Gs.* "the best poem of the best poet"; and James Thomson was called the "Eng. Virgil" on account of his hugely successful *The Seasons* (1726; Fr. tr. 1759). Thomson's far-reaching influence was felt even on the Continent. Even where the term "g." does not appear in their title, scores of 18th-c. poems were written which imitate Virgil's gs. in form and content—poems on the art of hunting, fishing, dancing, laughing, preserving health, raising hops, shearing sheep, etc. But the neoclassical g. manifested considerable changes from its Cl. models. It emphasized heterogeneous information rather than detailed instructions; it exalted landscape over work processes; and it invited the reader to feast on the native beauties of rural life, not to wring a living from the recalcitrant soil. And its attempts to elevate a lowly subject by exaggerated periphrases led many imitators to grotesqueries of style. Indeed, at times the serious imitation, as in William Cowper's *The Task*, can hardly be separated from the burlesque, as in Gay's *Trivia; or the Art of Walking the Streets of London* (1716). See BUCOLIC; DESCRIPTIVE POETRY; DIDACTIC POETRY; ECLOGUE; IDYLL; PASTORAL.

M. L. Lilly, *The G.* (1919); D. L. Durling, *G. Trad. in Eng. Poetry* (1935); R. Cohen, *The Art of Discrimination* (1964), *The Unfolding of* The Seasons (1970); D. B. Wilson, *Descriptive Poetry in France from Blason to Baroque* (1967); J. Chalker, *The Eng. G.* (1969); L. P. Wilkinson, *The Gs. of Virgil: A*

Critical Survey (1969); R. Feingold, *Nature and Society* (1978); J. G. Turner, *Politics of Landscape: Rural Scenery and Society in Eng. Verse 1630–1660* (1979); M. C. J. Putnam, *Virgil's Poem of the Earth* (1979); *Virgil's Ascraean Song*, ed. A. J. Doyle (1979); G. B. Miles, *Virgil's Gs.: A New Interp.* (1980); A. Low, *The G. Revolution* (1985); A. Fowler, "The Beginnings of Eng. G.," *Ren. Genres*, ed. B. K. Lewalski (1986); D. O. Ross, Jr., *Virgil's Elements* (1987); R. A. B. Mynors, *Virgil's Gs.: A Commentary* (1989); C. Perkell, *The Poet's Truth* (1989); *Handspan of Red Earth*, ed. C. L. Marconi (1991)—anthol. of Am. farm poems.
J.E.C.; T.V.F.B.

GERMAN POETICS. See MEDIEVAL POETICS; RENAISSANCE POETICS; BAROQUE POETICS; NEOCLASSICAL POETICS; ROMANTIC AND POSTROMANTIC POETICS; TWENTIETH-CENTURY POETICS.

GERMAN POETRY.

    I. ORIGINS TO 1750
    II. SINCE 1750

I. ORIGINS TO 1750. The emergence of an autonomous Ger. p. took place in a setting where it competed, on the one hand, with a living, highly sophisticated, and learned Med. Lat. culture and, on the other hand, with popular oral trads. often objectionable to the literate.

Charlemagne's biographer, Einhard, writes of the emperor's cultivation of his native lang., of his naming of the months and the winds in Ger., of his order to preserve in writing the *barbara et antiquissima carmina* of his people. His son, Louis the Pious, is reputed, perhaps unfairly, to have rescinded that order at the Synod of Inden (A.D. 817), reducing the written use of the vernacular to minor religious formulae. The sole survivor of these shifting policies seems to be the *Hildebrandslied* (The Lay of Hildebrand), a short narrative in irregular alliterative verse recorded at Fulda in the early 9th c. in a codex containing Old Testament materials. The *Hildebrandslied*, which has the distinction of being the oldest surviving example of heroic poetry in any Germanic dialect, is a tale of father and son on opposing sides in battle, of conflicting loyalties, and, presumably, of malevolent fate (the last lines have not survived). This poem begins the written record of Ger. p. Competitors of early date include the magical charms preserved in a 9th-c. ms at Merseburg (the *Merseburger Zaubersprüche*) of indeterminable pagan antiquity, with phrases dating back to IE times, and the fragmentary creation story in the *Wessobrunner Gebet* (The Wessobrunn Prayer) written down about the year 814 from an older source.

Like its Eng. and Scandinavian cousins, ancient oral Ger. p. employed alliteration rather than end rhyme (see GERMAN PROSODY, *Old Germanic*). The written record of Ger., however, provides but few instances of alliterative verse, which did not flourish in OHG as long as in OE. The conversion to end-rhyme (see RHYME) took place in the first hundred years of the written record, and was complete by the time of Otfried von Weissenburg's deliberately end-rhymed *Evangelienbuch* (ca. 868). His source was Med. Lat. hymnology (see HYMN). Such alliterative traces as survive Otfried color subsequent texts as *figurae* but no longer determine the form of poetic composition. The shift to end-rhyme points, together with the new knowledge of the identity of authors (Otfried is the first Ger. poet known by name), toward the foundation of a written vernacular lit. discrete from the dominant oral trad.

In the Carolingian period (752–911), the classes of lit. represented in the vernacular include: the poetic sermon (the *Muspilli*, in alliterative verse), gospel harmonies (the *Heliand* [The Savior] in Low Ger. alliterative verse, the *Evangelienbuch* in High Ger. rhyming verse), historical rhymed song (the *Ludwigslied* of 881), and hagiography (the *Georgslied*, ca. 896). As for Lat. written by Germans, the same period witnesses the prodigious hymnic output of Hrabanus Maurus (ca. 784–856), which seems to include "Veni creator spiritus," the lyrics of Gottschalk (ca. 805–69), a georgic (the *Hortulus*) of Walahfried Strabo (ca. 808–49), and the invention of the sequence (q.v.). One heroic epic survives in Lat., the *Waltharius* (of disputed date, but probably mid 9th c.), treating the Walther of Aquitaine materials.

The Ottonian and early Salian emperors who followed (918–1056) and who brought the Holy Roman Empire to the peak of its power and prestige presided over a period of neglect of the written vernacular. Lat., however, flourished, as in the works of the Saxon nun, Hrotswitha of Gandersheim (ca. 935–ca. 973), and the "Cambridge Songs" (recorded mid 11th c.), with instances of erotic, political, and farcical verses (see GOLIARDIC VERSE). Wipo, author of panegyric and historiographic poems (fl. 1039), composed the sequence "Victimae. paschalae laudes," which seems to have played a part in the gradual expansion of the Easter trope into full-fledged liturgical drama (q.v.). Two poetic epics with contacts to the unrecorded oral vernacular survive from the late years of this period, the beast epic (q.v.), *Ecbasis captivi* (The Escape of a Certain Captive), and the romance, *Ruodlieb*, which provides evidence of an indigenous courtly trad. in Germany by the mid 11th c.

A revival of written Ger. takes place in the wake of the Cluny reforms, which reached Germany around the middle of the 11th c. That revival is at the outset purely religious. Most of the poetic texts that survive treat *Heilsgeschichte* (the Hist. of Salvation), e.g. the *Summa theologiae, Das Anegenge* (The Beginning) of ca. 1060; *Ezzos Gesang,* sung on an ill-fated pilgrimage to the Holy Land, 1064–65; and *Das Leben Jesu* ("The Life of Jesus") by Frau Ava (d. 1127). The remaining documents are bib-

lical, homiletic, Marian, and hagiographic. The *Annolied* (ca. 1085) survives on account of a 1639 imprint ed. by the baroque poet and critic Martin Opitz. The work begins with a universal hist. then proceeds to an idealized biography of the powerful imperial magnate Anno, Archbishop of Cologne (d. 1075). It specifically attacks the oral lit. of the time, setting its religious truth against popular fiction. The biographer of Bishop Gunther of Bamberg, who commissioned the *Ezzolied*, reports that the Bishop had a weakness for the songs about Attila and the Amelungen (the Theodoric cycle).

The theological monopoly of written Ger. appears to have held sway until the middle decades of the 12th c. Even then, such secular materials as occur do so under the patronage of the Church. The *Alexanderlied* of the priest Lamprecht (mid 11th c.) contains fabulous materials, adventures, and conquests, but only as negative exempla, instances of immoderation and the vanity of earthly striving. The immediate source is a Fr. narrative by Alberich of Pisançon, of whose original only 105 lines survive. The importance of the *Alexanderlied* lies in its indication of two trends: an expansion of the spectrum of subjects in written Ger. and an openness to other vernacular materials, chiefly but not exclusively Fr. The priest Konrad's *Rolandslied* (ca. 1170), an adaptation of an early, lost version of the *Chanson de Roland* by way of Konrad's intervening Lat. tr. illustrates the progress of these trends.

Whereas the divine direction of history still permeates the *Rolandslied*, other epics once ascribed to wandering minstrels (*Spielmannsepos*) but now thought to be the product of clerics, came on the scene for the sake, it seems, of the sheer pleasure of story-telling. These include *König Rother* (ca. 1150–60) and *Herzog Ernst* (ca. 1180). The beast epic *Ysengrimus* (ca. 1150), of Flemish provenance, provides an analogue in Lat., as do the raucous songs of the Archpoet (ca. 1161). The period also witnessed the composition of a fiercely patriotic and partisan epic in Lat., the *Ligurinus* (1187), treating the wars of Frederick I Barbarossa.

The literary flowering in written medieval Ger. (MHG) unfolded in the decades surrounding the year 1200. Both the erotic and the highly stylized conventions of refined manners that characterize courtly poetry were available in indigenous trads. even as new conventions (e.g. the *alba* or "tagelied," qq.v.) and materials (Trojan and Arthurian) poured in from France (see OCCITAN POETRY). The bearers of this culture were no longer exclusively clerical but rather aristocratic or else those (the *ministerialis*) dependent on aristocratic patrons.

Still, the indigenous trads., the apparent receptiveness to influence from abroad, and the newly literate classes do little to explain the sudden arrival in Upper Austria around 1160 of the Ger. love lyric, fully formed in sophisticated meters, complex sentiment, and direct emotional appeal (see GERMAN PROSODY, *Middle High German*). The songs of Der von Kürenberg employed a stanza which the poet of the *Nibelungenlied* would soon thereafter use to write an epic (see NIBELUNGEN-STROPHE). The lyrics of this first generation, including those of Dietmar von Aist and Emperor Henry VI, are still accessible to modern tastes with little or no philological training. The second generation of "Minnesänger," as they were called, "singers of romantic love"—Friedrich von Hausen, Heinrich von Veldecke, Heinrich von Morungen, and the elder Reinmar—are even more accessible (see MINNESANG). This devel. culminates in the lyrics of Hartmann von Aue, Wolfram von Eschenbach, and, above all, Walther von der Vogelweide, the supreme lyric poet of the Ger. Middle Ages (fl. 1190–1230).

Narrative poetry shared this devel., often in the same persons. Heinrich von Veldecke was credited by his great successor Gottfried von Strassburg as "grafting the first slip on the tree of Ger. p." by his adaptation of the *Roman d'Eneas* into Ger., the *Eneit*, written 1174–90. Credit for such an infusion could as well go to the anonymous author of *Graf Rudolf* or to Eilhart von Oberg for his *Tristrant* (both ca. 1170). Hartmann (fl. 1180–1210) brought over into Ger. two of the romances of Chrétien de Troyes (*Erec*, ca. 1190, and *Iwein*, ca. 1202) and wrote his own manual on courtly love (*Das Büchlein* [The Little Book], ca. 1190), as well as two *legenda* (*Gregorius* and *Der arme Heinrich* [Poor Henry], ca. 1195). Gottfried's *Tristan* (ca. 1210) raises the discussion of courtly love to its highest level and remains one of the most perplexing and provocative explorations of romantic love. Wolfram (fl. 1200–20) took Chrétien's unfinished *Perceval ou conte del graal* and transformed the Arthurian romance in *Parzival*. These three—Hartmann, Gottfried, and Wolfram—represent the first rank of Ger. narrative poets.

Their number must be joined by the anonymous author of the *Nibelungenlied* (ca. 1200). Anonymity was probably required because the work was perceived, like *König Rother* and *Herzog Ernst*, to belong to oral lit.—which, as regards its sources, it did. The Ger. written record holds nothing that anticipates the scale of the work's spectacle of honor, loyalty, treachery, and revenge. In its own time it is matched or exceeded in scope and complexity only by Wolfram's *Parzival*. The *Nibelungenlied* preserves intact the archaic value system and countless motifs from Germanic antiquity. It is, nonetheless, a work of the years around 1200, adorned with a veneer of courtliness, barely acknowledging the fabulous backgrounds of Sigfried and Brunihilde and erasing all traces of the pagan pantheon. The Church does not, however, displace the old mythology. It is a secular universe that perishes in the concluding bloodbath in the great hall of the Huns.

As the 13th c. proceeded, social change was gradually reshaping the set of common presuppositions upon which courtly culture depended. A merchant could be a hero and could instruct an emperor in piety, as in Rudolf von Ems' *Der gute Gerhart* (Good Gerhart, ca. 1225). Although Gottfried was probably of urban middle-class origin, it becomes routine for the citizen to write *belles lettres* only from the time of Konrad von Würzburg (ca. 1225–87) onward. The period immediately following the flowering is characterized by the continuing dominance of courtly conventions both formal and substantive, but with a variety of transformations and the invention or resurgence of competing forms and subjects.

In one line of devel., the courtly narrative evolved toward vast, encyclopedic poems (Heinrich von dem Türlein's Arthurian *Die Krone* [The Crown], ca. 1230, 30,000 lines; Albrecht von Scharpfenberg's *Jüngerer Titurel*, after Wolfram, ca. 1270, over 6000 six-line stanzas; Ulrich von Eschenbach's *Alexandreis*, ca. 1287, some 30,000 lines; Konrad von Würzburg's *Trojanerkrieg*, broken off by his death in 1287 at over 40,000 lines). This devel., however, seems balanced by the introduction of written short narratives in verse by such poets as Der Stricker (probably of middle-class origins, ca. 1210–50) and Wernher der Gartenaere (fl. 1246–82) with his story of social decay, *Meier Helmbrecht* (Farmer Helmbrecht).

The lyric, with its elaborate courtly decorum, was susceptible to transformations, particularly but not exclusively parody (q.v.), even during the lifetime of the greatest masters. Thus Walther von der Vogelweide competed with the satirist Neidhart von Reuenthal (ca. 1190–1246), who employed peasant life as a foil to courtly conventions. As a reward, Neidhart himself was made the victim of peasant revenge throughout the vigorous subsequent trad. of farce (q.v.). The vocabulary of courtly love (q.v.) is summoned to higher purpose in the mystical writings of Mechthild von Magdeburg (1212–80) and lives on in a poetic trad. of mysticism that extends well into the 15th c. Courtly conventions undergo further transformation in the 13th c. as Ulrich von Liechtenstein (ca. 1200–75) and Der Tannhäuser (fl. 1228–60) contort "Minnedienst" (love service), the ordeals undergone for the unattainable object of love, into the grotesque. Heinrich von Meissen, called Frauenlob (The Singer of the Lady's Praises, fl. 1275–1318) both summarizes and repudiates the trad. with a learned and highly rhetorical style, which the subsequent urban middle-class "Meistersänger" (q.v.) would find congenial.

The rise of the bourgeoisie in the 13th c. brought with it a certain fondness for didactic poetry treating all manner of moral and practical problems. Freidank's collection of proverbs, *Bescheidenheit*, (Wisdom, ca. 1230) and Hugo von Trimberg's *Der Renner* (ca. 1290–1300) stand out for their great popularity in the late Middle Ages, that of the latter extending well into the 18th c.

This predilection also favored the continued devel. of short forms (the *Märe*, "story, tale"), easily moralized, anticipating and evolving alongside the short prose forms which come to prominence in the 15th and 16th cs. under It. and Fr. influence.

The last decades of the 13th c. also witness a revival of religious poetry. The pious returned to familiar biblical, moral, and allegorical materials, self-consciously looking back to MHG poetry of the 11th c.

In the 14th c., the great anthologies which preserve the courtly heritage are compiled in handsome mss., of which the most famous is the so-called Manesse ms. (before 1330). Compilatory works honor the memory of the Charlemagne materials (*Karlmeinet* [Little Charlemagne], ca. 1320). A pair of Strassburg citizens decided to fill in the perceived gaps in Wolfram's *Parzival* with 36,000 additional lines (1331–36). Competing genres in the middle of the 14th c. incl. vernacular liturgical poetry, "Geisslerlieder" (flagellant songs) associated with the plague years (1348–49), political poetry (Otto Baldemann and Lupold Hornburg), imperial panegyric in the court of Charles IV (Heinrich von Mügeln), and the beginnings of the minor genre of "Wappendichtung" (heraldic poetry: Peter Suchenwirt, fl. 1353–95). In the lyrics of Hugo von Montfort (1357–1423) at the end of the century, the fundamentally extramarital conventions of courtly poetry are thoroughly domesticated and applied strictly to the beloved spouse.

At the point of the apparent exhaustion of the courtly conventions, a poet and composer, Oswald von Wolkenstein (1377–1445), comes on the scene, exploring the breadth of the traditional courtly lyric, from lofty unrequited love to its bawdiest counterparts. The poet is alert to the renovations of the conventions from Italian sources, esp. Petrarch, whom he mentions by name. Oswald's obtrusive presence in many of his songs points toward a sense of self and of self-as-poet not at all in conformity with the self-effacing conventions of courtly poetry. He is the first Ger. poet (or composer) of whom a contemporary portrait survives.

Both Hugo and Oswald were of knightly class, whose dominance over the written lang. was coming to an end. An indication of the rise of popular forms is the satirical epic, set at a peasant wedding, known as *Wittenweilers Ring* (completed 1410). Sebastian Brant's widely translated *Narrenschiff* (Ship of Fools, 1494) provides evidence of how firmly entrenched the popular satirical trad. had become by the end of the 15th c.

After Oswald it is no longer possible to speak of continuity in the courtly trads. of the high Middle Ages. Attention to those trads. in the 15th c. may be characterized in the extremes as either antiquarian (Jakob Püterich von Reichertshausen, 1400–69) or revivalist (Ulrich Füetrer's *Buch der Abenteuer* [Book of Adventures], 1473–78). In be-

tween there are the countless knightly adventure stories coming into Ger. verse from Lat., Fr., and Dutch, and speaking directly to popular tastes. One translator thought enough of himself and his craft to compose a rhymed autobiography (Johann Grumelkut von Soest, 1448–1506). Among many important noble patrons of the revival, the most important is Emperor Maximilian I (1459–1519), without whose commission of the *Ambraser Heldenbuch* (the Ambras Book of Heroes) several of Hartmann von Aue's works and the *Gudrun*, a younger sister of the *Nibelungenlied*, would have been lost. The Emperor himself composed allegorical autobiographical epics (*Theuerdank* and *Weisskunig*) in a nostalgic spirit of appreciation for lost courtly trads. (or had his scribe do so in his behalf).

No fewer than five ms. anthologies of lyric poetry survive from the 15th c. In the 16th c., the number increases tenfold, with a similar number of printed books of songs for various occasions. This excludes hymnals. The lyric was an exceedingly popular form, serving all social classes and a wide array of occasions, public and private, secular and religious. The poems are largely anonymous, which led them later to be considered "folk songs," a misleading designation since many were composed for court and some evidence great sophistication. Like much of Ger. p., a few of these lyrics live on in modern times because of their link to music (e.g. "Innspruck ich muss dich lassen," set to music by Heinrich Isaak [d. 1519]).

The lyric texts of the finest Ger. poet of the 16th c., Martin Luther (1483–1546), live on in part for similar reasons, although this activity of Luther's is overshadowed by the reformer's other accomplishments. Luther addressed the Med. Lat. lyric (Notker's "Media vita in morte sumus," for "Mitten wir im Leben sind"), the courtly vernacular ("Sie ist mir lieb, die werde Magd"), the historical folksong, late med. hymnology, and the Psalms. Luther generally employed the popular four-stressed line in rhymed couplets, but also experimented with imitations of classical meters (iambic pentameters in the Ger. Sanctus, "Iesaia dem Propheten es geschah," from the Ger. mass of 1525). His early supporter, Ulrich von Hutten (1488–1523), wrote anti-papal satires, chiefly in Lat. but also in Ger. verse, and one *apologia*, "Ich hab's gewagt" (freely translating Caesar's "alia jacta est"), which was once considered the best poem in Ger. between Walther von der Vogelweide and Klopstock.

The most prolific verse writer in the period is Hans Sachs (1494–1576), who is at his best in praise of Luther ("Der Wittenbergsche Nachtigal"). Sachs, the most famous Ger. Meistersinger (q.v.), may stand for Ger. vernacular lit. of the 16th c. in general: formally simple (see KNITTELVERS), moralizing, jocular, anecdotal—in short, popular. With the possible exceptions of satire (Sebastian Brant, Ulrich von Hutten, but also Thomas

Murner's *Schelmenzunft* [Guild of Scoundrels], and *Narrenbeschwörung* [Conspiracy of Fools], 1512) and of the church hymn (Catholic, Lutheran, and Calvinist), *belles lettres* were almost exclusively in the hands of Humanists writing Lat. Conrad Celtis (1459–1508), who uncovered the works of Hrotswitha and the *Ligurinus*, wrote elegies, odes, and epigrams in imitation of the ancients. He is followed by poets of European reputation—Petrus Lotichius Secundus (1528–60), Paulus Melissus Schede (1539–1602), and Nathan Chytraeus (1543–98)—who constructed of elegies and epigrams a panegyric to Elizabeth I of England.

Toward the end of the 16th c., some signs both in criticism (e.g. Johannes Engerdus, *Prosodie*, 1583) and practice (Hans Leo Hassler, *Neue teutsche Gesang* [New Ger. Songs], 1596) point to dissatisfaction with the popular modes of expression in the Ger. vernacular. But it is not until the founding of the *Fruchtbringende Gesellschaft* (1617) in Weimar, the first of many literary societies, and the work of Martin Opitz (1597–1639), above all his *Von der deutschen Poeterei* (Concerning Ger. Prosody, 1624), that a genuine and permanent revolution overtakes Ger. p. Lat., It., Fr., and Dutch models are held up for imitation. With this devel., Lat. culture appears to triumph over "folk" trads. as the vernacular is molded to its standards, while in fact, Lat. begins to wane as the primary vehicle for lyric expression. The Ger. vernacular joins the international European style of the 17th c. known as "baroque" (q.v.), with its public posture and its highly rhetorical, reflective, and formalistic conventions. Perhaps precisely because of the rigidity of the forms, a remarkable amount of experimentation is undertaken, pressing the lang. for every kind of effect. The results occasionally appear bombastic or contrived to modern tastes, but many talented poets (e.g. Paul Fleming, 1609–40; Andreas Gryphius, 1616–64; Philipp von Zezen, 1619–89) employed the conventions with success. The epigram (q.v.), among the strictest of the forms, had one master, Friedrich von Logau (1604–55), who continued to be quoted in many langs. into recent times.

Both the conventions and the spirit of experimentation accorded well with the requirements of the poets of mysticism (e.g. Angelus Silesius, 1624–77; Katharina von Greiffenberg, 1633–94), who on occasion (e.g. Quirinus Kuhlmann, 1651–89), so pushed lang. to the limits of expression that they seem to anticipate the experiments of the 19th and 20th cs. The new genre of the oratorio evolved out of similar experimentation (Johann Klaj, 1616–56), later carrying the Ger. hymnology of this period (e.g. Johannes Rist, 1607–67; Paul Gerhardt, 1607–76) into the churches and concert halls of the world.

The conventions of baroque poetics (q.v.) collapsed quite suddenly at the turn of the 18th c. The collapse was signalled by the pub. of a multivolume retrospective anthol. (1695–1704) named by the editor, Benjamin Neukirch, for the poet Hoffmannswaldau (1617–79). The last poet to work wholly within the conventions was Johann Christian Günther (1695–1723), but his brief, brilliant, troubled career also points forward to the poetry of personal sentiment associated with the young Goethe. But the artifice and extravagance of baroque poetry offended Enlightenment theorists in Germany, both anglophile (Bodmer, 1698–1783, and Breitinger, 1701–76, who argued for "nature" and sentiment) and francophile (Gottsched, 1700–66, who argued for reason).

The rhetorical excesses, the grand theatrical panoply, and the thoroughly public posture of baroque poetry were quickly shaken off. The perspectives on nature provided by the mystical poets in particular and by the whole genre of the pastoral (q.v.) could not be so readily abandoned. The early "nature poetry" of the 18th c. (Brockes, *Irdisches Vergnügen in Gott* [Earthly Pleasure in God], 1721–1748; and Haller's *Alpen* [The Alps], 1729) follows in paths opened by the baroque. The same applies to the further exploration of nature, of friendship, and of wine, women, and song among the young poets who considered themselves successors of Anacreon (Hagedorn, 1708–54; Gleim, 1719–1803; Uz, 1720–96; Götz, 1721–81). They differ from their baroque predecessors by narrowing and sharpening the focus to the familiar, personal, and private. They are now perceived as immediate forerunners of the great flowering of Ger. p. that begins with the publication of the first three cantos of Klopstock's *Messias* (1748), written in Latinate hexameters but proving the Ger. vernacular tractable to any poetic task. See GERMAN PROSODY.

ANTHOLOGIES: *Deutsche Gedichte des elften und zwölfften Jahrhunderts*, ed. J. Diemer (1849); *Deutsche Dichtung des Barock*, ed. E. Hederer (1961); *Deutsche Lyrik des Mittelalters*, ed. M. Wehrli (1962); *Des Minnesangs Frühling*, ed. C. Kraus (1964); *Mittelalter*, ed. H. De Boor (1965); *Das Zeitalter des Barock*, ed. A. Schöne (1968); *Althochdeutsche Literatur*, ed. H. Schlosser (1970); *Spätmittelater, Humanismus, Reformation*, ed. H. Heger (1975–78); *Die Mittelhochdeutsche Minnelyrik*, ed. H. Schweikle (1977); *All mein Gedanken, die ich hab: Deutsche Lieder des 15. und 16. Jhs.*, ed. I. Spriewald (1982).

SURVEYS AND CRITICISM, *General*: Manitius; *Reallexikon I*; G. Ehrismann, *Gesch. der deutschen Literatur bis zum Ausgang des Mittelalters* (1955–59); *Reallexikon*; K. Conrady, *Lateinische Dichtungstrad. und deutsche Lyrik des 17. Jahrhunderts* (1962); M. Walshe, *Med. Ger. Lit.* (1962); W. T. H. Jackson, "Med. Ger. Lit.," in Fisher; *Gesch. der deutschen Literatur*, ed. H. De Boor and R. Newald (1966–87); P. Salmon, *Lit. in Med. Germany* (1967); G. F. Jones, *Walther von der Vogelweide* (1968); A. DeCapua, *Ger. Baroque P.* (1973); K. Dell'Orto, "Lyric P. of the Ger. Ren.," Diss., Johns Hopkins U. (1973); H. Segel, *The Baroque Poem* (1974); J.

Bostock, *A Handbook on OHG Lit.*, 2d ed. (1976); *Ren. and Reformation in Germany* (1977), *Ger. Baroque Lit.* (1983), both ed. G. Hoffmeister; W. Segebrecht, *Das Gelegenheitsgedicht* (1977); *Bibliographisches Handbuch der Barockliteratur*, ed. G. Dünnhaupt (1980); Sayce; W. Hinderer, *Gesch. der deutschen Lyrik* (1983); F. Spechtler, *Lyrik des ausgehenden 14. und 15. Jahrhunderts* (1984).

Special: K. Burdach, *Reinmar der Alte und Walther von der Vogelweide* (1928); M. Batts, *Gottfried von Strassburg* (1971); H. Bekker, *The Nibelungenlied* (1971), *Gottfried von Strassburg's Tristan* (1987); W. T. H. Jackson, *The Anatomy of Love: The Tristan of Gottfried von Strassburg* (1971); S. Jaeger, *Med. Humanism in Gottfried von Strassburg's Tristan und Isolde* (1977); H. Kuhn, *Minnelieder Walthers von der Vogelweide* (1982); J. Schultz, *The Shape of the Round Table: MHG Arthurian Romance* (1983); J. Goheen, *Mittelalterliche Liebeslyrik von Neidhart von Reuental bis zu Oswald von Wolkenstein* (1984); C. Jaeger, *The Origins of Courtliness* (1985); E. Haymes, *The Nibelungenlied: Hist. and Interp.* (1986); T. Anderson, *A Preface to the Nibelungenlied* (1987); A. Renoir, *A Key to Old Poems* (1988). F.L.B.

II. SINCE 1750. As in the 17th c., the unity of the modern Ger. literary trad. was in part consciously produced, an attempt to transcend the disunity and provincialism of mid 18th-c. Ger.-speaking societies. Friedrich Gottlieb Klopstock (1724–1803), with his rhapsodic monologues magisterially defining their own freedom, spoke for a literary culture waiting to be reborn. Until about 1750 there was no acknowledged genre of "the lyric," merely the subcategories (sonnet, song, ode, etc.) listed by Gottsched in his neoclassical *Critische Dichtkunst* (Critical Poetics, 1730). It was not until about 1850 that the lyric acquired, in a Ger. context, the dignity previously accorded to epic and drama.

Klopstock's innovations are not conceptual: his focus on Nature and God is traditional. But in his major poems, such as *Der Zürcher See* (Zurich Lake, 1750) and *Die Frühlingsfeier* (Celebration of Spring, 1764), he animates existing conventions in such a way as to transform them utterly. Thus, although Gleim had experimented inventively with imitations of classical meters, Klopstock deploys these meters seemingly effortlessly, as if they were native to the Ger. lang. (see CLASSICAL METERS IN MODERN LANGUAGES). And although the idea of "the sublime" (q.v.), derived from Longinus, was being widely promoted as preferable to didactic or descriptive nature-poetry, it is Klopstock who actually communicates sublimity through his verbal landscapes. Equally established was the ideal of friendship, of poetry affecting society through the elevating influence of the educated few. But Klopstock includes his friends expressly in the sublimity of Nature (q.v.); and his most devoted disciples, the *Göttinger Hain* which flourished in the early 1770s (Ludwig Hölty

[1748–76] was the most accomplished of the group), filled poetic friendship with a new "sensibility" (*Empfindsamkeit*; q.v.). Yet even as he invokes the lang. of friendship, Klopstock speaks as an inspired, necessarily isolated "bard," producing poetic truth through sheer intensity of experience. The "experience" is not subjective in any arbitrary sense; Klopstock presents himself not as a private individual but as an appointed singer, a cosmic representative of humanity.

The attribution of elevated meaning to every detail of Klopstock's world can make his intensity seem paradoxically abstract, even didactic. But the renewal of Nature was already receiving a new impetus from the theorist Johann Gottfried Herder (1744–1803), who, inspired by Bishop Percy's *Reliques of Ancient Eng. Poetry* (1765), developed a conception of the "lyrical" rooted in a new understanding of hist. Songs are, for Herder, direct expressions of a people's core experience; originally sung by bards, they survive in fragmentary form as folksongs. The definition of the folksong at this time was broad, however: Percy includes extracts from Shakespeare and other "named" poets. Herder's initiative crystallizes the key ideas of "lyric" and "nation," but with entirely different connotations from those familiar today. The nation is in no way self-contained: access to its past often involves other nations, e.g. the England, Wales, and Scotland of Herder's time. And the lyrical impulse is viewed as collective rather than private.

The quest for bardic voices was intense; the most influential of these "folk"-texts, Macpherson's *Ossian*, was revealed much later to be a forgery. But at this historical moment, the 1770s, the central project was the *creation* of a Ger. culture, not precise documentation of its past, and a genuine modern bard was ready to hand, Herder's close friend Johann Wolfgang von Goethe (1749–1832). So powerful was Goethe's personality that it is essential to recall the cultural elements blended into his poetics of nature and expressivity. The bardic voice speaks from the heart of things, but the idea of the sublime, elevating experience, as embodied in Klopstock's poetry, is vital to his speaking; so are the image of the aesthetic community and the matrix of complex metrical possibilities, deriving from Gr. and baroque models as well as from the newly prestigious folksong. What Goethe contributes to all this are two qualities decisive for all subsequent Ger. p. First, he takes the word "nature" literally: without in any way relinquishing the (inherited) sublime, Goethe pursues a lifelong quest for the organic, methodically articulating its rhythmic structures and locating the analogies to these structures in human lang. and experience. Second, he installs his own unique subjectivity at the center of his lyrical production; without abandoning the claim to representative experience (his theory of the organic sustains the claim), Goethe binds poetry to the intimate mood-shifts, the seemingly arbitrary perceptions of the private self. Goethe's poems in the 1770s range from the utter transformation of Anacreontic (q.v.) convention in *Mailied* (May Song) to the almost ruthless proclamation of personal autonomy in *Willkommen und Abschied* (Welcome and Farewell) and the bardic rhapsodies in emulation of Klopstock: *Ganymed, Prometheus, Wandrers Sturmlied.*

Goethe also wrote ballads in these years, the most famous of which are *Der König von Thule* (The King of Thule, 1774; sung by Gretchen in the earliest version of *Faust*) and *Erlkönig* (1782; widely known through musical settings by Schubert and Loewe). Ballads are a popular poetic form, found in the oldest Ger. lit. Herder's theory of the folksong thus provoked a flurry of ballad-writing by Goethe's young contemporaries in the so-called *Sturm und Drang* (q.v.) movement. The best known of these is *Lenore* (1773), a ghostly *Schauerballade* by Gottfried August Bürger (1747–94) compressing love, marriage, and death into a wild midnight ride. The blurring of the boundaries between "lyrical" expressivity and "epic" narration typifies Ger. p. at this time (the same applies to drama: Goethe's celebration of defiant genius, *Prometheus*, was originally spoken by the character Prometheus in a dramatic sketch). The lyric was to open new expressive possibilities for a lit. defining itself through images of its past.

Goethe wrote a series of ballads, notably *Die Braut von Korinth* (The Bride of Corinth), *Der Gott und die Bayadere*, and *Der Zauberlehrling* (The Sorcerer's Apprentice), in 1797 at the height of his friendship with Friedrich Schiller (1759–1805), but by then his goals had changed. In elaborately self-contained stanzas, these ballads shaped rather extreme, even perverse narratives into demonstration models of organic equilibrium. The famous "moderation" (*Mässigung*) of Goethe's genius is sometimes dated to the year 1786, when he suddenly left Weimar for Italy, later recording his discovery of "Classical" order in the *Römische Elegien* (Roman Elegies, 1788); in these 20 poems he blends a love experience into the myths, the architecture, the whole remembered imagery of Rome, playfully yet strictly deploying alternating hexameters and pentameters, the form of the Cl. elegiac distich. Returning to Weimar, Goethe began to develop a new, politically and socially stabilized fusion of the Cl. heritage with a scientific understanding of nature. Every variety of poetry was to be cultivated, incl. the epic: Goethe's *Hermann und Dorothea* (1797), an adaptation of "Germanic" values to a contemp. story of the Fr. Revolution and the resultant "refugee problem," became the model for numerous (unsuccessful) 19th-c. efforts to reinvent the Ger. verse epic.

To describe Weimar Classicism in terms of Goethe's personal devel. is both unavoidable (because of the way Goethe's personality imposed itself on Ger. lit. hist.) and misleading. Schiller was an equal partner in the collaboration until his death in 1805, and Schiller provided the central idea of this new "Classicism": *aesthetic education*. In this phrase are concentrated all the elements working productively through Klopstock and Goethe: the elevation of the individual through a fuller understanding of nature's laws as well as its "sublime" moment of grandeur, and the integration of individuals into a society governed by "beauty," i.e. the harmonious ethical functioning of the mental faculties. Schiller includes the idea of free play (*Spieltrieb*) in his vision, but it remains grave and serene nonetheless. The program is allegorized in his elegy *Der Spaziergang* (The Walk, 1795), in which self and landscape are fused at all experiential levels. Central to Schiller's experience is his contemplation of the loss of Gr. antiquity, an image of wholeness for which modernity is compelled to yearn in vain (*Die Götter Griechenlands* [The Gods of Greece], 1788). Aesthetic education can mitigate the loss, but within Weimar Classicism there remains a central contradiction, theorized by Schiller himself in 1794, between Goethe's "organic" absorption of history into his own life ("naive") and Schiller's own sense of exile ("sentimental"—see NAIVE AND SENTIMENTAL).

A far more radical version of exile is propounded by Friedrich Hölderlin (1770–1843), a disciple of Schiller whose later path took him into such isolation that his work is neither readily describable in historical terms nor, indeed, as yet exhausted in its impact on later lit. From the repertoire of poetic possibilities, Hölderlin fashioned a vision of his role as singer-bard for an irrevocably lost world (Greece). He works from the beginning with complex Gr. meters (e.g. the Alcaic, q.v.), contrasting subjective isolation with visions of natural and social fullness (e.g. *Abendphantasie* [Evening Fantasy], 1799), which speak always of the absence of the gods. The contentment of "the people" depends on their not knowing of this absence; only the singer knows, and his knowledge crowds out everything else, incl. all "moderating" hopes of aesthetic education. Hölderlin first published hymns and elegies in 1793; he is the very opposite of a hermit, being radically exposed to the immediacy of history, particularly the miseries of the wars following the Fr. Revolution. He also pursues the image of a Ger. nation, which however remains an ideal construct. In *Brod und Wein* (Bread and Wine), Hölderlin "travels" to ancient Greece in order to recapitulate the actual process of the withdrawal of the gods, of whom Jesus Christ is viewed as the last representative. Later hymns (e.g. *Patmos, Friedensfeier*, and *Germanien*) and fragments, written between 1800 and his insanity in 1806, strive to imagine a possible return of the gods.

A complexity of Ger. lit. hist. is that the decade of Weimar Classicism (1795–1805) coincides precisely with the most productive era of romanticism. Indeed Goethe was long called a "romantic" because of his paramount subjectivity. In fact there are linkages of all kinds: Goethe's study of natural phenomena, Schiller's and Hölderlin's sense of the gods as withdrawn from history—these notions are crucial to Friedrich von Hardenberg (1772–1801), who, under the pseudonym Novalis, became a major poet and theorist of romanticism. But the romantic program opposes both moderation and a Greek-centered view of culture. Novalis' *Hymnen an die Nacht* (1800) explicitly turn away from Greece towards the "Night," the mystique of death pervading medieval Christianity. The fascination with Ger. medieval culture leads to an intensive and now genuinely philological study of the Ger. past. This work culminated in the collection of folk poetry *Des Knaben Wunderhorn* (The Youth's Magic Horn, 1805–8), ed. by Achim von Arnim (1781–1831) and Clemens Brentano (1778–1842). Philological exactitude and philosophical sophistication combine to produce in the major romantic theorists, Novalis and Friedrich Schlegel (1772–1829), a very high level of linguistic self-consciousness, both serious and playful, now known as "romantic irony" (see IRONY). From this perspective the ideal modern poetic form was the fragment, a moment of history captured and sealed in and through irony. But apart from certain texts by Novalis, Brentano, and Ludwig Tieck (1773–1853), few romantic lyrics fulfilled this imperative in practice. Brentano's most successful texts (*Sprich aus der Ferne* [Speak from Afar] and *Schwanenlied* [Swansong]) do, however, achieve an extraordinary fusion of ecstatic subjectivity with "nature" as a symbolic totality of historical time. The writer who best embodies romantic poetics (q.v.) is from a slightly later generation, Joseph von Eichendorff (1788–1857). Eichendorff conveys both the intensity of a moment and an ironic distance from that intensity; his lang. is consciously stylized, with its medieval landscapes, its dawns and sunsets. Sudden discontinuities, from harmony to doubt, from darkness to light and vice versa, are Eichendorff's speciality; the reader experiences simultaneously a glimpse of fullness and a sense of exile within a specifically Ger. historical landscape. *Mondnacht* (Moonlit Night), *Zwielicht* (Twilight), *Sehnsucht* (Longing): the very titles of Eichendorff's most perfect poems convey a moment of danger for the self rendered vulnerable through its openness to history and beauty. Sometimes safety is reached (*Mondnacht*); sometimes the self is sustained on the margin through intense listening to or gazing at the aesthetic heart of things.

As in Herder's thinking, romantic "nationalism" opens up the world rather than closing it off. It is the older Goethe who coins the term "world lit."; indeed, Goethe's own later poetry draws extensively on Eastern models (*West-Östlicher Divan*, 1816, a homage to the Persian poet Hafiz; *Chinesisch-deutsche Jahres- und Tageszeiten* [Chinese-Ger. Seasons of the Years and the Day], 1830). In these creative explorations Goethe joins the new romantic philology, characterized by August Wilhelm Schlegel's (1767–1845) trs. of Shakespeare (1797–1810) and his brother Friedrich's investigations of Indian thought. This multiplying of poetic possibilities persists throughout the *Biedermeier* period (1815–48), but gradually a profound intellectual division becomes evident, controlling subsequent poetic devel. It is the dualism between private and public, between the increasingly subjective dream of Nature and the immediacy of technological, political, and social change.

The major *Biedermeier* (q.v.) poets, Eduard Mörike (1804–75) and Annette von Droste-Hülshoff (1797–1848), do indeed struggle to renew the Goethean synthesis of self and nature, but their perceptions are defined by romantic fascination with death as well as by the micro-worlds of the organic. Both explore natural environments with an intimacy often termed "realistic"; but lacking Goethe's "scientific" premises, each develops new versions of what constitutes nature. Mörike binds his shifting moods and meditations into such rigorously closed forms that the poem's actual shape, its verbal dimension, moves from being a secondary to a primary concern. The image of the poem as quasi-organic "object," as claiming physical presence, is implicit in Mörike's *Auf eine Lampe* (On a Lamp, 1846). Droste-Hülshoff risks extreme visions of dying and the collapse of time (*Im Moose* [In the Moss], 1842), and she survives them through an overt ritualizing of the seasons as defining the human year in counterpoint with religion. That such subjectivity was endangered in this period by its own freedom, a freedom without the cultural urgency of the 18th c., becomes obvious in the lesser poets such as August von Platen (1796–1835), who renews the sonnet trad. and codifies Eastern verseforms such as the *ghazal* (q.v.) into a protective aestheticism; Nikolaus Lenau (1802–50), who strives to merge his consciousness with the moments and seasons of nature; and Friedrich Rückert (1788–1866), who pursues the Orientalist trend and whose gloomy *Kindertotenlieder* (Songs on the Death of Children) are so emotionally exposed and fragile that they virtually demand the support of the musical setting they eventually receive from Gustav Mahler in 1904.

The cleavage between private and public worlds is wholly visible in the work of Heinrich Heine (1797–1856); indeed, his productivity seems to depend on it. On the one hand, his mastery of inherited romantic imagery enabled him to produce the most widely read volume of "romantic" texts, the *Buch der Lieder* (Book of Songs, 1827), though most of these poems either exaggerate the "sickness" of romantically stylized love or undercut elevated sentiments with an ironic final twist. On the other hand, Heine's sensitivity to the meaning of capitalism's new technologies (railtravel, stock exchange) was second to none. In voluntary exile in Paris from 1831 until his death,

Heine wrote vivid and sarcastic journalism and some famous political poems (*Atta Troll, Die schlesischen Weber*, 1844). Yet he always declared himself a lover of beauty, mocking the compromises and earnestness apparently endemic to political commitment. Heine's double-edged style seems in retrospect to epitomize the age from which he felt so alien. Early poems from *Lyrisches Intermezzo* (1822–23) were set to music by Robert Schumann in *Dichterliebe* (A Poet's Love, 1840); arguably Schumann misses the irony, yet his delicate near-sentimentality expresses the Heine his age chose to hear. *Die Nordsee* (The North Sea, 1825–26) contains Heine's most ambitious long poems, rhapsodic invocations of seascapes and vanishing myths in which the persistent irony is both emphasized and transcended by the sheer range of historical imagination. Heine's late poems, from the "mattress-grave" of his long final illness, achieve new intensities of pain, lucidity, and self-mockery: *Morphine* (ca. 1851), *Für die Mouche* (a long dream of death amid the confusions of Western mythology, addressed to his loyal mistress, 1856).

Political poetry began to be written before 1815, at the time of the struggle against Napoleon; Ernst Moritz Arndt (1769–1860) and Ludwig Uhland (1787–1862) adapted ballad forms to the patriotic cause. As "the nation" hardened into a reactionary and repressive institution, however, political poetry took on a new oppositional sharpness with the rise of the movement *Junges Deutschland* (Young Germany) in the early 1830s. Apart from Heine, the best known poets were Anastasias Grün (1806–76), Hoffmann von Fallersleben (1798–1874), Ferdinand Freiligrath (1810–76), and Georg Herwegh (1817–75). In the period before the Revolution of 1848 known as *Vormärz* (roughly 1840 to March 1848), their voices were briefly dominant.

Two poets who were to become major writers after 1848, Friedrich Hebbel (1813–63) and Gottfried Keller (1819–90), began to publish poetry before the Revolution. Hebbel, however, who felt strongly that a political poem was no poem at all, was influential in developing a theory of the "pure" lyric after 1848. There is a sad irony in the fact that the Ger. lyric, nurtured by multiple social aspirations, should have been codified and defined at this moment of political defeat. For, esp. after 1870 with the rapid expansion of the Ger. educational system, the lyric becomes fixed in the public mind, and in the textbooks, as something refined, private, devoted to the self's interactions with nature. Because of the fluidity of the trad. to this point, it was not difficult to read this definition back into the past, venerating Goethe while stylizing his poems as, in his own phrase so vulnerable to misreading, "fragments of a great confession."

Although provincialism dominates Ger. p. between 1850 and 1890 (typified by the popular success of Emanuel Geibel [1815–84]), important poems were written, particularly by three writers better known for their fiction: Keller, Theodor Storm (1817–88), and Conrad Ferdinand Meyer (1825–98). The contradictions of the *Biedermeier* period are intensified in their work. On the one hand, the sense of experience as intimate and fragile remains primary; on the other hand, the social impotence and passivity of the private self is felt inescapably. Meyer, a master lyricist, doubted the authenticity of his own texts, revising them ceaselessly and devoting much energy to the less exposed genre of the ballad. The implicit poetics of this endangered self is a complex fusion of "pure" temporal experience with a "pure" verbal construct. The poem is to be a "thing," an object made out of time and inserted into space. The text is justified not by any moral or personal interp. of experience but by its sheer being as a text: "In poetry every thought must move as visible form" (Meyer). Storm's intro. to his 1870 anthol. of Ger. p. expresses the new institutionalization of the lyrical experience. Readers are to be stirred not to thought or action but to a more intensive registration of their own moods. Schiller's aesthetic education of mankind has become the aesthetic self-enjoyment of the educated.

If refinement, chiseled perfection, is the poetic project of the late 19th c., it becomes a reality in the work of two writers, Hugo von Hofmannsthal (1874–1929) and Stefan George (1868–1933). Hofmannsthal's few poems are such exquisite expressions of the passive self, paralyzed by the sheer weight of time past, that they seem to anticipate their own attenuation into silence. Hofmannsthal ceased writing poems in 1902 (turning to the "public" modes of drama and opera libretti for Richard Strauss) after performing a self-diagnosis in his "Letter of Lord Chandos," written in the persona of a 17th-c. Eng. nobleman. Chandos' so-called *Sprachkrise* (lang. crisis) consists in his inability to translate either inner feelings or impressions of objects and events into lang. Words have become strange and alien. In contrast, Stefan George crystallized a doctrine of pure poetry to sustain a productivity lasting from *Hymnen, Pilgerfahrten, Algabal* (Hymns, Pilgrimages, Algabal, 1890–92) through *Der Stern des Bundes* (Star of the Covenant, 1914) to a final vision of the aesthetic "nation," *Das neue Reich* (The New Empire, 1928). The Nazi attempt to co-opt this refined concept led to George's refusal even to be buried in Ger. soil (he died in Switzerland). George's poetics was nourished by his reading of Friedrich Nietzsche (1844–1900). Nietzsche's few poems intensify late 19th-c. contradictions; suspicious of lang.'s metaphorical and masking structures, he yet sought to fill every lyrical word with intensity. Following Nietzsche, Stefan George turned to Fr. models, particularly Baudelaire, whose *Fleurs du mal* he translated into Ger., and the hermeticism of Mallarmé. George sought to develop a coded symbolic lang., with a specialized orthography and a repertoire of neopagan myths, incl. beautiful youths and autumnal parks. He also built up an aesthetic "community" of disciples, the "George Circle," in resistance to contemp. vulgarity. That vulgarity, the crude voice of the cities, was beginning to find some expression about 1890 in the "monumental" naturalist style of Arno Holz (1863–1929), the ballads and impressionistic precision of Detlev von Liliencron (1844–1909), and the "applied poetry" (*angewandte Lyrik*) and cabaret songs of Frank Wedekind (1864–1918).

The dominant ideal of the poetic object, already implicit in Mörike and ever more explicit in Meyer and George, is fulfilled in the *Neue Gedichte* (New Poems, 1907–8) of Rainer Maria Rilke (1875–1926). Rilke reaches the achievement of these poems by way of the three-part collection *Das Stundenbuch* (The Book of Hours, 1899, 1901, 1903) and *Das Buch der Bilder* (The Book of Images, 1902); these volumes recapitulate the religiosity, the rhapsodic celebration of creativity, and the dream of community which are stylistic gestures reaching back to Klopstock. In the New Poems, however, Rilke crystallizes a perfect fusion of the theory and practice of "objectivity." The theory is overtly derived from the visual arts, specifically the sculpture of Auguste Rodin (for whom Rilke worked briefly as secretary) and the painting of Paul Cézanne. Poems are to achieve the sheer "presence" of these visual texts. But this is done not through mimesis, through "imitation" (q.v.) of a physical object. Rather, the poem obeys its own laws as a temporal art: it records the momentary glimpse binding the poet's subjectivity to an object; and it embeds that moment both in the history of civilization which has accumulated in the poet's head and in the physical, even geometric connectedness of the object to its surroundings. Rilke calls this complex relationality *Bezug*; the objects chosen are primarily aesthetic (cathedrals, statues, graceful animals), but incl. the experience of the city of Paris (children, blind men, corpses) as well as an ethical urgency (the commandment to change one's life emitted by the archaic torso of Apollo). Rilke's aim, he said, was to translate the visible into the "invisibility" of lang. and, vice versa, to bring life's invisible richness and fragility into plain view.

This equilibrium could not be sustained. In 1911–12 Rilke entered a crisis of disjunction between lang. and the zones of subjectivity and world which its task was to mediate. The crisis was reminiscent of Hofmannsthal's, but Rilke was so totally a poet that he fought his way through it. After ten years of struggle and fragmentary achievement Rilke produced the astonishing abundance of Feb. 1922, the *Duineser Elegien* (Duino Elegies) and *Sonette an Orpheus* (Sonnets to Orpheus). In these texts the world of objects is blasted open and reconstituted in a poetological dimension unique to Rilke. The bardic vocation inherited from Klopstock and mediated through Rilke's reading of Hölderlin is reborn in the gestures of the "singer" who simultaneously celebrates the world of art

and nature and explores the death-realm through symbolic figures like the hero, the "young dead," and the dismembered Orpheus. This song is fused with a continuous meditation on the inadequacy of lang. as well as its transforming power. Like Goethe in his day, Rilke has had an irresistible impact on poetry in this century because of his virtual invention of a lyrical lang. The disquieting aspect of his influence derives not so much from the specifics of his subjective mythology as from the rhapsodic "overcoming" of technological, urban, and political reality. The Goethean image of harmonious nature is renewed by Rilke in the domain of sheer linguistic virtuosity. Although it is meaningless to blame Rilke for the seductions of his counter-world, his achievement has invited escapist imitation and has reactivated the struggle between nature and the city which characterized Ger. poetics before 1848.

The assault on the image of the poem as naturalized object was launched in the year of Rilke's lang.-crisis, 1911–12, by the generation known as expressionist, whose feelings towards Rilke's genius and prestige ranged from hostile to ambivalent (see EXPRESSIONISM). The publication in early 1911 of *Weltende* (End of the World) by Jacob van Hoddis (1887–1942) was widely felt to be the moment of a new poetics. The text consists of two stanzas of isolated lines, linked surreally through the passive act of reading a newspaper: "The bourgeois' hat flies off his pointed head, / the air re-echoes with a screaming sound. . . . The greater part of people have a cold. / Off bridges everywhere the railroads drop." The return of the repressed city is consummated apocalyptically in a mode of fragmentation and decay. The power of the established lang. of nature and the pure poem is such that no single counter-style is imaginable. The "grotesque" gestures of van Hoddis and Alfred Lichtenstein (1889–1914) exist in counterpoint with the "concrete" lyrics of August Stramm (1874–1915), who forced multiple meanings into single words, often neologisms.

The styles of the major expressionist poets are linked solely by the tonality of apocalypse. Georg Trakl (1887–1914) corrodes the lang. of nature poetry from within, peopling his landscapes with corpses and the streets of his native Salzburg with spots of decay; gradually his lang. uproots itself from all mimetic relations, evoking strange syntheses of corruption and purity, violence and passivity. Georg Heym (1887–1912) confronts urban life with a fanatical directness; the energy of his diseased world derives wholly from the impending moment of its disintegration. Ernst Stadler (1883–1914), on the other hand, who began publishing in 1904, strives to convert technological energy (e.g. railway trains) into imagery of Utopian transformation. His long rhapsodic lines, inspired by Walt Whitman, project a poetics that would fuse subject and object into a single rhythm of socio-political change. His was the style that became dominant: related expressionist voices incl. Franz Werfel (1890–1945), Johannes Becher (1891–1958), and Yvan Goll (1891–1950). *O Mensch* expressionism, poetry that proclaimed a "new man" in a new world, rapidly became bombastic and empty; much of the famous expressionist anthol. *Menschheitsdämmerung* (Twilight/Dawn of Humanity, 1919) has become unreadable.

A poet associated with expressionism, Else Lasker-Schüler (1869–1945) had begun publishing in 1902; her texts, with their strange linkage between religiosity, intense privacy, and surreal fantasy, suggest the deep fissures in expressionist poetics, the impossibility of a unified program such as emerged in England and France. expressionism immediately produced its ironic mirror-image, dada (q.v.), with an agenda of mockery and disruption formulated already in 1916. Some dada poets, with their delight in lang. games, their open display of the processes of text construction, have become more influential than the original expressionists, esp. Hugo Ball (1886–1927), Richard Huelsenbeck (1892–1974), George Grosz (1893–1959), Hans Arp (1887–1966), and Kurt Schwitters (1887–1948). The last three of these are better known as visual artists. Fusion of the arts was a project of this generation from the outset; the composer Arnold Schönberg (1874–1951), and the painter Wassily Kandinsky (1866–1944) were both involved in the redefinition of the lyric.

It is possible to define the years 1920–70 as a unified period, its continuities all the more apparent because of the rupture of the Nazi era, 1933–45, when all major poetic voices were forced into either exile or the silence of "inner emigration." What is not possible is to discern a single dominant poetics. Rather, one must distinguish three viable styles, with distinct aesthetic energies, which major authors frequently sought to combine. The first of these, the style of "international modernism," was the last to develop in Germany because of the political catastrophes. But after 1945 its potency was correspondingly great, as poets strove to reintegrate Ger. with European culture. And the poetological essays of Gottfried Benn (1886–1956) in the 1920s had already sketched its outlines: poetic lang. functions as a counterhistorical energy, shattering banal everyday reality (Benn's word is *Wirklichkeitszertrümmerung*) in order to reassemble the pure shards of lang., technological and mythical as well as emotional, into an "absolute" poem. Benn himself, a survivor of the expressionist generation (his first collection, *Morgue*, was published in 1912), briefly succumbed to the lure of Nazism before "emigrating inwardly"; with the publication of *Statische Gedichte* (Static Poems, 1948), he became a dominant figure in the postwar literary scene. His nihilistic view of everyday life represented an extreme against which others could define their perspectives. In his influential lecture *Probleme der Lyrik* (Problems of the Lyric, 1951), Benn codified his uncompromisingly aesthetic viewpoint: acknowledging his "unfriendliness" towards the world, he nevertheless insisted that poets wrest the "truth" from history by staying as close to it as the bullfighter does the bull.

Günter Eich's (1907–72) *Inventur* (Inventory, 1946), listing the minimal possessions of a prisoner-of-war, evokes a more urgent modernism. Poetry distills, strips down experience, but reconstitutes it as a warning or prophecy, sealed off yet far from neutral (*Botschaften des Regens* [Messages of the Rain], 1955). Paul Celan (1920–70) confronts the permanent, corrosive fact of the wartime death-camps not only in his *Todesfuge* (Death Fugue, 1945) but throughout his extremely hermetic later texts (his most powerful collection may be *Die Niemandsrose* [No One's Rose], 1963). Celan's modernism has a dialectical intention: the more obscure and seemingly exclusive their imagery, the more his texts seek to open a "dialogue" (his term) with history, a dialogue directed at the repression of the death-camps' meaning in postwar consumer society, at the truth that is slipping from us. Ingeborg Bachmann (1926–73) and Hans Magnus Enzensberger (b. 1929), in their poems of the 1950s, subvert the deluded harmonies of consumerism through sardonic and uneasy allegories. A frequent presence in Enzensberger's poems is radiation, the invisible destroyer which we prefer to ignore. Other major voices of this "critical" modernism are Nelly Sachs (1891–1970), whose work is strongly focused on the death-camps; Rudolf Hagelstange (b. 1912), whose sonnet-cycle *Venezianisches Credo* (Venetian Credo, 1946) confronts Nazi degeneracy through a militant formalism; Helmut Heissenbüttel (b. 1921), theorist and practitioner of a lang. liberated from conventional syntax and revealing "reality" to be a linguistic construct ("concrete poetry," q.v.); and Karl Krolow (b. 1915).

Krolow also has strong ties to the second major style of 1920–70, which seeks to maintain and redirect the trad. of nature poetry. Nature is no longer viewed as model or refuge. But just as Eichendorff could translate romantic clichés into a usable, transparent code, so these poets believe that the realities of 20th-c. experience can be read off from nature, using a lang. of shading and indirection. Wilhelm Lehmann (1882–1968), Oskar Loerke (1884–1941), and Elisabeth Langgässer (1899–1950) are important exponents of this style. Their deliberately conservative texts evoke landscapes with lang. that seems to "know" the other, banal, and degraded uses to which it is put. The posthumously published poems of Gertrud Kolmar (1894–1943), written largely in the 1930s, convey powerfully the ability of natural images to illuminate a denatured society. This trad. dominated East Ger. poetics, where coded writing was widely felt to be the only "free" kind. Peter Huchel (1903–81) and Johannes Bobrowski (1917–65) traverse wintry worlds that speak silently of war and despair. Sara Kirsch (b. 1935) and Bernd

Jentzsch (b. 1940) are prominent younger East Ger. poets who work in this style.

The third possibility of the years 1920–70 remained the production of an overtly political poetry, which had not achieved full stature in either *Vormärz* or expressionism. Almost single-handedly, Bertolt Brecht (1898–1956) realized this project within the modernist idiom, enabling political poetry to become central to the theory and practice of today's Ger. lit. Working eclectically, Brecht drew particularly on the ballad trad., which had been maintained in the 19th c. by regional and "storytelling" poets such as Meyer, Liliencron, and Theodor Fontane (1819–98). Brecht also adapted the epigrammatic and didactic poetics of the baroque and of China to a laconic or proverbial mode of social commentary. Not that Brecht neglected subjectivity; his long poems *Vom armen B. B.* (Of Poor B. B., 1921) and *An die Nachgeborenen* (To Posterity, 1938) present intense yet stylized autobiographical narrations, as if to reanimate Klopstock's projection of the representative self. The people Brecht represents, however, are those who have no cultural voice: soldiers who actually fight the wars, workers who actually build the palaces, and the unemployed. The complexities of publication "in dark times" meant that Brecht's poems were slow to exercise their full impact. A collection published in the Weimar Republic, *Hauspostille* (Homilies for Home Use, 1927) was followed by many poems written in exile and only gradually reassembled in the early 1950s. Important disciples were Erich Fried (b. 1921), who has specialized in the style of epigrammatic political engagement, notably at the time of the Vietnam war (*und Vietnam und*, 1966); and Wolf Biermann (b. 1936), an exiled East German, who has extended Brecht's explorations of ballad form and sought to revive poetry's ancient function through public performances.

As the modernist concept of the self-sufficient poem came to seem less viable about 1970, the goal of a political poetry became both desirable and imaginable. This does not at all mean that poems were henceforth "about" politics. Rather, a double realization was involved: that all inherited poetic lang., as mediated by the various modern styles, was the lang. of an elite; and that, in an age when everything, certainly incl. poetry, was a commodity to be bought and discarded, the poet must find ways simultaneously to confront and to evade consumerism. In practice this involved a reopening of all the issues of poetics, a guerrilla-like refusal to stay in one place. Thus Walter Höllerer (b. 1922) argued in 1965 for the merits of "long poems" as being in principle unpretentious, open to banality as well as pleasure, and shunning the preciosity and incipient commodification of the sealed-off short poem; the poems of Peter Handke (b. 1942), e.g. *Leben ohne Poesie* (Life without Poetry, 1972), seem to enact this program. Against it the case was made for brevity, for the neo-Brecht-

ian aggressive epigram. The label "new subjectivity" was applied to poets of the 1970s because of their absorption in the details of either momentary or habitual experience, experience potentially eluding consumerist expectations. But the phrase could be (and was) reversed into "new objectivity" because these poets never stopped with the self; they always strove to locate the experienced moment within the concealed structures of a society defined and still riven by no longer acknowledged prejudices, memories, and dreams.

A specific poetological innovation of the early 1970s was the adaptation, by Jürgen Becker (b. 1932) and Rolf Dieter Brinkmann (1940–75), of the technology of camera and tape recorder to the lang. of poetry: the moment is repeatable, reversible, can be "made strange" without any premature interp. or categorization. The struggle of poets to remain both inside and outside consumer society, resisting it without retreating from it, takes many forms. Ger. p. has again become social in both premises and aspirations, though hardly in Klopstock's sense; and many writers find the agenda challenging. A few whose achievement is already significant include Christoph Meckel (b. 1935), Günter Kunert (b. 1929), Nicolas Born (1937–79), Helga Novak (b. 1935), F. C. Delius (b. 1943), Ursula Krechel (b. 1947), Jürgen Theobaldy (b. 1944), and Karin Kiwus (b. 1942). As new blends of consumerism, democracy, and nationalism erase familiar political antinomies, incl. the coded lang. employed by East Ger. poets under communism, the social imagination assigns new tasks to the lyrical subject: the poetic self recalls the humane dream of the Ger. Enlightenment— but through the *via negativa* of imagery resisting all current "representative" experience, imagery of defeat, exclusion, withdrawal. In exploring these marginal zones poets seek to renew the Utopian impulse on which poetry ultimately depends. See also GERMAN PROSODY; ROMANTIC AND POSTROMANTIC POETICS; TWENTIETH-CENTURY POETICS, *French and German*.

ANTHOLOGIES IN GERMAN: *Menschheitsdämmerung*, ed. K. Pinthus (1919)—Expressionism; *De profundis*, ed. G. Groll (1946)—non-Nazi texts, 1933–45; *Ergriffenes Dasein: deutsche Lyrik 1900–1950*, ed. H. E. Holthusen and F. Kemp (1955); *Transit*, ed. W. Höllerer (1956); *Museum der modernen Poesie*, ed. H. M. Enzensberger (1960)—international modernism; *Lyrik des expressionistischen Jahrzehnts*, ed. G. Benn (1962); *Deutschland, Deutschland: Politische Gedichte*, ed. H. Lamprecht (1969); *17 Mod. Ger. Poets*, ed. S. S. Prawer (1971); *Deutsche Gedichte von 1900 bis zur Gegenwart*, ed. F. Pratz (1971); *Lyrik-Katalog Bundesrepublik*, ed. J. Hans, U. Herms, and R. Thenior (1978); *Ansichten über Lyrik*, ed. W. Schubert and K. H. Höfer (1980)—poetological poems and prose since Opitz; *Lyrik für Leser: Deutsche Gedichte der siebziger Jahre*, ed. V. Hage (1981); *Deutsche Gedichte 1930–60*, ed. H. Bender (1983); *Ger. P. of the Romantic*

Era, ed. O. Durrani (1986); *Ger. P.*, ed. M. Swales (1987).

ANTHOLOGIES WITH ENGLISH RENDERINGS: *20th-C. Ger. Verse*, tr. H. Salinger (1952); *Penguin Book of Ger. Verse*, ed. L. Forster (1957); *Anthol. of Ger. P. from Hölderlin to Rilke*, ed. A. Flores (1960); *The Ger. Lyric of the Baroque*, tr. G. Schoolfield (1961); *Mod. Ger. P. 1910–60*, tr. M. Hamburger and C. Middleton (1962); *20 Ger. Poets*, ed. W. Kaufmann (1962); *Anthol. of Ger. P. through the 19th C.*, ed. A. Gode and F. Ungar (1964); *East Ger. P.* (1972), *Ger. P. 1910–75* (1976)—both tr. M. Hamburger; *Ger. P. from 1750 to 1900*, ed. R. Browning (1984).

POETIC FORMS: K. Viëtor, *Gesch. der deutschen Ode* (1923); G. Müller, *Gesch. des deutschen Liedes* (1925); W. Kayser, *Gesch. der deutschen Ballade* (1936), *Kleine deutsche Versschule* (1946), *Gesch. des Deutschen Verses* (1960); F. Beissner, *Gesch. der deutschen Elegie* (1941); E. Staiger, *Grundbegriffe der Poetik* (1946), tr. J. C. Hudson and L. T. Frank as *Basic Concepts of Poetics* (1991); P. Böckmann, *Formgesch. der deutschen Dichtung* (1949), *Formensprache* (1966); F. Lockemann, *Der Rhythmus des deutschen Verses* (1960); W. Hinck, *Die deutsche Ballade von Bürger bis Brecht* (1968); W. Höck, *Formen heutiger Lyrik* (1969); K. Weissenberger, *Formen der Elegie von Goethe bis Celan* (1969); J.-U. Fechner, *Das deutsche Sonett* (1969)—anthol.; G. Storz, *Der Vers in der neueren deutschen Dichtung* (1970); W. Killy, *Elemente der Lyrik* (1972); W. Freund, *Die deutsche Ballade* (1978); H. Laufhütte, *Die deutsche Kunstballade* (1979); D. Breuer, *Deutsche Metrik und Versgesch.* (1981).

CRITICISM IN GERMAN: B. Markwardt, *Gesch. der deutschen Poetik*, 5 v. (1937–67); E. Staiger, *Die Zeit als Einbildungskraft des Dichters* (1938); W. Killy, *Wandlungen des lyrischen Bildes* (1956); *Wege zum Gedicht*, ed. R. Hirschenauer and A. Weber, 2 v. (1956–63)—v. 2 on the ballad; *Die deutsche Lyrik*, ed. B. v. Wiese, 2 v. (1957); T. W. Adorno, "Rede über Lyrik und Gesellschaft" and "Zum Gedächtnis Eichendorffs," *Noten zur Literatur, I* (1958); C. Heselhaus, *Deutsche Lyrik der Moderne* (1961); *Ars poetica: Texte von Dichtern des 20. Jahrhunderts zur Poetik*, ed. B. Allemann (1966)—51 essays; W. Naumann, *Traum und Trad. in der deutschen Lyrik* (1966); A. Schöne, *Über politische Lyrik im 20. Jahrhundert* (1969); *Doppelinterpretationen*, ed. H. Domin (1969); K. H. Spinner, *Zur Struktur des lyrischen Ich* (1975); J. Theobaldy and G. Zürcher, *Veränderung der Lyrik: Über westdeutsche Gedichte seit 1965* (1976); *Naturlyrik und Gesellschaft*, ed. N. Mecklenburg (1977); *Gesch. der politischen Lyrik in Deutschland*, ed. W. Hinderer (1978); W. Rey, *Poesie der Antipoesie* (1978); W. Hinck, *Von Heine zu Brecht. Lyrik im Geschichtsprozess* (1978); *Die deutsche Lyrik, 1945–75*, ed. K. Weissenberger (1981); H. T. Hamm, *Poesie und kommunikative Praxis* (1981); S. Volckmann, *Zeit der Kirschen? Das Naturbild in der deutschen Gegenwartslyrik* (1982); *Gesch. der deutschen Lyrik vom Mittelalter bis zur Gegenwart*,

ed. W. Hinderer (1983)—indispensable; H. Gnüg, *Entstehung und Krise lyrischer subjektivität* (1983); B. Sorg, *Das lyrische Ich* (1984); *Deutsche Lyrik nach 1945*, ed. D. Breuer (1988).

CRITICISM IN ENGLISH: S. S. Prawer, *Ger. Lyric P.* (1952); A. Closs, *The Genius of the Ger. Lyric*, 2d ed. (1962); J. Flores, *Poetry in East Germany* (1971); R. D. Gray, *Ger. P.* (1976); R. M. Browning, *Ger. P. in the Age of the Enlightenment* (1978); T. Ziolkowski, *The Cl. Ger. Elegy, 1795–1950* (1980); P. Bridgewater, *The Ger. Poets of the First World War* (1985); C. Waller, *Expressionist Poetry and its Critics* (1986); M. Hamburger, *After the Second Flood* (1986); J. Rolleston, *Narratives of Ecstasy: Romantic Temporality in Mod. Ger. P.* (1987); B. Peucker, *Lyric Descent in the Ger. Romantic Trad.* (1987); *Ger. P. through 1915*, ed. H. Bloom (1987). J.L.R.

GERMAN PROSODY.

I. OLD GERMANIC
II. MIDDLE HIGH GERMAN
III. MODERN

I. OLD GERMANIC. The prosodic system of the early Germanic (Gc.) peoples (1st–13th cs. A.D.), called *alliterative verse*, was remarkably homogeneous. Because all of their poetry observes it, in every dialect, and also because of references in the Roman historian Tacitus (*Germania*, ca. 98 A.D.), we assume that it developed in the period of Gc. unity (1st c. B.C.), prior to the Great Migrations. Poems were recorded, however, only after the introduction of the Lat. writing system by Christian missionaries (8th c. A.D.), and then only fragmentarily. As oral texts, the poems include elements indicating the flow of the content, but the verse is not strictly formulaic; it does not include the kind of fixed verbal sequence, called a *formula* (q.v.) by Milman Parry, which recurs in predictable metrical positions within the line, as can be seen in Homer (see ORAL POETRY; ORAL-FORMULAIC THEORY). Scholars who have applied the label "formulaic" to Old Germanic (OGc.) verse use the characterization in a weak sense.

No alliterative verse (AV) survives from Gothic, only two lays and some additional short poems from the Old High German (OHG) area. By historical report Charlemagne had old poems collected, but whether or not they were destroyed by his successor, Louis the Pious, they have not survived. In the Old Saxon (OS) of north Germany an epic of about 6000 lines, the *Heliand*, and a few short poems have been transmitted to us, but only fragments of legal texts survive from Old Franconian and Old Frisian. The greatest number of texts has come down from the margins of Europe, from England (OE), Scandinavia (ON), and esp. Iceland, where the form of AV did not go out of use after the introduction of rhymed verse on the model of Med. Lat. On the Continent, however, AV was replaced by the accentual-syllabic prosodic system of the Med. Lat. hymns (see HYMN) as early as 860 A.D. by the monk Otfrid in South Germany (see GERMAN POETRY)—the earliest such adoption in any European vernacular.

It was England, where AV was maintained for at least another century, and even later (past 1066) in a northern area, which preserved the greatest variety of genres (see ENGLISH POETRY, *Old English*). Among these are short heroic lays similar to the OHG *Hildebrandslied*, i.e. *Finnesburh, Waldere,* and *Widsith,* among others, as well as the OE heroic epic *Beowulf* and such religious epics as *Genesis, Exodus,* the works of Cynewulf, and shorter religious lays. Unmatched elsewhere are OE elegiac poems, among them *The Wife's Lament, Wulf and Eadwacer,* and *The Ruin,* as well as riddles and charms (qq.v.). In all of these, as in poems on the Continent, the metrical unit is the single line or "long line" divided into hemistichs (q.v.) or "verses." Only in Scandinavia were longer units introduced, namely stanzas of several types (see OLD NORSE POETRY; DROTTKVAET), yet even there the line is still the metrical unit.

The prosodic pattern of AV seems therefore to have already been in existence when there was little differentiation among the Gc. langs. On the background of this metrical system we can only speculate. If, however, we accept Antoine Meillet's hypothesis about the nature of IE prosody (q.v.), which had descendants in Sanskrit and Gr. lyric verse, the Germanic line may have been built on an inherited pattern. Aage Kabell, however, denying devel. from IE verse, sets the origin of "regulated alliterative poetry" within Lat.–OE culture around 700 A.D., possibly on the pattern of the Cl. Gr. Adonic (q.v.). Although he supports his hypothesis with great erudition, he fails to consider that the archaic lang. of poems such as *Beowulf* retains IE characteristics such as lack of chief metrical accentuation on verbs, except when clause-initial, not to mention the early runic texts.

If the Gc. prosodic pattern was developed on the basis of comparable IE lines when strong initial stress was introduced in Gc., the distribution of stress on long syllables may have led to the characteristic Gc. line. Evidence in support of this assumption is provided by maintenance of the metrical importance of the second halfline, which contains the key stressed alliterating lift. Moreover, the Gc. line continues to be somewhat irregular and unfixed in rhythm, admitting a varying number of short, weakly stressed syllables in the dips. The importance of stress in early European poetry is evident also in early Lat. and Celtic verse with alliteration, for these two branches also introduced a strong stress in the period before our era, perhaps as early as the 3d c. But in Lat. and Celtic the early verse with alliteration developed differently from the Gc. (see CLASSICAL PROSODY; CELTIC PROSODY).

Analyzing word-structure patterns in Gc., Jerzy Kurylowicz has demonstrated how the varying metrical patterns agree with them. Disyllabic

words like OE *eármum* consist of one stressed syllable followed by one unstressed, or the reverse, as in OE *gefeóll.* Trisyllabic compounds have in addition a syllable with strong secondary stress, as in OE *eagorstream, sorhfullne.* Like every vital verse, as others have pointed out, Gc. AV is thus clearly aligned with natural patterns in its lang.

Our earliest direct evidence of the form of AV is provided by runic inscriptions (see RUNE) such as that on the Gallehus horn, dated about 375 A.D.:

> *Ek Hlewagastiz holtijaz   horna tawido*
> (I Hlewagastiz of Holt   horn made).

This inscription exemplifies the essential metrical characteristics of AV: the line consists of an *on-verse* (first halfline) and an *off-verse* (second halfline), each with two *lifts* (equivalent to *ictus* [q.v.] in other metrical systems) on stressed syllables, and tied together by (structural) alliteration: the two lifts in the on-verse alliterate with the first in the off-verse, giving the basic pattern *a a a x.* (Other less common patterns are *a x a x* and *x a a x.*) Consonants (or certain consonant clusters) alliterate with each other; any vowel alliterates with any other. The *dips,* the runs of metrically nonprominent syllables, vary in extent. In the classic typology of verse-types given by Eduard Sievers in 1893, all the lines can be shown to fall into Five Types (see ENGLISH PROSODY, *Old English*), though the precise reasons for this are unclear; a single unifying principle which would produce these types still remains unknown. Sievers' taxonomy is thus accurate descriptively, but is not explanatory. Subsequent metrists, and even Sievers himself, searched for a unitary scheme for the line, as can be seen in other metrical proposals.

Perhaps the most prominent suggestion for such a scheme is the theory of Heusler that quantity not stress underlies a unitary pattern. Using musical notation, Heusler held that there are two segments per verse, each corresponding to one 4/4 measure. In interpreting the metrical quantities, a stressed long syllable counts as two fourths, and an unstressed as one fourth or even one eighth. Defective verses are filled with metrical rests (see REST). Heusler did not assume recitation of the poems to the accompaniment of a musical instrument, such as a harp, which might fill in the rests with a note. But in recent years, Heusler's musical scansion has not been favored: in an approach that now seems dubious, he extrapolated back to the earlier Gc. verse from scansion of later Ger. rhymed verse such as Otfrid's.

Other metrists later looked to pitch to provide a common basis. Such a metrical pattern would be most unusual, however. The major Western prosodies are based on one element: Gr. and Sanskrit on quantity alone, in complete disregard of pitch accent, and Lat. in disregard of stress accent. Subsequent European vernacular verse is based on accent alone. Nevertheless, it is difficult to avoid the assumption of a twofold basis for Gc. prosody—quantity and stress—however complex such a metrical basis may seem. It is this twofold basis which may account for the varying patterns Sievers found.

Metrists who consider alliteration the basic feature of Gc. verse fail to take into account the noncentral syllables that may alliterate with the central metrical syllables. Moreover, alliteration became widespread in ON legal texts only in the late 12th c. Like end rhyme in later verse, alliteration is a significant component of Gc. verse but not the primary metrical element, which is stress.

More complex patterns of alliteration in later works reveal an effort to maintain metrical prominence in spite of weakening of stress, a linguistic change that in the south of Germany was one characteristic leading to even rhythm and end rhyme. *Muspilli*, the later of the two OHG lays, incorporates rhyme and even rhythm while retaining the alliterative form. Its contemporary, Otfrid, deliberately adapted the rhythm and rhyme of Med. Lat. Church poetry, but still incorporates some alliterative lines and the uneven rhythm of AV. The few mss. of the next three centuries preserve little Gc. verse, and only at a pedestrian level. Yet that verse indicates that Otfrid's innovation did not lead to regular rhythm and perfect rhyme in Ger. poetry until strict standards were introduced in the late 12th c. under the strong influence of Occitan and OF poetry (qq.v.). See also ENGLISH PROSODY; GERMAN POETRY; GNOMIC POETRY; MEDIEVAL POETRY.—Sievers; A. Heusler, *Deutsche Versgesch.*, 3 v. (1925–29), *Die altgermanische Dichtung*, 2d ed. (1941); W. P. Lehmann, *The Devel. of Germanic Verse Form* (1956); W. Hoffmann, *Altdeutsche Metrik* (1967); J. Kurylowicz, *Die sprachlichen Grundlagen der altgermanischen Metrik* (1970), *Metrik und Sprachgesch.* (1975); J. K. Bostock, "Appendix on OS and OHG Metre," *Handbook of OHG Lit.*, 2d ed. (1976); H. Erhardt, *Der Stabreim in altnordischen Rechtstexten* (1977); A. Kabell, *Metrische Studien I: Der Alliterationsvers* (1978); J. B. Kühnel, *Untersuchung zum ger. Stabreimvers* (1978); D. Hofmann, "Stabreimvers," *Reallexikon* 4.183–93; Brogan, 616–40 and sect. K; S. Suzuki, "The IE Basis of Gc. AV," *Lingua* 75 (1988).   W.P.L.

II. MIDDLE HIGH GERMAN. The basic principle of MHG meter is the alternation of stressed and unstressed syllables. Normally metrical stress or ictus coincides with speech accent. The dominant rhythm is iambic, but trochaic rhythm also occurs. In classical MHG, alternating rhythm is the norm, but in the early epic and lyric there may be an accumulation of unstressed syllables. Two stresses may be juxtaposed (*beschwerte Hebung*).

Dactylic rhythm arises in the lyric from the accommodation of the Romance decasyllable to the Ger. 4-beat line. Thus, the same Romance model (see Frank 11) gives in Rudolf von Fenis 81,30 a 5-beat alternating line but in 83,11 a 4-beat dactylic line. In later poets alternating and dactylic rhythms may be combined (see LEICH).

There are two original types of line: the 7- or 8-beat line divided by a caesura, a devel. of the OHG alliterative long line, and a short line of somewhat variable length. The earliest named poets, i.e. from ca. 1150 (Kürenberg, Dietmar, Meinloh, Regensburg) use the long line almost exclusively, and it also occurs in the *Nibelungenlied* (see NIBELUNGENSTROPHE) and in related epic forms. The short line is found in 12th-c. epic, e.g. *König Rother*, anonymous examples of the lyric, and the earliest didactic poet (see SPRUCHDICHTUNG). Once Romance formal influence begins to prevail in the lyric (see MINNESANG), the long line is largely abandoned and the 4-beat line predominates, a development facilitated by its equivalence to the very common Romance heptasyllable and octosyllable (q.v.). Long lines may persist as one possible structural variant, or occasionally as the basis for a whole poem (e.g. Walther 124,1). The 4-beat line is also the medium of courtly romance, where it is the natural equivalent of its OF counterpart the octosyllable, and is used in other verse narratives, *Sprechspruch* (see SPRUCHDICHTUNG), and didactic treatises.

The strophic structures of the early lyric are very simple, made up of pairs or sets of long-line couplets, with the occasional insertion of a short unrhymed line (*Waise*). They are either isometric or virtually so. Under Romance influence, a tripartite stanza structure is introduced (see CANSO), with two metrically equivalent sets of lines (*Stollen*, together making up the *Aufgesang*), followed by a third, differing part (*Abgesang*), thus: AA/B. This remains the dominant type, and is introduced also into *Spruchdichtung*, though undivided, bipartite, and other structures also occur (see LEICH).

Whereas at first isometric stanzas predominate, on the pattern of early troubadour and trouvère lyric, later heterometric and polymetric forms become more common, and many poets have a preponderance of unique patterns. Particularly in the 13th c. and beyond, structures may be lengthened by the addition of a refrain, with a tendency in later poets, e.g. Oswald von Wolkenstein, towards longer stanzas and longer refrains.

In the earliest epic and lyric, only couplet rhyme, often assonating, is found. Later, different types of rhyme are introduced in the lyric, and pure rhyme gradually replaces assonance; couplet rhyme is characteristic of most of later epic, romance, and other verse narrative, *Sprechspruch*, and didactic treatises. Initially there may be only two rhymes in the lyric stanza, as in the early troubadours and trouvères, but later the number increases, so that some 13th-c. poets, such as Neifen and Winterstetten, have very high totals. A proliferation of rhymes is particularly characteristic of the *Leich*.

The main types of rhyme are triple rhyme, and in the *Leich* other monorhyme; internal rhyme, either linking the two hemistichs of a line or one line with the next; echoing rhymes (*Responsionen*); isolated rhyme (*Korn*), rhyming from one stanza to another; grammatical rhyme; punning rhyme, e.g. Neifen 32 *solt* "should": *solt* "reward"; *Pausenreim*, in which a word at the beginning of a line rhymes with an end-rhyme; *Schlagreim*, a rapid succession of the same rhyme, often combined with transitional rhyme, in which a word at the end of the line rhymes with the first word of the next.

Rarer types are *rims trencatz*, cutting across syllabic boundaries, e.g. Konrad von Würzburg 30; rhyme linking alternate stanzas (*coblas alternadas*), as in Neifen 7, or successive pairs of stanzas (*coblas doblas*), as in Neifen 21; reversed rhymes (*rims retrogradadatz*), e.g. Der Düring 1, which rhymes every word (*rims serpentis*) and has in its first section 25 rhymes repeated in reverse order. These rhyming devices, customarily designated by the Occitan technical terms above, are influenced by the Romance lyric. See also MINNESANG; TAGELIED.

A. Heusler, *Deutsche Versgesch.* (1925–29, rpt. 1956), v. 2; P. Habermann and W. Mohr, "Deutsche Versmasse und Strophenformen," *Reallexikon* 1.231–44; U. Pretzel and H. Thomas, "Deutsche Verskunst," *Deutsche Philologie im Aufriss*, ed. W. Stammler, 2d ed., v. 3 (1962); H. de Boor, *Kleine Schriften*, ed. R. Wisniewski and H. Kolb, v. 2 (1966); S. Beyschlag, *Altdeutsche Verskunst in Grundzügen*, 6th ed. (1969); G. A. Vogt, *Studien zur Verseingangsgestaltung* (1974); A. H. Touber, *Deutsche Strophenformen des Mittelalters* (1975); S. Ranawake, *Höfische Strophenkunst* (1976); W. Mohr, "Romanische Versmasse und Strophenformen (im Deutschen)," G. Schweikle, "Reim," *Reallexikon*; D. Breuer, *Deutsche Metrik und Versgeschichte* (1981); Sayce; O. Paul and I. Glier, *Deutsche Metrik*, 9th ed. (1983). O.L.S.

III. MODERN. If T. S. Eliot was right that "a different meter is a different mode of thought," one can note several shifts of metrical and thus also of conceptual paradigm in the devel. of Ger. verse. In fact its history could be described as a continual veering between two central trads.—an "art" trad. based on a syllabic principle (adapted from Cl. or Romance forms) and a "native" trad. based on an accentual principle (adapted from older Germanic forms). Modern Ger. pros. shows the co-existence and tenuous balance of these two principles (neither of which exists in pure form), and the relative prominence of one or the other accounts for many variations.

In contrast to the Ren. verseforms of the Romance countries and England, Ger. verse in the 16th c. reveals a modest continuation of late medieval forms such as the *Meistersang, Knittelvers* (qq.v.), church song, folksong, and Med. Lat. poetry. The beginning of modern Ger. pros. is often attributed to Martin Opitz (1597–1639), whose *Buch von der deutschen Poeterei* (1624) instituted the following reforms: (1) in reaction against the syllable-counting and concomitant distortion of word stress in the 16th c., Opitz reinstated stress

as the basis of Ger. verse; (2) in contrast to folk poetry, Opitz advocated strict alternation of stressed and unstressed syllables (i.e. only iambic and trochaic feet) and purity of rhyme; (3) he proposed the use of Fr. models, particularly the alexandrine (q.v.), which he adapted from the Pléiade (q.v.) by superimposing on the Fr. syllabic line the Ger. accentual principle. Although forms such as the madrigal (q.v.) and variations such as dactylic feet were soon introduced, the alexandrine remained the dominant meter for both lyric and dramatic verse in Ger. well into the 18th c., as exemplified by the sonnets and tragedies of Gryphius (1616–64).

Another 18th-c. revolution was the introduction of imitations of Cl. verseforms into Ger. poetry by Klopstock (1724–1803). Although Klopstock was not without predecessors, the first three cantos of his epic *Der Messias* (1748) were quickly perceived as a liberation from the monotonous alternation and rhyme of the alexandrine. In that work Klopstock adapted the dactylic hexameter (q.v.) of Homer by replacing the Gr. quantitative principle with the Ger. accentual principle, substituting trochees for spondees. He also introduced the Gr. lyric forms of the elegiac distich and the Alcaic, Asclepiadean, and Sapphic odes (qq.v.). The ode forms and esp. the hexameter were found to be compatible with Ger., and except for attempts by Voss and A. W. Schlegel to write spondaic verse, Cl. forms were used successfully by Hölderlin in his odes and elegies, by Goethe in his *Römische Elegien* and *Hermann und Dorothea*, and by Schiller. Klopstock's experimentation led further to the invention of new ode forms and to his most influential contribution to the trad., *freie Rhythmen* (q.v.). The free rhythm of *Die Frühlingsfeier* (1759) was regarded as a great innovation, with evident roots in Cl. trad. even though it displays no fixed line or stanza structure. Other sources of free rhythm, such as the Pindaric ode, the Hebrew Psalms, and the madrigal, as well as native Ger. forms, merged with this line as precedents for the free rhythm of Goethe's early hymns (e.g. *Prometheus*), Hölderlin's late hymns (e.g. *Der Rhein*), and Novalis' *Hymne an die Nacht*.

Weimar Classicism and romanticism brought further developments as modern Ger. poetry achieved the status of world lit. Blank verse (q.v.) was introduced from Eng. models in mid-century, and Lessing's *Nathan der Weise* (1779) quickly established its prominence as the standard meter for Ger. verse drama. The flexibility of blank verse encouraged a diversity of individual styles, ranging from Goethe's *Iphigenie* and *Tasso* to the dramas of Schiller and Kleist. The main exception is Goethe's *Faust*, which represents paradigmatically the integrative ability of the age by employing many different literary and folk forms. Around 1770 there arose a new interest in folk poetry, evident in the ballads of the Sturm und Drang (q.v.) poets and later the romantics. The influence of folk verse is evident in much of Goethe's early poetry, as well as in the major works of Brentano, Mörike, Uhland, Eichendorff, and Heine.

The Ger. romantics assimilated an amazing number of European and Oriental forms, among them It. ottava rima and terza rima (qq.v.), Sp. glosa (q.v.) and assonantal forms, and the Persian ghazal (q.v.). The sonnet was both revived and reborrowed, leading to a "sonnet rage." After the age of Goethe, poets refined the forms and trads. they had inherited. Blank verse remained the standard for verse drama. Although iambic pentameter was widely used, tetrameter lines predominated, either duple or triple meters and often in rhymed quatrains, revealing its folk origins (Rückert, Lenau, Droste, Storm, Keller, Meyer).

Free verse (q.v.) is by far the dominant mode in the 20th c., although the major modernist poets, such as George, Hofmannsthal, and Rilke, used or at least began with traditional forms. Rilke's *Duineser Elegien* (1922), for example, are based on the elegiac distich, but the form is modified almost beyond recognition. expressionist poets such as Trakl also used, modified, and ultimately rejected conventions in favor of free verse, which had gained impetus in the wake of Fr. symbolism. Two main lines of development are discernible. The first, which arrives at free verse by transformation of traditional meters, extends from the rediscovery of Hölderlin to Rilke, Trakl, Benn, Brecht, and Bachmann to Celan, confirming T. S. Eliot's observation that "the ghost of some simple metre should lurk behind the arras in even the 'freest' verse." In the second, the elevated tone of early free verse was dropped in favor of a prosaic or speechlike quality. The postwar period also produced concrete poetry (q.v.) and other types of visual poetry (q.v.), which are at the opposite pole from audible rhythm. Traditional forms are still a live option and were used a great deal during the middle decades of the century. But the cl. odes of Weinheber and Schröder are truly an exception, and the distance transversed becomes apparent when forms become available for ironic quotation or allusion, as in Brecht's recasting of the *Communist Manifesto* in hexameters. Although the study of prosody has been a very productive discipline in Ger. since the time of Opitz, it seems to stop short on the threshold of modern form. Free verse still seems difficult to define other than by negation, and much more work is needed even to identify its varied forms.

J. Minor, *Neuhochdeutsche Metrik* (1902); H. Paul, *Deutsche Metrik* (1905); A. Heusler, *Deutsche Versgesch.*, 3 v. (1925–29); P. Habermann, "Antike Versmasse und Strophen- (Oden-) formen im Deutschen," P. Habermann and W. Mohr, "Deutsche Versmasse und Strophenformen," and W. Mohr, "Romanische Versmasse und Strophenformen (im Deutschen)," all in *Reallexikon*—extensive bibls.; W. Kayser, *Gesch. des deutschen Verses* (1960), *Kleine deutsche Versschule*, 21st ed. (1982);

O. Paul and I. Glier, *Deutsche Metrik*, 9th ed. (1974)—best handbook; C. Wagenknecht, *Deutsche Metrik* (1981); D. Breuer, *Deutsche Metrik und Versgesch.* (1981). B.B.

GESELLSCHAFTSLIED. A song for several voices, written, composed, and performed by and for educated society, primarily in the baroque and rococo periods in Germany. It originated toward the end of the 16th c. and pursues a trad. distinct from that of the folksong. The first, musical impetus for the G. came with the adoption of It. song forms: the courtly, nonstrophic madrigal (q.v.), the strophic Neapolitan *villanella* (street song), and the *canzone* (q.v.). The pleasures and sorrows of love and convivial joys such as drinking and dancing are preferred subjects. There is a close affinity between the G. and the lyrical poem proper. Hence the high-flowering period of lyrical poetry from 1620–80 (e.g. Simon Dach, Martin Opitz, G. R. Weckherlin) had an ennobling effect upon the G., many of the composers writing their own texts (H. L. Hassler, Adam Krieger). From 1680–1740 the G. was overshadowed by the artistic aria, although the production of *Gesellschaftslieder* did not stop. The second great vogue of the G. occurred from 1740–80. Both the idea of "humanity" and renewed interest in the folksong now caused the artist to write in a more popular vein (J. A. Hiller, J. A. P. Schulz, J. André; J. F. Reichardt was the first to set Goethe's poems to music). After 1800, due to the renewed interest of Herder and the romantics in folk lit., the G. had to yield its place to the revived folksong, while compositions of high poetry (*Kunstlieder*) became monodic, required the art of the trained singer, and were reserved for the concert stage.—H. von Fallersleben, *Gesellschaftslieder des 16. und 17. Jhs.* (1860); A. Reissmann, *Das deutsche Lied in seiner historischen Entwicklung* (1861); F. W. von Ditfurth, *Deutsche Volks- und Gesellschaftslieder des 17. und 18. Jhs.* (1872); M. Friedlaender, *Das dt. Lied im 18. Jh.*, 2d ed., 2 v. (1908); R. Velten, *Das ältere dt. G. unter dem Einfluss der italienischen Musik* (1914); G. Müller, *Gesch. des deutschen Liedes vom Barock zur Gegenwart* (1925); H. Cysarz, *Deutsches Barock in der Lyrik* (1936); M. Platel, *Vom Volkslied zum G.* (1939); C. von Faber du Faur, *Ger. Baroque Lit.: A Catalogue* (1958); W. Flemming, "G.," *Reallexikon*; W. Kayser, *Gesch. des deutschen Verses* (1960). U.K.G.

GHAZAL. A monorhymed lyric poem, shorter than a *qaṣīda* (q.v.), common to Arabic, Persian, Turkish, Uzbek, Pashto, and Urdu lit. The rhyme scheme is aa ba ca, etc., and, after the 12th c., the poet mentions his name toward the end of the poem. Cl. gs. share a limited range of images and a fairly restricted vocabulary. The principal subject of the g. is earthly or mystical love, and the mood is melancholy, expressing sadness over separation from the beloved. The g. took its canonical form in Persian in the 11th–12th cs. The most famous of all g. poets were the Persians Sa‘di (d. 1292), Ḥāfeẓ (d.1389–90), and Ṣā’eb (d. 1677–78); and the genre developed in other lits. under strong Persian influence. Attempts to modernize the Urdu g. have met with some success and it continues to flourish in that lit. but has been mostly superseded by modern forms in the other lits. Tr. of Ḥāfeẓ inspired the Ger. romantic poets, esp. Goethe, whose *West-östlicher Divan* imitated Persian models. Platen wrote a large number of gs. Recently there has been something of a revival of interest in translating gs., with significant efforts being made by Am. poets such as Adrienne Rich and James Harrison. See also ARABIC POETRY; PERSIAN POETRY; TURKISH POETRY.—E. J. W. Gibb, *Hist. of Ottoman Poetry*, v. 1 (1900); D. Balke, *West-östliche Gedichtformen: Sadschal-Theorie und Gesch. des deutsches Ghasels*, Diss., Bonn (1952); A. Bausani, *Storia delle letterature del Pakistan* (1958); A. Pagliaro and A. Bausani, *Storia della letteratura persiana* (1960); *Encyclopaedia of Islam*, 2d ed., s.v. "G."; *Gs. of Ghalib*, ed. A. Ahmad (1971); *An Anthol. of Cl. Urdu Love Lyrics*, ed. D. J. Matthews and C. Shackle (1972); A. Schimmel, "The Emergence of the Ger. G.," *Studies in the Urdu Gazal and Prose Fiction*, ed. M. Memon (1979); W. Andrews, *Poetry's Voice, Society's Song* (1985). W.L.H.

GLOSA. A Sp. metric form, also called *mote* or *retruécano*, closely related to the *cantiga*, introduced in the late 14th or early 15th c. by the court poets. In its strict form it is a poem consisting of a line or a short stanza, called *cabeza* (also *mote, letra,* or *texto*), stating the theme of the poem, and followed by one stanza for each line of the *cabeza*, explaining or glossing that line and incorporating it into the explanatory stanza, often at the end as a refrain. Strophes may be of any length and rhyme scheme. Loosely, the g. is any poem expanding on the theme presented in the opening stanza and usually repeating one or more lines of that stanza. A famous late 16th-c. g. is one by Vicente Espinel beginning "Mil veces voy a hablar / a mi zagala."—H. Janner, "La g. española. Estudio histórico de su métrica y de sus temas," *RFE* 27 (1943); Le Gentil; Navarro. D.C.C.

GLYCONIC. Named after a Gr. poet named Glycon whose date and place are unknown, this metrical colon (x x – ◡ ◡ – ◡ –) was basic to Aeolic (q.v.) meters and so became common in Gr. and Lat. lyric poetry. It was used by the Gr. melic poets, Alcaeus and Sappho, and by later Gr. and Roman poets both for monody and choral lyric (see MELIC POETRY). In lyric, the number of syllables is fixed; in choral lyric and drama, resolution (q.v.) is permitted. Horace began his gs. with two long syllables.

The catalectic form of the g., x x – ◡ ◡ – – , is called the Pherecratean (q.v.) after the Gr. comic poet Pherecrates (fl. late 5th c. B.C.). Apart

from *anceps* (q.v.) in the final syllable, the P. permits resolution (q.v.) only in the quantities of the base (the first 2 syllables) and occurs, usually with one or more glyconics, chiefly in Anacreon, in the choruses of Gr. tragedy, and in Horace (in whom the base is regularly spondaic). An example is Horace's *Odes* 1.5.3. The hypercatalectic form of the g. (x x – ◡ ◡ – ◡ – –) is called the Hipponactean.—Wilamowitz, pt. 2, ch. 4; Maas; Koster; Dale; Halporn et al.; Snell; West; K. Itsumi, "The G. in Gr. Tragedy," *CQ* 78 (1984).
R.J.G.; P.S.C.; J.W.H.

GNOMIC POETRY. A gnome is a "short pithy statement of a general truth; a proverb, maxim, aphorism, or apothegm" (*OED*). The name "g." was first applied to a group of Gr. poets who flourished in the 6th c. B.C., incl. Theognis, Solon, Phocylides, and Simonides of Anorgos. But ancient Egyptian, Chinese, and Sanskrit lits. all attest to the long-standing and widespread popularity of the gnome. In the West, the first recorded Germanic gnome is given by Tacitus: "Women must weep and men remember." Old Ir. provides an example in *The Instructions of King Cormac MacAirt* and ON a particularly interesting one in the *Hávamál* (tr. D. E. M. Clarke, 1923). The popularity of gnomes among the Germanic peoples is also shown by the two OE collections, the *Cotton* and the *Exeter* gnomes. G. p. was later cultivated in England by Francis Quarles (*Emblems*, 1633) and in France by Gui de Pibras, whose *Quatrains* (1574) were a direct imitation of the g. poets and very successful. See EPIGRAM; PROVERB; RIDDLE.—B. C. Williams, *G. P. in Anglo-Saxon* (1914); K. Jackson, *Early Welsh G. Poems* (1935); R. MacG. Dawson, "The Structure of OE G. Poems," *JEGP* 61 (1962). R.P.A.

GOLIARDIC VERSE. The term *goliardus* or "Goliard" has been plausibly derived from the Germanic verb *goljan*, "sing, entertain," and seems to have been used of wandering entertainers. It came to be linked pseudo-etymologically with Lat. *gula*, "gluttony," and *Golias* or Goliath, commonly allegorized as a mocker and enemy of the Church; and in the 12th and 13th c. *goliardus* came to denote a member of the *familia Goliae*, the "wandering scholars" made famous by Helen Waddell, a restless student subculture around whom there developed the legend of a dissolute and anti-authoritarian guild or fraternity of scholar-poets, the *ordo vagorum*. Much of the finest Med. Lat. lyric, esp. that devoted to wine and women, was associated with this subculture, but the characteristic Goliard mode is satire, nearly always aimed at the Church establishment, and in ms. often attributed simply to "Golias." Its characteristic verseform is a stanza of four 13-syllable lines in feminine rhyme and sometimes ending with a hexameter called an *auctoritas* (a favorite device of Walter of Châtillon), which modern scholars call

"G. v." (Ger. "Vagantenstrophe"). The greater part of the lyrics is anonymous and is to be found in various collections, of which the most famous is the Benediktbeuern Collection (*Carmina Burana*), made probably in Bavaria early in the 13th c. The later 12th and early 13th c. is the great age of Goliard poetry, but its best products circulated throughout the medieval period, and the G. stanza was probably a model for vernacular verse-forms such as the Sp. *mester de clereçia*.

Most of the evidence adduced for the existence of an *ordo vagorum* comes from Goliard poetry itself. It is clear that the burgeoning schools of the 12th c. generated an "intellectual proletariat" (Bolgar), men of some learning but few worldly prospects, many of whom wrote poetry, and natural too that their poetry should often be critical of an establishment which denied them preferment. But there is no evidence that the best-known "goliard" poets, Hugh Primas, Walter of Châtillon, or even the "Archpoet," with his celebrated cough and Falstaffian failings, were "wandering scholars" in any literal sense. That the Goliard posture is wholly conventional is suggested by the fact that titles like "Primate," "Archpoet," and even "Walter" acquire a status virtually as fictional as that of Golias himself, and in the mss. are freely assigned to anonymous satires.

The mockery of established authority in G. satire takes many forms: the grandiose fiction of a Goliard "order," the assumption of a title like "Archpoet" (a sneer at the archbishops and archchancellors in his audience), and the quotation of biblical and Cl. texts as *auctoritates* in contexts which distort their meaning. In some of the finest poems the *persona* exhibits an engaging or shocking frankness about his reckless hedonism in tavern or bed which, like that of Falstaff or Chaucer's Pardoner, becomes a tool of the poet's satire as he makes it a measure of the corruption of his world.

T. Wright, *Lat. Poems commonly attributed to Walter Mapes*(1841); *Carmina Burana*, ed. J. A. Schmeller, 4th ed. (1907)—the only complete text, later ed. by A. Hilka and O. Schumann, though only v. 1, pts. 1–2, v. 2, pt. 1, and v. 3, pt. 1, have been pub. (1931–71); H. Waddell, *The Wandering Scholars*, 8th ed. (1938); *The Goliard Poets*, ed. G. F. Whicher (1949); *Hymnen und Vagantenlieder*, comp. K. Langosch (1954); Raby, *Secular*, v. 2; G. Fichtner, "The Etymology of Goliard," *Neophil* 51 (1967); A. G. Rigg, "Golias and Other Pseudonyms," *SMed*, ser. 3, 18 (1977); J. Mann, "Satiric Subject and Satiric Object in G. Lit.," *MitJ* 15 (1980).   W.W.

GONGORISM. See CULTERANISMO.

GRAMMAR AND POETRY. See SYNTAX, POETIC.

GRAMMATICAL RHYME (Fr. *rime grammaticale*, Ger. *grammatischer Reim*, It. *replicatio*), sometimes "etymological r." Rs. which employ related forms derived from a common root syllable or etymon, such as a verb and a noun, or otherwise play on the varying lexical forms of a stem, esp. by repeating the same r. word in a run of lines but in a different case each time, so with different inflectional endings: the effect is close to that of monorhyme (q.v.). This kind of rhyming would be regarded by most moderns as scarcely r. at all, for being too easy, but it was practiced in Occitan by the troubadours, in OF (Chrétien de Troyes), and by the *Rhétoriqueurs* (qq.v.), e.g. Rutebeuf and Mousket; it can be effective still in short runs. G. r. is not to be confused with homoeoteleuton (q.v.), "case rhyme," which is the Gr. term for agreement of inflectional endings on words, without any intent at r. strictly speaking: g. r. uses the identity of roots (whether obvious or not) counterpointed with the difference of endings precisely in a rhymelike fashion, though on the grammatical-category level, and expressly for a rhymelike effect: it is therefore a lexical analogue of (phonic) r., while homoeoteleuton is not (see RHYME). "Equivocal r." (Fr. *rime équivoque*), closely related and very popular among the *Rhétoriqueurs*, is discussed s.v. MOSAIC RHYME. The structure treated as g. r. in prosody is treated as "polyptoton" (q.v.) in rhetoric.—A. Tobler, *Le Vers français* (1885), 177–78; Patterson.   T.V.F.B.

GRAMMATOLOGY. See DECONSTRUCTION.

GRAMMETRICS. The writer has been correctly called the one who thinks sentences. Linguistics has not yet been able to go beyond the sentence to formulate a satisfactory text grammar, and literary hermeneutics (q.v.) has not, by and large, come down to study the sentence as a primary meaning-making unit in the text. G., esp. as it focuses on the relation of sentence and line in the poem, captures the mid-range theories and practices that lie between the disciplines of linguistics and hermeneutics. The philosophical justification for such a hybrid theory is that, on every level of the poem, and fundamentally, the notion of conflicting structural principles is a specific property of literary art. Meter is not a set of physical objects like fence-palings, but rather a system of relationships intersected by, and thus in rapport with, the other major system of verse, grammar. Meter and grammar occupy the same textual space, the same words in the poem. One blade of the shears is meter, the other grammar, and when they work against each other they divide the poem.

All competent readers use grammetrical habits of attention when they read poems. The practice (without the name) of g. was performed by Gerard Manley Hopkins a century ago, when he called poetry the figure that grammar makes, and by grammar-oriented prosodists in Russia in the 1920s—by Tynjanov in his studies of sentence-line coincidence and noncoincidence, and by Brik in studies of the dependence of rhythmical move-

GREEK POETRY

ment, besides phonetic factors such as stress distribution, on various types of syntactic ordering. G. was named and given empirical validation by Wexler in two studies of the Fr. alexandrine (q.v.) in the 1960s, and applied to free verse (q.v.) by Wesling in 1971. Other studies by Hrushovsky, Golomb, and Meschonnic examine the relationship between prosodic and grammatical units in the verse period.

Let us think of grammatical rank and metrical rank as pairs of coordinates:

Morpheme—Syllable
Word—Foot or Stress-Maximum
Group or Phrase—Caesura
Clause—Line
Sentence—Rhyme Pair or Stanza
Sentence Group—Whole Poem.

If we arrange these two columns of ranks along a vertical (*y*) axis and a horizontal (*x*) axis and draw the coordinate grid lines of the enclosed graph, we find that the most interesting intersections are at the points word–foot and sentence–line. These seem esp. privileged cutting-points, as we may suggest by a small example of line 10 of Shakespeare's Sonnet 129:

```
1    2 3   4   5   6   7 8   9  10
Had, hauing, and in quest, to haue extreame
w   s|w   s  |w   s  |w s  |w  s
Foot 1  |  Foot 2  |  Foot 3  |  Foot 4 | Foot 5
```

Here are three scissoring caesuras—one after syllable 1, one after syllable 3, and one after syllable 6—making four segments, which increase in size by increments from one to four syllables—a tidy progression made possible by the Elizabethan printer's commas. The other and more obvious progression is that of the verb conjugation, which in one line enacts in minature the sonnet's larger scheme of beginning—middle—end time frames, making up a rudimentary form of alliterative verse on the paradigm changes. Scansion of the line by traditional feet shows the first and second feet broken oddly by caesuras, playing stress against syntax to emphasize the time of the verb of lust which will, with the word *extreame*, soon be seen to be morally equivalent. More could be said about the line, and a great deal more about the whole poem from this point of view. Grammetrical analysis is inescapably interpretive, and ideally requires an accounting of the whole poem by such methods of description. G. loads stylistic concepts with semantic possibilities. Plainly, however, until we have stronger and more definitive explanations of both grammar and meter, the contributions of grammetrical analysis must remain provisional. See also SYNTAX, POETIC.

Y. Tynjanov, *The Problem of Verse Lang.* (1924), tr. M. Sosa and B. Harvey (1981); C. A. Langworthy, "Verse-Sentence Patterns in Eng. Poetry," *PQ* 7 (1928); O. Brik, "Contributions to the Study of Verse Lang." (1928), tr. in *Readings in Rus. Poetics*,

ed. L. Matejka (1978); G. M. Hopkins, s.v. "Poetry, Verse, Versification," in Index to *Note-Books and Papers*, ed. H. House (1959); B. Hrushovsky, "On Free Rhythms in Mod. Poetry," in Sebeok; P. Wexler, "On the G. of the Cl. Alexandrine," *Cahiers de lexicologie* 4 (1964), "Distich and Sentence in Corneille and Racine," *Essays on Style and Lang.*, ed. R. Fowler (1966); D. Wesling, "The Prosodies of Free Verse," *20th-C. Lit. in Retrospect*, ed. R. Brower (1971), *The New Poetries* (1985); H. Golomb, *Enjambment in Poetry* (1979); H. Meschonnic, *Critique du rythme* (1982); R. Cureton, "Rhythm: A Multi-Level Analysis," *Style* 17 (1985); E. Bollobás, "From Traditional Prosody to G.," *Studia Poetica* 8 (1985).
                                                                D.W.

GRAND STYLE. See STYLE.

GRAVEYARD POETRY. A type of meditative poetry, g. p. takes as its major themes a melancholy sense of mutability, the inevitability of death, and the hope of a future life, arriving at such moral generalizations as Gray's "The paths of glory lead but to the grave" and "Even from the tomb the voice of nature cries." Although there are some earlier examples (e.g. Andreas Gryphius' *Kirch-hof Gedancken* in the mid 17th c. in Germany), Thomas Parnell's *Night-Piece on Death* (1721) first develops the type that became fully established with Young's *Night-Thoughts* (1742), Blair's *The Grave* (1743), and Gray's *Elegy Written in a Country Churchyard* (1751). In the latter half of the 18th c., g. p. became widespread in Germany, Holland, Sweden, France, and Italy, the best known examples being von Creutz's *Die Gräber* and Foscolo's *I Sepolcri*.—P. von Tieghem, *Le Préromantisme*, 3 v. (1924–47); J. W. Draper, *The Funeral Elegy and the Rise of Eng. Romanticism* (1929); E. Sickels, *The Gloomy Egoist* (1932); C. A. D. Fehrman, *Kyrkogårdsromantik* (1954); H. Weinbrot, "Gray's *Elegy*: A Poem of Moral Choice and Resolution," *SEL* 18 (1978).   F.J.W.; A.PR.; L.MET.

GREEK ANTHOLOGY. See ANTHOLOGY.

GREEK POETICS. See CLASSICAL POETICS; ALEXANDRIANISM; BYZANTINE POETRY.

GREEK POETRY.

I. CLASSICAL
   A. *The Preliterate Period*
      (*ca. 2000–750* B.C.)
   B. *The Earlier Archaic Period*
      (*ca. 750–600* B.C.)
   C. *The Later Archaic Period*
      (*ca. 600–480* B.C.)
   D. *The High Classical Period*
      (*ca. 480–400* B.C.)
   E. *The Fourth Century* B.C
   F. *The Hellenistic Age*
      (*ca. 300–21* B.C.)

GREEK POETRY

G. *The Roman Imperial Period*
II. MEDIEVAL. See BYZANTINE POETRY.
III. MODERN

I. CLASSICAL. A. *The Preliterate Period (ca. 2000–750 B.C.).* The earliest Gr. verses preserved in writing date from the 8th C. B.C., and poetry has continued to be composed in Gr. from that time until the present day (for a view of the trad. as a whole, see Trypanis). But recent research (see ORAL-FORMULAIC THEORY) indicates that the Gr. poetic trad. is in fact far older than the introduction of writing. The nature of the word-groups of which the Homeric epics are largely composed (see FORMULA), as well as the content of those epics, implies a pre-existing oral trad. of heroic dactylic poetry extending back into the Bronze Age civilization of the Mycenaeans, which came to an end about 1100 B.C. (see ORAL POETRY). The Aeolic (q.v.) meters that are widely used in extant Gr. p., notably by Sappho and Alcaeus, presuppose an even more ancient oral trad. of song, for they show clear affinities with the meters of the Indian Vedas; their ultimate origins may therefore date back as far as about 2000 B.C. (see INDO-EUROPEAN PROSODY).

The introduction of an alphabet specifically adapted to the recording of Gr., which took place not later than the mid 8th C. B.C., was no doubt the most important single event in the history of Gr. p. Gr. (and European) *literature* begins here, at the point where the songs could be fixed in permanent form and transmitted to posterity. Yet for many centuries after, Gr. p. continued to bear the deep imprint of ancient oral trad., incl. two of its most distinctive characteristics: (1) its mythological and heroic content and (2) its long dependence on oral performance as the means of reaching its public. (1) Ancient Gr. p. in nearly all genres worked within a frame of reference provided by the traditional gods and the heroes of the Bronze Age. That mythic-legendary world afforded the poets both their basic story-patterns and their paradigms of conduct. Heroic epic, many forms of choral lyric, and tragedy directly represented characters and incidents drawn from that world; epinician and monodic lyric (see EPINIKION; MONODY) constantly evoked it as a standard against which the human condition might be measured. (2) For more than three centuries after the introduction of writing, Gr. p. continued as before to be enacted orally, often with the accompaniment of music or dancing or both, before audiences as small as dinner-parties and as large as the vast crowds at religious festivals—Plato (*Ion* 535d) mentions audiences of 20,000 for performances of epic at such festivals. Thus, Gr. p. of the archaic and high-Cl. eras combined features that may at first sight seem contradictory. It had the elaboration, finish, and durability that belong to book-poetry as opposed to oral poetry, and yet so far as its intended public was concerned it remained an oral and often even visual entertainment.

To this inheritance from the preliterate trad. may also be attributed certain other characteristics of archaic and high-Cl. Gr. p.: its richness in aural effects (the immense variety and musicality of its quantitative meters, for instance, are unmatched in any European poetry and perhaps in any poetry whatever); the prominent part it played in the cultural life of the society as a whole; and the wide range of its human appeal, particularly in its most popular genres the epic and the drama, ever since.

B. *The Earlier Archaic Period (ca. 750–600 B.C.).* Thanks (it seems) to the introduction of writing, a great number of poems dating from this period were known to the later Greeks. With the exception of the major poems attributed to Homer and Hesiod, however, most of this work survives only in quotations, summaries, and allusions, but these are enough to permit a sketchmap, at least, of a complex literary landscape. All the major non-dramatic genres of subsequent Cl. poetry are already in existence, but they tend to be associated with particular geographical regions. Of these regions four stand out: Ionia, Lesbos, Sparta, and Boeotia.

The Ionic-speaking region embraced the central part of the west coast of Asia Minor and the islands that stretch from there toward Greece proper. Here the most important and longest-lasting of all Gr. and Lat. verseforms, and quite possibly of all verseforms known to man—the dactylic hexameter ($- \smile \smile | - \smile \smile | - \smile \smile | - \smile \smile | - \smile$)—seems to have achieved its definitive form. The "formulae" of which the hexameters of Homer are largely composed show elements of several Gr. dialects, but the predominant and apparently latest stratum is Ionic. It is generally inferred that the trad. of hexameter composition, after passing through the bards of at least two other dialectal regions, culminated in Ionia; and in fact the oldest Gr. trads. concerning Homer place him in Chios or Smyrna, cities that belong to this region. Ionia, then, was the probable birthplace of the two great epics that later Greece, and later Europe, perceived as the fountainhead of their lit., the *Iliad* and the *Odyssey*. Since the 18th c., a debate has raged over the genesis, authorship, unity, and dates of completion of these poems (see the fourth section of the bibl., esp. the intro. to Parry). But one certainty at least remains: from the earliest period they stood as models of the poetic art, above all for the satisfying unity of their plots and for their brilliant technique of characterization through speeches.

Also from Ionia during this period come the first examples of iambic and elegiac (qq.v.) poetry. In both these genres the poems were relatively short monologues, predominantly concerned with war, political and personal invective, and love; but elegiac tended more than iambic to include a gnomic element, i.e. meditation and advice on various aspects of the human condition. Metrically speaking, "iambic" by the ancient Gr. definition embraced poems composed in the iambic trimeter (a three-metron or, in modern parlance, six-foot iambic line [$\smile - \smile - | \smile - \smile - | \smile - \smile -$]) and in the trochaic tetrameter catalectic ($- \smile - \smile | - \smile - \smile | - \smile - \smile | - \smile -$). These two were to have a rich afterlife in Cl. (and to some extent later European) lit., the former as the standard verseform for dialogue in drama, the latter in comic and popular verse. Elegiac poetry was composed in elegiac couplets (q.v.)—a dactylic hexameter followed by a dactylic pentameter, so-called ($- \smile - \smile - | - \smile \smile - \smile \smile -$); this meter also was to become an enormously important medium, not least in the epigrams of the *Greek Anthology* (see ANTHOLOGY).

The most famous and, so far as the Greeks were in a position to know, the first composer in both genres was Archilochus, of the Ionic island Paros (fl. 648 B.C.). Some Gr. authors actually put his poetry on a level with that of Homer, in its very different way; the intensity and metrical perfection of his surviving fragments seem to confirm that judgment. Archilochus was also the earliest known composer of a third variety of "iambic" poetry as anciently defined, the epode (q.v.), which consisted of alternating long and short lines predominantly in iambic or dactylic meters; this was a superb instrument for invective from Archilochus to the Roman Horace. Several other iambic and elegiac poets flourished in 7th-c. Ionia, esp. Semonides, Callinus, and Mimnermus. The only distinguished elegiac poet working on the Gr. mainland during this period was Tyrtaeus (fl. ca. 640 B.C.), whose poems, composed in Sparta, survive in several extensive fragments.

The poetry of the Ionian region in all its genres is remarkable for the clarity of its expression and metrical form (the repeated line and the repeated couplet are the only options available), and for a rather sophisticated realism. For lyricism during this period, one must turn elsewhere. Gr. lyric poetry by the ancient definition was *poetry sung to instrumental accompaniment*. In practice it fell into two broad categories: choral lyric, which was normally a dance as well as a song, and might be composed in an almost infinite variety of meters and stanza forms; and solo lyric (sometimes misleadingly called personal lyric), composed for accompanied singing only, in a more limited though still extensive range of meters, and falling into short stanzas, most often quatrains. Both kinds of lyric emerge from the mists of preliteracy during this period, primarily in two centers: Aeolic-speaking Lesbos and Doric-speaking Sparta.

From the late 8th into the early 6th c., a series of choral and solo lyric poets is recorded in the isle of Lesbos. Most of them, such as Terpander and Arion, are now scarcely more than sonorous names, but Sappho and Alcaeus, who both flourished ca. 600 B.C., have left many fragments of solo lyric poetry. Both composed in approximately the same range of Aeolic lyric meters (two of the most famous Aeolic stanza forms, the "Sapphic" and the "Alcaic" [qq.v.], are named after them), and in the same soft and musical Aeolic brogue; but in content and tone they are vastly unlike each other. For the power and beauty of her love-poetry Sappho has no peer in Gr. lit., and few in any lit. Alcaeus' songs on the turbulent politics of the island, his hymns to the gods, and above all his drinking-songs, if less elegantly crafted, were to prove of great influence on later European lyric.

Seventh-century Sparta was famed for the competitions in choral lyric at its great religious festivals, but the only one of its poets about whom anything significant is known is Alcman (second half of the 7th c.). From his numerous and in some cases quite substantial fragments it can be deduced that his choral lyrics already embodied the most striking characteristics of the choral lyric genre as it was later known. The long polymetric stanzas of his First Partheneion, for example, its extensively narrated examples from myth or saga, its gnomic passages in which the singers reflect on the universal meaning of their tale, can still find parallels in Pindar and Bacchylides a couple of centuries later.

In central Greece, Boeotia in this period saw the composition of a great number of poems; only three survive complete, the *Theogony*, the *Works and Days*, and the *Shield of Herakles*, but a fourth, the *Ehoiai* or *Catalogue of Women*, can now be restored to a considerable extent from papyrus fragments. Both the lost and the surviving poems of the Boeotian corpus were generally ascribed in ancient times to the great Hesiod, who seems to have flourished ca. 700 B.C., but most modern critics deny the authenticity of the *Shield*, and several that of the *Ehoiai*. In any case, all are composed in a medium that is virtually indistinguishable from that of the Homeric epics: the meter is the same, almost the same formulary is employed, and the same mixture of dialects is evident. But there the resemblance ends. The Hesiodic works show nothing of the architectonic skill of Homer, or of his genius for realizing character through speech. They are essentially episodic codifications of ancient lore. The *Theogony* presents the origin and history of the Gr. gods, organizing the material by generations; the *Ehoiai* followed the history of the heroic families by clans and, within clans, by generations; the *Works and Days* is a manual of the art of living, proceeding from ethical and political considerations to practical instruction in farming, navigation, and the rules of daily conduct. But this essentially catalogic principle of composition does not mean that Hesiod lacks art. Largely through the characteristically archaic techniques of ring-composition (q.v.) and significant repetition, he succeeds in making his topics and episodes cohere within themselves and between each other. Like Homer, Hesiod knows how to capture and hold his hearer, if by quite different means. One un-Homeric technique that appears in Hesiod for the first time in European lit. is that of the authorial "I": in the proem to the *Theogony* and through much of the *Works and Days* he builds up an impressive persona of "Hesiod," imparting both weight and liveliness to his teachings.

Much other hexameter poetry was composed in various regions of Greece during this period; the hexameter in fact seems early on to have become a kind of poetic *koine*. Particularly important in its time was the "Epic Cycle," a catena of medium-length epics by various hands that covered the entire Troy-saga. Other epics since lost are known to have told of the legendary history of Corinth, the story of the Argonauts, and the house of Oedipus. Other extant examples of early hexameter poetry are certain poems in the heterogeneous collection that has come down to us under the title of the *Homeric Hymns*: at least Hymns II (to Demeter), III (to Apollo), and V (to Aphrodite) probably belong to this period. It is a remarkable fact that by about 600 B.C. all the major nondramatic genres of Gr. p. were already in existence: heroic epic, iambic, elegiac, solo and choral lyric, and, at least in some sense, didactic (for Hesiodic poetry, though far wider in scope than the didactic poetry of later antiquity, was certainly its inspiration).

C. *The Later Archaic Period (ca. 600–480 B.C.)*. The diversity of later archaic Gr. p. was great, but two general trends may be distinguished: the major poetic genres become less tied to specific regions of Greece, and lyric poetry in particular shows a growing sophistication, metrically as well as intellectually. Several of the poets who worked in this period have left names famous throughout subsequent Western lit., despite the fact that none of their books has survived intact. Composition in epic hexameters continued in many parts of Greece; some poems of the Epic Cycle and of the Hesiodic corpus, as well as several of the Homeric Hymns, probably belong to the earlier part of this period. The most significant discernible devel. is the gradual disintegration of the system of formulae characteristic of the older epics. By the late 6th c. the first tentative signs of a "literary" or "secondary" epic may perhaps be made out in the work of Panyassis of Halicarnassus.

An outstanding exponent of both elegiac and iambic poetry was the statesman Solon (fl. 594 B.C.), the earliest recorded Athenian poet. The quite substantial fragments of his work are partly gnomic or personal in content—in this conforming to Ionian precedent—but the majority address political principles and issues connected with Solon's famous reforms of the Athenian economy and constitution. Across the Aegean, Hipponax of Ephesus (fl. 540 B.C.) culminated the Ionian trad. of iambic invective and lampoon. His favorite meter was one that now appears for the first time, the

scazon or limping iambic trimeter (⏕ – ⏑ – | ⏕ – ⏑ – | ⏕ – – ⏕ ; see CHOLIAMBUS). The last of the major archaic elegists, Theognis of Megara (second half of the 6th c.?), is represented by a large number of poems, predominantly gnomic in character, in the 1300-line anthology of elegiacs that somehow survived the Middle Ages and now goes under the title of *Theognidea*. Finally, the elegiac, iambic, and hexameter fragments of Xenophanes of Colophon (ca. 570–478 B.C.) open up a new dimension in poetry, the philosophic and scientific; his penetrating physical and ethnological observations and his criticism of Gr. anthropomorphic religion are expressed in lively and quite elegant verse. The two other Gr. poet-philosophers who followed him, Parmenides and Empedocles, belong rather to the history of philosophy than to that of poetry.

In lyric poetry there were spectacular developments. Recent papyrus discoveries (summarized in *CHCL* 1.6.3.) have greatly enriched our knowledge of Stesichorus of Himera in Sicily, who seems to have flourished in the first half of the 6th c. They fully confirm the ancient trads. that he composed songs very much in the epic manner, and even approaching the epic scale, and also that he adopted or perhaps invented the practice of composing choral lyric by triads (strophe, metrically responding antistrophe, nonresponding epode—qq.v.), which is the most striking formal characteristic of subsequent Gr. choral lyric. Ibycus of Rhegium in south Italy (fl. ca. 535 B.C.) and Simonides of the Aegean isle of Keos (556–468) have each left superb fragments of lyric. Simonides in particular seems to have been a great innovative master, turning his hand to many different varieties of choral lyric, incl. the epinikion (q.v.—which he may have originated) and the short epigram (q.v.) in elegiac couplets, a form which had an immense literary future before it.

Anacreon of Teos in Ionia (ca. 575–490) brought solo lyric poetry to heights of wit and technical polish that were matched in Cl. times perhaps only by the Roman poets Catullus and Horace. His many brilliant fragments sing mostly of love and wine, and only once or twice of the more somber themes of old age and death. Metrically he was not a great innovator, but he seems to have been the first poet to make extensive use of the catchy rhythm ⏑ ⏑ – ⏑ – ⏑ – ⏕, later called the Anacreontic (q.v.) after him. (This meter plays a great part in the extant collection of light verse datable from the Roman period that goes under the title *Anacreontea*, the poems of which had great popularity and influence in 16th- to 18th-c. Europe.)

The most momentous poetic devel. in this period was the introduction of poetic drama. Officially sponsored performances of tragedy at the Great Dionysia festival in Athens are first attested in ca. 534 B.C., and of comedy in 486. The ultimate origins of both genres, and their histories down to the time of the great Persian invasion of Greece in 480/79 B.C., are still problematic for want of adequate evidence; what is known, with some of the speculations on what is known, is collected in Pickard-Cambridge. Our extant examples of tragedy and comedy (qq.v.) date only from the ensuing period. Scarcely more than the names survive of the two earliest recorded tragedians, Thespis and Choerilus, and not very many fragments of the third, Phrynichus (active 511–476). But it is indisputable that well before the Persian Wars, at Athens, the decisive steps had been taken toward the creation of drama. That was Athens' supreme contribution to Gr. p., a contribution that was to transform the character of ancient lit. and deeply to affect the course of Western lit. as a whole.

D. *The High Classical Period (ca. 480–400 B.C.).* After the Persian Wars, Athenian power and splendor reached their peak. The years between 479 and Athens' defeat by Sparta in 404 saw the creation of a naval empire in the eastern Mediterranean, the Periclean democracy, the erection of the great buildings and sculptures on the Acropolis— and the composition of all the surviving masterpieces of Attic tragedy. Elsewhere in Greece, choral lyric seems to have been the only poetic genre that was still practiced with great success. Our first-hand knowledge of the tragic art depends almost exclusively on the extant plays of the three most famous Attic tragedians, Aeschylus (525–456 B.C.), Sophocles (496–406), and Euripides (484–406); the earliest surviving example, Aeschylus' *Persians*, was produced in 472. On the strictly *dramatic* aspects of the art, much is to be found elsewhere (see Lesky). Viewed in the context of Gr. p., tragedy is remarkable for the manner in which it combined and consummated the achievements of so many pre-existing poetic genres. In tragic tone, in characterization through speech, and to some extent even in plot construction, the tragedians picked up and developed precedents in Homeric epic (as Aristotle implies throughout the *Poetics*, e.g. 1449b17: "anybody who can tell a good tragedy from a bad one can do the same with epics"). In metric they owed less to the epic than to iambic, solo lyric, and choral lyric. They added little to the existing repertoire of Gr. meters but combining freely metrical elements that had previously been confined to separate genres. The result, esp. in the choral odes and the arias of tragedy, is a poetry of unprecedented richness and variety in tone, tempo, and rhythm. Fifth-century Attic tragedy is thus both the starting-point of European drama and the final synthesis of all the earlier modes of Gr. p.

Probably an art of such power and wide popular appeal was bound, in time, to overshadow the traditional genres of Gr. p., and by the end of the 5th c. this process had taken place. Elegiac and solo lyric continued to be practiced until the last few decades, but only falteringly. Choral lyric alone was still able to reach great heights, but even

that genre faded out of history with the death of Pindar of Thebes (ca. 518–438 B.C.). The most famous of all the choral lyricists, Pindar was master of a great range of song-types for a variety of occasions. When the Hellenistic scholars came to edit his complete poems, they grouped them under the headings of *hymns, paeans, dithyrambs, partheneia* (songs for girl-choruses), *hyporchemes* (dance-poems), *encomia, threnoi* (death-laments), and *epinikia* (victory-odes); the titles may not in every case have reflected Pindar's intent, but they give a vivid notion of the diapason of Gr. choral lyric. Of all these, only the *Epinikia*, praising the victors at the four great athletic festivals, have survived intact (see EPINIKION). Varying in length from one to thirteen triads, these odes concentrate not so much on the transient details of the athletic success as on its significance in the divine and human cosmos: the human victory is measured against mythological precedents the evocation of which—sometimes continuously, sometimes only in brief glimpses of matchless vividness—may occupy much of the ode.

Pindaric poetry is not easy reading. It may well have been more readily comprehensible in its original performance, when it was *heard* and its message was reinforced by music and choral dancing; its allusiveness, the intricacy of its word-placing and metric, and the never-failing originality and precision of its diction keep a reader in constant tension. But it is poetry of unsurpassed honesty, intensity, and profundity. Far more accessible is the choral lyric of Bacchylides of Keos, many of whose songs—mostly epinician odes and dithyrambs—have been discovered on papyri in modern times. Bacchylides was a younger poet than Pindar, but all his datable poems fall within the period 485–452 B.C., well before the end of Pindar's long career. Clarity and grace mark his poetry; his meters are simple and tuneful, his mythical narratives interestingly chosen and straightforwardly presented.

The first extant Gr. comedy is Aristophanes' *Acharnians*, produced in Athens in 425 B.C. Since antiquity it has been customary to divide the history of the Attic comic art into three phases, Old, Middle, and New. Old Comedy extended from the institution of the comic contests at the Great Dionysia in 486 B.C. until the opening decades of the 4th c., but most of our knowledge of it depends on Aristophanes' 11 surviving plays. Of all the poetry created by the Greeks, Old Comedy has the widest metrical and stylistic range and allows by far the freest play of fantasy. Its basic dialect is the local vernacular—colloquial Attic speech in all its vigor and explicitness, sexual and scatological. Further, the extant Aristophanic comedies display an extraordinary aptitude for the parody of every other poetic genre, and not least of tragedy. But Old Comedy's single most extraordinary feature was its total freedom to create characters and situations. In most Gr. p. up to that time, the basic narratives and characters were drawn from the ancient myths and sagas. The majority of Old Comic plots, however, seem to have been free fictions, some of them blossoming into poetic fantasies that might embrace Hades (as in Aristophanes' *Frogs*) or the entire universe (as in his *Birds*).

The last two or three decades of this period saw a revolutionary movement in Gr. p. and music which is known to us primarily from allusions in Old Comedy, from a partially preserved lyric text, the *Persians*, by Timotheus of Miletus (fl. ca. 450–360 B.C.), and from some of the songs in Euripides' last plays. The most remarkable technical features of this "New Music" were its total abandonment of the triadic arrangement of responding stanzas that had characterized all earlier lyric verse and the opening of a fatal split between the words and the melody of a lyric (see MUSIC AND POETRY). For the first time, the evidence suggests, one syllable, instead of being set to one note, might be extended over several notes, as in modern song. These and other similarly radical innovations in the instrumentation and performance of poetry effectively meant the end of the trad. of archaic and high Cl. lyric poetry that had flourished since at least the early 7th c.

E. *The Fourth Century* B.C. The outstanding event in Gr. lit. of this period is the triumph of prose. Prose as a literary medium had developed rather slowly in the outer regions of the Gr. world from the mid 6th c. B.C. onward. In Athens it did not establish itself until the second half of the 5th c.; only in the 4th c., and above all in the works of Isocrates, Plato, and Aristotle, did it acquire an unchallengeable position as the medium for the exploration of the deepest human concerns, philosophical, psychological, and political. Accordingly, the poet was gradually forced from his supreme role as universal teacher into the role of, at most, entertainer. The most flourishing variety of Gr. p. in the 4th c. was comedy. Aristophanes' last surviving play, the *Ploutos* (388 B.C.), is often taken to mark the transition from Old to Middle Comedy. Certainly the relative tameness of its central comic fantasy, its drastic reduction of the chorus' role, and its almost total elimination of any lyric element all seem to have been characteristics of Middle Comedy, which is conventionally dated ca. 380–320. New Comedy (ca. 320–250) is much more accessible to us, thanks to extensive papyrus discoveries over the past century. Most of these are plays by the most famous of the New Comic poets, Menander (ca. 342–291 B.C.). The New Comic plots continue the trad. of Old Comedy in that they are fictional and set in contemporary Greece, but the fictions are now much more restricted in imaginative range. On the other hand, Menander crafts exquisite plots and creates a long series of delicately shaded character studies. The predominant meter of his comedies is the iambic trimeter, occasionally varied with iambic or trochaic te-

trameters. Lyric now has no place in the fabric of the comedies, although they are divided into acts (regularly, it seems, five) by pauses in the scripts marked *Khorou*—"[song] of a chorus"—apparently songs unrelated to the dramatic action, and probably not composed by the playwright. It was this last traceable phase of Gr. poetic drama, through the Lat. adaptations by Plautus and Terence, which was to provide the formal model for both the tragedy and comedy of Ren. Europe: the five-act play in iambic verse.

Noncomic poetry of the 4th c. is reduced to pitifully few fragments. Tragedies continued to be produced in large numbers at the Great Dionysia in Athens, though, perhaps significantly, the masterpieces of the three great 5th-c. tragedians now began to be performed alongside the new compositions. The New Music movement in lyric poetry (see above) had apparently run its course by the middle of the century. The epic and elegiac poems by Antimachus of Colophon (fl. ca. 400 B.C.) had their admirers in later antiquity. But on the whole, the Gr. poetic impulse that had been sustained without break from preliterate times had temporarily exhausted itself. The stage was clear for a new kind of poetry.

F. *The Hellenistic Age (ca. 300–31 B.C.).* In Athens, New Comedy—the last survivor of any of the publicly performed Cl. genres—continued in full vigor during the earlier part of this period. Elsewhere the circumstances and character of Gr. p. changed radically. The conquests of Alexander the Great (d. 323 B.C.) had extended the power, and with it the lang., of the Greeks into the Near and Middle East, a shift soon followed by a shift in the focuses of literary activity. The newly founded Gr. metropolises, above all Egyptian Alexandria, attracted talent of every kind from wherever Gr. was spoken (see ALEXANDRIANISM). But the new poetic culture that arose in those vast cities, with their heterogeneous populations severed from the living traditions of the homeland, was necessarily a culture of the book; its audience was no longer the citizen in the marketplace. The result was a learned poetry of exquisite technical finish and literary allusiveness—a poetry, for the first time in this story, analogous to that of Virgil, Milton, or Eliot. At the same time, however, the Hellenistic poets were very conscious of the need to validate the new kind of poetry by ensuring the *appearance* of continuity with the older Gr. poetic trad. Many of the archaic genres were now revived in form, if transfigured in scope and tone. The most versatile of the Hellenistic poets, Callimachus (active in Alexandria ca. 280–245 B.C.), offers a good example of the process. His *Hymns* deliberately recall the Homeric Hymns of archaic Greece. Yet these Callimachean counterparts are not so much acts of piety as masterpieces of delicate wit and fantasy; and more than one of them incorporates a literary evocation of the festival at which it was to be *imagined* as delivered. Similar imitations and transpositions are to be found in Callimachus' *Iambi*, where Hipponax is an acknowledged model, and in his *Aetia*, where he invokes the precedents of Mimnermus and Hesiod.

In this general revival of the archaic genres it was impossible that Homer should be neglected, but he now elicited very diverse literary responses. To Callimachus and many other Hellenistic poets, notably Theocritus, the vast scale and heroic temper of Homeric epic were no longer achievable or even desirable, for these men aimed above all at brevity, polish, and realism. They devised their own brand of narrative poetry, the brief epic, adopting (with refinements) the Homeric medium, the hexameter, but limiting the scale to a few hundred lines. Within this space there could be no question of retelling a heroic saga; rather, the poet would illuminate a single heroic episode, bringing out its full color and detail. Examples of this form are Callimachus' fragmentary *Hekale*, Theocritus' *Idyll* 13 on Herakles and Hylas, and, at a later date, Moschus' *Europa*. A number of Hellenistic poets, however, did compose large-scale epics, though the only one that survives is the *Argonautica* of Apollonius Rhodius, a younger contemporary of Callimachus. In its versification, its lang., and its similes, this poem abundantly testifies to Apollonius' long study of Homer, yet in content and tone it is utterly un-Homeric. Apollonius' passive and hesitant hero, Jason, belongs rather to our world than to the world of Achilles and Odysseus, and the depiction in Book 3 of Medea's love for him is a breakthrough, at least in the epic context.

Hesiod was the alleged model for the many didactic poems composed in the Hellenistic period, though the wide human scope of Hesiodic poetry tended to be reduced simply to the versification of this technology or that. The most notable surviving example is Aratus' *Phainomena*, on astronomy and meteorology. The only altogether new genre created by the Hellenistic poets (or, if not created, adapted from subliterary songs and mummings of an earlier period) was pastoral (q.v.) poetry. The earliest known examples are the work of Theocritus, who was approximately a contemporary of Callimachus and Apollonius. The collection of his poems that has reached us under the title of *Idylls* consists of relatively short pieces, mostly in hexameters, but only a minority of them are pastorals, and one of Theocritus' most brilliant dialogue-poems, *Idyll* 15, is set in the hubbub of Alexandria itself. Both the nonpastoral and the pastoral poems display the Callimachean preference for brevity and precise detail, but in his control of verbal music Theocritus may be thought to surpass even Callimachus.

The great creative impetus of Hellenistic poetry was limited to the first half of the 3d c. B.C. Thereafter very little new ground was broken. The various genres that were then re-established or created continued to be practiced, but the surviving examples are of little poetic significance.

G. *The Roman Imperial Period*. With the battle of Actium in 31 B.C., Rome's empire over the Mediterranean and Near East was decisively established. Paradoxically, it was the *Roman* poets who henceforth most successfully exploited the legacy of Hellenistic Gr. p.; the three great poems of Virgil himself, for instance, would be inconceivable but for the precedents of Hellenistic pastoral, didactic, and epic. Though a great many poems were composed in Gr. under the Empire, none matches the work of the major Roman poets in intrinsic interest or influence on subsequent European poetry. Thus the trad. of ancient Gr. p., while competently perpetuated during this period, was gradually losing its momentum. Two slow but steady developments, one linguistic and the other social, were finally to bring that trad. to an end: a change in the pronunciation of Gr., whereby quantity is replaced by stress; and the triumph of Christian imagination over the pagan. From about the beginning of the Christian era, the distinction in colloquial Gr. speech between long and short vowel-quantities began to disappear, and the musical pitch-accent that had prevailed since archaic times began to be replaced by a tonic stress-accent similar to that of modern Gr. or Eng. Literary Gr. p. responded only very slowly to these changes, but by the 6th c. A.D., the characteristic Byzantine versification was well established, its guiding principle no longer syllable quantity but recurrent stress accent (see CLASSICAL PROSODY). In this fashion Gr. p. gradually lost the superb metrical system that in the hands of Pindar, the Attic tragedians, and Theocritus had generated such an incomparable wealth and variety of verbal music. Simultaneously, Gr. p. was also being gradually distanced from pagan mythology—from the rich intellectual and imaginative resource that had provided it with its themes since the preliterate era. As a consequence of these two developments, Gr. p. was no more the same art. No absolute date can be set to that final transformation, and exceptions to the general trend can always be found: for instance, scholars continued to compose verses in quantitative Gr. meters down through the Middle Ages and Ren. (see CLASSICAL METERS IN MODERN LANGUAGES). But effectively the change had taken place by the end of the 6th c. A.D.

Most of the Gr. p. that survives from the Imperial Roman period falls under one of three genres: didactic, epic, and epigram. Tragedy and comedy were no longer composed, and the few known examples of lyric poetry are not very striking either in substance or metric. The didactic poets followed closely in the steps of their Hellenistic predecessors, composing versified textbooks of varying interest and merit on such subjects as geography and fishing. Epic both mythological and panegyric (i.e. celebrating the exploits of some political figure) was very widely composed. Much the most interesting example is the

Dionysiaca composed by Nonnus of Panopolis in Egypt in the early 5th c. This story of the triumphant career of Dionysus, in 48 books (matching the total number of books in the *Iliad* and *Odyssey*), is the last major Gr. poem in hexameters.

Alone among the Gr. genres, the epigram (q.v.) never fell out of fashion. This kind of brief, finely worked, and pointed poem, somewhat comparable in finish and compactness to the haiku or the closed neoclassical couplet (qq.v.), most often took the form of one to four elegiac couplets (q.v.). The earliest examples are inscriptions (*epigrammata*) on gravestones or votive objects of the archaic period. During the 5th c. B.C. the form was increasingly adapted to literary purposes, and the range of its content was extended beyond the funereal and dedicatory to many other human concerns—above all, love, humor, and wine. The great surviving corpus of epigrams, the *Greek Anthology*, put together for the most part by the 10th c. A.D., is one of the most moving and impressive of all the monuments of ancient Gr. p. (see ANTHOLOGY). Within it are found epigrams by most of the famous poets, and philosophers too, composed over a span of something like 14 centuries.

See also AEOLIC; ALEXANDRIANISM; CHORUS; CLASSICAL POETICS; CLASSICAL PROSODY; CLASSICISM; COMEDY; DITHYRAMB; EPIC; EPINIKION; HEXAMETER; HYMN; INDO-EUROPEAN PROSODY; LATIN POETRY; LYRIC; MELIC POETRY; MONODY; ORAL POETRY; PAEAN; RECUSATIO; TRAGEDY; TRAGICOMEDY.

BIBLIOGRAPHIES: *L'Année Philologique: Bibliographie critique et analytique de l'antiquité gréco-latine* 1– (1927–); *The Cl. World Bibl. of Gr. Drama and Poetry* (1978); *Gr. and Roman Authors: A Checklist of Crit.*, ed. T. Gwinup and F. Dickinson, 2d ed. (1982)—covers 70 authors.

TEXTS: Bibliotheca Teubneriana series (1888–)—crit. texts without trs.; Loeb Cl. Library series (1912–)—texts, with facing trs., of all the major poets; J. M. Edmonds, *Lyra graeca*, 3 v. (1928; rpt 1952–58), *Elegy and Iambus*, 2 v. (1911; rpt 1979–82); *Callimachus*, ed. R. Pfeiffer, 2 v. (1949); *Theocritus*, ed. A. S. F. Gow, 2 v. (1950); D. L. Page, *Poetae melici graeci* (1962); M. L. West, *Iambi et elegi graeci ante alexandrum cantati* (1971–72); Oxford Cl. Texts series (1980–)—good critical texts without trs.; D. A. Campbell, *Gr. Lyric*, 4 v. (1982–)—texts with facing trs.

ANTHOLOGIES: *Oxford Book of Gr. Verse*, ed. C. M. Bowra et al. (1930); *Oxford Book of Gr. Verse in Tr.*, ed. T. Higham and C. M. Bowra (1938); D. A. Campbell, *Gr. Lyric Poetry* (1976); *An Anthol. of Alexandrian Poetry*, ed. J. Clack (1982); *Penguin Book of Gr. Verse*, ed. C. A. Trypanis, 3d ed. (1984).

GENERAL HISTORIES: F. Susemihl, *Gesch. der griechischen Literatur in der Alexandriner-Zeit*, 2 v. (1891–92); A. and M. Croiset, *Histoire de la litt. grecque*, 5 v. (1909–28); Schmid and Stählin; Trypanis; CHCL, v. 1.

HISTORY AND CRITICISM: D. L. Page, *Sappho and Alcaeus* (1955); A. E. Harvey, "The Classif. of Gr.

Lyric Poetry," *ClassQ* n.s. 5 (1955); R. Lattimore, *The Poetry of Gr. Tragedy* (1958); T. B. L. Webster, *From Mycenae to Homer* (1959), *Hellenistic Poetry and Art* (1965); A. Körte and P. Händel, *Die Hellenistische Dichtung* (1960); Bowra; A. Pickard-Cambridge, *Dithyramb, Tragedy and Comedy*, 2d ed. (1962); G. S. Kirk, *The Songs of Homer* (1962), *Homer and the Oral Trad.* (1975); W. B. Stanford, *The Sound of Gr.* (1967); Parry; B. Snell, *Poetry and Society* (1971); F. Cairns, *Generic Composition in Gr. and Roman Poetry* (1972); A. Lesky, *Die Tragische Dichtung der Hellenen*, 3d ed. (1972), tr. as *Gr. Tragic Poetry* (1983); K. J. Dover, *Aristophanic Comedy* (1972); M. L. West, "Gr. P. 2000–700 B.C.," *ClassQ* 23 (1973); G. M. Kirkwood, *Early Gr. Monody: The History of a Poetic Type* (1974); H. F. Fränkel, *Early Gr. P. and Philosophy*, tr. M. Hadas and J. Willis (1975); B. Peabody, *The Winged Word* (1975); W. G. Arnott, Intro. to Loeb ed. of Menander, v. 1 (1979)—comedy; H. White, *Essays in Hellenistic Poetry* (1980), *New Essays in Hellenistic Poetry* (1985), *Studies in Late Gr. Epic Poetry* (1987); R. Janko, *Homer, Hesiod, and the Hymns* (1982); D. A. Campbell, *The Golden Lyre* (1983); B. Snell, *Three Archaic Poets* (1983), *The Art of Bacchylides* (1985); W. G. Thalmann, *Conventions of Form and Thought in Early Gr. Epic Poetry* (1984); A. W. H. Adkins, *Poetic Craft in the Early Gr. Elegists* (1985); D. S. Carne-Ross, *Pindar* (1985); J. Herington, *Poetry into Drama* (1985); *The Iliad: A Commentary*, ed. G. W. Kirk, 6 v. (1985; v. 1, on *Iliad* 1–4); G. F. Else, *Plato and Aristotle on Poetry* (1987); M. W. Edwards, *Homer* (1987); R. L. Fowler, *The Nature of Early Gr. Lyric* (1987); B. Gentili, *Poetry and Its Public in Ancient Greece*, tr. A. T. Cole (1988); G. O. Hutchinson, *Hellenistic Poetry* (1988); R. Lamberton, *Hesiod* (1988); J. M. Snyder, *The Woman and the Lyre: Women Writers in Cl. Greece and Rome* (1989); R. Hamilton, *The Architecture of Hesiodic Poetry* (1989).

PROSODY: Wilamowitz; Koster; Maas; Dale; Halporn et al.; Snell; West.   C.J.H.

II. MEDIEVAL. See BYZANTINE POETRY; POLITICAL VERSE.

III. MODERN. After the fall of Constantinople to the Turks in 1453, and until the Gr. War of Independence (1821–28), poetry flourished mainly in Gr. lands under Venetian influence. The island of Crete was the most important center. In the 16th and first half of the 17th c. it gave birth to a poetry that, though depending on It. models, has a character of its own. The masterpiece of Cretan lit. is the *Erotokritos*, an epico-lyric poem of 10,000 rhyming 15-syllable political verses (q.v.) composed by Vitzentzos Kornaros. The story—the chivalrous love of Erotokritos for Aretousa and their union after long and arduous adventures—follows the Frankish romance *Paris et Vienne*, but at the same time, the influence of Ariosto and of the Cretan folk song is evident.

In the remainder of the Gr. world, then under Turkish rule, the only noteworthy poems composed were the folksongs. Their heyday was the 18th c., and many folk love songs, songs of travel, lullabies, and dirges are of a remarkable beauty and freshness, superior to any poetry in Gr. since the close of the 9th c. In the 18th c. we also find the first influence of Fr. lit. upon Gr. writing in the work of Athanasios Christopoulos and John Velaras, the two most important precursors of the poetry which followed the liberation of Greece.

The liberation, finally achieved in 1828, made Athens, the capital of the country, the center of all intellectual life. It was there that the Romantic School of Athens flourished, whose founder and leading spirit was Alexander Soutsos (1803–63). He was a fervent admirer of Victor Hugo and Byron, but his exuberant romantic and patriotic writings did not capture the spirit of their models. Though he is terse and vigorous as a satirist, the great influence he exercised upon Gr. p. was not always beneficial. The other main representatives of the Romantic School of Athens—Panagiotis Soutsos, Alexander Rizos Rangavis, George Zalokostas, Theodore Orphanidis, Elias Tantalidis, and John Karasoutsas—were all slaves of an exaggerated romanticism. They use a stilted and archaic form of Gr. (the *katharevousa*) and are painstakingly patriotic. Achilles Paraschos (1838–95) is the leading figure in the last period of the school. His contemporaries George Paraschos, Angelos Vlachos, Alexander Vyzantios, Demetrios Paparrhegopoulos, Spyridon Vasiliadis, and George Vizyenos were all overshadowed by his reputation, in spite of the greater sincerity and more delicate technique of many of their works.

The Romantic School of Athens with its rhetorical profuseness, hackneyed patriotism, and stilted, purist Gr. was superseded by the New School of Athens, which resulted from a fresh assessment of Gr. national values and the linguistic movement to introduce the spoken tongue (the *demotiki*, whence "demotic") into lit. The demotic had already been successfully used by the School of the Ionian Islands, of which the greatest representative was Dionysios Solomos (1798–1857). Like other members of the Ionian aristocracy of his day he was bilingual and, having received his education in Italy, wrote his first poems in It. His early works in Gr. were short lyrics, but the War of Independence stirred him to more ambitious projects. As the years passed, his philosophic approach to art and life deepened, coming to express itself in verses of unique delicacy and balance. His is a figure outstanding in the whole of European lit. because he finally succeeded in combining harmoniously the Classical and the romantic spirit. From the *Hymn to Liberty* (the first stanzas of which became the Gr. national anthem) to the *Free Besieged,* which sings of the heroic resistance of Missolonghi, we can trace the agony and artistic achievement of a highly spiritual nature. Unfortunately, however, most of his mature work exists as only partially completed texts. In the struggle that

continued from the Byzantine era between the *katharevousa* and the *demotiki* as the lang. of lit., Solomos marks a turning point. By choosing the latter he pointed the way which all subsequent Gr. p. worthy of the name was to follow. Moreover, he introduced into Gr. a number of Western metrical forms (the sestina, the ottava, the terza rima) which freed Gr. p. from the monotony of the 15-syllable verse.

Of the other poets of the Ionian School, the most important are Andreas Calvos (1792–1869) and Aristotle Valaoritis (1824–39). Calvos drew heavily on the Gr. classics to write an austere and often moralizing poetry in forms that inspired several important 20th-c. poets, such as Elytis and Karouzos. Valaoritis, though over-romantic and grandiloquent, was greatly admired in his day and became the link between the Ionian School, the "Demotic Movement," and the New School of Athens.

About 1880, a young group of poets, influenced by the violent criticism of E. Rhoides, formed the New School of Athens. They aspired to become the Gr. *Parnassians* (q.v.), masters of a restrained and objective art. The central figure was Kostis Palamas (1859–1943), a man of wide reading whose works blended not only the ancient and modern Gr. trads. but also the social and spiritual convulsions of the late 19th and early 20th cs. *The Dodecalogue of the Gypsy* is perhaps his central achievement. Its hero the Gypsy musician, a symbol of freedom and art, gradually deepens into the patriot, the Greek, and finally the "Hellene"—citizen and teacher of the world. This powerful epico-lyrical work, together with *The King's Flute,* an historical epic, and *Life Immovable,* the most important of his lyric collections, confirmed his influence on such contemporary poets as George Drosinis and John Polemis and on their successors: John Gryparis in his mastery of lang., Constantine Hatzopoulos in his sense of rhythm, Miltiadis Malakasis and Lambros Porfyras in their playful charm, and Costas Crystallis in his idyllic tone. It is the poets of this generation who also introduced symbolism and free verse (qq.v.) into Gr. p., which greatly enriched and enlivened it in the 20th c. After Palamas the most important figure of his school is undoubtedly Angelos Sikelianos (1884–1952). In his powerful verse, Gr. nature and history are seen in the light of a Dionysiac mysticism. This, together with a rich, incisive diction that brings landscape, the human form, and abstract thought into clear-cut relief, has produced some of the most striking lyrical poetry in the 20th c.

However, an equally important Gr. poet who remained untouched by the influence of Palamas was C. P. Cavafy (1863–1933). An Alexandrian both by birth and sensibility, Cavafy's major achievement was the creation of a mythical world of diaspora Hellenism dominated by irony, hedonism, and a tragic vision that celebrates those who face disaster with an honest self-awareness. The myth he created, though smaller in scale, parallels the imaginative worlds fashioned by eminent Anglo-Am. contemporaries such as Yeats, Joyce, Pound, and Eliot, and, along with his acute treatment of eroticism, eventually established his reputation as the most original and gifted Gr. poet of this century. Nikos Kazantzakis (1885–1957), well-known as a novelist, was also the author of a formidable 33,333-line modern sequel to the *Odyssey* in which the Odyssean hero, haunted by the idea of nihilism, searches for a personal belief among the various modes of thought that his new journey explores and ends in nihilism.

More significant than the poetry of Kazantzakis is that of Kostas Varnalis (1884–1974) and Takis Papatsonis (1895–1976). The former, with a strong political voice, was recognized as the last important traditional poet of his day, while the latter, esp. innovative in technique during the 1920s, wrote mystic religious poetry. The modernist movement known as the Generation of the Thirties is the most accomplished group of poets to have emerged in Greece during this century. Two of this group, George Seferis (1900–71) and Odysseus Elytis (b. 1911), were awarded the Nobel Prize in Lit. Seferis brought into Gr. p. a style, method, and vision that have often been compared to those of T. S. Eliot, and though he has been perhaps as influential in changing the course of poetry in his country as Eliot was in the Anglo-Am. trad., Seferis offers an image of the modern predicament that is deeply rooted in his own experience, in the Gr. landscape, and in Gr. lit., from Homer and the Attic tragedians through the 17th-c. Cretan renaissance and the Demotic Movement of the 19th and 20th cs. His major contributions have lain in creating a poetic lang. that is rich in nuance while spare in decoration, and a dramatic mode that makes use of mythical figures provided with a modern psyche and a contemporary habitation. Elytis was among those who introduced Fr. surrealism (q.v.) into Gr. p., though even in his earliest work, characterized by the yoking together of disparate images and a sometimes flamboyant lyricism reminiscent of Dylan Thomas, he projects a personal mythology that celebrates the natural and human features of his homeland. His most mature work includes the intricately constructed *The Axion Esti*, an extended secular hymn that draws on the Gr. Orthodox liturgy and the 19th-c. demotic trad. to evoke the spiritual dimension of those elements in the world of the senses that the poet feels to be most worthy of praise.

Three other poets of the same generation, Andreas Embirikos (1901–75), Nikos Engonopoulos (b. 1910), and Nikos Gatsos (b. 1912), confirmed the importance of surrealism in modern Gr. p. Embirikos was the most ambitious of the three, his use of the mode at times serving a large structure and an apocalyptic vision. Yannis Ritsos (b. 1909) and Nikiforos Vretakos (b. 1911), of the same generation, were more overtly political. Ritsos, the most prolific of the group, succeeded over the years in creating a broad if stylistically sparse poetic landscape in which the old gods no longer survive and in which their dispossessed creatures, wounded and still threatened by the tragic civilization they have inherited, move cautiously through ruined cities and across arid plains. Ritsos remains the most influential Gr. poet after Cavafy and Seferis, with wide international recognition.

The group of poets known as the First Post-War Generation found their principal resource in the Second World War and the Civil War that followed. Takis Sinopoulos (1917–81), writing in the shadow of Seferis, provided in his best work the sharpest portrait of the realities of war, attempting at the same time to enrich his vision with mythic analogies. Manolis Anagostakis (b. 1925), the most down-to-earth of the group, offered the bleakest prospect—poems in which irony is the only release from a pervasive mood of defeat, of man undone by the evil in him, often manifest through corrupt politics. Miltos Sachtouris (b. 1919) and Nikos Karouzos (b. 1926), both work in a post-surrealist mode. Sachtouris projects a nightmare image of a world that appears to have survived the destruction of humanity. Karouzos, making use of a highly personal idiom that is sometimes obscure or cryptic, draws on the pre-Socratics for philosophical sustenance, as does D. P. Papaditsas (1922–87), another post-surrealist with an esp. strong talent for promoting parallels between contemporaneity and antiquity.

The younger poets who followed these, known as the Generation of the Seventies, turned in a new direction, much under the influence of the Beat Generation in America. In style they exploited the full riches of colloquial speech, incl. imported terms. In content they called into question most orthodox beliefs and challenged most established positions, esp. those reflecting a particular political commitments. Their intention was to show the world as they truly saw it, without illusions, and to exhibit that world in a lang. as contemporary as the drifting scene they depicted. For some, this approach appeared to undervalue the traditional possibilities of poetry; for others, it appeared to rejuvenate dying modes of expression and thought by introducing vitally new, if changing, resources. The fact is that poetry has flourished in Greece in recent years as it had not since the 1930s, esp. poetry written by women, and prospects continue to be good, if still unsettled, as to who now coming to maturity will dominate the next generation. The fact is also, and more significantly, that in the last hundred years better poetry has been written in Greece than during the fourteen preceding centuries, and the Gr. p. produced in the 20th c., from Cavafy to Ritsos and Elytis, has a distinction equal to the best that has come from Greece's European neighbors.

ANTHOLOGIES: *Anthologia 1708–1933*, ed. E. N. Apostolidis (n.d.); *Poetry of Mod. Greece*, tr. F.

GYPSY POETRY

McFerson (1884); *Songs of Mod. Greece*, tr. G. F. Abbott (1900); *Mod. Gr. Poems*, tr. T. Stephanidis and G. Katsimbalis (1926); *Eklogae apo ta tragoudia tou Hellenikou Laou*, ed. N. Politis, 3d ed. (1932); *Med. and Mod. Gr. P.* (1951), *Penguin Book of Gr. Verse* (1984), both ed. C. A. Trypanis; *Mod. Gr. P.*, tr. K. Friar (1973); *Poitiki anthologia*, ed. L. Politis, 7 v. (1975–77); *Voices of Mod. Greece*, tr. E. Keeley and P. Sherrard (1981).

HISTORY AND CRITICISM: P. Sherrard, *The Marble Threshing Floor* (1956); A. Karantones, *Physiognomies* (1960), *Eisagoge ste neoteri poiese*, 4th ed. (1976); G. Seferis, *On the Gr. Style: Selected Essays in Poetry and Hellenism*, tr. R. Warner and T. D. Frangopoulos (1966); M. Vitti, *Storia della letteratura neogreca* (1971), *I Genia tou Trianda: Ideologia kai Morphi* (1979); C. T. Dimaras, *A Hist. of Mod. Gr. Lit.*, tr. M. Gianos (1972); *Mod. Gr. P.*, ed. K. Friar (1973); L. Politis, *A Hist. of Mod. Gr. Lit.*, tr. R. Liddell, 2d ed. (1975); A. Argyriou, *Neoteri poites tou mesopolemou* (1979); R. Beaton, *Folk Poetry of Mod. Greece* (1980); Z. Lorenzatos, *The Lost Center and Other Essays in Gr. P.* (1980); Trypanis; E. Keeley, *Mod. Gr. P.: Voice and Myth* (1983); G. Jusdanis, *The Poetics of Cavafy* (1987); V. Lambropoulos, *Lit. as National Institution: Studies in the Politics of Mod. Gr. Crit.* (1988); D. Ricks, *The Shade of Homer* (1989).   C.A.T.; E.K.

GREEK PROSODY. See CLASSICAL PROSODY.

GUATEMALAN POETRY. See SPANISH AMERICAN POETRY.

GUJARATI POETRY. See INDIAN POETRY.

GUSLAR (also *guslač, pevač, pesnik*). The Serbo-Croatian oral epic poet who flourished in various parts of present-day Yugoslavia from at least the 15th through the early 20th c., the trad. presently being in a state of decline. The term derives from the accompanying *gusle*, a (usually) one-stringed, lute-shaped instrument bowed by the singer, although some epic poets perform without the *gusle* (Murko 1951). Under the Ottoman Empire, gs. were attached to Turkish beys and pashas as court poets, but over the last century the number of professional poets has dwindled even in Moslem areas, with employment in the *kafana* (coffeehouse) during the holy season of Ramazan virtually the only paying position available. In the Christian areas, where the songs are shorter and customarily performed in a family context rather than in the coffeehouse, the epic poets have always been drawn from all occupations. The singer's craft, chiefly a masculine avocation, may be passed from father to son or from one g. to another; learning the singing trad. is an informal process, but one in which certain stages of private and public performance have been observed (Lord).

It was the gs. with whom M. Parry and A. Lord worked in evolving the oral-formulaic theory (q.v.), thus furthering a line of investigation begun by the ethnographer-linguist V. Karadžić (Koljević) and continued through the fieldwork and analysis done by Krauss (1908), Gesemann (1926), and Murko. The Parry-Lord gs. from Novi Pazar, Bjelo Polje, and elsewhere are selectively represented in the series *Serbo-Croatian Heroic Songs;* the most important modern g. is Avdo Medjedović, an illiterate singer who composed the 13,000-line *Wedding of Smailagi'c Meho.* On the role of the g. in the comparative study of oral trads., see Lord; Parry; and Foley 1985 (bibl.) and 1988 (esp. chs. 1–3).

F. Krauss, *Slavische Forschungen* (1908); G. Gesemann, *Studien zur südslavischen Volksepik* (1926); M. Murko, *La Poésie populaire épique en yougoslavie au début du XXe siècle* (1929), *Tragom srpsko-hrvatske narodne epike* (1951); A. B. Lord, "Yugoslav Epic Folk Poetry," *IFMJ* 3 (1951); *Serbo-Croatian Heroic Songs* (*Srpskohrvatske junacke pjesme*), coll., tr., and ed. M. Parry, A. B. Lord, and D. Bynum (1953–); Lord; Parry; S. Koljević, *The Epic in the Making* (1980); J. Foley, *Oral-Formulaic Theory and Research* (1985), *The Theory of Oral Composition* (1988).   J.M.F.

GYPSY POETRY. The G. left India some 900 years ago and migrated to Europe and, later, other parts of the world. Although generally regarded as a nomadic people, large numbers have been sedentary for many generations. Their lang., Romani, a close relation of Hindi and Punjabi, is still spoken by the majority of ethnic G. and is the vehicle of a large oral lit., chiefly folksongs, ballads, and tales. Poetry as such has only developed in this century. But there is no standard literary lang., and so each dialect has a life of its own.

The lyric first flowered in the newly founded Soviet Union, where the lang. was fostered up to 1934, after which time the Soviet government discouraged its use. Aleksandr German and O. Pankova were the outstanding names among Rus. G. writers who followed the state policy of discouraging nomadism and encouraging farm and factory work.

The Gypsies in Europe suffered alongside the Jews under Nazi persecution—a period recorded in contemporary and postwar songs and poetry such as Papusza's "Tears of Blood." Since the end of the War, increased settlement and educational opportunity at first produced writers who used the lang. of the country where they lived. These include Sandra Jayat (France), Dezider Banga (Czechoslovakia), Slobodan Berberski (Yugoslavia), and Károly Bari and József Kóvacs (Hungary), together with many in the USSR. But Romani has also developed as a written lang., though with numerous dialects. The nomadic nature of Gypsy life in the past promoted the elements of entertainment, spontaneity, and imagination in story, tale, and song. Now, greater integration with the host communities has meant the adoption of new cultural styles. In lit. the point of departure today is poetry and drama.

On a much smaller scale than before, a revival in the USSR has produced Satkevič and Leksa Manush, the latter influenced by Rus. and Fr. poets. He takes the life of his people as his main theme but looks upon that life with cold nonromantic eyes:

> Twentieth Century, what could you
>   give to the Romany people?
> Perhaps some of the bright sun, to
>   light their dark life.
> Or wipe the rush of tears falling from
>   the women's eyes
> Or lift their singing voices with a little
>   melody.
>
> (tr. Gillian Taylor)

In Poland emerged Papusza (Bronislaw Wajs, b. ca. 1909), who wrote abundantly for three years from 1950 until pressure from the local community to conform to the traditional role of a G. woman made her lay down her pen for some years. In Yugoslavia, where radio and periodicals foster the lang., a circle of poets developed in Skopje and the new town of Shuto Orizari, alongside a flourishing theater in Romani. Nowadays, however, the lyric writers of Kosovia are better known. Characteristic of this school is the creation of neologisms from Romani roots, rather than using loan words from Serbo-Croatian or Albanian. From a score of writers who have departed from the traditional folksongs handed down from generation to generation (and akin to those which inspired Strauss and Bartok), I will mention only three names, Dževad Gaśi (b. 1958), Iliaz Śabani, and Ismet Jaśarević (b. 1951). The last, in his (rhymed) autobiographical poem "Te džanel thaarako ternipe" (So that tomorrow's youth will know) tells of his hard struggle against poverty and illness.

Two poets independent of the mainstream are Ivan Nikolić and Rajko Djurić. The latter, a journalist in Belgrade, deals with philosophical concerns, which has led to his being more appreciated by educated Romanies abroad and in tr. than by his own community. G. poets in Hungary have seen their work appear both in the short-lived magazine *Rom Som* and in anthologies. Čoli Daroczi (b. 1939) takes his inspiration from Brecht and the Hungarian Jószef Attila, while Ervin Karsai is perhaps best known for his children's poems.

In Czechoslovakia the writers in Romani are often manual workers who have had little formal education. Worthy of mention are Bartolomyj Daniel (b. ca. 1931), Tera Fabiánová (b. 1930), František Demeter (b. ca. 1947), Elena Lacková (b. 1921; also a playwright), Vojtych Fabián (b. ca. 1944), and Ondrej Pešta (b. ca. 1922).

Vittorio Pasquale writes in the less used Sinti (Sindhi) dialect, and, together with Rasim Sejdić, has been published in Italy. There are other occasional poets—Mateo Maximoff, better known for his novels in Fr. and tr. of the Bible into Romani, Dimiter Golemanov, primarily a composer of songs, Rosa Taikon (Sweden), an artist in metal, and Ronald Lee (Canada), woodcarver and novelist. But the outstanding achievement of postwar Romani poetry is the full-length verse ballad "Tari thaj Zerfi" (Tari and Zerfi) by the Lovari-dialect writer Wladyslaw Jakowicz (b. 1915), recounting the story of two lovers. It has been published in Sweden with a glossary in the Kalderash dialect, making it accessible to a wider circle of Romani speakers. Romani poets, while hampered by the lack of a standard lang. and of a regular periodical lit., are at the same time part of the wider European trad. and vital instruments in the devel. of authentic G. culture.

ANTHOLOGIES: *Volksdichtungen der siebenbürgischen und südungarischen Zigeuner*, ed. and tr. H. Wlislocky (1890); *Csikóink kényesek* (1977); *Romské Písně* (1979); *Fekete Korall* (1981); *Jaga Vatre* (1984); *Tüzpiros Kígyócska*, ed. K. Bari (1985); *Romska Narodna Poezija* (1986).

JOURNALS: *Jour. of the G. Lore Society; Études Tsiganes; Lacio Drom.*

HISTORY AND CRITICISM: G. Black, *A G. Bibl.* (1914); *Leeds Univ. Romany Catalogue* (1962); J. Ficowski, *Cigianie na polskach drogach* (1965); M. Courthiade, "Jeunes poètes roms de Cassove," *Études Tsiganes* (1982–83); J.-P. Liégeois. *Gypsies: An Illus. Hist.* (1985). D.K.

H

HAIKAI. See RENGA; HAIKU; JAPANESE POETRY.

HAIKU (also called *hokku* and *haikai*). This Japanese poetic form was originally the opening section (hence *hokku*, "opening part") of *renga* (q.v.), which took shape in the 13th and 14th cs. as a sequential verseform that alternates up to fifty times 5-7-5- and 7-7-syllable parts composed in turn by two or more poets. The name *haiku* derives from the variety of *renga* known as *haikai*, "humorous." *Haikai* poets, most notably Matsuo Bashō (1644–94), rejected the poetic diction and lyricism of court poetry that prevailed in orthodox *renga* and found "humor" in describing the mundane. But they retained some basic features of orthodox *renga*, among them the inclusion of a *kigo*, a word or phrase that specifies the season of the composition.

Even though the *hokku* in units of 5-7-5 syllables was being written more or less independently by the 16th c., it was not completely severed from *renga* until the end of the 19th c. As it became an independent form, largely at the instigation of the reformist Masaoka Shiki (1867–1902), the name *hokku* was replaced by *haiku*. Some poets, such as Ogiwara Seisensui (1884–1976) and Ozaki Hōsai (1885–1926), went further and rejected the two basic requirements of the *hokku*, the syllabic pattern of 5-7-5 and the inclusion of a *kigo*. Some also departed from the one-line printing format, which was adopted as standard in the 19th c.—a practice which instilled in *haiku* writers a strong sense of the h. as a one-line poem. Such departures from the norm have not converted the majority, however.

Around 1900, h. began to attract the attention of Western poets, the Fr. being among the first to try to take up the form, calling it *haikai*. In the following decades, mainly under the influence of Fr. poets, a number of poets in the United States, in Latin America, and in other regions tried the form, writing their pieces mainly in three lines of 5-7-5 syllables. But they did not go much beyond experimentation. Imagism (q.v.), a literary movement linked with h., produced Ezra Pound's technique of "superposition" and otherwise had a considerable influence on the poetry of the time, and esp. on reducing discursiveness in Western poetry.

Outside Japan, interest in writing h. gained solid ground after World War II, esp. among Am. poets, as a result of a sudden increase in the number and quality of trs. of Japanese lit. and studies of Japanese culture. The works of three scholars have been seminal: Blyth, Yasuda, and Henderson. Of the three, Blyth's volumes displayed an intimate knowledge of the subject in relating h. to Zen Buddhism, thereby awakening interest in this form among poets, such as those of the Beat Generation, who were pursuing Eastern philosophies and religions during the '50s. Taking a contrasting secular approach, Henderson greatly helped to make the practical aspects of h.-writing understood during the '60s through his roles as adviser to the poets and as guiding hand in the formation of the H. Society of America in 1968. In 1963 *Am. H.*, the first magazine devoted to h. in Eng., began publication, followed by at least ten h. magazines over the next two decades. In 1974 *The H. Anthol.*, edited by Cor van den Heuvel, was published; a collection of h. by contemp. Am. and Canadian poets, it was the first notable anthol. in a non-Japanese lang. and was greatly enlarged in its 2d ed. (1986).

H. is now written in a great many langs., but receptivity to new ideas and experimentation seems strongest in North America. One indication of this is the writing of one-line h. that began in the mid-'70s largely in recognition of the one-line format employed by most Japanese h. writers and as a result of trs. of such Japanese h. in one line. This and other devels. make a definition of h. impractical, although at least the three-line format, if not the 5-7-5 syllable pattern, seems still to be regarded as the norm in many countries outside Japan. See also JAPANESE POETRY.

E. Miner, *The Japanese Trad. in British and Am. Lit.* (1958); R. H. Blyth, *H.*, 4 v. (1949–52), *A Hist. of H.*, 2 v. (1963–64); K. Yasuda, *The Japanese H.* (1957); *Haikai Dai-jiten* [The Great Dict. of Haikai], ed. Ijichi Tetsuo et al. (1957); H. G. Henderson, *An Intro. to H.* (1958), *H. in Eng.* (1967); G. L. Brower, *H. in Western Langs.: An Annot. Bibl.* (1972); M. Ueda, *Mod. Japanese H.* (Tokyo, 1976), *Basho and His Interpreters* (1991); R. Étiemble, "Sur une bibl. du h. dans les langues européennes," *CLS* 11 (1974); *Gendai H. Dai-jiten* [The Great Dict. of Mod. H.], ed. Azumi Atsushi et al. (1977); R. Figgins, "A Basic Bibl. of H. in Eng.," *Bull. of Bibl.* 36 (1979); *From the Country of Eight Islands*, ed. and tr. H. Sato and B. Watson (1981); H. Sato, *One Hundred Frogs* (1983), *Eigo H.* [H. in Eng.] (1987); *H. Rev. '84*, ed. R. and S. Brooks (1984); J. T. Rimer and R. E. Morrell, *Guide to Japanese Poetry*, 2d ed. (1984); S. Kodoma, *Am. Poetry and Japanese Culture* (1984); S. Sommerkamp, "Der Einfluss des H. auf Imagismus und Jüngere Moderne," Diss., Univ. of Hamburg (1984); *Anthologie Canadienne: H.*, ed. D. Howard and A. Duhaime

(1985); W. J. Higginson, *The H. Handbook* (1985).
H.S.

HAITIAN POETRY. The poetry of Haiti has exhibited two divergent tendencies: an emulation of the styles and movements of France, and an intense nationalism or racial pride. A corollary to this latter trad. of commitment is the sensitivity of H. p. to the political climate of the country. The production of poetry and the criticism of poetry have through the years been fostered to a great extent by Haiti's many literary and cultural magazines. The beginning of H. lit. is considered to coincide with the origin of the independent H. state in 1804, in the wake of the Fr. Revolution. Indeed, the first poets considered themselves the perpetuators of the ideals of that Revolution. It is not surprising therefore that the Fr.-educated poets Antoine Dupré, Juste Chanlatte, and Jean-Baptiste Romane intoned hymns and odes—replete with periphrasis, personifications, and invocations to Liberty and Independence—while Jules Solime Milscent, founder of Haiti's first significant literary magazine, *L'Abeille Haïtienne* (1817), wrote fables after the manner of La Fontaine.

With France's recognition of sovereignty (1925), poets became less intent on justifying independence, and an enthusiastic interest in the romantic movement led to a poetic production at first resembling the work of Lamartine in the case of poets such as Coriolan Ardouin and Ignace Nau. But while retaining the style of the Fr. romantics, H. poets soon began to introduce more of the tropical landscape and local ambience into their work. From the start, H. romanticism was characterized by a strong patriotism, but the patriotic current comes into its own after 1860, when poets such as Tertulien Guilbaud, Massillon Coucou, and Vendenesse Ducasse, in reaction to the numerous European and Am. detractors of the Black Republic and as apologists for Haiti's border wars with Santo Domingo, sang of the exploits of the heroes of Independence and anguished over Haiti's political and economic problems. Oswald Durand epitomizes H. romanticism, his work typically extolling the charms of the H. peasant girl but also concerned with the fate of the nation.

As the 20th c. opened, several journals, such as *Haiti littéraire et scientifique*, *Haiti littéraire et social* (later, *Haiti littéraire et politique*), and esp. *La Ronde*, served as forums for debate and illustration of both older romantic and newer nationalist and eclectic tendencies. Side by side with poets such as Georges Sylvain, who sought to infuse local color and a sense of the H. world-view into his rendering of La Fontaine's fables into creole (*Cric?-Crac!*), others, such as Etzer Vilaire, claimed the right to draw from all traditions in the quest for universality, while continuing to subscribe to the romantic tradition. And Léon Laleau (b. 1892) for several decades wrote carefully crafted poems ranging from delicate romanticism to complex racial awareness.

During the years 1925–27, a new group of poets emerged. Writing in *La Nouvelle Ronde* (1925), *La Trouée* (1927), and esp. *La Revue indigène* (1927), Emile Roumer, Philippe Thoby-Marcelin, Jacques Roumain, Carl Brouard, and others reacted against the Am. Occupation (1915–34), against what they perceived as a shallow portrayal of H. mores in the previous literary generation, and against the stilted formality of patriotism among some of their elders, who were reacting in their own way to the Am. occupation. Indigenism, as the movement came to be called, reaffirmed H. values and proposed to reflect them in lit. Although the theoretical writings seek a H. aesthetic, the poetry itself, while it speaks of vodun drums, peasant women, and the H. landscape, reflects the European revolutions in form and style of the first decades of the century: free verse, direct lang., surrealism, and the primacy of the image. Jean Price-Mars' critical study, *Ainsi parla l'oncle* (*Thus Spoke the Uncle*, 1928) did much to encourage greater expression of the Af. continuity in H. culture. In the early 1930s, a "new wave" of writers, among them Carl Brouard of the original *Revue indigène* group, sought to implement Price-Mars' ideas. Between 1938 and 1940, they published the journal *Les Griots*, the title of which evokes the poet-historians of Africa.

The period of the late 1940s and early 1950s was one of opened horizons. Marxism, democratic fervor, some restructuring of social institutions at home, the war and Fascism abroad, and the Négritude movement all combined to enlarge the H. poet's awareness of the common human struggle for social betterment. During the same time, race-consciousness acquired a global character which it had largely lacked in the Af.-oriented work of the 1930s. Jean Brierre, one of Haiti's most prolific poets, writes "to the memory of the lynched of Georgia" in his poem "Me revoici, Harlem" (Here I am again, Harlem): "And our footsteps across centuries of misery / Strike the same death knell on the same path." Within the same humanitarian context, poets such as René Despestre called for a revolutionary new order, Félix Morisseau-Leroy continued to validate and interpret H. culture and the ordinary folk, while others perpetuated a romantic poetry sometimes showing the influence of the newer perspective. Women (who achieved the right to vote in the 1950s and gained greater access to education) also became more vocal as poets.

With the institution of a particularly cruel and repressive dictatorship under François Duvalier in 1957, poets were among those who found it necessary to flee or take prudent leave, sometimes after torture or imprisonment. Some, such as Dépestre, energetically condemned the deterioration of Africanism into a tool of oppression in the hands of Duvalier. The exiled poets profited from cultural enrichment in Africa and North America while continuing to write of the H. experience, often using poetry as a liberating device, as in Anthony Phelps' *Mon Pays Que Voici* (This, My Country):

The Day will come . . .
when the dust of the pariahs
and the sweat of the homeless
will be no more in the new dawn
than images without reality
. . . .
But patience, my son
Sleep my child Sleep.

As the exodus continued over the next decade, the existence of an expatriate population large enough to support journals such as *Nouvelle optique* (Montréal) and *Présence haïtienne* (New York) and to justify the publication of poetry outside Haiti led to a bifurcation of H. lit. Inside Haiti, by the early 1960s, poetry and the literary magazine had been seriously impaired by repression. Nevertheless, romantic poetry continued to be produced in quantity, and several poets, such as Jeanine Tavernier Louis, Jacqueline Beaugé, René Philoctète, Rassoul Labuchin, Franck Etienne (later Frankétienne) and Marie-Ange Jolicoeur wrote poetry of substance, in much of which a social vision is evident. After the death of Duvalier in 1971, his 18-year-old son, Jean-Claude, same to power. Although repression continued, writers began to test the younger Duvalier's resolve. Magazines began to reappear, notable among them *Le Petit Samedi Soir*.

While it remains true that most H. p. has been written in Fr. (and, until recently, by members of the upper classes), a trad. of poetry in the Fr.-based creole of Haiti has also long existed, the most notable examples being by Oswald Durand, Georges Sylvain, and Félix Morisseau-Leroy. The practice of creole poetry gained ground in the 1970s and 1980s, its production swelled by younger voices such as Georges Castera Fils, Rudolph Müller, and Pierre-Richard Narcisse. Literary creole is not confined to verse, however; it has made a particular impact in the popular theater movement, in which many of the poets have participated. Creole has certainly not supplanted Fr., but it seems more and more to be viewed as a lang. capable of artistic expression.

In the years leading to the exile of Jean-Claude Duvalier in 1986, the liberating influence of poetry as a demystification (and esp. that written in creole because of its direct accessibility to the masses) was more and more exploited. Pierre-Richard Narcisse's *Dey ak lespwa* (Mourning and Hope) can serve as example: "My sun is cut into two pieces. / One for us, one for them." In the ensuing process of democratization, a freedom of expression hitherto largely unknown in H. letters came to exist, in which participated both returning exiles and those still overseas. H. p. continues to be directly related to the uncertain socio-political climate.

ANTHOLOGIES: *Anthologie d'un siècle de poésie haïtienne (1817–1925)*, ed. L. Morpeau (1926); *Panorama de la poésie haïtienne*, ed. C. Saint-Louis and M. Lubin (1950); *Poésie vivante d'haiti*, ed. S. Baridon and R. Philoctète (1978).

HISTORY AND CRITICISM: D. Vaval, *Histoire de la littérature haïtienne* (1933); G. Gouraige, *Histoire de la littérature haïtienne* (1960); N. Garrett, *The Ren. of H. P.* (1963); R. Berrou and P. Pompilus, *Histoire de la littérature haïtienne*, 2d ed., v. 1-3 (1975–77); D. Herdeck, et al., *Caribbean Writers: A Bio-Bibl.-Crit. Encyclopedia* (1979).   C.F.

HALF RHYME. See CONSONANCE; NEAR RHYME.

HAMARTIA. See TRAGEDY.

HARGA. See KHARJA.

HARLEM RENAISSANCE. A phrase traditionally used to designate the concentrated Afro-Am. artistic and intellectual activity that characterized New York's Harlem during the 1910s and 1920s. H. R. refers less to a rebirth of learning or a reclamation of a trad. than to a coming to fullness of impulses that had been at work in Afro-Am. culture from its inception in the 17th c. Specifically, the H. R. gave fuller voice to an impulse to found and sound an Afro-Am. national voice than any previous era of Afro-Am. cultural production. There was, however, no discontinuity between previous eras and the H. R., for the H. R.'s achievement of an Afro-Am. national voice was predicated upon the turn-of-the-century work of such Afro-Am. spokespeople as Booker T. Washington, W. E. B. DuBois, Ida B. Wells, Charles Chesnutt, Paul Laurence Dunbar, Frances E. W. Harper, and others. These artists, social activists, educators, and intellectuals all wished to define a national project for the masses of Afro-America. Their aim was to convert an impoverished, illiterate, agrarian, Southern, exploited aggregate of Afro-Americans numbering in the millions into an articulate, respected, and solvent nation.

James Weldon Johnson (1871–1938) produced the handbook for the new Afro-Am. national sound in *The Book of Am. Negro Poetry* (1922). In his long preface, Johnson asserts the cardinal tenet of H. R. faith: any group, race, or nation that has unequivocally demonstrated its artistic prowess will be respected and celebrated. Johnson also discusses longstanding forms of expression in Afro-America, repudiates a false trad. of dialect verse derived from white Am. minstrelsy, and hails the emergence of those Afro-Am. poets included in his collection. Many of his anthologized poets—Countee Cullen (1903–46), Claude McKay (1889–1948), Langston Hughes (1902–67), Jean Toomer (1894–1967)—are also included in another important and influential collection edited by Alain Locke (1885–1954), *The New Negro* (1925). Like Johnson, Locke was concerned to define the national sound of Afro-America in terms of both its traditional resonances and its most recent emergence.

Recently established periodicals such as *The Crisis*, the official publication of the *NAACP*, and *Opportunity*, the official organ of the National Urban League, sponsored literary contests and provided outlets for definitions of a distinctive poetics and for displaying the poetry of an emergent generation. Another journal, *Negro World*, the official publication of Marcus Garvey's Universal Negro Improvement Association, provided a firmly nationalistic and emigrationist (back to Africa) outlet. Such standard Am. magazines as *Poetry*, *Mercury*, and *New Masses* also opened their pages to various productions of what came to be called The New Negro.

During the H. R. it seemed to many that Countee Cullen represented the breath and finer spirit of the poet's work. Cullen was lauded by Afro-Am. and white Am. critics and periodicals for his genteel emulations of the second wave of 19th-c. British romanticism. He was also held in high esteem by some because he proclaimed his desire to be judged by nonracial criteria. He wanted to be "just a poet," not a Negro poet. John Keats was his poetic ideal. In volumes such as *Color* (1925), *Copper Sun* (1927), and *The Black Christ and Other Poems* (1929) he devoted most of his effort to lyrics that sing the bittersweet fortunes of life lived under the eternal threat of lost happiness and death. But there are, as well, strong, ironical moments in Cullen's *oeuvre*, moments when he sounds a distinctively racial note, as in "Yet Do I Marvel," which concludes with the lines: "Yet do I marvel at this curious thing: / To make a poet black, and bid him sing!"

In recent years the scales of evaluation have shifted, so that Langston Hughes is now widely considered the premier poet of the H. R. Hughes' manifesto "The Negro Artist and the Racial Mountain" (1926) begins with a repudiation of Negro poets who want to be judged by nonracial criteria. It continues by detailing an impulse in Afro-Am. culture to repudiate the sound and wisdom of the Afro-Am. masses in favor of Euroamerican cultural production. Hughes condemns this impulse, insists on the resonant importance of Afro-Am. vernacular modes of expression, and dedicates himself and his generation to a blues (q.v.) trad. In volumes of verse such as *The Weary Blues* (1926) and *Fine Clothes To The Jew* (1927), Hughes transforms the country as well as the cl. artistry of Afro-Am. blues into brilliant vernacular poetry.

The creative orientations of poets such as McKay, Toomer, Arna Bontemps (1902–73), and Sterling Brown (b. 1901) are all encompassed by the aspirations of Cullen and Hughes. McKay uses a standard sonnet form in the manner of Cullen to sound the most stridently nationalistic and bellicose sentiments in volumes such as *Harlem Shadows* (1922) and *Spring in New Hampshire and Other Poems* (1920). In his lyrical work of prose and verse entitled *Cane* (1923), Toomer employs a subtle lyricism to capture, sometimes as incantation or as call-and-response, the "souls of slavery." Brown is the clearest recipient of Hughes' legacy in his explorations of the lives and voices of the blues people. When his *Southern Road* appeared in 1932, one might argue that the H. R. had achieved its national ends. To the Afro-Am. vernacular/blues trad. the volume assimilates the poetics of such standard Am. writers as Edgar Lee Masters, Carl Sandburg, and Robert Frost.

One traditional view of the H. R. is that it comes to an end with the onset of the Great Depression in 1929. In fact, most of the poets of the H. R. were not yet in their prime in 1929, and Hughes' artistic life provides a more coherent and accurate view of the H. R. than the traditional chronological-period approach. Having arrived in Harlem during the Twenties, Hughes welcomed the famous Afro-Am. novelist Richard Wright when he took up residence there during the 1930s, and it was Hughes, as well, who introduced the Afro-Am. novelist Ralph Ellison to Wright when Ellison arrived in Harlem in the late Thirties. Continuity, a national sound, and a vernacular poetics are three major accomplishments of the H. R. See also AFRICAN POETRY, *In Portuguese.*—N. I. Huggins, *H. R.* (1971), ed., *Voices from the H. R.* (1976); *H. R. Remembered*, ed. A. Bontemps (1972); D. Lewis, *When Harlem Was in Vogue* (1981); *The H. R.: An Annot. Bibl. and Commentary*, ed. M. Perry (1982); B. Kellner, *The H. R.: A Historical Dict. for the Era* (1984); A. Rampersad, *The Life of Langston Hughes* (1986); H. Baker, *Modernism and the H. R.* (1987); G. T. Hull, *Color, Sex, and Poetry* (1987); *Shadowed Dreams: Women's Poetry of the H. R.*, ed. M. Honey (1989). H.A.B.

HAUSA POETRY. In the H. lang. as spoken in Nigeria, Niger, and parts of Ghana, the single term *waka* is applied to two closely related trads., song and the writing of poetry (verse). In Nigeria, H. poets and scholars have defined the one in terms of its difference from the other. Popular song and courtly praise-singing are oral, professional, and instrumentally accompanied, displaying complex interaction between lead-singer(s) and chorus. Poetry, on the other hand, is chanted without accompaniment, and reward for performance is not usually sought; poems are composed in Roman or in *ajami* (Ar.) script and often circulate in ms. or in printed form. Song displays rhythmic regularity deriving from the drum or other instruments; poetry can be scanned according to metrical patterns of heavy and light syllables that correspond to a number of Cl. Ar. meters. In song, the words of the lead-singer are interrupted by the refrains or repetition of the *amshi* (chorus); this may occasion considerable variation in the length of "verses" between choruses. Commonly, H. p. in couplets displays end rhyme, and in 5-line stanzas end rhyme in the final line is supplemented by internal rhyme in the first four lines. It has been shown that in some cases tonal rhyme can accompany syllable rhyme.

Of the Cl. Ar. meters, nine are found in H. p. (in descending order of frequency): *kāmil, mutadārik, mutaqārib, rajaz, basīṭ, wāfir, khafīf, ramal,* and *ṭawīl.* Claims for other meters require very liberal interp. of the meter to fit the poem. The suitability of Ar. prosody (q.v.) as a model for the description of rhythmic regularity in H. p. has come under question both from H. scholars, who argue that rhythmic patterns have often been taken directly from song, and from other scholars who have approached the performance of H. p. using a "beat and measure" system developed in unpublished work by A. V. King on the analysis of song. The "beat and measure" system, as opposed to the "syllable and feet" system, incorporates interlinear pauses, accounts for anomalous characteristics of H. poetic rhythms, and explains the systematic use of deviations not provided for in the Cl. Ar. system (see Schuh 1988).

Modern poetry in Roman script (1903 to date) developed from the trad. of Islamic religious verse in H. *ajami* of the 19th c. Since at least the time of the Islamic *jihād* (holy war) of Shehu Usman dan Fodio (1804), the propagation of the faith has involved the writing of H. p. that circulated both in ms. form and, among the common people, through the performances of religious mendicants, often blind. Such poetry fell broadly into the categories of theology, praise of the Prophet, biography of the Prophet and his companions, admonition and exhortation, religious obligations, law, and astrology. While strictly religious poetry continues to be written, particularly within the brotherhood organizations, the 20th c. has seen a great broadening in themes, now covering such diverse subjects as Western education, hygiene, the evils of drink, filial piety, Nigerian geography, and many topical subjects such as the population census and the introduction of new currency. Poetry writing along with song has been an important part of the political process during the 1950s with the approach of independence (1960) and the rise of political parties in Northern Nigeria, during the civilian political eras of the early 1960s and 1980s, and during the Civil War (1967–70). To a considerable extent H. p. retains, as its most prominent characteristics, a didacticism and a concern for social issues inherited from Islamic trad. Personal lyrical expression has traditionally been restricted to the category of *madahu* (praise of the Prophet), where the lang. of deep personal devotion, longing, and desire was both legitimate and appropriate. Recently, however, love poetry, which in the past had been private, has entered the public arena through the publication of an anthology, *Dausayin Soyayya.*

Modern H. p. has been published regularly in the newspaper *Gaskiya ta fi Kwabo* (founded 1939), and prominent poets such as Aƙilu Aliyu, Mudi Sipikin, Na'ibi Wali, Salihu Kwantagora, and others have reached a wider audience by being broadcast over the radio stations of the northern states of Nigeria. Poetry-writing circles have been formed and have also had access to radio. While the majority of poets have been men, women such as Hauwa Gwaram and Alhajiya 'Yar Shehu have written on contemp. social and religious issues, following in the footsteps of the poet and translator Nana Asma'u, daughter of Shehu Usman dan Fodio, leader of the *jihād* of 1804, and scholar in her own right.

ANTHOLOGIES: *Wakokin Mu'azu Hadejia* (1955); *Wakokin H.* [H. P.] (1957); *Wakokin Sa'adu Zungur* (1966); Mudi Sipikin, *Tsofaffin Wakoki da Sababbin Wakoki* [Old and New Poems] (1971); *Wakokin Hikima* [Poems of Wisdom] (1975); Akilu Aliyu, *Fasaha Akiliya* [The Skill of Akilu] (1976); *Zababbun Wakokin da da na yanzu* [Selected Poems of Yesterday and Today] (1979); *Dausayin Soyayya* [The Mellowness of Mutual Love] (1982).

HISTORY AND CRITICISM: J. H. Greenberg, "H. Verse Prosody," *JAOS* 69 (1949); D. W. Arnott, "The Song of the Rains," *AfrLS* 9 (1969); M. K. M. Galadanci, "The Poetic Marriage between Arabic and H.," *Harsunan Nijeriya* 5 (1975); M. Hiskett, *A Hist. of H. Islamic Verse* (1975); S. Baldi, *Systematic H. Bibl.* (1977); D. Muhammad, "Interaction Between the Oral and the Literate Trads. of H. P.," *Harsunan Nijeriya* 9 (1979), "Tonal Rhyme: A Preliminary Study," *AfrLS* 17 (1980); R. G. Schuh, "Préalable to a Theory of H. Poetic Meter," and N. Awde, "A H. Lang. and Ling. Bibl.," both in *Studies in H. Lang. and Linguistics,* ed. G. L. Furniss and P. J. Jaggar (1988)—bibl. esp. valuable for citation of unpub. dissertations on H.   G.F.

HEADLESS LINE. See ACEPHALOUS.

HEBRAISM.

    I. HEBRAISM AS A FORM OF LANGUAGE
    II. HEBRAISM AND HELLENISM
    III. HEBRAISM AS A CRITICAL TERM
    IV. MIDRASH AND KABBALAH

I. HEBRAISM AS A FORM OF LANGUAGE. A h. is a speech-form in common use which has its origin in the Bible, particularly in the OT. Such hs. are pervasive in all European langs., particularly Ger. and Eng. In Ger. this is to be accounted for by the powerful and continuing influence of Martin Luther's Bible tr. (1522, 1534); in Eng., the tr. and paraphrasing of books of the Bible goes back to the very beginnings of the lang. in OE and continues to the King James version of 1611 and beyond. The result is that Heb. speech-forms, ranging from brief phrases to proverbs, have become completely naturalized and are produced for the most part without users being aware of their Heb. origin. Examples are: to escape "by the skin of one's teeth," "to go from strength to strength," "the ends of the earth," "out of the mouths of babes," to "wash one's hands of," "to be clothed in scarlet," "no rest for the wicked," "the way of a man with a maid."

In literary lang., hs. are a constant presence for writers of all periods, but particularly concentrated use may be noted in Bacon, Bunyan, Blake, Wordsworth, and D. H. Lawrence. William Tyndale claimed that "the properties of the Heb. tongue agreeth a thousand times more with the Eng. than with the Lat." (*The Obedience of a Christian Man*, 1528). Even Addison, a writer of more Cl. taste, remarked that "it happens very luckily that the Heb. idiom turns into the Eng. tongue with a particular grace and beauty" (*Spectator* no. 405).

II. HEBRAISM AND HELLENISM. As an abstract noun, H. denotes the Heb. or biblical component in Western culture. H. is often perceived as the opposite of Hellenism. Matthew Arnold popularized and sharpened this distinction in *Culture and Anarchy* (1869). The Hellenic legacy, he claimed, is aesthetic, the Hebraic legacy moral. "The governing idea of Hellenism is spontaneity of consciousness; that of H., strictness of conscience." While the future of the human race is inconceivable without the passion for righteousness of the Heb. prophets, the exclusive emphasis on this aspect leads to the impoverishment of science, art, and lit. Arnold derived his ideal of Hellenism largely from the Ger. Hellenists, J. J. Winckelmann, Goethe, and his own contemporaries, Heinrich Heine and Wilhelm von Humboldt. But Arnold drew short of Winckelmann's radically anti-Christian sentiments and was not entirely comfortable with Humboldt's aim of ridding Christianity of its "Semitic" element in order to bring it closer to the Hellenistic ideal of human perfection to which he felt the IE peoples were naturally attuned.

Arnold's real target was evidently the Puritanism of the Victorian middle class, whom he spoke of as "Philistines"—borrowing the term from Heine. Their type of piety he said called for self-conquest—the Old Adam laboring under the burden of sin had to be "delivered from the body of this death." But it is questionable whether such evangelical piety—exemplified, as Arnold notes, by the Letters of the apostle Paul and the writings of St. Augustine—really characterizes the cultural and religious message of the Heb. scriptures. J. C. Powys had a truer sense of the essentials of H. when he spoke of "the human wisdom, the human sensuality, the human anger, the human justice . . . of this old shameless lit. of the OT." In this light, H. has at least as much reference to the Old Adam as to the regenerate man of Pauline Christianity.

Arnold modified his view of H. in *Lit. and Dogma* (1873), where he speaks of the prophets as using literary lang.; we must understand their words as human poetry rather than dogma. In fact, we need to bring to such texts an aesthetic taste no less refined than that required for the appreciation of the great texts of the Hellenic trad.

III. HEBRAISM AS A CRITICAL TERM. The use of H. in the general senses discussed above has often led to distortion. Critics have, however, also pointed to specific literary forms and modes of discourse associated with H. or derived from Heb. sources, an attention which, increasing in recent years, has yielded a more discriminating and finely gauged understanding of the nature of H. and its place in Western lit.

In the 3rd c., "Longinus" in a famous passage of his *Peri hypsous* had associated the sublime (q.v.) with H., pointing to the first verses of *Genesis* as an example of grandeur of vision and lang. With the awakening of interest in Longinus starting with Boileau (1674), increasing attention was given to Heb. examples of sublimity. Bishop Lowth in his lectures on Heb. poetry (1753) proposed biblical prophecy with its vehemence and passion as the perfect model of sublime poetry. Edmund Burke in defining the sublime (1757) cited passages from *Job* marked by power, darkness, and terror. Following Lowth's lead, the Ger. romantic philosopher J. G. Herder wrote a treatise (*Vom Geiste der hebräischen Poesie*, 1782) ardently praising the poetic genius of the Hebrews; he viewed the Bible as a body of national poetry which his own compatriots might emulate. Earlier he had written of the Song of Songs as an impassioned, oriental love-poem. H. in short provided a heady mixture of sublimity, primitivism, and orientalism to offset the neoclassical tenets of the 18th c. Blake went even further: revising Longinus, he dismissed Homer, Ovid, Plato, and Cicero and declared "the Sublime of the Bible" to be the only true standard (preface to *Milton*). He had in mind the "terrific" parts of his own longer poems, which consistently echo the lang. of the Heb. prophets and escape "the modern bondage" of rhyme and blank verse (preface to *Jerusalem*) to reproduce the effect of Heb. parallelism (q.v.). Coleridge in his *Table-Talk* likewise took it for granted that "Sublimity is Heb. by birth." H. thus defined helped to bring about a loosening of Cl. restraints, an increasing preference for emotional intensity, and a freer prosody in the romantic period.

While this appreciation gave Heb. poetry an important role in the hist. of European lit., the emphasis on sublimity suggests a somewhat limited understanding of H. Throughout his treatise, "Longinus" stressed "height of style," i.e. grandiloquence, finding his chief examples in Homer. The passage he chose from *Genesis* is from this point of view clearly untypical. "God said let there be light and there was light" is marked by extreme simplicity rather than grandiloquence. In the end, the rules and figures of rhet. listed by Longinus do not match such examples. And even when applied by Lowth and others to the more heightened examples of biblical poetry, something essential seems to be lost in the process of systematizing.

A different literary evaluation is that of Augustine, who in his *Confessions* (ca. 397) described how disagreeably low and simple he found Scripture on first encounter: "I could not bend down my neck to its humble pace." High though the meaning seemed to be, the lack of grandiloquence in the psalms and gospels offended his sense of decorum. Later, as Auerbach has shown (1965), Augustine came to appreciate the power of this "humility" which challenged the Cl. division of style into three types (high, middle, and low) as well as the artificial social structure which supported that division. The biblical style, combining as it did the sublime and the everyday, was thus an essentially subversive model, leading in the direction of a radical simplicity and realism both in prose and poetry. This model influenced the literary lang. of Europe in the Middle Ages and remained a latent force in the Ren. in spite of the moderating influence of other models and styles.

The Psalms in their simplicity and directness were perceived as a special example of this mode of H. Beginning with Petrarch (*Salmi penitenziali*, in Lat. [1347]), many leading poets turned to them as a primary lyric model (see PSALM). In the 16th c., Clément Marot in France, and Wyatt, Surrey, and Sidney in England found their poetic voices in their psalm paraphrases and trs. But the supreme achievement was that of the 17th-c. Eng. poets, George Herbert, Francis Quarles, and George Wither. Herbert's collection *The Temple* (1633) shows the subtlest and most pervasive use of the Psalter in this period. Responding to the dialogic character of the Psalms, Herbert achieved a dramatic tension lacking in other strains of lyricism in Eng.

> Look on my sorrows round!
> Mark well my furnace! O what flames,
> What heats abound!
> What griefs, what shames!
> Consider, Lord; Lord, bow thine eare,
> And heare!
> ("Longing")

In addition to other echoes, the last two lines of this example paraphrase the opening of Psalm 86. And yet what we hear is Herbert's personal, authentic voice.

Milton is a special case. Clearly, he is in many ways the most Hebraic of poets, and he too exercised his youthful powers in psalm trs. In *Paradise Lost* he addresses himself to the "heav'nly muse" who inspired Moses to speak of the creation of heaven and earth and claims a like inspiration for his own poem. But in fact the poem is written for the most part not in the biblical narrative mode but in the "high" epic style of Virgil and Homer. (Indeed, when later writers spoke of "the Sublime of the Bible," they often had Milton's poetry in mind.) Later, in Book 7, Milton announces that the second half of the epic will be "narrower bound / Within the visible Diurnall Sphere." From that

point on, the Heb. style of domestic realism makes its appearance, esp. in Adam's speeches, while the high oratory is assigned to Satan. In *Paradise Regained*, Book 4, his hero rejects the philosophy and poetry of the pagan world as "unworthy to compare with Sion's songs," but he does so in the lofty terms of that art which he is here condemning. The same paradox may be noted in *Samson Agonistes*, where his ambition to write a tragedy according to Gr. rules comes into conflict with the demands of a biblical narrative shaped by the upward curve of salvation history.

A certain unresolved tension thus marks the reception of H. in Western lit. Even Herbert, committed though he is to a Heb. austerity, cannot bring himself easily to forego the enchantment of richer fashions of lang.: "Farewell sweet phrases, lovely metaphors. / But will ye leave me thus?" ("The Forerunners"). Racine and Shakespeare betray similar ambivalence. As often noted, the subplot of *King Lear* is shaped by biblical categories, while the main plot exhibits the more fatal curve of tragedy. There is a certain structural disunity: while the heroes of the mainplot are doomed, Edgar, like Job, is a survivor and witness. The book of *Job* itself with its happy ending is a scandal to those who expect it to conform to a more tragic symmetry. Geoffrey Hartman has perceptively remarked that the lit. of the Bible is "generically impure." It also notoriously blurs the difference between prose and verse, as for instance in the Wisdom books, *Proverbs* and *Ecclesiastes*.

In short, the admixture of H. has often had a disabling effect on Western art and lit., the Heb. forms tending to undermine received genres. Nor does this seem to be merely a question of different tastes and standards. H. seems to question the status of lit. as such. "The Jewish imagination," declares Hartman, "fears . . . the abuse . . . that is inherent in lit. itself." James Kugel has claimed that "in some important ways the Bible is not lit." In it poetry and the distrust of poetry go together. This accounts for the tensions to which H. gives rise in the work of Herbert, Milton, and others.

IV. MIDRASH AND KABBALAH. A uniquely Heb. mode of discourse which has attracted critical attention in recent years is *midrash*. This term refers originally to the scriptural exegesis practiced by the Talmudic Rabbis, involving homilies, parables, and the imaginative interweaving of different texts. It was further developed in later centuries by the hasidic masters. Midrash is something between interp. and creative writing. Frank Kermode applies the term to the different versions of the passion narrative. Thus *Matthew* offers us a "midrash" on *Mark*: we have to do with retold tales, reinvented for new audiences. Such interpretive fiction is found in many literary genres. *Samson Agonistes* is a kind of midrash on *Judges* 13–16. The midrashic mode is of great importance for such modern Heb. writers as S. Y. Agnon (Israel) and Jorge Luis Borges (Argentina) and is manifestly the basis of the work of the Fr. writer Edmond Jabès. Frye speaks of Kafka's *The Trial* as a kind of "midrash" on *Job*. This model of interpretive or hermeneutic discourse is congenial to some modern theorists who welcome the merging of the critical and creative functions. It also sits well with the contemporary emphasis on intertextuality (q.v.). Meaning is thought to inhere not in texts but in the interrelations between them—as Harold Bloom has it (1973), "the meaning of a poem can only be another poem."

Viewed by the traditional formal standards of Western art, however, we have here once again an "impure" mode—the firm outlines of the poem or fable disappear, leaving us aware instead of a pattern of interrelations taking us back to an originary text susceptible of endless reinterp. This leads one to another basic feature of biblical lit., namely its denial of closure (q.v.). It operates by a pattern of recall and repetition (q.v.). The death of Saul has often been viewed as a tragic denouement, but in context it is much more the prelude to the emergent hist. of the house of David. Midrash may be seen as a crucial example of this aspect of H., each reading inviting and legitimating a further reading. The reader himself plays a key role in this process of continuing interp. Unity comes not from the formal coherence of the literary artifact, but from a covenantal bonding of generations sharing memories which join them to the past and future. Poems are from this point of view essentially "memorials" or "testimonies" (cf. *Deut.* 31:19, 21).

The last type of H. to be noted is *kabbalah*. In its origin, kabbalah is simply an esoteric form of midrash. Its classic text, the *Zohar* (Book of Splendor), is a commentary on the Pentateuch aimed at uncovering its occult meaning, which has to do with the dynamic structure of the divine world itself, and with primordial beginnings, rather than with history. It has links with gnosticism. Kabbalah aroused a great deal of interest among the humanists of the Ren., esp. Johann Reuchlin in Germany and Pico della Mirandola and Francesco Giorgi in Italy. Its ideas gained currency (though often in distorted form) in the 16th and 17th cs. in combination with elements of alchemy and Neoplatonism. However, claims that Spenser, Shakespeare, and Milton were significantly influenced by kabbalah have not gained scholarly acceptance. The first major poet to give powerful expression to kabbalistic ideas and symbols was Blake. His notion of the giant Albion is derived from the kabbalistic *Adam Kadmon*, who "anciently containd in his mighty limbs all things in Heaven and Earth," while the mythological drama involving Blake's "Zoas" and their female "Emanations" bears a striking resemblance to the sexual inner life of the kabbalistic *Sefirot*. Similarly kabbalistic is Blake's notion of a primordial Fall from which all evil flows in the divine and human realms. These ideas (drawn intermediately from Emanuel Sweden-borg and others) had a central influence on shaping Blake's poetry as a whole. Kabbalistic notions and images also emerged in the work of Victor Hugo, esp. his later, apocalyptic poems, and in the occult system developed by W. B. Yeats. In literary theory, kabbalah has been claimed by Harold Bloom (1975) as a crucial example of creative "misreading" and consequently as a model for "strong" poetry. Kabbalistic "misreadings" involving the radical subversion of normal lang. have also been seen as an anticipation of modern trends. Moshe Idel speaks of Abraham Abulafia as "deconstructing lang. as a communicative instrument into meaningless combinations of letters." New meanings are then discovered from the resulting verbal fragments by a kind of free association. See also HEBREW POETRY; HEBREW PROSODY AND POETICS; INTERPRETATION, FOURFOLD METHOD OF; CLASSICAL POETICS; CLASSICISM.

BACKGROUND STUDIES: *The Legacy of Israel*, ed. E. R. Bevan and C. Singer (1928); D. Daiches, "The Influence of the Bible on Eng. Lit.," and F. Lehner, "The Influence of the Bible on European Lit.," in *The Jews*, ed. L. Finkelstein, 3d ed. (1960); S. W. Baron, *A Social and Religious Hist. of the Jews*, 2d ed., v. 13 (1969): 160–201, v. 15 (1973): 141–55; *Literary Guide to the Bible*, ed. R. Alter and F. Kermode (1987)—esp. the appendix of General Essays.

SPECIALIZED STUDIES: J. C. Powys, *The Enjoyment of Lit.* (1938); Auerbach; D. Hirst, *Hidden Riches* (1964)—on occultism in Blake; H. Fisch, *Jerusalem and Albion* (1964)—on 17th-c. H., *Poetry with a Purpose* (1988); F. Secret, *Les Kabbalistes chrétiens de la Ren.* (1964); M. Roston, *Prophet and Poet* (1965)—on Lowth and the beginnings of romanticism; E. Auerbach, *Literary Lang. and its Public in Late Lat. Antiquity and in the Middle Ages* (1965), ch. 1; D. J. DeLaura, *Heb. and Hellene in Victorian England* (1969); A. A. Ansari, "Blake and the Kabbalah," *William Blake*, ed. A. H. Rosenfeld (1969); H. Bloom, *The Anxiety of Influence* (1973), *Kabbalah and Crit.* (1975); F. S. Heuman, *The Uses of Hs. in Recent Bible Trs.* (1977); F. Kermode, *The Genesis of Secrecy* (1979); J. L. Kugel, *The Idea of Biblical Poetry* (1981), "On the Bible and Lit. Crit.," *Prooftexts* 1 (1981); N. Frye, *The Great Code* (1982); S. A. Handelman, *The Slayers of Moses* (1982); G. H. Hartman, "On the Jewish Imagination," *Prooftexts* 5 (1985); C. Bloch, *Spelling the Word* (1985)—on Herbert and the Psalms; *Midrash and Lit.*, ed. G. H. Hartman and S. Budick (1986)—valuable bibl.; *Critics of the Bible 1724–1873*, ed. J. Drury (1989); M. Idel, *Lang., Torah, and Hermeneutics in Abraham Abulafia* (1989); E. Aizenberg, "H. and Poetic Influence," *Borges and His Successors*, ed. E. Aizenberg (1990); D. Boyarin, *Intertextuality and the Reading of Midrash* (1990).   H.F.

HEBREW POETICS. See HEBREW PROSODY AND POETICS; HEBRAISM.

HEBREW POETRY.

I. BIBLICAL AND MEDIEVAL
  A. *Biblical Poetry* (1150 B.C.–150 B.C.)
  B. *Extra-Canonical Works*
  C. *The Mishnaic and Talmudic Period* (ca. 100 B.C.–500 A.D.)
  D. *The Byzantine Period* (500–800 A.D.)
  E. *Moslem Spain* (10th–12th c.)
  F. *Christian Spain* (1200–1492)
  G. *Italian*
II. MODERN
  A. *The European Period* (1781–1920)
  B. *Palestinian Poetry* (1920–48)
  C. *Israeli Poets* (1948–87)

Heb. lit. spans three millennia and ranks among the world's oldest. Heb. p. began to appear at least by the 11th c. B.C. and is still being written today. Whatever gaps disrupted this almost continual literary flow are attributable more to the loss of linking texts than to so-called "dry periods" of creativity. At times, Heb. poets were not aware of their entire literary heritage, but most often they did have both a diachronic and synchronic knowledge of at least parts of it.

In every age, incl. our own, the Heb. Bible constituted the foundation and principal component of that heritage, a major source for literary forms, symbols, rhetorical tropes, syntactic structures, and vocabulary. There has been, however, no uniformity in metrical systems (see HEBREW PROSODY AND POETICS): these have varied from age to age and, following the biblical period, were usually adapted from those employed in the area where the Heb. poet happened to reside (see ARABIC POETRY; HISPANO-ARABIC POETRY; JUDEO-SPANISH POETRY). In the Persian period (5th–4th cs. B.C.), Aramaic began to replace Heb. as the vernacular in Palestine, continuing as the spoken lang. long into the Byzantine period (4th–7th cs. A.D.), while Gr. prevailed in the Mediterranean diaspora. With the rise of Islam in the 7th c., Arabic became the *lingua franca* for Jews of the Middle East, North Africa, and Spain. In Christian Europe the various IE langs. were adopted. From the Middle Ages until the early 20th c., Yiddish was the vernacular used by the majority of European Jewry as the centers of Jewish population shifted to Central and Eastern Europe (see YIDDISH POETRY). The interplay of these non-Hebraic langs. and lits. with Heb., the literary lang. of the Jews, broadened and altered Heb. p., affecting its syntax, vocabulary, themes, and genres.

The scope and variety of these phenomena make it as difficult to formulate a single comprehensive definition of Heb. p. as it is to formulate one that would be valid for world poetry. Still, the definition of poetry proposed by Barbara Herrnstein Smith is sufficient to accommodate the entire gamut of Heb. p.: "As soon as we perceive that a verbal sequence has a sustained rhythm, that it is formally structured according to a continuously operating principle of organization . . . we are in the presence of poetry and we respond to it accordingly, expecting certain effects from it and not others."

I. BIBLICAL AND MEDIEVAL. A. *Biblical Poetry* (1150 B.C.–150 B.C.). The Heb. Bible (or *Old Testament*) is an anthol. of sacred texts composed over the span of at least a thousand years. While modern biblical scholars have attempted to date its separate components with reasonable conjectures, no absolute date can be ascribed to the works forming the present canon. There has been a general consensus that the most salient feature of Heb. biblical p. is that which had been already perceived by med. scholars and formulated by Bishop Lowth in 1753 as *parallelismus membrorum*, or the parallelism (q.v.) of cola. The poetic line is usually composed of two cola (sequences of syllables, i.e. phrases or clauses)—sometimes three or four—which are parallel to each other either completely or partially in lexis or syntax. The words of the second colon repeat in different words the meaning of the first (*synonymous parallelism*); reverse, negate, or contradict its meaning (*antithetical parallelism*); or modify it (*synthetical parallelism*). Subsequent generations of scholars have added other categories to Lowth's list. Benjamin Hrushovski best summarizes the possibilities: "It may be a parallelism of semantic, syntactic, prosodic, morphological, or sound elements, or of a combination of such elements" (*Encyc. Judaica* 13.1200). James Kugel has argued that the basic function of the parallel colon or cola is sequential: "B (i.e. the second colon) by being connected to A (i.e. the first colon), carrying it further, echoing it, defining it, restating it, contrasting with it—*it does not matter which*—has an emphatic 'seconding' character, and it is this, more than any aesthetic of symmetry or paralleling, which is at the heart of biblical parallelism" (51). Indeed, the function of the subsequent parallel colon or cola is not merely to reiterate the contents of the first synonymously or antithetically in different words, but frequently to enhance or intensify the first statement.

Following the Rus. Formalist Victor Shklovsky, Robert Alter (*Art* 10) asserts that the principle of disharmony in an harmonious context is important in parallelism: "The general purpose of parallelism like the general purpose of imagery is to transfer the usual perception of an object into a sphere of new perception, that is, to make a unique semantic modification."

Kugel maintains that the use of parallelism in biblical prose passages precludes our identifying it as the major feature of biblical poetry, leading him to deny the very existence of biblical poetry, a rather specious contention. Like most other literary devices, parallelism can be used in prose as well as verse. What distinguishes its use in biblical poetry is that it becomes the constitutive device, whereas in prose it is "subordinate to the referential (or other) function" (Waugh 68). Adele Berlin has described the "elevated style" of biblical poetry as "largely the product of two elements: terseness and parallelism. It is not parallelism *per se* but the predominance of parallelism, combined with terseness, which marks the poetic expression of the Bible" (5).

There is, however, a more strictly prosodic element in biblical poetry, namely stress. While all attempts (e.g. Sievers') to "rediscover" a numerically fixed metrical system which might underlie the biblical text have so far proven futile, any sensitive reader of the Heb. original or even its better translations cannot fail to discern cadences. Hrushovski sees in these cadences "basic units" which are "not equal," but "almost never consist of one or more than four stresses," giving as a result "simple groups of two, three or four stresses" (in Sebeok, 189).

Stress, then, reinforces the parallelistic structure. Hrushovski again: "the basis of this type of rhythm may be described as semantic-syntactic-accentuation. It is basically free rhythm, i.e. a rhythm based on a cluster of changing principles. Its freedom is clearly confined within the limits of its poetics" (*ibid.*). While the number of stresses in each colon often varies, the numbers within a larger span are often equal or similar: "The condensed, laconic nature of biblical Heb. also contributes to the prominence of each word within the line ... the rhythm of major stresses is so strong that sometimes it may be the only support of the parallelism of two verses" (*Encyc. Judaica*, 13.1201–2).

Rhyme (q.v.) is occasionally employed in biblical poetry (Prov. 5:9–10), but consistent or fixed rhyme schemes are unknown in the Bible. Alliteration (q.v.) is a common technique: "ʾal tirʾúni sheʾaní sheharhóre / sheshshezaftani hashemesh" (Song of Songs 1:6). The stressed pun frequently has an emphatic or contrastive effect: "He hoped for justice [mishpat] and beheld injustice [mispaḥ; literally, a leprous growth] / for equity [ẓᵊdaqah] and beheld inequity" [zᵊʿaqah; literally, a cry of anguish] (Isa. 5:7).

Biblical poetry is replete with sophisticated tropes of every variety, incl. metaphor, simile, synecdoche, and metonymy (qq.v.). Psalms contains several hymns in the form of acrostics (q.v.— Ps. 4, 145; Ps. 119 is an eight-fold acrostic) and several refrains (Ps. 42, 103–4, 108); Ps. 136 was probably sung antiphonally. Other techniques such as anaphora and paronomasia (qq.v.) abound.

The Pentateuch and the Former Prophets are essentially prose works but contain the oldest strata of biblical poetry. Three types are used. (1) The short occasional poem is of very ancient provenance ("The Song of Lemekh" [Gen. 4:23], "The Song of the Well" [Num. 21:17–18], and Miriam's "Song at the Red Sea" [Exod. 15:21]— the latter may have served as the core around which Moses' "Song of Victory" [Exod. 15:1–18] was later composed). (2) A second type are the larger hymns or odes such as Moses' "Song" and "Deborah's Song" (Judg. 5), designated as *shirah* ("song," "long poem"[?]); Balaam's oracles (Num. 23:7–10, 18–25; 24:3–9, 15–24); and the song celebrating the victory over Moab (Num. 21:27–30)— this latter is designated as *mashal* (an imprecise term applied either to a poetic oration rich in allegory or metaphor [Num. 24:15 ff., for example] or later to an aphorism [much of the book of Proverbs]). (3) A third type are the early poems of blessing (Gen. 27:27–29, 39–40). These seem to mark a transition from the first type to the larger and perhaps later blessing-poems at the end of Genesis and Deuteronomy. The larger poems are sometimes called *shirah* in contrast to *shir*, but these terms are not precise: at least one shorter poem is labeled a *shirah*.

In the Former Prophets two new genres occur: David's elegy (*qinah*) over the death of Saul and Jonathan (2 Sam. 2:19–27) and Hannah's prayer (1 Sam. 2:1–10).

Few distinct poems appear in the Literary Prophets. Isa. 5:1–7 is labeled as *shirah* but follows the cadences of a prophetic peroration rather than the earlier *shirot* and *shirim*. Indeed, the peroration and oracle are the prevailing genres in these works. They employ parallelism, stresses, and other poetic conventions and are therefore sometimes defined as poetry.

It is clear that the ancient Heb. poets developed a more subtle and flexible versification and style than was elsewhere known in the ancient Near East. Nevertheless, the fundamental features of biblical poetry display a high degree of continuity with the poetry of second-millennium B.C. Canaan. Clay tablets unearthed at the Syrian coastal town of Ras Shamra beginning in 1928 reveal some of the epic and mythological poetry of the north Canaanite port of Ugarit. In a lang. closely akin to ancient Heb., three major epics and other texts employ a rather strict parallelism and a large number of Homeric-like formulae and word-pairs. Scores of the latter, such as "earth" / "dust," "head" / "pate," and "hand" / "right hand," are cognate to the same parallel usages in biblical poetry. A unique pattern known as "staircase parallelism" suggests a direct literary link between early Canaanite and biblical poetry. Ps. 92:10 ("Here, your enemies, O Lord, Here, your enemies shall perish, All doers of iniquity shall be scattered") would seem to be a demythologized variant of the following "staircase" from the Ugaritic Epic of Baal: "Here, your enemy, O Baal, Here your enemy you strike, Here you smite your adversary." However, one remarkable difference in function between Ugaritic (Canaanite) poetry and biblical poetry is that in the former, verse is used for all extant narratives, while in the latter verse never narrates at length, prose being used for that purpose.

Biblical poetry reaches its greatest sophistication in the Hagiographa (The Later Writings).

The 19th-c. view that these works were all post-exilic (i.e. after 586 B.C.) is now generally rejected. Poems in the *Hagiographa* fall into five categories: (1) the epithalamia (wedding poems) of the Song of Songs (probably all pre-exilic); (2) the hymns, personal prayers, and liturgical poems of Psalms; (3) the profound religious poems which make up the book of Job; (4) the dirges composed in commemoration of the destruction of Jerusalem in Lamentations; and (5) the aphorisms called *meshalim* in Proverbs and Ecclesiastes (here differing from the earlier usage).

The poems of the Song of Songs are highly erotic and rich in passionate imagery. Probably we will never know whether they are fragments of ancient cultic hymns or simply a compendium of nuptial songs.

The Psalter towers above any anthol. of religious poetry and makes up the very core of the liturgies of church and synagogue (see PSALM). Scholars have divided the Psalms into various genres either by attempting to define the technical terms in their superscriptions (these are probably later than the texts themselves and may have indicated instruments or some mode or melody to which a specific Psalm was chanted) or by classifying them according to structure or content. Classification according to content has been the more successful. Gunkel's (1967), while at times forced, is useful: hymns, songs of God's enthronement, national dirges, royal psalms, lamentations, prayers or songs of thanksgiving by individuals, pilgrims' songs, victory odes, national songs of thanksgiving, songs in praise of the Torah, wisdom psalms, antiphonal psalms, and liturgies.

Lamentations, traditionally (but dubiously) attributed to Jeremiah, and certain Psalms (e.g. 137) mourn the destruction of Jerusalem and are central in the liturgy for *Tishʿah Beʾav*, the fast day commemorating the destruction of both Temples.

Robert Pfeiffer (687) speaks of the author of Job as possessing "at the same time great poetic genius and incredible erudition. His command of lang. and powers of expression are unmatched at his time; he used the greatest vocabulary of any Heb. writer." The most sublime poems in Job appear in the closing chapters of the book (28–31, 38–42).

Proverbs and Ecclesiastes form what later scholars call wisdom lit. Although they are mainly epigrammatic in structure, they contain several poems (e.g. Prov. 5 with its description of the temptress, or the paean celebrating the good wife in Prov. 31:11–31). Ecclesiastes is a masterpiece of stoic rumination. Of particular poetic intensity are the opening chapters and the devastating poem on aging with which the book closes.

B. *Extra-Canonical Works* (i.e. works not included in the Heb. biblical canon). The book of Sirach (the sole Apocryphal work even partially preserved in the Heb. original) and the Dead Sea Scrolls discovered in 1947–48 indicate that poetic activity did not cease after the canonization of the Heb. Bible in the 2d c. B.C. Most scholars ascribe the Apocryphal works to the 2d or 1st cs. B.C., and their poetry is akin to that found in the wisdom lit. The author of Sirach at times displays a remarkable fluency and originality, as when he describes the High Priest's entry into the Holy of Holies on Yom Kippur:

> How glorious (he was) when he
>   emerged from the Sanctuary
> And stepped out from inside the curtain;
> Like a star shining through thick
>   clouds,
> Like a full moon on feast days,
> Like the sun combing the King's palace,
> Like a rainbow seen in the cloud,
> Like a lily by a flowing stream,
> Like a flower of Lebanon on a summer's day
> Like the fire of frankincense upon the
>   offering.
>   (50:5–9)

C. *The Mishnaic and Talmudic Period* (Roman-Byzantine, ca. 100 B.C.–500 A.D.). The lit. which has survived from the Mishnaic-Talmudic era is primarily legal or homiletic, but it contains several occasional poems celebrating important events in life: births, circumcisions, marriages, and epitaphs. These were not preserved for their aesthetic quality but because they honored important scholars. Stylistically, they mark a break with the biblical trad. Instead of parallelism, many use a four-colon line. The poems are not laced with biblical quotations, their vocabulary is a mixture of biblical and post-biblical words and their syntax is late Heb.

D. *The Piyyut* (500–800 A.D.). The Byzantine period witnessed the efflorescence of the *piyyut* (Gr. *poētēs*), a liturgical poem of a new type. Some scholars believe that it developed as a device to circumvent a decree by the emperor Justinian which forbade *deuterosis*, i.e. the teaching of the oral or Talmudic law as opposed to that in the Pentateuch. The *Hazanim* (Precentors), it is claimed, interlaced the liturgy of the synagogue with didactic hymns which expounded the prohibited teaching. Since the early *piyyut* antedates Justinian's decree, however, it is more likely that it evolved as an art form at first having the purpose of lending variety to the service and, after the liturgy was permanently fixed, simply of enriching the standardized ritual. The early authors are unknown. Unlike the *piyyutim* of the classical period, theirs were unrhymed; like the Talmudic poem, they employed word-stress and avoided parallelism. Some hymns were built around a single or multiple acrostic or reversed acrostic. Other techniques used were anadiplosis, the refrain (qq.v.), the repetition of a key word at the end of a colon or a stanza, and the introduction or closing of a poem with a biblical verse related to its subject.

Yose ben Yose is the first *paytan* whose name is known to us. He heads a line of major synagogue poets who wrote in Palestine between the 6th c. and the Moslem conquest of Jerusalem in 636 A.D., the more famous among them being Yannai, Simeon ben Megas, Eliezer ben Kallir, Haduta ben Abraham, Joshua ha-Kohen and Joseph ben Nisan. During the 6th c. the various *piyyut* forms became standardized and were usually inserted into key sections of the liturgy. The earliest types were the *kerovah*, which was linked to the ʿAmidah, and the *yotzer*, linked to the *Shemaʿ* sections of the Heb. liturgy. These varied on Sabbaths and holidays. As this lit. grew, subsections were given specific names. *Piyyutim* were also composed for festivals and fast days. An early type was the ʿAvodah describing the ritual at the Temple of Jerusalem on the Day of Atonement.

While the preclassical *piyyut* confined itself to a simple style, the classical *piyyut* is almost baroque, its lang. flowery and its diction involved, favoring intricate poetic structures. Poets succeeding Yose ben Yose introduced strict rhyme schemes (fixed rhyming seems to have been introduced by either the *Paytanim* or Syrian Christian poets). In addition to the earlier acrostic forms, some classical *paytanim* signed their poems with a nominal acrostic. They were daring coiners of new words, which they constructed by assuming that Heb. was based on biliteral roots. A common poetic device was the learned allusion. Isaac, for example, is referred to as the *haʿaqud* (the bound one). Such allusions can become very elaborate and are part of the aspect of "puzzlement" which pervades this lit.

The *piyyut* form spread to the diaspora communities of Moslem Iraq (Saadiah Gaon and his school, 11th c.), North Africa, Byzantine South Italy, and, finally, to Germany, where *paytanim* like the Qalonymos family enriched the ritual of the Ger. Jewish (*Ashkenazi*) trad.

E. *Moslem Spain* (10th–12th c.). The establishment of the Caliphate in Spain in the 10th c. led to the rise of the highly cultivated *Sephardic* (Sp. Jewish) trad. (see JUDEO-SPANISH POETRY). For the first time since the biblical era, secular Heb. p. reappears alongside the continuing trad. of religious verse. Although we can only surmise that the *paytanim* in Byzantine Palestine were influenced by Syriac and perhaps Gr. church poetry, it is patently clear that Sp. Heb. p. was the product of an extraordinary synthesis of Jewish and Ar. culture.

The poets of the Sp. Heb. "Golden Age" were frequently court poets maintained by Spain's Jewish aristocracy who, like their Moslem counterparts, took great pride in their patronage of the arts. We know that Ḥasdai ibn Shaprut, the Jewish advisor of the Caliph ʿAbd'ul Raḥman III of Cordova (mid 10th c.) maintained a coterie of Heb.

poets at his court. Foremost among them was Dunash ben Labrat, who, like many Jewish intellectuals of his day, had migrated to Spain from Iraq. Dunash adapted the Ar. quantitative meter (see ARABIC PROSODY) to the needs of Sp. Heb. p., whence it became the standard for subsequent verse. But it was not just the new metric forms which were borrowed from the Arabs: Heb. poets also adopted the rules of composition fixed by the Arab rhetoricians, their rhyme patterns, and their themes. They also favored the local Sp. popular poem, the *muwashshaḥ*. Only when they wrote sacred poetry did they sometimes adhere to the *piyyut* model. More often than not, they employed the Ar. structures and techniques even in the synagogue ritual. In terms of their Heb. diction, they eschewed the cavalier way by which the *paytanim* constructed words and phrases, considering these to be barbarisms.

If the Ar. rhetoricians had insisted that the lang. of the Qurʾān was the epitome of good writing, their Heb. counterparts adhered to the biblical models, though on rare occasions they allowed themselves to draw their vocabulary from Talmudic sources. Because Heb. and Ar. were both Semitic langs., they infused Heb. words with an Ar. connotation at times.

Secular poetry was written either by poets maintained by patrons or by scholarly members of the Jewish aristocracy. One of the most common genres was the Ar. ode, the *qaṣīda* (q.v.), which soon became the vehicle for occasional poems written to celebrate an important event or to praise a patron. Such poems would begin in a purely lyrical vein, describing the beauties of nature, a drinking party, or a meeting of friends, or would develop a philosophical meditation; the poet would then shift into a laudatory mode praising a patron or colleague.

The most common form of poetic line was divided into two cola. Both cola of the first line rhymed and then the same rhyme was used throughout the poem to link the end words of the second cola, i.e.

—a —a /
—b —a /
—c —a /, etc.

The poem could be of any length. Another type of poem was the stanzaic *muwashshaḥ*: each stanza was in monorhyme, the rhyme sound changing from stanza to stanza; in addition, each stanza concluded with a couplet of a new rhyme held constant throughout the poem, e.g. *aaabb cccbb*, etc. The last couplet of the poem was often written in either Ar. or Old Sp. and rhymed with the other Heb. couplets. These signatures were frequently drawn from popular song. Many other forms existed, particularly the *rubaiyat* ("quatrain"), used for love poetry, wine songs, and epigrams. Hundreds of poems from this period have been preserved.

Samuel ibn Nagrela (Hannagid, 9th–10th cs.) was a typical aristocratic poet. He was a statesman and soldier who served as prime minister of the small state of Granada. He is the author of almost every type of secular poem: wine and love songs, encomia, epigrams, dirges. Because of his military career, he wrote a great deal of war poetry, a feat never repeated by any other Jewish poet. While Samuel employed all the conventions of Ar. poetry, he often invented highly original figures of speech.

He was followed by Solomon ibn Gabirol (11th c.), a philosopher and highly gifted poet. If Samuel's personal poetry reflected the dangerous world of the soldier, ibn Gabirol's poems retold the struggle of a sickly young poet against his fate, and of his anger against the Philistines who failed to recognize his genius. Many of Gabirol's religious works give expression to his Neoplatonic philosophy. In his long poem *Keter Malkhut* (The Kingly Crown), he contrasts the glory of God the Creator with the tragic helplessness of man.

Moses ibn Ezra (11th–12th cs.) was the scion of an aristocratic family of Granada who lived to see the decline of his native city and the destruction of its affluent Jewish community. More than any other Heb. poet, ibn Ezra is an Arabophile. His work on Heb. rhet. is full of praise for the poetic genius of the Arabs. Yet he remained faithful to his own trad. Many of his religious poems form a part of the synagogue ritual, earning him the appellation of the *Sallaḥ*, the author of penitential poetry.

The greatest Heb. poet of the period was Judah Halevi (11th–12th cs.). Like Gabirol he was both philosopher and poet. Utilizing the conventions of both Heb. and Ar. poetry, he infused them with new meaning and demonstrated a linguistic agility unrivaled in postbiblical Heb. lit. Halevi also introduced two new genres: his *Zionides*, which sing of his personal longing for Zion, and his sea poems describing his voyage to Egypt from which he hoped to complete his pilgrimage to Palestine.

Sp. poets were medieval men. If their poetry was often highly sensuous and celebrated the pleasures of the flesh, at other times it reflected the somber religiosity and deep sense of sin which also permeated medieval culture. Their religious poetry indicates that they were aware of *paytanic* poetry even if they broke with its prescriptions.

Their philosophical training also led them to question the obsession of the *paytanim* with formal constructions and their paucity of original thought. Aware that they were composing poems for their community at large, the Sp. poets usually avoided complex philosophical ideas in their synagogue verse, but their religiosity is much more meditative than that of the *paytanim*. Moreover, as Kabbalah mysticism spread through Spain beginning in the 11th c., the Sp. poets introduced its early symbols and ideas into their verse.

F. *Christian Spain* (1200–1492). With the decline of Granada in the 11th c., the Golden period of Sp. Jewry ends. The centers of Jewish population shift to Christian Spain, whose monarchs unremittingly gnawed away at Moslem Andalusia. By the 15th c. the *Reconquista* was complete, and both Moslem and Jewish communities were liquidated either by exile or forced conversion.

Heb. p. in Christian Spain in the three centuries which preceded the Expulsion never equaled the quality of that attained in Moslem Andalusia. Here too a class of Jewish "nobles" served as the patrons of Heb. lit. However, class tensions often led poets to pen social satires against the powerful. Moreover, Heb. p. underwent a process of popularization, reaching a broader audience than it did in Andalusia. While the Ar. influence remained paramount, it was now transmitted through Heb. sources, since an increasing number of Jews no longer spoke Ar. The very process of translation led to a broadening of the Heb. vocabulary to include postbiblical forms and syntax. A new synthesis occurred between the Andalusian trad., which served as a formal and stylistic model, and the new Christian literary influences: troubadour and epic poetry, beast epics, allegories, and *chansons de geste* (qq.v.—see Pagis 1976).

The Heb. writers of Christian Spain adopted an Ar. literary form, the *maqamah*. Written mainly in rhymeprose (q.v.), the *maqamah* was a picaresque compendium which contained stories, aphorisms, essays, and poems. It takes as its frame-story a dialogue between a roguish wandering scholar and his foil. The ablest of several authors of the *Maqamoth* was Judah Alharizi (12th–13th cs.).

The most important Heb. poet of 12th-c. Christian Spain was Abraham Ibn Ezra (1092–1167), a philosopher, biblical commentator, and impoverished poet, trained in the Andalusian trad., who wandered through Spain and Italy and even reached England. His poetry already manifested the peculiarities that would soon be the hallmarks of the new cultural environment: sardonic humor, realistic self-deprecation, satire, and animal allegories. His long poem *Hai ben Meqits* adopts the frame-story of a journey to the outer universe under the guidance of a mysterious mentor, a genre prevalent in the Middle East and which first appears in the Apocrypha (*Enoch*, for example). In the allegory the author (the soul) leaves his birthplace (the domicile of souls) and meets a mysterious old man (Active Intellect) who warns him against his three evil companions (Imagination, Lust, and Anger). In other poems, ibn Ezra demonstrates a penchant for realistic detail. He laments his dire poverty and his wanderings; he writes satires about his torn cloak and swarms of flies that torment him. He is the author of a charming poem about the game of chess.

Other important poets in Christian Spain were Meshullam da Piera (1st half of the 12th c.), whose poems are written in a medley of biblical, Rabbinic, and Med. Heb. styles, and Todros ben

Abulafia (late 13th c.), who introduced motifs drawn from life in Christian Spain and composed a panegyric for King Alfonso X in the form of a troubadour *cançion*, using rhyme patterns hitherto unknown in Heb. p.

G. *Italian.* The It. Jewish community was established in Roman times. Although it was small in numbers, it was highly cultured and, until the 19th c., made important contributions to the corpus of Heb. p. The first It. poet known to us is Solomon of Verona (9th c.), who wrote *piyyutim* in the style of the Palestinian school which had dominated It. Heb. p. until the 12th c. Among Italy's leading *paytanim* were Shephatiah ben Amitai (d. 886) and Amitai ben Shephatiah (9th c.) of the Ahima'ats family, and also Meshullam ben Qalonymos (10th c.).

Between the 12th and 15th cs. the influence of Sp.-Heb. p.—its meter, subject matter, and structures—prevailed, but vernacular It. forms were gradually introduced, esp. the sonnet (q.v.) in the 14th and *terza rima* (q.v.) in the 15th c. The leading poets of this period were Benjamin ben Abraham delli Mansi (13th c.) and the renowned Immanuel of Rome (see below).

The final period begins at the close of the 15th c. and ends at the opening of the 20th. At first we feel the impact of the Sp. Jewish exiles who reached Italy after 1492. Religious poetry is now dominated by the Kabbalah (Jewish theosophy). Secular poetry, on the other hand, reflected the increasing contact with It. culture. More It. poetic forms are introduced: the *octava*, the *canzone* (q.v.), the *canzonetta*, the madrigal (q.v.), and blank verse (*versi sciolti*, q.v.). Heb. poetic drama appears in the 17th c., to be followed by many such works in the 18th–19th cs. Ar. quantitative meter is soon modified by the elimination of distinction between short and long syllables so that the lines began to resemble the It. *endecasillabo* (see HENDECASYLLABLE; Pagis 1976). The poet Natan Yedidiah of Orvieto (17th c.) even made an attempt to write poems in accentual meter, but the hendecasyllabic line prevailed.

Four poets stand out: Immanuel of Rome (1270?–1330?), Jacob and Immanuel Francis (16th c.), and Moses Luzzato (18th c.). Immanuel of Rome was undoubtedly the greatest of the Italians. His *Maḥberot Immanuel* (Immanuel's Compositions) is a *maqamah* containing 28 sections, the last of which, *ha-tophet / vehaʿeden* (Hell and Paradise), was inspired by Dante's *Divina commedia.* Immanuel first introduced the sonnet into Heb. p. His verse is amazingly supple and reflects the culture of the Ren. His bawdy verses are a rarity in Heb. letters. Immanuel composed a rhetorical work in which he described the new forms in It. verse and insisted that the *acutezza* (wit) of the poem's diction and subject matter must be primary. By this term he meant the use of *surprise,* either formally (oxymora) or conceptually (paradox), by strange and complex metaphors or un-

common conceits (qq.v.). In this he was faithful to the baroque school then current in Italy and Spain. Jacob and Immanuel Frances of Mantua wrote polemic satires against the supporters of Shabbatai Zevi (17th c.), the false Messiah.

Moses Hayyim Luzzato (18th c.) composed poems and allegorical closet dramas similar to the It. works of his day. His first play, *Migdal ʿOz* (Tower of Strength), was modeled after Guarini's *Pastor fido.* Luzzato combined an awareness of 18th-c. science with a deep Kabbalistic faith. His achievement lies on the border between a late Ren. and an early Modern world-view.

The Heb. p. produced by premodern Ashkenazi Jewry was almost totally religious, influenced by the Palestinian and It. schools. It consisted of liturgical hymns and dirges commemorating the massacres during the Crusades. A particular genre of martyrological poetry was the ʿaqedah, which celebrated the sacrifice of Isaac as a symbol of the martyrdom of Jews. Ephraim of Bonn (12th c.) has a fine example of this genre (Spiegel, *Last Trial* 129–52), and *Netaneh toqef,* a prayer attributed to the martyr Amnon of Mainz, still holds a prominent place in the Yom Kippur liturgy.

By the 16th c., the center of Ashkenazi Jewry had moved from Germany to Eastern Europe. The Jews in the Polish-Lithuanian kingdom expressed their piety by the meticulous observation of the *halakhah* (Jewish Law) and by the study of religious texts. They inhabited a cultural milieu which rarely resorted to the arts—not even to the composition of religious hymns.

II. MODERN. A. *The European Period* (1781–1920). The bulk of the Jews of Central and Eastern Europe (Ashkenazim) drew their vernacular (Yiddish) and their religious trads. from the Ger. Jewish communities of the Rhineland. Ashkenazi Jews were more culturally isolated from their non-Jewish neighbors than were the Sp. and It. Jews. Although "court Jews" functioned in the Ger. states, they rarely played the prominent role which the Sp. grandees had played in Portugal and Spain. We know of no Ger.-Jewish patron of Heb. p.

With the rise of the *Haskalah* (Enlightenment) in the 18th c., first (and for a short time only) in Germany and then in Eastern Europe, Ashkenazim began to write belles-lettres. The early *Maskilim* (Enlighteners) advocated the "modernization" of Jewish religious and social life and resorted to Heb., the only literary lang. known to their audience, to criticize the old order and propagandize for a radical transformation of Jewish life.

In Germany, a group of *Maskilim* whose mentor was Moses Mendelssohn (1729–86) created the first Heb. periodical, *Ha-ma'asef* (The Gatherer). None of the authors of the *me'asfim* produced Heb. p. of lasting value. However, both in *Ha-ma'asef* and in individual works they published didactic, epic, satirical, and epigrammatic poems motivated by the attempt to prove that poetry of distinction could be written in Heb. and by the desire to propagate their ideology.

The early *Maskilim* turned to the Bible for their vocabulary and symbols and to Ger. lit. for subject matter and genres. They developed an euphuistic Heb. (*melitsah*) which was a mosaic of biblical verses and phrases.

By the 1820s, the *Haskalah* had penetrated into Eastern Europe, first into Polish Galicia (annexed by the Austro-Hungarian Empire), and soon thereafter into Czarist Russia. The Heb. poets of Eastern Europe wrote imitations of Ger. poetry in Heb., but except for two, Micah Josef Lebensohn (1828–52) and Judah Leib Gordon (1831–92), all had scant literary talent. The poetic activity in Germany and Eastern Europe of the latter part of the 19th c. served as the training ground which ultimately enabled Heb. writers to develop a style sufficient for the writing of a poetry of significance, a stage they had reached by the turn of the century.

Following the Czarist pogroms of the 1880s, Heb. writers despaired of the hope that Rus. society would open up to the Jews and grant them civil emancipation, thus permitting a synthesis between Rus. and Jewish culture. Jewish nationalism arose, encouraged in part by other ethnic movements which appeared in the Rus. and Austro-Hungarian Empires. Heb. poets penned sentimental verse bewailing the Jewish condition and expressing nostalgic yearnings for the ancient homeland.

During this period, Yiddish was also legitimized as a literary lang. Although at that time only a few Rus.-Jewish authors ventured to express themselves in Rus., most had the option of composing their works in Heb. or in Yiddish (q.v.). Many actually wrote in both langs., and this bilingualism prevailed until World War II. The interrelation between Heb. and Yiddish lit. has recently become a major subject of interest in Heb. lit. crit. While Yiddish became the vehicle of those who dreamed of an autonomous Yiddish culture in pre-revolutionary Russia, Heb., which by the 1890s had become an adequate literary medium, quite naturally became the lang. of the Zionist writers who urged its revival as the lang. of a reconstituted Jewish commonwealth in Palestine.

Hayyim Nahman Bialik (1873–1934), the greatest figure in modern Heb. p., began publishing in 1888. He not only freed himself from the shackles of the *melitsah* but also replaced the cumbersome alexandrine meter which had been adopted by *Haskalah* poets with the accentual metrical system prevailing in Ger. and Rus. poetry. His output was relatively small: almost all of his major poems were written between 1900 and 1915. A neo-romantic lyricist, he gradually shifted from nationalist themes to personal poetry. Bialik usually employed the conventional poetic forms, but from time to time he experimented with prose poetry ("The Scroll of Fire") and wrote several works in which the cadences of the prophetic peroration override the underlying metrical pattern. These were his attempts to discover indigenous Heb. poetic forms. As a disciple of Ahad Ha'am, a positivist essayist, Bialik aimed at forging a new synthesis of the viable elements of Jewish trad. and European culture. But at the same time he had grave doubts as to whether this was possible.

His colleague Shaul Chernikhowsky (1874–1943) harbored none. Nurtured by Jewish Nietzschean ideas, he believed that symbiosis was impossible: there could be no reconciliation between modern hedonism and Jewish puritanism. He therefore sought to find links with that pre-Judaic paganism which preceded "the binding of God with the straps of phylacteries." Chernikhowsky introduced many European verseforms into Heb. and translated ancient Gr., Akkadian, and Finnish poems into Heb. Bialik and Chernikhowsky ultimately settled in Tel Aviv, but while Bialik wrote few "Palestinian" poems, Chernikhowsky composed many patriotic and landscape poems set in his new homeland. Both molded a modern Heb. poetic idiom often rooted in biblical diction, but bent it to their own needs, often giving traditional allusions an ironic twist.

B. *Palestinian Poetry* (1920–48). The school of Bialik dominated Heb. p. until the 1920s and 1930s. By then younger Heb. poets, many of whom had arrived in Israel following World War I and the Rus. Revolution, revolted against the linear and symmetrical poetry of the older poets with their traditional sources and themes. Now that Heb. had become a spoken lang., the new poetry was peppered with the vernacular. It also reflected the Socialist-Zionist ideology of the pioneer culture, which was far less "Jewish" in theme and permeated with the new Mediterranean landscape.

The prominent "pioneer" poets were Natan Alterman (1910–70) and Abraham Shlonsky (1900–73). Both were influenced by the Russian revolutionary poets Blok and Yesenin and by expressionism. The *ennui* of the disintegrating urban European culture, the destruction wrought by war, and the impending Holocaust vied with the enthusiasm for the daring novelty of the reborn homeland, its bright but uncompromising colors, its sand dunes, its sea.

A third poet broke with the Socialist-Zionist ideology and embraced a fiery quasi-racial Messianism. Uri Zvi Greenberg (1894–1981) reached Tel Aviv in the 1920s, disillusioned with European humanism. The "return" for him was a return to God's historic covenant, a rejection of the "false" morality of the gentiles and a dedication to the miracle of divine providence. Greenberg's style is often extravagantly Whitmanesque. He eschews foreign verseforms, preferring the cadences of the biblical peroration and *paytanic* verse. His vocabulary is sometimes drawn from Kabbalistic texts. *Rehovot Hanahar* (1951; *Streets of the River*) is an overpowering volume of verse inspired by the martyrdom of the Holocaust—swinging between agonized despair and exultant, almost hysterical faith.

Heb. writers of the Palestinian generation were much more "European" than the generation of Bialik. They were an uprooted generation who wandered through the capitals of Europe, absorbing the cultures of their temporary homes. Their poetry was open to all influences: Rus. and Ger. expressionism (q.v.), Rus. and Fr. symbolism (q.v.), the existentialism of Rilke and George, the Freudian and Jungian views of the arts (see PSYCHOLOGICAL CRITICISM).

C. *Israeli Poets* (1948–87). With Israel's War of Independence (1948), new poets make their appearance. These were either native Israeli poets or products of the excellent Heb. school system which the Zionists had established in Eastern Europe who arrived in Palestine as young pioneers prior to the outbreak of World War II. For them, Heb. was a vibrant spoken lang. and Israel's landscape the landscape of their youth, if not their infancy. Most no longer stemmed from the traditional religious world of Eastern Europe. They were less "learned" than their forebears.

The older writers of the Israeli generation who began as junior members of the Shlonsky-Alterman school remained committed to the Socialist-Zionist ideology (Haim Guri, for example). Following the War of Independence and the mass immigration into Israel, however, many discovered that there were no facile solutions to the problems their new society faced. Once independence was attained, the egoism which had been suppressed during the struggle broke loose. Subjectivism became the rule.

Poets such as Yehudah Amichai (b. 1924), Amir Gilboa (1917–85), and Abba Kovner (1918–87) abandoned the strict metrical and verse patterns to which the older generation adhered. Amichai chose his metaphors from quotidian experience: a newspaper headline, the terms of a contract, a cliche to which he gave an ironic twist, a fragment of an old prayer. Gilboa at first had a penchant for surrealistic, childlike imagery, but as he matured he eschewed figurative lang., preferring oblique allusion and experiments with sound.

By the 1950s, Israeli culture was well on the way to Americanization. Literary influences became increasingly less Ger. or Rus.-Polish and increasingly more Anglo-Am. Natan Zach (b. 1930), the theoretically-minded poet of the 1950's and '60s, attacked what he termed the monotonous rhythms of Alterman and called for a new poetry in which line and stanza should be freed from traditional rules, and for a new diction which should have semantic significance rather than mechanical regularity. Poems should not be neatly rounded to a close but be fluid and open-ended. Figurative lang. should be used sparingly. The poet should avoid "poetic lang." and draw upon everyday speech, incl. slang. Zach also attacked "objective" or "ideological" poetry: the artist should concentrate on the subjective, existential experience of a complex modern world.

Contemp. Heb. poets are in the main secular, yet are constantly confronted by the rich religious lit. of the past, particularly their biblical heritage. Amichai can still build an ironic poem on a prayer drawn from a requiem, and T. Carmi (b. 1925) can react to a Talmudic allusion. Indeed, much poetry is evoked by tension between the sacred classics and the profane experiences of the modern poet.

Israel remains a melting pot of many cultures. Heb. p. is enriched by the interplay between them: the middle European roots of Zach, Amichai, and Pagis (1929–86); the Rus.-Polish milieu from which spring Kovner and Gilboa; the Anglo-Am. influences on Carmi, Gabriel Preil (b. 1911), who lives in New York, and Simon Halkin (1898–1987); the Mediterranean world of Mordecai Geldman; and the Maghreb world of Erez Biton.

Few women poets published during the European period, but they were quite active in Mandatory Palestine. Rahel (1890–1931) was an early "conversationalist" poet whose lyrics were clearly influenced by Rus. acmeism (q.v.). Lea Goldberg (1911–70) was a sensitive and learned poet and a leading member of the Shlonsky-Alterman circle. Zelda Mishkowski (1914–84), a pious, orthodox woman, produced several volumes of imagist religious verse, a rare phenomenon in a lit. marked by its secularity. Three important contemp. women poets are Daliah Rabikowitz (b. 1935), a feminist poet whose very sophisticated *naif* poems have been widely acclaimed; Yonah Wallach (1944–85), whose verse has a decidedly Jungian bent; and Maya Bejerano, a bold experimenter with computer poetry (q.v.).

Since the rise of the right wing in Israel, and particularly as a consequence of the Lebanese War, Heb. poets have reverted to political poetry. In the wake of the war, several volumes of protest poetry appeared in which poets like Zach and Rabikowitz, once the apostles of subjectivism, have participated. See also HEBRAISM; HEBREW PROSODY AND POETICS.

BIBLIOGRAPHIES: Y. Goell. *Bibl. of Mod. Heb. Lit. in Eng. Tr.* (1968)—7500 items from 1880–1965, *Bibl. of Mod. Heb. Lit. in Tr.* (1975)—700 items since 1917 (comparative in scope); I. Goldberg and A. Zipin, *Bibl. of Mod. Heb. Lit. in Tr.* (1979–), this series providing current bibl. and extensive retroactive coverage.

ANTHOLOGIES: *In English: Apocrypha and Pseudepigrapha of the OT*, ed. R. H. Charles, 2 v. (1913); *Post-Biblical Heb. Lit.*, ed. B. Halper, 2 v. (1921); *The Bible*, Rev. Standard Version (1952); *A Treasury of Jewish Poetry*, ed. N. and M. Ausubel (1957); *An Anthol. of Med. Heb. Lit.*, ed. A. E. Millgram (1961); *The Mod. Heb. Poem Itself*, ed. S. Burnshaw, T. Carmi, and E. Spicehandler (1965); *Anthol. of*

Mod. Heb. P., ed. S. Y. Penueli and A. Ukhmani (1966); Mod. Heb. P., ed. and tr. R. F. Mintz (1966); The Psalms, tr. M. Dahood (1966–70)—intro. and notes; "Israel," Mod. Poetry in Tr., ed. R. Friend, (1974); Mod. Heb. Lit., ed. R. Alter (1975); The Dead Sea Scriptures, ed. T. H. Gaster, 3d ed. (1976); Fourteen Israel Poets, ed. D. Silk (1976); Contemp. Israeli Lit., ed. E. Anderson (1977); Mod. Heb. P., ed. and tr. B. Frank (1980); Penguin Book of Heb. Verse, ed. T. Carmi (1981)—with intro. on prosody; "Poetry from Israel," LitR 26, 2 (1983); Jewish Pub. Society, Tanakh (1985); Israeli Poetry: A Contemp. Anthol., ed. W. Bargad and S. F. Chyet (1986); Mod. Heb. Lit. in Eng. Tr., ed L. I. Yudkin (1987). In Hebrew: Mivḥar ha-Shirah ha-ʿIvrit be-Italia (1934)—Heb. p. in Italy, Ha-Shira ha-ʿIvrit bi-Sefarad u-vi-Provence, 2 v. (1954–56)—Heb. p. in Spain and Provence, both ed. J. Schirmann; Mivḥar ha-Shirah ha-ʿIvrit ha-Hadashah, ed. A. Barash (1938)—mod.; Sifruthenu ha-Yafah, ed. J. Lichtenbaum, 2 v. (1962)—mod.; Shirah Tseʾirah, ed. B. Yaoz and Y. Kest (1980)—Israeli.

HISTORY AND CRITICISM: In English: R. Lowth, De Sacra Poesi Hebraeorum (1753); G. B. Gray, Forms of Heb. P. (1915); S. Spiegel, Heb. Reborn (1930), The Last Trial (1967); R. H. Pfeiffer, Intro. to the OT, 2 ed. (1941); C. C. Torrey, The Apocryphal Lit. (1945)—concise handbook of Jewish postcanonical lit.; S. C. Yoder, Poetry of the OT (1948); The OT and Mod. Study, ed. H. H. Rowley (1951); M. Wallenrod, The Lit. of Mod. Israel (1956); M. Waxman, A Hist. of Jewish Lit., 5 v. (1960); H. Gunkel, The Psalms, tr. T. M. Horner (1967); B. H. Smith, Poetic Closure (1968); S. Halkin, Mod. Heb. Lit., 2d ed. (1970); D. Goldstein, The Jewish Poets of Spain (1971); B. Hrushovski, "Prosody, Heb.," Encyclopaedia Judaica, (1971–72), 13.1195–1240, and "On Free Rhythms in Mod. Poetry," in Sebeok; E. Spicehandler, "Heb. Lit., Mod.," Encyc. Judaica 8 (1971); I. Zinberg, A Hist. of Jewish Lit., ed. and tr. B. Martin (1972–78); E. Silberschlag, From Ren. to Ren., 2 v. (1973–77); J. Kugel, The Idea of Biblical Poetry (1981); N. Frye, The Great Code (1982); R. Alter, The Art of Biblical Poetry (1985); A. Berlin, The Dynamics of Biblical Parallelism (1985), Biblical Poetry Through Medieval Jewish Eyes (1991); R. Alter and F. Kermode, Literary Guide to the Bible (1987); H. Fisch, Poetry with a Purpose (1988); D. Pagis, Heb. P. of the Middle Ages and Ren. (1991). In Hebrew: J. Klausner, Historiyah Shel-ha-Sifrut ha-ʿIvrit ha-Hadashah, 6 v. (1930–50)—mod.; F. Lachover, Toldot ha-sifrut ha-ʿIvrit ha-Hadashah, 4 v. (1936–48)—mod.; A. Ben-Or, Toldot ha-Sifrut ha-ʿIvrit be-Dorenu, 2 v. (1954–55)—contemp.; D Miron, Arbaʾ Panim ba-Sifrut ha-ʿIvrit Bat Yamenu (1962)—contemp.; A. M. Habermann, Toledoth Hapiyyut Vehashir (1970); E. Fleischer, Shirath Haqodesh ha-ʿIvrit Biyemei Habeinayim (1975)—piyyut; D. Pagis, Hidush Umasoreth beshirath Hahol ha-ʿIvrit (1976), Heb. P. of the Middle Ages and Ren. (1991); E. Schirmann, Letoldoth Hashirah vehadramah ha-ʿIvrit (1979); L. Waugh, "The Poetic Function in the Theory of Roman Jakobson," PoT 2 (1980); R. Brann, The Compunctious Poet (1990).
E.SP.

HEBREW PROSODY AND POETICS.

I. BIBLICAL
II. MEDIEVAL
III. MODERN

I. BIBLICAL. A. Prosody. Approximately one-third of the Heb. Bible (to which discussion is here confined) in many editions is presented in a format which suggests that the content is to be viewed as verse. In fact, all talk of "verse" or "poetry" in the Bible is the result of modern scholarly hypothesis, so that no discussion of biblical pros. can be entirely descriptive. No trad. about the nature of biblical pros. has survived for the received Masoretic text. To be sure, a number of passages termed "song" (shirah), like the "Songs" of Miriam (Exod. 15), of Moses (Deut. 32), of Deborah (Judg. 5), and of David (2 Sam. 22), as well as a few Dead Sea texts, are so arranged as to suggest an effort at indicating verse. The special system of punctuation in the so-called "poetic books" (Psalms, Proverbs, and Job) as well as the format of their text in some biblical mss., incl. the Aleppo Codex (the earliest nearly complete form of the Masoretic text), may point in a similar direction; but we have no explicit statement of underlying prosodic principles. Early references by authors such as Josephus and the Church Fathers to Cl. meters like hexameters and pentameters in the Bible are simply apologetic in nature, designed to appropriate for the Bible the heritage of the Cl. Gr. trad., comprehensible to the Hellenistic audience and designed to elicit its respect.

Biblical study in the 18th and 19th cs. also attempted to force passages considered "poetic" into approximations of Cl. meters. But by the late 19th c., and despite the efforts of no less a metrist than Eduard Sievers, it was generally recognized that prospects for exact scansions were chimerical, not least because of uncertainties in regard to key aspects of ancient Heb. pronunciation. A loose working hypothesis was reached which, without claiming to be an adequate statement of biblical pros., still allowed prosodic considerations to play a role in practical exegesis.

An essential empirical fact is the general symmetry in clause length displayed in most passages which, on other grounds, might reasonably be termed "poetic." In books like Job or Psalms, most clauses consist of from two to six words, the majority having from three to five. (By contrast, in books like Genesis or Judges, mainly narrative in content, clause length seems to be random.) It is reasonable to suppose that passages with such symmetry form an expectation in the reader's mind that after a certain number of words a caesura or line break will occur. The specific phonetic, and therefore prosodic, aspect is the silence, real or potential, awaited at the limit of expectation, which usually corresponds to clause closure. The unit so delimited is the line (in other common terminologies, colon, stichos, hemistich, verset). So firm is the perceptual base that long clauses tend to be analyzed as two enjambed lines: *wa'ani nasakti malki / ál ṣiyyon har qodši* (For I have anointed my king / On Zion, my holy mountain [Ps. 2:6]).

Within lines a meter might potentially be either isosyllabic or accentual. Syllabic analysis has been attempted several times, esp. for some early verse (Freedman, Stuart). But even recourse to a reconstructed ancient pronunciation cannot remove the many examples of syllabic asymmetry between lines. The consensus has long been that the rhythmical basis for biblical pros. lies in the stresses of speech (the Ley-Sievers system). Heb. is a lang. with a strong stress accent which is phonemic (e.g. *qáma*, "she arose," vs. *qamá*, "rising" [participle]). The system may be summarized as follows: lines contain from two to six stresses, the great majority having three to five. Each metrical unit, or foot, receives a single stress, although long terms, usually of five or more syllables, may have two stresses. By "metrical unit" is meant in most cases what is commonly presented as a "word" in the Masoretic graphemic system.

The overall system has rightly been termed "semantic-syntactic-accentual" (Hrushovski). The essential device for linking verses or sense-units together within the system is parallelism (q.v.) of the couplet (in other terminologies, bicolon, distich, stichos). The great majority of couplets can be represented as 3:3, 2:2 (often doubled to 2:2::2:2, sometimes best analyzed as 4:4), and 3:2 (often analyzable as 5), where the numbers refer to words or stresses. Also present are slightly asymmetrical couplets like 2:3 or 4:3, etc. Extreme asymmetries like 4:2 or 2:4 are likely to be "regularized" by emendation *metri causa*, but the asymmetry may have been obscured in sung or chanted performance. A unit of three lines, the triplet (tricolon, tristich) is also common, as well as the quatrain. Larger units like strophes are frequently discernible in context. Biblical verse rarely employs a single meter throughout a poem, although 3:3 is so common as to appear dominant. Alternations of 3:3 and 2:2 seem to occur, esp. in early poems. Scansion of a given passage therefore often depends on one's assessment of the soundness of the text, one's interp. of the meaning, and one's willingness to view certain elements as "extra-metrical." For example, Isa. 1:1–2:

Hear O-heavens / And give-ear, O-
    earth,
For-YHWH has-spoken:
Sons I-have-reared and-raised,
But-they have-rebelled against-me!

may be scanned in several ways: as 2:2:2 + 3:3; or, if "For-YHWH has-spoken" is viewed as extrametrical, as 2:2 + 3:3; or, if one joins the monosyllabic preposition in the final line to its verb ("have-rebelled-against-me"), as 2:2 + 3:2. Such a loose system will never satisfy purists, who can point to passages in supposed "prose" that also scan quite regularly. Some have despaired of uncovering *any* biblical meter, and some have denied the very possibility of its existence. But since there are rhythmic symmetries accompanied usually by parallelism and a host of devices often associated with verse in other prosodies—alliteration, assonance, rhyme (all common if random in biblical verse), archaisms, and tropes—it has seemed to most scholars satisfactory as a general or working hypothesis to speak of biblical meter and pros.

Parallelism is commonly included in discussions of biblical pros. because of the constitutive role it clearly plays in the rhythm of biblical verse. Most scholars include both grammatical and semantic aspects in parallelism. Aside from sporadic examples of earlier awareness, the concept and term of parallelism were introduced by Bishop Robert Lowth in the mid.-18th c. Lowth recognized two aspects of "*parallelismus membrorum*": "constructive" (i.e. grammatical), or parallelism of form; and semantic, or parallelism of meaning. He isolated three categories: "synonymous," "antithetic," and (a catch-all) "synthetic." Despite the fact that the last category in particular was unclear, Lowth's classification remained basically unchanged until refined by G. B. Gray in the early 20th c.

The basic unit of parallelistic verse is the couplet, with its A and B lines (a triplet adds a C line, a quatrain a D line). Parallelism between individual members of the lines may be complete—a situation commonly represented by the schema *abc / a'b'c'* (each letter stands for a stressed metrical unit, those in the B line being marked with a prime)—but it is frequently partial or incomplete. The most common type involves ellipsis, or "gapping," of an A-line term in the B line, in the deep structure of which it is, however, still present or "understood" (O'Connor). Apparently from a desire to maintain general syllabic symmetry the approximate number of syllables in the gapped term may be "compensated" for by an expanded or longer B line parallel ("ballast variant"). A typical schema is *abc/b'c'2*.

Semantic correspondence between parallel terms extends from actual identity via repetition to varying degrees of synonymity and antonymity, to relationships that may be labeled complementary (*eat / drink*), merism (*heaven / earth*), whole-part or part-whole (*Pharaoh and his hosts / his chief officers*), metaphorical (*the wicked / chaff*), and epithetic (*God / the Holy One of Israel*), among others. Some parallel pairs, e.g. "silver" / "gold" or "heaven" / "earth," are so common as to become virtual formulae. Such A- and B-line "word pairs" may stem from oral composition, but in most biblical verse represent merely a form of poetic diction. Little work has been done on the history of biblical parallelism, although it is possible to discern a difference between an earlier, stricter form in which parallelism is mainly between individual constituents of the couplet, and a later, looser form in which whole lines, or even couplets, are merely general semantic equivalents of other lines and couplets, as in Ps. 23:3–6. In general, parallelism allows almost endless variation without obscuring its basic contours.

B. *Poetics*. The Bible contains no explicit statements about poetics in regard to the nature of either poetry or poetic composition. However, an implicit poetics may be inferred from the complaint of the prophet Ezekiel that people consider him a mere "maker of parables" (Ezek. 21:5), a singer of "love songs, sweetly sung and skillfully played" (Ezek. 33:32). "Parables" (Heb. *mashal*, the meaning of which extends from "proverb" to larger literary compositions of several types) and secular song were the province of Wisdom in Israel, as was elsewhere in the ancient Near East the trad. of science, intellect, and conscious literary art. Although the "wise" probably claimed some type of inspiration for their productions, their art was viewed predominantly as an expression of human skill. Prophets, on the other hand, although employing the forms of poetic expression cultivated by the "wise," were believed to be mere "mouths," passive transmitters of divine messages. To view their oracles as "art" violated their prophetic function, even though, as Fisch has observed, their message achieved its effect partly via the literary artifice employed. Implicit in the conflict between prophecy and poetry is a poetics of tension between aesthetics and religion that has had a profound influence on Western culture. Meir Sternberg has explored similar tensions in the poetics of biblical narrative. Related to this is the Bible's remarkably free use of genre. Although form critics long ago isolated most of the genres used by biblical authors and related them to their analogues in the ancient Near East, analysis often shows that the traditional forms have been "sprung" or "undermined" (Fisch) by introducing an element of tension, esp. in hymns, where myth is combined with history in a manner unattested elsewhere in the ancient world. F. M. Cross has explored the historicizing of myth in Heb. texts. For example, a key myth found in many places in the Heb. Bible centered on a cosmic battle between the deity and a sea monster (representing Chaos), followed by creation and, as a capstone, the erection of the divine palace, the shrine. ·These traditional elements are applied in a classical biblical hymn, the "Song of the Sea" (Exod. 15), to the formative events of the "creation" of Israel—the Exodus from Egypt and Conquest of Canaan. However, the old mythical motifs of the theme are radically redefined, so that the cosmic foe, the sea, becomes the natural agent of the destruction of Pharaoh and his army, while the conquest is described in quasi-mythic terms as the establishment of a shrine on the hills of Canaan. The ambiguity that arises from the indeterminancy of history and myth results in that tension which gives the poem, as so much of biblical poetry, its extra, transcendent dimension.

R. Lowth, Lecture 19, *De sacra poësi hebraeorum* (1753), "Preliminary Diss.",, *Isaiah* (1778); E. Sievers, *Metrische Studien* (1901–7)—attempt at a syllabic metrics based on stress; G. B. Gray, *The Forms of Heb. Poetry* (1915, rpt. 1972 with essential "Prolegomenon" [with bibl.] by D. N. Freedman); T. H. Robinson, "Basic Principles of Heb. Poetic Form," *Festschrift Alfred Bertholet*, ed. W. Baumgartner et al. (1950); P. B. Yoder, "Biblical Heb. [Versification]," in Wimsatt; B. Hrushovski (in bibl. to sect. II below); F. M. Cross, *Canaanite Myth and Heb. Epic* (1973); F. M. Cross and D. N. Freedman, *Studies in Ancient Yahwistic Poetry* (1975); D. Stuart, *Studies in Early Heb. Meter* (1976); S. Geller, *Parallelism in Early Biblical Poetry* (1979), Pt. 1 and App. B; J. Kugel, *The Idea of Biblical Poetry* (1981), incl. survey of theories in sect. 7.2; D. N. Freedman, *Pottery, Poetry, and Prophecy* (1980); M. O'Connor, *Heb. Verse Structure* (1980)—complex attempt to redefine categories; W. Watson, *Cl. Heb. Poetry* (1984)—survey of all devices with extensive bibl.; R. Alter, *The Art of Biblical Poetry* (1985)—intro. for general students of lit.; A. Berlin, *The Dynamics of Biblical Parallelism* (1985); M. Sternberg, *The Poetry of Biblical Narrative* (1985); *The Heb. Bible in Lit. Crit.*, ed. A. Preminger and E. Greenstein (1986); H. Fisch, *Poetry with a Purpose: Biblical Poetics and Interp.* (1988). S.A.G.

II. MEDIEVAL. Med. Heb. poetry comprises two distinct branches of verse, each governed by its own distinctive poetics and systems of versification. Generically speaking, these branches are *piyyut* (Gr. *poesis*, liturgical poetry) and nonliturgical or secular poetry. The poetic styles and verseforms developed by each branch varied widely according to epoch, historical school, and geographic center.

A. *Prosody*. Until the High Middle Ages, liturgical poetry predominated in Heb. writing to the complete exclusion of the secular. *Piyyut* emerged in Palestine (probably in the 4th c.) as a popular supplement to the increasingly standardized and fixed (prose) prayer. Additionally, complex poetic cycles (*yotser* and *qedushta*) whose themes were related to the weekly recitation of Scripture were incorporated into the synagogue service. The genres of *piyyut* were thus determined by specific liturgical contexts, and *piyyut* texts were always intended for public recitation. The rules pertaining to form (most *piyyutim* were strophic), structure, and rhyme were also closely tied to the liturgical function of the poem. Idiosyncratic and complex rhymes (initial, internal, and terminal) are characteristic of early *piyyut*, but end-rhyme eventually became the prevalent form. Acrostics (q.v.) based on the 22-letter Heb. alphabet or the poet's name constituted an important formal feature of nearly all *piyyut*.

Over the course of its long evolution, *piyyut* came to employ four distinct systems of versification. In its earlier phases it was composed in two verseforms similar to those found in the Heb. Bible, one based upon an equivalent number of words in parallel versets, the other an accentual system based on 3 to 5 word-stresses per line. Later, in a post-classical devel. (Spain, 10th c.), syllabic meters, which make no distinction in vowel length but fix the number of syllables per line (6 to 8 syllables per verset or line is common), were used extensively. Finally, the quantitative meters associated with secular poetry (see below) were employed sporadically in strophic liturgical verse after the 10th c.

Secular Heb. poetry emerged in Muslim Spain in the 10th c. as a subcultural adaptation of Ar. poetry (q.v.). Two main verseforms were cultivated. The predominant type, written in the classical mold of Ar. courtly poetry, forms one continuous sequence of lines, ranging from an epigrammatic couplet to a formal ode (*qaṣīda*, q.v.) of more than 50 lines. Regardless of length, this type of composition is governed by a single meter and end-rhyme which are carried through every line of verse without variation. Rhyme-words ending in a vowel include the consonant preceding the vowel (CV); for words ending in consonants, the rhyme must encompass the preceding vowel and antepenultimate consonant (CVC). See HISPANO-ARABIC POETRY.

The second type of secular composition was strophic in form and closely connected to musical performance. The *muwashshaḥ*, as it was known in Ar. (Heb. *shir ezor*, "girdle poem"), was usually devoted to the genre of love poetry or, in a secondary devel., to panegyric. Conservative Ar. literati tended to regard the *muwashshaḥ* with disdain because it did not meet the strict prosodic requirements of Cl. Ar. poetry. Jewish courtly circles, however, enthusiastically accepted it (11th c.), possibly on account of the prevalence of similar strophic forms in the pre-Andalusian *piyyut*. The *muwashshaḥ* employed the quantitative meters used in the cl. monorhyming poem, but did so in a highly irregular fashion; that is, the meter of the first part of a strophe often differed from that of the second part of the strophe. Additionally, the *muwashshaḥ* used quantitative meters in nonstandard patterns. Tonic elements may also have come into play, though this is a matter of dispute. *Muwashshaḥāt* also differed from poems of the cl. type in allowing great flexibility in the use of rhyme. One rhyme of the *muwashshaḥ* (that of the first part of the strophe) varies from strophe to strophe; a second rhyme (that of the last part of each strophe) remains fixed throughout the poem [e.g. *aaabb, cccbb, dddbb*]. In addition to its appealing rhyme schemes and often complex metrical patterns, a striking feature of the *muwashshaḥ* is its *kharja* ("exit"), or envoi. Heb. *muwashshaḥāt* frequently conclude with Romance or colloquial Ar. *kharjas* (in Heb. script), usually in the form of a quotation from a popular Old Sp. or Hispano-Ar. love song.

The quantitative meters employed in both types of secular composition, as well as in some liturgical poetry, were created by means of an artificial system which transposed the distinctive prosodic patterns of Ar. into Heb. In Ar., as in Cl. Gr., quantitative meters are based upon the distinction between long and short syllables. It is the pattern of long and short syllables that creates the different meters. A line of verse (Ar. *bayt*; Heb. *bayit*, "house") was typically composed of metrically equivalent versets made up of from two to four metrical feet (*camudim*). Since Cl. Ar. preserved the phonological values of long and short vowels to a greater degree than biblical Heb., the system required that certain liberties be taken with Heb. grammar and phonology. Twelve of the 16 basic Cl. Ar. meters were reproduced in simplified form, and with variants (lengthened or shortened metrical feet), the number of Heb. quantitative meters amounted to approximately 60. This Ar.-style quantitative prosody subsequently attained a normative status in various Near Eastern, European, and Mediterranean communities. It was still popular in Italy in the Ren., when Heb. poetry came under the influence of It. There, It. verseforms and poetic styles were assimilated into Heb.; eventually, quantitative metrics was exchanged for purely syllabic schemes akin to those employed in It.

B. *Poetics.* Secular poetry, which represented a fusion of Ar. form and style with biblical Heb. diction and imagery, was conventional in content and stylized in form. Its modes of expression and choice of themes were generally lyrical and descriptive (love and wine poetry as well as panegyric are well represented genres), and its purpose was to entertain and persuade. Manneristic virtuosity and rhetorical ornamentation were highly prized in secular verse, but, at least among the better poets, the importance attached to conventionality, rhetorical technique, and florid style did not preclude the expression of intense feeling, particularly in poems of a personal and occasional nature.

Piyyut, by contrast, was conceived as an ennobling poetry given over to the communal passion to draw closer to God. Until the 9th c. *piyyut* tended to be esoteric and elusive; it was suffused with arcane references to Talmudic texts and rabbinic interp. of Scripture and consciously lacking in metaphor and simile. After the 10th c., when liturgical poets of the Mediterranean lands were frequently engaged in the production of the prestigious secular verse, the pros. and style of secular poetry cross-fertilized *piyyut*. The old type of *piyyut* continued to be composed alongside newer, more intelligible *piyyutim*. The poets of Muslim Spain led the way, using many of the forms and genres of the post-classical Iraqi *piyyut* and creating some new ones of their own (notably the *rĕshut*, a short poetic meditation on the theme of the prose prayer), but they abandoned the eclectic and inventive lang. of early and cl. *piyyut* for the biblical purism they propagated in secular verse. Similarly, they revamped the austere poetics of the earlier *piyyut* trad., replacing it with the ornamental and decorative approach of their secular poetry. For most of the High and later Middle Ages, then, *piyyut* and secular poetry coexisted in "creative dissonance."—B. Hrushovski, "*Ha-shitot ha-ra'shiyot shel he-ḥaruz ha-ʿivri min ha-piyyut ʿad yameinu*" [The Major Systems of Heb. Rhyme from the Piyyut to the Present Day], *Hasifrut* 2 (1970–71), "Prosody, Heb.," *Encyclopaedia Judaica* (1971–72), 13.1203–24; E. Fleischer, *Shirat ha-qodesh ha-ʿivrit bi-ymei ha-beinayim* [Heb. Liturgical Poetry in the Middle Ages] (1975); D. Pagis, *Hiddush u-masoret be-shirat ha-ḥol ha-ʿivrit bi-ymei ha-beinayim* [Change and Trad. in the Secular Poetry: Spain and Italy] (1976); R. Brann, *The Compunctious Poet* (1990).

R.B.

III. MODERN. Heb. pros. has not stagnated over the past two hundred years. On the contrary, it has passed through stages of quick devel., and has changed to some extent at each of the major centers of Heb. poetry. From the beginning of the Ren., Heb. poetry—centered in Italy after the Jews were expelled from Spain—began to assimilate European poetic styles and conventions. Immanuel of Rome (ca. 1261–1332), a contemporary of Dante, used the It. sonnet form for lines written in Gr. meters. However, the natural accents of the Heb. lang. made it difficult to assimilate quantitative meter. Apparently, the pronunciation of long and short vowels in Heb. had been forgotten during the Middle Ages. The accepted substitution for the difference in length between parts of the foot, the *t'nua* (vowel) and the *yated* (one long and one short syllable), served Heb. poetry in Italy until the beginning of the 20th c. Hence for 600 years (until 1900), the accepted meter of the Heb. sonnet was a hendecasyllabic line with a stress on the penultimate syllable (Landau).

The harbinger of modern Heb. pros. was N. H. Weizel (1725–1805) in his *Shirey Tiferet* (1785–1805; Songs of Glory). Weizel sensed the strangeness of the meter used for Heb. poetry in Spain, and also the difficulty of assimilating Gr. meter. In his desire to write a Heb. epic in a form similar to the Gr. hexameter, he devised a line of 13 syllables with a strong caesura and penultimate stress. He used couplets separated by unrhymed lines and at times the envelope rhyme scheme, *abba*. This system remained in effect until the "Hibat Zion" period (1881–97), though with variations. After Weizel, all the common stanza forms of European lit. appeared in Heb. poetry (Shpan). But today this meter seems something artificial, for it does not distinguish between naturally accented syllables and those whose accent is weak. The blurring of the tonic differences renders this meter as monotonous as the Heb. Ar. meter of the Middle

Ages. Only during the period of Ḥayyim Naḥman Bialik (1873–1934) was a way found to absorb Gr. meter into Heb. poetry: accented syllables were treated as long, while unaccented syllables (or ones with a secondary accent) were treated as short.

During Bialik's generation, the dominant Ashkenazi vocalization of Heb. affected the poetry. This system stresses the penultimate vowel and pronounces certain vowels and consonants differently from the Sephardic pronunciation. For example, the vowel "o" is pronounced "oy," and the consonant "th" is pronounced "s." The tonic meter merged well with Ashkenazi pronunciation. One especially notes the flexibility of the amphibrach, well loved by Bialik (Benshalom). Use of the Sephardic pronunciation accepted in Israel today did not become widespread until the following generation (Shavit).

Saul Tchernikhovsky (1875–1943) translated Gr. epic poetry into Heb. and thereby created the Heb. dactylic hexameter, in which trochees take the place of spondees (Shpan). The following generation (Jacob Kahan [1881–1967] and Jacob Fichman [1881–1958]) preserved the traditional rhythms; only Uri Zvi Greenberg (1895–1981) and Abraham Shlonsky (1900–73) completely broke with the earlier framework. Greenberg abandoned regular meter and rhyme to create an extended rhythm, which was the only means, he felt, to create a poem with the pathos necessary to express this generation's pain (Hrushovski). Shlonsky, on the other hand, disregarded meter altogether. Jonathan Ratosh's (1908–61) poems are distinguished by a virtuoso rhythm built on repetition of sounds, words, and sentences that flow at a dizzying, intoxicating tempo. It is interesting that Nathan Alterman (1910–70), who is an extreme modernist with regard to lang., reverted to regular meter, esp. the anapest, and to regular rhyme (though a certain estrangement is expressed in his use of assonance), but found few disciples.

The poetics of modern Heb. has also been dynamic, changing from period to period in accord with its pros. Moshe Chaim Luzzato (1707–47) viewed lit. as "the creation of something good and pleasant," thus equating the artist with the aesthete. His conceptions of figurative lang. were derived from Cl. rhet. His explanations were based on the Bible, and they concur with the approach that views the arts as decorative. Shlomo Levisohn (1789–1821) regarded the Bible as an example of the poetics of the sublime. The tr. of the Bible into Ger., and the preparation of the "Commentary" during Moshe Mendelssohn's period (1729–86), created a poetics that also served the new poetry. Such poetry attempted to educate the Jewish nation, and therefore had to be expressed in Heb., for it alone was understood by all Jewish people. At first the poetry was composed in the lang. of the Bible, but this archaic diction reminded one more of ancient landscapes than of the current world. Words integrally linked in a poem proved to mean something else when taken out of context and thus distanced the poem from real life; the rhet. (*melitsa*) remained meaningless to most of its readers.

It was Bialik who created the synthesis of the lang. of the Bible, the Sages, and the Middle Ages; he even created new words. His symbols are rich and romantic. His lang. is not built on completely figurative elements taken from ancient sources: his sources are familiar to us, yet they do not stand out in his poetry. Greenberg created symbols, such as "Sinai," "Jerusalem," "Massada," "light," "yearning," and "sublime," which refer to national myths (Kurzweill). Shlonsky rebelled against the poetic conventions of Bialik's period. He opposed usage of biblical similes; he drew his imagery from his current surroundings. He created metaphors and similes open to variable interp., such as "breasts of the night" and "night like the altar stone." Yet despite his estrangement from Bialik's style, there are those who speak of "Shlonsky in Bialik's bonds" (Hagorni).

The World Wars, the Holocaust, and existentialism stimulated—though relatively late—the appearance of an expressionist poetics in modern Heb. poetry. In this mode, the sentence, the word, and even sense is broken, incomplete. Following Shlonsky and Greenberg, Amir Gilboa (1917–89) and others use ambiguity for effect: at times a word is linked to what precedes it as well as what follows, as for example, "Also in the city on sidewalks you will run from them." The expression "you will run" (a single word in Heb.) is linked to "sidewalks" as well as "from them" (Barzel). For the same reasons noted above, bathos is dominant in recent Heb. poetry, as in the poetry of Yehuda Amihai (b. 1924) who writes, "The memory of my father is wrapped in white paper / Like slices of bread for the working day." See also HEBRAISM; HEBREW POETRY; YIDDISH POETRY; cf. CLASSICAL POETICS.

B. Z. Benshalom, *Mishkalav shel Bialik* [Bialik's Meters] (1942); B. Kurzweil, *Sifrutenu Hahadasha Hemshekh o Mahapekha* [Our New Lit.—Continuation or Revolution] (1959); S. Shpan, *Masot Umehkarim* [Essays and Studies] (1964); N. Zakh, *Zeman Veritmus Etzel Bergson Uvashira Hamodernit* [Time and Rhythm in Mod. Poetry] (1966); D. Landau, *Hayesodot Haritmiyim shel Hashira* [The Rhythmic Elements of Poetry] (1970), *Hitpathut Hasonneta Basifrut Haivrit* [Devel. of the Sonnet in Heb. Lit.], Diss., Univ. Bar-Ilan, Israel (1972); B. Hrushovski, *Ritmus Harakhavut* [The Rhythm of Extensity] (1978); U. Shavit, *Hamahapekha Haritmit* [The Rhythmic Revolution] (1983); H. Barzel, *Amir Gilbo'a* (1984); A. Hagorni, *Shlonski Be'avotot Byalik* [Shlonsky in Bialik's Bonds] (1985).   D.L.

HEGEMONY. See CULTURAL CRITICISM; MARXIST CRITICISM.

HELLENISM. See CLASSICISM.

HELLENISTIC POETICS. See CLASSICAL POETICS; ALEXANDRIANISM.

HELLENISTIC POETRY. See GREEK POETRY.

HEMIEPES (Gr. "half-hexameter"). In Cl. Gr. poetry, the metrical sequence $-\cup\cup-\cup\cup-$, which corresponds to the first half of a dactylic hexameter (q.v.), before the penthemimeral caesura. This sequence took on a life of its own; it occurs alone and in various combinations with other cola in Gr. lyric verse. West (35) suggests that although it is conventional to think of the hexameter as six dactylic feet, in fact it might better be thought of as two cola, h. plus a paroemiac (q.v.), spliced together at the caesura with one long or two short syllables.—Wilamowitz; West.   R.J.G.; T.V.F.B.

HEMISTICH (Gr. "half line"). A half-line of verse; the two hs. are divided by the caesura. In Gr. it usually forms an independent colon (q.v.). The device is used in Gr. and subsequent drama whenever characters exchange half-lines of dialogue rapidly, giving the effect of sharp argument; in Gr., such a series is called *hemistichomythia* (see STICHOMYTHIA; SPLIT LINES). In other types of poetry an isolated h. may give the effect of great emotional or physical disturbance, e.g. Virgil's isolated half-lines in the *Aeneid* (1.534, 2.233), whence Shakespeare may have learned the device, but Dryden eschews isolated hs. as "the imperfect products of a hasty Muse" (Dedication to the *Aeneis*).

In Old Germanic poetry—i.e. in OE, OHG, and ON—the h. is the primary structural unit of the meter (see ENGLISH PROSODY, *Old English*; GERMAN PROSODY, *Old Germanic*; OLD NORSE POETRY). The first h. is technically called the a-verse (or on-verse), the second h. the b-verse (or off-verse). In the definitive typology of OE meter, Sievers showed that all the hs. in *Beowulf* could be reduced to orderly variations of only five types. Further, although each half-line in *Beowulf* generally contains metrical patterns that could occur in the other half (disregarding alliteration), hs. are by no means metrically interchangeable. A few hs. are exclusively first half-line types, (e.g. type A with a light first lift and the expanded type D), and studies have shown that certain combinations of first and second half-lines, while not prohibited, are avoided (e.g. two type As or two type Bs); consequently, the structure of the long line is far from being a random mixture of self-contained hs. All of this seems to imply that the poet put together hs. according to some definite principles as yet undiscovered. Recent studies have also shown the ME alliterative line to have a clearer hemistichic structure than has been assumed by most 19th- and 20th-c. scholars.—Sievers; J. L. Hancock, *Studies in Stichomythia* (1917); A. J. Bliss,

The Metre of Beowulf, 2d ed. (1967); T. Cable, "ME Meter and Its Theoretical Implications," *YLS* 2 (1988).　　　　　　　　　T.V.F.B.; R.A.H.; T.C.

HEN BENILLION (literally, old verses or stanzas). Traditional Welsh stanzas that have been preserved orally and are sung to the accompaniment of the harp. Sometimes several stanzas are strung together and deal with one theme, but generally they are single verses. Some are strongly didactic, functioning as verse proverbs; most give expression to familiar feelings with varying degrees of literary artifice. Of anonymous authorship, they cannot be very old, and they have been kept alive for their didactic and entertainment value. Their form has been adapted and imitated by some more conscious literary artists. The best-known collection is T. H. Parry-Williams, *H. B.* (1940). There have been fine translations by Glyn Jones, *When the Rosebush Brings Forth Apples* (1981) and *Honeydew on the Wormwood* (1984). See WELSH POETRY.　　　　　　　　　　　　　J.E.C.W.

HENDECASYLLABLE. A line of 11 syllables. The h. is significant in both the quantitative verse of Gr. and Lat. and in the accentual and syllabic prosodies of the modern Romance langs., though as different meters. In Cl. prosody (q.v.), the h. is the Phalaecean (q.v.), which has the pattern ∪ ∪ (or ∪ –; – ∪; – –) – ∪ ∪ – ∪ – ∪ – ∪ and is chiefly associated with Catullus. But in the Middle Ages, as the quantitative or "metrical" Lat. verse was transformed into the accentually based "rhythmic" verse of the vernaculars, the It. *endecasillabo* seems to have evolved from the Cl. Sapphic or iambic trimeter; its relation to the Fr. *décasyllabe* in the earliest stages is disputed. In *De vulgari eloquentia* (2.5, 2.12; ca. 1304), Dante defined the h. as the most noble line of It. prosody, the one most suitable for the highest forms of poetic expression in the vernacular and, as such, the preferred line for the *canzone* (q.v.), the most illustrious of lyric forms; the h. has been the staple line of It. poetry since the 13th c. The names of the lineforms in It. prosody are established by the place of the principal accent, and thus the normal h. has 11 syllables, with a fixed stress falling on the 10th (the *endecasillabo piano*; see VERSO PIANO); normally in this form of the meter the final word in the line is paroxytonic. Occasionally lines of 10 syllables occur (see VERSO TRONCO); these are the analogues of the Romance decasyllables and, in their unrhymed form (ENDECASILLABI SCIOLTI) and more distantly, the Eng. iambic pentameter. Lines of 12 syllables also occur, the final word being then pro-paroxytonic (see VERSO SDRUCCIOLO). In addition to the major stress on the 10th syllable, the It. h. is divided by a variable caesura into two hemistichs of unequal length, one a *settenario* and the other a *quinario*—with a corresponding secondary stress on either the 6th syllable (*endecasillabo a maiore*: "nel mezzo del cammín

/ di nostra vìta") or the 4th (*endecasillabo a minore*: "mi ritrovái / per una selva oscùra"). In the former, the *settenario* comprises the first hemistich, followed by the *quinario*, and vice versa in the latter. Given the large number of dispositions of the secondary stresses in the line, the h. is the most versatile meter in It. prosody, being used in virtually every genre (*canzone, ballata*, sonnet, *terza rima, ottava rima*, madrigal [qq.v.]) and for all subjects by most It. poets. A distinctive feature of many It. stanza forms is "the harmony of eleven and seven" (Ker), a mixing of hs. and heptasyllables which carried over into Sp. prosody as well.

The Marquis de Santillana (Íñigo López de Mendoza) adapted the h. to the Sp. sonnet form in 1444, and in general, the devel. of the h. in Spain followed the same pattern as that in Italy. Heine and Goethe imitated the It. h. in Germany. In Eng., the iambic pentameter (see DECASYLLABLE) was influenced in its early stages (i.e. in both Chaucer and Wyatt) by the It. *endecasillabo*, but 11-syllable lines in Eng. are usually simply pentameters with an (extrametrical) feminine ending (see MASCULINE AND FEMININE): true hs. in Eng. after the Ren. are usually trs. or imitations of Catullus, See also CLASSICAL METERS IN MODERN LANGUAGES; ITALIAN PROSODY; SAPPHIC; TRIMETER; VERSI SCIOLTI.

W. Thomas, *Le Décasyllabe roman et sa fortune en europe* (1904); F. D'Ovidio, *Versificazione italiana e arte poetica medievale* (1910); W. P. Ker, "De superbia carminum," *Form and Style in Poetry* (1928); M. Serretta, *Endecasillabi crescenti* (1938); A. Monteverdi, "I primi endecasillabi italiani," *Studi romanzi* 28 (1939); V. Pernicone, "Storia e svolgimento della metrica," *Tecnica e teoria letteraria*, ed. M. Fubini, 2d ed. (1951); M. Burger, *Recherches sur la structure et l'origine des vers romans* (1957); D. S. Avalle, *Preistoria dell'endecasillabo* (1963); G. E. Sansone, "Per un'analisi strutturale dell'endecasillabo," *LeS* 2 (1967); A. D. Scaglione, "Periodic Syntax and Flexible Meter in the *Divina Commedia*," *RPh* 21 (1967); L. Baldi, "Endecasillabo," *Enciclopedia Dantesca*, v. 2 (1970); P. Boyde, "The H.," *Dante's Style in his Lyric Poetry* (1971); A. B. Giamatti, "It.," in Wimsatt; Spongano; Wilkins; F. Caliri, *Tecnica e poesia* (1974); P. G. Beltrami, *Metrica, poetica, metrica dantesca* (1981); Elwert, *Italienische*.　　　　　　T.V.F.B.; C.K.; R.A.S.

HENDIADYS (Gr. "one through two"). The use of two substantives (occasionally two adjectives or two verbs), joined by a conjunction, to express a single but complex idea: one of the elements is logically subordinate to the other, as in "sound and fury" (*Macbeth* 5.5.27) for "furious sound." The figure appears in Gr. verse and prose but is not referred to before Servius (4th c. A.D.), who notes it in Virgil (e.g. *pateris libamus et auro*: we drink from cups and gold = from golden cups—*Georgics* 2.192). In Gr., according to Sansone, true h. typically shows a "reciprocal" relation between its two elements, "*either of which* could be logically and grammatically subordinated to the other": thus *pros haima kai stalagmon* (*A. Eumenides* 247) may mean both "the dripping of the blood" and "the dripping blood."

Virgil's h. sometimes involves two distinct ideas (Hahn)—from cups and from gold—as well as a third which fuses them. The sum is elusive and complex. Shakespeare, taking advantage of the figure's mysterious and anti-logical overtones, uses h. far more than any other Eng. writer, often in conjunction with other kinds of doublets, to cast doubt on the authenticity of ling. and social unions, couplings, contracts, and marriages, and to provide a ling. mirror for the internal agitation and ambivalence of troubled characters and plays (e.g. Gertrude's "Upon the *heat and flame* [for hot flame] of thy distemper" [*Hamlet* 3.4.123]). See esp. *Hamlet* (Wright, Kermode). Housman parodies Gr. h. in "I go into the house with *heels and speed.*"

A. E. Housman, "Frag. of a Gr. Tragedy," *Bromsgrovian* (1893), rpt. in *Parodies*, ed. D. Macdonald (1960); E. A. Hahn, "H.: Is there Such a Thing?" *CW* 15 (1921–22); G. T. Wright, "H. and Hamlet," *PMLA* 96 (1981); K. T. Loesch and Wright, "Forum: H.," *PMLA* 97 (1982); D. Sansone, "On H. in Gr.," *Glotta* 62 (1984); F. Kermode, "Cornelius and Voltimand," *Forms of Attention* (1985). G.T.W.

HEPHTHEMIMERAL. See HEXAMETER; CAESURA.

HEPTAMETER. This term means a line of 7 feet, but metrists have at times termed "hs." meters which have little resemblance to each other beyond syllable count, so the term is perhaps better avoided. It is occasionally used to refer to Cl. meters such as the Lat. *septenarius* (q.v.), which is a brachycatalectic line of seven trochaic feet, and it has been used by some prosodists for modern meters such as the Ren. fourteener (q.v.), as in Chapman's Homer, but this is not the same type of meter: it has a different rhythm and is used in radically different contexts. Still less is it an appropriate term for Eng. ballad meter (q.v.), which in its most common form is set in quatrains of lines of 4-3-4-3 accentual verse (q.v.). Schipper uses this term more or less synonymously with "septenary" for ME poems in 14–15 syllables such as the *Poema morale* and *Ormulum*, but here too terminology implies a derivation and structure that now seem problematic. In modern Eng. verse, the term is applicable mainly to the long line of William Blake's later Prophetic Books, a line which Blake said "avoided a monotonous cadence like that of Milton and Shakespeare" by achieving "a variety in every line, both in cadence and number of syllables." Syllable count actually ranges as high as 21. Blake's sources would seem to be the Bible (see VERSET), Macpherson, and late 18th-c. Ger. ex-

periments in long-lined verse such as those in Hölderlin's *Hyperion*, but Blake himself claimed the form was given him in automatic writing. Other 19th-c. instances: Wordsworth's "The Norman Boy" and "The Poet's Dream" (coupleted quatrains); Byron's "Stanzas for Music"; Scott's "The Noble Moringer"; E. B. Browning's "Cowper's Grave"; Whittier's "Massachusetts to Virginia."—A. Ostriker, *Vision and Verse in Wm. Blake* (1965); K. Raine, "A Note on Blake's 'Unfettered Verse,'" *Wm. Blake: Essays for S. Foster Damon*, ed. A. H. Rosenfeld (1969). T.V.F.B.

HEPTASYLLABLE. In most metrical systems, lines of 7 syllables are almost always variants of octosyllables (q.v.), not an autonomous meter. In Eng. such lines appear most prominently in the verseform known as "8s and 7s," as in Milton's *L'Allegro* and *Il Penseroso*. In Fr. they are one form of *vers impair* (q.v.), though the hs. in Ronsard's odes are a deliberate imitation of Pindar, whose odes were printed in short lines in the 16th c. Only in It. prosody (q.v.) is the h. or *settenari* a major line-form, being used in alternation with the hendecasyllable (q.v.), the *endecasillabo*. This mixing of lines of 7 and 11 syllables in stanzas is distinctive to It. prosody and very much exploited by It. poets. In Welsh *englynion* they were perhaps the original line length, later to be combined with 10s and 6s (see ENGLYN).—M. F. Moloney, "The Prosody of Milton's 'Epitaph,' 'L'Allegro,' and 'Il Penseroso,'" *MLN* 72 (1957); R. Nelli, "Remarques sur le vers heptasyllabique français et occitan," *Mélanges offerts à Rita Lejeune*, v. 1 (1968); B. Vine, "On the Heptasyllabic Verses of the *Rig-Veda*," *ZVS* 91 (1977): Elwert, *Italienische*. T.V.F.B.

HERESY OF PARAPHRASE. See PARAPHRASE, HERESY OF.

HERMANN'S BRIDGE. See BRIDGE.

HERMAPHRODITE RHYME. See MASCULINE AND FEMININE.

HERMENEUTIC CIRCLE. See HERMENEUTICS; THEORY.

HERMENEUTICS.

    I. MEANING OF THE TERM
   II. ANCIENT AND MEDIEVAL
  III. MODERN PHILOLOGICAL AND BIBLICAL
  IV. GENERAL AND PHILOSOPHICAL
   V. RELEVANCE TO POETRY AND POETICS

    I. MEANING OF THE TERM. H. is the art of interpreting texts, esp. via a body of rules, techniques, and a theory of literary, legal, or biblical exegesis. The term derives from Gr. *hermēneúein* ("to interpret"), which had three senses: to interpret poetry orally (to express), to explain, and to translate. Plato refers to the technique of oracle interp. as *hermēneutikē mantikē* (*Epinomis* 975c) and poets as *hermēnēs tōn theōn*, "interpreters of the gods" (*Ion* 534e). As a book title in antiquity, the term *hermēneía* refers to the capacity for expression and communication (Xenophon, *Mem.* 4.3.12; Aristotle, *Peri hermēneías*); *hermēneuticà Biblía* are glossaries (translations), while *hermēneía* titled many works of commentary or exegesis. The function of Hermes as message-bringer is referred to in antiquity as *hermēneúein*; a liminal god of margins and boundaries, Hermes guides the newly dead to the underworld; he is a god of sleep and transformation, of windfalls and "lucky breaks," and also a thief. H. in modern times is central to both Cl. and sacred philology; as such it is to be distinguished from textual crit. (q.v.), which establishes the text, whereas h. is the art of *understanding* the text thus established (see INTERPRETATION; EXPLICATION; ANALYSIS), and from lit. crit., which goes on to evaluate the text once understood (see CRITICISM; EVALUATION; METACRITICISM). The earliest recorded use of the term in Eng. dates from 1737 (*OED*). H. is often distinguished from exegesis: "the word '*hermeneutic*' implies the Science and Theory, the word *Exegesis* the Art and Practice of Scriptural Interp." (Farrar 1886). Hermes is identified with transformation in alchemy and the *Corpus hermeticum*; and h. is often associated with revealing the hidden (see HERMETICISM).

II. ANCIENT AND MEDIEVAL. The earliest treatise on interpreting dreams is an *Egyptian Dreambook* (ca. 2000 B.C.); probably the most extensive was Artemidoris' *Oneirocritica* (ca. 180 B.C.). Macrobius (ca. 400), in his commentary on Cicero's *Somnium scipionis*, distinguishes five types of dreams: enigmatic, prophetic, oracular, nightmare, and apparition. The last two, he says, "are not worth interpreting since they have no prophetic significance" (*Commentary on the Dream of Scipio*, tr. W. H. Stahl [1952], ch. 3; see Woods 1947). Oral interp. of Homer by rhapsodes dates from earliest historic times; Plato reflects on the status of such interp. in the *Ion*. The hermeneutic strategy of "demythologizing" (i.e. finding deeper meaning in myths when they can no longer be taken as literally true) used by the 20th-c. theologian R. Bultmann actually dates to the ancient Stoics, who, finding their behavior morally repugnant, interpreted the Homeric gods as allegories of the elements. Early Jewish and Christian interpreters of the Bible such as Philo, Origen, and Jerome applied a similar allegorical interp. to the Genesis narratives, and it is commonly applied to the poetry of the OT Song of Songs (see INTERPRETATION, FOURFOLD METHOD OF). Plato solves the same problem of interpreting offensive poetry not by reinterp. but by the blunter method of banning poets and Homeric poetry from the Republic altogether. Methods of textual interp. and theories of what it means to interpret a text are found in ancient Gr. and Roman rhet., pedagogy, and reflection on poetry (cf. Basil, "Address to Young Men

on Gr. Lit."). Plato is particularly rich in this regard, offering reflections on poetic exegesis (*Protagorus* 339a–47a); on names and things (*Cratylos* 433e–40e); on knowledge and perception (*Theaetetus* 151e–186e); on true and false rhet. (*Gorgias* 462b–465e, 521d); on dialectic (*Republic* 532b–534b); on true and false interps. of love (*Phaedrus* 231a–43e, 249d–57a); on varieties of madness—prophetic, cathartic, poetic, erotic (*Phaedrus* 244a–45b); and on the origin of writing (*Phaedrus* 274b–78b). Aristotle defined understanding in terms of grasping the structure and purpose of something: thus in the *Poetics* he looks at how comedy, epic, and tragedy are constructed and how they function. When he describes tragedy in terms of its cathartic effect (see CATHARSIS), Aristotle anticipates modern reader-response crit. (q.v.) and aesthetics of reception.

Biblical h. begins with the multiple layers and elaborate legalism of ancient Heb. Rabbinic interp. (Babylonian Talmud, Halacha, Haggada, 7 rules of Hillel, 13 rules of Ishmael; cf. Jacobs, Strack—see HEBRAISM); traditional Rabbinic forms of interpreting the OT are found in the NT (Heb. and Christian typological interp. must be distinguished from Gr. allegorical; cf. Bercovitch, Pépin). Origen (*De principiis* 4) offers the first set of Christian rules for allegorical interp., distinguishing three levels: literal, moral, and spiritual. Augustine (*De doctrina*) gives many rules, incl. the seven rules of Tichonius (3.31–38), and discusses three levels of allegorical interp. Subsequent medieval exegesis distinguishes four levels—literal, moral, allegorical, and anagogical—as described in the famous letter to Can Grande della Scala long attributed to Dante (see INTERPRETATION, FOURFOLD METHOD OF). Allegory (q.v.) as a literary form is certainly found in modern times, but the golden age of allegorical interp. is medieval, culminating in the four levels of exegesis. Nevertheless, allegorical interp. anticipates contemp. theories which elaborate the role of the reader and question the preoccupations with literal sense and with the desire to recover authorial intention (q.v.).

III. MODERN PHILOLOGICAL AND BIBLICAL. The term "h." as designating rules and methods for textual interp. comes into its own with the Reformation. The need in Protestant theology for methods of interpreting the Scripture apart from the trad. of episcopal authority, as well as the similar need for methods of treating texts from antiquity in Cl. philology, fostered the devel. of h. manuals. The first such manual to have the term "h." in its title is Dannhauer's *Hermeneutica sacra sive methodus exponendarum sacrarum litterarum* (Sacred H. or the Method of Explicating Sacred Lit., 1654). Reformation h. in Luther and Calvin marks a decisive shift away from allegorical interp. toward more literal and historical exegesis (cf. Ebeling, Dilthey). The goal of interp. now was less to construct layers of symbolic significance than to recover the intended meaning. Erasmus' edition of the Gr. NT brought a new sense of the historical foundations of the faith; Luther argued that the text of the Bible is clear, self-sufficient, and self-interpreting. Spurred by the availability of Luther's tr. of the Bible as well as of Scriptural tracts which were products of moveable-type printing, h. manuals began to appear which specifically set forth rules and principles for proper interp. of the Scripture. Between Luther's time (d. 1546) and the turn of the 19th c., several hundred such manuals were printed (Ebeling). Cl. philology and biblical h., previously separate, are closely intertwined in the 18th c., with the latter essentially accepting the methods of the former. F. A. Wolf (1759–1824) and F. Ast (1778–1841) are exemplars of the philological h. of the early 19th c.: Wolf defines the aim of h. as the effort "to grasp the written or even spoken thoughts of an author as he would have them to be grasped" and distinguishes three categories of *interpretatio*: *grammatica* (grammar), *historica* (history, background, incl. the author's biography), and *philosophica* (an overarching knowledge to conjoin the first two). This general trad. is continued by other interpreters in the 19th c., the greatest of whom is A. Boeckh (1785–1867). Boeckh distinguishes four components of interp.: the *grammatical* and *historical* (objective components), and the *individual* and *generic* (subjective components). H. as a methodology of philology and biblical interp. continues into the 20th c. (Wach, Szondi, Flashar et al., Müller-Vollmer), but a broader interp. of h. emerges in the romantic period with a line of devel. of its own.

IV. GENERAL AND PHILOSOPHICAL. At the beginning of the 19th c., Friedrich Schleiermacher (1768–1834) rebelled against the philological (and biblical) h. of Wolf, Ast, and Ernesti, labelling it a mere "aggregate of conflicting and contradictory rules" (*H.*, 1819, rpt. 1959, tr. 1978). He called for an *allgemeine Hermeneutik* ("general h.") that would hold for all cases of mutual understanding in dialogue. Schleiermacher defined h. very broadly, as the "art of understanding" whether of spoken words or written texts: h. is "what every child does in inferring the meaning of a new word" from its context and use. Arguing for a twofold "grammatical" (linguistic) and "technical" (psychological) interp., Schleiermacher also recognized a "divinatory" moment of understanding in which one apprehends the individuality of the author through his "style." "General" h. represented a decisive step beyond the traditional h. of philological rules for rightly interpreting Cl. and biblical texts and toward a h. that meditates on the nature and conditions of all understanding. See ROMANTIC AND POSTROMANTIC POETICS.

Life-philosopher W. Dilthey (1833–1910), a biographer of Schleiermacher (ed. M. Redeker, 1966), was to be the most important continuer of general h. Dilthey defined h. as the art of understanding *schriftlich fixierte Erlebnisausdrücke*, objects on which the human spirit had left its imprint. These might be works of art, a noble law, a poem, a sacred text, architecture, dance—every *sinnhaltige Form*, every form touched and shaped by the human spirit to convey sense. By explicating the process of *Erlebnis-Ausdrück-Verstehen* (Experience-Expression-Understanding) and by clarifying the contrast between empathic understanding in the human sciences and mere causal explanation in the natural sciences (*Verstehen* vs. *Erklären*), Dilthey hoped to provide a "critique of historical reason" which would give the same methodological foundation for the humanities and social sciences that Kant's *Critique of Pure Reason* had given for the natural sciences (*Selected Writings*, ed. H. P. Rickman [1976]; *Selected Works*, ed. R. A. Makkreel and F. Rodi, 5 v. [1985–]). Unfortunately, as Ricoeur has shown (*Conflit des interprétations*, 1968), this distinction is untenable with regard to separating the human and natural sciences. Yet in proposing that h. should be the methodological foundation for the humanities Dilthey greatly extended the scope and claims of h.

Martin Heidegger (1889–1976) wrote no book on h., and he discusses the term explicitly only in *Sein und Zeit* (Being and Time, 1927) and "Dialogue with a Japanese" (in *On the Way to Lang.*, 1959), yet his influence on 20th-c. philosophical h. has been seminal. In discussing his method in *Sein und Zeit*, Heidegger claims (*On the Way to Lang.*, sec. 7) that his explication of human existence will have the character of interp. (*hermēneúein*), because each human has a sense of the meaning of being. Explicating this sense "is h. in the original meaning of the word, which designates the business of interp. [*Auslegung*]." H. is here broadened to the widest possible extent: since the interpretive process is fundamental to being and goes on constantly, to exist is to interpret. By defining "understanding" in terms of existential self-understanding, Heidegger shifts the focus of h. from objects or texts in the world to the way in which each human interprets its own being-in-the-world to itself, which in turn forms the basis for interps. of texts. Heidegger radically changes the definition of the "hermeneutical circle," which traditionally had referred to the process of understanding a whole in terms of its parts and vice versa. Now the circularity is rooted in a prior existential understanding.

Hans-Georg Gadamer (b. 1900) in his magisterial *Wahrheit und Methode* (1960; tr. *Truth and Method*, 1975, rev. 1988) put forward a comprehensive "philosophical h." which offered a critique of prevailing views of aesthetic and historical consciousness as well as a new philosophical basis for literary and historical interp. A specialist in Plato, Gadamer made dialogic understanding central to his h. but otherwise generally followed Heidegger in emphasizing that all understanding is historical—not only in the sense of being situated at a moment in historical time but also in the sense that historically inherited concepts are always at work in our understanding. Interp. should not write off all trad. as dogma, as Enlightenment thinkers tended to do, but should renew what is valuable and challenge what no longer has warrant. Taking his lead from the later Heidegger, who saw lang. as the "house of being," Gadamer emphasizes the linguistic character of understanding, asserting that lang. is "the universal medium in which understanding finds its fulfillment," and the ontological priority of the work of art. Gadamer takes Heidegger's essay "Der Ursprung des Kunstwerkes" ("The Origin of the Work of Art," 1936) as his guide in challenging the "subjectivization of aesthetics since Kant," which has tended to reject any truth-claim in art, incl. poetry (see SUBJECTIVITY AND OBJECTIVITY). Gadamer argues that the truth-claims of art can be defended by grounding them in the being of the artwork; "truth" comes to stand preeminently in the work of art.

Almost immediately, Emilio Betti attacked Gadamer, protesting that objective interp. had been dumped overboard and calling for a return to the trad., to "h. as the general problematic of interp., that great general discipline which welled up so nobly in the romantic period as the common concern of all the humane disciplines, which commanded the attention of many great minds of the 19th c. This venerable older form of h. appears to be fading out of modern Ger. consciousness" (Betti 1962).

In America, E. D. Hirsch's *Validity in Interp.* (1967), following Betti and rejecting Gadamer, proposed to continue the trad. of a methodological h. oriented to objectively valid interp. But in Germany, many scholars found Heidegger and Gadamer more positive: Protestant theologians R. Bultmann, G. Ebeling, and E. Fuchs found in them a new direction for theological reflection on textual interp., and Gadamer's masterwork was embraced by Am. theologians J. Robinson and J. Cobb, who announced a "new h." in theology (see Robinson and Cobb). A group of Ger. literary scholars formed a "H. and Poetics Workgroup" which met biennially during the 1960s and '70s, among them P. Szondi, H.-R. Jauss, and W. Iser (see Amacher and Lange). Szondi (1975) began lecturing on the hist. of literary h., and both Szondi and Jauss issued manifestoes ("Über philologische Erkenntnis," 1967, tr. 1986; *Literaturgeschichte als Provokation*, 1970) calling for the radical reform of philology and of the study of lit. hist.

A contribution to h. second only to Gadamer's was made in France by the philosopher Paul Ricoeur. A translator of Husserl's *Ideen* (Ideas, 1913), Ricoeur applied phenomenology to interp. in *Histoire et vérité* (1955) and *La Symbolique du mal* (1960). In his *De l'interprétation: Essai sur Freud* (1964), he distinguished h. of suspicion (Marx, Nietzsche, and Freud) from h. of recovery of meaning (as in theological and philological h.). The former treats the text as embodying a false consciousness to be overcome, whereas the latter treats the text as a challenge to the false consciousness of the interpreter. Ricoeur endeavored to build bridges between h. and analytic philosophy, structuralism (q.v.), psychoanalysis, and theology, esp. in his *Le conflit des interprétations* (1968, tr. 1974), feeling that Gadamer's h. tended to justify trad., left too little room for critique, and failed to account for distorted communication (a criticism echoed by Habermas). Ricoeur also lamented that while h. in Heidegger and Gadamer offered a critique of the pretensions of method, this type of h. was not concretely useful as a methodology.

On the Continent in the early 1970s, the universal claims, the defense of "prejudice," and the lack of a critique of ideology in Gadamer's h. were assailed by his former student, social philosopher Jürgen Habermas (*Theorie des kommunikative Handelns* [1981, tr. 1983], *Der philosophische Diskurs der Moderne* [1985, tr. 1987], *Nachmetaphysisches Denken* [1988]) in a discussion that became the focus of considerable debate (see Apel et al.). In France, Ricoeur's work took a semiotic turn in *La Métaphore vive* (1975; tr. *The Rule of Metaphor* [1977]) and *Interp. Theory* (1976) which was continued in his imposing 3-vol. study, *Temps et récit* (1983–85, tr. *Time and Narrative* [1983, 1986, 1988]). From the late 1960s into the '80s, the poststructuralist writings of Jacques Derrida and Michel Foucault open up new dimensions of "textuality" (q.v.), linking themselves with Nietzsche's radical view of interp. as perspectival, postobjectivist, and inseparable from the power interests of the culture, which only a "genealogical" interp. can disclose (cf. F. Nietzsche, *On the Genealogy of Morals*, tr. 1969). While Foucault, for his part, explicitly rejected phenomenology to explore genealogically and archeologically the coercive interests and power structures concealed in knowledge, Derrida undertook an internal critique of Husserl's phenomenology and Heidegger's phenomenological ontology, showing a "metaphysics of presence" lurking not only in Husserl's view of lang. in the *Logische Untersuchungen* (1900; tr. *Logical Investigations*, 1970), but even within Heidegger's deconstructions of Western logocentrism. Using Saussure's insight into the differential structure of lang. while stripping it of its metaphysics of presence, Derrida, following Heidegger, posed a radical critique of Western metaphysics since Plato (*De la grammatologie* [1967, tr. 1976], *L'écriture et la différence* [1967, tr. 1978], *Marges* [1972, tr. 1983]). This *Verwindung* (curative overcoming) of logocentric metaphysics calls into question all hermeneutic theories and methods based on such metaphysics (incl. the whole history of lit. crit.), making them targets for what Heidegger terms *Destruktion* or *Abbau*, a term which Derrida translates and deepens as "*déconstruction.*" The consequences of Derridean deconstruction (q.v.) for lit.

crit. were explored during the 1970s by Yale critics Paul de Man, J. Hillis Miller, and Geoffrey Hartman, a development that continued through the 1980s (see TWENTIETH-CENTURY POETICS).

It remained for Am. pragmatist philosopher Richard Rorty to place h. at the center of Am. philosophical discussion with his *Philosophy and the Mirror of Nature* (1979; see also his *Consequences of Pragmatism*, 1982). Rorty found in h. an alternative to "foundationalism" (preoccupation with metaphysical or epistemological foundations for thought and interp.), viewing Kierkegaard, James, Dewey, Wittgenstein, Gadamer, and the later Heidegger as antifoundationalist, hermeneutic thinkers. Richard J. Bernstein, entering into dialogue with Gadamer, Rorty, and Habermas (see below), found in h. the basis for a "new conversation" that uncovers hitherto unseen dimensions of rationality; in *Beyond Objectivism and Relativism* (1983), Bernstein argued that h. continually points beyond itself to praxis.

In the h. discussions of the 1980s, the relevance of h. to Am. pragmatism was only one of several issues. More significant was the relation of h. to poststructuralism, which Gadamer, in his brief encounter with Derrida in Paris (1981), referred to as "the Fr. challenge" ("Text and Interp." in Michelfelder and Palmer). Toward the end of the 1980s, politics moved center-stage with Stanley Rosen's *H. as Politics* (1987)—incl. heated discussions of Heidegger's fascist inclinations centered on Victor Farias' *Heidegger and Nazism* (tr. 1989)— and with Derrida's work exploring the relation of deconstruction to politics (Derrida 1982, 1988).

V. RELEVANCE TO POETRY AND POETICS. Poetics and h. are closely related and even overlapping concepts. Poetics, taken either as "theory of poetry" or "theory of lit." (Aristotle), is as concerned with theories of poetic making as it is with interp., whereas h. is restricted to the theory and art of understanding. H. is significant for poetics, however, in that it offers a legacy of reflection from ancient times to the present on the task of interp. This legacy is particularly rich in the general and philosophical h. of the 19th and 20th cs., which emphasize the linguistic, historical, perspectival, and dialogical character of all understanding. The close ties of h. with 20th-c. philosophy, esp. phenomenology, also make it a source of insights potentially fruitful for poetics. For example, Heidegger's deconstruction of substance-metaphysics and its associated definitions of truth, hist., art, and lang. lead to Gadamer's critique of historical consciousness and of subjectivity aesthetics since Kant (*Wahrheit und Methode*, Part I, and *Poetik* [1977]). For Gadamer the poetic text is text in the eminent sense; it defines the highest potentialities of texts for pregnance of meaning, autonomy from authorial intention, and power within its speaking to use the deepest resources of the lang. ("Text and Interp.," in Michelfelder and Palmer [1989]). As with a sacred text, dialogue with a poetic text

reverses the direction of interrogation and puts the reader in question; it addresses and even places a demand on the reader. Gadamer's ontology of understanding in *Truth and Method* presents a complexly nuanced argument for the special status of poetry and its truth, and thus may be seen as a new poetics, though without a correlate theory of poetic production. It is possible to understand a poem without a theory of its production, but not without an implicit view of understanding, i.e., an implicit h. See also CRITICISM; HEBRAISM; INTERPRETATION, FOURFOLD METHOD OF.

HISTORIES: F. W. Farrar, *Hist. of Interp.* (1887)— dated and biased but still a valuable hist. of biblical interp.; W. Dilthey, "The Rise of H." [1900], in *Dilthey: Sel. Writings*, ed. H. P. Rickman (1976); J. Wach, *Das Verstehen: Die Hermeneutik im 19. Jahrh.*, 3 v. (1926–33); H. L. Strack, *Intro. to the Talmud and Midrash* (1931); R. L. Woods, *The World of Dreams* (1947)—extensive sampling of dream interp. ancient to modern; R. M. Grant, *A Short Hist. of the Interp. of the Bible* (1948); E. Betti, *Teoria della interpretazione*, 2 v. (1955), rev. and tr. as *Allgemeine Auslegungslehre als Methodik der Geisteswissenschaften* (1967)—multidisciplinary perspective, *Die Hermeneutik als allgemeine Methodik der Geisteswissenschaften* (1962), *Zur Grundlegung einer allegemeine Auslegungslehre* (1988); J. D. Wood, *The Interp. of the Bible* (1958); J. Pépin, *Mythe et allégorie* (1959)—ancient Gr. and Judeo-Christian allegory; R. E. Palmer, *H.: Interp. Theory in Schleiermacher, Dilthey, Heidegger, and Gadamer* (1969); S. Bercovitch, *Typology and Early Am. Lit.* (1972)—good bibl.; L. Jacobs, *Jewish Biblical Exegesis* (1974); P. Szondi, *Einführung in die literarische Hermeneutik* (1975); G. Scholem, *Kabbalah* (1978); H. Brinkmann, *Mittelalterliche Hermeneutik* (1980); S. A. Handelman, *The Slayers of Moses* (1983); J. C. Weinsheimer, *Gadamer's H.* (1985), *Philosophical H. and Literary Theory* (1991), *18th-C. H.* (1993); R. A. Makkreel, "H. and the Limits of Consciousness," *Nous* 21 (1987)—issues in contemp. philosophical h.; G. Warnke, *Gadamer: H., Trad., and Reason* (1987).

ENCYCLOPEDIA ARTICLES: "Hermenraetic [sic]," *Grosses Universallexikon aller Wissenschafften und Künste*, ed. J. S. Ersch and J. G. Gruber (1735); E. F. Vogel, "Hermeneutik," *Allgemeine Encyklopädie der Wissenschaften und Künste* (1829); C. F. G. Heinrici, "Hermeneutik," *Realencyklopädie für protestantische Theologie und Kirche*, 3d ed. (1899); E. Dobschütz, "Interp.," *Encycl. of Religion and Ethics* (1908); G. Ebeling, "Hermeneutik," *Die Religion in Gesch. und Gegenwart*, 3d ed. (1959); J. C. Joosen and J. H. Waszink, "Exegese," *Reallexikon für Antike und Christentum* (1966); L. Jacobs, "H.," *Encyc. Judaica* (1971); H.-G. Gadamer, "Hermeneutik," *Historisches Wörterbuch der Philosophie* (1974).

BIBLIOGRAPHIES: E. Betti (1967, above); N. Henrichs, *Bibliographie der Hermeneutik und ihrer Anwendungsbereiche seit Schleiermacher* (1972); W.

C. Gay and P. Eckstein, "Bibliographic Guide to H. and Critical Theory," *Cultural H.* 2 (1975); H.-G. Gadamer (1974, above); J. Bleicher, *Contemp. H.* (1980); R. E. Palmer, "Allegorical, Philological, and Philosophical H.," *Univ. of Ottawa Quarterly* 50 (1980), "H.," *Contemp. Philosophy*, ed. G. Fløistad, v. 2 (1982).

ANTHOLOGIES AND COLLECTIONS: *Hermeneutik und Ideologiekritik*, ed. K. Apel et al. (1971); *Hermeneutische Philosophie*, ed. O. Pöggeler (1972); *Rezeptionsaesthetik*, ed. R. Warning (1975); *Philosophische Hermeneutik* (1976), *Die Hermeneutik und die Wissenschaften* (1978), both ed. H.-G. Gadamer and G. Boehm; *Philologie und Hermeneutik im 19. Jahrhundert*, ed. H. Flashar et al. (1979); *Contemp. H.*, ed. J. Bleicher (1980); *Contemp. Literary H. and Interp. of Cl. Texts*, ed. S. Kresic (1981); *Klassiker der Hermeneutik*, ed. U. Nassen (1982); *Text und Interp.*, ed. P. Forget (1984); *H.*, ed. G. Shapiro and A. Sica (1984); *H. and Deconstruction*, ed. H. Silverman and D. Ihde (1985); *The H. Reader*, ed. K. Müller-Vollmer (1985)—intro. offers short mod. hist. of h.; *H. and Praxis*, ed. R. Hollinger (1985); *H. and Mod. Philosophy*, ed. B. Wachterhauser (1986); V. B. Leitch, *Am. Lit. Crit. from the Thirties to the Eighties* (1988), ch. 7; *Looking After Nietzsche*, ed. L. Rickels (1990).

HERMENEUTICS AND CONTEMPORARY THEORY: *The New H.*, ed. J. M. Robinson and J. B. Cobb (1964); M. Foucault, "The Discourse on Lang.," *Archeology of Knowledge* (tr. 1972), *Discipline and Punishment* (tr. 1977), *Power / Knowledge* (tr. 1980); T. Seebohm, *Kritik der hermeneutischen Vernunft* (1967), "Deconstruction in the Framework of Traditional Methodological H.," *Jour. Brit. Soc. Phenomenology* 17 (1985); G. Hartman, *The Fate of Reading* (1975), *Saving the Text* (1981); J. H. Miller, "The Critic as Host," *CritI* 3 (1977); *New Perspectives in Ger. Lit. Crit.*, ed. R. E. Amacher and V. Lange (1979); P. de Man, *Blindness and Insight* (1971), *Critical Writings* (1988); M. Frank, *Das Sagbare und das Unsagbare* (1980), *Was ist Neostrukturalismus?* (1983, tr. 1989)—Fr. neostructuralism; D. Tracy, *The Analogical Imagination* (1981)—hermeneutical theology; H. Dreyfus and P. Rabinow, *Michel Foucault: Beyond Structuralism and H.* (1983); M. C. Taylor, *Erring: A Postmodern A/ theology* (1987)—deconstruction and theology; J. D. Caputo, *Radical H.* (1987)—attempts to combine Heidegger and Derrida; *H. and Psychological Theory*, ed. S. B. Messer et al. (1988); *Hermeneutic Phenomenology*, ed. J. Kockelmans (1988); *Dialogue and Deconstruction: The Gadamer-Derrida Encounter*, ed. D. Michelfelder and R. E. Palmer (1989); R. R. Sullivan, *Political H.* (1989)—Gadamer's early politics; P. Carravetta, *Prefaces to the Diaphora* (1990)—h. in relation to the tension (*diaphora*) between poetry and philosophy; *The H. Trad. and Transforming the H. Context*, both ed. G. Ormiston and A. Schrift (1990).   R.E.P.

HERMETICISM. This translation of the It. term *ermetismo* (derived from the name of the Egyptian god Thoth, Gr. Hermes Trismegistus, the mythical author of occult texts) is used to refer to the most widely known autochthonous trend in 20th-c. It. poetry (q.v.), and extended by analogy to describe the general tendency of contemp. poetry toward inaccessibility of lang. and multivalence of meaning. The term gained wide critical currency after the 1936 publication of Francesco Flora's study *La poesia ermetica*, but the "school" had identified its origins in a group of poets gathered around the Florentine literary review *La voce* (1908–13), as well as in the "Orphism" (*orfismo*) professed by Arturo Onofri (1885–1928) and Dino Campana (1885–1932). The *Canti orfici* (1914) of the latter is now regarded as the first full manifestation of the new trend. The main exponents of the school between the two wars were Giuseppe Ungaretti and Eugenio Montale. Its third-wave representatives include Mario Luzi, Sandro Penn, Alfonso Gatto, and Piero Bigongiari. But h. has survived (although Bo, its most attentive commentator, has claimed 1945 as the date of its demise) into the present, disguised at first as "neorealism," later as various neo-avantguardist movements—all originally developed to oppose and replace h.

The *ars poetica* of the *ermetici* is hard to condense into a few tenets. Salient features are: a blind faith in the thaumaturgic virtues of the Word, often considered more as sound than as sense; a renewed awareness of the polysemous nature of all utterance; a reliance on the subconscious and irrational drives of the psyche; a partiality for mental processes based on intuition rather than logic and, hence, a favoring of oneiric techniques of description. The great tool of the hermeticist poetic discourse is the analogue, the art of the simile (q.v.), in the Aristotelian sense of the sudden grasp of "similarity in things dissimilar." Rimbaud and Trakl are figures often mentioned, esp. in relation to Campana's poetic chimaeras; less convincingly, the roots of the hermetic movement have been traced to Poe and Novalis. The parallels with Fr. symbolism (q.v.), esp. Mallarmé and Valéry, are evident.

In contemp. It. literary historiography, a sociological-political interp. of h. has taken hold. The only "form of rebellion" (Tedesco) available to the poet in totalitarian times is an "evasion into the self," a solipsistic *clausura*, "an island of salvation" (Bo). The historicist interp. has even been extended to the positing of a secret code, allegedly worked into hermetic texts by secretly antifascist authors. On the other hand, an equation of h. with Fascism (i.e. h. as a typically authoritarian art form) has also been proposed. It is unlikely that either of these interpretive lines will ultimately prevail or contribute significantly to our understanding of the texts. Parallel trends exist in countries with widely differing sociopolitical situations (e.g. Pound and Eliot; Lorca; Éluard; Mandelštam). Even less persuasive appears today the derivation from a generic "crisis of the liberal-bourgeois Western society," a tag applicable to everything, explaining nothing. H. was part of a cyclical recurrence of *trobar clus* (q.v.), a concept of poetry as magic and hypnosis, keyless mystery, Orphic descent into the dark nether regions of the soul. For discussion of the medieval version of h. see PLATONISM AND POETRY.

A. Onofri, *Il nuovo Rinascimento e l'arte dell'Io* (1925); F. Giannessi, *Gli ermetici* (1951, 1963); M. Petrucciani, *La poetica dell'ermetismo italiano* (1955); O. Ragusa, "Fr. Symbolism in Italy," *RR* 46 (1955); V. Orsini, *Ermetismo* (1956); S. Ramat, *L'ermetismo* (1969); N. Tedesco, *La condizione crepuscolare* (1970); L. Anceschi, *Le poetiche del novecento in italia* (1973); C. Bo, "Due testimonianze di letteratura contemporanea," *LI* 24 (1970); G. Cambon, *Eugenio Montale* (1972); Wilkins; R. West, *Eugenio Montale: Poet on the Edge* (1981); L. Woodman, *Stanza My Stone* (1983), ch. 3.   T.W.

HEROIC COUPLET. A rhyming pair of Eng. heroic (that is, iambic pentameter) lines, most often used for epigrams, verse essays, satires, and narrative verse, and the dominant form for Eng. poetry from ca. 1640 to ca. 1790. The English created the h. c. in the 16th c. by imposing a regular iambic stress pattern and a regular caesura (falling normally after the fourth, fifth, or sixth syllable) on the old Chaucerian decasyllabic line and by imposing on the Chaucerian couplet (called "riding rhyme" by Puttenham and Gascoigne) a regular hierarchy of pauses—respectively, caesural, first-line, and end-of-couplet—adapted from the Lat. elegiac distich. This form, in which the end of the couplet regularly coincides with the end of a sentence, would later be called "closed," as opposed to the "open" type, in which there is no such coincidence of line and syntax.

The transformation of the Chaucerian line into what Puttenham and Dryden called the "heroic" line was evolutionary, spanning the 16th c. from ca. 1520 to 1600 (Thompson). But the imposition of the hierarchy of pauses on the loose couplet inherited from Chaucer was more dramatic, taking place almost explosively between 1590 and 1600, when numbers of Eng. poets translated and adapted Lat. poems in elegiac distichs—chiefly the *Amores* and *Heroides* of Ovid and the *Epigrammaton* of Martial—achieving or approximating a correspondence of couplet to distich. Marlowe's tr. of the *Amores* accomplishes a virtually unexceptionable equivalence:

sive es docta, places raras dotata per
    artes;
  sive rudis, placita es simplicitate tua.
est, quae Callimachi prae nostris rus-
    tica dicat
  carmina—cui placeo, protinus ipsa
    placet.

est etiam, quae me vatem et mea
    carmina culpet—
  culpantis cupiam sustinuisse femur.
molliter incedit—motu capit; altera
    dur est—
  at poterit tacto mollior esse viro.

If she be learn'd, then for her skill I
    crave her,
If not, because shees simple I would
    have her.
Before *Callimachus* one preferres me
    farre,
Seeing she likes my bookes why should
    we jarre?
An other railes at me and that I write
Yet would I lie with her if that I might.
Trips she, it likes me well, plods she,
    what then?
Shee would be nimbler, lying with a
    man.

Other poets significant for the devel. of the form were Grimald (who preceded the wave), Harrington, Marston, Heywood, Hall, Drayton, Jonson, and Donne.

The immediate result of this structural imitation was the affixing onto Eng. couplets of the Lat. distich's hierarchy of pauses and of a correspondingly balanced rhet. Note the balances above between the sharply demarcated lines of single couplets—"If . . . / If not . . . "—and the sharply divided halves of single lines—"If . . . then"; "Trips . . . plods." Eng. rhyme, which had the same closural power as the recurrent half-line pattern in the pentameter of the Lat. distich, allowed the Eng. measure, once it outgrew its dependence on the Lat. model, to become much more flexible and thus absorb the modifications by which successive Eng. poets from Donne to Crabbe transformed it into a medium of great expressive power.

At the same time, the h. c. also endured a second major devel., beginning with Marlowe's *Hero and Leander* (1593) and extending until about 1660, in which the formal elements, the rhyme and all the pauses, were subsumed and all but concealed. This process, which Marlowe himself practiced cautiously, was carried further by Chapman in his tr. of the *Odyssey* (1614) and in Chamberlayne's long romance, *Pharonnida* (1659). This "romance" or "open" couplet pointedly rejected the emphasis and definition established by the closed couplet; here rhyme and syntax do not parallel and reinforce each other, and the formal elements work against sense, creating mystery and remoteness instead of clarity and precision. But the romance couplet vanished from Eng. poetry before the Restoration, to be revived—briefly, and appropriately—by such romantic poets as Keats (*Endymion*), Hunt (*The Story of Rimini*), and Moore (*Lalla Rookh*).

Meanwhile, the closed couplet was refined and extended in the 17th c. by such poets as Beaumont, Sandys, and Falkland, then Waller, Denham, and Cowley, and thus handed on to Dryden (practicing 1660–1700) and Pope (practicing ca. 1700–1745). The h. c. as all these poets understood it is both described and exemplified in the famous lines from *Cooper's Hill* (1642) that Denham addressed to the Thames:

> O could I flow like thee, and make thy
>   stream
> My great example, as it is my theme!
> Though deep, yet clear, though gentle,
>   yet not dull,
> Strong without rage, without ore-flow-
>   ing full.

As this widely known and widely imitated little passage illustrates, the closed couplet provides continuous support in its half-line, line, and couplet spans for certain rhetorical devices and corresponding intellectual procedures, particularly *parallelism* (q.v.; "deep . . . gentle . . . / Strong . . . full"), with which poets enforced systems of induction, and *antithesis* ("gentle . . . not dull"), with which they determined comparisons and refined analyses. They often intensified such patterns with the elliptical figures zeugma and syllepsis (qq.v.; "O could I flow like thee, and [could I] make thy stream") and with inversion ("Strong without rage, without ore-flowing full"). The argumentative and persuasive implications of such practices were esp. pertinent to an age empiricist in intellectual tendency and social in cultural orientation.

Dryden chiefly developed the oratorical possibilities of the h. c., addressing large, potentially turbulent groups: in theatrical prologues, men and women, or fops and gentlemen; in satires, Whigs and Tories, or Puritans and Anglicans. He projected himself not as an individual but as a spokesman, a representative of one faction or, if possible (as in the opening of *Astraea Redux*), of sensible Englishmen in general. In *Religio laici* he concludes his exposition of how Catholics and Protestants each in their own way abuse the Bible:

> So all we make of Heavens discover'd
>   Will
> Is not to have it, or to use it ill.
> The Danger's much the same; on sev-
>   eral Shelves
> If *others* wreck *us*, or *we* wreck our *selves*.

Notice, first, Dryden's use of the formal aspects of the closed couplet, the definitive use of caesura in the second and fourth lines, and the emphasis of the rhymes; and, second, the way he unifies the two sides, partially by using plural pronouns, himself taking the position of spokesman for both.

Pope developed the h. c. into a primarily social—as opposed to Dryden's political—instrument. He presented himself as a sensible gentleman addressing either an intimate friend—as in the opening lines of the Essay on Man—or an attentive society—as in the *Essay on Crit.*—or, as in

his mature essays and epistles, both at once. In this conversational exchange with his friend Dr. Arbuthnot, the sensible (if sensibly exasperated) gentleman asks who has been hurt by his social satire:

> Does not one Table *Bavius* still admit?
> Still to one Bishop *Philips* seems a Wit?
> Still *Sapho*—'Hold! for God-sake—
>   you'll offend:
> No Names—be calm—learn Prudence
>   of a Friend:
> I too could write, and I am twice as tall,
>
> But Foes like these!—One Flatt'rer's
>   worse than all;
> Of all mad Creatures, if the Learn'd
>   are right,
> It is the Slaver kills, and not the Bite.

Notice, first, the caesura-defined parallel in line 5, and the formally illuminated antithesis, dividing *both* "Foes . . . [and] Flatt'rer" *and* the two conversationalists, in line 6; and, second, Pope's and his friend's awareness, although they are in intimate talk, that the walls have ears. Dryden in his most characteristic achievements aimed at political harmony or what he called "common quiet." Pope aimed, rather, at generally shared understanding or what he called "common sense."

The h. c., modified in various ways, supported the generation of great poets who followed Pope, esp. Johnson, Churchill, Goldsmith, and Crabbe. And even when Eng. culture shifted its focus from general understanding to individual expression—and quite properly revived the open couplet—several poets, chief among them Byron, still found the closed couplet useful for public satire. It continues in occasional use to this day. Browning ("My Last Duchess") and Arnold used the h. c. in the Victorian period; Yvor Winters has produced several beautiful h. c. poems in our time; and Eliot composed an h. c. section for *The Waste Land*, which he wisely excised when Pound made him see that he could not compete with Pope. See also HEROIC VERSE; BLANK VERSE; PENTAMETER.

Schipper; F. E. Schelling, "Ben Jonson and the Cl. School," *PMLA* 13 (1898); G. P. Shannon, "Nicholas Grimald's H. C. and the Lat. Elegiac Distich," *PMLA* 45 (1930); R. C. Wallerstein, "The Devel. of the Rhet. and Metre of the H. C.," *PMLA* 50 (1935); G. Williamson, "The Rhet. Pattern of Neo-classical Wit," *MP* 33 (1935–36); E. R. Wasserman, "The Return of the Enjambed Couplet," *ELH* 7 (1940); Y. Winters, "The H. C. and its Recent Revivals," *In Defense of Reason* (1943); W. C. Brown, *The Triumph of Form* (1948); W. K. Wimsatt, Jr., "One Relation of Rhyme to Reason," *The Verbal Icon* (1954); J. Thompson, *The Founding of Eng. Metre* (1961); J. H. Adler, *The Reach of Art* (1964); J. A. Jones, *Pope's Couplet Art* (1969); W. B. Piper, *The H. C.* (1969), ed., *An H. C. Anthol.* (1977); G. T. Amis, "The Structure of the Augustan Couplet," *Genre* 9 (1976); H. Carruth, "Three Notes on the Versewriting of Alexander Pope," *MQR* 15 (1976); Brogan, 389 ff.   W.B.P.

HEROIC PLAY. The Eng. h. p., a type of high baroque tragedy or tragicomedy devised principally for the coterie audience at the court of Charles II, arose, flourished, and declined between 1660 and 1680. Plots were episodic, with many sudden reversals, and were concerned with warfare, revenge, chivalric generosity, illicit sexual passion, and the reconciliation, in balanced debate, of conflicting requirements of love and honor. The h. p. was set in distant lands among exotic cultures—Mexico or Morocco, Persia or Peru. Its heroes were indomitably courageous, rebellious, and erratic, its heroines flawlessly pure, its villains relentlessly malignant. Characters exchanged hyperbolic dialogue in rhymed heroic couplets, a style congenial to the then-current acting fashions of loud rant and sonorous "cadence." Dryden was foremost among critics who supported the heroic couplet instead of blank verse (qq.v.) as the proper measure for tragedy, an opinion he would adhere to until his abrupt return to blank verse in *All for Love* (1677).

As the h. p.'s most successful practitioner and apologist, Dryden approved the use of "improbabilities" like apparitions "or a Palace rais'd by Magick." Others—Orrery, Howard, Settle, Crowne, Tate, and Behn—agreed, and visionary objects abounded: new technology facilitated flying spectres, descending gods, and spectacular scenic effects. Costumes were magnificent; florid music by the Purcells and others accompanied soliloquies, symbolic dances, masques, religious rituals, and colorful "discoveries."

Dryden's dictum that an h. p. "ought to be an imitation, in little of an Heroick Poem: and consequently Love and Valour ought to be the Subject of it" was derived not from Homer and Virgil but from Ren. chivalric epics, esp. Tasso and Ariosto; he cited Sir William Davenant's semi-operatic drama *The Siege of Rhodes* (1656) as his principal source of inspiration. More recent critics have included in the genealogy of the h. p.: the tragicomedies of Beaumont and Fletcher; Senecan revenge drama; the "Herculean Hero" in Marlowe and Shakespeare; Fr. and Sp. romances; the political philosophy of Hobbes; and (for the catechistic ethical debates) manuals of theological and moral casuistry. Dryden's *The Conquest of Granada* exhibits the best and worst features of the type. Satire directed at the h. p. generally and Dryden personally in *The Rehearsal* (1671) may have hastened the demise of the h. p., but a more important factor was the growing popularity with middle-class audiences of the affective tragedies of Otway, Lee, Rowe, and Banks.—C. V. Deane, *Dramatic Theory and the H. P.* (1931); E. Waith, *The Herculean Hero* (1962), *Ideas of Greatness* (1971); A. Kirsch, *Dryden's Heroic Drama* (1965); E. Rothstein, *Restoration Tragedy* (1967); M. W. Alssid, *Dryden's Rhymed Heroic Tragedies*, 2 v. (1974); R. Hume, *Devel. of Eng. Drama in the Late 17th C.* (1976); C. Price, *Music in the Restoration Theatre* (1979); L. Brown, *Eng. Dramatic Form* (1981); D. Hughes, *Dryden's H.Ps.* (1981).   P.H.H.

HEROIC POETRY. See AFRICAN POETRY; EPIC; HEROIC VERSE.

HEROIC QUATRAIN. See ELEGIAC STANZA.

HEROIC VERSE, heroic meter. H. v. is the term which came to be used in the Middle Ages and after for epic (q.v.). Isidore of Seville in his *Etymologiae* (6th c. A.D.) defines h. v. (*carmen heroicum*) as being so named "because in it the affairs and deeds of brave men are narrated (for heroes are spoken of as men practically supernatural and worthy of Heaven on account of their wisdom and bravery); and this meter precedes others in status." In the Ren., Vida proclaims the subject of his *Ars poetica* (1527) to be h. v., though in fact it consists mainly of practical advice for poets derived from Horace and Quintilian. Torquato Tasso in his *Discorsi dell'arte poetica* (Discourses on the Heroic Poem, 1567–70; tr. I. Samuel and M. Cavalchini, 1973) advocated a more romantic conception of epic but also insisted on accurate depiction of historical reality; he also wrote "heroic sonnets" celebrating great men and events of the past. Dryden opens the Preface to his tr. of Virgil (1697) with the statement that "a heroick Poem, truly such, is undoubtedly the greatest Work which the Soul of Man is capable to perform."

H. m. is the meter characteristic of heroic poetry: in Cl. Gr. and Lat. this was of course the (dactylic) hexameter (q.v.). With the emergence of the Romance vernaculars from Low Lat., however, poets in each lang. sought a line-form which would represent the equivalent or analogue of the noblest meter of antiquity, the hexameter (q.v.), the canonical meter of the whole epic trad. These were the hendecasyllable (*versi sciolti*) in It.; first the alexandrine (q.v.) then the *décasyllabe* in Fr.; and first the fourteener (q.v.) then "blank verse" (q.v.), in Eng. Sebillet and Du Bellay brought into Fr. use the term *vers héroique* for the *décasyllabe*, but Ronsard, opposing the decasyllable, used it rather for the alexandrine.

"H. v." is still today the most neutral term for the 10-syllable, 5-stress line in Eng. otherwise called the "iambic pentameter" or decasyllable. Each of the latter two terms, while acceptable for general usage, carries with it connotations which are not historically accurate in every age, hence should be used with care. The former implies associations with Cl. prosody which many now feel inappropriate ("feet"), while the latter implies ones with Romance prosody that are equally inappropriate (syllabism as the chief criterion). It is certainly true that in the first half of the 16th c.,

when Eng. poets were "rediscovering" or simply constructing the line that was to become the great staple of Eng. poetry, most of them had been given training at school in Lat. metrics. Others, however, were very familiar with foreign verse models, chiefly It. and Fr., which offered a line of 10–12 syllables with variable stressing equally available for adaptation into Eng. The point is that all the Romance models were isomorphs of the Cl. line which adapted itself to the varying linguistic constraints of each new lang. into which it was imported. See also AFRICAN POETRY; CHANSONS DE GESTE; MEDIEVAL ROMANCE.—R. C. Williams, *The Theory of the H. Epic in It. Crit. of the 16th C.* (1921); Curtius, ch. 9; Weinberg; *Concepts of the Hero in the Middle Ages and Ren.*, ed. N. T. Burns and C. J. Reagan (1975); J. M. Steadman, *Milton and the Paradoxes of Ren. Heroism* (1987); *H. Epic and Saga*, ed. F. J. Oinas (1978)—surveys 15 national lits.; G. T. Wright, *Shakespeare's Metrical Art* (1988); O. B. Hardison, Jr., *Pros. and Purpose in the Eng. Ren.* (1989); W. J. Kennedy, "H. Poem before Spenser," and M. A. Radzinowicz, "H. Poem since Spenser," *The Spenser Encyc.*, ed. A. C. Hamilton et al. (1990).
T.V.F.B.

HETEROMETRIC, heterometrical, polymetric; technically, "anisometrical" (so Schipper). (1) Of stanzas taken singly or nonstanzaic poems: composed of lines of differing lengths and metrical structures. The Sapphic, the Lat. elegiac distich, and tail rhyme (qq.v.) are examples of stanzaic forms which mix longer and shorter lines. Variation of line length has been a significant factor in a number of lyric genres which have metrical form, certainly in Cl. and in Med. Lat. poetry, but particularly so after the flowering of Occitan poetry in the 12th–14th cs. (Elwert). The interplay between long lining and short may take three forms: alternation, as in the elegiac distich and one important type of ballad meter (q.v.); longer lines punctuated by short ones—the general phenomenon of "tailing"; and short lines closed by longer ones, as in the Spenserian stanza (q.v.). Fr. *vers mêlés* are h. (see VERS LIBRES CLASSIQUES). Sense (1) is the sense usually meant by the term "h." (2) Of stanzaic poems: heterostrophic—i.e. subsequent stanzas not in correspondence or responsion (q.v.) with the first. In strophic compositions which consist of more than one stanza, it is the norm that whatever metrical pattern is established in the first stanza will be duplicated in subsequent ones (they are said to *respond*). Most often the first stanza is isometric (q.v.), but even if it is h., all following stanzas in an isometric (isostrophic) poem are identical, i.e. h. in precisely the same way. In Eng. poetry the great masters of the isometric poem in h. stanza are Donne, Hardy, and Auden. Note that in the regular ode the *antistrophe* responds metrically to the opening *strophe* (qq.v.), and even in some free verse (q.v.), which is not metrical and is built on a base not

primarily aural but visual, the poet will establish a visual shape—the equivalent of a stanza—and then reiterate that shape exactly, giving a visually isometric effect. In some radical genres such as the *descort* (q.v.), however, each stanza is different metrically from every other—i.e. the poem as a whole is truly h. Admittedly such forms are rare, but one conspicuous example is the irregular or Pindaric ode (q.v.). In Cl. prosody, older terms for isometric and h. are "homoeomeral" and "polyrhythmic." It is deplorable that the kind of data collected by Vishnevsky on h. verse in Rus. has never been collected for Eng. See now DESCORT; RHYME COUNTERPOINT; STANZA.—Schipper; Elwert; K. D. Vishnevsky, "The Law of Rhythmical Correspondence in Heterogeneous Stanzas," *Metre, Rhythm, Stanza, Rhyme*, ed. G. S. Smith (1980).
T.V.F.B.

HEXAMETER (Gr. "of six measures").

    I. classical
    II. postclassical

I. CLASSICAL. The dactylic h. is the oldest Gr. verseform, the meter of Homeric and later epic poetry, Hesiodic and later didactic poems, Hellenistic epyllia, bucolic poetry, hymns, oracles, riddles, and verse inscriptions. It also forms the first verse of the elegiac distich (q.v.) and of the two "Pythiambic" *Epodes* of Horace. It was written in quantitative meter in Lat. through the Middle Ages, thereafter in accentual imitations and adaptations of quantitative meter in the vernaculars (see section II below). Linguistic evidence from the Homeric epics indicates its great antiquity; for a review of present thinking about its origin and prehistoric devel., see West 1973, Tichy 1981, and West 1982; see also INDO-EUROPEAN PROSODY and CLASSICAL PROSODY.

The Cl. Gr. and Lat. h. is a catalectic line which consists of six feet, five of which may be dactyls (– ‿ ‿) or spondees (– –), the sixth of which is always disyllabic—usually a spondee, but may show *brevis in longo* (– x ; see ANCEPS).

Caesura: The caesura in the Cl. h. occurs at one of three places: after 2 ½ feet (i.e. after the third longum in the line), after 2 ¾ feet (after the first breve in the third foot), or after 3 ½ feet (after the fourth longum in the line): the first of these is known as "penthemimeral" (q.v.; Gr. [after] "five half-feet") and the last as "hephthemimeral" (q.v.; Gr. "seven half-feet"); the second has no name. The first two types (i.e. in the third foot) greatly outnumber the third (of which only 14 instances occur in the *Iliad* and 9 in the *Odyssey*) and, between these two, the second (which might be said to have a "feminine" ending) slightly predominates over the first (with "masculine" ending) in the ratio of 4:3 (West). Conversely, hs. divided into equal three-foot halves are extremely rare, a fact which *may* lend support to the view sometimes advanced that originally the h. was not made up of six feet—as would appear from the traditional method for scansion of it—but rather of two *hemiepes* (q.v.)—i.e. the sequence – ◡ ◡ – ◡ ◡ – (which is the first 7 syllables, up to the penthemimeral caesura) joined together in the middle.

Contraction of *brevia* (– for ◡ ◡) is most common in the first two feet and decreases from the fourth to the third (because of the preference for the feminine caesura) to the fifth, where it is quite rare. The h. is subject to a complex of bridges regulating word boundary after trochaic segments and contraction (see BRIDGE); these bridges become more stringent in the Hellenistic period and later. Word boundary after a dactylic fourth foot is frequent and esp. favored in pastoral poetry, whence its traditional name, "bucolic diaeresis"; it too becomes more frequent over time.

The Gr. h. was adapted to Lat. by Ennius (239–169 B.C.) and employed, with the significant addition of satire, over the same range of genres as the Gr. The major differences from the Gr. h. are motivated by the Lat. stress accent. Disyllabic and trisyllabic words predominate at the end of the verse, ensuring, by the rules of Lat. stress, coincidence of linguistic stress and metrical prominence in the fifth and sixth feet. To prevent a monotonous coincidence throughout the line, however, the masculine caesura after the *longum* of the third foot is strongly preferred over the feminine, and, in those lines with a feminine caesura, word end after the second *longum* increases in frequency.

Variant Forms: (1) *Versus spondaicus,* "spondaic verse," refers to a h. whose fifth foot contains a spondee rather than a dactyl, thus causing the verse to end in at least two spondees, as in *Aeneid* 2.68. Spondaic verses appear only occasionally in Homer but are common in his Alexandrian imitators (esp. in lines which end with quadrisyllabic words: Catullus 64.78–80 has three in succession); they are however rarer in Lat. poets, and virtually disappear after Ovid. (2) *Versus Pythius* was another name sometimes used for the h., e.g. by Aphthonius (3d c. A.D.), because it was the meter used in the Pythian (i.e. Delphic) oracles. Combinations of hs. and iambic dimeters or trimeters were called *pythiambics* (q.v.). (3) *Meiurus* or *myurus* (Gr. "tapering," "mouse-tailed"; also called *teliambos*) refers to hs. in which the first syllable of the last foot is short instead of long. The classical example is: "Troes d' errhigesan, hopos idon aiolon ophin" (*Iliad* 12.208), translated by Terentianus Maurus as "attoniti Troes viso serpente pavitant," where in both cases the penultimate syllable in the line is naturally short. Mousetails were recognized by the ancients as a special verse. See also GREEK POETRY; HEMIEPES; HOMODYNE AND HETERODYNE; LATIN POETRY; METER; QUANTITY.

Wilamowitz, pt. 2, ch. 10; Hardie, ch. 1; T. F. Higham, *Gr. Poetry and Life* (1936); E. G. O'Neill, Jr., "The Localization of Metrical Word-Types in the Gr. H.," *YClS* 8 (1942); H. N. Porter, "The Early Gr. H.," *YClS* 12 (1951); C. G. Cooper, *Intro. to the Lat. H.* (1952); H. Drexler, *Hexameterstudien* (1953), *Einführung in die romische Metrik* (1967); E. Norden, "Die malerischen Mittel des Vergilischen Hs.," *Aeneis Buch VI,* ed. E. Norden, 4th ed. (1957); Maas, sects. 82–100; L. P. Wilkinson, *Golden Lat. Artistry* (1963); Koster; Crusius; G. E. Duckworth, *Vergil and Cl. H. Poetry* (1969); W. S. Allen, *Accent and Rhythm* (1973); M. L. West, "Indo-European Metre," *Glotta* 51 (1973), "Greek Poetry 2000–700 B. C.," *CQ* 23 (1973); G. Nagy, *Comparative Studies in Gr. and Indic Meter* (1974); B. Gentili, "Preistoria e formazione dell'esametro," *QUCC* 17 (1977); E. Liénard, *Répertoires prosodiques et métriques* (1978); *Lateinisches H.-Lexikon,* ed. O. Schumann, 6 v. (1979–83); Halporn et al.; E. Tichy, "Homerische *androtēta* und die Vorgesch. des daktylischen Hs.," *Glotta* 59 (1981); *H. Studies,* ed. R. Grotjahn (1981)—with annot. bibl. of statistical studies; Snell; West; W. G. Thalmann, *Conventions of Form and Thought in Early Gr. Epic Poetry* (1984); A. M. Devine and L. D. Stephens, *Lang. and Metre* (1984); M. W. Edwards, "Homer and Oral Trad.," *Oral Trad.* 1–2 (1986)—bibl.
A.M.D.; L.D.S.; T.V.F.B.; P.S.C.

II. POSTCLASSICAL. The quantitative Lat. h. continued to be written in late antiquity and during the Middle Ages, first by Christian writers such as Juvencus, Sedulius, Arator, and Avitus for epic, and later by clerics and secular poets for a variety of other kinds of poems as well (e.g. John of Salisbury's *Entheticus;* see Raby). But the loss of quantity in the Lat. lang. sometime around the 4th c. in favor of stress accent led to the rise of accentual, rhymed, medieval "rhythmical verse"; and though strict quantities continued to be written by scholastics well past the 12th c., for all practical purposes, quantity no longer mattered to popular poetry after the emergence of the hymn (q.v.)—written in iambic dimeters but based on stress—by Augustine, Ambrose, and Hilary in the 3d–4th cs. A particularly popular form of the h., esp. after the 9th c., is *leonine verse* (q.v.)—accentual hs. with internal rhyme.

When the Romance vernaculars emerged from vulgar Lat. as autonomous langs., poets sought to fashion meters equivalent to the h., but equivalent only insofar as the (quite different) phonological structure of each lang. permitted: thus emerged the *endecasillabo* (11 syllables) in It. and *alexandrine* (12) in Fr., and eventually the iambic pentameter (10) in Eng.—radically different in structure from, but meant as equivalents of, the Cl. h. In the Cl. langs., the h. might range from a theoretical minimum of 12 syllables (if all six feet were spondees) to a maximum of 18, though in practice, the most common form, five dactyls plus a spondee, has 17. But if the quantities are treated as temporal units, these 17 syllables comprise 24 "times" (one long equaling two shorts). Vernacular equivalents of the Cl. h. attempted to approximate these numbers: in Eng., the first analogue of the h. was the fourteener (14 syllables, 21 times), followed by the iambic pentameter (10 syllables, 15 times). The first blank verse (q.v.) in Eng. was Surrey's tr. of two books of Virgil's *Aeneid*. Most of the history of Western verse can be derived from the history of efforts to reproduce or find metrical equivalents for the Cl. h., meters which would rival its prestige and power as the great and sufficient meter for the greatest Western poetic form, the epic.

Early in the Ren., attempts were also made to return to the Cl. h., first written in Lat. then in the vernaculars, but meant as accentual imitations of Cl. quantitative verse, both in patterning of dactyls and spondees and also in claims for long and short syllables. These attempts first appear in It., in the *certame coronario* of 1441, where L. B. Alberti and Leonardo Dati introduced experimental *esametri italiani*, followed in the next century by Claudio Tolomei and other poets (see ITALIAN PROSODY; ITALIAN POETRY). In Fr., such verse first appears in the 16th c. and is associated with the movement known as *vers mesurés à l'antique* (q.v.; see also FRENCH PROSODY; FRENCH POETRY); similar efforts appear in Eng. (e.g. Harvey, Sidney, Stanyhurst, Webbe) and in Rus. (Maksim the Greek, *Maksimovshaja prosodija*, based on an artificial classification of long and short vowels).

In the 18th c., the quantitative experiments of Ger. poets—e.g. Klopstock's *Der Messias* (1748–73; cf. his *Vom deutschen H.*, 1779)), Voss's *Homer* and *Luise*, and Goethe's *Reineke Fuchs* and *Hermann und Dorothea* (1798)—inspired a new vogue which was widely influential both on the Continent and abroad for over a century. In Russia N. Gnedič's h. tr. of the *Iliad* at the end of the 18th c. was admired by Pushkin, who himself wrote much h. verse (Burgi). In England, in the 19th c., poets from Southey, Coleridge, Kingsley (*Andromeda*), Clough, Tennyson, Longfellow, Swinburne, and Bridges (*Ibant obscuri* [1916]) to a host of minor poets translated Homer or wrote other poems in several varieties of h. imitations 2(Omond). Even the first Eng. tr. of *Gilgamesh* (1927) was in hs. For fuller discussion, see CLASSICAL METERS IN MODERN LANGUAGES.

Meyer—for Med. Lat.; K. Wölk, *Gesch. und Kritik des englischen Hs.* (1909); Saintsbury 3.394 ff.; R. Bridges, *Milton's Prosody* (1921); Omond—still the fullest discussion for Eng.; H. G. Atkins, *Hist. of Ger. Versif.* (1923); J. S. Molina, *Los hexámetros castellanos* (1935); G. L. Hendrickson, "Elizabethan Quantitative Hs.," *PQ* 28 (1949); Raby, *Christian and Secular*; R. Burgi, *A Hist. of the Rus. H.* (1954); W. Bennett, *Ger. Verse in Cl. Metres* (1963); D. Attridge, *Well-Weighed Syllables* (1974); Brogan—fullest bibl., supp. in *Verseform* (1988); N. Wright, "The Anglo-Lat. H.," Diss., Cambridge Univ. (1981); Z. Kopczyńska and L. Pszczołowska, "Heksametr polski," *Pamietnik Literacki* (1983)—for Polish; Navarro—Sp.; Scherr—Rus.   T.V.F.B.

HEXASTICH. See SEXAIN.

HIATUS. The grammatical and metrical term for the gap which is created by pronunciation of contiguous vowels, either within a word or (more commonly) word-terminal and following word-initial. The effect of the juncture is a slight catch or pause in delivery. The alternative is to remove one vowel via elision (q.v.). In Eng. like other langs. the indefinite article (*a*) has an alternate form (*an*) which exists specifically to prevent h. In both prose and poetry h. has been deemed a fault since at least the time of Gorgias and Isocrates; Cicero and Quintilian (*Institutio oratoria* 9.4.34 ff.) discuss it at length. In the Cl. langs. (see CLASSICAL PROSODY), h. was common in Gr. epic poetry, with and without shortening of the first vowel, but rarer in Lat. Occitan had no strict rules about elision and h.; in OF, h. was generally tolerated until the 14th c.: there is no elision to prevent h. in the *Saint Alexis* (about 1040), but in Froissart there are 132 cases of elision against 5 of h. (Lote). In Fr. prosody (q.v.) since Malherbe (17th c.), the use of h. was proscribed. In It., h. is generally avoided, as it is in Sp., though in Sp. it was the rule into the late 14th c., after which time its frequency waned. Richter summarizes the Cl., Ren., and Fr. views, distinguishes nine types of h., and gives statistics and examples for each type. Pope's mimetic example, "Though oft the ear the open vowels tire" (*Essay on Crit.* 2.345), is more famous than it is offensive, and indeed the strict censuring of h. in Fr. and Eng. neoclassical crit. seems mainly genuflection to the Ancients, for elision is common in speech.

A. Braam, *Malherbes H. Verbot* (1884); A. Pleines, *Hiat und Elision im Provenzalischen* (1886); J. Franck, "Aus der Gesch. des H. im Verse," *ZDA* 48 (1906); Thieme, 370—cites 12 Fr. studies; R. Bridges, *Milton's Prosody* (1921); J. Pelz, *Der prosodische Hiat* (1930); W. J. H. Richter, *Der H. im englischen Klassizismus (Milton, Dryden, Pope)* (1934); Lote 3.87; A. Stene, *H. in Eng.* (1954); P. Habermann and W. Mohr, "H.," *Reallexikon*; Maas, sect. 141; Elwert, 62–67; Morier.   T.V.F.B.

HINDI POETRY. See INDIAN POETRY.

HIPPONACTEAN. See GLYCONIC.

HISPANO-ARABIC POETRY. Opinions are divided as to whether the Ar. poetry of Spain is truly distinctive within the general field of Ar. poetry (q.v.). Some scholars point to the prominence of specific themes, such as nature and descriptions of flowers and gardens, as well as to the two types of strophic poem that originated in Spain, as evidence of the distinctiveness of H.-Ar. p.; some (Pérès, García Gómez) claim that it reflects a native Iberian trad. preserved continuously from Roman times and reemerging later in Sp. poetry (q.v.). Others point to the continuity of the forms, rhetorical patterns, and themes prevailing in Spain with those of the Abbasid Empire: most poems are monorhymed, are set in quantitative meter according to certain canonical patterns, are phrased in classical Ar., and employ the rhetorical figures associated with Abbasid neoclassical verse.

The literary dependence of Andalusia on Iraq is epitomized in the career of Ziryāb, a court singer of Hārūn al-Rashīd (9th c.), who, arriving in Spain, used the prestige of his origins to set the court fashions in poetry, music, and manners in accordance with those of Baghdad in its glory. This dependent relationship of the Muslim West on the Muslim East corresponds to the political and trade links that connected the two ends of the Mediterranean world until the establishment of an independent caliphate in Cordoba by ʿAbd al-Raḥmān III (929). But by this time the *muwashshaḥa* ("girdle poem") had already emerged as a distinctive local contribution to Ar. poetry, the only strophic form ever to be cultivated to any great extent by poets writing in cl. Ar. It is said to have been invented by Muqaddam of Cabra (9th c.).

The *muwashshaḥa* has five to seven strophes, each in two parts (*ghuṣn* [pl. *aghṣān*] and *simṭ* [*asmāṭ*]). The *aghṣān* all have the same metrical and rhyming patterns, but the rhyme sound changes from strophe to strophe; the *asmāṭ* are uniform in meter and in rhyme sound throughout the poem. The poem usually begins with an opening *simṭ*. The final *simṭ*, around which the whole poem was probably composed, is the much-discussed *kharja*. The *kharja* is either in vernacular Ar., in Romance, or (commonly) Mozarabic, a form of Hispano-Romance, and is believed to be a quotation from vernacular songs otherwise lost. Of great interest to Romance linguists as the earliest attestations of lyric poetry in any Hispano-Romance lang., the *kharajāt* are thought by some to point to the existence of an Iberian popular poetry predating the Arab conquest (711 A.D.), supporting the theory of a continuous Iberian element in H.-Ar. p.; but aside from the *kharajāt* themselves, no such poetry is extant.

The metrics of the *muwashshaḥa* may also point to Romance origin. Though the poems can be scanned in conformity with the quantitative principles of Ar. poetry, the metrical patterns only rarely correspond to the canonical ones, and the *kharja* often resists quantitative analysis altogether. The metrical principle underlying the *muwashshaḥa* is now believed by many to be syllabic (García Gómez, Monroe), though others maintain that it is quantitative, having arisen through the evolution of the *qaṣīda* (q.v.). Hartmann and Stern pointed out that Eastern poets occasionally varied the *qaṣīda's* monorhyme by subdividing each of the two hemistichs with internal rhyme; the result was the pattern *bbba*, *a* representing the constant rhyme. When a whole poem has the *bbba* pattern, each line is a miniature stanza. Thus a

subtype of the *qaṣīda* may have developed into an entirely new verse type. This shift may have occurred under the influence of Romance verse-forms reflected in the *villancico* and the *rondeau* (qq.v.), for unlike cl. Ar. verse, the *muwashshaḥa* was sung, and Romance musical patterns seem to have played a part in shaping it.

Another class of poems thought to be derived from earlier Romance models has survived in the *urjūza* poems on historical themes by Ghazzāl ibn Yaḥya, Ibn ʾAbd Rabbihi, and others; these are long poems composed of rhyming distichs in a nonclassical quantitative meter known as *rajaz*. But neither the form nor the theme was an Andalusian invention, being rather a direct imitation of an Abbasid model, and these 9th- and 10th-c. poems do not seem to have created a lasting genre.

Though poetry is reported to have been an important feature of H.-Ar. culture, esp. in the Cordoban court, as it was throughout the Ar.-speaking world, little has survived from the 8th and 9th cs., and what has is conventional in themes, imagery, and verse patterns. But under the caliphate, Cordoba flourished as a literary center, and Andalusian poetry began to outshine that of the East. The bulk of the poetry was courtly panegyric and lampoon in *qaṣīda* form, but love poetry was extremely popular, as were descriptions of wine and wine drinking, gardens, and ascetic verse. The great names are Ibn Hānīʾ, Ibn Darrāj, and al-Sharīf al-Ṭalīq. The latter two cultivated flower poetry, which was to become a specialty of later Andalusian poets. They employ an increasingly ornate rhetorical style (*badīʿ*) that originated in the East in the 10th c. and is associated with the Abbasid master abu Tammām.

The decline of the Cordoban caliphate (1009–31) and the period of the Party Kings (1031–91) saw the greatest achievements of H.-Ar. p. Ibn Shuhaid composed a body of passionate and pessimistic verse, as well as an unusual treatise on the nature of poetry in which the narrator visits and converses with the familiar spirits of dead poets. In contrast to the prevailing doctrine of poetry as a learned craft of rhetorically ornamented speech, he propounds an idea of individual poetic inspiration. The theologian and legist Ibn Ḥazm (d. 1063) wrote mostly short love verses, more conventional in style, but embodying a spiritual ideal of love closely resembling that of the troubadours (q.v.) and worked out in detail in his prose treatise. Their younger contemporary Ibn Zaidūn composed a body of very individual poetry, esp. the odes arising out of his celebrated love affair with the princess Wallāda, which reflect the spiritual ideals of love developed by Ibn Ḥazm. It is from this period (late 11th c.) that *muwashshaḥa* texts are preserved.

Under the Party Kings, the city states of Spain vied with each other for pre-eminence in the arts, esp. poetry. Seville became the city of poets par excellence, boasting the presence of the mature

Ibn Zaidūn, Ibn ʿAmmār, Ibn al-Labbāna, and Ibn Ḥamdīs; its last Arab ruler, al-Muʿtamid Ibn ʿAbbad, the patron of all these, was himself a gifted poet. This efflorescence of poetry was partly made possible by a policy of religious tolerance common at the Sp. courts, but the Almoravids (1091–1145) introduced a fundamentalist regime that suppressed secular arts. A few great poets, trained in the earlier period, flourished, such as the nostalgic nature poet Ibn Khafāja, Ibn ʿAbdūn, the *muwashshaḥa* poet al-Aʿmā of Tudela, and the opaque Ibn al-Zaqqāq, but it was also an age of anthologists. Nevertheless, the period saw the invention, probably by Ibn Bājja (early 12th c.), of the *zajal* (see ZEJEL) and its full flowering in the works of Ibn Quzmān (d. 1160). These are strophic poems, similar to *muwashshaḥāt* in that the strophes have one element whose rhyme changes from strophe to strophe and another with constant rhyme, but the lang. is colloquial, the final *simṭ* is not different from the rest of the poem, and there may be more than seven strophes; the *asmās.t* have only half the number of lines in the opening *simṭ*. The vulgar lang. of the *zajal* complements its theme, the bawdy, colorful life of taverns and streets, observed and turned into lit. by sophisticated poets of aristocratic origin who mock the conventions of courtly love and courtly poetry. The form was probably adapted from vulgar poetry. Apparently as a secondary devel., a type of *zajal* arose resembling the *muwashshaḥa* in everything but lang. Both types are already present in Ibn Quzmān.

Under the Almohads (1145–1223) there was a revival of poetry; the great poets were al-Ruṣāfī, the converted Jew Ibn Sahl, Ḥāzim al-Qarṭājannī, whose work on the theory of poetry was also influential, and a famous woman poet, Ḥafsa bint al-Ḥājj. But the most original devel. was the mystical poetry of Ibn ʿArabī, which derived its imagery from secular love poetry and its diction from the highly metaphorical style of the age. The final phase of Islamic Spain, the Kingdom of Granada (1248–1492), produced a few important poets, incl. Ibn al-Khaṭīb, and Ibn Zamrak, whose poems embellish the Alhambra.

The similarity of some of the strophic patterns of H.-Ar. p. and the notions of love sung by the H.-Ar. poets to those of the troubadours (q.v.) has led some to see Ar. poetry as the inspiration of the troubadours (Nykl). The exact relationship of H.-Ar. p. to the troubadour lyric continues to be the subject of intense scholarly debate (Boaze; Menocal), as also is the problem of the *zajal's* influence on the *cantigas* (q.v.).

M. Hartmann, *Das arabische Strophengedicht* (1897); A. Cour, *Un poète arabe d'Andalousie: Ibn Zaïdoûn* (1920); H. Pérès, *La poésie andalouse en arabe classique au XIe siècle*, 2d ed. (1953), Sp. tr., *Esplendor de al-Andalus* (1983); R. Menéndez Pidal, "Poesía árabe y poesía europea," *Bulletin hispanique* 40 (1938); E. García Gómez, *Un eclipse de la poesía en Sevilla* (1945), *Poemas arábigoandaluces*, 3d ed. (1946), *Todo Ben Quzman* (1972), *Las jarchas de la serie árabe en su marco*, 2d ed. (1975), *El libro de las banderas de los campeones de Ibn Saʿid al Magribi*, 2d ed. (1978); A. R. Nykl, *H.-Ar. P. and Its Relations with the Old Prov. Troubadours* (1946); A. J. Arberry, *Moorish Poetry* (1953); Ibn Ḥazm, *The Ring of the Dove*, tr. A. J. Arberry (1953); P. Le Gentil, *Le Virelai et le villancico* (1954), "La Strophe zadjalesque, les khardjas et le problème des origines du lyrisme roman," *Romania* 84 (1963)—judicious review of research to 1963; S. Fiore, *Über die Beziehungen zwischen der arabischen und der fruhitalienischen Lyrik* (1956); W. Heinrichs, *Arabische Dichtung und Griechische Poetik* (1969); Ibn Shuhaid, *Treatise of Familiar Spirits and Demons*, ed. and tr. J. T. Monroe (1971); J. M. Solà-Solé, *Corpus de poesía mozárabe* (1973); J. T. Monroe, *H.-Ar. P.* (1974); S. M. Stern, *H.-Ar. Strophic P.* (1974); M. Frenk, *La jarchas mozárabes y los comienzos de la lírica románica* (1975), *Estudios sobre lírica antigua* (1978); R. Scheindlin, *Form and Structure in the Poetry of al-Muʿtamid Ibn ʿAbbād* (1975); R. Boase, *The Origin and Meaning of Courtly Love* (1976); L. F. Compton, *Andalusian Lyrical Poetry and Old Sp. Love Songs* (1976); R. Hitchcock, *The Kharja: A Critical Bibl.* (1977); R. Boase, *The Origin and Meaning of Courtly Love* (1977); S. G. Armistead, "Some Recent Devels. in Kharja Scholarship," *La Corónica* 8 (1980); GRLMA 2.1.46–73; M. R. Menocal, "The Etymology of Old Prov. *trobar, trobador,*" *RPh* 36 (1982–83), *The Ar. Role in Med. Lit. Hist.* (1987); Ibn Quzman, *El cancionero hispanoárabe*, tr. F. Corriente Córdoba (1984); D. C. Clarke, "The Prosody of the Hargas," *La Corónica* 16 (1987–88); B. M. Liu and J. T. Monroe, *Ten H.-Ar. Strophic Songs in the Mod. Oral Trad.* (1989).　R.P.S.

HISTORICISM. H. as a branch of historiography—the practices of the historian's art and science—queries the ways in which historians living at a given time and place may legitimately study the history of human actions occurring at another time and place. Arising out of the fundamental assumption that different cultures as well as different periods of the same culture are characterized by distinct and unique forms of human behavior and production, h. asks how it is possible for the historian, who is subject to the presuppositions of his or her own culture, to give an "objective" account of those of another culture. The problem lies in the deliberate or unwitting imposition of the historian's own cultural presuppositions on the culture he studies. H. poses these difficulties in the form of a dilemma: either the historian must reject his own cultural presuppositions wholly in favor of those he studies, or he is constrained to filter the latter wholly through the former.

This dilemma leads to h. being used to describe two opposed but related enterprises: the interp. of past history as something totally foreign to present perspectives; and the interp. of past history as wholly a function of present perspectives. As historicist thinking has developed from its late 18th-c. romantic origins in the thought of Herder and other Ger. thinkers (Pascal), through 19th-c. historians such as Von Ranke and Meinecke, to 20th-c. students of h. such as W. Dilthey, R. Collingwood, and H.-G. Gadamer, it has necessarily linked the problems of historiography to problems of interp. (Gadamer). The study of interp. (q.v.), broadly summarized under the study of hermeneutics (q.v.), concerns the meaning of human artifacts, whether these be political constitutions, philosophical systems, and scriptural texts, or artistic productions such as paintings and poetry. The linkages between h. and hermeneutics are complex and various, but they are reducible to this fundamental proposition: understanding historical events means understanding them as human productions. As Dilthey, Collingwood, and Gadamer have variously expressed these linkages, human history is the result of human thought and intention, so that to understand this history is to understand the thoughts and intentions that produced it. This implies for the student of poetry that a historical understanding of the literary productions of another culture or period requires discovery of the thoughts and intentions of its authors.

In the context of literary study, then, h. has attempted to interpret the lit. of a past period by discovering the kinds of meanings that a writer could possibly have intended (Hirsch), given the cultural presuppositions that govern his or her thought, as distinct from those which the author could not have intended—which were only available to writers of another period, incl. that of the literary historian himself. In this manner, literary h. has become a fundamental branch of lit. crit.

In the context of 20th-c. historiography, h. has usually set itself in opposition to claims that history should attempt a wholly "objective" account of past events. H. calls such attempts into question by emphasizing that the "present" historian cannot escape his own position in hist. and the cultural limitations endemic to this position (Danto). The h. of historiography then oscillates between attempts to overcome these limitations and an insistence that such attempts are futile (White, Nagel). Literary h. has shifted this oscillation to the argument between those who emphasize the literary work's meaning as primarily determined by the culture in which it was produced, and those who see its meaning determined primarily by its intrinsic structures (McCanles). Artistic productions such as poetry are not simply products of their culture, but are often original productions in their own right (see AUTONOMY), and that originality presents a fundamental obstacle to interps. that derive meanings wholly from the culture external to them.

The problem of h. in 20th-c. hist. and crit. has thus become one of relating cultural and social factors extrinsic to poetry to the purely formal structures and semantic effects intrinsic to individual poems. As a matter of interp., the meaning of a poem can be seen as reflecting either the ideas of the culture in which it was written or the ideas of the poet, which are in varying degree original, personal, and unique. Most 20th-c. critics recognize that, in general, the poem derives from both (Morris). But since h. has imposed on modern critical thinking a separation between individual poem (and poet) and the culture that produces and constrains both, the problem has been how theoretically to justify interps. that include and reconcile both dimensions.

It is possible to chart the major critical and theoretical positions that engage historicist categories according to the various ways in which they confront this dilemma. At one extreme are various types of formalism, which emphasizes the purely intrinsic dimension of poetry. These include Rus. Formalism (q.v.) and the various "structuralisms" that have descended from it: the Prague Linguistic Circle that flourished in the 1930s and the Fr. structuralism (q.v.) that exerted significant influence on Continental thought in the 1960s. Independent of European influences was Eng. and Am. New Criticism (q.v.) that developed between the 1930s and 1960s, which also shares, despite significant differences, a basic formalist orientation.

At the other extreme are various types of historical lit. crit. that treat poetry (and lit. in general) as documents essentially no different from nonliterary productions such as philosophical and political texts as all the products and manifestations of their own cultures. The ascendancy of Am. New Criticism was consistently challenged by "extrinsic" emphases typified by the school of "History of Ideas" historians centered at the Johns Hopkins University, though hardly limited to it (Lovejoy). Equally influential at mid-century were modern representatives of the 19th-c. Ger. romanticism in which h. had originated, incl. Ernst Cassirer, whose *Philosophy of Symbolic Forms* summarized a major historicist trend in contemp. thought: "with all their inner diversity, the various products of culture—lang., scientific knowledge, myth, art, religion—become parts of a single great problem-complex: they become multiple efforts, all directed toward the one goal of transforming the passive world of mere *impressions* . . . into a world that is pure *expression* of the human spirit" (1.80–81). A similar perspective, influenced by a Marxist emphasis on economic and class interests, has been developed by K. Mannheim.

Significantly, the quarrels between the historians and the critics were determined and, in a sense, predicted by the fissure inherent in h. itself. That aspect of h. which emphasized cultural determination funded the literary historians' arguments ("What we call the past is, in effect, a series of foreign countries inhabited by strangers" [Robertson]), while that aspect which saw poetry (along with all other human productions that constitute culture) as the product of human thought and intention funded the arguments of the critics (Brooks). A multi-sided debate developed in the 1930s involving, among others, Cleanth Brooks, F. W. Bateson, and F. R. Leavis in which the issue was whether the meaning of a poem could best be determined by historical and cultural investigation or intrinsic, formal analysis (McCanles). Like most genuine quarrels, this was a family argument.

By a kind of Hegelian reflex, these quarrels led to various attempts at a synthesis. The dominance of the New Criticism in America came to an end in the late 1960s with attempts at a "New H." which sought in various practical and theoretical ways to analyze poetry as both culturally-determined and original expression (Morris). Necessarily hobbling such attempts was the theoretical fact that both dimensions were the creatures of an h. that imposed the very oppositions that such a New H. sought to eradicate. What was required was a wholly new way of posing these questions, an approach that would rethink the whole nature of h. itself, so that poetry could be seen as at once product and producer of its culture, as something that cannot come into existence as original expression except through culturally determined categories (Weimann).

This new way of posing the question was the result of an explosion of critical theorizing that arose out of Fr. structuralism as practiced on both sides of the Atlantic, beginning with the 1960s and extending into the 1980s. Structuralism, though formalist in its immediate applications, nevertheless contained a powerful historicist component. Analyzing not the meanings of texts but the cultural and literary codes or "grammars" that make them possible—by analogy to linguistic grammars that "generate" the individual, distinct, and original sentences in a natural language (Saussure)—structuralism resituated extrinsic, cultural determination at the heart of the poetic text. The poem became, in this perspective, the locus of the complex intersection of codes shared by writer and reader. The production of the poem and its reception by its reader required that both share a common repertoire of codes, just as conversation between two speakers of the same language presupposes a shared grammar (Culler).

Structuralism led to various perspectives on poetry, on lit., and on human textual productions in general that extended and transcended the relatively limited goals structuralism had originally set itself. The most important perspectives that resituated historicist approaches to poetry are (1) semiotics (q.v.), (2) reader-response (q.v.) and reception theory, and (3) a second wave of "New H."

(1) Semiotics extends structuralism's concern with the codes that enable the production of verbal texts to the sign systems that produce all artifacts and practices that constitute a culture (Eco). Like natural languages, which were the focus of structural linguistics, cultures are, from a semiotic perspective, not merely the productions of specific agents, such as writers, nor only the results of cultural forces of influence and imitation (qq.v.), which were the dominant categories of traditional h., but are enabled by codes of signs and the rules that govern their combination. A semiotic view of culture envisions it as the collect of codes that all members of a culture share and in terms of which they communicate among themselves and perform actions and produce artifacts whose meaning and significance all members of a culture understand. In the context of literary crit., semiotics therefore recovers h.'s insistence on the cultural determination of poetry. Unlike traditional h., however, which investigates this determination by drawing connections between the contents of nonliterary documents and those of poetic productions, semiotics locates cultural determination in the codes which these productions share with all the other artifacts and practices which constitute its cultural setting. The most significant work on the semiotics of poetry is that of the Soviet semioticians led by J. Lotman, who have attempted a synthesis of cultural context and poetic structure that bypasses Marxist insistence on economic determination (see STRUCTURALISM, MOSCOW-TARTU SCHOOL).

(2) Reader-response and reception theory likewise recovers h.'s focus on cultural determination as a source of poetry's meaning, but does so by attempting to discover the expectations that its contemporaneous readers brought to it. These expectations are themselves the result of culturally determined understandings of what poetry is and does, the kinds of meanings it can convey, and the conventions that govern it, all peculiar to the specific time and place in which it was produced. Structuralism's influence is overt here, to the degree that a reader's capacity correctly to read a text depends on his or her sharing the linguistic, literary, and cultural codes that enabled its production (Culler). Reader-response and reception theory focuses on the signals internal to the poem by which the literary historian may infer and deduce the responses the work seems to have meant to posit and project for itself (Iser). Influenced by Collingwood and Gadamer, H. R. Jauss has sought to resituate the poetic text in its historical context by first recreating the literary climate within which it came into being and toward which it was directed. Extrapolating Collingwood's thesis that history is nothing but the re-enactment of past thought in the historian's mind, Jauss has renewed traditional h.'s emphasis on recreating the thoughts of the author, first projected by Schleiermacher, the founder of hermeneutics, and subsequently developed by Dilthey and Gadamer. Unlike traditional historicist crit., however, such theories proceed not only from extrinsic cultural constraints to in-

trinsic analysis. Like semiotics, they envision poetry as the producer of its culture as well as its product, and in this way bridge the gap between internal and external aspects created by the opposition between traditional formalism and h.

(3) The "New H." of the 1980s, unlike that of the 1970s which grew out of this opposition, appropriated the notion of culture as a composite of texts which was the legacy of structuralism and resituated the poem in an historical context that is already "textualized." That is, the poem differs only in degree of organizational complexity from the culture that produces it, not in kind. This is because the same creative, shaping forces of human intention and imagination that produce the poem, imbued and determined by the cultural codes that enable all meaning, likewise produce culture as well. The result is a crit. that radically historicizes poetry, and does so in the context of political, social, economic, and religious as well as artistic practices that are themselves contextualized historically, because all are equally textual productions. H. White's work has contributed significantly to the New H. of the 1980s by highlighting the ways in which traditional, mainstream historiography has been governed by a typology of literary genres (comedy, tragedy, romance, satire) and a repertoire of dominant tropes (metaphor, metonymy, synecdoche, irony).

The writer most influential in molding the thought of this latest form of literary h. has been M. Foucault, whose early structuralist writings (*Folie et déraison; Naissance de la clinique*) led to a major expansion of structuralist approaches beyond a concern with codes into a total revision of the history of ideas, which Foucault calls "the archaeology of knowledge" (*L'archéologie du savoir*). Sharing with other off-shoots of structuralism such as semiotics a radical reading of all culture as essentially "textual," Foucault's archaeology envisions all human verbal productions— poetry along with the "texts" of linguistics, biology, and economics (*Les Mots et le choses*)—as equally the products of the *épisteme* which dominates a historical period's thinking on these subjects. Unlike the Am. variety of History of Ideas (Lovejoy), Foucault's approach is less concerned with the contents of verbal documents than with the discursive practices that produced them. And unlike structuralism and semiotics, Foucault envisions discursive practices as radically decentered. That is, the discursive practices that produced the actual documents the historian works with do not form an unbroken stream of influence, but instead arise through unprepared-for and unforeseen ruptures between one practice and that which follows it. With Foucault, the categories and oppositions characterizing traditional h. are at once recapitulated and radically transformed. H.'s opposition between text and culture is turned inside out, so that "culture" consists of nothing but the texts and the discursive practices that produce them.

Authorial intentionality evaporates along with authors themselves, to the degree that "authorship" claims a spurious point of origin, replaceable by an origin that lies dispersed through the discursive practices that constitute the culture itself (ed. Bouchard).

In short, the structuralistically generated Hs. of the 1980s fuse intrinsic formalist analysis with extrinsic historicist research on the assumption that each individual text is part of the context of every other text. The distinction, endemic to the older h., between text and "background" disappears, leaving an interplay of poetic with other kinds of texts in which none is privileged because all are worthy of, and available to, both intrinsic and historical investigation.

Finally, the phrase "New H." also covers current studies derived from Foucault's later work on the politically coercive power of culturally dominant textual practices (Foucault 1975). In addition to the characteristics of "new h." delineated above under (3), adherents of new h. also espouse one or more of the following theoretical or interpretive positions: (a) a reaction against formalist approaches to textual interp., and a conscious resituation of texts in their historical context, where "historical context" is defined primarily in terms of hierarchies of power determined by gender, race, and class; (b) poetry as only one of many textual (nonliterary) productions of a society that reflect hierarchies of power in that society (see TEXTUALITY); or (c) literary study defined as part of an activist political agenda which is ideologically committed to the goal of the subversion of contemp. hierarchies of power. In these respects new h. shares certain positions and goals with contemp. feminist lit. crit. (see FEMINIST POETICS).

New h. as characterized by these positions does not locate itself within the tradition derived from 18th- and 19th-c. h., which is connected with problems of objectivity raised by differences in cultural presuppositions within literary work and literary student, respectively. In this respect, new h. is concerned less with the epistemological issues bequeathed by Ger. idealism than with the power struggles within social hierarchies as analyzed by Michel Foucault and by contemp. Western academic Marxism and feminism. Nevertheless, in arguing the bifurcation between individual poetic text and historical context, new. h. manifests its links with older hs. and to that extent commits itself to arguing once again their fundamental problematic. See also CANON; CRITICISM; HISTORY AND POETRY; INFLUENCE; THEORY.

F. Schleiermacher, *Hermeneutik* (1819); F. de Saussure, *Cours de linguistique générale* (1916); E. Cassirer *Philosophie der symbolischen Formen* (1923–29); K. Mannheim, *Ideologie und Utopie* (1929), and "Weltanschauung" and "H.," *Essays on the Sociology of Knowledge*, ed. P. Keckemeti (1952); A. Lovejoy, *The Great Chain of Being* (1936), *Essays in* the *Hist. of Ideas* (1948); *Philosophy and Hist.*, ed. R. Klibansky and H. Paton (1936); F. Meinecke, *Die Entstehung des Historismus* (1936); R. Aron, *Intro. à la philosophie de l'histoire* (1938); R. Collingwood, *The Idea of Hist.* (1946); C. Brooks, *The Well-Wrought Urn* (1947); R. Pascal, *The Ger. Sturm und Drang* (1953); Wellek and Warren; K. Popper, *The Poverty of H.* (1957); E. Nagel, "The Logic of Historical Analysis" and M. White, "Can Hist. be Objective?" *The Philosophy of Hist. in Our Time*, ed. H. Meyerhoff (1959); H.-G. Gadamer, *Wahrheit und Methode* (1960); W. Dilthey, *Pattern and Meaning in Hist.*, ed. H. P. Rickman (1961); M. Foucault, *Folie et déraison* (1961), *Naissance de la clinique* (1963), *Les Mots et le choses* (1966), *L'Archéologie du savoir* (1969), *Lang., Counter-Memory, Practice*, ed. D. Bouchard (1972), *Surveillir et punir: Naissance de la prison* (1975, tr. 1977); R. Wellek, *Concepts of Crit.* (1963); E. Hirsch, *Validity in Interp.* (1967); G. G. Iggers, "H.," *DHI*; D. Robertson, "Some Observations on Method in Literary Studies," *NLH* 1 (1969); Y. Lotman, *Struktura khudozhestvennogo teksta* (1970); W. Morris, *Toward a New H.* (1972); H. White, *Metahistory* (1973), *The Tropics of Discourse* (1978); J. Culler, *Structuralist Poetics* (1975); M. McCanles, *Dialectical Crit. and Ren. Lit.* (1975); U. Eco, *A Theory of Semiotics* (1976); W. Iser, *Der Akt des Lesens* (1976); R. Weimann, *Structure and Society in Lit. Hist.* (1976); S. Greenblatt, *Ren. Self-Fashioning from More to Shakespeare* (1980), *Shakespearean Negotiations* (1988); F. Jameson, *The Political Unconscious* (1981); H. Jauss, *Toward an Aesthetic of Reception*, tr. T. Bahti (1982); A. Danto, *Narration and Knowledge* (1985); R. D'Amico, *H. and Knowledge* (1988); *The New H.*, ed. H. A. Veeser (1989); J. R. De J. Jackson, *Historical Crit. and the Meaning of Texts* (1989); *The New H.*, ed. H. Veeser (1989); B. Thomas, *The New H. and Other Old-Fashioned Topics* (1991); *Theoretical Issues in Lit. Hist.*, ed. D. Perkins (1991); D. Perkins, *Is Lit. Hist. Possible?* (1992). M.M.

HISTORY AND POETRY. The terms for later discussion of hist. and p. are established in Aristotle's *Poetics*. As part of his argument that poetic unity consists not in the deeds of one man but in a single action, Aristotle says that the story (*mythos*) "must represent one action, a complete whole, with its several incidents so closely connected that the transposition or withdrawal of any one of them will disjoin and dislocate the whole" (1451a). A logical or quasi-logical unity thus draws p. away from the contingency of events and towards the probable or necessary as a formal principle for poems (see PLOT; FICTION). Hence "the poet's function is to describe, not the thing that has happened, but a kind of thing that might happen" (1451a). Rather than being distinguished by medium, i.e. verse or prose, hist. and p. are divided fundamentally according to the distinction between actual event and supposed event, prompting the further judg-

ment that historians are concerned with particulars, but poets with universals.

Thus considered, both p. and hist. are modes of discourse. Hist. is narrative conducted through real time, wherein incidents are strung together only by contiguity or contingency. Their philosophical significance is therefore limited. Because p. is structured logically, however, it is, in Aristotle's famous characterization, "more philosophic and of graver import than hist." (1451b). But Aristotle complicates his argument when he notes that although comic poets choose invented names for characters, tragedians still follow the old practice of the iambic poets and assign historical names to major characters, on the grounds that what convinces is the possible, and the possible is what has happened. Thus by referring to hist. as event, rather than as a form of discourse, Aristotle draws it back toward p. and establishes a relationship that has endured down through the entire hist. of Western literary theory (cf. Hardison 151–61).

In later antiquity, distinctions similar to Aristotle's constitute the standards used by literary and rhetorical theorists. *Rhetorica ad Herrenium* identifies three forms of narration, *fabula* (impossible events), *historia* (actual events), and *argumentum* (verisimilar events) (1.8.13). This and a similar triad in Quintilian (*Institutio* 3.4.2) anticipate Boccaccio's scale of poetic fiction ranging from that which has no appearance of truth to the verisimilar, which is like the truth and "more like hist. than fiction" (*Genealogia deorum gentilium* 14.9; cf. VERISIMILITUDE). However, the freedom to control the blend of fiction and fact and to fashion narrative time at will is essential to the poet, while the historian is constrained by the literal fact and the given chronology of events (14.13). The poet's privilege is in turn related to his need to link his images to meaning: the absence of the verisimilar encourages figurative readings, a point also made earlier by Augustine (*De doctrina christiana*, Bk. 3). By extension, p. becomes associated with metaphor (q.v.).

The most explicit codifications and extensive applications of the Aristotelian position occur in Ren. critical theory (see RENAISSANCE POETICS). Aristotle's logical probability is transformed into the ideal or the verisimilar, both common Ren. ways of defining the task of poetry. A related major effort of Ren. theory was to establish p. as a distinct genre comparable to, and in many instances the superior of, such discursive disciplines as rhet., philosophy, and hist. Modifications (or misinterpretations) were frequent, but for the most part, Aristotle was read as assigning to p. the verisimilar and limiting hist. to factual truth. This distinction flowered into a more elaborate set of differences and similarities, as in the *Ragionamento . . . de la historia* (1559) of Dionigi Atanagi: p. imitates, hist. does not; p. handles events as they should occur, hist. as they have occurred; p. treats the universal, hist. the particular; p. represents the single action of a single man, hist. many actions of many men; p. treats character as constant, hist. renders people as varied, unstable; p. is not limited by facts, hist. is; p. introduces gods and uses personification at will, hist. almost never; p. is freer in diction and *sententiae*, hist. is more restrained; p. may present allegorical meanings under the literal surface, hist. offers literal meanings only.

On the other hand, both are implicated in the postures and devices of rhetoric, as well as "proposition" and "narration." Both are subject to prudence and decorum; both describe ancient and distant subjects, peoples, and customs; both use sudden and unexpected accidents and changes of fortune leading to the expression of a wide variety of emotions; both use digression, amplification, and *varia* as well as figures of speech; and both are bound to represent things so graphically as to make them visible to the eye (both lists, Weinberg 40–44; for a full survey see Hathaway 129–202).

This summary testifies to the heavy dependence of lit. crit., first of all on Aristotle's disposition to give p. much greater richness and power as a kind of discourse, and second, on the terms and criteria of Cl. rhet. Perhaps the wittiest statement of the Ren. bias in favor of p. over hist. is Sidney's denigration of the historian's reliance not on known fact, but on his "bare was" and "old mouse-eaten records" (*Apology*). Records are unreliable because they depend on other documents, and the particular instance lacks the logical structure to connect it to universal truth. The poet, mediating between the abstractions of the philosopher and the particulars of the historian, is thus superior to both in coupling the abstract with the particular. This procedure in no way differs from the conventional understanding of rhetorical discourse.

It is worth noting, however, that Sidney, by this theory of the exemplary function of concrete particulars, in effect binds p. to hist. even as he seeks to distinguish them; and there were among It. Ren. critics those who granted much greater value to hist.'s contribution to poetic credibility. Chief among these was Castelvetro, who argued a dependence of p. on hist. and the consequent priority of hist. as an art and a kind of knowledge: "we cannot acquire the faculty of making right judgments about the adequacy and fidelity of representations and probabilities unless we first possess accurate and exhaustive knowledge of the things represented and the truth . . . p. borrows all its lights from hist." (tr. Bongiorno, 3–4). Arguing that the art of p. will remain obscure until rescued by an art of hist., Castelvetro wants a close symbiotic relationship between the two arts, for to be credible, p. must be grounded in hist. even to the extent of imitating the natural sequence of historical events (18, 76). Even more radically anti-Aristotelian is F. Patrizi, who argued that histories could be written in verse and had been from the beginning (Hathaway 182).

The substantial dependence of p. on hist. is also emphasized by Tasso, who insisted that the epic or heroic poet root his work firmly in historical reality before he embellishes and modifies (*Discorsi del'arte poetica* [1567–70]). Mazzoni, however, offers a rather different notion. He allows the poet to imagine the same kind of circumstantial particularity as the historian, but he makes distinctions on grounds of purpose rather than subject matter: the historian's aim is to recount what happened; the poet's is to make idols or images, that is, to imitate or represent (*La difesa della Commedia di Dante* [1572]). Bacon offers still another view of the relationship between p. and hist., one not necessarily generous to p.: it is, he asserts, "feigned hist.," but it caters to wish, to the world as we might like it to be, while hist. disciplines us to a more ordinary and more confining reality. Yet narrative p. is "mere imitation of hist.," and "representative" (i.e. dramatic) p. "is as a visible hist., and is an image of actions as if they were present" (*Advancement*, Bk. 2). Some neoclassical critics hold views similar to Bacon's, seeing hist. as either the origin of poetic narrative or the standard that controls and limits poetic fancy (e.g. Chapelain, "Lettre ou discours . . . Adone"; Hobbes, "Answer to Davenant's Preface to *Gondibert*." But apart from casual references to conventional distinctions between p. and hist., the topic is not central to neoclassical thinking.

A major exception is Giambattista Vico (1688–1744). His theory of hist., coupled to his theory of the origins of lang. in the expression of emotion rather than in the need to communicate, offers a very different view. Poetic expression is man's first reaction to his environment, and thus p. becomes the primary and essential mode of all discourse, incl. hist.: "The poets must therefore have been the first historians . . . all gentile histories have their beginnings in fables" (*La scienza nuova* [1725]). Hence, for Vico the names of deities represent the sky and the first of the gods simultaneously; they are identities rather than allegories. This early "poetic" stage of human hist. is one in which metaphysics is something "felt and imagined," in contrast to the more rational and abstract metaphysics of civilized culture, in which human experience is expressed differently (1.1). Vico thus turns p. into a moment in the broad sweep of hist.

One variant of romantic poetics (q.v.) sees human hist. in quasi-biblical terms, as a "fall" from innocence or, as Schiller put it, from a "naive" relationship to nature. P. reflects not just the beginnings but the broad pattern of hist., the "sentimental" kind recording our nostalgia as we measure the distance we have traveled from an unselfconscious past (see NAIVE AND SENTIMENTAL). For Schiller and some of his contemporaries, the ancient Gr. world and its culture offered the paradigm of a naive state in which nature functioned in human life as experience. Shelley, in contrast, sees p. as recovering hist. from the impermanence of the factual and particular whenever historians were able to offer "living images" ("A Defense of Poetry"). Thus, 19th-c. theories of hist. can be read as arguing that poetic resources such as metaphor and romance can be appropriated to the structure of historical narrative (White).

If p. can be understood as the better part of hist., hist. may be seen as both an index of the stages of p. and part of its subject matter. The grounding of poetic settings in historical event is traditional in both epic and tragic poetry. The epic typically concerns the historical destiny of whole peoples, and in such poems the legendary and providential are mingled with hist., often to bind the present to its origins, as in the *Aeneid* or the *Faerie Queene*. The latter esp., wherein Spenser claims to be following "antique poets historical," involves a complex mingling of veiled reference to contemp. hist., quasi-historical Romano-British legend, and a vision of the England of Queen Elizabeth as the fulfillment of Providence. Tasso, one of Spenser's many models, is Christian rather than nationalistic in orientation, but as much as possible he wanted his heroic poem *Gerusalemme liberata* to have the appearance of hist., and for later generations it acquired the status of a great national record.

The way in which distant historical settings are of concern to poets returns in the p. of Tennyson and Browning. In part, their interest in hist. can be understood as late-19th-c. antiquarianism, but it is more important to refer it to the contemp. theories of historical circularity, progress, and decline to which the major Victorian poets reacted. Not unlike Spenser, Tennyson in the *Idylls of the King* seems concerned to express a sense of decline and loss through contrast with the events and characters of a distant and legendary past. Browning, in his dramatic monologues and in *The Ring and the Book*, attempts to recover more recent pasts embodied in specific characters, an effort to define a *Zeitgeist* that in turn characterizes a Victorian awareness of the separate identities of historical periods. Both poets, as in "The Defense of Guinevere" and "My Last Duchess," seek to bring the past forward in the voices of historical characters speaking in the present tense to create the illusion of immediacy. Browning notoriously embodies the Victorian confidence in hist. as progress. William Morris, Matthew Arnold, and Thomas Hardy reflect more somber views of human devel., and witness a change from the role of hist. as a concept of the past or subject for poems. At mid-century, Arnold in "Stanzas from the Grande Chartreuse" perceives hist. as the occasion for internal division and conflict, as well as for reaction against traditional religious belief. Hist. offers to Arnold a picture of confusion and spiritual and social disorder, prompting his later stance of disinterestedness (q.v.) as a steadier intellectual position.

Arnold prepares the way for the modernist poets' even more self-conscious appropriation of hist. to their own purposes. The modernist "historical sense" is central to the p. of Yeats, Pound, and Eliot, as well as to their views of p. and the poet's task at large. Following the thought of such figures as Hegel, Dilthey, and Croce, Yeats, Pound, and Eliot appoint themselves interpreters of the significance of hist. for the present. Just as Dilthey says that the historian must himself be a historical being, so the poet, according to Yeats, experiences hist. personally: Yeats's mysticism is linked to Dilthey's historicism by "the belief in some kind of trans-historical spiritual world that encompasses all the elements of the past and the individual interpreter in the present" (Longenbach). Also, drawing on Hegel's theory of a general consciousness spanning recorded time, Yeats believed that the traces of the past in the present should be evoked by the poet; lit., he felt, must be saturated by the passions and beliefs of antiquity. This past is, however, remote, magical, mysterious, in other words mythical (see MYTH). For both Yeats and Pound the poet is engaged in a conversation with the dead, a bringing forward of the past because the identity of the present is fashioned from it. Yeats articulates the intersection of past and present in his elaborate cyclical theory of phases in which different civilizations undergo different stages of devel. within the same time period and yet eventually repeat similar moments of the cycle (*A Vision*).

In insisting on the poet as historian or as a vehicle for the awareness of hist., both Yeats and Pound react against what the latter calls "philology," the strict chronology of objective and inert fact. In Pound's *Three Cantos* the poet is seen as fashioning hist. for himself and in himself; hist. becomes an entity made by the mind and imagination of the poet, a concept that ties both poets to romanticism. The risk of subjectivism was vividly sensed by Eliot, whose answer is that the individual perceptions of poet and critic alike are valid only if they are prompted by the universalizing and objectifying historical sense, the realization of past and present as a system of relations. Tradition (q.v.), a concept of supreme value for Eliot, involves the historical sense, "and the historical sense involves a perception, not only of the pastness of the past, but of its presence. . . . This historical sense, which is a sense of the timeless and the temporal together, is what makes a writer traditional." What Eliot means by relation is the poet's awareness of his connections to the past, to other times and other poets, since the value of p. for Eliot is not in what makes an author distinctive but the way in which his work adapts to and modifies the collective body of "existing monuments" ("Trad. and the Individual Talent"). At the same time, Eliot echoes Dilthey in maintaining that the poet's personality and individual experience are the source of hist. and the means to its significance, a view realized in *The Waste Land* and in his remark in "Modern Tendencies in P." that "the capacity of appreciating p. is inseparable from the power of producing it . . . the present only keeps the past alive" (see Longenbach).

In addition to lit. hist., Eliot's p. often reveals an interest in hist. in much wider senses. "Gerontion" records his attempt to write p. so that it expresses hist. "as it is actually felt, a devastating force driving Europe toward cultural dissolution and moral despair" (Gross). Both the stance of the poet and the slant of the poem are prophetic, and prophetic commentary on the present is a major attitude in modernist p.

If pieces of hist. or theories of the design of hist. become part of the fabric of 20th-c. p., they do so in a much more complicated way than was the case either for medieval or Ren. writers or even for the historically more sophisticated Victorian poets. No doubt a major difference is the self-conscious use of theories of universal hist. by Yeats and his successors, but too, modernism has achieved a different sense of the role of the poet, who has come to be seen both as recording private experience and, more often than not, playing the part of a public and often political thinker. It is this often self-assumed cultural role that compels the poet to read hist. and use it, sometimes as a weapon, to measure his own times. There is also justification for tracing the poet's awareness of his special role to the mingled recollections and fashioning of pasts back to the Ren. (Toliver). This role has been called into question first by the New Critical effort to see poems as objects distinct from historical influences and contexts (see NEW CRITICISM) and later by poststructuralist and deconstructive decisions not to distinguish between poetic discourse and other modes of writing (see DECONSTRUCTION). As a result, the relations between p. and hist. are subordinated to a general skepticism about intelligible connections between lang. and the world or are assumed into comprehensive systems of cultural and political interp., esp. Marxist theories (Jameson).

One recent devel. in crit., "New Historicism," provides an alternative to poststructuralist judgment in encouraging critics to situate poetic and other texts historically, esp. as they are expressive of the interests of power and other historically based forces (see HISTORICISM). First directed at the Ren., New Historicist attention has sought to displace older views of the period which either looked at works of poetry as artistic forms detached from historical contexts or as more or less unambiguous repositories of, say, the dominant themes of humanism. One seminal study, an exercise in "cultural poetics," treats poems (and other texts) as they reflect the authors' efforts to construct identity and, ultimately, the ways in which various power interests shape authorial identity (Greenblatt). Thus poetry becomes, through its involvement in historical forces and circumstances, the reflex of social and psychological motives and furnishes the texts for social and cultural commentary (Wayne). The methods of the New Historicists, owing much to Michel Foucault, have begun to be applied to other periods. They result, at times, in something close to allegorization of poetic and other texts, and almost always, they mark a shift in critical attention from the work to its cultural and ideological origins.

E. Neff, *P. of Hist.* (1947); A. W. Gomme, *The Gr. Attitude to P. and Hist.* (1954); Wellek; Weinberg; B. Hathaway, *The Age of Crit.* (1962); T. R. Whitaker, *Swan and Shadow: Yeats's Dialogue with Hist.* (1964); B. Emrich, "Literatur und Gesch.," *Reallexikon* 2.111–43; H. Gross, *The Contrived Corridor* (1972); T. Tasso, *Discourses on the Heroic Poem*, tr. M. Cavalchini and I. Samuel (1973); H. White, *Metahist.* (1973); H.-D. Leidig, *Das Historiengedicht in der englischen Literaturtheorie* (1975); W. Dilthey, *Selected Writings*, ed. and tr. H. Rickman (1976); F. Jameson, "Marxism and Historicism," *NLH* 11 (1979), *The Political Unconscious* (1981); S. Greenblatt, *Ren. Self-Fashioning* (1980); *Aristotle's Poetics*, tr. O. B. Hardison, Jr., and L. Golden (1981); H. Toliver, *The Past That Poets Make* (1981); S. Smith, *Inviolable Voice: Hist. and 20th-C. P.* (1982); H. Adams, *Philosophy of the Literary Symbolic* (1983); G. Mazzoni, *On the Defense of the Comedy of Dante*, tr. R. Montgomery (1983); *Castelvetro on the Art of P.*, tr. A. Bongiorno (1984); D. Wayne, *Penshurst* (1984); *The Golden and the Brazen World*, ed. J. M. Wallace (1985); L. Martines, *Society and Hist. in Eng. Ren. Verse* (1985); "Studies in Ren. Historicism," spec. iss. of *ELR* 16 (1986); J. Longenbach, *Modernist Poetics of Hist.* (1987); G. M. MacLean, *Time's Witness: Historical Representation in Eng. Poetry, 1603–1660* (1990); L. Gossman, *Between Hist. and Lit.* (1990); J. Morse, *Word by Word* (1990).
R.L.M.

HISTORY PLAY is a term which may be loosely applied to any dramatic work based largely on hist. or what a given society accepts as history (which may include a good deal of myth and legend in cultures without a trad. of secular historiography). In a broad sense, then, the term can be used of most of the surviving Gr. tragedies. It can also refer to the mystery and miracle plays (see LITURGICAL DRAMA) of the Middle Ages and to such Shakespearean tragedies as *Hamlet, King Lear,* and *Macbeth.*

In practice, however, the term is normally reserved for plays that dramatize secular history and address issues broader than the fate of a single protagonist. Ordinarily a h. p. focuses on matters of state, and it normally does so in a way that relates exempla in the past to political, ethical, or philosophical concerns of the present. A h. p. will often come across as politically didactic, even when (as often seems the case with Shakespeare) the dramatist renders its "message" somewhat ambiguous. Because its canvas is broader than that of a tragedy, a h. p. will sometimes seem like the dramatic counterpart to epic poetry: mixing social classes freely, combining traits of tragedy and comedy in its atmosphere and structure and evoking themes of historical (usually national) destiny in its lang. and action.

The Persians by Aeschylus is usually accepted as the earliest extant h. p., and the only surviving instance from Gr. drama. The only extant Roman example is the *Octavia* attributed to Seneca. The flowering of the h. p. occurred in Ren. England under the influence of what Tillyard has called "the Tudor Myth." Drawing on such chroniclers as Geoffrey of Monmouth, Edward Hall, and Raphael Holinshed, playwrights like Bale (*King John*), Sackville and Norton (*Gorboduc*), and Marlowe (*Edward II*) dramatized significant episodes from Britain's past. By far the greatest achievement in the genre, however, was that of Shakespeare, who wrote ten plays on subjects ranging from the downfall of *Richard II* to the birth of Elizabeth in *Henry VIII*. In addition to his Eng. histories, Shakespeare also produced a second cycle based on Roman hist. (incl. *Julius Caesar, Antony and Cleopatra*, and *Coriolanus*).

After Shakespeare, histories were produced by 17th-c. playwrights such as Fletcher, Ford, and Dryden. In the late 18th c., Schiller achieved distinction with his *Wallenstein* trilogy and his *Maria Stuart*. And in the 19th and 20th cs., the genre has attracted such playwrights as Strindberg, Musset, Buchner, Brecht, and Miller.—E. M. W. Tillyard, *Shakespeare's H. P.* (1946); L. B. Campbell, *Shakespeare's "Histories"* (1947); I. Ribner, *The Eng. H. P. in the Age of Shakespeare* (1957); T. F. Driver, *The Sense of Hist. in Gr. and Shakespearean Drama* (1960); M. M. Reese, *The Cease of Majesty* (1962); H. Lindenberger, *Historical Drama* (1975); M. H. Wikander, *The Play of Truth and State* (1986); G. Holderness, *Shakespeare's Hist.* (1985), *Shakespeare: The Play of Hist.* (1988).   J.F.A.

HITTITE POETRY. The Hittites, who lived in Turkey in the second millennium B.C. and spoke an IE lang., have left a few poetic texts in the royal archives of their capital, Hattusa, modern Boghazkoy, 100 miles east of Ankara. The texts are written in cuneiform, a system of writing that the Hittites borrowed from Babylonia. It uses word signs and syllables; this causes the following difficulties for the reading of poetic texts: (1) clusters of two or more consonants at the beginning and end, and of three or more consonants in the interior of a word, had to be broken up by the addition of mute vowels; (2) the H. reading of some word signs is still unknown (such words will be rendered below by their Eng. equivalent in CAPITALS). The IE Hittites superseded an earlier population who spoke an unrelated lang., called Hattic by scholars and for the most part undeciphered. Among the Hattic texts used by the Hittites in the cult of the

gods of the land, there are some that are written in stanzas of 3 to 5 verses which are separated by horizontal rules. In contrast to these Hattic poems, H. poetic texts are not written in separate verses but rather consecutively, like prose. The oldest example is a short song contained in an historical text of the Old Kingdom (ca. 1700–1600 B.C.) and introduced by the words "Then he sings." Among texts of the New Kingdom (ca. 1400–1200 B.C.), some hymns and epics seem to be written in verse, e.g. a hymn to Istanu, the Sun God, which begins: "Istanui iskha-mi / 'ndants hannesnas iskhas" (Oh Istanu, my lord! / Just lord of judgment).

From the epic lit. of the New Kingdom we quote passages of The Song of Ullikummi. The first stanza of 4 verses, which was a prooemium of the type known from Homer, is mutilated; its last line reads: "dapiyas siunas attan Kumarbin iskhamihhi" (Of Kumarbi, father of all gods, I shall sing). The story itself begins in the fourth stanza:

11 man-tsa Kumarbis hattatar istant-
    sani piran das
    nas-kan kiskhiyats sara hudak arais
    kessarats STAFF-an das
    padas-sas-ma-tsa SHOES liliwandus
    huwan-dus sarkwit

15 nas-kan Urkisats happirats arha iy-
    annis
    nas ikunta luli-kan anda ar(a)s

11 When Kumarbi wisdom into (his)
    mind had taken,
    from (his) chair he promptly rose,
    into (his) hand a staff he took,
    upon his feet as shoes the swift winds
    he put;

15 from (his) town Urkis he set out,
    and to a cool(?) pond(?) he came.

Although both the lines and the stanzas have different length, and although it is impossible to establish a meter, it is clear from the term "song" used in the original title of the epic, as well as from the structure of the text, that we are dealing with some sort of bound lang. Occasional rhyme occurs (*das* in 11 and 13, perhaps *aras* in 16, if the *a* was pronounced; *arais* in 12 and *iyannis* in 15), but it is not systematically used throughout the text. The same is true of parallelism (q.v.) of the type found in the Bible: it is an occasional not an essential feature. Other devices of the epic style, such as standing epithets and repetition of standard lines and of whole passages, are common.

The Song of Ullikummi is one of a number of H. epic compositions which are based on originals in Hurrian, a non-IE lang. of north Syria and southeast Anatolia. Also of Hurrian background is an H. hymn to Ishtar, the goddess of love, with a clearly strophic structure. See also INDO-EUROPEAN PROSODY.

HÖRSPIEL

H. T. Bossert, "Gedicht und Reim im vor-griechischen Mittelmeergebiet," *Geistige Arbeit* 5 (1938), no. 18, 7–10: poetic texts in H. and other Mediterranean langs., with special emphasis on rhyme, "Zur Entstehung des Reimes," *Jahrbuch für Kleinasiatische Forschung* 2 (1951–53), 233 ff.; see also *Mitteilungen des Instituts fur Orientforschung* 2 (1954) 97 ff.

TEXTS discussed here and by Bossert: E. Tenner, "Zwei hethitische Sonnenlieder," *Kleinasiatische Forschungen* 1 (1930), 387–92 —text and tr. of Sun hymns analyzed by Bossert; H. G. Güterbock, *Keilschrifturkunden aus Boghazköi* 28 (1935), nos. 10–49, —cuneiform Hattic text; p. iv on stanzas, "The Song of Ullikummi," *Jour. of Cuneiform Studies* 5 (1951), 135–61, esp. 141–44 on form, continued in 6 (1952), 8–42—text and metrical tr. of the epic, "The Composition of H. Prayers to the Sun," *JAOS* 78 (1958)—text and tr. of Sun hymn quoted above, "A Hurro-H. Hymn to Ishtar," *JAOS* 103 (1983); I. McNeill, "The Metre of the H. Epic," *Anatolian Studies* 13 (1963); C. Watkins, "A Lat.-H. Etymology," *Lang.* 45 (1969)—Old Kingdom song. GENERAL: O. R. Gurney, *The Hittites*, 2d ed. (1954). H.G.G.

HÖRSPIEL. See SOUND POETRY.

HOKKU. See HAIKU; JAPANESE POETRY.

HOMERIC SIMILE. See SIMILE.

HOMODYNE AND HETERODYNE. Terms taken over from the science of radio waves by W. F. Jackson Knight in 1939 to describe the coincidence (homodyne) and conflict (heterodyne) between word-accent and (quantitative) verse ictus (q.v.) in the Lat. hexameter (q.v.) of Virgil, and from this usage expanded to refer to other patterns of alignment between accent and ictus in Gr. and Lat. poetry. Knight and others have argued these concords and discords were used by Virgil and other poets for expressive purposes, as instanced, for example, in the distinctive discord in the fourth foot of the Virgilian hexameter. Other scholars have questioned such a view, finding the coincidences and conflicts fortuitous. See ICTUS.—W. F. J. Knight, *Accentual Symmetry in Vergil*, 2d ed. (1950; rpt. with corrections, 1979); L. P. Wilkinson, *Golden Lat. Artistry* (1963), 89–134; W. S. Allen, *Accent and Rhythm* (1973). J.W.H.

HOMOEOMERAL. See ISOMETRIC.

HOMOEOTELEUTON (or *homoioteleuton*, Gr. "similar endings"; cf. *homoioptoton*). This term first occurs in Aristotle (*Rhetoric* 5.9.9; 1410b2) but (though the phenomenon may be found in Gorgias) is normally applied to Cl. Lat. (see Quintilian 9.3.77–80). It describes identical or similar inflectional case-endings on words in proximity, whether in prose or verse, as in Cicero's famous

"Abiit, abscessit, evasit, erupit," but most often the words are at the ends of cola (in prose) or lines (in verse). Aristotle distinguishes three types of sound similarity in endings. When h. occurs at the end of two or more lines in succession it becomes "case rhyme"—as when Cicero ends three consecutive hexameters with *monebant, ferebant,* and *iubebant.* But it should be understood that h. is not an instance of rhyme (q.v.) strictly speaking, for in inflectional langs. similarity of word-ending is the rule rather than the exception, so often can scarcely be avoided. In noninflected, positional langs. such as Eng., by contrast, the poet must labor for the phonic echo. Word-endings in h. bear grammatical information, but that is all. In a system where these do not exist, however, rhyme poses phonic similarity precisely to point up the semantic *difference* of the roots. H. is chosen by the lang.; rhyme is chosen by the poet. True rhyme first appears in the Christian Lat. hymns of the 3rd–4th c. A.D. Still, it is clear that h. was a distinct and intentional stylistic device and was capable of some range of effect. It is more common by far in Lat. than in Gr. By a curious turn, something of the same effect was later achieved in *rime grammaticale* as practiced in 15th- and 16th.-c. Fr. poetry by the *Rhétoriqueurs* (q.v.); see GRAMMATICAL RHYME.—P. Rasi, *Dell'omoeoteleuto latino* (1891); N. I. Herescu, *La Poésie latine* (1960); R. Lanham, *Handlist of Rhetorical Terms* (1968); E. H. Guggenheimer, *Rhyme Effects and Rhyming FIgures* (1972); Lausberg, 360–63; Norden. T.V.F.B.

HOMONYMIC RHYME. See IDENTICAL RHYME; RICH RHYME.

HORATIAN ODE. See ODE.

HOUSEHOLD POETS. See AMERICAN POETRY.

HOVERING ACCENT (Ger. *schwebende Betonung*). A term taken up by Jakob Schipper from Huemer and embraced by his students and a surprising number of otherwise sober 19th- and 20th-c. metrists (e.g. Sievers, Ten Brink, Gummere, Kaluza, Alden, La Drière, Malof, Attridge) for cases in scansion where stress seems to be equally disposed on two adjacent syllables. Originally the concept was offered to solve the problem of a word stress not in alignment with metrical ictus. Ten Brink confined "level stress" to equal manifestation of both stress and ictus "in delivery," but to later metrists it meant that "the stress seems to hover over two syllables, uncertain upon which it should alight" (G. R. Stewart), i.e. in scansion. Technically this is impossible: even if both syllables bore primary stress, or else one primary and one secondary, they can be scanned just so. Chatman has attacked it as a purely paper ambiguity, and it does look rather like simply a reluctance to make up one's prosodic mind. Gerard Manley Hopkins of course employs contiguous strong

- [538] -

stressing, but then his whole aim is to "spring" loose the alternating stresses of Eng. metrical verse. See ACCENT.—Schipper 1.91; Schipper, *History* 138; A. Eichler, "Taktumstellung und schwebende Betonung," *Archiv* 165 (1934): G. B. Erné, "Die schwebende Betonung als Kunstmittel in der Lyrik," Diss., Berlin (1944).   T.V.F.B.

HRYNHENT. An ON meter similar to *dróttkvætt* (q.v.) but distinguished from it by the use of eight syllables in each line rather than six. H. follows *dróttkvætt* in closing each line with a trochee and in general tends to be highly trochaic.

> Fyrri menn, er fræðin kunnu   forn ok
>   klók af heiðnum bókum
> slungin mjǫkt af sínum kóngum
>   sungu lof með danskri tungu

> (Former men, who learned ancient and
>   clever wisdom from pagan books,
> sang carefully crafted praise poems in
>   Danish about their kings.)

The extant h. verse is almost exclusively Icelandic and dates from the later Middle Ages. H. was employed in long *drápur* (see DRAPA) for both secular and sacred purposes and became the most important meter for religious poetry of the 13th and 14th cs. Three impressive *drápur* celebrating Bishop Guðmundr the Good, and numerous anonymous verses celebrating Mary and other saints, are among the major poetic monuments of the 14th c. The most famous is the 100-stanza *Lilja* [The Lily] of Eysteinn Ásgrímsson (d. 1361). Stylistically, these later h. poems share a tendency to eschew the kennings q.v.) and elaborate poetic diction typical of *dróttvkætt* poetry. See OLD NORSE POETRY.—G. Turville-Petre, *Scaldic Poetry* (1976).   J.L.

HUDIBRASTIC VERSE. Term for a specific form of octosyllabic verse with distinctive polysyllabic and mosaic rhymes, a satirical tone, and frequently impious imagery—widely imitated but never equaled—employed by Samuel Butler (1612–80) in his popular *Hudibras* (1663–78). The meter would appear joggingly monotonous were not the reader kept constantly engrossed in the wide-ranging, conversational, sparkling wit; and constantly alert for the unexpected rhymes, many of them feminine, which, as an anonymous writer has remarked, "seem to chuckle and sneer of themselves." Butler speaks, for example, of "Dame Religion,"

> Whose honesty they all durst swear for,
> Tho' not a man of them knew where-
>   fore;

of a time when

> The oyster women picked their fish up
> And trudged away to cry No Bishop;

and of Hudibras:

> He knew the seat of Paradise,
> Could tell in what degree it lies; . . .
> What Adam dreamt of, when his bride
> Came from the closet in his side; . . .
> If either of them had a navel;
> Who first made music malleable;
> Whether the Serpent, at the Fall,
> Had cloven feet, or none at all:
> All this, without a gloss or comment,
> He could unriddle in a moment. . . .
>   (Canto 1, Part 1)

See also MOCK EPIC.—G. Saintsbury, *Hist. of Eng. Pros.*, 3 v. (1906–10); E. A. Richards, Hudibras *in the Burlesque Trad.* (1937); I. Jack, "Low Satire: *Hudibras*," *Augustan Satire, 1660–1750* (1952); C. L. Kulisheck, "Swift's Octosyllabics and the H. Trad.," *JEGP* 53 (1954); L. S. Catlett, "An Odde Promiscuous Tone: A Study of the Prosody of *Hudibras*," *DAI* 32 (1971): 3244A.   L.J.Z.

HUITAIN. In Fr. poetry, an 8-line strophe (see OCTAVE) in 8- or 10-syllable lines, written on 3 rhymes with one of these appearing 4 times, and with the same rhyme for the fourth and fifth lines. The order is commonly *ababbcbc*, sometimes *abbaacac*. The h. may be a complete poem in 8 lines or it may be employed as the structural unit for longer poems. In the 15th c., François Villon wrote his *Lais* and the body of *Le grand testament* and most of its *ballades* (q.v.) in hs. The form was popular in France in the first half of the 16th c. (e.g. Marot), and it was sometimes employed in 18th-c. epigrams. In his *Petit traité de poésie française* (1872), Théodore de Banville regrets the abandonment of the h. by modern Fr. poets and calls it (with the *dizain*, q.v.) "perhaps the most perfect thing our lyric art has produced."—Kastner; Patterson.   A.G.E.

HUMANISM, NEW. See NEO-HUMANISM.

HUMORS. See COMEDY OF HUMORS.

HUNGARIAN POETRY. During the centuries of H. history before the establishment of the H. state (ca. 1000 A.D.), the cultural heritage of the tribal Hs. was completely oral, so we cannot consider it to be lit. strictly speaking, but rather folklore. The poetic works of ancient H. folklore were not preserved in their original form; we have only indications of their existence, such as the shamanistic songs (*regölés*). The chronicle writers of the 11th–14th cs. who wrote in Lat. made use of the content of several ancient legends and frequently recorded them (The Legend of the Miraculous Stag, The Legend of Álmos, The Legend of the White Horse). The trad. of the pagan bards gradually mixed with that of the jugglers, entertainers of the Middle Ages (see JONGLEUR). From the beginning of Lat. lit. in Hungary until the 16th c., the H. minstrels ensured the continuity of H. poetic trad., cultivating, perfecting, and polishing the oral forms.

During the Middle Ages and Ren., poetry continued to be written in Lat., the lang. used by Janus Pannonius (János Csezmiczei, 1437–72), the first significant H. poet. His humanism found expression in a variety of forms, from satiric epigrams to elegies ("Farewell to His Country," "When He Was Sick in the Army Camp"). The H. lang. was first used for poetry during the Reformation by three disciples of Erasmus, best known for their translations of parts of the Bible: Benedek Komjáthy, Gábor Pesti, and János Sylvester. During this period the most popular form was song verse. One of the most prominent Protestant songwriters was András Baitzi (1530–50). Péter Bornemissza (1535–85) first excelled as a songwriter but later wrote plays as well as a collection of sermons. The last great literary figure of the Reformation was Gáspár Károli (d. 1591), the first to translate the full text of the Bible into H. (1590), a tr. which is still in use.

During the 16th c. the most outstanding songwriter was Sebestyen Tinódi Lantos (d. 1556); his themes revolved around the anti-Turkish struggle (*Cronica*, 1554). During the last third of the 16th c. there appeared an increasing number of versified fictitious stories, the best known of which is "Miklós Toldi" by Péter Ilosvay-Selymes. The other notable work was the "Story of Argirus," based on an unknown It. "bella istoria" by Albert Gergei. The widespread cultivation of love poetry bore fruit in Bálint Balassi (1554–94), the first great lyricist of the H. lang. Son of Protestant aristocrats, he wrote poems about his courageous battles against the Turks ("In Praise of the Outposts," "Farewell to His Homeland") as well as love poems to Anna Losonczy, whom he called Julia ("To the Cranes," "Finding Julia He Greets Her Thus"); toward the end of his life he converted to Catholicism and wrote a number of religious poems. His poetry is distinguished by the richness of its forms. Balassi produced a new verseform, known as the Balassi-Stanza. He had many followers, the most remarkable among them being János Rimay (1569–1631), who later developed his own form of expression, representing the mannerist taste of the declining Ren.

At the beginning of the 17th c., baroque culture became predominant in Hungary. The most distinguished baroque poet was Miklós Zrinyi (1620–64), scourge of the Turks. His main work is a 15-song epic, "The Peril of Szigetvár." A contemporary of Zrinyi, István Gyöngyösi (1629–1704), wrote pseudo-epics describing everyday events instead of great historical moments and written in a captivating language ("The Marriage of Imre Thököly and Ilona Zrinyi," "Phoenix Risen from his Ashes"). Throughout the 17th c. appeared a steady stream of anti-Turkish, anti-Hapsburg, popular poetry, best of which is known as *kuruc* poems ("Song of Jakab Buga"; "Come on, Palkó";

"Outlaw's Song"). Many of these poems treat the person of Ferenc Rákóczi II, leader of the Kuruc struggles for freedom (1703–11). They include the famous Rákóczi-song, which was banned in 1848; the tune is related to Berlioz's "Rákóczi March."

During the 18th c., baroque slowly gave way to Enlightenment, clearly influenced by the Fr. Revolution. The H. Jacobin movement coincided with that of the innovators of the lang., Ferenc Kazinczy (1759–1831) and János Batsanyi (1763–1845). After the tragic fall of the Jacobin movement emerged the greatest H. lyricist after Balassi, Mihály Csokonay Vitéz (1773–1805). His poetry expresses anti-feudal ideas, and his love poems to Lilla are incomparable. He has some impressionist-rococo translucence in his work besides its symbolic power and musical qualities ("To the Echo of Tihany," "To Hope," "To the Butterfly"). The H. Enlightenment, a fascinating awakening of the nation, led to changes in values, as shown in the work of the last great poet of the nobility, Dániel Berzsenyi (1776–1836; "To the Hungarians," "The Approaching Winter").

H. romanticism, also called the Reform Age, is a period of social progress headed by the liberal nobility. Ferenc Kölcsey (1790–1838), the author of the National Anthem, and Mihály Vörösmarty (1800–55) were the greatest figures of this period. Vörösmarty wrote epic poems ("The Flight of Zalán," "Csongor and Tünde") as well as lyrics to his wife ("Dream," "To a Dreamer"). His desperation over the failure of the War of Independence is ever-present in his poem "The Old Gypsy." The most extraordinary figure of the time was Sándor Petöfi (1823–48). His enthusiastic patriotism is evident throughout his works, and in his narrative poems ("The Hammer of the Village," "John the Hero") he revealed his talent for storytelling. Much of his tender lyrism is dedicated to his wife, Julia ("What shall I call Thee," "'Twas a Poet's Dream," "At the End of September") and is heavily influenced by the style of folksongs. Many of his poems are still sung by the people. Petöfi had a legendary friendship with János Arany (1817–82), who wrote more epic poetry than lyric. His most famous work is the "Toldy Trilogy"; he also wrote beautiful ballads reviving historical events ("Szondi's Two Pages," "Bards of Wales"). His elegiac sadness at the failed War of Independence appears even in idyllic poems like "Family Circle" or "To My Son." His lyrics are particularly artful in his late poems ("Autumn Bouquet"). Moving from romanticism towards realism, the great lyric poet of the 19th c. was János Vajda (1827–97). After 1849, he entered a period of pessimism. ("Lamentations 1854–56"), but later his voice acquires a new tone in love poems for Gina, a fallen woman ("Twenty Years Past").

The 20th c. opened with a new generation of poets gathering around the literary review *Nyugat* (The West), most of whom were influenced by Fr.

symbolism (q.v.). Endre Ady published his first volume, a kind of fin-de-siècle parlor-poetry in which, however, his later genius is already manifested in some poems—the best are the ones describing his sorrow at the backwardness of his country ("At the Gare de L'Est," "Upward Thrown Stone," "Blood and Gold") or deal with his tormented relationship with Leda ("In an Old Wagon," "Beautiful Farewell Message"). Other poets of the same generation include Árpád Tóth (1886–1928), who classified himself as an Ady-follower ("a timid apostle of my mighty Lord"), which in fact he was not. He too evinces symbolist melancholy and a longing for a new and better world but in a quiet, pacifist way. The ill-fated Gyula Juhász (1883–1937), who was at the forefront of the Nyugat at the beginning, later slipped into the background. He carried within himself the weariness and decadence of the early 20th c., the fashionable Art nouveau. His love lyrics of hopeless desire, the Anna-cycle, are true masterpieces. The other two Nyugat poets, Babits and Kosztolányi, are examples of bourgeois humanism. Mihály Babits (1883–1941) was a poet, novelist, essayist, and moderately conservative representative of the H. intelligentsia, a great master of form, a *poeta doctus*, who contemplated with horror the detached brutality of World War I. His "Before Easter" is a masterpiece of antiwar poetry. On the other hand, Dezsö Kosztolányi (1885–1936) was a successful poet in his lifetime, a novelist, and a fashionable publicist. The child-cult of the era is mirrored in his "Laments of the Poor Little Child"—musical, tender pieces of poetry. He had no definite political views, but his playfulness and airiness became a protest in the midst of the War. Frigyes Karinthy (1888–1938) achieved wide popularity as a humorous writer, though he was the most versatile literary figure. His "The Way You Write" is a collection of superb pastiches, a satirical panorama of the literary world of his contemporaries. The only poet of war, Géza Gyóni (1884–1917), was to many critics an epigone of Petőfi.

During World War I emerged a new trend of lit. and a new generation of poets exemplified by Lajos Kassák (1887–1967). In his free verse, influenced by the It. futurists and Ger. expressionists, there was a new awareness of life. He opposed both the Social Democrats and the Communist Party and remained the most zealous propagandist of abstract lit. A significant and contradictory poet was Lörinc Szabó (1900–57); influenced by expressionism, he favored anarchical revolt against the existing order. His individualism slowly turned into self-centered isolation. This course is followed by the poetry of József Fodor (b. 1918), whose work moved in the direction of "symphonic poems." László Fenyö (1902–45), who died at the hands of the Nazis, and Lajos Áprily (1887–1978) were sensitive and accomplished poets. The mystical poetry of Jenö Dsida (1907–38) represented the Villonesque kind of fraternization with God and Death. On the other hand, Neo-Catholic lyricism is found in György Sárközi (1899–1945). József Berda (b. 1902) is the *enfant terrible* who praises in free verse the simple joys of life.

Between the two World Wars arose another generation of poets related to the Nyugat. Their poetry exhibits their depression at the rise of Fascism and also a high responsiveness to foreign cultures. A characteristic member of this generation is Sándor Weöres (b. 1913), a man of universal erudition influenced by Eastern philosophies and by T. S. Eliot, a brilliant versifier and a great master of form who created a new pattern in H. p. István Vas (b. 1910), a Socialist-sympathizer, keenly aware of the inhumanity of Nazism, protested against the barbarity of the period from the standpoint of pure reason. Zoltán Jékely (b. 1913) is a poet of romantic-mystic dream-imagery whose poetry reflects a certain melancholy, a longing for death. Gyula Illyés (1902–83), one of the leading figures of modern H. lit., started with expressionistic and surrealistic free verse during his exile in France. Upon his return to Hungary he lamented the poverty of the villagers ("Heavy Earth," "Second Harvest"). In the mid 1930s he joined the populist writers' movement ("Order Among Ruins"). After 1945 a dichotomy becomes increasingly apparent in his work: he praises the achievements of the people's democracy, while at the same time he worries about the fate of Hungary and H. culture.

The most creative poet in inter-war Hungary was undoubtedly Attila József (1905–37), a noble rival to Ady and Babits. He too visited Vienna and Paris, where he assimilated expressionism, coupling this with his highly concentrated technique of composition. He has an entire circle of surrealistic poetry ("Medals"), reality rigidified and turned grotesque. His major effort was to elevate H. working-class poetry to new heights ("Chop at the Roots"). His poems are mirrors of the increasing Nazism and his own growing psychosis ("Night in the Slums," "How It Hurts"). He took his own life at the age of 32.

After World War II, a new generation of populist poets emerged: Lajos Kónya (1914), Péter Kuczka (b. 1923), György Somlyó (b. 1920), and others. As a consequence of the social changes and Rákosi's personal cult during the 1950s, a new group of poets gathered around *Újhold* (New Moon) magazine: Ágnes Nemes-Nagy, György Rába, Sándor Rákos, István Jánosy, and János Pilinszky. They expressed their emotions and impressions in an objectified and very concise form. The greatest among them was Pilinszky (1921–81). The depth of his poetry is due to his apparent lack of poetical resources: he preferred short, epigrammatic poems, though on the other hand he also composed long poems with apocalyptic visions. The two greatest poets of our time are László Nagy (1925–78) and Ferenc Juhász (b. 1928). Their instinctive images go directly from impression to creation of a vision. Juhász wrote extensive epic poetry. His lyric mirrors the suffering of the troubled mind yet also turns towards great visions, a world-view of micro- and macrocosms. The richness of his association of ideas is quite unique, as is his extraordinary sense of rhythm. At the same time, Mihály Váci, Gábor Garay, and Mihály Ladányi tried to write a more politicized poetry without reducing the aesthetic quality of their work. They moved away from great visions to a style that is simple and direct. During the 1970s emerged a new trend, concrete poetry (q.v.); its major representative is Dezsö Tandory (b. 1938), who experiments with a new system of poetical signs of visual and musical quality sometimes at the expense of comprehensibility.

There have been several waves of emigration from Hungary during the 20th c. Western H. p. can be divided into three major groups: (1) Catholic; (2) poets in the Nyugat trad.; (3) emigrées of the Socialist period (1956). From the first group must be mentioned Béla Horváth (in Paris), influenced by the thought of Teilhard de Chardin, and Raymund Rákos (Vatican), author of several prayer books. Árpád Szélpál (Paris) represents the Nyugat trad., writing in both H. and Fr. György Faludy (England) writes a somewhat romantic "vagabond" poetry and has traveled extensively; his poetry is full of color and nostalgia. Emigration poetry is closed and introverted, a struggle to conserve a cultural identity in foreign surroundings. Tamás Tüz (Toronto) is one of the most tragic examples of this trend. In recent years there has been increasing dialogue between poets inside and outside of Hungary, leading to the creation of new modes of poetic expressionn and further enriching H. p. and culture. Political and social changes in Hungary during 1989–90 resulted in the democratic election of a new coalition government in April 1990, which eliminated all forms of censorship, thus opening endless possibilities for poetry among other forms of art. As the East-West exchange develops, hopefully more H. p. will be translated into different langs. so the world can discover the treasures of H. lit.

BIBLIOGRAPHY: *Bibl. of H. Lit.*, ed. Sándor Kozocsa (1959); A. Tesla, *An Intro. Bibl. to the Study of H. Lit.* (1964), *H. Authors: A Bibl. Handbook* (1970).

ANTHOLOGIES: *Magyar Poetry* (1908), *Mod. Magyar Lyrics* (1926)—both tr. W. N. Loew; *The Magyar Muse*, tr. W. Kirkconnell (1933); *Magyar versek könyve*, ed. J. Horváth (1942); *A Little Treasury of H. Verse* (1947); *H. P.*, ed. E. Kunz (1955); *Hét évszázad magyar versei*, ed. I. Király et al., v. 1–4 (1978–79).

HISTORY AND CRITICISM: G. Király, *Magyar ösköltészet* (1921); J. Horváth, *A Magyar Irodalmi Népiesség Faluditól Petöfiig* (1927), *A Magyar Irodalmi Müveltség Kezdetei* (1931), *A magyar vers* (1948), *Rendszeres magyar verstan* (1969)—systematic H. poetics; A. Schöpflin, *A Magyar Irodalom*

Története a XX. században (1937); T. Kardos, *Középkori Kultúra, Középkori Költészet* (1941), *A Magyarországi Humanizmus Kora* (1955); G. Lukács, *Irástudók Felelössége* (1945); T. Esze, *Magyar Költészet Bocskaytól Rákócziig* (1953); J. Waldapfel, *A Magyar Irodalom a Felvilágosoás Korában* (1954); A. Szerb, *Magyar Irodalomtörténet* (1958); J. Attila, *Sa Vie, son ouvre* (1958); A. Komlós, *A Magyar Költészet Petöfitöl Adyig* (1959); M. Bucsay, *Gesch. des Protestantismus in Ungarn* (1959); V. Tóth, *A Magyar Irodalom Története* (1960); L. Könnyü, *Az Amerikai Magyar Irodalom Története* (1961); A. Sivisky, *Die Ungarische Literatur der Gegenwart* (1962); *Kis Magyar Irodalomtörténet*, ed. T. Klaniczay et al. (1965); *A Magyar Irodalom Története*, ed. M. Szabolcsi, v. 1–4 (1966); P. Rákos, *Rhythm and Metre in H. Verse* (1966); A. Karátson, *Le symbolisme en Hongrie* (1969); A. Kerek, *H. Metrics* (1971); *L'Irréconciliable: Petöfi, poéte et révolutionnaire*, ed. S. Lukácsy (1973); M. Fajcsek, *Magyarországi irodalom idegen nyelven* (1975)— incl. bibl. 1944–68; T. Ungvári, *Poétika* (1976); M. Szegedy-Maszák, *Világkép és stílus* (1980); *Vándorének*, ed. M. Béládi (1981)—H. poets in Western Europe and overseas; *Pages choisies de la litt. hongroise des origines au millieu du XVIIIe siècle*, ed. T. Klaniczay (1981); B. Pomogáts, *A Nyugati Magyar Irodalom Története* (1982); *A Nyugati Magyar Irodalom 1945 után*, ed. M. Béládi et al. (1986).

S.M.N.

HYMN, an ancient Gr. liturgical and literary genre which assimilates Near Eastern and specifically Heb. trad. in the Septuagint tr. (LXX) of the Old Testament, is introduced into Christian trad. in the Gr. New Testament, the Lat. Vulgate Bible, and the Gr. and Lat. Fathers, and has continued to flourish in Western culture in both liturgical and literary trads. down to the 20th c. Other trads. represented in Oriental and in early Am. cultures, as well as in those of ancient Akkad, Sumeria, and Egypt which influenced Heb. trad., are undeniably important but lie beyond the scope of this entry.

The Gr. noun *hymnos* refers to a song, poem, or speech which praises gods and sometimes heroes and abstractions. Hs. are in lyric measures, hexameters, elegiac couplets, and even prose in late antiquity; the longest critical discussion of the h. by the rhetorician Menander, *Peri epideiktikōn* (3d c. A.D.), makes no distinction between prose and poetry. Most of the Gr. lyric hs. (mainly fragments by Alcaeus, Simonides, Bacchylides, Timotheus, and Pindar) were probably sung in religious worship. Similarly, the hexameter *Orphic Hs.* with their markedly theurgic emphasis may have been designed for religious purposes, although such abstractions as Justice, Equity, Law, and Fortune as well as the Stars, Death, and Sleep are subjects of praise. Thucydides refers to one of the hexameter *Homeric Hs.* as a prelude or preface; these presumably were literary introductions to epic recitations. The famous philosophic h. by the Stoic Cleanthes (4th–3d c. B.C.) is probably literary rather than liturgical in intention, as are the *Hs.* by the Neoplatonic philosopher Proclus (5th c. A.D.), although there is a significant theurgic element in the latter. The six extant *Hs.* of the Gr. poet Callimachus, in hexameters and elegaic couplets, are certainly literary emulations of the *Homeric Hs.*, and the long prose hs. of the apostate Emperor Julian (4th c. A.D.) could not have been used in worship.

When the LXX translators came to the Heb. Old Testament they used the nouns *hymnos, psalmos* (song or tune played to a stringed instrument), *ōdē* (song), and *ainesis* (praise), and the related verbs (*hymneō,* etc.) to translate a variety of Heb. words for praise, song, music, thanksgiving, speech, beauty, and joy. Several Psalms are identified in their titles as hs. (e.g. 53, 60), incl. sometimes the explicit use of both words, *psalmos* and *hymnos* (6, 75; see PSALM). The Psalms are also identified with odes/songs in several titles (e.g. 51), sometimes in the expression "a song of a psalm" (*ōdē psalmou,* 65), at others as "a psalm of a song" (*psalmos ōdēs,* 67 and 74). Psalm 136.3 connects *ōdē* and *hymnos,* and in two similar New Testament passages all three terms are mentioned together with the implication of rough equivalence (*Eph.* 5.19, *Col.* 3.16).

While literary hs. were not a popular or important genre in pagan Roman adaptations of Gr. literary forms, Lat. Christians of the 4th c., influenced by the h.-singing of the Eastern Church, revived and introduced both literary and liturgical hs. into the Lat. West. This revival is also reflected in Jerome's Vulgate tr. of the Bible, where the transliterations *hymnus* and *psalmus* are regularly employed (along with a more accurate and consistent translation of the Old Testament Heb.). In his *Confessions* (9.7), Augustine remarks on the introduction of the singing of hs. and psalms in Milan by Ambrose. Isidore's influential *Etymologiae* (7th c.) identifies the Psalms of David as hs. (1.39.17) and asserts that properly speaking they must praise God and be sung, although in another work he notes that Hilary of Poitiers (also 4th c.) first composed hs. in celebrations of saints and martyrs (*De ecclesiacis officiis* 1.7).

Ambrose's short hs. (8 quatrains of iambic dimeter) are explicitly Trinitarian and were intended to counteract Arian doctrine, which had itself apparently been fostered by hs. of an Arian bent. Considerable suspicion remained in the 6th and 7th cs. over the liturgical use of hs. composed by men as opposed to the divinely inspired Psalms of the Bible. But the unquestioned orthodoxy of Ambrose himself probably helped the h. become accepted as a regular part of the liturgy along with the Psalmody. As the Middle Ages progressed, many brilliant new hs. were added to the Lat. hymnody, from the great passion h. *Vexilla regis prodeunt* by Fortunatus (7th c.) and the *Veni, creator*

spiritus (tr. by Dryden) to Aquinas' hs. for Corpus Christi day and the Franciscan *Stabat mater.* Closely related to the h. is the medieval "prose" or sequence. Noteworthy are the works of Notker Balbulus (9th–10th cs.) and of Adam of St. Victor (12th c.), and the magnificent Franciscan *Dies irae.*

The Reformation renewed the suspicion of hs. among many Protestants. Although Luther composed hs. from paraphrases of the Psalms and other portions of the Bible, he also translated hs. from the Roman Breviary and wrote original ones. Calvin, on the other hand, who opposed the use of man-made hs. in congregational worship, retained the poet Marot to create a metrical psalmody or psalter in Fr., and the Calvinistic position strongly influenced the Anglican and Presbyterian churches in Great Britain in the 16th and 17th cs. The renderings of the Anglican Psalmody by Sternhold and Hopkins (2d ed., 1549), generally infelicitous but set in ballad meter (q.v.), may have prompted many Eng. poets of the Elizabethan and Jacobean periods to experiment with trs. of the Psalms (Milton translated 17 of them in a variety of verseforms), but in popular terms the Sternhold-Hopkins psalter was enormously successful.

The Roman Catholic Church experienced a different problem. The great influence of Ren. humanism led to a succession of more or less unfortunate revisions of the hymnody beginning with that by Leo X in 1525 and ending with Urban VIII's in the early 17th c. The motive was to turn the late-Cl. and Med. Lat. of the hs. and sequences into good Cl. Lat.

It remained for the Eng. Nonconformist minister Isaac Watts to revive the writing of original hs. in the 18th c. and turn the primary focus of hs. away from literary artistry back to the rugged emotional expression of strong religious beliefs (*Hymns and Spiritual Songs,* 1707–09). As the 18th c. progressed, there occurred an enormous outpouring of hs., along with new metrical versions of psalms, in the works of the Wesleys, Newton, Toplady, Perronet, the poet Cowper, and many others, some of which (e.g. those by Charles Wesley) have great lyric power.

This outpouring continued in the 19th c. The works of Fanny Crosby and Katherine Hankey and the musical arrangements of W. H. Doane are pre-eminent among those of literally hundreds of writers and composers. New hs. are still being composed to this day (e.g. by Gloria and William Gaither, Andraé Crouch, Stuart Hamblen, Ralph Carmichael, and Doris Akers), and new and revised hymnals are still being arranged.

At about the same time that Ambrose introduced congregational h.-singing to the Christian church in Milan, the Christian poet Prudentius (4th–5th c. A.D.) wrote Christian literary hs. in the manner of the pagan poets of antiquity. Although some of Prudentius' creations are brief enough to be sung congregationally, many of his hs. are much too long for worship, and all have obvious literary and poetic pretensions. The fine lyric measures in two of his collections (*Peristephanon* and *Cathemerinon*) celebrate mainly saints and martyrs.

The Cl. literary h. was revived during the Ren. in both its Christian/Prudentian and secular forms. Pope Paul II's 140-line Sapphic "Hymnus de passione" (15th c.) could have been written by Prudentius, but Pontano's (d. 1503) Sapphic "Hymnus in noctem", from his *Parthenopei* (*Carmina*, ed. J. Oeschger, 1948) imitates Catullus' lyric celebration of Diana. Pontano also wrote Christian literary hs. in Lat. elegaics. Another Neo-Lat. poet, Marco Antonio Flaminio (1498–1550), who wrote probably the best liturgical hs. of the Ren. (in Ambrosian dimeters), also composed a celebrated literary lyric, "Hymnus in auroram."

Michele Marullo's 15th c. *Hymni Naturales* (*Carmina*, ed. A. Perosa, 1951) were found by many in the Ren. to be too thoroughly pagan in subject and tone as well as form. There were other celebrated Christian literary hs. in the Ren., esp. those by Vida in the early 16th c. (*Hymni*, 1536). The later vernacular poets follow the lead of the Neo-Latinists. Ronsard, along with Marullo the most prolific writer of literary hs., composes both explicitly Christian and secular/philosophical hs. along with classical/mythological celebrations. The first two of Spenser's *Four Hs.* celebrate love and beauty in a Cl. philosophical (and Petrarchan) way, while the latter two celebrate heavenly (i.e. Christian) love and beauty.

These two trads. continue in Neo-Lat. and the vernacular lits., most notably in Chapman's two long hs. in *The Shadow of Night* (1594), in Raphael Thorius' celebrated *Hymnus tabaci* (1625), in several of Crashaw's long Christian literary hs., James Thomson's "A H. on the Seasons," Keats's "H. to Apollo," and Shelley's hs. "to Intellectual Beauty," "of Apollo," and "of Pan."

While liturgical hs. tend simply to start and stop, the literary h. frequently has an Aristotelian coherence—a beginning, middle, and end. Typically it begins with an invocation and apostrophe (qq.v.). The main body will narrate an important story or describe some moral, philosophic, or scientific attribute. A prayer and farewell provide the conclusion. The history of literary hs. is marked by great stylistic variation and rhetorical elaboration depending on the writer's object of praise and his conception of the relationship of style to content. The definitive survey of this trad. remains to be written. See LATIN POETRY, *Medieval*; see also ASSYRO-BABYLONIAN POETRY; EGYPTIAN POETRY; GREEK POETRY; HEBREW POETRY; INDIAN POETRY; LAUDA; SUMERIAN POETRY.

TEXTS AND ANTHOLOGIES: *Analecta hymnica*; *Mystical Hymns of Orpheus*, tr. T. Taylor (1896); *Lyra graeca*, ed. and tr. J. Edmonds, 3 v. (1922); *Early Lat. Hs.*, ed. A. Walpole (1922); *Proclus's Biography, Hs., and Works*, tr. K. Guthrie (1925); *Poeti Latini del Quattrocento*, ed. F. Arnaldi et al.

(1964); *Hymni latini antiquissimi XXV*, ed. W. Bulst (1975); *Hs. for the Family of God*, ed. F. Bock (1976); *New Oxford Book of Christian Verse*, ed. D. Davie (1981).

STUDIES: G. M. Dreves, *Aurelius Ambrosius* (1893); R. Wünsch, "Hymnos," in Pauly-Wissowa; Meyer, esp. 2.119, 3.145 ff.; Manitius; *Dict. of Hymnology*, ed. J. Julian, 2d ed., 2 v. (1907), s.v. "Psalters" *inter alia*; L. Benson, *Hymnody of the Christian Church* (1927), *The Eng. H.* (1962); P. Von Rohr-Sauer, *Eng. Metrical Psalms From 1600 to 1660* (1938); O. A. Beckerlegge, "An Attempt at a Classification of Charles Wesley's Metres," *London Quarterly Rev.* 169 (1944); H. Smith, "Eng. Metrical Psalms in the 16th C. and Their Literary Significance," *HLQ* 9 (1946); R. E. Messenger, *The Med. Lat. H.* (1953); Raby, *Christian*; *Reallexikon* 1.736–41; Bowra; J. Szövérffy, *Die Annalen der lateinischen Hymnendichtung*, 2 v. (1964–65), *Iberian Hymnody: Survey and Problems* (1971), *Guide to Byzantine Hymnography* (1978), *Religious Lyrics of the Middle Ages: Hymnological Studies and Coll. Essays* (1983), *Concise Hist. of Med. Lat. Hymnody* (1985), *Lat. Hs.* (1989); C. Maddison, *Marcantonio Flaminio* (1966); H. Gneuss, *Hymnar und Hymnen im englischen Mittelalter* (1968); P. Rollinson, "Ren. of the Literary H.," *RenP* (1968); C. Freer, *Music for a King* (1971); C. E. Calendar, "Metrical Trs. of the Psalms in France and England," *DAI* 33 (1973): 6863A; J. Ijsewijn, *Companion to Neo-Lat. Studies* (1977); *Menander Rhetor*, ed. and tr. D. Russell and N. Wilson (1981); P. S. Diehl, *The Med. European Religious Lyric* (1985). P.RO.

HYPALLAGE (Gr. "exchange"). A device of syntactic displacement which changes the reference of words in syntagms or sentences: a word, instead of referring to the word it logically qualifies, is made to refer to some other. As such, h. is one species of hyperbaton (q.v.). Henry Peacham, the Tudor rhetorician, gives "Open the day and see if it be the window." Shakespeare found many uses for the device; many of them exhibit, in the misplacing of the words, mental disturbance or confusion or (witty) dimness of wit. Bottom, appropriately, has several, incl. "I see a voice. Now will I to the chink, / To spy and I can hear my Thisby's face" (*Midsummer Night's Dream* 5.1.189–90). H. indicates the speaker's mental confusion in Slender's remark, "All his successors (gone before him) hath done't; and all his ancestors (that come after him) may" (*Merry Wives of Windsor* 1.1.13). The most common example of h. is the tranferred epithet, a figure characteristic of Virgil, Spenser, Shakespeare, and Milton, which has some effects of personification (q.v.). Lausberg, discussing "die metonymischen Epitheta," distinguishes syntactical and other varieties, e.g. Caesar's "This was the most unkindest cut of all" (*Julius Caesar* 3.3.188) and Othello's "Alas what ignorant sin have I committed?" (4.2.70). Eliot has "Winter kept us warm, covering / Earth in forgetful snow" (*The Waste*

HYPERBATON

Land). Many examples we would today be tempted to call Spoonerisms.—Sr. M. Joseph, *Shakespeare's Use of the Arts of Lang.* (1947); R. A. Lanham, *A Handlist of Rhetorical Terms* (1968); Lausberg; Morier; A. Quinn, *Figures of Speech* (1982). R.O.E.; T.V.F.B.; A.W.H.

HYPERBATON (Gr. "a stepping over," Eng. "inversion"). In rhet., the genus for several figures of syntactic dislocation, i.e. alteration of the normal (that is, prose) word order. Puttenham calls it the term for "all the auricular figures of disorder." Such dislocation may take several forms, may be ranked according to increasing severity, and may range from a single word moved from its accustomed place, to a pair of words simply reversed, to more extreme instances of disarray (Lat. *transgressio*), often used to depict extreme emotion. In Cl. rhet. h. would therefore subsume such figures as *anastrophe* (Lat. *inversio* or *reversio*), the reversal of a word-pair—this is one common meaning of the Eng. term "inversion"; *hypallage* (q.v.); and *hysteron proteron* (q.v.). Further, "normal (prose) order" is itself a problematic concept: simple cases are easy to analyze, but more complex structures are not. In inflectional langs., such as Gr. and Lat., where word-class is marked by ending, word order is, while very free, still not entirely free; and in positional langs., such as Eng., where inflections are almost entirely absent and word order determines case, still there may often be several acceptable ways of ordering many sentence elements. If, for example, one wants to insert the word "however" into the sentence "John disputed Smith's findings," there are five slots, and only one of them (between "Smith's" and "findings") is ungrammatical; but presumably this sort of optional placement is not what was traditionally meant by h. and its relatives. In Cl. rhet., dislocation was usually viewed not as displacement but either as the separation of two words normally belonging together or by simple reversal of the order of two adjacent words. Quintilian (*Institutio oratoria* 8.6.65) thus explains h. as the interposition of a foreign sentence element which has to be "stepped over", and restricts the term *anastrophe* (Gr. "a turning upside down") to the inversion of only two words, e.g. *mecum* for *cum me* or *quibus de rebus* for *de quibus rebus*. In any event, "normal" implies not a rule but a norm, i.e. statistical predominance; and the study of poetic syntax from a normative and statistical point of view is very much a modern phenomenon. All prose is stylized to some degree, so it is a problem to establish a base or zero degree against which to measure deviance, though extreme instances are obvious enough. Too, usage varies from age to age, allowing differing degrees of freedom in word order; this must be factored in. Nevertheless, it is undeniable that the several species of h. were recognized as rhetorical figures and exploited in poetry. Dionysius of Halicarnassus' *On Literary Composition* (ca. 10 B.C.) is actually on the placing of words; Sappho, Pindar, Sophocles, Euripides, and above all, Homer, are analyzed in detail. The example of Homer had the effect that h. increasingly came to be viewed as a specific stylistic feature of the high or grand style, suitable for heroic subjects—i.e. war and love—whence it passed from the epic trad. into the Ren. It. lyric and the sonnet: it is Tasso's favorite figure. Longinus (*On the Sublime*, ch. 22) applies the term h. to inversion of ideas rather than words, i.e. reversal of the expected or logical order of elements in an argument, pointing out what extra force a surprising order imparts to ideas that thus seem "wrung from" the speaker rather than "premeditated." Sister Joseph remarks that it "might almost be said to characterize the style" of Shakespeare's *Tempest* (54).

If we examine in particular the main line of syntactic sequence in Eng., i.e. subject–verb–object, some interesting facts emerge. In Eng. poetry the most common form of displacement is SOV, moving the verb to the end of the clause and line, often for the rhyme word; this is conspicuous in the heroic couplet (q.v.), but end-of-line is a point of maximum visibility in all verse. Milton uses normal SVO order 71% of the time, compared to 68% for Pope, 85% for Shelley, 86% for Shakespeare, and 88% for Tennyson; there are only 3 inversions in all of *The Waste Land* (Jespersen 7.60). Milton's chief inversions are OSV and SOV., e.g. "Him th'Almighty Power / Hurl'd headlong flaming . . . " (OSV; *PL* 1.44–45), and "They looking back, all th'Eastern side behold / Of Paradise . . . " (SOV; 12.641–42). But he relishes more complex h. as well: "ten paces huge / He back recoiled" (6.193–94); and esp. Miltonic is the placing of a word between two others which both modify it or both of which it modifies, such as a noun between two adjectives or other nouns, e.g. "temperate vapours bland," "heavenly forms angelic," or "Strange horror seize thee, and pangs unfelt before" (2.703). It was Miltonic inversions which Keats said were the reason for his abandoning *Hyperion*.

H. is thus exploited in poetry for a variety of useful ends, some rhetorical, some prosodic, but even in the latter, these extend far beyond the exigencies of meter or rhyme to include a number of strategies for emphasis, such as isolating, pointing, and conjoining. Thus Milton uses hyperbatic word-order more systematically so as to delay the narrative progression of the verse, thereby bringing the reader's attention to the phonic and rhythmic nuances of each line *qua* line. See also POETIC LICENSE; SYNTAX, POETIC.

O. Jespersen, *A Mod Eng. Grammar*, 7 v. (1909–49); M. Redin, *Word-Order in Eng. Verse from Pope to Sassoon* (1925); Sr. M. Joseph, *Shakespeare's Use of the Arts of Lang.* (1947); N. A. Greenberg, "Metathesis as an Instrument in the Crit. of Poetry," *TAPA* 89 (1958); S. R. Levin, "Deviation—Statistical and Determinate—in Poetic Lang.,"

Lingua 12 (1963); T. K. Bender, "Non-Logical Syntax: Lat. and Gr. H.," *Gerard Manley Hopkins* (1966); G. M. Landon, "The Grammatical Description of Poetic Word-Order in Eng. Verse," *Lang&S* 1 (1968); Lausberg; G. L. Dillon, "Inversions and Deletions in Eng. Poetry," *Lang&S* 8 (1975), "Literary Transformations and Poetic Word Order," *Poetics* 5 (1976); J. M. Lipski, "Poetic Deviance and Generative Grammar," *PTL* 2 (1977); F. Björling, "On the Question of Inversion in Rus. Poetry," *Slavica Lundensia Litteraria* 5 (1977), 7–84—on adj.–noun h. in Pushkin; W. P. Bivens, III, "Parameters of Poetic Inversion in Eng.," *Lang&S* 12 (1979); Morier, s.v. "Inversion"; Group Mu, 82–84; A. Quinn, *Figures of Speech* (1982); T. Eekman, "Some Questions of Inversion in Rus. Poetry." *Rus. Poetics* (1982); A. Clement, "The Technique of Hebraic Inversion in Eng. Lit.," *The Literary Criterion* 22 (1987); J. P. Houston, *Shakespearean Sentences* (1988); M. J. Hausman, "Syntactic Disordering in Mod. Poetry," *DAI* 49, 8A (1989): 2210; Corbett.　　T.V.F.B.

HYPERBOLE. (Gr. "overshooting," "excess"). A figure or trope, common to all lits., consisting of bold exaggeration, apparently first discussed by Isocrates and Aristotle (*Rhetoric* 1413a28). Quintilian calls it "an elegant straining of the truth" which "may be employed indifferently for exaggeration or attenuation" (*Institutio oratoria* 8.6.67) and exemplifies with Virgil's "Twin rocks that threaten heaven" (*Aeneid* 1.162). Shakespeare has "Not all the water in the rude rough sea / Can wash the balm off from an anointed King" (*Richard 2* 3.2.54–5). H. is thus any extravagant statement used to express strong emotion, not intended to be understood literally ("I've told you a million times not to exaggerate"). According to Puttenham, who understood the figure's ideological possibilities, h. is used to "advance or . . . abase the reputation of any thing or person" (*The Arte of Eng. Poesie* [1589]). Use of h. is common in Elizabethan drama from Marlowe (*Tamburlaine*) to Jonson, particularly for comic irony.

H., litotes (Gr. "plainness") and meiosis (Gr. "lessening"—qq.v.) belong in the "super-category" in rhet. which some rhetoricians have called "figures of thought." The latter organize other tropes or figures such as metaphor, metonymy, and synechdoche (qq.v.) to make ideological statements. Group Mu points out (132–38) that such super-figures refer to an "ostensive situation," i.e. to the pragmatic context of the utterance, and that it is only reference to this situation which makes possible communication of either exaggeration or understatement. The metaphoric assertion "this cat is a real tiger" can only be tested for truth-value or for its degree of "literalness" (as opposed to its "overstatement") by inspection of the individual member of the feline genus in question. Only such conventional h. as is found in adynaton (q.v.) based on obvious impossibility conditions evades

the necessity of reference to the ostensive situation. But h. certainly has a number of other functions as well.—A. H. Sackton, *Rhet. as a Dramatic Lang. in Ben Jonson* (1948); W. S. Howells, *Logic and Rhet. in England, 1500–1700* (1956); G. Genette, "Hs.," *Figures I* (1966); C. Perelman and L. Olbrechts-Tyteca, *The New Rhet.* (tr. 1969); B. Vickers, "The *Songs and Sonets* and the Rhet. of H.," *John Donne: Essays in Celebration*, ed. A. J. Smith (1972); Lausberg; Group Mu; Corbett.
　　　　　　　　　　　　　　　　R.O.E.; A.W.H.

HYPERCATALECTIC. See CATALEXIS.

HYPERMETRIC (Gr. "beyond the measure"). In prosody, a line which has an extra syllable or syllables which are not part of the regular metrical pattern but nevertheless appear regularly enough to seem clearly deliberate. There are none in Homer but 20 in Virgil; the 22 h. halflines in *Beowulf* have occasioned considerable prosodic dispute. H. lines contain an extra foot or colon, usually initial, and are to be distinguished from lines containing *extra-metrical* syllables, which are also not part of the meter but are usually single, e.g. extra syllables around the caesura (q.v.), or feminine endings, or Gerard Manley Hopkins's "outrides." In Old Germanic and OE poetry, the term denotes a line expanded by means of an additional initial foot or, according to the musical theory, by means of doubling the time given to it. In Cl. poetry, "hypermetron" denotes a line whose final vowel elides with the vowel beginning the following line, establishing metrical continuity or *synapheia* (q.v.). See ANACRUSIS; HYPOMETRIC.—Sievers; Hardie; J. C. Pope, *The Rhythm of Beowulf*, 2d ed. (1966); Koster; Brogan, sect. J.
　　　　　　　　　　　　　　　　R.A.H.; T.V.F.B.

HYPOGRAM. See ANAGRAM.

HYPOMETRIC (Gr. "less than a measure"). Poetic forms lacking in prosodic fullness in relation to the norm; contrast hypermetric (q.v.). The nature of the lack varies from prosody to prosody. Quantitative: in *Amores* 1, Ovid wittily announces he set out to write of heroic matters in hexameters, but Love stole a foot from every other line—so yielding the elegiac distich (q.v.) he had in mind all along. Accentual: Shakespeare's Sonnet 145 is in iambic tetrameter rather than in the conventional pentameter—the only h. sonnet in the sequence. Syllabic: early Japanese poetry often used lines shorter or longer than the normal 5s and 7s; from about the 9th c., however, the hypermetric (*ji amari*) was allowed, whereas the h. (*ji tarazu*) was proscribed, a rule followed rigorously until recent times. *Catalexis* (q.v.), by contrast, refers to a specific line or colon short on its end in an otherwise regular poem. See ACEPHALOUS; CATALEXIS; HYPERMETRIC.　　　　　　　　　　E.M.

HYSTERON PROTERON

HYPORCHEMA (pl. *hyporchemata*). Gr. choral song accompanied by dancing. H. was supposed to have been invented by Thaletas of Gortyn in Crete (ca. 7th c. B.C.), but Athenaeus found its origins in Homer (cf. *Odyssey* 8.261 ff.). It was characterized by its use of cretic (q.v.) measures. As a hymn, the h. was akin to the paean (q.v.) in honor of Apollo, as it was later to the dithyramb (q.v.) in praise of Dionysus. Pindar, for example, wrote both *hyporchemata* and paeans. In tragedy the term was applied by Eucleides, an authority cited by Tzetzes, to lyric passages where the chorus was evidently dancing. Consequently some modern scholars have unnecessarily imagined it as a kind of lively stasimon (q.v.), e.g. in several passages of Sophocles, where jubilation of the chorus at the arrival of glad tidings is followed by the catastrophe of the play.—E. Diehl, "H.," in Pauly-Wissowa; Schmid and Stählin; A. M. Dale, *Collected Papers* (1969), ch. 3; R. Seaford, "The *Hyporchēma* of Pratinas," *Maia* 29 (1977–78); Michaelides; A. W. Pickard-Cambridge, *The Dramatic Festivals of Athens*, 2d ed. rev. (1989).   R.J.G.; T.V.F.B.

HYPOTAXIS. See PARATAXIS AND HYPOTAXIS.

HYSTERON PROTERON (Gr. "the latter [as] the earlier"). A specific type of hyperbaton (q.v.) or syntactic dislocation: the figure in which the natural order of time events occur in is reversed, usually because the later event is considered more important than the former, e.g. Xenophon, "trophe kai genesis" (*Memorabilia* 3.5.10)—in Shakespeare's phrase, "for I was bred and born"; and Virgil, "Moriamur et in media arma ruamus" (*Aeneid* 2.353—"Let us die and rush into battle." Puttenham, recalling the Eng. proverb "the cart before the horse," calls it "the preposterous" (*Arte of Eng. Poesie* [1589], 170) but distinguishes between effective and ludicrous examples. "How wild a H. P.'s this, which Nature crosses, / And far above the top the bottom tosses" (Joseph Beaumont, *Psyche* 1.85). But in poetry especially the device may be highly effective without seeming preposterous, as, for example, in Shelley's "I die! I faint! I fail! ("The Indian Serenade"). Cf. the logical fallacy of *petitio principii.*—S. E. Bassett, "H. P. Homerikos," *HSCP* 31 (1920); Lausberg.   R.O.E.

I

IAMB. See IAMBIC.

IAMBE. A Fr. satiric poem of variable length in *rimes croisées* (*abab cdcd* etc.), in which alexandrines alternate throughout with octosyllables (qq. v.). The i., whose name is rooted in the satirical trad. going back to the bitter iambics of the Gr. poet Archilochus (8th or 7th c. B.C.), came into Fr. as a generic term with the posthumous publication of the *Iambes* of André Chénier (1762–94) and *Les Iambes* (1830–31) of Auguste Barbier. Isolated examples of the form are also to be found in Hugo (*La Reculade*) and Gautier (*Débauche*). Violent contrasts in rhythm from line to line make the Fr. i. a remarkably appropriate vehicle for satire; the brevity of the octosyllable interrupts the amplitude of the alexandrine with a sense of urgency and exasperation; the broad, oratorical movement of the longer line gives way to the looser rhythms and private voice-tones of the shorter one:

> Nul ne resterait donc . . .
> Pour cracher sur leurs noms, pour
>   chanter leur supplice?
> Allons, étouffe tes clameurs;
> Souffre, ô coeur gros de haine, affamé
>   de justice.
> Toi, Vertu, pleure si je meurs
>   (A. Chénier, *Iambes* XI).

Kastner; M. Grammont, *Le Vers français*, rev. ed. (1961), *Petit Traité de versification française*, 10th ed. (1982); A. Chénier, *Oeuvres complètes* (1958).
                                A.G.E.; C.S.

IAMBELEGUS. See ARCHILOCHIAN; DACTYLO-EPITRITE.

IAMBIC (Gr. *iambos*; Ger. *Jambus*). The chief type of meter in most Cl. and modern prosody, and perhaps in the world. In Lat. poetry, an iamb was a metrical unit, a foot (q.v.) consisting of a short syllable followed by a long; in Gr., however, it was a metron (q.v.) consisting of this plus a preceding *anceps* plus long, $x - \smile -$. The word *iambos* (pl. *iamboi*) first appears in Archilochus and is used for a distinct genre of poetry, namely invective (q.v.); this generic association was carried into Roman times. The name for the meter thus derived from the genre with which it was originally associated, not vice versa. There is evidence that praise and blame were intimately connected in IE and archaic Gr. Originally the word "i." may have arisen from the kind of occasion on which ritual songs (some of them lampoons) were sung and danced,

esp. cult festivals in honor of Dionysus; cf. *dithyramb* (q.v.) from *dithur-ambos*. West thinks such verses were explicitly sexual in nature and that i. was used for "verse of a scurrilous, lubricious or farcical character." Archilochus uses i. metra in trimeters, tetrameters and epodes (qq.v.); and the Ionian poets who preferred it have come to be known as "iambographers." To the practice of Archilochus, Hipponax added the device of using the variant *scazon* (see CHOLIAMBUS).

I. was thought in antiquity to be the rhythm nearest to common speech, and a clear distinction was made by the ancients between the supple i. rhythm and the heavier, more unstable trochaic (q.v.). Throughout Gr. and Lat. poetry, i. in trimeter and tetrameter is the standard meter for recitation forms, esp. dramatic dialogue; Epicharmus or Solon may have brought the i. from the Ionian trad. into Attic, where it flourished in comedy and tragedy (cf. Aristotle, *Poetics* 1449a21). The 3-metron Gr. trimeter became the 6-foot Lat. *senarius* (q.v.), and the 4-metron tetrameter the catalectic Lat. *septenarius* (q.v.). The Lat. i. dimeter became, with Augustine, Ambrose, and Hilary of Poitiers, the standard line for the early Christian hymn (q.v.), making it perhaps the chief meter of the Middle Ages and the ancestor of the modern tetrameter, very important in Rus. and second only to the pentameter in Eng. and Ger.—a very durable and versatile line form. It is an extraordinary fact that precisely the same claim has been made in modern times about Eng. as was made by the ancients about Gr. (Aristotle, *Rhetoric* Bk. 3)—namely that i. is the rhythm of common speech.

In modern verse, i. is overwhelmingly the most common meter in prosodies such as Ger., Rus., and Eng. which are based on word-stress rather than phrase-stress. Trochaic (hereafter "t.") and ternary meters are by comparison rare. Why this should be so is an important issue. It is not merely a question of the i. foot in metrical analysis, for units of measure in scansion (q.v.) may be thought arbitrary. Rather, we should look upon i. as one, and possibly the, fundamental type of rhythm in lang., hence in poetry. Many scholars believe that i. is the natural rhythm of Eng. speech; indeed; in Thompson's view, i. became the staple meter of Eng. poetry precisely on account of this fact, since for him, "what poetry imitates" is less the external world than "the structure of the lang. itself." I. sequences are indeed fairly easy to find in conversational speech, though not usually in long runs. But once a speaker grasps the pattern and its permissible variations, it is easy to manufacture ordinary sentences that scan perfectly well as i. pentameters, e.g. "I'll have a Whopper and a glass of Coke," or "Well, when you find the answer, let me know." Shakespeare apparently grasped the pattern, managing to preserve it, flexibly, through 37 plays and 151 sonnets, or 108,000 lines of verse.

This view—that much poetry is i. because lang. is i.—may be bolstered by the recognition that i. rhythm is, more simply, an alternating pattern, and that, given any system of two values (on—off, long—short, stressed—unstressed), alternation is the simplest pattern capable of being generated— a kind of primary rhythm which would automatically divide into i. metrical units in running series. Most modern theories of linguistics conceive lang. as binary and hierarchical in character; indeed, autosegmental or "metrical" phonology specifically treats groupings as "i." or "t." Presumably the brain encodes and processes all sense-data in binary form. Consequently, even though speakers may pronounce words with any degree of stress, for example, the phonological system reduces all degrees to only two—stressed or unstressed. Further, the regular spacing of stresses makes them easier both to articulate and to perceive: rhythm exerts a powerful force on speech and cognition. Spacing out events against a backdrop of nonevents makes it clear that they are events, which would be less apparent were they clumped in contiguous runs of two and threes. "I." as a rhythm, then, is thus simply another name for alternation, which is a fundamental pattern.

One may reasonably wonder, however, why t. rhythms could not make the same claim. Alternation describes t. meters as well as it does i., on the simplest level. T. is often treated as the opposite of i., but this is misleading. Several important psychological experiments early in the 20th c. showed that when auditors are presented with an alternating series of weak and strong tones that are perfectly isochronous (equidistant), they invariably *hear* them as grouped into binary units—i.e. i. or t., most often. When the intensity of the stress is increased, the units are perceived as t. When the stress is lengthened, the units are perceived as i. (Interestingly, longer tones are usually perceived as stressed—a revealing insight into the long dispute about quantity and stress in Western metrics.) When the interval after the stress is lengthened, the units are perceived as i. In general, when intervals are irregular, the series will be heard as t.

Fraisse in 1956 suggested that in any group of weak syllables containing one stress, two intervals are crucial, the one after the stress (the *effet accent*) and the one after the group (the *effet pause*). In t. series, these two intervals (pauses) are separate, and it would appear that the *effet pause* takes precedence over the *effet accent*. In i. verse, by contrast, the pause after the stress appears in exactly the same place as the pause ending the group, so that they reinforce each other. Woodrow says much the same thing: in i. series the pause

after the stress is heard as the longer one, whereas in t. series the pause after the weak syllable is longer. All the experiments suggest that "in the absence of any objective cue for rhythmic perception . . . a t. rhythm [will be] induced" (Vos; see Brogan for citations). In short, t. seems to be the most natural grouping-form.

But all these experiments report on only primary (simple) rhythmic series, not lang., which is a secondary rhythmic series where multiple rhythms are enacted, and interact, across the same space simultaneously. When the events are words, lang. imposes a secondary or counter-rhythm on top of the phonological rhythm of stresses and unstresses which is morphological and syntactic (see RISING AND FALLING); here word types and word boundaries matter. Morphological factors have been shown to be real and important forces in Cl. meters (see BRIDGE). We must realize that readers' and auditors' perceptions of lines as "i. or "t." depend on both phonotactics and morphotactics within the metrical frame. T. rhythms, which are brittle, are extremely sensitive to (1) the kinds of wordshapes used to fill the pattern (t. words are needed frequently) and (2) alteration of the beginnings or ends of the sequences (catalexis [q.v.] is important), whereas i. rhythms seem not to be sensitive to either: anacrusis (q.v.) is common in i. verse but virtually impossible in t., catalexis is unusual but not objectionable, and wordshapes are largely immaterial—i. verse accepts virtually any. The differentials between i. and t. verse are several and complex (see TROCHAIC). Halpern argues persuasively that i. meter is a more complex and subtle meter precisely because it is capable of effects of modulation not possible in any other meter, t., ternary, or purely accentual. I. meter, that is, is not the reverse of t. but rather in its own class altogether.

Disruption of an i. meter might be thought attainable in several ways: extra stresses in the line, missing stresses in the line, or extra unstressed syllables without loss of stresses (extra syllables). But i. generally tolerates occasional extra syllables and dislocations of stress-placement very well, esp. at major syntactic boundaries such as the beginning of the line and the caesura. In general, contiguous stresses are the most serious problem for i. meters. The general principles of rhythm (q.v.) apply: so long as the reader's perceptual frame, the "metrical set," is not broken, considerable variation is possible (see METER). Further, the lang. has an efficient mechanism for demoting heavy contiguous stresses and for promoting weak stresses in runs of unstressed syllables so as to even out the rhythm. Older prosodists who advocated the notion of t. "substitutions" in i. verse failed to grasp that such feet are not t.: so long as the i. metrical set is preserved: they are perceived as complications, not violations. This suggests that the terms "i." and "t." should be applied only to meters, not units of meters.

IAMBIC SHORTENING

Several important poets have felt that i. rhythm is tyrannous: Pound observed correctly that "the god damn iamb magnetizes certain verbal sequences" (*Letters* [1950] 260); for the *vers-librists* and imagists, then, "to break the pentameter, that was the first heave" (Canto 81); and the means were "to compose in the sequence of the musical phrase, not in sequence of a metronome" ("A Few Dont's by an Imagiste" [1913]), means Pound claimed to have found in Occitan poetry (q.v.) and Chinese. Breaking the i. rhythm is precisely the effect Gerard Manley Hopkins sought to achieve with "sprung rhythm" (q.v.).

For further discussion, with bibl., see BINARY AND TERNARY; DIPODISM; METER; PYRRHIC; RISING AND FALLING; SPONDEE; TROCHAIC.

Wilamowitz, pt. 2, ch. 6; J. M. Edmonds, *Elegy and Iambus* (1931); A. D. Knox, "The Early Iambus," *Philologus* 87 (1932); E. Pound, "Treatise on Metre," *ABC of Reading* (1934); Beare; J. Thompson, "Sir Philip and the Forsaken Iamb," *KR* 20 (1958), *Founding of Eng. Metre*, 2d ed. (1989); Maas; M. Halpern, "On the Two Chief Metrical Modes in Eng.," *PMLA* 77 (1962); Koster, ch. 5; Crusius; D. W. Cummings and J. Herum, "Metrical Boundaries and Rhythm-Phrases," *MLQ* 28 (1967); Dale, ch. 5; M. L. West, *Studies in Gr. Elegy and Iambus* (1974); G. Nagy, "Iambos: Typologies of Invective and Praise," *Arethusa* 9 (1976); *Oxford Cl. Dict.*, s.v. "I. Poetry" (1977); Halporn et al.; Brogan, esp. sects. D and E; Snell; West.　　　　　　　T.V.F.B.

IAMBIC SHORTENING or *brevis brevians* ("a short syllable shortening"). A linguistic phenomenon in Lat. whose consequences are of special importance for the metrics of early Lat. poetry. In the syllabic series ◡ – or ◡ – x , the syllable immedieately preceding or following the natural word accent may be counted short; thus ◡́ – may become ◡́ ◡ , as in Terence, *Eun.* 8: *ex Graecis bŏnīs*, where the final syllable of *bonis* (naturally long) counts as short because the word accent falls on *bo-*; or ◡ – x́ may become ◡ ◡ x́ , as in Terence, *Eun.* 22: *măgĭstrátus*, where the second syllable of *magistratus* though long counts as short because the natural word accent falls on the following *a*. A short monosyllable, or a disyllable with the first syllable short and the second elided, can alter a following long to a short, e.g. Plautus, *Aul.* 483: *ĕt ĭllae*. It is then a phenomenon of juncture (sandhi), and involves more than a preceding short.—W. M. Lindsay, *Early Lat. Verse* (1922); E. Fraenkel, *Iktus und Akzent im lat. Sprechvers* (1928); H. Drexler, *Plautinische Akzent Forschungen*, I, II (1932), *Index* (1933); O. Skutsch, *Prosodische und metrische Gesetze der lambenkürzung* (1934); C. Questa, *Introduzione alla metrica di Plauto* (1967), 31–70; W. Mańczak, "Iambenkurzung im Lat.," *Glotta* 46 (1968); W. S. Allen, *Accent and Rhythm* (1973); A. M. Devine and L. D. Stephens, "Lat. Pros. and Metre: Brevis Brevians," *CP* 75 (1980).　　　　　　　J.W.H.

IAMBOGRAPHERS. See IAMBIC.

ICELANDIC POETRY. (For I. p. prior to 1550 see OLD NORSE POETRY.) When one considers the degrading conditions in Iceland after its literary peak in the 12th to 14th cs., and esp. the period from 1600 to 1800, with its severe cold, epidemics, famines, volcanic eruptions, and harsh economic and political oppression from Denmark, it seems a miracle that there was any I. p. at all from this time. That there was, and in such excellent abundance, testifies to the extraordinary energy and love that Icelanders have devoted to poetry and the comfort and recreation they have derived from it. In perhaps no other country has poetry been so close to all the people, for there was a high rate of literacy as well as an almost universal custom of composing and memorizing and reciting verse, out of a fascination with the language's potential for intricate form and for producing an effect.

The introduction of paper in the 16th c. had more of an impact on I. p. than two other phenomena from the same period, the introduction of Danish Lutheranism and the beginning of printing (which was monopolized by the Church until 1772). Paper made it economically feasible for farmers and priests all over the country to copy manuscripts, and it was by means of these copies, as well as extensive memorization, that secular lit. was disseminated. The intensive copying and reciting activity also made for ling. and literary conservatism, with the result not only that a modern Icelander can read without difficulty his lit. from as far back as the 13th c.,but also that, at least until the recent advent of free verse, an I. poet felt a natural obligation to use alliteration according to the ancient fixed rules.

The most popular and enduring form of I. p. is the *rímur* (q.v.), and it is significant that Bishop Guðbrandur Þorláksson, in an attempt to appropriate this genre for spiritual uses, commissioned *rímur* on Ruth, Judith, Esther, Tobias, and Jesus Sirach for his *Vísnabók* (Book of Poems) of 1612. This remarkable book is not only the first volume of poetry (apart from hymns) printed in Iceland, but also by its very existence a comment on the strength of I. p. Whereas in countries such as Denmark and Germany clerical writings shaped the lang., in Iceland the Church had to rise to the level of the vernacular. Earlier translations of Lutheran hymns into I. had failed miserably in this respect. Bishop Guðbrandur, recognizing the problem, enlisted the service of the best poets he knew for this volume. Many of the poems in it are anonymous, but according to the preface the chief poet was the Reverend Einar Sigurðsson (1538–1626), among whose poems is a tender lullaby on the birth of Jesus, "Kvæði af stallinum Kristi" (Poem on Christ's Cradle) in the popular dance meter, *vikivaki*. His son, the Reverend Ólafur Einarsson (1573–1659), was also a notable poet who contributed a gloomy complaint on the times to *Vísnabók*.

ICELANDIC POETRY

In a rare instance of poetic genius passing from father to son through three generations, Ólafur's son Stefán Ólafsson (ca. 1619–88) became one of the leading poets of the 17th c. He wrote, as did his father, complaints on laborers and I. sloth, as well as love lyrics and poems about the pleasures of tobacco and drink and horses.

A poet who wrote little in this light, worldly vein was the Reverend Hallgrímur Pétursson (1614–74), indubitably the major poet of the 17th c., if not of all time in Iceland. A humble man who did not, like Stefán Ólafsson, mock the common people, he was not shy about attacking the ruling classes. At one point in his masterful 50-poem cycle, *Passíusálmar* (Passion Hymns), after commenting on Pilate's error in consenting to Jesus's death, Hallgrímur adds: "God grant that those in power over us avoid such monstrous offenses" (Hymn 28). An excellent shorter hymn, "Um dauðans óvissan tíma" (On the Uncertain Hour of Death) is still sung at funerals, a good example of the role that poetry of a high order has played in I. life. Hallgrímur also wrote three *rímur* cycles and other secular poems, such as "Aldarháttur" (Way of the World), contrasting the degenerate present with the glorious period of the I. commonwealth.

Two figures stand out in 18th-c. I. p. Jón Þorláksson (1744– 1819) wrote some popular short poems, including one on a dead mouse in church ("Um dauða mús í kirkju"), and long translations of Pope's *Essay on Man*, Milton's *Paradise Lost*, and Klopstock's *Messias*, the latter two in *fornyrðislag* (q.v.). Eggert Ólafsson (1726–68) was a child of the Enlightenment who, having studied natural history in Copenhagen and made a survey of Iceland, preached the beauty and usefulness of I. nature in poems such as "Íslandssæla" (Iceland's Riches) and the long *Búnaðarbálkur* (Farming Poem).

This positive attitude toward I. nature became, along with a yearning for independence, an important feature of I. romanticism, whose major poet was Jónas Hallgrímsson (1807–45). Apart from his lyrical descriptions of nature, as in "Ísland"— which begins "Iceland, frost-white mother, land of blessings and prosperity"—he is remembered for his poems on the pain of lost love and for his mastery of many poetic forms, including (for the first time in Iceland) the sonnet and terza rima. The other great romantic poet was Bjarni Thorarensen (1786–1841), who portrayed nature in similes and personifications and tended to glorify winter rather than summer, especially in his poem "Veturinn" (Winter). He also raised a traditional I. genre, the memorial poem, to a new height. Quite different from these Copenhagen-educated men was the poor folk poet and woodcarver Hjálmar Jónsson (1796–1875), known as Bólu-Hjálmar. His large body of verse includes personal invective, *rímur*, bitter complaints about poverty, and poems about death.

One of the greatest poets of the later 19th c. was Matthías Jochumsson (1835–1920), a free-thinking parson and newspaper editor who wrote excellent lyrics, hymns, and memorial poems and also made masterful translations of four of Shakespeare's tragedies.

From the abundance of good modern poets, three representatives will be mentioned here. Einar Benediktsson (1864–1940) was a powerful figure who, as a kind of latter-day Eggert Ólafsson, sought to improve Iceland by forming international corporations to mine gold and harness water power. He used lang. as he used wealth, to gain power over things, and his nature poems, like "Útsær" (Ocean), are rich with the imagery of opposing elements in nature and his view of the pantheistic force uniting all things.

Steinn Steinar (1908–58) came to Reykjavík as a poor youth in the late 1920s, and in his first collection (1934) produced poems of social protest, sympathizing with hungry workers who "don't understand / their own relationship / to their enemies." This same poem, "Veruleiki" (Reality), in free verse, goes beyond skepticism of the social order, however, to speak of the illusory nature of existence itself. This note of doubt, alienation, and nihilism became predominant in Steinn's finely pruned, paradoxical poems, the longest and most highly regarded of which is "Tíminn og vatnið" (Time and the Water), an enigmatic and symbolic meditation probably meant to be sensed rather than comprehended.

Hannes Pétursson (b. 1931) has produced sensitive and meticulously crafted lyrics on a variety of subjects including I. folklore, European places (the prison camp at Dachau, the Strasbourg cathedral), and Cl. figures like Odysseus. Hannes writes with a calm and firm voice on such themes as the emptiness of lang. and man's separation from nature. In "Stórborg" (Big City), he describes himself as sitting like a prisoner in a labyrinth of asphalt and stone from which he escapes, by the grace of a bird or trees or a fountain, "into another context, a bigger and more complex whole, a labyrinth where no one knows what lives deep inside."

BIBLIOGRAPHY: P. Mitchell and K. Ober, *Bibl. of Mod. I. Lit. in Tr.* (1975)—lists trs. of works since the Reformation period.

PRIMARY WORKS: *Bishop Guðbrand's Vísnabók 1612*, ed. S. Nordal (1937)—facsimile with valuable intro. in Eng.; *Hymns of the Passion by Hallgrímur Pétursson*, tr. A. C. Gook (1966); *Íslenzkt ljóðasafn*, ed. K. Karlsson, 6 v. (1974–78)—most comprehensive anthol.; *The Postwar Poetry of Iceland*, ed. and tr. S. Magnússon (1982).

SECONDARY WORKS: J. Þorkelsson, *Om digtningen på Island i det 15. og 16. århundrede* (1888); J. C. Poestion, *Isländische Dichter der Neuzeit* (1897)— begins with the Reformation; R. Beck, *Hist. of I. Poets 1800–1940* (1950); S. Einarsson, *A Hist. of I. Lit.* (1957); J. Hjálmarsson, *Íslenzk nútímaljóðlist*

(1971); T. M. Andersson, "The I. Sagas," *Heroic Epic and Saga*, ed. F. J. Oinas (1978).   R.CO.

ICON. See ICONICITY; ICONOLOGY; ONOMATOPOEIA; REPRESENTATION AND MIMESIS; SEMIOTICS, POETIC; SOUND.

ICONICITY. A natural resemblance or analogy of form between a word (the signifier) and the object it refers to (the signified). In the semiotics of Charles Sanders Peirce, every sign mediates between its referent and a meaning; the relation between signifier, signified, and meaning is in effect triangular. Three types or modes of representation are recognized, hence three possible relationships may obtain between the sign and its object. If the relation is cognitive (thought) but arbitrary, the sign is a *symbol*; thought is carried on in terms of signs, hence meaning itself is a sign relation. If the sign is in physical proximity to its object, then the sign is an *index*: smoke is an index of fire. If there is resemblance between sign and object, the sign is an *icon*: mimicry by a professional mime is iconic. Icons, like indices, are not genuine or full-bodied signs for Peirce but are inferior, though they may be common or even prolific; icons "can represent nothing but Forms and Feelings" (*CP* 4.544).

Peirce's concept of i. is important because it refutes the traditional critical denigration of mimetic sound effects in poetry such as onomatopoeia (q.v.) by showing that the mimetic function is a key component of the representational system itself. Mimetic effects in poetry may now be seen not as quaint aberrations or mere "poetical" devices but, rather, natural extensions of a process always at work in lang. There are other processes, certainly, but i. is one, and more one than allowed by Plato in *Cratylus*. Considerable linguistic research in the 20th c. has confirmed that i. operates at every level of lang. structure (phonology, morphology, syntax) and in virtually every known lang. worldwide. Beyond speech itself, i. also functions in visual representations of lang., e.g. sign lang. (particularly evident), and in several writing systems and writing-based picture-signs (hieroglyphs, ideograms, phonograms, the rebus). And verbal i. can be correlated with visual forms of i. operant in painting and poetic imagery.

In poetry, prosodic i. can be found operating at every level of the stratification of the text, from a wide range of mimetic sound effects (see SOUND) to expressive rhythms and "representative meter" (see METER), to iconic syntax; and in the visual mode of the poem, from mimetic subgenres such as pattern poetry and concrete poetry to mimetic strategies of deployment in free verse (see VISUAL POETRY).

See now REPRESENTATION AND MIMESIS; ICONOLOGY; IDEOGRAM; ONOMATOPOEIA; SEMIOTICS, POETIC.

C. S. Peirce, *Collected Papers*, ed. C. Hartshorne and P. Weiss, 8 v. (1931–58); D. L. Bolinger, *Forms of Eng.* (1965); R. W. Wescott, "Linguistic Iconism," *Lang* 47 (1971); S. Ullmann, "Natural and Conventional Signs," and T. Todorov, "Lit. and Semiotics," *The Tell-Tale Sign*, ed. T. A. Sebeok (1975); W. K. Wimsatt, Jr., "In Search of Verbal Mimesis," *Day of the Leopards* (1976)—eight types of verbal i.; T. A. Sebeok, "I.," *MLN* 91 (1976); Y. Malkiel, "From Phonosymbolism to Morphosymbolism," *Fourth LACUS Forum* (1978), supp. by D. B. Justice, "I. and Assoc.," *RPh* 33 (1980); R. Cureton, "e e cummings: A Case Study of Iconic Syntax," *Lang&S* 14 (1981); J. N. Deely, "Antecedents to Peirce's Notion of Iconic Signs," *Semiotics 1980*, ed. M. Herzfeld and M. D. Lenhart (1982); M. Nänny, "Iconic Dimensions in Poetry," *On Poetry and Poetics*, ed. R. Waswo (1985); J. Haiman, *Natural Syntax: I. and Erosion* (1985), ed., *I. in Syntax* (1985); W. Bernhart, "The Iconic Quality of Poetic Rhythm," *W&I* 2 (1986); W. Nöth, *Handbook of Semiotics* (1990).   T.V.F.B.

ICONOLOGY is the study of "icons" (images, pictures, or likenesses). It is thus, as E. H. Gombrich argues, a "science" of images, which not only "investigates the function of images in allegory and symbolism" (see ALLEGORY; SYMBOL) but also explores what we might call "the linguistics of the visual image," the fundamental codes and conventions that make iconic representation and communication possible. I. thus has links with philosophy, esp. the field of semiotics (see SEMIOTICS, POETIC) or the general science of signs, as well as with psychology, particularly the analysis of visual perception (Arnheim) and the imaginary (see IMAGE; IMAGERY; IMAGINATION). More modestly, i. may be described as a "rhetoric of images" in a double sense: first, as a study of "what to say about images"—e.g. the trad. of "art writing" that goes back to Philostratus's *Imagines* (ca. 220 A.D.) and is centrally concerned with the description and interp. of a work of visual art; second, as a study of "what images say"—i.e. the ways in which images speak for themselves by persuading, telling stories, or describing states of affairs.

I. also denotes a long trad. of theoretical and historical reflection on the concept of imagery, a trad. which in its narrow sense probably begins with such Ren. handbooks of symbolic imagery as Cesare Ripa's *Iconologia* (1592) and culminates in Erwin Panofsky's influential *Studies in I.* (1939). In a broader sense, the critical study of the icon extends to theological and philosophical concepts such as the biblical concept of the *imago dei*, the notion that man is created "in the image and likeness" of God. The Platonic concept of the *eikon* crops up in the notion of *eikasia* (cf. Eng. "icastic"), the perception of images, appearances, and reflections (*Republic* 509e), in the theory of art, where it is linked with *mimesis* (*Republic* 598e–599a; see IMITATION), and in basic models of being and knowing. F. E. Peters notes that, for Plato, "the visible universe is the *eikon* of the intelligible one."

The concept of the icon may best be understood as oscillating between a very general sense (the notion of "likeness" or "similitude") and a fairly specific reference to visual representations *by means of* likeness (e.g. paintings, statues, photographs). C. S. Peirce's semiotic theories and modern linguistic research provide the foundation for the modern understanding of iconicity (q.v.): in Peirce's theory, iconic signs would include such things as algebraic equations, diagrams, phonetic mimicry, and sugar substitutes. The notion of the icon enters poetics in both its general and specific senses. Theories of metaphor, figurative lang., and allegory, all of which involve the analysis of verbal analogies, similitudes, and comparisons, invoke the general sense of the icon as a relationship of likeness. The New Critical idea of the poem as a "verbal icon" (see Wimsatt) whose formal structure incarnates its propositional content is the formalist version of poetic iconicity. The more specific sense of the poetic icon conceives it as a poetic "image," not in the sense of similitude but as a verbal representation of a concrete (usually visual) object. Vivid descriptions of places, objects (see EKPHRASIS), and persons, while not themselves "iconic" in the general sense, are seen as eliciting mental images in the reader, evoking a kind of secondary visual representation. Sometimes the notion of an "iconic" poetic image may be reserved for highly charged symbolic objects (Keats's urn, Coleridge's albatross), but it may equally well be applied to more common materials. Experimental genres such as concrete, pattern, and visual poetry (qq.v.) which array the text into the visual shape of an object are of central interest for the ways they combine the general notion of iconic likeness with the specific strategies of visual representation.

Poetics often moves between these two senses without much critical self-awareness. Aristotle's *Rhetoric* (3.4) uses *eikon* in the general sense to denote comparison or simile; Quintilian calls it a kind of comparison "which the Greeks call *eikon* and which expresses the appearance of things and persons" (*Institutio oratoria* 5.11.24); Henry Peacham defines "icon" as a "forme of speech which painteth out the image of a person or thing by comparing forme with forme, quality with quality, one likeness with another" (*Garden of Eloquence*, 1577). As the Ren. interest in the naming and classifying of stylistic and rhetorical devices waned, the term "icon" almost disappeared from poetics. The all-purpose term "image" (q.v.) took its place in poetic theory until the modern revival of semiotics reopened the question of "iconicity" as a general problem.

Most early modern studies of literary or poetic i., e.g. Tuve, are compilations of specific symbolic motifs (see also Aptekar; Frye; Landow; Ziolkowski). These studies, which generally attempt to reconstruct the meanings associated with particular visual images, might better be called "iconographies", reserving the term "i." for studies which raise more general questions about the conditions under which poetic images acquire meaning, and of the nature of literary similitude, resemblance, and iconicity (see Panofsky, Bialostocki, and Mitchell for discussion of the distinction between iconography and i.). Most comparative studies of the "sister arts" of poetry and painting, regulated by the Horatian maxim *ut pictura poesis* (q.v.), are poetic "iconographies" that try to clarify the meaning of poems by reference to the pictorial scenes or works of art they describe. I. in its more general sense would raise questions about the status of iconic representation in the specific text, its genre, and its cultural context, as in Ernest Gilman's exemplary study, which not only provides a great deal of information about the iconographic resources of Eng. poetry in the 17th c., but situates this data in the context of the religious and political struggles over the relative value of visual and verbal representation.

I., then, is not just the interdisciplinary study of imagery in a variety of media, but a historical and theoretical inquiry into the nature of imagery, with special emphasis on the difference (as well as the similarity) between iconic and verbal representation. Images and words, despite their easy conflation in phrases like "poetic imagery" or "verbal icon," carry with them a history of radical differentiation, articulated in oppositions such as nature and convention (qq.v.), space and time, the eye and the ear. These oppositions are frequently associated with distinctions of class, race, gender, and political or professional identity (see Mitchell 1986). What Leonardo da Vinci (or his 19th-c. editors) called the *paragone* or contest of poet and painter, verbal and visual artist, often becomes a figure for competing if not antithetical modes of being and knowing, most fundamentally the gap between self and other.

I. thus comes to lit. and poetry with a sense of its own impropriety, as a discipline grounded in nonverbal forms of representation. It is the intrusion of the visual and pictorial into the realm of voice, hearing, and lang., the entrance of similitude into the (linguistic) territory of "difference," the colonization of writing by painting (or vice versa). The subject matter of i. is both the desire for and resistance to the merging of lang. and imagery. The political psychology and anthropology of iconic representation—the analysis of such phenomena as idolatry, iconoclasm, iconophobia, fetishism, scopophilia, voyeurism, and iconophilia—is as important to the discipline of i. as the meaning of any particular image. See also EMBLEM; FIGURATION; REPRESENTATION AND MIMESIS; SOUND; VISUAL ARTS AND POETRY.

C. S. Peirce, "The Icon, Index, and Symbol," *Collected Papers*, ed. C. Hartshorne and P. Weiss, 8 v. (1931–58), v. 2; C. Morris, "Aesthetics and the Theory of Signs," *Jour. of Unified Science* 8 (1939);

E. Panofsky, *Studies in I.* (1939), "Iconography and I.," *Meaning in the Visual Arts* (1955); J. C. Ransom, "Wanted: An Ontological Critic" (1941); rpt. in Ransom); E. H. Gombrich, "Icones Symbolicae: The Visual Image in Neo-Platonic Thought," *JWCI* 11 (1948), *Art and Illusion*, 2d ed. (1961); R. Arnheim, *Art and Visual Perception* (1954); W. K. Wimsatt, Jr., *The Verbal Icon* (1954); Frye; J. Hagstrum, *The Sister Arts* (1958), *William Blake: Poet and Painter* (1964); J. Bialostocki, "Iconography and I.," *Encyclopedia of World Art* (1963); H. Weisinger, "Icon and Image: What the Literary Historian Can Learn from the Warburg School," *BNYPL* 67 (1963); R. Tuve, *Allegorical Imagery* (1966); F. E. Peters, *Gr. Philosophical Terms* (1967); J. V. Fleming, *The* Roman de la Rose: *A Study in Allegory and Iconography* (1969); G. Hermeren, *Representation and Meaning in the Visual Arts* (1969); J. Aptekar, *Icons of Justice* (1969); U. Eco, *A Theory of Semiotics* (1976); T. Ziolkowski, *Disenchanted Images* (1977); W. J. T. Mitchell, *Blake's Composite Art* (1978), *I.* (1986), "I. and Ideology," *W&D* 11–12 (1988); *Ikonographie un Ikonologie*, ed. E. Kaemmerling (1979); B. Bucher, *Icon and Conquest* (1981); *Image and Code*, ed. W. Steiner (1981); G. C. Argan, "Ideology and I.," *The Lang. of Images*, ed. W. J. T. Mitchell (1982); G. Landow, *Images of Crisis: Literary I., 1750 to the Present* (1982); K. Moxey, "Panofsky's Concept of 'I.,'" *NLH* 17 (1986); E. Gilman, *Iconoclasm and Poetry in the Eng. Reformation* (1986). W.J.T.M.

ICTUS (Lat. "beat"). Long disputed as a term, the concept of i. goes by a variety of other less satisfactory names, esp. "metrical accent," "prosodic accent," "metrical stress," etc. As it is currently conceived, meter (q.v.) is a pattern of prominent and nonprominent, or marked and unmarked, positions which together form a distinct pattern, the line (q.v.). "I." is the most neutral term for each marked or prominent position. As an element of the abstract pattern which is meter, i. is marked in each verse-system by the phonological feature that is phonemic for its lang.—accent (q.v.) in stress-based langs., pitch (q.v.) in tone langs., length or duration (q.v.) in quantitative langs. In the Eng. iambic pentameter, for example, the five even syllables are ictic, meaning that in the most neutral or normative realization of this meter these syllables will be stressed. Some variations from this pattern were, according to the traditional account, allowed for, esp. reversing the stressing on the first and second syllables. It was disputed whether this should be accounted for at the level of realization, i.e. in the actual line (in which case a stress falls under nonictus and a slack under ictus) or at the level of meter, by positing the permissibility of "substitution" (a trochaic foot could be substituted for an iambic one, with stress now agreeably falling under ictus). The former option seems very undesirable, but the difficulty with the latter option lies in explaining why only some substitutions seem to be allowed and why their frequencies in the five feet of the line are very differential.

Neither option, however, infringes the fundamental distinction between meter, as an abstract pattern applicable to all lines, and rhythm, the actualization in each specific line. In the Cl. Gr. hexameter (q.v.), the first five of the six feet may be dactyls or spondees; the sixth must be a spondee. The number of syllables is thus variable, but the first position in each foot is ictic. On this analysis, it would seem that i. corresponds to the concept of *arsis* (in modern usage) and *thesis* in ancient usage, namely a subdivision of the foot (q.v.) into two elements (regardless of how many syllables occupy each element) of which only one is prominent (see ARSIS AND THESIS). In antiquity the terms "arsis" and "thesis" were used to describe the movement of the foot or the hand in keeping time with the rhythm of a verse; Roman writers like Horace and Quintilian, however, used them in the sense of a raising or lowering of the *voice* and so reversed their senses from Gr. usage, a confusion brought into the modern world by Bentley in the 18th c. and others. Nevertheless, "i." denotes the marked or prominent position in the foot.

It is important to remember that at the level of meter, all ictuses are equal, whereas in the rhythm of the actual line, stresses often vary considerably in their weights, some primary, some secondary, some even weaker. It was the signal accomplishment of modern metrics to articulate the relation between the latter and the former as the *relative stress principle* (q.v.): it does not matter how strong, in absolute terms, a stress under i. is so long as it is stronger—even if by a hair—than the syllable under nonictus. In the account given by structural metrists, stresses under nonictus can undergo *demotion* and weak stresses under i. *promotion*; effectually, this means that linguistic stresses are altered or adjusted in weight under the influence of the metrical grid.

In Cl. prosody, the term has been used in the 20th c. by scholars who held that the quantitative meter of Lat. poetry was in fact made audible not by length but by a stress accent. Beare, however, thinks that such an assumption "may be due merely to our craving to impose on quantitative verse a rhythm which we can recognize." Discussion of the controversy may be found in Allen. See now ARSIS AND THESIS; CLASSICAL PROSODY; HOMODYNE AND HETERODYNE.

C. E. Bennett, "What Was I. in Lat. Prosody?" *AJP* 19 (1898), with crit. by G. L. Hendrickson in 20 (1899): 198–210, and discussion, 412–34; E. H. Sturtevant, "The I. of Cl. Verse," *AJP* 44 (1923); E. Kapp, "Bentley and the Mod. Doctrine of I. in Cl. Verse," *Mnemosyne* 9 (1941); Beare, esp. chs. 5, 14; P. W. Harsh, "I. and Accent," *Lustrum* 3 (1958); P. Habermann and W. Mohr, "Hebung und Senkung," *Reallexikon* 1.623–28; A. Labhardt, "Le

IDEOGRAM

Problème de l'i.," *Euphrosyne* 2 (1959); 0. Seel and E. Pöhlmann, "Quantität und Wortakzent im horazischen Sapphiker," *Philologus* 103 (1959); H. Drexler, "Quantität und Wortakzent," *Maia* 12 (1960); L. P. Wilkinson, *Golden Lat. Artistry* (1963); W. S. Allen, *Accent and Rhythm* (1973), esp. 276 ff.; E. Pulgram, *Lat.-Romance Phonology: Prosodics and Metrics* (1975); Morier; Brogan; S. E. Traverse, "I. Metricus," *DAI* 41 (1981): 4697. T.V.F.B.

IDENTICAL RHYME, sometimes "tautological r." Increase in the "richness" or sonority of r. over the traditional form of end r., which repeats only the medial vowel and final consonants of the rhyming syllables, has usually been effected by repeating identically the initial consonant sound as well. This exact reiteration of syllable sound produces what has traditionally been called (in Eng.) "rich r." or (in Fr.) *rime riche,* as for example *down/down* (opposite of up; duck feathers). But the category "rich r." actually embraces several distinct forms of homonyms (words spelled or sounded identically but with differing meanings): for discussion and exemplification of these, see RICH RHYME. J. V. Cunningham entangles such a couple in a witty epigram: "God is love. Then by conversion / Love is God, and sex conversion." Beyond these forms, however, is the further class of words identical in sound (and perhaps spelling) and grammatical class *and meaning.* These are claimed by some theorists as examples of "i. r." (Ger. *rührende Reim,* though that term has not been applied consistently). In Eng., both rich and i. rs. are more common than is usually supposed—Chaucer uses them—but in other langs. they have been more freely accepted and more extensively cultivated at times, esp. in OF and MHG.

It is disputed whether i. r. is r. at all: strictly speaking, end r. requires phonic similarity (but *not* identity) amidst semantic difference. But the taxonomy of rich rhyming leads inexorably to i. r. and raises, thereby, the more interesting and fundamental question of whether or not a word can rhyme with itself. Abernathy argues in the negative, pointing out that identical word repetitions at line-end appear in some verseforms where r. is excluded, such as the blank verse of Browning's *The Ring and The Book* (Bk. 7), or Poe's "To Helen," or even Milton. And it may be pointed out that prosodic i. r. is in fact rhetorical *antistrophe* (q.v.). Scherr distinguishes rich from i. r. in Rus. poetry as "homonymic" vs. "repetend" r. (206). Scott takes the view that the phenomena here called i. r. constitute "terminal repetition" (237–39), which raises the issue of how r. is to be distinguished from repetition (q.v.). On the other hand, Lotman argues that no word repeated in verse is *ever* repeated with total identity, i.e. in precisely the same sense, by virtue of its appearance in a new semantic context: on these grounds one could say that identity of meaning is ruled out, so that i. r. is ultimately not separable from all the other categories of rich r. For Lotman, in i. r. semantic information is increased even if phonic is decreased, resulting in increased "richness" in the r. The status of i. r. bears on issues such as the formal specification of the sestina or villanelle (qq.v.), wherein words are repeated identically: are these rs. or, rather, repetitions? Wimsatt held the former, but Abernathy holds that the sestina "should be regarded as a special form of antirhymed verse." This would accord with the traditional view that a refrain (q.v.) word is not a r., and does not preclude Lotman's argument.

E. Freymond, "Über den reichen Reim bei altfranzösichen Dichtern bis zum Anfang des XIV Jh.," *ZRP* 6 (1882); A. Tobler, *Le Vers français* (1885), 167–76; J. Möllmann, *Der homonyme Reim im Französischen* (1896); C. von Kraus, "Der rührende Reim im Mittelhochdeutschen," *ZDA* 56 (1918); J. Fucilla, "*Parole identiche* in the Sonnet and Other Verse Forms," *PMLA* 50 (1935); A. Oras, "Intensified Rhyme Links in the *Faerie Queene,*" *JEGP* 54 (1955); P. Rickard, "Semantic Implications of OF I. R.," *NM* 6 (1965); R. Abernathy, "Rs., Non-Rs., and Antir.," *To Honor Roman Jakobson,* v. 1 (1967); J. Lotman, *Structure of the Artistic Text* (tr. 1977); Scott; Scherr; A. H. Olsen, *Between Earnest and Game* (1990)—homonymic rs. in Gower. T.V.F.B.

IDEOGRAM. In lang., a pictogram, a character in an alphabet which functions as an image for that to which it refers. In poetry, a field or matrix of juxtaposed words and images. The i. is the crux of Ezra Pound's "ideogrammic method," a new form of poetic structure which he hoped would allow Modernist poets to escape the traps of both late-Victorian vagueness, metaphor, and sentimentality, on the one hand, and the loss of immediacy created by the syntax of discursive, representational speech, on the other.

Pound's search for new poetic techniques led him, successively, into imagism and vorticism (qq.v.), but it was his discovery of the work of the Am. Orientalist Ernest Fenollosa (d. 1908) which provided the catalyst. Pound read Fenollosa's lecture notes (written ca. 1904) on the nature of Chinese pictograms in 1914, published trs. of Chinese poems based on Fenollosa's work as *Cathay* in 1915, and edited the notes into an essay which he published in 1919. Fenollosa's essay, *The Chinese Written Character as a Medium for Poetry,* may be fairly called the first and perhaps the most important *Ars poetica* of the 20th c.

In Chinese, said Fenollosa, the characters of the alphabet are, in greater or lesser degree, images or visual representations of the things they signify. Thus the i. for "East" is a synthesis of the is. for "sun" and "tree"—the sun in the trees. Here abstract concepts arise not out of abstract symbols but out of concrete particulars and the immediacy of experience. In the Western langs., by contrast, graphemes denote sounds which refer to objects purely by arbitrary convention. Fenollosa only contrasted Chinese and Western modes of thought; it remained for Pound to see how the pictogram could be formulated as a principle and developed into a poetic method.

The essence of the ideogrammic method is juxtaposition of separate objects or events so as to evoke a new matrix or constellation of meaning. The syntax is paratactic or asyndetic. But juxtaposition does not imply fragmentation or the mere "heaping together" of unrelated items. Rather, the poet still exercises selection and combination; separate items are juxtaposed so as to be re-integrated by the reader exactly as objects and events are integrated in ordinary perception of the external world: the reader's mind will organize the elements into a coherent pattern. The ideogrammic method thereby imitates perception itself, and in this respect, it is a mimetic strategy (see REPRESENTATION AND MIMESIS); is. are motivated signs. Further, emphasis shifts away from static description: now symbols are used to represent not objects but relations, motion, energy, and action. Now lang. has an immediacy of presentational form lacking in the discursive-descriptive-rationalist nature of Western writing.

Pound in fact misunderstood part of Fenollosa, but it was a terrifically fertile misprision. And Fenollosa himself was in error about Chinese: only 10% of its characters are pictographic; the vast majority are phonetic. Nevertheless, reading Fenollosa gave Pound the idea for a wholly new poetics, arguably a method which became more influential, in its several forms, than any other in the 20th c. Géfin claims that the principle of juxtaposition underlies much subsequent Am. poetry in the 20th c., incl. the Williams trad., Objectivism, free verse (qq.v.), "open form," Olson's "composition by field" (see PROJECTIVE VERSE), and Duncan's "collages." Pound seems to have intended *The Cantos* as a modern epic, though one organized not via narrative but via the ideogrammic method.—D. Perkins, *Hist. of Mod. Poetry*, 2 v. (1976, 1987); L. Géfin, *I.: Hist. of a Poetic Method* (1982). T.V.F.B.

IDEOLOGY. See CULTURAL CRITICISM; MARXIST CRITICISM; POLITICS AND POETRY.

IDYLL, idyl (Gr. *eidyllion* [diminutive of *eidos*, "form"], "short separate poem"; in Gr. a pastoral poem or i. is *eidylllion Boukolikon*). One of the several synonyms used by the Gr. grammarians for the poems of Theocritus, Bion, and Moschus, which at other times are called *bucolic* (q.v.), *eclogue* (q.v.), and pastoral (q.v.). Theocritus' ten pastoral poems, no doubt because of their superiority, became the prototype of the i. In the 16th and 17th cs., esp. in France, there was frequent insistence that pastorals in dialogue be called *eclogues*, those in narrative, *is.* In Ger., *Idylle* is the ordinary term for pastoral. Two biblical books—

Ruth and *The Song of Songs*—are sometimes called is., which may be taken to illustrate the latitude of the term. Note that Tennyson's *Is. of the King* 1859) is hardly pastoral. Perhaps Tennyson thought the use of the term was appropriate: each i. contains an incident in the matter of Arthur and his Knights which is separate (or framed) but at the same time is connected with the central theme; the contents treat the Christian virtues in an ideal manner and in a remote setting. But there is very little in Browning's *Dramatic Is.* (1879–80), which mainly explore psychological crises, to place them in the pastoral trad. The adjectival form, *idyllic*, is more regularly and conventionally applied to works or scenes which present picturesque rural scenery and a life of innocence and tranquillity, but this has little specific relation to any poetic genre. See BUCOLIC; ECLOGUE; GEORGIC; PASTORAL.—M. H. Shackford, "A Definition of the Pastoral I.," *PMLA* 19 (1904); P. van Tieghem, "Les Is. de Gessner et le rêve pastoral," *Le Préromantisme*, v. 2 (1930); P. Merker, *Deutsche Idyllendichtung* (1934); E. Merker, "Idylle," *Reallexikon* 1.742–49; J. Tismar, *Gestörte Idyllen* (1973); T. Lange, *I. und exotische Sehnsucht* (1976); R. Böschenstein-Schäfer, *Idylle*, 2d ed. (1977); K. Bernhard, *Idylle* (1977); V. Nemoianu, *Micro Harmony: Growth and Uses of the Idyllic Model in Lit.* (1977). T.V.F.B.; J.E.C.

IMAGE. "I." and "imagery" (q.v.) are among the most widely used and poorly understood terms in poetic theory, occurring in so many different contexts that it may well be impossible to provide any rational, systematic account of their usage. A poetic i. is, variously, a metaphor, simile, or figure of speech (qq.v.); a concrete verbal reference; a recurrent motif; a psychological event in the reader's mind; the vehicle or second term of a metaphor; a symbol (q.v.) or symbolic pattern; or the global impression of a poem as a unified structure (q.v.).

The term's meaning and use has also changed radically at various points in the history of Western poetics. It plays only a minor role in traditional rhetorical theory, where related notions such as "figure" and "trope" are the dominant terms. Frazer argues that the term first becomes important to Eng. crit. in the 17th c., perhaps under the influence of empiricist models of the mind. Hobbes and Locke use the term as a key element in their accounts of sensation, perception, memory, imagination, and lang., developing a "picture-theory" of consciousness as a system of receiving, storing, and retrieving mental images. The term continues to play an important role in neoclassical poetics (q.v.), usually in accounts of description. Addison, in the *Spectator* papers on the "Pleasures of Imagination" (nos. 411–21, 1712), argues that images are what allow the poet to "get the better of nature": "the reader finds a scene drawn in stronger colors and painted more to the life in his imagination by the help of words than by an actual survey of the scene which they describe."

In romantic and postromantic poetics (q.v.), the i. persists in a sublimated and refined form, and is often defined in opposition to "mental pictures" (Burke) or to the "merely descriptive" or "painted," ornamental images of 18th-c. poetry. Coleridge's distinctions between symbol and allegory ("living educts" versus a mere "picture lang.") and imagination and fancy (qq.v.; creative versus remembered images) consistently appeal to a difference between a "higher," inward, intellectual i. and a lower, outward, sensuous i. The notion of the poetic "symbol," along with the poetic process as an "expressive" rather than "mimetic" endeavor, helps to articulate the notion of the romantic i. as something more refined, subtle, and active than its neoclassical predecessor. Modernist poetics often combines (while claiming to transcend) the neoclassical and romantic concepts of the i., urging poets to make their lang. concrete and sensuous while articulating a theory of poetic structure that regards the entire poem as a kind of matrix or crystallized form of energy, as if the poem were an abstract i. Thus Pound: "The image is not an idea. It is a radiant node or cluster; it is a . . . VORTEX, from which ideas are constantly rushing" (Pound 81, 92).

It is not surprising, then, that "i." has been a key term in modern crit. An enormous bibliography of studies investigating "the imagery of X in Y" could be compiled, most of them employing some uncritical amalgam of the various usages mentioned above. Furbank has argued that the term is so vague and contradictory that it ought to be dropped altogether or else restricted to "its natural sense . . . as meaning a likeness, a picture, or a simulacrum." The revival of rhetorical terminology by structuralism, semiotics, and deconstruction (qq.v.) is in large part accomplishing a quiet retirement of traditional types of i. studies from literary scholarship. As the i. loses its function as a kind of universal solvent for poetic forms and elements, however, it may be taking on new interest as an object of critical investigation in its own right (see ICONOLOGY). Included in such an investigation would be some account of the historical shifts in the role of the concept of the i. in poetics; an analysis of the way it relies on philosophical, psychological, and aesthetic paradigms; and a critique of the values embedded in the application of a term like "imagery" to the specific problems of writing and reading.

A critique of the concept of the poetic i. would probably begin by noting that it tends to blur a distinction that underlies a large tract of poetics, namely, the difference between literal and figurative lang. An i. is, on the one hand, "the only available word to cover every kind of simile [and] metaphor" (Spurgeon); on the other hand, it is simply "what the words actually name" (Kenner), the literal referents of lang., concrete objects. The i. is, in other words, a term which designates both metaphor and description, both a purely linguistic relation between words and a referential relation to a nonlinguistic reality, both a rhetorical device and a psychological event. This confusion is most evident in theories of metaphor which follow I. A. Richards' influential distinction between "tenor" and "vehicle" (q.v.). Is Shakespeare's metaphor "Juliet is the sun" to be understood as an "i." because "sun" is a concrete noun that evokes a sensuous picture in the reader's mind? Or is the whole expression an i. because it insists on a "likeness" between two unlike things? Is an i., in short, a kind of bearer of sensuous immediacy and presence, or a relationship formed by the conjunction of two different words and their associated vocabularies? Is it a mode of apprehension or a rhetorical device? Whatever we may understand as the meaning of the term "i." in any particular context, it seems clear that the general function of the term has been to make this sort of distinction difficult if not impossible.

What could be at stake in perpetuating a confusion between metaphor and description, or between figurative and literal lang.? One possibility is that the figurative- vs. literal-lang. distinction is itself untenable, and the ambiguous use of the term "i." is simply a symptom of this fact. "I.," understood in its narrow and literal sense as a picture or statue, is a metaphor for metaphor itself (a sign by similitude or resemblance) and for mimetic representation or iconicity (q.v.). Since literary representation does not represent by likeness the way pictorial images do, literary representation is itself only and always metaphorical, whether or not it employs particular figures. (Goodman argues, for instance, that representation, properly speaking, only occurs in dense, analogical systems like pictures, and that a verbal description, no matter how detailed, never amounts to a depiction.) We might also note that the literal-figurative distinction itself appeals to an implicit distinction between "letters" (writing) and "figures" (images; pictures; designs or bodies in space).

The concept of "poetic imagery" is thus a kind of oxymoron, installing an alien medium (painting, sculpture, visual art) at the heart of verbal expression. The motives for this incorporation of the visual arts are usually clear enough: the whole panoply of values that go with painting—presence, immediacy, vividness—are appropriated for poetry. But there are equally powerful motives for keeping the incorporation of the visual under control, for seeing the visual arts as a dangerous rival as well as a helpful ally. Lessing, in *Laocoön* (1766), thought that the emulation of the visual arts by lit. would lead to static, lifeless description, while Burke (*A Philosophical Enquiry into the Origin of our Ideas of the Sublime and the Beautiful,* 1757) argued that visual imaging was a vastly overrated aspect of literary response, incompatible with the opacity he associated with true literary sublimity. The recurrent figure of the blind poet, whose blindness is a crucial condition of his insight and freedom from merely "external" visual images, reminds us that the boundaries between images and texts, figures and letters, the visual and the verbal are not so easily breached in Western poetics.

Another place where the contradictory tendencies of poetic imagery may be glimpsed is in the area of reader response. Here the i. plays the role of a supplement to the poetic text (Derrida 309). It opens an empty space to be filled by the activity of the reader's imagination. Ideally, it completes the text in the reader's mind, in the world it projects, in the "spaces" between its words, bringing the "vision" of the poem sensuously, perceptually alive; but it may equally well open a threatening space of indeterminacy (q.v.). Thus the voice and sound—phonetic "images" such as rhyme, rhythm, onomatopoeia, and tone (qq.v.)—are the first place to look for perfect iconicity in poetry. But what of the imperfect, secondary icons—the "mental pictures" that voice and sound produce, the imaginary spaces—theater, dream-vision, movie, map, or diagram—that arise out of the reading experience? Poetics discloses a certain ambivalence toward these phenomena. While visualization, for instance, is universally acknowledged as an aspect of reader response, there is still considerable resistance to treating it as a legitimate object of literary study. The supposed "privacy" and "inaccessibility" of mental images seems to preclude empirical investigation, and the supposed randomness of visual associations with verbal cues seems to rule out any systematic account. But mental imagery has taken on a whole new life in the work of post-behavioral cognitive psychology. Literary critics who want to talk about poetic imagery in the sense of readers' visual response would do well to consult the work of philosophers and psychologists such as Fodor, Goodman, Block, and Kosslyn, who have conducted experimental studies of visualization and mental imaging. Wittgenstein's critique of the "picture theory" of meaning (*Philosophical Investigations*, 1957) also ought to be required reading for those who think of images as private. If mental images are an essential part of the reading experience, why should it be any more difficult to describe or interpret them than the images offered in Freud's *The Interpretation of Dreams*?

At the same time, it might behoove psychologists experimenting in the field of mental imaging to attend to poets and critics who have dealt with this question. It seems obvious, for instance, that mental imaging cannot be a subject of laboratory investigation alone, but must be understood in the context of cultural history. Some cultures and ages have encouraged reader visualization far more extensively than others: "quick poetic eyes" and the "test of the pencil," for example, were the slogans of 18th-c. poetics, which urged the reader to match his or her experience with conventional, public models from painting and sculpture. We might ask ourselves why Shakespeare seems to have been singled out as the principal object of traditional i. studies in Eng. crit. One answer may be that the study of imagery is part of the transformation of each Shakespearean play from a prompt-book for the theater into a printed text for private reading. The first such study, Walter Whiter's *A Specimen of a Commentary on Shakespeare* (1794), was pub. in the same era that saw Shakespeare move from the playhouse to the study, and heard Charles Lamb's famous argument that "the plays of Shakespeare are less calculated for performance on a stage, than those of almost any other dramatist whatever" ("On the Tragedies of Shakespeare" [1811]; see CLOSET DRAMA). For Lamb, the inadequate visual and aural presence of mere actors on stage was to be replaced with "the sublime images, the poetry alone . . . which is present to our minds in the reading." Whatever its merits, Lamb's argument makes it clear that the issue of mental imaging is not solely a matter for experimental investigation but entails deeply disputed cultural values—the rivalry of visual and aural media (including the "breach" or "hinge" between written and spoken lang. explored by Derrida); the contest between art understood as a public, performative mode and its role as a private, subjective refuge; the notion of authorial intention (q.v.) as a mental representation ("vision" (q.v.) or "design") that stands before or behind the poem.

The very idea of the mental i. seems inextricably connected with the notion of reading as the entry into a private space (the Lockean metaphor of the mind as a *camera obscura* or "dark room" into which ideas are admitted through sensory apertures reinforces, with a kind of meta-image, this picture of mental solitude in an interior space filled with representations). It is not surprising, then, that the concept of the poetic i. in all its ambivalence holds part of the central ground of poetics, serving as both the mechanism of reference to and deferral of an external, imitated or projected reality; as the projection of authorial intention (but also of unauthorized "unconscious" meaning); as the linguistic ligature that composes figures of speech and thought and decomposes them into a general condition of lang. and consciousness; as the realm of polysemic freedom and dangerous uncertainty in reader response. Future crit. of the poetic i. must, at minimum, take account of the historical and conceptual variability of the concept and resist the temptation to dissolve poetic expression into the universal solvent of "the i."

See also DESCRIPTIVE POETRY; ENARGEIA; FIGURATION; IMAGINATION; IMITATION; REPRESENTATION AND MIMESIS; UT PICTURA POESIS; VISUAL ARTS AND POETRY.

H. W. Wells, *Poetic Imagery* (1924); S. J. Brown, *The World of Imagery* (1927); O. Barfield, *Poetic*

Diction (1928); J. Dewey, "The Common Substance of All the Arts," *Art as Experience* (1934); C. Spurgeon, *Shakespeare's Imagery and What It Tells Us* (1935); I. A. Richards, *The Philosophy of Rhet.* (1936); C. Brooks, "Metaphor and the Trad.," *Mod. Poetry and the Trad.* (1939); L. H. Hornstein, "Analysis of Imagery: A Critique of Literary Method," *PMLA* 57 (1942); C. D. Lewis, *The Poetic I.* (1947); R. B. Heilman, *This Great Stage: I. and Structure in* King Lear (1948); R. H. Fogle, *The Imagery of Keats and Shelley* (1949); W. Clemen, *The Devel. of Shakespeare's Imagery* (1951); Abrams; Wellek and Warren, ch. 15; F. Kermode, *The Romantic I.* (1957); Frye; H. Kenner, *The Art of Poetry* (1959); R. Frazer, "The Origin of the Term I.," *ELH* 27 (1960); M. Hardt, *Das Bild in der Dichtung* (1966); P. N. Furbank, *Reflections on the Word "I."* (1970); E. Pound, *Gaudier-Brzeska: A Memoir* (1970); J. Derrida, *Of Grammatology* (1974); N. Goodman, *Langs. of Art* (1976); T. Ziolkowski, *Disenchanted Is.* (1977); *The Lang. of Is.*, spec. iss. of *CritI* 6 (1980); S. Kosslyn, *I. and Mind* (1980); N. Block, *Imagery* (1981); M. A. Caws, *The Eye in the Text* (1981); *I. and Code*, ed. W. Steiner (1981); W. Steiner, *The Colors of Rhet.* (1982); *Articulate Is.*, ed. R. Wendorf (1983); P. de Man, "Intentional Structure of the Romantic I.," *The Rhet. of Romanticism* (1984); *Image / Imago / Imagination*, spec. iss. of *NLH* 15 (1984); W. J. T. Mitchell, "Wittgenstein's Imagery and What It Tells Us," *NLH* 19 (1988); W. J. T. Mitchell, "Tableau and Taboo," and E. Esrock, "Visual Imaging and Reader Response," *CEA Critic* 51 (1988). W.J.T.M.

IMAGERY.

    I. 16TH TO 19TH CENTURIES
   II. 20TH CENTURY
     A. *Mental Imagery*
     B. *Figures of Speech*
     C. *Cluster Criticism*
     D. *Symbol and Myth*
  III. RECENT DEVELOPMENTS
  IV. APPLICATION

Both the root meanings and broad implications of this term are akin to the word "imitate," and hence refer to a likeness, reproduction, reflection, copy, resemblance, or similitude. Its cognate terms, "icon" and "idol," often refer to objects of devotion and worship, manifesting the profound historical and cultural issues involved in i. The history of the term dates from at least the Old Testament, wherein are found the statement that humankind was made in God's image and the injunction against making graven images. The Judaic trad. took its stand firmly against the Many in favor of the One, Appearance in favor of Reality. Material representations of the Divine were seen as interfering with rather than enhancing humanity's realization of God.

Such dualisms are difficult to sustain, however, and later the Catholic Church perforce sanctioned the general use of images as an aid to worship. But the pendulum subsequently swung back with the Islamic rejection of the Trinity in the 7th c. A.D., the iconoclasm of the Catholic Church itself in the 8th and 9th c. A.D., and the Protestant rejection of images in the 16th and 17th c. It is during the Ren. and the Reformation that the history of lit. crit. in Eng. may be said to begin, and—although cl. critics such as Horace, Longinus, and Quintilian spoke of i. and its uses—here too begins the special consideration of i. in literary theory and practice (Frazer, Furbank, Legouis [in Miner], and Mitchell [1986]).

I. 16TH TO 19TH CENTURIES. The term i. itself, however, was not in general use during the Ren., where the emphasis fell on "figures" (q.v.)—of thought, of lang., and of speech—concepts largely derived from the Cl. rhet. of Greece and Rome. The underlying philosophy of this rhet. was that meaning is primary and manner of expression secondary. Thus the use of figures—e.g. metaphor, simile, allegory (qq.v.)—was viewed as ornamental and decorative, enlivening and enhancing a pre-existing meaning, and a premium was placed upon artificiality (artfulness) and technical virtuosity.

A primary example is Sir Philip Sidney's "Defence of Poesie" (1595). In characterizing a poem as a "speaking picture," a concept derived from Horace, and in claiming that the poet "nothing affirms, therefore never lieth," Sidney meant that the poet deals with what ought to be (the ideal) rather than with what is (the real)—a Platonized adaptation of Aristotle's distinction between poetry (the probable) and history (the actual) (*Poetics*, ch. 9). For Sidney the power of images lay in their ability to move us toward virtue and away from vice by means of their strong emotional appeal.

But with the growth of skepticism and empiricism in the late 17th and early 18th cs. there was a reaction against rhet. in favor of plainness and truth in lang. (Frazer). This left a vacuum which was filled by "image." The epistemology of Hobbes and the associationist psychology of Locke led to a new way of looking at poetry in which the image was seen as the connecting link between experience (object) and knowledge (subject). An image was defined as the reproduction in the mind of a sensation produced in perception. Thus, if a person's eye perceives a certain color, he or she will register an image of that color in the mind—"image," because the subjective sensation experienced will be ostensibly a copy or replica of the objective phenomenon of color.

But of course the mind may also produce images when not receiving direct perceptions, as in the attempt to remember something once perceived but no longer present, or in reflection upon remembered experience, or in the combinations wrought out of perception by the imagination (q.v.), or in the hallucinations of dreams and fever.

More specifically, in literary usage i. refers to images produced in the mind by lang., whose words may refer either to experiences which could produce physical perceptions were the reader actually to have those experiences, or to the sense-impressions themselves.

Thus, according to Frazer, the descriptive poetry of the 18th c. was new in that it focused more on the landscape itself than on that which it was supposed to represent. Creative power was assumed to reside in the "imagination," a storehouse of images in the empty mind. There was a shift, then, from the Ren. conception of the image as exemplum to the 18th-c. conception of the image as a basis for associative ruminating.

By the time of the romantic poets, however, the concept of "image" shifted once again. Given romantic transcendentalism, the world appearing as the garment of God, the abstract and general were seen as residing in the concrete and particular, and thus Spirit was felt to be immanent in Matter. Attempting to resolve the old dualism, they regarded Nature (q.v.) as Divine and nature poetry as a way to body forth the sacred. I., therefore, was elevated to the level of symbol (q.v.), to become thereby one of the central issues of modern criticism.

Meanwhile, several scientific and intellectual developments were underway during the latter 19th c. Max Müller put forth a theory of the growth of lang. (1861–64) which seemed to account for metaphorical imagery as an organic part of lang. rather than as an ornament or decoration. According to this theory, humanity, as it develops its conceptions of immaterial things, must perforce express them in terms of material things or images because its lang. lags behind its needs. So lang. as it expands grows through metaphor (q.v.) from image to idea. The word "spirit," for example, has as its root meaning "breath"; thus as the need to express an immaterial conception of soul or deity emerged, a pre-existent concrete word had to be used to stand for the new abstract meaning. Although Müller's thesis has been questioned (Barfield in Knights and Cottle), and although there may well be differences between ordinary and poetic metaphor, the implication that metaphor is created as a strategy for expressing the inexpressible is still influential today.

Sir Francis Galton reported in 1880 on his experiments in the psychology of perception. He discovered that people differ in their image-making habits and capacities. While one person may reveal a predominating tendency to visualize his reading, memories, and ruminations, another may favor the mind's "ear," another the mind's "nose," and yet another may have no i. at all. This discovery has also had some importance in modern crit. and poetry.

II. 20TH CENTURY. In what follows we shall trace out the modern devel. of four issues: (a) i. as a description of how part of the mind works, (b) i. as figure, (c) cluster criticism, and (d) symbol and myth.

A. *Mental Imagery.* Psychologists have identified seven kinds of mental images: visual (sight, then brightness, clarity, color, and motion), auditory (hearing), olfactory (smell), gustatory (taste), tactile (touch, then temperature, texture), organic (awareness of heartbeat, pulse, breathing, digestion), and kinesthetic (awareness of muscle tension and movement). These categories are preliminary to the other approaches to i., for they define the very nature of the materials.

Several valuable results have emerged from the application of these categories to lit. (Downey). In the first place, the concept of mental i. has encouraged catholicity of taste, for once it is realized that not all poets have the same interests and capacities, it is easier to appreciate different kinds of poetry. Much of Browning's i., for example, is tactile, and those who habitually visualize are unjust in laying the charge of obscurity at his door (Bonnell). Or again, the frequently-voiced complaint that Shelley's poetry is less "concrete" than Keats's suffers from a basic misconception, for Shelley's poetry contains just as much i. as Keats's, although it is of a somewhat different kind (Fogle). Second, the concept of mental i. provides a valuable index to the type of imagination with which a given poet is gifted. Knowing that Keats's poetry is characterized by a predominance of tactile and organic i., for example, or Shelley's by the i. of motion is crucial to an accurate appraisal of the achievement of each poet. Third, the concept of mental i. is pedagogically useful, for a teacher or a critic may encourage better reading habits by stressing this aspect of poetry.

But the disadvantages of the mental-i. approach almost outweigh its advantages. For one thing, there is an insoluble methodological problem, in that readers are just as different from one another in their i.-producing capacities as poets, and therefore the attempt to describe the imagination of a poet is inextricably bound up with the imagination of the critic who analyzes it. Second, this approach tends to overemphasize mental i. at the expense of meaning, feeling, and sentiment (Betts). And third, in focusing upon the sensory qualities of images themselves, it diverts attention from the *function* of these images in the poetic context.

B. *Figures of Speech.* It is evident that each of the key issues in the study of i. overlaps with the others and broadens out to encompass many areas of human knowledge and culture. For practical purposes, however, we may treat the second issue—the nature and function of i. in metaphor—as if it were a separable topic.

The figures of speech in common currency today have been reduced to seven: synecdoche, metonymy, simile, metaphor, personification, allegory, and—a different but related device—symbol (qq.v.). Each is a device of lang. by virtue of which one thing is said (analogue) while something else is meant (subject), and either the analogue, the subject, or both may involve i.—although most characteristically it is the analogue. Subject and analogue (or "tenor" and "vehicle" [q.v.] as I. A. Richards termed them) may be related with respect to physical resemblance—as when Homer compares the charge of a warrior in battle to that of a lion on a sheepfold, in which case the study of mental i. provides useful distinctions—here we may visualize the furious movement of the attack and perhaps imagine the roaring sound of rage. But many figures relate two different things in other ways: a lady's blush, in Burns's "my love is like a red, red rose," her delicate skin, or her fragrance may find analogues in the color, texture, or odor of a rose, but her freshness and beauty are qualities suggestively evoked by the rose rather than images displayed in it. Burns's speaker is saying that his lady is to him as June is to the world, in the sense of bringing rebirth and joy. The similarity, then, is that his lady makes him feel as spring makes him feel: the ground of comparison is an emotion, and the i. functions in relation to that purpose rather than to a physical object.

Furthermore, the two things related may each be images (as in the Burns example), or feelings or concepts; or the subject may be an image and the analogue a feeling or concept; or the subject may be a feeling or concept and the analogue an image. Some critics have asserted that the fundamental subject or tenor of a figure is in reality the relationship itself and that therefore the analogy or vehicle includes the two things related.

Thus, although the term i. is commonly used to refer to all figures of speech, as well as to literal images, further distinctions are obviously necessary. The kinds of things related and the nature and function of their relationship, as we have seen, provide grounds upon which these distinctions may be made. It was once common to claim that proper practice precluded mixing one's analogues in any one figure (Jennings), but more recent critics have argued that no such rule is universally valid, esp. in poetry (Brooks): it all depends on whether the mixture of analogues is consistent with the context and what their effect upon the reader is. Shakespeare is notoriously full of mixed metaphors, as in Hamlet's famous reflection on whether he should "take arms against a sea of troubles." Here we must either imagine some sort of demented warrior slashing at the sea with his sword, or we must imagine two separate metaphors—"feeling overwhelmed by troubles as by the inundation of the sea, and doing something about them as when a warrior arms himself and marches out to meet the enemy"—conflated. With such mixtures, when the figures flash by in rapid sequence, it is counterproductive to try to stop and picture each in our minds; the point is that they *seem* fitting and effective in context.

Or again, it was once considered good form to teach students to visualize figures, but not only are most metaphors constructed on bases other than on mental i. but also much mental i. is other than visual. In fact, persistent visualizing will break down the relationship between subject and analogue in many figures entirely—as in the Burns simile, for example: if we consider the rose further, we could imagine that there may be a worm buried within it, that it has thorns, and that its life is all too brief (qualities which have certainly been exploited in many other poems), we will have pretty much destroyed the image and the poem.

On the other hand, much attention was once focused on that kind of figure in which the difference between subject and analogue seems unusually great, the "metaphysical image" (Wells, Rugoff, Tuve, Miller)—a term and concept which go back to Dr. Johnson's essay on Donne, though Holmes has argued that such disparate figures were anticipated by the Elizabethan dramatists (see CONCEIT; METAPHYSICAL POETRY; and the discussion of the Donne image concluding TENOR AND VEHICLE). Thus, while the reader must beware of going too far with an image lest it break down into irrelevance, poets are licensed to challenge the reader with an image which at first appears far-fetched but which on closer inspection reveals its profounder core of significance.

Fourth, much was once made of the function of the "central" or "unifying" image in a poem, according to which the poet develops a sustained analogy which then serves as the structural frame of the poem. Ericson, for example, distinguishes among different sorts of i. patterns in a poem; in Herbert he finds that images may be extended, end-on-end, mixed, and so on, concluding that the extended image seems to be the most effective. But here again we can only conclude, as with mixed metaphors, visualized figures, and metaphysical images, that the central or unifying image is merely one possibility among many, and as such it has no special normative value but depends largely upon meaning and function in a particular context.

When such distinctions regarding the meaning and function of i. were adapted as the basis for theories about the nature of poetic lang., or the quality of the artistic imagination, i. became one of the key terms of the New Criticism (q.v.), which developed what it viewed as a radically "functional" theory of i., based on the assumptions that figures are the differentiae of poetic lang. and that poetic lang. is the differentia of the poetic art. This assumption was opposed to what the New Critics took to be the "decorative fallacy" of traditional rhet. and the "heresy" of modern positivist semantics, which claimed that logical statement is the only indicator of truth and all other forms of statement are untrue.

C. *Cluster Criticism.* The study of figurative i., therefore, anticipates and overlaps the subsequently developed study of symbolic i. In the latter approach the essential question is how *pat-*

terns of i.—whether literal, figurative, or both—in a work reveal facts about the author or the poem, on the basic assumption that repetitions and recurrences (usually of images but on occasion of word patterns in general) are in themselves significant. Hence the method involved the simple application (and sometimes distortion) of some elementary statistical principles. These patterns may appear either within the work itself or among literary works and myths in general (see ARCHETYPE) or both.

Assuming that repetitions are indeed significant, we must examine the nature of this significance. What exactly will counting image-clusters tell the critic? There developed at least five distinguishable approaches, each a bit more complex than the preceding: (1) texts of doubtful authorship can be authenticated (Smith); (2) some aspects of the poet's own experiences, tastes, temperament, and vision of life can be inferred (Spurgeon, Banks); 3) the causes of tone, atmosphere, and mood in a work can be analyzed and defined (Spurgeon); (4) the ways in which the structure of conflict in a play is embodied can be examined (Burke 1941); and (5) symbols can be traced out, either in terms of how image patterns relate to the author or how they relate to archetypes or both (Frye, Knight, Heilman).

The first two approaches relate to problems extrinsic to the work itself, although they seek internal evidence. The procedure involved counting all the images in a work or all the works of a given poet (and here the problems of what an image is, what kind it is, and whether it is literal or figurative had to be resolved anew by each critic doing the counting) and then classifying them according to the areas of experience these images represent: Nature—Animate and Inanimate, Daily Life, Learning, Commerce, and so on. Since these categories and their proportions represent aspects of the poet's perceptions and imagination, two inferences can be made on the basis of the resultant charts and figures: first, that the patterns are caused by the poet's personal experiences and therefore give a clue to the poet's personality and background; and second, that since they are unique—like fingerprints, no two minds have exactly the same patterns—they offer a means of determining the authorship of doubtful works. Perhaps the second assumption is sounder than the first, although both are dubious, for frequently images appear in a work because of literary and artistic conventions (q.v.) rather than because of the poet's personality or experience (Hornstein, Hankins).

The third and fourth approaches relate to problems intrinsic to the artistic organization of the work itself. Thus Kenneth Burke remarked, "One cannot long discuss imagery without sliding into symbolism. The poet's images are organized with relation to one another by reason of their symbolic kinships. We shift from the image of an object to its symbolism as soon as we consider it, not in itself alone, but as a function in a texture of relationships" (1937). Certain plays of Shakespeare, as Spurgeon showed, are saturated with one or another kind of similar images or clusters (usually figurative)—the i. of light and dark in *Romeo and Juliet*, or of animals in *King Lear*, or of disease in *Hamlet*—and it was reasoned that these recurrences, although they might not be consciously noticed by the ordinary reader or playgoer, are continually at work conditioning our responses as we follow the action of the play. Thus Kolbe, a pioneer of cluster crit. along with his predecessors Whiter and Spaulding, claimed in 1930: "My thesis is that Shakespeare secures the unity of each of his greater plays, not only by the plot, by linkage of characters, by the sweep of Nemesis, by the use of irony, and by the appropriateness of style, but by deliberate repetition throughout the play of at least one set of words or ideas in harmony with the plot. It is like the effect of the dominant note in a melody." Later critics added that clusters may form dramatic discords as well as harmonies.

From this argument it was but a small step to classifying images according to their relationship to the dramatic conflicts in the work. There are basically two sorts of clusters: the recurrence of the same image at intervals throughout the work, or the recurrence of different images together at intervals. If the same image recurs in different contexts, then it should serve to link those contexts in significant ways, and if different images recur together several times, then the mention of any one of them will serve to call the others to mind. Such notions of going below the surface to find associative patterns owed something, of course, to Freudian psychoanalysis as well.

D. *Symbol and Myth*. The next and fourth step was to reason once again from inside to outside the work, but this time ostensibly for the sake of greater insight into the work. According to Burke, a poem is a dramatic revelation in disguised form of the poet's emotional tensions and conflicts, and if, therefore, some idea of these tensions and conflicts can be formed, the reader will then be alerted to their symbolic appearance in the work. Thus Burke could make "equations" among Coleridge's image-clusters by comparing the poet's letters with the *Ancient Mariner* and could conclude that the albatross symbolizes Coleridge's guilt over his addiction to opium. This, he reasoned, illuminates the "motivational structure" of that particular poem.

It is not difficult, on the other hand, to equate image-clusters in a particular work with larger patterns found in other works and in myths instead of merely in the poet's personal life (a dream is the "myth" of the individual, a myth is the "dream" of the race), as does Frye, for example, and even Burke himself, for the "action" of which a poem is "symbolic" frequently resembles larger ritualistic patterns such as purgation, scapegoating, killing the king, initiation, and the like, though expressed on a personal level and in personal terms. Robert Penn Warren sees in the *Ancient Mariner* a symbol of the artist-archetype, embodied in the figure of the Mariner, torn between the conflicting and ambiguous claims of reason (symbolized by the sun) and the imagination (symbolized by the moon); thus the crime is a crime against the imagination, and the imagination revenges itself but at the same time heals the Mariner; the wandering is also a blessing and a curse, for the Mariner is the *poète maudit* (q.v.) as well as the "prophet of universal charity" (see Olson's review of this interp. in Crane). One may therefore find implicit images of guilt, purification, descent, and ascent running throughout a poem whose literal action may be of quite a different nature. Image clusters may form "spatial pattern" or even a "subplot" calling for special attention (Cook).

There are certain difficulties with cluster crit., however, which revolve primarily around the fact that it tends to reduce complex and individual works of lit. to simpler and more general paradigms. In emphasizing primarily certain aspects of a work for inspection, in finding similarities among all literary works, and in assuming that all recurrences have a certain kind of significance, this approach has been called seriously into question (Adams in Miner).

III. RECENT DEVELOPMENTS. More recently the literary study of i. has become at once more advanced and more problematic. There are a plethora of studies in speculative and experimental psychology, involving phenomenology, epistemology, and cognitive psychology, looking very closely at the question of what exactly mental i. is.

Block, for example, analyzes the recent objection that, although it seems as if we can see internal pictures, this cannot in fact be the case, for it would mean that we have pictures in the brain and an inner eye to see them with, and no such mental operations can be found. Images are, it is claimed, verbal and conceptual. Block concludes that there are two kinds of i., one which represents perception in roughly the same way pictures do, the other which represents as lang. does, i.e. conceptually, that some combine pictorial and verbal elements, and that the real question is what types of representation are possible.

Furbank, on the other hand, after giving a very useful history of the term "image" up to the imagists (q.v.), reveals the ambiguities and confusions involved in using the terms "image" and "concrete" to describe qualities of the verbal medium. We should not confuse "abstract" with "general" and "concrete" with "specific." "Concrete," for example, does not necessarily mean "sensuous," and that which is "specific" may very well also be "abstract." The only actual *physical* element of poetry is found in the subvocal or silent actions of tongue and larynx as a poem is recited or read. Furbank has suggested that we drop the term i.

altogether.

More inclusive is the work of Mitchell, who places the entire issue within the broad historical context of knowledge as a cultural product (see IMAGE; ICON AND ICONOLOGY). First, he has provided a chart of the "family of images" to indicate the different meanings of i.: in art history are found the graphic images (pictures, statues, designs), in physics the optical images (mirrors, projections), in philosophy and theology the perceptual images (sense data, "species," appearances), in psychology and epistemology the mental images (dreams, memories, ideas, fantasmata), and in lit. crit. the verbal images (metaphors, descriptions, writing).

Mitchell goes on to develop an argument concerning the nature and function of i. which is deliberately constructed to steer a middle course between the old-fashioned realism of empiricists such as John Locke and the recently fashionable nominalism of poststructuralists and deconstructionists such as Jacques Derrida. Both our signs and the world they signify are a product of human action and understanding, and although on the one hand our modes of knowledge and representation may be arbitrary and conventional, they are on the other hand the constituents of the forms of life—the practices and trads. within which we must make epistemological, ethical, and political choices. The question is, therefore, not simply "What is an image?" but more "How do we transfer images into powers worthy of trust and respect?" Discourse, Mitchell concludes, does project worlds and states of affairs that can be pictured concretely and tested against other representations.

Approaching the problem from a socio-political-historical perspective, Weimann would remind us that, while for modern critics the meaning of a poem is secondary to its figures, for Ren. and metaphysical poets the meaning was primary. Here he agrees with Tuve that modern interps., therefore, fail to do justice to the intentions and structures of earlier works. Metaphor, he says, is neither autonomous nor decorative; rather, it relates man and universe, and the link or interaction between tenor and vehicle (q.v.) is the core. History is part of the meaning of a metaphor. Shakespeare's freedom of linguistic transference reflects the social mobility of his era—an age of transitions and contradictions. That neoclassical critics did not value Shakespeare's over-rich i. but rather preferred plot over diction reflects their own view of man in society. This valuation was reversed during the romantic age, but even the romantics did not place form over meaning. Modernist poets and critics, Weimann argues, emphasizing the autonomy (q.v.) of a literary work and its spatial patterns, have removed lit. both from history and its audience (see MODERNISM; DECONSTRUCTION). In seeking liberation from time and space, and from history into myth, this trad. has rejected the mimetic function of lit. in Cl. crit. (see PO-

ETRY, THEORIES OF, *Mimetic Theories*), as well as the expressive principle of romanticism. Metaphor is now seen as an escape from reality and has become severed from its social meaning. In reply, Weimann calls for an integration of the study of i. within a more comprehensive vision of lit. hist. Other commentators more sympathetic to the achievements of modernism have held that, far from severing form and meaning, it sees meaning as a function of form; and far from seeking an escape from history, it seeks to redeem history. No more time-bound works can be imagined than those two monuments of modernism, Joyce's *Ulysses* and Eliot's *The Waste Land*.

Finally, Yu's analysis of Chinese i. suggests ways in which the study of poetic i. can be enriched further by means of comparative studies. She sees a fundamental difference between "attitudes toward poetic i. in classical China" and "those commonly taken for granted in the West." Western conceptions are based on the dualism of matter and spirit and upon the twin assumptions of mimesis and fictionality: poetry embodies concretely a transcendent reality, and the poet is a creator of hitherto unapprehended relations between these two disparate realms. The Chinese assumption, by contrast, is nondualistic: there are indeed different categories of existence—personal, familial, social, political, natural—but they all belong to the same earthly realm, and the poet represents reality both literally and by joining various images which have already been molded for him by his culture. Thus the Chinese poetic and critical trad. reveals the conventional correspondences used by the poets in their efforts to juxtapose images so as to suggest rather than explain meaning. One might point out, however, that these principles sound very much like those of the Western modernist poetic previously discussed, itself influenced by Oriental philosophy and poetry— namely, the objective correlative (q.v.) and the juxtaposition of images. Yeats, Pound, Eliot, and the imagists, not to mention Whitman before them, were all striving, each in his own way, to heal the split of Western dualism and achieve, in Yeats's phrase, Unity of Being. Whether they did so by means of a vision of transcendence or one of immanence, there are remarkable similarities in technique among them, as well as between them and the Chinese poets and critics so illuminatingly analyzed by Yu.

IV. APPLICATION. We may now ask what i. does in an actual poem. Although i. has come to be regarded as an essentially poetic device, many good poems contain little or no i. When i. *is* present, however, it is best viewed as part of the larger integral fabric of the poem's form and as having a variety of possible functions.

I. may be, in the first place, the speaker's subject, whether that thing is present in the situation or recollected afterwards, or simply the subject of a predication. Such subjects are, roughly speaking, people, places, objects, actions, and events. In Frost's "Come In," for example, the speaker, narrating in the past tense, represents himself as having come to a place of boundaries—a not uncommon situation in Frost—between the woods and field, night and day, earth and heaven. He heard a thrush's song echoing through the darkening trees, and he felt the pull of sorrow. He decided, however, to turn away from this invitation and to gaze, rather, at the stars.

The literal i. of subject here comprises the woods, the thrush music, the shades of darkness and light, and the stars. As for mental i., we may if we choose visualize the scene and "hear" the song of the thrush. Frost does no more than sketch it all in, however: he does not create a descriptive set piece; he merely names the objects and actions. Thus, although he presents a physical action and setting, he is much more concerned with their mood and atmosphere than their physical details, and so he presents just enough i. to create that effect. Nevertheless, all of the lang. of the poem, except perhaps for the last two lines, is involved in this physicality. In the concluding quatrain,

> But no, I was out for stars:
> I would not come in.
> I meant not even if asked,
> And I hadn't been.

The first two lines refer to action and setting, while the last two are ratiocinative and nonphysical. It does make sense, then, despite the problems of cognitive psychology, the strictures of Furbank, and the subtleties of Mitchell, to distinguish between imaginal and nonimaginal statements. Further, since economy is a fundamental artistic principle, we often expect to find that literal i. is converted into a second subject, becoming the symbol (q.v.) of something else as a result of the speaker's reflective and deliberative activity. Mere scenery is rarely enough to justify its presence in a poem. As we proceed through Frost's poem, these expectations begin materializing around a certain sort of symbolic structure: the sun has all but set, the speaker is hesitating between open field and enclosed woods, and he is pausing between going inside or staying outside. The speaker is not simply out for a pleasant evening walk; some more crucial issue is at stake.

Here is the penultimate stanza:

> Far in the pillared dark
> Thrush music went—
> Almost like a call to come in
> To the dark and lament.

Now we know something about the symbolic *significance* of the speaker's representation of this landscape: he is resisting the temptation of despair. Thus does the literal i. become symbolic, clustering around the poles of woods-inside-dark-birdsong-sunset-lamentation *versus* field-outside-dusk-stars-determination. The entire scene, therefore, and the speaker's response to it, are now symbolic of his inner struggle, which is his second or "real" subject—scene and act are now "vehicle" and inner struggle is the "tenor" of the basic "metaphor" which is the poem. And though most of the lang. of the poem is literal, in the third stanza the light of the sun is personified as having "died in the west," though it still "lived for one song more / In a thrush's breast." This figure is enfolded within another and more important one: the dying light of the sun is identified with the thrush's song. The thrush is singing, in other words, of the death of the day. All of these associations are reinforced by the i. of extremity which permeates the poem: "edge of the woods," "Too dark," "The last of the light," "Still lived for one song more," "I meant not even if asked." Everything seems just a bit desperate. But in the final two lines the speaker admits he realized the whole thing was a projection of his own despair: it was just a bird, and so we are led right out of the symbolic structure he has encouraged us to build—the same one he himself built. He has exorcised it. Are the "stars," then, an anti-symbolic symbol? Tension, irony, and ambiguity enough to satisfy any clever critic.

We could go even further, such is the skill and richness of this little lyric. Is there not the archetype of death-and-rebirth here? of the descent into the underworld and consequent ascent? of a ritual initiation in which the speaker-scapegoat tests himself against his own attraction-repulsion in relation to death? We could conclude with Mitchell that the i. in this poem is a representation of a cultural and literary convention rather than simply an unmediated piece of reality, and with Weimann that the poem's use of literal and figurative images embodies the social and historical realities of its time—1942. The literalism of the poem's i. reflects the modern suspicion of decorative figures and preference for implicit and symbolic i. The speaker's presentation of the experience as a matter of boundaries-hesitation-commit ment may be thought to reflect the nature of his society—its initial hesitation after the Depression in entering Word War II and its subsequent dedication to that task. In this view, the moods of Frost's speaker are not simply conventional poetic moods; they are, rather, the effects of a particular culture and history.

Thus, while we are not to regard the poem as embodying naked actuality, we are also not to ignore the fact that it springs from and refers back to an actuality, however mediated, and that the problem for the poet and the critic is to adjudicate among various representations of reality. The modernists did not believe that the autotelic nature of poetry either divorced it from history or revealed an "objective" truth about it. Realists such as Kermode and Weimann have exaggerated the influence of Fr. symbolism on 20th-c. Eng. and Am. poetry and poetics, while nominalists such as Kuhn, White, Rorty, and the deconstructionists (see Culler), have exaggerated the difficulty of matching mind to world through the agency of the Word. As Furbank says, a work is a self-contained "world" aesthetically so that it can refer to the world really. The entire enterprise has always been an attempt, whether successful or not, to define the way or ways in which Mind can come to know World other than simply factually, to balance our projections against what's out there, in the knowledge that we can never really finally say what it is. We know, on the one hand, that Mind mediates between ourselves and the World, and we seek, on the other, a validation-process for choosing among Mind's interpretations. The answer, as Frost's poem demonstrates—Stevens is another example, although without that literality—is to explore the boundary between them.

I. in poetry, therefore, may be seen to have the following uses. It may, in the first place, serve as a device for externalizing and making vivid the speaker's thoughts and feelings. It would have been much less effective had Frost's speaker simply stated, flatly, that he was tempted by despair and was seeking a way to resist it. In the second place, and consequently, since this scene serves to call up to the speaker's consciousness—and thereby becomes, as we have seen, the vehicle of—a problem which has been troubling him, it stimulates and externalizes further his mental activity. Mind and World are not simply being thought about, they are indeed confronting and interacting with one another—that is what the poem is "about," a *process* of thinking and feeling in relation to the environment rather than a set of "ideas" *about* it. Third, the poet's handling of i. serves to dispose the reader either favorably or unfavorably toward the various elements in the poetic situation. That Frost devotes four out of five stanzas on the thrush, for example, serves to indicate the magnitude of the temptation and hence the difficulty of turning away from it. I. may serve, in the fourth place, as a way of arousing and guiding the reader's expectations. Frost sets up the nature of the problem implicitly from the beginning via "edge," "outside," "inside," and so on. And finally, i. may serve to direct our attention, as we "slide," in Burke's term, from i. to symbolism, to the poem's inner meanings—realizing, in this case, that the speaker is testing himself against his despair and coming out the other side. See also ARCHETYPE; FIGURATION; ICONOLOGY; IMAGE; SYMBOL.

JOURNALS: *Journal of Mental Imagery; The Literary Image; Word & Image.*

HISTORICAL CONSIDERATIONS: R. Frazer, "The Origin of the Term 'Image'," *ELH* 27 (1960); P. N. Furbank, *Reflections on the Word "Image"* (1970); *17th-C. I.*, ed. E. Miner (1971); W. J. T. Mitchell, *Iconology* (1986).

MENTAL IMAGERY: F. Galton, "Statistics of Mental I.," *Mind* 5 (1880); G. H. Betts, *The Distributions* and Functions of Mental I. (1909); J. K. Bonnell, "Touch Images in the Poetry of Robert Browning," PMLA 37 (1922); E. Rickert, New Methods for the Study of Lit. (1927); J. E. Downey, Creative Imagination (1929); R. H. Fogle, The I. of Keats and Shelley (1949); Wellek and Warren, ch. 15; R. A. Brower, The Fields of Light (1951); J. Press, The Fire and the Fountain (1955); M. Tye, The I. Debate (1992).

FIGURES OF SPEECH: M. Müller, Lectures on the Science of Lang. 2d ser. (1894); F. I. Carpenter, Metaphor and Simile in Minor Elizabethan Drama (1895); G. Buck, The Metaphor (1899); J. G. Jennings, An Essay on Metaphor in Poetry (1915); H. W. Wells, Poetic I. (1924); O. Barfield, Poetic Diction (1928), "The Meaning of the Word 'Literal,'" Metaphor and Symbol, ed. L. C. Knights and B. Cottle (1960); E. Holmes, Aspects of Elizabethan I. (1929); I. A. Richards, The Philosophy of Rhet. (1936), Interpretation in Teaching (1938); M. A. Rugoff, Donne's I. (1939); C. Brooks, Mod. Poetry and the Trad. (1939); R. Tuve, Elizabethan and Metaphysical I. (1947); C. D. Lewis, The Poetic Image (1947); H. Coombs, Lit. and Crit. (1953); C. Brooke-Rose, A Grammar of Metaphor (1958); D. C. Allen, Image and Meaning (1960); M. Peckham, "Metaphor" [1962], The Triumph of Romanticism (1970); E. E. Ericson, "A Structural Approach to I.," Style 3 (1969); D. M. Miller, The Net of Hephaestus (1971); R. J. Fogelin, Figuratively Speaking (1988).

CLUSTER CRITICISM: W. Whiter, A Specimen of a Commentary on Shakespeare (1794); W. Spaulding, A Letter on Shakespeare's Authorship of The Two Noble Kinsmen (1876); S. J. Brown, The World of I. (1927); F. C. Kolbe, Shakespeare's Way (1930); C. F. E. Spurgeon, Shakespeare's I. and What it Tells Us (1935); U. Ellis-Fermor, Some Recent Research in Shakespeare's I. (1937); K. Burke, Attitudes Toward Hist. (1937), The Philosophy of Lit. Form (1941); G. W. Knight, The Burning Oracle (1939), The Chariot of Wrath (1942), The Crown of Life (1961); M. B. Smith, Marlowe's I. and the Marlowe Canon (1940); L. H. Hornstein, "Analysis of I.," PMLA 57 (1942); E. A. Armstrong, Shakespeare's Imagination (1946); Brooks; R. B. Heilman, This Great Stage (1948); D. A. Stauffer, Shakespeare's World of Images (1949); T. H. Banks, Milton's I. (1950); W. H. Clemen, The Devel. of Shakespeare's I. (1951); F. Marsh, Wordsworth's I. (1952); J. E. Hankins, Shakespeare's Derived I. (1953); Frye; J. W. Beach, Obsessive Images (1960); G. W. Williams, Image and Symbol in the Sacred Poetry of Richard Crashaw (1963); D. A. West, The I. and Poetry of Lucretius (1969); S. A. Barlow, The I. of Euripides (1971); R. S. Varma, I. and Thought in the Metaphysical Poets (1972); W. E. Rogers, Image and Abstraction (1972); J. Doebler, Shakespeare's Speaking Pictures (1974); J. H. Matthews, The I. of Surrealism (1977); V. N. Sinha, The I. and Lang. of Keats's Odes (1978); R. Berry, Shakespearean Metaphor (1978); V. S. Kolve, Chaucer and the I. of Narrative (1984); J. Steadman, Milton's Biblical and Cl. I. (1984); J. Dundas, The Spider and the Bee (1985).

SYMBOL AND MYTH: O. Rank, Art and Artist (1932); R. P. Warren, "A Poem of Pure Imagination," The Rime of the Ancient Mariner by Samuel Taylor Coleridge (1946); Crane; P. Wheelwright, The Burning Fountain (1954), Metaphor and Reality (1962); Frye; F. Kermode, Romantic Image (1957); H. Musurillo, Symbol and Myth in Ancient Poetry (1961); K. Burke, Lang as Symbolic Action (1966); 17th-C. I., ed. E. Miner (1971); A. Cook, Figural Choice in Poetry and Art (1985).

RECENT DEVELOPMENTS: T. S. Kuhn, The Structure of Scientific Revolutions (1962); R. Weimann, Structure and Society in Lit. Hist. (1976); H. White, Tropics of Discourse (1978); R. Rorty, Philosophy and the Mirror of Nature (1979); The Lang. of Images, ed. W. T. J. Mitchell (1980); I., ed. N. Block (1981); J. D. Culler, On Deconstruction (1982); P. Yu, The Reading of I. in the Chinese Poetic Trad. (1987).N.F.

IMAGINATION.

I. DISTINCTIONS FROM FANCY; GENERAL SCOPE
II. CLASSICAL AND MEDIEVAL
III. RENAISSANCE AND 17TH CENTURY
IV. 18TH CENTURY AND ROMANTICISM
V. LATER 19TH AND 20TH CENTURIES

I. DISTINCTIONS FROM FANCY; GENERAL SCOPE. I. derives from Lat. imaginatio, itself a late substitute for Gr. phantasia. During the Ren. the term "fancy" (q.v.)—connoting free play, mental creativity, and license—often eclipsed i., considered more as reproducing sense impressions, primarily visual images. By ca. 1700, empirical philosophy cast suspicion on fancy; i. seemed preferably rooted in the concrete evidence of sense data. Hobbes nevertheless retains "fancy" as is perhaps the last Eng. writer to use it to signify mind's greatest inventive range. Dryden describes i. as a capacious power encompassing traditional stages of composition: invention (q.v.), fancy (distribution or design), and elocution. Leibniz contrasts les idées réelles with les idées phantastiques ou chimériques (Nouveaux essais). Many, incl. Addison, use fancy and i. synonymously, but Addison calls his important Spectator series (nos. 409, 411–21) "The Pleasures of the I."

More susceptible to prosodic manipulation in actual lines of verse, the term "fancy" retains a higher place in poetic diction than in crit. (e.g. Collins' "Young Fancy thus, to me divinest name"). But in England and particularly in Germany, writers increasingly distinguish the terms long before Coleridge's definitions in Biographia literaria (1817). By 1780, Christian Wolff, J. G. Sulzer, J. N. Tetens, and Ernst Platner make explicit distinctions. Coleridge recognizes this by claiming himself the first "of my countrymen" to distinguish fancy from i. But several Eng. writers record distinctions between 1760 and 1800.

Since 1800, and to some degree before as well,

poets and critics have considered i. the chief creative faculty, a "synthetic and magical power" responsible for invention and originality (Coleridge). Writers have associated or identified i. with genius, inspiration (qq.v.), taste (q.v.), visionary power, and prophecy (see also EXPRESSION; INVENTION; IMITATION; ORIGINALITY). During the past three centuries, no other idea has proved more fruitful for poetics and critical theory, or for their intersection with psychology and philosophy. Before the watershed in the history of the idea during the 18th–19th cs., commentaries and poetics generally accord i. an important but ambivalent role: judgment or understanding must trim its vagaries and correct its wayward force.

Ancient poets, philosophers, and psychologists consider i. a strong and diverse power, but unregulated it produces illusion, mental instability (often melancholy), bad art, or madness. Yet i. nevertheless becomes the chief criterion of European and Am. romanticism. Even if we speak of romanticisms in the plural, i. is important to each one. Not only philosophers and psychologists, but critics and poets elevate it as the prime subject of their vital work. Wordsworth's *Prelude* proclaims i. as its main theme; Keats' *Lamia* and great odes debate in symbolic terms the function and worth of imaginative art. To a surprising extent, the transcendental or "critical" philosophy in Germany and America explores and elaborates the idea, spawning theories that champion the process and function of art as the final act and highest symbolic expression of philosophizing.

II. CLASSICAL AND MEDIEVAL. Aristotle advances in *De anima* the Cl. definition of i.: mental reproduction of sensory experience. In this elegant simplicity, i. registers sensory impressions that are immediately present in the act of perception. With sense data absent, i. becomes a form of memory, mother of the Muses. Aristotle discusses the role of i. in what Locke will call "the association of ideas," central to empirical psychology. Hume, Priestley, the associationists in general, Hazlitt, and to some degree Wordsworth will later view i. in terms of heightened associations of ideas (either unconscious in origin or determined by conscious choice) coexisting with feelings and passions, thus giving all associative operations a subjective and affective element. I. thus forms the basis of taste, by definition grounded in the perceiving subject, an argument Burke broaches in his *Enquiry into the Sublime and Beautiful* (1757) and later at the core of Kant's *Kritik der Urteilskraft* (Critique of Judgment, 1790).

But in the *Poetics*, where Aristotle pursues a structural or generic approach based on dramatic texts, he skirts the function of i. The audience's imaginative response projecting sympathy and identification (pity and fear) may be inferred, but Aristotle does not analyze i. as crucial to either reception or production.

Plato distrusts the artist's i. and assigns it only an essentially reproductive duty (copying a copy). In psychological terms, the soul passively receives an image, which reflects an idea. However, the Platonic *nous* (reason) carries a force similar to later conceptions of creative i. Sidney and Schelling, among others, will later interpret Plato's thought and image-laden writing to counter Plato's own condemnation of poetry and poets. For Plotinus, the i. (phantasy) is a plastic, constructive faculty which can change and alter experience, permit or realize a form of intellectual intuition or insight. Phantasy comes in two forms. The lower—linked to sense and the soul's irrational power—may harmonize with the higher, which reflects ideas and the rational. Plotinus and Proclus are among several who provide antecedents for Coleridge's "primary" and "secondary" i. As Plotinus considers nature an emanation of soul, and soul an emanation of mind, his thought adumbrates a large system of nature and sense, idea and soul, cosmos and mind, creator and creativity, all interconnected through imaginative power. Elements of this thought recur in the Hermetic philosophers, Jakob Boehme, Blake, Schelling, and Coleridge. Plotinus also provides broad implications for mimetic theory, and for a poetics that spills over into theodicy, where the external world is "the book of nature" or, as Goethe and others later express it (before the Rosetta Stone is deciphered), a divine "hieroglyphic." Using this general idea, Emerson and Thoreau develop their own angles of vision, as do the *Naturphilosophen* in their search for connections between the forces and laws discovered by natural science and poetry conceived as an inventive power creating its own related—but original—nature.

From the beginning, i. thus possesses roots both in empiricism based on sense experience and in transcendentalism. Its function may be seen in terms of natural and psychological phenomena, perception, acquisition of knowledge, creative production of art, and even, as Spinoza says, the prophets who receive "revelations of God by the aid of i." (*Tractatus theologico-politicus*, 1670). These manifestations are not mutually exclusive but interact, as in the thought of Giordano Bruno, who conceives of sense, memory, emotion, cognition, and the divine mind all linked through i. Many writers, in fact, divide the power into levels or degrees, with adjectives denoting particular functions (e.g. re/productive, *erste/zweite/dritte potenz*, primary or secondary, creative, sympathetic, perceptive). *The Prelude* traces a maturation of the power through different stages. The explosion of Ger. analytical terms for i. in the 18th c. is staggering (*Einbildungskraft, Phantasie, I., Fassungskraft, Perceptionsvermögen, Dichtungsvermögen* or *Dichtkraft*—with variants, and more). Since antiquity, then, images produced by this power have been variously considered as materially real, or simply as appearances and pure illusion, or even as idealized forms. Poetry, dreams, divine inspiration (madness and prophecy), delusion and emotional disturbances—all involve one or more activities of i. It therefore harbors the greatest potential not only for insight and intuition (q.v.) but for deception and illusion.

Horace, long influential in Western poetics, barely mentions i. in his *Ars poetica.* This absence, coupled with Platonic distrust of i. and later neoclassical emphasis on verisimilitude and decorum (qq.v.) in imitation (what much 18th-c. and romantic theory scorns as mere "copy"), diminishes the place of i. in poetic theory for centuries after Horace. Although Philostratus declares imitation inferior to phantasy and Quintilian connects i. (*visiones*) with raising absent things to create emotion in the hearer, not until the rediscovery in the 16th c. of the *Peri hypsous* (*On the Sublime*) attributed to Longinus do European critics turn more directly to the power he describes: "moved by enthusiasm and passion you seem to see the things whereof you speak and place them before the eyes of your hearers." Boileau translates Longinus; in England Dennis and Pope spread his views. The useful, if rough, distinction between "Aristotelian" and "Longinian" crit. stems largely from divergent emphases on i. and its corollaries for mimetic theory.

III. RENAISSANCE AND 17TH CENTURY. Pico della Mirandola's *De imaginatione sive phantasia* (ed. and tr. H. Caplan, 1971) collects from the Cl. and Med. trads., but stresses vision as the primary or archetypal sense, circumscribing the possibility of a larger poetics founded on i. Puttenham summarizes Ren. notions of i. in the production of poetry and emphasizes the link between poet as creator and a divine creator (see RENAISSANCE POETICS). Sidney and Scaliger call the poet a "creator" (Johnson calls him a "maker"), implying that such creation imitates or follows nature rather than copies it.

Hence a rigid dichotomy should not be established between imitation and creative i.; it is possible to ally them, as Coleridge does in *On Poesy or Art.* As Coleridge frequently says, to distinguish is not necessarily to divide. For even with Sidney (and later Leibniz, Reynolds, Shelley, and Carlyle), imitation is not so much a duplication of nature as an echo of divine creative power. The 19th-c. Platonist Joubert will claim that the poet "purifies and empties the forms of matter and shows us the universe as it is in the mind of God. . . . His portrayal is not a copy of a copy, but an impression of the archetype." Macaulay will call this the "imperial power" of poetry to imitate the "whole external and the whole internal universe." For Shaftesbury the poet is a "just Prometheus under Jove," and the variation on the Ovidian phrase—a god or daemon in us—becomes common in discussions of i.

During the *Sturm und Drang* (q.v.) and romantic eras, the theme of Prometheus further modifies the connection between divine creative energy and human poetry. In Blake's Christian vision these powers merge as the "divine-human i." Schelling calls genius (q.v.) "a portion of the Absolute nature of God." Poetry for Shelley elicits "the divinity in man." Coleridge considers the secret of genius in the fine arts to make the internal external and the external internal; in religious terms, Jesus is the living, communicative intellect in God and man—suggestively phrased in Emerson's "living, leaping Logos."

Ren. psychologists, among them Melancthon, Amerbach, and esp. Vives, advance increasingly sophisticated views of the mind wherein i. and the association of ideas play important roles. Sidney and Spenser consider imaginative power central to both theory and practice. Shakespeare uses i. (or fancy as its equivalent) suggestively, as in the Chorus of *Henry V.* In Eng. critical discussion of i., Theseus' lines in *A Midsummer Night's Dream* (5.1) become the most-quoted verses (*Paradise Lost* also figures prominently). Although close reading reveals Theseus' distrust of "strong" i. and its "tricks," identifying i. with madmen, lovers, and poets—whose tales may never be believed—Hippolyta reinterprets all the players and the night's action as a totalized myth which "More witnesseth than fancy's images, / And grows to something of great constancy."

Bacon's view of rhet. and poetry must be spliced together from his many writings. Two trends emerge. He splits rational or scientific knowledge from poetic knowledge, which is "not tied to the laws of matter." But this bestows greater freedom on i. to join and divide the elements of nature, to appeal to psychological satisfaction rather than verisimilitude (q.v.), and to permit the imitation of nature frankly to differ from nature itself not only in the medium of presentation but in its appeal to moral value—and to what would later be called aesthetics and the sublime (q.v.). Later these premises resurface often, incl. Addison's "Pleasures of the Imagination," Hume's "Of the Standard of Taste," and Reynold's *Discourses* (esp. 6, 7, and 13), where i. rather than the matter-of-fact becomes "the residence of truth." In *The Advancement of Learning* Bacon mentions an "imaginative or insinuative reason," a concept Addison repeats. But Bacon concludes, "I find not any science that doth properly or fitly pertain to the i."

Hobbes fails to see the capacious possibilities of Bacon's scheme for crit. or the arts, but his contributions to empirical psychology open other avenues and begin to supply the science Bacon found wanting. For Hobbes the "compounded i." forms "trains of ideas" or "mental discourse" which evolves into judgment or *sagacitas.* In "compounding" images and directing these associations to larger designs, the "contexture" of i. offers a picture of reality. This suggests what thinkers in the next century commonly express: i. subsumes judgment. In 1774 Alexander Gerard's *Essay on Genius* explicitly declares this.

Locke coins the phrase "association of ideas" in the *Essay Concerning Human Understanding* (4th ed., 1700). Originally he means idiosyncratic links between mental representations peculiar to an individual, a process Sterne explores in *Tristram Shandy*. But the phrase, like William James' "streams of consciousness," changes signification and soon stands for a pervasive habit of mind, both conscious and unconscious, akin to Hobbes' mental discourse and trains of compounded ideas. Locke receives little credit for recognizing i. as a strong faculty because he criticizes poetry and shows scant sympathy for art, and he distrusts figuration in lang. But the "tabula rasa" tag oversimplifies his epistemology and psychology. He states that "the mind has a power," an innate power (distinguished from innate ideas, which it never possesses) "to consider several" simple ideas "united together as one idea; and that not only as they are united in external objects, but as itself has joined them." As in Bacon, the active formation of complex ideas in "almost infinite variety" need not correspond to nature.

Replying to Locke's difficult arguments about innate ideas, Leibniz in his *Nouveaux essais* quotes Aristotle's *De anima*: "There is nothing in the mind not previously in the senses—except the mind itself." Here, as Santayana later notes, Leibniz uncovers the germ of Kant's critical philosophy. In Leibniz—and in Hobbes' and Locke's ascription of an active power forming complex ideas or trains of them—i. acquires a central position in a new, flexible faculty-psychology with its accompanying facultative logic.

IV. 18TH CENTURY AND ROMANTICISM. (See also paragraphs II.1,3,4 and III.1,3 above.) It is Joseph Addison who brings these concepts within the ken of critical theory and poetics. "The Pleasures of the I." arise from comparing our imaginative perception of nature with our perception of art, where art is itself an imitation of nature achieved through the artist's imaginative production which "has something in it like creation; it bestows a kind of existence. . . . It makes additions to nature." The interest rapidly becomes psychological and involves a projective faculty, active and passive, productive and reproductive. Like Pico, Addison emphasizes vision, but remarks that the pleasures of i. "are not wholly confined to such particular authors as are conversant in material objects, but are often to be met with among the polite masters of morality, crit., and other speculations abstracted from matter, who, though they do not directly treat of the visible parts of nature, often draw from them their similitudes, metaphors, and allegories. . . . A truth in the understanding is . . . reflected by the i.; we are able to see something like colour and shape in a notion, and to discover a scheme of thoughts traced out upon matter. And here the mind . . . has two of its faculties gratified at the same time, while the fancy is busy in copying after the understanding, and transcribing ideas

out of the intellectual world into the material." The material and the intellectual or passionately moral worlds thus fuse through i.; matter and spirit find a common faculty and may be represented by a single image.

In part derived from Addison's crit., Mark Akenside's popular poem *The Pleasures of the I.* combines empirical and Platonic elements. I. "blends" and "divides" images; its power can "mingle," "join," and "converge" them—phrases which anticipate Coleridge's "secondary" i. Collins and Joseph Warton reject satiric and didactic modes of verse; Warton proclaims that "invention and i." are "the chief faculties of a poet." Edward Young links originality and genius with i.; Gerard, whom Kant later praises as "the sharpest observer of the nature of genius," says, "it is i. that produces genius." Gerard, Priestley, and Duff extend associationist and empirical psychology to give a fluid model of the mind, not rigid or compartmentalized. Hazlitt concludes: "the i. is an *associating* principle" assuring "continuity and comprehension of mind," a definition allied with his remark that poetry portrays the flowing and not the fixed. Emerson eventually gives a twist to this organic process by hinting at a Neoplatonic foundation in "The Poet": "the endless passing of one element into new forms, the incessant metamorphosis, explains the rank which the i. holds in our catalogue of mental powers. The i. is the reader of these forms."

In Italy, L. A. Muratori advances a mutually beneficial combination of intellect and i. to produce "artificial" or "fantastic" images applied metaphorically and charged with emotion. Vico's *Scienza nuova* (3d ed., 1744) mentions a recollective *fantasia* but, more importantly, examines how poetic i. creates the basis for culture through the production of myth and universal patterns that shape understanding of both nature and human nature. Largely ignored during his lifetime, Vico produced ideas that have influenced historiography, anthropology, and imaginative writers since the early 19th c.

While Johnson and Hume generally distrust the i., they stress its pervasive ability to supplant reason. I. for Hume becomes the central faculty, and for Johnson, in his morality and psychology, the central concern. Both keenly appreciate the role of the passions in strengthening imaginative activity and the association of ideas. They yoke the Cl. theory of passions, further developed in the Ren., to empirical psychology. Hume sees i. as a completing power acting on suggestiveness; he claims that the elements a writer creates "must be connected together by some bond or tie: They must be related to each other in the i., and form a kind of *unity* which may bring them under one plan or view." This anticipates the romantic stress on organic unity. As Coleridge defines "the secondary" i., it "dissolves, diffuses, dissipates, in order to re-create; or where this process is rendered impossible, yet still at all events it struggles to idealize and to unify."

IMAGINATION

The associationists—among them Kames, Alison, H. Blair, Gerard, Hazlitt (to some extent), and others—stress imaginative association as pervasive; it determines taste. Images and sense data receive modifying "colors" of feeling and passion, a notion Wordsworth studies and uses widely. The emphasis on feeling fused with perception or cognition may be compared with I. A. Richards' later discussion of "emotive" versus "intellectual" belief (*Practical Crit.*), or T. S. Eliot's "dissociation of sensibility" (q.v.).

In Burke's *Enquiry* the imaginative arts become the "affecting arts." Because they trigger the completing i. of reader or audience, "suggestion" and "obscurity" (q.v.) attain positive value in poetry and visual art. This helps explain the growing interest in literary forms and genres not rigidly fixed but in metamorphosis, also the fascination in Blake, Novalis, and others for aphorism, and the importance of the literary fragment in the early 19th c. The i. of the reader becomes regarded as an important critical concept, too, ranging from Dryden's and Locke's "assent" to Coleridge's "willing suspension of disbelief." J. G. Sulzer, in his *Allgemeine Theorie der Schönen Künste*, notes, "the i. of those who hear or see the artist's work comes to his aid. If through any of the latent qualities in the work this i. takes on a vivid effect, it will thereupon complete what remains by itself."

Sensing rapid expansion of the idea, Burke claims in his *Enquiry*, (6th ed., 1770) that to i. "belongs whatever is called wit, fancy, invention, and the like." Hazlitt later remarks, "this power is indifferently called genius, i., feeling, taste; but the manner in which it acts upon the mind can neither be defined by abstract rules, as is the case in science, nor verified by continual unvarying experiments, as is the case in mechanical performances." Critics analyze passages of poetry as reflecting the pervasive operation of i., one aspect of what Coleridge first calls "practical crit.," a forerunner of the New Criticism (q.v.) in the 20th c.

Adam Smith bases his *Theory of Moral Sentiments* (1759) on the sympathetic identification that i. allows us to extend to others. As James Beattie says, "the philosophy of Sympathy ought always to form a part of the science of Crit." Hazlitt later states: "passion, in short, is the essence, the chief ingredient in moral truth; and the warmth of passion is sure to kindle the light of i. on the objects around it." The application to crit. is found in Wordsworth, Coleridge, and Keats, culminating rhetorically (along with much else) in Shelley's *Defence*: "the great secret of morals is love; or a going out of our own nature, and an identification with the beautiful . . . not our own. A man . . . must imagine intensely and comprehensively; he must put himself in the place of another and of many others. . . . The great instrument of moral good is the i.; and poetry administers to the effect by acting upon the cause. Poetry enlarges the circumference of the i." Applications of what Coleridge calls

"sympathetic i." are crucial to changes in dramatic crit. Before 1800, William Richardson, Thomas Whatley, and Maurice Morgann approach Shakespeare in this fashion, and Coleridge becomes the most brilliant exponent of such psychologically based crit., this too a forerunner of the psychological criticism (q.v.) of the 20th c.

The idea of imaginative sympathy also affects theories of poetic lang.: it should be "natural" and "spontaneous." Metaphor, personification (qq.v.), and figurative writing in general are now viewed less as ornament (q.v.) and more as essential to impassioned "natural lang." Theories of the primitive origin of lang. (Rousseau, Herder, Duff, Monboddo, and many recapitulations, incl. Shelley's and Hegel's) strengthen connections between i., poetry, early devel. of societies and their langs., and figurative speech in general (see ROMANTIC AND POSTROMANTIC POETICS). As Hazlitt says, exemplifying the connection between i. and the fascination with figurative lang., a metaphor or figure of speech requires no proof: "it gives *carte blanche* to the i." In the best poetry, images are "the building, and not the scaffolding to thought." What is true not only may but must be expressed figuratively, and is a specially valid form of knowledge. Hazlitt, neither a religious enthusiast nor transcendentalist, even says i. holds communion with the soul of nature and allows poets "to foreknow and to record the feelings of all men at all times and places."

Blake's emphasis falls heavily on i. as a power ultimately communicating and sharing with the holy power of creation, a vision that culminates in an Edenic state. "All things Exist in the Human I." "Man is All I.," so also "God is Man & exists in us & we in him." "The Eternal Body of Man . . . The I., that is, God himself," is symbolically "the Divine Body of the Lord Jesus." We are "Creating Space, Creating Time according to the wonders Divine of Human I."

Wordsworth's ideas of i. evolve from the Preface to the 2d ed. of *Lyrical Ballads* (1800), through its 1802 version, to a new preface and "Essay Supplementary" in 1815. In *The Prelude*, he describes the infant:

> . . . his mind
> Even as an agent of the one great mind,
> Creates, creator and receiver both,
> Working but in alliance with the works
> Which it beholds.—Such, verily is the first
> Poetic spirit of our human life.

Cf. Coleridge's definition of "primary" i.: "the living Power and prime Agent of all human Perception, and . . . a repetition in the finite mind of the eternal act of creation in the infinite I AM." Coleridge actually began the *Biographia* as a Preface to his own volume of verse, in part answering and modifying Wordsworth, but expanded it to a critical exposition and autobiography of his *liter-*

ary life that pivots on a reply to Wordsworth's published ideas concerning fancy and i. Coleridge considers that Wordsworth too closely links fancy and i. and explains i. too exclusively via associationism.

In the 1815 Preface, Wordsworth tries to explain how i. creates as well as associates. The power becomes for him so vast it challenges all conception, as with the apostrophe in *The Prelude* after crossing the Alps, or later: "I., which, in truth, / Is but another name for absolute power / And clearest insight, amplitude of mind, / And Reason in her most exalted mood." Wordsworth also claims: "I. having been our theme, / So also hath that intellectual Love, / For they are each in each, and cannot stand / Dividually." He uses his idea of i. to establish new grounding in poetic lang. and vindicates it in his practice (though not always in perfect conformity with his theoretical statements). He chooses not to exert a systematic philosophical concern for the idea as Coleridge does. He even considers that the word i. "has been overstrained . . . to meet the demands of the faculty which is perhaps the noblest of our nature."

Keats explores the idea of sympathetic i. and "negative capability" (q.v.), a search for truth or reality without any compulsive reaching after fact. Many of his letters and greater poems are undogmatic speculations on the value, "truth," and nature of the imaginative inner life. Shelley, regarding reason more in its deductive and experimental mode, contrasts it sharply with i., and on this distinction builds his *Defence of Poetry*. The essay recapitulates developments of the previous half century. He constructs his argument through powerful images and analogies rather than by Keats's "consequitive reasoning." Shelley's impassioned and figurative prose actualizes its own subject. He emphasizes the unconscious power of i. over the conscious will in poetic composition.

Coleridge, familiar with the philosophical developments in the idea since Plato and Aristotle, fuses and transforms them into the most suggestive and fruitful critical observations of Eng. romanticism. Though he never completes a systematic work that includes extended discussion of i., his theoretical pronouncements and practical insights provide rich ground for surmise. He combines British empirical psychology, Platonism and Neoplatonism (q.v.), scholastic and Hermetic philosophies, and Ger. transcendentalism. The result is more than an admixture: he crystallizes and connects issues of perception and constitutive or regulative ideas, of associationism, of theories of lang. and poetic diction, and of the function of i. into a *mimesis* that "humanizes" nature not only by reproducing natural objects and forms (the "fixities and definites" manipulated by fancy) but also by imitating the living process through which they exist and through which we feel and realize them. Unlike many contemp. Ger. writers (e.g. Fichte or Schelling), he applies the theory of i. at the level of phrase and individual image (q.v.) in the crit. of poetry.

Symbols for Coleridge are "living educts of the i., of that reconciling and mediatory power which, incorporating the reason in images of the sense, and organizing (as it were) the flux of the senses by the permanence and self-encircling energies of the reason, gives birth to a system of symbols, harmonious in themselves and consubstantial with the truths of which they are the conductors" (*The Statesman's Manual*). This definition is virtually identical to Bishop Lowth's discussion of "mystical allegory" in *De sacra poesi hebraeorum* (1753). Thus, even in the symbol as defined by Coleridge, we see elements of prophecy and its earlier critical devel. in the 18th c. Various romantic definitions of symbol, allegory, myth (qq.v.), and schema, whether from Kant, Schelling, Solger, Hegel, or others, all rely on i. Coleridge enlarges, reformulates, and applies the idea of i. in ways seminal for poetics. He may be regarded as the most important progenitor of the New Critical valuation of organicism and of unity (qq.v.).

The British devel. of the idea thus draws from both Platonic and Neoplatonic strains as well as from the line of 18th-c. empiricism initiated by Hobbes and Locke. With Coleridge, and to some extent Shelley and Carlyle, Ger. transcendental philosophy further enriches the Anglophone trad., just as British writing on the subject had vitalized Ger. thought in the 18th c. The Ger. background draws heavily on Spinoza, Locke, Leibniz, Wolff, Addison, Shaftesbury, the "Swiss Critics" Bodmer and Breitinger, Baumgarten, Hume, and the associationists (histories of associationism are written in 1777 by Michael Hissmann and in 1792 by J. G. E. Maass). In the later 18th c., Platner, Herder, and Sulzer extend discussion into psychology, lit., culture, and myth. Sulzer declares, "mythological poems must be considered as a lang. of i. . . . they make a world for themselves." Tetens, most eminent psychologist of the era, breaks the power of i. into different levels responsible for perception, larger associations and cognition, and ultimate poetic power. He profoundly influenced Kant, and Coleridge read him carefully.

The issue in Kant is central and vexing; his presentations of i. are multiple. Taking a less than clear-cut but prominent place in the *Critique of Pure Reason*, i. is "an active faculty of synthesis" operating on sense experience, "a necessary ingredient of perception itself" that mediates between senses and understanding. But "a transcendental synthesis of i." also exists, so that again, i. is both an empirical and a transcendental faculty or power. In the *Critique of Judgment* i. is vital to the analytic of both beauty and the sublime. It is not simply reproductive and operating under "the laws of association," but also "productive and exerting an activity of its own." Kant tries to reconcile empirical views of the "reproductive" i. with those derived from i. in its "pure" or "productive" mode;

this leads to a "tertium medium" joining the two, an idea Coleridge also suggests in the *Biographia*. In our perceptions, Kant claims, we "introduce into appearances that order and regularity which we name nature." In aesthetic theory he stresses the "free play" of i. and how, combined with taste, it draws an analogy between beauty and morality through the medium of the symbol.

Fichte proclaims "all reality is presented through the i." On the faculty of "*the creative i. . . . depends whether we philosophize with or without spirit . . . because the fundamental ideas . . . must be presented by the creative i. itself. . . . The whole operation of the human spirit proceeds from the i., but an i. that can be grasped no other way than through i.*" He elevates i. as the most important epistemological faculty and bases philosophy on it. In part to resolve potential contradictions or dualities in Kant, and to escape Fichte's more abstract epistemology, Schiller writes his *Ästhetische Erziehung* (1794–95), where free play of i. becomes *Spieltrieb* (the "play drive"). With antecedents of i. as "play" or "free play" in Bacon, Kant, Wieland, and Lessing, Schiller explores i. as an aesthetic state of being that oscillates (recalling Fichte's "schweben der Einbildungskraft") between "form" and "sense" drives. This aesthetic i. renovates the soul and permits it to be "fully human," opening a line of Utopian thought. An extensive transcendental poetics develops with Schiller, the Schlegels, and Novalis. They all hold i. to be of supreme importance in the psychological and epistemological grounding of art.

Schelling constructs his *System des tranzscendental Idealismus* (1800) on the idea of i., which in that and other works he carries further than perhaps any other thinker. It is central to his philosophy of nature and of mind as one larger system insured by the unifying revelation of the work of art. The *Kunstprodukt* combines the force of nature with that of mind into something that had not previously existed in either. I. creates the myths that secure all cultural and spiritual significance. Finally, the artist's i. generates the most comprehensive symbols; in them knowledge realizes its highest manifestation. Art becomes necessary to complete philosophy; philosophy's highest goal is the philosophy of art, ultimately based on i. in God, artist, philosopher, and audience.

Hegel's *Aesthetik* (1835) utilizes i. or "Geist" (spirit) as a key element for his historical and critical views but does not much enlarge the theory of i. Goethe emphasizes i., though in unsystematic fashion. The hermeneutic trad. from Schleiermacher through Dilthey and down to Gadamer relies on i. as an instrument of knowledge and interp., with Gadamer roughly retaining the older distinction between i. and discursive reason as that between *Wahrheit* ("truth") and *Methode* ("method"). See HERMENEUTICS.

Romantic writers provide the idea with its most extreme formulation and make the highest claims for i. It stands directly related to—and necessary for—perception, memory, images, ideas, knowledge, worldviews, poetry, prophecy, and religion. Santayana proclaims Emerson the first modern philosopher to base a system on i. rather than reason. Schelling or Coleridge may have a stronger claim, though Coleridge's later thought increasingly grasps a fuller reason, both discursive and intuitive, as subsuming imaginative power. Even a brief review of romantic manifestations of i. threatens to expand infinitely.

Perhaps the greatest "romantic" claim is that i. resolves all contradictions and unifies the soul and being of creator and receiver, writer and reader, subject and object, and human nature and *Naturgeist* alike. I., says Coleridge, "reveals itself in the balance or reconciliation of opposite or discordant qualities: of sameness, with difference; of general, with the concrete; the idea, with the image; the individual, with the representative. . . ." Coleridge, Schelling, Schiller, and Shelley all say that i. or poetry calls upon the "whole" soul or individual. To characterize this activity Coleridge coins two words: in an 1802 letter "co-adunating" (from the Lat. "to join" or "to shape into one") and in the *Biographia* the famous "esemplastic" (with its analogous Gr. basis). Schelling posits a fanciful etymology reminiscent of Herder: "In-Eins-Bildung" ("making into one") for "Einbildungskraft." The traditional way of expressing this unifying action, recognized in Neoplatonic and Hermetic circles, was to say, as Wordsworth does, that i. "modifies" or throws "one coloring" over all its productions. As the resolution of contradictions or antinomies, i. could be seen as a metaphysical, psychological, and artistic principle—as Kant said, a "blind power hidden in the depths of the soul"—that unifies noumenal and phenomenal, sensory and transcendental, mind and spirit, self and nature (e.g. Fichte's *Ich* and *Nicht-Ich*), even freedom and necessity. The power thus resolves Cartesian dualism and all subject/object, ego/world, Aristotelian/Platonic or Neoplatonic divisions. It drives all dialectical process and provides genuine knowledge.

V. LATER 19TH AND 20TH CENTURIES. Such full-dress syntheses left scant room for further analysis or higher claims. Arguably, i. had come to stand for many ideas, not one. The associated terms and adjectives grew confusing, and G. H. Lewes remarked: "there are few words more abused."

Ruskin posits three modes of i., and an elaborate, schematic division of fancy and i. He stresses the intuitive grasp of art rather than its reasoning or analysis. Pater echoes Coleridge to some degree, as Wallace Stevens will, but neither adds a new dimension to theory of i. In Germany Theodore Lipps' studies of *Einfühlung* or empathy (q.v.) are related to an imaginative grasp of living truth; in this connection Hopkins' "inscape" (q.v.) also suggests an intuition of object and the feelings it arouses. Oscar Wilde's simultaneous attacks on realism and on unrealistic romances in "The Decay of Lying" are playful defenses of what earlier had been called "feigning," now phrased in more provocative and paradoxical lang. than Sidney's or Shelley's.

Irving Babbitt, while unsympathetic to romanticism, nevertheless develops a theory of ethical i. similar to 18th-c. discussions. Croce's aesthetics and poetics lean heavily on a productive i. (*fantasia*) that acts under the influence of intuition and feeling to produce a unifying image. Though without extensive elaboration on the theory of i. as such, anthropological and psychological studies by Frazer, Lévi-Strauss, Freud, Jung, Eliade, and others have kept alive and deepened concerns voiced by Vico and Blackwell (see MYTH CRITICISM). The interest here, as to some extent with Cassirer's theory of the symbol, is more with the formation and importance of the individual image or myth (qq.v.) than with all the diverse powers once attributed to i. Richards, through his scholarship and crit. of late 18th-c. figures and esp. through *Coleridge on I.*, combines elements of a romantic aesthetic with modern psychology and helps create the New Criticism, indebted to Coleridge and the concept of organic unity.

R. G. Collingwood, positing i. as a mediating faculty between sense and intellect, refashions romantic theory and attempts to give it consistent shape. I. provides real knowledge guaranteed by the work of art, which raises perception, feelings, creation, and expression to consciousness through a concrete act. Collingwood jettisons higher claims and focuses on a comprehensive aesthetic, but the currency and effect of his views—fundamentally out of step with postmodernism—diminishes in the second half of the 20th c. More recently, neurophysiologists have attempted to analyze areas of the brain, while developmental psychologists have empirically studied artists' and children's creative activities to determine the functions played by brain hemispheres, biochemistry, the environment, habit, and association in the imaginative process, incl. poetry. Results have been mixed, with no single theory or explanation emerging.

But the notion of i. as creating unity is generally opposed to the spirit of literary modernism and postmodernism. Nor is it central to phenomenological approaches. More stress falls on the power of the individual image, or images juxtaposed, e.g. in imagism (q.v.) or the metaphysical revival. Claims for art to save and enlighten, or to provide special knowledge, are reduced. Detractors of the New Criticism simplify and attack the concept of organic unity. However, though less massively than in romantic poetics (q.v.), the idea of i. continues to play a role in postmodernism. Structuralism (q.v.) offers affinities with romantic organicism and an imaginative, intellectual reconstruction of reality, the creation of this "simulacrum" itself an imitation and not a copy. Deconstruction (q.v.) shuns any unifying power to resolve contradictions and builds itself—or rather deploys

its various moves and strategies—in part by exploiting those contradictions or divisions. But while deconstruction seems a polar opposite of imaginative unity and organic synthesis, the romantic theory of i. itself thrives on such contradictions and polarities. In one sense i. and deconstruction are allied: in crit. or philosophy they distrust any formal system or set of rules for either analysis or creativity; they rejoin poetry and philosophy through the medium of words and through a consideration of the nature and the history of writing in general, and figurative lang. in particular.

See also FANCY; GENIUS; INSPIRATION; INTUITION; INVENTION; ORIGINALITY; ROMANTIC AND POSTROMANTIC POETICS; ROMANTICISM; TWENTIETH-CENTURY POETICS; VISION.

I. Babbitt, *Rousseau and Romanticism* (1919); H. C. Warren, *Hist. of Association Psychology* (1921); G. Santayana, *Character and Opinion* (1921); B. Croce, *Aesthetic*, tr. D. Ainslie (1922), *Essays on Lit. and Lit. Crit.*, ed. and tr. M. E. Moss (1990); L. P. Smith, "Four Romantic Words," *Words and Idioms* (1925); Richards, esp. ch. 32; M. W. Bundy, *The Theory of I. in Cl. and Mod. Thought* (1927), "'Invention' and 'I.' in the Ren.," *JEGP* 29 (1930), "Bacon's True Opinion of Poetry," *SP* 27 (1930); R. Wellek, *Kant in England* (1931); A. S. P. Woodhouse, "Collins and the Creative I.," *Studies in Eng.*, ed. M. Wallace (1931), "Romanticism and the Hist. of Ideas," *Eng. Studies Today*, ed. C. Wrenn and G. Bullough (1951); I. A. Richards, *Coleridge on I.* (1934); S. H. Monk, *The Sublime* (1935); D. Bond, "'Distrust of I.' in Eng. Neoclassicism," *PQ* 14 (1935), "Neoclassical Psychology of the I.," *ELH* 4 (1937); R. G. Collingwood, *Principles of Art* (1938); C. D. Thorpe, *The Aesthetic of Hobbes* (1940); K. R. Wallace, *Bacon on Communication and Rhet.* (1943); W. J. Bate, "Sympathetic I. in 18th-C. Eng. Crit.," *ELH* 12 (1945), *From Classic to Romantic* (1946); W. J. Bate and J. Bullitt, "Distinctions between Fancy and I.," *MLN* 60 (1945); W. Stevens, *The Necessary Angel* (1951); Crane; Abrams; E. L. Fackenheim, "Schelling's Philosophy of the Literary Arts," *PQ* 4 (1954); Wellek, v. 1; M. H. Nicolson, *Science and I.* (1956); R. Cohen, "Association of Ideas and Poetic Unity," *PQ* 36 (1957); Wimsatt and Brooks; E. Tuveson, *The I. as a Means of Grace* (1960); E. D. Hirsch, Jr., *Wordsworth and Schelling* (1960); W. P. Albrecht, *Hazlitt and the Creative I.* (1961), chs. 1, 3, 5; B. Hathaway, *The Age of Crit.* (1962); R. Barthes, "The Structuralist Activity," (1963); F. Yates, *The Art of Memory* (1966); T. McFarland, *Coleridge and Pantheist Trad.* (1969), *Originality and I.* (1985); H. Mörchen, *Die Einbildungskraft bei Kant* (1970); T. Todorov, *Theories of the Symbol* (1977, tr. 1982); W. Wetherbee, *Platonism and Poetry in the 12th C.* (1972)—for i. and *ingenium*; R. Scholes, *Structuralism in Lit.* (1974), ch. 6; M. Warnock, *I.* (1976); E. S. Casey, *Imagining: a Phenomenological Study* (1976); J. Derrida, *Writing and Difference*, tr.

A. Bass (1978); J. Engell, *The Creative I.* (1981), ch. 1, 13; D. P. Verene, *Vico's Science of I.* (1981); de Man; E. Dod, *Die Vernünftigkeit der I.* (1985)—on Schiller and Shelley; M. Kipperman, *Beyond Enchantment* (1986)—Eng. poetry and Ger. idealism; C. G. Ryn, *Will, I. and Reason* (1986)—on Babbitt; R. Kearney, *The Wake of I.* (1988); *Coleridge, Keats, and the I.*, ed. J. R. Barth and J. L. Mahoney (1989); *Coleridge's Theory of I. Today*, ed. C. Gallant (1989).

J.E.

IMAGISM. A school of poetry which flourished in England and America between 1912 and 1914 and emphasized the virtues of clarity, compression, and precision. In 1912, Ezra Pound wrote of the "forgotten school of images" that formed around the Bergsonian philosopher T. E. Hulme, ca. 1908. Hulme was the founder of a Poets' Club which began meeting regularly in London in 1909, incl. Pound by April, and which was influenced by Hulme's speculations on literary lang. Hulme wrote in his essay "Romanticism and Classicism" that the lang. of poetry is a "visual concrete one.... Images in verse are not mere decoration, but the very essence of an intuitive lang."

As the founder of the "Imagist Movement," Pound was more interested in technique and even publicity than in theory. Hilda Doolittle recalls in her memoir of Pound that Pound named i. when he suggested revisions to her poem "Hermes of the Ways" and "scrawled 'H. D. Imagiste' at the bottom of the page" before sending it to *Poetry* magazine in October of 1912; in November Pound used the term "Imagiste" for the first time in print when he published the "Complete Poetical Works" of Hulme (five short poems) as an appendix to his *Ripostes*. Poems by "H. D., 'Imagiste'" were published in *Poetry* in January 1913, and in the March 1913 issue, F. S. Flint, quoting an unnamed "Imagiste" (Pound), listed these characteristics of the movement: (1) direct treatment of the "thing," whether subjective or objective; (2) use of absolutely no word that did not contribute to the presentation; (3) as regarding rhythm, to compose in the sequence of the musical phrase, not in the sequence of the metronome (see FREE VERSE). Flint wrote that there was a fourth principle, or a "certain 'Doctrine of the Image,'" which they had not committed to writing," perhaps referring to the complex influence of Hulmean philosophy. But in his "A Few Don'ts by an Imagiste" in the same issue of *Poetry*, Pound gave a one-sentence definition of the poetic image as "that which presents an intellectual and emotional complex in an instant of time" (see IDEOGRAM). The April issue of *Poetry* included the best-known and perhaps finest of the imagist poems, Pound's "In a Station of the Metro."

The climax of the movement came in the Spring of 1914, when Pound published in England and America an anthology of verse entitled *Des Imagistes*, which included poems by H. D., Richard Aldington, F. S. Flint, Amy Lowell, James Joyce, and William Carlos Williams. By this time, Lowell was assuming leadership of the movement and began publishing anthologies entitled *Some Imagist Poets* for the years 1915–17. But Pound repudiated "Amygism," declaring that it was a dilution of the original movement which violated the second imagist principle, and aligned himself rather with vorticism (q.v.).

By 1917 Lowell herself felt that the movement had run its course; but her anthologies had kept it alive, and her first two volumes contained prefaces which, along with the *Poetry* essays, constitute the most deliberate statements of imagist theory. Though the poems themselves may appear to have a merely casual relation to Pound's definition of the image, they place their values in clarity, exactness, and concreteness of detail; in economy of lang. and brevity of treatment; and in an organic basis for selecting rhythmic patterns, which is essential if only necessary words are to be used. H. D.'s "Storm" illustrates these values:

> You crash over the trees,
> you crack the live branch—
> the branch is white,
> the green crushed,
> each leaf is rent like split wood.

I. reacted against the verbose and abstract lang. into which much of the poetry of the 19th c. had declined. As a movement it thus parallels the romantic reaction a century earlier against the ossified poetic diction of neoclassicism. Its concentration on the object and realistic rendering of the external world recall similar principles in Wordsworth's "Preface" to *Lyrical Ballads*. A still deeper 19th-c. influence is the Fr. trad. of *symbolisme* (which the word *imagiste* echoed) from Baudelaire to Mallarmé (see SYMBOLISM).

The imagists' concern with poetic form and technique and their desire for the immediacy of effect that arises from the closest possible association of word and object were in part a program for improving the craft of writing which influenced the formalist poetics of critics like Eliot, Richards, and Ransom. But the imagist movement has more complex associations: its preoccupation with technique and with surfaces, light, and color links it with impressionism (q.v.); and Pound's concept of "presentation" recalls Henry James's insistence that the writer should "show" rather than "tell." Recent critics have seen i. as an attempt to create a poem as a single entity which, unlike a symbolic or allegorical poem, intensifies its objective reality rather than expressing the subjective feelings of the poet. The essential point about the influence and importance of i. was made by Stephen Spender: "the aims of the imagist movement in poetry provide the archetype of a modern creative procedure." See AMERICAN POETRY.

E. Pound, *Ripostes* (1912), *Letters*, ed. D. D. Paige (1950), *Literary Essays* (1954); F. S. Flint,

"Imagisme," *Poetry* 1 (1913), "The Hist. of I.," *The Egoist* 2 (1915); T. E. Hulme, *Speculations*, ed. H. Read (1924); S. K. Coffmann, *I.* (1951); W. C. Pratt, *The Imagist Poem* (1963); S. Spender, *The Stuggle of the Modern* (1963); F. Kermode, *Romantic Image* (1963); H. Gross, *Sound and Form in Mod. Poetry* (1964); H. Schneidau, *Ezra Pound* (1969); H. Kenner, *The Pound Era* (1971); J. B. Harmer, *Victory in Limbo: I., 1908–1917* (1975); D. Perkins, *A Hist. of Mod. Poetry*, v. 1 (1976), ch. 15; H. D., *End to Torment* (1979); J. T. Gage, *In the Arresting Eye: The Rhet. of I.* (1981); R. Taupin, *The Influence of Fr. Symbolism on Mod. Am. Poetry* (1985); Terras—Rus.; J. J. Wilhelm, *Ezra Pound in London and Paris, 1908–25* (1990).   T.M.; S.K.C.

IMITATION.

    I. FROM THE HISTORICAL PERSPECTIVE
    II. FROM THE MODERN PERSPECTIVE

I. FROM THE HISTORICAL PERSPECTIVE. Until the 20th c., when it was restored to the critical vocabulary by Auerbach and the members of the Chicago School (q.v.), "i." had been out of favor as a literary term since the 18th c. Its eclipse began with the neoclassical critical stirrings that led the way to romanticism, when "i." (Gr. *mimesis*; Lat. *imitatio*) was increasingly felt to be out of keeping with the new spirit of originality, spontaneity (qq.v.), and self-expression. Despite the fact that romantic poetics (q.v.) was preserved essentially intact well into the 20th c., interest in i. as a critical concept has been revived in recent years in connection with efforts to question the concept of representation in lang. and with a new interest in rhetoricity (see section II below).

The original connotation of *mimesis* (see REPRESENTATION AND MIMESIS) seems to have been dramatic or quasidramatic. Whether any theory of poetry as i. was developed before Plato is uncertain. Gorgias's notion of tragedy as a "beneficent deception" (*apate*) perhaps anticipated it in part; and Democritus certainly held that the arts in general arose out of i. of nature: singing, for example, from i. of the birds. The first place where we can actually grasp *mimesis* as a critical term is Plato's *Republic*, Books 3 and 10, though in Book 3, the context is political and pedagogical rather than literary. Plato's concern there is with the education of his elite corps of Guards, and he judges poetry strictly by that criterion. "I." is identified almost exclusively with the dramatic mode, i.e. with the direct impersonation of literary characters. This involves an identification of oneself with others which is perilous for the young; it may lead them to indiscriminate i. of low and unworthy persons. Hence poetry, but esp. the drama, must be banished from the professional education of the ideal ruler. In Book 10, Plato renews his attack on a broader front. I. is now identified as the method of *all* poetry, and of the visual arts as well. The poet, like the painter, is incapable of doing

more than counterfeiting the external appearance of things; Truth, the realm of Ideas, is inaccessible to him. In this second discussion (perhaps written later), Plato's attention has shifted from the method of i. to its object, and i.—i.e. art—is condemned not merely for its moral effects but because it cannot break through the surface of Appearance to the reality it ought to reproduce, Ideas.

This crushing verdict upon "i." does not result, as we might expect, in banishing the term from Plato's world of discourse; on the contrary, it permeates his thinking more and more in the later dialogues. In the *Sophist* (236) he hints at the possibility of a "true i." which would reproduce the real nature and proportions of its object. Indeed Plato came to think of the whole complex relation of Becoming to Being, Particular to Idea, as a kind of i. Thus the *Timaeus* (27 ff.) presents the universe itself as a work of art, an "image" of the world of Ideas made by a divine craftsman. From this it is only a step to conceiving visual art, and then poetry, as a sensuous embodiment of the ideal. The Neoplatonists (see Plotinus, *Enneads* 5.8; cf. Cicero, *Orator* 2.8–9) took this step, but Plato himself did not. The condemnation of poetry in the *Republic* was never explicitly revised or withdrawn (it is substantially repeated in the *Laws*, Books 2 and 7), and the developments just mentioned remain hints (highly fruitful ones for later thought) rather than a new and positive doctrine of poetic i.

Aristotle accepts i. (*Poetics* 4) as a fundamental human instinct—an *intellectual* instinct—of which poetry is one manifestation, along with music, painting, and sculpture. His real innovation, however, and the cornerstone of his new theory of poetry (see CLASSICAL POETICS), is a redefinition of *mimesis* to mean not a counterfeiting of sensible reality but a presentation of "universals." By "universals" he means not metaphysical entities like the Platonic Ideas but simply the permanent, characteristic modes of human thought, feeling, and action (9). It goes without saying, or at least Aristotle does not bother to say, that knowledge of such universals is not restricted to the philosopher. The poet can represent them, and his readers can grasp them, without benefit of metaphysical training. Poetic i. is of action rather than simply of men (i.e. characters). Tragedy (and, with certain reservations, the epic—qq.v.) is an i. of a single, complete, and serious action involving the happiness of an important human being. More specifically, the i. is lodged in the *plot* (*mythos*) of the poem; and by "plot" (q.v.) Aristotle means not merely a sequence but a *structure* (q.v.) of events, so firmly welded together as to form an organic whole. It follows that the poet's most important duty is to shape his plot. He cannot find it already given; whether he starts from mythical trad., history, or his own invention, he is a poet only so far as he is a builder (*poietes*, "maker") of plots. Thus "i." comes very close to meaning "creation." But the poet's creation is not of some "second nature" existing only in his fancy; it is a valid representation of the actions of men according to the laws of probability or necessity.

Aristotle's concept of i. was subtle and complex. His chief successors in crit. were men of another stamp, more literary than philosophical in their view of poetry. So far as i. remained a key term in the Hellenistic age (actually we do not hear a great deal about it), it seems to have been conceived as meaning the portrayal of standardized human types: the hot-headed man, the braggart soldier, the wild Thracian, etc. Aristotle's "probability" (*to eikos, verisimile*), and the even more characteristic concept of "appropriateness" (*to prepon, decorum*, q.v.), are now tailored to the measure of particular social standards and conventions more than to any permanent principles of human nature. At the same time Aristotle's insistence on action gives way to more relaxed and eclectic views: the object of i. may be character, thought, or even natural phenomena. Anything can be imitated, in accordance with the laws of the genre (q.v.) one has chosen, and the object, whether fable, fact, or fiction (q.v.), is tacitly assumed to have more or less the same status as a natural object.

Alongside the Aristotelian concept of i., thus denatured, another of very different provenience took on increasing importance in the Hellenistic and Roman periods. This was the relatively simple idea of imitating the established "classics" (the word is Roman, the concept Gr.), the great models of achievement in each genre. Its origin was rhetorical but it ended by spreading impartially over prose and poetry. The treatise of Dionysius of Halicarnassus *On I.* is lost except for fragments, but we can get some idea of the theme from the second chapter of Book 10 of Quintilian's *Institutio oratoria*. From these two authors, and more particulariy from "Longinus" (see SUBLIME), we can see that the doctrine had its higher side. I. of the great writers of the past need not and should not be merely a copying of devices of arrangement and style, but a passionate emulation of their spirit. Dryden (*Essay of Dramatic Poesy*) puts it very well: "Those great men whom we propose to ourselves as patterns of our i., serve us as a torch, which is lifted up before us, to illumine our passage and often elevate our thoughts as high as the conception we have of our author's genius." Here i. is united with its apparent opposite, inspiration. Nevertheless, both in antiquity and in the Ren., i. in the sense of emulation of models meant chiefly stylistic i., and thus helped to fortify the prevalent understanding of poetry as an art of words.

The Ren. inherited three major concepts of i. from antiquity: (1) the Platonic: a copying of sensuous reality; (2) the Aristotelian: a representation of the universal patterns of human behavior embodied in action; and (3) the Hellenistic and rhetorical: i. of canonized literary models. But each of these was further complicated by a deviation or variant interpretation: (1) the Platonic by the Neoplatonic suggestion that the artist can create according to a true Idea; (2) the Aristotelian by the vulgarization of Aristotle's "universals" into particular social types belonging to a particular place or time; and (3) the rhetorical by its rather adventitious association with "enthusiasm" and the *furor poeticus* (e.g. Vida's *Ars poetica* 2.422–44). That this mixed inheritance did not lead to complete critical chaos was due partly to the chronological accident that the *Poetics* did not become known in Italy until well after 1500, partly to the incorrigible syncretism of the humanists, and partly to the plain fact that the chief literary creed and inspiration of the It. Ren. was rhetorical. Humanism was an imitative movement in its very root and essence: the i. of Cl., and particularly Cl. Lat., lit. was its life-blood. Thus the burning question in the 15th c., and well into the 16th, was not "What is i.?" or "Should we imitate?" but "Whom [i.e. which Cl. authors] should we imitate?" The fiercest battle was waged over prose style, i.e. whether Cicero should be the sole and all-sufficient model.

A genuine theoretical interest in the concept of poetic i. as such could not arise, however, until Aristotle's *Poetics* had come to light again and begun to be studied (Gr. text 1508; Lat. trs. 1498, 1536; It. tr. 1549). Vida's *Art of Poetry* (1527) is still innocent of this new trend. It preaches the i. of "nature" (2.455) but for no other real purpose than to inculcate the i. of the ancient poets, and above all Virgil, who followed her to the best advantage. Daniello (*Poetica*, 1536) knows Aristotle's definition of tragedy as i. but hardly knows what to make of it since he draws only a faltering distinction between poetry and history. Robortelli, in his commentary on the *Poetics* (1548), allows the poet to invent things that transcend nature. Fracastoro (*Naugerius, sive de poeta dialogus*, 1555) pieces out Aristotle's concept of i. with the Platonic idea of beauty, identifying the latter with the universal. Scaliger (1561) recommends the i. of Virgil because Virgil had created a "second nature" more beautiful than the first; and Boileau gave the problem its definitive formulation for neoclassical theory: the surest way to imitate nature is to imitate the classics. But the real difficulty and challenge of Aristotle's idea of i. had not been grasped, much less solved. The later Ren. was as unable as the earlier to make an effective distinction between poetry and history on the one hand, and between poetry and rhet., on the other, because it could not seize and define any true "universal" as the object of poetic i., except in vague Platonic (Neoplatonic) terms, and so fell back into regarding poetry as essentially a special way of discoursing about "things."

Although i. was implicitly accepted down through the 18th c. as the goal and method of the fine arts in general, incl. poetry and painting, it began to slip into disrepute after 1770, being increasingly felt to imply a derogation of the artist's integrity. Edward Young sneered at "the meddling ape, I.," and Coleridge opined that "To admire on principle, is the only way to imitate without loss of originality." The revival of "i." in the 20th-c. has very little to do with either the Cl. or the neoclassical trad.; it goes straight to Aristotle, not through intermediaries, and views i. above all as a structural concept, the principle of organization of poetic wholes. G.F.E.

II. FROM THE MODERN PERSPECTIVE, i. refers to two different but related concepts: representation of external reality and copying or adaptation of artistic or literary models. Periods in which critical theory is privileged have tended to devalue the concept of i. in either sense and to stress, as its opposite, originality, influence, and intertextuality (qq.v.). Some recent theorists dismiss i. because it seems to rely on a rhet. of "presence" (insisting on "sameness" by suppressing the "difference" that haunts all representations); others point out that both in practice and in theory i. invokes that very "difference" which it is purported to suppress.

In Plato's articulation of two types of mimesis—as artistic reproduction of the physical object, and as inward representation of the idea—one activity represents the external world by means of lang. and the visual arts. The other is a conceptual activity, at once implicated in lang. yet presumably transcending its problematic elements, though this transcendence is put into question in the *Cratylus* and the *Theaetetus*, where lang. appears to be so intimately connected with thought itself that what is known and how it is known become inextricably entangled. Plato distinguishes poetry from philosophy in terms of their respective possibilities of representing the Idea, but if the act of representing can contaminate the Idea, then the claims of philosophy cannot readily be separated from the performance of poetry. Aristotle responds to Plato's debunking of mimesis by linking it to the concept of form (q.v.); in the *Poetics*, mimesis is governed by the rules of its form rather than by the accuracy with which it represents the object.

This shift in the concept of i. in antiquity in fact represents a broader divergence between affective and formalist theories of art that has endured to this day. Affective theories, such as Plato's, which recognize the power of the text to move the reader, tend to disregard i. (either of nature or of texts) as an adequate source of that power. Formalist theories, on the other hand, regard i. as a cognitive function made possible by the closure of form. A dramatic action with a beginning and an end, portrayed within the form of art, makes it possible for a text to yield to its reader knowledge which is both textual and human. In the formalist mimetic context, the order of lit. is also the order of nature. Once this representational link is established, mimesis slips into an i. of trad. Thus Horace (*Ars poetica*) asserts the propriety of i. because he does not see nature and art as disparate orders. Cl. accomplishments become rules (q.v.) for the production of lit., and the secret of good writing is learning (*sapere*). This connection between learning and originality remains important from the Ren. through the neoclassical period. When Dryden calls Jonson "a learned Plagiary" he means that Jonson has a profound knowledge of the classics: "he has done his Robberies so openly" and so authoritatively that the line between plagiarism and originality becomes blurred. Dante too echoes the importance of learning in i. ("the more closely we imitate those great poets, the more correctly we write poetry"), yet he engages at the same time in a theory of i. and a practice of invention (q.v.) by which the model (Virgil) is displaced in the *Commedia* and Paradise created. I. attempts to bridge the distance from its models, or more aggressively to suppress that distance, and in the process it slips into invention, creating a web of intertextual relations which make the link of "copy" to source problematic.

Ren. critical theory routinely grounded itself by referring to the Cl. trad., but the i. of those models only served to highlight the cultural and aesthetic distance between Ren. writers and their originals. In this respect i. forced upon Ren. critics a consciousness of historical change, and in turn this consciousness of their difference from the past compelled them to transform i. into an invention of beginnings (Greene). Thus i., which aims at the recuperation and presence of the originals, opens up the question of originality and poetic identity and drifts insensibly into the concerns of influence and intertextuality to which at first glance it appears to be opposed. The stability which accompanies the notion of i. is in this respect disrupted by the gap which i. as a practice opens, and this tension breaks into major debates in the 16th c. as to what i. means, who the models should be, and how the relation of nature to the classics should be defined.

At issue in this dispute was also the adequacy of the ancients' representation of nature—a question that remains in the foreground through the 18th c. The reliance on Cl. models produced a tension between i. of nature as external reality and i. of nature as represented in those models. In drama in particular this tension translated itself into a distinction between art as the i. of nature and art as an i. in which nature is elevated "to a higher pitch." Dryden (*An Essay of Dramatic Poesy*) suggests that the exact representation of nature must give way to an i. in which plot, characters, and description "are exalted above the level of common converse." This notion refers us back to Aristotle's statement in the *Physics* that art completes what nature leaves undone, or "imitates the missing parts" (2.8). The neoclassical period reaffirmed Aristotle's idea that art imitates not just actual nature but nature's potential form. When properly accomplished, i. is expected to reflect at once Cl. models and the nature which those models imitated: "Nature and Homer" become, in Pope's *Essay on Crit.*, "the same" (see CONVENTION).

In this way i. brings together two antithetical concepts: representation of reality, which assumes the priority of the object and demands of the work of art verisimilitude or accuracy of depiction, and formalism, which insists on the work of art "completing" its subject. Both concepts come to rest on a metaphysics of presence (though the notion of "completing" the model puts into question the fullness or presence of the original), and both idealize the nature of the artistic act. I. is made possible by assuming "sameness" to be the governing condition of lit. and life, and "difference" to be a mere departure from this central fact (Miller). The "sameness" of nature and model which Pope points to is affirmed in 18th-c. aesthetics through the painted image, which, as de Man suggests (1983), is supposed to restore the object to view and in that sense guarantee the continuity of its presence (see UT PICTURA POESIS). The possibility that the model might be absent is repressed.

Also repressed is the possibility that lang. might constitute its own fictions rather than represent, submissively, an external reality. The tension between nature as external reality and as potential totality conceals a deeper schism between theories of i. and theories of metaphor (q.v.), and consequently between formalist and affective theories of reading. Aristotle's view of metaphor as improper naming (*Poetics* 21) tends to put into question both the mimetic order that is assumed to exist between nature and art and the totality of form. When Longinus (*On the Sublime*) takes up the question of art's relation to nature, he develops a theory of the fragment which insures the priority of metaphor over the possibility of mimesis. Fragments rather than total forms strike fire from the reader's mind, and the power of the fragment resides not in i. of nature but in a figuration in which the argument is concealed (15). Affective theories of crit. in this way develop a line of argument antithetical to that of mimetic theories of crit., yet the two approaches are implicated in one another in the course of critical trads. Sidney (*An Apology for Poetry*) refers to Aristotle's mimesis at once as "representing" and "counterfeiting." Nature comes to be perceived as form in formalist readings, but power comes to be perceived as the breaking of that form. It may be that the felt need for "defenses" of poetry in the Ren. was a result of this tension between incompatible critical models.

Romantic writings engage in precisely this exploration of the limits of form and the inadequacies of i. For the romantics the text is merely a fragment of a larger vision, but this vision has less to do with nature as subject for i. than it does with the workings of consciousness itself. Both the Cl. and neoclassical periods privileged reason as the determining structure of consciousness, and this assumption made i. the proper method of interaction between text and world. But in romantic writings concealment plays such a large role (in its various guises as the unconscious, the "life of things") that nature becomes closed to the workings of reason, form, and i., and imagination (q.v.) comes to take their place; the visionary perspective now opposes itself to the mimetic one. At the same time, the neoclassical acceptance of i. as a practice of writing is displaced in romantic texts by a stress on originality (q.v.), a refusal to adopt inherited forms. At times this stress on newness is couched in the rhet. of i.—e.g. Wordsworth's desire to "imitate the very lang. of common men"—but romantic practice stresses a different rhet., built on the inescapable figuration that attends all knowledge "of ourselves, and of the universe." When Wordsworth looks down from a slow-moving boat into a lake he cannot tell apart what is at the bottom, what is reflected from the shore, and his own image: he finds he "cannot part / the shadow from the substance" (*Prelude* Bk. 4). The romantic subject is implicated in what he sees, and this implication undoes the possibility of a true, holistic, or transcendent representation of nature.

The 20th c. has witnessed both periods of formalism and antiformalism. The New Criticism (q.v.) repeated the gesture of associating form with a representation of idealized nature. In a different vein, Auerbach traces in *Mimesis* the history of the idea of representation in textual practice by assuming, in synecdochic fashion, the coherence between literary text and the culture it represents. But after 1960, in part as a result of the influx of Fr. crit. into America, the possibility of i. as representation has been put into question by the notion of textuality (q.v.): Derrida asserts the impossibility of representation that is not always already lang., and de Man terms representation "an ambivalent process that implies the absence of what is being made present again," an absence which "cannot be assumed to be merely contingent" (*Blindness and Insight* 123). For deconstruction (q.v.), mimesis is groundless repetition haunted by difference. The authority of representation is undermined in such theories by the perceived power of rhet. to constitute its object, that is, by the strange priority of effect over cause, thus reversing the traditional cause-and-effect relationship and taking the act of representation itself to be constitutive of the "origin" or cause which it supposedly mirrors. For deconstructive crit., "there are no originals; there are only copies," unavoidably repeated in their "failure to originate."

This upheaval in the structure and authority of i. is pursued on another front by Harold Bloom, who reverses the possibilities of i. of trad. by mapping out trad. as a battleground in which writers continually attempt to shake off or repress those precursors who would take away their freedom; in the process, these writers rewrite their precursors and become their cause.

Whether the term i. invokes Cl. models or nature, it rests on a metaphysics within which fulfillment is possible. But if the "original object" of i. is itself contaminated by the act of representing—if rhet. constitutes the object it purports to imitate—then i. shifts from the "re-presenting" of an "original" to a replication or doubling in which the original is displaced, inaccessible—imagined. The rhet. of presence and fulfillment opposes itself to the rhet. of desire, and loss; and the shift in the concept of i. from the one to the other aligns mimesis with violence (Girard). I. has become an important topic once again in critical theory precisely because it highlights the problematic relation to the "object" and the conception of history itself. It may well be, of course, that the very theoretical concerns which recognize the unstable play of i. and the problem of the original from Plato to Derrida are themselves instances of a mimetic replication by which theory constructs and realigns its models. See now F64044allusion; CRITICISM; CLASSICAL POETICS; CLASSICISM; CONVENTION; ICONICITY; INFLUENCE; INTERTEXTUALITY; INVENTION; ORIGINALITY; RENAISSANCE POETICS; REPRESENTATION AND MIMESIS; ROMANTIC AND POSTROMANTIC POETICS; SOUND; SPONTANEITY; TEXTUALITY; TRADITION.   H.R.E.

I. Scott, *Controversies Over I. of Cicero* (1910); S. H. Butcher, *Aristotle's Theory of Poetry and Fine Art*, 4th ed. (1911), ch. 2—suggestive, but overmodernizes; E. Nitchie, "Longinus and the Theory of Poetic I. in 17th- and 18th-C. England," *SP* 32 (1915); R. D. Havens, *The Influence of Milton on Eng. Poetry* (1922); U. Galli, "La mimèsi artistica secondo Aristotele," *Studi Ital. di Filol. Class.*, n.s. 4 (1926)—comprehensive, also covers Plato; J. W. Draper, "Aristotelian 'Mimesis' in 18th-C. England," *PMLA* 36 (1926); J. Tate, "I. in Plato's Republic," *ClassQ* 22 (1928), "Plato and I.," *ClassQ* 26 (1932); H. Gmelin, "Das Prinzip des *Imitatio* in den romanischen Literaturen der Ren.," *Romanischen Forschungen* 46 (1932); H. O. White, *Plagiarism and I. During the Ren.* (1935); R. McKeon, "Lit. Crit. and the Concept of I. in Antiquity," *MP* 34 (1936)—rpt. in Crane, and "I. and Poetry," *Thought, Action, and Passion* (1954)—discriminates types; M. T. Herrick, *The Fusion of Horatian and Aristotelian Lit. Crit, 1531–1555* (1946); H. F. Brooks, "The 'I.' in Eng. Poetry, Esp. in Formal Satire, before the Age of Pope," *RES* 25 (1949); W. J. Verdenius, *Mimesis* (1949); K. Burke, "A Dramatistic View of I.," *Accent* 12 (1952); Crane; Abrams, ch. 1–2; R. C. Lodge, *Plato's Theory of Art* (1953); R. R. Bolgar, *The Cl. Heritage and Its Beneficiaries* (1954); H. Koller, *Die Mimesis in der Antike* (1954)—ambitious but unreliable; Auerbach; Wimsatt and Brooks, ch. 10; G. F. Else, *Aristotle's Poetics: The Argument* (1957), "I. in the 5th C.," *CP* 53 (1958); V. F. Ulivi, *L'Imitazione nella poetica del Rinascimento* (1959); R. A. Brower, *Alexander Pope: The Poetry of Allusion* (1959); R. W. Dent, *John Webster's Borrowing* (1960); Weinberg; B. Hathaway, *The Age of Crit.* (1962); A. J. Smith, "Theory and Practice in Ren. Poetry: Two Kinds of I.," *BJRL* 47 (1964); G. Sorban, *Mimesis and Art: Studies in the Origin and Early Devel. of an Aesthetic Vocabulary* (1966); H. D. Weinbrot, "Translation and Parody: Towards the Genealogy of the Augustan I.," *ELH* 33 (1966); J. Derrida, *De la grammatologie* (1967), "La Mythologie blanche," *Marges de la philosophie* (1972), *La Dissémination* (1972); W. K. Wimsatt, Jr., "I. As Freedom—1717–1798," *NLH* 1 (1970); R. Girard, *La Violence et le sacré* (1972); J. Steadman, *The Lamb and the Elephant: Ideal I. and the Context of Ren. Allegory* (1974); *Mimesis*, ed. S. Agacinski et al. (1975)—esp. Derrida, "Economimesis"; G. Braden, *The Classics and Eng. Ren. Poetry* (1978); P. de Man, *Allegories of Reading* (1979); D. A. Russell, "De imitatione," *Creative I. and Lat. Lit.*, ed. D. West and A. Woodman (1979); G. W. Pigman, III, "Versions of I. in the Ren.," *RenQ* 33 (1980); L. Manley, *Convention 1500–1750* (1980); P. Ricoeur, "Mimesis and Representation," *Annals of Scholarship* 2 (1981); T. Greene, *The Light in Troy* (1982)—essential; J. H. Miller, *Fiction and Repetition* (1982); D. Quint, *Origin and Originality in Ren. Lit.* (1983); M. Ferguson, *Trials of Desire: Ren. Defenses of Poetry* (1983); De Man; B. J. Bono, *Literary Transvaluation From Vergilian Epic to Shakespearean Tragicomedy* (1984); J. Weinsheimer, *I.* (1984); N. Hertz, "A Reading of Longinus," *The End of the Line* (1985); J. L. Mahoney, *The Whole Internal Universe: I. and the New Defense in British Crit., 1660–1830* (1985); F. Stack, *Pope and Horace: Studies in I.* (1985); C. Prendergast, *The Order of Mimesis* (1986); G. B. Conte, *The Rhet. of I.*, ed. and tr. C. P. Segal (1986); S. K. Heninger, Jr., *Sidney and Spenser: The Poet as Maker* (1989); P. Lacoue-Labarthe, *Typography: Mimesis, Philosophy, Politics* (1989); R. W. Dasenbrock, *Imitating the Italians* (1991).   G.F.E.; H.R.E.

IMPAIR. See VERS IMPAIR.

IMPRESSIONISM. A term coined to identify a style of painting perfected in France during the later 1870s, most notably by Claude Monet, whose painting *Impression: Soleil Levant* (first shown in Paris, 1874) may have occasioned its first use. Its application to analogous phenomena in poetry soon followed, often in a manner that blurs the precise definition of critical categories. As the realization of an (unformulated) program, i. is one of several stylistic tendencies that emerged during the 1880s from the decline of realistic writing and its reliance on the mimetic function of lit. (see REALISM). I. thus came to share a penchant for subtle nuances, refined perception, and the ornamental use of "precious" images (see PRECIOSITE) with poetic Jugendstil (q.v.) and the decorative arts around 1900; its preference for the openness of allusive hints over conceptually fixed meanings and its fluid suggestion of atmosphere through a quick succession of sensory impressions were made possible at the expense of a clearly delineated world of concrete objects and have also been called "neoromantic." Were it not for their aversion to strict form and intense exactitude and thus to the principles of logical control, many impressionist poems might well be attributed to a symbolist aesthetic (see SYMBOLISM).

I. is fascinated with the spontaneous evocation of sensory and mental associations. It seeks to neutralize the mediating function of lang. (between the external world and the psyche) as well as its metaphorical qualities, which produced the concentrated meaning of the images in symbolist poetry, its inevitable successor. This preoccupation with fleeting sensations and their microscopic diversity is a response to a later 19th-c. crisis of identity and of personality of which Nietzsche had been the first analyst and the sensualist epistemology of Ernst Mach the popularized expression. It held to the notion that reality is its perception and that the individual is not a homogeneous unity but a complex agglomeration of reminiscences, nerve impulses, moods, and sensations. As a result, the most subtle and versatile practice of impressionist technique—in Verlaine's collections *Bonne chanson* (1870) and *Romances sans paroles* (1874), and in the religious verse of his *Sagesse* (1881), in the *vers libre* poems of Jules Laforgue, and in Mallarmé's *Après-midi d'un faune* (1887, illustr. by Manet and set to music by Debussy)—shows a predilection for synaesthesia and onomatopoeia (qq.v.) and for suggestive sound and rhythmic effects. Such attention to the subtlest nuances of lang. reveals an attitude of refined, often introspective observation, of ironic detachment, and of melancholy ambivalence. In Verlaine's *Art poétique* (1884), impressionist poetry was given its most congenial justification, without any attempt, however, at estabishing i. as a critical term. In general, most later European poetry, such as Stefan George's *Das Jahr der Seele* (1897) and Rainer Maria Rilke's *Neue Gedichte* (1907–8), resists subsumption under the essential definition of i., even though it retains some impressionist characteristics.

It is not advisable to extend the use of the label i. beyond its narrow application to a short phase of Ger. lit. hist. at the end of the 19th c. I. was neither a period style nor a school of poetry; there were only a number of marginal poets who practiced their craft to the limit of its potential. Of these, Detlev von Liliencron (1844–1909), the prolific Richard Dehmel (1863–1920), Max Dauthendey (1867–1918) with his preference for an exotic ambience, and Gustav Falke (1853–1916) deserve mention. Arno Holz (1863–1929) soon abandoned his naturalist beginnings and devoted much of his life to one hypertrophic book-length poem, *Phantasus* (1898). In this, the associative accumulation of myriad impressions, constant shifts in perspective, disparate arrangement of words around an imaginary "central axis," and elimination of conceptual prescience may have approached the ideal of impressionist versatility, but it soon turned into an amorphous panorama of trivia.

L. Thon, *Die Sprache des deutschen Impressionismus* (1928); C. Bally et al., *El Impressionismo en el Lenguaje* (1936); R. Moser, *L'Impressionnisme français* (1951); B. J. Gibbs, "I. as a Literary Movement," *MLJ* 36 (1952); W. Ramsey, *Jules Laforgue and the Ironic Inheritance* (1953); J. Lethève, *Impressionnistes et symbolistes devant la presse* (1959); K. Brinkmann, *Impressionismus und Expressionismus in deutscher Literatur* (1960); H. Sommerhalter, *Zum Begriff des literarischen Impressionismus* (1961); R. Hamann and J. Hermand, *Impressionismus* (1972). M.W.

IMPRESSIONISTIC CRITICISM. See CRITICISM.

IN MEDIAS RES (Lat. "into the middle of things"). The device of beginning an epic (q.v.) poem, drama, or work of fiction at some crucial point in the middle of a series of events which both initiates a subsequent chain of incidents and at the same time follows as the result of preceding ones. Thus the author may work forward and backward in time to narrate the story or action. The effect is to arouse the reader's suspense and interest quickly. The phrase is taken from Horace's *Ars poetica* (147–48): "Always [the poet] hastens to the outcome and plunges his hearer into the midst of events as though they were familiar, and what he despairs of treating effectively he abandons." The suggestion that a poet should not begin "at the beginning" derives from Aristotle's argument in the *Poetics* that a plot is a specific arrangement of incidents unified by probability and necessity, not sequence. Aristotle is recalling Homer: the *Odyssey* begins with the shipwreck of Odysseus after some ten years of wandering the Mediterranean, and the *Iliad* is not about the whole siege of Troy but a single episode in the last year of the war.

Horace's formulation became a standard convention and was discussed as such throughout the Middle Ages. During the Ren. *i. m. r.* was revived, critics distinguishing between "natural" (i.e. chronological) and "artificial" order. The effect of "artificial" order is to fold the time sequence of the narrative so that the poem opens at an especially dramatic moment and then, at a later moment, includes a "retrospective episode" that recounts the origin of the events. The events depicted in Milton's *Paradise Lost*, for example, begin chronologically with the rebellion of Satan, the War in Heaven, and the expulsion of the fallen angels, but the poem itself opens with the activities of the fallen angels in Hell (Books 1–2) after the expulsion. The plot moves forward from this point until Books 5 and 6, when Raphael tells Adam of the dire consequences of disobeying God's laws. In other words, the *i. m. r.* convention has made it more complex—more polyvalent.

By contrast, a simpler version of *i. m. r.* is invoked by Edmund Spenser in the "Letter to Raleigh" purporting to explain *The Faerie Queene*. There Spenser explains that the final meaning of all the adventures will be withheld until the last (12th) book of the poem—which, however, he never completed. The model of *i. m. r.* adopted by Ariosto in *Orlando Furioso* is a more complex variation on the convention: here "artificial" order justifies multiple plotting, frequent digressions, and a mosaic-like arrangement of flashbacks and continuing narratives.

After the neoclassical period the formal requirement of *i. m. r.* was ignored, but the precedent it established for complex foldings of narrative time is preserved in the device of flashback and the narrative reminiscence, as, for example, in Faulkner's *The Sound and the Fury*.—J. W. Draper, "The Narrative Technique of the *Faerie Queene*," *PMLA* 39 (1924); C. O. Brink, *Horace on Poetry*, 2 v. (1963–71); F. Quadlbauer, "Zur Theorie der Komposition in der mittelalterlichen Rhetorik und Poetik," *Rhet. Revisited*, ed. B. Stock (1982); O. B. Hardison, Jr., "*I. m. r.* in *Paradise Lost*," *MiltonS* 17 (1983).   O.B.H.; R.A.H.

IN MEMORIAM STANZA. A stanza of four lines of iambic tetrameter, rhyming *abba*; so called from its use in Tennyson's *In Memoriam* (1850):

> I hold it true, whate'er befall;
>   I feel it when I sorrow most;
>   'Tis better to have loved and lost
> Than never to have loved at all.

Although Tennyson believed he had invented the stanza, it may be found in 17th-c. poetry, notably Ben Jonson ("If Beauty be the Mark of Praise"), and Lord Herbert of Cherbury ("Ode upon a Question Moved, whether Love Should Continue for ever"). It is true however, that Tennyson exploited the inherent formal capacities of the stanza more extensively and with greater mastery than did his predecessors. In particular, he utilized its suitability for successive, mutually independent philosophical observations, each enclosed within its stanzaic "envelope," and its possibilities for special emphasis through the rhyme of first and fourth lines. Later uses of the stanza are rare; one is Oscar Wilde's "The Sphinx," in which the stanza is printed as two lines. See ALCAIC.—Schipper 3.546; Saintsbury 2.203–6; E. P. Morton, "The Stanza of I. M.," *MLN* 21 (1906), "Poems in the Stanza of I. M.," *MLN* 24 (1909).   A.PR.

INCA POETRY. See AMERICAN INDIAN POETRY, *South American*.

INCANTATION (Lat. *incantare*, to chant, bewitch, cast a spell). Use of a ritualistic formula spoken or chanted to produce a magical effect or charm (q.v.); more generally, a chant (q.v.) used in magi-

cal ceremonies or sorcery: "With nigromaunce he wolde assaile / To make his incantacion" (Gower, *Confessio amantis* 3.45). Also the magical spell itself: "Double, double, toil and trouble" (Shakespeare, *Macbeth*). Frazer discusses i. under homeopathic magic, though several of his examples are not magic but simply petitions to gods or spirits to undertake a desired action. Similar are other ancient examples such as the Babylonian is., which are ritualistic formulae associated with the act of burning images of one's enemies (the great Mesopotamian series of is. are known as the *Surpu* and *Maqlû*, both words meaning *burning*); the verbs are usually in the optative rather than the indicative mood (*may it happen* rather than *it will happen*), suggesting prayer rather than magic. In Hittite, at the dedication of a building a piece of copper is deposited in the foundation with the i., "As this copper is firm and sound, so may the house be firm and sound." Related are such voodoo practices as thrusting pins into a doll to cause pain or death, usually accompanied by an i. See also SOUND.—Sir J. Frazer, *The Golden Bough* (1890); B. Meissner, *Babylonien und Assyrien* (1920–25); G. Meier, *Die assyrische Beschwörungssammlung Maqlû* (1937).   R.O.E.

INCREMENTAL REPETITION. F. B. Gummere's phrase for a rhetorical device he believed to be a distinguishing feature of the Eng. and Scottish popular ballads (see BALLAD). In i. r. a line or stanza is repeated successively with some small but material substitution at the same crucial spot. A sequence of such repetition accounts for the entire structure of some few ballads, among them "Edward" and "Lord Randal"; the latter uses i. r. in the form of question and answer; "The Maid Freed from the Gallows" combines this with the "climax of relatives," another typical form. More commonly, though, i. r. spans a passage of only 3 or 4 stanzas, and it is frequently confined to the lines of a single quatrain, as in the following stanza from "Sir Hugh; or, The Jew's Daughter":

> Then out and came the thick, thick
>   blood,
>   Then out and came the thin;
>   Then out and came the bonny heart's
>   blood,
> Where all the life lay in.

This kind of repetition is different from the kind of additive repetition found in "This is the House that Jack Built" or "The Twelve Days of Christmas." Gummere thought i. r. a litmus test of a true oral ballad, but later scholars have demurred (Gerould); Bronson shows the influence of the music.

Though i. r. is common in the Eng. and Scottish ballads, it is also found in much oral or oral-derived poetry (see ORAL POETRY), from the ancient Sumerian epic *Gilgamesh*, to old Welsh poetry, to Portuguese folksong, to Zulu song, to songs of the

Teleut in Siberia, not to mention other Anglo-Am. folksongs that are not ballads. I. r. is but one of a number of devices characteristic of oral poetry and song that facilitate composition and memorization; and in audition it sometimes produces an effect of suspense or emotional intensification. In songs and ballads, it can enhance the music by reducing the density of the verbal component and by reinforcing parallels established by the repeated melody.—F. B. Gummere, *The Popular Ballad* (1907), esp. 117–24; L. Pound, *Poetic Origins and the Ballad* (1921)—sharply critical; G. H. Gerould, *The Ballad of Trad.* (1932), 105 ff.; K. Jackson, "I. R. in the Early Welsh Englyn," *Speculum* 16 (1942); D. K. Wilgus, *Anglo-Am. Folklore Scholarship Since 1898* (1959); R. D. Abrahams and G. Foss, *Anglo-Am. Folksong Style* (1968); W. F. H. Nicolaisen, "How I. Is I. R.?" *Ballads and Ballad Research*, ed. P. Conroy (1978). A.B.F.; E.D.; T.V.F.B.

INDETERMINACY. A term drawn from poststructuralist crit. which suggests the impossibility of stabilizing a text's (or word's) meaning. In traditional lit. hist., meaning is either inherent in the work or produced by context. But when context itself is drawn into the conditions of textuality, all connections one may make to "determine" meaning are open to this originary instability of lang. See AMBIGUITY; INTERTEXTUALITY; SIMPLICITY AND COMPLEXITY; TEXTUALITY.—M. Perloff, *The Poetics of I.* (1981); G. Graff, "Determinacy/I.," *Critical Terms for Literary Study*, ed. F. Lentricchia and T. McLaughlin (1990); B. J. Martine, *I. and Intelligibility* (1992). H.R.E.

INDEX. See REPRESENTATION AND MIMESIS; SEMIOTICS, POETIC.

INDIAN POETICS. Inviting as it might be, it would be misleading to see in Vedic lit. (ca. 1500–500 B.C.) a fully developed aesthetics. Certain terms, such as "rasa" ("taste, essence") or "alaṁkāra" ("making adequate, ornament") indeed occur in the Vedas, but they are not used there in any sense remotely suggestive of their centrality to the technically elaborate later systems. This does not mean, however, that we may not seek the origins of poetic theorizing in the Veda and its ancillary lit. Indeed, we should see in the *Mīmāṃsā* system of ritual exegetics (early first millenium A.D.) the first clear espousal of what was to become a leitmotif of I. cultural history—the notion that the Vedic *text* should be understood as having a self-defining reality. The *Mīmāṃsā*, then, is one of the earliest instances of literary theorizing known to us; it codified in unmistakable terms the cultural status of an entire lit. The end, though religious, should not be mistaken; as with any crit., the text is elevated above mundane expression and given the status of a communication available only to the elect.

In its technical apparatus too the *Mīmāṃsā* for-mulates a vocabulary and the conceptual outline of a poetics for the first time in I. history (see Śabara's commentaries to *Mīmāṃsāsūtra* 1.1.32 and 1.2.10 ff. [tr. G. Jha, *Śabara Bhāṣya*, 1933, 1.50, 58 ff.]; and Kumārila's commentary to 1.2.10 ff. [tr. G. Jha, *Tantra Vārttika*, 1924, 1.40 ff.]). Here we find both the distinction between the literal and the figurative and also the notion that figurative usages have a different kind of motivation, and must ultimately derive their authority (viz., their interpretation, their meaning) from a specific relation to the literal—ideas both fundamental to later I. poetics.

It should be made clear that we presume here the distinction between an implicit and an explicit poetics. The Vedic hymns give evidence of an elaborate and partly self-conscious practical poetics. Many hymns were doubtless composed by a professional class of poets (*kavi*), who frequently engaged in officially sanctioned competitions. The later hymns often have an academic cast and reflect conventions of composition that must have been evident to the cognoscenti (*sahṛdaya*). But despite all this inferential evidence, the beginnings of an explicit trad. of speculation *on* poetry—understood as a mode of expression and not simply in terms of some accident of its content, religious fervor or ritual inaccuracy—are found only in the cl. period (ca. 500 A.D. and later).

The I. epic *Rāmāyaṇa* (late first millennium B.C.), in a passage near the beginning of the poem (*Rām.* 1.2.9 ff.), also presents us with a myth accounting for the invention of poetry (*kāvya*)— by which is meant the *Rāmāyaṇa* itself—often styled the "ādikāvya," or "first poem." The bard Vālmīki identifies poetry not with the epic story, but with the form of its verse: *śloka*, the ubiquitous 8-syllable foot of Sanskrit didactic lit. Two other crucial themes are suggested in this myth: by a kind of pun, the *verse* (*śloka*) is associated with an *emotion* (viz., *śoka*, "grief"), and poetry as a kind of lang. is given a grounding in nature—it is the "sweet song" of the *krauñca* (cuckoo) grieving for its slain mate that Vālmīki transmutes into human song. The themes of the inextricability of convention with its natural basis, and with its proper response, are nowhere better formulated than in this simple tale, which again attributes a special character to the poet—still the "kavi," the quasi-magician who first "discovers" and best understands this semiological relation fundamental (i.e. which gives structure) to the universe.

The earliest extant text that begins to tie together these strains into a coherent and explicit poetics is the *Nāṭyaśāstra*, a compendium on theatrical theory and practice attributed to the sage Bharata which was composed over several centuries and edited in its present form about the end of the 6th c. A.D. But poetics still is ancillary to the larger purposes of the treatise, which seeks rather to give a comprehensive account of the stagecraft of the cl. Sanskrit drama. In the discussion of a suitable theatrical audience is formulated for the first time the notion of *rasa*,—now properly *aesthetic* "relish" (literally, "taste": the gustatory implication is etymologically correct), a characteristic emotional response to the drama which both serves as its proper end and integrates its elements—the story, the speeches, the actions, and even the scenery. At first, eight characteristic responses are defined: the amorous, the heroic, the comic, the pitiable, the violent, the disgusting, the fearsome, and the wondrous. Later a ninth, the peaceful, is added, and still later others, testifying to the increasing emotionalism of I. religions. From Bharata onwards, however, love, the amorous (*śṛṅgāra*), figures as the *rasa* par excellence.

Among the elements thus integrated, the lang. of the play is given prominent treatment; and for the first time is sketched a theory of what makes lang. poetic—still seen as *effective*, but whose purposes are neither religious nor didactic. Implicitly, what is being communicated is the novel emotion spoken of above, but our attention is drawn here to the equally novel techniques of that communication—those features of expression that define lang. as nonliteral, that direct the hearer away from the straightforward sense of the words to the many sided and always partly hidden context in which they are embedded. Bharata clearly understood simile (*upamā*) as the most important and perhaps the fundamental such expressive device. The use of this figure is for the early Indians coextensive with poetry, and what marks it as poetic is its persistent reference to another realm of discourse (*upamāna*) alongside of, but characteristically highlighting, the presumed "subject" of discourse (*upameya*). The relation between the two layers either immediately or ultimately brings the focus of the expression back to the context of the expression, which alone provides a proper motivation for the use of such elaborate lang. in the first place. Among possible determining contexts figures most importantly the mood, the emotional response, of the audience—esp. in the theater, where the audience is not just an abstraction, but a presence whose immediacy is a challenge: "moving" them is a first-level test of whether anything is happening on the stage.

In the lit. immediately following the *Nāṭyaśāstra*, these two themes seem to be taken up independently, defining two poetic trads.: the problem of the figures and nonliteral lang. preoccupies one (*alaṃkāraśāstra*: early texts date from the 8th to 11th cs.), whereas the question of the proper and integrating response is more and more the focus of the other (*rasaśāstra*, or *nāṭyaśāstra* proper: early texts date from the 10th and 11th cs.). Evidently a combination of historical developments underlay this separation. The performance trad. of Sanskrit theater suffered a decline with the lapse of Gupta patronage, causing Sanskrit *belles lettres* to take on a more exclusively literary aspect, which in turn awakened a need to understand a dramatic poetry that was only read and never performed—had, in effect, become a kind of *kāvya*. And to the extent that the integrating response can be separated from the actual technique of its evocation, it can serve as a general integrating principle for lit. as such.

For two or three centuries after the *Nāṭyaśāstra*, the *nāṭya* lit. is rather sparse; the *alaṃkāraśāstra* dominates the discussion. Well over one hundred figures are defined and examined by a series of authors, from Bhāmaha and Daṇḍin (probably 7th c. A.D., the latter being arguably the same Daṇḍin who composed the famous *Daśakumāracarita*, or *Hist. of the Ten Princes*) to Rudraṭa and Mammaṭa. The later writers also attempted to classify the figures into types and variations. Rudraṭa pursues the question most systematically, identifying four basic kinds of figurative lang., based on comparison, hyperbole, punning, and "the thing itself." The principle of the first is similitude, of the second, relations other than likeness, of the third, polysemy (relations grounded on the word alone), and of the fourth, obliteration of the relation between species and genus.

Most of what we know of the *rasaśāstra* strand of poetic theorizing during this period is gleaned from later commentaries, notably Abhinavagupta's *Bhāratī* (see below), and is best discussed in that connection. Several treatises, such as Dhanaṃjaya's *Daśarūpaka* (10th c.), survive which attempt to abstract from the *Nāṭyaśāstra* its core of theory, concerning on the one hand plot construction and characterization—suitable to the writing of plays—and on the other emotional response, which, separated from a concrete theatrical context, inevitably wears more and more a psychological guise. So too, it seems, did Sanskrit drama become an exclusively literary problem. Plays continued to be written but were rarely performed.

The most influential period of I. poetic theory is inaugurated by the Kāśmīra Ānandavardhana (early 9th c.), author of the *Dhvanyāloka* (the Illumination of Suggestion). The text is a gloss on the *kārikās* embedded in it, which are often attributed to an anonymous "Dhvanikāra." Some, however, believe Ānanda to be the author of the *kārikās* as well. In this work, the two divergent strands of post-Bharata speculation are brought together in a grand synthesis organized around the notion of the implicit meaning, which, it is claimed, is most characteristically (for poetry) its emotional message. The linguistic and expressionistic aspect of the theory is the more startling, however, for Ānanda claims that this emotional message—the *rasa*—is communicated by a semantic capacity of lang. other than and complementary to the generally recognized capacities of literal denotation and metonymy. This novel capacity he calls *dhvani*, which means literally "noise" or "sound," but by recursion (an instance of itself) "overtone," "suggestion." The notion of poetic context, always crucial in distinguishing poetic lang. from other kinds of speech, is here made the very center and soul of poetry, around which the ordinary capacities of lang. hover and which they serve. This synthesis not only reconciles theories of linguistic expressionism and emotional consequence; it also demonstrates the unity of the genres of poem and play (*kāvya* and *nāṭya*).

Abhinavagupta, a Kāśmīra of the 11th c. whose name is today synonymous with I. p., wrote commentaries on both *Dhvanyāloka* and *Nāṭyaśāstra*, called *Locana* and *Bhārati*, respectively, in which he rethought the entire problem of poetic lang. and poetic purpose in the light of an ancient truth that had again come to dominate Hinduism affected by the extreme devotionalism of the late medieval period: namely, that the most powerful forms of lang., and ipso facto, poetry, were the *via regia* to forms of experience that are not of this world. In effect, Abhinava proposed an even grander synthesis than Ānanda, for now the context of art is not so much differentiated from mundane modes of experience and signification as it is integrated wiht higher forms of religious experience, and in effect signifies them most truly. (Abhinavagupta is also the great theologian of Kāśmīra Śaivism, and author of the *Tantrāloka*).

Abhinava accomplishes this grand design in good I. fashion by reformulating the poetic trad. itself, most notably, the emotional and affective aspects of the theory focusing on *rasa*. Abhinava carries the inquiry, as might be expected, into truly psychological realms, concerning himself with questions of how and by whom the *rasa* is experienced, and what are its cognitive criteria. The notion of *rasa* is here given its classic formulation, for indeed *rasa* is reconceived *as* an experience (and not simply functionally, as a goal, or as a content of meaning), one that most closely resembles the liberating cognition (*mokṣa*) itself. Abhinava, commenting on the famous *rasasūtra* of Bharata, traces the history of speculation on *rasa* in the intervening period and shows how the notion evolved from that of a purely functional (quasi-realistic) effect (*Lollaṭa*), to that of an artifice achieved by imitation (*Śaṅkuka*), to that of an affect or emotion not really caused at all, but simply evoked (Abhinava's teacher Tauta). The crucial aspect of Abhinava's own theory is attributed to Bhaṭṭa Nāyaka, who first suggested that the status of *rasa* as an emotion had to be qualified in order to account for the peculiar power of drama to communicate. Emotions in the literal sense (termed *bhāva*) are private and particular to individuals and circumstances. In that sense, what the actor and the author and the audience experience is irremediably different, and no community of experience is implied. But the drama, the poem, now seen as a technique—thus updating Ānandavardhana's *dhvani*—by its very contrafactual status generalizes the conditions of emotion and consequently generalizes or abstracts emotion

itself—makes it into something essentially shared. *This* is Abhinava's *rasa*, emotion turned inside out—determining its conditions (the fictive play) rather than being determined by them (the real world)—and thus free of its conditions. Abhinava interprets this inversion as the experience of the *possibility* of experience itself, an experience that both cancels the boundaries separating men and kindles in them a desire for the essentially similar experience of liberation, seen as the Advaita inversion of cognitive point of view: the precondition of being is understood as more real than the particular manifestations of being.

Though Abhinava's *rasa* theory has become canonical, it has not exhausted the I. speculative spirit. Indeed, the emphasis on *rasa* as a kind of metaphysical bliss is neatly complemented by a renewed realism in other authors, who interpret *rasa* much more concretely as the bliss of love. In the Bengali Vaiṣṇava writers of the 16th c., notably Rūpagosvāmin, author of the *Ujjvalanīlamaṇī*, this is turned into a theology of loving God (*bhaktirasa*); in others, deriving from the encyclopaedist Bhoja (11th-c. king of Dhāra, author of the longest I. poetic work, the *Śṛṅgāraprakāśa*), *śṛṅgāra* itself, ordinary human amorousness, is elevated to the theoretical prominence it has always enjoyed in practice.

It is safe to say that the notion of *rasa*, however conceived, is the decisive achievement of I. p., and even today must be understood in order to appreciate not only the lit. but all the other art forms of the subcontinent—from Carnatic music to the films of Satyajit Ray—and this despite the introduction and sometime cultivation, in the 20th c., of Western literary modes. It is even more influential in the surviving folk idioms of India, and has been canonized in the aesthetic of the popular cinema, even when it thinks of itself as "realistic." Formal theories of aesthetics during the late medieval and modern periods, whether applying to Sanskrit or the vernacular langs., show little tendency to deviate from the concepts or terminology established by Abhinava or Bharata. (In the modern universities, of course, a quasi-Western aesthetics is cultivated.) The notion of *rasa* has many parallels in Western poetics, most notably among the "synaesthesists" (cf. C. K. Ogden, I. A. Richards, and J. Wood, *The Foundations of Aesthetics* [1925]; more recently, Suzanne Langer, *Feeling and Form* [1953]; also the theory of "detachment" espoused by José Ortega y Gasset).

S. K. De, *Hist. of Sanskrit Poetics*, 2d ed., 2 v. (1960), *Sanskrit Poetics as a Study of Aesthetic* (1963); V. Raghavan, *Bhoja's Śṛṅgāraprakāśa* (1963); K. C. Pandey, *Abhinavagupta* (1963); D. H. H. Ingalls, Gen. Intro., *An Anthol. of Sanskrit Court Poetry* (1965); E. Gerow, *A Glossary of I. Figures of Speech* (1971), *I. Poetics* (1977); K. Krishnamoorthy, *Ānandavardhana's Dhvanyāloka (1974)*; E. C. Dimock, Jr., et al., *The Lit. of India: An Intro. (1974)*; S. Dhayagude, *Western and I. P.: A Com-*

INDIAN POETRY

parative Study *(1981);* Theater of Memory, *ed. B. S. Miller (1984); V. K. Chari,* Sanskrit Crit. *(1990).*

E.G.

INDIAN POETRY.

I. OVERVIEW. The term "I. p." commonly refers to the immense and diverse body of usually metrical, often religious, and highly imagistic lit. produced on the I. subcontinent between about 1200 B.C. and the present. This region, which now consists mainly of India, Pakistan, and Bangladesh, is as large and varied as Western Europe. I. p. does not belong to a single, cohesive trad. but rather constitutes a constellation of numerous interacting trads. in about 20 major langs. and several hundred dialects, most of which are used widely in South Asia today.

The langs. of the I. subcontinent have preserved their poetic trads. in oral as well as written forms, using several different scripts both native and foreign. The langs. belong to four families: the Indo-Aryan (a branch of Indo-European, incl. Sanskrit, Hindi-Urdu, and Bengali), the Dravidian (the fourth largest lang. family in the world, containing 25 langs., particularly Tamil, which dates from the second century B.C.), the Austro-Asiatic (which includes many I. tribal langs.), and the Sino-Tibetan (incl. Burmese). The first two of these have dominated I. culture from the beginning. The oldest poetic trad. belongs to Sanskrit, which first achieved canonical status before 1000 B.C. and continued to flourish until the 18th c., while the youngest of the major lits. belongs to Urdu, which emerged only in the 16th c. This article covers the poetic trads. and cultural contexts in all the major Indo-Aryan and Dravidian langs., the primary subjects being Vedic, Sanskrit, Prakrit, Bengali, Hindi, Indian-English, Kannada, Marathi, Tamil, and Urdu poetry, with occasional examples from Gujarati, Malayalam, Panjabi, and Telugu. For more information on poetry in the last-mentioned set of langs., and in langs. we have not discussed—particularly Assamese, Kashmiri, Oriya, and Sindhi—the reader should consult the specialized works on these trads. listed in the bibl. (e.g. Gonda [1973–]; Zelliot; Heifetz and Narayana Rao;

Sarma; Kachru).

For the greater part of the present millennium, the Indo-Aryan and Dravidian mother tongues (which are vernaculars as distinct from literary or cl. Sanskrit) have been associated with specific regions of the subcontinent along surprisingly fixed lines. In addition, particular "foreign" langs., esp. Persian (between the 13th and 19th cs.) and Eng. (since the late 18th c.), have periodically come into widespread use, thus greatly complicating the issues of linguistic, regional, national, and cultural identity, as well as of literary style, artistic quality, and poetic trad. In addition to this regional linguistic complexity, itself intensified by the universal prestige enjoyed by Sanskrit in the cl. period and Persian in the middle, there is the greater complexity resulting from the fact that, over the past 1500 years, different langs. have exploded into exemplary creativity and affected the entire I. culture without really becoming nationally spoken langs.; examples of this are Tamil in the middle period and Bengali in the modern period.

The concept of "poetry" in the different I. trads. is reflected in the various native systems of poetic genres. For about 2500 years, I. theorists and literati have often used the word *kāvya* for poetry to distinguish it from other kinds of verbal composition. In its earliest and narrowest meaning (ca. 500 B.C.), the term *kāvya* was used to characterize the poetry of the *Rāmāyaṇa,* which is epic in scope, narrative in structure, and lyrical in effect. In this sense, *kāvya* (as distinguished from the *mantras* or formulaic hymns of the Vedas) signified poetry in the *śloka* meter (see INDIAN PROSODY), with relatively unadorned diction and simplified syntax; the term therefore could also be used to describe the poetic qualities of the other major epic of the period, the *Mahābhārata.* In its somewhat wider and slightly later meaning in the late cl. period, *kāvya* signifies composition in verse, intended to create the experience of *rasa* or a particular set of poetic emotions in the audience (see INDIAN POETICS). In this sense *kāvya* is of two basic kinds which will be further discussed below: (1) *mahākāvya,* great or major poetry, and (2) *laghukāvya,* short or minor poetry.

In its widest sense, popular around A.D. 700–1200, *kāvya* signifies the full range of imaginative composition, both in verse (*padya*) and prose (*gadya*) and mixtures of verse and prose (*miśra*). It now also includes dramatic or other texts meant for performance, which were composed in verse or prose or both and were often multilingual (in cl. Sanskrit drama, different characters speak different langs. or dialects, depending on their social and regional origins). *Kāvya* further includes prose narrative, both "fictional" (*kathā*) and "non-fictional" (*ākhyāyikā*), such as short stories, novellas and novels, moral tales, fables, biographies, and "true stories." The widest meaning of *kāvya* in the latter part of the ancient period thus coincides with the meaning of lit. itself (called *vāṇmaya* or *sāhitya*), although the term still does not cover the "total order of words" in the various langs. (Sanskrit, the Prakrits, and the several Jain langs. called the Apabhraṃśas) to which it is systematically applied. Because this conception of *kāvya* is so inclusive, I. theorists refine it by distinguishing between *dṛśya kāvya*, poetry that has to be seen in performance to be properly understood ("drama"), and *śravya kāvya*, poetry that needs only to be heard to be fully grasped ("epic," "lyric," "prose").

In the ancient period, *kāvya* was part of several distinct "Hindu" systems of genres, two of which are worth mentioning here. The first of these systems distinguishes between *śruti* and *smṛti*. The genre of *śruti* (hearing, that which is heard) consists of texts that record "original revelation," while the much larger and more varied genre of *smṛti* (recollection, that which is remembered) contains the "received trad." that has grown up around the *śruti*. Although much of the *śruti* (the Vedic texts) and the *smṛti* (authoritative discourse on religious, philosophical, mythological, social, and political matters, such as the *Manusmṛti* and the *Dharmaśāstras*) is composed in verse, it is considered sacred and canonical and falls outside the sphere of *kāvya*. By the end of the ancient period, however, some texts admitted into the category of *smṛti* (such as the *Mahābhārata* and the *Bhagavadgītā* within it) qualify as *kāvya*. As a consequence, what *kāvya* is in any of its narrow and wider senses also depends on the other types of discourse to which it is related and from which it is distinguished.

The second major system of genres distinguishes between *itihāsa*, *purāṇa*, and *kāvya*. An *itihāsa* is a received or traditional history, such as the *Mahābhārata*, a record and explanation of past, present, and predicted future events on an epic scale. A *purāṇa*, on the other hand, is an "old text," a more popular or sectarian account of affairs in the world, and is focused on a temple or religious community. In contrast, a *kāvya* is distinguished by its aesthetic qualities and purposes, its creation of poetic emotions and pleasurable fictions. If *itihāsa* and *purāṇa* are modes of discourse "about" the world, then *kāvya* remains suspended in a realm of imaginative effect and memorable entertainment, and stands only in a potential relation to the world of everyday experience. *Itihāsa* and *purāṇa* thus shift towards *smṛti* and *śruti* to constitute a broad continuum of culturally and ideologically authoritative or "true" discourse, while *kāvya* as *vāṇmaya* or *sāhitya* (lit.) stands apart as fictive discourse (Tripp).

These and other such concepts are discussed in greater detail in recent crit. on I. p. (Dimock et al., 1974; Ingalls). Here, we shall use a mixture of I. and Western theories of poetry to describe some of the most important poetic trads. of the subcontinent over three millennia, and esp. to show how

I. *kāvya* in its various senses changes, often irreversibly, and profoundly alters the ancient notion of *kāvya* itself. In our discussion of the ancient period, we shall concentrate on three different types of Sanskrit (verse) composition: (a) *śruti* or *mantra* (the Vedas); (b) *itihāsa* (the *Mahābhārata*); and (c) *kāvya* (from the epic *Rāmāyaṇa* to cl. *mahākāvya* and *laghukāvya* and their successors).

II. THE ANCIENT PERIOD (ca. 1200 B.C.–A.D. 1200). If we set aside the large lits. in the Buddhist lang. Pali and the Apabhraṃśas (the "fallen speech" varieties used by authors of the Jain religion towards the end of the ancient period), I. p. between about 1200 B.C. and A.D. 1200 was written chiefly in various forms of Sanskrit, the oldest of which (Vedic) reflects the patterns of a spoken lang. The 40 or more Prakrits that appeared later in this period probably evolved from the emerging common speech varieties of the subcontinent, and were closely related to Sanskrit in linguistic as well as literary terms.

A. *Vedic Poetry.* The Vedas, probably composed in the second half of the second millennium B.C. and redacted around 1000 B.C., contain the oldest surviving I. p. There are four Vedic collections (*samhitas*). The earliest (and best known in the West) is the *Ṛgveda* or the Veda of the Stanzas.

The *Ṛgveda* contains 1028 poems averaging ten verses in length, addressed to a wide variety of gods and treating a large assortment of themes. Among the gods it invokes in hymns, prayers, and supplications are Agni, Indra, Varuṇa, and Rudra, and among its recurrent themes are creation, birth, death, sacrifice, *soma*, earth, sky, water, dawn, night, women, and the horse of sacrifice. The verse is cryptic and the symbolism often obscure, but many of the *Ṛgvedic* poems are imagistic and disjointed, and even brilliantly surreal. The poems include natural descriptions, dramatized human and divine interactions, and condensed narratives and myths of various kinds, as well as riddles, epigrams, and spells. Although the context of these poems is ritual and the facts of performance are now complicated by the passage of time, many of them are poetically superb—strikingly fresh in imagery, dense in structure, memorable in sound and phrasing (O'Flaherty).

The second collection, the *Yajurveda* or the Veda of the Formulas, contains sacred formulas in verse which priests recite at the Vedic sacrifice. The third, the *Sāmaveda* or the Veda of the Chants, is mainly an anthol. of material found in the *Ṛgveda*. The fourth, the *Atharvaveda* or the Veda of the *atharvan* (a special kind of priest), brings together many sorts of prayers, incantations, spells, magic formulas, and songs. The Vedic verse collections are supplemented by three main kinds of later canonical discourse. The *Brāhmaṇas* are commentaries on the ritual aspects of the Vedas, while the *Āraṇyakas* are "books studied in the forests" (where early Hindu renouncers, sages, and seers seem frequently to have congregated);

both are written in expository and narrative prose. The third type of discourse consists of the *Upaniṣads*, collections of "esoteric equations," which are also largely in prose, although some of the later *Upaniṣads*, produced around 500 B.C., contain some of the earliest didactic poetry, a very significant genre in the I. trad.

The four Vedas, esp. the *Ṛgveda*, and the 13 principal *Upaniṣads* have exercised an enormous influence on Hindu and I. culture, at least among the dominant castes and classes. The primary literary influences of Vedic poetry, however, have been quite specific, among which three are particularly important. First, the anonymous Vedic poets, esp. of the *Ṛgveda*, "invented" a substantial amount of the I. poetic imagery that has undergone endless variation and amplification in the various I. langs. over the succeeding 3000 years— e.g. sun, fire, rivers, horses, cows, frogs, monsoon rain, flowers. Second, the Vedic poets established a simple formal and structural principle for non-narrative verse that dominated much I.-lang. poetry until the last quarter of the 19th c.: each verse must express one complete poetic thought. Third, Vedic poetic practice established the caesura that divides a line of premodern I. verse into two equal or unequal portions. Vedic meters provided the basis for the numerous simple and intricate meters that subsequently came to dominate Sanskrit and I.-lang. poetry (Keith; Lienhard; Dimock et al. 1974).

B. *Sanskrit Epic Poetry.* Between about 700 B.C. and A.D. 500, Sanskrit poets drew on a long trad. of bardic narrative, martial stories, and heroic tales, as well as popular accounts of specific historical events, to create the two major epics, the *Rāmāyaṇa* and the *Mahābhārata*. Although both these composite poems are traditionally attributed to specific I. authors, the latter, especially, clearly has been composed and edited collectively over a long period of time. The *Rāmāyaṇa*, attributed to Vālmīki—who may well have composed its central portion—was probably completed earlier, between about 600 and 300 B.C.; the *Mahābhārata*, attributed to Vyāsa ("the compiler"), is usually placed between about 500 B.C. and A.D. 500. The term "epic" can be applied only loosely to these works, however, for they have little in common with the conventions and structures of the Western epic trad. as defined by Homer, Virgil, Dante, and Milton. I. readers and theorists most often place the *Rāmāyaṇa* in the genre of *kāvya* (poetry, imaginative fiction) and the *Mahābhārata* in the genre of *itihāsa* (history, received trad.).

(1) The *Mahābhārata* is the longest poem in the world, running to about 100,000 verses in its canonical versions, nearly seven times the length of the *Iliad* and the *Odyssey* combined. It is divided into 18 major books (*parvans*) and concurrently into 100 minor books, each type of book being further divided into chapters (*adhyāyas*). The entire text with minor exceptions is in verse and employs a variety of meters, with the *śloka* predominating. The bulk of the poem, which would take nearly 25 days and nights to recite continuously at the rate of one verse per minute, is cast as a single dialogue between two characters, Vaiśaṃpāyana and Janmejaya. Vaiśaṃpāyana, the principal "reteller" of the story, is a student of Kṛṣṇa Dvaipāyana or Vyāsa, traditionally identified as the original author or compiler of the *Mahābhārata*. His listener and interlocutor, King Janmejaya, is a sixth-generation descendant of the principal characters of the *Mahābhārata*; it is on the occasion of a great snake sacrifice at his court that Janamejaya wishes to hear once again who his famous ancestors were and what they did.

Both outside and within this main frame of dialogue are embedded hundreds of complete, interlinked, separate, and overlapping narratives. Each of the embedded or lesser stories has its own particular teller (and sometimes its own interlocutors or listeners), so that somewhere between 300 and 400 "characters" serve as the work's "narrators within narratives." Many of the narratives nested inside the Vaiśaṃpāyana-Janmejaya dialogue are also structured as dialogues; a specific character or narrator tells a particular story or part of the main story to one or more listeners inside the fiction, so that narrator and audience, action and observation, story and dialogue become inseparable from each other and from the substance of the *Mahābhārata* throughout.

The *Mahābhārata* has at least three interrelated primary narrative lines or plots (van Buitenen, v. 1). The basic narrative framework involves over 50 major characters and spans half a dozen successive generations in an attempt to record and explain every aspect of the conflict between two branches of the Bhārata clan. The two branches are the Pāṇḍavas (the sons of Pāṇḍu) and the Kauravas (the descendents of Kuru), involved in a protracted struggle for power over the kingdom of Hastināpur (north of modern Delhi). The epic also includes a massive recounting of the long genealogy of the clan of the Bhāratas, mythological and cosmological accounts of all the significant events in the story, discussions of the ethics of the principal characters and their actions, and a general recapitulation (in poetic, narrative, and quasidramatic terms) of the entire known ancient I. world in its political, religious, philosophical, mythological, and cultural aspects. The poets of the *Mahābhārata* boldly claim: "What is found in the world is found in this book; what is not found here is not found in the world." Within its vast, epic perimeter, the *Mahābhārata* is also dialogic at the deepest level of meaning; every event, situation, and character anticipates a response and gives rise to multiple viewpoints, esp. in ethical terms, so that nothing crucial to the narrative remains unambiguous or uncontested.

Epic, heroic, and tragic in its scale and impact, the *Mahābhārata*, traditionally classified as an *iti-*

hāsa (a received history), also refers to itself as a *kāvya*, a great poem shaped by poetic insight into the nature of the human (I., Hindu) world. But the style of the work is often plain and even rough, and not always beautiful in comparison with later Sanskrit *kāvya*, esp. cl. *mahākāvya*. The *Mahābhārata* is also ultimately anagogic in meaning (in the Dantean sense), which complicates the generic status of the poem as well as the issue of how the text is to be interpreted. In this sense, the poem is understood as a discourse on *dharma* (right conduct, ethics, duty) and the many ambiguities in the story serve to outline the ethical dilemmas that define cl. Hindu civilization.

The generic confusion of the *Mahābhārata* has no easy solution, esp. because it contains within itself the *Bhagavad-gītā*, often regarded independently as one of the great poems of world lit. The *Bhagavad-gītā*, by now translated into all major langs., is a dialogue in 18 chapters (*adhyāyas*) that takes place on the battlefield of Kurukṣetra between Lord Kṛṣṇa and Arjuna, in which the ethical dilemmas posed by civil war are debated. Together with the *Mahābhārata* as a whole, which is sometimes treated as "a fifth Veda," the *Bhagavad-gītā* has exercised an influence on subsequent life and culture on the subcontinent that cannot be explained in terms merely of the generic conventions of *itihāsa*, *kāvya*, or *śāstra* (van Buitenen; Zaehner; Miller 1986).

(2) The *Rāmāyaṇa*, in contrast, is a relatively homogeneous text about one-fourth the length of the *Mahābhārata*. Traditionally called a *kāvya*, the poem also describes itself as an *itihāsa*, a history of the Raghuvaṃśa, the clan of Raghu to which King Rāma belongs. In fact, I. readers most often think of the *Rāmāyaṇa* as the *ādikāvya* or the first poem in the I. literary trad., and of its traditional author, the sage Vālmīki, as the *ādikavi* or first poet. Vālmīki is said to have invented the *śloka* meter, valued as the most poetic of the ancient meters, and the *Rāmāyaṇa* is the oldest and greatest poem composed in it. But because of its religious importance, and its concern with the themes of Hindu ethics, government, and family, the *Rāmāyaṇa* is also regarded as a devotional, discursive, and normative text. Like the *Mahābhārata*, then, the *Rāmāyaṇa* is a poem rich enough to belong simultaneously to several major genres, and to be sacred and poetic in several different senses.

Unlike the *Mahābhārata*, the *Rāmāyaṇa* basically tells one continuous story in a fairly straightforward manner. The story concerns the succession to the throne of the ancient republic of Kosala (now in northeastern Uttar Pradesh), and its protagonist is Rāma, the eldest in the line of succession. Although it contains many smaller stories embedded within the story of Rāma and his wife Sītā, these narratives function as episodes within the main action rather than as digressions or elaborations of the kind found in the larger work.

The central story line is complicated by the ethical issues and emotional dilemmas facing the main characters of the story: Queen Kaikeyī's ambitiousness and duplicity, her hold over Rāma's aging father King Daśaratha, Rāma's brother Lakṣmaṇa's decision to accompany Rāma and Sītā into exile, Sītā's abduction by Rāvaṇa, Sītā's faithfulness to Rāma while imprisoned in Laṅkā, and so on (Goldman et al.).

The *Rāmāyaṇa* is also very different in effect from the *Mahābhārata* because its main story is narrated in a single omniscient voice, which we associate with the implied presence of Vālmīki. The whole is organized into seven books (*kāṇḍas*) and divided into many short chapters (*sargas*), each of which tells one portion of the story progressively with sharpness, clarity, and concision. While the *Rāmāyaṇa* does not have the dialogue structure of the *Mahābhārata*, in the various Sanskrit forms in which it has come down to us it is fascinatingly self-reflexive. After a 14-year exile, Rāma returns to Ayodhyā as its rightful king. Sītā's likely violation by Rāvaṇa leads him to send her away to a hermitage in the forest which belongs to Vālmīki. There Sītā gives birth to twin sons, Lava and Kuśa, who learn and perfect the art of bardic recitation and singing. Vālmīki then teaches them—the sons of Rāma—the *Rāmāyaṇa* he has composed, and it is they who turn up at Rāma's court and sing the whole tale to the very men who are its heroes and characters. The *Rāmāyaṇa* thus contains its poet, performers, listeners, characters, and events in a closed poetic narrative of great power which is remarkably close to what W. B. Yeats called the "hermetic egg" of the poem that cannot break out of its shell.

C. *Classical Sanskrit Poetry.* Although the *Mahābhārata* and the *Rāmāyaṇa* probably continued to be edited and revised until around A.D. 500, by ca. A.D. 200 new kinds of Sanskrit poetry had begun to be composed. The new poetry, characterized chiefly by its forms, themes, and style, is usually called "classical" (as distinct from epic).

Western scholars frequently identify *kāvya* in its cl. phase as a style rather than as a genre (Keith; Seely et al.; Lienhard). This new style involved a conscious effort to create a verbal texture pleasing to both the ear and the mind. Heavily figural lang. (involving *alaṃkāra*, rhetorical embellishments or figures), strictly grammatical constructions, heavy use of nominal compounds (*samāsa*) instead of inflections, a display of learning in the arts and sciences, and a wide variety of complicated meters and verseforms all contributed to an overt show of poetic and rhetorical prowess. The cl. *kāvya* style was usually applied to subject matter provided by the earlier epics, to the creation of the specific poetic emotions (*rasas*), and esp. to the description of romantic love. In a large measure, these features gave cl. Sanskrit poetry its "impersonal" quality, analogous to the quality T. S. Eliot valorized in his theory of poetry. Among the masters of the cl. *kāvya* style were Aśvaghoṣa (2d c.), Kālidāsa (5th c.), Bhāravi (6th c.), Bhaṭṭi, Bāṇa, Kumāradāsa, Māgha, Daṇḍin, Bhartṛhari (all 7th c.), and Bhavabhūti (8th c.), as well as such later poets as Bilhaṇa, Śrīharṣa, and Jayadeva (all 12th c.). These poets and their lesser counterparts contributed to the formation and consolidation of the cl. *kāvya* style in the *mahākāvya* and *laghukāvya* genres.

(1) *Mahākāvya* (poetry in major forms) includes works that are several hundred (or even thousand) lines long, sometimes in a variety of meters. A *mahākāvya* is also referred to as a *sargabandha* poem because it is usually produced by binding together several or many *sargas* (cantos or chapters). The *mahākāvyas* by Kālidāsa, Bhāravi, Māgha, and Śrīharṣa are frequently regarded as model poems of their kind in Sanskrit poetry. The earliest surviving examples of the cl. style and the genre, however, are two *mahākāvyas* by the Buddhist poet Aśvaghoṣa (2d c.), the *Buddhacarita* and the *Saundarānanda*. The *Buddhacarita*, the complete version of which is known only through Tibetan and Chinese translations, describes in the extant Sanskrit portion the birth, childhood, and youth of Prince Gautama, leading up to the moment of his enlightenment as the Buddha. The *Saundarānanda* tells the story of how the Buddha converted his half-brother Nanda from the latter's deep love for his wife Sundarī and their worldly life together to a life of Buddhist monasticism. Both works contain numerous descriptions of natural and urban scenes, royal spectacles, amorous episodes, and theological and philosophical aphorisms—all of which were to become primary characteristics of *kāvya* over the next one thousand years.

The *mahākāvya*, however, achieved its mature form only with Kālidāsa. According to I. lore, Kālidāsa (5th c.) was originally an illiterate woodcutter but nevertheless found his genius as a poet and dramatist at the court of Candragupta Vikramāditya at Ujjain (now in Madhya Pradesh). Kālidāsa's plays include the *Śakuntalam*, probably the best known ancient I. work in the West other than the *Ṛgveda* and the *Bhagavad-gītā*. His epic poem *Meghadūta* and his two *mahākāvyas*—*Kumārasambhava* and *Raghuvaṃśa*—represent cl. Sanskrit poetry at its most refined.

Kālidāsa's *Meghadūta* (The Cloud Messenger), though technically not a *mahākāvya*, is an elaborate conceit of the *envoi* (q.v.) type. Here a *yakṣa* (a nature deity or demi-god) asks a cloud to carry a message to his beloved. The poem describes the cloud's journey in detail, mixing descriptions of scenic beauty with evocations of the emotions of separation and then union (Nathan). His *Kumārasambhava* (The Birth of Kumāra, the War God), a proper *mahākāvya*, describes the courtship and marriage of Lord Śiva and the daughter of the Himalayas, the goddess Pārvatī. The god of love, Kāmadeva, attempts to facilitate the union by distracting Śiva's attention while he is performing austerities; Śiva, angry, destroys Kāmadeva by opening his third eye; Pārvatī, however, succeeds where Kāmadeva failed by serving her lord faithfully; Śiva and Pārvatī marry, and on their wedding night conceive Kumāra. Kālidāsa's *Raghuvaṃśa* (The Dynasty of Raghu), his second *mahākāvya*, recounts the legends of the north-I. kings of the solar dynasty and retells the story of Rāma and Sītā.

Some of the other exemplary *mahākāvyas* in the Hindu trad., composed later, are based on material from the *Mahābhārata*. In Bhāravi's *Kirātārjunīya* (Arjuna and the Mountain Man, 6th c.) Arjuna fights a wild man who turns out to be Lord Śiva himself. Māgha's *Śiśupālavadha* (The Slaying of King Śiśupāla, 7th c.) draws on a different story from the same epic in which Śiśupāla insults Kṛṣṇa (an *avatāra* or incarnation of Lord Viṣṇu), and Kṛṣṇa then beheads him in combat. Śrīharṣa's *Naiṣadhacarita* (The Life of Nala, King of Niṣadha; 12th c.) is based on the Nala and Damayantī tale, perhaps the most famous of the stories embedded within the *Mahābhārata* (Keith; van Buitenen, v. 1). Two other significant *mahākāvyas* in the trad. from the same period are Bhaṭṭi's *Bhaṭṭikāvya* and Kumāradāsa's *Jānakīharaṇa*, the latter based on the episode of Sītā's abduction in the *Rāmāyaṇa*.

(2) *Laghukāvya*, a category of diverse poetry in minor forms, includes riddles, proverbs, and aphorisms; descriptive poems and seasonal verse; confessional poems; epigrams; erotic and love poems; devotional and religious lyrics; hymns and prayers to the natural elements; philosophical reflections and wisdom poems; verses on childhood, youth, and old age; didactic poems; imagistic observations; and even short dramatic monologues. In any of these kinds of poetry, a given piece may be in a particular metrical form or mixture of meters, often with an intricate prosodic pattern, and the category as a whole contains examples of virtually every well-known and obscure prosodic and formal variation possible in the lang. Other than brevity, the primary qualities of these poems are concreteness of imagery; exactness of description; powerful visual, aural, and emotional suggestion; refinement of expression and sensibility; and memorability. In most cases, a short poem of this kind evokes a very specific *rasa*, a poetic emotion or mood, presenting it in its purest and most concentrated form. The most highly valued *laghukāvya* verses in Sanskrit, and by extension in the Prakrit langs., are called *subhāṣita* or "well-fed, well-turned."

Much of the short lyric and didactic poetry from the ancient period of I. p., and esp. in cl. Sanskrit, is preserved in *kośas* (anthologies). A popular form of the *kośa*-style anthol. in the cl. Sanskrit period was the *śataka*, a "century" of verses. In the 7th c., four important *śatakas* of well-turned Sanskrit poems were compiled. One is the "Amaru collection" from Kashmir—attributed to a legendary author-editor, King Amaru—which served as a source for later anthols. such as Vidyākara's

Subhāṣitaratnakośa (An Anthol. of the Jewels of Well-Turned Verses; 12th c.). The other three are attributed to the poet Bhartṛhari, who organized them thematically: the first of his *śatakas* contains love poems; the second, epigrams of worldly wisdom; and the third, poems of dispassion or renunciation. Throughout the ancient period, such *kośas* drew on two kinds of material: short poems that were explicitly written as *laghukāvya*, and complete verses or series of verses extracted from longer works, esp. *mahākāvyas*, which could stand on their own (Ingalls; Miller 1967).

Some Sanskrit poetry written at the end of the ancient period or early in the middle period falls outside the categories of *mahākāvya* and *laghu-kāvya*. Two 11th-c. works esp. modify the genres of I. p. in important ways. Jayadeva's *Gītagovinda*, for instance, is structured in cantos like a *mahākāvya*, but its lang. is much more lyrical than its cl. antecedents. It intersperses short religious-erotic songs between the longer movements, and its overall theme is closer to the concerns of the short religious or devotional poems written in Sanskrit through much of the cl. period. It takes up the theme of Kṛṣṇa and Radha's love and turns Radha into an object of religious devotion within the Vaiśnava poetic trad. Jayadeva's variation on the subject has proved both memorable and extremely influential in I. p., music, dance, and painting (Miller 1977). Bilhaṇa's *Caurapañcāśikā* (Fifty Poems of a Thief of Love), on the other hand, brings together a series of short poems on a single theme, a remembered clandestine affair between a poet and a princess (Miller 1971). The great cycle (or series of cycles) of Sanskrit poetry from about 1200 B.C. to A.D. 1200 thus comes to a close remarkably different from its beginning in Vedic hymns.

D. *Prakrit Poetry.* Cl. Sanskrit, as we noted above, was probably based on a variety of common speech early in the ancient period, but soon acquired the characteristics of an elite, sophisticated literary lang. and served as the "official" lang. of court and state for a very long time. The common langs. of the people of the I. subcontinent during much of the first millennium A.D., and probably a little earlier, were the Prakrit langs., which appear in written form in central India around the 2d c. Over 40 Prakrit langs. are recorded; they are classified linguistically as Middle Indo-Aryan langs.

The Prakrit langs. were put to several kinds of literary uses. In multilingual Sanskrit plays of the cl. period, for instance, the common characters and most of the women (even the queens) speak in Prakrit, while the kings and courtiers (and an occasional female mendicant) speak in the more refined Sanskrit. At the same time, many of the love lyrics of the ancient period, esp. those describing the feelings of women, are composed in Prakrit. The Prakrits, simpler in imagery, style, and emotion, seem to have been the langs. of

choice for early I. song.

The most important Prakrit for lit. hist. is Maharashtri, which was used in central India in the 1st millennium A.D. King Hālā (ca. 3d c.) used Maharashtri to compose his *Sattasaī* or the *Gāthā Śaptaśadi*. It is an anthol. of about 700 short lyrics, broadly similar in content and convention to the cl. Sanskrit *laghukāvya kośas* of the kind described above. The Prakrit *gāthā*, together with the Sanskrit *kośa*, serves as the model for the collection of verses and short poems that dominates the middle period of I. p. in the Indo-Aryan vernaculars. Even in the modern period., a 20th-c. Marathi poet like P. S. Rege uses Hala's *gāthā* as a model for a collection of short, lyrical (often erotic and personal) poems.

E. *Classical and Epic Tamil Poetry.* The oldest non-Sanskrit lit. on the I. subcontinent belongs to Tamil, one of the four literary langs. of the Dravidian family found in the southern peninsular region. Early cl. Tamil lit. is called *cankam* lit., since it is believed to have been produced by three successive *cankams* or academies of poets. It is represented by eight anthols., ten long poems, and a grammar called the *Tolkāppiyam* (Old Composition). Nothing of the first *cankam* of writers has survived; the *Tolkāppiyam* is ascribed to the second *cankam*; and the anthols. and long poems are all said to be the work of the third *cankam* and probably belong to the first three centuries of this era. Together the eight anthols. and ten long poems constitute a body of 2,381 poems ranging in length from 4 to about 800 lines; about 100 of these poems are anonymous, but the rest are the work of 473 poets known by name or by epithet (Ramanujan 1986; Hart 1979).

In the *Tolkāppiyam*, a work that is crucial for the understanding of cl. Tamil poetry, and in the anthols. themselves, this body of verse is divided into two main *tiṇais* or genres whose features are completely independent of Sanskrit poetics: *akam* (interior) poetry and *puṟam* (exterior) poetry. *Akam* poems are highly structured love poems, while *puṟam* poems are heroic poems on war, death, social and historical circumstances, the characteristics of kings, and the condition of the poets. In the anthols. both types of poems carry colophons added by later commentators. The colophon to an *akam* poem identifies its speaker with a phrase like "What she said to her girlfriend" or "What his mother said to the neighbors," while the colophon to a *puṟam* poem usually identifies its speaker, the poet, and his patron (a chieftain or king). The poems thus function like dramatic monologues in very specific situations in the interior and exterior worlds of ancient Tamil culture.

The basic conventions of the two genres derive from a taxonomy of Tamil landscapes and the cultures associated with them. Using these conventions, the *akam* genre portrays an interior landscape of love, while the *puṟam* genre portrays an exterior landscape of war. Although the two genres are distinct, they parallel each other so that love and war become part of the same universe and metaphors for one another.

The taxonomy created by the ancient Tamil poets and their commentators is comprehensive and focuses on concrete particulars. The year is divided into six seasons and the day into six parts. The Tamil country is divided into five poetic landscapes (hill, seashore, forest and pasture, countryside, and wasteland); each landscape is then named after the flower or vegetation characteristic of it (*kuriñci, neytal, mullai, marutam,* and *pālai* respectively) and characterized by what it contains. Thus each landscape becomes a repertoire of images for the poets, and anything in it, whether a bird or drum, tribal name or dance, can then evoke a specific feeling. A favorite device for such evocation is *ullurai* (metonymy), in which the description of one thing evokes that of another associated with it in a particular landscape. The natural scene implicitly evokes the human scene; thus the image of bees making honey out of the *kuriñci* flower becomes a metonymic representation of the lovers' union.

In the *akam* genre, each of the five landscapes is matched metaphorically with the five phases of love, the times of day, and the season most appropriate to those phases: *kuriñci* (a white flower; hillside) is the landscape of union, at night in the cool season; *mullai* (jasmine; forest, pasture) is the landscape of patient waiting and domesticity, late in the evening and in the rainy season; *marutam* (queen's-flower; countryside, agricultural lowland) is the landscape of lovers' unfaithfulness and "sulking scenes," in the morning in all seasons; *neytal* (blue lily; seashore) is the landscape of anxiety in love and separation, at nightfall in all seasons; and *pālai* (desert tree; wasteland) is the landscape of elopement, hardship, separation from lover or parents, at midday and in summer. A similar but looser encoding of exterior situations occurs in the *puram* genre, where the landscapes are more inhospitable, often devastated by strife, battle, and destruction.

The *akam* poetry of cl. Tamil is found in five of the eight anthols.: the *Kuruntokai,* the *Narrinai,* the *Akanāṉūru,* the *Aiṅkuṟunūru,* and the *Kalittokai.* The poems of the *puram* genre are collected in three anthols.: the *Puranāṉūru,* the *Patirruppattu,* and the *Paripāṭal.* Taken together, these eight anthols. and the ten long poems give us a very detailed, highly structured, and intricately encoded picture of the cl. Tamil world, in which not only is the poet's lang. Tamil, but the landscapes, personae, moods, and situations are themselves a code of signifiers for Tamil culture. For five or six generations at the beginning of the first millennium A.D. the *cankam* poets spoke this common lang. with a passion, maturity, originality, and delicacy which may well be unique in the ancient I. world (Ramanujan 1986).

Between ca. A.D. 300 and 900, this *cankam* lit.

gave way to ancient Tamil epic poetry. The two main works in this trad. are the twin (interlinked) epics, the *Cilappatikāram* by Ilaṅkō Aṭikaḷ and the *Maṇimēkalai* by Cātaṉār, which draw on cl. Tamil poetics as well as on Sanskrit models. Aṭikaḷ's *Cilappatikāram,* composed in three books, tells a story not about kings but about Kōvalaṉ, a young Pukār merchant unjustly executed for a crime he did not commit, and his wife, the virtuous Kaṇṇaki, who acquires power through her unfailing faithfulness and becomes a goddess of chastity (Daniélou 1965).

Cātaṉār's *Maṇimēkhalai* (the last part of which is missing) continues the story of the *Cilappatikāram;* the heroine Maṇimēkalai, a dancer and courtesan like her mother Mātavi, (Kōvalaṉ's mistress), is torn between romantic love and spiritual longings. While the *Cilappatikāram* gives us a detailed picture of Tamil culture—its varied religions, towns, people (a mixture of Tamils, Arabs, and Greeks), performing arts, and daily life—using Tamil *cankam* poetics as well as Sanskrit poetics and folklore without any particular religious commitment, the *Maṇimēkhalai* is clearly a work influenced by Buddhism (Daniélou 1989).

After about the 6th c. A.D., Tamil poetry and lit. swerved increasingly towards the phenomenon called *bhakti,* intense personal devotion to a particular god, usually either Viṣṇu or Śiva, the two principal gods of ancient and subsequent Hinduism. The earliest Tamil *bhakti* poets were the 12 Nāyaṉār saints, devotees of Śiva, whose earliest representative was the woman poet Kāraikkāl Ammaiyār. The most important Nāyaṉārs were Appar and Campantar (7th c.), and Cuntarar (8th c.). Among the major works of Śaiva *bhakti* in Tamil is the collection of hymns called the *Tiruvācakam* by Māṇikkavācakar (9th c.), for whom Śiva was lover, lord, master, and guru. The Śaiva *bhaktas* were followed by the Tamil Vaiṣṇava saint-poets, called the Āḻvārs. Among the poets who worshiped Viṣṇu, one of the earliest was again a woman, Āṇṭāḷ (8th c.). The greatest of the Āḻvār poets was also one of the last, Nammāḻvār (9th c.), who expresses poignantly the pain and ecstasy of loving God (Ramanujan 1981).

As this discussion suggests, in what we have called the ancient period, I. p. evolved along several distinct lines (within Sanskrit and outside it), passed through a number of well-defined phases (in Sanskrit, from Vedic to epic to classical; in Tamil, from *cankam* to epic to devotional, etc.), and came to constitute a very large and multiform body of verbal composition. This body of poetry steadily became an immense reservoir of commonplaces for subsequent I. poets to draw upon. In the middle and modern periods it also became the canon against which poets and audiences could react, as they began to create new identities in lang., style, poetic theme, genre, religious orientation, and social and political ideology. As the ancient period drew to a close, I. poets started extending the domain of poetry or *kāvya* in ways that the cl. theorists and practitioners of verse could not have envisioned.

III. THE MIDDLE PERIOD (ca. A.D. 600–1500 TO 1800). The middle period of I. p. begins at different times in the different langs. and regions of the subcontinent. In Tamil poetry, it begins around A.D. 600, well before the ancient period of Sanskrit lit. comes to an end, whereas in the case of langs. like Urdu it begins only after 1500. Broadly speaking, however, the middle period comes to a close around 1800 for most of the Indo-Aryan and Dravidian mother tongues, even though clearly modern poetry, prose fiction, and drama do not appear in many of them until after about 1860. Although the absence of definite and uniform historical closure makes generalizations extremely difficult, it is nevertheless possible to say that during the middle period as a whole, esp. between about 1000 and 1500, Sanskrit and the Prakrits cease to be the primary medium of literary composition and give way gradually to the regional mother tongues. Sanskrit has continued to be used for scholarly and ritual purposes down to the present, but the last great original poets in it, such as Jayadeva, belong to the 12th c.

This large-scale linguistic and literary shift, which seems similar to the shift from Lat. to the vernaculars in Europe near the end of the Middle Ages, goes hand in hand in India with a selective but concerted devaluation of the ancient past, and particularly with the rise of a new chauvinism focused on the Indo-Aryan and Dravidian vernaculars and their native regions. The shift also accompanies very significant changes in the political complexion of the subcontinent (the Muslims arrive to stay after about 1200 and dominate much of India until the beginning of the 18th c.). But most importantly, the shift is part of a profound evolution in religious and literary theory and practice (Ramanujan 1981).

The first mother tongue to develop the new kind of poetry was a Dravidian lang., Tamil. Among the Indo-Aryan langs., Bengali in eastern India and Marathi near the western coast were the first to be written down (ca. 1000 A.D.). Between the 10th and 14th cs., poetry appeared for the first time on a significant scale in several other linguistic media: in Assamese, Oriya, Hindi, Rajasthani, Gujarati, and Kashmiri, among the Indo-Aryan langs.; and in Kannada, Telugu, and Malayalam, among the Dravidian langs. Between the 14th and 16th cs., poetry also appeared in Panjabi and Urdu, and by this time Arabic, Turkish, and Persian had also entered I. discourse as a result of Muslim political success on the subcontinent. By about 1600, all the native langs. mentioned had developed strong and continuous trads. of both oral and written poetry. Many of the particular genres of the middle period were associated with particular langs., social groups (esp. caste communities), and religious sects. Thus, from ca. 600–1600, more than a dozen

new major lits. and trads. of poetry appeared on the I. subcontinent, gradually displacing Sanskrit, Prakrit, and cl. Tamil poetry and changing radically the constitution of the world of I. poetic discourse (Dimock et al. 1974).

What poetry is in the middle period is itself an enormous problem, since the change of medium—from three or four main ancient langs. to about 15 new regional mother tongues—involves a transformation of the very notion of poetry and its various functions. Here the problems of historical continuity and difference will be addressed by limiting the discussion to the two main areas of I. p. in the middle period: the *bhakti* movement and Islamic poetry.

A. *Bhakti Poetry.* The most prominent literary, religious, and social movement of the middle period is *bhakti* ("devotion"), which began in the far south (in the Tamil-speaking area) after the 6th c. and spread with surprising success all over the subcontinent by the 16th c. Despite the linguistic fragmentation of India in this period, *bhakti* poetry in a dozen major langs. shares a considerable number of features, while of course revealing many regional variations and peculiarities (Zelliot).

Several thousand poets, variously called *bhaktas* and *sants*, are associated with the *bhakti* movement all over South Asia, but each of the major langs. and dialects has its own particularly valued figures. Among the most significant saint-poets associated with the various kinds of *bhakti* lit. are: the Nāyanār devotees of Śiva, the Śrivaiṣṇava Ālvārs, devotees of Viṣṇu in Tamil (Peterson; Cutler); the Vīraśaiva poets, esp. Basavaṇṇa, Dāsimayya, Allama Prabhu, and Mahādēviyakka, as well as the later *dāsas*, like Purandharadāsa and Kanakadāsa, in Kannada (Ramanujan 1973); Jñāneśvar, Nāmdev, Eknāth, Tukārām, and Rāmdās in Marathi (Kolatkar; Tulpule); Narasimha Mehtā and Mīrābāī in Gujarati, of whom the latter also belongs to the Hindi-Rajasthani trad. (Munshi; Hawley and Jurgensmeyer); Kabīr, Sūrdās, Rāidās, and Tulsīdās in Hindi (Vaudeville; Hess; Bryant; Hawley); Nānak in Panjabi (Hawley and Jurgensmeyer); Vidyāpati in Maithili and Candidās, Caitanya, and Rāmparsād in Bengali (Archer; Dimock and Levertov); and Śankardev in Assamese and Jagannāth Dās in Oriya. Over and above these individual poets, there are several sects or schools of *bhakti* poetry, each with its own tribe of saints and poets, such as the Vallabhācarya sect in the Braj Bhasa dialect of Hindi, the Dattātreya sect in Marathi, the Śaiva poets in Telugu, and the Vaiṣṇava poets in Malayalam.

Bhakti, frequently described as theism, centers on devotional poetry in which the poet expresses his or her intensely personal devotion to a particular god (or, occasionally, goddess) or seeks to be one with a god or an undifferentiated godhead. The many hundred *bhaktas* and *sants* (devotees, saint-poets) in the Indo-Aryan and Dravidian

INDIAN POETRY

trads. of the middle period fall roughly into three categories: (1) those who worship Viṣṇu, one of his ten *avatāras* (incarnations), or one of the numerous local I. gods absorbed into Vaiṣṇava mythology over the centuries; (2) those who worship Śiva, who has no *avatāras* but may be set in different regional and transregional contexts (both Viṣṇu and Śiva are *saguṇa* ["with qualities"]); and (3) those who remain in quest of a god or godhead "without qualities" (*nirguṇa*).

The *saguṇa* poets in the various *bhakti* trads. usually oppose the *nirguṇa* poets ideologically and politically; the former often tend to be conservative while the latter tend to be radical and satiric. Among the *saguṇa* poets themselves, the Vaiṣṇavas and the Śaivas often oppose each other; and among the Vaiṣṇavas, in turn, the worshipers of Rāma and the worshipers of Kṛṣṇa (the two most popular *avatāras* of Viṣṇu in this period) frequently mock and criticize each other. The goal of theistic devotion in the middle period is the same as the goal of ritualistic brahmanism (or even Buddhism) in the ancient period, but the means—ecstatic devotion—of attaining *mukti* ("liberation" from mundane existence) are now substantially different. As this suggests, a great deal remains in common across the great historical, ideological, and linguistic divide between Sanskrit and the later vernaculars. Consequently, many of the *bhakti* poets attempt to "vedicize" themselves and to take ancient Sanskrit texts, such as the *Bhagavad-gītā* and the *Bhāgavata Purāṇa*, as palimpsests to be over-written in the new langs.

Nevertheless, during its primary devel. over six or seven centuries, *bhakti* poetry and its large accompanying lit. (mainly the lives of the poets written in verse and prose and commentaries on the poems) substantially modified, reshaped, and even rejected the brahmanism and Hinduism of the ancient period. Many of the *bhaktas* and *sants* of the middle period were low-caste or "untouchable" men and women, although some of the important poets, such as Tulsīdās in Hindi, Bahiṇābāī in Marathi, and Basavaṇṇa in Kannada, were *brāhmaṇas*, administrators, statesmen, or scholars by birth and by profession. The traditional lives of the devotees of the middle period, mostly written late in the period, are full of miraculous deeds and transformations achieved against the greatest odds. These figures thus become larger-than-life "saints" because of their powerful devotion to their chosen gods and the reciprocal grace (*kṛpā*) those gods confer upon them, a combination that constitutes a major alternative to the ritual nature of "salvation" in ancient Hinduism. The typical poet of the ancient period is a royal sage in a forest, a worldly courtier, a learned priest, or a renouncing *yogi*, while the typical *bhakta* or *sant* in the middle period frequently puts on the persona of an outcast, a rebel, a rustic, or a reformer—sometimes illiterate but practically always divinely inspired.

In general, many of the *bhakti* poets of the middle period oppose the caste system, Vedic and later Hindu ritual, the notions of pollution and untouchability, and brahmanical learning and authority. They also seriously question the ancient hierarchy of genres, attacking the legitimacy of Vedic *śruti* or revelation, the hegemonic status of the brahmanical *śāstras* as cultural codes, and the pedantry involved in a refined (esp. cl. Sanskrit *kāvya*) style. Against the authority of the received trad. or canon they pose the authority of their own immediate experience (*anubhava*), their visions, their intense personal devotion (*bhakti*), and god's privileging grace (*kṛpā*). Despite a few superficial similarities, the I. *bhakti* poets use poetic strategies and function in cultural situations that differ immensely from those of the European and Anglo-Am. trads. of religious poetry. Jñāneśvar, for instance, has little in common with his contemporary Dante.

The *bhakta* or the *sant* often claims that true poetry must be spontaneous, urgent, personal, "divinely inspired," and composed in the simpler and more genuine vernacular rather than a remote and artificial lang. of refinement like Sanskrit. *Bhakti* poets and poems therefore tend to be more immediate, colloquial, autobiographical, confessional, and dramatic than many of their cl. counterparts. But since these qualities became conventionalized early in the *bhakti* movement, the bulk of *bhakti* poetry seems fairly routine and insipid rather than inspired. Though *bhakti* stands out as a "counterculture" in the great flow of I. p., it becomes, in turn, the norm against which subsequent poetic movements define themselves. Thus, by the end of the 18th c., many of the mother tongues (such as Hindi and Marathi) develop bodies of "academic" verse written by learned poets (*paṇḍit kavis*) modeled explicitly on Sanskrit poetry and poetics, which constitute countercurrents to the stream of *bhakti* writing.

Though a large portion of the lexicon, grammar, and prosody of the Indo-Aryan vernaculars is derived in some way from Sanskrit, and Sanskrit metrical verseforms often serve as the basic models for the new poetry, *bhakti* poetry swerves away from Sanskrit *kāvya* on a significant scale in more narrowly literary terms. For instance, as already indicated, if a significant portion of epic and cl. Sanskrit poetry is impersonal and attempts to create the experience of a particular *rasa* in its audience, then much of *bhakti* poetry aims at being personal in tone and serves as immediate self-expression for its authors. Even when the *bhaktas* and *sants* claim to create a *rasa*, they call it the *bhakti rasa* or "the poetic emotion of devotion," which falls outside the conventional list of poetic emotions proper to Sanskrit *kāvya*. Such reorientations acquire meaning and power on ideological grounds as well as within the context of form and genre.

Although the ancient and middle periods are intricately interconnected, their respective poetic forms and genres differ significantly. Many poets and poetic trads. within and outside *bhakti* are so strongly associated with particular vernacular verseforms that those forms acquire the status of genres, as did the sonnet in early modern Europe. For instance, the *mangalakābya*, which lies outside the *bhakti* movement, belongs uniquely to Bengali, the *vacana* to the Vīraśaiva poets in Kannada, the *ramainī* to the Hindi poet Kabir (15th c.), and the *ovi* and the *abhanga* to the Marathi poets from Jñāneśvar (late 13th c.) to Rāmdās (late 17th c.). Some genre names cut across several langs., regions, and trads., e.g. the *pada* ("verses, poem, song"), the *padāvalī* (a "string" of songs, very different in structure from a modern Western poetic sequence), and the *gāthā* (an anthol. or collection of poems, modeled on Sanskrit, Pali, and Prakrit antecedents). Besides these new and often precisely differentiated forms (a Hindi *pada*, a Kannada *vacana*, and a Marathi *abhanga* cannot be confused with each other), in the middle period the mother tongues also develop their own "oral epics" and varieties of "folk song," incl. martial sagas, romances, tragic love stories, ballad-like forms, work songs, etc., all of which affect the more canonical genres of poetry. Moreover, a very high proportion of the poetic forms of the middle period is designed for performance or is integrated with some of the performative arts—music, dance, folk or popular theater, dance-drama. As far as *bhakti* poetry itself is concerned, the various religious strands in the movement bring together lyric (short) forms and epic (long) forms, and further bring these forms together with performance of various types.

One common feature of lyrical *bhakti* poetry is a refrain-like pattern that becomes prominent in singing—the opening verse of a poem, often called a *ṭeka*, is repeated after each subsequent verse. The last verse usually identifies its author explicitly in its signature line (called *bhaṇita*) or, in cases like the Kannada *vacanas*, by a unique image, metaphor, or epithet that is clearly the "signature" of that particular poet. This important feature complements the rhetorical mode of many *bhakti* poems cast as dramatic monologues, in which the poet identified speaks in a particular voice, or through a particular persona, to a god or to an immediate audience of listeners. This form of direct address makes a *bhakti* lyric different from the imagistic or descriptive lyric of the *subhāṣita* kind in cl. Sanskrit *laghukāvya*, and differentiates its rhetoric significantly from the kind of speaker-listener drama we find in cl. Tamil *cankam* poetry in the *akam* genre.

Some *bhakti* poems are long, and they are frequently intertextual with long poems in the ancient period of I. p. For example, the earliest long poem in Tamil *bhakti*, the *Tirumurukaārruppaṭai*, which is about the god Murugan, has six sections and draws on earlier *cankam* images and ancient Sanskrit mythology. Tulsīdās's *Rāmacaritamānas* in

Avadhi (a major literary dialect of Hindi; 16th c.) is several thousand verses long and retells the story of the *Rāmāyaṇa*, but with all the characters now absorbed into a *bhakti* worldview. Rāma thus becomes Tulsīdās's chosen personal god. The poem is clearly epic in scope, tone, and structure, and its conventions derive from those in Vālmīki's Sanskrit *ādikāvya*, but its effect as a whole is very different: the omniscient voice of the narrator, for instance, is now interrupted by the poet-devotee's voice, expressing his devotion to the divine characters. Kampaṉ's *Rāmāyaṇa* in Tamil (12th c.) does something even more complex by accommodating the Sanskrit classic to a Dravidian lang. and its independent cl. trad.: his retelling of Rāma's story is shaped as much by the "interior" and "exterior" landscapes of *akam* and *puṟam* poetry as by the poetic conventions and emotional tones of Tamil Vaiṣṇava *bhakti* (Hart and Heifetz). All such changes connect I. p. of the middle period to the poetry and the poetics of the ancient period, but place many commonplace elements in entirely new combinations.

Many of the features of *bhakti* poetry already mentioned come together in a major poem like the Marathi *Jñāneśvarī*, one of the earliest and greatest works in the lang. of central and western India, and attributed to Jñāneśvar (13th c.), who is said to have achieved *mukti* before he turned 20. The *Jñāneśvarī* is intertextual with the *Bhagavadgītā*; it quotes each verse of the Sanskrit classic in the original lang., and then places several stanzas in Marathi before and after each quotation, thus building a new poem around and inside an old one (Tulpule).

The poetry of the *bhakti* movement coexists in the middle period of I. lit. hist. with a variety of other lits. Although *bhakti* does constitute a "counterculture" within Hindu society at this time, still it does not effectively replace older, continuing, or contemp. lits. Thus in Bengali, for instance, *bhakti* poetry inhabits a larger discursive world which also includes the genre of *mangalakābya* ("poetry of an auspicious happening"), consisting of narratives about and eulogies to local Hindu gods and goddesses, and the Bengali *mahākavya*, based on Sanskrit models (Sen). Similarly, in a Dravidian lang. like Malayalam, poetry written in the Vaiṣṇava trad. coexists with other types of poetic composition, such as the major genre of *pāṭṭu* (song), which combines linguistic and literary elements from Tamil, Sanskrit, and folk sources into a unique and complex trad. of its own after the 15th c. Moreover, *bhakti* lit. coexists with a substantial range of new court poetry, learned or academic poetry, and popular "oral epics" (Roghair; Heifetz and Narayana Rao; Blackburn et al.). In general, it also stands apart from such works and genres as the Hīr-Rānjhā tale in Panjabi, Chand Bardāī's *Prithvīrāj rāso* in Hindi, Malik Muhammad Jāyasī's *Padmāvat* in Avadhi, the Buddhist *caryā- padas* in Bengali, and the *lāvaṇi* and the *powāḍā* in Marathi.

Among the many such contexts of *bhakti* poetry in the middle period is the body of writing which we shall broadly call Islamic poetry.

B. *Islamic Poetry.* Islam first entered the South Asian region in the 8th c. with the conquest of Sind, and the first Islamic empire (the Delhi Sultanate) emerged early in the 13th c. Between the 13th and 18th cs., the courts of Muslim rulers, esp. in northern India, attracted refugee and immigrant men of letters from Persia and Central Asia (incl. Sufi poets) and also patronized local and regional writers who wrote in Arabic, Turkish, Persian (an Iranian relative of Sanskrit), and Urdu (a highly Islamicized version of Hindi), with the last two langs. becoming predominant. The presence of Islam on the subcontinent permanently influenced many of the Indo-Aryan langs. Modern Hindi, Marathi, and Bengali, for example, derive substantial portions of their lexicons from Arabic and Persian roots (Rypka; Sadiq).

Among the Muslim writers who played important roles in the regional lits. of the subcontinent are: Lallā (14th c.) in Kashmiri; Shāh ʿAbdul-Latīf (17th–18th cs.) in Sindhi; Wāris Shāh (18th c.) in Panjabi; Daulat Qāzī and Ālāol (17th c.) in Bengali; and Malik Muḥammad Jayası, Rahīm, Manjhan (all 16th c.), and ʿUsman (17th c.) in the Avadhi and Braj Bhasha dialects of Hindi. Sufi ideas and poetics, esp. the doctrine of monotheism, clearly influenced the *nirguṇa sant* poets of north India, esp. Kabīr and the various poets in the Sikh *guru* trad. (particularly Guru Nānak, 16th c.), whose poems in a mixture of Panjabi, Hindi, Urdu, and other langs. are included in the canonical text of the Sikh religion, the *Ādigranth* or *Guru Granth Sāhib.*

The trad. of Persian writing in India, which is different from the trads. of Muslim writing in Urdu and in other I. mother tongues, goes back to the 11th c.; its first major poet was Amīr Khusrau (13th–14th cs.), who composed poetry in Persian, Urdu, and early Hindi (Hindui or Hindavi). The most important poet in this trad. was ʿAbdul Qādir Bēdil (17th c.), who wrote 16 volumes of poetry. The I.-Persian trad. introduced the *maṣnavī, qaṣīda,* and *ghazal* (qq.v.) genres into I. lit.; the *ghazal* in particular became very popular by the end of the middle period. In the 19th and 20th cs., the *ghazal* has spread, principally from Urdu models, to langs. like Panjabi and Marathi.

The poetic trads. of Urdu have their beginnings in Persian as well as in the various I. langs. of the subcontinent. Urdu poetry first appeared in central India at the courts of Bijapur and Golconda in the 16th c. In the early 18th c., Aurangabad in the Deccan became a notable center; from there, Urdu poetry spread to the courts at Delhi and Lucknow in the north, where it acquired an unusual preeminence at the end of the middle period. Two of the characteristic institutions of Urdu poetry emerged during this period: the practice of novice-poets choosing an *ustād* or master from whom they learned the craft of poetry, and the practice of poets gathering in a private or semiprivate setting to read or recite their poems (meetings called *mushaʿirahs*).

The genres of poetry that appeared in Urdu during the middle period were the *qaṣīda* (panegyrics in praise of high or holy personages); the *ḥaju* (personal and other satires; epigrams on contemporaries); the *shahr-āshūb* (poems lamenting the decline or destruction of a city and its culture); the *marsiyah* (an elegy for the martyred family and kinsmen of Husayn [Muḥammad's grandson]); the *maṣnavī* (the preferred genre for long narrative and descriptive poems); and the *ghazal* (a short, metrical, rhymed lyric on a variety of themes, esp. erotic love, Sufi love, and metaphysics). All these forms and genres in Urdu are related to specific antecedents in Persian, Arabic, and Turkish lit., and though they are not all primarily "religious" in function they are never far from the central tenets of various branches of the Muslim faith. The masters of the *qaṣīda* are Saudā and Inshāʿ (18th c.), and Zauq and Ghālib (19th c.); of the *marsiyah*, Mīr Anīs and Mīrzā Dabīr (19th c.); of the *maṣnavī*, a very widely practiced genre, Mīr, Mīr Hasan, Dayā Shankar Nasīm, and Mīrzā Shauq (18th–19th cs.); and of the *ghazal,* Mīr Taqī Mīr (18th c.) and Mīrzā Ghālib (19th c.). As these dates clearly show, the greatest phase of Urdu poetry in the middle period was the 18th through early 19th cs., overlapping with the beginning of the modern period (Ali; Ahmad; Russel and Islam; Russell).

Between ca. 1400 and 1800, *bhakti* poetry and Islamic poetry in India influenced each other extensively. The *nirguṇa sant* poets in the Hindu and Sikh trads., for example, were affected deeply by such elements in the Muslim faith as monotheism, the rejection of all forms of idol-worship, and belief in an egalitarian society; and the Muslim religious poets, esp. the ecstatic poets in the Sufi trad., were in turn affected by *bhakti* performative practices, esp. communal singing in places of worship.

Although we have described the middle period of I. p. mainly in terms of two of its components, the nature of *bhakti* and Islamic poetry, their interrelations, and their divergence from the older I. past should have indicated the kinds of change that took place on the subcontinent between about 600 and 1800. The shift from Sanskrit, the Prakrits, and cl. Tamil (as well as Pali and the Jain Apabhraṃśas) to the major Indo-Aryan and Dravidian mother tongues for literary purposes, the creation and dissemination of new genres and new principles of poetic composition, and the introduction of new beliefs, values, and worldviews added numerous features to I. p. that did not previously exist on the subcontinent. In fact, the middle period not only brought fresh resources into the common stock of I. p., but also became a part of the "traditional" I. world against which the writers of the modern period reacted. In this composite "trad.," *bhakti* poetry (but not Islamic poetry or the poetry of the folk and oral trads.) also came to be referred to as *kāvya*, thus extending the field of canonical poetry well beyond that of Sanskrit *kāvya*.

IV. THE MODERN PERIOD (SINCE CA. 1800). In the conventional view of India's lit. hist., the division between the "traditional" and the "modern" is marked by the establishment of the British colonial empire on the I. subcontinent. Two precise dates are significant: 1757, when the East India Company effectively gained control of Bengal following the Battle of Plassey; and 1818, when the British acquisition of I. territories was practically completed. In the course of the 60 years between these two dates, deeply traditional I. society began to "modernize," affecting not only the "manners and customs" of the natives but also their langs. and—often unknowingly—their lits.

A. *Colonialism and Modernization.* Western-style education first became available on a significant scale to Indians late in the 18th c. with the establishment of a number of influential missionary schools and colleges; after Macaulay's famous "Minute on Education" (1834), Eng.-lang. education became quite commonplace in the cities and towns and among the I. middle and upper classes. In the later 19th c., Indians all over the country began encountering European and Anglo-Am. literary works and reading Eng. translations of Gr. and Roman lit. and the modern European, Eng., and Am. classics. Many I. poets of the 19th c. then began consciously to imitate their Western predecessors and contemporaries, thereby creating one major kind of modern I. p. in the I. mother tongues. Thus Bengali writers started a Bengali trad. of modern epic in verse, just as Marathi poets began composing sonnets, odes, and pastoral elegies, and Hindi poets started writing romantic lyrics. These "imitative innovations" significantly changed the formal, thematic, and generic complexion of the lits. of the subcontinent. The Westernization of India under British rule also went one step further: it created the kind of poet who wanted to write poetry of the Anglo-Am. kind directly in the Eng. lang.

However, contrary to the common claim, the modernity of modern I. writing does not consist entirely in its Westernization, and I. writers did not become modern merely by imitating the qualities invented originally by European or Western writers. In many of the modern Indo-Aryan langs. the 18th and 19th cs. were largely periods of very complex and innovative interaction among the various local, national, and international trads. In Hindi and Marathi, for instance, the transitional decades between the middle and the modern periods (roughly 1775–1875) were dominated by many *paṇḍit-kavis* ("learned" or "academic" poets). These *brāhmaṇa* writers worked with Sanskrit and Persian as their cl. langs., and in the 19th c. also with Eng. as one of their official langs., but

used their own vernaculars and local dialects as the actual media of literary composition. Their often voluminous poetry comes in several interlinked genres that cross the boundaries usually erected between derivative and original writing: (1) close translations of Sanskrit poems, plays, and narratives into modern I. mother tongues; (2) loose adaptations, retellings, or imitations of Sanskrit, Persian, and Arabic literary works; (3) "new" works in the modern mother tongues that basically rework old materials from the cl. langs. and from the older lit. in the mother tongues; and (4) genuinely original poems in their own langs. which explicitly adopt the norms and values of Sanskrit (and sometimes Persian-Arabic) poetics. Thus the *paṇḍit-kavis*, as the men who prepared the way for modern poetry without actually practicing it, produced works like Hindi and Marathi translations of Kālidāsa, adaptations of tales from the Arabic *Thousand and One Nights*, modern versions of old Hindi and Marathi poems and tales, and original poems modeled closely on Sanskrit erotic poetry (Dharwadker 1989, v. 2).

This mixed body of writing provided the ground in which Eng. and broadly European influences, both modern and cl., took root. The Western influences first became noticeable in the mid 19th c. when the *paṇḍit-kavis* gave way to the first two generations of writers educated in schools where Eng. was the medium of instruction and the valorized lang. The work of the new Westernized poets of these two generations falls into two main categories: (1) I.-lang. translations of Eng., Am., and some European poetry, such as the works of Shakespeare, Milton, the romantics, Thomas Hood, William Cowper, Tennyson, and Longfellow; and (2) original poems in the I. langs. that involved conscious imitation of Eng. poetic genres from the Ren. onwards, in verseforms that used Sanskrit prosodic principles and meters but had rhyme schemes, stanzaic structures, and thematic elements drawn clearly from Western models and sources. In the long run, this layer of material interacted in complicated ways with the somewhat earlier work done by the *paṇḍit-kavis*, producing mixed prosodic, formal, and generic practices that have become commonplace in the I. langs. of the 20th c. (McGreggor 1974; Schomer).

The pivotal shift from the middle to the modern period, accomplished in a surprisingly short time considering the number of langs. and cultures involved, thus brought together several lines of translation, adaptation, imitation, and original writing, as well as two very different types of poets and writers: native scholars trained in the "purely I." way (mainly in non-Western langs., incl. Persian and Arabic), and "Westernized" natives with bilingual training (mainly in Eng. and their native I. vernaculars). The historical transformation was further shaped by the print media, which introduced a factor of common access, esp. after ca. 1800, that was missing earlier. The transformation, however, was not uniform. In terms of time, the effects of modernization varied a great deal: distinctly modern I. p. appeared first in Eng. (1820s) and Bengali (1840s), and then in langs. like Marathi, Tamil, Panjabi, Gujarati, and Malayalam (1860s–90s), followed by langs. like Hindi, Urdu, and Oriya (1900s–20s) (Dimock et al. 1974; Srinivasa Iyengar; McGreggor 1974; Kopf; Schomer; Dimock 1986; Naik).

The overall effect of colonization on I. p. was thus clearly multifaceted and far-reaching: the encounter with cultures of European origin drove I. poets to experiment with varieties of poetry markedly different from anything the I. trads. themselves had invented so far; it went hand in hand with a renewed interest among I. poets in their own trads. of the ancient and middle periods, incl. Islamic lit.; and it introduced yet another literary lang. into the I. babel—Eng. These effects have continued from the early 19th c. down to the present, and the grafting of Western "influences" onto "native" sensibilities has resulted in a hybrid lit. that has broken away sharply from many of the patterns set up in I. p. over the preceding 3000 years. Ādhunik kāvya or urvācīn kāvya (modern poetry) swerves away in complicated ways from prācīn kāvya (ancient or old poetry), whether that of cl. Sanskrit or of the bhakti movement, and pushes the notion of kāvya or kavitā (poetry) across new frontiers.

B. *The Modern Poetic Genres.* The shift away from the poetry and poetics of the middle period was signaled by a concerted change in poetic forms, themes, conventions, images, metrical frames, and structural principles, as well as by radical changes in the conception of who the poet (*kavi*) is, what his or her functions are, and how his or her audience is constituted. Moreover, the new situation of the I. poet in the 19th and early 20th cs. evoked new attitudes, concerns, tones, and voices. Bengali, Hindi, Marathi, Kannada, and Tamil poets, for example, began experimenting with enjambed lines, imitations of Elizabethan blank verse, Eng. epic conventions, Miltonic similes, greater romantic lyrics, and specific European and non-I. verseforms grafted onto Sanskrit-based prosody, as well as with themes of nationalism, cultural chauvinism, and social and religious change (some of the important early modern I. poets were former Hindus who had recently converted to Christianity). This complex shift led to writing which, when placed beside I. p. of the early periods, strikes a very clearly cosmopolitan, "modern" note. However, as already suggested above, the newness of 19th- and 20th-c. I. p., whether in the native langs. or in Eng., does not emerge simply out of a rejection of the I. past.

Interestingly enough, the earliest modern poetry by writers of I. birth appeared in Eng. (in the 1820s and '30s), and not in one of the regional langs. The first I.-Eng. poet was Henry Derozio, whose sonnets and odes are virtually the earliest

documents of I. nationalism. The first modern poetry in the I. langs. was written in Bengali (in the 1830s and '40s), and includes the work of bilingual poets like Michael Madhusudan Dutt, who began as a writer in Eng. and then turned to his native Bengali by conscious decision at age 35 (Srinivasa Iyengar; Parthasarathy). This is practically the earliest modern writing by non-Western writers in the world, preceding by several decades the corresponding instances in Japanese and Chinese and in the African langs. Modern I. p. in Eng. and Bengali soon gave way to a flood of similar poetry across the entire subcontinent, with self-consciously modern poetry appearing in Panjabi, Gujarati, Marathi, Tamil, Malayalam, and in the Braj Bhasha, a dialect of Hindi, from 1850 to 1900, and in Khadi Boli (modern standard Hindi), Urdu, Oriya, Dogri, Sindhi, Kashmiri, Telugu, and Kannada from 1900 to 1930. This literary expansion coincided with a number of historically and politically crucial events: the "I. Mutiny" of 1857, the subsequent dismantling of the East India Company, the formal absorption of India into Queen Victoria's Empire in 1877, the formation of the I. National Congress in 1885, and the launching of the I. freedom movement under Mahatma Gandhi's leadership at the end of World War I.

The specific poetic genres that have emerged from these developments in the colonial and postcolonial decades are worth mentioning in some detail because they demonstrate the distance modern I. p. has covered since the end of the middle period. Among the more notable modern genres are: the long philosophical or speculative poem, often epic in size and scope, which attempts to formulate a new poetic worldview (e.g. Aurobindo Ghose's *Savitri* in Eng., G. M. Muktibodh's *Andhere men* in Hindi); the nationalist or chauvinist epic, quite frequently cast as a retelling of an ancient Hindu myth or story, often from the *Rāmāyaṇa* or the *Mahābhārata* (e.g. Michael Madhusudan Dutt's *Meghanād-vadh* in Bengali, Jaishankar Prasad's *Kāmāyanī* in Hindi); the long sequence of short poems, whether religious, philosophical, satiric, or personal in theme, modeled on the Western poetic sequence as well as on premodern I. sequences (e.g. Rabindranath Tagore's *Gitanjali* in Bengali, Subramania Bharati's "prose poems" in Tamil, Arun Kolatkar's *Jejuri* and R. Parthasarathy's *Rough Passage* in Eng.); the short metrical lyric in modern rhymed stanza form, sometimes set to music, as well as the modernized lyric based on premodern I. and foreign verseforms (e.g. Tagore's songs in Bengali, Mahadevi Varma's in Hindi, Faiz Ahmed Faiz's *ghazals* and *nazms* in Urdu, B. S. Mardhekar's and Vinda Karandikar's *abhangas* in Marathi, numerous *haikus* in Kannada, Buddhadev Bose's sonnets and Bishnu De's imitations of folksongs in Bengali); and the "free verse" poem, varying in length from a few lines to several hundred and ranging in theme from autobiographical and confessional to mythological, political, and historical (e.g. the later love poems of P. S. Rege in Marathi; the political poems of Dhoomil, Sarveshwar Dayal Saxena, and Raghuvir Sahay in Hindi; the landscape poems of Keki N. Daruwalla and the surreal poems of Arvind Krishna Mehrotra in Eng.; the poetry of bilingual poets like A. K. Ramanujan in Eng. and Kannada and Arun Kolatkar in Eng. and Marathi; protest poetry, Dalit poetry, and contemp. feminist and women's poetry in a number of langs.).

Among these, the genre of free verse poetry is esp. crucial to the changes in I. p. in all the major langs. in the late-colonial and the postcolonial periods. Modern I. poets "invented" free verse in the I. langs. in the second and third quarters of the 20th c., following the examples of the Anglo-Am. imagists and high modernists. But the freedom of free verse has meant different things in different langs.—for instance, in Bengali, freedom from the overwhelming presence of Tagore's modernity; in Urdu, freedom from the domination of the *ghazal* form in lyric poetry; in Hindi, freedom from the cloying lyricism of the early 20th-c. *ādarś avād* and *chāyāvād* poets; in Marathi, freedom from the sentimental songs of the early moderns; in Kannada and Malayalam, freedom from the rhetorical public poetry of the national freedom movement. Since the 1960s, a very high proportion of the poetry written in the various langs.—incl. Telugu, Oriya, Dogri, Sindhi, Panjabi, and Gujarati, besides those mentioned in the examples above— has appeared in free verse. Much of this poetry reveals the influence of international poetic movements that originated in Europe or the West in the 19th and 20th cs., incl. symbolism, modernism, futurism, expressionism, dada, Beat poetry, and even concrete poetry (qq.v.) and Zen writing. Among the important Western poets of the past 200 years that I. poets working primarily in free verse (and Western forms) allude to are: Whitman, Baudelaire, Rimbaud, Mallarmé, Valéry, Apollinaire, Cesare Pavese, Vasko Popa, hans magnus enzensberger, Pablo Neruda, Nicanor Parra, Aimé Cesaire, Allen Ginsberg, and the Soviet socialist poets. As with other trads. in the world, the domination of free verse in modern I. p. since the 1940s has generally involved a major shift in poetic sensibility, from the "musical phrase" to the "colloquial phrase" as the basis of composition.

It is also noteworthy that early in the modern period (ca. 1775– 1850), the colonial reconstitution of India led to the creation of specific genres of discourse which involved both colonizers and their colonial subjects in mutual tension, and altered the immediate and the future generic shapes and literary environments of I. lit. One of the striking facts about the colonial modernization in the I. case (as also in many African cases) is that a very large amount of modern I. p. is social rather than personal or confessional. For the modern I. *kavi* or poet, who is a very different person from the *bhakti* poet or the ancient I. poet de-

scribed above, social poetry is so important because it exercizes his or her citizenship in the modern world. As a loosely integrated body of writing appearing in all the I. literary langs., modern I. social p. branches out into several genres, two of which are of particular significance. The first is antinationalistic or "satiric poetry," ridiculing specific aspects of I. society, history, culture, and lit., past and present. The second is nationalistic or "heroic poetry," attempting to counter the satirists by praising things Indian, concentrating on the achievements of ancient I. culture and lit. as well as on future possibilities. Satiric discourse has generated a large body of poetry in the 19th and 20th cs. criticizing particular I. beliefs, customs, and institutions such as caste, brahmanical ritual, female infanticide, widow-immolation, child-marriage, and untouchability. In contrast, the conventions of heroic discourse have enabled I. poets to retell stories from the Sanskrit and mother-tongue classics, to create new nationalistic epics, and to write about freedom from colonial rule (Dharwadker 1989, v. 2).

Broadly speaking, in the last 150 years I. p. has undergone cyclical interchanges between these two modes of writing. Between ca. 1825 and 1900, I. poets largely practiced a mixture of satiric and heroic discourse; thus Derozio in Eng., K. K. Dāmle in Marathi, Bhāratendu Harīshchandra in Hindi, and Rabindranath Tagore in Bengali, for instance, attacked certain features of I. society for being backward, exploitative, and inhuman, and at the same time also patriotically praised I. culture and values. From ca. 1900 to 1940, I. poets practiced the heroic mode, in keeping with the massive nationalist movement, esp. under the leadership of Mahatma Gandhi. In this phase, poets like Maithili Sharan Gupta and Mahādevī Verma in Hindi, Subramaniam Bhāratī in Tamil, Tagore in Bengali, Umā Shankar Joshi in Gujarati, G. Shankara Kurup in Malayalam, Bendre and Putappa in Kannada, and Muhammad Iqbal in Urdu turned explicitly to nationalistic and culturally chauvinistic themes, praising and revalorizing the content of native I. trad. and helping to transform India into "Mother India," Bengal into "Our Golden Bengal," and so on (*Daedalus*; Schomer; Dimock et al. 1974).

By about 1940, however, disillusionment with the freedom movement and its politics led to a new surge of satiric and antinationalistic poetry. With Suryakant Tripathi and G. M. Muktibodh in Hindi, B. S. Mardhekar in Marathi, and the later work of Jibananada Das in Bengali, I. poets began once again to ridicule and attack the state of contemp. India and the hist. of I. cultural institutions. This satiric phase continued into the poetic preoccupations of the early postcolonial period (beginning with freedom from British rule in 1947), in which I. poets quite concertedly attacked the negative features of the I. past and present. Between the 1960s and '80s, social poetry in most of the langs.

has arrived at yet another mixture of the satiric and heroic modes, now based on new regional, communal, ideological, and national concerns (Rubin; Jussawalla; Daruwalla; Dharwadker 1990; Dimock 1986).

The contemp. variations are most apparent in several specific phenomena: the long-term success of the Progressive (left-wing) movement in langs. like Urdu (in present-day Pakistan and Bangladesh, as well as in India), Hindi, Marathi, and Bengali (in both India and Bangladesh); "protest" movements like those involving the Hungry Generation poets in Bengali, the *pratirodhī kavis* ("oppositional poets") and *akavis* ("anti-poets" in Hindi, the Dalit poets in Marathi, the "naked poetry" writers in Telugu, and protest poets in Tamil and Malayalam; a strong upsurge of women poets in Bengali, Hindi, Marathi, Oriya, Panjabi, and Kannada; and the national prominence achieved by the poets of the 1960s and '70s in Oriya and Kannada. They are also evident in the reputations particular "modernist" poets have acquired in the various I. langs., e.g. Muktibodh, Dhoomil, Agyeya, Sahay, Saxena, Kedarnath Singh, and Shrikant Verma in postcolonial Hindi; Das, Bose, De, Nirendranath Chakrabarti, Sunil Gangopadhyay, and Subhas Mukhopadhyay in Bengali; Rege, Mardhekar, Karandikar, Kolatkar, Indira Sant, Mangesh Padgaonkar, Namdev Dhasal, Narayan Surve, and Dilip Chitre in Marathi; Chandrashekhar Kambar, Gopalkrishna Adiga, and K. S. Narasimhaswami in Kannada; N. Picamurti, Shanmuga Subbiah, and Gnanakoothan in Tamil; and Nissim Ezekiel, A. K. Ramanujan, Jayanta Mahapatra, Daruwalla, Adil Jussawalla, Mehrotra, Parthasarathy, Gieve Patel, Kamala Das, Eunice de Souza, Chitre, and Kolatkar in Eng. Although this list of poets and langs. (and most of the foregoing discussion) is limited to contemp. India, corresponding claims can be made for poets in Pakistan writing in Urdu, Panjabi, Sindhi, and other langs., as well as for poets in Bangladesh working in the Bengali and Urdu trads.

In the course of these fluctuations, the tensions between modernity and trad., Indianness and Westernization, have played a shaping role. Like many of their 19th-c. counterparts, 20th-c. I. poets reject certain aspects of their own past, but at the same time make use of it, achieving a modernity in which Westernization and Indianness stand in a constant and constantly productive conflict. As a result, modern I. writers, critics, and common readers now refer to all the varieties of poetry surveyed in this article as *kāvya* or *kavitā*, although they sometimes reserve the former word for the high canonical poetry of the ancient and middle periods (or, more rigorously, for only cl. Sanskrit poetry) and the latter term for the verse of the past 200 years. In its broadest 20th-c. usage, *kāvya* thus embraces a vast quantity of writing in about 20 major langs. produced over about 3000 years. As our survey indicates, the word is now capable of

signifying trads. as different as those of the Valmiki *Rāmāyaṇa* and cl. Tamil *akam* and *puṟam* poetry, *bhakti* lyrics and religious epics in the middle period, Telugu "Vedas" and Bengali "mangalakābyas," Urdu or Marathi sonnets and condensed allegories in Hindi free verse, ancient Hindu Buddhist works, as well as contemp. Marxist poetry and protest poetry by former untouchables. See also INDIAN POETICS; INDIAN PROSODY.

GENERAL: A. B. Keith, *A Hist. of Sanskrit Lit.* (1928); H. H. Gowen, *A Hist. of I. Lit.* (1931); S. N. Dasgupta and S. K. De, *A Hist. of I. Lit.* (1947); M. Winternitz, *A Hist. of I. Lit.*, 3d ed. (1962)—original Ger., 3 v., 1908–22; A. K. Warder, *I. Kāvya Lit.* (1972); *A Hist. of I. Lit.*, ed. J. Gonda, 1–(1973)—uneven but indispensible multivolume reference in progress, all langs., genres, and periods; E. C. Dimock et al., *The Lits. of India* (1974)—excellent intro.; C. Seely et al., "South Asian Peoples, Arts of," *Encyc. Britannica* (1974)—useful overview; E. Gerow, *I. Poetics* (1977); C. P. Masica, *The Indo-Aryan Langs.* (1989); *Columbia Book of I. P.*, ed. B. S. Miller et al. (forthcoming)—trs. from 15 langs.

SERIALS: *Annals of the Bhandarkar Oriental Research Institute [ABORI]* (1919–); *Bahuvachan* (1988–); *Harvard Oriental Series* (1883–); *Illustrated Weekly of India* (1929–); *I. Horizons [IndH]* (1952–); *I. Lit. [IndL]* (1957–); *Jour. of Asian Studies [JASt]* (1941–); *Jour. of South Asian and Middle Eastern Studies* (1977–); *Jour. of South Asian Lit. [JSoAL]* (1963–); *Jour. of the Am. Oriental Society [JOAS]* (1843–); *Mod. Asian Studies* (1967–); *Quest* (1950–); *South Asian Digest of Regional Writing* (1972–); *Vagartha* (1974–79); *Chandrabhaga* (1979–); *Indian P.E.N.* (1934–); *Toronto South Asia Review* (1987–).

ANCIENT PERIOD: A. A. MacDonnell, *A Hist. of Sanskrit Lit.* (1900)—useful for Vedic lit.; E. W. Hopkins, *The Great Epic of India* (1901); *The Ramayana and the Mahabharata*, tr. R. C. Dutt (1910); *The Bhagavad Gita*, tr. F. Edgerton (1944); S. N. Dasgupta and S. K. De, *A Hist. of Sanskrit Lit., Cl. Period*, 2d ed. (1962)—full inventory of the lit.; *The Shilappadikaram*, tr. A Daniélou (1965); *An Anthol. of Sanskrit Court Poetry*, tr. D. H. H. Ingalls (1965)—from Vidyākara's *kośa*, extremely influential; C. V. Narashimhan, *The Mahabharata* (1965)—handy abridgment; B. S. Miller, *Bhartrihari* (1967), *Phantasies of a Love-Thief* (1971)—on Bilhana, *Love Song of the Dark Lord, Jayadeva's Gitagovinda* (1977), *The Hermit and the Love Thief* (1978); A. K. Ramanujan, *The Interior Landscape* (1967)—important text, tr., commentary; *The Mahābhārata*, tr. J. A. B. van Buitenen, 3 v. (1973–80)—unfinished but indispensible; W. Buck, *The Rāmāyaṇa* (1974)—unreliable yet useful retelling; L. Sternbach, *Subhāṣita, Gnomic and Didactic Lit.* (1974); *The Cloud-Messenger*, tr. L. Nathan (1974)—*Kalidasa*; J. Gonda, *Vedic Lit.* (1975); G. L. Hart, *The Poems of Ancient Tamil* (1975), *Poets of the Tamil Anthols.* (1979); R. Panikkar, *The Vedic*

Experience (1977); B. A. van Nooten, "The Sanskrit Epics," *Heroic Epic and Saga*, ed. F. J. Oinas (1978); W. D. O'Flaherty, *The Rig Veda* (1981); S. Lienhard, *A Hist. of Cl. Poetry* (1984)—Sanskrit, Pali, Prakrit; *The Rāmāyaṇa of Vālmiki*, tr. R. Goldman et al. (1984–)—essential, in progress; *The Bhagavad-Gītā*, tr. B. S. Miller (1986)—major new tr.; *Poems of Love and War*, tr. A. K. Ramanujan (1986)—excellent, indispensible; *The Forest Book of the Ramayana of Kampaṇ*, tr. G. L. Hart and H. Heifetz (1988)—Tamil; *Maṇimekhalai*, tr. A. Daniélou (1989).

MIDDLE PERIOD: R. D. Ranade, *Mysticism in India* (1933); S. Sen, *A Hist. of Bengali Lit.* (1960); M. Mansinha, *Hist. of Oriya Lit.* (1962); *Love Songs of Vidyāpati*, ed. W. G. Archer (1963); *In Praise of Krishna*, tr. E. D. Dimock and D. Levertov (1967); K. M. Munshi, *Gujarat and Its Lit. from Early Times to 1852*, 3d ed. (1967); K. M. George, *A Survey of Malayalam Lit.* (1968); R. Russell and K. Islam, *Three Mughal Poets* (1968); J. Rypka, *Hist. of Iranian Lit.* (1968)—section on "Persian Lit. in India"; G. V. Sitapati, *Hist. of Telugu Lit.* (1968); L. H. Ajwani, *Hist. of Sindhi Lit.* (1970); *Ghazals of Ghalib*, ed. A. Ahmad (1971); *Ghalib*, ed. R. Russell (1972); *The Golden Trad.*, tr. A. Ali (1973)—Urdu; A. K. Ramanujan, *Speaking of Śiva* (1973)—Kannada, excellent; C. Vaudeville, *Kabīr*, v. 1 (1974); K. Zvelebil, *Tamil Lit.* (1974); S. Sarma, *Assamese Lit.* (1976); E. Zelliot, "The Medieval Bhakti Movement in Hist.," in *Hinduism*, ed. B. L. Smith (1976)—essential bibl.; K. E. Bryant, *Poems to the Child-God* (1978); S. G. Tulpule, *Cl. Marathi Lit. from the Beginning to 1818* (1979); B. B. Kachru, *Kashmiri Lit.* (1981); *Hymns for the Drowning*, tr. A. K. Ramanujan (1981); A. Kolatkar, "Translations from Tukaram and Other Saint-Poets," *JSoAL* 17 (1982); G. H. Roghair, *The Epic of Palnāḍu* (1982)—Telugu oral epic; *The Bijak of Kabīr*, tr. L. Hess and S. Singh (1983); J. S. Hawley, *Sūr Dās* (1984); R. S. McGreggor, *Hindi Lit. from its Beginnings to the 19th C.* (1984); M. Sadiq, *A Hist. of Urdu Lit.*, 2d ed. (1984); N. Cutler, *Songs of Experience* (1985); *For the Lord of the Animals—Poems from the Telugu*, tr. H. Heifetz and V. Narayana Rao (1987); *Songs of the Saints of India*, ed. and tr. J. S. Hawley and M. Juergensmeyer (1988); *Poems to Śiva*, tr. I. V. Peterson (1989)—Tamil; *Oral Epics in India*, ed. S. H. Blackburn et al. (1989).

MODERN PERIOD: *Collected Poems and Plays of Rabindranath Tagore* (1956); *Green and Gold*, ed. H. Kabir (1958)—Bengali; *A Tagore Reader*, ed. A. Chakravarty (1961); *Mod. Hindi Poetry*, ed. V. N. Misra (1965); *An Anthol. of Marathi Poetry, 1945–65*, ed. D. Chitre (1967); D. McCutchion, *I. Writing in Eng.* (1969); *Poems by Faiz*, tr. V. G. Kiernan (1971)—Urdu; *Contemp. I. P. in Eng.*, ed. S. Peeradina (1972); K. R. Srinivasa Iyengar, *I. Writing in Eng.*, 2d ed. (1973); *New Writing in India*, ed. A. Jussawalla (1974); R. S. McGreggor, *Hindi Lit. in the 19th and Early 20th Cs.* (1974); *I Have Seen Bengal's Face*, ed. S. Ray and M. Maddern (1974);

Ten 20th-C. I. Poets, ed. R. Parthasarathy (1976); *A Season on the Earth*, tr. D. Rubin (1976)—Hindi; *Considerations*, ed. M. Mukherjee (1977); D. Kopf, *The Brahmo Samaj and the Shaping of the Mod. I. Mind* (1979); *Two Decades of I. P., 1960–1980*, ed. K. N. Daruwalla (1980); *Contemp. I. Eng. Verse*, ed. C. Kulshreshtha (1980); *India: An Anthol. of Contemp. Writing*, ed. D. Ray and A. Singh (1983); K. Schomer, *Mahadevi Varma and the Chhayavad Age of Mod. Hindi Poetry* (1983); R. Tagore, *Selected Poems*, tr. W. Radice (1985); E. C. Dimock, *The Sound of Silent Guns* (1986); B. King, *Mod. I. P. in Eng.* (1987), ed., *Three I. Poets* (1991); M. K. Naik, *Studies in I. Eng. Lit.* (1987); *The True Subject*, tr. N. Lazard (1988)—Faiz; "India," *Nimrod* 31 (1988); *Contemp. I. Trad.*, ed. C. M. Borden (1989); V. Dharwadker, "The Future of the Past," 3 v., diss., Univ. of Chicago (1989); "Another India," *Daedalus* 118 (1989); "29 Mod. I. Poems," tr. V. Dharwadker, *TriQ* 77 (1990); *Another India*, ed. M. Mukherjee and N. Ezekiel (1990); *100 Mod. I. Poems*, ed. V. Dharwadker and A. K. Ramanujan (forthcoming)—14 langs.

V.D.; B.S.M.; A.K.R.; E.A.H.

INDIAN PROSODY.

I. THE CLASSICAL LANGUAGES: SANSKRIT, PRAKRIT, AND TAMIL
II. THE MODERN VERNACULARS

I. THE CLASSICAL LANGUAGES: SANSKRIT, PRAKRIT, AND TAMIL. I. metrics is one of the world's most complex prosodic trads. Though perhaps best treated historically, it must in an article such as this be surveyed formally. I. meters fall into three main types: (a) those that fix the quantity of each syllable (*varṇavṛtta*), (b) those that fix the total quantity of each line (*mātrāvṛtta*), and (c) those that appear to mix the two types (*śloka*). Like the metrics of Gr. and Lat., I. is based on a prosodic distinction between *heavy* and *light* syllables. A heavy syllable contains a long vowel, or a short vowel followed by two or more consonants. A light syllable contains a short vowel followed by at most one consonant. The distinction of vowel quantity is inherent in the phonology of Sanskrit and the other I. langs.

A. *Fixed-syllable meters.* The elegant meters of cl. Sanskrit poetry are of this type. The general formula calls for four usually identical feet (*pāda*), which in practice may vary from 8 to 21 or more syllables each. *Mandākrāntā* (the meter of Kālidāsa's *Meghadhūta*) may be taken as an example. Each of its four 17-syllable feet realizes the following pattern: G G G G L L L L L G / G L G G L G x (G = *guru*, or heavy syllable; L = *laghu*, or light syllable; x = a syllable of variable quantity; "/" marks the *yati*, or caesura). Less common meters may vary identical first and third feet with identical second and fourth feet, or may have four different feet, but the principle remains the same: the quantity of each syllable is predictable and the sequence or pattern is fixed. In recitation, a chanting intonation is usually employed, modeled on the quantitative sequence of the line. Though some common recitative patterns are noticeable, each reciter may also cultivate a personal style. The names of the meters generally scan in the meter and often suggest appropriate associations: "mandākrāntā," "(a lady) slowly approaching."

B. *Fixed-line or moric meters.* Here the quantity of the total line is fixed by considering a *laghu* worth one "measure" (*mātrā*; cf. Lat. *mora*) and a *guru* two. Free variation of syllables within the line is however restricted by several conventions, which demonstrate the influence of a regular beat—indicating that these meters were probably sung. It is forbidden, for instance, that the beat fall on the second half of a *guru* syllable. If we assume one beat every four *mātrās* (three, five, and six are also possible), this convention will in effect articulate the line into groups (*gaṇa*) of four mātrās each, which have only the shapes G G, G L L, L G L, L L G, or L L L L, each signaled by an initial beat. The *āryā*, which probably originated in popular, non-Sanskritic milieux and remained the meter of choice for cl. Prakrit poetry, may serve as a typical example: it is composed of two lines, the first of which must contain 30 *mātrā*, the second 27. The simple tetramoric pattern (above) is however complicated (and syncopated) by adding to seven of these *gaṇas* an eighth of two *mātrās* (for a total, in the first line, of 30), and, further, in the second line, by reducing the sixth *gaṇa* to a single *laghu* (i.e. 27). Convention also restricts the kinds of *gaṇas* that do in fact occur in given loci in the verse; for example, in the *āryā*, L G L is possible only for the second and fourth *gaṇas*. The meters of the songs of the *Gītagovinda* (13th c.) and those employed in middle Indic devotional poetry and in the modern north I. langs. are generally of the moric type, which is subject to extreme variation. Beginning with the *Gītagovinda*, end-rhyme is frequently associated with moric meter, and later vernacular poetry is regularly rhymed. Alliteration, though not unknown in earlier poetry, also becomes an increasingly prominent feature of moric verse. As may be surmised, the correlation of moric meter with song is in the modern period even more marked.

The meters of the Dravidian langs. of the south (Tamil, Telugu, Kannada, Malayalam) are based on a somewhat more complicated scansion (in certain circumstances treating as light even a syllable containing a long vowel), but during the long course of coexistence and mutual contact, there has been a give and take of both theory and practice with the Sanskritic north. The oldest Dravidian (viz., Tamil) meters greatly resemble the moric meters of the Prakrits, employ alliteration with great effect, and are definitely rhythmical (cf. again the *Gītagovinda*). On the other hand, they often feature initial rhyme, based on the first interior consonant of the line—virtually unknown

in the north. Lines most commonly consist of four feet (*cīr*) comprising two or three syllables (*acai*). The earliest treatise on pros. in the Dravidian langs. is the *Ceyyuḷiyal* chapter of the Tamil *Tolkāppiyam* (3d c. B.C.?). The classical meters prevailed up to the end of the first millennium A.D., when folk meters were popularized by devotional poets.

C. *Śloka.* The most common Sanskrit meter is partly fixed, partly free. *Śloka* (viz., "praise"— doubtless referring to a usual context of Sanskrit poetry) is both a type and a species, deriving in its special epic and later form (after 500 B.C.) from the meters found in the oldest extant Indic text, the *Ṛgveda* (ca. 1500–1000 B.C.). The cl. *śloka* is like type (a) in that it is composed of 4 feet, each of which must have 8 syllables; but it is like (b) in that its line appears to fall into two 4-syllable halves, the first of which is quantitatively quite free (though x L L x does not normally occur), the second of which is obligatorily L G G x in odd feet and in even feet L G L x. A "trochaic" cadence thus alternates with an "iambic." Many variations on this pattern are however found. The older Vedic meters (*chandas*) are composed generally of feet with 8, 11, or 12 syllables. Of the 8-syllable meters, some have three feet (*gāyatrī*), some four (*anuṣṭubh*). This latter is evidently the ancestor of the cl. *śloka*, but it lacks, along with the other Vedic meters, the contrast between even and odd feet. Its usual shape is x G x G / L G L x. The 11-syllable meters (*triṣṭubh*) generally have the same attack and the same cadence, but add a middle sequence of L L L G (/). The *jagatī* adds a syllable to the *triṣṭubh* but is otherwise like it. Like the *anuṣṭubh*, the *triṣṭubh* and *jagatī* have descendants in the cl. metrics—the family of 11-syllable meters called *upajāti*, and 12-syllable meters such as the popular *vaṃśastha* and *drutavilambita*. The style of *śloka* recitation is more or less uniform over all of India, testifying to its antiquity. The Vedic meters have been deformed by the superimposition of later prosodic features, such as the obligatory sandhi (linguistic junctures) of the cl. lang., and are only dimly perceivable in the (otherwise) beautiful ritual chanting of the Vedic priest, itself the likely precursor of cl. I. music.

The *śloka* is not "poetic" in the usual Western sense, however. Though it is metrical, it is functionally the equivalent of our "prose," in that it is the mode of choice for an entire range of literate composition, from epic (*Mahābhārata, Rāmāyaṇa*) and fable (*Kathāsaritsāgara*) to grammar (*Vākyapadīya*) and astronomy (*Sūryasiddhānta*)—doubtless reflecting the importance of memorization in I. religious and cultural trad.

The study of prosody is very old in India, being counted as one of the six "ancillaries of the Veda" (*vedāṅga*). A *sūtra* attributed to Piṅgala, portions of which may be as old as 600 B.C. (the rest as late as 500 A.D.), describes about 160 meters, but surprisingly not the *śloka* that we know. In the late cl. period (after A.D. 900), an elaborate technical lit. (*chandaḥśāstra*) grew up, based on Piṅgala, wherein were defined the various meters in actual use and, with mathematical completeness, many meters merely possible. Associations with moods, time of day, and colors were sometimes also made, testifying to an effort to integrate metrics into the larger domain of aesthetics. See also INDO-EUROPEAN PROSODY; CLASSICAL PROSODY; GREEK POETRY; INDIAN POETICS.   E.G.

II. THE MODERN VERNACULARS. Throughout the medieval and early modern periods the end-stopped rhyming couplet is the preferred medium of expression for poets in the New Indo-Aryan langs. (Hindi, Punjabi, Gujarati, Marathi, Bengali, Assamese, and Oriya). As in Cl. Sanskrit, lines are usually divided by caesurae into two, three, or four feet (*pāda* or *caraṇ*). The most popular verseform for the vast number of devotional lyrics produced in this period is the *pad*, a stanza of from 4 to 8 lines (but often extended to several more), all having the same metric structure and frequently the same rhyme. Often the lyric begins with a shorter line which in performance serves as a refrain. Alliteration is prevalent throughout the medieval period; among the poets of Rajasthan it becomes obligatory.

On the whole, Hindi poets favored moric meters, esp. those with a tetramoric pattern. It appears that the poets normally had a specific rhythmic cycle (*tāla*) in mind when they chose the meter. Often this was a cycle of 16 beats divided into 4 equal sections, the common time of I. music. The majority of lyrics have 16 morae in the first foot of each line and from 10 to 16 in the second.

The *dohā* is a rhyming couplet commonly used for aphorisms as well as for longer narrative and didactic poetry. The first foot of each line has 13 morae and the second 11. In the case of Kabīr and other Sant poets it is called *sākhī*, and in the *Ādigranth* of the Sikhs it is termed *salok* (from Sanskrit *śloka*, of which it was the vernacular equivalent). The basic unit of the narrative poems composed in the Avadhī dialect of Hindi (notably the Sufi romances and the *Rāmcaritmānas* of Tulsīdās) was a stanza of from 5 to 8 distichs in the 16-moric *caupāī* meter followed by a *dohā*.

Hindi poets also used syllabic meters, the most common being two types of quatrains called *savaiyā* and *ghanākṣarī*. The former has lines of 22–26 syllables with a trisyllabic rhythm and a medial caesura; the *ghanākṣarī* line has three feet of 8 syllables and a fourth of 7 or 8. The tetrasyllabic rhythm of the latter prevailed in other vernaculars which used mainly syllabic meters. The most common meter in Eastern India (Bengali, Assamese, and Oriya) was the *payār*, a rhyming couplet used for both lyric and narrative poetry. Here, each line has 14 syllables divided 8 + 6 but subdivisible into a 4 + 4 + 4 + 2 structure. Another popular couplet form was the *tripadī*, of which each line has two feet of equal length, often with

end rhyme, followed by a third that is slightly longer, e.g. 6 + 6 + 8 or 8 + 8 + 10.

Similar to the *payār* are the *abhaṅga* and the *ovī*, the most popular forms used by Marathi poets. The shorter type of *abhaṅga* is composed of rhyming octosyllabic sections; the longer *abhaṅga* has lines of four feet (6 + 6 + 6 + 4 syllables) with the second and third rhyming. The *ovī* is considered a folk-meter from which the *abhaṅga* derived. Its first three feet are of equal length and have end rhyme, while the fourth is slightly shorter and rhymeless.

These are the most common types of meter. The theorists describe many more, of which several are adaptations of Sanskrit meters or permutations of the basic vernacular ones, but the more recondite meters are usually confined to the work of scholastic court poets. Poetry in Urdu stayed within the Perso-Arabic trad., using principally the *ghazal* and *maṣnavī* (qq.v.) forms.

Medieval and modern Tamil poets retained their purely indigenous meters; those who composed in the other Dravidian langs. (Kannada, Telugu, Malayalam) more readily assimilated the meters and vocabulary of Sanskrit. Kannada and Telugu poetry, of which the earliest examples emerged about a thousand years ago, used meters derived from Sanskrit as well as Dravidian meters that are found earlier in Tamil, adapting some of them to the Sanskrit method of scansion. Though Telugu poets were stricter in observing metrical rules, they modified the Sanskrit meters more than their Kannada counterparts and also accepted enjambment. Many of the meters used in Malayalam bear Sanskrit names but are freer than Sanskrit in their syllabic structure.

A form of prose poetry in Kannada is found in the short *vacana* ("utterances") of Basavaṇṇa (12th c.) and subsequent Vīraśaiva poets of Karnataka. Comparable, though more regular, are the *vākh* of the Kashmiri female saint Lallā (or Lāl Ded; early 14th c.): these are quatrains of approximately seven syllables and four stresses in each line with occasional rhyme. In the 19th c., familiarity with Eng. poetry encouraged Bengali poets, and later those writing in other langs., to experiment with blank verse and enjambment. Rabindranath Tagore, besides writing blank and free verse, also maintained the moric trad. but simplified the rules for measuring quantity by giving all open syllables the value of one mora and all closed syllables two.   A.W.E.

E. W. Hopkins, *The Great Epic of India* (1901), esp. ch. 4; E. V. Arnold, *Vedic Metre* (1905)—still the standard authority; A. B. Keith, *A Hist. of Sanskrit Lit.* (1920), esp. ch. 20, sect. 3–4; H. Weller, "Beiträge zur Metrik der Veda," *Zeitschrift für Indologie und Iranistik* 12 (1922), "Metrica," *Beiträge zur indischen Philologie und Altertumskunde* (1951); J. Hermann, Über die älteste indischer Metriker und ihr Werk," *IndLing* 3 (1933); H. D. Velankar, "Apabhraṁśa Metres," *Jour. of the Univ.*

of Bombay (Arts) (1933), 32–62, (1936), 41–93, "Prosodical Practices of Sanskrit Poets," *Jour. of the Bombay Branch of the Royal Asiatic Society* n.s. 24–25 (1948–49), ed., "Chandaḥkośa," *Jour. of the Univ. of Bombay (Arts)* (1933)—repub. as App. 2 to his *Kavidarpaṇa* (1960); A. C. Chettair, *Advanced Studies in Tamil Poetry* (1943); H. N. Randle, "Sanskrit and Gr. Metres," *Jour. of Oriental Research* 17 (1947); V. Raghavan, "Sanskrit and Prakrit Metres," *Jour. of the Madras Univ.* 23 (1952–53); L. Renou, *L'Inde Classique*, v. 2 (1953), App. 2, and "Sur la Structure du Kāvya," *JAsiat* 247 (1959); M. Sinha, *The Historical Devel. of Med. Hindi Pros.* (1964); A. K. Warder, *Pali Metre* (1967); A. D. Mukherji, "Lyric Metres in Jayadeva's Gītagovinda," *Jour. of the Asiatic Society of Bengal* (1967, pub. 1969); H. Jacobi, *Kleine Schriften* (1970)—his coll. essays; P. Kiparsky, "Metrics and Morphophonemics in the *Rigveda*," *Contribs. to Generative Phonology*, ed. M. K. Brame (1972); D. Matthews and C. Shackle, "Note on Prosody and Metre," *An Anth. of Cl. Urdu Love Lyrics* (1972); *I. Lit.*, ed. A. Poddar (1972); N. Sen, *Early Eastern New Indo-Aryan Versif.* (1973); W. S. Allen, *Accent and Rhythm* (1973); G. Nagy, *Comparative Studies in Gr. and Indic Metre* (1974); S. Pollock, *Aspects of Versification in Sanskrit Lyric Poetry* (1977); S. Subrahmanyan, *The Commonness in the Metre of the Dravidian Langs.* (1977); J. F. Vigorita, "The Trochaic Gāyatrī," *ZVS* 93 (1979); C. E. Fairbanks, "The Devel. of Hindi Oral Narrative Meter," *DAI* 42 (1982), 4452A; S. Lienhard, *A Hist. of Cl. Poetry: Sanskrit—Pali—Prakrit*, v. 3 of *A Hist. of I. Lit.*, ed. J. Gonda (1984); E. Gerow, "Jayadeva's Poetics and the Cl. Style," *Essays in Honor of Ernest Bender*, spec. iss. of *JAOS* 109 (1989).   E.G.; A.W.E.

INDO-EUROPEAN PROSODY. Like the IE lang. itself (the common ancestor of most of the langs. of Europe and of India, dating to ca. 4000 B.C.), IE pros. is lost and must be reconstructed. Since the work of Meillet in 1923, conclusions have been based on analyses of Sanskrit and Gr. verse, with subsequent attention to Slavic, Germanic, and Celtic, using the comparative method. Recent research on the phonological pattern of IE has, however, resulted in changes in our views of the conservatism of Sanskrit and Gr. in the IE family; the pros. proposed by Meillet may then require revision. In the meantime, his conclusions, built on those of earlier scholars, notably Wilamowitz, represent our best hypotheses about the prosodic pattern of IE verse.

IE verse is assumed to have consisted of short lays, songs of praise to gods and men, charms, and other small pieces; epic verse like the Homeric is considered a subsequent form taken from Mediterranean genres. Initial impetus for the assumption of IE verse came from Kuhn's comparison of a number of Atharvavedic and Germanic charms of striking similarity. Typically these portray a situation, such as riders on horses one of which suffers a broken or sprained leg, then apply an incantation (itself surviving into recent use) such as "bone to bone, sinew to sinew, blood to blood, flesh to flesh." While some doubts have been expressed on typological grounds about Kuhn's postulation of an IE charm of this type, the common characteristics are sufficiently comparable and complex to justify the assumption of historical continuity.

Other grounds for assuming continuity of poetic trad. are found in diction. Thieme has examined passages in the *Rigveda* and other early verse for their use of poetic terminology such as derivatives of the Sanskrit root *vat* (its simplest sense, "blow," was extended to "inspire"; derivatives refer to "poet" [Lat. *vates*, Old Irish *faith*, Old Slavic *vetija*], to the name of the Germanic god of poetry [*Wotan*], and to other Indic, Iranian, and Gr. terms concerned with poetry). Like other poetic terms, forms of this root bear the record of a trad. of poets maintained, much as were later poets at Germanic, Celtic, and Indic royal courts, to remind their rulers of past glory and to preserve their own deeds of valor in memory.

Phrases provide a third basis for positing IE verse. The most widely cited such phrase consists of adjective + noun, a sequence found in many Vedic and Homeric formulae. The oldest example, appearing three times in the *Rigveda*, is *ákṣiti śrávas*, lexically equivalent to Gr. *áphthiton kléos*; though cited in a late form, the phrase is demonstrably archaic. IE poetry as oral verse (see ORAL POETRY) has also been assumed to contain formulae such as those made up of the words for "sacred" in Vedic and early Gr. But application of proposed formulae to prosodic reconstruction has been complicated by extension of the term (to "theme") beyond the classical definition given by Milman Parry in 1930 (see FORMULA). Homeric formulae are characteristically found in the final syllables of the line, which is indeed a central prosodic characteristic of IE verse: the line is most strongly regulated at its end. Other assumed characteristics are constant number of syllables per line, freedom of quantity except in the cadence preceding a final syllable either long or short (i.e. an anceps), and a mandatory internal break or caesura around the fifth syllable of the line.

Vedic lines based on the IE pattern (see INDIAN PROSODY) consisted of 12 or fewer syllables with only slight regulation of the distribution of long and short syllables, but a generally iambic rhythm in the initial segment. Examples are the *Jagatī* meter of 12 syllables, $x - x - | x \cup x | - \cup - \cup x$, and the *Triṣṭubh* meter of 11 syllables, in two schemes, $x - x - \cup \cup - | - \cup - x$ and $x - \cup - x \cup \cup | - \cup - x$. These have been compared with Gr. aeolic (q.v.) lines such as Sappho's of 11 syllables, $x x - \cup - \cup \cup | - \cup - x$. Because the section after the caesura is the most strictly regulated, it gives basic structure to the line. The Gr. paroemiac (q.v.), of varying length but generally of 9 or 10 syllables with free distribution of quantity before a fixed cadence ending ⌣ ⌣ – x, has also been considered a direct descendant of IE verse. Jakobson also ascribes the Slavic line of 10 syllables to inheritance from IE; Watkins suggests continuation through linguistic change into Celtic. Earlier, Sievers had proposed that an IE line of 8 syllables may be the precursor of the Vedic *Gāyatrī*, of the pattern x ⌣ x ⌣ | ⌣ – ⌣ x, and of the Germanic alliterative long line. On the other hand, Kurylowicz with other metrists rejects any continuity into the dialects and accordingly denies the possibility of reconstructing IE prosody.

But even those who posit the existence of IE verse and its direct transmission into the subgroups assume that its prosodic structure was relatively free. The dialects of the sub-groups modified IE metrical principles in accordance with the linguistic modifications they themselves underwent, such as the introduction of stress accent in Germanic, Celtic, Italic, and other late dialects. In view of the persistence of quantity as a metrical device in the early dialects, IE prosody must have been based on it, and also on isometrical lines within a poem. See now CLASSICAL PROSODY; GERMAN PROSODY, *Old Germanic*; GREEK POETRY, *Classical*; INDIAN PROSODY.

A. Kuhn, *Indische und Germanische Segenssprüche* (1864); R. Westphal, *Allgemeine Metrik der indogermanischen und semitischen Völker* (1892); Sievers; Wilamowitz; A. Meillet, *Les Origines indo-européennes des mètres grecs* (1923); P. Thieme, *Die Wurzel vat* (1954); M. Durante, *Untersuchungen zur Vorgesch. Griechischen Dichtersprache* (1962); C. Watkins, "IE Metrics and Archaic Ir. Verse," *Celtica* 6 (1963); R. Jakobson, "Slavic Epic Verse: Studies in Comparative Slavic Metrics," in Jakobson, v. 4; R. Schmitt, *Dichtung und Dichtersprache in indogermanischer Zeit* (1967); *Indogermanische Dichtersprache*, ed. R. Schmitt (1968)—incl. the articles of Kuhn and Thieme cited above; J. Kurylowicz, "The Quantitative Meter of IE," *IE and Indo-Europeans*, ed. George Cardona et al. (1970), *Metrik und Sprachgesch.* (1975); Parry; M. L. West, "Lydian Metre," *Kadmos* 11 (1972), "Gr. Poetry 2000–700 B.C.," *ClassQ* 23 (1973), "IE Metre," *Glotta* 51 (1973); W. S. Allen, *Accent and Rhythm* (1973); G. Nagy, *Comparative Studies in Gr. and Indic Meter* (1974); J. F. Vigorita, "IE Comparative Metrics," *DAI* 34 (1974), 7216A; B. Peabody, *The Winged Word* (1975), ch. l; V. N. Toporov, *Die Ursprünge der indoeuropäischen Poetik* (1981); West.   W.P.L.

INDONESIAN POETRY, like contemp. Malay poetry (q.v.), is rooted in older and folk Malay poetry. *Bahasa indonesia*, the I. lang., formally divided itself from the Malay lang. in 1928; I. p. began to assume its separate course in 1917.

One of the first of the modern I. poets was Mohammad Yamin (1903– 62), an active politician. Strongly patriotic, romantic, and distinctly sentimental, Yamin was much influenced both by European (esp. Dutch) poetry and the work of Rabindranath Tagore, as well as by older and folk Malay poetry. He introduced the sonnet into I. p. His contemporaries, Rustam Effendi (1903–79), Sanusi Pané (1905–68), and Sutan Takdir Alisjahbana (1908–86), were somewhat more successful at integrating Malay, European, and oriental strands into stronger, less derivative poetry. Effendi in particular experimented with the devel. of new forms; he also tried to "find a new poetic manner" and to make *bahasa indonesia* capable of the wry, dry tone of European poetry. Pané (who also wrote in Dutch) and Alisjahbana were influenced primarily by Malay and oriental poetry. Pané had studied at Tagore's Santiniketan University. His *Puspa Mega* (Cloud Flowers, 1927) features quiet, lyrical poems of high polish but no great substance. Alisjahbana's *Tebaran Mega* (Scattered Clouds, 1936), written in memory of his first wife, is his only major work of poetry; most of his other writing is heavily European-influenced social, linguistic, and philosophical crit.

Pané, Alisjahbana, and Amir Hamzah (1911–46) jointly founded *Pujangga Baru* (The New Writer), a journal the most significant contributor to which was Hamzah, the outstanding I. poet before World War II. Scion of an aristocratic Sumatran family, he was deeply religious and just as deeply steeped in the older Malay trad. His *Nyanyi Sunyi* (Songs of Loneliness, 1937) is largely autobiographical. Chairil Anwar (see below) exclaimed: "What a bright light he shone on the new lang.," though the mystical and complex qualities of Hamzah's work sometimes make him difficult to understand. In 1939 Hamzah published a coll. of translations from other oriental lits., *Setanggi Timur* (Incense from the East).

The break with Dutch colonialism begun by the Japanese Occupation (1942–45) and formalized, on August 17, 1945, by the declaration of I. independence helped bring into being the *Angkatan 45* (Generation of '45), led by the greatest of all I. writers, Chairil Anwar (1922– 49). Others of the Generation of 45 incl. Asrul Sani (b. 1926) and Rivai Apin (b. 1927), both associated with Anwar in the tripartite *Tiga Menguak Takdir* (Three Against Fate or Three Against Takdir Alisjahbana), and Sitor Situmorang (b. 1924). Led by Anwar, these and other writers broke with romanticism; their work features blunt lang., emphatic syntax, strong components of irony and social crit., and, in Anwar's case, a passionate lyricism and strength:

> She winks. She laughs
> And the dry grass blazes up.
> She speaks. Her voice is loud
> My blood stops running.
>   (*Lagu Biasa* [An Ordinary Song])

> When my time comes
> I want to hear no one's cries
> Nor yours either
> Away with all who cry!
>   (*Aku* [Me], tr. Raffel)

INFLUENCE

His three collections, all posthumous, incl. *Deru Campur Debu* (Noise Mixed with Dust) and *Kerikil Tajam dan Yang Terampas dan Yang Putus* (two books in one: Sharp Gravel; Plundered and Broken). Many I. writers first realized the true literary possibilities of *bahasa indonesia* reading Anwar's poetry.

Anwar's effect has been almost as strong on the literary generations which have followed, though I. p. has expanded far beyond the boundaries of any one influence. Contemp. I. p. has become one of the world's most vital bodies of lit., incl. among others the work of W. S. Rendra (b. 1935), Ayip Rosidi (b. 1938), Taufiq Ismail (b. 1937), Goenawan Mohamad (b. 1942), Subagio Sastrowardoyo (b. 1924), Toeti Heraty (b. 1942), I.'s leading woman poet, Sutardji Calzoum Bachri (b. 1940), and Darmonto (b. 1942). Rendra is the senior and most noted poet of this group:

> Fire has gutted the forest:
> Charred logs curse at the sky
> That runs across the world.
>
> Overhead, the moon, shining with
> blood,
> Drips orange tears from its eyes.
> (*Koyan Yang Malang* [Koyan the Unfortunate], tr. Raffel)

But the range and strength of contemp. I. p. as a whole is remarkable.

> Sleep, child, on the earth which never
> sleeps
> Sleep on the grass, on the sand, on the
> bed
> Sleep with the butterflies, the waves of
> the sea and the bright lights,
> Which sing, slowly sing
> (Goenawan Mohammad, *Nina-bobok*
> [Lullaby])
>
> We are the people with sad eyes, at the
> edge of the road
> Waving at the crowded buses
> We are the tens of millions living in misery
> Beaten about by flood, volcano, curses
> and pestilence
> Who silently ask in the name of freedom
> But are ignored in the thousand slogans
> And meaningless loudspeaker voices
> (Taufiq Ismail, *Kita adalah pemilik
> syah republik ini* [The Republic is
> Ours], tr. Aveling)

ANTHOLOGIES AND TRANSLATIONS: *Poeisi Baru*, ed. S. T. Alisjahbana (1946); *Pujangga Baru*, ed. H. B. Jassin (1962); *Anthol. of Mod. I. P.*, ed. B. Raffel (1964); *Complete Poetry and Prose of Chairil Anwar*, ed. and tr. B. Raffel (1970); *Ballads and Blues: Sel. Poems of W. S. Rendra*, ed. and tr. B. Raffel

and H. Aveling (1974); *Contemp. I. P.* (1975), *Arjuna in Meditation* (1976), both ed. and tr. H. Aveling.

HISTORY AND CRITICISM: H. B. Jassin, *Chairil Anwar, pelopor Angkatan 45*, 2d ed. (1945), *Amir Hamzah, Raja Penyair Pujangga Baru* (1962), *Kesusastraan Indonesia modern dalam kritik dan esei*, 2 v. (1962); W. A. Braasem, *Moderne Indonesische Literatur* (1954); R. B. Slametmuliana, *Pöezie in Indonesia* (1954); A. Teuw, *Pokok dan tokoh dalam kesusteraan Indonesia baru*, 3d ed., 2 v. (1955); A. H. Johns, "Chairil Anwar: An Interp.," *Bijdragen tot de taal-, land-en Voklenkunde* (1964); B. Raffel, *The Devel. of Mod. I. P.* (1967); H. Aveling, *A Thematic Hist. of I. P. 1920 to 1974* (1974).   B.R.

INFLUENCE. Traditionally, i. has been associated with imitation (q.v.) and most often understood as the result of learning and technique. Horace counsels writers to follow trad.; "Longinus" considers imitation of earlier writers as a means to sublimity; Dante urges writers to first drink of Helicon before taking up their singing instruments. I. is a beneficent and necessary corollary of creative genius, routinely addressed and acknowledged up until the late 18th c. romantic poetry and poetics instead stress originality (q.v.), taking the latter to be the direct opposite of the former. A trad. of "affective" crit. then arises in both the poetry and crit. of the 19th c. which proceeds to reread earlier critical texts, such as Longinus, in terms of the struggle between, on the one hand, the techniques steeped in learning and imitation and, on the other, the sublime and wholly original power of genius. Genius (q.v.), however, cannot be fully separated from learning, and the notion of i. develops as a way of negotiating the distance between the two. In the 4th c., i. had referred to the stars, and later came to be associated with the exercise of power. It signals an influx or flowing in, and thereby relates the imitation of earlier writers to the power that such writers exert on the trad.

This concept of "tradition" (q.v.), of an ideal order of lit., has had a considerable impact on the hist. of i. as traced by critics in the 20th c. Northrop Frye, for example, repeats Eliot's ideal order by reading the lines of filiation (of i.) between one writer and another in terms of myth and archetype (qq.v.), knowledge of which makes possible an understanding of the "total form" of lit. Each work is a synecdoche (q.v.) for the whole. The myth constitutes an origin (*arché*) outside of time and lang., and each creative act becomes a "fable of identity." Both Frye and Eliot perceive lit. as a totality, present in space and expressed through form.

This model of i., articulated within the framework of traditional lit. hist., has produced many other solid scholarly works. R. D. Havens' *The I. of Milton on Eng. Poetry* (1922), for example, traces the 18th and 19th centuries' indebtedness to Milton by a meticulous inventory of repetitions and echoes of Milton's style. Havens refers, for instance, to Wordsworth's poems about Milton as well as his conscious stylistic borrowings from Milton, incl. his lofty diction and "organ tone." Several assumptions underwrite such studies as Havens': (1) the earlier poet functions as an undisputed and stable "source," a foundation or origin itself not open to question; (2) i. is conscious and explicit, not hidden; (3) the scholarly study of i. observes the boundaries of the discipline, eschewing interactions with other disciplines such as philosophy and psychoanalysis; and (4) literary trad. works in cumulative fashion and holds out the promise of further riches, so that i. (such as Milton's) is both powerful and beneficent.

It is W. J. Bate (1970) who for the first time emphasizes the difficulty that a rich trad. produces for each poet who comes after. He sees the past as a "burden," though he suggests that this burden is a recent phenomenon ("the product of the last 50 years"). Bate is explicit that the strength of the past in no way indicates the weakness of the future, a condition which only a self-fulfilling prophecy could bring about. An idealizing, humanistic strain informs *The Burden of the Past*, with the assertion of human freedom and human choice its paramount concern. For Bate the rich heritage of the past points the way to our own "identities," the way "to be ourselves."

These conceptions of i. rest on the traditional view of lit. hist. as a stable context with determinate cause and effect relations, recognizable sources, and a reliably straightforward chronology. Literary relations, in this scheme of things, are equally straightforward and determinable. Their determinacy is built on the premises of traditional crit., but these premises were put into question by the advent of theoretical crit. originating in France in the 1950s and '60s. "Textuality" and "intertextuality" (qq.v.) disrupt the stability of the "work" and its meaning, deny its "origin" and "originality," and open up infinite and random connections between texts.

The concept of the origin is problematic long before the advent of "textuality," however. Poststructuralist critics note that the history of Western metaphysics is haunted by the impossibility of establishing a system of knowledge authorized by a cause external to the system, and after poststructuralism the study of causes and effects between texts often goes by the name of "genealogy." The name suggests a genesis which is already a metaphor within the system rather than the cause of it. Gregory Jay defines genealogy as "charting, between writers and texts, those often unauthorized relationships that nonetheless belong to the literary lineage of an essay or poem" (1983). Genealogy rereads the simultaneous order as a figure for textuality itself. Relations with the history of texts may shift, but genealogy does not produce an origin: it already knows that beginnings do not trace a history but constitute instead a metaphor

for such a history (Riddel).

Poststructuralist critics suggest that the absent origin punctuates a history of texts stretching from Plato to the present. Three writers within this history place particular emphasis on the problematics of the origin. That is, in the terms outlined above, three writers are repeatedly drawn out of a history of texts to function as a genealogical locus and exemplar for the problem: Giambattista Vico (1668–1744), Friedrich Nietzsche (1844–1900), and Sigmund Freud (1856–1939).

Vico's major work, *Scienza Nuova* (*The New Science*, 1725, tr. 1744) asks how human beings first began to think humanly, a question prefaced by an account of the difficulty Vico encountered in reaching back to inaccessible origins which he could "imagine only with great effort." The text dealing with origins enacts the problematic for which it seeks to account. Vico's response to the question he poses is that thought begins in metaphor. The first human beings begin to think humanly when, in response to fear, they create a world out of themselves and assign to it the names of gods. This is the "imaginative metaphysics" born of ignorance and fear and needing no authority other than its own creation. We might say that it is born out of need, and functions as defense. Vico traces a later "rational metaphysics" which emphasizes learning and which he describes as a fall from the first. Imaginative metaphysics is a metaphysics of power: it imagines the origins it needs in order to survive. Rational metaphysics recognizes the tropological nature of those origins and the groundlessness of all understanding.

This double attitude is echoed by Nietzsche in "Über Wahrheit und Lüge im aussermoralischen Sinn" ("On Truth and Lying in their Ultramoral Sense" [1873]), which notes two significant moments in thought: the creation of "truth" through metaphor ("truth is a mobile army of metaphors") and the forgetting of the fact of that creation. The first points to an epistemological impasse, since we cannot know anything in its essence, only in the relations posited by lang. The second points to a will-to-power by which an artist creates out of the "delicate material of ideas." Nietzsche denigrates the "impulse to truth" crucial to a metaphysics of presence, since it promotes a false sense of understanding and security. Understanding for Nietzsche is built on metaphor and cannot claim a privileged point of reference beyond it. There is no metalanguage or external reference point from which to view the whole. Identity is a fiction, cause and effect relations an illusion, and origin an imagined thing; this is the frightening world without rational order, without bottom, that art reveals to us when it tears for a moment "the woof of ideas." It is the power of art to witness the abyss that underlies human thinking, and it is also the power of art to create the illusion of origin and poetic identity.

Nietzsche's "forgetting" is Freud's "repression."

INFLUENCE

Though Freud is perceived as a scientist, and his initial gestures are in that direction, his theories lead him further away from the world of real causes and events and into the area of "phantasy." The case history of the Wolf Man proposes "cause" as phantasy. At first Freud surmises that the Wolf Man's trauma is caused by a "primal scene" in which the child, at one and a half years of age, watches his parents copulating. Yet it is not until the child is four years old that another event triggers the memory of the primal scene and renders it traumatic. Freud terms this phenomenon "Nachträglichkeit" (retroactive meaningfulness). In this case cause and effect so contaminate one another that the rational chronology of events (the kind of chronology that would be employed in "normal" lit. hist.) does not apply. The later even could well be said to be the cause of the earlier one, or rather the cause of its "meaning." Freud further suggests that even the "primal scene" is a phantasy, constructed out of the child's experience on a farm and the stories he was read. In place of origin, then, we have imagined construct. In the beginning is another metaphor or text.

In the wake of Vico, Nietzsche, and Freud, deconstruction assumes the problematic nature of the origin, and in so doing it undermines the logocentric and rationalist Western metaphysics upon which presence, continuity, and the notion of fulfillment are based. Following Nietzsche, Paul de Man emphasizes "the tropological structure that underlies all cognitions, incl. knowledge of the self" ("Autobiography as De-facement"). Far from making any totalization possible, rhet. suggests that even the ultimate self-understanding (autobiography) comes to rest on a figure. Through his discussions of irony (q.v.) and prosopopoeia, de Man points to the "rigorous unreliability" of literary lang. and to the "systematic undoing of all understanding." Irony is the recognition that conflict cannot be reduced to logic, and prosopopoeia (the giving of a face) is the *giving* of a face to that which is otherwise faceless. Such a rhetorical (ironic) reading undoes the possibility of lit. "hist." or of a "genetic" study of i., since neither history nor lit. would be generative processes (de Man speaks of the literary text's repeated failure to originate). Deconstruction makes impossible the reading of lit. in terms of periods, dismantles the notion of "lit. hist.," and dismisses the vision of a trad. as an aggregation of great works. Lit. hist. conceived along the lines of rhetorical figures and aporias would be a halting phenomenon, accounting "at the same time for the truth and falsehood of the knowledge lit. conveys about itself" (1983).

While the controversy over traditional lit. hist. vs. deconstruction was raging, Bloom published in 1973 *The Anxiety of I.*, followed by three subsequent books (1975, 1975, 1976) setting forth a theory of i. which opposed both the idealizing views of traditional lit. hist. and the deconstructive readings of Derrida and de Man. Three more books followed (1976, 1982, 1982), refining and extending these theories. Together the seven studies have made Bloom the major modern theorist on the subject. Bloom rejects the view of trad. as a "handing over" from precursor to later poet and argues for a reading of trad. as a series of struggles in which the later poet attempts to turn his lateness into earliness. The informing rhetorical figure for Bloom is metalepsis (q.v.)—the "trope-reversing-trope" which reverses cause and effect. Bloom rejects the conventional view of trad. as an inclusive order in which space is always made for the newcomers. Trad. is the force that takes potential originality away from a poet, always rendering the space available more limited and more exclusive. Originality in this view is a moment of freedom which the poet must achieve by creating discontinuity and thus turning loss into the illusion of origins. Bloom's story of influence-relations is one of power, violence, and appropriation, since these will be the marks of a poet's strength. He has no compunctions about dividing poets into strong and weak: weak poets accept the "handing over" and are silenced by it; strong poets react against it and their reaction is mapped out by Bloom into specific "revisionary ratios." The later poet "swerves" from the precursor by finding where the earlier poet went wrong, establishes discontinuity with the precursor, and rewrites the parent poem in such a way that, far from appearing to be influenced by the earlier, the later poet now appears to have created the earlier poet's work.

Bloom's approach to texts is not entirely unlike intertextual conceptions. For him, texts have neither closure nor meaning: meaning wanders between texts, and the meaning of a poem lies in its reaction to another poem. This wandering of meaning is a key concept in Bloom's theory of i., and when it becomes appropriation it merits the term "misreading." Misreading is the necessary condition of all strong poetry and all strong crit., for it describes a swerving away from the precursor's poem which in turn makes possible the strength of the belated poet. Misreading points to a practice which Bloom terms "antithetical crit." and which refuses to distinguish between poetry and crit. In the predicate that there are no right or wrong readings, only strong or weak readings, misreading opens up the space of persuasion, "the domain of the lie." Bloom attacks the humanistic and New Critical procedures which would make crit. an ancillary activity, and which, like Auerbach's "figura," would make the later reading a fulfillment of the earlier one. Strong crit. and strong poetry constitute a lie against time, granting the poet for a moment the illusion that he is self-begotten. Though he draws from poststructuralist theories of intertextuality, however, Bloom insists finally on "figures of willing" against "figures of knowing." Epistemology tells us that all origins are metaphors; Bloom's readings of Freud and Vico remind us that origins can be imagined. It is the power of great poetry to achieve the latter, and Bloom's seven books on i. are an account of the strategies by which a poet turns his belated "authority" into imaginative "priority," or the illusion of originality. Deconstruction transforms i. into intertextuality because the poet is himself an effect of a system of lang. in which he is inscribed. Bloom denies on the one hand a self that is not the construct of a poem, but on the other hand insists on the figurative creation of a poetic self. He argues that repression and forgetting (embedded in his theory of i.) offer a much more realistic account of the relations between one text and another and of the ways in which a text finally comes to read itself than deconstruction's emphasis on epistemology. In this way he insists on the importance of psychic strategies of reaction and defense as opposed to the epistemological concerns of deconstruction. Within a single poem, the condition of belatedness expresses itself as a series of disjunctive moments, and the "crossings" between these moments are defined as a repression of i., a leaping over time, and an image of voice. Voice (q.v.) is a term drawn from traditional crit., but Bloom's use of it is directed against purely rhetorical readings that focus on an impasse rather than a metaleptic leaping over that leads to self-begetting.

Self-begetting can be achieved in other ways. Geoffrey Hartman links quotation with the creation of a poetic self. A poet has to "overhear" and work through the ghostly echoes or allusions which haunt him, and in poets like Wordsworth quotation turns into self-begetting. Intertextuality (and its implication that the poem cannot complete itself) becomes *intra*textuality, with the poet finally quoting not Milton or the classics, but himself.

The arguments over i. over the past quarter century continue unabated. De Man refers to Bloom's scheme of a father-son struggle as a genetic model and hence a "rhetorical mystification." But while the issues between the priority of epistemology in deconstruction and the priority of the psyche in Bloom's theories will continue to affect the way in which i. is understood, it is clear that these concerns have radically transformed the study of i., turning it away from any simplistic kind of "source-study" toward more elaborate patterns of allusion.

Far from attempting to define a text's origin or cause, i. has shifted to a concern with the problematic wanderings between texts and has taken on the shape of theory. It is no longer possible to distinguish, in an age of theoretical self-consciousness, the objective literary relations between writers from the critical articulations that shape those relations, so that the study of i. engages the critical history through which i. is articulated. In a 1987 collection suggestively entitled *Re-membering Mil-*

ton, Robin Jarvis begins with a meditation on Havens' study and takes us to an "i.-theory" that argues the self-divided, androgynous, effeminate nature of poetic fathers and their texts, "shored against an otherness which inscribes them in the irrecuperable ebb of meaning." In contemp. theory the paternity of the text is an illusion, and i. and intertextuality address the complex wandering and dismemberments and the critical "rememberings" of the orphaned text. In the realm of theory, there are no last words, only further articulations. In this respect the theories of the past 20 years have, in transforming the understanding of i., opened up space for other work to follow. See also ALLUSION; ECHO VERSE; METALEPSIS; POETRY, THEORIES OF, *Recent Developments.*

T. S. Eliot, "Trad. and the Individual Talent" (1917), rpt. in *Essays*; S. Freud, "Aus der Gesch. einer infantilen Neurose" (1918), rpt. in *Standard Works*; R. D. Havens, *The I. of Milton on Eng. Poetry* (1922); N. Frye, "The Archetypes of Lit.," *KR* 13 (1951); J. Derrida, *L'Écriture et la différence* (1967); W. J. Bate, *The Burden of the Past and the Eng. Poet* (1970); C. Guillén, "The Aesthetics of Literary I.," *Lit. as System* (1971); H. Bloom, *The Anxiety of I.* (1973), *A Map of Misreading* (1975), *Kabbalah and Crit.* (1975), *Poetry and Repression* (1976), *Figures of Capable Imagination* (1976), *Wallace Stevens* (1976), *Agon* (1982), *The Breaking of the Vessels* (1982); E. Said, *Beginnings* (1975); *The New Nietzsche*, ed. D. Allison (1977); P. de Man, "Shelley Disfigured," in *Deconstruction and Crit.* (1979), *Blindness and Insight*, 2d ed. (1983), "Autobiography as De-facement," *The Rhet. of Romanticism* (1984); J. Riddel, "Decentering the Image," *Textual Strategies*, ed. J. Harari (1979); F. Lentricchia, *After the New Crit.* (1980)—critique of Bloom; S. M. Gilbert and S. Gubar, *The Madwoman in the Attic* (1980); G. H. Hartman, "Words, Wish, Worth: Wordsworth," in *Deconstruction and Crit.* (above); J. Hollander, *The Figure of Echo* (1981); J. Culler, *On Deconstruction* (1982); J. Guillory, *Poetic Authority* (1983); G. S. Jay, *T. S. Eliot and the Poetics of Lit. Hist.* (1983); *The Anxiety of Anticipation*, spec. iss. of *YFS* 66 (1984); C. Baker, *The Echoing Green* (1984); P. Brooks, "Fictions of the Wolf Man," *Reading for the Plot* (1984); D. Fite, *Harold Bloom* (1985); J. P. Mileur, *Literary Revisionism and the Burden of Modernity* (1985); N. Lukacher, *Primal Scenes* (1986); *Re-membering Milton*, ed. M. Nyquist and M. Ferguson (1987); H. R. Elam, "Harold Bloom," *Mod. Literary Critics 1955 to the Present*, ed. G. Jay (1988); *Intertextuality, Allusion, and Quotation: An Internat. Bibl. of Crit. Studies*, ed. U. J. Hebel (1989); L. A. Renza, "I.," *Critical Terms for Literary Study*, ed. F. Lentricchia and T. McLaughlin (1990); *I. and Intertextuality in Lit. Hist.*, ed. J. Clayton and E. Rothstein (1991).   H.R.E.

INITIAL RHYME. See ALLITERATION.

INITIATING ACTION. See PLOT.

INSPIRATION

INSCAPE AND INSTRESS. Inscape is Gerard Manley Hopkins' term for the pattern of attributes in a physical object that gives it at once both its individuality and its unity. In his critical study, Peters defines inscape as "the outward reflection of the inner nature of a thing, or a sensible copy or representation of its individual essence" (2). Gardner (1970) concurs: inscape denotes "those aspects of a thing, or *group* of things, which constitute its individual and 'especial' unity of being, its 'individually-distinctive beauty'" which is the "very essence of its nature" (xx). Hopkins later found confirmation of his conception of inscape in the Scotist notion of *haecceitas* or "thisness," namely that which uniquely differentiates each thing from all other things. Cf. ENARGEIA.

Closely related to inscape, the principle of individuation, is instress, which is "that energy or stress of being which holds the 'inscape' together", and, as a projective force, "carries it whole into the mind of the receiver," being "ultimately the stress of God's Will in and through all things" (Gardner xxi). See *Letters* 66, *Note-books* 98.—*The Letters of G. M. H. to Robert Bridges*, ed. C. C. Abbott (1935); *Note-books and Papers of G. M. H.*, ed. H. House (1937); W. A. M. Peters, *G. M. H.: A Critical Study* (1948); W. H. Gardner, *G. M. H.: A Study of Poetic Idiosyncrasy in Relation to Poetic Trad.*, 2 v. (1948–49), "G. M. H. and the Poetry of Inscape," *Theoria* 33 (1969); *Immortal Diamond*, ed. N. Weyand (1949); A. Heuser, *The Shaping Spirit of G. M. H.* (1959); A. J. McCarthy, "Toward a Definition of Hopkins' Inscape," *UDR* 4 (1967); *Poems of G. M. H.*, ed. W. H. Gardner and N. H. MacKenzie, 4th ed. (1970); P. Milward, *Landscape and Inscape* (1975); L. Cochran, "Instress and Its Place in the Poetics of G. M. H.," *HQ* 6 (1980). S.H.; T.V.F.B.

INSCRIPTION. See EPITAPH.

INSPIRATION (Lat. "breathing in"). Every poet recognizes that, during poetic composition, material emerges—words, images, figures, rhythms—from sources which lie beyond the pale of consciousness. Conscious effort and craft may indeed produce such material, and certainly they will shape all material, but at least some material seems to come into the mind from that place which we know only as *other*. In most cultures, poets, esp. those of religious conviction, have believed this source, this other, to be divine, the "breath" of the god or God blown into the recipient poet, who becomes the vehicle of godhead. In the West, the doctrine of i. has deep roots in both Hellenic and Hebraic cultures, from which streams it fed into Christianity and so was transmitted to the modern world, where it still holds sway: the concept of production by other-than-the-conscious-self has survived all radical alterations in attribution of its source.

At least as early as Homer, i. holds a central place in Gr. poetics, both as invocation to the gods or, more often, the Muses (see MUSE) for the gift of memorable speech, and also as claim that when the god does take possession, the poet enters a state of transcendent ecstasy or frenzy, a "poetic madness" (q.v.) or *furor poeticus*. Throughout most of archaic Gr. thought, the creation of art is associated with ritual, religion, and substance-induced *ecstasis*. In *Odyssey* 22.347–48, the bard Phemius acknowledges that the god has put songs into his heart. Hesiod and Pindar also invoke divine i., as does Theocritus, though with the latter perhaps the invocation has already become conventional. Plato refers to i. and to the doctrine of poetic madness often (*Laws* 719c), sometimes at length (*Symposium* 197a; *Phaedrus* 244–45). In the *Ion*, Plato suggests, borrowing from Democritus, that just as iron filings become magnetized by the magnet, so the poet is inspired through divine power, which power is conveyed by him in turn to the professional rhapsodes (q.v.) and their audiences. Aristotle repeats Plato's view in the *Poetics* (cf. *Rhetoric* 3.7) but seems uninterested in pursuing it; and the Peripatetic *Problemata* (Bk. 30; ca. 250 B.C.) offers an alternative, organic explanation, the four "humors."

Virgil's invocation to the Muse at *Aeneid* 1 is well known, and Ovid also refers to i. (*Ars amatoria* 3.549; *Fasti* 6.5). Longinus, one of the key texts of antiquity, treats i. from the reverse direction: the litmus test of great lit. is sublimity, and in all works which are sublime, the reader is transported, carried out of herself, expired as it were into divinity. Cicero discusses i. in his *On Divination* (1.18.37), *On the Nature of the Gods* (2.66: "No man was ever great without divine i."), *On the Orator* (2.46.194), and *The Tusculan Disputations* (1.26). Modern Eng. trs. of these passages use the word *i.*, but Cicero's Lat. terms are *afflatus, instinctus*, and *concitatio*: *inspiratio* does not appear until the late Lat. period. *Afflatus* in particular long survived as a synonym for i.

I. has, if anything, even more central a position in Hebraic poetics, as the poets and prophets of the Old Testament freely acknowledged (*Joel* 2:28–30, *Ezekiel* 2:1–10), though for them possession was by no means always willed, desired, or ecstatic (*Jeremiah*). When Christianity emerged triumphant over the other Roman mystery cults, it appropriated the notion of the Muses to the Christian God as the source of i., making not the breath of the god but divine grace the inseminating force. The Church Fathers—Jerome in particular—often referred to David as the perfect poet-prophet, inspired by God. St. Paul's claim that "all scripture is given by i. of God" (*2 Timothy* 3:16) was reasserted by literalists for millennia thereafter. I. became a central tenet of Neoplatonism, which transmitted it through the Middle Ages (see PLATONISM AND POETRY). The emergence of science in the 17th c. and of psychology in the 18th, however, transferred the locus of i. from outer to inner: now the source is the subconscious mind—

creative and energetic, but also appetitive and unstable. In this form, i. becomes, along with spontaneity (q.v.), one of the principal tenets of romanticism (q.v.), and is given the fixative, for the 20th c., by Freud (see PSYCHOLOGICAL CRITICISM). But the two loci, outer and inner, should not be taken as mutually exclusive, for even in the religious view the mind itself is a divine creation: the issue is only whether i. is directly given or mediate and proximal. Nor, similarly, should the two dimensions of poetic production—i. and craft, or seeing (see VATES) and making—be taken as mutually exclusive: the only question is whether the materials which appear are already fully formed and finished, or require subsequent shaping.

In its most extreme form, the doctrine of i. makes of the poet a passive receptacle and mere mouthpiece. This would reverse Auden's remark, elegizing Yeats, that poetry is only a mouth and makes nothing happen, for even there the saying itself is attributed to the poem; literalist i., by contrast, strips even the poet of creative capacity. Composition becomes now merely automatic writing, as Yeats reported of his wife, or Blake reported of himself. It is Blake who says, "I have written this Poem from immediate Dictation, 12 or sometimes 20 or 30 lines at a time, without Premeditation & even against my Will," and "I dare not pretend to be any other than the secretary the Authors are in Eternity." And we may recall that Socrates in the *Thaetetus* (149–50) claims that even the philosopher is merely the midwife of truth, possessing no wisdom in himself. Subsequent examples incl. Bede's account of Caedmon (*Ecclesiastical History* 4.24); Dante, *Purgatorio* 1.1–20; Boccaccio, *Genealogy of the Gods* 14, 15.39, 15.99, etc.; J. C. Scaliger, *Poetics libri septem* 1.2; Bacon, *Advancement of Learning*; and Ben Jonson, *Discoveries*. The most significant example in Eng. poetry is found in Milton's invocations of the Muse in *Paradise Lost* (e.g. 9.24). Milton's Muse is a source of enlightenment comparable to the Protestant "inner light" and equated with the spirit from whom Moses received the Ten Commandments.

This sort of theory finds its strongest modern statement in romantic poetics (q.v.): preromantic and romantic examples incl. Young's *Conjectures on Original Composition* ("genius" is "the god within"); Blake's letter to Thomas Butts of April 25, 1803; Wordsworth's conclusion to "The Recluse"; Coleridge's account of the origin of "Kubla Khan"; Poe's "Poetic Principle"; and Emerson's "The Poet." The doctrine will be found full blown [sic] in Shelley's *Defence of Poetry* (1821) and "Ode to the West Wind." But study of the notebooks and working habits of the romantic poets (incl. Shelley; cf. the preface to *Prometheus Unbound*) shows unequivocally that one should regard i. as more a part of the mythology of romanticism than of its praxis, for the romantics recognized the necessity of composition after—or without—i.: even Blake admitted that "without practice noth-

ing can be accomplished." To say this is to acknowledge the importance of craft, of what Horace called "the labor of the file," i.e. the application of effort and skill in the acquisition of technique—practiced, learned, remembered, repeated. Thus the concepts of i. and making may come to be seen as antinomies, which mutually entail and illuminate each other; and in the heat of sustained and complex poetic composition, a good poet, asked to distinguish the two, might not be able to say. It is of interest to notice that, in the *Iliad* and *Odyssey*, on every occasion when Homer appeals to the Muses, the appeal is for matter of a factual nature rather than for form. That is, Homer always asks for i. concerning what to say, never how to say it.

Less extreme forms of i. would probably be acceptable to many poets, particularly if the locus is left unspecified or if the nature of the infusion is seen as less systematic, less direct (the Aeolian harp, the correspondent breeze), or simply occasional. And if the joint effect of romanticism and Freudian psychology was ultimately to shift the locus of i. from external divinity to internal psyche, the mystery of the process of production itself was not thereby lessened. See also GENIUS; IMAGINATION; INVENTION; POETIC MADNESS; SPONTANEITY; WIT.

W. Dilthey, *Die Einbildungskraft des Dichters* (1887); Patterson, esp. 507–20; C. D. Baker, "Certain Religious Elements in the Eng. Doctrine of the Inspired Poet During the Ren.," *ELH* 6 (1939); E. A. Armstrong, *Shakespeare's Imagination: A Study of the Psychology of Association and I.* (1946); G. Grigson, *The Harp of Aeolus* (1947); J. C. Simopoulous, "The Study of I.," *JP* 45 (1948); R. E. M. Harding, *An Anatomy of I.*, 3d ed. (1948); G. Kleiner, *Die I. des Dichters* (1949); B. Ghiselin, *The Creative Process* (1952); J. Prévost, *Baudelaire* (1953); Abrams; C. M. Bowra, *I. and Poetry* (1955); M. C. Beardsley, "On the Creation of Art," *JAAC* 23 (1964–65); A. Anvi, "I. in Plato and the Heb. Prophets," *CL* 20 (1968); E. N. Tigerstedt, *Plato's Idea of Poetical I.* (1969); B. Vauter, *Biblical I.* (1972); P. Milward, *Landscape and Inscape* (1975); H. Mehnert, *Melancholia und I.* (1978); K. K. Ruthven, *Critical Assumptions* (1979), ch. 4; C. Fehrmann, *Poetic Creation* (tr. 1980); P. Murray, "Poetic I. in Early Greece," *JHI* 101 (1981); A. J. Harding, *Coleridge and the Inspired Word* (1985); *CHLC*.   T.V.F.B.

INSTRESS. See INSCAPE AND INSTRESS.

INTENSITY, although chiefly a romantic standard of poetic excellence, has a long history. Its most famous Cl. statement is in Longinus' *On the Sublime* (1st c. A.D.), with its emphasis on the superiority of original genius to trad., of strong emotion to restraint. Sir Philip Sidney's *An Apology for Poetry* (1595) similarly underlines the superiority of the poet to the philosopher, "for he yieldeth to the powers of the mind an image of that whereof the philosopher bestoweth but a wordless description: which doth neither strike, pierce, nor possess the sight of the soul so much as that other doth." Dryden's recognition of the i. of Shakespeare's imagery in *An Essay of Dramatic Poesy* (1668) can be seen in Neander's observation that "when he describes anything, you more than see it, you feel it too." Hobbes and Locke among other British empirical philosophers did much to challenge 18th-c. rationalism and to emphasize the power of sensation. Boileau's tr. of Longinus in 1674 stirred wide interest in literary circles; but Burke's treatise *On the Sublime and the Beautiful* (1757) was even more influential, with its characterization of the sublime as "productive of the strongest emotion which the mind is capable of feeling" or as producing "astonishment."

It is among the romantics that i. receives its fullest expression. Wordsworth speaks of poetry as "the spontaneous overflow of powerful feelings" ("Preface" to *Lyrical Ballads*, 1800). Shelley contends that it is impossible to read the most celebrated writers of his day "without being startled with the electric life which burns within their words" (*A Defence of Poetry*, 1821). Hazlitt's "gusto" embodies one of the most powerful descriptions of i. in art—"power or passion defining any object" ("On Gusto," 1816). His emphasis on poetry's need for a firm grasp of reality is reflected in Keats's idea of negative capability (q.v.)—"the excellence of every art is its i. capable of making all disagreeables evaporate from their being in close relationship with Beauty and Truth" (Letter of 1817).

Poe's attraction to i. is evidenced in his requirement that poems be short, that stories be such that they can be read in one sitting. "The value of the poem," he contends, "is in the ratio of this elevating excitement. But all excitements are, through a psychical necessity, transient" (*The Poetic Principle*, 1848). Subsequent 19th-c. advocates of art for art's sake continued this trad., with Pater searching for "the focus where the greatest number of vital forces unite in their purist energy," arguing that "to burn always with this hard, gemlike flame, to maintain this ecstasy is success in life" ("Preface" to *The Ren.*, 1873).

But in general the late 19th c. saw a marked shift away from the emphasis on i. in art. Major examples incl. Arnold's praise for great human actions and his unhappiness with situations where "suffering finds no vent in action" ("Preface" to *Poems*, 1853); the more scientific methodology of Sainte-Beuve and Taine in studying connections between work and author, work and the spirit of the age; and Tolstoy's stress on the social responsibility of art. More notable still is the critical writing of T. S. Eliot, with its focus on trad., on objectivity, on intelligence in the poet, and on the idea of the "objective correlative" (q.v.). The increasingly scientific and textually oriented approaches of the Am. New Critics downplayed i. in favor of irony

and structure, while poststructuralism, and esp. deconstruction (q.v.), questions fundamental presumptions of authorial presence and textual meaning, offering, instead of perceived i., delight in the play of lang. See also SUBLIME.—T. R. Henn, *Longinus and Eng. Crit.* (1934); S. Monk, *The Sublime* (1935); W. J. Bate, *From Classic to Romantic* (1946); Abrams; W. Jackson, *Immediacy: The Devel. of a Critical Concept from Addison to Coleridge* (1973); J. Engell, *The Creative Imagination* (1981); J. L. Mahoney, *The Whole Internal Universe* (1985); P. Veyne, *Roman Erotic Elegy* (tr. 1988), Epilogue; T. McFarland, *William Wordsworth: I. and Achievement* (1992). J.L.M.

INTENTION. The question of the relevance and value of i. has been at the center of debate in literary theory for close to half a century, and the controversy is far from reaching a satisfactory resolution. In Anglo-American literary theory, the debate has found its central terms in W. K. Wimsatt and Monroe Beardsley's well-known essay, "The Intentional Fallacy" (*SR* 54 [1946]; rpt. in Wimsatt's *The Verbal Icon* [1954]). Here Wimsatt and Beardsley characterize all crit. which takes account of authorial i. in the production of a work, insofar as this is known, as committing a serious "fallacy," and resolve the question in favor of New Critical formalism.

Wimsatt and Beardsley do not deny the presence of an element of i. in the structure of a poem; rather, they deny the usefulness of any genetic analysis of the concept of i. A genetic analysis attempts to give a causal explanation of how works of art are created, and many genetic theorists claim that their accounts also provide criteria for deciding whether or not a poem is successfully realized by the poet and, in such criteria, a more valid (because more objective) methodology for the appreciation and judgment of the poem. It is in order to reject this latter claim that Wimsatt and Beardsley argue that intentionalist crit. commits a fallacy.

The anti-intentionalist position denies that knowledge of a poet's i. is necessary to the proper critical appreciation and judgment of a poem. And it extends this denial to the romantic claim for the relationship of the poet's personality to his poems. Wimsatt and Beardsley give their position further support by arguing that poems are verbal structures made out of public lang., which is governed by the conventions of a lang. community; what ambiguity or obscurity (qq.v.) there may be in a poem occurs not because a private lang. has crept into the poem but because the conventions of a lang. community permit it, since it adds to the aesthetic richness of the poem. Anti-intentionalists (e.g. Wimsatt and Beardsley) argue that a great deal of crit. confuses inquiries beginning with "why" (our reasons for finding a poem interesting and successful) with inquiries beginning with "how" (the way the poem came about). In order to keep these two inquiries separate, Wimsatt and Beardsley would rewrite romantic poetics (q.v.):

> It would be convenient if the passwords of the intentional school, 'sincerity,' 'fidelity,' 'spontaneity,' 'authenticity,' 'genuineness,' 'originality,' could be equated with terms such as 'integrity,' 'relevance,' 'unity' [q.v.], 'function,' 'maturity,' 'subtlety,' 'adequacy,' and other more precise terms of evaluation—in short if 'expression' [q.v.] always meant aesthetic achievement. But this is not always so.

The rejection of intentionalist crit. is part of a more comprehensive attack on romanticism launched earlier in this century by T. E. Hulme and T. S. Eliot. For the modernists, the romantic critics (e.g. Pater, Sainte-Beuve, and Taine) are the antagonists whose method of appreciation and judgment of poetry is genetic. The romantic writers and critics place great emphasis on individual experience and inner vision, which constitute for them the nature of the work an artist produces. Consequently, artists no longer have a common set of problems which critics can understand and appraise. Given the emphasis on the peculiar qualities of the poet's vision, sincerity, originality, spontaneity, and adequacy become the romantic criteria of crit.

Anti-intentionalists reject *adequacy* and *originality* (q.v.) as criteria of expression on the grounds that one can argue for the adequacy of a poem only when we compare the poem to the poet's original experience. But in fact we have no verifiable access to that experience. And at what stage, they ask, is the experience original and the expression adequate to it? As T. S. Eliot trenchantly put it, "the 'experience' in question may be the result of a fusion of feelings so numerous and ultimately so obscure in their origins, that even if there be communication of them, the poet may hardly be aware of what he is communicating; and what is there to be communicated was not in existence before the poem was completed."

As for *sincerity* and *spontaneity* (qq.v.), anti-intentionalists argue that the first is relevant only when considering content, while the second is relevant only when considering process, but neither is adequate. Consequently, although the romantic criteria are usable, they are inadequate because they are neither necessary nor sufficient for crit., which needs a criterion of value. Hence the insistence by Eliot, the New Critics, and others that crit. ought to concern itself with the verbal structure of a poem.

Further, anti-intentionalists argue, in the process of writing, poets often abandon their original i. or include elements not central to that i. If there is a change in i. in the course of writing a poem we can no longer consider the original i. as the standard for judging. "'Intentions' of the author are always *a posteriori* ratiocinations, commentaries which certainly must be taken into account but also must be criticized in the light of the finished work of art" (Wellek). Moreover, in the case of anonymous poetry, Homer, Shakespeare, and most other poetry of the past, there is no way of determining the poet's i. And finally, there is the Socratic argument about the inherent unreliability of the poet's capacity to explain his i.

The controversy over the role of i. is part of a larger dispute on more fundamental questions about what a work of art is and what is proper to crit. The anti-intentionalist position conceives the theoretical problems of creativity and crit. as definitional and conceptual problems to be settled by rigorous logical scrutiny; thus Wimsatt and Beardsley argue that "it is not so much a historical statement as a definition to say that the intentional fallacy is a romantic one."

Romanticism, however, is a historical phenomenon which gives rise to a host of conceptual and definitional problems not resolvable by some unitary and objective logical procedure. Moreover, intentionalists such as E. D. Hirsch, Jr., question Wimsatt and Beardsley's distinction between poetic lang. and ordinary lang. Hirsch insists that all uses of lang. "are ethically governed by the i. of the author." On this view, the author is the determiner of the meaning of her work, because without that we have no compelling normative principle for validating one interpretation (q.v.) and rejecting others. Without some knowledge of what an author set out to do, we cannot reasonably judge how well she did it, for otherwise a critic is liable to condemn the work merely for not being the kind of work the critic happens to approve of—i.e. the kind of work the author never set out to create in the first place.

In sum, anti-intentionalists give considerable logical power and coherence to their position and its formalist and organicist criteria, and they succeed in showing the limitations of romantic criteria. Yet they cannot succeed in showing that intentionalists are entirely wrong, for there are always numerous ways by which other critics can show how art and personality, art and consciousness are indissolubly linked together, inevitably requiring the critic to take into account historical and biographical contexts for the proper interp. and judgment of literary works. See also SUBJECTIVITY AND OBJECTIVITY; THEORY.

T. S. Eliot, *The Use of Poetry and the Use of Crit.* (1933); *The Critic's Notebook*, ed. R. W. Stallman (1950), ch. 8; Abrams; I. Hungerland, "The Concept of I. in Art Crit.," *JP* 52 (1955); Wellek and Warren; M. C. Beardsley, *Aesthetics* (1958), *The Aesthetic Point of View* (1982), ch. 11; E. D. Hirsch, Jr., *Validity in Interp.* (1967), *The Aims of Interp.* (1976); R. Maier, "'The Intentional Fallacy' and the Logic of Lit. Crit.," *CE* 32 (1970); J. Derrida, *Speech and Phenomenon* (1973)—critique of authorial i. in the phenomenology of Husserl; G. Hermeren, "I. and Interp. in Lit. Crit.," *NLH* 7 (1975); W. K. Wimsatt, Jr., "Genesis: An Argument Resumed," *Day of the Leopards* (1976); *On Literary I.*, ed. D. Newton-de Molina (1976); J. W. Meiland, "Interp. as a Cognitive Discipline," *P&L* 2 (1977); K. K. Ruthven, *Critical Assumptions* (1979), ch. 9; S. Raval, "I. and Contemp. Literary Theory," *JAAC* 38 (1980); P. D. Juhl, *Interp.* (1980); J. M. Ellis, "Wittgensteinian Thinking in Theory of Crit.," *NLH* 12 (1981); J. Searle, *Intentionality* (1983); H. P. Grice, *Studies in the Way of Words* (1989); A. Patterson, "I.," *Critical Terms for Literary Study*, ed. F. Lentricchia and T. McLaughlin (1990); J. T. Shawcross, *Intentionality and the New Traditionalism* (1992).   S.R.

INTENTIONAL FALLACY. See INTENTION.

INTERLOCKING RHYME. See CHAIN RHYME.

INTERLUDE, enterlude (Lat. *interludum*, It. *intermedii*, Fr. *entremets*) was formerly considered a light break between acts of a longer didactic play or between courses in a banquet. The term has always been ambiguous and generally has been used as a catchall or generic term for a great variety of secular and nonsecular, short and long, comic and serious plays. Yet many mss. and early printed editions of the plays refer to themselves specifically as interludes. (e.g. *Ralph Roister Doister, Gammer Gurton's Needle*, and several of John Bale's plays), though later critics "correct" the term to the more commonly accepted morality (q.v.) or "moral play." The earliest reference to the i. is probably Robert Brunne's *Handlyng Synne* (1303), which includes "enterludes" of singing, tabor-playing, and piping as household entertainments, demonstrating the early connection between the i. and private patronized performance. The 14th-c. fragment "Interludium de clerico et puella," a bawdy secular play in the fabliau trad., is the first extant i.

Early references suggest that Tudor audiences and theater personnel considered the i. an indoor, private entertainment performed for a small audience by patronized players; it is tempting to suggest that the i. was perhaps commissioned by a patron for his players, unlike the mystery, miracle, and morality plays, which were in the hands of the parish or city clerks, or the stage-plays, which were the province of unpatronized and later professional troupes. By the time of Elizabeth, i. comes to refer to short plays in general.

In addition to indoor performance, small casts, select audience, and certain forms and themes characterize these plays. Frequently the i. is similar in structure to the "morality" or "moral play," but is concerned with social, political, pedagogical, and religious values in the guise of theological lessons. For example, *The I. of Youth* and *Hickscorner* (1514) are frequently called moralities because of their innocence-sin-redemption, battle-of-virtue-and-vice-paradigms, but *Youth* concerns ideological and specifically noble interests, and *Hickscorner* contains political satire.

Humanistic is. of the first half of the 16th c. are commonly written in loose four stress couplets (called "cantilevered verse" by Bernard), though other verseforms such as rhyme royal are often used as well. Many are debates or adaptations of Fr. farce whose purposes vary from amusement to instruction. John Redford's *Wit and Science*, (ca. 1530) considers education; John Rastell's *Of Gentleness and Nobility* (ca. 1530) debates the nature of true nobility, and his *Nature of the Four Elements* (ca. 1518) discusses contemporary natural science, including the doctrine of the roundness of the earth. John Heywood, the most prolific of the i. writers, composed *The Play Called the Four PP* (ca. 1525), a farcical presentation much influenced by Chaucer. See also MORALITY PLAY; FARCE.—D. Bevington, *From "Mankind" to Marlowe* (1962); *Tudor Drama and Politics* (1968); E. K. Chambers, *The Med. Stage*, 2 v. (1903), *The Elizabethan Stage*, 4 v. (1923); J. E. Bernard, *The Prosody of the Tudor I.* (1939); T. W. Craik, *The Tudor I.* (1958); G. Wickham, *Early Eng. Stages*, 3 v. (1959–81), *The Med. Theatre*, 3d ed. (1987); S. R. Westfall, *Patrons and Performance* (1990).   S.R.W.

INTERMEDIA. See CUBISM; PERFORMANCE; VISUAL ARTS AND POETRY; SOUND POETRY.

INTERNAL RHYME (Ger. *Inreim, Binnenreim*; It. *rimalmezzo*) is the Eng. cover-term for a variety of rhyming structures which have to do with rhyming words solely at line end but line-internally. Terminology is not at all standardized across prosodies, but the typology of forms includes: (1) rhyming (a) a word at line end with a word or words in the same line or (b) in another, or (2) rhyming (a) words within a line with each other but not with the end, or (b) words within one line with those in another but without ends. Types (1a) and (2a) occur within a single line, types (1b) and (2b) usually in two consecutive lines. Type (1a), Ger. *Inreim* or *Mittelreim*, Fr. *rime léonine* or *renforcée*, most often rhymes the word at line end with the word at the caesura: this is form developed in the Middle Ages known as leonine rhyme (q.v.) and the form which in Eng. prosody is usually meant by the phrase "i. r." Type (2a), Ger. *Binnenreim*, most often rhymes two words inside the same line and is sometimes in Eng. called "sectional r."; if the rhyming in a long-line couplet is ——a ——a —— b / ——a ——a ——b, splitting into short-line verse will give *tail rhyme* (q.v.). Type (1b), Ger. *Kettenreim* or *Mittenreim*, Fr. *rime batelée*, most often rhymes the line-end word of one line with the caesural word of the next, or vice versa; Eng. prosodists sometimes call this "caesura r." Type (2b) is rare. In Fr. *rime brisée*, caesura rhymes with caesura and end with end; this was already developed in leonine verse and is treated here as "cross

INTERPRETATION

rhyme" (q.v.). Both Fr. and Ger. forms developed from Med. Lat.; Meyer gives a full taxonomy of types. The Fr. terms for these elaborately interlaced sound patterns were developed mainly by the *Grands Rhétoriqueurs* of the late 15th and early 16th cs. See AICILL.—K. Bartsch, "Der innere Reim in der höfischen Lyrik," *Germania* 12 (1867); Meyer; Patterson; W. Vogt, "Binnenreime in der Edda," *Acta Philologica Scandinavica* 12 (1938); H. Forster, "Der Binnenreim (Reimformel)," *Sprachspiegel* 37 (1981); Brogan.   T.V.F.B.

INTERPRETATION. The entry for HERMENEU-TICS treats the history of interp., with attention to the broader meanings of this term and the philosophical issues they entail. The medieval systems of Jewish and Christian interp. are treated in the entry following the present one, INTERPRETATION, FOURFOLD METHOD OF. The present entry concerns the interp. of poetry written in modern langs., which did not become a central concern of crit. until the 20th c.

   I. TERMINOLOGY: THEORY VS. PRACTICE
  II. THEORETICAL ORIENTATIONS
     A. *Intrinsic Interp.*
     B. *Intentional Interp.*
     C. *Referential Interp.*
     D. *Structuralist and Semiotic Theories*
     E. *Reader-Response Theories*
 III. PHILOSOPHY, HERMENEUTICS,
     AND DECONSTRUCTION

I. TERMINOLOGY: THEORY VS. PRACTICE. Interp. begins when we have difficulty understanding a poem. "Explanation"—achieved by obtaining extratextual information about an allusion, for example—may solve the problem. If the relevance of an allusion (q.v.) is not apparent or a metaphor (q.v.) is hard to fathom, "explication" (q.v.)—elucidation of the meaning through analysis (q.v.)—will be necessary. In Fr. crit., *explication de texte* includes explanation and explication. The Ger. *erklären*, to explain, is often opposed to *verstehen*, to understand, the former being characteristic of the natural sciences, the latter of the human sciences. *Explizieren* means to explicate, in the limited sense; *auslegen*, like *interpretieren*, means to explicate and to interpret. As in Ger., the Eng. term "interp." includes explanation and explication but goes beyond them: the purpose of analysis is to understand the meaning of the poem as a whole (see THEME; MEANING, PROBLEM OF).

Some critics (e.g. Hirsch) hold that there is, in principle, a single correct interp. of a poem, notwithstanding the fact that it may have varied kinds of significance in connection with one or another situation. Critical pluralists argue that different theories of lit. can produce different interps. of a poem, all of which are legitimate (see CHICAGO SCHOOL; Pasternack 1975). "Syncretists" would draw together the useful parts of other theories to produce an encompassing interp. (Hermand and

Beck). One school of Ger. crit. has undertaken detailed studies of the evidence and logic that critics use in interp. The results are disappointing: critics' methods often prove to be haphazard and sometimes even contrary to their own theories. Attempts to create formal procedures for interp. based on principles taken from the philosophy of science, while revealing, have not proved influential (Göttner; Schmidt; Kindt and Schmidt; Pasternack 1979). Those who look on the multiplicity of interps. not as a defect but as a necessary result of literary study, one that cannot be explained or contained by pluralism or syncretism, are often called relativists or skeptics. But these terms are products of the very philosophical and critical trads. they would call into question.

Theories of interp. often seem remote from interpretive practice, which cannot be reduced mechanistically to a set of rules or a method. But arguments about interp., beginning with reasons, lead toward theoretical conclusions, and, as in philosophy, the quest for meaning becomes one for certainty, for knowledge grounded on indubitable premises. Some interpreters avoid this problem by rejecting theory (Knapp and Michaels), and some theorists seem determined to eschew praxis at all costs, concentrating instead on the study of literary conventions and textual structures. But this separation of theory and philosophy from interpretive praxis cannot be sustained, as de Man (1982) points out. In identifying a phrase as a metaphor, for example, we are unavoidably interpreting it, not merely describing it, and at the same time invoking poetics (the interp. depends on a theory of figures). This reciprocal relation between theory and praxis encompasses all aspects of interp. If we find a poem ambiguous, we can either appeal to a theory that provides methods of reducing ambiguity (q.v.), on the assumption that it is a fault in the poem or the interp.; or we can invoke a theory that explains why poems should be ambiguous, after which we might seek ambiguity where we had not noticed it before. The history of crit. shows that methods used in interpreting one type of poetry tend to be generalized into a theory that is then applied to other genres, in the same way that theories developed in other disciplines have been used to interpret poetry.

Two conceptual schemes discussed in other entries provide a useful means of classifying theories of interp. The first is Jakobson's communication model (see SEMIOTICS, POETIC; POETIC FUNCTION). On a horizontal axis, left to right, an "addresser" sends a "message" to an "addressee." The transmission depends on three factors named on a vertical axis over "message": the "context" (a situation and its realities), the "code" (in this case, lang.), and "contact," a means of communication (e.g., speech and hearing, or print and reading). This diagram corresponds to a simpler one in the entry for POETRY, THEORIES OF: a poet produces a poem for an audience, and the poem refers, in a

INTERPRETATION

general sense, to reality.

Intrinsic theories of interp. derive the meaning of a poem (Jakobson's "message") from its lang., isolating it from the poet, variations of audience, and other factors. In 20th-c. poetics (q.v.), such theories have been termed formalist or New Critical (see RUSSIAN FORMALISM; NEW CRITICISM). Other theorists emphasize the connection between the poem and other terms in the communication model; while not necessarily rejecting poetics, their allegiances are with rhet., linguistics, semiotics, or the social sciences. *Intentional* theories concern the relation of the poem to the consciousness of the poet or "addresser" (see INTENTION). *Referential* theories, which emphasize the poem's connections with reality (the "context"), include traditional literary historians, biographers, and social and political critics, as well as psychoanalytic and myth critics (who hold that poems embody encoded references to reality). The codes and conventions important in interp. are emphasized in structuralist and semiotic theories (see STRUCTURALISM; SEMIOTICS, POETIC); in research these are concerned with the history of ideas. *Reader-response* theories show how variations in the audience ("addressee") affect interp. (see READER-RESPONSE CRITICISM).

This classification is heuristic; for other purposes, it could be constellated differently. Some critics and philosophers see the communication model, based on the idea that we mentally encode and decode messages in specifiable contexts, as itself an erroneous interp. of how lang. works. The last section of this entry treats this view.

II. THEORETICAL ORIENTATIONS. In the 19th c., Arnold and Taine could refer to poetry as an interp. of life; in our century, the burden of interp. has shifted from the poets to the critics. For the emergence of significant theories of interp., three factors seem crucial. The 20th c. inherited a high esteem for the lyric (q.v.) from romanticism (q.v.). The enigmatic texts of modernist poets, the progeny of symbolism, imagism, and surrealism (qq.v.), required new interpretive methods (see OBSCURITY). A third factor contributing to the rise of intrinsic interp. was the growing importance of modern lits. in the universities. For an understanding of Gr., Lat., and Heb. texts, linguistic and historical knowledge had been paramount; modern poetry presented entirely different problems.

A. *Intrinsic Interp.* 19th-c. philosophy had provided a place for poetry in the scheme of things without indicating how it should be interpreted (see TWENTIETH-CENTURY POETICS). Poetry, said Kant, unites "a concept with a wealth of thought to which no verbal expression is completely adequate"; it is peculiarly suited to express feeling and the inner life, according to Hegel, and can do so without reliance on representation of the outer world (see EXPRESSION). As a mode of discourse, it is opposed to rhet.; it is not heard, but overheard (Mill); when produced by genius, it seems to flow

from nature (q.v.), not the poet's intentions (Kant). Similar ideas can be found in Coleridge. While not in agreement about what a poem is, these thinkers nevertheless all assume that it is *not* a "message" that the poet transmits to readers to inform or persuade them, as in ordinary discourse. For modern Fr. and It. critics, Bergson and Croce provided philosophical grounds for a conception of poetry as a special use of lang.

Drawing on these philosophical resources, a broad range of 20th-c. critics developed methods of poetic analysis that are fundamentally intrinsic or formalist (see CONTEXTUALISM; CONCRETE UNIVERSAL). The assumption that the meaning of poetry is entangled in its concrete and figural lang.—so ambiguous, paradoxical, ironic, and polysemous that it is not reducible to paraphrase (q.v.)—is most obviously applicable to modern poems. Because modern poets were influenced by a poetics that advocated impersonality and discouraged mimetic representation, early advocates of intrinsic interp. often found in practice what they held in principle: modern poems were self-sufficient entities, complex verbal structures creating meanings that could not be recovered from the poet's biography or historical circumstances. Mallarmé, Valéry, Rilke, the late Hölderlin, Eliot, and Wallace Stevens were poets ideally suited to intrinsic interp., as were some metaphysical poets, *Culteranismo* (q.v.), Scève, and Dante's *canzoni*.

In order to apply intrinsic interp. to poetry written between the 17th and 20th cs., it was necessary, as Cleanth Brooks said, to read "the intervening poems . . . as one has learned to read Donne and the moderns." Confirmation of the intrinsic theory required the discovery of complexity in poems that appeared simple (Staiger). Originally a method for the interp. of obscure lyrics, the immanent approach now became a theory that determined how *all* poetry should be read: poems not displaying the features it esteemed were correspondingly devalued.

The faults of intrinsic crit., which have been more than adequately exhibited, should be balanced against its pedagogical achievements. As Richards showed, the wildly disparate interps. produced by students often resulted from an inability to recognize the basic conventions of poetry, quite apart from the ambiguity that could be imputed to it (Empson). Influential textbooks led to the improvement of exegetical skills (Brooks and Warren; Kayser), and cogent accounts of the logic underlying intrinsic interp. (Wimsatt; Burckhardt) provided later generations of critics with a theoretical awareness that helped them pinpoint the deficiencies of the theory.

B. *Intentional Interp.* Intrinsic interp. achieved such widespread acceptance that even politically conscious critics (Bakhtin; Sartre) did not challenge it; conceding the autonomy (q.v.) of poetry, they devoted their critical energies to socially relevant prose forms. Those who opposed intrinsic interp. in the 1950s, despite their differences, agreed on one thing: poems are not self-contained entities cut off from their authors, readers, and reality. Though distinctive in some structural or textual respects, in other respects they do not differ in kind from other forms of verbal communication.

To separate the poet from the poem, intrinsic interp. had argued that the speaker should always be construed as a dramatized persona (q.v.), a poetic voice (q.v.), never to be identified with the flesh-and-blood author. Apart from the difficulties that this position presents with respect to poems that are obviously personal, it glosses over important theoretical issues. Unlike organisms (see ORGANICISM), poems have meaning because someone intends them to mean something. To interpret them, it is helpful to consider the poet's intentions (see INTENTION) insofar as they are manifest or latent in his or her other writings and inferable from biographical study.

From this premise, *intentional* theorists diverge along several lines. Philosophers have distinguished nine meanings of "intention," three of which are important here. Some critics use the word in its everyday sense but add to it a concept from phenomenology: meaning *as such* is intentional (Hirsch; Juhl). A poem therefore means what the poet intended it to mean, in general and in every particular, though we are unlikely ever to know exactly what that meaning was. In a more fully phenomenological sense, intentionality is not just a matter of conceptual meaning; it is that property of consciousness whereby objects are constituted in all their experiential dimensions. Interp. from this point of view is a matter of assimilating all of a poet's writings in order to replicate his or her mode of experiencing the world—sensory and emotional as well as intellectual and volitional. In intrinsic crit., image (q.v.) and idea are the parts that constitute the unity (q.v.) of the poem; for "critics of consciousness," the poet's mind is the unity to be interpreted, and images taken from various poems become parts used to reconstitute that whole (see GENEVA SCHOOL).

C. *Referential Interp.* When the relationship between the poet and the poem is the focus of interp., intention and meaning may become nearly synonymous. But the latter terms are often opposed to each other in ordinary usage. Like other mortals, poets may intend to conceal facts (representing as a general situation some incident that has a specific biographical basis) and may unintentionally convey meanings that they do not try to communicate. *Referential* or mimetic theories emphasize the importance of concrete circumstances in determining what a poem means. They recover from history and biography the facts or situations to which poems directly or indirectly refer. In a similar manner, we interpret what friends say in light of what we know of them; and to understand other cultures, we must know what

they assume about the world as well as what they "intend" to say about it. To interpret a poem from the past, we must understand not just its words but its pastness; its distance from us becomes part of its meaning.

To these traditional methods of interp. the 20th c. has added others based on the assumption that references to reality in lit. can themselves be encoded. Todorov refers to these as symbolic or "finalist" theories; they are exemplified in the entries for ARCHETYPE, MYTH, and PSYCHOLOGICAL CRITICISM. He includes Marxist interps. in this category, but their interpretive decoding usually connects poetry to the facts of history rather than to an individual or transhistorical psyche (see MARXIST CRITICISM). Jameson bridges the gap between psyche and history by positing a "political unconsciousness" that contains an imaginary replication of one's socioeconomic circumstances.

The success of referential theories is inseparable from their weakness (see HISTORICISM). The wholeness of meaning they reconstruct is that of a life, an epoch of history, or a racial unconscious; poems are merely parts useful in creating these wholes. That a poem is a product of its time is undeniably true; but it is easier to posit connections between the two than to confirm or refute them. Rather than providing a factual basis for interpretive inference, historiography produces different histories, which are themselves interps.; the same is true of biography and psychology. Some recent literary critics have tried to resolve this dilemma by treating all the events and writing of a period as a "social text." From this point of view, history is not the cause or source of lit.; acts and texts are both embodiments of cultural powers and practices (Greenblatt; Pechter). Alternatively, one may find conceptual configurations emerging in poetry before they are registered elsewhere in culture (Fineman).

D. *Structuralist and Semiotic Theories.* In the traditional opposition of intrinsic to extrinsic interp. and of language-bound meanings to facts independent of linguistic embodiment, what is lacking is attention to the mediating terms through which these antitheses interact: the conventions and codes that bind poet, poem, lang., and reality together in shared systems of signification. An emphasis on the distinctive *codes* of poetry is characteristic of Rus. Formalism and structuralism (qq.v.). Shklovskij conceived them as purely formal structures: "The purpose of the new form is not to express new content, but to change an old form which has lost its aesthetic quality." Jakobson isolated the "poetic function" (q.v.) in phonetic, syntactic, and grammatical features (see EQUIVALENCE). Like the formalists, some structuralists and poststructuralists have argued that the purpose of literary study should not be to produce still more interps. but "to advance one's understanding of the conventions and operations of an institution, a mode of discourse" (Culler).

INTERPRETATION

Semioticians argue that social and cultural codes are as important as linguistic and literary conventions in the interp. of poetry. Challenging traditional methods of extracting a theme from a poem, J. Mukařovský held that *all* of its features, including sound, are endowed with meaning, and that poetry refers not to reality as such, but to the "total context of so-called social phenomena, for example, philosophy, politics, religion, economics, and so on." The Prague School (q.v.) structuralists found in poems a dialectical tension between the poet and others of his era; between inherited and innovative forms; between lit. and society. Interp. thus becomes an inclusive project that moves back and forth between text and culture, correlating the semiotic configurations of the text with the cultural contexts in which they take on one or another significance. In its final phase, this school began to explore the ways in which interp. depends upon the assumptions, habits, and expectations of readers in different historical periods (see Galan).

E. *Reader-response Theories.* Phenomenological critics, structuralists, and semioticians all hold that a poem exists as an object of interp. only when it is read; in this sense they recognize the importance of the reader. But they are usually interested in finding what remains constant in varied instances of interp. rather than in determining why these vary. Riffaterre, for example, criticized Jakobson and Lévi-Strauss for disregarding the reader when identifying patterns in poetry, but he did not go on to argue that readers could legitimately find different meanings in poems. His semiotic approach assumes that there is only one valid interp. of a poem, that it involves not "meaning" (reference to reality) but "significance" (semantic coherence within the poem), and that all deviations from clear meaning are generated by a commonplace or cliché that serves as the poem's matrix. "All of the reader's possible reactions to the text" constitute for him the audience; this inclusiveness insulates his theory from individual and historical differences.

Reader-response (q.v.) critics explore the ways in which interp. depends upon the audience. Their answers to the following questions are crucial: (a) Who is the reader? For structuralists and semioticians, the reader is anyone who has acquired "competence" in understanding literary codes and conventions. From an empirical point of view, however, the reader is a particular person who may produce a unique interp., or simply disregard the exegetical labors undertaken by interpreters to enjoy the poem (see TASTE). Other critics posit an ideal reader or the kind of reader implied by the text as the appropriate interpreter of its content. (b) To what extent does the poem exercise control over the interp.? The phenomenologist's assertion that a text exists only as it is perceived and understood can correct a naive belief that the meaning lies "in" the words, inde-

pendent of interp., but it can also lead to the conclusion that meaning is in the reader, independent of any corrigible experience of words. Interps. that cannot plausibly be related to the words of a poem may serve as evidence for this conclusion, but it has had little effect on the practices of interpretive communities, which produce tacit (and evolving) criteria governing how readings will be justified. (c) What is "interp."? As Ricoeur and Ray point out, critics at one extreme hold that it is an act, the process of experiencing a text, which may cancel as many meanings as it creates (Fish); at the other extreme is the traditional view that the purpose of interp. is to reconstitute a stable meaning after the experience of reading.

Jauss tries to accommodate these differences in his inclusive model of reader response. In his view response comprises three phases: understanding (the act of reading), interp. (reflective constitution of meaning), and application (relating the interp. to other knowledge and experience). He distinguishes the *Wirkung* or effect of a poem, which the structure of the text lays out for the reader, from its *Rezeption* or reception, the actualization of its meaning conditioned by the reader's social and personal existence. Despite their differences, readers from a particular period have much in common. The history of literary reception shows that poems survive because they remain open to varied interps. governed by needs and expectations that could not have been imagined when they were written. Other critics would add that interp. can thus be seen as a product of "interpretive communities," institutional practices, and social structures that will determine whether or not an innovative reading is acceptable (Fish; Kermode).

III. PHILOSOPHY, HERMENEUTICS, AND DECONSTRUCTION. The shift from intrinsic interp. to theories based on the communication model corresponded to a shift in interest from lyric poetry to narrative modes in literary study. Consideration of how literary codes, reality, and readers determine the meaning of texts seemed to provide a sound basis for interp. of lit. within a general theory of communication (e.g. Jakobson's); while disagreements about interp. persisted, it was at least possible to point out their sources within the framework of the model. Beginning in the 1970s, however, the model itself was called into question—either because it failed to account for specific features of literary lang. or because of its philosophical presuppositions.

If poets intend to convey clear messages, they are remarkably unsuccessful in doing so; the variety of interps. elicited by their works suggests that they have other aims. Bloom holds that their intention is to attain literary immortality and that their poems are misinterpretations of earlier poems, created to clear a space for their own meanings in the trad. (see INFLUENCE). In a similar manner, the "strong" reader or critic proposes a new interp. of a poem to assert priority over other readers and, indeed, over the poem itself.

The assumption that literary lang. is a deviation from ordinary lang., one in which conventions (the use of figures and sound effects) add ambiguity and pleasure to messages that could be transmitted without them, is likewise questionable. Intrinsic critics held that poetry unites meaning (codes) and being (reference); de Man argued that allegory reveals the gap between the two, and that rhet. cannot be contained within the tidy codes of linguistics and semiotics (see TWENTIETH-CENTURY POETICS, sect. II). Despite their differences, intrinsic and subsequent critics agree that poets explore the relationship between lang. and reference, rather than assuming it to be unproblematic.

The communication model presupposes that, on the basis of reliable knowledge about intentions, history, literary conventions, and lang., we can elucidate the less evident meanings contained in poems. But that purportedly reliable knowledge is *itself* an interp., based on philosophical and linguistic assumptions that are far from certain (see HERMENEUTICS, sect. IV). Interp. is always caught in the hermeneutic circle: rather than using facts to determine meaning, we cannot help but let our anticipations of meaning determine what "facts" (themselves prior interps.) we will select to support it (see Fish 1980).

Linguists, philosophers, and critics who employ the communication model treat speech as the typical instance of lang. use. In a particular context, at a certain moment, someone says something for a specifiable purpose. When this model is applied to written poetry, interp. becomes a matter of recovering information we lack about the poet, the audience, and a unique moment of inscription. Writing is seen as an impoverished version of speech, since it has been torn from a presence that made it meaningful. It is possible, however, to construe writing as a distinct method of creating meaning, in which case interp. becomes a very different activity.

As Ricoeur says, writing severs lang. from the writer and "opens it to an indefinite range of potential readers in an indeterminate time." An interp. that would confine the meaning of a poem to the historical moment of its creation is at odds with the poet's intentions, and denial that poems written in earlier centuries have meaning in our world is at odds with our desires. If, in the case of writing, the "context" and "addressee" of the communication model continually change, interp. cannot be invariant. The different interps. of a poem we inherit from the past may themselves become part of its meaning for us (Jauss).

For deconstruction (q.v.), the instability of meaning apparent in the case of writing results not just from the text's survival in changing circumstances but from the character of lang. itself. Phi-

losophers have argued that problems of interp. result from literary uses of lang. (e.g. metaphor and polysemy) that could be eliminated in a systematic literalism. Deconstructive critics reply that philosophers also make use of these "supplementary" aspects of lang. in building systems that themselves contain paradoxes and contradictions. Literary lang. and the interpretive difficulties it poses can be seen as characteristic of lang. in general. As a self-reflexive unfolding of the figural and rhetorical constituents of meaning, poetry explores and exemplifies the impossibility of attaining a univocal interp. of words and the world. From this point of view, the critic's task is to discover the patterns underlying alternative readings of a poem and the points at which they intersect to create an impasse or dilemma.

By discovering a diversity of interpretive possibilities in the lang. of poetry, deconstruction confers on the poetic text a richness denied it in intentionalist, referential, structuralist, and reader-response theories. Miller suggests that the impossibility of univocal interp. is implied in poems that he interprets—a paradoxical conclusion that can only be as correct as his interp. Many critics admit or assert that there is no single correct interp. of a poem; yet when themselves engaged in interp., they very often urge the superiority of theirs; and almost always cannot help but imply that the poem has one range of meanings rather than another, referring to its formal features to substantiate their arguments. Thus theory and praxis, while interdependent, remain dialectically at odds with each other in the critical acts of reading and writing. See also CRITICISM; POETRY, THEORIES OF; THEORY; TWENTIETH-CENTURY POETICS, *American and British*.

I. A. Richards, *Practical Crit.* (1929); Brooks; Empson; W. K. Wimsatt, Jr., *The Verbal Icon* (1954); E. Staiger, *Die Kunst der Interp.* (1955); Wellek and Warren; M. C. Beardsley, *Aesthetics* (1958); A. Child, *Interp.: A General Theory* (1965); S. Sontag, *Against Interp.* (1966); *Immanente Ästhetik—Ästhetische Reflexion*, ed. W. Iser (1966); Jakobson; E. D. Hirsch, Jr., *Validity in Interp.* (1967), *The Aims of Interp.* (1976); symposium on Hirsch 1967 in *Genre* 1,3 (1968), with his reply in 2,1; S. Fish, *Surprised by Sin* (1972), *Is There a Text in This Class?* (1980); H. Bloom, *The Anxiety of Influence* (1973); H. Göttner, *Logik der Interp.* (1973); J. Hermand and E. T. Beck, *Interpretive Synthesis* (1975); G. Pasternack, *Theoriebildung in der Literaturwiss.* (1975), *Interp.* (1979); L. Pollmann, "Lyrikinterp. heute," *Sprachen der Lyrik*, ed. E. Köhler (1975); S. J. Schmidt, *Literaturwiss. als argumentierende Wiss.* (1975); W. Kindt and S. J. Schmidt, *Interpretationsanalysen* (1976); J. A. Coulter, *The Literary Microcosm* (1976)—Neoplatonic theories of interp.; J. Mukařovský, "Art as Semiotic Fact," *Semiotics of Art*, ed. I. R. Titunik et al. (1976); P. Ricoeur, *Interp. Theory* (1976); J. W. Meiland, "Interp. as a Cognitive Discipline," *P&L* 2 (1977);

W. Kayser, *Das Sprachliche Kunstwerk*, 18th ed. (1978); M. Riffaterre, *Semiotics of Poetry* (1978); T. Todorov, *Symbolism and Interp.* (1978); F. Kermode, *The Genesis of Secrecy* (1979), *The Classic* (1983); H. Bloom et al., *Deconstruction and Crit.* (1979); P. de Man, *Allegories of Reading* (1979), Intro. to Jauss (below); S. Greenblatt, *Ren. Self-Fashioning* (1980); P. D. Juhl, *Interp.* (1980); *Text und Applikation*, ed. M. Fuhrmann et al. (1981); J. Culler, "Beyond Interp.," *The Pursuit of Signs* (1981); F. Jameson, *The Political Unconscious* (1981); Fowler; H. R. Jauss, *Toward an Aesthetic of Reception* (1982), *Aesthetic Experience and Literary Hermeneutics* (1982); S. Knapp and W. B. Michaels, "Against Theory," *CritI* 8 (1982); de Man; K. Mueller-Vollmer, "Zur Problematik des Interpretationsbegriffs," *Erkennen und Deuten*, ed. M. Woodmansee et al. (1983), and "Understanding and Interp.," *Lit. Crit. and Philosophy*, ed. J. P. Strelka (1983); W. E. Rogers, *The Three Genres and the Interp. of Lyric* (1983); S. Schmidt, "Selected Bibl. on Interp. (1970–1982)," *Poetics* 12 (1983); F. Galan, *Historic Structures* (1984); W. Ray, *Literary Meaning* (1984); J. H. Miller, *The Linguistic Moment* (1985); J. Fineman, *Shakespeare's Perjured Eye* (1986); E. Schauber and E. Spolsky, *The Bounds of Interp.: Linguistic Theory and Literary Text* (1986); E. Pechter, "The New Historicism and Its Discontents," *PMLA* 102 (1987); A. Barnes, *On Interp.: A Critical Analysis* (1988); J. M. Ellis, *Against Deconstruction* (1989); P. B. Armstrong, *Conflicting Readings: Variety and Validity in Interp.* (1990); S. Mailloux, "Interp.," *Critical Terms for Literary Study*, ed. F. Lentricchia and T. McLaughlin (1990); U. Eco, *The Limits of Interp.* (1990).   W.M.

INTERPRETATION, FOURFOLD METHOD OF. This phrase, or any of a number of variations on it, refers to the classical system of biblical interp. dominant in the Middle Ages and Ren., and derived from Patristic theorizing on and systematizing of biblical hermeneutics (see HERMENEUTICS). The common fourfold system—the literal (historical) level, the allegorical (typological or figural) level, the tropological (moral) level, and the anagogical (eschatological) level—was not widely developed among Christian exegetes until the 12th c.; a similar yet different fourfold hermeneutic was first articulated among Jews in the late 13th c. One of the best known examples, in the letter to Can Grande that is prefixed to the *Paradiso* and was once attributed to Dante, illustrates the fourfold method with respect to the Israelite exodus from Egypt: on the literal level, the Hebrews celebrated Passover and left Egypt; allegorically, members of the Church are redeemed through Jesus; tropologically, Christians are transformed from sinfulness to grace; anagogically, the soul passes from material bondage to eternal existence. At no time was the formula slavishly applied, nor does it suit all or even most biblical verses, and not all theories of biblical interp. in either the Patristic or later periods were classified in a fourfold way.

A more fundamental bipartite division contrasts literal and spiritual (or fuller ["plenior"]) meaning, both of which were themselves subdivided variously. The basic argument in the NT for the genuineness of Jesus' claim to divinity was based on the notion of a deeper meaning in the OT to be discovered in the fullness of time. Interp. of a highly regarded text was also allegorized to preserve its currency. Classical Judaism posited an oral trad. that interpreted written scripture through the hermeneutic of *midrash* to derive contemp. law and express current values. Similarly, Hellenistic scholars in Alexandria developed a systematic exegesis of Homer in order to keep the Cl. epics up to date. Alexandria, carrying on this pagan and Rabbinic trad., esp. in Philo (d. ca. 54 A.D.), produced a lively school of biblical exegesis which was Christianized largely by Origen of Alexandria (d. 254). This school came to emphasize the spiritual or allegorical sense, while the interpretive school of Antioch tended to stress philologically determined meaning. Allegory (q.v.) within the NT is usually typological or figural, in which the actions and events of the OT are seen to foreshadow true events in the NT and in the future, a kind of "horizontal" allegory. Allegory on the Bible, by contrast, is more frequently "vertical," in which one, two, three, or four levels are found. However, a strict distinction between the two types of allegory is not always possible.

Here we can only briefly trace the devel. of biblical exegesis. Cl. Rabbinic interp. employed a network of hermeneutic techniques—midrash—for discovering divine revelation in scripture. Legal midrash, for practical reasons, had to arrive at a single authoritative interp., but homiletical midrash could proliferate alternate meanings. The Jewish sect at the Dead Sea (2d c. B.C.–1st c. A.D.) and the later Rabbis explained prophetic and other biblical texts according to a contemp. esoteric meaning as well as a historical one. Such esoteric interp. harks back to Joseph's interpreting of his dream and Daniel's deciphering of the writing on the wall in the Bible. Allegorical interp. was applied early among Jews and then Christians to the Song of Songs, ostensibly personal love poetry but also interpreted as expressions of devotion between God and Israel or God and the Church.

Indeed, Paul and the early Church Fathers understood the NT to represent a fulfillment of the figures and "types" of the OT. A "type" is a character, institution, or concept that is taken symbolically. Types of the OT, in this view, prefigure "antitypes" of the NT that realize or replace them. For example, the paschal lamb offering of *Exodus* 12, of which no bone was to be broken, prefigures the divine sacrifice of Jesus on the cross; and the tabernacle of God in the Sinai wilderness "becomes" the incarnation of God in Jesus. Jewish midrash may generally be distinguished from Christian typological interp. by the former's exegetical dependence on the actual (Heb.) lang. of its scriptural base.

Origen had a threefold system—somatic, psychic, and pneumatic—based on Hebraic and Gr. psychology. Augustine in his *De doctrina christiana* provided the canonical justification to the high Middle Ages for the use of allegorical methods, even though his own system usually refers to the way Jesus Himself taught rather than to current biblical exegesis. He did distinguish, however, the spiritual from the literal sense, and he provided an aesthetic of allegory in which the beauty of figurative and obscure biblical lang. is praised. Gregory the Great (d. 604), esp. in his *Homilies on Ezechial* and *Moralia* (a moralized commentary on Job), proposed a threefold method which become more influential than Augustine's in med. biblical allegorizing.

Various medieval schools of exegesis flourished and carried on the trad.: the Ir. Monastic School, the Benedictines, the School of Laon, the Victorine School, the school of Scholastic exegesis, and, above all, from the 12th c. on, a "scientific" school, culminating in Nicholas of Lyra of the 14th c., who unified all the exegetical trads. for subsequent Christianity. Among Jews, the 12th c. Franco-German school of Rashi (Rabbi Solomon Itzhaki) distinguished contextual ("peshat") from rabbinic exegetical ("derash") meaning. Sp. Jewish exegetes developed allegory to bring scripture into congruence with rational or philosophical truth; in the 13th c., they adopted mystical doctrines as well. Accordingly, in 1291, Bahya ben Asher employed a fourfold system of interp. which soon became known as "*pardes*" (Heb. for "orchard")—an acronym for "peshat" (contextual, philological level), "remez" (rational or philosophical level), "derash" (rabbinic, midrashic), and "sod" (mystical, kabbalistic).

In modern literary theory, the medieval and Ren. use of the so-called fourfold system of interp. in lit. has been much debated. Is there a "fourfold" meaning to the *Romance of the Rose*, or in Chaucer or Chrétien de Troyes, and so on? Some have thought so. That biblical symbolism and exegesis had influence on medieval and Ren. works is beyond doubt, but the degree and extent of that influence is difficult to establish. Typological and allegorical levels of meaning have been plausibly attributed to such explicitly Christian poets as Milton, Herbert, and Blake. In the 20th c., typological models of crit. have been proposed in particular by Protestant biblicists and by Northrop Frye. See also ALLEGORY; FIGURATION; HEBRAISM; HERMENEUTICS; INTERPRETATION; MEDIEVAL POETICS.

F. W. Farrar, *Hist. of Interp.* (1886); J. Tate, "Plato and Allegorical Interp.," *ClassQ* 23–24 (1929–30), "On the Hist. of Allegorism," *ClassQ* 28 (1934); B. Smalley, *The Study of the Bible in the Middle Ages*, 2d

ed. (1952); G. W. H. Lampe and K. J. Woollcombe, *Essays on Typology* (1957); E. Auerbach, "Figura," *Scenes from the Drama of European Lit.* (1959); H. de Lubac, *Exégèse médiévale*, 4 v. (1959–64); *Critical Approaches to Med. Lit.*, ed. D. Bethurum (1960); D. W. Robertson, Jr., *A Preface to Chaucer* (1962); H. Hailperin, *Rashi and the Christian Scholars* (1963); *Cambridge Hist. of the Bible*, ed. P. R. Ackroyd et al., 3 v. (1963–69)—esp. 2.155–279; R. Tuve, *Allegorical Imagery* (1966); H. R. Jauss, *Entstehung und Strukturwandel der allegorischen Dichtung* (1968); D. C. Allen, *Mysteriously Meant* (1970); *Anagogic Qualities of Lit.*, ed. J. Strelka, spec. iss. of *YCC* 4 (1971); J. Pépin, *Dante et la trad. de l'allégorie* (1971); M. W. Bloomfield, "Allegory as Interp.," *NLH* 3 (1971–72); S. Bercovitch, *The Puritan Origins of the Am. Self* (1975); *Literary Uses of Typology*, ed. E. Miner (1977); G. Marshall, *The Tempering of Allegory* (1982); M. Saperstein, *Decoding the Rabbis* (1982); F. Talmage, "Apples of Gold," *Jewish Spirituality from the Bible through the Middle Ages*, ed. A. Green (1986); *A Guide to Contemp. Hermeneutics*, ed. D. K. McKim (1986); *Mikra*, ed. M. J. Mulder (1988); J. Saly, *Dante's Paradiso: An Interp. of the Anagogical Meaning* (1989); *CHLC*, 85 ff.; U. Eco, "Two Models of Interp.," *The Limits of Interp.* (1990).

M.W.B.; E.L.G.

INTERTEXTUALITY refers to those conditions of textuality (q.v.) which affect and describe the relations between texts, and in most respects is synonymous with textuality. It originates in the crisis of representation and the absent origin that would guarantee meaning, centrality, and reference. Without an ultimate referent that would make possible the self-presence and meaning of a text, texts are by definition fragments in open and endless relations with all other texts.

In traditional models of influence (q.v.), a text comes to rest on a prior text which functions as a stable source which is retrieved and made present by a study of allusion (q.v.), quotation, and reference. Relations between texts are thus straightforward and determinate. Their determinacy is the result of five premises of traditional crit.: (1) that lang. has the capacity to create stable meaning; (2) that such meaning exists within the confines of form; (3) that the artist is in control of meaning; (4) that a work has closure (q.v.), its tensions, ambiguities, and ironies coming to a point of resolution; and (5) that crit. is an ancillary activity, separate from lit. These premises tend toward totality (either in the mode of "the work itself" [see AUTONOMY; NEW CRITICISM] or Frye's mode of the "total form of lit." [see MYTH CRITICISM]), and the concepts of stable meaning and the artist's control of it are basic to the humanistic trad. of learning, which affirms and emphasizes the notions of human self and human will.

In the late 1950s and '60s, however, as a result of the influx of Fr. crit. into America, the premises upon which the study of lit. had been carried out changed dramatically, and the conceptual approach to literary relations underwent an equally radical transformation. With structuralism (q.v.) and poststructuralism (see DECONSTRUCTION), the concept of "influence" was discarded in favor of the concept of "i." Seven major premises now come into play: (1) Lang. is not a transparent medium of thought or a tool in the service of communication; it is arbitrary and dense, and its very excessiveness leads to an infinite number of interps. (2) Texts are fragments, without closure or resolution. No text is self-sufficient; each text is fraught with explicit or invisible quotation marks that dispel the illusion of its autonomy and refer it endlessly to other texts—like the entries in this *Encyclopedia*, referring parenthetically to other references, except that there is no way to contain all possible references in any encyclopedic "whole." (3) Given the above, no writer can ever be in control of the meaning of the text. I. does away with the concept of "author" in its conventional meaning (authority, property, intention), supplanting it with the concepts of "author-function" (Foucault) or "subject" (Lacan). (4) Meaning is supplanted by the notion of "signification" (a sign is composed of signifier and signified, but in poststructuralist thinking the signified is lost, leaving the signifier in search of a referent it can never find). Poststructuralism thus discards the humanistic version of human beings as creators of meaning, and proposes them instead as creatures (effects) of lang. (5) Crit. is no longer an ancillary activity, but is now considered part of the poem, creative of its meaning or signification. In formalism and humanism, the task of crit. is "explication" (q.v.), which distinguishes the reading subject from the literary object and defines lit. as a discipline and a mode of knowledge. I. stands in direct opposition to explication, with its explicit distinction between primary and secondary texts, and instead opens up literary, critical, and indeed many other texts to illimitable relations. (6) Disciplinary boundaries are erased: such fields as philosophy and psychoanalysis are all considered discursive practices and ultimately inseparable from lit. (7) Finally, poststructuralist crit. defies the rules of reason and identity and suggests instead the idea of contradiction. "Contradiction," says Adorno, "indicates the untruth of identity, the fact that the concept does not exhaust the thing conceived." Adorno's "contradiction" is very close to Derrida's "*différance.*"

I. is marked by two key features: the absence of an origin and the function of randomness. Traditional ("logocentric") critics consider lit. as a privileged mode of communication, expressive of human nature in its highest form. For these critics a transcendent referent (the "transcendental signified") organizes all lang. and experience, making possible a "self" which expresses itself in terms of "voice" (q.v.). Poststructuralist crit. "steals" that

ultimate referent. In the place of a privileged origin it finds a trace of something prior, which is lang. (writing) itself. Derrida speaks of the absence of a center or origin which would "arrest and ground the play of substitutions" because the sign which replaces the center "supplements" it and thus underscores its lack. *Différance* is the name for this unnamable absence of origin and for the "chain of differing and deferring substitutions" which it unleashes. In this respect textuality is precisely synonymous with i., in that it signals the impossibility of boundaries or borderlines that would adequately frame a "work" and its "meaning," and points instead to writing's "dissemination." Under these conditions, there could be no metalanguage, no privileged point that would make reference and knowledge possible, that would not "always already" be implicated in the tropological relations it would seek to describe. This submission to the legislature of lang. transforms the nature of intertextual relations and thereby the relations between crit. and lit. In the absence of an origin that would guarantee presence, meaning, and voice, there can be no originals—only copies. And without a univocal and transcendental referent, all texts refer to one another—translate one another—in infinite and utterly random ways.

Representation and reference, the mainstays of traditional humanism, underwrite a patriarchal "logocentric" order (Derrida terms it "phallogocentric") in which a work or a referent functions as a stabilizing ("seminal") source and provides the authority of meaning. Explicit in i. is the dismantling ("dissemination") of paternity. Barthes claims that "there is no father-author"; Derrida argues that "writing is an orphan." I. underwrites a critique of logocentrism and of patriarchy, substituting for patriarchal self-presence the feminizing "otherness" of intertextual "lapses."

These lapses which signal lost and irrecuperable meaning have altered the very shape of the "book." Notable as an effect of i. is the number of quotation marks deployed across texts, indicating "other" or alien contexts in which the words in question might be understood. The book, as a concept and as an entity, has undergone a similar transformation. While it still appears to us as words between two covers, the traditional rules by which prefaces functioned as openings, introductions introduced, and afterwords or epilogues closed are often missing. A preface may be termed a "pre-text" or "prefatory material"; a conclusion may well be a "postscript" or an "afterword" (or both, in sequence); "interchapters" or "interstices" point to the fragile relations between parts; and footnotes will sometimes constitute a parallel text, as in Derrida's "Living On . Borderlines," where the essay is entitled "Living On" and the long footnote threading its way through the essay is entitled "Borderlines." The latter does not function in submission to or as a subtitle to the former, so even the punctuation between them for routine reference becomes problematic. All of these strategies point to the impossibility of a text's wholeness or self-presence, and to the changed relations i. has wrought between reading and writing. See now ALLUSION; DECONSTRUCTION; ORGANICISM; STRUCTURALISM, *Moscow-Tartu School*; TEXTUALITY.

J. Derrida, *De la grammatologie* (1967, tr. 1976)—with essential preface by G. Spivak, "Signature, Event, Context," *Marges de la philosophie* (1972), *La Dissémination* (1972), *Glas* (1974, 1981, tr. 1986), "Living On . Borderlines," *Deconstruction and Crit.*, ed. H. Bloom (1979); J. Kristeva, *Séméiotikè* (1969), *La Révolution du langage poétique* (1974, tr. 1984); *Poétique* 27 (1976)—spec. iss. on i.; M. Riffaterre, *Semiotics of Poetry* (1978), *Text Production* (tr. 1983), *Fictional Truth* (1990); *Textual Strategies*, ed. J. Harari (1979)—excellent intro., bibl.; J. Culler, "Presupposition and I.," *The Pursuit of Signs* (1981), *On Deconstruction* (1982); *Untying the Text*, ed. R. Young (1981); *The Question of Textuality*, ed. W. Spanos and P. Bové (1982); *Displacement*, ed. M. Krupnick (1983); *The Anxiety of Anticipation*, spec. iss. of *YFS* 66 (1984); G. Atkins and M. Johnson, *Writing and Reading Differently* (1985); G. Jay and D. Miller, *After Strange Texts* (1985); *Intertextualität: Formen, Funktionen, anglistische Fallstudien*, ed. U. Broich et al. (1985); A. McHoul and D. Wills, "The Late(r) Barthes: Constituting Fragmenting Subjects," *Boundary 2* 14, 1–2 (1985–86); C. Chase, *Decomposing Figures* (1986); M. Nyquist, "Textual Overlapping and Dalilah's Harlot-Lap," *Literary Theory / Renaissance Texts*, ed. P. Parker and D. Quint (1986)—on textual "lapses"; S. Weber, *Demarcating the Disciplines*, ed., (1986), *Institution and Interp.* (1987); R. Dasenbrock, "Accounting for the Changing Certainties of Interpretive Communities," *MLN* 101 (1986); *Poems in Their Place: The I. and Order of Poetic Collections*, ed. N. Fraistat (1986); C. Norris, *Derrida* (1987); R. Goodkin, "Proust and Home(r): An Avuncular Intertext," *MLN* 104 (1989); *Autour de Racine: Studies in I.*, spec. iss. of *YFS* 76 (1989); *I. and Contemp. Am. Fiction*, ed. P. O'Donnell and R. Davis (1989)—esp T. Morgan, "The Space of I."; *I., Allusion, and Quotation: An Internat. Bibl. of Crit. Studies*, ed. U. J. Hebel (1989); G. Jay, "Paul de Man: Being in Question," *America the Scrivener* (1990); *I.: Theories and Practices*, ed. M. Worton and J. Still (1990); *Influence and I. in Lit. Hist.*, ed. J. Clayton and E. Rothstein (1991); *I.*, ed. H. F. Plett (1991). H.R.E.

INTONATION. See PITCH; ACCENT; DURATION.

INTUITION.

   I. IN AESTHETICS AND POETICS
   II. IN POETRY

I. IN AESTHETICS AND POETICS. The term "i." owes its importance in 20th-c. poetics to Benedetto Croce's use of it in his *Aesthetic as Science*

of Expression and General Linguistic (1902, tr. D. Ainslie, 2d ed., 1922), where he identifies it with expression (q.v.). Rejecting as naive the popular view of i. as a completely subjective phase of the cognitive process, Croce lays down the warning: "it is impossible to distinguish i. from expression in this cognitive process. The one appears with the other at the same instant, because they are not two, but one." Also: "to intuit is to express; and nothing else (nothing more but nothing less) than to express" (Ainslie 8–11). In 1915, Croce acknowledged that his own dissatisfaction with his 1902 account of i. had led to its "conversion" into the "further concept of pure or lyrical i." Under the influence of Giovanni Gentile (*Philosophy of Art*, tr. G. Gullace, 1972) as well as Vico and Hegel, Croce had delivered his Heidelberg lecture in 1908 on "Pure I. and the Lyrical Character of Art," where the term's meaning deepens to include the "successful union of a poetic image with an emotion."

By the time he is done, Croce has given an aesthetic theory of i. which is a theory of expression and of imagination (q.v.) as well. By identifying it with expression and imagination, Croce was able to give his use of i. a measure of variety and novelty it probably could not have sustained on its own. Croce nearly makes us forget that, before Kant took it up with fresh insight, the concept had already had a long history in Med. Lat. as *intuitus*, and an even longer history in its original Gr. form, *nous*.

It was C. S. Peirce who pointed out that the Lat. term *intuitus*—which Kant puts in parentheses after the Ger. equivalent, *Anschauung*—first occurs as a technical term in St. Anselm's *Monologium* (11th c.; tr. S. N. Deane 1903). Anselm, Peirce explains, had tried to draw a clear distinction between seeing things through a glass darkly, (*per speculum*) and knowing them "face to face," calling the former *speculation* and the latter *intuition*. In a famous passage of the *Monologium*, Anselm says: "to the supreme Spirit, expressing [*dicere*] and beholding through conception [*cogitando intueri*], as it were, are the same, just as the expression of our human mind is nothing but the i. of the thinker." Some students of Pound's *Cantos*, commenting on the so-called St. Anselm canto (105), have suggested that the entire *Monologium* may be read as an adumbration of what Eliot called the "objective correlative" (q.v.).

In the *Proslogium*, St. Anselm would later attempt to show that, in the concept of God intuited through Christian faith, enough is contained to "prove" discursively that anything so conceived must not only be thinkable but also exist. Pressing his argument (against the fool who has said in his heart "there is no God"), Anselm compares human i. of God with a painter's i. of a painting he has actually painted, as contrasted with his i. of the same before he has painted it. This so-called ontological "proof" of God's existence, later advanced by Descartes, Leibnitz, and Spinoza, prompted many later critics to attack Anselm. And foremost among them has been Immanuel Kant.

I. lies at the heart of Kant's entire intellectual paradigm. In his first critique, the *Critique of Pure Reason* (1781), Kant is at pains to distinguish two kinds of i.: first, a *receptive* kind, which enables the understanding (*Verstand*) to take in phenomenal sensations in the *a priori* forms of space and time, and as related to one another causally; and second, a *nonreceptive* kind, which Kant does not hesitate to characterize as a "productive imagination." It provides the understanding with a contents of supersensory things-in-themselves, not knowable through sensory experience. A proper name for it, says Kant, is "intellectual i." The chief supersensory ideas it provides are soul, world, and God. However grand their suggestiveness, those ideas have no empirical validity: they belong entirely to intellectual i.; the understanding cannot "prove" to itself whether they exist or not.

In Kant's second critique, the *Critique of Practical Reason* (1788), the entire context of his argument derives from one of the three supersensory ideas provided by intellectual i., namely the soul or human psyche. As the subjectivity of reason, the soul is made "aware" of itself not in the process of trying to know itself, but in that of being or willing itself. Kant's critique shows that, for the practical reason, the will can in no sense be a phenomenon related by laws of necessity to other phenomena; on the contrary, it is a noumenon or thing-in-itself, unaffected by anything external to it, and therefore completely free, answering only to itself for how it responds to the *a priori* "categorical imperative" by which its ends are determined intuitively.

But i. rises to a still higher level in Kant's third essay, the *Critique of Judgment* (1790; ed. K. Vorländer 1923, tr. J. C. Meredith, 1911, 1928). At the outset, Kant speaks of a "great gulf" yawning between the two previous critiques, "between the realm of the natural concept, as the sensible, and the realm of the concept of freedom, as the supersensible." What is needed, he says, is "a third mediating principle," an *a priori* intuitive synthesis of the opposed perspectives of nature (which mind comprehends only through its phenomenal impressions on the understanding) and freedom (where mind is at home with itself in its inner, noumenal reality). A table at the beginning of the third critique shows it is "art and beauty in general" that must "bridge the gap" between the two.

Only art or aesthetic experience, Kant explains, can provide the needed *a priori* intuitive synthesis, precisely because it is neither natural nor free in itself, and yet participates, at least apparently, in both. In nature, our mind seeks knowledge; in freedom, it wills or desires; in art, it neither seeks knowledge nor wills, but rather finds itself viewing things intuitively—Wordsworth in his *Excursion* (4.1295) will call it a "passionate i."—so as to link the realms of nature and freedom together in what amounts to a great metaphor or intuitive synthesis. Despite his Humean skepticism, Kant allows himself to speak of the "divine mind" as author of that "highest synthesis of the critical philosophy." Having identified it as "that reason which creates the content at the same time with its forms," Kant adds that it here appears at last as "intellectual perception or intuitive understanding."

It was Hegel who remarked that, in rising through his three critiques to the concept of intellectual i. or intuitive understanding as the governing principle of the experience of purposiveness and beauty in nature and art, Kant merits the kind of praise Aristotle accorded Anaxagoras in Gr. antiquity. When Anaxagoras first said that *nous* (understanding in general or reason) rules the world, "he appeared," says Aristotle, "like a sober man among drunkards." Awed, like Kant, by the spectacle of the night sky with its "undisturbed circling of countless worlds," Anaxagoras had concluded that it could only be the result of a mind or *nous*, a divine intuitive reason which sorts out the original constituents of things in order to join like to like in a well-ordered whole (*kosmos*). Still, as Aristotle notes, Anaxagoras wavers between assigning his *nous* completely to man's thinking soul (like Kant in his first critique) and proclaiming its total objectivity as the "soul-stuff" of the sensory world of nature.

In Plato and, even more, in Aristotle and the Neo-Platonists, the *nous* of Anaxagoras retains its original significance as the divine mind that gives order to all things. It comes finally to be conceived as a pure act of "thinking thinking about thinking" (*nóesis noéseos nóesis*). The human soul or psyche, like everything else that is, "imitates" or "participates" in that pure act in the measure of its natural potencies. The psyche receives intuitively—quite as Kant will later explain it—the principles of its theoretical, practical, and productive kinds of rational activity. Through rational making, men and women build the cities or states in which they are able, individually and collectively, to behave rationally. And it is only when their making and behaving have acquired habitual excellence that human beings can have the experience of sharing, however briefly, in the divine existence of thinking thinking about thinking, which is the height of *sophia* or wisdom. The good habit or virtue of making well is *techne* or art; of behaving well, it is *phronesis* or prudence; of explaining well, it is *episteme*, or excellence in discursive reasoning. *Nous* or intuitive reason is what ultimately activates all three; but when the three become one at the pole, like the meridians on the globe, it is *sophia*, the highest intuitive reason joined with the highest discursive reason, that absorbs the other two (the highest good and the highest beauty) in its highest truth.

Through St. Jerome, St. Augustine, and St. Thomas, the form of rational i. that activates practical reason will get a special name: *synderesis*. But it will be left to Dante to do the same for the productive reason, or fine art. Dante will dare to say that his whole *Commedia*, in which he sought to "write like God," was for him a metaphoric, intuitive vision, completed to perfection in his "creative imagination" (*alta fantasia*) before he applied himself to the task of writing it down. Love, he says, helped him to turn his vision into poetry by dictating words in his heart (see INSPIRATION). Fortunately, he had native talent—*ingenium* or genius (q.v.)—and had acquired the traditional poetic skills (*ars*) through long practice (*usus*), to be able to do some justice to love's divine dictation; otherwise, as he says, his trying to write like God might have looked rather like the efforts of a goose to fly like an eagle.

For a rounded view of the importance of i. as an aesthetic concept that does full justice to its long history, one must turn to Hegel (*Aesthetics*, tr. T. M. Knox 1975). Hegel makes use of i. to distinguish the three great kinds of art that have characterized the civilizations of ancient Greece, the Near and Far East, and European Christendom. The three are the Classical, with its ideal reciprocal adequacy of content and form; the Symbolic, which falls short of that ideal, presenting a reciprocal inadequacy of constituents, the results of which are sometimes ugly but sometimes tremulously sublime (q.v.) in Kant's sense of the term; and the Romantic, which transcends the classical reciprocal adequacy—as Shakespeare does in his characterizations of Falstaff and Hamlet, and Dante does at the close of his *Paradiso*, where, after telling us that his creative imagination finally experienced a vast intuitive power-shortage (*all'alta fantasia qui mancò possa*), he permits us to share with him, intuitively, the dizzying heights of art in the process of transcending itself as art.

The same insight permits Hegel to treat comprehensively the great epic, lyric, and dramatic genres or voices of poetry, and to predict that poets of the future in the Western world are apt to find the lyric voice more vital than the other two voices of poetry. As a living experience, epic poetry belongs to the beginnings of a people's national history, just as dramatic poetry does to the decades of its full maturity. Lyric poetry has no special time in a people's history, and therefore its voice is never silent. From that Hegelian vantage point, it is possible to explain why theorists of art since Kant who have counted on i. to tell them what is actually living for them in aesthetic experience have tended to emphasize the ideal of the lyric in poetry and of musical subjectivity among all the arts. That has been so from Schopenhauer and Nietzsche down through Henri Bergson (*The Creative Mind*, tr. 1946) and Jacques Maritain (*Creative I. in Art and Poetry*, 1953). René Wellek has seen in it a tendency to abolish the "whole concept of art as one of the distinct activities of man" by collapsing the rich legacy of traditional artistic distinctions into a crude "unity of experience" that makes all things subjectively and intuitively one. Still, Hegel's best insights permit us to say on Croce's behalf that, when he faithfully scrutinized his personal aesthetic experience, he found indeed that its depths resounded, for him at least, with a voice of singularly lyrical intuitive inspiration. A.P.; H.P.

II. IN POETRY. Theories of poetry as a form of i. are even today somewhat alien to our ways of thinking. G. N. G. Orsini observes that Am. literary critics are profoundly distrustful of their intuitive capacities and, one might add, of the intuitive power of poetry itself. Am. histories of aesthetics do contain clear descriptions of theories of poetry as i., but their clarity depends on their remoteness from that which they are describing. Even when most objective, they seem to suggest that such theories are simply untenable. Of course, the theories may in truth be untenable. But because they have emerged in cultures with much richer conditions of poetry and art than our own, we should reject them only with extreme caution.

In its most fully developed form, the theory of poetry as essentially intuitive is based on the belief that lines like the following are exemplary: "the dry sound of bees / Stretching across a lucid space" (Hart Crane, "Praise for an Urn") and "As a calm darkens among water lights" (Wallace Stevens, "Sunday Morning"). To be sure, any line of verse, according to this theory, is poetic only if it is intuitive. But the two lines just quoted seem to exhibit what is meant by poetic i. with unusual clarity and vividness. Even these lines, it is true, do not force the reader to respond to them intuitively. The lines may be taken to be imitative of certain natural events or as illustrations of visual illusions or even as instances of rhetorical catachresis (q.v.). But if the reader takes these lines in as they really are—or so the theory goes—then the reader will experience them as poetic intuitions, as immediate fusion of feeling and image. The reader is pulled into a new place and time and becomes one with its desperate beauty. If the reader mediates within this intuitive moment, it will enfold his whole world; Crane's world will become the reader's world, and he will see everything afresh, colored by a pain and lucidity as never before. In experiences such as this, life, lang., the world, and the word are irrefrangibly one. The experience one has of the poetry and one's knowledge of the experience are identical. The poetry creates the experience—as a fusion of world as experienced and of the person as experiencing—and gives knowledge of the experience as an identity of world and person in a single, seamless act of i.

This theory does not equate poetry with creative acts such as the primal creative act of God, for it views poetic i. not as a creation out of nothing but as the creation of a poetic maker and the world, of lang. and being, out of a material which is its prior condition. But this condition is utterly formless; it is only a hum and buzz, a pure flux of sensation. In effect, then, poetic i. discovers only what it creates: it knows that which it itself makes. Moreover, in this theory, poetry as we ordinarily think of it is only the highest form of that creative experience in which each of us becomes a human being, both sentient and verbal, living in a world.

Poetic i. differs from sensation because it is neither passive nor psychological; it is a oneness of person and world expressed in lang. In the other arts its lang. may be song or shape or gesture. It is knowledge, but of an immediate kind, and thus is prior to conceptual, judgmental, discursive knowledge. There is no claim in poetic i. that its world is either real or unreal or that that world and the experiencing person are distinct; because it is not a self-conscious experience, it does not even contain the claim that it is itself poetic i. Although it is possible to extract concepts and abstract ideas from a poem, in the poem experienced as a poem, these ideas are fused within the i.

Vico, who may be credited as the originator of this conception of poetry, argued that Homer conceived of Achilles not as a courageous individual or as an example of courage or as courage itself, but as an utter fusion of all of these. In poetic i., in other words, individuality and universality are identical (cf. CONCRETE UNIVERSAL). Poetic i., moreover, is radically distinct from perception, which is the basis of empirical knowledge. If one perceives "the blue spot here and now," one observes it as part of a spatial and temporal and chromatic framework, a structure already composed by conceptual thought. It is, of course, possible to perceive rather than intuit poems, to consider their space and time as part of some large, conventional structure within which we live our days. But to do so is to miss the poems as poems. Space and time are abstractions by means of which we think and perceive the world. But poetic i. creates the world and with it our living sense of space and time. The crudeness or fineness of our very ideas of space and time is thus derivable from the quality of our poetic, intuitive experience. Finally, in its purest form, the concept of poetry as i. is at odds with the idea of poetry as self-expression. In a poetic i., self and world, subject and object, are immediately identical. This is the way the world begins. This is the way the self begins. On its basis alone we construct our distinctions, self and world, space and time, real and unreal, truth and error, even beauty and ugliness.

M.E.B.

After Croce, theories of i. in the 20th c. have been pursued from directions he might never have anticipated, but with results which in some cases at least he would have found congenial. Expressionist theories of poetry, which are the last inheritors of romanticism (q.v.) and of which poetic i. is one, have had surprising strength through much of the 20th c. In Italy, the publication of Gentile's *Philosophy of Art* in 1932 effectively put an end to the currency of Crocean expressionism, but in Switzerland and France, the rise of the Geneva School (q.v.) of critics during the same decade produced a strong form of intuitivist crit. This, however, is based now on Bergson, existentialism, and (esp.) phenomenology. Here too the operating assumption is that a reader will, through inseeing or i., come into a rapport with the imaginative space of the text, and through it that of the poet, the authenticity of which is taken as guaranteed. On the basis of this guarantee one can then say that the ordinary category boundaries between subjective and objective are indeed dissolved, and along with them the usual concerns of critics with the gaps or spaces between the world and the world as embodied in words. In such i., one is literally seeing through words into the very life of things. Eng. translations of Geneva-School phenomenological crit. brought its methods into currency in America in the 1960s. The subsequent assaults on referentiality and determinate meaning that were associated with deconstruction (q.v.), however, sought to dissolve all possibility of intuitive readerly rapport with the text, much less with the poet, as convenient but vain delusions built upon a fictive metaphysics. But in denying the possibility of stable meaning, deconstruction reduced its own position to merely one voice among all the rest, and not one on which any productive or even viable cultural practice could be built.

Much more productive were developments in reader-response criticism (q.v.), which sought to reestablish links between individual readers and texts, at least, and perhaps even to restore links among readers themselves, and so guarantee intuitive authenticity, via the concept of readerly and social convention (q.v.). Nevertheless, intuitivist theories of poetry, like phenomenological philosophy, provides the most radical alternative to traditional Western dualist metaphysics. Most of the great Western poets have indicated implicitly or explicitly their belief in the power of i. to bypass the circuits of feeble human rationality and fickle human perception, going straight to the source. "If a sparrow come before my window," said Keats, "I take part in its existence and pick about the gravel." Whether such entering-in upon the conscious lives of other selves, other beings not human, and even events beyond all selfhood be dream or truth is a question that seems, finally, less important than the evident fact that it proceeds from a human capacity certain beyond cavil, and one which poetry above all arts, for some reason, makes central. See also GENEVA SCHOOL; IMAGINATION; INVENTION; SUBJECTIVITY AND OBJECTIVITY; VISION.—G. N. G. Orsini, *Benedetto Orsini* (1961); M. E. Brown, *Neo-Idealistic Aesthetics: Croce, Gentile, Collingwood* (1966); M. R. Westcott, *Psychology of I.* (1968).

T.V.F.B.

INUIT POETRY.

INUIT POETRY

The Inuit (pl. form; sing. Inuk), commonly called Eskimos (a name the Inuit consider offensive), live along some five thousand miles of Arctic coastline, so comments about any one aspect of their culture are generalizations, but unlike Namerindians, the Inuit have a strong linguistic connection throughout the circumpolar world. The I. lang. belongs to the Eskalutian family, which has two branches: I., spoken in Greenland, Canada, and Alaska, and Yupik, spoken in Alaska and Siberia. Until relatively recently, I. p. belonged to oral trad. and was usually sung or chanted, often to the accompaniment of drum, choral background, or dance. Its agglutinative nature makes translation of I. p. particularly rewarding, for although a single word may require 100 characters to spell, it will contain a fully developed image.

I. TRADITIONAL SONG AND POETRY. Traditional Inuit believed in the literal power of the word (hence everyone was a singer and to some extent a poet) and thought it as imperative to work on lang. as on skins or ivory. As hunter-gatherers, they had to sing and compose in order to control the universe—to catch a seal, break a fever, or cut the weather. I. p. was very special, possessing supernatural powers, but it was also very commonplace, a part of everyday life.

Knud Rasmussen, the Greenlandic poet and scholar who collected literary material from across the circumpolar world, identified four categories of I. p.: charms, mood songs, hunting songs, and songs of derision. These four categories are not mutually exclusive, however, for they were occasionally integrated in traditional myths and legends as well as sung on their own.

A. *Mood Songs* are songs of reflection which do not involve a central story or action, but like imagist poems try to give a visual impression which involves the perception of relationships. These short poems have a strong literal meaning; they may describe a bird perched on a rock or a man waking in the morning, but tied into the simple description of the moment is a subtext concerned with the poet's emotional response to the bird or his perception of his place in the universe.

B. *Charms and Incantations*, often fragmented, incomprehensible, or in supernatural lang., are similar to nonsense verse, sound poetry, or even concrete poetry (qq.v.), where form dominates meaning, but they have added depth in that they have magical powers. A charm can be capable of drying blood in a wound, attracting a fish to the hook, or killing an enemy. These poems were thought by some to be so powerful that it was dangerous to give them to strangers, so words were sometimes changed before charms were offered to collectors. Simply reciting the words of a chant was often enough to put a person into a shamanistic trance. The use of obscure or archaic diction frequently makes the chants incomprehensible even to native speakers.

C. *Hunting Songs* can be reflective but are more likely to be narrative, in keeping with the subject. Rasmussen notes the difficulty of separating hunting songs from mood songs because so many touch on the joys and disappointments of the hunt; they also often use the lang. of incantation. Frequently the circumstances described in the poems are familiar to the audience, and mnemonic phrases are included to fill out the song.

D. *Derisive Songs*. Sometimes referred to as *nith* songs, drum songs, song duels, or satirical songs, these are the most interesting to readers outside the culture, perhaps because a common denominator is an ironic element of criticism. These monologues or dialogues are like medieval flytings (q.v.): verbal assault is part of the game. The poet can aim the derision at himself, at another, at a group of people, or at a type of behavior. The song may only be part of an attack, or it may be a response to an attack by another singer; it may be a cheerful, loving correction or it may be a vicious assault on a reputation. The song duel, in which two singers exchange reproaches, has a judicial function in that each is allowed to voice complaints against the other in public, each is given an opportunity to respond, and the loser either acknowledges his fault or leaves the community. The song duel varies greatly from one area to another, occasionally involving boxing or head butting, and is usually also considered entertainment.

II. MODERN SONG AND POETRY. As long as the Inuit were nomadic, they had no real need for a written lang., but in the 18th c. they came in contact with European explorers, and Christian missionaries soon followed. Although writing did not develop indigenously, it was accepted quickly. Orthographies as diverse as Cyrillic, syllabic, hieroglyphic, and Roman were used across the Arctic coast as printing presses and schools were established.

Today, highly individualistic forms of I. p. such as throat music—in which the distinctive sounds are produced through gutteral, nasal, and breathing techniques—are extant, but song dueling has virtually disappeared. Although the traditional forms are seldom performed or read in the I. lang. they have gained credibility outside the culture as written translations. Modern I. p. and song is not so widely admired, but is also gaining acceptance. Most I. composers and writers now draw heavily on European musical and literary structures while still retaining some elements of the ancient forms. The themes are often different and the tone intervals are more familiar to Western ears than they would be to the ancient Eskalutians, but the lang. dictates certain rhythmic patterns peculiar only to I., so comparisons must be circumscribed. In general terms, however, poetry from the written trad. can be grouped into units similar to those Rasmussen identified in the oral modes.

A. *Mood Poems*. Still popular with both old and

young authors, though now they often refer to settlement life and modern technology, these short, vivid lyrics attempt to capture emotions related to the senses, such as the joy of seeing the sun come up, the taste of meat or a steaming mug of tea, or an awareness of the passage of time. Often these brief poems will be worked into photographs, drawings, or prints so that illustration and text are indivisible.

B. *Religious Hymns and Poems.* Magic chants and incantations are no longer evident, but Christian hymns, tr. or adapted from Eng. and Danish or composed originally in I. are widely promulgated. The hymns of Rasmus Berthelsen are known throughout Greenland, while in Canada, Armand Tagoona is the best known composer of Christian songs. Occasional poems on the Incarnation or the nature of the Creator appear, but there is no significant body of lay Christian religious writings comparable in quality to that lit. which emerged from the old shamanistic beliefs.

C. *Contemporary Hunting Poems.* Although written poems about hunting are still emerging in the circumpolar world, they have taken on a romantic or spiritual importance that is quite different from those in the oral trad. While the old songs tended to be narrative and reminiscent, the new ones emerge as imaginative speculation written in many cases not by hunters but by young urban Inuit who are reluctantly tied to office jobs but regard hunting as the only fit occupation for a true Inuk. The works often urge people to return to the ways of their ancestors, or describe the need to protect the land and animals for future generations. The old hunting poems frequently explored man's sense of fragility and insecurity, with images of the land providing a sense of continuity and stability, but modern poets are more concerned with the survival of the land itself.

D. *Political Poetry.* The song duels and derisive poems generally do not exist in a pure form in modern I. p., having been banned by Christian missionaries, but certain elements have survived. The question-answer sequence, or the repeated use of the interrogative, is a feature of contemp. I. political poetry, though the respondent is as likely to be a garbage can or an alien from Mars as a snowy owl or an offended husband. The devel. of the epic is a major innovation in modern I. p.; Frederik Nielsen's trilogy on Qitdlaussuaq traces the 18th-c. I. migration from Canada to Greenland; Alootook Ipellie's long poem "The Strangers" describes the I. occupation of the Arctic from ancient times and examines the effect of European contact; Villads Villadsen's Christian epic *Nalusuunerup Taarnerani* (In Heathen Darkness) describes the death of the last Norseman in Greenland and the eventual conversion and baptism of Aattaaritaa the exorcist. The politically inspired poems are sometimes purely didactic but are more frequently satiric and ironic. Since the Inuit traditionally had no political structure, poetry has been

used as an impetus to social activism by writers many of whom are politicians. There is a large body of popular music concerned with political and social issues to be found in all the I. regions. To date, there is not a wide body of I. p. available outside the culture, but inside the culture the trad. is flourishing and continues to develop.

H. Rink, *Eskimoiske Eventyr og Sagn*, 2 v. (1866–77), tr. as *Tales and Trads. of the Eskimo* (1875); W. Thalbitzer, "Old Fashioned Songs," *Phonetical Study of the Eskimo Lang.* (1904); H. Roberts and D. Jenness, *Songs of the Copper Eskimos* (1925); K. Rasmussen, *Report of the Fifth Thule Expedition, 1921–24*, 7–9 (1930–32); *Anerca*, ed. E. Carpenter (1959); *I Breathe a New Song*, ed. R. Lewis (1971); *Eskimo Poems From Canada and Greenland*, ed. T. Lowenstein (1973); *Kalaallit Taallaataat Nutaat INUIT Ny Gronlandsk Lyrik*, ed. K. Norregaard (1980); *Paper Stays Put*, ed. R. Gedalof (1980); *Poems of the I.*, ed. J. R. Colombo (1981); C. Berthelsen, *Gronlandsk Litteratur* (1983); *Alaska Native Writers, Storytellers and Orators*, spec iss. of *Alaska Quart. Rev.* (1986); *Northern Voices*, ed. P. Petrone (1988).

history and criticism: S. Frederiksen, "Henrik Lund, A National Poet of Greenland," *PAPS* 96,6 (1952), "Stylistic Forms in Greenland Eskimo Lit.," *Meddelser om Gronland* 136,7 (1954); E. Carpenter, "Eskimo Poetry: Word Magic," *Explorations* 4 (1955); H. Lynge, "The Art and Poetry of Greenland," *Greenland Past and Present*, ed. K. Hertling et al. (1971); R. Wiebe, "Songs of the Canadian Eskimo," *CanL* 52 (1972); R. McGrath, *Canadian I. Lit.* (1984); R. Pedersen, "Greenlandic Written Lit.," *Handbook of North Am. Indians*, V, ed. D. Damas (1984); C. Berthelsen, "Greenlandic Lit.: Its Trads., Changes, and Trends," *Arctic Anthro.* 23 (1986).   R.McG.

INVECTIVE. A personal attack or satire, often scurrilous, a lampoon, formerly written mainly in verse. I. is to be differentiated from satire (q.v.) on the grounds that it is personal, motivated by malice, and unjust; thus John Dennis remarks that satire "can never exist where the censures are not just. In that case the Versifyer, instead of a Satirist, is a Lampooner, and infamous Libeller." I. is as old as poetry, and as widespread; in the West it appears (if not in the Homeric *Margites*) at least as early as Archilochus, who wrote an i. against Lycambes; other notable Gr. examples include those by Hipponax against Bupalus, by Anacreon against Artemon, and others by Xenophanes, Timon of Phlius, Sotades (see SOTADEAN), Menippus, and (less virulently) Callimachus. Indeed, iambic meter itself (see IAMBIC) is in its earliest, Ionian form so called specifically because of its association with i., which has the specific characteristics both of a speaker giving vent to personal hatred and of common speech for its vehicle, to which iambic meter was thought by the ancients to conform. In Lat., i. is written, though in a wider variety of meters, chiefly by Catullus (see SCAZON), Ovid (*Ibis*), Martial, and Varro. In the Middle Ages, Petrarch's i. against doctors, *I. contra medicum*, is notable; in the Ren., the scope of personal i. is expanded considerably by the invention of printing, which provided broadsides, bills, and ballads particularly well suited for rapid and wide dispersal of political i. and satire. Eng. i. of this sort abounds particularly in the Restoration and 18th c.; indeed, the Eng. word "lampoon" (from the Fr. slang term *lamper*, "to guzzle, swill down") dates only from mid 17th c. Rochester's *History of Insipids, a Lampoon* (1680) is but one of many of his, and others'. Dryden, a master of i., nevertheless deplores it in his "Discourse concerning the Original and Progress of Satire" (1693) as both illegal and dangerous. After 1750, however, verse i., like other verse genres such as narrative poetry (q.v.), rapidly gave ground to prose as the medium of choice, except in the (remarkably durable) trad. of the epigram, incl. scurrilous and vindictive epigrams, which have been produced in the 20th c. most notably by J. V. Cunningham. See also DOZENS; EPIGRAM; FLYTING; SATIRE; TOAST.

J. Addison, *Spectator*, no. 23; *An Anthol. of I. and Abuse*, and *More I.*, both ed. H. Kingsmill (1929, 1930); C. Reichley, "Lampoon: Archilochus to Byron," *DAI* 32 (1971), 2703A; J. C. Manning, *Blue I.* (1973); *The Book of Insults, Ancient & Modern*, ed. N. McPhee (1978); G. Nagy, *The Best of the Achaeans* (1979), chs. 12–13; *Tygers of Wrath: Poems of Hate, Anger, and I.*, ed. X. J. Kennedy (1981); A. Richlin, *The Garden of Priapus* (1983); *The Devil's Book of Verse*, ed. R. Conniff (1983); *The Blasted Pine: An Anthol.*, ed. F. R. Scott and A. J. M. Smith (1965)—Canadian; R. M. Rosen, *Old Comedy and the Iambographic Trad.* (1988); H. Rawson, *Wicked Words* (1989); G. J. van Gelder, *The Bad and the Ugly: Attitudes towards I. Poetry* (Hija') *in Cl. Arabic Lit.* (1989); K. Swenson, *Performing Definitions* (1991); L. Watson, *Arae: Curse Poetry in Antiquity* (1991). T.V.F.B.

INVENTIO. See INVENTION; RHETORIC AND POETRY.

INVENTION (Gr. *heurēsis*, Lat. *inventio*). Ancient theories of rhet. commonly identified five steps in construction of an oratory or composition of a literary work: *inventio* (i. or discovery, "the devising of matter"), *dispositio* (arrangement), *elocutio* (expression or style), *pronuntiatio* (delivery), and *memoria* (memory). *Inventio*, the most complex and important of the five steps, refers to the nature and source of *what* is said rather than to *how* it is said: it concerns the preliminary tasks of collecting, exploring, discovering, or creating materials for use. Important discussions are to be found in Aristotle, *Rhetoric*, Bks. 1–2; the anonymous *Rhetorica ad Herennium* 1.2.3; and Cicero, *De inventione* 1.7.9 (cf. Cicero, *De oratore* 1.31.142, 2.19.79; Quintilian 3.3.1).

The first three of these rhetorical divisions have also been widely employed in poetics to distinguish not only the tasks and faculties involved in writing poems but also the elements of poems themselves. Here "i." most often refers to finding, or otherwise producing, the subject matter or "content" of poems. But the concept has also been used to indicate the production of poetic form or structure (e.g. Aristotle's *Poetics*, ch. 14), or of poetic lang. or style (Du Bellay's *Deffense et illustration de la langue françoyse* 1.8 [1549]; the passages on Homer's "expression" in the Preface to Pope's *Iliad* [1715]), or of poetry in general (Boccaccio's *Genealogia deorum gentilium* 14.7 [ca. 1365]), or specific poetic kinds (Scaliger's *Poetices libri septem* 1.1 [1561]), or a particular whole work of art (A. Gerard's *Essay on Genius* 1.3 [1774]).

The special meanings given to the term within this general usage have been numerous. Sometimes i. is contrasted with "imitation" (q.v.) of prior models, thus signifying originality (q.v.) and independence in the production of subject matter (Horace, *Ars poetica* 119–20; Quintilian, *Institutio oratoria* 10.2.12; Johnson, *Rambler* no. 121 [1751]; E. Young, *Conjectures on Original Composition* [1759]). Sometimes it is contrasted with "judgment," and thus refers to the native power of producing poetic substance as opposed to the control of that power by reason, convention, or skill (Pope, *Essay on Crit.* 1.114 [1711], Preface to the *Iliad*). Sometimes it refers to the production of things "fanciful" or incredible (Johnson, *Rambler* no. 4 [1750]); sometimes it means the production of "fiction" (q.v.) as opposed to historical truth; sometimes it indicates the artful combination of historical truth and imaginative falsehood.

Basic differences in the conception of poetic i. are in large part functions of more general differences in poetics regarding what is necessary or desirable in poetic subject matter, and why. In most mimetic theories in Western poetics (see POETRY, THEORIES OF), poetic i. is conceived primarily as a matter of the proper imitation (q.v.) of nature (in one or another of the several senses of that term), since the desired effects of poetry, it was argued, are possible only through images or likenesses of real or natural things (Plutarch, *Moralia* 17–18; Aquinas, *In libros posteriorum analyticorum expositio* 1, Lectio 1; Ronsard, *Abrégé de l'art poétique françois* [1565]; Dryden, *Parallel betwixt Poetry and Painting* [1695]; Johnson, Preface to *Shakespeare* [1765]). "Imitation of nature," however, has been a very inclusive concept, and in some theories in this trad., poetic i. legitimately embraces the powers of "imagining" things and hence of producing visionary, supernatural, and "marvelous" subjects (see IMAGINATION).

On the other hand, there have been a number of theories (incl. those of some of the Stoics and Neoplatonists, and of preromantics and romantics like Shaftesbury, Akenside, Herder, and Coleridge) in which poetic i. is conceived as the production of subject matter which transcends "ordinary" human images or ideas of nature and the natural, often on the grounds that the poet is one who rivals or reflects a higher, "creative" being. Sir Philip Sidney's statement is characteristic: "only the poet [of all human artists] . . . lifted up with the vigor of his own i., doth grow in effect another nature, in making things either better than nature bringeth forth, or, quite anew, forms such as never were in nature" (*Apologie for Poetrie* [1583; 1595]). In some theories in this trad. (Shelley, Emerson), the emphasis is on the poet's special inspired or intuitive "vision" of ultimate reality (see INSPIRATION; INTUITION; VISION), and poetry is justified by its provision of a superior kind of cognition to that available via ordinary human discourse. In others (A. W. Schlegel, Wordsworth), the emphasis is on the poet's power of supremely great or original thought and feeling (see ORIGINALITY); here poetry is defended not as primarily depictive or imagistic but rather as a superior mode of "expression" (q.v.). Some later theories stress the need for a coalescence of two or more transcendent powers (Croce, Maritain, Wimsatt, Vivas, Wheelwright). The most significant recent devel. in the history of the concept has been a general shift of emphasis, beginning in the 18th c., away from the principle that the poet produces subject matter (and form and style) by deliberate acts of learned technique, incl. the imitation of prior works and of nature, to the converse principle that poetry is generated in the poet's mind—whether consciously, via intuition, or by any other organic process—by God or nature.

It has traditionally been said that, while the original meaning of "i." involved primarily the idea of "finding" subject matter (even by imitating or borrowing from other writers), the term later came to suggest, through association with the concept of imagination, not so much finding as "creating." This observation has considerable validity, but it ought not obscure the fact that there never was a time in the history of Western crit. when poetic i. was not conceived by someone in terms of the poet's creative or imaginative ability to transform given or discovered materials, for better or worse. It was romanticism which fixed in the modern mind the valorization of creativity and purely original i. over the wider concept of antiquity. "Outside of God," Victor Hugo remarked, "Shakespeare invented most."

See now RHETORIC AND POETRY, sect. II.

C. S. Baldwin, *Ancient Rhet. and Poetic* (1924), *Med. Rhet. and Poetic* (1928); M. W. Bundy, "'I.' and 'Imagination' in the Ren.," *JEGP* 29 (1930); W. G. Crane, *Wit and Rhet. in the Ren.* (1937); F. Solmsen, "The Aristotelian Trad. in Ancient Rhet.," *AJP* 62 (1941); Sr. M. Joseph, *Shakespeare's Use of the Arts of Lang.* (1947); R. McKeon, "Imitation and Poetry," *Thought, Action, and Passion* (1953); W. S. Howell, *Logic and Rhet. in England, 1500–1700* (1956); W. J. Ong, *Ramus, Method and the Decay of Dialogue* (1958); Weinberg; G. A. Kennedy, *The Art of Persuasion in Greece* (1963); C. Vasoli, *La dialettica e la retorica dell'Umanesimo: 'Invenzione' e 'metodo' nella cultura del XV e XVI secolo* (1968); Lausberg; L. Jardine, *Francis Bacon: Discovery and the Arts of Discourse* (1974); Murphy; L. D. Martin, "Literary I.," *CritI* 6 (1980); P. Bagni, "L'Inventio nell'ars poetica latino-medievale," *Rhet. Revalued,* ed. B. Vickers (1982); S. Crowley, *The Methodical Memory* (1990).   R.M.; T.V.F.B.

INVERSE RHYME. See REVERSE RHYME.

INVERSION. See HYPERBATON.

IONIC. The metrical unit $\smile \smile - -$, and meters composed in such metra or derived from it. In Gr. poetry, pure I. meters found wide use in monody (esp. Anacreon), choral lyric, and the choruses of Gr. tragedy (particularly Euripides) and comedy. For other varieties of I. rhythms, see GALLIAMBUS and ANACREONTIC. Aeolic (q.v.) and I. meters are closely related and were often confused with one another by the ancient grammarians. Pure Is. are found in Horace, *Odes* 3.12 (probably an imitation of Alcaeus, fr. 108 [Lobel-Page]), but mixtures of Is. and other meters are found in Plautus. The pure I. is sometimes called the "lesser I." or I. *a minore.* The so-called "greater I." or I. *a maiore* ($- - \smile \smile$) is a later Hellenistic devel., found particularly in the Sotadean (q.v.), which also had its Lat. imitators; an example is provided by Varro, *Satirae Menippeae* 489. Accentual imitations of lesser Is. in Eng. poetry incl. Browning's "In the midnight, in the silence of the sleep-time" and John Frederick Nims' "The Young Ionia" (*Knowledge of the Evening* [1960]). Some modern metrists have entertained the idea that the sequence xx// in the first four syllables of the Eng. iambic pentameter is a kind of analogous I. foot—Wimsatt calls it a "crescendo foot"—but this is a confusion of rhythm with meter (see Brogan).—Hardie; Wilamowitz, pt. 2, ch. 9; Crusius; Dale; Koster, ch. 9; Dale, ch. 8; Halporn et al.; West.   J.W.H.; T.V.F.B.

IRANIAN POETRY. See PERSIAN POETRY.

IRISH LITERARY RENAISSANCE. See IRISH POETRY.

IRISH POETRY.

    I. POETRY IN GAELIC:
        6TH–19TH CENTURIES
    II. POETRY IN ENGLISH: YEATS
        AND THE CELTIC REVIVAL
    III. IRISH POETRY AFTER YEATS

I. POETRY IN GAELIC: 6TH–19TH CENTURIES. From its origins to the present, the form and content of Ir. p. have been enmeshed with the evolution of Ir. hist. and society. Poetry in Gaelic belongs to one of the oldest vernacular lits. in

Europe, extending from the 6th c. A.D. to the present. In the pre-Christian oral culture, Ir. poets (*filidh*, sing. *fili* [q.v.]) had for long constituted a privileged professional class; they were not only repositories of traditional knowledge but also seers and prophets with magical powers. With the displacement of their druidic religion by Christianity in the 5th c., the *filidh* apparently ceded their magical functions but maintained their identity as scholars and poets. It was the Lat. learning that accompanied Christianity that enabled Gaelic verse to be written down. The poetry of the *filidh* consisted typically of genealogies, histories, and praise for noble patrons. As Christianity was established in Ireland, the *filidh* coexisted, perhaps even intermingled with, the monastic clerics who constituted another class of learned men. The early Ir. church was organized, unusually, on a monastic structure, and such monasteries as Glendalough and Clonmacnoise were centers of learning akin to modern colleges: it was this system that gave Ireland its Golden Age in the 7th and 8th cs. Ireland became known as the island of saints and scholars, as missionary Ir. monks founded monasteries all over Europe. One official duty of clerics in the Ir. monasteries was to copy sacred texts, but they also compiled the pre-Christian lit. of Ireland—the ancient myths and epic tales which recount the exploits of the heroes Cuchulainn and Finn. They were also responsible for a body of lyric poetry, some of it as formulaic as the poetry of the *filidh*, but some charged with a fresh and numinous sense of the natural world.

The economy, precision, and delicacy of early Ir. nature poetry at its best can be seen in such delightful poems as "The Scribe in the Woods," the poem from the Fenian Cycle that begins *scel lem duib*, and "The Blackbird of Belfast Lough." Seamus Heaney gives this tr. of the latter poem: "The small bird / let a chirp / from its beak: / I heard / woodnotes, whin- / gold, sudden. / The Lagan / blackbird!" The style of poetry from the 6th to the 12th c., virtually all of it anonymous, is for the most part an intricate formalism. Complex rhyming syllabic meters gradually incorporated and displaced the technique of the earliest Ir. verse, which was cadenced and unrhymed and originated in the same IE system as did Sanskrit and Gr. verse (see CELTIC PROSODY; INDO-EUROPEAN PROSODY; and see Watkins). It was long thought that the rhyming, syllabic meters of Ir. verse were formed under the influence of late Lat. verse, but more recent scholarship argues just the opposite—that the versification of early Ir. p. influenced Med. Lat. verse. Certainly Lat. verse in medieval Ireland would seem to reveal the impress of Celtic models in its technique; the most famous collection of poems in this style by the Ir. Latinists is *Hisperica Famina* (7th c.). This hisperic or rhyming style was subsequently employed in the OE rhyming poem.

Bardic or Classical Ir. p. is usually dated from 1200–1600. With the Norman invasion in the 12th c. and the decline of the the monastic system, poetry became the hereditary vocation of the professional poets, inheritors of the *filidh* trad., who trained for many years in an academy and were employed by noble families, Gaelic or Norman. Before this period the distinction between *fili* and *bard* derived from the more elevated function of the *fili* as druidic prophet and seer as well as poet; the *bard* was merely a poet or versifier who specialized in eulogy and satire. During the bardic period, however, this distinction disappears, and the term *bard* paradoxically is rarely used as the title for poet. What seems to have happened is that the once separate functions of *fili* and *bard* have merged as the *fili* shed his sacred attributes and assumed some of the functions of the *bard*. The poets of the bardic period would have been known as *filidh*; their social function and their poetry is devoid of the romanticism attached to the word "bard" in the 19th c. (see BARD). Some authorities would date this period earlier, from the 8th c., to coincide with the devel. of *dán díreach* ("strict verse"), the generic name for the new syllabic meters which were to be the hallmark of Ir. p. until the 17th c. Much of the verse of the bardic period is encomiastic, consisting of formal eulogies and elegies composed in the strictest of meters, court poetry written for noble patrons. Religious verse of the period is also written in this strict style.

But if virtuosity and artifice, learned lang. and ornateness were prized in all the verse of this period, there was a considerable amount of poetry in which less elaborate forms were employed. To begin with, there is a body of love poetry in the European convention of courtly love (q.v.), imported into Ireland by the Normans. Pierce Ferriter (d. 1653) and Gerald Fitzgerald (d. 1398) are among the better known authors of these *dánta grádha* (love poems). There is also a category of poems on the lore of places (*dinnseanchas*), lyric and narrative verse that elaborates on the tales about Finn and Oisin, and finally, an amount of more personal poetry. If it is the somewhat less formal and more personal poetry which appeals to the modern reader, there is still a high degree of craft and technical virtuosity in such poems as Giolla Brighde MacNamee's prayer for a son (13th c.) or Gofraidh Fionn Ó Dálaigh's poem on a child born in prison (14th c.), or Muireadach Ó Dálaigh's "On the Death of his Wife," which begins "I parted from my life last night, / A woman's body sunk in clay: / The tender bosom that I loved / Wrapped in a sheet they took away" (13th c.; tr. Frank O'Connor).

With the military defeat of the Ir. Chieftains at Kinsale in 1601, the Cromwellian settlements of 1652–54, and the defeat of James II in 1690, the old Ir. social and cultural organization which supported the privileged status and function of the poet was broken. Thus much of the poetry of the 17th and 18th cs. is overtly political, a poetry of defiance, of mourning for the old order and contempt for the new. The collapse of the old order was experienced in a very personal way by the poets of the 17th c. Dáibhí Ó Bruadair (1625–98), Aogán Ó Rathaille (1675–1729), and others inherited a residual social endorsement of the aristocratic and scholarly role of the poet which in their own lifetime was suddenly withdrawn. Both went from positions of privilege and status to impoverishment and misery; Ó Bruadair ended up as an agricultural laborer.

The form and content of post-bardic poetry reflected the massive social and political upheaval of the 17th c. It is still ornate and intricate, but composed in accentual rather than syllabic verse; it employs assonance but not rhyme, uses more colloquial lang., and is dramatic in utterance. The political context obviously provided the prevailing themes of lament for Ireland's defeat and hope for its political redemption, but it probably also generated the new form of the *aisling*. Ó Rathaille is credited with inventing this political dream-vision in which a beautiful young woman, the personification of Ireland, appears to the poet, complains of her captivity and (sometimes) prophesies salvation. Perhaps the most famous of these *aisling* poems is Ó Rathaille's "Gile na Gile" (Brightness of Brightness).

With the 18th c. and the penal laws, Gaelic culture became the culture of an impoverished and oppressed peasantry. Poets were reduced to employment as hedge-school masters, minstrels, or agricultural laborers. Poetry moved closer to the people and the oral trad., and frequently employed song meter (*amhrán*). In the figures of the blind poet/musicians Turlough O'Carolan (1670–1738) and Anthony Raftery (1784–1835) may be seen the merging of literary style with folk music and ballad. Two masterpieces produced in the 18th c. are Brian Merriman's bawdy and comic *The Midnight Court* and Eibhlin Dubh O'Connell's tragic "Lament for Art O'Leary." *The Midnight Court* has affinities both with Ir. folk poetry and the European medieval poetic genre of the Court of Love; in it a court of Ir. women indict, humorously yet savagely, the various sexual failures of Ir. men. The occasion for the second poem was the murder of Art O'Leary, a casualty of the penal laws. The "Lament" is a poem of passionate grief written by the dead man's wife; it is in the keening trad., but made memorable by its sustained and moving eloquence.

There is also a large body of anonymous folk poetry written in the 17th and 18th cs. which is written mainly in accentual meters and is technically quite sophisticated. "Roisin Dubh," "Kilcash" and "Fair Donncha" are three of the better-known examples.

II. POETRY IN ENGLISH: YEATS AND THE CELTIC REVIVAL. The decline of poetry in Gaelic is obviously a result of the historical and social circumstances also responsible for the decline of the lang.

in the 18th and 19th cs. By the 19th c., Eng. was rapidly becoming the vernacular lang. of Ireland, a process accelerated by the famine of the 1840s and the massive emigration that followed. While verse continued to be written in Gaelic in the 19th c., it is by and large undistinguished. The idea of Celticism was a product of Eng. romanticism, a way of explaining the difference in temperament and character of the Ir., Scots, and Welsh from the Eng. This idea supposed the spirit of these "Celts," but esp. the Ir., to be in its essentially wild and imaginative nature utterly different from (and more interesting than) that of the stolid "Anglo-Saxons." The attempt to recover the native trad. in Ireland was fueled by this assumption of cultural difference—and superiority—to England. In the first half of the 19th c., Moore, Mangan, and Ferguson attempted in various ways to absorb and reconstitute the Gaelic trad. Although Moore's enormously popular melodies sentimentalized their originals, and his lyrics were facile if charming, he did transmit some sense of what Ir. culture had been and might be again. Mangan's "translations" (he knew little Ir.) of old Ir. poems such as "Róisín Dubh" (Dark Rosaleen) and "O'Hussey's Ode to the Maguire" somehow captured if also transformed their passionate qualities and thereby become the classic Eng. versions. Ferguson's translations from Ir. heroic and mythic material were a recovery of much that had been inaccessible but that was later to become an important part of Ir. cultural and political nationalism.

In the latter part of the 19th c., Anglo-Ir. writers, scholars, and antiquarians continued this attempt to recapture the Ir. Gaelic past and to write a distinctively Ir. lit. in the Eng. lang. William Allingham (1824–89) and William Larminie (1850–1900) are both significant contributors to this effort, but Douglas Hyde (1860–1949) and George Sigerson (1839–1925) were more influential through their translations from the Ir.

William Butler Yeats (1865–1939) was born into the Anglo-Ir. class, the Protestant landowning class that was rapidly losing its power and privilege in the late 19th c. Yeats subscribed to the efforts of the Celtic Revival; his sense of his own Irishness derived, initially, from his 19th-c. predecessors and contemporaries engaged in the enterprise of the Revival. Yeats's poetry before 1900, in such volumes as *The Wind Among the Reeds* (1899), is Ir. in its use of mythology and folklore in narrative and ballad forms, although Yeats had no first-hand knowledge of Gaelic. To a great extent, this cultural and political nationalism in Yeats and his contemporaries can be seen as a reaction to the scientific and industrial ethos of the late Victorian world. But even in this first phase of his work, Yeats's poetry cannot be dismissed as mere belated romanticism based on the notion of the superiority of things "Celtic." It is a poetry remarkable not only for its music and imagery but also for its self-conscious awareness that the quest for transcendence is unduly limiting: see, for example, "The Man Who Dreamed of Faeryland."

After 1900, in part because of Yeats's involvement in founding and running the Ir. national theater (the Abbey), the lang. of his verse became a great deal more energetic and colloquial. Most remarkably in the love poems of the volumes *In the Seven Woods* (1904) and *The Green Helmet* (1910), the stylized if beautiful rhet. of the earliest phase of Yeats's verse has been transformed into passionate and dramatic utterance: "Heart cries, 'No, / I have not a crumb of comfort, not a grain. / Time can but make her beauty over again'" ("The Folly of Being Comforted"). With the volume *Responsibilities* (1914), there is yet another change as Yeats began to write a poetry of engagement with the social and political life of his country, emerging as the chronicler of modern Ireland who spoke, in his poetry, for and about Ireland with great authority. The poems of *Michael Robartes* (1921) and *The Tower* (1928) are haunted by the nightmare of contemporary history in Ireland and Europe. It was this phase of Yeats's work, with its apocalyptic view of history, that had most in common with the work of such modernists as T. S. Eliot and Ezra Pound: "Things fall apart; the centre cannot hold; / Mere anarchy is loosed upon the world" ("The Second Coming"). In the last decade or so of Yeats's life, esp. in *Last Poems* (1936–39), the dominant note is a tragic affirmation of life defiantly expressed in the teeth of time and the worst that life can offer: "All things fall and are built again, / And those that build them again are gay" ("Lapis Lazuli").

Yeat's verseforms are the traditional ones of Eng. poetry and not the revolutionary new forms associated with Pound and Eliot: his preference is for various quatrain, sestet, and octave stanzas in iambic and trochaic measures, and he employs rhyme extensively.

Associated with Yeats and the Revival is a group of poets writing in the earlier part of the 20th c.: George Russell, also known as AE (1867–1935), Oliver St. John Gogarty (1878–1957), Padraic Colum (1881–1972), and James Stephens (1882–1950). The great folk dramatist John Millington Synge (1871–1909) is also affiliated with this group. The term "Ir. Literary Renaissance" (q.v.) may be employed to include the Celtic Revival and the later poetry of Yeats (which makes him not only Ireland's greatest poet, but the greatest poet of the modern world); it also includes the prose fiction of James Joyce (1884–1941), surely the greatest of the modernist prose writers, and the drama of Sean O'Casey (1880–1964).

III. IRISH POETRY AFTER YEATS. The vitality of Ir. p. after Yeats is remarkable. Poetry in Eng. may be divided, for simplicity's sake, into two categories. The first shares the broad theme of exploration of cultural identity: it reflects the individual's experience of the social life of the Ir. people in the 20th c., esp. as they emerge from a traditionally rural way of life to confront modern urban experience. This poetry is written by a very different class from the one to which Yeats belonged, and is based on a very different social experience from his. The major figures are Austin Clarke (1896–1974), Patrick Kavanagh (1904–67), Thomas Kinsella (b. 1928), John Montague (b. 1928), and Seamus Heaney (b. 1939). (Of contemporary Ir. poets only Richard Murphy hails from Yeats's Anglo-Ir. background.) This poetry by and large shares a certain sense of history, place, lang., and religion. Indeed, the theme of Ir. history as an urgent personal issue, felt in the blood, supersedes the present conflict in Ulster, and takes as its domain all of Ir. history, including the archaeological past. There is little sense of the aestheticizing of history or the creation of heroic myth that one finds in Yeats. Much of this poetry is shaped to various degrees by an awareness of Ir. lang. and lit.; except for Kavanagh, all the major figures have effected a substantial repossession of poetry in Ir. through tr. into verse in Eng. which captures more authentically the spirit of the original than did the trs. of the Revival writers. Contemporary poets have also incorporated, in various ways, this linguistic awareness into their verse in Eng. The sense of place in their poetry is frequently atavistic in its recovery of an Irishness which has been hidden from the present. The common attitude toward religion resists the oppressive aspects of the Catholic Church as a social institution in Ireland, yet the poetry is frequently imprinted with a vision of nature as sacramental, of poetry as prayer, of the artist as a sacerdotal figure.

The second category of poetry after Yeats vigorously disputes the agenda set by the first, stressing modernity rather than Irishness. There are two main groups, as well as numerous individuals: The European-Ir. poets—Samuel Beckett (b. 1906), Thomas MacGreevy (1893–1967), Brian Coffey (b. 1905), Dennis Devlin (1908–59)—constitute one group, and a number of the Ulster poets, pre-eminently Derek Mahon (b. 1941), who look to Louis MacNeice (1907–63) as exemplar, constitute the other. Both groups are possessed of a cosmopolitan sensibility, modern feelings of loss and alienation, a view of hist. informed by modern European and world hist. (rather than Ir. hist.), and a conviction that the European langs. and the classics are more significant than Ir. lang. and lit. They distrust the idea of an Ir. poet, as opposed to a poet who happens to be Ir.

The technique of Ir. p. in Eng. after Yeats, as in poetry in Eng. elsewhere in the same period, has tended to reject the traditional forms within which Yeats worked. The example of Pound and Williams (and behind both, Whitman) has been particularly liberating for Ir. poets in their struggle to emerge from Yeats's colossal shadow. But this is not the whole story. There is also, and esp. among poets from Ulster, a disposition toward a more traditional sense of form, akin to the notion of the well-made poem fostered by The Movement in Britain. There is an occasional reversion to older forms, as in Seamus Heaney's sonnet sequences; and at least one Ir. poet, Austin Clarke, has sought to import into Eng. the complicated and ornate technique of poetry in Gaelic, an undertaking which he described thus to Robert Frost: "I load myself with chains and try to get out of them." Conventional forms in Ir. may also be used unconventionally in contemporary poetry in Eng., as in the parodic appropriation of *immram* (voyage poem) and the *aisling* in the work of Paul Muldoon (b. 1951).

One index to the vitality and accessibility of recent poetry in Gaelic is the fact that it is being translated by contemporary Ir. poets who write in Eng. In the earlier generation of poets writing in Gaelic, the names to reckon with are Seán Ó Ríordáin (1917–77), considered by some to be the finest poet writing in Ir. since the 18th c., Máirtín Ó Direáin (b. 1910), and Máire Mhac an tSaoi (b. 1922). The present generation includes a host of writers, from whom may be singled out Michael Hartnett (b. 1941), who also writes in Eng., Michael Davitt (b. 1950), and Nuala Ní Dhomhnaill (b. 1952). What characterizes this most recent resurgence of poetry in Gaelic is not only individual talent, but the fact that writing in Gaelic no longer precludes an acceptance of the modern world, nor does it require the employment of the strict poetic forms of the past.

If contemporary poets writing in Eng. or Gaelic do not enjoy quite the same privilege as the *filidh*, they do, like their ancient counterparts, tend to stand as a group in intimate relation to the national life of their country. By and large, they are known, respected, and listened to when they speak or write on history, society, or politics, as well as on more personal subjects. *Aosdána*, the state-supported association of writers, is obviously based in part on the conviction that the dignity and prestige enjoyed by the poets of ancient Ireland ought in some measure to be accorded to the poets of contemporary Ireland.

See also AI FHREISLIGI; AICILL.

BIBLIOGRAPHIES: R. I. Best, *A Bibl. of Ir. Philology and of Printed Ir. Lit.* (1913); K. G. W. Cross and R. T. A. Dunlop, *A Bibl. of Yeats Crit. 1887–1965* (1971); R. Bromwich, *Med. Celtic Lit.: A Select Bibl.* (1974); M. Lapidge and R. Sharpe, *A Bibl. of Celtic-Lat. Lit., 400–1200* (1985); K. P. S. Jochum, *W. B. Yeats: A Classified Bibl. of Crit.* (1990).

ANTHOLOGIES IN ENGLISH AND TRANSLATIONS FROM GAELIC: *The Love Songs of Connacht*, and *The Religious Songs of Connacht*, ed. and tr. D. Hyde (1893; 1906); *Bards of the Gael and Gall*, ed. and tr. G. Sigerson (1897); *Sel. from Ancient Ir. P.*, ed. and tr. K. Meyer (1911); *An Anthol. of Ir. Verse*, ed. P. Colum (1922); *Love's Bitter-Sweet*, ed. and tr. R. Flower (1925); K. A. Jackson, *Studies in Early Celtic Nature Poetry*, (1935), *A Celtic Miscellany* (1951); *1000 Years of Ir. P.*, ed. K. Hoagland (1947); *Ir. Poets*

of the 19th C., ed. G. Taylor (1951); *Early Ir. Lyrics*, ed. and tr. G. Murphy (1956); *Kings, Lords and Commons*, ed. and tr. F. O'Connor (1959); *Love Poems of the Ir.*, ed. and tr. S. Lucy (1967); *The Penguin Book of Ir. Verse*, ed. B. Kennelly (1970); *The Book of Ir. Verse*, ed. J. Montague (1974); *An Duanaire 1600–1900*, ed. and tr. T. Kinsella and S. O'Tuama (1981); *Early Ir. Verse*, ed. and tr. R. Lehmann (1982); *Poets of Munster*, ed. S. Dunne (1985); *The Bright Wave*, ed. D. Bolger (1986); *The New Oxford Book of Ir. Verse*, ed. T. Kinsella (1986); *Contemp. Ir. P.*, ed. A. Bradley (1988).

HISTORY AND CRITICISM: E. O'Reilly, *A Chronological Account of Nearly Four Hundred Irish Writers* (1820, rpt. 1970); E. A. Boyd, *Ireland's Literary Ren.* (1916); D. Corkery, *The Hidden Ireland* (1924); A. De Blacam, *Gaelic Lit. Surveyed* (1929); R. Flower, *The Ir. Trad.* (1947); M. Dillon, *Early Ir. Lit.* (1948); E. Knott, *Ir. Syllabic Poetry 1200–1600* (1957); C. Watkins, "IE Metrics and Archaic Ir. Verse," *Celtica* 6 (1963); *Early Ir. P.*, ed. J. Carney (1965); C. Donahue, "Med. Celtic Lit." in Fisher; P. L. Henry, *The Early Eng. and Celtic Lyric* (1966); P. Power, *A Lit. Hist. of Ireland* (1969); O. Bergin, *Ir. Bardic Poetry* (1970); H. Bloom, *Yeats* (1970); J. E. Stoll, *The Great Deluge: A Yeats Bibl.* (1971); T. Brown, *Northern Voices: Poets from Ulster* (1975); *Two Decades of Ir. Writing*, ed. D. Dunn (1975); R. Finneran, *Anglo-Ir. Lit: A Review of Research* (1976); D. Perkins, *Hist. of Mod. Poetry*, 2 v. (1976, 1987); S. O'Neill, "Gaelic Lit.," *Dict. of Ir. Lit.*, ed. R. Hogan et al. (1979); G. J. Watson, *Ir. Identity and the Literary Revival* (1979); R. Welch, *Ir. P. from Moore to Yeats* (1980); *The Pleasures of Gaelic Poetry*, ed. S. MacReammoin (1981); A. N. Jeffares, *Anglo-Ir. Lit.* (1982); S. Deane, *Celtic Revivals* (1985), *A Short Hist. of Ir. Lit.* (1986); D. Johnston, *Ir. P. After Joyce* (1986); P. L. Marcus, *Yeats and the Beginning of the Ir. Ren.*, 2d ed. (1987); R. Garratt, *Mod. Ir. P.* (1986); E. Longley, *Poetry in the Wars* (1986); D. Donoghue, *We Irish* (1988); R. F. Garratt, *Mod. Ir. P.* (1989). A.BR.

IRISH PROSODY. See CELTIC PROSODY.

IRONY (Gr. *eironeia*, Lat. *dissimulatio*, esp. through understatement).

A. *Classical I.* In Gr. comedy the *eiron* was the underdog, weak but clever, who regularly triumphed over the stupid and boastful *alazon*. In Theophrast's *Characters*, the ironist appears as a deceitful hypocrite pursuing his own advantage. The cl. image of i. as a lofty, urbane mode of dissimulation, practiced in conversation and public speech and without one's own advantage in mind, finds its origin in the Platonic Socrates (hence the term "Socratic i."). In front of his conversational partners who claim to know, Socrates professes not to know, but through insistent questioning proves them also not to know, thereby finding a common basis for their quest for knowledge. Hence Socrates dissimulates not for his own advantage but for the sake of truth. Aristotle (*Rhet.*, Bk. 3) presents i. as "a mockery of oneself": "the jests of the ironical man are at his own expense; the buffoon excites laughter at others" (1419b7). In the *Nicomachean Ethics* Aristotle conceives of i. as "the contrary to boastful exaggeration; it is a self-deprecating concealment of one's own powers and possessions; it shows better taste to deprecate than to exaggerate one's virtues" (1108.19–23). In the same work Aristotle discusses *eironeia* and *alazoneia*, understatement and boastfulness, as deviations from truth, holding that i. is a noble form because it deviates not for the sake of one's own advantage but from a dislike for bombast and a desire to spare others the feeling of inferiority. The prototype of this genuine i. is Socrates (1127b22–26).

Cl. rhetoricians distinguished several varieties of i. In i. proper, the speaker is conscious of double meaning and the victim unconscious; in *sarcasm* both parties understand the double meaning. Other forms incl. *meiosis* and *litotes* (understatement); *hyperbole* (overstatement); *antiphrasis* (contrast); *asteism* and *charientism* (forms of the joke); *chleuasm* (mockery); *mycterism* (the sneer); and *mimesis* (imitation [q.v.], esp. for the sake of ridicule). Cicero termed i. "that form of dissimulation which the Greeks named *eironeia*" (*Academica posteriora* 2.5.15) and also considered Socrates the prototype of this witty and refined art of conversation (*De officiis* 1.30.108). Quintilian assigned i. its position among the tropes and figures discussed in Books 8 and 9 of his *Institutio oratoria*. For Quintilian the common feature in all rhetorical forms of i. is that the intention of the speaker is different from what he says, that we understand the contrary of what he says (9.2.44).

In late antiquity, the Middle Ages, the Ren., and neoclassicism, the cl. delineation of i. was varied and enriched by including other rhetorical forms and elaborating a more complex system of figures, but the basic meaning remained the same. The Fr. *Encyclopédie* of 1765 summarizes the various nuances of i. found in numerous critical handbooks of the time by defining i. as "a figure of speech by which one indicates the opposite of what one says" (8.905). To this one should add that, according to cl. opinion, in order to distinguish i. from mere lying, the entire tenor of speaking, incl. intonation, emphasis, and gesture, is supposed to reveal the intended meaning. One should also recollect that authors (Boccaccio, Cervantes, Shakespeare) whom today we consider ironic in their literary creations were not viewed so in their time; this term remained confined to the field of rhet. until late in the 18th c.

B. *Romantic I.* The most significant change in meaning took place in 1797, when Schlegel observed in his *Fragments*: "there are ancient and modern poems which breathe throughout, in their entirety and in every detail, the divine breath of i." Schlegel's most constant description of i. in its literary and poetic forms is that of a consistent alternation of affirmation and negation, of exuberant emergence from oneself and self-critical retreat into oneself, of enthusiasm and skepticism. In Ger. romantic poetry (Tieck, Jean Paul, Hoffmann, Heine), i. became a conscious form of literary creation, although its prototype was seen, as is now fully recognized, in older European authors such as Boccaccio, Cervantes, and Shakespeare. Particular points of ironic contrast, of creation and annihilation, were the relationships of illusion and reality, subjective and objective, self and world, the inauthenticity and authenticity of the self, the relative and the absolute. A new dimension was introduced when these relationships were viewed not only in terms of artistic playfulness (Schlegel) but also in terms of melancholy and sadness as the *mal du siècle* (Fr. romanticism), the transitoriness of life (Keats), or the perishing of the divine in this world (Solger). See ROMANTIC AND POSTROMANTIC POETICS.

C. *Tragic I.* was introduced by Connop Thirlwall in 1833, who based it on a distinction among three basic types of i.: verbal, dialectic, and practical. Verbal i. establishes, as in cl. rhet., a contrast between what is said and meant; dialectic i. relates to works of lit. and thought in which i. permeates the entire structure. Practical i., however, is the most comprehensive form, present throughout life in individuals as well as in the history of states and institutions, and constitutes the basis for tragic i. The contrast of the individual and his hopes, wishes, and actions, on the one hand, and the workings of the dark and unyielding power of fate, on the other, is the proper sphere of tragic i. The tragic poet is the creator of a small world in which he reigns with absolute power over the fate of those imaginary persons to whom he gives life and breath according to his own plan.

D. *Cosmic I.* I. took on a new and more comprehensive dimension with Hegel, who strongly opposed romantic i. because of its "annihilating" tendency, seeing in it nothing but poetic caprice. Yet in *The History of Philosophy*, Hegel sensed in the "crowding of world historical affairs," in the trampling down of the "happiness of peoples, wisdom of states, and virtue of individuals," in short, in his comprehensive view of history, an ironic contrast between the absolute and the relative, the general and the individual, which he expressed by the phrase, "general i. of the world." Later we find this phrase in Heine and Kierkegaard. In Kierkegaard, however, i. becomes an absolute and irreconcilable opposition between the subjective and objective. Heine uses terms such as "God's i." and "i. of the world" to express the disappearance of reasonable order in the world. The ultimate extension of Hegel's concept was made by Nietzsche, who asked what would happen if all our ultimate convictions would become "more and more incredible, if nothing should prove to be divine any more unless it were error, blindness, lie—if God himself should prove to be our most enduring lie."

E. In *Verbal I.* (see paragraph 2 above), one meaning is stated and a different, usually antithetical, meaning is intended. In understatement the expressed meaning is mild and the intended meaning often intense, e.g. Mercutio's comment on his death-wound, "No, 'tis not so deep as a well, nor so wide as a church door; but 'tis enough, 'twill serve." Overstatement, esp. common in Am. folk humor, effects the reverse. The i. of a statement often depends on context. If one looks out of his window at a rain storm and remarks to a friend, "Wonderful day, isn't it?" the contradiction between the facts and the implied description of them establishes the i. When Hamlet rejects the idea of suicide with the remark, "Thus conscience does make cowards of us all," his remark is ironic because *conscience* is a sacramental word associated with moral goodness, whereas *coward* is a pejorative. The same kind of i. is illustrated in Comus' seduction speech, where a true principle (natural fertility) is used to prove an untrue doctrine (libertinism). Thus, i. can arise from explicit or implicit contradiction, as when Marvell begins his proposition to his coy mistress with the remark that time is short, but ends with the observation that love can make time pass more quickly.

F. *Dramatic I.* is a plot device according to which (a) the spectators know more than the protagonist; (b) the character reacts in a way contrary to that which is appropriate or wise; (c) characters or situations are compared or contrasted for ironic effects, such as parody; or (d) there is a marked contrast between what the character understands about his acts and what the play demonstrates about them. Foreshadowing is often ironic: Hamlet's speech on the fall of the sparrow has one meaning in its immediate context and a somewhat different one in Hamlet's own "fall" at the end of the scene. Tragedy is esp. rich in all forms of dramatic i. The necessity for a sudden reversal or catastrophe in the fortunes of the hero (Aristotle's *peripeteia*) means that the fourth form of i. (form d) is almost inevitable. *Oedipus Rex* piles i. on i. Form (a) is present because of the fact that the audience becomes increasingly conscious as the play progresses that Oedipus is rushing blindly to his doom. Form (b) is present in Oedipus' insistence on pursuing his investigation to its bitter climax (the fact that his basic motivation is a desire for justice and public welfare is a further i.—his fall is in part caused by his nobility). Form (c) is illustrated in the parallel between blind Tiresias (who can "see" morally) and the figure of Oedipus when he, too, has gained "vision" after blinding himself. Form (d) is, of course, present in the contrast between what Oedipus hopes to accomplish and what he finally does accomplish.

G. *Poetic I.* An important new step in the crit. hist. of i. can be noticed with the literary theory elaborated by the New Criticism (q.v.), esp. in the work of I. A. Richards, Cleanth Brooks, and Robert Penn Warren, equating i. with poetry as such. For Brooks in particular, i. is considered the "principle of structure" in literary works, a reconciling power fusing the ambiguity, paradox, multiplicity, and variety of meaning in a work into the unity, wholeness, and identity which constitutes its modes of being. On this basis, but by way of reversal, Paul de Man conceives of i. in terms of a discrepancy between sign and meaning, an absence of coherence or gap among the parts of a work, and an inability to escape from a situation that has become unbearable. In this sense i. practically coincides with the notion of deconstruction (q.v.). In all its forms of expression, cl. and modern, i. functions as an agent of qualification and refinement. But during the modern period esp., beginning with romanticism, i. has become inseparable from literary and poetic expression itself.

S. Kierkegaard, *The Concept of I.* (1841), tr. L. M. Capel (1965); J. A. K. Thomson, *I., an Historical Intro.* (1926); G. G. Sedgwick, *Of I., Esp. in the Drama* (1935); C. Brooks, *Mod. Poetry and the Trad.* (1939), *The Well Wrought Urn* (1947), "I. as a Principle of Structure" (1949), in *Literary Opinion in America*, ed. M. W. Zabel (1951); D. Worcester, *The Art of Satire* (1940); A. R. Thompson, *The Dry Mock: A Study of I. in Drama* (1948); R. P. Warren, "Pure and Impure Poetry," *Critiques and Essays in Crit.*, ed. R. W. Stallman (1949); R. B. Sharpe, *I. in the Drama* (1959); N. D. Knox, *The Word I. and its Context, 1500–1755* (1961); V. Jankelevitch, *L'Ironie* (1964); E. M. Good, *I. in the Old Testament* (1965); A. E. Dyson, *The Crazy Fabric: Essays in I.* (1965); N. D. Knox, "I.," *DHI*; B. Allemann, *Ironie und Dichtung*, 2d ed. (1969); B. O. States, *I. and Drama: A Poetics* (1971); E. Behler, *Klassische Ironie, Romantische Ironie, Tragische Ironie* (1972), *I. and the Discourse of Modernity* (1990); W. C. Booth, *A Rhet. of I.*, 2d ed. (1974); D. H. Green, *I. in the Med. Romance* (1979); D. Simpson, *I. and Authority in Romantic Poetry* (1979); A. K. Mellor, *Eng. Romantic I.* (1980); Morier; D. C. Muecke, *I. and the Ironic*, 2d ed. (1982); U. Japp, *Theorie der Ironie* (1983); L. R. Furst, *Fictions of Romantic I.* (1984); E. Birney, *Essays on Chaucerian I.*, ed. B. Rowland (1985); D. J. Enright, *The Alluring Problem: An Essay on I.* (1987); M. Yaari, *Ironie paradoxale et ironie poétique* (1988); C. D. Lang, *I./Humor: Crit. Paradigms* (1988); R. J. Fogelin, *Figuratively Speaking* (1988); F. Garber, *Self, Text, and Romantic I.* (1988), ed., *Romantic I.* (1989); S. Gaunt, *Troubadours and I.* (1989); L. Bishop, *Romantic I. in Fr. Lit.* (1990); D. Knox, *Ironia* (1990); J. A. Dane, *The Critical Mythology of I.* (1991). W.V.O'C.; E.H.B.

ISOCHRONISM or ISOCHRONY refers to the rhythmic organization of speech into equal intervals of time. Most modern discussions derive from Kenneth Pike's distinction between "stress-timed" and "syllable-timed" langs. Proponents of i. claim that in *stress-timed* langs. (incl. Eng.), i. operates in such a way that the distance between stressed syllables is held constant in speech regardless (within limits) of the number of syllables between them; unstressed syllables between stresses are either lengthened or shortened in timing in order to keep the intervals isochronous. (Notice that i. is operative in music: musical bars are all equal in duration regardless of how many notes actually fill each one, and by convention the first note in every bar bears a stress.)

Opponents of i. note that objective evidence is slim: Bolinger showed that interstress intervals in continuous speech can vary as much as 6:1. However, within certain more localized contexts, i. does seem to occur. And it may not be necessary that the intervals be objectively equal, so long as they are *perceived* to be equal. Acoustic measurements have failed to confirm perfect i. in speech production, but there is evidence that listeners do impose rhythmic structure on sequences of interstress intervals. In the "syllable-timed" langs., by contrast, such as Fr., it is the syllables than are evenly spaced. Here i. comes closer to having both objective and subjective reality.

Some temporal prosodists, who hold that timing rather than stressing is the basis of meter, have applied the concept of i. to the scansion of Eng. poetry. This approach has not worked well on accentual-syllabic verse, but most types of accentual verse (q.v.), by contrast, probably show some degree of i., because they are not far removed from song. A good example is ballad meter (q.v.): since ballad texts were originally almost always set to music, the i. probably derives from the residue of the musical structure. However, some metrists insist that i. can only be a feature of performance (q.v.), never of meter.

C. Patmore, "Eng. Metrical Critics," *North Brit. Rev.* 27 (1857); P. Verrier, *Essai sur les principes de la métrique anglaise,* 3 v. (1909–10)—esp. v. 3; J. W. Hendren, W. K. Wimsatt, Jr., and M. C. Beardsley, "A Word for Rhythm and a Word for Meter," *PMLA* 76 (1961); Y. Shen and G. G. Peterson, *I. in Eng.* (1962); D. Bolinger, *Forms of Eng.* (1965), 164–71; *Intonation and Its Parts* (1986), ch. 5; J. E. Duckworth, "An Inquiry into the Validity of the Isochronic Hypothesis," *DAI* 26 (1966), 5424A; E. M. Kafalenos, "Possibilities of I.: A Study of Rhythm in Mod. Poetry," *DAI* 35 (1974), 2273A; C. L. Coleman, "A Study of Acoustical and Perceptual Attributes of I. in Spoken Eng.," *DAI* 35 (1975), 4724A; M. Sumera, "The Concept of I.: Some Problems of Analysis," *SIL* 25 (1975); J. S. Hedges, "Towards a Case for Isochronous Verse," *1975 Mid-Am. Linguistics Conference Papers,* ed. F. Inglemann (1976); I. Lehiste, "I. Reconsidered," *Jour. of Phonetics* 5 (1977). T.V.F.B.; I.L.

ISOCOLON (Gr. "equal length") and **PARISON.** P. (Gr. "almost equal") is the figure which describes syntactic members (phrases, clauses, sentences; or lines of verse) showing parallelism (q.v.) of structure. In short, they are identical in grammar or form. I. denotes members that are identical in number of syllables, or in scansion. Two members could show p. without i.: the number and types of words would match identically, but the words themselves would not match in number of syllables. Conversely, two members could be isosyllabic and even identical rhythmically without having exact correspondence of members. But normally p. implies i. as well. Sometimes an obvious word is elided in the second member: "The ox hath known his owner, and the ass his master's crib." I. is particularly of interest because Aristotle mentions it in the *Rhetoric* as the figure which produces symmetry and balance in speech, and thus creates rhythmical prose or even measures in verse; cf. Quintilian 9.3.76. In rhythmical prose it is important for establishing the various forms of the cursus (q.v.). Vickers gives examples of p.: "As Caesar lov'd me, I weep for him; as he was fortunate, I rejoice at it; as he was valiant, I honour him; but as he was ambitious, I slew him" (*Julius Caesar* 3.1.24); and of i.: "Was ever woman in this humour woo'd? / Was ever woman in this humour won?" (*Richard 3* 1.2.227). The p. by Nathaniel in *Love's Labour's Lost* (5.1.2) is famous.—Norden; A. Quinn, *Figures of Speech* (1982), 77–79; B. Vickers, *In Defence of Rhet.* (1988), *Cl. Rhet. in Eng. Poetry,* 2d ed. (1989). T.V.F.B.

ISOMETRIC, isometrical; in Cl. prosody, "homoeomeral." Stichic verse is by definition i.: every line is of the same length and meter. Most stanzaic poems are i.: the metrical structure of the first stanza is repeated identically in subsequent ones. A few—e.g. tail rhyme and the Sapphic (qq.v.)—are not. In nonstanzaic poetry (consisting of only one stanza not repeated, e.g. the sonnet [q.v.]), by contrast, a significant number are heterometric (q.v.)—some lines are shorter than others. It is not known whether most forms in Western poetry are i. See now HETEROMETRIC; STANZA. T.V.F.B.

ITALIAN POETICS. See MEDIEVAL POETICS; RENAISSANCE POETICS; BAROQUE POETICS; NEOCLASSICAL POETICS; ROMANTIC AND POSTROMANTIC POETICS; TWENTIETH-CENTURY POETICS.

ITALIAN POETRY.

    I. DUECENTO: THE 1200S
   II. TRECENTO: THE 1300S
  III. QUATTROCENTO: THE 1400S
   IV. CINQUECENTO: THE 1500S
    V. SEICENTO: THE 1600S
   VI. SETTECENTO: THE 1700S
  VII. OTTOCENTO: THE 1800S
 VIII. NOVECENTO: THE 1900S

I. DUECENTO: THE 1200S. The Middle Ages, from the fall of the Roman Empire to the 1300s, were long regarded as merely an epoch of barbarism. Modern historiography, however, has rediscovered the period from Charlemagne to the birth of the Romance vernacular lits. as a time of fervent incubation, a preparation for the cultural rebirth of the 13th and 14th cs. During this period the autonomous existence of the neo-Lat. langs. became evident. The first documents of It. lang. and lit., from the doubtful "Veronese Riddle" (9th c.) and the "Laurentian Verse" (ca. 1150) to St. Francis's "Hymn," Jacopone's poems, and the Sicilian and Tuscan love lyrics, should be examined in the light of three conditioning facts: (1) the political conformation of the It. peninsula—the constant tension between temporal and ecclesiastical power and its result, the Guelph-Ghibelline wars; (2) the influence of Fr. and Occitan literary models—the Fr. lang. precedes It. by a century or more; the delay usually being attributed to a tenacious survival of Lat., though it also owes to the absence of a central power, hence a slower evolution of feudal structures in the peninsula; and (3) the widespread religious revival beginning around the year 1000 and its vast influence throughout the 1300s.

Directly related to the latter is the monastic order founded by Francis of Assisi (1182–1226), who is also the first It. poet worthy of note. His "Cantico delle creature" (Song of the Creation), a thanksgiving hymn by and for the creature to the Creator, reflects a spirit of humility and simple faith as well as a new-found wonder at the beauty of the creation and an implicit refusal to see earthly life as a mere valley of tears. The primitive diction should not mislead the reader: Francis is a conscious creator of poetry. This can be seen in the careful structure of the hymn, in the purposeful ambivalence of word choice, and in the celebrated adjectival series which define each "member" of the grace-giving choir.

The genre of the *lauda* (q.v.; the "Canticle" is also known as "Laus creaturarum"), enriched by the example of Med. Lat. liturgical lit., was endowed with high poetry by Jacopone da Todi (1236?–1306), an attorney spiritually reborn after the tragic death of his wife. Jacopone vigorously opposed the power plays of Pope Boniface VIII (Dante's arch-enemy), and was excommunicated and imprisoned by him; a number of the approximately 100 extant *laude* by Jacoponi are against the simony of the Church (e.g. "O Papa Bonifazio"). Jacopone's best poetry is inspired by his feeling of singularity and isolation in his mystical passion. "There's wisdom and rank methinks no higher / than the madness of love for the fair Messiah," Jacopone sings in "Senno me pare"; holy insanity pervades his poems. The primitive diction is, in part, poetic artifice. In "O iubelo del core" (O Heartfelt Joy), a rough-hewn *ars poetica*, the poet seems to give his program: "the tongue in your mouth stutters, / it knows not what it says." His masterpiece, the "Donna del Paradiso" (Lament of Mary), is a short dramatization of Christ's passion seen through the eyes of the Mother. Here Jacopone reaches lyric heights never before attained in It. p. The Madonna's cry to her Son, the "Lovely Lily," ("O figlio figlio figlio / figlio amoroso giglio") is supreme religious poetry, equalled only in Dante's *Paradiso.*

Jacopone had no direct following. Among Dante's indirect predecessors was the late 13th-c. flowering of religious verse in Northern Italy on the theme of the Beyond: the excessive realism of Giacomino da Verona's "Infernal Babylon" and "Heavenly Jerusalem" (620 stammering verses), and the *ex-voto*-like "Threefold Book" by Bonvesin de la Riva (1240–1313). The actual forerunners of Dante's lyric poetry were the poets of the "Sicilian School" (q.v.), the first matrix of It. literary trad. Centered at the Palermo court of Frederick II (1194–1250), the group devolved from the Occitan troubadour (q.v.) trad. It superimposed the rituals of feudal bondage and court protocol onto a concept of love, its only topic, in which the perfect submission by the Platonic lover corresponded to the heavenly perfection of the lady. The school, of vast cultural importance but wanting in invention, produced no great poetry. Among its members were Giacomino Pugliese, Rinaldo d'Aquino, and Pier delle Vigne. The reputed "inventor" of the sonnet (q.v.), the notary Jacopo da Lentino (mid 1200s), is mentioned by Dante as the foremost poet of the "Magna Curia"; he was a faithful adapter of the *trouvères'* schemata of *fin amor.*

The Emperor Frederick, himself a poet, had vainly attempted to unify his Ger. and It. domains against violent ecclesiastical opposition. During his reign arose the Ghibelline (Imperial) and Guelph (Papal) factions, antagonists for over a century in It. politics. After the battle of Benevento (1266) the practice of poetry survived but was transplanted to the North. Its first noteworthy heir, Guittone d'Arezzo (1225–93), a Guelph exiled from his homeland, renewed and enriched the Siculo-Occitan trad. by extending its topics to ethical and social concerns. Guittone's hermeticism is an exasperation of the *trobar clus* (q.v.) of Fr. minstrelsy; his poems sound cold and artistically stifling. Although poets such as Chiaro Davanzati and the abstruse Monte Andrea shared his taste for technical complexity, Guittone had no direct disciple. His songbook is a bridge, or rather a hurdle to be overcome between the Sicilians and the first great flowering of It. lyric, the school of Dante's Sweet New Style, the Dolce stil nuovo (q.v.).

The very existence of such a "school," posited only by a vague reference in *Purgatory,* is unsure. Certain, however, is a common conception of Love as "dictator" (inspirer and despot). The Bolognese judge Guido Guinizzelli (ca. 1240–76), praised by Dante as the father of the style *dolce* ("sweet," not bitterly harsh, as in Guittone) and *nuovo* ("original"), left a celebrated summary of the new amorous *ars poetica* in his *canzone:* true nobility is not of lineage but of virtue; love is a positive force:

through the lady, admired from afar, the lover of "noble heart" attains spiritual perfection. Guido's Songbook (about 20 extant texts) shows a youthful vitality and a springtime acerbity, also present in Dante's *Vita nuova.* Among the numerous adepts of the Sweet New Style we can but mention Lapo Gianni, Gianni Alfani, Dino Frescobaldi, Bonagiunta Orbicciani; an anonymous Compiuta Donzella ("Accomplished Maiden"; her three sonnets show poetic skill and sincere passion); and the prolific Cino da Pistoia (d. 1336), usually characterized as a hyphen between Dante and Petrarch. The maturity of the school is represented by Guido Cavalcanti (d. 1300), Dante's "primo amico." Legend depicts him as a haughty loner, an image probably inspired by his poems (52 extant), his *ars poetica,* and theory of love. Cavalcanti's interest in the mechanics of feelings, esp. the anguish of love, gives him a "morbid and mournful" air; he seems to be an observer of his own soul. In his concept of love the image of a "real" woman stimulates the lover to create an idea of beauty which pervades his soul and, in turn, prods him to strive vainly toward the "original." Cavalcanti's masterpiece, "Ballatetta" (ca. 1300), was written in exile.

Parallel to *stilnovo* a school of jocose (or "bourgeois") poetry developed. The "Contrasto" by a Cielo d'Alcamo (1250?) is a highly artistic, lively "script" of amorous bickering, ending in bed, between a cynical minstrel and a clever country lass. The Sicilian court poets' recurrent topics (praise, submission) and artful linguistic *koiné* are the ironic subtext to this still enjoyable little masterpiece. Parody of *stilnovo* results in shrill outbursts in Cecco Angiolieri (1260–1313), the skilled Sienese sonneteer (about 100 extant poems) whose themes incl. wild quarrels with his lady (Becchina—who is no lady), tavern brawls, the sorry state of his purse, and the stinginess of his parents, who are reluctant to die. Cecco is no "It. Villon," as he has been called. His texts are meant for recital in the inn or brothel; the punchlines are ideally completed by guffaws from the guzzlers. A gentler realism inspires the sonnets of Folgòre, poet of San Gimignano (early 14th c.), reflecting the chivalric ceremonies of polite society. The frank pursuit of pleasure here is tempered by a code of behavior based on good taste. Folgòre's tenuous poetry harks back, as *stilnovo* does, to the courtly poets of Provence.

II. TRECENTO: THE 1300S. In retrospect, the first hundred years of It. lit. appear as preparation for Dante's poetry. This perception, philologically speaking, is quite correct. Aesthetically, however, a veritable chasm separates *Duecento* poetry from *The Divine Comedy.* For valid parallels one must turn to the fine arts and Giotto, or to philosophy and Thomas Aquinas.

Little is known of Dante Alighieri's life. Born in 1265 in Florence into a Guelph-leaning family of lesser nobility, he studied rhet. with Brunetto Latini. His attendance at Bologna University is doubt-ful; service in the wars of the *Commune* in 1289 is attested. Lasting influences upon his youth included his friendship with Guido Cavalcanti, his discovery of his own talent for poetry, and, esp., his love for a Bice Portinari, wife of the banker Bardi ("Beatrice" for the poet who remained devoted to her in her life and after her death.) Their lop-sided love story is told in his youthful novel, the *Vita nuova,* but in his *magnum opus,* written to honor this young woman who died at 25, Beatrice is present from beginning to end. No mention is ever made of wife Gemma and their three or four offspring (two, Jacopo and Pietro, become exegetes of their father's work). After 1295 documents attest Alighieri's participation in the civic life of his city; in 1300 he became one of six "priori" (cabinet members) in a Florence torn between two Guelph parties: Blacks, subservient to Rome, and Whites, anti-imperial but resistant to Papal hegemony. Alighieri sided with the latter. In 1301 he was sent by his party, then in power, as ambassador to Pope Boniface VIII, who promptly detained him while the Blacks, with French and Papal help, seized power in Florence. Dante, sentenced *in absentia* to be burned at the stake, never again set eyes on his city. In exile over 20 years, he hoped at first to deserve recall on the strength of his learning: he produced works on linguistics (*De vulgari eloquentia,* a fragment in Lat.), exegesis (*Convivio,* unfinished), and political science (*De monarchia*). Scholars date the composition of *The Divine Comedy* from 1307 to the year of Dante's death in Ravenna, 1321.

The *Vita nuova* (1292–93) is a collection of poems connected by prose passages relating a tenuous love story from the meeting between Dante and Bice, both aged nine, to her death in 1290 and beyond. It is a story made up of abstract emotions, the most daring "real" event being Beatrice's one-time reciprocation of Dante's greeting. *Vita nuova* is neither autobiography nor total fiction: it is rather a typology of youthful love, pervaded by a quasi-religious, mystical solemnity and by an oneiric vagueness of detail. Poems not fit for inclusion in the "Vita," and those written after 1293, make up Dante's *Canzoniere* (or *Rime* [Songbook]). Here, besides the early and later experiments with styles and forms, we find the *canzoni* of Dante's maturity and exile; closest to the inspiration of the *Comedy* is the poem "Tre donne" (Three Women).

The 15,000 verses of the *Comedy* (for Dante, "comedy" as opposed to tragedy meant a story beginning badly but ending well; "divine" was added by posterity) took 15 years to compose. *Grosso modo,* he wrote an average of one strophe a day: 33 syllables (three hendecasyllables); hence the impression, predominant among his good readers for over six centuries, of an extraordinary density, a continually unfolding and renewed inner richness. The poet claimed at different times different purposes for his enterprise: in addition to the glorification of Beatrice and the exile's wish to show his worth, Dante seems to claim, in a letter (*Epistle* XIII) of doubtful attribution, the messianic mission "to lead the living out of a state of misery into a state of bliss." The purpose the poet did accomplish was poetic: to create with words a world which in its miraculous credibility vies with God's own creation. The reader must keep constantly in mind that the *Comedy* is a fiction, not a world, the work of a poet and master storyteller, not of the Holy Spirit. This *lapalissian* truth sets a limit to symbolic interp., even though the medieval practice of allegory (q.v.) is ever-present in the text. Consider, however, what distinguishes Dante's from earlier transcendental journeys. His unreadable predecessors are *all* allegory; we read Dante after seven centuries for what we find beyond his didactic purposes. Allegory is a premise of the *narratio*, flexible and often ambiguous: it is part of the plurivalence genetic to all enduring poetry. Beatrice and Virgil are, respectively, "theology" and "reason," but we believe and love them primarily because Dante "forgot," more often than not, their roles as abstractions.

The grand architecture of the poem is universally known. The *Comedy* is the fictive, visionary account of a redemptive journey through Hell and Purgatory to Paradise and God, by a pilgrim who both is and is not Dante Alighieri, guided at first by Virgil and later by Beatrice. Allegorically the trip is Everyman's progress through suffering and purgation to salvation and bliss; narratively it is an immensely, mysteriously moving story of an exploration of an unknown universe. The first realm holds the souls of the damned, distributed into nine "circles" set up according to Aristotle's categories of sin (intemperance, violence, fraud—with heresy, unknown to the Greek, thrown in). The realm of purgation is segmented into the seven deadly sins of Christian dogma (with Ante-Purgatory and Earthly Paradise bringing the number of divisions to nine). The blessed regions comprise the nine heavens of Ptolemy's geocentric universe, from the sphere of the Moon through the planets and the Sun to the fixed stars and the Empyrean, abode of all the souls happy in the sight of God. The recurrence of the number 3 and its multiples, as well as other divisions in the edifice, such as the 100 *canti*, or the strophic scheme of 3 lines of 11 syllables each—*terza rima* (q.v.)—or the canto and episode parallelisms and contrasts at corresponding "locations" in the three *cantiche* are the cross and delight of Dante exegesis (see NUMEROLOGY). Hints at the Trinity?—certainly. But first and foremost, these are self-imposed "difficulties," order-creating limits with which the poet circumscribes and regulates the excesses of his boundless imagination.

Of the three canticles (34+33+33 *canti*), *Inferno* is the most dramatic and suspenseful. Memorable characters and events dominate several *canti*: Francesca's story of love and death, Farinata's "war

memoirs," Chancellor Pier's suicide, Ulysses' last voyage, the prison "cannibalism" of Count Hugolin of Pisa. Purgatory is the reign of elegy, subdued sadness, and hopeful yearning: it is the *cantica* most "earthly" and peaceful. Feelings of brotherly affection dominate here; the middling tone fits well the characters on the mountainside. It is a mild crepuscular setting, in contrast to the purple-dark violence of Hell and the soul-searching beams of the last domain. *Paradise* is the triumph of Beatrice, who is a symbol and yet a real woman, with her individualized intonation, choreography, and even mannerisms. Among the blessed, absolute equality is the rule: no character should emerge; but a hymnal choir clearly cannot satisfy the playwright in Dante. The sequence of Heavens is transformed into a transcendental fireworks of growing intensity. Humanity is never absent from the rarefied mysticism signalling God's presence. And the great Saints appear in person to test, prod, warn, and guide the Pilgrim toward fulfillment. God, thanks to the magnificent intuition of Dante's genius, is depicted here not as the bearded elder of Judaeo-Christian iconography but as a blinding point of light immeasurably far and immeasurably near. In *Paradise* Dante is at his most sublime; it is the soaring flight of his mature genius.

In "Limbo" the pilgrim meets the six great poets of Cl. antiquity, and there, in a prideful aside, he reports how he was made an equal among them. Some readers detect immodesty here. In truth, Dante's claim is rather modest. Two of the six, Ovid and Lucan, through respectable storytellers, are certainly not in the same league with Homer, Horace, and Virgil (and Dante). In fact, the author of *The Divine Comedy* has in world lit. fewer than five equals: he is in that most select club which has so far admitted only Homer, Virgil, Shakespeare, and Goethe.

Dante's robust spirituality, unshaken religious convictions, and firm belief in the continuity of social structures were rooted in the apparent stability of the "old" world, the thick Ages in the Middle. The *curriculum vitae* of Francesco Petrarca (1304–74) coincides with a historical moment of accelerated change and crumbling certainties. Petrarch appears much closer to us than Dante, closer than the generation or two that actually separate these two quasi-contemporaries. The "modern" lability of Petrarch's psychic makeup is manifest in his vast correspondence, in his treatises (e.g. on "solitude," on the "remedies against Fortune"), and esp. in his Lat. "Confessions" (*Secretum*), which is a microscopic analysis of that nameless something that forever anguished his soul. Born in Arezzo of a Florentine bourgeois family in exile, Petrarch was brought up in Southern France. He studied jurisprudence at Montpellier and Bologna. On April 6, 1327, his destiny was redirected by his meeting in Avignon, Laura, the unidentified Provençal girl whom he loved in life and in death (she died of the plague in 1348) and whom he immortalized in his poetry. Petrarch is the forefather of humanism, the revival of Graeco-Roman culture that dominates the next century. His work in Lat. is immense; it (mainly the epic in hexameters, *Africa*) procured him the Poet Laureate (q.v.) title and crown conferred by the Senate of Rome in 1341. The uncontested arbiter of European lit., Petrarch lived the latter half of his life mainly in Italy.

Petrarch expected enduring fame from his Lat. work; immeasurably superior are his modestly titled (with affected scorn) *Rerum vulgarium fragmenta* (freely rendered, "It. bits and pieces") or *Canzoniere*. In spite of his expressed desire to burn the collection, he kept revising and perfecting the ms. to his dying day. The 366 poems (317 sonnets, plus *canzoni*, sextets, ballads, and madrigals) record the earthly (not at all merely spiritual) passion inspired by Laura, even after her "flight to heaven." This last great representative of the troubadour trad. (afterwards there will be epigones and "Petrarchism") breaks with its "Platonic" incorporeality. Some critics have doubted the very existence of Laura, assuming her to be a composite of the poetic trad. And the "love story" behind the stylized abstractions is clearly an unrequited love. But the human passion of the poet, with its ebb and flow over the years, with its emotional flotsam and jetsam of brief joys and long despair, with its cries and silences, with its phases of resignation and of rebellion, recreates, albeit perhaps *ex nihilo*, the anonymous Beloved, body and soul. A curious double process takes place: Petrarch veils and stylizes his earthly model, but the living warmth of his words makes the reader mentally recreate Laura. There is no direct description of her in the Songbook, yet we never lose sight of her.

There is something artful if not artificial in this process—the something that made F. De Sanctis remark that, while Dante was more poet than artist, Petrarch was more artist than poet. It is true, however, that readers have always privileged the poems written about Laura and the self-analytic pauses. Set aside the recantatitive opening and closing pieces as well as the few non-directly "Laura" poems, and what remains engraved in memory are the dreamy evocation of the memorable day (no. 2), the Proustian simile of the old pilgrim (16), a *solo e pensoso* walk across the fields (35), the tired prayer of the penitent (62), a lovely shape made of transparencies (90 and the famous 126), the *cameretta* [little room] of the poet (234), and, in the death of Laura, the inexorable march of days and years (272), the useless return of spring (310), and the sad song of a nightingale telling us that "nothing here below delights—and lasts" (311). A certain repetitiousness has been observed in the *Canzoniere*, but in fact the work was meant to be sampled by fits and starts, rather than by continued perusal. A monochrome uniformity is genuine in Petrarch's only other "vul-

gar" (i.e. It.) verse work, the later *Trionfi*. Heavily allegorical, unfinished and unrefined, these series of Dantesque *terzine* sing the "triumphs" of Love, Modesty, Death, Fame, Time, and Eternity.

Among the minor *Trecentisti* poets one should mention at least the late *stilnovista* Fazio degli Uberti, from Pisa; the courtly poet Antonio Beccari from Ferrara; the Florentine prolific polygraph, popularizer of vernacular lit., Antonio Pucci (d. 1388); and the fine author of ballads, Franco Sacchetti (d. 1400). The third component of the great *Trecento* triumvirate, Giovanni Boccaccio (1313–75), father of modern storytelling, was an uninspired but evidently inspiring versifier. Known is Chaucer's vast and undervalued debt to his *Filostrato* (1336?; the romance of Troilus in octaves) and *Teseida* (1341?, an epic, the Palamon and Arcite story). Boccaccio's own "Vita nuova" (*Commedia delle ninfe*, 1341) and allegorical vision in *terzine* (*Amorosa visione*, 1343?) influenced in turn Petrarch's *Trionfi*. There are some 100 lyric compositions also attributed to Boccaccio, counting the "day"-divider ballads from the frame of the *Decameron*. The real poetry of the *Decameron*, however, is to be looked for rather in some of the stories construed more according to the compositional norms of a poem (strophic architecture, anaphoric insistences, gigantic "rhymes," echoes and refrains) than of a short story (e.g. Zima, Federigo and his falcon, the rhythmical tale of the baker Cisti, or, esp., the wondrous ballad of Isabetta and her "pot of basil").

III. QUATTROCENTO: THE 1400S. The sudden blossoming of vernacular lit. in the 14th c. carried in it the seeds of decadence, or rather of exhausted retrenchment during the first half of the next century. Petrarch and Boccaccio (and protohumanist Dante) were indeed the fountainhead of the cultural movement called humanism, essentially an enthusiastic revival of Lat. lit. (as opposed and "superior" to It. lit.). The trend, initially a passion for Cl. learning and a rediscovery of many major texts of Lat. and Gr. antiquity, by degrees became a belief in the panacea of Cl. education, capable of "freeing" man. The main creative tenet of this new classicism was *imitatio* (see IMITATION), theorized by Petrarch and basis for the later "Petrarchism" (q.v.). The new blooming of Lat. lit. highlights such well-known humanists as Pico della Mirandola, Lorenzo Valla, Coluccio Salutati, Giovanni Pontano, and Marsilio Ficino. Far from being slavish imitators, the humanists in fact ended by "dethroning the ancients from their exalted position" (Guarino, in Bondanella) by reexamining under the microscope of philology old texts and by historicizing classicism. Humanism was nothing short of a discovery of history in the modern sense of the word (see RENAISSANCE POETICS).

Poetry in It. continued to be produced, marginally as it were, often in its "lower" species as imitations of popular song. The Venetian patrician

Leonardo Giustinian (1338–1446) became a sort of bestseller on account of his talent for reproducing the sonorities and easy grace of the *canzonette* sung by gondoliers on the *laguna*. The same taste for the simple diction of popular genres inspired the Florentine Luigi Pulci (1432–84), but with a different result. Pulci is a "humorist" in the true sense of the word: for him life was a "harmonious mixture of sweet and bitter and a thousand flavors." His mock-heroic "epos" *Morgante*, a rewriting of the *Chanson de Roland*, is not merely a parody on the solemnities of the Fr. *chansons de geste,* it is the amusing product of a whimsical comic genius. Its rough model is enriched by characters *alive* on the page—in spite of their irrational capriciousness. In addition to the usual types, Pulci introduced Morgante, the giant, inspirer of Rabelais, the ribald monster Margutte who dies of immoderate laughter at a gross practical joke, and the amusing "logician" fiend, Astaroth, spokesman for Pulci's religious doubts and occult leanings. Byron read and translated part of this weird epic; it may have been among the inspirations for *Don Juan.*

Matteo Maria Boiardo (1441–94) made reference in a serious vein to the same material. Pulci's attitude toward the Carolingian sources had reflected popular Tuscan city-bred tastes; Boiardo brought to them the conservative provincial atmosphere of Northern courtly life. The incomplete *Orlando innamorato* (The Loves of Roland) injects Arthurian elements into the chivalric material: all-conquering love now presides over the knights' and ladies' adventures. The poem is a whirlwind of disparate episodes, unified, if at all, by overwhelming passion and vigorous action. The idiom, of strong regional flavor, hindered wide diffusion of the original; up to the 19th c. *Orlando* was read in Tuscanized remakes by Berni and others.

Florence, transformed from Dante's *Commune* into a *Signoria* under the Medicis, reacquired its cultural centrality during the second half of the century. Pulci's lord protector, Lorenzo de'Medici (1449–92; known as "Il Magnifico"), was himself a poet of great versatility. Critical appraisals of the Magnifico's poetry range from enthusiastic endorsement of his artful masquerades to viewing his output as the pastime of a statesman, the amusement of a dilettante. In truth, Lorenzo was simply one of the many skillful literati of his court. His principal merit, other than his all-important patronage, lies in his vigorous defense of literary It.: Lorenzo contributed in a decisive way to the final prevalence of the Tuscan-Florentine trad. and the decline of creative writing in Lat., almost in abeyance during the Ren.

Still, it may well be that Lorenzo's most enduring achievement was the discovery of the poetic talent of Politian (Poliziano), pseudonym of Agnolo Ambrogini (1454–94) from Montepulciano (hence the name). Politian became a leading humanist rediscoverer and editor of ancient texts. Apart from his poetry in Lat. and Gr., Politian wrote *canzoni* and other lyric poems; his masterwork is the unfinished *Stanze* ("Strophes"), the allegorical retelling, in *ottave,* of the meeting between Giuliano de' Medeci, a youth devoted to pleasure and adventure, and the nymph of unearthly beauty Simonetta (Vespucci). The airy lightness of the *Stanze* is a poetic miracle. Every octave is a contexture of reminiscences, references, and reminders (Homer, Horace, Virgil, Dante, Petrarch, and dozens of lesser classics), but the resulting quilt appears perfectly natural. Moments of noble melancholy accent the translucid text, mementos of the fragility and transience of all that is earthly. Politian is the first poet of modern times whose subject is poetry; a poet's poet, he saw lit. as the essence of life.

Composed during the last two decades of the century, the *Arcadia* of Jacopo Sannazaro (1458?–1530) has enjoyed a plurisecular fortune, cyclically renewed and, in a way, enduring into our own times of recurrent ecological lamentation. On the model of Boccaccio's *Ameto, Arcadia* is a mixture of prose tales and pastoral songs. "Antimetropolitan" yearnings (anachronistic already at inception) for a nonexistant rural simplicity, together with the immemorial myth of a lost Golden Age, inspire this early environmental manifesto. It is also a stylistic miracle: there is hardly a sentence in its loose quilt that is without a source in Cl. lit.

IV. CINQUECENTO: THE 1500s. The *Rinascimento,* the It. Ren., is the age of artistic and literary splendor between the age of humanism and the advent of baroque. Its poetic practice is pervaded by the heritage of the great *Trecento,* esp. of Petrarch (Dante was considered, by this age of refinement, a "primitive"), filtered through the classicism that prevailed in the 15th c. The *Rinascimento* is the age of Petrarchism (q.v.), an age not only of servile imitation of the themes and style of the *Canzoniere,* not only the fashionable organization of one's poetic output into an ideal love story, but also an adherence to the Platonic ideal of love (see PLATONISM AND POETRY) and to the linguistic ideal of purity, harmony, and elegance of expression, which later deteriorated into mere technical virtuosity. The patron saints of the European 1500s were Petrarch and Plato; however, Aristotle's *Poetics* was also rediscovered and deeply, at times obsessively, studied—and in part misconstrued. The tenet of *imitatio* became paramount. Literary genres were rigidly codified, just as social behavior came to be governed by a code—its great documents are Castiglione's *Courtier* and Machiavelli's *Prince.* At the threshold of this great age stands the historically important but poetically insignificant Cardinal Pietro Bembo (1470–1547), friend of Lorenzo and Politian. Bembo, as codifier of Petrarchism and Platonism, is the embodiment of the Ren. His *Rime* (Poems) are little more than textbook examples to illustrate his theories, but his treatise on the *Prose della volgar lingua* (It. Prose Style, 1525) became something of a bible for the literati of the century. This inclusive codification of literary taste and linguistic choice had a decisive influence on the diction of authors from Ariosto to Tasso.

The essence of the *Rinascimento* is best revealed in the epic romance *Orlando furioso* (The Frenzy of Roland), whose creator, one of the most likeable figures in the annals of It. lit., is Ludovico Ariosto (1474–1533). Ariosto's minor work illustrates the frustrations of a harried existence. His lyric poetry was inspired by his lifelong devotion to Alessandra Benucci, whom he married secretly so as not to forfeit ecclesiastical benefits. The *Satire* (seven *capitoli* on the model of the Horatian *sermo*) recounts his travels and reflections. The last years of his life were devoted to the definitive revision of his poem (pub. 1532 in 46 *canti*). *Orlando*, 30 years in the making, pools the experience of the minor work, the warmth and immediacy of the love poetry, the detached and smiling wisdom of the *Satire*, and the character-sketching of his theatrical pieces. The external occasion for the poem was the unfinished *Orlando innamorato*: the *Furioso* completes the story, closely following Boiardo's sources in the Carolingian epic cycle and the Celtic Arthurian legends in narrative detail, but renewing the material with poetic license. This master storyteller holds hundreds of threads in hand at once and unerringly weaves them into an immense coherent tapestry. Some critics, disturbed by the artifice of the complex plotting, posit an improbable network of allegories behind the *narratio*. The great movers of the threefold plot are Ariosto's passions: first, love conceived as an earthy emotion, frankly sensual; second, the forms of knightly behavior and of court ritual; third, an insatiable appetite for adventure. Voltaire noted that Ariosto is always "superior" to his material: he tells his story "jokingly"—taking seriously and yet mocking his inventions. Hence the frequent authorial intrusions (comments, tongue-in-cheek explanations, ironic misdirection); hence the fable-like and dreamy atmosphere around Ariosto's errant knights and ladies. Painstaking realism of detail fuses with an oneiric vagueness of context. The description of Atlante's castle and the invention of the lunar travels of Astolfo are emblematic of this attitude.

The form of the *Orlando furioso* is nothing short of prodigious. The octaves of narrative poetry—woody and lagging in Boccaccio's youthful poems, prosily stammering in Pulci's *Morgante*, loosely dressing Boiardo's laborious inventions—coincides here, for the first time in It. p., with the "breathing" of author and reader. Ariosto thinks, nay, lives in his octave, in the six (the alternately "sonorized" verses) plus two (the clinching couplet) pattern of his strophe, each one a microcosm, in its perfectly controlled and yet wondrously airy architecture, of the entire magnificent construction.

Ariosto's Petrarchan love lyrics are undistinguished products of the age, similar to myriads of contemp. songbooks. Little talent emerges from the crowd of the *Cinquecento Petrarchisti*. Monsignor Giovanni della Casa (1503–56), remembered for his *Galateo* (Book of Manners), shows a nostalgia for robust emotions and monumental imagery. Casa is an expert architect of resonant verse; his skilled enjambments still provide examples of the device in prosodic treatises. Two women poets introduce a welcome variation in a field dominated by the stylized male psychology of emotions: Vittoria Colonna (1492–1547), of aristocratic family and patroness of artists, authored a conventional songbook; Gaspara Stampa (1523–54), probably of low social standing, occasionally allows life to show through her imitative verse. Even more creatively, the feverish and disordered rhythms of a passionate existence seem to influence her songs, which are suggestive of entries in a love diary.

Intimations of the incipient baroque taste have been detected in Luigi Tansillo (1510–68). His too-easy sonorities, abuse of color, predilection for horrid landscapes, and colloquial touch seem, indeed, to point toward Marino. But more noteworthy than the lyric output of the age and its vast and forgotten epic feats (the best are Trissino's *Italy Freed from the Goths*, Alamanni's *Avarchide*, and Bernardo Tasso's *Amadigi*) is its humorous or light verse (q.v.). Two cultivators of this genre had vast influence throughout the following century. Francesco Berni (1498–1535), Tuscan refurbisher of Boiardo's epic, is the wellhead of the *bernesco* poem, still jokingly cultivated in Italy—a buffoonery or "sitcom" heavy on puns. Written in an irresistibly funny It. modeled on Lat. (or a Lat. bastardized by It.), the mock-heroic epic *Baldus* by Merlin Cocai (pseudonym of the rebellious Benedictine monk Teofilo Folengo [1491–1574]) extends Pulci's *Morgante* by recounting the farcical adventures of Baldus, a descendant of Rinaldo.

The last great poetic voice of the Ren. has long been considered to be Torquato Tasso (1544–95), spiritual forerunner of baroque poetics (q.v.). Most likely inheriting a psychic disorder, he became distraught by the mental effort required to produce his masterwork, the epic *La Gerusalemme liberata* (Jerusalem Delivered, 1575). Episodes of irrational behavior at the court of Ferrara and aimless excursions across the peninsula eventually led to Tasso's confinement for seven years in the dungeon asylum of Sant'Anna. Pirated editions of his poem, attacks from pedantic critics, and obsessive religious doubts exasperated his illness; he died in Rome. His minor work alone would be sufficient to give him a high rank among the Petrarchists and epic poets of his century. The *Rime* (Verses), nearly 2000 lyrics, is a workshop in which the poet perfected techniques and experimented with sentimental situations; these are interspersed with lyrics of admirable invention and masterful execution, esp. his madrigals, a genre congenial to Tasso's evanescent moods. The Petrarchan model here appears at one remove, filtered through the Petrarchists of the early 1500s—Bembo, Casa—as indeed Petrarch will be read through Tasso by the next generation of lyricists, Marino and his school. The chivalric poem *Rinaldo* (12 *canti* of *ottave*) betrays the adolescent's hand as well as features that will later govern the inspiration of his epic. Already here the war chronicle of the sources is constantly squeezed out by the courtly love. Tasso first favored the idyll, and his pastoral play *Aminta* is rightly spoken of in the same breath with his lyric output: its theatrical pretext gives way to the emotional situations and flights of pathos experimented with in the *Rime*.

Whether *La Gerusalemme liberata* is the first full poetic manifestation of the incipient baroque age (some critics hold that the very terms "baroque" and "Marinism" [qq.v.] are misnomers for "Tassism" and "Tassomania"), or, inversely, the last bloom of the "sane" *Rinascimento* is an academic question, and interestingly, it parallels the great 17th-c. controversy (which engaged Galilei) on the relative worth of the two great narrative poems of the preceding age, Ariosto's and Tasso's. Tasso's epic, its pretext the last phase of the 1099 Crusade, has a cast made up on the one hand of lifeless historical characters and, on the other, of fictive *personae* of the poet himself, each endowed with throbbing life. To Ariosto's objectivity, detachment, and irony, Tasso opposes his subjectivity, participation, and sentimentality. All the great passionate characters of the oft-abandoned plot are facets of Tasso's psychic makeup, exhibiting the excesses and morbidity that landed their creator in Sant'Anna. The *Gerusalemme* is in this sense that *unicum*: a truly autobiographical epos. Long traverses through Aristotle's poetics and the theory of the epic preceded and accompanied the feverish composition, but the rules reaffirmed were soon discarded by Tasso's prepotent sentimental inspiration. The Crusade cedes place to the multiple, strangely disturbed love stories of the variously and wrongly assorted couples. The whole is immersed in an overheated atmosphere of gratuitous heroism, white and black magic, cliffhangers *cum* heavenly intervention, duels to the death, and battle scenes of vast confusion. In the *Orlando furioso* the goodnatured "colloquial" voice of Ludovico the Amiable constantly tended to over-dub the narrator, while in the *Gerusalemme* Torquato's falsetto breaks through, fitfully as it were, to lend his creations a hundred diverse intonations of emotional disorder.

Tasso's *ottava*, ordered into obsessive parallelisms and chiastic contrasts, offers an ineffable musicality and a psychomimetic finesse never before heard. It is masterfully torn by the high drama of enjambments—much more so than Ariosto's peaceful, at times lumbering gait would allow. And yet Boileau's objection to the *clinquant*

du Tasse, as well as the sometimes violent antipathy for the *Gerusalemme* shown by excellent readers, points at a fact recent Tasso crit. has placed into light: the poem is addressed to a new audience of a new age and sensibility, that of the Counter-Reformation, an age of earthshaking upheavals. This critical view allows us to reevaluate Tasso's reworking of *Gerusalemme conquistata* (Jerusalem Recovered), a text of vaster and more solemn architecture, characterized by a baroque heaviness of pace and expression and universally judged until quite recently a complete failure. The characteristics of *Gerusalemme conquistata* are in evidence in Tasso's late poem *Il mondo creato*, a ponderous account of the Creation similar in flavor to an overripe fruit.

V. SEICENTO: THE 1600s. The 17th c., a Golden Age in Góngora's and Cervantes' Spain, in Racine's and La Fontaine's France, and in the England of the metaphysical poets (q.v.), was long considered to have been an age of decadence in Italy, a "century without poetry." Its dominant Tassesque aesthetics certainly revealed the exhaustion of a long-mined vein, an exasperation of the drive for outward perfection yearned for by the Ren. The age frittered away its heritage in an obsessive search for originality and "marvels." Foreign (Sp.) and Papal domination in the peninsula, the newborn religious dogmatism imposed by the Counter-Reformation, the general lowering of ethical standards owing perhaps to the riches from the New World, and the universal instability of ideas in this age of scientific revolution have all been pointed to as causes for the alleged poetic aridity of the age. In truth, an equation of the beautiful with the difficult has prevailed in all silver ages of culture (Hellenistic Greece, later Imperial Rome, our own 20th c.). The baroque age in Italy adopted the *ars poetica* of the late Ren., developing Tasso's theories and example toward a concept of poetry as a nonrational activity, and it endorsed a view of literary production and appreciation based on taste (q.v.) and feeling.

Giambattista Marino (1569–1625), a Neapolitan, became the high priest of the new school of writing usually called Marinism (q.v.; also *Seicentismo*, conceptism [see CULTERANISMO], and *manierismo* [see MANNERISM]). He was the theorizer and the most prolific practitioner of the poetics of *meraviglia* (of astonishment—at all costs), a style in search of the arduous and the complex. A genre loved by Marino and the *Marinisti* was poetry on art (e.g. his collection *Galleria*), a species of poetry feeding on itself (his *Lira* [Lyrics]) and pillaging all preexistent lit.—as does Marino's masterpiece the *Adone* (Adonis), in almost every one of its 40,000 verses. The poem is truly a miracle of words growing fungus-like on words and never managing to cover the void under them. The enthusiasm for the poem among Marino's contemporaries was followed by three centuries of almost total critical rejection, though *Adone* is being reevaluated.

Among Marino's contemporaries, two poets sought independence from the master: Gabriello Chiabrera (1552–1638), whose Anacreontic songs are another "reading" of Tasso, and Alessandro Tassoni (1565–1635), remembered for his mock-heroic *Secchia rapita* (The Ravished Pail, 1622). The most notable recovery of recent crit. is the poetry of the philosopher Tommaso Campanella (1568–1639), whose work closely parallels the metaphysical songs of Donne, Herbert, and Crashaw. This Calabrese monk suffered a monstrous fate, 30 years in prison (several years in the flooded underground dungeon of St. Elmo with hands and feet chained) for heresy and rebellion. Campanella's speculative output was immense, notwithstanding, and involved all branches of the *scibile*. His poems, owing to their forbidding complexity of concepts and diction, were judged by their rare readers almost devoid of interest. But today these *canzoni*, esp. the beautiful "Hymn to the Sun," composed in the depth of St. Elmo, strike us as the "missing link" in It. baroque poetry. In his translucent verses the chained poet attains the lyrical height for which Marino always strove but rarely reached.

VI. SETTECENTO: THE 1700S. The latter half of the 1600s produced a general decadence in poetry. The anti-baroque backlash came as a call to "return to nature," to observe the limits of good taste and common sense, and to renew *imitatio* and the cult of the classics. The adepts of this neoclassical revival congregated in the *Academy of Arcadia* (a loose association of literati, self-defined "shepherds"), founded in 1690 by Queen Christine of Sweden, then in exile in Rome. *Arcadia* promoted pastoral poetry, sobriety of lang., and faithfulness to trad., discarding the whole Marinist century to hark back to Sannazaro's *Cinquecento*. However, this school too in turn became the matrix of mediocre versifiers of derivative bucolic idylls. An intermittently genuine poetic voice is heard in the tenuous lyrics of the great libretto dramatist Metastasio (pseudonym of Pietro Trapassi; 1698–1782), poet-in-residence for most of his life at the Hapsburg court in Vienna. His many melodramas (e.g. *Didone abbandonata, Olimpiade, Demoofonte,* and *Demetrio*) are deservedly famous. In his *Canzonette* (Songs), Metastasio introduced a facile sentimentalism and an evanescent lyricism which he, unlike his predecessors, couched in down-to-earth lang.

Descartes' rationalism influenced practically all intellectual trends in 18th-c. Italy. The influence of the Fr. encyclopedists, Voltaire, Montesquieu, and Diderot, on the one hand, and of the Ossian craze, with the nocturnal/sepulchral fashion it brought with it, on the other, became paramount. The first civic poet of Italy, the Lombard Giuseppe Parini (1729–99), represents the sober awakening of the age leading to the earthquake of the Fr. Revolution. A seriousness of ethical purpose and a sense of mission in his social crit. distinguish this Catholic priest, editor, and schoolteacher. His early lyrics show the Arcadism prevalent at the time; his later odes from "Alla Musa" to "Messaggio" are the meditations of a political moderate. Parini is remembered, however, for his long and unfinished poem of bitter social comment, *Il giorno*, depicting one day in the life of a "giovin signore," a young man about town. The satire, ferociously allusive and resentful, and seldom attenuated by the smile of superior comprehension, seems at times shot through by a secret nostalgia for the world of fashion and elegance. Parini is the first in the history of It. p. to have obtained from the "short" hendecasyllable effects vying with those of the flexible Cl. hexameter.

The essence of pure poetry—as opposed to the practically ambitious *engagé* verse of Parini—is represented by the domineering figure of the preromantic playwright Vittorio Alfieri (1749–1803), scion of an old aristocratic family from Italy's Piedmont region. After a stint, customary for his class, at the military academy, and the grand tour, the rich nobleman settled in the capital of Savoy to act out, as it were, Parini's recipe for the useless existence of the high-society youth of his day. Alfieri dated his conversion from 1775, with the sudden realization that the aimless, incessant agitation of his soul could be channelled into artistic creation. The first fruit of his illumination, the tragedy *Cleopatra*, was followed by a feverishly fertile decade of dramatic production (1776–86): 18 more tragedies, dramatic verse in dialogue form. The Alfierian hero, a pure revolutionary, acts out the abstract libertarian rebellion of the poet's soul, scornful of any pragmatic effort at real social progress. Alfieri's stay in Tuscany afforded him time to refine, to "Tuscanize," his Piedmontese, Frenchified linguistic and cultural background. In Paris in 1789, he was at first wildly enthusiastic about then bitterly disappointed in the Fr. Revolution. In 1792 he escaped the Terror to spend his last years in Florence writing six comedies, his violent anti-French persiflage *Il misogallo* (The Francophobe), and his celebrated *Vita* (Memoirs), with its relentlessly, almost breathlessly drawn portrait of the poet-hero.

Alfieri represents the *Sturm und Drang* (q.v.) of It. p. His collection of lyrics (*Rime*) amounts to a spiritual autobiography of a soul tormented by dreams of immensity. The idealized and idolized figure of the poet, alone, in haughty solitude, looms large. The Petrarchan subtext of these poems signifies a return to the source; it is the manifestation of a genuine "elective affinity" rather than the obligatory imitation of an earlier century. However, the greatest lyric poetry of this "lion of Asti" is to be found in his tragedies, texts of a lyrical essentiality, of an elliptic diction, a barebones structure, and an unrelenting pace. By critical consensus, Alfieri's most acclaimed tragic pieces, *Saul* (1882) and *Mirra* (Myrrha, 1887), are staged poems on the sublime.

VII. OTTOCENTO: THE 1800s. The Arcadian trend had sown the seeds of a rebirth of taste for Cl. ideals of beauty. In Italy these preromantic stirrings coincide with a short period of neoclassical predominance in art (Canova) and lit. concurrent with the Napoleonic age. The two movements, Arcadism of the late 1700s and neoclassicism of the early 1800s, shared an attention to form, an aesthetics based on the renewed concept of the sublime (q.v.), a taste for the genuine and primordial, and a purism in the medium of art. Ippolito Pindemonte (1735–1828), remembered for his *Poesie campestri* (Rustic Verses), and Vincenzo Monti (1745–1828) were the most coherent adepts of the new trend. Monti's inborn flexibility and susceptibility to influences favored his art as a translator (his 1810 *Iliad* is a masterpiece) as well as the eclectically occasional nature of his poetic output—the centerpiece of it being his anti-republican *Basvilliana* (1791).

The poetic genius of the imperial *intermezzo* was Ugo Foscolo (1778–1827). His poetry fuses the classicist's love for perfection of form with the heritage of Parini and Alfieri and with European romanticism. Born of a Gr. mother on the Ionic island of Zante, Foscolo's classicism was, so to speak, a congenital trait in his psychic makeup. His tempestuous age provided the background for a truly romantic curriculum of wars and turbulent loves. In 1802 he published the "Vita nuova" of It. romanticism, the *Ortis* (The Last Letters of Jacopo Ortis), an epistolary novel of love and suicide inspired by Goethe's *Werther*. Foscolo's shorter poems are exemplary of the short-lived It. *Sturm und Drang*. His 12 sonnets (among them the masterpieces "Alla Musa," "A Zacinto," "Alla sera," and "In morte del fratello Giovanni") and his two major odes (1800–03) are perfect expressions of the Cl. ideal implanted in a romantic soul. His principal claim to posthumous glory should have been the *poemetto*, or three-part hymn, "Le Grazie" (The Graces), a vast corpus of fragments composed over the course of 20 years. The immaterial lightness of diction and verse can only increase our regret at the structural sketchiness of the magnificent torso. Though 20th-c. exegesis, with its bias for the fragmentary, has rediscovered this great mass of poetic wreckage, attempts at a coherent reconstruction have not been wholly convincing. The entire experience of the poet's "life in art" is the true theme of the poem.

Foscolo remains best known for his *Dei sepolcri* (Tombs, 1806), written in 295 blank verses. The theme, occasioned by the Napoleonic decree prohibiting burial within urban limits, is left behind, replaced by a poetic meditation on life and death, on the immemorial rites of burial, on fame surviving the tomb, and on the great men of the past and their sepulchers. The evocation of the nocturnal cemetery, the "triumph" in the Petrarchan sense of posthumous glory over death, the celebration of memory as a cenotaph to greatness, the motif of tears and consolation—all are close to the central topics of romanticism (q.v.). In his *Sepolcri*, Foscolo emerges most cleary as the "father of It. romanticism."

The new mode of conceiving the human condition given by romanticism, with its components of Enlightenment rationalism and Restoration historicism, with its taste for the unsophisticated and primordial, and with its repertory of lugubrious themes, came of age in Italy in the 1820s. It. romantics, who first gathered around the Florentine periodical *Conciliatore* (1818–19), distinguished themselves from their fellows in Germany and England by their concern with the social and ethical role of lit. The *Risorgimento* (It. national "Resurgence," a movement which would result in 1870 in the birth of a unified modern Italy) was an important factor, mainly through the educative influence of such protagonists as the patriot Giuseppe Mazzini, the publicist Vincenzo Gioberti, and the literary historian Francesco De Sanctis.

The great models, Schiller, Byron, Chateaubriand, and Scott, had only limited direct influence on literary works. The most conventional It. romantic poet, Giovanni Berchet (1783–1851), left a thin collection of songs and ballads which is a veritable index of the items dear to European romanticism. Berchet's theoretical *Semi-Serious Letter* had a lasting impact on the reception of romantic ideology. A more interesting figure is Niccolò Tommaseo (1802–74), the blind lexicographer and Dante scholar and author of lyric poetry of "cosmic nostalgia" and a prophetic tone. The bitterness of a bleak existence inspired the Tuscan Giuseppe Giusti (1809–50), who wrote poetry marked by sarcasm and despair. His mimic talent is at its best when fixing on the page a gesture or attitude; his cerebral diction has lost its popularity. Alessandro Manzoni (1785–1873) is best known for his great novel *The Betrothed*; his verses are marginal products, but his five "Hymns" (1812–22), of deep religious inspiration, his commemorative poems, and the choral passages from his plays *Carmagnola* (1820) and *Adelchi* (1822) show the great novelist's precise diction as well as the characteristic undercurrent of *I promessi sposi*: compassion for the humble, the disinherited, and the marginal.

The realistic penchant of the romantic movement in Italy, its bias for the popular and immediate, favored the flowering of dialect poetry (q.v.). The traits of dialectal speech included a down-to-earth tone, a direct documenting of life, and a built-in smile owing to the use of dialectal variation as a vehicle of low humor. The two greatest It. dialect poets lived in the heyday of the romantic *querelle*; both show the taste for the "slice-of-life," for a ready plebeian wit, and for the antiliterary spirit congenital to the realistic facet of romanticism. Carlo Porta (1775–1821) derived some of his inspiration from the decidedly nonpoetic contacts through his clerk's window in the Milan tax offices. He is one of those humble "chroniclers without pretense who end by preserving for posterity the portrait of a whole epoch" (Momigliano). His masterworks are versified *novelle*: the "disasters" of a semi-derelict (the "Giovannin Bongee" stories), the "lamentations" of a poor street fiddler (bow-legged "Marchionn"), and the tale of a streetwalker ("Ninetta del Verzee"). Porta's laughter never becomes a sneer; behind his smile one often senses the sadness of the wise. The encounter with Porta freed Giuseppe Gioachino Belli (1791–1863) from his failed attempts at It. verse and opened up the dialect of the Roman *plebs* as inspiration. A minor cleric, Belli left behind about 2000 sonnets (pub. in the 1880s) inspired by a violent anticlericalism, irreverent and often obscene. He too is a poet of metropolitan low-class life—vagrants and beggars, monks and spies, flunkeys and whores—with an infusion of prelates. His immense rogues' gallery, with its lightning-fast character sketches, infernal settings, and cynicism of expression, has been compared to Dante's characterizations in the *Inferno*. Belli's tone is more virulent than Porta's, but like Porta's, his art of portraiture, imitation of colloquial speech, and mastery of detail all point to future literary developments—to the narrative art of the naturalist school, to great Verga, and to *verismo*.

The greatest poet of modern Italy, Giacomo Leopardi (1798–1837) was born to an impoverished aristocratic family in Recanati. The poet's professed revulsion for his backward hometown and his disciplined upbringing (esp. the conservatism of his father) have been made much of in critical attempts to trace the roots of his cosmic pessimism. Recanati, however, acted as the almost exclusive locus of the poet's inspiration; there he wrote most of his poetry, and there, placed at the child-prodigy's disposal, was his father Count Monaldo's extensive library. Young Giacomo spent his adolescence in obsessive studies, amassing an astonishing amount of writing: verses, plays, and learned (though all compilative) essays and treatises, almost blinding himself in the process. Though merely the products of a pedantic youth, the early works have been shown to contain the germ of Leopardi's later and most persistent *leitmotif*: the attraction to illusions and delusions, the heroic striving toward an abstract glory marking one's passage on earth (for Leopardi, man's only existence). These motifs are recurrent in the immense notebook collection, *the Zibaldone* (1815–32). The clash of nature and reason, dominant theme of the Enlightenment, was at first given by young Leopardi a Rousseauian solution (benign nature vs. the ills brought on by human reason), but the contrary prevails in his later work: hostile nature, a "stepmother" for mankind, undermines all human endeavors. The romantic elements influencing Leopardi's system underwent a characteristic transformation: the denial of the poet's

social role (and the belief in pure poetry, anticipating the "decadent" poetics to come), a materialistic worldview, a refusal of almost all nonlyric content, and a bias for the "pathetic" based on "immediacy" of feeling.

The concepts of "infinity" and "remembrance" are the cornerstones of Leopardi's best verse and are strongly present in his poetry until 1821, when the poet "escaped" from Recanati. "Rimembranze" (Recollections) and "Appressamento della morte" (Nearness of Death), written at age 18; experiments with fashionably lugubrious topics; a number of *engagé* compositions; and poetic meditations—show Leopardi's search for his poetic voice. He discovers it in the idyll "Vita solitaria" (Life of Solitude) and esp. "Sera del dì di festa" (Sunday Night). The tension is maintained through the whole (short) poem in the admirable "Alla luna" (To the Moon); however, "Infinito" (Infinite), a poem of a mere 15 lines written before the poet's flight from his family, is universally recognized as his masterwork—it is, with Dante's "Tanto gentile," the most renowned It. lyric. Its contents are of a lightness and evanescence which elude paraphrase. Its last line, with its sign of *cupio dissolvi* (the "sweetness of shipwreck"), ties Leopardi to such key texts of modern poetry as Rimbaud's "Bateau ivre" and Mallarmé's "Brise marine."

The years 1822–28, a period of uneasy independence interrupted by desperate returns to Recanati, mark an intermission in Leopardi's poetry. He fitfully produced the *Operette morali* (Little Moral Exercises, 1824), pensive and ironic dialogues on ontological questions, in this pause, a gathering of strength before his second creative period (ca. 1828–1830), an economically forced return to Recanati for 16 months of *ennui*. The cosmic meditation of "Canto notturno" (Nocturn of a Nomadic Shepherd in Asia) is "one of the supreme modern songs of existential anguish" (Perella, in Bondanella). "A Silvia" (written in Pisa, "perhaps the most poignant elegy in the It. lang."), "Ricordanze" (Memories), and "Sabato del villaggio" (Saturday in the Village) are the most characteristically Leopardian texts in his collection of *Canti* (1831), with their tone of thoughtful melancholy and disconsolate contemplation of the nullity of all things under the empty heavens. The elegy "Quiete dopo la tempesta" (The Calm After the Storm) looks for happiness in death.

The great idylls are Leopardi's true *operette morali*, meditations couched in immortal verse, liberated from the bitterness and animosity often prevailing in his prose dialogues. Leopardi lived to see his *Canti* published in a definitive edition in 1836. Their themes have a common denominator: the loss of dreams—of youth, of happiness, of heroic existence—a loss restated with calm despair in the cruel light of cold and godless reality. The meter is a kind of early free verse: discarding the strophic models of the past, Leopardi relied on a loose rhythm, now expanded freely, now sud-

ITALIAN POETRY

denly restrained. While the incisive "A se stesso" (To Himself) is a pitiless spiritual self-portrait, the poet facing his bleak universe and murmuring his final renunciation, the late elegies "Amore e morte" (Love and Death) and "Tramonto della luna" (Moon Setting), as well as his last poem, "La ginestra" (The Desert Flower), seem to be not only the conclusion of an experience but also a hint at another incipient search for new directions.

The reaction to the excesses of romanticism, such as the lachrymose sentimentalism of the Prati-Aleardi school, took place in Italy under a double flag, realism and classicism. The call for a return to the sanity of everyday life as the master theme of literary mimesis was spread by a largely Lombardian group of poets known as "Scapigliati," ("the 'unkempt' ones")—a movement parallel to the Fr. *bohème*. The salient figures of the movement, the Boito brothers, Camillo and Arrigo (the latter is also remembered for his librettos), Emilio Praga, and Carlo Dossi professed an *ars poetica* based on the "slice of life." For the most part they produced "little proses in verse," unwittingly turning upside down Baudelaire's ambition of *petites poèmes en prose*.

The classicists' reaction, on the other hand, to the romantic mania for originality had at first a rather ineffectual leader in Giacomo Zanella (1820–88), who revived the minor neoclassical trad. of Monti and Pindemonte, a trend largely exhausted by mid century. The heritage of classicism in Alfieri and Foscolo, and even in the young "civic" Leopardi, was pressed into the service of anti-romanticism by Giosuè Carducci (1835–1907), a poet of vast authority who was the uncontested focal point of It. *fin de siècle* poetry. Carducci attempted to confer dignity and discipline on a field that, by his maturity, had lost or refused both. Carducci, chair of It. at Bologna, was "the last great *literatus*" Italy had. His professed ideal of a "sane, virile, strongwilled" lit. has lost most of its appeal in modern times; his reclaiming for the poet the immemorial function of *vates* has an archaic flavor. Carducci himself, after a youthful phase of loud and heathen Jacobinism, became something like a mouthpiece for the powers that were and for prevailing public opinion. His lyric production in traditional form appeared in the collections *Levia gravia* (Light and Heavy, 1861–71), *Giambi ed epodi* (Iambs and Epodes, 1867–69), and *Rime nuove* (New Verses, 1861–87). Carducci believed in the possibility of transplanting Graeco-Lat. metrics into It. versification; while probably overrated as a prosodic experiment, it makes an interesting *curiosum* out of his most discussed volume, *Odi barbare* (Barbaric Odes, 1877–89). It is likely that Carducci will survive his current eclipse by virtue of a few nonprogrammatic compositions, usually deeply autobiographical, such as his *Pianto antico* (Old Grief), about a personal loss.

VIII. NOVECENTO: THE 1900s. The last hundred years exemplify Viktor Shklovsky's observation on "schools." Apparently antithetical trends may long coexist until one of them by manifesto rises to predominance—only to cede its shortlived hegemony to its successor, which usually claims direct opposition to it but, in fact, dialectically presupposes and continues it. Thus currents as diverse as positivism and decadence, the "Voce" and the "Ronda" groups, the "Twilight" poets and the futurists, hermeticism and neorealism, not only coexist but in retrospect appear to be interdependent elements of the same whole. Two monumental figures, D'Annunzio and Pascoli, preface and condition contemp. poetry; neither strictly belongs to a "school," but each recapitulates and anticipates several.

Carducci today appears firmly rooted in the century of Leopardi and Manzoni, while the poetry of Giovanni Pascoli (1855–1912), his successor at Bologna, stretches far into our own. It foreshadows trends as distant from and seemingly alien to it as the neo-avant-garde of the 1960s and the postmodern verse of the 1980s. Pascoli is the first It. poet to "wring the neck" of eloquence. Some of his best-known pieces from *Poemetti* (1897–) and *Canti di Castelvecchio* (1903–) most surely have been swept away by the tears shed over them (e.g. "Cavallina storna" [The Dappled-Gray Pony], memorized by generations of schoolchildren). But his thin first collection, *Myricae* (1891), remains the cornerstone of modern It. p. The title "Tamarisks" hints at the "lowly shrubs" of the Fourth Eclogue, but this "last descendant of Virgil" is not merely a poet of simple rustic scenes, as his themes seem to suggest. His quaint syntax and vocabulary, invasive onomatopoeia, dialect and Lat. words, and exotic and technical terms, for example, signal the complexity underlying his deceptively simple landscapes. Pascoli's interest never fixes on the positive spectacle of human labor in the fields; his rural tableaux radiate a mysterious feeling, an almost religious stupor. G. A. Borgese recommended an impressionistic reading of Pascoli, with eyes "half-shut," and called *Myricae* the most heterogeneous book of It. p. However, a pattern in Pascoli's constructions may be discerned: a rural view is sketched out by broad brush strokes, then filtered and "un-defined" through some optical disturbance: haze, mist, fog (*tremulo* is a favorite adjective). A minimal sign of life appears, slowed at once almost to a standstill (*lento*, "slow," appears frequently in Pascoli's concordance). The cadence remains "the beating of his own heart" (Garofalo, in Bondanella)—though with the constant sinking feeling of skipped beats. At last a tiny acoustic element is added to the landscape—the chirping of a bird, the rustle of leaves, a snatch of faraway singing. That is all, but the whole remains miraculously suspenseful, suggestive not of something "else" but of itself. Even the most allegorical-seeming texts of Pascoli, e.g. his best *poemetti*, "Il vischio" (Mistletoe) and "Digitale purpurea" (Foxglove),

ITALIAN POETRY

suggest, rather than a meaning, an abstract horror, a visionary experience of Evil. The tragedy of Pascoli's life, the unsolved murder of his father in 1867, fixed his poetic age at 12: there is a sense of bewildered wonder in front of an uncomprehended world, the urge to escape, the need for refuge—a need he soon identified with poetry. In the poet's psyche, the unknown assassin assumes the features of mankind, driven on by the eternal enigma of evil. In an 1897 essay, "Il fanciullino" (The Child), Pascoli shaped this very concept into an *ars poetica*. Leopardi was the last It. poet to have, in a poetic sense, a geocentric view of man's habitat. Pascoli's universe, by contrast, is heliocentric, or rather centerless: a cold immensity in which the poet sees himself as a "tiny wanderer / lost on a star among the stars."

If Pascoli's "life in art" had few events, Gabriele D'Annunzio (1863–1938) construed his life as a work of art. A cross between Nietzsche's "superman" and Huysman's Des Esseintes (*À rebours*, 1884), this last *vates* of It. lit. devoted only his talent to his work, reserving, like Oscar Wilde, his genius for his life. In appraisals the latter crowds out the former with the memorabilia of this master self-promoter: his heroics as a flying ace, his well-publicized loves, his public switch from extreme right to extreme left, his bankrupt flight to France. "More a rhetorician than poet" (Sapegno), a "dilettante di sensazioni" (Croce), D'Annunzio titled his mature collection *Laudi* (1903–4). Composed of three parts, *Maia, Electra*, and *Alcyone*, it is a *laus vitae*, a celebration of life, in which he seems intoxicated by his own exultation: his poetry is the "inventory of his delights" (Momigliano). His extraordinary imitative skill fills his writing with disparate echoes: some from the Fr. and Eng. Parnassians and Preraphaelites, some deliberate impersonations of *stilnovo* and OF masters. This mimetic bent reflects D'Annunzio's principal characteristic, the musicality of his verse. As Debussy "paints" with music, so his friend uses words as musical notes. But D'Annunzio's music at its best is not imitative but abstract— vaguely allusive, suggestively obsessive, as in the airy curlicues of *Alcyone*, "texts without a topic." The best of D'Annunzio is often his most extreme: poems in which the thematic pretext is at its baroque flimsiest and the text an orgy of polyphony, as in "Undulna" (the nymph "regulating" the ideal line the sea "writes" on the shore), or texts in which the poet's decadent attraction to the morbid is released. D'Annunzio's art had no perceptible devel., no "early" or "late" period: his is a verse of a curious immobility.

In a 1910 article ("Poets on the Wane," in De Bernardi) Borgese defined as *crepuscolari* a group of young poets whose cult of quotidian themes and slipshod expression seemed to signal the end of a great lyric trad. The term took root without its negative connotation and today denotes a tone shared by most verse published in the decade preceding World War I. Not a formal school, "Waning Poetry" was as much a derivation from as a reaction to Pascoli's mystic rusticism and D'Annunzio's pompous alexandrinism. Given its popularity, it is probably not so much a product of its age as a producer of the contemp. fashion of skepticism and sadness. *Poems written with a pencil* (M. Moretti), *Harmonies in Gray and Silence* (Govoni), *Useless Booklet* (Corazzini), *Conversations*— the very titles of these slim volumes announce deliberate colorlessness and monotony, everyday emotions about banal objects: sleepy old gardens, hospital wards, convent walls, creaky weathervanes, bells tolling, yellowed photographs, dried flowers, nuns, invalids, beggars. These poets delight in diminutives and limited horizons: views are cut out by a small window or filtered by a dusty pane, often with some distorting defect. The most versatile member of the group was Corrado Govoni (1884–1965), who later became a futurist. Dying at 20, a consumptive, Sergio Corazzini (1886–1907) declined the title of poet for that of a "weeping child" who "knows nothing but how to die." His free verse ebbs and flows with his desolate sobbing, and imminent death confers a vicarious authenticity on his sadness. Two poets of the first rank are customarily included here: Aldo Palazzeschi exceeds all labeling and warrants treatment apart; Guido Gozzano (1883–1916) survived tuberculosis long enough to see the success of his *Colloqui* (1911). Not since the *secentisti* did a verbless list have the evocative power of Gozzano's catalogues of "good old things in atrocious taste." Gozzano's mild irony blends with his mild yearning: he mocks what he loves and loves only what he mocks. His great trick is faking with sincerity. Gozzano's only mode is the idyll, a slightly addled idyll with its melodramatic element gone bad; the smell, voluptuously inhaled, is often that of kitsch.

Historically, "Crepuscularism" and futurism (q.v.) rise from the same impulse, the need to escape D'Annunzio's dominance and Pascoli's classicism. Futurism springs not from the "perception of a chaotic universe" (a formula applicable to most movements of the past thousand years) but from the adolescent rebelliousness which sustains all cyclical recurrences of *Sturm und Drang*— hence the interest in it by the New Vangard of the 1960s. It burst on the scene with the 1909 manifesto of F. T. Marinetti (1887–1944), a first-rate polemicist and a fourth-rate poet. Marinetti trumpeted activism at all costs, adventure and aggression, speed and the triumph of the Machine, destruction of the past, war as the "hygiene" of history, and scorn for women and sentiment. The very scope of its ludicrous claims killed the school; after its disintegration (1915), however, futurism was adopted by National Socialism, Marinetti becoming a sort of Poet Laureate of the regime. Still, Marinetti's poetics had a vast and, on the whole, salutary influence. His main thesis, simultaneity of impression and expression (hence fusion of object and image), influenced Apollinaire's calligrammes, dada, cubism (qq.v.), and Majakovskij. In Italy, futurism's best adherents soon developed in different directions, turning against its ontological claims (Lucini, Ardengo Soffici) or deriving from its libertarian impulse a ludic concept of poetry (Govoni, Palazzeschi).

Gian Pietro Lucini (1867–1914), between his early Parnassian sonnets and his late anti-futurist stance, published his theory of free verse in Marinetti's review ("Poesia," 1908) and then his *Revolverate* (Gunshots, 1909). His *Antidannunziana* (1914) satirizes D'Annunzio's superman poses. Resistance to time attests to the greatness of Aldo Palazzeschi (1885–1974), a much appreciated novelist. The production of his "poetic" decade (1905–15) differs from the humorless declamation of mainline futurists. Its wit and charm is seen in his celebrated phonomimetic "Fontana malata" (Ailing Fountain). His "L'incendiario" (The Arsonist) records the urge to break with trad.—without the obsessive need for activism or linguistic anarchy. The title of his "poetics," "E lasciatemi divertire!" (Well, I want to have fun!) describes well the zany wit of his poems. But Palazzeschi's endurance is assured by his great myths, created out of airy nothings ("Ara Mara Amara," "Oro Doro Odoro Dodoro," "Rio Bo"), and by his poems commemorating the grotesque in everyday life (Contini).

A flourishing literary culture in the years preceding World War I gave rise to a number of periodicals, many of them Florentine. The most influential, *La voce* (1908–13), was directed by the grand "impresario of culture," Giuseppe Prezzolini, who gathered together a heterogeneous group of collaborators. *La voce* became associated with nearly all the trends in vogue during its run. It offered a first forum to the best known autochthonous poetic movement in 20th-c. Italy, later called "Hermeticism" (q.v.). The forefather of this novel *trobar clus*, Dino Campana (1885–1932), came to notice after the "school" had gained notoriety with Ungaretti and Montale. Campana is often compared to Rimbaud and Trakl for his aimless wanderings over the world, interrupted only by his stays in mental asylums (he was permanently committed in 1918), and for his poetics of total faith in the magic of the Word. The *Canti orfici* (1914) refer to Orpheus: here poetry is a descent into Hell and a religion for initiates. The poems, marvels of fragmented verbal obsession (or drugged hallucinations), show for all that echoes of Carducci and D'Annunzio. In them syntax is not (futuristically) eliminated; it is replaced by cadences (see "L'invetriata" and the irrational "logic" of Campana's oneiric chimeras: "La Chimera" is perhaps his best known poem).

Two other influential poets who matured in the *La voce* context produced poetry in a vein related to Campana's. The existential adventure of Clemente Rébora (1885–1957), not less erratic than Campana's, took place all *within*, as a lifelong struggle with his own soul and a periodically despairing search for superior truth. Not given to theorizing, Rébora's only inspiration is his need to find the all-encompassing Word. His aptly titled *Frammenti lirici* (1913) and *Canti anonimi* (1922) record in their daring analogies, in Rébora's characteristic "imagine tesa" (taut imagery), a "sort of transcendental autobiography" of powerful originality (Contini). Camillo Sbàrbaro (1888–1967) sang the "monotonous recurrence of indifferent life," withdrawing from the bustle into his private drama. *Resine* (Amberdrops, 1911) and *Pianissimo* (1914) sound at first curiously old-fashioned—as if in the midst of a dodecaphonic revolution a humble songwriter kept on modulating his simple *lieder* on his flute—but Montale shows in *his* complex tunes the impact this withdrawn predecessor had.

The review *La ronda* (1919–23) welcomed the voices of reaction to the cult of originality in prewar poetry. Its founder, Vincenzo Cardarelli (1887–1959), advocated a return to the classics (esp. Leopardi and Manzoni), i.e. to syntax, logic, and immediate comprehension. The progress of Hermetic poetry, supported by parallel trends abroad among the Fr. and also in Eliot and Pound, proved irresistible. Its principal exponents are less typical of its program than its lesser adepts (S. Quasimodo, A. Gatto, M. Luzi, L. Sinisgalli, V. Sereni). All share the quasi-mystical concept of "poetry as life," as a magic formula capable of revealing, under the semblances of this phenomenal world, "universal reality" (Manacorda).

Giuseppe Ungaretti (1888–1970) will be long appreciated for his prosodic innovation, based on the lesson of Rimbaud's *Illuminations* and Mallarmé's "Un Coup de dès." Fragmenting the *vers libre* of his futurist beginnings, he paralleled the jocose cough of Palazzeschi's "Ailing Fountain" and Majakovskij's "staircase" poems in his trademark one-word verse (imitated even today by would-be poets). It acts as a "macroscope" for the word, harshly isolating it (Ungaretti eliminated punctuation) and transforming poetic diction into a series of fragments lit up by intermittent floodlights. In spite of disclaimers, Ungaretti is heir both to futurism and to Waning Poetry, but while these trends merely raised or lowered their volume, Ungaretti is a master of tonal modulation. His first book of verse, *Allegria* (1916; repub. 1923 with a preface by Mussolini) remains the overture to a new phase of It. p. The title of his collected poems, *Vita d'un uomo* (A Man's Life), points to his dominant theme, the sublimation of his experiences, though these, esp. in the verse of the 1930s and '40s, at times remain untranslated into poetry.

When the blurbs have yellowed and the promotion died down, Eugenio Montale (1896–1981) may well be perceived as the true heir to Pascoli. His poetry is Pascolian in its resignedly hopeless scrutiny of the "ontological mystery," its vague desire for an escape route from the "male di vivere" (both "pain of life" and "evil of living"), for a "broken seam / in the net that constrains us." Pascolian too is Montale's characteristic of transforming emotion into landscape. Pascolian is, in his epoch-making *Ossi di seppia* (Cuttlefishbones, 1925), Montale's metaphysical and baroque mythmaking, soberly desolate as it is. Much has been made of the political texts by antifascist Montale (from *Occasioni*, 1939, to *Satura*, 1971), endlessly deciphered by immense and often too-Hermetic exegesis.

Variously related to Hermeticism are four poets whose assessment is still pending: Umberto Saba (1883–1957), Cesare Pavese (1908–50), Sandro Penna (1906–77), and Pier Paolo Pasolini (1922–75). Saba was in a sense pre-hermetic; his *Canzoniere* (Songbook) "reads as a 19th-c. work" (Debenedetti). Its Petrarchan ambition signals the "only major contemp. poet wholly free from experimentalism." His simplicity and trite diction prompted critics to see in him an authentically popular poet. It slowed recognition and led Saba to publish a *Chronicle* (1948) effectually advertising his own songbook. His bias for the humble shows no trace of Gozzano's worldly irony; instead, we find warm participation, an almost childlike *amor vitae*. A typical motif is animal life related to human behavior. Pavese offered a model of anti-Hermetic poetry in his realistic and matter-of-fact *poesie-racconto* (story-poems), but the project failed both in this role and as a matrix of poetry, despite Pavese's great (but mostly extraliterary) popularity with the young. His *Lavorare stanca* (Work Makes You Tired, 1936; ineptly tr. as *Hard Labor*) is a curiosity. Interest is still inspired by this often politically and culturally "misappropriated" writer, a suicide at 42.

The populist search for the "primitive" drew another blank with Penna. "Hermetic" in a special sense ("coding" for this gay poet was a must), Penna's only topic is love, *dolce pena*, "cross and delight," "strange joy" (the last two are titles of collections). This "vigorous outsider" was also an *ermetico* in his refusal of easy legacies, in his ironclad rule of conciseness, and in his stenographic imagery. Penna sings of joy and pain with a Matisse-like luminosity of vision. His best poems, always centered on his beloved *ragazzi*, are prodigies of a balanced moment suspended in timelessness. Everything is burned off in the white heat of the poet's dogged hammering at the "right word." Penna, the self-defined "penny-a-dozen [sex]fiend" has, incongruously, an almost virginal chastity of poetic voice. Pasolini, the filmmaker, whose 1957 *Le ceneri di Gramsci* (Gramsci's Ashes) is widely acknowledged as one of the most important collections of poetry published in the postwar period, had a different and more tragic purity of voice. Paroxysms of paradox interrupt his song. The popular brand of Marxism he professed never overcame his bourgeois values. Pasolini took idiosyncrasy for ideology: the pangs of libido appear in some of his purposely controversial and perhaps less enduring pieces as the stirrings of History.

Around the critic Luciano Anceschi and his influential periodical *Il Verri* sprang into being the self-styled *Gruppo 63* (so called from its founding meeting at Palermo in 1963). Three poets associated with it are likely to mark the last decades of this century with their names: Antonio Porta (1935–89), Andrea Zanzotto (b. 1921), and Edoardo Sanguineti (b. 1930). In their verse the linguistic revolution begun by Pascoli comes full circle; his weakening of the tie between signifier and signified reaches the final stage of divorce. The movement has been compared in its sound and fury to futurism; however, the poetry initially born out of and later in some cases opposed to *Gruppo 63* is distinguished by a theoretical rigor unknown to Marinetti *et Cie*. Porta was first brought to critical notice by the collective volume *I novissimi* (1961). His poems reveal a strongly individual voice and have an eerie capacity to suggest, behind a deliberately gray diction, vast threatening conspiracies by unknown objects and persons. Porta has since gone beyond his *novissimi* origins and alliances. Some critics distinguish his poetry as the first real novelty after Hermeticism.

Zanzotto "joined" the group after the fact, as it were. His early collections, *Dietro il paesaggio* (Behind the Landscape, 1951), *Elegia* (1954), *Vocativo* (1957), and *IX Egloghe* (1962), are characterized by traditional form (Zanzotto even wrote Petrarchan sonnets, the only 20th-c. poet to do so outside of parody). Zanzotto's arcane Arcadia suggests spectral visitations, séances of literary ghost-evoking. Lang. acts here as a trance-inducing drug. New revolutionary techniques appear with *La beltà* (Beauty, 1968) and subsequent collections of ever-increasing textual complexity.

An original member of the Palermo group, Sanguineti had anticipated in his *Laborintus* (1956) its ideological and technical characteristics. A shocked Pavese refused to consider seriously Sanguineti's early samples, and Zanzotto later called them the "record of a nervous breakdown." Sense in *Laborintus* is replaced by obsessive paranomasia. Segments read as if they were a medieval treatise on alchemy, a textbook on sociology, yesterday's newspaper, and Freud's *Traumdeutung*, all put through a shredder and reassembled at random. But Sanguineti's collected poems, *Segnalibro* (Bookmark, 1982), and esp. his *Novissimum Testamentum* (1986), rank him with the best of contemp. European poets.

Among the poets active in the last two decades, Franco Fortini and Paolo Volponi, *engagé* writers of the older generation, deserve more than a summary listing, as well as Luciano Erba, Maria Luisa Spaziani, Giovanni Raboni, Dario Bellezza, and Fabio Doplicher. Curiously, while the dialects of the peninsula had seemed doomed by 20th-c.

mass education and media diffusion, poetry in dialect shows no sign of decadence. Among its practioners, heirs to Meli, Porta, and Belli, one must mention the first-rate poets Virgilio Giotti and Giacomo Noventa. See also FROTTOLA AND BARZELLETTA; ITALIAN PROSODY; LAUDA; RITORNELLO; ROMANTIC AND POSTROMANTIC POETICS; TWENTIETH-CENTURY POETICS, *Italian.*

GENERAL HISTORIES: F. De Sanctis, *Storia della letteratura italiana* (1870), tr. J. Redfern, *Hist. of It. Lit.* (1968); A. Momigliano, *Storia della letteratura italiana* (1936); F. Flora, *Storia della letteratura italiana*, 4 v. (1940–41); N. Sapegno, *Compendio di storia della letteratura italiana*, 3 v. (1954); J. H. Whitfield, *A Short Hist. of It. Lit.* (1960); *Storia della letteratura italiana*, ed. E. Cecchi and N. Sapegno, v. 8–9 (1969); *I classici italiana nella storia della critica*, ed. W. Binni, 3 v. (1971–77); B. Croce, *La letteratura italiana per saggi*, ed. M. Sansone, 4 v. (1972), *Essays on Lit. and Lit. Crit.*, ed. and tr. M. E. Moss (1990); *Dizionario critico della letteratura italiana*, ed. V. Branca (1973); Wilkins; *Orientamenti culturali: La Letteratura italiana: I maggiori*, I–II; *I minori*, I–IV; *Le correnti*, I–II; *I contemporanei*, I–VI (1975–); *Dictionary of It. Lit.*, ed. P. and J. C. Bondanella (1979); *Letteratura italiana, profilo storico*, ed. I. De Bernardi et al., 3 v. (1980); M. Puppo, *Manuale critico bibliografico per lo studio della letteratura italiana* (1985).

SPECIALIZED HISTORIES AND STUDIES: E. Underhill, *Jacopone da Todi, Poet and Mystic* (1919); E. Garin, *Il Rinascimento italiano* (1941); F. Flora, *La poesia ermetica* (1947); C. Calcaterra, *Il Barocco in Arcadia* (1950); A. Momigliano, *Saggio sull'Orlando Furioso* (1952); M. Fubini, *Ritratto dell'Alfieri* (1967), "Arcadia e Illuminismo," *Dal Muratori al Baretti* (1975), *Ugo Foscolo* (1978); *Marino e marinisti: opere scelte*, ed. G. Getto, 2 v. (1954); A. Bobbio, *Parini* (1954); A. Galletti, *Il Novecento* (1954); *Lirici del Settecento*, ed. B. Maier (1960); A. Viscardi, *Storia della letteratura italiana dalle origini al Rinascimento* (1960); *Poeti del Duecento*, ed. G. Contini (1960); E. H. Wilkins, *The Life of Petrarch* (1961); J. H. Whitfield, *Leopardi's Canti* (tr. 1962), *Giacomo Leopardi* (1964); G. Santangelo, *Il secentismo* (1962); M. Bishop, *Petrarch and His World* (1963); J. V. Mirollo, *The Poet of the Marvelous: Giambattista Marino* (1963); G. Petronio, *Il Romanticismo* (1963); A. Del Monte, *Le origini* (1964); B. Maier, *Il Neoclassicismo* (1964); G. Singh, *Leopardi and the Theory of Poetry* (1964); *Complete Poems and Sel. Letters of Michelangelo*, tr. C. Gilbert (1965); T. G. Bergin, *Dante* (1965), *Petrarch* (1970); C. P. Brand, *Torquato Tasso . . . and His Contrib. to Eng. Lit.* (1965), *Ludovico Ariosto: A Preface to the Orlando Furioso* (1974); G. Pozzi, *La poesia italiana del Novecento* (1965); *Am. Critical Essays on the Divine Comedy*, ed. R. Clements (1967); *Dante's Lyric Poetry*, ed. K. Foster and P. Boyde (1967); G. Getto, *L'interpretazione del Tasso* (1967), *Carducci e Pascoli* (1977); P. Nardi, *La Scapigliatura* (1968); G. Manacorda, *Storia della letteratura italiana con-*temporanea (1968); G. Contini, *Letteratura dell'Italia unita, 1861–1968* (1968); W. Binni, *Saggi alfieriani* (1969); P. Dronke, *The Med. Lyric* (1969); *Tasso's* Jerusalem Delivered, tr. J. Tusiani (1970); *Enciclopedia dantesca*, ed. U. Bosco, 5 v. (1970–78); A. Vallone, *Dante* (1971); L. Anceschi, *Le poetiche del Novecento in Italia* (1973); M. Marti, *Storia dello stil nuovo* (1973); G. Debenedetti, *Poesia italiana del Novecento* (1974); R. Griffin, *Ludovico Ariosto* (1974); *Ariosto's* Orlando Furioso, tr. B. Reynolds (1975–77); *F. Petrarch Six Centuries Later: A Symposium*, ed. A. Scaglione (1975); A. Seroni, *Il decadentismo* (1975); *Petrarch's Lyric Poems*, tr. R. Durling (1976); U. Bosco, *Petrarca* (1977); *Il Novecento*, ed. G. Grana, 10 v. (1980); *The New It. P.: 1945 to the Present*, ed. and tr. L. R. Smith (1981)—bilingual anthol. T.W.

ITALIAN PROSODY.

I. METER
II. RHYME
III. POETIC FORMS

At its beginnings in the 13th c., It. poetry (q.v.) imitated many of the themes and forms of the earlier trads. of Occitan and Fr. poetry (qq.v.). Med. Lat. rhythmical verse also exerted a strong formal influence on many of the nascent vernacular lyrical modes in Italy. In addition to his preeminence as Italy's leading poet, Dante Alighieri (1265–1321) was the first among many well known theoreticians of prosody. In the *Vita nuova* (ch. 25), Dante expresses his views on the history of poetic composition in the European vernaculars and argues that, on the model of their Gr. and Lat. predecessors, It. poets should be granted the use of rhetorical figures. He also evidences his recognition not only of the seriousness of lit., but also of his own role as a creative artist and of his place in the literary trad.

Dante's literary career essentially retraces the trajectory of lyric poetry in 13th-c. Italy, from the Sicilian School (q.v.) through the Dolce stil nuovo (q.v.), and thus his remarks on and practice of versification are of particular importance for the It. poetic trad. In his unfinished treatise, *De vulgari eloquentia* (On Eloquence in the Vernacular, ca. 1302–5), Dante situates poetic praxis within a more theoretical discussion of the nature of poetic lang., esp. the search among the various It. dialects for a sufficiently noble literary lang., one that would be, in his terms, "illustrious, cardinal, courtly, and curial" (1.17.1). Such a lang. would be the proper medium for refined lyric poetry in the "high" or "tragic" style on one of the three noble themes: prowess in arms, love, and virtue (2.2.7). From the "question of lang.," Dante passes to an extended discussion of metrical forms (2.3.1–3), particularly the construction of the canzone (q.v.): the grammatical structure of the verse period, the qualities of individual words, varying line lengths, the AAB structure of the canzone stanza, and the particular nature of rhyme words and rhyming devices. While intending to treat this last point in the (unwritten) fourth book of the treatise, Dante discusses the ordering of the canzone through placement of rhymes and discourages certain practices: excessive use of the same rhyme, equivocal rhymes, and rhymes on harsh sounds. Not extant—if they were ever written—are sections on the *ballata* and sonnet (q.v.), both of which belong to the "middle" style. Nevertheless, Dante's codification of It. prosody served as a touchstone for centuries of both praxis and and crit.

I. METER. It. metrics is based both on number of syllables and on the position of the primary accent in the line; the latter is the more important factor for determining meter. Syllables are counted only up to the last accent; if any follow it, they are ignored. Hence the hendecasyllable (q.v.; It. *endecasillabo*), the most excellent of meters according to Dante and the one most appropriate for subjects in the high style, is not necessarily determined by the presence of 11 syllables, as its name implies, but rather by the placement of the primary accent on the 10th syllable and secondary stresses on either the 4th or 6th. While a "normal" hendecasyllable (*endecasillabo piano*; see VERSO PIANO) adheres to the 11-syllable model, it may have as few as 10 syllables (*endecasillabo tronco*; see VERSO TRONCO) or as many as 12 or 13 syllables (*endecasillabo sdrucciolo* or *bisdrucciolo*; see VERSO SDRUCCIOLO). Vowels in hiatus (q.v.) must often be elided (see ELISION) for a verse to scan, via either synalepha or synaeresis (qq.v.). At other times, such vowels must be pronounced separately, via dialefe (across a word boundary) or diaeresis (q.v.; within a word).

After the hendecasyllable, the 7-syllable line (*settenario*) is the most popular It. meter, with the principal stress always on the 6th syllable, as in "Il Cinque Maggio" by Alessandro Manzoni (1785–1873). Dante notes that verses with an odd number of syllables (3, 5, 7, 11) are generally to be preferred, and thus we find verses in all periods of It. lit. with 5 syllables (*quinario*: major stress on the 4th), as, for example in "La pioggia nel pineto" by Gabriele D'Annunzio (1863–1938). Although in early It. poetry the *trisillabo* (major accent on the 2nd syllable) is generally found only as a rhyming component (internal rhyme: *rimalmezzo*) of a longer verse, it sometimes appears as a separate verse. The *trisillabo*, however, does occur with some frequency in modern poets, as in D'Annunzio's "La pioggia nel pineto" (14–15), where he combines a *quinario* with a *trisillabo*. Dante holds the 9-syllable line (*novenario*: major accent on the 8th syllable) in contempt for giving "the impression of being three lines of three syllables" (*D.V.E.* 2.5.6; tr. Haller), but it has been used by Chiabrera (1552–1638), Redi (1626–1698), Carducci (1835–1907), Pascoli (1855–1912), and D'Annunzio.

Dante considers lines with an even number of syllables decidedly less noble (2.5.7), perhaps because the regularity of the stress pattern led to a monotonous cadence. There are, nevertheless, numerous examples of octosyllabic verse (*ottonario*, accent on the 7th syllable), esp. in poems of popular inspiration; similarly, we have examples of 6-syllable verses (*senario*, accent on the 5th syllable) and 4-syllable verses (*quadrisillabo*, accent on 3rd).

Many early narrative poems were written in stanzas composed of 14-syllable lines, *alessandrini*, which imitate OF verses; these are essentially double septenaries (*doppi settenari*, accents on the 6th and 13th syllables) with a caesura (q.v.) after the first *settenario*. They were also called *versi martelliani*, after Pier Jacopo Martelli (1661–1727), who composed tragedies in this meter based on the model of Corneille and Racine, and were used subsequently by Goldoni (1707–93) and Giacosa (1847–1906) in their comedies and by Carducci in his *Rime nuove*. Decasyllables (*decasillabi*, accent on 9th syllable) also were first modeled on OF meters; these enjoyed a certain popularity in the 19th c. with Manzoni, Berchet (1783–1851), Giusti (1809–50), and Pascoli.

Both in the Ren. and in the 19th c. we find examples of the imitation of Cl. meters (see CLASSICAL METERS IN MODERN LANGUAGES). The first conscious attempts were made by Leon Battista Alberti (1404–72) and Leonardo Dati, who composed It. hexameters for the poetry contest—the *certame coronario*—of 1441. Ariosto (1474–1533) tried his hand at reproducing the Lat. iambic trimeter in hendecasyllables. In the 16th and 17th cs., Claudio Tolomei (1492–1555) and Chiabrera attempted to resolve the conflict between the Lat. quantitative and the It. accentual systems. Carducci also experimented with "barbarian" poetry (*metrica barbara*)—for such it would have appeared and sounded to the ancients—based on accentual imitations of Cl. meters, e.g. Virgilian hexameters and Catullian elegiac distichs. In his *Odi barbare*, Carducci is esp. indebted to Horace.

II. RHYME. Rhymes in It. are exact. Rhyme sounds are identical from the major stress to the end of the word: *amóre/dolóre; compí/sentí; cántano/piántano*. Eye rhymes (q.v.; *rime all'occhio*), which are apparently but not actually identical, are infrequent (*pálmi/sálmi/almí*; Dante, *Inf.* 31.65–69). Examples of composite rhymes (*rime composte*; see MOSAIC RHYME) may be found in early poetry (*chiome/oh me, Inf.* 28:121–23) and esp. in the poetry of Guittone d'Arezzo (ca. 1225–93) and his followers. Other unusual sorts of rhyme found among the early lyrics include (1) equivocal rhyme (q.v.; *traductio*), where the word is the same but has a different meaning; (2) derivative rhyme (*replicatio*; see GRAMMATICAL RHYME), where the rhyme words have the same root; (3) and rich rhyme (q.v.; *rima cara, ricca*), where an uncommon word form is used.

In the early lyrics there is a phenomenon known as "Sicilian rhyme" (*rima siciliana*), which refers to words which in the dialect of the Sicilian poets would have rhymed because of the identity of the vowels *e* and *i*, and *o* and *u*. Thus *diri* (= *dire*) and *taciri* (= *tacere*), as well as *tuttu* (= *tutto*) and *muttu* (= *motto*), rhyme in Sicilian, but not in It. When the Sicilian lyrics were copied into manuscripts by late 13th-c. Tuscan scribes, these forms were "Tuscanized," i.e. regularized orthographically, and thus emerged matches of the sort *ride/vede* (Sicilian *ridi/vidi*) and *ascoso/incluso* (Sicilian *ascusu/inclusu*), which are "Sicilian rhyme."

Generally speaking, most medieval It. poetry is rhymed, although we do find occasional examples of assonance or consonance, as for example in the *Laudes creaturarum* of St. Francis of Assisi (1182–1226), and some examples of *versi sciolti* (q.v.), poems with unrhymed lines, the first example of which is the anonymous 13th-c. poem, "Il mare amoroso." This It. variety of blank verse (q.v.) was reintroduced in the Ren., first by Trissino (1478–1550) in his epic, *L'Italia liberata dai Goti*.

III. POETIC FORMS. For Dante, the canzone represents the height of artistic perfection. It developed in Italy under the direct influence of the Occitan *canso* (q.v.), the OF *chanson*, and the Ger. Minnesang (q.v.). Canzoni generally have several strophes composed mainly of *endecasillabi* and *settenari*, all of which follow the same structure (a one-stanza canzone is called a *cobbola*). The mix of 11s and 7s is distinctive. Canzoni composed entirely of shorter meters are called by the diminutive *canzonette*; these were esp. privileged in the 17th and 18th cs. by Chiabrera, Frugoni (1692–1768), Parini (1729–99), and Metastasio (1698–1782).

The essential division of the canzone strophe is bipartite, the first part being termed the *fronte* and the second the *sirma*. The fronte usually divides into two (sometimes three) equal parts called "feet" (*piedi*); the sirma sometimes divides into two equal parts called *volte* or *giri*. The passage from *fronte* to *sirma*, which marks the change from one musical pattern to another, is generally known as the *diesis*. Some canzoni conclude with a *commiato* (see ENVOI), a short stanza generally having the same pattern as the *sirma* (or a part of it), in which the poet sometimes addresses his composition and instructs it where it should go, with whom it should speak, what it should say, and so on.

These rules were followed rigidly until the 17th c., when the rise of the *canzone libera* signaled the abandonment of prosodic uniformity among strophes. Poets were thus presented with two possibilities: following the older, traditional forms or the newer, freer models. While some poets adhered in part to the earlier modes (Alfieri [1749–1803], Monti [1754–1828], Foscolo [1778–1827], Manzoni, Carducci), most followed the newer forms, perhaps best exemplified by Leopardi (1798–1837) in his *Canti*.

Other important forms include the *ballata* (see FROTTOLA AND BARZELLETTA), which arose in the mid 13th c. as a song to accompany a dance and has essentially the same form as the canzone, except that the ballata begins with a refrain, the *ritornello* (q.v.) or *ripresa*, which in performance was repeated after each stanza, and the last rhyme(s) of which recur(s) at the end of each stanza. The *ballata* was very popular in the Middle Ages and Ren. and found illustrious practitioners in Dante, Petrarch (1304–74), Lorenzo de' Medici (1449–92), Poliziano (1454–94), and Bembo (1470–1547). It was revived briefly in the late 19th c. by Carducci, Pascoli, and D'Annunzio. The *lauda* (q.v.) adopted the metrical form of the secular *ballata* under the guidance of its first great practitioner, Jacopone da Todi (1236–1306), but its very popular use for religious subjects did not extend past the 15th c. In imitation of the Occitan troubadour Arnaut Daniel (fl. 1189), Dante introduced the sestina (q.v.); later practitioners include Petrarch, Michelangelo, Carducci, D'Annunzio, and Ungaretti (1888–1970). The 14th c. saw the advent of other lyrical modes, esp. the madrigal (q.v.) and caccia (q.v.). In the 16th and 17th cs., the madrigal became the preferred form to be set to music, e.g. by Palestrina (ca. 1525–94) and Monteverdi (1567–1643); the caccia disappears after the 16th c.

The sonnet, arguably the single most important creation of It. prosody, was apparently invented in the second quarter of the 13th c. by Giacomo da Lentini, a notary at the court of Frederick II in Sicily. Although perhaps formed by the reduction of two *strambotti* (q.v.), it more likely developed in imitation of the strophe of the canzone. In early It. lit., the rhyme schemes of the quatrains and tercets are more flexible than later. It was also used as the vehicle for verse epistles in the *tenzone* (q.v.). Under the influence of Petrarch, perhaps its most important practitioner, and Petrarchism (q.v.), the sonnet sequence (q.v.) spread throughout Europe. It. poets who have cultivated the sonnet include Michelangelo (1475-1564), Tasso (1544-1595), Alfieri, Foscolo, Carducci, and D'Annunzio, although its popularity has steadily diminished since the 17th c.

In narrative poetry, *ottava rima* (q.v.), used first by Boccaccio (1313–75) for his verse narratives (*Teseida*; *Filostrato*; *Ninfale fiesolano*), became the staple for both the epic and the popular cantare, which had for its subject matter Cl. and medieval myths and legends, as well as contemp. political events and humorous tales. Following Boccaccio's lead, the great epic poets of the Ren. used ottava rima for their chivalric poems (Boiardo [1441–94], *Orlando innamorato*; Ariosto, *Orlando furioso*; and Tasso, *Gerusalemme liberata*), as did other poets such as Pulci (1432–84, *Morgante*), Poliziano (*Stanze per la giostra*), Marino (1569–1625, *Adone*) and Tassoni (1565–1635, *La secchia rapita*).

Allegory, didactic poetry, and the dream vision (qq.v.) generally followed the great model of Dante's *Divine Comedy*, with its intricate concatenation (q.v.) of hendecasyllables in a pattern known as *terza rima* (q.v.). It was used by Boccaccio in the *Amorosa Visione*, by Petrarch in the *Trionfi*, and by Fazio degli Uberti (ca. 1307–70) in the *Dittamondo*. In later centuries *terza rima*, often in the form of the *capitolo* (q.v.), was incorporated by poets for a variety of compositions: satires (Ariosto, Berni, Alfieri, Leopardi), historical (Machiavelli), eclogues (Lorenzo de' Medici), amorous elegies (Ariosto, Foscolo, Carducci), and political allegories (Monti).

The rules of It. prosody were essentially fixed for subsequent poets in the first two centuries of It. lit., thanks to the great example of Dante, Petrarch, and Boccaccio and to the work of early compilers of metrical treatises such as Francesco da Barberino (*Documenti d'amore* [1306–13]), Antonio da Tempo (*Summa artis rithimici vulgaris dictaminis* [1332], ed. R. Andrews [1977]), and Gidino da Sommacampagna (*Trattato dei ritmi volgari* [1381–84], ed. G. B. C. Giuliari [1870]). To be sure, metrical innovation has always taken place, particularly in the 20th c. with literary movements such as futurism and hermeticism (qq.v.). Nevertheless, while prosodic forms are no longer followed strictly, poets still imitate, albeit unconsciously, the cadences of traditional verse.

P. E. Guarnerio, *Manuale di versificazione italiana* (1893); F. Flamini, *Notizia storica dei versi e metri italiani* (1919); R. Murari, *Ritmica e metrica razionale ital.* (1927); V. Pernicone, "Storia e svolgimento della metrica," *Problemi ed orientamenti critici di lingua e di letteratura italiana*, ed. A. Momigliano, v. 2 (1948); *La metrica*, ed. R. Cremante and M. Pazzaglia (1972); A. B. Giamatti, "It.," in Wimsatt; D'A. S. Avalle, *Sintassi e prosodia nella lirica italiana delle origini* (1973); F. Caliri, *Ritmica e metrica: le origini: nozioni ed esempi* (1973); Spongano; M. Fubini, *Metrica e poesia*, 3d ed. (1975); *Lit. Crit. of Dante Alighieri*, ed. and tr. R. S. Haller (1977); L. Castelnuovo, *La metrica italiana* (1979); Dante Alighieri, *Opere minori*, ed. P. V. Mengaldo (1979); M. Shapiro, *Hieroglyph of Time: The Petrarchan Sestina* (1981); Brogan—bibl. to 1981, supp. in *Verseform* (1988); Elwert, *Italienische*. C.K.

ITHYPHALLIC (Gr. "erect phallus"). An iambo-trochaic colon of the form $- \cup - \cup - \times$, which can be regarded as the remainder of a catalectic iambic trimeter after the caesura after the second anceps. According to the scholia to the ancient metrist Hephaestion, the i. received its name from its use in the procession of the phallos at the festival of Dionysus (cf. Aristophanes, *Acharnians*). It is often used as a colon or a closing element (clausula) in the iambic songs in Gr. drama (see DACTYLO-EPITRITE); in Aristophanes' *Wasps* (248–72) it is used with a colon consisting of an iambic dimeter. It is also used in the epodes (q.v.) of Archilochus and the epodic forms Horace derived from him. An i. of the form $- \times - \times - -$ is often used by Plautus with cretics ($- \cup -$), and sometimes it is used as a clausula in a short cretic system (*Pseudolus* 921) or together with iambic quaternarii (*Curculio* 103–04).—W. M. Lindsay, *Early Lat. Verse* (1922); Maas; Dale; C. Questa, *Introduzione alla metrica di Plauto* (1967); Halporn et al.; Snell; West. J.W.H.

J

JAKOBSONIAN POETICS. See RUSSIAN FORMAL-ISM; SEMIOTICS, POETIC; STRUCTURALISM; EQUIVALENCE; POETIC FUNCTION.

JAPANESE POETICS.

    I. CLASSICAL (TO A.D. 1868)
    II. MODERN (AFTER 1868)

I. CLASSICAL (TO 1868). The most important features of J. p. derive from its definition out of lyricism augmented by a certain kind of history. There is a parallel with, and some differences from, Chinese poetics (q.v.). In fact, all of the world's poetic systems but one appear to have been defined out of lyric as the privileged genre. The exception is the Western, which used drama to produce mimesis (see IMITATION), but even this was later supplemented by the affectivism of Horace (see CLASSICAL POETICS). Varying ideas of lit. produce varying discourses. Ki no Tsurayuki begins his preface to the *Kokinshū* (10th c.):

> The poetry of Japan takes the human heart as seed and flourishes in the countless leaves of words. Because human beings possess interests of so many kinds, it is in poetry that they give expression to the meditations of their hearts in terms of the sights appearing before their eyes and the sounds coming to their ears. Hearing the warbler sing among the blossoms and the frog that lives in the waters—is there any living thing not given to song? It is poetry which, without exertion, moves heaven and earth, stirs the feelings of gods and spirits invisible to the eye, softens the relations between men and women, calms the hearts of fierce warriors.

Here is affectivism (all are moved), expressivism (all sing), and realism: all is possible because the world is real. This poetic accounts for poet, reader, world, and expression.

Lit. (at least *bun* or *fumi*) also included mythical history from the age of divinities to the sovereigns who succeeded them on earth. Much in the two J. histories, the *Kojiki* (A.D. 712) and *Nihon Shoki* (720), is fabulous, much dynastic self-justification. Significantly, prose yields to lyric verse when a divinity or sovereign is deeply moved. These are lyricized narrative histories.

History also strengthened the realist presumptions. Fact and fiction are not extremes; either may be used to literary ends without Western anxiety. J. affectivism differs from Chinese and from the Horatian in being nondidactic: J. poetry is very rarely moralistic.

Tsurayuki's chief terms are heart or conception (*kokoro*), words or subjects (*kotoba*), technique or style (*sama*), and total form (*sugata*). These terms or equivalents last through cl. J. p. Some terms were borrowed from China: e.g. elegance (*fūryū*; Ch. *feng-liu*), with a native equivalent, courtly beauty (*miyabi*). Elegance was esteemed variously, so that *fūryū* is a word with a long, complex history. To be possessed of a right heart or conception was designated by *kokoro aru* and by the Sinified *ushin*. An ideal of mystery and depth (*yūgen*) was distinguished in terms of conception (*kokoro yūgen*), expression (*kotoba yūgen*), and total effect (*sugata yūgen*). But *yūgen* later signified beauty. *Sabi* is disputed by J. critics but seems to mean desolation, deterioration, silence, esp. later in the cl. period.

Naturally there was some prescriptive crit.: one should avoid hypometric (*ji tarazu*) lines, poetic ills (*kahei*) of various kinds, and repetition (*rin'e, rinne*) esp. in linked poetry (see RENGA). Other slogans, e.g. "Old lang., new conceptions" (*kotoba furuku, kokoro atarashi*), found some who disagreed with one part or the other. Rudely put, early poetry tends to be more factual. Fictionalizing accompanied esteem of elegance, yielding to beauty in linked poetry and *nō* (q.v.). In later linked poetry (*haikai*; see HAIKU), beauty was poised with desolation (*sabi*), elevation with humor, etc. The dominant *waka* used purely J. diction, eschewing Sinified: as if, in Eng., we used "amorous," "bishop," and "rigor" in prose but in verse "loving," "overseer," and "hardness." Earlier linked poetry (*renga*) continued the choice; later (*haikai*) did not.

Numerous distinctions existed, but formally poet and audience were interchangeable: poetry was not entertainment but transmission of what was found moving and might elicit reply—competition in a poetry match (*utaawase*; see POETIC CONTESTS), or another poet's added stanza (*tsukeku*) in linked poetry. *Waka* moves from communication to composition on topics, often in competition. Linked poetry moves from joint composition of sequences to that of individual stanzas (*hokku*). Poetry remains, however, an art open to all, since a poet is not one specially inspired but rather one moved.

Poetic training also differs from its Western equivalent. Writing practice (*tenarai*) commonly

- [655] -

involved calligraphy less than setting down old, or composing new, poems expressive of one's concerns (see "Writing Practice" in *The Tale of Genji*). Poetry was learned from example, not precept. Numerous collections of exemplary poems (*shūka, shūku*) were made. Tutelage by a poetic authority normally involved marking compositions as good or bad; reflection was left to the composer.

Crit. involved general treatises, but less often than in the West, because one wrote for potential equals and always for people of taste. Certain critical emphases recur, incl. increasing attention to the dicta of esteemed poets. Classification involved forms, topics (*dai*), and other distinctions. As suggested, some crucial terms (*kokoro, kotoba, sugata*) remained stable in meaning; others (*yūgen, fūryū, sabi*) changed, and most were initially metaphorical. In poetry matches (incl. *renga awase*), judgments and reasons were commonly supplied, as were commentary, anecdotes (e.g. *utagatari*), and tales of poems (e.g. *utamonogatari*). Comparisons were frequent, as in matches and emulations. Alternative styles were distinguished in varying numbers, e.g. the lofty style (*taketakaki yō*), the style possessing heart (*ushintei*), etc. Rulebooks (*shikimoku*) emerged for linked poetry setting forth elaborate canons designed to control the rapid composition in alternation by several poets. Historical assumptions emerge very early; as a sense, the historical exists from the beginning of poetic collections. The sense of generations or ages begins with Tsurayuki. Historical and cultural relativism comes with prose (see "Fireflies" in *The Tale of Genji*). The historical devel. of J. p. involves the enlargement, but not the displacement, of the affective-expressive system, first by literary prose narrative, and then by drama. (For bibl., see below.) E.M.

II. MODERN (AFTER 1868). With the Meiji Restoration and the coming of the West, J. p. began to show a number of new developments. The history of modern J. p. can be recounted in terms of Western-inspired literary movements that successively came to dominate the J. poetic scene. As romanticism, symbolism, naturalism (qq.v.), and other Western literary movements were introduced, poets tried to adopt the imported ideas in a manner appropriate to their lang. and culture as well as to their individual creative needs. They were, as before, inclined toward lyricism and formal brevity, yet they knew that in order for their poetry to become part of a world culture they would have to be informed of, and respond to, new poetic movements emerging in other parts of the world, esp. Western Europe. Meanwhile, scholars searched for ways to reinterpret traditional ideas in the light of imported poetics and incorporate them into some general conceptual scheme that would encompass both Eastern and Western aesthetics.

Romantic ideas of poetry reminiscent of Words-worth, Byron, and Heine, which came into vogue in Japan around the turn of the 20th c., were soon overshadowed by other Western theories such as symbolism and naturalism (see JAPANESE POETRY, *Modern*), although all such foreign concepts were modified. J. romanticism, for instance, extolled free love more loudly than its European counterpart in order to reach those who were still in the shadow of feudal morality. J. symbolists showed more confidence in nature than in art for a medium through which to probe the mystery at the heart of the universe. Western naturalism was transformed into a kind of autobiographical realism that emphasized the author's personal observations and feelings, not far from the type of realism implied in Ki no Tsurayuki's preface to the *Kokinshū* (see JAPANESE POETRY, *Classical*).

In general, modern J. poets have shown a tendency to adore Western ideas of poetry in their youth but to return to their own literary heritage as they grow older. Some of their most interesting poetics emerge in mid-career, when they struggle to reconcile the two poetic trads. A typical case is Hagiwara Sakutarō (1886–1942), who admired European symbolist poetry early in his career but later became an avid reader of *waka* and *haikai*. In the process of that transition he formulated a unique poetic that centered upon the idea of "nostalgia," a modern poet's instinctive longing for his existential homeland. A similar transition is seen in Takahashi Shinkichi (1901–87), who considered himself a disciple of Tristan Tzara during his youth but soon abandoned dada (q.v.) in favor of Zen Buddhism. His conception of poetry is highly individual: he tried to combine an intellectual verseform imported from the West with an Eastern religion that defies intellect. The case is more complex with Shaku Chōkū (real name, Orikuchi Shinobu, 1887–1953), who started as a traditional *tanka* poet but proceeded to follow the worldwide trend during the 1920s toward proletarian lit. His second book of poetry shows a radical break from *tanka* convention in both theme and technique. When that phase passed, he resumed writing *tanka* in a more traditional manner, drawing on materials that reflect his lifelong interest in ancient J. mythology and folklore. His concept of poetry is characterized by his attempts to modernize *tanka* through a kind of cultural primitivism.

Poetics in premodern Japan had been largely unsystematic. With the newly acquired knowledge of European philosophy, modern J. scholars began to reinterpret traditional ideas from a new angle and to try to make them part of a coherent scheme. Mori Ōgai (1862–1922), for example, proposed to elucidate the implications of *yojō* (overtones) against the background of Eduard von Hartmann's aesthetics. Watsuji Tetsurō (1889–1960) analyzed *mono no aware*, a cl. literary ideal implying sad awareness of life's ephemerality, by using a philological method learned from European scholars like Gilbert Murray. Perhaps the most ambitious of all such attempts was made by Ōnishi Yoshinori (1888–1959), who reinterpreted *yūgen* and *sabi* from the viewpoint of Ger. phenomenology. It does not seem, however, that more recent theorists feel as much urge to internationalize J. p., probably because they have become more confident of their own trad. Or else they are already so much a part of the international poetic community that they feel no need to insist on their national identity.

ANTHOLOGIES AND TRANSLATIONS: *Nihon Koten Bungaku Taikei* [Great Compendium of Cl. J. Lit.], ed. I. Takagi, 102 v. (1957–68); *Nihon Kagaku Taikei* [Great Compendium of J. Poetic Treatises], ed. N. Sasaki, 10 v. (1956–63), and *Bekkan* [Supplement], ed. N. Kyūsojin, 4 v. (1959–80); *Nihon Koten Bungaku Zenshū*, ed. K. Akiyama et al., 51 v. (1970–76)—full collection of J. lit.; *Kindai Bungaku Hyōron Taikei* [Great Compendium of Mod. Lit. Crit.], ed. S. Yoshida et al., 10 v. (1971–77).

HISTORY AND CRITICISM: S. Hisamatsu, *Nihon Bungaku Hyōronshi* [Hist. of J. Lit. Crit.], 5 v. (1936–50); A. Yasuda, *Nihon no Geijutsuron* [J. Treatises on the Arts] (1957); M. Ueda, *Literary and Art Theories in Japan* (1967), *Mod. J. Poets and the Nature of Lit.* (1983); T. Matsui, *Kindai Haironshi* [Hist. of Haiku Crit. in the Mod. Period] (1973); S. Yoshida, *Kindai Bungei Hyōronshi* [Hist. of Lit. Crit. in the Mod. Period], 2 v. (1975); D. Keene, *World Within Walls* (1976–)—J. lit. 1600–1868, part of a continuing hist.; H. Shino, *Kindai Tanka Ronsōshi* [Hist. of Tanka Controversies in the Mod. Period], 2d ed., 2 v. (1981); J. Konishi, *A Hist. of J. Lit.*, 5 v. (1984–); *Principles of Cl. J. Lit.*, ed. E. Miner (1985); Miner et al., esp. parts 1A, 4, 6A, I, J, and K.
                                                                    M.U.

JAPANESE POETRY.

    I. CLASSICAL (TO 1868)
        A. *Genres and Characteristics*
        B. *History*
    II. MODERN (AFTER 1868)

I. CLASSICAL (TO 1868). This account treats poetry written in J. by those racially J. on the main archipelago. That is, it excludes Ainu and Ryukyuan poetry and J. composition in Chinese. This is the usual implicit, limited definition. The prosody of J. p. comes to consist of lines constituted by 5+7 or 7+5 morae in alternation, a mora being a formally or conceptually conceived syllable. Some modern haiku poets conceived of their poems as single lines and, like Chinese poetry, J. has been written or printed without typographical breaks for lines, except for modern editions reproducing *chōka* (see below). The following terms are assumed:

  (1) *waka* (*yamatouta*): J. p., particularly
      (a) *chōka* ("long poem"), alternating 5- and 7-syllable lines with a last 7- added; and

      (b) *tanka* (q.v.; "short poem"), of 5, 7, 5, 7, 7 syllables respectively (also used as envoys [*hanka*] for *chōka*): *kami no ku* ("upper-lines part"), the 5, 7, 5 of *tanka*, and *shimo no ku* ("lower-lines part"), the 7, 7 of *tanka*.
  (2) *renga* (q.v.; "linked poetry"), particularly
      (a) *renga*, using pure J. diction of *waka*; typically composed by three or four poets alternating stanzas of the upper and lower parts of *tanka* to a total of 100 (50 each), but 100-stanza units could be multiplied to 1000- or 10,000-stanza lengths; and
      (b) *haikai* ([*no*, q.v.] *renga*; modern designation, *renku*), introducing Sinified words of lower decorum and of the same typical alternate composition and length, although the 36-stanza form (*kasen*) was most favored by Bashō.

A. *Genres and Characteristics.* Song has always been an activity of both individual and communal importance in Japan. The divinities and sovereigns in the two J. mythical histories (*Kojiki*, ca. 712; *Nihon Shoki*, 720) deliver their strongest feelings in verse. These pieces were not sung in the modern sense but were delivered in heightened voice, often as spells (*kotoage*). The court enjoyed various kinds of songs. *Kagura* were associated with Shinto and dance. *Saibara*, originally folksongs, were taken up by the court and modified by *gagaku*, stately music imported from China (lost there but preserved in Japan). *Imayō* ("present styles") incl. many kinds of song compiled around 1169. Kinds proliferate and names with them, e.g. *nagauta* and *meriyasu*, music in *kabuki*; the former is instrumentally accompanied and is fundamental to the stage; the latter is unaccompanied and was only briefly in vogue. Both kinds were also performed in pleasure quarters, where minute discriminations existed for songs. The verse portions of *nō* are cantillated in a manner approaching singing.

Comic, parodic, and satiric verse flourished ca. 1650 ff. The two major kinds were *kyōka* (*mad waka*) and *senryū*. The latter developed out of *haikai* and eventually took on the 5, 7, 5-syllabic form of opening stanzas in linked poetry. Numerous other kinds came and went as vogues.

The main line of J. p., *waka* (including esp. *chōka* and *tanka*) originated with the court but was open to all. Its earliest examples appear in *Kojiki*. It used pure J., i.e. excluded the Sinified diction increasingly used in prose. Early prosody consisted of inconsistent alternation of shorter with longer lines which gradually became settled as 5s and 7s, with hypersyllabic but not hyposyllabic lines permitted. The verse sections of *nō* and some other writing are in units of 7s and 5s; some songs are in 8s and 6s.

J. lit. seldom demonstrates the strong oppositions of its Western counterparts. Significantly, fact and fiction do not conflict, both being drawn on equally by poets. There is, however, a growing tendency for *waka* to be fictionalized. Poems might be composed to go with paintings on screens. As poetic contests (q.v.; *utaawase*) became a chief venue for formal poetry, it became necessary for matching poems to be on the same topic (*dai*). Poets perspiring in August might write on "Snow in a Mountain Village," or old male poets of a young woman's love yearning. Topics were also necessary for sequences, commonly of 100 poems (*hyakushuuta*), for presentation. Informal poetry addressed to friends or lovers, or formal poetry on actual occasions, remained factual. The opening stanzas of linked poetry (see below) were required to deal with the actual setting, the rest to be fictional; but both requirements could be violated. In brief, fact is often embellished, and fiction often based on fact, with factual elements often dominant in modern poetry.

Brevity is a central feature. Poetic units not long to begin with grow shorter. The longest extant *chōka* of consequence is also the only one describing a battle, a poem by Kakinomoto Hitomaro (d. 708–15), only 149 lines long. By the late 17th c. it was common to compose opening stanzas (*hokku*) for *haikai* that were meant to stand alone, hence formally the same as modern *haiku* (q.v.). No complete explanation exists for this attachment to brevity. One factor involves the closely knit nature of composing groups. The more intimately poets know each other, the less necessity and good manners require lengthiness, a fact the converse of which is the weak opposition between poet and reader. A person who is one now will be the other another time. These roles are codified in J. linked poetry, where poets compose in alternating roles as poets and audience according to complex canons. In effect, they make an integrated collection as poets-audience on the spot.

Collections (q.v.) are another conspicuous feature of J. p. The most prestigious, although not always the greatest, were the 21 royally commissioned *nijūichidaishū*, beginning with the *Kokinshū* (905–15) and ending with the *Shinzokukokinshū* (1439). Their typical 20-scroll form divides into halves: the first begins with the seasons (1–2 spring, 3 summer, 4–5 autumn, 6 winter) and the second with love (11–15 or so). Other scrolls involve travel (*tabi no uta*), congratulations (*ga no uta*), and complaints (*jukkai*). More and more comes to be made of a miscellaneous category in which no single topic predominates (*kusagusa no uta*, *zōka*), thereby allowing poets to introduce fact or avoid topics they thought timeworn. Seasonal poems open with spring's beginning and close with winter's end. Love poems present a stylized version of courtly love (q.v.); the man's view dominates early on, the woman's more thereafter. Love (*koi*) means loving or yearning for someone else, not being loved, although happy consummation (*au koi*) is treated. Love is, then, particularly agi-

tated, and in the collections undergoes many fluctuations. Travel scrolls progress through the geography of central Japan, if not farther, and the trip never returns to the capital. There is considerable codification of topics, a tendency fully realized in the rule books (*shikimoku*) for linked poetry: haze represents spring; the moon is an autumn moon unless qualified; drizzle (*shigure*) belongs to both autumn and winter, although first drizzle (*hatsushigure*) belongs to winter.

As progressions became more skilled, associations were devised to integrate them more closely. Group associations, such as runs of anonymous poems and older (recent) poems, come first. Subtler associations involve conception (*kokoro*) or diction (*kotoba*). Conceptually, a poem on making a pillow in travel (a frequent topos) might precede one on a dream of home. The poem *de rigueur* for a man to send a woman after a love meeting might precede one where the woman wonders if her lover will come again the next evening. Frost imagery in one poem connects with withered plants in the next, or dew in one with leaves changed in color in the next (dew and frost were considered agents of change). The common association of winds with peaks could lead to a poem on wind following one on mountains. By the time of the eighth collection, *Shinkokinshū* (ordered 1201), another principle functions. Not merely selecting the best poems, compilers used lesser to set off greater to give a pleasing variety and to honor the J. aesthetic canon of asymmetry. Somewhat later, two poems might be juxtaposed with no apparent association until one realized that together they constituted an allusive variation (*honkadori*) on an older poem. Modern sequential composition (*rensaku*) offers similar forms of integration.

As these procedures imply, progressions and associations usually derive not from individual poets but from compilers, who were themselves distinguished poets. A poet with a dozen poems in a collection would find them scattered, situated according to stated or inferrable topics, progression, or association. The result is a force countervailing brevity: hence the *Shinkokinshū* can be read as a complex, varied poem of upwards of 10,000 lines. A *renga* 10,000-stanza unit (*manku*) would involve 25,000 lines. The poet Ihara Saikaku (1642–93) produced extraordinary numbers of *haikai* stanzas in a single day and night, his prodigy being 23,500 (nearly a thousand per hour, more than 15 per minute). Nobody has read this; Saikaku exhausted his scribes. Such bravado aside, the collective principle holds remarkable strength in Japan, surely the only country whose first writing system, *man'yōgana*, was named after the collection employing it, the *Man'yōshū*—although in fact it was first used in the *Kojiki* and was probably adapted from a Korean model.

In Japan verse has been unusually hospitable to prose and vice versa. Still, they are distinguished since the introduction of writing in J.: a distinct kind of *man'yōgana* was used for verse in the *Kojiki*, whose narrative in prose is interspersed with lyrics. Again, a people's rites show what they devote to the divine, and in Japan almost 30 Shinto pieces are prosimetric. Some lines are in verse, some in prose, a distinction immediately evident and ultimately baffling. Why is a line of 5 or 7, or even 4 or 8, syllables verse, whereas one of 3 or 9 is prose?

The royal collections provide two kinds of information. The second is the poet's name (or "Poet Unknown"). The first is its subject (or "Subject Unknown," not quite a title). The subject may be: (1) a flower or bird; (2) topics, e.g. "Love by the seaside"; (3) topics and occasions such as "'A distant spring view' for *The Poetry Match in Six Hundred Rounds*"; or (4) headnotes. Headnotes may show that one poem is a message or statement, the next poem a reply. Extended headnotes give a narrative setting to an exchange. In fact, with slight alteration the headnoted exchange could become an episode in the "tales of poems" genre, e.g. *The Tales of Ise*. Essentially collections of brief stories about poems, these tales show again the urge to collect, to make larger integers from smaller. Given J. poetics, readers wish to know the poet in the poem; and at court, poetry was a form of social communication. In *The Tale of Genji*, the characters exchange about 800 poems, nearly 4000 lines, alluding to yet other poems in Chinese as well as J. and to songs.

Throughout cl. J. lit., verse and prose are compatible, even if distinct and even if changing in nature over time. Poetry is the idealized member: an early term exists for J. p. (*yamatouta*), but not for prose. The term "J. lang." (*yamatokotoba*) implied idealizing of J. (as opposed to Chinese) lang. and poetry, with J. taken as the purer and truer. Chinese poetry must be written in Chinese characters; J. can be written in the cursive syllabary (*hiragana*), the standard medium of literacy for women, hence called "woman's hand," vs. the man's for Chinese. Although in practice both sexes wrote in both hands, J. p. goes back to the divinities headed by the sun goddess.

Idealizing gradually led to codifications (those for moons, haze, and travel were mentioned above), incl. poetic placenames. One visited places for poetic associations, not actual sights. In visiting Sayo no Nakayama on a clear day, one thought of the night, storms, clouds, and moon associated with the place. The Bay of Sleeves, Sode no Ura, was a godsend to poets indulging in the one excess in J. p.—superabundant tears. When *renga* master Sōgi (1421–1502) wrote of a place in Kyushu lovelier than a famous one near the capital, he rejects what he sees: what has not been celebrated in verse is, he says, no worthier of attention than poems by someone whose status is unattested by family trad. or study with a famous master.

The precedented and the customary have very strong appeal to people in traditional societies. In both Japan and China, socially esteemed art is precedented art, which is why innovation is often cast as appeal to a pristine past. Circumvention and innovation were, however, possible by experiment, and the eccentric in one generation might set precedent in another, or old Chinese precedents innovate on J. practice. All else failing, the few great innovators and exception-makers could intervene. Change in cl. and modern poetry alike also reflects engagement with, or revulsion from, valued foreign lits. (Chinese for cl., Western for modern).

The two major subjects of J. p. are nature and love. Nature has been treated in terms of the progression of seasonal phenomena, and progressively ordered so in collections. Love has been conceived of chiefly as longing, and at court involved taste more than physical beauty: lovers met in the dark. The erotic was expressed by images of wetness and women's tangled hair and symbolized by spring, dream, and color. These associations have endured. Male homosexual love became a frequent poetic topic, although not female until very recently. But a trad. of the passionate woman has endured from early times to Yosano Akiko (1878–1942). Nature tends to give assurance and love to agitate, particularly in linked poetry.

B. *History*.

Period	Genre
Oral to 13th c.	*Waka* (*chōka, tanka*)
13th–19th cs.	Linked poetry (*renga, haikai*)

J. lit. hist. is periodized, although as elsewhere the logic and terminology are inconsistent. Only two basic divisions distinguish what follows, with the second also divided in two. The dividing principle is the poetry which flourishes most, although genres of all kinds have continued to be practiced.

1. *Waka* Period. The last date assignable a *Man'yōshū* poem is A.D. 759; its first poem is assigned to Yūryaku (regnal dates unclear; he sent an embassy to China in 478). The *Kojiki* (ca. 712) may have some songs from the 3rd c. By the end of the 13th c., compilation rights for a royal collection are vested in descendants of Fujiwara Teika (1162–1241). The final four royal collections were compiled by royal order on request of the military aristocracy: power was dispersing as the nation fell into chaotic wars.

Even beyond the *waka* period proper, *waka* was associated with the divinities, with the monarchs who continued their line, and with all Japanese. *Yamatouta* is J. p. in a special sense: it is the sole literary art never on probation and from the outset the possession of all, including the illiterates.

The *Man'yōshū* selects from previous collections now otherwise lost. It includes poems from all levels of society, even a few attributed to animals. Its greatest achievement, reflecting a time over a century prior to 759, lies in the work of Kakinomoto Hitomaro (d. 708–15), a middling courtier, a kind of poet laureate, and one of the great J. poets. His occasional poems on royal affairs are public in the highest sense; his personal poems render the individual universal. Dynastic causes mingle with humane observation in his poems on the bloody Jinshin War (671), on the death of its hero Prince Takechi, and on the poet's visit to the ruined capital of the defeated rival. His poems on parting from, or mourning, wives are unforgettable. His masterpiece recounts seeing a dead man on a rocky shore after he himself has barely survived a typhoon. The world in which we die is divine—one of many kind ironies, as in the second envoy:

From open sea the waves
Break upon a rugged coast
  Become your bedding
For the pillow you have made,
And so, my lord, your rest is here.

"Become your bedding" renders a pillow-word (*makurakotoba*), an evocative fixed epithet of which Hitomaro is the unquestioned master.

His *chōka* show a skill in complex, alternating parallelism derived from Chinese practice. Otherwise he seems to ignore anything foreign. That is truer still of melodious Yamabe Akahito (fl. 724–37), who features greenery, hills, streams—whatever is "pure"—an unsullied world ignoring the suffering Hitomaro knew defined the goodness of life.

Yamano(u)e Okura (d. 785) visited China. Not surprisingly, Buddhism and even Confucianism enter *chōka* like his "Dialogue on Poverty." Emotional generalization, homely imagery, and broken syntax make his styles unmistakable. That syntax shows tellingly in the envoy to a poem mourning a son:

He is still too young
And cannot know the road to take.
  I will pay your fee.
Courier to the realms below—
Bear him there upon your back!

Ōtomo Yakamochi (d. 785) and his family are most fully represented in the collection. Perhaps the last compiler, Yakamochi sought out interesting poems from the remote and humble. His own show mastery of both poetic inheritance and new thought. He lacks the differing intensities of the other three, but his fluency and range exceed theirs.

The first of the early royal collections, the *Kokinshū* (905– 15), has poems credited to *Man'yōshū* poets, anonymous subsequent poets, and the more recent Six Poetic Sages dominated by Ariwara Narihira (825–80) and Ono no Komachi (fl. ca. 833–57), both legendary lovers. Narihira's conceptions seem to find words inadequate. Komachi's words defined her conceptions, as her famous use of pivot-words (*kakekotoba*) reveals in the double or triple meanings she infuses. The

single most famous *tanka* is his:

There is no moon!
Nor is this spring the spring that was
  In those days bygone!
I myself being the sole one
Remaining the thing it was. . . .

A paradoxical poem reflecting Buddhist transience, it was known so well by later poets that its words were thought too familiar to be used for allusion.

The compilers, particularly Ki no Tsyrayuki (882–945?), defined the *Kokinshū* ethos. His generation gave Japan its first poetic, its first poetic diary, its *art*. Accommodating Chinese wit to J. sensibility, he also accommodated poetry to painting, vastly enlarging its fictional scope while retaining fact. Precisely because technique (*sama*) was his standard, he most prized the human heart (*kokoro*) as conceiver, and purity of lang. (*kotoba*) as means. His greatness towers over any single achievement, and the collection he led still affects assumptions concerning poetry's relations to the rest of life.

The next six collections imitated, then innovated on, the *Kokinshū*. Izumi Shikibu (b. 976?) was the occasion, and probably the author, of an important poetic diary. Her position in poetry was unrivaled in her time, when women created the greatest J. lit. Intense, subjective, various, and difficult, her poetry is still not adequately comprehended. After her, most of the best poets are men who extended poetic understanding, leading to the eighth royal collection, the *Shinkokisnhū*, with the profoundest poetry of these centuries.

Poetic arbiter of the age, Fujiwara Shunzei (1114–1204) imparted depth by adapting Buddhist meditation to poetry. Priest Saigyō (1118–90), beloved in Japan, and the sensitive, intense Princess Shokushi (d. 1201) are excelled in the age only by Fujiwara Teika, Shunzei's brilliant, difficult son. Poetic fiction now required learning and intellectual effort to define feeling. Many chapters have been written on two of Teika's poems:

Looking out afar,
What need is there for cherry flowers
  Or colored autumn leaves?
Along the cove the humble huts
Yielding to the autumn dusk.

The brief spring night,
Its floating bridge of dreams
  Breaks all apart,
And from the peak there takes its leave
A cloudbank into open sky.

Teika's heirs disputed his legacies. One line offered subtle variations on the familiar, the two others new conceptions. Novelty lay in subjective manipulation through patterning, synaesthesia, and metamorphosis in seasonal poems often consisting entirely of images, in love poems without images, and in miscellaneous poems fusing the alternatives. These are represented in the 14th (*Gyokuyōshū*, 1313) and esp. the 17th (*Fūgashū*, 1349) of the 21 collections. The outstanding poets incl. the ambitious Kyōgoku Tamekane (Tamekanu, 1254–1332) and three royal figures: Fushimi (1265–1317), Eifuku Mon'in (1271–1342), and Hanazono (1297–1348). *Waka* and royalty were still associated, even after the age of *renga* had begun.

2. *Linked Poetry*. As politics turned toward chaos in the 13th c., linked poetry (*renga*, 13th–16th cs.) achieved greatness. Linked poetry employed as stanzas alternations of the *kami no ku* (upper-lines part) and *shimo no ku* (lower-lines part)—the 5–7–5 and the 7–7 syllable lines making up a *tanka*. Two or more poets usually took part in alternating composition according to elaborate rules and canons. *Renga* proper used elevated diction not unlike that of *waka*, and a 100-stanza length was most common. The nobleman Nijō Yoshimoto (1320–88) accorded *renga* premier status with a semi-royal collection, the *Tsukuba Shū* (1357). A *renga* boom had begun (even illiterates were composing it) which lasted through the 16th c. The *renga* masters knew *waka* thoroughly; Shinkei (1406–75) composed brilliantly in both kinds. Frequently difficult, Shinkei resembles in *renga* Teika in *waka*. But the peak of *renga* came with Sōgi, who made the whole sequence rather than stanzas the aim of poetry. Caught up in wars, he fled the capital and taught *renga*, receiving teaching in classics that raised him from unknown origins to an unrivaled height as lecturer and *renga* master. Inevitably he also collected *renga*. His solo of a hundred stanzas (1499) is thought the greatest *renga* sequence, but solo composition over four months is abnormal for *renga*, so that two trios—with the noble Shōhaku (1443–1527) and Sōchō (1448–1532), son of a smith—are always praised. Sōchō's performance in *The Hundred Stanzas at Minase* sometimes lags, but perfection was subsequently achieved in *The Hundred Stanzas at Yunoyama*.

As long as *renga* was composed at court, women participated. They did less when warcamps and temples were the sites. The last impressive *renga* master, Satomura Jōha (1524–1602), made *renga* into a house art taught to the military aristocracy. Ossification had begun.

The art of *renga* can be suggested by three stanzas from the Minase sequence. Shōhaku (76) and Sōchō (77) demonstrate *renga* connectedness. Master Sōgi (78) shows how to vary, imparting beauty to desolation:

(76)　Shrubs never cultivated by the owner
　　　　stand thick by the wattled door
(77)　in that vicinity
　　　the overgrown field by the hedgerow
　　　covers the neglected hoe

In that vicinity
the overgrown field by the hedgerow
covers the neglected hoe
(78)　the traveler returns dim in haze
　　　brought by twilight in light rain.

Haikai (*haikai renga*, 16th–19th cs.) brought a lower decorum, beginning in play with diction extended by the Sinified, the humble, and the otherwise unwakalike. Conceptions were also lower. The problem was to make this mixture fundamental to human experience. It is too easy to treat Matsunaga Teitoku (1572–1653) and Nishiyama Sōin (1605–80) as frivolous predecessors of grand Matsuo Bashō (1644–94), most loved of J. poets. Actually, Teitoku effected the transition from *renga* to *haikai*, and Sōin's Danrin school had survival value in its spirited practicality. Bashō's seriousness with the low and lighthearted made *haikai* the most difficult poetic art in cl. Japan. No wonder his oeuvre is small or that he turned to an easier style when late success required frequent composition. No wonder the glory of his school ended with him.

Japan's foremost poet-painter, Yosa (Taniguchi) Buson (1716–83), led the *Haikai* Revival. Bashō sometimes nods, Buson seemingly never. Yet the common judgment seems correct: Bashō risked more of self and art, achieving a human profundity not achieved by Buson's greater accuracy and beauty. Also, by Buson's time Bashō's sequential art yielded to brilliant stanzas (cf. Shinkei) and often to separate *hokku* very like *haiku*. Kobayashi Issa (1763–1827) made a virtue of this defect by interspersing stanzas in the prose of many poetic diaries. They are moving, if not the equal of Bashō's *Narrow Road Through the Provinces*.

Two quotations must suffice to show the precarious meaningfulness of *haikai*. In *Poetry Is What I Sell* (1682), Bashō is joined for a duo by the irrepressible Enomoto (Takarai) Kikaku (1661–1707), who composes the different-seeming stanzas 34 and 35. Bashō's conclusion (36) joins Kikaku's last in violating the rule of nonrecollection in linked poetry: they echo their first two stanzas (capitals designate J. treated as Chinese):

(34)　Horses may neigh at dawn like cocks
　　　　announcing freshly fallen snow
(35)　　poetry is what I sell
　　　flowers not my debts concern me
　　　so I drink all the time

　　　　Poetry is what we sell
　　　flowers not our debts concern us
　　　　so we drink all the time
(36)　as sun sets on THE SPRINGTIME LAKE
　　　AND PLEASURE HAS BROUGHT
　　　HOME OUR POEM.

A quite different, religious mood governs a passage in *At the Tub of Ashes*, a foursome. From Mukai Kyorai (1651–1704) (31) to Okada Yasui (1658–

1743) (32) to Bashō (33), the rise in tone is remarkable; so is the skillful shift by Nozawa Bonchō (d. 1714) (34):

(31) The strolling peddler
loudly calls his wares in shortened names
as he passes by
(32) no more than cover from a shower
is human life in ceaseless flux

No more than cover from a shower
is this world in ceaseless flux
(33)   sleeping at noon
the body of the blue heron
poised in·nobility

Sleeping at noon
the body of the blue heron
poised in nobility
(34) trickle trickle go the waters
where rushes sway in utter peace.

Bashō's heron, head under wing, asleep on one leg, is a figure of human enlightenment. A painterly counterpart by Buson is secular, not noticeably figurative of the human, but exact in its sequence of images:

The evening breeze
blows waters to the blue heron
whose legs are rippled.

All these quotations exemplify the opening sentence of Tsurayuki's preface to the *Kokinshū*: "The poetry of Japan takes the human heart as seed and flourishes in the countless leaves of words." E.M.

II. MODERN (AFTER 1868). Poetry since the Meiji Restoration has been dominated by three major forms:

(1) *tanka*, with the same pattern as in the cl. period, but no longer used as envoys;
(2) *haiku*, normally incl. a season word, originating in but distinct from *hokku* (first stanza of *haikai*); and
(3) *kindaishi* ("modern poetry"), particularly
(a) *shintaishi* (new-style poetry, typically consisting of 7+5 or 5+7 syllable lines and written in cl. J.) and
(b) *jiyūshi* (free-style poetry, evolved from *shintaishi* but without a fixed syllable scheme and usually written in modern J.).

Renga and *haikai* became virtually extinct in the late 19th c., surviving only among a small number of literati. *Senryū* has come to be viewed more as epigram or playful commentary than as poetry.

Like the rest of modern J. culture, poetry since 1868 has developed under the influence and stimulation of the West. It has had to respond not only to Western literary currents but to internal political and social changes caused by rapid modernization. To early modern poets, traditional verseforms seemed so outmoded that several poets, incl. Masaoka Shiki (1867–1902), went so far as to predict their total disappearance in the near future. *Shintaishi* emerged in response to the new need. Yet poets working in *tanka* and *haiku* did not give up; they endeavored to modernize those forms, and eventually succeeded in doing so.

Modernization of J. p. involved a number of innovations aimed at overcoming what early modern poets saw as the main weaknesses of cl. verse, such as brevity of form, lack of social awareness, and inability to embody sustained reasoning. One early Meiji scholar, after reading European poetry, observed: "Their poetry is closer to our prose fiction than to our poetry." The task of modern J. poets, then, was to bring poetry closer to prose, to a type of lit. flexible enough to reflect the ever-increasing complexity of modern civilization. Those who opted for *kindaishi* had little problem overcoming the deficiencies, but those who persisted in writing in premodern forms had a stiff challenge on their hands.

One scheme adopted by a number of modern *tanka* and *haiku* poets has been a method known as *rensaku* (sequential composition), in which the poet strings together two or more poems written on a common topic. The method is reminiscent of *renga* and *haikai*, except that it uses thematic rather than tonal qualities to attain structural unity and is composed by a single poet. Individual *tanka* or *haiku* grouped together would become like stanzas of a Western poem, showing progression of thought or feeling from one to the next within the group. A complex topic that cannot be done justice in a short form receives more adequate treatment by use of the *rensaku* technique. Even a topic that demands sustained thinking can be dealt with.

Other schemes devised to help overcome the brevity of traditional forms exploit visual qualities of the lang. Kawahigashi Hekigodō (1873–1937), for example, once tried what he called *ruby haiku*—haiku that has *furigana* (J. phonetic symbols, called "ruby" in typography) alongside Chinese ideograms. The poet would use unconventional *furigana*, so that added meaning would emerge from the surprising juxtaposition of J. syllabary and Chinese characters. Ishikawa Takuboku (1886–1912) had many of his later *tanka* printed in three lines, sometimes utilizing indentation for poetic effect:

My wife today
behaves like a woman unleashed.
I gaze at a dahlia.

The new typographical format shocked contemp. readers, because a *tanka*, though consisting of five syllabic units and often translated as a five-line poem, had always been printed in a single or run-on line in J. Similarly, J. readers had known of *haiku* as a one-line poem, but Takayanagi

Shigenobu (1923–83) began writing *haiku* like Western visual poetry:

> blooming
> flaming
> ash's
> swirling
> circle
> lone island's
> roses

Both poets observed the 31- and 17-syllable rules, but not the line conventions of the genres.

In another attempt to modernize traditional forms, some radical poets advocated "free-style *tanka*" and "free-style *haiku*." The basis of their argument is the same as in Western free verse (q.v.): the form of each poem should be determined by its unique subject matter, not by predetermined prosody. In effect, their work was short free verse, yet they insisted it was *tanka* or *haiku* on the basis of nonformal elements. For instance, Ogiwara Seisensui (1884–1976), leader of the freestyle *haiku* movement, argued that even though his poems did not follow the 5+7+5 syllable pattern they should be considered *haiku* because their subject matter was confined to nature and their structure concentric rather than linear. Such arguments did not convince many fellow poets, however, who believed that any poem that refused conventional prosody was free verse. Although free-style *haiku* gained wider support than its counterpart in *tanka*, both declined in popularity with time and all but disappeared in the second half of the 20th c. In his last years, Seisensui himself began calling his poems free verse.

Incorporating social awareness into *tanka* and *haiku* proved an easier challenge. Already in the 19th c. Shiki had shown a strong dislike for the confinements of cl. aesthetics and advocated enlargements of theme, tone, and imagery. Later poets, esp. those who came under the influence of Western naturalism, positively sought to draw on plebeian life. This trend reached a peak with proletarian *tanka* and *haiku* in the 1920s and '30s. The following 31-syllable poem by Ōkuma Nobuyuki (1893–1977) on the subject of J. Labor Day is typical:

> Amidst the dust
> Rising from the earth,
>   A red flag—
> The sight in my memory
> Forever unblottable.

Efforts to link poetry to social issues went to the other ideological extreme during World War II, when many poets wrote *tanka* with ultranationalistic overtones. After the war, leftwing poetry became popular again, but this time poets were more careful not to let their political beliefs impinge on the artistic autonomy of their work. Also, the social upheaval of the postwar period wrought changes on readers' sensibilities, so that they no longer expected contemp. *tanka* and *haiku* to have *aware*, *sabi*, or other such traditional tones. Using the 31- or 17-syllable forms, today's poets can treat most political, social, or intellectual issues without appearing experimental or avant-garde.

All such problems that plagued *tanka* and *haiku* poets were largely unknown to those who chose to write *kindaishi*, for their verseform had all the flexibility of the Western poetry it was modeled on. Their major challenge lay in finding a way to naturalize the alien form, which had centuries of cultural trad. behind it. Esp. troublesome was the problem of lang.: Western poetry fully exploited the various musical qualities of lang., whereas modern J., mingling native and Sinified words, seemed a lang. woefully lacking in music. Devoid of accent, meter was nonexistent in J.; alliteration and rhyme were not effective poetic devices because they abounded in ordinary usage. The only usable scheme was the syllable pattern, so early poets wrote *shintaishi* in 5+7 or 7+5 syllable lines; yet repetition of such lines brought monotony in long poems. Hagiwara Sakutarō (1886–1942), who tried harder to solve the problem than most other poets, believed that the only solution would be to mix 5+7, 6+4, 8+5 and other syllable patterns in a single poem, which would be the same as writing a poem in prose. "In J.," he concluded, "the more prosaic the lang. is, the closer it approaches to verse."

Later *kindaishi* poets tried to exploit the visual features of the lang. and thereby compensate for the lack of musical quality in their work. They skillfully combined letters from the three different scripts available in their lang.: angular and seemingly artless *katakana*, cursive and graceful *hiragana*, and ideogrammic and dignified *kanji*. They would make use of *furigana* in the same way Hekigodō did in *ruby haiku*. Going beyond visual effects, they arranged words, images, and ideas in such a way as to create an "emotive rhythm," a rhythm which is more sensory than phonetic. To cite a short example, a *jiyūshi* entitled "Horse" by Kitagawa Fuyuhiko (b. 1900) consists of just one line: "It has a naval port in its intestines." This prose sentence creates no noticeable musical rhythm. Its emotional impact, however, arising almost entirely from the interplay of images and associations, is similar to that of a surrealist painting. And, in general, *jiyūshi* has become more imagistic than traditional Western poetry.

Another way in which *kindaishi* attempted to compensate for lack of inherent musical quality was by bringing in vocal and instrumental music in performance. Recordings by several early poets show that in reading *kindaishi* they sang out with a certain melody, somewhat in the manner in which *tanka* poets recite before an audience. It was as if these poets did not feel *kindaishi* would sound poetic enough when recited with the intonation of ordinary speech. Later, some famous *kindaishi* were transformed into songs by professional composers, who wrote special melodies for them. "Moon over the Ruined Castle" by Tsuchii Bansui (1871–1952) and "Coconut" by Shimazaki Tōson (1872–1943) are two notable examples. In a sense, this practice was an extension of the cl. cultural practice that had produced many instances of happy union between lit. and music. It has continued to the present day, and provides a good opportunity for the general public to come into contact with *kindaishi*.

Despite different problems confronting *tanka*, *haiku*, and *kindaishi*, the history of modern J. p. shows that in each of its phases there was a centripetal force bringing together a large number of poets regardless of the verseform in which they specialized. The earliest phase, extending to the first few years of the 20th c., was one of romanticism (q.v.), during which time many poets worked under the influence of European romantic writers. The promoter of the movement, Kitamura Tōkoku (1868–94), wrote two long *shintaishi* inspired by Byron's *The Prisoner of Chillon* and *Manfred*, but the full potential of the new form was not revealed until Shimazaki Tōson published a collection of short lyrics called *Young Herbs* in 1897. Tōson's two predominant themes were romantic love and the anxiety of youth, and he expressed them in a delicate, exquisitely beautiful lang. that was to become a model. The theme of romantic love also found eloquent expression in the *tanka* of Yosano Akiko (1878–1942), whose *Tangled Hair* (1901) shocked contemp. readers by its bold affirmation of female sexuality. For *haiku*, Shiki published an essay called "Buson the Haiku Poet" (1897), giving lavish praise to Buson's poetry for its bright, fanciful, sometimes startling beauty.

Romanticism was succeeded by J. symbolism (q.v.), most notably in *kindaishi*, after *The Sound of the Tide* was pub. in 1905 by Ueda Bin (1874–1916). This book of translations introducing the works of many Fr. symbolists made a great impact on the J. poetic scene, inspiring a new movement led by Susukida Kyūkin (1877–1945) and Kanbara Ariake (1876–1952). One reason why such difficult European poetry appealed to J. poets lay in its emphasis on the idea of "correspondence" (cf. Baudelaire), which was common in cl. J. verse. The symbolist movement reached a peak with Kitahara Hakushū (1885–1942), who, with his decadently modern sensibility and colorfully rich vocabulary, created in J. a type of poetry reminiscent of European *fin-de-siècle* lit.

Haiku poets were the least attracted to romanticism or symbolism during these years, mainly because their leader Shiki advocated in his later years the principle of *shasei* (sketch from life). This principle was advanced further by his two leading disciples, Takahama Kyoshi (1874–1959) and Hekigodō, esp. as naturalistic realism became a dominant force in J. fiction shortly after the turn of the century. Some major *tanka* poets, such as Itō Sachio (1864–1913) and Nagatsuka Takashi

(1879–1915), came under the spell, too, and wrote 31-syllable poems that purported to copy life objectively. Others, like Maeda Yūgure (1883–1951) and Takuboku, focused on copying plebeian life in their *tanka*, thereby paving the way for proletarian poetry. Principles of modern European realism also attracted some *kindaishi* poets, notably Kawaji Ryūkō (1888–1959), who published a collection of naturalistic poems entitled *Flowers on the Roadside* in 1910.

J. p. entered a new stage of maturity when its writers became more fully awakened to their modern identity. Western neo-humanism (q.v.) had begun to permeate the depths of J. consciousness in the early years of the 20th c., and poets gradually came to seek out their inner selves, trying to give them poetic expression. Of several major poets who did this, Takamura Kōtarō (1883–1956) was the most intensely ethical. In his first book of *kindaishi*, *The Journey* (1914), he powerfully asserted the potential of humanity and pleaded for elevating it to its highest level by rigorous disciplining of the self. A similar longing for exalted life pervades the *tanka* collected in *Red Light* (1913) by Saitō Mokichi (1882–1953), but life as conceived by him seems more primordial and biological, presuming a powerful force flowing in the depths of all living things. In sharp contrast, the self as seen by Hagiwara Sakutarō is lonely, ailing, and anxiety-ridden. His first book of *kindaishi* was called *Howling at the Moon* (1917), the title suggesting spiritually starved modernists forever longing for unreachable ideals. The celebration of the self did not touch *haiku* until later, possibly because the form traditionally focused on depicting external nature rather than expressing the inner self. The publication of *Katsushika* in 1930, a collection of *haiku* by Mizuhara Shūōshi (1892–1981), belatedly announced the arrival of the age of individualism in that verseform.

The 1920s and '30s saw a number of new Western ideas flowing into Japan and inducing poets to respond in varying ways. The most pervasive of such ideas was Marxism; however, except for the *jiyūshi* of Nakano Shigeharu (1902–79), few poems written by Marxist sympathizers have stood the test of time. More productive was interaction between other European movements and young *kindaishi* poets, such as between dada (q.v.) and Takahashi Shinkichi (1901–87); between surrealism (q.v.) and Nishiwaki Junzaburō (1894–1982); between imagism (q.v.) and Murano Shirō (1901–75); and between modernism and Kitazono Katsue (1902–78), Anzai Fuyue (1898–1965), and others. The only major poet largely free of Western influence during this period was Miyazawa Kenji (1896–1933), who turned to Buddhism and agrarianism for inspiration. Although imported ideas had less impact on poets writing in traditional forms, they still spurred the emergence of such short-lived movements as "proletarian *tanka*" and "modernist *haiku*."

After the barren years of the War, J. p. made a fresh start and, with the nation's rapid economic recovery, in time attained a new height of prosperity. Poets who established themselves in the postwar years can be classified in two categories. One was a school that stressed the social significance of poetry. Its founders were Ayukawa Nobuo (1920–86), Tamura Ryūichi (b. 1923), and other *jiyūshi* poets who in 1947 started a poetry magazine called *The Waste Land* with the aim of "discovering a ray of light in the dark empirical awareness and hopeless realization that we live in a waste land." They were joined by leftwing poets like Kaneko Mitsuharu (1895–1975), Sekine Hiroshi (b. 1920), and others, who tried to discover in the energy of the masses a hope for reclaiming the "waste land." Their poetry, unlike that of prewar proletarian poets, appealed to a wide audience because it was artistically more satisfying. *Tanka* by Kondō Yoshimi (b. 1913) and *haiku* by Kaneko Tōta (b. 1919), among many others, also showed awareness of contemp. social issues to an unprecedented degree, freely treating such topics as atomic bombing, the Tokyo Trial, and the U.S.-Japan Mutual Security Treaty.

The other school of postwar poets emphasized the importance of more universal issues. It was sometimes called the "art school" because of its high regard for the artistic perfection of the poem. Among its earliest promoters were Nakamura Shin'ichirō (b. 1918), Katō Shūichi (b. 1919), and other *kindaishi* poets, who in 1948 initiated the "matinée poétique" movement to introduce modern Fr. poetics to J. p. Although Nakamura and Katō soon stopped writing poetry, and the movement itself was short-lived, poetry concerned with basic human nature gained support when younger poets with no direct war experience began writing in the 1950s and '60s. Most prominent among these are Tanikawa Shuntarō (b. 1931) and Ōoka Makoto (b. 1931), who write meditative lyrics of serene intellect and restrained diction. Tanikawa is the first poet who has successfully transplanted the sonnet (q.v.) form into J. p. He and his associates have also been active as literary and social critics; their activities extend far beyond the conventional role of the poet.

What is known as "the poetry boom" arrived in the late 1960s. Perhaps the general anti-establishment attitude of the younger generation during that decade stirred interest in poetry, a medium that otherwise seemed to be becoming obsolete. Another factor may have been the ready availability of washing machines and other household appliances which freed women from many daily chores and gave them time to read and write. For whatever reason, numerous books of poetry by both old masters and new experimenters appeared. As the nation's affluence continues, "little magazines" publishing poetry have proliferated, as have books of poetry that are privately published. Poetry no longer enjoys the kind of high social prestige it once did, but it continues to fulfill its social and personal functions in Japan. See JAPANESE POETICS. M.U.

BIBLIOGRAPHIES: *The P.E.N. Club News* (1958–71); Japan P.E.N. Club, *J. Lit. in European Langs.* (1961); *Kokubungaku Kenkyū Bunken Mokuroku* [Bibliographical Materials for the Study of J. Lit.] (1971–76); J. T. Rimer and R. E. Morrell, *Guide to J. P.* (1975); *J. Lit. Today* (1976–); Internat. House of J. Library, *Mod. J. Lit. in Tr.* (1979); *Kokubungaku Nenkan* [J. Lit. Annual] (1977–); *JASt*—annual bibl.

ANTHOLOGIES AND TRANSLATIONS: Nishiyama Sōin, *Sōin Toppyaku Koi no Haikai* (1671)—J. p. on heterosexual and male homosexual love; Yosano Akiko, *Midaregami* (1904)—daring love poetry; *The Man'yōshū, 1000 Poems* (1940); R. H. Blyth, *Senryū, J. Satirical Verses* (1950), *Edo Satirical Verse Anthols.* (1961); J. Konishi, *Haiku: Hassei Yori Gendai Made* [*Haiku*: From Its Origins to the Present] (1952); T. Ninomiya and D. J. Enright, *The P. of Living J.* (1957); *Nihon Koten Bungaku Taikei* [The Great Compendium of Cl. J. Lit.], ed. I. Takagi et al., 101 v. (1957–68); K. Yamamoto, *Nihon Shiikashū* [Anthol. of J. P.] (1959); *Nihon no Shiika* [J. P.], ed. S. Itō et al., 31 v. (1967–70); H. C. McCullough, *Tales of Ise* (1968), *Kokin Wakashū* (1985), *Brocade by Night* (1985); *Nihon Koten Bungaku Zenshū* [A Full Collection of J. Lit.], 51 v. (1970–76); H. Kijima, *The P. of Postwar J.* (1975); M. Ueda, *Mod. J. Haiku* (1976); J. Kirkup, *Mod. J. P.* (1978); E. Miner, *J. Linked P.* (1979); E. Miner and H. Odagiri, *The Monkey's Straw Raincoat and Other Poetry of the Bashō School* (1981); H. Sato and B. Watson, *From the Country of Eight Islands* (1981); *The Ten Thousand Leaves*, tr. I. Levy, v. 1, *Man'yōshū*, 1–5 (1981); *Shimpen Kokka Taikan* [Newly Edited Great Canon of J. P.], 3 v. in 6 (1983–85); *Kyōka Taikan* [The Great Canon of Mad Waka], 3 v. (1983–85); L. R. Rodd, *Kokinshuū* (1984); *Waiting for the Wind: 36 Poets of Japan's Late Medieval Age* (1989), *Traditional J. P.*, tr. and ed. S. D. Carter (1991).

HISTORY AND CRITICISM: *Kindai Tankashi* [A Hist. of Mod. Tanka], ed. U. Kubota et al., 3 v. (1958); J. Konishi, "Association and Progression," *HJAS* 21 (1958), *Sōgi* (1971), *A Hist. of J. Lit.*, 5 v. (1984–), with J. version, *Nihon Bungeishi* (1985–); R. H. Brower and E. Miner, *J. Court P.* (1961), *Fujiwara Teika's Superior Poems of Our Time* (1967); K. Yamamoto, *Gendai Haiku* [Mod. Haiku] (1964); *Kōza Nihon Gendaishi Shi* [Lectures on the Hist. of Mod. J. P.], ed. S. Murano et al., 4 v. (1973); D. Keene, *World Within Walls* (1976), *Dawn to the West*, 2 v. (1984); M. Ueda, *Mod. J. Poets and the Nature of Lit.* (1983); S. Yamada, spec. iss. of *Koku Bungaku Kaishaku to Kanshō* (1983)—on erotic writing and art; Miner et al., esp. parts 1, 6A, F, J, K, 7H, 8K. E.M.; M.U.

JARCHA. See SPANISH POETRY.

JAVANESE POETRY

JAVANESE POETRY.

    I. A.D. 732–928
   II. A.D. 929–1527
  III. CA. A.D. 1500–1625
  IV. CA. A.D. 1578–1940

J. p. was in the beginning closely linked to religion and politics. In the Hindu-J. period, poets were members of the Brahman caste or Buddhist clergy, working either as priests and teachers in the service of the monarch or in monasteries patronized by the court.

I. A.D 732–928: the dynasty of Mĕḍang in South Central Java. Period I is dominated by Śivaite and Buddhist rulers, presumably of mixed Indian and J. blood. *Kakawin* lit. originates in this period. A *kakawin* is a sizable epic poem in Old J. composed in the metrical rules of the Indian *mahākāvya* and mostly dealing with topics borrowed from Indian mythology. The oldest dated poetry in Old J. idiom and in Indian meters is preserved in a stone inscription of 29 stanzas dated A.D 856. The oldest and largest complete poem is the *Rāmāyaṇa-kakawin*, comprising 2783 stanzas in 81 different meters and also believed to date from the 9th c. The author must have known by heart Bhaṭṭi's *kāvya Rāvaṇa-vadha*, which treats the same theme but is meant as a textbook of grammar and *alaṃkāra*.

J. art in this period adheres strictly to Indian rules. This also applies to *kakawin* prosody. In principle the *kakawin* stanza is built up of four lines of similar length and showing the same pattern of long and short syllables. Thus the metric formula of the popular Old J. meter *śārdūla-vikrīḍita*, for example, is as follows:

– – – | ᴗ ᴗ – | ᴗ – ᴗ | ᴗ ᴗ – | – – ᴗ | – – ᴗ | ᴗ

Although in J. phonology vowel-length is not phonemic, the aesthetic effect of *kakawin* poetry must have been very distinctive, the text being sung, each meter to its own melody. Poetry in Java was from its inception something to be sung before an audience, not read in private.

II. A.D. 929–1527: the dynasties of Kĕḍiri, Singhasari, and Majapahit in East Java. In period II a strong tendency toward "Javanization" occurred in the plastic arts and in lit. Around A.D. 1000, the great Indian epics together with some Purāṇa's and other religious texts were translated into Old J. prose, and an efflorescence of *kakawin* lit. followed. *Kakawins* were composed for royal marriages, victories in war, and funeral rites. The authors most often used existing Indian themes but transformed them into J. stories, changing the plots radically to fit the needs of the moment and to suit the tastes of their highly placed patrons. The *Nāgarakṛtāgama* by Prapanca, a panegyric in praise of King Hayam Wuruk which contains a description of Majapahit in its heyday, is an exception, however.

Old J. must have become a dead lang., used only for literary purposes, by the end of the 13th c. if not earlier. It is not surprising therefore that the Majapahit era (1294–1527) witnessed the emergence of a new poetic trad., the *kidung* lit. A *kidung* is a sizable epic poem in Middle J., composed in indigenous meters and treating indigenous themes. Most frequently the *kidungs* contain a *ruwat* story or deal with local historical trad. or a variant of the *Panji* theme. *Ruwat* stories relate how a person or group was once freed of a curse or safeguarded against evil. They are sung or performed on the *wayang* (shadow theater) stage as part of a conjuration ceremony. *Panji* stories relate how a prince of Koripan, who is an incarnation of Vishṇu, is united after many vicissitudes with his niece, a princess of Daha (Kĕḍiri) who, being an incarnation of Śrī, was predestined to become his bride.

Kidungs ("songs") are, just as *kakawins*, sung to an audience, though on different occasions, and are composed in *tengahan* or *macapat* meters. A stanza consists of a fixed number of lines (different for each meter) of mutually different but otherwise fixed length, each ending in a certain vowel. Thus the structure of the *tengahan* meter *wukir* can be summarized in the following formula: 10–u, 6–e, 8–i, 7–u, 8–u, 8–e, 8–u, 8–a, 8–a; which means that a stanza consists of 9 lines, the first of which has 10 syllables with *u* in the final one, etc. After the downfall of the Majapahit empire in 1527, the poetic trads. in Old and Middle J. were perpetuated on the island of Bali.

III. CA. A.D. 1500–1625: the petty kingdoms on the North Coast (Pasisir). Important cultural changes occurred in Java's third period. In the prosperous cities along the North coast, a new Islamic elite had sprung up, speaking an early form of Modern J. and interested in the Arab and Indo-Persian stories that came to Java with the Qur'anic trad. The *wayang* remained popular, serving to perpetuate the Indian epic trad. Out of the *kidung* trad., new forms of poetry evolved, using the Modern J. idiom, treating new topics, and exhibiting an outspoken preference for *macapat* meters which, though technically obedient to the same rules of prosody as the older *tengahan* meters, were used in such a way that each meter with its specific melody was supposed to suggest the particular atmosphere prevailing in the canto. Included in this Modern J. p. are J. stories on topics borrowed from the international Islamic trad., original didactic poems on tenets of Islamic faith, often concerning questions of orthodox or heterodox mysticism (the *suluk* lit.), adaptations of older stories from the pre-Islamic period, wanderer stories, and compilations called *serat kanṇḍa* in which the cycles of tales forming the repertoire of the shadow theater were brought together.

IV. CA. A.D. 1578–1945: the dynasty of Mataram in South Central Java. In period IV, poetry once again became "court poetry." The new genres generated during the Pasisir period were refined. In addition, a new genre became important: the

- [666] -

chronicle (*babad*). A modern type of *Panji* story was developed. A renewed interest in the cl. heritage led to the creation of Modern J. versions of the most important *kakawins*. New epic poems, some of them hundreds of pages long, were created, along with many shorter didactic-moralistic poems. The court poets played an important role, and even members of the royal house took an active part in poetry writing.

After Indonesian Independence in 1945, traditional J. p. ends. Western genres written in modern idiom and dealing with modern topics, such as the novel, the short story, free verse, and modern forms of the drama, all of which have developed since 1900, now hold the field.

HISTORY AND CRITICISM: E. M. Uhlenbeck, *A Crit. Survey of Studies on the Langs. of Java and Madura* (1964); C. Holt, *Art in Indonesia, Continuities and Change* (1967); T. Pigeaud, *Lit. of Java: Mss. in the Library of the Univ. of Leiden*, 4 v. (1967–80); P. J. Zoetmulder, *Kalangwan: A Survey of Old J. Lit.* (1974).   J.J.R.

JAZZ POETRY. See MUSIC AND POETRY.

JE NE SAIS QUOI ("I know not what"). A term of aesthetic response in 17th- and early 18th-c. France closely related to charm, taste (q.v.), and (to some extent) the sublime (q.v.). As the phrase implies, j. n. s. q. indicates the failure of lang., rational discourse, or any critical system to capture the totality of aesthetic perception. In contrast to the (neo)classical conventions of objectivity in art, the j. n. s. q. asserts an ineffable residuum of personal response—personal, certainly, but not idiosyncratic, since it supposes a community of readers with good taste and shared standards. The j. n. s. q. is posited beyond formal and generic rules as a certain quality, a particular combination of formal aspects, or a relationship between form and content which can only be sensed, not defined or articulated. The very evasiveness inherent in the term led to abuse, affectation, and ridicule (Molière, *Les Femmes savantes* 3.3).

The Lat. *nescio quid* (Augustine), It. *non so che* (Dante, Ariosto, Tasso), and Sp. *no sé qué* (Juan de la Cruz, Gracián) were generally disparate, and applied to Neoplatonic love or metaphysics. The concept entered France in this context (Corneille, *Rodogune* 1.4; Pascal, *Pensées* 162) but developed as a critical term (Ogier, *Apol. Balzac*, 1628; Mairet, *Préface à Silvanire*, 1631). It received greatest examination in the fifth conversation of Abbé Bouhour's *Entretiens d'Ariste et d'Eugène* (1671). Rapin compared it to poetic rhythm (*Réflexions*, 1674) and Marivaux equated it with voice (*Cab. du phil.*, 1734). The Fr. term entered Eng. (Blount, 1671) and appears in Congreve (*Double Dealer*, 1694) and Shaftesbury (*Characteristicks*, 1711). Cf. Pope's "grace beyond the reach of art." Montesquieu (*Essai sur le goût*) and Feijóo (*El no sé qué*) also analyzed it in the 18th c., but since then the

j. n. s. q. has not been a vital concept in lit. crit. Jankelevitch has explored the concept in his phenomenological investigations. See BAROQUE POETICS.—E. B. O. Borgerhoff, *Freedom of Fr. Classicism* (1950); E. Haase, "Zur Bedeutung von 'J. n. s. q.' im 17. Jh.," *ZFSL* 67 (1956); Saisselin; E. Köhler, *Esprit und Arkadische Freiheit* (1972); F. Schalk, "Nochmals zum 'j. n. s. q.,'" *RF* 86 (1974); V. Jankelevitch, *Le j. n. s. q. et le presque-rien* (1980); L. Marin, "Le Sublime dans les années 1670: Un J. n. s. q.?" *Actes de Baton Rouge* (1986).   A.G.W.

JINGLE (ME *gyngle*). Any verse which pleases the ear by its catchy rhythm and by pronounced sound repetition (q.v.), e.g. rhyme or alliteration (qq.v.), often at the expense of sense. *Eeny meeny miny mo* and *Hickory dickory dock* are js. Because they are easily memorized and repeated, js. are often as enduring as the loftiest poetry, though in a different register. Mark Twain in "Punch, Brothers, Punch" (*Tom Sawyer Abroad*) humorously describes his "catching" and passing on a contagious newspaper j. Modern advertising js.—usually one phrase or sentence, heavily formulaic if not close rhymed (q.v.), and set to a single melodic phrase—use the same devices of repetition for the same mnemonic end. Since the 16th c., the term has also been applied depreciatively to any poetry which makes pronounced use of sound effects. Addison (*Spectator* no. 297) criticizes Milton for often affecting "a kind of J. in his Words" in *Paradise Lost*, but Milton himself in the note on "The Verse" prefixed to *PL* had referred to rhyme scornfully as the "jingling sound of like endings." This catches, in its sense of "mingled metallic sounds" (e.g. bells, coins), very precisely the structural conditions of rhyme and the tinny effect of excessive alliteration.—*Oxford Book of Nursery Rhymes*, ed. I. and P. Opie (1951).   L.P.; T.V.F.B.

JOC PARTIT. See PARTIMEN.

JONGLEUR (Fr. *jongleur*, Occitan and Catalan *joglar*, Sp. *juglar*, Port. *jogral*, It. *giullare*). A medieval minstrel (q.v.) in France, Spain, or Italy. Although the word dates only from the 8th c., js. seem to have existed in France from the 5th c. to the 15th. In the earlier period the name was applied indiscriminately to acrobats, actors, and entertainers in general, as well as to musicians and reciters of verse. From the 10th c. on, however, the term is confined to musicians and reciters of verse, evidencing the importance of the distinction between the composer and the performer of verse. Cf. the OE *scop*, the ON *skald*, and the Celtic *bard* (qq.v.).

The Occitan *joglar* performed lyrics composed by a troubadour (q.v.) whom he served as a singing messenger, perhaps accompanying himself with an instrument or alternating song with instrumental performance. The troubadour might name the j. in the *tornada* (q.v.), with instructions to take the song to an addressee who could be expected to reward him for it. Thus a given song was usually entrusted to one j., but the troubadour might commission several js. with different songs during his career, occasionally revising a given song for a second performer. During the 12th and 13th c. the frequency of such mentions of js. declined steadily, suggesting that oral diffusion was being gradually replaced by written transmission.

The OF j. performed not only the lyrics of the *trouvères* (q.v.), but also *chansons de geste* (q.v.), medieval romances (q.v.), saints' lives, and other narratives. The *chansons de geste* were originally performed to a simple melody, and according to the oral-formulaic theory (q.v.) were composed in performance by a technique similar to that of the 20th-c. illiterate Yugoslavian *guslar* (q.v.; see Lord, Duggan); but other scholars maintain that the js. read the *chansons de geste* from a book even in the earliest times, as they certainly did later on, and as they must have normally read romances and hagiographic texts.—E. Faral, *Les Js. en France au moyen âge* (1910); Jeanroy; R. Morgan, "OF Jogleor and Kindred Terms," *RPh* 7 (1954); R. Menéndez Pidal, *Poesia juglaresca y origines de las literaturas románicas* (1957); Lord; J. Duggan, *The Song of Roland* (1973); W. A. Quinn and A. S. Hall, *J.: A Modified Theory of Oral Improvisation* (1982); W. D. Paden, "The Role of the Joglar," *Chrétien de Troyes and the Troubadours*, ed. P. S. Noble and L. M. Paterson (1984). W.D.P.

JUDEO-SPANISH POETRY is that poetry sung, recited, or written in the Judeo-Sp. (Judezmo, Ladino) dialect, in the various post-diasporic sanctuaries of the Sephardic Jews—North Africa (Morocco, Algeria) and the Eastern Mediterranean (the Balkans, Greece, Turkey, Israel)—after their exile from Spain in 1492. By contrast, in Western European centers such as Amsterdam, Bayonne, and Leghorn, there were Jewish authors who did not write in the Judeo-Sp. dialect but continued to form part of the Hispanic (Sp. or Port.) literary trads. (see HEBREW POETRY; SPANISH POETRY). Judeo-Sp. p. can be organized into the following generic categories: *complas* (popular religious or didactic songs), *cantigas* (q.v., lyric songs), *romansas* (traditional ballads), *endevinas* (riddles), and *refranes* (q.v., proverbs). *Complas* can be considered essentially written lit.; the other genres are oral. Following World War II, a special sub-genre of Sephardic poetry, written in Judeo-Sp. and in Fr., commemorated the tragic events of the Holocaust.

Complas (Sp. *coplas*, q.v.) are strophic poems usually of paraliturgical content, by both known and anonymous authors, and are the most characteristic Sephardic genre. Typically they are sung and often are acrostic (q.v.) poems presenting the letters of the Hebrew alphabet or of the author's name. Since they are essentially part of a written trad., they are generally sung by men, unlike the *romansas*, which are usually performed by women. Among the most traditional *complas* are those for the festivity of Purim, composed in the 18th and 19th cs., that relate the biblical story of Esther or evoke the joys of the holiday in strophes of varying lengths, with short or long verses in zejelesque rhyme (*aaab*), often incl. a refrain. Other *complas* celebrate the festivities of Hanukkah, Passover, Pentecost, the Sabbath, the Rejoicing of the Torah, and Arbor Day. There are also dirgelike *complas* (*Quinot*) that commemorate the destruction of the Temple (70 A.D.) and other tragic events in ancient Jewish history. Other *complas* of a moralizing, admonitory bent (*complas de castiguerio*) preach the glories of God and warn against the illusory nature of worldly attractions. *Complas del felek* ("destiny") present the life and customs of late 19th- and early 20th-c. Sephardic Jewry from a satirical or humorous perspective. In *complas de Tebariá* are celebrated the praises of the city of Tiberias, of venerable sages who lived there, and of miracles concerning its Jewish population. M. Attias has published another group of poems, *Complas de 'Aliyá* ("Songs of Return to Zion"), which give voice to the Jews' longing for redemption and return to Jerusalem in all its glory. Those *complas* by Abraham Toledo, devoted to the life of Joseph and first published in 1732—part of a subgenre designated as *complas hagiográficas*—constitute for I. M. Hassán perhaps the single greatest poem in Judeo-Sp. In reworking the biblical account of Joseph's life (Genesis 37, 39–45), Toledo used numerous elements from folklore, rabbinical commentaries, and traditional life, presented with lyrical verve, lexical versatility, and rhetorical strength. In comparison with such genres as ballads and proverbs, which have strong Hispanic connections, the study of *complas* has, until recently, been gravely neglected.

Cantigas are traditional lyric songs, frequently of Hispanic origin in form and content, but, in the Eastern trad., with significant Gr. and Turkish lexical, structural, and thematic influences. Although love in all its vicissitudes is the predominant theme, there are also lyric songs devoted to various functions in the traditional life cycle: *cantigas de boda* (wedding songs), *de parida* (birth songs), and *endechas* (dirges). Many Sephardic lyric songs, esp. in the Eastern communities, are of relatively recent origin (late 19th and early 20th c.) and often consist of quatrains in couplets with assonance; some are modeled on Gr. originals and others even imported on phonograph records from Spain or Sp. America. But other lyric songs attest to a venerable Sephardic trad. going back to medieval Hispanic origins. The parallelistic rhymes of some Eastern poems and of many Moroccan wedding songs—similar to that of the primitive Sp. and Port. lyric—confirm the medieval character of the Judeo-Sp. *cantiga* trad.

Romansas (Sp. *romances*, q.v.) are traditional ballads in assonating octosyllabic verse. In content they are essentially similar—in some cases, genetically related—to narrative poetry current in other European communities. No other Sephardic genre is so closely linked to its medieval Hispanic origins, and none has received as much scholarly attention. Judeo-Sp. ballads can be documented from as early as 1525 through verses used as tune indicators in Heb. hymnals. Several 18th-c. mss. are known, and numerous Eastern ballads were collected and printed in popular Heb.-letter chapbooks in the late 19th and early 20th c. There are Sephardic ballads derived from medieval Sp. and Fr. epics; others concern events in Sp. and Port. hist. or tell stories from the Bible, Cl. antiquity, or medieval romances; still others concern a variety of topoi (prisoners and captives, the husband's return, faithful or tragic love, the unfortunate wife, the adulteress, amorous adventures, tricks and deceptions). Some ballads function as wedding songs, others as dirges, still others as lullabies. Though a majority of Sephardic ballads have med. or 16th-c. Sp. counterparts, others can be shown to derive from modern Gr. narrative poetry; some were undoubtedly created in the exile communities by the Sephardim themselves. P. Bénichou's studies of oral trad. as a creative artistic process are essential to ballad crit.

Endevinas (riddles) are often rhymed and, like proverbs, should count as a part of Sephardic traditional poetry. Of all genres, the riddle (q.v.) has been the most gravely neglected by scholarship. Little fieldwork has been done to collect riddles, and the known Eastern repertoire is still radically limited. Nothing is presently known of the Moroccan Sephardic riddle trad. As far as origins are concerned, a preliminary assessment indicates that Eastern Judeo-Sp. riddles are about evenly divided between texts of medieval Hispanic origin and adaptations from Turkish and Gr. However, in many cases it is impossible to point to a specific origin.

Refranes (proverbs) have been abundantly collected in Heb.-letter chapbooks since the late 19th c. by the Sephardim themselves and also by Western scholars. Some Sephardic proverbs agree exactly with their Sp. counterparts, while others have obviously been taken over from Gr., Turkish, or biblical Heb. sources.

M. Attias, "Shelôshah shîrê Tsîyôn," *Shevet va-'Am* 4 (1959), *Cancionero* (1972); P. Bénichou, *Creación poética* (1968); M. Alvar, *Endechas* (1969), *Cantos de boda* (1971); S. G. Armistead and J. H. Silverman, *Folk Lit.* (1971–86), "El antiguo romancero," *NRFH* 30 (1981), *En torno al romancero* (1982), "Adivinanzas," *Philologica M. Alvar* (1983); E. Romero, "Complas de Tu-Bishbat," *Poesía: Reunión de Málaga*, ed. M. Alvar (1976), "Las coplas sefardíes," *Jornadas*, ed. A. Viudas Camarasa (1981); L. Carracedo and E. Romero, "Poesía admonitiva," *Sefarad* 37 (1977), "Refranes," *Sefarad* 41 (1981); S. G. Armistead et al., *El romancero en el Archivo Menéndez Pidal* (1978); I. Hassán and E.

Romero, "Quinot paralitúrgicos," *Estudios Sefardíes* 1 (1978); P. Díaz-Mas, "Romances de endechar," *Jornadas*, ed. A. Viudas Camarasa (1981); I. Hassán, "Visión panorámica," *Hispania Judaica*, ed. J. M. Solà-Solé (1982); *And the World Stood Silent: Sephardic Poetry of the Holocaust*, tr. I. J. Lévy (1989). S.G.A.; J.H.S.

JUDEZMO POETRY. See JUDEO-SPANISH POETRY.

JUGENDSTIL. A term originally applied to the "new style" in the decorative arts and crafts that flourished around 1900, and soon broadened to include other phenomena effected by the same spirit of refinement and rejuvenation. At first used synonymously with "Art Nouveau," J. more specifically refers to the Ger. and Austrian characteristics of a European stylistic reorientation (*Modern* or *Yachting Style, stile modernista, Nieuwe Kunst, Mouvement Belge*, etc.) that sought to free the applied arts from imitative eclecticism and historicism. The Munich journal *Die Jugend*, established in 1896 by Georg Hirth to popularize the cult of beauty and vitalism among the "youthful" middle-class at the end of the economic recession (1873–96), gave the "new style" its name; periodicals like *Pan* (1895), *Ver Sacrum* (the publication of the Vienna Secession, 1898), and *Die Insel* (1899) addressed a readership of connoisseurs. The satirical weekly *Simplicissimus* (1896–1944) subsequently became famous for its cartoons and for its almost carnevalesque irreverence toward political solemnities. The most widely influential propagator of J. in Germany was the Belgian designer and architect Henry van de Velde, the director of the Weimar *Kunstgewerbeschule* (School of Arts and Crafts) from 1902 to 1912.

The aims and techniques by which the visual arts and lit. of the time constructed a delicately and vibrantly beautiful reality were the same, but it was only after the rediscovery of *fin-de-siècle* culture in the early 1960s that it became popular to speak of J. lit. Similar characteristics were discovered among virtually all writers who came into prominence at the turn of the century: a coexistence of creative exuberance and morbid preoccupation with sterility, decay, and death; a wavering between ecstatic profusion resulting from a naive trust in the spontaneity of lang. and debilitating skepticism about all media of communication; the linguistic release of desires for powerful action disguising an alienation from most social purposes; the search for vital coherences between all people and things in dreamlike fantasies as opposed to the experience of rigid isolation; the longing for emotional elevation as an antidote to functional abstraction; visionary intuition, often erotically stimulated and producing orgiastic sensations of the infinite and of a fusion with excited masses, as an answer to the narcissistic retreat into artificial paradises. During its most intense phase (1895–1905), J. tried to rediscover the hidden unity of all things before critical consciousness had fragmented and technological materialism had destroyed it.

Though most easily identifiable by its use of highly stylized ornament, J. neither followed a coherent program nor dominated the art of its time, which speaks against using the noun as a period term. It shows affinities to other concurrent styles (impressionism, symbolism, revivals of mannerism) as well as a multitude of contradictory impulses that defy definition. In its simplest form it is a playful combination of decorative details; in its most ambitious purpose it is an attempt to overcome life's contradictions by aesthetic means.—*J.: der Weg ins zwanzigste Jahrhundert*, ed. H. Seling (1959); D. Jost, *Literarischer J.* (1969); *J.*, ed. J. Hermand (1971); E. Hajek, *Lit. J.: Vergleichende Studien zur Dichtung und Malerei um 1900* (1971); *Theorie des lit. J.*, ed. J. Mathes (1984).   M.W.

JUNGIAN OR ARCHETYPAL CRITICISM. See ARCHETYPE; MYTH CRITICISM; PSYCHOLOGICAL CRITICISM.

K

KABBALAH. See HEBRAISM.

KANNADA POETRY. See INDIAN POETRY.

KASA. See KOREAN POETRY.

KASHMIRI POETRY. See INDIAN POETRY.

KENNING (pl. *kenningar*). A multi-noun substitution for a single noun, e.g. "din of spears" for battle. Although found in many poetries, the k. is best known from Old Germanic verse. Ks. are common in West Germanic poetry, and scholars have recognized a k. in the expression of "corpse-sea," i.e. "blood," on the Eggjum runic inscription from Western Norway, ca. 700 A.D. ON Eddic poetry also makes use of ks., but their greatest importance was in skaldic poetry.

In medieval Icelandic rhet., the verb *kenna* (*við*), "make known (by)," was used to explain these expressions: "din" (the "base word" in modern analysis) is "made known" as battle by "of spears" (the "determinant"). The determinant may be in the genitive case, as here, or may attach to the base word to form a compound ("spear-din"); the base word takes the morphological and syntactic form of the concept the k. replaces. In skaldic poetry the determinant could in turn be replaced by another determinant; if "flame of battle" means "sword," then "flame of the din of spears" makes an acceptable k. Snorri Sturluson, the 13th-c. poet and man of letters and the first to attempt a rhetoric of ks., called this example *tvíkennt* ("twice-determined") in the commentary to *Háttatal* in his *Edda*. If another determinant were added, to make a four-part k., he would call it *rekit*, "driven." Snorri cautioned against "driven" ks. with more than six parts.

The relationship between the base word and determinant(s) could be essentially metonymic, as in "Baldr's father" for Odin, or metaphoric, as in the examples above. The ks. of West Germanic poetry, frequently used in connection with variation, tend toward the first category, those of skaldic poetry toward the second. Many skaldic ks. rely on Norse mythology or heroic legend for the links between the parts; thus poetry is the "theft of Odin" because he stole it from the giants. In skaldic poetry the number of concepts for which ks. may substitute is limited to about one hundred, among which warrior, woman, weapons, and battle are well represented. Since the base words tend to be fairly stereotyped (ks. for "woman" often have the name of a goddess as base word, for example), the system is relatively closed, but ks. make up nearly all the nouns in skaldic poetry, and the verbs are not important. Having imposed on themselves this closed system, the skalds exploited it brilliantly. In skaldic poetry the sum of the ks. is, to be sure, greater than their parts, but the best skalds made every word count. See also OLD NORSE POETRY.

As the following ks. for "sea" from *Beowulf* show, ks. enabled poets to express various aspects of an underlying noun: *ganotes bæð* "gannet's bath": a shoreward salt-water area where the sea-fowl fishes, sports, and bathes; *floda begang* "expanse of the floods or currents": emphasizes the vast extent of the oceans, esp. between the lands of the Geats and the Danes; *lagustræt* "path of the sea": the sea on which men sail their ships from one port to another; *windgeard* "enclosure or home of the winds": the sea, its storms, a watery expanse marked off from and enclosed by land, to be compared with *middan-geard* "middle enclosure," the land surrounded by the sea. See also LEXIS.—R. Meissner, *Die Kenningar der Skalden* (1921); H. van der Merwe Scholtz, *The K. in Anglo-Saxon and ON Poetry* (1927); *Edda Snorra Sturlusonar*, ed. F. Jónsson (1931); C. Brady, "The Synonyms for 'Sea' in *Beowulf*," *Studies in Honor of A. M. Sturtevant* (1952); H. Lie, *"Natur" og "unatur" i skaldekunsten* (1957); R. Frank, *ON Court Poetry* (1978); E. Marold, *Kenningkunst* (1983); M. Clunies Ross, *Skáld-*

skaparmál (1986). J.L.

KHARJA. See HISPANO-ARABIC POETRY; SPANISH POETRY.

KIND. See GENRE.

KNITTELVERS (also *Knüttelvers, Knüppelvers, Klippelvers*). Since the 18th c. the term "K." (originally a Ger. designation for Lat. verse in leonine hexameters) has been used to describe two types of 4-stressed rhymed couplets in Ger. and Scandinavian poetry. "Free K." (*freier K.*) consists of lines varying in number of syllables (usually 6–15 per line); "strict K." (*strenger K.*), primarily a 16th c. phenomenon sometimes called "Hans-Sachs-Vers," consists exclusively of 8-syllable masculine and 9-syllable feminine lines in couplets. K. can be traced back to Otfrid, who, using Lat. verse as a model, introduced couplets into Ger. verse in the 9th c. Free K. predominates in the Shrovetide plays (*Fastnachtsspiele*) of Hans Rosenplüt and Hans Folz in the 15th c.; strict K. prevails from the late 15th to the late 16th c. (e.g. Sebastian Brant, Hans Sachs, Johann Fischart). Led by Martin Opitz, 17th-c. poets rejected both forms and used "K." as a derogatory term to refer to the unwieldy rhythms and crude subject matter—usually humorous or satirical, often earthy and pithy, sometimes even obscene—of these 16th-c. couplets.

In the 18th c., free K. was revived by J. C. Gottsched and used later by Goethe (*Hanswursts Hochzeit, Jahrmarktsfest zu Plundersweilern*, and parts of *Urfaust, Faust*, and the *West-östlicher Diwan*), Schiller (*Wallensteins Lager*), and other poets (Herder, Bürger, Lenz), e.g.:

> Hab nun, ach, die Philosophei,
> Medizin und Juristerei,
> Und leider auch die Theologie
> Durchaus studiert mit heiBer Müh.
> Da steh ich nun, ich armer Tor,
> Und bin so klug, als wie zuvor.
> (Goethe, *Urfaust*)

In general, the metrical form of 19th-c. K. (as in Eichendorff, Heine, Mörike, Hebbel, Storm, Keller, and Fontane) and turn-of-the-century K. (Liliencron, Dehmel, Holz, Schnitzler) is quite similar to that written in the late 18th c. In the 1780s, however, Goethe's contemporary Karl Arnold Kortum developed a new form of K. (*Die Jobsiade*, 1784, 1799) consisting of quatrains in which a masculine couplet is followed by a feminine couplet. Many lines are extremely long (15 or more syllables), with the result that syllables bearing word-stress often occur in metrically unstressed positions:

> / / / /
> So kann man nur hier das Rätsel lösen
> / /
> Was die *Kapitel* sechs und sieben

> / /
> beschreib'ne Krankheit gewesen
> (*Die Jobsiade*)

Kortum's variant of K. was later imitated by Wilhelm Busch, Julius Bierbaum, and, most successfully, by Frank Wedekind (*Santa Simplicitas; Politische Lieder*), but it has not been used since.

In the 20th c., Gerhart Hauptmann, Hugo von Hofmannsthal, Max Mell, Peter Weiss, and Peter Hacks have used K. in dramatic works, and poets such as Bertolt Brecht, Karl Kraus, Peter Huchel, Wolf Biermann, and Christoph Meckel have written short poems in this verseform. K. was used by Kurt Tucholsky for a number of cabaret texts and a long political-satirical poem (*Die verkehrte Welt in Knüttelversen dargestellt von Kaspar Hauser*, 1922). Today K. continues to be used as a medium for political and social satire and parody, and to depict middle- and lower-class people in burlesque, mock-heroic, and tragicomic situations. These couplets are often used in children's verse and are spoken at Carneval festivities (*Fasching*) in Mainz and elsewhere in local dialects as well as in standard Ger.

O. Flohr, *Gesch. des K. vom 17. Jahrhundert bis zur Jugend Goethes* (1893); E. Feise, *Der K. des jungen Goethe* (1909); A. Heusler, *Deutsche Versgesch.* (1925–29), v. 3; W. Kayser, *Gesch. des deutschen Verses* (1960); H.-J. Schlütter, "Der Rhythmus im strengen K. des 16. Jahrhunderts," *Euphorion* 60 (1966); H. Heinen, *Die rhythmisch-metrische Gestaltung des K. bei Hans Folz* (1966); D. Chisholm, *Goethe's K.* (1975). D.H.C.

KNOWLEDGE, POETRY AS. See CRITICISM; DECONSTRUCTION; FICTION, POETRY AS; MEANING, POETIC; POETRY, THEORIES OF; REPRESENTATION AND MIMESIS; SCIENCE AND POETRY; SEMANTICS AND POETRY; SEMIOTICS, POETIC.

KOREAN POETRY.

I. SILLA DYNASTY (57 B.C.–A.D. 935)
II. KORYO DYNASTY (A.D. 918–1392)
III. CHOSON DYNASTY (1392–1910)
IV. JAPANESE OCCUPATION (1910–1945)
V. AFTER THE LIBERATION (1945–)

Although the K. lang. belongs to a ling. family totally different from Ch., cl. Ch. was the primary written lang. of Korea until the invention of the K. alphabet in the mid 15th c. After that point, most learned men wrote both in Ch. and K., but more often in Ch. Earlier, an ingenious system was devised by the Silla people to transcribe the current spoken lang. using Ch. graphs; used from the 6th c. on, it was through this means that the extant Old K. poems, or *hyangga*, were preserved. This article, however, considers only K. poetry written in the vernacular.

There are four major native poetic forms in traditional Korea: *hyangga*, ("native song," 6th–

10th c.); *pyŏlgok* or *changga* ("long song," 11th–14th c.); *sijo* ("current tune," 15th c. on); and *kasa* ("song words," 15th–19th c.). Another poetic form that flourished briefly is the *akchang* ("eulogy," 15th c.), the most representative of which is the *Songs of Flying Dragons* (1445–47), a cycle compiled in praise of the founding of the Chosŏn dynasty.

I. SILLA DYNASTY (57 B.C.–A.D. 935). *Hyangga* were written in 4-, 8-, and 10-line forms; the 10-line form comprising two quatrains and a concluding couplet was the most popular. The poets were either Buddhist monks or *hwarang*, knights trained in civil and military virtue in preparation for national service. Seventeen of the 25 extant *hyangga* are Buddhist in inspiration and content. Most *hyangga* gain their resonance through verbal felicity and symbolism. The "Ode to Knight Kip'a" (8th c.) by Master Ch'ungdam, for example, begins with a symbolic equation between the moon that pursues the white clouds and the speaker seeking the depths of his friend's mind, and concludes with a correspondence between the knight and the pine that "scorns frost, ignores snow." Like the pine tree, the knight represents the principle of growth and order, an emblem of continuity of society and culture. "Requiem" (8th c.) by Master Wŏlmyŏng uses the ancient trope comparing human generations with the scattering of leaves. The eleven devotional poems by Great Master Kyunyŏ (923–73) recall Western religious poetry in their imagery and symbolism. (As passion's flame scorches and destroys the fabric of human nature, so the ignorant mind suffers the blight of affliction.) Only the Buddha's sweet rain of truth can cause the withered soul to yield the grass of spiritual regeneration, bringing forth the golden fruit of knowledge. This harmonious state of the mind is expressed by the single metaphor of "a moonlit autumn field," the full moon of enlightenment.

II. KORYO DYNASTY (A.D. 918–1392). The interplay of Buddhist and native beliefs continued to inspire popular culture. Koryŏ lyrics, the *pyŏlgok* or *changga*, a blend of folk and art songs rooted in the indigenous culture, were composed and sung to music. Their refrains combine verbal and musical rhythms with nonsense syllables and onomatopoeic representation of the sound of the drum to create tension, suspense, and an incantatory quality. The refrain establishes the tone that carries the melody and spirit of the poem or unites a poem comprised of discrete parts. The theme of most of these anonymous poems is love, the joys and torments of which are expressed in frank and powerful language—the sadness of parting, revulsion at betrayal, renewed desire, grief at abandonment. The nameless poets were at war with time, love's chief enemy. In "Ode on the Seasons," a woman likens the stages of her love to the four seasons; in "Spring Overflows the Pavilion," a woman laments a blighted spring in her heart; and in "Winter Night" she compares the agony of de-

sertion to a stormy night that scatters sleet and snow. But the poets say they can make the river stand still, they are content to be dissolved by fire, and they are able to transform the icy bamboo hut into a love grotto.

III. CHOSON DYNASTY (1392–1910). The *sijo*, the most popular, elastic, and mnemonic of K. poetic forms, is a 3-line poem (in tr. usually a 6-line stanza is used). The *sijo* meter is formed by an ordered sequence of metric segments comprising syllables within a set range (2–7, commonly 3–4). Each line consists of four syllable groups, with a minor pause occurring at the end of the second group and a major at the end of the fourth. An emphatic syntactic division, usually introduced in the third line in the form of a countertheme, paradox, resolution, judgment, command, or exclamation, indicates a shift to subjectivity. The interplay of sound, rhythm, and meaning is the soul of the *sijo*, the basis of its organic structure. Writers of the *sijo* in the first half of the Chosŏn dynasty were mainly the lettered class and *kisaeng*, women entertainers, while in the second half, beginning from the 18th c., they were commoners. *Sijo* are still written, an oral art for the lettered and unlettered alike. Any subject is permissible, but favored ones include praise of virtue, complaints of desertion, fear of death, the beauty of friendship, and the simplicity of rural life. A long form, called *sasŏl sijo*, evolved in the latter part of the dynasty. Written mainly by commoners, it is marked especially by onomatopoeia (q.v.), a tendency to catalogue, striking imagery, and a bold twist at the end. It is frank and humorous, often satirical and running to burlesque, and explores the resources of the vernacular.

> Is it a cuckoo that cries?
> Is it the willow that is blue?
> Row away, row away!
> Several roofs in a far fishing village
> Swim in the mist, magnificent.
> Chigukch'ong chigukch'ong ŏsawa!
> Boy, fetch an old net!
> Fishes are climbing against the stream.

This is the fourth poem in the spring cycle from *The Angler's Calendar* (1651) by Yun Sŏndo (1587–1671). Yun adds two envois to the form characteristic of the fisherman's songs: a set of verbs connected with boating, and three 3-syllable onomatopoeic expressions simulating the movements and sounds of rowing. The poem opens with two lines that question the reliability of the senses of hearing and sight. Next, we see something in the distance, barely visible in the mist, but confirming the reality of the uncertain vision. The last two lines are brief and forceful, bespeaking a practical and more immediate connection with nature. In an ordered progression, then, the poem presents nature's mystery, beauty, and bounty in terms of illusory loveliness, real visual beauty, and life-sustaining reality, food from the stream. The poem not only suggests the felt transcendence of the vision, but reveals a consciousness of the transience of earthly joy and beauty. Yun Sŏndo achieves clarity and richness of vision with the simplest vocabulary and utmost economy.

The *kasa* that emerged as a new form toward the middle of the 15th c. can be compared to the Ch. rhymeprose (q.v.), the *fu*. It is characterized by a lack of stanzaic division, varying lengths, a tendency toward description and exposition, at times lyricism, and by verbal, syntactical parallelism. Its norm is a group of two 4-syllable words, or alternating groups of 3 and 4 syllables, forming a line often employing syntactic and semantic parallelism.

> in.seang.ŭn yu.han.han.dae
> si.ram.do kŭ.ji.ŏp.ta
> Life has an end:
> Sorrow is endless.

Earlier examples dealt with topics such as the loyalty to the king, celebration of the virtues of retired life (Chŏng Ch'ŏl, 1536–93; Pak Inno, 1561–1643), and the sorrows of unrequited love (Hŏ Nansŏrhŏn, 1563–89). The subject matter of the 18th-c. anonymous *kasa* by women was the daily life of the middle and lower classes. The themes of later examples of definite authorship include records of officials to Tokyo and Peking, praise of institutions, the farmer's works and days, and the sorrow of banishment. From the 19th c., the *kasa* became didactic, patriotic, or nostalgic. The "Song of Seoul" (1844), which details the institutions and glories of the Chosŏn dynasty, was popular among women.

IV. JAPANESE OCCUPATION (1910–45). The "new poetry" movement dates back to the publication of "From the Sea to Children" (1908) by Ch'oe Namsŏn (1890–1957). Written in free verse, the poem's inventions include the use of 106 punctuation marks, hitherto not used in cl. poetry, stanzaic forms of unequal length, topics of the sea and children also previously little used, and onomatopoeia in the first and seventh lines of each stanza. The first collection of translations from Western poetry was *Dance of Anguish* (1921) by Kim Ŏk, the principal transmitter of Fr. symbolist poetry. Two major poets in the 1920s were Han Yongun (1879–1944) and Kim Sowŏl (1902–34). With *The Silence of Love* (1926), comprising 88 Buddhist poems, Han became interpreter of the plight of the colonized peoples by creating a poetics of absence. Kim Sowŏl, the nature and folk poet, effectively used simplicity, directness, and terse phrasing. Unfulfilled love, or unquenchable longing, permeates his work. Perhaps the most influential modern poet before 1945 was Chŏng Chiyong (b.

1903), a student of William Blake and Walt Whitman. Chŏng rendered details with imagistic precision, as in his *White Deer Lake* (1941), symbolically representing the progress of the spirit to lucidity, the fusion of man and nature. Yi Yuksa (1904–44) and Yun Tongju (1917–45), major resistance poets, perished in Japanese prisons.

V. AFTER THE LIBERATION (1945–). Major poets writing after the liberation of 1945 include Sŏ Chŏngju (b. 1915) and Pak Tujin (b. 1916). Sŏ is credited with exploring hidden resources of the lang. from sensual ecstasy to spiritual quest, from haunting lyricism to colloquial earthiness. Capable of a wide range of moods, Pak uses sonorific intricacies and incantatory rhythms, revealing a strong historical and cultural consciousness. Some poets younger than Sŏ and Pak were determined to bear witness to the events of their age; some sought to further assimilate traditional K. values; others drew variously on Western traditions to enrich their work. Hwang Tonggyu (b. 1937) has drawn his material not only from personal experience but from the common predicament of his people. In his fifth collection, *Snow Falls in the South* (1974), Hwang studies modern K. history to determine the root of the K. tragedy, esp. its division and attendant instability, in images of barbed wire besieging his consciousness and snowflakes falling from the sky. In their search for order, for what Frost called "a momentary stay against confusion," modern poets affirm their situations by bold articulation of their human condition. Like their predecessors, they do not jettison cognitive claims or social functions for poetry but give that sense of purpose and coherence that only poetry can provide. Thus they have delved into the tradition to redeem the past and to affirm the new world they have created.

ANTHOLOGIES: *Kranich am Meer: Koreanische Gedichte* (1959), *Poems from Korea: A Hist. Anthol.* (1974), *The Silence of Love: 20th C. K. P.* (1980), *Anthol. of K. Lit.: From Early Times to the 19th C.* (1981), *Pine River and Lone Peak* (1991), all ed. P. H. Lee; *Contemp. K. P.*, ed. Ko Wŏn (1970); R. Rutt, *The Bamboo Grove: An Intro. to Sijo* (1971).

HISTORY AND CRITICISM: P. H. Lee, *Songs of Flying Dragons: A Crit. Reading* (1975), *Celebration of Continuity: Themes in Classic East Asian Poetry* (1979); D. R. McCann, "The Structure of the K. Sijo," *HJAS* 36 (1976); Chŏng Pyŏnguk, *Hanguk kojŏn sigaron* [Studies in Classic K. P.] (1977); M. Sym, *The Making of Mod. K. P.* (1982); Cho Tongil, *Hanguk munhak t'ongsa* [Gen. Hist. of K. Lit.], 5 v. (1982–88). P.H.L.

KVIÐUHÁTTR. See FORNYRTHISLAG.

L

LADINO POETRY. See JUDEO-SPANISH POETRY.

LAI (OF; Eng. *lay*; Ger. *leich*). A short narrative or lyric poem, perhaps based on Celtic material but primarily Fr., most often secular and usually set to music. (1) In OF the oldest narrative *lais*, almost always written in octosyllables (q.v.), are the *contes* or short romantic tales originated by Marie de France in the late 12th c. Most of them have Breton themes, chiefly love but also the supernatural. Marie's dozen *lais* take as their central interest true love, even if adulterous, in the face of marriages of convenience and abusive husbands. Later the term *l.* become synonymous with *conte*. (2) The oldest lyric *lais* are by Gautier de Dargies, who flourished in the first third of the 13th c. The lyric *l.* is addressed to an earthly lady or to the Virgin, but it differs from other poems of this theme by varying the rhymes and syllable counts in its stanzas, without refrain. One of the most interesting, by Ernoul le Vieux, has no love theme; it is the *L. de l'ancien et du nouveau testament*. The OF *l.* may be related to the Occitan *descort* (q.v.; "discord"). In the 14th c., Machaut standardized the form; half this century's 57 extant *lais* are by him. (3) The term "Breton lay" was applied in 14th-c. England to poems set in Brittany, written in a spirit similar to that of Marie's, or, often, applied the term to themselves. About a dozen Breton lays are extant in Eng., among them *Sir Orfeo*, *Sir Launfal*, *Emare*, and Chaucer's *Franklin's Tale*. Since the 16th c. "lay" has been used for song; in the early 19th c. the term was sometimes used for a short historical ballad, e.g. Scott's *Lay of the Last Minstrel*. See LEICH.—F. Wolf, *Über die Lais, Sequenzen, und Leiche* (1841)—still sound; *Lais et descorts fr. du XIIIe siècle*, ed. A. Jeanroy et al. (1901); H. Spanke, "Sequenz und L.," *Studi medievali* 11 (1938); G. Reaney, "Concerning the Origins of the Med. L.," *M&L* 39 (1958); J. Maillard, *Évolution et ésthetique du l. lyrique* (1961); H. Baader, *Die Lais* (1966); M. J. Donovan, *The Breton L.: A Guide to Varieties* (1969); K. W. Le Mée, *A Metrical Study of Five Lais of Marie de France* (1978); R. Hanning and J. Ferrante, *The Lais of Marie de France*, 2d ed. (1982); G. S. Burgess, *The Lais of Marie de France* (1987).
U.T.H.; T.V.F.B.

LAISSE. The OF epics or *chansons de geste* (q.v.) are divided into sections or group of lines of no specified length called ls.; in the *Chanson de Roland* they range from 5 to 35 lines. Technically ls. are not strophic because there is no response (q.v.) of form from one l. to the next; the length of each depends upon how much emphasis the poet wishes to give its subject. Each l. links together its lines with terminal assonance or—in later poems—rhyme (qq.v.); the distinction between masculine and feminine (q.v.) is observed. Sometimes the content of a l. is repeated item for item in one or two following ls., though with differing assonance or rhyme; such repetitions are called *ls. similaires*. The modern analogue is the verse paragraph (q.v.), though this is unrhymed.—J. Rychner, *La Chanson de geste* (1955), ch. 4; A. Monteverdi, "La L. epique," in *La Technique littéraire des chansons de geste* (1959); B. Schurfranz, "Strophic Structure versus Alternate Divisions in the *Prise d'Orange*," *RPh* 33 (1979); R. M. Johnston, "The Function of L. Divisions in the *Poema de mio Cid*," *Jour. of Hispanic Philol.* 8 (1984); E. A. Heinemann, "Measuring Units of Poetic Discourse," *Romance Epic*, ed. H.-E. Keller (1987).
U.T.H.; T.V.F.B.

LAKE SCHOOL, L. Poets, Lakers. A derogatory term applied to Wordsworth, Coleridge, and Southey. In the first number of the *Edinburgh Rev.* (Oct. 1802, 63–83), the hostile critic Francis Jeffrey referred to these three as a "sect" of poets which in 1807 he coupled with "the Lakes of Cumberland." A December 1809 review calls them "The Bards of the Lake"; other terms applied included "Naturals" and "Simple Poets." The expressions "Lake Poets" and "Lakers" first appear in 1814; the term "L. S." does not actually appear until 1817. The terms themselves and other close variants were obviously in conversational use ca. 1813 and are common in print thereafter. Hence, despite the common assumption, Jeffrey himself did not coin the phrase "L. S.," and in fact other references to the idea of a "new school" appear as early as 1797 (in a review by Canning in the *Anti-Jacobin* parodying Southey). At first the jibes are aimed against the new poets' political principles, but after the pub. of the 2d ed. of *Lyrical Ballads* in 1802, with Wordsworth's and Coleridge's names now on the title page, the focus shifts to the radical innovations in poetics— simplicity (q.v.) in diction, novelty in meter, and, in content, the effort to naturalize the supernatural and make transcendent the natural. The association via geography in the terms was a metonym meant to imply vulgar rusticity. It is certainly true that nature figures large in Wordsworth's poetry, though descriptive verse (q.v.) strictly defined was hardly his sole aim, and his claims in the "Preface" concerning diction were quickly punctured. And

- [674] -

the differences in philosophies, temperaments, and production among the three poets far outweigh their similarities. Cf. COCKNEY SCHOOL.—P. A. Cook, "Chronology of the 'L. S.' Argument: Some Revisions." *RES* 28 (1977).   T.V.F.B.

LAMENT (Ger. *Klagelied, Totenklage, Trost*). In its largest sense, l. is an expression of grief at misfortune, esp. at the loss of someone or something, and occurs throughout poetry in most genres. There are ls. in Sumerian poetry (e.g. over the fall of Sumer and Ur) and in *Gilgamesh*, Homer (e.g. *Iliad* 22.477–514), and the Heb. Bible (e.g. Lam.; Isa. 47; Ps. 44; Job 3). Ls. are a common feature of Gr. tragedy in the form of a monody (q.v.) or *kommos* (Alexiou). In Gr. choral lyric poetry (see MELIC POETRY), Simonides developed the *threnos* or dirge (q.v.), followed by Pindar, of whose book of dirges only fragments remain (Smyth). Theocritus introduced l. into pastoral (q.v.) poetry (*Idyll* 1), foll. by Bion ("L. for Adonis") and Virgil (*Eclogue* 5). Pseudo-Moschus' "L. for Bion" is the precursor of numerous ls. or elegies (see ELEGY) for poets, incl. Virgil's l. for Gallus (*Eclogue* 10), Ovid's for Tibullus (*Amores* 3.9), Garnier's for Ronsard, Spenser's for Sidney, Carew's and Walton's for Donne, Milton's *Lycidas* for Edward King, Shelley's "Adonais" for Keats, Arnold's "Thyrsis" for Clough, and Auden's "In Memory of W. B. Yeats."

Standard topics in ls. incl. a summons to and list of mourners, praise of the deceased, depiction of the death, contrast between the past and the present, the *ubi sunt* topos, and complaints about the cruelty of fortune, the purposelessness of life ("What boots it?"), and the finality of death (Menander Rhetor; Hardison; Alexiou; Race). In pastoral ls., nature is often depicted as mourning.

Poetic ls. or elegies over deceased individuals, most often including various topics of consolation or "comforting" (Wilson), are legion in virtually all langs. A sampling includes: *Hebrew*: David's l. for Saul and Jonathan at 2 Sam. 1.19–27; *Greek*: *Iliad* 24.748–59, Hecabe's l. for Hector; *Latin*: Catullus 101 for his brother; Propertius 3.18 for Marcellus; and Geoffrey of Vinsauf, *Poetria nova* 368–430, for Richard the Lionhearted; *French*: Ronsard's *Epitaphes*; *English*: *Deor's L.* (OE); Jonson's "On My First Son"; Donne's *Epicedes and Obsequies*; Whitman's "When Lilacs Last in the Dooryard Bloom'd"; and Dylan Thomas's "Do Not Go Gentle Into That Good Night"; *Italian*: Foscolo's "In morte del Fratello Giovanni" and Carducci's "Piano Antico"; *German*: Schiller's "Nänie"; *Spanish*: Manrique's "Coplas por la muerte de su padre" and García Lorca's "Llanto por Ignacio Sánchez Mejías." See now COMPLAINT; DIRGE; ENDECHA; ELEGY; EPICEDIUM; EPITAPH; MONODY; PLANH.

H. W. Smyth, *Gr. Melic Poets* (1900); *Wilson's Arte of Rhetorique*, ed. G. H. Mair (1909); R. Kassel, *Untersuchungen zur griechischen und römischen Kon-* *solationslit.* (1958); R. Lattimore, *Themes in Gr. and Lat. Epitaphs* (1962); O. B. Hardison, *The Enduring Momument* (1962); N. K. Gottwald, *Studies in the Book of* Lamentations (1962); V. B. Richmond, *Ls. for the Dead in Medieval Narrative* (1966); G. Davis, "*Ad sidera notus*: Strategies of L. and Consolation in Fortunatus' *De gelesuintha*," *Agon* 1 (1967); H.-T. Johann, *Trauer und Trost* (1968); J. B. Pritchard, *Ancient Near Eastern Texts* (1969); P. von Moos, *Consolatio: Studien zur mittellateinischen Trostliteratur*, 2 v. (1971–72); M. H. Means, *The* Consolatio *Genre in ME Lit.* (1972); M. Alexiou, *The Ritual L. in Gr. Trad.* (1974); *Menander Rhetor*, ed. and tr. D. A. Russell and N. G. Wilson (1981); Terras; W. H. Race, *Cl. Genres and Eng. Poetry* (1988).   W.H.R.

LAMPOON. See INVECTIVE.

LANDSCAPE POEM. See DESCRIPTIVE POETRY; VISUAL ARTS AND POETRY.

LANGUAGE POETRY emerged in the mid 1970s as both a reaction to and an outgrowth of the "New Am. Poetry" as embodied by Black Mountain, New York School, and Beat (q.v.) aesthetics. Within the pages of little magazines like *Tottel's, This, Hills*, and the Tuumba chapbook series, poets such as Ron Silliman, Barrett Watten, Charles Bernstein, Lyn Hejinian, Bruce Andrews, Bob Perelman, and Robert Grenier developed modes of writing that implicitly criticized the bardic, personalist impulses of the 1960s and explicitly focused attention on the material of lang. itself. This practice was supplemented by essays in poetics, pub. in journals like *L=A=N=G=U=A=G=E, Open Space, Paper Air*, and *Poetics Jour.*, or presented in "talk" series conducted at lofts and art spaces. The general thrust of this critical discourse has been to interrogate the expressive basis of much postwar Am. poetry, esp. the earlier generation's use of depth psychology, its interest in primitivism (q.v.) and mysticism, and its emphasis on the poetic line (q.v.) as a score for the voice (q.v.). While l. p. has derived much from the process-oriented poetry of Charles Olson, Robert Creeley, and John Ashbery, it has been skeptical about the claims of presence and participation (see PROJECTIVE VERSE) that underlie such practice.

The response of l. p. to expressivism has taken several forms, most notably a deliberate flattening of tonal register and extensive use of non-sequitur. Experimentation in new forms of prose, collaboration, proceduralism, and collage have diminished the role of the lyric subject in favor of a relatively neutral voice (or multiple voices). L. poets have endorsed Victor Shklovsky's notion of *ostranenie* or "making strange," by which the instrumental function of lang. is diminished and the objective character of words foregrounded. The poetry of Rus. Futurism and Am. objectivism (qq.v.) has been influential. Far from representing a return to an impersonal formalism, l. p. regards its defamiliariz-

LANGUE

ing strategies as a critique of the social basis of meaning, i.e. the degree to which signs are contextualized by use. In order to defamiliarize poetic lang., l. p. has had recourse to a variety of formal techniques, two in particular. The first involves the condensation and displacement of linguistic elements, whether at the submorphemic level (as in the poetry of David Melnick, P. Inman, or Steve McCaffery) or at the level of phrases and clauses (Charles Bernstein, Bruce Andrews, Barrett Watten). Bernstein, for example, condenses what appear to be larger syntactic units into brief, fragmentary phrases:

Casts across otherwise unavailable
    fields.
Makes plain. Ruffled. Is trying to
    alleviate his false: invalidate. Yet all is
"to live out," by shut belief, the
    various, simply succeeds which.

Although the title of this poem, "Sentences My Father Used," implies some autobiographical content, there is little evidence of person. The use of sentence fragments, false apposition, and enjambment displaces any unified narrative, creating a constantly changing semantic environment.

A second prominent feature of l. p. has been extensive work in prose. In the most influential essay, "The New Sentence," Ron Silliman calls for the organization of texts on the level of sentences and paragraphs. The "new" sentence refers less to deformations of normal sentences as to alternate ways of combining them within larger structures. Lyn Hejinian's *My Life*, for example, consists of 37 paragraphs of 37 sentences, each one of which leads to the next by the substitution or replacement of materials from the previous one or by mutiple forms of association.

The issues raised by such writing are not simply aesthetic but involve the social implications of literary reception. By blurring the boundaries between poetry and prose, everyday and literary lang., theory and practice, l. p. has attempted to establish a new relationship with the reader, one based less on the recuperation of a generically or stylistically encoded work and more on the reader's participation in a relatively open text. By thwarting traditional reading and interpretive habits, the poet encourages the reader to regard lang. not simply as a vehicle for preexistant meanings but as a system with its own rules and operations. However, since that system exists in service to ideological interests of the dominant culture, any deformation forces attention onto the material basis of meaning production within that culture. If such a goal seems utopian, it has a precedent in earlier avant-garde movements from symbolism (q.v.) to futurism and surrealism (qq.v.). Rather than seeking a lang. beyond rationality by purifying the words of the tribe or by discovering new langs. of irrationality, l. p. has made its horizon the material form rationality takes. See also SOUND POETRY; AMERICAN POETRY.

ANTHOLOGIES: *The L=A=N=G=U=A=G=E Book*, ed. B. Andrews and C. Bernstein (1984); *Writing / Talks*, ed. B. Perelman (1985); *In the Am. Tree*, ed. R. Silliman (1986); *"Lang." Poetries: An Anthol.*, ed. D. Messerli (1987).

CRITICISM: B. Watten, *Total Syntax* (1985); M. Perloff, *The Dance of the Intellect* (1985), ch. 10; S. McCaffery, *North of Intention: Crit. Writings 1973–1986* (1986); C. Bernstein, *Content's Dream: Essays 1975–1984* (1986); L. Bartlett, "What is 'L. P.'?" *CritI* 12 (1986); R. Silliman, *The New Sentence* (1987); J. J. McGann, "Contemp. Poetry, Alternate Routes," *CritI* 13 (1987); A. Ross, "The New Sentence and the Commodity Form: Recent Am. Writing," *Marxism and the Interp. of Culture*, ed. C. Nelson and L. Grossberg (1988); G. Hartley, *Textual Politics and the L. Poets* (1989). M.D.

LANGUE. See DECONSTRUCTION; SEMIOTICS, POETIC; SOUND; TEXTUALITY.

LAPIDARY VERSE. See EPITAPH; EPIGRAM; SCULPTURE AND POETRY.

LATIN AMERICAN POETRY. See AMERICAN INDIAN POETRY, *Central American, South American*; BRAZILIAN POETRY; SPANISH AMERICAN POETRY.

LATIN POETICS. See CLASSICAL POETICS; CLASSICISM; MEDIEVAL POETICS.

LATIN POETRY.

    I. CLASSICAL
        A. *Origins*
        B. *Preclassical*
        C. *Late Republican*
        D. *Augustan*
        E. *Post-Augustan*
    II. MEDIEVAL
    III. RENAISSANCE AND POST-RENAISSANCE

I. CLASSICAL. Lat. p. is commonly censured as derivative. The Lat. poets wrote in meters originated by the Greeks, employed a more or less assimilated Gr. mythology as a poetic vehicle, and confined their efforts, for the most part, to genres already well established when Rome was little more than a barbarous village. Yet despite this real dependence, there remains nothing less Gr. than the masterpieces of Lat. p., whose imitation of the Gr. was never slavish, and whose trad. was a double one. On one side stood the centuries of developed Gr. lit., a lit. of infinite variety and vast achievement, supplying Lat. poets with models and sanctions, and the more valuable for being foreign without being alien. On the other stood the developing corpus of Lat. lit., steadily informing the cultural context within which a given Roman poet lived and wrote. Between these two trads. the tension was lively and fruitful for Republican poetry esp.; if earlier Lat. poetry can be generally divided between a "Romanizing" school on the one hand and a "Hellenizing" school on the other, for later poets the problem was one of preserving the double loyalty they felt without doing damage to either trad. This double loyalty was not maintained by the simple mechanical act of domesticating Gr. meters and forms or adapting them to a specifically Roman sensibility, but by the far more delicate operation of blending the strengths and virtues of both sensibilities in a common form. This marriage of two trads. was the achievement of Virgil more than any other Lat. writer; and for Virgil's followers his example loomed so large that their problem was less whether they should be Greeks or Romans than whether they should be Virgilians or something else.

Further governing the finished Lat. poem were two states of mind almost completely alien to Cl. Gr. poetry. The first was the Lat. poet's *consciousness* of his trad. and his place in it. Like the Roman historian, the Lat. poet was intensely aware of and intensely loyal to his trad.; at times his humility before his tradition's authority approaches servility. It is this intense loyalty that most nearly explains the small range and variety of Lat. p. when measured against Gr. or Eng. poetry. Trad. for the Lat. poet early acquired an enormous authority, extending to subject, conventions, form, and even rhetorical modes; it was something to be exploited, but the exploitation was an exercise in humility and craft, a constant refinement of a more or less dominant mode. Rarely does the Lat. poet rebel against his trad., though he may reject one of its modes for another. In poetry as in character the virtue of *pietas* (dutiful loyalty) is central, and *continuity* is therefore one of the dominant features of Lat. p.: in all essential respects the poetics of Virgil and the poetics of Claudian four cs. later are the same. For the same reason that Lat. p. exhibits a restricted range, it also exhibits much less flagrant sensationalism and striving after originality; yet it would be a mistake to suppose that Lat. poets were indifferent innovators or that their style is somehow impersonal. Nowhere is sensationalism of rhet. and situation more prevalent than in Lat. p., esp. in post-Virgilian verse; but it needs to be observed that formal rhetorical innovation is almost always marginal, an elaborate, sometimes frigid, refinement of the dominant rhet. of the lang. Almost never is there revolution at the core or rejection of the cardinal principles of traditional poetics. Combined with consciousness of the trad., the second dominant characteristic of Lat. p. was the passion for *utility* in lit., for its application to some patriotic or instructive end—a passion never really absent, even in the hyperesthetic pieces where the poet emphasizes its existence by his determined avoidance of it. But it is not difficult to see how the poetry that emerged from the juggling of these elements was completely different from any Gr. poetry ever written.

A. *Origins.* Traces of wholly indigenous Lat. lit. are almost nonexistent. There were rude farces in the Saturnian (q.v.) stress meter before the irruption of Gr. culture into Latium, but we possess no fragments. This meter, however, was employed in the first Lat. poem of which we have even the barest knowledge—a tr. of the *Odyssey* written about the mid 3d c. B.C. by Livius Andronicus, a Gr. ex-slave. He handled the jigging, heavily accented movement of his verse with little distinction, but he had the incalculable advantage of being first; his work was used as a school text for more than two centuries. His younger contemporary Gnaeus Naevius represents a further stage in the transition. His versified chronicle of the First Punic War was done in the same meter, but he seems to have owed much to Homer, while he also wrote tragedies and comedies on Attic models wherein he employed quantitative Gr. meters based on quantity rather than stress. But the towering figure of the early years is Quintus Ennius (239–169 B.C.), in the wreck of whose work we may discern the roots of most subsequent Lat. p. He wrote tragedies, comedies, didactic poems and epigrams, all largely derived from the Greeks, but his most important work was the *Annals*, an epic chronicle recording the history of Rome from the arrival of Aeneas down to Ennius' own times.

The fragments of this work—which established the dactylic hexameter as the medium of Lat. epic—still serve to illustrate the peculiar nature of Lat. p. Based openly on the Homeric poems, and in some sense a continuation of them, the work also seems to have been influenced by Hellenistic poetic histories, and it fused these two sources, separated by cs. in time and outlook, into something distinctly Roman by its dedicated patriotic and didactic bias. Ennius' somewhat older contemporary, Titus Maccius Plautus (250–184 B.C.) set a number of plays of the Gr. New Comedy into Lat., but his debt to the rough native dramatic tradition is probably quite great, as the rather tired comedy of manners of the late Hellenic and Hellenistic ages suffers a sea-change, becoming excellent bawdy farce. The 21 Plautine comedies which survive are rude, colloquial, and frankly aimed at the pit, but they are funny and vital as well.

B. *Preclassical.* The 2d c. B.C. saw Rome's first literary-philosophical coterie, a gathering of philhellenes around the younger Scipio Africanus for the purpose of serious study and adaptation of Gr. culture. Two great poets of the c. were friends and clients of Scipio. The first was Terence (Publius Terentius Afer, at work 166–59), whose six verse-comedies show a definite reaction from the "excesses" of his predecessors, such as Plautus, back to the pure Menandrean ideal of the Gr. New Comedy. The purity and beauty of Terence's Lat. is a definite landmark; but more important are the implications of his subtlety. In stressing form, expression, and relationships at the expense of strength, character, and humor itself, he clearly turned away from the general public to address the educated classes—a situation that had not occurred in Greece until the beginning of the Hellenistic Age. It was a necessary step toward grafting a sophisticated Gr. trad. onto a crude but vital Roman one. Henceforth, with few exceptions, Lat. p. was composed by learned poets for a more or less learned audience. The other great name was Gaius Lucilius (180?–102 B.C.), considered the father of satire (q.v.), the only genre to which the Romans laid fair claim—though the satirical attitude has a long history in Greece, and Lucilius was well acquainted with its examples in mock-epic, comedy, and diatribe. His work, 30 books of miscellanies, or *saturae,* ranged over the experiences of educated Romans in a world that was becoming increasingly Romanized and politicized, and his strong personal statements and versatile colloquial style established the mode of Roman satire. We possess numerous fragments of his works—he fixed on the hexameter for verse-form—but none, unfortunately, of any length.

C. *Late Republican.* The lst c. B.C. witnessed the rise of rhet. and the fall of the Roman Republic, both of them events of prime importance for poetry. The first important poem of which we possess any considerable remnants was the tr. by the orator Cicero (106–43) of the *Phaenomena* of Aratus of Soli, an Alexandrian didactic work on astronomy and meteorology that combined "science," devout Stoicism, and literary art. Cicero was no great poet, but his contributions to poetic lang. and metrical polish should not be minimized. A far greater poet, who used Cicero's developments but argued passionately for Epicureanism, was Lucretius (Titus Lucretius Carus, at work 65–55). In six hexameter books he composed his remarkable poem *De rerum natura* ("On Nature"), a memorable exposition of his love of nature and its essential creativity and his passionate belief in Epicurean natural philosophy as it bears upon primary human anxieties, superstition, and the fear of death.

But the *De rerum natura* is not completely isolated. Lucretius' protest against the disturbances of politics and imminent civil war and his acceptance of the poetic challenges of didactic hexameter ally him with the interests of the revolutionary "New Poets.170 (see NEOTERICS). These rejected Roman politics and social issues and adopted the standards and forms of Alexandrian crit. and performance, preferring the brief, highly-wrought genres—epyllion, lyric, epigram, elegiac (qq.v.)— to full-scale epic and didactic with their traditional themes. Our sole survivor from this learned group is Gaius Valerius Catullus (84?–54?), whose range was remarkably wide. He wrote epyllia in the Hellenistic fashion which brilliantly manifest variety and beauty of texture, care for responsion (q.v.) and juxtaposition, and dismay at contemporary pressures, as witnessed in *The Marriage of Peleus and Thetis,* a marvelous exhibition of unity

in layered diversity. In his intenser, shorter pieces, however, he turned from Gr. practice—though not from Gr. theory—employing (like Lucilius) the full range of colloquial Lat. in experimental Gr. lyric meters to greet friends, damn enemies, and celebrate or abuse his mistress Lesbia (a name invented to evoke Sappho). These, and esp. the last group, are not the simple effusions that romantic crit. has dotingly supposed: Catullus in love is a learned poet still, and to say that he conveys the immediacy of passion more directly than any other Lat. poet is not to deny the learned intricacy of even his shortest poems.

D. *Augustan.* The Hellenizing New Poets never succeeded in making—if they ever intended—a full break with the didactic-patriotic trad., and their achievements significantly affected the superb and subtle poetry of the next age. This is best shown in the work of Rome's greatest poet, Virgil (Publius Vergilius Maro, 70–19 B.C.). His first major work was the *Eclogues* or *Bucolics* (qq.v.), a collection of ten pastoral (q.v.) poems which observe the New Poets' architectonic structure, intense attention to the word, and approved Hellenistic sources—in this case, Alexandrian Theocritus. But the difference is significant: Virgil's shepherds are not Gr., but It., and his pastorals treat overtly and covertly the way war, love, and literary politics threaten the serenity of the bucolic world. The same tendency is heightened in the *Georgics,* a poem starting from the didactic farming-poem of the Gr. Hesiod, the *Works and Days,* but transforming its agricultural poetics into a representation of human beings (particularly Romans) at the painful task of wringing a living from Nature, now gratified, now defeated, but ultimately heroic in their dedication.

This troubled dedication becomes the central focus of Virgil's *magnum opus,* the *Aeneid.* Ostensibly returning to Homeric epic, Virgil builds upon, not imitates, Homer, and his whole poem functions, in form and subject alike, to marry the hitherto divided trads. of Gr. and Roman sensibility. The achievement of the *Aeneid*'s is the willful creation of a culture, fusing apparently disparate and warring trads. into the full *mythos* of Lat. culture, and this synthesis is perfectly mirrored and supported in the almost miraculous union of form and subject. Poetry and history meet in the *Aeneid* and in the New Rome which is its subject, and the formulation is so perfect that it almost came to be final as well. Virgil, that is, almost usurps the entire trad., for his example (and the prestige of his success) was so great that it practically compelled subsequent poetry into its path and rendered it impossible by its exhaustion of the ground. The poem is strongly but realistically patriotic. It shows the New Rome of Augustus Caesar to be the product of ineluctable fate, but (in line with the New Poets) it deplores the losses to cities and people, both guilty and innocent, that imperial success entails. Aeneas, who embodies the painful dedication of the hero, finally emerges as a tragic and flawed character, and Virgil ends the epic by picturing him as a ruthless killer rather than a creative statesman. Inasmuch as Aeneas represents in mythical terms the achievements of Augustus, there can be no question about Virgil's attitude toward imperial propaganda. He and all the other Augustan poets did not scruple to distance themselves pointedly from the negative tendencies of Augustus' despotism.

Horace (Quintus Horatius Flaccus, 65–8 B.C.) is another example of restrained commitment. His earliest works—the *Epodes*—polished iambic poems based on the Gr. Archilochus—and the *Satires*—much more skillful, polished, and kindly developments of Lucilius' genre—define his mixed view of revolutionary Rome in their survey of human foibles. But in his transfer of the forms of Sappho and Alcaeus into Lat., *Odes*, Books I–III, Horace became both a great poet and the lyric voice of Augustan tensions. These lyrics (written ca. 30–23 and dedicated to Augustus' loyal aide Maecenas) treat, in various Gr. meters, in a felicity of lang. equaled only by Virgil, and in exquisitely formal precision, love and wine lightly, life and death deeply, reflecting the continuing dialogue in Rome between engagement and disengagement, Stoicism and Epicureanism.

Horace's later works consist of a fourth book of *Odes*, where this dialogue is overshadowed by the tensions of approaching old age; an important collection of ethically oriented epistles; the famous *Ars poetica*, a highly problematic versification of literary doctrines attributed to the 3d-c. Gr., Neoptolemus, which formulated for all time the basic Roman literary tenet: the successful poet must mix the useful (*utile*) with the pleasing (*dulce*)—see CLASSICAL POETICS; and, lastly, a Roman centennial ode.

The mixture of, or tension between, the useful and the pleasing exhibits a different and entertaining blend in another genre. Though Gr. elegiac poetry is various in theme, Roman elegy, which derived from Catullus, Alexandrian elegy, and Gr. and Roman New Comedy, was largely restricted to one theme—love—not in the light Horatian sense, but as the most important thing in the world. The spare-dictioned, deceptively simple elegies of Albius Tibullus (54?–19 B.C.) treat, with flowing structure, only of his mistress (Delia or Nemesis, significantly Gr. names), his farm, peace, and occasionally the praise of his patron, Augustus's disenchanted lieutenant Messalla. Sextus Propertius (ca. 50–after 16), the most violent and original of Augustan poets in his structure, lang., and imagery, also shows little willingness to compromise his amatory world for politics. From the intense, introspective poems on his mistress Cynthia which comprise his earliest collection, he moves to the odd sort of Roman poetry found in his fourth and last book, where, adapting an interest of Gr. Callimachus, he mixes patriotism and amatory themes. It is a mix where love often overshadows heroism or subverts it, where Roman trads. yield to a modern elegiac irony.

Propertius prepares the way for Ovid, with his much more obvious irreverence for Roman conventions and his almost total engagement with the values he perceives in love. Publius Ovidius Naso (43 B.C.–A.D.17?) utilized every bit of his formidable rhetorical training in his poetry, seeking, even at his wittiest, to elicit the underlying reality by an intense exploration of the conventional poses of the amatory elegist. Thus, in his love elegies, the *Amores* and *Heroides* (verse letters cleverly imagined as written by famous women of Gr. mythology to their absent, usually faithless lovers), and even in his double-edged satirical treatments of didacticism and love-practice (*The Art of Love* and *The Remedy of Love*), he develops the unheard-of concept of equality between the partners in a love affair. But erotic poetry (q.v.) won him no favor with Augustus. When Ovid's greatest work, the *Metamorphoses*, potentially a patriotic epic in its size and use of heroic meter, the hexameter, turned out to be an interweaving (on the thread of "form-changing") of 250-odd stories and epyllia, which, in typical elegiac manner, exalted the individual and personal feelings at the expense of temporal and divine authority, Augustus had had enough. Ovid, already compromised by the supposed lasciviousness of *The Art of Love*, committed some accidental political indiscretion and was summarily banished to Tomi on the Black Sea—an event which brought to a premature end his *Fasti*, an irreverent elegiac poem on the Roman calendar. His last collections, the *Tristia* (Sorrows) and *Epistulae ex Ponto* (Letters from the Black Sea), return to the elegiac lament, protesting his bitter life among Latin-less barbarians but at the same time showing his independence, in spite of his suffering, as poet and man of feeling.

E. *Post-Augustan.* The last considerable age of Cl. Lat. p. shows only too clearly the cramping effects of authoritarianism and the changes made in the social life of poetry by despotism. Rhet., already a danger to poetry, now often became an end rather than a means. The literary past, both Gr. and Roman, assumed enormous prestige and became an inhibiting power—esp. the example of Virgil, whose great success with epic tended to demote other genres by comparison.

Characteristically, Silver Lat. p. exhibits a spectacle of uprooted rhet. that flourishes for its own sake or supports grandiose mythological (Gr.) structures lacking almost any social or political relevance to the times. Socially, it is the age when gifted poets beg for patronage, rich aristocrats dabble in poetry, and both types perform their works in public recitations. Many of the subjects focus on horror, perverse crimes, cosmic disorder, and the apparent triumph of evil, but they have a convenient distance as myths or long-past Roman history. In satire, however, Silver Lat. verse engages itself with contemporary immorality with great vigor and power, and its colloquial or unorthodox style combines with rhetorical techniques in an especially successful way.

Much of this poetry may be dismissed as little more than pious imitation of Virgil, as in the Virgilian pastorals of Calpurnius Siculus (under Nero) or the wretched Virgilian epic on the career of Scipio Africanus, the 17-book *Punica* of Silius Italicus (late 1st c.). Usually, however, Ovid has also exerted his influence, and the blend of Virgil, Ovid, and exuberant rhet. focused on a demonic theme appeals to the tastes of many a subsequent age, notably that of Elizabethan England and our own. The court of Nero (54–68) stimulated many poets, notably Seneca, Persius, and Lucan. Seneca, perhaps while he was tutor, then advisor to young Nero (49–63), perhaps after he prudently retired from the court, produced a series of tragedies on violent, irrational crimes from Gr. myth, which feature malevolent deities, ruthless and unpunished villains, and helpless victims—situations that negate the Stoic order and implicitly call for a new assertion of Stoic values. Aules Persius Flaccus (34–62) wrote satires saturated with Stoic conviction and a passionate appeal to the Roman conscience in a uniquely crabbed style. And Lucan (39–65), Seneca's nephew, at first a favorite then a hated rival of the artistically pretentious Nero, reacted so violently to the despotic emperor that he turned his magnificent epic, the *Civil War* (ostensibly about the conflict between Julius Caesar and the Senate in 49–6 B.C.), into a platform for shrill editorial rhet. against the political system that spawned and protected Nero. He too appeals to Stoicism and the heroic resistance to the tyranny that has enslaved Romans.

After another Civil War in 68–69, another imperial family came to power for nearly 30 years, and in its last member, the unstable and cruel Domitian, it promoted the fortunes of Statius and Martial, both men of nonRoman and unaristocratic backgrounds, and both in desperate need of patronage. Statius (ca. A.D. 40–95), son of a schoolmaster, wrote much occasional verse, published in a collection called the *Silvae*, while devoting his main efforts over 12 years to his epic the *Thebaid* (on the senseless tragedy of the Seven Against Thebes). In the end, he did not feel that Rome had adequately rewarded his poetic efforts and retired to Naples to die. Martial (ca. 40–102) came to Rome from Spain, with high hopes of capitalizing on the Sp. friends of Nero, but he found himself struggling under the new dynasty, with some success though he likes to portray himself as a needy client, until the murder of Domitian in 96 put the poet in trouble with the angry men who came to power. He too was obliged to retire to his native Sp. town. But his epigrams are a fine, genial legacy of the period, sentimental or witty, often naughtily so, about life in the most brilliant and corrupt city of antiquity.

In the next "liberated" generation appears Juvenal (at work 100–30), who starts from the theme of violent Roman reaction against the tyrant Domitian but develops his own themes, Roman and general, as time passes. His tight and memorably phrased indictments of human pretense and weakness are Rome's greatest, wittiest, and angriest satires, an able use of the rhetorical techniques that had overwhelmed others' efforts. For the next three cs., Virgil, Ovid, and rhet. variously influenced Lat. p., and capable writers of Lat. verse came from all parts of the Empire to Rome or wherever the emperor made his residence. In the 3d and 4th cs., the poets began to divide over conservative Roman religion and the new Christianity. Contemporaries, Claudian from Africa was a staunch pagan, while Prudentius from Spain wrote only on Christian topics as Alaric approached, to bring Cl. Lat. p. to an end, bereft of a home, and to turn Rome into a symbolic topic for medieval poets.

See also GREEK POETRY, *Classical.*

BIBLIOGRAPHY: *L'Année philologique* 1–(1927–); *The Cl. World Bibl. of Roman Drama and Poetry* (1978); *Gr. and Roman Authors: A Checklist of Crit.*, ed. T. Gwinup and F. Dickinson, 2d ed. (1982)—covers 70 authors.

GENERAL: W. Y. Sellar, *Roman Poets of the Augustan Age*, 2 v. (1897); H. E. Butler, *Post-Augustan Poetry* (1909); T. Frank, *Life and Lit. in the Roman Republic* (1930); J. F. D'Alton, *Roman Lit. Theory and Crit.* (1931); H. J. Rose, *A Handbook of Lat. Lit.*, 2d ed. (1949); J. W. Duff, *A Lit. Hist. of Rome*, ed. A. M. Duff, 3d ed., 2 v. (1953, 1964); G. Williams, *Trad. and Originality in Roman Poetry* (1968), *Change and Decline: Roman Lit. in the Early Empire* (1978); *CHCL*, v. 2; *Nouvelle Histoire de la littérature latine*, ed. R. Herzog and P. L. Schmidt (1990).

SPECIALIZED STUDIES: P. Nixon, *Martial and the Mod. Epigram* (1927); M. M. Crump, *The Epyllion from Theocritus to Ovid* (1931); A. L. Wheeler, *Catullus and the Trads. of Ancient Poetry* (1934); H. F. Fraenkel, *Ovid: A Poet Between Two Worlds* (1945); L. P. Wilkinson, *Horace and His Lyric Poetry* (1945), *Ovid Recalled* (1955), *Golden Lat. Artistry* (1963); G. E. Duckworth, *The Nature of Roman Comedy* (1952); G. Highet, *Juvenal the Satirist* (1954); F. O. Copley, *Exclusus Amator: A Study in Lat. Love Poetry* (1956); E. Fränkel, *Horace* (1957); K. Quinn, *The Catullan Revolution* (1959); S. Commager, *The Odes of Horace* (1962); V. Pöschl, *The Art of Vergil*, tr. G. Seligson (1962); C. O. Brink, *Horace on Poetry*, 3 v. (1963–82); B. Otis, *Virgil; A Study in Civilized Poetry* (1963), *Ovid as Epic Poet* (1970); N. Rudd, *The Satires of Horace* (1966); E. Segal, *Roman Laughter* (1968); W. S. Anderson, *The Art of the Aeneid* (1969), *Essays on Roman Satire* (1982); G. Luck, *The Lat. Love Elegy* (1969); D. O. Ross, Jr., *Style and Trad. in Catullus* (1969), *Backgrounds to Augustan Poetry: Gallus, Elegy and Rome* (1975); D. West, *The Imagery and Poetry of Lucretius* (1969); M. C. J. Putnam, *The Poetry of the Aeneid* (1965),

Virgil's Pastoral Art (1970), *Virgil's Poem of the Earth* (1979), *Essays on Lat. Lyric, Elegy, and Epic* (1982), *Artifices of Eternity* (1986); E. H. Guggenheimer, *Rhyme Effects and Rhyming Figures* (1972); D. Vessey, *Statius and the* Thebaid (1973); *Seneca*, ed. C. D. Costa (1974); J. Wright, *Dancing in Chains: the Stylistic Unity of the Comoedia Palliata* (1974); G. K. Galinsky, *Ovid's Metamorphoses: An Intro. to the Basic Aspects* (1975); F. M. Ahl, *Lucan. An Intro.* (1976), *Metaformations: Soundplay and Wordplay in Ovid and Other Cl. Poets* (1985); M. Coffey, *Roman Satire* (1976); F. Cairns, *Tibullus: A Hellenistic Poet at Rome* (1979); R. O. A. M. Lyne, *The Lat. Love Poets* (1980); R. Jenkyns, *Three Cl. Poets: Sappho, Catullus, Juvenal* (1982); M. Morford, *Persius* (1984); R. L. Hunter, *The New Comedy of Greece and Rome* (1985); H.-P. Stahl, *Propertius: "Love" and "War": Individual and State under Augustus* (1985); F. Verducci, *Ovid's Toyshop of the Heart: Epistulae Heroidum* (1985); R. Kilpatrick, *The Poetry of Friendship: Horace, Epistles I* (1986); S. Goldberg, *Understanding Terence* (1986); P. Veyne, *Roman Erotic Elegy* (tr. 1988); J. K. Newman, *Roman Catullus* (1990).   W.A.; D.S.P.; W.S.A.

II. MEDIEVAL. Early evidence of Christian Lat. poetry is sparse and random. If Commodian, who offers doctrine and exhortation in an accentual approximation of the Cl. hexameter, was indeed a 3d-c. African, he is an isolated phenomenon. Indicative of things to come are two short narratives, on Jonah and on the destruction of Sodom, written in skillful hexameters (ca. 300), and the beautiful *Phoenix* attributed to Lactantius (ca. 310), wholly pagan in detail but to the early Middle Ages plainly a celebration of the Resurrection.

A coherent Christian Lat. trad. emerges in the 4th c., deliberately conceived as an alternative to the pagan classics on which all learned Christians had been reared, but in effect an extension of the cl. trad. The *cento* of Proba (mid 4th c.) is a mere pastiche of tags from Virgil. What is innovative in Juvencus' hexameter rendering of the Gospels (ca. 330) and the freer version in Sedulius' *Carmen paschale* (ca. 430) is their ingenuity in adapting Virgilian style to Christian purposes; and Paulinus of Nola (353–431) expresses his resolve to repudiate pagan models and write a new kind of poetry in verse richly evocative of Virgil, Ovid, and Horace. Prudentius (348–405), master of many cl. styles and genres, was a brilliant original whose complex attitude toward both Christian and pagan culture we are only beginning to fathom. His *Psychomachia*, a short epic on the conflict of virtue and vice in the human soul, greatly influenced medieval iconography, and his elaborate hymns were incorporated in simplified form into the Church liturgy.

The Christian Lat. poets were to coexist with, and even displace, the great pagans in the school curriculum of the early Middle Ages, but they had few imitators. More significant for Med. Lat. poetry was the hymnody which appeared as Lat.

replaced Gr. as the lang. of the liturgy. The cumbersome, dogmatic verse of Hilary of Poitiers (310–66) can hardly have had a liturgical function, and the rhythmical prose of the great *Te Deum*, despite its early and abiding popularity, was not imitated; Med. Lat. hymnody begins with Ambrose (340–97), who provided his Milanese congregation with meditations appropriate to the liturgical hours and calendar couched in 4-line strophes of iambic dimeter (see HYMN). Psychologically profound, and written in beautiful and surprisingly cl. Lat. , the Ambrosian hymns were widely imitated and came to form the nucleus of the medieval hymnaries; their form, 4-stress lines in quatrains, has been preserved with only minor variations down to the present day, as may be seen in the Metrical Index of any hymnal.

The upheavals of the later 5th c. left their mark on the Christian Lat. trad. The bookish verse of Sidonius Apollinaris (d. 480) reflects its survival in an attenuated form in Gaul; the "epic" trad. of Prudentius and Sedulius enjoys a late flowering in the *De laudibus Dei* of Dracontius (ca. 450–500); and the verse in Boethius' *Consolation of Philosophy* (ca. 524), a prosimetrum (q.v.) including a range of meters imitated from Horace and Seneca, is a last manifestation of inherited familiarity with Cl. culture. The verse epistles and occasional poems of Fortunatus (535–604), charming and often brilliantly innovative, show a marked loss of syntactic and metrical fluency, though his passion-hymns *Vexilla regis* and *Pange, lingua* are among the greatest of Christian hymns. The Cl. trad. is still alive in the poems of Eugenius of Toledo (fl. ca. 650) and resurfaces with the Carolingian court poets, but new developments were also taking place. Rhyme and accentual meters begin to appear, most notably in Ir. hymnody, evidently influenced by native Celtic verseforms and the rules of rhythmical prose formulated by the Lat. grammarians, culminating in the *Altus prosator* of Columbanus (d. 597). Correct Lat. verse in quantitative meters continued to be taught in schools and written by the learned past the 16th c., but accentually measured Lat. verse is the rule after the 4th c., paving the way for the accentually based prosodies of the vernaculars (Beare). The riddles of Aldhelm (d. 709), which inaugurated a popular genre, imitate the African Lat. poet Symphosius, and the metrical life of Cuthbert by Bede (673–736) is couched in a fluent hexameter shaped by 4th-c. Christian models, but the high points of 8th-c. It. Lat. poetry are a rhythmical poem in praise of the city of Milan (ca. 738) and the accentual verse experiments of Paulinus of Aquileia (d. 802). Paulinus' somber lament on the death of Eric of Friuli (799) is an early and influential example of the *planctus* (see LAMENT), which became a popular form and may reflect the influence of vernacular trad.

The poets who came to the court of Charlemagne brought their culture with them; much of the poetry of Paul the Deacon (d. 802) was written before he left Italy, and Theodulf (d. 821) and Alcuin (d. 804) were products of thriving schools in Spain and England. But Charles and his court inspired new poetry. Panegyric epistles by Alcuin and Theodulf, and the *Karolus Magnus et Leo Papa* (ca. 800) attributed to Einhard, celebrate Charles as the champion of political and cultural renewal, and Aachen as a new Rome. The poetry of the court includes charming occasional poems by Paul the Deacon and Theodulf's satire on the courts of law, but its finest product is the Christian Lat. pastoral, best illustrated by Alcuin's nightingale poems, his *O mea cella*, and a "Conflict of Winter and Spring," probably his, which is both a pastoral and perhaps the first example of the debate-poem or *Streitgedicht*, a form imitated in Sedulius Scotus' "Contest of the Lily and the Rose" (ca. 850) and the "Eclogue" of the pseudonymous "Theodulus" (9th–10th c.), and widely popular in later centuries, e.g. "The Owl and the Nightingale" in ME (see POETIC CONTESTS).

The later 9th and 10th c. produced further new departures. The hexameter narrative of an anonymous "Poeta Saxo" (ca. 890) celebrates the deeds of Charlemagne as an example for the Emperor Arnulf, and Abbo of St. Germain combines war poetry with moral reflections on the state of France in a poem on the Norman siege of Paris (ca. 897). The remarkable *Waltharius*, commonly attributed to Ekkehard of St. Gall (900–73) but possibly earlier, balances the impulsive and bombastic heroism of Attila against the less heroic but more sophisticated behavior of Walter of Aquitaine and his companions, providing a perspective at once sympathetic and detached on the trad. of Germanic heroism and heroic poetry that it evokes. Vernacular culture is probably reflected also in the *Ecbasis captivi* (ca. 950), a rambling beast-fable in leonine (q.v.) hexameters apparently written for the edification of young monks; in the mid 11th-c. *Ruodlieb*, the adventures of a wandering knight, based partly on an oriental tale, provide an early foretaste of chivalric romance (see MEDIEVAL ROMANCE).

This period was also a time of innovation in religious music, its most significant form being the sequence, sung at Mass between the Epistle and the Gospel, in which the emotional and dramatic scope of religious lyric is greatly expanded. The origins of the sequence are much debated, though the impulse it reflects is present in emotionally expressive poems like the *Versus de Lazaro* of Paulinus or the *O mi custos* of Gottschalk (ca. 825). A shaping influence (formerly thought to be the originator of the sequence) was Notker of St. Gall (d. 912), whose *Liber hymnorum* expresses a range of spiritual feeling, often in striking dramatic monologues and set forth in rhythmically parallel phrases designed for antiphonal singing. His work anticipates the religious poetry of Peter Damian and Peter Abelard and the great achievements of Franciscan hymnody.

The devel. of the secular lyric is even harder to trace, but as early as the mid 10th c. the lang. of the *Song of Songs* was being used to celebrate an idealized beloved in a way which clearly anticipates the courtly lyric of the 12th c. (see COURTLY LOVE). The mid-11th-c. "Cambridge Songs" ms. includes the sophisticated *O admirabile veneris idolum*, addressed to a beautiful boy; *Levis exsurgit Zephirus*, which dwells on the interplay of emotion and natural setting in the manner of high medieval lyric; and the magnificent *Iam dulcis amica venito*, here a passionate lovesong but found elsewhere in a form adapted to religious use. The 12th c. saw a great flowering of secular love-lyric, ranging from imitations of popular song to elaborate essays in love-psychology and *courtoisie* by poets such as Walter of Châtillon (b. 1135) and Peter of Blois (ca. 1135–1212). Many of the best of these are gathered in collections such as the early 13th-c. *Carmina Burana*, which also includes drinking songs, narrative love-visions like *Phyllis and Flora* and *Si linguis angelicis* (which anticipate the *Romance of the Rose*), and satire in the trad. of "Goliardic" verse (q.v.), in which poets such as Hugh Primas (fl. ca. 1150) and the anonymous "Archpoet" of Cologne (fl. 1160s) make their own misfortunes and dissipations, real or imagined, occasion for discussing the ills of the world.

Religious poetry, too, appears in new forms in this period. The sequence form, now evolved into accentual verse with a regular rhyme scheme, provided a model for the powerful series of *planctus* in which Abelard (1079–1142) dramatizes the sufferings of such Old Testament figures as Samson, Dinah, and the daughter of Jepthah. In the sequences of Adam of St. Victor (d. 1177–92), subtle allegorical and theological arguments appear in forms as intricate as any lyric poetry of the period, and the sonorous rhyming hexameters of the *De contemptu mundi* of Bernard of Morlas (ca. 1140) give a new force to religious satire.

Side by side with these new departures is a steadily evolving trad. of "learned" Lat. poetry based on Cl. models. Already in the late 11th c., Marbod of Rennes (1035–1123), Hildebert of Le Mans (1056–1133), and Baudri of Bourgueil (1046–1130) had produced a new, urbane poetry, Ovidian in form and manner and devoted to such topics as friendship and the cultivation of relations with noble patrons. The renewal of Cl. studies in the 12th-c. cathedral schools led to more ambitious exercises. Bernardus Silvestris' *Cosmographia* (ca. 1147) and the *De planctu naturae* (ca. 1170) of Alan of Lille, philosophical allegories in the trad. of Boethius and Martianus Capella, exhibit a new assurance vis-à-vis the great authors of antiquity. Alan's *Anticlaudianus* (1182–83), on the creation of the perfect man, announces itself as a new kind of epic, and the *Alexandreis* of Walter of Châtillon (1182), Joseph of Exeter's *Ilias* (1188–90), and John of Hanville's virtually all-encompassing Juvenalian satire *Architrenius* (1184) re-

LATIN POETRY

flect similar ambition, while Geoffrey of Vinsauf provided a latter-day equivalent to Horace's *Ars poetica* in his *Poetria nova* (1216). Later critics such as John of Garland (d. 1258) and Hugh of Trimberg (fl. ca. 1280) could claim these writers as modern *auctores* worthy of the respect and study accorded the ancients. In addition, the 12th and early 13th cs. produced a range of school-poetry in less ambitious but widely popular forms: topical satires like the mock-visionary *Apocalypse of Golias*, aimed at ecclesiastical corruption, and the *Speculum stultorum* of Nigel de Longchamps, an elaborate beast-fable allegorizing monastic ambition; narrative imitations of ancient comedy like the *Pamphilus*, which had a lasting influence on love-narrative in several langs.; and a body of pseudo-Ovidian poetry incl. the mock-autobiographical *De vetula*, which was long considered an authentic Ovidian work.

A number of the greatest examples of medieval religious poetry date from the later 13th c., notably the *Philomena* of John Howden (d. 1275), a meditation on the power of love as exemplified in the lives of Christ and the Virgin; the hymns and sequence for the feast of Corpus Christi traditionally attributed to Thomas Aquinas (1229–74), the highest achievement of theological poetry in the trad. of Adam of St. Victor; and the work of a number of Franciscan poets, above all the *Dies irae* and *Stabat mater dolorosa* associated with the names of Thomas of Celano (d. 1255) and Jacopone da Todi (1230–1306). But in other areas the great proliferation of vernacular lit. led to a decline in the production of Lat. poetry, and the typical 13th-c. works are didactic treatises, designed to systematize and compress the materials of the traditional curriculum, secular and religious, in accordance with the needs of a newly compartmentalized system of education. Examples include the *De laudibus divinae sapientiae* of Alexander Nequam (d. 1217), an encyclopedic review of Creation as a manifestation of divine wisdom; the *Aurora*, a versified biblical commentary by Peter Riga (d. 1209); and the *Integumenta Ovidii* of John of Garland. The 14th c. produces such late flowerings as the devotional verse of the Eng. mystic Richard Rolle (d. 1349) and the powerful anatomy of the social ills of England in the *Vox clamantis* (1380–86) of John Gower, but the most significant work of this period, the Lat. verse of Dante, Petrarch, and Boccaccio, belongs to the history of the Ren.

See also BYZANTINE POETRY; GOLIARDIC VERSE; LEONINE RHYME; MEDIEVAL ROMANCE; MEDIEVAL POETRY; MEDIEVAL POETICS; RENAISSANCE POETICS.

ANTHOLOGIES AND TEXTS: MGH, *Poetae latini aevi Carolini*, ed. E. Dümmler, L. Traube, P. von Winterfeld, and K. Strecker, 5 v. (1881–1937); Migne, *PG* and *PL*—the fullest collection of texts; *Analecta hymnica*—the fullest collections of hymns; *Carmina Burana*, ed. J. A. Schmeller, 4th ed. (1907)—the only complete text, later ed. by A. Hilka and O. Schumann, though only v. 1, pts. 1–2, v. 2, pt. 1, and v. 3, pt. 1, have appeared to date (1931–71); *Early Lat. Hymns*, ed. A. S. Walpole (1922); *Med. Lat. Lyrics*, 5th ed. (1948), *More Lat. Lyrics from Virgil to Milton* (1977), both ed. and tr. H. Waddell; *The Goliard Poets*, ed. and tr. G. F. Whicher (1949); F. Brittain, *The Med. Lat. and Romance Lyric*, 2d ed. (1951); *Oxford Book of Med. Lat. Verse*, ed. F. J. E. Raby (1959); *Hymni latini antiquissimi xxv*, ed. W. Bulst (1975); *Seven Versions of Carolingian Pastoral*, ed. R. P. H. Green (1980); *Poetry of the Carolingian Ren.*, ed. P. Godman (1985)—long intro.

HISTORY, CRITICISM, AND PROSODY: Keil—collects the principal Med. Lat. grammarians and prosodists; Meyer; Manitius—the standard lit. hist.; H. Walther, *Das Streitgedicht in der lateinische Literatur des Mittelalters* (1920); Faral; Lote; Curtius; Raby, *Christian* and *Secular*; D. Norberg, *Poésie latine rythmique* (1954); Beare—good survey; M. Burger, *Recherches sur la structure et l'origine des vers romans* (1957); K. Strecker, *Intro. to Med. Lat.*, tr. and rev. R. B. Palmer (1957)—with excellent intro. and bibl., and "Mittellateinische Dichtung in Deutschen" in *Reallexikon I*; Norberg—best account of Med. Lat. prosody; Norden—artprose; A. C. Friend, "Med. Lat. Lit." in Fisher; M. R. P. McGuire, *Intro. to Med. Lat. Studies* (1964); J. Szövérffy, *Annalen der lateinische Hymnendichtung*, 2 v. (1964–65), *Weltliche Dichtungen des lateinische Mittelalters*, v. 1 (1970), *Lat. Hymns* (1989); Dronke; Lausberg—rhet.; Murphy—survey of med. rhet.; F. Brunhölzl, *Geschichte der lateinischen Literatur des Mittelalters*, 1–(1975–; Fr. tr., 2 v., 1990); P. Dronke, *The Med. Lyric*, 2d ed. (1978), *The Med. Poet and His World* (1985); C. Witke, *Numen litterarum* (1971); P. Klopsch, *Einführung in die mittellateinische Verslehre* (1972); J. Stevens, *Words and Music in the Middle Ages* (1980); *The Interp. of Med. Lat. P.*, ed. W. T. H. Jackson (1980); Brogan, 720 ff.; P. Godman, *Poets and Emperors* (1987); O. B. Hardison, Jr., *Prosody and Purpose in the Eng. Ren.* (1989)—incl. Med. Lat. W.W.; T.V.F.B.

III. RENAISSANCE AND POST-RENAISSANCE. The Ren. turned away from medieval varieties of rhythm and rhyme in Lat. p. towards versification based on a closer study and understanding of the forms of Cl. Antiquity. The result, from the 14th to the early 17th c., was not only a flood of poetry in the vernacular langs. and meters imitating Cl. themes and forms, and poetry in vernacular langs. imitating Cl. meters (see CLASSICAL METERS IN MODERN LANGUAGES), but also an immense output of Lat. verse itself. Petrarch (1304–74) showed the way with hundreds of hexameters on personal and intimate themes in his three books of *Epistolae metricae* (Metrical Letters, 1333–54). Petrarch also attempted a hexameter epic on the Punic Wars, *Africa* (1338–41), left incomplete after many revisions, and 12 eclogues, *Bucolicum carmen* (Pastoral Songs, 1346–68), that allegorize his ideas on poetry and politics. Similar incursions into epic and pastoral marked the history of Lat. p. in the 15th c., e.g. the incomplete *Sforzias* by Francesco Filelfo (1398–1481) about the author's Milanese patrons; a supplementary 13th book of the *Aeneid* by the humanist Maffeo Veggio (1406–58); and ten widely admired eclogues by Mantuan (Battista Spagnoli, 1447–1516) that recall models by Virgil and Petrarch while yet evincing a distinctive piety, humor, and satire.

Further, some of the best Ren. Lat. p. appeared in Cl. forms that Petrarch did not use, such as epigram, elegy, and ode (qq.v.). Panormita (Antonio Beccadelli, 1394–1471) initiated Naples' Golden Age with his *Hermaphroditus* (1425), two books of licentious epigrams that out-Martial Martial. His protégé, Giovanni Pontano (1429–1503), wrote with skill in many genres, incl. four sets of elegies in the Ovidian manner, the early *Parthenopeus* for his mistress Fannia, the mature *De amore coniugali* for his beloved wife Adriana, the late *Eridanus* for young Stella, and finally *De tumulis* (Burial Mounds) for deceased loved ones.

The finest Ren. Lat. p. is supremely conscious of its imitative debt to Cl. texts, and it gains a characteristic resonance from the explicit recall of ancient poetry. At the Florentine Academy, Angelo Poliziano (1454–94) urged poets by precept and example in five verse essays, *Silvae* (Forests, 1475–86), to cultivate Cl. allusions. Poliziano himself produced some of the finest Ren. epigrams in a Cl. vein in his *Epigrammata* (1498), as did his friend and later rival Michael Marullus (ca. 1453–1500) in four books of short poems on his exile from Constantinople and his love for his mistress Neaera. But Marullus's greatest work was his four books of *Hymni naturales* (Hymns of Nature) in various meters—hexameter, Alcaic, Sapphic, iambic—proclaiming the tenets of Neoplatonic philosophy. Two high points of creative imitation were attained by the Neapolitan Jacopo Sannazaro (1458–1530): the *Piscatoriae* (Piscatorial Eclogues, 1526) that adapt to a seaside setting conventional rhetorical structures of pastorals (q.v.) by Virgil, Calpurnius, and Nemesianus; and an epic on Christ's nativity, *De partu virginis* (Virgin Birth, 1526), that appropriates formulas, expressions, and even whole lines from the epics of Virgil, Ovid, Claudian, and others.

The more Ren. humanists sought to recover the past, the greater they realized their distance from it. Their imitations of ancient poetry only drew attention to incontrovertible differences between pagan Classicism and Christian humanism. One consequence was an effort to develop new forms and thus expand the repertory of Lat. p. The disillusioned Venetian historian Andrea Navagero (1483–1529), e.g., destroyed his own didactic verse, but his heirs managed to publish his lively experiment in 47 pastoral epigrams, *Lusus pastoralis* (Pastoral Diversions, 1530), with great impact on both Lat. p. and the vernacular. In yet another notable departure, Girolamo Fracastoro (1483–1553), a professor of medicine at Padua, wrote *Syphilis* (1530), three books attributing the origins of venereal disease to the New World and proposing a cure.

The Reformation in the North and the Counter-Reformation in Italy accentuated the religious intensity of much Lat. p. Marcantonio Flaminio (1498–1550), e.g., renounced his own early pastoral diversions in order to devote himself to paraphrases of the Psalms in Cl. meters, *Davidis psalmi* (1546), and other *Carmina sacra* (1551). After publishing an influential versified *De arte poetica* (1527), Marco Girolamo Vida (1485–1566) composed a hexameter epic on the life of Jesus, *Christias* (1535), and a collection of Christian *Hymni* (1550).

The devel. of Ren. Lat. p. beyond the Alps followed similar patterns, confirming the use of Lat. as a truly international lang. The Hungarian poet Janus Pannonius (1434–72) and the Ger. poet Conrad Celtis (1459–1508) wrote elegies, epigrams, hexameters, and hendecasyllables about their education in Italy and their efforts to bring humanist teachings to the North. The Fr. poet Salmon Macrin (1490–1557) graced the courts of Francis I and Henry II with a vast output of elegies, hymns, epithalamia, and assorted political verse. The Dutch poet Joannes Secundus (1511–36) displayed metrical and ling. virtuosity in odes, epigrams, epistles, and three books of elegies, but he earned fame throughout Europe for his *Basia* (Kisses), 19 voluptuous songs for a mistress named after Marullus's beloved Neaera, at once appropriating the erotic lyric from antiquity and announcing his competition with It. Ren. poets.

With the devel. of the vernaculars and the prestige of their lits. throughout Europe in the 16th c., many poets who wrote superb Lat. lyrics turned to their own langs. for more ambitious projects. Lodovico Ariosto (1474–1533) in Italy, Joachim Du Bellay (ca. 1525– 60) in France, Jan Kochanowski (1530–84) in Poland, and John Milton (1608–74) in England exemplify the trend. Notable exceptions include two 17th-c. Jesuit poets, Maciej Kazimierz Sarbiewski (1595–1640) in Poland and Jacob Balde (1604–68) in Germany, who wrote exquisite religious lyrics that accommodate scriptural poetics to Cl. meters. Though vernacular lit. finally gained ascendance, the composition of Lat. p. has survived even until our own day in schools and universities as an accomplishment proper to a Cl. scholar. See also IMITATION; RENAISSANCE POETICS.

ANTHOLOGIES: *Poeti latini del quattrocento*, ed. F. Arnaldi et al. (1964)—with It. trs.; *Lateinische Gedichte deutscher Humanisten*, ed. H. C. Schnur (1967)—with Ger. trs.; *Musae reduces*, ed. P. Laurens, 2 v. (1975)—with Fr. trs.; *An Anthol. of Neo-Lat. P.*, ed. F. J. Nichols (1979)—with Eng. trs.; *Ren. Lat. Verse*, ed. A. Perosa and J. Sparrow (1979).

EDITIONS AND TRANSLATIONS: Johannes Secun-

LATVIAN POETRY

dus, *Love Poems,* ed. and tr. F. A. Wright (1930), and in *The Lat. Love Elegy,* ed. and tr. C. Endres (1981); G. Fracastoro, *Syphilis,* ed. and tr. H. Wynne-Finch (1935); Conrad Celtis, *Selections,* ed. and tr. L. Forster (1948); M. K. Sarbiewski, *Odes,* tr. G. Hils (1646), ed. M.-S. Roestvig (1953); J. Sannazaro, *Arcadia and the Piscatorial Eclogues,* tr. R. Nash (1966); J. Milton, *Variorum: Lat. and Gr. Poems,* ed. and tr. D. Bush et al. (1970); A. Navagero, *Lusus,* ed. and tr. A. E. Wilson (1973); Petrarch, *Bucolicum carmen,* ed. and tr. T. G. Bergin (1974), *Africa,* tr. T. G. Bergin (1977); M. G. Vida, *De arte poetica,* ed. and tr. R. G. Williams (1976), *Christiad,* ed. and tr. G. C. Drake and C. A. Forbes (1978); *Ren. Lat. P.,* ed. and tr. I. D. McFarlane (1980).

HISTORY AND CRITICISM: L. Bradner, *Musae Anglicanae: A Hist. of Anglo-Lat. Poetry 1500–1925* (1940); P. Van Tieghem, *La Lit. lat. de la Ren.* (1944); L. Spitzer, "The Problem of Lat. Ren. Poetry," *SP* 2 (1955); G. Ellinger and B. Ristow, "Neulateinische Dichtung im Deutschlands im 16. Jh.," *Reallexikon* 2.620–45; J. Sparrow, "Lat. Verse of the High Ren.," *It. Ren. Studies,* ed. E. F. Jacob (1960); W. L. Grant, *Neo-Lat. Lit. and the Pastoral* (1965); J. Ijsewijn, *Companion to Neo-Lat. Studies* (1977); W. J. Kennedy, *Jacopo Sannazaro and the Uses of Pastoral* (1983). W.J.K.

LATIN PROSODY. See CLASSICAL PROSODY.

LATVIAN POETRY. The beginnings of L. p., indeed its very roots, are to be found in L. folksongs called *dainas.* Most of the dainas date from the days of serfdom and express the L. ethos that has changed little over the cs.: respect for nature, a work ethic, attitudes that edify family ties, forebearance, emotional restraint. These motifs are often found in L. p.

L. lit. proper begins in the middle of the 19th c. with the so-called National Awakening movement, a movement primarily initiated by L. intellectuals, some of them gifted poets who, inspired by the Fichtean notion of *Volksseele,* turned to indigenous sources (national history, folklore, mythology) for the inspiration and subject matter of their poetic efforts. Juris Alunāns (1832–64) inaugurates L. p. with his opuscule, *Dziesminas* (Ditties), in 1856, which set a precedent. The volume, however, is distinctly a notch above the devotional verse offered up to that time by well-meaning Ger. pastors whose knowledge of L. was very minimal. This generation of committed poets, most of them students at the University of Tartu, set the tone for what was to become known as "national romanticism." Among them: Auseklis (pseudonym of Mikelis Krogzems, 1850–79), a fiery poet much inspired by Schiller; Andrējs Pumpurs (1841–1902), who in imitation of the Finnish and Estonian national epics attempted a similar feat with his *Lāčplēsis* (The Bearslayer), though with limited success; Krišjānis Barons (1835–1923), known

for his labors to collect and classify dainas, the number of which now reaches two million.

A rival intellectual impulse came with Marxism in the 1880s, precipitating a movement called the New Current and thereby an ideological schism that runs deep in L. lit. A syncretic vision, however, is proffered by Jānis Rainis (pseudonym of Jānis Pliekšāns, 1865–1929). The national past and mythology are often sources of his poetry, yet his philosophical thought extends beyond the fold of nationalism to embrace a religion of all humanity. His wife Aspazija (pseudonym of Elza Rozenberga-Pliekšāne, 1868–1943), the first L. feminist, combined in her poetry a flamboyant neoromantic nationalism with a social conscience that inveighs against social and economic injustices and bourgeois prejudices and complacency. Close to Aspazija's emotional intensity in some respects are Fricis Bārda (1880–1919) and Jānis Poruks (1871–1911), poets of lyrical moods and subtle tonalities. Other poets who became popular before World War I include Plūdonis (pseudonym of Vilis Lejnieks, 1874–1940), a master of robust rhymes and rich images, sometimes á la impressionism; Kārlis Skalbe (1879–1945), a popular poet of simple forms, with affinities to the dainas; and Anna Brigadere (1861–1933), best remembered as the spokesperson of the humble and the young.

With L. national independence in 1918, L. p. became more susceptible to the literary currents of Western Europe. Edvarts Virza (pseudonym of Lieknis, 1883–1940) studied and translated Fr. poetry and became the official voice of the new authoritarian regime installed by a coup d'etat in 1934. His most celebrated work is an extended prose poem, *Straumēni,* that praises the virtues of bucolic life on a L. farmstead. Expressionism left an impact on Pēteris Ērmanis (1893–1969), the first L. poet to experiment with free verse. The coup d'etat brought to the fore a group of staunchly patriotic poets. Jānis Medenis (1903–61) tried to adapt folk meters to modern verse. Zinaīda Lazda (1902–61) became much admired for her lyrical landscapes, her celebration of simple life á la dainas. But there were also poets who deviated from the officially sanctioned poetics. Ēriks Ādamsons (1907–47) was an essentially urban poet, introspective and complex, ironic and refined, scornful of rural simplicities. Aleksandrs Čaks (pseudonym of Čadarainis, 1902–50) is considered the most original modernist and the one whose legacy to the following generation of poets is most felt. Forceful and iconoclastic, mocking and ironic, insisting on the importance of rhythm over rhyme, he shocked the traditionalists and fascinated the young.

In the late 1930s, as Europe was in the throes of apocalyptic events, a new generation of poets came of age. When the Soviet Armies occupied Latvia in 1944, most of them preferred to go into exile. Veronika Strēlerte (pseudonym of Rudīte Strēlerte-Johansone, b. 1912) is a poet of profound meditative moods and restrained patriotic feelings, much appreciated for her finely sculpted verse. Andrējs Eglītis (b. 1912), the widely proclaimed national bard, popular and prolific, is most celebrated for his thunderous poem, "God, Thy land is aflame." Velta Toma (b. 1912), a somewhat controversial figure for her nonconformist ideas, cultivates a forceful personal expression. Velta Snikere (b. 1920), a multifaceted personality, grafts new sensibilities of surrealist penchant onto the folkloric traditions.

Exile nurtured a new generation of poets, who share a certain aversion to loud political commitment and to emotion-drenched rhet. and a distrust for traditional poetic forms. The first cénacle was formed in Manhattan's Hell's Kitchen to become known as the Hell's Kitchen Poets. Among them: Linards Tauns (pseudonym of Arnolds Bērzs, 1922–63), an urban poet fascinated by the Babel of New York City, a visionary seeking more heightened forms of existence; Gunars Salinš (b.1924), who interweaves urban with rural images, folkloric patterns with jazz rhythms; Baiba Bičole (b. 1931) who celebrates, in rites sacred and erotic, encounters with the physical world; Aina Kraujiete (b. 1923), intellectual and erudite, given to ontological adventures, exploring alternate states of being. Outside the cénacle, but aesthetically affinitive, are Astrīde Ivaska (b. 1926), whose subtle tonalities celebrate the preciousness of lang., weaving nuance to nuance, connecting sound and sense in configurations familiar and yet original; and Olafs Stumbrs (b. 1931), whose existential anguish and loneliness subtend the satire of the social scene, much laced with black humor and sarcasm. Andrējs Irbe (b. 1924), living in Sweden, probes the ever-evanescent inner self that intimates affinities with the mysterious Nordic landscape that too escapes finality.

In the homeland, the coevals of the exiles lived on the native soil and among their people, whose lang. constantly replenishes their work. But they also created under duress, never knowing the official level of tolerance for deviation from Soviet doctrine. Vizma Belševica (b. 1931) was first hailed, then silenced, then rehabilitated for her poetry, so often characterized by ontological introspection and contemplation of the collective destinies of the L. people. Imants Ziedonis (b. 1933), prolific and immensely popular, subject to contrapuntal moods, celebrates the beauty of the land and the vitality of the people and mourns the effacement of the past through urbanization and industrialization. Ojārs Vācietis (1933–83), frequently dubbed "the L. Yevtushenko," versatile and impulsive, always managed to remain in the good graces of the Soviet authorities, while not sparing his caustic wit. Māris Čaklais (b. 1940), intensely personal and very popular among the young, combines the rustic and the refined, the spontaneous and the analytic, giving his verse a wide tonal range and a fine filigree texture. Next to these poets another generation, both abroad and in the homeland, has already come to the fore, generally more polyphonic, more acerbic, more experimental than their elders. Most recently, the advent of openness (*glasnost*) and the collapse of the Soviet Union in 1989 are not only certain to leave a lasting impact on the present and future generations but will also necessitate a revaluation of those poets whose works, long suppressed, are now being published.

ANTHOLOGIES: *Latvju modernās dzejas antologija*, ed. A. Čaks and P. Kikuts (1930); *Latviešu tautas dziesmas*, ed. A. Švābe et al., 12 v. (1952–56); *Latvju sonets 100 gados 1856–1956*, ed. K. Dzilleja (1956); *Lettische Lyrik*, ed. E. Eckard-Skalberg (1960); *Dzejas un sejas / Latviešu dzeja svešumā*, ed. T. Zeltinš et al. (1962); *Poetry from Latvia*, ed. J. Anerauds, 3 v. (1982); *Lettische Lyrik*, ed. E. Zuzena-Metuzala (1983); *Contemp. L. P.*, ed. I. Cedrinš (1984).

HISTORY AND CRITICISM: E. Virza, *La Littérature lettonne depuis l'époque de réveil national* (1926); A. Johansons, *Latviešu literatūra* (1953); J. Andrups and V. Kalve, *L. Lit.* (1954); M. Dombrovska, *Latviešu dzeja* (1966); A. Ziedonis, *The Religious Philosophy of Janis Rainis, L. Poet* (1969); R. Ekmanis, *L. Lit. under the Soviets: 1940–1975* (1978).
J.S.

LAUDA (Lat. "praise"). It. genre of religious origin and content. It was first created probably as a vernacular equivalent or adaptation of the Med. Lat. hymn (q.v.), e.g. the *Stabat mater* and the *Dies irae*. Its devel. is connected with the 13th-c. cult, esp. widespread in the Umbrian region of Italy, the confraternity of the Scourgers (*Flagellanti*). Umbrian in origin is its earliest surviving example, the *Laudes creaturarum* ("Praise of the Creation"; in Lat., ca. 1224) of Francis of Assisi. The greatest cultivator of the l., Jacopone da Todi (1236?–1306), set its range of topics (from simple thanksgiving to complex multivocal dramatizations of liturgical themes) and meters (of great freedom and variety, but the typical form was the *ballata* with a 2-line *ripresa* [*xx*] and a 4-line monorhymed stanza [*aaax bbbx*, etc.] composed generally of *ottonari*, hendecasyllables [q.v.], and *settenari*). Jacopone's ca. 100 surviving *laude* found no direct imitators of note, but the genre survived into the 16th c.—G. Ippoliti, *Dalle sequenze alle laudi* (1914); P. Dronke, *The Mediaeval Lyric* (1969); M. Fubini, *Metrica e poesia*, 2d ed. (1970); Wilkins; D. L. Jeffrey, *The Early Eng. Lyric and Franciscan Spirituality* (1975), ch. 4; Elwert, *Italienische*, sect. 90–91; P. S. Diehl, *The Med. European Religious Lyric* (1985). T.W.; C.K.

LAUREATE. See POET LAUREATE.

LECTURE. See DECONSTRUCTION; SOUND; TEXTUALITY.

LEICH. Poem in unequal stanzas, cultivated in

Ger.-speaking areas in the 13th and 14th cs. Music survives for a few examples. The term l. originally designated an instrumental melody, a sense which persists in addition to that of "non-isostrophic poem," a semantic loan on the pattern of OF *lai* first attested in Ulrich von Liechtenstein (mid 13th c.). The l. has affinities with the Med. Lat. sequence, Occitan and OF *descort*, OF *lai*, Occitan *estampida* and OF *estampie* (qq.v.). Like sequence and *lai* (but unlike *descort*), the l. may be used for religious as well as secular subjects.

There are considerably more examples of the secular l. Its themes are in the main those of *Minnesang* (q.v.). A new devel., not paralleled in the Romance analogues, is the intro. of a dancing section into the l. in Heinrich von Sax, Ulrich von Winterstetten, and Tannhäuser; this is associated with dactylic rhythms (*Tanzl.*). Tannhäuser is unique in introducing into the l. the didactic themes of princely panegyric and lament for dead rulers.

The l. is usually considerably longer than most isostrophic poems. A high proportion of unique strophes is characteristic of the religious l. and the *Tanzl.* There may also be contiguous or noncontiguous repetitions of strophic patterns, or partial or approximate responsion between sections. There is a proliferation of short rhyming units, with a high incidence of different types of rhyme. The l. is frequently divided into two halves, but in the *Tanzl.* a ternary division is also found; internally, the strophes are frequently bipartite, less often tripartite. The religious l. has affinities with Lat. sequence, but in the main the l. is more closely akin to its Romance analogues. See also MINNESANG; GERMAN PROSODY, *Middle High German.*

F. Wolf, Über die Lais, Sequenzen und L. (1841); O. Gottschalk, *Der deutsche Minnel.* (1908); R. J. Browne, *Stylistic and Formal Hist. of the MHG L.*, Diss., Yale (1955); K. H. Bertau, *Sangverslyrik* (1964); H. Kuhn, "L.," *Reallexikon*; I. Glier, "Der Minnel. im späten 13. Jahrhundert," *Werk-Typ-Situation*, ed. I. Glier et al. (1969); J. Maillard, "Lai, L.," *Gattungen der Musik*, ed. W. Arlt et al. (1973); H. Spanke, *Studien zu Sequenz, Lai und L.* (1977); Sayce.　　O.L.S.

LENGTH. See DURATION.

LEONINE RHYME, VERSE. "Once rhyme invaded the hexameter," John Addington Symonds remarked, "the best verses of the medieval period in that measure are l." Also the worst (Raby). Ordinarily the term l. r. refers to internal rhyme in the Med. Lat. hexameter (i.e. the word at line-end rhyming with the word preceding the caesura); technically it denotes an oxytonic word-ending (a "feminine" rhyme; see MASCULINE AND FEMININE). Though there are examples in Cl. Lat. poetry (e.g. Ovid, *Ars amatoria*) and epitaph verse, l. r. flourished in Med. Lat. after the 9th c., being so popular it was imitated in Ir., Eng. (the OE

Rhyming Poem), Ger., and (esp.) Fr. It is regularly mentioned in the medieval prosody manuals of *ars metrica* and *Séconde rhétorique* (q.v.). Presumably the device came into verse from one of the clausulae of rhythmical prose, the *cursus leoninus*, though the origin of the term is uncertain: some trace it to Pope Leo the Great, others to Leoninus, a 12th-c. Benedictine canon of Paris (fl. 1135; see Erdmann).

Leonine verse refers to a hexameter-pentameter couplet (not always rhymed), as in Eberhard's *Laborintus*—the meter known to antiquity as the elegiac distich (q.v.). Both in these couplets and in hexameter couplets more elaborate schemes of internal rhyming quickly developed both in Occitan and OF, such as rhyming the lines' first two hemistichs together and last two together (Lat. *versus interlaqueati*, Fr. *rime enterlacée*, "interwoven rhyme"); or a double rhyme in the first line, a second double rhyme in the second, and a third binding the ends of the two lines—which by breaking gives the *aabccb* scheme of Fr. *rime couée*, "tail rhyme" (q.v.). Thus the partitioning of long-line Lat. verse via internal rhyme paved the way for a multitude of short-line lyric stanzas in the vernaculars.

W. Wackernagel, "Gesch. des deutschen Hexameters und Pentameters bis auf Klopstock," *Kleinere Schriften*, v. 2 (1873); E. Freymond, "Über den reichen Reim bei altfranzösischen Dichtern," *ZRP* 6 (1882); Schipper 1.305 ff; Kastner; Meyer, 2.267; K. Strecker, "Leoninische Hexameter und Pentameter im 9. Jahrhundert," *Neues Archi für ältere deutsche Geschichtskunde* 44 (1922), 213 ff.; C. Erdmann, "Leonitas," *Corona Quernea: Festgabe Karl Strecker* (1941); Lote, 2.141 ff.; Curtius, 8.2–3; Raby, *Secular*, 1.228, 2.1; Norden.　　T.V.F.B.

LESBIAN POETRY. See LOVE POETRY.

LETRILLA (diminutive of *letra*, a short gloss). A Sp. poem generally written in short lines, often having a refrain, and usually written on a light or satiric topic. Such poems can be found as early as the 14th c. at least, but were apparently not given the name *l.* until much later. Famous examples are Góngora's *Ándeme yo caliente, y ríase la gente* ("As long as I am comfortable, let people laugh if they wish") and Quevedo's *Poderoso caballero es don Dinero* ("A powerful gentleman is Sir Money").—Navarro.　　D.C.C.

LETTER, VERSE. See VERSE EPISTLE.

LETTRISME. A movement which first gained prominence in Paris following World War II. Founded by the Romanian expatriot Isidore Isou, who wished to reduce lang. to its constituent elements, L. sought to displace surrealism (q.v.) as the leading avant-garde movement. Since the early 1950s, Maurice Lemaître has been L.'s principal theorist and chief organizer; Jean-Paul Curtay has introduced several innovations. L. derives from the It. futurists' *parole in libertá* ("liberated words"), from the Rus. futurists' exploration of transrational lang. (*zaum*—see FUTURISM), and from the dadaists' experiments with opto-phonetic poetry. Like dada (q.v.), L. is a violently antagonistic movement that attacks the foundations of bourgeois society through the medium of the written word by reducing the letters of the alphabet to a series of phonetic or visual counters. By emphasizing the autonomy of the individual letter at the expense of the larger word, L. aims to destroy signification itself. Meaning is not only fragmented but totally effaced.

In theory (and to some extent in practice) the principles underlying L. may be applied to all forms of human endeavor. While Letterists have become involved in such areas as politics, economics, erotology, and even pharmacy, their more significant contributions have been in the realm of the arts. Of these, poetry and the plastic arts have provided the most fertile ground for experimentation. L. originally focused on sound poetry (q.v.), combining letters in various fashions according to their phonetic values, then visual poetry (q.v.), varying the size and shape of letters to produce the graphic equivalent of drawing. Usurping the traditional prerogatives of painting, graphic conventions were placed at the service of the visual composition, and the concept of visual poetry gave way to that of visual art.

An inherently interdisciplinary genre, L. juxtaposes elements such as letters, photographs, miscellaneous signs, and pictorial images in an attempt to transcend the limits of traditional representation. The linguistic sign is stripped of its linguistic function: letters are powerless to assert themselves, and the whole field of signs is reduced to the status of random marks on the page. The only recourse left to the spectator is to focus on the letters' visual properties. Lacking verbal identity, the letters function exclusively as pictorial signs, with the result that their significance derives according to the rules governing abstract art.—I. Isou, *Intro. à une nouvelle poésie et à une nouvelle musique* (1947), *Les Champs de force de la peinture* (1964); M. Lemaître, *Qu'est-ce que le L.?* (1954), *Bilan lettriste* (1955), *L. et hypergraphie* (1966); J.-P. Curtay, *La Poésie lettriste* (1974); D. Seaman, *Concrete Poetry in France* (1981); *VLang* 17 (1983)—valuable bibl.   W.B.

LEXIS. The term "l." (Gr. "diction"), was accepted as Eng. usage by the *OED* in the 2d ed. (first citations 1950, 1957 [Frye]) and defined as "the diction or wording, in contrast to other elements, of a piece of writing." "L." is a more useful term than "diction" because more neutral. Even where "the diction of poetry" is distinguished from "poetic diction" (esp. in the 18th-c. sense), "diction" may elicit only the question of unusual lang. rather than all questions concerning the lang. of

poetry. L. in poetics is further to be differentiated from 1. in linguistics (*OED*, sense 1.2).

The primary rule for thinking about 1. is that words in a poem always exist in relation, never in isolation: "there are no bad words or good words; there are only words in bad or good places" (Nowottny 32). Otherwise, classifying 1. can be a barren exercise, just as concentrating on isolated words can be barren for a beginning poet. Consistency within the chosen area of 1. is necessary for a well-made poem, and consistency is not necessarily easy to achieve (Johnston). Ascertaining the consistency of 1. in a poem enables the reader to hear moves outside that range (e.g. Kenner on Wordsworthian 1. in Yeats's "The Tower" [*Gnomon* (1958)]). Great skill in 1. implies that a poet knows words as she or he knows people (Hollander 228), knows how "words have a stubborn life of their own" (Elton), and knows that words need to be "at home" with the "complete consort dancing together" (Eliot, *Little Gidding* 216–25, the best modern poetic description of 1. "that is right").

Some useful categories for studying 1. may be drawn from the *OED* (preface on "General Knowledge"), where vocabulary is classified as follows: (1) *Identification*, incl. usual spelling, pronunciation, grammatical part of speech, whether specialized, and status (e.g. rare, obsolete, archaic, colloquial, dialectal); (2) *Morphology*, including etymology, and subsequent word-formation, including cognates in other languages; (3) *Signification*, which builds on other dictionaries and on quotations; and (4) *Illustrative quotations*, which show forms and uses, particular senses, earliest use (or, for obsolete words, latest use), and connotations. Studies of 1. might test these categories for any given poem. It should be remembered that in common usage "meaning" refers to definition under category (3), but "meaning" as defined by the *OED* includes all four categories. And "meaning" in poetry, fully defined, includes all functions of the word (see MEANING, POETIC).

L. includes all parts of speech, not simply nouns, adjectives, and verbs. Emphasis on what is striking tends to isolate main parts of speech and imposes a dubious standard of vividness (though see ENARGEIA) analogous to Arnold's critical method of reading "touchstones" (q.v.). Even articles matter (Browning sometimes drops them; cf. Whitman and Forster on passages to India). Verb forms matter (see James Merrill's *Recitative* [1986] 21 on the prevalence of first-person present active indicative). The metaphorical force of, for example, prepositions must be remembered as well as their double possibilities (e.g. "of," as in "the love of three oranges," a favorite device of Stevens). Different langs. offer different possibilities for plurisignation and ambiguity according to their grammatical structures (see SYNTAX, POETIC).

Discussions of 1. often tend more toward polemics than poetics. It may be impossible to separate the two, but the effort is essential (Nowottny is exemplary). Coleridge's dictum should be kept in mind: that every great and original author "has had the task of creating the taste by which he is to be enjoyed" (cited in Wordsworth 1815), a task that perforce includes polemics. Thus Eliot's attacks on the Keats-Tennyson line of l., esp. as developed by Swinburne, are better read generically in terms of charm and riddle (qq.v.), as Frye does (1976; and see Welsh), rather than in Eliot's terms. Similarly, readers and critics must be vigilant so as not to read modern assumptions about l. back into older poetry. Thus, says Strang, "the reader of Spenser should approach the text as being in Spenser's lang., which is a very different matter from reading him as if he were writing modern Eng. with intermittent lapses into strange expressions which require glossing." Here critics must avail themselves of the results of historical scholarship on the contemporaneity or archaism (q.v.) of words—often a difficult assessment.

There are only a few general questions concerning l., and they have remained for centuries. The most fruitful may be the more particular ones. One longstanding general issue is whether a special l. for poetry exists, or should exist. This in turn depends on what poetry is thought to be, or what type of poetry is in question. Of discussions in antiquity, those by Aristotle, Dionysius of Halicarnassus, Horace, and Pseudo-Longinus are the most important. Aristotle's few remarks remain pertinent: poetic l. should be both clear and striking, "ordinary words" should be used for clarity, and "unfamiliar terms, i.e. strange words, metaphors" should be used to make l. shine and to avoid l. that is inappropriately "mean." There should be a mixture of ordinary and unfamiliar uses of lang. (*Poetics*, tr. Bywater [1909]). In the Middle Ages and early Ren., the issue of diction takes on particular importance as Med. Lat. gives way to the vernaculars. Dante's *De vulgari eloquentia* (Of Eloquence in the Vernacular, ca. 1303; tr. R. S. Haller [1973]) is the central text in the *questione della lingua*; Dante debates this same division at some length, setting l. in the context of the disputes on the suitability of the vernaculars for elevated expression, on the biblical origins of lang., and on prosody. He judges the best l. to be "illustrious," "cardinal," "courtly," and "curial" (i.e. well-balanced, as in a law-court). In *DVE* 2.7, Dante gives detailed criteria for those words that are suitable for "the highest style." Some are as specific as those constraining Valéry's well-known search for "a word that is feminine, disyllabic, includes P or F, ends in a mute syllable, and is a synonym for break or disintegration, and not learned, not rare. Six conditions—at least!" (Nowottny 2). Here Dante classifies words in the "noble vernacular" as "childish" (too elementary), "feminine" (too soft in sound, and unelevated), and "manly"; only the last type will serve for poetry. These last, in turn, are either "rustic" or "urban," and only the urban will serve for poetry. And of the urban words, some are "smooth-haired or even oily" while others are "shaggy or even bristly." Only words that are "smooth-haired" or "shaggy" are suitable for the high style in poetry, as, for example, in tragedy; words that are "oily" or "bristly" are "excessive in some direction." Dante sees that the main question, as so often, is appropriateness or decorum (q.v.), but not simply for a given type of writing. He also stresses appropriateness for the person using a given l., a criterion unfamiliar to many current writers. Only those with sufficient natural talent, art, and learning should attempt the most demanding l., says Dante, for l. has its own implicit demands. Even today it remains true that the use of l. reflects a poet's judgment, for good or ill.

The term "poetic diction" is strongly associated with 18th-c. poetry, largely because of Wordsworth's attacks on it in the "Preface" to *Lyrical Ballads* (3d ed., 1802; see also the "Appendix on . . . Poetic Diction" and "Essay, Supplementary to the Preface" [1815]). Wordsworth remarks that "there will be found in these volumes little of what is usually called poetic diction," by which he means the epithets, periphrases, personifications, archaisms (qq.v.), and other conventionalized phrases all too often employed unthinkingly in Augustan poetry. As against Thomas Gray, for example, who wrote that "the lang. of the age is never the lang. of poetry" (Letter to R. West, April 1742), Wordsworth advocated using the "real lang. of men," esp. those in humble circumstances and rustic life. But Wordsworth's many conditions governing such "real lang." in poetry must be kept clearly in mind (e.g. men "in a state of vivid sensation," the lang. adapted and purified, a selection only).

Coleridge, with his superior critical mind, saw that "the lang. of real life" was an "equivocal expression" applying only to some poetry, and there in ways never denied (*Biographia literaria*, chs. 14–22). He rejected the argument of rusticity, asserting that the lang. of Wordsworth's rustics derives from a strong grounding in the lang. of the Eng. Bible (the Authorized Version, 1611) and the liturgy or hymn-book. In any case, the best part of lang., says Coleridge, is not derived from objects but from "reflection on the acts of the mind itself." By "real," Wordsworth actually means "ordinary" lang., the "lingua communis" (cf. *OED*, Pref.), and even this needs cultivation to become truly "communis" (Coleridge cites Dante). Wordsworth's real object, Coleridge saw, was to attack assumptions about a supposedly necessary poetic diction. The debate is of great importance for l. It marks the shift from what Frye calls a high mimetic mode to a low mimetic one, a shift still governing the l. of poetry today. (In Fr. poetry, the shift comes a little later and is associated with Hugo [1827].)

Coleridge disagreed with Wordsworth's contention that "there neither is, nor can be any *essential* difference between the lang. of prose and metrical composition." Though there is a "neutral style" common to prose and poetry, Coleridge finds it "a singular and noticeable fact . . . that a theory which would establish the *lingua communis* not only as the best, but as the only commendable style, should have proceeded from a poet, whose diction, next to that of Shakespeare and Milton, appears to me of all others the most *individualized* and characteristic." To be sure, some words in a poem may be in everyday use; but, he adds, "are those words *in those places* commonly employed in real life to express the same thought or outward thing? Are they the style used in the ordinary intercourse of spoken words? No! nor are the modes of connections; and still less the breaks and transitions" (*Biographica literaria*, ch. 20). In Coleridge's modification of Wordsworth's well-intentioned arguments, readers may still find essential principles applicable to questions of poetic l.

The 20th c. has, in one sense, taken up Wordsworth's words, steadily removing virtually every restriction on diction. The 20th c. now generally bars no word whatever from the l. of poetry, at least in the Germanic and Romance langs. Struggles over appropriate l. in the 19th c. included attacks on the romantics, Browning, and Whitman. Attempts by Bridges and others to domesticate Hopkins' extraordinary l. are well known. In the early 20th-c., Edwardian critics with genteel notions of poetry objected to Brooke writing about seasickness and Owen's disgust at the horrors of World War I (Stead). Wordsworth's "real lang. of men" was twisted by some into attacks on any unusual l. whatsoever—difficult, local, learned—a problem to this day, though now less from genteel notions than egalitarian ones inappropriately extended to the l. of all poetry. Yet the l. of poetry may still be associated with the lang. of a certain class—see Tony Harrison's poems playing Standard Eng. against working-class Eng. But if poetry now generally admits all types of l., it remains true that the l. of poetry—of the Bible, Shakespeare, and the ballads, for example—needs to be learned; otherwise most older poetry, as well as much contemporary, cannot be well read at all (Vendler 56). The l. of the Authorized Version and of the Gr. and Lat. classics has been influential on Eng. poetry for centuries, and the manifold strategies and effects of allusion (q.v.) must not be overlooked. Virgil's l. in eclogue, georgic, and epic was admired and imitated well past the Ren. (see IMITATION; INFLUENCE).

Historical changes in the lang. make the use of good dictionaries mandatory. In Eng., the *OED* (both eds.) is the most generous and its quotations invaluable, but other dictionaries are also needed (e.g. of U.S. Eng., for etymology; see Kenner on Pound's use of Skeat). The elementary philological categories of widening and narrowing, and raising and lowering, in meaning are useful. (Cf. "wanton," where solely modern senses must not be applied to Milton's use, or even as late as Bridges'

"Wanton with long delay the gay spring leaping cometh" ("April, 1885"); "gay" is well known.) Hidden semantic and connotative changes must be esp. watched, along with favorite words in a given time (Miles) and key words whose meaning was assumed and so not defined (Becker). The l. of some modern poets pays attention to historical linguistics, while that of others is largely synchronic; readers should test.

Etymologies are stories of origins. The etymologist cares whether they are true or false, but a poet need not (Ruthven); mythologies are for the poet as useful as histories. Philology may include certain assumptions about poetic l. (see Barfield against Max Müller). Etymologies may include histories of war and struggle (for nationalism involves lang. just as class does). Poets may exploit the riches of etymology (see Geoffrey Hill's *Mystery of the Charity of Charles Péguy* on Eng. and Fr. l.). Etymology may function as a "mode of thought" (Curtius) or as a specific "frame for trope" (see Hollander on Hopkins) or both. Invented or implied etymologies can also be useful ("silva" through Dante's well-known "selva" links by sound and sense with "salveo," "salvatio," etc.). Milton plays earlier etymological meaning against later meaning, such play functioning as a trope for the fallen state of lang.: the prelapsarian "savage" hill, for example, is closely connected to its Lat. root "silvaticus" and Eng. "silvan," but with post-lapsarian "savage . . . obscur'd" solitude, the later meaning of "savage" as "barbaric" is implied (*PL* 4.172, 9.1085). Eng. is unusually accommodating, combining as it does both Latinate and Germanic words. Other important word-roots should also be noted (cf. the etymological appropriateness of "sherbet" in Eliot's "Journey of the Magi").

L. may be considered along an axis of old to new, with archaism (q.v.) at one end and innovation (neologism being one part) at the other. Archaism may be introduced to enlarge the l. of poetry, sometimes through native terms (Spenser, Hopkins). Or it may be used for certain genres (e.g. literary imitations of the oral ballads) or for specific effects, ironic, allusive, or other. Innovation may remain peculiar to one poet or may enlarge the stock of the poetic lexicon. Neologisms (new-coined words) tend now to be associated with novelty more than freshness, and sometimes with strained effects. The very word indicates they are not common currency. Some periods are conducive to expanding l. in general (the mid 14th c.; the late 16th c.) or to expanding l. in some areas (computer terms, nowadays, though they have yet to be entered in general poetic l.).

Where poets do not invent or resuscitate terms, they draw on vocabulary from different contemporaneous sources (see the *OED* categories). Foreign, local, and dialectal words are noted below. The precision of terms drawn from such areas as theology, philosophy, or the Bible must not be underestimated, for controversy can center on one

- [690] -

word. Studies working outward from single words (e.g. Empson; Lewis; Barfield on "ruin") are valuable reminders of historical and conceptual significance in 1.

Shakespeare has contributed most to the enlargement of our stock of words; critics regularly note how often he provides the first example of a given word in the *OED*. His many mintings incl. adaptations from the stock of both Eng. (e.g. "lonely," presumably from Sidney's "loneliness") and other langs. ("monumental," from Lat.), apparent inventions ("bump"), shifts in grammatical function ("control" as a verb rather than a noun), and other strategies. His mastery of 1. is seen above all in his boldness and innovation. He possesses easily the largest known vocabulary of any poet (by some calculations, about 21,000 words, as against Milton's 8,000), but it is his extraordinary *use* of so large a word-hoard (as against ordinary recognition of a large reading or speaking vocabulary) that is so remarkable (Jespersen).

Most new words are now generally drawn from scientific or technical sources, though poetry makes comparatively little use of them. In the 18th c., poets could say that "Newton demands the Muse" (see Nicholson), but poets today do not generally say that "Einstein demands the Muse." A. R. Ammons is one of the few modern poets exploiting the possibilities of new scientific 1.— e.g. "zygote" (1891, *OED*) rhymed with "goat"; "white dwarf" (1924, *OED* 2d ed.); and "black hole" (1969). Of the large stock of slang and colloquial expressions, many are evanescent or inert, though special uses may be effective. Shakespeare's gift for introducing colloquial 1. is a salutary reminder not to reject colloquialisms per se.

Along the axis of old to new, the most interesting question is why and how some 1. begins to sound dated. Archaisms and innovations alike are easy to hear. What is it the 1. we designate as, say, 18th-c. or Tennysonian or Whitmanian. But what is it that distinguishes the poetic 1. of a generation ago, and why do amateur poets tend to use the 1. of their poetic grandparents? The aging of words or the passing of their claim on our allegiance is of continuing interest to poets as part of the diachronic aspect of their art.

Different types of poetry require different lexical praxis, though such requirements vary according to time and place. Oral poetry (q.v.) makes use of stock phrases or epithets (q.v.) cast into formulae (see FORMULA). Some of Homer's epithets became renowned, e.g., "polupholoisbos" ("loud-roaring") for the sea (see Amy Clampitt's echo of this). Compound epithets in OE poetry are known by the ON term "kenning" (q.v.) and sometimes take the form of a riddle. Different genres also require different praxis (Fowler 71), a requirement much relaxed today. Epic (q.v.) required a high-style 1., as did the sublime (qq.v.; see Monk). Genres of the middle and low style drew from a different register. Satire (q.v.) usually works in the

middle style but allows much leeway, esp. in Juvenalian as against Horatian satire. Any 1. may become banal—e.g. that of the 16th-c. sonneteers or that of some pastoral (q.v.) writers (cf. Coleridge, *Letters*, 9 Oct. 1794: "The word 'swain' . . . conveys too much of the Cant of Pastoral"). Connotation (q.v.) or association is governed partly by genre, and is all-important for 1.

L. also depends partly on place. The largest division in Eng. is between Great Britain and the U.S.A., but poetry from elsewhere (Ireland, Africa, Asia, Australasia, Canada, the Caribbean) also shows important differences. Establishing a distinctive poetic style in a new country with an old lang. presents peculiar problems which novelty in itself will not solve. Within a country, 1. will vary locally, and poets can make memorable uses of local terms (Yeats of "perne" in "Sailing to Byzantium," Eliot of "rote" in *The Dry Salvages*; Whitman uses native Amerindian terms). The question of dialect shades into this. Burns and Hardy draw on local and dialectal words. Hopkins' remarkable 1. derives from current lang., dialectal and other, as well as older words; a few (e.g. "pitch") have specific Hopkinsian usage (see Milroy). Foreign words, a special case, work along a scale of assimilation, for standard 1. includes many words originally considered foreign. Considerable use of foreign 1. (apart from novelties like macaronic verse [q.v.]) implies a special contract with the reader, at least in societies unaccustomed to hearing more than one lang. L. may also vary according to class (see above). It is still a matter of dispute how far it varies according to gender.

Interpretive categories are numerous, and readers should be aware of them as such; even taxonomies are interpretive. Beyond the categories already mentioned, 1. may be judged according to the degree of "smoothness" (Tennyson as against Browning is a standard example; see Frye 1957), "smoothness" (recollect Dante above) centering on the large and important question of sound in 1. (cf. Seamus Heaney on Auden: "the gnomic clunk of Anglo-Saxon phrasing . . . pulled like a harrow against the natural slope of social speech and iambic lyric" [*The Government of the Tongue* (1989) 124]). Or 1. may be judged by the degree of difficulty (Browning, Hopkins, Eliot, Stevens), though once-difficult 1. can become familiar. Strangeness in 1. can contribute to the strangeness sometimes thought necessary for aesthetic effect (Barfield) or for poetry itself (Genette, arguing with Jean Cohen, also compares the *ostranenie* of the Rus. Formalists, and the lang. of a state of dreaming). Some poets are known for difficult or strange 1. (e.g. Spenser, the metaphysical poets, Whitman, Browning) but readers should also note consummate skill in quieter effects of 1. (e.g. Frost, Larkin, Bishop).

A distinctive praxis in 1. is part of what makes a poet familiar, and the 1. of an individual oeuvre may be studied in itself (see Fowler 128–29). The discipline of the art of l. is still best apprehended by studying the comments and revisions of good poets.

See also ARCHAISM; AUREATE DICTION; DENOTATION AND CONNOTATION; EPITHET; PERIPHRASIS; POETIC LICENSE; SYNTAX, POETIC.

GENERAL STUDIES: O. Elton, "The Poet's Dictionary," *E&S* 14 (1929); C. Becker, *The Heavenly City of the 18th-C. Philosophers* (1932), esp. 47–63 on key words; O. Jespersen, *Growth and Structure of the Eng. Lang.*, 9th ed. (1938); W. Empson, *The Structure of Complex Words* (1951); D. Davie, *Purity of Diction in Eng. Verse* (1952); Curtius; B. Groom, *The Diction of Poetry from Spenser to Bridges* (1955); Frye; C. S. Lewis, *Studies in Words* (1960); W. Nowottny, *The Lang. Poets Use* (1962)—essential reading; J. Miles, *Eras and Modes in Eng. Poetry*, 2d ed. (1964); K. K. Ruthven, "The Poet as Etymologist," *CQ* 11 (1969); O. Barfield, *Poetic Diction*, 3d ed. (1973)—essential reading; F. W. Bateson, *Eng. Poetry and the Eng. Lang.*, 3d ed. (1973); A. Sherbo, *Eng. Poetic Diction from Chaucer to Wordsworth* (1975); N. Frye, "Charms and Riddles," *Spiritus Mundi* (1976); A. Welsh, *Roots of Lyric* (1978); M. Borroff, *Lang. and the Poet* (1979); G. Genette, *Figures of Literary Discourse* (tr. 1982), esp. 75–102; G. Johnston, "Diction in Poetry," *CL* 97 (1983); Fowler—excellent on l. and genre; J. Boase-Beier, *Poetic Compounds* (1987); C. Ricks, *The Force of Poetry* (1987); A. Ferry, *The Art of Naming* (1988); J. Hollander, *Melodious Guile* (1988); H. Vendler, *The Music of What Happens* (1988).

SPECIALIZED STUDIES: S. H. Monk, *The Sublime* (1935); V. L. Rubel, *Poetic Diction in the Eng. Ren.* (1941); M. H. Nicolson, *Newton Demands the Muse* (1946); J. Arthos, *The Lang. of Natural Description in 18th-C. Poetry* (1949); M. M. Mahood, *Shakespeare's Wordplay* (1957); Wimsatt and Brooks, ch. 16; A. Ewert, "Dante's Theory of Diction," *MHRA* 31 (1959); C. K. Stead, *The New Poetic* (1964); G. Tillotson, *Augustan Poetic Diction* (1964); W. J. B. Owen, *Wordsworth as Critic* (1969); H. Kenner, *The Pound Era* (1971), esp. 94–191; J. Milroy, *The Lang. of G. M. Hopkins* (1977); N. Hilton, *Literal Imagination: Blake's Vision of Words* (1983); M. H. Abrams, "Wordsworth and Coleridge on Diction and Figures," *The Correspondent Breeze* (1984); R. W. V. Elliott, *Thomas Hardy's Eng.* (1984); E. Cook, *Poetry, Word-Play, and Word-War in Wallace Stevens* (1988); C. Ricks, *T. S. Eliot and Prejudice* (1988) R. O. A. M. Lyne, *Words and the Poet* (1989)—Virgil; B. M. H. Strang, "Lang.," *Spenser Encyc.*, ed. A. C. Hamilton et al. (1990). E.C.

LIED. See SONG.

LIGHT VERSE. The term l. v. is an *omnium gatherum*; although it once referred principally to *vers de société*, its meaning in the 20th c. includes a wide variety of verse: folk poetry, nonsense verse (q.v.), ribald verse, comic poems, and kitsch. If the earlier meaning of the term was too narrow, it has now been stretched so far that it has lost its shape.

While the word "light" has been applied to lit. or music to mean "requiring little mental effort; amusing; entertaining" since the 16th c. (*OED*), the first serious attempt to define the term l. v. came in the 19th c., when Frederick Locker-Lampson compiled the anthology *Lyra elegantiarum* (1867). An earlier anthology, Thomas D'Urfey's *Pills to Purge Melancholy* (1719), is considered the first l. v. collection in Eng. As the title implies, Locker-Lampson was less interested in comic verse than in *vers de société*, verse distinguished by its wit and polish and intended to amuse polite society. In the 20th c., a series of anthologists broadened the term to include poetry that is homely or comic. In *The Oxford Book of L. V.* (1938), W. H. Auden held that l. v. meant any poetry that is "simple, clear, and gay." He included performed poems, nonsense verse, and poetry of ordinary life; l. v. was no longer aristocratic. While Auden was influential, however, not everyone followed his lead. In 1941 Michael Roberts explicitly distinguished between comic verse, and "l. v. or *vers de société*." In 1958, Richard Armour defined l. v. as "poetry written in the spirit of play," then added that l. v. "can safely be limited to what is called *vers de société*: humorous or witty verse that comments critically on contemp. life. It is usually to some degree funny." Such anthologists as G. Grigson and W. Harmon have extended the definition of l. v. even further to include bad poetry, for example, or Cole Porter's lyrics. Matters have been further complicated by Kingsley Amis, who in the *New Oxford Book of Eng. L. V.* (1978) argued that the best l. v. is necessarily conservative; in this he followed a view set forth by D. Macdonald in his 1960 parody anthology.

One result of this widening and blurring of meaning is that the term l. v. is sometimes used pejoratively to mean trivial or unimportant poetry. Because some critics now include the magnificently dreadful verse of such writers as William McGonigal or Julia Moore, the term is also sometimes used to mean any bad verse. Yet no one would dismiss Chaucer's tales, Jonson's epigrams, Pope's *The Rape of the Lock*, Byron's *Don Juan*, Rossetti's *Goblin Market*, or Eliot's cats—all of which find a place in both standard anthols. and in collections of l. v. Thus the term seems, however, to have retained favorable connotations for sophisticated readers who know enough about what is "weighty" to recognize and enjoy what is "light." Some critics fear this audience may be diminishing. Grigson says that nonsense verse "is in danger now because it does demand an accepted idea of the nature of verse in general, a widely shared idea of the ways in which poetry works."

Many varieties of l. v. depend on whether one defines the term principally by reference to technical virtuosity or by reference to content. Among the important types of l. v. as defined by technique are limericks, clerihews, and double dactyls (qq.v.). The limerick is the oldest of these; the clerihew is the most anarchic, with its formalized irregularity; the double dactyl has attracted distinguished poets. Arguably the Japanese form of *senryū* also fits in this category. If one does not insist on the comic nature of l. v., then other polished fixed-term poems would be included: ballads, double ballade, rondeau, sestina, and triolet (qq.v.). Finally, there is poetry distinguished by clever use of certain techniques: verse with interlocking rhymes like Edward Lear's limericks; acrostics (q.v.) like Jonson's "Argument" to *Volpone*; verse with extensive alliteration or assonance (qq.v.), as was occasionally practiced in the Middle Ages—e.g. poems where every word in the line begins with the same letter. (A modern example of alliterative ingenuity is the poem by Alaric Watts which begins "An Austrian army awfully arrayed / Boldly by battery besieged Belgrade" and proceeds through the alphabet.) There is also visual poetry, pattern poetry, and concrete poetry (qq.v.) such as Lewis Carroll's "Mouse's Tail" in *Alice in Wonderland*. In all such verse the sophistication of the craft—ingenuousness, skill, and polish—is apparent, the technique serving as foil to the content. But the problem with defining l. v. *solely* on technical grounds is that it then seems to include poetry not usually considered light. George Herbert's "Easter Wings" is shaped as craftily as Carroll's "Mouse's Tail," while Gerard Manley Hopkins' "Spring and Fall: To a Young Child" plays with words in much the same punning way as many limericks do. But neither is l. v.

If one turns from technique to content, however, other problems arise. Auden focuses on content in his three categories of l. v.: "poetry written for performance, to be spoken or sung before an audience"; "poetry intended to be read, but having for its subject-matter the everyday social life of its period or the experiences of the poet"; "such nonsense poetry as, through its properties and technique, has a general sense of appeal." His first category includes folk poetry such as riddles, folksongs, or the songs of Thomas Moore or Ira Gershwin. Yet one might object that all poetry is intended to be spoken to an audience, even if the audience is the reader speaking to himself. The lyrics W. S. Gilbert wrote for Arthur Sullivan's music are hardly folksongs, although clearly l. v. Furthermore, the boundary between folksongs and popular songs or between popular songs and light opera is no longer clear, as the careers of Bob Dylan and Stephen Sondheim demonstrate. Auden's category of nonsense verse, however, is uncontroversial, for nonsense is among the oldest of l. v. As Grigson points out, "The moment lit. develops, nonsense lit. must be expected as both a counter-genre and an innocent game."

One of the few points on which most critics agree is that l. v. requires the formal confines of verseform. If one transmogrifies a limerick or dou-

ble dactyl into prose, one destroys part of its essence. Nonsense verse cast into prose may retain its humor, but it is no longer l. v. The poet Ogden Nash illustrates this point: he regularly stretches metrical forms with his irregular line length, yet his work depends on the reader's recognizing the rules he violates. In "Very Like a Whale," for example, his mock-attack on the lang. of poets is made more effective by the insistent rhymes nestled among the aggressively antimetrical lines. If the complaint were paraphrased in prose, it would be prosaic in every sense of that word, but in verse it amuses, felicitously.

Auden's other category is verse rooted in everyday life. Cl. Gr. offers the verse inscriptions—epigrams and epitaphs—collected in *The Gr. Anthology*; today one might include clever graffiti. Occasional verse (q.v.) would also fit in this category, from Thomas Gray's "On a Favourite Cat Drowned in a Tub of Goldfishes" to William McGonigle's poem on the beaching of the great Tay whale. Clearly the slighter the occasion, the lighter the verse. And because their targets are quotidian, satire, burlesque, and mock-heroic (qq.v.) could also be considered l. v. One might of course object that mere homeliness or topicality does not in itself make a work l. v., that not all comic verse is light, and that not all l. v. is comic or *vers de société*. While most readers recognize l. v. as poetry that amuses by reflecting an aspect of their everyday lives in a clever way, probably none would agree on a body of works that meet a univocal set of criteria defining them as l. v.; rather, the works merit inclusion in the class by what Wittgenstein calls "family resemblances." The criteria are diverse and overlap, so that not every poem need meet every criterion.

ANTHOLOGIES: *Wit and Mirth, or Pills to Purge Melancholy*, ed. T. D'Urfey (1719); *Lyra elegantiarum*, ed. F. Locker-Lampson (1867); *Speculum Amantis, Musa Proterva*, both ed. A. H. Bullen (1888, 1889); *A Vers de Société Anthol.*, ed. C. Wells (1900); *Oxford Book of L. V.*, ed. W. H. Auden (1938); *Faber Book of Comic Verse*, ed. M. Roberts (1942); *What Cheer*, ed. D. McCord (1945); *The Worldly Muse*, ed. A. J. M. Smith (1951)—serious l. v.; *Penguin Book of Comic and Curious Verse*, ed. J. M. Cohen (1952); *Silver Treasury of L. V.*, ed. O. Williams (1957); *Parodies: An Anthol.*, ed. D. Macdonald (1960); *New Oxford Book of Eng. L. V.*, ed. K. Amis (1978); *Faber Book of Epigrams & Epitaphs* (1978), *Faber Book of Nonsense Verse* (1980), *Oxford Book of Satirical Verse* (1980), all ed. G. Grigson; *Oxford Book of Am. L. V.*, ed. W. Harmon (1979); *The Tygers of Wrath*, ed. X. J. Kennedy (1981); *Norton Book of L. V.*, ed. R. Baker (1986).

GENERAL: L. Untermeyer, *Play in Poetry* (1938); R. Armour, *Writing L. V.*, 2d ed. (1958); T. Augarde, *Oxford Guide to Word Games* (1984).   F.T.

LIMERICK. The most popular form of comic or light verse (q.v.) in Eng., often nonsensical and frequently bawdy: in a famous joke, when Bennett Cerf, then head of Random House, was asked how they chose the winner of their l. contest, he said it was simple: they threw out all that were indecent, and the winner was the one that was left. The verseform of the l. is very exacting: 5 lines of accentual verse (q.v.) rhyming *aabba*, the first, second, and fifth lines having 3 stresses, the third and fourth 2; the rhythm is effectually anapestic or amphibrachic. The first syllables of each line (and unstressed syllables elsewhere in the lines, though less frequently so) may be omitted. The pattern, once caught, is unforgettable (slashes denote stresses, and *x*s weak syllables):

    (x) x ⁄ x x ⁄ x x ⁄
    (x) x ⁄ x x ⁄ x x ⁄
    (x) x ⁄ x x ⁄
    (x) x ⁄ x x ⁄
    (x) x ⁄ x x ⁄ x x ⁄.

It may be that the third and fourth lines are actually hemistichs, so that the form is actually 4 lines of 3-3-4-3 stresses, i.e. the form of hymn meter known as *Short Measure*, though the rhythm is not the same. Also possible is that lines 1–2 are hemistichs of a 6-stress long line and lines 3–5 the sections of a 7-stresss long line, the long-line couplet having 6 + 7 stresses, i.e. *Poulter's Measure* (q.v.), though again, the rhythm differs (see BALLAD METER).

The l. is unique in that it is the only Eng. stanza form used exclusively for light verse. It was popularized by Edward Lear (*A Book of Nonsense* [1846]); however, the etymology of the term "l.," never used by Lear, is unknown. Theories concerning its origin range from the belief that it was an old Fr. form brought to the Irish town of Limerick in 1700 by returning veterans of the Fr. war, to the theory that it originated in the nursery rhymes (q.v.) pub. as *Mother Goose's Melodies* (1791). What is certain is that the l. may be found in a volume entitled *The History of Sixteen Wonderful Old Women* (1821) and in *Anecdotes and Adventures of Fifteen Gentlemen* (1822), possibly by R. S. Sharpe. Lear cites the latter volume as having given him the idea for his ls. Whatever its origin, the l. has a secure place in the history of Eng. verse. In the wake of Lear, such notable authors as Tennyson, Swinburne, Kipling, Stevenson, and W. S. Gilbert attempted the form, and by the beginning of the 20th c. it had become a fashion. The chief tendency in the modern l. has been the use of the final line for surprise or witty reversal, in place of the simply repeated last line of Lear's day. See also CLERIHEW; NONSENSE VERSE.—L. Reed, *The Complete L. Book* (1925); *Oxford Book of Nursery Rhymes*, ed. I. and P. Opie (1951); A. Liede, *Dichtung als Spiel*, v. 2 (1963); W. S. Baring-Gould, *The Lure of the L.* (1972); *The L.: 1700 Examples* (1970, 1974), *The New L.* (1977), both ed. G. Legman; C. Bibby, *The Art of the L.* (1978); G. N. Belknap, "Hist. of the L.," *PBSA* 75 (1981); *Penguin Book of Ls.*, ed.

E. O. Parrott (1984).   T.V.F.B.; A.PR.

LINE (Sanskrit *pāda*, Gr. *stichos* [q.v.], Lat. *versus* "verse"). The concept of the l. is fundamental to the concept of poetry itself, for the l. is the differentia of verse and prose: throughout most of recorded history, poetry has been cast in verse, and verse set in ls. (see VERSE AND PROSE). That is, verse is cast in sentences and ls., prose in sentences and paragraphs. The sense in prose flows continuously, while in verse it is segmented so as to increase information density and perceived structure. It is impossible that there could be verse not set in ls. It is possible there could be poetry not set in ls., if one defines poetry in terms of content or compression of content; and certainly there are hybrid forms such as rhythmical prose (see PROSE RHYTHM) and the prose poem (q.v.). But we must assume that the preponderance of the world's poetry has been cast in verse precisely to take advantage of those resources which verse—for which l. is a virtual metonym—has to offer (see PROSODY).

Structure. Readers and auditors of poetry perceive the l. as a rhythmical unit and a unit of structure. As a unit of measure (q.v.), it is linked to its neighbors to form higher-level structures, and as a structure itself, it is built of lower-level units. In metrical verse the l. is usually segmented into elements—hemistichs (q.v.), measures (q.v.) or metra (see METRON), or feet (see FOOT)—but it is the l. which generates these intralinear units and not vice versa. Ls. are not made simply by defining some unit of measure such as a foot and then stringing units together, because the units are susceptible of differential constraint at differing points in the l. The l., that is, has a shape or contour, and a structure as a whole, over and above the sum of its constituent elements. In various verse systems these elements are bound together in differing ways, such as structural alliteration in OE. It is true that, in the handbooks, meters are usually specified by the type of foot and number of feet per l.—i.e. monometer (a l. of 1 foot), dimeter (2 feet), trimeter (3 feet), tetrameter (4 feet), pentameter (5 feet), hexameter (6 feet), heptameter (7 feet; see the separate entries on each of these). But these simplistic descriptors do not capture the internal dynamics of a l. form such as the Gr. hexameter.

How do readers and auditors recognize the l. as a rhythmical unit? In isometric (q.v.) verse, meter measures out a constant spacing, either of a certain number of events or a certain span of time (depending on one's theory of meter) which the mind's internal counter tracks in cognition; meter also provides predictable internal structure. The l. can also be bound together by syntactic and rhetorical structures such as parallelism and antithesis (qq.v.) which have their own internal logic of completion; these structures may or may not be threaded into meter: in biblical Heb. verse they

LINE

are, in Whitman they are not.

Line End. But probably the most common strategy is to mark the *end* of the l., since without some sort of signal, we would not know where one l. ended and a second one began. Traditionally the signal has been thought to be a "pause" (q.v.), though not a metrical (l.-internal) one but rather some kind of rhetorical or performative one. (Some have suggested that its duration is something like "half a comma.") But this claim derives not from prosody (verse theory), or from claims made in poetics (q.v.) about the nature or ontological status of poetry as sound (q.v.), but rather from assumptions put in play about performance (q.v.), about the reading aloud of verse. On this account, performers of poetry recognize the l. as a unit (by seeing it as such when read from the page) and mark its end in delivery with a linguistic pause or paralinguistic cue such as elongation of the final syllable. Auditors hear these cues, which cross or ignore syntax, as boundary markers.

An alternative conception of the signal, which depends rather on assumptions about the status of poetry as a visual text on a page, is "white space to the right of the l." This is perceived in reading, is irrelevant to performance, and *may* by taken not only as a terminal marker but even as a part of structure (see below).

But both these answers specify phenomena *after* the l. ends. A more powerful conception of the signal, not committed to any doctrine about either performance or text, would be, "some kind of marker," not after the final syllable of the l. but *in* the final syllables of the l. In Gr. and Lat. poetry, where the meter is quantitative, auditors could recognize the ends of ls. because they were marked by an alteration in the meter, either an increase in the formality in its closing syllables, a *cadence* (q.v.), or unexpected shortening at l.-end, *catalexis* (q.v.). In the hexameter, for example, the l. closes on a spondee—two heavy syllables in succession—rather than a dactyl, a closural pattern which is obligatory. In post-Cl. verse, l.-ends have been most often marked by some distinctive sound echo, chiefly rhyme (q.v.), though important also are the several other strategies of sound-repetition which approach rhyme (are rhyme-like) or exceed rhyme: homoeoteleuton, assonance, identical rhyme (qq.v.). Short ls. in particular seem to demand the support of rhyme, else they will be mistaken for the cola that are parts of longer ls.; this is a major factor in the devel. of the lyric (q.v.). Also important are strategies for end-of-l. semantic emphasis: Richard Wilbur, for example, sometimes employs the strategy of putting important words at l.-end, words which may offer an elliptical synopsis or ironic commentary on the argument of the poem. All these strategies, taken together as devices for end-fixing, i.e. *marking* or *weighting* l.-ends so as to highlight or foreground them perceptually, constitute one of the most distinctive categories of metrical universals, conspicuous in a wide range of verse systems.

The phenomenon of extra syllables at l.-end is fairly extensive and is taken account of in several prosodies: l. endings are classified depending on whether the last stress falls on the final syllable of the l. (a "masculine" ending) or the penultimate one (a "feminine" one; see MASCULINE AND FEMININE). The distinction dates from at least Occitan poetry, and may date from ancient Gr. Classifying types of l. endings was also one of the central "metrical tests" which several British and Ger. Shakespeare scholars of the later 19th c. hoped would yield a definitive chronology of the plays. Spedding in 1847 suggested the "pause test," which tabulated frequencies of stopped vs. enjambed ls. Bathurst (1857), Craik, and Hertzberg discussed "weak endings"; Ingram (1874) distinguished types of these as "light" endings (enjambed ls. ending on a pronoun, verb, or relative bearing only secondary stress, plus a slight pause) and "weak" (enjambment on a proclitic, esp. a conjunction or preposition, allowing no pause at all—see Brogan for citations). But statistical evidence which is purely internal is vulnerable to textual criticism and, where not supported by other types of evidence, vulnerable altogether.

Line and Syntax. The syllables of the l. are the arena for deploying meter or rhythm; they are also of course the ground of syntax and sense: these two structures overwrite the same space. Some verse-forms regularly align l. units with sense units; such ls. are known as *end-stopped.* The ("closed") heroic couplet (q.v.), for example, ends the first l. at a major syntactic break and the second at a full stop (sentence end). But few meters do so *every* l.: the demands of narrative or discursive continuation are simply too strong. Systematic contrast or opposition of l. units and sense units (l. end and sentence flow) is the complex phenomenon known as *enjambment* (q.v.). In enjambed verse, syntax pulls the reader through l.-end into the next l., while the prosodic boundary bids pause if not stop. In reading, the mind makes projections, in that pause, based on what has come before, about what word is most likely to appear at the beginning of the next l., expectations which a masterful poet will deliberately thwart, forcing rapid rereading: in Milton such error is the emblem of man's postlapsarian state. Certainly in modern times, at least, it has been thought that one of the chief functions of l. division is to stand in tension with or counterpoint to the divisions of grammar and sense, effecting, in the reader's processing of the text, multiple simultaneous pattern recognition. Most of the time this results in heightened aesthetic pleasure, but it may also work in reverse: in Gwendolyn Brooks' poem "We Real Cool," the severe and reiterated rupture of subjects from predicates across l.-end dislocates sentences, emphasizing subjects (pronouns) severed from action (verbs), generating extreme discomfort. Even in enjambed verse, the word at l.-end, which the

French call the *contre-rejet* (see REJET), receives some sort of momentary foregrounding or emphasis. This is not a matter of the word marking the end but of the end marking the word.

Aural Line and Visual Line. Since the advent of writing in Greece, ca. 750 B.C., and certainly since the advent of printing in the West, ca. 1450 A.D., the l. has had a visual reality in poetry as seen, but long before that time and without interruption throughout print culture it has continued to have an auditory reality in poetry as heard. This gives the l.—poetry itself—a fundamentally duality, in the eye and ear, as seen/heard (Hollander), a duality complicated, however, by the appearance of free verse (q.v.). Arguments about the historical or ontological precedence of the aural over the visual l. therefore miss the point: these forms are, for us, now, both realities; the important question is how they interaffect each other—whether, for example, the break at l.-end demands an auditory pause in performance. Levertov has argued that there must be linkages of this sort, so that print texts of poems are in fact "accurate scorings" of them as read aloud. Margaret Atwood concurs when she calls the l. "a visual indication of an aural unit."

Line Forms. Up to the advent of free verse, l.-forms and -lengths are mainly determined by genre specification, so that a poet who wishes to write, say, in elegiac distichs (hexameter plus pentameter) knows or learns, by reading her predecessors, what forms have already been tried, for what kinds of subjects, with what kinds of tone, and with what success. In metrical verse, that is, l.-forms were mainly determined by history and convention, by the interplay of tradition and the individual talent; and the prosody which generated them was aurally based. Free verse, by contrast, foregrounded visual space and posited the l. within a two-dimensional matrix where blanks, white spaces, drops, gaps, vectors, and dislocations became possible. This is not to say that free verse abandoned aurality, for some poets, such as the Beats, Olson with his "projective verse," and the proponents of Sound Poetry (q.v.) and "Text-Sound," continued to speak programmatically of the l. as based on the energy of the breath. It is only to say that visual prosody (q.v.) was made central to free verse at least in claim, and if aural prosody was at the same time not dispensed with, no poet seemed to wish or prosodist to be able, at least for the first century of free-verse practice, to give a coherent account of the relations of the one to the other.

To think, however, that the free-verse l. can function solely as visual prosody, without the resources of aural prosody to aid it, is to commit what Perloff calls the "linear fallacy," making some free verse indistinguishable from prose chopped up into ls. The sonic and rhythmic devices of aural prosody offer poetry effects *not available* to prose: and if these are to be discarded, visual prosody must provide others, else the distinction between prose and verse collapses. One might respond that several Eng. poets—Jonson and Pope, to name but two—wrote out drafts of their poems first in prose before versifying them; and verse translators routinely work through intermediary prose versions. But this shows simply that they wished to clarify the argumentative or narrative structure first to get it out of the way, so as to concentrate on *poetic* effects—else why versify at all.

Whether or not visual prosody has been able to generate other devices, and whether or not free verse in fact abandons aural prosody, are disputed questions. It is often held that visual prosody can do much with "placing"—i.e. framing or highlighting words or phrases by isolating them as ls. The l. is thus reduced to the measure, though in a differing sense (if that is possible), since measure traditionally implied regularity (see VARIABLE FOOT). But probably few would hold that the visual l. does not affect the aural l. at all. Levertov says that the free-verse l.-break affects both rhythm and intonation: it is both "a form of punctuation *additional* to the punctuation that forms part of the logic of completed thoughts," which introduces "an a-logical counter-rhythm into the logical rhythm of syntax," and also, more importantly, a device which affects "the *melos* of the poem" by altering pitch patterns, since "a pitch pattern change *does occur* with each variation of lineation" (italics original). If so, then linkage between the two prosodies is preserved. Again, the full demonstration of these matters still remains to be given.

But what, after all, is the status of the visual l.? In the days of the mechanical typewriter, l.-end seemed a right-hand terminus: the next l. could only begin by the long carriage return to the left-hand margin and down. But on the computer, we learned, ls. are stored in a file in one continuous row of characters, with a special character between each l. which is recognized by the computer as a command to return to the left-hand margin *for formatting on screen* (i.e. on the page). This shows that the visual display of the ls. was merely epiphenomenal—a function of the medium of presentation—not inherent to the nature of the thing itself. Is this an analogy for cognition? We know that, in perception, ls. are processed sequentially. The l. is a frame, and frames are arrayed seriatim. In cognition, however, their semantic content is rearranged in short-term memory so as to make possible synchral (aserial) recognition of information. The articulation (jointure) of the frames one to the next is subject to some flexibility (thus extrametrical syllables at the end of one l. and inversions at the beginning of the next are allowed); at the same time, there is good evidence that the ends of the frames are usually more highly constrained than their beginnings, a fact which supports the frames as perceptual units, not mere arbitrary sectionings of the Heraclitean flow. It is these articulated frames across which sentences are stretched to make the distinctive discourse which is verse.

See now FREE VERSE; METER; PROSODY; STANZA; STICHOS; VERSE AND PROSE; VERSIFICATION; VISUAL PROSODY.

C. A. Langworthy, "Verse-Sentence Patterns in Eng. Poetry," *PQ* 7 (1928); J. S. Diekhoff, "Terminal Pause in Milton's Verse," *SP* 32 (1935); A. Oras, "Echoing Verse Endings in *Paradise Lost*," *So. Atlantic Studies S. E. Leavitt* (1953); C. L. Stevenson, "The Rhythm of Eng. Verse," *JAAC* 28 (1970); D. Crystal, "Intonation and Metrical Theory," *TPS* (1971); C. Ricks, "Wordsworth," *EIC* 21 (1971); B. Stáblein, "Versus," *MGG*, 13.1519–23; H. McCord, "Breaking and Entering," and D. Laferrière, "Free and Non-Free Verse," *Lang&S* 10 (1977); J. Lotman, *The Structure of the Artistic Text* (tr. 1977), ch. 6; D. Levertov, "On the Function of the L.," *ChR* 30 (1979); *Epoch* 29 (1980), 161 ff.—symposium; M. Perloff, "The Linear Fallacy," *GaR* 35 (1981), response in 36 (1982); Brogan; J. C. Stalker, "Reader Expectations and the Poetic L.," *Lang&S* 15 (1982); P. P. Byers, "The Auditory Reality of the Verse L.," *Style* 17 (1983); R. Bradford, "'Verse Only to the Eye'?: L. Endings in *Paradise Lost*," *EIC* 33 (1983); S. A. Keenan, "Effects of Chunking and L. Length on Reading Efficiency," *VisLang* 18 (1984); *The L. in Postmodern Poetry*, ed. R. Frank and H. Sayre (1988). T.V.F.B.

LINE ENDINGS. See LINE; MASCULINE AND FEMININE.

LINGUISTICS AND POETICS. We are concerned here with the two senses of the term "poetics" (q.v.; hereafter p.) which have been developed since about 1960: p. as a theory of the essential property of lit., "literariness"; and p. as the theoretical or systematic study of the texts, and genres of texts, which fall under the category of lit. The intellectual bases for the conjunction of l. and p. were laid in Switzerland and in Russia in the early years of this century by the linguistic theory of Ferdinand de Saussure, reconstructed by two of his Geneva students from their notes of his lectures and pub. in 1916 as *Cours de linguistique générale* (see STRUCTURALISM); by the aesthetic theory of the Rus. Formalists (see RUSSIAN FORMALISM), articulated most memorably in Victor Shklóvsky's essay "Art as Technique" (1924); and by the narrative analysis of Vladimir Propp, *Morphology of the Folktale* (1928), which is procedurally relevant to poetry as well as to narrative in offering a model for the application of l. to poetry (see PLOT). But the period of greatest activity in l. and p. began in the 1960s, when these works became available in translation—Saussure (Eng. tr. 1959), Shklóvsky and the Formalists (Eng. and Fr. trs. 1965), Propp (Fr. 1957, Eng. 1958). The climate in l. in the 1960s was one of great ambition and confidence, and p. was blessed with the attention of some creative thinkers, notably Roman Jakobson and Roland Barthes; the work of the anthropologist Claude Lévi-Strauss, adapting Propp's model for the structural analysis of myth (q.v.), was also important in showing the way for one kind of linguistic analysis of lit. The 1960s saw the birth of what came to be known as "structuralist p." (see Culler), embodying general theory of lit. and also linguistic theories of both poetry and narrative as genres, with the devel. of linguistic methodologies for analysis of the genres. This period moreover saw the foundation of a more pragmatic, less theoretical discipline of "stylistics" (q.v.) or "linguistic crit." devoted to the linguistic analysis of literary texts.

Citing the Formalists and Jakobson as his authorities, Tzvetan Todorov, the Fr. translator of the Formalists, argued that the business of p. was not the crit. or interp. of individual works but the articulation and codification of the abstract properties which make every literary work possible and which make it "literary." P. then was to be a general science devoted to identifying the defining quality of the literary work. There is an act of idealization in this definition of the goals of p. which is strikingly similar to that proposed at the time by Chomsky in his definition of the goals of l.: the linguist is ultimately concerned with abstract universals of lang., not with individual sentences, which are regarded merely as manifestations of underlying structural principles. The distinction, in l. and in p., derives ultimately from Saussure's separation of *langue* (lang. as system) from *parole* (utterance). The generative analogy caught on with the structuralists, who extrapolated a concept of "literary competence" presumed to be a cognitive property of readers who had "internalized" the universal rules of lit.

What is the substance of literary universals? The most powerful suggestion came from Roman Jakobson ("L. and P.," in Sebeok). A literary work is first and foremost a "verbal message": p. seeks that which makes it literary, given that it is inherently verbal. His proposal, natural enough for one who was essentially a linguist rather than a literary scholar or an aesthetician, is conceived in terms of a specific kind of deployment of the structural resources of lang. (see POETIC FUNCTION). The power and facility of Jakobson's synthesis are clear in his theory of metaphor and metonymy (qq.v.), which are seen as poetic figures based on the same structural principles which allow us to understand the nature of two kinds of aphasic disorder (and, so abstract are these principles, much else in "ordinary lang."). These principles, drawn ultimately from Saussure and fundamental to all modern l. and semiotics (q.v.), are what are generally called "paradigm" and "syntagm" or, by Jakobson, "selection" and "combination": in a memorable dictum, "*the poetic function projects the principle of equivalence from the axis of selection into the axis of combination.*" This superficially cryptic formula is quite simple in its meaning. Language-users, constructing phrases, sentences, and texts, are obliged to perform two operations: to *select* units from sets of alternatives—"cat" rather than "kitty," "rug" rather than "mat," "white" rather than "black," the phoneme /i/ rather than /a/, and so on—and to *combine* their selections sequentially along the syntagmatic chain according to the structural rules of the lang.: "The white cat purred on the rug." An utterance becomes poetic when a language-user selects items which have some paradigmatic relationship (Jakobson's "equivalence" [q.v.], but it could be any systematic relationship, even opposition) and lays them in an extra level of patterning along the same syntagm, the paradigmatic equivalences being salient. In "The white cat sat on the black mat," the subject and object phrases are equivalent syntactically, Determiner + Adjective + Noun, making them parallel; the adjectives are antonyms made even more contrastive by the parallelism; the three words "cat," "sat," and "mat" are phonologically equivalent by virtue of being monosyllables sharing the phoneme /a/. Jakobson's example is "I like Ike." When such patterns draw attention to the verbal texture of the message itself, lang. becomes poetic.

These structural principles form the basis of many traditional prosodic and rhetorical devices, e.g. oxymoron, chiasmus, alliteration, rhyme (qq.v.); Jakobson illustrates them copiously in the seminal "L. and P." But this is only part of the point. Jakobson's theory encouraged structural thinking in general and the application to literary forms of notions such as binary opposition, underlying system, syntagmatic ordering, and transformation. The same intellectual conditions that produced Jakobson and Lévi-Strauss's minute structural (but minimally interpretive) analysis of Baudelaire's "Les Chats" also made welcome the story-grammar model of Propp, and thereby grounded, through the combination of Propp and l., the structuralist narratology of the 1960s.

To return to Jakobson's "poetic principle," his proposal hypothesizes the *effect* as well as the mechanics of poetic structure. "The set (*Einstellung*) [this gloss could be construed in the sense of 'orientation,' a term he uses elsewhere in the paper] toward the MESSAGE as such, focus on the message for its own sake, is the POETIC function of lang." The linguistic form of the text is "foregrounded" (Mukařovský), made perceptually salient. The poetic function of lang., "by promoting the palpability of signs, deepens the fundamental dichotomy of signs and objects." The brilliance of this comment lies in its synthesis of Saussurean l. and formalist aesthetics: at a stroke Jakobson has provided a linguistic mechanism for the perceptual difficulty and the distancing of meaning which Shklóvsky—a central figure in Jakobson's first intellectual milieu, pre-Revolutionary Russia—specified as conditions for the aesthetic effect of "defamiliarization": "The technique of art is to make objects 'unfamiliar,' to make forms

difficult, to increase the difficulty and length of perception because the process of perception is an aesthetic end in itself and must be prolonged. *Art is a way of experiencing the artfulness of an object; the object is not important*" (1924). Jakobson's l., then, supports the importance of Shklóvsky's aesthetics as a reference-point in modern p.

One of the most controversial aspects of Jakobson's poetic theory is his claim that p. is *part of* l.: "P. deals with problems of verbal structure. . . . Since l. is the global science of verbal structure, p. may be regarded as an integral part of l. . . . Insistence on keeping p. apart from l. is warranted only when the field of l. appears to be illicitly restricted." Setting aside the questions of whether l. could in principle by itself provide an adequate p., and whether Jakobson's p. is itself adequate, we may consider in what sense his p. is part of l. according to his own definitions. Certain basic structural principles, expressed at an extreme level of generality, are repeatedly found manifested in details of linguistic form at the different levels of phonology, syntax, and semantics. Certain configurations—alliteration, for example—are said to be "poetic"; they are found in some texts, such as poems by Baudelaire and Shakespeare, in respect of which the designation "literary" is given and unquestioned, and in certain other texts such as "I like Ike" which would not be called literary—the poetic function is a relative rather than an absolute matter. The same linguistic principles, or variants of them, are found in other linguistic domains, but without the "projection of the principle of equivalence from the axis of selection into the axis of combination." Conceived thus, p. could be said to be a part of l., since its defining concepts and procedures are solely derived from l.; but so could aphasiology, phonology, and the other fields that Jakobson treated in this brilliantly rational yet reductive way.

The analyses of poems given by Jakobson and his co-authors employ linguistic theory literally; when Jakobson identifies something as a feminine rhyme or an indefinite article, the grammatical designation is literal. However, other branches of structuralist p. appeal to linguistic concepts in a less direct, more metaphorical way. For example, Propp's *Morphology of the Folktale* (1928, tr. 1958) describes the general structure of stories on the *analogy* of grammatical structure; and that is explicitly the procedure of the structural narratology of Barthes, A. J. Greimas, and Todorov. The appropriation of linguistic concepts for the description of larger structures in lit., in myth, and in other fields such as architecture, fashion, and cinema—areas for which no adequate metalanguage had previously existed—was the central feature of structuralism in the 1960s. This movement embodies a second relationship of l. and p., a second way in which the appeal to l. has progressed and refined literary theory.

Saussure had maintained that the l. he sketched

was only one part of a more general discipline, "sémiologie," devoted to "the life of signs within society." Roland Barthes, half a century later, developed the general framework of "semiology," instanced some of the social constructs and conventions which belonged in this field, and proposed a positioning for both lang. and lit. within this framework. The implication in Saussure is that lang. and l. form just one of the fields within semiology, but what emerges from Barthes is that lang. and l. are privileged, paradigmatic branches of semiology (or what we would now call "semiotics"). Structure in other branches was modeled on linguistic structure, so the procedural assumption followed that linguistic methods and concepts which had been developed for the study of lang. could be extended to other semiotic fields: thus paradigm, syntagm, constituent structure, and transformation could be found in culinary conventions, fashion, etc. Obviously this was a significant methodological gain, allowing the instant foundation of new disciplines with their metalanguage ready-made. The most highly developed of these was literary structuralism.

Lit., on that model, relates to lang. in two distinct ways. First, it *is* lang., literally, in that its medium is words and sentences. And it is also *like* lang., in that it is a second-order semiotic system patterned on higher units which mirror the structure of the lang. medium. The plot of a narrative text, for instance, is not actually a sentence (though of course it is mediated through sentences), but it can be presented as sentence-like in structure, the actions which advance the story being like verbs, and the characters who perform these actions being like nouns in grammatical functions such as subject and object. The work of Barthes, Greimas, Todorov, and others illustrates the use of l. as a source of structural analogies for the constitutive elements of poetry and of narrative. Although this analogical, basically semiotic procedure is easiest to illustrate with reference to "syntactic" studies of plot, it has been followed fruitfully in theorizing on other dimensions of lit. and on the nature of lit. (Eco; Lotman).

The applications of l. to lit. reviewed so far have been bold and fruitful, and rightly prominent in scholarly debate. It might be said that the main contribution of structural and semiotic p. has been to present certain postulates about l. and p. with such notable force and clarity that metatheoretical debate in the field has been wonderfully facilitated. But such clarity of definition is bought at the price of deliberate limitation of goal, and structuralist p. does not exhaust the range of linguistic contributions to the study of lit. A major restriction is the decision to limit attention to the *formal* aspects of lang.—to syntactic, phonological, and (structural) semantic patterns. Little consideration is given to the pragmatic, functional, or social dimensions of lang. in lit. Lang. is not only formal pattern, it is also *discourse*, mediating social

and personal roles and relationships, constructing and reproducing ideology, historically and culturally situated. To cope with such factors—which after all have been among the traditional concerns of literary studies—we need a kind of l. which both the Saussurean and the Chomskyan schools have excluded, a l. of *parole*. This sort of l. has begun to be developed on several fronts in recent years. In fact, the need for such a l. to counter the restrictions of formalist p. had already been argued by Bakhtin/Voloshinov (perhaps one and the same person) in Russia around 1930. Saussurean l. was strongly attacked, and a notion of lang. as the interplay of socially and ideologically accented voices was developed. The Bakhtinian model has proved very fruitful since translations made it available to the West in the early 1970s; the technical l. of discourse has only recently begun to catch up.

A wider and more catholic range of connections between l. and p. is found if we extend the field to work in what is often generally called "stylistics" or "linguistic crit." This work is trans-generic, and many writings on fiction and drama are also relevant to poetry because the discussion often concerns general theory and methodology. In the 1960s there was heated debate about the propriety of applying l. to lit., the linguists making such a proposal meeting the same Anglo-Saxon critical opposition that resisted Fr. structuralism. But in the last 20 years there has nevertheless been published a considerable body of work in linguistic crit. giving practical demonstration of the value of l. to the student of lit. There have been empirical studies of every aspect of lang. in lit., written from the points of view of a wide diversity of linguistic models. Almost always there have been new descriptive insights and new analytic terminology. Some of the more conservative work, which is eclectic in selecting tools from l. and linking them with time-honored rhetorical concepts, has been among the most useful in practical yield. But most linguistic critics have been less eclectic, choosing to focus a particular linguistic model on some specific dimension of poetic structure.

Our understanding of Eng. metrical forms, for example, has been enhanced by a number of technical studies using different phonological theories, e.g. the 4-stress-level suprasegmental phonology of Trager and Smith (Chatman) or the generative phonology of Chomsky and Halle as developed by analogy in generative metrics (q.v.). At the level of poetic syntax (q.v.), there have been a number of applications of transformational grammar—e.g. Ohmann's treatment of style in terms of deep and surface structure (in Chatman and Levin, eds., 1967); Freeman's and Austin's studies of transformational preferences as the constitutive elements of artistic design (in Freeman, ed., 1981); and Thorne's generative studies of e e cummings and of Donne (in Freeman, ed., 1970)—initiating debates on linguistic deviation in poetry and the proposition that a poem autonomously creates its own lang. or at least a special dialect. Semantic and pragmatic structures have also been explored, e.g. Levin's comparison of componential semantics and speech-act theory (q.v.) in relation to metaphor—which requires a more thoroughly interdisciplinary approach—or Riffaterre's work on the semiotics of poetry, analysis which focuses intensely on semantic structure (and which is grounded in a sophisticated devel. of Jakobson), or Pratt's approach using the concepts of speech act and of natural narrative.

These are but a few examples of a broad range of studies which were valuable in advancing the theory and procedures of linguistic crit. and of p. Of course it must be conceded that, in a period when l. itself was rapidly changing, it was inevitable that some linguistic critics committed themselves to theoretical models that became outmoded. However, this area of l. and p. has made many permanent contributions by debating issues and testing analyses in the lang. of poetry. The continuing liveliness of linguistic crit. has more recently been attested by completely new orientations, reaction against the predominant formalism of earlier research, and a growing concern with the social contexts and functions of literary discourse. These new interests come at a stage in the devel. of l. when pragmatics (Sperber and Wilson), discourse analysis (specifically the analysis of belief systems), and functional grammar (Halliday) offer theories and methods for further advances in the conjunction of l. and p.

See also DISTINCTIVE-FEATURE ANALYSIS; METER; POETICS; SEMIOTICS, POETIC; SOUND; SPEECH ACT THEORY; STRUCTURALISM; STYLISTICS; SYNTAX, POETIC.

F. de Saussure, *Cours de linguistique générale*, (1916), 5th ed. (1955), crit. ed., ed. R. Engler (1967–74), tr. R. Harris (1983); V. Shklóvsky, "Art as Technique" (1924), rpt. in *Rus. Formalist Crit.*, ed. and tr. L. Lemon and M. Reis (1965); M. Bakhtin, *Problems of Dostoevsky's P.* (1929, tr. 1973); V. Voloshinov, *Marxism and the Philosophy of Lang.* (1929–30, tr. 1973); G. Trager and H. L. Smith, *An Outline of Eng. Structure* (1951); "Eng. Verse and What It Sounds Like," spec. iss. of *KR* 18 (1956); C. Lévi-Strauss, *Structural Anthropology* (1958, tr. 1968); R. Jakobson, "L. and P.," in Sebeok, rpt. in Jakobson, v. 5; Sebeok; F. L. Utley, "Structural L. and the Literary Critic," *JAAC* 18 (1960); S. R. Levin, *Linguistic Structures in Poetry* (1962), "The Conventions of Poetry," *Literary Style: A Symposium*, ed. S. Chatman (1971), *The Semantics of Metaphor* (1977); R. Jakobson and C. Lévi-Strauss, "Charles Baudelaire's 'Les Chats'" (1962), rpt. in *The Structuralists from Marx to Lévi-Strauss*, ed. R. and F. DeGeorge (1972); R. Barthes, *Elements of Semiology* (1964–67), *S/Z* (1970, tr. 1975); S. Chatman, *A Theory of Meter* (1965); A. J. Greimas, *Sémantique structurale* (1966); J. Mukařovský, "Standard Lang. and Poetic Lang." and R. Ohmann, "Lit. as

Sentences" in Chatman and Levin, eds. (1967); N. Chomsky and M. Halle, *The Sound Pattern of Eng.* (1968); G. N. Leech, *A Linguistic Guide to Eng. Poetry* (1969); *L. and Literary Style, Essays in Mod. Stylistics*, both ed. D. Freeman (1970, 1981); T. Todorov, *The Poetics of Prose* (1971, tr. 1977); *Literary Style: A Symposium*, and *Approaches to P.*, both ed. S. Chatman (1971, 1973); R. Fowler, *The Langs. of Lit.* (1971), *Lit. as Social Discourse* (1981), *Linguistic Crit.* (1986); S. Chatman and S. R. Levin, eds., *Essays on the Lang. of Lit.* (1967), "L. and Lit.," *Current Trends in L. X*, ed. T. A. Sebeok (1973); P. Kiparsky, "The Role of L. in a Theory of Poetry," *Daedalus* 102 (1973), rpt. in *Lang. as a Human Problem*, ed. E. Haugen and M. Bloomfield (1974); Culler; U. Eco, *A Theory of Semiotics* (1976); A. A. Hill, *Constituent and Pattern in Poetry* (1976); T. Hawkes, *Structuralism and Semiotics* (1977); J. Lotman, *The Structure of the Artistic Text*, tr. R. Vroon (1977); M. Pratt, *Toward a Speech Act Theory of Literary Discourse* (1977); M. Riffaterre, *Semiotics of Poetry* (1978); Brogan, items E709–827—comprehensive list of work in structural and generative metrics to 1981, with numerous other studies in the linguistic analysis of lit. listed *passim*; J. Culler, "Lit. and L.," *Interrelations of Lit.*, ed. J.-P. Barricelli and J. Gibaldi (1982); M. Halliday, *An Intro. to Functional Grammar* (1985); D. Sperber and D. Wilson, *Relevance* (1986); *The L. of Writing*, ed. N. Fabb et al. (1987); D. Birch, *Lang., Lit. and Critical Practice* (1989); *Lang., Discourse and Lit.*, ed. R. Carter and P. Simpson (1989); K. Wales, *A Dictionary of Stylistics* (1989).   R.F.

LIRA. A Sp. stanza form of 4, 5, 6, or, rarely, more than 6 Italianate hendecasyllables and heptasyllables, the term denoting loosely any short-strophe *canción* (q.v.) in Italianate verse. The name was first applied to the form *aBabB* (capitals denote hendecasyllabic lines) and was taken from the end of the first line of Garcilaso's *A la flor de Gnido*. Garcilaso (1501?–1536) supposedly imitated it from Bernardo Tasso, who is credited with its invention. This form is sometimes designated the *l. garcilasiana* and has also come to be known as *estrofa de Fray Luis de León, l. de fray Luis de León*, and *quintilla de Luis de León* for being popularized through Fray Luis de León's works and later being replaced in popularity by other forms, particularly the *l. sestina* (*aBaBcC*, also called *media estancia*).—Navarro.   D.C.C.

LITERARINESS. See LINGUISTICS AND POETICS; POETICS; RUSSIAN FORMALISM.

LITERARY HISTORY. See CRITICISM; HISTORICISM; INFLUENCE; THEORY; TRADITION.

LITHUANIAN POETRY. Written lit. arose in Lithuania during the Reformation and Counter-Reformation. Before that, the poetic heritage of the nation was sustained by anonymous folk songs

LITHUANIAN POETRY

(*dainos*), mentioned in medieval sources. These *dainos*, of which about 200,000 have now been recorded, are best represented by lyrical love songs. The lyrical nature of poetic expression is characteristic of *dainos* in general, and it is strongly evident even in the war songs and ballads, while mythological songs are rare and epic narratives are altogether lacking. The most typical of the *dainos* exhibit numerous diminutives and employ highly developed parallelisms and a rather intricate, basically erotic, symbolism. Because the text and melody are integrally connected in the *dainos*, the rhythm is of great importance, and, as a result of the free stress in L., it is variable and often mixed. The rhyme, however, is not essential. The stanzas have mostly two, three, or four lines, either with or without refrain. Some older songs have no stanzas at all. The earliest collection of *dainos* (1825) is by Liudvikas Rėza (Rhesa, 1776–1840), the largest (4 v., 1880–83) by A. Juškevičius (1819–80); much more extensive collections are now being assembled by the L. Academy of Sciences. The trad. of folk poetry became a strong factor in the formation of the distinctly national character of L. p.

Written L. p. begins in the 16th c. with versions of canticles and hymns (qq.v.), incl. those of Martynas Mažvydas (Mosvidius, d. 1563), who also prepared in Königsberg the first printed L. book, *Catechismusa prasti szadei* (The Plain Words of the Catechism, 1547), a tr. of the Lutheran catechism, and prefaced it with a rhymed foreword. The most outstanding 18th-c. work was Kristijonas Donelaitis's (Donalitius, 1714–80) poem *Metai* (The Seasons, 1765–75, pub. 1818), a 3000-line poem in hexameters which exhibits in forceful lang. a keen love and observation of nature and depicts vividly the life and character of the common people. Imbued with the Pietist spirit, the poem transmits a moving sense of the sacredness of life and of the earth. At some points it can be compared with the work of James Thompson and Ewald von Kleist.

A more active literary movement appeared at the beginning of the 19th c., marked first by pseudo-classicism and sentimentalism (q.v.) and later by the influence of romanticism (q.v.) and a growing interest in L. folklore. The latter trend was particularly evident in the poetry of Antanas Strazdas, who was one of the first to merge the folksong trad. with personal expression. The next peak in the devel. of L. p. was Antanas Baranauskas (1835–1902), whose picturesque poem *Anykščiu šilelis* (The Grove of Anykščiai, 1858–59) is a veiled lament for Lithuania under the Rus. czarist regime. Baranauskas was esp. successful in creating a melodious flow of lang. using the traditional syllabic versification that is not very well suited to L. The pre-20th-c. devel. of L. p. was concluded by Maironis (pen name of Jonas Mačiulis, 1862–1932), the creative embodiment of the ideals of the national awakening and a foremost lyric poet (cf. his collection *Pavasario balsai* [Voices of

Spring], 1895). His formal and structural innovations, particularly the introduction of syllabotonic versification, had great influence on the growth of the new L. p. Two other poets writing in a lyrical mode in some respects similar to that of Maironis were Antanas Vienažindys (1841–92) and Pranas Vaičaitis (1876–1901).

At the beginning of the 20th c., the general relaxation of Rus. political pressure and the ever growing cultural consciousness increased literary production and widened its horizon. New approaches were inspired by literary movements abroad. Already evident before World War I, these trends were fulfilled during the period of independence (1918–40) when L. p. reached high standards of creative art. Symbolism (q.v.) left a strong imprint on the early period, best represented by Balys Sruoga (1896–1947), also an outstanding dramatist; Vincas Mykolaitis-Putinas (1893–1967), later a leading novelist as well; Faustas Kirša (1891–1964); and Jurgis Baltrušaitis (1873–1944), who, after achieving distinction among the Rus. symbolists, began to publish verse in his native L. around 1930. In the 1920s, the more conservative trends were countered by modernist poets who, led by Kazys Binkis (1893–1942), formed the group *Keturi vėjai* (Four Winds). Somewhat later, neoromanticism, neosymbolism, aestheticism (q.v.), and expressionism (q.v.) appeared on the scene, while the group *Trečias frontas* (Third Front) advocated poetry of leftist orientation.

These trends were transcended, however, by the individual achievements of the four leading poets of the second generation: Jonas Aistis (1904–73), a highly intimate poet and a master of subtle and refined expression; Bernardas Brazdžionis (b. 1907), whose poetry, sometimes stylistically innovative, sometimes rhetorical and of prophetic overtones, is a synthesis of national trads.; and Antanas Miškinis (1905–83) and Salomėja Neris (pen name of S. Bačinskaitė-Bučienė [1904–45]), both of whom have transformed the best qualities of the *dainos* into their own personal expression. The transitional features leading to the poetry of the next generation were best reflected in the verse of Vytautas Mačernis (1920–44).

The annexation of the country by the USSR during World War II was responsible for the schism that divided L. p. On the one hand, L. p. was haunted until 1989 by the paralyzing specter of Socialist Realism, and on the other, it has been learning to speak in the many modes of Western culture of many things, first of all of the pain and righteousness of exile. While some poets at home became eulogists of the Soviet system, and others, mostly of the older generation, retreated carefully into their ultimate long silence, new authors came forth to claim the favors of both the Muses and the regime and, in recent years, of the Muses alone. Eduardas Mieželaitis (b. 1919), paradoxically a loyal Communist of philosophical bent, did much to help Soviet L. p. break through to a more modern idiom. Justinas Marcinkevičius (b. 1930), also important as playwright, is perhaps the most popular poet today, speaking with great devotion, though at times with a forked tongue, of love for his country and people. Judita Vaičiūnaitė (b. 1937) sings of love in intimate urban settings and of myth in dreams of the past. Sigitas Geda (b. 1943) transforms both nature and myth into a single magical presence, his vision of the country and its soul. Marcelijus Martinaitis (b. 1936) mostly converses with his own and the nation's conscience about history, myth, and the responsibility of being human. Janina Degutytė (1928–90) is an intensely personal, lyrical poet of great integrity and noble dedication to humanity.

A number of prominent artists, writers, and intellectuals found themselves in the forefront of the national movement for independence beginning in 1989. One might say that their first obligation has become to create for themselves a free country, a fitting home for their Muse. Thus history has come full circle, returning to the situation at the end of the 19th c., when the poet's voice was also first of all a clarion for freedom.

In the West the foremost poet is Henrikas Radauskas (1910–70). He speaks in lucid and calmly measured cl. verse of the beauty of the world seen as a carnival of love and death. His loyalty, however, is not with that world but with the enchanting mysteries of poetic speech that it engenders. Jonas Aistis and Bernardas Brazdžionis continue in their previous vein, except that both have adopted a voice of outrage at their nation's destiny. Kazys Bradūnas (b. 1917) looks inward and into the past to awaken the ancient spirits of his native earth and engage them in an ongoing dialogue with Christianity and history in the native land. Jonas Mekas (b. 1922), one of the moving spirits of the "underground cinema" in New York, also writes nostalgic and pensive verse full of self-questioning and yearning for the truthful life. Algimantas Mackus (1932–64) found his own truth in a radical confrontation with the fact of exile which required him to transform all the images of hope and faith from the traditional cultural heritage into grim totems of death. Liūnė Sutema (pen name of Zinaida Katiliškienė, b. 1927) chooses the opposite task of allowing the alien world to grow into the very tissue of her soul to rejuvenate both her and the land of remembrance she carries within. Her brother Henrikas Nagys (b. 1920) embraces both emotional expressionism and Neo-romanticism. Alfonsas Nyka-Niliūnas (pen name of Alfonsas Čipkus, b. 1919), a cosmopolitan existentialist of a deeply philosophical bent, contemplates the large and bleak presence of Cosmos through the window of Western civilization.

ANTHOLOGIES: *The Daina*, ed. U. Katzenelenbogen (1935); *Aus litauischer Dichtung*, ed. and tr. H. Engert, 2d ed. (1938); *Litauischer Liederschrein*, ed. and tr. V. Jungfer (1948); *L. Folksongs in America*, ed. J. Balys (1958); *The Green Oak*, ed. A. Landsbergis and C. Mills (1962); *Lietuviu poezija*, v. 1–2, ed. V. Vanagas, v. 3, ed. K. Bradūnas (1969–71); *Litovskie poety XX veka*, ed. V. Galinis (1971); *Selected Post-War L. P.*, ed. J. Zdanys (1978); *L. Writers in the West*, ed. A. Skrupskelis (1979); *The Amber Lyre: 18th–20th-C. L. P.* (1983); *Chimeras in the Tower: Selected Poems of Henrikas Radauskas*, tr. J. Zdanys (1986).

HISTORY AND CRITICISM: B. Sruoga, "L. Folksongs," *Folk-Lore* (London) 43 (1932); J. Mauclere, *Panorama de la litt. lithuanienne contemporaine* (1938); A. Vaičiulaitis, *Outline Hist. of L. Lit.* (1942); J. Balys, *L. Narrative Folksongs* (1954); A. Senn, "Storia della letterature lituana," *Storia della letterature baltiche*, ed. G. Devoto (1957); A. Rubulis, *Baltic Lit.* (1970); R. Silbajoris, *Perfection of Exile* (1970); P. Naujokaitis, *Lietuviu literatūros istorija*, 4 v. (1973–76); *Istorija litovskoj literatury*, ed. J. Lankutis (1977); *Baltic Drama*, ed. A. Straumanis (1981). R.S.

LITOTES (Gr. "plainness," "simplicity"). A form of meiosis (q.v.) employing (1) affirmation by the negative of the contrary ("Not half bad"; "I'll bet you won't" meaning "I'm certain you will") or (2) deliberate understatement for purposes of intensification ("He was a good soldier; say no more" for a hero). Servius, commenting on Virgil's *Georgics* 2.125, says, "non tarda, id est, strenuissima: nam litotes figura est" (not slow, that is, most brisk: for the figure is l.). L. is used so frequently in *Beowulf* and other OE, ON, and Old Germanic poetry that it has become (with the kenning [q.v.]) one of its distinguishing features, e.g. "þæt wæs god cyning" (that was a good king), following a passage telling how the king flourished on earth, prospered in honors, and brought neighboring realms to pay him tribute. Chaucer's Cook is described as "nat pale as a forpyned goost. / A fat swan loved he best of any roost" (Gen. Prol. 205–6). Milton has: "Nor are thy lips ungraceful, Sire of men, / Nor tongue ineloquent" (*Paradise Lost* 8.18–19). Pope has more sophisticated subtleties, using l. as an effective satiric instrument.

Like meiosis, hyperbole, irony, and paradox (qq.v.), l. requires that the reader refer to the ostensive situation, i.e. to the utterance's pragmatic context, in order to perceive the disparity between the words taken literally and their intended sense. Group Mu distinguishes l. from meiosis, or "arithmetical" understatement ("one says less so as to say more") by restricting l. to the "double" negation of a grammatical and lexical contrary. So Chimène's conciliatory remark to her lover, "Go, I do not hate you" (Corneille, *Le Cid* 3.4), negates the lexeme "hatred," while at the same time the negative assertion posits the opposite series of statements referring to the degrees between loving and not hating. Thus the seemingly negative construction of the l. not only suppresses a positive seme, replacing it with the corresponding negative one, but also replaces any one of a series of negative semes (133–38, 147). Corbett illustrates how l. may function in forensic rhet. with an example of the lawyer who assists his client "by referring to a case of vandalism as 'boyish highjinks.' A rose by any other name will smell as sweet, but a crime, if referred to by a name that is not too patently disproportionate, may lose some of its heinousness" (488). L. in this instance functions like euphemism by reducing the resistance of the audience. In logic the device corresponding to l. is *obversion.*

The distinction between l. and meiosis is that, in the former, calling a thing less than it is is done so as to make evident that it is actually larger, whereas in the latter, calling it less is meant to make it less.—K. Weyman, *Studien über die Figur der L.* (1886); 0. Jespersen, *Negation in Eng. and Other Langs.* (1917); A. Hübner, *Die "Mhd. Ironie" oder die L. im Altdeutschen* (1930); F. Bracher, "Understatement in OE Poetry," *PMLA* 52 (1937); L. M. Hollander, "L. in ON," *PMLA* 53 (1938); Sr. M. Joseph, *Shakespeare's Use of the Arts of Lang.* (1947); C. Perelman and L. Olbrechts-Tyteca, *The New Rhet.* (tr. 1969); Lausberg; Morier; Group Mu, 138, 147; Corbett.   R.O.E.; A.W.H.; T.V.F.B.

LITURGICAL DRAMA. Other terms for a religious play performed in a med. church may distinguish certain aspects of the play form—e.g., mystery, miracle, Lat. play, medieval drama—but *liturgical* seems best to categorize the ceremonial site and seedbed of the l. ds. These plays were regarded as appropriate ("Proper") in every kind of service from a monastic hour to the Introit of the Mass, and were chronologically arranged according to seasonal religious feasts. The great Easter drama, the *Visitatio sepulchri,* in its mature versions was usually performed after the third responsory of the Easter Matins service, and was immediately followed by the closing hymn of that service, the *Te Deum laudamus.* Similarly, three of the St. Nicholas "miracle" plays at Fleury were grafted onto one or another monastic office for the feast of St. Nicholas, and the fourth came between the end of Matins and the beginning (Introit) of the Mass for that feast. Most medieval playscripts of the 12th and 13th cs. include the incipit of the traditional concluding hymn or antiphon of the service as the epilogue of the play, even when the play is preserved in a nonl. ms.

Since the Easter and Christmas Matins services were—and are—the most elaborate of the church year, they could include a play more readily than could the central service, the Mass.

The audience for the l. ds. was generally the cloistered monastic community, neither very large nor very lay. Sometimes present were members of a royal or noble court who were patrons of that church; Eleanor of Aquitaine and Louis VII spent Christmas of 1137 at Limoges, where two existing l. plays are known to have been performed in the

Church of St. Martial in that period. There is a widely received opinion that the purpose of the plays was to instruct the illiterate, in the same way that the Gothic cathedral was the people's Bible in stone. The circumstances of medieval monastic life and contemporary records, however, favor a nonpopular definition of the audience. The plays seem to have been the possession of sophisticated, vocational monks who knew the Bible and liturgy and were fluent in Med. Lat. Pope Gregory IX, clarifying a 1207 ruling by Innocent III, mentions a number of plays by their titles, and states that they "lead men to conscience . . . and are performed to excite to devotion" (*Ad devotionem excitandam*).

The lang. of the mature plays is from three-fourths to nine-tenths Lat. verse, the remainder l. antiphons (lines sung by one choir in response to another). The verse is in a wide range of meters and stanza forms, the antiphons in traditional Lat. nonmetrical form. Most scholars agree that the melodies for the verses were composed in measures, not in the free-rhythm of plainchant. The musical meter was derived from that of the verses, care being taken to avoid false word-accents. This aesthetic is found also in the secular compositions of the troubadour and trouvère composers of the same period. In fact, the styles of the religious pieces and the secular songs are so similar that without the accompaniment of lang., a given melody can hardly be distinguished as religious or secular.

The melodic style of the great Easter sequence, *Victimae paschali,* is similar to that of contemporary, through-composed, secular pieces, and its words and music were often incorporated in the more complex *Visitatio* dramas. Verbal material of the famous hymn, *Stabat mater,* is likewise shared with the dialogue of the Cividale play, *Planctus Mariae.* Often surfacing in the heads of the l. d. composers were analogues of musical and verbal phrases from the large repertory of medieval hymns, some of which had been in circulation for 700 years.

Because the authors of the l. ds. composed for the glory of God, like other religious craftsmen, their names and ranks are entirely unknown—with the exception of the wandering scholar Hilarius, whose works are in dramatic form but without music. The names of song-makers to the Fr., Eng., and Ger. courts of the same period, on the other hand, are on most of the secular mss. that have survived. There is little evidence of church borrowing melodies from court, or vice versa, both kinds of composers being melodically prolific. The identity of the church composers can only be inferred from consideration of the role of the choirmaster, the director of the *schola cantorum,* the most experienced musician in the community. He was in the right place to compose, rehearse, and perform the plays with his choir of men and boys. He was in charge of the performance of l.

music for every service of the year, and required his group of singers to learn by rote the many hundreds of l. items for these services. The Lat. name for the choir, *chorus*, appears in the rubrics (stage directions) of surviving mss. and suggests its dramatic function as commentator on the action of the play, most frequently by an "Alleluia!" or two; otherwise, it was involved mainly with the choral hymns or antiphons that framed the play as prologue and epilogue.

The action of the plays, while centered in the Choir area, included the entire church, with processions to various locations for scenes, and with frequent travel scenes, as in the Shepherds' journey from the fields to the Manger, the Magi's similar quest through the length of the nave, the Apostles' meeting with the Christus on the road and their journey with him to the inn at Emmaus, the many journeys in the *Lazarus* play, and the long approach of the Marys to the Sepulcher in the *Visitatio*.

The acoustics of the stone and glass envelope of the medieval church maintained the ancient trad. of monophonic vocal music, the "live" and reverberative quality of sound therein being more hospitable to the single melodic line than to polyphonic compositions for voices or instruments. Singers, then as now, had no problem "playing the building," and the medieval chorister-actor must have taken those acoustics for granted.

Background and props for the play were supplied by the building and its furniture—altar, chancel, nave, pulpit, and so forth. No scenery was used, though on occasion medieval gadgeteers contrived an "anastasis" to house the Sepulcher, outlined a lions' den for Daniel, and built a prison facade from which St. Paul escaped. All in all, the emphasis was symbolic, in contrast to modern representational naturalism.

Only in the costuming of the actors was a consistent effort made at verisimilitude, as exemplified vividly by the rubric in the Fleury *Lazarus* that requires Magdalene to be dressed "*in habitu . . . meretricio*" (in the dress of a whore). The early playwrights appear to have improvised costumes from the ecclesiastical wardrobe, in the manner of a 10th-c. *Visitatio* from Winchester, in which the three monks playing the roles of the Marys are directed to wear copes with the hoods on top of their heads to make them appear less tonsured, more feminine. The move toward verisimilitude was thus slow, but inevitable, as the scale of theatrical effort enlarged, so that eventually we find Norman chain-mailed soldiers guarding the Sepulcher at the beginning of the *Visitatio*, as they had long been depicted in the visual arts. While this was a strong drift toward naturalism, the anachronism of the chain mail was not distasteful to the medieval audience, salvation history being eternally in the present. As Hardison observes, "anachronism was a form of verisimilitude."

The content of the plays is derived from Old and New Testament narratives, l. antiphons and hymns, and saints' legends. New Testament narratives and saints' legends are favored, owing to the fact that the feast days of the medieval church were devoted exclusively to the celebration of the events of Christ's life and the lives of his saints. L.d. used narratives appropriate to the occasion. The only two surviving, producible plays with Old Testament affiliations are the Beauvais *Play of Daniel*, attached to the Advent season because Daniel is a prophet of Christ, and the Limoges *Procession of Prophets* (of Christ). Not until the 14th c., with the appearance of cycles of plays to be performed for a popular audience in celebration of the newly created feast day, Corpus Christi, were Old Testament stories used extensively, and by then the dramatic form had radically changed. The lang. was vernacular, the dialogue was spoken rather than sung, and many of the playlets were significant mainly as links in a series of events stretching from Creation to the Day of Judgment.

In their heyday, the plays portrayed dramatically the life of Christ from the Annunciation to the Ascension. The most substantial cluster of plays dealt with the Resurrection: the lament of Mary at the cross, the visit of the other Marys to the Sepulcher (more than a thousand local versions), and the *Peregrinus* (the risen Christus in disguise at Emmaus and afterward revealed to Doubting Thomas and the other disciples). There is likewise a fine group of Nativity plays, concerned either separately or in combination with the Shepherds, Midwives, Magi, Herod, Joseph and Mary, and the Innocents. On each side of this cluster are the additional Marian plays of the Annunciation, Purification, and Assumption. Other producible plays for the New Testament are the *Resuscitation of Lazarus*, the *Sponsus* (Wise and Foolish Virgins), and the *Conversion of St. Paul*.

A final category of medieval church plays deals with miraculous events in the lives of the saints, a category formerly considered separate and called Miracle Plays. This distinction now seems invalid inasmuch as the l. circumstances of their production and the aesthetics of their form are identical with those of the other music-dramas of the 12th and 13th cs.

The scarcity of records has made the history of l. d spotty and rife with speculation and scholarly controversy. The place and date of origin, or simultaneous origins, may never be objectively determined, though we can generalize with some confidence about the process by which the l. plays came into being. The practice of troping—expanding l. chants with additional melodic and verbal material—beginning in the 9th c. invited dramatic and theatrical expression. Although there is no direct evidence for the evolution of the *Visitatio* from tropes of the Easter *Quem quaeritis* antiphons, this may have happened during the Carolingian Renaissance. As to what transpired between the very simple versions and the emergence of the most artistic versions of the *Visitatio* and others, we have little reliable information. See, however, Hardison for a quite different theory.

K. Young, *The Drama of the Med. Church*, 2 v. (1933); O. B. Hardison, Jr., *Christian Rite and Christian Drama in the Middle Ages* (1965); F. Collins, *The Production of Med. Church Music-Drama* (1972), *Med. Church Music-Dramas: A Repertory of Complete Plays* (1976); M. H. Marshall, "Aesthetic Values of the L. D.," *Med. Eng. Drama*, ed. J. Taylor and A. H. Nelson (1972); C. Flanigan, "The L. Context of the *Quem queritis* Trope," *CompD* 8 (1974); W. Lipphardt, *Lateinische Osterfeiern und Osterspiele*, 7 v. (1975–); W. L. Smoldon, *The Music of the Med. Church Dramas*, ed. C. Bourgeault (1980); J. Stevens, "Med. Drama—Music Drama," *New Grove*; S. Sticca, *Il Planctus Mariae nella tradizione drammatica del medio evo* (1984); *The Fleury Playbook: Essays and Studies*, ed. T. P. Campbell and C. Davidson (1985); *The Saint Play in Med. Europe*, ed. C. Davidson (1986); M. Stevens, *Four ME Mystery Cycles* (1987); H.-J. Diller, *The ME Mystery Play* (tr. 1992). F.C.

LJÓÐAHÁTTR. ON Eddic meter. Stanzas of l. contain two 3-line segments, each of which makes up a syntactic whole. The first two lines of each segment resemble *fornyrðislag* (q.v.) and the Germanic long line: they have two stresses each, are linked by alliteration, and are separated by a caesura. The "even" (third and sixth) lines, in a Scandinavian innovation, have three (according to some scholars only two) stresses, but each alliterates within itself, and there is no caesura.

> Vígríðr heitir á, er finnaz vígi at
> Surtr oc in sváso goð

> (That river is called Vígríðr, where
> Surtr and the sweet gods will meet
> in battle.)

L. means literally "meter of songs," and it is generally used for verse in dialogue and didactic poetry. Addition of a second "even" line creates *galdralag*, a meter traditionally associated with magic chants. See OLD NORSE POETRY.—*The Poetic Edda*, tr. H. A. Bellows (1923) and L. M. Hollander, rev. ed. (1962); W. P. Lehmann, *The Development of Germanic Verse Form* (1956); P. Hallberg, *Old Icelandic Poetry* (1975). J.L.

LOCUS AMOENUS. See DESCRIPTIVE POETRY; EKPHRASIS; TOPOS.

LOGAOEDIC. A term used sporadically by ancient metrists to refer to verses consisting of single long syllables in alternation first with double then with single shorts: ∪ ∪ – ∪ ∪ – ; – ∪ ∪ – ∪ ∪ – ∪ – x , etc. Some 19th-c. metrists took the term to imply actual rhythmical equivalence between double and single short and applied it to a much larger class of ancient forms consisting (so they believed) of isochronous metra (see ISOCHRONISM) in which the normal time-values of longs and shorts were altered in such a way that dactyl, spondee, trochee, and single long syllable were all durational equivalents. The asclepiad (q.v.) in its Horatian form would accordingly be analyzed as a hexameter (p equals pause): – – | – ∪ ∪ | – p | – ∪ ∪ | – ∪ | – p . Though now generally rejected in favor of some sort of choriambic or aeolic (qq.v.) analysis of the sequences once called l., the theory still has occasional defenders, particularly among Classicists who are also musicians. It encourages us to find in a piece of Gr. verse the equidistant strong stresses that one might look for in trying to set it to music, or that an Eng. or Am. reader would be inclined to introduce when reciting it. And it becomes, with the elimination of the spondee and the addition of the first paeon to its repertory of isochronous metra, the "sprung rhythm" (q.v.) of Gerard Manley Hopkins. But in general the term has not been used by modern metrists in reference to mixed binary-ternary (iambic-anapestic or trochaic-dactylic) meters in modern Eng. verse, nor is it clear that such usage would be at all appropriate, since even its Cl. sense is problematic, and it is by no means an obviously necessary term: thoughtless transference of concepts and terms from Cl. to modern metrics is one of the greatest dangers in prosody.— P. Shorey, "Choriambic Dimeter and the Rehabilitation of the Antispast," *TAPA* 38 (1907)—favors the term; J. W. White, *The Verse of Gr. Comedy* (1912)—opposes. A.T.C.; T.V.F.B.

LOGOCENTRISM. See DECONSTRUCTION; INFLUENCE; INTERTEXTUALITY; TEXTUALITY.

LOGOPOEIA. See MELOPOEIA, PHANOPOEIA, LOGOPOEIA.

LOGOS. See DECONSTRUCTION; ETHOS; PATHOS.

LONG. See DURATION; QUANTITY.

LONG METER, LONG MEASURE. See BALLAD METER; HYMN.

LONG POEM. See EPIC; MODERN LONG POEM; NARRATIVE POETRY.

LOVE POETRY.

    I. WESTERN
    II. EASTERN
        A. *Arabic and Persian*
        B. *Egyptian*
        C. *Hebrew*
        D. *Indian*
        E. *Chinese*
        F. *Japanese*

    I. WESTERN. In evaluating l. p., we must ask first

whether the lang. is private and original or formulaic and rhetorical. Is the poet speaking for himor herself, or is the voice a persona (q.v.)? The poem, if commissioned by friend or patron, may be a projection into another's adventures, or it may be an improvised conflation of real and invented details. A love poem cannot be simplistically read as a literal, journalistic record of an event or relationship; there is always some fictive reshaping of reality for dramatic or psychological ends. A love poem is secondary rather than primary experience; as an imaginative construction, it invites detached contemplation of the spectacle of sex.

We must be particularly cautious when dealing with controversial forms of eroticism like homosexuality. Poems are unreliable historical evidence about any society; they may reflect the consciousness of only one exceptional person. Furthermore, homoerotic images or fantasies in poetry must not be confused with concrete homosexual practice. We may speak of tastes or tendencies in early poets but not of sexual orientation: this is a modern idea.

L. p. is equally informed by artistic trad. and contemp. cultural assumptions. The pagan attitude toward the body and its pleasures was quite different from that of Christianity, which assigns sex to the fallen realm of nature. The richness of Western l. p. may thus arise in part from the dilemma of how to reconcile mind or soul with body. Moreover, the generally higher social status of women in Western as opposed to Eastern culture has given l. p. added complexity or ambivalence: only women of strong personality could have produced the tormented sagas of Catullus or Propertius. We must try to identify a poem's intended audience. In antiquity the love poet was usually addressing a coterie of friends or connoisseurs; since romanticism, however, the poet speaks to him- or herself, with the reader seeming to overhear private thoughts. We must ask about pornographic material in l. p. whether it reflects the freer sensibilities of a different time or whether the poet set out to shock or challenge his contemporaries. Much l. p. is clearly testing the limits of decorous speech, partly to bring sexual desire under the scrutiny and control of imagination. In the great Western theme of the transience of time, vivid sensuous details illustrate the evanescence of youth and beauty; the poet has a godlike power to defeat time and bestow immortality upon the beloved through art. Romantic impediments give the poem a dramatic frame: the beloved may be indifferent, far away, married to someone else, dead, or of the wrong sex. However, difficulty or disaster in real life is converted into artistic opportunity by the poet, whose work profits from the intensification and exploration of negative emotion.

The history of European l. p. begins with the Gr. lyric poets of the Archaic age (7th–6th cs. B.C; see MELIC POETRY). Archilochus, Mimnermus, Sappho, and Alcaeus turn poetry away from the grand epic style toward the quiet personal voice, attentive to mood and emotion. Despite the fragmentary survival of Gr. solo poetry, we see that it contains a new idea of love which Homer shows as foolish or deceptive but never unhappy. Archilochus' account of the anguish of love is deepened by Sappho, whose poetry was honored by male writers and grammarians until the fall of Rome. Sappho and Alcaeus were active on Lesbos, an affluent island off the Aeolian coast of Asia Minor where aristocratic women apparently had more freedom than later in classical Athens. Sappho is primarily a love poet, uninterested in politics or metaphysics. The nature of her love has caused much controversy and many fabrications, some by major scholars. Sappho was married, and she had a daughter, but her poetry suggests that she fell in love with a series of beautiful girls, who moved in and out of her coterie (not a school, club, or cult). There is as yet no evidence, however, that she had physical relations with women. Even the ancients, who had her complete works, were divided about her sexuality.

Sappho shows that l. p. is how Western personality defines itself. The beloved is passionately perceived but also replaceable; he or she may exist primarily as a focus of the poet's consciousness. In "He seems to me a god" (fr. 31), Sappho describes her pain at the sight of a favorite girl sitting and laughing with a man. The lighthearted social scene becomes oppressively internal as the poet sinks into suffering: she cannot speak or see; she is overcome by fever, tremor, pallor. These symptoms of love become conventional and persist more than a thousand years (Lesky). In plain, concise lang., Sappho analyzes her extreme state as if she were both actor and observer; she is candid and emotional yet dignified, austere, almost clinical. This poem, preserved for us by Longinus, is the first great psychological document of Western lit. Sappho's prayer to Aphrodite (fr. 1) converts cult-song into love poem. The goddess, amused at Sappho's desperate appeal for aid, teasingly reminds her of former infatuations and their inevitable end. Love is an endless cycle of pursuit, triumph, and ennui. The poem, seemingly so charming and transparent, is structured by a complex time scheme of past, present, and future, the ever-flowing stream of our emotional life. Sappho also wrote festive wedding songs and the first known description of a romantic moonlit night. She apparently invented the now-commonplace adjective "bittersweet" for the mixed condition of love.

Early Gr. l. p. is based on simple parallelism between human emotion and nature, which has a Mediterranean mildness. Love-sickness, like a storm, is sudden and passing. Imagery is vivid and luminous, as in haiku (q.v.); there is nothing contorted or artificial. Anacreon earned a proverbial reputation for wine, women, and song: his love is not Sappho's spiritual crisis but the passing diversion of a bisexual bon vivant. L. p. was little written in classical Athens, where lyric was absorbed into the tragic choral ode. Plato, who abandoned poetry for philosophy, left epigrams on the beauty of boys. The learned Alexandrian age revived l. p. as an art mode. Theocritus begins the long literary trad. of pastoral (q.v.), where shepherds complain of unrequited love under sunny skies. Most of his *Idylls* contain the voices of rustic characters like homely Polyphemus, courting the scornful nymph Galatea, or Lycidas, a goatherd pining for a youth gone to sea. Aging Theocritus broods about his own love for fickle boys, whose blushes haunt him. In his *Epigrams*, Callimachus takes a lighter attitude toward love, to which he applies sporting metaphors of the hunt. In Medea's agonized passion for Jason in the *Argonautica*, Apollonius Rhodius tries to mesh l. p. with epic. Asklepiades adds new symbols to love trad.: Eros and arrow-darting Cupid. Meleager writes with equal relish of cruel boys and voluptuous women, such as Heliodora. His is a poignant, sensual poetry filled with the color and smell of flowers.

The *Greek Anthology* demonstrates the changes in Gr. l. p. from the Alexandrian through Roman periods. As urban centers grow and speed up, nature metaphors recede. Trashy street life begins, and prostitutes, drag queens, randy tutors, and bathhouse masseuses crowd into view. Love poets become droll, jaded, less lyrical. Women are lusciously described but given no personalities or inner life. For the first time, l. p. incorporates ugliness, squalor, and disgust: Leonidas of Tarentum and Marcus Argentarius write of voracious sluts with special skills, and Antipater of Thessalonika coarsely derides scrawny old lechers. Boy-love is universal: Straton of Sardis, editor of an anthol. of pederastic poems, celebrates the ripening phases of boys' genitals. By the early Byzantine period, however, we feel the impact of Christianity, in more heartfelt sentiment but also in guilt and melancholy.

The Romans inherited a huge body of Gr. l. p. Catullus, the first Lat. writer to adapt elegy (q.v.) for love themes, is obsessed with Lesbia, the glamorous noblewoman Clodia, promiscuously partying with midnight pickups. "I love and I hate": this tortured affair is the most complex contribution to l. p. since Sappho, whom Catullus admired and imitated. The poet painfully grapples with the ambiguities and ambivalences of being in love with an aggressive, willful Western woman. He also writes tender love poems to a boy, honey-sweet Juventius. There is no Roman l. p. between adult men. Propertius records a long, capricious involvement with capricious Cynthia, a fast-living new woman. There are sensual bed scenes, love-bites, brawls. After Cynthia dies (perhaps poisoned), the angry, humiliated poet sees her ghost over his bed. Tibullus writes of troubled love for two headstrong mistresses, adulterous Delia and greedy

Nemesis, and one elusive boy, Marathus. In Virgil's *Eclogue 2*, the shepherd Corydon passionately laments his love-madness for Alexis, a proud, beautiful youth; the poem was traditionally taken as proof of Virgil's own homosexuality. Horace names a half dozen girls whom he playfully lusts for, but only the rosy boy Ligurinus moves him to tears and dreams. In the *Amores*, Ovid boasts of his sexual prowess and offers strategies for adultery. *The Art of Love* tells how to find and keep a lover, including sexual positions, naughty words, and feigned ecstasies. *The Remedies for Love* contains precepts for falling *out* of love. The love-letters of the *Heroides* are rhetorical monologues of famous women (Phaedra, Medea) abandoned by cads. Juvenal shows imperial Rome teeming with effeminates, libertines, and pimps; love or trust is impossible. The Empress prowls the brothels; every good-looking boy is endangered by rich seducers; drunken wives grapple in public stunts. Martial casts himself as a facetious explorer of this lewd world where erections are measured and no girl says no. The *Dionysiaca*, Nonnus' late Gr. epic, assembles fanciful erotic episodes from the life of Dionysus. Also extant are many Gr. and Lat. *priapeia* (q.v.): obscene comic verses, attached to phallic statues of Priapus in field and garden, which threaten thieves with anal or oral rape.

In medieval romance (q.v.), love as challenge, danger, or high ideal is central to chivalric quest. From the mid 12th c., woman replaces the feudal lord as center of the militaristic *chansons de geste* (q.v.). Fr. aristocratic taste was refined by the courtly love (q.v.) of the Occitan (Provençal) troubadours (q.v.), who raised woman to spiritual dominance, something new in Western l. p. (see OCCITAN POETRY). Amorous intrigue now lures the hero: to consummate his adultery with Guinevere, Chrétien de Troyes' Lancelot bends the bars of her chamber, then bleeds into her bed. The symbolism of golden grail, bleeding lance, and broken sword of Chrétien's *Perceval* is sexual as well as religious. Wolfram von Eschenbach's Ger. *Parzival* is vowed to purity, but adulterous Anfortas suffers a festering, incurable groin wound (see MINNESANG). Sexual temptations are specifically set to test a knight's virtue in the Fr. romances *Yder* and *Hunbaut* and the ME *Sir Gawain and the Green Knight*. The adultery of Gottfried von Strassburg's Tristan and Isolde, with their steamy lovemaking, helped define Western romantic love as unhappy or doomed. The Trojan tale of faithful Troilus and treacherous Cressida was invented by Benoît de Sainte-Maure and transmitted to Boccaccio and Chaucer. Heavily influenced by Ovid, *The Romance of the Rose* (Guillaume de Lorris and Jean de Meun) uses dreamlike allegory (q.v.) and sexual symbols of flower, garden, and tower to chart love's assault. The pregnancy of the Rose is a first for European literary heroines. Abelard wrote famous love songs, now lost, to Heloise. Dante's youthful love poems to Beatrice in the *Vita nuova* begin in troubadour style, then modulate toward Christian mysticism. In the *Inferno*'s episode of Paolo and Francesca, seduced into adultery by reading a romance of Lancelot, Dante renounces his early affection for courtly love. Med. Lat. lyrics express homoerotic feeling between teacher and student in monastic communities. There are overtly pederastic poems from the 12th c. and at least one apparently lesbian one, but no known vernacular or pastoral medieval poetry is homosexual. The goliardic (q.v.) *Carmina Burana* contains beautiful lyrics of the northern flowering of spring and love, as well as cheeky verses of carousing and wenching, some startlingly detailed. The Fr. *fabliau* (q.v.), a ribald verse-tale twice imitated by Chaucer, reacts against courtly love with bedroom pranks, barnyard drubbings, and an earthy stress on woman's hoary genitality. Villon, zestfully atumble with Parisian trollops, will later combine the devil-may-care goliard's pose with the fabliau's slangy comedy.

Ren. epic further expands the romantic elements in chivalric adventure. Boiardo, Ariosto, and Tasso open quest to an armed heroine, a motif adopted by Spenser, whose *Faerie Queene*, emulating Ovid's *Metamorphoses*, copiously catalogues incidents of normal and deviant sex. Petrarch, combining troubadour lyricism with Dante's advanced psychology, creates the modern love poem. His Laura, unlike saintly Beatrice, is a real woman, not a symbol. Petrarch's nature, vibrating to the lover's emotions, will become the romantic pathetic fallacy (q.v.). His conceits, paradoxes, and images of fire and ice, which spread in sonnet sequences (q.v.) throughout Europe, inspired and burdened Ren. poets, who had to discard the convention of frigid mistress and trembling wooer (see PETRARCHISM). Ronsard's sonnets, addressed to Cassandre, Marie, and Hélène, first follow Petrarchan formulas, then achieve a simpler, more musical, debonair style, exquisitely attuned to nature. In the *Amoretti*, Spenser practices the sonnet (introduced to England by Wyatt and Surrey), but his supreme love poem is the *Epithalamion*, celebrating marriage. Like Michelangelo, Shakespeare writes complex l. p. to a beautiful young man and a forceful woman: the fair youth's homoerotic androgyny is reminiscent of Shakespeare's soft, "lovely" Adonis and Marlowe's longhaired, white-fleshed Leander, romanced by Neptune. Richard Barnfield's sonnets and *Affectionate Shepherd* openly offer succulent sexual delights to a boy called Ganymede, a common Ren. allusion. The traditional allegory, based on the Song of Songs, of Christ the bridegroom knocking at the soul's door, creates unmistakable homoeroticism in Donne's Holy Sonnet XIV, George Herbert's "Love (III)," and spiritual stanzas by St. John of the Cross. In ardent poems to his fiancée, later his wife, Donne, with Spenser, demonstrates the new prestige of marriage: before this, no one wrote l.

p. to his wife. Furthermore, Donne's erudition implies that his lady, better educated than her medieval precursors, enjoys flattery of her intellect as well as of her beauty. Aretino's sonnets daringly use vulgar street terms for acts of love. Marino's *Adonis* makes baroque opera out of the ritualistic stages of sexual gratification. Waller and Marvell use the *carpe diem* (q.v.) argument to lure shy virgins into surrender; the Cavalier poets adopt a flippant court attitude toward women and pleasure. Carew's "A Rapture" turns Donne's ode to nakedness into a risqué tour of Celia's nether parts. Libertines emerge in the late 17th c.: Rochester, a Restoration wit, writes bluntly of raw couplings with ladies, whores, and boys. Milton's *Lycidas* revives the Cl. style of homoerotic pastoral lament. *Paradise Lost*, following Spenser and Donne, exalts "wedded Love" over the sterile wantonness of "Harlots" and "Court Amours" (4.750–70).

The Age of Reason, valuing self-control and witty detachment, favored satire over l. p. Rousseau's delicate sentiment and pagan nature-worship created the fervent moods of "sensibility" (q.v.) and woman-revering romanticism. Goethe, identifying femaleness with creativity, writes of happy sensual awakening in the *Roman Elegies* and jokes about sodomy with both sexes in the *Venetian Epigrams*, with its autoerotic acrobat Bettina; withheld pornographic verses imitate ancient *priapeia*. Schiller dedicates rhapsodic love poems to Laura, but his hymns to womanhood sentimentally polarize the sexes. Hölderlin addresses Diotima with generalized reverence and reserves his real feeling for Mother Earth. Blake calls for sexual freedom for women and for the end of guilt and shame. Burns composes rural Scottish ballads of bawdy or ill-starred love. Wordsworth's Lucy poems imagine woman reabsorbed into roiling nature. In *Christabel* Coleridge stages a virgin's seduction by a lesbian vampire, nature's emissary. The younger Eng. romantics fuse poetry with free love. In *Epipsychidion* Shelley is ruled by celestial women radiating intellectual light. Keats makes emotion primary; his maidens sensuously feed and sleep or wildly dance dominion over knights and kings. Byron's persona as a "mad, bad" seducer has been revised by modern revelations about his bisexuality. In the "Thyrza" poems, he woos and changes the sex of a favorite Cambridge choirboy; in *Don Juan* his blushing, girlish hero, forced into drag, catches the eye of a tempestuous lesbian sultana. Heine's love ballads are about squires, shepherd-boys, hussars, and fishermaidens; later verses record erotic adventures of the famous poet wined and dined by lady admirers.

The Fr. romantics, turning art against nature in the hell of the modern city, make forbidden sex a central theme. Gautier celebrates the lonely, self-complete hermaphrodite. Baudelaire looses brazen whores upon syphilitic male martyrs; sex is torment, cursed by God. Baudelaire's heroic, defiant lesbians are hedonistically modernized by Verlaine and later rehellenized by Louys. In *Femmes* Verlaine uses vigorous street argot to describe the voluptuous sounds and smells of sex with women; in *Hombres* he lauds the brutal virility of young laborers, whom he possesses in their rough workclothes. He and Rimbaud co-wrote an ingenious sonnet about the anus. Mallarmé's leering faun embodies pagan eros; cold, virginal Herodias is woman as castrator. In contrast, Victorian poetry, as typified by the Brownings, exalts tenderness, fidelity, and devotion, the bonds of married love, preserved beyond the grave. Tennyson and the Pre-Raphaelites revive the medieval cult of idealized woman, supporting the Victorian view of woman's spirituality. Tennyson's heroines, like weary Mariana, love in mournful solitude. His *Idylls* retell Arthurian romance. *In Memoriam*, Tennyson's elaborate elegy for Hallam, is homoerotic in feeling. Rossetti's sirens are sultry, smoldering. Swinburne, inspired by Baudelaire, reintroduces sexual frankness into highbrow Eng. lit. His Dolores and Faustine are promiscuous *femmes fatales*, immortal vampires; his Sappho, sadistically caressing Anactoria, boldly proclaims her poetic greatness. Whitman broke taboos in Am. poetry: he names body parts and depicts sex surging through fertile nature; he savors the erotic beauties of both male and female. Though he endorses sexual action and energy, Whitman appears to have been mostly solitary, troubled by homosexual desires, suggested in the "Calamus" section of *Leaves of Grass*. Reflecting the Victorian taste for bereavement, Hardy's early poetry features gloomy provincial tales of love lost: ghosts, graveyards, suicides, tearful partings. Homoerotic Gr. idealism and epicene fin-de-siècle preciosity characterize the poems of Symonds, Carpenter, Hopkins, Wilde, Symons, and Dowson. Renée Vivien, the first poet to advertise her lesbianism, writes only of languid, ethereal beauty.

L. p. of the 20th c. is the most varied and sexually explicit since Cl. lit. T. S. Eliot diagnoses the sexual sterility or passivity of modern man. Yet Neruda writes searing odes to physical passion, boiling with ecstatic elemental imagery. D. H. Lawrence similarly roots the sex impulse in the seasonal cycles of the animal world. Recalling long-ago, one-night pickups of handsome, athletic youths, Cavafy declares sex the creative source of his poetry. For Yeats, woman's haunting beauty is the heart of life's mystery; in "Leda and the Swan," rape is the metaphor for cataclysmic historical change. Rilke contemplates the philosophical dilemma of love, the pressure upon identity, the tension between fate and freedom. Valéry makes lang. erotic: the poet is Narcissus and, in *La Jeune Parque*, the oracle raped by her own inner god. Éluard sees woman erotically metamorphosing through the world, permeating him with her supernatural force. Lorca imagines operatic scenes of heterosexual seduction, rape, or mutilation,

and in "Ode to Walt Whitman" denounces urban "pansies" for a visionary homosexuality grounded in living nature. Fascinated but repelled by strippers and whores, Hart Crane records squalid homosexual encounters in subway urinals. Amy Lowell vividly charts the works and days of a settled, sustaining lesbian relationship, while H. D. projects lesbian feeling into Gr. personae, often male. Edna St. Vincent Millay is the first woman poet to claim a man's sexual freedom: her sassy, cynical lyrics of Jazz Age promiscuity with anonymous men are balanced by melancholy love poems to women. Auden blurred the genders in major poems to conceal their homosexual inspiration; his private verse is maliciously bawdy. William Carlos Williams is rare among modern poets in extolling married love and kitchen-centered domestic bliss.

For Dylan Thomas, youth's sexual energies drive upward from moldering, evergreen earth. Theodore Roethke presents woman as unknowable Muse, ruling nature's ghostly breezes and oozy sexual matrix. Delmore Schwartz hails Marilyn Monroe as a new Venus, blessing and redeeming "a nation haunted by Puritanism." The free-living Beat poets (q.v.), emulating Black hipster talk, broke poetic decorum about sex. Adopting Whitman's chanting form and pansexual theme, Allen Ginsberg playfully celebrates sodomy and master-slave scenarios. In "Marriage," Gregory Corso imagines the whole universe wedding and propagating while he ages, destitute and alone. The Confessional poets weave sex into autobiography. Robert Lowell lies on his marriage bed paralyzed, sedated, unmanned. Anne Sexton aggressively breaks the age-old taboo upon female speech by graphically exploring her own body in adultery and masturbation. Sylvia Plath launched contemp. feminist poetry with her sizzling accounts of modern marriage as hell. With its grisly mix of Nazi fantasy and Freudian family romance, "Daddy," after Yeats' "Leda," may be the love poem of the century. John Berryman's *Sonnets* records a passionate, adulterous affair with a new Laura, her platinum hair lit by the dashboard as they copulate in a car, the modern version of Dido's dark "cave." *Love and Fame* reviews Berryman's career as a "sexual athlete" specializing in quickie encounters. The sexual revolution of the 1960s heightened the new candor. Hippie poetry invoked Buddhist avatars for love's ecstasies. Denise Levertov and Carol Bergé reverse trad. by salaciously detailing the hairy, muscular male body. Diane di Prima finds sharp, fierce imagery for the violent carnality of sex. Charles Bukowski writes of eroticism without illusions in a tough, gritty world of scrappy women, drunks, rooming-houses, and racetracks. Mark Strand mythically sees man helplessly passed from mother to wife to daughter: "I am the toy of women."

The 1960s also freed gay poetry from both underground and coterie. James Merrill, remembering mature love or youthful crisis, makes precise, discreet notations of dramatic place and time. Paul Goodman, Robert Duncan, Frank O'Hara, Thom Gunn, Harold Norse, and Mutsuo Takahashi intricately document the mechanics of homosexual contact for the first time since Imperial Rome: cruising, hustlers, sailors, bodybuilders, bikers, leather bars, bus terminals, toilets, glory holes. Gay male poetry is about energy, adventure, quest, danger; beauty and pleasure amidst secrecy, shame, and pain. Lesbian poetry, in contrast, prefers tender, committed relationships and often burdens itself with moralistic political messages. Adrienne Rich and Judy Grahn describe intimate lesbian sex and express solidarity with victimized women of all social classes; Audre Lorde invokes Af. myths to enlarge female identity. Olga Broumas, linking dreamy sensation to Gr. sun and sea, has produced the most artistically erotic lesbian lyrics. Eleanor Lerman's *Armed Love*, with its intellectual force and hallucinatory sexual ambiguities, remains the leading achievement of modern lesbian poetry, recapitulating the tormented history of Western love from Sappho and Catullus to Baudelaire.

ANTHOLOGIES: *Poetica erotica*, ed. T. R. Smith (1927); *Erotic Poetry: The Lyrics, Ballads, Idylls, and Epics of L.*, Cl. to Contemp., ed. W. Cole (1963); *The Body of L.: An Anthol. of Erotic Verse from Chaucer to Lawrence*, ed. D. Stanford (1965); *Dein Leib ist mein Gedicht: Deutsche erotische Lyrik aus funf Jahrhunderten*, ed. H. Arnold (1970); *Sexual Heretics: Male Homosexuality in Eng. Lit. 1850–1900*, ed. B. Reade (1970); *An Anthol. of Swahili L. P.*, ed. and tr. J. Knappert (1972); *The Gr. Anthol.*, ed. P. Jay (1973); *The Male Muse: A Gay Anthol.*, ed. I. Young (1973); *A Book of L. P.*, ed. J. Stallworthy (1974); *The Woman Troubadours*, ed. M. Bogin (1976); *Eros baroque: Anthologie de la poésie amoureuse baroque 1570–1620*, ed. G. Mathieu-Castellani (1979); *Penguin Book of Homosexual Verse*, ed. S. Coote (1983); *Priapea: Poems for a Phallic God*, tr. W. H. Parker (1988); *Gay and Lesbian Poetry in Our Time*, ed. C. Morse and J. Larkin (1988); *The Song of Eros: Ancient Gr. L. Poems*, tr. B. P. Nystrom (1991); *Games of Venus*, ed. P. Bing (1991).

HISTORY AND CRITICISM: O. Waser, "Eros," Pauly-Wissowa 1.6.484 ff.; R. Reitzenstein, *Zur Sprache der lateinischen Erotik* (1912); H. Brinkmann, *Gesch. der lateinischen Liebesdichtung im Mittelalter* (1925); M. Praz, *The Romantic Agony* (1933); Lewis; A. Day, *The Origins of Lat. Love-Elegy* (1938); J. H. Wilson, *The Court Wits of the Restoration* (1948); D. L. Page, *Sappho and Alcaeus* (1955); G. W. Knight, *The Mutual Flame* (1955); D. de Rougemont, *L. in the Western World*, 2d ed. (1956); M. J. Valency, *In Praise of L.: An Intro. to L.-P. of the Ren.* (1958); H. Bloom, *The Visionary Company* (1961); A. Lesky, *A Hist. of Gr. Lit.* (1963); D. Bush, *Mythology and the Ren. Trad. in Eng. Poetry*, 2d ed. (1963); J. B. Broadbent, *Poetic L.* (1964); G. E. Enscoe, *Eros and the Romantics* (1967); Dronke; S. Minta, *L. P. in 16th-C. France* (1977); T. A. Perry,

Erotic Spirituality: The Integrative Trad. from Leone Ebreo to John Donne (1980); J. H. Hagstrum, *Sex and Sensibility: Ideal and Erotic L. from Milton to Mozart* (1980), *The Romantic Body: L. and Sexuality in Keats, Wordsworth, and Blake* (1985); R. O. A. M. Lyne, *The Lat. L. Poets from Catullus to Horace* (1981); P. J. Kearney, *A Hist. of Erotic Lit.* (1982); A. Richlin, *The Garden of Priapus: Sexuality and Aggression in Roman Humor* (1983); P. Veyne, *Roman Erotic Elegy: L., Poetry, and the West* (1983, tr. 1988); I. Singer, *The Nature of L.*, v. 1, *Plato to Luther*, 2d ed. (1984), v. 2, *Courtly and Romantic* (1984), v. 3, *The Mod. World* (1987); A. J. Smith, *The Metaphysics of L.: Studies in Ren. L. P. from Dante to Milton* (1985); G. Woods, *Articulate Flesh: Male Homoeroticism and Mod. Poetry* (1987); D. O. Frantz, *Festum voluptatis: A Study of Ren. Erotica* (1989); A. R. Jones, *The Currency of Eros: Women's L. Lyric in Europe, 1540–1620* (1990); *The Song of Eros: Ancient Gr. L. Poems*, tr. B. P. Nystrom (1990); C. Paglia, *Sexual Personae: Art and Decadence from Nefertiti to Emily Dickinson* (1990).   C.P.

II. EASTERN. A. *Arabic and Persian*. Ar. l. p. in the pre-Islamic period is found chiefly in the extended ode (*qaṣīda*, q.v.), which typically begins with expressions of nostalgic longing for departed loved ones, or incorporates accounts of amorous conquests which serve the predominant mode of *fakhr* (boasting of personal achievements). In the Islamic period l. p. (generically termed *ghazal*, q.v.) was raised to independent status by the urban poets of the Hijaz (e.g. ʿUmar ibn Abī Rabīʿa [d. 711]) and the ʿUdhri poets of the desert (e.g. Jamīl [d. 710] and the semi-legendary Qays of the Banī ʿAmr, better known as Majnūn, "the madman"), who introduced the motif of the dedicated love-service to an often capricious lady. L. p. flourished under the early Abbasid caliphs (750–850) with Abū Nuwās (d. 813?), who mingled bacchic with erotic motifs and excelled in obscene l. p. (*mujūn*), both hetero- and homosexual, and al-ʿAbbās ibn al-Aḥnaf (d. ca. 808), the celebrated poet of courtly love (q.v.) at the court of Hārūn al-Rashīd. In later periods erotic motifs were generally incorporated into the panegyric *qaṣīda*; but independent l. poems are found in the mystical poetry of Ibn al-Fāriḍ (d. 1235) and Ibn al-ʿArabī (d. 1240), who adapted the lang. of secular bacchic and l. p. to express the mystical longing for union with the divine beloved. In Andalusia and Sicily l. p. retained its independent status, particularly in the Andalusian *muwashshaḥa* and *zajal*.

Persian l. p. first appears both in the exordium of the panegyric *qaṣīda* and in brief, independent lyrics (*ghazal, tarāna*) usually composed to be sung. The *ghazal* was adapted by Sanāʾī (d. 1130–31) for themes of mystical love and was later used extensively for this purpose, notably by Fakhr al-Din ʿIrāqī (d. 1289) and Jalāl al-Dīn Rūmī (d. 1273); the *ghazals* of Ḥāfiẓ (d. 1389) incorporate both secular and mystical topics to create deliberate ambiguity. The Persian verse romance (*mas̱-*

navi, q.v.), which centers on the love quest, was also adapted to mystical purposes, chiefly by Jāmī (d. 1498).

Both Ar. and Persian l. p. deal primarily with the sufferings and aspirations of the lover; with few exceptions (notably in the *kharjas* of some Andalusian *muwashshaḥāt*) the female voice is absent, and lesbian love does not furnish a poetic theme. Homoeroticism is more prominent in Persian l. p., where it is generally depicted in the context of idealized love, than in Ar., where it is largely confined to *mujūn*, which often deals explicitly with sexual matters; similarly, mystical l. p. is more widespread in Persian than in Ar., and mystical overtones come to permeate secular poetry in later periods.   J.S.M.

L. p. has re-emerged in the 20th c. as a privileged theme. Among contemp. Arab poets particularly known for erotic poetry are the Lebanese poets Saʿīd ʿAql (b. 1912) and Nizār Qabbānī (b. 1923). The oeuvres of the Syrian-Lebanese poet Adūnīs (ʿAlī Ahmad Saʿīd, b. 1930) and the Palestinian Tawfīq Ṣāyigh (1923–71) include important love poems.

In Persian poetry there are major erotic themes in the poetry of Ahmad Shamlu (b. 1925) and Mahdi Akhavāni Sālis (1928–90), but Furūgh Farrukhzād (1935–67) is the most innovative and forthright love poet of modern times, with an unprecedented, autobiographical treatment of erotic themes. Her collection *Another Birth* (1964) has been particularly influential.   M.B.

Ibn al-ʿArabī, *The Tarjumān al-Ashwāq*, tr. R. A. Nicholson (1911, rpt. 1978); Ibn al-Fāriḍ, *The Mystical Poems*, tr. A. J. Arberry (1956); *The Seven Odes*, tr. A. J. Arberry (1957); Jalāl al-Dīn Rūmī, *Mystical Poems*, tr. A. J. Arberry, 2 v. (1968, 1979); J. T. Monroe, *Hispano-Ar. Poetry* (1974); L. F. Compton, *Andalusian Lyrical Poetry and Old Sp. Love Songs* (1976); A. Karimi-Hakkak, *Anthol. of Mod. Persian Poetry* (1978); A. Schimmel, *As Through a Veil: Mystical Poetry in Islam* (1982); M. C. Hillmann, *A Lonely Woman: Forugh Farrokhzad and Her Poetry* (1987); S. Jayyusi, *Mod. Ar. Poetry: An Anthol.* (1987).   J.S.M.; M.B.

B. *Egyptian*. Extant from the Ramesside period (ca. 1305–1080 B.C.) of the New Kingdom are four small collections totaling about 60 poems, noteworthy because they are among the few examples of clearly personal and secular lyric poetry to survive from ancient Egypt. They are also one of the first clear instances of human female speakers (as opposed to deities) in the lit.; though most likely written by males, about half of the poems are spoken by women young or old. The authors in all cases are unknown. The speakers of both sexes in most cases appear to be young, expressing the full range of love situations between the sexes (never between members of the same sex). There is the catalogue of the beloved's attributes, head to toe; the lovelonging for the absent lover ("I love you through the daytimes, / in the dark, / Through all the long divisions of the night"); the depths of emotion ("Love of you is mixed deep in my vitals, / like water stirred into flour for bread"); the game of love ("I think I'll go home and lie very still, / feigning terminal illness"); the love ecstasy; the broken heart ("Whose turn is it now / making soft eyes up into his face?"). The range of emotion extends from the chasteness, simplicity, and tentativeness of a first love, like that of Romeo and Juliet ("A girl's sleepy feelings wakened by you— / you've made a whole world for me!"), on through the frankly physical attractions of love, directly and sensuously expressed, to at times the openly erotic ("Would your fingers follow the line of my thighs, / learn the curve of my breasts, and the rest?"). In general the love songs are romantic, idyllic, humorous, even satirical, sometimes naive, almost always graceful. Since most of the moves on the chessboard of love are represented, these songs seem broader in scope than the poems in the biblical Song of Solomon (see below), with which they are often compared, but which they antedate by a thousand years.—J. L. Foster, *Love Songs of the New Kingdom* (1974).   J.L.F.

C. *Hebrew*. Only one ancient Heb. love poem is extant, the biblical Song of Songs (also known as the Song of Solomon and the Canticles). In traditional Jewish exegesis, the Song was interpreted as an allegory of God's love for Israel (in Christian exegesis—God's love for the Church). It is, however, a secular, erotic love song of the sort well known from Egyptian l. p., which it resembles and from which Israelite l. p. probably derives. In both places, such songs were probably sung by professional singers as entertainment at private festivities. Traditionally the Song was attributed to King Solomon (mid 10th c. B.C.E.). Scholars are divided on its actual dating, but its lang. seems to belong to the 4th–3d c. B.C.E. Also at issue is the Song's unity, with some commentators regarding it as a collection of short love poems, others viewing it a unified work. The uniform style and the frequent appearance of repetends (q.v.) imply single authorship, though there is no clearly unifying structure. The speakers in the Song are an unmarried couple; since both lovers speak, they are best regarded as personae. The main voice is that of the young woman who speaks to and about her love, praising his beauty in a series of sometimes startling similes and expressing her desire in bold and sensual terms; he responds in kind. The song as a whole is a dialogue in which the words of the lovers often intermesh closely and echo each other. The lovers' relationship is surprisingly egalitarian and their eroticism quite unabashed. No other ancient Heb. l. p. is extant. Ezekiel 33:32, however, refers to a singer of a "song of desire," and Isaiah 5:1–4 seems to be based on a love-song theme.—M. H. Pope, *Song of Songs* (1977); M. Falk, *Love Lyrics from the Bible* (1982); M. V. Fox, *The Song of Songs and the Ancient Egyptian Love Songs* (1985).   M.V.F.

Medieval Heb. liturgical poetry continued the old trad. of treating God and Israel as lovers or spouses. Secular l. p., imitating the Ar. *ghazal* (q.v.), appeared in 10th-c. Spain, particularly by Samuel the Nagid (993–ca. 1055), Moses Ibn Ezra (ca. 1055–ca.1135), and Judah Halevi (ca. 1075–1141). Many poems are apparently homoerotic; but the sex of the lovers is not stressed, for the poems focus more on love than on sexuality, and on the poet's adoration of ideal beauty embodied in the beloved. The erotic prelude to formal panegyric (*nasīb*) was also adopted from Ar. In strophic poems (*muwashshah*), love may be the theme of the whole poem or an intro. to panegyric. In the 11th c. the (usually strophic) epithalamium appears; though intended for the wedding feast, such poems are sometimes unexpectedly erotic. They were composed in the Middle East until the present century.

Liturgical poets in Spain and later in other Mediterranean countries added Ar. love themes to those deriving from the *Song of Songs*. Such poems enjoyed immense popularity, esp. in the Ottoman Empire, where, from the 16th c., mysticism inspired a rich poetic lit. In medieval Castile, Todros ben Judah Abulafia (1247–ca. 1298) continued the trads. of Ar. courtly l. p., but also wrote hedonistic verse as well as spiritual l. p. In Italy, Immanuel of Rome (ca. 1260–1328) introduced the sonnet into Heb.; though influenced by the *dolce stil nuovo* (q.v.), he also contributed some truly salacious verse. In 17th-c. Italy, the brothers Immanuel (1618–1710) and Jacob (1615–67) Frances introduced baroque taste into Heb. l. p.

Except for Mica Joseph Lebensohn (1828–52), who was influenced by the Ger. romantics, the first period of modern Heb. lit. (*Haskala*, 1781–1881) was nearly devoid of lyrical l. p. The "Love of Zion" movement (1870–1900) generally subordinated love to the Zion-allegory. Only with Ḥayyim Naḥman Bialik (1873–1934) did Heb. poetry free itself from Haskala rhet. and sentimentality. Yet even his l. p. rejects erotic union, the beloved being portrayed as madonna or whore. In the poetry of Nathan Alterman (1910–70), the most outstanding of the modernist poets who rebelled against Bialik's poetics, erotic union is seen only as a transcendental certainty after death, remaining tragically unachievable in the lovers' lifetime. Only with the political and linguistic normalization of the Israel period (1948–) did Heb. l. p. become deromanticized and normalized. Under the influence of Eng. poetry, the poets of the "Generation of the State," esp. Yehuda Amichai (b. 1924), used a lower diction and dealt with real-life relationships, not only as an object of longing but also as a solution and a refuge for the individual.

S. Burnshaw et al., *The Mod. Heb. Poem Itself* (1965); *Penguin Book of Heb. Verse*, ed. T. Carmi (1981); *Wine, Women, and Death: Med. Heb. Poems on the Good Life* (1986), *The Gazelle: Med. Heb.*

Poems on God, Israel, and the Soul (1990), both ed. R. P. Scheindlin. R.P.S.

D. *Indian.* The luxuriant dreamworld of erotic romance that first comes to mind when we think of Indian l. p. is but one aspect of the complex universe of love represented in the vast body of poetry that exists in various Indian langs. such as Sanskrit, Prakrit, Tamil, Hindi, and Bengali.

Indian poets realized the unique power and aesthetic potential of the emotions of passionate sexual love. The erotic mood that emerges from such love was expressed in the antithetical modes of "separation" and "consummation." To experience this mood in the interplay of its two modes was considered the height of aesthetic joy. In Indian poetry, an act of remembering is the focal technique for relating the antithetical modes of love-in-separation and love-in-consummation. This conception of love is dominant throughout the trad.: one finds it in verses scattered through the anthologies, as well as in longer poems and dramas.

The emotions of erotic love are close to the intensity of religious devotion. The poets Kālidāsa (5th c.) and Bhartṛhari (7th c.) address their poems to the god Śiva, the erotically potent divine ascetic. Erotic poems thus become religiously powerful. The lyric poems of medieval devotional lit., which exist in every Indian lang., give expression to a religion that is predominantly emotional. For example, the Bengali devotional cults focus chiefly on episodes in the early romantic life of Kṛṣṇa, as they are described, not in the *Mahābhārata*, but in medieval sectarian epics known as *purāṇas.*

In the devotional poetry addressed to Kṛṣṇa, the emphasis is on complete surrender to his love, accompanied by all the emotions of attachment. What makes Indian devotional poetry unique is the notion that the god may be enticed by the love of the devotee and reciprocate in passionate ways. The idea of incarnation makes it possible to think of the god in human ways and in human relationships.

Although the promise of Kṛṣṇa's embrace exists, what inspires the poets is not the satisfaction of love, but the passionate yearning of a lover separated from his beloved—a suffering of such intensity that it liberates the devotee from worldly concerns. Jayadeva's Sanskrit poem *Gītagovinda* and the devotional lyrics of *bhakti* poetry exemplify how completely religious, erotic, and aesthetic meaning is integrated in this popular trad.
B.S.M.

E. *Chinese.* Chinese l. p. in the ancient elite trad., whether in the form of short lyrics expressing agonized passion for women or of longer *fu* celebrating the erotic pursuit of goddesses, was often read as political and moral allegory (see CHINESE POETRY, *Classical*). But explicit love themes, heightened by sexual images of flowers, seasons, etc., are central to certain types of popular song such as *yuefu*. The personae of popular love songs are almost always female, singing the joys of spring and youth. Such erotic motifs were incorporated, with vividly described love scenes, into the elite Palace Style Poetry of the Six Dynasties (4th–6th c. A.D.). Prince Xiao Gang (503–51) wrote about seductive sleeping beauties and even gave detailed accounts of a catamite engaged in a homosexual act. Later in the Tang Dynasty, Li Shangyin's (ca. 813–58) l. p. fused allusive lang. with emotional suggestiveness, creating ambiguities in sharp contrast to the explicit Palace Style verse. In the Song Dynasty (960–1279), a new form of poetry, *ci* (see LYRIC, *Chinese*), noted for its romantic themes and association with courtesan culture, became the lyric of emotion *par excellence*. But the *ci* was viewed as a "dying genre" from ca. 1300 to ca. 1600. Late in the Ming Dynasty it was revived by the Yunjian School of *ci* under the impetus of the poet Chen Zilong (1608–47). Chen exchanged many poems with his lover, the woman poet and courtesan Liu Shih (1618–64). Their vivid and dramatic "alternating poems," framed as personal letters, tell the story of a passion felt by two equally talented authors. The idea that Cl. Chinese poetry does not deal with love is a myth. Love remains an important theme for both male and female poets since the 17th c., except that eroticism in poetry was usually interpreted by the Qing (1644–1911) readers as political allegory. The woman poet Wu Zao (fl. 1800) broke taboos in Chinese poetry: she celebrates intimate lesbian love and introduces sexual frankness into *ci* lyric. But in general, gay and lesbian love is not a poetic subject, though it appears frequently in prose fiction and memoirs from the late Ming on.

J. Scott, *Love and Protest* (1972); H. Frankel, *The Flowering Plum and the Palace Lady* (1976); *New Songs from a Jade Terrace*, tr. A. Birrell (1982); *Women Poets of China*, tr. K. Rexroth and L. Chung, rev. ed. (1982); K. S. Chang, *The Late-Ming Poet Ch'en Tzu-lung* (1991). K.S.C.

F. *Japanese*. Early Japanese versions are distinctive in involving violations of the incest taboo. Cl. Japanese poets found erotic potential in wetness, women's tangled hair, Spring, dreams, and color. Since at court men visited women after dark, lovers saw each other indistinctly or not at all until the relation lasted on. Physical description was replaced by poetic or other good taste as erotic attraction. Courtesans and prostitutes first appear with *haikai* (see RENGA), which also features male homosexuality. The female is not a poetic subject, but does appear in prose and erotic pictures. In the performing arts, cross-dressing is important. Exceptions to these generalizations include the trad. of the passionate woman from ancient to modern times and eccentric individuals like the high cleric Ikkyū Sōjun. In general, however, even today eroticism is tolerated in private rather than public versions. See also JAPANESE POETRY.— Nishiyama Sōin, *Sôin Topphyaku Koi no Haikai*

(1671); Yosano Akiko, *Midaregami* (1904); R. H. Brower and E. Miner, *Japanese Court Poetry* (1961); E. Miner, *Japanese Linked Poetry* (1979); "Himerareta Bungaku," ed. S. Yamada, spec. iss. of *Koku Bungaku Kaishaku to Kanshō* (1983)—on erotic writing and art. E.M.

LÜ-SHIH. See CHINESE POETRY.

LUSOPHONE AFRICAN POETRY. See AFRICAN POETRY, *In French*.

LYRIC.

I. ORIGIN AND DEFINITIONS
II. HISTORICAL DEVELOPMENTS
   A. *The Ancient Middle East and the Western Tradition*
   B. *Russia and Eastern Europe*
   C. *Africa*
   D. *Asia*
III. CONTEMPORARY DEVELOPMENTS

I. ORIGIN AND DEFINITIONS. L. is one of the three general categories of poetic lit., the others being narrative (or epic) and dramatic (qq.v.). Although the differentiating features between these arbitrary categories are sometimes moot, l. poetry may be said to retain most prominently the elements which evidence its origins in musical expression—singing, chanting, and recitation to musical accompaniment (see SONG). Though drama and epic may also have had their genesis in a spontaneously melodic expression which adapted itself to a ritual need and thus became formalized, music in dramatic and epic poetry was at best secondary to other elements, being mainly a mimetic or mnemonic device. In the case of l., however, the musical element is intrinsic to the work intellectually as well as aesthetically: it becomes the focal point for the poet's perceptions as they are given a verbalized form to convey emotional and rational values. The primary importance of the musical element is indicated in the many generic terms which various cultures have used to designate nonnarrative and nondramatic poetry: the Eng. "l.," derived from the Gr. *lyra*, a musical instrument; the Cl. Gr. *melic*, or *mele* (air, melody); the Ch. *shi* or *ci* (word song).

To speak of the "musical" qualities of l. poetry is not to say that such poetry is written always to be sung. Neither does the appellation of "musical" indicate that l. possesses such attributes as pitch, harmony, syncopation, counterpoint, and other structural characteristics of a tonal, musical line or sequence—though such terms have often been (loosely) applied. To define the quality of lyricism in this way is to limit a l. to the manner of its presentation or to its architectonic aspects. This is largely the approach which Cl. critics have taken in their treatment of l. poetry. On the other hand, equating poetic lyricism with the nonarchitectural or "emotional" qualities of music is even less profitable, because it leads to such question-begging definitions of the l. as "the essence of poetry," "pure poetry," or, most vaguely, "poetry." To declare that "the characteristic of the l. is that it is the product of the pure poetic energy unassociated with other energies, and that l. and poetry are synonymous terms" (Drinkwater) is as extreme a definition of lyricism as the converse claim that a passage is lyrical simply because it possesses "the quality of metrical construction or architecture" (Murray). Both are extreme.

Most of the confusion in the modern critical usage of "l." (i.e. usage after 1550) is due to an overextension of the term to cover a body of poetic writing that has radically altered its nature over the centuries of its devel. The first critical use of the word *mele* by the Greeks was for the purpose of broadly distinguishing between various nonnarrative and nondramatic types of poetry: the melic poem was intended to be sung to musical accompaniment, in contrast to the iambic and elegiac poems, which were chanted. The first general use of "l." to characterize a selection of poetic lit. encompassing several genres did not come until the Alexandrian period, when "l." became a generic term for any poem which was composed to be sung; it was this meaning which "l." largely retained until the Ren. The preoccupation of pre-Ren. critics with the metrics of melic or l. poetry was entirely appropriate to the principle upon which the category was established.

But with the Ren., poets began suiting their work to a visual as well as an auditory medium; even while such critics as Minturno, Scaliger, Sidney, and Puttenham were formulating their discussions of l. poetry, the l. was becoming something quite different from the Cl. melic poem. No longer a performing bard, scop, skald, or troubadour (qq.v.), the poet ceased to "compose" his or her poem for musical presentation but instead "wrote" it for a collection of readers. The l. poem, nominal successor to a well-established poetic method, inherited and employed specific themes, meters, attitudes, images, and myths; but in adapting itself to a new means of presentation, the l. found itself bereft of the very element which had been the foundation of its lyricism—music.

At the time the l. was undergoing this crucial metamorphosis, 15th- and 16th-c. critics chose either to ignore the genre or to treat it by the same quantitative or metrical criteria as the classicists had done. Until the end of the 17th c., therefore, critics failed to distinguish between the true or melodic l., such as the "songs" of Shakespeare, Campion, and Dryden, and the nonmusical, verbal ls. of Donne, Marvell, and Waller. Both the straightforward, plain song-poem and the more abstrusely phrased print-poem were called "l." The neoclassical concern in 18th-c. France and England with the tragic and epic genres was sufficiently overwhelming that the l. receded as a topic of critical discussion; and when the romantic

movement came, with its championing of lyrical modes, terminological confusion continued in the equation of "l." with "poetry" by Wordsworth, Goethe, Coleridge, Poe, and other poets and theorists. The 19th-c. devel. of scientific methodology, with consequent insistence on accuracy of terms and precision of generic distinctions, translated itself in lit. crit. into a concern with the intrinsic and characteristic nature of the l. The definitions by Drinkwater and Murray given above represent the overinclusive and overexclusive criteria which resulted from this concern; and critical attempts to re-establish the melodic or musical substance of l. poetry were a third, and equally unsuccessful, method of dealing with the paradoxical nature of a "musical" poetry which was no longer literally "melodic." Such, in greatly simplified lines, is the history of the verbal ambiguity by which post-Ren. critics concealed their basic failure to define both the precise aspects of the l. genre which distinguish it from narrative and dramatic poetry and those which justify the inclusion under one term of all the disparate types of poem commonly called "lyrical."

Critical attempts to define l. poetry by reference to its secondary (i.e. nonmusical) qualities have suffered by being descriptive of various historical groupings of ls. rather than definitive of the category as a whole. Among the best known and most often cited proscriptions regarding the l. are that it must (1) be brief (Poe); (2) "be one, the parts of which mutually support and explain each other, all in their proportion harmonizing with, and supporting the purpose and known influence of metrical arrangement" (Coleridge); (3) be "the spontaneous overflow of powerful feelings" (Wordsworth); (4) be an intensely subjective and personal expression (Hegel); (5) be an "inverted action of mind upon will" (Schopenhauer); or (6) be "the utterance that is overheard" (Mill).

Though the attributes of brevity, metrical coherence, subjectivity, passion, sensuality, and particularity of image are frequently ascribed to the l., there are schools of poetry obviously l. which are not susceptible to such criteria. Milton's *L'Allegro* and *Il Penseroso*, as well as the most famous Eng. elegies, are "brief" in only the most relative sense. Much of the *vers libre* of the present age contradicts the rule of metrical coherence. Imagist ls. are hardly "empassioned" in the ordinary sense of the word. The "lucubrations" of the metaphysicals are something less than sensual in the romantic sense of the term. The problem of subjectivity must always plague the critic of the Elizabethan love l. And, finally, the common artistic admission that the universal can be expressed best, and perhaps solely, through the particular image largely invalidates any distinction between the l. and nonlyric on a metaphoric or thematic basis.

The irreducible denominator of all l. poetry must, therefore, comprise those elements which it shares with the musical forms that produced it.

Although l. poetry is not music, it is representative of music in its sound patterns, basing its meter and rhyme on the regular linear measure of the song; or, more remotely, it employs cadence and consonance to approximate the tonal variation of a chant or intonation. Thus the l. retains structural or substantive evidence of its melodic origins, and this factor serves as the categorical principle of poetic lyricism.

In the 20th c., critics, predicating the musical essence of l. as its vital characteristic, have come close to formulating an exact and inclusive definition of l.: "Words build into their poetic meaning by building into sound . . . sound in composition: music" (R. P. Blackmur). "A poet does not compose *in order to* make of lang. delightful and exciting music; he composes a delightful and exciting music in lang. *in order to* make what he has to say peculiarly efficacious in our minds" (Lascelles Abercrombie). Lyrical poetry is "the form wherein the artist presents his image in immediate relation to himself" (James Joyce). "Hence in lyrical poetry what is conveyed is not mere emotion, but the imaginative prehension of emotional states" (Herbert Read). It is "an internal mimesis of sound and imagery" (Northrop Frye). Thus, in modern critical usage it may be said that "l." is a general, categorical, and nominal term, whereas in the pre-Ren. sense it was specific, generic, and descriptive. In its modern meaning, a l. is a type of poetry which is mechanically representational of a musical architecture and which is thematically representational of the poet's sensibility as evidenced in a fusion of conception and image. In its older and more restricted sense, a l. was simply a poem written to be sung; this meaning is preserved in the modern colloquialism of referring to the words of a song as its "ls."

II. HISTORICAL DEVELOPMENTS. However useful definitions of the l. may be, they cannot indicate the great flexibility of technique and range of subjects which have helped this category to comprise the preponderance of poetic lit. There are literally dozens of l. genres, ranging from the ancient *partheneia* to modern *vers libre*, leaving no topic, whether a cicada or a locomotive, untreated. Though it is manifestly impossible to say everything about the historical devel. of the l. in short, certain general facts prove interesting as pieces in an evolving pattern of theories about and treatment of the lyrical mode between various ages, cultures, and individuals. The l. is as old as recorded lit., and its history is that of human experience at its most animated.

A. *The Ancient Middle East and the Western Tradition.* It is reasonable to suppose that the first "lyrical" poems came into existence when human beings discovered the pleasure that arises from combining words in a coherent, meaningful sequence with the almost physical process of uttering rhythmical and tonal sounds to convey feelings. Both the instinctive human tendency to hum or intone as an expression of mood and the socialization of this tendency in primitive cultures by the chanting or singing of nonsense syllables in tribal rites are well-documented. At that remote point in time when the syllables ceased to be nonsense and took on meaning, the first l. was composed, though in what Neanderthal or Cro-Magnon cave this took place, no one will ever know. This impossibility, however, has scarcely impeded speculation about the folk origins of lit., ranging from those of Herder to A. B. Lord and Andrew Welsh. The earliest recorded evidence of l. poetry suggests that such compositions emerged from ritual activity accompanying religious ceremonies and were expressive of mystical experience. Scholars have found evidence to support a theory of the religious derivation of poetry in general and the l. in particular in such lits. as Eskimo, American Indian, and Polynesian.

1. *Sumerian.* The earliest ls. in the Middle East were composed in Sumer (modern Iraq). The Old or Cl. Sumerian Period (2300–2000 B.C.) produced the divine invocation; the New Period (2000–1700 B.C.) added further lyrical riches in the form of proverbs, hymns, lamentations, incantations, and lovesongs. Begun in a much earlier oral trad., the ls. were set down ca. 2500 years ago. Preserved on clay tablets in cuneiform, Sumerian ls. were precursors of the more famous Heb. songpoems. One of the earliest of all lovesongs is the Sumerian "To the Royal Bridegroom" (ca. 2025 B.C.):

> Bridegroom, dear to my heart,
> Goodly is your beauty, honeysweet,
> Lion, dear to my heart,
> Goodly is your beauty, honeysweet.

The poetic devices of these lines—parallelism, inversion, repetition—characterize Sumerian l. poetry and the trads. derived from it. (See SUMERIAN POETRY.)

2. *Assyro-Babylonian* poetry includes such l. types as hymns and prayers: to Ishtar, to Sin the Moon God, to Shamash the Sun God, to Gula the goddess of healing, and other deities. Lyrical elements are also present in the *Gilgamesh* epic. Samples of folk poetry preserved in texts of magic or healing also exhibit a characteristic parallelism. (See ASSYRO-BABYLONIAN POETRY.) The Hittites, who spoke an Indo-European lang. and lived in modern Turkey, borrowed cuneiform from the Babylonians, their neighbors in Mesopotamia. The earliest of their known ls. from the Old Kingdom (ca. 1700–1600 B.C.) is a short song. The New Kingdom (ca. 1400–1200) produced an extant hymn to Istanu the Sun-God and other ls. embedded in epics. (See HITTITE POETRY.)

3. *Egyptian.* The most complete written evidence of early l. activity is Egyptian: the Pyramid Texts (ca. 2600 B.C.) include specimens of the funeral song (elegy—q.v.), song of praise to the king (ode—q.v.), and invocation to the gods

(hymn—q.v.); tomb inscriptions from the same period include work songs of shepherds, fishers, and chair bearers. Also among the earliest l. writings of the Old Kingdom are the dialogue, proverb, and lament or complaint (qq.v.). The Middle Kingdom (ca. 1950–1660 B.C.) proliferated these l. types, esp. the hymn, and added victory song. Prophecies, proverbs, and encomia were popular. Works from the New Kingdom (ca. 1570–1070 B.C.) incl. songs of revelry, love songs, and the epitaph. "Harpers' songs" contained elements of the *carpe diem* theme. Although relatively uncomplex, the Egyptian l. contained in nascent form many elements which were to become characteristic of later l. poetry. The lines seem to have some form of free rhythm without meter. Alliteration and parallelism were frequently used, as was paronomasia. Irony and paradox were present in a primitive form; and these first of all lyrics were already treating such subjects as death, piety, love, loneliness, jealousy, martial prowess, and joy. Furthermore, the personal tone of the l., though not ubiquitous, was apparent in such poems as those enclosed in *The Dispute with His Soul of One Who Is Tired of Life*. Remains of other ancient lits. do not show much advancement over the Egyptian. (See EGYPTIAN POETRY.)

4. *Hebrew.* The most complete of the ancient bodies of l. poetry is the Heb., which, while owing something to Egyptian and Babylonian sources, nevertheless marked a distinct advance in l. technique. These ls., well known to modern readers because of their religious associations and important for their effect on the patristic lyricists of the Middle Ages, are among the most strikingly beautiful ever written. Though textual evidence indicates that some Heb. l. poetry was written as early as the 10th c. B.C. (notably the *Song of Deborah*), many poems were of much later date; and the earliest Jewish lit. crit. dealing with the l. was as late as the 1st c. A.D. Philo Judaeus (ca. 20 B.C.–A.D. 50) claimed Egyptian origin for some Heb. l. techniques by declaring that Moses was taught "the whole theory of rhythm, harmony, and meter" by the Egyptians. Flavius Josephus (ca. A.D. 37–95), discussing the hymn of Moses in Exodus 15:1–2 said that it was written in hexameters, and the hymns and songs of David in other Cl. meters. Later discussions of Heb. meters were carried on by Origen, Eusebius, and Jerome; Gr. metric nomenclature was overlaid on Heb. prosody not because it accurately fit but because Heb. prosody was poorly understood while Gr. metrics was prestigious: indeed, the ancient Heb. l. meters are only partially understood even today (Gray). It is known, however, that the ls. were accompanied by such instruments as the harp, sackbut, and cymbals; and suggestions of the manner in which hymns, elegies, songs of joy, and victory songs were composed and performed may be found in 1 Samuel 16:23 and 2 Samuel 1:17–27, 6:5, and 15–16. (See HEBREW PROSODY.)

The ancient Heb. poets were proficient in the use of paronomasia, parallelism, and alliteration (qq.v.), perfecting and using these devices in a variety of ways. Parallelism is obvious in such ls. as Psalm 19 ("The heavens declare the glory of God, and the firmament sheweth his handiwork") and Proverbs 21:17 ("He that loveth pleasure shall be a poor man: he that loveth wine and oil shall not be rich"); but it is also more subtly used, as in Jeremiah 6:24 ("Anguish hath taken hold of us, and pain, as of a woman in travail"). The use of tropes is highly developed, with simile and metaphor predominating; the apostrophe and hyperbole increase the personal tone of the l. far beyond the Egyptian. Many of the ls. seem intensely subjective, e.g. Psalm 69, but even these poems reflect what Frye has called "the sense of an external and social discipline." Yet the personal tone remains and is essential to the lyricism of such passages as Isaiah 5:1, Psalm 137, and 2 Samuel 1:19.

The Heb. lyricists developed a number of types and subtypes of the l. genre, which are classified by method of performance, source of imagery, and subject matter. These include the psalm (q.v.; from Gr. *psallein*, "to pull upon a stringed instrument"); the pastoral (q.v.), which draws heavily upon the agrarian background of Heb. culture; and the vision or apocalyptic prophecy, which employs the indirection of the trope. Other types incl. the proverb, the epigram (qq.v.), and similar forms of "wisdom" lit.; the descriptive love l.; the triumph; various sorts of threnody; the lament; panegyrics of different kinds; and even a lyrical dialogue (or "drama") in the Book of Job. Some overlapping of types is obvious (the triumph was frequently a panegyric on the hero), but the ambiguity is an historical one and terminological distinctions have yet to be drawn. (See HEBREW POETRY; HEBRAISM.)

5. *Greek* l., like Egyptian and Hebrew, had its origins in religious activity; the first songs were probably composed to suit an occasion of celebration or mourning. Gr. ls. were chanted, sung, or sung and danced; each mode is traceable to some form of religious practice. The dithyramb (q.v.), for example, may have been composed to commemorate the death of some primitive vegetable god or the birth of Dionysus; in any case, it was originally sung to the accompaniment of the flute playing a melody in the Phrygian mode, which the Greeks considered the most emotional. In time, the dithyramb took on a more particular form, with formalized dance steps corresponding to passages in the text: these rhythmical and thematic patterns may have been the prototype of the fully developed ode, or song of celebration, with its divisions of strophe, antistrophe, and epode (qq.v.) as written by Pindar, Sophocles, and others. Similar tracings of the devel. of other lyrical modes in Greece from the Heroic Age to the Homeric to the Periclean have been attempted. The essential element of the Gr. l. was its meter,

which was of two kinds: the stichic, that spoken or recited; and the melic, that suited for singing or singing and dancing (see MELIC POETRY). Stichic meters were well demarcated lines of equal length and repetitive rhythm that can be divided into units (feet, metra). Melic meters were composed of phrases of varying length or movement; each phrase, called a colon (q.v.) could be combined into a unit rhythmically complete or rounded, the *periodos* (see PERIOD). Some cola are rhythmically repetitious in themselves and may be broken into dimeter or trimeter; but in the melic poems, it was the period or stanza that constituted the l. unit (Dale). Melic meters were obviously subject to wide adaptation, and most of the best known Gr. l. meters are named for the poets who developed and customarily used them: the Sapphic, Alcaic, Anacreontic (qq.v), and Pindaric. The earliest Gr. ls. may emerge from the mists of oral tradition, but even in Homer and Hesiod there is an artistic concern with the l. mood and subjects. In the *Iliad*, for instance, there are such embryonic ls. as Helen's laments, Achilles' speech at the death of Patroklos, and the elegiac speeches at Hector's funeral. But it is the hymn which is perhaps the first developed of the definably l. genres, being composed in significant numbers before 700 B.C. The Homeric Hymns from this period indicate the religious nature of the first ls.: they are addressed to Artemis, Dionysus, Heracles, Helios, *et al.*, and the pattern of some became a distinct type of l. hymn (e.g. the "paean," a hymn to Apollo). The hymns employ devices appropriate to the apostrophe but are not very expansive in their tropes, chiefly using the attributive epithet, as in this hymn to Hera: "I sing of golden-throned Hera, whom Rhea bare. Queen of the immortals is she, surpassing all in beauty" (tr. Evelyn-White).

The Homeric epigrams are attributed to this period also, thereby setting up an archetype for the later iambics. The period from 700–500 B.C. saw the rise of elegiac and political verse, written by Solon among others, and the personal lampoon in iambics, by Archilochus, Hipponax, and Simonides of Amorgos. After 660 B.C., melic poetry developed, primarily in two strains: the Aeolian, or personal, ls. written at Lesbos by Sappho and Alcaeus; and the Dorian, or objective, by Alcman, Arion, Stesichorus, and Ibycus. This group of ls. may also be categorized by method of performance as solo or choral, but the dividing line is not sharp. Although the ancient distinctions of melic poetry on the basis of meters may indeed indicate separate categories, the modern definition of the l. would be hard pressed to differentiate between a number of poems by Alcman, Ibycus, and Sappho.

The 5th c. in Greece produced some of the best of l. poets, Simonides, Pindar, and Bacchylides; it was then too that the l. found such magnificent expression in the choral odes of Sophocles, Aeschylus, and Euripides. Melic poetry became national in tone, with the Dorian mode prevailing; there was an abundance of such l. types as the hymn, paean, dithyramb, processional, dance song, triumph, ode, and dirge. Other popular genres were the *partheneia* (songs sung by virgins to flute accompaniment); *nomos* (war song); *kommos* (a dirge sung in Attic drama by an actor and the chorus alternately); *prosodion* (processional song of solemn thanksgiving); *hyporcheme* (q.v.; dance song); *epinikion* (q.v.; victory song); *threnos* (dirge); wedding songs for men; and the *scolion* (q.v.—banquet song accompanied by the lyre).

Gr. critics were less concerned with l., or melic, poetry than with tragedy and the epic; the few extant comments predicate the musical nature of the genre. Plato's denunciation of all poetry, esp. "representational" tragedy, included the melic, which Plato considered "untrue" or false in its depiction of reality. Stripped of musical coloring and laid bare as ideas, Plato says, the melic poems reveal the ignorance of the poet, which clothes itself in "rhythm, meter, and harmony." (*Republic* 10.4). Aristotle, however (*Poetics* 1–4), remarked the absence of a generic term which might denote such nonepic and nondramatic kinds of poetry as the works in iambic, elegiac, and similar meters, which imitated "by means of lang. alone," as contrasted with the melic poems, which used rhythm, tune, and meter "all employed in combination." This statement indicates the existence of poetry, l. in the modern sense, which was not melic in the Gr. sense; but the Alexandrian use of "l." to indicate such disparate types as the dithyramb, iambics, elegies, and Sapphics (qq.v.), while a broad attempt to repair the deficiency noted by Aristotle, was inexact and only resulted in confusion. (See GREEK POETRY.)

6. *Latin.* Roman critical remarks on the l. would indicate that the term was used in the sense of melic poetry or poetry sung to the lyre. Horace shows a belief that l. poetry is less substantial in content than epic poetry, being the *jocosa lyra*, a view with which Quintilian concurred, though for him the ode might be worthy of more significant themes. To Horace's mind, the "dainty measures" were suited to "the work of celebrating gods and heroes, the champion boxer, the victorious steed, the fond desire of lovers, and the cup that banishes care"; they included the iambic and elegiac distich. These general criteria for form and content were adopted by most Lat. commentators following Horace—Ovid, Petronius, Juvenal, Pliny the Younger—so that, as for l. theory, the Romans were advanced but little beyond the Greeks.

In practice, Roman poets tended to imitate the Alexandrian l. poets, who composed works primarily meant to be read rather than performed. Hadas has pointed out that this practice tended to produce ls. more enigmatic and allusive than earlier "sung" poems had been; and it may be generally observed that Roman l. poets are more notable as formulators of a "personal" or subjective poetry than are the Greeks. While Roman poets modeled their poems on the hymns of Callimachus, the Idyls of Theocritus, the epigrams of Anacreon, and the elegiac laments of Bion and Moschus, they adapted the l. to produce a more subjective or autobiographical utterance. Conventional and minor Roman lyricists were content with the school of "fastidious elegance" which kept them copying the Greeks, and which Catullus mocked, but the Roman genius emphasized particularized experiences—Propertius in his observations, Catullus in his amours, Virgil in his rustic pleasures, Ovid in the sorrows of his exile, Tibullus in his love pangs, Martial and Juvenal in their private asperities. The private insight, the subjective focusing of experience is more keenly apparent in Roman ls. than in other ancient works: e.g. in Ovid's *Tristia* 1.8 ("To their sources shall deep rivers flow"); Martial's *Epigrams* 1.8 ("Thou hast a name that bespeaks the season of the budding year, when Attic bees lay waste the brief-lived spring"); Catullus' *To Hortalus* 65 ("Though I am worn out with constant grief and sorrow calls me away"); and Tibullus, *To Delia* 1.2 ("More wine; let the liquor master these unwonted pains"). Coincidentally, there are many more "occasional" ls. among the Roman poets which celebrate private rather than public festivals, with a greater proportion of such genres as the prothalamium and epithalamium (wedding songs), the *vale* (farewell), the epigram, the satire, and the epistle.

The strict approach to meter which typifies the l. writers of the pre-Augustan and Augustan periods of Roman lit. began to weaken by the middle of the 1st c. A.D., and greater flexibility of form resulted. The rigid preoccupation of the Horatian and Virgilian schools with the exact meters dictated by the Gr.-derived system of quantitative verse was probably an attempt to substitute precision of metrics for the abandoned melodies of the true l. In any case, the ls. of Petronius, unlike the formal measures of the Statian odes, are experimental in form; and during the 2d c., Lat. l. moves toward a nonquantitative or accentual form of verse. The earliest extant examples appear in Christian hymns. In the 3d c., the completely new principle of rhyme (q.v.) can be found in the verses of Commodian; it was then that the principles which were to guide not only Med. Lat. verse but all subsequent vernaculars—accent, isosyllabism, and rhyme—were established.

Like the Hebrews and the Greeks, the patristic critics chose to discuss long established forms and practices rather than treating contemp. ones. Patristic l. crit. throws little light on the practice of the times. Eusebius, Jerome, and Origen were concerned with analyzing Heb. l. modes in the categories and terms of Gr. metrics; and the anthologer Isidore of Seville discussed Heb. and Gr. meters in conventional fashion, noting the musical element of l. poetry, but still failed to make any distinctions among the various genres.

Not suprisingly, the first ls. of the Church were hymns patterned on the Heb. Psalter and the Gr. hymns. The earliest were those of St. Hilary of Poitiers, who probably used meter for its mnemonic effectiveness, and who employed the *versus quadratus* or trochaic tetrameter catalectic, subsequently a favorite meter of Prudentius, Fortunatus, and Thomas Aquinas, and the basis for several of the medieval sequences (Beare). St. Ambrose developed the use of iambic dimeters grouped in quatrains (the "Ambrosian" stanza), which became the basis for all modern stanzas of four 4-beat lines; St. Jerome made Lat. more flexible as the lang. of poetry; and Augustine wrote a didactic psalm against the Donatist heretics which may contain the embryo of all Med. Lat. versification. The Rule of St. Benedict (6th c.) required hymns to be sung at all the canonical hours, an edict which spurred on numerous lyricists. Once more, ls. were composed to be sung or chanted; the indissoluble rapport between the Lat. words and meters and the melodic line must not be forgotten. The sequence or trope depended on the repetition of phrases both verbal and musical; and the involved meters as well as the simple rhymes of the hymns which Abelard wrote for Heloise and her nuns to sing both derive from their avowedly musical nature:

> Christiani, plaudite,
> (Resurrexit Dominus)
> Victo mortis principe
> Christus imperat.
> Victori occurite,
> Qui nos liberat.

The Church hymns of the 12th and 13th cs. are among the most perfect ls. ever produced in the history of liturgical lit.: the *Stabat mater* and *Dies irae* must be included in any list of the world's great ls., and there are numerous other examples of accomplished l. art: sequences, *cantiones*, nativities, and a variety of hymns. The importance of patristic songs cannot be exaggerated in the history of the l. (See LATIN POETRY.)

7. *Arabic.* From its origins in the late 5th c. A.D., Ar. poetry was predominantly lyrical. Recited by a *rāwī* and accompanied by music of some kind, Ar. ls. assumed mantic powers in their expression of public rather than personal perceptions. The earliest ls. praised the tribal chief's virtues with the eulogy and *rithā* (elegy) and scorned tribal enemies and vices with satire. Wine, women, spirited horses, and brotherhood were lauded in eulogies. Professional bards, tribal and court poets at the Sassanian, Ghassanid, and Lakhmid courts favored the *gita* and *qaṣīda*. The arrival of Islam in the 7th c. changed Ar. poetry only slightly. Subsequently, the traditional *qaṣīda* was modified for panegyric purposes. Other forms included hunt poems (*tardiyat*), wine poems (*khamriyat*), and ascetic and homiletic poems. *Ghazal* or love poetry also developed, sometimes becoming linked with

the love-death theme. A widely accepted version of the Qu'rān in the 7th c. encouraged the collection of various kinds of ls. as well as formal analysis of Ar. verse. A "new" awareness of style in poetry (*badī*) similarly led to a critical analysis of figurative and tropic devices in the 10th c. This era of Cl. Ar. poetry produced some noted writers of the *qaṣīda* and its primary topic, the *madih* (panegyric); two strophic genres, *muwashshaha* and *zéjel* (q.v.), Hispano-Ar. forms, were not admired by the classicists but were popular nonetheless.

Ar. l. poetry between the 13th and 18th cs. has been considered decadent by some modern critics, given its elaborate poetic figures and verbal excess. Since the Ottoman Empire governed Ar.-speaking people much of this period, Ar. writing therefore was directed at an elite audience. Popular trad., however, led to expansion of the collected tales of *The Thousand and One Nights*, which contains many examples of l. poetry. In the 19th and 20th c., influenced by European poets, some Ar. writers tried to recapture the splendor of the Cl. Ar. period in theatrical and occasional verse. Their counterparts, the poets of *al mahjar*, or the emigré school in the Americas, were exponents of Ar. romanticism. The romantic ideal also affected Ar. poets in Lebanon, Egypt, Syria, and the Sudan during the 1930s and '40s. The establishment of the State of Israel after World War II stirred the Arab peoples; the romantic and symbolist poets were termed detached and elitist. Arab awareness demanded a poetry of "commitment," which Palestinian poets in particular supplied, developing in the process new forms utilizing free verse (*al-shīʿr al-hurr*). In tones ranging from bitter to compassionate, poets such as Khalīl Hāwī, Nizār Qabbānī, and Adūnīs comment lyrically on Ar. concerns with brothers and enemies, noble heroes and contemptible foes, creating a poetry of commitment and political involvement symptomatic of modern Ar. lyricism. (See ARABIC POETRY.)

8. The *Mozarabic* poetry of Spain appears to be the earliest vernacular poetry in Europe. Mozarabic writers inherited from the Visigoths the hymns of various Church Fathers—Hilary, Prudentius, Ambrose—transcribed into Gothic characters. Maurico, the compiler of Mozarabic ls. in the 10th and 11th cs., collected a large number of hymns and songs written by Mozarabic poets of earlier periods. The Mozarabic l. include hymns, psalms, pleas, and occasional poems (e.g. from the ordination of bishops). Though in time the Mozarabic l. adapted itself to the characteristic cultural themes and attitudes of its era and came to be written in the vernacular, it remains one of the most complex and least known of all bodies of European l. poetry. (See HISPANO-ARABIC POETRY; SPANISH POETRY.)

9. *Persian*. The 9th c. witnessed the beginning of cl. Persian poetry, which replaced earlier Pahlavi practices with adapted Ar. and Persian forms and meters. Typical lyric devices (parallelism, punning, metaphoric allusions) informed the prescribed meters of the Persian *ghazal* and *qaṣīda*. Recited in public, the *qaṣīda* was useful for praising, congratulating, elegizing, meditating, or hurling invective. After the Mongol invasions, however, the *qaṣīda* was largely supplanted by the *ghazal*; here unrequited love was a favorite theme sometimes combining with a mystical mode of spiritual or ecstatic love. The *ghazal* enjoyed popularity for centuries. Another Persian lyric form, the *rubaʿi* (pungent epigrams), was made familiar by Edward Fitzgerald's tr. of Omar Khayyam. Its imagery of minarets, flowers, pottery, war drums, birds, fire, wine, and wilderness epitomizes for many Western readers the Persian l., though the 20th c. has witnessed innovative themes and techniques being tried by modern Persian poets. (See PERSIAN POETRY.)

10. *Old English*. The centuries between 300 and 1200 A.D. produced Anglo-Saxon (OE) poetry, with its antecedents in Scandinavian (esp. Danish) lit. and analogues with Icelandic poetry (q.v.). Anglo-Saxon poetry (see ENGLISH POETRY) is interesting as a folk or communal lit. transmitted through religious channels. The verseform, perhaps composed for harp accompaniment to be presented by bards or scops (qq.v.), consisted of hemistichic lines of four metrical stresses bound together by structural alliteration (see ENGLISH PROSODY). Somewhat redolent of Heb. poetry in its use of parallelism and alliteration, the verse also relied on poetic diction and tropes, esp. the kenning (q.v.). Though Anglo-Saxon poetry as a whole is not predominantly lyrical in either structure or tone, the range of Anglo-Saxon ls. includes gnomic and runic verse, the lament, the complaint, the elegy, and the hymn. *The Wanderer* and *The Seafarer* touch on the highly emotional and personal, and *Caedmon's Hymn* reflects the influence of the patristic hymn on the vernacular.

11. *European Vernaculars*. In Europe, the 12th and 13th cs. saw the growth in popularity of the wandering minstrel (q.v.): the quasi-ecclesiastical goliards who wrote secular songs in Lat. (see GOLIARDIC VERSE); the *trouvères* (q.v.) in northern France and troubadours (q.v.) in the south; the Minnesinger (see MINNESANG) in Germany. The l. was widely sung, or sung and danced. The troubadours, composing in the vernacular, produced the *chanso* (song, often of love), *sirventes* (topical songs of satire, eulogy, or personal comment), the *planh* (complaint), *tenso* (debate), *pastorela* and *pastourelle* (pastoral episode), *alba* or *aube* (dawn song), and the *balada* and *dansa* (dance songs—qq.v.). Much study has been devoted to the differences between the *chansons courtois* and *chansons populaire*, the *caroles* (see CAROL) and *rondets* for dancing, and the chansons designed for singing only, the *chansons de toile* (work songs), and their subspecies. Medieval ls. survive in abundance, exerting a special charm for the modern reader in their mixture of naïveté and sophistication. They

range from slapstick "macaronic" songs (multiple langs.) to the simple understatement of "Foweles in the frith"; from the direct but delightful "Sumer is icumen in" to Chaucer's complex rondeau, "Now welcom somer, with thy sonne softe," and ballade, "Hyd, Absalon, thy gilte tresses clere." Although this period produced such masters of the written "art-lyric" as Chaucer, Bertrand de Born, Chrétien de Troyes, Walther von der Vogelweide, Rutebeuf, Pierre Vidal, and Sordello, l. poetry was still a thing of the people, composed to be sung and enjoyed. The melodic element of the l. genre in the medieval period has not been equaled since the dawn of the Ren.

12. *Renaissance.* After 1400 the l. and music became increasingly disassociated, as evidenced by the rise of such primarily melodic forms as the madrigal, glee, catch, and round, which subordinated the words to the music. Despite the efforts of later writers who were primarily poets and not composers, such as Swinburne, Hopkins, and Yeats, the l. since the Ren. has remained a verbal rather than a musical discipline, and the traces of its melodic origin have become largely vestigial. The influence of the Lat. metrists on the It. and Fr. lyrical theorists of the Ren. may have helped to produce the latter-day emphasis on meter as a substitute for melody. In any event, Ren. lyricists, writing for an aristocratic audience (of readers), adapted their forms to a different medium, and the l. suffered a sea change after the 15th c.

Ren. ls., diffused as they are through several countries and centuries, nevertheless share characteristics which evidence their common origin in the Occitan ls. of the troubadours. In Spain, l. poets fused their Mozarabic and Occitan trads. to perfect some older forms (the *cantiga* [qq.v.] and possibly the *cossante*) and to develop some new ones (the *bacarola, bailada,* and others). After its inception at the Sicilian court of Frederick II, the *sonetto* (see SONNET) rose to full flower in Dante's *Vita nuova* and Petrarch's sonnets to Laura. Petrarch's *Canzoniere,* the prototype of It. l. poetry, contained sonnets, sestinas, ballatas, and even a few madrigals (qq.v.). In his sonnets, Petrarch struck the passionate thematic chords that were to echo for centuries in the ls. of countless imitators in Italy, France, and England (see PETRARCHISM). Despite excellent *canzoni* written by Ariosto and others, it is Petrarch whose name remains synonymous with Ren. It. artverse. More popular vernacular verse—e.g. the *strambotto* and *rispetto* (qq.v.)—was also composed in Italy in great quantity.

What Petrarch was to l. poetry in Italy, Ronsard was to the poetry of Ren. France. The leader of the *Pléiade* (q.v.), a stellar group of poets incl. Joachim du Bellay, Ronsard pub. his version of the sonnets to Laura in *Les Amours* in 1552, and the *Sonnets pour Hélène* in 1578. Ronsard also composed odes, mythological and philosophical *Hymnes,* and elegiacs and pastorals. Scorning the older forms of the rondeau and rondelle, Ronsard explored the whole gamut of lyric images and emotions in his sonnet cycles. Though the earlier sonnets contained frank Petrarchan notes (e.g. "Cent et cent fois penser un penser mesme"), the later works were perfectly Ronsard's own ("Adieu, cruelle, adieu, je te suis ennuyeux").

In England, the publication of Tottel's Miscellany in 1557 marked the beginning of the most lyrical of England's poetic eras. A collection of songs, sonnets, and other kinds of verse, the Miscellany evidenced the musicality of earlier Eng. poetry and established a form, the miscellany (see ANTHOLOGY), to be imitated repeatedly, from *The Phoenix Nest* (1593) and *Englands Helicon* (1600) to the eventual broadside ballads (q.v.) and Bishop Percy's *Reliques* (1765). Wyatt and Surrey were among the first in England to test the possibilities of the sonnet's thematic and metrical subtleties; and dozens of Eng. sonneteers—Sidney, Daniel, Spenser, Shakespeare *et al.*—pub. lengthy sonnet sequences (q.v.) more or less directly patterned on Petrarch's. Certain old forms of the lyric were redeveloped in England, e.g. the prothalamium and epithalamium (q.v.); and adulation for Horace and other Lat. l. poets created a widespread vogue for the ode (q.v.). The song (q.v.) also remained popular, both in its melodic and ballad forms, being written by such poets as Sidney, Shakespeare, Campion, and Jonson.

In general, it may be said of Ren. l. poetry that it was a succinct example of the philosophy of humanism (see RENAISSANCE POETICS). The l.'s preoccupation with the subjective self dovetailed neatly with the humanistic interest in the varied forms of human emotion; and the new geographical concerns of the Ren. supplemented the pastoralism of the traditional l. to produce an imagery that fused scientific and poetic perspectives. The effect of printing on the l. poets was also central; and though the shifting nature of l. poetry was not apparent to those Ren. critics who discussed that "divine" art—Minturno, Scaliger, Tasso, Sebillet, Gascoigne, Sidney—the changes were fundamental for poetic practice as well as theory (see RENAISSANCE POETRY).

13. *Modern.* Although the past 300 years in the history of the Western l. may be divided into certain chronological "periods" (i.e. Ren., Restoration, Augustan, *Fin de siècle*) or certain distinctive "movements" (metaphysical, neoclassical, romantic, symbolist, modernist), these terms reveal little about the true nature of l. theory and practice. Far more accurate is the designation of all l. poetry after 1600 as "modern." The range of this body of ls., from the most objective or "external" to the most subjective or "internal," may be included in three chief l. types: (a.) the Lyric of Vision or Emblem, (b.) the Lyric of Thought or Idea, and (c.) the Lyric of Emotion or Feeling.

a. The L. of Vision or Emblem, although it has its antecedents in Cl. Gr., Anglo-Saxon, and

Ch. poetry, is nevertheless fundamentally the product of the Age of Type. It is this sort of visual poetry (q.v.) that Ezra Pound called "Ideograms" and Apollinaire called "calligrammes" (qq.v.). This is the most externalized kind of l., utilizing the pictorial element of print to represent the object or concept treated in the poem. The visual l. therefore exists in itself, without reference to a private sensibility, whether of poet or reader. The first use of the visual in the modern l. came in the Ren., when poets printed poems in the shape of circles, spires, and pillars (see PATTERN POETRY). Later, George Herbert showed wings, altars, and floor patterns in poems on these subjects; and the prevalence of pictorial ls. among Fr. and Eng. poetasters of the 17th and 18th cs. drew Dryden's scorn in *MacFlecknoe* and Addison's laughter in *The Spectator*. In the later 19th c. the symbolists were influenced by this practice; in the 20th c. the imagists explored it under Ch. influence, and more recent Am. poets, under the influence of dada (q.v.), incl. Amy Lowell, H. D., William Carlos Williams, e e cummings, May Swenson, and John Hollander.

b. Somewhat more personal but still objective in tone and method is the L. of Thought or Idea, which may be divided into the expository or informative and the didactic or persuasive (even though some critics believe "l." and "didactic" to be contradictory terms). This school of lyricists is classically oriented, believing with Horace that poetry must be *utile* as well as *dulce*, and consequently emphasizing musicality of form to balance prosaic content. Expository L. writers incl. Boileau, Dryden, Cowper, Schiller, Tennyson, and such modern poets as Rainer Maria Rilke in his early descriptive works, Juan Ramón Jiménez, Jorge Guillén, Rafael Alberti, St. John Perse, T. S. Eliot, Robert Lowell, and Elizabeth Bishop. The preoccupation of 19th- and 20th-c. poets with sound and verseform has produced *vers libre* (q.v.), which is as obvious an effort to accompany poetic statement with musical techniques as are the heroic couplets (q.v.) of the neoclassical poetry of statement.

The didactic or persuasive l. includes the allegorical, satiric, exhortatory, and vituperative species. L. allegory (q.v.) is apparent in the animal myths of La Fontaine, Herrick's use of Cupid, Mandeville's bees, Heine's Atta Troll, Arnold's merman, Davidson's dancers in the house of death, and Frost's departmental ants. The satiric l. includes, of course, the l. parody, such as Lewis Carroll's burlesques of Wordsworth and Swinburne's mockery of Tennyson; but it also includes directly satiric verse: Donne's verses on women, Majakovskij's *Bedbug*, Bertolt Brecht's acrid observations on romantic love (see SATIRE). The exhortatory l. is often patriotic or moralistic, as in the Elizabethan panegyrics on England, Burns's call to the Scots, Gabriel D'Annunzio's fervent championing of life and freedom, or Kipling's tributes to

Britannia. The vituperative l. aims its darts everywhere: against critics (Pope's *Epistles*), convention (Rimbaud's *Illuminations*), war (Owen and Sassoon), poverty and suffering (Antonio Machado's *Del Camino*), a parent (Sylvia Plath's "Daddy"), or the world in general (Allen Ginsberg's *Howl*). Pound's *Cantos* seem to combine all of the subtypes—allegory, satire, exhortation, and vituperation—uniquely.

c. The most subjective or "internal" strain of modern l. poetry is the L. of Emotion or Feeling. It is this type which has in the modern world become synonymous with "poetry" through the agency of romantic poetics (q.v.). The L. of Emotion comprises three major groups: (i.) the sensual l., (ii.) the "imaginative" l. (which intellectualizes emotional states), and (iii.) the mystical l. The mystical l. is antipodal to the l. of emblem: these two varieties of "vision" l., one literal and the other metaphorical, mark the extreme limits of objectivity and subjectivity.

(i.) The sensual l. enjoys an unbroken continuity from the 16th c. to the 20th in the sonnets of Ronsard and the *Pléiade*, the love poetry of the Elizabethans and metaphysicals, the erotica of the Restoration and 18th c., the synaesthetic images of Keats and the romantics, the symbolist glorification of the self and its peculiar sensations, the neurotic sensualism of the Nineties, and the "new" sensualism of the Lost Generation, the existentialists, and the Beat Generation. Ranging in theme from *carpe diem* to *memento mori*, the sensual trad. is sustained in differing forms by Shakespeare, Donne, Collins, Herder, Heine, Baudelaire, Mallarmé, Whitman, D'Annunzio, Millay, and Dylan Thomas. (ii.) The "imaginative" or "intellectualized" L. of Emotion furnishes a host of examples. The Ger. lyricists provide a large number (notably Goethe, Schiller, Rilke, Hauptmann, and George). The "verbalized feelings" of the Eng. romantics and the Fr. symbolists have their modern counterparts in the ls. of Apollinaire and Valéry as well as in the poetry of Garcia Lorca and the It. hermetics Ungaretti and Montale. Many of the ls. of Puškin and Pasternak fall into this category. Writers of British ls. of this type are Auden, MacNeice, Empson, Spender, and Larkin; Americans include Emerson, Dickinson, Frost, Jeffers, MacLeish, Stevens, Moore, Wilbur, and Hecht. (iii.) Finally, the poetry of mysticism is significant in modern l. hist., perhaps as an attempt to find some substitute for the Gr. myths which provoked the Cl. l., or for the Christian mythography which stimulated the med. l. Foremost among the mystical lyricists are Herbert, Vaughan, Traherne, Smart, Blake, Hopkins, Thompson, Baudelaire, Claudel, Yeats, and Rilke.

B. *Russia and Eastern Europe.* Like the Byzantine poetry from which some of it derived, the l. of Eastern Europe often mixed native trads. with Western (Ger., Fr., It.) and Eastern (notably Rus.). Just as the military incursions and domination of

Western nations affected the lits. of Africa and Asia, the incursions of Russia into Baltic, central European, and Balkan areas have had a strong impact on the l. practices of these areas.

1. *Russian* l. began in the 11th c. with folk poetry performed to musical accompaniment, songs attached to harvest ceremonies, worship, and wedding. *The Lay of Prince Igor's Campaign* (1185) has strong elements of lyricism. Liturgical songs and folk satires appeared in the 13th–16th cs.; and a new syllabic verse found its best expression in the poems of the monk Simeon Polotsky (1629–80). After the Reforms of Peter the Great introduced European poetic practices into Russia, Lomonosov (1711–65) perfected a system of versification based on Ger. prosody that made Western metrics the basis of most future Rus. verse. He also wrote odes and meditations and prescribed styles for various l. genres: "high" for odes, "middle" for ls., "low" for songs. Sumarokov's *Epistle on Writing Poetry* (1747) emphasized the song; and his own tragic love-lyrics, transformed from songs, became the model for the genre. His near-contemporary, Derzavin, "the supreme poetic genius of the 18th c.," however, indiscriminately called all of his poems "odes." In the Rus. Golden Age, Žukovskij's moody and emotional romantic ls. introduced polysemy, and Batyuškov's ls., faintly erotic, strove for concrete objectivity; Bobrov wrote philosophical and nature ls. But the towering genius of the Golden Age was Alexander Puškin (1799–1837), whose masterpiece, *Eugene Onegin*, is made up of 400 lyrical episodes or digressions; and his other extensive ls. are notable for the remarkable decorum of their diction. His contemporary Fyodor Tyutčev (1803–73) composed a small number of soul-searching ls. and love poems darkened with tragedy, an intensely personal poetry countered by Nekrasov's (1812–78) concern with peasant life. An "art for art's sake" movement produced Afanasy Fet's (1820–92) l. proclamations that the poet sees and reveals the beauty of a "poetic" world to lesser mortals. Fr. symbolism was transformed into its Slavic version through characteristically Rus. symbols; and with the collected poems of Alexander Blok, the l. entered the 20th c.

The emergence of the acmeists (e.g. Anna Axmatova, Osip Mandelštam) and the futurists (e.g. Xlebnikov, Majakovskij) heralded the decline of symbolism. The former stressed a pictorial l., clear, plastic, and ecumenical in knowledge, while the latter made for more radical experiments with form. In the 1920s imagist poetry occupied some poets, but in the Stalinist era, many poets were shot as subversives, while others like Boris Pasternak "wrote for the drawer." His *Doctor Zhivago*, the last section of which is a l. cycle, was finally published in the West in 1957, whereupon it won a Nobel Prize. With the end of Stalinism, some young, internationally known poets (Evtušenko, Voznesenskij) were free to publish; others used tape recorders in their revival of l. performance. The leading proponent of the "barracks" school of l. realism, Josef Brodsky, went into exile in the West. Those who remained in Russia styled themselves poets of a "Bronz Age," indicating their pessimistic view of the future. (See RUSSIAN POETRY.)

2. The earliest *Czech* ls. are vernacular hymns of the 12th c. Ls. based on Med. Lat. were composed in the 14th c., as were satiric verses and the Fr.-inspired *aubade* in Bohemia. The Counter-Reformation increased the number of hymns and prayers; by the end of the 18th c., ls. of praise and idylls abounded, and a burgeoning Pan-Slavism quickened sonnet writing and folk-inspired ls. A Czech strain of romanticism developed in the early 19th c., producing the greatest Czech poet, K. H. Mácha (1810–36). But the 1848 Revolution ended romanticism and strengthened Pan-Slavism; the technical aspects of verse were subsequently polished in the ls. of Vrchlichy, whose values grew increasingly aesthetic. His successors variously stressed musicality, imagery, and Whitmanesque rhapsodies. Czech independence in 1918 was followed by intensified poetic activity: "Proletarian" poets were sympathetic toward the Soviets; "poetism" (pure poetry) eschewed politics for dada; "futurism" and "vitalism" also had their proponents striving to convey their joy in life, in the city, and in technology. In this and later poetry, the influence of Czech folk ls. and the literary ballad was evident. But the 1968 Russian invasion of Czechoslovakia effectively terminated the publication of Czech poetry until 1990. (See CZECH POETRY.)

3. *Ukrainian* poetry has met a similar fate. Originating in the 13th c. from old Kievan sources, Ukrainian oral poetry (ballads, elegies) was sung by *dumy* or composed by wandering minstrels in the 14th c.; 16th-c. trs. of Byzantine hymns are the first written evidence of lyricism. The establishment of an autonomous Cossack state in the mid-17th c. was accompanied by a bilingual lit. (Ukrainian and Polish) in which panegyrics, laments (*Kyry*), satires, and seasonal verses were composed. Even the edict of Peter the Great forbidding writing in Ukrainian did not entirely suppress l. poetry. In the 18th c. Skovoroda's *The Garden of Divine Songs*, a collection of devotional ls., was the outstanding accomplishment, while in the 19th c. emergent Ukrainian romanticism revived interest in folk lyrical trads. Shevshenko's *The Minstrel* evidences this, along with very intimate and personal ls. In the 20th c. the policy of "Ukrainization" allowed schools of symbolist, futurist, and constructivist poets to flourish, but Stalin crushed all these. More recent poets (Symonenko, Kostenko, Pavlychko) have shown their concern for a more concentrated lyricism. (See UKRANIAN POETRY.)

4. *Polish.* The first, and best, example of written Polish lyricism was the "Mother of God," a

13th-c. hymn. In the 14th–15th cs., ls. of devotion derived from the Lat. (carols, hymns, Easter songs) were often innovative. The fragmentary specimens of oral lit. show little ability. In the "Polish Golden Age," which began in the 1560s, Mikolaj Rej (1505–69), the "father of Polish lit.," wrote robust epigrams; Jan Kochanowski (1530–84), called the greatest of Slavic poets, wrote songs, Anacreontics, psalms, and "Threnodies," a moving series of laments for his daughter. Other poets composed religious sonnets, pastorals, and devotional ls. In the 17th c. a Westernized form of baroque was prominent. Andrzej Morsztyn (1621–93) wrote ls. about love's paradoxes and metaphysical fear. The *Ruthenian Maidens* (pub. 1654) by Szymon Zimorowic (ca. 1608–29) was a sequence of lyrical monologues. Later, Wespazjan Kochowski (1633–1700) published his *Unleisurely Leisure* (1674), a collection of epigrams and ls. The early 18th c. witnessed a decline in creativity, but the latter part of the century brought a purer lang. and descriptive ls., odes, epistles, fables, and epigrams. After the partition of Poland in 1795, the *wieszcz* or bard-prophet exhorted the Polish spirit. A central figure was Adam Mickiewicz (1798–1855), a poet steeped in romanticism. His odes and ballads united folklore with the fantastic and supernatural; the later *Crimean Sonnets* dealt with passionate love, the isolated hero, and tragic sacrifice. His contemporary, Juliusz Selowacki (1809–49) composed l. confessions and a booklength *Beniowski*, a "poem of digressions" which has been compared to *Don Juan* and *Eugene Onegin*. In the 1860s romanticism declined under the impact of positivism. Symbolism was used innovatively by Boleslaw Lesmian (1878–1937) in his fantastic ballads and metaphysical ls. of "becoming." The "Young Poland" movement at the turn of the century valorized the poet as primeval man, whose act of perceiving creates the world; and the period of Polish Independence (1918–39) gave rise to the five "Skamander" poets, epitomized by Julian Tuwim (1894–1953). Since 1946, Polish poets have included the former Catastrophist, Czeslaw Miłosz (b. 1911), who was awarded the Nobel Prize in 1980. Tadeusz Roozewicz (b. 1921) has evolved a new style of ascetic lyricism spoken with "an anonymous voice." Other movements—Revisionism, neoclassicism, "lyrical linguism," and "liberation of the imagination"—sustained the vigor of Polish l. during the difficult era of Soviet domination, which ended in the 1980s. (See POLISH POETRY.)

5. *Yugoslavian.* The distinct regions and ethnic cultures of Yugoslavia have produced separate forms of l. expressions. The earliest ls. appeared in the 13th–14th cs. as ritual folksongs and Byzantine-inspired hymns in Serbia. It. forms were imported into Ren. Dalmatia. Croatian fisherman songs and pastorals were widespread in the 16th c., and It. l. meters were introduced into Ragusan poetry, which reached its Golden Age in the poems of Gundulic (1589–1638). In the late 18th c., Karadzik (1787–1864) set a romantic standard for later Serbian and Croatian poets with a collection of folk ballads. Vraz (1810–51) brought the sonnet to Croatia, and Preseren (1800–49) refined Slovenian and prepared the way for a very strong lyrical heritage. At the same time in Serbia and Croatia, lyricism became the dominant mode with some outstanding practitioners: Levstik, Ilie, Jenko, and Petrovic. The 20th c. has produced a wide variety of l. experimentation in style and theme. Symbolism and surrealism had their exponents; Eng. and So. Am. influences became notable; and after existing underground for centuries, Macedonian poetry emerged. Civil war in the 1990s, however, deepened ethnic divisions. (See YUGOSLAVIAN POETRY.)

6. In the *Balkans*, national l. trads. are recent. In Bulgaria, centuries of ecclesiastical trad. (Old Slavonic and Gr.) and foreign domination (the Ottomans, the Russians) discouraged much beyond folksongs and ballads before the 18th c.; since then Bulgarian poets have reflected Western practices. In Hungary, after centuries of similar influences and folk genres, the first poet to write Hungarian ls. in the 16th c. was Balassa; the modern term for "poetry" (*kolto*) was not used before the 18th c. Since then, Western influences have been pronounced, though the themes of freedom and defiance are definably Hungarian. Romanian ls.—psalms, elegies, odes, and epigrams based on Western models, or indigenous folksongs (*doinas*)—date from the 17th c. In the late 18th c. Hungarian poetry imitated Western neoclassical odes, romantic ballads, and even the Ger. Biedermeyer verse. Romanian poets of the present century have explored the l. potential of expressionism, symbolism, and dada. (See BULGARIAN POETRY; HUNGARIAN POETRY; ROMANIAN POETRY.)

7. In the *Baltic* republics the form of l. is also recent. In Latvia, the so-called National Awakening in the mid-19th c. supplemented the native *dainas* (folksongs) with romantic-style ls. Independence in 1918 made Latvian poets susceptible to Western modes, incl. free verse. Descriptions of nature, apocalyptic visions, and ironic verse were muted by the Soviet invasion in 1944, and Latvian poetry was forced into exile (e.g. the Hell's Kitchen Poets in Manhattan) until the collapse of the Soviet Union in 1989. Lithuanian l. originated in folk *dainos* before the 18th c., mainly canticles and hymns. In the 19th c., neoclassicism and sentimentalism were succeeded by romanticism, symbolism, and modernism, and in the 20th c. by melding of these approaches. The imposition of Socialist Realism by Rus. annexation left Lithuanian poets, such as exile Jonas Mekas, to continue the native trad. abroad. Estonia has a native trad. of oral ls. and a written trad. of poetry based on Ger. prosody. Effectively starting in the 19th c., Estonian poets then wrote Pindarics, folk verse, and patriotic ls. Toward the end of World War I, a

new group, the *Siuru*, began a new outburst of l. creativity that was sustained until Sovietization in World War II. After that, Estonian poetry existed only in exile until 1989. In Finland, vernacular l. poetry from oral trad. was collected in the 19th c. in the *Kalevala*. These folk poems reflected ritual origins and showed erotic, festive, and lamentative themes. The folk trad. inspired Finnish poets, and romanticism had a discernible effect. After centuries of Swedish domination ended, the Finns then faced Russian attack (but not defeat) in World War II. Subsequently, the increase of poetry in Finnish has matched the decline of that in Swedish. Unlike their Baltic neighbors, the Finns have successfully established a lyricism free of domination by either West or East. (See LATVIAN POETRY; LITHUANIAN POETRY; ESTONIAN POETRY; FINNISH POETRY.)

C. *Africa.* From its origins in the practices of ancient Egypt to its present-day diversification across the continent, the l. in Africa has a history of interrelation between oral and written trads. Closely allied with music through singing and the dance, the oral l. is also an integral part of Af. heroic and epic poetry. The ancient social purpose of Af. poetry—voicing the beliefs of a people about themselves and their rulers within contexts of the past—continues into the 20th c., whether in the largely oral and pastoral ls. of Somalia, in the printed explorations of *Négritude* by the francophone poets of Senegal, the Congo, and Ivory Coast, or in the celebrations of *Uhuru* by post-colonial writers in East and South Africa.

The devel. of the Egyptian l. from 2700–1086 B.C. suggests a close connection between the different l. genres in their performed and recorded versions. In Ethiopia, the ancient literary lang., Ge'ez, was used in the cl. *genē*, epigram, praise poems, and long hymns. Highly compact and allusive, based on ambiguities, the *genē* evidences its academic and literary origins. Later Ethiopian poetry, written in Amharic, can be traced to oral sources in the 14th c.: recitations at weddings, funerals, or other public occasions; love songs; and patriotic verse. Like much folk-derived poetry, Amharic ls. often rely on puns and verbal play. (See EGYPTIAN POETRY; ETHIOPIAN POETRY.)

Although it existed in Africa for many generations, the oral trad. of lyricism has been recorded by researchers only recently. From dirge to lament, *jeu d'ésprit* to panegyric, langs. as diverse as the San, Mbuti, Ewe, Xhosa, Yoruba, and Dinka express l. themes through music and images drawn from the landscape: moon and sun, birds, wild animals, reptiles, and domesticated beasts. Repetition, reiterative expansion, and body movements in the dance are common devices for lyrical devel. Emotions of joy and grief, desire and exultation—both political and personal—animate these poems. Af. oral heroic poetry (episodic narratives dominated by lyrical elements) is sometimes recited by professionals, the *griot* or *imbongi*.

In heroic poetry, the emotional and imagistic forces of the l. are aimed at describing tribal leaders, both admirable and not, comparing them with their predecessors. Similarly, the oral epic celebrates the continuity of a people lyrically expressed in the collective events of their past.

Many Af. oral trads. were affected by the Arab invasion of the continent in 641 A.D. As Islam and the Ar. lang. spread, such l. types as odes, the Ar. *qaṣīdas* (q.v.) and panegyrics were introduced by the *rāwīs* (reciters or memorizers). This reinforcement of a combined oral/literary trad. readily adapted to Af. practice; and the Berbers quickly adopted the Ar. lyric-panegyric (war chants, praise of heroes), taking it with them into Iberia. Timbuktu in West Africa became the center of Islamic learning in the 14th c.; its spread into the Hausa states resulted in a blending of the Ar. *qaṣīda* with the indigenous Hausa *kīraṅ*. The two lyrical and panegyric trads. were easily reconciled, as in the Hausa "Song of Bagauda." The Swahili oral trad., with its combination of l., epic, and panegyric, was equally hospitable to Islamic influence. The Malagasy poets were somewhat less affected, the chief of them electing to write not in Ar. but Fr. and Malagasy.

In later times, Western influences (primarily through colonial settlement and Christian missionaries) affected the Af. l. most deeply. Western religious forces encouraged the writing of hymns, such as the Xhosa l. of praise by the convert Ntsikana in the 1820s. Many outstanding Xhosa poets followed him, but the racial clashes in South Africa during the later 19th c. produced less lyrical pietism and more statements of anguish, hope, alienation, and political aspiration. The Zulu followed a similar poetic course, first adopting their ancient bardic trad. of the oral *izibongo* to more literary forms, incl. ls. about apartheid and the feelings it creates. African ls. written in Fr. (francophone) or Eng. (anglophone) during the 1950s and '60s were anti-colonial in theme and emotion; those of the postcolonial period in the 1970s and '80s continue to explore the social and political themes that have characterized Af. poetry from the beginning. Today, both oral and written l. poetry thrive in Africa, sustaining each other as they have for centuries. The former preserves long-standing trads. of form and performance while the latter confronts new dimensions, personal and collective, of the historical legacy of the continent. (See AFRICAN POETRY; HAUSA POETRY; SOUTH AFRICAN POETRY; SWAHILI POETRY.)

D. *Asia.* 1. *Indian* lit. written in Sanskrit is among the oldest in the world, dating from the 3rd c. B.C. The Vedic hymns to various deities of nature are early specimens of the l. mode. Many anonymous ls. between 200 B.C. and 400 A.D. have been lost, but Kalidasa's love l., *Cloud Messenger*, became the model for numerous imitations. The other outstanding Sanskrit l. is Jayadeva's *Song of Lord Govinda* (ca. 1200 A.D.), also widely imitated.

Other Sanskrit ls. include prayers, praises, and psalms. Ls. in the Prākrits dialects include a collection of 700 lovepoems, the *Gāthā-Sapaśatī* (ca. 200 A.D.). Other Indian dialects were used to translate and imitate Sanskrit and Prākrits ls. after the 11th c. Marathi writers developed the *lavani* form of lovelyric. Gujarati religious songs were sung throughout India. Punjabi ls. included religious songs and, later, ballads. Kashmiri lovepoems, often mystic, show Persian influences.

Hindi, in time the federal lang. of India, began out of other dialects with a bardic trad. of poetry. In the 11th c. the Gypsies left India, taking with them the Romani lang. (related to Hindi and Punjabi) and a trad. of oral lyricism. Outstanding Hindi ls. include the 700 couplets (*satsai*) of Biharila (1603–63). Other dialects (Urdu, Tamil, Bengali, et al.) contained l. derivations from Sanskrit, and all were affected by Western new forms (e.g. the sonnet) and Western schools of l. writing (neoclassicism, romanticism) after the 18th c. (See INDIAN POETRY.)

2. *Chinese* l. poetry can be traced to the 11th c. B.C.; the first anthol. was made after 600 B.C. Attributed to Confucius, the *Shi-jing* contains 305 poems (folk and court songs, hymns) that were originally sung or chanted. In their themes and prosodic techniques, these *shih* (poems) established l. precedents for later poets. Somewhat later, the *Songs of Chu* showed Shamanist imagery and attitudes while emphasizing the musical nature of the l., grouping the poems in "nines," a musical term. The stylistic pattern called *sao*, identified with "China's Pindar," Qu Yuan, the first known poet, was established in this collection. From the *sao* derived the *fu* (rhapsodies) and *yongwu fu* (*fu* on objects) popular in the Han dynasty, together with the *yuefu* (hymns, ballads). About the 2d c. B.C., the 4-line *shi* gave way to the 5-line and to poetry of deep reflection and meditation. Death and separation were common l. topics, treated in a restrained manner that became widely used. In the 4th–6th cs., *Shanshui* (mountains and waters) poetry emphasized the physical world and the genuineness of the poet's feelings.

During the Tang period (618–907 A.D.), considered the Golden Age of Ch. poetry, *Lu-shih*, or regulated verse, opened new poetic themes: the l. moment in time, the merging of self and nature. Li Bo (701–62) and Du Fu (712–70) are the poetic geniuses of this school of lyricism. Bo Juyi (772–816) revived and renewed the *yuefu*, and near the close of the Tang era, imported musical tunes from Central Asia encouraged a new genre of l., the *ci*, highly suitable for expressing the ecstasy and misery of romantic love. Li Yu (837–978) wrote *ci* at once intensely personal and humanly universal. In the Song Dynasty, Liu Youg (978–1053) freed the *ci* from its musical origins, making it a literary medium suitable for a range of poetic emotions. *Shi* poems became more philosophical, more "plain" and "calm." In the Yuan period

(1280–1386), the irregular and colloquial *sangu* sometimes took a quasi-dramatic, sequential form. The painter-poets increased during the Ming and Qing dynasties; they combined the *shi* with calligraphy. In the 17th c., *ci* poetry regained a favor that continues to the present day. Through the centuries of its history, Ch. l. poetry has maintained its ancient presuppositions about the poet and nature while constantly searching for the genres, meters, and images that best embody their eternal relationship. (See CHINESE POETRY.)

3. Primordial *Japanese* ls. composed before 685 A.D. and preserved in chronicles included work and play songs, laments, occasional poems, and songs of praise. Between 685 and 1350, court poets defined two major l. forms, the *tanka* (also *uta, waka*) and the *chōka* (also *nagauta*). The great Hitomara (fl. ca. 680– 700) wrote elegies and imbued travel and occasional poems with lyrical qualities. The *chōka* declined in favor toward the 8th c. Between 784 and 1100, the *tanka* was paramount. Under Ch. influence, the Japanese l. became very subjective, inventive, even passionate. Twenty-one imperial anthols. were collected, the most important being the *Kokinshū* (ca. 905). Use of such poetic devices as the "pillow-word" and "pivot-word" set up standards for future l. practice. The decline of court influence from 1100–1241 and the example of somber Ch. poets raised new themes—loneliness, autumnal scenes and moods, travel sadness—to be explored by Japanese lyricists. A return to earlier practices also marked one of several neoclassical revivals. Fujiwara Shunzei (1114–1204) combined these several strains and focused the poetic interests of his age.

From 1241 to 1330, court poetry stagnated, but two imperial anthols. contained poems original in their concentration on moments of intensity or minute particulars, their purely imagistic seasonal poems, and their love-poems. The desire to experiment led to synaesthetic poems and the use of innovative images such as decaying hovels and barking dogs. The end of the Feudal Period (1350–1867) saw the growth of new forms (the *No* plays), the formation of new Zen-influenced "linked" forms of earlier genres (*renga, haikai*), and the evolution of the first stanzas (*hokku*) of the *haikai* toward a form perfected in the modern period: the *haiku* (q.v.). The stellar poet of the Late Feudal Age was the great Bashō (1644–94). Since 1868, Japanese poetry has been dominated by the *tanka, haiku,* and *kindaishi* (or modern poetry), which is subdivided into *shintashai* (new style poems written in Cl. Japanese) and *jiyushi* (free style poems written in modern Japanese). The *senryū* is considered an epigram rather than a poem, and both the *renga* and *haikai* are practically extinct except for a small number of traditionalists. The rapid appearance of new forms and the disappearance of old ones are evidence of the radical changes wrought on Japanese culture in the aftermath of World War II; Japanese l. poetry has undergone a correlate metamorphosis. (See JAPANESE POETRY.)

4. *Korean* poetry was less sweepingly changed. Before the invention of written Korean in the mid 15th c., the earliest vernacular poetry, or *hyangga*, was preserved in Ch. graphs from the 6th c. on. Composed by Buddhist monks or professional warriors between 57 B.C. and 935 A.D., the *hyangga* used extensive nature symbols (pine trees, clouds, snow, the moon, rain, fruit, grain) to convey spiritual values. From 918 to 1392 *pyŏlgok* or *changga* ls.—a blend of art and folk song—were sung to music. Songs of love, parting, grief, betrayal, and desire, the *changga* used onomatopoeia, nonsense syllables, and incantation for their effects. From 1392 to 1910 the *sijo*, a form of poetry written first by the educated classes and later by commoners, dealt with love, virtue, death, nature, and rural life. In common mouths, the longer *sasol siji* was often humorous, frank, earthy, with an unexpected ending. *Sijo* are still being composed in Korea. In the 15th c. the Korean *kasa*, analogous to the Ch. *fu*, emerged as words to *kasa* tunes. The Japanese Occupation (1910–45) produced "new poetry," with such innovations as punctuation marks and unequal stanza lengths. Western poetry and Fr. symbolist writers were translated into Korean, and poets wrote feelingly of alienation and exile. Since the Liberation in 1945, l. poets have borne witness to the "Korean tragedy" and showed a new historic and national consciousness. (See KOREAN POETRY.)

III. CONTEMPORARY DEVELOPMENTS. The popularity of l. poetry in the 20th c. has increased with its employment in the causes of self-expression, feminism, and racial and social equality. The abundance of l. writing has been accompanied by a plethora of critical analyses and theories. The most influential critical approaches to the l. in the decades after World War II have been those of scholars and academic critics in America and Europe.

During the 1940s and '50s, the "New Critics" in America emphasized the formal integrity of the poem and its self-containment, diminishing the importance of authorial reference and reader response. Their emphasis on paradox and irony, lucubration, and the poem qua poem led to a critical neglect of lyricism. At the same time, in Europe the influence of Ferdinand de Saussure on words as signs and langs. as systems (see STRUCTURALISM) pointed the way to deeper analyses of poetic lang., such as those by Roman Jakobson, and to the deconstructionist approaches of Jacques Derrida.

When deconstruction (q.v.) was imported to America, critics began reexamining the l. mode. Finding unconvincing and inadequate the critical postulation that the speaker of the l. was the poet himself, or even a fictive persona, such critics as Jonathan Culler declared that "the fundamental aspect of l. writing . . . is to produce an apparently phenomenal world through the figure of voice." Paul de Man expanded this to say, "the principle of intelligibility, in l. poetry, depends on the phenomenalization of the poetic voice (which is) the aesthetic presence that determines the hermeneutics of the l." The I-Speaker of the l. thus ceases to be Shelley, Valéry, Li-Bo, or Bashō—or even a mask for or a Joycean image reflective of the poet. The speaker is a device for making the invisible visible. De Man replaces such standard terms as "personification" with "catachresis" (qq.v.) in order to explain the function of the frequent trope of address ("apostrophe" [q.v.]) in l. poetry. The poet-surrogate is replaced by the figurative voice, a mantic or shamanistic presence that makes the verbal world of the l. a visible world to the mind of the reader.

Thus, from its primordial form, the song as embodiment of emotion, the l. has been expanded and altered through the centuries until it has become one of the chief literary instruments which focus and evaluate the human condition. In flexibility, variety, and polish, it is perhaps the most proficient of the poetic genres. In the immediacy and keenness of its expression, it is certainly the most effective. These qualities have caused the 19th and 20th cs. to look upon the l. as largely their own, but l. poetry has belonged to all ages.

See also DRAMATIC POETRY; EMOTION; EPIC; GENRE; LYRIC SEQUENCE; NARRATIVE POETRY; PERSONA; POETRY; VOICE.

F. B. Gummere, *The Beginnings of Poetry* (1901); J. Erskine, *The Elizabethan L.* (1903); F. E. Schelling, *The Eng. L.* (1913); J. Drinkwater, *The L.* (1915); G. B. Gray, *The Forms of Heb. Poetry* (1915); A. Erman, *The Lit. of the Ancient Egyptians,* tr. A. M. Blackman (1927); P. S. Allen and H. M. Jones, *The Romanesque L.* (1928); G. Murray, *The Cl. Trad. in Poetry* (1930); J. Pfeffer, *Das lyrische Gedicht als aesthetisches Gebilde* (1931); Manitius, 3.III.F; K. Kar, *Thoughts on the Med. L.* (1933); Jeanroy; H. Färber, *Die Lyrik in der Kunsttheorie der Antike* (1936); F. Brittain, *The Med. Lat. and Romance L. to A.D. 1300* (1937); G. Errante, *Sulla lirica romanza delle origine* (1943); E. K. Chambers, *Early Eng. Ls.* (1947); Le Gentil; C. M. Ing, *Elizabethan Ls.* (1951); J. Wiegand, *Abriss der lyrischen Technik* (1951); G. M. Kirkwood, "A Survey of Pubs. on Gr. L. Poetry, 1932–53," *CW* 47 (1953), foll. by D. E. Gerber for 1952–67 and 1967–75 in *CW* 61 (1968), 70 (1976); G. Benn, *Probleme der Lyrik* (1954); M. Hadas, *Ancilla to Cl. Reading* (1954); A. E. Harvey, "The Classification of Gr. L. Poetry," *ClassQ* n.s. 5 (1955); *The Harley Ls.*, ed. G. L. Brook, 2d ed. (1955); H. Friedrich, *Die Struktur der modernen Lyrik* (1956)—influential; G. Murphy, *Early Irish Ls.* (1956); J. L. Kinneavy, *A Study of Three Contemp. Theories of L. Poetry* (1956); Beare; Frye; Bowra; R. Dragonetti, *La Technique poétique des trouvères dans la chanson courtoise* (1960); R. Kienast, "Die deutschsprachige Lyrik des Mittelalters," *Deutsche Philologie im Aufriss,* ed.

W. Stammler, 2d ed., v. 2 (1960); L. Nelson, *Baroque L. Poetry* (1961); C. S. Lewis, *Eng. Lit. in the 16th C.* (1962); J. M. Cohen, *The Baroque L.* (1963); B. Markwardt, "Lyrik (Theorie)," *Reallexikon* 2.240–52; Jeanroy, *Origines; Zur Lyrik-Diskussion*, ed. R. Grimm (1966); F. Goldin, *The Mirror of Narcissus in the Courtly Love L.* (1967); P. Boyde, *Dante's L. Poetry* (1967), *Dante's Style in his L. Poetry* (1971); Y. Winters, "The 16th-C. L. in England: A Critical and Historical Reinterp.," *Elizabethan Poetry*, ed. P. J. Alpers (1967); Dronke; Dale; R. Woolf, *The Eng. Religious L. in the Middle Ages* (1968); *Forms of L.*, ed. R. Brower (1970), esp. P. de Man, "L. and Modernity"; J. Mazzaro, *Transformations in the Ren. Eng. L.* (1970); R. Oliver, *Poems Without Names* (1970); B. Watson, *Ch. Lyricism* (1971); W. Killy, *Elemente der Lyrik* (1972); H. M. Richmond, *Ren. Landscapes* (1973); J. J. Y. Liu, *Major Lyricists of the Northern Sung* (1974); Bec; H. A. Stavan, *La Lyrisme dans la poésie française de 1760 à 1820* (1976); A. Welsh, *Roots of L.* (1978); D. Woolf, *The Concept of the Text* (1978); H. Parry, *The L. Poems of Gr. Tragedy* (1978); B. K. Lewalski, *Protestant Poetics and the 17th-C. Religious L.* (1979); S. Cameron, *L. Time* (1979); *The Interp. of Med. L. Poetry*, ed. W. T. H. Jackson (1980); S. Owen, *The Great Age of Ch. Poetry* (1980); K. S. Chang, *The Evolution of Ch. T'zu Poetry* (1980); Trypanis; Sayce; W. R. Johnson, *The Idea of L.: L. Modes in Ancient and Mod. Poetry* (1982); Fowler; D. A. Campbell, *Gr. L.*, 4 v. (1982–), *The Golden Lyre* (1983); I. H. Levy, *Hitomaro and the Birth of Japanese Lyricism* (1983); W. E. Rogers, *The Three Genres and the Interp. of L.* (1983); H. Spanke, *Studien zur lateinischen und romanischen Lyrik des Mittelalters* (1983); *Gesch. der deutschen Lyrik vom Mittelalter bis zur Gegenwart*, ed. W. Hinderer (1983); *Lyrik des Mittelalters: Probleme und Interpretationen*, ed. H. Bergner et al., 2 v. (1983); A. Williams, *Prophetic Strain: The Greater L. in the 18th C.* (1984); M. H. Abrams, "Structure and Style in the Greater Romantic L.," *The Correspondent Breeze* (1984); *CHCL*, v. 1, chs. 6, 8; J. Herington, *Poetry into Drama* (1985); T. G. Rosenmeyer, "Ancient Literary Genres: A Mirage?" *YCGL* 34 (1985); D. Lindley, *L.* (1985); R. Alter, *The Art of Biblical Poetry* (1985); *L. Poetry: Beyond New Crit.*, ed. C. Hošek and P. Parker (1985); P. S. Diehl, *The Med. European Religious L.* (1985); *The Vitality of the L. Voice*, ed. S. Lin and S. Owen (1986)—Chinese; R. L. Fowler, *The Nature of Early Gr. L.* (1987); Hollier; G. Kaiser, *Gesch. der deutschen Lyrik von Goethe bis Heine: Ein Grundriss in Interpretationen*, 3 v. (1988); D. Lamping, *Das lyrische Gedicht* (1989); A. R. Jones, *The Currency of Eros: Women's Love L. in Europe, 1540–1620* (1990); M. Perloff, *Poetic License: Essays on Modernist and Postmodernist L.* (1990), esp. ch. 1; *Ls. of the Middle Ages*, ed. J. J. Wilhelm (1990); M. Dickie, *L. Contingencies* (1991). J.W.J.

LYRIC CAESURA. See CAESURA.

LYRIC SEQUENCE.

I. RENAISSANCE TO ROMANTIC
II. MODERN BRITISH AND AMERICAN

I. RENAISSANCE TO ROMANTIC. A collocation of lyrics, the l. s. is generally thought to have gained its vernacular identity in the Ren. and after from Francis Petrarch (1304–74), who wrote and arranged his s. called *Rime sparse* or, alternatively, *Canzoniere* over 40 years. Both titles ("Scattered Rhymes" and "Songbook") ironically point away from the rigorous ordering of Petrarch's 366 amatory and devotional lyrics, which manifests several patterns at once (formal, fictional, calendrical) to establish a continuum—or dis-continuum, considering the new-found structural importance of the white space between the lyrics—that greatly exceeds the unities of earlier lyric collections. Petrarch's diverse models included the Book of Psalms; the lyric volumes of Catullus, Propertius, and other Augustan poets; Dante's prosimetric *Vita nuova* (ca. 1292–1300) and his short s. *Rime petrose* (ca. 1296); and the 12th- and 13th-c. *chansonniers* of the Occitan troubadours.

For two centuries after Petrarch's death the possibilities opened by the l. s.—to write lyric *in extenso*, allowing each poetic integer to hold its autonomy as it participates in a larger unity—attracted the efforts of poets in all the countries of Europe; Wilkins lists most of these, an astonishing array. The l. s. effectively became to lyric (q.v.) what tragedy was to drama, or what the novel would be to narrative—not merely a "form" but a complex of generic capacities. Some particularly interesting l. ss. are written at the margins or in the hiatuses of the convention: the 24-sonnet s. (1555) by the Fr. poet Louise Labé dissents from the sexual politics of Petrarchism (q.v.); the Italians Giovanni Salvatorino and Girolamo Malipiero, believing Petarch's speaker insufficiently Christian, adapt the forms and much of the lang. of the *Rime sparse* to purely devotional experience in their respective works *Thesoro de sacra scrittura* (ca. 1540) and *Il Petrarca spirituale* (1567); and, near the end of the century, after most European cultures had temporarily exhausted the s., a generation of Eng. sonneteers between Thomas Watson's *Hekatompathia* (1582) and Michael Drayton's *Idea* (1600) undertook a frenzy of experimentation, refinement, and superstitious imitation of Petrarch (see SONNET SEQUENCE). While a number of poets essentially non-Petrarchan in topics and ideology are attracted by the l. s. (e.g. George Gascoigne, the first to use the term "s." in Eng. in *Alexander Nevile* [1575], and Ben Jonson in *The Forrest* [1616]), nearly every s. in this period interprets some aspect of Petrarch's rich achievement. Even such monuments of their vernaculars as Pierre de Ronsard's *Sonnets pour Hélène* (1578, enl. 1584), Luís de Camões' *Rimas* (pub. posthumously 1595, though written as early as the 1540s), and Shakespeare's *Sonnets* (ca. 1593–99, pub. 1609) are, in the first analysis, responses to the *Rime sparse* as a compendium of organizational strategies—formal, characterological, devotional, political, speculative.

The principal trend in the 17th-c. l. s. develops its religious dimensions. Virtuoso events include Jean de la Ceppède's *Théorèmes* (1613, 1622), George Herbert's *The Temple* (pub. 1633), and John Donne's *Holy Sonnets*, incl. "La Corona," a 7-unit crown of sonnets (1633; see CORONA). The first major North Am. l. s., Edward Taylor's *Preparatory Meditations* (written 1682–1725), arrives near the end of this line. The 18th and 19th cs., perhaps because of an attenuation of the formal resources of Petrarchism, perhaps from ineluctable shifts in European poetics and ideologies, produce little of compelling interest in the form of the l. s. itself (though much important poetry within the form). The romantics composed numerous l. ss., but the unities of these works are generally looser than those of earlier specimens; one notices the tendency, as in Novalis and Wordsworth, for example, to announce a l. s. to be in effect a single poem, thus affirming the idea of its unity but waiving the actual tensions generated between strong integers and an equally strong unifying structure.

The most successful 19th-c. European and Am. l. ss. tend to be like Tennyson's *In Memoriam* (1850) in that they do not imitate Petrarch's outward forms and gestures but find contemporary analogues for his inventions—which perhaps inevitably means discarding the sonnet (q.v.) in favor of other constituents. Walt Whitman's *Leaves of Grass* (1855, frequently enl.) is the most visionary of these versions; his influence on the l. s. is virtually that of a New World Petrarch, and has led to an extraordinary abundance of works in the modern period, esp. in the U.S. and in Latin America. See also ANTHOLOGY; COLLECTIONS, POETIC; RENGA.

E. H. Wilkins, "A Gen. Survey of Ren. Petrarchism," *Studies in the Life and Works of Petrarch* (1955); G. T. Warkentin, "*Astrophil and Stella* in the Setting of its Trad.," *DAI* 34 (1974): 5211A; C. T. Neely, "The Structure of Ren. Sonnet Ss.," *ELH* 45 (1977)—limited to Eng.; *Arethusa* 13 (1980)—five essays and bibl. on the Augustan volumes; H. Vendler, *The Odes of John Keats* (1983)—the Odes as a l. s.; N. Fraistat, *The Poem and the Book* (1985)—on Eng. romantic collections, ed., *Poems in Their Place* (1986); J. Freccero, "The Fig Tree and the Laurel," *Literary Theory / Ren. Texts*, ed. P. Parker and D. Quint (1986); Hollier; T. P. Roche, Jr., *Petrarch and the Eng. Sonnet Ss.* (1989)—esp. on the religious elements of the early modern s.; R. Greene, *Post-Petrarchism* (1991); *The Ladder of High Designs*, ed. D. Fenoaltea and D. L. Rubin (1991). R.GR.

II. MODERN BRITISH AND AMERICAN. The modern poetic (or lyric) s. (m. p. s.) is a grouping of mainly lyric poems and passages (or fragments), usually heterogeneous in form, that tend to interact as an organic whole. Although a m. p. s. may well include narrative, dramatic, and ratiocinative elements, its structure is finally lyrical. That is, it is comparable to the characteristic structure of the modern lyric as it has evolved under symbolist, surrealist, and imagist transformations. Its dynamics are primarily emotive and associative, the result of strategic juxtaposition of separate poems and passages without a superimposed logical or fictional continuity. It is, in fact, a modern lyric poem writ large, its several parts providing the same sort of emotive or apperceptive thrusts of affective lang. in relation to the whole as do the shifts of tonal coloration and intensity in a single lyric. The m. p. s. was developed all but unconsciously by poets in search of longer structures that would be both true to inner associative process and responsive to the moral uncertainties and violent disruptions of the age. It has evolved into the dominant modern mode for longer poetic structures and often has an epic or tragic function.

The m. p. s., whose first fully achieved examples in Eng. are Whitman's *Song of Myself* and at least some of Dickinson's fascicles, is the genre in which major poets have excelled: Hardy (*Poems of 1912–13*), Yeats (the Irish Civil War poems, *Words for Music Perhaps, Last Poems and Two Plays*), Pound (*Homage to Sextus Propertius, Hugh Selwyn Mauberley, A Draft of Thirty Cantos, Pisan Cantos*), Eliot (*The Waste Land*, "The Hollow Men," "Ash Wednesday," *Four Quartets*), MacDiarmid (*A Drunk Man Looks at the Thistle*), Williams (*Paterson*), Stevens ("Auroras of Autumn"), Auden (*Look, Stranger!*, "Hora Canonicae"), Lowell (*Life Studies*). Other ss. incl. some of the best work of Hart Crane, Olson, Guthrie, Berryman, Ginsberg, Plath, Sexton, and Kinnell in America, and Bunting, Jones, Kinsella, Hill, Montague, and Hughes in Britain and Ireland.

The formal character of the m. p. s. is unusually protean. On the one hand, it is generally distinguished from the modern "long poem" (q.v.) by its free deployment of different prosodic forms and shifting focal points. (True, Tennyson's *Maud* offers far more shifts of form, tone, and intensity than do Stevens' "Auroras of Autumn," Auden's "Sonnets from China," and Berryman's *Dream Songs*; but its narrative framework contains it within the limits of an extended dramatic monologue). On the other hand, the m. p. s. presents a more psychologically evocative dynamic than a "linked series" does (see section I above). Such a series—whether formally consistent, as in Shakespeare's or Donne's sonnet ss. or as in Tennyson's *In Memoriam*, or whether more varied, as in Herbert's *The Temple*, Blake's *Songs of Innocence and Experience*, or Housman's *A Shropshire Lad*—may exhibit a certain redundancy or overly thematic slant that interferes with true lyrical structure. And frequently such linked series lack a strong sense of initial (or psychological) pressure—i.e. a directive source of disturbance and response energizing the process of association and realization. In any case, they lack the means to sustain, redirect, or counter that pressure with full responsiveness and control.

The m. p. s. frees us to look at poems of all periods, long and short, in a new way, for its dynamics are those of lyrical structure itself, defined as the overall directive energy of movement—the progression, juxtaposition, and interrelation of all the lyric centers, dynamic shifts, and tonal notes— in a poem or s. The object of lyrical structure is neither to resolve a problem nor to conclude an action but to achieve the keenest, most open realization possible. The best ss. depend for their life on the interrelation of lyric centers—units that present specific qualities and intensities of emotionally and sensuously charged awareness in the *lang.* of a passage, not in the supposed feelings of the author or of any implied "speaker." In the modern period, such centers may be juxtaposed freely. From this perspective, the m. p. s. is a true descendant of the Pindaric ode (q.v.), Shakespearean dramatic poetry (q.v.), and Coleridgean organicism (q.v.) in its formal and dynamic openness, yet uniquely modern in its associative and improvisatory aspects. See now MODERN LONG POEM; AMERICAN POETRY.—M. L. Rosenthal and S. M. Gall, *The M. P. S.* (1983); D. A. Sloane, *Aleksandr Blok and the Dynamics of the L. Cycle* (1988). M.L.R.; S.M.G.

M

MACARONIC VERSE usually refers to the mixing of words, sometimes whole lines, of more than one lang. in a poem, most often for comic or satiric effect though sometimes (and more recently) with serious intent. When m. v. first appeared in earnest in the 12th c., vernacular (Fr.) phrases were interspersed in Lat. verses, but by far the more common practice has been the reverse, salting a poem in a vernacular lang. with Lat. or other foreign phrases (cf. abbreviaions in scholarly prose, and marginal glosses in medieval mss., a practice to which m. v. may be related). Medieval examples may be found in OF and It., are copious in MHG, and are more copious still in ME, though isolated earlier examples exist, notably the OE *M. Poem* (Krapp-Dobbie 6.69–70). In Italy the name of Tisi degli Odassi is associated with the invention of m. v. (*Carmen maccaronicum*, 1488), but Teofilo Folengo gave m. v. its renown through his famous mock-epic *Maccaroneae* (1517–21); Folengo's anonymous Fr. translator in 1606 describes Folengo as the "prototype of Rabelais." According to Folengo the name "m. v." indicates a crude mixture—like that of flour, cheese, and butter in macaroni—and its burlesque appeal. The classic Fr. m. poet was Antoine de la Sablé; in Eng., some of John Skelton's verses are m. But it was Ger. which maintained an affinity for m. v. (Ger. *Nudelverse*) past the Middle Ages the longest.

Strictly speaking, m. v. entails not inserting foreign words but giving words of the poet's native tongue the inflectional endings of another lang. (Lat.), yielding a comic mock-Lat. One of the rare examples of true m. v. in post-medieval Eng. is the short 17th-c. epic ascribed to William Drummond, *Polemo-Middinia*, in which Lat. terminations are skillfully tacked on to the Lowland Scots vernacular. Because it is multilingual and often plays upon carryovers of both sound and sense from one lang. to another, m. v. is most often a learned production, not a species of nonsense verse (q.v.); its comic element usually has a satiric edge. Its learned character has other import: in the ME examples, whole lines of Lat. are frequently inserted as quasi-refrains (see REFRAIN), and since the meter of both langs. often matches, m. v. may have been an important vehicle for transporting the accentual rhythms of Med. Lat. into Eng. Scholarly interest in the form revived in the early 19th c. (citations in Morgan). In modern times, both Ezra Pound (*The Cantos*) and T. S. Eliot (*The Waste Land*) have transformed the m. into a serious and important technique of poetic composition, allusion, and structure.

F. W. Genthe, *Gesch. der maccaronischen Poesie* (1829); M. O. Delepierre, *Macaronéana ou mélanges de litt. macaronique* (1852); J. A. Morgan, *M. Poetry* (1872); *Die Floia und andere deutsche maccaronische Gedichte*, ed. C. Blümlein (1900); Sr. C. Sullivan, *The Lat. Insertions and the M. V. in* Piers Plowman (1932); W. O. Wehrle, *The M. Hymn Trad. in Med. Eng. Lit.* (1933); U. E. Paoli, *Il latino maccheronico* (1959); B. Ristow, "Maccaronische Dichtung in Deutschland," *Reallexikon*; L. Forster, *The Poet's Tongues: Multilingualism in Lit.* (1970); P. S. Diehl, *The Med. Eur. Religious Lyric* (1985); T. Folengo, *Macaronee minori*, ed. M. Zaggia (1987).

T.V.F.B.; U.K.G.

MACEDONIAN POETRY. See YUGOSLAV POETRY.

MACRON. See QUANTITY; SCANSION.

MADNESS AND POETRY. See POETIC MADNESS.

MADRIGAL. A name given to an It. poetic and musical form in the 14th c. and to a different form in the 16th c. and later. The early m., of which Petrarch's "Nova angeletta" (*Rime* 106) is an example, consisted typically of two or three 3-line stanzas with no set rhyme scheme followed by a couplet or *ritornello* (q.v.). The lines often comprised eleven syllables, sometimes seven. Musical settings used two or three voices, the lower of which may have been performed on an instrument. The same music was repeated for the stanzas, with different music for the *ritornello*.

In the 16th c., the musical m. used various kinds of poetic forms—the *canzone*, the *ballata*, the sonnet (qq.v.)—as well as the m. proper, which had become a very free monostrophic verseform of about a dozen 7- and 11-syllable lines with no fixed order or rhyme scheme, although it usually ended in a couplet. The musical settings varied considerably but usually consisted of three to six voices in a mixture of polyphonic and homophonic textures. Many 16th-c. musical mss., notably those by Luca Marenzio, made a point of illustrating the sense or emotion of the text by means of musical conventions, so each phrase of the text was set to its own music. The subjects tended to be pastoral and amatory. Many of these texts are anonymous, but m. verses by Guarini, Bembo, Alamanni, and Sannazzaro were set, as well as sonnets from Petrarch and stanzas from the narrative poems of Ariosto and Tasso.

This later style of m. influenced the Sp. *villancico* (q.v.) and was adopted by composers in Germany, Poland, Denmark, and the Netherlands. Italianate ms. flourished especially in England. Although ms. were imported as early as the 1530s, the Eng. seem not to have begun composing their own until after the publication in 1588 of *Musica Transalpina*, an anthol. of It. music with words in Eng. translation. The It. models made feminine rhyme a consistent feature of these translations. The earliest Eng. poem called a m. appears in Sir Philip Sidney's *Old Arcadia* (ca. 1577–80), a 15-line poem of mixed six- and ten-syllable lines with masculine rhymes. Some later Eng. writers such as Barnabe Barnes use the term m. loosely to designate lyrics in various forms (see also *Englands Helicon*, 1600). Eng. m. composers set verses in many forms, some of which did resemble the It. m.

By the middle of the 17th c., the musical m. was dead in England, and in Italy had been transformed by Caccini, Monteverdi, and others into "concertato"-style pieces with instrumental continuo which would rapidly evolve into the baroque aria. But amateur singers in England revived some ms. as early as the mid-18th c. They have been performed ever since.

K. Vossler, *Das deutsche M.* (1898); E. H. Fellowes, *The Eng. M. School*, 37 v. (1913–24), rev. as *The Eng. Madrigalists* (1956–76), *Eng. M. Composers*, 2d ed. (1948); A. Einstein, *The It. M.*, 3 v. (1949); A. Obertello, *Madrigali Italiani in Inghilterra* (1949); N. Pirrotta et al., "M.," *MGG*; J. Kerman, *The Elizabethan M.* (1962); *Eng. M. Verse*, ed. E. H. Fellowes, 3d ed. rev. F. W. Sternfeld and D. Greer (1967); B. Pattison, *Music and Poetry of the Eng. Ren.* 2d ed. (1970); J. Roche, *The M.* (1972); Wilkins; P. Ledger, *The Oxford Book of Eng. Ms.* (1978); A. Newcomb, *The M. at Ferrara 1579–1597*, 2 v. (1980); K. von Fischer et al., "M.," *New Grove*; J. Chater, *Luca Marenzio and the It. M.*, 2 v. (1981); J. Haar, *Essays on It. Poetry and Music in the Ren.* (1986); W. Maynard, *Elizabethan Lyric Poetry and its Music* (1986); E. Doughtie, *Eng. Ren. Song* (1986); I. Fenlon and J. Haar, *The It. M. in the Early 16th C.* (1988). E.D.

MAGYAR POETRY. See HUNGARIAN POETRY.

MAITHILI POETRY. See INDIAN POETRY.

MAKARS. See SCOTTISH CHAUCERIANS; SCOTTISH POETRY.

MAL MARIÉE. An OF lyric genre, within the larger class of women's songs, in which a woman complains of her marriage, often arranged by her father against her will, or of her boorish husband. The poet overhears her lament, or witnesses an argument between her and her husband, or sees her meet her lover, or attempts to console her himself, or hears two women confiding in one another. In a variant type a nun wishes her lover would deliver her from the convent. The metrical form is variable, incl. motets, rondeaux, ro-

trouenges, ballettes, and chansons (qq.v.). Numerous examples are attested among OF lyrics of the 13th c., in the 15th–16th cs., and among modern folksongs; the medieval genre is also well represented in It. and, more rarely, in Occitan (where it is termed the *gilozesca*), Galician, Sp., and ME. The heroine finds a counterpart in Chaucer's May of the *Merchant's Tale*. For Bec, the origin of the m. m. is to be sought among Fr. popular songs of the Middle Ages which must have co-existed with the early artistic versions.—Bec; D. Evans, "Marie de France, Chrétien de Troyes, and the *m. m.,*" *Chrétien de Troyes and the Troubadours*, ed. P. S. Noble and L. M. Paterson (1984). W.D.P.

MALÁHÁTTR. See FORNYRÐISLAG.

MALAY POETRY.

    I. OLDER AND FOLK MALAY POETRY
    II. MODERN MALAY (MALAYSIAN) POETRY

I. OLDER AND FOLK MALAY POETRY is highly romantic and usually derivative of Persian, Indian, Urdu, and Arabic forms, telling tales of aristocratic life and adventures. It does not possess great formal variety. The *shair*, the verscform for narrative poetry, employs monorhymed quatrains and dates from ca. 1600 A.D. In addition to romantic narrative, *shair* also record local conflicts and, in some instances, impart religious knowledge. More enduring, and therefore more important, is M. folk poetry, which is composed of three principal genres: *sesmomba* or *bahasa berirama*, a kind of unrhymed rhythmical verse usually of magical origin and utility; *peribahasa* (proverbs); and *pantun* (q.v.), constructed of two couplets, rhyming *abab*, the first (known as the *sampiran*) more or less general and the second in some way a narrowing or application of the first. *Bahasa berirama* is probably the oldest of the three genres; it survives today largely in Minangkabau (Sumatran) poetry. It is chanted by a *pawang* (reciter of spells):

> Ha, you disturber of the peace,
> Noise-maker,
> Iron pins grow on my arms,
> Copper pins grow on my legs,
> I've snake poison in my beard,
> Crocodiles hold open my mouth,
> Tigers roar my roar,
> Elephants trumpet with my voice.

M. proverbs are intensely metaphorical and, because the lang. is highly compressed, can be powerfully effective. *Jang rebah, dintidih*: He that falls is pushed farther down. *Anjing ditepak kepala menjengkit ekor*: Pat a dog's head and his tail stands up. "Not even in Fr. is it possible to be so polite, or so rude, or to say such rude things with every appearance of exaggerated courtesy" (*M. Sayings*).

The most commonly employed and most influential M. folk poetry form is the *pantun* (q.v.—the Eng. and Fr. spellings are "pantoum"):

Where have you gone to, where were
you from?
Weeds grow taller than grain.
What year, what month will time have
spun
Around to when we meet again?

Both sung and recited as well as read, the *pantun* continues to be employed in rural Malaysia and exercises a significant influence on modern M. p. (below).

II. MODERN MALAY POETRY is very different from Indonesian poetry (q.v.), which like it draws from M. roots. Indonesian poetry is largely directed toward a small, highly educated, urban elite; modern M. p. seeks to be read and appreciated by all who speak Malay, whether urban or rural, and who have at most a secondary education. It is on the whole more open and accessible than Indonesian poetry, simpler and brighter in word-choice and metaphor, though also (esp. to Western tastes) much less subtle and frequently sentimental. The leading poet of contemp. Malaysia is Usman Awang (b. 1929), whose humanistic commitment and poetic bad taste is revealed in lines like "My child and all our children, / Let not their hearts be injured with weapons / Let love bloom on their faces and in their hearts / For a peaceful world, a prosperous life!" (tr. Asraf and J. Kirkup). The "Generation of the Fifties" was followed by a group of writers more interested in imagistic development (and often in religion) than in messages of social transformation. Noor S.I.: "My cup is pure / Drink, my love"; A. S. Amin: "My new life is lighted / By a friend / On the battlefield"; Salmi Manja: "The silent dusk comes alone. / The tabuh beats, the prayer call comes, / And we remember God."

The writers of the 1970s, incl. Latiff Mohidin (b. 1941), Muhhamad Haji Salleh (b. 1942), and Baha Zain (b. 1941), attempt to expand M. p. in more sophisticated directions. Baha Zain Latiff, also a visual artist, works with a vivid poetic vocabulary: "a village of rafts / Floating on the water's skin / A hundred families gathered together / Like leaves of watercress." Salleh, trained in Eng. and Am., probes the nature of M. cultural identity in a time of rapid social change: "The city builds thin walls / Around reality, / Beside canals of acid. / We cannot base civilization / On supply and demand / And old tin mines" (tr. Aveling).

None of these poets, however, has as yet solved the problems of reconciling pressing social and spiritual issues with the demands of a truly effective modern poetry. There is some hope for the future in the increased use of the M. lang. among non-M. communities, and in the government's regular and often generous support of poetry publications. Public interest, too, is high, but the outcome remains uncertain.

ANTHOLOGIES AND TRANSLATIONS: *Pantun Melayu*, ed. R. J. Wilkinson and R. O. Winstedt, 2d ed. (1955); *Kesusteraan Melayu*, ed. R. O. Winstedt, 6 v. (1958); *M. Sayings*, ed. C. C. Brown, 2d ed. (1959); *Mod. M. Verse, 1946–61*, ed. O. Rice and A. Majid (1963); *Selections from Contemp. Malaysian P.*, ed. M. H. Salleh (1978); *Malaysian P. 1975–1985*, ed. A. K. Abdullah, tr. H. Aveling (1987).

HISTORY AND CRITICISM: R. O. Winstedt, *A Hist. of Cl. M. Lit.*, 2d ed. (1961); M. T. Osman, *An Intro. to the Devel. of Mod. M. Lang. and Lit.* (1961); A. Teeuw, "The Origins of the M. *Shair*," *BKI* 122 (1966); U. Junus, *Perkembangan puisi melayu modern* (1970); A. H. Johns, *Cultural Options and the Role of Trad.* (1974); M. H. Salleh, *Trad. and Change in Contemp. M.-Indonesian P.* (1977). B.R.

MALAYALAM POETRY. See INDIAN POETRY.

MANNERISM in lit. has long had the general meaning of affected or excessive use of a peculiar style; recently, in imitation of art history, it has been used to designate a period style between Ren. and baroque. In tracing the origin of the word we must go back to Vasari (1511–74), who used the word *maniera* to mean "impressive and distinctive quality," and more particularly, the ability to join together single beauties into a beautiful whole. In the 17th c. it came to mean affected style, and when it appeared in the form of an "–ism" in the chief European langs. around 1800, it meant more or less artistic affectation. In the 20th c. a major effort in art history has succeeded in imposing a relatively neutral and chronological meaning on the word. Between Michelangelo and Rubens lies the trajectory of a whole period within which flourished artists such as Parmigianino, Bronzino, Caravaggio, Cellini, Breughel, Tintoretto, and El Greco.

If m. were applied to a similar period in European lit. it would include authors like Antonio de Guevara (1480?–1545) and John Lyly (1554–1606), and perhaps others such as D'Aubigné and Tasso. In the case of the first two, the difficulty would lie in distinguishing their style from similar styles in late antiquity and the Middle Ages; and, in the case of the latter two, from baroque. An ambitious scheme deriving from the art-historical concept of mannerist style was attempted by Wylie Sypher in *Four Stages of Ren. Style* (1955). In Donne and *Hamlet*, e.g., Sypher finds a kind of instability which, according to the scheme, existed between the two syntheses of Ren. and baroque. Since 1955, there has been a steady output of monographs, symposia, and syntheses in which m. in European lit. has been proclaimed, argued, and disputed as a major period concept (see esp. ch. 1 and the bibl. in Mirollo). M. is now an established period designation in art history. But its application to lit. still remains insecure, and many prefer to use it in the most general sense of lit. heavily dependent on overly elaborate or ingenious ornamentation in tropes and syntax. Prime examples would be the elaborately balanced or antithetical styles of

Guevara and Lyly, the lush ornate style of Marino, the evocative sensual style of D'Annunzio and Valle-Inclán, and numerous artificial styles in poetry since Mallarmé. Among rhetorical devices used in abundance by mannerists are, to follow E. R. Curtius, hyperbaton, periphrasis, paranomasia, and affected metaphors; among verseforms, lipograms and pangrams, pattern poetry (q.v.), and correlative verse (q.v.).—Curtius, ch. 15; G. R. Hocke, *Manierismus in der Literatur* (1959); R. Daniells, *Milton, M. and Baroque* (1963); A. Hauser, *M.: The Crisis of the Ren. and the Origin of Mod. Art*, 2 v. (1965)—esp. Part Two in v. 1, ch. 3 and 4; J. Shearman, *M.* (1967); G. Weise, *Il Manierismo: bilancio critico del problema stilistico e culturale* (1971), *Manierismo e letteratura* (1976); *The Meaning of M.*, ed. F. W. Robinson and J. G. Nichols, Jr. (1972); M. Praz, *Il Giardino dei sensi: studi sul manierismo e il barocco* (1975); *Problemi del manierismo*, ed. A. Quondam (1975); C. G. Dubois, *Le maniérisme* (1979); G. Gillespie, "Ren., M., Baroque," *Ger. Baroque Lit.: The European Perspective*, ed. G. Hoffmeister (1983); J. V. Mirollo, *M. and Ren. Poetry* (1984); J. Greenwood, *Shifting Perspectives and the Stylish Style: M. in Shakespeare* (1988); J. M. Steadman, *Redefining a Period Style* (1990).
L.NE.

MAORI POETRY. See NEW ZEALAND POETRY.

MARATHI POETRY. See INDIAN POETRY.

MARINISM can usefully be accorded three ranges of meaning: the poetic style of Giambattista Marino (1569–1625); the style of a number of It. poets who may be considered his direct disciples (*marinisti*); and the general influence Marino had on other poets in Europe in the baroque period. As a species of baroque (q.v.) poetic style, m. is closely related to *preciosité* and gongorism (see CULTERANISMO), but less so to euphuism.

Marino's several collections of lyrics, *La Lira* (1602–14), *La Galleria* (1620), and *La Sampogna* (1620), show the baroque gamut of subject matter from sensuality to religiosity. His knowledge of It. poetry was considerable; one finds esp. the influence of Ariosto and Tasso. There is, however, less direct Petrarchan influence than among the socalled *antimarinisti;* instead of ideal, nostalgic, tender love, Marino celebrates actual, languid, sensual lovemaking. His great reservoir, particularly for his most imposing work *L'Adone* (1623), is the whole of polished or sentimentalized mythology to be found in poets like Ovid and Claudian. The "fable" of this enormous poem (5123 octaves) is, in Marino's own words, "narrow and incapable of incident"; nevertheless, he manages to "lengthen it with digressions and other luxuriances." His means are an unsparing use of catalogues, processions, tableaux, and miscellaneous descriptions. The style is characterized by rambling syntax, correlative clauses, inexorably

pursued metaphors; moreover, the lang. is highly adjectival and sensually suggestive.

Granted, within its narrow limits Marino's poetry has a variety and mellifluousness remarkable even in It. poetry. There is also merit in the satirical and burlesque poems, esp. in the *Murtoleide* (1619), directed against the poetaster Gaspare Mùrtola. It is there that we find the supposed "poetics" of Marino ("Fischiata XXXIII"): "The poet's goal is wonder (I speak of the excellent and not the clumsy poet): he who does not know how to astonish, let him take up the currycomb!"

During Marino's stay in Paris (1615–23), there is no evidence that he frequented the Hôtel de Rambouillet (see PRECIOSITE); yet one of its habitués, Jean Chapelain, wrote a "Lettre ou Discours" in extravagant praise of the poet, which he later modified, however, saying that the poem was "a bottomless and edgeless sea and that no one but Saint-Amant has been able to survey it completely." In Italy, of course, Marino's influence was pervasive. His best known direct disciple is Claudio Achillini; yet even his opponents, such as Tommaso Stigliani and Gabriello Chiabrera, could hardly escape his impress. Elsewhere, in England, his love lyrics had a certain vogue, and were translated or imitated by such poets as William Drummond of Hawthornden, Thomas Carew, Edward Sherburne, and Thomas Stanley, though his greatest influence was on Richard Crashaw, who translated, under the title *Sospetto d'Herode* (1637), the first book of Marino's *Strage degli Innocenti* (1632). In Germany Marino's chief debtor was Christian Hofmann von Hofmannswaldau. In Spain the situation was, in a sense, reversed; not only did Góngora occupy any possible place Marino might have taken, but Marino even found himself tempted to borrow from Lope de Vega.

B. Croce, *Lirici marinisti* (1910), *Storia dell'età barocca in Italia* (1925); M. Praz, *Selcentismo e marinismo in Inghilterra* (1925); *I Lirici del Seicento e dell' Arcadia*, ed. C. Calcaterra (1936); *Marino e i marinisti*, ed. G. G. Ferrero (1954); J. V. Mirollo, *The Poet of the Marvelous* (1963); H. Friedrich, *Epochen der italienischen Lyrik* (1964); M. Guglielminetti, *Tecnica e invenzione nell'opera di Giambittista Marino* (1964); C. Jannaco, *Il Seicento*, 2d ed. (1966); C. Colombo, *Cultura e tradizione nell'Adone di G. B. Marino* (1967); D. Alonso, *En torno a Lope* (1972)—Marino's borrowings from Lope de Vega; F. J. Warnke, *Versions of Baroque* (1972); Wilkins; G. Weise, *Manierismo e letteratura* (1976); J. M. Rozas, *Sobre Marino y España* (1978).
L.NE.

MARXIST CRITICISM. In spite of the radical changes that Marxist (hereafter M.) thought has undergone, esp. since the 1960s, the abiding spirit of the crit. associated with the M. trad. can still be traced to Marx's 11th thesis on Feuerbach: "The philosophers have only *interpreted* the world in various ways: the point is to change it." Consequently, M. crit. ought to be seen as more than just another critical approach or interpretive method for analyzing cultural texts. It is concerned, finally, with linking critical interp. to social practice and social change in a world in which men and women recognize and live out their subordination or domination through the everyday experience of cultural forms. While M. critics have always tried to reveal how lit. reproduces existing relations of power, they have also argued that it is a place where power can be contested, resisted, and redefined. Power, at least in modern capitalist societies, is not exercised through coercion but through consent, and so the realm of culture and the expression of ideas in cultural forms have come to be seen as a primary medium for maintaining rule through consent, rather than as an epiphenomenon of power relations that are legislated elsewhere.

In this respect, lit., defined as a canonical body of texts each invested with immense cultural authority, can be seen as an institution for legitimizing and preserving the dominant interests that have historically enjoyed such authority, interests that are usually described as Western, white, male, heterosexual, and recognizably ruling-class. M. crit. has been instrumental in the critique of lit. as an institution and has supported the critical movement to expand the literary canon (q.v.) and curriculum to incl. not only popular lit. and socially engaged lit. (traditional fields of M. interest) but also poems either produced by or explicitly associated with women, people of color, and sexual minorities. So too, the growth of M. attention to film, media studies, and popular music has helped to challenge the canonical centrality of lit. that is traditionally accorded the status of "high" culture. The result of this institutional critique is not only a greatly expanded definition of "lit." and "culture," but also an erosion of the real power of cultural authority that was hitherto concentrated in a small body of texts.

Generally speaking, M. crit. is concerned with the relationship between cultural texts and the social conditions under which they are produced (see HISTORICISM). It proceeds from Marx's perception, no different from commonsense materialism, that "it is not men's consciousness that determines their social existence, but their social existence that determines their consciousness." Thus M. crit. includes many of the concerns traditionally covered by a sociological crit. of lit.: levels of literacy; modes of publication, distribution, and consumption; composition of audience; constituents of taste; questions of censorship, copyright, and propaganda; effects of new cultural technologies; changes in the legal institutions of authorship and in the professional codes of crit., and so on. The more specific aim of M. crit., however, is to demonstrate, in accord with the principles of historical materialism, how cultural texts are a particular kind of product of historical conditions,

and how they contain a particular kind of knowledge about those conditions. While this claim places a strong emphasis on the social determination of culture, it also shares the assumption of classical aesthetics that art, esp. "great" or "genuine" art, somehow harbors the capacity to transcend its moment of social origin and thereby escapes its being defined as ideology. While there are many different definitions of the latter term to be found in the work of Marx and Engels, ideology is generally viewed as the realm of false or distorted consciousness, i.e. ideas which are the intellectual property of the ruling class and whose production is historically specific but which are presented as "universal" and "natural," and thus serve to mask the true relations of ruling-class power.

The early history of M. crit., often referred to as orthodox, reductionist, mechanistic, economic, or "vulgar," is characterized by *reflectionist* theory; Lenin wrote, for example, that Tolstoy held up a mirror to the social contradictions that led to the Rus. revolution. This kind of approach could be described as a sociogenetic version of mimesis, whereby the features of a cultural text are strictly determined by the economic and social conditions of its production and by the class status of its author (transcended in the case of great poets like Dante, Shakespeare, Goethe, and Byron, whom Trotsky, for example, judged to have risen above the "spirit" of their class). Yet despite the many scattered observations about lit. and culture in Marx's and Engels' published work, neither offered anything like a systematic body of aesthetic theory to serve as an orthodox method of M. crit. It was left to their followers, e.g. Antonio Labriola, Franz Mehring, Georg Plekhanov, and even Leon Trotsky, to reduce their by-no-means-strict and often contradictory observations about cultural determination and ideology to a fixed set of interpretive principles, under which texts were seen as ideal emblems of historical processes, mechanistically determined by the social base or economic foundation. Reflectionist theory reached its zenith in the Thirties' espousal of "Socialist Realism" as an officially approved doctrine of crit. and aesthetic practice.

Since then, the bulk of M. crit. has evolved in disagreement with or in opposition to the orthodoxy of economic determinism. The fledgling work done on semiotics (q.v.) in the Twenties by Rus. Formalists such as Viktor Shklovskij, Boris Eichenbaum, Roman Jakobson, and Jurij Tynianov (and later, the more historically and socially minded "school" of Mikhail Bakhtin) called attention to the failure of classical M. crit. to address literary or textual specificity, or what Jakobson called "the autonomy of the aesthetic function." The *literariness* of lit.—its codes of signification, its generic conventions—could not be explained by classical M. theories of direct causality. The synchronic structure of textual relations was as important to consider as the diachronic dimension of historical relations. While Rus. Formalism (q.v.) was later to prove an important influence on poststructuralist Marxism in the 1970s, it was criticized in its day as unhistorical, and therefore stands apart from what is often referred to as the Western M. trad., associated with the cultural crit. of Georg Lukács, Ernst Bloch, Walter Benjamin, Bertolt Brecht, Theodor Adorno, Antonio Gramsci, Galvano della Volpe, Jean-Paul Sartre, Lucien Goldmann, Herbert Marcuse, Raymond Williams, Louis Althusser, Pierre Macherey, Fredric Jameson, Stuart Hall, and Terry Eagleton.

In contrast to reflectionism, Western Marxism has been characterized by theories of *mediation*, which offer more complex explanations of the determinist relation between economic base and ideological superstructure. In mediation there is no direct or easily apparent similarity, but rather an essential homology or correspondence of structures that can be revealed by hermeneutic analysis. Culture *represents* society according to its own laws of cultural production. The meaning of a text's relation to historical processes lies buried, and often transformed or disfigured beyond immediate recognition, at a deeper level of textual production.

In the Hegelian strain of this emphasis on mediation, revived by Georg Lukács, history figures as the ultimate author of the text, moving towards "objective rationality" or the "self-realization of the World-Spirit." Generic or formal features of the text are seen to express or typify the totality of the social process in world-historical terms. Genres such as the epic, the romance, or the realistic novel arise at specific moments to express the contradictions of a particular historical era. "Decadent" forms like those of experimental modernism are associated with a class in decline and herald the erosion of bourgeois individualism. While Christopher Caudwell's critical method owes as much to reflectionism as to mediation, the most sustained attempt to provide such an historicist account of poetic forms is his *Illusion and Reality* (1937), which exhaustively traces the social and political significance of successive technical characteristics in poetry from Shakespeare to the Popular Front.

If, for Caudwell, poetry embodies the "clotted social history" of the period of bourgeois individualism, it also offers access to the collective dream of emancipation promised by historical materialism, in which Freedom is wrested from the necessity of Nature. A more fully developed treatment of this hermenuetic reading of the utopian narrative of history can be found in Fredric Jameson's concept of the "political unconscious." For Jameson, history is an absent cause available only in a mediated, textual form that is itself further transformed by the narrative paradigms of cultural genres. If these generic narratives are ways of organizing, managing, or resolving real social contradictions in symbolic form, they also embody a utopian function because of their appeal to collective fantasies about a better world. It is the task of M. crit. to reveal the allegorical structure of these narratives by reconstituting the link between the collective fantasies they generate and the "unity of a single great collective story," which is the grand narrative of history itself. So too, it falls to M. crit. to "correct" all other critical modes of interp. by returning them to history and thereby completing the tasks they set for themselves. Jameson's conclusion—that the absolute horizon of interp. is always political in the largest sense—is consistent with Lukács's emphasis on the hermenuetic discovery, in each casual detail of cultural form, of traces of social totality.

The theory of *hegemony*, associated with Antonio Gramsci, preserves the interpretive framework of social totality while providing an explanation of the more immediate and local ideological role played by cultural forms in winning consent for the interests of ruling groups. Far from being imposed mechanistically, hegemony saturates and suffuses everyday consciousness as embodied in the "common sense" of most people. It is an unstable process which, to be successful, must include ideas other than the dominant ones—contradictory and often oppositional ideas that are constantly being incorporated, contained, and redefined to suggest a settled consensus. The task of the Gramscian critic is to locate and foreground these oppositional or alternative tendencies as part of the struggle to renegotiate the currently hegemonic definitions of cultural life. Gramscian theory has been particularly important to the influential British trad. of Cultural Studies, which includes the work of Raymond Williams and Stuart Hall (see CULTURAL CRITICISM).

Rejecting the Hegelian critical trad. of "expressive causality," whereby a part expresses the whole, Louis Althusser emphasizes "structural causality," which postulates the relative autonomy of superstructural features from the economic base. Culture is accorded its own effectivity, and can react upon the base. More important for cultural crit., art is understood to be partly independent of ideology. The critics associated with the Althusserian school, incl. Pierre Macherey and Terry Eagleton, affirm this precept, which can be found in Marx, that art has a privileged relation to ideology; in Althusser's terms, it is "internally distanciated" from ideology. What the text does is to transform the raw materials of ideology, illuminating some of the historical conditions of its production but being forced to keep quiet about others. If the text lets us "see" ideology in a transfigured light, it is because it contains gaps and silences suggestive of unspoken events and ideas. The task of the Althusserian critic is (1) to reconstruct the formal processes through which the text has transformed its ideological materials, and (2) to locate the silences and contradictions in the text that signify what it cannot say about social relations. The result is a more scientific critical knowledge of the historical conditions of the text's making: "to know the text as it cannot know itself."

The contradictions which pervade Milton's *Paradise Lost*, for example, can be read in terms of the poem's reworking of Puritan ideology's attempt to cover up some of the truths about the tyranny of its God. Written in the death throes of the Eng. Revolution, the poem has trouble reconciling its author's intention "to justify the ways of God to men" with the need to explain the failure of (God to direct) the Revolution. The opposition between Milton's harsh, cruel, and unappealing God, and the cavalier and heroic Satan, leader of the sympathetic, restorationist cause of the Devils, cannot be directly translated into any reflective opposition among the real historical events that pitted the Puritan rebels against the monarchy. So too, the tyranny of Milton's God is suggestive of the absolute sovereignty of the monarch, yet his structural claim in the poem is to represent Absolute Good and explain the course of hist. to the populace. What can the poem of an honest Puritan revolutionary be allowed to say about a God who had shown himself to be as much a tyrant as the king who claimed his sanction by divine right? This is the question which the poem cannot answer fully because it is ideologically silenced; instead of a direct answer we are left with a palimpsest of suggestive contradictions and incomplete correspondences.

Influenced by poststructuralist ideas about textuality (q.v.), Althusserian and post-Althusserian crit. rejects the binary opposition between text and experience, or culture and society, where each term is given *a priori* and where the reading subject comes to the text with universally assumed resources, competences, and experiences. Experience and subjectivity are shown to be products, effects, or constructions of cultural texts. It is but a short step from here to what is often referred to as the post-M. notion that there is no necessary relation between a text and its meaning at any particular time and in any particular context. The meaning of texts and the power relations that are brought into play by inflecting the text's meaning in different ways are *articulated* differently from moment to moment, and often depend upon the institutional contexts of a reading—i.e. whether a poem is read in a prison or an Ivy League university, whether it is interpreted for a professor or a lover, whether it is quoted in a presidential address or at a family Thanksgiving dinner. In this shifting universe of power and meaning, often associated with the thought of Michel Foucault, the traditional parameters of M. crit.—committed to explaining the relation between culture and society in a systematic way—are barely recognizable. It is in the micropolitical dimensions of such a universe that poetry, long neglected by the epic overviews of classical M. crit., demands closer examination, since poetry expressly calls attention to the questions of subjectivity and its psychosexual/social construction (addressing the long history of syntheses of Marxism and psychoanalysis), lang. and its contingent effects, the body and its circuits of desire, and the surface details and rhythms of everyday life. Increasingly, M. crit. has come to recognize that these more *specific* features of cultural life are as important to the modern understanding of power as once were the *universal* grand narratives of class struggle to a world in which the relationship between culture and society was understood in more objective terms. See also CRITICISM; POETRY, THEORIES OF; THEORY; TWENTIETH-CENTURY POETICS, *American and British*.

BIBLIOGRAPHIES: L. Baxandall, *Marxism and Aesthetics: A Sel. Annot. Bibl.* (1968); D. Peck, "The New M. Crit.: A Bibl.," *MinnR* 2–3 (1974), 7 (1976), 12 (1979), *Am. M. Lit. Crit. 1926–1941* (1975), "M. Lit. Crit. in the U.S., 1941–1966," *BB* 35 (1978); C. Bullock and D. Peck, *Guide to M. Lit. Crit.* (1980); W. Cohen, "M. Crit. in the Eighties," *Mediations* 12, 1–2 (1987–88).

COLLECTIONS: *The Politics of Lit.*, ed. L. Kampf and P. Lauter (1970); *Marxism and Art*, ed. B. Lang and F. Williams (1972); *Radical Perspectives in the Arts*, ed. L. Baxandall (1972); *Marxists on Lit.*, ed. D. Craig (1975); *Weapons of Crit.*, ed. N. Rudich (1976); *Marxism and Art*, ed. M. Solomon (1979); *Feminist Crit. and Social Change*, ed. J. Newton and D. Rosenfelt (1985); *Lit., Politics & Theory*, ed. F. Barker et al. (1986); *Marxism and the Interp. of Culture*, ed. C. Nelson and L. Grossberg (1987); *Universal Abandon? The Politics of Postmodernism*, ed. A. Ross (1988).

HISTORY AND CRITICISM: G. Lukács, *Gesch. und Klassenbewusstsein* (1923), tr. R. Livingstone as *Hist. and Class Consciousness* (1971), *Der historische Roman* (1955), *Writer and Critic* (1971); V. N. Volosinov, *Marksizm i filosopfija jazyka* (1929), tr. L. Matejka and I. R. Titunik as *Marxism and the Philosophy of Lang.* (1973); E. Wilson, *Axel's Castle* (1931); C. Caudwell, *Illusion and Reality* (1937), *Studies in a Dying Culture* (1938); W. Benjamin, *Illuminationen* (1955), *Charles Baudelaire: Ein Lyriker im Zeitaler des Hochkapitalismus* (1969); V. I. Lenin, *O lit. i iskusstve* (1957), tr. as *On Lit. and Art* (1967); R. Barthes, *Mythologies* (1957); L. Trotsky, *Lit. and Revolution* (1960); L. Althusser, *Pour Marx* (1965), *Lenin and Philosophy* (1971); M. Bakhtin, *Tvorchestvo Fransua Rable i narodnaia kultura srednevekovia i Renessansa* (1965), tr. H. Iswolsky as *Rabelais and His World* (1968); P. Macherey, *Pour une théorie de la production littéraire* (1966), with E. Balibar, "Lit. as an Ideological Form," *Praxis* 5 (1980); P. Demetz, *Marx, Engels, and the Poets* (1967); A. Gramsci, *Selections From the Prison Notebooks*, ed. Q. Hoare and G. Nowell-Smith (1971), *Selections From Cultural Writings* (1985); F. Jameson, *Marxism and Form* (1971), *The Prison-House of Lang.* (1972), *The Political Unconscious* (1981), *The Ideologies of Theory*, 2 v. (1987); *Marx and Engels on Lit. and Art*, ed. L. Baxandall and S. Morawski (1973); J. Kristeva, *La Revolution du langage poétique* (1974); T. Eagleton, *Crit. and Ideology* (1976), *Marxism and Lit. Crit.* (1976), *Literary Theory* (1983); S. S. Prawer, *Karl Marx and World Lit.* (1976); R. Weimann, *Structure and Society in Lit. Hist.* (1976); R. Williams, *Marxism and Lit.* (1977), *Problems in Materialism and Culture* (1980); H. Marcuse, *The Aesthetic Dimension* (1978); E. Bloch et al., *Aesthetics and Politics* (1978); F. Mulhern, *The Moment of* Scrutiny (1979); T. Bennett, *Marxism and Formalism* (1979); *Culture, Media, Lang.*, ed. S. Hall et al. (1980); V. Erlich, *Rus. Formalism*, 3d ed. (1981); M. Ryan, *Marxism and Deconstruction* (1982); E. Said, *The World, the Text, and the Critic* (1983); *The L=A=N=G=U=A=G=E Book*, ed. B. Andrews and C. Bernstein (1984); Wellek, v. 6, ch. 5; G. Spivak, *In Other Worlds* (1987); V. B. Leitch, *Am. Lit. Crit. from the Thirties to the Eighties* (1988), ch. 1; P. Goldstein, *The Politics of Literary Theory: An Intro. to M. Crit.* (1990). A.RO.

MASCULINE AND FEMININE endings, lines, or rhymes (Ger. *männlicher* and *weiblicher*, or *stumpfer* and *klingender*). A m. rhyme joins two oxytonic words (i.e. words whose final syllables are stressed), a f. rhyme, two paroxytonic words (penultimate syllables stressed, final syllables unstressed). The terms first appear in troubadour poetry of the 14th c. and are first mentioned in a prosody manual by the Second Rhetorician Jacques Legrand ca. 1405; prior to that time, the usual term for f. rhyme in Med. Lat. and Fr. is *leonine* (q.v.). Both terms derived from the declension of adjectives in Occitan, but they long survived the decay of the inflectional systems of OF and ME as purely technical terms in prosody, so that they now have nothing to do with grammatical gender: in Fr. verse a f. noun by gender if oxytonic will make a m. rhyme.

In Fr. prosody (q.v.), any line which ends in mute *e* (*e atone*) or mute *e* foll. by *s* or *nt* is f.; all others are m. The *e atone* is by convention extrametrical, i.e. not counted for metrical purposes regardless of whether it is pronounced. About its acoustic status opinions differ, some (e.g. Grammont) holding that it has no auditory reality at all, others that it is a true syllable. This ambiguity means that a distinction can still be made between m. and f. endings: the only question is where it cuts. On these grounds a 12-syllable Fr. line whose ending is m. and a 13-syllable line whose ending is f. are both correct alexandrines; but an 11-syllable line is not. In It., by contrast, word-endings of both grammatical genders are so commonly paroxytonic that in It. meters, syllables are counted for metrical purposes as if *every* line-end were f., regardless of whether one, two, or no unstressed syllables actually appear after the final stress. The greatest It. meter, the *endecasillabo*, has 11 syllables including its paroxytonic ending (*verso piano*

[q.v.]), but the 10-syllable *verso tronco* and 12-syllable *verso sdrucciolo* varieties (qq.v.) are also considered metrically hendecasyllabic. In short, the distinction between m. and f. endings does not exist in It. metrics.

Eng. meters, like Fr., ignore the extra syllable of a f. ending as part of the meter strictly speaking. But f. *rhymes* have a different character in Eng.: in Fr., the auditory difference between m. and f. rhymes is, as we have seen, slight at best and nonexistent at worst. But terminal syllables are pronounced in Eng., so carry weight even if slight. Further, since Eng. has lost nearly all of its inflectional system, the f. endings that remain often fall on polysyllables, abstract words that give a more studied effect when used frequently at line-end. Normally in Eng., f. rhymes are true double rhymes, both syllables echoing (*balance/talents, double/trouble*). F. endings have, however, been used in place of rhymes, as Eliot does in the second movement of *Little Gidding*, concatenating the terzines of the *terza rima* by alternation of m. and f. endings (see below).

The preservation of inflections in Fr., however, provided such a wealth of both forms of rhyme that, by the Ren., further regulation was felt needed; hence in cl. Fr. verse from Ronsard to Baudelaire there is a rule that m. and f. rhymes may rhyme only with each other, i.e. prohibiting the rhyming of a m. word with a f. one (*mer, mère*). Further, there is a rule, originating with Saint-Gelais (fl. ca. 1500) but canonized by Ronsard, requiring "alternation of rhymes" (Fr. *alternance des rimes*, Ger. *Wechsel der Reim*), i.e. a rule that once a m. rhyme has been made, the next rhyme in the scheme must be f., the next m., then f., etc. From Fr. practice this rule passed into Ger. and then Polish, whence it passed into Rus. poetry in the 1730s, where its influence was long felt. A number of Eng. Ren. poets (e. g. Wyatt, Peele, Chapman, Donne) experimented with rhyming m. with f. words (*blóws, fúrrows*)—an interesting effect sometimes called "hermaphrodite" (Tatlock's curious term; it rather implies that true end r. is homoerotic) or "Simpsonian" rhyme (see RHYME)—but extensive usage declined in the 18th c. in Eng., largely not canonical, as in Welsh *cywydd* [q.v.] couplets, since the 14th c.) Nonetheless, Eng. poets have never ceased experimenting with f. rhymes. In dramatic verse, they give a sense of colloquialism to speech (very common in Jacobean drama, nearly obsessive in Fletcher); in narrative and lyric verse they have been generally reserved for moments of special poignancy, on account of their conventional ethos, a "dying fall." Spenser avoids them scrupulously in Books I–III of the *Faerie Queene*, then reverses his practice in Book IV. Harington uses them copiously in his tr. of *Orlando Furioso*, but this is to imitate the effect of the It. Shakespeare uses them about 20% of the time, on average (e.g.

MASK

MND 5.1.158), and steadily throughout his career. They have also been used for delightful comic effects (Byron). Edwin Arlington Robinson gives a mesmerizing exhibition of their power in the haunting syntactic frames of "Eros Turannos." See now LINE.—Schipper, *History* 275; P. W. Timberlake, *The F. Ending in Eng. Blank Verse* (1931); A. Oras, *Blank Verse and Chronology in Milton* (1960); Scott, ch. 4; Chambers; H. Suhamy, *Le Vers de Shakespeare* (1984), 243 ff., 309 ff.; M. Tarlinskaja, *Shakespeare's Verse* (1987). T.V.F.B.

MASK. See PERSONA.

MASNAVĪ (Mathnawi). A Persian prosodic form used for narrative and didactic poems in which each verse (*bayt*) consists of two metrically identical rhyming hemistichs (*miṣrāʿ*). Persian m. may represent a blending of indigenous Middle Persian verseforms with Ar. prosodic schemes. A similar form called *muzdawij* was developed in Ar. poetry but never achieved widespread popularity. M. was used for epic and heroic poetry and courtly romance. Epic is best represented by Firdawsī's (d. ca. 1025) *Shāhnāmah* (Book of Kings), a history of Iranian monarchy incorporating didactic and romance materials. Courtly romance, in which the central theme of love often serves as a means for conveying profound ethical issues, reached its peak with Niẓāmī Ganjavī (d. 1209); his four romances and one homiletic poem, later known as the *Khamsa*, found many imitators. Of these, Amīr Khusraw of Delhi (d. 1325) expanded the genre to include topical materials, while Jāmī (d. 1492) adapted its themes to present a mystical conception of love. In the devel. of didactic and homiletic m. Sanāʾī (d. ca. 1130) played a seminal role. His *Sayr al-ʿibād ilā al-maʿād* (The Believers' Journey Toward the Eternal Return) depicts the soul's progress toward spiritual perfection; his *Hadīqat al-ḥaqīqa* (Garden of Truth) uses exemplary stories to illustrate religious and moral topics. Later poets adapted or varied these two models: Farīd al-Dīn ʿAṭṭār's (d. 1220?) *Manṭiq al-ṭayr* (Conference of the Birds) embeds exemplary tales within an allegorical narrative of the birds' pilgrimage in search of a king; Jalāl al-Dīn Rūmī's (d. 1273) *Maṣvī-yi maʿnavī* (Spiritual M.) uses stories to illustrate aspects of mystical belief; in Saʿdī's (d. 1292) *Būstān* (The Garden) exemplary tales are followed by moral glosses. Awḥadī Marāghī (d. 1338) employed an epistolary format in his *Manṭiq al-ʿushshāq* (Lovers' Converse); ʿUbayd-i Zākānī (d. 1371) used m. for satirical purposes. M. was adapted into Turkish and Urdu lit., where it also acquired considerable popularity. See also PERSIAN POETRY; ARABIC POETRY; TURKISH POETRY.

"Mathnawī," *Encycl. of Islam*, 1st ed. (1913–34); J. al-Dīn Rūmī, *The Mathnawī.*, ed. and tr. R. A. Nicholson, 8 v. (1925–40); E. Benveniste, "Le Mémorial de Zarer, poème pehlevi mazdéen," *Jour. Asiatique* 220 (1932); G. E. von Grunebaum, "On the Origin and Early Devel. of Ar. *Muzdawij* Poetry," *JNES* 3 (1944); M. Molé, "L'Epopée iranienne après Firdōsī," *La Nouvelle Clio* 5 (1953); P. J. Chelkowski, *Mirror of the Invisible World* (1975); W. L. Hanaway, Jr., "The Iranian Epics," *Heroic Epic and Saga*, ed. F. J. Oinas (1978); J. T. P. de Bruijn, *Of Piety and Poetry* (1983); F. al-Dīn ʿAṭṭār, *The Conference of the Birds*, tr. A. Darbandi and D. Davis (1984). J.S.M.

MASQUE. The m. is primarily a Ren. form brought to perfection in England. It drew upon various kinds of entertainment that had arisen throughout Europe in the Middle Ages, and in England upon the mummings and disguising that had become popular amusements on festive occasions, put on in the streets as well as in halls and courts. The character of such productions took form in Italy when masked and ornately costumed figures presented as mythological or allegorical beings entered a noble hall or royal court, singing and dancing, complimenting their hosts and, in the course of the entertainment, calling upon the spectators to join them in dancing. In bringing the royal and noble personages into the company of beings of a supernal nature, the entertainments were in effect affirming the relation of royalty to divinity.

The ambitiousness of such a purpose was taken to justify very great expenditures for these productions. In Italy Brunelleschi and Leonardo were called upon to design scenery and to devise machines providing spectacular effects, creating heavenly and on occasion infernal vistas. The masques offered at the Eng. court matched these in splendor.

The It. term used for these entertainments, *maschere*, was taken over by the Eng. as *maske* as early as 1513. While spectacle and song dominated, we should regard the dance as the fundamental impetus, so that there is a point to characterizing both Stuart and earlier masques as substantially invitations to a dance.

Ben Jonson is credited with inventing the anti-m., a briefer entertainment ordinarily preceding the main one, and offering effectually the other side of the coin—comic treatment of the unruly forces and elements monarchy subdues, the grotesque persons contrasting with the gorgeous ones of the main m.

Circe, a *ballet de cour* produced in Paris in 1581, helped set the mode for later Eng. masques in providing greater dramatic and thematic unity than had previously been usual. Jonson's conception of the m. as primarily the work of the poet went further in aiming for dramatic unity; in the preface to *Hymenaei* (1606), he speaks of the theme and words of the m. as its soul, the spectacle and mime and dancing its body. Inigo Jones, however, continued to stress the spectacular, and after ceasing collaboration with Jonson in 1631 was free to give full scope to the most elaborate visual effects. The Stuarts supported his and others' work generously—Shirley's *Triumph of Peace* (1634) was as richly produced as anything under Henry VIII. The interest in thematic and dramatic unity, however, continued, and was strengthened by the new custom of concentrating the action on a stage at one end of the hall.

The Elizabethan theater had made some place for maskings; the informal, improvised kind that was apparently very popular is briefly represented in *Romeo and Juliet*. More elaborate forms are present in *Cymbeline*, *The Winter's Tale*, and *The Tempest*. But the conventions which developed for combining music and dancing with allegory and spectacle excluded the tensions of drama; much of the controversy between Jonson and Inigo Jones concerned the question of how far the presentation of character and meaning were to challenge the choreography. In the Jacobean period the establishment of the proscenium arch led to the devel. of a special form that has been called the "substantive theatre m." With the Restoration, masques were often assimilated in the new operatic works but were also sometimes offered as a special kind of opera, as one may think 18th-c. productions of *Comus* were produced.

Over the past two decades, research on masques has taken new directions, stressing their political content and arguing that they offer representations more emblematic than mimetic. Ignorance of such emphases may lead one to mistake sophistication for quaintness or pragmatic statement of policy for fulsome flattery. Ren. courts did not use masques simply to praise and amuse themselves, but rather to explore in a quasi-mystical way the sources and conditions of power. And while critics have analyzed in some detail how masques are expressions of royal power, they have paid less attention to such expressions by the commons in civic pageantry. To correct this deficiency, some scholars have begun to study how masques are connected to the pageant form, whether in the commercial theater or in civic shows. Work also continues on iconographic understanding of the masques, on actual production techniques, and on the relationship between the elements of lang., dance, and music.

E. K. Chambers, *The Med. Stage* (1903); A. Solerti, *Musica, ballo e drammatica alla corte medicea dal 1600 al 1637* (1905); H. Prunières, *Le Ballet de cour en France avant Benserade et Lully* (1914); *Designs by Inigo Jones for Masques and Plays at Court*, ed. P. Simpson and C. F. Bell (1924); E. Welsford, *The Court M.* (1927); A. Nicoll, *Stuart Masques and the Ren. Stage* (1938); J. Arthos, *On a Mask Presented at Ludlow Castle* (1954); A. Sabol, *Songs and Dances for the Stuart M.* (1959); S. Orgel, *The Jonsonian M.* (1965), *Illusions of Power* (1975); J. G. Demaray, *Milton and the M. Trad.* (1968); A. Fletcher, *The Transcendental M.* (1971); *Twentieth-C. Crit. of Eng. Masques, Pageants and Entertainments*, ed. D. M. Bergeron (1972); S. Orgel and R. C. Strong, *Inigo Jones*, 2 v. (1973); R. C. Strong, *Splendor at Court*

(1973), *Art and Power* (1984); D. J. Gordon, *The Ren. Imagination* (1976); G. W. G. Wickham, *Early Eng. Stages, 1300–1660*, 2d ed. (1980); M. C. McGuire, *Milton's Puritan M.* (1983); S. P. Sutherland, *Masques in Jacobean Tragedy* (1983); S. Kogan, *The Hieroglyphic King* (1986); J. Limon, *The M. of Stuart Culture* (1990). J.A.; F.T.

MASTERSINGERS. See MEISTERSINGER.

MEANING, POETIC. Theories of poetry usually recognize a fictive quality in poetic lang. that distinguishes it from ordinary discourse. Nonetheless, most of these theories also insist on the capacity of poetry to make meaningful statements about the world and the whole range of human activity in it. "M." thus occupies a central role in poetics (q.v.), but its function is more complicated than the simple referential relation of word to thing that characterizes the traditional conception of pragmatic use of lang. in everyday life. For some critics, these complications have mainly concerned debates about the truth or falsity of poetic statements (see SEMANTICS AND POETRY). For other critics, they have involved more sweeping epistemological claims about the special nature of poetic insight or intuition (q.v.). More recent theories of p. m. have evinced skepticism about the capacity of lang. to "mean" anything at all; in these theories, m. is treated merely as an effect of broader semiotic or ideological forces at work in society at large.

I. The simple referential view of p. m. was not seriously challenged before the end of the 18th c. because poetics was dominated until then by mimetic theory, i.e. the theory of "imitation" (q.v.). Whether critics approved of poetry, as Sir Philip Sidney did, or disapproved, as Plato did, they agreed about its ability to make meaningful statements about the world. They did differ, however, regarding the object of poetic imitation. One side invoked Plato's example of the artist holding a mirror up to nature and argued that the words of the poem must correspond to things as they are. The other side, often citing the same example but drawing upon Aristotle's more complex theory of imitation, argued that the words of the poem ought to correspond to things as they should be, not necessarily to things as they appear in the world around us.

This second position was much more influential and accounts for most justifications of poetry before the 19th c. At times, the two versions of mimetic theory reinforced one another, as in Sidney's claim that the poet could combine the concrete example of the historian's "facts" with the general truth of the philosopher and so lead people to desire the good that the philosopher could only define. More typically, though, the literal or "realistic" object of imitation was subordinated to a more universal truth. The poet "does not number the streaks of the tulip," Imlac says in Samuel

Johnson's *Rasselas* (1759); while no detail is too small for the poet's attention, images must be selected from the world around us exclusively for "the enforcement or decoration of moral or religious truth."

Thus for Johnson, and finally for Sidney as well, the poem exists primarily for its message or paraphrasable m., with its propositional content irrevocably separated from its form, which serves merely as a suitable "decoration." Until very recently this attitude toward p. m. was shared by most of the major theorists of Western poetics: Horace, medieval writers such as Dante and Boccaccio, most 16th-c. It. writers, and neoclassicists such as Dryden, Boileau, Addison, and Pope. Even in the 20th c., when Victorian didacticism has been largely displaced by an organic insistence on the fusion of form and content, we may detect an affinity for this theory of p. m. in the Neohumanists, to a lesser extent in the work of Yvor Winters and the aesthetician T. M. Greene, and in the early work of E. D. Hirsch.

II. Around 1800, however, the mimetic trad. was challenged by the growing importance of Ger. idealism, which led to an expressive theory of p. m. (see POETRY, THEORIES OF, *Expressive Theories*). For the idealist, the pure mental expressions of the poetic genius served as a measure of ultimate reality more trustworthy than the limiting illusions of the external world. Disdaining the work of the reason and the analytic, scientific m. that reason discovered in everyday experience, the romantic theorist praised the work of the imagination (q.v.), which Coleridge claimed "dissolves, diffuses, dissipates, in order to recreate" perceptions of the external world in the poetic symbol (q.v.). Drawing upon the work of F. W. J. Schelling, Coleridge argued that, in the symbol, the imagination joins form and content in an organic whole where "the figure, and the real thing so figured, exactly coincide." Rather than decorating the truth—a function Coleridge consigns to allegory—the symbol *is* that truth, the highest form of truth, in that it "always partakes of the reality which it renders intelligible" (see ROMANTIC POETICS).

This connection between theories of expressive m., Coleridge's imagination, and philosophical idealism is significant, for it emphasizes the monistic metaphysics underlying those theories: obviously, the organic m. associated with poetry in romantic poetics is quite different from the propositional m. of mimetic aesthetics, which must endorse some form of Platonic dualism to distinguish between the poem and its referent. Nevertheless, both of these theories assume that some kind of m. accrues to the poetic experience.

III. Other critics, however, have argued that poetry has nothing to do with any kind of m. at all. Most of these critics have rejected any link between the work and the world and instead located the function of poetry solely in its affective impact on the reader. The simplest versions of this position may be characterized as psychological or, following Aristotle's theory of catharsis (q.v.), therapeutic; and they tend to focus on the form of poetry rather than on its content or m. This position was argued by a few 16th-c. It. critics, notably Castelvetro and Mazzoni, and affective theory played an important role in the aesthetics of such later writers as Addison, Du Bos, Hume, and Diderot.

This emergent interest in both the expressive and affective aspects of p. m. substantially weakened the hold of mimetic theory throughout the 17th and 18th cs., and it presaged the more extreme challenge posed by the later 19th-c. aestheticist movements in France and England. Following Gautier's slogan, "l'art pour l'art," the poets of Fr. symbolism (q.v.) and British aestheticism (q.v.) defended the pleasure of poetry as its own justification, an attitude also reflected in 20th-c. formalist movements such as the neo-Aristotelian crit. of Elder Olson and the Chicago School (q.v.) of the 1950s.

In the 1960s this attitude was revived in a very different form in the work of the Fr. writer Roland Barthes. Barthes rejected any attempt to restrict a text to a single m. as the mere "consumption" of writing, proposing instead an experience of pure *jouissance* as the end of reading. Resistant to the restrictive norms of m. as they govern the rest of our lives, the sheer "pleasure of the text" disseminates m. in an infinite plurality that is purely and deliberately "superficial," giving up the security of the signified for the unfettered play of the signifier. For Barthes, as for many of the writers associated with this attitude toward p. m., this freedom takes on a liberating and even revolutionary potential in the face of oppressive social practices, and this potential grants to art an indirect political function that justifies this position against charges that it fosters an empty relativism or that it is impressionistic, irresponsible, and useless.

IV. Other critics have stopped short of the extremity of Barthes' position by proposing forms of coherence for poetic discourse that organize the text without subordinating it to the world through referential or mimetic m. In the early 20th c., I. A. Richards distinguished between the referential discourse of science and the "emotive discourse" of poetry. According to Richards, scientific lang. yields a propositional truth through signs that correspond closely to the things they represent, but poetic discourse makes no such truth-claims. Instead of statements, the emotive lang. of poetry contains "pseudo-statements" (q.v.), collocations that may look like statements about the world but are in fact intended only to arouse emotional impulses in the reader. Thus emotive discourse does not literally *mean* anything; it finally points only to itself. Ambiguity may be allowed and even encouraged, since the denser the discourse, the more complexity it has, and the more effective its organization of our impulses.

Richards' distinction between science and poetry (q.v.) left poetry vulnerable to attacks by more positivistic philosophers and critics. In the 1940s and '50s, however, a different defense of poetic lang. was mounted by antipositivist critics—principally the New Critics (see NEW CRITICISM; CONTEXTUALISM). Writers such as Allen Tate, Cleanth Brooks, and John Crowe Ransom transformed the elements of Richards' dichotomy in order to restore m. to poetic lang. For them, p. m. does not resemble the propositional truth of referential discourse, which they associated not only with science but also with philosophy and all other conceptual systems that made abstract generalizations about the world. Such generalizations try to reduce the complexity of human experience to their own categories of m., these critics argued, and in so doing fail to render the particularities of what Ransom called "the world's body" as it is experienced in all its ambiguity and multivalence. These particularities can be rendered only through the balanced tensions of the poetic context (see TENSION; PARADOX; IRONY). Unlike the abstractions of science, the verbal complexities of poetic discourse come closer to rendering experience in all its fullness.

The purely contextual m. of the poem is neither propositional nor intuitive in an idealist sense; it does not directly tell us about the world around us, nor does it break through to some transcendental reality of a noumenal world. In contrast to referential m., the m. yielded by the poetic context might be termed "presentational m.," which would as Brooks said be an experience "rather than any mere statement about experience or any mere abstraction from experience" (see PARAPHRASE, HERESY OF).

The contextualist emphasis on m. as depending on an autotelic poetic object contrasts sharply with the affective critics' interest in the reader's own subjective experience. For phenomenological critics such as Georges Poulet and Roman Ingarden, however, literary works are situated somewhere between these two poles, where the reader bestows m. upon the work as an "intentional object" that cannot be reduced to the status of either an empirical object or pure consciousness (see Ray). For Ingarden, m. is only one of several "strata" which comprise the "ontically heteronomous . . . work" (362). Each of these strata functions discretely within the "polyphony" of the literary work, Ingarden says, but he claims that m. determines our access to the other strata and "provides the structural framework for the whole work" (29, 100). In addition, m. establishes the literary experience as intersubjective. Although it obviously depends on the reader's cognition of the work, m. transcends the subjective limit of the isolated act of reading by "actualizing" at least part of an "ideal concept" that may be shared by both author and reader (362–64). Thus, although a literary m. cannot be matched to any external standard, nevertheless it can be shared and reproduced consistently, within the limitations of each reader's particular fund of images and associations. According to Ingarden, this reproducible aspect of m. is what makes linguistic communication possible—a view later echoed by Hirsch, who argued that the very possibility of a "valid" interp. of a literary work depends on the willingness of readers to measure their readings against the "normative principle" of authorial m.

V. In a series of works beginning in the late 1960s with *Speech and Phenomenon*, a critique of intentionality in Husserl, Jacques Derrida challenged both the mimetic and phenomenological accounts of m., replacing m. with the differential function of the sign. In the '70s Am. critics quickly extended Derrida's deconstructive critique of "presence" in lang. and the "logocentric" character of Western metaphysics (see DECONSTRUCTION).

Derrida's critique, based largely on the work of the Swiss linguist Ferdinand de Saussure, split the sign into two elements which Saussure called the *signifier* (the material aspect of the sign itself) and the *signified* (the mental image or concept associated with the signifier). Signification or m. is produced by the relation between the signifier and the signified. In every lang. that relation is arbitrary, but it is regulated by the system of lang. (*langue*) in which the signifiers function, wherein the m. of any single signifier is purely differential, deriving solely from *differences among* the signifiers rather than from any positive relation between the signifier and the signified.

Saussure's theory of the sign was immensely influential among linguists and, later, anthropologists and literary theorists in the fields of structuralism (q.v.) and semiotics (q.v.). Saussure's focus on the relations among signifiers led critics to pay particular attention to the structural systems governing specific utterances, gestures, images, and sounds; and in this respect European structuralism often resembles the Am. formalism of New Criticism and other contextualist critics. Like the formalists, structuralists argued that m. is entirely determined by the structural context in which a word functions. The most significant difference between these movements is the structuralists' generalization of structure to include all forms of human social organization and human artifacts, not just poetry. This more universal notion of structure was the antithesis of the specific, entirely local nature of poetic context as described by the Am. formalist critics; and it assumed a continuity among all symbolic systems that contradicted the formalists' insistence on the utterly unique nature of poetic discourse.

Similar as they were, these two contemporaneous formalisms might never have confronted one another without Derrida's seminal critique of structuralism. In "Structure, Sign, and Play," Derrida attacked structuralism for its assumption that the idea of structure itself did not share the contingent, differential character of other concepts, which are constituted through the structural relations of signifiers. "Centering" structure in this way, Derrida claimed, required an essentially metaphysical ground somewhere beyond the structural forms of human expression, an untenable assumption that had always been disguised under the transcendental forms of God, truth, history, and m. Derrida claimed that the propositional truth-claims of any discourse are simply effects produced by particular strategies of reading, and that the "presence" in the text of any sort of truth, whether that of Platonic forms, romantic spirit, or the experiential world of scientific positivism, is merely an illusion that constrains what would otherwise be the "free play" of the signifier in the field of writing. Invoking Saussure's differential theory of m., Derrida argued that "presence" operates in the text only against a corollary "absence," and that this opposition "decenters" m. into an endless proliferation of signification generated by what Derrida calls the textual principle of *différance* (the Fr. term carries at once the sense of both "differ" and "defer").

Derrida's deconstructive critique of m. was adopted by many critics in the United States during the 1970s and '80s, who applied it to literary texts. Paul de Man, Geoffrey Hartman, and J. Hillis Miller turned deconstruction into a technique of analysis that sought in the poem moments at which lang. called attention to the limits and illusions of m. and resisted the aspiration toward absolute closure and coherence. Formalism had identified such moments as the unique characteristics of poetic discourse, but Derrida showed that they were essentially tropological effects inherent in all forms of discourse. Consequently, if deconstructive critics distinguished poetry from other forms of discourse at all, they praised the poem's tendency to undermine the forms of m. imposed on lang. through various strategies of philosophical mystification and ideological constraint.

VI. This association between m. and ideology appears in many forms of contemp. literary analysis, and it has transformed the problem of m. into a more general question of social practice. As a result, critical approaches to that problem today often bear little resemblance to more traditional forms of semantic or textual analysis. A principal source for such crit. is the work of Michel Foucault, who identified the production of knowledge with the exercise of power and argued that the m. of any discourse was merely a consequence of social regulation. Foucault claimed that m. was produced and supported by a "discursive apparatus," the entire array of rhetorical conventions, legal authorizations, and institutional practices that determine who gets to say what to whom in any particular society. In the work of New Historicists (see HISTORICISM) such as Stephen Greenblatt, Foucault's approach results in detailed and specific analyses of the many forms of discourse current at any given moment, esp. as they intersect to produce the m. of a literary text written and read at that time.

VII. Foucault has also influenced many feminist critics, who argue that the m. attributed to some literary works and denied to others has historically been used as a means of excluding texts written by women from serious consideration as lit. Some feminists see this exclusion as purely political, the willful imposition of a set of values (e.g. clarity, consistency, or complexity) as a means of limiting access to power. In this attack on ideological exclusion, the feminist argument resembles the case made by many other kinds of critics for noncanonical writing from a variety of ethnic and racial minorities. Other feminists, however, have argued that the effect of m. involves an even more fundamental relation between the symbolic order of lang. and the gender identity of the individual. Drawing upon the work of the Fr. psychoanalyst Jacques Lacan, these critics claim that the phenomenon of signification in lang. necessarily involves the individual assuming the place of a sexed being who is subject in and to the laws of the symbolic order. Not only is m. governed by an order beyond the individual that controls the operation of lang., that same order actually constitutes the individual's sense of self and his or her position in the social hierarchy. This is why critics such as Hélène Cixous have treated traditional forms of m. as repressive not only of women's writing but even of women's very existence as social beings (see FEMINIST CRITICISM).

VIII. The interaction between individual subjectivity and the symbolic order of lang. is also linked to the production of m. by reader-response crit. (q.v.), though in different ways. Wolfgang Iser, for example, argues that what we usually call the m. of a literary text is produced in a relation established between the text and the reader as the reader responds to gaps or indeterminacies in the work. Iser, drawing on Ingarden's phenomenological theory of literary m., argues that the reader's response is structured by the lang. of the text yet not contained in it. Instead, that response is genuinely dialectical, the product of an endless series of modifications that include some meanings and exclude others in order to grasp the text.

Another form of reader-response crit. has been proposed by Stanley Fish, who, unlike Iser, discounts the importance of textual features and argues that the m. of a literary text is entirely dependent on the "interpretive community" in which it is read. Readers trained to read in one way will "find" a m. in the text that may be entirely different from the m. described by readers trained to read in another way. Influenced by Foucault's work but also indebted to the speech-act theory (q.v.) of John Searle and J. L. Austin, Fish treats m. not so much as a property of the text as a form of behavior, an "act" that is governed by the rules that are constitutive of the community in which that m. is evoked. While both Fish and Iser situate m. somewhere within the relation between the text and the reader, they differ greatly on how that relation is governed and on the relative importance of social and textual constraints on what readers read as the m. of the literary work. See also BELIEF AND POETRY; CONNOTATION AND DENOTATION; DECONSTRUCTION; FICTION, POETRY AS; INTENTION; INTERPRETATION; INTERTEXTUALITY; POETRY, THEORIES OF, *Cognitive Theories*; PSEUDO-STATEMENT; SEMANTICS AND POETRY; SEMIOTICS, POETIC; SIMPLICITY AND COMPLEXITY; TEXTUALITY; THEORY.

Richards; T. M. Greene, *The Arts and the Art of Crit.* (1940); J. C. Ransom, *The World's Body* (1938); E. Olson, "A Symbolic Reading of the Ancient Mariner," in Crane; Brooks; S. Fishman, "M. and Structure in Poetry," *JAAC* 14 (1956); R. Ingarden, *The Literary Work of Art* (1965; tr. 1973); E. D. Hirsch, Jr., *Validity in Interp.* (1967); P. Wheelwright, *The Burning Fountain*, 2d ed. (1967); J. Derrida, *Of Grammatology* (1967; tr. 1976), *Speech and Phenomenon* (1967; tr. 1973), "Différance," *Théorie d'ensemble*, coll. *Tel Quel* (1968), "Structure, Sign, and Play," *The Structuralist Controversy*, ed. R. Macksey and E. Donato (1972); M. Foucault, *Archaeology of Knowledge* (1969; tr. 1972); G. Graff, *Poetic Statement and Critical Dogma* (1970); R. Barthes, *The Pleasure of the Text* (1973, tr. 1975); P. M. Wetherill, *The Literary Text* (1974); M. Krieger, *Theory of Crit.* (1976); W. Iser, *The Act of Reading* (tr. 1978); P. de Man, *Allegories of Reading* (1979); H. Cixous, "Laugh of the Medusa," *L'arc* (1975), tr. *Signs 1* (1976); S. Fish, *Is There a Text in This Class?* (1980); W. Ray, *Literary M.* (1984); S. Greenblatt, *Shakespearean Negotiations* (1988); J. K. Sheriff, *The Fate of M.* (1989). M.K.; M.CL.

MEASURE. (A) Since "meter" and "m." both derive from Gr. *metron* (q.v.), which itself means m., they are often used nearly synonymously, in a general sense, to refer to the system of organization in a poem or the units which comprise that system; thus in hymnody "common m." is also frequently referred to as "common meter" (see BALLAD METER). (B) In musical theories of prosody (see METER; PROSODY), which are based on the analogy of the verse m. to the bar in music, the metrical unit always begins with a stress and is usually referred to as a m. (C) Historical meanings of m. include "tune," as early as the 14th c., and "dance," as early as the 16th.

(D) However, there is another sense in which the terms "meter" and "m." are more divergent in reference, the latter associating itself more closely with "rhythm" (q.v.) in a broader and looser sense than the more precise senses that the term "meter" suggests. In a regular meter there is but one base foot or metrical unit, variations being strictly controlled, but in loose metrical verse or free verse (q.v.), the ms. may vary considerably in size and shape depending on how they are scanned. Indeed, the crucial point to recognize about all systems of scansion which employ ms. rather than feet is that the successive ms. in the line are dissimilar, disparate, and frequently unpredictable, unlike the predictable regularities of foot verse. Prior to the advent of free verse in Eng., the m. was mainly associated with music or musical scansion ([B] above). It is precisely because "m." connotes regular ordering that free-verse ms. must be based on principles radically divergent from traditional prosody if they are to avoid being found simply a contradiction in terms (see VARIABLE FOOT).

(E) In other langs., however—most of the Romance prosodies, for example (see Scott)—the m. has long been a fundamental and constitutive element of metrical analysis. In these systems the verse ms. conform to the natural phrasal groupings of the lang., each phrase having its dominant phrase-stress and demarcated by pauses of differing degree (see FRENCH PROSODY; METER).

(F) In the largest sense m. is a general trope for poetic order, even poetic epistemology, acknowledged by critics and poets alike: both W. K. Wimsatt, Jr., and William Carlos Williams held that verse must be measured in order to be verse. Indeed, m. is the key concept in Williams' thought. It is only by the act of measuring, Williams insisted, that we come to know the world. When we encounter something unknown, our standard of measurement can only be what we already know; hence the measurements of cognition necessarily entail recognition. The operations of m. in verse reflect this epistemological repetition, in that m. involves the structuring of lang. to come by reference to lang. that has already passed. I. A. Richards attributes this backward-looking aspect of verse to "the influence of past words." When poets measure lang., they allow earlier words to determine the organization of later ones. The more tightly the organization of earlier words controls that of later ones, the more regular the pattern and the more likely it is that the m. is a meter.

In any event, it is incontrovertible that measuring is a fundamental principle of verse-structure, and that such m. in verse realizes itself in and through the line (q.v.); measurement seems to inhere in the very concept of lineation. Perhaps a poet's m. is a meter which, through counting syllables or stresses or both, determines structure within the line; perhaps it is something looser which, through reliance on syntactic repetitions, visual patterns, or the intermingling of end-stopped and enjambed lines, develops patterns between or among lines. Either way, no matter how tightly the influence of past words controls its own internal structure, the line itself measures out lang. in ways that are essential and unique to verse. See now COLON; COUPE; FOOT; GRAMMETRICS; METRON.—P. Habermann, "Takt," *Reallexikon I*; H. Nemerov, "On the M. of Poetry," *CritI* 6 (1979); Scott; S. Cushman, *William Carlos Williams and the*

Meanings of M. (1985).   S.C.; T.V.F.B.

MEDIEVAL POETICS. Like Aristotle before them and Sidney after, the philosophers and poets of med. Europe speculated about the nature, the kinds, and the functions of poetry in order to illuminate an art they cherished. Their claims for it were, for the most part, comparatively modest. The notion of a poetic imagination (q.v.) which could supplant nature's brazen world with a golden one was not given to them. Artistic originality (q.v.) was often equated in Platonic thought with falsification (see FICTION). Lit. was praised for its didactic efficacy, its ability to offer salutary instances of good and evil (see DIDACTIC POETRY), but nobody imagined that it could modify the moral sensibilities of an audience in the Aristotelian manner. Nevertheless, many learned and engaged minds applied themselves during the Middle Ages to questions bearing on p. They kept the intellectual trad. of Cl. p. (q.v.) alive and prepared the ground for the great theoretical undertakings of Ren. p. (q.v.).

At Byzantium, accurate and perceptive reflections on Aristotle's *Poetics* appear in the *Suda* (late 10th c.). These did not, however, reach the West until the 16th c., and indeed, an accurate text of the *Poetics* was not available in the West until 1500 (Gr. text 1508, trs. into Lat. 1498 and 1536, and into It. 1549). The substance of Aristotle's *Rhetoric*, considerably simplified, was preserved in Cicero's *De oratore* and *Topica*. Throughout late antiquity, rhet. had as large a role as grammar—which meant basically the study of poetry—in generating theoretical reflections about lit. By the 4th c., rhetoricians, teachers of the arts of persuasion, were claiming that Virgil really belonged to them and that the *Aeneid* was an argumentative, lawyerly defense of its hero's actions. This emphasis on rhet. maintained itself into the Ren. The text on p. best known in the Middle Ages, Horace's *Ars poetica*, was regularly quoted, and in the 12th c. it occasioned a certain amount of emulation, but it does not seem to have inspired much reflection.

The allegorical interp. of poetry was practiced in Cl. antiquity and, following a complicated series of Jewish and Christian adaptations, magisterially applied to Scripture by Augustine. The first half of Augustine's *De doctrina christiana* is devoted to a grammatical analysis of the Bible, the second to a rhetorical one. Under the heading of grammar, he gives classic expression to the theory, developed earlier by the Egyptian schools of Scriptural exegesis, that the Old Testament was allegorical throughout and that all interpretive difficulties could be resolved by an appeal to a hidden Christian significance placed in the text by God (see INTERPRETATION, FOURFOLD METHOD). Elsewhere he grounds this view in a theory of history, asserting that God has installed meanings not only beneath the words of the Old Testament but within the historical facts it relates. An emphasis on exploring these hidden meanings pervades the med. sense of textuality (q.v.). Lactantius and others had maintained earlier that the *Aeneid*, Book Six in particular, contained Christian allegory (q.v.), though for the most part this was ascribed to God's purposes rather than Virgil's. In the 6th c., Fulgentius' *De continentia Vergiliana* proposed that Virgil hid profound philosophical truths in the poem and analyzed it as a vast allegory describing the three ages of man and the passage from nature to wisdom to felicity.

Grammar and rhet. are the announced subjects of the first two chapters ("De metris" and "De poetis") of Isidore of Seville's *Etymologiae* (ca. 560–636), a conscientious but poorly informed digest of Greco-Roman, late antique, and Patristic doctrine, distantly related to Aristotelian mimetic theory, and med. Europe's most influential encyclopedic statement about poetry. This is a work of conservation rather than original thought, an effort to preserve and order the remnants of a shattered trad. Defining a *carmen* as a metrical composition, Isidore offers a shaky generic classification and settles, for purposes of definition, on the distinction between poetry, history, and fable. History deals with what actually happened, poetry with what might have happened, fable with what could not possibly have happened. Isidore (rather inconsistently) follows Lactantius in defining the poet as one who disguises historical fact in a gracefully indirect, figurative manner. Not every metrical composition is a poem. Comedy deals with joyous events and private persons of low moral character with the aim of reprehending vice. Tragedy is a mournful song which tells of the deeds and the crimes of ancient kings "while men look on." It employs "fictional plots fashioned to an image of truth." In drama the characters speak and the author does not. Only the author speaks in the *Georgics*. In the *Aeneid* both author and characters speak. Despite its manifest inadequacies, the *Etymologiae* remained a major source of information throughout the Middle Ages, and was cited with great respect into the Ren.

Comparatively well informed Carolingian comments on drama appear in the 8th-c. Terentian scholia. These contain, untypically, bits of solid information on staging and dialogue. Their moral doctrine is somewhat more inclusive than Isidore's: drama instructs by offering images of both vice and virtue to be avoided or emulated. This view made a more spectacular appearance in the distorted Lat. tr. of Averroes' commentary on Aristotle's *Poetics* made by Hermannus Alemannus in 1256. (The *Poetics* itself was tr. in 1278 by William of Moerbecke, but appears to have received almost no notice.) Averroes had never seen a play and probably never read one. He supposed that a tragedy was a narrative poem recited in public, and so rigorously transposed all of Aristotle's dramatic terms into strictly ethical ones, beginning by translating tragedy as "praise" and comedy as "blame." Tragedy imitates the deeds of virtuous men in order to inspire virtue in the audience. (The tragic flaw is not mentioned.) Comedy imitates evil actions in order to reprehend vice and encourage avoidance. Averroes was read in the Middle Ages and even into the Ren., though evidently not very widely; the extent of his influence is disputed.

In the 13th c., Vincent of Beauvais' *Speculum doctrinale* situates Isidore's traditional claims for poetry next to a revolutionary one extracted from Alfarabi's *De divisione naturae*: "Alfarabi says that it is proper to poetry to cause by discourse something which is not really fair or foul to be imagined as such by an auditor so that he will believe and either shun it or accept it, since although it is certain that it is not thus in truth, still the souls of the auditors are stirred to shun or desire the thing imagined" (3.109). Imagination—*imaginatio* or *ingenium*—figures prominently elsewhere in 12th-c. Lat. speculation about the powers of the soul, but Vincent's citation is the first med. European text to connect it with the appeal of poetry. He does not explore the connection, however, and concludes by reformulating Evanthius' 4th-c. observation that tragedy begins in joy and ends in misery, while comedy does the opposite.

He also says that Alfarabi took poetry to be the least reliable branch of logic, producing a simulacrum of proof. Alfarabi had in fact removed poetry from Aristotle's class of productive arts and placed it in the Organon, thus associating it with the operations and powers of the mind. This is what Aquinas, a fine poet himself, had in mind when he called poetry the lowest of the sciences and when he observed that it had very little of the truth about it. The poet, he says, "leads the mind aside" by his metaphors and figures. This is not a derogation of poetry but a reference to its imaginative origins and a crucial advance from the unreflectively mimetic assumptions of prescholastic comments on art, like those of Hugh of St. Victor, which tend to treat the poet's craft in much the same terms as the tinker's. It is also a corollary of the scholastic view that truth was *formalissima*, obtained from the scrutiny of abstract essences and not from images of everyday reality or the stuff of concrete experience, and not far removed from 16th-c. notions about poetry as a tissue of enthymemes or "weak proofs."

During the 12th and 13th cs., the texts known collectively as the *artes poeticae* ("arts of poetry"; the major texts are collected in Faral) employ a strictly rhetorical vocabulary to describe the composition of a poem. The poet, like the orator of Aristotle and Cicero, invents material by consulting the topics or commonplaces (*inventio*). He thereupon disposes it (*dispositio*) and decorates the result with appropriate tropes (*elocutio*). The best known *ars poetica*, Geoffrey of Vinsauf's *Poetria nova*, strongly emphasizes premeditation: the poet proceeds like an architect, drawing a plan before building the house. One great resource of art is *amplificatio* (see AMPLIFICATION), the process of turning a short poem into a long one and a long poem into one even longer. He has little to say about endings and nothing about middles or about coherent devel. in general. John of Garland's *Parisiana poetria* offers a list of topics along with advice on amplifying. He recommends the diagrammatic aids to memory which Cicero borrowed from Aristotle and provides a diagram of his own—the so-called Wheel of Virgil—for help in finding images appropriate for each level of style, high, middle, and low. As Bede had done long before in his *De arte metrica*, John offers information not only about Cl. meters but about contemporary accentual ones. These treatises were, to be sure, written for schoolboys, but so was the logical treatise of Peter of Spain which represented the state of the art. Despite their practical tenor, the treatises were presented and regarded as major statements. Other important specimens of the genre include Alexander of Ville Dei's *Doctrinale*, Matthew of Vendome's *Ars versificatoria*, and the *Laborintus* of Eberhard the German.

The most popular format for 12th- and 13th-c. literary commentary and analysis was provided by the *accessus ad auctores*. These were partly biographical, partly interpretive schoolroom introductions to major authors, with antecedents in the prologues of Servius. The richest example is the 12th-c. *Dialogus super auctores* of Conrad of Hirschau. Among the ancients, Conrad says, seven things were required for the sufficient discussion of a book: author and title, type of poem, intention of the writer, order and number of books, and explanation. The moderns, however, favor another scheme: material treated, author's intention, final cause of the work, and branch of philosophy to which it belongs. In the 12th c., the branch of philosophy was customarily ethics. An *accessus* to Ovid's *Epistles*, for example, would class it as a work of moral philosophy, maintaining that the author's intention throughout was to praise chaste love, reprehend shameful love, and invite us to live chastely ourselves. In the 13th c., by contrast, the branch of philosophy is frequently logic. Much 12th-c. Scriptural commentary adopts the pattern of the secular *accessus*, a tendency now thought to be related to the increasing concern of the time with the literal and historical significance of the Old Testament.

Bernardus Silvestris, one of the leading spirits of the 12th-c. Neoplatonic revival, followed Fulgentius in claiming that Virgil was an allegorist who hid profound philosophical truths beneath the beauty of his poetry. He was no doubt thinking of his own cosmological epic *De mundi universitate* when he distinguished Scriptural *allegoria* as a vehicle for revealed truth from *integumentum* or *involucrum*, his terms for a hidden philosophical wisdom. This sapiential emphasis continued and culminated in the poetry of Dante, who distinguishes in the *Convivio* between the allegory of the poets and the allegory of the theologians, claiming that he had covertly installed profound philosophical statements beneath the surface of his *canzone* to the *donna gentile*, poems which the rest of the world had erroneously taken to be expressions of mere passion. The *Vita nuova* describes the invention of the *dolce stil nuovo* (q.v.), which he regarded as a recovery of the practice of the ancients, who were both poets and sages. The foundations of the *dolce stil* were, he maintained, assiduity in art and the cultivation of knowledge.

In the 24th canto of the *Purgatorio*, Dante explains the difference between his verse and that of his Sicilian predecessors, themselves the continuators of the troubadour (q.v.) trad. The Occitan poets had invented or perhaps borrowed from the Arabs an entirely novel theory of poetic inspiration (q.v.), locating it in the exalted joy and vigor which was paradoxically kindled by a socially refined but sexually passionate love for an unattainable lady. Dante appears to have seen their exaltations and laments as insufficiently reflective and analytical. His own verse, he claims, is a precisely observed transcription of the emotions inspired by Love. This is what his friend Guido Cavalcanti had in mind when, in his canzone "Donna mi prega," he refused to write about affairs of the heart without *naturel dimostramento*, "scientific demonstration." The true poet is passionately and accurately wise, and it is this kind of wisdom which, in Limbo, made Dante the sixth member of a company which includes Virgil, Homer, Lucan, Ovid, and Horace.

The dedicatory epistle to the *Paradiso*, addressed to Dante's patron Can Grande della Scala, is in outline a traditional *accessus*, though it is probably not by Dante. Its definition of comedy and tragedy is traditional, its account of allegory Augustinian. Perhaps its most Dantesque assertion concerns the method of treatment, which balances five logical modes against five literary ones (poetic, fictive, descriptive, digressive, metaphorical).

Genuine or not, this allusion to an imaginative realization of philosophical truth is basic to Dante's conception of art. In his unfinished *De vulgari eloquentia* (ca. 1303), he conducts a search for an It. poetic lang. appropriate to verse which aspires to the same lasting fame as that of the ancients. This would be a standard dialect divested of provincial peculiarity and worthy to be spoken at the royal court of Italy, if only Italy had a royal court. The subjects—lofty ones—fit for such a lang. are considered. The matter of form and style leads to an unprecedented analytical survey of contemp. poetic practice in Italy, Provence, and France. This expertly principled and engaged account of verse writing in Dante's time decisively transcends the med. speculative trad. and indeed makes much 15th-c. It. theorizing and commentary seem dim by comparison.

See now MEDIEVAL POETRY. For discussion of Med. Lat. poetry see LATIN POETRY, *Medieval*. For discussion of the transition from Med. Lat. poetry and p. to the vernaculars, see FRENCH PROSODY; ITALIAN PROSODY; SPANISH PROSODY; SECONDE RHETORIQUE; then see ENGLISH PROSODY; GERMAN PROSODY. See also HEBRAISM; HEBREW PROSODY AND POETICS; HERMENEUTICS; INTERPRETATION, FOURFOLD METHOD; RENAISSANCE POETICS.

PRIMARY WORKS: Migne, *PL*; Migne, *PG*; Keil—texts of the chief Med. Lat. prosodists and grammarians; Bernardus Silvestris, *De mundi universitate libri duo*, ed. C. S. Baruch and J. Wrobel (1876), *Commentary on the First Six Books of* The Aeneid, ed. E. Schreiber and T. Maresca (1979); Fulgentius, *De Virgiliana continentia*, ed. R. Helm (1898); Isidore of Seville, *Etymologiae sive originum libri*, ed. W. M. Lindsay, 2 v. (1911); E. Faral, *Les arts poétiques du XIIe et du XIIIe siècles* (1924)—texts of the major Med. Lat. treatises on p. with commentary; K. Abbott, *Prolegomena to an Ed. of the Pseudo-Servian Commentary on Terence*, Diss., Univ. of Illinois (1934); Hugh of St. Victor, *Didascalion*, ed. C. H. Bottimer (1939); Conrad of Hirschau, *Dialogus super auctores*, ed. R. B. C. Huygens (1955); Dante, *De vulgari eloquentia*, ed. A. Marigo, 3d ed. (1957), tr. with commentary M. Shapiro (1990); Augustine, *De doctrina christiana*, ed. G. M. Green (1963); Hermannus Alemannus, *Averrois Cordubensis commentum medium in aristotelis poetriam*, ed. W. F. Boggess, Diss. Univ. of No. Carolina, (1965); Vincent of Beauvais, *Speculum doctrinale* (1624, rpt. 1965); John of Garland, *Parisiana poetria*, ed. and tr. T. Lawler (1974); *Cl. and Med. Lit. Crit.*, ed. A. Preminger et al. (1974)—trs. with good commentary, esp. Hardison on Averroes.

SECONDARY WORKS: C. S. Baldwin, *Med. Rhet. and Poetic to 1400* (1928); G. Pare et al., *La Ren. du XIIe siècle* (1933); H. I. Marrou, *St. Augustin et la fin de la culture antique* (1938); B. Smalley, *The Study of the Bible in the Middle Ages* (1941); E. de Bruyne, *Etudes d'esthétique médiévale*, 2 v. (1946); W. F. J. Knight, *St. Augustine's* De musica: *A Synopsis* (1949); Curtius—magisterial; R. R. Bolgar, *The Cl. Heritage and Its Beneficiaries* (1954); E. Auerbach, "Figura," *Scenes from the Drama of European Lit.* (1959), *Literary Lang. and Its Public in Late Lat. Antiquity and the Middle Ages* (1965); P. Zumthor, *Langue et techniques poétiques a l'époque romane* (1963), *Essai de poétique médievale* (1972); Murphy; E. Vinaver, *À la récherche d'une poétique médiévale* (1971); W. W. Wetherbee, *Platonism and Poetry in the 12th C.* (1972); J. Allen, *Ethical Poetics in the Later Middle Ages* (1983); W. Trimpi, *Muses of One Mind* (1983); Norden; L. Ebin, *Vernacular Poetics in the Middle Ages* (1984); A. J. Minnis, *Med. Theory of Authorship* (1984); B. Stock, *The Implications of Literacy: Written Lang. and Models of Interp. in the 11th and 12th Cs.* (1986); *Med. Literary Theory and Crit., ca. 1100–1375: The Commentary Trad.*, ed. A. J. Minnis and A. B. Scott (1988); M. Shapiro, De vulgari eloquentia: *Dante's Book of Exile* (1990).

P.D.

MEDIEVAL POETRY.

"Medieval poetry" is not a definite term. Some critics have worked to discover and describe latent unity in the lit. of med. western Europe in studies of genres like hymnography, dramaturgy, and mythology, or of the arts of prosody, music, and rhet., while some aestheticians and historians like de Bruyne, Curtius, Auerbach, and Bezzola have tried to distinguish an essentially med. poetic vigor. Still others look upon med. poetry as de-based classicism (q.v.) or a primitive stage of the several national lits.

Except for fragments of oral poetry (q.v.) caught up in letters, our heritage from the Middle Ages consists of works designed to be read or to be recited in accordance with a script. It is therefore literary poetry. The roots of literary poetry are Lat. to bedrock. Lat. Christianity introduced from the Alps to Iceland an alphabet, writing materials, schools and libraries, and an idiom primarily developed for religious expression by a clerical class. It fused elements of Semitic and Hellenic diction, syntax, and figure with the Roman imperial lang. This Christianity embraced Celtic, Teutonic, and Scandinavian peoples who had developed indigenous oral poetries; and it was affected, too, by the Arab world and, lightly, by Byzantium. In the course of ten centuries Western social systems changed radically both as a whole and regionally. Consequently there are marked diversities, first as the exclusive cultures acquired the Lat. arts, then as vernaculars, now Latinized in varying degree, became literary and spread from clerical to noble and bourgeois classes. Particularly from the 7th to the 12th c. did regional poetry receive its Lat.-Christian impress, which makes the "Western trad."

I. LATIN POETRY. Esp. in the century following the Nicene Council (A.D. 325), brilliant, rhetorically trained Romans devoted themselves to developing and disseminating Christian doctrine and liturgy. They supplied the lang. of med. poetry, primarily in prose: Ambrose's hymns and addresses, Jerome's trs. of Scriptures (the basis of the Vulgate) and Augustine's doctrinal works expressed insensible realities in sensible terms. At the same time, Roman versifiers like Prudentius and Paulinus turned Hebrew-Christian poetry into traditional Lat. genres. This patristic writing, the staple of early med. schools and libraries, was popularized in sermons, liturgy, and paraliturgy as a unified body of doctrine, trad., legend, and myth which was, or might be, poetical.

A. *Prosody and Verseform*. Med. verse evolved from quantitative meters (technically called "metrical verse" in the Middle Ages) to accentually based meters ("rhythmical verse," "rhythms") and rhyme. The great influx of foreigners, at first from the east and later from the north, affected Lat. metrical purity as early as the 2d c.; by the end of the 4th c., Augustine stated that his students could no longer distinguish between long and short syllables, and the transition from quantity to accent had been completed. Though learned poets continued the composition of quantitative meters throughout the Middle Ages, popular poets developed patterns derived in part from Lat. artprose (see Norden), which had taken on "Asian" flourishes including such homophony as alliteration, homoeoteleuton, and rhyme (qq.v.).

Isosyllabism (as in Augustine's *Psalm Against the Donatists*), which restricted the greater variation inherent in the quantitative system, aided memory and helped to preserve the text. Such Cl. meters as had been isosyllabic (e.g. the trochaic septenarius [q.v.] and iambic dimeter [q.v.]) acquired additional popularity as being simultaneously traditional and modern; at the same time, isosyllabic substitutes were developed for popular Cl. meters like the heroic hexameter, elegiac distich, and Sapphic (qq.v.). Emphasis upon linear units of thought (as in Ambrose's hymns), partly because of choral antiphony, stimulated the growth of patterned terminal rhythms, which became stressed in the Teutonic regions. By the end of the 7th c., homoeoteleuton and assonance, were common, and as Lat. increasingly became a scholastically acquired second lang., these figures of sound increased: by the 12th c., complex di- and trisyllabic rhymes are found often.

Strophic patterns seem to have followed these patterns of rhyme and rhythm. Long lines broke into hemistichs at their rhymed caesuras; thus the dactylic hexameter became *leonine verse* (q.v.). Versifiers learned to double or triple the number of lines with the caesural rhyme. The septenarius was another long verse which evolved into a cadenced stanza. Refrains (q.v.) became more common and more complex. Thus internal rhyme (q.v.) in long-lined verse led to the complex rhyme schemes (q.v.) of short-lined stanzas.

Vernacular and Med. Lat. verse tended to interchange sound patterns, but eventually Lat. predominated. There are a few early attempts to compose Lat. verses in Teutonic stress rhythms. But the Lat. isosyllabism, rhyme, and patterned terminal accent became the Romance vernacular standard. The octosyllable (q.v.) developed from the Ambrosian iambic dimeter; the decasyllable (q.v.) and It. hendecasyllable (though long thought to be Fr.) probably partly from the dactylic tetrameter catalectic and partly from the Horatian Sapphic. However, once the principles were established, both Lat. and vernacular versifiers tried every variation. The sequence, which began from the 9th c. as musical prose, introduced flexibility. By the middle of the 13th c., composers in Lat. had ceased to invent; the vernaculars now led the development.

B. *Characteristics.* The clergy preserved selected classics esp. adaptable to the schools, but Scriptures, including ancillary apocryphal writings and hagiography, were primary. Before about A.D. 1050, the word "poet" or "maker" was hardly ever used for a contemporary writer or versifier, even if he composed learnedly in meters; God was the sole Creator. It was applied to Cl. poets somewhat pejoratively, though Virgil became *Poeta* as Aristotle eventually became *Philosophus*. *Author* was similarly affected. Versifiers were apt to designate their work as *rhythmi, versus, carmina,* but not *poemata.* Reverence for scriptures, that is, lit., exalted the science of *grammar,* and dislike of pagan eloquence (as prideful) depressed *rhet.* Words needed to reveal simultaneously (according to traditional interp.) the highest exaltation and the most mundane sensibility. The polysemous allegory (q.v.) which developed would have been ambiguous beyond understanding were its interp. not anchored in a common doctrine (see INTERPRETATION, FOURFOLD METHOD). This doctrine had to be carried in the mind, for books were expensive and literacy uncommon; hence mnemonic formulas strongly determined med. aesthetics, including use of *carmina figurata* (see PATTERN POETRY), number symbolism (see NUMEROLOGY), etymologies, and topics. The Cl. distinction between the content of poetry and prose disappeared. An author quite customarily wrote the same matter twice, once in prose for meditation and once in verse for recitation. Sometimes, in the model of Martianus and Boethius, he would alternate prose and verse, the form called *prosimetrum* (q.v.), e.g. Sedulius Scotus, *Liber de rectoribus christianis,* and Boccaccio, *Ameto.* Contrast and color, more than formal unity, were desired.

Consequently, genres are difficult to identify. At the early centers of literacy, the basic modes were hymnody, hagiography, and scholastic verse.

1. *Hymnody* was the heart of lyric poetry, and scriptural psalms and canticles its muscle. Hymns (q.v.), defined as songs of praise, were admitted to the Office on sufferance after Hilary and Ambrose led the way. Later, sequences developed in the Mass from extension of Hebraic jubilations like the *Alleluia.* Their melodies spread to the marketplaces as paraliturgy. Med. love of parody and inversion grew with adaptation of these religious pieces to profane use.

From the 10th c., liturgical drama (q.v.) developed slowly out of hymnody by expansion of tropes and use of processionals, until extensive representations of scriptural narrative in the form of Passion and Nativity Plays and Cycles (see PASSION PLAY) came to be presented by the laity as popular entertainment. Concurrently a more secular drama based on legends ("miracles") developed, quite possibly in the schools, since the earliest (Hildesheim) plays are scholastic. Dramatized allegories ("moralities"; see MORALITY PLAY) and professional entertainments ("interlude" and "farce," qq.v.) do not appear to have become conventional before the late 14th c.

2. *Hagiography,* which in the late Cl. period had arisen as *acta martyrum* and *vitae patrum,* was designed for edification; in various proportions it combines Semitic narrative, epideictic eloquence, and "Gr. romance" in pious tales for conversion, meditation, and instruction in manners (see DIDACTIC POETRY). Because in cloisters it was employed for reading in nocturnal office and in refectory as well as for private meditation, demand and supply were high. The Oriental trad. of monasticism determined that Oriental narratives and narrative devices should predominate. The romantic narrative trad. (see MEDIEVAL ROMANCE) is markedly hagiographical: poetized knighthood takes its start from the Pauline arming of the Christian warrior in *Ephesians;* chivalry from the beast and saint of, for instance, Jerome's *Malchus;* peerage (the Twelve Peers of France) from discipleship; quests (*quaerere*) from Oriental seekers, and gestes (*gesta* is hagiographical synonym for *virtutes* and *miracula*) from superhuman accomplishments; love and joy from *amor Dei* and *gaudia christi;* and courtliness from *cohors* (cognate *garden*), which in hagiography combined notions associated with Eden, the pastoral Canticles, the *locus amoenus* ("lovely spot"; cf. Horace, *Ars poetica* 17; Isidore, *Etymologiae* 14.8.33) and the cloister (see DESCRIPTIVE POETRY).

3. *Scholastic verse* was ancillary to the other two, but helped to preserve Cl. trad. for useful adaptations. The scholars, as the only literates, composed occasional verse—epistles, eclogues, epigrams, panegyrics (qq.v.), processionals, and the like—usually in quantitative meters. Secular drama (e.g. the Nicholas plays) developed from exercises based on Terence, a model of style. Scholastic imitations of Roman epics (Abbo's *Siege of Paris*) doubtless affected narrative verse (q.v.). Even textbooks were sometimes cast into meter, partially as models. A most fruitful activity was student composition. Walafrid's *Visio wettini* (9th c.) is a prototype of Dante's *Commedia.* The *Waltharius* may be called the first chivalric epic; it phrases a Teutonic tale in the lang. of Virgil and Prudentius. The *Ecbasis captivi* is a progenitor of beast epics (q.v.), and *Ruodlieb* of the type of psychological tale found in *Parzival.* Scholars provided the often quite imaginative verse chronicles and the *specula* or "mirrors" for leaders of church and state; these ranged from manners and advice to sheer trifles for amusement, in verse or prose.

As the West produced more scholars than the church could absorb, the marked increase in vagrants and wits became an issue, though they had always existed (see Augustine's *De opere monachorum*). They converted ecclesiastical art to a wider public, composing esp. parodies, drinking and love songs, and scurrilities often called goliardic verse (q.v.). Esp. as they located posts in civil life as chaplains or chancellors, they were prime agents in adapting the forms, imagery, idiom, and melody of Lat. verse to the emergent vernaculars of the secular classes. The mendicant orders, esp. the Franciscans (13th c.), composed some of the most moving lyrics (*Stabat mater, Dies irae*) of all time.

Petrarch represents the entire middle age in regarding Lat. as the lang. of true poetry; Dante's exaltation of the *eloquentia vulgaris* as a fit poetical medium is exceptional.

II. VERNACULAR POETRY. A. *Celtic*. The earliest recorded C. poetry dates from the 6th and 7th cs. in Ireland and the 9th c. in Wales (see IRISH POETRY; WELSH POETRY). The tiny remnants of Med. Cornish and Breton poetry (qq.v.) date from the later Middle Ages but show similarities to the Welsh poetry of the same period. No Gaulish or Celtiberian poetry survives, and Scottish Gaelic (q.v.) and Manx must be viewed as dialectal variants of Ir. until modern times. C. poetry shows evidence of direct descent from earlier IE poetic forms (see CELTIC PROSODY; INDO-EUROPEAN PROSODY) and was largely produced, even in the later Middle Ages, by a semi-hereditary class of professional bards (q.v.) whose forebears are the druids and seers spoken of by Caesar (*Gallic Wars* 6). The corpus of Old and Middle Ir. poetry (7th to 14th cs.) is large and varied, that of Welsh smaller but of generally high quality. Surviving C. poetic materials from the early period include eulogy and panegyric as well as legal, onomastic, vatic, gnomic, and historical texts, and possibly some narrative fragments. In 9th-c. Ireland there was a lively trad. of monastic lyric. Whether it had a secular counterpart is open to question.

As in IE, the earliest Med. C. verseforms are structured by line-ending cadences, although these soon developed into or were replaced by syllabic meters. Alliteration and rhyme appear early as ornaments and later become complex and obligatory characteristics of many meters. Both stichic and stanzaic forms occur early and continue to be used. Rhyme seems to have been a native devel. and may in fact have been transmitted to Med. Lat. from C.; the earliest rhyming Lat. verse was produced by Celts. Devels. in prosody during the Middle Ages include, in Ir., the elaboration of a system of generic rhyme (q.v.), and, in Welsh, the systematization of *cynghanedd* (q.v.— "chiming" or "harmony"), in which sequences of initial sounds in stressed words alliterate with their counterparts in the second halfline or subsequent lines.

The extreme complexity of 11th- to 15th-c. Ir. and Welsh professional bardic poetry, comparable to that of the ON court meters (see OLD NORSE POETRY), is often viewed by modern readers as aesthetically sterile. It should be remembered, however, that apparent complexity at the surface does not necessarily imply difficulty of composition or unintelligibility to an initiated audience.

B. *Teutonic*. The verse of the Goths, Franks, Germans, and Eng. was primarily mytho-historical, but they were also given to charms, riddles (qq.v.), and convivial songs. The few genres seem to have been customarily composed in lines of 4 stresses with structural alliteration (see GERMAN PROSODY; ENGLISH PROSODY). The Teutons lacked the lyricism of the Celts: Tacitus speaks kindly of their heroic songs, but Fortunatus complains of the dull thump of their conviviality. King Theodoric, reared at Constantinople, worked as king of the Goths and the Romans to transmit Cl. culture to the Teutonic races; he lived on in Ger. poetry (q.v.) as the hero Dietrich.

The earliest vernacular documents are Eng. and are contemporaneous with Bede's description (*Historia ecclesiastica* 4.22) of Caedmon, the earliest identifiable Germanic poet (fl. ca. 670). According to Bede, Caedmon dreamed a hymn to the Maker of Heaven and Earth; thereafter, monastic doctors taught him Scripture, which he converted to verse for their transcription. Early Germanic verse was adapted transcription (*Widsith, Beowulf*), transference (*Genesis*), or imitation (*Phoenix*) of great poetic power. After the outhurst in the century following Caedmon, OE poetry declined; the later survivals draw nearer Lat. models. Only after the Norman conquerors and their lang. and poetry had been absorbed (12th c.) did a ME poetry emerge. Though fecund and, in Chaucer's verse, magnificent, and though provincial versifiers revived and for a time enlivened some elements of native trad. in the so-called "alliterative revival" (*Piers Plowman, Pearl, Gawain*), this late med. verse depended greatly upon France and, later, Italy for themes and forms.

The early Eng. missionaries on the Continent transmitted Caedmon's art; during the 9th c., Ger. poets followed the methods of their Eng. relatives. The *Hildebrandslied* survives incompletely in a monastic codex as the only transcription of native song; but Otfrid's *Gospel Book*, the *Muspilli*, and the *Heliand* show how Caedmon's trad. was transplanted. Late in the century, the *Ludwigslied* followed the trend of Lat. secular panegyric. Verse gave way to prose until the century after A.D. 1175. That glorious period under the Hohenstaufen emperors is marked by the lyrics of the Minnesinger (see MINNESANG), with Walther von der Vogelweide at the head, and by the beast epic *Reinhart Fuchs*, the courtly tales of Hartmann von der Aue and Gottfried von Strassburg, the psychological and symbolical *Parzival* of Wolfram von Eschenbach, and the epic *Nibelungenlied*. Almost certainly, noble patronage and the exhilaration of crusade and discovery fertilized this bloom, which quickly withered. The 14th and 15th cs., dominated by Meistersinger (q.v.), are crabbed in comparison.

C. *Scandinavian.* Though it acquired a life of its own, Scandinavian may be regarded as a branch of Teutonic (see ICELANDIC POETRY; OLD NORSE POETRY). The lyrics are largely preserved in the Icelandic collections formed in the 13th c. by Snorri Sturluson and his nephews and now known as the Eddas, but were also incorporated in long narrative works known as sagas; these are a rich and independent form, though in some debt to the Ir. Unversified, designed for recitation with appropriate formal conventions of diction, they more resemble poetry than eloquence. Their clear-eyed simplicity and accuracy of observation add force and conviction to heroic tales strongly historical. Composed by the governing class, they were written down after Christianization in the 11th c., apparently without notable change in form. From the 13th c., many poets went to the Continent for education, and their works became romanticized. But the borrowing was not reciprocal, and only in the 19th c. when antiquarians revived the poetry—e.g. the Finnish *Kalevala*—did it measurably affect the Western stream.

D. *Romance.* The earliest verses in the Romance vernacular (ca. 880) are a paraliturgical exaltation of an early virgin martyr *Eulalie* in unevenly decasyllabic assonanced lines (see FRENCH PROSODY). That same codex contains both a Lat. *Eulalia* with lines borrowed from Prudentius and also the *Ludwigslied*; this suggests that monks supplied the matter and form and Teutons the incentive for vernacular composition. A line through the *St. Eulalie* and the *Alexis* (11th c.) to the *Chanson de Roland* (12th c.) indicates the secularization of liturgical form in Fr. *épopées* (see CHANSONS DE GESTE); Bédier and followers have, somewhat overzealously, described how the content accrued around shrines. The approximately 80 chansons, nearly all in assonanced decasyllables, were recited, chanted, and possibly mimed at fairs, markets, and camps. The *Poema de mio Cid* (12th c.), of similar genre, inaugurates Sp. poetry (q.v.). Heroic in the 12th c., the chansons declined later to sheer buffoonery.

A parallel form of narrative was the courtly tale, which seems to have been secular edification growing out of scholastic verse, of which *Waltharius* is a prototype (see MEDIEVAL ROMANCE). The consolidation of feudality in castles and manors, burgeoning of schools, and spread of literacy to the counties induced poetry for a noble class almost as cloistered as the monks. For manorial festivals, clerks composed recitations in *roman,* commonly in rhymed octosyllabic couplets. The content was described by Bodel, one such *trouvère* (q.v.), as matter of Rome, France, or Britain—that is, tales drawn from scholastic classics about Troy, Alexander, or Caesar; or tales of Charlemagne and his peers; or Celtic tales of King Arthur and his knights. Centered in Northern France, these romances spread in all directions, to become poetic models for diverse nations. As might be expected,

the profanity, secularity, and glorification of the individual man on horseback and the *dames* of castellar pallor contrast with the often patriotic and religious fervor of the early chansons, though the genres overlap. Emphasis upon the *tale,* which now attracted an avid audience, resulted in ransacking all sources; the Crusades, not only in Palestine but throughout eastern Europe, Byzantium, and Muslim Spain and Africa, were a fertile supply.

The first extant Romance lyrics were composed by Duke William IX of Aquitaine (d. 1127), and the 12th c. witnessed an outpouring of lyrics in *langue d'oc* (see OCCITAN POETRY). Comparative peace and isolation in the 11th and 12th c. bred, as it were, a group of wealthy prisoners, and their verse, like prison lit., emphasized forms, enigmas, ambiguities, acuity, and surprise, with restricted content. New stanzaic structure for each song, within the further restrictions of rhyme and rhythm, became requisite. The subjects were *salus, venus, virtus* ("safety, love, virtue"; cf. Dante, *De vulgari eloquentia* 2.2.70).

The fruits of this cultivation ripened elsewhere. As civil war and other Occitan disruptions interfered with the art of poetry at home, the poets stimulated others elsewhere, esp. the trouvères of Northern France, the Ger. Minnesinger, the Portuguese, the Eng., and the Italians. The It. lyric began at the Sicilian court of Frederick II (see SICILIAN SCHOOL) but soon burst out in the north, eventuating in the *dolce stil nuovo* (q.v.) of Guido Guinicelli and then Dante and his contemporaries—a spiritualizing and, in some ways, Platonizing of an earthbound trad. Dante's *Vita nuova* and his critical *De vulgari eloquentia* demonstrate that vernacular poetry was coming of age. The *Commedia* was indeed in many respects the voice of ten silent centuries; for if there is a middle age, that poem is at once its fittest representative and supreme achievement. Through long vicissitude Italy had lost but never forgotten its Roman heritage; the new bourgeoisie of Tuscany and Lombardy held the pass from the cultivated barbarism of the north to Rome and even India (see ITALIAN POETRY).

Dante, with transalpine scholasticism and cisalpine catholicity, bound in one volume the scattered leaves of the med. world. His two great Tuscan successors, Petrarch and Boccaccio, in their quite different ways catching Dante's high conception of the poet's function, returned to earth his exalted vision. Petrarch, primarily a rhetorician, but a priest of poetry, revived antiquity in receiving the laurel; his Lat. epic *Africa* was archaeology, but his *Canzoniere,* replete with feeling and perception, imposed a stamp, not always felicitous, upon modern verse (see PETRARCHISM; LYRIC SEQUENCE). Boccaccio, father of It. prose but meriting attention as font for Chaucer and many another, composed as his own epitaph, *studium fuit alma poesis* ("My study was nourishing poetry"). Medieval poetry had moved on from the days when *poeta* was an opprobrious word.

See also BYZANTINE POETRY; LATIN POETRY, *Medieval*; ARABIC POETRY; HISPANO-ARABIC POETRY; LEONINE VERSE; MEDIEVAL POETICS; POLITICAL VERSE.

BIBLIOGRAPHY AND REFERENCES: W. Stammler and K. Langosch, *Die deutsche Literatur des Mittelalters: Verfasserlexikon*, 5 v. (1931–55); *CBFL*, v. 1, *The Middle Ages*, ed. D. C. Cabeen (1947); F. Baldensperger and W. P. Friederich, *Bibl. of Comp. Lit.* (1950); R. Bossuat, *Manuel bibliographique de la littérature française du moyen âge* (1951) and supps.; W. Bonser, *An Anglo-Saxon and Celtic Bibl.*, 2 v. (1957); K. Strecker, *Intro. to Med. Lat.*, ed. and tr. R. B. Palmer (1957); Fisher—reviews research 1930–1960 on 9 med. lits.; *A Manual of the Writings in ME, 1050–1500* ed. J. B. Severs and A. E. Hartung, 7 v. (1967–86); *International Med. Bibl.*, 1– (1967–); R. Bromwich, *Med. Celtic Lit., A Select Bibl.* (1974); *New CBEL*, ed. G. Watson, v. 1, *600–1660* (1974); S. B. Greenfield and F. C. Robinson, *A Bibl. of Publications on OE Lit. to the End of 1972* (1980); Brogan, sects. J and K and App.; *Dict. of the Middle Ages*, gen. ed. J. R. Strayer, 13 v. (1982–).

COLLECTIONS OF AND INDEXES TO TEXTS: Migne, *PL*, 221 v. (1844–64); *MGH: Auctores antiquissimi*, 15 v. (1877–1919), *Poetae Latini medii aevi*, 5 v. (1881–1939), *Scriptores*, 32 v. (1886–1934); *Analecta hymnica medii aevi*, ed. G. Dreves, C. Blume, and H. Bannister, 55 v. (1886–1922); *Rerum Britannicarum medii aevi scriptores*, "Rolls Series," 99 titles in 254 v. (1887–96), esp. *The Anglo-Lat. Satirical Poets*, ed. T. Wright, 2 v. (1872); *The Index of ME Verse*, ed. C. Brown and R. H. Robbins (1943), *Supp.*, ed. R. H. Robbins and J. L. Cutler (1965); *Corpus christianorum, series latina*, 176 v. (1953–65), *series graeca*, 1– (1977–); *Initia carminum ac versuum medii aevi posterioris latinorum*, 2d ed., ed. H. Walther (1969).

ANTHOLOGIES: *Med. Lit. in Tr.*, ed. C. W. Jones (1950); *Med. Romances*, ed. R. S. and L. H. Loomis (1958); *Lyrics of the Middle Ages*, ed. H. Creekmore (1959); *Oxford Book of Med. Lat. Verse*, ed. F. J. E. Raby (1959); *An Anthol. of Med. Lyrics*, ed. A. Flores (1962); *Deutsche Lyrik des Mittelalters*, ed. M. Wehrli (1962); *Med. Epics*, tr. W. Alfred et al. (1963); *Oxford Book of Med. Eng. Verse*, ed. C. and K. Sisam (1970); *Med. Song and Lyrics of the Middle Ages*, both ed. J. J. Wilhelm (1971, 1990); *An Anthol. of Med. Ger. Lit.*, ed. A. K. Wimmer (1987).

HISTORY AND CRITICISM: *Hist. littéraire de la France*, 38 v. (1865–1949)—reaches beyond Fr. lit., use indexes; E. K. Chambers, *The Med. Stage*, 2 v. (1903); Manitius—the fullest reference on Med. Lat. through the 12th c.; J. Bédier, *Les Légendes épiques*, 3d ed., 4 v. (1926–29)—still useful though theories discounted; G. Ehrismann, *Gesch. der deutschen Literatur bis zum Ausgang des Mittelalter*, 2d ed., 2 v. in 4 (1932); K. Young, *Drama of the Med. Church*, 2 v. (1933)—with Lat. texts; Jeanroy; Patterson; J. de Ghellinck, *Litt. latine au moyen âge*, 2

v. (1939), *L'Essor de la litt. latine au XIIe siècle*, 2d ed. (1955); R. R. Bezzola, *Les Origines et la formation de la litt. courtoise en occident*, 3 v. (1944–63); G. Graf, *Gesch. der christl. arabischen Literatur*, 5 v. (1944–53); Lote; Curtius—still essential, and N.B. the list of his monographs, p. 600; Le Gentil; Lote; F. Brittain, *The Med. Lat. and Romance Lyric*, 2d ed. (1951); Auerbach; Raby, *Christian* and *Secular*; H. A. W. de Boor, *Gesch. der deutschen Literaturn*, v. 1, 2, 5 (1955–62); E. Köhler, *Ideal und Wirklichkeit in der höfischen Epik* (1956), *Troubadourlyrik und höfische Roman* (1968); *Le Origini*, ed. A. Viscardi et al. (1956); G. Murphy, *Early Ir. Lyrics* (1956); Beare; Norberg—versif.; F. Artz, *Mind of the Middle Ages*, 3d ed. (1958)—survey and bibl.; W. T. H. Jackson, *The Lit. of the Middle Ages* (1960)—useful bibl., *Med. Lit.: A History and a Guide* (1966)—concise survey, ed., *The Interp. of Med. Lat. P.* (1980); R. Menéndez-Pidal, *La Chanson de Roland et la trad. des Francs* (1960); R. Dragonetti, *La Technique poétique des trouvères dans la chanson courtoise* (1960); M. D. Legge, *Anglo-Norman Lit. and Its Background* (1963); 0. H. Green, *Spain and the Western Trad.*, v. 1 (1963); P. Courcelle, *Hist. littéraire des grandes invasions Germaniques* (1964); E. Auerbach, *Literary Lang. and Its Public in Late Lat. Antiquity and the Middle Ages* (1965); Jeanroy, *Origines*; *Gesch. der deutschen Literatur*, ed. H. de Boor and R. Newald (1966–87); *GRLMA*—most extensive modern effort; J. Rychner, *La Chanson de geste* (1968); Dronke; P. Klopsch, *Einführung in die mittellateinische Verslehre* (1972); S. M. Stern, *Hispano-Ar. Strophic Poetry* (1974); A. Hamori, *On the Art of Med. Ar. Lit.* (1974); L. M. Paterson, *Troubadours and Eloquence* (1975); R. Boase, *The Origin and Meaning of Courtly Love* (1976); D. Rieger, *Gattungen und Gattungsbezeichnungen der Trobadorlyrik* (1976); D. Pearsall, *OE and ME Poetry* (1977); R. Hannig, *The Individual in 12th-C. Romance* (1977); R. Jauss, *Alterität und Modernität der mittelalterlichen Literatur* (1977); J. Stevens, *Words and Music in the Middle Ages* (1980); Sayce; G. Wickham *The Med. Theater*, 3d ed. (1982); W. D. Paden, Jr., "Europe from Lat. to Vernacular in Epic, Lyric, Romance," *Performance of Lit. in Historical Perspectives*, ed. D. W. Thompson (1983); Chambers; Norden; *Poetry of the Carolingian Ren.*, ed. P. Godman (1985); B. Stock, *The Implications of Literacy* (1986); J. Stevens, *Words and Music in the Middle Ages* (1986); M. R. Menocal, *The Ar. Role in Med. Lit. Hist.* (1988); O. B. Hardison, Jr., *Prosody and Purpose in the Eng. Ren.* (1989)—much on medieval; Hollier.   C.W.J.; T.V.F.B.; P.D.

MEDIEVAL PROSODY. See MEDIEVAL POETRY.

MEDIEVAL ROMANCE. In the primary sense, stories of adventure and love which flourished from the mid 12th to the end of the 14th c. The meaning of the term "r." is complicated by the fact that both in med. and modern times it has been used loosely. In France, where it originated, it was applied at first to a lang.—i.e. vernacular Fr. (as opposed to Lat.)—and thence its lit. Later it came to refer to a genre, i.e. imaginative works in verse whose subject matter was felt to be fictional or nonhistorical. By the 13th c., however, any tale of adventure, whatever the origin of its matter and whether in verse or prose, could be r. The earlier examples are mainly in verse; hence med. rs. are often called "metrical rs.," though after 1400, variant forms, continuations, or new subjects were mostly in prose, the dominant medium from the 13th c. They differ from earlier narrative genres such as the saint's life and epic (*chanson de geste* [q.v.], *Volksepos*) by their focus on the individual hero who emerges from his communal background (often a royal court, hence the importance of courtly and chivalrous ideals) and journeys alone, seeking adventure. The quest motif is fundamental. In the best rs. he (and sometimes the lady) grows in self-knowledge and achieves fulfillment through the overcoming of obstacles. Women always play important roles, allowing authors to depict, analyze, and celebrate matters of the heart. Indeed, love often ennobles the hero, spurring him on to deeds of prowess which confirm him as the ideally chivalrous knight, wonderfully good-mannered, brave beyond belief, acutely conscious of honor and loyalty, ever merciful to his enemies, helpful to the oppressed (see COURTLY LOVE). In general, r. is distinguished from the older epic forms by its less heroic tone, its greater sophistication, its use of interlace, and its apparently looser structure and less obvious unity of action.

Traditionally, scholars group rs. into three cycles according to their subject matter: (1) "The Matter of Britain" (subdivided into "Arthurian Matter"—rs. derived from Breton lays—and "Eng. Matter," e.g. *King Horn*); (2) "The Matter of Rome" (stories of Alexander, the Trojan war, Thebes, and the Orient); (3) "The Matter of France" (stories of Charlemagne and his knights). The earlist rs. are the OF *romans d'antiquité* of the "Matter of Rome" cycle, so called because their authors retell tales from Cl. Antiquity, even though their tone and ethos is thoroughly med. In some long rs. the love element is severely limited, as in the *Roman de Thèbes* (ca. 1150), which draws on Statius' *Thebaid*; and even more so in the *Roman d'Alexandre* (after 1100) which recounts episodes in the life of Alexander of Macedonia and which lent its name to its meter, the *alexandrine* (q.v.). Others, much briefer, concentrate almost entirely on a largely tragic sentimental affair: e.g. the story of *Pyramus and Thisbe* (ca. 1150) and that of Danae and *Narcisus* (ca. 1190), both expanded versions of tales from Ovid's *Metamorphoses*. Of major importance is the *Roman d'Enéas* (ca. 1160), which draws heavily on the *Aeneid*—it becomes a love story, with the destructive love (Dido) spurned and true love (Lavinia) finally triumphant. Benoît de Sainte-Maure's *Roman de Troie* (ca. 1165),

based on the Lat. account of Dares Phrygius, tells of the Trojan war. The love interest centers on Paris and Helen, Achilles and Polyxena, and (perhaps invented by Benoît) Troilius and Cressida, whose story was to be retold often, notably (in prose) by Boccaccio (*Il Filostrato*, ca. 1350) and brilliantly (in verse) by Chaucer (*Troilus and Criseyde*, ca. 1385).

The most important group of rs. comes under the heading *matière de Bretagne*, the "Matter of Britain," and are mostly Arthurian. An early subgroup treats Tristan and Isolda's tragic, all-consuming passion for each other. The earliest fragments are Fr. and of two kinds: one is more earthy and robust, the other more aristocratically courtly and restrained, with greater interest in emotion and states of mind. France and Germany give us one of each kind. Béroul's *Tristan* (ca. 1180) and Eilhart von Oberg's *Tristant* (ca. 1180) are the more earthy versions; Thomas's *Tristan* (ca. 1170) and Gottfried von Strasburg's *Tristan und Isolt* (ca. 1210) are the more courtly.

Controversy has raged over the origins of Arthurian r.; were they Celtic or Fr.? Whatever they were, the earliest extant Arthurian rs. (and some of the finest) are those of Chrétien de Troyes, writing in the second half of the 12th c. (see FRENCH POETRY). *Erec et Enide*, *Cligès* (a Byzantine r., sometimes described as "anti Tristan"), *Lancelot* (*The Knight of the Cart*), *Yvain* (*The Knight of the Lion*), and the unfinished *Perceval* (*The Grail Story*) are all that have come down to us. *Erec*, *Cligès*, and *Yvain* are about married love; *Lancelot* is about adulterous love. Most of Chrétien's rs. have parallels in other langs., notably the Welsh prose *mabinogion*. In MHG, Hartmann von Aue reworked two stories to produce his polished, courtly *Erec* (ca. 1185) and *Iwein* (before 1205; see GERMAN POETRY). There is a Norwegian prose *Yvain* on which a Norwegian and a Swedish verse retelling are based. Also in Ger., Wolfram von Eschenbach retold and completed the Grail story using Chrétien and other material to produce his masterpiece, *Parzifal* (ca. 1210). With this, verse r. scales its highest spiritual levels while retaining its essential characteristics—adventure and love intrigue combined with idealized chivalry.

The Perceval–Gawain–Grail stories of Chrétien's last r. had an enduring fascination and were frequently reworked in both verse and prose. In the Fr. *Continuation Gauvain*, the Grail episodes occupy only 1200 of the 22,000 lines of verse. In the *Continuation Perceval* (13,000 lines) Perceval proves his superiority to Gauvain but fails to end the quest for the Grail. This is achieved only in a third (the Manessier) continuation (and another 10,000 lines) in which Perceval succeeds his uncle, the Fisher King. Finally, in France, Robert de Boron, whose piety was greater than his poetic talent, composed a series of Grail rs., the most important being the *Roman de l'Estoire dou Graal* (also known as *Joseph d'Arimathie*). Thereafter, most further treatments of the legend were in prose, though the 15th-c. ME *Sir Perceval of Galles* is an interesting exception.

Gawain is in fact prominent in a number of Eng. rs., most notably in the alliterative *Sir Gawayne and the Grene Knight* (late 14th c.), full of the supernatural and amorous intrigue in which courage, loyalty, and courtesy are severely tested. The beheading motif, found in numerous tales, is superbly handled here. Also belonging to the Gawain cycle are the ME *Avowing of Arthure* and *Awntyrs of Arthure*.

In a class of their own are the Arthurian tales featuring the *fier baiser* (brave kiss), of which the best and earliest is the Fr. *Le Bel Inconnu* (*The Fair Unknown*) by Renaud de Beaujeu (ca. 1190). This is a forerunner of many a Beauty-and-the-Beast story. *Jaufré* (late 12th c.) is of interest as one of only two surviving Occitan Arthurian rs.

Also belonging to the *matière de Bretagne* are those mini-rs. sometimes called lais (q.v.). Among the best are those of Marie de France (ca. 1165), who concentrates on the realistic and psychological aspects of her material rather than on the fantastic. *Lanval*, her only Arthurian lai, is perhaps her masterpiece, while *Chievrefeuil* belongs to the Tristan legend. There is a charming group of ME mini-rs. based on Breton lais: *Sir Launfal, Sir Degare, Le Freine,* and perhaps *Sir Orfeo,* all in 14th-c. mss.

Sir Thomas Malory's misnamed *Morte d'Arthur* is best known in the form in which Caxton rearranged it. It is a final accounting of the Arthurian cyle, with a strong feeling for the fate which the sin of adultery brought to the world of chivalry.

Finally, there are those "independent" rs. of adventure belonging to none of the groups identified thus far (though some have links with them), such as *Partonopeu de Blois* (before 1188), which betrays the influence of *Enéas* and *Thèbes*, and has affinities with *Lanval.* This was tr. into six other langs., incl. Eng. *Floire et Blancheflor* (ca. 1150) is a romantic idyll and a model for many others which tell how two very young lovers are separated only to be re-united after a long series of misadventures often taking place in north Africa or Spain. This particular r. had a long history in France, Norway, Denmark, Holland, England, Germany, Spain, and Italy. A unique and beautiful relation is the prosimetric *Aucassin et Nicolette* (ca. 1200?; see CHANTE-FABLE; PROSIMETRUM). Hue de Rotelonde composed ca. 1180 two lively love stories: *Ipomedon* (cf. the ME *Lyfe of Ipomydon,* ca. 1400) and *Protesilaus. Horn,* ca. 1170 (cf. *King Horn* [ca. 1225], interesting, along with *Havelok the Dane* [ca. 1275], as one of the earliest explicit ME minstrels' lais) is unusual for its versification: monorhymed *laisses* of varying length in alexandrines. Gautier d'Arras composed ca. 1178 both *Ille et Galeran,* the story of a man divided between two women, and *Eracle* (adapted in Ger. by Otte, *Eraclius,* ca. 1210), a Byzantine story in which the hero passes from slavery to become Emporer of Rome. The legend of the Seven Sages of Rome, destined to become extremely popular throughout Western Europe, was turned from Lat. prose into Fr. verse ca. 1200. Its basic structure bears some resemblance to that of the *Thousand and One Nights.* Mention should finally be made of several 13th-c. masterpieces in Fr., e.g. the *Chastelaine de Vergi,* one of the few tragic love stories of the age; the lively rs. of Jean Renart; the *Castelain de Couci* (which contains the motif of the eaten heart); Philippe de Remi's *Manekine* (king falls in love with daughter); and *Jehan et Blonde* (Fr. boy wins Eng. girl against all odds).

The trads. of r. lingered on, though often in distorted and even parodied form, into the Ren. Ariosto's *Orlando furioso,* the *Teuerdank* of Maximilian I, and *Amadis de Gaule* all show the conventions of chivalry; and the humor of *Don Quixote,* as well as its tragedy, depends on the recognition of r. conventions. See also NARRATIVE POETRY.

REFERENCE: A. H. Billings, *Guide to the ME Rs.* (1900); *The Arthurian Encyclopedia,* ed. N. J. Lacy (1986); J. A. Rice, *ME R.: An Annot. Bibl., 1955–1985* (1987).

COLLECTIONS: *ME Metrical Rs.,* ed. W. H. French and C. B. Hale (1930); *Med. Rs.,* ed. R. S. and L. H. Loomis (1957).

HISTORY AND CRITICISM: W. P. Ker, *Epic and R.,* 2d ed. (1908); E. Faral, *Recherches sur les sources latines* (1913); R. S. Crane, *The Vogue of Med. Chivalric R. in the Eng. Ren.* (1919); C. B. Lewis, *Cl. Myth and Arthurian R.* (1932); Lewis; *CBFL,* v. 1; E. C. Pettet, *Shakespeare and the R. Trad.* (1949); *The Continuations of the OF Perceval of Chrétien de Troyes,* ed. W. Roach, 3 v. (1949–52); F. E. Guyer, *Romance in the Making* (1954); R. R. Bezzola, *Les Origines et la formation de la litt. courtoise en occident,* 5 v. (1958–67); A. C. Baugh, "Improvisation in the ME R.," *PAPS* 103 (1959); J. Frappier, *Le Roman breton* (1959); R. S. Loomis, *Arthurian Lit. in the Middle Ages* (1959), *The Grail from Celtic Myth to Christian Symbol* (1963); L. A. Hibbard, *Med. R. in Eng.,* 2d ed. (1961); M. J. C. Reid, *The Arthurian Legend* (1961); A. Johnston, *Enchanted Ground* (1964); B. E. Perry, *The Ancient Rs., a Lit.-Hist. Account of their Origins* (1967); J. Frappier, *Chrétien de Troyes* (1968); *Pastoral and R.: Mod. Essays in Crit.,* ed. E. T. Lincoln (1969); G. Beer, *The R.* (1970); E. Vinaver, *The Rise of R.* (1971); J. Stevens, *Med. R.: Themes and Approaches* (1973); *Epic and R. Crit.,* ed. A. Coleman, 2 v. (1973); P. A. Parker, *Inescapable R.* (1976); N. Frye, *The Secular Scripture: A Study of the Structure of R.* (1976); R. W. Hanning, *The Individual in 12th-C. R.* (1977); D. H. Green, *Irony in the Med. R.* (1979); P. Boitani, *Eng. Med. Narrative* (1982); L. C. Ramsey, *Chivalric Rs.* (1983); J. A. Schulz, *The Shape of the Round Table: Structures of MHG Arthurian R.* (1983); *The R. of Arthur,* ed. J. J. Wilhelm and L. Z. Gross (1984); *R.: Generic Transformation from Chrétien de Troyes to Cervantes,* ed. K. and M. S. Brownlee (1985); D.

Pearsall, "The Devel. of ME R.," *Studies in ME Rs.: Some New Approaches*, ed. D. Brewer (1988); P. Parker, "R.," *The Spenser Encyc.*, ed. A. C. Hamilton et al. (1990); D. Kelly, *The Art of Med. Fr. R.* (1992). See also the annual *Bulletin bibl. de la soc. internat. arthurienne* (1949–). K.V.

MEDITATIVE POETRY. See METAPHYSICAL POETRY; RELIGION AND POETRY.

MEIOSIS (Gr. "lessening"; Lat. *extenuatio*). A figure employing understatement, usually to convey that a thing is less in importance (or size) than it really is; the opposite of *auxesis* (q.v.). M. is often confused with *litotes* (q.v.), which, properly understood, affirms or increases the importance, usually by negating the contrary. Litotes, however, is laudatory in intent; m. is derogatory. It is m. which should be considered the genus, the more general term. Scaliger (*Poetices libri septem* 3.81) says that "true *extenuatio* is a form of crit., not mere understatement." Group Mu reminds us that, as a metalogism, m. functions, like hyperbole, litotes, irony, and paradox (qq.v.), by implicit reference to an ostensive situation, i.e. to the extra-linguistic, pragmatic context of the utterance (132–38).

Quintilian discusses m. as an abuse or fault of lang. which characterizes obscure style rather than one lacking ornament, but indicates that, deliberately employed, m. may be called a figure (*Institutio oratoria* 8.3.50). Puttenham distinguishes the function of m. more particularly: "If you diminish and abbase a thing by way of spight . . . , such speach is by the figure M. or the disabler" (*The Arte of Eng. Poesie*). The startling simplicity of a powerful m. is arresting in narrative; e.g. Dante's famous "quel girono più non vi leggemmo avante" (We read no more that day) from the Paolo and Francesca episode (*Inferno* 5); or the concluding lines of Wordsworth's *Michael*. M. may be used as a structuring device in a poem, as in Housman's "Long for me the rick will wait, / And long will wait the fold, / And long will stand the empty plate, / And dinner will be cold" (*A Shropshire Lad* 8.21–24); or it may dominate an entire poem, as in Auden's "Musée des Beaux Arts" and "The Unknown Citizen." Note also that in Shakespeare's later tragedies, esp. *Lear*, understatement often marks the most dramatic moments. In modern times, however, what is unquestionably a valuable rhetorical device has fallen into some cultural disfavor, in part because of its abuse as a nearly obsessive Victorian locution: understatement is now viewed as virtually the hallmark of the British temperament.—Sr. M. Joseph, *Shakespeare's Use of the Arts of Lang.* (1947); L. A. Sonnino, *Handbook to 16th-C. Rhet.* (1968), 95; Lausberg; Group Mu; Corbett. R.O.E.; T.V.F.B.

MEISTERSINGER. Late med. Ger. burgher poets (14th–16th cs., some attested as late as the 18th c.) who traced their ancestry traditionally to twelve *Meister* among the Minnesinger (see MINNESANG), including such figures as Walther von der Vogelweide, Wolfram von Eschenbach, and Frauenlob, reputedly the founder of the first *Singschule* (Singing School), in Mainz; the catalogue of 12 Meister was first mentioned by Lupold Hornburg in ca. 1340. Unlike many of the earlier poets, however, whose themes were often erotic, they concentrated largely on didactic material, mainly moral, religious, and political themes. To some extent *Meistersang* developed from the didactic *Spruchdichtung* (q.v.) of the 13th and 14th cs. It was primarily intended for solo vocal performance. The *Meistersang* is transmitted in over a hundred mss., some with melodies, including those ascribed to earlier poets such as Walther but furnished with new texts.

From the end of the 14th c. on, the M. were characterized by their organization into guilds, by their adherence to a system of rules and categories, and by the rigidly formalistic nature of their productions. Some scholars believe the guilds originated in groups of laymen organized by the church to sing on public occasions. Before becoming a *Meister*, an aspirant was obliged to work his way up through a series of grades from *Schüler* (pupil) through *Dichter* (poet) to the highest rank, *Meister*, yet even he was restricted in his choice of material and technique. At the *Schulsingen*, or formal meetings, he could treat only religious subjects; at the *Zechsingen*, however, informal meetings frequently held in taverns, a wider range of material was permissible, although amorous themes were not permitted for the songs until the 16th c.

In technique, the M. were restricted to a certain set of *Töne*, or patterns of tune and meter; the metrical form was determined by the number of syllables and may have disregarded the natural accents of speech; often these forms display great intricacy. In fitting words to the *Töne*, the M. followed the *Tabulatur*, an extensive and pedantic code of rules which differed from School to School. The M. took over from the *Minnesang* a tripartite division of the stanza into two *Stollen* (together constituting the *Aufgesang*) followed by a third, differing section (the *Abgesang*)—structurally, A/A//B (see CANSO)—which became a staple form. They called their songs *Bar* or *Par* and codified them in *Tabulaturen*.

Famous M. include Hans Folz (d. ca. 1515), who successfully established the right of the Nuremberg Meister to introduce new metrical patterns and melodies in place of the established forms; Lienhard Nunnenpeck (d. after 1515); Adam Puschmann (d. 1600); and, above all, Hans Sachs (1494–1576), the most prolific and the first to introduce *Buhllieder* (love songs). Goethe rediscovered Sachs in 1776 (see KNITTELVERS), and later Wagner made him the hero of his opera *Die M. von Nürnberg*, a work which gives a generally accurate (though somewhat idealized) picture of the M. but which incorrectly ascribes appreciation of their art to the wider public and to the ruling class, whereas in fact such appreciation was confined almost entirely to their own social sphere. Although *Meistersang* is predominantly didactic lyric poetry, the later M. (Folz, Sachs, Jörg Wickram, Wolfhart Spangenberg) also composed short stories and shrovetide plays.

The M. flourished for the most part in the Rhineland, Swabia, Franconia, and the Ger. lands east of the Elbe. There were some individual *Meister* in the north, but the characteristic guild organization seems to have existed neither there nor in Switzerland.

COLLECTIONS: *Die Meisterlieder der Kolmarer Handschrift*, ed. K. Bartsch (1862); *Die Singweisen der Kolmarer Handschrift*, ed. P. Runge (1896), facsimile ed. U. Müller et al. (1976); H. Folz, *Meisterlieder*, ed. A. L. Mayer (1908); *Die Jenaer Liederhandschrift*, facsimile ed. H. Tervooren and U. Müller (1972); *Repertorium der Sangsprüche und Meisterlieder des 12. bis 18. Jahrhunderts*, ed. H. Brunner and B. Wachinger (1986–87).

HISTORY AND CRITICISM: A. Taylor, *Lit. Hist. of Meistergesang* (1937); C. H. Bell, *Georg Hager, a M. of Nürnberg*, 4 v. (1947), *The Meistersingerschule at Memmingen* (1952); B. Nagel, *Der deutsche Meistersang* (1952); R. W. Linker, *Music of the Minnesinger and early M.* (1962); *Der deutsche Meistersang*, ed. B. Nagel, 2d ed. (1971); A. L. Burkhalter, *Minstrels and Masters* (1968); H. Brunner, *Die alten Meister* (1975); B.-F. Schultze, *Der Augsburger M. Onoferus Schwartzenbach* (1982); F. Schanze, *Meisterliche Liedkunst zwischen Heinrich von Mügeln und Hans Sachs*, 2 v. (1983–84); R. Hahn, *Die löbliche Kunst* (1984); N. Henkel, "Die zwölf alten Meister," *Beiträge zur Gesch. der deutschen Sprache und Lit.* 109 (1987). A.C.

MEIURUS, MYURUS. See HEXAMETER.

MELIC POETRY (Gr. *melos*, "member," "song"). Later called lyric poetry (q.v.) by the Alexandrians, m. p. refers loosely to Gr. poetry composed from the 7th through 5th cs. B.C., exclusive of epic, dramatic, elegiac, and iambic. M. p. was sung to the accompaniment of a lyre or woodwinds or both and was divided into two broad categories, monodic and choral. Monodic m. p. (see MONODY), whose chief representatives were Sappho, Alcaeus, and Anacreon, was sung by a solo voice and often consisted of short stanzas, the two most important of which became known as Sapphic and Alcaic (qq.v.). Monodic m. p. reflected Aeolic and Ionian trads., and its lang. tended to be more conversational and personal (Kirkwood, Bowra). Choral m. p., whose chief composers were Alcman, Stesichorus, Ibycus, Simonides, Pindar, and Bacchylides, was sung and danced by a chorus and was often arranged in triads consisting of strophe, antistrophe, and epode (qq.v.). In contrast to monodic m. p., its character was more public, and it employed a highly artificial lang. with strong Doric coloring. Choral m. p. was classified by Alexandrian editors into various genres, the most important being hymns, paeans, dithyrambs, *prosodia, partheneia, hyporchemata*, encomia, dirges, and *epinikia* (qq.v.). Although we have fragments from all the major choral poets (ed. Edmonds, which must be supp. by many recent papyrological additions), the most important extant representatives are Pindar (45 *epinikia*) and Bacchylides (14 *epinikia* and 6 dithyrambs). See AEOLIC; GREEK POETRY.

H. W. Smyth, *Gr. Melic Poets* (1900); Bowra; H. Färber, *Die Lyrik in der Kunsttheorie der Antike* (1936); J. E. Sandys, *The Odes of Pindar*, 3d ed. (1937); *Lyra graeca*, ed. J. M. Edmonds, 3 v. (1952), now being superseded by D. A. Campbell, *Gr. Lyric*, 4 v. (1982–); D. L. Page, *Sappho and Alcaeus* (1955); G. M. Kirkwood, *Early Gr. Monody* (1974); Trypanis; *CHCL*, v. 1 (1985); R. L. Fowler, *The Nature of Early Gr. Lyric* (1987); M. Davies, "Monody, Choral Lyric, and the Tyrany of the Handbook," *CQ* 82 (1988). W.H.R.

MELOPOEIA, PHANOPOEIA, and LOGOPOEIA are the three poetic modes by which, in Ezra Pound's formulation, lang. is "charged or energized." M. charges words "over and above their plain meaning, with some musical property, which directs the bearing or trend of that meaning." Pound further distinguishes three kinds of m.: "(1) that made to be sung to a tune; (2) that made to be intoned or sung to a sort of chant; and (3) that made to be spoken." L. "employs words not only for their direct meaning, but it takes count in a special way of habits of usage, of the context we *expect* to find with the word, its usual concomitants, of its known acceptances, and of ironical play." It occurs to a limited degree in 17th- and 18th-c. satire and particularly in the Fr. poet Jules Laforgue. P. is "a casting of images upon the visual imagination." (See IMAGISM.) Chinese poets have excelled in the use of p., which can be readily tr. from one lang. to another. Although the poetic qualities of m. are rarely translatable, Pound studied them in his versions of Arnaut Daniel, Propertius, and Cavalcanti. L. does not translate, but "the attitude of mind it expresses may pass through a paraphrase," as in these lines from Pound's *Homage to Sextus Propertius*: "The Cytherean brought low by Mars' lechery / reigns in respectable heavens. . . ."—E. Pound, "How to Read," *Literary Essays* (1954); J. P. Sullivan, *Ezra Pound and Sextus Propertius: A Study in Creative Translation* (1964); H. N. Schneidau, *Ezra Pound: The Image and the Real* (1969); Michaelides. T.J.M.

MELOS. See EUPHONY; MELOPOEIA, PHANOPOEIA, LOGOPOEIA; MUSIC AND POETRY; SOUND; SOUND EFFECTS IN POETRY.

MEMORIA. See RHETORIC AND POETRY.

MESOSTICH. See ACROSTIC.

METACRITICISM.

    I. RELATION TO LITERARY CRITICISM,
        HISTORY, AND THEORY
    II. THE CLASSIFICATION OF CRITICAL
        STATEMENTS
    III. PROBLEMS OF METACRITICISM
    IV. METACRITICISM AS PHILOSOPHY

The prefix "meta-" marks a step upward in lang. level, often characterized by contemp. philosophers and logicians as a second-order discourse about a first-order discourse. Philosophy itself is meta-discourse: philosophy of history is metahistory, and philosophy of science is metascience. Thus m. is critical and theoretical discourse about the nature and ends of crit. (q.v.). Fluidity of terminology, however, makes crit. and literary theory (q.v.) hard to distinguish from each other, and sometimes from m., esp. when some poems are implicitly "metapoetic" or self-referential (see Colie), or when some literary theories are metapoetic (see Steiner). Nevertheless, the distinctions among lit. crit., literary theory, and m. are no less crucial than in fields such as philosophy, science, and mathematics, where they were first developed and are most firmly entrenched.

The task of m. is the critical examination of crit.—its technical terms, its logical structure, its fundamental principles and presuppositions, and its broader implications for cultural theory. When a critic makes an observation about a literary work, the metacritic or theorist will characteristically ask: How does the critic know this? What sorts of evidence could establish such an observation? Is a particular concept, analogy, or method sufficiently articulated, or adequate, to serve as a critical tool? Why is the presence of, say, an archetype, symbol, tension, irony, or paradox in a literary work a criterion of value, i.e. a reason for judging it to be good or great? These questions lie beyond the scope of the practical critic, who is concerned primarily with explication and interpretation (q.v.) of the work itself.

I. RELATION TO LITERARY CRITICISM, HISTORY, AND THEORY. Lit. crit. can be said to consist of the class of all existing statements about literary works of art. And this class can be considered the subject matter of m. But a further distinction within this class has come to be widely acknowledged, that between "internal" and "external" statements. Among the remarks made about literary works are two external sorts: (1) *comparative* statements, noting the likenesses and differences of literary works or of literary works and other cultural products, and (2) *causal* statements about the influence of antecedent conditions, about the effects of literary works on individual readers or social processes, and about the ways in which literary works may be symptoms of underlying conditions. These external statements are frequently assigned to the prov-

ince of *literary history*, which is thus distinguished from crit. defined, in its narrower sense, as consisting of statements about the internal properties of literary works. This distinction need not commit us to any assumptions about the logical connections, or lack of logical connections, between critical statements and the statements of lit. hist. (see HISTORICISM). The task of the critic would then be to tell us what he knows about the form and content of individual works, and that of the literary historian to trace their conditions and consequences. It is a matter of debate, inviting metacritical scrutiny, whether, to what extent, and in what ways the performance of either task depends on the completion of the other.

Although crit. consists primarily of singular statements about particular works of lit., critics do frequently wonder whether their statements can be brought together into a system in which some principles are logical consequences of other more fundamental ones. The theory of lit., sometimes called "poetics" (q.v.), attempts to discover and, if possible, unify such principles. Aristotle's *Poetics*, René Wellek and Austin Warren's *Theory of Lit.* (1956), Northrop Frye's *Anatomy of Crit.* (1957), Barbara Herrnstein Smith's *Poetic Closure* (1968), and Jonathan Culler's *Structuralist Poetics* (1975) are examples of this genre. In attempting such a theory, the theorist is still on the same lang. level as the critic; the former has merely moved from the particular to the general, from isolated and intermittent generalizations to system. How far crit. can be, or ought to be, systematized in this way is itself an important (metacritical) question; but it is a fact of the hist. of crit. that no eminent and productive critic has been content to utter only singular statements without suggesting more general principles and making an effort to justify them by appeal to other general principles.

Literary theory, moving toward the highest generality of which it is capable, impinges on music theory (e.g. Meyer), art theory (e.g. Gombrich), and, ultimately, aesthetics as a branch of philosophy. Aesthetics encompasses the general and fundamental problems of m. But at least one species of aesthetics attempts to articulate a criterion of art, and it therefore remains controlled by certain normative considerations about what does, and what doesn't, constitute art. Thus in its endeavors to examine the logic of critical reasoning, aesthetics is the same as m., though when it claims to possess a norm of meaningfulness or goodness, it functions as a prescriptive analytic inquiry. In the view of those who reject such inquiry, all attempts to examine other theories and to show their serious limitations are not metacritical, although they may involve metacritical analysis. Such a view implies that m. does not seek to offer an indubitably true theory of crit., or a theory of crit. as such, but rather shows the historical, institutional, and therefore changing nature of crit. and its concepts. Its objective is to enable us to understand the basis of lit. crit. by seeking to countervail parochial attitudes, and it helps us to perceive the complexity of the form of critical life. Metacritical inquiry is not directed toward literary works themselves; it is directed toward the possibilities of lit. and crit.

Crit., literary theory, and m. are all logically independent of each other, but the distinctions among them are not precisely marked, and every question raised does not allow for instantly recognizable classificatory categories. Questions such as—what gives the experience of reading a literary work its value? why prefer one poem to another? how or why is this experience better than another? why is one opinion about literary works not as good as another? what is a literary work? what is value?—are not always easy to classify without more context, and by treating them as if they are of the same order one is liable to lump diverse sorts of inquiry together. Sorting them out is extremely important because it clarifies the scope and limits of each of these inquiries in given contexts. Certainly, "Why prefer Pope's *Rape of the Lock* to Tennyson's *Locksley Hall*?" is precisely a question for the critic. But "What makes one opinion about a poem better than another?" is a metacritical question, since it inquires into the logic of critical judgment. And "What is a poem (i.e., what is the word 'poem' best taken to mean)?" is also a metacritical question, though once the class of poems has been marked out (if that can be done), then the question about other properties poems always, or generally, have in common is a question for literary theory. When critics engage in philosophical analysis of the problems of crit. and literary theory, they are then functioning as metacritics. Like the advocate of a theory seeking to modify and refine that theory or to improve or change a critical practice, the metacritic can point up confusion or significance in a particular theory or practice. Unlike literary theorists, however, who attempt to provide foundations for a theory or practice, the metacritic does not intend to provide such a foundation, though he or she may certainly examine and explore the logical and conceptual bases of various theories and practices of crit.

II. THE CLASSIFICATION OF CRITICAL STATEMENTS. Crit. encompasses a variety of types of statements, each giving rise to different metacritical problems. So the preliminary task of the metacritic is to find the basic categories into which all critical statements can be sorted. Of these there appear to be at least three:

A. *Description.* A critic may say that a poem contains certain words in certain syntactic structures, a certain pattern of meter or rhyme, certain metaphors or rhetorical figures, certain imagery (see ANALYSIS). More complex descriptions are those that classify literary works into certain *genres*, e.g. sonnet, tragedy, pastoral elegy, epic (Hernadi; see GENRE).

B. *Interpretation.* If the term "interp." (q.v.) may be said to encompass any statement that purports to say what a literary work means, we can distinguish several interpretive tasks, each having its own special features and problems: (1) unraveling an obscurity or complexity (qq.v.) in a text by showing, for example, how a syntactic construction is to be read, or by unpacking the meaning of a metaphor; (2) interpreting implicit motives or traits of character in the fictional world of a literary work; (3) interpreting the symbols (q.v.) in a literary work or identifying its themes; (4) saying what implicit propositions—e.g. philosophical, political—are dramatized in a work; (5) explaining what "artistic acts" are performed in a work— e.g. that the author evinces a certain attitude toward certain characters or events (he or she has treated them coldly, compassionately, with calm detachment, or with moral indignation—see Sircello). These tasks are not always distinguishable from one another, however; indeed they are often closely intertwined: by explicating a syntactic obscurity or complexity, for example, the critic may uncover larger themes or symbols which in turn disclose larger philosophical or political propositions dramatized in the work.

C. *Evaluation.* To say that a literary work is good or bad, or better or worse than another, is to offer an evaluation (q.v.). To say, on the other hand, "I like this poem," or "I prefer this poem to that" is not to evaluate but rather merely to express one's subjective preferences, or taste (q.v.), though in certain contexts such remarks may suggest that the speaker is not merely evincing his personal feelings but is making, or is prepared to make, a judgment of literary value.

These categories are distinct only at an analytic level, for in practice, the three activities are too closely integrated to allow for any easy or absolute separation. The critic who identifies certain syntactic patterns in a poem also interprets and values them in certain crucial ways, and when he interprets certain thematic concerns or philosophical propositions in a poem he also places them in a certain evaluative context in the sense of remarking on the artist's success or failure in realizing them (see EXPRESSION; INTENTION).

III. PROBLEMS OF METACRITICISM. The problems of m. arise from analysis of the grounds and implications of making particular critical claims. The following list is a representative selection of such problems, one that explains briefly the concerns and methods of m.

A. When explications conflict, as will happen, questions arise which m. seeks to explore and, if possible, answer. The first question concerns the possibility of deciding whether one of the incompatible explanations is correct; the second concerns which procedures the critic may employ to decide whether a particular explication is correct; and the third focuses on the implications for crit. if the impossibility of deciding conclusively between two or more incompatible interps. is accepted. The problem of interp. is highly controversial: some theorists (e.g. Hirsch) argue for the importance of reading literary works in terms of their authors' intended meanings, whereas others (e.g. Gadamer) reiterate the inevitability and limitations of our own cultural horizons and contexts of presuppositions in making interps. of (historically and culturally) alien literary works. This is a central metacritical issue still open to further analysis. It leads to fundamental questions in the philosophy of lang. such as the nature of meaning (see SEMANTICS; MEANING; SEMIOTICS), and to the consequent question of how such meaning is expressed in poetry.

B. Although the grammatical and syntactic forms of literary lang. are similar to those found in other lang. uses, in other respects literary lang. appears to differ in crucial ways (see POETIC FUNCTION). What are the distinctive features of literary lang., and how do they differ from nonliterary lang.? This has been one of the central topics of structuralism (q.v.). It is also a matter of dispute (and metacritical relevance) whether ordinary lang. is indeed ordinary in relation to literary lang. And there is the question of the propositional truth or falsity of the sentences in works of lit.: are they "true" in the same way declarative sentences setting forth facts in a newspaper are true, or are they neither true nor false, but exempt from ordinary semantic categories (see SEMANTICS)?

C. When evaluations conflict, as very often seems to happen, is there an objective procedure by which one judgment can be shown to be more reasonable or more acceptable than another? Those who hold one or another version of relativist metacritical theory deny that any such procedure exists, esp. since disputants may frequently differ from one another even concerning description and interp., not to mention cultural values or personal tastes. Nonrelativist metacritical theory, on the other hand, stresses the role of reason in critical discussion. The problem of resolving conflicting evaluations becomes more intractable, however, when the question is raised whether critical evaluations can be supported by genuine reasons. This is a question that leads to fundamental axiological problems about the nature of value, esp. the kind of value sought in lit., and its relation to literary response and critical practice.

D. Whether or not the specific sentences of a literary work are taken to be true or false, referentially, works seem to embody implicit theses of a more general sort—philosophical, political, religious (see PHILOSOPHY AND POETRY). The problem of truth in lit. is a problem of whether the truth or falsity of such embodied propositions has any logical bearing on the literary goodness or badness of the work. This problem is closely connected with, though not identical to, the problem of belief (q.v.) which deals (roughly) with the relation between the reader's beliefs antecedent to experiencing the work, the effect of that experience on those beliefs, and his or her consequent evaluation of the work. Analysis of these problems depends in part on what has become known as hermeneutics (q.v.).

E. Also analogous to the problem of truth is the problem of the relation between art and morality: whether any facts or implications about the moral aspects of a literary work (undesirable political effects of propaganda, for example, or asocial actions resulting from pornography) have a bearing on its *literary* goodness. Though the issues involved here trouble the metacritic less today than at earlier periods, they have perennial features and continually arise in new forms.

F. Finally, there is the problem of the nature of the world portrayed (realized, reflected, imagined) in literary works—in philosophical terms, the problem of the ontological status of art, its mode of being. Are there explicit, unique, and constant purposes embodied in literary works, and if so, are there stable means of realizing such purposes? If, on the other hand, literary works exhibit purposes and means of realizing those purposes which are undefinable or ever-changing, what is an adequate ontology of lit.? These questions have been answered in a variety of ways over the history of critical theory, from Plato and Aristotle to New Criticism, structuralism, and deconstruction (qq.v.). M. examines the logic and presuppositions underlying these theories and explores the implications of the conflicts and consonances among them.

IV. METACRITICISM AS PHILOSOPHY. Broadly speaking, i.e. construed as philosophy of crit., m. deals with all aspects of crit. requiring or inviting philosophical scrutiny: its lang., its procedures, the scope and function of its presuppositions and theories, its functions and values. M. may undertake a systematic classification of critical approaches or methods, or in its prescriptivist form devise and propose new strategies, for example the "modes" of crit. distinguished by McKeon. But its central concern is with the *logic of criticism*, wherein problems fall into two groups: those arising in an attempt to understand and clarify the *meaning* of the key terms in which crit. is conducted, and those arising in the attempt to analyze and appraise the *logical soundness* of the critic's arguments in support of his statements.

If there is no such thing as a logic of crit., as some theorists have held, then m. (on one view) becomes fairly limited. However, some theorists argue, rather, that there is simply no single logic of crit.—that critical practices and concepts are grounded in specific cultural, gender, historical, and institutional contexts which undergo change, all of which undermine the notion of any unitary and monolithic logic we might otherwise ascribe to crit. It has sometimes been suggested that critical statements work in a special way and that critical argument is not argument in the usual sense. Objectivist metacritics reject this stance as depriving critics of any important critical function at all, since it would strip crit. of genuine statements altogether.

The metacritic's first enterprise—the analysis of meaning—raises a conflict within m. concerning the scope and limits of m. *Semantic descriptivists* take the technical terms of crit. as the critic uses them and are content merely to study and make explicit the way these terms are used, modified, and refined by critics. *Semantic revisionists* are uneasy about stopping there: they consider it part of the metacritic's job to point out where critical vocabulary goes astray and, where possible, to recommend clearer definitions or new terminology. They do not necessarily have any intent to standardize all critical lang., but they think that critical discussion would be improved and much less discussion wasted if critics at least used key terms in the same clear, explicit, and agreed-on senses. A broader and historically more informed form of m. would embrace the tasks of both descriptivists and revisionists, seeking to show why critical vocabulary cannot be standardized or improved (in the sense of being logically grounded) beyond a point, and how a sound and intelligent critical practice need not remain strictly bound by a particular set of criteria. This form of metacritical analysis discloses the historically situated and changing nature of crit. and its theories and acknowledges the internal modifications and refinements within them.

The metacritic's second enterprise—the logical appraisal of critical reasoning—raises a second conflict within m. about the ultimate relationship between crit. and philosophy. Does crit. rest on more general aesthetic foundations, and must it be justified by philosophical arguments? The *autonomist* view is that crit. is independent of philosophy and needs no justification. M., on this view, attempts to make clear the actual reasoning underlying various critical practices, bringing out their tacit assumptions and thereby helping critics better understand what they are doing. The *heteronomist* view is that crit. necessarily rests on philosophical foundations whose truth, or at least reasonableness, can be established only by philosophical inquiry. If explication presupposes certain propositions about the nature of meaning, if evaluation presupposes certain propositions about the nature of truth and value, then (on this view) the critic may talk nonsense, or go wildly astray in his or her work, unless the propositions presupposed are philosophically sound. The *historicist* (or *pragmatist*) view, on the other hand, considers crit. and its theories to be quasi-autonomous rather than fully autonomous, and shows them to be situated in particular historical, institutional, and cultural contexts. See now ANALYSIS; CRITICISM; EVALUATION; INTERPRETATION; POETICS; THEORY.

S. C. Pepper, *The Basis of Crit. in the Arts* (1945); R. McKeon, "The Philosophical Bases of Art and Crit.," in Crane, "Imitation and Crit.," *Thought, Action and Passion* (1954); Abrams, ch. 1; W. K. Wimsatt, Jr., *The Verbal Icon* (1954), *Hateful Contraries* (1965); L. B. Meyer, *Emotion and Meaning in Music* (1956); Wellek and Warren; M. C. Beardsley, *Aesthetics* (1958)—esp. Intro., *The Possibility of Crit.* (1970); *Aesthetics and Lang.*, ed. W. Elton (1959); J. Stolnitz, *Aesthetics and Philosophy of Art Crit.* (1960); E. H. Gombrich, *Art and Illusion*, 2d ed. (1961); J. Margolis, *The Lang. of Art and Art Crit.* (1965); J. Casey, *The Lang. of Crit.* (1966); E. D. Hirsch, Jr., *Validity in Interp.* (1967); *Lit. and Aesthetics*, ed. M. C. Beardsley (1968); R. Colie, *"My Echoing Song": Andrew Marvell's Poetry of Crit.* (1970); R. Wellek, *Discriminations* (1970); F. Jameson, "Metacommentary," *PMLA* 86 (1971); *In Search of Literary Theory*, ed. M. W. Bloomfield (1972); P. Hernadi, *Beyond Genre* (1972); G. Sircello, *Mind and Art* (1972); J. M. Ellis, *The Theory of Lit. Crit.* (1974); H.-G. Gadamer, *Truth and Method* (1975); W. C. Booth, *Critical Understanding* (1979); S. Fish, *Is There a Text in This Class?* (1980); S. Raval, *M.* (1981); C. Norris, *Deconstruction* (1982); J. Culler, *On Deconstruction* (1983); P. Steiner, *Rus. Formalism: A Metapoetics* (1984).

M.C.B.; S.R.

METALEPSIS or TRANSUMPTION (Gr. *metalepsis* [*metalambano*, to partake in, take in another sense, "take after," interpret], Lat. *transumo*, to adopt, assume). In Quintilian (8.6.37) and later rhetoricians, an obscure and minor trope, variously defined, "a change from one trope to another," often moving through an associative chain. Since Fletcher's ascription to it of the figuration of poetic allusiveness, the term has become widely used to designate a moment or turn of revisionary, reinterpretive allusiveness (Fletcher 241n; see ALLUSION). Bloom (83–105) associated t. with his revisionary "ratio" of *apophrades*. Originally this referred to the spooky sense we have of the presence, in a poem, of the voice of a later poetic descendant; but Bloom later came to extend the concept to cover the role of the allusive relation in the rhetorical surface of the later poem, particularly with respect to the images of early- and-lateness (see INFLUENCE). In an attempt to associate strong poetic stances toward precursors with Freudian psychic choreography and tropological terms from Cl. rhetoric as reinterpreted by Vico and, later, Kenneth Burke, Bloom's taxonomy invoked t. variously as a figure, a style, and a whole rhetorical strategy. Bloom's psychologized rhetoric associates t. with the Freudian nonrepressive mechanisms of defense, projection, and introjection, whereby t. becomes a type of *Verneinung* (Negation) which frees the poet cognitively from the literary past while continuing the emotive consequences of repressing that past.

Hollander followed Fletcher in linking m. with allusiveness and suggested its name for that of a previously undiagnosed trope of diachrony—a rhetorically defined moment or unit of poetic echo (q.v.) which he distinguished from outright quotation or manifestly stated allusion.

In all three of these critics, the revisionary, interpretive force of m. or t. (today the Gr. and Lat. terms are used interchangeably) is at central issue. In recent decades, t. has come to designate a range of allusive devices at a number of rhetorical and textual levels, whether of particular word or phrase, trope, formal mode, or genre. Thus the revisionary relation of Theocritus' hexameter line in his new genre of pastoral idyll to Homer's hexameter; that of many of the *Canterbury Tales* to canonical genres of medieval story; Shakespeare's revisions of dramatic subgenres—all of these exhibit that transcendental (in Schlegel's sense) or subversively analytic quality which is so much deeper than mere elegant exemplification of a genre or mode. Increasingly they are being called transumptive in this broadest sense.

Narratology presents a seemingly different but parallel usage for m.; Genette's structuralist approach to narrative form develops another traditional use of the term. In narrative discourse, a m. occurs when the story jumps from one voice-level to another, transgressing the boundaries between "the world *in* which one tells and the world *of* which one tells" (1972). Genette instances Julio Cortazar, who "tells the story of a man assassinated by one of the characters in the novel he is reading." Narrative ts. may resemble Diderot's address to the reader: "If it gives you pleasure, *let us set* the peasant girl back in the saddle behind her escort, *let us let* them go and *let us come back to* our two travellers" (italics added). For Borges, continuous narrative illusionism breaks down metaleptically, so that "if characters in a story can be readers or spectators, then we, their readers and spectators, may be fictitious." Such radically disorienting switches in the planes and levels of narrative reality are the transumptive or metaleptical hallmark of the great precursors of late 20th-c. fiction, such as D'Urfé or Sterne.

Narrative m. parallels allusive m. in that both violate normal expectations established within the standard "voiced" boundaries of any discourse. Transumptive allusion shocks because it violates expectations of the separateness of "early" and "late." Such allusions do not belong where they are, but rather float, like echoes, rebounding from some disconnected pre-text. Similarly, narrative m. breaks the storyteller's stance of continuous epic relation to his story; *his* story abandons him and begins to narrate its own narration, as the change of Genette's "voice" transgresses the borders between the telling and the told. The effect is often uncanny, since the poet has now made "his" what is simultaneously "not his," allowing for what one might call "textual alienation." For a history of the use of the term "t." by Cl. and later rhetoricians, with some observations on the Cl. examples traditionally cited, see Hollander 133–

49.—A. Fletcher, *Allegory* (1964); G. Genette, *Narrative Discourse* (1972); Lausberg, sect. 571; H. Bloom, *Kabbalah and Crit.* (1975); J. Hollander, *The Figure of Echo* (1981), App.   J.HO.; A.F.

METAPHOR.

    I. DEFINITIONS
    II. CRITICAL VIEWS
    III. HISTORY
    IV. CONTEMPORARY THEORIES
        A. *Linguistics and Semiotics*
        B. *Pragmatics*
        C. *Philosophy*
        D. *Other Extensions*
        E. *Summary*

I. DEFINITIONS. M. (Gr. "transference") is a trope, or figurative expression, in which a word or phrase is shifted from its normal uses to a context where it evokes new meanings. When the ordinary meaning of a word is at odds with the context, we tend to seek relevant features of the word and the situation that will reveal the intended meaning. If there is a conceptual or material connection between the word and what it denotes—e.g. using cause for effect ("I read Shakespeare," meaning his works) or part for whole ("give me a hand," meaning physical help)—the figure usually has another name (in these examples, metonymy and synecdoche [qq.v.] respectively). To understand ms., one must find meanings not predetermined by language, logic, or experience. In the terminology of traditional rhet., these figures are "tropes of a word," appearing in a literal context; in "tropes of a sentence," the entire context is figurative, as in allegory, fable, and (according to some) irony (qq.v.). For further treatment of these distinctions, see FIGURE, SCHEME, TROPE.

Following I. A. Richards, we can call a word or phrase that seems anomalous the "vehicle" of the trope and refer to the underlying idea that it seems to designate as the "tenor" (see TENOR AND VEHICLE). An extended m., as the name implies, is one that the poet develops in some detail. A conceit (q.v.) is an intricate, intellectual, or far-fetched m.; a diminishing m., one of its types, uses a perjorative vehicle with reference to an esteemed tenor. An extreme or exaggerated conceit is a catachresis (q.v.). Mixed m., traditionally derided because it jumbles disparate vehicles together, has recently found some critical acceptance (see Richards). Dead m. (q.v.) presents fossilized ms. in ordinary usage (e.g. "he *missed* the *point*").

What Quintilian said of tropes remains true today: "This is a subject which has given rise to interminable disputes among the teachers of lit., who have quarreled no less violently with the philosophers than among themselves over the problem of the genera and species into which tropes may be divided, their number and their correct classification." To say that m. is any trope that cannot be classified as metonymy, hyperbole (qq.v.), etc., is to provide only a negative definition. Any attempt to define m. positively—e.g. "the application of a word or phrase to something it does not literally denote, on the basis of a similarity between the objects or ideas involved"—will inevitably apply to other tropes.

Some critics accept this consequence and call all tropes ms. But even this definition begs the question of how to distinguish the figurative from the literal, or at best relegates it to accepted usage. If two species are members of the same genus on the basis of similarity, are they not "like" the genus and therefore like each other? Extension of this argument leads to the conclusion that all figures should be understood literally. On the other hand, every object is unique; "it is only the roughness of the eye that makes any two persons, things, situations seem alike" (Pater). Perfect literalness might be achieved by giving each object a unique name. In relation to that standard, a common noun is a m. because it provides a name that can be applied to different entities on the basis of a likeness between them. Hence "literal" lang. can be considered metaphorical.

Despite these arguments and repeated attempts to create a more satisfactory classification of figures, the principal definitions of the major tropes have remained unchanged since the Cl. period. The most innovative attempts to clarify the status of m. have come from philosophers, linguists, and historians, who have explored m.'s relation to propositional truth and meaning (q.v.), to the origins of lang. and myth (q.v.), to world views, scientific models, social attitudes, and ordinary usage. For their purposes, conventional and dead ms. provide adequate examples for analysis. Scholars and literary critics, less concerned with theory than with practice, have usually accepted the imprecise accounts of m. handed down by trad. since the 5th c. B.C. and focused their attention on its effects in particular poems. To say this is not to claim that the uses of m. in poetry are categorically different from those in other domains of lang. use, but simply to call attention to the institutionalized character of poetry. One learns to construe and even create poetic ms. through training at school, and the expectations in place when one starts reading a poem differ from those active in reading a newspaper or conversing. A summary of what critics have usually said about m., with some account of objections to traditional views, will provide a context for a brief discussion of historically important theories of m. and contemp. treatments of the subject.

II. CRITICAL VIEWS. Aristotle's discussion of simile (q.v.) in the *Rhetoric* was until recently the starting-point for most treatments of m. In saying that Achilles "sprang at the foe as a lion," Homer used a simile; had he said "the lion sprang at them," it would have been a m. In one case, according to Aristotle, the comparison is explicit (using "like" or "as"); in the other, the word "lion"

is "transferred" to Achilles, but the meaning is the same. Quintilian endorsed Aristotle's view of metaphor as a condensed simile: "in the latter we compare some object to the thing which we wish to describe, whereas in the former the object is actually substituted for the thing." What Max Black calls the "comparison view" of m. is based on the grammatical form "A is B"; m. is seen as a condensed simile, meaning that A is (like) B. The "substitution view," as Black says, takes "the lion sprang" as the paradigmatic form of m.: rather than predicating a likeness, m. uses a figurative word in place of a literal one. Both of these views are compatible with the reductive conception of m. as "saying one thing and meaning another," thus implying that the poet has gone out of the way to say something other than what was meant (perhaps in the interests of decorating an ordinary thought), and suggesting that in reading poetry, one must dismantle ms. in order to find out what the poem "really means."

A different conception of m. is necessary to sustain Aristotle's claim, endorsed through the centuries, that m. is the most significant feature of poetic style: "that alone cannot be learnt; it is the token of genius. For the right use of m. means an eye for resemblances." New ms. are said to spring from the poet's heightened emotion, keen perception, or intellectual acuity; their functions are aesthetic (making expression more vivid or interesting), pragmatic (conveying meanings concisely), and cognitive (providing words to describe things that have no literal name, or rendering complex abstractions easy to understand through concrete analogies). Emphasis on the value of concreteness and sensory appeal in m. is frequent. Some modern critics treat m. under the general rubric "imagery" (q.v.; *Bild* has a corresponding importance in Ger. crit., as does *image* in Fr. crit.).

Opposing the comparison and substitution views, 20th-c. critics and philosophers developed more intricate accounts of the verbal and cognitive processes involved in metaphoric usage. Despite their differences, the "interaction" view (Richards and Black), "controversion theory" (Beardsley), and "fusion" view (espoused by New Critics) all hold that m. creates meanings not readily accessible through literal language. Rather than simply substituting one word for another, or comparing two things, m. invokes a transaction between words and things, after which the words, things, and thoughts are not quite the same. M., from these perspectives, is not a decorative figure, but a transformed literalism, meaning precisely what it says. Fusion theorists argue that it unifies the concrete and abstract, the sensual and the conceptual in a concrete universal (q.v.) or symbol. An entire poem, if it is organically unified, can therefore be called a m.

A less audacious explanation of the uniqueness of m. will be discussed in the next section (for a defense of the traditional view, see Fogelin); at present, let us simply note what problems this view solves, and what ones it creates. Treating all tropes as ms., the fusion theory frees crit. from the inconsistent classification systems handed down from antiquity. Synecdoche (q.v.), as a species—genus or part—whole relation, can be imputed to any comparison whatever (everything being "like" everything else in some generic respect, or part of it, if the level of abstraction is high enough). Metonymy can be an empirically observed association (cause—effect), an entailment (attribute for subject), or a contingent relation (object for possessor). Since no single principle of classification governs these distinctions, one figurative expression can exemplify two or more tropes, as Foquelin observed (*La Rhétorique françoise* [1555]). Fusion theorists eliminate this problem and seek the new meanings released by m., rather than reducing them to uninformative categories.

This freedom from pedantry can, however, entail a loss of precision leading to the neglect, if not the dismissal or misperception, of many tropes. The blurring of traditional distinctions leads to changes in the ways figures are construed. "Pale death," which would now be considered a trite m. involving personification, was in the Ren. a metonymy (death, not personified, is the cause of the effect paleness). The verbal vitality created by tropes other than m. is categorized as "imagery" (q.v.) if it is sensory, and "style" (q.v.) if it is not. Similes, otherwise identical to ms., are automatically accorded a lower status merely because they use the word "like" or "as"—a sign of timidity in the eyes of the fusion theorist, who may see in simile new possibilities for describing the nature of lang. (see Brogan).

Singleminded emphasis on the meaning of m., apart from the semantic and grammatical details of its realization, can lead both modern theorists and traditionalists to questionable interpretive practices. In most textbooks, the only examples of m. provided are in the form "A is B," despite the fact that this is not the most common grammatical form, "the A of B" ("th'expense of spirit") and "the A B" ("the dying year") being more frequent (see Brooke-Rose). When they encounter metaphorical verbs, adjectives, and adverbs, critics who seek new meanings in poetry are tempted to transfer the figuration of these word classes over to the nouns with which they are associated. If a speaker snarls a reply or has a green thought, the critic concludes that the poet has said that the speaker is a dog or wolf, and that the thought is a plant. Johnson's line describing those who gain preferment—"They mount, they shine, evaporate, and fall"—may be clarified through reference to mists and May flies (ephemerae, living for a day), but its power and meaning evaporate if one concludes that the metaphoric verbs are a roundabout way of saying that the rich and famous are like insects. The alternative assumption would be that the poet wanted to connect figurative attributes to a noun that remains literal; the nominal "A is B" equation was after all available to the poet, along with the other grammatical forms that create identity (apposition, demonstrative reference) and presumably would be used if that were the meaning. The tendency to think that ms. always equate or fuse entities (nouns) reduces the varied effects of m. in poetry to a single register. Poets may intend their figurative renderings of process, attribute, and attitude to evoke a range of relations, from suggestiveness to total fusion. If so, they are not well served by theorists who translate every figurative velleity into a declaration of equivalence.

The affective and aesthetic functions of m., usually mentioned in traditional accounts, have been emphasized by a few modern critics who oppose the assumption that the purpose of m. is to convey meanings. Forrest-Thomson argues that "the worst disservice crit. can do to poetry is to understand it too soon." Modern poets in particular try to forestall this haste by using ms. that do not lend themselves to assimilation by the discursive elements of the text. Thus they try to preserve poetry from reduction to paraphrastic statement. Shklovsky goes further, asserting that the purpose of new ms. is not to create meaning but to renew perception by "defamiliarizing" the world: unlikely comparisons retard reading and force us to reconceive objects that ordinary words allow us to pass over in haste.

III. HISTORY. Four approaches have dominated all attempts to improve on the account of m. provided by the rhetorical trad. Some writers propose more logical classifications of the tropes. Others undertake semantic analysis of the ways in which features of a word's meaning are activated or repressed in figurative usage. These two modes of analysis blend into each other, but they can be distinguished from treatments of m. that emphasize its existential entailments—its relation to reality and to hist. rather than to logic and lang. The crudity of this fourfold classification must justify the brevity of the following discussion, which touches on only those treatments of m. that, from a contemp. perspective, seem crucial.

For Aristotle, m. has two functions and two structures. In the *Poetics*, its function is to lend dignity to style, by creating an enigma that reveals a likeness, or by giving a name to something that had been nameless ("the ship *plowed* the sea"). But in the *Rhet.*, m. appears as a technique of persuasion, used to make a case appear better or worse than it is in fact. Modern critics would say that "kill," "murder," and "execute" have the same denotation but differ in connotation (q.v.); for Aristotle, one of the three words would be proper in relation to a particular act, and the other two would be ms. It is from its rhetorical uses that m. acquires its reputation as a dangerous deviation from the truth, being for that reason castigated by Hobbes, Locke, and other Enlightenment philosophers.

The four kinds of m. distinguished by Aristotle in the *Poetics* are of two structural types. One results from substitution (of species for genus, genus for species, or species for species), the two terms having a logical or "natural" relation to each other. The other type has an analogical or equational structure: A is to B as C is to D. Although only two of the four terms need be mentioned (A and D, or B and C), we must infer the other two in order to derive the meaning: "the evening of life" enables us to reconstruct "evening is to day as X is to life." Here we find the bifurcation that will henceforth characterize discussions of tropes: one type is based on accepted conceptual relationships (here, genus—species), and the other type includes all tropes that cannot be so defined. Species—genus and species—species relations are part of common knowledge; to cross from genus to genus, we need four terms that create what might be called a hypothetical likeness, one not given by logic or nature.

The species—genus relation is one of many that make it possible to infer the tenor from the vehicle. Identification of other such relations (e.g. cause—effect, quantitative change) led to the proliferation of names for the tropes in rhet. Once they separated themselves from Aristotle's generic term "m.," it was necessary to define m. in such a way that it would not include the other tropes. Quintilian's solution—to say that m. is a substitution involving any permutation of the terms "animate" and "inanimate"—is not as unreasonable as it first appears. The dividing-line between these two domains, which is a fundamental feature of lang. and culture, cannot easily be crossed by species—genus, part—whole, or subject—adjunct relations. Furthermore, animate—inanimate ms. are strikingly frequent in poetry, as are animate—animate ms. involving humans and nature.

Looking back on Quintilian from the perspectives provided by Vico, the romantic poets, and semioticians, we can see that his untidy classification (which defines m. by reference to its subject matter, the other tropes by reference to "categorical" relationships) reveals something about the role of m. that escapes notice in any purely formal analysis. But when subject matter becomes the primary basis of classification, as it is in 19th- and 20th-c. studies such as those of Brinkmann, Konrad, and Spurgeon, the specificity of the tropes dissolves in the all-embracing category "imagery."

For the Ren., Quintilian's *Institutio oratoria* (pub. 1470) provided an orderly exposition of rhet. in place of the patchwork syntheses inferrable from other Cl. texts; it was Quintilian's renown that made him one target of Ramus's campaign to reform the curriculum. To provide a rational classification of the tropes, Ramus correlated them with Aristotle's ten "categories," the most general ways in which any subject may be described (Howell). Aristotle had himself defined m. by appeal to the category species—genus. Ramus concluded that there were four basic tropes: metonymy, irony ("a change in meaning from opposites to opposites"), m. ("a change in meaning from comparisons to comparisons"), and synecdoche. In Vico's *New Science* (1725 et seq.; tr. 1977), these four become the basis of a history of lang. and civilization. In the age of the gods, metonymy ruled: lightning and thunder were a great effect of unknown origin, and mankind imagined the agent Jove as the cause. The age of heroes was one of synecdoche: men who held themselves to be sons of Jove embodied his abstract attributes. The age of men is the age of m., in which likenesses are taken from bodies "to signify the operation of abstract minds"; and philosophy gives rise to what we call "literal" meaning.

Ramus is the precursor of modern attempts to reduce tropes to a rationale, and Vico occupies the same position in relation to modern discussions of m.'s importance in the devel. of lang., though their successors are not always aware of this lineage. That lang. was originally metaphorical, mythic, and poetic is a common theme in romanticism—e.g. in Rousseau, Herder, Schelling, and Shelley—but there is little evidence that Vico was their source (the idea can be found in Lucretius, among others). Müller, Werner, and Cassirer exemplify the Ger. thinkers who have developed this theory; Langer and Wheelwright contributed to its popularity in Am. crit. On the basis of recent research on the asymmetry of cerebral functions, Jaynes argues that the visions of Old Testament prophets and the voices of the gods heard by heroes in the *Iliad* came from the brain's right hemisphere; when processed by the left hemisphere, they became the ms. that marked the birth of human consciousness. Nietzsche's contrary thesis—that lang. was originally concrete and literal in reference, and that the abstract vocabulary now considered literal is in fact metaphorical—has recently attracted critical attention (de Man). But as Vico pointed out (par. 409), it makes little sense to speak of lang. as either literal or metaphorical before it incorporates a distinction between the two. Even Gadamer's carefully worded claims about the historical and conceptual primacy of m. cannot escape Vico's objection (Cooper).

The theories of m. proposed by Richards, Black, and Beardsley, which incorporate insights into the workings of lang. and meaning derived from 20th-c. analytic philosophy, provide an alternative to traditional accounts of m. as a substitution, comparison, or fusion of meanings. Sentences, Richards says, are neither created nor interpreted by putting together words with unique meanings. Any ordinary word has several meanings and a number of loosely associated characteristics; often it will be both noun and verb, or noun and adjective. The varied traits or semes of a word's meaning are sometimes sorted into two groups—denotations (characteristics essential to a distinct sense of the word) and connotations—but in practice this distinction is hard to maintain. (In his precise and revealing analysis of this issue, Mac Cormic describes words as "fuzzy sets.") Only when placed in a context does a word take on one or more meanings, at which time some of its traits become salient and others are suppressed. It is often difficult to decide when we have crossed the line between literal and figurative usage. In the series *green dress, green field, green memory, green thought*, the adjective gradually moves from one denotation to another and then takes on a connotative emphasis (that may or may not be listed as a "meaning" in the dictionary) before becoming clearly metaphorical.

Richards looked on m. as a "transaction between contexts," in which tenor and vehicle combine in varied ways to produce meanings. The distinction between literal and figurative is of little importance in his theory. Beardsley makes it more precise by discussing the apparent contradictions that lead us to identify a m. and to seek connotations relevant to the construction of an emergent meaning. He argues persuasively that m. is intensional: we find it in words, not in the objects to which they refer. Black's "interaction theory" contains an important distinction between the "focus" and "frame" of a m. (the figurative expression and the sentence in which it occurs). The focus brings with it not just connotations but a "system of associated commonplaces"—what Eco will later call "encyclopedic knowledge"—that interacts with its frame to produce implications that can be shared by a speech community. To say "Achilles is a lion" can mean that Achilles is courageous only by virtue of the position that the lion occupies in common lore (a hunter, not an herbivore; sociable with its own kind, unlike the tiger, but not a herd animal; monogamous; a lone hunter, unlike the wolf). The lion cannot represent courage until, through a prior mapping of culture on nature, he is the king of beasts. Black emphasizes the "*extensions* of meaning" that novel ms. bring to lang., but his theory has proved most useful in understanding the inherited and dead ms. that structure a society's way of thinking and talking about itself.

IV. CONTEMPORARY THEORIES. Every innovative critical theory of the past two decades has generated a new delineation of m.—either as the "other" of its own conceptual domain, or as the very ground of its new insights. One of the most influential innovations has been Jakobson's opposition of m. to metonymy. In his view, m. results from the substitution of one term for another; it is characteristic of poetry and some literary movements, such as romanticism and symbolism (qq.v.). Metonymy, based on contiguity, appears more frequently in prose and typifies realism. Though they often cross disciplinary boundaries, recent theories of m. can be classified as (a) linguistic or semiotic (based on intralinguistic relationships, or relations between signs of any sort);

(b) rhetorical or pragmatic (involving a difference between sentence meaning and speaker meaning); (c) philosophical (emphasizing relations between words and reality, or sense and reference); and (d) extended (treating nonlinguistic relationships in other disciplines).

A. *Linguistics and Semiotics*. The most ambitious recent attempt to identify ling. features of m. appears in *A General Rhet.*, produced by "Group Mu" of the University of Liège. They treat all unexpected suppressions, additions, repetitions, or permutations of ling. elements, from phonemes to phrases, as figures, the nonfigurative being a hypothetical "degree zero" discourse from which rhet. deviates. M. results from an implicit decomposition of words into their semes (lexical features), some of which will be cancelled, and others added, when one word is substituted for another. The natural route for such substitutions is through species and genus, as Aristotle observed, and Group Mu concludes that a m. consists of two synecdoches, the progression being either species—genus—species (the intermediate term being a class that incl. the first and last terms) or whole—part—whole (here the central term is a class formed where the first and last overlap). S. R. Levin, using a more flexible scheme for the transfer and deletion of semantic features, shows that there are six ways to interpret a m. (his example is "the stone died"). He points out that the grammatical structure of many ms. allows for the transfer of features in two directions: "the brook smiled" can either humanize the brook or add sparkle and liquidity to the idea of smiling. Although he analyzes m. as an intralinguistic phenomenon, Levin recognizes that Aristotle's fourth type, analogy, often depends upon reference to reality—a fact that Group Mu overlooked. Thus m. appears to escape formalization within a system. Umberto Eco's semiotic solution to this problem is to imagine an encyclopedia that describes all the features of reality not included in the semanticist's dictionary. For Riffaterre, mimetic reference is only a feint that the literary text makes before refocusing itself in a network of semiotic commonplaces.

B. *Pragmatics*. Proponents of speech-act theory (q.v.) hold that m. cannot be explained through reference to relationships between words and their ling. contexts. They make a categorical distinction between "word or sentence meaning" and "speaker's utterance meaning." M., in their view, arises from a disparity between the literal meaning of the words used and what is intended by the speaker or writer. Words always retain their invariant "locutionary" definitions, but when used to make ms., the hearer notices that there is something odd about them and infers unstated suggestions or meanings. As evidence for this theory, Ted Cohen says that a speaker's intention may lead us to infer that a literally true sentence is a m. (e.g. "no man is an island"). As evidence against it, L. J.

Cohen (in Ortony) points out that speech acts lose their speaker-meaning in indirect discourse ("Tom told George he was sorry" is not an apology), but ms. remain ms. when repeated ("Tom said George was a fire-eater"), indicating that the meaning of a m. is in the words, not in the occasion of their use. Grice's theory of "conversational implicature" provides a set of rules and maxims for normal talk that, when violated, may alert us to the fact that someone is speaking figuratively. His theory, like Searle's, locates m. in a difference between utterance meaning and speaker meaning—the domain of "pragmatics"—and is subject to the same sorts of crit. that speech-act theory has elicited (see Sadock in Ortony; Cooper).

C. *Philosophy.* Searle and Grice are philosophers, but their theories entail empirical claims of relevance to linguists. Davidson's treatment of m. is more strictly philosophical. Meaning, in his view, involves only the relation between lang. and reality. He is willing to accept the pragmatic "distinction between what words mean and what they are used to do," but he denies the existence of metaphoric meaning: "ms. mean what the words, in their most literal interp., mean, and nothing more." To this one might reply that if we did not realize they were patently false, we would not know they were figurative. Recognizing them as such, we may discover truths about the world, but this is not a consequence of some meaning inherent in the words. Nelson Goodman disagrees. In *Langs. of Art* (1979), he conceives of m., like many other activities, as exemplification. Rather than applying a label to a thing, we use the thing as an example of the label, as when the lively appearance of the literal brook is seen as an instance of smiling (above). This reverses the direction of denotation: the example refers to the word, rather than vice versa, and the word may bring with it a whole schema of relationships that will be sorted anew in the metaphorical context. Goodman concludes that m. is "no more independent of truth or falsity than literal use."

D. *Other Extensions.* Postponing discussion of deeper philosophical differences that divide theorists, one cannot help but note that they tend to privilege different moments in the interpretive process. At first glance, or outside time, m. is false (Davidson). Realizing that the creator of a m. means something else, one might create a theory of the difference between sentence and speaker meaning (Searle, Grice). When engaged in deciphering, a reader enacts the interaction theory—discovering new meanings—and the falsity of m. is forgotten. Truth usually results from testing many examples to find one rule; in m., meaning emerges from repeated consideration of a single example, uncovering all its possibilities; and a hypothesis or generalization is the product of the process, not its inception. In accordance with information theory, the low probability of a word or phrase in a particular context implies that it carries a great deal of meaning.

This improbable interaction of conceptual domains has also attracted the attention of theorists in other disciplines, leading them to transport the figure outside its usual literary domain. Like ms., scientific models serve heuristic functions when familiar structures are used to map uncharted phenomena. Mary Hesse and Thomas Kuhn have extended Black's discussion of this subject, which has also attracted the attention of Fr. philosophers of science. Citing the work of Bachelard and Canguilhem, Derrida suggests that the function of m. in science is not merely heuristic; Boyd (in Ortony) argues that "ms. are *constitutive* of the theories they express, rather than merely exigetical." Lakoff and Johnson show how pervasive ms. are in organizing personal and social experience. For example, words used to describe arguments ("he *attacked* my *position* and he was *right on target*") show that we conceive argument as a form of warfare. A few dozen such equations generate countless ms. in ordinary usage. In such cases the occurrence of a particular m. is less significant than the model ("frame," "schema," "system of commonplaces") that it evokes. When employed to order understanding of the past or to plan for the future, metaphoric analogies take on a narrative dimension (see Schön and Sternberg [in Ortony] for discussion of their influence on social policy). Pepper's *World Hypotheses* (1942), which treats most philosophic systems as elaborations of four "root ms.," proved useful to Hayden White (1973), who argues that a poetic "prefiguration" based on one of the four tropes identified by Ramus and Vico underlies the methods of explanation used by modern historians.

E. *Summary.* The figural use of "m." in modern theory, through which it assimilates not only all other tropes (as in Aristotle) but models, analogies, and narrative methods as well, leads back to the question of whether the literal and figurative can properly be distinguished from one another at all. The simplest and in some ways most logical answers are that all ling. meaning is literal (Davidson) or all figural (Nietzsche). Children do not discriminate between the two in lang. acquisition, and there is little evidence that adult comprehension of literal and metaphorical usage involves different psychological processes (Rummelhart). Rather than attempting to identify rules capable of accounting for literal usage and then explaining figures as transformations or deviations from this set, one can begin from an inclusive set of semantic features from which literal and figurative usage can be derived by imposing further constraints (Weinreich; van Dijk). Alternatively, one can treat literalness "as a limiting case rather than a norm" and develop a pragmatic theory of meaning in which ms. need not be considered different from other usage (Sperber and Wilson).

While contributing to an understanding of its ling. features and conceptual implications, recent theories of m. show that it is not simply one critical problem among others, notable only for the number of disagreements it causes. As that which lies outside the literal, normal, proper, or systematic, m. serves as the topic through which each system defines itself: m. is not simply false, but that which marks the limits of the distinctions between true and false, or between meaningful and deviant. As Derrida says (1972), "each time that a rhet. defines m., not only is *a* philosophy implied, but also a conceptual network in which philosophy *itself* has been constituted." Thus agreement about the status of m. will be deferred until all other philosophical disputes have been resolved. In *The Rule of M.*, the best available survey of the subject, Paul Ricoeur integrates many of the views discussed above in a synoptic theory that preserves while subsuming the oppositions on which they are based. To do so, he is forced to assign literary m. (despite its virtues) a subordinate position in relation to the "speculative discourse" of philosophy, within which m. can reveal the nature of being. Showing how little has changed since Plato described the quarrel between philosophy and rhet., Ricoeur's work has served as a stimulus for a more penetrating analysis of the conceptual operation that gives rise to the distinction between being and textuality (q.v.), and hence to that between the literal and the figurative (Derrida 1978). See now FIGURATION; METALEPSIS; PSYCHOLOGICAL CRITICISM; SIMILE.

BIBLIOGRAPHIES: W. A. Shibles, *M.: An Annot. Bibl. and Hist.* (1971); M. Johnson, "Selected Annot. Bibl.," *Philosophical Perspectives on M.* (1981); A. Haverkamp, "Bibliographie," *Theorie der Metapher* (1983)—covers ca. 1870–1981; W. Bohn, "Roman Jakobson's Theory of M. and Metonymy: An Annot. Bibl.," *Style* 18 (1984); J.-P. van Noppen et al., *M.: A Bibl. of Post-1970 Pubs.* (1985).

STUDIES: M. Müller, *Lectures on the Science of Lang.*, 2.ser. (1862, 1865); F. Brinkmann, *Die Metaphern* (1878); V. Shklovsky, "Art as Technique" (1916), tr. in *Rus. Formalist Crit.* (1965); H. Werner, *Die Ursprünge der Metapher* (1919); C. Spurgeon, *Shakespeare's Imagery and What It Tells Us* (1935); I. A. Richards, *The Philosophy of Rhet.* (1936); W. B. Stanford, *Gr. M.* (1936); G. Bachelard, *La Formation de l'esprit scientifique* (1938); H. Konrad, *Étude sur la métaphore* (1939); S. Pepper, *World Hypotheses* (1942); S. Langer, *Philosophy in a New Key* (1942); E. Cassirer, *Lang. and Myth* (1946); M. Foss, *Symbol and M. in Human Experience* (1949); W. Empson, *The Structure of Complex Words* (1951); W. S. Howell, *Logic and Rhet. in England, 1500-1700* (1956); R. Jakobson, "Two Aspects of Lang. and Two Types of Aphasic Disturbances" (1956), rev. in Jakobson, v. 2; C. Brooke-Rose, *A Grammar of M.* (1958); *M. and Symbol*, ed. L. C. Knights and B. Cottle (1960); H.-G. Gadamer, *Wahrheit und Methode* (1960, tr. 1975); T. Kuhn, *The Structure of Scientific Revolutions* (1962); M. C. Beardsley, "The Metaphorical Twist," *PPR*

22 (1962); M. Black, *Models and Ms.* (1962); Jakobson; P. Wheelwright, *M. and Reality* (1962); J. Cohen, *Structure du langage poétique* (1966); M. Hesse, *Models and Analogies in Science* (1966); H. Weinreich, "Explorations in Semantic Theory," *Current Trends in Linguistics*, v. 3 (1966); M. B. Hester, *The Meaning of Poetic M.* (1967); G. Canguilhem, *Études d'histoire et de philosophie des sciences* (1968); N. Goodman, *Langs. of Art* (1968); D. C. Allen, *Image and Meaning: Metaphoric Trads. in Ren. Poetry* (1968); Group Mu; C. Turbayne, *The Myth of M.* (1970); T. Hawkes, *M.* (1972); J. Derrida, "La mythologie blanche," *Marges de la philosophie* (1972, tr. 1982), "The *Retrait* of M.," *Enclitic* 2 (1978); T. A. van Dijk, *Some Aspects of Text Grammars* (1972), "Formal Semantics of Metaphorical Discourse," *Poetics* 4 (1975); Lausberg; H. White, *Metahistory* (1973); H. P. Grice, "Logic and Conversation" [1975], *Studies in the Ways of Words* (1989); P. Ricoeur, *La Métaphore vive* (1975, tr. as *The Rule of M.*, 1977); T. Cohen, "Figurative Speech and Figurative Acts," *JP* 71 (1975); J. Jaynes, *The Origin of Consciousness in the Breakdown of the Bicameral Mind* (1976); S. R. Levin, *The Semantics of M.* (1977), *Metaphoric Worlds* (1988); R. Berry, *Shakespearean M.* (1978); D. Davidson, "What Ms. Mean," and P. de Man, "The Epistemology of M.," in "Spec. Iss. on M.," *CritI* 5 (1978); V. Forrest-Thomson, *Poetic Artifice* (1978); M. Riffaterre, *Semiotics of Poetry* (1978); M. Black, "How Ms. Work," and N. Goodman, "M. as Moonlighting," *CritI* 6 (1979); D. Rummelhart, "Some Problems with the Notion of Literal Meanings," and J. Searle, "M.," in *M. and Thought*, ed. A. Ortony (1979); P. de Man, *Allegories of Reading* (1979); *On M.*, ed. S. Sacks (1979); G. Lakoff and M. Johnson, *Ms. We Live By* (1980); J. Culler, "The Turns of M.," *The Pursuit of Signs* (1981); Morier; U. Eco, "The Scandal of M.," *PoT* 4 (1983); G. Bouchard, *Le Procès de la métaphore* (1984); L. Gumpel, *M. Reexamined* (1984); *The Ubiquity of M.*, ed. W. Paprotté and R. Dirven (1985); E. R. Mac Cormac, *A Cognitive Theory of M.* (1985); J. V. Brogan, *Stevens and Simile: A Theory of Lang.* (1986); D. E. Cooper, *M.* (1986); D. Sperber and D. Wilson, *Relevance* (1986); E. Kittay, *M.* (1987); *M., Communication, and Cognition*, ed. M. Danesi, Monograph Series of the Toronto Semiotic Circle 2 (1988); M. C. Haley, *The Semeiosis of Poetic M.* (1988); R. J. Fogelin, *Figuratively Speaking* (1988); C. Hausman, *M. and Art* (1989); G. Lakoff and M. Turner, *More than Cool Reason* (1989).　　　　W.M.

METAPHYSICAL POETRY. A term applied to the poetry written by John Donne, George Herbert, Andrew Marvell, Henry Vaughan, and other 17th-c. Eng. poets, distinguished by ingenuity, intellectuality, and sometimes obscurity. Recent scholarship (de Mourgues, Warnke) has extended application of the term to Continental poets of the same period, so that m. p. is now often seen as an international phenomenon of the baroque (q.v.)

or, as some would have it, of mannerism (q.v.) (Sypher). Use of the term to designate a recurrent constant rather than a specific historical phenomenon has at best only a metaphorical or impressionistic validity, however. M. p. of the 17th c. is characterized by a strong dependence on irony and paradox (qq.v.) and by the use of the conceit (q.v.) as well as such figures as catachresis and oxymoron (qq.v.). Its strategy of address is typically dramatic rather than narrative or descriptive. In its earlier manifestations (e.g. the *Songs and Sonets* of Donne), m. p. was further distinguished by highly original attitudes toward sexual love. Donne rejected not only Petrarchan rhetoric (see PETRARCHISM)—except in a partially ironic manner—but also the pose of abject worship of the mistress which 16th-c. poets had inherited, via Petrarch, from the troubadours. A new sexual realism, together with introspective psychological analysis, thus became an element in the m. fashion.

Realism, introspection, and irony remained dominant features in Eng. as well as Continental m. p., but many of the greatest of Donne's successors—Herbert, Crashaw, Vaughan—generally chose to articulate those qualities in a religious rather than an amorous context. A great deal of m. p. is devotional; some of it is mystical. Although some scholars regard the term "m. p." as a misnomer, pointing out that its practitioners are seldom concerned with questions of metaphysics or ontology (Leishman), others have maintained that the distinctive quality of m. p., the occasion of its technique, is precisely that the subject—love, death, God, human frailty—is presented in the context of some m. problem (J. Smith). Such a justification was not, however, in the mind of Dryden when he suggested the term in a reference to Donne (*Discourse Concerning the Original and Progress of Satire*, 1692): "He affects the metaphysics not only in his satires, but in his amorous verses, where nature only should reign, and perplexes the minds of the fair sex with nice speculations of philosophy." (In Donne's own lifetime William Drummond of Hawthornden had referred scornfully to poems in which "m." diction is employed.) It remained for Dr. Johnson to supply the first analysis of m. imagery and to establish the term "m." permanently in Eng. crit. Johnson described the basis of m. imagery as a kind of *discordia concors* through which "the most heterogeneous ideas are yoked by violence together," criticizing the school therefore for its lack of naturalness.

Favoring a kind of imagery which requires the mediation of the intellect for full comprehension, m. p. shows relatively little interest in sensuous imagery. There are, however, some poets (e.g. Crashaw in England, Gryphius in Germany) who manifest aspects of both the m. and the "high baroque" manners. The assumption made by many earlier critics (Williamson, White), that Eng. m. p. derives primarily from attempts to imitate Donne, has been refuted by modern scholarship, which has demonstrated not only the notable individuality of poets such as Herbert and Marvell but also the fact that many features of m. style are present in much poetry written either shortly before or during the time when Donne wrote his *Songs and Sonets,* by such poets as Southwell, Greville, and Alabaster (Martz), not to mention the fact (noted above) that many poets on the Continent, predecessors and contemporaries of Donne, wrote poems in the m. style. Such poets as La Ceppède in France, Huygens and Revius in Holland, and Quevedo in Spain seem certainly to deserve the name "m. poets." If there can be said to be a "School of Donne" in England, it consists of such minor amorous lyrists as Lord Herbert of Cherbury, Carew, and Suckling, not of the great devotional poets.

Poets and critics during the heyday of m. p. had almost no awareness of that kind of poetry as a distinct stylistic phenomenon; most theorists of the age continued to describe poetry in the traditional terms of Ren. poetics (see BAROQUE POETICS). However, some It. and Sp. writers—particularly Baltasar Gracián—did offer the doctrine of "universal analogy" as a basis for the conceit, and "strong lines" was a phrase used by Eng. critics to designate the intricate intellectual quality of Donne and many of his contemporaries.

Dominant in England until the Restoration (1660) and the associated triumph of neoclassicism, m. p. went into eclipse throughout the 18th and 19th cs. (Continental m. p. had a similar destiny.) Although such poets as Coleridge and Browning admired Donne, he and his successors were generally regarded as frigid and pretentious purveyors of intentional obscurity. But the turn of the 20th c. ushered in a revaluation, heralded in England by the publication of Sir Herbert Grierson's great ed. of Donne's *Poetical Works* (1912) and coinciding with the Ger. rediscovery of baroque poetry and the Sp. rehabilitation of the reputations of Góngora and Calderón. The age of modernism (ca. 1920–ca. 1960) privileged m. p. with particular intensity. T. S. Eliot, the most influential modernist poet-critic in the Eng.-speaking world, saw in its practitioners, as in the Jacobean dramatists, a sensibility that had not suffered "dissociation" (q.v.), a capacity for "devouring all kinds of experience" which he contrasted with the singleness of tone of the romantics and Victorians. For the first time since the 17th c., the m. poets became a vital influence on living poets.

Some critics of the 1920s and 1930s went too far in stressing the modernity of the m. group, but balance was subsequently restored by studies that demonstrated the links between m. p. and the phenomena of its own age and its intellectual heritage—such phenomena as scholastic philosophy, Ren. logic and rhet., the "new science" of the 17th c., and Reformation and Counter-Reformation theology (Tuve, Nicolson, Martz, Lewalski). Especially rewarding has been the examination of the relationship between m. p. and the practice of formal religious meditation as formulated by Ignatius of Loyola. Some scholars (see Martz) have found in Ignatian meditation a basis for both the union of thought and feeling so often ascribed to m. p. and the markedly dramatic qualities of that poetry. Martz and others have suggested that the term *meditation* might be extended to cover an entire poetic mode rather than the 17th-c. phenomenon alone, and that meditation is one of the psychological bases of lyric composition (Warnke). Meditation has also been studied in the m. p. of France, Spain, and Holland.

If modernism exaggerated the modernity of the m. poets, however (and it should be noted that in the decades after 1960 scholarly attention tended to shift from Donne and the ms. to Spenser and Milton), the fact remains that the age did feel a special affinity with them. It may be that in our own century, under the disturbing impact of scientific relativity, social fragmentation, and political confusion, many artists and intellectuals were bound to feel a kinship with an age in which, in Donne's phrase, "new philosophy call[ed] all in doubt." The m. style, in its introspective and realistic orientation, its wide-ranging metaphor, and its daring rhet., aimed at wresting a precarious unity from the scattered materials of an existence which had become puzzling and unfocused. The poets of modernism may have felt their own task as similar. Similarity, however, is not identity (H. Block, for example, has convincingly refuted the supposed parallel between m. and symbolist poetry), and the m. poets are best approached with a clear sense of their historical uniqueness.

S. Johnson, "Life of Cowley," *Lives of the Eng. Poets* (1781); H. J. C. Grierson, *M. Lyrics and Poems* (1921); G. Williamson, *The Donne Trad.* (1930); J. Smith, "On M. P.," *Scrutiny* 2 (1933); J. B. Leishman, *The M. Poets* (1934); H. C. White, *The M. Poets* (1936); R. Tuve, *Elizabethan and M. Imagery* (1947); Brooks; T. S. Eliot, "The M. Poets" and "Andrew Marvell," *Essays* (1950); L. Unger, *Donne's Poetry and Mod. Crit.* (1950); O. de Mourgues, *M., Baroque and Précieux Poetry* (1953); S. L. Bethel, "Gracián, Tesauro, and the Nature of M. Wit," *Northern Miscellany of Lit. Crit.* 1 (1953); W. Sypher, *Four Stages of Ren. Style* (1954); J. E. Duncan, *The Revival of M. P.* (1959); M. Nicolson, *The Breaking of the Circle*, 2d ed. (1960); R. Ellrodt, *L'Inspiration personelle et l'esprit du temps chez les poètes métaphysiques anglais*, 3 v. (1960); L. Nelson, Jr., *Baroque Lyric Poetry* (1961); F. J. Warnke, *European M. P.* (1961), *Versions of Baroque* (1972); L. L. Martz, *The Poetry of Meditation*, 2d ed. (1962); J. Bennett, *Five M. Poets*, 2d ed. (1964); H. M. Block, "The Alleged Parallel of M. and Symbolist Poetry," *CLS* 4 (1967); T. C. Cave, *Devotional Poetry in France* (1969); E. Miner, *The M. Mode from Donne to Cowley* (1969); L. E. Hoover, *John Donne and Francisco de Quevedo* (1978); *M. P.*, ed. M. Bradbury and D. J. Palmer (1970); J. H. Summers, *The Heirs of Donne and Jonson* (1970); B. K. Lewalski, *Protestant Poetics and the 17th-C. Religious Lyric* (1979); A. J. Smith, *M. Wit* (1992).   F.J.W.

METER (Gr. *metron* "measure").

    I. OVERVIEW
    II. TYPOLOGY
    III. METER AND RHYTHM
    IV. METER AND LANGUAGE
    V. COMPLEXITY AND METRICALITY
    VI. FUNCTIONS
    VII. THEORY
    VIII. HISTORY
    IX. EMPIRICAL STUDIES
    X. COMPARATIVE METRICS
    XI. METRICAL VERSE AND FREE
    XII. SUMMARY

I. OVERVIEW. The oldest and most important device of verseform, m. selects one phonological feature of lang. (stress, pitch, length) and reduces its several levels or degrees in ordinary speech (3 or 4 levels of stress; high, mid, and low pitch; various durations) to a simple binary opposition ("stress" vs. "unstress"; "level" vs. "inflected" pitch; "long" vs. "short") which may be generalized as "marked" vs. "unmarked." Regular patterns of these contrastive features create units of structure (feet, measures, metra, cola) which in turn comprise the line (q.v.) of verse. Within each unit, the marked element or position is called the ictus (q.v.), the unmarked, nonictus. The size and shape of the units vary from one verse system to another, but normally they are binary or ternary (q.v.). Some ms. repeat units identically; others mix. Poets who write metrical verse thus select one aspect of the sound of words and organize it systematically; such a form then becomes an instrument which enables semantic and rhythmic effects not otherwise possible.

Many readers treat m. as a metonym for poetry itself ("So far as I'm concerned," said J. V. Cunningham, "poetry is metrical writing. If it's anything else, I don't know what it is"). But this view is too narrow: there are stricter and looser varieties of metrical verse, as well as several types of nonmetrical verse which have prosodic structure (see PROSODY). The concept of poetic m. comes down to us from the Greeks, who had a more sophisticated practice—but a much more primitive theory—than we have now. All Western metrical praxis (and theory) derived from Gr. and Lat. models up to ca. 1850 (see section VIII below). But ancient Chinese and Sanskrit verse is also metrical, as is IE verse, at least in part; indeed, the preponderance of all poetry written in the history of the world has been metrical. This is prima facie evidence that the range of expressive resources in metrical verse is greater than that in nonmetrical. Chatman's definition of m.—"a systematic literary convention whereby certain aspects of phonology are organized for aesthetic purposes"—is admirable; to it one need add only that what is ordered orders, so that metrical structuring on the phonological level has pervasive effect on all other levels of poetic lang.—morphology, syntax, discourse. These effects have long been recognized, albeit unsystematically, by metrists. Lacan calls m. "parallelism of the signifier," and in so doing gestures toward the still-unexplained power of repetition (q.v.), i.e. form, in human cognitive processing: m. makes repetition into system.

It is essential to keep separate the m. itself, with its associated terms, definitions, rules, and processes, and the linguistic resources for the realization of the m., which vary from lang. to lang. The province of the former is metrical theory, that of the latter linguistics. Confusion of these is fatal, but so is blindness to either, a lesson most linguists learned but slowly. In some respects, m. obviously shadows or mirrors linguistic processes closely. But in other respects, purely metrical rules (such as end-fixing and catalexis; see section X below) do not derive from the lang.; rather, they derive (in part) from the general laws of rhythmicity applicable to all rhythmic series (see RHYTHM), and in part they are purely arbitrary and conventional, being determined by the forces of literary history. How, how much, and how well a m. can be instantiated in a given lang. depends on its linguistic structure but is only made manifest (and can be expanded) through the invention (q.v.) and skill of poets.

The first distinction is therefore that between the phonological feature used as the marker of the m. and the pattern made by those markers. The marked positions in m. are filled by some kind of linguistic prominence such as stress; how such prominence is achieved varies from lang. to lang. depending on its phonology. The abstract pattern is capable of being notated by graphic symbols (see SCANSION). Historically, enormous confusion has been created by failure to distinguish the metrical pattern from the linguistic markers that fill it, most particularly in usage of the terms "long" and "short." This seems easy to say, but in fact the clarification took nearly two millennia, most of it achieved only within the past century. Much remains unclear still.

Twice in the history of Western poetry have entirely new metrical systems come into existence: once in the IE or archaic Gr. era, and once again around the 3d–4th c. A.D. The markers in these systems have been, respectively, quantitative and accentual. In IE, Sanskrit, and Gr., the marker was length—syllables were defined as either "long" or "short" based on the syllable ending (open or closed) and on vowel length. (The Gr. lang. had a natural pitch accent as well, but this was not the marker.) In the quantitative meters (hereafter "ms.") of Cl. prosody (q.v.), therefore, ictus is normally filled by a long syllable, nonictus by a short (see QUANTITY); rules for resolution and substitution (qq.v.) control exceptions. The author-

ity and prestige of the Cl. langs. ensured that the notion of longs and shorts was retained in Western metrical theory down to the 19th c., even though the actual linguistic phenomenon of phonemic length disappeared from Lat. around the 4th c. A.D. What replaced it, in some epochal linguistic shift, was intensity or stress (see ACCENT). It is stress which is the marker for the poetries of Med. Lat. and virtually all the subsequent Western vernaculars. But even this thumbnail history is too simple: there was an early, native Lat. m., the Saturnian (q.v.), which was apparently based on stress; and there is one modern theory that Gr. itself was based on stress accent (Allen). The linguistic facts are by no means well understood even now: pitch is known to correlate highly with perceived prominence (stress), for example, and a number of metrists since the Ren. (e.g. Bright) have held that pitch matters as much as if not more than stress for m. Several scholars in the 20th c.—e.g. Eikhenbaum, Mukařovský, Crystal, Fowler—have argued for the importance in m. of intonation more broadly conceived.

The choice of the marker is not primarily up to the poet at all; it is controlled almost entirely by the lang., and so subject to the phonological processes at work in every lang. over time. The poet may certainly choose another marker—as Ren. poets tried to choose length so as to imitate Cl. quantitative ms.—but if the feature is not phonemic in the lang. (as quantity is not in Eng.), the poetry will be only an exercise or erudite diversion at best (see CLASSICAL METERS IN MODERN LANGUAGES).

The patterns too are not entirely under the control of the poet, though they are not, like the markers, controlled by the lang.; rather, they are controlled, except in cases of genuine innovation, by convention or tradition (qq.v.). When a great poet achieves something substantial in a particular metrical form, that form becomes canonical for that genre, and often others, in that trad., or lang., or even other langs., often for centuries, sometimes for millennia. Thus Homer writes the *Iliad* and the *Odyssey* in the (dactylic) hexameter (q.v.) in the 8th c. B.C.; and for two millennia thereafter, through Virgil, Dante, Tasso, Spenser, and Milton, every poet who aspired to greatness aspired to write an epic, and to write it in the canonical m., the hexameter, or its modern vernacular equivalents, the It. *endecasillabo*, the Fr. alexandrine, or the Eng. iambic pentameter.

The invention of a wholly new m. is relatively rare; what is not rare, and is vastly more important, is the discovery of what a m. borrowed from one lang. can be made to do in another, based on the particular kinds of sound clustering (phonological rules), characteristic word shapes (morphological patterns), and sentence constructions (syntactic rules) possible in the target lang. Within that m. and in that lang., the poet will find what is possible. Equally important is the poet's discovery of what new effects an existing m. is capable of, namely its extension into new lexical registers (see LEXIS), semantic fields, and stanza forms (see STANZA). Consequently, the poet's art lies not so much in the choice of a form as in showing how successfully that form can be employed as an instrument to say something important and to make a design. The poet is always to double business bound, making and saying, using words as opaque objects woven into a design, and words as meaning shaped by that design.

It is characteristic of every great m., says Wright, that "strong poets of every period have not merely learned to use it efficiently, refining their knowledge of it into a skill which they come to manipulate almost instinctively, but . . . wrestle with it, compel it to perform new work, and tune it to their own distinctive energies." A m. is a means, a tool, but even more than that, it is a "keyboard a young poet learns to master, exploring its range and subtleties, stretching its capabilities of harmony and expressiveness" (17–18). Lesser poets imitate it; competent poets master it; great poets find its edge, turn it to new uses.

Despite scansions, a m. is not a mathematical equation but rather a cognitive shape, one way of thinking in words. The fitting of natural-lang. phrasing into any given m. isn't as impossible as it might seem; once the mind catches the rhythm, it is not difficult to compose ordinary sentences which scan perfectly: "I'll have a burger and a glass of Coke"; "Well, when you find the answer let me know"; "I never saw my father in my life." These are all iambic pentameters; the last one, it happens, belongs to Shakespeare, who wrote over a hundred thousand of them. It was Eliot who said that "a different m. is a different mode of thought" and that the poet who invented a new m. expanded the sensibilities of the age (*KR* 14 [1952]).

II. TYPOLOGY. Understanding the typology of ms. depends on distinguishing clearly between categories and levels of analysis. Jakobson in 1958 set forth two crucial distinctions between *verse design* and *verse instance*, and *delivery design* and *delivery instance*; Fowler in 1968 added one more, between *verse type* and *metrical set*, giving the ordered hierarchy:

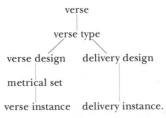

This schema assumes that design precedes, underlies, and controls all particular manifestations (lines). Verse type is determined by the phonological feature that is phonemic in the lang. Verse design, i.e. m., is the pattern set as invariant for the poem as a whole; variations occur at the level of verse instance, which is the specific line *as apprehended* (not in its linguistic form). "Metrical set" (Chatman's term), the disposition to read ambiguous cases as fitting the meter rather than not, may amount to "reading design," or else silent reading and oral recitation are variant modes of delivery. Delivery instance is a specific performance (q.v.). How a reader's apprehension of verse design is translated into a style of delivery ("delivery design") has never yet been made explicit.

As for verse design, i.e. the nature of the metrical patterns possible and the principles governing them, most of the typology may be seen in modern verse. We may begin by identifying two criteria of metrical organization in the line, count of syllables and count of prominences (in most modern verse, stresses), either of which may be determinate (fixed) or indeterminate (variable). Crossing the two forms of the one against the two of the other gives four categories: "accentual verse," also called "tonic" or "strong-stress" verse (number of stresses fixed, number of syllables variable); syllabic verse (syllables fixed, stresses variable); "accentual-syllabic" or "syllabotonic" verse (both fixed); and free verse (both variable)—for schema, see Brogan 319.

Accentual verse (q.v.) is the type for much popular verse, folk poetry, and oral poetry, and also for the Eng. and Scottish ballads (though not ballads in other langs.; see BALLAD). Isochronous timing (see ISOCHRONY), the use of metrical rests (see PAUSE), and the phenomenon known as dipodism (q.v.) are all characteristic of such verse and reveal its direct origin in or close association with song (q.v.). Syllabic verse (q.v.), conversely—lines metered solely by count of syllables—is esoteric (Jakobson claimed to find it in Mordvinian); most metrists deny its existence altogether, arguing that m. is impossible without some kind of pattern. Accentual-syllabic verse is usually held to be the type for all modern literary ms., though Halpern has argued that iambic verse is the only genuine m. of this type; trochaic (q.v.) and all ternary ms. he views as accentual. As for free verse (q.v.), any verse having neither count nor patterning obviously lacks m., but this term covers a complex set of verseforms little understood and never yet mapped (see section XI below). The Greeks had lyric ms.; the moderns think lyric exceeds m.

On this analysis, only accentual and accentual-syllabic verse look to be ms., strictly speaking. The question then is how these differ. On the traditional account, in accentual verse only the number of stresses in the line is regulated. If then syllables too are regulated, one would think, accentual-syllabic verse will arise automatically. But this analysis ignores the *placing* of the stresses in the line: syllabotonic ms. have specific patterns of stress, while accentual ms. do not. This suggests that counting is merely a first-order constraint, necessary but not sufficient for m., though counting certainly has an ancient pedigree in the concept of number (q.v.), Lat. *numerus* (see RHYTHM). Alternatively, we may view syllable counting as an epiphenomenon, the automatic effect of the imposition of strict pattern.

Relevant here is the argument of Bridges (*Milton's Prosody*, 1901) that accentual and accentual-syllabic verse are in fact two radically different species. Bridges points out that in accentual verse "the stresses must all be true speech-stresses": only words naturally stressed in speech count for marking the m. This is not true in accentual-syllabic verse, where it is the function of the m. to preserve in the mind's ear a paradigm such that, if the line itself does not supply the requisite number of stresses *in the requisite places,* the mind, via "metrical set," will adjust the stressing to fit via the strategies of promotion and demotion (see below). Number of syllables is subject to some variability so long as the pattern is not effaced or distorted into another pattern. In short, in accentual verse, the pegs mark the rhythm: the syllables merely provide the ground. In syllabotonic verse, by contrast, the number and relative weight of the unmarked syllables are made significant to the design. Accentual m. projects upward from the lang., while accentual-syllabic m. projects downward from the paradigm; both jointly form a gradient of types. Indeed, in some modern and many medieval poems a sharp boundary between the two is hard to draw. And some verse trads. make finer distinctions, allowing species of accentual verse which are stricter and freer in constraint: these include *Knittelvers* and *Freie Rhythmen* in Ger. and *dol'nik* (qq.v.) in Rus.

Even in accentual verse, however, if the aggregations of proclitic and enclitic syllables around a phrasal stress harden into recognizable units, they then become formulae, metrical and usually also lexical (see FORMULA). If the poetry is oral, it is then susceptible of composition via oral-formulaic techniques (see ORAL POETRY; ORAL-FORMULAIC THEORY), but formulaic cola in reduced form are visible in several written poetries as well. If hemistichs come to be formulaic, the number of formulae is likely to be reduced to a small corpus of distinct types, as are the Five Types of OE halflines identified by Sievers.

The categories and levels of metrical typology as given by Jakobson generally match those which were recognized in traditional metrics, though terminology varied so wildly from one set of theories to another that the problem of correlating them seemed all but insurmountable. Most scholars understand that m. can be represented as (1) one abstract pattern which is the simplest and most general description; (2) a small subset of permissible, variant subpatterns (in a poem, a poet, a trad., an age) which are manifested in (3) actual lines if not (4) performances. These four levels form a hierarchy from the one general pattern through descending levels of increasing specificity to the actual line read or heard. Allen identifies the first three, respectively, as metrical *form,* metrical *structure,* and *composition.* Most Am. metrists have usually called the first two categories *meter* and the third *rhythm* (see section III below). Rus. metrists, however, sometimes call the second—more precisely, the national or period variants of a m.—*rhythm.* Elements at levels (1) or (2) are structural; other elements and variations in actual lines (3) are not. Yet another class of variants manifested at level (4) (pitch patterns, pausing, paralinguistic cues) obtain only in each delivery instance and are irrelevant to m.

Level (2) has sometimes occasioned difficulties. Most major ms. develop a relatively small number of principal subtypes: the alexandrine, for example, developed the *tetramètre* and the *trimètre* (qq.v.). For Allen, metrical structure is "the particular choice of the alternatives offered within the general form." The number of variations is limited and is controlled by some internal rule: "there must always be some general principle of arrangement underlying the variety of structure."

The general principle controlling metrical variation was given as early as 1889: "any variation is allowable that does not obscure or equivocate the genus; but any that suggests another genus is not allowable" (W. H. Browne 198; see Brogan). This has long been understood as a general rhythmical law, though most of the efforts to formalize it have not succeeded. In strict metrical verse, "small variations count for a great deal" (Wright); that is the virtue of strictness: it heightens attention on significant events that would seem random or trivial in loosely metrical or nonmetrical verse.

A "m." may thus be seen as a range of permissible patterns all constrained by one *rule* but showing frequent approximation to a common *norm.* Wimsatt in his later writings moved to this position, and Wright likens our awareness of lines to our knowledge of dogs: we do not hold up all dogs to some one type but see in all of them overlapping sets of similar features. These, we might add, collectively amount to something very much like Wittgenstein's "family resemblances."

Some critics have had difficulty viewing m. as a single pattern when that specific pattern doesn't very often appear: the irregularities or variances seem greatly to outweigh the regularities. The paradigm of the iambic pentameter (x x́ x x x́ x x́ x x x́ x x́), for example, is not statistically preponderant—it appears only about 25% of the time. But the principles of perceptual psychology and information theory show that once a pattern is recognized, even if unconsciously, it need be reproduced only often enough to reconfirm it, and even then not always wholly. As Allen puts it, "the ideal line may occur in composition only rarely—or conceivably not at all; it may simply be intuited as that structure which comprises the most regular recurrence of the structural elements" (110).

One answer to this problem has been to distinguish rigidly between m. and rhythm, abstract frame and real entities filling it (see section III below). McAuley speaks of "the essential duality of our experience of the line" and says that the metrical "pattern is never actually embodied with complete equality and uniformity in any line, but is felt as a constant behind ever line." C. S. Lewis called this phenomenon "double audition": the mind "hears" the pattern as it "hears" the line, simultaneously, continuously recording the fit. Lewis implied there is pleasure in such recognitions. Others have treated the evident discrepancy in the great majority of lines between the pattern and the filling of the pattern as "counterpoint" or "tension" (qq.v.). Others consider the former of these a faulty analogy from music.

Another more sophisticated answer is based on cognitive psychology, i.e. on an implicit theory of pattern recognition. In this view, the pattern must only be made manifest at the very outset of a poem, and repeated thereafter only as often as necessary for the pattern not to become blurred or forgotten. To insist that every line conform to one pattern is to misunderstand what the mind requires for pattern recognition: monotony is fatal. But in fact not even setting the pattern at the outset may be necessary; experienced readers in an established trad. often have a good idea what the m. of a poem is before they even begin it: this is part of their literary competence.

Knowing the pattern means having expectations which one actively applies in reading lines, a readerly strategy which has come to be called the "metrical set" (Ger. *Zwang*). Such expectations, whether established by explicit training or from the unconscious internalization of regularities in poetry as a result of long reading, create a disposition to perceive the pattern wherever possible. In iambic verse, pairs of syllables need not all be stressed 4-1 (4 denoting weakest, 1 strongest stress): 4-3, 3-2, and 2-1 are iambic, and even successive syllables equally weighted (4-4, 3-3, 2-2, 1-1) will not be felt as disconfirming the pattern. Shakespeare has numbers of iambic pentameters beginning "Out, out," "Come, come," "Hark, hark," "Die, die," "No, no," "Sir, sir," "Aye, aye," "Cease, cease"; all these will be heard as iambic.

Increasingly, modern metrists have come to realize that it is unproductive to overemphasize the pattern at the highest level of generalization, thus treating m. as a single, abstract, Platonic form. The idealized form is a mere set of unrealized possibilities, emptied of meaning, expressiveness, and effect. Wright says of the iambic pentameter that it "is best understood not as a single form with such-and-such weak and strong positions . . . but as a changing syllabic design of alternating greater and lesser stresses, with changing internal and external phrasal and clausal relationships, a complex unstable pattern that is realized differently in every line and that engenders in poets habits of arrangement that change from work to work and from one phase of a career to another. A poet thus does not write 'in iambic pentameter' but 'in *an* iambic pentameter.'" And I. A. Richards held that poetic rhythm that "cannot be judged apart from the sense and feeling of the words out of which it is composed nor apart from the precise order in which that whole of sense and feeling builds itself up" (*Practical Crit.* 230).

One cannot say, therefore, in any exact sense that a poet in one lang. and one in another use the *same* m.: the differences between national-poetry forms of a m. are fundamental; indeed, the differences between a m. in the hands of two major poets in the same lang.—say, Donne and Browning—are so extensive as to weaken the very idea of a monolithic m. The differences between a m. used for dramatic and nondramatic verse are far more sweeping than one might suspect; and the changes in the use of a m. in the hands of only one poet over the course of a long career of experiment, discovery, and refinement are normally so extensive that accurate description requires a book. T. S. Eliot doubted "whether, in the 18th c., could be found two poems in nominally the same metre so dissimilar as Marvell's *Coy Mistress* and Crashaw's *Saint Teresa*, the one producing an effect of great speed by the use of short syllables, and the other an ecclesiastical solemnity by the use of long ones" ("The Metaphysical Poets").

III. METER AND RHYTHM. The distinction between m. and rhythm is ancient and fundamental. Precise accounts of the distinction vary, but in general, rhythm becomes manifest in speech (as well as prose and verse) when elements are repeated in series close enough together so as to be noticed, even if the repetition is variable and irregular (see REPETITION). In that they show grouping, hierarchy, and repetition, ms. are simply species of rhythm (q.v.), as was recognized by Aristotle (*Poetics* 1448b21; cf. *Rhet.* 1408b29), namely the most regular, strict, or rigid species. As Bede pointed out, "all m. has rhythm, but not all rhythm has m." Rhythm is harmony unsystematized; m. is harmony by order made systematic.

Theories of rhythm provide the framework for events to happen in, and so specify both events and spaces; theories of m. specify only events. If all the spaces are filled in, the only question is how conspicuous the events are. Pauses are not metrical because they cannot be counted or measured like events. This is the view taken by Quintilian (*Institutio oratoria* 9.4.45–57), who restricts all timing effects to rhythm and order of feet to m. Rhythm distinguishes time intervals without concern for events within those intervals; from a rhythmic point of view, a dactyl is equivalent to a spondee, since two plus one plus one equals two plus two: the one can just as well be substituted for the other. From the metrical point of view, by contrast, a dactyl is manifested in three events, a spondee two, and the one has a very different shape from the other (9.4.48). This suggests that all temporalist theories of m. are actually theories of rhythm.

But if m. is a species of rhythm, m. also contains rhythms within it as major subtypes (see section II above). In this sense m. is better thought of as a set of rhythms all driven by a single rule than as any one single pattern. The essence of any m. is not the pattern but the principle or principles which generate that pattern (and its subtypes) but exclude all other patterns.

"Rhythm" is traditionally derived from the Gr. word for "flow"; "m." derives from *metron* "measure." For the Greeks, rhythm was movement, whereas in Lat. it became arithmetical, as number, and so was confused with counting. The concept of measure is the bridge. For definitions of "rhythm" the *OED* gives "the measured flow of words and phrases" (II.4.d)—a definition really better suited to m.—and, more helpfully, "due correlation and interdependence of parts, producing a harmonious whole" (II.6).

Besides being used in the sense of timing (event spacing versus events), "rhythm" is also used in a linguistic sense, to refer to actual lines of poetry and their full linguistic structure. M. is a binary system based on only one phonological feature, while linguistic (phonological) rhythm in its fullest sense embraces pitch or intonation patterns, stressing, vowel lengths, timing, and juncture. At the level of linguistic rhythm, the Eng. iambic pentameter may contain only 4, or 3, or even 6, 7, or 8 stresses ("Rócks, cáves, lákes, féns, bógs, déns, and Shádes of déath"—Milton, *PL* 2.621). At the level of m., it contains only 5 ictuses—no more, no less.

The consequences of the abandonment of the distinction between m. and rhythm are such that to most modern metrists, that has seemed all but unthinkable. To abandon it would mean scansion of lines of metrical verse not in terms of fixed units but in terms of looser measures which mirror the irregular phrasal groups in the lang. itself. It would mean settling for a "phrasal prosody" of "word-group cadences" for Eng. verse rather like that in Fr. prosody (q.v.), in which syntactic junctures alone are allowed to separate words into groupings often unpredictable in size and stress pattern. This approach has appealed to some metrists (Nott on Surrey; Southworth and Robinson on Chaucer; Nist; Wesling; see Brogan). But the traditional view has been that the verse systems of Eng. and Fr. differ radically; that the analytic units for each cannot be applied to the other; and that regularity of structure is, beyond all else, fundamental to m.

Still, one may cheerfully admit that traditional metrics, taken over wholesale from Cl. prosody as once understood, did not work. The weakness of foot theory was that it classified feet as distinct rhythms and presumed ms. were mere accumulations thereof, so that change of foot meant change of m. This is not so. The trochee as an isolated foot looks like the reverse of an iamb, but in an iambic line "trochaic substitutions" are not and never were felt to be violations of the iambic m., but simply complications in the rhythm of the line. Trochaic m.—whole trochaic lines in succession—*was* recognized to be fundamentally different from iambic m., but that is a very different matter. As Gummere said over a century ago, the old terms for the various feet are best used simply to characterize the general movement of verse. Ms. are whole line-forms, not foot-types strung together.

IV. METER AND LANGUAGE. It has been recognized since antiquity that the two forces at work in m. are lang. and convention. The traditional view had always been that m. is an arbitrary pattern imposed on words—that, as Gurney put it, "metrical rhythm is imposed upon, not latent in, speech" (1880). It seems indubitable that m. is in some sense a filter or grid superimposed on lang. But 20th-c. linguistics has shown convincingly that many aspects of poetic form are merely extensions of natural processes already at work in lang. itself. This would suggest the schematic representation L > T < M, where L is the lang. system, M the m., and T the poetic text, i.e. verse line.

Much structural metrics of the 1950s and 1960s assumes this model, as in Fowler's influential distinction between "prose rhythm" and m. The stressing or intonation of the line is not what it would be were it ordinary speech or prose, but is altered under the pressure of metrical convention, which is in large part arbitrary. The line thus becomes the site for interplay between linguistic rules and poetic conventions. McAuley (1966), in a still valuable handbook, makes this interaction graphic, marking two levels of stress above each line, one the prose rhythm (the stressing that the line would get in ordinary speech), and the other the resultant of the interaction of the prose rhythm with the m., i.e. the *scansion* (q.v.) of the line; the metrical pattern itself is presumed.

But the situation is almost certainly more complex than this. Lotman argues that since there are always some elements of m. that are found identically in lang., "metrical sequences are initially mapped onto linguistic ones, and only later are the forms of the metrical strings so produced represented as texts." M., that is, always already writes itself through lang. Additionally, if we take m. as but one species of rhythm—rhythm being a cognitive process for the perceptual organization of periodicity—this model, which shows how rhythms are manifested in the verbal medium, will fit into wider models of rhythmicity (see RHYTHM). Too, on this model one can say, with Lotman, that m. affects different levels of poetic lang. differently, thereby creating different prosodies. If lang. is composed of stratified rule systems constraining phonology, morphology, syntax, and semantics, metrical organization can interact with any or all of these. The synthesizing power of such a model is appealing.

Linguistic support for such a view appears in

the theory of autosegmental or "metrical" phonology developed in America since the late 1970s. Here the framework and terminology of traditional metrics (e.g. feet, iambic, trochaic) are appropriated for the description of phonology: in effect, lang. itself is now held to be metrical. The equation should now read: M > L > T. On this account, rhythmical forces—segmentation, relativity of stress, hierarchy—act as a filter on lang., simplifying the intonational patterns of the lang. into a binary code, where all intermediate cases—weak syllables under ictus, strong syllables outside ictus—are pushed in one direction or the other. Now m. seems fundamentally a reduction of processes already present in the lang., not an arbitrary convention, and the filtering is double: once to produce speech, and once again to produce versified speech. After all, poets do not invent ms. out of the blue, or if they do, they soon find that only those that fit the structure of the lang. offer sufficient resources to yield a prosody that is durable, flexible, and powerful.

Following the work of Wesling, we may say that the elements inherent in both lang. and m. are not only hierarchical but congruent, so that there is a systematic homology between the two domains:

discourse	poem
paragraph	stanza; verse paragraph
sentence	line
clause	hemistich
phrase	measure, metron, colon
word	foot
morpheme	arsis-thesis; lift–dip
syllable	position
phoneme	sound

If these two series are set as the x and y axes of a Cartesian graph (as Wesling shows), the points of intersection will form a grid which maps all the possible strata on which structural linguistic and poetic organization can interact; Wesling calls this the "scissoring" of grammar and m. (cf. Lotman). Blocks of the grid will represent those areas of metrical style implicitly staked out by verse trads. such as OE, Fr., ballad m., etc. How the elements in each system are matched on each level will be discussed in the rest of this section.

Adjustments within the lang. to fit the syllabic requirements of the m. mainly involve the several devices for syllabic compression or expansion, particularly "doublets," (modern *because, 'cause, probably, probly*; Ren. *heaven, heavn*—see Sipe), pleonastic forms of the auxiliary *do*, alternate preterites, etc. Adjustments in the m. to accommodate stress patterns in the lang. mainly involve the strategies of promotion and demotion of stressing on (respectively) nonictus and ictus so as to bring a larger span of natural linguistic rhythms into conformity with the metrical frame (Wimsatt's "tilting").

As a binary code, m. functions by reducing the multiple degrees of prominence in the lang. to one

opposition, on-off, yes-no, 1-0, marked-unmarked, ictus-nonictus. Traditional grammar, for example, held that Eng. had 3 degrees of stress; Trager-Smith structural linguistics held that it had 4. How are the 3 or 4 levels of stress in lang. reduced to 2 in m.? "Absolutists" would say that in an iambic pentameter line, on a 4-level scale of stress (1 being strongest, 4 weakest), 1s and 2s count as metrically strong, 3s and 4s as weak. Hence sequences such as 4-3 and 3-2 count as pyrrhics as much as 4-4 and 3-3, while 2-1 counts as a spondee along with 2-2 and 1-1 (so Pyle, Wright, Ramsey). Only 4-1, 3-1, and 4-2 seem iambs. "Relativists," however, accept the principle of relativity of stressing first noted by Sievers (*Grundzüge der Phonetik*) and Jespersen (see RELATIVE STRESS PRINCIPLE). What is interesting about relativist scansion is that it creates almost entirely iambs and trochees, since it is stress *differentials* that are emphasized.

But modern metrics also holds that strong syllables outside ictus are "demoted" and weaker syllables under ictus "promoted" under the influence of the m. Promotion of weak syllables under nonictus weights and slows the line, adding power. Demotion of stresses under ictus gives a quicker and lighter line. This is not a purely metrical mechanism; it shadows the normal phonological process by which alternation of weak and strong, and strong and stronger, is effected automatically in polysyllables. Of the two, promotion is in some sense more important than demotion, in that it uses the m. to heighten emphasis on syllables that would normally be skimmed over in speech. This is very valuable for poets who want to increase both the subtleties of inflection in and semantic density of the line. Wright shows efficaciously how Shakespeare highlights the meaning in minor words such as prepositions by positing them under ictus, a strategy also well known to Chaucer, Donne, and Frost. Poets who reserve substantive words for ictus and function words for nonictus simply don't know much about what m. is capable of.

V. COMPLEXITY AND METRICALITY. What makes a line unmetrical? How far may variation extend into increased line complexity before it passes into a form that is unacceptable? Is unmetricality specifiable by rule, or do readers' judgments vary? If we look at metricality via set theory, we may envision all metrical lines as falling within the first two of four concentric circles, each successively larger. The smallest circle contains the set of the most frequent variants of the m. developed in each national-poetry trad. Outside the first circle, but still in the second circle, lie all less common (but still metrical) variants, including the pattern itself. The edge of this second circle is the limen of metricality: outside it (circle three) lie all those lines that are unmetrical. The third circle is of interest because it contains failed—but still recognizable—attempts at this particular m. Outside its pale, in circle four, lie other recognizable ms. and, beyond that, the sphere of everything else that is verbal but ametrical: free verse, rhythmical prose, prose, speech.

Set theory may mislead, however, insofar as it suggests sharp boundaries between circles (categories of perception). Several metrists (e.g. Tsur) have sought to develop a numerical gradient or quantitative index of metricality, a "scale of delicacy" for gradations of complexity. Generative metrics (q.v.) devoted extensive attention to specific procedures for differentiating metrical from unmetrical lines. Traditional metrics was aware of complexity: the setting of metrical units against grammatical units in verse has been variously characterized as "counterpoint," "tension," syncopation (qq.v.), or "scissoring," but often these terms have been used very loosely. Note that Gerard Manley Hopkins' "counterpoint rhythm" (q.v.) is quite different from the more common conception of the "counterpoint" of m. against syntax, line against sentence.

Experienced readers sense increase of complexity from lines such as Shakespeare's "Of hand, of foot, of lip, of eye, of brow" (Sonnet 106.6) or "Here's snip and nip and cut and slish and slash" (*Shrew* 4.3.90) to "Sans teeth, sans eyes, sans taste, sans everything" (*AYL* 2.7.166) and "'Tis not so sweet now, as it was before" (*TN* 1.1.8), to the much more complex but still metrical "Let me not to the marriage of true minds" (Sonnet 116), not to mention "Never, never, never, never, never" (*Lear* 5.3.309).

But it is not clear that even experienced readers recognize degrees of metricality in minute gradations, and since significant differences of judgment about metricality do obtain among readers, the boundary between acceptably complex and unacceptable lines may in fact be blurred not distinct. We must not reify a finely articulated spectrum of numerical discriminations that even sophisticated readers may not have. "Who is to say," one critic pointed out, "whether a weak syllable in a strong position produces one-fourth or one-half or even the same complexity as a strong stress in a weak position?" No such evidence has ever been adduced; it is questionable whether it can be adduced. Tarlinskaja's data on the Eng. iambic pentameter from the 14th–19th cs. showed that, on average, ictuses are stressed about 75–85% of the time, and nonictuses are unstressed 79–93% of the time. Therefore, no more than 25% of the ictuses in the line may be unstressed or 21% of the nonictuses stressed. But these aggregates offer no explanations as to *why* a given pattern is unmetrical.

What breaks a m.? In accentual-syllabic ms. such as the iambic pentameter, contiguous stressing can break the alternating pattern, "springing" it, as Hopkins said, into another mode, usually accentual verse. A lexical (word-) stress in a nonictic position flanked by weaker syllables in ictic positions also wrenches the pattern (the "Stress Maximum" of generative metrics). Presence of occasional extra syllables in the line or shortage of the requisite number of syllables is a less serious offense than stress (pattern) dislocation. But frequent extra syllables do disrupt stressing (the pattern): the establishment of a ternary rhythm in a binary m. for a significant period of time will break it and establish a new metrical set (see BINARY AND TERNARY).

VI. FUNCTIONS. In general, the functions of m. fall into three categories: generic, cognitive, and aesthetic. The first function is to mark written discourse as literary and, within that, poetic, by identifying it as a versified text. Hollander (ch. 7) discusses this function under the rubric of the "metrical frame," that invisible border or limen which, like the frames on pictures, defines the interior space as aesthetic rather than quotidian. Further, m. is the emblem of literariness in representing the most extensive means available to poets for heightening the degree of order in their texts. Ms. strengthen the cohesion of the line and intensify reader perception of it as an integral unit (Kurylowicz). Ms. enable the system of variation-against-the-norm or pattern against ground, which increases information load without increasing the number of words, indeed quite the contrary: with the minimum number of words.

The cognitive functions of m. all serve to mark, highlight, or point up certain syllables or words in the line, either by bringing unexpected words under ictus or moving strong words outside of ictus, and so draw attention to them. M. can draw attention to syllables of lesser strength that in ordinary speech would be lost in the rush but that still carry important nuances of meaning: when these are set between even weaker syllables, they gain strength, relatively. This sort of pointing counts for a great deal. The linguistic device of contrastive stress (see ACCENT) and the rhetorical strategy of "arsis-thesis variation" (Melton; see Brogan) are enabled by m., creating striking effects of repetition, opposition, and balance. M. *used with skill* deautomatizes poetic lang., preventing habituated or perfunctory responses by the reader, forcing her back to the text with sharpened attention. The segmentation of lang. by m. yields additional contexts in which meanings can multiply, producing polysemy. But m. may also qualify, alter, and undercut meanings, thereby delimiting ranges of meaning and improving the process of interp.

Within the line, nearly all metrical effects of interest are local, subtle, and semantic (expressive). In a strict m., a good poet can maneuver as little as one syllable so as to keep conformity with the m. yet at the same time say something striking, rhetorically powerful, and memorable. At the beginning of *Twelfth Night*, Valentine reports on Olivia's despondency at the drowning of her brother, saying that she weeps for "A brother's dead love, which she would keep fresh, / And lasting in her sad remembrance." A lesser poet might have said, "A dead brother's love"; this would emphasize the literal fact, but in fact the death is doubly diremptive: Olivia is also bereft of his love. This hyperbaton (q.v.) both speaks doubly and scans. Such fitting of memorable phrase to line is almost the whole art of traditional metrical verse.

The aesthetic functions of m. result from the fact that it is doubly a test of verbal skill to make words speak memorably and at the same time fall under some submorphemic principle of order. Readers experienced in the nature of poetic conventions and the particular literary trad. take successful movement within a constrained medium as perhaps the chief index of poetic accomplishment. In every literary culture, the recognition of heightened order accomplished seemingly without effort, of polish and finish, of artifice well contrived, and of semantic complication skillfully wrought, gives pleasure. It is, as Hopkins says, "the achieve of . . . the mastery." This is a legitimate criterion for literary evaluation.

One other important function is mimetic or representational. When Sidney says, "With how sad steps, O Moone, thou clim'st the skies," the first four syllables enact the lunar ascent itself in a pattern of successively increasing stress (Trager-Smith 4-3-2-1)—perfectly metrical, yet also mimetic. More mimetic still are these two lines from Shakespeare's sonnet 130: "I grant I never saw a goddess go—/ My mistress, when she walks, treads on the ground." The first line is perfectly regular. The second is more complex—more physical, one might say—but still metrical. And the contrast, which is the point, is made not in the words but in the m.

Metrical mimesis Dr. Johnson called "representative m.," criticizing it for its inability to do much more than imitate effects of sound or motion (*Lives of the Eng. Poets* [1779], 1.51, 2.314; *Rambler* 92, 94). This is too severe: these effects convey the tempo, pace, movement, rhythm, or shifts and sudden turns in the experience of the line, and are mainly impossible in prose. Even Blake, whose metric is radical, acknowledged metrical mimesis or decorum: "the terrific numbers are reserved for the terrific parts" (Preface to *Jerusalem*). And Donne, said Grierson, is not simply "willing to force his accent, to strain and crack a prescribed pattern; he is trying to find a rhythm that will express the passionate fullness of his mind, the fluxes and refluxes of his moods; and the felicities of verse[form] are as frequent and startling as those of phrasing" (1921, xxiii).

Various critics have explored these functions in greater detail (Chatman, ch. 7; Hollander). Wright (ch. 16) finds at least six motives in Shakespeare's metrical practice: variety, grace, energy, elevation, verisimilitude (making the line speechlike), and expressiveness. M. in verse drama he sees as a clue to the expression of general emotions made by characters, as a figure for natural speech itself,

and as a symbol for the forces of rebellion and authority, creativity and limitation, in both the human and cosmic spheres.

VII. THEORY. What should a metrical theory do? The minimum criteria are six: (1) it must develop neutral categories, concepts, and terms applicable to the description of all metrical systems in the world, not merely Gr. or Eng.; (2) it must map out the links between metrical systems and the entire range of quasi-metrical and nonmetrical prosodies; (3) it must distinguish rigorously between purely metrical operations and elements, purely linguistic ones, and ones which arise only in the convergence of the two; (4) it must provide a simple, clear, but powerful formalization for describing a m. and for showing how a m. changes from poet to poet, genre to genre, and age to age; (5) it must explain what happens to a m. when translated, adapted, or imitated in another, often quite different, lang.; and (6) it must show the typology of means by which metrical structures and effects shape and create meaning.

For any given m., i.e. all ms., metrical theory must identify at least four principles: (1) one which selects the marker used to inscribe the pattern; (2) one which determines how the markers may be grouped into intralinear units; (3) one which specifies how many and what kinds of groups will be allowed in a line-form; and (4) one which controls whether or not some units may be replaced by others and why.

Since antiquity, m. has been identified with the concept of measure (q.v.), and ms. have often been described by identifying one unit (e.g. foot) having a particular shape (rhythm) and specifying how many times the unit occurs in the line, e.g. dactylic hexameter, iambic trimeter. West calls these the "two coordinates of rhythm and amount." This is a very misleading taxonomy, however, for it suggests precisely that ms. are built by choosing one type of foot and then stringing feet together, which is very far from the truth. The hexameter, for example, while analyzable as five dactyls and a spondee, may well have been composed as hemiepes + paroemiac (qq.v.), i.e. as two halfline shapes which occur elsewhere as independent cola. The foot (q.v.) was recognized as a unit of metrical structure as early as Plato and Aristophanes, but the units in m. are no more strung together end to end than are words in lang. (so Chomsky): both systems employ grouping and hierarchy constitutively and systematically. Grouping, however, is the corollary of segmentation. Verseform segments discourse into lines and lines into units, i.e. m.

It is one of the central tenets of modern verse theory that verse, like lang. and all information delivery processes, segments the soundstream into units which are set in a relation of correspondence (De Groot) or equivalence (Jakobson), and so organized into hierarchies. By this, increased amounts of information can be carried in the channel, increasing semantic density and economy: more is said in less. The units in verse are, first, lines, then intralinear units. It is simple fact that if one inspects lines of metrical poetry, one finds demonstrable intralinear patterns: feet, metra, and cola in Cl. prosody; feet, traditionally, in Eng. and Ger. prosody; measures in Fr. prosody. The first issue is therefore how many types are to be recognized, and on what principle—i.e. a principle controlling how to generate any measure. Insofar as there has been any modern consensus on such a principle, it would seem to be that units are made of one marked element plus at least one unmarked, possibly more, e.g. a stress with its attendant clitic unstressed syllables. The unit must have heterogeneous members, hence pyrrhics, spondees, and "monosyllabic feet" are excluded. The units must be short and simple; larger structures are composites. In fine, the unit must contain at least two elements, and these must differ. In binary and ternary forms we will have, then, only five types of units: iambic, trochaic, dactylic, anapestic, and amphibrachic. But the latter three are not only rare but difficult to differentiate in running series; in practice, ternaries all amount to one m., as argued by Halpern. If iambic and trochaic are accepted as genuinely different rhythms, then we end up with two binary rhythms and one ternary; if not, then one of each. For more extensive discussion, see FOOT.

What is certain about defining intralinear units is that it will not do to take over the whole panoply of Gr. feet, (which even in antiquity formed at least three radically different regional verse trads. that evolved over more than a millennium) and apply them wholesale to any subsequent poetry simply on account of the cultural hegemony of Gr. and Lat. poetry in the West down to romanticism. From the point of view of comparative metrics, Gr. has no *a priori* authority over any other verse system except insofar as it contains metrical structures demonstrable in lits. which derived from it directly or demonstrable in all lits. because they are metrical universals. As for the latter, Gr. is not a representative case: it is the most complex and sophisticated metrical system presently known. The categories of Gr. metric do not apply at all to some verse systems such as Germanic and Romance. A viable theory must be built comparatively and neutrally, not privileging any one verse system. Only thereby will it avoid the distortions and legacies of error historically created by writing the concepts and terms of one metrical system over another which they do not fit, without due consideration of the innate differences between the ms. or the langs. from which they are formed.

VIII. HISTORY. One would think that, like most other subjects, m. would have its history (which poets used what ms. when) and its theory (explanation of how m. works). But if history has a theory, theory has a history: the theory we are able to give of a phenomenon, as we know it at any point

in time, is but one moment in the history of our theories about the phenomenon. This does not mean that facts cannot be established, for they can; nor that theories are not capable of successively greater approximation to the data, for they are. It only means that every history entails a theory and vice versa. Every age, says Taylor, has had its appropriate theory, and "in each stage metrical law is defined in a distinctive way—as classical law, as mechanical law. as musical law, as organic law, as dialectical law, as statistical law, as structural law, as generative law." This localizing view of theory, in which "definitions reflect the character of the age in which they were proposed," runs counter to the 19th-c. mythos of prosody as "scientific."

There is at present no comprehensive and reliable history of the devel. of metrical practice in the West, not even for any one lang., mainly because there never developed, and there still does not exist, any adequate theory for explaining that history. Histories of the evolution of Western verse, insofar as we have them at present, are each built on some specific theory, hence vulnerable at the demise of that theory, or else histories of theories about the evolution of Western verse, which is not at all the same thing.

Nor does any history of the devel. of metrical theory in the West presently exist, not even competent accounts for any one lang. In part this is because there seems to be no secure place to stand outside of any theory from which to critique and synthesize all other theories. In part, linguistics is still too new a science. But much of what one wants to know about metrical theory can still be gleaned from patient sifting of earlier metrists, who had many acute perceptions but no tools with which to articulate what they felt.

The basic facts about Western metrical theory are however simple to state: the ancient authorities are almost no help at all, and unfortunately nearly everything else came from them. Paul Maas's famous judgment in 1923 that "ancient metrical theory offers nothing but superficial description, mechanical classification, and unprofitable speculation" would seem the *coup de grace*—except that the ancient categories and terms are still in use. The main story to be told is simply one of the wholesale appropriation of the categories and terms of Cl. prosody, overlaid onto all subsequent Western verse systems. It took about two millennia to be able to see whether they fitted or not.

There are two classes of metrical theorists: those who do not consider time a part of m., and those who do (see Brogan 142 for schema). In antiquity these were known, respectively, as *metrici* and *rhythmici* (q.v.). There were two strains of *metrici*, an earlier (older) and a later (younger) school. The earlier school, Alexandrian Gr., derives from Philoxenus, Juba, Heliodorus, and (esp.) Hephaestion (2d c. A.D.); after the 3d c. it influenced

Roman and, later, Byzantine metrists. It analyzed ms. by constituents and postulated 8 (later 9) prototype ms. from which all others were derived. The later school, stemming from Varro (1st c. B.C.) and Caesius Bassus, influenced Roman metrists up to the 3d c., analyzed by colometry, and attempted to derive all ms. from the heroic hexameter and the dramatic (iambic) trimeter. The Lat. grammarians, as Allen remarks, "slavishly misapplied" the "whole detailed system of Gr. accentuation" to Lat. (151). The Med. Lat. grammarians (collected in Keil) mostly digest or repeat their predecessors, when they understand them aright. Ren. prosody, recoiling from the sterility of medieval grammar, turned back to the Classics, incl. Cl. prosody; the scholastics still attempted to apply the ancient system, while the poets knew better. Cl. prosody on a sounder basis emerges in the 18th c. with Bentley and in the 19th with Hermann and Boeckh, but as Cl. Philology gained ascendancy in Germany through the 19th c., its concepts and terms were simply mapped over the vernaculars in the subsequent devel. of Germanic, Romance, and English Philology (so Schipper). With the emergence of acoustic phonetics and experimental psychology, many thought the secrets of m. were to be unvelied at last via scientific experiment. Acoustic metrics held sway through the first three decades of the 20th c. in Britain and America, and in France even longer, as in the work of Faure and Morier. But its final value for metrics would seem to be neutralized by Jakobson's 1933 dictum that it is "not the phone, but the phoneme as such [which] is utilized as the cornerstone of verse."

All temporal theories of m. (see Brogan, 142, 193–232) assume that in one way or another, m. organizes timing. Barkas observes, astutely, that it makes a difference whether one measures temporal intervals as beginning from syllable boundaries or peaks; on this basis he distinguishes between four types of temporal theories (Barkas 10, 39, 62), depending on whether the units run from stress to stress or are defined in some specific pattern (e.g. iambic; notice that trochaic qualifies for both), and whether or not the internal elements of these units have fixed durational relationships to each other (as in music and quantitative ms.). One school, influential from the late 18th c. (esp. Steele 1775) to about 1930 (Patmore, Lanier, Verrier, Thomson, Wilson), held that verse is identical in temporal organization to music in showing isochronism (q.v.) and letting stresses begin measures. Another school sought to apply the results of acoustic and psychological experiments to metrics (see esp. Brown 1908 and others in Brogan). Linguists pointed to Pike's claim that Eng. is a "stress-timed" lang. Some even looked back to the quantitative system of Cl. prosody, believing that since Gr. poetry and music were once united in the dim mists of antiquity, longs and shorts represented real timing.

But objections to temporalist theories are weighty. The Cl. rules, "one long equals two shorts" and "length by position," were purely metrical conventions. It is logically impossible to support both quantitative and temporal theories simultaneously, since the timing theory entails equality of metrical units regardless of how they are filled, whereas the quantitative theory entails the equality of the constituents of the units, so that longer units are longer. The equality of lines varying in length would be unthinkable in the Cl. system. The consensus in the later 20th c. has been that theories which specify rules of timing mistake m. for performance: they overspecify features of lengthening, shortening, tempo, and pausing that will inevitably vary among readers, so cannot be m. Temporalists, that is, do not respect the fundamental distinction between m. and rhythm (see section III above). Theories of rhythm provide the framework for events to happen in, and so specify both events and spaces; theories of m., however, specify only events. Pauses are not metrical because they cannot be counted or measured like events.

In the 20th c., it was the textually based New Critics, esp. Richards, Ransom, and later Wimsatt (aided greatly by Brooks and Warren's *Understanding Poetry*), who rescued the study of m. from the pedantic, Classicizing obfuscation of Saintsbury and the crudely mechanistic methods of Ger. Philology and made it central to exegesis. Unlike the Germans, the New Criticism interested itself almost entirely in expressiveness, i.e. in what scansion could reveal about the semantic structure of the line and so contribute to the interp. of poetry.

The structural metrics of the mid 20th c. (e.g. Whitehall, Lotz, Chatman, Levin; see Brogan), spurred by the rise of structural linguistics, brought fresh winds to the study of poetic m. This work took place from the late 1940s through 1966, when Generative Metrics (q.v.) appeared, a vigorous but mainly unproductive effort to apply the concepts and methods of transformational syntax to the phonological environment constrained by literary convention that is poetic m. This latter movement had a vogue from 1966 into the early 1980s. Modern metrists have embraced every new theory in linguistics and thereby suffered their fate, as theories in linguistics were proposed then discarded in the 1970s and '80s with increasing rapidity. And the emergence of "theory" in Anglo-Am. crit. in the 1970s and '80s heralded a wide movement toward cultural studies—race, class, gender, power—which had little interest in literary texts. Crit. following Derrida and Heidegger denied the value, if not the very existence, of verbal reference, stable meaning, and accurate interp., ends which metrics attempts to validate. Rus., Polish, and Czech metrists in the 1920s and again in the 1960s developed elaborate statistical methods for verse analysis, though with scant integration of their results into a wider theory of crit. In short, the Anglo-Am. critics pursued theory without facts, the Slavic scholars facts without theory.

IX. EMPIRICAL STUDIES. Metrics in the 20th c. moved from the impressionism of Saintsbury—whose theory was bankrupt—through Am. (and later Rus.) formalism to enthusiastic interest in the descriptivism of structural linguistics to the excessively abstract theorizing of generative linguistics without any intermediary stage which would provide the empirical data on which a theory could be tested, nor with a sufficient determination to keep linguistic insights separate from metrical theory itself. Both Am. lit. crit. (the New Criticism and all its successive rivals) and linguistics (after Chomsky 1957) denigrated the collection of large corpora of data. This is all the more ironic because metrics is one of the few areas of poetics where empirical verification actually applies, and can be used to prove (and disprove) theories. Some bodies of data are slowly emerging, though few or none has yet been made available in a standardized electronic format so that hypotheses could be widely tested by scholars.

Early empirical work such as the many Ger. dissertations of the latter 19th c. is mostly vitiated by having been based on faulty texts. The example of Sievers' work on OE is, however, distinguished. Some Eng. metrists—Mayor, Bridges, Young, Pyle—showed awareness of the problem; later, scansion algorithms were attempted by Dilligan and other data collected by Chisholm and others.

The "Rus. linguistic-statistical method" is based on the assumption that, at the level of m., all ictuses are equal, but in the stressing of the line, not all stressed syllables are equally strong. "Stress profiles" are then compiled which tabulate the stressing on each position in the line and express the result as a percentage. These data in effect show poets' metrical "fingerprints"—the characteristic weightings of their lines—and thus can be used to identify a poet's metrical style and changes thereto from work to work, dramatic verse to nondramatic, poet to poet, age to age, or literary movement to movement (see Tarlinskaja 1987). Such methods, based on the work of Tomaševskij and Gasparov in Russia and applied to Eng. by Bailey and Tarlinskaja in the 1970s and '80s, differed radically from the Anglo-Am. trad., where prosody was employed mainly for close reading of texts, and where quantification and scientific method were repudiated under the antipositivist aegis of the New Criticism. The Rus. method is mathematical and scientific: it draws conclusions from enormous masses of data. The Am. formalist method was localized, semantic, and heuristic: typically it dealt with only one line at a time and allowed us to see what choices a poet made, what problems she solved, what triumphs, what evasions.

The empiricist approach has limitations. One is that researchers must, in order to classify and count, define the stress on words as categorical or absolute rather than relative: such methods deprive themselves of the insights deriving from the relative stress principle and the idea that m. influences or tilts normal prose stressing in the line. That is, stress-profiling does not directly yield *metrical* information. Another is that the method is aggregatory: it may show, for example, that some feature occurs 25 times out of every 100 lines in one Shakespearean play but 30 in another. This fact may or may not be significant, and it will still be the critic who determines which.

All this means simply that critical and theoretical operations are always already in play in empirical work: there is no such thing as empirical data without theory. The notion of naive or pure empirical research is a fiction: what one collects depends on what one chooses to collect, i.e. defines as objects both capable and worthy of collection. These definitions and tacit choices amount to a theory.

X. COMPARATIVE METRICS. If great ms. are deeply related to or even emblematic of their langs., the transplantation or adaptation of a m. from one lang. into another via translation (q.v.) becomes an important issue in comp. lit. One might think that most langs. would develop their own ms. or that ms. would not translate very well into other langs. whose phonologies differ markedly, but in fact metrical transference has been, overwhelmingly, the rule rather than the exception in the history of world poetry. Some of the most successful ms. in the world have sustained themselves by adaptation to langs. for which they were not originally well suited. This is particularly the case for Eng. (see Legouis). Most poets learn m. from imitating their great predecessors, and the majority of those predecessors have written in other langs. The force of literary trad., of the canonization of key texts, is very great: the force of the example of Homer was great enough to impel the dactylic hexameter into Lat. and Med. Lat. poetry and to produce countless accentual imitations in all the Western vernaculars down to the end of the 19th c., despite the fact that the dactyl is not a pattern natural to any of them.

Four of the five most influential langs. in the history of the world—Lat., Eng., Ar., and Rus.—adopted either verseforms or metrical theories or both from other langs. and wrote them over their own poetries without full understanding of the one or the other or both. Lat. after Ennius took over the principles of Gr. metric wholesale; Eng. imported Romance verseforms in the 14th c. to map onto an amorphous and shifting morphological base built upon Ger. and Lat.; Rus. adopted Polish metrical conventions in the 18th c. via the Ukraine; Ar. poetry assimilated Persian metrical theory (Elwell-Sutton) and later Hispano-Romance song refrains when the Arabic empire overran Spain (see HISPANO-ARABIC POETRY). In many cases the poets themselves tell us their models, or reveal them via allusive imagery or diction or borrowed plot. But the exact mechanism by which a m. is assimilated into a new lang. is not yet well understood across many langs.

"One lang.," insisted Dr. Johnson, "cannot communicate its rules to another" (*Rambler* 88). This is very misleading: many langs. *have* communicated them, and many rules have been received, regardless of how well they fitted. Both poets and prosodists have taken over principles from other langs. and imposed them on their own, sometimes by alteration, sometimes not, often with little consciousness of the differences between the langs. Sometimes the results are disastrous, but sometimes spectacular: in praxis, creative misprision counts for as much as true understanding. The lang. itself will determine whether the imported form will work well, or at all, or can be altered to fit. *Pace* Dr. Johnson, the imitation and adaptation of ms. are processes crucial to lit. hist.

Here, however, one might want to emphasize that a m. is not a monolithic pattern, that ms. turn out to be very different things when actualized in the differing phonological environments of various langs. The 10-syllable line in the Germanic langs. (incl. Eng.) is very different from the Fr. *décasyllabe* (see FRENCH PROSODY), much less its functional metrical analogue, the 11-syllable It. *endecasillabo* (see ITALIAN PROSODY), which functions on principles similar to those of the Fr. 12-syllable alexandrine (q.v.), which itself is radically unlike the 12-syllable line in Eng. *Analogue* is the operative term here: line length is a trivial criterion of m. in comparison with other principles. The ms. in each national poetry come to be much more than mere variants of one basic pattern: they are fundamentally distinct forms, alternative realizations related by the historical actualities of tr. and imitation at the hands of poets. Each of the ms. just mentioned above was developed in its own lang. as the "heroic" (q.v.) line, the vernacular equivalent of the hexameter; in effect they are three versions of a metrical archetype.

All these issues have important implications for our ability to describe metrical forms comparatively, perhaps eventually to discover metrical universals. As the study of linguistics developed in the 20th c., the accumulation of substantial amounts of comparative data quickly led to the question of linguistic universals—specific constants of form or function which could be found in every lang. since necessary to the functioning of *any* lang., i.e. constitutive of lang. itself. One is naturally led to wonder if analogous types of universals may be found in verse systems. One example might be a cadential rule (see CADENCE), which would hold that the ends of metrical strings are in general more highly constrained than their beginnings. Such a rule in widely attested in IE, Sanskrit, and Gr.; even in the Eng. iambic pentameter the fifth foot is the most highly constrained. Another would be a catalexis (q.v.) rule: ends of metrical lines may be optionally shortened without affecting perception of the pattern.

Gayley and Scott's 1902 remark that "metric as a comparative study is still in its infancy", less severe than Maas's 1923 judgment that "at present no comparative science of metric exists," is still largely true, despite much progress, nearly a century later. Despite fundamental spadework by comparativists such as Jakobson, Kurylowicz, Sievers, Meillet, Parry, Gasparov, Watkins, Allen, and Scott, most Eng. metrists are still unacquainted with the most advanced modern work on other verse systems, e.g. stress profiling, rhythmical figures, word-boundary distribution, and grammatical analysis of m. Constraints on the positioning of word boundaries, for example, have been studied intensively in Cl. metrics, where they are the basis for rules such as Hermann's Bridge and Porson's Law (see BRIDGE), but they have been scarcely studied at all in the modern prosodies.

XI. METRICAL VERSE AND FREE. The advent, after 1850, of the several nonmetrical prosodies known collectively as free verse (q.v.) represented not merely the abandonment of m., as its critics lamented, but rather a more fundamental transition from not one but two entire prosodic modes. First, poetry moved away from metrical verse to a range of experimental prosodies of considerable variety, no one of which prevailed; and indeed no full taxonomy of free-verse types has ever been given. Some types were quasi-metrical, others loosely rhythmical but not metrical. Second, the locus of prosodic deployment chosen after 1855 was not aural, as in the metrical poetry of the last two millennia, but visual; and this latter came to represent an overlay, or complication, of the aural effects and rhythmic structures which could still be discerned in much free verse. Visual structures now seemed used primarily for effects of grouping and delay, also for a scissoring of syntax in ways that particularly create surprise—that is, for the disruption and thwarting of expectation. White space became a structural element rather than the transparent background (see VISUAL POETRY); space now took on a positive reality that silence in the delivery of a line does not have. Yet it must also be remembered that all the postmodernist modes of nonmetrical poetry have emphasized performance: this is the latent schizophrenia of all visual prosodies mapped over aural.

What free verse lost in giving up m. was the resource of modulation. Even beyond the resource of variation against the norm—which is capable of far greater subtlety and power than is commonly supposed—free verse lost devices for highlighting and compounding meaning. It has been argued, most directly by Yvor Winters, that modern poetry thereby lost all hope of forging a medium equal to traditional verse. This is not to say that all metrical verse was of superior quality: great masses of it were mediocre. Great masses of poetry in any age are mediocre. But Eliot's point is still telling: "free" verse isn't free; no verse is free.

There is no escape from form, and a reaction to form can only be expressed in another set of forms. Lang. itself is form. The only question then is what a given form is capable of. Verse, to be distinguished from prose, must have some principle of differentiation, namely lineation; and there must be some reason why the lines are constituted as they are and not as other things. That principle might change in a poem; conceivably, it might even change from one line to the next, so long as a reader could infer from one line to the next what the principle is. But in verse where the principle is held constant throughout, reader attention is freed for maximum focus, line by line, on precisely those ends the principle is capable of effecting. This is the source of the power of metrical verse.

Critics who attack metrical poetry as false to the ethos of an age of violence, alienation, and cultural decay confuse the code with the message. It is certainly true that m. imposes order on experience—all art does that, indeed all lang. does that. A code can convey disorder, but cannot itself be incoherent, else nothing will be transmitted at all. If this be thought a paradox, it is nevertheless one beyond which we cannot go. In speech the orders of the code are transparent; in art they are made opaque—hence the double message.

XII. SUMMARY. M. is a species of rhythm, and so subject to the general laws of rhythmicity; it is manifested in lang., which is subject to linguistic processes. Our understanding of the general nature of rhythmicity has advanced very little over the past three thousand years, not for want of effort but because rhythm is a sophisticated cognitive process that operates across media. Lang. too turns out to be extraordinarily subtle and complex. An accurate understanding of the phonological structure of lang. did not begin to appear until the 18th c. Linguistics did not move beyond description until the 20th c., and theoretical work is still in its early stages, full of confusion and contention. Metrical theory itself has followed linguistics closely in the 20th c., which is both understandable and unfortunate. Some central concepts of m. are now clear, but there is as yet no general theory in place and shockingly little available data. An accurate comparative metrics is visible only dimly, as an alluring distant prospect. In general, modern work has dissolved the old notions of m. without yet having anything solid to put in their place. The old age has passed away, but the new age has not yet begun.

Literary critics have often chafed at the narrow bounds of metrics, wanting instead a broader theory of rhythm that would also apply to other arts (dance, music), other speech modes (ordinary lang., oratory, song), perhaps even perceptual processes. A general field theory of rhythmicity might eventually be able to give rules unifying all these extremely diverse phenomena, but certainly not without extensive accommodation of their differentiae. To date we know a little about the latter

and nearly nothing about the former. Some impetus may come from elaborate efforts such as that by Meschonnic (1982)—who remarks, amusingly, that "la métrique est la théorie du rythme des imbéciles" (143). It is useful to clarify the failures of past theories while we try to envision a successful future one.

All told, it is fair to say that traditional metrics, which dealt with the rhythmic pattern of the line by dividing it into constituent members then naming and counting them, never moved beyond mechanism to rhythmics as line-flow and flow-effects. "The flow of thought and the structure of verse are of course different," says Weismiller. Yet every prosodist since antiquity has sought to describe or explain the flow—somehow—in terms of structure. More importantly, however, "no theory can explain the structure of a line that was not written to embody, to actualize, that theory. That is, verse laws are real, not theoretical." Our graphic notation of a m. (i.e. scansion) is our attempt, however clumsy, to describe a real process at work in verse.

But scansion is only one method for describing m.; there are certainly others, some yet remaining to be developed. It was not until the 18th c. that an explicit technical vocabulary developed for describing what poets and readers had felt in poetry since the 4th c.; not until the 20th c. that linguistics moved past purely descriptive adequacy to ask for explanations; not until the latter 19th c. that textual criticism (q.v.) made reliable texts available for the first time; not until the latter 20th c. that pros. could be seen afresh in the contexts of comparative poetics and critical thinking about theory; and not until the late 20th c. that computers of sufficient power were affordable to scholars for collection of large corpora of data and testing of hypotheses. Linguistics, texts, theory, and data—these are the essential preliminaries. At the turn of the 21st c., pretty much everything still remains to be done.

For surveys of the major metrical traditions, with extended bibliographies, see ARABIC PROSODY; CELTIC PROSODY; CLASSICAL PROSODY; ENGLISH PROSODY; FRENCH PROSODY; GERMAN PROSODY; HEBREW PROSODY AND POETICS; INDIAN PROSODY; INDO-EUROPEAN PROSODY; ITALIAN PROSODY; SLAVIC PROSODY; SPANISH PROSODY. For specific meters see esp. MONOMETER; DIMETER; TRIMETER; TETRAMETER; PENTAMETER; HEXAMETER; OCTOSYLLABLE; and DECASYLLABLE. See also ACCENT; ACCENTUAL VERSE; ACEPHALOUS; ALLITERATIVE VERSE IN MODERN LANGUAGES; ANACRUSIS; ANCEPS; ARSIS AND THESIS; BALLAD METER; BINARY AND TERNARY; BLANK VERSE; BRIDGE; CAESURA; CHRISTABEL METER; CLASSICAL METERS IN MODERN LANGUAGES; COLON; COUPE; COUPLET; DIPODISM; DISTINCTIVE FEATURE ANALYSIS; DOLNIK; DURATION; ELISION; EPIPLOKE; EQUIVALENCE; FOOT; FREE VERSE; GENERATIVE METRICS; GRAMMETRICS; HEMIEPES; HEMISTICH; HEROIC COUP-

METER

LET; HETEROMETRIC; HOMODYNE AND HETERO-
DYNE; HOVERING ACCENT; HYPERMETRIC; HYPOMET-
RIC;̇ IAMBIC; IAMBIC SHORTENING; ICTUS; ISO-
CHRONISM; ISOMETRIC; KNITTELVERS; LINE;
LINGUISTICS AND POETICS; MEASURE; METRICAL
TREATMENT OF SYLLABLES; METRICI AND RHYTH-
MICI; METRON; MUSIC AND POETRY; NUMBER; PAUSE;
PERFORMANCE; PERIOD; PITCH; PROSE RHYTHM;
PROSODY; PYRRHIC; QUANTITY; RELATIVE STRESS
PRINCIPLE; RESPONSION; RHYTHM; RISING AND
FALLING RHYTHM; RULES; SCANSION; SECONDE
RHETORIQUE; SOUND; SOUND EFFECTS IN POETRY;
SPONDEE; SPRUNG RHYTHM; STICHOS; SUBSTITU-
TION; SYLLABIC VERSE; SYLLABLE; SYNAPHEIA;
SYNCOPATION; SYNTAX, POETIC; SYSTEM; TRO-
CHAIC; VARIABLE FOOT; VERS LIBRE; VERSE AND
PROSE; VERSET; VERSIFICATION.

BIBLIOGRAPHIES: Omond—lengthy discussions
of metrists; Thieme, esp. ch. 3 and 361–64—in-
dexes Fr. works, 1364–1913; Brogan—fullest com-
parative survey to date, supp. in *Verseform* (1988),
the latter incl. citations of bibls. and bibl. rev.
essays for specific langs.

HISTORIES: All the major standard histories, e.g.
Schipper, Kastner, Saintsbury, Atkins, Heusler,
Lote, and Allen (see Brogan), are out of date and
need to be redone. Navarro is still useful on Sp.;
Chambers is recent on Occitan; Pretzel and Kan-
zog (below) offer good summaries of Ger.

TERMINOLOGY: *Classical*: O. Schroeder, *Nomen-
clator metricus* (1929); J. B. Hoffmann and H.
Rubenbauer. *Wörterbuch der grammatischen und
metrischen Terminologie*, 2d ed. (1963); West; and
see bibl. for RHYTHM. *Modern*: none wholly reli-
able.

STUDIES: S. Daniel, *A Defense of Rhyme* (1603),
rpt. in Smith; T. Tyrwhitt, *Essay on the Lang. and
Versif. of Chaucer* (1775); J. Steele, *Prosodia ration-
alis*, 2d ed. (1779); E. Guest, *Hist. of Eng. Rhythms*
(1838), ed. W. W. Skeat (1882); Keil—collects
Med. Lat. treatises; A. J. Ellis, *On Early Eng. Pro-
nunciation* (1869–89); T. S. Omond, "Is Verse a
Trammel?" *Gentleman's Mag.* 14 (1875); Schipper;
C. M. Lewis, *The Foreign Sources of Mod. Eng. Versif.*
(1898); O. Jespersen, "Notes on M." [1900], rpt.
in his *Linguistica* (1933); J. B. Mayor, *Chapters on
Eng. M.*, 2d ed. (1901); H. Gleditsch, "Rhythmis-
che und metrische Theorie der Alten," *Metrik der
Griechen und Römer*, 3d ed. (1901); Meyer, esp.
3.130–45—Med. Lat.; Schipper, *History*; R.
Bridges, *Milton's Pros.* (1921)—still essential;
Wilamowitz, esp. ch. 3—capsule history of Cl.
metrical theories; B. V. Tomaševskij, *Russkoe
stixosloženie: Metrika* (1923), *O stixe* (1929); A.
Meillet, *Les origines indo-européennes des mètres grecs*
(1923); E. Legouis, *A Short Parallel between Fr. and
Eng. Versif.* (1925); P. Habermann, "Metrik,"
"Metrum," *Reallexikon I*, 2.342–51; I. A. Richards,
"Rhythm and M.," *Principles of Lit. Crit.* (1925),
"Poetic Form," *Practical Crit.* (1929); T. Taig, *Rhy-
thm and Metre* (1929); G. R. Stewart, Jr., *The Tech-
nique of Eng. Verse* (1930); P. Barkas, *Critique of
Mod. Eng. Pros.* (1934); E. Pound, "Treatise on
Metre," *ABC of Reading* (1934); Patterson; J. W.
Hendren, *A Study of Ballad M.* (1936); Y. Winters,
"The Influence of M. on Poetic Convention,"
Primitivism and Decadence (1937); A. W. de Groot,
Algemene Versleer (1946); W. F. J. Knight, *St.
Augustine's* De musica: *A Synopsis* (1949); I.
Baroway, "The Accentual Theory of Heb. Pros.,"
ELH 17 (1950); K. Taranovski, *Ruski dvodelni rit-
movi* (1953); V. Hamm, "M. and Meaning," *PMLA*
69 (1954); P. Fussell, *Theory of Prosody in 18th-C.
England* (1954); "Eng. Verse and What It Sounds
Like," *KR* 18 (1956); W. P. Lehmann, *The Devel. of
Germanic Verse Form* (1956); W. K. Wimsatt, Jr., and
M. C. Beardsley, "The Concept of M.," *PMLA* 74
(1959); Sebeok, esp. essays in Part 5 with following
"Comments," and R. Jakobson, "Linguistics and
Poetics"; C. S. Lewis, "Metre," *REL* 1 (1960); J.
Thompson, *The Founding of Eng. M.* (1961); G. B.
Pace, "The Two Domains: Rhythm and M.," *PMLA*
76 (1961); *Coventry Patmore's "Essay on Eng. Metri-
cal Law": A Crit. Ed.*, ed. Sr. M. A. Roth (1961); W.
B. Yeats, "A Gen. Intro. to My Work," *Essays and
Introductions* (1961); U. Pretzel, "Deutsche Vers-
kunst," *Deutsche Philologie im Aufriss*, ed. W.
Stammler, 2d ed., v. 3 (1962); M. Halpern, "On
the Two Chief Metrical Modes in Eng.," *PMLA* 77
(1962); Maas; S. Chatman, *A Theory of M.* (1965);
J. O. Perry, "The Temporal Analysis of Poems,"
BJA 5 (1965); C. S. Brown, "Can Musical Notation
Help Eng. Scansion?" *JAAC* 23 (1965); V. Žirmun-
skij, *Intro to Metrics: The Theory of Verse*, ed. and tr.
E. Stankiewicz and W. Vickery (1966); J. McAuley,
Versif.: A Short Intro. (1966); R. Fowler, "'Prose
Rhythm' and M.," *Essays on Style and Lang.* (1966),
The Langs. of Lit. (1971), esp. "What Is Metrical
Analysis?"; P. Habermann and W. Mohr, "Hebung
und Senkung," W. Mohr, "Rhythmus," and P.
Habermann and K. Kanzog, "Vers, Verslehre, Vers
und Prosa," *Reallexikon*; Dale, ch. 2; A. M. Dale,
"Speech-rhythm, Verse-rhythm and Song," *Coll. Pa-
pers* (1969); H. Kuhn, *Sprachgesch., Verskunst*
(1969); J. Malof, *A Manual of English Ms.* (1970);
G. W. Meyers, "Mod. Theories of M.: A Critical
Rev.," *DAI* 30 (1970), 3912A; C. L. Stevenson,
"The Rhythm of Eng. Verse," *JAAC* 28 (1970);
M. Sumera, "The Temporal Trad. in the Study of
Verse Structure," *Linguistics* 62 (1970)—capsule
hist.; D. Crystal, "Intonation and Metrical Theory,"
TPS (1971); *Mathematik und Dichtung*, ed. H.
Kreuzer and R. Gunzenhäuser, 4th ed. (1971); J.
Lotz, "Elements of Versif.," in Wimsatt, and "Met-
rics," *Current Trends in Linguistics, 12*, ed. T. A.
Sebeok (1974); S. R. Levin, "The Conventions of
Poetry," *Literary Style*, ed. S. Chatman (1971); J.
Levý, "Contrib. to the Typology of Accentual-Syl-
labic Versif.," rpt. in his *Paralipomena* (1971); E.
R. Weismiller, "Studies of Verse Form in the Minor
Eng. Poems" and "Studies of Style and Verse Form
in *Paradise Regained*," *A Variorum Commentary on
the Poems of John Milton*, ed. M. Y. Hughes, v. 2, 4
(1972, 1975); W. S. Allen, *Accent and Rhythm*

(1973), esp. ch. 9; S. Marcus, *Mathematische Poetik* (1973); M. L. West, "Gr. Poetry 2000–700 B.C.," *CQ* 67 (1973); M. Pazzaglia, *Teoria e analisi metrica* (1974); A. W. Bernhart, "Complexity and Metricality," *Poetics* 12 (1974), "The Iconic Quality of Poetic Rhythm," *Word & Image* 2 (1986); D. Attridge, *Well-Weighed Syllables* (1974), "The Lang. of Poetry," *EIC* 31 (1981), *The Rhythms of Eng. Poetry* (1982); J. E. Thiesmeyer, "Prosodic Theory: A Critique and Some Proposals," *DAI* 35 (1974), 1064A; M. L. Gasparov, *Sovremennyj russkij stix* (1974), *Očerk istorii russskogo stixa* (1984); Terras; A. T. Gaylord, "Scanning the Prosodists: An Essay in Metacriticism," *ChR* 11 (1976); M. G. Tarlinskaja, *Eng. Verse: Theory and Hist.* (1976), *Shakespeare's Verse* (1987)—statistical methods; L. P. Elwell-Sutton, *The Persian Metres* (1976); R. Tsur, *A Perception-Oriented Theory of M.* (1977); J. Lotman, *The Structure of the Artistic Text* (tr. 1977), 112 ff., 136 ff., 155 ff.; M. Dłuska, *Studia z historii i teorii wersyfikacji polskiej*, 2d ed., 2 v. (1978); H. J. Diller, "The Function of Verse in Byron's *Don Juan*," *Constance Byron Symposium* (1978); D. Laferrière, "The Teleology of Rhythm in Poetry," *PTL* 4 (1979); P. Barry, "The Enactment Fallacy," *EIC* 30 (1980); Scott; West—best account of Cl. at present; R. Lewis, *On Reading Fr. Verse* (1982); B. de Cornulier, *Théorie du vers* (1982), "Versifier: Le Code et sa règle," *Poétique* 66 (1986); J. Herington, *Poetry into Drama* (1985); Hollander; Chambers—Occitan; J. Stevens, *Words and Music in the Middle Ages* (1986); Scherr; *Hephaestion on Metre*, ed. and tr. J. M. van Ophuijsen (1987); G. T. Wright, *Shakespeare's Metrical Art* (1988); O. B. Hardison, Jr., *Pros. and Purpose in the Eng. Ren.* (1989); G. M. Hopkins, "Author's Preface," *Poetical Works*, ed. N. H. MacKenzie, 5th ed. (1990); Aristoxenus, *Elementa rhythmica*, ed. L. Pearson (1990).

COMPARATIVE METRICS: W. Mitford, *Inquiry into the Principles of Harmony in Lang. and the Mechanism of Verse, Ancient and Modern* (1804); E. Du Meril, *Essai philosophique sur le principe et les formes de la versif.* (1841); R. Westphal, *Allgemeine Metrik* (1892); M. Kawczinski, *Essai comparatif sur l'origine et l'histoire des rythmes* (1889); Sievers; E. V. Arnold, *Vedic Metre in its Historical Devel.* (1905); Thieme 365–66, 371; "Metrica," *Encyclopedia italiana*, v. 23 (1934), 102–13—covers 7 lits.; E. Olson, "Gen. Pros.: Rhythmik, Metrik, Harmonics," Diss., Univ. of Chicago (1938); M. Burger, *Recherches sur la structure et l'origine des vers romans* (1957); Beare; Norberg; J. C. La Drière, "The Comparative Method in the Study of Pros.," *Comp. Lit.*, ed. W. P. Friederich (1959); Lord; Jakobson, esp. v. 5, *On Verse: Its Masters and Explorers* (1979), v. 3, *Poetry of Grammar and Grammar of Poetry* (1981), v. 4, *Slavic Epic Studies* (1966), and v. 8 (1988); C. Watkins, "IE Metrics and Archaic Ir. Verse," *Celtica* 6 (1963): Parry; G. Martini, *Tecnica poetica e metrica comparata* (1972); Wimsatt; G. Nagy, *Comparative Studies in Gr. and Indic M.* (1974); E. Pulgram, *Lat.-Romance Phonology: Prosodics and Metrics* (1975); J. Kurylowicz, *Metrik und Sprachgesch.* (1975); M. L. Gasparov, *Očerk istorii evropejskogo stixa* [Outline of the History of European Versif.] (1989). T.V.F.B.

METONYMY (Gr. "change of name," Lat. *denominatio*). A figure in which one word is substituted for another on the basis of some material, causal, or conceptual relation. Quintilian lists the kinds usually distinguished: container for thing contained ("I'll have a glass"); agent for act, product, or object possessed ("reading Wordsworth"); cause for effect; time or place for their characteristics or products ("a bloody decade," "I'll have Burgundy"); associated object for its possessor or user ("the crown" for the king). Other kinds are sometimes identified: parts of the body for states of consciousness associated with them (head and heart for thought and feeling), material for object made of it (ivories for piano keys), and attributes or abstract features for concrete entities. In common usage, one subset of m. is synecdoche (q.v.).

Because metonymies are common in ordinary usage and new ones are often easy to decipher, they have attracted less critical attention than metaphor (q.v.). When the effect of m. is to create a sense of vividness or particularity—as in Gray's "drowsy tinklings" of sheep (the sound of their bells), or Keats' "beaker full of the warm South"—the figure is often treated as an instance of imagery (q.v.). But the metonymies "drowsy" and "South" are not concrete images. Auden's lines "the clever *hopes expire* / Of a *low* dishonest *decade*" show that a clear surface meaning can arise from metonymic associations of cause, attribute, and effect that are far from simple. Conversely, m. can create riddles, hard to fathom but clear once understood, as in Dylan Thomas's "Altarwise by owl-light," the title of which suggests facing east in the dark.

Some linguists argue that m. and synecdoche can often be understood as nonfigurative expressions that result from verbal deletions intended to reduce redundancy (Ruwet). "A glass of Burgundy wine" becomes "a glass of Burgundy," or simply "Burgundy" or "a glass" when the sentence or context implies the rest. In "I just read (a novel by) Balzac," the phrase in parentheses can be deleted because the context conveys its sense.

Attempts to produce a definition of m. that would show what generic features its different types have in common have been part of the larger project of deriving a systematic rationale underlying tropes (see FIGURE, SCHEME, TROPE). The meaning assigned to m. in such cases is determined by the categorical features used to define the tropes (e.g. linguistic, logical, semiotic, psychological) and the number of tropes considered fundamental. Ramus, Vico, and their modern followers hold that there are four; Bloom retains six; Jakobson treats two, m. and metaphor. The meaning of m. expands as the number of tropes decreases.

In the fourfold classification, the other three are synecdoche, metaphor, and irony (qq.v.). Ramus (*Arguments in Rhet. Against Quintilian*, 1549) limited m. to "a change in meaning from causes to effects, from subjects to adjuncts, or vice versa." Some argue that these two types of m. can be equated with Aristotle's four causes: efficient (which would explain metonymies of agent for act), material (encompassing metonymies of time, place, matter, and container), formal (m. of abstract for concrete, attribute for subject), and final. Among modern adherents of fourfold classification, Kenneth Burke would limit m. to "reduction" (incorporeal and corporeal); Hayden White defines it as part-whole reduction; Bloom treats it as a change from full to empty. In these three definitions, m. is not reversible: to substitute incorporeal for corporeal, or empty for full, would be another trope (synecdoche, for Burke and Bloom). These critics use the names of the tropes figuratively, applying them to passages or to entire texts.

In practice, it is often difficult to distinguish m. from synecdoche (part for whole, genus for species, or the reverse). Some hold that synecdoche entails a "one—many" substitution, or, in logical terms, a change of extension, whereas m. is a one-for-one replacement involving a change of intension (definition; see Henry). Finding no satisfactory means of distinguishing the two, many critics use "m." as a generic term for both and contrast it with metaphor on one of several grounds.

Boris Eichenbaum (*Anna Akhmatova*, 1923) held that metaphor operates at a "supra-linguistic" level, that of the idea: a word is pulled from its semantic field to superimpose a second level of meaning on the literal level. M., he said, is a displacement, or lateral semantic shift, that lends words new meanings without leaving the literal plane. Jakobson (1935) extended the dichotomy, suggesting that frequent use of metaphor unites the poet's mythology and being, separated from the world. Poets who prefer m., on the other hand, project their being on an outer reality that their emotion and perception displace from the normal. The shifting, sequential character of m., he said, was more common in prose than in poetry (see Lodge).

Reworking the distinction in 1956, Jakobson described metaphor as a metalinguistic operation (roughly speaking, a process through which an idea or theme is actualized in words). M., he said, was a change that operated on the hierarchy of linguistic units, either affecting their order or substituting part of a word's meaning, or one associated with it, for the word itself. Both tropes can result from substitution of one word for another (on the paradigmatic axis) or from combination (the succession of words on the syntagmatic axis— see EQUIVALENCE). In metaphor, for example, a single word can be substituted for another, or the two can be successive ("A is B"). A series of meta-phors may point toward a single theme, as in Shakespeare's sonnet that successively likens old age to autumn, sunset, and a dying fire. The same possibilities exist in m., but in the latter, there is no metalinguistic idea unifying the chain of metonymies.

Jakobson held that these two tropes could be used to classify mental disorders (e.g. aphasia), literary movements (romanticism and symbolism being based on metaphor, realism on m.), styles in painting and cinematography, operations of the unconscious (Freud's "identification and symbolism" being metaphor, whereas "displacement" and "condensation" are m.), and cultural practices (e.g. the two types of magic identified by J. G. Frazer—one based on similarity, the other on contiguity). Adapting Jakobson's taxonomy to his own psychoanalytic theory, Lacan treated discourse as a continuous m., displaced from the real, in which metaphoric, unconscious signifiers sometimes appear (see Ruegg and Vergote).

Attempts to revise or simplify the m.–metaphor opposition as conceived by Jakobson and Lacan have taken several forms. Henry defines m. as the result of a psychological focus that substitutes the name of one of a word's semantic elements (semes) for the word itself; metaphor in his view is a combination of two metonymies. Le Guern argues that the "contiguity" of Jakobson's m. involves reference to reality, whereas metaphor is the product of a purely linguistic or conceptual operation. De Man pushes this difference further, seeing m. not only as referential but as contingent or accidental, in opposition to the pull toward unification of essences that underlies most uses of metaphor. Bredin agrees that m. refers to the world but sees such "extrinsic relations" as "a kind of ontological cement holding the world together," not as contingencies. Metaphor is also referential in his view, both figures being opposed to the "structural" or intralinguistic relations underlying synecdoche.

In seeking a logic underlying m. and other tropes, theorists are forced to redefine them, reassigning some of the types they have traditionally included to other tropes and discarding yet others. In so doing, they represent tropes as rule-governed transformations of literal usage. The theoretical clarity thus obtained results from treating rhet. and poetics as branches of philosophy or linguistics.

R. Jakobson, "Marginal Notes on the Prose of the Poet Pasternak" (1935) rpt. in *Lang. in Lit.* (tr. 1987), "Two Aspects of Lang. and Two Types of Aphasic Disorders," *Fundamentals of Lang.* (1956), rev. ver. in Jakobson, v. 1; K. Burke, "Four Master Tropes," *A Grammar of Motives* (1945); J. Lacan, *Écrits: A Selection* (1966, tr. 1977); A. Henry, *Métonymie et métaphore* (1971); Lausberg; M. Le Guern, *Sémantique de la métaphore et de la métonymie* (1973); H. White, *Metahistory* (1973); N. Ruwet, "Synecdoches et métonymies," *Poétique* 6 (1975); H. Bloom, *A Map of Misreading* (1975), *Wallace Stevens* (1977); D. Lodge, *The Modes of Mod. Writ-*

ing (1977), Pt. 2; P. Ricoeur, *The Rule of Metaphor* (1977); P. de Man, *Allegories of Reading* (1979); M. Ruegg, "Metaphor and M.," *Glyph* 6 (1979); J. Culler, "The Turns of Metaphor," *The Pursuit of Signs* (1981); G. Genette, *Figures of Literary Discourse* (1982), ch. 6; A. Vergote, "From Freud's 'Other Scene' to Lacan's 'Other,'" *Interpreting Lacan*, ed. J. Smith and W. Kerrigan (1983); H. Bredin, "M.," *Poetics Today* 5.1 (1984); W. Bohn, "Jakobson's Theory of Metaphor and M., An. Annot. Bibl.," *Style* 18 (1984); J. Hedley, *Powers in Verse* (1988).   W.M.

METRIC FIGURES. See METRICAL TREATMENT OF SYLLABLES.

METRICAL REST. See PAUSE.

METRICAL ROMANCE. See MEDIEVAL ROMANCE.

METRICAL TREATMENT OF SYLLABLES. Most meters are based on a count of recurring features of lang. Thus the Old Germanic meters require the occurrence in each line of four syllables carrying major stress (there are of course accompanying requirements), while the number of syllables in the line is relatively less constrained (see GERMAN PROSODY); the Romance meters, in comparison, regulate the number of syllables more strictly (see FRENCH PROSODY). The accentual-syllabic or syllabotonic meter adapted to Eng. first by Chaucer and again by Wyatt and Surrey from Fr. and It. syllabic models was during the first centuries of its use in England principally a syllable-counting meter with secondary constraints on stress (see ENGLISH PROSODY).

The concept of the "syllable" (q.v.) is somewhat theoretical and conventional, a point which may be illustrated in the words "higher" and "hire," hardly distinguishable in pronunciation, though the first is usually considered of two syllables, the second of one. Nonetheless the native speakers of a lang. tend to feel that they know how many syllables there are in a given word, and therefore how many syllables a given line of verse contains. The traditional definition of the syllable as a cluster centered in a vowel that may be preceded or followed by a consonant or consonants, provided that the whole remains capable of articulation in a single impulse of the breath, is not technically exact, but it will provide us with a reasonably satisfactory background against which we may view the syllable-counting practice of Eng. poets from the mid 16th c. to the beginning of the romantic period. During this time span, verse writers were as part of their craft counting syllables, and in this they were affected by the state of the lang. in their time and by conventions that had arisen or were arising having to do with what was thought correct or appropriate or aesthetically pleasing in the handling of syllables.

Gr. and Lat. quantitative meters, based on a count of *times* (two short syllables being held equal to one long, the nature of shorts and longs being conventional—see CLASSICAL PROSODY), provided Western verse with models for the—somewhat artificial—metrical treatment of syllables. The next-to-the-last foot of the Lat. dactylic hexameter, for example, is always a dactyl, a long followed by two short syllables; the last foot is always a spondee, two long syllables. The first four feet of the hexameter may be either dactylic or spondaic in any combination, so that the line, always 24 "times," will contain no fewer than 13 syllables (11 long, 2 short), and no more than 17 (7 long, 10 short).

To see how a strict count of syllables functions formally in the syllabotonic line of a vernacular poetry, we may consider the It. *endecasillabo*, a line of 11 syllables intermediate between the Lat. iambic trimeter and the Eng. decasyllable (or iambic pentameter). In the first dozen lines of Dante's *Inferno*, the first line—but only the first—is of 11 syllables without adjustment; in all the other lines, various kinds of metrical compression or other artifices are employed to reduce the number of syllables to 11 or to bring them into the required stress pattern, i.e. a stress on the tenth and on either the fourth or sixth syllables.

Many of the syllable-adjusting devices of It. were adaptable to Eng., and—at first by Chaucer, later by Early Modern Eng. poets from Wyatt and Surrey through Milton—were so adapted. What may in general be referred to simply as *elision* (q.v.) is familiar to readers of 16th- to 18th-c. verse in such forms as "gainst," "twixt," "th'eternal," "th'art," "t'advance," "t'have," "see'st," "fly'st," "low'st," "dev'lish," "pois'nous," "murm'ring," "med'cine," and the like. The first two of these are examples of *aphaeresis* (the dropping of a word-initial vowel or syllable; q.v.), the last four (at least) of *syncope* (suppression of a word-internal vowel; q.v.), and such (early) forms as monosyllabic "i'th'," "o'th'," "to th'," and "by th' " are fairly clear examples of *apocope* (excision of a word-final vowel; q.v.), which is illustrated also in the second word of Spenser's line "Callèd Fidess', and so supposd to bee" (*Faerie Queene* 1.4.2.4). But the terminology, the elaborate technical vocabulary, would seem useful only if identification of the nature or means of achieving syllabic loss in a given instance were absolutely crucial. Terms such as *aphaeresis, apocope, synaeresis, synaloepha* (qq.v.), and *synizesis* no doubt have their application to Eng. forms; all things considered, however, the ordinary reader is perhaps better off using a simple explanatory vocabulary as accurately as she or he can, and no more precisely than the situation requires.

Coalescence of contiguous vowels, the first stressed, is illustrated in Early Modern Eng. verse in such forms as monosyllabic "prayer," disyllabic "déity," "píety," "póesy." The fact that primary stress in Eng. has tended to move back toward the beginning of polysyllables perhaps accounts for the paucity in Eng. of disyllabic forms such as "Biánca" and "Iágo" (*Shrew* 2.1.346; *Othello* 4.1.3); but Milton gives us tetrasyllabic "humiliation" in *Paradise Lost* and *Paradise Regained*; and the situation may arise between words, as in monosyllabic "the eare" (if the first *e* is not elided), trisyllabic "any other," monosyllabic "to have," etc. The blending of adjacent vowels neither one of which is stressed is very common in Eng.; everywhere in Early Modern Eng. verse one finds such forms as disyllabic "hideous," "valiant," "worthiest," "glorying," "many a" (in all of which [ɪ] is converted to consonantal [j] before a following vowel, the two together being pronounced [je] or [jɪ]) as well as "echoing," "follower," "shadowy," "sensual," "influence" (in which *o* or *u* is assimilated or converted to consonantal [w] before a sequent vowel). Poets from Chaucer through Milton imitated this process by blending into a single syllable a final syllabic liquid or nasal and a vowel beginning a following word, e.g. disyllabic "temple and," "open his," "river of."

In syllable-counting verse, forms that may be contracted may equally, of course, be used in full, and forms normally short may be extended; *diaeresis* (q.v.), that is, is as much a resource of the poet as *synaeresis*. When Milton writes "Whispering new joyes to the milde Ocean" (*On the Morning of Christ's Nativity* 66), having prepared us for trisyllabic "O-ce-an" with its rhyme word "began" in line 63, we find contraction (disyllabic "Whispering") and extension in the same line; and, indeed, many 16th- and 17th-c. poets thought it a beauty of verse to use the same word twice in a single line or in adjacent lines, once contracted, once in full. Contraction (or extension) may or may not be signalled by spelling in 16th- to 17th-c. Eng. verse; often it cannot be. When Spenser uses "air" and "fire" as disyllables, it is true, he spells them "aier" and "fier"; but with some obvious exceptions, specifically metrical spellings (even where these would be possible) are less and less common in the work of later poets.

Considering that in any event not all words are now pronounced as they were pronounced by the great poets of the past, inevitably we ask ourselves whether, and how, to perform the metrical compressions and extensions of earlier poetry, some of which now fall very oddly on the ear. Such instances as Milton's *Nativity Ode* rhyme, however, or Spenser's unusual spelling, suggest that the extensions illustrated were *meant* to be read, were intended to preserve the meter *actually*, not merely theoretically. As for contractions, many of those found in verse of the 16th to 18th cs. occur in prose as well, and so are not specifically "poetic," the motivation for their use being not solely metrical. Alternative linguistic forms such as "wandring" or "threatning" are not contractions at all. Genuinely contracted forms used commonly by educated speakers and writers of formal verse must have been thought appropriate to such verse, and it is

scarcely to the point for irrelevant modern tastes to decree them, retrospectively, inappropriate, and thus unlikely to have been performed. In general, the unexpected full forms and the metrical compressions of 16th- to 18th-c. verse seem either to have come from speech at an appropriate level or to be phonologically analogous to attested speech forms, and must have been written to be pronounced—though readers of a later period may shudder, or refuse, to think so.

Of course, pronunciations change, usage changes. Speech contractions, after the lang. discards them, become "poetic" if they continue to be used in verse—e.g. "o'er," "e'en," "ope." Less obviously—but more importantly—the model used by Eng. poets from Wyatt through Milton to regulate number of syllables was basically It.; after the Restoration the model was, rather, Fr. Italianate synaloepha (the blending or coalescence of vowels at the end of one word and the beginning of the next, as in "the eare," "only in," "yellow as") and the Eng. imitation of this process involving syllabic semivowels dropped out of use after Milton. From Dryden on, the syncopations and other contractions lying within the narrowed range considered acceptable were on the whole required, so that one finds in late 17th- and 18th-c. verse relatively far fewer alternative metrical forms than appeared in, and indeed characterized, earlier verse.

Late 20th-c. prosodists, concerned with meter primarily as an abstraction, tend to argue that the Eng. iambic pentameter is a line with a base of ten positions alternately weak and strong, and that any of these positions may be occupied by one *or* two syllables—or in exceptional circumstances by none—and that one may read apparent contractions or not, as one chooses, whatever the period of the verse in question. Doubtless it does not matter greatly if one reads "Whispering" as a light trisyllable in Milton's *Nativity Ode* line 66, and doubtless most of us would forgive the actor who, delivering *Julius Caesar* 3.2.101–3,

> I thrice presented him a kingly crown,
> Which he did thrice refuse. Was this
>   ambition?
> Yet Brutus says he was ambitious,

reads the last line as of nine syllables—a tetrameter with a feminine ending—as the previous line is a pentameter with a feminine ending. A modern audience is likely to be put off by [am-bi-si-əs] or [am-bi-ši-əs]. Yet Shakespeare's verse contains thousands upon thousands of lines which are clearly decasyllables, and few textually certain lines of nine syllables. One view of meter is precisely that it tells us *how to read* where otherwise varying possibilities would exist.

But the subject is complex and poses more problems than can be solved here. We *can* say that, from the time of the romantics on, Eng. poets increasingly admitted to the familiar decasyllabic line extra unstressed syllables which did not allow of contraction:

x x

Migration strange for a stripling of the hills
   (Wordsworth, *Prelude* 3.34)

x   x   x x   x x

Like the skipping of rabbits by moonlight—
three slim shapes
   (Browning, *Fra Lippo Lippi* 59),

whereas poets of the 16th, 17th, and 18th cs.—
nondramatic poets, at any rate—seem on the
whole not to have written lines containing extra
syllables (the feminine ending excepted) which
could not be resolved phonologically. This prob-
ably says something about the intended perform-
ance, the intended *sound*, of the earlier verse. And
sound, including tautness or relaxation of rhythm,
is sufficiently a part of the meaning of verse that
we do well to take seriously the apparent inten-
tions of the poet regarding it.

The basic music of verse in the great Eng. trad.,
the verse of Chaucer, of Spenser, of Shakespeare,
of Milton, of Dryden, of Pope, and of all the other
poets who have used consciously the meter they
used, depends to a significant degree upon the
artifices for metrical treatment of syllables de-
scribed above. They reflect the lang. of their
times. And to the degree that the difference be-
tween that lang. and our own is of importance, we
must do what we can to understand them. See also
ELISION; METER.—E. J. Dobson, *Eng. Pronunciation
1500–1700*, 2d ed., 2 v. (1968); H. Kökeritz, *Shake-
speare's Pronunciation* (1953); A. C. Partridge, *Or-
thography in Shakespeare and Elizabethan Drama*
(1964); D. Sipe, *Shakespeare's Metrics* (1968).

                                          E.R.W.

METRICAL VARIATION. See METER.

METRICI AND RHYTHMICI (Gr. *metrikoi*, stu-
dents of metrics, *rhythmikoi*, musical theorists).
Among the ancient Greeks there were two schools
of metrical theorists. The m. were primarily gram-
marians; they held that only long and short sylla-
bles need to be considered in scansion (q.v.), and
that a long syllable was always twice the length of
a short; actual variations were ignored. The chief
exemplar is Hephaestion (2d c. A.D.), whose
Enchiridion ("Manual," ed. Consbruch 1906; tr.
van Ophuijsen 1987), originally in 48 Books, has
survived in a one-book abridgment. In opposition
to this group, the r., chiefly the musical theorist
Aristoxenus of Tarentum (pupil of Aristotle, fl. 4th
c. B.C.; see Westphal, Pearson), viewed poetry as
allied to music, maintaining that long syllables
differ greatly from one another in quantity, and
that even short syllables may differ to some de-
gree, thus demanding more complicated methods
of analysis.

Certainly much early Gr. poetry was sung to the
accompaniment of flutes or pipes (see MELIC PO-
ETRY), as were the songs in Gr. drama, though
strictly recited verse such as monody (q.v.) cer-
tainly existed, and the dialogue portions of drama
were metrical. At issue among the theorists is not
the question of performance mode but the more
fundamental issue of whether meter is in ontologi-
cal terms a structural phenomenon or a temporal
one: essentially, m. count the occurrence of events,
while r. also insist on taking account of the timing
of those events. But on the extant evidence we
ought not overstate the clarity or depth of ancient
theory: the m. are mechanistic and oversimple,
the r. extremely difficult.

In fact, however, this plane of cleavage between
competing theories of the nature of verse extends
straight through the history of Western prosody
up to the present. The musical–rhythmical view is
carried into the Middle Ages by Augustine (*De
musica*, 389 A.D.); later it is transformed into
claims that quantitative verse could be written in
the European vernaculars (see CLASSICAL METERS
IN MODERN LANGUAGES)—a vestige of the linger-
ing authority of Lat. which persisted until the
emergence of Cl. Philology in the 19th c., and is
revived in modern times in the "musical" theories
of prosody of Joshua Steele (18th c.), Sidney
Lanier (19th c.), Andreas Heusler, and John C.
Pope (in the 20th c., for Ger. and OE), and a host
of epigones, as well as in other temporal theories
not strictly musical (e.g. Omond, Stewart, At-
tridge)—for schema, see Brogan 142. Allied are
those who deny that modern verse is metrical at
all, such as G. F. Nott (1815) and J. G. Southworth
(1954). By contrast, the m. incl. Aristotle, the Lat.
grammarians (texts collected in Keil, v. 6), Bede,
Sidney, Daniel, Mitford, Tyrwhitt, Guest, Schip-
per, Mayor, and most modern prosodists such as
Wimsatt and Wright.

Keil; R. Westphal, *Die Fragmente und Lehrsätze der
griechischen Rhythmiker* (1861), "Die Trad. der al-
ten Metriker," *Philologus* 20 (1863), ed., *Scriptores
metrici graeci*, 2 v. (1866), ed., *Aristoxenos von Tar-
ent: Melik und Rhythmik*, 2 v. (1883–93)—with com-
mentary; J. Hadley, "Gr. Rhythm and Metre," *Es-
says Philological and Critical* (1873); T. D. Goodell,
Chapters on Gr. Metric (1901); C. Williams, *The
Aristoxenian Theory of Musical Rhythm* (1911);
Wilamowitz, pt. 1, ch. 3—still the best survey of
ancient theory; H. D. F. Kitto, "Rhythm, Metre,
and Black Magic," *ClassR* 56 (1942); Brogan; West;
Aristoxenus, *Elementa Rhythmica*, ed. L. Pearson
(1990).

                                        T.V.F.B.

METRON (pl. metra). In Cl. Gr. and Lat. prosody,
a unit of measurement in the metrical analysis of
a period (q.v.) which is attested as early as Hero-
dotus. Metra are recurring and equivalent units of
from 3 to 6 long and short syllables. Verseforms
that can be analyzed in terms of metra are said to
be organized *kata metron*, i.e. in measure (q.v.);
such verse includes stichic forms such as the iam-
bic trimeter and dactylic hexameter (recitation

meters); verse that is measured by cola (singular form "colon" [q.v.]), by contrast, are said to be measured *ou kata metron* (see AEOLIC). The ancient grammarians and metrists also analyzed metrical units in terms of feet (see FOOT). In some Gr. meters—e.g. dactylic and ionic—a m. is equivalent to a foot, while in others—e.g. iambic, trochaic, anapestic—it is equivalent to two feet (hence the older term "dipody"). Thus the dactylic hexameter has six feet, but the iambic trimeter has three metra (scanned x − ∪ −). It is best to measure Gr. verse in iambs, trochees, and anapests in metra primarily because verse composed in these three genres always consists of an even number of feet and certain features are restricted to the second foot. In the recited verse of Lat. comedy, however, there is no distinction between the two parts of iambic or trochaic metra, hence these meters are measured in feet (see SENARIUS; SEPTENARIUS; OCTONARIUS). When the concepts and terms of Cl. prosody were revived in the Ren. for the description of modern meters, however, these subtleties were lost, hence it was the foot rather than the m. which became the basis for prosodic description of intralinear metrical units. See also COLON; FOOT; MEASURE; METER; PERIOD; SYSTEM.—Wilamowitz, 103, 441 ff.; Beare, 76–77; Maas, sects. 52, 61–66; Koster, 16–17; Dale, chs. 1–2, and *Collected Papers* (1969), ch. 4; W. S. Allen, *Accent and Rhythm* (1973); West 4–6, 198, 200.

J.W.H.; T.V.F.B.

MEXICAN AMERICAN POETRY. See CHICANO POETRY.

MEXICAN POETRY. See SPANISH AMERICAN POETRY.

MIDRASH. See HEBRAISM; INTERPRETATION, FOURFOLD METHOD OF.

MIME (Gr. "imitation"). In the Cl. sense of the term, a type of drama in which players rely mainly on gestures to tell a story. Found in ancient Greece and Rome, the m. probably arose, as its name implies, from the natural impulse to imitate persons or scenes from daily life. As a literary genre, however, it developed in Sicily and southern Italy, where Sophron of Syracuse (5th c. B.C.) wrote, in colloquial prose, realistic scenes which border on the gross. Subsequently Herodas (3d c. B.C.) used meter for his *mimiambi*, which in turn influenced the Alexandrian poetry of Theocritus, the Lat. poets Plautus, Terence, and Horace (*Epodes, Satires*), and the Roman m. writers Decimus Laberius and Publilius Syrus (1st c. B.C.), of whose works only fragments survive. Lat. actors performed m. without masks and spoke in prose. Originally comic, the m. came to be closely associated with farce (q.v.), which it supplanted at the ends of tragedies. Ribaldry and burlesque (q.v.) were its chief ingredients and its source of great popularity. Consequently the Church waged war on the m. and its actors, so that finally in the 5th c. A.D. all who took part in it fell under ban of excommunication. As a genre it again became popular in the *commedia dell' arte* of 16th-c. Italy, whence it spread to France and England. In 19th-c. France, *L'Enfant Prodigue*, a three-act m. play, culminates the history of the genre.

In the modern sense of the term, which is distinct from the Cl., m. or *pantomime* refers to a performance which relies exclusively on gesture and forsakes words entirely, though it may be accompanied by music. This form was also known to the Romans, being introduced by Pylades of Cilicia in 22 B.C., but became a sophisticated and refined form of performance with masks, in contrast to the increasingly vulgar m. described above. A famous late literary example is the Dumb Show in *Hamlet*; popular pantomime was revived in the 20th c.—H. Reich, *Der Mimus* (1903); O. Crusius, *Die Mimiamben des Herondas* (1926); A. Körte, *Hellenistic Poetry* (1929); A. Nicoll, *Masks, Mimes and Miracles* (1931); W. Beare, *The Roman Stage*, 2d ed. (1955); J. D. A. Ogilvy, "Mimi, Scurrae, Histriones: Entertainers of the Early Middle Ages," *Speculum* 38 (1963); Trypanis, ch. 10; T. Leabhart, *Mod. and Post-Mod. M.* (1989).

R.A.H.; T.V.F.B.

MIMESIS. See REPRESENTATION AND MIMESIS; CLASSICAL POETICS; IMITATION; SOUND.

MINIMALISM. The principle of intentional reduction, whether formal or semantic, with respect to the size, scale, or range of a given poetic composition. The term m. may refer to poems that are very short and condensed, to poems that use short lines or abbreviated stanzas, or to poems that use a severely restricted vocabulary. But m. is not a term used to refer to just any short poem: it is not, for instance, applied to the haiku or epigram (qq.v.). Rather, m. is a late 20th-c. designation for a poetics that holds that spareness, tautness, understatement, and reduction are emblematic of poetic authenticity. As such, m. is an offshoot of phenomenology (see GENEVA SCHOOL), with its trust in the principle that William Carlos Williams called "no ideas but in things."

The use of the term "m." to designate poetic features is quite recent, it having been coined originally to define specific movements in the visual arts and in music, respectively. Richard Wollheim's 1965 essay "Minimal Art" was probably the first to define "a class of objects" that "have a minimal art-content, in that either they are to an extreme degree undifferentiated in themselves and therefore possess very low content of any kind, or else the differentiation that they do exhibit . . . comes not from the artist but from a nonartistic source, like nature or the factory." Wollheim cites the black canvases of Ad Reinhardt and the readymades of Marcel Duchamp, but the more common reference of the term is to the primal geometric sculptures of Donald Judd, Sol LeWitt, and Robert Morris, as well as to the abstract color-field paintings of such artists as Frank Stella, Kenneth Noland, and Elsworth Kelly.

In music, the term "m." was first used to refer to compositions that use a minimum of material, such as John Cage's *4'33'* or La Monte Young's *Composition 1960 #7*, which contains only the notes B and F# with the instructions "to be held for a long time." But since the early 1970s, m. specifically refers to the work of Philip Glass and related composers whose tonal works restrict progression (movement from one chord to the next) so as to explore the static development of sonorities.

When m. is transferred to poetry, it thus refers to such abbreviated lyrics as Robert Creeley's "The Box" (1967):

Three sides,
four
windows. Four

doors, three
hands.

Other poets whose m. is often discussed are François Ponge (France), Ernst Jandl (Austria), Tom Raworth (Britain), and, in the U.S., William Carlos Williams, the early H.D., the objectivists Louis Zukofsky and George Oppen (whom Hugh Kenner calls "the geometers of minima"), David Ignatow, Gary Snyder, James Laughlin, Clark Coolidge, Aram Saroyan, and Bruce Andrews. But the greatest practitioner of m., Samuel Beckett, is primarily a writer of prose: such "residua" as *Imagination Dead Imagine*, *Ping*, and *Fizzles* permutate a rigidly circumscribed set of words and phrases in minimal units of great tension and complexity.—J. Cage, *Silence* (1962); R. Wollheim, "Minimal Art," *Arts Magazine* 39 (1965); *Minimal Art*, ed. G. Battcock (1968); H. Kenner, *A Homemade World* (1975); C. Gottlieb, *Beyond Modern Art* (1976); R. Kostelanetz, "An ABC of Contemporary Reading," *Esthetics Contemporary* (1978); D. H. Cope, *New Directions in Music* (1981); M. Perloff, Preface, *Contemporary Poets*, 3d ed. (1985); E. Brater, *Beyond M.: Beckett's Late Style in the Theatre (1987)*.   M.P.

MINNELIED. See MINNESANG.

MINNESANG. The collective designation for lyrics on themes of love (*minne*) produced in German-speaking areas from the 12th through the early 14th cs. The M. is considerably influenced by the poetry of the troubadours and trouvères (qq.v.) and forms part of a European trad. which spread also to Sicily, north Italy, and Spain. In the 12th c., the poets were of knightly origin, but in the 13th c. there are also professional poets of lower social status. The songs (*Minnelied*, pl. *Minnelieder*) were intended for vocal performance be-

fore a courtly audience, but very little music survives. There is some evidence for indigenous lyric trads. in a few anonymous poems and named Austro-Bavarian poets probably active from ca. 1150, which indicates that the woman's stanza (*Frauenstrophe*), the woman's complaint of absence, desertion, or rivals (*Frauenklage*), and the indirect exchange between lovers (*Wechsel*) are native types, depicting the woman as subordinate to or equal with the man. The poems have simple structures and are predominantly monostrophic, though occasionally two, or more rarely three, stanzas may be loosely linked. (For details of the metrical structure of these and other forms described below, see GERMAN PROSODY, *Old Germanic*.) All the poets in this group whose names are known to us, and esp. Meinloh von Sevelingen, fuse native trads. with thematic features derived from knowledge of the Romance lyric—e.g. the lover's submission to his lady, the complaint of ill-wishers—but remain uninfluenced by Romance forms.

I. THE LATER 12TH CENTURY. From ca. 1170 the thematic and formal influence of the Romance lyric, transmitted originally through a group of Rhineland and Western poets, becomes pervasive. The dominant type of poem, the equivalent of the Romance *canso*, is the first-person reflection on love, which may be combined with an apostrophe of Love or the lady. Love service is presented in feudal terms as an arduous but ennobling aspiration, addressed to a lady who is a paragon of beauty and virtue. A minor variant (*Kreuzlied*) expresses the conflict between love and crusading duty. On the pattern of the Romance lyric, polystrophic poems and tripartite stanza forms made up of short lines (see CANSO) become the norm; new types of rhyme are introduced, pure rhyme replaces assonance, and dactylic rhythms occur for the first time. The connection between stanzas is often loose, reflecting the original predominance of the monostrophic poem.

In the period up to 1200, precise textual and formal borrowings from Occitan and OF poets may be traced in Friedrich von Hausen, Rudolf von Fenis, Bernger von Horheim, and Ulrich von Gutenburg (Frank); thereafter, direct imitation is rendered superfluous by widespread knowledge of Romance conventions and forms. However, poets such as Albrecht von Johansdorf and Reinmar, writing in areas more remote from Romance influence, those in which the lyric is first attested, also retain certain archaic features, e.g. women's stanzas, examples of the *Wechsel*, and long and unrhymed lines.

II. THE 13TH CENTURY. Because the main collective mss. were compiled at the end of the 13th or beginning of the 14th c. in southern Germany and Switzerland, the bulk of the material preserved belongs to the 13th c., and to areas close to the places of compilation. Thus, whereas there are only some 16 to 20 poets who can be assigned to the 12th c., about 130 belong to the 13th c., mostly the latter half, and on occasion beyond. The transmission undoubtedly gives a distorted picture of the frequency and geographical distribution of poetic production at each stage, but nonetheless bears witness to the immense popularity of the M. over a long period.

The most original poets belong to the turn of the 12th c., when established trads. allowed scope for innovation. Walther von der Vogelweide is unique in his thematic and formal range and in his synthesis of native, Romance, and Med. Lat. trads. Wolfram von Eschenbach is the first major exponent of the dawn song (see TAGELIED). Neidhart creates two new and formally distinct types of poem depicting summer and winter festivities and dancing, in which the poet vies with peasant rivals for his lady's favor. Both realistic details of setting, clothing, and proper names, and also elements of parody and satire are juxtaposed with M. conventions. Like Walther, Neidhart is familiar with Med. Lat. and probably also with the OF *pastourelle* (q.v.). There are other major 13th-c. poets with a substantial oeuvre, some like Walther with a wide repertoire, incl. the *Leich* (q.v.) and the didactic lyric, but also a host of minor poets.

Particularly in the first half of the 13th c., there are survivals of earlier features—single and women's stanzas, examples of the *Wechsel* and of crusading themes, and simple isometric forms—but in the main the 13th c. is characterized by new developments, largely in a second wave of Romance influence. The genres of dawn song, *Leich*, and dialogues in the manner of the Occitan *tenso* are introduced, and there is a marked increase in the use of refrains, a phenomenon very rare in the 12th c. but paralleled in the 13th-c. OF lyric. The nature-introduction, also rare in the 12th c. except in Heinrich von Veldeke, becomes common, on the pattern both of OF and Neidhart, who uses it in virtually every poem. The schematic description of beauty, often reduced to the single symbolic feature of the red mouth, is widespread, and is particularly characteristic of Gottfried von Neifen. There is a strong tendency, already present in Walther, to treat love themes didactically, which results in generalized praise of women. From Neidhart on, realism, parody, and satire form one strand in the M. Because the traditional themes had become so worn, there is increasing emphasis, particularly in the later 13th c., on formal virtuosity, manifested in complex structures, displays of rhyming skill, and combinations of alternating and dactylic rhythm, a feature first found in Heinrich von Morungen and Walther.

See also SPRUCHDICHTUNG.

EDITIONS: *Die Schweizer Minnesänger*, ed. K. Bartsch (1886); *Trouvères et Minnesänger*, ed. I. Frank, [v. 1] (1952), v. 2, *Kritische Ausgabe der Weisen*, ed. W. Müller-Blattau (1956); *Liederdichter des 13. Jahrhunderts*, ed. C. von Kraus, 2d ed. (1978); *Des Minnesangs Frühling*, ed. H. Moser and H. Tervooren (1982).

MUSIC: W. Müller-Blattau (above); B. Kippenberg, *Der Rhythmus im M.* (1962); U. Aarburg, "Melodien zum frühen deutschen M.," *Der deutsche M.*, ed. H. Fromm (1963); *Ausgewählte Melodien des Minnesangs*, ed. E. Jammers (1963); R. J. Taylor, *Die Melodien der weltlichen Lieder des Mittelalters* (1964), *The Art of the Minnesinger* (1968); *Deutsche Lieder des Mittelalters*, ed. H. Moser and J. Müller-Blattau (1968); the series *Litterae, Göppinger Beiträge zur Textgeschichte*, ed. U. Müller et al. (1971–)—facsimiles of mss. with music and transcriptions; Frauenlob, ed. K. Stackmann and K. Bertau (1981); *Die Berliner Neidhart-Handschrift c (mgf 779)*, ed. I. Bennewitz-Behr and U. Müller (1981).

GENERAL: K. Wesle, *Frühmittelhochdeutsche Reimstudien* (1925); H. Kolb, *Der Begriff der Minne und das Entstehen der höfischen Lyrik* (1958); *Der deutsche M.*, ed. H. Fromm, v. 1 (1963), v. 2 (1985); H. Kuhn, *Minnesangs Wende*, 2d ed. (1967); *Walther von der Vogelweide*, ed. S. Beyschlag (1971); H. de Boor, *Die deutsche Literatur im Spätmittelalter*, 4th ed. (1973); *Die deutsche Lit. des Mittelalters, Verfasserlexikon*, ed. K. Ruh et al., 2d ed. (1978–); P. Wapnewski, *Hartmann von Aue*, 7th ed. (1979); H. de Boor, *Die höfische Literatur*, 10th ed., rev. U. Hennig (1979); P. Hölzle, *Die Kreuzzüge in der okzitanischen und deutschen Lyrik des 12. Jahrhunderts* (1980); J. Bumke, *Wolfram von Eschenbach*, 6th ed. (1981); Sayce; U. Müller, "Die mhd. Lyrik," *Lyrik des Mittelalters*, ed. H. Bergner et al. (1983); K. H. Halbach, *Walther von der Vogelweide*, 4th ed., rev. M. G. Scholz (1983); H.-H. S. Räkel, *Der deutsche M.* (1986); *Neidhart*, ed. H. Brunner (1986); J. F. McMahon, *The Music of Early M.* (1989). O.L.S.

MINNESINGERS. See MINNESANG.

MINOR EPIC. See EPYLLION.

MINSTREL. The general term for a professional performer of medieval lyric or narrative poetry, incl. the Med. Lat. *histrio* (specifically an actor) and *joculator* (jester); the OE *scop* (q.v.) and ME *minstrel*; the Fr. *jongleur* (q.v.) and Occitan *joglar*; the Ger. *Spielmann*; and the Rus. *skomorokh*.

As popular entertainers, minstrels moved in a world of travelling musicians, actors, mimes, acrobats, clowns, beggars, and others of more dubious character. Christian moralists expressed disapproval of their wicked lives from Tertullian (2d c.) through Aquinas, who was the first to deny that their profession was intrinsically sinful. Many minstrels travelled great distances, either as messengers or as wanderers, but others were more sedentary, particularly those whose service had been rewarded with a gift of property.

Scholars differ over the degree of literacy which may be ascribed to the minstrels; partisans of the oral-formulaic theory (q.v.) of epic composition argue that they composed by a technique similar to that of the 20th-c. unlettered Yugoslavian *guslar* (Lord, Duggan). The troubadour Guiraut Riquier distinguished four classes of Occitan joglars: the lowly buffoon; the court musician and singer, or joglar in a strict sense; the composer of melody and words, or troubadour (q.v.); and the teacher, or doctor of composition—a title which Guiraut claimed for himself. Med. Lat. *ministerialis* applied to any servant active in a noble, royal, or episcopal household, or to a messenger, whether or not he performed music or poetry. See also GOLIARDIC VERSE; OCCITAN POETRY.

E. Faral, *Les Jongleurs en France au moyen âge* (1910); E. K. Chambers, *Eng. Lit. at the Close of the Middle Ages* (1945), ch. 3; R. Menéndez Pidal, *Poesía juglaresca y orígenes de las literaturas románicas* (1957)—esp. on Spain; Lord; J. Duggan, *The Song of Roland* (1973); P. Dronke, *The Med. Lyric*, 2d ed. (1977); C. Bullock-Davies, *Menestrellorum multitudo* (1978)—on England; R. Zguta, *Rus. Minstrels* (1978); W. Hartung, *Die Spielleute* (1982)—historical sociology; K. Sutherland, "The Native Poet: The Influence of Percy's M. from Beattie to Wordsworth," *RES* 33 (1982); W. Salmen, *Der Spielmann im Mittelalter* (1983)—esp. on musicians; J. Southworth, *The Eng. Med. M.* (1989). W.D.P.

MIRACLE PLAY. See LITURGICAL DRAMA.

MISCELLANY. See ANTHOLOGY.

MISREADING. See INFLUENCE.

MOCK EPIC, MOCK HEROIC. Terms used in a broad sense to describe a satiric method in poetry and prose and, more specifically, a distinct subgenre or kind of poetry which seeks a derisive effect by combining formal and elevated lang. with a trivial subject. The m.-h. poem consciously imitates the epic style, follows a Cl. structure and heroic action for deflationary purposes, and employs some of the standard paraphenalia of the epic (q.v.), e.g. invocations, dedications, celestial interventions, epic similes, canto divisions, and battles. But the neoclassical form is not a subtype of epic nor even a mockery of epic, but rather, in Warren's terms, an "elegantly affectionate homage offered by a writer who finds it irrelevant to his age."

The Homeric *Batrachomyomachia* (Battle of the Frogs and Mice) served as a model for many an 18th-c. battle in m.-e. strain. The 1717 ed. of this work by Thomas Parnell belongs with many such neoclassical, burlesque battles of pygmies or cranes or rats or hoops or books or sexes. Chaucer had employed the m.-h. style in *The Nun's Priest's Tale*, but Boileau's *Le Lutrin* is commonly viewed as the most influential modern poem magnifying a trivial subject on an ambitious scale. Dryden's *Mac Flecknoe* and Pope's *Rape of the Lock* and *Dunciad* are classic examples of Eng. m.-h. poetry

aiming their shafts at literary pretense and social folly. Mock odes, mock elegiacs (Gray's ode "On the Death of a Favourite Cat"), and mock eclogues abound in Eng. poetry, but the m. h. held supremacy among them until it blended with later burlesque (q.v.) and satiric modes.—R. P. Bond, *Eng. Burlesque Poetry, 1700–1750* (1932); A. Warren, *Rage for Order* (1948); K. Schmidt, *Vorstudien zu einer Gesch. des komischen Epos* (1953); G. deF. Lord, *Heroic Mockery* (1977)—on mockery in epic; M. Edwards, "A Meaning for M.-H.," *Poetry and Possibility* (1988); U. Broich, *The 18th-C. M.-H. Poem* (1990); G. G. Colomb, *Designs on Truth: The Poetics of the Augustan M.-E.* (1992).

R.P.F.; T.V.F.B.

MODE. See GENRE; VERSE AND PROSE.

MODERN LONG POEM. Ezra Pound's 1909 definition of the epic (q.v.) as "the speech of a nation through the mouth of one man" points as well to the central tension which animates the 20th-c. l. p. Typically, the m. l. p. attempts to identify and synthesize the various voices and details of a culture or "tribe" but, unlike the traditional epic, finds itself, "in a society no longer unified by a single, generally accepted code of values . . . justifying its argument by the direct appeal of the author's own experiences and emotions" (Bernstein). Such an appeal brings about both an inevitable foregrounding of the poet as "hero" and an almost ritual acknowledgment of limitation that follows when the desire to speak for a culture stands revealed as a drive toward self-portraiture as well. This tension also generates the technical innovations for which these poems are noted; if no single narrative exists to explain a culture, then it follows that such discontinuous yet accumulative forms as cantos, letters, catalogs (q.v.), songs, notes, passages, dreams, or journal entries might be useful in tracking a repeatedly engaged, non-guaranteed movement toward an explanatory tale. Individual cantos or letters themselves often become strikingly tentative arrangements of the shifting, resistant materials of a culture.

The most influential example of this "modern" form dates, however, from the 19th-c.: Whitman's "Song of Myself" (1855). Whitman's attempt in that poem to sing the "Me myself" through embracing the many-featured world not only gave his culture a possible articulation ("through me many long dumb voices") but also called attention to itself as a single, still unfinished "call in the midst of the crowd" (Miller). The most striking 20th-c. example of the l. p., Ezra Pound's *Cantos* (1925–72), painfully highlights that tension. In working out an extraordinary number of linguistic rituals through which to gather, juxtapose, and give voice to the "luminous details" of our culture's religious, political, and literary heritage, Pound's poem has become a sourcebook for poets. Yet in their tragic acknowledgment of the limits of one person's ability to gather a "live trad.," the *Cantos* have been a sober warning as well. Shorter but no less ambitious, T. S. Eliot's *The Waste Land* (1922), deliberately juxtaposing the voices and tags of a culture in order to expose the intimate workings of a tormented psyche, has been an equally significant model for poets drawn to the personal implications of the form. William Carlos Williams' *Paterson* (1946–58) offers a clear statement of yet another line of devel. Responding to Pound and Eliot, Williams gathered the half-heard voices of his poem from local New Jersey culture. In so doing, he insisted that the question of the source of one's luminous details must also be asked.

Individual responses to the pull between self-portraiture and cultural synthesis, or between the resistances of local speech and those of a broader trad., vary. Hart Crane's *The Bridge* (1930), David Jones's *The Anathémata* (1952), and James Merrill's *The Changing Light at Sandover* (1983) tend toward synthesis while also bearing traces of the poet's foregrounded hand. The different structural models of these poems—the curve of Brooklyn Bridge suggesting a possible "mystical synthesis of America"; a meditative dream during a celebration of the Mass opening out to the interlocking cycles of history and prehistory; or voices gathered from an ouija board first playfully then insistently dictating a Manichean view of the universe—acknowledge as well individual sources for each gathering. Conversely, l. ps. framed as self-portraits and struggling therefore to chart such concerns as the interplay of multiple voices within a psyche (John Berryman's *Dream Songs* [1969]), or the intricate overlap of self, family, and world (Louis Zukofsky's *"A"* [1927–79]), or the "curious" ways the "shipwreck of the singular" is linked to a larger world (George Oppen's *Of Being Numerous* [1968]), or the rich, if inevitable distortions of the act of portraiture itself (John Ashbery's "Self-Portrait in a Convex Mirror" [1975]) are also important clusters of cultural information.

Other l. ps. highlight the struggle to read and interpret. H. D.'s description of London during World War II, compiled as *Trilogy* (1944–46), leaps from a world in which structures are shattered and remade by nightly bombing into a new sort of reading which itself takes shattered elements of the world's stories and "alchemizes" them into something new. The same range is displayed in Robert Duncan's "Passages" (1968–87), where the struggle to weave himself into what he calls the "grand ensemble" of humanity's made things— poems, debates, religious heresies, and fantasies—is foregrounded. Equally notable l. ps. have been written that seek to read deeply into one locality: Hugh MacDiarmid's reply to Eliot, *A Drunk Man Looks at the Thistle* (1926), a rapidly moving meditation on the thorny flowering of Scotland; Charles Olson's investigation of the manifold historical implications of Gloucester,

Mass. in *The Maximus Poems* (1960–75); or Basil Bunting's autobiographical account in *Briggflatts* (1966) of leaving a landscape and an early love and circling back, years later, to read both with a gathering, resonant intensity. For further discussion of modern poetic forms see FREE VERSE; LYRIC SEQUENCE PROSE POEM; see also AMERICAN POETRY; ENGLISH POETRY; EPIC; NARRATIVE POETRY.

R. H. Pearce, *The Continuity of Am. Poetry* (1961), ch. 3; L. S. Dembo, *Conceptions of Reality in Mod. Am. Poetry* (1966); H. Kenner, *The Pound Era* (1971); J. E. Miller, *The Am. Quest for a Supreme Fiction* (1979); M. A. Bernstein, *The Tale of the Tribe* (1980); C. Nelson, *Our Last First Poets* (1981); M. L. Rosenthal and S. Gall, *The Mod. Poetic Sequence* (1983); M. Perloff, *The Dance of the Intellect* (1985), ch. 1, *Poetic License* (1990), ch. 6; B. Rajan, *The Form of the Unfinished* (1985); M. Dickie, *On the Modernist L. P.* (1986); T. Gardner, *Discovering Ourselves in Whitman* (1989); J. Walker, *Bardic Ethos and the Am. Epic Poem* (1989); S. Kamboureli, *On the Edge of Genre* (1991); J. Conte, *Unending Design* (1991). T.G.

MODERN POETIC SEQUENCE. See LYRIC SEQUENCE.

MODERN POETICS. See ROMANTIC AND POST-ROMANTIC POETICS; TWENTIETH-CENTURY POETICS; POETICS.

MODERNISM AND POSTMODERNISM. Part description, part normative projection, and part self-promoting distortion, concepts of m. and p. have become fundamental for isolating a distinctive experimental trad. in postromantic art and then positing imperatives for change within it. As David Antin puts it, "From the m. you choose you get the p. you deserve."

Writers and artists had to make such choices because they needed systematic and comprehensive alternatives to the dominant ideals of cultural m. best represented by Enlightenment thinkers who emphasized a secular rationality promoting empiricism, material progress, and increasing democratization. Unfortunately, however, the myths of lucidity and progress also exacted an exorbitant price by fostering social and psychological economies that threatened all those humane values elaborated by the displaced aristocratic culture. Therefore, in the 19th c., artists began to develop their own account of what it meant to be modern. That concept of m. proposed much more individualist and stylized versions of Enlightenment lucidity which might resist its mythology of progress, its commitment to empiricist and utilitarian values, and above all its affiliations with a sensationalized and superficial popular culture. The noblest acts of mind would be those resisting the triumphant bourgeois order by positing forms of spiritual activity that neither fell back on religious superstition nor curried the favor of the newly dominant audiences. A century later, p. would find itself obliged to posit various ways of undermining those ideals of self-legislation, forcing the arts back into their uncomfortable social contexts and foregrounding their intersections with "popular culture."

If we begin our account with this project of resisting the Enlightenment in the name of Enlightenment ideals, we can see how romanticism could at once make the crucial break with traditional art and become the blocking force against which m. in the arts would eventually define itself. Kant provides the necessary ground by offering romanticism a model of mind that casts scientific rationality as merely a practical mode of understanding bound to appearances and unable to reflect upon the productive energies giving value to those appearances. Once such limits are cogently established, it becomes feasible to explore alternative accounts of mental powers capable of preserving the authority of philosophy for many of the values sustained by religious thought. Kant's scrupulous system would soon be invoked to justify a range of claims that artists could articulate dynamic energies of spirit which cannot be rendered within any mode of representation committed to appearances. But no romantic artist could sufficiently break from those appearances, despite the cult of genius. Thus figures like Flaubert and Baudelaire would make the critique of romantic natural symbolism sanctioned by Christian interpretive allegories their rationale for insisting on a much more overtly ironic and self-reflexive art. Irony would free the mind from both the scenic and the narrative continuities of romantic art, and the self-reflexive features would allow the full legislative energies of the work of art to serve as direct testimony to spiritual powers irreconcilable with the realm of appearances. Where romantic art sought to harmonize mind and nature, these writers would exacerbate the differences between productive mind and passive nature in the hope that the spirit would be enabled to appreciate its own energies and the needs they generate. The composed meditative voice of the romantic lyric then yields to a theatricalized yet overrefined nervous sensibility seeking an ironic distance which will both give vent to its alienation and free desires to dwell in the alternative world produced by the work's formal structures. Ultimately, writing characterized by such intricate internal relations might even establish principles of individual self-creation that writers like Wilde dreamed would provide new cultural ideals.

But the most acclaimed instances of high modernist art are not content with ironic gestures. Rather, they use ironic strategies to undo the expectations elicited by representational art and then focus attention on the capacity of the work's own syntactic intensity to demonstrate the significance of certain powers for engaging and interpreting experience. In poetry, that constitutive project relied on two fundamental principles. First, "realization" had to replace description, so that instead of copying the external world the work could render it in an image insisting on its own distinctive form of reality. The poem defines what Hugh Kenner calls "the gestalt of what it could assimilate" because the conditions of imaginative visibility become part of the constructed object. Images like Rilke's "Der Panther" or Williams' "black eyed Susan" combine the fluid, attentive sensibility of impressionism with a symbolist concern to place the object in a site where one senses its participation in a play of permanent energies given reality by the poem's dense formal patternings. Second, the poets develop collage techniques for intensifying that sense of productive immediacy: it becomes the spaces between images that offer the audience its access to the mode of spirit defined by the work. Thus Eliot's *The Waste Land* makes the failure to integrate the multiple layers within Western culture the poem's access to strange psychic states in which neurotic obsession borders on giving the mind access to the emotional conditions at the core of all self-transcending rituals. And at the other pole, poets as diverse as Pound, Apollinaire, and late Rilke use syntactic gaps to articulate the powers of will or pure concentration to compose new models of self: cubist simultaneity and transformations of perceptual into conceptual realities provide the basis for imagining that the encounter with history can take on an intensity in the present, enabling one to "schufst du ihnen Tempel im Gehör" (build [your] temple deep inside hearing). Baudelaire's alienated withdrawal inside the intricacy of form now opens the way for rebuilding a formal site where the spirit learns to dwell reflexively within its own deepest powers and, for some of the poets, to project from such states the Orphic task of building a truly habitable city.

That city, however, seemed to depend all too often on the most appalling politics. And those politics would combine with two other factors to undermine high m. and create a cultural stage for a variety of ps. First, there occurred the astonishing interp. of m. provided by surrealism and dada (qq.v.). Each in its own way took literally claims that were intended metaphorically and thereby managed simultaneously to parody modernist idealism and to open new imaginative territories in which formal energies were inseparable from unrepresentable forces in dizzying contradiction with one another. If the image really conveys a distinctive reality, if collage articulates a poetic logic unencumbered by discursive rationality, and if the activity of the work somehow establishes an ethos with the power to reform society, it makes perfect sense to devote oneself to the unconscious, to cultivate startling, apparently random connections among particulars, to experiment with automatic writing or other strategies for disclosing aspects of that authorial presence occluded by common sense, and to insist on art as the theatrical disruption of bourgeois hopes and convictions. In this context, modernist idealism seemed a tepid evasion of the work, and the pleasure, of engaging that alienating bourgeois culture. And m.'s insistence on refined, concentrated intelligence seems better suited for repressing poetic logic than for making it a social force.

Second, the versions of m. reconstructed after World War II in both painting and lit. were as tepid as surrealism was radical. Ignoring the artists' claims for the semantic significance of their formal experiments, Clement Greenberg cast them as seeking autonomous, self-contained states earned by following the Kantian imperative to concentrate on the properties distinctive to the medium. Painting became the expressive use of color, line, and volume as it addressed the demands of bringing working space to the flatness of the canvas. The New Criticism (q.v.) was by no means so radically formalist. But it stressed a similar concern that formal closure earn the work an autonomy from empirical desires. Narrowing Yeats and Eliot to their self-doubts and virtually ignoring Stevens, Williams, and Pound, these critics translated the modernist desire to have art produce direct testimony to values into an account of aesthetic experience which subordinated everything to the exposure of internal ironies and paradoxes. M. then became tragic resignation to the failures of Enlightenment optimism.

These are the reductive ms. that confident ps. are made on. By the late 1950s, painters like Johns and Rauschenberg were in the process of reversing the late m. of the abstract expressionist painters championed by Greenberg. In the place of such lonely sublime efforts to purify passion into the structural intensities afforded by painting's two-dimensional surface, the younger painters projected tauntingly indeterminate, playfully ironic examples of the contradictory pulls of canvas and experience, intelligence and the unspeakable needs that blindly drive it. More important, they showed that John Cage's Zen-inspired rejection of the idealist synthetic ego could carry a great deal of artistic weight. Greenberg's flat surface constituting the support structure for the painting could be converted into a metaphoric flatbed that had the task of gathering to itself a diverse range of cultural materials. Now the support would consist in the sly intelligence that showed how art could playfully spin rhymes within the world that constantly imposed itself upon it. A similar sense of poetic openness to worldly contingencies and a similar rejection of the self-ennobling artist entered poetry about the same time from three radically different sources—Ginsberg's emotional immediacy cast as direct demotic speech, Olson's blend of eager anthropologist and crackerbarrel philosopher, and Lowell's rejection of contemplative impersonality in favor of the contradictions inherent in self-exposure. The several self-con-

sciously postmodernist movements that emerged from this conjunction all shared a foregrounding of personal immediacy; a denial of elaborate thematic and verse patterning in favor of speech rhythms, quotidien situations, and the semantic textures of popular culture; and a quest for release from Western rationality that encouraged experiments with ideals of immanence and modes of serial structure developed in Eastern thought.

Another war, this time in Vietnam, brought the postmodernist confidence to an end. Embarrassed by the failure of projected spiritual revolutions, all the arts in the 1970s withdrew into a defensive pluralism suspicious of all theoretical claims and anxious to align with mainstream cultural values. But by the end of the decade a new p. was emerging, this time with an intellectual base that may be sufficient to make it a more challenging rival to modernist values. This p. was defined first by architects resisting modernist functionalism by experiments in a playful and theatrically allusive eclecticism, then by the popularization of Fr. poststructuralist philosophy (see DECONSTRUCTION). Where m. sought to purify all its disciplines by elaborating complex formal models which could abstract from the confusing noise of daily life in order to isolate its underlying principles and explore what could be constructed upon them, p. seeks, in Vincent Descombes' formulation, to concentrate attention on the irreducible aspects of that noise in order to dramatize the impure interests and suggestive slippage at the core of all idealized projects. In epistemology, for example, the efforts of Russell and the early Wittgenstein to establish a truth-functional lang. give way to Derrida's demonstration that the very ideal of a "proper sense" for words is based on metaphors that reintroduce the notions of property and propriety which the project seeks to banish. Confronted by such contradictions, whose suppression often serves property and propriety, we are less in need of new proposals than of ways to negotiate the complex confusions we learn to hear.

M. based its heroic sense of constructivist genius on the capacity of the art work to gather diverse properties within an intensely unified field of balanced forces. In p., emphasis falls instead on those features of textuality (q.v.) that distribute the compositional forces into processes of weaving and unweaving meanings as a divided judgment tries to understand the competing desires imposed upon it by the various cultural codes shaping its imaginary investments. And that view of agency then projects a very different sense of the social roles art must play. Two Fr. philosophers have so far offered the most influential accounts of those roles. Jean Baudrillard has argued that rather than build the new city, one must understand how contemporary information-based economies change the very idea of human relationships, because the traditional idea of signs representing objects has given way to a sense of signs as primarily simulacra, i.e. as phenomena defined only by their relations to other signs and the screens that mediate them. The result of having to read who one is from a computer screen is a psychological economy in which "the loss of public space occurs simultaneously with the loss of private space. The one is no longer a spectacle, the other no longer a secret." And the art that expresses this condition can do little more than devote itself to exposing the effects of media images on our deepest sources of emotional intensity—art itself is simulacrum writ large. Jean-Francois Lyotard is somewhat more optimistic because he sees in this global order the ironic possibility of generating new versions of the artist hero. Instead of concentrating on genius giving form to the unrepresentable and thereby disclosing hidden universals, Lyotard suggests that this very quest for universals has been the major factor in the undoing of m. Where the master narratives of a Freud or a Marx had been, there we must learn to thrive on stories that are legitimated only by their relation to specific "tribal" interests or lang. games. And where Kant had postulated an unrepresentable other to the lang. of understanding, a new art can locate the sublime within the play of forces that separates the mind from its own products and disperses its energies among the noises it tries to organize.

An art so implicated in social forces and so suspicious of all idealizing efforts to project ethical and explanatory universals or even envision coherent selfhood must confront political issues. For example, the L=A=N=G=U=A=G=E poets (see LANGUAGE POETRY) argue that the primary task of poetry is to make us hear the ways in which the media pervade the most intimate recesses of psychic life so that we learn to develop other ways of understanding our subjective investments. Consequently, their poetry becomes a political struggle to expose the alienating imposition of cultural codes and to exemplify the freedoms offered by an art, and a self, willing to devote itself to recombining the textual codes that it loosens. But when everything is simulacra, when there are neither criteria for judgment nor shared goals for shaping audiences, and when serious gestures seem inseparable from self-advertisement, p. finds it difficult to distinguish resistance to the dominant social order from complicity in its hunger for media events. Sympathetic critics in turn have enormous difficulty in deciding which features of the art are genuinely "oppositional"—either as counterassertions or as exposures of basic contradictions in the established order—and which actually reinforce the subjectivist multiplicity on which late monopoly capitalism feeds. Such difficulties then allow others to criticize p. as little more than an inflated repetition of outmoded avant-garde strategies. Thus movements like L=A=N=G=U=A=G=E poetry are castigated as the last enervated gasp of m.'s experimental and oppositional fantasies: such decadence is ample evidence that poets should return to the traditional roles of providing pleasure and consolation to a genteel audience. Similarly, p.'s politics becomes for Jürgen Habermas merely a sceptical withdrawal from those Enlightenment traditions of critical lucidity and social responsibility which have allowed the arts to serve as a major liberating force in Western culture.

We are left with four basic normative positions on the relation between m. and p. If one stresses formal commitments, one can say either that p. carries out certain experimental strategies that m. withdrew from, or one can say the p. exposes the fundamental poverty of an art that, in Lukacs' terms, replaces "the concrete universal by an abstract particularity" and pursues the doomed sublimity of hoping that art can realize values no longer accessible to religion or philosophy. The situation is even more complex politically: if m. offers a significant critique of bourgeois values, then one must consider it a living source of oppositional energies that can be exercised against an increasingly commodified social and artistic culture. However, one can argue just as well that modernist opposition is an elitist quest for aesthetic autonomy which must be rejected in favor of an art willing to accept the responsibility to the people basic to any future revolution. Perhaps the ultimate test of p. is whether one thinks these confusions are to be resisted or embraced.

ANTHOLOGIES: D. M. Allen, *The New Am. Poetry* (1960); *The Mod. Trad.*, ed. R. Ellman et al. (1965); *Theories of Mod. Art*, ed. H. Chipp (1968); *The Idea of the Mod. in Lit. and the Arts*, ed. I. Howe (1968); *M.: 1890–1930*, ed. M. Bradbury and J. McFarlane (1978); *Mod. Art and M.*, ed. H. F. Frascina and C. Harrison (1982); *The Anti-Aesthetic: Essays on Postmodern Culture*, ed. H. Foster (1983); *Code of Signals*, ed. M. Palmer (1983); *Art After M.*, ed. B. Wallis (1984)—good bibl.; *The L=A=N=G=U=A=G=E Book*, ed. B. Andrews and C. Bernstein (1984); *Critical Theory Since 1965*, ed. H. Adams and L. Searle (1986).

MODERNISM: C. Brooks, *Mod. Poetry and the Trad.* (1939); M. Krieger, *The New Apologists for Poetry* (1956); R. Shattuck, *The Banquet Years* (1958); C. Greenberg, "Modernist Painting," *Arts Yearbook* 4 (1961), *Art and Culture* (1961); J. H. Miller, *Poets of Reality* (1965); M. Fried, "Art and Objecthood," *Minimal Art: A Crit. Anthol.*, ed. G. Battcock (1968); M. Raymond, *From Baudelaire to Surrealism* (1970); P. de Man, "Lyric and Modernity," in de Man; H. Kenner, *The Pound Era* (1971), *A Homemade World: The Am. Modernist Writers* (1975); D. Antin, "M. and P.," *Boundary 2* 1 (1972); L. Trilling, *Sincerity and Authenticity* (1972); G. Lukacs, "The Idealogy of M.," *Marxism and Human Liberation*, ed. E. San Juan (1973); O. Paz, *Children of the Mire*, tr. R. Phillips (1974); M. Beebe, "What M. Was," *JML* 3 (1974)—bibl. essay; J. N. Riddel, *The Inverted Bell* (1974); E. Said, *Beginnings: Intention and Method* (1975); G. Bornstein, *Transformations*

of Romanticism in Yeats, Eliot, and Stevens (1976);
E. Bloch et al., *Aesthetics and Politics* (1977)—collects debates of Lukacs, Brecht, Benjamin, and
Adorno; W. Steiner, *Exact Resemblance to Exact Resemblance* (1978), *The Colors of Rhet.* (1982); M.
Perloff, *The Poetics of Indeterminacy* (1981), *The
Futurist Moment* (1986); A. Wilde, *Horizons of Assent* (1981); M. Berman, *All That Is Solid Melts Into
Air* (1982); M. Levenson, *A Genealogy of M.* (1984);
R. Schiff, *Cézanne and the End of Impressionism*
(1984); D. Walker, *The Transparent Lyric* (1984);
C. Christ, *Victorian and Mod. Poetics* (1984); A.
Jardine, *Gynesis: Configurations of Woman and Modernity* (1985); R. J. Quinones, *Mapping Literary M.*
(1985); C. Russell, *Poets, Prophets and Revolutionaries* (1985); S. Schwartz, *The Matrix of M.* (1985);
A. Gelpi, *A Coherent Splendor* (1987); C. Altieri,
Infinite Incantations of Ourselves (1988), *The Contemporaneity of M.* (1991); S. Gaggi, *Modern/Postmodern* (1989); A. Eysteinsson, *The Concept of M.*
(1990).

POSTMODERNISM: R. Venturi, *Complexity and
Contradiction in Architecture* (1966, 2d ed. 1977); I.
H. Hassan, *The Dismemberment of Orpheus* (1971, 2d
ed. 1982), "Ideas of Cultural Change," *Innovation
/ Renovation*, ed. S. Hassan and I. H. Hassan
(1983); C. Molesworth, *The Fierce Embrace* (1979);
C. Altieri, *Enlarging the Temple* (1979), *Sense and
Sensibility in Contemp. Am. Poetry* (1984); J. Baudrillard, *For a Critique of the Political Economy of the Sign*,
tr. C. Levin (1981), *Simulations*, tr. P. Foss et al.
(1983); J. Habermas, "Modernity versus Postmodernity," *NGC* 22 (1981); V. Descombes, "An Essay
in Philosophical Observation," *Philosophy in France
Today*, ed. A. Montefiore (1983); J. Holden, "Postmodern Poetic Form: A Theory," *NER* 6 (1983); A.
Huyssen, "Mapping the Postmodern," *NGC* 33
(1984); C. Owens, "The Allegorical Impulse," *Art
After M.*, ed. B. Wallis (1984); J.-F. Lyotard, *The
Postmodern Condition*, tr. G. Bennington and B.
Massumi (1984); A. Williamson, *Introspection and
Contemp. Poetry* (1984); C. H. Newman, *The Post-Modern Aura* (1985); H. Foster, *Recodings* (1985);
M. Perloff, *The dance of the intellect* (1985); Terras;
C. Bernstein, *Content's Dream* (1986); A. Ostriker,
Stealing the Lang. (1986); D. Harvey, *The Condition
of Postmodernity* (1989); J. McGowan, *P. and Its
Critics* (1991); C. Norris, *What's Wrong with P.*
(1991); M. A. Rose, *The Post-Modern and the Post-Industrial* (1991); F. Jameson, *P.* (1991). C.A.

MODERNISMO. A complex artistic movement
which gave new freedom to Hispanic letters, M.
originated in Sp. America in the 1880s and spread
to Spain, in large part due to the influence of the
Nicaraguan poet Rubén Darío (1867–1916). M. is
a modern renaissance from which Hispanic lit.
today is derived. According to the poet Juan
Ramón Jiménez, M. was both an epoch and a
decisive attitude in art, lit., and thought. It was
also a technique and a form. After the wars of
Independence in South America, the new nations

attained some stability, and lit. ceased being primarily a political and social force to become an art
form.

The fundamental importance of M. is twofold.
First, it represented a total renovation which enriched and perfected form as well as content,
returning vitality to the Sp. lang. Second, M. produced a group of poets whose work was on a par
with the former excellence of Hispanic poetry,
stunted since the 17th c. The starting point is
generally accepted as 1882, when the Cuban José
Martí published *Ismaelillo*. Another date frequently given is 1888, the year Darío's *Azul* appeared in Chile, its short stories written in a new,
refined prose. It is more difficult to establish the
exact date of M.'s demise, since as aesthetic lesson
and ling. renewal it transcends strictly chronological frameworks, extending for some critics beyond
1920. M. implies prosodic experimentation, altered accentual patterns, but also the flexibility of
established verses such as the alexandrine (q.v.).
It was a necessary step for the formulation of the
vanguard soon to follow. An antipositivistic movement that rejected the practical and utilitarian, it
privileged intuition and the senses. In M. all 19th-c. literary schools were reflected, even to some
extent realism and naturalism (qq.v.), which
would seem contrary to its artistic aims. Nor were
certain qualities of romanticism rejected.

For many years, M. was considered to be merely
escapist, concerned mainly with form and filled
with aristocratic symbols: royal swans, princesses,
exotic flora and fauna. Nothing could be further
from the truth in the authentic poets. The beautiful aesthetic symbols were arms to combat materialism and bourgeois values. Among the modernists existed a desire to surpass the exterior facets
of daily life to create a world of uncontaminated
beauty. The ivory tower was adopted as a defense,
not simply to seek isolation. The modernists opposed vulgarity and convention and felt superior
to their circumstances. Almost all the writers were
interested in occult sciences and religions. Their
thought turned toward analogy and *correspondances* to recapture a lost cosmic unity. Influenced
by a vague Pythagorism, they sought to penetrate
the mysteries of life as a spiritual quest.

M. was a movement of youth and enthusiasm.
Spain was still immobilized in the realistic trad.,
but in America a new flexibility permitted the
fledgling nations to be receptive to cosmopolitan
and universal tendencies in lit. and art. Paris was
the constant dream. Nevertheless, the importance
conceded to exclusively Fr. literary influence has
been exaggerated, though it is true that the Sp.
Am. poets learned much from the Parnassian
school (q.v.), adopting to their use the doctrine of
art for art's sake. In the search for formal perfection they gave new plasticity to their poetry, which
they filled with beautiful art objects and mythological allusions. From the decadents and symbolists (q.v.) they took a vague, suggestive music and

created a personal, sometimes obscure imagery. Some modernists cultivated the rare and artificial, using morbid elements fused with erotic sensations. A studied satanism was often combined with a new mystical search both erotic and perverse. The influence of such poets as Gautier, Baudelaire, Verlaine, and Samain, and even Victor Hugo, was obvious. Not only does M. represent new verbal refinement, but also, as in France, a notable fusion of prose and poetry.

Currently critics distinguish two generations of modernist writers. In the first group are Martí, Casal, Gutiérrez Nájera, and Silva, all of whom died prematurely by 1896, leaving Rubén Darío as undisputed leader. Around him was formed the second modernist generation: Lugones, Nervo, Herrera y Reissig, Tablada, González Martínez, et al. M. triumphed in Buenos Aires. The center moved to Mexico when Darío left for Europe, where he spent most of the final 15 years of his life. A great poet and musical genius, Darío also created a program of reform, although he constantly reminded poets not to imitate him. He proclaimed a libertarian theory of art; years later Manuel Machado equated M. with anarchy. The creation of an individual artistic personality is a basic belief shared by all modernists, hence their extreme subjectivity. In 1896 Darío published his epoch-making *Prosas profanas*, which dazzled readers with its voluptuous form. For many years M. was associated with the gardens of Versailles, the elegant *fêtes galantes* à la Watteau, Classical and Oriental mythology, and other decorative or exotic elements. This hedonistic poetry, born in the library and the museum, in Darío soon gave way to a more profound expression, far removed from the luxurious trappings of *Prosas profanas*. In 1905 he published what is generally considered his best book, *Cantos de vida y esperanza*. In it he appears as a poet deeply preoccupied by existential questions and, occasionally, socio-political themes. Pure aestheticism was in crisis. In Spain, both Antonio Machado and Juan Ramón Jiménez were early disciples of Darío, and until 1920 the writing of Valle-Inclán showed his friend's influence. Manuel Machado, despite his roots in popular Andalusian forms, was an enduring modernist, as were so many Sp. poets of the time. In the early years of the century the influence of Darío was everywhere. Even Unamuno, who attacked the modernists and wished to remain aloof, could not escape entirely.

The renovation of poetry went hand in hand with prose, which was elaborated with the same aristocratic and artistic ideals. Actually, the movement began in prose, which was brilliant and highly stylized, esp. so in the prose poem.

ANTHOLOGIES: C. García Prada, *Poetas modernistas hispanoamericanos* (1956); H. Castillo, *Antología de poetas modernistas hispanoamericanos* (1966); G. Brotherston, *Sp. Am. Modernist Poets* (1968); R. Yahni, *Prosa modernista hispanoamericana* (1974);

J. O. Jiménez and A. R. de la Campa, *Antología crítica de la prosa modernista hispanoamericana* (1976), *Antología crítica de la poesía modernista hispanoamericana* (1985); R. Gullón, *El m. visto por los modernistas* (1980); J. E. Pacheco, *Poesía modernista: Una antología general* (1982).

HISTORY AND CRITICISM: A. Vela, *Teoría literaria del m.* (1949); G. Díaz Plaja, *M. frente a Noventa y ocho* (1951); R. A. Arrieta, *Introducción al m. literario* (1956); M. P. González, *Notas en torno al m.* (1958); B. Gicovate, *Conceptos fundamentales de literatura comparada: Iniciación de la poesía modernista* (1962); M. Henríquez Ureña, *Breve historia del m.* (1962); N. J. Davison, *The Concept of Modernism in Hispanic Crit.* (1966); M.-J. Faurié, *Le Modernisme hispano-americain et ses sources françaises* (1966); I. Schulman, *Génesis del m.* (1968); *Estudios críticos sobre el m.*, ed. H. Castillo (1968); A. Rama, *Rubén Darío y el m.* (1970); R. Gullón, *Direcciones del m.* (1971); *El m.*, ed. L. Litvak (1974); O. Paz, *Children of the Mire: Mod. Poetry from Romanticism to the Avant-Garde* (1974); *Estudios críticos sobre la prosa modernista hispanoamericana*, ed. J. O. Jiménez (1975); S. Yurkiévich, *Celebración del m.* (1976); F. Perus, *Literatura y sociedad en América Latina: El M.* (1976); Navarro; G. Kirkpatrick, *The Dissonant Legacy of "M."* (1989).   A.W.P.; K.N.M.

MODULATION. See METER.

MOLOSSUS. In Cl. prosody, a metrical foot consisting of 3 long syllables: $- - -$. It is found very rarely as an independent foot and never in a connected series. Sometimes it replaces an Ionic (q.v.) *a minore* by the contraction of the first 2 short syllables, and less often an Ionic *a maiore* or a choriamb (q.v.). West suggests that, like the spondee (q.v.), it derived from slow, solemn chants where every syllable is fully intoned.—D. Korzeniewski, *Griechische Metrik* (1968); West, 55–56.
    P.S.C.; T.V.F.B.

MONGOLIAN POETRY. The chief source of early M. p. is an imperial chronicle of Genghis Khan's house, the *Secret History of the Mongols* (A.D. 1240), which contains many rough-hewn verses of irregular length. Some later historical chronicles of the 17th c., such as the *Erdeni-yin Tobči* (Jewelled Summary), contain sophisticated and polished quatrains of even length and fixed form, particularly at points of direct discourse in the narrative.

The bulk of native literary expression is in the form of *üliger's*, orally transmitted verse epics, which may reach 20,000 verses in length and are recited from memory by bards. They relate the adventures of real or legendary heroes and villains such as Genghis Khan, Erintsen Mergen, Gesser Khan, and Janggar. These heroes struggle against the many-headed *manggus*, who is defeated in the end. The internal structure of the poems is quite stylized and may be diagrammed as a series of rounds between the hero and his adversary.

M. verse is alliterative (although rhyme is found in a few instances, such as the Sino-M. inscription of 1362). This alliteration chiefly occurs on the initial syllable (the entire syllable, not just the first phoneme), but internal alliteration is also found. There is no set pattern of repetition for the initial alliterating syllables. In epic poetry, alliteration is in couplets or is irregular; in lyric poetry (here used in the strict sense of the word, "composed for the lyre," hence in stanzas), it is in quatrains. The best-styled verse has 7 to 8 syllables with 3 or 4 stresses, but this is only a general guide to its construction. One may also encounter in texts the so-called graphic alliteration, by which some letters of identical shape in the Mongolian script (as t/d, o/u) may alliterate (cf. Eng. "eye rhyme").

The most characteristic formal feature is parallelism (q.v.), the same idea reiterated in slightly different words in succeeding verses. This usage is very similar to the Hebraic parallelism made familiar by the Old Testament Psalms. The chief theme of M. p. has been the great epic legends, with their elaborate descriptions of heroic deeds, royal palaces, and maidenly beauty. There are also shorter poems with themes of love, nature, and religion.

One of the finest poems in M. is the *Lament of Toghon Temür,* six well-polished stanzas uttered by that ruler when he was driven from Khubilai's palace and the throne of China in 1368. In bemoaning the loss of that residence, he draws on an accretion of M. legends which were likewise used by Marco Polo in his description. This account was later taken by Purchas for his travel book, whence it filtered through Coleridge's subconscious to emerge as *Kubla Khan.*

The following free translation of M. verse employs both initial alliteration as well as end rhyme to convey the nature of the original, although rhyme is not present there. The parallelism between the stanzas will be evident.

> Sitting in their hillside bowers (are)
> Seven sorts of hillside flowers;
> Seven sorts of stories, too,
> Soon I'll say in song to you.

> Garlands of the gloomy swamp,
> Grow eight flowers in their pomp;
> Games and gladness, eight kinds too,
> Give I gladly now to you.

N. Poppe, *Mongolische Volksdichtung* (1955), "Der Parallelismus in der epischen Dichtung der Mongolen," *Ural-Altaische Jahrbücher* 30 (1958), *Khalkha-mongol'skii geroičeskii epos* [The Heroic Epic of the Khalkha Mongols], 2d ed. (1979); K. Grønbech, "Specimens of M. P.," *The Music of the Mongols* (1943); Damdinsüren, *Monggol uran joki-yal-un degeji jagun bilig orusibai* [One Hundred Extracts from M. Lit.] (1959); J. R. Krueger, "Poetical Passages in the *Erdeni-yin Tobči,* a M. Chron-

icle of the Year 1662," *Central Asiatic Studies* 7 (1961); F. W. Cleaves, *The Secret Hist. of the Mongols* (1982)—see also the poetic adaptation by P. Kahn (1984) of the same title; *Fragen der mongolischen Heldendichtung,* ed. W. Heissig (1983–). J.R.K.

MONK'S TALE STANZA. An octave (q.v.) of iambic pentameter devised by Chaucer: it is simply an isolated octave from the 3-octave Fr. *ballade* (q.v.). The rhyme scheme is *ababbcbc,* as in the *ballade,* though in Fr. the lines are octosyllables. Chaucer uses the true *ballade* for several of his early lyrics; he uses the isolable *ballade* octave (which had been used in OF for narrative verse first by Oto de Granson), for others, e.g. *An A.B.C.,* his earliest extant poem, and *The Former Age.* (The *Complaint of Venus* uses a variant *ababbccb.*) In *The Canterbury Tales* he returns to it for *The Monk's Tale*—whence the name—where it is used in groups of from 1 to 16 stanzas, though end-stopping is heavy and the meter somewhat monotonous. The stanza had some popularity in the 15th c.; apparently it served as the inspiration for the Spenserian stanza (q.v.), which simply adds an alexandrine as a ninth, *c*-rhymed line. T.V.F.B.

MONODY. Early Gr. melic poetry (q.v.) is divided into two general classes, the choral ode, sung to flute accompaniment with a dancing chorus—e.g. threnodies, paeans, maiden songs, wedding songs, expressive dances (*hyporchemata*), processional songs (*prosodia*), dithyrambs, praises of great men (*enkomia*), and victory songs (*epinikia*)—and solo song or m.—originally an ode sung by a single voice, e.g. by one of the characters in a tragedy, or to a more private audience, as at a symposium. The Sapphic and Alcaic (qq.v.) are the principal subgenres. Its themes were wider in scope than those associated with modern lyric—they include politics and satire, for example—but it came to be associated with the lamentation of a single mourner and hence came to refer a dirge (q.v.) or funeral song. In metrical form the strophes are isometric (q.v.), i.e. repeated without variation. In Eng. poetry, Milton's *Lycidas* is referred to (in the epigraph) as a m., though in fact it is written in irregular Eng. *canzoni* rather than in regular strophes. Matthew Arnold titled his elegy on A. H. Clough "Thyrsis, A M." See GREEK POETRY; LAMENT.—G. M. Kirkwood, *Early Gr. M.: The Hist. of a Poetic Type* (1974); Trypanis; CHCL, v. 1; M. Davies, "M., Choral Lyric, and the Tyranny of the Hand-Book," *CQ* 82 (1988). T.V.F.B.; R.A.H.

MONOLOGUE is used in a number of senses in discussing poetry, all of which suggest the idea of a person speaking alone, with or without an audience. Thus prayers and laments are ms., as are many lyric poems. At the same time, m. has a clearly dramatic element, since no speaker ever speaks in complete isolation. All vocalization, indeed all lang., implies an audience, either external or internalized, but m. characteristically emphasizes the subjective and personal element in speech. The term is also often used to refer to sections from longer works that emphasize a single voice representing a unitary point of view. M. is not therefore restricted to a specific genre but rather a point of view, and it may describe any sustained speech by a single person. In ordinary usage the term often suggests lang. used to preclude other speech or to prevent conversation.

In poetry, m. has clear connections to drama. Thus Strindberg's play *The Stronger*, which consists of but one speech by a single character, involves the audience directly in dramatic revelations about the personalities of three people in a love triangle. Similar single-voiced revelations derive from characters as diverse as Sophocles' Oedipus, Marlowe's Tamburlaine, and Beckett's Hamm. "Soliloquy" refers to a form of m. in which an actor speaks alone on the stage. It represents a character's attempt to verbalize his thoughts, consciously or distractedly, as in Othello's self-revelations and Hamlet's meditative speeches. In some cases, characters address the audience directly, as in Falstaff's address on honor. Numerous plays, notably Marlow's *Doctor Faustus*, Goethe's *Faust*, and Byron's *Manfred*, open with an overheard speech by the main character. Thus ms. either heard or overheard produce a complex semantic interplay between character and audience. Some of the most powerful passages in dramatic poetry (q.v.) are cast in m. form.

The technique is ancient, but too closely connected with the ritualistic origins of drama to have a distinguishable origin. Elegies, diatribes, and comic harangues often have strongly monologic elements, while epistles and philosophical poems do not, since they are meant to be read rather than spoken. Significant biblical examples include *The Song of Deborah*, Jeremiah's lament for Jerusalem, and the Psalms. Prophetic utterances were often cast in m. form, focusing attention on the connection between impassioned verse and prophecy. Lengthy speeches in a refined, direct rhet. appear in Gr. epics and odes. Gr. drama includes numerous examples. Some miming included single-voiced speech, although dialogue (q.v.) was the preferred mode. Theocritus' idylls, and the resulting emphasis on first-person speakers, produced admirable examples of m., as did elegiac poems by Propertius. All types of rhet. involving declamation encouraged m. The prosopopoeia (q.v.), an ancient rhetorical form that impersonated the speech of an actual or imagined person, found its way into poems like Ovid's *Heroides*.

M. tends always to emphasize the personal and potentially ironic element in poetry. Germanic lit. and its OE derivatives, such as *The Wanderer* and *The Wife's Lament*, employ the subjectivity often associated with the form. Devotional and meditative poetry in all trads. tends to canonize m., as in speeches by the Virgin to the Cross or direct addresses to deity, to the point that such orations become fixed subgenres. In the later Middle Ages and the Ren., variations on the classical "complaint" (q.v.) and "address" increase the dramatic element of earlier religious verse. Dunbar, Lindsay, and Skelton continue Chaucer's earlier use of such forms. Imitations of Horace and Ovid develop these trads. even further. M. appears throughout the 16th c. in works by Wyatt, Gascoigne, Raleigh, and Drayton. Elizabethan dramatic verse as in Shakespeare, Marlowe, and Corneille achieves part of its power from the uncompromising directness of m. and its elements of internal dialogue. Milton's *L'Allegro* and *Il Penseroso* point up the tendency for m. to imply or demand a response. The form is weakened by the social tendencies of Restoration and Augustan verse, while romantic poetry de-emphasizes the ironic element of m. by identifying the poet directly with the speaker of the poem. The dramatization of the lyric "I" in poems like Coleridge's *Frost at Midnight* and Wordsworth's "Tintern Abbey" suggests a possible separation between poet and speaker, pointing toward the ironic ms. of the Victorians.

Such emphasis on the subjective posture of the poem's voice, and a new element—impersonation—are characteristic of the best later examples of m. Partly for this reason, the dramatic ms. of Robert Browning represent the most significant use of the form in postromantic poetry. Browning himself called poems like *My Last Duchess* and *Porphyria's Lover* "dramatic lyrics," emphasizing the blurring of genres implied in the form. Browning's use of m. derives its power from his ability to depict in detail powerful situations in remarkably few lines. His stanzaic ms. draw on the ballad trad., while his blank-verse masterpieces derive directly from dramatic models. The dramatic m. gains additional force from the fact that a silent auditor often constrains or controls the speaker's words, contributing to complex levels of irony within the poem. Browning's ms. have sometimes been regarded as brief closet dramas (q.v.) with a single speaker, while the term "monodrama" has been used to describe poems by Tennyson, such as *Ulysses* and *Tithonus*, which present the varying emotions of a single mind rather than a powerfully conceived dramatic situation. Matthew Arnold, William Morris, the Rossettis, and Swinburne all wrote powerful lyrics "spoken" by dramatic voices, but it is clearly Browning's use of the m. that has had the most significant impact on subsequent poetry.

In the 20th c., Browning's dramatic form of the m. has been adopted most directly by Ezra Pound, who also noted his debt to Propertius. T. S. Eliot, in poems like *The Love Song of J. Alfred Prufrock* and *Gerontion*, creates a m. spoken without a direct dramatic auditor. This form is directly related to the rise of the persona (q.v.) or mask in modern poetry. In recent years one critic has called such poems "mask-lyrics" (Rosmarin). Poems by Pound and Eliot, for example, provide a monologic and dramatic speaker like Tennyson's, one more closely identified with the lyric voice of the poet than with the dramatic voice of an imagined character. Such poems can be distinguished from strictly dramatic ms., which set up a necessarily ironic distance between poet, speaker, and reader. E. A. Robinson, Edgar Lee Masters, and Robert Frost all contributed variations on the form; Robert Lowell, Sylvia Plath, John Ashberry, and Diane Wakowski subsequently employed a monologic mode that reveals a tension between the poet and the speaker of the poem. M. is a characteristic of all poems that strive to deny dialogue or control possible responses to the utterance. While recent speculation has suggested that all lang. contains a dialogical aspect that denies the possibility of pure m. (Bakhtin), poets continue to explore the implications of a single voice speaking alone and advocating a unitary, determinate position.

F. Leo, *Der Monolog im Drama* (1908); E. W. Roessler, *The Soliloquy in Ger. Drama* (1915); I. Hürsel, *Der Monolog im deutsche Drama von Lessing bis Hebbel* (1947); I. B. Sessions, "The Dramatic M.," *PMLA* 62 (1947); H. Schauer and F. W. Wodtke, "Monolog," *Reallexikon*, v. 2; R. Langbaum, *The Poetry of Experience*, 2d ed. (1974); A. D. Culler, "Monodrama and the Dramatic M.," *PMLA* 90 (1975); R. W. Rader, "The Dramatic M. and Related Lyric Forms," *CritI* 3 (1976); A. Sinfield, *Dramatic M.* (1977); J. Blundell, *Menander and the M.* (1980); K. Frieden, *Genius and M.* (1985); L. D. Martin, *Browning's Dramatic Monologues and the Post-Romantic Subject* (1985); P. Parker, "Dante and the Dramatic M.," *SLRev* 2 (1985); A. Rosmarin, *The Power of Genre* (1985), ch. 2; W. Clemen, *Shakespeare's Soliloquies* (1987); J. T. Mayer, *T. S. Eliot's Silent Voices* (1989); E. A. Howe, *Stages of Self: The Dramatic Ms. of Laforgue, Valéry, and Mallarmé* (1990).　　　　　　　　　　　　　　B.A.N.

MONOMETER. A metrical line consisting of one measure, either a foot (in the modern langs.) or a metron (in Cl. verse). Poems in m. are rare, the shortness of the lines making for severe segmentation of syntax. The best known Eng. example is Herrick's "Upon his Departure Hence," an epitaph of 15 lines beginning "Thus I / Passe by / And die."　　　　　　　　　　　　　T.V.F.B.

MONORHYME (Ger. *Reimhaufung*) refers to a passage, stanza, or entire poem in which all lines have the same end rhyme, i.e. the rhyme scheme *aaa*. . . . In Western poetry, prior to the advent of the modern preference for complex rhyme schemes inaugurated by the troubadours, Med. Lat. poets took greater interest in m., which may be found, for example, in the poems of Commodian, in a psalm by St. Augustine of 288 lines (all ending in *-e* or *-ae*), in the sequences of Notker

(echoing the *-a* of the Alleluia), in the *Dies irae*, and in the poems of Gottschalk. It was also used by the Goliards in stanzas of four 13-syllable lines (see GOLIARDIC VERSE). In the OF *chansons de geste* (q.v.), the *laisses* (q.v.) of irregular length are unified by assonance (q.v.) having the effect of m.; later this is restricted to quatrains and tercets which, in turn, were imitated in Spain in the *cuaderna via* of Berceo and the *tercetos* of Pedro de Verague's *Doctrina cristiana*. In modern Fr., m. has been employed by Voltaire, Lefranc de Pompignan, and Théophile Gautier. Ger. examples of m. (*gehäufter Reim*) are rare, as they are in Eng. (Skelton; Hardy, "The Respectable Burgher"; Frost, "The Rose Family"). In Arabic poetry, however, m. is the rule not the exception, as in the *ghazal* and *qasīda* (qq.v.), and can be carried on for hundreds of lines. This is parallel to the case in OF except that Ar. m. is true rhyme while OF assonance is not. Case rhyme or homoeoteleuton (q.v.) is also excluded. Linguistically speaking, if the medial vowel and final consonant of a syllable are fixed, e.g. *-at*, the number of permissible initial consonants or clusters in any given lang. is relatively small (in Eng., 20), so could not long be maintained, and many of the rhymes thus generated are not appealing anyway (drat, splat, brat). Hardy manages 35.—M. C. Lyons, "The Effect of M. on Ar. Poetic Production," *JArabL* 1 (1970). T.V.F.B.

MONOSTICH. It is an interesting question whether a one-line poem is possible. Prior to the advent of modern free verse (q.v.), a single line would have to have been metrical to qualify as a recognizable instance of verse; and there are certainly a considerable number of extant gnomes, epigrams, proverbs, and funerary inscriptions extant from the ancient world, both Cl. Gr. and Celtic, which are metrical so presumably were thought of as, in some sense, poetic (see EPIGRAM). The Delphic Oracle spoke thus. The several collections of ms. attributed to Menander, who used ms. both seriously and ironically in his plays, fall into this category, too, though probably few of the 800-odd extant lines are genuinely his. Cf. the *Greek Anthology*, 11.312. See STICHOS.—W. Görler, *Menandrou gnomai* (1963).　　T.V.F.B.

MONOSYLLABIC FOOT. See FOOT.

MORA. See DURATION; QUANTITY.

MORALITY AND CRITICISM. See CRITICISM; ETHICS AND CRITICISM; EVALUATION; PLURALISM.

MORALITY PLAY. The term m. p. is in fact not originally Eng. and does not appear during the medieval or Ren. periods in any association with the plays we have come to regard as "moralities"; taken from the 18th-c. tr. of Luigi Riccoboni's *Reflexions historiques . . . theatres de l'Europe*, the term has been applied to plays as divergent as the

MOSAIC RHYME

huge outdoor *Castle of Perseverance* (ca. 1405–25) and Marlowe's *Dr. Faustus* (1588–92). Contemporary mss. and printed copies, when they mention genre at all, generally refer to such plays as "enterludes" (interludes—q.v.), or "moralls" (moral plays).

Scholars of the 19th c. attempted to distinguish and classify types of m. p. generally by chronology, calling the pre-16th-c. plays "moralities" and the later ones "moral plays" or "moral interludes." This notion subtly reinforced the popular theory that theatrical productions became more secularized between the 14th and late 16th cs. through comedy and nonliturgical themes, but the theory has subsequently been disproven since various types of plays continued to coexist through the 17th c.

Consequently, later scholars have preferred to classify medieval and Ren. dramas by structure and content, limiting the list of plays called moralities to *The Pride of Life, Everyman,* and the Macro Plays (*The Castle of Perseverance, Mankind,* and *Wisdom Who Is Christ*). Other plays which bear some resemblance to these and are frequently mentioned in the same context include Medwall's *Nature, The Nature of the Four Elements, Hykescorner,* and *Mundus et Infans.* As the 16th c. advanced, such plays became increasingly secular and comic, and the allegorical devils and vices developed into more specifically social, political, and moral evils on their way to becoming the villains of the comedies and tragedies of the public stage. The political form of m. p. is illustrated by John Skelton's *Magnificence* (ca. 1515) and John Bale's *King John* (ca. 1535).

In sum, we may say that the m. p. is now generally understood to be an allegory in dramatic form produced from the 14th through the 16th cs. that is religiously didactic, enacting pilgrimages through man's temporal and spiritual life in order to instruct the community in Christian doctrine and to encourage repentance. Rather than re-creating what the audience would perceive as Christian historical events, as the mystery and miracle plays attempted, the m. p., growing perhaps out of the sermon and adapting some of its rhetorical techniques, sought to enact universal spiritual patterns in concrete experience.

The structures of m. ps. fall into three categories: (1) the fate of human beings on earth, usually expressed as a pilgrimage through life, a moral struggle of good and evil based on free will, and an individualized microcosm of the Creation-to-Doomsday structure of the Cycle plays; (2) the "Dance of Death," exemplified by *Everyman* and the fragmentary *Pride of Life,* which enact repentance, divine forgiveness, and Christian death; and (3) the *psychomachia,* often including a "parliament in Heaven," wherein the seven deadly sins, with attendant vices and devils, battle the seven virtues for the possession of the soul of a human being (variously called Everyman, Mankind, Humanus Genus, Infans) who through free will has fallen victim to sin. *The Castle of Perseverance,* being the longest and most complex of the genre, comprises all three paradigms and thus became a prototype for the m. ps. that followed.

In order to differentiate the m. p. from "moralls" or interludes, we can point to three criteria: an allegorical structure, abstract characters, and a pedagogical objective (Mackenzie). Later, as the structures and characters become more concrete and the lessons more generalized, the functions of the plays clearly changed from religious didacticism to social and political argumentation. For example, Medwall's *Fulgens and Lucrece* (1497) is too specific in character and structure and too secular in its argument to be considered a m. p.; similarly, Heywood's farces are not allegorical; and Bale's virulent plays, while they employ allegorical structures and abstract characters, intend to communicate polemics rather than specific lessons. *Godly Queen Hester* (1527) is concrete in structure and character and political in intent; *The Three Ladies of London* (ca. 1580) and its sequel are allegorical but social in their themes.

Critics have frequently dismissed the m. p. as a necessary evil in the "progress" of drama from trope to tragedy. Citing the poor literary quality of the plays as dramatic texts, they have continually ignored or underestimated the quality and sophistication of the plays as theatrical events, in the process conveniently suppressing copious evidence of their great and continued popularity until the closing of the theaters in 1640. Verseforms, stanzaic structure, and diction may indeed be "uncertain and poor," as Hardin Craig has charged, but more damage has been done by scholarly bowdlerization of "unsuitable" passages. More recently, scholars have begun applying new techniques to investigate the nonverbal langs. of the stage, stressing the pageantry, spectacle, social function, and semiotics of the plays. This process has to some extent redeemed the reputation of the m. p. as an exciting theatrical form that fulfilled the expectations of its original audiences. See also LITURGICAL DRAMA.

E. K. Chambers, *The Med. Stage* (1903), *The Elizabethan Stage* (1923); W. R. Mackenzie, *The Eng. Ms.* (1904); C. F. Tucker Brooke, *The Tudor Drama* (1912); H. Craig, *Eng. Religious Drama of the Middle Ages* (1955); G. Wickham, *Early Eng. Stages,* 3 v. (1959–81), *The Med. Theatre,* 3d ed. (1987); D. Bevington, *From Mankind to Marlowe* (1962); O. B. Hardison, Jr., *Christian Rite and Christian Drama in the Middle Ages* (1965); P. J. Houle, *The Eng. M. and Related Drama: A Bibl. Survey* (1972); R. Potter, *The Eng. M. P.* (1975); A. Dessen, *Shakespeare and the Late Moral Plays* (1986). S.R.W.

MOSAIC RHYME (Occitan *rim trencatz,* Ger. *gespaltener Reim,* It. *rime composte*), sometimes "broken r.," "split r.," rarely "heteromerous r." (so

Harmon). The "piecing together" of two or more short (often monosyllabic) words to rhyme with one longer (usually polysyllabic) one. Cases where both of the rs. are made out of more than one word, e.g. *pray thee / slay thee, greet me / meet me* (Whittier), are viewed by some as m. but by most as simply double or feminine rs. (see MASCULINE AND FEMININE). Traditionally, r. concerns the phonological structure of one or more syllables but respects morphological categories; m. rs., by contrast, transgress word boundaries in order to effect the r., highlighting that fact in the r. by the contrast between the r.-fellows. Thereby they expand the range of the r. device. Byron has the famous m. r. *intellectual/ hen-peck'd you all.* James Russell Lowell has: "Unqualified merits, I'll grant, if you choose, he has 'em, / But he lacks the one merit of kindling enthusiasm." Browning, who was partial to the device, has 16 out of a possible 37 in "A Grammarian's Funeral," including such novelties as *fabric / dab brick, far gain / bargain, all meant / installment, failure / pale lure, soon hit / unit, loosened / dew send.* Gerard Manley Hopkins has "*I am and / diamond.*

Since polysyllables are, despite greater commonality of endings, more difficult to rhyme, and since Eng. as a Germanic lang. has a greater stock of monosyllables than the Romance langs., one might think that this sort of rhyming would be limited in scope and confined mainly to Eng. But the effect is striking, and this is not the case: the m. technique, which takes advantage of compounding in morphology and which can be combined with other strategies, has been popular in several langs. Occitan, Fr., and Ger. developed a variety of m. rich or identical r. in which two words rhyme with one, both members having the same spelling and sound but different senses, e.g. *a roi/ aroi, des cors/ descors.* This is known in Fr. as *rime équivoque;* first attested in Gautier de Coincy (13th c.); it was very popular among the *Grands Rhétoriqueurs* of the late 15th–early 16th cs., e.g. Badouin and Jean de Condé, and even Clement Marot in some *épitres.* Apollinaire rhymes *Ah, Dieu* with *adieu;* Aragon develops the technique, which he calls *rime complexe.* Cognate is Ger. *rührende Reim,* in which one of the rhyming words is a compound of the other, e.g. Ger. *zeigen/ erzeigen,* or Eng. *mortal/ immortal,* though these are not, strictly, m.—A. Tobler, *Le Vers français ancien et moderne* (1885); Patterson 168–69 and Index; L. Schourup, "M. R.," *Lang&S* 21 (1988).   T.V.F.B.

MOSCOW-TARTU SCHOOL. See STRUCTURALISM.

MOTE. A Sp. poem consisting of a single line or couplet, rarely more, containing a complete thought. Usually, but not always, this thought is glossed in verse, the whole composition then being called either *m.* or *glosa,* occasionally *villancico* or *letra.* One *m.* may be glossed by several poets or by the same poet in several versions. The m. was particularly popular in the 15th c.—Le Gentil; Navarro.   D.C.C.

MOTIF. See THEME; THEMATICS.

MOVEMENT, THE. See ENGLISH POETRY.

MOZARABIC LYRICS. See SPANISH POETRY.

MULTIPLE RHYME. See RHYME; TRIPLE RHYME.

MUSE. One of the nine Gr. goddesses who preside over poetry, song, and the arts, invoked by male poets from Cl. times through the Ren. and after to grant them inspiration (q.v.). So Homer begins the *Iliad*: "Sing, Goddess, the wrath of Achilles, Peleus' son." A psychological explanation of this ancient convention is offered by Jacoby: the Muse is the image of the poet's "unconscious creative potentiality" which "is not in his own power." As a symbol she is thus "an image of the mysterious woman in the psyche of the man" and is "associated with the remembrance of primeval creation, of the last and deepest mysteries." In the terms proposed by Jung, the Muse represents the poet's anima: "immortal," she is "disguised under the many names we give to creative impulses and ideas."

In Gr. antiquity the Muses, daughters of Zeus and Mnemosyne (goddess of memory), originally indefinite in number, were first celebrated in Thrace near Mt. Olympus and Pieria; hence, that peak was regarded as their home and the Pierian Spring as the fount of learning. Probably before Homer's time their worship had spread southward to Helicon and thence to Delphi, eventually to become a common feature of Gr. religious culture. By the 3d c. B.C. the festival of the Heliconian Muses at Thespai was patronized by Athens and the important guild of artists of Dionysus; here all the poetic and musical talent of Greece was consecrated. Elsewhere, observance of the Muses became attached to the worship of Apollo. The attribution of particular arts to each Muse is a late devel., and there is some duplication. The Muses are: Calliope (epic or heroic poetry); Clio (history, lyre-playing); Erato (love poetry, hymns, lyre-playing); Euterpe (tragedy, flute-playing, lyric poetry); Melpomene (tragedy, lyre-playing); Polymnia or Polyhymnia (hymns, pantomime, religious dancing); Terpsichore (choral dancing and singing, flute-playing); Thalia (comedy); and Urania (astronomy, i.e. cosmological poetry).

With the recovery of Cl. writings in the later Middle Ages, the trad. of invoking the Muse was revived. In Dante (where Beatrice herself fulfills the Muse's role), there are references to the Muses of antiquity (*Inferno* 2.7 ff., 32.10 ff.; *Paradiso* 2.8, 18.82 ff.). Milton invokes the pagan Muse but transforms her into a specifically Christian inspiring power:

MUSIC AND POETRY

Descend from Heav'n, *Urania*, by that
name
If rightly thou art call'd . . .
            . . . for thou
Nor of the Muses nine, nor on the top
Of old *Olympus* dwell'st, but heav'nly-
born . . .
Thou with Eternal Wisdom didst con-
verse
            (*Paradise Lost* 7.1 ff.)

For other Ren. poets the Muses of antiquity could be accepted without relinquishing their pagan attributes. Thus Spenser commences *The Faerie Queene*: "Me, all too meane, the sacred Muse areeds / To blazon broad amongst her learnèd throng: / Fierce warres and faithfull loues shall moralize my song" (1.7–9). The unnamed "sacred Muse" is either Clio (history) or Calliope (epic). The Petrarchan love poets, too, invoked their inspiring spirit: "Fool, said my muse to me, look in thy heart and write" (Sidney, *Astrophil and Stella* 1.14). In much other Ren. poetry influenced by Petrarchism (q.v.), and even more in poetry after the Ren., the beloved herself assumes the role of Muse for male poets. Their trad. of invoking the Muse for inspiratory power lingered into modern times (Thomas Gray, *The Progress of Poesy*; W. H. Auden, *Homage to Clio*).

A provocative history of poetic homage to the Muse from ancient to modern times was proposed by Robert Graves in 1948. Since then, women poets and critics influenced by feminism have raised objections to the identification of the Muse by male poets as the solely feminine embodiment of the poet's creative principle or as an idealized yet erotic image of a woman beloved by a man. For women poets in the 19th c., the poetic trad. was embodied in the work of male forebears; thus Diehl suggests that for Emily Dickinson, the poetic canon itself supplied the image of the "other," the source of her creativity, yet this "composite father" is also an adversary whose "priapic power" she fears. Diehl finds a similar etiology in the work of Christina Rossetti and Elizabeth Barrett Browning. Feminist commentators protested Diehl's assumption that "women poets are invariably heterosexual" and her failure to examine female relationships in Dickinson, but Diehl maintained that "Dickinson confronts her masculine precursors to wrest an independent vision. No woman need ever feel so alone again."

The interdependence of later women poets on one another is examined more extensively by DeShazer. She charts how her chosen poets were "sisters woven in a complex web of creative reciprocity": "Louis Bogan served as an often rigorous muse and mentor for May Sarton; H.D.'s woman-centered poems inspired Adrienne Rich: Rich and Audre Lord offer a feminist model of literary interdependence." These affiliations, esp. strong among lesbian poets, are not, however, universal among women. Anna Akhmatova in "The Muse" asks, "Was it you who dictated to Dante / The pages of *The Inferno*?" She replies: "It was I." The Muse is a legendary presence for Carolyn Kizer, who speaks for those "who must act as handmaidens / To our own goddess" ("A Muse of Water," *Mermaids in the Basement*, 1984); Denise Levertov, too, associates her Muse with water and with legend, seeing her "gliding . . . in her barge without sails" across a lake, but "I know no interpretation of these mysteries" ("The Well," *Jacob's Ladder*, 1961). See also FEMINIST POETICS; POETIC MADNESS.—L. R. Farnell, *The Cults of the Gr. States*, v. 5 (1909); L. B. Campbell, "The Christian Muse," *HLB* 8 (1935); Curtius, ch. 13; W. F. Otto, *Die Musen und die göttliche Ursprung des Singens und Sagens* (1955); R. Graves, *The White Goddess*, 3d ed. (1958); E. Barmeyer, *Die Musen* (1968); G. Snare, "The Muse as a Symbol of Literary Creativity," *YCC* 4 (1971); M. Jacoby, "The Muse and Literary Creativity," *Anagogic Qualities of Lit.*, ed. J. P. Strelka (1971); J. F. Diehl, "An Exploration of Woman Poets and Their Muse," *Signs* 3 (1978), foll. by L. Faderman and L. Bernikov in *Signs* 4 (1978); M. K. DeShazer, *Inspiring Women: Reimagining the Muse* (1986); E. R. Gregory, *Milton and the Muses* (1989); I. Tayler, *Holy Ghosts: The Male Muses of Emily and Charlotte Brontë* (1990).   D.HO.

MUSIC AND POETRY (Gr. *mousike*, "the art of the Muses"). Our best evidence about primitive song suggests that melodies and rhythms precede words, that the first step toward p. was the fitting of words to pre-existent musical patterns. Primitive cultures did not make the distinctions we now make between m. and p.: the Egyptian "hymn of the seven vowels," for example, appears to have exploited the overtone pitches present in the vowels of any lang. The ancient Gr. linguistic system of pitch accents was strikingly similar to the tetrachordal system of ancient Gr. m. Spoken Gr. moved between two stable pitches, a high pitch (indicated in post-Alexandrian texts by the acute accent) and a low pitch (indicated by the absence of accent); these pitches framed an area from which the sliding pitch indicated by the circumflex accent arose; the grave accent may also indicate such a medial pitch. Gr. m. also moved between two fixed pitches; these tones, a perfect fourth apart, framed a middle area containing two sliding microtonal pitches. The linguistic pitch system operated independently from the rhythmic system we now call quantitative meter; high-pitched syllables did not necessarily correspond with long positions in the meter. But the scraps of ancient m. we possess do show a general correspondence between pitch-accent and melodic shape, and studies of "accentual responsion" in the lyrics of Sappho and Pindar suggest that the poet's choice of words in an antistrophe may have been constrained by an attempt to have those words correspond to the melodic pitch-pattern established in the strophe.

The Greeks used the same word, *moûsike*, to describe dance, m., p., and elementary education. *Moûsike* was essentially a "mnemonic technology," a rhythmic and melodic way of preserving the wisdom of the culture; alphabetic writing, the next advance in mnemonic technology, forced changes. It was adopted as a musical notation soon after its introduction, with letters of the alphabet written above the vowels in a poetic line to indicate pitches. Thanks to the quantitative conventions of Gr. meter, no separate rhythmic notation was necessary. The visual separation of pitches and words in the new notation began to separate the once unified arts; alphabetic writing led to both rhetorical and musical theory, the latter of which, thanks to Pythagorean mysticism, quickly became concerned with advanced theoretical and mathematical problems virtually divorced from performance.

Roman p., in which the normal word-accents of Lat. words were arbitrarily distorted as those words were wedged into what had once been the rhythms of Gr. m., was another step in the separation. What began as *moûsike*, an organically unified art, had now become not two but four elements: performed m., m. theory, p., and rhetorical theory. Christian thought altered the relative prestige of the four elements: the Church fathers embraced the elaborate mathematical m. theory of the ancient world and allegorized its numbers; they banished instrumental m. from the Church and sought to alter and control vocal m.; on the literary side, by contrast, pagan p. itself had to be saved by allegory, while rhetorical theory was treated with suspicion. The drift in Lat. p. away from quantitative verse toward accentual-syllabic verse, in which the hymns of Ambrose and Augustine are important documents, was a motion away from writing Lat. words to Gr. tunes toward writing Lat. words to Christian tunes whose origin was probably Hebrew.

In the early Middle Ages, liturgical chant became longer, more complex, and more ornate, despite attempts by Charlemagne and Gregory to arrest its devel. When the lengthy melismatic passages sung to the last *a* of the word *alleluia* proved hard to memorize, because church singers had a much less accurate notational system than the now-forgotten letters of the ancient Greeks, monks began writing words for them; the resulting works were called *sequences* or *proses*, though they employ many devices we would call poetic. By fitting new words to a pre-existing melody, such sequence poets as Notker Balbulus (ca. 840–912) again altered poetry, moving it still closer to modern stanzaic form, including rhyme. The troubadours and *trouvères* (qq.v.), composer-poets writing in the vernacular, took over and extended the formal innovations of the sequence, producing increasingly complex stanzaic forms with elaborate rhyme schemes. In their art, poetic form was more complex than musical form, and by the time Dante

defined p. as a combination of m. and rhet., "m." had become a somewhat metaphorical term. Not only were the It. poems in forms derived from the troubadours normally written without a specific tune in mind, but poetic form itself had become sufficiently demanding to occupy the attention once devoted to making words fit a pre-existing tune.

Musicians, who were now increasingly called upon to compose settings of pre-existing words, made an important technical advance in the invention of polyphony. They may have gotten the idea of combining two or more melodies from the literary notion of allegory, realizing that the mystical simultaneity of an Old Testament story and its New Testament analogue could become, in m., actual simultaneity. One result, oddly parallel to the dropping away of m. from the troubadour trad., was that texts became less audible in polyphonic vocal m. than in the monodic singing of all previous m. In early polyphony, the *tenor* or lowest part often sustained one vowel for many long notes, while the more rapidly moving upper parts sang as many as 40 short notes on one vowel. Predictably, these upper parts often picked up new texts, including Fr. texts glossing or commenting ironically on the liturgical Lat. text being sustained in the lower part.

Influenced by Christian versions of the ancient Gr. numerological theory, in which the universe was conceived as created and ordered by numbers, medieval poets and composers frequently constructed their pieces by complex, mystical, mathematical formulae. Fr. isorhythmic motets, tricky crab canons in which one line is the other sung backwards, anagram poems concealing the names of mistresses—all elaborate forms whose principles of construction cannot be heard in performance—flourished as representations of the numerical mystery of the universe, or (for adepts in both arts) as secret displays of technical ingenuity. In the service of such causes, musicians treated texts as a tailor treats cloth: they cut them up, stretched them out, redistributed their rhythms in ways that entirely destroyed the original poetic form, obscured the rhyme scheme, and made the content impossible to hear—esp. in motets, where three different texts in two different langs. were sung simultaneously. Guillaume Machaut (1300–77), who was at once the leading composer and the leading poet of his period, wrote such motets, but also simpler monodic songs such as *chansons*, *virelais*, and *lais* (qq.v.) in which expression of the text was an artistic concern.

In Ren. p. and m., techniques initially developed as virtuoso modes of construction, such as rhyme in p. and chordal harmony in m., began to acquire expressive values. A new rereading of the ancient poets and rhetoricians, with fresh interest in persuasion, emotion, and the moral force of sounds, was an important factor. Medieval composers had often worked out their m. before pasting in a text, but Ren. composers normally started with a text and worked in various ways at animating or expressing it. Josquin des Prés (ca. 1450–1521), who used dissonant harmonies at painful moments in the text, pointed the way toward the witty rhetorical musical expression of the It. madrigal school, which developed a number of harmonic and melodic "word-painting" conventions for setting words dealing with running, weeping, dying, and so forth. When Cardinal Bembo's edition of 1501 restored Petrarch as a model for lyric p., composers of secular songs were compelled to increase the musical sophistication of their settings, and in searching for musical equivalents of Petrarchan oxymorons (q.v.)—"freezing fires" or "living deaths"—they developed a more expressive use of harmony. Despite this general motion toward expression, however, the highly elaborate methods of construction typical of medieval art survived, as virtuosity or mysticism, in both arts, esp. in England, where the hidden numerical schemes of Spenser's p. and the abstract patterns of John Bull's keyboard fantasias provide extreme examples.

The increased attention to the rhet. and meaning of p. on the part of composers did not satisfy the literary reformers now called the "musical Humanists" (the *Camerata* of Bardi in Florence and the *Académie* of Baïf in Paris). Fired by ancient myths concerning the capacity of m. to arouse various passions, these men concluded that it would do so most effectively by submitting to the rule of the text: they opposed independent musical rhythm, arguing that m. should exactly follow the rhythm of the poem; they opposed the staggered declamation typical of the madrigal, favoring homophonic, chordal singing or monody. Such composers as Monteverdi paid lip service to the aims of this reform program, but did not allow it to deprive their art of the techniques it had developed since the Middle Ages. Operatic recitative is the most familiar legacy of musical humanism, but Monteverdi's operas show as much attention to musical construction as to literary expression. By the later 17th c., opera singers had become more important in the public view than either composers or librettists, and arias designed for vocal display became a central part of operatic practice.

While most Ren. poets possessed some technical understanding of m., thanks to the importance of m. in the traditional school curriculum, poets in later centuries often lacked such knowledge, and their mimetic theories of musical expression proved increasingly inadequate. In 18th-c. vocal m., such composers as Bach continued to employ versions of the mimetic "word-painting" techniques of the madrigal; Pope's witty lines on "sound and sense" in the *Essay on Criticism* are a poetic analogy. But composers, unlike poets, were able to use materials that originated in such local mimesis as building-blocks from which to construct a larger structure. Trained by such rhetorically organized texts as Fux's *Gradus ad Parnassum* (1725), a treatise on counterpoint praised by Bach, they were also learning to combine canonic procedures with an increasingly stable tonal grammar; these devels. liberated instrumental m., which could now embody several kinds of purely musical meaning. The willingness of later 18th-c. concert-goers to attend purely instrumental performances demonstrated once and for all the inadequacy of Ren. theories that had maintained that music's only legitimate function was to animate texts. Mimetic theorists, however, shifted their ground. No longer able to maintain that composers were imitating words, they now insisted that they were imitating or expressing feelings, a doctrine that led to the *Affektenlehre*, a systematic catalogue of musical formulae for expressing passions.

Two fundamentally opposed conceptions of m. were now coexisting uneasily: poets and philosophers continued to insist on the mimetic function of m., now calling it a lang. of the passions, but composers and some theorists, by developing the tight musical syntax we now call the tonal system, had given m. a grammar of its own, a meaning independent of imitation that made possible such larger forms as the "sonata-allegro." The romantic poets, just as ignorant of musical technique as their Augustan predecessors, now embraced m. for the very qualities that had made it unattractive to those older poets, its supposed vagueness, fluidity, and "femininity." They sought in their p. to imitate these myths about m., not the logical, witty m. actually being written by such composers as Haydn. In the cause of a more "musical" p., the romantics loosened Eng. syntax while Haydn and Mozart were tightening and refining musical syntax. But eventually these romantic and literary myths about m. began to affect composers, and in the m. of Berlioz, Liszt, and Wagner, all of whom acknowledge literary influences, a similar loosening of musical syntax takes place. Later 19th-c. composers frequently embraced poetic aims: "program" m., the idea of the "leitmotif," the revived claim that m. could express emotions and tell stories.

Wagner's opponent Eduard Hanslick insisted on the autonomy of m., espousing the revolutionary idea that musical structure itself was the real subject of m. Contemporaneous poetic theories of autonomy were somewhat similar in their drive to separate p. from its subject matter. But while Hanslick rejected all attempts to describe m. as a lang., the poetic autonomists (Poe, Wilde, Pater) claimed to want to make p. more like m. Fr. symbolist p., in its fascination with sound and its attempt to maximize the extent to which words in a poem acquire their meaning from that particular poetic context alone, attempts to realize the program announced in Verlaine's familiar declaration: "De la musique avant toute chose." Still, the waning of the tonal system in 20th-c. m. and Schönberg's success in devising a new system for composition suggested again the limitations of attempts to describe m. in ling. terms. 20th-c. relations between the arts have often followed the old axes of numerical construction: Schönberg was profoundly influenced by the mathematical constructive procedures, in p. and m., of Machaut; in his "expressionist" period, he used poetic line-lengths to determine musical structure; Berg organized his "Lyric Suite" on a sonnet by Mallarmé, but suppressed the text; Auden, in seeking a musical sophistication of technique, invented poetic forms closely related to the serial techniques of modern m. Despite the large differences in the way m. and p. are practiced in the modern world, Pound's cranky insistence that "poets who will not study m. are defective" acknowledges the advantages of a long and fruitful partnership.

See also AIR; BALLAD; CACOPHONY; DITTY; EUPHONY; LYRIC; MADRIGAL; SONG; SOUND; SOUND EFFECTS IN POETRY; cf. SCULPTURE AND POETRY; VISUAL ARTS AND POETRY.

BIBLIOGRAPHIES: *A Bibl. on the Relations of Lit. and the Other Arts 1952–1967* (1968); S. P. Scher, "Literatur und Musik: Eine Bibliographie," *Literatur und Musik: Ein Handbuch zur Theorie und Praxis*, ed. S. P. Scher (1982).

STUDIES: G. Reese, *M. in the Middle Ages* (1940), *M. in the Ren.*, 2d ed. (1954); T. S. Eliot, *The M. of P.* (1942); B. Pattison, *M. and P. of the Eng. Ren.* (1948); C. S. Brown, *M. and Lit.: A Comparison of the Arts* (1948), "Musico-Literary Research in the Last Two Decades," *YCGL* 19 (1970), ed., spec. iss. of *CL* 22 (1970); *Source Readings in M. Hist.*, ed. O. Strunk (1950); A. Einstein, *Essays on M.* (1956); J. Hollander, "The M. of P.," *JAAC* 15 (1956), *The Untuning of the Sky: Ideas of M. in Eng. P., 1500–1700* (1961), *Vision and Resonance*, 2d ed. (1985), esp. chs. 1, 2, 4; G. Springer, "Lang. and M.: Parallels and Divergencies," *For Roman Jakobson*, ed. M. Halle (1956); *Sound and P.*, ed. N. Frye (1957); D. Feaver, "The Musical Setting of Euripides' *Orestes*," *AJP* 81 (1960); J. Stevens, *M. and P. in the Early Tudor Court* (1961), *Words and M. in the Middle Ages* (1986); C. M. Bowra, *Primitive Song* (1962); A. Wellek, "The Relationship between M. and P.," *JAAC* 21 (1962); K. G. Just, "Musik und DIchtung," *Deutsche Philologie im Aufriss*, ed. W. Stammler, 2d ed. (1962), 3.699–738; F. W. Sternfeld, *M. in Shakespearean Tragedy* (1963); D. T. Mace, "Musical Humanism, the Doctrine of Rhythmus, and the St. Cecilia Odes of Dryden," *JWCI* 27 (1964); H. Petri, *Literatur und Musik: Form- und Strukturparalleln* (1964); G. Reichert, "Literatur und Musik," *Reallexikon* 2.143–63; M. Pazzaglia, *Il verso e l'arte della Canzone nel De vulgari Eloquentia* (1967); S. P. Scher, *Verbal M. in Ger. Lit.* (1968), "Lit. and M.," *Interrelations of Lit.*, ed. J.-P. Barricelli and J. Gibaldi (1982), ed., *M. and Text: Critical Inquiries* (1991); L. Lipking, *The Ordering of the Arts in 18th-C. England* (1970); E.

Wahlström, *Accentual Responsion in Gr. Strophic P.* (1970); J. M. Stein, *Poem and M. in the Ger. Lied from Gluck to Hugo Wolf* (1971); P. Johnson, *Form and Transformation in M. and P. of the Eng. Ren.* (1972); H. Van der Werf, *The Chansons of the Troubadours and Trouvères* (1972); D. J. Grout, *A Hist. of Western M.*, 2d ed. (1973); R. Hoppin, *Med. M.* (1978); Michaelides; *Dichtung und Musik*, ed. G. Schnitzler (1979); D. Hillery, *M. and P. in France from Baudelaire to Mallarmé* (1980); J. A. Winn, *Unsuspected Eloquence: A Hist. of the Relations between P. and M.* (1981); E. B. Jorgens, *The Well-Tun'd Word* (1982); W. Mullen, *Choreia: Pindar and Dance* (1982); L. Kramer, *M. and P.: The 19th C. and After* (1984); L. Schleiner, *The Living Lyre in Eng. Verse from Elizabeth through the Restoration* (1984); B. Stimpson, *Paul Valéry and M.* (1984); J. Neubauer, *The Emancipation of M. from Lang.* (1986); D. M. Hertz, *The Tuning of the Word* (1988); G. Comotti, *M. in Gr. and Roman Culture*, tr. R. V. Munson (1989); M. L. Switten, *M. and Lit. in the Middle Ages: An Annot. Bibl.* (1990); *The Jazz Poetry Anthol.*, ed. S. Feinstein and Y. Komunyakaa (1991); C. O. Hartman, *Jazz Text* (1991). J.A.W.

MUSIC OF POETRY. See EUPHONY; MELOPOEIA, PHANOPOEIA, LOGOPOEIA; SOUND; SOUND EFFECTS IN POETRY.

MUWASHSHAH. See HISPANO-ARABIC POETRY.

MYSTERY PLAY. See LITURGICAL DRAMA.

MYTH.

    I. FUNCTIONS AND DIFFUSION
    II. MEANING AND SIGNIFICANCE
    III. MYTH AND LITERATURE
        A. *Formal*
        B. *Causal*
        C. *Historical*
        D. *Psychological*

I. FUNCTIONS AND DIFFUSION. M. is a narrative or group of narratives which recount the activities of a culture's gods and heroes. These narratives are the product of communal and (often) sacred impulses to sanction and reflect the cultural order existing at the time of their creation. As such, they arouse, at least initially, large-scale beliefs concerning either their veracity or meaningfulness. Prior to—and indeed for long after—the introduction of writing (in Greece, in the 7th c. B.C., for example), the transmission of myths was an important function of oral trad. So far as is known, there has been no culture which has not generated a set of myths uniquely its own.

Originating as it appears to do in the oral stage of human culture, m. constitutes the culture's effort to retain through the exercise of memory its knowledge of itself. Much if not all of oral poetry (q.v.) originates in ritual functions and purposes, and ritual is essentially a physical rendering or equivalent of m. Perhaps the most graphic instance of this is the Babylonian *enuma elish*, a creation m. whose ritual recitation at the New Year was thought to be simultaneously an enactment of the original events of the m. and a celebration of those events designed to restore life to the dead god Marduk. Oral poetry and m. in many cultures often treat the same subjects—the nature of the gods, the origin of the world, man, society, law. For example, the Japanese account in the *Kojiki* of the three Kami emerging from a white cloud, the Australian stories of variously named Supreme Beings who existed in *alcheringa* (dream) time and produced plants and animals while wandering the earth, the ancient Gr. narratives of Cronos and Zeus, and the North Am. Indian tales of Coyote and his animal helpers, all purport to tell how gods came into being, how the world was created, and how ancestors emerged.

Lit. as it is known today, regardless of lang. or national identity, appears to have developed out of or to have grown up in close relation to m. as exemplified by those myths held and venerated by individual ethnic and national groups. Thus, Gr. lit. is shot through with mythic materials—characters, subject matter, plots, and actions. Thus Sophocles, in the most celebrated instance from antiquity, takes up mythic materials and narratives already familiar to his audience about the ill-fated Oedipus to be reworked and given visual embodiment in his dramatic trilogy. In Asia, traditional literary forms such as Japanese *No* drama are rooted in ancestral legends and rites. In Africa, contemporary artists such as Amos Tuotola deliberately reach back to retrieve and renew the myths of their region.

As a result of cultural diffusion, a culture's mythic materials also incorporate motifs, figures, and incidents from other regions, then are given other forms in their subsequent lives when transmitted through the lits. of later cultures. Mythic figures such as Ulysses, Prometheus, Hercules, and Orpheus have been traced in subsequent manifestations throughout much of Europe, particularly in Ger., Fr., and Eng. lit. Hence, while any national lit. may be closely linked to its cultural myths, it is not exclusively wedded to them. Cultural pluralism and historical stratification rather than geographical or ethnic purity condition both m. and lit., perhaps most particularly in their nascent states. Eng. Ren. lit., for instance, would not be what it is but for its reliance on Cl. myths and the lit. which recorded while also modifying them. Shakespeare's *Venus and Adonis* is an obvious example. Corneille and Racine, like Vittorio Alfieri later, in works such as *Medee, Polyeucte, Andromeque,* and *Phedre* develop their literary versions of Gr. myths just as do Heinrich von Kleist and E. T. A. Hoffmann later. The same is true of non-Cl. instances, such as Cain and Abel, Moses, and Joseph from the Bible, Faust and Tristan from medieval mythography, and Cuchulain, Finn, and

Taliesin from Celtic mythology: all these appear in one guise or another in many of the world's lits.

The cultural centrality of myth's chief characters encourage expansion and connection of myths to produce groups of narratives, e.g. the labors of Hercules, the exploits of Zeus, and the adventures of Finn Mac Cool. Myth's inclination to embrace the entire lives of its characters expands in lit. into epics such as *Beowulf* and *Gilgamesh*, as well as into other narrative genres such as the *Bildungsroman*. Another common trait of m. is the manifest impossibility of many of the events and beings described. Fifty-headed monsters, shape-changing deities, talking animals, descents to the underworld, and chariot-drawn flights through the sky all testify to myth's characteristic concern with experiences beyond the normal or natural, a concern extended into the numerous subsequent literary genres which treat of the marvelous and incredible.

II. MEANING AND SIGNIFICANCE. The meaning and significance of m. have occupied thinkers as far back as recorded history. The Gr. Sophists regarded myths as allegorical or symbolic means of conveying truths about nature and the world, as well as human ethics. Euhemerus (3d c. B.C.) saw myths rather as covert accounts of purely naturalistic or historical occurrences and personages. Philo Judaeus and St. Augustine manifest the inclination of Christian and Hebrew theologians to adopt both a literal and an allegorical approach to the myths of the Old Testament (see ALLEGORY) while viewing pagan myths as falsehoods. Christian humanists of the Ren. in Europe blurred this by concentrating upon the iconic nature of Christian sacred narratives and upon the poetic and metaphoric character of other myths. A reaction to this accommodation and celebration of m. occurred with the 18th c.: Voltaire, for example, attacked both Christian and pagan m. as superstition founded upon a failure of human reason, but inability to explain why such a failure should occur led him to view m. as a means used by a particular social class (for Voltaire, unscrupulous priests of any religion, but particularly Christianity) for maintaining its power by manipulating the ignorance of the lower classes.

At almost the same time, Giambattista Vico's *Scienza nuova* (1725) provided an approach to m. which blended the allegorical and the euhemeristic. Vico saw society as existing in several emergent stages based upon dominant attitudes, and the figures of m. as constituting class symbols of society. The effect was an attitude toward m. combining the literal and the symbolic. This book became seminal to romantic theorists, particularly Goethe and Herder in Germany. They found m. to be a self-sustaining structure of the human spirit which is a necessary and essential mode of belief and of conceiving reality. In the 20th c., Ernst Cassirer's *Philosophy of Symbolic Forms* continues this outlook while making it conform to neo-Kantian philosophy. In essence, Cassirer argues that m. as product is the result of m. as process. The latter is a mode of mental operation radically different from the familiar norm of subject-object relations, material causality, and rational inference. For him as for a number of modern thinkers, m. is man's original way of looking at the world. Its cornerstone is the general intuition that things, the undifferentiated entirety of the natural world, possess an inherent power that is both magical and extraordinary. This condition of consciousness is the spirit's teleological endeavor to shape and determine the nature of spiritual reality.

III. MYTH AND LITERATURE. Equal in importance to these theories of the nature and significance of m. are the persistent entwinements of m. and the world's lits. Four interrelated strands may be discerned in this relationship: formal, causal, historical, and psychological.

A. *Formal.* The formal relation of m. and lit., as suggested above, encompasses the innumerable shared traits of narrative, character, image, and theme. Prometheus' exploits, for example, are rendered by Apollodorus as well as Aeschylus and Shelley. Without confusing one account with any other, the similarities are obvious. All are accounts of certain events befalling certain individuals whose character traits determine the action. Each is also marked by the presence of images and ideas which lend meaning or significance to the tales. The nailing of Prometheus to Mount Caucasus, the self-blinding of Oedipus, and the wily deceitfulness of the Am. Indian trickster resonate in m. as much as in literary works such as *Prometheus Unbound, Oedipus at Colonus,* or Ted Hughes' recent *Crow.*

Such affinities as these, however, are matters only of similarity and not of identity. From the formal standpoint, the resemblances occur in a less explicit and less sustained fashion in m. than in lit. Actions are more arbitrary, motivation simpler and more enigmatic, and continuity and form marked more by the perfunctory and the ruptured than by design and resolution. The lack of formal identity of traits can be seen in the contrast between, say, the biblical tale of Samson and the developed genre of the short story. The fullest and most resourceful example of this sort of approach is found in the work of Northrop Frye, esp. his *Anatomy of Crit.* (1957), *Fables of Identity* (1963), and *The Great Code* (1982; see MYTH CRITICISM).

B. *Causal.* Both the welter and the persistence of resemblances between m. and lit. raise the obvious question of a causal connection. Since the origins of m. and the generic forms of oral lit. are lost in prehistory, any answer is only provisional if not speculative. Nevertheless, the number, degree, and diversity of similarities between specific myths and individual works of lit. argues a reasonably high probability that at least some, perhaps many, are matters neither of accident or coincidence. One way of viewing this relationship would be to regard m. as logically and temporally prior

to lit. This approach sees the formal properties of m. mentioned above as simple, elementary forms which gradually become more complex and diverse as the societies which preserve them develop and transform, and as individual authors come to replace anonymous communal narrators. Such a view, which treats m. as man's earliest expressive mode, is the one most fully developed by Cassirer, Susanne Langer, and Philip Wheelwright. Lit. together with religion, science, history, and philosophy then emerge historically from myth. It is as if a group of undifferentiated iron filings were over time sorted out into various different patterned groupings through the introduction of a number of magnets. The causality implicit in this view is a form of pluralistic teleology.

Another view focuses on their temporal or logical coincidence rather than the temporal priority of one over the other. For scholars such as E. A. Havelock, Milman Parry, and A. B. Lord, the oral stage of human culture is of great importance. This view stresses oral memory as being both different from and greater than that found in the literate stage of cultures. The assistance metrical lang. provides to remembering laws, genealogies, and cultural practices puts it at the very heart of oral culture. Consequently, oral poetry (q.v.) with its conspicuous formulaic, rhythmic, and paratactic traits perpetuates not only the stories but the knowledge of a people. Scholars have drawn evidence of this from such disparate sources as pre-Socratic philosophy, Babylonian law tablets, and Bulgarian folk epics. In serving to reinforce social knowledge, such poetry perpetuates the narratives themselves, particularly when the two are not sharply differentiated. In short, the oral culture possesses in its myths, legends, and folktales what is essentially a lit., except for the absence of a definitive, recorded text. M. and lit., according to this view, are functionally differentiated in that they have different sociological roles stemming from technological transformations. M. is sacred, at least so long as believed by the culture at large, whereas lit. is secular or profane in the original sense. The role of the former is to encourage and render possible actual worship, while the latter provides entertainment in a manner which includes moral reinforcement, social responsibility, and religious piety. The two come together in the concept and act of celebration which unites work and play, activities later separated by literate cultures.

C. *Historical.* A third relationship is one in which m. serves both directly and indirectly as source, influence, and model for lit. The most familiar instance of this, of course, is the extent to which Western European lit. is permeated by Cl., and particularly Gr., myths. In addition to the sheer multitude of such instances, esp. striking is the variety of forms which the relationship is capable of taking. In the hands of Aristophanes, the bawdy yet solemn women's fertility festivals provide the material for his satiric and parodic genius in *The Thesmophoriazusae*, while in the 20th c., mythic heroes like Prometheus and Orpheus focus the moral satire, wit, and irony of iconoclastic writers such as André Gide and Jean Cocteau.

Lit. often draws on m. as a direct source for events and characters, in which case the relationship is one of transcriptive retelling. It also, and more frequently, uses m. to stimulate original conceptions and formulations. Thus the original legend of Faust dealt with a knave, but in Goethe's hands he becomes a figure representative of man's aspirations, while Thomas Mann later made of the same mythic protagonist a much more enigmatic and morally ambiguous figure. The range of the diffusion of m. throughout its own culture and into other cultures is impressive. Equally striking is the lack of a single direction or migratory pattern for this diffusion. Writers are frequently drawn to their own culture's myths, but they are also fascinated with the structural, thematic, and narrative possibilities in myths quite alien to their immediate culture.

D. *Psychological.* The fourth relationship between m. and lit. embraces the affective dynamics of production and response. Linguistically, neither m. nor lit. is an empirically accurate record of historical events. Yet both are taken seriously and held to possess meaning and significance. Belief or something similar to belief seems to be involved in both cases, though not in the way of reportorial accuracy or truth. Even members of a culture holding or revering a particular m. are not always prepared to assert its absolute veracity even when convinced of its centrality as a model or paradigm of past or future events. And persons outside a particular culture are likely to view its myths as obviously either false or else fictions, tales capable of socio-religious reinforcement, psychological arousal by way of imaginative curiosity, or intrapsychic explorations. As such, myths are substantially of the same psychological order as are works of lit. Both underscore the overwhelmingly central role of fictions in human affairs (see FICTION) and the need to define and classify their manifold functions. Each is the product of the affective and constructive powers of the human psyche. Lit. impinges on its reader or audience through its capacity to construct persons, scenes, and even worlds which arouse responses uncircumscribable by rational knowledge or empirical description. The same is true of m. Its roots in religious ritual and the convictions they arouse suggest that one of myth's central functions is to provide narratively and dramatically human contact with that trans-rational but experiential power variously called "mana," "orenda," or the numinous. Though largely secular in function and role, lit. still preserves the emotional core of myth's spiritual power. Both are capable of perpetuating and focusing the significance of those sensations of awe, wonder, and, above all, vitality which are mankind's response to the nature of experience, both external and internal.

F. Cornford, *Thucydides Mythistoricus* (1907); J. Harrison, *Themis* (1912); O. Rank, *The M. of the Birth of the Hero* (1914); B. Malinowski, *M. in Primitive Psychology* (1926), *Sex, Culture, and M.* (1962); *M. and Ritual*, ed. S. Hooke (1933); J. Thomson, *The Art of the Logos* (1935); F. R. R. S. Raglan, *The Hero* (1936); D. Bush, *Mythology and the Romantic Trad. in Eng. Poetry* (1937), *Mythology and the Ren. Trad. in Eng. Poetry*, 2d ed. (1963); E. Cassirer, *Lang. and M.* (1946), *The Philosophy of Symbolic Forms*, 3 v. (tr. 1953–57); H. Frankfort et al., *The Intellectual Adventure of Ancient Man* (1946); J. Campbell, *The Hero with a Thousand Faces* (1948), *The Masks of God*, 4 v. (1959); C. Jung and C. Kerenyi, *Essays on a Science of Mythology* (1949); T. Gaster, *Thespis* (1950); E. Fromm, *The Forgotten Lang.* (1951); E. Neumann, *The Origins of the Hist. of Consciousness* (1954); Wimsatt and Brooks, ch. 31; Frye; S. Langer, *Philosophy in a New Key*, 3d ed. (1957); *M.*, ed. T. Sebeok (1958); M. Eliade, *The Sacred and the Profane* (1959), *M. and Reality* (1963); *M. and Mythmaking*, ed. H. Murray (1960); C. Bowra, *Primitive Song* (1962); J. de Vries, *Heroic Song and Heroic Legend* (1963); *M. and Lit.*, ed. J. B. Vickery (1966); N. Frye, "Lit. and M.," *Relations of Literary Study*, ed. J. Thorpe (1967)— with bibl.; P.-M. Schuhl, "M. in Antiquity," F. L. Utley, "M. in Biblical Times," J. Seznec, "M. in the Middle Ages and the Ren.," B. Feldman, "M. in the 18th and Early 19th Cs.," M. Eliade, "M. in the 19th and 20th Cs.," and F. Hard, "M. in Eng. Lit.: 17th and 18th Cs.," all in *DHI*; M. Slochower, *Mythopoesis* (1970); G. S. Kirk, *M.: Its Meaning and Functions* (1970), *The Nature of Gr. Myths* (1975); P. Maranda, *Mythology* (1972); K. K. Ruthven, *M.* (1976); A. Cook, *M. and Lang.* (1980); J. B. Vickery, "Lit. and M.," *Interrelations of Lit.*, ed. J.-P. Barricelli and J. Gibaldi (1982); H. Adams, *Philosophy of the Literary Symbolic* (1983); *Sacred Narrative*, ed. A. Dundes (1984); *M. in Lit.*, ed. A. Kodjak et al. (1985); H. Blumenberg, *Work on M.* (1985); J. Puhlvel, *Comparative Mythology* (1987); P. Veyne, *Did the Greeks Believe in Their Myths?* (1988).

J.B.V.

MYTH CRITICISM.

    I. THE ANTHROPOLOGICAL PERSPECTIVE
    II. THE PSYCHOLOGICAL PERSPECTIVE
    III. THE PHILOSOPHICAL PERSPECTIVE
    IV. PRINCIPLES

The explicit interest of literary critics in m. crit. is of relatively recent vintage, dating essentially from the mid-20th c., though in preceding eras figures such as Vico, Herder, Schelling, and Goethe generated enormous interest in the cultural role and significance of myth (q.v.). By the term "m. crit." is meant the interp. of works of lit. in the light of patterned resemblances to figures, actions, plots, meanings, or significances associated with myths or the culturally sanctioned tales of a civilization's gods and heroes. Naturally, its practitioners also exhibit a strong interest in the more general lines of relationship between m. and lit., but the bulk of their work and influence focuses on individual texts.

In pursuing mythic modes of thinking and forms of expression, critics had their perceptions and approaches shaped by a number of extra-literary perspectives either antedating or coinciding with them, the most important of which were anthropological, psychological, and philosophical.

I. THE ANTHROPOLOGICAL PERSPECTIVE. Two different subsets of the anthropological perspective provided formative ideas. The first and earliest of these is the so-called Cambridge School of Sir James Frazer (1854–1941), Jane Harrison (1850–1928), Gilbert Murray (1866–1957), and F. M. Cornford (1886–1950), which derived from the evolutionary views of E. B. Taylor (1832–1917). Its central contention was that m. had a ritual character; that is, ritual expresses in action an emotion or complex of emotions which in m. is expressed in words. Frazer's *The Golden Bough* (1st ed., 1890) employed the comparative method in a loose but very wide fashion: the epochal 3rd ed. ranged over the globe—from Australia to Africa, Asia, the Americas, and Europe—and throughout history—from Cl. and pre-Cl. times to modern customs and beliefs—in its effort to show the universality of m. and ritual and their fundamental similarities despite differences in place and time of occurrence (see ANTHROPOLOGY AND POETRY).

This broad approach to recurring figures and forms of action encouraged literary critics to focus on limited but seminal resemblances between aspects of literary texts and subsumptive conceptual patterns rooted—according to Frazer and others—in m. and ritual. Examples of such patterns are the dying and reviving god, the scapegoat, the mother goddess, the sacred prostitute, and the sacrificial virgin. The mythic approach also served, with the advent of the New Criticism (q.v.), to loosen the grip of the older scholarly historicism (q.v.) on critical thinking and to prepare, implicitly, for the structuralist juxtaposition of synchrony and diachrony (see STRUCTURALISM).

The Cambridge School was also inclined to regard m. as becoming etiological when the original emotions giving rise to ritual lost their immediacy and recognizability. This view also encouraged critics, albeit indirectly, to find meanings and significances not likely to have been historically associated with texts by either their authors or original audiences. In so doing, these scholars were implicitly following the lead of Harrison, whose use of the ideas of anthropologists like Frazer and philosophers like Bergson to interpret Gr. festivals, sculpture, and art broke new ground in Cl. studies. The same was true of Murray, who not only interpreted Olympic festivals and celebrations as ritual performances but treated Shakespeare's Hamlet

as akin to a mythic deity of natural fertility and sacrifice on the basis of dramatic structure and imagery. Similarly, Cornford argued that the historical narratives of Thucydides were strongly shaped by mythic considerations. Much later, such approaches influenced John Speirs' interpretation of *Sir Gawain and the Green Knight* (1957), and Francis Fergusson's *The Idea of Theater* (1949), a study of drama from Sophocles to Shakespeare.

A more recent anthropological perspective on m. which has both directly and indirectly influenced many modern literary critics is that associated with structuralism (q.v.). Pre-eminent here is the name of Claude Lévi-Strauss, although in differing ways such Continental scholars as Marcel Detienne, Roland Barthes, A. J. Greimas, and Georges Dumézil are also involved. Drawing on Marx, Saussure, and Freud, this view argues that m., regarded as the sum of its versions, consists of a set of binary polar relationships, assertions, or implications. These polar contradictions or tensions are progressively mediated through other concepts introduced into the situation until a provisional or conditional resolution is achieved. The lang. of m. expands the context of the original contradiction or problem so that it is absorbed in socially structured solutions embedded in the culture.

This process conforms to a rigorous underlying logic which can be detected beneath myth's surface narrative, which is full of discontinuity, arbitrariness, and repetitiveness. Like Frazer, Lévi-Strauss finds m. exhibiting many similarities throughout cultures remote from one another. But unlike Frazer, who attributes this to the uniform workings of the human mind, Lévi-Strauss sees it as due to an underlying structural pattern which is both synchronic and diachronic. It is detectable in all manifestations of m. because of its tendency to multiply similarities of narrative sequence, figures, and traits. Essentially, the structuralist approach to m. regards myths as cohering in a kind of system in which their latent structure is at least as important as their manifest content. They also function on various levels—social, psychological, economic, and cosmological—but always in the same fundamental fashion.

For literary critics, the structuralist approach to m. offers a methodology of reading in terms of deep structures of meaning—a stratification of functional levels which permits interpretive or ideological pluralism—and an opportunity to focus on the synchronicity of lang. As a result, structuralist m. crit., as exemplified by Eric Gould's *Mythical Intentions in Modern Lit.* (1981), focuses on specific authors—here, modern writers like Eliot, Joyce, and Lawrence—but scarcely attend at all to specific myths from particular cultures. What the structuralist approach does not do of itself is to assist in dealing with the issue of the interpretive untranslatability of lit., esp. poetry. This follows from its regarding m. as essentially a means for translating one set of relations or concerns into another without regard to a hierarchical or culturally prioritized structuring of problems, concepts, or langs.

II. THE PSYCHOLOGICAL PERSPECTIVE. Another major influence on m. crit. is the complex of psychological ideas concerning m. developed by Sigmund Freud (1856–1939), Carl Jung (1875–1961), and their followers. Early analysts called m. the dream of the race and thought it functioned culturally much as did the dreams of an individual. Both m. and dream were seen as symbolically constructed messages from the unconscious concerning its problems, needs, and desires. The Freudian view sees m. as representing the basic elements of human existence as developed by the ego of the child and persisting in some measure into adulthood. Occurrences such as urination, defecation, masturbation, menstruation, and copulation, coupled with the feelings of aggression, anxiety, pleasure, disgust, and pride they arouse, are projected into fantasy form. Early theorists like Otto Rank regarded such projections, which reverse actual interpersonal relations, as paranoid. Later, m. and folklore were viewed as providing individuals and groups escape mechanisms from socially imposed repressions such as taboos on incest or polygamy as well as from blockages of drives other than sexual. A key role in the emergence of this view was played by the advocates of ego psychology.

The Jungian view, on the other hand, regards m. as a function rooted in the structure of the human mind. Freud emphasized libidinal impulse, the unconscious as analyzable, and the psyche as structurally determined in infancy. Jung stresses psychic maturation in response to recurring challenges, the unconscious as an irreducible symbolic structure common to all men but not directly accessible (like Kant's *noumenon*) to inspection, and the psyche as capable of continuous development through time. The inclination of the first is to draw the critic in the direction of the individual and hence of psychoanalytic biography, whereas the Jungian emphases push the critic toward conceptual generalities and philosophical resolutions so that the texts become transpersonal mediations of cultural conditions and crises of civilization. Because of, among other things, the anonymity of myths' authorship, the postwar fissures in spiritual authority, the dominance of formalism in critical practice, and the metamythic nature of the archetypal, literary critics were inclined to find more that was congenial to their interests in Jungian views, even though many were cautious and even skeptical of its methodology, logic, and entailed metaphysic (see PSYCHOLOGICAL CRITICISM).

III. THE PHILOSOPHICAL PERSPECTIVE. The third influence of major significance on m. crit. is the philosophical work of the neo-Kantian Ernst Cassirer (1874–1945), Susanne K. Langer (1895–1985), and Philip Wheelwright (1901–1970). Cassirer came to m. as a result of his epistemological interest in the problems of subject and object and perception and reality. Out of them he developed a view of m. as an autonomous symbolic expression of the human spirit related to but not reducible to other cultural forms of expression such as lang., art, and science. These philosophical problems also led him to conclude that m. is not only a mode of narrative but also a mode of thinking which is a basic and ineradicable activity of human consciousness. It is, however, neither rational nor intellectual, but a function of will and emotion. Mythic perceptions, Cassirer holds, are affect-saturated, and issue in active projections objectified as real though nonexistent entities such as demons or divinities. By objectifying emotions in image and symbol, m. generates for mankind a shared conviction of social and natural unity.

For m. critics, the stress upon the persistence of m. as a form of thinking provides an assurance of its continued relevance to emergent literary forms and expressions. Similarly, the notion of its coalescence around images and symbols carrying an aura of preternatural significance and power reinforces these critics' concern for cultural and epistemological sanctions for lit. And finally, the notion of m. being a primary mode of human perception and expression, in which image and entity, ideal and real, exist undifferentiated, provides a more than rhetorical ground for lit.'s linkage to metaphor (q.v.) and the inexpungibility of both from the human economy. The best example of this dimension of m. crit. is Philip Wheelwright's *The Burning Fountain* (1954), which deals with the symbolic and sacramental resonances in works as diverse as the *Oresteia* and *Four Quartets*. Alan Watts' *Myth and Ritual in Christianity* (1954) merges the influences of Jung and Cassirer in interpreting celebrations such as Easter and Christmas, ceremonies such as the Mass, and concepts such as the Eucharist. More heavily Jungian and doctrinaire is Maud Bodkin's seminal *Archetypal Patterns in Poetry* (1934), which explores the workings of mythic archetypes of rebirth (in Coleridge's "The Rime of the Ancient Mariner"), of woman (in *Paradise Lost* and *The Divine Comedy*), and of the hero (from *Othello* to D. H. Lawrence, Virginia Woolf, and *The Waste Land*).

IV. PRINCIPLES. Despite this spectrum of influences and shaping forces, m. critics do not constitute anything resembling a school. Their unity, such as it is, derives from a shared interest in m. as a narrative, symbolic, and structural phenomenon which significantly impinges on lit. and its interp. Nevertheless, most m. critics would subscribe to the following general principles. First, the creating of myths, the mythopoeic faculty, inheres in the thinking process itself and satisfies a basic human need. Second, m. constitutes a matrix out of which lit. emerges both historically and psychologically. As a result, literary plots, characters, themes, and images are essentially complications and displacements of similar elements in ms. and folktales. Third, the concepts and patterns found in m. not only inform and stimulate the artist's consciousness but also serve as useful heuristic and structural principles for critical interp. In recognizing that mythic features reside beneath as well as on the surface of literary works, m. crit. differs substantially from earlier historical treatments of the mythological in lit. Fourth, m. critics locate the affective power of lit. in its residual mythic quality, its affinities with primordial responses to the mystery of existence. In the face of the protean manifestations and representations of this last, the human world perennially has responded with awe, delight, or terror. Fundamentally, then, m. critics see the function of lit. to be the continuation of myth's basic and ancient endeavor to create a meaningful place for man in a world oblivious to his presence.

Loose and extrapolative though these principles are, they nevertheless shape both the practices and the goals of m. critics. For them, knowledge of and receptivity to m. as a cultural form and force, as provided by such seminal works as Joseph Campbell's *The Hero with a Thousand Faces* (1949), materially sharpens the critic's perception of theme, structure, imagery, and character. Recognition of the pattern of ritual *sparagmos* in Goethe's *Faust*, the protagonist's rites of passage in *Beowulf, The Faerie Queene*, and *Prometheus Unbound*, or the roles of the divine king and scapegoat in *The Waste Land* uncovers significant aspects of these works that other forms of crit. slight. Such patterns can be observed both in specific works and throughout an author's canon. Thus the elegiac form of *Lycidas* has been related to the archetype of the dying and reviving god. Such literary concepts as theme, structure, character, and imagery are also crucial to tracing the transmogrifications of a single motif, such as the injured or crippled hero, or a single figure, such as Orpheus, Oedipus, or Ulysses, in one historical period or across several. Similarly, awareness of m. contributes materially to genre crit., as in modern Continental drama: Theater of the Absurd owes much of its cultural role and tone to its skeptical or comic deployment of m., which it simultaneously asserts and calls into question. Myth's cultural role is even more important for critics who trace the preoccupations and responses of an entire historical period, school, or lit. as the embodiment of culturally or historically dominant m. or concatenation of myths. Particularly fruitful explorations of this sort have been conducted in such disparate areas as the Eng. Ren. and Am. lit.

Finally, the understanding of m. as both primordially originary and psychologically emergent is capable of shaping an entire theory of lit., as exemplified most conspicuously in the work of Northrop Frye, which seeks to define narrative types, poetic forms, character types, and patterns of imagery in relation to cycles of m. These cycles are viewed as paradigms of possible literary formulations rather than as static or predetermined subject matter. For Frye, m. in general constitutes the structural principles or meaning of lit.

In *Anatomy of Crit.* (1957) Frye suggests that all literary forms may be subsumed under four categories or "generic plots," labeled romantic, tragic, comic, and ironic, and which stand to one another as the points of a compass. These four *mythoi* consist of six phases, each having a parallel with one of the other *mythoi*, thereby creating a continuum of structural relationships between individual works of lit. These relationships are a function of the interaction of generic structures of imagery, narrative, form, and mode. All four *mythoi* are, for Frye, aspects of a central quest m. or fiction dealing with occurrences of literal or metaphoric conflict; catastrophe; dismemberment or disappearance; and recognition or discovery, and are called, after the Cl. paradigm, *agon, pathos, sparagmos,* and *anagnorisis* respectively. Each of these dominates the theme and narrative of one of the *mythoi*.

Frye's theory of the nature and structure of lit. models itself and draws on Frazer's *Golden Bough*, with its emphasis on the centrality of the m. of the dying and reviving god for ancient cultures. Thus, he treats the four generic plots as akin to distinct phases clearly perceivable in this and related primordial myths. This fourfold schema reflects, corresponds to, or is structurally equivalent to the same general pattern found in the diurnal and seasonal cycles, as well as the movement of water from sky to earth and back again, and the progression of human life from infancy to old age. These resemblances lead Frye to suggest that the *mythoi* are basic patterns within which the imagination operates and that these patterns are seen most clearly in the great myths of all cultures. There the human impulses of common concern—toward desire or wish-fulfillment, freedom or liberty, law or necessity, and rejection or recoil—are seen paradigmatically.

As lit. emerges historically as a distinctive cultural expression, it modifies and adapts the basic patterns of m. in a variety of ways. These adaptations result from: a mimetic tendency to verisimilitude and accuracy; an inclination to recreate earlier, already employed plots or characters or themes; and a disposition to reflect or absorb, either positively or negatively, current social and cultural values. No matter how extensive this process of modification or displacement, as Frye calls it, the lineaments of m. are still perceptible. The reason for this is twofold. First, since the *mythoi* are inherent functions of the imagination, they are inevitably replicable by creative artists. And second, since they exist not only in a linear continuum but in a cyclical relationship, which may be loosely historical as well as conceptual, they keep emerging both thematically and narratively.

The cardinal significance of Frye's work in m.

crit. lies not only in its bold effort to frame an entire theory of the nature of lit. and crit. It also shifted the concern of m. critics in general away from the effort to detect latent individual ms. or para-ms. in individual texts toward the particular and individual ways in which m. merges with texts. Function rather than identification became the focus for the study of the relation of m. and lit. Instead of arguments and relationships grounded in analogy, m. crit. after *Anatomy of Crit.* increasingly probed the character and roles of homology in charting the connections between m. and lit. At the forefront of this effort were, among others, Frye's own subsequent works, such as *Fables of Identity* (1963) and *Spiritus Mundi* (1976). And with this came a new sense of the ability of m. crit. to do full justice to both synchronic and diachronic concerns.

See also ARCHETYPE; CRITICISM; THEORY.

E. Cassirer, *Philosophy of Symbolic Forms*, 3 v. (1923–29; tr. 1953–57); C. Still, *The Timeless Theme* (1936); R. Chase, *Quest for M.* (1949); H. Smith, *Virgin Land* (1950); H. Watts, *Hound and Quarry* (1953); H. Weisinger, *Tragedy and the Paradox of the Fortunate Fall* (1954), *The Agony and the Triumph* (1964); W. Stanford, *The Ulysses Theme* (1954); Frye; C. Barber, *Shakespeare's Festive Comedy* (1959); R. Elliott, *The Power of Satire* (1960); D. Hoffman,

Form and Fable in Am. Fiction (1961), *Barbarous Knowledge* (1967); R. Hathorne, *Tragedy, M. and Mystery* (1962); N. Frye, *Fables of Identity* (1963); *M. and Lit.*, ed. J. B. Vickery (1966); H. Matthews, *The Hard Journey* (1968); P. Wheelwright, *The Burning Fountain*, 2d ed. (1968); R. B. Gottfried, "Our New Poet: Archetypal Crit. and *The Faerie Queene*," *PMLA* 84 (1969); P. Merivale, *Pan the Goat-God* (1969); T. Porter, *M. and Mod. Am. Drama* (1969); H. Slochower, *Mythopoeis* (1970); L. Feder, *Ancient M. in Mod. Poetry* (1971); P. Hays, *The Limping Hero* (1971); R. Slotkin, *Regeneration Through Violence* (1973); J. Vickery, *The Literary Impact of the Golden Bough* (1973), *Ms. and Texts* (1983); W. K. Wimsatt, "Northrop Frye: Crit. as M.," *Day of the Leopards* (1976); R. Richardson, Jr., *M. and Lit. in the Am. Ren.* (1978); E. Gould, *Mythical Intentions in Mod. Lit.* (1981); V. B. Leitch, *Am. Lit. Crit. from the Thirties to the Eighties* (1988), ch. 5; M. Manganaro, *Myth, Rhet., and the Voice of Authority* (1991).   J.B.V.

MYTHOPOEIA. See MYTH.

MYTHOS. See PLOT.

MYURUS. See HEXAMETER.

N

NAGAUTA. See Japanese poetry.

NAIVE-SENTIMENTAL is an antinomy developed by Friedrich Schiller in the last of his aesthetic philosophical essays, "Ueber naive und sentimentalische Dichtung" (1795–96). The n. was already an established category, having been treated recently by Mendelssohn, Diderot, Sulzer, and Kant, but by opposing it to the s., Schiller insisted on the relative or perspectival character of both conceptions. The natural becomes n. only when it is contrasted with art or artifice. The n. is thus a moral, not an aesthetic, pleasure (as Kant defined the terms) since it is mediated by a concept. In the first installment of Schiller's essay, the n. thus seems closer to the s. than to traditional ideas of the n., in effect because he focuses on our interest in the n., not on how things would seem to a n. poet. The difference is that, viewed as n., nature (q.v.) puts art to shame, while from the s. perspective (which is only introduced in later installments), artificiality and culture have value of their own which compensates for a loss of naturalness. When Schiller in the first installment contrasts the Greeks, who felt or experienced naturally, to the moderns, who experience nature, offering Werther's response to Homer as an example, it is an instance of being moved by the n., but it is not what Schiller means by s.

When he comes to contrast n. and s. types of poets, Schiller levels his conception of n., as in the contrast: the n. poet *is* nature, the s. poet *seeks* it. This has led to a common reductive understanding of his intentions in drawing the contrast. He did not characterize Goethe as a n. poet in the sense Homer was (or is now for us), but as a modern poet drawn to imitate the manner if not the mentality of the Greeks, in contrast to his own poetic stance, which acknowledges the reflective break with nature and the resulting modern tension between feelings and principles, but which seeks its strength in that tension and in the "abstract" ideas and ideals which perpetuate it (see his letters to Goethe, Aug. 23, 1794; to Wilhelm von Humboldt, October 26, 1795; and to Herder, November 4, 1795). In a later installment of the essay, Schiller remarks that in much of Werther, Tasso, *Wilhelm Meisters Lehrjahre*, and in the first part of *Faust*, Goethe is clearly a s. poet. Given Schiller's complex and changing development of these ideas, it was perhaps inevitable that their influence would proceed from a reduced version. His comments on genius as a property of the n. resonated throughout romanticism, while on a deeper level his (scrupulously qualified) contrast of the cultural situations of the Cl. (Gr. but not Roman) and the modern poet subsequently proved important for Hölderlin, the Schlegels, Hegel, Matthew Arnold, and others. See now primitivism; romantic and postromantic poetics; cf. sentimentality.— U. Gaede, *Schillers Abhandlung ueber n. und sentimentalische Dichtung* (1899); H. Meng, *Schillers Abhandlung ueber n. und sentimentalische Dichtung* (1936); H. Cysarz, "N. und sentimentalische Dichtung," *Reallexikon*; O. Sayce, "Das Problem der Vieldeutigkeit in Schillers ästhetischer Terminologie," *Jahrbuch der deutschen Schillergesellschaft* (1962); H. Jäger, *Naïvität* (1975); H. Koopmann, *Friedrich Schiller*, v. 2 (1977), 25–27—overview of the secondary lit.   J.B.

NARRATIVE POETRY.

   I. definition
   II. history
  III. theory and versification

I. definition. N. is a verbal presentation of a sequence of events or facts (as in *narratio* in rhet. and law) whose disposition in time implies causal connection and point. Traditionally, a distinction has been made between factual or literal and fictive or literary n. (Bacon's "Feigned History"; see fiction), though in recent years such distinctions have come to seem harder and harder to draw. But it is perhaps still useful, whatever our philosophical doubts, to note that we continue to act as though there are kinds of n., judged so, if not according to generic standards, at least according to standards of intention and context. Thus we do not confuse legal arguments or histories of photography with what are called literary works, fictions, ns. that may in fact exploit legal arguments or histories of photography for their own ends. So we can, at least practically, talk about literary n. as a subtype of n. in general, and, further, talk of subtypes of literary n.: prose fiction and n. p. The grammatical emphasis on poetry in the latter phrase suggests that we must also say that the impact of versification (q.v.) is crucial to the total effect of n. poems.

II. history. Except in relatively short stretches, n. p., exclusive of epic, does not warrant a history in the sense of evolution or even continuity in change. But unfortunately, epic (incl. the issue of oral trad. versus written composition) cannot always be excluded. It may lie at the roots of medieval romance (q.v.) and conditions the so-called epyllion (q.v.) in its nonepic permutations (see below). Its dominance is everywhere visible in the ancient world, even in work that has no connection with it. Poets who write in other modes feel called upon to excuse themselves, sometimes ironically (Ovid and Horace), sometimes irritably (Callimachus). Prudentius, 4th-c. Christian, feels compelled to open his *Psychomachia* with an epic invocation to Christ, his muse (q.v.). And it does not stop there, or centuries later with Milton or Pope or Wordsworth (*The Prelude*), but enters Pound's modernist Homerics that open *The Cantos* and sends a faint Virgilian echo through *The Waste Land* ("A Game of Chess," 1.92-93).

If a history of epic and its impact on western lit. can be written (see, for example, Greene), that is not the same thing as writing a history of n. p. The question here for a historian of other-than-epic modes is where epic ends and something else, still n. p., begins. There is no precise answer, only a sense of local intention in the context of a particular cultural trad. Many n. poems draw heavily for their effects on epic convention (*Batrachomyomachia*, *The Rape of the Lock*) and probably belong very much to epic history; but many others merely gesture toward epic conventions, out of deference to literary habit or irony, and belong to some other mode of n. p. (Chaucer in *Troilus and Criseyde*). Perhaps the *locus classicus* of the dismissively ironic gesture is found in *Eugene Onegin*, where the narrator waits until the end of the next-to-last canto to invoke the epic muse, and adds, with a Byronic yawn: "Enough! The burden's off my back, / My debt to classicism paid, / Though late, my introduction made" (7.55). But works like Ovid's *Metamorphosis* (and perhaps *The Faerie Queene*) seem to belong both to epic history and to the history of other modes of n. p.

What are some of these other modes? One would surely be the folkloric and tendentious beast-fable in verse (see BEAST EPIC; FABLIAU), exploited by sophisticated poets—Horace in the fable of the town and country mice (*Satires* 2.6), Chaucer in the "Nun's Priest's Tale," La Fontaine and Gay in their fables, and perhaps, in a violent, near-surreal, and particularly modern form, Ted Hughes in *Crow* (1971).

Another mode is found in poems whose interest is less suspenseful action than highly figured erotic description and lyric pathos—"Hero and Leander," "The Rape of Lucrece," "Endymion"— poems whose lineage can be traced back through Ovid, Catullus, and Virgil to Callimachus and Theocritus, to Alexandrian modes like "n. elegy" (Wheeler 120 ff.) and the elegantly stylized, mythic tale termed by some modern scholars the epyllion, "little epic" (Williams 242 ff.).

Still another mode, exemplified in the cl. Sanskrit n. poem, is based on ancient works, the *Mahābharata* and the *Vālmīki Rāmāyaṇa*, but, like the epyllion, became something quite different from its ancestors. Here the term "epic" intervenes to complicate if not confuse the issues. The

term is often applied to *Mahābharata* and *Rāmāyana*, and in some ways fits, but in important ways does not if the model is Homer or Virgil. And the term for the later, literary n. poems, *mahākāvya*, has been translated both as "great poem" and "court epic," suggesting a problem of classification. Here again, the term "epic" can mislead as to poetic intention, though this mode takes for its subject the doings of heroes and gods.

Histories of poetic trads. like the Chinese and Japanese must account for the fact that, as Levy puts it, "lyric and n. modes of expression interpenetrate to a far greater extent than they do in European literary trads." (3). Indeed, the history of Japanese court poetry must explain why n. played so subordinate a role in literary culture. Describing the ethos of this trad., Miner observes that "the characteristic figure of cl. Western lit. is the orator, and of the Japanese the diarist" (9). The poetry that emerges from private meditation on personal feelings in the presence of nature and the divine is likely to be overwhelmingly lyrical.

The concept of interpenetration of modes suggests yet another category of n. poems that consciously exploit a sort of hybridization, namely *verse novels*. In Eng. one thinks first of Elizabeth Barrett Browning's *Aurora Leigh*, the aim of which is, according to Edmond, "to give that attention to everyday life which the novel manages so easily, without relinquishing the manner, power, and concentration of poetry" (131). A far more complex example is Nabokov's *Pale Fire*, set forth as a long poem swathed in the apparatus of commentary, the effect being like nesting n. within n. within n., the poetry absorbed into the larger, prose whole. Interpenetration takes place, too, beginning with the Eng. romantics, between the ballad (q.v.) and the lyric. If romantic ballads often take on the pathos of the personal lyric ("Peter Bell"), the lyric often assimilates the apparent directness, objectivity, and simplicity of the ballad (the "Lucy" poems; Coleridge's "conversation poems"). It would be hard to underestimate the effect of the latter kind of interpenetration on the lyric to this day. It could be argued that a characteristic type of poem by James Wright exemplifies a late version of romantic ballad-like lyric. It is plain that a hist. of the ballad would have to navigate genres other than the n., which suggests the difficulty of doing a history of any literary mode.

To sum up: a history of n. p. has to be plural, and rooted in local intention, not framed as a problem of genre (q.v.). Where genre (or any typal concept) is involved, history must be concerned with shared intentions, not necessarily with shared forms or terminological correctness.

III. THEORY AND VERSIFICATION. Early Western theorists like Plato and Aristotle approached n. p. as a problem in classification, and specifically, the exact classification of epic. This approach was bound to raise difficulties. Plato noticed that the epic was partly n., partly dramatic. He might just as easily have noticed that other "purer" modes were likewise and inevitably mixed as artistic exigency required. N. entered tragic drama with the messenger who had a tale to tell, and entered Pindar's epinikia as mythic "evidence" to refute or affirm received opinion. Much of the problem would have disappeared had theory allowed for a view of n. as part of a continuum of poetic discourse in which one or another mode dominated according to poetic intention, others being called into play as needed.

Though we have not wholly profited from the confusions of our forebears, we have recently become considerably more sophisticated and systematic in our approach to the topic of n. Martin has noted that in less than two decades "the theory of n. has displaced the theory of the novel as a topic of central concern in literary study" (15). In the process, our sense of discourse of all kinds has complicated itself immensely; this is reflected in the daunting multiplication (and sometimes duplication) of technical terms meant to sort out and define micro- and macrocosmic elements of discourse in general and literary n. in particular. For example, each aspect of the tripartite division of ancient Western critical trad.—author, text, audience—has been further subdivided into a complex cluster of elements. Thus, in a fairly common model (no one theory or terminology wholly dominates the field), author has been analyzed into actual author, implied author, and n. speaker or persona (q.v.); these, like a set of Rus. nesting dolls, give definition and point(s) of view to the voice (q.v.) or voices implied by the text, itself analyzed into discourse, story, plot or narration, description, argument (q.v.), and grammatical, semantic and (deep or surface) structural patterns that create the effects associated with literary n. These effects are actively experienced or received by (ideally competent) readers and analyzed into the mirror image of the authorial cluster.

This model by no means exhausts theoretical interest. The dynamics of composition and of reading (or listening) are important topics of a n. theory, as is time (actual reading time as against time within the n.) and its ordering. And it should come as no surprise to find narratological theory much engaged with the topics of epistemology and method, which call into question theory itself and its actual powers to describe. The long struggle of lit. crit., since the 19th c., to free itself from subjectivity has never been fiercer or crossed so many disciplines. Thus modern theory calls upon anthropology, sociology, psychology, and philosophy to give its methods stable grounds.

Insofar as it is a subclass of literary n., n. p. is subject to analysis in all the categories noted above. When verse is added to the mix, attention is apt to focus on stylistic, grammatical, and semantic patterns, and on the figures and tropes most often associated with poetic discourse. But

theory, were it to stop here, would miss what seems to be the real differentia of poetry, measure (q.v.), which is that which most clearly marks off verse from prose. Before dismissing this as a self-evident proposition, it is well to remind ourselves that keeping time, however simply, makes a difference, even in the banality of Johnson's little parody:

> I put my hat upon my head,
> And walked into the Strand
> And there I met another man
> Whose hat was in his hand.

Here, meter (q.v.) rouses expectation, and expectation conditions the experienced meaning of the verse. Nor is it merely that the best thing about doggerel (q.v.) is that we remember it; some of the strongest comic effects in *Hudibras* are built on such minimal versifying.

But n. poems in general deploy other prosodic and figurative elements to play on, and with, the constant of measure and the expectation it rouses. Measure, in fact, invites such devices as caesura, enjambment, rhyme, assonance, stanza, anaphora, and metonymy (qq.v.); it allows, positively encourages, linguistic behavior much less frequently found in prose. Though it is easy to recall prose that is more "poetic" than some poetry, it is hard to imagine the following locution outside a poem: "The future fearing, while he feels the past" (Crabbe, *The Elder Brother*). In this, by one of the most prosaic of Eng. poets, meter is joined with alliteration, assonance, antithesis, and chiasmus to create the effect. If such symmetries are seldom found in prose, how much less so are those of more richly textured n. poems—this, for example, from Yeats's "The Wanderings of Oisin": "Wrapt in the wave of that music, with weariness more than of earth, / The moil of my centuries filled me" (3.69–70). Measure then, tends to be the differentia that provides the ground for other differentiae that we associate with poetry, and this is as true for n. as for lyric and dramatic poetry.

Useful as this distinction might be, it is yet so general that it can only be the beginning of analysis in the face of the immense variety found in n. p. John Clare's "The Badger" and Kālidāsa's *Kumārasambhava* (The Birth of the War God) are both n. poems, but while the former is close to reporting (however highly charged), the latter, working in the cl. Sanskrit poetic trad., depends heavily on elaborate lyrical description. Clare drives his audience with unrelenting momentum to the brutal end, compelling them to experience the logic of the cruelty he depicts; Kālidāsa slows his audience down so that they will experience the intricate but static beauty of the ideal world, the subject of his poem. What Bruno Snell has said about the Virgil of the *Eclogues* could be fittingly applied to Kālidāsa: "he does not narrate facts or events at all; he is more interested in the unfolding and praising of situations" (*Discovery of the Mind* [1953], 291).

NARRATIVE POETRY

The variety of n. p. is such that it must defeat any attempt to sort it into a manageable taxonomy. Evidence to suggest the futility of classification: in 1819, Wordsworth published "The Waggoner" and Byron the first cantos of *Don Juan*, while Shelley composed "The Mask of Anarchy" and Keats "Lamia." What besides verse measure and the fact that they are in Eng. brings these poems within the compass of a definition more specific? And more useful? The distance between Crabbe's deliberate plainness and Keats's deliberate brilliance suggests that, if these poems are members of the same family, they are so in Wittgenstein's sense, as A and Z are members of the same family, sharing "family resemblances."

This much conceded, we can examine some of the positive effects that measure can have on the impact of the ns. that unfold within its patterns. Among the simplest, measure can—by jolting expectation—underscore, or create, the tone of surprise, as in this from Byron's "The Corsair": "He thought of her afar, his only bride: / He turn'd and saw—Gulnare, the homicide!" (3.13). The sudden pause, the contrast between what was thought and what is seen: these effects are heightened by the regular meter, which yet contains the disruption in the expected flow of events. More complex effects are found everywhere—e.g. in these two lines from James Dickey's "The Shark's Parlor," where tremendous intensity is built by the tension between a halting measure (a word or clusters of words isolated from each other by abnormally wide spacing and sometimes syntactic disjunction) and the forward thrust of the action:

> The front stairs   the sagging boards
> still coming in   up   taking
> Another step   toward the empty house
> where the rope stood   straining
> (*Buckdancer's Choice* [1965], 41)

Movement can be quickened as well as slowed, however, as in the famous chase in Burns' "Tam O'Shanter."

Measure itself not only controls pace and expectation—and in units as small as a single word—it also provides the ground for other effects from relatively simple anaphora to the most complex of tropes. It is highly unlikely that the following lines from the Radin-Patrick (1937) tr. of Puškin's *Eugene Onegin* would sit comfortably in prose:

> The cuckold with the pompous port,
> Completely satisfied with life,
> Himself, his dinner, and his wife.
> (1.12).

The zeugma (q.v.) here very much depends on strict metrical regularity. But it also depends on rhyme, and the force of the little catalogue (q.v.) that peaks at the last word—all these symmetries heighten the asymmetry of "dinner" and "wife."

This is to say that, grounded in meter, the n. poem has at its disposal virtually all the means available to dramatic and lyric poetry. There are indeed instances where modes blend perfectly—for example, Herbert's "The Pilgrimage," about which one might (momentarily) be tempted to emulate Polonius and find designations like "allegorical n. lyric."

Poems like "The Pilgrimage" lie at the approximate center of a very broad spectrum, ranging from very plain to very elaborate style. On the one side, there are the ns. of the medieval biblical paraphrasts, Chaucer of "Sir Thopas," Butler, Crabbe, Wordsworth on occasion, Scott, Byron, and, in our own time, George Keithley (*The Donner Party* [1972]). On the other, there are the ns. of Ovid, of the author of *Sir Gawain and the Green Knight*, of Shakespeare, Keats, Arnold, and Christina Rossetti (in "Goblin Market"). But even this broad classification breaks down before a poem like *Troilus and Criseyde*, which, in its amplitude, incorporates both plain and elaborate styles and all the genres and modes, lyric, n., dramatic, descriptive—proof, if any were needed, that pure types are not likely to keep their purity over any distance, and that types, depending on need, comfortably assimilate one another.

The best modern theory is cognizant of the complexity lying beyond terms like genre (q.v.), type, and mode, and is cognizant, too, that the dynamics of composing, performing, reading, hearing, and analyzing forbid the satisfying symmetries of taxonomy. Even categories not long ago taken as given—authorship and audience—have been opened to admit complex functions and qualifications. If modern theorists of n. have mostly concentrated their efforts on prose, it is perhaps because analysis of prosody (q.v.), as of figures, schemes, and tropes (q.v.), has customarily been applied to the lyric (q.v.). If it is understood that n. poems are susceptible of the same kind of analysis, with the difference that prosodic effects feed into the general effect produced by a particular narration, then we can approach individual texts unworried by classificatory anxieties, reasonably confident that we are looking at real similarities and equally real differences.   L.N.

See also AFRICAN POETRY; BEAST EPIC; BALLAD; CHANSONS DE GESTE; DRAMATIC POETRY; DREAM VISION; EPIC; EPYLLION; FABLE; FABLIAU; GENRE; LYRIC; MEDIEVAL ROMANCE; MODERN LONG POEM; MYTH; ORAL-FORMULAIC THEORY; ORAL POETRY; PASTORAL; PLOT; PROSE POEM; STRUCTURE.

A. L. Wheeler, *Catullus and The Trads. of Ancient Poetry* (1934); L. R. Zocca, *Elizabethan N. P.* (1950); Frye; Lord; T. Greene, *The Descent from Heaven* (1963); R. Scholes and R. Kellogg, *The Nature of N.* (1966); *Elizabethan N. Verse*, ed. N. Alexander (1967); F. Kermode, *The Sense of an Ending* (1967), *The Art of Telling* (1983); Kālidāsa, *The Kumārasambhava*, tr. M. R. Kale (1967); *Sanskrit Poetry: From Vidyākara's Treasury*, tr. D. H. H. Ingalls (1968); E. Miner, *Intro. to Japanese Court Poetry* (1968); G. Williams, *Trad. and Originality in Ro-*

man Poetry (1968); N. P., ed. C. L. Sisson (1968); Jour. of N. Technique 1–(1970–); M. H. Abrams, Natural Supernaturalism (1971); E. Vinaver, The Rise of Romance (1971); K. D. Uitti, Story, Myth, and Celebration in OF N. P., 1050–1200 (1973); E. Miner et al., To Tell a Story: N. Theory and Practice (1973); E. S. Rabkin, N. Suspense (1974); P. H. Lee, Songs of the Flying Dragons: A Critical Reading (1975); Kālidāsa, The Transport of Love: The Meghadūta, tr. L. Nathan (1976); D. Perkins, Hist. of Mod. Poetry, v. 1 (1976), ch. 4; S. Chatman, Story and Discourse (1978), Coming to Terms (1990); Finding The Center: N. P. of the Zuni Indians, tr. D. Tedlock (1978); G. Genette, N. Discourse (tr. 1980), N. Discourse Revisited (tr. 1988); W. J. T. Mitchell, On N. (1981); D. A. Russell, Crit. in Antiquity (1981); P. Boitani, Eng. Med. N. in the 13th and 14th Cs. (1982); M. Perloff, "From Image to Action: The Return of Story in Postmodern Poetry," ConL 23 (1982); The Ballad as N., ed. T. Pettitt (1982); J. M. Ganim, Style and Consciousness in Middle European N. (1983); Oxford Book of N. Verse, ed. I. and P. Opie (1983); R. Alter, "From Line to Story in Biblical Verse," PoT 4 (1983); D. Bialostosky, Making Tales: The Poetics of Wordsworth's N. Experiments (1984); A. S. Gamal, "N. P. in Cl. Ar. Lit.," Quest of an Islamic Humanism, ed. A. H. Green and M. al-Nowaihi (1984); P. Ricoeur, Time and N. (1984); C. Christ, Victorian and Mod. Poetics (1984); "The Music of What Happens: A Symposium on N. P.," NER/BLQ 8 (1985); I. M. Kikawada and A. Quinn, Before Abraham Was (1985); B. Connelly, Arab Folk Epic and Identity (1986); W. Martin, Recent Theories of N. (1986); H. Dubrow, Captive Victors: Shakespeare's N. Poems and Sonnets (1987); H. White, The Content of the Form (1987); D. Damrosch, The N. Covenant (1987)—biblical genres; D. J. Levy, Chinese N. P.: Late Han through T'ang Dynasties (1988); R. Edmond, Affairs of the Hearth (1988); J. Walker, Bardic Ethos and the Am. Epic Poem (1989); Expansive Poetry, ed. F. Feirstein (1989); M. J. Toolan, N. (1989); H. Fischer, Romantic Verse N. (tr. 1991).   T.V.F.B.

NARRATOLOGY. See NARRATIVE POETRY; PLOT.

NARRATOR. See PERSONA.

NATURALISM. There are two principal ways in which this contradictory term is used in the study of poetry: one emphasizes a set of romantic principles concerning description of nature and their extension throughout most of the Victorian era, while the other, narrower, identifies an aesthetic program that is based on an essentially anti-romantic system of philosophical-scientific doctrines. Walter Pater has the former concept in mind when, in the "Preface" to The Renaissance (1873), he mentions Wordsworth's naturalistic vision as "that strange, mystical sense of a life in natural things, and of man's life as a part of nature." N. here refers to the poetic evocation of a

vital reciprocity between man and his living natural environment, an experience that may allow intimations of a transcendent realm to emanate from this close sympathy between private sensibilities and the domain of organic life. Tennyson's view of nature as "red in tooth and claw," on the other hand, is predicated on the contrary notion—that man's existence is a constant "struggle for life," dominated by morally indifferent compulsions and subject to a blind dynamism of regeneration undone by destruction. Nature appears as an impediment to virtuous self-fulfillment, to humane civilization, and to ennobling vision. In either case, whether nature is perceived as a benign source of value or agent of rapacious destiny, the term "n." refers to an abiding preoccupation with nature as the essential determinant of life. More restrictively, however, n. in poetics is closely associated with the mechanistic and deterministic assumptions developed by late 19th-c. science. In this context the term refers to the programmatic systematization of a literary aesthetic that sought to reconcile the aims of art and science by subordinating creative individualism to the laws of causality.

Critical convention, though, tends to equate n. ahistorically with a particular stylistic norm that, as a radical type of modern realism (q.v.), is characterized by meticulous attention to the details of the world used to convey a sense of the given work's distinctive social milieu and psychological peculiarity. Such a definition also emphasizes the elimination of image-making, rhetorical embellishments, and metaphorical allusiveness in favor of unadorned directness of diction and description.

To be sure, the implications of scientific materialism need not be the only criteria on which to base a definition of n. But there are advantages to retaining an essential distinction between realism and n. and to accepting the Ger. trad. of using the former to denote a way of looking at things artistically, and the latter a literary movement. This movement started with an aggressive rebellion against the official Prussian culture of the 1870s, the Gründerjahre, and a concomitant preference for eclectic imitations of earlier styles. The mass-produced proliferation of an insipidly conventional, though technically accomplished poetry contrasted glaringly with the ubiquitous destruction of the "old world" during a decade of accelerated urbanization and industrialization after 1871. In protest against the inevitable displacement of poetry by the commodities of an indiscriminate capitalistic market, small groups of university students in Munich and Berlin propagated a revolutionary modernism. At first arousing little more than curiosity, they became a challenge to bourgeois taste when the repeal of the law prohibiting socialist agitation in 1890 also removed the restrictions on the circulation of socialist poetry.

N. came into its own in 1885, with the appearance of M. G. Conrad's Munich weekly *Die Gesellschaft* (1885–1902), and of the anthol. *Moderne Dichter-Charaktere*, a diffuse sampling of work by 22 poets instigated by the brothers H. and J. Hart, authors of *Kritische Waffengänge, 1882–84* (1884). That same year, Arno Holz, the most original and prolific naturalist, brought out his *Das Buch der Zeit: Lieder eines Modernen*, which marked the beginning of five years of intensive poetry writing (collections by C. Alberti, Conrad, O. Kamp, J. H. Mackay, B. Wille, Henckell, Conradi), before the Freie Bühne (1889, with 1000 subscribing members) and the Freie Volksbühne (1890) in Berlin introduced n. to the stage. Holz's poetics as formulated in *Die Kunst: Ihr Wesen und ihre Gesetze* (2 v., 1891–93) developed from a critical encounter with the inductive, experimental method of Émile Zola. He argued for as complete and consistent a transformation of art into nature (i.e. the full compass of physical reality) as lang. would allow. His "Sekundenstil" (a term coined by A. von Hanstein) tried to recreate reality with stenographic precision. This insistence on logical exactitude also informs his *Revolution der Lyrik* (1899), a treatise written to accompany his *Phantasus* (1898), an ever-growing verse collection that he considered, on analogy to Homer and Dante, the "world poem of the modern age." Both books were published, however, several years after n. had exhausted its potential for poetic innovation.—S. A. Brooke, *N. in Eng. Poetry* (1920); R. Hamann and J. Hermand, *Naturalismus* (1959); *Literarische Manifeste des Naturalismus 1880–1892*, ed. E. Ruprecht (1962); R. Leppla, "Naturalismus," *Reallexikon*; G. Mahal, *Naturalismus* (1975); J. Schutte, *Lyrik des deutschen Naturalismus, 1885–1893* (1976); R. C. Cowen, *Der Naturalismus*, 3d ed. (1981). M.W.

NATURE.

I. IN POETRY
II. IN CRITICISM

To deal with n. in poetry is, in some sense, to deal with nearly the whole task of poetry, for poetry is, to paraphrase Dryden, the "image of n." All theories of poetry have made some allowance for both terms ("image"—a thing in itself, a construct; "n."—what the poem imitates or speaks about), however much a given theory may stress some particular aspect of the many interconnections, or however much a theory may deny text or image or n. "When me they fly, I am the wings." To speak is to speak, to make a text claiming some truth about what is without the text. Hence, n., both as subject and as one component in poetic theory, is central in poetry.

It is symptomatic of our times, semantics being in some measure a product of the Cartesian and Kantian divisions and romantic doubts about n., that "n." is so often thought of by modern writers as primarily an ambiguous word. But the situation is not quite so desperate as might appear from,

say, the articles of Lovejoy and Wilson. For the galaxy of meanings there adduced do have a center—reality, manifested in this way or that—and the crucial differences in meaning are more ontological than semantic.

Man has puzzled much about his relation to n. throughout the history of thought. People have felt that man is in, but not of, n.; or of, but not quite in, n.; or, in any case, that he is a very special part of n. The late Ren. with its enthusiasm for science felt that man had found and discovered "almost a new n."; the romantics in Europe and in England celebrate n. as the "nurse and guardian" of one's being, and with that celebration assert the primacy and rights of self and self-expression as against n. and natural law (see ROMANTICISM). In the 20th c. the result of such assertions and of the Humean division of fact and value—a scientific n. without value, a human world with only subjective valuing and with nothing truly to be valuable—is often anomie, fragmented denials of self and n., postmodernism. The fear of, or hostility to, or indifference toward science is widespread: the celebration of science, which Dryden advocated and practiced, is rare. From the earlier semireligious, semimaterialistic speculations about the n. of things, lit. and men's views about n. have been mutually though not exclusively causative, and considerably complicated.

I. IN POETRY. This essay attempts a historical survey of some views of n. But it is good to remember that n., though it has its own history, is, *vis-à-vis* much human history ahistorical; and much that happens in n. poetry is recurrent rather than historically caused. Celebratory and spirited descriptions of n. recur in many places: for instance, in the special discipline of the Japanese *haiku* (q.v.), such as a famous example from Moritake: "See the leaf flutter / Upward, and light on a branch! / No! a butterfly." So does the longing for a home, as in Rosalia de Castro's "Sweet Galician Breezes," where breeze "banishes sorrow, / charms the waters . . . / and in green corn dances / with silken rustle." N. is, in many poems, intricate with love and with memory, as in Henrik Ibsen's *Musician*, in which the musician has great success but has lost his lady: "Now I play my music, applauded / In great churches and mansions. / My grief remains in the alders / In the late light of summer." Poetry is permanent and human as well as historical.

In Homer, n., though mythic and under the sway of supernatural beings, is a large, solid, brilliantly lighted world of objects, and every episode is presented in detail, forcibly, with precision (Auerbach 1–20). Life and n. are accepted and presented in their own right. In the Old Testament, n. is rigorously subordinated to God; details are given never for their own sake, but for the sake of religious truth. They may be simple exterior parts of the story briefly, sometimes naively, put forward (the bear and the children, the events in Kings and

NATURE

Chronicles, important because Jewish history is uniquely sealed by God); or they may have supernaturally illumined potency (the burning bush), or may be poetically magnificent responses to God and created beauty (the Psalms, the Song of Solomon).

In Daniel and Revelations, prophetic imagery, however interpreted, achieves a sometimes obscure grandeur, a surrealism. In Job, n. is explored with agony and complexity of thought: its logistics are godly, hence those who suffer *must* have sinned; it is a province of Satan, who walks abroad carrying forth his malice and carrying out God's providence. The Voice from the Whirlwind offers perhaps the most magnificent psalm of praise of n., showing God's creative power and authority, yet also showing that logistics are real and require *hesed*—loving kindness—and forgiveness. Job is restored only when reconciled in forgiveness to his friends who offered their partially true arguments in sincerity if also in pride.

In Gr. thought and lit., n. becomes many things: god-haunted, a goddess herself, a demiurge, a Heraclitean flux, an unreal world of appearances, an unceasing and godless play of atoms. Usually, however, she keeps a more substantial independence (even when conceived as unreal) than in Jewish ontology, because the Jews, unlike the Greeks, think of n. as created. Heraclitus sees the world as change, transformation, and flux (though he apparently also accepts a divine order behind the flux), an idea that has influenced poets from Ovid (*Metamorphoses*) through Gerard Manley Hopkins and T. S. Eliot (*Four Quartets*). In Sophocles' *Oedipus Rex*, man and n. are joint heirs of weal and of woe; the plague, caused by Oedipus' wicked deeds, falls on land and people alike: n. is subject to the (partly unknowable) moral order.

Parmenides and Plato, in their different ways, found the world to be delusive. Scholars and literary critics still disagree whether Plato finally rejects poetry and poets, but it is clear enough that he does reject most poetry from the ideal kingdom, as appertaining to the lesser world. But the idea of n. as appearances, with its subsidiary idea of the ladder of reality, is among the most telling ideas in hist., in poetry and crit. as in religion and ethics. It comes through Plotinus, the Neoplatonists, and Christian theology and is a Ren. commonplace, however powerful the contrary impulse (in science, for example) to accept, explore, and control a thoroughly real natural world. It informs Sidney's great sonnet, "Leave me, O love, that reachest but to dust," and Spenser's four Hymns, and reappears in Wordsworth's *Peele Castle* and Shelley's *Hymn to Intellectual Beauty*.

But n. is not only the world-view which a poet assumes or wrestles with: it was, and is, place—the rocks, streams, hills that women and men can admire, live among, and fancifully rearrange. In the pastorals of Theocritus and Virgil, a gentle, special world is selected *from* n. to serve as a counterpoise of spirit for man's hectic life in courts and cities and to serve the perpetually recurring theme of (and need for) innocence and freshness (see PASTORAL). But the genre is no simple one, and it grows: it includes elegy (q.v.), disguised autobiography, battles of wit, half-mocking or tender praises of love; it can deepen to allegory (q.v.), drama, passion, and prophecy. An overlapping trad. is found in the shepherds' plays of the Middle Ages, rediscovered in the Ren. and developed by such writers as Politian, Mantuan, Sannazaro, the *Pléiade* poets, Tasso, Guarini, and Spenser. It takes various forms: (1) the pastoral novel of Sidney, Honoré d'Urfé, and others; (2) the pastoral play or masque (q.v.; e.g. Fletcher and Jonson, as well as the Shakespeare of *As You Like It* and scenes from *The Winter's Tale* and *The Tempest*); (3) the more common pastoral eclogue (see ECLOGUE). The trad. culminates, but does not end, in *Lycidas*. In pastoral, n. is refined, humanized, decorated, elaborated, simplified; yet this recreated n. can have, as in Virgil and Milton, a deeply natural and quickening power of its own. "Pathetic fallacy" and "decoration" or projection, or relativism or subjectivism will not do to describe or explain away the dense reality and interplay between man, n., and God in *Lycidas*, in the "bright shoots of everlastingness" felt through n. in Vaughan or in many another mystical poet.

The *Georgics* of Virgil (which are founded largely on the poems of Hesiod) show n. in a special view. In one sense an agricultural manual, they nonetheless reflect a deeply humanized n. impregnated by civilization, by man's rational and earnest cultivation, that in turn gives to man rootedness and stability and accord with the past. The world is stubborn and requires appropriate logistics; so does poetry. In the *Aeneid*, n. keeps the qualities of the *Georgics*, though deepened, made more dignified, pious, and stately. The epic simile though presumes man's separation from the natural world, the orderliness of n., and dignifies man and natural world alike.

N. was often for the Greeks and Romans a goddess, and remained so for centuries, at least in lit. Even Lucretius, whose materialism is stubborn and basic, hymns Venus, the creative power of n., in verse nearly religious in quality, and achieves a poetic naturalism whose closest modern parallel is perhaps some of the philosophic prose of George Santayana. "Natura" (or "Physis") as a generative and intervening goddess appears in poetry from Ovid through Claudian and the Orphic hymns of the 3d and 4th cs., down through such medieval writers as Bernard Silvestris (*De universate mundi*) and Alan of Lille (*De planctu naturae* and *Anticlaudianus*). In the process of partially Christianizing the pagan goddess, there derives a new poetic genre, the philosophical-theological epic, in which the Christian view of the world provides the frame and end for the story, but various pagan or semipagan deities and demigods are the actors. This trad. worked against obstacles, in part because of the multiple Christian attitudes toward n.: n. is created, hence good; n. is fallen, hence evil, esp. so as involved in sensuality. As innocent or as redeemed, n. can be lovely and holy. In the Middle Ages (and of course the Middle Ages are not entirely Christian), various Christian attitudes to n. appear, esp. in the complex trad. of courtly love (q.v.). In the two parts of the 14th-c. *Romance of the Rose* there are two "natures," both quite medieval, incorrigibly different. In the first part, by Guillaume de Lorris, n. is gardenlike and delicate of bloom; in Jean de Meun's second part, n. means rank and sprawling sensuality.

The n. in the lit. of the semi-Christian and courtly world of the Middle Ages is different in kind and emphasis from the n. found in poems of the semi-Christian and courtly world of Old English. In such poems as *Beowulf, The Wanderer,* and *The Seafarer,* the most successful natural descriptions are of the bleak and great and spare: the bitter sea of exile, the fens and fastnesses where demons walk, a great and lonely funeral pyre. But in the medieval *Sir Gawain and the Green Knight,* n. is magnificent, various, and brilliantly colored, even when expressive of grim fears; and in the *Pearl,* as in many medieval carols and lyrics, the loveliness of the landscape is dipped in supernatural hues. Chaucer is a master of natural description, of n. in many moods and features: symbolically black rocks, the delicacy of Love's gardens (a delicacy paralleled in Fr. n. poets: Deschamps, Machaut, Froissart), the natural and vigorous earth the pilgrims travel over, the invented and phantasmagoric landscape (or airscape) of many spheres rising toward God spheres (the *Knight's Tale; Troilus and Criseyde*). He learned much, borrowed much, and transformed much from Dante, who, though his greatest poem is almost entirely set in supernature, has perhaps the most exact eye for physical detail of any poet. Light in the *Paradiso* becomes the most eloquent of all literary symbols (for mind is there illumined by the supernatural); yet he uses similes with a businesslike attention to the point of the resemblance, that presumes the genuine importance of the intellect in its own capacity and the Thomistic reliance on the senses, the plainly visible.

Petrarch praises God in n. and praises the lady whose light shines for transcendent and painful years on him, his joy and pain. Natural similes are *for* the lady but truly seen: through "sharp seas" his ship sails (Poem 189). In Petrarch's poem the stars are clearly the eyes of Laura; in Wyatt's great translation the analogy is subdued, the suffering made real and universalized in n.: "The stars be hid that led me to this pain."

The great poets of the Eng. Ren.—Shakespeare, Spenser, Milton—share some fruitful, if tangled, assumptions about n.: that n. is created, hierarchical, symbolic, full of personal-social-physical-theological correspondences, struck with sin, pow-

erfully threatened; and these assumptions appear whether they write of real or imaginary fields (Agincourt or the Bower of Acrasia). One of their great motifs is the overthrow of n., physical n. being stubbornly involved in the moral world; and the supreme correspondences of man and n. are expressed in *King Lear.*

The medieval trad. of meditation on the features of the world (as image of God's glory, or symbols of temporal vanity; or to express the coinherence of the church and the mystical life) is kept alive in the devotional poetry of Southwell, Donne, Herbert, Vaughan, Crashaw, and Dryden. In general, Dryden keeps the theory of a symbolical and hierarchical world, but relaxes the practice except in moments and in the semi-Miltonic *Absalom and Achitophel.* For Pope, the more traditional view has faded. N. exists to serve philosophical argument, for primitivistic sentimentalizing, for faint pastoral or fainter Christian pastoral; but Pope speaks with power and in pungent detail when he deals with bugs, worms, toads, or chicks in satiric attack or when he sees, in the bitterness and magnitude of the *Dunciad*'s close, the wreck of a former world. In Voltaire, n. exists almost exclusively for argument (even Candide's garden to be cultivated is as much an example as an exception), to "prove" the existence of the deistic God by its noble and orderly design or to "disprove" Christian providence by its cataclysmic and meaningless evils.

Shaftesbury's and Rousseau's optimistic benevolism and antirational associationism (n. conceived as innately good and sponsoring social as well as sentimental feeling) rules much of the 18th c. and to some degree the 19th, even though Miltonic diction for describing a well imagined literary n. has its influence too; and the long-standing epideictic trad. (poetry as praise of God through praise of the natural creation) shows attractively in Thomson's *The Seasons,* magnificently in Smart's *A Song for David,* and deistically and thinly in Addison's *Hymn.* Gray, Collins, and Blake achieve some unique and beautiful effects of natural description.

The theory of "general n.," as expressed by Rapin and Boileau and vividly by Johnson when he advises against numbering the streaks of the tulip, is never completely obeyed by its proponents, but Blake contemns the idea ("To Generalize is to be an Idiot"—itself a generalization!) and seeks knowledge inhering in and through particular images of the poetic vision. Wordsworth has some excellent passages of particular description, but his landscapes are more apt to be generalized, important for their effect on the soul or their philosophical and religious meaning. His poetic theory insists more on the general than the particular. In Goethe, n. shows range, but not a return to the Ren. Whether serving as a mirror for the sorrows of a young poet, or as the ground for man's reclamation in the second part of *Faust,* n. is essentially passive and, by romantic projection and by engineering, bears humanity's stamp.

Wordsworth and Coleridge, however much they differ in specific poetic ideas, are, like a number of Continental poets of the period, very seriously puzzled about n. (see ROMANTICISM). Earlier poets widely believed in, or simply assumed, spiritual power in or behind n.; they frequently gave n. human qualities without embarrassment (they had rhetorical terms, prosopopoeia or personification [qq.v.], for such devices). Coleridge, Wordsworth, Shelley, and Keats are at once more passionate and more uncertain about physical n. The term "pathetic *fallacy*" (q.v.) is, significantly, a 19th-c. invention. The question of projection vs. perception was perhaps the most agonizing that these poets dealt with, and they strongly feared the negative conclusion (that men merely read meaning into a deterministic and meaningless world). All of them have, like the Victorians after them, their moments of great doubt. They also have their moments of great vision. Wordsworth perhaps came off best in the struggle. In the latter part of the century, the problem was intensified by the Darwinian concept of n. as blindly evolving, in Tennyson's phrase, "red in tooth and claw."

In 19th-c. Fr. poetry, this reduced view of n. appears in at least three different ways: the praise of n. as admirably alien from man; the re-creation of a "Parnassian" n. from refined natural elements; and the belated and desperate attempt of the symbolists to achieve the medieval view of analogy by a desperate leap of the "angelical imagination" (a phrase Tate uses in speaking of Poe, the hero of the symbolists). The first and second ways combine beautifully in such a poem as de Lisle's *Les Eléphants*, the second and third ways magnificently in the poems of Baudelaire, with their mixture of romantic charlatanism and a revived and deadly sense of sin (inherited in some part from the meditative and powerful Jansenism of Racine). And in passages of such poems as De Vigny's *La Maison du Berger* or *La Mort du loup* (as in Tennyson's *In Memoriam*), there is a rediscovery of the meditative trad., only drawing strength and profundity from doubt rather than faith, "questioning all with inquietude" (as De Vigny says in another context).

The typical n. of 20th-c. poetry is that of T. S. Eliot's *The Waste Land* and Hart Crane's *The Bridge*, where the natural—and human—world is conceived as shattered, fragmentary, painful. Eliot's poem attempts to express this confusion: Crane's does express the confusion in the very failure of his attempt to unify Am. experience (but achieves much coherence within the partially broken frame). Wallace Stevens broods freshly the projection-perception puzzle, with faint hope, ironic irresolution, loud and deliberately literary creations of an elegant or amusing n., or with the starkest vision of a world devoid of meaning except for the motion of naked particularity. In Valéry, n. is pre-

sented with an almost pitiless brilliance of detail and a highly subtle ambivalence of feeling and belief. Auden handles natural imagery imitatively (i.e., of the n. of OE poetry), or with journalistic aplomb, or so as to express the *oddness* of particularity. Less commonly and more seriously, he offers redemptive glimpses of supernature through n. or celebrates n. lyrically. Yeats bridges the chasm: his natural imagery is magical, hieroglyphic, wavering; or it is solid and Irish: it can serve for savage espousal of the harshest naturalism or for images that beget images of supernature. R. P. Warren is bold with the pathetic fallacy and attains a nightmarish intensity at times, at rare times a beauty of light and color, but he seems to feel the fallacy as fallacy and commits it stridently. In much minor poetry, n. is interior, contrivedly Freudian, uglily symptomatic, appearing only in prosaically casual bits of description, or academically tentative. In some of the best free verse (q.v.), e.g. W. C. Williams, the very shape of the line expresses the fragmentation of n., though seen with a fresh, loving, and particular eye. Some poets, such as St.-John Perse and Dylan Thomas in some moods, attempt in the Whitman trad. to make n. a paradise by dithyrambic lyricism and by harmonizing conscious and unconscious meanings of natural symbols.

Allen Tate in *Ode to the Confederate Dead* presents in great bitterness an alien and deadly n. which undoes man's best hopes and visions. In his later poem *The Swimmers*, n. serves him for symbols of moral and psychological depth, but is also the place where the action occurs and has the wholeness and resonance of places of boyhood remembered and, though distinct from man, is like man under the aegis of the moral law. Robert Lowell and Anne Sexton present n. brilliantly, almost solipsistically, while yet focusing moral and religious as well as personal problems. Postmodern trendiness, obscure imagery, prosaic rhythms, and epistemically hopeless uncertainty sought as an ideal, will pass.

II. IN CRITICISM. Western critical theory since Plato has centered in ideas of n. Platonic theories of the world and the "image" have influenced crit. as well as poetry, despite Plato's (at least partial) rejection of poetry as an imitation of the world of appearances and as baneful moral influence. Modern "Platonic" theories (those of the Abbé Bremond, Wallace Fowlie, to some degree Maritain) conceive of art as imitating or somehow partaking of, at least by analogy, the transcendent world, a privilege reserved in Plato for the trained and morally good philosopher. The doctrine in the *Ion* of the poet as inspired seems to be ironic, but it has extended a major influence, not ironic.

The central theory of crit. has been, however, Aristotelian, whose primary concept is poetry as the imitation of n. I would contend, in the teeth of some vivid denials and contempt for the trad., that it remains and shall remain the central trad., because it is true. In this theory n. enters into both terms, since the imitation is not only of n. (man's n., primarily), but is natural (according to n.), since it is natural for men to delight in imitation and to respond to the joys and terrors of men not unlike themselves. As developed by Cicero and Quintilian, who insist on the propriety of the three styles, high, middle, and low, to various subject matter, and reinterpreted by Ren. critics (who yoke, with some violence, Horace's *Art of Poetry* to Aristotle's *Poetics*), the theory has been *the* Western critical trad., and its major concepts—imitation and decorum (qq.v.)—though rejected in most modern theory, are still unavoidably *used* in most practical crit.

In this theory, "n." means the subject of imitation; the foundation of accords between emotion, idea, and subject; and the poet's inborn talent ("n." as opposed to "art," "art" meaning the cultivation of one's powers by judgment and practice). The consistency and intelligibility of n. is the ground for the "rules" (q.v.). The 17th-c. theory of the rules is often misunderstood, however. Dryden puts the case clearly: there is only one primary rule, as certain as reason itself—that good poetry should be in accordance with n., both as an imitation (that is, poems should have verisimilitude [q.v.]) and as something made (poems should be in accord with moral and aesthetic law and immutable human n.—else they cannot long please). All other rules are secondary and uncertain, and therefore judgment, trad., mediation, and good sense are permanent essentials of crit.

In the last two centuries, the ideals of imitation and propriety have been widely replaced by the Coleridgean (and Ger. romantic) ideals of imagination and organicism (qq.v.). In this view, poetry is *like* n. rather than an image of it or proper to it. Poems and physical n. are, according to Coleridge, created by different but analogous acts of human imagination. But the newer theory sometimes conceals the old. The notion of lit. as a proper imitation of n. is a hardy plant, and critics nowadays (sometimes in the teeth of their theories) let us know what poetry does or should represent: the organic biological essence of life (Susanne Langer); the harmonizing of emotions (the earlier I. A. Richards); God by analogy and intuition (Wallace Fowlie); the poet's soul (many); Jungian archetypes (Elizabeth Drew); the ambiguous uncertainty of life (Cleanth Brooks); the desperate struggle with forebears achieving the sublimity of blankness (Harold Bloom); the particulars in which reside and vanish all truth (W. C. Williams and Ezra Pound in some moods). In some theories, organic form is the chief good because it better fits (is more *proper* to) the idea of natural evolution than older theories. Or it is sometimes argued, in flamboyant self-inconsistency, that a dynamic, nonmimetic theory is proper to the modern notion of a purposeless n., since value must come from within the human mind rather than from n.

Wallace Stevens' aesthetic is based on a perpetual and desperate philosophical and poetic vacillation—what is agony to him becomes doctrine for some of his followers: poetry should express fragments of confusion, of radical disconnection with God and with n.

See also CONVENTION; DESCRIPTIVE POETRY.

C. V. Deane, *Aspects of 18th-C. N. Poetry* (1935); L. Welch, *Imagination and Human N.* (1935); A. O. Lovejoy and G. Boas, *Primitivism and Related Ideas in Antiquity* (1935)—distinguishes 61 senses of the term "n."; J. W. Beach, *The Concept of N. in 19th-C. Poetry* (1936); D. B. Wilson, "Some Meanings of 'N.' in Ren. Literary Theory," *JHI* 2 (1941), *Ronsard, Poet of N.* (1961); T. Spencer, *Shakespeare and the N. of Man* (1942) H. Trowbridge, "The Place of Rules in Dryden's Crit.," *MP* 44 (1946); W. V. O'Connor, "N. and the Anti-Poetic in Mod. Poetry," *JAAC* 5 (1946); A. O. Lovejoy, "N. as Aesthetic Norm," *Essays in the Hist. of Ideas* (1948); N. MacLean, "From Action to Image," in Crane; Auerbach; Curtius, ch.10; L. L. Martz, *The Poetry of Meditation* (1954); Wellek; R. Tuve, *Images and Themes in Five Poems by Milton* (1957); R. Langbaum, "The New N. Poetry," *ASch* 28 (1959); C. S. Lewis, *Studies in Words* (1960); P. Van Tieghem, *Le Sentiment de la n. dans le préromantisme européen* (1960); P. Ramsey, *The Lively and the Just* (1962), *The Truth of Value* (1985); N. Frye, "N. and Homer," *Fables of Identity* (1963); E. W. Taylor, *N. and Art in Ren. Lit.* (1964); *New Essays on Plato and Aristotle*, ed. R. Bamborough (1965); G. Boas, "N.," *DHI*; A. J. Close, "Commonplace Theories of Art and N. in Cl. Antiquity and the Ren.," *JHI* 30 (1969); F. W. Leakey, *Baudelaire and N.* (1969); L. Manley, *Convention, 1500–1700* (1970); Saisselin; J. Gitzen, "British N. Poetry Now," *MQ* 15 (1974); O. Barfield, *The Rediscovery of Meaning and Other Essays* (1977); I. Berlin, *Concepts and Categories* (1979); *The Feeling for N. and the Landscape of Man*, ed. P. von Hallberg (1980); L. Wittgenstein, *Culture and Value*, ed. G. H. Wright, tr. P. Winch (1980); *Approaches to N. in the Middle Ages*, ed. L. D. Robert (1982); *Relativism*, ed. M. Krausz and J. Meiland (1982); R. Modiano, *Coleridge and the Concept of N.* (1985); C. E. Hummel, *The Galileo Connection* (1986); I. Wylie, *Young Coleridge and the Philosophers of N.* (1988); G. Rotella, *Reading and Writing N.* (1990); M. Oelschlaeger, *The Idea of Wilderness from Prehistory to the Present* (1991); J. Bate, *Romantic Ecology* (1991). P.R.

NAVAHO POETRY. See AMERICAN INDIAN POETRY.

NEAR RHYME, generic r., half r., imperfect r., oblique r., off r., parar., partial r., slant r. There is no standard term in Eng.; "n. r." will be used here as a cover term for several varieties of rhyming practice which are related to yet neither fulfill the canonical definition of r. (see RHYME) nor exceed it, as in rich r. (q.v.). Judgmental adjectives were better avoided, for they carry the pejorative implication that a n. r. is a failure to achieve true r., either on account of deficiency of lang. resources or incompetence of the poet—equally dubious assumptions, both. "N." must be taken, therefore, not in the sense of "imperfect" but rather of "approximate," i.e. close to the narrow band of instances qualifying as canonical end r. but outside it, in the wider field of "related but alternative forms of sound correspondence" (Scherr). Within the Eng. taxonomy, most forms of n. r., of which there are several, amount to various complex types of consonance (q.v.) and produce such rs. as *justice/hostess* (Swift), *port/chart* (Dickinson), *grope/cup, maze/coze, drunkard/conquered*. Žirmunskij distinguishes the forms of r. as *exact, augmented* (by deletion or addition), and *altered* (by both, meaning substitution), a typology accepted and extended by Gasparov.

In judging rs., it is important not to be misled by shifts in historical phonology, whereby rs. that now seem only n. were actually true in their day, e.g. Pope's *obey/tea*. Further, it is important that n. r. not be conceived solely in terms of Eng. practice, for since the early 20th c., the status of "n. r." in Eng. has been problematized, while in Rus., for example, prosodists since Žirmunskij have recognized both "approximate" and "inexact" r. as part of the standard definition of r. (see Scherr). In Celtic prosody (q.v.), too, esp. Ir. and Welsh, n. r. has been recognized and approved as an important and constructive element of rhyming technique since the Middle Ages under the rubric of *generic r.* (q.v.; see also CELTIC PROSODY); and indeed, n. r. first appears in Eng. deliberately in Vaughan, in imitation of Welsh prosody. In Fr. prosody of the early 20th c., the term *accord* was proposed by J. Romains (Louis Farigoule [1885–1972]) and G. Chennevière, poets and theorists of the movement known as *Unanimism*, for a variety of forms of consonance and n. r. The accords of Romains were attacked by Grammont but may have influenced the "parar." of Wilfred Owen.

In fact, n. r. has played an important role in most of the major Western prosodies of the late 19th and early 20th cs.—not only British (Hopkins, Yeats, Owen, Auden, Day Lewis, Spender, Mac-Neice, Dylan Thomas) and Am. (Dickinson—from whom much of the later Am. practice derives), but esp. Rus. (Blok, Bryusov, Mayakovskij, Pasternak). In Eng., the trad. of canonical r. was old but not deeply established, having always had to contend with the enormous force of Shakespearean and Miltonic blank verse and, after 1855, free verse. But Rus. never developed extensive trads. of either blank or free verse, so that in the 20th c., Rus. modernist poets experimented extensively with new and variant r. forms—as many as 50% of Mayakovskij's rs. are noncanonical. In the West, the avant-garde prosodies sought to dispense with both meter and r., but in Russia it was only the former: r. practice was not abandoned but

expanded. Experiments with the one went hand in hand with experiments with the other, but renunciation of the one did not necessarily entail the other as well. In Eng., free verse of course dropped r., but several major poets who retained traditional verseforms and meters, e.g. Yeats and Auden, also chose to explore n. r.: Yeats's practice includes rs. such as *push/rush* and *up/drop* in a sonnet, for example ("Leda and the Swan"). Wilfred Owen developed what he called "parar.," a kind of frame r. in which the initial and final consonants are repeated while the vowel is varied—e.g. *killed/cold, mystery/mastery, friend/frowned*—deliberately to express the wrenching sensation of war. This sort of effect is explored also by Dickinson and Hopkins, as it had been by Vaughan.

In much late-Victorian and Edwardian crit., one finds frequent attacks by reactionary prosodists on all less-than-correct rhyming as decadent, degenerate, and incompetent, attacks epitomized in Saintsbury and Brander Matthews. But in retrospect such practice is to be seen not as a falling-away from a standard but as a redefinition of that standard. In a radical age, the breaking of conventions is an expansive and creative act. N. r. is in this sense not an abandonment of r. in defeat but an opening up of the r. canon—not supplanting r. but enriching it.

There is evidence from Rus., if any were needed, that each poet develops her or his own distinctive idiolect in n. r., preferring to explore not the entire range of possibilities, but rather only certain types. But no extensive and reliable set of data on r. has yet been collected. The practice of n. r. in artverse is of course the primary interest, but it has also been used extensively and probably for much longer in light verse, satire, and (perhaps) dialect poetry (qq.v.).

K. Meyer, *Primer of Ir. Metrics* (1909); V. Žirmunskij, *Rifma* (1923), ch. 3; J. Romains and G. Chennevière, *Petit traité de versif.* (1923); J. Hytier, *Les techniques modernes du vers français* (1923), rev. by Grammont in *RLR* 62 (1923); T. W. Herbert, "Near-Rimes and Paraphones," *SR* 14 (1937); L. Pszczołowska, *Rym* (1972); B. P. Gončarov, *Zvukovaja organizatsija stixa i problemy rifmy* (1973); M. Shapiro, *Asymmetry* (1976), ch. 4; W. E. Rickert, "R. Terms," *Style* 12 (1978); M. L. Gasparov, "Towards an Analysis of Rus. Inexact R.," *Metre, Rhythm, Stanza, R.*, ed. G. S. Smith (1980); Scott 233–36; W. Frawley, "A Note on the Phonology of Slant R.," *Lang&S* 17 (1984); Scherr, ch. 4; B. J. Small, *Positive as Sound* (1990)—Dickinson.

T.V.F.B.

NEGATIVE CAPABILITY is Keats's phrase for a power of sympathy and a freedom from self-consciousness which peculiarly characterize the artist. It occurs in a letter of 22 December 1818: there is a quality that goes "to form a Man of Achievement esp. in lit. & which Shakespeare possessed so enormously—I mean *N. C.*, that is when man is capable of being in uncertainties, Mysteries, doubts, without any irritable reaching after fact & reason." The quality has to do as well with a capability "of remaining content with half knowledge." Elsewhere, speaking of the "poetical Character" in general, Keats observes that "it has no character—it enjoys light and shade; it lives in gusto, be it foul or fair, high or low, rich or poor, mean or elevated—It has as much delight in conceiving an Iago as an Imogen. What shocks the virtuous philosopher delights the camelion Poet."

Keats found a clue for many of these speculations in the writings of Hazlitt—particularly the essays "On *Gusto*" and "On Imitation" and the lecture "On Shakespeare and Milton." The character of the artist is there said to be so absorbed in the act of creation that it subsists only inside the act. In the process of imagining, all the self-regarding data of ordinary life seem to vanish. Thus the artist's curious attentiveness to other persons and things, like that of the chameleon or the ventriloquist, may outwardly resemble the selflessness of one who has no character. The work of art, in turn, elicits our attention in a way that requires the giving up of ordinary selfish and social concerns. It leaves in suspense our usual interest in moral judgment for the sake of a new interest in beauty and truth.

In late romantic and modernist usage, n. c. separates into the rival doctrines of sincerity (q.v.) and "the truth of masks" (see PERSONA). Wilde illustrates the change concisely: "what people call insincerity is simply a method by which we can multiply our personalities." The artist still "has as much delight in Caliban as in Ariel, in rags as he has in cloth of gold, and recognizes the artistic beauty of ugliness." But Wilde has in view a self-conscious stance very remote from Keats's. The modernist precept in favor of "impersonality" seems to have arisen partly as a reaction against this, yet it too carries a trace of its origin in the idea of n. c. Poetry, writes Eliot, is "a continual extinction of personality." But, he adds, "only those who have personality and emotions know what it means to want to escape from these things." See also EMPATHY AND SYMPATHY.—W. J. Bate, *John Keats* (1963), ch. 10; N. C. Starr, "N. C. in Keats's Diction," *KSJ* 15 (1966); D. Bromwich, *Hazlitt* (1983).   D.B.

NÉGRITUDE. See AFRICAN POETRY, *In French*; SOMALI POETRY.

NEOCLASSICAL POETICS.

I. GENERAL SURVEY. N. p. concerns the literary aspect of that broad movement in European culture and the arts extending from the early 17th c. to approximately the mid 18th c. Separate literary cultures offer individual attitudes and varying emphases, but in terms of what is more widely shared, n. p. is first of all a set of interests deriving from an effort to imitate and reconstitute the literary values of ancient Greece and Rome, continuing the attention of humanism to those values (see RENAISSANCE POETICS) but doing so in reaction against what were thought the stylistic indiscipline and excessive invention (q.v.) of Ren. poets, esp. the *concettismo* of the Italians and the Eng. metaphysicals. This reactive mood also sets n. p. against other artistic tendencies in the late 17th and early 18th cs., esp. efforts at verbal wit, exotic fiction, and contemp. realism. Two general criteria influenced n. crit. with respect to its championing of the ancients: first, the belief that their poems were a more direct and faithful representation of nature (q.v.), esp. human nature, than has usually been achieved since; and second, the conviction that the restraint, simplicity, and impersonality in style observable in the best Roman poets were more likely to please an audience. These two values were the principal grounds for an embattled polemic mounted against what was called a barbaric or "gothic" taste (Bouhours, *Conversations of Aristo and Eugene* [1671]; Addison, *Spectator*, nos. 58–63 [1711]).

According to Ben Jonson, who cites Horace, imitation (q.v.) properly exercised consists in assimilating the best of ancient poetic forms and style to a personal idiom, "to draw forth out of the best and choisest flowers, with the Bee, and turne all into Honey" (*Timber* [1620–35]). This concept developed into an adherence to Cl. ideas of decorum and genre (qq.v.), but there are various shadings of opinion. Bouhours warns against "larceny" and limiting oneself to Cl. models, while La Bruyère gloomily announces that the ancients have already said everything worth saying (*Characters* [1687]). Samuel Johnson on the other hand recommends caution on the grounds that a copy is almost always inferior to its model (*The Rambler* 121 [1751]).

The cult of imitation, however much its partisans might insist upon assimilation and adaptation, nevertheless tended to imply the inimitable mastery of Homer and Virgil, and to a lesser extent of the Gr. and Roman dramatists and lyric poets. It thus gave rise to debates over the relative worth of ancient and modern writers (see QUERELLE DES ANCIENS ET DES MODERNES) that often took the form of quarreling over which group had the better contact with nature. Boileau, for example, mocks the literal realism of Saint-Amant, who has the fish watching the Israelites marching between the parted waters of the Red Sea (*Art poétique* [1674], Canto 3), and Swift in *The Battle of the Books* (1710) charges the moderns with spinning matter out of their own entrails, like spiders. The ancients, having discovered the natural "laws" governing literary genres, which in turn realize the various forms of human social organization and universal (as opposed to particular) experience, thereby stood as a model to be followed by all but the most exceptionally imaginative genius (Pope, *Essay on Crit.* [1711]). This argument depends upon a view that associates the ancients with common sense, nature, and the rules (q.v.) of composition, though it must be noted that the rules were often understood as practical guides. Such is the lesson Corneille hoped to teach in his three "Discours" introducing the 1660 ed. of his works. These essays, his belated answer to the Fr. Académie's adverse judgment of *Le Cid* (1637), set common sense and the artistic judgment of the poet against the arbitrary authority of the state and trad. At the same time, the natural, far from being the detailed recording of current actuality, is seen as manifested in the typical and in that which transcends temporal and cultural difference (Wellek 1.15–16). The value of such imperatives is that they help to make the works of the past in some sense contemporary. The disadvantage, as the partisans of the modern pointed out, is the discouraging of contemp. talent, the elimination of freshness and variety, and the hardening of poetic forms into fixed genres. One result is the paradox that the most conventional literary forms are considered the closest to nature.

This view needs to be reconciled with the 17th- and 18th-c. interest in science, marked by a shift from a concept of nature as a set of metaphysical laws to physical processes of cause and effect, a shift first articulated by Bacon (*Advancement of Learning* [1605]). Nature became the object of observation, of something seen, itemized, tested, and understood so it could be exploited and used. This "scientific" attitude had a number of consequences for 17th- and 18th-c. critical doctrine, among them a belief in some quarters that the "dynamic" processes found in the world of things might also be discovered in the world of man. Less drastically, n. p. was encouraged by the 17th-c. interest in science to identify the laws of lit., literary structure, creation, and affect—in other words to provide a rational system for poetry and the other arts (Wellek 12–14).

The concept of probability, which for Aristotle had governed the structure of plot (q.v.) and guaranteed the universality of poetry, formed the heart of this system and was justified on the grounds that inventions that were fantastic or divergent from common experience would be unwelcome to an audience (see VERISIMILITUDE). The unities are defended by many critics on the grounds that not to observe them is to violate the audience's sense of the correspondence between stage events and likely events. As Crites in Dryden's *An Essay of Dramatic Poesy* (1668) remarks, "that play is thought to be the nearest imitation of nature, whose plot is confined within [24 hours]." The rules, together with severe judgments on any evidence of stylistic excess or gratuitous ornament, had the effect of imposing strict limitations on poetic invention or exuberance, but their implications in n. p. go well beyond their apparent status as arbitrary, conventional, and restrictive. They belong to a system of probability that offers credibility to plot and the signs by which action and character are expressed (Patey 90–133). Even so, it escaped no one's notice that from Homer to Milton there were a few exceptional figures whose works could be seen to exemplify the very faults of logic or sense which n. critics liked to enumerate or whose genius seemed to have nothing to do with the observance of established conventions. Moreover, the general n. preference for the epic (q.v.) as the first among genres is evident in comments testifying to its scale and abundance, e.g. Boileau's approval of its lavish use of trope and myth (*Art poétique*), Le Bossu's insistence on the greatness and importance of its action (*Traité du poème épique* [1675]), Hobbes's seconding of the "majesty" of the heroic style (*Answer to Davenant's Preface to* Gondibert [1650]), and Dennis's enthusiastic endorsement of *Paradise Lost* as "the greatest poem ever written" (*The Grounds of Crit. in Poetry* [1704]). And despite Le Bossu's position that epic poems are rationally planned, tightly structured, and basically didactic works, what Pope called "a grace beyond the reach of art," and the French termed "je ne sais quoi" (q.v.), the inexplicable, was widely acknowledged. Some 20th-c. scholars argue that this acknowledgement in critics such as Dryden or Boileau or Johnson reflects a commendable effort to offer a balanced theory of poetics (e.g. Mahoney 22–32; Engell 15–43), but it can also be seen as a reflection of a profound distrust of the contemporary and of the subjective, a view bolstered by the tendency in 17th- and 18th-c. critical theory to subordinate the writer to his task and his audience, to caution him against vanity and self-indulgence, charges from which Johnson does not exempt Shakespeare, however generous his praise. Nevertheless, contemp. poetry had strong defenders, e.g. Dryden early in his career (*An Essay of Dramatic Poesy*), Charles Perrault ("Le Siècle de Louis Le Grand" [1687], and Addison (*Spectator* 160 [1711]).

If it is to offer its audience images of nature, then, as John Dennis asserted, "the speech by which poetry makes its imitation must be pathetic" (*The Advancement and Reformation of Poetry* [1701]). For all the n. claims to a rational, commonsensical, orderly poetic system, it is nevertheless the case that the prerogatives of form exist side by side with a firm belief that the central appeal of poems, plays, and works of fiction is their representation of human emotion (q.v.) or their providing the audience with an emotional rendering of human events. This means that n. p. invests in the passions as the objects of representation (q.v.) and in emotional response as the portion of the audience, though such orthodox thinkers as Corneille and Rapin also suppose that by the end of a tragedy the spectator's mind must be, as Corneille remarks, "serene."

N. and 18th-c. attention to emotion has further implications. Aristotle proposed as the source of the audience's emotion the movement of tragic action from ignorance to knowledge. This gives way to a mode of action as conflict between irreconcilable claims, and the audience is prompted to respond to the drama of inner conflict, moving away from Aristotle's priority of action to that of character (Corneille, "Essay on Tragedy" [1660]). Two separate but related lines of thought about the impact of tragedy (q.v.) may be noted. On the one hand, there is a reiteration and partial rethinking of the Aristotelian notion of tragic pleasure. Catharsis (q.v.), according to Rapin (*Réflexions sur la Poétique d'Aristote* [1674]), is the spectator's total absorption into the feelings of tragic characters, so that the soul is "shaken" and the mind is cured of its fears; earlier, Boileau had simply required strong emotionalism, and Corneille had seen the tragic emotions as a kind of warning to the audience. Dryden argues that emotions other than pity and fear are common in modern tragedies ("Heads of an Answer to Rymer" [1677]), and Rymer himself assents that the effectiveness of tragedy lies in its management of poetic justice ("Tragedies of the Last Age Considered" [1678]). Generally, in the early 18th c., there is an increasing emphasis on sympathy or compassion (see EMPATHY) as the spectatorial response to suffering; this is perhaps a reaction to the partial displacement of strictly Cl. forms by domestic pathos.

The second feature of tragic crit. is what has been called the "Lucretian return upon ourselves," the argument that spectacles of distress and suffering are tolerable and pleasurable because the spectators are themselves exempt, onlookers only (Hathaway). Such a view often equates spectacles such as public executions, in which people actually suffer and die, with theatrical representations. But Du Bos, for one, argued that no one ever mistook a play for real events (*Réflexions critiques sur la poésie et la peinture* [1719–33]). Perhaps the most sophisticated (though not an influential) theory is Hume's proposal that the formal properties of the tragedy as a work of art transform and shape events and emotions so that the responses of spectators are themselves different than they would be to an actual event: "the fiction of tragedy softens the passion, by an infusion of new feeling" ("Of Tragedy" [1757]; cf. Cohen).

Interest in kinds of audience response also centers in the *sublime* (q.v.). The term had been used in the Ren. to characterize the grand style (see STYLE), which was thought to prompt the strongest emotion. Boileau's tr. of *On the Sublime* (1674), and esp. his introduction and subsequent com-

ments ("Réflexions"), served to promote an entirely different concept, emphasizing grandness of conception translated by simple and understated lang. The sublime rapidly became a popular subject of critical thought in England and Germany (less so in France and Italy), eventually extending well beyond theories of style or literary representation to include the arts and the experience of landscape, esp. features of overwhelming grandeur such as the Alps (Monk; Nicolson). As a theory of emotional experience, the sublime served n. p. precisely because it envisaged a transcendence of the limits, visual and imaginative, central to n. aesthetics, offering a contrast of scale by which to differentiate types of aesthetic experience. Artistic representations observing human scale and clearly perceived limits were the province of *beauty*, a difficult term in that it evoked debate over whether aesthetic experience was entirely subjective or was the consequence of particular properties in the viewed object (de Crousaz, *Traité du beau* [1685]; Hutcheson, *Inquiry into the Origin of Our Ideas of Beauty and Virtue* [1725]). Implicated in the debate over the nature of beauty, which was usually defined as unity in multiplicity and as symmetry or its perception, was the troubled question of taste (q.v.). Apart from the rather obvious effort of late 17th- and 18th-c. critics to argue for a universal standard of taste, based either in the authority of Cl. models or the theories of Johnson and Hume that time reveals universal excellence, taste reveals the n. hunger for an experience of art as spontaneous and uncalculated as possible, joined to a recognition that a superior taste requires study, experience, and civilized company (Burke, *A Philosophical Enquiry into the Origin of Our Ideas of the Sublime and the Beautiful* [1757]; Hume, "Of the Standard of Taste" [1757]).

The n. interest in measurable limits shows in a concern for the sensory, and esp. the visual, as a component of lang. New significance was given in 17th- and 18th-c. theory to the ancient rhetorical notion that lang. could render objects as if present to the sight. Locke's theory that lang. represents "ideas" (i.e. mental images) of objects, rather than objects themselves, results in an emphasis on mental "seeing" as a process, as opposed to a static, quasi-pictorial representation (Burke; Hagstrum [1958]). A word may prompt us to recall an object, or more properly the idea of an object, but our individual experience, as described by associationist psychology, entails that what we recall is a context. This complicated the n. desire for clarity of representation by suggesting variability of meaning, a problem intensified by the post-Lockean doctrine that words have arbitrarily, not naturally, assigned meanings or referents. It was also eventually to trouble the effort to establish a universal standard of taste, as well as the persistent effort to discover in lang. a means to reconnect the mind with essential nature, that is, with states of sympathetic feeling.

These tendencies combine in the n. interest in the ancient formula, *ut pictura poesis* (q.v.). This emerged at first in efforts to make fairly simple parallels between the plastic and verbal arts (Dryden, "A Parallel of Poetry and Painting" [1695]), and then, beginning with Du Bos' *Réflexions* and culminating in Lessing's *Laocoön*, developed into a countermovement concentrating on the psychological and aesthetic consequences of the radical differences between these media. Poetry was seen to be conditioned by the temporal linearity of lang., and painting and sculpture understood to represent frozen moments in a narrative—notions which for both Du Bos and Lessing guarantee the superiority of poetry. At the same time, the critical effort involved in these and similar discussions continued to regard words as vehicles rather than objects. In moving from a debate over style to theories of perception and affect, the attention to lang. also produced extensive efforts, such as those of Condillac, to establish the origins of lang., an activity continued in preromantic and romantic critical theory (see ROMANTIC AND POSTROMANTIC POETICS). Yet behind the awareness of lang. as a dynamic system of representation, there lingers the n. desire for a vision of universal and permanent forms and fixed truths (Aarsleff), a desire suggested by the wide interest in the visual and also by the efforts in 17th- and 18th-c. crit. to refine and settle vernacular styles into enduring modes.

II. NATIONAL LITERATURES. A. *French.* France is generally conceded to have established the main outlines of n. p. to which the rest of Europe responded and referred. One of the earliest critics to offer prescriptive standards for poetry, Jean Chapelain censures Marino's *Adone* for its lack of verisimilitude (what ought to be) and its promotion of the marvelous in excessive ornament (q.v.): both, he argues, distract the reader to secondary and inessential features of the poem. His approach is neo-Aristotelian and Horatian: he prescribes utility joined to pleasure, proclaims the natural origin of the rules and conventional genres, and insists on a style limited to what the subject matter dictates ("Letter . . . Conveying His Opinion of *Adone*" [1623]). Chapelain is famous for having attacked Corneille's handling of the unities in his *Sentiments of the Academy on the Cid* (1638), which eventually prompted Corneille's *Three Discourses on the Dramatic Poem* (1660), in which the playwright generally adhered to a version of Cl. rules while significantly modifying them. Racine offered a more strictly correct dramatic practice, one that combined severe formal restraint enclosing powerful emotional conflict. The 17th c., which saw the appearance of the major writers of Fr. Classicism (see CLASSICISM), Corneille, Racine, Molière, and La Fontaine, has been described as a time when poetry achieved an especially concentrated analysis of the human character (Peyre 87), but it should also be understood as a period of primary critical attention to the impact of poetry on its audience.

Strictness of generic form and prescriptions for style are the twin poles of Fr. Classicism as urged by the two most influential critics of the later 17th c., Bouhours and Boileau. Bouhours crystallized the reaction against *concettismo* and baroque support of verbal ornament (q.v.), arguing for restraint in metaphor and a congruity of subject matter and expression. He thus established the influential view that verbal ornament by itself is vain, that it can be tolerated only by logical indebtedness to a prior and authorizing concept. Boileau expressed similar views in arguing for a reasoned and calculated exercise of the established poetic genres, though his comments on the sublime propose less obvious relationships, and his instructions for tragic drama, in contrast to the pedantic d'Aubignac, allow room for elevated diction and strong metaphor as agencies of powerful emotional effect. Generally the tone of Boileau's treatise is reasonable, but his critical procedure accepts the inevitability of genres and the aim of pleasing as requiring the knowledgeable artist, that is, a man of taste (Brody 51). Some modern crit. tends to emphasize the sanity, rational freedom, even the wise conformity of the major Fr. Classicist critics and poets (Borgerhoff; Peyre 36–41). Although there is a tendency to see Classicism as dissipated in the early 18th c. under pressure from Enlightenment thinking (Peyre), Voltaire continues the standard views of tragic form, and Du Bos, who explores the topic of pleasure, can be seen as extending n. interests in theatrical spectacle. Rapin's neo-Aristotelian writings were widely echoed, among other things in maintaining the doctrine of illusion in conformity with "bienséance" (decorum, q.v.) and verisimilitude (q.v.; Hobson 34). If one wants to witness the dissolving of orthodox n. p., perhaps the best place to look is Diderot's dramatic crit. (*Entretiens sur le fils naturel* [1757], *De la poésie dramatique* [1758], *Le Paradoxe sur le comédien* [1770–77]) which argues against the maneuvers of illusionism and the theatricality of rules and poetic lang. Nevertheless, the triumph of Fr. Classicism lies in its concern for the theatrical both as genre and as a basis for theoretical speculation.

B. *English* n. p. has its foreshadowings in Jonson and extends nearly to the end of the 18th c. (Crane), but its maturity owes much to the Fr. example, however often Eng. critics deplore Fr. pedantry and rigidity. Dryden translated Boileau's *Art poétique*, and though he was sensitive to a variety of critical views, the burden of his dramatic crit. is to argue with Fr. theories with Fr. examples in mind. Thomas Rymer, the translator of Rapin, is the most obviously orthodox of the Eng. n. critics, demanding strict attention to the unities and rigid probability, as his negative account of *Othello* indicates ("A Short View of Tragedy"). Addison's view of Eng. tragedy is scarcely more generous, measuring the local taste for "butchery" on stage against superior Continental delicacy (cf. *Spectator* nos. 42, 44). Many critics in spite of their allegiance to Classicist standards accepted what were considered the obvious deviations of Shakespeare—Dryden, Pope, and Johnson are the critics most often cited—while others, such as Addison, sought to accommodate Milton to n. standards (*Spectator*, no. 279).

More broadly viewed, Eng. n. p. is a continuing effort to reduce lit. and its crit. to a system governed by a theory of pleasure derived from empirical psychology and responsive to what Addison calls a "polite" imagination (*Spectator* nos. 409–10). On the one hand, this disposition shares in the Fr. distaste for excesses of stylistic ornament and penchant for powerful emotional affect; on the other hand, it anticipates the extensive Eng. and Scottish interest in aesthetics. Addison, though himself most unsystematic, with an assist from Shaftesbury, is the key figure, raising the issues of taste, imagination (q.v.), and visual and verbal affect that were taken up by Hutcheson, Burke, Hume, Gerard, and Lord Kames, to name the more obvious.

Dennis's interest in emotionalism (*The Grounds of Crit. in Poetry* [1704]), Addison's discussion of the sublime in *Spectator* no. 412, and Akenside's incoherent but immensely popular poem, *The Pleasures of the Imagination* (1774), helped make the sublime a central topic of Eng. crit. throughout the 18th c. Burke's definition of the sublime as terror of the unseen links it to tragedy, and it has from the time of Hobbes been tied to heroic poetry, esp. by Dennis and Addison. Although the sublime was generally supposed as a result of Boileau's theory to be a category of experience and thought beyond lang., it was nevertheless seen to result in the lang. of transport. At the same time, its devel. in Eng. was closely linked to an interest in landscape.

For many modern critics, Samuel Johnson represents the most mature and flexible representative of n. thought in his insistence on a timeless, universal critical standard ("Preface to Shakespeare" [1765]), his belief that the poet's task is to record the typical (*Rasselas*, ch. 10 [1759]), and his dislike of romance. Consistently, he censures the metaphysicals for a lack of logic, while conceding their learning, and praises Shakespeare while depriving him of everything local, Elizabethan, and idiosyncratic (*Life of Cowley* [1779]; "Preface to Shakespeare").

C. *German* n. p. has two phases. The first, exemplified by J. C. Gottsched's *Versuch einer kritischen Dichtkunst* (1730), is deeply indebted to Boileau and Fr. Classicism, and characterized by their doctrines of imitation, style, and genre (qq.v.). The second and aesthetic phase, which owes something to Gottsched's concept of beauty as the perfection of the poem, begins in J.

Winckelmann's *Thoughts on the Imitation of the Painting and Sculpture of the Greeks* (1755) and culminates in the critical reflections and early work of Goethe. Ger. neoclassicism overlaps substantially with romanticism (q.v.), sometimes in the same writer. Both strains are powerfully philosophical, n. p. being grounded in the rationalism of Leibniz and the Cartesian psychology of Wolff. There is a consistent and conscious line of critical theorizing from A. G. Baumgarten, G. Friedrich Meier, and M. Mendelssohn to Lessing that argues for a poetics following the general laws of reason, probability, and internal consistency deduced from the nature of the representational faculties. This theory links the poem to beauty as a relation between the object, its representation, and the effect in the soul. Since the relationship is all important, the verbal sign must be transparent. Lessing develops this theory by proposing that the object of aesthetic enjoyment is not the words of the poetic text but the imaginative concepts they prompt (*Laocoön*, ch. 17). Ger. n. aestheticism flourished in the context of the Hellenism popularized by Winckelmann, for whom the Gr. concept of beauty was supposed "noble simplicity and tranquil grandeur" (42), a view challenged by Lessing's theory of narrative and dramatic dynamism.

The Classicism of Schiller and Goethe proposes a new direction, beginning with Schiller's idea of an absolute value for the work of art independent of its effect on the reader or spectator. Schiller opposes mimetic emotional immediacy and requires an artistic idealizing (review of Bürger's poems, 1791; Hohendahl 80–81). Goethe supplements Schiller by a concept of style that universalizes and objectifies, producing the Cl. symbolic form as a cognition of essences; he thus moves toward a concept of lit. as autonomous. (Hohendahl 85).

D. *Italian* n. p. is complicated by the 17th-c. Fr. attack on Ren. It. poets, esp. Tasso and Marino, which divided the sympathies of It. critics drawn to n. doctrine. With the arrival of G. B. Gravina, however, a spirit of undivided neoclassicism took over, a reaction against Marino having taken root in the founding of the academy named "Arcadia" at Rome in 1690. Dedicated to the propagation of "buon gusto" and the establishment of the laws of poetry manifested in generic orthodoxy and simplicity of style and feeling, the influence of the Arcadian Academy reached well into the 18th c. Gravina's attention to the ties between science and art included an interest in the early hist. of poetry, esp. the Homeric poems, but unlike Vico, who looked on early poetic expression as a necessary feature of barbaric humanity (see ROMANTIC AND POSTROMANTIC POETICS, I.D.), Gravina finds in them an expression of Gr. life. Another Arcadian, G. M. de'Crescimbeni, links the vernacular to Gr. poetry and prescribes an internal spiritual beauty against external, superficial ornament. Somewhat differently, the familiar topics of the beautiful and the true as the objects of imitation, as well as the problem of taste, appear in G. Spalletti's *Saggio sopra la bellezza* (1765). An empiricist, Spalletti contends that beauty is determined by repeated sensory observation and that aesthetic pleasure has its source in human *amour propre* (self-regard). The Enlightenment interest in lit. hist. emerges in the extensive antiquarian studies of L. A. Muratori, who with Gravina sought in promoting visual representation and probability to recover the best elements of It. Ren. poetry from the indiscipline of the baroque (q.v.). A different side of It. neoclassicism appears in the work of M. Cesarotti. An admirer of Gravina, he was familiar with British empiricism, argued against Du Bos and Hume about tragic emotion, praised Lucian over Homer, and produced important essays on the philosophy of linguistic change.

E. *Spanish.* The effects of European n. p. and of neoclassicism in general are belated in Sp. culture and co-exist with vestiges of baroque styles during the early 18th c. and with sentimental and preromantic impulses somewhat later. As elsewhere, Fr. Classicist doctrine was imported to combat what some saw as excessive and lawless habits of expression. A beginning is illustrated in the Real Academia Espanol's effort to regularize the vernacular in its dictionary (1714), and the attempt at encouraging a standard marks the *Poética* (1737) of I. Luzan, a Boileau-like manifesto urging moral purpose in lit. by means of common sense, clarity and simplicity of style, restraint of the imagination, verisimilitude, and the imitation of nature. A member of the symptomatically named Academia del Buen Gusto, Luzan belonged to an anti-Góngora set in reaction to baroque style, much as had their Fr. predecessors Bouhours and Boileau. The Benedictine essayist B. J. Feijoo (1676–1764) was perhaps the most instrumental figure in urging Northern European culture on Spain. His volumes entitled *Teatro critico universal* (1726–39) and *Cartas eruditas y curiosas* (1742–60) involved every conceivable subject while focusing on ignorance and superstition, encouraged literary rules, but conceded the exemption of genius (*no sé qué*).

Later 18th-c. Sp. n. p. is exemplified by N. de Moratin, editor of the periodical *El Poeta* (1764–) and a tragedian. His work argued for traditional values and historical and patriotic subjects, but like much Sp. n. tragedy at this time, it reflected the taste of the court rather than the theatre-going population at large. His son, L. F. Moratin, produced comedies and within a n. framework developed a form of comedy featuring contests between the forces of reason and unreason. Besides the obvious influence of writers such as Boileau, Voltaire, and Rousseau, educated Sp. taste was conversant with the works of André, Batteux, Du Bos, Diderot, and Marmontel, as well as Hutcheson, Addison, Pope, Shaftesbury, Burke, and Blair. And

as in the countries from which Sp. n. crit. drew its examples, it gave way at the end of the century to preromantic and romantic tendencies with which it had coexisted in its later stages, tendencies that in various ways dissipated concerns for critical rationalism, rules, imitation, stylistic moderation and simplicity, and various forms of restraint.

F. *Russian.* Almost entirely derivative from Fr. and Eng. models, Rus. n. p. was encouraged by Peter the Great's efforts to modernize Rus. culture. It largely took shape as an interest in the standard literary genres and their rules or features, as presented in Boileau's *Art poétique.* Much translated into Rus. in the 18th c., this work was seminal in encouraging judgment, discrimination, and simplicity of style, though M. Lomonosov, with some affinity for the strain of préciosité (q.v.) in 17th-c. Fr. lit., and influenced in part by Ger. baroque aesthetics, in part by the work of the Jesuit N. Caussin, offered a more emotive and rhetorically ornamental version of the ode. At the same time, he accepted the Cl. rhetorical doctrine of three levels of style. A more thoroughly conventional adaptation of Fr. doctrine informs the Kiev Academy lectures of F. Prokopovich on poetics and rhetoric (1705–7). These insisted on imitation of Gr. and Lat. models for style and repeated the usual Horatian imperatives of delight and utility.

The central figure in Rus. neoclassicism is A. P. Sumarokov. Using Boileau to propagate the concept of dramatic rules, Sumarokov wrote in some detail on the genres and unities and discussed the major figures in Fr. Classicism, as well as exhibiting some acquaintance with Shakespeare, Milton, Tasso, and Camoës. In all he wrote nine tragedies, imitating Racine, Corneille, and Voltaire, a practice that indicates that n. imitation was as much an effort to adapt nearly contemporary models as it was a conformity to Gr. or Roman originals (Brown 119–23). Other features of the Rus. movement may be seen in the ode on taste of V. I. Maikov, a follower of Sumarakov's, and in the didacticism of G. R. Derzhavhin. Although the dominance of neoclassicism in Rus. lasted only a brief time (ca. 1747–70), when the drift towards romanticism begins, it is important in Europeanizing and modernizing Rus. lit. and critical thinking and in providing examples and concepts that significantly broadened and sophisticated Rus. letters. See also CLASSICISM; NAIVE-SENTIMENTAL; PREROMANTICISM; ROMANTIC AND POSTROMANTIC POETICS; RULES; SENSIBILITY; SENTIMENTALITY; SUBLIME.

GENERAL STUDIES: K. Borinski, *Die Antike in Poetik und Kunsttheorie,* 2 v. (1914–23); S. Monk, *The Sublime: A Study of Critical Theories in 18th-C. Eng.* (1935); B. Hathaway, "The Lucretian 'Return upon Ourselves' in 18th-C. Theories of Tragedy," *PMLA* 62 (1947); J. Hagstrum, *Samuel Johnson's Lit. Crit.* (1952), *The Sister Arts* (1958); R. S. Crane, *The Langs. of Crit. and the Structure of Poetry* (1953); Wellek; Wimsatt and Brooks; M. H. Nicolson,

Mountain Gloom and Mountain Glory (1959); R. Cohen, "The Transformation of Passion: A Study of Hume's Theories of Tragedy," *PQ* 41 (1962), "The Augustan Mode in Eng. Poetry," *ECS* 1 (1967); L. Lipking, *The Ordering of the Arts in 18th-C. England* (1970); Saisselin; T. Jones and B. Nicol, *N. Dramatic Crit., 1560–1770* (1976); H. Aarsleff, *From Locke to Saussure* (1982); D. Patey, *Probability and Literary Form* (1984); J. Mahoney, *The Whole Internal Universe: Imitation and the New Defense of Poetry* (1985); J. Engell, *Forming the Critical Mind: Dryden to Coleridge* (1989); R. L. Montgomery, *Terms of Response* (1992).

NATIONAL LITERATURES: A. *French*: R. Bray, *La Formation de la doctrine classique en France* (1931); E. Borgerhoff, *The Freedom of Fr. Classicism* (1950); *CBFL*, v. 4, 4a; J. Brody *Boileau and Longinus* (1958); H. Peyre, *Qu'est-ce que le classicisme?*, rev. ed. (1965); *Fr. Classicism: A Critical Miscellany*, ed. J. Brody (1966); M. Hobson, *The Object of Art* (1982); Hollier.

B. *English*: J. W. H. Atkins, *Eng. Lit. Crit.: 17th and 18th C.* (1951); R. Crane, "Eng. N. Crit.," in Crane; R. Cohen, "The Augustan Mode in Eng. P.," *ECS* 1 (1967); P. Stone, *The Art of Poetry: 1750–1820* (1967); J. Johnson, *The Formation of Eng. N. Thought* (1967); E. Marks, *The Poetics of Reason: Eng. N. Crit.* (1968); R. Stock, *Samuel Johnson and N. Dramatic Theory* (1973).

C. *German*: K. Borinski, *Die Antike in Poetik und Kunsttheorie*, 2 v. (1914–23); B. Markwardt, *Gesch. der deutschen Poetik*, 5 v. (1937–67); E. Cassirer, *The Philosophy of the Enlightenment* (1951); A. Nivelle, *Les théories esthétiques en Allemagne de Baumgarten à Kant* (1955); H. Allison, *Lessing and the Enlightenment* (1966); K. Scherpe, *Gattungspoetik im 18. Jahrhundert* (1968); D. Wellbery, *Lessing's Laocoön: Semiotics and Aesthetics in the Age of Reason* (1984); H. Nisbet, "Intro.," *Ger. Aesthetic and Lit. Crit.: Winckelmann, Lessing, Hamann, Herder, Schiller and Goethe*, ed. H. Nisbet (1985); K. Berghan, "From Classicist to Cl. Lit. Crit., 1730–1806," *A Hist. of Ger. Lit. Crit., 1730–1980*, ed. P. Hohendahl (1985); B. Bennett, *Goethe's Theory of Poetry* (1986).

D. *Italian*: H. Quigley, *Italy and the Rise of a New School of Crit. in the 18th C.* (1923); M. Fubini, *Dal Muratori al Baretti* (1946); B. Croce, *La letteratura italiana del Settecento* (1949); *Antologia della critica letteraria*, ed. G. Petronio, v. 2 (1967); J. Whitfield, *A Short Hist. of It. Lit.* (1960); G. Petrocchi, *Questioni di critica letteraria* (1970); G. Natali, *Il settecento*, v. 1, ch. 6 (1973); Wilkins.

E. *Spanish*: J. Cook, *N. Drama in Spain: Theory and Practice* (1959); R. Chandler and K. Schwartz, *A New Hist. of Sp. Lit.* (1961); N. Glendinning, *A Lit. Hist. of Spain: The 18th C.* (1972); J. Stamm, *A Short Hist. of Sp. Lit.* (1979).

F. *Russian*: D. Cizevskij, *Hist. of Rus. Lit. from the 11th C. to the End of the Baroque* (1970); *The 18th C. in Russia*, ed. J. G. Garrard (1973); R. Neuhauser, *Towards the Romantic Age: Essays on Sentimental and Preromantic Lit. in Russia* (1974); *Rus. Lit. in the Age of Catherine the Great*, ed. A. Gross (1976); W. E. Brown, *A Hist. of 18th-C. Rus. Lit.* (1980); *Cambridge Hist. of Rus. Lit.*, ed. C. A. Moser (1989). R.L.M.

NEOCLASSICISM. See CLASSICISM.

NEOGONGORISM. A term used to designate a brief but significant 20th-c. Sp. poetic trend stemming from a revival of the 17th-c. baroque poet Luis de Góngora (1516–1627) on the tricentennial of his death. His style, characterized by brilliant if extravagant metaphors and convoluted or Latinate syntax, created a new interest in the formal possibilities of lang., which also led to the publication of modern editions of his work and of important stylistic studies of his poetry. Among the contributors to this vogue are Dámaso Alonso, Gerardo Diego, and Cossío. Renewed enthusiasm for Góngora was esp. reflected in the poets of the Generation of 1927, whose name may be attributed to the commemoration they organized in that year. One of this group, F. García Lorca, composed a remarkable prose piece in which he studied poetic imagery with specific references to Góngora. In part, the 20th century's interest came from Góngora's identity as an unassimilated or "different" poet, with his techniques of linguistic structure that, in a way paradoxically similar to that of the avant-garde movements emerging at the same time, sought a fundamental renovation of creative expression. See also CREATIONISM; ULTRAISM; SPANISH POETRY.

H. Friedrich, *Die Struktur der modernen Lyrik* (1956); P. Salinas, *Reality and the Poet in Sp. Poetry* (1966); C. B. Morris, *A Generation of Sp. Poets, 1920–1936* (1969); J.-C. Mainer, *La edad de plata (1902–1939)* (1981). A.W.P.; K.N.M.

NEO-HUMANISM. A movement in Am. crit. which had greatest impact in the years 1915–1933. N. had no direct relationship to Ren. humanism or to other expressions of humanism in letters and philosophy except to emphasize human dignity, moral strenuousness, and exercise of the will and reason. Primarily, n. defended conservative ethical, political, and aesthetic standards against 19th-c. romantics, liberals, empiricists, and their 20th-c. counterparts. Irving Babbitt (1865–1933), in *Lit. and the Am. College* (1908), formulated its program, which remained essentially unchanged; Paul Elmer More (1864–1937) was his associate.

Despite their emphasis upon reason, the neo-humanists felt that intuition was ultimately the source of philosophical truth. Certain permanent, distinctively "human" qualities, they said, could be ascertained by looking within; they thus took over the neoclassical concept of ethical and aesthetic universals. They repudiated not only all formal philosophies based upon nature, like those of Dewey, William James, and Bergson, but also the romantic nature-worship of the 19th-c. poets such as Wordworth, Coleridge, Emerson, Goethe, and Whitman. They also condemned a negative approach to nature like that of Thomas Hardy. To ethical emphases in these and other writers, the neo-humanists were, however, sympathetic; and they tended to judge lit. by ethical rather than by aesthetic criteria. Drawing heavily on Christian moral trad. while opposing Christian dogma and formal theology, the neo-humanists pictured man in a continuing, dualistic struggle between lower and higher impulses, between expansive natural desires and the inner check or "will to refrain." Many of these views and attitudes the neo-humanists derived from Matthew Arnold. At the end of his life, Paul Elmer More came to feel that the absolute nature of his values required the additional sanction of revealed religion.

In lit. the neo-humanists were hostile to the concept of original genius. In his best book, *Rousseau and Romanticism* (1919), Babbitt flayed Rousseau and the romantic poets for their primitivism, optimism, and uncontrolled emotionalism. As classicists, the neo-humanists stressed the rational rather than the emotional; perfection of form rather than experimentalism; and serenity and repose rather than manifestations of undisciplined creative energy, in art as in life. In emphasizing the need for selection of detail, they were hostile to realism in poetry and fiction. In their aversion to literary realism; in their evasiveness about sexual experience; in their emphasis upon the identity of the good, the true, and the beautiful; and in their moralism they deserved George Santayana's crit. that they were merely an atavism of the genteel trad. in Am. culture. The neo-humanists, however, repudiated genteel ideality and optimism. In Babbitt's *Democracy and Leadership* (1924) and More's *Aristocracy and Justice* (1915), anti-democratic, antihumanitarian, and anti-individualistic tendencies are evident.

From the beginning of World War I until about 1924, Stuart P. Sherman (1881–1926) was chief spokesman for n. After his accidental death in 1926, the chief popular and academic publicist for the movement was Norman Foerster (1887–1972) in *Am. Crit.* (1928), *Toward Standards* (1930) and the anthol. he edited, *Humanism and the Am.* (1930). C. Hartley Grattan attacked the neo-humanists in another anthol., *The Critique of Humanism* (1930). With the publication of these anthologies and with Babbitt's death in 1933, the movement had spent its force. The principal issues in "the great critical debate" between neo-humanists and their liberal and radical opponents in the 1920s and early 1930s were the extent of the artist's freedom to create without restriction, the relationship between the absolute and the relative, and the relevance of philosophical naturalism to the spiritual life.

For lasting significance in crit. and aesthetics, the neo-humanists were too negative, too concerned with the ethical, too inflexible in applying their formulas, and too unsympathetic to modern lit. In their insistence upon standards for literary judgment, in challenging the deterministic implications of lit. naturalism, and in emphasizing—like Pound and Eliot later—the philosphical inadequacies of romanticism, they had an important and beneficial influence. More's critical instincts were sounder than Babbitt's, and at his best he achieved Arnold's fusion of discriminating sensibility with moral insight. In *The Shelburne Essays*—the chief contribution to lit. by the neo-humanists—More exposed incisively the ideological weaknesses of the Eng. romantic and Victorian poets. From the neo-humanists Eliot in part developed his conservative and classical bias, and his censure of the romantic poets in *After Strange Gods* (1932) reveals the strong influence of Babbitt. Eliot repudiated, however, the aesthetic insensitivity of the neo-humanists and their rejection of formal Christianity. Either directly or through Eliot, other critics and poets like the Southern Agrarians (Ranson, Tate, Donald Davidson) and Yvor Winters were influenced to adopt conservative aesthetic, moral, and religious standards. At a time when literary studies in Am. ran to impressionistic appreciation or to philology, the neo-humanists stressed the experiential aspects of lit., its contribution to the life of the mind, its expression of crucial ideas, and its relevance to world culture.

In the 1980s, a resurgence of n. occurred. It was associated with fears about the decay of Am. education and concern that students were not learning enough about "the Western trad." Much of the concern centered on the humanities curriculum (see CANON). The most important critical work taking a generally neo-humanist position was Alan Bloom's *The Closing of the Am. Mind* (1987).

L. J. A. Mercier, *Le Mouvement humaniste aux États-Unis* (1928), *The Challenge of Humanism* (1933); *I'll Take My Stand* (1930)—Ransom, Tate et al.; T. S. Eliot, "The Humanism of Irving Babbitt" and "Second Thoughts on Humanism," *Selected Essays* (1932); R. Schafer, *Paul Elmer More and Am. Crit.* (1938); *Irving Babbitt, Man and Teacher*, ed. F. A. Manchester and O. Shepard (1941); A Kazin, *On Native Grounds* (1942); Y. Winters, *In Defense of Reason* (1947); R. E. Spiller, "The Battle of the Books," *A Lit. Hist. of the U.S.*, v. 2 (1949); J. H. Raleigh, *Matthew Arnold and Am. Culture* (1957); R. M. Davies, *The Humanism of Paul Elmer More* (1958); A. Warren, "'The New Humanism' Twenty Years After," *Modern Age* 3 (1959); A. H. Dakin, *Paul Elmer More* (1960); H. Levin, *Irving Babbitt and the Teaching of Lit.* (1961); F. X. Duggan, *Paul Elmer More* (1966); J. D. Hoeveler, *The New Humanism* (1976); T. R. Nevin, *Irving Babbitt: An Intellectual Study* (1984); Wellek, v. 6. ch. 2; S. L. Tanner, *Paul Elmer More: Lit. Crit. as the Hist. of Ideas* (1987).   F.P.W.M.

NEOLOGISM. See LEXIS.

NEW CRITICISM

NEOPLATONISM. See PLATONISM AND POETRY.

NEOTERICS. In Lat., *poetae novi* and *cantores Euphorionis*, and in Gr., *neoteroi* are terms applied by Cicero to the members of the fashionable trend in Roman poetry to which he belonged himself in his younger period, influenced by Alexandrian Gr. poetry and its later devels. The most famous example of them is Catullus, but others whose work survives in fragments are Laevius, Calvus, Cinna, Cornificius, Furius Bibaculus, and Ticidas. Alexandrianism (q.v.) as the mere display of technical cleverness was a recurring temptation in Lat. lit., and made itself apparent, for example, in the poets around Nero, in Statius, and in Claudian. A notable instance is a group, often called the *poetae novelli*, flourishing in the 2d c. A.D. See LATIN POETRY.—J. de Ghellinck, "Neotericus, n.," *ALMA* 15 (1940); E. Castorina, *I "Poetae novelli"* (1949), *Questioni Neoteriche* (1968); R. O. A. M. Lyne, "The Neoteric Poets," *ClassQ* 28 (1978); W. V. Clausen, "The New Direction in Poetry," *CHCL*, v. 2; J. K. Newman, *Roman Catullus* (1990).   J.K.N.

NEW CRITICISM, THE. When John Crowe Ransom published *The New Criticism* in 1941, he apparently meant no more by the title of his book than to designate the crit. then current. Either he was not aware of, or not concerned with, the fact that Joel E. Spingarn had preempted the term in a different connection in an address delivered at Columbia University in 1910. The critics with whom Ransom was primarily concerned were I. A. Richards, William Empson, T. S. Eliot, and Yvor Winters. But Ransom's book was a sustained, though respectful, attack on these four figures; and the critic that he desired to see, an "ontological critic," was conspicuous by his absence from the modern scene. The book closed with an invitation for such a critic to appear. Ransom showed himself fully aware of the sharp differences in assumptions and method among the four critics he discussed, and he did not insist on such traits as they held in common. Yet with the publication of his book, the "New Crit." as the name of a species gained immediate currency, and has been used constantly, if not always very responsibly, ever since.

There are significant reasons for the persistence of the term. One is that the increased critical activity in our time has brought about the need for a term that would characterize a kind of literary interest which, though difficult to define sharply, seems to many people clearly to exist. Certain polemicists and antiformalist critics have been content to use the term to mean simply "that crit. that I don't like." On the other hand, critics such as Allen Tate, R. P. Blackmur, and Kenneth Burke—not to mention those discussed in *The New Criticism*—have resisted acceptance of the term and would have great difficulty in recognizing themselves as the members of a critical guild.

One aspect of the New Crit. which is often seized upon as central is the "close reading" of poetry, and certainly a concern for nuances of words and shades of meaning has characterized much modern crit. since 1941. But "close reading" as such is by no means the most distinctive trait of the New Crit. The Fr. *explication de texte* (see EXPLICATION) involves close reading, yet few would call it "New Crit." Much depends on what one intends to do with a text and on what one regards as an adequate reading of it. The application of semantics to literary study, a devel. which owes much to critics like I. A. Richards and William Empson, was an important aspect of the New Crit. and has taken on even greater importance in subsequent decades (see SEMANTICS AND POETRY). Yet the early Richards' affective bias and Empson's inveterate psychologizing about both writer and reader run quite counter to the antiexpressionistic tendencies of a T. S. Eliot, for example, or to the insistence on a *cognitive* crit. by other "New Critics."

A more crucial premise is that literary art contains a distinct kind of knowledge. Yet that knowledge is not essentially a matter of "statement"; rather, the poem, drama, or fiction renders an experience, and in describing the nature of such an experience, many of the New Critics rejected the old dualism of form and content. (Here Ransom was a notable exception.) The way in which something is said often significantly affects the meaning of what is said. "Form" becomes an integral part of "content." Thus, such factors as metaphor, tone, and even rhythm (qq.v.) cannot be dismissed as mere incitements to emotion (q.v.); they have a bearing on meaning itself. Besides, in significant experiences of all kinds, thought and emotion are united.

A related aspect worth noting is the New Critics' concern for the unity (q.v.) of the literary work: many of them championed a strenuously achieved unity. They argued that the most mature literary art was not content to associate like with like but sought to bring into meaningful relation materials that we commonly think of as quite unlike. In all poetry (and, we may add, in all lit.), as T. S. Eliot wrote in 1921, there is a "degree of heterogeneity compelled into unity by the operation of the poet's mind." Eliot is here looking back at Dr. Johnson's crit. of the metaphysical poets, but he knows and therefore must also be looking forward to Coleridge's celebrated praise of the power of the imagination (q.v.) to synthesize and reconcile apparently discordant particulars into a new whole.

This "fusion of opposites" can be put in simpler terms. Coleridge described Wordsworth's intent in the *Lyrical Ballads* as being one to remove the "film of familiarity" from the objects of our everyday world so that we will see them as new and strange. The ordinary is thus revealed by the poet as fresh and wonderful. But wonder and irony are akin; in both there is a reversal of expectations and usual habits of mind.

A literary work in which such reversals are powerfully present can be regarded as "tensional" poetry: one is conscious of resistances acknowledged and overcome (see TENSION). The New Critics tended to regard such a quality as a hallmark of all great poetry, and if they found it in Donne and Marvell, they claimed to find it also in Wordsworth and Keats.

Yet the hallmark of the New Critics themselves continues to be close reading," a strategy very often taken to be their limitation: that is, obsessed with their microscopic examination of the text in hand, they never looked beyond it. Thus they had no regard for the fact that literary works are written by human beings. Actually, there was little likelihood that the New Critics could forget the importance of the author, since most of them had undergone the literary training of the earlier day, which was chiefly a study of lit. hist. and of the lives and times of the canonized authors, a study in which the standards of literary evaluation (q.v.) were by and large extrinsic to the text itself. The New Critics countered that a study of the author and his or her background, ambience, and sources will throw a great deal of light on the genesis of a work and may be absolutely necessary for an understanding of it, but such information cannot determine its literary merit. Thorough knowledge of Abraham Cowley will not establish him as a great poet. Nor will evidence of a poem's resounding impact on a huge number of readers prove it a literary masterpiece. If we are interested in lit. per se, we shall—in spite of all difficulties of definition—in the end have to appeal to the text.

This is the upshot of the much-maligned and ill-understood "intentional fallacy" (see INTENTION). Wimsatt and Beardsley did not dismiss as of no consequence the author's intentions or—more captiously still—deny that the author had any intentions at all. Rather, they insisted that what counted were achieved intentions—those that are manifest in the work itself.

There is no reason why a critic should not be involved in all three concerns: with the writer, with what the writer has written, and with its effects on the reader. In fact, most of the New Critics were so concerned. But it is very important that the critic remain aware of the distinctions.

The New Critics also stressed the importance of the written work, against a long season of mainly biographical and historical studies, because they believed that literary excellence is not merely relative to a particular cultural era. They believed, for example, that Dante and Shakespeare still speak to our own century, and that their works have universal value, including literary value.

In our own age such a view is not easily maintained. Yet if all "literary" judgments are merely relative, lit. crit., both "New" and age-old, becomes radically changed. All lit. crit. henceforth is reduced to "historical" studies indeed, and, as

in current writing, to socio-psychological studies of popular taste.

See also ANALYSIS; AUTONOMY; CHICAGO SCHOOL; CLOSURE; CONCRETE AND ABSTRACT; CONCRETE UNIVERSAL; CONTEXTUALISM; CRITICISM; EVALUATION; FORM; INTERPRETATION; INTERTEXTUALITY; IRONY; MEANING, POETIC; ORGANICISM; PARAPHRASE, HERESY OF; PARADOX; POETICS; POETRY, THEORIES OF; SCIENCE AND POETRY; STRUCTURE; TEXTUALITY; TEXTURE; THEORY; TWENTIETH-CENTURY POETICS, *American and British*.

J. C. Ransom, *The New Crit.* (1941); Brooks; W. K. Wimsatt, Jr., *The Verbal Icon* (1954), *Day of the Leopards* (1976), esp. "Genesis: An Argument Resumed"; S. Hyman, *The Armed Vision*, 2d ed. (1955); Wellek and Warren; M. Krieger, *The New Apologists for Poetry* (1956); D. Daiches, *Critical Approaches to Lit.* (1956, rev. 1981); J. P. Pritchard, *Crit. in America* (1956); Wimsatt and Brooks; R. J. Foster, *The New Romantics* (1962); W. J. Handy, *Kant and the Southern New Critics* (1963), ed., *Symposium on Formalist Crit.* (1965); L. T. Lemon, *The Partial Critics* (1965); G. Graff, *Poetic Statement and Critical Dogma* (1970); D. M. Miller, *The Net of Hephaestus* (1971); T. D. Young, *Gentleman in a Dustcoat* (1976)—on Ransom; *The Possibilities of Order*, ed. L. P. Simpson (1976)—on Brooks; R. Wellek, "The N. C.: Pro and Contra," *CritI* 4 (1978), reply and rejoinder, 5 (1979); G. Webster, *The Republic of Letters* (1979); Ransom; F. Lentricchia, *After the New Crit.* (1980), ch. 6; de Man; C. Brooks, "In Search of the N. C.," *Am Scholar* 53 (1984); Wellek, v. 6, ch. 8; J. Jones, *Wayward Skeptic* (1986)—on Blackmur; V. B. Leitch, *Am. Lit. Crit. from the Thirties to the Eighties* (1988), ch. 2; J. P. Russo, *I. A. Richards* (1989), ch. 20. C.B.; T.V.F.B.

NEW FORMALISM. A reaction, in late 20th-c. Am. poetry, against free verse (q.v.) and a return to metrical verse and fixed stanza forms.

In the great paradigm shift of the later 19th and early 20th cs. inaugurated by romanticism (q.v.) and carried forward by symbolism (q.v.) into the several movements collectively known as modernism (q.v.), poets turned away from the canons of traditional prosody (meter, rhyme, stanza) toward alternative forms of verse which were looser metrically if metrical at all, freer rhythmically, or constructed on the basis of visual prosody (q.v.) rather than aural. These new prosodies of "open form" take their origin in Fr. *vers libre* (q.v.) of the 1880s and after and run, via modernist free verse, Beat poetry, concrete poetry, prose poetry, sound poetry, and language poetry (qq.v.), into the 1960s and '70s. In its later stages, such work is collected in anthologies (q.v.) like Hall's 1960 *The New Am. Poetry* (covering 1945–60), Berg and Mezey's 1969 *Naked Poetry*, and Halpern's 1975 *New Am. Poetry Anthol.*

This is not to say that poetry in traditional forms was not being written in America in the 1940s,

'50s, '60s, and '70s, however; some poets, like Lowell, Hecht, Merrill, and Berryman, never strayed far from strict form, and others, esp. John Hollander, turned to it increasingly over time. Nor was it a question of liberals versus conservatives—of political Left vs. Right—for both Pound and Eliot were staunch conservatives in politics while radical in poetics; conversely, both Auden and Lowell were leftist in ideology while formalist in prosody. The only issue was whether the form of the poem was to be given by trad. (q.v.) or the moment (see ORGANICISM).

Hence a more scrupulous history of 20th-c. Am. verse would say that modernist free verse was succeeded by several versions of formalist verse (itself following in the wake of New Criticism [q.v.]), which in turn provoked the reaction of the San Francisco Ren. Consequently the New Formalist movement of the '80s is more directly a response to the Sixties. Its impetus may be found in books like Charles Martin's *Room for Error* (1978), Timothy Steele's *Uncertainties and Rest* (1979), and Brad Leithauser's *Hundreds of Fireflies* (1982); it found its own codification in anthologies like Dacey and Jauss's *Strong Measures* (1986) and Lehman's *Ecstatic Occasions, Expedient Forms* (1987); and it evoked new journals like *The Formalist* (1990–).

In retrospect, what the modernists repudiated was not so much a set of worn-out forms as, more deeply, the social attitudes and literary conventions that legitimized those forms and held them in place. Modernist poets sought, for the most part, not to destroy poetic form but to Make It New. Yet even in revolt the more technically scrupulous of the modernists, e.g. Pound, still took inspiration from some of the most elaborate prosodies of *l'ancien régime*, e.g. Occitan and OE. All of them soon discovered, however, that having rejected old forms, they had no choice but to invent new ones in order to go on at all: there is no escape from form, and the reaction to form can only be expressed in another set of forms; for not to have form is not to have any means by which to express the reaction one wants to articulate. No Form, No Speech.

Free verse is thus no more or less artificial than traditional metered verse; the choice of any form is a priori the same: the choice of form. And, in time, with the old attitudes and old moralities manifestly gone, gone altogether, poets discovered they could return to traditional forms once again, forms which a generation of poets who came of age in the Sixties never knew. By 1980, Gioia remarks, "for the first time in the history of modern Eng., most published young poets could not write with minimal competence in traditional meters" since "most of the craft of traditional Eng. versification had been forgotten." The revival of Formalist modes thus became a new initiative amid the general poverty of Am. poetry in the 1980s. In this initiative, old forms were Made New

in a very real sense: stripped by time of much of their associative baggage, they became simply opportunities, strategies—ways of proceeding. See FORM; VERSIFICATION.—A. Shapiro, "The N. F.," *CritI* 14 (1987); D. Wojahn, "Yes, But: Some Thoughts on the N. F.," *Crazyhorse* 32 (1987); D. Gioia, "Notes on the N. F.," *HudR* 40 (1987); *Expansive Poetry*, ed. F. Feirstein (1989). T.V.F.B.

NEW HISTORICISM. See HISTORICISM; HISTORY AND POETRY.

NEW HUMANISM. See NEO-HUMANISM.

NEW NORSE. A Norwegian lang. norm constructed by Ivar Aasen (1813–96) from the less adulterated rustic dialects in order to give his country a lang. directly descended from ON and to provide the rural population, constrained by Dano-Norwegian, with a natural medium of literary expression. In a modest way Aasen proved the poetic viability of his *landsmaal* (now called *nynorsk*—i.e. N. N.). Formally notable is *Haraldshaugen* (The Mound of King Harold), in which he achieved a masterly recreation, with addition of end rhyme, of the ON alliterative measure *fornyrðislag* (q.v.). Of later poets who helped to create the national N. N. poetry envisaged by Aasen may be mentioned Aasmund Vinje, Arne Garborg, and Olav Aukrust, who demonstrated the remarkable power and rich melody of the new medium. In present-day Norway, N. N. enjoys the same official status as the *bokmål*, a misnomer ("literary lang.") for Dano-Norwegian. See NORWEGIAN POETRY.—O. J. Falnes, *National Romanticism in Norway* (1933); *Norske dikt*, ed. J. A. Dale et al. (1960); L. S. Vikør, *The N. N. Lang. Movement* (1976); *Målreising i 75 år*, ed. O. Almenningen et al. (1981); I. Stegane, "The N. N. Literary Trad.," *RNL* 12 (1983); *N. N. Lit. in Eng. Tr., 1880–1982*, ed. J. Fet (1985)—with bibl. S.LY.

NEW YORK POETS. See AMERICAN POETRY.

NEW ZEALAND POETRY must be seen as comprising several overlapping trads., beginning with a Maori (indigenous Polynesian) oral poetry composed of chants, songs, and choric-dance pieces. This develops alongside, and is influenced by, an intrusive Pakeha (European) presence, partly in missionary (above all, London Missionary Society and Anglican, but also Roman Catholic) hymn writing. Along with sentimental colonial imitations in Eng., there is a Maori poetry of an overt pedagogical and religious nature. Meanwhile, moving toward the 20th c., Pakeha N. Z. verse moves through partial awareness of late Victorian and Georgian conventions in Britain, and only recently, along with openness to influences from Continental Europe and America, becomes receptive to Maori traditional content and rhythmic forms. Until the mid-1960s, British dominance maintains a false separation of Pakeha (in Eng.) and Maori (in Maori and Eng.) poetry.

Although it is essentially true that Pakeha poetry did not begin to mature until after World War I, it began to exist over a century ago. The early settlers were often cultured men, and some wrote verse, like Alfred Domett's Maori epic *Ranolf and Amohia* (1872), which imitates the more popular romantic and Victorian poets. A trad. of vernacular rhyming survived in colonial laureates like John Barr of Craigilee; but the country inherited little that was validly traditional. "Serious" verse, such as that of the journalist Thomas Bracken, was fluent but undistinguished; and the real sense of historic events—exploration, settlement, gold rushes—remained unexpressed. Even when the colonists wrote best, on the country's impressive landscapes, the work was often falsely colored by nostalgia for their Eng. "home."

The 1890s brought modest prosperity, and second-generation settlers became conscious of themselves as a people. William Pember Reeves, Parliamentarian and reformer, spoke in easy and popular verse for the idea of N. Z. as "social laboratory"; the work of Jessie Mackay and Blanche Baughan showed a stronger and more genuine talent. But, on the whole, the anxious desire for a distinctive national lit. did not begin to be realized for another generation.

Early 20th-c. Pakeha writers shared the mediocrity of contemp. Eng. poets who were often their models, but some achieved significant poetry without radical innovations of manner—Arnold Wall (1869–1966), Alan Mulgan (1881–1962), J. C. Beaglehole (1901–71), and, even more, Ursula Bethell ((1874–1945) and Eileen Duggan (1894–1972), Walter D'Arcy Creswell (1896–1960), and R. A. K. Mason (1905–71). Bethell described the Canterbury scene with virtuosity and an intense contemplative affection. Duggan evolved independently the concrete and energetic idiom of her later poems. Creswell and Mason both articulated striking attitudes toward their country: Creswell's, more highly mannered, expresses the ambivalent emotion of a kind of exasperated love affair; Mason's is that of a Roman stoic looking on the brevity of life and the fall of empires.

Although many of the poems collected in *Kowhai Gold* (1930) were still feeble, changes had begun in the 1920s. It is only roughly true to say that the achievements of modern N. Z. p. began in the 1930s, and to connect them with the depression, political ferment, and social anger of a growing community finding its place in a disturbed world. N. Z. poets came abreast of European writers—not only the younger Eng. poets (e.g. Auden, MacNeice) with whom they seemed to have most in common, but older masters such as Eliot, Pound, and Rilke. It was, however, a transformation rather than a revolution. The whole process can be seen in the work of the versatile "Robin Hyde" (Iris Wilkinson, 1906–39), which develops

from the late romantic aestheticism to a contemp. idiom; another kind of example is the accomplished traditional verse of John Russell Hervey (1889–1958) and Basil Dowling (b. 1910).

From the end of World War II down to the late 1960s, there has been a conscious and sometimes factitious reaction against this "myth of insularity." In practice this means that certain writers have widened their range of reference to include more of the urban scene and to accept the influence of European and Am. poets (e.g. Baudelaire, Hart Crane, Robert Lowell, Dylan Thomas). A similar indication is the growing tendency toward the longer poem or sequence, as in Alistair Campbell's (b. 1925) *Elegy*, Keith Sinclair's (b. 1922) *Ballad of Half-Moon Bay*, or Pat Wilson's (b. 1926) *Staying at Ballisodare*. Yet this new work often represents an extension rather than an extinction of the island-myth and what it signifies, as can be seen in the poetry of Kendrick Smithyman (b. 1922), Mary Stanley, Ruth Dallas (b. 1919), and others whose work is represented in Louis Johnson's (b. 1924) annual anthology. Most of all, it appears with varied range and tone in James K. Baxter (1926–72), who combines the attitudes of the *poète maudit* (q.v.) and the bard. "Hemi," as Baxter was known in his last days, moved from the early romanticism of his youth to a poetry that was at once satirical and religious, and in his *Jerusalem Sonnets* and *Autumn Testament*, he creates a mystical, even apocalyptic vision of N. Z.

While some of the older British-model writers such as Allan Curnow (b. 1911), Keith Sinclair, C. K. Stead (b. 1932), and Kendrick Smithyman, continue through the Muldoon Era of the late 1970s and into the '80s, the new period is marked by increasing Am. influence, esp. after the visit by Robert Creeley (of Black Mountain fame), and in the last several years by a shift toward the word-games of postmodern poetry. Above all, it is a period marked by the assertive presence of women writers, from Lauris Edmond (b. 1924), Elizabeth Smither (b. 1941), and Riemke Ensing (b. 1939) to Marina Makarova, with her imported Slavic intensities in the University of Hawaii's Pacific Poetry Award-winning *For Yesterday* (1984). Yet some N. Z. poets move "home" to England still, like Fleur Adcock (1934), though overseas writers also establish themselves in "the land of the long white cloud," writers such as Michael Harlowe (b. 1937), Norman Simms (1940), and Don Long. These movements signal the new dynamic in N. Z. society and verse. While brash young men like Ian Wedde (b. 1946) experiment with diction to discover the discourses of a deconstructionist N. Z. , the octogenarian shepherd-poet Vaughan Morgan (1907–87) creates what George Ewart Evans calls lapidary verse in "Anthoxanthum Odoratum":

After the cutting
and the tedding

and the windrowing,
after the drying
and the gathering of harvest;
after labour; not till then does the
vernal,
sweetest of all grasses,
yield the meadow scent in hay.

Maori and other Pacific Island poets also begin to move into the mainstream of N. Z. verse during this decade. Hone Tuwhare (b. 1922) had initiated the Polynesian trend with his *No Ordinary Sun* in 1964 but moved into his stride with *Come Rain Hail* in 1973 and *Something Nothing* (1974). Now one finds either the delicacies of Katerina Mataira or the harsh forcefulness of Apirana Taylor, whose *Eyes of the Ruru* (1979) leaps from street bluntness to true literary power. Samoan-born Talosaga Tolovae's *The Shadows Within* (1985) offers a subtle new blending of European and Polynesian myths with a delicate ear for voice rhythms. Listen to Tolovae echo and develop the rhythms of Hone Tuwhare in his "Poem in Spring":

Come hail
Come rain
let time and the hour rattle
the grown up children
like the wind
amongst the brittle ribs
of virgin trees.

N. Z. p. in the late 1980s is diverse and exciting, with a future brighter than at any time in the recent past. Though still a provincial trad., it nevertheless has more than its fair share of interesting poets. See also POLYNESIAN POETRY.

ANTHOLOGIES: *N. Z. Verse*, ed. W. F. Alexander and A. E. Currie (1906), rev. without preface as *A Treasury of N. Z. Verse* (1926); *Kowhai Gold*, ed. Q. Pope (1930); *Lyric Poems of N. Z. 1928–42*, ed. C. A. Marris (n.d.); *A Book of N. Z. Verse, 1923–45*, 2d ed (1950), *Penguin Book of N. Z. Verse*, both ed. A. Curnow (1959); *N. Z. P. Yearbook*, ed. L. Johnson (1951–); *Anthol. of N. Z. Verse*, ed. R. M. Chapman and J. Bennett (1956)—comprehensive and up-to-date; *Private Gardens*, ed. R. Ensing (1977)—N. Z. women poets; *Fifteen Contemp. N. Z. Poets*, ed. A. Patterson (1980); *Oxford Book of Contemp. N. Z. P.*, ed. F. Adcock (1982); *Into the World of Light: An Anthol. of Maori Writing*, ed. W. Ihimaera and D. S. Long (1982); *Oxford Anthol. of N. Z. Writing Since 1945*, ed. M. P. Jackson and V. O'Sullivan (1983); *Penguin Book of N. Z. Verse*, ed. I. Wedde and H. McQueen, rev. ed. (1985); *Anthol. of 20th-C. N. Z. P.*, ed. V. O'Sullivan, 3d ed. (1987).

HISTORY AND CRITICISM: E. H. McCormick, *Letters and Art in N. Z.* (1940), *N. Z. Lit., a Survey* (1959); J. C. Reid, *Creative Writing in N. Z.* (1946)—two chs. on poetry; M. H. Holcroft, *Discovered Isles* (1951); J. K. Baxter, *Recent Trends in N. Z. P.* (1951), *The Fire and the Anvil* (1955); K. Smithyman, *A Way of Saying* (1965); F. McKay, *N.*

Z. P. (1970); M. R. Longa, *La poesia neozelandese: delle origin inglesi a contemporanei* (1977); C. K. Stead, *In the Glass Case* (1981); N. Simms, *Silence and Invisibility* (1986), *Who's Writing and Why in the South Pacific* (1989); A. Curnow, *Look Back Harder: Critical Writings 1935–1984*, ed. P. Simpson (1987). The long-overdue *Oxford Hist. of N. Z. Lit.* is still in preparation.   N.S.

NIBELUNGENSTROPHE, *Kürenbergstrophe*, the most important stanza of MHG epic poetry. The N. is named from its use in the *Nibelungenlied* (ca. 1200–10), although its earliest recorded use is by Der von Kürenberg (fl. 1150-70). It is composed of 2 pairs of lines (*Langzeilen*). For a long time Heusler's somewhat conjectural analysis of the N. was accepted as authentic: a line consists of 2 hemistichs (*Kurzzeilen*), of which the first usually contains 4 stresses, the third and fourth stresses occurring in the same word (*klingende Kadenz*), while in the second hemistich the fourth stress is replaced by a metrical pause (*stumpfe Kadenz*) except for the last hemistich of the stanza, which has 4 stressed syllables. Thus, ending with a full cadence, the stanza has the character of a distinct formal unit. Its basic scheme is as follows:

x / x / x / x / \ | x / x / x / p
x / x / x / x / \ | x / x / x / p
x / x / x / x / \ | x / x / x / p
x / x / x / x / \ | x / x / x / x /

The rhyme scheme for hemistichs 2, 4, 6, 8 is *aabb*; caesural rhyme occurs occasionally.

Modern prosodists confine themselves to a more cautious, purely descriptive formula, according to which hemistichs 1 to 7 contain three stresses each, and the eighth 4; further, 1, 3, 5, and 7 as a rule show feminine and 2, 4, 6, and 8 masculine (q.v.) endings. A recent study (Wakefield) rejects the "performance based" metrics of Heusler and most of his successors with its concomitant notion that the verse of Ger. poetry is essentially four-stressed. Basing his description on a statistical study of the distribution of syllables in the strophes in Ms. B, he describes verses 1, 3, 5, and 7 of the N. as belonging to a long realization of the verse and verses 2, 4, and 6 as belonging to a short realization. Both realizations tend to show an alternation of stressed and unstressed syllables, particularly toward the cadence. Verse 8, however, follows a quite different pattern, called "dipodic" by Wakefield, which exhibits two cadential structures rather than one.

The use of the N. has continued over the centuries in many variants, e.g. among the *Meistersinger* (q.v.) as "Hönweis," in the church hymn (P. Gerard, *O Haupt voll Blut und Wunden*), and in the modern secular *Lied*, esp. among the romantics (L. Uhland, *Des Sängers Fluch*), and even in the drama (Z. Werner, *Die Söhne des Thals*, [1803]). See also GERMAN POETRY.—A. Heusler, *Deutsche Versgesch.*, 3 v. (1925–29, rpt. 1956), *Nibelungensage und Nibelungenlied*, 6th ed. (1965); P. Habermann, "N.," *Reallexikon I*; F. Panzer, *Das Nibelungenlied* (1955); U. Pretzel and H. Thomas, "Deutsche Verskunst," *Deutsche Philologie im Aufriss*, 2d ed., ed. W. Stammler, v. 3 (1957); H. de Boor, "Zur Rhythmik des Strophenschlusses im Nibelungenlied," *Kleine Schriften*, ed. R. Wisniewski and H. Kolb (1966), "Die 'schweren Kadenzen' im Nibelungenlied," *BGDSL* (T) 92 (1970); R. M. Wakefield, *Nibelungen Prosody* (1976); E. Stutz, "Die Nibelungenzeile: Dauer und Wandel," *Philologische Studien: Gedenkschrift R. Kienast*, ed. U. Schwab and E. Stutz (1978); G. J. H. Kulsdom, *Die Strophenschlüsse im* Nibelungenlied (1979).

U.K.G.; E.R.H.

NICARAGUAN POETRY. See SPANISH AMERICAN POETRY.

NIL VOLENTIBUS ARDUUM (Nothing is Difficult to the Willing). A society of Dutch poets founded at Amsterdam in 1669 by Lodewijk Meyer, Andries Pels, and others. The major concern of the society was the establishment of Fr. neoclassical artistic principles in Dutch dramatic poetry. The members of the N. V. A. interpreted these principles so strictly that they condemned not only the decadent and sensational drama of Jan Vos and Blasius but also the earlier classical drama of Hooft and Vondel, since regarded as one of the high points of Dutch poetry. Like its earlier counterpart, Samuel Coster's *Duytsche Academie*, N. V. A. also exerted its influence by giving courses in grammar and philosophy. The writings of its members include Andries Pels' *Horatius' Dichtkunst op onze tijden en zeden gepast* (Horace's Art of Poetry revised to fit our times and customs, 1677). In 1681, after the death of Meyer and Pels, the society began to decline in influence.—A. J. Kronenberg, *Het kunstgenootschap N. V. A.* (1875); J. Bauwens, *La Tragédie française et le théâtre hollandais au XVIIe siècle* (1921).

F.J.W.

NŌ. This relatively short Japanese dramatic form, employing poetry, prose, patterned movement, dance, and music, was perfected in the 14th c. Adapting with some variations the traditional syllabic 5s and 7s, the poetry is highly allusive and elevated. Such elevated richness, the religious subjects, and the slow tempo of most nō create a drama akin to the Gr., which it further resembles in its use of traditional materials, masks, male performers, and a chorus (that takes no part in the action).

Nō has broadly influenced Western drama, nondramatic poetry, and lit. crit. since Ezra Pound first received (1914), studied, revised, and published (1916) Ernest Fenollosa's notes and rough translations. Pound felt that nō showed how to write a long Vorticist poem (see VORTICISM; IMAGISM), since he saw in it a technique by which crucial images could be used to unify passages or

whole plays. He used both allusions to nō and this technique of "Unity of Image" to unify the *Cantos* by employing certain recurring, archetypical images—e.g. light, the literary journey, and the heavenly visitor to earth. Often these images take on an additional oriental dimension, since the heavenly visitor to earth may be the central character of the nō *Hagoromo* as well as Diana; or it may be the Sino-Japanese character for "brightness" combined with other imagery of light.

Pound had discussed a number of his interests with Yeats, who became so absorbed that he completely reshaped his later dramaturgy in the image of nō. On the Japanese model, he fashioned an "aristocratic form" employing a bare stage, masks, dance, a few rhythmic instruments, a chorus not part of the action, and other elements characteristic of nō. Some of his "Noh plays," as he called them, have elements borrowed from specific nō: the blue cloth centrally onstage in *At the Hawk's Well*, for example, is modeled on the brocade cloak of *Aoi no Ue* and *Words Upon the Window-Pane* and *The Dreaming of the Bones* borrow the *Nishikigi* motif of unmarried ghostly lovers from the distant past. But Yeats seems to have come upon the unifying-image technique in nō independently of Pound, using it to give coherence to such plays as *The Only Jealousy of Emer*, *Calvary*, and *A Full Moon in March*, through dramatic focus on an object onstage (Cuchulain's body; Christ hanging on the cross) or an imagistic pattern (of moon and cat's eyes). The importance of nō to Yeats can be measured by his use of it to form a new poetic drama, by his use of images and techniques related to it in his nondramatic poems, and by his statement that the Japanese dramatists were more like modern Western man than either Shakespeare or Corneille.

The Fenollosa-Pound adaptations, Yeats's enthusiasms, Arthur Waley's translations and commentaries, and the monumental studies of Noel Peri in *Cinq Nô* (1929) and *Le Nô* (1944) have influenced many other playwrights, esp. those concerned with the poetic or semiprivate theatre. Yeats induced his friend T. Sturge Moore to write "Noh plays," and such others as Gordon Bottomley and Laurence Binyon soon followed. In Germany, Berthold Brecht conceived his two didactic plays, *Der Jasager* and *Der Neinsager*, in the light of Waley's translation of *Taniko*; and in France, Paul Claudel, who had seen nō performed in Japan, borrowed techniques for his marionette plays. Similarly, Thornton Wilder modeled the bare-stage technique of *Our Town* in part upon nō and adapted the *waki* (deuteragonist) and the chorus of nō into a *raisonneur* for many plays. Other lesser known writers such as S. Foster Damon and Paul Goodman have written plays modeled on nō; and Stark Young's *Flower in Drama* uses earlier ideas about nō as antinaturalistic dramatic criteria. If haiku (q.v.) has influenced more Western poets than any Japanese or other non-European form in this century, the nō may be credited with having produced a larger amount of first-rate lit., esp. in Eng., through its influence upon dramatists and poets. See also JAPANESE POETRY.—W. B. Yeats, Introd. to *Certain Noble Plays of Japan* (1916); A. Nicoll, *World Drama* (1949); D. Keene, *Japanese Lit.* (1953); E. Miner, *The Japanese Trad. in British and Am. Lit.* (1958); M. J. Smethurst, *The Artistry of Aeschylus and Zeami: A Comparative Study of Gr. Tragedy and Nō* (1989); K. Yasuda, *Masterworks of the Nō Theater* (1989). E.M.

NONSENSE VERSE. Some readers consider that any poetry which tells a fantastic story or which describes a fictive world in which the natural laws of the world as we know it do not operate (comparable to the prose example of Lewis Carroll's *Alice in Wonderland*) is n. v. And there are certainly, in the world's poetries, ample numbers of bizarre, fantastic, mythic, or surreal stories in verse which describe some autonomous world which clearly operates according to a set of laws which have their own internal logic. The impossibility trope is common to the rhetorical figure of adynaton (q.v.) and to medieval absurdity-genres such as *coq-à-l'âne*, *frottola*, and *barzelletta* (qq.v.). Any versified account that is nonreferential or unrealistic to a considerable degree could be called n.

These certainly have their interest. It is however naive to believe that n. v. does not "make sense"; much of it does, in its own way. "N.," a modern critic has remarked, "is not no-sense." Rather, we must say, n. v. is verse which does not yield the *same kind* of denotative sense that sentences do in ordinary lang. or prose or even most poetry, where the words chosen are of known lexical meaning (as recorded in dictionaries; see LEXIS) and are arranged in normal syntax. N. v. may in fact yield sense in only vestigial, disconnected, or centrifugal ways, or it may yield sense in unexpected, unpredictable, or hitherto unknown ways. But these are shard-sense or new-sense, not no-sense, which would be the verbal equivalent of a series of random numbers. Users of lang. live in meaning, and will create sense wherever conceivably possible.

Still, the term "n. v." is more properly reserved for verse in which the dislocation is less that of plot or fictive world than of lang. itself. N. v. is most often constituted by unusual words—e.g. neologisms, portmanteau words—or unusual syntax or both. But even a poem which presented wholly unrecognizable morphemes in a wholly unrecognizable syntactic order would evoke at least some threads of sense. The reason is writ large in linguistic competence. All native speakers of a lang. know, intuitively, the phonotactics of their particular lang.: these are the vowel-and-consonant patterns which are permissible in that lang. vs. those which are not, e.g. initial *pl-*, *pr-*, *ps-*, or *st-* in Eng. but not *pf-* or *pg-* and only rarely *skl-* or *sv-*. Even the invention of new words is not carried on in a

vacuum; such words automatically suggest vestiges of meaning which their component vowels or consonant patterns carry over from familiar words having similar ones (Bolinger). Further, every lang. develops intricate constellations of synchronic meaning, based on the associations words come to have with each other, quite apart from the diachronic affiliations they have, based on their family histories (Malkiel). So, for example, many Eng. words (though certainly not all) beginning *gl-* are associated with light, e.g. *glisten*, *gleam*, *glitter*, *glow*, *glower* (but not *gland*, *glitch*). Also of importance are the rules of morphotactics, namely the rules by which words may be formed in a lang.—e.g. compounding, prefixing, and suffixing. These rules also are finite, specified, and internalized by native speakers.

Of relevance too are the rules of syntax. Whether a lang. is positional or inflectional or some mixture of both, readers have expectations for word order which they maintain even when the words that fill the syntactic slots are unknown. Eng. readers, for example, normally expect the syntactic sequence Subject—Verb—Object, and they expect sentences to be complete and to be drawn from the inventory of only nine patterns available in Eng. Readers are much less disoriented by unfamiliar words in familiar syntax than by the opposite. This explains why most n. v., in which the object is to create amusement or delight not confusion or alienation, relies mainly on novelty in phonotactics and morphology rather than syntax. N. v. draws upon and requires linguistic competence, i.e. the complex of information about sound-combinations, word-formation, and syntactic order which is part of the ordinary processing skill of all native speakers. N. v. simply extends these rules in order to create new semantic structures.

The classic example of n. v. in Eng. is Lewis Carroll's "Jabberwocky," esp. its famous opening:

> 'Twas brillig and the slithy toves
> Did gyre and gimble in the wabe;
> And mimsy were the borogroves
> And the mome raths outgrabe.

The gloss of this poem provided by Humpty Dumpty in ch. 5 of *Through the Looking Glass* is only partly enlightening: many readers would have felt on their own that "slithy" implies both "lithe" and "slimy," or that "gyre" means "to go round and round like a gyroscope," as it does in Yeats. Dumpty reports that "toves" are "something like badgers . . . something like lizards . . . something like corkscrews," and that a "rath" is "a sort of green pig," but these denotations are arbitrary; readers are free to devise their own creatures for these words regardless of whether they take these nouns as having expressive sound patterns (see ONOMATOPOEIA). It is of interest that, of the 23 words in the four lines above, only 11 are novel: the syntax, while paratactic, is perfectly normal

Eng.: four main clauses in sequence, the second one, for example, consisting of N + V + V + PrepP.

The affiliations between n. v. and other verseforms still remain to be mapped out, as do relations on the level of content, given the caveat in paragraph two of this entry. As for the former, n. limericks are a well established form. N. v. may also be related to some types of visual poetry (q.v.). One thinks of the fragmented shapes of e e cummings' poems, for example, but the deep structures of these poems turn out to be traditional—a great many of them are exploded sonnets. As for the latter, the connections are much wider: children's verse covers a range of forms which obviously pertain, and numerous other forms of verse which are highly imaginative or the result of various states of altered consciousness also employ dislocated, reconstructed, or novel lang. The line between n. and the verbal products of dada, surrealism, and cubism (qq.v.), for example, is virtually impossible to draw. The verse generated by computer programs which reassemble lexical items in ordinary syntax to create new poems, or else use the same process to parody famous poems of the past, is also n. v.—of a sort. But is it poetry? We will not ask that here. See COMPUTER POETRY; LIGHT VERSE.

N. Verses: An Anthol., ed. L. Reed (1925); E. Cammaerts, *The Poetry of N.* (1926); A. L. Huxley, *Essays New and Old* (1927); *Surrealism*, ed. H. Read (1936); D. K. Roberts, *Nonsensical and Surrealist Verse* (1938); L. E. Arnaud, *Fr. N. Lit. in the Middle Ages* (1942); E. Partridge, *Here, There and Everywhere* (1950); E. Lear, *The Complete N. of Edward Lear*, ed. H. Jackson (1951); *Penguin Book of Comic and Curious Verse*, ed. J. M. Cohen (1952); E. Sewell, *The Field of N.* (1952); G. Orwell, *Shooting an Elephant* (1954); *Anthol. du n.*, ed. R. Benayoun (1957); *A N. Anthol.*, ed. C. Wells (1958); *A Book of N. Songs*, ed. N. Cazden (1961); W. Forster, *Poetry of Significant N.* (1962); D. F. Kirk, *Charles Dodgson, Semeiotician* (1962); A. Liede, *Dichtung als Spiel*, 2 v. (1963); D. Bolinger, *Forms of Eng.* (1965); D. Sonstroem, "Making Earnest of Game: G. M. Hopkins and N. Poetry," *MLQ* 28 (1967); *The N. Book*, ed. D. Emrich (1970); R. Hildebrandt, *N.* (1970); A. Schöne, *Englische N. und Gruselballaden* (1970); D. Petzoldt, *Formen und Funktionen englische N.* (1972); Y. Malkiel, "From Phonosymbolism to Morphosymbolism," *Fourth LACUS Forum*, ed. M. Paradis (1978); S. Stewart, *N.: Aspects of Intertextuality in Folklore and Lit.* (1979); J.-J. Lecercle, *Philosophy Through the Looking-Glass* (1986); G. Deleuze, *The Logic of Sense* (tr. 1989).   T.V.F.B.

NORSE PROSODY. See GERMAN PROSODY, *Old Germanic*; OLD NORSE POETRY.

NORSKE SELSKAB, DET (The Norwegian Society). A social-literary club of Norwegian students, teachers, and writers resident in Copenhagen,

1772–1812. It carried on the inheritance from Fr. neoclassicism and Eng. Empiricism in opposition to Klopstock and his Danish adherents. Some poets associated with it were Johan Nordahl Brun (1745–1816), Claus Frimann (1746–1829), Thomas Rosing de Stockfleth (1743–1808), Johan Herman Wessel (1742–85), and Jens Zetlitz (1761–1821). The poetic endeavors of the members ranged over most of the neoclassical genres, from heroic drama and fables in verse to elegy and epigram. Worthy of note as Norway's first national-historical play is Brun's *Einar Tambeskielver* (1772). By the emphasis it placed on the use of Norwegian subject matter in poetry and on a national manner of treatment, the society laid the foundations for the literary renascence that came with Henrik Wergeland. See NORWEGIAN POETRY.—F. Bull, *Fra Holberg til Nordal Brun* (1916); A. H. Winsnes, *Det n. S., 1772–1812* (1924).   S.LY.

NORWEGIAN POETRY. At the height of the Middle Ages (ca. 1250), when the trad. of Old Norse poetry (q.v.) had virtually ceased to be productive, the vogue of versified Fr. romances and Occitan poetry (q.v.) replaced original creativity in the vernacular. The chief N. poetic monuments of the age are the folk ballads, which derived their new, nonalliterative style from troubadour verse. *Draumkvæde* (The Dream Ballad), a remarkable visionary poem, successfully blends elements of pagan and Christian myth. Petter Dass (1647–1707), the first important N. poet, remains close to folk poetry, representing a kind of people's baroque. Though indebted to the Dane, Anders Arrebo, a bishop of Trondheim whose epic *Hexaëmeron* (1661) contained descriptions of North Norway (see DANISH POETRY), Dass's *Nordlands Trompet* (The Trumpet of Nordland, ca. 1700, pub. 1739; Eng. tr. 1954) is original in style and tone. In the hymns and other poems by Dorothe Engelbretsdatter (1643–1716), the artificial lang. of the baroque (q.v.) is feminized through domestic imagery, and the religious feeling expressed toward Christ is tinged with a dreamy eroticism, at times lending a very engaging personal tone to her verse.

Ludvig Holberg (1684–1750) was the first N. writer to attain European stature. Holberg established an enduring conception of poetry as crit. of life and offered his countrymen, still Danish subjects, a brilliant example. However, the N. poets failed in their first ambition, namely, to create a viable poetic tragedy in the Fr. neoclassical style. Their attempts are remembered chiefly because of the parody *Kierlighed uden Strømper* (Love without Stockings, 1772) by Johan Herman Wessel (1742–85), whose ironic satire in graceful alexandrines put an end to the imitation of It. opera and Fr. tragedy. In his comic narratives Wessel effectively alternates living dialogue with rhymed epigrams. The descriptive poem was another favorite genre with the poets of this period. Like Wessel, most of them belonged to *Det norske Selskab* (q.v.;

The N. Society) in Copenhagen.

Whereas Denmark and Sweden had produced great romantic poetry by the first and second decades of the 19th c., respectively, romanticism reached Norway only in the 1830s and '40s. Despite the political independence of Denmark held since 1814, Norway was still under Danish cultural hegemony. In the 1830s a "culture feud" occurred between those who followed the Danish romantics and those who wanted to build a lit. on native grounds. Henrik Arnold Wergeland (1808–45), leader of the Patriots, had prodigious gifts and inexhaustible energy, which he expended on politics and popular education as well as on literary creation. His production ranges from satirical farces and cosmic dramas to intimate lyrics. As one to whom poetry meant rapture and organic form, he was the exact opposite of the Intelligentsia Party's leader, Johan Sebastian Welhaven (1807–73), a poet of quiet reflection and chiseled form who adopted the aesthetic of the Danish poet-critic J. L. Heiberg. The trads. established by these two figures have coexisted in N. p. down to the present day, though tending to converge since 1900.

Wergeland defies literary classification. While a child of the Enlightenment, he is also Norway's first great romantic poet. His vast lyric drama *Skabelsen, Mennesket og Messias* (Creation, Man and Messiah, 1830) expresses a philosophical rationalism tinged with pantheism à la Shelley. Welhaven, who found the work formless and turgid, subsequently wrote *Norges Dæmring* (The Dawn of Norway, 1834), a series of epigrammatic sonnets showing up the Patriots' uncritical cultural nationalism as well as Wergeland's artistic faults. Narrative poems such as *Jøden* (The Jew, 1842), *Jødinden* (The Jewess, 1844), and *Den engelske Lods* (The Eng. Pilot, 1844), however, escape these strictures. Wergeland's lyric genius reached its apex as he neared death, in poems like "Til min Gyldenlak" (To My Wallflower) and "Til Foraaret" (To Spring), the latter in free verse.

Romanticism underwent change in the 1840s as N. poets discovered the values inherent in their folk culture. Native ballads were collected by Jørgen Moe (1813–82) and M. B. Landstad (1802–80); the latter's *Norske Folkeviser* (N. Folk Ballads, 1853) exerted a broad influence on poetry. The pioneering work of Ivar Aasen (1813–96) in creating the New Norse (q.v.) lang. was another manifestation of National Romanticism. Most of the important poets—Welhaven, Vinje, Ibsen, Bjørnson—contributed to the movement. Welhaven's poetry of recollection eventually embraced the entire nation and its heritage, which he celebrated in the tone of ballad or romance, and his nature poems featured fairies and trolls of a distinctly N. character. To the romantic output of the New Norse poet Aasmund Vinje (1818–70) belongs the first authentic N. mountain poetry. National Romanticism came to full fruition with Ibsen and

Bjørnson, besides Wergeland the greatest N. poets of the 19th c.

Henrik Ibsen (1828–1906) is an exponent of the Welhaven trad., both in his National-Romantic and his satirical phases. His condensed lyric poetry, often cryptically symbolic, employs a minimum of imagery. Ibsen's chief contribution to National Romanticism was the drama *Gildet paa Solhaug* (*The Feast at Solhaug*, 1856), a historical idyll influenced by the ballad. *Kjærlighedens Komedie* (*Love's Comedy*, 1862) marks the beginning of realism. Its variously rhymed, skipping iambic pentameters abound in caricature and paradox. In *Brand* (1866; Eng. tr. 1898) and *Peer Gynt* (1867; Eng. tr. 1892), the satirist blends with the National Romantic; for while exposing the faults of the N. national character, both plays envelop the N. landscape—its rivers and lakes, its mountain peaks and fabled fjords—in a romantic aura. In *Peer Gynt*, moreover, Ibsen portrays dramatic symbols of universal import. Its major theme—a selfish, morally flawed hero ultimately saved, if saved at all, through a noble woman's love—recalls the *Divine Comedy* and *Faust*. And the play's metrical variety, by contrast with the *knittelvers* (q.v.) used in *Brand*, produced verse capable of a vast range of effects, from idle daydreaming to physical abandon, from the lightest banter to funereal solemnity. As a group, Ibsen's verse dramas demonstrated the strengths of N. as a medium for dramatic poetry (q.v.).

Bjørnstjerne Bjørnson (1832–1910) saw himself as literary heir to Wergeland. His saga dramas *Halte-Hulda* (Lame Hulda, 1858), *Kong Sverre* (1861), and *Sigurd Slembe* (1862; Eng. tr. 1888) were undertaken to give Norway a gallery of heroes matching those of the other European nations, an ambition in line with the National-Romantic program. The chief merits of these plays are historical verisimilitude and their epic tone. Bjørnson was an excellent narrative and lyric poet. *Arnljot Gelline* (1870; Eng. tr. 1917), a narrative cycle of 15 romances in various measures, is a N. counterpart to Oehlenschläger's *Helge*, Tegnér's *Frithiofs saga*, and Runeberg's *Kung Fjalar*. The imagery is rich, the diction colloquial and varied, and the meter, mostly trochaic and dactylic, attuned to the changing moods. Bjørnson's lyric poems define him as a figure of European stature. Their structure is often dramatic: "Olav Trygvason" and "Bergljot" (in *Digte og Sange* [Poems and Songs], 1870) present an entire tragic action within a few dramatically taut scenes. Worthy of special mention is "Salme II," a hymn to ever-resurgent life that marks the highpoint of Bjørnson's poetic achievement.

When, after the prose-dominated 1870s and '80s, poetry again gained prominence, it had acquired a more personal note, one attuned to nature, mysticism, and fantasy. Nietzsche, Edvard Munch, and the Fr. symbolists—largely as mediated by Danish and Swedish neoromantic poetry—were important sources of inspiration. The chief exponents of neoromantic *fin de siècle* moods were Vilhelm Krag (1871–1933) and Sigbjørn Obstfelder (1866–1900), the former expressing a rather conventional melancholy, the latter evoking bizarre moods of anxiety and wonder in a highly original form marked by pauses, repetitions, abrupt transitions, and incompleteness. Symbolist in conception, Obstfelder's poetry, with its free verse and urban imagery, anticipates Scandinavian modernism. By contrast, Nils Collett Vogt (1864–1937) possessed a robust sensibility, celebrating in dithyrambic accents an individualistic Cl. paganism à la Swinburne. New Norse poetry was revived by Arne Garborg (1851–1924) and Per Sivle (1857–1904). Garborg's *Haugtussa* (The Elf Maiden, 1895) and *I Helheim* (In Hel's Home, 1901) give voice to the dark, uncanny forces in man and nature while expressing a profound religious nostalgia. The poetry of Knut Hamsun (1859–1952) is also neoromantic in inspiration. *Det vilde Kor* (The Wild Chorus, 1904) showed Hamsun as a lyric poet of considerable range, handling national and personal themes with equal mastery. Best known is the poem "Skjærgaardsø," an exquisite lyric with mystical intimations.

About 1910 a lyric revival occurred, due in large part to Herman Wildenvey (1886–1959) and Olaf Bull (1883–1933). Inspired by Hamsun's verse, Wildenvey's *Nyinger* (Bonfires, 1907) alternates between seductive love lyrics and pantheistic nature poetry. His novel diction, mixing biblical and ballad idioms with jargon and slang, and his conversational yet musical anapestic line were apt vehicles for his troubadour talent. Bull, Wildenvey's opposite in sensibility and craft, was the leading N. poet of his time. To him, as to fellow symbolists like Rilke and Valéry, the purpose of poetry was to transmute fugitive moments of experience into what Yeats called the "artifice of eternity." "Metope" (1927), one of his most famous poems, is a moving meditation on love and destructive time. Bull's deeply personal verse is focused on the tensions of inward experience. Only through an arduously achieved perfection of form was he able to blend the disparate elements within his creative impulse: perception and memory, image and abstraction, reality and fantasy, picture and sound, spontaneous feeling and discursive thought. Starting with but few sensory data, his poems gather substance from a visionary imagination and an intellect schooled in contemp. science and philosophy. His metapoems illuminate the condition of the imagination in a world without transcendence. New Norse poetry found worthy practitioners in Olav Aukrust (1883–1929), Tore Ørjasæter (1886–1968), and Olav Nygard (1884–1924). Aukrust and Ørjasæter treated religious and philosophical themes in a national spirit using forms derived from the Edda and the ballad. Aukrust's main work, *Himmelvarden* (The Cairn Against the Sky, 1916), is a visionary poem based on a quasi-mystical experience. Its sonorous verse,

vivid imagery, and mythic symbols evoke a spiritual struggle of cosmic dimensions. Both Nygard and Aukrust superbly demonstrated the evocative potential of New Norse as a poetic medium.

Though the period between the wars generated new themes and original voices, there was a dearth of formal innovation. Arnulf Øverland (1889–1968) realized his poetic mission in the wake of World War I, as evidenced in *Brød og vin* (Bread and Wine, 1919). Much of his work springs from a religiously conceived Socialist ideal, often presented in biblical symbols. *Den røde front* (The Red Front, 1937) is devoted to proletarian songs and other texts with a political message. Notable monuments to the 1930s are the poems "Guernica," inspired by Picasso's famous painting, and "Du må ikke sove" (You Must Not Sleep). His best collection, however, is *Hustavler* (House Tablets, 1929), which ranges from politics to themes such as love, death, and self. Though Øverland was awarded the national honor of dwelling in Wergeland's house after the Liberation, his restrained fervor, laconic form, and austere diction place him decidedly in the formal trad. of Welhaven and Ibsen. By contrast, Nordahl Grieg (1902–43), ceaselessly active on many fronts, is reminiscent of Wergeland. Novelist, playwright, and poet, Grieg chiefly wrote socially oriented patriotic lyrics in a style of impassioned eloquence. His greatest poetic success was the collection of war poems entitled *Friheten* (Freedom, 1943; Eng. tr. *All That Is Mine Demand*, 1944), where his rhetorical pathos is poetically justified. Gunnar Reiss-Andersen (1896–1964), whose sheer formal talent has no equal in N. p., combined a brooding introspection with sensitivity to a world in crisis. During the war he was an important spokesman for his country. One of the poems written in Swedish exile, "Norsk freske" (N. Frieze), from *Dikt fra krigstiden* (Wartime Poems, 1945), is remarkable for its imaginative scope, rhythmical virtuosity, and colorful imagery; it deserves a place beside the best poems of Grieg and Øverland.

Modernism had to wait until about 1950 to make an impact on N. p., despite the fact that in some ways Wergeland was a modernist long before Whitman's *Leaves of Grass* (1855) or before Mallarmé and Rimbaud changed the concept of poetry in Europe. Wergeland's idiosyncratic form, adapted to the changing flow of consciousness, had no counterpart in N. p. until Obstfelder. It was Welhaven's classical conception of form which prevailed, even in the 20th c.: Wildenvey, Bull, and Øverland, all very influential, were formally conservative. Their avatars were not only prolific but excelled in their craft. Inger Hagerup (1905–85) wrote condensed love lyrics reminiscent of Øverland, as well as eloquent war poems (e.g. *Aust-Vågøy*, 1941); André Bjerke (1918–85) showed his technical versatility in highly finished verse, elegantly sensuous or introspective. With the exception of Kristofer Uppdal (1878–1961), who had written some expressionist poetry early in the century, the New Norse poets were all traditionalists.

From the 1930s on, however, various features of modernism became manifest. Emil Boyson (1897–1979) mediated the poetics and the preoccupations of Fr. symbolism. Claes Gill (1910–73) knew Yeats and T. S. Eliot; an ecstatic imagist, he admired Wergeland among others. His verse disregards ordinary syntax and follows a logic of suggestion, dynamic, surprising, often paradoxical. Rolf Jacobsen (b. 1907), who received an impetus from both Fr. and Am. poetry, used free verse and technical imagery early on to evoke urban civilization in *Jord og jern* (Earth and Iron, 1933) and *Vrimmel* (Throng, 1935), but by 1951 his emphasis had shifted to the natural landscape, and in *Hemmelig liv* (Secret Life, 1954) technology is seen as a sinister force. Jacobsen is basically an imagist, and his modernism is largely limited to free verse and rapid shifts in point of view. In *Headlines* (1969) and *Pass for dørene—dørene lukkes* (Watch the Doors—The Doors are Closing, 1972), which contain much social criticism, he presents a kaleidoscope of contrasting moods, effects, and angles of vision—pathos and humor, the commonplace and the cosmic, sensory vividness and symbolic resonance. Jacobsen's poetry is quite accessible and has been widely translated.

The 1950s witnessed a debate between the traditionalists—headed by Øverland, the uncrowned poet laureate—and the modernists. The latter looked for inspiration, like Carl Keilhau (1919–57), to Rilke and modern Danish poets, or, like Erling Christie (b. 1928) and Paal Brekke (b. 1923), to T. S. Eliot. Tarjei Vesaas (1897–1970), an established New Norse novelist who had adopted a moderate modernism in his poetry, provided an important example. But the leading spirit was Brekke, whose Swedish exile during the war had exposed him to *fyrtiotalisterna* (q.v.). In 1949 appeared his tr. of *The Waste Land* and other Eliot poems, along with his own first collection, *Skyggefektning* (Shadow Boxing). Brekke, also a critic and an innovative novelist, did more than anyone else to promote the new poetics. His own production is polarized between a fragmented, chaotic reality and a dream of renewed wholeness, with ironic satire as a prominent feature. He employs a richly allusive, fractured lang., with abrupt shifts in usage levels, mood, rhythm, and point of view—sentimental cliché alternating with fervent invocation, pathos with black humor, personal recollection with glimpses of a world at risk, quotidian banality with the mythic sublime. His best work, *Roerne fra Itaka* (The Oarsmen from Ithaka, 1960), is a poetic cycle in which Brekke, like Eliot, juxtaposes contemporary actuality with Cl. myth. Other important poets who responded to the new signals were Gunvor Hofmo (b. 1921), Arnold Eidslott (b. 1926), Astrid Hjertenæs Andersen (1915–85), and Harald Sverdrup (b. 1923).

Hofmo and Eidslott treat religious themes; Andersen evokes erotic rapture and *participation mystique*; Sverdrup, endowed with a liberated imagination à la Dylan Thomas, celebrates the body and excoriates societal complacencies.

By 1960 the new lang. of poetry was taken for granted and many new voices were heard. Chief among them were Stein Mehren (b. 1935) and Georg Johannesen (b. 1931). Mehren is a writer of wide range—novelist, playwright, and cultural critic as well as poet. His entire *oeuvre* forms part of a philosophical-religious quest for authenticity. The problem of lang. is a central theme: how can poetic lang. mediate reality rather than merely be a reflection of consciousness? The answer, to Mehren, seems to be a quasi-mystical concept of the imagination, a transcendental aesthetic which envisages the poetic process as noetic and tropes as rooted in the reciprocal relation between subject and object in the act of cognition. In *Aurora, Det Niende Mørke* (Aurora, the Ninth Darkness, 1969) the quest theme is traced through the mythic motif of the great journey. Other noteworthy collections are *Den usynlige regnbuen* (The Invisible Rainbow, 1981) and *Corona* (1986). The work of Johannesen is sociopolitically oriented; stylistically and otherwise he is Mehren's contrary. Whereas Mehren's poems often seem like a torrential stream of images, the style of Johannesen—who was deeply influenced by Brecht—is condensed and elliptical, characterized by bizarre contrasts and mordant irony. *Ars Moriendi eller de syv dødsmåter* (Ars Moriendi or the Seven Ways of Death, 1965), his main collection, treats the seven deadly sins—modes of false, inauthentic life—within a strict, semi-scholastic format, in dialectical opposition to its often surrealist imagery.

In the late 1960s new tendencies became evident, as seen in the work of Jan Erik Vold (b. 1939). Vold began as a self-conscious experimentalist preoccupied by solipsism, and his early work includes forays into emblematic verse and concrete poetry. *Hekt* (1966), framed by a document from the Vietnam War, creates a world poised on nightmare through grotesque imagery that evokes the uncanny. Subsequently, under the influence of William Carlos Williams and contemporary Swedish poets, Vold moved toward a "new simplicity," anecdotal and confessional in *Mor Godhjertas glade versjon. Ja* (Mother Goodheart's Glad Version. Yes, 1968), almost purely visual and objective in *spor, snø* (tracks, snow, 1970), where he adapts haiku form. An older poet, Olav H. Hauge (b. 1908), who decades earlier had started out in the Aukrust mode, progressively simplified his style until, with *Dropar i austavind* (Drops in the East Wind, 1966), he was writing about everyday things in an unadorned idiom akin to his Chinese and Japanese models. Hauge became a favorite with the young poets dissatisfied with late symbolism and eager to bring poetry closer to actuality. He and Jacobsen are the grand old men of contemp. N. p. Two other poets with similar aims are Paal-Helge Haugen (b. 1945) and Kolbein Falkeid (b. 1933). The former's work has been influenced by Anglo-Am. rock music and pop poetry. *Steingjerde* (Stone Fences, 1979; Eng. tr. 1986), an autobiographical work, is notable for its narrative elements, regional color, and a mood of nostalgic recollection. Falkeid, whose poetry expresses a deep ecological concern, envisages the poem as an extension of everyday lang.; his diction has distinct anecdotal features.

In the 1970s the literary scene in Norway became intensely politicized. Several feminist poets appeared, continuing their production into the 1980s. Among important figures whose profiles were defined in the course of the decade may be mentioned Arvid Torgeir Lie (b. 1938), Eldrid Lunden (b. 1940), Annie Riis (b. 1927), Halvor Roll (b. 1929), and Arne Ruste (b. 1942). Among those whose production belongs mainly to the 1980s, the following seem very talented: Erik Bystad (b. 1952), Jo Eggen (b. 1952), Ellen Einan (b. 1931), Liv Lundberg (b. 1944), Karin Moe (b. 1945), Håvard Rem (b. 1959), and Tor Ulven (b. 1953).

N. p. today shows a variety of tendencies. Old-style lyrics flourish, but so do innovative texts that experiment with multi-media effects—"sound sculptures," "picture poems," and so forth—which blur genre distinctions. Yet the two central N. trads. of Welhaven and Wergeland persist. Satire, too, continues to hold an important place, as does national and religious pathos—all elements that have been present in N. p. from the beginning. The same applies to visionary poetry, an important strain in the work of 19th- and 20th-c. figures like Wergeland, Aukrust, Bull, and Mehren, as well as in Old Norse poetry and the medieval *Dream Ballad*. There is also a living folk poetry, made extremely popular by Alf Prøysen (1914–70). Others whose work contains elements of ballad and folksong are Einar Skjæraasen (1900–66), Jacob Sande (1906–67), Hans Børli (b. 1918), and Arnljot Eggen (b. 1923).

Finally, a special kind of poem, exemplified by Hamsun's *Munken Vendt* (The Monk Vendt, 1902) and *Driftekaren* (The Drover, 1908) by Hans E. Kinck (1865–1926), has had a deep fascination for N. writers. Dramatic in form, it has a legendary basis and a loose, episodic structure reminiscent of the picaresque. The hero, an incurable wanderer, is a great teller of tales and lives by his wits. These works adumbrate a N. epic genre. A marginal example is *Jonsoknatt* (St. John's Eve, 1933, rev. 1965) by Hans-Henrik Holm (1896–1980), a quest epic based on the ethos of National Romanticism. This ambitious, immensely difficult poem was designed as a folk epic. But the "folk" prefer more accessible fare and have received that from the troubadour poets with their simple, melodious lyrics.

WORKS AND ANTHOLOGIES: B. Bjørnson, *Poems and Songs* (1915); *Oxford Book of Scandinavian Verse*, ed. E. W. Gosse and W. A. Craigie (1925); H. Wergeland, *Poems*, tr. G. M. Gathorne-Hardy et al. (1929); *Anthol. of N. Lyrics*, tr. C. W. Stork (1942); *Norsk lyrikk gjennom tusen år*, 2d ed., ed. E. Kielland, 2 v. (1950)—comprehensive anthol.; *Norsk folkedikting*, ed. O. Bø and S. Solheim, 2d ed., 7 v. (1958–64); *Norsk lyrikk*, ed. G. Johannesen (1966); *The Literary Rev.* 12, 2 (1968–69)—N. issue; *Micromegas*, ed. F. Will, 4, 3 (1971)—New Norse issue; T. Vesaas, *30 Poems*, tr. K. G. Chapman (1971) and *Land of Hidden Fires*, tr. and intro. F. König and J. Crisp (1973); *Draumkvæde*, ed. M. Barnes (1974); *Five N. Poets*, spec. issue of *Lines Rev.*, ed. R. Fulton, 55–56 (1976); *Dannemarks og Norges poesi 1600–1800*, ed. I. Havnevik (1981); *Mod. N. Writing*, spec. iss. of *Stand* 23, 3 (1982); *Mod. Scandinavian Poetry 1900–1975*, ed. M. Allwood (1982); *20 Contemp. N. Poets*, ed. T. Johanssen (1984); O. H. Hauge, *Don't Give Me the Whole Truth*, tr. R. Fulton and J. Greene (1985); R. Jacobsen, *The Silence Afterwards*, ed. and tr. R. Greenwald (1985); *Moderne norsk lyrikk*, ed. K. Heggelund and J. E. Vold (1985).

HISTORY AND CRITICISM: E. W. Gosse, *Northern Studies* (1890); K. Elster, *Illustreret norsk litteraturhist.*, 2 v. (1923–24), "Three Lyric Poets of N.," *ASR* 13 (1925); F. Bull, "Bjørnsons lyrikk," *Streiftog i norsk litt.* (1931); F. Bull et al., *Norsk litteraturhist.*, 6 v. (1924–55); H. Beyer, *A Hist. of N. Lit.*, ed. and tr. E. Haugen (1956)—best survey in Eng.; G. C. Schoolfield, "The Recent Scandinavian Lyric," *BA* 36 (1962); W. Dahl, *Ordene og verden* (1967); H. Lie, *Norsk verslære* (1967); E. Beyer, "Et dikt mot verden," *NLÅ* (1968)—about Brekke; H. Næss, "Stein Mehren," *BA* 47 (1973), *N. Lit. Bibl. 1956–70* (1975); I. Havnevik, "Norsk lyrikk etter 1945," *NLÅ* (1974); I. Stegane, *O. H. Hauges dikting* (1974); *Norges litteraturh.*, ed. E. Beyer, 6 v. (1974–75)—most recent comprehensive lit. hist.; W. Baumgartner, "Die Dezentralisierung der n. Poesie," *Aspekte der skandinavischen Gegenwartslit.*, ed. D. Brennecke (1978); H. and E. Beyer, *Norsk litteraturhist.* (1978)—good bibl.; J. E. Vold, *Det norske syndromet* (1980); P. T. Andersen, *Stein Mehren—en logos-dikter* (1982); M. K. Norseng, *Sigbjørn Obstfelder* (1982); *Norway*, ed. S. Lyngstad, spec. iss. of *RNL* 12 (1983); S. Lyngstad, "Olav Bull," *News of Norway* 41 (1984); A. Aarseth, "The Modes of N. Modernism," *Facets of European Modernism*, ed. J. Garton (1985). S.LY.

NOVAS (RIMADAS)—used in the plural, even for a single composition. Occitan nonlyric poems (verse novels) ordinarily written in rhymed octosyllabic couplets. Although the words were sometimes applied to poems with a strong didactic element, they normally designated some kind of narrative, the most famous examples being the verse novels *Jaufré* and *Flamenca*; the latter in particular is one of the gems of Occitan lit.—Chambers. F.M.C.

NUMBER(S) (Lat. *numerus*). (a) The traditional metonym for metrical feet, meter (q.v.), and hence verse. Originally derived from the quantitative prosodies of the Cl. langs. (see CLASSICAL PROSODY), the notion of "ns." involved the idea of mathematical proportion in meter (chief among which was 1 long = 2 shorts) and was linked to the proportions of musical harmonies, and, through that, to cosmology itself, i.e. the "harmony of the spheres," which music was thought to represent (see Hollander). In Lat., references to *numerus* are common, e.g. Cicero *Orator* 170, 199, 204, 207 ff., 228, and *Brutus* 8, 34; and Quintilian 9.4.55–57; Augustine's discussion carries it into the Middle Ages. In the Ren. and after, "ns." usually denotes either metrical feet or verse in general. But the extension to musical composition was also invoked: "E. K." in Spenser's *Shepheardes Calender* says Plato held that "the mynd was made of certaine harmonie and musicall nombers" (Gloss to "October" 27); and Milton has "In full harmonic n. joined" (*Paradise Lost* 4.687). In the 17th c. the musical and metrical senses converge in the doctrine of "harmony of ns.," still influential in the 18th c. (e.g. F. Manwaring, 1744; J. Mason, 1749 [see Brogan]). Usage declined in the 19th c. with the demise of all forms of a classicizing approach to metrics, i.e. syllable arithmetic.—W. F. J. Knight, *St. Augustine's* De musica: *A Synopsis* (1949); Lote, pt. 1, bk. 2, ch. 3; C. M. Ing, *Elizabethan Lyrics* (1951); D. T. Mace, "The Doctrine of Sound and Sense in Augustan Poetic Theory." *RES* 2 (1951); G. S. Koehler, "Milton on Ns.," *SP* 55 (1958); J. Hollander, *The Untuning of the Sky* (1961); A. Primmer, *Cicero Numerosus* (1968); Brogan; J. Stevens, *Words and Music in the Middle Ages* (1986); K. Meerhoff, *Rhétorique et poétique au XVIe siècle en France* (1986).   T.V.F.B.; J.H.

NUMEROLOGY is a theory of composition whereby authors order their works according to numerical patterns—when number itself becomes, in Jakobson's phrase, "the constitutive device of the sequence." The items arranged may be almost anything countable, whether substantive (events of a narrative, days of its action) or formal (chapters, stanzas, lines). Equally various are the possible patterns: they range from complex arrays of Platonic numbers or numbers bearing special religious significance—such as 3 in Christianity—to simple round-number counts or mere allusions—like the 200s that refer to Carolus Calvus (CC in Roman numerals). The art of intricate n. (as of its concealment) can achieve effects of great subtlety.

Much medieval and Ren. n. derived from the Bible, which itself offered models for such organization, notably in Lamentations and the acrostic (q.v.) Psalms. These examples exerted immense authority through the trads. of biblical poetics and of Heb. poetics (q.v.): the letter total of the Heb. alphabet, for example, used in Psalms 119, became a favorite compositional number. Indeed, handbooks of number symbolism (arithmology), such as Pietro Bongo's *Numerorum mysteria* (1591), most often based a number's symbolisms on the contexts of its biblical occurrences. But it is important to recognize that n. could nevertheless be mimetic, since creation itself was thought to reveal patterns of number symbolism. A much-quoted authority was Wisdom of Solomon 11:20: "Thou hast ordained all things by measure and number and weight."

Philo Judaeus gave a decisive turn to number symbolism when he interpreted Genesis in terms of Pythagorean number theory (e.g. the six days of creation made a perfect number). Subsequently, biblical numbers mingled with Pythagorean-Platonic symbolisms like the *tetraktus* (1 + 2 + 3 + 4 = 10) and the *lambda* series (1, 2, 4, 8; 1, 3, 9, 27). Such principal symbolic numbers informed patterns throughout Western culture: they appear in early medieval Celtic romances and 17th-c. ecclesiastical music, in biblical commentaries and lyric poems, in masque dances and cathedral architecture.

Ren. writers emulated the symmetries and Pythagorean proportions of architecture fairly directly, so that a doctrine of *ut architectura poesis* developed, comparable with the more familiar *ut pictura poesis* (q.v.). In particular, poets liked to form symmetries emphasizing an array's central position, which carried associations of sovereignty or dignity. Thus Dante treats divine love in the central canto of the *Divina commedia* at the center of a symmetrical array of line totals: 151 / 145 / 145 / 139 / 145 / 145 / 151. Texts like Gen. 3:3 and Exod. 8:22 ("I am the Lord in the midst of the earth") authorized such procedures. Consequently, in approaching a late medieval or Ren. poem, it is worth counting to find what lies at its center: in *Paradise Lost*, for example, Messiah ascends his throne in the central lines of the first edition's 10,550 (exact n. was often confined to the *editio princeps*).

Another common sort of n. is calendrical. Here again there was biblical authority in texts like Psalm 90:12 ("teach me to number my days"). Petrarch took these to heart, structuring his *Canzoniere* as a calendar and noting the astrological circumstances of composition of individual poems. In the Ren. it is Spenser who followed this trad. most extensively: his *Epithalamion* represents a celebrated instance of n., rediscovered by Hieatt. Many Elizabethan sonnet sequences have calendrical n., e.g. Spenser's *Amoretti*. Alternatively, they may use allusive numbers such as the 108 of the Penelope Game in Sidney's *Astrophil and Stella* and Alexander Craig's *Amorous Songs, Sonnets and Elegies* (1606).

Most Ren. poems of any formal pretensions are organized numerologically. And certain mannerist poets (such as Chapman) reach a *ne plus ultra* if not a *reductio absurdum* of self-conscious intricacy in this regard by continual references to their own n. But this is far from obvious, since they assiduously finesse by "concealing" their secrets—e.g. by using totals one more or one less than the significant number.

In the Middle Ages and the Ren., numerical composition was taken for granted; it formed part of the poetic craft or "mystery"—like that whereby the rules of prosody are still handed down. Few Ren. writings about n. have survived, and these are not on a high plane of critical interest. In the 18th c., with the spread of a new world view, number came to be assigned a less symbolic function, and interest in n. declined. The romantic movement brought a rupture with the older compositional trad., so that n. had to be rediscovered by the pre-Raphaelite D. G. Rossetti, by devout students of medieval Catholicism, by early 20th-c. Dante scholars, and by hermetic modernists like Joyce. In the 1960s and early '70s, n. enjoyed something of a vogue, perhaps in part because of the excitement of rediscovery, perhaps as a signal instance of the kind of arbitrary, historically conditioned coding system to which structuralists liked to draw attention. Since then, n. has gone out of critical fashion (its intentional patterns are hardly consonant with free play of meaning), but it has taken its place as a regular part of historical scholarship. Like prosody, n. is indispensable to a full appreciation of earlier poetry, and sometimes (particularly where allusive numbers are involved) it can aid interpretation decisively. There is still no comprehensive study of the subject.—Curtius, Excursus 15; A. K. Hieatt, *Short Time's Endless Monument* (1960); A. Fowler, *Spenser and the Numbers of Time* (1964), *Triumphal Forms* (1970); W. Haubrichs, *Ordo als Form* (1969); C. Butler, *Number Symbolism* (1970)—wide-ranging primer; *Silent Poetry*, ed. A. Fowler (1970); M. Hardt, *Die Zahl in der Divina commedia* (1973); E. Hellgardt, *Zum Problem symbolbestimmter und formalästhetischer Zahlenkomposition in mittelaltericher Literatur* (1973); *Fair Forms*, ed. M.-S. Røstvig et al. (1975); R. G. Peterson, "Critical Calculations," *PMLA* 91 (1976); C. D. Eckhardt, *Essays in the Numerical Crit. of Med. Lit.* (1980); J. MacQueen, *N.* (1985)—the best intro., esp. valuable for the earlier periods; J. J. Guzzardo, *Dante: Numerological Studies* (1988); A. Dunlop, "Number Symbolism, Mod. Studies in," and M.-S. Rostvig, "Number Symbolism, Trad. of," *The Spenser Encyc.*, ed. A. C. Hamilton et al. (1990).
A.FO.

NURSERY RHYMES. A n. r. may be defined as a rhyme or verse preserved in the world of children. Examples are:

> Humpty Dumpty sat on a wall,
> Humpty Dumpty had a great fall—
> All the King's horses and all the King's
> men

Could not put Humpty Dumpty together again.

and

> Rain, rain, go away,
> Come again another day.

The origins of the n. r. are manifold, but except for lullabies and verses which accompany infant games ("This little piggy"), very few originated in the nursery. Material from adult life was introduced to children either for reason or by accident, often simply because of its memorability; that material which proved popular with the children survived, and with surprisingly little alteration—despite the fact that some of it disappeared from print for two centuries at a time—being handed down efficiently and continuously through oral trad. Metrically, most n. rs. are in accentual verse (q.v.), particularly one or another form of ballad meter (q.v.).

It is certain that n. rs. are ancient. Peter Opie estimates that at least one fourth, and probably one half, of the n. rs. known to Eng.-speaking children today are more than 200 years old. It is impossible to be precise about the age of most of the verses. "White bird featherless" appears in Lat. in the 10th c., "Two legs sat upon three legs" in Bede, "Thirty days hath September" in Fr. in the 13th c., "Matthew, Mark, Luke, and John" in Ger. in the 15th c.; but it is likely that these n. rs. existed many, perhaps hundreds, of years before they were written down. References in Gr., Lat., and Oriental lits. show that children's games and verses analogous to ours were known in these cultures, and some scholars believe that some "classic" n. rs. (e.g. "Buck, buck," "Humpty Dumpty") are thousands of years old. This theory is supported by the prevalence of a number of specific n. rs. and their analogues throughout Europe. Probably many n. rs. were carried from country to country by armies, travelers, missionaries, and translators; many Eng. n. rs. have been translated into Hindustani, Malayan, Rus., etc. But the possibility exists that some of the lore came down in an unbroken line from the ancient world.

It is possible to trace the sources (or define the types) of many of the later n. rs.—those of the last 300 years. Some of these sources are: (1) *Songs.* These include ballads (q.v.) and folksongs (e.g. "One misty moisty morning"); drinking songs ("I've got sixpence"); war songs ("The King of France went up the hill"); songs from plays ("There was a jolly miller"—but probably this song existed before it was incorporated in *Love in a Village*); romantic lyrics ("Where are you going, my pretty maid?"); popular songs of recent date ("Where, o where has my little dog gone?"); lullabies ("Rockabye, baby"). (2) *Street cries* ("Hot Cross Bun"). (3) *Riddles* (q.v.; "Little Nancy Etticoat"). (4) *Proverbs* (q.v.; "Needles and Pins"). (5) *Custom and ritual* ("London Bridge"). (6) *Religious and antireligious poetry* ("Matthew, Mark, Luke, and John," "Good morning, Father Francis"). (7) *Rs. about historical figures* ("Lucy Locket"; the Robin Hood ballads). (8) *Poems by recent authors* ("Twinkle, twinkle, little star," by Jane Taylor). (9) *Songs or chants for children's games* ("Here we go round the mulberry bush"). (10) *Counting out rs.*, many of which seem to have derived from old Celtic numbers preserved among the illiterate classes in England and still used for counting sheep, fish, stitches in knitting, etc. ("Eena, meena, mina moe," "One-ery, two-ery," and originally "Hickory Dickory Dock"). These classifications are rough and do not account for all n. rs.; they serve, however, to show from what a variety of sources the lore of the nursery is culled.

"Mother Goose" n. rs. were introduced in Europe by a Frenchman, Charles Perrault, in his *Histoires ou contes du temps passé* in 1697. His *contes de ma mère l'Oye* were immediately popular, being tr. into Eng. by Robert Samber in 1729. A new collection, *Tommy Thumb's Pretty Song Book*, appeared in 1744; there is extant in the British Museum a single copy of the second of its two volumes, containing about 40 songs. In ca. 1781 appeared *Mother Goose's Melody, or Sonnets for the Cradle* (earliest extant copy 1791); in 1784 came *Gammer Gurton's Garland*. In America, *Songs for the Nursery, or Mother Goose's Melodies for Children* was published in 1819; no copies survive. There is an apochryphal story that the printer named the book after his mother-in-law, née Elizabeth Goose. The n. rs. are usually called "Mother Goose Rs." in America even though the origin of that phrase is not British. The term "n. r." was not used in England until the 19th c.; before that, n. rs. were "Tommy Thumb's songs." During the past century and a half, hundreds of collections have appeared.

The first scholar to explore the material was James O. Halliwell, whose collection of 300 n. rs., most of them still popular today, was published in 1842. His work has been superseded in the 20th c. by that of Iona and Peter Opie, whose *Oxford Dict. of N. Rs.* contains 550 entries, with many variants, important notes, and a valuable introduction. Scholars have offered two main theories concerning the n. r. One of these, the *historical* theory, tries to identify the "real personages" of the verses: e.g. Old King Cole is a British king of the 3d c., or

the father of St. Helena, or the father of Finn McCool; Georgie Porgie is George I, or the Duke of Buckingham; the Queen the pussy-cat went to see is Elizabeth I. Although some of these identifications can be only wild surmise, there is evidence for the historicity of a number of the characters: Elise Marley was a famous alewife, Lucy Locket and Kitty Fisher courtesans of the time of Charles I, and Jack Horner probably a steward of the Abbot of Glastonbury, whose "plum" was a deed to valuable property still in the Horner family.

Henry Bett believes that the n. r. (as well as many children's tales and games) reflects nature myths ("Jack and Jill" is about tides), custom ("London Bridge" echoes the rite of human sacrifice necessary to appease the water over which a bridge was built), and history ("John Ball"). James Joyce owned a copy of Bett's book, and *Finnegans Wake* contains references to about 70 rs. Joyce sees the rs. as embodying myths which express the experiences of the human race. In this, Joyce illustrates what may be called the *psychoanalytic* theory, a theory subsequently applied to folk material in general by Joseph Campbell in *The Hero with a Thousand Faces*. See also ACCENTUAL VERSE; BALLAD; CHANT.

J. Ritson, *Gammer Gurton's Garland: or, the N. Parnassus* (1784); J. O. Halliwell, *The N. Rs. of England*, rev. ed. (1843); H. C. Bolton, *The Counting Out Rs. of Children* (1888); A. B. Gomme, *The Traditional Games of England, Scotland, and Ireland*, 2 v. (1894–98); *The Book of N. Songs and Rs.*, ed. S. Baring-Gould (1895); P. B. Green, *A Hist. of N. Rs.* (1899); W. W. Newell, *Games and Songs of Am. Children*, rev. ed. (1903); L. Eckenstein, *Comparative Studies in N. Rs.* (1906); H. Bett, *N. Rs. and Tales* (1924); D. E. Marvin, *Historic Child Rs.* (1930); B. A. Botkin, *The Am. Play-Party Song* (1937); V. M. Sackville-West, *N. Rs.* (1947); *Oxford Dict. of N. Rs.*—best general survey, *Oxford N. R. Book*, both ed. I. and P. Opie (1951, 1955); *The Authentic Mother Goose Fairy Tales and N. Rs.*, ed. J. Barchilon and H. Pettit (1960); P. H. Evans, *Rimbles* (1961); *Hogarth Book of Scottish N. Rs.*, ed. N. and W. Montgomerie (1964); A. M. Stevens, *The N. R.: Remnant of Popular Protest* (1968); *Counting-Out Rs.: A Dict.*, ed. R. D. Abrahams and L. Rankin (1980).   M.P.W.

O

OBJECTIVE CORRELATIVE. The phrase comes from T. S. Eliot's 1919 essay "Hamlet and His Problems": "the only way of expressing emotion in the form of art is by finding an 'o. c.'; in other words, a set of objects, a situation, a chain of events which shall be the formula of that *particular* emotion; such that when the external facts, which must terminate in sensory experience, are given, the emotion is immediately evoked." Eliot used the formula to pronounce *Hamlet* "an artistic failure" on the grounds that Hamlet suffers from an emotion "he cannot objectify"; and that this dramatic difficulty is a "prolongation" of Shakespeare's inability to express his own feelings satisfactorily by writing the play. Hamlet's "disgust" exceeds its object (his mother's incestuous remarriage) just as the Hamlet story is an inadequate vehicle for the emotion ("by hypothesis unknowable") that prompted Shakespeare to use it for his play.

Eliot's essay has not convinced many critics to consider *Hamlet* a failure, but the phrase "o. c." has passed into general usage as a tool of aesthetic judgment. When we feel that an image (or any other element) in a work fails to embody the "*particular* emotion" required, or when we feel that an emotion is being described rather than "presented," we say that the artist has not found an o. c. And when we suspect that some emotion of the artist's has not been expressed or satisfied, we say that the work itself is an inadequate o. c. Both usages are suggested by Eliot's essay, but each comes wrapped in a different theoretical package. Eliot's formula—with its implicit attack on romantic "excess"—has a modernist flavor, but the requirement that a poem evoke emotion by the representation of sensory experience was conventional in the 19th c. Antecedent instances of Eliot's prescription have been identified in Pater (DeLaura); Washington Allston, in whose *Lectures on Art* (1850) the phrase appears (Stallman); Coleridge (DiPasquale); and Schiller (Wellek) among many others. In fact, Eliot's formula reproduces a standard definition of 20th-c. imagism. Ford Madox Ford, reviewing Pound's *Cathay* (1915), cites "the theory that poetry consists in so rendering concrete objects that the emotions produced by the objects shall arise in the reader"—a phrase Eliot quotes in *Ezra Pound: His Metric and Poetry* (1917). The o. c. thus marks one of the points at which 20th-c. modernism aligns itself with the 19th-c. aesthetic values it was ostensibly designed to supplant.

In "Trad. and the Individual Talent" (1919) and elsewhere, Eliot suggests that the satisfactory construction of the poem relieves the poet of a psychic distress—a "personal" emotion that need have no connection with the emotions expressed in the poem. The poet "expresses" his own feelings only in the sense of "escap[ing]" from them by producing the poem. This psycho-biographical aspect of the o. c. has no necessary relation to its imagist aspect; Eliot's yoking of the two in the *Hamlet* essay—Hamlet's "problem" reproduces Shakespeare's—is logically factitious.

Although the o. c. has proved useful for sympathetic readings of Eliot's own poetry (e.g. Matthiessen's), its theoretical standing is not high. Eliot's formulation verges on tautology—"the emotions evoked by a work of art must be the product of elements in that work" is a possible paraphrase. The imagists' suggestion that an object has an inherent emotional value, cashable by its correct representation, depends on an epistemology no longer fashionable, and the idea that naming an object in a poem presents the reader with a concrete sense-experience—in effect, with the object itself—is one that structuralist and poststructuralist critics have rejected: they are more likely to regard lit. as writing "about" the impossibility of such referentiality. But because it names things intuitively felt about art, "o. c." seems one of those terms destined to survive their philosophical supersession. See also SUBJECTIVITY AND OBJECTIVITY.—F. M. Hueffer [Ford], "From China to Peru," *The Outlook* 35 (1915); F. O. Matthiessen, *The Achievement of T. S. Eliot* (1935), ch. 3; T. S. Eliot, "Hamlet and His Problems" in *The Sacred Wood* (1920), rev. as "Hamlet" in *Essays*, "Trad. and the Individual Talent" (1919), rpt. in *Essays*, "Mod. Tendencies in Poetry," *Shama'a* (1920); E. Vivas, "The O. C. of T. S. Eliot," *The Critic's Notebook*, ed. R. W. Stallman (1950); Wellek, v. 1; F. Kermode, *Romantic Image* (1957); G. Hough, *Image and Experience* (1960); D. J. DeLaura, "Pater and Eliot: The Origin of the O. C.," *MLQ* 26 (1965); P. DiPasquale, Jr., "Coleridge's Framework of Objectivity and Eliot's O. C.," *JAAC* 26 (1968); L. Brisman, "Swinburne's Semiotics," *GaR* 31 (1977).
                                                                    L.ME.

OBJECTIVISM. A term used to designate what some have regarded as a movement in Am. poetry in the early 1930s, based on the work of the poets published in the February 1931 issue of *Poetry*, guest-edited by Louis Zukofsky, in *An "Objectivists" Anthol.*, ed. by Zukofsky and pub. by TO, Publishers, in 1932, and in books issued by the Objectivist

OBSCURITY

Press in 1933–36. In wider application, that part of modern Am. poetry (1) which has not followed in the trad. of symbolism (q.v.) but has developed out of imagism (q.v.); (2) which presents concrete objects not in order to convey abstract ideas but for the sake of their sensuous qualities and haecceity; (3) which reflects the poet's primary interest in composing a structure of relationships apprehensible as a whole, rather than in offering interpretations of experience; and (4) which uses lang. more literally than figuratively. The poets most frequently associated with O. are Zukofsky (1904–78), George Oppen (1908–84), Charles Reznikoff (1894–1976), Carl Rakosi (b. 1903), Lorine Niedecker (1903–70); also the Eng. poet Basil Bunting (1900–85). The Am. modernists W. C. Williams and Ezra Pound were also affiliated with the younger objectivists for part of their careers.

Since these poets differ widely from each other and since, though most of them had personal ties to each other, they never worked together as a group, it is not surprising that some critics have denied that O. was a movement at all. Zukofsky himself denied the existence of O. as a movement; the term he coined was "objectivist," which he meant to designate only individual poets. But other critics have treated O. either as a unitary phenomenon or as a designation for a particular kind of poetry, taking Zukofsky's essay "Sincerity and Objectification" as an articulation of its principles. In that essay Zukofsky argues that sincerity is manifested in details of seeing and wording and that the perfected deployment of poetic structure can result in the objectification of the poem. To Reznikoff and Rakosi the goal of poetic craft was, rather, a clear, precise naming of things, serving to evoke emotions associated with them, a view that suggests the influence of imagism (q.v.), of Eliot's notion of the objective correlative (q.v.), and of oriental poetry (see EXOTICISM). The objectivists produced a considerable diversity of styles, ranging from the intricate sound-play of Zukofsky and Niedecker to the nearly transparent sentences of Reznikoff, from the multiple possibilities for parsing in Oppen's late poetry to the clarifying articulation of syntax through lineation in Rakosi's recent work. If one generalization could be made about all the objectivists, it would probably be that they sought to "think with things as they exist" (Zukofsky's phrase), to extend the principles of imagism while retaining its respect for things and for craft, and to allow thought and history into the poem. Cf. DINGGEDICHT.

Poetry 37, 5 (1931), *An "Objectivists" Anthol.* (1932), both ed. L. Zukofsky; W. C. Williams, *Autobiography* (1951); L. S. Dembo, "The Objectivist Poet: Four Interviews," *ConL* 10 (1969); S. Faucherau, "Poetry in America: O.," *Ironwood* 6 (1975); "Lorine Niedecker Issue," *Truck* 16 (1975); R. Schiffer, "Die Poetik und Lyrik der Objektivisten," *Die amerikanische Literatur der Gegenwart*, ed. H. Bungert (1977); C. Altieri, "The

Objectivist Trad.," *ChiR* 30 (1979); *Louis Zukofsky* (1979), *Basil Bunting* (1981), both ed. C. F. Terrell; *George Oppen*, ed. B. Hatlen (1981); R. Silliman, "Third Phase O.," *Paideuma* 10 (1981); L. Zukofsky, "An Objective," *Prepositions*, 2d ed. (1981); *Charles Reznikoff*, ed. M. Hindus (1984); N. M. Finkelstein, "What Was O.?" *Am. Poetry* 2 (1985); "George Oppen: A Spec. Iss.," *Ironwood* 26 (1985); M. Heller, *Conviction's Net of Branches* (1985); S. Sandbank, "The Object-Poem," *PoT* 6 (1985). E.B.

OBJECTIVITY. See SUBJECTIVITY AND OBJECTIVITY; POETICS.

OBLIQUE RHYME. See NEAR RHYME.

OBSCURITY in poetry has had a long history. One of the earliest and most significant forms of o. appears in medieval allegory (q.v.). The basic impulse behind allegorical o. in the Middle Ages seems to lie in the recoding of the Old Testament in a modified figural system which could be used by readers of the New, based on the premise that the subject matter of OT texts held a second, concealed meaning to be fulfilled in the future (see INTERPRETATION, FOURFOLD METHOD). Characteristically, medieval theorists did not always foreground the intrinsic elements of the text in a discernible formal arrangement but rather interpreted the fragmentary signs and traces embedded in OT texts as veiled disclosures of a mysterious God's half-illuminated messages. Because the subject matter was obscure, the deeper meaning of original OT texts was assumed to be still hidden and subject to interp. Dante's *Divina commedia* is the best example of allegorical o. in medieval lit. In it the annunciatory signs and residues of previous texts are taken as an obscure manifestation of God's veiled, sacred message. To the same category belongs the esoteric and obscure poetry of the *dolce stil nuovo* (q.v.; Guinizelli, Cavalcanti). Interestingly, obscure poetry was attacked in the 14th c. because it was thought to be unneccessarily incomprehensible and opaque. Such narrow crit., failing to discern the meaning concealed beneath the artistry of the poem's surface, is but one indication of a persistent hostility towards the hermetic work of art. Nevertheless Boccaccio defended poetry in *De genealogia deorum gentilium* when he argued that the value of a poem is heightened by the obstacles that stand in the way of its decipherment.

In Ren. England, following the increased censorship of the 1580s, disguised political commentary and theories were concealed in a double-voiced allegorical o. whose meaning was hard to formulate—e.g. Spenser's *Shepheardes Calender* and Sidney's *Arcadia*. The devel. of o. in Ren. poetry was also influenced by Hermeticism (q.v.) and the writings of Hermes Trismegistus (ca. 100–200 A.D.) disseminated in Elizabethan England by

Giordano Bruno. The exceedingly complex and intricate occult symbolism which Hermeticism introduced into Ren. poetic lang. clearly contributed to the power and richness of Ren. poetry. In *The Faerie Queene*, for example, Spenser uses stellar symbolism and cosmology adapted from Hermetic iconography. Other surviving remnants of Hermetic o. are evident in a large number of Ren. works such as Jonson's masques, Milton's *L'Allegro* and *Il Penseroso*, Lovelace's *Aramantha*, and the lyrics of Vaughan and Traherne.

A somewhat different type of o. takes shape in 17th-c. metaphysical poetry (q.v.), where several heterogeneous elements combine to produce o.: hyperbole and conceit (qq.v.); deliberate syntactic inversions; and abstruse diction employing terminology from alchemy, scholastic philosophy, astronomy, mathematics, and geography. Moreover, the primary concern of the metaphysical poets with probing the validity of appearance and exploring contradictory, not easily assimilated ideas lends their poetry a dense intellectual difficulty.

The o. of much 20th-c. poetry is also characterized by a number of distinctive features: disjointed syntax, broken lines, rupture, and dissonance; deliberate stress on allusions, sometimes cryptic; exaggerated metaphors and unreal images; and a renunciation of the referential and communicative functions of lang. Such o. of lang. distinguishes modern poetry from 18th- and 19th-c. poetry, which seems relatively clear and transparent in comparison. In contrast to earlier objective and emotional modes of expression, the intricate wordplay of those forms which developed under the influence of symbolism, futurism, dada (qq.v.), and other avant-garde movements is strange, unfamiliar, and esoteric. Its impersonal poetic universe dissolves prosaic reality into an artificial structure of enigmatic associations. The poetry of Yeats, esp. the early collections, *The Rose* and *The Wind Among the Reeds* exemplifies such o. in its inscrutable, mysterious symbolism derived from Celtic mythology, Rosicrucianism, Theosophy, and occultism.

The formal devel. of o. has been accompanied by a proliferation of programmatic and justificatory statements: "There is a certain glory in not being understood" (Baudelaire); "I utter the word in order to plunge it back into its inanity" (Mallarmé); "I have no language, only images, analogies, symbols" (Yeats). In "The Metaphysical Poets" T. S. Eliot explains the o. of the modern poem as reflective of its social context: "We can only say that it appears likely that poets in our civilization, as it exists at present, must be *difficult*." Delmore Schwartz, concerned with the isolation of the modern poet, finds the o. of modern poetry to originate in the dissociation of sensibility (q.v.) from intellect that Eliot held took place during the 17th c., in which emotions and sensibilities became subordinate to the instrumental categories of science. There thus emerges a mechanistic rationality which reaches its full devel. in the sterile classificatory schemas of 19th-c. science. This impoverishment of experience is ultimately responsible for the poet's isolation. A poetic sensibility rooted in a common lang. can no longer exist in such a society; the poet's idiom and a dehumanized existence become opposed to each other. If the poet is unable to express himself in normal linguistic usage, he must slip into an idiosyncratic and specialized discourse.

John Crowe Ransom, however, reformulates Eliot's dissociation in terms of the poet's conscious decision to withdraw from the drab realities of the public sphere: "modern poets," Ransom tells us, "have formed a compact to unclasp the chaplet from their brows, inflicting upon themselves the humility of delaureation, and retiring from public responsibility and honors." Ransom distinguishes two dominant styles in modern poetry: "pure" style and "obscure" style. In the first type, the poem tends towards complicated wordplay and technical audacities (Wallace Stevens' "Sea Surface Full of Clouds" is his example). In the second type, the poem tends toward an effect of controlled o. (Allen Tate's "Death of Little Boys").

More recent critical discussion focuses less on a social diagnosis of the factors contributing to o. in modern poetry than on an identification of those interpretive codes through which the critic tries to decipher the poem. Michael Riffaterre has suggested that a "hermeneutic model" is at work within the poetic object, helping the reader unravel the structural peculiarities of the text. As an interpretive paradigm, it "offers a frame of thought or a signifying system that tells the reader how or where to look for a solution, or from what angle the text can be seen as decipherable." Significantly, Riffaterre's model hinges on "the word, phrase, sentence or text that resists deciphering, or whose reason for being is hard to judge." Hence the essential motivation of his method is precisely the unique resistance or excessive difficulty presented by the complicated verseforms of obscure poetry.

Discussions about the o. of modern poetry are not limited to Western crit. William Tay has shown that controversy about o. (*menglong*) in poetry extends to post-Maoist China. In the 1970s and '80s, poets such as Gu Cheng, Wang Xiaoni, and others have created a corpus of work whose special kind of expression resembles imagist poetry. This Chinese debate about the unintelligible or hermetic character of the modern poem raises anew theoretical questions about the status of o. in poetry. See also CULTERANISMO; HERMETICISM; NEO-GONGORISM; PLATONISM AND POETRY.

E. Holmes, *Henry Vaughan and the Hermetic Philosophy* (1932); H. Read, "O. in Poetry," *Coll. Essays* (1938); J. C. Ransom, "Poets Without Laurels," *The World's Body* (1938); D. Schwartz, "The Isolation of Mod. Poetry," *KR* 3 (1941); R. Daniells, "Eng. Baroque and Deliberate O.," *JAAC* 5 (1946);

W. V. O'Connor, "Forms of O.," *Sense and Sensibility in Mod. Poetry* (1948); T. S. Eliot, "The Metaphysical Poets," in Eliot, *Essays*; Auerbach, ch. 8, and *Dante*, tr. R. Manheim (1980); Curtius; *G. Boccaccio on Poetry*, tr. C. E. Osgood (1956); J. Press, *The Chequer'd Shade* (1958); F. Warnke, *European Metaphysical Poetry* (1961); D. C. Allen, *Mysteriously Meant* (1970); F. Yates, *Giordano Bruno and the Hermetic Trad.* (1978), *The Occult Philosophy in the Elizabethan Age* (1979); K. K. Ruthven, *Critical Assumptions* (1979), ch. 3; D. Brookes-Davis, *The Mercurian Monarch* (1983); M. Riffaterre, "Hermeneutic Models," *PoT* 4 (1983); de Man, ch. 9; A. Patterson, *Censorship and Interp.* (1984); W. Tay, "Obscure Poetry," *After Mao: Chinese Lit. and Society, 1978–81*, ed. J. C. Kinkley (1985).　　P.M.

OCCASIONAL VERSE. All literary works are occasioned in some sense; o. v. differs in having not a private but a public or social occasion. From Pindar's odes to Whitman's "When Lilacs Last in the Dooryard Bloom'd," poets have found public occasions for writing: e.g. the memorial pieces in honor of Edward King, among which *Lycidas* was one; the odes expected of a poet laureate (q.v.); tributes to a poet placed at the beginning of his volume, esp. in the 16th and 17th cs.; epithalamia, such as those by Spenser and Donne; funeral elegies, respectful or ironic; sonnets or odes memorializing some state occasion or historic event; or the prologues and epilogues to 17th- and 18th-c. plays. Counterparts abound in modernist and contemp. poetry; W. B. Yeats, Ezra Pound, and William Carlos Williams have written a good deal of o. v. Some modern occasional poems are Hardy's "On an Invitation to the United States," Yeats's "Easter 1916," and Auden's "September 1, 1939." Although o. v. is often associated with poets from the Ren. through the Enlightenment, that is too narrow a view, as is also the restriction to European writers. Islamic poetry is rich in panegyrics founded on occasion, as is Korean. With their strong assumption of the historical and of the historical bases of poetry, Chinese poets typically write o. v.; Japanese poems of the court period specify occasions, if only fictional, in their headnotes. In short, although o. v. is often taken to be ephemeral or trivial or public, it is difficult to devise theoretical terms to distinguish rigorously between *Lycidas*, Dickinson's imaginary occasions of her own death, Lowell's *On the Union Dead*, and various Asian examples. On the other hand, to be dismissive is to violate the most serious conceptions of much of the world's lyric poetry; even narrative and drama may arise from occasion. See also ELEGY; ENCOMIUM; EPIDEICTIC POETRY; EPINIKION; EPITHALAMIUM; ODE.—R. Haller, "Gelegenheitsdichtung," *Reallexikon*; P. Matvejevic, *La poésie de circonstance et l'engagement en poésie*, Diss., Paris (1967); E. M. Oppenheimer, *Goethe's Poetry for Occasions* (1974); W. Segebrecht, *Die Gelegenheitsgedicht* (1977); M. Z. Sugano, *The Poetics of the Occasion* (1992).　　E.M.; A.J.M.S.; T.V.F.B.

OCCITAN POETRY. The root of the term O. is the word *oc*, "yes," in the lang. of medieval southern France, in contrast to OF *oïl* (Modern Fr. *oui*) and It. *si*; this triple distinction was made by Dante in *De vulgari eloquentia* (ca. 1305). The lang. has been called "langue d'oc," "Provençal," and other names since the 13th c. "Provençal" was long preferred, esp. in Eng. and Ger., but has the disadvantage that it seems to refer specifically to Provence (Lat. "Provincia romana," the region of Gaul nearest to Rome), i.e. the area east of the Rhône and home of the 19th-c. poet Mistral (see below), which is only one part of the larger area where the lang. is spoken; "Languedoc" refers to another part of the territory, west of the Rhône. "O." is free from both such misleading connotations and enjoys increasing acceptance, although it was introduced comparatively recently in both Fr. (since 1886) and Eng. (since 1940).

The annals of O. p. begin about A.D. 1000 with the *Boeci*, a fragmentary paraphrase of Boethius' *Consolation of Philosophy*, and continue to about 1050 with the *Chanson de Sainte Foy*, a saint's life. From ca. 1100–1300 were the halcyon days of the troubadours (q.v.), lyric poets who sang of courtly love (q.v.) and a range of other subjects. Scholars debate whether William IX, Duke of Aquitaine and Count of Poitiers (1071–1126), was the first troubadour or merely the first whose works have been transmitted to us. William's eleven (or ten) extant poems include some expressing the humility and devotion of courtly love, but also others of explicit eroticism (one has been called a *fabliau* [q.v.]) and one in which he says goodbye to earthly power, perhaps because of an imminent departure on crusade or because he expected to die soon. The next generation included the moralist Marcabru (fl. 1130–49), who scourged the sexual license of married men and women, while in other songs he depicted encounters of the first-person narrator with a young girl; in one of these, the prototypical *pastorela* (see PASTOURELLE), the narrator attempts to seduce the girl but she steadfastly refuses.

In the middle years of the 12th c., Peire d'Alvernhe (fl. 1149–68) developed a theory of difficult style, or *trobar clus* (q.v.—closed composition), which involved elaborate play on rhymes and sounds with obscure vocabulary and syntax; Raimbaut d'Aurenga (d. 1173) advocated such abstruseness in a debate with Giraut de Bornelh (fl. 1162–99), who defended *trobar leu*, or the easy style. Bernart de Ventadorn (fl. 1147–70?), considered perhaps the greatest love poet among the troubadours, sang with a deceptive air of simplicity about his adoration for a lady, the joy of his love and the grief of his yearning, and, less frequently, about his ecstasy in sexual fulfillment.

By about 1170 the troubadours developed a set of generic concepts. In terms of this system, the

2500-odd extant poems comprise about 1000 *cansos* (q.v.) or love songs; about 500 are *sirventes* (q.v.) or satires; about 500 are *coblas* (see COBLA) or individual stanzas; and those remaining comprise a number of genres, incl. the *pastorela*, the *alba* (q.v.) or dawn poem, debate-poems such as the *tenso* and the *partimen* (qq.v.), and the *planh* (q.v.) or funeral lament.

Bertran de Born (ca. 1150–1215), whose castle of Altafort was besieged and captured by Richard Lionheart, sang of political passions with the commitment of a feudal lord dedicated to warfare as a source of moral stature. The feudal mentality also informs the *chanson de geste* (q.v.) *Giraut de Roussillon* (ca. 1150), written in an artificial blend of O. and Fr., and the parodic romance *Jaufre* (late 12th c.).

In the early 13th c., the O. region was the scene of the Albigensian Crusade, waged in the service of the pope by a Fr. leader, Simon de Montfort, against the heretical Cathars centered at Albi. According to one interpretation, the crusade destroyed the courtly society which had nourished the troubadours, and destined O. p. to inevitable decline; but it is not certain that this conflict, one among many, played so decisive a role. Peire Cardenal (fl. 1205–72) criticized the Roman Catholic Church for the failings of its unworthy priests, incl. members of the Inquisition, while expressing his own orthodox piety. Perhaps in the mid 13th c. was composed the delightful romance of *Flamenca*, whose heroine succeeds, despite the cruelty of her jealous husband, in enjoying the love of a perfect knight. Late in the century, Guiraut Riquier (fl. 1254–82) complained of the insecurity of the courtier's life and lamented that he had come among the last of the troubadours.

Though we have the melodies of only one-tenth of the troubadour poems, it is assumed that virtually all of them were set to music. The troubadour wrote both text and melody, which were performed by the joglar (see JONGLEUR). Joglars and troubadours travelled widely, William IX on crusade to Syria, Marcabru and Guiraut Riquier to Spain, Bernart de Ventadorn to England, Bertran de Born to Northern France. Peire Vidal (fl. 1183–1204) ventured as far as Hungary. These travels contributed to the diffusion of the artform into other langs. such as Northern Fr., starting at the end of the 12th c. (see TROUVERE); Ger. (see MINNESANG); It., at the court of the Emperor Frederick II in Sicily; and Galician-Portuguese (see GALICIAN POETRY). The heritage of the troubadours was acknowledged by Dante and Petrarch, who extended their indirect influence throughout the Europe of the Ren. (see PETRARCHISM) and beyond. Poets of the 20th c. who have returned to the troubadours incl. Ezra Pound, Paul Blackburn, Jacques Roubaud, and W. D. Snodgrass.

Meanwhile, a trad. of commentary on the troubadours and their songs had begun in the early 13th c. with Raimon Vidal's *Razos de trobar* (Principles of Composition) and continued with the *Donatz proensals* (Provençal Grammar) of Uc Faidit. Uc and other writers also compiled the *razos*, brief prose commentaries on individual songs, and the *vidas*, or lives of the troubadours (see VIDAS AND RAZOS). Around 1290 Matfre Ermengau attempted to reconcile the love sung by the troubadours with love of God in his lengthy verse *Breviari d'amor* (Breviary of Love).

During the 14th and 15th cs., O. p. fell into decline. The trad. was maintained at Toulouse by the Consistòri de la Subregaya Companhia del Gay Saber, or Academy of the Most Joyful Company of the Joyful Wisdom, which regularly awarded prizes for the best compositions in various troubadour genres (see POETIC CONTESTS). The regulations of these contests were codified in a meticulous taxonomy of troubadour practice called *Las Leis d'amor* (ca. 1341), understood as equivalent to a Code of Poetry. We are still indebted to *Las Leis d'amor* for definitions of the genres and for distinctions such as those among *coblas unissonans*, in which all the stanzas of a song have the same rhyme-sounds; *coblas singulars*, in which the rhyme-sounds change with every stanza; *coblas doblas*, in which given rhyme-sounds are maintained for two stanzas; *coblas ternas*, in which they are maintained for three stanzas; and *coblas quaternas*, in which they are maintained for four. In *coblas capcaudadas* the first line of one stanza uses the rhyme-sound of the last line of the preceding stanza, whereas in *coblas capfinidas* the first line of one stanza repeats a key word from the last line of the preceding stanza. In *coblas retrogradadas* the rhymes of one stanza repeat those of the preceding stanza but in reverse order.

On the other hand, the authority of the *Leis* has obscured evolutionary developments in troubadour practice. We are only beginning to realize that the earliest troubadours used no generic distinctions among types of song, hence that the development of the generic system requires explanation. Another fundamental evolution occurred in the practice of metrical imitation, or *contrafacture*, which only gradually became characteristic of the *sirventes* but was adopted in the *Leis* as its timeless defining trait. The elaborate rhyme-patterns of the troubadours analyzed by the *Leis*, which have attracted the scorn of critics averse to formal experimentation, are in fact only a few of the endless variations of their technique.

Only one poet of this period, Raimon de Cornet (fl. 1324–40), has left an extensive body of work incl. lyrics, verse letters, didactic texts, and two poems in Lat. The fate of O. in this period may be illustrated in the career of Count Gaston Fébus of Foix (1331–91). Although he requested the translation of an encyclopedia from Lat. into O., called the *Elucidari de las proprietatz de totas res naturals* (Elucidarium of the Properties of All Natural Things), Gaston Fébus composed his own treatise on hunting in Fr. and a collection of prayers in Fr. and Lat.—but only a single love song in O. The 14th-c. *Jeu de Sainte Agnès* shows verve in its elaboration of the traditional story and in its use of music, but two cycles of mystery plays from the 15th and 16th cs. are less successful. When the edict of Villers-Cotterêts (1539) established Fr. as the lang. of administration in the Midi, it simply recognized, and did not cause, the decline of the local vernacular.

Historians of O. p. speak of a first Ren. in the 16th c., illustrated by the Gascon Protestant Pey de Garros (d. 1581), the Provençal Bellaud de la Bellaudière (d. 1588), and Pierre Godolin of Toulouse (d. 1649); and a second Ren. in the 19th c. marked by the group of seven poets called Félibrige (q.v.). Through the annual publication of the *Armana provençau* (Provençal Almanac), the group strove to reform O. spelling, to renew the lang., to compose great poetry, and to revive O. culture. The greatest of the *félibres*, Frédéric Mistral, won high praise from Lamartine for his narrative poem *Mirèio* (Mireille) and received the Nobel Prize in 1905. Despite continuing factional disputes, O. p. has grown broader in appeal during the 20th c. with the work of Max Rouquette, Bernard Manciet, and Henri Espieux. A number of contemporary figures, such as R. Nelli, C. Camproux, P. Bec, and R. Lafont, are both practicing poets and troubadour scholars. The poet and singer Claude Marti, who has recorded troubadour songs, allied O. p. with the regionalist movement during the 1970s. See also HISPANO-ARABIC POETRY; FRENCH POETRY.

BIBLIOGRAPHIES: A. Pillet and H. Carstens, *Bibl. der Troubadours* (1933); P. Berthaud and J. Lesaffre, *Guide des études occitanes* (1953), supp. by J. Lesaffre and J. Petit, *Bibl. occitane 1967–1971* (1973) and *Bibl. occitane 1972–1973* (1974); C. A. Knudson and J. Misrahi in Fisher; F. Pic, *Bibl. des sources bibliographiques du domaine occitan* (1977); R. Taylor, *La Litt. occitane du moyen âge* (1977); F. Zufferey, *Bibl. des poètes provençaux des XIVe et XVe siècles* (1981).

ANTHOLOGIES: *Trouvères et Minnesänger*, ed. I. Frank (1952); *Les Troubadours*, ed. R. Lavaud and R. Nelli, 2 v. (1960–66); *Anthol. de la poésie occitane 1900–1960*, ed. A. Lafont (1962); *Anthol. of Troubadour Lyric Poetry*, ed. A. Press (1971); *La poesia trobadorica in Italia*, ed. G. Folena and M. Mancini (1971); *La lirica religiosa en la literatura provenzal antigua*, ed. F. J. Oroz Arizcuren (1972); *La Poésie occitane*, ed. R. Nelli (1972); *Lyrics of the Troubadours and Trouvères*, ed. F. Goldin (1973); *Anthol. of the Provençal Troubadours*, ed. R. Hill and T. Bergin, 2d ed., 2 v. (1973); *Los Trovadores*, ed. M. de Riquer, 3 v. (1975); *The Women Troubadours*, ed. M. Bogin (1976)—popularization; *Anthol. des troubadours*, ed. P. Bec (1979); *Mittelalterliche Lyrik Frankreichs, I: Lieder der Trobadors*, ed. D. Rieger (1980); *A Med. Songbook*, ed. F. Collins, Jr. (1982); *Intro. à l'étude de l'ancien provençal*, ed. F. Hamlin

et al., 2d ed. (1985); M. Switten et al., *The Medieval Lyric*, 3 v. (1987–88).

TRANSLATIONS: E. Pound, *Personae* (1926); A. Bonner, *Songs of the Troubadours* (1972); W. D. Snodgrass, *Six Troubadour Songs* (1976); P. Blackburn, *Proensa* (1978).

VERSIFICATION AND MUSIC: Patterson 1.1.2; Lote; F. M. Chambers, "Imitation of Form in the Old Provençal Lyric," *RPh* 6 (1952–53); I. Frank, *Répertoire métrique de la poésie des troubadours*, 2 v. (1953–57); F. Gennrich, *Das musikalische Nachlass der Troubadours*, 3 v. (1958–65), "Troubadours, trouvères," *MGG*, v. 13; H. van der Werf, *The Chansons of the Troubadours and Trouvères* (1972); *Las cançons dels trobadors*, ed. I. Fernandez de la Cuesta (1979); P. Bec, "Le problème des genres chez les premiers troubadours," *CCM* 25 (1982); *The Extant Troubadour Melodies*, ed. H. van der Werf and G. Bond (1984); Chambers; U. Mölk, "Zur Metrik der Trobadors," *GRLMA*, v. 2.1.

HISTORY AND CRITICISM: "Prov. Versif.," *North Brit. Rev.*, 53 (1871); Jeanroy; Patterson; K. Vossler, "Die Dichtung der Trobadors und ihre europäische Wirkung," *RF* (1937); Lote; C. Camproux, *Hist. de la litt. occitane* (1953); H.-I. Marrou (under pseud. H. Davenson), *Les Troubadours* (1961); M. Lazar, *Amour courtois et "fin'amors" dans la litt. du XIIe siècle* (1964); R. Lafont and C. Anatole, *Nouvelle Hist. de la litt. occitane*, 2 v. (1970); J. J. Wilhelm, *Seven Troubadours* (1970), *Il Miglior Fabbro: The Cult of the Difficult in Daniel, Dante, and Pound* (1982); C. Marks, *Pilgrims, Heretics, and Lovers* (1975)—popularization; L. M. Paterson, *Troubadours and Eloquence* (1975); L. Topsfield, *Troubadours and Love* (1975); N. B. Smith, *Figures of Repetition in the Old Prov. Lyric* (1976); R. Boase, *The Origin and Meaning of Courtly Love* (1976); D. Rieger, *Gattungen und Gattungsbezeichnungen der Trobadorlyrik* (1976); P. Makin, *Provence and Pound* (1978); W. D. Paden, "Pound's Use of Troubadour Mss.," *CL* 32 (1980), ed., *The Voice of the Trobairitz: Perspectives on the Women Troubadours* (1989); U. Mölk, *Trobadorlyrik* (1982); J. Gruber, *Die Dialektik des Trobar* (1983); P. Miremont and J. Monestier, *La Litt. d'oc des troubadours aux Félibres* (1983); M. Mancini, *La gaia scienza dei trovatori* (1984); M. R. Menocal, *The Ar. Role in Med. Lit. Hist.* (1987); L. Kendrick, *The Game of Love* (1988); S. Gaunt, *Troubadours and Irony* (1989); Hollier; S. Kay, *Subjectivity in Troubadour Poetry* (1990); A. E. van Vleck, *Memory and Re-Creation in Troubadour Lyric* (1991).
W.D.P.

OCTAVE (rarely, octet). A stanza of 8 lines. Os. appear as isolable stanzas, such as particularly the It. *ottava rima* (rhyming *abababcc*) and the Fr. *ballade* (*ababbcbc*—qq.v.), as well as the single o. in Fr. called the *huitain* (q.v.) and the single *ballade* stanza in Eng. called the "*Monk's Tale* stanza" (q.v.) after Chaucer, who probably also derived his 7-line "rhyme royal" (q.v.) from the o. of the *ballade*. The o. is the stanza of the first rank in Occitan

OCTONARIUS

poetry (q.v.), a favorite of the troubadours; and although the *trouvères* of northern France are less exclusive, they still show a decided preference for the o.: roughly a third of all extant OF lyrics are set in one or another form of o. In Sp. the o. of octosyllables rhyming *abbaacca*, less often *ababbccb* or *abbaacac*, is called the *copla de arte menor*, that of 12-syllable lines the *copla de arte mayor*. In It., the Sicilian o. (q.v.), in hendecasyllables rhyming *ababab*, first appears in the 13th c. In ON skaldic poetry, the most important stanzas are *drottkvætt* and *hrynhent* (qq.v.), os. of 6- and 8-syllable lines, respectively, bound tightly by alliteration, stressing, and rhyme.

Os. are also important components of larger stanzas: the first eight lines of the sonnet (q.v.) are also called an o. Shelley uses os. for *The Witch of Atlas*, as does Keats for "Isabella." "I Have finished the First Canto, a long one, of about 180 os.," says Byron in a letter, of *Don Juan*. Gerard Manley Hopkins uses the scheme *ababcbca* for *The Wreck of the Deutschland*. John Berryman uses heterometrical os. in *abcbcbca* for *Homage to Mistress Bradstreet* (1953). Louis Zukofsky's *80 Flowers* is a sequence of 81 os.—Schipper; R. Beum, "Yeats's Os.," *TSLL* 3 (1961); R. Moran, "The Os. of E. A. Robinson," *CLQ* 7 (1969).   T.V.F.B.

OCTONARIUS. The Lat. equivalent of the Gr. acatalectic tetrameter, iambic, trochaic, or anapestic, used in Roman comedy, and of which the units are feet not metra. The iambic o. of Plautus has two forms: the first with a medial diaeresis (q.v.), with the seventh position short, and with the eighth allowing *brevis in longo* (see ANCEPS), with the effect of creating two iambic *quaternarii*; the second has a caesura after the ninth position. This meter is rarely used as stichic verse but often in cantica (see CANTICUM AND DIVERBIUM). The trochaic o. is only a meter of cantica. Having medial diaeresis, it too might be regarded as a system of trochaic *quaternarii*, as might the anapestic.— Beare, 137–40; Crusius; C. Questa, *Introduzione alla metrica di Plauto* (1967); Halporn et al.J.W.H.

OCTOSÍLABO. See OCTOSYLLABLE.

OCTOSYLLABLE. A line of eight syllables, one of the two most popular line forms in the European vernaculars: the chief line form in Sp. poetry, the oldest in Fr., and the second most important in Eng. It derives presumably from the iambic dimeter line of Med. Lat. hymnody, established by Ambrose in the 4th c. and pervasive in the later Middle Ages. In Fr., the o. first appears in the 10th c. in the *Vie de Saint Léger* (40 sixains in couplets) and is the most popular meter of OF and Anglo-Norman narrative poetry (excluding the *chansons de geste*, which adopted first the decasyllable then the alexandrine [qq.v.]) of the 12th through 15th cs.—i.e. chronicles, romances (e.g. Wace), saints' lives, *lais*, *fabliaux*, and *dits*—and was esp. favored

(along with the decasyllable) for the courtly love lyric (esp. *ballades* and *rondeaux*) and popular lyric genres (*chansons de toile, pastourelles*) from the 14th to the mid 16th c. It is also common in medieval drama. Finally, it is the staple meter of folkverse, of poetry of the oral trad., as in the late medieval ballads. In succeeding centuries the o. never lost the close connections thus established to hymnody, song, and orality, and (esp. in couplets) to narrative.

After 1500, Ronsard and Malherbe made it the meter of the ode, but in post-Ren. Fr. poetry, the o. became associated with light verse (q.v.): even as late as the 18th c., Le Sage, Piron, and Voltaire used it for popular appeal. Its lability and the swift return of its rhymes have given it a reputation for alertness, impertinence, and zest. In rhythmical structure, the *octosyllabe* is mercurial and often ambiguous: it has only one fixed accent, on the eighth syllable, either one or two secondary accents, and no caesura. This ambiguity derives from the fact that it is caught uneasily between the three-accent norm of the decasyllable and the two-accent norm of the hexasyllable, thus frequently inviting both a two-accent and a three-accent reading, e.g. Banville: "Quand je baise, pâle de fièvre" (3+5 syllables or 3+2+3). Whereas the alexandrine is the line of sustained discourse, usually enjoying a certain syntactic completeness, the o. parcels syntax into a series of fragmentary tableaux or near-autonomous images which can stand in a variety of potential relationships with each other. These are the qualities which attracted Gautier (*Emaux et camées*, 1852) and the symbolist poets to octosyllabic verse.

Spain received os. (normally in varied rhyme schemes rather than couplets) in the 14th c. (Juan Ruiz, *Libro de Buen Amor*) from the Occitan troubadours (q.v.) by way of Galician-Portuguese sources; these reinforced a native tendency toward the o. in earlier Sp. poetry. By the 15th c. the Sp. *octosílabo*, was firmly established through collections of courtly lyrics (e.g. the *Cancionero de Baena*) and since that time has come to be the national meter par excellence in Spain (see SPANISH PROSODY). There is no set rhythmical pattern: the only requirement is that the line contain from 7 to 9 syllables (endings vary) with stress on the seventh.

In Eng. the o. is, in the Latinate terminology of foot metrics, commonly called iambic tetrameter (see TETRAMETER); in Ger. it is called *Kurzzeile*, or *Kurzvers*. Occasionally it is trochaic, and when so, often catalectic, the 8s and 7s giving a special (and powerful) effect, as in the stanzas of Auden's elegy to Yeats beginning "Earth receive an honored guest." It forms the staple line of several stanzas, such as the Long Meter of the ballads and the *In Memoriam* stanza (qq.v.), but is more commonly associated with couplets. Byron's reference to "the fatal facility of the octo-syllabic meter" alludes to the danger of singsong monotony, a danger offset, however, by the rapid movement of the line, which makes it an excellent medium for narrative verse. But in the hands of a skilled craftsman, monotony is not difficult to avoid, as evidenced by Milton's *Il Penseroso* and Goethe's *Selige Sehnsucht*.

In England, the influence of the Fr. o. in the 12th and 13th cs. through Anglo-Norman poets such as Gaimar, Wace, and Benoit led to a refinement in the syllabic regularity of the indigenous ME four-stress line used for narrative verse (Layamon; *The Owl and the Nightingale*; *Sir Orfeo*; Barbour's *Bruce*). Chaucer translated part of the *Romance of the Rose*, which is in octosyllabic couplets, from which, according to the received theory, he learned to adapt, *mutatis mutandis*, the metrical structures of the OF line to the exigencies of the Eng. lang. The os. of *The Book of the Duchess* and *The House of Fame* yield to the decasyllables of the *Canterbury Tales*. Chaucer's successors, however, esp. Gower (*Confessio amantis*), could not equal his flexibility. The o. finds heavy use in the miracle and morality plays, but a lessening use in the 16th c. (chiefly songs). After 1600 the tetrameter becomes the vehicle of shorter poems, descriptive or philosophical, by Jonson, Milton (*L'Allegro* and *Il Penseroso*), Marvell ("To His Coy Mistress"), Gay, Prior, Swift (his favorite meter, e.g. "Verses on the Death of Dr. Swift"), Collins and others; the jogging, satiric os. and polysyllabic rhymes of Samuel Butler's *Hudibras* (1663–78) canonized the name as a generic—"Hudibrastic verse" (q.v.). In the 19th c., narrative verse both serious and whimsical was again written in 8s as Burns, Wordsworth, and Coleridge (*Christabel*, in couplets), but esp. Byron, Scott, Keats, and William Morris ("The Earthly Paradise") brought the tetrameter couplet to a height it had not seen since ME.

However, it must be emphasized that it is dangerous to treat all 8-syllable lines as a class, without due adjustment for the differences in metrical systems of each national poetry. One cannot treat the Sp. *octosílabo*, the Fr. *octosyllabe*, the Lat. *octonarius*, and the Eng. iambic tetrameter, for example, as automatic equivalents—i.e. as having the same structure or effects. Each resides within a distinctive verse system dependent *in part* on the lang. in which it operates. As Grimaud has put it, "eight is a different number" in langs. such as Fr. and Eng.

C. M. Lewis, *The Foreign Sources of Mod. Eng. Versif.* (1898); E. P. Shannon, "Chaucer's Use of the O. Verse," *JEGP* 12 (1913); Thieme, 373 ff.; P. Verrier, *Le Vers français*, 3 v. (1931–32); P.-A. Becker, *Der gepaarte Achtsilber in der französischen Dichtung* (1934); E. N. S. Thompson, "The Octosyllabic Couplet," *PQ* 18 (1939); D. C. Clarke, "The Sp. O.," *HR* 10 (1942); J. Saavedra Molina, *El octosílabo castellano* (1945); Lote; M. D. Legge, *Anglo-Norman Lit. and Its Background* (1963); F. Deloffre, *Le Vers français* (1969); Navarro; Elwert; C. Scott, *A Question of Syllables* (1986); E. B. Vitz, "Rethinking OF Lit.: The Orality of the Octosyllabic Couplet," *RR* 77 (1986); J. Kittay, "On Octo," *RR* 78 (1987). T.V.F.B.; C.S.

ODE (Gr. *aeidein* "to sing," "to chant"). In modern usage the term for the most formal, ceremonious, and complexly organized form of lyric poetry, usually of considerable length. It is frequently the vehicle for public utterance on state occasions, e.g. a ruler's accession, birthday, or funeral, or the dedication of some imposing public monument. The ode as it has evolved in contemporary lits. generally shows a dual inheritance from classical sources, variously combining the measured, recurrent stanza of the Horation ode, with its attendant balance of tone and sentiment (sometimes amounting to a controlled ambiguity, as in Marvell's "Horation Ode" on Cromwell), and the regular or irregular stanzaic triad of Pindar, with its elevated, vertiginously changeable tone (as in Collins' "Ode on the Poetical Character"), in interesting manifestations as late as Robert Bridges and Paul Claudel. Both forms have frequently been used for poems celebrating public events, but both have just as frequently eschewed such events, sometimes pointedly, in favor of private occasions of crisis or joy. The serious tone of the ode calls for the use of a heightened diction and enrichment by poetic device, but this lays it open, more readily than any other lyric form, to burlesque (q.v.).

In Gr. lit., the odes of Pindar (522–442 B.C.) were designed for choric song and dance (see MELIC POETRY). The words, the sole surviving element of the integral experience, reflect the demands of the other two arts. A *strophe*, a complex metrical structure whose length and pattern of heterometric lines varies from one ode to another, reflects a dance pattern, which is then repeated exactly in an *antistrophe* (the dancers repeating the steps but in the opposite direction), the pattern being closed by an *epode*, or third section, of differing length and structure. The ode as a whole (surviving examples range from fragments to nearly 300 lines) is built up by exact metrical repetition of the original triadic pattern. These odes, written for performance in a Dionysiac theater or perhaps in the Agora to celebrate athletic victories, frequently appear incoherent in their brilliance of imagery, abrupt shifts in subject matter, and apparent disorder of form within the individual sections. But modern crit. has answered such objections, which date from the time of Pindar himself, by discerning dominating images, emotional relationships between subjects, and complex metrical organization. The tone of the odes is emotional, exalted, and intense; the subject matter, whatever divine myths can be adduced to the occasion.

Apart from Pindar, another pervasive source of the modern ode in Gr. lit. is the cult-hymn, which derived from the Homeric hymns and flourished during the Alexandrian period in the work of Callimachus and others. This sort of poem is notable not for its form but for its structure of argument: an invocation (q.v.) of a deity (later of a personified natural or psychological entity), followed by a narrative genealogy establishing the antiquity and authenticity of the deity, followed by a petition for some special favor, and concluding with a vow of future service. A complete modern instance of this structure is Keats's "Ode to Psyche." Yet another source of the modern ode's structure of prayerful petition is the Psalms and other poems of the Hebrew Bible (see HEBREW POETRY), which increasingly influenced Eng. poetry by way of Milton, the crit. of John Dennis, the original and translated hymns of Isaac Watts (see HYMN), and Bishop Robert Lowth's *Lectures on the Sacred Poetry of the Hebrews* (1753; see HEBREW PROSODY).

In Lat. lit., the characteristic ode is associated with Horace (65–8 B.C.), who derived his forms not from Pindar but from less elaborate Gr. lyrics, through Alcaeus and Sappho. The Horatian ode is tranquil rather than intense, contemplative rather than brilliant, and intended for the reader in his library rather than for the spectator in the theater. Horace himself wrote commissioned odes, most notably the *Carmen saeculare* for Augustus, all of which more closely approximated the Pindaric form and voice, but his influence on modern poetry is felt more directly in the trad. of what might be called the sustained epigram (q.v.), esp. in the period between Jonson and Prior. Among the Eng. poets of note, only Mark Akenside habitually wrote odes in the Horatian vein, but in the 17th c. poets as diverse as Herrick, Thomas Randolph, and—most important among them—Marvell with his "Cromwell Ode" wrote urbane Horatians.

The third form of the modern ode, the Anacreontic (q.v.), is descended from the 16th-c. discovery of a group of some 60 poems, all credited to Anacreon, although the Gr. originals now appear to span a full thousand years. In general the lines are short and, in comparison with the Pindaric ode, the forms simple, the subjects being love or drinking, as in the 18th-c. song "To Anacreon in Heaven," whose tune was appropriated for "The Star-Spangled Banner."

Throughout Europe the history of the ode commences with the rediscovery of the classic forms. The humanistic ode of the 15th and earlier 16th c. shows the adaptation of old meters to new subjects by Fifelfo in both Gr. and Lat., and by Campano, Pontano, and Flaminio in Neo-Latin. The example of the humanistic ode and the publication in 1513 of the Aldine edition of Pindar were the strongest influences upon the vernacular ode in Italy; tentative Pindaric experiments were made by Trissino, Alamanni, and Minturno, but without establishing the ode as a new genre. More successful were the attempts in France by members of the *Pléiade* (q.v.): after minor trials of the new form by others, Ronsard in 1550 published *The First Four*

Books of the Odes, stylistic imitations of Horace, Anacreon, and (in the first book) Pindar. Influenced by Ronsard, both Bernardo Tasso and Gabriele Chiabrera later in the century succeeded in popularizing the form in Italy, where it has been used successfully by, among others, Manzoni, Leopardi (in his *Odicanzone*), Carducci (*Odi barbare*, 1877), and D'Annunzio (*Odi navale*, 1892). In France, the example of Ronsard was widely followed, notably by Boileau in the 17th c. and by Voltaire and others in formal occasional verse in the 18th. The romantic period lent a more personal note to both form and subject matter, notably in the work of Lamartine, Musset, and Victor Hugo. Later, highly personal treatments of the genre may be found in Verlaine's *Odes en son honneur* (1893) and Valéry's *Odes* (1920). In Sp., odes have figured in the work of Pablo Neruda (1904–73), who wrote three volumes of them: *Odas elementales* (1954), *Nuevas odas elementales* (1956), and *Tercer libro de las odas* (1957).

The ode became characteristically Ger. only with the work of G. R. Weckherlin (*Oden und Gesänge*, 1618–19), who, as court poet at Stuttgart, attempted to purify and refashion Ger. letters according to foreign models. In the mid 18th c. Klopstock modified the classical models by use of free rhythms, grand abstract subjects, and a heavy influence from the Lutheran psalms. Later Goethe and Schiller returned to classical models and feeling, as in Schiller's "Ode to Joy," used in the final movement of Beethoven's Ninth Symphony. At the turn of the century, Hölderlin in his complex, mystical, unrhymed odes united classical themes with the characteristic resources of the Ger. lang. Since Hölderlin, few noteworthy odes have been written in Ger., with the possible exception of those of Rudolf Alexander Schröder (*Deutsche Oden*, 1912).

The few attempts at domesticating the ode in 16th-c. England were largely unsuccessful, although there is probably some influence of the classical ode upon Spenser's "Fowre Hymnes," "Prothalamion" and "Epithalamion." In 1629 appeared the first great imitation of Pindar in Eng., Ben Jonson's "Ode on the Death of Sir H. Morison," with the strophe, antistrophe, and epode of the Cl. model indicated by the Eng. terms "turn," "counter-turn," and "stand." In the same year Milton began the composition of his great ode, "On the Morning of Christ's Nativity," in regular stanzaic form. The genre, however, attained great popularity in Eng. only with the publication of Abraham Cowley's *Pindarique Odes* in 1656, in which he attempted, like Ronsard and Weckherlin before him, to make available to his own lang. the spirit and tone of Pindar rather than to furnish an exact transcription of his manner. Cowley was uncertain whether Pindar's odes were regular, and the matter was not settled until 1706, when the playwright William Congreve published with an ode of his own a "Discourse" showing that they were indeed regular. With the appearance in 1749 of a scholarly tr. of Pindar by Gilbert West, the fashion for Cowleyan Pindarics died away. With Dryden begin the great formal odes of the 18th c.: first the "Ode to the Memory of Mrs. Anne Killigrew," and then, marking the reunion of formal verse and music, the "Song for St. Cecilia's Day" and "Alexander's Feast." For the 18th c. the ode was the perfect means of expressing the sublime (q.v.). Using personification (q.v.) and other devices of allegory, Gray and Collins in the mid-18th c. marshall emotions ranging from anxiety to terror in the service of their central theme, the "progress of poetry," making the ode a crisis poem that reflects the rivalry of modern lyric with the great poets and genres of the past.

The romantic ode in Eng. lit. is a poem written on the occasion of a vocational or existential crisis in order to reassert the power and range of the poet's voice. It begins with Coleridge's "Dejection: An Ode" (1802) and Wordsworth's pseudo-Pindaric "Ode: Intimations of Immortality" (written 1802–4, pub. 1815). Wordsworth's "Intimations Ode," with its varied line lengths, complex rhyme scheme, and stanzas of varying length and pattern, has been called the greatest Eng. Pindaric ode. Of the other major romantic poets, Shelley wrote the "Ode to the West Wind" and Keats the "Ode on a Grecian Urn," "Ode to a Nightingale," and "To Autumn," arguably the finest three odes in the lang. They are written in regular stanzas derived not from Horace but from Keats's experiments with the sonnet form. Since the romantic period, with the exception of a few brilliant but isolated examples such as Tennyson's "Ode on the Death of the Duke of Wellington," the ode has been neither a popular nor a really successful genre in Eng. Among modern poets, the personal ode in the Horatian manner has been revived with some success, notably by Allen Tate ("Ode to the Confederate Dead") and W. H. Auden ("In Memory of W. B. Yeats," "To Limestone").

See also EPINIKION; GREEK POETRY; LATIN POETRY; STANCE; STASIMON.

Schipper, v. 2, sects. 516–25, and *History* 366 ff.—on the Pindaric; G. Carducci, "Dello svolgimento dell'ode in Italia," *Opere*, v. 16 (1905); E. R. Keppeler, *Die Pindarische Ode in der dt. Poesie des XVII und XVIII Jhs.* (1911); R. Shafer, *The Eng. Ode to 1660* (1918); I. Silver, *The Pindaric Odes of Ronsard* (1937); G. N. Shuster, *The Eng. Ode from Milton to Keats* (1940); G. Highet, *The Cl. Trad.* (1949); N. Maclean, "From Action to Image: Theories of the Lyric in the 18th C.," in Crane; C. Maddison, *Apollo and the Nine: A Hist. of the Ode* (1960); Bowra; K. Viëtor, *Gesch. der deutschen Ode*, 2d ed. (1961); A. W. Pickard-Cambridge, *Dithyramb, Tragedy and Comedy*, 2d ed. (1962); S. Commager, *The Odes of Horace: A Critical Study* (1962); K. Schlüter, *Die englische Ode* (1964); H. D. Goldstein, "*Anglorum Pindarus*: Model and Milieu," *CompLit* 17 (1965); P. Habermann, "Antike Versmasse und Strophen- (Oden-) formen im Deutschen," and J. Wiegand and W. Kohlschmidt, "Ode," *Reallexikon*; J. Heath-Stubbs, *The Ode* (1969); G. Hartman, "Blake and the Progress of Poetry," *Beyond Formalism* (1970); G. Otto, *Ode, Ekloge und Elegie im 18. Jahrhundert* (1973); J. D. Jump, *The Ode* (1974); Wilkins; M. R. Lefkowitz, *The Victory Ode* (1976); P. H. Fry, *The Poet's Calling in the Eng. Ode* (1980); Morier; J. Culler, *The Pursuit of Signs* (1981), ch. 7; K. Crotty, *Song and Action: The Victory Odes of Pindar* (1982); W. Mullen, *Choreia* (1982); H. Vendler, *The Odes of John Keats* (1983); M. H. Abrams, *The Correspondent Breeze* (1984), ch. 4; J. W. Rhodes, *Keats's Major Odes: An Annot. Bibl. of Crit.* (1984); Terras; A. P. Burnett, *The Art of Bacchylides* (1985); D. S. Carne-Ross, *Pindar* (1985); N. Teich, "The Ode in Eng. Lit. Hist.," *PLL* 21 (1985); S. Curran, *Poetic Form and British Romanticism* (1986), ch. 4; W. Fitzgerald, *Agonistic Poetry: The Pindaric Mode in Pindar, Horace, Hölderlin, and the Eng. Ode* (1987); Hollier, 198 ff.; *Selected Odes of Pablo Neruda*, ed. and tr. M. S. Peden (1990); G. Davis, *Polyhymnia* (1991).   S.F.F.; P.H.F.

ODL (Celtic "rhyme"). Both end rhyme and internal rhyme are features of Welsh poetry (q.v.) from the beginning (6th c.), esp. the complex internal rhyming of cynghanedd (q.v.). Repetition of final unstressed vowels together with the consonants which follow them is adequate in Welsh verse (as in Eng. *father*/*sister*), for all vowels are distinct, stress accent is not very strong, and the rhyming of final syllables was established before the shift of accent from final to penultimate syllables. Rhyming of stressed with unstressed syllables (*stick* / *ecclesiastic*) is also common in Welsh, and in some meters (*englyn* and *cywydd*, qq.v.) is obligatory. There are two kinds of partial rhyme in Welsh: (a) "Irish" rhyme, as in Gaelic, where only the vowels correspond and the consonants following them need only belong to the same phonetic group; and (b) *proest*, where the consonants following the vowel correspond exactly and the vowels (or diphthongs) need only be of the same length, short to short or long to long (e.g. *an, in, on*). Nostalgia, or a sense of loss or incompleteness, can be very effectively conveyed thus. Wilfred Owen made much use of *proest* in Eng., which he called "pararhyme." See also WELSH POETRY.—Morris-Jones; Parry, *History*.   D.M.L.

OFF RHYME. See NEAR RHYME.

OLD GERMANIC PROSODY. See GERMAN PROSODY, *Old Germanic*.

OLD NORSE POETRY. The poetry of the Viking Age and medieval West Scandinavia. Although verse was composed throughout Viking Scandinavia, England, and the Western Islands, all ms. recordings are from Iceland, where they began no earlier than the end of the 12th c. Only runic inscriptions preserve alliterative lines (perhaps just rhythmic prose) from Denmark and Sweden; the most important periods are the late 10th and 11th cs. ON p. descended from common Germanic prosody (See GERMAN PROSODY, *Old Germanic*; INDO-EUROPEAN PROSODY) but introduced a number of important innovations, of which the most important were a shift from stichic to stanzaic structure and the introduction of syllable-counting and rhyme in some meters. The stanzas have eight lines (four Germanic long lines) in nearly all meters, and there is always a syntactic break in the middle of the stanza. Stylistically, ON p. developed the metaphoric and metonymic aspects of Germanic poetry, whereas West Germanic poetry relied more heavily on variation (q.v.). Nothing in ON p. approaches the length of the West Germanic epics *Beowulf* and *Heliand*. Although a few poems exceed 800 lines (e.g. *Hávamál, Lilja*), most are far shorter.

The basic formal principle is structural alliteration (q.v.). In *fornyrðislag* (q.v.), the meter most like what can be reconstructed for common Germanic, pairs of lines (each pair is equivalent to one Germanic long line) are linked by alliteration. It occurs in one or both of the two stressed syllables of the odd lines and regularly in the first stressed syllable of the even lines. In this system, consonants alliterate with identical consonants. Only the first consonant of a cluster is relevant for alliteration, except that *sp, st*, and *sk* function as single units. Any vowel, however, alliterates with any other vowel. Unstressed syllables and those in anacrusis are metrically irrelevant.

An important Norse innovation to this system is *ljóðaháttr* (q.v.), in which the even long lines in effect are shrunk into a single line. One stress (at least) is lost, but the alliteration remains. The anonymous mythological and heroic poems are in these meters and their variations.

A second important departure was the introduction of syllable-counting. Coupled with internal rhymes, it was particularly exploited in the meter *dróttkvætt* (q.v.). Besides the four pairs of lines linked by alliteration (with two alliterations required in the odd lines) and the syntactic break after the second pair, *dróttkvætt* employs a strict count of six syllables per line, with the last two forming a trochee, and with internal half-rhymes in odd lines and full rhymes in even. Here is an example:

> út munu ekkjur líta,
> allsnúðula, prúðar
> —fljóð séa reyk—hvar ríðum
> Rǫgnvalds í by gǫgnum
> (Sighvatr Þórðarson, *Austrfararvísur*
>   12a).

> (The fair women will look out—the ladies see smoke—as we ride furiously through Rǫgnvaldr's village.)

Here the first couplet employs vowel alliteration (the syllables út, ekk, and all); the second *r, út*, and *lít* provide half rhyme, *snúð* and *prúð* full rhyme, *fljóð* and *ríð* half rhyme, and *Rǫgn* and *gǫgn* full rhyme. The two unstressed short syllables in *munu* resolve to one syllable.

This half-stanza contains two words for "women," neither of which is the ordinary prose term. ON p. relies heavily on noun substitution for its stylistic effect, either through metonymy (e.g. *ekkjur*, literally, widows or unmarried women) or use of an elevated vocabulary (e.g. *fljóð*,) found only in poetry. The latter is an *ókennd heiti* or "unexplained appellative." If an appellative is "explained," it is part of a *kenning* (from the verb *kenna*, "teach, make known"), a figure employing two or more nouns, like "horse of the sea" for "ship." Kennings (q.v.) can be grammatical compounds or employ the genitive case for the determining noun ("of the sea" in the above example). It was possible to build up kennings by replacing the determining noun with another kenning ("horse of the paths of the whale"); kennings with up to six parts are attested. Given the complex metrical requirements of *dróttkvætt* and related meters and the highly inflected nature of ON, word order is far from that of ON prose. How far remains an open question.

Dróttkvætt and its numerous variations tended to be used by poets whose names survived with their work. Often such poetry was of an occasional nature. Later scholars called such poets "skalds" (q.v.) and their verse "skaldic."

The earliest known skald is thought to be Bragi Boddason the Old, who flourished during the latter half of the 9th c., perhaps in Norway, Sweden, or even Viking Russia. No ON p. is demonstrably older than his, and some scholars have seen in Bragi the originator of *dróttkvætt*. ON mythology has a god of poetry named Bragi. The skald Bragi and over 200 others were active from the late 9th c. through the end of the Middle Ages. During the Viking Age, they were often attached to the courts of kings or other rulers, and much of their surviving verse is encomiastic, focusing particularly on royal battles and employing the form of the *drápa* (q.v.). Skalds composed verse on many other topics, however, ranging from *níð* (insults, often of a sexual nature), through love poetry, boasts, challenges, and topical comments to deep emotion (e.g. Egill Skallagrímsson's *Sonatorrek*). With the conversion to Christianity, ca. 1000 A.D., skalds began to compose on Christian topics, and these became increasingly important, although the other topics never disappeared. The major verse of the 13th and 14th cs. is mostly religious (e.g. *Lilja*, the stately poems on the Icelandic bishop Guðmundr the Good, and numerous verses on Mary and other saints), but the 13th-c. Icelandic chieftain Áron Hjǫrleifsson was the subject of at least three poems of which fragments still remain.

Later religious poetry, which was often in the meter *hrynhent* (q.v.), avoided the kennings and obscure diction of earlier *dróttkvætt* poetry.

The earliest written lit. in West Scandinavia was historical, and authors frequently cited individual skaldic stanzas rather than whole poems as evidence. As a result, the transmission of the early skaldic corpus is fragmentary, although some occasional stanzas (*lausavísur*, "loose stanzas") were intended to stand alone. The Icelandic family sagas contain many such verses, some of which, however, may have been composed later, perhaps even by the saga authors, and placed in the mouths of the early skalds.

Ca. 1220, Snorri Sturluson, a member of a leading Icelandic family, composed *Háttatal* ("enumeration of meters") as an encomium to the young Norwegian king Hákon Hákonarson and his guardian regent, Jarl Skúli. The poem was a metrical and stylistic *tour de force*: 101 stanzas each of which exhibited a named variation of meter or diction. It was not the first such ON poem; the Orkneyan Jarl Rǫgnvaldr Kali Kollsson and the Icelander Hallr Þórarinsson had composed their *Háttalykill* ("metrical key") during the 1140s. Snorri, however, augmented his poem with a prose commentary that has remained the foundation of ON poetics. Poem and commentary now make up the last section of a longer work, a handbook on poetics, all attributed to Snorri. Later called *Edda* (perhaps a neologism on Lat. *edo* with the sense "compose verse"), Snorri's *Edda*, now sometimes also called the "Prose Edda" or "Younger Edda," contains a Prologue, a section setting forth the mythological narratives on which many kennings are based (*Gylfaginning*, "The Deluding of Gylfi"), a section on poetic diction (*Skáldskaparmál*, "The Language of Poetry"), and *Háttatal*, the metrical catalogue and commentary. *Skáldskaparmál* is richly illustrated with examples and is a major repository of skaldic poetry. Snorri's *Edda* is not the only rhetorical work from medieval Iceland—there are four grammatical treatises, from the 12th c. through the 14th c., and the third and fourth esp. are important for poetics, but Snorri's work is in a class by itself.

In *Gylfaginning* and in the opening sections of *Skáldskaparmál*, Snorri quotes extensively from anonymous poems in *fornyrðislag* and *ljóðaháttr*, and when a ms. of such poetry turned up in the 17th c., Reformation scholars called it the *Edda* of Sæmundr Sígfússon the Learned, the 12th-c. founder of Icelandic historiography. In fact, the book dates from the later 13th c., and its written antecedents go back no further than to the end of the 12th c. Nevertheless, this ms. is still called *Codex Regius of the Poetic Edda*, sometimes also the *Elder Edda*, and its poems are termed "Eddic," as opposed to the "skaldic" poems that are mostly occasional and in *dróttkvætt* or related meters. As the existence of another ms. fragment of some of these poems shows, *Codex Regius* was a carefully planned book. It begins with *Vǫluspá*, which presents the full curve of mythic history. The following mythological poems treat, respectively, Odin, Freyr, Thor, and beings from the lower mythology (*Vǫlundarkviða* and *Alvíssmál*). Heroic poems follow. Again the redactor placed synoptic poems before those dealing with smaller aspects of the whole story. He presents, roughly speaking, two heroic cycles, those of Helgi and of the Nibelungs, from the career and death of Sigurðr through the aftermath of his demise to the final moments of death and destruction in *Hamðismál*). In all, *Codex Regius* contains some thirty poems and a lacuna whose probable contents scholars continue to debate. Another half-dozen or so Eddic poems have been found outside *Codex Regius*, and A. Heusler and W. Ranisch gathered similar verse from the mythic-heroic *fornaldarsagas* under the title *Eddica Minora*, which has by now acquired something of the status of a generic term.

Particularly in the heroic section, many of the Eddic poems tell the same or similar stories (e.g. the apparently older *Atlakviða* and younger *Atlamál*), and the role of oral trad. in their transmission remains an important research question. At least some of the poems must have been composed centuries before they were written down; each poem by now has an extensive research history discussing possible provenience. Guesses range over five centuries from Greenland to Viking Russia.

Snorri wrote his *Edda* at least in part as an attempt to defend the older skaldic style from modish dance songs, perhaps ballads (see BALLAD). It is certain at least that ballads reached Scandinavia by the later Middle Ages, although serious recording did not begin until after the Reformation. Ballads certainly existed in Iceland, too, but there the proper heirs to the older poetry were the *rímur* (q.v.).

BIBLIOGRAPHY: L. M. Hollander, *A Bibl. of Scaldic Studies* (1958); P. Schach, "ON Lit.," in Fisher; R. Frank, "Skaldic Poetry," and J. Harris, "Eddic Poetry," in *ON–Icelandic Lit.: A Crit. Guide*, ed. C. J. Clover and J. Lindow (1985).

EDITIONS: *Eddica Minora*, ed. A. Heusler and W. Ranisch (1903); *Den norsk-islandske skjaldedigtning*, ed. F. Jónsson, 4 v. (1912–15)—standard ed. of skaldic poetry; *Edda Snorra Sturlusonar*, ed. F. Jónsson (1931); *The Poetic Edda*, v. 1: *Heroic Poems*, ed. U. Dronke (1969)—with tr. and commentary; *Edda: Die Lieder des Codex Regius nebst verwandten Denkmälern*, ed. G. Neckel, rev. H. Kuhn, 5th ed. (1983)—standard ed. of Eddic poetry; *Háttatal: Edda, Part 3*, ed. A. Faulkes (1991).

TRANSLATIONS: *The Poetic Edda*, tr. H. M. Bellows (1923); *The Skalds*, tr. L. M. Hollander (1945); *The Poetic Edda*, tr. L. M. Hollander, rev. ed. (1962).

HISTORY AND CRITICISM: W. P. Lehmann, *The Devel. of Germanic Verse Form* (1956); S. Gutenbrunner, "Beiträge zur germanischen Terminologie der Metrik," *ZDP* 86 (1967): P. Hallberg, *Old Ice-*

landic Poetry (1975); G. Turville-Petre, Scaldic Poetry (1976); G. Kreutzer, Die Dichtungslehre der Skalden, 2d ed. (1977); R. Frank, ON Court Poetry (1978); K. von See, Skaldendichtung (1980); H. Kuhn, Das Dróttkvætt (1983); E. Marold, Kenningkunst (1983); Frank and Harris in Clover and Lindow (above).   J.L.

OMAR KHAYY'ÁM QUATRAIN or Rubaiyat stanza (from Persian: originally Ar., rubā'iyyāt [pl.], quatrains). In Eng. poetry, a quatrain of decasyllabic lines rhyming aaba (rarely aaaa). The term is taken from Edward FitzGerald's famous collection, Rubáiyát of Omar Khayyám (1859), which is a free adaptation of a selection of poems by the Persian poet 'Umar al-Khayyām (d. 1122), whose major reputation within the cl. Ar. trad. is as an algebraist. There is considerable doubt as to the attribution of a large part of al-Khayyām's poetry, but about 50 poems are clearly authentic while a large number of others are also thought to be so. The wide popularity of Fitzgerald's versions must be seen in the context of an extraordinary vogue in the 19th c. for Oriental exoticism (q.v.). While many of the subtleties of imagery and lang. in the original Persian escaped FitzGerald, his renderings clearly presented a new and different poetic voice. Whereas Ar. and Persian poetry in qaṣīda (q.v.) form uses monorhyme (q.v.), the rubā'iyyāt break the rhyme in the third line of each stanza, and FitzGerald follows this rhyme scheme in his versions: "I sometimes think that never blows so red / The rose as where some buried Caesar bled; / That every hyacinth the Garden wears / Dropt in its Lap from some once lovely Head." Enjambment is common in the initial couplet. Swinburne's imitation in Laus veneris links third lines in pairs. See also PERSIAN POETRY.—W. L. Hanaway, Jr., "Persian Lit.," The Study of the Middle East (1976); Reallexikon 2.824; V.-M. D'Ambrosio, Eliot Possessed (1989).   R.M.A.A.

ONEGIN STANZA. The stanza form which the Rus. poet A. S. Puškin created for his novel in verse Evgenij Onegin (1825–31). The 14 lines in iambic tetrameter have the rhyme scheme AbAbCCddEffEgg, which consists of three differently rhymed quatrains and a couplet. According to Toma-ševskij, each stanza constitutes a "small chapter": the first quatrain presents the main idea, the second and third quatrains develop the theme, and the couplet often contains a witty or aphoristic conclusion. The o. s. is admirably suited for the varying tone of the ironic and playful author-narrator, who frequently indulges in urbane chatter, lyrical digressions, and comments about poetry.—B. V. Tomaševskij, Stix i jazyk (1959); A. Puškin, Eugene Onegin, tr. V. Nabokov, v. 1 (1964). J.O.B.

ONOMATOPOEIA (Ger. Klangmalerei, Lautsymbolik) is the traditional term for words which seem to imitate the things they refer to, as in this line

from Collins' "Ode to Evening": "Now the air is hushed, somewhere the weak-eyed bat / With short shrill shriek flits by on leathern wing." In the strict sense, o. refers to words which imitate sounds (e.g. dingdong, roar, swish, murmur, susurrus), but other qualities such as size, motion, and even color may be suggested; and the term is most often used with wider reference, to denote any word whose sound is felt to have a "natural" or direct relation with its sense. Since their phonetic shape seems motivated rather than arbitrary, onomatopoeic words exert significant limitations on Saussure's doctrine of the arbitrariness of the sign. Both Jespersen and Sapir showed evidence that Saussure greatly overstated his case.

O. is one of four types of verbal effects which in poetics are usually called "expressive" or "mimetic" but which in linguistics are widely referred to as instances of "phonetic symbolism" or "sound symbolism." All four terms are objectionable: the first begs the question, the second explains little, and the third and fourth are simply confused: expressive and onomatopoeic words are, in the terminology of Charles Sanders Peirce, icons rather than symbols; it is precisely the point that they are not symbolic in the way ordinary words are. Beyond terminology, however, the four types of effects are closely interrelated: these are (1) o. itself (wordsounds imitate sounds in nature); (2) articulatory gesture or kinesthesia (movements of the vocal or facial muscles or the shape of the mouth is suggestive; see SOUND); (3) synaesthesia, phonesthemes (qq.v.), and other associative phenomena (heard sounds trigger other sensory impressions); and (4) morphosymbolism and iconic syntax (see below).

It has long been fashionable among literary critics to disparage o. as a crude and over-obvious poetic device, but the linguistic evidence for iconicity as an important process at work in langs. worldwide is formidable. There is good evidence that certain iconic effects operate across a wide spectrum of langs. and may be linguistic universals. Jespersen's astonishingly long list of words having the unrounded high front vowel /i/ and all connoting "small, slight, insignificant, or weak" is famous; in Eng., this phoneme is used almost universally by babies if not parents as a suffix for small, familiar, or comforting things (e.g. mommy, daddy, baby, teddy, beddie, dooggie, kitty, ouchie, munchie). Woodworth's analysis of deixis in 26 langs. revealed a "systematic relationship between vowel quality and distance," namely that a word having proximal meaning has a vowel of higher pitch than one having distal meaning.

Further, iconic effects in lang. have been shown to be not merely phonological but also morphological and syntactic. O. is therefore simply the most conspicuous instance of a broad range of natural linguistic effects, not a merely "poetic" device. In ordinary speech, sound is motivated by sense: once sense is selected, sound follows. But in iconic speech, sense is motivated by sound: words are chosen for their sound, which itself determines meaning. When Pope says that "the sound must seem an echo to the sense," he means, says Dennis Taylor, not merely that sound follows sense but that "the sense makes us read the sound as confirming the sense." Now meaning proceeds from the very mouth of lang.

It is usually said of o. that the sound of the word imitates a natural phenomenon in the world which the word represents, because the thing is itself a sound, such as *whirr*. But the sound of the word is not often precisely the sound of the thing. As Chatman shows, the connection is not exact: a word cannot enact even a natural sound if that sound is not an available phoneme in the lang. itself, and most onomatopoeic words are only approximations of the natural sounds. Even the words which we tell our children are the sounds the animals make are highly conventionalized in every lang.: Americans teach their children that dogs say "Bow, wow" or "Arf, arf" or "woof," but the Fr. say their dogs say "Ouah, ouah." In Eng., pigs are said to say "oink, oink" (though every adult knows better), while in Flemish they say "gron, gron" (which is closer). The conventionality inherent in every lang. can never be entirely filtered out, and the confusions are legion.

But o. is not solely a relation between words and things, for this formulation leaves out sense. The relation between words and things in the world has not two poles but four. The horizontal, linear relation linking the poles of words and things is crossed by the vertical line linking the poles of sense and sound. Since o. only operates through the agency of words, iconic effects in lines of poetry are created by words which always already bear meaning. "The pattern of sound does not reinforce an already established meaning," says Stein, "so much as it helps shape and modulate that meaning." Dr. Johnson complained that the "same sequence of syllables" can convey very different senses, and both I. A. Richards and John Crowe Ransom constructed "dummies" of onomatopoeic lines to show that alterations of wording without radical alteration of the underlying sound pattern of the line produce wildly different meanings.

The point is that sound-symbolic effects do not operate without words to trigger them, words which first establish the semantic field. Sibilants are often described as sonorous or soft, but they may also be used to convey sinister connotations (the hissing of snakes, slithering through the grass), sadness, and lubricious sexuality. Sounds can never precede meaning: they can only operate on meanings already lexically created. Dr. Johnson's criticism is still trenchant: "it is scarcely to be doubted, that on many occasions we make the musick which we imagine ourselves to hear; that we modulate the poem by our own disposition, and ascribe to the numbers the effects of the sense" (*Rambler*, nos. 94, 92; cf. *Idler* 60; *Life of Pope*).

In general, it may be said that all forms of sound symbolism operate by analogy or association of the physical properties of sound to the physical properties of real objects, as the former are constrained by the conventions specific to each lang., and to meanings. It was Lord Kames who observed in 1762 that "in lang., sound and sense being intimately connected, the properties of the one are readily communicated to the other."

From the wider perspective of sound symbolism or iconicity, o. is part of a much larger set of associative relations between word(sound)s and meanings. Here one feature of a word, its sound, becomes an analogue, a correlate in another mode, for a feature of some other word or natural process. Now "relationships between sounds will map relationships of sense" (Kenner), a point made by Shelley in the *Defense of Poetry*. This is a much more satisfactory heuristic within which to map out a typology of iconic effects in that it will link seemingly unrelated effects. Such associative processes are no less real than the physical features of objects; once codified as conventions, they become facts of behavior and are taken as fact by speakers of a lang.

The process of association operates in both directions. Once speakers associate a certain sound with a certain meaning or field(s) of meaning, words of similar sound come to be associated with those meanings, and words of similar meaning conversely will come to use similar sounds over time. It is one of the axioms of verse structure that similarity in word-sounds implies some similarity in meanings; all sound-marking devices (e.g. alliteration) and sound patterns in poetry use sound to connect meanings. And similarity is apparently preferentially selected over contrast: Benjamin Lee Whorf pointed out that auditors are likely to notice if words for a certain experience share similar characteristics with it, but usually do not notice a relation of contrast or conflict. Indeed, contrasts will be overlooked: Jakobson pointed out the interesting phenomenon whereby words denoting roughly the same concept often form binary pairs with opposed vowels: tip—*top, slit—slot*. There is extensive linguistic evidence that certain associations and, more significantly, oppositional structures operate across langs., generating such contrasts as "dark" vs. "bright" vowels. Jakobson attributed such binary oppositional forms to the nature of cognition itself.

Associative processes operate extensively among words themselves, particularly in morphology, though also in syntax. The sound shape of a word is almost never created *ex nihilo*: it is most often formed in relation to some existing word; and after it comes into existence, it is continuously subject to influence from other words in the lang. system not only diachronically but also synchronically. Any entity, no matter how arbitrary when it enters the system, is thereafter subject to continuous accommodation to and influence by all the other entities in the system. Many writers use the term "o." for what in fact amounts to "reverse o." (Bolinger's term): here "not only is the word assimilated to the sound, but the sound is also assimilated to the 'wordness' of the word." Bolinger identified a series of morphosemantic processes based mainly on association wherein the form influences the meaning or the meaning influences the form of words. Constellations of words form over time, all having similar meanings and similar sound: one example is the series of Eng. words beginning with *gl-* which have to do with light; another is the set of words ending in *-ash*. All this evidence strongly suggests that any word "assumes all the affective and associative privileges enjoyed by the most obvious o." (Bolinger). Malkiel has also mapped some of this terrain, arguing that the phenomenon of phonosymbolism is flanked by a parallel and even wider field of "morphosymbolism," namely iconic or mimetic processes at work in word-formation, phrase formation, and syntax. His many examples suggest that lang. encompasses "form symbolism as against sound symbolism," and that there is a steady gradation between the two: phonic and morphic processes of iconicity "work in unison." Consequently, "when we speak of sound-suggestiveness, we speak of the entire lang., not just of a few imitative or self-sufficient forms" (Bolinger). Iconic syntax has only recently been examined (Haiman), but clearly some structures are mimetic, e.g. any sentence which refers to a situation where items appear in sequence and presents its lexical terms in the same sequence.

The subject of iconicity in lang. was a topic of lively interest to the ancients. It is of course central to Plato's *Cratylus*, and it also appears in Aristotle (*Rhet.* 3.9), Demetrius (*On Style*), Dionysius of Halicarnassus (*On Literary Composition*), and Quintilian (*Institutio oratoria* 9.3, 9.4), among others. In Canto 32 of the *Inferno*, Dante seeks the sorts of appropriate words (*s'io avessi le rime aspre e chiocce*) which he classifies in his prose treatise on diction and prosody, *De vulgari eloquentia*. Saussure impressed indelibly upon the mind of the 20th c. the idea that the relation between word and thing is arbitrary. But of course desire cuts so much deeper than fact. As Ransom repeatedly said, poetic lang. aspires to the condition of nature: it "induces the provision of icons among the symbols." Poets continually desire to make lang. appropriate, so that words partake of the nature of things. And the agency is the fact that words *are* things, have physical bodies with extension in space and duration in time, like people, like things.

For fuller discussion of the several types of expressive sound in poetry, see SOUND. See also CACOPHONY; DISSONANCE; EUPHONY; ICONICITY; PHONESTHEME; REPRESENTATION AND MIMESIS; SYNAESTHESIA; TIMBRE.

G. von der Gabelentz, *Die Sprachwissenschaft* (1891); M. Grammont, "Onomatopoées et mots expressifs," *Trentenaire de la société pour l'étude des langues romanes* (1901); A. H. Tolman, "The Symbolic Value of Eng. Sounds," *The Views About* Hamlet (1904); O. Jespersen, "Sound Symbolism," *Lang.* (1922), "Symbolic Value of the Vowel *I*," *Linguistica* (1933); J. R. Firth, *Speech* (1930), "Modes of Meaning," *E&S* 4 (1951); J. C. Ransom, *The World's Body* (1938), "Positive and Near-Positive Aesthetics," *KR* 5 (1943), both rpt. in Ransom; E. Sapir, *Sel. Writings* (1949); D. T. Mace, "The Doctrine of Sound and Sense in Augustan Poetic Theory," *RES* 2 (1951); A. Stein, "Structures of Sound in Milton's Verse," *KR* 15 (1953); H. Wissemann, *Untersuchungen zur Onomatopoiie* (1954); Wellek and Warren, ch. 13; W. T. Moynihan, "The Auditory Correlative," *JAAC* 17 (1958); P. Delbouille, *Poésie et sonorités*, 2 v. (1961, 1984); Z. Wittoch, "Les Onomatopées forment-elles une système dans la langue?" *AION-SL* 4 (1962); L. P. Wilkinson, *Golden Lat. Artistry* (1963); I. Fónagy, *Die Metaphern in der Phonetik* (1963); G. Bebermeyer, "Lautsymbolik," *Reallexikon* 2.4–8; C. Ricks, "Atomology," *Balcony* 1 (1965); D. Bolinger, *Forms of Eng.* (1965), esp. "The Sign Is Not Arbitrary," "Word Affinities," and "Rime, Assonance, and Morpheme Analysis"; S. Chatman, *A Theory of Meter* (1965); L. B. Murdy, *Sound and Sense in Dylan Thomas's Poetry* (1966); M. B. Emeneau, "Onomatopoetics in the Indian Linguistic Area," *Lang.* 45 (1969); J.-M. Peterfalvi, *Recherches expérimentales sur le symbolisme phonétique* (1970); A. A. Hill, "Sound-Symbolism in Lexicon and Lit.," *Studies in Ling. G. L. Trager* (1972); J. D. Sadler, "O.," *ClassJ* 67 (1972); J. A. Barish, "Yvor Winters and the Antimimetic Prejudice," *NLH* 2 (1970); G. L. Anderson, "Phonetic Symbolism and Phonological Style," *Current Trends in Stylistics* (1972); J. Derbolav. *Platons Sprachphilosophie im Kratylos und in den späteren Schriften* (1972); D. H. Melhem, "Ivan Fónagy and Paul Delbouille: Sonority Structures in Poetic Lang.," *Lang&S* 6 (1973); E. L. Epstein, "The Self-Reflexive Artefact," *Style and Structure in Lit.*, ed. R. Fowler (1975); W. K. Wimsatt, Jr., "In Search of Verbal Mimesis," *Day of the Leopards* (1976); P. L. French, "Toward an Explanation of Phonetic Symbolism," *Word* 28 (1977); Y. Malkiel, "From Phonosymbolism to Morphosymbolism," *Fourth LACUS Forum* (1978), supp. by D. B. Justice, "Iconicity and Association," *RPh* 33 (1980); L. I. Weinstock, "O. and Related Phenomena in Biblical Hebrew," *DAI* 40 (1979): 3268A; R. Jakobson and L. Waugh, "The Spell of Speech Sounds," *The Sound Shape of Lang.* (1979), rpt. in Jakobson, v. 8; D. A. Pharies, "Sound Symbolism in the Romance Langs.," *DAI* 41 (1980): 231A; R. A. Wescott, *Sound and Sense: Essays on Phonosemic Subjects* (1980); M. Borroff, "Sound Symbolism as Drama in the Poetry of Wallace Stevens," *ELH* 48 (1981), "Sound Symbolism as Drama in the Poetry of Robert Frost," *PMLA* 107 (1992); Morier; Brogan, 97–108—survey of studies; R. Lewis, *On Reading Fr. Verse* (1982), ch. 7; N. L. Woodworth, "Sound Symbolism in Proximal and Distal Forms," *Linguistics* 29 (1991).   T.V.F.B.

ONTOLOGY OF POETRY. See POETRY; PROSODY; SOUND.

OPEN COUPLET. See COUPLET; HEROIC COUPLET.

OPEN FORM. See AMERICAN POETRY; FREE VERSE.

OPOJAZ. See RUSSIAN FORMALISM; STRUCTURALISM.

OPSIS. See VISUAL POETRY; VISUAL ARTS AND POETRY.

OPUS GEMINATUM. See PROSIMETRUM.

ORAL INTERPRETATION. See PERFORMANCE.

ORAL POETRY, esp. oral traditional poetry (o. t. p.), is poetry composed and transmitted mainly but not exclusively by people who cannot read or write. O. p. is traditional when each generation has received it orally from the preceding one, back to the dawn of poetry, and transmits it to the next as long as the trad. lives. O. t. p. has its own methods of composition and transmission which differentiate it from written lit. We should, however, exclude from this category poetry composed in the manner of written lit. "for oral presentation" (see PERFORMANCE). Such poetry, though delivered orally, does not differ from written poetry in its manner of composition. The origins of o. p. are those of poetry itself and are to be sought in ritual; for the rhythms, sound patterns, and repetitive structures of poetry help to support and give power to the words and actions of ritual.

There are three general divisions by genre: ritual, lyric, and narrative. The non-narrative types of o. t. p. include, under ritual: (a) incantation, (b) lullabies, (c) wedding ritual songs, (d) laments, (e) songs for special festivals, and (f) praise poems, or eulogies. Lyric songs are preeminently love songs.

The two main types of oral traditional narrative poetry are epic and ballad (qq.v.). The epic is stichic, the same metric line being repeated with some variation for the entire song; whereas the ballad is stanzaic. Consequently, the tempo of narration of epic is rapid, but that of the ballad is slower. The epic tends to be longer than the ballad, because it tells its story from beginning to end, often with a fullness of detail which is typical. The ballad concentrates frequently on the most intense or dramatic moment of a story, and some ballads consist entirely of dialogue. Although there are comic ballads, the genre as a whole has

an elegiac tone. Some of the great oral traditional epics, such as the *Iliad* or the *Chanson de Roland*, are tragic or have tragic overtones, but on the whole, traditional epic is optimistic; the hero generally triumphs gloriously over the enemy.

The most distinctive characteristic of o. t. p. is its variability or fluidity of text, but in some cultures a certain degree of word-for-word memorization is reported, particularly in the shorter forms. In the longer songs, such as epics, the absence of a fixed text makes word-for-word memorization impossible, there being nothing stable to memorize. In the shorter songs the text tends to become more stable in the practice of a single singer and in a song which is frequently sung. In the case of magic incantations, it is sometimes said that the exact reproduction of a text is necessary to make the magic effective, but the existence of variants seems to indicate that sometimes only certain sound patterns such as alliteration and assonance, or certain types of words or word-combinations, are preserved rather than an entire poem, however short. When traditional singers tell us that a text must be repeated exactly, word-for-word, we know from comparison of performances that they mean essential characteristic for essential characteristic, for their concept of a word is different from that of lettered people.

In those cultures where fluidity of text is attested beyond any doubt, where the absence of a fixed text is well documented, the singer-poet learns in the course of years a special technique of composition by "formula" and "theme" (see ORAL-FORMULAIC THEORY). It would be misleading to call it improvisation, which implies creating a story or song on the spur of the moment. It would seem, of course, that there are such oral traditional improvisations of both content and text. They are generally topical in nature. Some scholars maintain, however, that even these "improvisations" are traditional and hence composed in the formulaic technique.

The formula (q.v.) is "a word or group of words regularly used under given metrical conditions to express a given essential idea" (Parry). The most often used phrases, lines, or even couplets—those which a singer hears most frequently when he is learning—establish the patterns for the poetry, its characteristic syntactic, rhythmic, metric, and acoustic molds and configurations. In time the individual practitioner of the art can form new phrases—create formulas—by analogy with the old as needed. When he has become proficient in thinking in the traditional patterns, incl. the traditional phrases and everything else like them, he is a full-fledged singer of o. t. p. In essence, he has learned to speak—or to sing—the special lang. of that poetry. He composes naturally in the forms of his trad., unconsciously, and often very rapidly, as a native speaker speaks a lang.

O. p., of whatever genre, is paratactic (see PARATAXIS AND HYPOTAXIS). Its style has been called an "adding" style, because the majority of its lines *could* terminate in a period, insofar as their syntax is concerned; instead, however, another idea is often "added" to what precedes. A comparatively small percentage of necessary run-on lines, in contrast to the number of cases of nonperiodic enjambment, is therefore another distinctive and symptomatic feature of oral traditional style. This does not mean that the traditional singer only adds ideas, however; he can develop them as well, and he can return to themes introduced earlier.

Even as the formulas and their basic patterns make composing of lines possible in performance, so the associative use of parallelism (q.v.) in sound, syntax, and rhythm aids the oral poet in moving from one line to another. A line may suggest what is to follow it. Thus clusters of lines are formed and held together by sound, structure, and association of meaning. Such units are easily remembered. At times the complexity of structural interconnections between verses in oral traditional style is so great that it seems that one could have attained it only with the aid of writing. The truth is that these intricate architectonics of expression were developed first in oral traditional verse, establishing from very archaic times the techniques which man with writing inherited and then believed himself to have "invented" with the stylus, the quill, and the pen. The lang. of o. t. p., formulaic though it be, is in fact a dynamic, organic lang., an organism of man's imaginative life.

Because poems composed in the formulaic style have no fixed text, they are not, and cannot be, memorized, for the text is never the same even in performances by the same singer. There may be changes in the narrative or other context as well. To say that the text remains "essentially the same" or "more or less the same" over time is not to say that the text is fixed.

Although there are many repeated incidents, scenes, and descriptions, these too remain flexible, susceptible to expansion or contraction; a journey may be related briefly or with copious details—the description of armor may occupy one line or fifty and still be termed the same "theme," as such repeated incidents and descriptions are called. A "theme" is not merely a repeated subject, however, but a repeated *passage*. It has a more or less stable core of lines or parts of lines, surrounded by various elements adapting it to its context.

The theme is multiform and has existence only in its multiforms. Habit and frequent use may give its form in the practice of a single singer some degree of stability, but no given form of it is sacrosanct. Themes, like formulas, are useful in any song in which the incident or description may belong. The journey framework may be employed in any number of stories; the assembly of men or of gods is common to many tales in song. In learning a song which the singer hears for the first time, he does not think of the text; he constructs his own. He need remember only the names of persons and places and the sequences of events. In formulas and themes he has the building blocks and techniques for rapid composition.

There are "themes" in ritual and lyric songs as well. Recent research has demonstrated that nonnarrative o. t. p. composed formulaically has passages consisting of a more or less stable core of lines and parts of lines that are used in several songs. For such research to be meaningful, it is necessary to have a large body of texts for comparison, since many variants of songs are possible.

In the o. t. p. of some cultures in India and Africa there is reportedly more memorization than in those discussed above, although it is said that they too are composed formulaically. An analysis of some sample texts has indicated, however, that they also exhibit a more or less stable core with surrounding variations.

It is not surprising that a special manner of composition and transmission would influence in a profound way the poetic structure and the poetics of o. t. p. One of the most obvious ways in which this is manifested is in the repetitions of formulas. Written poetry does not tolerate a high degree of repetition, but nothing is more characteristic of o. t. p. than repetition, because it is endemic in the method of oral formulaic composition itself. Translators of Homer, for example, normally avoid Homer's repetitions of noun-epithet formulas, using several different epithets where Homer used only one. In this they are tacitly acknowledging the difference between the poetics of written poetry and that of o. t. p. Another device in some o. p. is to repeat on occasion the second half of a line at the beginning of the next line. This is not acceptable as a regular phenomenon in written poetry, but it is natural to o. t. p. On the other hand, one must stress that rhetorical devices such as anaphora and epiphora, and figures of speech such as similes, metaphors, and even ring composition (qq.v.) were used in o. t. p. before the invention of writing and were inherited by written poetry from its predecessor.

The configuration of themes that forms a song in oral formulaic traditional composition is similar to the single theme in its fluidity. Like the themes that make it up, the song, reflecting the desires of the singer at the moment of performance, may be sung long or short, even as tales can be told at length or in brief. It may be ornamented to greater or lesser degree. It too has multiforms, which are usually called variants or versions. The term "multiform" is more accurate than "variant" or "version," terms which imply an "original" that has undergone some kind of change resulting in the text before us.

In o. t. p. one can distinguish three meanings of the word "song," not only in the narrative genres but also in ritual and lyric. The first is that of any performance, for each performance is unique and valid in its own right. The second might be called that of the specific subject matter; for example, the song of the capture of Bagdad by Sultan Selim, which would be designated by a title, "Sultan Selim Captures Bagdad." Combining the first and the second, one can say that there will be as many texts of the specific song as there are performances, whether they are recorded or not. The third meaning of "song" could be called the "generic." The story of the capture of Bagdad (the specific song) falls into the category of a number of stories dealing with the capture of cities, just as the *Odyssey*, for example, falls into the generic category of songs recounting the return of the hero after long absence from home. The texts of this particular generic song are very numerous and reach far back into the depths of human history.

The generic song is of considerable importance in o. t. p. It is not merely a convenient method of classification; it represents the significant core of ideas in a song that survive reinterpretation and specific application to "history," a core held together by tensions from the past that give a meaning to the song not apparent on its surface, no matter how lowly or local any given performance may be. Because of this core, one might say that every song in oral trad. retains the essence of its origins within it, in this way reflecting the origin of the very genre to which it belongs.

In o. t. p. the question of authorship is complicated, yet it is clear that, to use the first of the three meanings of song given above, the performer, the traditional singer, is the "author" of his particular performance. In this case the performer is composer as well. One has, therefore, multiple authors, even as one has multiple texts, of any specific or generic song. From that point of view, there are as many authors as there are performances. But of any given text there is but one author, namely its performer-composer. This is a different concept of multiple authorship from that historically employed in Homeric and other epic criticism since Wolf. Moreover, this concept should not be confused with the theory of "communal" authorship once put forth by scholars of the romantic period.

The date of any text of an oral traditional poem is, consequently, the date of its performance, that being the date of its composition. The date of the specific song would be the date on which some traditional singer for the first time adapted existing themes and configurations to other specific people and events—that is to say, the date of the first performance. This is ordinarily beyond our ken. The date of the generic song is lost in prehistory.

In some cultures there are poems, or songs, usually topical in nature, made up on the spot on demand or composed in live contests of poetry. The poems in this category are ephemeral, created for the moment and usually not transmitted to anyone else. Therefore, since they are improvised for a specific circumstance and do not "enter into tradition," they might be called "oral non-traditional" poems. Because the practice of "improvising" such poems has long existed, however, some scholars feel that the style of these ephemeral creations can also be traditional.

O. p. long played an integral role in the life of human beings and social communities; its practice provided that spiritual activity necessary to man's existence; its bonds with everyday life were manifold and close. Its deeper qualities are becoming clear as they are sifted from the transitional periods in which they were first recorded. The knowledge of how o. t. p. is composed and transmitted has brought with it new modes for its evaluation. And these modes have led back to the symbols and meanings of poetry itself in its origins.

The study of o. p. begun by Milman Parry in the 1930s has engendered many other studies, and debate continues. His theory consisted of first making as exact a description as possible of the process of composition and transmission of oral traditional narrative poetry in order to determine its basic and necessary characteristics, and then applying that knowledge to texts from ancient and medieval times for which there is little or no information about how they were composed. He concentrated on the living practice of oral traditional epics in Yugoslavia, but he also collected a large number of oral traditional lyric songs as well. A description of the collecting and a digest of the contents of the collection can be found in the intro. to v. 1 (1954) of *Serbocroatian Heroic Songs*, ed. by Albert B. Lord. More details on singing and collecting are given in David E. Bynum's Prolegomena to v. 6 (1980) and 14 (1979), ed. by him. The music of a selection of the lyric songs was transcribed by Béla Bartók and pub. with a full study of them by him in 1951.

Parry died in 1935; Lord's book *The Singer of Tales*, published in 1960, gave a description of the Yugoslav practice and applied the principles gained from its study to the Homeric poems, the Anglo-Saxon *Beowulf*, the *Chanson de Roland*, and the medieval Gr. epic of *Digenis Akritas*. Later the theory was applied to other poetries as well, incl. the works of Hesiod and the Homeric Hymns in ancient Gr. trad., the MHG *Nibelungenlied*, the med. Sp. *Cantar de mio Cid*, Eng. and Scottish ballads, Pre-Islamic and Cl. Arabic poetry, Chinese traditional lyrics, the quatrains of Latvian *dainas*, and many others.

Subsequent scholarship focused largely on the definitions of o. p. and of the formula, the problem of composition by formula and theme vis-a-vis improvisation, memorization, and the context of performance. Ruth Finnegan has advocated a broad definition of o. p. with emphasis on the literal meaning of "oral" and on performance. Among reports of o. p. in various parts of the world, those of Jeff Opland on praise poetry among the Xhosa in South Africa have contributed to a deepening understanding of the place of that kind of poetry in the general scheme of o. p.

Opland has also applied his experience with African o. p. to Anglo-Saxon poems and their possible indebtedness to eulogy. Biblical and Near Eastern studies have been influenced by the approach of scholars in the field of o. t. p. Robert C. Culley and William Whallon were among the pioneers in applying oral-formulaic theory to the Old Testament, and the work of Werner H. Kelber is a valuable contribution to the study of the Gospels from that same point of view. Ching-Hsien Wang broadened the field to include Chinese traditional lyrics. James T. Monroe has written on the oral composition of Pre-Islamic poetry, and Michael J. Zwettler's book, in addition to its main subject, has an excellent intro. on oral-formulaic theory. A thorough bibl. of the scholarship on the theory with full intro. is available in Foley (1985).

Parry's work was concerned primarily with oral traditional epic song. He was also interested in the way of life of the people who practiced that kind of poetry, and he was very much aware of the importance of the circumstances of performance and the role of the audience. These aspects of o. p. have been written about by both anthropologists and others concerned with social studies. A special philosophical branch of studies of orality—rather than oral lit.—has also developed from Parry's writings. It includes the work of Eric A. Havelock, H. Marshall McLuhan, and Walter J. Ong. These scholars have examined the effect of literacy and mass media on the way in which humans view the universe and the world in which they live, as well as how they think. Their writings have some pertinence to the study of o. p. See also AFRICAN POETRY; ANTHROPOLOGY AND POETRY; GREEK POETRY, Classical; NARRATIVE POETRY.

BIBLIOGRAPHY: J. M. Foley, Oral Formulaic Theory and Research: An Intro. and Annot. Bibl. (1985). JOURNAL: Oral Tradition (1986–). STUDIES: B. Bartók and A. B. Lord, Serbo-Croatian Folk Songs (1951); R. H. Webber, "Formulaic Diction in the Sp. Ballad," Univ. of Calif. Pubs. in Mod. Philology 34 (1951); C. M. Bowra, Heroic Poetry (1952); A. B. Lord, The Singer of Tales (1960), "Perspectives on Recent Work on Oral Lit.," Oral Lit.: Seven Essays, ed. J. J. Duggan (1975), Epic Singers and Oral Trad. (1991); H. M. McLuhan, The Gutenberg Galaxy (1962); E. A. Havelock, Preface to Plato (1963); G. S. Kirk, The Songs of Homer (1962); R. C. Culley, Oral Formulaic Lang. in the Biblical Psalms (1967); M. Curschmann, "O. P. in Med. Eng., Fr., and Ger. Lit.: Some Notes on Recent Research," Speculum 42 (1967); J. B. Hainsworth, The Flexibility of the Homeric Formula (1968); N. K. Chadwick and V. Žirmunskij, Oral Epics of Central Asia (1969); A. C. Watts, The Lyre and the Harp (1969); W. Whallon, Formula, Character, and Context: Studies in Homeric, OE, and OT Poetry (1969); Parry; J. T. Monroe, "Oral Composition in Pre-Islamic Poetry," JArabL 3 (1972); J. Duggan, The Song of Roland: Formulaic Style and Poetic Craft (1973); M. N. Nagler, Spontaneity and

Trad. (1974); C.-H. Wang, The Bell and the Drum: "Shih Ching" as Formulaic Poetry in an Oral Trad. (1974); B. Peabody, The Winged Word (1975); Oral Lit. and the Formula, ed. B. A. Stolz and R. S. Shannon, III (1976); R. Finnegan, O. P.: Its Nature, Significance, and Social Context (1977), ed., World Treasury of O. P. (1978); M. J. Zwettler, The Oral Trad. of Cl. Arabic Poetry 1978; D. E. Bynum, The Daemon in the Wood (1978); G. Nagy, The Best of the Achaeans (1979); V. Vikis-Freibergs and I. Freibergs, "Formulaic Analysis of the Computer-Accessible Corpus of Latvian Sun-Songs," CHum 12 (1979); J. Opland, Anglo-Saxon O. P. (1980), Xhosa O. P.: Aspects of a Black South-Af. Trad. (1983); Oral Trad. Lit.: Festschrift for A. B. Lord, ed. J. M. Foley (1981); W. J. Ong, Orality and Literacy (1982); R. Janko, Homer, Hesiod and the Hymns (1982); W. A. Quinn and A. S. Hall, Jongleur (1982); W. H. Kelber, The Oral and the Written Gospel (1983); V. Vikis-Freibergs, "Creativity and Trad. in Oral Folklore," Cognitive Processes in the Perception of Art, ed. R. Crozier and A. J. Chapman (1984); J. F. Nagy, The Wisdom of the Outlaw (1985); S. A. Sowayan, Nabati Poetry: The O. P. of Arabia (1985); P. Zumthor, La Lettre et la voix de la litt. médiévale (1987), O. P.: An Intro. (tr. 1990); A. Renoir, A Key to Old Poems: The Oral-Formulaic Approach to the Interp. of West-Germanic Verse (1988); J. M. Foley, The Theory of Oral Composition: Hist. and Methodology (1988), Traditional Oral Epic (1990), ed., Comparative Research in Oral Trads. (1988). A.B.L.

ORAL-FORMULAIC THEORY. Also known as the Parry-Lord theory of oral composition, o. f. t. designates an approach to oral and oral-derived texts that explains the performance and transmission of folkloristic and literary material through a series of structural units: formula (q.v.), theme, and story-pattern. The formula is a substitutable phrase that provides the performer with a malleable, ready-made idiom that simplifies the task of oral composition in performance; the theme and story-pattern amount to formulas at the higher levels of the typical scene and tale-type, respectively. The theory has evolved from its original derivation in ancient Gr. and South Slavic epic to an application to more than a hundred lang. trads.

Anticipators of o. f. t. have been many, starting from the Jewish priest Josephus in the 1st c. A.D. through the amateur classicists F. Hédelin and R. Wood in the 18th c., but the true antecedents are the Ger. philologists and Rus. and other Slavic ethnographers, chiefly of the 19th c. Of the former, the most significant are F. Wolf (1795), who offered archaeological proof that writing was not available to Homer, and the linguists J. Ellendt (1861), H. Düntzer (1872), and others, all of whom studied the relationship of Homeric phraseology and meter. As for the ethnographers, V. Radlov's report (1885) of fieldwork among the central Asian Kara-Kirghiz, which treated the questions of improvisation versus memorization, the units of composition, the role of the audience, and the multiformity of tales, had special interest for Milman Parry. Also extremely influential were M. Murko's accounts (1929, and the posthumous masterwork of 1951) of his experiences among the Yugoslav epic singers or *guslari* (see GUSLAR). It was to this "living laboratory" in Yugoslavia that Parry was eventually to travel in order to confirm the discoveries he had made through analysis of the Homeric texts.

As early as his 1923 Master's thesis, one can glimpse Parry's vision of a long-standing *trad.* of ancient Gr. singers that led eventually to Homer. His explanation, which superseded the contemporary debate in Cl. Philology between Unitarians and Analysts (one or many Homers) over the authorship of the Gr. epics, was a radical proposal: in his 1928 theses he showed that the lang. and style of Homer were neither an original creation nor the composite work of redactors, but rather the bequest of traditional poets who over generations had assembled an adaptable diction and a flexible narrative repertoire. Thus Parry conceived of the formula as "a group of words which is regularly employed under the same metrical conditions to express a given essential idea" (272); the "formulaic system" consisted of a set of formulas that shared a common pattern of phraseology. A singer's formulas and systems together comprised something akin to a set of phraseological equations, some of them constant and others with variables, that could be called upon to solve whatever compositional problem arose. There simply was no narrative situation that could not be handled by recourse to this plastic diction. Parry also showed that the noun-epithet phrases (e.g. "swift-footed Achilles" or "wily Odysseus"), a species of formula, exhibit a kind of *thrift*, in that each hero or god is customarily assigned only one such phrase for a given part of the hexameter verse, and that Homer tended to avoid enjambment, his thought being either complete in a single hexameter line or optionally continued to the next line. These and other findings led him to posit a formulaic diction in which individual aesthetic choice is subservient to metrical expediency, and in which the kind of creative artistic effect so cherished by modern crit. is much less likely than traditional values epitomized through traditional structures.

From the hypothesis of *trad.* Parry moved, at the suggestion of Murko and Parry's mentor Antoine Meillet, to the further and complementary hypothesis of *orality*. In his studies of 1930 and 1932, he argued that Homer's formulaic diction must also have been oral, since nothing less than the pressure of composition in performance could have stimulated the production and maintenance of this special verse idiom. Parry's field trips to Yugoslavia in 1933–35 with Albert B. Lord were intended to provide a comparison between the ms. texts of Homer and the living oral trad. of the South Slavs. With the discovery of formulaic diction in the Yugoslav songs, as recorded in the partially published Cor Huso, the o. f. t. as a comparative approach was born.

With Parry's premature death in 1935, the completion and extension of his work was undertaken by Lord, who made trips to Yugoslavia and Albania in 1950–51 and, with D. Bynum, in the 1960s. First in importance among Lord's works, and in the field at large, stands *The Singer of Tales*, in which he brings the Yugoslav analogy to bear on ancient Gr., OE, OF, and Byzantine Gr. narrative. This volume also saw the elaboration of the concepts of *theme* (e.g. arming the hero, feasting, boasting) and *story-pattern* (e.g. the Return Song, the Wedding Song), which together with formula offered an explanation of oral traditional multiformity at all levels of epic verse. Crucial to the extension of o. f. t. to other trads. was his concept of "formulaic density," through which, following Parry's famous analyses of passages from the *Iliad* and *Odyssey*, he claimed that one could determine whether a text was orally composed by calculating its percentage of formulas and systems. Also important has been the publication of the South Slavic songs (Parry et al., 1953–) gathered during fieldwork, particularly the 13,000-line *The Wedding of Smailagic Meho* by Avdo Medjedović. His later comparative research has treated Rus., Latvian, Finnish, Ukrainian, Bulgarian, and other oral trads. As the two "Perspectives" articles (1974, 1986) illustrate, Lord has brought the o. f. t. from a revolutionary but narrowly applied method to a discipline of broad comparative importance.

This history and rapid expansion are chronicled in *The Theory of Oral Composition* (Foley 1988) and bibliographically surveyed in *O. F. T. and Research* (Foley 1985). Among the most significant issues and points of disagreement have been (a) the question of how far comparison can be extended and how binding are proofs by analogy (e.g. Kirk 1962, Watts 1969); (b) the problem of the seemingly mechanistic nature of o. f. t. and its impact on aesthetic crit. of the works involved (e.g. Vivante 1982); (c) the legitimacy of the "formulaic density" criterion (e.g. Benson 1966); (d) the phenomenon of "transitional texts" that reveal signs of both oral and written provenance; and (e) the respective roles of fieldwork and textual analysis in the study of oral trads. (e.g. Finnegan 1977). A number of related and parallel areas have taken on considerably greater prominence, among them philosophical and historical treatments of oral trad. (e.g. Havelock 1963; Ong 1967, 1982). In order to provide a central forum for the interdisciplinary debate surrounding the area, the journal *Oral Trad.* (1986–) and the Lord monograph series (1987–) were established. See also ANTHROPOLOGY AND POETRY; ORAL POETRY.

F. Wolf, *Prolegomena ad Homerum* (1795; Eng. tr. 1985); J. Ellendt, *Über den Einfluss des Metrums* (1861); H. Düntzer, *Homerische Abhandlungen*

(1872); V. Radlov, *Der Dialect der Kara-Kirgisen* (1885); M. Murko, *La Poésie populaire épique en Yougoslavie au début du XXe siècle* (1929), *Tragom srpsko-hrvatske narodne epike* (1951); *Serbo-Croatian Heroic Songs (Srpskohrvatske junacke pjesme)*, coll., ed., and tr. M. Parry, A. B. Lord, and D. Bynum (1953–); Lord; G. S. Kirk, *The Songs of Homer* (1962); E. Havelock, *Preface to Plato* (1963); L. Benson, "The Literary Character of Anglo-Saxon Formulaic Poetry," *PMLA* 81 (1966); W. Ong, *The Presence of the Word* (1967), *Orality and Literacy* (1982); A. C. Watts, *The Lyre and the Harp* (1969); Parry; A. B. Lord, "Perspectives on Recent Work on Oral Lit.," *FMLS* 10 (1974), "Perspectives on the Oral Traditional Formula," *OT* 1 (1986); R. Finnegan, *Oral Poetry* (1977); P. Vivante, *The Epithets in Homer* (1982); J. M. Foley, *O. F. T. and Research* (1985), *The Theory of Oral Composition* (1988), ed., *Comparative Research in Oral Trads.* (1988), *Traditional Oral Epic* (1990), *Immanent Art* (1991); *Oral Trad.* (1986–); Albert Bates Lord Studies in Oral Trad. monograph series (1987–); A. Renoir, *A Key to Old Poems* (1988).   J.M.F.

ORGANICISM. Many critics, from Aristotle and Longinus to Emerson, Croce, Dewey, Brooks, and Ingarden, have claimed that some insight into the origin, nature, or value of artistic works can be gained by describing them by analogy to living things. Their use of the organic analogy has been strongly influenced both by their conceptions of the kinds of properties possessed by living things and by their decision as to which of these properties best illuminates human experience with art. For some critics the analogy was little more than a rhetorical flourish (e.g. "the spirit that suffuses an author's works," "the body and soul of a poem," "a poem demands a living response"), but other critics, particularly the Ger. romantics and Coleridge, used the analogy to help them formulate a nonmechanistic aesthetics and psychology of the creative process. The poem, the romantics said, begins as a "seed" or "germ" in the creative imagination (q.v.) of the poet; its growth, to a large extent a spontaneous and unconscious process, consists in assimilating foreign and diverse materials to itself and adapting them to its needs; its devel. and final form are self-determined in accord with a "Power or Principle" that inheres in the seed. The result is an artwork whose parts have the kind of necessity, functional interdependence, and subordination to the whole which is characteristic of living things like plants or trees.

In 20th-c. poetics, the organic analogy has been particularly attractive to those theorists who argue that a poem must be experienced in isolation from other objects for the sake of its intrinsic values. A poem is an autonomous, autotelic object which, properly apprehended, produces in the reader a unique kind of "aesthetic" experience which has been variously described as having such qualities as absorbed but disinterested contemplation; a pervasive hedonic tone of considerable intensity; a heightening of consciousness inspired by beauty or other aesthetic qualities; and a sense of inner coherence, completeness, and harmony. The evocation of aesthetic experience is primarily dependent on perceiving the poem as an integrated ("organic") whole or gestalt (see UNITY). The whole is prior to the parts; it selects, determines relevance and order, shapes, and establishes interrelationships among the parts (see ANALYSIS); thus the parts in consort acquire synergistic qualities, meanings, and effects which they would not have separately. Hence the most important excellence that can be attributed to any of the parts is to show that it is a necessary element of the whole.

An important difference among organicists lies in their conception of the nature of the synthesizing (or formal) principle that integrates the parts of a poem into a whole (see NEW CRITICISM; CONTEXTUALISM; CHICAGO SCHOOL; RUSSIAN FORMALISM; STRUCTURALISM). An organicist like Croce may argue that every poem has an utterly unique synthesizing principle which must be discovered by the reader via intuition (q.v.). Other organicists (e.g. the Chicago Critics) have tried to establish broad categories of synthesizing principles from inductive study of the intentions of poets as these appear in their works. Culler (1975) enumerates six basic "models of totalities" that structuralist critics have proposed for describing the unity of lyric poems. Other theorists, such as Coleridge, see the same abstract principle reflected in all poetry, e.g. the fusion of opposites (particular and universal, good and evil, material and spiritual), the reduction of the many to one, or repetition with difference.

Organicists also differ in the delimitation of the whole to which organic categories are then applied. The organic analogy was used by Longinus to specify and relate the elements that give even a verbal fragment the power to generate a moment of sublime transport. And though it has been used often by formalist critics, it has also been used by social theorists to analyze the devel. and structure of institutions, cultures, and historical periods; such theorists hold that there is an organic connection, an indivisible continuity, among all elements of reality. In myth and transcendental philosophy the universe itself has been characterized as a living thing whose parts are controlled by a World Soul.

Over the long history of poetics, unity (q.v.; and associated concepts such as completeness, coherence, synthesis, integration, and wholeness) has almost always been considered a positive quality in a poem, though the degree of importance ascribed to it has varied. Organic unity in the most radical sense has been used by only a small number of theorists (e.g. Pater, Croce), who have regarded unity as the indispensable criterion of aesthetic value. But most theorists recognize that unity exists in degrees and that aesthetic value

ORIGINALITY

depends on other qualities as well (see EVALUATION). Thus Aristotle says that the rank of a poem, when it is compared with other poems, depends not only on the degree of its unity but also on the richness and diversity of the materials that it succeeds in integrating into its structure. And Beardsley argues that the depth or "magnitude" of aesthetic experience depends on such qualities as complexity and intensity (qq.v.), qualities that might be diminished by too strict an emphasis on unity. Most nonformalist critics (like the typical Ren. or neoclassical critics), while not denying the value of unity, have preferred a "loose" (nonorganic) conception of unity which permits the inclusion of digressions, episodes, subplots, or other types of narrative figuration to provide "variety" or "surprise" or "comic relief." These critics recognize a number of different values that lit. can convey. These values may be reflected by the whole poem, but they may also appear in its parts (e.g. original metaphors, ornamental diction, harmonious versification, multiplicity of interesting characters, or aphorisms or more extended moral commentary). Such parts are then evaluated by criteria other than their contribution to the whole. Indeed, in extreme cases the structure of the poem is regarded simply as providing a framework for the exhibition of a variety of pleasing or instructive elements. It may be hard to appreciate, say, *The Rubáiyát of Omar Khayyám* in any other way.

In the latter 20th c., some theorists have become skeptical about the desirability or even possibility of achieving unity (tight or loose) in works of art. It is said that even though o. may reflect the human attempt to bring order to an otherwise chaotic existence, it also parallels the undesirable values of totalitarian systems of government or repressive cultural conventions. Order is desirable, but humans also need freedom, innovation, and differentiation. Thus there has been a tendency to admire openness rather than closure (q.v.). The study of poetry from this perspective has shown the presence in it of ambiguities, incoherences, indeterminacies, and gaps which o., with its commitment to the ideal of tight unity, tended to ignore or denigrate. Thus some modern poets compose works deliberately incorporating discontinuities, obscurities, irrelevancies, and inner contradictions, devices that frustrate a traditional reader's expectation that the work should make sense and be an integrated whole. The reader is invited to abandon the constraints on reading imposed by the convention of o. and enjoy other values: a sense of free play, active participation in the creation of a poem, release from the restrictions of linguistic and genre conventions, and a discovery of the fluid, contingent nature of existential reality when it is stripped of the forms imposed on it by culture. Such recommendations are in part the result of deconstruction (q.v.), which claims that no text can have a determinate, totalizable meaning reflecting a "centered" structure or synthesizing principle. From this point of view a poem is more properly analogous to a labyrinth with no exit than to a plant or tree.

See now FORM; INTERTEXTUALITY; STRUCTURE; TEXTUALITY; UNITY.

C. Brooks, "The Poem as Organism," *Eng. Institute Annual* (1941), "Implications of an Organic Theory of Poetry," *Lit. and Belief* (1958); J. C. Ransom, "Art Worries the Naturalists," *KR* 7 (1945); J. Benziger, "Organic Unity: Leibniz to Coleridge," *PMLA* 66 (1951); Abrams; R. S. Crane, *The Langs. of Crit. and the Structure of Poetry* (1953); R. H. Fogle, "Organic Form in Am. Crit., 1840–1870," *The Devel. of Am. Lit. Crit.*, ed. F. Stovall (1955), *The Idea of Coleridge's Crit.* (1962); S. J. Kahn, "Towards an Organic Crit.," *JAAC* 15 (1956); M. C. Beardsley, *Aesthetics* (1958); *Parts and Wholes*, ed. D. S. Lerner (1963); C. Lord, "Organic Unity Reconsidered," *JAAC* 22 (1964); G. N. G. Orsini, "The Organic Concept in Aesthetics," *CL* 21 (1969), "O.," *DHI, Organic Unity in Ancient and Later Poetics* (1975); *Organic Form: The Life of an Idea*, ed. G. S. Rousseau (1972)—excellent bibl. to 1970; M. Perloff, *The Poetics of Indeterminacy* (1981); O. Kenshur, *Open Form and the Shape of Ideas* (1986); E. Rothstein, "'O.,' Rupturalism, and Ism-ism," *MP* 85 (1988); M. Krieger, *A Reopening of Closure: O. Against Itself* (1989); R. Shusterman, "Organic Unity: Analysis and Deconstruction," *Redrawing the Lines*, ed. R. W. Dasenbrock (1989); G. Sircello, "Beauty in Shards and Fragments," *JAAC* 48 (1990). F.GU.

ORIENTALISM. See CULTURAL CRITICISM; EXOTICISM; PRIMITIVISM.

ORIGIN. See DECONSTRUCTION; INFLUENCE; INTERTEXTUALITY; TEXTUALITY.

ORIGINALITY. The most typical use of o. is to indicate some degree of difference in matter or form that a new work exhibits when compared with some specified body of existing lit. Thus o. is opposed to plagiarism, copy, and imitation (q.v.); to translation and paraphrase (qq.v.); to "rules," conventions, and tradition (qq.v.); to the cliche and the stereotype. It is usually associated with change, novelty, exoticism (q.v.), freedom, experimentation, revolt, spontaneity (q.v.), individuality, uniqueness.

O. is attributed to a work if it reflects novelty in diction, imagery, prosody, rhet., style, or technical or structural devices; if it modifies an existing genre or establishes a new genre; if it treats of some aspect of nature or human life that had hitherto escaped literary treatment; if it describes a make-believe world, wonderland or nightmare, with little or no relation to reality; if it re-evaluates a historical, mythological, or fictional person, object, or event; if it reflects the individuality of the author, esp. by presenting an interp. of life (or some aspect of it) from a fresh perspective; if it is designed to evoke novel effects in the reader; or if it uses lang. to create a unique structure of organically interrelated meanings independent of any immediate external reference.

In nonnormative uses, o. is a key concept for the literary historian or thematist tracing the innovations, the rise and fall of conventions, the repetitions and differences that have occurred in authors' use of literary forms and materials over the course of time. It may also appear nonnormatively in psychological analyses of the nature and operation of genius, imagination (qq.v.), creativity, and invention (q.v.).

Normative uses of o. occur frequently in poetics and practical crit., though critics do not agree as to whether o. should carry positive or negative value and, if positive, to what degree it is desirable and in which aspects of a poem it should be reflected. Extreme positions have been defended. Coomaraswamy, speaking from a metaphysical perspective, severely condemns the search for individuality and novelty that has increasingly characterized the work of artists since the Ren.: Eternal Truth does not change; the artist's function is to provide a guide for the contemplation of Eternal Truth; any novelty in the artist's work—any exhibitionism—is therefore a distraction and an embodiment of error; "true o." is a return to the spiritual origin or source from which the transcendental forms reflected in a good work of art are derived. Vigorous defenses of the opposite extreme—the more o. the better (in art and in life)—can be found in the pronouncements and practice of authors rebelling against the "exhausted" conventions still supported by the literary establishment of their times (see, e.g., CULTERANISMO; STURM UND DRANG; DECADENCE; DADA; CUBISM; SURREALISM), in the work of authors feeling "the burden of the past" or "the anxiety of influence" (Bate, Bloom), or in authors committed to an unqualified version of expressionist poetics, which demands that a poem reflect an author's "original genius" or unique vision (q.v.).

Most critics take a position somewhere between these extremes. A good example is Coleridge, for whom o. is of crucial importance; however, he also insists that in a great poem o. must be balanced by its opposite—the familiar. In the *Biographia literaria* he says that one of the ways in which the poetic imagination reveals itself is in the reconciliation of a "sense of novelty and freshness with old and familiar objects." In the poems of *Lyrical Ballads*, he and Wordsworth intended to unite the "two cardinal points of poetry": "the power of exciting the sympathy of the reader by a faithful adherence to the truth of nature, and the power of giving the interest of novelty by the modifying colors of imagination."

Some theorists have argued that o. ought not be considered an aesthetic norm. Beardsley, for example, points out that since a poem can be origi-

nal and good or original and bad, o. cannot be a valid standard. Of course repetition (q.v.) usually creates boredom, and thus o. will catch and hold the reader's attention. But o. must not be allowed to obscure the values that traditionally have been found in poetry: o. is perhaps a reason for admiring the poet but should not be used to justify a value judgment on the work.

I. Babbitt, "On Being Original," *Lit. and the Am. College* (1908); J. L. Lowes, *Convention and Revolt in Poetry* (1919); T. S. Eliot, *After Strange Gods* (1934), *On Poetry and Poets* (1957); E. L. Mann, "The Problem of O. in Eng. Lit. Crit., 1750–1800," *PQ* 18 (1939); A. K. Coomaraswamy, *Why Exhibit Works of Art?* (1943); M. C. Nahm, *The Artist as Creator* (1956); M. C. Beardsley, *Aesthetics* (1958), "The Relevance of Reasons in Art Crit.," *The Aesthetic Point of View* (1982); W. J. Bate, *The Burden of the Past* (1970); H. Bloom, *The Anxiety of Influence* (1973); M. Krieger, *Theory of Crit.* (1976); R. Mortier, *L'Originalité: une nouvelle catégorie esthétique au siècle des lumières* (1982); D. Quint, *Origin and O. in Ren. Lit.* (1983); P. Phillips, *The Adventurous Muse: Theories of O. in Eng. Poetics 1650–1760* (1984); T. McFarland, *O. and Imagination* (1985).   F.GU.

ORIYA POETRY. See INDIAN POETRY.

ORNAMENT. An accessory or embellishment, an element added to some object. It may or may not contribute to the structure (q.v.) or effective functioning of that object, but it must have some kind of independent interest, and most often this is an aesthetic one. An o. adorns, or adds charm, splendor, or beauty to the object; it fascinates by its refinement or exoticness; or it challenges perception and stimulates comprehension by its intricacy or grotesqueness. An o. may also have instrumental values—cognitive, rhetorical, social, moral, religious: it may identify an object or person's social status, for example, or it may have magical or symbolic values. All cultures have used o., but opinions have differed widely as to the functions, types, and amounts appropriate. Taste in o. has ranged from classical simplicity to baroque (q.v.) intricacy. There have also been anti-ornamentalists, who value only the practical and strictly functional and who regard any o. as a sign of superficiality, waste, and even decadence.

The term "o." has appeared regularly over the long trad. of Western poetics, particularly in those forms of pragmatic crit. that see a close relationship between poetry and rhet. (see POETRY, THEORIES OF, *Pragmatic Theories*). In Cl. rhet., o. is a part of the vocabulary of discussions of style (q.v.). After the content of a speech has been invented and outlined, it is dressed in lang. and, if desirable, decked out in appropriate o. An ornate style such as the baroque is defined as an artistic deviation of considerable degree from ordinary usage in word choice or word order. The means for heightening style that apply in oratory apply even more fully to poetry. Cl., medieval, and Ren. theorists (e.g. Puttenham) spent much time identifying and classifying the "flowers," "gems," and "colors" of expression. Distinctions were made between schemes and tropes, figures of speech and figures of thought, and "difficult" and easy os. Although there have always been practitioners and admirers of the florid (a style which since Cl. times has been known as "Asiatic"), most theorists sought to develop a set of principles for guiding an author in the tasteful and effective use of o. These principles involved considerations of genre and, most important, appropriateness to an author's subject, purpose, and audience (see DECORUM). Thus, the justification in medieval and Ren. theory for figurative lang. stressed the functional as well as the ornamental values of figures (Tuve). Figures are good because they catch the reader's attention, sustain a state of pleasurable anticipation, and delight the imagination. They can also assist the persuasive process by clarifying and vivifying the abstract, by generating emotion, and by moving the will.

Neoclassical critics continued to find use for the term "o." to refer not only to figurative lang. but also to other parts of a poem. The musical qualities of lang. are now seen as pleasing accessories or added embellishments. Dryden speaks of adorning a poem with noble thoughts. Sometimes the plot of a dramatic poem is regarded as a naked structure which is ornamented with a variety of interesting characters, moving episodes (incl. digressions), and finely wrought speeches. Indeed, almost any aspect of a poem which could be isolated could be called an o. Even neoclassical critics who stressed instruction, the second of the Horatian twin aims of poetry, continued to speak of the "beauties" or "os." of poetry. Pleasure, though a secondary aim, is the necessary sugarcoating to get the audience to swallow the pill of instruction.

During the 19th c., the notion of o. quickly lost currency. Romantic poetics (q.v.) postulated as a fundamental premise the irrefrangibility of form and content, so that the very idea of poetic o., with its connotation of adventitiousness, was no longer imaginable. In this most of the poetic theories of the 20th c. have followed suit. Most versions of formalism insist on both the unity of form and content (see ORGANICISM) and a principle of artistic economy whereby every element serves a purpose in the semantic and affective economy of the poem: no element is wasted or somehow "extra." Even in structuralist theories like Lotman's, every element contributes on a variety of levels. The notion that thought could be separated and specified apart from the specific verbal articulation of it, which seemed so easy to Pope, now seems impossible.

Still, the appeal of o. seems universal; human beings have always loved to decorate themselves, their artifacts, and their places of power. There are some signs that late 20th-c. taste is shifting away from functionalism and minimalism in the arts; there is new praise for copiousness, variety, novelty, and a recognition of the multiple values that may inhere in a poem. Indeed, radical critics even hold that ornamentalism may subvert or contradict the function or structure of the object to which it has been added. To such theorists there is no clear-cut distinction between what is essential and what is marginal in a text.

G. Puttenham, *The Arte of Eng. Poesie* (1589), esp. Bk. 3, "Of O."; L. Cooper, "The Verbal 'O.' in Aristotle's Art of Poetry," *Cl. and Med. Studies Edward Kennard Rand*, ed. L. W. Jones (1938); A. Coomaraswamy, *Figures of Speech or Figures of Thought* (1946); Brooks; R. Tuve, *Elizabethan and Metaphysical Imagery* (1947); W. S. Howell, *Logic and Rhet. in England, 1500–1700* (1956); Weinberg; Saisselin; M. E. Hazard, "An Essay to Amplify 'O.,'" *SEL* 16 (1976); E. H. Gombrich, *The Sense of Order* (1979); R. Jensen and P. Conway, *Ornamentalism* (1982); W. Steiner, "Postmodernism and the O.," *Word & Image* 4 (1988); R. B. Gordon, *O., Fantasy, and Desire in 19th-C. Fr. Lit.* (1992); O. Grabar, *The Mediation of O.* (1992).   F.GU.

OTTAVA RIMA (or *ottava toscana*; Ger. *stanze*; Rus. *oktava*). In It. prosody, an octave stanza in hendecasyllables (q.v.) rhyming *ababab cc*. Its origin is obscure, being variously attributed to development from the stanza of the *canzone* (q.v.) or the *sirventes* (q.v.) or to imitation of the Sicilian *strambotto* (q.v.). Wilkins suggested that what we today call o. r. was a popular borrowing in the 14th c. on the part of some minstrel or minstrels of the *strambotto* form for long poems (*cantari*) of less than epic length. However, it was in use in the religious verse of late 13th-c. Italy, and it was given definitive artistic form by Boccaccio in his *Filostrato* (1335?) and *Teseida* (1340–42?). Becoming almost immediately the dominant form of It. narrative verse, o. r. was developed in the 15th c. by Politian, Pulci, and Boiardo and reached its apotheosis in the *Orlando Furioso* (1516) of Ariosto, whose genius exploited its potentialities for richness, complexity, and variety of effect. Later in the same century, Torquato Tasso (*Gerusalemme liberata*) showed his mastery of the form. In subsequent centuries o. r. was employed in Italy by Marino (*Adone*), Tassoni (*La secchia rapita*), Alfieri (*Etruria vendicata*), Tommaseo (*Una serva, La Contessa Matilde*), and Marradi (*Sinfonia del bosco*).

In the broader European context, the poets of Ren. Spain and Portugal followed the It. example in adopting the form for narrative purposes. Notable epics in o. r. are Ercilla's *La Araucana* in Sp. and Camões' *Os Lusíadas* in Port. The form was explored by Eng. Ren. poets, e.g. Wyatt (some 15 poems, most monostrophic), Sidney (*Old Arcadia* 35, 54), Spenser, Daniel (*Civil Wars*), Drayton, Greville, Harington (*Orlando Furioso*), and Fairfax (his Tasso). Milton uses it for the coda of *Lycidas*.

OULIPO

But it was not until the romantic period that the form found a true Eng. master in Byron, whose tr. of a portion of Pulci's *Morgante Maggiore* (if not J. H. Frere's *The Monks and the Giants*) seems to have made him aware of the stanza's possibilities. He employed the stanza in *Beppo, The Vision of Judgment*, and, with greatest success, in *Don Juan*. Shelley used it after 1820, chiefly for *The Witch of Atlas*; Keats used it for *Isabella*; Yeats used it for several major works (see below). It was popularized in Rus. poetry by Puškin on the model of Byron.

The work of the great masters of the stanza—Ariosto, Byron, and Yeats—suggests that o. r. is most suited to work of a varied nature, blending serious, comic, and satiric attitudes and mingling narrative and discursive modes. Byron, referring to Pulci, calls it "the half-serious rhyme" (*Don Juan* 4.6). Its accumulation of rhyme, reaching a precarious crescendo with the third repetition, prepares the reader for the neat summation, the acute observation, or the epigrammatic twist which comes with the final couplet:

And Julia's voice was lost, except in sighs,
  Until too late for useful conversation;
The tears were gushing from her gentle eyes,
  I wish, indeed, they had not had occasion;
But who, alas! can love, and then be wise?
  Not that remorse did not oppose temptation:
A little still she strove, and much repented,
And whispering "I will ne'er consent"—
    consented.
             (Don Juan 1.117)

At 8 lines (cf. the Spenserian of 9), the o. r. stanza is long enough to carry the thread of narrative but not so long that it becomes unmanageable, and it allows ampler room for exposition and elaboration than do quatrains. Yeats, the greatest modern master of o. r., uses it for some 15 of his poems, incl. "Sailing to Byzantium" (with near rhymes), "Among School Children," and "The Circus Animals' Desertion." Significantly, Yeats develops the form precisely at the same time (1910–19) that the dreamy style of his early period is evolving into the more realistic, colloquial style of the great poems of his middle period. See also ITALIAN PROSODY; STRAMBOTTO; SICILIAN OCTAVE.—Schipper; P. Habermann, "Stanze," *Reallexikon I*; G. Bünte, *Zur Verskunst der deutschen Stanze* (1928); V. Pernicone, "Storia e svolgimento della metrica," *Problemi ed orientamenti critici di lingua e di letteratura italiana*, ed. A. Momigliano, v. 2 (1948); G. M. Ridenour, *The Style of Don Juan* (1960); A. Limentani, "Storia e struttura dell'o. r.," *Lettere italiane* 13 (1961); A. Roncaglia, "Per la storia dell'o. r.," *CN* 25 (1965); R. Beum, *The Poetic Art of W. B. Yeats* (1969), ch. 10; E. G. Etkind, *Russkie poety-perevodchiki ot Trediakovskogo do Pushkina* (1973), 155–201; Spongano; Wilkins; Elwert, *Italienische*; I. K. Lilly, "Some Structural Invariants in Rus. and Ger. O. R.," *Style* 21 (1987).   A.PR.; C.K.; T.V.F.B.

OULIPO is the acronym for "Ouvroir de littérature potentielle," which was founded in 1960 by a group of ten writers and mathematicians led by Raymond Queneau and François Le Lionnais. Later additions included Georges Perec and Jacques Roubaud, as well as correspondents from abroad, notably Marcel Duchamp and Harry Mathews (USA), and Italo Calvino (Italy). Although Duchamp and Queneau constitute links between dada (q.v.), surrealism (q.v.), and the O., the latter movement has emphasized its autonomy. The procedures based on chance which Tristan Tzara devised for generating dada poems aimed essentially at demolishing traditional notions of aesthetic value. Surrealism proceeded on the belief that chance is controlled by surreal forces which, as in the case of automatic writing, work through the unconscious. The O., on the other hand, rejects both chance and the unconscious as valid tools for literary creation. It is primarily interested in the conscious elaboration and the systematic application of text-generating methods.

The O. has experimented with existing forms—the Occitan sestina (q.v.), rhopalic verse (q.v.), lipograms (texts in which one or more letters may not be used), tautograms (each word must begin with the same letter), holorhyming verse (every syllable in the line must rhyme), permutational poems (lines can be read in any order)—and created new variants in the process. The "quenine," for instance, extends the structure of the sestina to stanzas with larger numbers of lines. In the "avalanche," a variant of the rhopalic poem, the increment for each line is not one letter, but one word. Unlike the surrealist "proverbes mis au goût du jour," Oulipian "perverbs" retain only the poetic structure of traditional aphorisms. The O. has also invented many original forms often based on mathematical concepts or operations: Boolean poems (e.g. if two poems are considered as sets, a new poem is generated by their intersection, i.e. the words common to both sets), Fibonaccian poems (if a poem is broken up into *n* fragments, the number of new poems generated by recombining noncontiguous fragments is given by Fibonacci's formula), S+7 poems (a new poem is generated by replacing each noun S in an existing poem by the noun which ranks seventh after it in a given dictionary), etc. Finally, it has used the computer for the automatic generation of poems.

The first major creation of Oulipian poetry was Queneau's *Cent mille milliards de poèmes* (1961), in which a matrix of ten sonnets generates 100 trillion poems. The 361 poems in Roubaud's ε (1967) correspond to the 361 pawns in the Japanese game of *go* and can be read in four different ways. Other collections based on Oulipian techniques include Jean Lescure's *Drailles* (1968), Noël Arnaud's *Poèmes Algol* (1968), Harry Mathews' *Trial Impressions* (1977), and Georges Perec's *La Clôture* (1980).

In 1982, four Oulipians joined a group of writers, mathematicians, and computer scientists to found the ALAMO, or "Atelier de littérature assistée par la mathématique et les ordinateurs," a very active offshoot of the O. taking part in major exhibits and training educators and writers in its methods.

Raymond Queneau complained in 1963 that the O. found no echo in literary circles, but similar experiments soon took place in France and elsewhere, e.g. the combinatory poems of Michel Butor, or the computer poetry (q.v.) of Margaret Masterman, Marie Borroff, and Louis T. Milic. Robert Pinsky's *Mindwheel* (1986) is probably the most sophisticated creation in this line.—Oulipo, *La Littérature potentielle* (1973), *Atlas de littérature potentielle* (1981); P. Fournel, *Clefs pour la littérature potentielle* (1978); J. Bens, *O. 1960–1963* (1980); *O.: A Primer of Potential Lit.*, ed. W. F. Motte, Jr. (1986).   R.G.

OUTRIDE. See HYPERMETRIC; SPRUNG RHYTHM.

OXYMORON or *synoeciosis* (Gr. "pointedly foolish"; Lat. *contrapositum*). A figure of speech which yokes together two seemingly contradictory elements. O. is thus a form of condensed paradox (q.v.). Shakespeare has "O heavy lightness! serious vanity! / Mis-shapen chaos of well-seeming forms! / Feather of lead, bright smoke, cold fire, sick health!" (*Romeo and Juliet* 1.1.178–80). Although o. has been a recurrent device in poetry at least since the time of Horace ("concordia discors rerum"—the jarring harmony of things [*Epistulae* 1.12.19]), it was an important device in the poetry of Petrarchism (q.v.) and was the trope of the baroque (q.v.) era par excellence. Such poets as Marino in Italy, Góngora in Spain, and Crashaw in England made it a primary vehicle of the 17th-c. sensibility:

> Welcome, all wonders in one sight!
> Eternity shut in a span,
>   Summer in winter, day in night,
> Heaven in earth, and God in man!

As this quotation shows, o. is particularly effective in evoking religious mysteries or other meanings which the poet feels to be beyond the reach of logical distinction or ordinary sense. Its popularity in the late Ren. owes something to the heightened religious concerns of that period, and something, too, to the revival of the habit of analogical thinking. Milton uses the figure often in the early books of *Paradise Lost*, in part to evoke the unimaginable glories of God. Note, however, that o., which reveals a compulsion to fuse all experience into a unity, is to be distinguished from antithesis (q.v.), which tends to divide and categorize elements of experience. Significantly, the latter figure, with its basis in rationality, dominates the poetry of the 18th c., a period which regarded the figures of the baroque poets as examples of "bad taste" and "false wit." But o. returns in many passages in Keats, who also uses it to express the paradoxes of sensuous experience.

O. is a complex figure best understood by placing it in the group formed by the other related figures of contrast such as antithesis, antiphrasis, and paradox; Ren. rhetoricians distinguished 11 of these. Ducrot and Todorov define o. as the "establishment of a syntactic relationship between two antonyms" (278). Group Mu attempts (with only partial success) to distinguish o. from the other complex figures of contrast by analyzing the semantic elements in the oxymoric conjunction: "the contradiction is absolute because the negation takes place in an abstract vocabulary: 'harmonious discord,' 'black sun.' We have, therefore, a figure in which one term is a nuclear seme (semantic trait, element of meaning) negating a classeme (the generic element indicating the class to which individual semes belong, e.g. the same *color* for the word *red*) of the other term." For example, in the well known Miltonic o., "darkness visible," "'darkness' imposes the classeme *obscure* which is cancelled by *visible*" (123). Thus o. is a "*coincidentia oppositorum*" in which the antithesis is denied and the contradiction fully assented to." O. differs from antiphrasis, a "metalogism [figure of thought] by repetition (*A* is not *A*)," because o. 2"violates the code and belongs *de facto* to the class of metasememes [tropes]" (124). Group Mu does not discuss the difference between o. and paradox. Dupriez distinguishes between o. (words), oxymoric sentences, and oxymoric sentiments and ideas.

O. is by no means reserved, however, for religious experience or even love's contradictions; the modern world abounds in them even for quotidian existence—e.g. "amicable divorce," "free pet," "painless dentistry," "airline food," "life insurance," "friendly fire," "boneless ribs," "married life," "sight unseen," "nonworking mother"—and Hegel has, we recall, "concrete universal" (q.v.). Finally, one may note that in *1984*, o. is the very basis of "doublethink," that process of holding two opinions simultaneously, "knowing them to be contradictory and believing in both of them." This way not higher unification of opposites but madness lies. See also CATACHRESIS; SYNAESTHESIA.—H. J. Büchner, "Das O. in der griechischen Dichtung von Homer bis in die Zeit des Hellenismus," Diss., Tübingen (1950); E. McCann, "Oxymora in Sp. Mystics and Eng. Metaphysical Writers," *CL* 13 (1961); E. Weber, "Das O. bei Shakespeare," Diss., Hamburg (1963); Lausberg; W. Freytag, *Das O. bei Wolfram, Gottfried und andern Dichtern des Mittelalters* (1972); O. Ducrot and T. Todorov, *Encyclopedic Dict. of the Sciences of Lang.* (tr. 1979); B. Dupriez, *Gradus* (1980), s.v. "alliance"; Morier; Group Mu; W. Blumenfeld, *Jumbo Shrimp* (1986), *Pretty Ugly* (1989); Y. Shen, "On the Structure and Understanding of Poetic O.," *PoT* 8 (1987); B. Vickers, *In Defence of Rhet.* (1988); Corbett.
                              F.J.W.; A.W.H.; T.V.F.B.

P

PAEAN. A type of Gr. hymn whose name derives from *ié paián*, a cry addressed to Apollo as the god of healing, which often forms the refrain (cf. Homer, *Hymn to Apollo* 517). Ps. were sung on numerous occasions: to Apollo in his role as healer or protector (e.g. *Iliad* 1.473), as a song of hope before going into battle (Pindar, *Paeans* 2) or of joy after victory (*Iliad* 22.391), and at the beginning of a symposium (Alcman, fr. 98; Ariphron, "P. to Health"). Ps. were addressed to gods other than Apollo (e.g. Zeus, Poseidon, Dionysus, and Hygeia) and even, in the late 5th c. and Hellenistic period, to victorious generals (e.g. Lysander and Titus Flamininus). Composed for both choral and monodic performance, ps. were accompanied by lyres or woodwinds or both. The ancient debate whether Aristotle's poem to Hermias was a p. or a *skolion* (q.v.) shows that the distinctions between p. and other lyric genres were not precise (Harvey).

Although many early Gr. lyric poets wrote ps., the only substantial remains are papyrus fragments of 22 ps. by Pindar, of which *Paeans* 2, 4, and 6, written for Abderitans, Ceans, and Delphians, respectively, are the best preserved (tr. Sandys). A number of Hellenistic ps. surviving as inscriptions are collected in Powell. Although some poems of Horace (e.g. *Odes* 4.5) resemble ps., the genre was moribund by his time, and in modern usage p. refers loosely to any song of joy or triumph. See also GREEK POETRY, *Classical.*—A. Fairbanks, *A Study of the Gr. P.* (1900); H. W. Smyth, *Gr. Melic Poets* (1900); J. U. Powell, *Collectanea Alexandrina* (1925); H. Färber, *Die Lyrik in der Kunsttheorie der Antike* (1936); J. E. Sandys, *The Odes of Pindar* (1937); Pauly-Wissowa; A. E. Harvey, "The Classif. of Gr. Lyric Poetry," *ClassQ* 5 (1955); Michaelides. W.H.R.

PAEON. In Cl. prosody, a metrical unit which is formed of one of the four permutations of 1 long and 3 short syllables: these are called first p. (– ◡ ◡ ◡), second p. (◡ – ◡ ◡), third p. (◡ ◡ – ◡), and fourth p. (◡ ◡ ◡ –). The first and the fourth ps. are, in effect, cretics (– ◡ –) by resolution of their last and first syllables respectively. The second and the third, however, are to be found only in ancient metrical theory, and the fourth is quite rare. But the first p., esp., is found in Gr. poetry and drama (more frequently in comedy than in tragedy). Cretics and ps. may occur in combination (cf. Aristophanes, *Acharnians* 210 ff.). Forms of ps. are also common as clausular cadences in Gr. rhythmical prose. But only the most resolutely Classicizing of metrists would find these Gr. rarities in Eng. meter, which is founded on a different basis.—J. W. White, *The Verse of Gr. Comedy* (1912); Wilamowitz, pt. 2, ch. 8; B. Ghiselin, "Paeonic Measures in Eng. Verse," *MLN* 57 (1942); Dale, ch. 6; West; Norden. D.S.P.

PAINTING AND POETRY. See VISUAL ARTS AND POETRY.

PALIMBACCHIUS. See BACCHIUS.

PALINDROME (Gr. "running back again"). A word ("Eve"), sentence, or verse (whence *versus cancrinus*, "crab verse") which reads alike backward or forward. There are several varieties: (1) in the canonical form, the sentence or verse reads alike in either direction letter by letter; but (2) another variety reverses only word by word. Puttenham's example (*Arte of Eng. Poesie*, Bk. 1, ch. 7), which he calls *Verse Lyon* (from the Fr.), merely reverses the order of the words.

The reputed inventor of the p. was Sotades, a minor Alexandrian poet of the early 3d c. B.C. who wrote virulent invective (q.v.) and obscene verses (see SOTADEAN); there are no extant examples from the Cl. Gr. period. The best known p. in post-Cl. Gr. is *nipson anomemata me monan opsin* ("wash my transgressions, not only my face"), attributed to Gregory of Nazianzus (329–89) and often inscribed on fonts in monasteries or churches. Other familiar ones in Lat. are: "Roma tibi subito motibus ibit amor" and the so-called devil's verse, "Signa te, signa, temere me tangis et angis." William Camden illustrates type (2): "Odo tenet mulum, madidam mappam tenet Anna." Ps. were esp. popular in Byzantine times, and we possess a number of them written by the emperor Leo the Wise (10th c.). Ger. ps. were written by J. H. Riese in the 17th c.; and in 1802 Ambrose Pamperis published in Vienna a pamphlet containing 416 ps. recounting the campaigns of Catherine the Great. Among the best known examples of ps. are: "Madam, I'm Adam" and "Able was I ere I saw Elba," the latter attributed to Napoleon.

The metrical analogue of the p. is *reciprocus versus*, a line which scans identically forward and backward, either letter-by-letter or word-by-word. Sidonius Apollinaris (5th c. A.D.) mentions *versus recurrentes* (*Epistulae* 9.14) which, when read backward, retain the same order of letters and meter (*Roma tibi . . .* above): this is a p. both in sense and meter. And Virgil's "Mūsă, mǐ|hī cāu|sās mĕmŏ|rā quō | nūmǐně | lāesō" (*Aeneid* 1.8) is still a dactylic hexameter when the order of the words is reversed: "lāesō | nūmĭnĕ | quō mĕmŏ|rā caū|sās mĭhĭ̄, | Mūsa." See Keil 1.516.24–517.14, 6.113.11–114.10.

K. Krumbacher, *Gesch. der byzantinische Lit.*, 2d ed. (1897); K. Preisendanz, "Palindrom" in Pauly-Wissowa; A. Liede, *Dichtung als Spiel*, 2 v. (1963); H. Bergerson, *Ps. and Anagrams* (1973); West 65; P. Dubois, "(Petite) histoire des ps.," *Littératures* 7 (1983); T. Augarde, *Oxford Guide to Word Games* (1984); G. Freidhof, "Schuttelreim, Anagramm, Palindrom," *Aspekte der Slavistik* (1984); W. Irvine, *Madam I'm Adam* (1987).   T.V.F.B.; R.J.G.

PALINODE. Originally a term applied to a lyric by Stesichorus (early 6th c. B.C.), in which he recanted his earlier attack upon Helen as the baneful cause of the Trojan War—hence any poem or song of retraction. The p. as a theme, or a conceit, in lit. has been common in love poetry since Ovid's *Remedia amoris*, supposedly written to retract his *Ars amatoria*. It appears in medieval lit. in *The Romance of the Rose* and in courtly love poetry. Chaucer uses it as a device throughout his poems and as the reason for his *Legend of Good Women*, written to retract the effect of *Troilus and Criseyde*. The notion of recantation also underlies the palinodic form, wherein two metrically corresponding members (e.g. strophe and antistrophe) are interrupted by another pair of similarly corresponding members. Thus the strophes are arranged in the pattern *a b b' a'*, with *a b* the "ode" and *b' a'* the "p."; *a* and *a'* are strophe and antistrophe and *b* and *b'* are the second strophe and antistrophe. The term is now used of any such arrangement in any poetry and may also be applied to single lines in such a pattern. See RECUSATIO.—U. von Wilamowitz-Moellendorff, *Sappho und Simonides* (1913).   R.A.H.

PANEGYRIC (Gr. *panegyrikos*) originally denoted an oration delivered at one of the Gr. festivals; later it came to designate a speech or poem in praise of some person, object, or event. Much oral poetry (q.v.) is p. in nature, consisting of the praises of heroes, armies, victories, and states; and in most cultures particular subgenres developed for specific occasions, such as the Gr. *epinikion* (q.v.), a victory ode, or the *epithalamium* (q.v.), a marriage song. P. is closely related to, and may have developed from, the eulogy, a speech or poem in praise of the dead. In Greece, p. was originally a rhetorical type belonging to the epideictic category of oratory. Its rules are given in the rhetorical works of Menander and Hermogenes, and famous examples include the *Panegyricus* of Isocrates, the p. of Pliny the Younger on Trajan, and the 11 other *XII Panegyrici latini* (4th c.). Pindar's odes have sometimes been described as ps. After the 3d c. B.C., when much of rhetorical theory was appropriated for poetics, p. was accepted as a formal poetic type and its rules were given in handbooks of poetry. Significant Western examples of ps. incl. Apollinaris Sidonius' poems on the Emperors Avitus, Majorian, and Anthemius; Claudian's on the consulships of Honorius, Stilicho, Probinus, and Olybrius; the p. on the death of Celsus by Paulinus of Nola; Aldhelm's *De laudibus virgitate*; and innumerable Christian Lat. poems in praise of Mary, the cross, the martyrs, etc. It remained popular through the Middle Ages both as an independent poetic form and as an important *topos* (q.v.) in longer narrative poems, esp. epic (q.v.); and like other such forms persisted into the Ren., with perhaps more emphasis on the praise of secular figures and institutions. Scaliger (*Poetices libri septem* [1561]) distinguishes between p., which tends to deal with present men and deeds, and encomium (q.v.), which deals with those of the past, but in general the two are indistinguishable. The p. underwent a brief revival in 17th-c. encomiastic occasional verse, e.g. Edmund Waller's 1655 "Panegyrick to My Lord Protector." For further discussion of the Western trad., see now EPIDEICTIC POETRY; for Arabic, see QASIDA; for African, see bibl. below.

Pauly-Wissowa 5.2581–83, 18.2340–62; T. Burgess, *Epideictic Lit.* (1902); Curtius; R. Haller, "Lobgedichte," *Reallexikon*; *XII Panegyrici latini*, ed. R. A. B. Mynors (1964); T. Viljamaa, *Studies in Gr. Encomiastic Poetry of the Early Byzantine Period* (1968); J. Stuart, *Izibongo: Zulu Praise-Poems*, ed. T. Cope (1968); A. Georgi, *Das lateinische und deutsche Presigedicht des Mittelalters* (1969); B. K. Lewalski, *Donne's Anniversaries and the Poetry of Praise* (1973); J. D. Garrison, *Dryden and the Trad. of P.* (1975); A. C. Hodza, *Shona Praise Poetry*, ed. G. Fortune (1979); *Leaf and Bone: African Praise-Poems*, ed. J. Gleason (1980); R. S. Peterson, *Imitation and Praise in the Poems of Ben Jonson* (1981); S. MacCormack, *Art and Ceremony in Late Antiquity* (1981); A. Hardie, *Statius and the Silvae* (1983); G. W. Most, *The Measures of Praise* (1985); W. Portmann, *Gesch. in der spätantiken Panegyrik* (1988); A. B. Chambers, *Andrew Marvell and Edmund Waller* (1991); L. Kurke, *The Traffic in Praise* (1991).   O.B.H.; T.V.F.B.

PANJABI POETRY. See INDIAN POETRY.

PANTUN (Eng. and Fr. spelling *pantoum*). A Malay verseform (see MALAY POETRY), usually in 4 but sometimes in 6 to 12 lines. The basis of the form is internal opposition, usually in two end-stopped couplets rhyming *abab*. The first couplet, the *sampiran*, tends to be highly charged and evocative, while the second couplet soars, sometimes obscurely, on the basis of the first: a M. proverb declares "a p. is like a hawk with a chicken, it takes its time about striking." Western writers have necessarily altered and adapted the p. Introduced to the West by the Fr. orientalist Ernest Fouinet and established by the practice of Victor Hugo in his notes to *Les Orientales*, the form enjoyed a vogue in France and England in the later 19th-c. revival of Fr. fixed forms. In Fr. the form was effectively used by Théodore de Banville, Louisa Siefert, Leconte de Lisle (5 ps.), and, with considerable variations, by Baudelaire, in Eng. by Austin Dobson among others. As altered and adapted into these langs., the p. became a poem of indeterminate length composed of quatrains in which the second and fourth lines of each stanza serve as the first and third lines of the next, through the last stanza, where the first line of the poem reappears as the last and, in some Eng. pantoums, the third line of the poem as the second. Thus the pantoum begins and ends with the same line and, throughout, the cross rhymes scissor the couplets, different themes being developed concurrently, one in the first couplet and the other in the second of each quatrain. Brewster finds analogues to the p. in several European poetries.—Kastner; P. G. Brewster, "Metrical, Stanzaic, and Stylistic Resemblances between Malayan and Western Poetry," *RLC* 32 (1958); R. Étiemble, "Du 'Pantun' malais au 'pantoum' à la française," *ZRL* 22 (1979).   T.V.F.B.; A.PR.; B.R.

PARABASIS (Gr. "a coming forward"). In Gr. Old Comedy, a choral performance, composed mainly in anapestic tetrameters. During an intermission in the action, the chorus, alone in the *orchestra* and out of character, came forward without their masks to face the audience and delivered, in song or recitative, views on topics such as politics or religion about which the dramatist felt strongly. The parts of a complete p. were said to be *kommation* (introductory song), *parabasis* (properly called), *makron* or *pnigos* (to be recited in one breath), strophe or ode (*melos*), and *epirrhema* ("that said afterwards"). This last, a speech (usually in trochaic tetrameters) whose content was satiric, advisory, or exhortative, was delivered by the leader of one half of the chorus after an ode had been sung by that half; the other half then sang a responding *antode* (set in lyric meters corresponding metrically to the ode) and *antepirrhema*. Such an arrangement of lyrics by the chorus and speech or dialogue by a character is found in the plays of Aeschylus and Sophocles as well as of Aristophanes.—J. W. White, *The Verse of Gr. Comedy* (1912); G. Norwood, *Gr. Comedy* (1931); H. Herter, *Vom dionysischen Tanz zum komischen Spiel* (1947); Aeschylus, *Agamemnon*, ed. E. Fraenkel, v. 3 (1953); E. Burkardt, *Die Entstehung der Parabase des Aristophanes* (1956); A. M. Dale, *Collected Papers* (1969); G. M. Sifakis, *P. and Animal Choruses* (1971); A. M. Bowie, "The P. in Aristophanes," *ClassQ* 32 (1982); T. K. Hubbard, *The Mask of Comedy* (1991).   R.A.H.

PARADOX. A daring statement which unites seemingly contradictory words but which on closer examination proves to have unexpected meaning and truth ("The longest way round is the shortest way home"; "Life is death and death is life"). The structure of p. is similar to the oxymoron (q.v.), which unites two contradictory concepts into a third ("heavy lightness"), a favorite strategy of Petrarchism (q.v.). Ps. are esp. suited to an expression of the unspeakable in religion, mysticism, and poetry. First discussed in its formal elements in Stoic philosophy and cl. rhet., the p. became more widely used after Sebastian Frank (*280 Paradoxa from the Holy Scriptures*, 1534) and has always retained an appeal for the Christian mode of expression, as in Luther and Pascal. In the *Concluding Unscientific Postscript* (1846), Kierkegaard considered God's becoming man the greatest p. for human existence.

The most famous literary example of sustained p. is the *Praise of Folly* by Erasmus (1511). In the baroque (q.v.) period, p. became a central figure; it is particularly important in metaphysical poetry (q.v.), esp. the poetry and prose of Donne, who makes frequent use of p. and paradoxical lang. in the *Paradoxes and Problems* and *Songs and Sonets* (1633, 1635). The p. is manifest in the lit. of the 17th and 18th cs. in its antithetical verbal structure (see ANTITHESIS) rather than as argument. Diderot in his late dialogue *Le Paradoxe sur le comédien* (1778)—on the art of acting but with far-reaching implications for poetry—holds that an actor should not feel the passion he expresses but should transcend direct imitation and rise to the conception of an intellectual model. Everything in him should become a controlled work of art, and the emotional state should be left to the spectator. In the romantic period, Schlegel (*Fragments*, 1797) called the p. a basic form of human experience and linked it closely with poetry and irony (q.v.). De Quincey in his *Autobiographical Sketches* (1834–53) argued that the p. is a vital element in poetry reflecting the paradoxical nature of the world which poetry imitates. Nietzsche made p. a key term of human experience and of his own literary expression. In the lit. of the 20th c., p. often fuses with the absurd, which can be interpreted as an intensified expression of the p.

The term p. is widely employed in 20th-c. crit., esp. in the work of the New Criticism (q.v.). Cleanth Brooks discusses it in *The Well Wrought Urn* (1947, esp. ch. 1) as a form of indirection which is distinctively characteristic of poetic lang. and structure. As his example, Wordsworth ("Composed Upon Westminster Bridge"), illustrates, Brooks does not use p. in the strict antithetical sense but gives it an unusually broad range by showing that good poems are written from insights that enlarge or startlingly modify our commonplace conceptions and understandings, esp. those residing in overly simplistic distinctions; this "disruptive" function of poetic lang. is precisely what Brooks calls paradoxical. Since the degree of paradoxical disruption is an index of poetic meaning, p. and poetry assume a very close affinity with one another. Subsequently, this New Critical emphasis on p. was taken up in deconstruction (q.v.). Paul de Man argued that the insistence by the New Critics on the unity, harmony, and identity of a poetic work was irreconcilable with their insistence on irony, p., and ambiguity—or rather, that the insistence on unity was the "blindness" of the New Criticism, whereas the insistence on irony and p. was its "insight." Theory thus establishes a close relationship between p. and irony.—Brooks; A. E. Malloch, "Techniques and Function of the Ren. P.," *SP* 53 (1956); W. V. Quine, *The Ways of P. and Other Essays* (1966); R. L. Colie, *Paradoxia Epidemica: The Ren. Trad. of P.* (1966), "Literary P.," *DHI*; De Man; *Le Paradoxe au temps de la Ren.*, ed. M. T. Jones-Davies (1982); J. J. Y. Liu, *Lang.—P.— Poetics: A Chinese Perspective*, ed. R. J. Lynn (1988). E.H.B.

PARALIPSIS (Gr. "a passing over"; Lat. *praeteritio, occultatio*). The figure by which a speaker emphasizes an idea by pretending to say nothing of it even while giving it full expression, e.g. "I'm not going to tell you what I know but. . . ." The difference is explained by Gregory of Corinth (12th c.) in his commentary on Hermogenes' *Peri deinotetos*, ch. 7.—*Rhetores Graeci*, ed. C. Walz, 9 v. (1832–36). T.V.F.B.; A.W.H.

PARALLELISM (Gr. "side by side"). The repetition of identical or similar syntactic patterns in adjacent phrases, clauses, or sentences; the matching patterns are usually doubled, but more extensive iteration is not rare. The core of a p. is syntactic; when syntactic frames are set in equivalence by p., the elements filling those frames are brought into alignment as well, esp. on the lexical level (thus the term "semantic p."). Meter and rhyme have both been recognized as species of p. on the phonological level. In a formulation of Jakobson, parallel syntax "activates" p. on other linguistic levels. The extreme case of similarity (Jakobsonian *equivalence*, q.v.) is repetition (q.v.); alternatively, p. can be considered the most significant subtype of repetition.

There is nothing which restricts p. (or the cognate trope in Cl. rhet., *isocolon*, q.v.) as a grammatical phenomenon to verse, and it is common in certain forms of elevated prose, notably oratory, prayer, and, in Chinese, letter-writing. Further, it is a complex question whether p. is properly a trope (or master trope) or, again, strictly a matter of only grammar or also rhet. and logic. In Jakobson's later work p. came to hold a place of ever-increasing importance. The variety of grammatical domains over which p. can work is tremendous. A series of examples from Eng. Ren. verse will illustrate some common features of parallelistic usage. The domain may be a phrase: "Light of my life, and life of my desire"; "Oft with true sighes, oft with uncalled teares, / Now with slow words, now with dumbe eloquence" (Sidney, *Astrophil and Stella* 68, 61).

In the first example, two possessive noun phrases are parallel (as are the components, *light/ life, life/ desire*), while in the second, four temporal phrases are matched. Within the second example, the first two phrases involve repetition (*oft=oft*), as do the second two, though the sequence *now . . . now* has a distinct sense, "alternately." Thus the line has an internal reading, and another reading suggested by the p. In each case the short item comes first: *life* (1 syllable), *desire* (2 syllables); *true sighes* (2 syllables), *uncalled teares* (4 syllables); *slow words* (2 syllables), *dumbe eloquence* (4 syllables).

The unit of p. may be simple clauses: "I may, I must, I can, I will, I do . . . " (*AS* 47). Here the parallels are perfect, *subject + verb*; but greater variety is equally effective: "My mouth doth water, and my breast doth swell, / My tongue doth itch, my thoughts in labour be" (*AS* 37). In more complex structures, the individual entities are themselves likely to be more complex:

> Let Fortune lay on me her worst disgrace,
> Let folke orecharg'd with braine
> against me crie,
> Let clouds bedimme my face, breake
> in mine eye,
> Let me no steps but of lost labour trace,
> Let all the earth with scorne recount
> my case.
> (*AS* 64)

The line here is the unit of p.; at the same time, these are lines 3–7 of a sonnet, and as a block they cut across the two opening quatrains.

Complex sentences may show p., e.g. embedded noun clauses and *if/then* structures:

> I saw that teares did in her eyes appeare;
> I saw that sighes her sweetest lips did part.
> (*AS* 87)

> If he do love, I burne, I burne in love:
> If he waite well, I never thence would move:
> If he be faire, yet but a dog can be.
> (*AS* 59)

In tight p., where the grammatical texture of the parallel entities is identical, it is common to find a reversal of position, as *object + adverb* here: "I curst thee oft, I pitie now thy case" (*AS* 46). This is one variety of the scheme of chiasmus (q.v.).

These examples are drawn from literate poetry, and the great variety displayed in them is in part due to that circumstance. In most poetries exhibiting p., however, the ways in which the scheme is disposed are relatively few. These poetries tend to be either oral or early-literate; the later typological category is important: the poetry of the Heb. Bible began to be written down two and a half millennia ago, while Finnish folk poetry has only been recorded for a century and a half, but cl. Heb. and Finnish poetry are comparably close to the oral poetic situation and comparably far from the literate setting.

P. is well represented in traditional poetry in Chinese (and its literary offspring, Vietnamese), in Toda (but not in the other Dravidian tongues), in the Semitic langs. (in addition to ancient Semitic texts in Heb., Ugaritic, and Akkadian, there are several types of "parallel prose" in Arabic), in the Uralic langs. (incl. Finnish), in the Austronesian langs. (Rotinese is the best known), and in the Mayan langs., both medieval and modern. Rus. folk poetry is parallelistic, as is some Altaic (Mongol and Turkic) verse.

Biblical Heb. is the best know system of p., first described by Bishop Robert Lowth in 1753. In Heb. verse (and related ancient Near Eastern poetries) p. plays a role in structuring the line (see HEBREW POETRY; HEBREW PROSODY AND POETICS). Most scholars believe that the verse of the Bible is distinct from its prose, although parallelistic coloring is found in the prose as well (e.g. the fable in Judges 9). J. L. Kugel has argued that there is in fact no real dividing line between prose and verse, but his remains a minority view. He takes the two halves of a parallel unit as having an augmentative relationship: the first element is assertive and the second has the force "not only that, but also this." Another minority view holds that there is a strictly recoverable metrical component to the poetry of the Heb. Bible (e.g. Eduard Sievers), but it is more generally assumed that there is an unrecoverable or opaque metrical element in the verse.

More recently, scholars have recognized syntactic regularities as structural features of the verse (O'Connor): "He-led the-east-wind out-of-heaven. / He-guided out-of-his-power the-south-wind" (Psalms 78:26). Lowth's traditional scheme distinguishing three types of biblical parallel verse— "synonymous", "antithetical", and "synthetic"—is of only limited usefulness. The example above would be synonymous, based on the notion that the elements *led* and *guided*, *east-wind* and *south-wind*, and *heaven* and *power* can be regarded as synonyms. But the idea of synonymy has been exaggerated in Heb. philology; many 20th-c. trs. of the Bible are seriously marred by a reliance on the false principle of "synonymy." As the term "synonymous p." is used, it means that the lines in question refer to (more or less) identical things. This conception can be made to cover a wide range of biblical verse, but there is much left over. Of the rather large latter category, some sets of parallel lines can be taken as "antithetical," either because they mean the opposite or because they use opposed or antithetical pairs:

> In many people is the glory of a king,
> but without people a prince is ruined.

> Slowness to anger is great under-
>   standing,
> but a hasty temper is an exaltation of
>   folly.
>   (Proverbs 14:28–29)

In the first pair of lines the sense of the first line is the opposite of the second, and the range of reference is the same; in the second pair of lines, the opposed pairs *anger/understanding* and *temper/folly*, are lined up, but the reference is to two quite different types of people. This diversity, combined with the fact that antithetical p. occurs largely in so-called wisdom lit. (notably the Book of Proverbs), makes it suspect as an independent category. Even more suspect is "synthetic p.," which was the category meant to catch all remaining examples of p.; and some more narrowly defined subtypes have also been proposed to supplement the typology of biblical p. In fact, the traditional scheme originated by Lowth has outlived its value. Rather, p. needs to be approached as a syntactic phenomenon more or less independent of the semantic features that overpower Lowth's approach.

One particular difficulty posed by Heb. verse is the actual domain of p.: many accounts suggest that the poetry is made up exclusively of parallelistic couplets, but in fact this is true only of wisdom lit.; in other poetic books, esp. those of the prophets, single lines, triplets, and quatrains are common. Thus the practice of some scholars to refer to a single line as a halfline leads to great confusion when it is applied to the bulk of Heb. verse. The line (or colon or stich) can be defined on bases largely distinct from p.

In general, the relationship between the metrical unit and the parallel entity can take on numerous forms. In traditional poetries all (or nearly all) verse discourse may be parallelistic. The basic domain of p. may then be the line (Rotinese, Mayan) or the half-line (Finnish and some other Uralic poetries), or a variable range (Toda). In Chinese verse, largely isosyllabic, with tonal patterning, the rules governing p. vary widely according to genre; *fu* ("parallel prose"; see RHYME-PROSE) is more loosely parallelistic than the central couplets of *lü shi* ("regulated verse"), the most constrained variety of p. known.

In European poetry since the Ren., biblical influence has reinforced the use of p. to the point that few major verse texts are without some p. William Blake and Christopher Smart both use quasi-biblical p. extensively. A decisive break comes with Walt Whitman's choice of biblical structures to supplant the metrical basis of Eng. prosody itself:

> The prairie-grass accepting its own spe-
>   cial odor breathing,
> I demand of it the spiritual correspond-
>   ing,

Demand the most copious and close
   companionship of men,
Demand the blades to rise of words,
   acts, beings,
Those of the open atmosphere, coarse,
   sunlit, fresh, nutritious,
Those that go their own gait, erect,
   stepping with freedom and com-
   mand, leading, not following,
Those with a never quelled audacity,
   those with sweet and lusty flesh
   clear of taint, choice and chary of
   its love-power,
Those that look carelessly in the faces
   of Presidents and governors, as to
   say, *Who are you?*
Those of earth-born passion, simple,
   never constrained, never obedient,
Those of inland America.
         ("Calamus," *Leaves of Grass*)

Nearly as important is Paul Claudel's use of the *verset* (explicitly acknowledged as biblical in origin; q.v.) as an avenue between the Fr. alexandrine and the prose-poem mode established by Whitman's contemporary, Baudelaire. Because romantic, modernist, and esp. postmodern lit. reflects awareness of a world-wide range of poetry, it was unavoidable that various traditional types of p. would be imitated in European lit.: the many modes of Chinese imitation, from Pound and Amy Lowell on, are well known; Longfellow's *Hiawatha* (1855) and John Ashbery's "Finnish Rhapsody" (*April Galleons*, 1987) are each narratives in the style of then-current Eng. trs. of the *Kalevala*.

Whatever the particular ways that p. is disposed in verse discourse, schemes of equivalence, often associated with metaphor, juxtaposition, and near repetition, take on distinctive force in a parallelistic context. Gestures of signification and logic are represented and carried out in ways that often elude linearly based discourse. An important key to understanding p. lies in acknowledging that parallel structures can operate in both prose and verse and over spans from phrase to entire poem.

R. Lowth, *De sacra poesi Hebraeorum praelectiones academicae Oxonii habitae* (1753), tr. *Lectures on the Sacred Poetry of the Hebrews* (1787); E. Sievers, *Metrische Studien I–II* (1901–07); Jakobson, esp. v. 3; R. D. Fraser, "Verbal P. in Ballad and Med. Lyric," *DAI* 33 (1973), 6869A; J. J. Fox, "Roman Jakobson and the Comparative Study of P.," *Roman Jakobson: Echoes of His Scholarship*, ed. D. Armstrong and C. H. Van Schooneveld (1977); M. O'Connor, *Heb. Verse Structure* (1980); J. L. Kugel, *The Idea of Biblical Poetry* (1981); A. Berlin, *The Dynamics of Biblical P.* (1985); Terras; D. Pardee, *Ugaritic and Heb. Poetic P.* (1988); M. R. Lichtmann, *The Contemplative Poetry of G. M. Hopkins* (1989).   M.O'C.

PARAPHRASE, HERESY OF. Cleanth Brooks de-fines the h. of p. in the concluding chapter of *The Well Wrought Urn* (1947). Following I. A. Richards' formulation, he insists on the essential difference between scientific statements (which are paraphrasable) and poetic statements (not paraphrasable): in the former, the "same" content can be expressed in other words; in the latter, form and content are inseparable, so that any change of wording is a change of meaning, and the poem cannot be reduced to a prose *précis*.

There is no denying that the critic must sometimes resort to discursive summary statements about the meaning of a poem. However, such plain statements are always put into question by the formal structure of the poem itself. As Brooks puts it, "whatever statement we may seize upon as incorporating the 'meaning' of the poem, immediately the imagery and rhythm [qq.v.] seem to set up tensions with it, warping and twisting it, qualifying and revising it."

This "warping and twisting" process is the indispensable structural principle from which the very meaning of the poem is derived. For Brooks the poem is not a clear-cut and ready-made scientific proposition: it is "a structure of gestures and attitudes" that constitutes an autonomous poetic universe (see AUTONOMY).

In this sense the poem resembles dramatic structure: "the poem does not merely eventuate in a logical conclusion. . . . It is 'proved' as a dramatic conclusion is proved: by its ability to resolve the conflicts which have been accepted as the *données* of the drama." Thus a poem has a "meaning" because a dramatization of experience is enacted structurally within the poem: its tensions are set in motion; its elements are played one against the other; its conflicts are embodied in metrical pattern and metaphors.

This dynamic process—modifications, qualifications, revisions—comprises the inner fabric and meaning of poetry. It is not through logical proof, abstract symbols, and discursive statements, but through irony, ambiguity, and paradox (qq.v.), Brooks holds, that the poem speaks.

Certainly the elaboration of new modes of reading poetic texts after New Criticism (q.v.) seem to suggest that the concept of the h. of p. no longer has the theoretical urgency it once had. Yet it is no less clear that Brooks' formulation, with its implications about the nature of poetic meaning, remains a fundamental contribution to the formalist analysis of poetry. See also MEANING; STRUCTURE; TEXTURE; SCIENCE AND POETRY; THEME.—Brooks; M. Krieger, *The New Apologists for Poetry* (1956).   P.M.

PARARHYME. See NEAR RHYME.

PARATAXIS AND HYPOTAXIS. P. is a stylistic term referring to a relative paucity of linking terms between juxtaposed clauses or sentences, often giving the effect of piling up, swiftness, and sometimes compression. A paratactic style is one in which a lang.'s ordinary resources for joining propositions are deliberately underused; propositions are set one after another (Gr. *para* + *tassein*) without the expected particles, adverbs, or conjunctions. The effectiveness of p. varies relative to a lang.'s structure, since langs. differ widely in their means of joining clauses. Within a single lang., genres also vary in degree of p.: in cl. Chinese, verse is more paratactic than prose, and traditional verse (*shi*) is more paratactic than other verse genres such as *fu* and *ci*. It seems likely that verse in general is more paratactic than prose simply because verse has other structural determiners to rely on. Rynell argues that oral poetry esp. favors p. Short-lined verse tends to be more paratactic than verse in long lines, a difference that may account in part for the slightly rushed feeling of Eng. tetrameters over pentameters, and for the languor of hexameters.

P. can be humorous: "Pride, Malice, Folly against Dryden rose, / In various shapes of Parsons, Critics, Beaus" (Pope, *Essay on Criticism*); the faults and enemies can be taken in single pairs, *Pride* and *Parsons*, etc., or in the two groups; an effect the use of *and* might blur. Syllogistic or pseudo-syllogistic compression also issues in p.: "A hatefull cure with hate to heale: / A blooddy helpe with blood to save: / A foolish thing with fooles to deale: / Let him be bob'd that bobs wil have" (Sidney, "From the Old Arcadia 25"). The effect can also be one of courtly formality: "In silver robes the moone, the sunne in gold, / Like young eyes peaking lovers in a dance, / With majestie by turns retire, advance" (Wm. Drummond, "Teares on the Death of Moeliades").

P. is a major stylistic resource in the poetry of the Old Germanic langs., in which it works alongside both wordcompounding (effectively, p. on the lexical level) and the larger dynamics of syntactic parallelism (q.v.) and scene juxtapositions. Its units are frequently nominal (and adjectival) appositions of the type technically called "variations." *Beowulf* takes such p. to an extreme; the conjunction *ond* occurs only about once in every 10 lines, but even then joins single words rather than clauses. Robinson argues that the p. is the basis for the poet's "controlled equivocations," balancing the admiration and regret that Saxon Christians felt for their pagan ancestors.

Most European trs. of biblical Heb. prose are paratactic in reproducing Heb.'s extensive use of the simple conjunction *wĕ*, "and." The Heb. is not itself paratactic; rather, the stylistic imitation of it in langs. with more complex systems of linkage leads to p. Such a style is often judged "vigorous" or "pure" on the basis of the p., but such judgments actually arise from other bases. The Vulgate tr. of Jerome is notable for preserving the Heb. shape, with two important consequences for later Lat. (Auerbach). The paratactic style provides Augustine with a resource that enables him to

stand apart from the baroque usage of most late antique Lat. writers. Too, the biblical text furnishes a texture against which an argument or ethical appeal can be set: the paratactic exemplar shines in a plainer context. Thus p. plays a complex role in the devel. of the mixed Christian Lat. style of the Middle Ages. Adorno attributes the p. in Hölderlin's verse in part to the influence of Pindar.

There is no proper antonym of p. (see Rynell). The term h. refers to subordination; as a stylistic term, *hypotactic* describes a style in which extensive subordination takes place, thereby allotting a major role to logical or temporal sequencing; both uses are evident in, for example, the prose of Thucydides. See also IDEOGRAM; SYNTAX, POETIC.—A. Rynell, *P. and H. as a Criterion of Syntax and Style, Esp. in OE Poetry* (1952); E. Auerbach, *Mimesis* (1953); T. W. Adorno, "P.: Zur späten Lyrik Hölderlins," *Noten zur Literatur III* (1965); J. Notopoulos, "P. in Homer," *TAPA* 80 (1969); F. Robinson, Beowulf *and the Appositive Style* (1985); J. P. Houston, *Shakespearean Sentences* (1988).
M.O'C.

PARISON. See ISOCOLON.

PARNASSIANS. The "Parnassiens" were the group, or groups, of Fr. poets who were born about 1840 or 1850 and gravitated around Leconte de Lisle. They treated a number of nonpersonal themes taken from history, science, philosophy, nature, or contemp. life; but some were mainly lyricists. They respected and often followed their elders, used traditional verseforms, and regarded the cult of poetry as a religion. *Le prémier Parnasse contemporain* (1866) was followed by other *recueils* in 1871 and 1876, but the works of individual P. covered the period from 1865 to the end of the century, representing an important trend in Fr. poetry between the Romantics and the Symbolists.

The movement was initiated by Catulle Mendès and L.-X. de Ricard in the early 1860s, when the P. first met in Lemerre's bookshop and in the salon of the Marquise de Ricard; later they gathered in the salon of Mme. Leconte de Lisle, whose formidable husband was regarded as a manner of oracle. Of the 50 or more poets called P. only a few can be mentioned here. Among the more independent, Albert Glatigny (1839–73) was a wit and virtuoso who took his cue from Banville. Sully-Prudhomme (1839–1907) explored the secrets of the inner life in verses as poignant as Heine's but without Heine's bitterness. He wrote philosophic poems using a delicate imagery drawn from the natural sciences. François Coppée (1842–1908) described the life and problems of humble folk and, like Sully-Prudhomme, was sensitive to the writer's moral responsibilities. The followers of Leconte de Lisle respected traditional morals, but worshiped "Art." Gautier as well as Banville remained a potent influence. Léon Dierx (1838–

1912) wrote tragic poems on historical themes and struck a note of despair. Jean Lahor (1840–1909) exhaled his melancholy in Buddhistic verses. J.-M. de Heredia (1842–1905) drew inspiration from the Gr. myths, from the epigrams of the *Greek Anthology* and from the Lat. poets. He was something of a scholar and paleographer, but above all a finished artist. Most of his *Trophées* (1895) are sonnets, and he is one of the outstanding sonneteers of late 19th-c. France. Anatole France (1844–1924) was more independent: although a versatile neo-Hellenist, he was also, in his *Poèmes dorés*, an able nature poet. Jules Lemaître (1853–1914), the critic and literary historian, was a *conteur* and poet who achieved formal eloquence.

Though some of them underwent the influence of Ménard, the P. were not primarily Hellenists, nor were they as a whole impassive or impersonal. If they had anything in common, it was a love of precision, a devotion to formal beauty, the cult of rhyme, and, beyond that, "un romantisme assagi et mitigé" (Henri Peyre), which left a mark on such great poets as Mallarmé and Verlaine and, to a lesser extent, on a few figures of the following generation like Paul Valéry in his *Album de vers anciens*. In England the work of Banville and others inspired a vogue for Fr. fixed forms such as the villanelle, sestina, and triolet (qq.v.).

C. Mendès, *La Légende du Parnasse contemporain (1884); R. Canat, La Ren. de la Grèce antique (1911); M. Ibrovac, J. M. de Heredia: Sa vie, son oeuvre (1923); T. Martel, Le Parnasse (1923); F. Desonay, Le Rêve hellénique chez les poètes parnassiens (1928); E. Estève, Le Parnasse (1929); A. Therive, Le Parnasse (1929); A. Schaffer, Parnassus in France (1930), The Genres of P. Poetry (1944); M. Souriau, Hist. du Parnasse (1930); H.-M. Peyre, Louis Ménard (1822–1901) (1932), Bibl. critique de l'hellénisme en France de 1843 à 1870 (1932), Qu'est-ce le Symbolisme (1974); F. Vincent, Les Parnassiens (1933); M. G. Rudler, Parnassiens, symbolistes et décadents (1938); Z. Rosenberg, La persistance du subjectivisme chez les poètes parnassiens (1939); A. L. Sells, "Heredia's Hellenism," MLR 37 (1942); V. Errante, Parnassiani e simbolisti francesi (1953); M. Decaudin, La Crise des valeurs symbolistes (1960); P. Martino, Parnasse et Symbolisme (1964); A. Racot, Les Parnassiens (1968); R. T. Denommè and H. T. Moore, The Fr. P. Poets (1972); L. Decaune, La Poésie parnassienne (1977); The Symbolist Movement in the Lit. of European Langs., ed. A. Balakian (1982); Hollier.* A.L.S.

PARODY.

    I. DEFINITION
   II. CRITICAL ISSUES
  III. HISTORY

I. DEFINITION. P. imitates the distinctive style and thought of a literary text, author, or trad. for comic effect. Some critics distinguish between critical (satiric) and comic p., while others prefer

to speak of p. as the dominant comic form and pastiche as the subordinate, more solemn form. In other words, when the imitation of another work is an end in itself, the result is pastiche; when the imitation serves to mock another work, the result is p. An example of pastiche is the player's speech about Pyrrhus in *Hamlet*, a speech that imitates the style and subject of Marlowe's *Dido, Queen of Carthage* (2.1) but is not intended to make the audience smile. A Shakespearean p. is Falstaff's imitation of John Lyly's euphuistic style in the tavern scene in *1 Henry 4*:

> Harry, I do not only marvel where thou spendest thy time, but also how thou art accompanied: for though the camomile, the more it is trodden on the faster it grows, yet youth, the more it is wasted the sooner it wears.

This speech clearly imitates Lyly's passage:

> Though the camomile the more it is trodden and pressed down, the more it spreadeth; yet the violet the oftener it is handled and touched the sooner it withereth and decayeth (*Euphues*, 1578).

Unlike Lyly, who is being sententious, Falstaff is being marvelously ironic in his questioning of the errant Prince of Wales. We laugh because the imitation is so accurate and, in Falstaff's mouth, so inappropriate.

One can distinguish between pastiche and p. on the grounds of purpose; distinguishing between p. and burlesque (q.v.) is more difficult. The usual distinction is said to be method: p. strives for congruence in imitation, burlesque for incongruity. Thus a burlesque may imitate a formal style but use it as a vehicle for vulgar or topical content. P., on the other hand, imitates both style and subject, so that the reader's amusement comes from recognizing how closely the p. follows the subject. As Dwight Macdonald sums up the matter, "If burlesque is pouring new wine into old bottles, p. is making a new wine that tastes like the old but has a slightly lethal effect" (559).

II. CRITICAL ISSUES. Some critics have viewed p. as a more important literary form than burlesque, but traditionally p. was regarded as a species or subclass of burlesque. P. at its best deals with sophisticated stylistic techniques, while burlesque is often cheerfully vulgar. One wonders if it is the overly serious critics who prefer the former. P. is attractive not only for considerations of taste, but also because it is more interesting in the challenges it presents, in its nature as a "meta-fiction" (Rose) which raises questions about such theoretical issues as the process of writing, the role of the reader, the role of authority, and the social context of the text (187). Because the success of p. depends not only on the reader's understanding of the text, but also on the recognition of the source-text it is based on and the comical twist or reversal of those cultural values embedded in the source-text, the readerly transaction is complex. And the p. itself of course reinstantiates the source at the same time that it subverts it.

The nature of p. continues to be a matter of discussion. On the one hand, it is seen as a highly reflexive form that celebrates textuality (q.v.). Macdonald praises p. as "an intuitive kind of lit. crit, shorthand for what 'serious' critics must write out at length. It is Method Acting, since a success-ful parodist must live himself, imaginatively, into his parodee. It is *jiujitsu,* using the impetus of the opponent to defeat him, although 'opponent' and 'defeat' are hardly the words. Most parodies are written out of admiration rather than contempt" (xiii). His positive view of the form is not universal, however, even among those who enjoy p.: Brett warns that "one must never forget the dependent nature of p. It is a parasitic art and, though it can hold up the eminent to ridicule, without them it could not exist" (25). To some extent the reaction that a p. draws depends on the critic's opinion of the work it imitates. It may also depend on the critic's attitude toward current ideology, for it is undeniable that p. is a subversive form. Freund defines p. as "a literary instrument of ideological crit. P. destroys established ideologies, such as the heroic or fascistic, by searching them for sympto-matic, verbally and structurally fixed constructs and tearing these structures down along with the ideologies manifested in them" (13).

So understood, p. is uniformly subversive, even when affectionate. There is also, however, sacred p.: this takes secular themes such as erotic love and transforms them to divine purposes. Both Virgil's incorporation of the two Homeric epics and also much East Asian practice are forms of elevating p., and Milton uses dissimiles and com-parisons of "small things to great" to serious ends.

III. HISTORY. P. was originally "a song sung be-side," i.e. a comic imitation of a serious poem. Aristotle (*Poetics* 1448a12) attributes its origin to Hegemon of Thasos (5th c. B.C.), who used epic style to represent men not as superior to what they are in ordinary life but as inferior. Athenaeus (15.699a) states that Hegemon was the first to introduce parodies into the theater, but elsewhere quotes Polemo as saying that p. was invented by the iambic poet Hipponax (6th c. B.C.), who had himself been the victim of caricature at the hands of the sculptors and painters; we have a few lines of his mock-epic on a glutton. Much earlier than these examples of p. was the pseudo-Homeric *Margites,* known to Archilochus, which set forth in hexameters with intermingled iambics the story of a fool. We still have the *Battle of the Frogs and Mice,* which parodies Homer.

But the supreme parodist of antiquity was Aris-tophanes, who may be thought to have reached his highest level in the *Frogs,* where he parodies the styles of Aeschylus and Euripides. But almost every passage of Aristophanes contains a touch of p. In later comedy this element dwindles. Plato imitates the styles of several prose writers with amusing effect; in the *Symposium* (194e–197e) he puts into Agathon's mouth a speech in the manner of Gorgias. Lucian has a good many touches of p. or burlesque: in Dialogue 20, the *Judgment of Paris,* for example, the comic effect is achieved by mak-ing the divine characters talk in the lang. of ordi-nary life.

Roman humor had a strong element of p.; the phlyax pots and the performances which they presumably illustrate must have appealed to the Romans. In Lat. comedy we find occasional bur-lesque of the tragic manner, as in the prologues to the *Amphitryon* and the *Rudens,* the mad scene in the *Menaechmi,* and Pardalisca's mock-tragic out-burst (*Casina* 621 ff.)—passages which, whatever the original may have been, owe their effect to lang. and meter. A more delicate irony is shown in Syrus' mocking reply to the sententious words of Demea (*Adelphoe* 420 ff.). Lucilius parodies such stylistic techniques of the Roman tragedians as Pacuvius' unusual words and awkward com-pounds. The fourth poem of Catullus is closely parodied in *Catalepton* 10. Persius ridicules by imitation the styles of Pacuvius and other poets. Petronius gives us a long hexameter poem on the Civil War, parts of which may be meant as a cari-cature of Lucan.

In the later days of the Empire, the Roman mime parodied the rites of the Christian church. During the later Middle Ages, ps. of liturgy, well-known hymns, and even the Bible were popular. Ren. authors, when not embroiled in the polemics of the Reformation, preferred to parody the clas-sics or such "gothic" phenomena as medieval ro-mance and scholasticism; these include Pulci's *Morgante Maggiore* and Cervantes' *Don Quixote* (p. of romance); Giambattista Gelli's *Circe,* Tassoni's *La Secchia Rapita* and Scarron's *Virgile Travesti* (p. of the classics); and Erasmus' *Praise of Folly* and Rabelais' *Gargantua and Pantagruel* (p. of scholasti-cism). Of these authors, Rabelais is the most univer-sal, the richest, and the most difficult to classify.

P. became institutionalized during the 17th c. The existence of academies and distinct literary movements, particularly in Italy, France, and Eng-land, encouraged debates in which p. was used as a weapon of satire. Boccalini's *Ragguagli di Par-nasso* (1612) was the origin for a whole genre employing p. as a device for criticizing contemp. authors.

Eng. p. of the late Middle Ages is employed in the cycle plays, where a scene of common life (e.g. the Mak episode in *The Second Shepherd's Play*) provides comic relief. Chaucer's *Sir Thopas* paro-dies the grandiose style of medieval romance (q.v.). Shakespeare burlesqued his own romantic love plots with *rustic amours,* and John Marston, in turn, wrote a rough, humorous travesty of *Venus and Adonis.* One of the best-known 17th-c. ps. was the Duke of Buckingham's *The Rehearsal* (1671), which leveled its shafts mainly at Dryden's *The Conquest of Granada* and at the grand manner of the heroic play (q.v.). In 1701 John Phillips (*The Splendid Shilling*) used the solemn blank verse of Milton to celebrate ludicrous incidents. Later in the century, Sheridan's *The Critic* (1779) revived dramatic p. Exceptions to the general rule that p. rarely outlives the text or trad. parodied, both *The Rehearsal* and *The Critic* have been revived in the 20th c.

The Golden Age of p. in Eng. poetry paralleled the rise of the romantic and Transcendental movements. Canning, Ellis, and John Hookham Frere produced a series of ps. in the *Anti-Jacobin Journal* (1790–1810). Here the Southey-Wordsworth brand of Fr. revolutionary sympathy for knifegrinders and tattered beggars provided good anti-Jacobin sport. Blake's *Vision of Judgment* and Shelley's *Peter Bell* likewise parodied Southey, Wordsworth, and "elemental" poetry. James Hogg in 1816 took off most of the Eng. romantics, and in 1812 James and Horace Smith published *Rejected Addresses*, a landmark in Eng. p., in which the styles of Scott, Wordsworth, Byron, Coleridge, Samuel Johnson, and others were skillfully but not uproariously parodied. In the later 19th c., names and titles continue to multiply. Tennyson, Browning, Longfellow, Poe, Swinburne, and Whitman become the chief targets for such p. artists as J. K. Stephen, C. S. Calverly, J. C. Squire, Lewis Carroll, Swinburne (who not only produced *The Higher Pantheism in a Nutshell* à la Tennyson, but also parodied himself in *Nephelidia*), and Andrew Lang. Best of all was Max Beerbohm. In America the names of Phoebe Cary, Bret Harte, Mark Twain, Bayard Taylor, H. C. Bunner, and J. K. Bangs were most prominent before 1900. In the 20th c. *The New Yorker* has carried on the trad. established in the last century by *Punch* and *Vanity Fair.* During the 1920s, p. found a highly congenial locus in the temperaments of such talented practitioners as Corey Ford, Louis Untermeyer, Frank Sullivan, Donald Odgen Stewart, Wolcott Gibbs, James Thurber, Robert Benchley, and E. B. White. There has been less p. since then, but it continues in the work of such writers as Kenneth Tynan, Tom Stoppard, Veronica Geng, and Frederick Crews. After 25 centuries, p. seems unlikely to fade as a comic and critical form. But the existence of sacred p. and of Asian counterparts, for example, should be taken as reminders that amusement is not the sole end of p. Seriousness of parodic ends is fundamental to works like Joyce's *Ulysses*. In addition, the mingling of sacred and profane (or erotic) in Indian poetry (q.v.) makes p. almost inseparable from the most serious of nonparodic lit. See also BURLESQUE; MOCK EPIC; SATIRE.

COLLECTIONS: *Ps. of the Works of Eng. and Am. Authors*, ed. W. Hamilton, 6 v. (1884–89); *A P. Anthol.*, ed. C. Wells (1904); *A Book of Ps.*, ed. A. Symons (1908); *A Century of P. and Imitation*, ed. W. Jerrold and R. M. Leonard (1913); *Am. Lit. in*

P., ed. R. P. Falk (1955); *Ps.: An Anthol.*, ed. D. MacDonald (1960); *20th-C. P., Am. and British*, ed. B. Lowrey (1960); *The Brand X Anthol. of Poetry*, ed. W. Zaranka (1981); *Faber Book of Ps.*, ed. S. Brett (1984).

HISTORY AND CRITICISM: A. T. Murray, *On P. and Paratragoedia in Aristophanes* (1891); A. S. Martin, *On P.* (1896); C. Stone, *P.* (1915); E. Gosse, "Burlesque," *Sel. Essays* (1928); G. Kitchin, *A Survey of Burlesque and P. in Eng.* (1931); A. H. West, *L'Influence française dans la poésie burlesque en Angleterre entre 1660–1700* (1931); R. P. Bond, *Eng. Burlesque Poetry, 1700–1750* (1932); L. L. Martz, *The Poetry of Meditation*, 2d ed. (1962)—sacred p.; G. Highet, *Anatomy of Satire* (1962); P. Lehmann, *Die lateinische Parodie im Mittelalter*, 2d ed. (1963); J. G. Riewald, "P. as Crit.," *Neophil* 50 (1966); U. Weisstein, "P., Travesty, and Burlesque," *Proc. IVth Congress of the ICLA* (1966); P. Rau, *Paratragodia* (1967); U. Broich, *Studien zum Komischen Epos* (1968); G. D. Kiremidjian, "The Aesthetics of P.," *JAAC* 28 (1969–70); "P., Gr.," and "P., Lat," *Oxford Cl. Dict.*, ed. N. G. L. Hammond and H. H. Scullard, 2d ed. (1970); G. Lee, *Allusion, P., and Imitation* (1971); W. Karrer, *Parodie, Travestie, Pastiche* (1977); A. Liede, "Parodie," *Reallexikon*; M. Rose, *P.//Meta-Fiction* (1979); W. Freund, *Die Literarische Parodie* (1981); J. Hartwig, *Shakespeare's Analogical Scene: P. as Structural Syntax* (1983); L. Hutcheon, *A Theory of P.* (1985); J. A. Dane, *P.: Critical Concepts vs. Literary Practices, Aristophanes to Sterne* (1988); K. Gravdal, *Vilain and Courtois* (1989); E. G. Stanley, "P. in Early Eng. Lit.," *Poetica* 27 (1988).

R.P.F.; F.T.

PAROEMIAC (Gr. "proverbial"). In Cl. prosody, the term for an anapaestic dimeter catalectic, common in proverbs and popular expressions: it has the metrical form ◡◡ – – ◡◡ – ◡◡ – – and was used in series as a march rhythm and as a close to anapestic systems. It finds related use in the cantica of Plautus (see CANTICUM AND DIVERBIUM) and was used later as a stichic line by Med. Lat. poets such as Boethius.—Crusius; Dale; *Oxford Cl. Dict.* (1970), s.v. "Paroemiographers"; Halporn et al.; West 53. J.W.H.

PAROLE. See DECONSTRUCTION; SEMIOTICS, POETIC; SOUND.

PARONOMASIA. See PUN.

PARTIMEN (also *joc partit*, Fr. *jeu parti*). In Occitan, a specialized variety of *tenso* (q.v.) in which one poet proposes two hypothetical situations (e.g. whether it is better to love a lady who does not love you, or to be loved by a lady whom you do not love). The second poet chooses and defends one of these alternatives, while the first poet upholds the other. After each has had his say in the same number of stanzas (usually three), all identical in structure, the poets commonly refer the debate to one or more arbiters for settlement. There are also ps. involving three poets and three choices, but these are far less frequent. It seems certain that these ps. really represent the cooperative work of two or more poets; but in view of the difficulties involved, it is unlikely that they were actually improvised, as they purport to be. Sometimes it is even clear from the poem itself that the poets were writing back and forth over a considerable distance.—A. Långfors, *Recueil général des jeux-partis français*, 2 v. (1926); S. Neumeister, *Das Spiel mit der höfischen Liebe* (1969); E. Köhler in *GRLMA*, v, 2.1B.16 ff.   F.M.C.

PASSION PLAY. Dramatizations of Christ's redemptive sufferings and death developed centuries later than Easter plays, possibly because the Mass itself was understood as a daily representation of the Passion; some medieval commentators even explained the actions of the Mass in dramatic and theatrical terms. Little evidence remains for the performance of p. ps. from the Gr. Byzantine trad. Notable is a 13th-c. scenario of a text, probably of Cypriot origin, from which we can reconstruct a p. p. that opens with the Raising of Lazarus and concludes with the scene of the Doubting Thomas. Conversely, the disputed *Christos paschōn* is now recognized as a skillful literary exercise rather than a true play. Cycles of dramatic homilies, some of very early date, include Passion material, but it is not clear how these were presented.

Evidence for the performance of Med. Lat. p. ps. is more substantial, but few texts survive. The earliest is probably the mid 12th-c. monastic music-drama from Monte Cassino that introduces a vernacular *planctus* (see LAMENT) of the Virgin Mary at the foot of the Cross. A later fragment from Sulmona suggests a related, considerably longer play. The famous *Carmina Burana* ms. from Benediktbeuern contains two p. ps. dating from the 12th or 13th c.: the shorter *Ludus* (play) composed entirely of Lat. prose probably draws on a Gospel harmony; the longer *Ludus* is a complex drama combining spoken and sung text in prose and verse, incl. significant passages in Ger.

Vernacular p. ps. flourished in Western Christianity from the early 14th until the late 16th c. Authors, often clerical, employed established as well as experimental verseforms and also prose. Some plays constituted true music-dramas; others contained occasional hymns, songs, and instrumental music. Sources of the various episodes incl. the Bible, apocryphal and legendary material, narrative poems, lyric laments, and meditative texts. Allegory, humor, ribaldry, and farce were introduced. P. ps. were also influenced by the iconography of the visual and plastic arts, for which they in turn inspired further developments. The production of p. ps. could call upon the resources and organizational efforts of religious orders, lay confraternities, trade guilds, even entire towns. They were acted, often with considerable spectacle, in or near churches, along processional routes, in public squares, in earthen amphitheaters in Cornwall, and in the Colosseum at Rome. Performance time varied from under an hour to several days, in extreme cases to 20 or 25 days. The plays were usually presented during Holy Week and Easter Week, on or around the warm-weather feasts of Whitsun and Corpus Christi.

In Italy, brief music-dramas based closely on Gospel accounts formed the original nucleus of the extensive repertory of the flagellant confraternities that came to embrace dramatizations for the main feasts of the Liturgical Year. From the 15th c., such groups tended to specialize in producing a small number of plays, such as the influential Roman p. p.

In France, the 15th c. was the great age of spectacular p. ps. The Passion of Semur dramatizes material from Creation to Ascension in numerous relatively short scenes. The longer Passion of Arras, attributed to the rhetorician Eustace Mercadé, deals only with the Life of Christ but frames it with scenes of the Debate of the Four Daughters of God. But the most accomplished Fr. p. p. is that by Arnoul Gréban, theologian and choirmaster at Notre Dame de Paris.

In the Sp. trad., brief vernacular plays were performed in conjunction with the ceremonies of Holy Week; such a play may have made use of the famous articulated figure of Christ in Burgos Cathedral. Plays on Passion material were also among those presented with the use of pageant wagons during Corpus Christi rituals and processions. Missionaries brought p. ps. to Sp. America, where they merged with native trads.

The great Eng. cycle plays connected with the celebrations and processions of Corpus Christi dramatize salvation history from Creation to Doom. Of central importance are the pageants devoted to events of the Passion; noteworthy among these are the compositions of the so-called "Wakefield Master" and "York Realist."

The term p. p. is sometimes used with special reference to the Ger. trad., which is particularly rich. The p. p. from St. Gall, considered the most complete and typical of 14th-c. works, shows the persistence of Lat., which is employed symbolically for the speeches of the most sacred characters. Later Ger. plays parallel the Fr. in complexity and spectacle; texts often provide detailed instructions for staging, as those from Alsfeld, Donaueschingen, and Lucerne. Most widely known is the controversial Oberammergau p. p., a product of the Catholic Reform but still performed periodically to this day. Recent years have witnessed a burgeoning of interest in p. ps. of all national trads.; and performances by professional and amateur groups have confirmed the realization that these are not just works of literary art but true dramas that must be brought to life in order to be appreciated.

See also LITURGICAL DRAMA; MEDIEVAL POETRY.

BIBLIOGRAPHIES AND REVIEWS OF SCHOLARSHIP: C. J. Stratman, *Bibl. of Med. Drama*, rev. ed. (1972); W. Michael, "Das deutsche Drama und Theater vor der Reformation," *DVLJ* 47 (1973); G. A. Runnals, "Med. Fr. Drama," *RORD* (1978–79); *The Present State of Scholarship in 14th-C. Lit.*, ed. T. D. Cooke (1982); K. C. Falvey, "It. Vernacular Religious Drama from the 14th through the 16th Cs.," *RORD* (1983).

STUDIES: V. De Bartholomaeis, *Origini della poesia drammatica italiana*, 2d. ed. (1953); G. Frank, *The Med. Fr. Drama* (1960); N. D. Shergold, *A Hist. of the Sp. Stage from Med. Times until the End of the 17th C.* (1967); R. Steinbach, *Die deutschen Oster- und Passionsspiele des Mittelalters* (1970); S. Sticca, *The Lat. P. P.* (1970); R. Woolf, *The Eng. Mystery Plays* (1972); M. Stevens, *Four ME Mystery Cycles* (1987).   K.C.F.

PASTICHE. See BURLESQUE.

PASTORAL.

    I. HISTORY
    II. THEORY

I. HISTORY. The p. is a fictionalized imitation of rural life, usually the life of an imaginary Golden Age, in which the loves of shepherds and shepherdesses play a prominent part; its ends are sometimes sentimental and romantic, but sometimes satirical or political. To insist on a realistic presentation of actual shepherd life would exclude the greater part of the works that are called p. Only when poetry ceases to imitate actual rural life does it become distinctly p. It must be admitted, however, that the term has been and still is used loosely to designate any treatment of rural life, as when Louis Untermeyer speaks of Robert Frost as a "p." poet. Many critics might agree with Edmund Gosse that the "p. is cold, unnatural, artificial, and the humblest reviewer is free to cast a stone at its dishonored grave." But there must be some unique value in a genre that lasted 2,000 years (and has generated the bibliography below).

For all practical purposes the p. begins with Theocritus' *Idylls*, in the 3d c. B.C. (see IDYLL). Though the canon of Theocritus' work is unsettled, enough of the poems in the collection made by Artemidorus are certainly his to justify the claim that Theocritus is the father of p. poetry. No. 11, for example, in which Polyphemus is depicted as being in love with Galatea and finding solace in song, becomes the prototype of the love lament; no. 1, in which Thyrsis sings of Daphnis' death, sets the pattern and, to no small degree, the matter for the p. elegy (see below); no. 5 and no. 7 introduce the singing match conducted in *amoebaean verses* ("responsive verses"), whereby verses, couplets, or stanzas are spoken alternately by two speakers. The second speaker is expected not only to match the theme introduced by the first but also to improve upon it in some way (see Koster). And no. 7, in the appearance of contemporary poets under feigned names, contains the germ of the allegorical p. Theocritus wrote his ps. while he was at Ptolemy's court in Alexandria, but he remembered the actual herdsmen of his boyhood and the beautiful countryside of Sicily, so he, like the p. poets who followed him, was a city man longing for the country. But perhaps no other p. poet has ever been able to strike such a happy medium between the real and the ideal.

Virgil's *Eclogues* refine and methodize Theocritus' idylls (see ECLOGUE). Expressing the sentiment inspired by the beauty of external nature in her tranquil moods and the kindred charm inspired by ideal human relationships (love in particular) in verse notable for its exquisite diction and flowing rhythm, they consolidate and popularize the conventions of p. poetry. During the Middle Ages, the p. was chiefly confined to the *pastourelle* (q.v.), a type of vernacular dialogue (q.v.) first developed in Occitan poetry (q.v.), and to a few realistic scenes in the religious plays. The vast body of post-medieval p.—that is, p. elegy, p. drama, and p. romance—is a direct outgrowth of Ren. Humanism.

The p. elegy, patterned after such Cl. models as the *Lament for Adonis*, credited to Bion, the *Lament for Bion*, traditionally ascribed to Moschus but most probably by a disciple of Bion, and Theocritus' first idyll, became conventional in the Ren. Its traditional machinery included the invocation, statement of grief, inquiry into the causes of death, sympathy and weeping of nature, procession of mourners, lament, climax, change of mood, and consolation. Marot and Spenser (*Astrophel* [1595], for Sidney) produced important Ren. examples, and numerous other p. poets, including Pope, Ambrose Philips, and Gay tried their hand at the genre. Milton's *Lycidas* and Shelley's *Adonais* conform rather closely to the classical conventions, of which vestiges can be seen even as late as Arnold's *Thyrsis*. In the Eng. trad. it is *Lycidas* which unquestionably holds the first position.

The p. drama was latent in the idylls and eclogues, for the brief dialogue was easily expandable. Even as early as Boccaccio's *Ninfale feisolano* the dramatic intensity of the eclogue was considerably heightened. With the addition of the crossed love plot and secret personal history, the p. drama emerged, and it grew in popularity as the medieval mystery plays lost ground. Poliziano's *Favola di Orfeo* (1472) is perhaps more correctly classified as an opera, but p. elements are prominent. Agostino de' Beccari's *Il Sacrificio* (1554), the first fully-developed p. drama, led to the heyday of the p. drama in Italy during the last quarter of the 16th c. Tasso's *Aminta* (1573), an allegory of the court of Ferrara, is no doubt the greatest of the kind and has exerted the most far-reaching influence on the trad. Second only to it is Guarini's

Il pastor fido (The Faithful Shepherd, 1580–89), the first important tragicomedy (q.v.). In France, the most famous drama is Racan's *Les Bergeries* (1625), founded on d'Urfé's *Astrée*. It was followed by countless *bergeries*, which, after the mode of *Astrée*, were so filled with *galant* shepherds and beautiful nymphs that the type wore itself out with its own artificiality. England's first noteworthy p. dramas, Lyly's *Gallathea* and Peele's *Arraignment of Paris*, were both published in 1584, and the most excellent, Fletcher's *Faithful Shepherdess* (imitating Tasso's *Aminta*), in 1610. In general, the Eng. plays differed from their predecessors in that, in the former, the p. setting and elements are merely a backdrop to courtly characters engaged in courtly intrigues. Because of the constant pressure of Eng. empiricism and the austerity of the Puritan taste, the p. drama in England never reached the extravagant artificiality that it attained on the Continent. The last p. drama in England was the belated *Gentle Shepherd* by Allan Ramsay in 1725. Written in Lowland Scots, detailing Scottish scenes, and using "real" shepherds, it was highly praised by the early romantic poets and critics.

The p. romance usually takes the form of a long prose narrative, interspersed with lyrics, built on a complicated plot, and peopled with characters bearing p. names. In antiquity it is represented by Longus' charming story of sexual initiation, *Daphnis and Chloe*. The modern genre, while anticipated by Boccaccio's prosimetric *Ameto* (1342), is usually dated from Sannazaro's *Arcadia* (1504), a remarkable work, written in musical prose and filled with characters who live in innocent voluptuousness. Popular imitations are Montemayor's *Diana* (1559?) in Portugal and Cervantes' *Galatea* (1585) in Spain. In France the indigenous *pastourelle* held back the p. romance; but Rémy Belleau's *Bergerie* (1572) established the type, and in d'Urfé's *Astrée* the baroque p. romance found its most consummate example, as nymphs bedizened in pearls and satin cavort with chivalric shepherds. The most celebrated Eng. p. romance is Sir Philip Sidney's *Arcadia* (the "Old Arcadia," written ca. 1580; rev. 1584, the "New Arcadia," pub. 1590). Its lofty sentiment, sweet rhythm, ornate rhetoric, elaborate description, and high-flown oratory display one aspect of the Italianate style of Elizabethan courtly lit. In spite of the riddle of its plot, in which the strange turns of fortune and love make all the virtuous happy, it is still good reading as a romance of love and adventure. The literary influence of the *Arcadia* was pervasive: Greene and Lodge, for example, imitated it; Shakespeare drew from it for the character of Gloucester in *King Lear*; on the scaffold Charles I recited an adaptation of a Pamela's prayer; in translation the *Arcadia* contributed to the elaborate plots of the Fr. romances; and traces of it may perhaps be seen even in Richardson and Scott. The sustained elaboration of its structure marks another step in the devel. of the novel away

from the short story and the picaresque tale. Robert Greene's *Menaphon* (1589), conventional and imitative, adds little to the genre except some delightful lyrics. Thomas Lodge's *Rosalynde* (1590), in the style of Lyly's *Euphues* but diversified with sonnets and eclogues, was dramatized with little alteration by Shakespeare in *As You Like It*.

Early in the 14th c., the p. eclogue was profoundly influenced by the new learning, when Dante, Petrarch, and Boccaccio wrote Lat. eclogues after the mode of Virgil. They continued the allegory of their master, extended its political and religious scope, and introduced the personal lament. About the turn of the 15th c., Baptista Spagnuoli Mantuanus exploited the satirical possibilities of the p. by using rustic characters to ridicule the court, the church, and the women of his day. Late in the century, the It. poet Marino (1569–1625) developed a style paralleling gongorism and euphuism (see MARINISM). His Fr. p. idyll, *Adone* (1623), filled with affected wordplay and outrageous conceits, represents a baroque (q.v.) aberration of the genre comparable to the contemporaneous *Astrée*. The *Pléiade* (q.v.) transplanted the classical eclogue into France, where Marot and Ronsard and many imitators produced conventional eclogues. In England, the eclogue makes its first appearance in the work of Alexander Barclay (*Egloges* [1515?, pub. 1570]) and Barnabe Googe (*Es., Epitaphs, and Sonnets* [1563], ed. J. M. Kennedy [1989]), but important p. poetry effectually dates from Spenser's *Shepheardes Calender* (1579), which inspired a host of late 16th-c. imitations. Though Spenser follows the conventions of the classical eclogue, he aims at simplicity and naturalness by making use of rustic characters speaking country lang. During the last quarter of the 16th c., England continued to produce much p. poetry in imitation of Spenser. According to modern taste and judgment, those of most merit are Michael Drayton's *Shepherds Garland* (1593) and William Browne's *Britannia's Pastorals* (1613–16). In his *Piscatory Eclogues* (1633), Phineas Fletcher imitated Sannazaro, who may have taken his cue from Theocritus' fisherman's idyll, no. 21.

The swan song of the p. was sung by the Eng. poets of the 18th c. Revived by Pope and Philips, whose rival ps. appeared in Tonson's *Miscellany* in 1709, the p. attracted a surprising amount of interest. Pope, inspired by Virgil's *Eclogues*, produced one of the showpieces of rococo art—a part of "Summer" being so tuneful that Handel set it to music. Philips, under the rising influence of Eng. empiricism, tried to write pastorals that came closer to the realities of Eng. rural life. The followers of neither poet wrote any p. worthy of mention, and the genre soon died of its own inanition. So artificial and effete had it become that Gay's *Shepherd's Week*, in broad burlesque, was sometimes read as a p. in the true Theocritean style. The outstanding examples of the romantic p. are Ger.:

Salomon Gessner's *Daphnis* (1754), *Idyllen* (1756), and *Der Tod Abels* (1758). Wordsworth's *Michael*, reflecting the empirical element of Eng. romanticism, well marks the end of serious attempts in the genre.

II. THEORY: Sustained criticism of the p. begins with the essays of the Ren. Humanists, the most important being Vida's *Ars poetica* (1527), Sebillet's *Art poétique françoys* (1548), Scaliger's *Poetices libri septem* (1561), and "E. K."'s epistle and preface in 1579. The interest of these critics in the p. sprang from their desire to enrich the vernacular by imitating the "ancients" in this genre and to exploit its allegorical potential.

But mere imitation of Theocritus and Virgil did not long suffice, as the debate over Guarini's tragicomedy *Il pastor fido* illustrates. In his *Discorso* (1587), Jason Denores attacked this play because, he argued, it is a bastard genre, unauthorized by Aristotle. In *Il verato* (1588), and *Il verato secondo* (1593), Guarini secured the new form against his adversary, thereby widening the scope of the genre. D'Urfé, in *L'Autheur à la bergere astrée* (1610), further extended the bounds of the p. when he turned critic to defend his baroque romance. The extravagances of Marino's *Adone* made him the main target of neoclassical attack.

In France, critical discussion of the p. followed in the course of the *Querelle des anciens et des modernes* (q.v.). In 1659, René Rapin argued that p. poets should return to the ancient models, and to his *Eclogae sacrae* he prefixed "Dissertatio de carmine pastorali," wherein he declares that he will gather all his theory from "*Theocritus* and *Virgil*, those great and judicious Authors, whose very doing is Authority enough," since "*Pastoral* belongs properly to the Golden Age." The most significant rebuttal to Rapin's theory is Fontenelle's "Discours sur la nature de l'eglogue" (1688). Whereas Rapin looked for his fundamental criterion to the objective authority of the ancients, Fontenelle, like his master Descartes, sought a subjective standard in and expected illumination from "the natural light of Reason." Fontenelle's method is deductive. He starts with a basic assumption, the self-evident clarity of which he thinks no one will question: "all men would be happy, and that too at an easy rate." From this premise he deduces the proposition that p. poetry, if it is to make men happy, must present "a concurrence of the two strongest passions, laziness and love."

The quarrel between the ancients and the moderns was transferred directly to England; Rapin was translated by Thomas Creech in 1684, and Fontenelle was "Englished by Mr. Motteux" in 1695. The clash between the objective authority of the classics and the subjective standards of reason divided the critics into two schools of opinion, which are best denominated as neoclassical and rationalist. The immediate source of the basic ideas of the Eng. Neoclassical critics of the p.—the

chief of whom are Walsh, Pope, Gay, Gildon, and Newbery—is Rapin's "Treatise." Pope, in practice as in theory, epitomizes the neoclassical ideal.

The immediate source of the basic ideas of the Eng. rationalist critics—the chief of whom are Addison, Tickell, Purney, and Johnson—is Fontenelle's "Discours." But the Eng. followers of Fontenelle insist that the p. conform to experience as well as to reason. Though Dr. Johnson's *Rambler* essays on the p. observe both Rationalist and empirical premises: his definition of a p. is that it is simply a poem in which "any action or passion is represented by its effects on a country life."

Romantic p. theory evolved from Rationalist theory. As the critics became more certain of their empirical grounds, they showed more freedom to disregard the form and the content of the traditional p.; to look on nature with heightened emotion; to endow primitive life with benevolence and dignity; and to place a greater value on sentiment and feeling. For example, in *An Essay on the Genius and Writings of Pope* (1756), Joseph Warton, by arguing that Theocritus was primarily a realistic poet and that the Golden Age depicted in his poetry may be equated with 18th-c. rural life, substitutes cultural primitivism for chronological. In "Discours préliminaire" to *Les Saisons*, Jean-François de Saint-Lambert disregards the distinction between the p. and descriptive poetry (q.v.) and speaks with enthusiasm of the beauty of fields, rivers, and woods and of the felicity of rural life as he knew it in his childhood. In *Lectures on Belles Lettres* (1783), Hugh Blair singles out Salomon Gessner's *Idyllen* as the poems in which his "ideas for the improvement of P. Poetry are fully realized." Blair's essay, along with Wordsworth's *Michael* (which exemplifies much of Blair's theory), ends serious consideration of the p. After that poem and Blair's essay, the genre belongs to the academics.

See also BUCOLIC; DESCRIPTIVE POETRY; ECLOGUE; GEORGIC; IDYLL; PASTOURELLE; RENAISSANCE POETICS.

T. Purney, *A Full Enquiry into the True Nature of P.* (1717), rpt. with intro. by E. Wasserman (1948); N. Drake, "On P. Poetry," *Literary Hours* (1798); E. Gosse, "Essay on Eng. P. Poetry," *Works of Spenser* (1882); J. Marsan, *La Pastorale dramatique en France* (1905); E. K. Chambers, *Eng. Ps.* (1906); W. W. Greg, *P. Poetry and P. Drama* (1906); J. Marks, *Eng. P. Drama* (1908); H. A. Rennert, *The Sp. P. Romances* (1912); J. P. W. Crawford, *Sp. P. Drama* (1915); Torquato Tasso, *Aminta: A P. Drama*, ed. E. Grillo (1924)—good intro.; M. K. Bragg, *The Formal Eclogue in 18th-C. England* (1926); J. Hubaux, *Les Thèmes bucoliques dans la poésie latine* (1930); W. P. Jones, *The Pastourelle* (1931); W. Empson, *Some Versions of P.* (1935); A. Hulubei, *L'Eglogue en France au XVIe siècle* (1938); T. P. Harrison, *The P. Elegy* (1939); E. F. Wilson, "P. and Epithalamium in Lat. Lit.," *Speculum* 23 (1948); M. I. Gerhardt, *La Pastorale* (1950)—It., Sp., Fr.;

J. E. Congleton, *Theories of P. Poetry in England 1684–1798* (1952); *Eng. P. Poetry*, ed. F. Kermode (1952); H. Smith, *Elizabethan Poetry* (1952); Curtius, 183 ff.; E. Merker, "Idylle," *Reallexikon* 1.742–49; J. Duchemin, *La Houlette et la lyre* (1960); W. L. Grant, *Neo-Lat. Lit. and the P.* (1965); Koster—for amoeban verse; T. G. Rosenmeyer, *The Green Cabinet: Theocritus and the European P. Lyric* (1969); R. Cody, *The Landscape of the Mind* (1969)—Tasso and Shakespeare; M. Friedman, *Marvell's P. Art* (1970); P. V. Marinelli, *P.* (1971); H. E. Toliver, *P. Forms and Attitudes* (1971); T. McFarland, *Shakespeare's P. Comedy* (1972); L. Lerner, *The Uses of Nostalgia* (1972); D. Young, *The Heart's Forest* (1972); N. B. Hansen, *That pleasant place* (1973); R. Williams, *The Country and the City* (1973); R. L. Colie, *Shakespeare's Living Art* (1974), chs. 6–7; Wilkins; R. Poggioli, *The Oaten Flute* (1975); *A Book of Eng. P. Verse*, ed. J. Barrell and J. Bull (1975); H. Cooper, *P.: Med. into Ren.* (1977); N. J. Hoffman, *Spenser's Ps.* (1977); *Schäferdichtung*, ed. W. Vosskamp (1977); R. Böschenstein-Schäfer, *Idylle*, 2d ed. (1977)—Ger.; R. Feingold, *Nature and Society* (1978)—18th-c. Eng.; *Survivals of P.*, ed. R. F. Hardin (1979); C. Hunt, *Lycidas and the It. Critics* (1979); P. Alpers, *The Singer of the Eclogues* (1979), "What is P.?" *CritI* 8 (1982); *Seven Versions of Carolingian P.*, ed. R. P. H. Green (1980); R. Mallette, *Spenser, Milton, and Ren. P.* (1981); C. Segal, *Poetry and Myth in Ancient P.* (1981); Fowler; D. M. Halperin, *Before P.: Theocritus and the Ancient Trad. of Bucolic Poetry* (1983); W. J. Kennedy, *Jacopo Sannazaro and the Uses of P.* (1983); *Milton's* Lycidas, ed. C. A. Patrides, 2d ed. (1983); J. Blanchard, *La Pastorale en France aux XIVe et XVe siècles* (1983); A. V. Ettin, *Lit. and the P.* (1984); D. R. Shore, *Spenser and the Poetics of P.* (1985); S. C. Brinkmann, *Die deutschsprachige Pastourelle: 13. bis 16. Jh.* (1985); P. Lindenbaum, *Changing Landscapes: Anti-P. Sentiment in the Eng. Ren.* (1986); L. Metzger, *One Foot in Eden* (1986)—Romantic ps.; A. Patterson, *P. and Ideology* (1987); C. M. Schenck, *Mourning and Panegyric* (1988); J. D. Bernard, *Ceremonies of Innocence* (1989)—Spenser; O. Schur, *Victorian P.* (1989); S. Chaudhuri, *Ren. P. and its Eng. Devels.* (1989); S. Burris, *The Poetry of Resistance* (1990)—Seamus Heaney; K. J. Gutzwiller, *Theocritus' P. Analogies* (1991).

J.E.C.; T.V.F.B.

PASTORAL DRAMA. See PASTORAL.

PASTORAL ELEGY. See ELEGY; PASTORAL.

PASTORAL ROMANCE. See PASTORAL.

PASTOURELLE. A genre of lyric poetry most frequent in OF. In the classical type the narrator, who is sometimes identified as a knight, recounts his meeting with a shepherdess and his attempt to seduce her. Sometimes the narrator is humiliated, even beaten, or the shepherdess makes a clever escape; in other poems they make love, either with the consent of the shepherdess or by rape. Less frequent subgenres include the "augmented" p., which adds a shepherd lover or other members of the cast, with appropriate developments in the plot (the girl quarrels with Robin and the poet takes her away, etc.); the *bergerie*, in which the poet recounts his meeting with a group of peasants who dance and quarrel; and the *pastoureau*, in which the poet meets a shepherd and talks with him.

The Fr. term shows influence of Occitan *pastorela* in the retention of the *s* and in the treatment of the vowel spelled *ou*, and the genre seems to have originated in Occitan. There are antecedents or analogs in Med. Lat., among the Romance *kharjas* (q.v.), and in Chinese around the 2d c. A.D., but the classical p. took form with the troubadour Marcabru in the early 12th c. He was imitated in the same century in Occitan, Lat., and Fr. In the 13th c. the p. flowered in Fr.; continued in Occitan, with a hiatus around mid-century after which it was perhaps reintroduced under Fr. influence; was practiced in Lat. until the *Carmina Burana* (ms. ca. 1230); and was introduced into Ger., It., and Galician-Portuguese. Fourteenth-c. Fr. poets dropped the p., but it inspired the invention of the *serranilla* (q.v.) in Sp.; more were written in Ger. and It., and a few in Gascon, Eng., and Welsh. We have 15th-c. ps. in Fr., Ger., Franco-Provençal, and *serranillas* in Sp. After the Middle Ages, the p. has been cultivated in poetry and folksong in Fr., Gascon, Catalan, Sp., and Eng.

The lyric genre has influenced other forms such as the *Jeu de Robin et Marion* (ca. 1283) by Adam de la Halle, which is a dramatization of a p., Mahieu le Poirier's narrative *Court d'amours* (ca. 1300), and the *Dit de la pastoure* (1403) by Christine de Pisan. A shepherdess named Pastorella figures in an episode of Spenser's *Faerie Queene* (6.9–12) which is reminiscent of an augmented p. In Shakespeare's *Tempest* the wooing of Ferdinand and Miranda recalls the cl. p., and the masque of reapers recalls the *bergerie*. Molière's *Dom Juan* seduces two country girls in the medieval manner.

ANTHOLOGIES: *Romances et ps. françaises des XIIe et XIIIe siècles*, ed. K. Bartsch (1870); *La P. dans la poésie occitane du Moyen Age*, ed. J. Audiau (1923); *Ps.*, ed. J.-C. Rivière, 3 v. (1974–76)—anonymous OF ps.; *The Medieval P.*, ed. and tr. W. D. Paden, 2 v. (1987)—all the classic ps.

HISTORY AND CRITICISM: M. Zink, *La P.* (1972); Bec—study and texts; E. Köhler in *GRLMA*, v. 2.1.B.3 (1979). W.D.P.

PATERNITY. See FEMINIST POETICS; INFLUENCE; INTERTEXTUALITY.

PATHETIC FALLACY. A phrase coined by John Ruskin in v. 3, ch. 12 of *Modern Painters* (1856) to denote an old and enduring practice in Western lit., the tendency of poets and painters to imbue the natural world with human feeling. For Ruskin it becomes an important criterion of artistic excellence. The fallacy, due to "an excited state of the feelings, making us, for the time, more or less irrational," creates "a falseness in all our impressions of external things." The offending example is taken from a poem in Charles Kingsley's novel *Alton Locke*: "They rowed her in across the rolling foam— / The cruel, crawling foam." Ruskin declares that "the foam is not cruel, neither does it crawl," the author's state of mind being "one in which the reason is unhinged by grief."

For Ruskin there are two classes of poets, "the Creative (Shakspere [sic], Homer, Dante), and Reflective or Perceptive (Wordsworth, Keats, Tennyson)"; it is one of the faults of the latter group that it admits the p. f. But Ruskin was unconcerned with the psychological origins of the p. f., and his ideas should not be applied indiscriminately to other lits. B. F. Dick contends that the "origins of the p. f. probably lie in a primitive homeopathy . . . wherein man regarded himself as part of his natural surroundings." In older lits., the p. f. does not automatically have the pejorative implications that Ruskin's definition established. Dick considers the Babylonian epic *Gilgamesh* an early and important source of the p. f.: in a climactic passage, all of nature weeps for the death of the warrior Enkidu; since Enkidu embodies the ideals of the natural man, nature as the universal parent must reflect the joys and sorrows of her children. Homer, for Ruskin one of the first order of poets, occasionally employs the p. f., but he characteristically attributes human feelings to weapons instead of the natural world—a standard convention of the war-epic. It is generally agreed that in the *Iliad* Homer falls prey to Ruskin's censures only once, when the sea rejoices as Poseidon passes overhead in his chariot (13.27–29). Yet even in this case Homer strictly curtails the passage, avoiding the indulgences Ruskin would later criticize.

Based on various Cl. models, the pastoral elegies of the 16th and 17th cs. provided Eng. poetry with a natural arena for the p. f. The early Eng. translators—e.g. Sir William Drummond, who translated the sonnets of the It. poet Jacopo Sannazaro in 1616—were among the first poets to provide the Eng. trad. with flowers, lillies, and columbine that would bow their heads in sympathetic response to the poet's grief; the p. f.'s earliest appearance is thus not the result of native invention but of the preservation of a pastoral convention.

Although he was unconcerned to invent a name for it, Samuel Johnson recognized the phenomenon in the 18th c. and complained 100 years earlier than Ruskin that the phrase "pastoral verse" referred simply to poetry in which, among other things, "the clouds weep." Johnson was reacting to the excesses of sentimentality in 18th-c. verse, but the device continued to be employed: it appears with varying frequency throughout the work of Collins, Cowper, Burns, Blake, Wordsworth, Shelley, Keats, Tennyson, and Hopkins. Wordsworth, justifying its usage, argued that "objects . . . derive their influence not from properties inherent in them . . . but from such as are bestowed upon them by the minds of those who are conversant with or affected by these objects." Tennyson, on the other hand, was well schooled in the scientific issues of his day, and his descriptions of natural objects are often clinically precise: after 1842 his verse reveals a markedly less frequent usage of p. f. (Miles), and *In Memoriam* offers a striking revision of the device by evoking its essential effect without indulging its excesses ("Calm is the morn without a sound. / Calm as to suit a calmer grief" [XI]).

During the 20th c., the most vigorous applications of the p. f. have been self-consciously designed to explore the epistemological issues implied by the technique. Modern usage of the p. f. ironically emphasizes the loss of communion between the individual and the natural world; and in its implied envy of an older world where such communion once existed, it resurrects yet another remnant of its ancient origin, pastoral nostalgia. See NATURE; PERSONIFICATION; SENTIMENTALITY.—F. O. Copley, "The P. F. in Early Gr. Poetry," *AJP* 58 (1937); J. Miles, *P. F. in the 19th C.* (1942); B. F. Dick, "Ancient Pastoral and the P. F.," *CL* 20 (1968); J. Bump, "Stevens and Lawrence: The Poetry of Nature and the Spirit of the Age," *SoR* 18 (1982); D. Hesla, "Singing in Chaos: Wallace Stevens and Three or Four Ideas," *AL* 57 (1985); A. Hecht, "The P. F.," *YR* 74 (1985). S.BU.

PATHOS (Gr. "suffering," "passion"). Evoking an audience's emotions in order to use them as a means of persuasion. In the *Rhetoric* (Book 1;1356a) Aristotle distinguishes three types of persuasive appeal: ethical (*ethos* [q.v.]); emotional (*pathos*), which depends upon putting the audience into a fit state of mind; and logical (*logos*), which depends upon the forms of proof or apparent proof. The orator has to study the emotions in order to know how to arouse them; toward that end Aristotle provides one of the first systematic treatments in the West of emotions and of the types of audience-members with which they are associated and consequently in which they are most readily aroused. As should be evident, there is a close relation between *ethos* and p., which continued to be exploited in the long trad. of writing "characters"—brief moral-psychological essays usually meant to assist orators with audience analysis. Too, the study of p., as seen in Aristotle and in later writers on religion and "physics," is relevant to discussions not only of the "soul" (*psyche*) but also of medicine; in the latter the subject became assimilated to the "humors"—mainly physical elements which gave a character or personality-type a propensity toward certain behaviors. With the rise of 18th-c. science, the newly established discipline of psychology began drawing to itself these formerly dispersed treatments of the emotions and contributed to the narrowing of the sense of the term "p." to merely the pitiable or sad. It is this abuse of the original sense of p. which is more properly linked to sentimentality (q.v.). The importance of p. as a means of persuasion—or as it is commonly referred to today, audience appeal—has never diminished in the study of rhet., or in rhetorical approaches to poetry. In the latter study, the traditional link between p. and the figures of speech—Aristotle, for example, claims that anger demands hyperbole (q.v.; Bk. 3; 1413a)—undergirds such modern stylistic approaches as "reader response" crit. (q.v.) and "rhet. of affect." The *locus classicus* of the general link between poetry and p. remains the Aristotelian theory of catharsis (q.v.), but here it is theorized that the arousing of emotions (pity and fear) in an audience at a tragedy (q.v.) is aimed not so much at persuasion toward an argumentative point as at purgation of the emotions themselves. See RHETORIC AND POETRY.—Sr. M. Joseph, *Shakespeare's Use of the Arts of Lang.* (1947), ch. 5, 9; J. de Romilly, *L'Évolution du pathétique d'Eschyle à Euripide* (1961); B. R. Rees, "P. in the *Poetics* of Aristotle," *Greece and Rome* (1972); S. Fish, *Self-Consuming Artifacts* (1972), *Doing What Comes Naturally* (1989); Lausberg; H. Plett, *Rhetorik der Affekte—Englische Wirkungsästhetik im Zeitalter der Ren.* (1975); C. Gill, "The Ethos/P. Distinction in Rhetorical and Lit. Crit.," *ClassQ* 34 (1984); Corbett, esp. 86–94.   T.O.S.

PATRIARCHY. See FEMINIST POETICS; INTERTEXTUALITY.

PATTERN POETRY, known also as "shaped poetry" (Gr. *technopaigneia*, Lat. *carmina figurata*), is premodern verse in which the letters, words, or lines are arrayed visually to form recognizable shapes, usually the shapes of natural objects. While the origins of p. p. in the West are unknown (a Cretan piece dating from ca. 1700 B.C. and some Egyptian pieces dating from 700 B.C. are not certain p. p.), there are six surviving p. poems by Gr. Bucolic poets, shaped as an axe, an egg, wings, two altars, and a syrinx. In late Cl. Lat. there is a panegyric cycle by P. Optatianus Porfyrius (fl. 325 A.D.) praising the Emperor Constantine the Great, whose court poet Optatian was. These poems are for the most part rectilinear or square, with "intexts" woven into or canceled out from the main text (hence their names *carmina quadrata* and *carmina cancellata*). This subgenre, revived at the Merovingian court by Fortunatus, was also popular in the Carolingian Ren. (Boniface, Alcuin, Josephus Scotus) and was the dominant form of the subgenre through the Middle Ages and into the 12th c., when the popularity of p. p. waned. Extant intexts are shaped as a galley with oars (Optatian) and a crucified Christ (Hrabanus

Maurus [784–856]; texts in Migne, *PL*, 107.133 ff.); about 70 late Cl. and Med. pieces are known.

A second and larger wave of p. p. began in the 16th c., initially written mainly in Lat. and Gr. by learned poets in imitation of the pieces in the *Greek Anthology*, but, later, in virtually all the langs. of Europe and in Hebrew as well, in such new shapes as suns, circles, pyramids, and columns, and in dozens of less common and unique shapes (see Puttenham, Bk. 2 ch. 12). By the 17th c., p. p. had become associated, for the most part, with occasional verse and was used to celebrate such occasions as births, marriages, ordinations, and funerals, though in Eng. such major poets as George Herbert (1593–1633) and Robert Herrick (1591–1674) wrote serious p. p.; Herbert's "The Altar" and "Easter wings" are the best-known examples in the lang. While from this period nearly 2000 pieces are known, a reaction against p. p. set in with the spread of neoclassical poetics (q.v.) in the late 17th c. It is difficult for a modern reader to understand the vehemence of the caustic comments heaped on p. p. in the 18th and early 19th cs., e.g. by Addison in *Spectator* no. 58. When p. p. was accepted at all, it was taken as suitable only for comic verse, e.g. "The Tale of the Mouse" in *Alice in Wonderland*.

But late in the 19th c., serious poets turned once more to visual poetry (q.v.), as in Stéphane Mallarmé's "Un coup de dés" and Apollinaire's *Calligrammes* (q.v.); and thousands of modern works have been composed in its several subgenres. However, modern visual poems are usually associated with avant-garde movements and assume some degree of originality, unlike p. p., which is usually mimetic and less abstract in shape than other modern forms of visual poetry such as concrete poetry (q.v.). Further, the shapes of p. p. often have their accrued traditions which the reader in older times would have known but which modern scholars are only now rediscovering (Ernst). Still, some modern poets, such as Dylan Thomas and John Hollander, have successfully experimented with p. p.

Close analogues to p. p. exist in many non-Western poetries, such as *hüi-wen* in Chinese (from the late Han, 2d c. A.D., up to modern times), *ashide-e* in Japanese (esp. in the early Tokugawa, 16th c.), and *citra-kāvyas* in Sanskrit (from the 7th c. A.D. onward) and other langs. of the Indian subcontinent. These latter are particularly interesting since, like Western p. poems, they are composed in traditional shapes and classified by these into *bandhas*, with each *bandha* having its own associations and traditions.

G. Puttenham, *Arte of Eng. Poesie*, ed. G. D. Willcock and A. Walker (1936); *Bucoli graeci*, ed. A. S. F. Gow, 2 v. (1958)—the *Greek Anthology*; Curtius; J. Addison, *Spectator*, ed. D. F. Bond (1965), nos. 58, 63; K. Jhā, *Figurative Poetry in Sanskrit Lit.* (1975); U. Ernst, "Die Entwicklung der optischen Poesie in Antike, Mittelalter und

Neuzeit," *GRM* 26 (1976), "Europäische Figurengedichte in Pyramidenform aus dem 16. und 17. Jahrhundert," *Euphorion* 76 (1982); C. Doria, "Visual Writing Forms in Antiquity: The *Versus intexti,*" *Visual Lit. Crit.*, ed. R. Kostelanetz (1979); G. Pozzi, *La Parola depinta* (1981); D. W. Seaman, *Concrete Poetry in France* (1981); J. Adler, "*Technopaigneia, carmina figurata,* and *Bilder-Reime,*" *YCC* 4 (1982); W. Levitan, "Dancing at the End of the Rope," *TAPA* 115 (1985); J. Hollander, "The Poem in the Eye," in Hollander, and *Types of Shape,* 2d ed. (1991); E. Cook, *Seeing Through Words* (1986); *P. P.: A Symposium,* ed. D. Higgins, Spec. Iss. of *VLang* 20, 1 (1986); D. Higgins, *P. P.: Guide to an Unknown Lit.* (1987). D.H.

PAUSE. Terms such as *p., rest, unrealized beat, implied offbeat, silent stress,* and *hold* have a confused history in prosody because (1) they are used inconsistently to refer to two quite distinct phenomena, one linguistic, the other metrical, and because (2) one major group of metrical theorists, those who scan by syllables and stresses rather than by measuring timing, usually deny that the metrical p. actually exists in meter *per se,* assigning it instead to the corollary domain of "performance" (q.v.). Everyone agrees on the normal linguistic p., determined by syntax and rhet.; ps. or junctures of varying durations are an essential component of speech, and since they are very imperfectly captured in orthography by punctuation (q.v.), linguists have devised several systems for more exact transcription. The question is whether a unit of time can replace a missing syllable or syllables in a *metrical* structure. This narrow question is the key to understanding one of the central disputes in metrical theory, that between the "timers" and "stressers."

A metrical p. can coincide with a syntactic p.:

x / x / (x) / x / x /
Pull off my boots: harder, harder: so
(*King Lear* 4.6.177).

But a metrical p., in temporal analyses, may also occur where we do not normally think of ps. occurring:

/ x / (x) / x / x / x /
As a huge stone is sometimes seen to lie
(Wordsworth, *Resolution and Independence* 57).

Recent phonological studies have confirmed what timers such as Coventry Patmore and Egerton Smith always maintained—that two adjacent stresses, even in prose, require either a separating beat or subordination of one of the stresses (Liberman and Prince; Selkirk).

If one accepts the existence of these two kinds of p., terminology might usefully be divided as follows: the metrical element is a *metrical p.,* a *rest,* or an *unrealized beat,* the syntactic and rhetorical element a *juncture, caesura,* or *extrametrical p.. Si-*

lence is probably misleading for both types of p., because no metrist insists on a complete absence of phonation after a preceding syllable for either type, and no one wants to specify as a relevant feature the point at which phonation stops. Some temporal analyses also hold that a p. can replace a stressed syllable, but this substitution is much rarer than that of a p. for an unstressed syllable. See also CAESURA; DURATION; ISOCHRONISM; METER.

T. S. Omond, *A Study of Metre* (1903); A. L. F. Snell, P. (1918); W. Thomson, *The Rhythm of Speech* (1923); E. Smith, *Principles of Eng. Metre* (1923); G. R. Stewart, Jr., *The Technique of Eng. Verse* (1930); I. Fónagy, "Die Redenpausen in der Dichtung," *Phonetica* 5 (1960); *Coventry Patmore's Essay on Eng. Metrical Law,* ed. M. A. Roth (1961); E. K. Schwartz et al., "Rhythm and 'Exercises in Abstraction,'" *PMLA* 77 (1962); M. Liberman and A. Prince, "On Stress And Linguistic Rhythm," *LingI* 8 (1977); Michaelides, s.v. *chronos, parasemantike*; D. Attridge, *The Rhythms of Eng. Poetry* (1982); E. Selkirk, *Phonology and Syntax* (1984). T.C.

PAYADA. An Argentinian song or ballad, generally anonymous, in simple meter, sung by popular poets who wandered the pampas. These modern troubadors were called *payadores,* and their improvisations were generally accompanied by the guitar. Its types included *vidalitas, cielitos, tristes,* and *milongas.* They began to appear in print in the 18th c. As in the Middle Ages, the p. was most often a poetic debate in the form of questions and answers, known as *contrapunto,* played before an audience which was both witness and judge. The famous mythical *payador* Santos Vega, so legend tells us, conquered the Devil in such a contest. The most celebrated p. takes place in the second part of *Martín Fierro* (*The Return,* Canto 30 [1879]), a long narrative gaucho poem by José Hernández and one of the masterpieces of Argentinian lit. This competition has highly dramatic overtones, as Martín Fierro is challenged by *El Moreno,* a man wishing to avenge the murder of his brother. This p. in *contrapunto* is not an improvisation but an integral episode of the poem (itself highly realistic) wherein the two contestants forget their rustic antecedents and sing of abstract ideas and supernatural themes.—F. Page, *Los payadores gauchos* (1897); L. Lugones, "El payador" (1916)—a well known essay; F. de Onís, "El 'Martín Fierro' y la poesía tradicional," *Homenaje ofrecido a Menéndez Pidal* (1925); R. Porter de la Barrera, "Los payadores de antaño," *En viaje* (1941); E. F. Tiscornia, "Orígenes de la poesía gauchesca," *Boletín de la Academia Argentina de Letras* (1943); I. Guerrero Cárpena, "Santos Vega y Poca Ropa, payadores ríoplatenses," *Boletín de la Academia Argentina de Letras* (1946). A.W.P.; K.N.M.

PEDES. See CANZONE; CAUDA.

PENTAMETER. In Cl. prosody, this term should denote a meter of five measures or feet, as its name says, but in fact the Gr. p., which is dactylic, does not contain five of any metra: it consists of two hemiepes (q.v.) with an invariable caesura: $- \cup \cup$ $- \cup \cup - | - \cup \cup - \cup \cup -$. Contraction of the shorts in the first half of the line is common; the second half runs as shown. P. is the conventional name for the second verse in the couplet form called the elegiac distich (q.v.), though this is probably a hexameter shortened internally (West calls it "an absurd name for a verse which does not contain five of anything"). The Cl. Gr. and Lat. p. should not be confused with the Eng. "iambic p.," despite the fact that the Ren. prosodists derived that name from Cl. precedent, for the Eng. line had been written in great numbers for two centuries (Chaucer) before it was given any Cl. name, and the internal metrical structures of the two meters are quite distinct—this follows form the deeper and more systematic differences between quantitative and accentual verse-systems (see PROSODY). Other terms lacking Cl. connotations which were formerly and are sometimes still used for the staple line of Eng. dramatic and narrative verse include "heroic verse" and "decasyllable" (qq.v.; see also BLANK VERSE; HEROIC COUPLET); which term of these three one chooses depends on what genealogy one assumes for the Eng. line (Cl., native, Romance, mixed) and what featuers of the line one takes as constitutive—feet, stress count, syllable count, or the latter two, or the latter two as creating the first one (feet). Despite the fact that trochaic tetrameters (see TETRAMETER; RISING AND FALLING) are fairly frequent in Eng., trochaic ps. are extremely rare—Shakespeare's famous line "Never, never, never, never, never" (*King Lear*) notwithstanding; virtually the only sustained example is Browning's "One Word More."—Wilamowitz; Crusius; Halporn et al.; Snell; West.   J.W.H.; T.V.F.B.

PENTHEMIMER (Gr. "of five halves," i.e. 2 1/2 feet). In Cl. poetry, a colon of the form $x - \cup - x$, which is the first half of the line in the iambic trimeter when the main caesura occurs after the fifth position. The corresponding first half of the dactylic hexameter with caesura also after the fifth position ($- \cup \cup - \cup \cup -$) is called *hemiepes* (q.v.). In both meters this caesura after the first half of the third foot is known as *penthemimeral*, while caesura amid the fourth foot (much rarer) is known as *hephthemimeral*. See HEXAMETER.— West.   T.V.F.B.

PERFECT RHYME. See RHYME.

PERFORMANCE (Lat. *recitatio*; Ger. *Vortrag, Rezitation*). The recitation of poetry either by its author, a professional performer, or any other reader either alone or before an audience; the term normally implies the latter.

I. THEORY
II. HISTORY

I. THEORY. The p. of poetry entails a performer, a setting, an audience, and a p. style. The term itself implies focus on the person performing, but in fact nearly all critical discussions (including this one) mainly concern the audience and its responses. Though poets naturally seem the most likely performers, from ancient times to at least the Ren., a class of professional performers or singers has usually been available for p. who have trained in delivery (see RHAPSODE; JONGLEUR; MINSTREL; SCOP; GUSLAR). The setting for p. may be a literary *salon*, a poetry workshop, a ceremonial civic or state occasion, or a quasi-theatrical p. at which a poet, poets, or performers address a wide public. By extension to electronic audio and visual media, ps. can also be disseminated via radio or television broadcasts; phonograph records, audio tapes, or compact disks; and videotapes or movies. A distinction should be made here between ps. which are live and static recordings thereof: the latter are merely fixed copies of but a single p. reduced in form and recoded into some machine lang..

It is also essential to distinguish between the p. of a poem and its composition. These two processes may or may not overlap. In the first case, the poetry presented in p. has already been transcribed as a written text, whether manuscript, scribal copy, or published book. This is the condition of nearly all modern, literary poetry: composition has been completed and the work has passed into textuality (q.v.). Here p. and composition are separated in temporal sequence.

In the second case, namely oral poetry (q.v.), no distinction exists between composition and p.: the "text" is spontaneously composed during p. by illiterate bards. Such a "text" is unique in every p. and is not normally recorded in any written form or even on tape except perhaps by scholars from Harvard. Successive recitations by even the same bard may draw upon the same story pattern, but the construction of scenes and selection of verbal details is different in every case; the choice of wording and phrasing is both controlled by—and assists—a stock of relatively fixed "formulas" (q.v.). These are at once both narrative and metrical building blocks, serving to construct both metrical lines and a coherent story. Here the written mode is simply absent. Even if one were to transcribe a recitation, the written record would be palpably derivative from only a single p. It should be noted that, in historical terms, the second class of course preceded the first—i.e. orality preceded the invention of writing, print technology, and the spread of literacy (reading). But even in modern literate cultures where written texts are widely published, spontaneous composition has re-emerged as a species of "secondary orality."

The audience is the least understood component of all performative arts: Western poetics has taken virtually no interest in this subject. It is obvious, however, that audiences often bring with them significant sets of expectations about subject, diction, tone, and versification. As Wordsworth remarked, the poet who would write in a new style must create the audience by which it will be appreciated—or perish. Some audiences are trained, but most are not. The exact degree of audience comprehension of oral texts is unknown: some verse traditions, such as OE, apparently helped auditors recognize meter with musical chords, for example. In general, it would seem reasonable to assume that audiences cannot quickly process archaisms or unusual words, complex meters or heterometric stanza forms, or distanced rhymes or elaborate sonal interlace. On the other hand, sound patterns are very much obscured by orthography, particularly in a lang. such as Eng. Sound patterning can certainly be recognized *as* elaborate in p. even when it is not evident *how*, exactly, the sounds are structured. It is a question just how much of poetic form is perceived in oral transmission.

In one respect, however, audiences have an easier time with the recognition of meaning in oral texts. Chatman isolates a central difference between the reading and scansion of poems on the one hand and their p. on the other: in the former two activities, ambiguities of interp. can be preserved and do not have to be settled one way or the other ("disambiguated"). But in p., all ambiguities have to be resolved before or during delivery. Since the nature of p. is linear and temporal, sentences can only be read aloud once and must be given a specific intonational pattern. Hence in p., the performer is forced to choose between alternative intonational patterns and their associated meanings.

P. styles are one of the most interesting subjects in prosody and have direct connections to acting and articulation in the theater. Jakobson has distinguished between "delivery design" and "delivery instance," the former set by verseform, the latter representing the features that are specific to each individual p. But between these lies the realm of expressive style. The two general classes of styles are realistic (naturalistic) and oratorical (declamatory, dramatic, rhapsodic, incantatory). C. S. Lewis once identified two types of performers of metrical verse: "Minstrels" (who recite in a wooden, singsong voice, letting scansion override sense) and "Actors" (who give a flamboyantly expressive recitation, ignoring meter altogether). And early in the 20th c., Robert Bridges argued that verses should be scanned in one way but read aloud another—clear Minstrelsy.

The triumph of naturalistic technique in modern drama has obscured the fact that artificial modes of delivery are well attested in antiquity, as reported by the grammarian Sacerdos (Keil 6.448). The evidence adduced by W. S. Allen (338–46) for "scanning pronunciation" and the demonstration of Ren. pedagogy by Attridge suggest that the practice of reciting verses aloud in an artificial manner has been more the rule than the exception in the West. Nevertheless, for dramatic verse which is metrical, particularly Shakespeare, actors learn that attention to scansion (qq.v.) will elucidate nuances of meaning in lines that a literal or natural delivery style will not manifest (see Hardison). Consequently, great actors learn how to convey both sense and meter together, so that each supports the other.

II. HISTORY. In Oriental poetry, the trad. of poetry presentation is esp. important in Chinese and Japanese poetry (qq.v.) and continues in 20th-c. Japan. Occidental poetry readings from the Greeks to the 19th c. have mainly favored invitational ps. in courtly settings. It is likely that ps. of poetry took place at the Alexandrian court of the Ptolemies (ca. 325–30 B.C.) and, at Rome, in the aristocratic residences of C. Cilnius Maecenas (d. 8 B.C.), who encouraged the work of Virgil, Horace, and Propertius. In Petronius' *Satyricon*, Trimalchio first writes, then recites, his own "poetry" to the guests at his banquet.

The fifth of the five great divisions of Cl. rhct., after *inventio* (discovery), *dispositio* (arrangement), *elocutio* (style), and *memoria* (memorization), was *pronuntiatio* or delivery. This was less developed in antiquity than the first four subjects, though Aristotle discusses it, as do Cicero (*De inventione* 1.9) and the *Rhetorica ad Herennium* (3.9), treating, like most subsequent rhetoricians, voice control and gesture. Quintilian devotes a lengthy chapter to the subject (*Institutio oratoria* 11.3). The practice of reciting Lat. verses was encouraged by all the Med. Lat. grammarians and central to Ren. education.

The Occitan troubadours (q.v.) retained professional performers to recite their verses (see JONGLEUR), though the poets of the Minnesang (q.v.) did not; other itinerant minstrels (q.v.) maintained themselves by recitation throughout the Middle Ages. Written poetry was recited at the 13th-c. court of Frederick II (see SICILIAN SCHOOL), in the Florentine circle of Lorenzo de'Medici (late 15th c.), and in the late 17th-c. *salons* of the Princes de Condé. In the 18th c., however, the patronage system gave way to one of public consumption of published books, and p. accordingly changed from a courtly to a public function. As a young poet of the late 1770s, Goethe read his work at the Weimar Court; on the occasion of a production of *Faust* to commemorate his 80th birthday in 1829, he personally coached the actors in the delivery of their lines. The 18th c. also witnessed the emergence of elocution as an important part of the theory of rhet.

In the 19th c., public recitations by both poets and their admirers became commonplace. The format was generally quasi-theatrical. Edgar Allan Poe in America, Victor Hugo in France, and Alfred, Lord Tennyson in England are examples of major poets noted for the dramatic quality of their readings. Tennyson is the earliest poet for whom we have an extant recording of a poet reading his own works. The work of Robert Browning was recited in meetings of the Browning Society (founded 1881), an organization which produced hundreds of offshoots in the U.S. in the 1880s and 1890s. A *Goethe Gesellschaft* (founded 1885) held readings in places as distant as St. Petersburg and New York. Wagner's opera *Die Meistersinger von Nürnberg* (musical version, 1867), based on the historical figure of Hans Sachs, brought the late medieval Ger. trad. of p. by members of craft guilds (*puys*) to an international audience. Elocution was even further popularized in the 19th c.; the practice of reading aloud from lit. after dinner in Victorian households was widespread, since they were not yet subjected to the brutalities of television and stereo. Elocution led to the emergence in the 20th c. of "oral interp." as a formal activity in Am. university departments of speech.

The p. of poetry is central to symbolist poetics (see SYMBOLISM). Mallarmé read his poetry to a select audience on designated Tuesdays at which the poet himself played both host and reader in oracular style. While Mallarmé's poetry was anything but spontaneously written, his ps. both personalized and socialized the work. Stefan George's mode of delivery was consciously influenced by Mallarmé: the audience was restricted to the poet's disciples (*Kreis*), and the occasion was perceived as cultic and sacral. George read from manuscript in a strictly rhapsodic style which disciples were required to follow.

In the 20th c., naturalistic or realistic delivery styles have owned the field. W. B. Yeats was much concerned with having his work sound spontaneous and natural. Though his delivery style was dramatic and incantatory, he deliberately revised some poems so that they would sound like an ordinary man talking (see VOICE). By contrast, T. S. Eliot's ps. were aristocratic in style and tonally flat. The Wagnerian prescription of having the performer seem spontaneous in expression but personally remote had its best 20th-c. exemplar in Dylan Thomas, whose dramatic, incantatory style contrasted sharply with the plain, conversational style of Frost and Auden. Frost's "sentence sounds" are the intonational patterns of colloquial speech, esp. as frozen into idioms—precisely the kind of speech effects that would be likely to come across well to audiences on Frost's frequent reading tours. The many recordings of 20th-c. poets have by now defeated the instinctive belief of many that the poet will be his own best interpreter, or that the poem will open up at last when once we have heard it aloud. Several poets—Pound, Eliot—read in a monotone specifically intended to thwart those expectations.

Politically motivated poetry readings early in the 20th c. served as models for others to come in the second half of the century. Now the poetry p. is the vehicle for political resistance and social activism. In post-revolutionary Russia, Vladimir Majakovskij sang the praises of the October Revolution in lyrics written to be read aloud; his dramatic ps. attracted mass audiences both in Western Europe and the U.S. (see RUSSIAN POETRY). Avant-garde movements of the 1920s and '30s such as dada and surrealism (qq.v.) generated ps. of poetry staged simultaneously with music, dance, and film, and so adumbrated the intermedia ps. later in the century. Poetry readings of the 1950s and '60s often took the form of multi-media presentations and random artistic "Happenings." Prominent innovators of the poetry p. in the 1950s were the Beat poets (q.v.), notably Allen Ginsberg, Gregory Corso, and Lawrence Ferlinghetti, all instrumental figures in the movement now known as the San Francisco Renaissance (see AMERICAN POETRY). Orality and p. were foregrounded in the poetics of Charles Olson, who conceived of the poem as a "field of action" and made his unit of measure the "breath group." Olson's "projective verse" (q.v.) found followers in Robert Duncan, Robert Creeley, and Denise Levertov.

Since 1960, New York and San Francisco have been the two major Am. poetry p. centers, with London, Amsterdam, and West Berlin their European counterparts. In New York City, the poetry-reading movement of the 1960s generally associated with the name of Paul Blackburn served as a stimulus for a new vogue of poetry readings in other parts of the country, esp. in Chicago and the West Coast. Further experimentation with elements of recitation, music, song, digitized or synthesized sound, drama, mime, dance, and video, which are mixed, merged, altered, choreographed, or improvised in seriatim, simultaneous, random, or collage order, characterized the phenomena variously called sound poetry, language poetry (qq.v.), intermedia, or sometimes "p. art" of the 1970s and '80s. David Antin called his improvisations "talk poems."

Since the 1950s, then, the p. of poetry in America has undergone a resurgence. Its tone ranges from conversational idioms to street lang. Poetry readings by one poet have become increasingly rare: "open poetry readings" are events to which anyone may bring work to read. Jazz or rock music, electronic audio and visual effects, and spontaneous dramatic presentations often accompany recitation. Consumption of alcohol or other drugs during the p. is not unknown. The ethos in intermedia events such as these is one of experimentation, liberation, and spontaneity. Like all postmodern literary genres, poetry retains a strong interest in p. as a reaction to academic formalism and its fixation on the text. It remains a paradox, however, that the new oral poetry has by and large chosen to disseminate its own works not on cassette or even video tapes but rather in traditional print—book—form.

The heritage of all the various forms of post-modernism in America has been a turning away from the autonomy (q.v.) of the text and the presumption that a text presents one determinate meaning (see INDETERMINACY) or its author's intended meaning (see INTENTION) toward the more fluid, less determinate, free play of readerly responses to texts. Hence critical interest has shifted from written documents to ps. as *experiences*. It should not be thought, however, that meaning is therefore removed: rather, it is merely relocated from the more patient and reflective process of reading and coming-to-understand a poem on the page to the more immediate, rapid, sequential process of trying to follow the poem when delivered aurally. Whether the meaning that is thus provided in p. is more or less extensive or fulfilling to auditors as opposed to readers is a judgment that only auditors and readers may make. Nevertheless, many audiences still consider the p. of poetry a communal, nearly sacral event for heightened speech, investing the poet with the transportive powers of the *vates* (q.v.). And many readers and teachers of poetry continue to believe that poetry achieves its body only when given material form, as sound (q.v.), in the air, aloud.

See also BOUTS-RIMES; EISTEDDFOD; POETIC CONTESTS.

JOURNALS: *Lit. in P.* 1– (1980–); *Text and P. Quarterly* 1– (1981–).

STUDIES: Thieme 377–78—lists 19th-c. Fr. works; F. K. Roedemeyer, *Vom künstlerischen Sprechen* (1924); E. Drach, *Die redenden Künste* (1926); T. Taig, *Rhythm and Metre* (1929); R. C. Crosby, "Oral Delivery in the Middle Ages," *Speculum* 11 (1936), "Chaucer and the Custom of Oral Delivery," *Speculum* 13 (1938); W. B. Nichols, *The Speaking of Poetry* (1937); S. F. Bonner, *Roman Declamation* (1950); D. Whitelock, *The Audience of* Beowulf (1951); K. Wais, *Mallarmé*, 2d ed. (1952); E. Salin, *Um Stefan George*, 2d ed. (1954); F. Trojan, *Die Kunst der Rezitation* (1954); S. Chatman, "Linguistics, Poetics, and Interp.," *QJS* 43 (1957), "Linguistic Style, Literary Style, and P.," *Monograph Series Langs. & Ling.* 13 (1962); Y. Winters, "The Audible Reading of Poetry," *The Function of Crit.* (1957); C. S. Lewis, "Metre," *REL* 1 (1960); R. Jakobson, "Linguistics and Poetics," in Sebeok; Lord; S. Levin, "Suprasegmentals and the P. of Poetry," *QJS* 48 (1962); F. Berry, *Poetry and the Physical Voice* (1962); J. M. Stein, "Poetry for the Eye," *Monatschefte* 55 (1963)—against p.; K. T. Loesch, "Literary Ambiguity and Oral P.," *QJS* 51 (1965), "Empirical Studies in Oral Interp.," *Western Speech* 38 (1969); D. Levertov, "Approach to Public Poetry Listenings," *VQR* 41 (1965); D. Norberg, "La Recitation du vers latin," *NBhM* 66 (1965); *The New Rus. Poets, 1953–1968*, ed. G. Reavey (1966); Dale, ch. 13; W. C. Forrest, "The Poem as a Summons to P.," *BJA* 9 (1969); G. Poulet, "Phenomenology of Reading," *NLH* 1 (1969); H. Hein, "P. as an Aesthetic Category," *JAAC* 28 (1970); P. Dickinson, "Spoken Words," *Encounter* 34 (1970); *The East Side Scene*, ed. A. De Loach (1972); S. Massie, *The Living Mirror: Five Young Poets from Leningrad* (1972); *P. in Postmodern Culture*, ed. M. Benamou et al. (1977); M. L. West, "The Singing of Homer," *JHS* 101 (1981); Brogan, sect. IV—bibl.; B. Engler, *Reading and Listening* (1982); K. Quinn, "The Poet and His Audience in the Augustan Age," *Aufstieg und Niedergang der römischen Welt*, ed. W. Haase, v. 2 (1982); B. Rowland, "*Pronuntiatio* and its Effect on Chaucer's Audience," *SAC* 4 (1982); O. B. Hardison, "Speaking the Speech," *ShQ* 34 (1983); E. R. Kintgen, *The Perception of Poetry* (1983); D. A. Russell, *Gr. Declamation* (1983); W. G. Thalmann, *Conventions of Form and Thought in Early Gr. Epic Poetry* (1984), ch. 4; J. Herington, *Poetry Into Drama* (1985)—Gr.; D. Wojahn, "Appraising the Age of the Poetry Reading," *NER/BLQ* 8 (1985); J.-C. Milner and F. Regnault, *Dire le vers* (1987); B. Bowden, *Chaucer Aloud* (1987); E. Griffiths, *The Printed Voice of Victorian Poetry* (1988); R. Schechner, *P. Theory*, 2d ed. (1988)—theatrical; M. Davidson, *The San Francisco Ren.* (1989); D. Oliver, *Poetry and Narrative in P.* (1989); G. Danek, "Singing Homer," *WHB* 31 (1989); H. M. Sayre, *The Object of P.: the Am. Avant-garde since 1970* (1989), "P.," *Critical Terms for Literary Study*, ed. F. Lentricchia and T. McLaughlin (1990); S. G. Daitz, "On Reading Homer Aloud," *AJP* 112 (1991); D. Cusic, *The Poet as Performer* (1991); P., spec. iss. of *PMLA* 107 (1992). T.V.F.B.; W.B.F.

PERIOD. I. IN PROSODY. In Cl. prosody (q.v.), a term used to refer to (1) any rhythmic sequence which is whole and complete in itself—i.e. capable of constituting an entire poem, but also of being used as one element alongside others in some higher-order rhythmic structure; or (2) any sequence separated from what precedes and follows by a break in synapheia (q.v.)—i.e. some sort of pause. Form (1) is thus what modern metrists would call a verse paragraph (q.v.) or a poetic sequence ending in closure (q.v.), and seems a much narrower category than (2). The latter includes not only stanzas and their major subdivisions, in stanzaic verse (see STANZA), but the individual lines in stichic verse (see STICHOS), as well as sequences such as the pentameter (q.v.) in the elegiac distich (q.v.) and a number of even shorter lyric segments which, unlike stichic units such as hexameter and trimeter (qq.v.), are never found as isolated, independent poetic utterances. The nature of the pauses to which such breaks in synapheia correspond and the reasons for their distribution within a composition are imperfectly understood: reinforcing closure is obviously one purpose, but probably not the only one. Caution in the use, and interp., of the term "p." is therefore in order. Dale distinguishes (1) and (2) as "major" and "minor" ps., Rossi as "p." and "verse." But not all metrists are so careful. See also COLON; FOOT;

METRON; PUNCTUATION; SYSTEM.—Wilamowitz, esp. 441 ff.; Maas, sect. 52; Dale 11–13; L. E. Rossi, "Verskunst," *Der kleine Pauly*, v. 5 (1975); T. C. W. Stinton, "Pause and P. in the Lyrics of Gr. Tragedy," *CQ* 71 (1977); Halporn et al., 6, 66; West, 4–6, 198.

A.T.C.

II. IN RHETORIC. The term "p." was taken over into rhet. from prosody for discussion of prose style. Cicero (*Orator* 174 ff.) credits Thrasymachus with the introduction of poetic rhythms into prose, Gorgias with the devel. of the figures or schemes, and Isocrates with combining the two, so that a rhetorical p. came to have both metrical and schematic form.

Aristotle (*Rhetoric* 3.9) differentiates between "periodic" or "rounded" style and nonperiodic or "continuous," the latter the more sophisticated form. He defines the p. in both structural (logical) and rhythmical terms, as a sentence "which has a beginning and end in itself, and a size which can be seen as a whole." Periodic style is pleasing because "the hearer thinks always he has a grip on something, because there is always a sense of completion," and comprehensible "because it is easily remembered; this is because the periodic style has number. . . . The p. must be completed also with the sense. . . . The p. may be either composed in cola or simple. A sentence in cola is one which is complete, has subdivisions, and is easily pronounced in a breath" (tr. Fowler). The end of the p. thus completes at once the sense and the metrical figure, but more the former than the latter, apparently; Aristotle recommends marking the beginning and end with a distinct metron such as the paean, but he discourages extensive use—even the paean he thinks unobtrusive—and none of his examples uses paeans at both ends.

Aristotle permits only two cola per period—this too came from metrics—perhaps because he emphasizes structures of antithesis, but later writers such as Demetrius quite reasonably allow more, and Aristotle allows periods of only one colon, denied by most later writers. The crucial point, however, is that good style is rhythmic, and that these rhythms flow either continuously or in periods, segments that are short enough to be perceived as a whole, complete themselves in sense, and are marked rhythmically as distinct segments. It is this segmenting and shaping which allows auditors to perceive structure. As Theophrastus puts it (Cicero, *De oratore* 3.184), one can count falling drops of water, but a flowing stream cannot be measured.—J. Zehetmeier, "Die Periodenlehre des Aristoteles," *Philologus* 85 (1930); R. L. Fowler, "Aristotle on the P.," *ClassQ* 32 (1982); Norden.

T.V.F.B.

PERIPETEIA. See PLOT.

PERIPHRASIS. A circumlocution, a roundabout expression that avoids naming something by its most direct term. Since it is constituted through a culturally perceived relationship to a word or phrase that it is *not*, p. has no distinctive form of its own but articulates itself variously through other figures, esp. metaphor (q.v.). Quintilian (*Institutio oratoria* 8.6.59) subdivides it by function into two types: the euphemistic or "necessary," as in the avoidance of obscenity or other unpleasant matters (Plato's "the fated journey" for "death"— cf. the modern "passing away"); and the decorative, used for stylistic embellishment (Virgil's "Aurora sprinkled the earth with new light" for "day broke"). The descriptive kind includes most periphrases which approximate a two-word definition by combining a specific with a general term ("the finny tribe" to signify fish). Pseudo-Longinus considered it productive of sublimity but, like Quintilian, warned against its excesses, such as preciosity or pleonasm (28–29). Later writers have characterized it as representing a term by its (whole or partial) definition, as in the expression "pressed milk" for "cheese." P. also appears in poetry that tries to translate culture-specific concepts from one lang. to another without neologism.

Though it is unlikely that any movement or era in poetry has succeeded in suppressing p. altogether, some styles favor it more than others. Curtius (275 ff.) associates it, like other rhetorical ornaments, with mannerism (q.v.) and marks stages in its use and abuse. Oral traditions frequently build formulas around periphrases, as in the patronymic "son of Tydeus" for "Diomedes"; these have important metrical functions and are not ornament (see FORMULA; ORAL POETRY).

While widely used in biblical and Homeric lit. and by Hesiod, the devel. of p. as an important feature of poetic style begins with Lucretius and Virgil, and through their influence it became a staple device of epic and descriptive poetry (qq.v.) throughout the Middle Ages and into the Ren. Classified by medieval rhetoricians as a trope of amplification (q.v.), p. suited the conception of style which emphasized *copia* and invention (q.v.). The OE poetic device of variation (q.v.) typically employs multiple periphrastic constructions, as does the kenning (q.v.), the characteristic device of Old Germanic and ON poetry, which in its more elaborate forms illustrates the connection between p. and riddle (q.v.).

Given new impetus through the work of the Pléiade (q.v.), p. proliferated in 17th-c. diction, particularly as influenced by the scientific spirit of the age, and even more so in the stock poetic diction of the 18th c., where descriptive poetry often shows periphrastic constructions (Arthos). Since the 18th c., the form has lost much of its prestige in the romantic and modern reaction against rhetorical artifice; more often than not it survives only in inflated uses for humorous effect, as in Dickens. Yet its occasional appearance in the work of modernists such as T. S. Eliot ("white hair of the waves blown back" for "foam") suggests that, insofar as directness of locution is not always the preferable route (direct speech being, most often, shorn of semantic density and allusive richness), p. has an enduring poetic usefulness. See also LEXIS.—P. Aronstein, "Die periphrastische Form im Englischen," *Anglia* 42 (1918); J. Arthos, *The Lang. of Natural Description in 18th-C. Poetry* (1949); Curtius; D. S. McCoy, *Trad. and Convention: A Study of P. in Eng. Pastoral Poetry from 1557–1715* (1965); Lausberg—fine compendium of Cl. citations; A. Quinn, *Figures of Speech* (1982).

W.W.P.; J.A.

PERSIAN POETRY.

   I. PROSODY AND RHETORIC
   II. GENRES
   III. MOVEMENTS AND SCHOOLS
   IV. CRITICAL TOPICS
   V. POETRY AND OTHER AESTHETIC DOMAINS

P. p. is that written in the New P. lang., after the Islamic conquest of Persia in the 7th c. The formal aspects of this poetry changed little until after World War I, and the poetry written in the traditional styles is generally called "classical."

I. PROSODY AND RHETORIC. In the period preceding the Islamic era, poetry was written in Pahlavi, or Western Middle Iranian, but its prosodic system is not clearly understood. Pahlavi meters were probably based on syllable-counting combined with a pattern of stresses. Some fragments of epic and didactic verse survive. With the coming of Islam to Persia, the Pahlavi meters fell out of use and Persians began writing poetry, probably in Arabic (hereafter Ar.) at first but soon in P. as well. When they began writing in P., they used the prosody, rhet., and forms familiar from Ar. Although Elwell-Sutton has argued convincingly for P. precedents for some of the borrowed meters, the prosodic system (Ar. *ʿarud*, P. *ʿaruz*) of cl. P. p.—i.e. the theory of prosody, the terminology, and many of the meters used by the Persians—was borrowed from Ar. trad. The traditional *ʿaruz* is based on 16 meters derived from patterns of vowelled and unvowelled consonants. The Arab prosodists (likewise the Persians) never conceptualized the syllable. Particular sequences of consonants and vowels were grouped into various three- or four-syllable "feet." Such "feet" were then used to build hemistichs (*miṣrāʿ*) of equal metrical length, two hemistichs forming a line (*bayt*) of poetry. Because of morphological differences and the fact that Ar. has a higher percentage of four- and five-syllable words than has P., the Ar. system of prosody did not fit the P. lang. perfectly and had to be adapted. The Persians did not use all the Ar. meters available to them, and also created a number of meters not found in Ar. poetry (q.v.). P. p. has end rhyme and occasionally internal rhyme at the mid-point of a 4-foot hemistich.

  The highly evolved array of P. rhetorical devices is divided into verbal devices (e.g. parallelism, paronomasia) and devices of meaning (e.g. metaphor, allusion) and bears some relation to the rhetorical systems of Gr. and Lat. poetry. Some common Western devices such as alliteration and consonance are not part of the P. rhetorical system, while others such as punning are more highly developed than in most Western poetry. Even in narrative poetry, each line should be a grammatically and syntactically complete and independent unit; enjambment is very rare.

II. GENRES. A. *Lyric Forms*. Poetic genres are defined by their content as well as form. The *qaṣīda* (q.v) is a poem in monorhyme (q.v.) the main subject of which is other than love. By the late 15th c., prosodists were describing the *qaṣīda* as a poem having more than 15 lines, where the first two hemistichs rhyme, and then each line carries this rhyme to the end of the poem, thus: *aa, ba, ca,* and so on. Some *qaṣīdas* run to over a hundred lines. The *qaṣīda* is an occasional poem, generally meant to be declaimed in public. Subjects can include praise, congratulations, invective, celebration, elegy, or religious or philosophical meditation. Many *qaṣīdas*, following the Ar. model, begin with an amorous prelude or a description of nature, then move to the main purpose of the poem.

The principal sources of poetry in the premodern period were royal and provincial courts and Sufi centers. Poets were important members of a ruler's entourage, and poetry was part of most public and private occasions. Most court poets of the cl. period wrote *qaṣīdas*, while the mystical poets, generally not part of courtly life, tended to write fewer of these poems. Popular or folk poetry, sometimes in syllabic meters, was also produced, but little survives, and much of that is in dialects.

Qaṣīdas were written from the very beginnings of Islamic P. p. Rudaki (d. ca. 940), the earliest poet from whom we have a substantial body of work, wrote *qaṣīdas* in a fully developed style which he used with complete confidence. This indicates that a considerable trad. of P. p. preceded him, though almost none of it has survived. Other early poets who wrote mainly *qaṣīdas* were Farrokhi Sistani (d. 1037–38) and Manuchehri (d. ca. 1040), of the Ghaznavid court. Naser-e Khosrow (d. 1072–77) wrote somber, contemplative *qaṣīdas* strongly colored by his Ismaili beliefs. By the 12th c. the poetic style was beginning to change, and the *qaṣīdas* of the Seljuk period were often vehicles to display the erudition of the poet. Anvari (d. 1189–90?) and Khaqani (d. 1199) were the most prominent poets writing on secular themes during this period. After the Mongol period, as Sufi thought began to permeate P. lit. and patterns of patronage began to change, the *qaṣīdas* gave place to the *ghazal* as the most popular P. poetic form.

The *ghazal* (q.v.) is a monorhymed poem, the subject of which is love. Amorous preludes to *qaṣīdas* were sometimes called *ghazals* as well. By the late 15th c., the *ghazal* was described as having

7 to 15 lines, and it resembles the *qaṣīda* in its rhyme scheme. The poet generally mentions his name toward the end of the poem. If the *qaṣīda* can be considered "public" poetry, then the *ghazal* is "private" poetry. Most P. p. is meant to be performed rather than read silently, and the *ghazal*, which is intended to be sung to music in an intimate gathering, expresses best of all many of the literary and aesthetic values of the Persians. The subject of the *ghazal* is love, and the prevailing mood is one of sadness, for love is not a joyful state in P. p. Longing in separation from the beloved, the brevity of moments of union, and the pain of unrequited passion are themes that dominate the *ghazal*, and the music to which it is sung reflects this sadness perfectly. As with the *qaṣīda*, the *ghazal* displays a certain unity, the nature of which is a matter of critical debate. The ms. trad. of a cl. *ghazal* is likely to show considerable variation in both the number and order of lines, although the first two and the last lines are usually fixed. In performance, lines are often repeated and are frequently separated from each other by musical passages, giving the listener time to savor the "point" of the line and the elegance of its expression.

The *ghazal* began to flourish in the 12th c. Two distinct paths, secular and mystical (with some overlapping and deliberate ambiguity in all periods), can be traced in its devel. The secular *ghazal* continued the course of secular love poetry and had as its subject earthly love. The speaker is the male lover. The P. lang. does not formally distinguish gender, however, and unless specific male or female attributes are mentioned, the sex of the beloved is ambiguous. This causes problems when translating P. *ghazals* into Eng., and translator's decisions about the sex of the beloved often reflect the mores of the period. The customary way of portraying the lovers in *ghazals* results in the creation of conventional types and roles, where the focus is much more on the use of lang. than on the expression of personal emotion. The secular *ghazal* reached its highest level of devel. in the work of Saʿdī of Shiraz (d. 1292).

The great flowering of mystical thought which began in the 12th c. produced some of Persia's finest poetry. The first important writer of mystical *ghazals* was Sanāʾī (d. 1130–31). The scope and imagery of the mystical *ghazal* were greatly expanded by ʿAṭṭār (d. ca. 1220) and brought to their highest level by Jalāl al-dīn Rūmī (d. 1273). Rūmī's *ghazals* are ecstatic poems of spiritual love expressed in the vocabulary of earthly love, a convention familiar to Western mystical poetry. Hence mystical poetry developed an elaborate symbolic vocabulary of wine and physical beauty, along with the imagery of earthly love.

In the 14th c., the two streams of the *ghazal* began to merge, a movement which culminated in the poetry of Ḥāfiẓ of Shiraz (d. 1389–90). Using lang. in a way unparalleled in the P. trad., Ḥāfiẓ extended and combined the imagery of secular and mystical poetry and created *ghazals* with multiple levels of meaning, all simultaneously present and inseparable. Read wherever P. culture was influential, Ḥāfiẓ's *ghazals* also made a profound impression in Europe, where they inspired Goethe's *West-östlicher Divan*.

The remaining sorts of lyric poems are distinguished by form. A favorite small genre of P. p. is the *robaʾi* or quatrain. A 4-hemistich epigrammatic poem rhyming *aaaa* or *aaba*, the quatrain was written by almost all poets and by most educated persons. The *robaʾi* meters are thought to be an indigenous devel., not derived from the ʿ*aruz* meters. The P. quatrain was made famous in the West by Edward FitzGerald, who translated a collection of unrelated quatrains attributed to Omar Khayyam (d. 1122) and made them into a narrative (1859, 1868, 1879; see OMAR KHAYYAM QUATRAIN). The *qetʾa* is a monorhymed poem except that the first two hemistichs do not rhyme. The principal strophic forms are: the *tarjiʾ band*, where *ghazal*-like stanzas are linked by the same rhyming couplet; the *tarkib band*, in which the same sort of stanzas are linked by couplets of different rhyme; and the *mosammat*, a typical form of which rhymes *aaaaax, bbbbbx, cccccx*, etc. The strophic forms are used in the same fashion as *qaṣīdas*.

B. *Narrative Poetry*. P. narrative poetry stands out among the Islamic literary trads. by virtue of its quantity, its range of subject matter, and its refinement. Written in the *maṣnavī* (q.v.) form (closed rhyming couplets), P. poetic narratives fall into the general categories of *epic, romance*, and *didactic*, subgenres produced continuously from the 10th c. to the 20th.

C. *Epic Poetry*. P. epic poetry is best exemplified by the *Shahnama* of Abu al-Qasem Firdawsī (d. ca. 1020–25). Using written and oral sources, Firdawsī cast a large part of the Iranian national legend into a poem of ca. 50,000 lines. The meter he used became so identified with the *Shahnama* that it was used for all subsequent poems in the epic style. By the time Firdawsī was writing the *Shahnama*, the P. literary lang. had become somewhat Arabicized, but Firdawsī apparently made a conscious effort at a style as purely P. as possible, and thus he is credited with preserving not only the national trad. but the P. lang. as well.

D. *Romances* were written in Persia long before the coming of Islam, and the trad. continued vigorously in the Islamic period. Produced in a courtly milieu, the P. romances had royal figures as their principal characters and emphasized the military and amorous adventures of the hero. Apart from romances within the *Shahnama*, the first important example of the genre is *Vis va Ramin* by Fakhr al-Din Gorgani (fl. 1054). Thought to be a recasting in New P. of an earlier Iranian story, *Vis va Ramin* has striking affinities with the story of Tristan and Isolde. But the most famous of the P. romance writers is Niẓāmī (d.

1209), whose five long poems were assembled into a *khamsa* (Quintet) that set a pattern imitated by many later poets. Four of these poems are romances about the lives of pre-Islamic figures: the Arab lovers Leyli and Majnun, the Iranian royal couple Khosrow and Shirin, the monarch Bahram V, and Alexander the Great. Niẓāmī was a master storyteller who wrote in a rich, complex, and subtle lang. far removed from that of Firdawsī. Niẓāmī's principal imitators were Amir Khosrow of Delhi (d. 1325) and Jāmī (d. 1492).

Horace's dictum that the poet should aim to blend instruction with delight could well have been said about P. p., whose *didactic* aspect is nowhere better developed than in extended narrative poems. *Shahnama* has its share of it, as do the romances, but there are many long poems of a deliberately didactic nature. The most popular ones are the Sufi narratives, beginning with Sanā'ī's influential *Hadīqat al-ḥaqīqa* (The Garden of Truth) and ʿAṭṭār's *Manṭiq al-ṭayr* (The Parliament of the Birds), an allegory of the soul's progress on the path to union with the Divine. The greatest of the mystical narratives is Rūmī's *Maṣvīyi maʿnavī* (The Spiritual *Masnavi*), a heterogeneous poem in 27,000 lines containing Sufi philosophy and ethics, meditations, anecdotes, and tales of all kinds. A work of more secular, practical ethics is Saʿdī's *Bustan*.

III. MOVEMENTS AND SCHOOLS. The trad. of cl. P. p. was conservative, although not rigid. Great stress was laid on adherence to the canonical poetic forms, from which no deviation was allowed. Innovation, as understood today in the West, was not valued. The subject matter of poems was restricted, the stock of traditional images was relatively limited, and a sense of decorum prevailed. Poetic style did evolve, but only by refining ever more subtly the received trad. In spite of what seem to be excessive constraints, P. poets were able to achieve an unparalleled elegance and refinement of lang. in both sense and sound.

P. p. is traditionally classified in four broad period styles. The Khorasani style prevailed in Eastern Persia from the 10th c. until the 13th and is characterized by a simple and relatively unarabicized diction. After the Mongol invasion in the early 13th c., the center of P. civilization shifted to western Iran, which was more under the influence of Ar. culture and lang. than was the East. The 'Iraqi style developed here in the 12th c. and continued until sometime in the 15th c. The Safavid dynasty gained control of Persia in 1500 and succeeded in converting most of the Sunni population to Shiite Islam. Thereafter, patronage for secular court poetry declined, and many poets left Persia for the more receptive courts of central Asia and Moghul India, where P. had become the lang. of culture and diplomacy. In this period the elaborate and complicated Indian style prevailed. In Central Asia and India in particular, but also in Ottoman Turkey, P. p. flourished greatly, and in-

deed, Indian style poetry was still being written in the Subcontinent well into the 20th c. In the mid 18th c. within Iran, a reaction to the Indian style set in, and there was a return to writing poetry in imitation of the Khorasani and 'Iraqi styles, a movement that lasted until the Constitutional Revolution of 1906. With the Revolution and World War I came a change in the relation of the poet to society. Court patronage almost disappeared, and poets found their new audience in an expanding middle class.

The Modern style began in 1921 with the publication of Nima Yushij's long poem "Afsana" (Legend), and soon Persians began writing poetry influenced by Western styles. In this context, "modern" implies not only experiments with line length, meter, rhyme, and larger form, but the presence of an individual voice in the poem, a striving for structural unity, and personal and social concerns as subject matter. A fierce battle between modernists and traditionalists raged until after World War II, when the modern style became firmly established. Some poets threw over all restraints of form and lang. and wrote poetry that acknowledged no debt to trad.; others developed an imagery that was almost hermetic in its private symbolism. By the 1960s, voices of the generation following Nima Yushij began to be heard. Ahmad Shamlu, Mehdi Akhavan Sales, Nader Naderpur, and Forugh Farrokhzad were the leaders of this generation. Each made his or her accommodation with the past while extending the range of poetry toward the future. A younger generation, more distant from Nima, were looser with rhyme and meter, and many struggled between demands for a socially committed, activist poetry and one more private, sometimes even mystical. But the Islamic Revolution of 1979 put an end to these movements and sent many poets into exile in Europe and the United States, where an active P. literary life soon emerged.

IV. TOPICS OF CRITICAL ATTENTION. Traditional P. crit. was essentially connoisseurship, demanding highly cultivated taste in the listener and formal orthodoxy on the part of the poet. Among modern critics, P. and Western, the production of reliably edited texts has been of the first priority. Studies of the artistic devel. of individual poets writing in the cl. style are practically impossible because poems are arranged in *divans* (collections; see COLLECTIONS, POETIC) alphabetically by the rhyme consonant, making chronological ordering almost impossible except where there are internal historical references. There has been some attention to the question of unity, particularly in *ghazals*, but it is by no means clear what, in aesthetic terms, P. poets considered to be a well-made poem. The question of the role of the poet in society occupied many critics in the 1970s.

V. POETRY AND OTHER AESTHETIC DOMAINS. Poetry was, until the 20th c., considered the primary literary medium; prose was held to be a workaday form suitable for scientific discourse but incapable of achieving the authority of poetry. Therefore prose was generally interlarded with verse, which served two main functions—either to confirm a point made in the prose or to serve as decorative embellishment. Poetry is most commonly found in the works of historians and bellettrists, and there is a special mixed genre of poetry and prose called *maqama*, of which Saʿdī's *Golestan* is the most prominent example. The relation of poetry and music has been mentioned above. Poetry and painting are closely connected by virtue of many poetic texts being illustrated with miniature paintings. Oral narrators recounting epic or religious stories, generally in verse, sometimes use large paintings as illustrations for their performance. Finally, the aesthetics of poetry and painting have some common features. For example, the worlds of the poem and the painting are often idealized and frozen in time, a garden where nature is at its most beautiful and changeless. Persons too are usually abstracted and not individualized, representing idealized beauty in a world lacking shadows. Often poetry is also used as part of decorative programs in architecture.

ANTHOLOGIES: *Sokhanvaran-i-Iran*, ed. M. Ishaque, 2 v. (1933–37); *P. Poems*, ed. A. J. Arberry (1954); G. Lazard, *Les Premiers Poètes persans*, 2 v. (1964); B. Foruzanfar, *Sokhan va sokhanvaran*, 2d ed. (1971); *Anthol. of Mod. P. P.*, ed. A. Karimi-Hakkak (1978); *LE&W* 20 (1976 [pub. 1980]).

PROSODY, RHETORIC, AND STYLISTICS: H. Blochmann, *Pros. of the Persians* (1872); F. Ruckert, *Grammatik, Poetik und Rhetorik der Perser* (1874); M. T. Bahar, *Sabk shenasi*, 3 v. (1942); M. Raduyani, *Tarjoman al-balagheh* (1949); Shams-e Qeys al-Razi, *al-Moʾjam* (1959); M. J. Mahjub, *Sabk-e khorasani* (1966); W. Heinz, *Der indische Stil in der persischen Literatur* (1973); L. P. Elwell-Sutton, *The P. Metres* (1976); F. Thiesen, *Manual of Cl. P. Pros.* (1982).

HISTORY AND CRITICISM: E. G. Browne, *Lit. Hist. of Persia*, 4 v. (1902–24), *Press and Poetry of Mod. Persia* (1914); T. Nöldeke, *Das iranische Nationalepos* (1920); Shebli No'mani, *She'r al-ʾajam*, 5 v. (1935–48)—P. tr.; Z. Safa, *Hamasa sara'i dar Iran* (1954), *Tarikh-e adabiyat dar iran*, 5 v. (1956–85); E. Yarshater, *She'r-e farsi dar ahd-e Shahrokh* (1955); I. S. Braginskii, *Iz istorii Tadzhikskoi narodnoi poezii* (1956); A. J. Arberry, *Cl. P. P.* (1958); A. Pagliaro and A. Bausani, *Storia della letteratura persiana* (1960); F. Machalski, *La littérature de l'Iran contemporain*, 3 v. (1965–80)—deals only with poetry; R. Baraheni, *Tela dar mes* (1968); M. Boyce, "Middle P. Lit.," *Handbuch der Orientalistik*, ed. B. Spuler, pt. 1, v. 4 (1968); J. Rypka, *Hist. of Iranian Lit.* (1968), "Poets and Prose Writers of the Late Saljuq and Mongol Periods," *Cambridge Hist. of Iran*, v. 5 (1968); Y. Aryanpur, *Az Saba ta Nima*, 2 v. (1971); M. R. Shafi'i Kadkani, *Sovar-e khiyal dar she'r-e farsi* (1971); A. Schimmel, *Islamic Lits. of India* (1973), *As Through a Veil* (1982); W. L.

Hanaway, "P. Lit.," *The Study of the Middle East*, ed. L. Binder (1976), "The Iranian Epics," *Heroic Epic and Saga*, ed. F Oinas (1978); J. D. Yohannan, *P. P. in England and America* (1977)—bibl. of trs.; J. Clinton, "Esthetics by Implication," *Edebiyat* 4 (1979); J. S. Meisami, "Arabic and P. Concepts of Poetic Form," *Proc. of the Xth Congress of the Internat. Comp. Lit. Assoc., 1982* (1985), *Med. P. Court Poetry* (1987); H. Javadi, *Satire in P. Lit.* (1988); *P. Lit.*, ed. E. Yarshater (1988).   W.L.H.

PERSIAN PROSODY. See PERSIAN POETRY.

PERSONA. An ancient distinction, explicit in Plato and Aristotle, is that between poems or parts of poems in which a poet speaks in her own voice and those in which characters that she has created are speaking. This distinction, refined and expanded in various ways, has been used throughout the hist. of crit. as a criterion for making discriminations among literary works and as a guide to the formulation of conventions for their interp. The term *dramatis personae* (or, more simply, "persons") has long been used to refer to an author's created characters, esp. as they appear in a drama.

Some 20th-c. critics have asked whether it is ever desirable to say that a poem—even a first-person poem—is the direct utterance of its author. Modern formalist and objectivist critics, who recommend that a poem be read as an autonomous verbal artwork, argue that the concept of a poem as an expression of its author's vision (q.v.), which dominated romantic views on the nature of poetry, distracts critics from their proper concern with a poem's internal relations; it sends them off on wild-goose chases after authors' intentions (q.v.) and forces them to raise the unresolvable issue of authors' sincerity (q.v.). It may be of great interest to discover how accurately a poem reflects its author's experience, attitudes, or beliefs; but this is a question that belongs to biography not to crit. Hence objectivist critics recommend that any poem, even a brief lyric, be regarded as "a little drama" (Brooks) and that the dramatic term "p.," rather than the name of the author, be used to refer to the narrator or speaker of the poem. Thus the lyric, which in the 19th c. meant a poem "directly expressing the poet's own thoughts and sentiments" (*OED*), becomes assimilated to the dramatic monologue (q.v.), and in thoroughgoing objectivist crit. the term "p." is applied indiscriminately to the speakers in Browning's "My Last Duchess," "Rabbi Ben Ezra," "By the Fireside," and "To Edward FitzGerald."

The use of "p." in this extended sense has been frequently attacked by critics committed to critical perspectives that stress expression or communication (see Elliott). But some of these critics have found other uses for p. Thus p. is sometimes used to refer to a speaker who, though obviously not the poet, is a spokesman for the poet. The poet either creates a fictional character (Browning's

The Last Ride Together or Newman's *The Dream of Gerontius*) or, more commonly, selects a historical or mythological figure (Tennyson's *Ulysses*; Browning's *Abt Vogler* or *A Death in the Desert*) and presents the experiences and utterances of this person in such a manner that the reader is led to assume a high degree of identification between that person's attitudes and those of the poet. The advantages that accrue to the poet from the use of such a p. or "mask" were discussed early in the 20th c. by Ezra Pound, W. B. Yeats, T. S. Eliot, and others. The mask permits the poet to say things that for various reasons she could not say in her own person or could say only with a loss of artistic detachment; it permits the poet to explore various perspectives without making an ultimate commitment; it is a means for creating, discovering, or defining the self; it prevents the poet from being hurt by self-exposure or being led astray by the limitations of her own vision; it is a means for expressing anxieties and frustrations, or ideals that the poet may not be able to realize in her own life but to which she is committed.

A third use of "p." in current crit. parallels that found in recent psychological and sociological studies of the self. (The bibliography of such studies in now immense.) Numerous attempts have been made to formulate theoretical models of "self," "personal identity," "role-playing," "sincerity," and related concepts. Depth psychologists use "p." to talk about the relations between the conscious and unconscious parts of the psyche; Jung opposes the p., the self a person assumes in order to play a social role, to the anima, a person's true inner being. Behavioral psychologists and sociologists stress the importance of role-playing—adopting appropriate ps.—for personality growth and successful performance in social situations. In these studies, distinctions like the following almost inevitably appear: the inner and outer; the hidden and the overt; the individual and the social; reality and appearance; the authentic and the put-on; the true self and the p. Similar concerns about the self are found in some versions of expressionist crit. Such theorists have held that one of the most important functions of poetry is to help resolve a poetic identity crisis; in this view, the best poetry reflects a process of exploration that leads to the discovery of the authentic self hidden under the disguises of various socially imposed ps. Readers of a poem are invited to inquire which self—the true self or a p.—a poet is projecting in a particular poem and are advised to assign less value to a poem whose speaker is only a conventional p. or whose image has been carefully crafted by the poet to produce certain desired effects on the audience. Innovation and originality (q.v.) become signs of authenticity; what oft was thought belongs to ps. In many ways these positions simply reflect the ancient quarrel between the values of individuality and conformity, freedom and restraint, and rebellion and order.

"P." is a polysemous term in 20th-c. crit. It refers to one of the speakers whose voice (q.v.) is heard in a literary work. The speaker may be dramatically present, or her presence and message may have to be inferred. Modern critics distinguish the voices of the real-life author, the implied author, the narrator, and dramatized characters (finer discriminations are possible; see Rorty). Furthermore, the voice may be that of a conscious empirical being; or it may arise from the depths of the individual or collective unconscious; or, as in Orphic song, it may be that of a transcendent being. It may also be a voice from the past, an echo or a resonance produced by a poet's use of allusion (q.v.) or quotation. It is unusual for a poem to present the utterance of only a single speaker (Bakhtin has suggested the term "heteroglossia" to refer to the multiple voices or langs. heard in literary works). There is no agreement among critics as to which (if any) of these speakers should be called a p. or as to what her relations to the other voices should be. Other difficulties are raised by theorists who wonder whether it makes any sense to speak of a "true self" (rather than just to "aspects" of a "decentered" subject); or whether, if such exists, a true self can ever be discovered (a reminder of Matthew Arnold's unsatisfactory search for his "buried life"); or whether, finally, it is possible or even desirable for the true Self to present itself to the Other on all occasions. See ETHOS.

W. K. Wimsatt and M. C. Beardsley, "The Intentional Fallacy," *SR* 54 (1946); Brooks; R. Ellman, *Yeats* (1949); M. Mack, "The Muse of Satire," *YR* 41 (1951); T. S. Eliot, "The Three Voices of Poetry," *On Poetry and Poets* (1957); R. Langbaum, *The Poetry of Experience* (1957), *The Mysteries of Identity* (1977); M. C. Beardsley, *Aesthetics* (1958); G. T. Wright, *The Poet in the Poem* (1960); P. Cruttwell, "Makers and Persons," *HudR* 12 (1960); R. P. Blackmur, "The Masks of Ezra Pound," *The Double Agent* (1962); W. J. Ong, *The Barbarian Within* (1962); N. Frye, *Fables of Identity* (1963); J. O. Perry, "The Relationships of Disparate Voices in Poems," *EIC* 15 (1965); D. Geiger, *The Dramatic Impulse in Mod. Poetics* (1967); L. Trilling, *Sincerity and Authenticity* (1972); J. Kirchner, *The Function of the P. in the Poetry of Byron* (1973); I. Ehrenpreis, "Personae," *Literary Meaning and Augustan Values* (1974); V. Buckley and R. Wilson, "P.: The Empty Mask," *Quadrant* 19 (1975); R. W. Rader, "The Dramatic Monologue and Related Lyric Forms," *CritI* 3 (1976); A. O. Rorty, "A Literary Postscript: Characters, Persons, Selves, Individuals," *The Identities of Persons* (1976); W. C. Booth, *Critical Understanding* (1979), *The Rhet. of Fiction*, 2d ed. (1983); M. M. Bakhtin, *The Dialogic Imagination*, ed. M. Holquist, tr. C. Emerson and M. Holquist (1981); R. C. Elliott, *The Literary P.* (1982); M. M. Winkler, *The P. in Three Satires of Juvenal* (1983); R. Selden, *Crit. and Objectivity* (1984), ch. 7; D. A. Lawton, *Chaucer's Narrators* (1985); C. Bedient, *He do the*

PERSONIFICATION

Poetics of Impersonality (1987).   F.GU.

PERSONIFICATION, as a manner of speech en-
dowing nonhuman objects, abstractions, or crea-
tures with life and human characteristics, has
been a feature of European poetry at least since
Homer and has been used in painting and sculp-
ture in every age. In rhet. this device is treated
under the term prosopopoeia (q.v.). Psychologically
and rhetorically, it may be described as "a means
of taking hold of things which appear startlingly
uncontrollable and independent" (Webster). But
the famous ps. of Strength and Force in Aeschylus'
Prometheus Bound parallel and challenge the fig-
ures of the gods in Cl. myth (q.v.); and, according
to the 20th-c. theory supported by Cassirer, Corn-
ford, and others, ps. replaced mythical figures
when rational attitudes superseded the primitive
imagination. The disposition for p. was reinforced
by the Stoic doctrine that abstractions when per-
sonified communicate demonic power.

In the early Christian era and in the Middle
Ages, the history of p. is closely associated with the
rise of allegory (q.v.), as in the Psychomachia of
Prudentius, The Romance of the Rose, and Piers Plow-
man. It was almost equally important in the devel.
of mythological poetry in the Ren. (e.g. Poliziano,
Spenser). Here, too, as in Ariosto's descriptions of
war and in Spenser's Mutabilitie Cantos, the ps.
aspire to the power and automatism of mythical
figures. Such is the central p. of Spenser's Hymn
to Love: "For Love is lord of truth and loyalty." The
apostrophe (q.v.) is a related figural trad.: Donne
addresses the p. directly in his apostrophizing
sonnet "Death, be not proud."

In the 18th c., ps. lost much of their emotional
and quasi-mythical power to the degree that po-
etry subscribed to the anthropomorphism of deis-
tic philosophy, but their vogue increased even as
they became, as in much nature poetry, barely
more than abstractions themselves. The following
enumeration of abstractions in Gray's "Ode on a
Distant Prospect of Eton College" shows how such
ps. had lost their capacity to produce emotional
effects like those in medieval morality plays or in
Milton:

> These shall the fury Passions tear
> The vultures of the mind,
> Disdainful Anger, pallid Fear,
> And Shame that skulks behind;
> Or pining Love shall waste their youth,
> Or Jealousy with rankling tooth,
> That inly gnaws the secret heart,
> And Envy wan, and faded Care
> Grim-visaged, comfortless Despair,
> And Sorrow's piercing dart.
> (61–70)

The devel. of symbolist poetry in the later 19th
c. (see SYMBOLISM) largely smothered this use of
p. as a figure in which the rational element is the

determining character. But it returned to fashion
again in Auden ("At the Grave of Henry James"),
while the more nearly mythological forms have
been employed in the 20th c. by Dylan Thomas
("The force that through the green fuse drives the
flower") and Ted Hughes ("Life is trying to be
Life"). See also ALLEGORY; DESCRIPTIVE POETRY;
MYTH; PATHETIC FALLACY.

H. Usener, Götternamen (1896); J. Tambornino,
De antiquorum daemonismo (1909); R. Hinks, Myth
and Allegory in Ancient Art (1939); B. H. Bronson,
"P. Reconsidered," ELH 14 (1947); E. R. Wasser-
man, "The Inherent Values of 18th-C. P.," PMLA
65 (1950); R. Trickett, "The Augustan Pantheon:
Mythology and P. in 18th-C. Poetry," E&S 6
(1953); T. B. L. Webster, "P. as a Mode of Gr.
Thought," JWCI 17 (1954); C. F. Chapin, P. in
18th-C. Eng. Poetry (1955); N. Maclean, "P. but not
Poetry," ELH 23 (1956); N. D. Isaacs, "The Con-
vention of P. in Beowulf," OE Poetry, ed. R. P. Creed
(1967); A. D. Nuttall, Two Concepts of Allegory
(1967); P. Valesio, "Esquisse pour une étude des
ps.," LeS 4 (1969); Lausberg; D. Davie, "P.," EIC 31
(1981); L. Griffiths, P. in Piers Plowman (1985);
S. Knapp, P. and the Sublime (1985); D. A. Harris,
Tennyson and P. (1986); Corbett.   J.A.; T.V.F.B.

PERUVIAN POETRY. See SPANISH AMERICAN PO-
ETRY.

PETRARCHISM. In the broadest sense of the
word, P. is the direct or indirect imitation of the
Lat. or It. writings of Francesco Petrarca (1304–
74), whether in prose or verse. However, it is in
connection with his It. poetry that the term has
most commonly been employed, alluding almost
exclusively to later imitations of or derivations
from his Canzoniere (or "Song-book"), composed
over most of his adult life and completed in its
present form in the year of his death.

Petrarch learned much from Dante, most esp.
the technique of playing off a complex, often
Latinate syntax against the various rhyme schemes
of the It. sonnet (q.v.). He drew on thematic ma-
terials employed by the poets of the dolce stil nuovo
(q.v.), incl. love through vision, the power of the
lady's glances, her angelic purity, her dazzling
beauty, and the anguish of unfulfilled desire, the
struggle set up in the poet's soul between admira-
tion of her purity and the desire to possess her
because of her physical beauty. From Dante's Vita
nuovo, perhaps, he learned the placing of individ-
ual lyrics in a cycle or lyric sequence (q.v.) depict-
ing the gradual victory of virtue over vice as a
result of the lady's influence. Petrarch also drew
on and developed many standard topics (see
TOPOS) of love, incl. the catalogue of lovely fea-
tures—e.g. hair like golden wires, eyes as blue as
the sky and sparkling like diamonds, lips of coral,
bosom white as snow (see BLASON)—and meta-
phors such as the eyes as windows of the soul;
precious metals, flowers, and jewels as symbols of

aspects of the lady's beauty; and fire as metaphor for lust and ice, its opposite, for chastity. Particularly important is Petrarch's fondness for word and image play—later termed "conceits" (q.v.)—illustrated esp. by paradox and oxymoron (qq.v.), e.g. the experience of love described as an "icy fire," and by images (e.g. love as a stormy voyage) elaborated over several lines or a whole sonnet.

The *Canzoniere* was an immediate literary success; poetic borrowing began even during Petrarch's lifetime in the 14th c. (e.g. Boccaccio, Ricciardo da Battifolle, Lorenzo Moschi, Cino Rinuccini, Chaucer), reached considerable proportions in the last half of the 15th c. (Poliziano, Sannazaro, Boiardo, the Marquis of Santillana), and became the predominant mode of poetic expression in the 16th c. not only in Italy but throughout most of Western Europe, with survivals even into the age of romanticism. Most of the lyric poets of the 16th c. and after, and they were legion, wrote under the influence of P. In Italy they include such first-rate artists as Ariosto, Della Casa, Michelangelo, Gaspara Stampa, Vittoria Colonna, Tansillo, and Torquato Tasso; in France, Maurice Scève, Louise Labé, Ronsard and his fellow-poets in the *Pléiade* (q.v.), and Desportes; in Spain, Boscán, Garcilaso de la Vega, Cetina, the Argensola brothers, Herrera, Lope de Vega, Quevedo, and Góngora; in Portugal, Sá de Miranda, Camoës, Bernardes, and Antonio Ferreira; in England, Wyatt and Surrey, Sidney, Daniel, Drayton, and Shakespeare, among many others.

In the 16th c. the cult of Petrarch spread from Italy to Spain, France, England, and elsewhere. Although the age celebrated revivals of such classicizing forms of poetry as the elegy, the ode, the pastoral, and the satire (qq.v.), and denigrated romance forms like the rondeau and the ballade (qq.v.), the sonnet was regularly cited as a brilliant form entirely compatible with the newer poetic trends, largely because of its association with Petrarch. Among Italians of the early 16th c., Pietro (later Cardinal) Bembo was a key figure. Bembo offered his own synthesis of Platonic love-philosophy in his dialogue *Gli Asolani* (1505); in his *Prose della volgar lingua* (1525) he called Petrarch's sonnets the ideal models for vernacular It. poetry and provided a close analysis of the Tuscan dialect in which they are written. Bembo also wrote Petrarchan sonnets of his own embodying his ideas about the ideal lang., love-philosophy, and rhetorical technique for vernacular lyric poetry. It is significant that he played down the Christian elements in Petrarch's sequence and reduced Petrarch's emphasis on complex syntax and conceit. Bembo was extremely influential. Among his immediate It. followers are two important women, Veronica Gambara and Vittoria Colonna. Later in the century sonnet-writing continued to proliferate. An important devel. is Torquato Tasso's writing of "heroic sonnets"—individual sonnets celebrating a great man or historical event—a form with precedent in Petrarch but quite different from the typical sonnet sequence (q.v.) of the age.

P. was introduced into Spain by the Marquis de Santillana (d. 1458) but did not become an established fashion until the 16th c.; the sonnets of Góngora mark the beginning of Sp. emphasis on the poetry of *ingenio* ("wit"). In France, although Clément Marot and Mellin de Saint-Gelais wrote Petrarchan sonnets in the earlier 16th c., the first sonnet sequence was Du Bellay's *L'Olive* (1549), followed by sequences by Ronsard, Desportes, and others. An argument has developed (see Simone) as to whether the Fr. sonnets reflect Fr. dependence on Italy or in some sense constitute a declaration of independence, in spite of their use of It. conventions.

In England, P. begins in the 16th c. with the translations from the *Canzoniere* between 1520 and 1540 by Sir Thomas Wyatt and Henry Howard, Earl of Surrey. After 1540, sonnet writing declines, although Petrarchan conventions continue to be used in other lyric forms. The revival of P. at the end of the century begins with Sir Philip Sidney's *Astrophil and Stella* (written ca. 1580; pub. 1591). Among the major sonnet sequences of the 1590s are Samuel Daniel's *Delia* and Edmund Spenser's *Amoretti*, the latter varying Petrarchan convention not by leading to worship of the lady in death but by pointing toward marriage. Shakespeare's sonnets appear after the major phase of Eng. P. (1609), and although they use Petrarchan conventions, they use them freely, being addressed for the most part to a young man rather than a lady and being concerned with themes like the need to beget children, poetic immortality, quarrels over an unfaithful mistress, and the aging of the poet. At times (most notably in the sonnet "My mistress' eyes are nothing like the sun"), Shakespeare experiments with anti-P., a style explored in Italy by Pietro Aretino among others. In the early 17th c., interest revived in Petrarch's use of conceits and his "wit" (*ingenio*; see WIT). At this point P. became an important contributing—perhaps even a shaping—influence on It. *concettismo*, and on such related movements as Gongorism in Spain, *préciosité* (q.v.) in France, and metaphysical poetry (q.v.) in England. P. characterizes the love poetry of John Donne and even carries over into his *Holy Sonnets*, which use Petrarchan motifs to explore religious themes.

On the whole, it may be said that Petrarch's followers, esp. in the 16th c., appreciated his inventiveness and correctly assessed the superlative lyric value inherent in the poems. Subsequent critical opinion of their work has generally held that (1) the "true" poets among these followers were able to use the collection as a model and still rise to lyric heights with a minimum of violence to their own artistic personalities, and that (2) numerous other poets indulged in imitation (q.v.) merely because it was a literary fad. Here, as elsewhere, the excesses of imitation in the hands of inferior poets led to a mannerism that became the object of ridicule. As a corrective to the disparagement of their work, however, Forster has argued that, given the social and literary motives for the widespread currency of imitation in the Ren., it "seems unreasonable to reproach them with imitating precisely those aspects of Petrarch's poetry which were imitable and with neglecting those which were not." In point of fact, P. represents one of the most revolutionary advances in the hisory of modern poetry.

See also COURTLY LOVE; LOVE POETRY.

J. Vianey, *Le Pétrarquisme en France au XVIe siècle* (1909); A. Meozzi, *Il petrarchismo europeo* (1934); E. H. Wilkins, "An Introductory Petrarch Bibl.," *PQ* 27 (1948), "A General Survey of Ren. P.," *CL* 2 (1950); C. Calcaterra, "Il Petrarca e il petrarchismo," *Problemi ed orientamenti critici di lingua e letteratura italiana*, ed. A. Momigliano, v. 3 (1949); L. Baldacci, *Il Petrarchismo italiano nel Cinquecento* (1957); G. Spagnoletti, *Il petrarchismo* (1959); J. G. Fucilla, *Estudios sobre el petrarquismo en España* (1960), *Oltre un cinquantennio di scritti sul Petrarca (1915–1973)* (1982); B. T. Sozzi, *Petrarca* (1963); D. L. Guss, *John Donne, Petrarchist* (1964), "Wyatt's P.," *HLQ* 29 (1965); J.-U. Fechner, *Der Antipetrarkismus* (1966); G. Watson, *The Eng. Petrarchists: A Crit. Bibl. of the* Canzoniere (1967), "Petrarch and the Eng.," *YR* 68 (1979); L. Forster, *The Icy Fire: Five Studies in European P.* (1969); A. Quondam, *Petrarchismo mediato* (1974); Wilkins; *Petrarch's* Canzoniere in the Eng. Ren., ed. A. Mortimer (1975); M. Guglielminetti, *Petrarca e il petrarchismo contemporaneo* (1975); F. Simone, "Italianismo e anti-Italianismo nei poeti della Pléiade," *La Pléiade e il rinascimento italiano* (1977); T. M. Greene, *The Light in Troy* (1982); T. P. Roche, Jr., *Petrarch and the Eng. Sonnet Sequences* (1989); R. Greene, *Post-P.* (1991).   O.B.H.; J.G.F.; C.K.

PHALAECEAN. In Cl. prosody (q.v.), a hendecasyllabic line which has the pattern x x – ◡ ◡ – ◡ – ◡ – x , so called after the Gr. poet Phalaikos (4th c. B.C.?). It is used at times by Sophocles (*Philoctetes* 136, 151) and Aristophanes (*Ecclesiazusae* 942 ff.); the Alexandrian poets employed it for whole poems, e.g. Theokritos (*Epode* 20), Phalaikos (*Anthologia Palatina* 13.6). In Lat. it is attempted by Laevius and Varro, but finds its deepest roots in Catullus (84–54 B.C.?), e.g. Ădēste ēndĕcăsyllăbī, quŏt ēstīs. Forty of his 113 extant poems are in hs., ranging in subject from love to invective. These have been imitated in modern accentual form in Ger. by Conrad Gesner (*Mithridates*, 1555) and in Eng. by Sidney (*Arcadia* no. 36), Coleridge (who makes [intentionally?] the opening trochee a dactyl) in "Hear, my beloved, an old Milesian story," W. S. Landor, Tennyson in "O you chorus of indolent reviewers" and "All composed in a meter of Catullus" (*Enoch Arden*, 1864), Swinburne in "In the month of the long decline of roses" (*Poems and Ballads*, 1866), and Hardy ("The Temporary the All," "Aristodemus the Messenian"). The rhythm is basically that of a trochaic pentameter. Nearly all these examples fall within the Catullan strain of Cl. imitations.—Hardie, pt. 1, ch. 8; Wilamowitz, pt. 2, ch. 1; Halporn et al.; West.   T.V.F.B.; R.A.S.

PHALLOCENTRISM. See FEMINIST POETICS; INTERTEXTUALITY; DECONSTRUCTION.

PHANOPOEIA. See MELOPOEIA, PHANOPOEIA, LOGOPOEIA.

PHENOMENOLOGY. See GENEVA SCHOOL.

PHERECRATEAN. See GLYCONIC; AEOLIC.

PHILIPPINE POETRY. A strong oral tradition—expressed as riddles and rituals in verse for planting and harvest cycles, war songs (*kumintang*), plaintive love lyrics (*kundiman*), and boat songs (*talindao*)—has kept alive the Indonesian-Malayan origins of Filipino culture. Typically, these have been characterized by quatrains built on 8-syllable lines; or 7- in the case of *tanaga*, whose core is the cryptically imagistic *talinghaga*. One of the most popular forms of entertainment during fiestas in rural Tagalog barrios is *balagtasan* (called *crissotan* in Pampango, *bukanegan* in Ilokano), spontaneous debating in verse that tests wit rather than reason. As relief during lengthy wakes, dramatic competitions in rhyme, the *duplo* and *karagatan*, are held. Losers forfeit objects which can be reclaimed only after a *loa*, a declamation similar to a riddle.

Two days are required to recite the epics of the Ifugaos, heirs to the ancient mountain rice-terraces. The *Hudhud* connects the tribal ancestors with the world's creation; the *alim* describes collective life among the gods. Muslim epics (*darangen*)—e.g. *Bantugen* and *Bidusari*—which require a week of chanting are valued for their absence of Western intrusions, whereas the Ilokano *Lam-ang* betrays the influence of 17th-c. Christian fathers. Among upland tribes scores of epics continue to assimilate modern events into ancient narratives.

No Sp. theme or form, despite 300 years of colonialism, successfully resisted local adaptation. The *pasyon*, for example, a dramatic singing of scriptural hist. at Eastertide, was originally introduced to pacify Filipinos through Christianization. Over time, however, it came to encourage nationalism because it stressed Christ's redemption of all people. Similarly, as early as the 17th c. the celebration-dance of converted Muslims inspired *moro-moro* plays (*komedya*) portraying costumed conflicts between Muslims and Christians in which religious differences gave way to poetic expression of festive tournaments and courtship. Filipinos developed extravagant translations of the Sp. *awit* (a chivalric-heroic romance in monorhymed 12-syllable quatrains) and *korido* (a legendary or religious tale in monorhymed 8-syllable quatrains). The most famous *awit*, *Florante at Laura* (ca. 1838), was situated in Albania in order to enable Francisco Baltazar (known as Balagtas) to describe Sp. tyranny without being censored. So effective is this concealment that the *awit* is as often remembered for the felicity of its Tagalog (the principal vernacular) as for its anticolonialism.

The elitism of Sp. rule prevented Filipinos from publishing verse in Sp. until late in the 19th c. Pedro Paterno's *Sampaguitas y Poesias Varias* (1880), the first collection of a Filipino-Sp. poet, had to be printed in Europe. More permanent has been Jose Rizal's "Mi Ultima Adios," a patriotic lament composed in Manila the day before his execution in 1896, an event which ironically helped provoke the revolution he had tried to prevent. For a time Rizal had lived in Spain with other Filipino *ilustrados* of the Propaganda Movement, which attempted, through Marcelo del Pilar's satirical verses, for example, to halt the Foreign Office's oppression in the colony. Fernando Ma. Guerrero, in *Crisalidás* (1914), carried on Rizal's libertarian views in Sp. but turned them against the new occupying force, the United States, which could not decide on a date for the islands' independence. For the same purpose, Tagalog was used by Jose Corazon de Jesus (called "Batute" for his romantic poems) when he wrote his 443-stanza allegorical narrative, *Mga Gintong Dahon* (The Golden Leaves, 1920) against Western imperialism.

In 1940, Manuel L. Quezon as first president of the Commonwealth awarded national prizes for lit. in Sp., Tagalog, and Eng. Zulueta da Costa's prize poem, *Like the Molave*, praises the nation about to be born in the declamatory style of Walt Whitman. Even simpler are the short poems of Carlos Bulosan, about troubled migrant workers like himself on the West Coast of the United States and, later, his wartime hymns. Far more experimental are the imagery and internal rhymes of Jose Garcia Villa, an expatriate in New York whose self-assertions find radiant expression, often compared with William Blake's, in *Have Come, Am Here* (1943) and *Volume Two* (1949). The latter contains his "comma poems," with spaces between words replaced by a regular filigree of commas, to enforce a stately and incandescent measure. Wordplay as encrusted correlatives of the perceiver's sensibility occurs as well in Virginia Moreno's "batik poems," Ophelia Alcantara Dimalanta's *Montage* (1974), and Edith Tiempo's *The Tracks of Babylon* (1966).

In Tagalog the counterparts of these opposing poetics—the socially committed and the resplendently self-expressive—have been Amado V. Hernandez, whose *Isang Dipang Langit* (A Measure of Sky, 1961) and *Bayang Malaya* (Free Land, 1969)

describe the struggle of a labor leader, later a political prisoner, to liberate the peasantry from poverty; and Alejandro G. Abadilla, whose free-verse *Piniling mga Tula ni AGA* (Selected Poems of AGA, 1965) is a protest in the name of personal independence.

Such contrasts signify the multiple heritage of the Filipino writer and, sometimes, bilingual skill. "Mestizo" poems by Rolando Tinio try to combine Asian and Euroamerican heritages by alternating lines in different langs. or providing a pastiche of langs. in a single line. *Sitsit sa Kuliglig* (Chitchat with a Cricket, 1972) and *Dunung-Dunungan* (Pretending Knowledge, 1975) include reminiscences of Tinio's childhood in Manila's slums and complaints against the neo-colonialism which keeps the Filipino economically dependent. Other writers have produced poems or books in alternating langs. Alejandrino Hufana supplemented the epic portraits in *Poro Point* (1961) and his long narrative *Sieg Heil* (1975) with occasional lyrics and Ilokano lullabies. To Cirilo Bautista's early volumes—*The Cave* (1968), an Orphic descent into the "minotaur" caves of Lascaux in the Pyrenees; *The Archipelago* (1970), a chronicle of the *conquistadores*; and *Telex Moon* (1981)—have been added *Sugat na Salitâ* (Wounds of Words, 1986). Marra Pl. Lanot devotes a third of *Passion and Compassion* (1981) to poems of social protest in Filipino, the national lang. Her themes typify the liberal-radical defiance of writers during the dictatorial rule (1965–86) of Ferdinand Marcos. A variety of such poems appear in the multilingual volume, *Versus*, edited by Salanga and Pacheco (1986).

No poet writes in more langs. or on more diverse themes then Federico Licsi Espino, Jr., whose chapbook output has been prolific, exemplified by *In Three Tongues* (1963), *Dark Sutra* (1969), and *In the Very Torrent* (1975). Among persons working in Filipino, Virgilio S. Almario (Rio Alma) ranks foremost, as his translations into Eng., *Selected Poems 1968–1985*, (1987), demonstrate. His *Doktrinang Anakpawis* (Worker's Manifesto, 1979) sacrifices nothing of difficult art to its identification with the oppressed and impoverished. More understated and conversational but equally nonconformist politically are Jose F. Lacaba's poems in *Mga Kagilagilalas na Pakikipagsapalaran* (Feats of Chance, 1979).

Ricaredo Demetillo, almost alone, has regularly resisted the trend to identify ethnic pride with either the national lang. or the eight dominant vernaculars. Since *No Certain Weather* (1956), he has published only in Eng., incl. the spiritual pilgrimage *La Via* (1958); the epic encounter of dissidents from Brunei with pygmy aborigines on Panay in the 13th c., *Barter in Panay* (1961), *The Heart of Emptiness in Black* (1974); the crosscultural mural of literary and visual artists, *Masks and Signatures* (1968); and his meditations on morality, in *The Scarecrow Christ* (1973) and *Lazarus, the Troubadour* (1974).

Politicization of P. p. has been inevitable, given centuries of uneasy acquiescence to foreign rule. Poetry served resistance movements determined to achieve national self-definition. Critics and anthologists memorialize these efforts over and above hundreds of transitory love lyrics, even when suffering and loss animate both. Yet only occasionally have they failed to distinguish between naked manifesto and poetic merit; and despite recurrent appeals for the exclusive use of Filipino, the cosmopolitanism of so many writers due to the confluence of cultures regularly demonstrates the Filipinos' ability to adapt opportunities from abroad to their own perceived needs.

ANTHOLOGIES: *New Writing from the Philippines*, ed. L. Casper (1964); *Walong Dekada ng Makabagong Tulang Pilipino*, ed. V. Almario, (1981); *P. Lit.*, ed. B. and C. N. Lumbera (1982).

HISTORY AND CRITICISM: V. Almario, *Ang Makata sa Panahon ng Makina* (1972); O. Dimalanta, *The P. Poetic* (1976); R. Ileto, *Pasyon and Revolution* (1979); *Salimbibig*, ed. J. Galdon (1980); *Balagtasismo vs. Modernismo*, ed. V. Almario (1984); B. Lumbera, *Tagalog Poetry, 1570–1898* (1986); L. Casper, *Firewalkers* (1987); R. Demetillo, *Major and Minor Keys* (1987); D. L. Eugenio, *Awit and Corrido: P. Metrical Romances* (1987). L.C.

PHILOSOPHY AND POETRY (hereafter ph. and p.). The activity of philosophical reflection or disputation can hardly be identical with the activity of composing a poem. But a text can embody the outcome of both activities. The trad. of contrasting p. with ph. as two distinct forms of discourse stems from Plato's *Republic*, which insists on an "ancient war" between them. A persistent trad. in rhetorical theory, however, denies the validity of the contrast, arguing that every text has an intelligible content ("philosophy"), a formal structure ("poetry"), and a practical standpoint ("rhetoric"), and that any discourse in which these are pursued exclusively or independently is necessarily impoverished and perverted. But the conceptual and practical conflict envisaged by Plato still remains recognizable 2500 years later.

A philosophical text may be written in verse form for any of a number of reasons. The author may judge that rhyme or metrical form will add an attraction to the philosophical content; or it may be felt that the dignity of the subject requires the dignity of verse; or there may be a standing convention, not further explained, that philosophical texts should be in verse; or the author may rely on an expectation that verse will be read more attentively than prose. But Aristotle claimed (*Poetics*) that the fact that a philosophical (or any other) text was written in verse did not suffice to impart a poetical character to that text. Any text may, however, be poetic in two further senses. First, the text may resist literal interp. altogether—may have no determinate prose meaning.

Second, the text may be deeply figurative in texture, or in structure, or in both. In the second kind of case, the poetic aspect of the text may be thought of as adding a dimension to a discourse that might have existed without it. In such a case, the philosophical content of the poem may be potentially or actually statable in a nonpoetic form (see THEME; cf. PARAPHRASE, HERESY OF). If so, the ph. may be that of an individual author (who may be the poet himself, as with Bridges' *Testament of Beauty*, or someone else, as with Lucretius' *De rerum natura*), or may consist of beliefs or problems more widely diffused (as with Pope's *Essay on Man* or Tennyson's *In Memoriam*).

In the West, philosophical works that resist literal or prosaic reading are rare. One example is the poem of Parmenides, of which both the structure and the grammar defy paraphrase. Similarly, Blake's "prophetic" writings, and much of Nietzsche contain what seems to be a definite philosophic teaching until one attempts to paraphrase it. More generally, myths of origin in many civilizations may be read as equally poetic and philosophic, imagery and cosmology having equal cogency, though it is often argued that such myths are neither true p. nor true ph. Other works (Ezra Pound's *Cantos*, Edward Dorn's *Gunslinger*) are didactic in manner without it being quite possible to say what doctrine is imparted (see DIDACTICISM). Most often, a poem may lack a specifiable philosophic content and yet employ its full linguistic, rhythmic, imagistic, and figurative resources to open up new insights into values, relationships, and significant possibilities such as could not be restated without gross distortion outside the particular poetic structure that expresses them. Shakespeare's *King Lear* and Keats's "Ode on a Grecian Urn" illustrate this last type.

Even where an explicit ph. serves as the main subject or theme of the poem, it is never identical with the whole of the integral ph. that is being poetically expressed. Success in conveying explicit ph. in good p. usually comes from using lang. in such a way as to generate implicit thoughts, adumbrated by poetic rather than logical means, so as to deepen and enliven the explicit teachings that furnish the scenario of the poem. In *De rerum natura*, the very opening line of the poem— "Aeneadum genetrix, hominum divumque voluptas" (O Mother of the race of Aeneas, the delight of men and of gods)—announces the philosophical themes to follow by doing three things at once: it sets a Roman tone for the poem by its reference to Aeneas; it invokes Venus in her dual aspect of desirable femininity and bounteous motherhood; and it acknowledges the power of the goddess, by arousing love, to produce and sustain life. The poem thus introduced transforms the dry mechanism of Epicurean atomism, of which nothing is sacrificed or falsified, into a drama of political alliance, sentimental attraction, creative fecundity, and longing, the whole expressing a fervor of intellectual allegiance.

The foregoing distinction between explicit and implicit ph. finds a counterpart in T. S. Eliot's distinction ("Dante," 1929, rpt. in Eliot, *Essays*) between the intellectual lucidity that compels belief and the poetic lucidity that commands "poetic assent." In Dante's *Divine Comedy*, where the philosophical beliefs are logically and overtly those of the theologians of the day, the assent of someone adequately responding to the poem must be different from the "belief attitude" of the same person reading the *Summa theologiae* of Aquinas. Eliot points out that the *Commedia*, unlike the *Summa*, is constructed according to a "logic of sensibility" representing "a complete scale of the depth and height of human emotion": the poetic assent, which is to say the total belief attitude, of Dante and his reader is inseparable from the elaboration of images which are "not merely antiquated rhetorical devices, but serious and practical means of making the spiritual visible." Eliot's distinction between two forms of persuasion and assent, both involving the intellect, is not to be confused with I. A. Richards' distinction between poetic meaning, which works on the emotions, and scientific meaning, which calls for the allocation of truth values (*Principles of Lit. Crit.* [1924], ch. 34).

The view that ph. and p. have something important in common was first stated by Aristotle in his remark that "p. is more philosophical than history, for p. deals with universals, history with particulars" (*Poetics*). In this, Aristotle is no doubt responding to the Platonic allegation that ph. and p. are at war. P. works on the emotions, and is thus useful in the moral training of children and in the promotion of socially desirable attitudes; but in its reliance on emotion and imagery it works against the philosophical reasoning on which truth and sound policy must rest. Ph. deals with intelligible essences that are nowhere perfectly exemplified; p. deals, not even with the deeds that imperfectly manifest the personalities that imperfectly exemplify those essences, but with only so much of those deeds as can be put into words. A literary education thus offers, says Plato, attractive illusions in place of truth. Aristotle, on the other hand, holds that essences are realized in the natural world itself, though in any particular case the realization will be imperfect and overlaid with accidental features. The poet, whose creations eliminate such accidents, is accordingly closer in fact to the truth than an unimaginative chronicler.

Plato's criticism of Homer's portrayal of the gods ran afoul of his evident reverence for the poet's literary power. The resulting tension was taken up and given new meaning in the first centuries of the present era, when it seemed necessary to reconcile the inviolable wording of a sacred text (Homer, the Bible) with the tenets of a doctrine held to be certainly true (Neoplatonic metaphysics; the doctrines of revealed religion). The attempt at reconciliation called for intensive inquiry into the forms and functions of symbolism and allegory (q.v.). Some schematic paragraphs of Macrobius (*Commentary on the Dream of Scipio*, 4th c. A.D.), apparently derived from Porphyry's recent commentary on Plato's *Republic*, laid down guidelines in this regard that remained influential throughout the Middle Ages. Such excogitation of rules for finding predetermined meanings in texts whose apparent meaning is something quite different seems to have little to do with p. or ph. as such. But the prevailing philosophical and theological doctrines argued that the ultimate realities of the universe must transcend conceptual thought, so that a fantastic narrative (such as the *Odyssey*) that could not be read naturalistically might after all be the best way to achieve such representation of those realities as is possible. The argument is powerful though hard to apply convincingly since reading ineffable truths into unintelligible texts is a tricky business at best.

Aristotle, unlike Plato and his followers, nowhere suggests that p. either rivals or assists ph. But he holds that "art" generally, in the sense of systematic exercises of human skill, "partly imitates nature and partly carries to completion what nature has left incomplete" (*Physics* 2). Later adapters of Aristotelian principles were accordingly able to think of p. as "imitating" nature, not only by representing a "golden" world free from irrelevances but by creating alternative realities and by expressing, not the essences of things as nature produces them (*natura naturata*), but the creative principles by which nature operates (*natura naturans*).

This idea that p. at once reflects and develops the activity of creative nature takes on special significance in the romantic era, esp. in Germany. The decisive influence seems to have been that of J. G. Hamann (1730–88), who taught that "The whole world is the lang. of God, and p. is therefore nothing but the imitation of this lang." Poetic knowledge, archetypally exemplified in myth (q.v.), is the paradigm of all knowledge and hence, by implication, of ph.

The equation of p. with ph. was adopted by many Ger. writers, though to effect the equation they had to divest one or the other if not both terms of their usual meaning. J. G. Herder (1744–1803) reduced Hamann's ideas to a human scale. The paradigm of p. was now not myth but lyric (q.v.), the function of which was to forge the imagery (q.v.) which was the basic form of lang. and hence the foundation of all human thought (*Abhandlung über den Ursprung der Sprache* 2[1770]). According to A. W. Schlegel (1765–1845), the practice of p. re-enacts on a higher level the creation of lang. itself (*Vorlesungen über schönen Literatur und Kunst* [1884]). Goethe (1746–1832) held that the true role of the mind in understanding the world is not to impose its own laws on an alien reality, but a "thinking in objects" (*gegenständliches Denken*) that discovers the harmonies and analogies between the creative processes of nature and art, and thus comes to grasp archetypes (q.v.) that are present in both of them. Unlike the Platonic "Form," however, the Goethean archetype exists only in and through particulars, and thus can be known only by one who is responsively open to the sensuously living world. Among the sensuous, the mind is to discover "eminent instances," each of which is "a living-moment disclosure of the inscrutable"—a disclosure that would never have been made were it not for just this individual manifestation. P. thus has, by its very nature, something of the character of revelation, not because it proclaims universal truths as such but because "by grasping the particular in its living character it implicitly apprehends the universal along with it" (see CONCRETE UNIVERSAL).

Goethe, unlike Herder, has no distinctive theory of p. as opposed to art in general. His idea that p. grasps a universal tendency through a characteristic instance survives to form the animating idea of Marxist aesthetics, and finds elaborate expression in the neo-Marxist theory of art formulated by G. Lukács (1885–1971). The belief that such insights amount to ph. was, however, implicitly opposed by F. Schiller (1759–1805) under the influence of Kant's *Critique of Judgment* (1790). Schiller rejects the very idea of philosophical p., contrasting the conceptual articulation of philosophical lang. with the imaginative presentations of p.: "P. wants intuitions; lang. offers only concepts."

The contrast between ph. and p. was rearticulated formidably by G. W. F. Hegel (1770–1831). He argued that the function of the fine arts had always been to achieve beauty by finding an adequate expression of the Divine in sensuous form—the Divine being, in effect, the essence of humanity as self-conscious reality. Sculpture is the "classically" beautiful art, in which human perfection is made as visible as it can be, but sculpture cannot actually give form to the human spirit. Hence, the highest arts are the "romantic," in which the visible form suggests what it cannot embody, and of these p. is the highest because its sounding fabric is itself inherently symbolic—the medium of p. is, as Schiller had suggested, pure imagination (q.v.): "P. is adequate to all forms of the beautiful and extends over all of them, because its proper element is beautiful imagination, and imagination is indispensable for every beautiful production, no matter to what form of art it belongs" (Intro. to *Ästhetik* [1834]). Even in p., however, though the ideas expressed them, the systematic work necessary to grasp the Absolute is not essayed: "At this highest stage art now transcends itself, in that it forsakes the element of a reconciled embodiment of the spirit in sensuous form and passes over from the p. of the imagination to the prose of thought." Hegel's critics wonder whether ph., in surpassing p. in this way, has really superseded

rather than complemented it. The question is taken up by B. Croce (1866–1952), among others.

Other writers in the Ger. romantic trad. (including the Schlegel brothers and F. W. J. von Schelling [1775–1854]) assimilated poetic vision to philosophic understanding, but without providing suitably clear notions of what p. and ph. respectively are. In England, Coleridge borrowed and adapted their way of relating poetic insight to the Neoplatonic trad. in Christian thought. All imagination is "a repetition in the finite mind of the eternal act of creation in the infinite I AM" (*Biographia literaria* [1817], ch. 13); and to unite themselves with that act is the mission of all such minds. But the imagination takes two forms: the primary imagination, the "living power and prime agent of all human perception" (much the same as Kant's "transcendental unity of apperception"), the general ground of our ability to grasp the world as a world, and the "secondary imagination" whereby the poet envisages and brings into being artistic worlds that symbolize the real world in the process of which they share. There is thus a firm continuity between the genuine philosophical insights of poets and their poetic creations. That poets are "philosophers of the very loftiest power" was also asserted by Shelley (1792–1822), but his eloquent restatement of some main themes from Ger. romanticism adds nothing distinctively his own (*A Defence of P.* [1821]).

Subsequent attempts to relate p. to ph., such as that of Schopenhauer (1788–1860), mostly sought to establish a more general relationship between ph. and art, which p. merely exemplifies. One influential exception has been M. Heidegger (1889–1976), in whose later thought ph. is regarded as an activity of deep reflection in which a space is cleared for Being to appear (*Einführung in die Metaphysik* [1935]). Heidegger's deepest roots are in Ger. literary romanticism, and it seems that the kind of meditation he has in mind is better exemplified by the p. of Hölderlin than by any professed philosopher. The difference between poetic creation and philosophic reflection is hard to make out, but corresponds roughly to the traditional claim (derived from Plato) that ph. seeks to establish the nature of objective reality whereas p. explores the subjective world of experience (see SUBJECTIVITY AND OBJECTIVITY). Philosophic reflection (*Denken*) lays itself questioningly open to Being, the putative ground of all beings; in p. (*Dichtung*), the lang. in which we dwell lays us correspondingly open to the ground of our indwelling in the world: earth, heaven, home. "The thinker *says* Being, whereas the poet *names* the holy" (Kockelmans).

Heidegger's distinction between philosophic affirmation and poetic invocation represents the widespread survival into our own day of the theory of Herder and Schlegel, which assigns to p. a cognitive role in the origination of lang. Before langs. can combine lexical items in syntactic structures, the mental items to which words will correspond must be formulated. At the basis of ph. lies the poetic intuition, expressed in a symbol (q.v.), a unified complex of thought and feeling (as envisaged in the poetic theories of symbolism and imagism [qq.v.]). Ph. is thus dependent on p. This theory is extended to apply to art in general, but it fits p. best. Croce, its most articulate and influential exponent, increasingly came to regard lyric p. as the paradigm of art.

A rapprochement between lit. and ph. is characteristic of 20th-c. existentialism. This ph. proceeds from the insight that we have access to reality in two ways, both by observing and encountering it and by living it, and that the latter mode of being ("existence") must take priority in any ph. that is not self-deceiving. In the work of A. Camus (1913–60) and J.-P. Sartre (1905–80), and earlier in the work of S. Kierkegaard (1819–55; *Synspunktet för min Forfatter-Virksomhed*, tr. as *The Point of View for My Work as an Author* [1859]), the imaginative presentation of modes of experience in literary form seems to be a major tool of ph. But the lit. in question is prose narrative or drama, not p. as such. Prose effects communication, p. expresses despair of communicating, says Sartre, who further contrasts philosophical with literary works and the uses of lang. appropriate to each.

The contrast between philosophic and poetic texts, with the lang. appropriate to each, has been undermined since about 1960 by a number of Fr. writers—notably the philosopher J. Derrida (b. 1930)—on the basis of the theory of general linguistics worked out by F. de Saussure (1857–1913). In this view langs. operate by internal differentiation and are self-contained systems, and all culturally meaningful behavior is codified in much the same way. Anything in which we find meaning is meaningful, hence is a text, and every text is decodable in the terms of whatever code may be found in it: among this plethora of meanings the subset through which the author may have thought to create a poetic image or to propound a philosophic theory can have no privilege, if it can be identified at all (see DECONSTRUCTION).

In general, a review of the material surveyed in this article suggests that the various accounts of the relation between p. and ph. are to be viewed less as attempts to resolve a single problem or to analyze a single relationship than as a variety of discussions of topics that are but loosely related to each other.

For discussion of the ontological status of p., see POETRY; PROSODY; SOUND. See also HERMENEUTICS; MEANING, POETIC; SEMANTICS AND POETRY; SEMIOTICS, POETIC; THEORY.

G. Santayana, *Three Philosophical Poets: Lucretius, Dante, Goethe* (1910); G. Boas, *Ph. and P.* (1932); K. Burke, *Ph. of Literary Form* (1941); W. Stevens, *The Necessary Angel* (1951); F. M. Cornford, *Principium sapientiae* (1952); Curtius, ch. 11; Crane; S. K. Langer, *Feeling and Form* (1953), ch. 1–2; J. Maritain, *Creative Intuition in Art and P.* (1953); Wellek, v. 1–2; Wellek and Warren, ch. 10; E. W. Knight, *Lit. Considered as Ph.: The Fr. Example* (1957); K. Hoppe, "Philosophie und Dichtung," *Deutsche Philologie im Aufriss*, 2d ed., ed. W. Stammler (1962), 3.751–1098; A. W. Levi, *Lit., Ph., and the Imagination* (1962); P. Wheelwright, *Metaphor and Reality* (1962); B. Croce, *Ph. P. Hist.*, ed. C. Sprigge (1966); J. Derrida, *De la grammatologie* (1967), *Marges de la philosophie* (1972); M. Heidegger, *P., Lang., Thought*, ed. A. Hofstadter (1971); J.-P. Sartre, "L'Écrivain et sa langue," *Situations* 9 (1972); M. Riffaterre, *Semiotics of P.* (1975); T. McFarland, "Lit. and P.," *Interrelations of Lit.*, ed. J.-P. Barricelli and J. Gibaldi (1982); H. Zeltner, "Philosophie und Dichtung," *Reallexikon*, v. 3; W. Trimpi, *Muses of One Mind* (1983); F. Sparshott, "Text and Process in P. and Ph.," *P&L* 9 (1985); J. Kockelmans, *Heidegger on Art and Art Works* (1985); B. Lang, *P. and the Art of Writing* (1983); *Lit. and the Question of P.*, ed. A. J. Cascardi (1987); *Philosophers' Poets*, ed. D. Wood (1990); T. Gould, *The Ancient Quarrel between P. and Ph.* (1991). P.WH.; F.S.

PHONEME. See PROSODY; SOUND.

PHONESTHEME, phonaestheme. Apparently coined by Firth (1930) for a phenomenon related to or included in onomatopoeia (q.v.) and sound symbolism, the term p. signifies a specific sound that seems to be "shared by a group of words which also have in common some element of meaning or function" (Firth). Although many students of lang. consider such a theory tentative, others agree on the existence of ps. but warn against excesses in discovering them. That is, since a given phone or combination of phones does not always force a given cognitive reaction, a p. to be effective as a stimulant to the mind or the emotions must be aided by lexical associations in context.

Nearly every p. so far discovered by count or by psychological tests is an initial or final consonant or consonant cluster and—it is claimed—aids cognition when employed in alliteration or consonance (qq.v.). A convincing argument has been made by Bolinger for the morpheme *-ash*, which in stressed syllables of 21 of 48 possible forms signifies "headlong," "hit," or the result of hitting, as in *splash, lash*. The cluster *st-* often begins words suggesting firmness or arrest in Germanic langs., e.g. *stand, stable*, or *Stark, stecken*, and has been a favorite of poets wishing to stress those notions, as in Hopkins' "underneath him steady air and striding / High there." Other consonantal ps. argued for are *gl-* for visual phenomena (*glare, gleam, glow, glitter*), *sk-* for swiftness, *l-* for softness, and *tw-* for twisting motions—e.g. Dryden's "twine / The sallow twigs." Perhaps more convincing are theories about *s* and *z* for whistling or buzzing; the Greeks and Romans, Wilkinson says, "thought an excess

PHONETIC SYMBOLISM

of sibilants cacophonous" (see CACOPHONY).

Although less has been claimed for vowels, Grammont, Chastaing, and other Fr. prosodists offer theories about vowel symbolism, while Jespersen and others in Eng. conclude that the vowel in Ger. *licht* and Eng. *bit* universally reflects lightness and smallness. In Eng. the vowel in *no* has been popular for death and melancholy, not just with Poe in the theory about "nevermore" and throughout "Lenore" but with Pope in "Eloisa" and "Elegy to . . . an Unfortunate Lady" and with Tennyson in "Ballad of Oriana" and the song of "The Dying Swan," whose voice "With a music strange and manifold / Flow'd forth on a carol free and bold." The Am.-Eng. low mid vowel of *dull* and *blood* is, Masson claims, Wilfred Owen's "great discovery in assonance" and presents "the sensuous and spiritual desert of war," but that p. was anciently employed by Shakespeare, Dryden, Shelley, and others to suggest ugliness, disgust, clumsiness, and sulky states of mind, as in Pope's attack on Lady Mary in *Epistle II* and, again and again, in the *Dunciad*. But in identifying ps., one must remember the cautions of Jakobson and others (incl. Pope) that the thought or emotion must fit the sound. See now SOUND.

M. Grammont, *Le Vers français* (1913); O. Jespersen, "Sound Symbolism," *Lang.* (1922), "Symbolic Value of the Vowel I," *Linguistica* (1933); E. Sapir, "A Study in Phonetic Symbolism," *Jour. Exper. Psych.* 12 (1929); J. R. Firth, *Speech* (1930), "Sounds and Prosodies," *TPS* (1948); M. M. McDermott, *Vowel Sounds in Poetry* (1940); W. B. Stanford, *Aeschylus in His Style* (1942), *The Sound of Gr.* (1967); D. L. Bolinger, "Rime, Assonance, and Morpheme Analysis," *Word* 6 (1950); L. P. Wilkinson, *Golden Lat. Artistry* (1963); M. Chastaing, "Dernières Recherches sur le symbolisme vocalique de la petitesse," *Revue philosophique* 155 (1965); G. M. Messing, "Sound Symbolism in Gr. and Some Mod. Reverberations," *Arethusa* 4 (1971); P. G. Adams, *Graces of Harmony* (1977); Brogan, esp. 97–108; P. Delbouille, *Poésie et sonorités, II* (1984). P.G.A.

PHONETIC SYMBOLISM. See ICONICITY; ONOMATOPOEIA; PHONESTHEME; SOUND.

PHONOSTYLISTICS. See EUPHONY; SOUND; STYLISTICS.

PIE QUEBRADO. Although this Sp. metrical term may occasionally mean any half-line used with its corresponding whole line (as the heptasyllable or the pentasyllable with the hendecasyllable, the hexasyllable with the dodecasyllable), p.q. usually denotes the tetrasyllable (or equivalent) used in combination with the octosyllable, particularly in the *copla de p. q.* (see COPLA). The use of the p. q. has been common in Sp. poetry since at least the early 14th c., when it appears in the *Libro de buen amor* of Juan Ruiz, Archpriest of

Hita.—Le Gentil; Navarro. D.C.C.

PINDARIC ODE. See ODE.

PITCH. In speech, the frequency of a sound, represented on an oscilloscope by the number of sound waves in a given duration, but represented in music and perceived by auditors as higher vs. lower. P. is one of the three intonational features of sound, the others being intensity or stress (see ACCENT for more extended discussion) and length (see DURATION). Sound frequency is measured in number of sound waves or cycles per second (quantified in acoustics as Hertz [Hz; 1000 Hz = 1 Millihertz (Mhz)]; the median frequency for male voices is ca. 140 Hz and for female ca. 200; the range of the human ear is ca. 20–20,000 Hz). Research in articulatory phonetics and acoustics has shown that the sound produced by human vocal cords is actually not single but a complex band or bands of frequencies called "formants"; p. is therefore often represented in linguistics as "fundamental frequency."

Before the advent of 20th-c. linguistics and phonetics, with their technologies for recording, graphing, and analyzing sound (e.g. the sound spectrograph, not developed until the 1940s), p. was, literally for millennia, not clearly differentiated from stress, and with good reason: research shows that stress on syllables correlates highly with raised pitch (and increased length as well); indeed, stress itself seems to be mainly a function of raised p. The precise nature and relations of the concepts of p. and stress are still not wholly understood even now. The Ren. grammarians and prosodists, who drew their concepts from antiquity, speak of "tone" as a raising or lowering of the voice but differentiate "grave," "acute," and "circumflex"—i.e. three degrees of stress. It is not until the 18th c., in the work of prosodists such as Sir Joshua Steele, that real advances begin to be made in developing a terminology that accurately described what critics and readers of poetry had heard for centuries, but could not adequately notate in print and so express.

In most of the Western langs., particularly those based on Germanic, stress is used as the marker of emphasis, contrast, and meaning at the word level. P. in relation to single words is generally referred to as "tone"; the pattern of p. (and stress) across a sentence is its "intonational contour." Note, though, that p. is thus a perceptual phenomenon while tone is a linguistic phenomenon; and p. is determined by acoustic criteria while stress is a motor activity (Allen 260). In the terminology of structural linguistics (Trager-Smith), p. is marked in 4 degrees from 1 to 4 (highest), and speech is divided into clauses each of which begins and ends on a p. and contains at least one peak (primary stress). All changes in p. are marked, giving an intonational contour for the whole utterance. In Eng., such p. patterns are used to differentiate questions (rising contour at the end) from statements (falling), as in "You need help," which can either confirm or query depending on how inflected. P. can even change within a word: every child knows the difference between Nos which are Nos and those which are Maybes. This shows that p. ·can counter lexical meaning—or, more precisely, that a word can have more than one p. pattern, hence more than one meaning, since intonation is one generator of meaning. But for the most part, p. in stress-based langs. applies more to the whole utterance than the word.

Stress in one form or another (lexical or phrasal) is the basis of most Western prosodies, though this fact was not widely endorsed by prosodists until the 19th c. Nevertheless, since the 18th c. a small but steady succession of scholars (e.g. Bright, Bolinger, Crystal) has held that, in fact, p. coincides with if not comprises the major constituent of accent, and so holds a more important place in the structure of meter (q.v.) than accentual prosodists (who see stress as the basis of meter) have been willing to admit. The accentualists readily admit that p. is a major component of verse-structure, but only for the performance (q.v.) and interp. of verse; for them, p. lies outside the domain of meter strictly speaking, in the wider realm of effects concerning tone and voice (qq.v.). For them, p. patterns and intonational contours are deployed by poets to achieve a wide range of tonal effects in their poetry such as irony, hyperbole, litotes, or paradox (qq.v.); Donne is a superb example.

But if the lang. today known the most widely in the world—Eng.—is based on stress, over half the world's four thousand langs. are based on p. In p.-based langs., syllables (words) are not stressed or unstressed but rather high, mid, or low in p., or level, rising, or falling in tone, or some complex of these p. levels or changes, such as level-falling or rising-falling. Each different tonal or p. pattern constitutes a different meaning. Consequently the poetries of these langs.—esp. Chinese and Japanese—use p. level or p. change as the basis of their prosodies. The nature of these prosodies has only begun to emerge in the latter part of the 20th c.; for further discussion, see CHINESE POETRY. In the West, an important p.-based lang. was Cl. Gr., which, according to the ancient grammarians and their modern successors (though see Allen), used p. for accentuation but syllabic length or quantity for metrical patterning, making Gr. prosody inherently more complex than the modern prosodies, which use as the marker in meter the same feature used for markedness in the lang. (stress).

In short, present doctrine holds that p. is the marker of meter in several of the world's major langs. and one of the if not the most important secondary effects in those langs. which mark their poetic meters by stress. A detailed comparison of the characteristic metrical patterns of the former with those of the latter still remains to be made.

In the West, there have been a few claims over the past century that it is possible to recover the distinctive melodic pattern or intonational contour exhibited by every poet, particularly the theory of "Schallanalyse" by the great Ger. metrist Eduard Sievers, now nearly forgotten, and that by Berry. The more recent and more important work of Mukařovský and Crystal on the role of intonation in stress-based prosodies also has yet to be assessed.

See now ACCENT; DURATION.

J. Steele, *Prosodia rationalis*, 2d ed. (1775); J. W. Bright and R. D. Miller, *Elements of Eng. Versif.* (1910); E. Sievers, *Rhythmisch-melodische Studien* (1912); P. Habermann, "Ton," *Reallexikon I*; K. L. Pike, *Tone Langs.* (1948); T. W. Herbert, "Tunes of Poetry," *Emory Univ. Q.* 16 (1960); F. Berry, *Poetry and the Physical Voice* (1962); D. L. Bolinger, "A Theory of P. Accent in Eng.," *Forms of Eng.* (1965), *Intonation and Its Parts* (1986), esp. ch. 1, *Intonation and Its Uses* (1989); I. Lehiste, *Suprasegmentals* (1970); D. Crystal, *Prosodic Systems and Intonation in Eng.* (1969), esp. the history in ch. 2, and "Intonation and Metrical Theory" in *The Eng. Tone of Voice* (1975); W. S. Allen, *Accent and Rhythm* (1973), esp. ch. 6; I. Maddieson, "An Annot. Bibl. of Tone," *UCLA Working Papers in Phonetics* 28 (1974)—551 items; *Studies in Tone and Intonation*, ed. R. M. Brench (1975); J. Mukařovský, "Intonation as the Basic Factor of Poetic Rhythm," *The Word and Verbal Art*, ed. and tr. J. Burbank and P. Steiner (1977); *Tone: A Linguistic Survey*, ed. V. A. Fromkin (1978); D. R. Ladd, Jr., *The Structure of Intonational Meaning* (1980); Morier, s.v. "Mélodie"; Brogan 119–20; J. J. Ohala, "Crosslang. Use of P.: An Ethological View." *Phonetica* 40 (1983); A. C. Gimson, *Intro. to the Pronunciation of Eng.*, 4th ed. (1989). T.V.F.B.

PIYYUT. See HEBREW POETRY.

PLANH. Occitan funeral lament. In form it may be considered a specialized variety of *sirventes* (q.v.). Of the 40-odd *planhs* preserved, three-fourths bewail the death of some distinguished person, normally a patron or patroness; only 10 are laments for close friends and loved ones. The poem ordinarily consists of conventional and hyperbolic eulogies of the departed (he was generous, hospitable, gracious, chivalrous, well-mannered, wise, brave, all to a supreme degree), plus a prayer for his soul and a statement of the poet's sense of loss, the sincerity of which is sometimes open to question. See DIRGE; ELEGY; LAMENT.—S. C. Aston, "The Prov. p., I, II" in *Mélanges offerts à Rita Lejeune*, v. 1 (1968) and *Mélanges de philologie romane . . . Jean Boutière* (1971); D. Rieger, *Gattungen und Gattungsbezeichnungen der Trobadorlyrik* (1976), and in *GRLMA* 2.1B.83 ff.; P. H. Stäblein, "New Views on an Old Problem: The Dynamics of Death in the P.," *RPh* 35 (1981). F.M.C.

PLATONISM AND POETRY.

I. PLATONIC VIEWS OF POETRY
   A. *Poetry as Education*
   B. *Poetry as Imitation*
   C. *Poetry as Inspiration*
   D. *Poetry as Hermetic Symbolism*
   E. *Allegory*
II. HISTORY

Plato's most famous critical judgment is the banning of poets from the *Republic*. Yet Plato has been a powerful influence on Western poetry and poetics from the 4th c. B.C. to the present. To understand this paradox, it is necessary to consider the several facets of the Platonic view of poetry and to review the history of the influence of P.

I. PLATONIC VIEWS OF POETRY. A. *Poetry as Education* (*Paideia*). In the *Republic* (2), citizens are instructed in moral and civic virtue from earliest childhood. But poets like Hesiod and Homer tell fables that depict the gods as lustful, vindictive, capricious, and cruel. Since the divine is by definition perfect, poets who tell such fables are guilty of lying and should therefore be banned from the Republic. Only those able to understand the poet's apparently subversive fables as allegories of deeper truths are permitted to read them. The influence of poetry is understood as a kind of emotional contagion, and the state uses censorship to prevent it.

In *Protagoras* (325–26) Plato shows how poetry can educate citizens by creating exemplary images of gods and noble heroes. Thus poets who sing "hymns to the gods and encomia of famous men" are admitted to the Republic (*Rep.* 10.607), a concession repeated in the *Laws* (8.801). Plato's doctrine is simply the didactic theory of poetry, a doctrine repeatedly exemplified between his time and ours (see DIDACTIC POETRY).

B. *Poetry as Imitation* (*Mimesis*—see REPRESENTATION AND MIMESIS). Related to the charge that poets encourage immorality is the idea that they create imperfect imitations of the real. In the *Republic* (10.595) Socrates argues that the true form of each material thing is its "idea." A bed, for example, exists first as a perfect idea and only later, and in a secondary way, as a particular wooden frame made by a carpenter. A poet's description of a bed is even further removed from the idea than the carpenter's bed; hence, poetry is an imitation of an imitation. At best it is a shadow of truth; more typically it is a falsification.

Two answers have been offered to this charge. In the *Poetics* Aristotle accepted and extended Plato's idea that poetry is imitation (q.v.). However, Aristotle argued that the poet uses "probability and necessity" to construct imitations, rendering poetry "more philosophical" than history (*Poetics* 9) and closer to truth. Poetry is therefore educational, and the pleasure it gives arises from the fact that all men enjoy learning (*Poetics* 4).

Both of these arguments reply directly to Plato's charges that poetry distorts and corrupts.

Subsequent Neoplatonists took a different tack. Beginning with Plotinus (d. 270), they argued that artistic (incl. poetic) imitation transcends the world of appearances and imitates divine truth directly. The ideal poet imitates the idea of the bed rather than the bed made by the carpenter, and his poetry is a form of mystic vision. In his commentary on the *Timaeus*, Proclus (d. 485) explains that the soul has three faculties—fantasy, which deals with appearances, reason, which seeks causes behind appearance, and mind, which is capable of a direct vision of truth. The three faculties account for three kinds of poetry, all of which Homer uses in the *Iliad* and *Odyssey*.

C. *Poetry as Inspiration* (*Enthousiasmos*). Like the theory that poetry is vision, the theory of inspiration (q.v.) was drawn from Plato's own dialogues. In the *Ion* Plato satirizes a rhapsodist whose recitations of Homer move the audience but who cannot explain the source of his ability. Socrates suggests that poets and rhapsodists are inspired by a supernatural power that speaks through them. Their words are by definition supra-rational, and inspired poets seem to the uninitiated to behave like drunkards or madmen (see POETIC MADNESS). Elsewhere (e.g. *Phaedrus*) Plato seems to argue that true poetry cannot be produced without inspiration, a theory at variance with the idea of poetry as twice-removed imitation set forth in the *Republic*. Neoplatonists stressed the theory of inspiration since it explained how the poet could transcend the limits of ordinary reason. Both the ancient association between poetry and prophecy preserved, for example, in the Lat. word for poet (*vates*, "prophet") and the equally ancient convention of an invocation (q.v.) to the muse at the beginning of a poem appeared to support this explanation. In Christian culture, the example of David and the psalms seemed equally persuasive, and Christian poets regularly invoked the Holy Spirit for guidance.

D. *Poetry as Hermetic Symbolism*. Throughout the *Dialogues* Plato uses myths, emblematic images, and symbols to express his ideas. The following are typical: number and geometric symbolism (*Timaeus*); the idea of the One and the Many (*Timaeus*); the equation of light and Truth (*Republic, Parmendies*); the equation of music and the divine order, the music of the spheres (both in *Timaeus*); the golden chain of creation (*Timaeus*); the Platonic ladder or stair and Platonic love (*Symposium*); the soul as the body's prisoner, the soul as a charioteer drawn by a light and dark horse (*Phaedrus*).

Neoplatonists extended this collection by absorbing materials from the works of Hermes Trismegistus, the mystery religions, Egyptian and Near Eastern mythology, and astrology and alchemy.

The theories of imitation and inspiration as

developed by the Neoplatonists tended to emphasize the mystic and occult elements in poetry. Carried to an extreme, they encouraged poetry which was consciously obscure. This obscurity (q.v.) is perhaps the most obvious feature of Hermetic writing from Hermes Trismegistus through Pico della Mirandola down to Blake and Yeats. It results from the conscious use of esoteric symbols which are explained in two ways: first, the poet is by definition trying to convey a more than human vision (the divine archetypes). Since normal lang. is inadequate, he must resort to symbols. Second, the poet's symbols and allegories create a veil which only the initiated can penetrate, and which conceals his knowledge from the profane who would abuse it. The theory of symbolism as protective veil is evident in Fulgentius's reading of the *Aeneid*, in Dante's *Convivio*, in Boccaccio's *Genealogy of the Gods*, and in numerous Ren. critical works (see HERMETICISM).

E. *Allegory.* Plato's tendency to regard the visible world as an appearance concealing the real is given definitive statement in "the allegory of the cave" (*Rep.* 7), where earthly life is compared to life in a cave, and visible reality to shadows on the cave's wall. This view encouraged readers of poetry to differentiate between the literal meanings of a text and its hidden or mystical meanings. Allegorical interp. was further encouraged by the idea that truth is beyond the capacity of ordinary lang. The inspired poet can only convey his vision through enigmas and allegories. Concealing certain truths from the uninitiated provides another theme associated with allegory: since the literal sense of a poem veils its true meaning, the poem may seem uninteresting or obscure at first but may reveal hidden depths of meaning when read with proper understanding. The Bible is written in a style quite different from the style to which classically educated readers were accustomed in the 3d and 4th cs. Both St. Jerome and St. Augustine admit to having found many parts of it plain and uninteresting until they came to understand the truths lurking under its literal surface. From this point of view, obscurity is a virtue; obscurity may also be a desirable aesthetic quality, in that the work of discovering the hidden truth makes finding it all the more pleasurable (see ALLEGORY).

II. HISTORY. Although P. has never ceased to be an influence on Western poetry, its influence has fluctuated. Four periods of strong influence are late Cl., high medieval, Ren., and romantic.

In the late Cl. period, P. influenced understanding of poetic texts. A succession of pagan philosophers beginning with Plotinus emphasized the mystical and otherworldly elements in the *Dialogues*. The result for poetry was an emphasis on inspiration and hidden wisdom, and for crit., a fascination with allegorical interp. In the 3d. c., Porphyry explained in "On the Cave of the Nymphs" that Homer's episode (*Odyssey* 13.102–12) is an allegory of the soul's fall into the world

and of the eventual escape of virtuous souls from that dark cave. In the Lat. West, parallel interps. are found in the commentary of Macrobius (4th c.) on the *Dream of Scipio* and the interp. by Fulgentius (6th c.?) of Virgil's *Aeneid* as an allegory of the education of the ideal man.

Early biblical interpreters were equally fascinated by allegory. Philo Judaeus (d. ca. 50 A.D.), an Alexandrian Jew, wrote an immense allegorical interp. of *Genesis* along Platonic lines. Christian interp. followed the lead of Philo and often borrowed from him directly or through intermediaries, a point of view evident in the work of Origen in Gr. and St. Ambrose and others in Lat.

After the 4th c., the Lat. West lost touch with the Gr. sources of P. Only the *Timaeus* (tr. Calcidius, ca. 350 A.D.) and a few fragments of the other dialogues were available in Lat. For the most part, the Middle Ages relied on second- and third-hand sources, incl. St. Augustine's commentary on *Genesis*, Macrobius' commentary on *The Dream of Scipio*, and Boethius' *Consolation of Philosophy*.

The second phase of Platonic influence began with the 9th-c. tr. by Scotus Erigena of the *Mystical Theology, On the Divine Names*, and *Heavenly Hierarchy* of Dionysius the Areopagite. Dionysius claimed to be contemporary with St. Paul, but his works were composed in the 6th c. under the influence of Plotinus and Proclus. They led to a revival of mysticism in western Europe. Their insistence that normal lang. is unable to express higher truth led to the use in poetry of rhetorical strategies and symbolic imagery associated with "negative imagery" (the *via negativa*), a practice evident in the poetry of the Victorine sequences and in descriptions by mystics such as St. Bonaventura and Bernard of Clairvaux of the mind's ascent to transcendent vision. The same strategies carry over into the lyrics and lyrical prose of such authors as St. John of the Cross and St. Teresa of Avila.

The hierarchical understanding of creation adopted by Dionysius from Plotinus encouraged renewed interest in the order and beauty of the Book of Nature and in images of the glorious hierarchy of heaven. Thus P. helped to shape two quite different kinds of poetry in the high Middle Ages. On the one hand, there is the sensual and worldly vision of life embodied in poems like the *De planctu naturae* of Alan de Lisle and the *De mundi universitate* of Bernard Silvestris (both 12th c.). On the other, there is the image of the soul's ascent through the hierarchy of heavenly beings to final communion with God that forms the third part (*Paradiso*) of Dante's *Divine Comedy*.

Although P. yielded to Scholasticism in the later Middle Ages, it was vigorously revived in Florence at the end of the 14th c. at the so-called Platonic Academy led by Marsilio Ficino. The history of P. in the Ren. has been traced many times (see Kristeller, Robb, Merrill, and Ellrodt). Among its results for poetry were (1) a renewed emphasis on the didactic theory of poetry; (2) a general emphasis on the idea of "Platonic love," esp. in lyric poetry; and (3) frequent appeal to the idea of inspiration—most notably, perhaps, in Milton's *Paradise Lost*, where the invocations blend P. with the radical Protestant habit of asking the Holy Spirit for guidance in spiritual matters. The latest flowering of European P. was the work—esp. the poetry—of the so-called "Cambridge Platonists," in particular, Henry More and Ralph Cudworth.

During Milton's lifetime, scientific materialism was displacing P. as a guiding principle of philosophy and science. However, in the later 18th c., Kant's argument that the perceived world is "phenomenal" and that reality is forever beyond the reach of the mind seemed to many artists, esp. poets, to echo P. Wordsworth's "Ode on Intimations of Immortality" repeats many P. ideas—the pre-existence of the soul, the image of the soul trapped in a prison-house, birth as a "forgetting." But both Blake and Shelley are more consistently Platonic than Wordsworth. Blake tends to the Hermetic side of P. and was influenced by the tr. of the major Neoplatonic writers into Eng. by Thomas Taylor, "the Platonist." According to the most famous image of Shelley's *Adonais*, life is "a dome of many-coloured glass that stains the white radiance of eternity." In Germany, Hölderlin shows the influence of P., while in America, Emerson interpreted Plato in the key of Transcendentalism, and Poe taught that poetry creates symbols in lang. of unattainable realities—a theory incorporated by Baudelaire, with modifications, into the poetics of Fr. symbolism.

P. continued to influence European poetry in the later 19th and 20th cs. Among 20th-c. poets esp. indebted to P. are Ranier Maria Rilke and William Butler Yeats, both of whom draw on the Hermetic trad. and the idea of inspiration, and Wallace Stevens, whose P. comes via Ger. idealist philosophy and the Transcendentalism of Emerson. At present, P. is challenged by the skepticism of deconstruction (q.v.) and the materialism of much modern science. However, P. is a hardy philosophy; it will doubtless survive these as it has so many other challenges in the past.

See now ALLEGORY; CLASSICAL POETICS; HERMETICISM; IMITATION; INSPIRATION; PLOT.

L. Winstanley, *P. in Shelley* (1913); T. Whittaker, *The Neo-Platonists* (1918); C. E. Rott, *Dionysius the Areopagite*, On the Divine Names *and* The Mystical Theology (1920); N. Robb, *P. in the It. Ren.* (1935); R. Klibansky, *The Continuity of the Platonic Trad. in the Middle Ages* (1939); M. dal Pra, *Scoto Eriugena ed il neoplatonismo medievale* (1941); W. J. Verdenius, *Mimesis: Plato's Doctrine of Imitation* (1948); I. Samuel, *Plato and Milton* (1949); P. Kristeller, *Il Pensiero filosofico di Marsilio Ficino* (1953); E. Cassirer, *The Platonic Ren. in England* (1953); R. V. Merrill and R. J. Clements, *P. in Fr. Ren. Poetry* (1957); Wimsatt and Beardsley, ch. 7; R. Ellrodt, *P. in the Poetry of Spenser* (1960); B. Smalley, *The Study of the Bible in the Middle Ages*, 2d

ed. (1961); J. E. Baker, *Shelley's Platonic Answer to a Platonic Attack on Poetry* (1965); B. Feinstein, "Hermeticism," A. H. Armstrong, "Neo-Platonism," G. M. A. Grube, "P., Rhetorical and Literary Theory in," J. Fisher, "P. in Philosophy and Poetry," and J. C. Nelson, "P. in the Ren.," all in *DHI*; A. N. Rich, "Plotinus and the Theory of Artistic Imitation," *Mnemosyne* 13 (1969); R. Harriott, *Poetry and Crit. before Plato* (1969); G. Harper, *The Neoplatonism of William Blake* (1961); L. Whitbread, *Fulgentius the Mythographer* (1971); W. Wetherbee, *P. and Poetry in the 12th C.* (1972); S. K. Heninger, Jr., *Touches of Sweet Harmony* (1974); J. A. Coulter, *The Literary Microcosm: Theories of Interp. of the Later Neoplatonists* (1976); J. A. Elias, *Plato's Defence of Poetry* (1984); G. F. Else, *Plato and Aristotle on Poetry*, ed. P. Burian (1986); S. Gersh, *Middle P. and Neoplatonism*, 2 v. (1986); E. Bieman, *Plato Baptized* (1988); E. D. Kabitoglou, *Plato and the Eng. Romantics* (1990).   O.B.H.

PLÉIADE. This term, which refers to the small group of poets of the Fr. Ren. led by Pierre de Ronsard, originated in 1556 in an elegy in which the latter welcomed a new member to the group: "Belleau, qui viens en la brigade / Des bons, pour accomplir la septiesme P." (Laumonier). This was Ronsard's only use of the term in this sense. Until that time he had used the term *Brigade,* which had been hospitable to a much larger number of poets than the expression that replaced it. Probably with no rigid intention of thereby creating an exclusive circle of poets limited in membership to seven, Ronsard adopted the expression *P.* from the well-known Alexandrine group of poets who in antiquity had gone by that name.

Although membership in the P. varied with the years, it did not at any time surpass seven. In 1556, along with Remy Belleau and Ronsard himself, the group included Joachim du Bellay, Pontus de Tyard, Jean-Antoine de Baïf, Jacques Peletier, and Étienne Jodelle. According to Ronsard's first biographer, Claude Binet, the name of Peletier was eventually replaced by that of the poet's teacher, Jean Dorat, one of the great Hellenists of the Fr. Ren. Within a few years of its first and last mention by Ronsard, the term P. had been found so convenient as a designation of the group immediately associated with the poet that Henri Estienne is able to use it in his *Apologie pour Hérodote* (1566) in confident expectation that it would be understood to refer to the contemp. group of Fr. poets.

Three members of the P. were influential contributors to Fr. poetic theory of the Ren.: Peletier, du Bellay, and Ronsard himself. As early as 1541, Peletier had published a tr. of the *Ars poetica* of Horace prefaced by remarks of his own in which the fundamental principle later to be adopted by Ronsard and his associates was clearly enunciated: that Fr. writers should *defend* and *illustrate* (i.e. render illustrious) their own lang. by writing in Fr., not Lat. or Gr. In 1555 Peletier published an *Art poëtique* in which he reaffirmed the position he had adopted in the preface to the *Ars poetica* of 1541, insisted upon the divine nature of poetry, and discussed the relationship between technique and native endowment, the function of imitation, the varieties of poetic subjects, and genres (see Patterson; see also RENAISSANCE POETICS).

Both du Bellay and Ronsard may be called, in matters of theory, disciples of Peletier. The former published in 1549 the renowned *Deffence et illustration de la langue françoyse* which, though it followed by eight or more years Peletier's preface, became, because it arrived precisely at the right moment, and because of the intensity of its lang., the manifesto of the new school. Du Bellay blames the alleged poverty of the Fr. lang. of his time on the unwillingness of earlier generations of Frenchmen to devote their energies to its cultivation. Intrinsically, he says, it is capable of the highest reaches of poetic and philosophic expression, and need not bow in these respects before any of the langs. of antiquity or modern times. This is the essence of his *deffence*. As for the *illustration*, du Bellay rejects the position that tr. of the great classics into Fr. can of itself suffice to raise Fr. lit. to a status of equality with Gr., Lat., or It. What the Fr. poet needs is so intimate a knowledge of the classics and of the more important modern lits. that their substance will become part of his own, and that ideally his imitation (q.v.) of them will result not so much in a conscious effort to reproduce their thought and feeling as in their natural assimilation and transformation into a form congenial to the Fr. lang. and acceptable to cultivated Frenchmen.

The *Abbrégé de l'art poëtique françois* of Ronsard (1565) is a brief practical handbook intended for the young beginner in poetry. Like Peletier and du Bellay, Ronsard's fundamental premise is that the poet must write in Fr., although he too demands that the would-be writer possess as profound a Cl. instruction as possible. He demands that the poet, who for him is the inspired prophet of the Muses, should hold them "in singular veneration and never reduce them to a position of dishonorable servitude" (Laumonier 14.10).

To form a clear idea of the contribution of the P. in the area of poetic practice, it is useful to consider which of its members were the most successful, and in the works of these poets, which features proved to be the most creative and enduring. De Baïf, although innovative in many ways, lacks suppleness of expression. Belleau obtains striking and picturesque effects, but these are accompanied by a mannered style that tends to be insipid in the treatment of love. With the exception of Ronsard, du Bellay outstrips the other members of the P. in his mastery of the sonnet (q.v.), in the music of his syllables, and in expressiveness of inner feeling, esp. the nostalgia of the *Regrets*. The range and the quality of the poetic activity of Ronsard, however, place him head and shoulders above his colleagues. As McFarlane has aptly observed, "the achievement of the P. is primarily that of Ronsard himself" (325).

Ronsard's sense of the dignity of his poetic calling is reflected in the Cl. and It. forms that he chose: the ode, the sonnet, the elegy, the eclogue (qq.v.). The technical mastery which he amply demonstrates in these is matched by sound placement, concrete word choice, grace of expression, and rhythm in a wide variety of metric forms. His sure taste seized upon the alexandrine (q.v.) and demonstrated for all time its peculiar suitability to the Fr. tongue. To embellish his verse Ronsard made bold and broad use of the abundant resources of Cl. mythology. He imparted renewed validity to the legends of antiquity by adopting them as his principal mode of figurative expression, at a time when these myths were still perceived by some with mistrust. Ronsard's erudition and imagination are manifest not only in his frequent references to the Muses, Apollo, and other deities associated with the arts, but also by the fact that in his hands myth becomes the means of exploring the many facets of human experience.

If Ronsard's leadership of the P. springs from the wider range of form and theme that he deploys, it is nevertheless as a poet of love that he excels. In this key area he seeks and finds originality by adroit exploitation of both Petrarchan and Neoplatonic *topoi*, through which devices he expresses his sufferings on the one hand and idealizes the object of his love on the other (see PETRARCHISM; PLATONISM AND POETRY). With Ronsard, however, the evocation of feminine beauty is often more sensual, the suffering more specifically portrayed, than in Petrarch. Yet, over and above the traditional erotic imagery, Ronsard weaves into his love-poetry a perception of nature which is at once fresh and intimate. Few poets have been able to capture the exquisite mingling of beauty and ephemerality that haunts the celebrated *Ode à Cassandre*. A feature of this poem, and indeed of his best love poetry, is a certain tone of discretion, a controlled and elegant diction, a graceful fusion of intellect and feeling. At this level Ronsard achieves his goal of rivaling the ancient poets, while leaving for posterity a practical aesthetic.

The "revolution" of Malherbe (1605) was, in reality, the regularization, perhaps the excessively rigid codification, of tendencies already clearly apparent in Ronsard and his colleagues. With the end of the Malherbian dispensation, as the romantic period begins, qualities of subjective lyricism, equally present in the poets of the P. but somewhat neglected during the period of Fr. Classicism, come once more to the fore. The influence of the P. was thus durable and pervasive, and it is fair to say that the principles laid down by Peletier, du Bellay, and Ronsard have not lost their vigor except among poets for whom harmony and sonority take precedence over communication. See also FRENCH POETRY; RENAISSANCE POETRY.

C. Binet, *Vie de Ronsard*, ed. P. Laumonier (1910); Patterson—still essential; H. Chamard, *Hist. de la P.*, 4 v. (1939–41); R. J. Clements, *The Crit. Theory and Practice of the P.* (1942); F. Simone, "I poeti della P. ed i loro predecessori," *GIF* 2 (1949); *Crit. Prefaces of the Fr. Ren.*, ed. B. Weinberg (1950); F. Desonay, "Les Manifestes lit. du XVIe siècle en France," *BHR* 14 (1952), *Ronsard, poète de l'amour*, 3 v. (1952–59); H. Weber, *La Création poétique au XVIe siècle en France* (1956); R. V. Merrill and R. J. Clements, *Platonism in Fr. Ren. Poetry* (1957); J. Bonnot, *Humanisme et p., l'hist., la doctrine, les oeuvres* (1959); I. Silver, *Ronsard and the Hellenic Ren. in France*, v. 1: *Ronsard and the Gr. Epic*, (1961), v. 2: *Ronsard and the Grecian Lyre*, Part I (1981), Part II (1985), Part III (1987), *The Intellectual Evolution of Ronsard*, v. 1: *The Formative Influences* (1969), v. 2: *Ronsard's General Theory of Poetry* (1973), v. 3: *Ronsard's Philosophic Thought* (in progress); G. Castor, *P. Poetics* (1964); D. Stone, *Ronsard's Sonnet Cycles* (1966); F. Gray, *Anthologie de la poésie française au XVIe siècle* (1967); E. Armstrong, *Ronsard and the Age of Gold* (1968); H. W. Wittschier, *Die Lyrik der P.* (1971); G. Demerson, *La Mythologie dans l'oeuvre de la P.* (1972); *Ronsard the Poet*, ed. T. Cave (1973); M. B. Wells, *Du Bellay, a Bibl.* (1974); I. D. McFarlane, *Ren. France, 1470–1589* (1974); F. Hallopeau and H. Longnon, *À la recherche de Ronsard* (1985); M. McGowan, *Ideal Forms in the Age of Ronsard* (1985); Hollier; I. Y. Bellenger, *La P.: La Poésie en France autour de Ronsard* (1988). I.S.; I.J.W.

PLOCE, ploche (Gr. "plaiting"; Lat. *iteratio*). The genus of figures for word repetition, with or without intervening words, generally in close proximity, i.e. within the clause or line. Cl. and Ren. rhetoricians distinguished between p., as the "speedy iteration of one word but with some little intermission by inserting one or two words between" (Puttenham) and *epizeuxis*, repetition with no words intervening (Quintilian, *Institutio oratoria* 9.3.40–44; Herodian [2d c. A.D.] in Walz 8.603). Examples of p.: Euripides' "O mortal man, think mortal thoughts," Sidney's "Even those sad words in sad me did breed" (*Astrophil and Stella* 58), and Pope's "Where Wigs with Wigs, with Sword-knots Sword-knots strive, / Beaus banish Beaus, and Coaches Coaches drive" (*Rape of the Lock* 101–2). Examples of epizeuxis are Shakespeare's "Never, never, never, never, never," "Tomorrow and tomorrow and tomorrow," "O horror, horror, horror," "Then kill, kill, kill, kill, kill, kill"; and Tennyson's "Break! Break! Break!" Susenbrotus says that epizeuxis is valuable "for the sake of greater vehemence" in speech, imitating the iterations natural to moments of great emotion. Sometimes the meaning of the word may be altered in the repetition, or its word-class, but technically these are the province of other figures; most immediately, p. concerns simple iteration of a word without a shift in its grammatical form or meaning (see POLYPTOTON). Milton deploys "stood/fell" 10 times in 21 lines of *Paradise Lost* at 4.561–81; Book 4 is esp. dense in p. These and other examples give us some reason to think that when Milton reported that he meant to have "the sense variously drawn out from one Verse to another," he had in mind not only enjambment (q.v.) but also the several figures of verbal iteration which may be characterized as p.

Other more complex rhetorical figures which deploy word repetition in syntax—i.e. at the beginnings and endings of phrases and clauses—and in meter as well—i.e. to begin or end lines or stanzas, or at caesurae—are *anaphora* (word-repetition at beginnings), *epistrophe* (at ends), *symploce* (combination of the two preceding, i.e. one word repeated at beginnings, another at ends—see ANAPHORA), *epanalepsis* (q.v.; same word repeated at beginning and at end), and *anadiplosis* (word at end of one member repeated at beginning of the next; q.v.). These figures take advantage of the heightened visibility offered by edges in syntax and meter, i.e. of the special status of boundaries in the flow of discourse. Their presence is more conspicuous, but at the same time usually limited to less extensive repetition, than p., which allows the weaving of verbal repetitions throughout a passage more subtly and more extensively without overstraining the reader's sense of satiation.

C. Walz, *Rhetores graeci*, 9 v. (1832–36); Sr. M. Joseph, *Shakespeare's Use of the Arts of Lang.* (1947), 84–85, 306; A. Quinn, *Figures of Speech* (1982), 77, 80–81; L. A. Sonnino, *Handbook to 16th-C. Rhet.* (1968), 64, 174; B. Vickers, *In Defence of Rhet.* (1988), *Cl. Rhet. in Eng. Poetry*, 2d ed. (1989), 138–39, 144–46; Corbett. T.V.F.B.

PLOT may be defined as the pattern or structure of events within a text. Conceptions of p. vary, but common to most of them is the notion of a sequence of actions related implicitly or explicitly by chronology and perhaps also by causality. While some New Critics used the term "p." to designate any textual design, p. is more commonly considered a feature of temporal structures. Although p. has traditionally been associated with drama and narrative, it may figure in any genre, from a single sonnet (e.g. Milton's "Methought I saw my late espoused saint") to the visual arts (Hogarth's "Rake's Progress").

P. is an element of a text's "deep structure": it is not dependent on the precise lang. or surface form of a work but may be abstracted, translated or transferred to another medium. Thus a single p.—say, Figaro's marriage—could be represented in a prose summary, a drama, an opera, a story, a film, a verse narrative, or a lyric. Though technically p. may refer to any sequence of actions in a text, it is usually associated with those event structures that can be related to a text's themes. Indeed, as Frye conceives it, p. is theme in movement; theme (q.v.) is p. at rest. Yet p. cannot be

PLOT

reduced to a theme or "point": simply because p. develops its messages through temporal succession, it offers "a specific mode of human understanding" (Brooks) that differs from the kind of knowledge created by purely spatial forms.

Up to the 20th c., analyses of p. have been framed almost entirely within the terms given by Aristotle in the *Poetics*. Aristotle defines p. (*mythos*) as "the imitation of the action" and "the arrangement of the incidents," stressing at once the content and its representational form. For Aristotle p. was the most essential element of dramatic art. Aristotle's aesthetic gives primacy not only to p. itself but to certain forms of p. The best ps., he says, are "whole and complete," are of sufficient scope to have a "beginning, a middle, and an end," and involve a change of fortune that seems probable or inevitable rather than accidental or mechanical. Aristotle dislikes the loosely structured "episodic" p. and holds to a strict unity (q.v.) of action: "the various incidents must be so constructed that, if any part is displaced or deleted, the whole p. is disturbed and dislocated. For if any part can be inserted or omitted without manifest alteration, it is no true part of the whole." The best p. develops its movements conjointly through recognition (*anagnorisis*) and reversal (*peripeteia*): recognition involves a change from ignorance to knowledge, reversal a corresponding change of situation to its opposite. In "simple" ps., change occurs without recognition or reversal; Aristotle prefers "complex" ps. like that of *Oedipus Rex*, in which the reversal of the hero's fortunes occurs at the moment he realizes that he has indeed fulfilled the terrible prophecies he thought he had avoided. Particularly when events are "unexpectedly interconnected," the well-wrought tragic p. creates the experience of pity and terror which Aristotle sees as the goal of tragedy (see CATHARSIS). Aristotle also believes that different genres necessitate different forms of p.: a "double p." is appropriate to comedy, in which "the good are rewarded and the bad punished," while in tragedy, a "single" p. entails a hero's suffering. Although Aristotle values the capacity of the epic to represent broad and sometimes simultaneous sequences of events, he insists that the epic p. maintain the strict organic unity that is his dramatic ideal.

Although p. does indeed dominate the literary forms which Aristotle analyzes, his privileging of p. over character has been controversial. Esp. in discussions of modern lit., with its focus on individual psychology and the inner life, character has been considered more important than p., and the construction of p. has even been seen as a deterrent to the "natural" representation of character. A famous comment by Henry James in "The Art of Fiction" mediates the argument: "What is character but the illustration of incident? What is incident but the revelation of character?"

In the early decades of the 20th c., a new atten-

tion to "close reading" and hence to the lang. of texts led some scholars to consider p. scarcely worthy of critical analysis. New life was brought to the analysis of p. by Vladimir Propp and Northrop Frye, who, though they approached the subject differently, both investigated it in structural terms. Propp's *Morphology of the Folktale* (1927) identifies in the Rus. folktale a series of 31 functions occurring in invariant order but not necessarily in invariant number in every tale. Frye created in 1957 a complex and widely influential system attempting to categorize the whole of lit. through intersecting typologies; one element of his *Anatomy* was the identification of four *mythoi* or generic ps.: the romantic, the tragic, the comic, and the satiric or ironic. For Frye, comedy typically involves movement from one society to another, usually through the agency of marriage; romance is structured on the adventure or quest p.; tragedy emphasizes the individual and entails the disintegration of family or society because of a hero's fall; and irony and satire represent struggles between societies or social norms (see MYTH CRITICISM).

For some 20th-c. theorists, however, the Aristotelian concept of p. is not a universal definition but one specific to a particular culture and world view. The tightly wrought, logical p. assumes a world that, while it may not be controllable, may at least be known and explained, and develops a corresponding aesthetic of closure and unity (qq.v.). These theorists also reject the association of p. with causality and argue that temporal sequence alone is sufficient to constitute a p., since some cultures assume an arbitrary or random universe or elide the question of motivation entirely. Similarly, some feminist critics (Brewer; Miller; De Lauretis) suggest that men and women have constructed ps. on different premises, in accordance with traditional differences in men's and women's experiences of the world. What Aristotelian poetics may have called "plotless" or "poorly plotted" discourse is, under such newer conceptions of p., encompassed within new definitions of p.; what for Aristotle was a failing becomes simply a manifestation of literary and cultural diversity. In such a framework, theorists are less interested in prescribing and evaluating ps. than in identifying their distinguishing structural features.

One result of this challenge to the Aristotelian notion of p. has been a shift in the terminology through which critics talk about event structures. The distinction between "p." (causal sequence of events) and "story" (mere temporal succession of events), given its classic formulation in E. M. Forster's *Aspects of the Novel*, has yielded to a distinction, initiated by Rus. Formalism (q.v.), between events as ordered in the content of the story (*fabula*) and events as the text arranges and presents them (*sjuzet*), a distinction which Fr. structuralism (q.v.) more or less replicates in the terms *histoire* and *récit*. Within this framework, p. comes to be a function of the relationship between the story's chronological events (*histoire*) and the order and manner in which they are revealed in the temporality and spatiality of the text (*récit*). P. is then understood as a complex structure in which many textual elements participate: order, time, pace, point of view. P is "the intelligible whole that governs a succession of events in any story" (Ricoeur); it is finally the interrelationship among all these textual elements that constitutes the p.

The work of early analysts such as Propp was continued in the Fr. structuralism of the 1960s as narratologists (those studying the structures of narrative) sought to identify the specific mechanisms or "grammar" of p. Abstracting from Propp's notion of functions, which are actions undertaken by characters (hero, villain, helper) and "defined from the point of view of [their] significance for the course of action of the tale as a whole," theorists such as Todorov, Greimas, Bremond, Prince, Pavel, and Costello define p. in terms of actions or "verbs." Greimas is interested in the simultaneously temporal and thematic reversals that a p. effects. In Bremond's formulation, initiating events or "kernels" are amplified, delayed, or maintained by "catalysts," and small sequences intersect to form larger ones. Costello speaks of p. as constituted by paired statements, often widely separated in the text, that together function as units of prediction and fulfillment. Pavel formulates p. in terms of "moves," each of which is defined as "the choice of an action among a number of alternatives" in a rule-governed situation. Thus Lear has the alternative to banish or not to banish Cordelia, and his choice sets in motion another series of moves.

These investigations seem to assume a set of structures inherent in the text. For many critics, however, p. is a construction engaged in by readers according to a set of conventions learned in the practice of reading texts. As Culler puts it, "the reader must organize the p. as a passage from one state to another and this passage or movement must be such that it serves as a representation of theme. The end must be made a transformation of the beginning so that meaning can be drawn from the perception of resemblance and difference." These theorists argue that p. is at least in part a reading-effect that may be imposed upon even very unconventional texts in order to render them intelligible and orderly.

But recent interest in p. by psychoanalytic theorists suggests a still more complex understanding of the nature of p. and of its relationship to reading. In light of Freud and Lacan, ps. are understood to embody unconscious as well as conscious elements: the forms of our ps. articulate both the conscious and unconscious forms of our desire. *Oedipus Rex* exposes the unconscious nature of desire as Oedipus himself is taken over by the discourse of the oracle and actually lives out what horrifies his consciousness. Thus there is a p. beneath the p., a chaotic story of desire that

threatens to disturb the coherence of the traditional p., which becomes in turn an effort both to repress and to articulate desire. The reader's construction of p. may be seen as a response not simply to learned conventions but to deeper desires, desires for certain kinds of revelation, repetition, and control. Thus, in ways that evoke Aristotle's notion of catharsis (q.v.), psychoanalytic critics see p. as inscribing structures of human desire, drawing the reader into an enactment of her or his own desires, incl. the desire for a mastery that can never be attained. And since it is in the nature of desire itself that it will be endlessly repeated, never completely fulfilled or understood, people will always be "reading for the p."

See ARGUMENT; NARRATIVE POETRY; STRUCTURE.

E. M. Forster, *Aspects of the Novel* (1927); V. Propp, *Morphology of the Folktale* (1927); Frye; R. Scholes and R. Kellogg, *The Nature of Narrative* (1966); A. J. Greimas, *Du Sens* (1970); R. Barthes, *S/Z* (1970); C. Bremond, *Logic du récit* (1973); E. T. Costello, "Modality and Narration," *DAI* 36 (1975), 6654A; Culler; S. Rimmon-Kenan, *Narrative Fiction* (1983); M. Brewer, "A Loosening of Tongues," *MLN* 99 (1984); P. Brooks, *Reading for the P.* (1984); P. Ricouer, *Time and Narrative* (1984); *Lacan and Narration*, ed. R. C. Davis (1984)—good bibl.; N. Miller, "Emphasis Added: Plots and Plausibilities in Women's Fiction," *The New Feminist Crit.*, ed. E. Showalter (1985); T. Pavel, *The Poetics of P.* (1985)—application to Ren. drama; T. De Lauretis, *Alice Doesn't* (1986); T. Leitch, *What Stories Are* (1986); E. Belfiore, *Tragic Pleasures* (1992). S.S.L.

PLURALISM. The term "pl.," invented less than a hundred years ago, is now used to cover a variety of beliefs, esp. in philosophy, lit. crit., religion, and politics. The most controversial of these beliefs is the claim that not only is there a plurality of philosophical, critical, religious, or political theories and practices—a fact obvious to everyone—but that in principle there must be at least two (and probably many more) legitimate ways of grasping or working with any intellectual domain, ways that cannot be reduced to any one purer or truer way. In this view, the rivalry among "modes of thought" ("langs.," "systems," "schools," "approaches," "perspectives," "analytical schemes," "mental worlds"—the labels are controversial) is in principle inescapable, not just because of present limitations in our knowledge but for all time, since no way of thinking, no "mode," can fully describe or encompass the interests and procedures of all the others. In this view, a mode justifies itself not by its capacity to refute the others but rather by its success in answering questions that in other modes are either distorted or ignored.

This kind of pl., a kind of meta-mode applied in both philosophy and crit., should be distinguished from political pl., where the term refers to a vari-

PLURALISM

ety of democratic and anti-totalitarian beliefs, esp. the claim that states are healthiest when they encompass a plurality of power bases. Critical and philosophical pl. are much more closely akin; here their principles will be treated as roughly identical.

Pl. as a meta-mode can be usefully distinguished from four other ways of addressing modal rivalries: (1) mutual toleration: live and let live, rejoice in multiplicity; (2) monism (sometimes but not always combined with a courteous toleration), which claims that some one mode is uniquely true and legitimate—either one already now in hand or one to be hoped for in the future; (3) eclecticism, which offers to winnow the true from the false in each mode, often in the hope of producing a new synthesis free of falsehood—thus transforming itself into another monism; (4) skepticism, which claims that no mode is really true or legitimate because every mode is refutable by one or more of its rivals. In crit., one version of skepticism, usually called relativism but also found among some who call themselves "new historicists" or partisans of "cultural crit." (q.v.), argues that each mode reveals nothing other than the training, personal preferences, political aspirations, or historical situation of those who profess it; the truth of all human statements is relative to the historical situation or character of the claimer. This claim can be extended to "full" or "utter" relativism or skepticism: what is true is only whatever is true for you, and whatever is true for you is true. The number of truths is thus identical with the number of perspectives—in extreme form, the total number of human beings. This view implies that it is not the contradiction among modes that makes them untrue: in fact, there can be no genuine contradiction, because there is no general standard for determining what is contradictory.

These ways of accepting or rejecting manifold modes exist under a variety of names. Way (2) in its more assertive forms is dogmatism, or even fanaticism or fascism. Way (3) is sometimes called pl., or "qualified relativism," or operationalism— some forms of rhetorical theory are essentially eclectic. Way (4) is often called relativism or, in its extreme forms, "utter skepticism" (Pepper). Modal pl., the effort to provide a meta-mode that offers an unqualified embrace of many modes, will here count as way (5).

A paradox about (5), sometimes used by its opponents as proof that it is incoherent, is that pluralists cannot be pluralistic about the other views of plurality. Though they may tolerate (2), (3), and (4) as providing some partial truth, in the end the pluralist believes that only (5) gets at the truth about plurality itself. In contrast, monists, eclectics, and skeptics can be equally monistic, eclectic, or skeptical about all the positions, thus presenting what may look like a coherence not possible for the pluralist.

Modal pl. can be distinguished from or com-

bined with several claims about a radical plurality at the heart of reality; none of the following rejects the possibility of a knowledge which, though irreducibly plural, is genuine:

(a) The goods in the world cannot be reduced to one good or one scale of goods; many goods and scales of better and worse are real, both in human and nonhuman existence; some of these may well conflict in forms that are permanently irreducible (e.g. total liberty conflicts with order as a good; in art the beauty of concision conflicts with the grandeur of eloquence). The search of philosophers like Kant for one supreme moral good is inherently misguided.

(b) There is actually a plurality not just of goods in this world but of overlapping or parallel worlds or perhaps even of totally independent worlds, only one of which we can hope to know (Pavel, esp. his bibl.). Each of these worlds may or may not have its own first principles, standards of beauty or morality, prime substance, ultimate reality, or God.

(c) Though there is only one world, it is radically divided into irreconcilable aspects or prime substances, two or more ultimate principles or Gods. Historically the most prominent pl. of this kind was in fact a dualism—the Manichean belief that good and evil are co-equal as principles in the universe. All dualisms are by definition pluralistic in this limited sense. In crit., this version of pl. claims that "the poem" is really and irreducibly many poems. It is not just that each critical mode takes a different aspect; the thing itself is many different things.

Modal pl. need not choose among these versions of what might be called substantive pl. For modal pluralists, the key point is that human beings cannot escape a plurality of philosophical systems or critical perspectives, regardless of whether or not the universe (or poem) is in itself single or manifold. Some modal pluralists have argued that with sufficient skill in translation, the truth of each valid mode could be translated into any other valid mode. But most see that hope as vain, or as a task suited only for the mind of God.

Among philosophers, there have been four influential modal pluralists. (1) William James speculated vigorously about the reasons for rejecting all monistic modes of thought and about the possibilities in substantive pls. (a), (b), and (c). (2) Stephen Pepper argued that every philosophy is based on one of five "root metaphors," formism, contextualism (q.v.), organicism (q.v.), mechanism, and purposivism: each of these can be developed to account—to the true believer—for everything in the world, which is yet in some sense "one." (3) Richard McKeon showed how every philosophy or critical theory chooses one of many possibilities within each of four main variables: a purpose, a definition of the "real," a method of argument and proof, and a first principle. Since each of these variables offers many possible variants, there are in principle an infinite number of modes of philosophizing, many of them capable of yielding a comprehensive view of the world that will seem, from inside that mode, to account for everything. (4) Nelson Goodman argues that our multiple "worlds" are symbolic "versions," each of which can only be tested by reference to the "fit" its parts exhibit toward each other—the truth of each version is relative not to some common ground shared by all versions but only to the terms in which the versions are set up. Goodman assumes that some versions are inherently better than others; like the others he is not an utter relativist.

Other philosophers, each of whom has had critical followers, can be said to be pluralistic in various senses: Aristotle, because he believed that we must practice a plurality of methods on diverse subject matters; Kant, because he believed that our efforts to know cannot be reduced to pure reason or practical or aesthetic judgments; Hegel and other dialecticians because they believe that everything must be taken into account and that nothing ever gets fully canceled out; Bakhtin and other "dialogic" critics because they see the world of inquiry as a fluid intermingling of multiple langs.; and various deconstructionists because they see all lang. as in infinite flux and every statement as depending on other statements in a potentially infinite regress. But all these, when viewed in the perspectives of the four above, will appear as (complex) monists: each believes that his system is all that we need. The modal pluralists believe—this is why pl. is confused with relativism—that every mode is radically constrained by its vision or perspective or lang.: those who work within its terms can see only what that mode can reveal.

Because pl. in lit. crit. is essentially a philosophical way of addressing the diversity of critical modes, what has been said about philosophical pl. applies to the relations of rival literary studies, whether we think of those studies as poetics, theory, aesthetics, linguistics, semiotics, semantics, or crit. The history of such studies presents the same sort of rivalry among schools and the same range of pleas in response: (1) for easy tolerance—the stance of some anthologists of the history of crit.; (2) for the unique validity of some one (usually highly complex) mode (e.g. Frye, some deconstructionists); (3) the eclectic raiding of all versions for whatever tools are useful (Burke); and the skeptical rejection of the essential truth claims of all, because genuine truth in these domains is unattainable (Fish). Though many of these have on occasion applied the term "pl." to their work, few have asserted direct indebtedness to any of the philosophers mentioned above. The fullest developments of way (5) in literary studies can be found in the line of descent from McKeon—the so-called Chicago School (q.v.)—and in Abrams.

There is little evidence that a full modal pl. will ever be widely embraced. To believe its claims requires, as a first step, a kind of total embrace of at least two modes for long enough to recognize their radically distinct and irreducible powers. It thus seems probable that the critical world, like the philosophical world, will always find more enthusiasts for monist, eclectic, and skeptical claims. Perhaps the most that anyone who cares about improved understanding among rival positions can hope for is that some critics will continue at least to tolerate their rivals (way [1]) while others choose to continue a warfare that miraculously always falls short of killing off the critical enterprise entirely.

See now CRITICISM; POETICS; THEORY.

W. James, *Pragmatism* (1907), *A Pluralistic Universe* (1909); J. Dewey, *The Quest for Certainty* (1929); S. Pepper, *World Hypotheses* (1942); R. McKeon, "The Philosophic Bases of Art and Crit.," *MP* 41 (1943–44), "Philosophy and Method," *J. of Philos.* 48 (1951); E. Cassirer, *Lang. and Myth* (tr. 1946), *The Philosophy of Symbolic Forms* (tr. 1953); Abrams; R. S. Crane, *The Langs. of Crit. and the Structure of Poetry* (1953); Frye; K. Burke, *Lang. as Symbolic Action* (1966); D. Tracy, *Blessed Rage for Order: The New Pl. in Theology* (1975); N. Goodman, *Langs. of Art*, 2d ed. (1976), *Ways of World-Making* (1978); E. Olson, *On Value Judgments in the Arts* (1976); W. A. Davis, *The Act of Interp.* (1978); R. Rorty, *Philosophy and the Mirror of Nature* (1979); W. C. Booth, *Critical Understanding* (1979), *The Company We Keep* (1988); S. Fish, *Is There a Text in This Class?* (1980); J. Phelan, *Worlds from Words: A Theory of Lang. in Fiction* (1981); M. M. Bakhtin, *The Dialogic Imagination* (tr. 1981); T. G. Pavel, *Fictional Worlds* (1986); R. Rorty, *Contingency, Irony, and Solidarity* (1989); E. Rooney, *Seductive Reasoning* (1989); P. B. Armstrong, *Conflicting Readings: Variety and Validity in Interp.* (1990); J. L. Battersby, *Paradigms Regained* (1991); I. Berlin, *The Crooked Timber of Humanity* (1991).   W.C.B.

PLURISIGNATION. See AMBIGUITY; SEMANTICS AND POETRY.

POEM. See POETRY; VERSE AND PROSE.

POEMA. See EPIC.

POESIS, POIESIS. See POETICS; POET; CLASSICAL POETICS.

POET (Gr. *poietes*, "maker," from *poiein*, "to make"; Lat. *poeta*).

    I. PERSON AND MAKER
   II. SEER AND MAKER
  III. SOCIAL ROLE

I. PERSON AND MAKER. The first thing to say is that the p. is a maker of poems, and that the maker is not the same as the person. The quality of the maker's productions is not diminished by his or her personal shortcomings or failings in life, and conversely, the successes or social privilege of the person do not improve mediocre poetic productions: all that is *ad hominem*. The person, in the course of coming into and passing through adulthood, forms a self out of life's experiences, but the maker is formed specifically out of a decision to write poetry, to practice ("Without practice," says Blake, "nothing is possible"), to learn technique, and to continue to write. Lipking has written an elegant and absorbing essay on that moment in the lives of several persons when they first determined to become poets. The decision may or may not be entirely conscious—as everywhere else, that does not matter very much. Thus the p. develops a second self, emergent from the first yet supersessive to it; from such augmentation come enhanced opportunities for complex psychic relations. The maker is able to quarry the person (i.e. memory and sensibility) for experiences, reflections, insights, sensations, ambiguities, ambivalences, feelings, and thoughts—all potential threads to be woven into the emergent fabric of the poem. Most importantly, the maker can take advantage of these complex psychic interactions by creating a speaker for the poem, a persona (q.v.) that is quite distinct from the person.

One may reasonably wonder if it is even possible to say when one is the one self and when the other. The person is a person ever, obviously, but the maker is only a maker in the act of composing verse. W. H. Auden has attested to this belief and the accompanying fear that, when the p. has completed a poem, he or she may never successfully complete another again. Obviously, technique is precisely the resource one would rely on to overcome such a fear and write another poem, except for the fact that technique is always learned about another problem in another poem, so that to repeat it is not to confront a new poem, wholly, but merely to repeat gestures from the past. On the romantic and organicist theory of poetry, to which there have been many 20th c. free-verse adherents, every poem is unique. Still, without the accrual of learned technique, poems and ps. would never improve. The inferior p. is owned by technique; the great p. seeks, masters, alters, and extends technique (see VERSIFICATION).

The p. is only a maker in the act of composition, then, but we must not construe "composition" too narrowly as merely the act of writing lines. The act of making words, and making words make lines, is a process that may well extend over long periods of time and be carried on, according to the vagaries of thought and passion and the exigencies of circumstance, in several episodes, some conscious, some unconscious, many partly both. "Emotion recollected in tranquility" is too elliptical a description of the true nature of poetic genesis, incubation, articulation, and—most importantly—revision. The maker may mine the person (life) simply and directly: here autobiographical material is taken over directly into the poetry, subject only to the shaping that all verbal material undergoes when cast into verseform. But much more likely, in the long-standing view in Western poetics, is that the p. is not limited to her own experiences but will build up, via imagination (q.v.), a second reality quite other than the external world we know. The experiences of the person may be merely the springboard for extensive creative worldmaking, in exactly the same way that, in Freud's account of dreams, the dream work effects a virtually complete transformation of the latent content of the dream—the raw materials, the stimulus—into the manifest content, the actual dream—which in the case of poetry is the poem itself. Here one may recall Coleridge's distinction between fancy and imagination: it is not the copious generation of images but rather the selection and arrangement of them—along with thought, emotion, memory, and perception—within the frames of meter and stanza that constitutes the art poetical.

The obvious source to consult on making would be the p. But even if one were to ask a p. about the nature of her methods of composition, it is as much a question whether the answer would emerge from the maker or the person, as whether the methods of the one are ever entirely known to the other. Eliot is a prime example of this: despite his many theoretical pronouncements about impersonality, we always emerge from his poetry with the conviction that he is one of the most autobiographical of poets. In general, theorizing by ps. (e.g. Horace, Sidney, Pope, Coleridge, Eliot, Valéry) about poetry is suspect if not compromised, particularly if they build a theory out of their own work. Most ps. are notoriously unreliable as critics of themselves. Some may know what they are doing, in terms of technique and purpose, carry it out, and report on it accurately. Others may "know," in some less conscious sense, what they are doing but not be able to articulate it theoretically or analytically—this is very common. Still others may not even "know" what they are doing, even in the process of doing it, and for a variety of legitimate reasons, most of which follow from Chomsky's distinction between competence and performance. Some ps. may even know what they are doing but choose to be evasive about it to others—again, for a variety of reasons.

One might assume that utterances from a p. are reliable when confined to the subject of the versecraft. Utterances on all other subjects made by a p. are being made by the person and carry no greater authority than those made by any other citizen. Granted, the p. as person may well have an unusually perceptive or talented or complex personality compared to most; certainly many readers have felt that the lives and personalities of artists are worth knowing. It does not diminish the truth of this to urge, along with it, the corollary that such knowledge alone tells us nothing about the poetry—that, in other words, "biographical crit." is an oxymoron if not a contradiction in terms. What one wants to know is what the artist made, what she had available to work with, and how readers subsequently have responded to it. These are the realms, respectively, of textual and lit. crit., linguistics and stylistics, and reader-response crit. (qq.v.).

But makers make poems, and poems are made, of course, out of words. Hence any p. who wishes to perfect her art must be a student of lang.— words, sounds, rhythms—and of forms. Only by thorough knowledge of the materials and their permissible combinations can she master the craft. The p. who aspires to learn technique will study what forms have been shown to have expressive power by the great ps. of the past; the p. who knows that in every age the p. who wishes to be heard must find new means to express a new sensibility will experiment. Between these two poles lies all the dialectic of tradition (q.v.) and the individual talent that Eliot spoke of. In such study she will learn, in the simplest terms, *what is possible*, for the artist always works in and with a medium, taking advantage of what the medium offers, working around what the medium denies or restricts.

II. SEER AND MAKER. Since the Greeks, there have been two conceptions of the role of the p.: p. as seer, and p. as maker. That is to say, nearly all the metaphors and analogies that have been offered to describe the nature of *poiesis* concern either the poet's eye or the poet's hand. The former concerns mental representation (eidetic creation and alteration) while the latter concerns the physical aspects of text production. These two descriptive modes are inextricably intertwined throughout the history of Western poetics.

In the first conception, poet as seer (Lat. *vates* [q.v.], Ir. *fáith*, Welsh *gwawd*), the primary emphasis falls on origination, the chief assumption being that ideas, images, phrases, and words come to the p. from some source outside or beyond herself. From antiquity up to the 18th c., this notion was formulated as the doctrine of divine inspiration (q.v.), first in a kind of frenzy, a "poetic madness" (q.v.) given by the Muses to Gr. poets, then, for Christian poets, in a state of receptiveness to gifts from God. With the advent of romanticism, however, this conception was replaced by the doctrine of imagination (q.v.); now outer is replaced by inner as the point of origination for mental imagery (q.v.). The p. is now seen not as passive instrument but as creator, and the locus of origin is reduced to the self. All modern psychological investigation derives from the romantic and post-romantic focus on inner life. The imagination throws up new images before the poet's mind: the p. is "seer" of forms and modes of reality not apprehensible to normal sight. Perhaps such seeing is the product of some altered state of experience—dream, reverie, or trance, natural or induced—but the older sense of such states as *given*,

bestowed by some higher power, is gone. In such accounts the act of making and the role of technique are minimized. This is not to say they are denied; certainly the ps. themselves, at least, knew better. But in extreme formulations of the doctrine of inspiration, the p. is a mere mouthpiece for not only images but wording and even whole poems—as Blake claimed, as Coleridge reported about "Kubla Khan," as Poe would have liked for us to believe, and as Yeats and the surrealists alleged about "automatic writing."

Despite the frequency of references to poetic imagination, however, there are equally frequent appeals to recognize the poet's work as a skilled craft. The oldest metaphors in the world for the poet's work are those of weaving. Even the Greeks conceded the importance of skill at craft. Pindar acknowledges it very early. In the *Iliad* and the *Odyssey*, on every occasion when Homer appeals to the Muses, the request is for matter of a factual nature rather than for form. That is, Homer always asks for inspiration concerning what to say, never how to say it. Apparently divine possession may provide information, for Homer, but the p. must rely on her own accrued technical skill for the making of the song. This union of special knowledge and technical skill is the distinctive mark of the p. in Homer. And the ancient Gr. concept of the p. as maker is given greater authority by Horace, whose insistence on the importance of "the labor of the file" (revision) made the *Ars poetica* a central text throughout the Middle Ages. The "Scottish Chaucerians" [q.v.] writing in Middle Scots refer to themselves as "Makars," a usage echoed in the early Ren. by references to Wyatt and Surrey as the "Courtly Makers" (q.v.). In the 120th c., it finds echo in Ezra Pound's injunction to modernist poets to "Make It New."

Ultimately, of course, there is no simple division between having ideas and shaping them as words, between envisioning and revising: composition does not divide neatly into two distinct activities, separate and sequential. Both proceed simultaneously, interpenetrating each other so extensively that, at any given moment, one probably could not say whether a bit of phrasing or an image has just been invented *ex nihilo*—if such be possible—or was remembered from prior reading of some earlier p. (see INFLUENCE) or the newspaper or, indeed, anything. The mind's reception of words and ideas, and their retention in memory and the subconscious, and their alteration both consciously and subconsciously both at inception and later, is so complex a process and so little available to conscious inspection that simplistic dichotomies of origination and alteration seem worse than simplistic. And the role of the word itself, in this process of envisioning, arranging, and casting into verbal form, then verseform, is, while pivotal, nevertheless little understood (see POETRY).

III. SOCIAL ROLE. In the West, the poet's status, prestige, and cultural authority have changed radically in the long transition from preliterate, oral, monarchical societies to literate, written, democratic ones. In tribal societies, the p. naturally moved in the retinue of the chief, king, or ruler because he was invested with the same kind (though perhaps not the same amount) of cultural authority as the king and spiritual authority as the priest. Indeed, the roles of priest and p. become indistinguishable in sacred chant, ritual, and incantatory speech. As the adviser and chronicler of the king, the p. finds his task largely eulogistic (see Opland), praising the present and past deeds of the tribe and its heroes, preserving information (e.g. genealogical, medical) and proverbial lore, offering spiritual advice. Infused with divine sight and speech by the gods, the p. provides words that surpass the ordinary function of lang. to communicate ordinary knowledge. The p. is the carrier of tribal wisdom, the accumulated knowledge and experience of the race; and the poetry which embodies it, more tightly bound, becomes transcendent speech. The OE *scop* (q.v.) is still carrying on these functions into and past the 8th c. A.D. As tribal and nomadic societies become geographically established, however, both the ruler and the poet become institutionalized. Court poetry and the recording thereof replace bardic improvisation. In the Middle Ages, academic skill at versifying was crowned with a laurel wreath, a practice which was soon transferred to the court: Petrarch was crowned "poet laureate" (q.v.) in 1341, an honorary title preserved in England and eventually America up to the present. In modern times the communal and sacral function of the p. has been repeated in the call, by Mallarmé echoed by Pound, for the p. to "purify the dialect of the tribe."

W. H. Auden reminds us that much of the role of the p. is culturally defined. Some cultures make a formal social distinction between the sacred and the profane; others do not. In those that do, the p. has a public and sacral status as the conveyor of wisdom and knowledge of a very high order. In those that do not, however—which includes all modern Western industrial societies—the p. can present only knowledge that is personal and private, appealing to his or her readers, in essence, to judge for themselves whether or not the knowledge and experience described is not also their own. Now the poet's calling is merely a profession, valued highly by some, viewed with curiosity or skepticism by many.

The poet's cultural and spiritual authority have always had to be balanced against the practical exigencies of making a living; the disparity between the two indeed suggests that the former are more indirect, if not more illusory, than we would like to think. The poet's association with a monarch or a member of the aristocracy for financial support, most often by composing occasional verse (q.v.) on demand, lasted from ancient times until the 18th c., when the patronage system gave way—

its end might almost be dated precisely in Dr. Johnson's letter to Lord Chesterfield—to public consumption of printed books. This in turn lasted into the 20th c., when public preference for other artforms (the novel, cinema) forced many ps. to seek their livelihood in "creative writing" positions in universities or on the lecture circuit, as with Frost's very popular and profitable reading tours. In truth, the public for poetry has been small in every age: the more advanced the sensibility, the smaller the circle. But that market, if small, is on the other hand most often the most influential, appreciative of the arts, and possessed of the greatest means. The very notion of a literary *career* oscillates between the development of a reputation, among those competent to judge, for skill at the craft of verse and the utterance of words worth remembering, and, on the other hand, of the cultivation of a readership which will reward the making sufficiently to provide the necessary leisure for creative work in the future. It fell to Wordsworth to articulate the dilemma for the poet seeking to Make It New—that he or she must create the very audience by which the work may adequately be judged.

Further, since the 18th c., as the capacity for empathy, intensity, and imagination (qq.v.) increasingly came into conflict with the values of an urban, industrial, polluted, capitalist, and intolerant society, alienation came to be the primary characteristic of the poet's condition. This is made central to the ethos of romanticism—both Blake and Byron saw the p. as an isolated figure, a visionary, prophet, and political radical. Byron, however, like many other 19th-c. Eng. ps., did not have to struggle for existence. But as the 19th c. wore on, alienation became more than merely romantic, witness Baudelaire ("The Albatross") and the symbolists. The p., too sensitive, too verbal, too aestheticized, becomes the *poète maudit* (q.v.), "the p. defeated by life," brutalized by the vulgar tastes of the bourgeoisie. By the 20th c., with its triumph of media for the masses, alienation is simple fact. Perhaps to some degree it was always fact: ps. who do not consciously define themselves as following in a tradition (q.v.) must of necessity work to escape the burden of the past and the overbearing pressure of the great accomplishments of their predecessors (Bloom). But in modern times this private and psychological resistance-in-order-to-create has been overwritten with a more extensive resistance to the brutalities of modern culture, or what passes for culture.

Finally, we must recognize the deeper, more systemic, hence less visible forms of marginalization of ps., those which apply not individually but categorically, on account of gender, race, nationality, dialect, and class. Modern feminist critics have demonstrated in detail the kinds of disfigurements suffered by women poets who have had to exist in a patriarchal system which controls the means of production and of social recognition.

See also BARD; FILI; GENIUS; GUSLAR; SCOP; SKALD; TROUBADOUR; TROUVERE; see also PERFORMANCE; PERSONA; VOICE. For discussion of professional performers as distinct from ps. as composers, see GOLIARDIC VERSE; JONGLEUR; MINSTREL; RHAPSODE.

T. Carlyle, *On Heroes, Hero-Worship, and the Heroic* (1841), lecture 3; O. Behaghel, *Bewusstes und Unbewusstes in dichterische Schaffen* (1906); I. Zangerle, *Die Bestimmung der Dichters* (1949); W. Muschg, "Dichtertypen," *Festschrift F. Strich* (1952); Abrams; Curtius, Excursus 7; M. C. Nahm, *The Artist as Creator* (1956); A. F. Scott, *The Poet's Craft* (1957); P. Crutwell, "Makers and Persons," *HudR* 12 (1960); G. T. Wright, *The P. in the Poem* (1960); R. Jakobson, "Linguistics and Poetics," in Sebeok, rpt. in Jakobson, v. 2; W. H. Auden, "Making, Knowing, and Judging," *The Dyer's Hand* (1962); J. W. Saunders, *The Profession of Eng. Letters* (1964); P. Vicaire, *Recherches sur les mots désignant la poésie et le poète dans l'oeuvre de Platon* (1964); A. Kambylis, *Die Dichterweihe und ihre Symbolik* (1965)—concepts of the poet's calling in antiquity; J. K. Newman, *The Concept of Vates in Augustan Poetry* (1967); R. Schmitt, *Dichtung und Dichtersprache in indogermanischer Zeit* (1967), ed., *Indogermanische Dichtersprache und Namengebung* (1973); E. N. Tigerstedt, "The P. as Creator," *CLS* 5 (1968); T.-T. Chow, "The Early Hist. of the Chinese Word *Shih* (Poetry)," *Wen-lin: Studies in the Chinese Humanities* (1968); A. D. Skiadas, "Über das Wesen des Dichters im platonischen *Ion*," *Symbolae Osloenses* 46 (1971); K. K. Ruthven, *Critical Assumptions* (1979), ch. 5; H. Moisl, "Celto-Germanic *Watu-/Wotu-* and Early Germanic Poetry," *N&Q* 225 (1980); J. Opland, *Anglo-Saxon Oral Poetry* (1980); L. Lipking, *The Life of the Poet* (1981); K. Quinn, "The P. and His Audience in the Augustan Age," *Aufstieg und Niedergang der römischen Welt*, ed. W. Haase. v. 2 (1982); R. Helgerson, *Self-Crowned Laureates* (1983); M. Ellmann, *The Poetics of Impersonality* (1987); M. W. Bloomfield and C. W. Dunn, *The Role of the P. in Early Societies* (1989)—Ir., Welsh, Gaelic, ON, and OE; A. Balakian, *The Fiction of the P.* (1992). T.V.F.B.

POET LAUREATE. About to be seized by Apollo, Daphne turns into a laurel tree. Apollo takes the laurel for his emblem and decrees that its branch or bay shall become the prize of honor for poets and victors (Ovid, *Metamorphoses* 1). The line from Apollo to the Eng. poets l. follows the custom of kings and chieftains to maintain a court poet to sing heroic and glorious achievement. The Scandinavian *skald* (q.v.), the Welsh *bard* (q.v.), and the Anglo-Saxon *scop* (q.v.) resembled the poets l. in being attached to a ruler's court and serving his purposes. Professional entertainers like William I's *ioculator regis* or Henry I's *mimus regis* develop into the *versificator regis* who is part of Henry III's royal household in England. The *versificator* suggests an official l. not only by his regular payment

in money and wine but also in his being ridiculed, as were, later, Jonson, Davenant, Eusden, Cibber, Pye, and even Tennyson.

The actual term "l." arose in the medieval universities, which crowned with laurel a student admitted to an academic degree in grammar, rhet., and poetry. In time the word applied to any notable poetic attainment and was used as a standard compliment to Chaucer and, more formally, Petrarch, who was crowned p. l. at Rome in 1341. In a trad. of loosely bestowing the title "l." we find the names of Gower, Lydgate, Skelton, and Bernard Andreas, the Augustinian friar under Henry VII who anticipated Dryden's later double appointment as court poet and historiographer royal. Spenser, Drayton, and Daniel shared in various court activities receiving official recognition, while Ben Jonson thought of himself as a formal l., having received two pensions and much popular acclaim. Davenant seems to have enjoyed tacit recognition as p. l. under both Charles I and II, but held no official patent. The office was finally authorized with the appointment of John Dryden as the first "p. l." in 1668, and historiographer royal in 1670. The two offices were separated in 1692, and the emolument of l. was fixed at 100 pounds a year, where it has in effect remained ever since.

Since Dryden's removal in 1688, 17 poets have been made p. l.: Thomas Shadwell, 1689–92; Nahum Tate, 1692–1715; Nicholas Rowe, 1715–18; Laurence Eusden, 1718–30; Colley Cibber, 1730–57; William Whitehead, 1757–85; Thomas Warton, 1785–90; Henry James Pye, 1790–1813; Robert Southey, 1813–43; William Wordsworth, 1843–50; Alfred Tennyson, 1850–92; Alfred Austin, 1896–1913; Robert Bridges, 1913–30; John Masefield, 1930–67; C. Day Lewis, 1968–72; Sir John Betjeman, 1972–84; and Ted Hughes, 1984–. A number of poets have sought the laureateship in vain, incl. Johnson's friend Richard Savage, the "volunteer l.," William Mason, Leigh Hunt, and Lewis Morris (when, after Tennyson, a period of four years elapsed without a choice being made). The position has been refused by Gray, Scott, and Wordsworth (once, before accepting it), and by Samuel Rogers at the death of Wordsworth.

Traditionally the l.'s duty was to write eulogies, elegies, and other occasional verse (q.v.) for important events. In this sense, Tennyson's "Ode on the Death of the Duke of Wellington" (1852) emerges as the ideal performance. In practice, the laureateship from its beginning with Dryden falls into three periods. Dryden, Shadwell and Tate had no stated duties and could make of the office what they chose. In Dryden's case this was to speak brilliantly and with entire conviction for the royal cause, making *Absalom and Achitophel* in its way the ideal l.'s poem. In the early 18th c., the l. became a member of the royal household, charged with writing annually a New Year's Ode and a Birthday Ode to be set to music and sung before the king. The office became something of a joke until the annual odes were abandoned in the tenure of Southey. The modern phase has restored dignity to the position, with Wordsworth symbolically and Tennyson actively standing for the best that poetry is capable of.

In America an unofficial poet laureateship has existed since 1937, though no emolument was attached until 1985, when the honorific title of "Poetry Consultant to the Library of Congress" was changed to "P. L. Consultant in Poetry." The first official Am'. p. l. was Robert Penn Warren (1905–89), who on his resignation for reasons of health in 1987 was succeeded by Richard Wilbur (b. 1921), followed in turn by Howard Nemerov (b. 1920), Mark Strand (b. 1934), and Joseph Brodsky (b. 1940). The Am. position is for one year only, though with possibility of renewal, and begins in May; official duties comprise one poetry reading and one public lecture.—W. S. Austin, Jr., and J. Ralph, *The Lives of the Poets L.* (1853); W. Hamilton, *The Poets L. of England* (1879); K. West, *The Ls. of England from Ben Jonson to Alfred Tennyson* (1895); W. F. Gray, *The Poets L. of England* (1914); E. K. Broadus, *The Laureateship* (1921); K. Hopkins, *The Poets L.*, 3d ed. (1973); R. Helgerson, *Self-Crowned Ls.* (1983)—related. B.N.S.; T.V.F.B.

POÈTE MAUDIT. A phrase that mirrors the widening gulf in 19th-c. France between the gifted poet and the public upon which his survival might depend. It was given currency by Verlaine's *Les poètes maudits* (1884), a collection of essays on poets hardly known at the time, such as Corbière, Rimbaud, and Mallarmé. A half-century earlier, Vigny's *Stello* (1832) had developed, in successive tales on Gilbert, Chatterton, and André Chénier, the idea that poets ("the race forever accursed [*maudite*] by those who have power on earth") are envied and hated for their superior qualities by society and its rulers who fear the truths they tell. Thereafter, a sick, impoverished or dissolute poet of significant but generally unrecognized talent came to be seen in these terms as doubly victimized by a hostile and insentient society.   A.G.E.

POETIC AUTONOMY. See AUTONOMY, POETIC.

POETIC CLOSURE. See CLOSURE.

POETIC COLLECTIONS. See COLLECTIONS, POETIC.

POETIC CONTESTS.

    I. WESTERN
    II. EASTERN

I. WESTERN p. cs. are formal, agonistic exchanges in verse that display some or all of the following characteristics: (1) two or more poet contestants, (2) physically present to each other,

(3) in a public setting before witnesses, (4) engaging in a verbal duel or debate that (5) treats a conventionalized or prestipulated subject matter (often of an *ad hominem* variety), (6) undertaken for the sake of a prize, material or spiritual, and (7) resolved through appeal to external judgment. Since all seven elements seldom obtain in a single work, the class of p. c. is heterogeneous, encompassing several subgenres and defying precise circumscription. Indeed, the poetic contest itself is not a genre at all but rather the verbal expression of a general mode of human interaction—the aggressive and agonistic—whose roots extend deep into biology and psychology. The distinction between "real" and "imaginary" (or, more precisely, extratextual and intratextual) p. c. is fundamental though not inviolable. Historically actual p. c. (such as the Athenian Dionysia) may occasion the composition of poems that contain no contestual elements; fictional p. c. (such as the *Canterbury Tales*), on the other hand, may be dramatized in poems that were not themselves products of a contest. Yet the line may be blurred, as when a real poetic contest results in poetic texts with contestual elements recognizable only by audiences who knew the original performance setting. It should be recollected that p. c. are usually rooted in the world of orality that assumes greater interdependence between poem and presentational context than is customary in the poetries of highly literate societies.

Verbal-contest forms akin to p. c. flourished in ancient civilizations. Ancient Gr., Arabic, and Celtic legends feature poet-magicians whose satirical verses could produce a range of woes from the raising of blisters to death; occasionally such versifiers match off in supernatural contests. In heroic poems such as the *Iliad, Mahabharata, Beowulf,* and *The Song of Roland,* warrior pairs hurl boasts and insults prior to battle. In such exchanges the spoken word poetically cast is perceived as an extension of the personal vitalic energy, martial prowess, or moral worth of the speaker. The poetic contest emerges spectacularly into the foreground of Western lit. hist. in the great dramatic festivals of Cl. Athens (5th c. B.C.). While this contest setting is not directly reflected in the content of Gr. tragedy, Aristophanes made it the subject of *The Frogs,* where Aeschylus and Euripides compete posthumously before Dionysus for the laurel crown. From Hellenistic times, singing matches begin to make their appearance in pastoral (q.v.) poetry, first in Theocritus' *Idylls,* later in the eclogues (q.v.) of Virgil and Ren. poets. Some of the verse satires of Horace and later writers in the satiric trad. are cast in argumentative, dialogic frames.

It is in the Middle Ages, however, that p. c. both fictive and actual are most abundantly represented. Med. Lat. poems of *conflictus* feature altercations between character types or allegorical personifications such as summer and winter, wine and water, body and soul, rustics and clerics, or a Moslem, a Jew, and a Christian, subjects that recur in several vernacular lits. In the 12th c., love emerges as a major topic, as in the *Altercatio Phyllis et Florae*. In the same period in Fr. and Occitan lit. emerges the *tenso* (q.v.), in which troubadours (q.v.) debate in alternating strophes on matters of politics, morality, poetics, or, above all, love and women. Perhaps derived from the *sirventes* (q.v.), a political or satirical diatribe, and incorporating such subgenres as the *partimen* (q.v.), the *tenso* is the dominant medieval verse-debate form, although debate elements appear in other genres as well, such as the *pastourelle* (q.v.), the It. *lauda* (q.v.) and *contrasto*, and the 14th- to 15th-c. Sp. *pregunta* (q.v.). The purest and most dramatic medieval p. c. is the 13th-c. MHG *Wartburgkrieg*, in which five poets are pitted against a magician in a riddle competition, with death as the penalty for losing. Several Eddic poems feature verbal contest between such adversaries as Thor and Odin. ME produced a classic *débat* in the late 12th- or early 13th-c. *The Owl and the Nightingale*. Chaucer's *Canterbury Tales* represents a full-blown peregrine poetic contest with some thirty contestants, a judge, and a prize. The flamboyant *flytings* (q.v.) of 15th- to 16th-c. Scotland feature volleys of fantastical invective (q.v.) and abuse between noted contemporary poets, possibly as court entertainment.

The scope and longevity of these forms should be taken as an index of the wide popularity of verbal contesting in the Middle Ages in circles both courtly and popular. Rival troubadours and *Minnesingers* such as Gottfried von Strassburg and Wolfram von Eschenbach traded barbs by alluding to each other, by name or epithet, in their works. Cultivating independence from courtly patronage, Fr. poets and minstrels in the 13th c. began to form associations (*puys*) that trained apprentices in the craft and sponsored competitions for prizes. Meistersinger (q.v.) guilds in 14th- to 16th-c. Germany served similar functions. Several such associations and annual festivals still survive, such as the Jacs Florals in Toulouse and the National Eisteddfod (q.v.) in Wales.

After the Ren., p. c. witnessed a decline both as poetic topic and social custom—despite its allusion to the laurel crown of Cl. contests, official poet laureateship (q.v.) became a reward for political loyalties more than poetic skill—although debate features have persisted in the pastoral, Ren. and neoclassical drama, and other genres. Racine, Corneille, and Voltaire asserted their superiority over their rivals in the prologues of their plays, and Dryden's *MacFlecknoe* and later Augustan satires register through thinly veiled fictions real social and poetic rivalries.

In the contemporary era, though real p. c. are a regular feature of the literary landscape, the resultant poetry is seldom agonistic in style or subject. Yet p. c. remain vital in third-world and popular culture. Such poetic or semi-poetic modes as "playing the dozens" (see DOZENS), "toast" (q.v.), "signifying" (q.v.), and "rapping," widely in evidence among contemporary American blacks and often realized as verbal duel, feature verbal pyrotechnics and a marked facility for extemporization. Other instances of p. c. attest to their contemporary cross-cultural popularity and diversity: Greenland Inuit resolve quarrels through drum-and-song duels adjudicated by the tribe; obscene dueling genres flourish among Turkish and Guatemalan adolescents; European television broadcasts a yearly *Saengerkrieg*, taking its title from the "war of singers" at the Wartburg.

H. Knobloch, *Die Streitgedichte im Provenzalichen und Altfranzösischen* (1886); H. Jantzen, *Gesch. des deutsches Streitgedichtes* (1896); B. Petermann, *Der Streit um Vers und Prosa in der französischen Literatur des 18. Jhs.* (1913); H. Walther, *Das Streitgedichte in der lateinischen Lit. des Mittelalters* (1920); H. Pflaum, *Die religiöse Disputation in der europ. Dichtung des Mittelalters* (1935): Jeanroy; J. Huizinga, *Homo Ludens* (1944); R. Elliott, *The Power of Satire* (1960); J. G. Cummins, "Methods and Conventions in Poetic Debate," *HR* 31 (1963); W. Labov, *Lang. in the Inner City* (1972); G. Bebermeyer, "Streitgedicht," *Reallexikon* 4.228–45; C. Lindahl, *Earnest Games* (1987); *Med. Debate Poetry: Vernacular Works*, ed. and tr. M.-A. Bossy (1987); A. Pickard-Cambridge, *The Dramatic Festivals of Athens*, 2d ed. rev. (1989); W. Parks, *Verbal Dueling in Heroic Narrative* (1990); R. Osmond, *Mutual Accusation* (1990); T. L. Reed, *ME Debate Poetry and the Aesthetics of Irresolution* (1990). W.H.; W.W.P.

II. EASTERN. Japanese p. c. are the world's most elaborated. They began in the late 19th c. as one of a variety of matches on objects ranging from iris roots to paintings, and were largely social; the low-ranking nobility commonly writing the poems did so for presentation by their betters. But in time, social distinctions became less important, and competition keener, often bitter. One or more judges decided the outcome. To facilitate judgment, topics were increasingly given out in advance and became more detailed as well as fictionalized, e.g. "Cherry Blossoms at a Mountain Temple," "Love Consummation Unconsummated." Because p. c. were a major form of publication, and because of increasing rigor, standards of judgment were conservative, being based on precedent. But standards altered, and the judgments at p. c. provide important insights into poetic theory as well as praxis. At the Japanese court, two of the most important p. c. are *The Poetry Match in 600 Rounds* (i.e. 1200 poems; 1193 A.D.) and *The Poetry Match in 1500 Rounds* (3,000 poems; 1202). There were also p. c. by one person, pitting poems on the same topic against each other for judgment by an esteemed critic, e.g. Monk Saigyō's *Mimosusogawa Poetry Match* (1187). There were numerous other variants. Closest to the kind, and indeed often part of it, 100-poem sequences were often the unit of competition. Subsequently other kinds of matches occurred, chiefly those of linked poetry (*renga*, q.v.) and nō (q.v.). Beginning in the 9th c., p. c. of various kinds are a major feature of Japanese lit. until about 1600, after which only modified and attenuated versions exist. But during these six or seven centuries, p. c. are a more important feature of Japanese lit. than of any other.—R. H. Brower and E. Miner, *Japanese Court Poetry* (1961).　　E.M.

POETIC DICTION. See ARCHAISM; AUREATE DICTION; CONCRETE AND ABSTRACT; CONNOTATION AND DENOTATION; EPITHET; KENNING; LEXIS.

POETIC DRAMA. See DRAMATIC POETRY.

POETIC FORM. See SOUND; VERSE AND PROSE; FORM.

POETIC FUNCTION. In a classic analysis of the act of verbal communication formulated by Roman Jakobson in 1958, every such act involves six elements: an *addresser*, an *addressee*, a *context* referred to; a *code* common to addresser and addressee as encoder and decoder of the message; a *contact*, i.e. "a physical channel and psychological connection between the addresser and the addressee"; and the *message*, i.e. the actual spoken or written discourse in all its linguistic particulars. Each element corresponds to one of six functions of lang.: the *emotive* or expressive (orientation toward the addresser, aiming at a direct expression of his or her attitude); the *conative* (oriented toward the addressee, and often expressed grammatically through the vocative case of a noun designating the addressee and through the imperative mood of verbs); the *referential* (toward the context); the *metalingual* (speaking about lang., toward the code); the *phatic* (toward the contact, aimed at establishing, maintaining, or prolonging communication); and the *poetic* (toward the message). In short, the p. f. is "[t]he set (*Einstellung*) toward the message as such, focus on the message for its own sake."

The p. f. of lang., Jakobson stressed, is not restricted to poetry, nor are the other functions absent from poetry. In any act of verbal communication several functions may be realized, having different degrees of importance, one being predominant. However, the terms Jakobson uses to define the p. f. he elsewhere employs to describe poetry, and others have used his definition of the p. f. as the basis for distinctions between poetry and prose, and between literary and ordinary lang.

The predominant function is, for Jakobson, the primary determinant of the verbal structure of the message, so, presumably, the analyst can deduce the function from the structure. Where the p. f. is predominant, "the principle of equivalence" (q.v.) is projected "from the axis of selection into the axis of combination." That is, words in the text are related to each other not only syntagmatically, by contiguity, but also paradigmatically, i.e. as they are related to other words that could be substituted for them. Where the p. f. is predominant, then, the words present in the text will have the same kinds of relations to each other as they do to the words from which they were chosen, those absent from the text. These relations include phonological identity (whence meter and rhyme), grammatical parallelism, and semantic synonymy or antithesis.

This definition of the p. f. of lang. has important implications for stylistics (q.v.); the task of the stylistician becomes that of analyzing exhaustively the linguistic structure of a text, and thereby discovering patterns of equivalences. Jakobson himself practiced such stylistic analysis on poems in several langs.; esp. controversial have been studies of Baudelaire's "Les Chats" and of Shakespeare's Sonnet 129. In these analyses, different parts of the poem are contrasted in terms of the presence or absence of features in binary opposition, revealing multiple symmetries. Jakobson's methodology and results have been challenged by Riffaterre, who has argued that a given linguistic equivalence is not necessarily stylistically relevant unless or until it becomes perceptible to readers (other than trained linguists). Similarly, Werth has argued that recurrence will be found in any text, that its perceptibility and effects depend in part on the nature of the repetition and of the units involved (whether phonological, lexical, or syntactic), that binary oppositions can be generated at the whim of the analyst, that it is pointless if not impossible to attempt an analysis that is exhaustive at all levels, and that semantic analysis is properly a prerequisite to analysis of other aspects of text structure.

Jakobson was not the first scholar to discriminate different functions of lang. use in a way that bears on the analysis of poetry. As early as 1925, I. A. Richards distinguished between the scientific use of lang., for the sake of reference, and the emotive use, for the sake of the emotion produced. His emotive function, being concerned with production of attitudes in the audience, is unlike Jakobson's, which concerns the expression of emotion by the addresser. Richards' functions derive not from analysis of the act of communication, like Jakobson's, but simply from an attempt to categorize the kinds of work a sentence can do. By 1949 he was distinguishing six such jobs, three of them—*indicating*, *characterizing*, and *realizing*—referential in function, two—*appraising* and *influencing*—emotive. Only the sixth, *structuring*, resembles Jakobson's p. f. See also INTERPRETATION.

Richards; R. Jakobson, "Linguistics and Poetics," in Jakobson, v. 5; R. Jakobson and C. Lévi-Strauss, "*Les Chats* de Charles Baudelaire," *L'Homme* 2 (1962); R. Jakobson and L. G. Jones, *Shakespeare's Verbal Art in "Th'Expense of Spirit"* (1970); M. Riffaterre, "Describing Poetic Structures," *Structuralism*, ed. J. Ehrmann (1970); Culler, ch. 3; E. Holenstein, *Roman Jakobson's Approach to Lang.*, tr. C. and T. Schelbert (1976); P. Werth, "Roman Jakobson's Verbal Analysis of Poetry," *JL* 12 (1976); T. J. Taylor, *Linguistic Theory and Structural Stylistics* (1980), ch. 3; L. R. Waugh, "The P. F. in the Theory of Roman Jakobson," *PoT* 2, 1a (1980); J. P. Russo, *I. A. Richards* (1989).

E.B.

POETIC LICENSE. This phrase originally referred to the freedom allowed the poet to depart in diction, grammar, or subject matter from the norms of prose discourse or, later, from poetic "rules" (q.v.). "P. l." is still a popular phrase in common usage, but in crit. it is now chiefly a historical term used to describe the creative management of historical fact—Virgil's decision to make Dido the contemporary of Aeneas, for example. But many other rhetorical ploys once fell under its aegis, among them the use of archaic words or pronunciations (see ARCHAISM) and inversions of syntax (see HYPERBATON). Both Aristotle and Horace thought it feasible for poets to coin, lengthen, shorten, alter, or import words that might distinguish their lang., and Aristotle even encouraged p. l. to enhance verisimilitude (q.v.): "for poetic effect a convincing impossibility is preferable to that which is unconvincing but possible" (tr. Butcher). The notion of a "l." itself implies, however, a fairly strict set of rules or norms of generic or structural specification which the poet is given permission to ignore, and modern critical theory has refined and altered considerably the ideas that pertain to the nature of literary genres and the authority of convention (q.v.). Genre studies have questioned the integrity of the various rules that once governed the assignment of a text to the ranks of poetry or prose; and the confidence that once allowed a critic to identify an instance of p. l. is of very limited use in describing the prose poem (q.v.), as Arthur Rimbaud implicitly demonstrated in *A Season in Hell*. In conceptualizing poetic making as either deviation from strictly defined "rules" (which do not exist) or as lawless freedom to create, the phrase distracts attention from the the specific and important functions that innovation and invention (q.v.) can serve. Paul Celan was one of the most innovative poetic neologists of the 20th c., but his coinages are very poorly served by being described as p. l., because they were not designed to create effects simply by violating standard Ger. vocabulary. Rather, by taking advantage of the natural affinity of Ger. for making compounds, Celan was able to combine neology and etymology for constructing a critique of lang. and its influence on perceptions of reality.

In modern stylistics (q.v.), similar characterizations of unusual lexical and syntactic constructions are occasionally found; these too are unfortunately cast in negative terms rather than positive. In prosody (q.v.) it was sometimes said that p. l. allowed the poet freedom to alter lexis or syntax so as to meet the stricter requirements of meter, but this amounts to an indictment of the competence of the poet, who on this account is not master of the meter for her or his own purposes but is mastered by it. This too is inapt: prose norms of lexis or order have no precedence or authority such that poetry should be judged against that standard.

T.V.F.B.; S.BU.

POETIC MADNESS (Gr. *mania* or *enthousiasmos*; Lat. *furor poeticus*). Up to the Ren., the central component of the Western conception of poetic composition was that of divine inspiration (q.v.)—literally, a "breathing in." The notion that the poet may become "possessed" by a frenzy or ecstasy bequeathed by a god in order to create poetry descends from the Greeks. In the earliest Gr. poetry, the voice of the poet is simply the stringed instrument of the Muses (q.v.), who impart information which he either could not know himself or is not able to remember. Homer several times appeals to the Muses for factual information, though the notion of divine inspiration for poetic *form*, by contrast, is nonexistent in Homer. The first extant reference to p. m. is by Democritus (fr. 17, 18), who says that no one can be a poet without "divine breath."

Plato in the *Phaedrus* (244a–245a, 265a–b,) identifies four types of m., prophetic, ritual [Dionysiac], poetic, and erotic, a formulation surviving from archaic times, when the boundaries between religious ecstasy, drunkenness, mystical prophecy, and poetic creation were blurred if not nonexistent. Subsequently Plato's four types were reduced to three, which is the number two millennia later in Shakespeare, (*MND* 5.1), when the Duke confirms that "the lunatic, the lover, and the poet / Are of imagination all compact." Socrates asserts that poets cannot succeed without p. m. In the *Ion* both poet and critic are described as so possessed that they no longer consciously control their words—clear evidence of the Platonic denigration of craft, for in fact Plato's purpose is to show that poetry, being wholly *given*, is no art at all. The Roman poets and critics also accepted p. m.: Horace says that drink improves poetic creation; Cicero says that no one can be a poet "who is not on fire with passion and without a certain touch (*afflatus*) of frenzy" (*De oratore* 2.46); Ovid remarks that "a god is within us; when he urges, we are inspired." Thereafter the concept was appropriated by Neoplatonism.

All of these references amount to claims that (1) a heightened state of consciousness or intensity of experience is the necessary condition or effect not only of genuine madness (insanity) but also of artistic creativity and erotic transport, and that (2) category divisions between these states are largely immaterial. "Great wits are sure to madness near allied," says Dryden, "And thin partitions do their bounds divide." The belief that the genius (q.v.; "spirit") and lunatic ("driven by the Moon") are fed from the same springs has never departed Western culture.

In the subsequent history of Western poetics, major alterations in this conception are but two: with the advent of Christianity, transfer of the locus of generation from pagan gods to a Christian God, and with the advent of secular psychology, from external inspiration to internal creation. And while Plato clearly distinguishes between m. which is divinely inspired and that caused by physical disease ("our greatest blessings come to us by way of m.," says Socrates, "provided the m. is given us by divine gift" [tr. Dodds]), the subsequent devel. of the concept of m. has served mainly to call the very notion into question.

The phrase *furor poeticus* is however not Cl. but Ren. Lat.; in Ficino's 1482 It. tr. of Plato, the *Ion* is given the subtitle, *De furore poetico*; thereafter the term is a commonplace of Ren. poetics (q.v.). The doctrine of divine inspiration first appears in Fr. in *L'Instructif de la seconde rhétorique* (1501) and forms an important part of the poetic theories of both Ronsard and Montaigne (Patterson). But in England its reception was cooler: Sidney in the *Defence* mouths the traditional (Neoplatonist) line but also insists on the power of the poet as maker, and in *Astrophil and Stella* (74) rejects p. m. outright. The notion of divine origination and control of poetic creation ran counter to the emergent Ren. spirit of scientific rationalism, as well as the profound Humanist distrust of the irrational and immoral. To a Humanist, it would be sacrilege to assign to mere mortals qualities of the divine.

But in romantic poetics (q.v.), the role of the poet is given new primacy as both visionary (see VISION) and tormented outcast (see POETE MAUDIT). And though inspiration is now dissociated from divinity for some of the romantics, or else transferred to a pantheistic source, the aesthetics of spontaneity, originality, and imagination (qq.v.) all affirm intensified consciousness. To poems the result of intoxication or hallucination are now added poems given in a dream or reverie—Coleridge's "Kubla Khan," Poe's "The Raven"—though Coleridge himself calls "Kubla Khan" a "psychological curiosity."

Modern reformulations of the idea of p. m. derive almost entirely from the emergence of psychology in the late 19th c. The connection to the concept in antiquity is simply the new belief that creativity is the work of the id not the ego. To Freud (in his essay "The Relation of the Poet to Day-Dreaming" and elsewhere), the artist is neurotic and his work is a by-product and symbolic statement of his disturbance, particularly so in that, for Freud, the unconscious itself works by processes that are tropological. But for Jung, creative activity puts the poet in touch with the primal source of human vitality, the energy welling up from the collective unconscious; it synthesizes id as eros and ego as will to power in a productive act.

All this is only to say that poets who really are mad, like Lucretius, Villon, Marlowe, Collins, Smart, Blake, Nerval, Hölderlin, Nietzsche, and Pound, or, at the very least exhibited marked personality disorders, nevertheless seem able, thereby, to access regions of creativity not available to others. The question of who is mad thus begins to seem really the question of who gets to define the criteria: on aesthetic criteria, it is bourgeois materialism and philistinism which seem mad.

The issue of whether art is neurotic or emblem of deeper health has been explored by Thomas Mann, Kenneth Burke, Lionel Trilling ("Art and Neurosis"), and esp. by Edmund Wilson: in *The Wound and the Bow* (1941), "wound" refers to the artist's neurosis, and "bow" to the art which is its compensation. Now poetry like all art is a catharsis (q.v.) for the poet, whereas for the Greeks it was one for the audience. Even I. A. Richards' theory of poetry was originally neurologically based, emphasizing interinanimations, synergism, and wholeness, though few now remember that. P. m. was for the Greeks a myth. It still is. Poetic creativity was a mystery. It still is.

G. E. Woodberry, "P. M.," *The Inspiration of Poetry* (1910); F. C. Prescott, "P. M. and Catharsis," *The Poetic Mind* (1922); R. Graves, *Poetic Unreason* (1925); A. Delatte, *Les Conceptions de l'enthousiasme chez les philosophes présocratiques* (1934); L. Trilling, *The Liberal Imagination* (1950); E. R. Dodds, *The Greeks and the Irrational* (1951); Curtius, Excursus 8; J. C. Nelson, *Ren. Theory of Love* (1958); Weinberg, s.v. "Furor" in the Index; B. Hathaway, *The Age of Crit.* (1962); G. Bruno, *The Heroic Frenzies*, tr. P. E. Memmo, Jr. (1964); *Intoxication and Lit.*, ed. E. R. Peschel (1974); E. Fass, *Shakespeare's Poetics* (1986); J. Britnell, "Poetic Fury and Prophetic Fury," *Ren. Studies* 3 (1989); A. Rothenberg, *Creativity and M.* (1990). T.V.F.B.

POETIC PRINCIPLE. See POETIC FUNCTION; EQUIVALENCE.

POETICS.

 I. WESTERN
 A. *Theoretical*
 B. *Historical*
 II. EASTERN
 A. *Theoretical*
 B. *Historical*

I. WESTERN. A. *Theoretical.* The term "p." has been used in the West in several senses. In recent decades it has been applied to almost every human activity, so that often it seems to mean little more than "theory" (q.v.); such usage is the most general and least useful. Applied to the works of authors, as in "the p. of Dostoevskij," it means something like "implicit principles"; for discussion of the relation between extrinsic theory and intrinsic principles, see RULES. More narrowly, the term has been used to denote "theory of lit.," i.e. "theory of literary discourse": this usage is more productive because it remains framed within theory of (verbal) discourse and it specifically retains the concept of the literary, i.e. the distinction between literary and nonliterary. Critics who have denied that distinction, extending "textuality" (q.v.) beyond the realm of the verbal, hold a minority view. This is the sense used by Aristotle, who bases the *Poetics* on verse drama, and by most 20th-c. theorists, e.g. Jakobson, operating after the collapse of the Cl. theory of genres. Part of the virtue of this usage is that it will allow concepts such as "the p. of prose." For Northrop Frye, p. is "theory of crit." (*Anatomy* 22), which is one level up from "theory of lit."; for discussion of p. as theory of crit., see METACRITICISM.

Granting the distinction of the literary, the most specific sense of "p." denotes "theory of poetry." Taking the term in this sense entails the claim that there is a fundamental distinction between the modes of verse and prose (q.v.). There have been two views taken, in the hist. of crit., on whether the mode or form of verbal discourse is essential to category distinctions within the "literary" or, indeed, to "the literary" (lit.) itself. Aristotle holds that it is not metrical form which makes for poetry but rather *mimesis*—a skillfully contrived imitation (q.v.) of actions that is *convincing*. Texts set in versified form but which lack this motive, such as Empedocles' versified history, are not poetry for Aristotle (*Poetics* 1). For him, "poetry" inheres in the purpose not the form (though cf. *Rhet.* 3.1.1404a). And so Sidney and Shelley after him: "poetry" can be written in prose, and many versified texts are not worthy of the name of "poetry." So too, in our time, Wallace Stevens, for whom "poetry is not the lang. of poetry but the thing itself, wherever it may be found. It does not mean verse any more than philosophy means prose" (*Opus posthumous*). Most such critics are implicitly Longinian, ascribing to "poetry" some transcendent mode of thought, imagination (q.v.), or insight which prose form could also convey.

The opposing view is that verseform matters, that form makes an irrevocable difference to poetry. The 5th-c. Sophist, Gorgias, in the *Defense of Helen*, holds that poetry is but one lang.-use among several for persuasion (or delusion): the differentia is the verseform. Subsequent critics who take verseform to be not ornamental but constitutive have included Scaliger, Coleridge, Jakobson, and the Rus. and Am. formalists (see VERSE AND PROSE). Such critics recognize the additional resources afforded for expression of transcendent thought, imagination, or insight by increased pattern or design, in aural prosody, and by strategies of deployment in visual prosody. Jakobson in his 1958 white paper on "Linguistics and P." asserts that p. "deals primarily with the question, 'what makes a verbal message a work of art?'" His answer, which is the Rus. Formalist answer, is that

self-referentiality—the "poetic function" (q.v.)—is the one characteristic of poetic lang. Admittedly, this function also operates in other patterned forms of speech such as political slogans and advertising jingles ("I like Ike"). But in other lang.-use, sound patterning is secondary, whereas in poetry it is made "the constitutive device of the sequence" (see PROSODY). Prose, "where there is no dominant figure of sound," Jakobson likens to "transitional" linguistic forms. *Pace* Aristotle, the overwhelming majority of critics and readers in the history of the world's poetries have believed that verseform is an essential differentia of poetry which enables effects not otherwise obtainable in prose.

P., then, is in the most specific sense a systematic theory of poetry. It attempts to define the nature of poetry, its kinds and forms, its resources of device and structure, the principles that govern it, the functions that distinguish it from other arts, the conditions under which it can exist, and its effects on readers or auditors. The term itself derives from the title of Aristotle's work on verbal making, *Peri pioetikē*—fragmentary and perhaps only lecture notes to begin with—which is the prototype of all later treatises on the art of poetry, formal or informal (e.g. Horace, Dante, Sidney, Shelley, Valéry).

There have been two formal models produced within the past half-century which pertain to p. The most comprehensive taxonomy, given by Abrams in 1953 (see POETRY, THEORIES OF), posits a model which has four orientations poetic theories may take: toward the work itself (objective or formalist theories), toward the audience (pragmatic or affective theories), toward the world (mimetic or realistic theories), and toward the poet-creator (expressive or romantic theories). All literary theorists recognize these orientations; they only disagree about their respective valuations. The communication model mapped by Jakobson, more complex but not essentially different in its premises from Abrams', identifies six components of any verbal discourse: the transactional continuum of course runs from speaker (poet) through message (text) to audience (auditor, reader), but the text itself must also comprise the context, contact type, and code (lang.) which make it possible. For Jakobson like most others it is the nature of the code which is the major issue: it is lang. which has been the model and trope for the major intellectual inquiries in the 20th c.

Western p. over the past three millennia has moved in three major waves (see section IB below). P. in the Aristotelian trad. was overwhelmingly objectivist and formalist down to the 18th c., with a lesser, Horatian strain being more affective and rhetorical but consonant with Aristotle (Howell); the literary mode valorized was the epic. Subsequently, romantic p., expressivist, restored the perceiving subject, consciousness, emotion (q.v.), and the Longinian sublime (q.v.) to the frame of what poetry presents; romantic p. exerted influence on poetic praxis (though not on theory) well into the 20th c.: its mode was the lyric. In the 20th c., p. moved steadily toward the metacritical or theoretical. In the first half of the century, p. was again objectivist and formalist (Rus. Formalist, Am. New Critical, Structuralist), with an affectivist undercurrent in phenomenology (Ransom drew upon Hegel; Wellek's definition of poetry derives from Ingarden). In the last half of the century, however, literary theory has retreated from the work of crit. common to all Western critics from Aristotle through the mid 20th c.—articulating a p. inductively, on the basis of critical praxis—to the metacritical task of asking, rather, what would constitute an adequate p., what questions it must answer, and what entailments those answers have. In so doing, postformalist crit. has called into question most of the major assumptions of Western p., though in practice it has continued the close reading of texts while moving further into readerly affectivism. In general, we may say that Western p., unlike the several Eastern p. which have mainly concerned themselves with the expressive and affective powers of lit. (see section II below), has mainly taken as its central problem the issue of the reliability of verbal representations of the external world, i.e. *mimesis* (see REPRESENTATION AND MIMESIS; IMITATION). The main issue has been dispute over the nature and (objective) veracity of a work's depiction of "reality," whatever that is taken to be.

Put another way, the great specter haunting Western p. has been the issue of subjectivity. There have been repeated efforts since ancient times to establish p. on an objective basis, either as science or philosophy, and repeated counterefforts to deny it that status; the dispute concerns what kind of activity p. is and what its objects are. There have been strong proponents on both sides (see Hrushovski). On the objectivist side have stood all who view p. as a science: Classicists and philologists; the Rus. Formalists; the Czech, Fr., and Am. structuralists; nearly all linguists; critics who admit empirical methods in psychological crit. or stylistics (qq.v.); and critics who use statistical analysis or mathematical modeling. Other objectivist critics such as I. A. Richards and the New Critics (esp. Wimsatt) have insisted on an exclusive orientation to the text while yet adamantly opposing poetry to science. Nonobjectivist critics ("subjective" is too limited) treat art not primarily as an object but as an *experience*, subjective or intersubjective, whether in the making (see EXPRESSION) or the reception: such critics include phenomenologists (see GENEVA SCHOOL), reader-oriented critics (see READER-RESPONSE CRITICISM), and, significantly, Aristotle himself (see below).

Jakobson, for example, held that since poems are verbal works of art, their rules fell within the purview of linguistics, as the global science of all verbal behavior. But others (e.g. Brogan, Intro.) have argued that this is the wrong plane of cleavage: poems are verbal works of *art*, hence their study falls within the domain of aesthetics rather than science, science being, strictly speaking, only a procedure for empirical verification of hypotheses which are objectively verifiable. The objects of study in science are objective phenomena the truth values of which constitute "facts"; the objects of literary study, on the other hand, are intersubjective meanings and values generated from an object which is itself a structure of forms (lang.), not marks on pieces of paper (see POETRY).

But this question about p. really amounts to the question of what, exactly, a *poem* is, i.e. whether it is an objective entity capable of being understood or analyzed with methods such that the results will be the same regardless of the reader, or whether the perception of a poem and the construction of meanings in and through it by readers results in inevitable and irreducible variability of response, making "the poem" seem more an interpersonal transaction or process than an object. In this latter view, the structures of poetry turn out to be not inherent in "the poem" itself but the rules or procedures of cognition as yet largely undiscovered by cognitive science, but incl. the conventions of meaning-making and legitimization which are constructed by communities of readers. But all this eventually comes to but a single question, the issue of how much variability in interpretation (q.v.) is permissible, and what factors control the process of interp. The most immediate answer would be that *structures in the text* are the primary determinants (see PROSODY), though obviously not the only ones; some critics hold that cultural values (defined by these critics, stipulatively, as "ideologies") control lang. hence control authors who write texts hence control reader response. But the link between reader and text is not determinate: historically, lit. has nearly always been perceived as a subversive act, which is why totalitarian governments always seek to suppress lit. Regardless of which position one takes on any of these issues, the nature of the process of interp. becomes central to p.

Seamon suggests that scientific p. and hermeneutics (interp.) are fundamentally opposed, and that the former is always undone by the latter: interp. by its nature—always incomplete, always generative—creates variability of response, whereas if the interp. of literary works were susceptible to scientific method, a computer could do it. More productively, we should see this opposition as antinomian, both processes being necessary and productive so long as each is reconciled to the fact of the other. Olsen shows that while interp. denies p. its dream of objectivity, it will always be necessary, for the critic's judgments are irreplaceable. Scientific analysis—witness some of Jakobson's own—will produce a virtual infinity of facts about a poem, most of which are irrelevant. It is only the critical mind that selects the few significant details from the mass of trivial ones. Interp. always involves the collection of evidence from a text so as to support a pattern of meaning or value seen by a critic; interps. are therefore arguments and can be countered by argument: essentially they are rhetorical. On the other hand, some questions about lit. which are admittedly important ones are undeniably factual; certain textual, philological, stylistic, and prosodic questions can only be answered definitively with facts, "facts" being patterns in the available evidence which no other analysis can presently contravene. What is most of importance is to see that these are not two kinds of answers to the same questions but two answers to two different kinds of questions which derive from two differing strata of the text. Literary theory runs to excess in believing it need not be grounded in texts; textual analysis runs to excess in denying the necessity of critical judgment in analysis (see METER, section IX).

The study of poems is always carried out on the basis of implicit assumptions about what is there and how it is to be taken: this means the reading of poetry always already assumes some kind of a theory. Conversely, theory requires poems to substantiate it, else it is mere speculation. Insofar as one believes that verbal art is more directly art than verbal, then p. must be viewed as a subset of aesthetics. Insofar as one views verbal art as more verbal than art, one can invalidate the distinctions between the literary and the nonliterary and between rhetoric and p.

Poetry being the art of words cast in verseform, every p. must therefore be based, either explicitly or implicitly, on a theory of lang. and, behind that, on a theory of mind, mind being the maker of lang. The philosophy of lang. on which Western p. is based, and the epistemology underlying it, derives from the Greeks. Aristotle opens the *Peri hermeneias* (On Interp.) with the first principles that "spoken forms are symbols of mental impressions, and written forms are symbols of the spoken forms. And just as letters are not the same everywhere, so are not the vocal forms; but what all these forms [i.e. both spoken and written] are originally symbols of, the mental impressions, they are the same everywhere, and what the latter are likenesses of, the things, they are also the same" (tr. H. Arens). This account posits a four-level hierarchy running (if we reverse the sequence) from noumena (things-in-themselves) to phenomena, i.e. mental impressions (sense data decoded/constructed in consciousness and cognition) to speech (lang. as sound) to writing.

This account rightly recognizes the arbitrariness of lang. as a symbol system by making convention (q.v.) central to it (both writing systems and phonologies vary from one lang. to another; they are "not the same everywhere"), and it posits the inferiority of written lang. to spoken that was traditionally accepted and still is mainly accepted by linguists but denied by philosophical sceptics such as Derrida (see DECONSTRUCTION). However, it is the assumption that the phenomenal aspect of a thing, as perceived in the mind, is the same for every perceiver which constitutes the most fundamental divergence of modern epistemology from Aristotelian doctrine, for the joint effects of Cartesian dualism, 18th-c. empiricism, the romantic doctrine of the imagination (q.v.), 20th-c. psychology, and modern information theory have made this claim seem all but impossible. And the final principle, that things prior to perception are unitary, will seem, variously, either obvious and indubitable or else unknowable to we who are merely mortal.

For p., the central issues are the latter two of the three relations between the four levels, namely those of cognition to speech and speech to writing. Both address directly the fundamental nature of lang., i.e. *verba* as *res*. The latter of these two relations, that of written lang. to spoken lang., includes the issue of which mode of the two has ontological priority (see SOUND; POETRY), which Derrida used as one of the axioms of deconstruction. The former relation, that of mental representation to verbalization, concerns the question of whether lang., when it recodes sense data or cognitive data (incl. memory) or both into externalized forms (sound shapes, letters) subject to social use, produces a modeling system which is mainly mimetic (accurately descriptive, perhaps imitative) of the phenomenal or even (possibly) noumenal world (see REPRESENTATION AND MIMESIS), or rather mainly constructive and fictive (see FICTION), fashioning a "world" like enough to the one presented to each individual by sense data so as to be verisimilar (see VERISIMILITUDE), yet which is of course in itself different by nature of the symbolic coding systems involved. In either case, it is certain that whatever descriptive adequacy or "realism" is achieved by lang. is conveyed by a mechanism that is fundamentally artificial and alien to the original sensory stimuli, yet which is nevertheless able to generate, by such wholly indirect and *other* means, an analogue that is, if defective in some respects ("blue" is not an attribute of objects but imposed in perception; hence the word should be a verb not an adjective), nevertheless accurate in others and seemingly adaptable, on the whole, to a wide variety of representational tasks.

When, now, lang. is used for narrative and dramatic lit. (esp. prose fiction), what is added is the construction of fictive situations and characters, devices which only deepen the representational and mimetic functions of lang. Even style is meant to represent the shape, pace, or direction of thinking or the states of sensibility, hence is ultimately mimetic. The lang. itself, as medium, is still held transparent. What is added when lang. is used for poetry is that lang. is wrought to a greater degree of design or pattern, thickening the medium— words and the sounds of words—into a palpable density, opacity, or texture (Hegel, Ransom) which is also brought into consciousness along with the semantic character of words and made contributory to meaning. The reader is aware not only of words' meanings but also of words' bodies, the symbols becoming concretized objects in their own right, things to be felt, valued, and weighed while, simultaneously, understood. The semantic structures built from the words taken lexically and syntactically are made more complex by the addition of excess pattern or form, achieved via rhythm and repetition (qq.v.). The reader's cognitive responses to the poem are thereby enriched twice over, once by addition of kinesthetic texture, once by semantic intensification and compression through form.

Some of the soundest observations of the 20th c. on p. were given by Northrop Frye in the "Polemical Intro." to his *Anatomy of Crit.* (1957). Frye had little interest in the linguistic and structural p. of the half-century before him, and subsequent critics have not been inclined to follow his grand mythmaking, so he now seems something of an isolated figure. And, indeed, the synthesizing, "synoptic view of the scope, theory, principles, and techniques of lit. crit." which Frye sought to give—or, more precisely, sought to furnish reasons for—has in succeeding decades seemed increasingly less of a goal for critics. After 1967, many critics retracted from all belief in objective knowledge about or determinate meaning from texts. Many postformalist and deconstructive critics posited the locus of interpretive authority in each reader, denying any standards of value by which to sift and prefer some interps. among the babble of them all (though they themselves certainly did). The "too enormous" gaps which Frye recognized in his own theory were subsequently valorized rather than filled. Many cultural critics, Marxists, and feminists investigated social phenomena—gender, race, class, power—as manifested in lit., though not, primarily, so as to deepen our understanding of the nature of lit. as, rather, to effect social change. Consequently lit. itself came to be devalued in "theory" as only one discourse among many, and a suspect one at that. But lang. serves all ends, some reactionary, some radical, some oppressive, some liberating. The idea of disinterested inquiry (see DISINTERESTEDNESS) is at present simply absent in crit., rejected on the claim that every inquiry is motivated by a "political" purpose. Two millennia of Western philosophy did not think so.

The weakness of socially committed crit. is precisely that of the formalist crit. it attacked. All single-issue and one-sided theories, said Frye, are engaged in "substituting a critical attitude for crit., all proposing, not to find a conceptual framework for crit. within lit., but to attach crit. to one of a miscellany of frameworks outside it"—no one of which has any *theoretical* precedence over any other. "There are no definite positions to be taken in chemistry or philology, and if there are any to

be taken in crit., crit. is not a field of genuine learning. . . . One's 'definite position' is one's weakness." The proper framework, for Frye, must be derived solely from "an inductive survey of the literary field." For Frye, as for Leo Spitzer, all "systematic study alternates between inductive experience and deductive principles," of which study p. furnishes half, but not more. Some theorists, far more knowledgeable about theory than lit., have eagerly approved Frye's remark that, even now, "we have no real standards to distinguish a verbal structure that is literary from one that is not" (13). But Frye also insisted that "crit. cannot be a systematic study unless there is a quality in lit. which enables it to be so."

Frye in 1957 despaired of any "consolidating progress" in crit. Nearly a half century later, after a profusion of new approaches, crit. seems to have borne out his prediction with a vengeance. All this work notwithstanding, the fundamental matrices within which any p. must be framed remain the same. It is as certain that we cannot know a thing, fully, without inquiry into its relations with the other things in the world with which it interacts, as it is that these interactions, much less the other things, are not the thing itself. The theory Frye sought, a "coherent and comprehensive theory of lit.," which would explain, of literary works, why they are so and not otherwise, still lies before us. It will not be a scientific theory, and it must make a place for the reader's interp. of texts within both cognitive and cultural frames. It must resolve the continuing problematic—unstable, antinomian— of subjectivity and objectivity (q.v.) posed for the modern world by Kant. It must give a better account of what meaning itself is. But it must also recertify the simple fact that common readers automatically certify fictive and patterned texts as literary and aesthetic rather than utilitarian (or ideological), and that they look upon these as delivering a certain version of "truth" superior to history—as Aristotle himself held. The insight of Aristotle was that poets show us true universals in fictive particulars (see CONCRETE UNIVERSAL). Theory must rediscover the author and the concept of expressiveness. Lang. itself may no longer be the model for such a synthesis, though the nature of verbal representation will be a key component of any account of *poiesis*, for all representation whether visual or verbal is a making, a constructive activity, a *poiesis*.

For more extended discussion of the foundation of Western p. in mimesis, see REPRESENTATION AND MIMESIS; IMITATION. For alternatives thereto, see GENEVA SCHOOL and ROMANTIC AND POSTROMANTIC POETICS. For the relation of theory to poems, see POETRY; PROSODY; RHETORIC AND POETRY; THEORY. For discussion of the ontological status of poetry, see POETRY; for the theoretical basis of p. in poetic form, see VERSE AND PROSE; PROSODY; SOUND. For typology of the critical orientations in Western p. concerning poetry, see

POETICS

POETRY, THEORIES OF. Modern criticism is surveyed in TWENTIETH-CENTURY POETICS and analyzed in CRITICISM and METACRITICISM. See also MEANING, POETIC; INTERPRETATION; PHILOSOPHY AND POETRY; FEMINIST POETICS; LINGUISTICS AND POETICS; ETHICS AND CRITICISM; PLURALISM.

T.V.F.B.

B. *Historical.* Scattered commentary on poetry as entertainment and didactic instrument appears in the West as early as Homer (e.g. *Iliad* 2.484, *Odyssey* 8) and Hesiod. Commentary on poetic making first appears in Pindar, who emphasizes skill and technique. The 5th-c. Sophists, attacked by Plato as deceivers, studied verbal effects extensively, though for a rhetorical end, persuasion. But Western p. begins with, and is still framed largely in the terms established by, Plato and Aristotle.

Plato's views on poetry are inconsistent, but in general they derive directly from his metaphysics: the world of material reality presents appearances that are only an imitation of the truth of things as manifested in the world of ideal Forms. Poetry as a made object consequently produces images that are copies of copies and so twice removed from reality. Truth inheres only in nonmaterial Forms, then poems deceive. This makes them dangerous. And if only Forms contain Being, then poems have, in fact, only diminished Being if any at all. At *Republic* 10, Plato uses *mimesis* to denote all artistic activity as imitation of reality, though elsewhere he uses it in the sense of "discourse." In the *Phaedrus* Plato seems to espouse the doctrine of poetic inspiration (q.v.) by the Muses, i.e. the doctrine of "poetic madness" (q.v.); on this account the poet is a mere mouthpiece for the gods, making p., as Tigerstedt remarks, superfluous.

Aristotle is the first writer in the West known to have constructed a taxonomy for the systematic study of lit. Like Plato, Aristotle recognizes *mimesis* as imitation, but conversely he treats it as a natural, pleasurable, and productive human drive. Too, the emphasis falls not on the veracity of the mimesis in the end or even on the kinds of things it produces but on the skillfulness of it at the hands of the poet and its convincingness: *poietike* is not a class of objects but *techne*, i.e. "making." Aristotle is not directly concerned with "the nature of poetry" in the *Poetics*: rather, he is concerned with the *art* of poetry, the skill of making poetry that will succeed in moving its audience (Else). Aristotle reverses the attribution of Being from another world to this one: now the poem itself has Being; the ideas it "contains" or evokes are of only secondary reality. Further, form for Aristotle is not extrinsic to things, as it was for Plato, but intrinsic: the acorn contains the pattern for the oak.

Aristotle is not much concerned to discriminate categories or kinds. The modern concept of "lit." only arose in the 18th c., and the modern conception of rigidly defined genres, which the Ren. attributed to Aristotle, is a misunderstanding of him—in short, a modern invention (Rosenmeyer).

The *Poetics* lays down a rudimentary schema of genres at the outset, though the account seems incomplete or mutilated; what the modern reader notices most is that Aristotle gives very little attention to what we think of the lyric. His interest is the chief artform of his time, verse drama. Consequently mimesis is for Aristotle "an imitation of actions, shaped into special forms by the techniques of a skilled artisan" (Adams). Had he taken a wider view or had in front of him an extensive lyric trad., he might have framed his definition of *mimesis* more widely, as the portrayal of an external object through the skillful manipulation of a medium—in drama, action, in poetry, rhythmical speech. In either case, features of extrinsic form are not much of interest to Aristotle, who presumably would have approved the modern doctrine of the inseparability of form and content.

Hence Aristotle minimizes the boxes-with-labels approach to literary form: *poiesis* is a making, a process, and the point of the *Poetics* is the artful and successful carrying out of that process, not its ends, which will never emerge in precast or predictable forms. "The forms of the process of making are the various technical ways in which the process of composing can be worked out. What matters is the art," not the products thereof (Rosenmeyer). In this process, mimesis is a means not an end. Aristotle conceives poetry as the making of fictions that achieve verisimilitude (q.v.) through imitation. And the chief means to that end is *structure*, or plot (q.v.), not character, thought, diction, melody, or spectacle. The aim of the *Poetics* is not to copy nature or even, so much, to move audiences but rather, as Howell says, "to discover how a poem, produced by imitation and representing some aspect of a natural object—its form—in the artificial medium of poetry, may so achieve perfection of that form in the medium that the desired aesthetic effect results" (46).

As for the "aesthetic effect," Aristotle is obviously aware of the issue, since the *Poetics* discusses the effects of tragedy on the emotions of the audience. We can only wish he had framed it more widely. Aristotle's account of *catharsis* (q.v.), which seems to be taken over from ancient medical speculation, concerns the arousal of certain emotions in the audience, apparently so as to purge them. But this is not the major issue, and if it were, rhet. would be indistinguishable from poetic. As Howell points out, Aristotle clearly makes a distinction between rhetoric and p., on which subjects he wrote two different treatises: the distinction seems to be essentially that poetic works are mimetic—they create their effect by the telling of a fictional story—whereas rhetorical works are nonmimetic—they affect their audience by presenting factual evidence, logical argument, and persuasive appeals. The orator achieves credibility and acceptance by making statements and offering proofs which his audience sees as directly relevant to the circumstances at hand and based on facts, while the poet produces a story which does not pertain, literally, to the situation at hand and is clearly not factual but from which they are to *extract universals by inference* (57; italics added).

In Roman times, lit. declined while forensic rhet. flourished as the vehicle of civic discourse; rhetoricians nevertheless encouraged the study of literary works for figuration (so Quintilian on Homer). Horace follows Aristotelian concepts closely in his letter to the Piso family on the art of poetry (*Ars poetica*); however, he places greater emphasis on craft and revision, and he identifies the ends of verbal art as not merely aesthetic but also didactic: to delight and to instruct. Horace was read and his *Ars poetica* imitated widely throughout the Middle Ages. Aristotle was however lost throughout the Middle Ages, preserved only in Alemanni's mistranslation (1256) of Averroes' Middle Commentary (1147) on an Arabic tr. of the Gr. text. In the early Middle Ages, poetry was treated under the aegis of grammar, though after the 12th-c. Ren., the study of poetry was again taken up under rhet. in the *artes poetriae* of John of Garland, Matthew of Vendome, and Geoffrey of Vinsauf (see RHETORIC AND POETRY). But even here the distinction between rhet. and p. is thin: what is distinctively poetic is prosody. Vernacular treatises on the art of poetry all take their example from Dante's *De vulgari eloquentia* (ca. 1303–5), which argued that the range and power of poetry in the vernaculars was equal to that in the Cl. langs., but these are few, esp. in Occitan. In late medieval France, p. is associated once again with music (see VERS MESURES).

With the Ren. came the recovery of texts of Plato (tr. 1484), Aristotle (Lat. trs. 1498 and 1536, Gr. text 1508, It. tr. 1549), Cicero, and Quintilian. The Ciceronian tripartite division of styles (high, middle, low) and the concept of decorum (q.v.) were restored. After Robortelli's commentary (1548), critics mix Aristotelian concepts with Horatian (Herrick). The premises on which Ren. p. (q.v.) proceeds are not foreign to Aristotle: the ends are Horatian—to delight and instruct—and the means are mimetic. The "rules" (q.v.) hardened into prescriptive doctrine, most particularly in the case of the "Dramatic Unities," epitomized in Boileau's *Art of Poetry* (1674). Pope's art of poetry, the *Essay on Crit.* (1711), was inspired by Boileau. The 18th-c. emphasis on "imitation" (q.v.), as in the classicizing crit. of Dr. Johnson, is however not mimetic but formal: "Nature" (q.v.) is now more than the world perceived by the senses. The insistence by Ramus in the Ren. that invention and arrangement belonged to logic left to rhet. only the study of style and delivery. Hence 18th-c. rhetorical treatises on elocution are monuments of a discipline reaching its end. The most powerful thinking about lang. and mind—Locke, Leibnitz, Condillac, Hume, Rousseau—no longer takes place in the domain of rhet., which is reduced to a confused classification of figures and tropes (see FIGURE, SCHEME, TROPE).

It was not until the turn of the 19th c. that Western p. began to detach itself, fully, from Aristotelian and mimeticist premises. The rise of aesthetics as a branch of philosophy in the 18th c. (A. G. Baumgarten, *Reflections on Poetry*, 1735, tr. 1954) had strengthened the objectivist approach to p., but not enough to withstand the effects of Kant and Hegel, who develop a new metaphysics in which the object is conceived in terms of its cognitive representation by the subjective perceiver, making "objective" and "subjective" mutually permeable fields (see ROMANTIC AND POSTROMANTIC POETICS). Romantic p. turns away altogether from the conception of poetry as an imitation of the external world, in favor of a more creative emphasis on the poet's expression of a vision which transcends the merely personal, based on a creative conception of mental imagination (q.v.). Poems now no longer conform to the neoclassical theory of genres but may each grow organically (see ORGANICISM). The romantics revolted against what they saw as the inert and mechanical formalism of neoclassical rhet., esp. ossifications such as "poetic diction" (see LEXIS), though in their poetry they continued to exploit the resources of verbal figuration. Key romantic accounts of p.: A. W. Schlegel's Berlin lectures on the theory of art (1801–2), Wordsworth's "Preface" to the third ed. of *Lyrical Ballads* (1802); Coleridge's *Biographia literaria*, esp. ch. 13 (1817), Shelley's Platonic *Defense of Poetry* (1821), and Hegel's lectures on aesthetics (1820–29; pub. 1835, 1842; tr. T. M. Knox 1975). Romantic p. lasted for over a century, having a late manifestation in the expressionistic theory of Croce (see EXPRESSION).

In the first half of the 20th c., movements in lit. crit. foregrounded the distinction between literary and nonliterary discourse. Rus. Formalism (1919–30; q.v.) reacted against postromantic vagueness in lit. and against psychology with a return to the word, to the literary device (Šklovskij), and to structural *relations* as opposed to features, making *literariness* the defining characteristic of verbal art. Most of their work consequently came round to verse-theory (see PROSODY). In Am. crit., literary and rhetorical analyses were deeply intertwined: New Critical close reading usually subsumed rhet., and Kenneth Burke treated lit. as explicitly rhetorical, a kind of modeling system for human emotion and action. Aristotle himself is revived in the 20th c. by the critics of the Chicago School (q.v.), inspired by Richard McKeon and R. S. Crane.

These movements were opposed in the second half by movements wherein the distinction between literary works and nonliterary is dissolved, usually in favor of a larger and more synoptic account of discourse. Now discourse was studied as a *system*, and the effort was to discover processes that apply across the board, not merely in lit. Increasingly, the concept of "text" was extended to everything: all human artifacts and institutions were textualized. Structuralism (q.v.), which was first Czech then influenced Fr. anthropology before migrating to Am. lit. crit. in the 1960s and '70s, was developed on the model of linguistics, hoping to discover the underlying rules and conventions which make lit. possible for the members of a culture in the same way that grammatical rules make speech itself possible. Jakobson himself in an influential early study identified two traditional rhetorical figures, metonymy and metaphor (qq.v.), as two fundamental cognitive modes, dysfunctions of which appear in aphasics. Efforts to revivify traditional rhetorical theory such as that by Group Mu approached the same synthesis from the other direction, also aiming at a larger account of discourse.

Fr. structuralists such as Roland Barthes, Gérard Genette, and Tzvetan Todorov make clear that the focus of p. has shifted from the literary work itself as text to the system that makes it possible. "The work is a fragment of substance," says Barthes, but "the Text is a methodological field" (*Image* 156). What is wanted in a structuralist p., says Culler, is not yet another interp. of *Moby Dick* but rather an understanding of how the institution of lit. functions at all. Now it is the "study of the institution rather than participation in it that is the proper business of p." (Seamon). For Barthes, the "science of lit. can never be a science of content, but only of the *conditions* of content"; its aim is not to discover meanings but "to know how meaning is possible, at what cost and by what means" (*Partisan Rev.* (1967) 87). This work led naturally into theory of signs or semiotics (q.v.), where meaning becomes a system of relations, not a set of entities.

But the analogy from grammar did not work out: the constraints on interp. turn out to be social conventions (see CONVENTION), which are very different from linguistic rules. And it was but a step from meaning-as-relations to Derrida's appropriation of Saussure so as to claim that all meaning is endlessly deferred, never capable of being fixed. Deconstruction (q.v.) aimed to show that literary works do not control their meaning but are in fact partly controlled by forces of which they are unable to speak. In such a condition, critics must therefore revert to rhetorical analysis, which De Man made central, as "rhetorical crit.," to deconstructive praxis. Like its predecessors, deconstruction too foregrounded the nature of figuration in lang., but now to show not design, coherence, or unity of meaning but rather the reverse, incompletion and incoherence, the generation of meanings other than or antithetical to those intended by a writer. One prominent Yale critic was led into musings on nihilism, and fascist associations by both de Man and Heidegger were discovered. Derrida's original aim, if it was to authorize new voices, ended up authorizing no voices at all. Marxist literary critics watched the swift collapse

of virtually all the Soviet-influenced Marxist economies. In the rapid collapse of systems, voices grew shrill.

Still, deconstruction rested on only one model of lang.; and like all theories, and in line with its own tenets, it must necessarily be blind to its own premises. De Man allied it to formalism as but one more type of close reading. From the vantage of the next century, deconstruction may come to seem a mere emetic, a fast-acting purgative for the mimetic excesses and textual fixations of New Critical and structuralist formalism, which excluded all reasonable consideration of persons, situations, history, life as lived. The decade of the 1980s witnessed a reversion in crit. to issues of gender, race, culture, power, ideology, and history. From the vantage of the next century, these movements should be seen as having restored some of the richness of literary experience to an excessively arid, insulated, and theoretical crit. wherein the text became a mere pretext. But in the stimulus of turning away from the word toward culture and history, we must not forget that we have not, thereby, solved the problems of meaning and interp. that have repeatedly been shown to be central to the very nature of lang. and lit.: those problems still remain, still await answers. Too many critics have forgotten what F. R. Leavis once said in his book of the same title: that lit. is a way of knowing; that it is distinct from other ways of knowing and not to be subsumed in any other *modus cogitandi*; and that if we ignore lit., we turn away from not merely our greatest cultural artifacts but from a centrally human mode of recognition, from ourselves.

See now CLASSICAL POETICS; MEDIEVAL POETICS; RENAISSANCE POETICS; BAROQUE POETICS; NEOCLASSICAL POETICS; ROMANTIC AND POSTROMANTIC POETICS; TWENTIETH-CENTURY POETICS.

C. M. Gayley and F. N. Scott, *Intro. to the Methods and Materials of Lit. Crit.* (1899); B. Tomaševskij, *Teorija literatury: Poetika* (1927); M. Dragomirescu, *La Science de la litt.* (1929); M. T. Herrick, *The P. of Aristotle in England* (1930), *The Fusion of Horatian and Aristotelian Lit. Crit., 1531–1555* (1946); R. Ingarden, *The Literary Work of Art* (1931, tr. 1973); W. L. Schwartz, "Some 20th-C. Arts poétiques," *PMLA* 47 (1932); Patterson—Fr. arts of peotry, 1328–1630; E. Staiger, *Grundbegriffe der Poetik* (1946, tr. 1991); P. van Tieghem, *Petite hist. des grandes doctrines littéraires en France de la Pléiade au Surréalisme* (1946); A. H. Warren, *Eng. Poetic Theory, 1825–1865* (1950); Auerbach; Abrams; Curtius; W. K. Wimsatt, Jr., "Rhet. and Poems," *The Verbal Icon* (1954)—enumerates five relations of theory to poems; F. L. Will, "The Justification of Theories," *Phil. Rev.* 64 (1955); M. Weitz, "The Role of Theory in Aesthetics," *JAAC* 15 (1956); Wellek; Wellek and Warren; *L'Art poétique*, ed. C. Charpier and P. Seghers (1956); B. Markwardt, *Gesch. der Deutschen Poetik*, 2d ed., 5 v. (1956–67), "Poetik," *Reallexikon* 3.126–57; Frye; G. F. Else,

Aristotle's Poetics: The Argument (1957), Plato and Aristotle on Poetry, ed. P. Burian (1986); F. Martini, "Poetik," Deutsche Philologie im Aufriss, ed. W. Stammler, 2d ed. (1957), 1.223–80; Weinberg; R. Wellek, "Literary Theory, Crit., and Hist.," "The Term and Concept of Lit. Crit.," Concepts of Crit. (1963), "Evolution of Lit.," "Lit. and Its Cognates," DHI; Poetica Pre-platonica, ed. G. Lanata (1963); P. O. Kristeller, "The Modern System of the Arts," Ren. Thought II (1964); K. Borinski, Die Antike in Poetik und Kunsttheorie, 2d ed., 2 v. (1965); E. N. Tigerstedt, "Poetry and P. from Antiquity to the Mid-18th C.," DHI; R. Harriott, Poetry and Crit. Before Plato (1969); R. E. Palmer, Hermeneutics (1969); E. Leibfried, Kritische Wiss. vom Text (1970); C. Guillén, Lit. as System (1971), ch. 9; Lausberg, sect. 1156–1242; J. Buchler, The Main of Light (1974); F. Svejkovsky, "Theoretical P. in the 20th C.," Current Trends in Linguistics, 12, ed. T. A. Sebeok (1974)—esp. for Ger., Rus., Czech, and Polish; W. S. Howell, P., Rhet., and Logic (1975); G. Pasternack, Theoriebildung in der Literaturwiss. (1975); S. H. Olsen, "What Is P.?" Philos. Q. 26 (1976); B. Hrushovski, "P., Crit., Science," PTL 1,1 (1976); W. K. Wimsatt, Jr., "In Search of Verbal Mimesis," Day of the Leopards (1976); J. Lotman, The Structure of the Artistic Text (tr. 1977); P. D. Juhl, Interp. (1980); U. Margolin, "The (In)dependence of P. Today," PTL 4 (1980); Brogan; Group Mu; T. Todorov, Intro. to P. (1981); F. E. Sparshott, The Theory of the Arts (1982); W. J. Verdenius, "The Principles of Gr. Lit. Crit.," Mnemosyne 4 (1983); H. F. Plett, Englische Rhetorik und Poetik, 1479–1660: Eine systematische Bibl. (1985); T. G. Rosenmeyer, "Ancient Literary Genres: A Mirage?" YCGL 34 (1985); Comparative P. / Poétiques comparées: Proc. 10th Congress, ICLA, ed. C. Guillén (1985); R. Barthes, Crit. and Truth (tr. 1987); R. Seamon, "P. Against Itself," PMLA 104 (1989); L. Dolezel, Occidental P. (1990).   T.V.F.B.

II. EASTERN. A. Theoretical. A systematic p. emerges in a culture when lit. is viewed as a more or less autonomous subject and is defined (by a major critical mind) on the basis of a single literary kind—drama or lyric. (No known p. is defined out of narrative solely or primarily.) In the West, the Gr. concept of the Muses (see MUSE) did not directly lead to a p. because no single kind was isolated as a model, and nonliterary kinds like dance (Terpischore) and astronomy (Urania) were commingled with more literary kinds. Subsequently, however, as the titles of Aristotle's works show, p. was considered autonomously among the other domains of thought such as politics, ethics, and metaphysics. And although the Homeric poems existed as an important Gr. literary model, Aristotle chose drama for his definition, appropriately concentrating on its representation of action and thereby producing a mimetic p. (see REPRESENTATION AND MIMESIS; IMITATION). The Poetics does give attention to narrative (which Plato had labelled diegesis), but it defines lit. on the radical basis of drama.

Unlike Western poetic systems, other systematic p. among the lits. of the world are explicitly defined out of lyric, and yet others without a formal, explicit p. are lyric by implication. (The complex Indian example requires later mention.) Lyric p. are affective and expressive, being concerned with the affected poet and/or reader and the words of the expressive medium. Instead of concern with representation of the world or of universals, and hence preoccupation with issues of fiction (q.v.), the various affective-expressive p. focus on the primacy of the affected poet, the words chosen to give expression to what has proved moving, and the reader/hearer who is affected in turn, sometimes being moved to further expression, as when a Chinese poet responds to a poem by a friend by using the same rhyme pattern as in the affecting poem.

In their traditional versions, both affective-expressive and mimetic p.—unlike deconstruction (q.v.)—presume a real, knowable world available to knowledge and treatment. This philosophical realism might be threatened historically by extremes of idealism, nominalism, or Buddhist antiphenomenalism. In the enduring version, the realism is dominant—sufficiently so that, in east Asia, for example, it is assumed that, in the absence of evidence to the contrary, lit. is necessarily factual. Because drama alone is necessarily fictional (the players acting the roles of people they are not), it poses a problem to affective-expressive p. Drama is simply absent from major cultures such as the Islamic and Semitic. In China it is slow to achieve prestige. In Japan it does achieve early prestige by being adapted to, or assimilated into, lyric criteria. In east Asia, the philosophical realism of the affective-expressive system is heightened by the inclusion (along with dominant lyricism) of certain prized kinds of history in the category which is the counterpart to Western "lit.": Ch. wen, Japanese bun or fume, and Korean mun.

Affective-expressive p. offers a more complete account of lit. than the mimetic, in the sense of accounting for all four principal radicals of a p.: the poet, the poetic expression, the reader, and the world. To Plato and Aristotle, the affected reader or hearer could not be a differentia of poetry (in spite of catharsis [q.v.]) because affectivism was also a property of (Sophistic) rhet. and (Academic) philosophy, with philosophy considered paramount (see, for example, Plato, Phaedrus). Western p. was not complete in recognizing the affected reader until Horace created an affective-expressive p. from his practice of odes and satires, writing, like Japanese critics, of words or lang. and of affectivism in crucial passages of his Ars poetica, the Epistula ad Pisones (46–72, 99–118, 309–22, 333–44).

These fundamental distinctions between affective-expressive and mimetic p. are more complex in historical practice. Something like a p. based on narrative emerges, under affective-expressive dominance, in the "Fireflies" ("Hotaru") chapter of the greatest work of Japanese lit., *The Tale of Genji* (*Genji Monogatari*), and elsewhere in the author's writing, where the models of history and the Buddha's teaching are invoked. This was within a century of the affective-expressive definition of lit. out of lyric in the prefaces to the *Kokinshū* (ca. 1010 A.D.) and modeled in part on the "Great Prefaces" to the Ch. *Classic of Poetry* (*Shi jing*). In India, the earliest major treatise, the *Nātyaśastra*, concerned drama, but the strong religious emphasis continuing for centuries (and making distinction between sacred and profane impossible) prevented the emergence of a mimetic p. Mimesis was considered, but rejected as psychologically untenable; the dominant emphasis on affect (*rasa*), expressive figures (*alaṃkāra*), and suggestion (*dhvani*, a kind of *tertium quid*) led finally to a p. affective-expressive in major emphasis (see INDIAN POETICS). Even in the West, the loss of Aristotle's *Poetics* until ca. 1500 led to the dominance throughout most of the Middle Ages of the Horatian affective-expressive model: "drama" was considered to be the Ciceronian dialogue and "tragedy" the narrative *De casibus* kind.

Affectivism has proved the dominant element in world p. In the West it has sometimes led to a didacticism mainly unconcerned with expressivism. But affectivism itself has been conceived differently in different cultures and times. In east Asia, it was conceived in relation to both the poet and the reader/hearer, whereas Horace's emphasis falls only on the latter. There are also differences in the relative importance of moral as opposed to all other kinds of affectivism. Horace was concerned with both teaching and delight ("dulce et utile," "audesse . . . prodesse"). Guided by Confucianism, Ch. and Korean views tended to emphasize the moral line while allowing for nondidactic delight (see CHINESE POETICS). Japanese views have not been without moral concern, particularly after the official adoption of a neo-Confucian ideology early in the 17th c. But motivated more fundamentally by Shinto happiness and anguish, and reinforced by the Buddhist sense of evanescence, Japanese poets are seldom didactic, and have even rebelled as far as possible against neo-Confucian orthodoxy (see JAPANESE POETRY). Islamic love and mystical poetry (see LOVE POETRY; PERSIAN POETRY) are also highly affective in their differing ways. And whatever the difficulties of defining Indian p., all would agree that the codified emotions (*rasa*) are central to understanding Indian views of the divine and human.

The results of any description or comparison depend on scale. Considered alone, Eng. or Japanese p. seems highly various and given to change. Compared with Ch. alternatives, however, Japanese p. seems more consistent and very different from Ch. When Eng. (or some other Western) p. becomes the basis of comparison, Japanese and Ch. seem very much alike. The reason is that, in spite of the medieval dominance of Western p. by Horatian affective-expressive principles, Western p. became centrally mimetic with the recovery of Aristotle in the Ren. ("Representation" in Eng. or Fr. and "Darstellung" or "Vorstellung" in Ger. are the revealing terms, as concern with fictionality is the betraying concept.) Nothing makes Western p. seem more distinct, or parochial, than its mimetic character. Even poets supposedly liberated from their mimetic assumptions—Mallarmé, Eliot—look very like their European predecessors in comparison with their Ch. counterparts. Antimimetic European writing itself differs from that written in an affective-expressive p.; it differs in terms of the definitions and the relative importance of the major poetic constituents (poet, reader, expression, world), differs in the expectations held for the aims as well as the reception of poetry, and differs in the standards of the necessary and valuable in poetry.

B. *Historical.* See ARABIC POETICS; CHINESE POETICS; HEBREW PROSODY AND POETICS; INDIAN POETICS; JAPANESE POETICS.

E. Gerow, *Indian P.* (1977); E. Miner, "The Genesis and Devel. of Poetic Systems," *CritI* 5 (1979), *Comparative P.* (1990); Miner et al., Part 1A.   E.M.

POETICS AND RHETORIC. See POETICS; RHETORIC AND POETICS.

POETRY (Lat. *poema, poetria*, from Gr. *poiesis*, "making," first attested in Herodotus).

    I. MEANS AND ENDS
   II. SOUND AND MEANING
  III. HEARD AND SEEN
  IV. ONTOLOGY

I. MEANS AND ENDS. A poem is an instance of *verbal art*, a text set in verse, bound speech. More generally, a poem conveys heightened forms of perception, experience, meaning, or consciousness in heightened lang., i.e. a heightened mode of discourse. Ends require means: to convey heightened consciousness requires heightened resources. Traditionally these have been taken as the ones offered by pros., i.e. verseform: lineation, meter, sound-patterning, syntactic deployment, and stanza forms. Except for the three or four hybrid forms so far developed in the West—the prose poem, rhythmical prose and rhymeprose, and the prosimetrum (qq.v.)—p. has traditionally been distinguished from prose by virtue of being set in verse (see VERSE AND PROSE). What most readers understand as "p." was, up until 1850, set in lines which were metrical, and even the several forms of *vers libre* and free verse (qq.v.) produced since 1850 have been built largely on one or another concept of the line. Lineation is therefore central to the traditional Western conception of p. (see LINE). Prose is cast in sentences; p. is cast in sentences cast into lines. Prose syntax has the shape of meaning, but poetic syntax is stretched across the frame of meter or the poem's visual space (see PROSODY), so that it has this shape as well as meaning. Whether the pros. of the poem is primarily aural or visual or mixed (see below), it creates design.

If either of the criteria indicated by the two words italicized in the first sentence of this entry is removed, texts become "poetic" only in looser, more general, and metaphorical senses. (1) *Verbal* but not *artful*: any verbal text or piece of verbal discourse, even if not meant as "art," can be called "poetic" if it seems to exhibit intensified speech—an impassioned plea, a stirring speech, a moving letter. Often these texts partake of the resources offered by traditional rhet., i.e. devices of repetition and figuration (qq.v.). They become more highly figured and patterned than ordinary speech or prose, and so take on the term "poetic" as a metonym, since verse characteristically deploys these features. (2) *Artful* but not *verbal*: any object skillfully made or intended as art though not a verbal text can be called "poetic" in the metaphorical sense—an intense moment in a play or movie, a romantic gesture, a painting, a piece of music. These foreground the act of attention itself, which is the paradigmatic criterion of aesthetic events.

We may identify these two criteria with the *means* and *ends* of p. The means are verbal and the end is the aestheticization of the experience of the object. The means primarily involve design, or increase of order, particularly (1) repetition and patterning of words and phrases (the province of rhet.) and (2) repetition and patterning below the level of the word (the province of pros.; see SOUND). Means of type (1) comprise rhet.; means of type (2) can occur frequently in rhet. but are made systematic in pros. In p., that is, phonological patterning is made "the constitutive device of the sequence" (Jakobson) and so comes to represent a genuine differentia.

The ends, however, are more difficult to define: in the West, the ends of p. have traditionally been seen as instruction and delight—that is, learning (increase of knowledge) and aesthetic pleasure (the nonutilitarian pleasure of such learning or of contemplation of the object, and the appreciation of a thing well made). But some critics have upheld other ends, such as expression or communication or even promotion of didactic content; and some have denied that p. has any specifiable ends at all. Anti-intentionalist critics would say we can never know the end the poet had in mind in creating the poem, and reader-oriented and deconstructive critics would say that even if we could it would make no difference: each reader creates her own meaning in the act of interpretation (q.v.). If, however, one cannot at least say, on objective grounds, that the end is *not* persuasion, then p. cannot be distinguished from rhet. Some of these ends p. shares with religious, political,

oratorical, and ludic (recreational) forms of discourse; and sometimes it may also share some of the first set of means. But not the second.

Aristotle in the *Poetics* identifies four "causes" of art: the formal, material, efficient, and final. In sculpture, these are the shape of, stone used in, sculptor of, and reason for making the sculpture. In p. these are verseform, words (their soundshapes, visual shapes), the poet, and the purposes for which poets write and readers read. But p. differs from the other arts in that the material cause is not in itself semantically neutral—as are stone in sculpture, sound in music, and color in painting—but always already semanticized. The webs of meaning which words create naturally when brought into conjunction with each other are compressed and given additional order when subjected to verseform, effects which are also semantic, increasing the semantic density in p. over prose.

II. SOUND AND MEANING. To understand p., therefore, we must understand words and the word. We might bear in mind the remark made by Mallarmé to Degas—which, had it not existed, it would have been necessary to invent—that poems are not made out of ideas, they are made out of words (P. Valéry, *Art of Poetry* [1939]). Critics who treat p. merely as a structure of ideas, imagery, metaphor, or figurative lang. do not, thereby, fundamentally identify anything "poetic" except perhaps by degree, nor do they distinguish verbal art from other verbal texts which are nonart. Critics who take meaning or "theme" (q.v.) as the essence of p. are encouraged, of course, by our automatic response to the referential and semantic character of words, so strong in ordinary lang. use. But they neglect the medium. In all the arts the medium is mere substance, alien and opaque to expression; and in this respect words appear in p. as pure sound—sounds in and of themselves, having aural textures, and sounds patterned, qua pattern. It is for this reason that Wimsatt remarked that "p. approximates the sensuous condition of paint and music not by being less verbal, less characteristic of verbal expression, but actually by being more than usually verbal, by being hyperverbal" ("The Domain of Crit."). Sound must be taken as sound in p., but also as the creator of meaning. Neither can erase the other, since each requires the other in order to exist. These two dimensions of the word are constant interinanimations of each other in verse.

The verbal medium in p. is not, therefore, a fully physical medium, as is sculpture, nor is it pure meaning, as in prose. It is irrefrangibly a bivalent or double medium, which critics separate at their peril. The critic will seek to show how the physical (aural) and semantic dimensions of words are related in both directions (Levý). Few Western critics except some very recent ones have embraced philosophical scepticism so wholly as to claim that the meanings readers derive from the reading of poems are not in some way directly determined by their material elements, words: the presumption of at least some kind of relation between text structures and reader effects is fundamental to all critical discourse whatsoever (see PROSODY). The only issues—and they are great ones—are what kinds, and how.

The two dimensions of words in p. (meaning, sound) have produced, historically, two traditions or lines of descent, two kinds of poetries which in their pure forms one might for simplicity call extrinsic and intrinsic, or centrifugal and centripetal. The first emphasizes the referential, propositional, and mimetic aspect of lang., and leads to descriptive and narrative p. (qq.v.), esp. epic but also lyric (qq.v.). The Western doctrine of mimesis held that the poem was an imitation (q.v.) of reality; this function works best when the physical bodies of words become purely transparent, the words dissolving into pure meaning. In this mode we see straight through words into interior visualization. While these kinds of poems are obviously referentially false or fictive (see FICTION), they are nonetheless taken as true at a deeper level (see REPRESENTATION AND MIMESIS), leading Richards to his famous but ineffectual attempt at a synthesis, "pseudo-statements" (q.v.; see also MEANING, POETIC). In this line of descent, imitation takes on primary importance, though this concept must not be understood in any naive sense: "representation" would be better, for the ability of lang. to represent extralinguistic events is simply assumed, as "signifier" entails "signified." The prosodic means, the kinds of opportunities afforded by verseform, are in this trad. minimized.

In the second line of descent, reference is minimized, ignored, or denied, and words become wholly of interest in themselves, as pure sound form or visual form or both. This trad. embraces a variety of aural and visual poetic modes never yet mapped out by critics but which include, at the very least, pure p., language p., and sound p. (qq.v.), and perhaps some types of concrete p. and pattern p. (qq.v.) as well. Now lang. focuses on itself, and Jakobson's poetic function (q.v.) is not only foregrounded but becomes the limiting condition of lang. The medium, made (or claimed to be) transparent in the first trad., is now made opaque. The full range of prosodic devices is exploited, sometimes to excess. This p. approaches the condition of music; its medium becomes the purely sensuous medium of the other arts. Meaning is not suppressed (which is impossible) but is made, at best, derivative from sound- and wordplay. P. in this trad. seeks to naturalize its signs, to generate an Adamic lang. where the relation of signifiers to signifieds is not arbitrary but rather motivated; or at least it seeks to produce the *illusion* that they are so.

But these are not mutually exclusive modes of *poiesis*: the great majority of poems written in the history of the world show some characteristics of both, and the great majority of poets have viewed the second set of features as simply the differentia of p. itself, i.e. that set of enabling conditions which validates the distinction between verse and prose at all. Focus on the verbal medium, in other words—on design or pattern in sound—is for these critics the route to the extension and intensification of meaning which p. makes possible.

III. HEARD AND SEEN. Of all the arts, consequently, p. may well seem the most schizophrenic. This was much less apparent before 1450, when the printing press revolutionized modern consciousness. In ancient Greece, and even in the Middle Ages, written texts were relatively rare and often intended simply as transcriptions of oral performances. But with the spread of literacy and then the ubiquity of print, visual texts become not merely superimposed on but actually correlate to, quasi-independent from, aural ones. By the 16th c., p. had become an artform manifesting itself in two separate and distinct, though mutually permeable, media, (heard) speech and (seen) print. There is the poem in the ear, as Hollander remarks, and there is the poem in the eye, the poem heard and the poem seen, even if only in the mind's ear (mind's eye). The material cause of p., which was originally and for long aural, is now aural-visual mixed.

It is the point of view taken here that these two representational modes are not entirely congruent and that, more centrally, the visual text is not a mere transcript or notation-system for the oral text. Rather, they are two versions of the prior, originary, abstract entity called "the poem." Neither has ontological precedence. Rather, they are, irremediably, two—interrelated, certainly, even deeply and complexly, perhaps even unstably. "The poem" is not to be identified with a recitation (as against a written text) nor, alternatively, with a written text (as opposed to a performance). Much in each recitation is individual and idiosyncratic, and written texts can always be destroyed. "The poem" logically precedes both of these manifestations. As Fowler puts it, the performance of a poem "is not to be viewed as an implementation of the written record . . . but as an independent realization; because the written record is not the poem, but is itself only an implementation of it. The distinction is not between the poem on paper and the reading of it but between the poem (an abstraction) and two ways of realizing it." Poetic texts, that is, "may exist in both types of substantial realization—phonic and graphic." This follows from the nature of lang. itself: "lang. is *form*, not the physical representation of form." Hence "neither the linguist nor the literary critic is interested in mere differences of substance" (7–9). In sum, "the poem" is a twin thing, a bivalent entity, brought together only in acts of consciousness, whether aural performance, silent reading, or heard reading. The audience of oral p. (q.v.) in preliterate cultures heard p. only as aural experience, but the modern reader confronts the poem both visually and aurally, and as both object and experience—i.e. as an ontologically bivalent verbal sign.

IV. ONTOLOGY. Form, then, precedes realizations of form. The realization modes are heard form (oral recitation) and seen form (written text). But these modes are apprehended in radically different ways. The question of *what* a poem is may be more adequately unpacked by asking, rather, *where* a poem is: this is a question about the ontological location or *situs* of the poem. In the chief model of Western poetics, i.e. that given by Abrams (cf. the more complex but not essentially different model of communication mapped by Jakobson), the correlative processes of writing and reading p. are conceived along a transactional continuum which essentially runs from poet through text to reader or audience. And lit. crit. in the 20th c. has followed this line, steadily shifting its focus of attention rightward from biographical crit. (the author) to formalist crit. (the text; see NEW CRITICISM) to reception theory (the reader). The text stands in the center of the two processes as (what would seem) an object. But the issue, as we have seen in the paragraphs above, is what kind of object, for it is evident that the object has its existence for us only *as experienced*. Many postformalist critics have naively assumed that formalism posited the poem solely as an aesthetic object, with no quarter given to the aesthetic experience evoked by that object. But this is an inaccurate characterization. Formalist crit. certainly emphasized the focusing of critical attention squarely on the aesthetic object (text) so as to avoid the vagaries and distractions of impressionistic, belle-lettristic, and biographical crit. But formalism never held that meaning was literally "in" the text; rather, most of the New Critics held that certain structures and strategies in the text, once apprehended, would generate strategies of interp. which would guarantee some commonality among reader responses. Readerly freedom in interp. was not expressly denied, but on the other hand it was not granted unlimited license, either. Even René Wellek's influential definition, in *Theory of Lit.* (first ed., 1947), of the poem and its "mode of existence" as a structure of norms is in fact not objectivist but rather phenomenological (see GENEVA SCHOOL), having been derived from the work of the Polish phenomenologist Roman Ingarden, as Wellek himself later reiterated (*CritI* 4 [1977] 203).

Postformalist, reader-oriented theories posit "the poem" as something created within the interobjective space between the verbal text—itself dumb, mute—and the active consciousness of the reader. Some would hold that this is true for every reader, so that a hundred readers create a hundred unique "poems" by reading the same print text. The text then becomes something like, but perhaps less stipulative than, a musical score, a set of directions for performance. Deconstruction (q.v.) embraced the notion that the text can never control its own meaning since meaning resides in the interstices between words (the "free play of the signifiers"), so that every reader constructs meaning out of the inert materials offered by a text. But this way anarchy lies. In some other readerly theories the infinite proliferation of "poems" from a single text by readers is greatly reduced by the claim that all readers are well socialized members of speech or reading communities, so that they bring to bear, in reading, extensive (if unconscious) sets of conventions (tacitly agreed-upon rules) for interp. (see CONVENTION; READER-RESPONSE CRITICISM).

In the 20th c., rapid progress in linguistics and prosody has had the very salutary effect of showing us just how extraordinarily complex the verse situation really is. To say that lang. structures are overlaid with prosodic ones in verse, and to see how, is to see that we are still very far from a full and satisfying exegesis of what an intricate complex of formal relations a poem is and, concomitantly, what precisely is involved in a reader's cognition and interp. of a poem. "Reading" is still the great undiscovered country of lit. crit., mentioned by many but mapped by few. One reason may be the evident fact that "reading" covers not one situation but three or four: what happens when a reader reads a poem aloud differs radically from what happens when she reads it silently, or listens to someone else read it aloud, or engages the poem in that backward-and-forward movement of reflection and study which Leo Spitzer once described astutely as the "hermeneutic circle." About the detailed nature of these readerly engagements we have at present only minimal knowledge. About the immense effect that patterning has on perception, verbalization, and cognition even psychology knows only a little. Lit. crit. is not psychology, nor even epistemology, but it must go hand in hand with both.

J. W. Mackail, "The Definition of P.," *Lectures on P.* (1911); R. Ingarden, *The Literary Work of Art* (1931, tr. 1973), *The Cognition of the Literary Work of Art* (tr. 1973); J. C. Ransom, "P.: A Note in Ontology," *The World's Body* (1938), "Wanted: An Ontological Critic," *The New Crit.* (1941); M. T. Herrick, *The Fusion of Horatian and Aristotelian Lit. Crit., 1531–1555* (1946), esp. ch. 4; J. J. Donohue, *The Theory of Literary Kinds*, v. 2 (1949); E. C. Pettet, "Shakespeare's Conception of P.," *E&S* 3 (1950); Abrams; Curtius 152–53; R. Wellek, "The Mode of Existence of the Literary Work of Art," in Wellek and Warren; C. L. Stevenson, "On 'What Is a Poem?'" *Phil. Rev.* 66 (1957); S. Hynes, "P., Poetic, Poem," *CE* 19 (1958); R. Jakobson, "Linguistics and Poetics," in Sebeok, rpt. in Jakobson, v. 2; N. A. Greenberg, "The Use of *Poiēma* and *Poiēsis*," *HSCP* 65 (1961); V. M. Hamm, "The Ontology of the Literary Work of Art," *The Critical Matrix*, ed. P. R. Sullivan (1961)—tr. and paraphrase of Ingarden, continued in *CE* 32 (1970); R. Fowler, "Linguistic Theory and the Study of Lit.," *Essays on Style and Lang.* (1966); J. Levý, "The Meanings of Form and the Forms of Meaning," *Poetics—Poetyka—Poetika,* ed. R. Jakobson et al. (1966); E. M. Zemach, "The Ontological Status of Art Objects," *JAAC* 25 (1966–67); J. A. Davison, *From Archilochus to Pindar* (1968); R. Harriott, *P. and Crit. Before Plato* (1969); R. Häussler, "Poiema und Poiesis," *Forschungen zur römischen Literatur,* ed. W. Wimmel (1970); D. M. Miller, "The Location of Verbal Art," *Lang&S* 3 (1970); T. McFarland, "P. and the Poem," *Literary Theory and Structure,* ed. F. Brady et al. (1973); J. Buchler, *The Main of Light* (1974); E. Miner, "The Objective Fallacy and the Real Existence of Lit.," *PTL* 1 (1976); J. Margolis, "The Ontological Peculiarity of Works of Art," *JAAC* 36 (1977); M. P. Battin, "Plato on True and False Poetry," *JAAC* 36 (1977); S. Fish, "How to Recognize a Poem When You See One," *Is There a Text in This Class?* (1980); E. H. Falk, *The Poetics of Roman Ingarden* (1981); A. L. Ford, "A Study of Early Gr. Terms for P.: 'Aoide,' 'Epos,' and 'Poesis,'" *DAI* 42, 5A (1981): 2120; J. J. McGann, "The Text, the Poem, and the Problem of Historical Method," *NLH* 12 (1981); W. J. Verdenius, "The Principles of Gr. Lit. Crit.," *Mnemosyne* 4 (1983); G. B. Walsh, *The Varieties of Enchantment: Early Gr. Views of the Nature of P.* (1984); R. Shusterman, *The Object of Lit. Crit* (1984), ch. 3; Hollander; T. Clark, "Being in Mime," *MLN* 101 (1986).　　　　　　　　　　　　T.V.F.B.

POETRY, THEORIES OF (WESTERN).

    I. MIMETIC THEORIES
    II. PRAGMATIC THEORIES
    III. EXPRESSIVE THEORIES
    IV. OBJECTIVE THEORIES
    V. RECENT DEVELOPMENTS
    VI. THE USES OF POETIC THEORY

There is no uniquely valid way to classify theories of poetry; that classification is best which best serves the particular purpose at hand. The division of theories presented here is adopted because it is relatively simple; because it stresses the notable extent to which later approaches to poetry were expansions—although under the influence of many new philosophical concepts and poetic examples—of Gr. and Lat. prototypes; and because it defines in a provisional way certain large-scale shifts of focus during 2500 years of Western speculation about the nature of poetry, its kinds, and their relative status, the parts, qualities, and ordonnance of a single poem, and the kinds of criteria by which poems are to be evaluated. But like all general schemes, this one must be supplemented and qualified in many ways before it can do justice to the diversity of individual ways of treating poetry.

Most theories take into account that poetry is a fabricated thing, the product of *technē* (Gr. "skill, craft"), not found in nature, and therefore contingent on a number of factors. A *poem* is produced by a *poet,* is related in its subject matter to the *universe* of human beings, things, and events, and is addressed to, or made available to, an *audience* of hearers or readers. But although these four elements play some part in all inclusive accounts of poetry, they do not play an equal part. Commonly a critic takes one of these elements or relations as cardinal and refers the poem either to the external world or to the audience or to the poet as preponderantly "the source, and end, and test of art"; or alternatively, she or he considers the poem as a self-sufficient entity best analyzed in theoretical isolation from the causal factors in the universe from which the poem derives its materials, or the tastes, convictions, and responses of the audience to which it appeals, or the character, intentions, thoughts, and feelings of the poet who brings it into being. These varied orientations give us, in a preliminary way, four broad types of poetic theory, which may be labeled *mimetic, pragmatic, expressive,* and *objective.*

I. MIMETIC THEORIES. In Plato's *Republic* (Bk. 10), Socrates argues that poetry is mimesis, or "imitation," and illustrates its relation to the universe by a mirror which, turned round and round, can produce an appearance of all sensible things. Plato thus bequeathed to later theorists a preoccupation with the relation of poetry to that which it imitates, and also the persistent analogy of the reflector as defining the nature of that relation. But in the cosmic structure underlying Plato's dialectic, the sensible universe is itself an imitation, or appearance, of the eternal Ideas which are the locus of all value, while all other human knowledge and products are also modes of imitation. A poem therefore turns out to be the rival of the work of the artisan, the statesman, the moralist, and the philosopher, but with the disadvantage that it is an imitation of an imitation, "thrice removed from the truth," and composed not by art and knowledge but by inspiration, at a time when the poet is not in his right mind (*Ion;* see POETIC MADNESS). Plato thus forced many later critical theorists into a posture of defense, in a context in which poetry necessarily competes with all other human enterprises and is to be judged by universal criteria of truth, beauty, and goodness. (See also IMITATION.)

In Aristotle's *Poetics* the various kinds of poetry are also defined as "modes of imitation" of human actions. Aristotle attributes the origin of poetry to our natural instinct to imitate and to take pleasure in imitations, and grounds such essential concepts as the different species of poetry, the unity of a poem (since an imitation "must represent one action, a complete whole"), and the primacy of plot in tragedy (for "tragedy is essentially an imitation not of persons but of action and life") in large part on the kinds of subjects which are imitated. But Aristotle's use of the term "imitation" sharply differentiates his theory of poetry from that of Plato. In Aristotle's scheme, the forms of things do not exist in an other-worldly realm but are inherent in the things themselves, so that it is in no way derogatory to point out that poetry imitates models in the world of sense. On the contrary, poetry is more philosophic than history, because it imitates the form of things, and so achieves statements in the mode of "universals," whereas those of history are singulars." Furthermore, "imitation" in Aristotle is a term specific to the arts, distinguishing poems from all other activities and products as a class of objects having their own criteria of value and reason for being. And by exploiting systematically such distinctions as the kinds of objects imitated, the media and manner of imitation, and the variety of emotional effects on an audience, Aristotle implements his consideration of poetry as poetry by providing means for distinguishing among the poetic kinds—e.g. tragedy, comedy, epic—and for discriminating the particular parts, internal relations, power of giving a specific kind of pleasure, and standards of evaluation proper to each type of poem. (See also FICTION; PLOT.)

Later the eclectic Cicero (*Ad M. Brutum orator* 2) and Plotinus (*Enneads* 5.8) demonstrated that it was possible to assume a world-scheme which includes Platonic Ideas yet to allow the artist to short-circuit the objects of sense so as to imitate, in Plotinus' phrase, "the Ideas from which Nature itself derives." In accordance with this strategy, later critics used building blocks from Plato's cosmos to construct aesthetic theories which could raise poetry from Plato's inferior position to the highest among human endeavors. The claim that poetry imitates eternal Forms was developed by It. Neoplatonists in the l6th c., occasionally echoed by neoclassical critics (including, in England, Dennis, Hurd, and Reynolds), and played a prominent part in the writings of Ger. romantic philosophers such as Schelling and Novalis. Diverse cognitive claims for poetry as approximating verities beyond sense-experience are also found in the Eng. romantics Blake, Coleridge, and Carlyle. Shelley, in his eloquent *Defence of Poetry*, demonstrates the reductive tendency of an uncompromising Neoplatonic theory. Since all good poems imitate the same Forms, and since these Forms, as the residence of all values, are the models for all other human activities and products as well, Shelley's essay all but annuls any essential differences between poem and poem, between poetic kind and poetic kind, between poems written in various times and in various places, and between poems written in words and the poetry of all other men who "express this indestructible order," incl. institutors of laws, founders of civil society, inventors of the arts of life, and teachers of religion. In our own day, a formal parallel to such critical monism is to be found among the critics who, after Jung, maintain that great poems, like myths, dreams, visions,

and other products of the collective unconscious—or else of the generic imaginations compelled by enduring human needs and desires—all reproduce the same limited set of archetypal paradigms, and ultimately the whole or part of that archetype of archetypes, the cycle of the seasons and of death and rebirth (P. Wheelwright, *The Burning Fountain* [1954]; N. Frye, *Anatomy of Crit.* [1957]).

However, the concept that art reproduces aspects of the sensible world has been much more common in mimetic theories than the Neoplatonic or transcendental variant. The doctrine that poetry and the arts are essentially imitations of this world, in a variety of systematic applications, flourished through the Ren. and well into the 18th c. In *Les Beaux Arts réduits à un même principe* (1747), Charles Batteux found in the principle of imitation the "clear and distinct idea" from which he undertook to deduce the nature and rules of the various arts. The Englishman Richard Hurd declared that "all poetry, to speak with Aristotle and the Gr. critics (if for so plain a point authorities be thought wanting) is, properly, *imitation* . . . having all creation for its object" ("Discourse on Poetical Imitation," 1751). And Lessing's classic *Laokoön* (1766), although it set out to substitute an inductive method for the blatantly deductive theories of Batteux and other contemporaries, still discovered the "essence" of poetry and painting to be imitation, and derived the bounds of the subjects that each art is competent to imitate from the differences in their media.

Since the 18th c. the mimetic doctrine has been more narrowly employed by proponents of artistic realism (q.v.), or in theories limited to the more realistic literary genres. In the Ren. there had been many echoes of the saying Donatus had attributed to Cicero that dramatic comedy is peculiarly "a copy of life, a mirror of custom, a reflection of truth." In the early 19th c., when prose fiction had superseded comedy as the primary vehicle of realism, Stendhal put the mimetic mirror on wheels: "a novel," he said, "is a mirror riding along a highway." Since that time representational theories have been voiced mainly by exponents of naturalistic fiction and imagist poetry, as well as by Marxist critics who claim that great lit. "reflects" (or at least ought to reflect) the "objective" reality of our bourgeois era.

The mimetic approach to lit., accordingly, has been used to justify artistic procedures ranging from the most refined idealism to the rawest realism. What the various theories have in common is the tendency to look to the nature of the given universe as the clue to the nature of poetry, and to assign to the subject matter which is represented—or which ought to be represented—the primary role in determining the aims, kinds, constitution, and criteria of poems. The key word in mimetic definitions of poetry, if not "imitation," is another predicate which aligns the poem in the same direction: the poem is an "image," "reflection," "feigning" (see FICTION), "counterfeiting," "copy," or "representation." The underlying analogue for a poem, which often comes to the surface as an express comparison, is Plato's mirror, or "a speaking picture" (see UT PICTURA POESIS), or a photographic plate. The focus of attention is thus on the relation between the imitable and the imitation, and the primary aesthetic criterion is "truth to nature" or "truth to reality." In purely representational theories, the patent discrepancies between the world as it is and the world as it is represented in poems tend to be explained, not by reference to the psychology of the poet or the reader, or to the conventions and internal requirements of a work of art, but by reference to the kinds or aspects of reality which are to be imitated. Transcendental theorists maintain that poetry represents the poet's intuitions of models existing in their own supramundane space (see INTUITION). This-worldly theorists claim that poetry represents, or should represent, a composite of the beautiful and moral aspects of things, or "la belle nature," or the statistical average of a biological form, or the universal, typical, and generically human, or the quotidian, the particular, the unique, and "the characteristic," or the conditions of bourgeois reality. In all these instances, however opposed, the objects or qualities are conceived to be inherent in the constitution of the universe, and the genius (q.v.) of the poet is explained primarily by his acuity of observation, enabling him to discover aspects of reality hitherto unregarded, and by his artistic ingenuity, enabling him to select and arrange even the more familiar elements into novel combinations which surprise us by their truth.

II. PRAGMATIC THEORIES. The pragmatic scheme sets a poem in a means-end relationship, regarding the matter and manner of imitation as instrumental to producing certain effects in the reader. "Poesy therefore," declared Sidney in a typical formulation which assimilates mimesis to a pragmatic orientation, "is an art of imitation . . . a speaking picture: with this end, to teach and delight."

Ancient rhetorical theory provided the conceptual frame and many of the terms for this approach to poetry, for it was held that the aim of rhet. is to effect persuasion, and there was wide agreement (e.g. Cicero, *De oratore* 2.28) that this end is best achieved by informing, winning, and moving the auditor.

But the great prototype for the pragmatic view of poetry was Horace's *Ars poetica*, with its persistent emphasis that the aim of the poet, and the measure of poetic success, is the pleasure and approval of the contemporary Roman audience and of posterity as well (see CLASSICAL POETICS). Aristotle has been more often quoted, but Horace has in fact been the most influential critical exemplar in the Western world.

The pragmatic orientation, exploiting the mode of reasoning and many of the concepts and topics presented in Horace's short epistle, dominated lit. crit. through the Ren. and most of the 18th c., and has made frequent reappearances ever since.

"Aut prodesse volunt, aut delectare poetae," Horace declared, although pleasure turns out to be the ultimate end, with instruction requisite only because the graver readers will not be pleased without moral matter. Later critics added from rhet. a third term, "movere," to sum up under the three headings of instruction, emotion, and pleasure the effects of poetry on its audience. Most Ren. humanists, like Sidney, made moral profit the ultimate aim of poetry; but from Dryden through the 18th c. it became increasingly common to subordinate instruction and emotion to the delight of the reader as the defining end of a poetic composition. Samuel Johnson, however, continued to insist that "the end of poetry is to instruct by pleasing," and that "it is always a writer's duty to make the world better" (*Preface to Shakespeare*). In the 19th c. the influential reviewer Francis Jeffrey deliberately justified writing in such a way as to please the least common denominator of public taste, and in this procedure he has been followed by later peddlers of formulae for achieving popular success. Neoclassic pragmatists, however, justified the sophisticated preferences of the classically trained connoisseurs of their own day by the claim that these accorded with the literary qualities of works whose long survival prove their adaptation to the aesthetic proclivities of man in general (Johnson's "common reader"), and that works written in accordance with these principles have the best chance to endure. The renowned masters, John Dennis said, wrote not to please only their countrymen; "they wrote to their fellow-citizens of the universe, to all countries, and to all ages."

We recognize pragmatic critics of poetry, whatever their many divergences, by their tendency to regard a poem as a made object, the product of an art or craft, which (after due allowance for the play of natural talent, of inspired moments, and of felicities beyond the reach of art) is still, for the most part, deliberately designed to achieve foreknown ends; we recognize them also by their tendency to derive the rationale, the chief determinants of elements and forms, and the norms of poetry from the legitimate requirements and springs of pleasure in the readers for whom it is written. Thus the *ars poetica* (the artistry in making a poem) looms large in this theory, and for centuries was often codified as a system of prescriptions and "rules" (q.v.). "Having thus shown that imitation pleases," as Dryden summarized the common line of reasoning, "it follows, that some rules of imitation are necessary to obtain the end; for without rules there can be no art" (*Parallel of Poetry and Painting*). These rules were justified inductively as essential properties abstracted from works which have appealed to the natural preferences of mankind over the centuries; in the 18th c., esp. in such systematic theorists as Beattie, Hurd, and Kames, they were also warranted by a confident appeal to the generic psychological laws governing the responses of the reader. Through the neoclassical period, most critics assumed that the rules were specific for each of the fixed genres, or kinds, but these poetic kinds in turn were usually discriminated and ranked, from epic and tragedy at the top down to the "lesser lyric" and other trifles at the bottom, by the special moral and pleasurable effects each kind was thought most competent to achieve. Poetic deviations from the truth of fact, which in strictly mimetic theories are justified by their conformity to objects, forms, and tendencies in the constitution of the universe, are warranted pragmatically by the reader's moral requirements and, even more emphatically, by his native inclination to take delight only in a selected, patterned, heightened, and "ornamented" reality. In 1651 Davenant (Preface to *Gondibert*) attacked the trad. use of pagan machinery and supernatural materials on the mimetic assumption that the poet undertakes to "represent the world's true image," a point of view which Hobbes at once abetted by proscribing all poetic materials that go "beyond the conceived possibility of nature" (*Answer to Davenant*). To this mimetic interp. of poetic probability as correspondence to the empirical constitution and order of events, pragmatic critics responded by shifting the emphasis from the nature of the world to the nature of man, and by redefining poetic probability as anything which succeeds in evoking pleasurable responsiveness in the reader. "The end of poetry is to please," Beattie wrote in his *Essays on Poetry and Music* (1776), and "greater pleasure is . . . to be expected from it, because we grant it superior indulgence, in regard to fiction," than if it were "according to real nature." Later, Thomas Twining justified for poetry "not only impossibilities, but even absurdities, where that end [of yielding pleasure] appears to be better answered with them, than it would have been without them" (Preface to *Aristotle's Treatise on Poetry*, 1789).

III. EXPRESSIVE THEORIES. The mimetic poet is the agent who holds the mirror up to nature; the pragmatic poet is considered mainly in terms of the inherent powers ("nature") and acquired knowledge and skills ("art") which she or he must possess to construct a poetic object intricately adapted, in its parts and as a whole, to its complex aims. In the expressive orientation, the poet moves into the center of the scheme and himself becomes the prime generator of the subject matter, attributes, and values of a poem. The chief historical source for this point of view is the treatise *On the Sublime* attributed to Longinus. In this treatise the stylistic quality of sublimity is defined by its effect of *ekstasis*, or transport, and is traced to five sources in the powers of the author (see SUBLIME). Of these sources, three have to do with

expression and are amenable to art; but the two primary sources are largely innate and instinctive and are constituted by the author's greatness of conception and, most important of all, by his "vehement and inspired passion." Referring the major excellence of a work to its genesis in the author's mind, Longinus finds it a reflection of its author: "Sublimity is the echo of a great soul."

The influence of Longinus' essay, after it became generally known in the third quarter of the 17th c., was immense, and its emphasis on thought and passion, originally used to explain a single stylistic quality, was expanded and applied to poetry as a whole. The effect on poetic theory was supplemented by primitivistic concepts of the natural origins of lang. and poetry in emotional exclamations and effusions, as well as by the rise to high estate of "the greater lyric," or Pindaric ode, which critics (following the lead of Cowley) treated in Longinian terms. By 1725 the boldly speculative Giambattista Vico combined Longinian doctrines, the Lucretian theory of linguistic origins, and travelers' reports about the poetry of culturally primitive peoples into his major thesis that the first lang. after the Flood was dominated by sense, passion, and imagination, and was therefore at once emotional, concrete, mythical, and poetic. In Vico is to be found the root concept of the common expressive origin and nature of poetry, myth, and religion, a concept which was later exploited by such influential theorists as Herder, Croce, and Cassirer; this mode of speculation is still recognizable in the recent theories of Suzanne Langer and Philip Wheelwright, among many others.

In the course of the 18th c. there was a growing tendency to treat poetry, though still within a pragmatic frame, as primarily an emotional (as opposed to a rational) use of lang., esp. among such Longinian enthusiasts as John Dennis, Bishop Lowth, and Joseph Warton (see Warton's *Essay . . . on Pope*, 1750–82). By the latter part of the century, unqualifiedly expressive theories of poetry as grounded in the faculties and feelings of the poet are to be found in Sir William Jones's "Essay on the Arts Called Imitative" (1772), J. G. Sulzer's *Allgemeine Theorie der schönen Künste* (1771–74), and Hugh Blair's "Nature of Poetry" (*Lectures on Rhet. and Belles Lettres*, 1783). Ger. romantic theorists such as the Schlegels, Schleiermacher, and Tieck formulated the expressive view in the terminology of post-Kantian idealism; Novalis, e.g., said that "poetry is representation of the spirit, of the inner world in its totality" (*Die Fragmente*). In France, Mme. de Stael announced the new outlook on poetry in *De L'Allemagne* (1813), and in Italy it manifested itself, later on, in some of Leopardi's speculations on lyrical poetry.

Wordsworth's "Preface" to *Lyrical Ballads* is the heir to a century of developments in this mode of thinking, and became the single most important pronouncement of the emotive theory of poetry.

His key formulation, twice uttered, is that poetry is "the spontaneous overflow of powerful feelings." The metaphor "overflow," like the equivalent terms in the definitions of Wordsworth's contemporaries—"expression," "uttering forth," "projection"—faces in an opposite direction from "imitation," and indicates that the source of the poem is no longer the external world but the poet himself; and the elements which, externalized, become the subject matter of the poem are, expressly, the poet's "feelings." The word "overflow" also exemplifies the water-language in which feelings are usually discussed and suggests that the dynamics of the poetic process consists in the pressure of fluid feelings; later John Keble converted the water to steam and described the poetic process as a release, a "safety valve" for pent-up feelings and desires. The poetic process, therefore, as Wordsworth says, is not calculated, but "spontaneous." Wordsworth still allows for the element of "art" by regarding the success of spontaneous composition to be attendant upon prior thought and practice, and takes the audience into account by insisting that "poets do not write for poets alone, but for men." But in the more radical followers and successors of Wordsworth, incl. Keble, Mill, and Carlyle, the art of affecting an audience, which had been the defining attribute of poetry in pragmatic theory, becomes precisely the quality which invalidates a poem. "Poetry," wrote Mill, "is feeling, confessing itself to itself in moments of solitude." And when the utterance "is not itself the end, but a means to an end . . . of making an impression upon another mind, then it ceases to be poetry, and becomes eloquence" ("What is Poetry?" 1833). Later writers adapted the concept of poetry as emotive expression to a communicative, or pragmatic, frame of reference. That poetry is emotional communication is the basic principle of Tolstoy's "infection theory" of art (*What is Art?* 1898), as well as of the earlier writings of I. A. Richards, who claimed that emotive lang. is "used for the sake of the effects in emotion and attitude produced by the reference it occasions," and that poetry "is the supreme form of emotive lang." (*Principles of Lit. Crit.*, 1924).

Feelings overflow into words, so that it is characteristic of Wordsworth and later emotive theorists, through the school of I. A. Richards, to give to the nature and standards of poetic diction, or "language," the systematic priority which earlier critics had given to plot, character, and considerations of form. In earlier discussions of poetry as an imitation of human actions, the chief forms of poetry had been narrative and dramatic, and the usual antithesis to poetry had been history, or the narration of events that have actually transpired. But Wordsworth, Hazlitt, Mill, and many of their contemporaries, conceiving poetry as the lang. of feeling, thought of the lyrical poem, instead of epic or tragedy, as the exemplary form, and replaced history as the logical opposite of poetry by

what Wordsworth called "matter of fact, or science." This romantic innovation, positing poetry as an antithesis to "science," has become a common theoretical gambit in the 20th c. (e.g. Richards and Ransom); and, as we shall see, both Continental formalists and Am. New Critics tend to establish the essential nature of poetry by systematic opposition to the features attributed to the lang. of science.

Among expressive theorists of the 19th c., the old criterion of truth to objective or ideal nature was often reinterpreted as truth to a nature already suffused with the poet's feelings or reshaped by the dynamics of desire. More commonly still, the criterion was turned around in the demand that poetry be "sincere"; it was in this period that "sincerity" (q.v.) became a cardinal requirement of poetic excellence. "The excellence of Burns," as Carlyle said, clearly revealing the reversal of the standard of "truth," is "his *sincerity*, his indisputable air of truth . . . . The passion that is traced before us has glowed in a living heart." Or as Mill asserted, in a phrasing anticipating the theory of later symbolists and expressionists, poetry embodies itself "in symbols which are the nearest possible representations of the feeling in the exact shape in which it exists in the poet's mind." The mirror held up to nature becomes a mirror held up to the poet, or else it is rendered transparent: Shakespeare's works, according to Carlyle, "are so many windows, through which we see a glimpse of the world that was in him." Correspondingly, the elements constituting a poem become in large part qualities which it shares with its author: feelings, imagination, spirit, and (in Matthew Arnold, for example) such traits of character as largeness, freedom, benignity, and high seriousness.

As Carlyle shrewdly observed as early as 1827, the grand question asked by the best contemporary critics is "to be answered by discovering and delineating the peculiar nature of the poet from his poetry." Essays on Shakespeare, Milton, Dante, and Homer became to a singular degree essays on the temperament and moral nature of the poet as manifested in his work. The most thorough exponent of poetry as self-expression was John Keble in his *Lectures on Poetry* (1832–41), whose thesis was that any good poem is a disguised form of wish-fulfillment—"the indirect expression," as he said in a review of Lockhart's *Scott*, "of some overpowering emotion, or ruling taste, or feeling, the direct indulgence whereof is somehow repressed"—and who specified and applied a complex set of techniques for reversing the process and reconstructing the temperament of the poet from its distorted projection in his poems. In both critical premises and practice, Keble has hardly been exceeded even by critics in the age of Freud, who, like Edmund Wilson, hold that "the real elements, of course, of any work of fiction, are the elements of the author's personality: his imagination embodies in the images of characters, situations, and scenes the fundamental conflicts of his nature" (*Axel's Castle*, 1936). A more recent devel. is that of the Geneva School (q.v.) of phenomenological crit., or "critics of consciousness." These critics conceive a literary work, in its elements and form, to be an objectified embodiment of the unique mode of consciousness of its author, and propose that the chief aim of the reader should be to re-experience this immanent consciousness. As Georges Poulet wrote, in "Phenomenology of Reading" (1969): "When I read as I ought . . . my consciousness behaves as though it were the consciousness of another." So early as 1778 J. G. Herder had declared: "This *living reading*, this divination into the soul of the author, is the *sole* mode of reading, and the most profound means of self-development." The quotation reveals the extent to which consciousness-criticism, although employing phenomenological concepts derived from the philosopher Husserl, is rooted in the romantic conception that a work of lit. is the expression of a unique self.

The principal alternative, in 19th-c. expressive theory, to the view that poetry is the expression of the feelings, or unrealized desires, of an individual personality was Coleridge's view that "poetry" (the superlative passages which occur both in poems and other forms of discourse) is the product of "that synthetic and magical power, to which we have exclusively appropriated the name of imagination" (q.v.; *Biographia literaria*, 1817). The creative imagination of the poet, like God the Creator, is endowed with an inner source of motion, and its creative activity, generated by the tension of contraries seeking resolution in a new whole, parallels the dynamic principle underlying the created universe. Following the lead of post-Kantian Ger. theorists, esp. Schelling and A. W. Schlegel, Coleridge opposes the organic imaginative process to the mechanical operation of the fancy (q.v.); that is, he deals with it in terms that are literal for a growing plant and metaphoric for imagination, as a self-organizing process, assimilating disparate materials by an inherent lawfulness into an organic unity that is revealed "in the balance or reconciliation of opposite or discordant qualities" (see ORGANICISM). Coleridge thus inaugurated the organic theory of poetry in England, as well as the aesthetic principle of inclusiveness, or the "reconciliation of opposite or discordant qualities" which became both the basic conception of poetic unity (q.v.) and the prime criterion of poetic excellence in I. A. Richards and many of the New Critics.

One other variant of the expressive theory deserves mention. Longinus had attributed the sublime quality esp. to the stunning image, or to brief passages characterized by "speed, power, and intensity," comparable in effect "to a thunderbolt or flash of lightning" and recognizable by the transport or "spell that it throws over us." Many expressive theorists, assuming the lyric to be the paradigm of poetry, depart from the neoclassical emphasis on distinct and hierarchically ordered poetic kinds by minimizing other genres and by applying to all poems qualitative and evaluative terms which are independent of their generic differences. Joseph Warton and other 18th-c. Longinians went still further by identifying the transporting short poem, or the intense image or fragment in a longer poem, as "pure poetry," "poetry as such," or "the poetry of a poem." In the 19th c., there emerged the explicit theory that the essentially poetic is to be found only in the incandescent and unsustainable short poem or passage, originating in the soul, unachievable by art and unanalyzable by critics, but characterized by the supreme aesthetic virtue of "intensity" (q.v.). This mode of thinking is to be found in Hazlitt's treatment of "gusto"; in Keats's concept that "the excellence of every art is its *intensity*"; in Poe's doctrine (picked up by Baudelaire) that "a poem is such, only inasmuch as it intensely excites, by elevating, the soul, and all intense excitements are, through a psychal necessity, brief," so that a long poem is a contradiction in terms ("The Philosophy of Composition," 1846); in Arnold's use of fragmentary touchstones (q.v.) for detecting "the very highest poetical quality"; in the Abbé Bremond's theory of "la poésie pure" (see PURE POETRY); and more explicitly still, in A. E. Housman's subsequent *The Name and Nature of Poetry* (1933).

IV. OBJECTIVE THEORIES. Aristotle, after defining tragedy as an imitation of a certain kind of action with certain characteristic "powers," or effects, showed the way to the further consideration of the tragic poem as an entity in itself, subject to internal requirements (such as unity, probability, progression from beginning through complication to catastrophe) which determine the selection, treatment, and ordering of the parts into an artistic whole. Despite their persistent appeal to Aristotle as exemplar, however, most later critics in effect assimilated Aristotle to the Horatian theoretical frame, aligning the poem to its audience. In the 18th c., however, a radical shift occurred in the approach to poetry as to the other arts. Since Cl. times the theoretical framework had been a construction paradigm, in which the enterprise was to discover and describe the "art," or what Ben Jonson had called "the craft of making" a good poem, which would then serve to inform critics how to judge whether a poem was good, or well-made. In the 18th c. this often gave way to a perceptual paradigm in which a perceiver confronts a completed poem, however it got made, and analyzes the features it presents to his attention and "taste," or sensibility. Addison's *Spectator* papers on "The Pleasures of the Imagination" (1712) comprise an innovative document in the theory of art, above all because, by adopting the general stance of Locke's epistemology, it substitutes for the old view of the *poeta* as "maker" and the *poema* as a "made thing" the stance of a perceiver to the poem as a given object. Within this altered paradigm, or theoretical stance, two critical models for the nature of a poem were exploited during the 18th c. until they effected a shift among philosophies of art from the earlier mimetic or pragmatic theories to an objective theory of poetry-as-such. One of these is the heterocosmic model, in which each work constitutes a unique, coherent, and autonomous world (see AUTONOMY). The other is the contemplation model, in which each work is a self-sufficient object that is contemplated disinterestedly for its own sake.

The figurative model of a poem as its own created world had been inaugurated by thinkers of the It. Ren.—Cristoforo Landino, Tasso, Scaliger—who proposed that the poet does not imitate God's world but, like the God of Genesis, creates his own world, and, it was sometimes suggested, *ex nihilo*, "out of nothing." Such high claims, however, served at first merely as a passing topic of praise within an overall pragmatic view of poetry, used in order to counter the ancient Platonic derogation of poets on the charge that their fictions are lies. With this aim Sidney, for example, glorified poetry above all other human achievements by claiming that the poet alone, "lifted up with the vigor of his own invention, doth grow in effect into another nature," when "with the force of a divine breath he bringeth things forth far surpassing her doings." Sidney at once turns, however, to his basic formulation that poetry is an "art of imitation" that is designed "to teach and delight" (*Defence of Poesie*, ca. 1580). The revolutionary possibilities of the concept that the poet is the creator of a new world began to be exploited only when it became necessary to justify poetry against the claim, by writers in the age of the "new philosophy", that (as Hobbes put it in "Answer to Davenant") since poetry is "an imitation of human life," the poet may not go "beyond the conceived possibility of nature." Addison's counter-claim, in defending "the fairy way of writing" (*Spectator* 419), is that in such products of the poet's "invention" and "imagination" (qq.v.) we "are led, as it were, into a new creation," and that in its nonrealistic components, poetry "makes new worlds of its own, shows us persons who are not to be found in being." The young Ger. philosopher, Alexander Baumgarten, in *Philosophical Reflections on Poetry* (1735), developed this concept that some kinds of poetry are a new creation by translating into poetics the cosmogony of Leibniz, according to which God, in creating this "best of all possible worlds," chose from an indefinite number of "possible worlds," each constituted by "compossible" (mutually coherent) elements, and each ordered by unique internal laws. In Baumgarten's poetics, the nonrealistic elements in a poem, which he calls "heterocosmic fictions," are justifiable in that they are capable of co-existing in another "possible" world; he also, in an important theoretical move, extends

the heterocosmic analogue to account for the "interconnection" of elements in all poems whatever: "the poet is like a maker or creator. So the poem ought to be like a world"; hence each poetic world, since it is governed by its own system of laws, manifests a "poetic" truth that is not one of correspondence to the real world but of internal coherence. The adaptation to poetry of Leibniz's philosophy of divine creation effected similar conclusions in the Swiss-German critics, Bodmer and Breitinger. As Breitinger summarized this view in his *Critische Dichtkunst* (1740), the poetic imagination finds its originals "not in the actual world, but in some other possible world-structure. Every single well-invented poem is therefore to be regarded in no other way than as the history of another possible world. In this respect the poet alone deserves the name of *poietes*; that is, of a creator." The consequence, as Bodmer put it, is that "poetic truth," within the distinctive world of a poem, differs from "rational truth" in that its probability consists not in correspondence to the existing world, but "in its coherence with itself" (*Von dem Wunderbaren*, 1740). In England, critics who adopted Addison's metaphor of a poem as a new creation achieved parallel results, though in less detail and without the underpinning of Leibnizian cosmogony. In explicit refutation of Hobbes, for example, Richard Hurd (*Letters on Chivalry and Romance*, 1762) affirmed that "poetical truth" is independent of "philosophical or historical truth" on the grounds that "the poet has a world of his own, where experience has less to do, than consistent imagination."

The alternative model—the concept that a poem, like other works of art, is a self-bounded object that is to be contemplated disinterestedly and for its own sake—also had a theological origin, but one quite different from that of the poem as an alternative to God's creation. The historical roots of this concept lie in Plato's assertion in the *Symposium* that the highest good of life consists in the "contemplation of beauty absolute" (that is, of the Idea of Ideas), as seen "with the eye of the mind"; also in Plotinus' derivative claims in the *Enneads* that the Absolute, or One, is "wholly self-sufficing," "self-closed," and "autonomous," and that the ultimate aim of the human soul, impelled by "love," is to "contemplate Absolute Beauty in its essential integrity" and thus achieve a peace without "movement," "passion," or "outlooking desire." In the early Christian centuries various Church Fathers conflated the self-sufficient Absolute of Plato and Plotinus, however incongruously, with the personal God of the Bible. St. Augustine, more than any other, fixed these ideas in Christian thought in his reiterated claims that all the good and beautiful things in this world of sense are to be loved only for their "use," but that God alone, as "the Supreme Beauty," and thus self-sufficient, is to be loved not for use but for pure "enjoyment," as His own end and for His own sake. And in this life, Augustine says, the highest manifestation of love is an "enjoyment" of God which is a *visio*, or contemplation by the mind's eye, of God in His supreme beauty. It was the third Earl of Shaftesbury, in his *Characteristics* (1711), who introduced the theological terms "contemplation" and "disinterested" into the context of a discussion of the way we apprehend beautiful earthly objects, incl. works of art; but Shaftesbury dealt with such sensible beauties only as ancillary to his Neoplatonic ethical and religious philosophy, which permitted no essential distinction between religious, moral, and aesthetic "contemplation." It remained for Shaftesbury's philosophical successors in Germany, where he enjoyed an enormous vogue, to secularize and specialize the terms "contemplation," "disinterested," and "for its own sake," by transferring their application from God to works of art and by using these terms specifically to differentiate aesthetic experience from religious and moral, as well as from practical and utilitarian, experience.

The young Ger. thinker Karl Philipp Moritz was the first to propound an unqualifiedly objective theory of art and poetry, and in so doing he deployed both the contemplation model and the heterocosmic model of art in a way that evidenced the degree to which the two were in fact conducive to similar artistic concepts and criteria. In his "Essay on the Unification of All the Fine Arts" (1785), Moritz attacks the reigning views that the arts aim at an "imitation of nature" with the "end" of giving pleasure to an audience. Only the mechanical, useful arts, Moritz asserts, have an "*outer* end." "In the contemplation of the beautiful object [of art], however . . . I contemplate it as something which is *completed . . . in its own self*, which therefore constitutes a whole in itself, and affords me pleasure *for its own sake*" (italics original). Three years later, in his essay "On the Formative Imitation of the Beautiful," Moritz buttresses these views by adverting to the heterocosmic model of a work of art as its own creation: the "formative power" of the artist dissolves reality in order to "form and create" what nature has left unrealized into a "self-sufficient whole." In this way the artist's power "creates its own world, in which . . . every thing is, in its own way, a self-sufficient whole" that has "its entire value, and the end of its existence, in itself."

It is evident that when, only a few years later, Kant published his epochal *Critique of Aesthetic Judgment* (1790), he assumed the perceiver's, instead of the maker's, stance to a work of art; further, that he adopted, but greatly subtilized, the contemplation model and its attendant philosophical vocabulary descended from the Neoplatonists and Augustine that we have traced in Moritz. According to Kant the "pure judgment of taste" (that is, the normative aesthetic perception) "combines delight or aversion immediately with the mere *contemplation* of the object irrespec-

tive of its use or any end"; it is "the one and only disinterested and *free* delight," in that it is "purely contemplative," "without desire," and free of reference to the "external" ends of use or moral good; and it "pleases for its own sake" (*für sich selbst gefällt*). Like Moritz, Kant also conjoins the contemplative to the heterocosmic model: "The [productive] imagination is a powerful agent for the creation, as it were, of a second nature out of the material supplied to it by actual nature," in which, "following, no doubt, laws that are based on analogy," the materials are worked up into "what surpasses nature."

Various of these Moritzian and Kantian concepts of art as such were assimilated by Schiller, the Schlegels, Schopenhauer, and others, to become elements in the mainstream of professional aesthetics. In the mid 19th c., similar views emerged among practicing poets and critics, when the concept that a poem, as an autonomous object to be contemplated for its own sake, became a common tenet among Fr. proponents of *l'art pour l'art*. One source of this view was, through Baudelaire as intermediary, Poe's laudation in "The Poetic Principle" (1848–49), of the "poem *per se*—this poem which is a poem and nothing more—this poem written solely for the poem's sake" and offering a "pure" pleasure "from the contemplation of the Beautiful." Another important source was a popularized version of Kant's aesthetic ideas in Victor Cousin's lectures on *The True, the Beautiful, and the Good*, available in numerous editions first published 20 years after they had been delivered in 1817–18. "The mere imitation of nature," as Gautier wrote in 1847, "cannot be the end of the artist." The purpose of the modern school of *l'art pour l'art* "is to seek beauty for its own sake with complete impartiality, perfect disinterestedness" (q.v.).

This concept of disinterested contemplation, as in the latter 18th c., was often merged with that of a literary work as its own created world. To Flaubert, for example, the relation of an author to his second creation should be like that of God to his original creation, both immanent and transcendent: "An author in his book must be like God in the universe, present everywhere and visible nowhere. Art being a second Nature, the creator of that Nature must behave similarly"—a view that Stephen Dedalus echoes in Joyce's *A Portrait of the Artist as a Young Man*, in asserting that "the artist, like the God of the creation, remains within or behind or beyond or above his handiwork, invisible, refined out of existence, indifferent, paring his fingernails." In his 1901 essay "Poetry for Poetry's Sake" (*Oxford Lectures on Poetry* [1909]), A. C. Bradley undertook, he said, to salvage the basic truths within the exaggerated claims of art for art's sake. The experience of poetry, he declared, "is an end in itself," and "*poetic* value" is "this intrinsic worth alone," independently of a poem's "ulterior worth" as means to ends outside itself; for a poem is not "a part, nor yet a copy of the real world," but "a world by itself, independent, complete, autonomous," and the reader must "conform to its laws." Poetry and reality "are parallel developments which nowhere meet . . . they are analogues." And the reciprocal of this concept, from the standpoint of the reader, is that the poetic otherworld exists solely for our disinterested contemplation; as Bradley puts it, the poem "makes no direct appeal to those feelings, desires, and purposes [of our life in this world], but speaks only to contemplative imagination."

The objective conception of poetry-as-such, expressed in one or another idiom, became the dominant mode of thinking for many literary theorists and critics, as well as for many major authors, in the half-century or so beginning in the 1920s. The Russian Formalists set up a fundamental opposition between literary (or poetical) lang. and ordinary "practical," "referential," or "scientific" lang. Whereas ordinary lang. communicates by references to the outer world, literary lang. is self-focused, exploiting various devices in order to "foreground" the utterance itself, to "estrange" it from ordinary discourse, and to draw attention from outer relations to its own formal features, the inter-relationships among the linguistic signs themselves (see RUSSIAN FORMALISM). The loose-boundaried critical movement of Fr. structuralism, beginning in the 1950s, absorbed some formalist concepts but viewed a literary work as primarily a second-order signifying system; that is, it uses lang., the first-order system, as its medium, and thus is itself to be analyzed on the model of the linguistic theory propounded by Ferdinand de Saussure in his *Course in General Linguistics* (1915). Structuralism (q.v.) opposes the views that lit. imitates reality, or expresses the subjectivity of an author, or is a mode of communication between author and reader; instead, it regards a work as a mode of writing (*écriture*) which, like the linguistic system that precipitates it, is a self-determining structure of inter-relations constituted by a play of specifically literary conventions and "codes." The general aim of structuralist critics, as Jonathan Culler has put it, is to "construct a poetics which stands to lit. as linguistics stands to lang."—that is, as the general laws of a *langue* stand to a particular utterance or *parole*.

Among Am. literary theorists between 1930 and 1960, the most widely accepted formulations were that a literary work is "autotelic," and that we must consider poetry "primarily as poetry and not another thing" (T. S. Eliot); or that the first law of crit. is to "cite the nature of the object" and to recognize "the autonomy of the work itself as existing for its own sake" (J. C. Ransom); or that the essential task of the critic is the "intrinsic," not the "extrinsic" study of lit. (Wellek and Warren). The acute and learned critics of the "Chicago School" (q.v.) while acknowledging the usefulness of an "integral criticism" that considers poetry in an inclusive context as sharing essential features with other human products, themselves advocate and pursue a "differential crit." that deals with a poem as such, in its distinctive internal characteristics. This they do by expanding upon a procedure they attribute to Aristotle: they view each poem as an artistic whole that is formally constructed to achieve a particular "working or power"; the elements, inter-relations, and structure of the poem are systematically analyzed as internal causes of that power—causes that are theoretically separable from the extra-artistic causes of a poem in the nature of an individual author, in the audience addressed, or in the state of the lang. that the author inherits (see the Intro. to Crane).

The most widespread and commonly applied theory of poetry in the quarter-century between the mid 1930s and 1960 was that named by Ransom in 1941 "the New Criticism" (q.v.); it became the reigning point of view in Am. colleges and schools esp. after the publication in 1938 of Cleanth Brooks' and Robert Penn Warren's widely influential textbook, *Understanding Poetry*. These critics differ in the details of their theory but share the concept that poetry in the large (with little or no attention to diverse poetic genres) is to be considered as a special mode of lang. which is defined by positing for poetry features that are systematically contrary to the abstract, literal, and conceptual nature, the empirical claims, and the referential and practical purposes attributed to the lang. of "science." A poem thus becomes its own world—a distinctive universe of discourse—which is set against representations of the ordinary world of things, people, and events; and the integrity and boundaries of the former, the world of the poetic "object," are carefully guarded by prohibitions against the "personal heresy," "the heresy of paraphrase" (q.v.; Brooks), and what W. K. Wimsatt, Jr., and Monroe Beardsley called the "intentional fallacy" (reference to the purpose and state of mind of the author) and "affective fallacy" (reference to the responses of the reader). The sole end of a poem is the poem itself as a self-sufficient "structure of meanings." The New Critics developed a formidable apparatus for their most innovative and distinctive procedure, the detailed "explication" (q.v.) or "close reading" of individual poems as a totality of "logical structure" and "local texture" (Ransom), or an equilibrium of multiple "tensions" (Tate), or an "organic unity" of ironies, ambiguities, paradoxes, and image-patterns (Brooks). The attempt was often made to reconnect the poem-as-such to the ordinary world by positing as its organizing principle a "theme" (q.v.), which is embodied and dramatized in the poem's evolving imagery and "symbolic action" (qq.v.), and is to be judged by such tests as "seriousness," "maturity," "profundity," and the subtlety of the "moral awareness" that the poem manifests. (See Brooks's "Irony as a Principle of Structure" and the influential writings of F. R.

Leavis, which are in parallel with many of the assumptions and practices of his Am. contemporaries.) But as Wimsatt stresses in *The Verbal Icon*, such reassertions of the thematic and moral aspects of a poem are to be understood not in an expressive or pragmatic but in an objective orientation: "Neither the qualities of the author's mind nor the effects of a poem upon a reader's mind should be confused with the moral quality expressed by the poem itself." The same shift of orientation to the poem in itself is evident in the assertions of Ransom and other New Critics—in opposition to the positivists' claim that valid knowledge is the sole prerogative of science—that poetry is "cognitive" and provides, as Tate says, a "special, unique, and complete knowledge" ("The Present Function of Crit."). It turns out that the knowledge yielded by a poem is not that of correspondence to the world, but that of the concrete and bounded world of the poem itself. "It is sufficient," as Tate puts it, "that here, in the poem, we get knowledge of a whole object." And as in the earlier applications of the heterocosmic concept, the mimetic truth of correspondence is replaced by a truth of coherence that is coterminous with the poem. As Wimsatt puts this view, a poem does not mirror the world but, by the multiplicity of its internal relationships, becomes an object which is itself densely physical, hence isomorphic with the world to which it stands in the relation of an "icon" or (in the term earlier used by A. C. Bradley) an analogue: "The dimension of coherence is . . . greatly enhanced and thus generates an extra dimension of correspondence to reality, the symbolic or analogical."

Resistant, in this century, to the theories of poetry-as-such have been Freudian critics who, whatever the refinements they introduce, continue to treat poetry as primarily a product (under a variety of cunning disguises) of the poet's unconscious desires (see PSYCHOLOGICAL CRITICISM). Another counter-theory is that of Marxist critics, who in recent decades have produced complex and subtle versions of the basic view that lit. both expresses and reflects an ideology which derives, in the final analysis, from the structure and conflict of classes attendant upon the means of economic production in any given era; the special emphasis is on the literary "reflection," in the modern bourgeois era, of the class conflicts, contradictions, crippling intellectual conditions, and human alienation under capitalism (see MARXIST CRITICISM). Another major challenge to reigning views was mounted by Northrop Frye's archetypal theory, announced in *Anatomy of Crit.* (1957) and elaborated in a number of later writings (see MYTH CRITICISM; ARCHETYPE). Frye substitutes for the autonomous single work of the New Critics an all-inclusive autonomous realm, the "self-contained literary universe," which has over the ages been bodied forth by the generically human imagination so as to humanize an inhuman reality by incorporating it into persisting mythical forms that serve to satisfy enduring human needs and concerns. The four radical *mythoi* (structural principles) are the primary genres of comedy, romance, tragedy, and satire; but within each genre, individual works inevitably play variations upon many other archetypes, or inherited imaginative forms, that lit. shares not only with other "discursive verbal structures" and myths but also with ritualized forms of social activities.

V. RECENT DEVELOPMENTS. Since the mid 1960s, the traditional frames of reference for dealing with poetry have been thrown into considerable disarray by a number of new developments, usually called "critical theories." These are not, however, theories of poetry, in the traditional sense of setting up definitions, categories, and criteria for identifying, classifying, and analyzing works of poetry. Instead, they are general theories of "reading," or interp.; in fact, their common tendency is to deny that there are stable criteria for differentiating poetry, or lit. generally, from other forms of discourse, including the discourse of lit. crit. itself. A number of these theories also claim that poetry, like other forms of discourse, is radically indeterminate, or undecidable, in it meanings, hence that there is no valid way to establish "the right reading" for any poem or poetic passage (see INDETERMINACY; INTERPRETATION; TEXTUALITY).

In *The Anxiety of Influence* (1973) and a number of later books, Harold Bloom proposes that a poet, as a reader, experiences some poem, or group of poems, of a precursor as a threat to his own imaginative autonomy (see INFLUENCE). The consequent anxiety brings into play a variety of psychic defenses which unconsciously distort the precursor-poem even as the later poet re-embodies the precursor into his own "belated" poem; these distortions serve to yield the later poet the precarious illusion of being "prior" to his predecessor both in psychological time and in imaginative reality. But readings of the later poem, whether by poets or by critics of poetry, are in turn bound to be "defensive," hence distortive, with the result that, as Bloom says, all "reading is . . . misprision—or misreading."

In essays written during the 1970s and collected in *Is There a Text in This Class?* (1980), Stanley Fish established himself as a radical and highly articulate exemplar of the international movement of reader-response crit. (q.v.)—that is, of a form of critical theory which, in place of conceiving of a literary work in the traditional way as an achieved structure of meanings, conceives of the work and its meanings as produced by the evolving responses of a reader to a given text. In his earlier essays in this collection, Fish proposed that the poetic text is simply a set of stimuli to which a reader, putting into play one or another "interpretive strategy," "creates" all the formal features and meanings that constitute a poem, incl. its postulated author and that author's supposed intentions to mean something determinate. In the later essays of the collection, however, Fish stresses that a reader is not an isolated individual but a member of an "interpretive community." Members of such a community have been trained to share interpretive assumptions, habits of reading, and standards of judgment and so will agree, approximately at least, on the features and meanings that they find in a poem, as well as in the modes of critical reasoning by which they undertake to resolve such disagreements as may occur. In essays after 1980, Fish has especially emphasized the role of the shared practice that constitutes, for the time being, the "discipline" of lit. crit., in determining the way that one reads and analyzes a text. Although current "theorists" may insist on the radical indeterminacy (q.v.) of poetic boundaries, features, and meanings, Fish asserts that when they turn to the applied crit. of a particular poem, they have no option except to work in accordance with boundaries, as well as with the determination of what will count as poetic facts and meanings, that are effected by the "constitutive rules" of the current "game," or disciplinary practice, that we call lit. crit. (see Fish, "Consequences," in *Against Theory* [1985]).

Most prominent in the 1980s, esp. in America, has been deconstructive theory, based primarily on the writings, beginning in the latter 1960s, of the poststructuralist Fr. thinker Jacques Derrida (see DECONSTRUCTION). Derrida views all Western writing, incl. poetry and lit., as "logocentric," in that it presupposes a "logos" or "presence"—an absolute "ground," or a "transcendental signified"—which exists outside of, and is unmediated by, the lang. system that it is presumed to underwrite. In the inevitable lack of such an absolute ground, Derrida asserts, all modes of writing "deconstruct" themselves by "disseminating" in a suspension of significations that are undecidable, and that inevitably involve "aporias"—that is, deadlocks of conflicting or contradictory meanings. Derrida insists that "deconstruction has nothing to do with destruction." He acknowledges that the play of differences that constitutes a lang. indeed produces the "effects" of intentionality, of determinate meanings, and of other features on which the common practice of reading depends, and he asserts that a deconstructive reading cannot simply cancel, but must recognize and "respect" the "exigencies" that determine this common reading. What a deconstructive reading goes on to do, however, is to "reinscribe" or "resituate" such seemingly decidable meanings within the differential play of lang. so as to make clear their status as no more than "effects" of such a play, and to reveal their inability to master the "surplus of signification" by which a text goes on, inexorably, to disseminate itself into self-conflicting undecidabilities.

A number of Am. critics—among whom Paul de Man, J. Hillis Miller, Barbara Johnson, and Cynthia Chase are prominent—have adapted what Derrida calls his "critical reading" (that is, his deconstructive analysis) of short textual passages to that "close reading" of individual poems or literary works which had been the innovative and distinctive practice of the New Criticism in America. Although these critics differ in emphasis and procedure, they all follow Derrida in insisting that the linguistic medium is not simply transparent to meaning but opaque and operative, and also in focusing on the ways that the internal play of differences in lang. inevitably frustrates any attempt to establish fixed boundaries between poetry and nonpoetry, or between lit. and crit., as well as any possibility of fixing upon straightforward assertions or decidable meanings in a text. As Barbara Johnson has put it in *The Critical Difference* (1985), the deconstruction of a text proceeds "by the careful teasing out of warring forces of signification within the text itself." In *Allegories of Reading* (1979), Paul de Man conducted a series of close deconstructive readings of passages in prose and verse in his enterprise of demonstrating how in a text the "rhetoric" (the play of tropes and figures) disrupts and subverts the claims of its "grammar," with the result, as he says, that the reader ends in a "state of suspended ignorance" about what the text signifies or asserts; de Man's further claim is that any literary text, whatever the subject-matter that it seemingly represents, can be read as an "allegory" of its own self-baffling workings. In *The Linguistic Moment* (1985), J. Hillis Miller concurs that through "an intrinsic necessity of lang.," any literary work will manifest a "plurality of meanings" which are "undecidable" except by a reader's arbitrary choice. In an essay on Wallace Stevens, Miller describes deconstructive crit. as the attempt to find "the element in the system studied which is illogical, the thread in the text in question which will unravel it all. . . . Deconstruction is not a dismantling of the structure of a text but a demonstration that it has already dismantled itself."

VI. THE USES OF POETIC THEORY. The multiplicity of competing theories of poetry and lit., and their power of survival despite what seem their mutual contradictions, has occasioned a variety of attacks against the validity of any theory in crit. Some philosophers of aesthetics, for example, have described theories of poetry as logical mistakes, in that they are impossible attempts to establish an "essentialist" definition—that is, a definition of the essence, or else of the necessary and sufficient properties, of all poems (see, e.g., *Aesthetics and Lang.*, ed. W. Elton [1954]). More recently, Steven Knapp and Walter Benn Michaels have incited considerable controversy by their essays "Against Theory" (in *Against Theory* [1985]). That these authors direct their attack primarily against the "theories" of interp. current since the 1960s is indicated by their stipulating a definition of theory as "the attempt to govern interps. of particular texts by appealing to an account of interp. in general." They claim that such an account rests on a mistake and is bound to fail, therefore cannot entail consequences for the crit. of particular texts, whether to validate a determinate interp. or (as in the theories described in the preceding section of this article) to deny the possibility of determinacy or correctness in interp.; they therefore conclude that "the whole enterprise of critical theory is misguided and should be abandoned."

To counter the claims of these antitheorists that a valid theory is neither possible nor consequential for critical practice, we need to look past what they say theorists try to do—and even what some theorists claim that they do—to the actual history of critical practice in the 2500 years since Aristotle. A comparative study of the enduring masters of crit. reveals that their distinctive and systematic differences in practice have been fostered by differences in their general theories, and that the test of the soundness and survival-value of a theory is the profitability that it has demonstrated for the applied crit. of individual works of lit. A profitable theory, although it is empirical in the sense that it begins and ends with an appeal to the purported properties of poems, is not a science of lit. but an enterprise of artistic discovery—what Coleridge called a "speculative instrument." In practice, that is, a sound theory—whether or not put forward as a definition of the essential nature of poetry or of lit. in general—has served as an indispensable device for blocking out the area of discourse that the critic proposes to investigate and for establishing a point of vantage over that area, as well as a frame of reference for developing concepts to deal with single literary works. The diverse theories of poetry described in the course of this article—however contradictory an assertion excerpted from one may seem when set against an assertion excerpted from another—have in fact served as alternative and complementary procedures for carrying out the critical enterprise, each theory, from its elected vantage, yielding distinctive kinds of insights into the structures and features of poems and their relations to each other and to their enabling conditions and contexts. Crit. without some understructure of theory—whether the theory, as in Aristotle and Coleridge, is prior and explicit or, as in Johnson and Arnold, is merely implied, or adverted to only as occasion demands—is made up of desultory impressions and concepts that are supposedly given by common sense but in fact turn out to have been inherited from earlier and greater critics, in whose writings they were implicated in precisely those principles, distinctions, categories, and frame of reasoning that constitute what has traditionally been known as a poetic theory.

For further discussion of poetic theory see CRITICISM; INTERPRETATION; METACRITICISM; REPRESENTATION AND MIMESIS; and THEORY. For fuller discussion of specific types of crit., see esp. IMITATION; HISTORICISM; EXPRESSION; RUSSIAN FORMALISM; STRUCTURALISM; PSYCHOLOGICAL CRITICISM; NEW CRITICISM; CHICAGO SCHOOL; ORGANICISM; CONTEXTUALISM; MYTH CRITICISM; LINGUISTICS AND POETICS; GENEVA SCHOOL; HERMENEUTICS; INFLUENCE; INTUITION; MARXIST CRITICISM; CULTURAL CRITICISM; READER-RESPONSE CRITICISM; DECONSTRUCTION; FEMINIST POETICS; ETHICS AND CRITICISM; and PLURALISM; see also MODERNISM AND POSTMODERNISM. The major periods of Western poetics are discussed in greater detail in CLASSICAL POETICS; MEDIEVAL POETICS; RENAISSANCE POETICS; BAROQUE POETICS; NEOCLASSICAL POETICS; ROMANTIC AND POSTROMANTIC POETICS; and TWENTIETH-CENTURY POETICS. Non-Western trads. in poetics are surveyed in ARABIC POETICS; CHINESE POETICS; HEBREW PROSODY AND POETICS; INDIAN POETICS; and JAPANESE POETICS. For overview of the Western and Eastern trads. in poetics, see POETICS.

CONVENIENT ANTHOLOGIES OF POETIC THEORY: *Elizabethan Crit. Essays*, ed. G. G. Smith, 2 v. (1904); *Crit. Essays of the 17th C.*, ed. J. S. Spingarn, 3 v. (1908–9); *Crit. Essays of the 18th C.*, ed. W. H. Durham (1915); *Eng. Crit. Essays, 19th C.*, ed. E. D. Jones (1916); *Kunstanschauung der Frühromantik*, ed. A. Müller (1931); *Lit. Crit. Plato to Dryden*, ed. A. H. Gilbert (1940); *Crit.: The Major Texts*, ed. W. J. Bate (1948); *Critiques and Essays in Crit., 1920–1948*, ed. R. W. Stallman (1949); *Crit. Prefaces of the Fr. Ren.*, ed. B. Weinberg (1950); *Mod. Lit. Crit.*, ed. I. Howe (1958); *The Continental Model: Selected Fr. Crit. Essays of the 17th C. in Eng. Tr.*, ed. S. Elledge and D. S. Schier (1960); *18th-C. Crit. Essays*, ed. S. Elledge, 2 v. (1961); *Mod. Fr. Poets on Poetry*, ed. R. Gibson (1961); *Mod. Continental Lit. Crit.*, ed. O. B. Hardison, Jr. (1962); *Mod. Crit. in Theory and Practice*, ed. W. Sutton and R. Foster (1963); *Crit. Theory Since Plato*, ed. H. Adams (1971); *Ancient Lit. Crit.*, ed. D. A. Russell and M. Winterbottom (1972); *Cl. and Med. Lit. Crit.*, ed. A. Preminger et al. (1974); *Textual Strategies: Perspectives in Post-Structuralist Crit.*, ed. J. V. Harari (1979); *Critical Theory Since 1965*, ed. H. Adams and L. Searle (1986); *Contemp. Lit. Crit.: Literary and Cultural Studies*, ed. R. C. Davis and R. Schleifer, 2d ed. (1989).

SELECTED SECONDARY WORKS: J. E. Spingarn, *Hist. of Lit. Crit. in the Ren.* (1899); G. Saintsbury, *Hist. of Crit. and Literary Taste in Europe*, 3 v. (1900–4); C. M. Gayley and B. P. Kurtz, *Methods and Materials of Lit. Crit.* (1920); R. Bray, *La Formation de la doctrine classique en France* (1931); J. W. H. Atkins, *Lit. Crit. in Antiquity*, 2 v. (1934), *Eng. Lit. Crit.*, 3 v. (1943–51); Patterson; S. C. Pepper, *Basis of Crit. in the Arts* (1946); M. T. Herrick, *The Fusion of Horatian and Aristotelian Lit. Crit., 1531–1555* (1946); S. E. Hyman, *The Armed Vision* (1948); Crane; M. H. Abrams, *The Mirror and the Lamp* (1953)—provides, together with *Doing Things with Texts* (1989), an expanded treatment of much of the material in this article; Wellek; Wellek and Warren; M. Krieger, *The New Apologists for Poetry* (1956); B. Markwardt, *Gesch. der deutschen Poetik*, 2d ed., 5 v. (1956–67); S. K. Langer, *Philosophy in a New Key*, 3d ed. (1957); Wimsatt and Brooks; Weinberg; R. Foster, *The New Romantics, a Reappraisal of the New Crit.* (1962); R. Wellek, *Concepts of Crit.*, ed. S. G. Nichols (1963); R. Marsh, *Four Dialectical Theories of Poetry* (1965); S. Lawall, *Critics of Consciousness* (1968); J. Culler, *Structuralist Poetics* (1975), *On Deconstruction* (1982); J. J. Y. Liu, *Ch. Theories of Lit.* (1975); G. Webster, *The Republic of Letters: A Hist. of Postwar Am. Literary Opinion* (1979); Ransom; F. Lentricchia, *After the New Crit.* (1980); *Against Theory*, ed. W. J. T. Mitchell (1985); L. Dolezel, *Occidental Poetics* (1990).   M.H.A.

POETRY AND FINE ARTS. See DESCRIPTIVE POETRY; EKPHRASIS; ENARGEIA; MUSIC AND POETRY; SCULPTURE AND POETRY; VISUAL ARTS AND POETRY.

POETRY AND HISTORY. See HISTORY AND POETRY.

POETRY AND MUSIC. See MUSIC AND POETRY; SONG.

POETRY AND PHILOSOPHY. See PHILOSOPHY AND POETRY.

POETRY AND PROSE. See PROSE POEM; VERSE AND PROSE.

POETRY AND RELIGION. See RELIGION AND POETRY.

POETRY AND SCIENCE. See SCIENCE AND POETRY.

POETRY AND SEMANTICS. See SEMANTICS AND POETRY; SEMIOTICS, POETIC.

POETRY AND SOCIETY. See CULTURAL CRITICISM; SOCIETY AND POETRY.

POETRY AND THE OTHER ARTS. See MUSIC AND POETRY; SCULPTURE AND POETRY; VISUAL ARTS AND POETRY.

POETRY AS TRUTH. See CRITICISM; DECONSTRUCTION; FICTION, POETRY AS; MEANING, POETIC; POETRY, THEORIES OF; REPRESENTATION AND MIMESIS; SCIENCE AND POETRY; SEMANTICS AND POETRY; SEMIOTICS, POETIC.

POETRY READING. See PERFORMANCE.

POETRY THERAPY. See PSYCHOLOGY AND POETRY.

POINT OF VIEW. See PLOT.

POLISH POETRY.

    I. THE MIDDLE AGES
    II. RENAISSANCE
    III. BAROQUE
    IV. ENLIGHTENMENT
    V. ROMANTICISM
    VI. POSITIVISM AND NEOROMANTICISM
    VII. THE INTERWAR PERIOD AND THE WAR YEARS
    VIII. THE POSTWAR PERIOD

I. THE MIDDLE AGES. As a consequence of Poland's adoption of Christianity in its Western form in A.D. 966, Lat. served as the dominant literary lang. for at least three centuries. Some oral folk poetry in P. must have existed at this early stage, but nothing has been preserved in written form. Oddly enough, the first recorded poem in P. is the most refined literary product of the entire medieval period. "Bogurodzica" (Mother of God), an anonymous religious hymn from the 13th c. preserved in a 15th-c. ms., consists of two stanzas with a highly complex parallel construction and sophisticated verse structure.

Throughout the 14th and 15th cs., P. p. is characterized by a prevalence of religious topics. Within devotional poetry, the epic is still poorly represented: "Legenda o św. Aleksym" (The Legend of Saint Alexis), e.g., is unexceptional verse hagiography, drawing on foreign sources and rather primitive in form. By contrast, devotional lyricism flourished in numerous Lenten and Easter songs, Christmas carols, and hymns to the Virgin, mostly adaptations from Lat. Some of these poems are quite innovative. "Żale Matki Boskiej pod Krzyżem" (Lament of the Mother of God at the Foot of the Cross), a first-person monologue, forsakes allegorical commonplaces for an individualized point of view and emotional intensity. "Pieśń o Męce Pańskiej" (Passion Song) represents an early attempt at syllabic regularity. As a rule, however, the verse structure of medieval P. p. is based on a loose system of relative syllabism, with uneven lines equal to clauses and approximate rhymes.

Secular P. p. of the Middle Ages, far less abundant, consists of poems and fragments written for various purposes with similarly various aesthetic results. Some of them are merely mnemonic devices, while others are didactic and satiric; there are several timid attempts at erotic poetry as well. The most interesting lay poem of the period is the 15th-c. "Rozmowa Mistrza ze Śmiercią" (A Dialogue between Master and Death); one of many variations on the medieval theme of *memento mori*, it stands out by virtue of its vivid, if macabre, imagery and humor.

II. RENAISSANCE. Western European humanism had its representatives in Poland as early as the second half of the 15th c., but only the 1560s ushered in the "Golden Age" of the P. Ren. Meanwhile, a few transitional figures emerged. The first P.-lang. poet whose identity is at least partly established is Biernat of Lublin (ca. 1465–ca. 1529). His major poetic work is *Żywot Ezopa* (The Life of Aesop, ca. 1522), the first part of which is a rhymed account of the life of the legendary slave, while the second part presents the collection of fables. Another early humanist, this time much closer to the Ren. mentality, is Mikołaj Rej (1505–69), traditionally called the father of P. lit. A country squire with almost no formal education, he wrote in P., not in Lat. Rej's exclusive use of the vernacular was deliberate: it had much to do with the awakening of a sense of national identity in the beginnings of the Ren. His poetry is mostly didactic, descriptive, or satiric; it ranges from enormous versified treatises or dialogues to brief epigrams. As a poet, Rej undeniably lacks subtlety and artistic balance; his strengths are his passion for the particulars of life and his robust style.

Against the background of his predecessors, but also of his contemporaries, the work of Jan Kochanowski (1530–84) appears as the culmination of the P. Ren. as well as one of the crowning achievements of all Slavic poetry before the 19th c. An educated humanist, Kochanowski was indebted to the Cl. heritage as well as to contemporary It. and Fr. lit., but he gave his writing a national specificity and personal perspective. The bulk of his mature work is written in P., which he raised almost single-handedly to the rank of a literary lang. His P. output consists of the collections *Fraszki* (Trifles, 1584), *Pieśni* (Songs, 1586), and *Treny* (Threnodies, 1580); a masterly poetic adaptation of the Psalms, *Psałterz Dawidów* (1578); several epic poems; and a Cl. tragedy in verse, *Odprawa posłów greckich* (The Dismissal of the Grecian Envoys, 1578). If the Anacreontic *Fraszki* and Horatian *Pieśni* present Kochanowski as an orderly and well-balanced mind that enjoys the *aurea mediocritas* of everyday life, his *Treny* is marked by a radically different tone. This sequence of laments over the death of his little daughter encompasses a wide range of shifting feelings, from utter despair and doubt to final reconciliation with God's decrees; the poet's usually lucid and tranquil style acquires a pre-baroque complexity and tension.

Kochanowski's influence on subsequent phases of P. p. was both enormous and varied. Perhaps his most durable legacy was his contribution to the devel. of P. verse. The revolution he carried out consisted in replacing the remnants of the medieval system of relative syllabism with a strictly syllabic system, incl. exact rhyme, stabilized caesura, and paroxytonic cadence. This rigor allowed him the freedom to employ enjambment and thus create an interplay between syntax and verse structure. In addition, he was able to introduce a bewildering variety of meters and stanza patterns. Despite the 19th-c. success of the more songlike

syllabotonic system, Kochanowski's syllabism remains one of the basic verse systems of P. p.; only since the beginnings of the 20th c. has it been rivaled seriously by tonic verse and *vers libre*.

As early as the second half of the 16th c.—that is, at the zenith of the Ren.—some literary innovations were already foreshadowing the arrival of the baroque. Mikołaj Sęp Szarzyński (1550–81), who died three years before Kochanowski, was a full-fledged baroque poet *avant la lettre*. His only collection, *Rytmy abo wiersze polskie* (P. Rhythms or Verses; pub. posthumously in 1601), has been rediscovered only in recent decades, after centuries of oblivion. Szarzyński did not write much, but what he wrote reveals an extraordinary personality, a profoundly metaphysical poet. In particular, a handful of his religious sonnets, in which tortuous syntax, violent enjambment, and oxymoronic imagery portray a mind torn asunder by spiritual torment, bear comparison with the best of John Donne or George Herbert.

These two giants, Kochanowski and Szarzyński, dwarf the other poets of the P. Ren., yet several are not without artistic merit. Sebastian Grabowiecki (ca. 1543–1607) was an author of refined devotional lyricism. Sebastian Fabian Klonowic (ca. 1545–1602) wrote descriptive and didactic poems that abound with picturesque details. Szymon Szymonowic (1558–1629) left behind a collection of half-bucolic, half-realistic *Sielanki* (Idylls, 1614), an important link in the evolution of the pastoral genre.

III. BAROQUE. In P. p. of the 17th c. the new baroque style soon evolved into two different manners, sociologically demarcated by the cultural horizons of a royal or aristocratic court on the one hand and, on the other, those of the petty gentry's manor. While court poetry, more cosmopolitan, strongly resembled the Western European baroque of Marino and Góngora, the latter manner, often called the Sarmatian Baroque, was much more provincial and conservative.

The "Westernized" brand of the P. baroque had its most brilliant exponent in Jan Andrzej Morsztyn (1621–93). A courtier and political intriguer, he was close to Fr. libertinism in outlook, and he considered his writing a kind of entertainment (his two collections of poems were never published in his lifetime). His chief concern in poetry was not so much "worldly happiness" *per se* as its inherent self-contradictions. In particular, the paradoxes of love are illuminated in Morsztyn's poetry by a wide variety of striking conceits, in which there is as much frivolity as metaphysical fear. Beside him, the P. "line of wit" was represented by, among others, Daniel Naborowski (1573–1640), perhaps the most typical Marinist among poets of the early baroque, and J. A. Morsztyn's distant relative Zbigniew Morsztyn (ca. 1627–89), author of erotic poetry as well as devotional emblems.

While the court poets excelled in lyric and epigrammatic forms, the Sarmatian baroque was more diversified in its choice of genres and styles, which ranged from brief songs and lyrics to immense epic poems. The lyric branch is best represented by Szymon Zimorowic (ca. 1608–29), whose only book, *Roksolanki* (Ruthenian Maidens, 1654), appeared many years after his premature death. An ingeniously composed sequence of songs or lyric monologues by different speakers, the collection sounds the psychological mysteries of love with subtle simplicity. Kasper Miaskowski (ca. 1550–1622) was the most gifted representative of early baroque poetry of nature.

The middle and late phases of the Sarmatian baroque were characterized, however, by the poets' taste for moralism, didacticism, satire, and historical epic. The poet who exemplified all of these inclinations was Wacław Potocki (1621–96), a provincial nobleman who, in the seclusion of his country manor, wrote an immense amount of verse, incl. the epic *Wojna chocimska* (War of Chocim, 1670) and the collections *Moralia* (1688) and *Ogród*... (A Garden; pub. only in 1907). Samuel Twardowski (ca. 1600–61) was another poet who wrote in this vein, producing a historical epic, a mythological tale in verse, and a poetic romance. Krzysztof Opaliński (1609–55) can be considered the most prominent representative of the satirical bent in baroque poetry. Finally, Wespazjan Kochowski (1633–1700) was the central figure of the late baroque; his collection of lyrics and epigrams, *Nieprόżnujace prόżnowanie* (Unleisurely Leisure, 1674), surpasses the average production of those years in its technical finesse, and his long poem in biblical prose, *Psalmodia polska* (P. Psalmody, 1695), is an early manifestation of messianic P. historiosophy.

The first 60 years of the 18th c. marked a catastrophic decline in P. culture. P. p. of this period, still continuing the line of the Sarmatian baroque, was becoming increasingly monotonous in its treatment of devotional topics and its reliance on worn-out conceits. The last great triumph of baroque style—a much belated one, to be sure—occurred in 1768, when the so-called Confederacy of Bar, a gentry rebellion, produced a wave of anonymous religious and patriotic verses.

IV. ENLIGHTENMENT. In the mid 1760s, however, new tendencies began to occupy the center of the cultural stage. Under the reign of the last P. king, Stanisław August, the ideology of the Enlightenment rapidly gained ground along with a renewal of interest in Western (esp. Fr.) literary novelties. In poetry, the last decades of the 18th c. marked a resurgence of neoclassicism. The purification of lang. went hand in hand with a return to discipline and clarity in writing. Cl. genres, incl. descriptive poems, mock epics, odes, epistles, satires, fables, parables, and epigrams, were revived and cultivated.

Among the circle of poets close to the royal court, the most outstanding was Bishop Ignacy Krasicki (1735–1801). In 1778 he published anonymously his *Monachomachia*, a mock epic in ottava rima (q.v.) ridiculing the obscurantism and indulgence of monks. As a satiric poet, he reached his climax in *Satyry* (Satires, 1779–84), a series of penetrating ironic observations on contemporary morals which, thanks to brilliant dialogue and dramatic monologue, succeeded in being didactic without indulging in intrusive rhetoric. Another of his masterpieces is the collection *Bajki i przypowieści* (Fables and Parables, 1779), in which the old genre of the animal fable acquires a new form close to the epigram and characterized by clarity and conciseness as well as a bitter and disillusioned, if humorous, vision of humanity.

Another great master of witty verse was Stanisław Trembecki (1739?–1812). A libertine and courtier, he wrote political odes honoring the King and obscene erotic poems with equal ease. His highest achievements are his poetic fables, his rococo anacreontics, and his descriptive poem *Sofiόwka* (Sophie's Garden, 1806).

By and large, though, poets of the P. Enlightenment pursued the stylistic ideals of either strict neoclassicism or preromantic sentimentalism. A good example of the former is the work of Bishop Adam Naruszewicz (1733–96); its belated extension can be seen in the conservative and rigid stance of the last generation of neoclassicists, incl. Kajetan Koźmian (1771–1856), Ludwik Osiński (1775–1838), and Alojzy Feliński (1771–1820). During the first decades of the 19th c., Sentimentalism, on the other hand, surfaced in the works of Franciszek Dionizy Kniaźnin (1750–1807) and Franciszek Karpiński (1741–1825), who, in their songs and eclogues, offered many fine examples of simple and emotionally direct lyricism. Another link between the Enlightenment and romanticism can be discerned in the work of the versatile writer Julian Ursyn Niemcewicz (1758–1841), the first to popularize the ballad through both his translations and his original poetry.

V. ROMANTICISM is a pivotal epoch in P. lit. hist. The historic upheavals beginning with the final partition of Poland in 1795 created a sociopolitical situation in which lit., and particularly poetry, became a substitute for other means of shaping the nation's mentality. The term *wieszcz* (a bard, but also a prophet) came into being to denote the new role of the poet as spiritual leader. However, one of the most conspicuous features of P. romanticism is the enormous disparity between a few great "bards" and hundreds of minor poets, both for artistic innovation and actual influence. It is also significant that all the giants of P. romanticism achieved their prominence in exile; their works, of unprecedented value to the cultural survival of the oppressed P. nation, were written and published mostly in Paris.

The period of greatest achievement in romantic poetry is framed by the dates of two abortive insurrections against Czarist Russia, 1830–31 and

1863. But the starting point of P. romanticism in a broader sense is 1822, the year that saw the debut of Adam Mickiewicz (1798–1855). Mickiewicz began to write as a student at the University of Wilno and immediately became the central figure of the rapidly emerging romantic movement. His early work still owed a great deal to the spirit of the Enlightenment: "Oda do młodości" (Ode to Youth), for example, is a peculiar combination of Cl. rhet. and the new *Sturm und Drang* (q.v.) ideology. Well read in Goethe, Schiller, and Byron, Mickiewicz soon developed his own romantic style. His first volume, *Ballady i romanse* (Ballads and Romances), was an audacious manifestation of a specifically P. version of early romanticism in which references to native folklore helped to introduce elements of fantasy and the supernatural and to express the "living truths" of the heart. Mickiewicz's debut was hailed as a literary breakthrough by his own generation, but it met with ridicule from his elders the Classicists. The ensuing strife between the romantics and the Classicists was fueled by Mickiewicz's subsequent publications during the 1820s. Two tales in verse, *Grażyna* (1823) and *Konrad Wallenrod* (1828), two parts of the poetic drama *Dziady* (Forefather's Eve, 1823), and the exquisite sequence of *Sonety krymskie* (Crimean Sonnets, 1826), all offer an entirely new set of values, such as frenetic love, the tragic loneliness of the hero, and individual sacrifice.

Mickiewicz's leading role at this stage becomes apparent when contrasted with the output of other early romantics. Antoni Malczewski (1793–1826) left behind only one major work: the Byronic tale in verse, *Maria* (1826). Bohdan Zaleski (1802–86) was an author of serene, songlike imitations of folk poetry. Seweryn Goszczyński (1801–76) gained notoriety as a bard of social protest.

Esp. after the 1831 defeat of the November Insurrection, when many P. intellectuals, incl. Mickiewicz, settled in France as political refugees, Mickiewicz's position of leadership became indisputable. His theme of patriotic struggle and heroic sacrifice now acquired new, metaphysical dimensions, while in his poetic art he constantly sought new forms of expression. Part 3 of *Dziady* offered a new vision of Poland's destiny as well as a new step in the devel. of romantic drama; the work is a masterpiece of innovative construction, style, and versification. Only two years later, Mickiewicz published a completely different book, yet another masterpiece, *Pan Tadeusz* (1834), a Homeric epos on the poet's homeland, the P.-Lithuanian province at the time of the Napoleonic wars, in which nostalgia and sorrow mix with warm humor and discreet irony. In the subtlety of its narration (the interplay of the narrator's identification with and distance from the reality presented) and its stylistic richness, *Pan Tadeusz* remains to this day the crowning achievement of P. epic poetry. After its publication, Mickiewicz,

increasingly absorbed in mystical soul-searching and political activity, lapsed into silence as a poet, interrupted only by the brief sequence of the so-called Lausanne poems (written in 1839), purely lyric in character and strikingly innovative in their use of indirect symbolic lang.

Mickiewicz's fellow-exile and main rival, Juliusz Słowacki (1809–49), was less appreciated by his contemporaries. Yet his voluminous output spans a great many genres from lyric poems to poetic dramas to tales in verse and visionary epics, and his plays are a crucial factor in the evolution of P. romantic poetry as well as theater. Written mostly in verse, they experiment with both versification and dramatic construction; their settings are variously realistic, historical, legendary, dreamlike, or symbolic. In his poems, Słowacki felt equally at ease in epic description or in lyric confession, in complex stanza patterns or in biblical prose. His book-length poem in ottava rima, *Beniowski* (1841), is a magnificent example of the genre of the "poem of digressions" and of romantic irony, close in its style to Byron's *Don Juan* and Puškin's *Evgenij Onegin*. The last, "mystical" period in Słowacki's short life yielded an immense (even though unfinished) poem, also in ottava rima, *Król-Duch* (King-Spirit, 1847), a mythopoetic vision of P. destiny shown through consecutive reincarnations of the nation's spirit. Sélowacki's significance lies not only in his matchless technical virtuosity but also in that in his last phase he was an early forerunner of modern trends in poetry, incl. symbolism. Characteristically, his fame grew rapidly in the 1890s and 1900s.

Critical opinions, concerning the other two poets of the 19th-c.'s "great four" have become diametrically opposed in the 20th c. Zygmunt Krasiński (1812–59), for some time labeled "the third bard," today is admired mostly as an author of fascinating letters and two excellent political plays. Possessing a perspicacious and complex mind, Krasiński nevertheless lacked both Mickiewicz's poetic force and Słowacki's craftsmanship.

The posthumous reputation of the work of Cyprian Kamil Norwid (1821–83) presents a stark contrast with Krasiński's diminishing appeal. Forgotten and isolated in his lifetime and rediscovered only several decades after his death, today he is considered the philosophic and artistic harbinger of modern P. p. One generation younger than Mickiewicz, Norwid developed his art both under the influence of and as a polemic with P. romanticism. He replaced the prevalent attitude of nationalistic messianism with his original version of humanistic universalism, a concept of modern man as heir to the great civilizations of the past. From this perspective, Norwid attempted to dissect the most essential problems of contemp. history, politics, and culture. Although he employed a wide variety of genres and forms, he was most successful in his brief lyrics, distinguished by their highly intellectual content. In particular, his collection of 100 such poems titled *Vade-mecum* (written before 1866 and never published in his lifetime) offers an amazingly modern model of semantically dense and ironic poetry.

In contrast to the four great emigrés, among the multitude of "domestic" poets of the 19th c. only a few authors achieved some distinction—Kornel Ujejski (1823–97) with patriotic poems, Ryszard Berwiński (1817–79) with a call for social revolution and with ironic observations on contemp. morals, Teofil Lenartowicz (1822–93) with lyrics based on stylistic references to folklore, and Władysław Syrokomla (1823–62) with verse tales employing the voice of a peasant speaker.

VI. POSITIVISM AND NEOROMANTICISM. The 1863 defeat of the January Insurrection generated a distrust of romantic ideology and undermined the authority of romantic "bards": the ensuing epoch of positivism was a programmatically anti-poetic age. In lit. there was a general shift toward realistic and naturalistic fiction and drama; only a few names of relative significance emerged in the field of poetry. Adam Asnyk (1838–97) left behind a number of lyrics, postromantic in style and ranging from the erotic to the philosophic. Maria Konopnicka (1842–1910) was one of the most vocal proponents of social reform in the spirit of positivism; her poetry written in defense of the oppressed is characterized by its skillful use of folklore and its introduction of a speaker from the lower classes. In the last decade of the 19th c., the prosaic epoch of positivism gave way to another era of poetry. This new trend, variously called Young Poland, modernism, or neoromanticism, was strongly influenced by Western European symbolism and the philosophy of Schopenhauer and Nietzsche, but it also gave expression to specifically P. problems. The most influential exponent of the new "decadent" mood was Kazimierz Przerwa Tetmajer (1865–1940), who in his lyric poems published in the 1890s set up an emotional model for the whole generation of Young Poland—a norm of sensitivity consisting of pessimism, individualism, and distrust of any dogma. Other poets of this period underwent a more complicated devel. Jan Kasprowicz (1860–1926), for example, started with naturalistic depictions of peasants' poverty and after intermediary stages of symbolist spleen and expressionist rebellion ended as a serene poet of reconciliation with God and the world. From the technical point of view, his late poems are an important contribution to "tonism," a system of accentual versification based on an equal number of stresses rather than syllables (see SLAVIC PROSODY).

Stanisław Wyspiański (1869–1907), best known as a prolific playwright, was perhaps the most romantic of all poets of Young Poland. His visionary, half-romantic, half-symbolist plays refer to both P. history and contemp. events, mingling mythological or legendary figures with historical or present-day characters. Tadeusz Miciński (1873–1918), also an innovative dramatist, was the author of an important collection of poems, *W mroku gwiazd* (In the Darkness of Stars, 1902), in which he anticipated expressionism. Leopold Staff (1878–1957) lived long enough to participate in three consecutive literary epochs; within Young Poland, he represented a trend opposing "decadence" and favoring Cl. lucidity.

The greatest poet of Young Poland emerged quite unexpectedly when the epoch was already in decline. Bolesław Leśmian (1878–1937) published his first collection only in 1912, and his next two books appeared as late as 1920 and 1936. Nevertheless, he must be considered a belated symbolist, and only the striking originality of his lang. obscures this genetic link. Leśmian's poetic style is a direct consequence of his philosophy. A follower of Bergson, he saw the world as a field of incessant conflict between inert Matter and the creative force of Spirit; since this conflict cannot be resolved, the world is always *in statu nascendi*. The task of poetry is to convey this instability. Its rhythm should express the world's *élan vital*, and its imagery should reflect reality's metamorphoses. The poet himself should assume the cognitive stance of primeval man, whose act of perception creates, as it were, the world perceived.

VII. THE INTERWAR PERIOD AND THE WAR YEARS. The 20 years of Independent Poland (1918–39) can be visualized as a gradual turn from light to darkness, from initial optimism and hope to final catastrophe. This change found its reflection in the evolution of poetry. The tone for the first decade of the interwar period was set by an explosion of new, mostly avant-garde programs and a multitude of poetic groups, periodicals, and even cabarets around 1918. Many of these initiatives were ephemeral, but some of them developed into influential trends. There was, however, only one poetic group that managed to hold sway over public opinion for two decades, if not longer. The five poets who formed a group called Skamander—Julian Tuwim (1894–1953), Antoni Słonimski (1895–1976), Jan Lechoń (1899–1956), Jarosław Iwaszkiewicz (1894–1980), and Kazimierz Wierzyński (1894–1969)—owed their popularity to the fact that their poetry was original and innovative while also far more comprehensible than the works of their avant-garde contemporaries.

Skamander's only program consisted of rejecting traditional concepts of poetry's "duties" and enjoying artistic freedom; accordingly, the group abandoned all neoromantic conventions and turned to contemp. reality and a refreshingly direct style. But the differences among the five poets were to increase as their work developed. Tuwim soon became a master of verbal magic and explosive lyric force. Słonimski's poetry was rationalistic, discursive, and rhetorical. Lechoń, obsessed with P. history, combined references to the romantic trad. with a Cl. style. Iwaszkiewicz, after his brief fascination with expressionism, chose aestheticism (q.v.) as his principal attitude.

Wierzyński, initially a joyful vitalist, was to reach his peak in his bitter post-1945 poetry, written in exile and much modernized in form. Within the wide circle of Skamander's influence, some other poets followed their individual paths. Władysław Broniewski (1897–1962) managed to combine his Communist ideology with close ties to the P. romantic trad. In her concise, aphoristic poems, Maria Pawlikowska (1891–1945) aimed to formulate modern woman's perspective on the theme of love. Jerzy Liebert (1904–31) was an original poet of religious experience.

While Skamander dominated the poetic scene, numerous avant-garde groups propounded more radical programs of new poetry. The P. futurists, incl. Bruno Jasieński (1901–39) and Aleksander Wat (1900–67), did not win a great following, but they prepared the ground for the program of the so-called Cracow Avant-garde, the most prominent representatives of which were Tadeusz Peiper (1891–1969) and Julian Przyboś (1901–70). As opposed to the futurists' poetic anarchism, the Cracow Avant-garde advocated constructivism (q.v.) and rigor based on metaphor and syntax.

The 1930s, marked by economic, political, and ideological crisis, brought about the so-called Second Avant-garde—not so much a poetic group as a new generation of poets who prophesied the approaching global catastrophe. Konstanty Ildefons Gałczyński (1905–53), who later was to become one of the most popular P. poets, did so by use of the grotesque and mockery. Józef Czechowicz (1903–39), initially a poet of idyllic provincial landscapes, in his later poems expressed his Catastrophist fears using his own avant-garde technique of metaphoric condensation. Czesław Miłosz (b. 1911), the greatest living P. poet and the winner of the 1980 Nobel Prize for Lit., underwent a complicated evolution from his prewar Catastrophism to his present poetry of metaphysical theme and polyphonic construction.

The atrocities of World War II confirmed the premonitions and predictions of Catastrophist poetry; the theme of "Apocalypse come true" was central to the work of a new generation of poets, most of whom died young as underground fighters or soldiers in the 1944 Warsaw Uprising. Such was the fate of Krzysztof Kamil Baczyński (1921–44), who left behind a brilliant lyric oeuvre, visionary and symbolist in style.

VIII. THE POSTWAR PERIOD. After the end of World War II and the imposition of Communist rule in Poland, many of its poets worked in exile. Despite a censorship ban, a great deal of emigré lit. found its way into the country and enjoyed a remarkable popularity, to mention only the examples of Miłosz, Wierzyński, and Wat. Those poets who have remained in Poland or have been repatriated faced a situation of more or less limited freedom of speech until the 1980s. In spite of that, post-1945 P. p. scored many artistic successes. Tadeusz Różewicz (b. 1921) offered a new, ascetic style employing "the anonymous voice" of a survivor. After the years of Stalinism (1949–55), one of the first harbingers of the approaching "thaw" in cultural policy was the publication in 1955 of Adam Ważyk's much-discussed "Poemat dla dorosłych" (Poem for Adults), followed by similarly "revisionist" poems by Mieczysław Jastrun (1903–83) and others.

The year 1956 marked the beginning of a genuine eruption of new names, trends, and poetic programs. The poetry of the late 1950s and 1960s was characterized by the coexistence of a strong current of ironic moral reflection, as found in the works of Zbigniew Herbert (b. 1924), Wisława Szymborska (b. 1923), Artur Międzyrzecki (b. 1922), Julia Hartwig (b. 1921), Wiktor Woroszylski (b. 1927), and Stanisław Jerzy Lec (1909–66), and an equally powerful trend of linguistic experimentation, exemplified by Miron Białoszewski (1922–83), Tymoteusz Karpowicz (b. 1921), Witold Wirpsza (1918–85), and Jerzy Ficowski (b. 1924). Stanisław Grochowiak (1934–76), Tadeusz Nowak (b. 1930), and Jerzy Harasymowicz (b. 1933) contributed to the post-1956 "liberation of imagination" by building their private worlds of imagination and fantasy. Ernest Bryll (b. 1935) offered his own version of a return to the romantic trad., and Jarosław Marek Rymkiewicz (b. 1935) propounded his program of modern neoclassicism.

In the early 1970s, a new generation of P. poets came to the fore, drawing upon the experiences of both the older "moralists" and "linguists" in order to find a new poetic lang. for antitotalitarian protest and existential reflection. Ryszard Krynicki (b. 1943), Ewa Lipska (b. 1945), Adam Zagajewski (b. 1945), Julian Kornhauser (b. 1946), and Stanisław Barańczak (b. 1946) are representative of this trend, joined in the 1980s by promising younger poets such as Jan Polkowski (b. 1953) and Bronisław Maj (b. 1953).

ANTHOLOGIES: Od Kochanowskiego do Staffa, ed. W. Borowy (1930); Poeci renesansu, ed. J. Sokołowska (1959); Zbiór poetów polskich XIX wieku, ed. P. Hertz, 7 v. (1959–75); Five Cs. of P. P., ed. and tr. J. Peterkiewicz and B. Singer (1962); Poezja polska 1914–39, ed. R. Matuszewski and S. Pollak (1962); Poeci polskiego baroku, ed. J. Sokołowska and K. Zukowska, 2 v. (1965); Poezja polska, ed. S. Grochowiak and J. Maciejewski, 2 v. (1973); Poezja polska XVIII wieku, ed. Z. Libera, 2d ed. (1976); Poezja Młodej Polski, ed. M. Jastrun (1976); Kolumbowie i współcześni, 2d ed. (1976), Ze struny na strune (1980), both ed. A. Lam; Antologia polskiego futuryzmu i Nowej Sztuki, ed. Z. Jarosiński and H. Zaworska (1978); Średniowieczna pieśń religijna polska, ed. M. Korolko, 2d ed. (1980); Świat poprawiac—zuchwałe rzemiosło, ed. T. Kostkiewiczowa and Z. Goliński (1981); Postwar P. P., ed. C. Miłosz,

3d ed. (1983); *Poeta pamieta*, ed. S. Barańczak (1984); *P. P. of the Last Two Decades of Communist Rule*, ed. S. Baranczak and C. Cavanagh (1992).

HISTORY AND CRITICISM: J. Krzyżanowski, *P. Romantic Lit.* (1930), *A Hist. of P. Lit.* (1980); W. Borowy, *O poezji polskiej w wieku XVIII* (1948), *O Norwidzie* (1960); W. Weintraub, *The Poetry of A. Mickiewicz* (1954), *Rzecz czarnoleska* (1977); M. Kridl, *A Survey of P. Lit. and Culture* (1956); C. Zgorzelski, *O liryce Mickiewicza i Słowackiego* (1961); K. Wyka, *Pan Tadeusz*, 2 v. (1963); M. R. Mayenowa, *Strofika: praca zbiorowa* (1964), *O sztuce czytania wierszy*, 2d ed. (1967); J. Trznadel, *Twórczość Leśmiana* (1964); J. Sławiński, *Koncepcja jezyka poetyckiego Awangardy Krakowskiej* (1965); *Obraz literatury polskiej XIX i XX w.*, 11 v. (1965–79); H. Zaworska, *O nowa sztuke* (1965); J. Błoński, *M. Sep Szarzyński, a poczatki polskiego baroku* (1967), *Odmarsz* (1978); K. Wyka, *Modernizm polski*, 2d ed. (1968), *Rzecz wyobraź ni*, 2d ed. (1977); S. Jaworski, *U podstaw Awangardy* (1968); M. Podraza-Kwiatkowska, *Młodopolskie harmonie i dysonanse* (1969), *Symbolizm i symbolika w poezji Młodej Polski* (1975); M. Janion, *Romantyzm* (1970); M. Giergielewicz, *Intro. to P. Versification* (1970); Z. Łapiński, *Norwid* (1971); I. Opacki, *Poezja romantycznych przełomów* (1972); J. Kwiatkowski, *Klucze do wyobraź ni*, 2d ed. (1973); G. Gomori, *C. Norwid* (1974); A. Witkowska, *A. Mickiewicz* (1975); T. Kostkiewiczowa, *Klasycyzm, sentymentalizm, rokoko* (1975); C. Zgorzelski, *O sztuce poetyckiej Mickiewicza* (1976); A. Sandauer, *Poeci czterech pokoleń* (1977); J. Stradecki, *W kregu Skamandra* (1977); *Słownik literatury polskiego Oświecenia*, ed. T. Kostkiewiczowa (1977); M. Dłuska, *Studia z historii i teorii wersyfikacji polskiej*, 2d ed., 2 v. (1978); S. Barańczak, *Etyka i poetyka* (1979), *A Fugitive from Utopia* (1987); J. Ziomek, *Renesans*, 4th ed. (1980); M. Klimowicz, *Oświecenie*, 4th ed. (1980); H. Markiewicz, *Pozytywizm*, 2d ed. (1980); J. Pelc, *J. Kochanowski* (1980); C. Hernas, *Barok*, 4th ed. (1981); M. Głowiński, *Zaświat przedstawiony* (1981); M. G. Levine, *Contemp. P. P., 1925–75* (1981); E. Balcerzan, *Poezja polska w latach 1939–65*, v. 1 (1982); *Poeci dwudziestolecia miedzywojennego*, ed. I. Maciejewska, 2 v. (1982); R. Przybylski, *Klasycyzm* (1983); C. Miłosz, *The Hist. of P. Lit.*, 2d ed. (1983); B. Carpenter, *The Poetic Avantgarde in Poland, 1918–39* (1983); T. Nyczek, *Powiedz tylko słowo* (1985); *Poznawanie Miłosza*, ed. J. Kwiatkowski (1985); F. W. Aaron, *Bearing the Unbearable: Yiddish and P. P. in the Ghettos and Concentration Camps* (1990). S.B.

POLISH PROSODY. See SLAVIC PROSODY.

POLITICAL VERSE (Gr. *politikos stichos*, "the verse of the polis and its citizens"). A Byzantine meter of 15 syllables, accentually based and iambic. P. v. first appears in the 10th c. A.D. and is the standard meter for Mod. Gr. poetry from at least the 12th c. to the present day. It consists of two cola of 8 and 7 syllables with a caesura after the eighth syllable, each colon having one main accent, on the eighth or sixth syllable in the first and on the fourteenth in the second. Maas gives the scansion xx/xxx/x/ x/x/x/x as common. The origin of the verse is uncertain; some imperial dirges of ca. A.D. 912 are in p. v., and the hymns of Symeon the New Theologian (A.D. 1000) include some five thousand lines of it. The Byzantine grammarian Eustathios thought it originated in the Cl. trochaic tetrameter, Krumbacher in a mixture of the Cl. iambic and trochaic tetrameter, but all such hypothesized connections to antiquity seem remote. From the beginning it is the medium of oral poetry and popular verse. See GREEK POETRY.—K. L. Struve, *Ueber den politischen Vers der Mittelgriechen* (1828); K. Krumbacher, *Gesch. der byzantin. Lit.*, 2d ed. (1897), 651 ff.; P. Maas in *Byz. Zeitschrift* 18 (1909); Maas; I. Ševčenko in *Dumbarton Oaks Papers* 23–24 (1969); H. G. Beck, *Gesch. der byzantin. Volkslit.* (1971), 15 ff.; M. J. Jeffreys, "The Nature and Origins of the P. V.," *Dumbarton Oaks Papers* 28 (1974); Trypanis, 454 ff. T.V.F.B.

POLITICS AND HERMENEUTICS. See HERMENEUTICS.

POLITICS AND POETRY. In 1968 the poet James Merrill was asked about the relationship between poetry and "political realities." "Oh dear," he answered, "these immensely real concerns do not produce *poetry*." *L'art pour l'art* was at that moment more a posture than a tenable position, though 20 years earlier many poets and critics had operated on the assumption that poetry in fact suffers from contact with political subjects. At that time, skepticism about political subjects derived largely from a strong postwar anti-Stalinist impulse among Western literary intellectuals, who had been sympathetic to Soviet Marxism until the Nazi-Soviet pact of 1939. Am. and Western European critics knew that the major controversy among Rus. poets was the role of private rather than public subject matter. On the one hand was Majakovskij, who gladly accepted every practical writing assignment given him by the Soviet bureaucracy; on the other was Anna Akhmatova, disciplined for refusing to write plainly political poems. Her refusal was a gesture of resistance within the Soviet Union; and the devel. of an exalted lyric, antipolitical poetic in the West after the Second World War was one literary aspect of the Cold War. Then too, the political record of the High Modernist poets was discouraging to Western intellectuals: from 1945 to 1958, Ezra Pound was incarcerated in a Washington insane asylum because of charges of treason. All this immediate postwar context has by now been forgotten, and the alleged incompatibility of pol. and p. is now discussed abstractly, as if the difficulty were exclusively theoretical.

The history of poetry, as Tom Paulin has demonstrated, is full of different kinds of successful political poems in every period of literary distinction: medieval peasant's songs, the *Divine Comedy*, Marvell's Horatian Ode, Milton's political sonnets, Dryden's "Absalom and Achitophel," Blake's "London," Andre Chenier's "Iambes VIII," Wordsworth's *Prelude*, Yeats's "Easter 1916," Davie's "Remembering the Thirties," Heaney's "Punishment," and Douglas Dunn's "Green Breeks." The lineaments of heroism, the limits of national or tribal solidarity, the power of persuasion, the forceful imposition of authority, and war—these Homeric themes have long been traditional to poetry. Political subjects churn at the center of poetry, and toward the periphery the lesser genres—seduction songs, epithalamia, nature poems—now seem, though less obviously, still fascinatingly political. Among traditional subjects, only the coming of spring and the going with old age do not seem inherently political to us now.

What counts as a political subject is a question of audience. Poems like Brecht's "The God of War" seem only vaguely political in peacetime, but in time of war such a poem would be understood to be insistently partisan. Therefore, we may say, all that can be changed by social consensus or external authority is properly called political. The possibility of change itself, certainly not the state, is after all the source of political passion. Political poems concern situations that might be otherwise. Causes and consequences, choices—these are the special concerns of political poets. This sounds rationalistic, yet political writing concerns the possibility of deliberate action rather than unsought revelation. Dryden's "Absalom and Achitophel," for instance, ends not with action but instead with King David's announced resolution to punish the conspirators; although Dryden said he could not bring himself to "show *Absalom* Unfortunate," narration of the events would have been superfluous.

Critics of the 1970s and '80s have shown repeatedly how subjects formerly thought not to be political are in fact importantly so, partly because the range of social change that can be envisaged has expanded. The literary representation of women is an obvious example. The description of landscape is a less obvious one: Raymond Williams has shown that the landscapes of Eng. poetry are political figurations of the prerogatives of wealth and class. Other critics have focused on all that is taken for granted in poetry, for that is where political issues are treated as already somehow settled. As Empson noted, figurative lang. can shut off inquiry by suggesting that some political or historical event is natural, no more in question than an ocean or mountain. Neo-Marxist interpreters set themselves the task of counteracting the alleged effort of poets to render politics invisible. One weakness of this approach is the presupposition that once political intent has been unveiled, a critic's job is done, as though the

revelation that poetry is politically motivated were itself a critical achievement. These critics presume, on implicitly ethical grounds, that the values and objectives of their political adversaries cannot be maintained in the light of day. Those with experience in democratic political controversy or struggle know that adversarial views must be not only revealed but argued down one by one, again and again, or else accommodated.

Mythological figures are more obviously political than natural ones, since they bear both a weight of hermeneutical trad. and explicit cultural authority. When Dryden characterized Charles II as King David, the Duke of Monmouth as Absalom, and the Earl of Shaftesbury as Achitophel, the political significance of the poem was set forth explicitly. Invocations of myth, history, or scripture to structure contemp. political events are different from other sorts of figures, however, in that the criterion of aptness is counterbalanced by one of audacity. The choice of a framing myth, esp. in satire, is usually outrageous: Charles II as David? Lenin as Christ, in Hugh MacDiarmid's "First Hymn to Lenin"? Eisenhower as Satan, in Robert Duncan's "The Fire"? But that is where the controversial aspect of these poems is sharpest; what David, Absalom, and Achitophel are made to say is much less tendentious. The pleasure and success of such poems depend on the framing myth seeming audaciously afield yet, finally, acute. Mythological figures also bear the weight of utopian hope for poets, like Blake, Adrienne Rich, or Judy Grahn, who want to imagine some future social order radically different from the actual one that provokes satirists.

The supposed strain between pol. and p. is actually more a strain between pol. and the evaluative criteria of crit. Mod. crit. has only limited access to a didactic view of poetry (see DIDACTICISM). Didactic poems are esteemed according to a universality or generality criterion, whereby a poem succeeds insofar as it speaks to the conditions of life in different historical contexts. By this measure satire either derives from an overall moral norm or it counts as a minor genre, because it names names and deeply loves its historic moment. Johnson's "Preface to Shakespeare" blocks the access of modern critics to a contemporaneity criterion that can treasure the minute particulars of a local social milieu. Dryden, Pope, the Pound of Cantos XIV and XV, and, among contemporaries, Turner Cassity express a kind of curiosity and, beyond the satire, fondness for very specific details of their time. Crit. needs a way of esteeming this poetry, not because the details are heterogeneous, but because they are thorny and abundant evidence of a citizen's passionate engagement less in a party than in a particular moment.

Michael McKeon argues that ideological comprehensiveness is the apt criterion for political poetry: political poets succeed by comprehending a wide range of the demands and conflicts of their time, not by rising above their historical moment. This view addresses the apprehensions of New Critics, such as Cleanth Brooks, in the face of partisan leftist poetry of the 1930s: leftist poems employed, in Kenneth Burke's terms, a rhetoric of exclusion. Those circumstances or considerations that did not fit a leftist ideological perspective were ignored, not incorporated into the poem as a sign of faith with the historical moment. The result, Brooks argues, was a sentimental appeal to a reader's political beliefs.

The relationship between particularity and generality is esp. troublesome in political poetry, as it is in political discourse generally. Which experiences typify a class of experiences? How are exceptions to general practice to be recognized? Soviet writers from 1943 to 1953 were routinely censured for attending too closely to the allegedly exceptional negative aspects of social experience. Whose experience stands for that of large social groups or classes? These questions constantly arise in political discussions, and poets answer them. Furthermore, poets claim that metaphors have great explanatory power, that some particular vehicle stands for a larger tenor; poets derive authority by claiming to speak to universal issues, or for some group of people. And, beyond representation, poets use lang. to suggest some not yet realized idea; in this sense, particulars stand for ideals in poetry. Georg Lukacs constantly defended the power of realistic fiction to characterize not just individuals but types, and thereby to invoke ideas that transcend historical actualities. As Peter Demetz has argued, every concept of type, biblical or not, is at base theological, because it presumes a transcendent order whereby particular phenomena are measured. Lukacs imagined that order to be the future that socialism would bring, or the meaning of history. From Engels to the present, Marxist criticism (q.v.) has insisted on the need for poetry to be not merely specific but typical too.

Pindar's songs in praise of Gr. tyrants provide the most obvious archaic example of Western political poetry (the political significance of the *Iliad* is more abstract). Although Robert Lowell wrote praise-poems for Senators Eugene McCarthy and Robert Kennedy during the 1968 Am. Presidential campaign, and Gary Snyder wrote sympathetically about California Governor Jerry Brown in the late 1970s, modern poets have been generally disinclined to employ their art to praise the state in any form. What we now appreciate in Pindar is less his capacity to praise, which Pound dismissed as a big bass drum, than the back of his hand: his clever management of myths to warn the tyrants against the abuses of power. The most admired praise-poem in Eng., Marvell's Horatian Ode, is esteemed for its mix of praise and blame. Mod. poems of sheer blame, such as Robert Bly's "Asian Peace Offers Rejected Without Publication" and Adrienne Rich's "Rape" have been far more widely appreciated. But poems of true praise are much harder for critics to esteem. More importantly, the middle ground between praise and blame has been badly eroded by an oversupply of extremist crit. Thomas Edwards argues that the best political poems express mixed feelings, if outrage then also complicity, if contempt then also sympathy. This view draws support from two considerations: (1) an ambitious poem should do more than gild the monolith of an ideology; and (2) political issues are often more complicated than one or another party suggests.

However, modern poets and critics tend to admire, even more than mixed feelings, frankly oppositional poems. Indeed political poetry, if not poetry in general, is commonly (and too narrowly) understood now to be oppositional by definition. Even a centrist critic like Frank Kermode has argued that "lit. which achieves permanence is likely to be 'transgressive' . . . [the art] of the stranger in conflict with the settled order." "In his heart of hearts," Auden wrote, "the audience [the European poet] desires and expects are those who govern the country." Most contemp. political poems, however offensive they would be to those who do not read them, are consoling to those who do. Am. poets write about the possibility of civic change, but their poems are—quite rightly—no longer of interest to politicians, statesmen, and political administrators, because few Am. poets begin from a belief in political processes or agents as worthy of sustained scrutiny. They rarely take pol. seriously enough in political terms, nor do they present political problems as difficult to solve, or as ethically problematic. Am. poets like Bly, Duncan, and Ginsberg attribute mean motives and low intelligence to their political adversaries, as though virtue or cleverness could make a great difference. When Am. poets now attempt to extend sympathy to politicians, they invoke a psychoanalytic frame, in which no one is really guilty, but the sympathy is clinical and well outside of pol. Critics might credit as oppositional only that political poetry that challenges the political opinions of its audience and condemn those poems that extend the blunt discourse that is routine in political controversy.

Probably well before Milton's prefatory note to *Paradise Lost* readers sensed an analogy between social and prosodic order. Departure from prosodic norms has been loosely likened to political liberty, and discussions of poetic form have thereby been burdened by political polemics. One of the paradoxes of this sort of thinking is that the modernist poets responsible for breaking the force of metrical convention were not champions of political liberty. F. T. Marinetti, Ezra Pound, and T. S. Eliot were staunchly on the political right, though their efforts in free verse (q.v.) made it difficult for younger poets to continue writing in meter. Donald Davie has suggested that there is indeed a deep connection between the literary modernism of Pound and his attraction to authoritarian pol. Pound, Eliot, and other modernists felt unconstrained by the pressure of immediate poetic precedent, by the desire of readers to find continuity from one generation to the next, or by the daily secular experiences of their readers. These poets made a radical break with the conventions of late 19th-c. British and Am. verse. They dealt with historical subject matter very selectively and from a bird's-eye view, skipping over that which did not engage them. And together with Yeats they asserted claims to supranational revelations. The willfulness that Pound displayed in lit. crit. and admired in the poetry of Dante he also admired in totalitarian pol. of the right.

Under the influence of Fr. and Rus. literary theory, academic critics in England and America have begun to locate the oppositional effort of poetry not in ideas or statements so much as in technical expressions of noncompliance with the referential and discursive features of descriptive, narrative, and expository prose—all of which supposedly underwrite the prevailing capitalist economic and social order. For many critics, a poet's breaking of genre conventions is itself an admirable act of political defiance. Some critics, such as Cora Kaplan, hold that particular rhetorical figures, such as metonymy, have political significance and value for women writers and readers whose "experience [has been] suppressed in public discourse." The Am. "Language Poets" of the 1970s (see LANGUAGE POETRY) have argued that the undermining of narrative structure and the disruption of syntactic expectations are the most responsible ways in which poets can contribute to large-scale social change: "lang. control = thought control = reality control," Charles Bernstein has said. "Poetry, like war," his collaborator Ron Silliman writes, "is the pursuit of pol. by other means." These poets see their writing as a poetic and expressly Marxist part of a broad intellectual movement in literary theory and philosophy that includes Derrida, Barthes, Jameson, and Rorty. One major objection to this approach to the nexus of pol. and p. is that it appeals only to academics who see it as a demonstration of the practical implications of literary theoretical texts that have achieved currency, as well as one way of reconciling these theories with neo-Marxism. Also, these poets reduce the political significance of poetry from a wide range of statements made by poets throughout history to but one mode of exemplification, based on an analogy of poetic form and political action.

New Historicist critics (see HISTORICISM) have pushed well beyond broad analogical arguments by identifying ways in which political motives determine the writing not just of poets or even of imaginative writers, but rather of all sorts of writers within a culture; they discover intentional connections between particular discursive practices and specifiable political positions. Richard Helgerson has shown how the controversy of the 16th and 17th cs. about quantitative verse in Eng. was understood then to be part of a debate about the kind of nation England would become, the kind of civil laws it would establish. John Barrell has argued that conditions of patronage fostered a particular kind of periodic structure in Ren. Eng. praise-poems. In reconstructing the political significance of poetic forms, this devel. in lit. crit. is restoring continuity to a view of poetry that was distinguished until very recently by the work of poet-critics such as Empson and Davie, who insisted always that a poet's formal choices expressed political considerations alive at the time of writing. But by close historical methods, New Historicists have refined connections between poetic form and ideology and located those connections not only in lang. itself but in entire cultural systems.

There is a need for critics to maintain a broad range of interpretive and, especially, evaluative principles for analyzing the relations of pol. to p., so that the political significance of poetry not be confined either to prophecy or to satire. The obligations of a citizen of a state are various, according to circumstances, and a citizen's prerogatives are usually many. The need is for a crit. that does not see the role of political poets as excluding, whether in the name of eloquence, literary trad., or higher truth, any of the duties or options of citizens. See also CULTURAL CRITICISM; THEORY.

ANTHOLOGIES: *Political Poems and Songs Relating to Eng. Hist.*, ed. T. Wright (1859); *Poems on Affairs of State*, ed. G. deF. Lord et al., 7 v. (1963–75); *Marx and Engels on Lit. and Art*, ed. L. Baxandall and S. Morawski (1973); *Carrying the Darkness: The Poetry of the Vietnam War* (1985), *Unaccustomed Mercy: Soldier Poets of the Vietnam War* (1989), both ed. W. D. Ehrhart; *P. and Pol.*, ed. R. M. Jones (1985); *Faber Book of Political Verse*, ed. T. Paulin (1986); *Pol. and Poetic Value*, ed. R. von Hallberg (1987).

HISTORY AND CRITICISM: W. Empson, *Some Versions of Pastoral* (1935); K. Burke, *Attitudes Toward Hist.* (1937); C. Brooks, *Mod. Poetry and the Trad.* (1939); A. P. d'Entrèves, *Dante as a Political Thinker* (1952); D. V. Erdman, *Blake: Prophet against Empire* (1954); C. V. Wedgwood, *P. and Pol. Under the Stuarts* (1960); B. Snell, *Poetry and Society in Ancient Greece* (1961); H. Swayze, *Political Control of Lit. in the USSR, 1946–1959* (1962); M. Adler, *P. and Pol.* (1965); C. M. Bowra, *P. and Pol. 1900–1960* (1966); P. Demetz, *Marx, Engels, and the Poets*, tr. J. L. Sammons (1967); J. M. Wallace, *Destiny His Choice* (1968); M. Mack, *The Garden and the City: Retirement and Pol. in the Later P. of Pope* (1969); G. Lukacs, *Writer and Critic*, tr. A. D. Kahn (1970); C. Woodring, *Pol. in Eng. Romantic P.* (1970); T. R. Edwards, *Imagination and Power* (1971); K. W. Klein, *The Partisan Voice: A Study of the Political Lyric in France and Germany, 1180–1230* (1971); V. J. Scattergood, *Pol. and P. in the 15th C.* (1971); L. C. Knights, *Public Voices* (1972); S. N. Zwicker, *Dryden's Political Poetry* (1972), *Pol. and*

Lang. in Dryden's Poetry (1984); E. J. Brown, *Mayakovsky, A Poet in the Revolution* (1973); D. Davie, *Thomas Hardy and British Poetry* (1973), *Czeslaw Milosz and the Insufficiency of Lyric* (1986); R. Williams, *The Country and the City* (1973); J. F. Mersmann, *Out of the Vietnam Vortex* (1974); N. Reeves, *Heinrich Heine: P. and Pol.* (1974); M. McKeon, *Politics and Poetry in Restoration England* (1975); *Gesch. der politischen Lyrik in Deutschland*, ed. W. Hinderer (1978); W. Mohr and W. Kohlschmidt, "Politische Dichtung," *Reallexikon* 3.157–220; M. Calinescu, "Lit. and Pol.," *Interrelations of Lit.*, ed. J.-P. Barricelli and J. Gibaldi (1982); C. G. Thayer, *Shakespearean Pol.* (1983); J. K. Chandler, *Wordsworth's Second Nature* (1984); D. Norbrook, *P. and Pol. in Eng. Ren.* (1984); T. Olafioye, *Pol. in Af. Poetry* (1984); *P. and Pol. in the Age of Augustus*, ed. T. Woodman and D. West (1984); R. von Hallberg, *Am. Poetry and Culture, 1945–1980* (1985); C. Bernstein, *Content's Dream* (1986); D. Davie, *Czeslaw Milosz and the Insufficiency of Lyric* (1986); C. Kaplan, *Sea Changes* (1986); P. Breslin, *The Psycho-Political Muse* (1987); P. Godman, *Poets and Emperors: Frankish Pol. and Carolingian P.* (1987); J. Montefiore, *Feminism and Poetry* (1987); R. Silliman, *The New Sentence* (1987); P. S. Stanfield, *Yeats and Pol. in the 1930's* (1988); T. Des Pres, *Praises and Dispraises* (1988); B. Erkkila, *Whitman the Political Poet* (1988); R. Helgerson, "Barbarous Tongues," *The Historical Ren.*, ed. H. Dubrow and R. Strier (1988); *"The Muses Common-Weale": P. and Pol. in the 17th C.*, ed. C. J. Summers and T.-L. Pebworth (1988); A. Patterson, *Pastoral and Ideology* (1988); F. Kermode, *Hist. and Value* (1989).

R.V.H.

POLYNESIAN POETRY. Cultural and linguistic homogeneity, both in poetry and prose, is sufficiently marked, despite interisland diversity, to designate Polynesia a distinctive cultural area of the Pacific. This area extends south from the Tropic of Cancer, which passes through the Hawaiian Islands, and east of the 180th meridian, except for New Zealand and Tuvalu (formerly called Ellice Islands). Westward in Melanesia and Micronesia are scattered P. enclaves. Because Polynesia, like these other areas, was nonliterate prior to European contact, knowledge was mainly transmitted orally and by demonstration, usages which are both of continuing importance. An exceptionally verbal society, Polynesia elevated oral art to a high level of beauty and subtlety. The limited number of sounds in P. langs. also shaped P. verbal style, with Hawaiian having the fewest (five long and five short vowels and only eight consonants— *p, k,* glottal stop, *h, m, n, l, w*). Consequently, poets used numerous homonyms, puns, repetitions, reduplication, and alliteration and, unlike modern listeners, enjoyed frequent reiterations of sound. Grammar also favored repetition.

The earliest knowledge of P. p.—its themes, styles, forms, functions, performances, and composers—that came from late 18th-c. Western explorers provides a baseline for charting post-European change and retention. Initially Western culture—Christianity, literacy, printing, mores, technology, and political organization—introduced by 19th-c. missionaries, settlers, colonial officials, and voyagers stimulated poetic creativity by adding new concepts and symbols without, however, the traditional art losing its indigenous identity. Although the subsequently increasing Westernization led to cultual attenuation of the traditional, more than "memory culture" of poetics survived. With modifications to allow for foreign stimulus, the past tense used here to characterize P. p. can frequently be replaced by the present tense.

Poetry, integral to personal life from birth to death and to both religion and entertainment, was frequently entwined with ritual, vocalization, and dance to express values, give aesthetic pleasure, transmit knowledge, and affirm the affinity of human beings with nature and the supernatural. P. cultural traits of personifying nature with gods and spirits (many regarded as ancestors) and of reacting emotionally to changing aspects of landscape led to minute observation, vivid description, and extensive naming of places and natural forces.

The value given to artistic and imaginative manipulation of lang. within recognized patterns ensured that any individual with creativity, a good memory, and a good voice could win social and material rewards. Fame was not limited by sex, age, occupation, or social position either in a populous, class-structured archipelago or a small, less formally organized atoll. A bard of commoner status received gifts from audiences and, even better, might be added to a chief's retinue. Chiefs and chieftesses, however, were the most prolific composers, priding themselves on their poetic talent and erudition. Their elite status, assuring them of recognition and opportunity for performance, made poetry a predominantly aristocratic art. Oral trad. and publication have preserved texts of poems, many composers' names, and information about styles of delivery, circumstances of composition, and the significance of elliptical allusions.

Poetry and music being inseparable, each adding power to the other, a poet composed text and melody at the same time. Each category of poetry had its characteristic modes of rhythmic oral delivery, the principal modes being song or recitative, with variations and combinations of each. Hawaiians, for example, distinguished between an *oli* and a *mele* but adapted a poem to either. An *oli* was a dignified recitative, most often a solo, with limited gestures and occasional percussion accompaniment, for dirges, prayers, eulogies, and genealogies, each class with its special *oli* style. The basic style was a rapid, guttural, vibrating monotone on a single pitch that required a strong, deep voice trained to hold the breath through long phrases often ending with a trill. Continuity of sound was essential because breath carried the *mana*-filled words, and a break or hesitation except at appropriate places was believed unlucky in a secular poem and fatal in a sacred. A *mele* was sung or chanted to the accompaniment of dance (*hula*), pantomime, and instruments (not always the three together); a subtype was performed either with or without dance for love songs, name songs honoring individuals, or genital chants celebrating their generative powers. A *mele*, customarily performed with a chorus whose leader sang solo parts, had marked, repeated rhythmic patterns if danced and a wider range of pitch and freedom than the *oli*. Missionary hymns brought melody, which Polynesians called *hīmeni* and combined with old styles of delivery for new poems, not necessarily sacred, but not danced. While music changed as Westerners introduced their folk and work songs, texts retained many traditional themes and devices. The same was the case in other achipelagos beside the Hawaiian.

A new poem that met an audience's approval was performed repeatedly and might become a classic passed on for generations. Change came, however, from variations and distortions in delivery and from other poets combining the new poem with existing poems, adding or eliminating verses, replacing proper names, and adapting the poem to different social uses. The recurrence of certain themes, images, phrases, and lines was not considered plagiarism because poets shared the same culture, formulaic lang., and poetic diction; genius lay in fresh and innovative rearrangement or reinterpretation.

Islands frequently restricted rights of performance, esp. if the poem was a gift or part of the intangible treasure of a chiefly lineage. It could be performed only in the owner's presence or with permission, and at death was bequeathed to a relative. A 101-line poem was the condolence gift ("My poem is but poor yet take it") that Chief Fisherman Ulamoleke, a petty Tongan chief, composed and chanted to his bereaved friend Falepapalangi, a renowned professional poet, who thanked him by immediately repeating the entire poem.

Samoan chiefs (but not commoners) could sing a *solo* (the Samoan term for a recitative epitomizing a myth or legend) of the subcategory *fa'ali'i*—royal, concerning a royal lineage. A politically important trad., for example, centered on Sanalālā: when his canoe was swept to sea from Tonga to Samoa, his father's land, his Tongan mother, Chieftess Fitimaupaloga, composed a 21-line *solo fa'ali'i* considered "exceedingly beautiful." A chief was much admired when he sang it with a plaintive cadence while accompanying himself on a type of drum only certain chiefly families could use (Freeman). The first three lines of its introduction below are repeated as epilogue:

See the morning cloud arise.

Where in that crimson cloud
Is Oneata's lovely bay?
The bay where is my child,
My child makes my heart breathless.

Illustrated are such common P. poetic devices as inspiration from nature and place; irregular but rhythmic lines; repetition of sounds, words, and syllables; and (peculiarly in western P.) deliberate rhyming and terminating sets of lines with a certain sound.

Hawaiian, Marquesan, and Tuamotuan ruling families owned sacred creation and genealogical chants which only senior males and high priests could intone in consecrating a chief's primary wife's firstborn son and on other occasions. Numerous resemblances with other chants elsewhere prove the chants share the same P. heritage. Their fundamental function concerned procreation and the continuity of life through the chief, on whom, as the closest link to the gods, the fertility of nature and people depended. Starting with creation, a chanter connected the infant to his divine and earthly kin and thereby confirmed his rank, privileges, taboos, territory, and power. Because words had power to produce action, an error or hesitation negated a sacred chant.

An example is the Hawaiian *Kumulipo* (Origin in Deepest Darkness), a 2,102-line masterpiece of the type called *ku'auhau*, "pathway-lineage," property of the family of Kalākaua and his sister Lili'uokalani, the last rulers in the 19th c. of the monarchy established by Kamehameha I in 1795. When priests ca. 1700 A.D. chanted the *Kumulipo*, each name activated the latent *mana* (supernatural power) of High Chief Keawe's son and heir, named Lono-i-ka-makahiki because he was born during the annual Makahiki festival for Lono, god of peace and prosperity. It may have been recited in 1779 over Captain Cook as the returned god Lono.

Over half of the chant lists genealogical pairs. Of its sixteen odes the first seven are in the period of Pō (Darkness, Night) when earth emerged and generating couples bore named descendants in each class of plant and animal species of sea, sky, and land. The remaining nine odes are in the era of Ao (Light, Day, Reason) when gods, demigods, and their sacred descendants were born. The chant carried the spark of life and *mana* down to Lono-i-ka-makahiki, who would continue this ancestral line. Hawaiians differ on the inner meaning (*kaona*) of the chant. A political interpretation is that it symbolizes migration, population growth, and the rise of rival chiefs who established branch family lines and seized lands. A favored *kaona* is that the child's development parallels that of the cosmos, born from night and ocean; conception, birth, and early growth occur in Pō, and adolescence and sexual and social maturity in Ao. Here is the prologue to Ode One:

At the time when the earth became hot

At the time when the heavens turned
  about
At the time when the sun was darkened
To cause the moon to shine
The time of the rise of the Pleiades
The slime, this was the source of the
  earth
The source of the darkness that made
  darkness
The source of the night that made
  night
The intense darkness, the deep dark-
  ness
Darkness of the sun, darkness of the
  night
  Nothing but night
The night gave birth. . . .
                  (Beckwith)

A secular text and sometimes its music might come to a poet during dreams, visions, trances, and solitude, aided by supernatural beings after prayers and offerings. Narrators of prose sagas used supernatural, legendary, and fictitious characters as surrogates to pour out poems, more stable over time than the plots. The New Zealand fairy folk Patupaiarehe sang in an archaic dialect, and the Hawaiian goddess Hi'iaka, the most prolific poet of all, composed incomparable *mele, ole,* and other forms during a journey (a favorite P. device for unifying songs) for her sister Pele, volcano goddess. Chants in sagas about pan-Polynesian mythical or legendary chiefs like Rata and Tahaki are sometimes attributed to other characters in the plots.

Poets composed alone, with a companion, or in a group. Each poet in a conclave, composing at a chief's order for a special event, contributed lines which after revision became part of the whole that everyone memorized so as to preserve. A Hawaiian ruler who had his *haku mele* (weavers of songs) compose name chants celebrating his expected child's ancestry, then perform them widely, believed, as did others, they contributed to a favorable outcome.

Among numerous festivals that central Polynesians held between 19th-c. wars was Chief Poito's dusk-to-dawn entertainment to please two gods of Mangaia Island. For a year, six poets worked on 20 songs and presentations while the people raised food for guests. In the local style the poets structured solos and choruses with an introduction, "foundation," "offshoots," and finale. Some required drums and precision choreography with as many as 200 performers. In Pukapuka three villages set aside a festival day to face each other in poetic contests (q.v.) with old and new insulting songs and dances.

Eastern P. chiefs and priests, who were educated in sacred houses of learning, excelled in technical skill at composition and erudition. Marquesan and Mangarevan masters served rulers as organizers and directors of ceremonies, determined official versions of sacred chants and history, and recited the most sacred parts of chants. A Marquesan tribal Master of Chants, outranked only by the ruler and the inspirational priest, might be deified at death. Nonetheless, if another tribe's Master challenged him, he had to compete successfully before an audience, exhibiting his learning, quickness in composition, and ability in other oral arts at the risk of losing his title or even his life. Many P. islands had such contests of wit and learning.

A Samoan chief's talking chief, also a master of ceremony and subject to challenges from a rival, upheld his chief's and village's prestige, esp. on official visits to other villages, by his command of the complex art of oratory, learning, composition, and knowledge of procedure and etiquette due each titled man present. Tonga, on the other hand, had a class of professional poets, generally untitled but with status roughly equivalent to a ruler's ceremonial attendants. A poet, though honored, was entirely dependent on his patron chief, and usually insecure even as to his life. At one time contests between poets became so bitter they had to be discontinued.

Travelling entertainment troupes, dependent on the largesse of chiefs and donations from audiences, danced and sang popular songs and put on humorous skits at public gatherings and festivals. Islands like Mangareva and the Cook Islands and Marquesas had informally organized groups, mostly young people with an older leader. Hawaiian hula troupes, more organized, underwent taboo-regulated education in schools, each with its own customs but all emphasizing prayers and invocations to gods and goddesses. Most organized of all was the progressively graded Arioi Society of male and female entertainers serving the god 'Oro in the Society Islands; all except members of the highest grades in inherited positions had to kill children born to them or leave in disgrace (Luomala).

One cannot generalize as yet for all Polynesia as for New Zealand about differences between men's and women's compositions. Maori women, who as a group predominated as composers, were more likely than men to compose songs about frustrated love ("Would I were a broken canoe that might be mended") and short, informally arranged, intensely personal laments with simple but appealing imagery ("Like the tides within Tirau forever rising and falling / Is my wild lamentation within Houhangapa"). Maori men were more likely to compose longer, more formally structured laments, filled with elaborate imagery to emphasize that the whole tribe had lost a great man ("like a star shining apart in the Milky Way," or "a sheltering rata tree from the north wind"). That men composed most of the priestly songs may apply to Polynesia as a whole; however, little is known about compositions by priestesses (Ngata; Mead). See NEW ZEALAND POETRY.

The West has fostered both retention and change through its printing press, transportation, education, and lang. Foreigners, the first to collect and publish traditional lore in island langs., occasionally translated and discussed it in their national langs.— Eng., Fr., or Ger. Vernacular newspapers and magazines since the 19th c. have published literate islanders' collections of "old" lore and their creations of novels, plays, and poems combining traditional and Western themes. Festivals of song and dance reviving older forms and inspiring new that were once limited to a single island or archipelago now bring audiences, composers, and performers from an increasingly wider area; air travel has made them pan-Pacific. An elite group of University-educated literary artists that emerged during the 1960s and 1970s, consciously or not, draws inspiration from oral art to write creatively in Eng. and to develop a Pacific-wide "new lit."

Collections of texts of chants, most with translations, some with music, and all with ethnographic discussion, appear in the bulletins, memoirs, and special publications of the Bernice P. Bishop Museum (Honolulu) and in the journals, memoirs, and Maori texts of the P. Society (Wellington). See Bishop Museum *Bulletin* 8, 9, 17, 29, 34, 46, 48, 95, 109, 127, 148, 158, 183, *Memoirs* IV, V, VI, *Special Pubs.* 2, 51, 61; P. Society *Memoirs* 3, 4, 5, 41; *Maori Texts*: A. T. Ngata, *Nga Moteatea*, Part I (1959), and A. T. Ngata and P. Te Hurinui, Part II (1961); *MANA*, Univ. South Pacific Publ. (1973–).

W. W. Gill, *Myths and Songs from the South Pacific* (1876), *Historical Sketches of Savage Life in Polynesia* (1880); M. W. Beckwith, Intro., *The Hawaiian Romance of Laieikawai* (1919), *The Kumulipo, a Hawaiian Creation Chant* (rpt. 1972); S. H. Elbert, "Chants and Love Songs of the Marquesas, Fr. Oceania," *Jour. P. Society* 56 (1947), "Hawaiian Literary Style and Culture," *Am. Anthropologist* 53 (1951); J. D. Freeman, "The Trad. of Sanalālā," *Jour. P. Society* 56 (1947); M. K. Pukui, "Songs (Meles) of Old Ka'u, Hawaii," *JAF* 62 (1948); D. Christensen and G. Koch, *Die Musik der Ellice-Inseln* (1964); S. M. Mead, "Imagery, Symbolism, and Social Values in Maori Chants," *Jour. P. Society* 78 (1969); B. Mitcalfe, *Maori Poetry: The Singing Word* (1974); M. McLean and M. Orbell, *Traditional Songs of the Maori* (1975); N. B. Emerson, *Unwritten Lit. of Hawaii: Sacred Songs of the Hula* (rpt. 1977), *Pele and Hiiaka, a Myth from Hawaii* (rpt. 1978); Subramani, *South Pacific Lit. from Myth to Fabulation* (1985); K. Luomala, *Voices on the Wind: P. Myths and Chants*, rev. ed. (1986).
K.L.

POLYPHONIC PROSE. (1) Amy Lowell's term for a type of poetic prose or prose poem (q.v.) which she developed from Fr. poetry, based on the *versets* (q.v.) of Paul Fort, and which first appeared in *Can Grande's Castle* (1918). Fort used the alexandrine as the base for his prosodic variations; Lowell experimented with blank verse as an Eng.

analogue but found it insufficiently flexible. Still, as she says in her preface, "to depart satisfactorily from a rhythm it is first necessary to have it." The form had a brief vogue and was imitated by John Gould Fletcher but has never subsequently been studied. Artprose is of course ancient, as Norden has shown (see VERSE AND PROSE).

(2) Mikhail Bakhtin's term for a type of "dialogic" prose in which more than one narratorial voice appears, not simply because an author has created several characters with distinguishable voices (though all spoken from the one "monologic" authorial voice) but because a profoundly pluralistic narratorial voice is displaced into a polyphony of heterogeneous, discordant, or antithetic character voices which never are and never can be synthesized into one authorial vision/ voice. See DIALOGUE; VOICE.—A. Lowell, "Paul Fort," *Six Fr. Poets*, 2d ed. (1916); M. Bakhtin, *Problems of Dostoevsky's Poetics* (1929, tr. 1973); Norden; G. S. Morson and C. Emerson, *Mikhail Bakhtin* (1990).
T.V.F.B.

POLYPTOTON (Gr. "word in many cases"; Lat. *traductio*). Related to the varieties of simple word-repetition or iteration, which in Cl. rhct. are treated under the genus of *ploce* (q.v.), is another class of figures which repeat a word or words by varying their word-class (part of speech) or by giving different forms of the same root or stem. Shakespeare takes great interest in this device; it increases patterning without wearying the ear, and it takes advantage of the differing functions, energies, and positionings that different word-classes are permitted in speech. Schaar says Shakespeare uses p. "almost to excess," "using derivatives of more than a hundred stems" in the *Sonnets*. Some of these are but natural in the amplification of any theme, e.g. *love—lov'st—beloved—loving—love's— lovers*, though it is obvious in other cases that the figuration is intentional, as in sonnet 43:

> And darkly bright, are bright in dark directed.
> Then thou, whose shadow shadows doth make bright—
> How would thy shadow's form form happy show
> To the clear day with thy much clearer light.
>
> (4–7)

To Shakespeare's hundred forms in 154 sonnets compare Sidney's 45 in the 108 of *Astrophil and Stella*, Spenser's 27 in the 88 *Amoretti*, and Ronsard's 63 in the 218 of *Amours* I. Despite his penchant, however, Shakespeare never uses p. to excess, as does Sidney: "Sweete kisse, thy sweetes I faine would sweetly indite, / Which even of sweetnes, sweetest sweeter art" (*Astrophil and Stella* 79).

Transferred to prosody, p. at line-end becomes, *mutatis mutandis*, a type of rhyme which also avails itself of grammatical categories, which was known to the *Rhétoriqueurs* (q.v.) as *rime grammaticale* (see GRAMMATICAL RHYME). To us now this does not seem true rhyme, but standards for acceptability in rhyming have varied from age to age (see IDENTICAL RHYME).

Very similar to p. is *antanaclasis*, repetition of a word with a shift in meaning. By using two forms of a word, antanaclasis can play on two senses of it and thereby generate homonymic puns. Shifting the meaning of the word *without* repeating it, the shift being entailed by a second predicate or modifier, is the function of the elusive *syllepsis* (q.v.). Recognition of all these forms suggests that we should construct a taxonomy of the varieties of word repetition as given (albeit often confusedly) in Cl. and Ren. rhet. Four types seem distinguishable: repetition of the same word, in the same grammatical form, with the same meaning (*ploce* and *epizeuxis*); same word, same form, different meaning (*antanaclasis*); same word, different form, same meaning (*polyptoton*); same word, different form, different meaning (sometimes called *antanaclasis*, sometimes *polyptoton*). Here, however, one must define "word" and "form" carefully. Also related is *anthimeria* (q.v.)—another favorite of Shakespeare's—the turning of one part of speech into another, particularly the making of verbs out of nouns.

Some rhetoricians have used *traductio* not in the sense of p. but in the sense of *ploce*, or direct word-repetition (see Quintilian, *Institutio oratoria* 9.3.68–73); one should therefore be explicit about definitions when using any of these terms.

Sr. M. Joseph, *Shakespeare's Use of the Arts of Lang.* (1947), 83–84, 306; C. Schaar, *An Elizabethan Sonnet Problem* (1960); L. A. Sonnino, *Handbook to 16th-C. Rhet.* (1968), 24, 193; Group Mu, 124–26; A. Quinn, *Figures of Speech* (1982), 74–77; B. Vickers, *In Defence of Rhet.* (1988), *Cl. Rhet. in Eng. Poetry*, 2d ed. (1989), 129–30, 146–48; Corbett 447.   T.V.F.B.

POLYRHYTHMIC. See HETEROMETRIC.

POLYSYLLABIC RHYME. See RHYME; TRIPLE RHYME.

POLYSYNDETON (Gr. "much compounded"). The repetition of conjunctions, normally *and*; the opposite of asyndeton (q.v.), which is the omission of conjunctions; common in all kinds of poetry. Quintilian (*Institutio oratoria* 9.3.51–54) remarks, however, that "the source of [both figures] is the same, as they render what we say more vivacious and energetic, exhibiting an appearance of vehemence, and of passion bursting forth as it were time after time," citing, as an illustration, "Both house, and household gods, and arms, and Amyclaean dog, and quiver formed of Cretan make" (Virgil, *Georgics* 3.344–45). Longinus discusses both figures, differentiating them. Modern rhetorical theorists point out that, in addition to a

sense of breathlessness, p. may add emphasis to the items in an enumeration, or may represent the "flow and continuity of experience" (Corbett 436). Conversely, Quinn observes that by slowing down a sentence, p. may add "dignity" to it, or produce an incantatory effect (13). The latter usage may explain the numerous examples of p. often cited in the Bible (e.g. Gen. 1:24–25; Rev. 13:1). Examples may be found in Horace, *Odes* 15; in Petrarch, sonnet 61 (p. is a major structuring device in Petrarch's poetry); in Shakespeare, sonnet 66; in Whitman; and in T. S. Eliot's "Journey of the Magi" (11–15). Group Mu, which classifies p. among metataxes, i.e. as a figure of repetitive addition affecting syntax, explain the effect in the Eliot passage as "responsible for the harmony of the sentence and the metrical scheme of the verse. This is not by chance, since . . . harmony and metrics are systematic groups of practices and rules, two vast syntactic figures that proceed by addition and repetition" (75). In some cases, then, the p. may contribute to rhythm. Although p. in Eng. poetry mainly involves the repetition of *and*, examples do occur in which other conjunctions repeat, as in Eliot's "Love Song of J. Alfred Prufrock" (101–2), though these are disputed, since they do not give the same effect; cf. Milton, whose Satan "pursues his way / And swims or sinks, or wades, or creeps, or flies" (*Paradise Lost* 2.949–50), or *Othello* 3.3.77–80, where a series of *or*'s offer logical alternatives. See also PARATAXIS AND HYPOTAXIS.—Group Mu; A. Quinn, *Figures of Speech* (1982); J. P. Houston, *Shakespearean Sentences* (1988); Corbett.   T.V.F.B.; A.W.H.

PORSON'S LAW. See BRIDGE.

PORTUGUESE POETRY. P. lit. has its origins in the *cantigas* (q.v.) which arose in Galicia toward the end of the 12th c. In the earliest period, Galician and P. p. cannot be satisfactorily separated (see GALICIAN POETRY). Gradually the center of gravity of this common poetry moves south with more identifiable P. names among the *trovadores* (troubadours of upper classes), *segreis* (lower-born, paid composers), and *jograis* (musicians of humble birth) represented in the three great *cancioneiros*. Although these collections contain much monotonous verse revealing poverty of ideas and highly conventional vocabulary, there are poetic gems of clearly personal inspiration and technical perfection, esp. among the *cantigas de amigo* based on indigenous folk *cossantes* rather than on Occitan types. Some of the better known P. poets are Joan Zorro, Vasco Gil, Joan Soares Coelho, Airas Perez Vuitorom, Lourenço Jogral, King Diniz (1261–1325) and his natural sons Afonso Sanches and Pedro Conde de Barcelos. After the death of Diniz, who was the most prolific, the Galician and P. langs. gradually separate, and the troubadouresque tradition declines.

Much of the poetry written during the 15th c. is contained in the *Cancioneiro Geral* (General Songbook, 1516), published by Garcia de Resende (1470?–1536) with compositions by nearly 300 poets. This court poetry shows greater metrical variety and more sophisticated form than the Galician-P. compilations. Sp. influence predominates—some poems are in this lang. (Indeed, most P. poets up to the 18th c. are bilingual.) Much space is devoted to such trivia as poetic competitions, collective poems on ladies, petty satire, and poetic glosses of more social or sociological than literary interest. There are, however, Garcia de Resende's *Trovas* on the death of Inês de Castro; João Roiz de Castelo Branco's *Cantiga, partindo-se* (Song of Parting); the satirical work of Alvaro de Brito Pestana; Duarte de Brito, who reveals some It. influence; and poets who became famous later in the 16th c. One of these, Gil Vicente (1465?–1536?), the father of P. theater, included in his popular drama many lyric passages, *cantigas de amigo*, and other songs of medieval and folk inspiration in Sp. and P.

Resende's *Cancioneiro* already shows some Italianate influences, but Francisco Sá de Miranda (1495–1558), after his stay in Italy (1521–26), introduced into Portugal the sonnet, *canzone*, Dante's tercets and Ariosto's ottava rima, and many Ren. features that characterized the *Quinhentistas* (poets of the 1500s). Sá de Miranda was a painstaking craftsman, but the moral tone and formal innovations of his work are more important than its artistic qualities. His friend Bernardim Ribeiro (1482–1552), author of a highly sentimental pastoral novel *Menina e moça* (Young and Maiden), favored bucolic poetry and wrote the first eclogues in P. (*Jano e Franco*, etc.). This form would be greatly exploited for the next century, perhaps most successfully in the *Trovas de Crisfal* by Cristóvão Falcão (1518–57?).

The Ren. imitation of Cl. genres inspired Luis de Camões (ca. 1524–80), author of the greatest literary epic of the Iberian Peninsula, *Os Lusíadas*, and the outstanding P. lyric poet of all time. His *canções* and sonnets show a rare mastery of form and inspiration:

My sweet soul who departed so soon,
discontent with this life,
rest eternally in heaven
and let me live always sad on this earth!

The Lusiads, in ten ottava rima (q.v.) cantos, is perhaps the most typically national of all epics. Vasco de Gama's memorable expedition to India (1497–98) represents the principal subject; the hero of the poem is the P. people. Historical events (the founding of the P. kingdom, the battle of Aljubarrota, the death of Inês de Castro, etc.) and legendary ones (the "Twelve of England"), episodes from voyages (the fictitious Island of Love), and, through prophecy, Lusitanian accomplishments of the 16th c. are all magnificently described. The mingling of pagan mythology and Christianity, prosaic lines, and abuse of Cl. allusions in this poem have been criticized, but they are amply compensated for by the grandeur of conception, quotable lines, sincere patriotism, erudition, and reflections of the personal experiences of a very eventful life.

Other contemporaries still popular are two brothers, Diogo Bernardes (ca. 1530–1605?) and Frei Agostinho da Cruz (1540–1619). Bernardes wrote religious verses and bucolic poems that show a sincere love for P. nature in their descriptions of the Lima River. Agostinho destroyed his profane verse but left some profoundly religious songs.

The 17th c. could not but represent an anticlimax. In literary terms, its chief distinction lies in the great prose that contributed to the devel. of the modern P. lang. The poetry, much of which was collected in the five-volume *A Fénix Renascida* (1716–28), suffered from excesses inspired by Sp. Gongorism and *culteranismo* (q.v.). Francisco Rodrigues Lobo (1580?–1622), however, continued the Ribeiro trad. with simple, gentle, yet colorful eclogues. Sóror Violante do Céu (1601–93), a Dominican nun, was much admired for her ingenious conceits imbued with mystic fervor, occasionally in a somewhat incongruous fashion. Francisco Manuel de Melo (1608–66), bilingual in Castilian and P., is better in prose, but has left eclogues and epistles of technical excellence. Throughout the century there were many epics, but all were overshadowed by Camões' work. Perhaps in no other country has such a large part of the national poetic effort gone into the production of epics.

The best poetry of the 18th c., particularly from the latter half, is produced by Arcadians who rejected Sp. influence of the 17th c. in favor of Fr. neoclassicism. The poetry from this period that is still remembered owes its reputation more to style and philosophical content than to its lyric qualities. Many of the poets belonged to the "Arcadia Lusitana" (or "Acad. Ulissiponense," from 1756) or the "Nova Arcádia" (from 1790). Each poet adopted the name of a shepherd celebrated in antiquity, and often such pseudonyms became better known than the real names. Pedro António Correia Garção (1724–72) is remembered for his reforms and for elegant poems such as *A cantata de Dido*. Nicolau Tolentino de Almeida (1740–1811) is the principal satirical poet. The most personal love lyrics of the century were written by a poet claimed by both Portugal and Brazil, Tomás António Gonzaga (1744–1810). His *Marília de Dirceu*, a lyric exception among many volumes of moralizing neoclassic verse of the age, has enjoyed exceptional popularity, as demonstrated by the great number of editions (probably second only to Camões). This is due not only to its melodiousness and sincerity, but also to the poet's romantic personal tragedy, his involvement in the Minas Conspiracy in Brazil (1789) and subsequent exile to Mozambique, which frustrated his love for

"Marília." Among the New Arcadians, José Agostinho de Macedo (1761–1831) attracted contemporary attention by his irregular life and his bitterly polemic and philosophic verse. More important was Manuel Maria Barbosa du Boccage (1765–1805), a bohemian whose life has given rise to many *piadas* (anecdotes) but whose production includes, among much that is trivial, contentious, satirical, and improvised, sonnets of a perfection to be found only in Camões and Antero de Quental.

Romanticism in Portugal borrowed many features from France and elsewhere but represents a less spectacular break with the 18th c. than in other countries. Politically, events in Portugal tended to make its proponents patriotic and liberal. The beginning of the movement is usually dated from 1825, with the publication of *Camões*, an epic on the neglect of genius, by João Batista da Silva Leitão de Almeida Garrett (1799–1854). Almeida Garrett's neoclassical background prevented him from falling into romantic excesses. He contributed to literary nationalism with his collection of ballads, *Romanceiro* (1843). His best lyric verse is contained in *Folhas caídas* (Fallen Leaves, 1853)—ardent, elegant poetry among the best love songs in the lang. He is more restrained and more modern than many contemporaries. With his interest in the national past, his politically liberal enthusiasms, his great versatility, and his mastery of all genres, Almeida Garrett personifies P. romanticism, coming as close to being a oneman movement as is possible. Contrasting with him in personality and works, Alexandre Herculano (1810–77) wrote his best poetry in *A harpa do crente* (The Harp of the Believer, 1838), imbued with an austere, Christian spirit. Herculano, best known for his histories and historical novels, is a master of the lang. but produced more prosaic poetry than Garrett.

Another romantic, António Feliciano de Castilho (1800–75), remained more detached from the political agitation of the time because of his blindness. He, too, began as a neoclassic and possesses formal perfection with occasional inspiration. Usually, however, he must substitute mastery of lang. and patient craftsmanship for imagination and sensibility.

Among the "ultra-romantics," Soares de Passos (1826–60), translator of Ossian, is characterized by an emotive melancholy and morbid imagination. João de Deus (Ramos, 1830–96) combines some of the best features of the romantics with bourgeois sentiment and optimistic unselfishness. His effervescent *Campo de flores* (Field of Flowers, 1869, 1893) expresses best *o amor português*: fresh, chaste, and simple love.

The reaction against Castilho, who had come to represent all that was trivial and traditional in romanticism, gave rise to the "Questão Coimbrã" (1865), a pamphlet war led by Antero de Quental (1842–91), Teófilo Braga (1843–1924), and other Coimbra students. Although interested in liberal political and philosophical ideas, they also were more fertile in genuine poetry. Antero's *Sonetos* are unique in P. lit., presenting a diary of the poet's pessimism and his agonized struggle to attain a faith reconciling materialism and the spirit, a struggle the failure of which culminated in his suicide. Abílio Manuel Guerra Junqueiro (1850–1923), occasionally reminiscent of Victor Hugo in his fiery rhetoric, attacks church and state in *A velhice do Padre Eterno* (The Old Age of the Eternal Father, 1885) and *A Pátria* (The Motherland, 1896), but shows some transition to symbolism in *Os simples* (1892) with episodes from the simple, virtuous life of country people. Also often iconoclastic and satirical, António Duarte Gomes Leal (1848–1921) has genial moments when he avoids the declamatory. José Joaquim Cesário Verde (1855–86), in the posthumous *Livro de Cesário Verde*, has left a collection of increasing popularity. His chief quality is an adaptation of naturalism or realism to poetry, painting in concrete details the monotony of bourgeois life, with some inclination to the unusual and grotesque.

António Nobre (1867–1900) lived and published his *Só* (Alone, 1892) in Paris and was familiar with current literary movements there, but he is intensely P. in his introspective subjectivity. His suffering is communicated with gentle sensitiveness and almost morbid *saudade*. Sebastianism, P. folklore, a wealth of images, and metrical freedom lend to his work an enduring fascination. Fausto Guedes Teixeira (1872–1940) and Augusto Gil (1873–1929) may be compared in their tenderness and simple lyric qualities.

Some of these poets display traits of Fr. symbolism, but usually Engénio de Castro (1869–1944) is given credit for introducing this movement and Sp.-Am. modernism (see MODERNISMO) into Portugal. Castro, who became the country's best known poet abroad, prefaced his manifesto to *Oaristos* (Intimate Dialogues, 1890). He advocated greater freedom of form, varied and often eccentric vocabulary, unusual rhymes, alliteration, and emphasis on the aesthetic and sensual rather than the social uses of poetry. Beginning as a refined and aristocratic poet for the elite, in *Horas* (1891) and *Salomé e outros poemas* (1896), he later became more restrained and national in such works as *Depois da ceifa* (After the Harvest, 1901) and *Constança* (1900). Camilo Pessanha (1867–1926) wrote the delicate, symbolistic *Clépsidra* (1920). Through his long residence in Macao he learned to translate Chinese poetry and to endow his own work with an exquisite imagination, a musicality and formalistic daring greatly admired by the next generation. From Olhão in the extreme south came João Lúcio (Pousão Pereira, 1880–1918), who has some admirable moments, esp. when singing of his native region. Joaquim Pereira Teixeira de Vasconcelos ("Teixeira de Pascoaes," 1878–1952) invented Saudosism to epitomize the Lusitanian genius, a melancholy and pantheistic solidarity with all things. From his nationalistic theories sprang the traditionalist *Renascença Portuguesa*, a society organized in Oporto in 1910 to promote public awareness and civic-mindedness. Its mouthpiece was the journal *Águia*. Florbela Espanca (1894–1930), "Sóror Saudade," continues to enjoy great popularity because of the formal perfection of her sonnets, which depict personal tragedy, unfulfilled yearnings, and a deep despair.

With the publication of the Vanguard journal *Orpheu* (1915), P. p. underwent a total renewal. Instead of nationalistic isolationism, the journal proposed internationalism; instead of traditional forms and themes, its poetry incorporated such European literary trends as futurism and cubism (qq.v.). Launched by a group of young poets, some still symbolists, *Orpheu* revealed an innovative quality due principally to the work of three poets: Fernando Pessoa (1888–1935), Mário de Sá-Carneiro (1890–1916), and José de Almada Negreiros (1893–1970). These poets broke away from the lyrical trad. to embrace the dramatic. Showing an overriding commitment to poetry, they directed their talent toward technical experimentation and their boundless energy against the fossilized, well-entrenched writers whose work reflected parochial nationalism. Because their poetry was iconoclastic, the young modernists of *Orpheu* were for many years identified with scandalous, insane behavior.

Fernando Pessoa is the most extraordinary poet of *Orpheu* and the most astonishing P. poetic phenomenon of this century. His influence dominated the next three generations of poets and continues to be felt. Wanting to deviate from traditional lyricism, he stepped outside the self into four poets, one designated by his own name, the others by other names, each with a unique style and a particular philosophical outlook, a different way of looking at the world. Yet in spite of the multifaceted self, Pessoa's poetry is a composite whole, the totality made clear by each contributing self.

Mário de Sá-Carneiro (1890–1916), the other dominant poetic figure to emerge from *Orpheu*, is known by two books of poetry, *Dispersão* (Dispersion, 1914) and *Indícios de Ouro* (Traces of Gold, 1937), both revealing an extraordinary inventiveness combined with exquisite images. Pessoa is the fabulous architect of a poetic cathedral, each altar exhibiting on all sides contrasting magical glass windows of luminous brightness. Sá-Carneiro, on the other hand, is more instinctive and musical as he creates in a sheaf of metaphors the myth of his deep-felt despondency. By contrast, José de Almada Negreiros (1893–1970), better known as a painter than as a poet—his poetry was confined to the *Orpheu* period—is visibly exterior. He wrote long, free-verse poems criticizing P. society, venting his spleen against social hypocrisy and pseudo-intellectualism. The youngest of the group, his combativeness and public posture was the most outrageous; behind the pose, however, loomed a great talent, manifested not only in poetry but also in painting and fiction.

The next movement centered on the magazine *Presença* (1927–40), begun by a group of young students at the University of Coimbra who valued lit. above political militancy through the arts. As such, they reverted to the model set by *Orpheu*, resurrecting that journal from oblivion and ostracism. The most important poet of the group was José Régio (pseudonym of José Maria dos Reis Pereira, 1901–69), also an important novelist, dramatist, and critic. As a poet, Régio dwells on deep, psychological probings, as in *Poemas de Deus e do Diabo* (Poems of God and the Devil, 1925), which dramatizes the conflict between good and evil. Miguel Torga (b. 1907), another *presencista*, reaffirms in his poetry the hegemony of the visible self as he grapples tortuously with the question of Christ's presence on earth; his mysticism is rooted in the crags and arid valleys of Northern Portugal, the harsh, inhospitable region of his birth. Adolfo Casais Monteiro (1908–72) also emphasizes the telluric, intimating the intangible at times without pursuing it. Monteiro and esp. Carlos Queiroz (1907–49) already reflect the impact of Pessoa's poetry, whose influence began to mold every major movement and poet in Portugal after 1943–49, when his posthumous works began to be known.

After *Presença* ceased publication in 1940, world events as well as internal politics demanded that poets become politically committed. The Neorealist movement had as its principal representatives Carlos de Oliveira (b. 1921) and Manuel da Fonseca (b. 1911), whose poetry reflected social problems and national folk themes. One of the few poets whose work derives from a trad. preceding the Pessoa phenomenon, Vitorino Nemésio (1902–78) depicts the P. scene through surrealist imagery in precise, careful lang. Pessoa's legacy is particularly noticeable in the surrealist poets Alexandre O'Neill (1924–86) and Mário Cesariny de Vasconcellos (b. 1923). The former uses colloquialisms and slang to express vociferously a satirical poetic bent; the latter is an exceptional, intellectually profound poet, as seen in the much anthologized "You are Welcome to Elsinore." *Cadernos de Poesia* (Poetry Notebooks), a poetic movement popular in the 1940s, brought together poets who, besides admiring Pessoa, read the Anglo-Am. poetry of Pound and Eliot. Of these, the better known are: Eugénio de Andrade (b. 1923), whose poems are metaphorical and intensely musical; Sophia de Mello Breyner (b. 1919), who depicts in images of singular beauty the transcendence of things real; and Jorge de Sena (1919–78), who taught for 18 years in the United States and was a novelist and short-story writer as well as a critic and poet. His poetry is erudite, sometimes passionate, other times delicate, but marred by bitter denunciation.

In the 1950s, P. p. continued its fascination with Pessoa, esp. with the poems subscribed by the self, which conceptualize the ineffable. The magazine *Árvore* (1951–53) introduced two important poets who, following Pessoa, pursued luminous transcendence, albeit with a greater degree of emphasis on linguistic innovation. António Ramos Rosa (b. 1924) attempts to capture a fragmented reality through words, ultimately the only reality. Egito Gonçalves (b. 1922), on the other hand, much more telluric than visionary, wavers between eroticism and social commitment, love and satire. Still tied to surrealism (q.v.), Herberto Helder (b. 1930) blends surrealistic metaphors to the point of losing sight of any referent.

Concretism is represented in Portugal by E. M. de Melo e Castro (b. 1932), whose poems reflect the emphasis placed by recent poets on the intricacies of the text.

ANTHOLOGIES: *Poems from the P.*, ed. A. F. G. Bell (1913); *Portugal—An Anthol.*, ed. G. Young (1916); Antero de Quental, *Sonnets and Poems*, tr. S. G. Morley (1922); E. de Castro, *Dona Briolanja and Other Poems*, tr. L. S. Downes (1944); L. Vaz de Camões, *The Lusiads*, tr. W. C. Atkinson (1952); *The Oxford Book of P. Verse*, ed. A. F. G. Bell, 2d ed., ed. B. Vidigal (1953); *P. Poems with Trs.*, ed. J. B. Trend (1954); *Líricas portuguesas*, 1st ser., ed. J. Régio (n.d.), 2d ser., ed. J. Cabral de Nascimento (1945), 3d ser., ed. J. de Sena (1958); *Presença da literatura portuguesa*, ed. A. A. S. Amora, M. Moisés, and S. Spina, 2d. ed., 5 v. (1967); *Contemp. P. P.*, tr. J. Longland (1966); *Contemp. P. P.*, ed. H. Macedo and E. M. de Melo e Castro (1978); J. de Sena, *The Poetry of Jorge de Sena*, ed. F. G. Williams (1980); E. de Andrade, *Inhabited Heart*, tr. A. Levitin (1985); F. Pessoa, *Selected Poems*, tr. E. Honig and S. M. Brown (1986).

HISTORY AND CRITICISM: T. Braga, *História da litteratura portugueza* (1896–)—many vols. deal specifically with different phases of poetry; A. F. G. Bell, *Studies in P. Lit.* (1914), *P. Lit.* (1922; P. tr. 1931); *Historia da literatura portuguesa ilustrada*, ed. A. Forjaz de Sampaio et al., 4 v. (1929–42)—lavishly illustr., with bibl.; Le Gentil; F. de Figueiredo, *A épica portuguesa no século XVI* (1950), *Lit. portuguésa*, 3d ed. (1955)—also available in Sp.; J. G. Simões, *Fernando Pessoa* (1950), *Itinerário histórico da poesia portuguesa* (1964); G. Le Gentil, *La littérature portugaise*, 2d ed. (1951)—the best brief intro.; H. V. Livermore et al., *Portugal and Brazil, An Intro.* (1953)—with bibls. of studies by E. Prestage and A. F. G. Bell and of trs. from P. to Eng.; *Dicionário das literaturas portuguesa, galega e brasileira*, ed. J. do Prado Coelho (1960)—entries on individual poets and works, versification, and movements; T. R. Hart, "Med. P. Lit.," in Fisher; *Portugal and Brazil in Transition*, ed. R. Sayers (1966); A. J. Saraiva and O. Lopes, *História da lit. portuguesa*, 5th ed. (1967); H. Cidade, *Lições de cultura e lit. p.* (1968); T. F. Earle, *Theme and Image in the Poetry of Sá de Miranda* (1980), *The P. of António Ferreira* (1988); *The Man Who Never Was*, ed. G. Monteiro (1982); L. N.

Rodrigues, *Garrett and the Eng. Muse* (1983); F. Bacarisse, "A Alma Amortalhada," *Mário de Sá Carneiro's Use of Metaphor and Image* (1984), N. Andrews, Jr., *The Case Against Camões* (1988); T. F. Earle, *The Muse Reborn: The Poetry of António Ferreira* (1988).　　　　L.A.S.; A.E.S.

POSTCOLONIALISM. See CULTURAL CRITICISM.

POSTMODERNISM. See MODERNISM AND POSTMODERNISM.

POSTROMANTICISM. See ROMANTIC AND POSTROMANTIC POETICS.

POSTSTRUCTURALISM. See CRITICISM; DECONSTRUCTION; INTERTEXTUALITY; POETICS; POETRY, THEORIES OF, *Recent Developments*; TEXTUALITY; TWENTIETH-CENTURY POETICS.

POULTER'S MEASURE. In Eng. Ren. verse, a heterometric rhymed couplet consisting of one line of 12 syllables followed by one of 14. The term seems to be a quaint moniker coined by George Gascoigne, who alleges a proverbial practice among poultrymen of giving 12 eggs for the first dozen and 14 for the second (*Certayne Notes of Instruction* [1575]; see Smith 1.59). It is used by Wyatt, Surrey, Sidney, Grimald, and others, and after Tottel (1557) it is almost the staple meter of the 1560s and '70s: G. says it is "the commonest sort of verse which we use now adayes." Some metrists think it also appeared in quatrain form having lines of 3, 3, 4, and 3 stresses, i.e. the "short meter" of the Eng. hymns (see BALLAD METER), hence that these are the same meter whether printed in long lines or short. Short Meter derives from song, hence is accentual verse (q.v.) by nature, and isochronous: missing stresses are filled by pauses. But it is not clear that P. M. is this: the usual charge laid to it is its rigidity of caesura and syllable counting. Saintsbury (*Hist. Man.*) says correctly that P. M. "is not a very good form" but that Short Meter "has not been ineffective in hymns." Context may be all. P. M. is not related to Eng. imitations of the elegiac distich (pentameter + hexameter; q.v.); and its second line is perhaps to be distinguished from the fourteener (q.v.) as used in narrative verse.—Schipper, 2.429 ff.; Smith; C. S. Lewis, *Eng. Lit. in the 16th C.* (1954); J. Thompson, *The Founding of Eng. Metre* (1961); J. Malof, *Manual of Eng. Meters* (1970).　　T.V.F.B.

PRACTICAL CRITICISM. See ANALYSIS; CRITICISM; EVALUATION.

PRAGMATICS. See STYLISTICS.

PRAGUE SCHOOL. See STRUCTURALISM.

PRAISE POETRY. See AFRICAN POETRY; EPIDEICTIC POETRY; SOUTH AFRICAN POETRY.

PRAKRIT POETRY. See INDIAN POETRY.

PRAXIS. See VERSIFICATION.

PRÉCIOSITÉ. Deliberate pursuit and "prizing" of refinement in manners, dress, lang., and lit. Bray (among others) has traced the history of p. from medieval courtly love (q.v.) to the present (Mallarmé, Giraudoux), but as a significant cultural phenomenon it is most pertinently applied to 17th-c. Fr. salons and polite society (1630–60). In 1608 the Marquise de Rambouillet, disgusted by the licentious court of Henri IV, retired to her Parisian manor, noted for its "chambre bleue"; as a salon, it reached its height from 1630 to 1645. Elegance in clothing and manners, decorum and modesty in behavior, and witty conversation were cultivated. Love and lit. were the topics of discussion. Honoré d'Urfé's pastoral novel *Astrée* was analyzed and imitated; authors (incl. Corneille) read aloud their works. The poet and epistolist Vincent Voiture (1598–1648) animated the group and epitomized the delicate, ludic tone of the "précieux" style. In the 1650s, p. appeared in several salons, most notably that of Mlle. de Scudéry, renowned for her lengthy novels. P. became widespread and fashionable in polite ("mondaine") society. Some critics (Lathuillère) consider this decade the only true period of p. By the time of Molière's satiric attack in *Les Précieuses ridicules* (1659), it was already beginning to wane.

As an attitude and endeavor, p. is characterized by reductionism, purity, artifice, and abstraction. In terms of lang., it continued Malherbe's task of rejecting the cacophonous Latinate neologisms of the Ren. The "précieux" lang. of the "ruelle" (an alcove in the salon) stressed exaggerated metaphors, clever "pointes" (puns, witticisms), and paraphrase. Objects could not be crudely designated by their vulgar, common names: in Somaize's *Dictionnaire des précieuses* (1660), a mirror is a "counselor of the graces," cheeks are the "thrones of modesty." Platonic love interests were encouraged, which gave rise to the minor literary forms valued by p.: the epistle, ode, sonnet, rondeau, epigram, and madrigal (qq.v.). But the more popular p. became, the clearer and more frequent were the abuses of extravagance and pretension (esp. among the bourgeois). Burlesque poetry and realistic novels were linked, inversely, to "précieux" thought.

An element of the Fr. baroque (q.v.), p. had several earlier European analogues of idealized refinement: Euphuism, Gongorism, Marinism (q.v.). Yet it did not seek the periodic style of Euphuism, the Latinate vocabulary of Gongorism, or the rambling syntax of Marinism. The influence of p., restricted to Fr. lit., was considerable, since the psychological analysis of love, expressed by "galant" terms (but without florid images or an excessive style) is evident in Mme. de Lafayette, the *Lettres portugaises*, and La Rochefoucauld.—R.

Bray, *La P. et les précieux* (1948); O. de Mourgues, *Metaphysical, Baroque and Precious Poetry* (1953); G. Mongrédien, *Les Précieux et les précieuses* (1963); Y. Fukui, *Le Raffinement précieux* (1964); R. Lathuillère, *La P.*, v. 1 (1966); J.-M. Pelous, *Amour précieux, amour galant* (1980). A.G.W.

PRECURSOR. See INFLUENCE.

PREGUNTA. The "p." or *requesta* (question) with its corresponding *respuesta* (answer) was a form of poetic debate practiced principally by Sp. court poets of the late 14th and 15th cs. One poet presented his question—often on such themes as morals, love, philosophy, or religion—in a poem, and another poet gave the answer in a poem of identical form, including the rhymes. Sometimes answers in identical form were given by more than one poet. Occasionally an answering poet was unable to follow the rhymes of the p. and might excuse himself for his substitutions.—Le Gentil; J. G. Cummins, "Methods and Conventions in Poetic Debate," *HR* 31 (1963); Navarro. D.C.C.

PRE-RAPHAELITE BROTHERHOOD. A group of young Eng. artists who banded together in London in 1848 to protest the academicism and formalism of the classic trad. and lead Eng. painting back to what they called "Nature"—i.e. a sincere and unpretentious representation of the subject through precise attention to detail. Because they professed to find their ideal in the It. painters before Raphael, they called themselves "P.-R." and their organization the P.-R. B. Dante Gabriel Rossetti, William Holman Hunt, and John Everett Millais were the leading spirits of the group, which ultimately numbered seven. As an organization it lasted only into the early 1850s, but the movement it inspired entered a second phase in 1856, when Rossetti met William Morris and Edward Burne-Jones, who had similar aspirations. The group remained active through the 1880s and contributed importantly to aestheticism and symbolism (qq.v.).

From the beginning, Pre-Raphaelitism had a literary side which manifested itself in two short-lived "little magazines," *The Germ* (1850) and *The Oxford and Cambridge Magazine* (1856). Unlike their painting, however, the poetry of the P.-Rs. was not a reaction against the trad. but a continuation and devel. of the romanticism of Keats, Blake, Poe, Whitman, and the early Tennyson, with influences from Dante, Chaucer, Malory, and the Eng. ballads. The chief P.-R. poets were Rossetti, Morris, and Swinburne; also Christina Rossetti, Coventry Patmore, and Meredith. Despite their original aim of symbolic realism, the P.-R. poets tended ultimately toward the creation of a poetic realm in which medievalism, musicality, vague religious feeling, and a dreamlike atmosphere combined to give a narcotically escapist effect. Their central symbol was often a woman whose spiritualized eroticism was highly ambiguous. This aspect of their work was violently attacked by Robert Buchanan in 1871 in an article entitled "The Fleshly School of Poetry" (q.v.). Despite this and other attacks, the movement succeeded in establishing, in the face of mid-Victorian complacency and materialism, the idea of a religion of beauty and the alienated artist which was extremely important for Yeats, Pound, and the modernist movement. Though Ruskin originally inspired the group, it was Pater who most sensitively delineated its ideals.

In 1863 a group of artists in New York City organized an Am. counterpart to the P.-R. B.—the Society for the Advancement of Truth in Art. There were also followers of the movement on the Continent, and for a time the term "P.-R." was used loosely as the equivalent of "aesthetic."

W. Pater, "Aesthetic Poetry" (1868), "Dante Gabriel Rossetti" (1889); W. H. Hunt, *Pre-Raphaelitism and the P.-R. B.*, 2 v. (1905–6); G. Hough, *The Last Romantics* (1949); D. H. Dickason, *The Daring Young Men: the Story of the Am. P.-Rs.* (1953); W. E. Fredeman, *Pre-Raphaelitism: A Bibliocrit. Study* (1965); J. D. Hunt, *The P.-R. Imagination* (1968); T. Hilton, *The P.-Rs.* (1970); L. Stevenson, *The P.-R. Poets* (1972); *Pre-Raphaelitism*, ed. J. Sambrook (1974); W. M. Rossetti, *The P.-R. B. Jour.*, ed. W. E. Fredeman (1975); *Jour. of P.-R. Studies*, 1–(1980–); Tate Gallery, *The P.-Rs.* (1984); *P.-R. Papers*, ed. L. Parris (1984); L. S. Ferber and W. H. Gerdts, *The New Path: Ruskin and the Am. P.-Rs.* (1985); *P.-R. Poets: Mod. Crit. Views*, ed. H. Bloom (1986).   A.D.C.

PREROMANTICISM. Since 1923, when the Fr. term *préromantisme* was introduced, *préromantique* and "preromantic" (1934—*OED*) have been convenient labels for features of 18th-c. writing that reveal a turning away from neoclassicism, even though not all genres—e.g. middle-class drama—were to be important to romantic poetics or lit. (The Ger. equivalent of p., *Vorromantik*, is not frequently used, probably because of the strong connotations of aestheticism, philosophical idealism, and sociopolitical conservatism that attach in Ger. to the root-word *Romantik* but are not important for p.) In rococo (q.v.) poetry there are some preromantic elements, but more appear in genres newly developed in the 18th c. or undergoing radical modification: the exotic and the sentimental novel (Defoe, Prévost, Marivaux, Richardson, Rousseau, Goethe); bourgeois drama and nonmusical melodrama (Lillo, Diderot, Sedaine, Mercier, *Sturm und Drang* [q.v.] playwrights, Schiller as author of *Die Räuber* and *Kabale und Liebe*); and poetry of individual observation and personal experience (Brockes, Haller, the authors of "Seasons"; Günther, Young, Klopstock, Goethe, Bürger, A. Chénier, Blake).

With its doctrines of progress and relativism and its valuation of experiment and individuality, the Enlightenment created an atmosphere favorable to expressions of political and social crit. as well as to the use of nonclassical mythology (Gray, Klopstock, and other Nordic and Bardic poets), of primitive and exotic motifs (the Noble Savage of Rousseau and others, the cult of the untutored poet in England and Germany), and of forms and themes from popular lit. (secular folk song and ballad; drama inspired by folk plays and by Shakespeare's histories; Gothicism and medievalism). It also justified such novelties as prose idylls (Gessner), novels in dialogue (Diderot), tragedies in prose or prose-and-verse (de la Motte, Lessing, *Sturm und Drang* playwrights), and unrhymed, often "Pindaric" odes in Gr. meters or free rhythms (Klopstock, Goethe). By allotting an important place to feeling and instinct, and by ignoring larger metaphysical issues and so perhaps abetting the spread of religious enthusiasm and cryptomystic societies, philosophic speculation fostered sentimentality (*comédie larmoyante*, the sentimental novel and lyric—see SENTIMENTALITY) and sensationalism (Gothic and horror novels, much *Sturm und Drang* writing). The religion of Nature's God directly accessible to Human Reason permeated religious and moral speculation; in the absence of special revelation it was widely held that Virtue subjectively felt could be objectively revealed only as feeling expressed, so that Deism, no less than occultism and such movements as Pietism and Methodism, favored irrational subjectivism and sentimentality.

Historical relativism led to the interp. of Homer and the Old Testament as primitive or early national poetry (Young, Herder) and to the overvaluing of Ossian (Blair, Herder). With rural life thought to be closer to God-Nature than urban civilization, sentimental and realistic idylls, sometimes entirely in dialect, enjoyed wide popularity (Haller, Gessner, E. von Kleist, Thomson, Gray, Goldsmith, Cowper, Burns, Voss, Müller). Poetry of religious feeling, strongly reflective in tone, was given renewed life by Young, Klopstock, and those they inspired. Anticlassical critical theories were expounded ever more vigorously (Bodmer, Breitinger, J. E. Schlegel, Lessing, Young, Diderot, Rousseau, Gerstenberg, Herder, Goethe, Mercier); in varying degrees such theories favored the characteristic" or individuated as opposed to the "ideal" or normative, so that Fr. and Ger. plays consciously executed under their influence, no less than the novels of Lesage, Sterne, or Smollett, may properly be considered preromantic. The concepts of the organic growth of national lits. (Herder) and of the organic structure of the work of art (Goethe) were also developed (see ORGANICISM). Because the unique and the particular were considered precious, literary lang. was enriched by neologisms (Klopstock), archaic forms (Chatterton), and dialectal or otherwise uncommon words (Burns, Goethe), esp. in Germany, where Hamann and Herder demanded a revitalization of poetic speech.

An inept blending of disparate stylistic elements (e.g. simplicity and sublimity, realistic detail and neoclassical epithet, vulgarism and sentimental pathos, ballad form and insistent rhetoric) is evident in much preromantic writing. Not until conscious romanticism (q.v.) with its ironic self-awareness—Goethe's early works are important exceptions—was unity of tone or the successful harmonizing of dissimilar styles generally achieved. P. is thus more than a breaking away from neoclassicism; it is a series of ideological and technical developments that liberated imagination from reason and so prepared the ground for the triumph of romanticism.

See GENIUS; NEOCLASSICAL POETICS; ROMANTIC AND POSTROMANTIC POETICS; ROMANTICISM; STURM UND DRANG.

J. G. Robertson, *Studies in the Genesis of Romantic Theory in the 18th C.* (1923); P. van Tieghem, *Le Préromantisme*, 3 v. (1924–47); P. Trahard, *Les Maîtres de la sensibilité française au XVIIIe siècle*, 4 v. (1931–33); K. Wais, *Das antiphilosophische Weltbild des französischen Sturm und Drang* (1934); W. J. Bate, *From Classic to Romantic* (1946); Wellek, v. 1; R. Ayrault, *La Genèse du romantisme allemand*, 2 v. (1961); S. Atkins, "Zeitalter der Aufklärung," *Fischer-Lexikon: Literatur*, v. 2 (1965); A. Monglond, *Le Préromantisme français*, 2d ed., 2 v. (1966); F. Gaillard, "Le Préromantisme constitue-t-il une période?," *Hispanic Studies in Honour of Joseph Manson*, ed. D. M. Atkinson and A. H. Clarke (1972); G. S. Smith, "Sentimentalism and P. as Terms and Concepts," *Rus. Lit. in the Age of Catherine the Great*, ed. A. G. Cross (1976); P. Arnaud and J. Raimond, *Le Préromantisme anglais* (1980); M. Brown, *P.* (1991).
S.A.

PRESENCE. See DECONSTRUCTION.

PRIAMEL. A Ger. form of Lat. *praeambulum* ("prelude," "introduction"); the term originally referred to a subgenre of epigrammatic poems composed primarily in Germany from the 12th through the 16th c. and characterized by a series of seemingly unrelated, often paradoxical statements cleverly brought together at the end, usually in the final verse. Numerous collections of *priameln* survive, but the author most noted in the genre is the 15th-c. Nuremberg poet, Hans Rosenplüt. The first to study the p. not as a form of the *Spruch* (q.v.) but as a separate genre were G. E. Lessing and J. G. Herder in the 18th c. The first to study the form of the p. in world lit. was F. G. Bergmann (1868), who, however, restricted his survey to didactic verse (e.g. *Proverbs* 30.21-23).

In Cl. studies since the pioneering work of F. Dornseiff and the diss. of his student W. Kröhling (1935), the p. refers to a poetic (and rhetorical) form which occurs throughout Graeco-Roman poetry but has received the most attention in connection with Pindar (Bundy) and Horace (Nisbet and

Hubbard). As it is currently defined, the p. consists of two basic parts, the "foil" and "climax." The function of the foil is to introduce and highlight the climactic term by enumerating or summarizing a number of other instances which then yield (with varying degrees of contrast or analogy) to the particular point of interest or importance. A brief example is Sappho, fr. 16.1–4: "Some say an array of cavalry, others of infantry, and others of ships is the most beautiful thing on the black earth, but I say it is whatever a person loves." Here various military arrays are foils to the real subject of the poem, "whatever a person loves." There are hundreds of examples in Gr. and Lat.; modern examples can be found in Shakespeare (Sonnet 91), Baudelaire ("Au Lecteur"), Yeats ("An Irish Airman Foresees his Death"), and Auden ("Law Like Love").

F. G. Bergmann, *La Priamèle dans les différentes littératures anciennes et modernes* (1868); W. Uhl, *Die deutsche Priamel und ihre Entstehung und Ausbildung* (1897); K. Euling, *Das P. bis Hans Rosenplüt* (1905); F. Dornseiff, *Pindars Stil* (1921); W. Kröhling, *Die Priamel (Beispielreihung) als Stilmittel in der griechisch-römischen Dichtung* (1935); E. L. Bundy, *Studia Pindarica* (1962); R. G. M. Nisbet and M. Hubbard, *A Commentary on Horace, Odes Book I* (1970); U. Schmid, *Die Priamel der Werte im Griechischen von Homer bis Paulus* (1964); W. H. Race, *The Cl. P. from Homer to Boethius* (1982), *Cl. Genres and Eng. Poetry* (1988); H. Kriepe, *Die Nürnberger P.-Dichtung* (1984)—controversial. W.H.R.

PRIAPEA. In Alexandrian Gr. and Lat. poetry, short erotic poems honoring the god of fertility, Priapus, whence the name. Euphronius of Chersonesus (3d c. B.C.) is traditionally said to be the inventor of the P., but it was Leonidas of Tarentum who set the fashion. These poems use a distinctive meter called the Priapean, consisting of a glyconic and a pherecratean (see GLYCONIC) separated by a diaeresis. This was used by Anacreon and other Gr. erotic poets and is also found in dramatic poetry, esp. the chorus of satyr plays. In Lat., it is found in Catullus (e.g. Catullus 17.1) and in the anonymous P., of which some 80 examples survive. See also ITHYPHALLIC; LOVE POETRY.—M. Coulon, *La Poésie priapique dans l'antiquité et au moyen âge* (1932); Dale; Koster; Crusius; V. Buchheit, *Studien zum Corpus Priapeorum* (1962); Halporn et al.; West; A. Richlin, *The Garden of Priapus* (1983); *P.: Poems for a Phallic God*, tr. W. H. Parker (1988).
P.S.C.; T.V.F.B.

PRIMITIVISM. The critique of one's own society through comparison with a less culturally or technologically "advanced" way of life; sometimes the expressed preference for such a state or the advocacy of a return to it. P. idealizes a mythical Golden Age, a prehistorical "savage" state, a rural or "pastoral" existence within one's society, or an allegedly primitive society elsewhere in the world or in an imagined Utopia.

Many lits. nostalgically celebrate or lament an Edenic past or an Arcadian world elsewhere, e.g. the topos of a Golden Age in Cl. and Ren. poetry. In the modern period p. emerges as a meaningful concept with the rise of a more eclectic (if not relativistic) historicism in the 18th c., along with the cultural relativism or at least skepticism inspired by increased contact with "uncivilized" societies: Montaigne's anticipatory "Des Cannibales" and Diderot's *Supplément au voyage de Bougainville*, for example, are inspired by early accounts of Brazil and Tahiti. Both contributed, along with Rousseau's speculations regarding the "savage" state in his two *Discours* and other works, to the topos of the "noble savage" in 18th- and early 19th-c. lit. Schiller celebrated the "naive" perfection of both childhood and Gr. poetry in *Über naive und sentimentalische Dichtung* (1796–97; see NAIVE-SENTIMENTAL); Goethe's *Leiden des jungen Werthers* (1774) typifies *Sturm und Drang* (q.v.) lit. (and Eng. "sensibility"; q.v.) in its ascription of intuitive wisdom and a fuller emotional life to women, children, and peasants, and in Werther's predilection for Homer, Ossian, fairytales, and a "patriarchal" rural existence. Wordsworth celebrated the "elementary" and "permanent" qualities of rustic life and lang., and described in his poetry the "primal" emotional experience of rustics, children, and the mentally deranged or "simple." P. accounts in large part for the romantic and Victorian poets' interest in the Middle Ages, in Gr. antiquity, in "Oriental" cultures and societies, and in the Am. Indian.

P. affected poetics no less than poetry throughout the 18th and 19th cs. Rousseau and Herder among others saw "Oriental" and "savage" langs. as more ancient, more emotional, and more poetic than modern langs. Critics such as Blair and Lowth opposed the spontaneity, wildness, and stronger emotional tones of Homer, the Old Testament, and "Oriental" poetry to the regularity and rigidity of neoclassical taste. "Primitive" poetry of various kinds was collected (Percy's *Reliques of Ancient Eng. Poesy* in 1765, Arnim and Brentano's *Des knabens Wunderhorn* in 1805), recovered (the Eddas, the *Niebelungenlied*, the *Chanson de Roland*), translated (the *Bhagavad Gita* in 1784), fabricated (Macpherson's "Ossian," Chatterton's "Rowley"), and imitated (Wordsworth and Coleridge's *Lyrical Ballads*, Scott's *Lay of the Last Minstrel*). "Peasant poets" such as Robert Burns and John Clare acquired a special status. The Pre-Raphaelites (q.v.) in the later 19th c. aimed for a naive, "medieval" effect in their poetic style as in their painting, and linguistic primitivists like William Barnes sought to purge the Eng. lang. of all but its Anglo-Saxon elements.

In the 20th c. the anthropological and psychological theories of Frazer, Freud, and Jung brought the "primitive" into new prominence as a latent force in culture and as an instinctive, unconscious, or "archetypal" presence in psychic life. A number of modern poets (most prominently Yeats, Eliot, and Rilke) incorporated motifs from myth (q.v.) and ritual; D. H. Lawrence sought to revitalize poetry through a "blood-consciousness," influenced by his reading of Frazer and anticipated by Rimbaud ("Le sang païen revient!"); poets affiliated with surrealism and dada (qq.v.) experimented with "automatic writing" and self-consciously primitive poetry. Unconscious or anti-rational modes of understanding have more recently appealed to poets as diverse as Ted Hughes, W. S. Merwin, and Gary Snyder, while a strong romantic interest in rural life and customs, the archaic, and Celtic myth characterizes the work of Seamus Heaney.

P. was attacked early in the 20th c. by Irving Babbit as escapist and anti-humanist. The rise of modern anthropology has radically reshaped our conceptions of culture and cultural change—we have learned all too well that advances in technology do not themselves constitute advances in culture—and modern linguistics flatly denies that any lang. is "superior" to any other. More recent critiques reject the concept "primitive" altogether as ethnocentric if not racist and view the collection of primitive artifacts and texts as both an instance of cultural imperialism and an index of the desiccation of modern Western culture. See also ANTHROPOLOGY AND POETRY; CULTURAL CRITICISM; EXOTICISM; MARXIST CRITICISM; THEORY.

I. Babbitt, *Rousseau and Romanticism* (1919); H. N. Fairchild, *The Noble Savage* (1928); L. Whitney, *P. and the Idea of Progress* (1934); A. O. Lovejoy et al., *P. and Related Ideas in Antiquity* (1935); E. A. Runge, *P. and Related Ideas in Sturm und Drang Lit.* (1946); G. Boas, *Essays on P. and Related Ideas in the Middle Ages* (1948); D. Hoffman, *Barbarous Knowledge* (1967); G. Boas, "P.," and A. O. Aldridge, "P. in the 18th C.," *DHI*; M. Bell, *P.* (1972); J. B. Vickery, *The Literary Impact of The Golden Bough* (1973); A. Welsh, *Roots of Lyric* (1978); J. R. Cooley, *Savages and Naturals* (1982).
A.R.

PRIORITY. See INFLUENCE.

PROCELEUSMATIC (Gr. "rousing to action beforehand"). In Cl. prosody, a resolved anapest, i.e. a metrical foot of 4 short syllables. It is found among the lyric anapests of Gr. drama and in Lat. drama, esp. comedy, as a resolution in iambs and trochees as well, though with certain restrictions.—W. M. Lindsay, *Early Lat. Verse* (1922); Crusius; D. Korzeniewski, *Griechische Metrik* (1968); West.
P.S.C.

PRODELISION. See APHAERESIS.

PROEST. See ODL.

PROJECTIVE VERSE. A term coined by the Am. poet Charles Olson in an influential 1950 essay on poetics to designate verse composed in open forms resulting from the poet's taking the stance of an object among other objects, rather than imposing himself upon content or materials. This mode of composition Olson also calls "open composition" or "composition by field," and the stance he designates "objectism," a coinage free of the connotations conveyed by "objectivism" (q.v.) that it is simply the opposite of "subjectivism." The result Olson envisions—that the poet's work will have "a seriousness sufficient to cause the thing he makes to try to take its place alongside the things of nature"—is essentially "the objectification of the poem" which Louis Zukofsky spoke of in his introduction to the special "Objectivists" issue of *Poetry* (1930). The verse produced by this method and from this stance supposedly registers the breathing of the poet as he writes and conveys to the reader the energy transfusing the poet.

P. v. belongs in a trad. of organic form that can be traced back to Coleridge's notion of "form as proceeding" (as opposed to "form as superinduced"). In the Am. line, it has its roots in the poetics of Emerson and Whitman. Already in Emerson one finds a sense not only of poetic form as organic but of the primacy of process over product and of the process as dynamic. Olson's warning that "the descriptive functions generally have to be watched" because observation prior to "the act of the poem" tends to drain its energy is reminiscent of Pound's 1913 dictum to "use no superfluous word, no adjective, which does not reveal something" ("A Few Don'ts by an Imagiste"). It differs, though, in its emphasis on energy as the prime requisite for poetry.

Olson's emphasis on the kinetics of verse and verse composition owes much to Ernest Fenollosa's treatise on "The Chinese Written Character as a Medium for Poetry" (1920), which Pound had published and promoted. In particular, Fenollosa's insistence on the "inseparability of actions and things" and his celebration of the transitive sentence as corresponding to the "universal form of action in nature," the "transference of power" from agent through act to object, influenced Olson's notion of the poem as a means of energy transfer.

Though Olson credits principally Pound, Williams, cummings, and, among his contemporaries, Robert Creeley and Edward Dahlberg, with contributing to the theory and practice of p. v., his account of poetic composition is reminiscent of Eliot's in "Trad. and the Individual Talent" (1919), and his complaints about the dominance of conceptual reason over perceptual experience recall Eliot's about the "dissociation of sensibility" (q.v.).

Olson's poetic answer to Eliot's "Waste Land," "The Kingfishers," has been called "the central poem in the Projectivist School of poets." Numerous drafts showing extensive revision and rearrangement evidence that "the poem was a long process" and, more generally, that "Olson's poetics

is not just spontaneity" (Butterick).

Especially characteristic of p. v. is the open sequence, exemplified by Olson's *Maximus* poems, Creeley's *Pieces*, and Duncan's "Structure of Rime" and "Passages" series. But the process—the stance and method—of p. v. can produce very different poetic products, as is evidenced by the great contrast between Olson's long poems (esp. the later *Maximus* poems), arranged across the full width of wide pages, and Creeley's poems in short lines arranged in short stanzas.

The practice of p. v. can be seen as raising questions that would ultimately be addressed by "language poetry" (q.v.). When poets put themselves "in the field," pay attention to each syllable, and listen to their own speech, sooner or later they come up against the problem of how lang. mediates meaning. Even in their reaction against projectivism's unproblematized view of speech and reference, then, language poets can be seen as carrying its principles to their logical conclusion.

C. Olson, *Human Universe*, ed. D. Allen (1967); *Poetics of the New Am. Poetry*, ed. D. Allen and W. Tallman (1973); M. Perloff, "Charles Olson and the Inferior Predecessors," *ELH* 40 (1973); *The Gist of Origin*, ed. C. Corman (1975); S. Paul, *Olson's Push* (1978); R. von Hallberg, *Charles Olson* (1978); P. Christensen, *Charles Olson* (1979); G. Butterick, "Charles Olson's 'The Kingfishers,'" *AmerP* 6 (1989). E.B.

PRONUNCIATION. See PERFORMANCE.

PROPOSITIONAL STATEMENTS. See MEANING, POETIC; PSEUDO-STATEMENT.

PROSE AND POETRY. See PROSE POEM; VERSE AND PROSE.

PROSE POEM. The extreme conventions of 18th-c. Fr. neoclassicism, with its strict rules for the differentiation of "poetry" from "prose," are to be blamed for the controversially hybrid and (aesthetically and even politically) revolutionary genre of the p. p. With its oxymoronic title and its form based on contradiction, the p. p. is suitable to an extraordinary range of perception and expression, from the ambivalent (in content as in form) to the mimetic and the narrative (or even anecdotal). Or rather, they are to be thanked, since the p. p. occasions even now a rapidly increasing interest. Its principal characteristics are those that would insure unity even in brevity and poetic quality even without the line breaks of free verse: high patterning, rhythmic and figural repetition, sustained intensity, and compactness.

In the p. p. a field of vision is represented, sometimes mimetically and often pictorially, only to be, on occasion, cut off abruptly; emotion is contracted under the force of ellipsis, so deepened and made dense; the rhapsodic mode and what Baudelaire called the "prickings of the un-

PROSE POEM

conscious" are, in the supreme examples, combined with the metaphoric and the ontological: the p. p. aims at knowing or finding out something not accessible under the more restrictive conventions of verse (Beaujour). It is frequently the manifestation of a willfully self-sufficient form characterized above all by its brevity. It is often spatially interesting (D. Scott). For some critics, it is necessarily intertextual (Riffaterre), for others, politically oriented (Monroe). It is, in any case, not necessarily "poetic" in the traditional sense and can even indulge in an engaging wit.

The p. p. is usually considered to date from Aloysius Bertrand's *Gaspard de la Nuit* (1842), though he was writing p. ps. earlier, and to be marked by heavy traces of Fr. symbolism (q.v.), and conditioned by the stringency of the Fr. separation of genres. Among its antecedents are the poeticized prose trs. of the Bible (see VERSET), of classical and folk lyrics, and of other foreign verse; the poeticized prose of such romantics as Chateaubriand and the prose passages of Wordsworth's *Lyrical Ballads*; and the intermixtures of verse and prose in Maurice de Guérin's "Le Centaure," Tieck's *Reisegedichte eines Kranken* and Sainte-Beuve's *Alexandrin familier.* Characteristically, it was the romantics who came to the defense of this hybrid: Hugo's plea for the *mélange des genres* in his preface to *Cromwell* is the natural counterpart to Barbey d'Aurevilly's apology for the p. p.

But the most celebrated example of the p. p. is Baudelaire's *Petits Poèmes en prose*, or *Le Spleen de Paris* (begun 1855, pub. 1869), in which he pays tribute to Bertrand for originating the genre. Baudelaire's texts can complicate figuration to the point of "figuring us" as reader (Johnson, in Caws and Riffaterre). His "Thyrse" offers female poetic windings and arabesques around an upright male prose pole as the highly eroticized primary metaphor of mixing, while the *Petits poèmes* themselves are at once anecdotal and intimate, to the point of mixing the self with the subject. Rimbaud's *Illuminations* (1872–76) celebrate with extraordinary intensity the emergence of poems from less intimate matter, a newness dynamic in its deliberate instantaneity, yet the precursor of the aesthetic of suddenness practiced by Hoffmannsthal in his *Philosophie des Metaphorischen*—the speed of the metaphor is an "illumination in which, for just a moment, we catch a glimpse of the universal analogy"—and by imagists such as Pound. Rimbaldian confusion of first- and third-person perspective ("the lyric process of undergoing oneself and the more properly novelistic business of mapping out a behavior"—C. Scott) sets up, together with his notational rapidity, a kind of vibratory instant (Shattuck). Mallarmé's *Divagations* (begun 1864, pub. 1897) with their intricate inwindings of metaphor, Lautreamont's *Chants de Maldoror* (the first canto in 1868, the rest pub. posthumously in 1890) lush with a sort of fruity violence, Gide's *Nourritures terrestres* (Earthy Eats, 1897), and

Claudel's *Connaissance de l'est* (The East I Know, 1900), nostalgic and suggestively pictorial, lead to Valéry's *Alphabet* (1912), whose form has been compared to what Valéry later calls, speaking of the dual function of discourse, "the coming and going between two worlds" (Lawler).

Elsewhere, the p. p. flourishes with a different cast: early on, in Switzerland, with Gessner (*Idylls*, 1756); in Germany, with Novalis and Hölderlin, then Stefan George, Rilke, Kafka, Ernst Bloch, and recently, in former East Germany, Helga Novak; in Austria, Hofmannsthal, Altenberg, and Polgar; in Belgium, Verhaeren; in England, De Quincey, Beddoes, Wilde, and the imagists; in Russia, Turgeney and the Rus. futurists, esp. Xlebnikov; in Italy, the cubo-futurists such as Marinetti (see FUTURISM); in Spain, Bécquer, Jiménez, and Cernuda; in Latin America, recently, Borges, Neruda, and Paz; in Denmark, J. B. Jacobsen.

Modernist writing as practiced in France after symbolism and postsymbolism increasingly problematized the genre; the so-called cubist poets Max Jacob, Reverdy, and Blaise Cendrars (see CUBISM) each gave his own slant to the p. p., emphasizing respectively its "situation," its strangely reticent irresolution, and its simultaneous perceptions. The Fr. surrealists Eluard, Breton, and Desnos provide a rich nostalgia and revelatory illumination by means of a startling juxtaposition of images; Gertrude Stein's "Tender Buttons" reaches a height of the lyric and the everyday held in tension, taking its energy from the androgynous. Among recent 20th-c. Fr. poets, René Char, St.-John Perse, and François Ponge, and then Ives Bonnefoy, Dupin, and Deguy prove the sustained vigor of the genre, proved equally in America by such prose poets (after Whitman) as James Wright, Robert Bly, W. S. Merwin, Russell Edson, John Ashbery, and John Hollander, and such language poets (after Gertrude Stein and W. C. Williams) as Charles Bernstein. See also POLYPHONIC PROSE; RHYME-PROSE; VERS LIBRE; VERSE AND PROSE; VERSET.

V. Clayton, *The P. P. in Fr. Lit. of the 18th C.* (1936); G. Díaz-Plaja, *El poema en prosa en España* (1956); S. Bernard, *Le Poème en prose de Baudelaire jusqu'à nos jours* (1959); M. Parent, *Saint-John Perse et quelques devanciers* (1960); U. Fülleborn, *Das deutsche Prosagedicht* (1970), *Deutsche Prosagedichte des 20. Jahrhunderts* (1976), *Deutsche Prosagedichte vom 18. Jahrhundert bis zur letzten Jahrhundertwende* (1985); D. Katz, "The Contemp. P. P. in Fr.: An Anthol. with Eng. Trs. and Essay on the P. P.," *DAI* 31 (1970), 2921A; *The P. P.: An Internat. Anthol.*, ed. M. Benedikt (1976); R. Edson, "The P. P. in America," *Parnassus* 5 (1976); C. Scott, "The P. P. and Free Verse," *Modernism*, ed. M. Bradbury and J. McFarlane (1976); D. Lehman, "The Marriage of Poetry and Prose," *DAI* 39, 8A (1979): 4938; K. Slott, "Poetics of the 19th-C. Fr. P. P.," *DAI* 41, 3A (1980), 1075; J. Holden, "The Prose Lyric," *Ohio Rev.* 24 (1980); D. Keene, *The Mod. Japanese*

P. P. (1980); B. Johnson, *The Critical Difference* (1981), ch. 3; S. H. Miller, "The Poetics of the Postmodern Am. P. P.," *DAI* 42 (1981), 2132; *The P. P. in France: Theory and Practice*, ed. M. A. Caws and H. Riffaterre (1983)—13 essays on Fr. and Eng.; R. E. Alexander, "The Am. P. P., 1890–1980," *DAI* 44, 2A (1983), 489; D. Scott, "La structure spatiale du poème en prose," *Poètique* 59 (1984); M. Perloff, *The Dance of the Intellect* (1985); D. Wesling, *The New Poetries* (1985), ch. 6; S. H. Miller, "John Ashbery's P. P.," *Am. Poetry* 3 (1985); M. S. Murphy, "Genre as Subversion: The P. P. in Eng. and Am.," *DAI* 46 (1986): 1932A; J. Monroe, *A Poverty of Objects: The P. P. and the Politics of Genre* (1987); J. Kittay and W. Godzich, *The Emergence of Prose* (1987); R. G. Cohn, *Mallarmé's P. Ps.* (1987); J. Simon, *The P. P. as a Genre in 19th-C. European Lit.* (1987); R. Silliman, *The New Sentence* (1987); S. Fredman, *Poet's Prose*, 2d ed. (1990); M. S. Murphy, *A Trad. of Subversion* (1992); S. Stephens, *The Poetics and Politics of Irony in Baudelaire's* Petits poèmes en prose (1993).   M.A.C.

PROSE RHYTHM.

  I. OVERVIEW
  II. CLASSICAL AND MEDIEVAL
  III. MODERN

I. OVERVIEW. In the simplest and most general sense, all prose has rhythm, at least insofar as lang. itself has shorter or longer rhythms of phonological, morphological, and syntactic structuring; and virtually all prose, regardless of how artful or utilitarian, is more formal and more structured than virtually all speech, certainly than ordinary quotidian discourse, which is typically fragmentary in character. (In structural metrics [see METER], the term "p. r." was used to denote simply the ordinary pronunciation that a line would receive were it spoken aloud or read as prose, without influence from meter.) But even speech normally becomes stylized and rhythmical in rhetorical situations (political orations, sermons), in situations of extreme emotion, and in cases of speech or cerebral disorders. Rhythmicity in prose for strictly utilitarian purposes—newspapers, technical manuals, reports—is actively discouraged in the modern world, since the aesthetic effect of the poetic function—in Jakobson's terms, lang. oriented toward itself—is to give pleasure by thickening the transparency of the sign and thus distracts from the communication of information.

  Since "rhythm" etymologically means "flow," almost any prose which seems satisfying to the ear may be said to be rhythmic. But if, in the stricter sense of the term, rhythm is taken to refer to grammatical elements or members of equal size or length (see ISOCOLON), disposed at equal distances, or delivered with equal or approximately equal timing (see ISOCHRONISM), then "p. r." refers to those species of artprose wherein rhythmic effect is deliberately sought. Such ornamentation or figuration has been cultivated in nearly all cultures with written records, some of these traditions being very extensive and of great antiquity. Prose itself, so far as the most ancient evidence indicates, is a secondary or derivative mode—some would say, poetry *manqué*—but it too has been cultivated as an artform for the powerful effects that rhythmicity (see RHYTHM) and sound patterning (see SOUND) can bestow.

  Prose which develops sound patterning, incl. such devices as alliteration, assonance, echo (qq.v.), or the more complex but less easily described forms of sound interlace and architectonics is often grouped with more specifically rhythmical prose under the latter term. In the West, however, sound-patterned forms developed most extensively the device of rhyme (q.v.) in the several forms known collectively as *rhymeprose* (q.v.). This form has had a significant history in Arabic, less so in Med. Lat. In the East, it has been cultivated for a much longer period in Chinese. But rhyme itself must be recognized as but one form of phrasal or clausal end-marking with close relatives in homoeoteleuton (q.v.), strict lexical repetition such as refrains and identical rhyme (qq.v.), and the more strictly rhythmic forms such as the *cursus* (see below). This is only to say that the general principle on which p. r. relies is operative on all levels of the linguistic text, from phonological through syntactic if not discursive, yielding congruent or cognate forms on each level of the hierarchy (so Lotman). In the usual sense of "p. r.," it is the phonological level which is referred to.

  Prose which cultivates rhythmical effects comes in two species: either the patterns are smaller and exact (even if short), controlling the number of syllables and patterning of quantity (q.v.) or stress strictly, or else larger and inexact. The first species includes Gr. and Lat. artprose, which is quantitative and regulates the ends (last few syllables) of syntactic periods (known as the "cadence" or "clausula"), and Med. Lat. accentual forms apparently derived therefrom. The second species covers most modern forms of rhythmical prose, which employ syntactic parallelism, anaphora, and amplification (qq.v.); at various times such sentencing has been referred to as periodic, balanced, or "Attic" style.

  Giving figuration or perceived shape to prose utterances so as to enhance their recognition, persuasion, and memory was in fact the chief purpose of Cl. rhetoric, which developed an extensive inventory of sound and syntactic shapes; these are the familiar rhetorical figures, variously classed as schemes or tropes. Once a syntactic form was established, such as "reversal" in *chiasmus* (q.v.) or "reiteration" in parallelism (q.v.), it only remained to require an equal number of syllables in each member to make the sequence rhythmical, exactly as in verse. In the terminology of Cl. rhet., syntactic members (phrases or clauses) which are equal in shape or structure are treated under the figure *parison*, those equal in number of syllables and quantitative pattern *isocolon* (q.v.).

Owing to the structure of lang., words have a natural tendency to come in set patterns of number of syllables and stress-pattern ("the course of the river," "a gift for your sister," "I'll come in a minute"). The poet adopts these natural patterns, fitting them into the metrical scheme. Verse, of course, comes in lines, prose in paragraphs, but if the single crucial formal feature of verse, lineation, is removed, rhythmic prose and versification are distinguishable only in degree of rhythmicity, and may well not be distinguishable at all, as for example in Pope's (in)famous line, "Most women have no character at all," which could as well be prose—so Matthew Arnold. Most of the ancients held that rhythmic patterning in prose should be present and felt but only occasional and various, not regular, else it becomes obtrusive—and prose becomes verse. "Prose must have rhythm but not meter," says Aristotle, "for then it will be poetry." Lack of regularity bodes well for readers—it makes for a supple and expansible medium—but augurs ill for analysts.

The most common method for identifying varieties of p. r. has been by breaking down sentences or phrases into syllables, then by analyzing quantitative or accentual patterns by poetic scansion (q.v.). Since the structure of any lang. will generate some rhythmic patterns naturally, statistical analysis must take these patterns as the ground against which to measure variation. Scholars have taken a number of texts, portions of texts, and speech forms as possible grounds for analysis, with only mixed results. A further issue is whether to analyze clausulae in terms of feet, without regard to word-boundaries, or to analyze by word-types, or both.

II. CLASSICAL AND MEDIEVAL. P. r. was an accepted part of ancient rhetorical theory; the major texts are Aristotle (*Rhetoric* 3.8–9), Demetrius, Dionysius (*On Literary Composition*, chs. 25–26), Quintilian, and Cicero (*De oratore* 3.173–98, *Orator* 168–236). In Aristotle, discussion of rhythmicity is conflated with that of periodic structure, and treatment of the rhythm of the whole sentence with that of merely the sentence-end (clausula), neither of which issues were distinguished clearly by subsequent theorists. Since variety was emphasized, close analysis of sentence-rhythm produced few regularities, but marked patterning of the closing syllables (the "cadence") of the syntactic period (q.v.) was both possible and effective. Marking the end of the member with one of only a small class of fixed patterns is one of the most distinctive laws of rhythmical structure (see RHYTHM; CATALEXIS). Cicero particularly emphasizes clausulae.

The ancients believed the Sophist rhetorician Thrasymachus of Chalcedon (fl. ca. 430–400 B.C.) to have been the first to cultivate quantitative patterns in Gr. prose, as did, later, Gorgias and Demosthenes. Plato uses them, esp. in *Phaedrus*, but also objects to them and parodies them in the *Symposium*; Thucydides, by contrast, is unrhythmical. After the shift from quantity to accent, later Gr. and Byzantine writers cultivate accentual clausulae. Cicero takes over the Gr. quantitative system into Lat. (though without recognizing the differences between the two langs.) and develops a clear system of preferences for clausulae which he seeks—principally the clausula – ⌣ – – x and its resolutions, all elaborated from cretics—or else avoids. His example provoked wide imitation—Seneca, Suetonius, Nepos, Quintilian, Pliny, Tertullian—though he was not followed by Sallust and Livy.

Cicero's clausulae also show significant coincidences of accent and quantity; purely accentual clausulae first appear in the work of the Africans Minucius and Cyprian in the early 3d c. A.D., and by the late 4th c. have supplanted quantitative clausulae altogether. In the 11th c., the system of accentual clausulae or *cursus* was taken up by the professional scribes of the Roman Curia as an obligatory stylistic feature for Papal correspondence, specific rules for which were formulated by Pope Gregory VIII. Clausulae could be written in only three patterns: (1) *planus* (plain): x́xxx́x ; (2) *tardus* (slow): x́xxx́xx; and (3) *velox* (fast): x́xxxx́x; these continued to be described by the older quantitative terms (respectively, [1] dactyl plus spondee, [2] dactyl plus dactyl, [3] dactyl plus dispondee) though they were in fact accentual. The two chief features of all forms of the *cursus* are that runs of three or more short syllables are avoided (Blass's Law) and that the number of syllables between accents is a multiple of 2 (Meyer's Law). The *cursus* held long currency among the learned: Petrarch and Dante were familiar with it, and evidence from it has been used to deny Dante's authorship of the famous letter to Can Grande prefixed to the *Paradiso* espousing the fourfold method of interpretation (q.v.).

Cl. and medieval p. r. evoked a flurry of work from ca. 1880 to 1930, much of it outdated and only now beginning to be reexamined. It still remains for these various studies of Gr., Lat., and Med. Lat. to be brought into one locus, mapped out, synthesized, and appraised definitively in the light of modern linguistics, statistical methods, and prosodic theory.

III. MODERN. Strict or clausular p. r. did not survive the Middle Ages: Ren. interest in artprose developed the full range of rhetorical figuration, as in Euphuism and Mannerism (q.v.), but did not codify any practice into set forms. By far the most influential rhythmical prose to emerge from the Ren. was that of the Authorized Version (1611), which sought to import into Eng. prose the chief prosodic hallmark of Hebrew verse, parallelism (see HEBREW PROSODY). Indeed, many readers object to modern translations of the Bible which are in fact more accurate lexically because such versions lose most of the periodic and rhythmical effects which were so deliberately sought by King James's translators, and which have by now become part of the cultural memory for Eng. readers. Deriving from this fountainhead is the trad. of 17th-c. devotional prose, as in the sermons of Donne and essays of Sir Thomas Browne. Later stylists such as Gibbon, Macaulay, and perhaps the Faulkner of *Absalom, Absalom* can be found rhythmic in places, some of which have become purple patches, but the scanning of long passages by pedants such as Saintsbury is misguided. The rhythmicity of Hebraic verse prosody and Eng. biblical prose was reintroduced into Eng. verse by Whitman. See CADENCE; CHANT; PARALLELISM; PERIOD; POLYPHONIC PROSE; PROSODY; REPETITION; RHYMEPROSE; VERSE AND PROSE.

L. Havet, "La Prose métrique de Symmaque et les origines métriques du cursus," *Bibliothèque de l'École des Hautes Études* 94 (1892); T. Zielinski, *Das Clauselgesetz in Ciceros Reden* (1904), *Der constructive Rhythmus in Ciceros Reden* (1914)—pioneering survey, with charts still useful; Meyer, v. 2, chs. 7–8—criticizes Havet; H. Bornecque, *Les Clausules métriques latines* (1907)—fullest collection of ancient theory; C. Zander, *Eurhythmia*, 4 v. (1910–14); A. C. Clark, *The Cursus in Med. and Vulgar Lat.* (1910), *P. R. in Eng.* (1913); P. Fijn van Draat, *R. in Eng.* (1910), "Voluptas aurium," *Englische Studien* 48 (1915); R. L. Poole, *Lectures on the Hist. of the Papal Chancery* (1915); W. M. Patterson, *The R. of P.* (1916); M. W. Croll, "The Cadence of Eng. Oratorical Prose," *SP* 16 (1919); H. D. Broadhead, *Lat. P. R.* (1922); G. Saintsbury, *A Hist. of Eng. P. R.* (1922); K. Polheim, *Die lateinische Reimprosa* (1925); A. W. De Groot, *La Prose métrique des anciens* (1926)—scientific but polemical; L. Laurand, *Études sur le style des discours de Cicéron*, 3d ed. (1928), "Bibl. du *cursus* lat.," *REL* 6 (1928), 12 (1934); F. Novotny, "État actuel des recherches sur le rythme de la prose latine," *Eus supplementa* 5 (1929); M. G. Nicolau, *L'Origine du cursus rythmique et les débuts de l'accent d'intensité en lat.* (1930)—balanced; A. Schiaffini, "La tecnica della prosa rimata nel medio evo latino," *Studi romanzi* 21 (1931); N. Denholm-Young, "The Cursus in England," *Oxford Essays in Med. Hist. H. E. Salter* (1934); D. Seckel, *Hölderlins Sprachrhythmus* (1937); F. Di Capua, *Il ritmo prosaico nelle lettere dei Papi nei documenti della cancellaria romanza dal IV al XIV secolo*, 3 v. (1937–46), *Fonti ed esempi per lo studio dello "stilus curiae romanae" medioevale* (1941); A. Classé, *The R. of Eng. P.* (1939); M. Schlauch, "Chaucer's P. Rs.," *PMLA* 65 (1950); P. F. Baum, *The other harmony of prose* (1952); M. M. Morgan, "A Treatise in Cadence," *MLR* 47 (1952); Beare, ch. 16; W. Schmid, *Über die klassische Theorie und Praxis des antiken Prosarhythmus* (1959); G. Lindholm, *Studien zum mittellateinischen Prosarhythmus* (1963); L. P. Wilkinson, *Golden Lat. Artistry* (1963), chs. 5–6, App. 2; A. Primmer, *Cicero Numerosus: Studien zum Antiken Prosarhythus* (1968);

Lausberg, sect. 977; T. Janson, *P. R. in Med. Lat. from the 9th to the 13th C.* (1975); H. Aili, *The P. R. of Sallust and Livy* (1979); Morier, s.v. "Prose cadencée"; Brogan, 125 ff.; Norden; S. M. Oberhelman and R. G. Hall, "A New Statistical Analysis of Accentual Prose Rhythms in Imperial Lat. Authors," *ClassP* 79 (1984); T. Habinek, *The Colometry of Lat. Prose* (1985); S. M. Oberhelman, "Hist. and Devel. of the *Cursus Mixtus* in Lat. Lit.," *ClassQ* 82 (1988); R. G. Hall and M. U. Sowell, "*Cursus* in the Can Grande Epistle: A Forger Shows His Hand?" *Lectura Dantis* 5 (1989).   T.V.F.B.

PROSIMETRUM. A text composed in alternating segments of prose and verse. The p. is widely attested in both Western and Eastern lits. and apparently appears worldwide. Typically the verse portions serve as lyric, emotive, or personal insets within a philosophical or narrative frame, often with connectives between prose and verse sections, but in fact there are several varieties still not thoroughly understood: the definitive cross-cultural study yet remains to be written. Differentia of variables include: whether the sections alternate regularly or irregularly; whether the number and form of the sections is controlled by a larger architectonic structure (i.e. the principle of mixture); whether the one form is a paraphrase of the other, or not, and whether by the same author, and whether at the same time; whether there is more than one narrator or, if two, whether both speak in both modes or are kept separate; whether the content of the two modes is similarly kept separate (e.g. philosophical vs. lyric); whether differing subgenres (philosophy, fictional narratives, drama) differ categorically in structure; and whether variety of meters is required in the verse sections.

In Chinese, prosimetric form is manifested in the *Fu* ("rhymeprose"; see CHINESE POETRY) and in some 10th-c. *Pien-wen* (narratives); in Japanese it is used for the collection of mythical history known as the *Kojiki* (ca. 712 A.D.); in Sanskrit is is a major component of Vedic narrative poetry, as evidenced in the *Mahabarata*, the long dynastic epic containing the *Baghavad Gita* (see NARRATIVE POETRY), among many others. Indeed, some have seen the lyric itself as emergent from these emotive or sung inserts in epic narratives.

In the West, the earliest exemplars are the satires of the Gr. writer Menippus (3d c. B.C.), from which developed the Lat. *satura* (later "satire" but originally "medley") and the *Satyricon* of Petronius; extant too are four Gr. texts in a ms. of the 2d c., two of which seem to be romances. Both satire and the prose romance retained long association with prosimetric form. But the central text which established the popularity of the p. for the Middle Ages was Boethius' *De consolatione philosophiae* (ca. 524 A.D.), five Books of alternating, numbered segments called "Metrum" and "Prosa" and set within a larger numerological structure.

The *Consolation* moves from emotive complaint to metaphysical contemplation: the male prisoner-narrator and female personified Philosophy speak both the first two metra and the last prosa. Polymetry in the verse segments is emphasized (some two dozen meters). The influence of Boethius' p. on the later Middle Ages was extensive and prolonged, even though subsequent translators and imitators did not all retain the prosimetric format: the OE *Meters of Boethius* attributed to King Alfred, the OF tr. by Jean de Meun, and Chaucer's *Boece* are entirely in prose; the Occitan *Boëce* (11th c.), the Anglo-Norman *Roman de fortune*, and the one other surviving ME version are entirely in verse.

Also influential, though less so, was Martianus Capella's *De nuptiis philologiae et mercurii*, an odd work in nine Books wherein the Seven Liberal Arts become the bridesmaids at the wedding of Learning and Eloquence: here the verse insets are arranged irregularly. The p. was revived in the 12th c. in Lat.—as instanced in Bernard Silvestris' *De universitate mundi* (ca. 1150) and *Cosmographia*, which return to regular alternation of segments and free use of both modes by all characters, and Alan of Lille's *De planctu naturae*, a complaint on sodomy—and then the vernaculars. Very similar in form are the Occitan *vidas* and *razos*—biographical story-collections including poems meant to be sung; these, along with Boethius, influenced Dante, whose *Vita nuova* (1293), 31 poems introduced and connected with prose, and *Convivio*, esp. interesting in that one narrator recounts all, the verse segments being, he says, from his own earlier writings. Boccaccio's *Ameto* (1342) provides a frame story in which seven stories are told and seven songs sung, a structure leading directly to the *Decameron* and Chaucer, where the regular alternation of segments is lost. But it is retained in the pastoral romance, esp. Jacopo Sannazaro's *Arcadia* (1485; 12 prose segments and 12 verse) and Sidney's *Arcadia* (1590), with its inset eclogues and experiments in Eng. quantitative verse.

Fr. also explored the p.: from the 13th there are 13 extant OF versions of Boethius, some of them prosimetric. The anonymous author of the 13th-c. *Aucassin et Nicolette* calls his text a *chante-fable* (q.v.) or "song-story," showing that the verse segments had moved from lyric into song. This development made natural the extension of prosimetric form into medieval drama, where inset songs, if occasional, provided relief from dialogue and narrative in prose—a practice later evident not only in Shakespeare but even in modern times. Other Fr. ps.: Froissart's *Prison amoureuse* and Machaut's *Voir-Dit*, where prose letters and love poems are set in a verse frame.

Other medieval lits. knew the p.: the Arabic *maqāmāt*, which originated around 1000 A.D.; the Celtic epic *Taín*; some of the Icelandic sagas; and the Turkish epic known as *The Book of Dede Korkut*. Snori Sturlusson's *Edda* (ms. ca. 1300) is in prose but includes a 100-meter catalogue of Icelandic verseforms. The relations of prose and verse in the Middle Ages were more fluid than today (Curtius 147 ff.); within the range of mixed forms, the p. is but one hybrid form among several, e.g. rhythmical prose (see CURSUS) and rhyme-prose (q.v.). A related genre is the *opus geminatum* or "twinned work," written once in prose and then versified or vice versa, the prose for recitation in church, the verse for private meditation. This takes its origin in the rhetorical doctrine of *conversio* or paraphrase, and emerges in Caelius Sedulius' *Carmen paschale* and *Opus paschale* of the mid 5th c., foll. by Aldhelm (*De virginitate*, 60 chapters of prose transformed into a *Carmen de virginitate* of 3000 hexameters), Bede, and Alcuin among others.

H. R. Patch, *The Trad. of Boethius* (1935); Curtius; H. Scheible, *Die Gedichte in der* Consolatio philosophiae *des Boethius* (1972); E. Walter, *Opus geminatum* (1973); M. Dillon, *Celts and Aryans* (1975), 147 ff.; R. A. Dwyer, *Boethian Fictions* (1976); P. Godman, "The Anglo-Lat. Opus geminatum," *MÆ* 50 (1981); C. D. Eckhardt, "The Medieval P. Genre," *Genre* 16 (1983); Norden 2.755 ff.; J. Kittay and W. Godzich, *The Emergence of Prose* (1987), ch. 4. T.V.F.B.

PROSODY (Gr. *prosodia* "tune"; Lat. *ad + cantus, accentus* [a calque] "song added to speech") is the traditional term for what is now called verse theory, which is the study of verseform, i.e. structures of sound patterning in verse, chiefly meter, rhyme, and stanza (qq.v.).

I. OVERVIEW. Pros. is that branch of poetics which treats what Aristotle called the material and formal causes of art, i.e. its medium and the forms into which that medium can be shaped. In the plastic arts, the aesthetic material is formless and solid, but in verbal art the medium is the word, which has both a material form (sound) and (always already) meaning, even in nonsense verse (q.v.). In prose the medium is transparent, but in poetry it is made opaque (so Hegel) and given design. The situation in poetry is thereby made double, for its medium is apprehended as meaning, of course, but meaning given figured and textured shape. Pros. is thus the study of the means by which verbal material is made over into verbal art in texts set in verseform, and more particularly the study of those extensions, compressions, and intensifications of meaning of which bound speech becomes capable by increase in formal structure.

In Western poetics, the fundamental conception of the poem is not of a page-bound entity but rather of a structure of equivalences (q.v.) held together as an aural shape, i.e. as sound (q.v.), whether virtual or actual. Traditional pros. therefore held that verse structure operated below the level of the word in patterning of sound, i.e. the phonological features of lang. These features—using for the moment the terminology of structural linguistics—include the so-called sound "segments" themselves (vowels and consonants) as well as the "suprasegmentals" (pitch, stress, duration), which are not marked in orthography so are invisible in print but are nevertheless heard in all recitations of poetry. Pros. is therefore not textually oriented: it considers writing a limited and imperfect transcription of speech; properly, it is based on sounded speech, where two syllables are often elided into one, for example, regardless of how they are represented orthographically.

Verse theory asks questions about what kind of thing a poem is, in ontological terms (its locus or site); about how verbal texts used for aesthetic ends (verbal art) differ from those used for communication or play or any other function (verbal nonart); about how verse differs from prose (see VERSE AND PROSE) and intermedia such as rhymeprose and the prose poem (qq.v.); about what resources verseform offers for expression not available in prose or speech; about what form is, what kinds of forms are possible, what effects forms have (see METER), and what happens to verbal material when it is laid into artistic forms; about the relation of acoustic features to semantic ones in verse; and about the relation of text features to reader reception and cognition. Pros. is therefore not merely formalist; central to its method is the nexus between text structures and readerly effects (see below). Its first assumption is that cognitive equivalences arise from formal equivalences.

II. BOUND SPEECH. Two facts about the condition of poetry are immediately obvious to anyone. First, poetry is made out of words. When Degas complained to Mallarmé that he was having trouble coming up with any noble sentiments or profound thoughts to put into a poem, Mallarmé replied that poetry isn't made out of ideas; it is made out of words. All artists create art out of the materials available—in painting, canvas and paint; in sculpture and the plastic arts, stone or plastic or metal; in drama and cinema, action; in poetry, lang. This is not to say that what is made is wholly limited by the medium—to say that would be to close down the whole concept of expression. It is precisely the great interest of art that it *seems* capable of extending or transcending the medium. But art nevertheless inexorably arises from the medium, hence attention to the opportunities and constraints that the medium offers will tell us much about what art is capable of. As A. M. Clark observed, "the artist's experience is conceived in terms of his medium"; his "desire to create is directed to, and conditioned by, the possibilities and the resistances of the medium" (171).

In the art world, it would never occur to anybody to deny the value of inquiry into the concepts of formal structure and expressiveness. But in poetics, close attention to the medium has often been disparaged as too mechanical, too artificial—too alien, somehow, to the "spirit" of *poetry*. Many sensitive readers of poetry have recoiled from close prosodic analysis, muttering, as they retreated, Wordsworth's "we murder to dissect." And it is certainly true that pros. as practiced in the late 19th and early 20th cs. was handled badly, with nearly obsessive interest in mere counting and terminology. But in the second half of the 20th c., mainly as a result of major new work in comparative metrics, the theory of verse has taken on the status of a fundamental component of literary theory, alongside issues of reader response and cultural conditioning.

Second, in most poems there are very few words. An average sonnet probably contains not many more than a hundred words. Yet one of the most widely held beliefs about poetry is that poems "say" more than prose. If so, then each word must find ways of bearing more meaning than it would in prose. Every possible resource the word offers must be exploited—its sound shape, its size and weight, its visual shape, its position, its effects on its neighbors. In the most general terms, poetry does more with less by heightening the degree of design or order. Verseform gives to the lang. of poetry, on account of this excess of design, a supercharged quantity of meaning, a semantic density not found in ordinary prose. As Pound said, the function of pros. is simply "to charge words with meaning to the utmost possible degree" (*ABC* 36). Poetry enriches meaning by compounding form even as it compacts lang. This idea, that verse is more ordered, more tightly bound than ordinary lang., is ancient, and applies to forms as diverse as runic inscriptions, sacramental chants, incantations, epics, verse dramas, all manner of lyrics and songs, pattern poems (q.v.), even "language poetry" (q.v.). Verse is "bound speech" (Ger. *gebundene Rede*), lang. subjected to additional constraint. It was Cicero who said, "things that are bound together have much more force than things that are loose." Since the ordering in poetry is mainly submorphemic, we may say that, in the main, phonological constraints are increased in poetry while syntactic constraints are relaxed.

But the notion that verse compounds order is not the aspect of poetry which first occurs to most readers: they think of poetry first as the expression of emotion—i.e. as lyrical. There is little reason to cavil at this: it is obvious that poetry most often concerns moments of heightened emotion, heightened consciousness, more intense life—moments that might well seem the most removed from order. Yet it is one of the great imponderables of conscious life, as mysterious as indisputable, that "intense emotion causes pattern to arise in the mind" (Pound). Utterances which seem the most "natural" often have the most internal structure, repetition, and design. In all moments of heightened emotion, joyous or grieving, we are given to instinctive and automatic repetition when we speak. Most of Cl. rhetoric is built on this fact, which public speakers, clergymen, and politicians know well: the orator is taught the devices for the figuration of lang. which will make it seem most like spontaneous and impassioned speech. "Under the inspiration of high imaginings," says Omond, man has always "expressed himself in regular periods." And this law of "rhythmical expression" has nothing to do with lineation or even print; the proper distinction, as Shelley said, is not between verse and prose, but simply between "measured and unmeasured lang." In short, some sort of formal design or measuring principle is the *sine qua non* of verse.

Nevertheless, there is a general belief that the forms of verse—meter, rhyme, stanza—are an impediment to expression, and that such forms merely make poetry "difficult." Recalling that all art takes place in a medium, which is by definition alien to expression, we may well agree with Clark that "artistic incarnation of any kind is always the result of struggle against the obstruction offered by the medium on the one hand and against the formal limitations on the other. An artist's creativeness thus functions within constraint and through opposition" (172).

What could be the use of constraint and opposition? One answer that has been suggested is that diverting attention away from the problem of what to say on the larger semantic or thematic level to the strictly verbal problem of, say, finding a rhyme frees the mind to work out the problems of conception and expression more creatively. "In each art the difficulty of the form is a substitute for the difficulty of direct apprehension and expression of the object" (Richard Wilbur). Another theory suggests that it is precisely the poet's having to conform to a pattern such as rhyme that leads to the discovery of new verbal avenues not previously apprehended, one of which will almost certainly turn out to be productive. Third, from the perspective of information theory, the superimposition of further order on verbal series compounds the codes in the channel and thereby increases the amount of information delivered in the same time. Fourth, increase of text complexity increases reader attention. Viktor Shklovsky, the Rus. Formalist, held that "the technique of art is to make objects 'unfamiliar,' and so increase the difficulty and length of perception, because the process of perception is an aesthetic end in itself and must be prolonged. Art is a way of experiencing the artfulness of an object; the object is not important" (1924).

Verseform, then, is no constraint, or if it is, only for an inferior poet. For a more inventive poet, forms become, rather, opportunities, ways of proceeding, routes for mapping meaning. "It is clear," says Baudelaire, "that systems of rhet. and prosodies are not forms of tyranny arbitrarily devised, but a collection of rules required by the very organization of the spiritual being: prosodies and systems of rhet. have never prevented originality from manifesting itself distinctly. The opposite would be far more true, that they have been a help to the blossoming-forth of originality" (*L'Art romantique* [1885], tr. Maritain).

III. STRUCTURES AND EFFECTS. Much of the justification for the study of verse- and text-structure is given by Quintilian (ca. 90 A.D.), whose defense of the uses of *compositio* or "artistic structure" (*Institutio oratoria*, Bk. 9, ch. 4) is still one of the most important accounts ever given. Quintilian opposes the claim of those who hold that ordinary or spontaneous speech is the most "natural": "What does not ripen with cultivation? Why do we train the vine? . . . No, that which is most natural is that which nature permits to be done to the greatest perfection. How can a style which lacks orderly structure be stronger than one that is welded together and artistically arranged?" Hence "all the best scholars are convinced that the study of artistic structure is of the utmost value, not merely for charming the ear, but for stirring the soul. For in the first place nothing can penetrate to the emotions that stumbles at the portals of the ear, and secondly man is naturally attracted by harmonious sounds." This is as true in music as in rhet. Word choice is certainly important to the orator, but "however important the selection of words for the expression of our thoughts, the structural art which wields them together in the body of a period or rounds them off at the close, has at least an equal claim to importance. . . . In fact, if we break up and disarrange any sentence that may have struck us as vigorous, charming, or elegant, we shall find that all its force, attraction and grace have disappeared."

This last point—that the ordering of words (sounds) is at least as important as the words themselves—justifies Quintilian's central claim, which is that artistic structures create effects. There is linkage between text features and reader response. The ancient rhetoricians developed elaborate theories about the effects of specific structures, even down to such minute elements as vowel-and-consonant combinations. Modern prosodists do not recognize such specificity of linkage, even as modern musicians no longer accept the theory of modes, and nearly all readily acknowledge some variance of response even among informed readers, but none has suggested abandoning altogether the principle of linkage itself. And to poets, the efficacy if not the necessity of prosodic structure is simple fact.

Indeed, the elaborate machinery of analytical pros.—e.g. scansion—is simply an attempt to make explicit the agency of the nexus between structures and effects. The mechanism of, say, metrical feet may not explain the dynamics of rhythms, but it is at least one way—even if an awkward one—of talking about them. Quintilian himself concludes his inventory of combinations of metrical feet with the reminder that what is important ultimately is not the machinery of analysis but the resultant understanding of the instinctive and natural process which produced rhythmic structure to begin with: "Prose-structure, of course, existed before rhythms were discovered in it, just as poetry was originally the outcome of a natural impulse and was created by the instinctive feeling of the ear for quantity and the observation of time and rhythm, while the discovery of feet came later. . . . It is possible to have an inadequate understanding of what it is precisely that makes for severity or charm, but yet to produce the required effect better by taking nature for our guide in the place of art: nonetheless there will always be some principle of art underlying the promptings of nature." Prosodic rules (q.v.) may often be clumsy in conception or notation. But that they are attempts to formulate processes which do exist is, as Quintilian insists, beyond question.

Such analytic machinery as scansions and rhyme schemes also sometimes give the impression that the forms pros. treats are "abstract." But it is as unproductive to deal for very long with forms as abstractions as it is to make a naive distinction between "content" and "form." Sound itself is form, a waveform imposed on the air. Lang. is a set of forms, not any specific medium for them, not even sound—witness sign lang. All linguistic meaning is therefore already a set of forms, not something apart from form. As W. S. Johnson remarks, "there is no pure and independent form"; "while formal relationships can be perceived without reference to the semantic function of lang. . . they cannot be *determined*, nor can they be analyzed, without referring to the meaning of words." Poetic form is not external to meaning, and "a regular verse form is not a ready-made container into which an emotion is poured" (Irwin). Though abstract schemas have their uses, most of the effects of interest in poetry are local and semantic (see Wright). Even when one focuses on only one prosodic form—e.g. the iambic pentameter—most of the effect depends on how it is filled. The iambic pentameter line in Eng. has a very different texture than it does in Ger. or Rus., not to speak of its analogues in the Romance langs.

IV. VERSEFORM. It is verseform which enables the distinction between verse and prose (q.v.), key terms in any discussion of poetry. It was reportedly Jeremy Bentham who said that he knew poetry when he saw it: the words did not run all the way to the right-hand side of the page. But this seems a little confused: surely Bentham was not talking about *poetry* but rather *verse*. Verseform is the mode of presentation of lang. which segments speech into *lines*, which on the printed page do not fill all the space to the right, or in recitation are marked at their ends for aural recognition (see LINE). Poetry, most of us would say, is something else, something less definite. Poetry is memorable speech, the tale of the tribe (Pound), the best words in the best order (Coleridge), the thing that makes you cut yourself, shaving, when you remember the best of it (Housman). Yet everyone can think of passages of prose which seem memorable, incantatory, powerful, "poetic." We have, then, not two terms, poetry and prose, but three—poetry, prose, and verse. Pros. poses these terms as an equation and asks a simple question: why is poetry written in verse? What is it about verseform that causes speech to be perceived as "poetic"? Since it is palpable that no single feature can be identified which is present in poetry though not in prose or speech, the differentia can only lie in degree of order, which leads to difference in kind. Patterns bind up segments into wholes. Division into lines is one form of segmentation, and the several devices of sound patterning within lines (e.g. meter) and across lines (rhyme) are merely extensions of the same principle deeper into the fabric of lang.

In speech and prose, segmentation is motivated by semantics and expressed in syntax: in general, phrases and clauses are as long as speakers want them to be. Repetition, rhythm, sound patterning, and rhetorical ornament are discouraged in modern expository prose, where the aim is to make meaning transparent. In oratorical and art prose such as Cicero's speeches, Gibbon's *Decline and Fall of the Roman Empire*, Lincoln's Gettysburg Address, or Churchill's wartime speeches, such devices are encouraged, but even here only in moderation. Verse however makes rhythm or repetition (q.v.)—what De Groot calls correspondence and what Jakobson calls *equivalence* (q.v.)—its principle, whether based on phonological features (meter, rhyme) or syntactic ones (parallelism [q.v.]).

In verse, the cutting, *découpage* (Cohen), or scissoring (Wesling) of the syntagm is handled so that the segments are equivalent to each other not semantically or syntactically but by virtue of an arbitrary phonological pattern. If sound and sense are coterminous in speech and prose, they are set into equipoise in verse. Many theorists have testified to their sense that the segmentation of verse-structure in some way runs across, or in counterpoint (q.v.) to, that of prose, and hence that all lines of verse are necessarily "to double business bound." Cognitive and aesthetic structures overwrite each other. "The figure of grammar in a poem," says Wesling, "occupies the same poetic space as the figure of rhythmic sound," with the result that "gathering rhythmic and lexical power in a word makes meaning burst forth." Cohen suggests that the differential nature of the lang. system pointed out by Saussure is reversed by the homophony in poetic lang., which doubles the message and so becomes an altogether different mode of discourse (87, 99). "Literariness," therefore, is not a question of any particular form, nor even solely a matter of the degree to which forms are applied, but rather a question of forms being made systematic and so altering fundamentally the nature of the system.

Since verseform therefore produces effects not obtainable in prose, or obtainable (at best) only to a limited degree, we must say, against most of the Ren. critics, that poetry is not an imitative art but a constitutive art. Prosodic effects are not primarily mimetic, hence pros. is not confined to any mimetic theory of crit. (see POETRY, THEORIES OF). Prosodic structures, unlike lexical, semantic, logical, figural, or imagistic, make little effort to be representational of objects or processes in the external world. Granted, mimetic effects are more extensive than most readers suspect (see Wimsatt 1976), and Dr. Johnson's strictures against "representative meter" are excessive (see METER), but on the whole they are not central to verseform. Prosodic structures do not, mainly, stand for or point to things, they *do* things. The rhythm of a line is not an imitation of a rhythm in life or even in speech so much as it is a framework which controls, inflects, paces, and nuances the meanings of the words it is carried by. It is not even a description of a rhythm: it is an *enactment* of a rhythm that is delivered for cognitive processing at the same time that lexical or emotive or imagistic information is delivered. Therefore what a theory of rhythm (or meter) treats is not the representational or referential character of signifiers but rather relations between signifiers generated directly— i.e. presentationally—in the performance or reading of the poem.

This is not, as Krieger would have it, the illusion of presence, but in fact presence itself, for sounds are being chosen now not out of the differential system of lang. but out of the equivalential system of verse, in which representation gives way to presentation. The choice of signifiers (sounds) in verse is motivated not primarily on grounds of representation but on account of other sounds in the system, all of which act in consort to create a design. One might think this no improvement, but the net of words does not capture by virtue of its holes— which are frequent, in fact predominant—but by virtue of its cords. Meter, rhyme, and sound-patterning motivate and naturalize words that would in prose seem arbitrary and dislocated.

Most generally, the functions of verseform are four: to attract attention, to please the ear, to make meaning more dense, and to make speech worth remembering. Dr. Johnson called verbal music "that harmony that adds force to reason, and gives grace to subtlety, that shackles attention, and governs passions" (*Rambler* 88). All verse devices function to deautomatize the reading process, heightening attention, intensifying perception, and preventing habituated response. Lineation of discourse is a generic marker identifying it as verse

if not "poetry" and adumbrating intensified speech, wherein meaning is compacted. In general, sound patterning establishes semantic relationships, either of similarity or contrast, other than those generated lexically, and so provides a second stratum of meaning, thereby drawing readerly attention to semantic links between words that might not otherwise be noticed. So in Shakespeare's sonnets, for example, essential semantic relations are established in homophonic echoing of such paired terms as *tombe—wombe* (86.4), *hunted—hated* (129.6), and *captive-good attending Captain ill* (66.12; see Booth). Sound patterning of all sorts is normally perceived as pleasurable, as is the perception of all design so long as it does not overwhelm meaning.

V. THEORY. The structure of the theory of verse rests upon a series of initial distinctions concerning (1) text versus experience of the poem, i.e. latent form versus realization; and (2) elements which are essential to the design of the poem itself hence cannot vary from one reader to another, and elements which permissibly vary among readers. In Jakobson's schema (1960), the fundamental distinction is one between design and instance, both of the verse itself as a text or else series of norms, and of any performance (or reading) of it. "Verse design" and "verse instance" therefore flank "delivery design" and "delivery instance"; for further discussion, see METER, section II.

Traditional pros. had three components: (1) rhythmics, or theory of rhythm (rhythmicity as a perceptual mode; the kinds of rhythmic forms and their modes of combination), which includes metrics, meter being simply one type of rhythm; (2) sonics or harmonics, or theory of sound-patterning, its types (particularly rhyme) and effects (see SOUND; EUPHONY; RHYME); and (3) strophics (see STANZA), the theory of the forms poetry may assume above the level of the line. Unfortunately, however, these components—meter, sound patterning (incl. rhyme), and stanza—were treated as if they were independent and virtually unrelated topics. Indeed, enormous effort has been wasted in the past producing studies in only one area which duplicate work in other areas, or use inconsistent terminology or methods, or fail to integrate such work within a wider field theory of versestructure.

Of the three components, rhythmics (metrics) historically has been far more extensively discussed than the other two; indeed, many critics think of metrics and pros. as synonymous. But theory of rhythm is still in a very rudimentary state (see RHYTHM; METER), and metrics only a little less so, much ink having been spilled over the single issue of metrical "feet" (see FOOT). It is obvious, however, that rhythms can be constructed in only a few ways. The simplest is to establish a single unit of structure and repeat it identically, joining units end to end; only slightly more complex is concatenation (q.v.). Some "dovetailing" of one type of colon to another type with a complementary end (e.g. masculine and feminine) is also possible. Headlam suggested that early Gr. lyric was constructed of rhythmical phrases, each distinctive in aural shape to the audience, and that the whole art of the lyric consisted "in passing from one rhythm to another while keeping the movement going all the time." He identified three devices which effected transitions: link, echo, and overlapping (216). West identified some basic principles for producing more complex metrical forms out of simpler ones in his outline of eight "procedures by which successive verses are generated" in Gr. odes (64–65).

Our understanding of sound patterning and of stanza is even less developed than of metrics, in part because intralinear structures are often more vestigial and localized, in part because the relations of sound to meaning have been more difficult to describe systematically, in part because structures such as rhyme seemed discrete. Rhyme was traditionally treated as sound equivalence between line-terminal syllables. De Cornulier, however, has argued that rhymes do not exist merely at the end of the line, in isolation from the rest of the line's structure: they arise from and in turn deeply affect that structure and so must be said, strictly speaking, to be spread over the entire line. Rhymed verse, in short, is not rhymeless verse with the jingle of like endings added, but a fundamentally different mode of verse structure throughout.

To date, the most extensive and sophisticated effort to map out the relationships between sound (acoustic structures) and meaning (semantic effects) is the schema given by Levý in 1961. Here the three basic principles of serial ordering are identified as discontinuity, hierarchy, and irregularity, along with their opposites, continuity, equivalence, and regularity. These are the forms of linear arrangement of sound. Since meaning, too, is effectually linear, i.e. sequentially revealed, the three physical principles of linear arrangement correspond to three semantic ones, namely incoherence, intensity, and unexpectedness, along with their opposites, coherence, lack of intensity, and predictability. These are the "forms of meaning." But sound also has some "inherent acoustic meanings" or "a priori semantic values" which are mimetic or expressive (see ONOMATOPOEIA; TIMBRE); these are manifested in the direction, rate, and change of articulation itself, and may be measured on scales of semantic space such as Osgood's semantic-differential test. These comprise the "meanings of form." Most generally, "the relations between the acoustic and semantic levels [in verse] consist not in a one-to-one relation between segments of both levels, but in a parallel morphology of the two systems as wholes," i.e. a systematic homomorphism.

If verse theory is articulated at a sufficiently general level, i.e. as a "general field theory" of verse, where the issues are ones simply of segmentation (see FOOT; METER) and repetition (q.v.) on the formal level, and of structure and effect on the semantic level, all three types of phenomena—meter, sound, stanza—might be shown to follow from one set of principles which apply at all levels of verseform (Lotman), i.e. which apply for verse to be verse at all (Olson). Some writers would say that such a theory amounts to a theory of repetition, others of rhythm, but these are merely terminological difficulties in describing objective phenomena and the subjective perception thereof. If rhythm and repetition overwrite the same verbal space, we may see both as deriving from the same underlying problem in epistemology. The problem of rhythm in fact has roots that tap directly into the bedrock of Western metaphysics. If rhythm is the perceptual (subjective) structuring of a series of repeated (objective) events, then its nature is essentially phenomenological. But so, surely, is that of repetition. During the cognitive processing of the text in reading, what was, in the past, a present moment is retrieved and re-enacted. Repetition re-instantiates the present at successive intervals and, in so doing, thwarts the hegemony of mere successiveness, which is entropic. Serial experience is overwritten with synchral. In *Four Quartets*, Eliot's speaker wonders how "words, after speech, reach / Into the silence." The answer seems to be that "Only by the form, the pattern, / Can words or music reach / The stillness." In order to be able to use words to reach into the silence, we seem to need a pattern to extend in front of us. Pattern is achieved by repetition, and repetition functions by suspending sequence.

In a fully deployed theory of verse structure, all forms of figuration would be synthesized and schematized into one grid, with layering for the phonological, morphological, syntactic, and perhaps discursive levels of lang., lexical choices and semantic effects being seen simply as manifestations of such figuration (Lotman). Such a grid or typology would derive all the manifold varieties of metrical, sonal, rhymic, and stanzaic structures from only a few fundamental processes which apply at differing positions in the line (verse syntagm) or at differing levels of lang. structure (verse paradigm).

VI. CRITERIA. Given the fact that no comprehensive theory presently exists, it is worth trying to specify what such a theory must do. There are nine requirements for a unified field theory of verse:

(1) It must address the fundamental issue of the ontological status or situs of poetry—whether oral/aural or written/visual, or both, and if both, how—and the ensuing distinctions must be reflected explicitly in all definitions (e.g. "line"), methodologies, and conclusions. Since the advent of writing some three millennia ago and the invention of printing a scant half millennium ago, poetry has had two modes for its auditors/readers, one aural, the other visual. But these are not finally independent, and a general theory of pros.

must give an account of both and of their complex interrelations. Much older work does not clearly distinguish poetry's two modes—the poem seen and the poem heard—and draws evidence or arguments indiscriminately from the one or the other as convenient (but see Hollander). Many prosodic concepts depend on recognizing both— "eye rhyme," for example. But it is manifest that the modes of apprehension for the poem heard are not those for the poem seen. The 17th- and 18th-c. quarrel about blank verse being "verse only to the eye," for example, rested on a conception of line-ends as aural entities which would be indistinguishable if not marked by rhyme. The deeper issue concerned the definition of "line."

(2) It must be comparative. It must not privilege any verse-system, modern or Cl., as the paradigm, but place all in a neutral typology which will reveal the differences between superficially similar systems and the hidden similarities between seemingly diverse systems. It is as dangerous, says Olson, to build a theory on any one, lang.-specific pros. as it is to assume "that a difference of lang. entails a difference of principle." A form in one lang. may well have very different effects from its analogue in another, but some metrical principles—e.g. catalexis (q.v.)—apply across langs. Arguably the worst mistake that poets and prosodists have made, historically, has been to read the metrical rules of one lang. onto another *tout court* without due consideration of the systematic differences between the two systems. (Note, however, that this may imply the nonexistence of metrical universals analogous to linguistic universals [see METER]). The paradigm for all Med., Ren., and post-Ren. prosodic theory was Cl. In the 20th c., it has mainly been Eng. But Eng. is not obviously a very representative case, for Eng. verse in its historical devel. was a complex hybrid form (see Legouis).

Since verse theory in the West took about two millennia to shake off the stifling effects of Classicism, and since linguistics did not mature as a science until the 20th c., it would be reasonable to conclude that the comparative study of pros. on sound literary *and* linguistic principles is, as Maas held in 1923 and La Drière reasserted in 1959, still in a nascent stage. We do not yet have a comprehensive theory of verse; we do not even have an adequate description of the verse-system most familiar to us, Eng. The main outlines are known, but several key issues are still uncertain and many details are largely a mystery. We know somewhat more for Rus., but less for Fr., little for Chinese, and virtually nothing for most African langs. Over the past century, though, important research toward a general field theory has been produced by comparativists such as Parry, Kurylowicz, Watkins, and Gasparov, as well as by researchers in national poetries cognizant of the comparative perspective—e.g. Scott and de Cornulier in Fr.; Sievers, Lehmann, and Kuhn in Ger.; and Jakobson among many other Rus., Czech, and Polish scholars. This research continues to await integration with the work of theorists such as Lotman and Levý. Only when we know much more about many verse trads. and have a theory in which to frame them will we be able to give a comprehensive explanation of how poetry works.

Verse theory, that is, must incorporate difference as a principle of typology. It must accept the differences between verse systems as fundamental and irrefrangible. It is a mistake, for example, to treat all 8-syllable lines as a class, to assume that the Lat. *octonarius*, the Sp. *octosílabo*, the Fr. *octosyllabe*, and the Eng. or Rus. iambic tetrameter are automatic equivalents—i.e. that they have the same structure or give the same effects—for they are not: each resides within a metrical system which controls those structures and effects and so must be taken into account. Pros. must explain the devel. of these systems themselves; historical phonology must explain the evolution of the langs. on which they are built. Analogous or correlate forms in different verse systems have a different "feel": they generate a different set of semantic associations and generic expectations. This is not to say that commonalties between systems do not exist— they do—but only that systemic differences cannot be swept under the rug of generality. They must be built into the theory.

(3) It must re-establish its rapport with Cl. pros., not on the old bases but on new ones, viewing Cl. Gr. as but one verse-system among the world's many, albeit perhaps the most sophisticated one. Most of the late 19th- and early 20th-c. work in Eng. pros. drew heavily on Cl. pros. as then understood. But Cl. pros. itself after Wilamowitz, Maas, Parry, and Dale replaced some key concepts. If the Eng. metrists of Saintsbury's day followed the Cl. system too readily, fifty years later there were few if any Eng. metrists who had any thorough familiarity with recent developments in Cl. pros. at all. Disciplinary specialization had taken its toll.

(4) It must make a place for syntax. Traditional pros. was based on phonology: it assumed that the phonological elements of lang. were the elements organized by verse-structure. This made metrics and sound patterning the central components. Nonmetrical prosodies such as free verse were consequently problems for pros., which had no taxonomy or general field theory within which they could be treated. Such avant-garde prosodies were therefore disparaged by reactionary prosodists like Saintsbury. Verse syntax was recognized in traditional pros. in such phenomena as enjambment and the verse paragraph (q.v.), but only indirectly and derivatively. In the wake of Chomsky's 1957 revolution of grammar, linguists began to study syntax then phonology as a set of hierarchies of elements constrained by rules for change, but the interaction between phonology and syntax continued to elude full understanding, despite

important studies such as Selkirk (*Phonology and Syntax* [1984]). At the same time, it became increasingly clear to literary prosodists that any adequate field theory of verse-structure would have to incorporate syntax—witness the devel. of "grammetrics" (q.v.)—i.e. would have to be framed more widely than traditionally conceived, so as to provide an explanatory matrix for all verse prosodies, metrical and nonmetrical, even aural and visual, and the (relatively common) prosodies which mix aspects of both.

(5) It must build theory on all possible facts about the distribution of prosodic features in the major poets of each lang., based on accurate historical phonology (e.g. for rhymes) and made available in electronic format (esp. databases along with texts) for use and expansion by scholars worldwide. If we accept the notions of a variorum edition of a poet and a variorum commentary, we should also want to have variorum metrical indices giving data on rhymes, stanza forms, and scansions, with computer programs included for further analysis and comparison. Accurate prosodic facts are the first requisite for integration of formal information in any interp. of poetry.

It is shocking to realize that even today we still do not have complete and reliable information about such obvious matters as meters, rhymes, and stanza forms for more than a handful of poets. Empirical and mathematical work on meter has been prominent in Slavic pros., esp. in the work of Tomaševskij, M. Lotman, and Gasparov, as well as in the exported Eng. version, the so-called "Rus. linguistic-statistical method" of Tarlinskaja (see METER), but only certain kinds of data have been collected and a very great deal still remains to be done. As for rhymes and stanzas, some few older works are still of value (e.g. Martinon 1912), but most are obsolete, and most of the empirical work in 19th-c. Ger. dissertations was based on poor texts or weak theory or both. Only since Frank's pioneering work on Provençal (1953–57) have reliable stanza indexes begun to appear. Some stanza indexing has been done for Fr. and Ger. (see Brogan 1989), but none, astonishingly, for Eng. This is a statement about what the late 20th-c. vogue for literary "theory" has done to crit. Few would hold that collection of facts is the sole end of scholarship, certainly. But without modes of verification, theories may proliferate ad infinitum with no grounds for preferring one over any of the others. The validity of a theory is determined not by how many people happen to hold it at any one point in time but rather by how well it fits the corpus of available evidence at that time.

Empirical research, however, must not be treated naively. Some empirical prosodists at work today have denied they have any theory, claiming their conclusions only arise from the data. But empirical data is never innocent of theoretical presuppositions, for in collecting data a researcher has already implicitly answered the prior questions of what categories exist, what count as entities to collect, and which of these are significant and which not—in short, what counts as a "fact." These answers constitute a theory. Pros. is therefore no less theoretical or critical than any other area of poetics; the only difference lies in the fact that claims advanced in pros. are susceptible of proof according to how well they fit the data. This does not consign all prosodic inquiry to the realm of the scientific; data is meaningless until interpreted, and it is critical judgment not distribution patterns in the data which determines which facts about a poem we will take as significant. If many older prosodists erred in thinking pros. a science, many modern critics and theorists err in forgetting facts or denying judgment.

(6) It must settle the issue of the status of psychological and reader-response studies. On the one hand, there is serious question what status psychological studies should have in poetics. Many formalist critics (e.g. Wimsatt) showed unrelenting resistance to such work, denying that it has any validity at all for a theory of crit. Psychological theories, they say, come and go; texts remain. Such critics have held that asking readers about their perception of meter is a waste of time, for the answers by definition apply only at the level of rhythm, not meter. If meter is abstraction and rhythm actualization, these critics maintain, psychological studies cannot tell us about meter. At the very least, one may concede, asking *uninformed* respondents is unproductive, for meter is governed by a complex set of conventions that must be learned. On this account, metrical verse is a skilled craft, hence only *trained* readers count as informants.

On the other hand, it is obvious that we want to know much more than we presently do about how readers perceive and read (process) verse. Some features of sound patterning, for example—such as the widely dispersed rhymes in *Paradise Lost*—simply lie below the threshold of perceptibility and so are not noticed by readers even though they exist. Some of the older psychological studies of pros. still seem sound, but many now look to be flawed beyond repair—and not a few modern ones along with them (see Brogan). The emerging discipline of cognitive science may yet hold promise of a synthetic approach which will conceive the bases for perception and cognitive processing more comprehensively than those of the old psychology and so give us a "cognitive poetics" (so Tsur). Says Wesling: "when lit. crit. can complete linguistic metrics, and when it can in turn be completed by being deepened with a cognitive psychology of the reader, and when it can be fully historicized—then we shall have a pros. adequate to the greatness and range of poetry."

(7) It must differentiate linguistics from poetics, recognizing that the former is merely instrumental to the latter. *Pace* Jakobson, aesthetics is not a subcategory of linguistics simply treating one

type of lang.-use; it is axiomatic of verse theory that poetic lang. is a wholly different mode of discourse from ordinary speech (see below). "Literary pros.," says La Drière, "is not directly concerned with the use which lang. makes of rhythm for linguistic ends; it is more properly concerned with the use which rhythmic impulse makes of lang. for its own ends, when those are involved with the processes or forms of rhet. and poetry." Linguistics cannot subsume literary pros. for several reasons. One is that it has never been shown that the distribution of linguistic systems in the world is congruent with the classification of verse-systems; most likely it is not. Both Ir. and Welsh are Celtic langs., but their verse-systems developed quite different characters. Another is the fact that verse imposes on lang. structures additional constraints which are purely conventional and aesthetic. Many forces come to bear on the devel. of a verse-system other than merely what the lang. makes possible. Study of linguistics tells us about lang.-structures, not about the nature, history, or interp. (q.v.) of poetry, on which stylistics and semiotics (qq.v.) have more direct bearing. The interest taken by linguists in poetic texts in the 20th c. did not directly lead to a deeper understanding of poetry but rather to a more shallow one, for to them poems were only data. Having no grasp of literary convention, they committed the "linguistic fallacy"—assuming that the rules of lang. are the only rules that control poetry. Poetry being the art of words, pros. rightly makes use of linguistic information, but only to know what lang. makes possible, not what art makes possible.

On this view, all linguistic and psychological studies of lang. and rhythm are merely preliminary. They can never tell us more than half the story. It is true that verbal devices in poetry are simply extensions and foregroundings of processes already at work in lang. itself (see Brogan, sect. C). But the nature of poetic lang. is fundamentally different. Verbal signs in poetry are not pointed toward signifieds nor even simply raised to a higher pitch: by being given pattern, they become presentational and constitutive in their own system. That is why the use of poetic devices in prose only causes confusion: such devices momentarily thicken the transparency of the sign and thereby divert the reader's attention away from sense to the play of the pattern.

(8) It must remove the artificial distinction within poetics between rhetoric and pros. Traditionally, sound patterning and metrics were both treated s.v. "pros.," while lexical selection and syntactic patterning were not: syntactic figures were treated, if at all, as rhetorical schemes. But of course metrical patterns and rhetorical figures unfold simultaneously: they overwrite the same verbal space. This has led to considerable confusion and duplication across the two disciplines. Concatenation (q.v.), for example, is a general structural device or form which can manifest itself

as pros., rhet., lexical repetition, or semantics. In pros. it is Eng. *chain rhyme* (q.v.), Ger. *Kettenreim*; in rhet., *anadiplosis* and *climax* (qq.v.); in lexical repetition, *ploce* and *echo* (qq.v.); and in semantics and logic, *sorites*. Similarly, chiasmus (q.v.) in rhet. is "reverse rhyme" (q.v.) in pros. Eventually it should be possible to give a synthetic taxonomy of forms of figuration such as the one Group Mu gives for rhet. (Group Mu, 45) subsuming all the terms used in different disciplines for the same structural processes at work on each level of the stratification of the text.

(9) It must reclaim its position as an irrefragable component of poetics, the only road to any adequate semiotics of poetry (Grimaud). Locally, within each line, verse structure is always semantic in nature: it shapes, alters, and adds to lexical meaning, hence it is an indispensable component of any theory of interp. or hermeneutics (qq.v.). Lotman says that "all types of secondary equivalences lead to the formation of supplementary semantic units in a text. The phenomenon of structure in a line always, in the final analysis, turns out to be the phenomenon of meaning" (119). Since all form is semantic, a formal system is a secondary semantic system, 'secondary" meaning not derivative but doubled. Verseform, in short is a multiplier of meaning, and "the movement of the verse," as Richards said, "becomes the movement of the meaning" (*Coleridge* 119). Here the work of Levý (see above) mapping out the relations of sound to meaning is central.

VII. HISTORY OF THEORY. No full, reliable, comparative history of Western verse theory has yet been written. The difficulty in writing one is not merely the number of langs. involved, nor even the uncertainties of rhythmic theory, but also the fact that it must cover more ground than merely poetry. Historically, the prosodic aspects of lang. have been common ground for three areas of critical discourse—grammar, music, and rhet. All three have contributed extensive theorizing, some of it confused in itself, and even more so when set against the other areas; there is no common terminology. Still, there is a great deal to be learned by patient sifting of ancient texts.

There were two schools of prosodists in antiquity, the *metrici* and *rhythmici*, i.e. grammarians and musical theorists. The former school analyzed verse by identifying and counting units, the latter by specifying time values for the durations of units (see METER). Chief among the former is Hephaestion, and among the latter Aristoxenus of Tarentum. St. Augustine's *De musica* represents a late conflation of both schools. Cl. rhet. (e.g. Quintilian, Cicero) included treatment of prosodic issues mainly under the rubric of prose rhythm (q.v.), carried into medieval rhet. as the *cursus*, but in the main, literary pros. strictly speaking was treated under the aegis of grammar up to the 12th c. Thereafter, medieval interest in verse structure is taken up again in rhet., in the *artes poetriae* (see

Hardison) and the Fr. *Seconde Rhétorique* (q.v.), then in musical theory, as in *vers mesurée* (q.v.). In the Ren., the locus of interest reverts to grammar (see Brogan 1981, Intro.).

Up to the 20th c., most of the analytic machinery of pros. was still heavily Cl. Some crucial linguistic terminology necessary to describe prosodic phenomena (esp. stress) did not develop until the 18th c. Romanticism made much—in theory, though not in praxis—of the repudiation of conscious craft and the study of technique. The 19th c. was dominated by the rise in Germany of Cl. Philology, followed by Germanic, Romance, Celtic, and finally Eng. Numbingly empiricist at times, wholly committed to the scientific method, and inflexibly Cl. in its fundamental categories and terms, philological pros. all too often produced studies that were both tedious in detail and impoverished in conception. Saintsbury wrote three volumes on pros. evincing an almost complete (and willful) obtuseness about theory. The legacy of such work was the widespread perception of verse theory as mechanistic, pseudo-scientific, and eccentric, leaving the work of more sophisticated scholars (Bridges, Omond, Taig, Stewart) marginalized or ignored. One of the great ironies of the history of pros. is that a coherent understanding of it did not emerge until after the system itself had collapsed. The division among the ancients was in fact carried down to the 20th c.: it betokens a more fundamental uncertainty in poetics about the ontological status of poetry—whether object or experience. These latter are not, however, two answers to the same question but rather answers to two related but different questions.

Arguably, the most important prosodic work of the 20th c. was carried on under the aegis of Rus. Formalism (q.v.), whose chief tenet was that "if literary scholarship is to become a discipline, then it must make the literary device its only champion, for the object of literary scholarship is not lit. but literariness, that is, that which makes a given work a work of lit." (Jakobson). The Formalists and Prague-School structuralists (see STRUCTURALISM) sought in "the device" a criterion which would distinguish between poetic lang. and other types of discourse, just as the Am. New Critics sought to contrast the langs. of poetry and science. The only difficulty was that no single device or set of devices could be isolated as the invariable differentia of verse; all appear in vestigial form in prose and mixed modes. The Formalists therefore drew the conclusion that poetic lang. was heightened in degree of structure and had a different, self-referential function (Jakobson's "poetic function"), the New Critics that devices (or tropes) such as irony, paradox, and tension (qq.v.) privileged its status as an autonomous "verbal icon." But Jakobson buried the artfulness of verbal art in linguistics, and New Critical verse analysis was too conservative and dogmatic to entertain study of the cultural conditioning or cognitive processing of texts

by readers—both essential to any fully developed poetics.

Philological and impressionistic pros. were dead ends, but the work of Rus. Formalism did not become widely known in the West until the Sixties. In the interim, a fresh approach first appears in the 1940s with the application of structural linguistics to metrics (Lotz, Whitehall) and extends into the Sixties, followed by "generative metrics" (q.v.), which sought to apply the framework of transformational grammar and had a vogue from 1966 to ca. 1980. Linguistic approaches dominated the secondary lit. of pros. for nearly three decades (see Brogan). Indeed, most literary prosodists made the mistake of eagerly embracing every new theory in linguistics and so suffered their fate, as theories proliferated rapidly, leaving in their wake a long stream of obfuscatory publications rapidly outdated. It is to the credit of linguistics, however, that it dispatched many old ghosts of prosodic theory—esp. quantity (q.v.)—and established sound factual bases for the analysis of poetic lang.

Subsequent antiformalist approaches in crit. sought to dissolve the boundaries between literary and other "texts," or backed away from defensible interp. of any text altogether, or located the sense of *literariness* in conventions shared by readers. Nonetheless, antiformalist critics almost instinctively turned to explicating texts to prove their theories, showing that formalism was not a critical position to be demolished but rather a method necessary to be assimilated so as to be built upon. It was an irony that repetition (q.v.) came to hold a central position in postmodernist crit. as the only recourse in the absence of reference.

VIII. HISTORY OF VERSEFORMS. There is no comprehensive history of the devel. of prosodic practice in the West in existence. Very few scholars command all the requisite langs., are well grounded in linguistics, and understand the full range of prosodic conventions minutely. Still, the main outline is now reasonably clear, and a short outline is worth giving. In general, we may say that indigenous linguistic change and the importation of foreign models are the two great forces driving prosodic transformation, and that the great limens in the history of Western poetic forms have been three: the devel. of the quantitative hexameter in archaic Greece, the emergence of accent in the 3d–4th cs. A.D., and the emergence of rhyme from the hymn and sequence. From the latter two of these all modern verse forms follows.

In Cl. verse, the metrical form of narrative verse—the dactylic hexameter for epic—was established in archaic times, and that of drama—the iambic tetrameter—in the 5th c. B.C. The meters of Gr. lyric—choral and monodic being archaic, dramatic being 5th-c.—were much more complex. The marker of meter was quantity; the footpattern, dactylic, was apparently not entirely congenial even to Gr., much less Lat., and certainly not to any mod. lang., but was preserved nonetheless from at least Homer's day until Med. Lat. gave way to the vernaculars. Both marker and patterns were taken over wholesale from Gr. by Lat. and preserved down to the 4th c., when quantity was replaced by accent. The hexameter was preserved in the Middle Ages for epic and narrative verse, though altered by leonine rhyme (q.v.), which broke long-line stichic verse into short-lined stanzaic verse (see below). The only major new form of the Middle Ages is the iambic dimeter of the Ambrosian hymn—first quantitative but soon accentual—which developed into the octosyllabic *abab* quatrain, the great staple stanza meter of all modern vernacular song. Outside of quatrains, octosyllables proved exceedingly durable for popular and song verse through Lat. into all the vernaculars, Romance and Germanic, incl. Eng. As for high artverse, the hexameter gave way to a line of 11–12 syllables in It. and Fr., though now with only one fixed accent in each hemistich and no strict metrical feet. It. influenced, first through Chaucer, then again (the metric of Chaucer being lost in the Great Vowel Shift) through Wyatt and Surrey, the emergence of the heroic decasyllable or iambic pentameter line in Eng. The influence of Milton authorized the rhymeless pentameter for narrative verse (Wordsworth, Tennyson, Browning) until the deluge after 1855. In dramatic verse, the pentameter was perfected by Shakespeare but silenced by the closing of the theaters; after 1660 dramatic verse follows the age.

Apart from meter, the only other characteristic of modern verse, rhyme, developed in Med. Lat. (whence Otfrid brought it into Ger. in the 8th c.) and first flowered in the vernaculars (succeeding assonance) in the 12th c., in the short-lined lyrics of elaborate rhyme schemes in Occitan poetry (q.v.). The invention of the sonnet (q.v.) in Italy drew most lyric verse into that form until the 17th c. Thereafter, Fr. and then Eng. Classicism revived the couplet (q.v.); the 19th c. suscitated pre-neoclassical forms. After 1850 (Whitman, Symbolism), verse detached itself from meter for experiment with looser rhythmic forms and attempted gropingly to combine aural prosodies with visual ones.

IX. SUMMARY. Over the past century, there has been a general perception that pros. is a desiccated subject, a stony little patch of ground frequented only by eccentrics, fanatics, and pedants. The indictments are easy to finger: verse theory took nearly two millennia to free itself from the detritus of Cl. pros.; it has never been able to give even an adequate theory of meter; it has been unable to agree on not merely concepts and terms but underlying assumptions about the nature of poetry itself (text, performance, experience); it has been unable to generate a flexible and powerful hermeneutic methodology; it has been too willing to base theory on whatever version of linguistics happened to be current; it has too often

failed to distinguish linguistic processes from artistic conventions; it has misconceived the nature of rules (q.v.); and it has too often claimed to offer factual, even scientific knowledge about poetry rather than what it does in fact offer, namely precise tools for the exercise of critical judgment. Consequently it has not succeeded in convincing all critics of its importance for the theory and crit. of poetry. Yet the failure to give final answers is no proof that the questions are trivial; quite the contrary: it is proof that the questions asked and the issues they concern are the hardest ones. It is not important that the answers have so far been unsatisfactory—this is equally true in other areas in crit. The copiousness of discussions of pros. in the history of crit. is such that we must say that verse structure lies at the very core of our understanding of poetry.

It is the task of verse theory to show how particular poetic forms come about, how well they suit their particular lang., what happens to them when transplanted into another lang., and what effects they are capable of. Langs. differ in what resources they make available to poets, and even within one lang., the resources vary from one age to another, so that a verse system will undergo change over time. Differing verse systems may also be present in a lang. simultaneously, and the conventional definitions of verse and prose also change, so that a variety of mixed modes and intermedia may arise and subside. In some respects, verse systems are profoundly conservative, and often lag decades or even centuries behind changes in pronunciation. The rules for the use of masculine and feminine (q.v.) rhyme, for example, were retained in Fr. pros. for four centuries after they ceased being phonetic realities. But in other respects change can be quite sudden: particularly at moments of transition in a lang. (in Eng., the Conquest, the Restoration), poets in search of forms have often turned to models already developed in other langs., regardless of whether the rules developed for that lang. applied to their own lang. well or even at all. Model borrowing and superimposition do not necessarily lead to disaster, of course; quite the contrary. Romance models were mapped onto Eng., a Germanic lang. having radically different phonotactics, leading to very different—but ultimately very productive—results.

Edward Weismiller once remarked that poets who have no interest in the formal powers of their medium to release, inflect, and modulate meaning are not poets at all—a remark we may take to mean that for the traditional poet, at any rate, meter, sound-patterning, and other prosodic effects are the chief vehicles of verbal art. To study these things is to be brought near that place where mere strategies—devices and the learned techniques of craft—are taken up and transformed into the dynamics of art. To study pros. is to study the nature of working in a medium; its aim is to unravel the apparently seamless web of finished art so as to reveal the separable strands of material and the techniques used in weaving them, techniques which other minds can imitate, learn from, assimilate, and extend.

What poetry achieves by being cast in verse is access to resources of formal organization and meaning-release not available outside of verseform. These are structures, forms of order. What is achieved thereby is transmission of the maximum amount of information in the minimum space. And since poetic texts are *art*, what readers and critics want to know, first, is what the poet's materials were, so as to be able to judge what she made of them, what she did with what she had. And what she had, always, were the sounds of words, the rhythm of sentences, the resources of syntax, the forms offered by poetic trad., and the happy discoveries of invention. That is what is possible. In fact, that is all there is.

For discussion of the theoretical bases of poetic form in poetics, see VERSE AND PROSE. For surveys of major prosodic traditions, see ARABIC PROSODY; CELTIC PROSODY; CHINESE POETRY; CLASSICAL PROSODY; ENGLISH PROSODY; FRENCH PROSODY; GERMAN PROSODY; HEBREW PROSODY AND POETICS; INDIAN PROSODY; INDO-EUROPEAN PROSODY; ITALIAN PROSODY; OLD NORSE POETRY; PERSIAN POETRY; SLAVIC PROSODY; SPANISH PROSODY. For more extended discussion of the chief components of aural pros., with extensive bibliographies, see METER; RHYME; RHYTHM; SOUND; SOUND EFFECTS IN POETRY; STANZA. For discussion of visual pros., see esp. FREE VERSE; VERS LIBRE; VISUAL POETRY. For more extended discussion of etymology and of theory vs. praxis, see VERSIFICATION. See also EQUIVALENCE; LINGUISTICS AND POETICS; RULES.

BIBLIOGRAPHIES: Brogan—comprehensive coverage of Eng. incl. OE and ME to 1981 and extensive coverage of other langs. in appendices, supp. to 1988 in *Verseform* (1989), incl. citations of bibls. for other langs.

COLLECTIONS OF PRIMARY AND SECONDARY TEXTS: Keil—texts of Med. Lat. prosodists; E. Langlois, *Recueil d'arts de seconde rhétorique* (1902)—texts of med. Fr. prosodists; Smith—texts of Ren. prosodists; E. Faral, *Les Arts poétiques du XIIe et du XIIIe siècles* (1924)—Med Lat. *artes poetriae*; Sebeok; *Poetics—Poetyka—Poetika*, ed. D. Davie et al. (1961); *Poetics—Poetyka—Poetika*, ed. R. Jakobson et al. (1966); *Teorie Verše I/Theory of Verse I/Teorija stixa I*, ed. J. Levý (1966); *Essays on Style and Lang.*, ed. R. Fowler (1966); *Essays on the Lang. of Lit.*, ed. S. Chatman and S. R. Levin (1967); *Teorie Verše II/Theory of Verse II/Teorija stixa II*, ed. J. Levý and K. Palas (1968); Wimsatt; *La metrica*, ed. R. Cremante and M. Pazzaglia, 2d ed. (1976); *Issledovanija po teorii stixa*, ed. V. N. Žirmunskij et al. (1978); *The Structure of Verse*, ed. H. Gross, 2d ed. (1979); *Rus. Poetics*, ed. T. Eekman and D. S. Worth (1983); *Rhythm and Meter*, ed. P.

Kiparsky and G. Youmans (1989); *Rus. Verse Theory*, ed. B. P. Scherr and D. S. Worth (1989).

GENERAL STUDIES: W. Wordsworth and S. T. Coleridge, "Preface," *Lyrical Ballads*, 3d. ed. (1802); G. W. F. Hegel, *Aesthetics* (1835–38), tr. T. M. Knox, 2 v. (1975); T. S. Omond, "Is Verse a Trammel?" *Gentleman's Mag.* 14 (1875); W. Headlam, "Gr. Lyric Metre," *Jour. Hellen. Stud.* 22 (1902); Wilamowitz; Quintilian, *Institutio oratoria*, tr. H. E. Butler, (1921), Bk. 9, ch. 4; P. Habermann, "Metrik," "Prosodie," *Reallexikon I*; W. P. Ker, *Form and Style in Poetry* (1928); C. S. Baldwin, *Medieval Rhet. and Poetic to 1400* (1928); T. Taig, *Rhythm and Metre* (1929); Patterson; E. Olson, "Gen. Pros.: Rhythmik, Metrik, Harmonics," Diss., Univ. of Chicago (1938); T. S. Eliot, "The Music of Poetry" (1942); A. W. de Groot, *Algemene Versleer* [Gen. Pros.] (1946); A. M. Clark, *Studies in Literary Modes* (1946); A. D. Culler, "Edward Bysshe and the Poet's Handbook," *PMLA* 63 (1948); W. F. J. Knight, *St. Augustine's De musica: A Synopsis* (1949); I. Baroway, "The Accentual Theory of Heb. Pros.," *ELH* 17 (1950); J. R. Firth, "Modes of Meaning," *E&S* 4 (1951); R. Wilbur, "The Bottles Become New, Too," *QRL* 7 (1953); J. C. La Drière, "Prose Rhythm." "Pros.," *Dict. of World Lit.*, ed. J. T. Shipley (1953), "The Comparative Method in the Study of Pros.," *Comp. Lit.: Proc. 2d Congress ICLA*, ed. W. P. Friederich (1959), "Structure, Sound, and Meaning," *Sound and Poetry*, ed. N. Frye (1957); W. S. Johnson, "Some Functions of Poetic Form," *JAAC* 13 (1955); S. Fishman, "Meaning and Structure in Poetry," *JAAC* 14 (1956); R. Wellek, "Euphony, Rhythm, and Metre," in Wellek and Warren; Beare; M. Burger, *Recherches sur la structure et l'origine des vers romane* (1957); Norberg; P. Valéry, *The Art of Poetry* (tr. 1958); Maas; L. P. Wilkinson, *Golden Lat. Artistry* (1963); H. Gross, "Pros. as Rhythmic Cognition," *Sound and Form in Mod. Poetry* (1964), recanted in Gross (1979) above—the expressivist theory; A. Ostriker, "Song and Speech in the Metrics of George Herbert," *PMLA* 80 (1965)—song-mode and speech-mode; H. Meyer, "On the Spirit of Verse," *Disciplines of Crit.*, ed. P. Demetz (1968); J. O. Perry, "The Temporal Analysis of Poems," *BJA* 5 (1965); I. Fónagy, "Form and Function of Poetic Lang.," *Diogenes* 51 (1965), *La vive voix* (1983); J. Levý, "The Meanings of Form and the Forms of Meaning," *Poetics—Poetyka—Poetika* (1966, above), *Paralipomena* (1971)—his coll. papers; V. N. Žirmunskij, *Intro. to Metrics: The Theory of Verse* (tr. 1966); J. Cohen, *Structure du langage poétique* (1966); S. Booth, *An Essay on Shakespeare's Sonnets* (1969); K. Lea, "The Poetic Powers of Repetition," *PBA* 55 (1969); A. M. Dale, "Speech-rhythm, Verse-rhythm and Song," *Coll. Papers* (1969); *Mathematik und Dichtung*, ed. H. Kreuzer and R. Gunzenhäuser, 4th ed. (1971); W. S. Allen, *Accent and Rhythm* (1973), esp. ch. 1; S. R. Levin, "The Conventions of Poetry," *Literary Style: A Symposium*, ed. S. Chatman (1971); J. Lotz, "Elements of Versif.," in Wimsatt (1972, above); V. Forrest-Thompson, "Levels in Poetic Convention," *Jour. European Studies* 2 (1972); Dante, *De vulgari eloquentia*, tr. R. S. Haller (1973); P. Kiparsky, "The Role of Linguistics in a Theory of Poetry," *Daedalus* 102 (1973): J. T. Irwin, "The Crisis of Regular Forms," *Sewanee Rev.* 81 (1973); E. D. Polivanov, "The General Phonetic Principle of Any Poetic Technique," *Sel. Works*, ed. A. A. Leontev (1974); D. Laferrière, "Automorphic Structures in the Poem's Grammatical Space," *Semiotica* 10 (1974); G. L. Beccaria, *L'Autonomia del significante* (1975); M. Black, "Why It Is So, and Not Otherwise," *NLH* 6 (1975); A. Gaylord, "Scanning the Prosodists," *ChR* 11 (1976); D. I. Masson, "Poetic Sound-Patterning Reconsidered," *PLPLS, LHS* 16 (1976): W. K. Wimsatt, Jr., "In Search of Verbal Mimesis," *Day of the Leopards* (1976); J. M. Lotman, "Elements and Levels of the Paradigmatics of the Artistic Text," *The Structure of the Artistic Text* (tr. 1977); P. Habermann and K. Kanzog, "Vers, Verslehre, Vers und Prosa," *Reallexikon* 4.677–98; R. Jakobson, *On Verse: Its Masters and Explorers* (1979), esp. "Linguistics and Poetics"; D. Wesling, *The Chances of Rhyme* (1980), *The New Poetries* (1985); Scott; Group Mu; D. Attridge, "The Lang. of Poetry: Materiality and Meaning," *EIC* 31 (1981); West; B. de Cornulier, *Théorie du vers* (1982); Ransom; J. Hollander, *Vision and Resonance*, 2d ed. (1985), *Melodious Guile* (1988); J. Stevens, *Words and Music in the Middle Ages* (1986); O. B. Hardison, Jr., *Pros. and Purpose in the Eng. Ren.* (1989); D. Oliver, *Poetry and Narrative in Performance* (1989); M. L. Gasparov, *Očerk istorii evropejskogo stixa* (1989); M. Grimaud, "Versification and Its Discontents," *Semiotica* 88 (1992).   T.V.F.B.

PROSOPOPOEIA (Gr. *prosopon* "face," "person," and *poiein* "to make"). The speech of an imaginary person. A term still used for personification (q.v.)—the attribution of human qualities to animals or inanimate objects—to which it is closely allied. P. is one of the few figures discussed by Aristotle (*Rhetoric*, Book 3), who views it as promoting vividness in a discourse. Lausberg defines it as a "figure which gives the ability to act and move to insensate things, as well as speech to absent or present persons or things, sometimes even to the dead" (2.936). The example given by Quintilian (9.3.89), "Avarice is the mother of cruelty," shows, however, that p. also exists as a trope at the basic levels of metaphor or axiom. As a means of making a speech "vivid" or lively, Lausberg's definition agrees with that of the Tudor rhetoricians, who placed p. in the list of figures which included *prosopographia, characterismus, ethopoeia* (which together give us our notions of fictional portraiture); mimesis of gesture, pronunciation, and utterance; and *dialogismus* or *sermocinatio*, by which an imaginary person is given the ability to speak, even to answer questions.

In antiquity, *prosopopoeiae* were school exercises

in which writers took on the persona (q.v.) of a famous historical or mythological figure in a composition with the end of exhibiting his character; hence the figure often spoke in the first person (cf. Quintilian 3.8.49). To *address* an imaginary person as if present engages the figure of *apostrophe* (q.v.). C. Perelman (*The New Rhet.* [tr. 1969]) also remarks that the combination of devices like apostrophe with personification produces imaginary addressees and a more "stable" illusion of dialogue, as in Sidney's sonnet "With how sad steps, O Moon, thou climb'st the skies" (*Astrophil and Stella* 31).

M. Grimaud, "P. de sainte Sophie, patronne des poéticiennes," *Poétique* (1980); P. de Man, "Autobiography as De-Facement," *The Rhet. of Romanticism* (1984); M. Riffaterre, "P.," *YFS* 69 (1985); Corbett.   T.V.F.B.; A.W.H.

PROVENÇAL POETRY. See OCCITAN POETRY.

PROVERB. A traditional saying, pithily or wittily expressed. Proverbial expression is traditionally given to customs, legal and ethical maxims, "blasons populaires," superstitions, weather and medical lore, prophecies, and other categories of conventional wisdom. Ps. are among the oldest poetic expressions in Sanskrit, Hebrew, Germanic, and Scandinavian lits. "Learned" ps. are those long current in lit., as distinct from "popular" trad. The former come into Western European lit. both from the Bible and the Church Fathers and from such Cl. sources as Aristophanes, Theophrastus, Lucian, and Plautus. Erasmus' *Adagia* (1500) was instrumental in spreading Cl. p. lore among the European vernaculars. The first Eng. collection was John Heywood's *Dialogue conteining . . . all the ps. in the Eng. lang.* (1546). But ps. had been commonly used by OE and ME writers, particularly Chaucer. The Elizabethan delight in ps. is evident in John Lyly's *Euphues* (1578–80) and in countless plays—as it is in Shakespeare. The genres of lit. in which ps. frequently occur are the didactic (e.g. Chaucer's *Tale of Melibeus*, Ben Franklin's *Way to Wealth*, and Goethe's "Sprichwörtliches"); the satirical (Pope); works depicting folk characters (*Don Quixote*, J. R. Lowell's *The Biglow Papers*); works reproducing local or national characteristics (E. A. Robinson's "New England"); and literary *tours de force* (Villon's "Ballade des proverbes").

What distinguishes ps. from other figures such as idioms or metaphors, G. B. Milner proposes, is their structure of "four quarters" in a "balanced relationship . . . both in their form and content." This configuration, evident in "Waste/not, // Want/not" or "Qui seme/le vent // Recolte/la tempete," appears in ancient and non-European as well as in modern langs. Milner associates this balanced four-part form with Carl Jung's paradigm of the structure of the mind. Milner's analysis, however, is found inadequate by Alan Dundes

(1981), who proposes the p. as "a traditional propositional statement consisting of at least one descriptive element" which consists of "a topic and a comment." Ps. which contain "a single descriptive element are non-oppositional" while those with two or more "may be either oppositional or non-oppositional." Dundes relates proverbial structures to that of riddles; however, "ps. only state problems, in contrast to riddles which solve them." Dundes calls for empirical testing of his hypothesis with ps. from various cultures. See also DIDACTIC POETRY; EPIGRAM; GNOMIC POETRY; PAROEMIAC; REFRAN.

W. Bonser, and T. A. Stephens, *P. Lit.: A Bibl.* (1930); A. Taylor, *The P.* (1931, reissued with Index, 1962); B. J. Whiting, *Chaucer's Use of Ps.* (1934); W. Gottschalk, *Sprichwörter des Romanen,* 3 v. (1935–38); G. Frank, "Ps. in Med. Lit.," *MLN* 58 (1943); S. Singer, *Sprichwörter des Mittelalters,* 3 v. (1944–47); W. G. Smith, *Oxford Dict. of Eng. Ps.,* 2d ed., rev. P. Harvey (1948); M. P. Tilley, *Dict. of the Ps. in England in the 16th and 17th Cs.* (1950); O. E. E. Moll, *Sprichwörterbibliographie* (1958); H. Weinstock, *Die Funktion elisabethanischer Sprichwörter und Pseudosprichwörter bei Shakespeare* (1966); D. MacDonald, "Ps., Sententiae, and Exempla in Chaucer's Comic Tales," *Speculum* 41 (1966); F. Seiler, *Deutsche Sprichwortkunde,* 2d ed. (1967); C. G. Smith, *Shakespeare's P. Lore,* 2d ed. (1968), *Spenser's P. Lore* (1970); G. B. Milner, "What is a P.?" *New Society* (6 Feb. 1969), and "De l'armature des locutions proverbiales: Essai de taxonomie semantique," *L'Homme* 9 (1969); A. W. Weidenbrück, *Chaucer's Sprichwortpraxis,* Diss., Bonn (1970); *Oxford Cl. Dict.,* s.v. "Paroemiographers" (1970); F. A. de Caro and W. K. McNeil, *Am. P. Lit.: A Bibl.* (1970); M. I. Kuusi, *Towards an Internat. Type-system of Ps.* (1972); W. R. Herzenstiel, *Erziehungserfahrung im deutschen Sprichwort* (1973); P. Zumthor, "L'épiphonème proverbial," *RSH* 41 (1976); R. W. Dent, *Shakespeare's Proverbial Lang.: An Index* (1981), *Proverbial Lang. in Eng. Drama Exclusive of Shakespeare, 1495–1616: An Index* (1984); A. Dundes, "On the Structure of the P.," *The Wisdom of Many: Essays on the P.,* ed. W. Mieder and A. Dundes (1981); W. Mieder, *Internat. P. Scholarship: An Annot. Bibl.* (1982), *Supplement 1* (1990), *Supplement 2* (1992), comp., *Prentice-Hall Encyc. of World Ps.* (1986); G. Bebermeyer, "Sprichwort," *Reallexikon* 4.132–51; *Proverbium 1–* (1984–); H. and A. Beyer, *Sprichwörterlexikon* (1985); B. J. Whiting, *Mod. Ps. and Proverbial Sayings* (1989); W. Mieder, *Am. Ps.: A Study of Texts and Contexts* (1989). D.HO.

PRYDDEST. This term, resulting in a misreading of *prydest,* first appears in a Welsh dictionary compiled by John Davies in 1632 and is explained as *poësis, poëma, encomium, encomiasticum.* It was used by William Williams (Caledfryn) in his *Drych Barddonol* (1839) in the plural (*pryddestau*) to refer to long poems without *cynghanedd* (q.v.), either with or without rhyme. The Eisteddfod (q.v.) at Cardiff in 1834 held a competition for the best *pryddest ddiodl,* i.e. a long poem without rhyme in the form of an elegy on a clergyman, and again at London in 1841 for the best *p.* on "Dirwest" (Temperance). In 1860 at Rhuthin the modern practice of awarding the "Chair" for the best *awdl* (q.v.) and the "Crown" for the best *p.* was begun. Long poems in the "free meters" had certainly been composed in Welsh poetry (q.v.) before the modern Eisteddfod came into being, but they were not called *pryddestau,* and the term is still more or less limited to the entries in free meters or *vers libre* in the competition for the "Crown" at the National Eisteddfod, a competition and a prize considered to be less prestigious than that for the best *awdl* for the "Chair." Still, some of the most notable Welsh poetic productions of the 20th c. have been Eisteddfodic *pryddestau,* e.g. "Y Ddinas" (The City) by T. H. Parry-Williams, "Y Briodas" (The Marriage) by Caradog Prichard, and "Difodiant" (Extinction) by Euros Bowen.—Intro., *Pryddestau Eisteddfodol Detholedig 1911–1953,* ed. E. G. Millward (1973); Jarman and Hughes; Stephens. J.E.C.W.

PSALM. The poetic form of the p., at least as it has come down to us in the Western literary trad., is an invention of the ancient Near East. P.-writing, associated with temple cult, was an important literary activity in Mesopotamia, Egypt, possibly Ugarit (in present-day Syria), and, one may assume, despite the lack of surviving texts, in Canaan. The p.-poets of ancient Israel took over the form from the surrounding cultures, not hesitating to borrow images, phrases, and even whole sequences of lines, but also refashioning the p. to make it an adequate poetic expression of the new monotheistic vision of reality. The collection that constitutes the biblical *Book of Ps.* is an anthology (q.v.)—or more precisely, a conflation of what were originally four smaller anthologies—assembled sometime in the Second Temple period, but that includes poems probably composed over a span of several hundred years, going back to the beginning of the first millennium B.C. There are certain minor shifts in lang. and poetic structure over the centuries, but far more striking are the continuities of style and convention in the whole biblical lit. of ps.

The term for these poems current in Western langs. is derived from Gr. *psalmos,* a song sung to the accompaniment of a plucked instrument. The two Heb. terms, which are sometimes used in conjunction, are *mizmor,* simply indicating "song," without the necessary implication of instrumental accompaniment, and *tehillah,* "praise" (the plural, *tehillim,* is the usual Heb. title of the biblical book). The two predominant subgenres of ps. in the biblical collection are in fact ps. of praise and supplications. Together these make up more than two-thirds of the *Book of Ps.* There are other subgenres, such as wisdom ps., royal ps., and historical ps., but each of these is represented by only a few instances in the traditional collection and none has exerted the post-biblical influence of the supplication and the p. of praise.

Some of the Heb. ps. are clearly marked for liturgical performance on specified occasions or at specified moments in the temple rite. A view promulgated by Mowinckel holds that many ps. are texts for an annual rite of the enthronement of YHWH, but this notion is no more than a conjecture. Other ps. seem intended to be recited by individuals in moments of anguish or exaltation. This double nature of the ps., alternatively collective and personal, has been a source of their relevance both to the institutional and the individual lives of Christians and Jews ever since. At least some of the ps., to judge by the orchestral directions set at their head, were framed for musical performance, and most of them exhibit symmetries of form far beyond the norm of biblical poetry in other genres. Some ps. are cast as alphabetic acrostics (see ABECEDARIUS). One encounters refrains or refrain-like repetitions, antiphonal voices, and most common of all, "envelope structures," in which the conclusion explicitly echoes images, motifs, or even whole phrases from the beginning (see ENVELOPE; RING COMPOSITION).

This fondness for envelope structures is combined with a recurrent concern with the efficacy and power of lang. in general and of poetic lang. in particular. Thus the typical supplication begins with a foregrounding of the act of supplication ("From the depths I called to Thee, O Lord," etc.) and concludes by recapitulating the initial phrases, usually with the implication: "since I have called to Thee, Thou must surely hear me." The typical thanksgiving p. (the most common subcategory of ps. of praise) begins with a declaration of intent to sing out to the Lord, to tell His praises, and concludes by again affirming the act of praise or thanksgiving, now completed in the symmetrical structure of the poem.

It should also be noted that there is a certain fluidity among the psalmodic subgenres. Every supplication looks toward the possibility of becoming a thanksgiving p., and a few are turned into that retrospectively by the confident affirmation at the end. Even within one subgenre, there are striking differences in emphasis: a supplication may stress sin and contrition, the speaker's terror in a moment of acute distress, a reflective meditation on human transience, and much else.

The beautifully choreographed movements and the archetypal simplicity of style of the biblical ps. have made them a recurrent source of inspiration to later poets. For obvious reasons, the *Book of Ps.* has repeatedly influenced Jewish and Christian liturgical poetry through the ages. With the resurgence of interest in the Bible after the Reformation, adaptations of ps. became widespread. In France, the versions of Clément Marot are particularly noteworthy. The apogee of psalmodic verse

in Western langs. was reached in Ren. England, where the Bible in its new vernacular version became central to the culture. A variety of Eng. poets, from Wyatt and Sidney to Herbert and Milton, tried their hand at metrical versions of ps. In the signal instance of Herbert, the poet's original production owes something abiding in its diction, imagery, and sense of form to the model of the biblical ps. Modern Eng. poetry continues to evince a deep interest in ps. Dylan Thomas's work is strongly marked by ps., as is Donald Davie's *To Scorch or Freeze* (1988). See also HEBRAISM; HEBREW PROSODY AND POETICS; HYMN.

J. Julian, *A Dict. of Hymnology* (1925); *The Psalmists*, ed. D. C. Simpson (1926); I. Baroway, "'The Lyre of David,'" *ELH* 8 (1941); H. Smith, "Eng. Metrical Psalms in the 16th C. and Their Literary Significance," *HLQ* 9 (1946); J. Paterson, *The Praises of Israel: Studies Literary and Religious in the Ps.* (1950); C. S. Lewis, *Reflections on the Ps.* (1958); S. Mowinckel, *The Ps. in Israel's Worship*, 2 v. (tr. 1962); C. Westermann, *The Praise of God in the Ps.* (1965); J. Gotzen et al., "Psalmendichtung," *Reallexikon*; L. Finscher, "P.," *MGG*; H. Gunkel, *The Ps.: A Form-Critical Intro.*, tr. T. M. Horner (1967); R. C. Cully, *Oral-Formulaic Lang. in the Biblical Ps.* (1967); A. L. Strauss, *Bedarkhei hasifrut* (1970), 66–94; C. Freer, *Music for a King* (1972)—Herbert and metrical ps.; R. Lace, "Le Psaume 1—Une Analyse structurale," *Biblica* 57 (1977); E. Werner et al., "P.," and N. Temperley et al., "Ps., Metrical," *New Grove* 15.320–35, 347–82; C. Bloch, *Spelling the Word: George Herbert and the Bible* (1985); P. D. Miller, Jr., *Interpreting the Ps.* (1986); R. Alter, *The Art of Biblical Poetry* (1985), "Ps.," *Literary Guide to the Bible*, ed. R. Alter and F. Kermode (1987); E. L. Greenstein, "Ps.," *Encyc. of Religion*, ed. M. Eliade, v. 12 (1987); L. A. Schökel, *A Manual of Heb. Poetics* (1988). R.A.

PSALTERS, METRICAL. See HYMN; PSALM.

PSEUDO-STATEMENT. Nowhere in *Science and Poetry* (1926) does I. A. Richards provide an exact formal definition of p.-s. In spite of this, however, a relatively coherent formulation may be extracted from the following comment, which strikingly illustrates the way Richards conceives the term: "A p.-s. is a form of words which is justified entirely by its effect in releasing or organizing our impulses and attitudes . . . ; a statement, on the other hand, is justified by its truth, i.e. its correspondence, in a highly technical sense, with the fact to which it points." Richards uses this distinction between propositional statements (which aim to express truth about the external world) and the "pseudo"-statements of poetry (which do not) to posit a deeper opposition between poetic lang. (emotive) and scientific lang. (denotative). For him, an identical sequence of words or phrasing would be propositional in scientific lang. but emotive in poetic lang. The function of a poem is not to supply a repertoire of verifiable facts but to impart "a perfect emotive description of a state of mind." What separates the "truth" of poetic p.-s. from that of scientific statement is its special ability to organize experience in richly complicated and imaginatively stimulating ways. The whole of p.-s. is epitomized by this complex organization of feelings and impulses in the emotive utterance. Of course, logical argumentation is sometimes present in the devel. of "subtle, finely compounded attitudes." But ultimately the emotional organization of poetic p.-s. differs from the ordinary referential function of lang.

P.-s. occasioned much debate in the 1930s and '40s. Since the term is equivocal (see Murry) and since it privileges the emotive over the cognitive, Richards' formulation did not find favor with a number of critics. Allen Tate, for example, made the point that poetic value is much more related to "the knowing mind" than to a "projection of feeling." Although Richards continued to be preoccupied with the question of belief and poetry (q.v.), it appears that in practice he ceased to make use of the controversial term. After the emergence of structuralism (q.v.) in the 1960s and '70s, the distinction between scientific and emotive lang. seems to have lost its importance. The new structuralist model eliminates the older distinction between literary and scientific forms of expression, both being subsumed under the more comprehensive framework of discourse. Generally speaking, the term p.-s. is best viewed as one of Richards' attempts to furnish crit. with an adequate technical vocabulary and with systematic critical principles. See also MEANING, POETIC.—I. A. Richards, *Science and Poetry* (1926), *Practical Crit.* (1929), esp. 186–188; J. M. Murry, "Beauty is Truth," *Sym* 1 (1930); A. Tate, "Lit. as Knowledge," *SoR* 6 (1941); P. Wheelwright, *The Burning Fountain*, rev. ed. (1968); G. Graff, *Poetic Statement and Critical Dogma* (1970); J. P. Russo, *I. A. Richards* (1989). P.M.

PSYCHIC DISTANCE. See AESTHETIC DISTANCE.

PSYCHOLOGICAL CRITICISM.

    I. PSYCHOANALYTIC PSYCHOLOGY
    II. ARCHETYPAL PSYCHOLOGY
    III. OTHER PSYCHOLOGIES

Crit. using a formal model from psychology to analyze the writing or reading or content of literary texts; more generally, the application to literary problems of psychology. When Plato speaks of poetry enfeebling the mind or composition as poetic madness (q.v.), when Aristotle writes of catharsis (q.v.) or Coleridge of imagination (q.v.), they are making psych. statements. All crit. is in a sense psych. crit., since all crit. and theory proceed from assumptions about the psychology of humans who make or experience or are portrayed in lit.

Lit. both embodies the psych. assumptions of its makers and is realized through the psych. assumptions of its interpreters. Even critics who posit an "objective" text are making a psych. assumption, namely that the perception of that text can be independent of the activities of the perceiver's mind. Historical critics may explore the psych. beliefs of the Ren. to explicate the plays of Shakespeare. Modern critics also have psych. assumptions. Some leave these assumptions tacit, deriving them from common sense or philosophy, not the discipline of psychology as such. Since the devel. of psychoanalysis, however, most 20th-c. critics make their psych. assumptions formal and explicit.

Near the end of the 19th c., Freud began to develop psychoanalytic psychology. At the same time, academic psychology was changing from a branch of philosophy to a science. Psych. crit., properly so called, dates from the first efforts to use these now-separated experimental, clinical, or "scientific" psychologies instead of aesthetic or philosophical statements about the nature of the human. From that time to the present, psych. crit. has drawn primarily on three psychologies: psychoanalytic (Freudian), archetypal (analytic or Jungian), and cognitive. Psychologies, however, deal in the first instance not with poems but with persons. Psych. crit. will discuss the author, some member(s) of the author's audience, a character, or the lang. (usually meaning a character or some psych. process represented in the lang.).

I. PSYCHOANALYTIC PSYCHOLOGY. By far the largest body of psych. crit. draws on psychoanalytic psychology, perhaps because from the very beginning Freud was concerned with the exact wording of a patient's free associations, a slip of the tongue, or the telling of a dream or joke. Hence, one can use psychoanalytic psychology to study details of poetic lang. Also, since the 1960s, psychoanalysis has become more and more a general psychology, as theorists have drawn on anthropology, experiments, neuroscience, and such modern theories as semiotics (q.v.) and information theory. Controversies that loomed large in the 1920s, such as Freud vs. Jung, now seem small as psychoanalysis has become a psychology of the self.

One can think of psychoanalysis in three phases: a psychology of the unconscious (1897–1923), ego psychology (1923–), and a psychology of the self (ca. 1950–). The later phases build on and include the earlier, enlarging the field of human behavior that psychoanalysis attempts to explain. The most recent thinking in psychoanalysis incorporates and generalizes much (but not all!) of Freud's earliest work. One can define these three phases by the polarity used to explain events: conscious and unconscious, ego and non-ego, or self and not-self.

The first stage grew directly from Freud's most fundamental discovery. If a patient free associates in connection with a symptom, i.e. says whatever comes to mind, sooner or later the patient will enunciate (over strongly felt resistance) a repressed thought or feeling that the symptom expresses. Similarly, if a patient free associates to a dream, the patient will become aware (also against resistance) of a previously unconscious wish. So too, Freud found, with slips of the tongue or pen, lapses of memory, forgettings, or jokes. In all these odd, marginal behaviors, free association reveals a resisted latent or unconscious content underneath the tolerated manifest or conscious behavior. Once Freud realized this manifest-latent pattern occurred in so many spheres of mental activity, he concluded that he had arrived at something fundamental to human nature itself, a general principle of psych. explanation, the struggle between "the" conscious and "the" unconscious.

In this "classical" phase, Freud thought of conscious and unconscious as opposed forces, as systems or even places. He and his first followers explained human behaviors as either repressions or expressions of unconscious material when psychic energy shifted from one state to the other. The other major devel. of the first phase was their understanding of child devel. as having specific stages leading to adult life. In particular, adult character developed from the child's resolution of its Oedipus complex. That is, a style of adult relations to other persons grew out of the way the child coped with its love and hate toward mother and father as the child grew into a world divided into male and female and parent and child. Even earlier, the child developed character from the way it learned to adapt internally to adult concerns about the management of the child's body in feeding, defecating, urinating, walking, masturbating, etc. Within this first framework, Freud developed ideas of great generality about the working and structure of the mind, although psychoanalysis often focused primarily on special behaviors such as neurosis and dreams.

Lit. played a key role in Freud's discoveries. In a letter of October 15, 1897, in which he announced that he had found love of the mother and jealousy of the father in his self-analysis, he went on to identify this complex with the "gripping power" of *Oedipus Rex* and the unconscious forces behind Shakespeare's writing of *Hamlet*, as well as that prince's inability to act. He thus addressed all three of the persons of psych. crit., although in this first phase he confined his writings largely to author and character.

In "Creative Writers and Day-Dreaming" (1908), Freud developed a powerful model of the literary process. The writer, stimulated by a present wish, enriches it unconsciously with wishes from childhood and embodies it in a literary form that entices an audience (who in their turn take the text as stimulus and elaborate it with *their* unconscious wishes). Using this model, he wrote studies of Leonardo da Vinci and Dostoyevsky and his longest literary analysis, an interp. of the dreams in Jensen's novel *Gradiva*. He also analyzed a variety of literary characters: Hamlet, Macbeth and Lady Macbeth, Ibsen's Rebecca West, and Falstaff (see Strachey).

Freud's writings prompted other early psychoanalytic figures to lit. crit. Typical were Ernest Jones' study of *Hamlet*, Marie Bonaparte's of Poe, and Phyllis Greenacre's of Swift and Carroll. Characteristically, these first-phase critics used only such early psychoanalytic concepts as unconscious content or the Oedipus complex or the phallic and anal stages of child development. They relied heavily on Freud's lists of symbols in the 1914 additions to *The Interp. of Dreams* or the first set of *Introductory Lectures* in 1915–17, a tactic that resulted in some bizarre crit. and a bad reputation for psychoanalytic studies among conventional literary critics.

Perhaps because it was so novel, this earliest style, the search for latent content, set the image of psychoanalytic crit. in literary circles. Also, a number of prominent literary critics of the 1930s, '40s, and '50s began to use this first-phase theory, esp. William Empson, Edmund Wilson, Lionel Trilling, Kenneth Burke, and Leslie Fiedler (see Phillips). Hence work continues in this vein (Crews; Kaplan and Kloss). Some of this work remains highly effective precisely because of the simplicity of its theory. Harold Bloom's influential theory of poetic influence (q.v.), for example, rests on Freud's early version of the Oedipus complex.

Freud himself, however, found that a quarter-century of clinical experience required him to revise his first theories. In the second phase of his thought, Freud complicated the simple division of the mind into conscious and unconscious by mapping it onto the "structural" hypothesis of a mind whose workings consisted of the interaction of id, superego, reality, and repetition compulsion under the governance of a presiding ego. Id, one would define today as the psychic representation of biological drives; superego, the internalized commands of one's parents, both to do and not to do, violation of which leads to guilt or depression; repetition compulsion, the tendency to try old solutions even on new problems; the ego, the synthesizer and executive that chooses strategies and tactics that best balance these competing needs. Freud and his colleagues of the 1930s expanded their inventory of defense mechanisms from repression to other strategies such as reversing anger into kindness and projecting one's own impulses onto others. Although Freud had largely ceased writing on lit. by 1923, some of his earlier works illustrate what his second-phase writing might have been like: studies of jokes and humor, the legend of the Medusa's Head, the theme of beauty's transience (an essay prompted by Rilke), or the "uncanny" in ghost stories. These writings all have less to do with author or character and more with the audience and an assumed collective response to a literary stimulus.

Second-phase psychoanalytic theory made possible a more powerful poetics. Kris and Mauron were able to integrate the new ego-psychology of multiple defense into studies of the writing process. Sharpe and Rogers showed how the new theories could explicate the psych. function of metaphors and poetic lang. Kris, Lesser, and Holland used ego psychology to study the response to literary texts (see READER-RESPONSE CRITICISM). Reflecting the new complexity in the theory of defense, Kris approached lit. as "regression in the service of the ego." Lesser showed how lit. variously appeals to id, ego, and superego. Holland developed a model of lit. as a fantasy modified by poetic forms (analogous to psych. defenses) toward a meaning. Where first-phase critics felt they could only talk about persons, second-phase critics could use the new theories to consider forms such as lyric poetry. Thus, "Dover Beach" denies a primal scene fantasy; "The Second Coming" splits a fantasy of omnipotent rage. Psycholanalytic studies of writers could become more realistic with biographers like Edel, Kaplan, Meyer, Fruman, or Wolff. The anthols. by Ruitenbeek, the Manheims, and Tennenhouse sample this phase.

The third phase took place largely after Freud's death in 1939. Psychoanalytic psychology went beyond the ego to address the self in the largest sense and, finally, all of human behavior. As early as 1930, in the first chapter of *Civilization and Its Discontents*, Freud ushered in this phase: "Originally the ego includes everything; later it separates off an external world from itself." Nazi persecutions forced the emigration of Freud and his circle from Vienna and spread second- and third-phase psychoanalysis all over the world.

British theorists, during the 1940s and '50s, replaced Freud's biological determinism from innate drives with learning based on interpersonal encounters between the child and its significant others ("object relations"). Concentration on these pre-Oedipal experiences led to a more comprehensive account of the themes in a child's devel. that persisted in the adult's style. The Oedipus complex was only one among several critical events, and indeed the child's first-year relation to the mother overshadowed what Freud had thought dominant, the relation to the father in the third year and after. In particular, both theory and observation indicated a crucial period early in life when the child felt it was not yet separate from its mother, and Holland (1968) showed how this early experience could explain "absorption" in lit. later in life. From this "object-relations school," theories of "potential space" and "transitional object" (Winnicott) have had an important influence on literary theory (Schwartz, Hartman, Grolnick and Barkin), evidenced, for example, in current work on Shakespeare (Schwartz and Kahn).

In response to developments in the 1960s in identity theory, Holland showed how personal style (or identity) controlled the actual (as opposed to the assumed) response to lit. (1973, 1975, 1988) and to jokes (1982); this became an important theme in reader-response crit. (q.v.). A number of literary critics in the U.S. have built on the work of Karen Horney, who focused early on defensive patterns and object relations. By accenting early childhood and sexuality less than other psychoanalytic critics, third-force psych. critics have been able to write more realistically about authors and characters, adding importantly to mimetic crit.

In France, under the influence of Jacques Lacan (after ca. 1965), psychoanalysis turned toward understanding conscious and unconscious experiences as an entry into a linguistic culture. Lacan wrote in an arcane, metaphorical way, describing concerns of the third phase of psychoanalysis (object relations or personal style) in the lang. of the first phase (phallus, castration). Although much Lacanian literary writing simply explicates Lacan, Lacan himself posited important psychoanalytic ideas on analyses of "The Purloined Letter" and *Hamlet*, and some critics have begun to work on specific texts (see Bersani, Felman, and the Davis and Felman anthols.). Current crit. appears in the journal *Littoral*. In some versions, Lacanian psychoanalysis meshes with the work of such Fr. thinkers as Roland Barthes, Michel Foucault, and Jacques Derrida, who treat lang. as an active, autonomous system and the speaker as passive. Psychoanalytic psychology in this form is more widely read in literary circles (in the U.S., U.K., France, and South America) than earlier versions were, though, paradoxically, it reduces the importance of the actual free associating on which psychoanalysis rests.

A particularly vigorous current in 1980s psych. crit. is feminist psychoanalytic crit., this despite Freud's boyish theories about women. Feminists sometimes re-read Freud as if he were a literary text; sometimes they use Freud to understand a patriarchal society (Mitchell); sometimes they rewrite him into a more sophisticated psychology (Chodorow). Some feminist critics draw on Fr. theory (Irigaray; Marks and de Courtivron). Others draw on Anglo-Am. ego-psychology and object-relations theory (Gilbert and Gubar; Garner). All have found in psychoanalytic psychology both a challenge and a resource (see FEMINIST CRITICISM).

Most recently, in the U.S., Heinz Kohut among others has developed a "self-psychology" based on the devel. of the individual's capacity for realistic self-love alongside the traditional account of child devel. through libidinal stages. These new theories have become highly influential among Am. therapists, and have led to one anthol. of lit. crit. based on the theory of narcissism (Layton and Schapiro). Thus, this latest current continues the pattern psychoanalytic crit. has followed from the beginning: new theory based on clinical experience which then leads to new modes of thinking about lit. which may in turn shed light on psycho-analytic theory.   N.N.H.

II. ARCHETYPAL PSYCHOLOGY. Archetypal psychology has been a significant force in critical theory since the 1920s. Its theoretical foundation derives from the work of the Swiss psychoanalyst Carl Jung, esp. his idea that archetypal structures are the primary factors organizing human personality (see ARCHETYPE). For Jung, the personal unconscious consists of memories and images (*imagos*) collected in the course of an individual life. The collective unconscious, on the other hand, is limited to the imposition of structural laws—*archetypes*. The personal unconscious is like a lexicon where each of us accumulates an individual vocabulary; these lexical units, however, acquire value and significance only in so far as they are archetypally structured. If the unconscious activity of the psyche consists in imposing structures (*archetypes*) upon content (*imagos*), and if these structures are fundamentally the same for all personalities, then to understand and interpret a literary text it is necessary to analyze the unconscious structures underlying the text itself. This is the model used in traditional Jungian crit.

Jung published the first archetypal analysis of a literary text in 1912 in "Wandlungen und Symbole der Libido," an extensive treatment of the structures underlying Longfellow's *Hiawatha*. Here Jung introduced his interpretive method know as *amplification*. Earlier, Freud had demonstrated the importance of free association for understanding the unconscious motivation and meaning of a person's dreams. Jung extended this idea not only to the personal associations of the dreamer but also to intertextual associations within the dreamer's cultural canon and, in some cases, cross-cultural associations as well. By establishing a larger intertextual context for the dream image through philological, iconological, mythological, and historical research, Jung showed, the process of amplification deliteralizes the image, cultivating an attitude which psychologically questions the naive, literal level of lang. and image in order to expose its more shadowy, metaphorical significance.

Analysis of archetypal structures and the phenomenological amplification of images has characterized archetypal crit. from the 1920s to the mid 1960s, esp. in the early work of Maud Bodkin, John Thorburn, Herbert Read, and Elizabeth Drew, through the later Kathleen Raine and Graham Hough, and culminating in the prodigious writings of Northrop Frye. See also MYTH CRITICISM; MYTH.

In the 1970s revolutionary changes in archetypal crit. came from two areas: (1) expansion of clinical analysis to a phenomenological study of imagination and lang., and (2) study of the depth-psychological dimension of religion and lit. The most influential figure has been Jungian psychoanalyst James Hillman. To extend Jungian psychol-ogy beyond clinical practice to a study of Western imagination, Hillman calls for a "postanalytic consciousness" committed to an articulation of the "poetic basis of mind." Hillman's phenomenological view of mind holds fantasy images to be the means by which consciousness and self-consciousness are possible and through which the world is imagined. Work with images, whether in therapeutic, cultural, or literary analysis, has thus become as much a work on the process of seeing as on the object seen.

The shift from Jung to Hillman may be illustrated in their differing approaches to alchemy. Where Jung writes an "objective" and "empirical" psychology of alchemy, Hillman tries instead to provide an experiential closeness to the alchemical images and tropes themselves. In writing about "silver and the white earth," Hillman intends his writing, like a poem, to bear traces of "silver," to become a "silver mine," unearthing and performing the images' tropological structure. The metaphor of silver "author-izes" the actual style of writing and internal logic of the text. As a mode of psych. crit., Hillman's new archetypal psychology assumes that a literary work brings with it the very hermeneutics (imagos and tropes) by which it can be interpreted. In the late 1970s, Paul Kugler further developed the interrelation between alchemy and the poetic dimension of lang. by focusing on the interrelation between consciousness, lang. (texts), and imagos. Consciousness is continually being imagined (imaged, in-formed) by the metaphors in the very text it is writing or reading.

In the 1980s, archetypal crit. has drawn upon the philosophy of the later Heidegger, Derrida, and the notions of nothingness and emptiness from Zen Buddhism to further deepen the imaginal hermeneutic toward semiotic and postmodern literary theory. Important in this postmodern phase are Miller's essays on the motifs of "play" and the "vanishing angel," Patricia Berry-Hillman's *Echo's Subtle Body*, work by Michael Adams, and Robert Avens' *The New Gnosis*.   P.K.K.

III. OTHER PSYCHOLOGIES. Except for I. A. Richards' and Morse Peckham's somewhat eclectic use of psychology, an occasional nod to a Gestalt psychologist like Kurt Koffka, or a mention of Piaget's work on the devel. of play and symbolic thought in children, academic psychology did not attract the attention of theorists on poetics until the 1970s. Since then, a number of literary theorists have begun to explore artificial intelligence, developmental and cognitive psychology, and other subfields of the cognitive sciences that deal with poems, stories, humor, metaphor, and general symbolic activities. *Poetics* (1971–), ed. by Dutch narratologist Teun van Dijk, was the first journal to provide a forum on theory for both literary scholars and scientists of *les sciences de l'homme* and spurred three other jours., *Spiel* (1982–), *Empirical Studies of the Arts* (1983–), and

Metaphor and Symbolic Activity (1986–).

Van Dijk and others continued the multidisciplinary research program on lang. and lit. begun by Rus. Formalists and continued by Fr. structuralists and Ger. text-grammarians. For example, psychologist Colin Martindale examined trends in Eng. and Fr. poetry, showing how their evolutions (due to the socio-psychological pressure toward novelty) differed. The use of certain poetic features increased in linear fashion while the use of other conventions seemed best described as cyclical. Robert Brooke has shown the complementarity of some models of reading (using a poem by W. Stafford).

Metaphors We Live By, a 1980 book by cognitive linguist George Lakoff and philosopher Mark Johnson, has been equally influential among cognitive scientists and literary scholars. More recent books by Lakoff and Turner show how poetry builds on the established metaphors of a culture. For example, from *life is a journey* Emily Dickinson can generate *death is a coachman*. Theorists on poetics have paid less heed to Roger Schank's 1982 book on *Dynamic Memory*. This artificial-intelligence researcher argued that much of remembering (and therefore thinking) is a kind of reminding, which functions according to story-like scenarios. Taken together, Lakoff's and Schank's research suggests that if metaphors, stories, and remindings are basic to the structure and functioning of the human conceptual system, then the literary and rhetorical phenomena of everyday life must be central to any worthwhile general psychology, incl. a psychology of lang. and lit.

Discourse analysts study people alongside texts, focusing on thought processes leading to the product as well as on the poem itself. Such analysts study how a child acquires the skills needed to produce and understand rhymes, metaphors, jokes, or stories; what emotional and cognitive structures and processes are involved once this competence is established; what happens when the processes break down because of brain damage; what people remember, and what they prefer, and why.

Consider a metaphor, "white butterflies" for "snowflakes." Both children and adults can produce or understand it, but (psychologists have shown) by different processes. A psychology of metaphor (q.v.) must first be able to distinguish the adult's and the child's mental representations of the images, concepts, and words for "white butterflies" and then be able to specify the different mental steps both took in order to arrive at the production or comprehension of snowflakes as "butterflies." This process-oriented approach to thinking leads artificial-intelligence researcher Jerry Hobbs to model metaphor comprehension in four stages. First, when the metaphor is new, "snowflake" is analyzed as a potential member of the category of things known as "butterfly." Second, when the metaphor is met again it can be analyzed easily. Third, it becomes an automatic routine, still analyzable but no longer analyzed (clichés or tired metaphors like the "foot" of a mountain). Finally, the metaphor dies: neither analyzed nor analyzable, only specialists can recapture its historical motivation ("muscle": small mouse—see DEAD METAPHOR).

To a psychologist, some 20th-c. literary theory uses formalisms that do not validly describe how people think and feel. For example, how do readers go about understanding genres? Formalists try to classify text types in Aristotelian fashion, but this procedure provides a psychologically meager representation of what people know when they are said to know a genre. Contrast psychologist Eleanor Rosch's "reference point reasoning." For her, categorizing does not always involve a minimal set of shared features but can include non-necessary but frequent traits as well as prototypical models or exemplars. Instead of listing necessary conditions that define pastoral elegy, one could simply say *Lycidas, Adonais, Thyrsis*. Artificial-intelligence work shows that "common sense" succeeds where logic-bound machines fail. Out of this realization has come a new respect for the poetic and metaphorical ways in which we think. Putting this insight into practice is the challenge for cognitive poetics, indeed for all of psych. crit. See also CRITICISM; INTERPRETATION; POETIC MADNESS; THEORY. M.G.

OVERVIEWS: F. J. Hoffman, *Freudianism and the Literary Mind* (1957); J. Strachey, "List of Writings by Freud on Aesthetic Subjects," *Standard Ed.*, v. 21 (1961); M. Grimaud, "Recent Trends in Psychoanalysis," *Sub-Stance* 13 (1976), "Part Three," *Saint / Oedipus* (1982); N. N. Holland, "Literary Interp. and Three Phases of Psychoanalysis," *Psychoanalysis, Creativity, and Lit.*, ed. A. Roland (1978); D. Bleich et al., "The Psych. Study of Lang. and Lit.," *Style* 12 (1978)—bibl.; M. A. Skura, *The Literary Use of the Psychoanalytic Process* (1981); E. Winner, *Invented Worlds* (1982); M. Schwartz and D. Willbern, "Lit. and Psychology," *Interrelations of Lit.*, ed. J.-P. Barricelli and J. Gibaldi (1982); E. Wright, *Psychoanalytic Crit.* (1984); J. Natoli and F. Rusch, *Psychocrit.* (1984)—bibl.

PSYCHOANALYTIC PSYCHOLOGY I: E. Wilson, *The Wound and the Bow* (1929); M. Bonaparte, *Edgar Poe* (1933); W. Empson, *Some Versions of Pastoral* (1935); K. Burke, *The Philosophy of Literary Form* (1941), *Lang. as Symbolic Action* (1966); E. Jones, *Hamlet and Oedipus* (1949); S. Freud, *Standard Ed. of the Complete Psychological Works of Sigmund Freud*, ed. J. Strachey, 24 v. (1953–74); L. Trilling, "Freud and Lit.," *The Liberal Imagination* (1953), "Art and Neurosis," *Art and Psychoanalysis*, ed. W. Phillips (1963); P. Greenacre, *Swift and Carroll* (1955); Wellek and Warren, ch. 8; *Psychoanalysis and Literary Process*, ed. F. C. Crews (1970); M. Kaplan and R. Kloss, *The Unspoken Motive* (1973); H. Bloom, *The Anxiety of Influence* (1973).

PSYCHOANALYTIC PSYCHOLOGY II: E. F. Sharpe,

Coll. Papers on Psycho-Analysis (1950); E. Kris, *Psychoanalytic Explorations in Art* (1952); L. Edel, *Henry James* (1953–72), *Literary Biography* (1959); S. O. Lesser, *Fiction and the Unconscious* (1957); C. Mauron, *Des Métaphores obsédantes au mythe personnel* (1963); *Psychoanalysis and Lit.*, ed. H. Ruitenbeek (1964); *Hidden Patterns*, ed. L. and E. Manheim (1966); J. Kaplan, *Mr. Clemens and Mark Twain* (1966), *Walt Whitman* (1980); B. C. Meyer, *Joseph Conrad* (1967), *Houdini* (1976); N. N. Holland, *The Dynamics of Literary Response* (1968, 1989); N. Fruman, *Coleridge, the Damaged Archangel* (1971); *The Practice of Psychoanalytic Crit.*, ed. L. Tennenhouse (1976); C. G. Wolff, *Feast of Words* (1977), *Emily Dickinson* (1986); R. Rogers, *Metaphor* (1978).

PSYCHOANALYTIC PSYCHOLOGY III: K. Horney, *Neurosis and Human Growth* (1950); J. Lacan, *Le Séminaire* (1953–75), *Écrits* (1966); D. W. Winnicott, *Playing and Reality* (1971); H. Kohut, *The Analysis of the Self* (1971); Fr. Freud, Spec. Iss. of *YFS* 48 (1972); J. Mitchell, *Psychoanalysis and Feminism* (1974); M. Schwartz, "Where is Lit.?" *CE* 36 (1975); N. N. Holland, *Poems in Persons* (1973, 1989), *5 Readers Reading* (1975), *Laughing* (1982), *The Brain of Robert Frost* (1988); C. G. Wolff, *A Feast of Words* (1977); L. Bersani, *Baudelaire and Freud* (1977), *The Freudian Body* (1986); L. Irigaray, *Ce sexe qui n'en est pas un* (1977); S. Felman, *Lit. and Psychoanalysis* (1977), *La Folie et la chose littéraire* (1978); *Between Reality and Fantasy*, ed. S. A. Grolnick and L. Barkin (1978); N. Chodorow, *The Reproduction of Mothering* (1978); *Psychoanalysis and the Question of the Text*, ed. G. Hartman (1978); *Psychoanalysis, Creativity, and Lit.*, ed. A. Roland (1978); S. M. Gilbert and S. Gubar, *The Madwoman in the Attic* (1979), *No Man's Land* (1988); *New Fr. Feminisms*, ed. E. Marks and I. de Courtivron (1980); *Representing Shakespeare*, ed. M. Schwartz and C. Kahn (1980); *Psychology and Lit.*, Spec. Iss. of *NLH* 12, 1 (1980); R. P. Wheeler, *Shakespeare's Devel. and the Problem Comedies* (1981); *The Fictional Father*, ed. R. C. Davis (1981); R. Silhol, *Le Texte du désir* (1984); *The (M)other Tongue*, ed. S. N. Garner et al. (1985); B. J. Paris, "Horney, Maslow, and the Third Force," *Third Force Psychology and the Study of Lit.* (1986); *Narcissism and the Text*, ed. L. Layton and B. A. Schapiro (1986).

ARCHETYPAL PSYCHOLOGY: M. J. Thorburn, *Art and the Unconscious* (1925); M. Bodkin, *Archetypal Patterns in Poetry* (1934); C. Jung, *Collected Works*, Bollingen Ser., 20 v. (1956–79), *The Structure and Dynamics of the Psyche* (1960); Frye; H. Read, *Poetry and Experience* (1967); K. Raine, "Poetic Dynamics as a Vehicle of Trad.," *Eranos Jahrbuch* (1970); G. Hough, "Poetry and the Anima," *Spring* (1973); J. Hillman, *Re-Visioning Psychology* (1975), *Archetypal Psychology* (1983); P. Berry-Hillman, *Echo's Subtle Body* (1982); P. Kugler, *The Alchemy of Discourse* (1982); R. Avens, *The New Gnosis* (1984); M. Adams, "Deconstructive Philosophy and Imaginal Psychology," *Jour. of Lit. Crit.* 2 (1985).

OTHER PSYCHOLOGIES: I. A. Richards, *Principles of Lit. Crit.* (1924); J. Piaget, "The Secondary Symbolism of Play," *Play, Dreams and Imitation in Childhood* (1962); M. Peckham, *Man's Rage for Chaos* (1965); C. Martindale, *Romantic Progression* (1975); *The Arts and Cognition*, ed. D. Perkins and B. Leondar (1977); T. van Dijk, "Advice on Theoretical Poetics," *Poetics* 8 (1979); E. Rosch, "Prototype Classification and Logical Classification," *New Trends in Conceptual Representation*, ed. E. K. Scholnick (1983); J. Hobbs, "Metaphor Interp. as Selective Inferencing," *Empirical Studies of the Arts* 1 (1983); R. Brooke, "Three Models of Narrative Comprehension," *Empirical Studies of the Arts* 2 (1984); G. Lakoff, *Women, Fire, and Dangerous Things* (1987); G. Lakoff and M. Turner, *More than Cool Reason* (1989).

JOURNALS: *Am. Imago; Empirical Studies of the Arts*—cognitive; *Eranos*—archetypal; *IPSA Abstracts* [Institute for Psych. Study of the Arts]—annual bibl. and abstracts; *Littoral*—Lacan; *Metaphor and Symbolic Activity; Ornicar*—Lacan; *Poetics; Psychiatry and the Humanities; Psychoanalytic Quarterly; Lit. and Psychology; Spiel*—cognitive; *Spring*—archetypal. N.N.H.; P.K.K.; M.G.

PUERTO RICAN POETRY. The historical devel. of the art of poetry in Puerto Rico dates back to the Taino Indians. On his second voyage in 1493, Columbus discovered Puerto Rico, which was called *Borinquen* by the Indians. The Sp. chroniclers described the *Areyto* of the Tainos as a choral ritual of magical and aesthetic significance. Oral poetry, songs, and dances merged in recitation, movement, and music. In the 16th c., *Areyto* remnants mingled with folklore and popular poetry brought by Spaniards and Africans to their new home.

The *Sixth elegy* of Juan de Castellanos' (1522–1607) *Elegías de Varones Ilustres de Indias*, dedicated to Juan Ponce de León and his conquest of Borinquen, is comparable to Ercillas' *La Araucana*. The impact of the Golden Age on the cultural life of Puerto Rico centered on the seven years that Bishop Bernardo de Balbuena (1561–1627) lived on the island until his death. His work and his library in San Juan were so esteemed that Lope de Vega mentioned this fact in *Laurel de Apolo*. The first native poet, the priest-scholar Francisco de Ayerra y Santamaría (1630–1708), spent his adult life in Mexico. Found in his elaborate baroque poetry is an exceptional sonnet dedicated to Sor Juana Inés de la Cruz at her death.

By the mid 19th c., poetry had emerged as the preferred medium for expression of the creative spirit in the island's artistic and literary life. Youth collected their own prose and poetry in anthologies called *aguinaldo, album*, or *cancionero*. Poets recited and improvised verse in public and official gatherings. Founded in 1876, the *Ateneo Puertorriqueño* became an intellectual center. Neoclassical and romantic poets lectured, recited, and celebrated *juegos florales*. The influence of Sp. and Latin-Am. poetry was pervasive in the late 19th c.: romanticism dominated, from the most passionate nuance to the most subtle and refined. Themes of love and patriotism flourished in the works of such talented writers as Alejandro Tapia y Rivera (1826–82), Lola Rodríguez de Tío (1843–1924), and José Gautier Benítez (1851–80). Tapia exalted the past in *La Sataniada*, the most extensive P. R. poem of the 19th c. The 30 cantos in 8-line stanzas are reminiscent of Espronceda's *El Diablo Mundo*. Lola Rodríquez de Tió, the first recognized outstanding woman writer, created love poetry and patriotic verse charged with vigor and fire. As a political exile, she lived in Caracas, New York City, and finally in Cuba until her death. Among her contributions to her homeland's culture are the revolutionary lyrics of *La Borinqueña*, the national anthem. Gautier Benítez excelled in writing love and patriotic verse similar to the verse of Byron and Bécquer. His lyrical expressions of nostalgic absence and joy at the return to the shores of Borinquen attest to his essential romanticism.

At the turn of the century, the impact of the Sp.-Am. War (1898), with the subsequent transferral of Puerto Rico from the colonial orbit of Spain to that of the U.S., created social and artistic unrest. This "fear and trembling" gave the poetry of the pre-World War I period (until 1918) a special character within the prevalent modernismo (q.v.). The struggle to preserve the vernacular and to survive as a Sp.-Am. cultural entity gave poetry a strongly romantic accent. Even so, the poets adopted the aesthetic credo, metrical innovations, and stylistic freedom that the Nicaraguan master Rubén Darío was disseminating in his new verse throughout the Sp.-speaking world. Among the first innovators of P. R. p. was José de Diego (1866–1918), celebrated both for his patriotic and love poems: in 1915 he became the torchbearer in defense of the Sp. lang.

Modernismo denounced the perils of colonialism under the new master, while searching for universal values. Examples abound in the poetry of Luis Lloréns Torres (1878–1944), Virgilio Dávila (1869–1943), Evaristo Ribera Chevremont (1896–1976), and Luis Palés Matos (1899–1959). Lloréns Torres, together with Nemesio Canales (1878–1923), the prominent author of *Paliques*, founded the literary magazine *Revista de las Antillas* in 1913. This opened the way for the avant-garde movements following World War I. The defense of Hispanic roots and the ideal of Antillean union dominated the work of thinker-patriot Eugenio María de Hostos (1839–1903). In turn, these thoughts inspired some of Lloréns' best poems: "Song of the Antilles" and "Mare Nostrum." Besides those major works he wrote *décimas* and *coplas* (qq.v.) of extraordinary beauty, reviving "criollo" motifs in a search for identity. Virgilio Dávila chanted the beauties of country life and

smalltown tempo with a sense of humor and graceful criticism in *Pueblito de Antes* (1916) and *Aromas del Terruño* (1917). Introducing post- and ultramodern tendencies from Spain, Ribera Chevremont's poetry offers a new transition. *Tú, Mar y Yo y Ella* (1946) and *El Hondero lanzó la piedra* (1975) are two of his best books.

The avant-garde movements had captured the minds and imaginations of the poets around 1930. Luis Palés Matos, outstanding exponent of Afro-Antillean themes, created the masterpiece *Tun Tun de Pasa y Grifería* (1937), considered as significant as the Cuban poetry of Ballagas and Nicolás Guillén. Palés devised his own mythology of black culture which exploits onomatopoeic rhythms with magical cadence and carries a satirical, social protest. He identifies Caribbean islands with subtlety and refinement:

> Cuba—ñáñigo y bachata
> Haití—vodú y calabaza
> Puerto Rico—burundanga.

The movement and dance of the "African soul" in the Caribbean is expressed in some of his poems:

> Calabó y bambú bambú y calabó
> Es el sol de fuego que arde en Tumbuctú
> Es la danza negra de Fernando Poo
> El alma africana que vibrando está
> En el ritmo gordo del mariyandá.

The avant-garde movements, short-lived but impressive, followed the pattern set by European and Latin-Am. ultra-modern trends. Ultraism, cubism, dada (qq.v.) and many other philosophical, artistic, and anti-artistic tendencies (like existentialism) have left their mark on 20th-c. P. R. p. Some of the more significant are: "Noismo," based on the concept of negation; "transcendentalismo," suggesting the metaphysical; "atalayismo," boldy emphasizing the extravagant side of every possible idea.

According to the ideology, imagination, and personality of the writer, a variety of lang. and a search for originality typify 20th-c. P. R. p. Prominent scholar-poet José A. Balseiro (b. 1900) published his first books under the influence of Rubén Darío. His favorite themes have been love, art, music, and a sentimental patriotism. His *El Ala y el Beso* (1983) has the charm of a classic and the surprise of a youthful approach to life. In his youth, Luis Muñoz Marín (1898–1980), politician and creator of the "Estado Libre Asociado" (Commonwealth status), wrote excellent poems in Eng. and Sp. denouncing misery and social injustice.

The Nationalist Party, led by Pedro Albizu Campos, has generated since the 1930s a political poetry of protest and denunciation of colonialism. Many poets wrote in defense of the poor, demanding social justice. Francisco Manrique Cabrera (1908–78), in *Poemas de mi Tierra, Tierra* (1936), stressed a "neocriollismo," characterized by a telluric and mysterious symbiosis with the soil, the "tierra, tierra" of one's birth with its strongly patriotic and emotive overtones. Juan Antonio Corretjer (1908–85), in *Amor de Puerto Rico, Alabanza en la Torre de Lares* and other books, expressed his militant, Marxist ideas and his ideological fusion of history, geography, and patriotism within a comprehensive poetical whole.

Women came to the fore as excellent poets in the 1930–50 period. Clara Lair's (1895–1973) passionate accent compares to the erotic frenzy of the Uruguayan Juana de Ibarbouru and the Argentinian Alfonsina Storni. *Arras de Cristal* (1937) and *Trópico Amargo* (1950), together with *Cuaderno* (1961), represent her best work. Julia de Burgos (1914–53) combines a telluric, "neocriollista" love of nature with a patriotic and cosmic love of freedom. She expresses in tender, brave accents the struggles of a person suffering love, loneliness, and death in tragic circumstances. Her famous poem *Rio Grande de Loíza* is a biographical song in which self and river are intertwined through symbolic myth. Critics laud her books: *Poemas en Veinte Surcos* (1938), *Canción de la Verdad Sencilla* (1939), and *Mar, tú y Otros Poemas* (1954).

Since 1960, there has been a rich output of anthologies, literary reviews, and performances. So-called "canta-autores" sing their poems to the accompaniment of music, popularizing their own work and that of the past. The quantity and quality of creative lyrical minds, whose militant voices mingle in gradations of artistic and humanitarian themes, form a pattern of multiple tones and meanings. They include the denunciation of colonialism and identification with "Third World" struggles and Latin-Am. woes.

Francisco Matos Paoli (b. 1915), author of *Elogio de la Locura* and candidate for both the Nobel and Cervantes Prizes, is the most prolific 20th-c. poet to date. His lang., his faith, the metaphysical search for the unknown, and his total dedication to poetry deserve the high esteem he commands. Paoli's best known book is *Elogio de la Locura*. Luis Hernández Aquino (1907–88), a scholar, linguist, and poet, writes about hist. and the Sp. and Taino components of the P. R. identity. He founded *Bayoán*, one of the finest poetry reviews (1950–51, 1961–65), and wrote *Isla para la Angustia*, one of the best books of contemporary P. R. p.

Some P. R. poets have done their work in the U.S., esp. in New York City. Though some may have spent most of their lives there, they continue to write in Sp. and to express their attachment to the homeland. Among the best are: Diana Ramírez de Arellano (b. 1919), Juan Avilés (b. 1904), Clemento Soto Vélez (b. 1905), and Graciany Miranda Archilla (b. 1910). A younger generation, known as "Neo-Ricans," write poetry in Eng. and mixed Sp. and Eng. similar to that published by the Chicanos. This new speech pattern exploring new areas of expression is characteristic of Víctor Hernández Cruz (b. 1949) and of Pedro Pietri (b.

1944), who has written movingly about the New York Puerto Ricans in *P. R. Obituary*. One of the best translators of Eng. poetry to Sp. is César A. Portala (b. 1914), a P. R. poet also living in New York.

Vehicles for post-1950 poetry and crit., the new but short-lived reviews represent a chain of aesthetic and ideological stages that trace the process of poetic devel. in modern P. R. The most important are: *Bayoán* (1950–51, 1961–65); *Guajana* (1962–66); *Mester* (1966); *Orfeo* (1954–56); *Pegaso* (1952); *Versiones* (1966); *Ventana* (1975); *Alero* (1982–86); and *Mairena* (1979–87). Other general magazines open to poetry and poetics have been *Asomante*, *Sin Nombre*, and *Zona de Carga y Descarga*. Probably the best critic of poetry, and a poet himself, is Juan Martínez Capó (b. 1923). Author of *Viaje* (1961), for years he has maintained a regular weekly article in one of the leading newspapers, *El Mundo*.

Since 1980, the younger and older generations have upset the age barrier, establishing and maintaining a closer relationship in public recitals and literary meetings. Consequently, the discussion of "poetry and poetics" has broadened in scope. *En Una Sola Torre (50 años de Poesía Puertorriqueña)* (1986) includes a great variety of poets. Among them is the work of Angela María Dávila (b. 1944), author of *Animal Fiero y Tierno* (1977). Also represented is 90-year-old Manuel Joglar Cacho (b. 1898), author of such works as *La Sed del Agua* (1965), *Soliloquios de Lázaro* (1956), and *Cien Campanas en una Sola Torre* (1986). Martínez Capó considers this "exceptional anthology" of "diverse context" a magnificent compendium of 50 years of P. R. p. The influences on current P. R. p. are many, but chiefly Sp. poetry of the generation of 1927 (Lorca, Alberti, Alonso, et al.) and Latin-Am. poetry from Darío onward (Neruda, Vallejo, Borges, et al.). Furthermore, today's poetry, in lang. and in theme, reflects the impact of modern technology on an unwary humanity, drug addiction, the women's liberation movement, and obscenity. Contemporary P. R. p. lends itself to a wide range of critical approaches. See also SPANISH POETRY; SPANISH-AMERICAN POETRY.

ANTHOLOGIES: *The P. R. Poets*, ed. A. Matilla and I. Silén (1972); *BORINQUEN*, ed. M. T. Babín and S. Steiner (1974); *Poesía militante Puertorriqueña*, M. de la Puebla (1979); *Herejes y mitificadores: Muestra de poesía Puertorriqueña en los Estados Unidos*, ed. E. Barradas y Rafael Rodríguez (1980); *Inventing a Word: An Anthol. of 20th-C. P. R. P.*, ed. J. Marzán (1980); *Antología de la poesía de la mujer Puertorriqueña*, ed. T. Ortiz (1981); *Antología general de la poesía Puertorriqueña: Tradición y originalidad*, ed. L. Ríos (1982); *En una sola torre (50 años de poesía Puertorriqueña)* (1986).

HISTORY AND CRITICISM: L. H. Aquino, *Movimientos literarios del siglo XX en P. R.* (1951), *Nuestra aventura literaria* (1966); J. R. de Alvarez, *Literatura Puertorriqueña: Su proceso en el tiempo*

(1983); J. E. González, *La poesía contemporánea de Puerto Rico, 1930–60* (1986). M.-T.B.

PUN. Every art form knows ps. Painting and sculpture have visual ps. (e.g. optical illusions), and music has melodic, rhythmic, and harmonic ps. (e.g. the "deceptive cadence"), but they are most deeply involved with lang. and literary art. Verbal ps. play with sound and meaning: identical or similar sounds bring together two (or more) meanings. The p. "works" when the context gives both meanings significance. In the lang. of poetry we find lexical ps., grammatical ps., and the sophisticated form of p. based on words or phrases which simultaneously belong to disparate levels of diction, situation, or experience. A lexical p. turns on an ambiguous word: Shakespeare's witty Mercutio, mortally wounded, says that by tomorrow he will be "a grave man" (*Romeo and Juliet* 3.1.96), and melancholy Hamlet, asked by Claudius why the "clouds" of mourning still hang on him, replies that on the contrary he is "too much in the sun" (and "son"; *Hamlet* 1.2.67). Although Noah Webster called punning "a low species of wit," it can be a powerful instrument of poetic lang. when it reveals that two things which bear the same name, i.e. the same phonic sequence, also share deeper affinities. John Donne, meditating on the Crucifixion, used Hamlet's p. to embrace profound religious paradox: "There I should see a Sunne, by rising set, / And by that setting endlesse day beget" ("Goodfriday, 1613. Riding Westward").

A grammatical p. turns on some ambiguity in morphology or syntax, e.g. ambiguous parts of speech. Milton describes Eve eating the forbidden fruit with a chilling p. of this type: "Greedily she ingorg'd without restraint, / And knew not eating Death" (*PL* 9.791–92)—i.e., Eve did not know that with the apple she was eating death, and also did not yet know of the ravenous figure of Death soon on its way to devour *her*.

The third form of p. appears at its simplest in those joking tales in which the punchline plays off a familiar idiom, proverb, or slogan ("shaggy dog" stories). A long tale about a bear wearing tennis shoes who is caught stealing a Chinese man's lumber ends with the man shouting "Stop! Boyfoot bear with teak of Chan!" In poetry this form is the basis for what Ezra Pound called *logopoeia* (q.v.). Early Gr. lyric frequently used epic diction in distinctly nonheroic contexts: e.g. taking Homer's *lusimelēs* ("limb-loosening," "limb-relaxing"), an epithet of sleep in the *Odyssey*, and applying it to desire (Archilochos) or love (Sappho). In OE poetry certain words such as "lord," "joy," and "glory" can have double reference—one pagan and heroic, the other Christian and homiletic: e.g. "There is no man on earth . . . whose *dryhten* [earthly lord] is so gracious that he never worries as to what *dryhten* [heavenly Lord] will bring about for him" (*The Seafarer*). Many lines in modernist poems such as T. S. Eliot's *The Waste Land* and Ezra

Pound's *Hugh Selwyn Mauberley* reverberate with this device. Involving both allusion and irony (qq.v.), such ps. bring together different views of human experience for analogy and contrast.

The word *p.* first appeared in Eng. ca. 1650; its origins are not clear. At the same time, neoclassical taste conceived a dislike for ps. in literary lang. which lasted until modernism. Dryden wrote that Shakespeare's comic wit too often degenerated into "clenches," or ps. (*An Essay of Dramatic Poesy* [1668]); Addison attacked ps. as "false wit" (*Spectator* no. 61 [1711]); Dr. Johnson complained about Shakespeare's fatal "quibbles," ps. again ("Preface to Shakespeare" [1765]). Before that, however, the p. had long been treated seriously as a topic in Cl., medieval, and Ren. rhet., where it was known as the figure of speech called *paronomasia* (Gr.) or *adnominatio* (Lat.). The rhetoricians were primarily interested in the figure which *repeated* words of identical or similar sounds. Roman rhetorical treatises such as the anonymous *Rhetorica ad Herennium* (4.13–23) and Quintilian's *Institutio oratoria* (9.3) developed elaborate (if inconsistent) categories and nomenclature for this and other figures—distinguishing, for example, whether the sound-repetition brought with it a completely different word, a secondary or extended meaning of the same word, the same word with a different prefix or vowel-length (in Gr. and Lat.), a different word with the same ending (*homoeoteleuton*), the same word in a different grammatical form or function in the sentence, etc. Such figures were considered useful "ornaments" of lang. when kept under control by decorum, and were most valuable, Aristotle suggested (*Rhet.* 3.11), when they supported structural and conceptual meaning, using aural repetition to help define a revealing antithesis or powerful metaphor. Emily Dickinson inherits that trad. when she repeats different grammatical forms of the verb *stop* (*for*), varying at the same time the emphases on its colloquial and literal meanings ("call for" and "cease"): "Because I could not stop for Death— / He kindly stopped for me—" (no. 712). Milton also draws on the rhetorical trad. when he has Adam address Eve as "Sole Eve, Associate sole" (*PL* 9.227): forewarned of an enemy in the Garden, Adam wishes to dissuade Eve from going off alone, first by reminding her she is both the "only" Eve he has and "alone" Eve without him, then by saying his "only" associate is also an associate "soul"—a complex paronomasia which discovers all that is at risk. See also ALLUSION; AMBIGUITY; ANAGRAM; IDENTICAL RHYME; RIDDLE; WIT.

Sr. M. Joseph, *Shakespeare's Use of the Arts of Lang.* (1947); Empson; L. Spitzer, "P.," *JEGP* 49 (1950)—etymology; P. F. Baum, "Chaucer's Ps.," *PMLA* 71, 73 (1956, 1958); J. Brown, "Eight Types of P.," *PMLA* 71 (1956); M. M. Mahood, *Shakespeare's Wordplay* (1957); S. B. Greenfield, *The Interp. of OE Poems* (1972), ch. 4; T. W. Ross, *Chaucer's Bawdy* (1972); Lausberg, 322–36; H. A. Ellis, *Shake-*

speare's Lusty Punning in Love's Labour's Lost
(1973); Murphy; A. Jolles, "Witz," *Einfache Formen*,
5th ed. (1974); W. C. Carroll, *The Great Feast of
Lang. in* Love's Labour's Lost (1976); Morier, s.v.
"*paronomase,*" "*annomination*"; E. Le Comte, *A Dict.
of Ps. in Milton's Eng. Poetry* (1981); Jakobson, v. 3;
F. Rubinstein, *A Dict. of Shakespeare's Sexual Ps. and
Their Significance* (1981); W. Redfern, *Ps.* (1984);
M. Foucault, *Death and the Labyrinth* (tr. 1986); E.
Cook, *Poetry, Word-play, and Word-war in Wallace
Stevens* (1988); *On Ps.,* ed. J. Culler (1988); B.
Vickers, *Cl. Rhet. in Eng. Poetry*, 2d ed. (1989),
143–44; E. Partridge, *Shakespeare's Bawdy*, 3d ed.
(1990).   A.W.

PUNCTUATION (Lat. *punctus,* "point"). A system
of nonalphabetical signs that express meaning
through implied pauses, pitch shifts, and other
intonational features. For prose, in Western
Europe, p. began as a pedagogical and scribal
guide to reading aloud. It evolved to mark syntax
for silent readers, as urged by Aldo Manuzio in
Orthographiae ratio (1566) and Ben Jonson in *The
Eng. Grammar* (ca. 1617, pub. 1640). For poetry,
however, the diachronic shift from oral delivery to
silent reading had less impact on comprehension,
because in poetry—whether its sound (q.v.) is
actual (heard) or virtual (read)—sound helps cre-
ate sense.

Both pedagogy and performance (q.v.) loom
large in the history of p. Speech seems continuous;
thus the earliest Gr. inscriptions do not separate
words. Points occasionally separate longer phrases,
and Aristotle mentions a horizontal line, the *para-
graphos*, used to introduce a new topic. At the
Museum in Alexandria, ca. 200 B.C., the librarian
Aristophanes proposed terms and marks (not cor-
responding to their modern counterparts) to dis-
tinguish a short section (*comma*) from the longer
and longest textual sections (*colon, periodos*). His
terms survived via the Roman grammarians, nota-
bly Donatus in the 4th c. A.D., and via early Chris-
tian teachers such as Jerome, who devised p. *per
cola et commata* ("by phrases") specifically to facili-
tate reading aloud of his new Vulgate tr. of the
Bible. Over the next millennium, various writers
developed systems of p., adapting musical nota-
tion (neumes) to indicate pitch shifts as well as
pauses. Thus authorities long dead could con-
tinue to prescribe correct oral recitations of sacred
texts.

For secular poetry, early printers (e.g. Caxton)
and theorists (e.g. Puttenham) emphasized the
practical functions of p.—esp. breath breaks—
rather than syntax or prescriptive interp. During
the 17th c., syntactic p. became the norm for
imaginative as well as expository prose, whereas
drama and poetry tended to retain sound-based
flexibility. Before John Urry (1721), for instance,
no editor preparing Chaucer for print punctuated
ordinary line ends. Similarly, readers of Shake-
speare's plays as scripts for performance could

realize that no amount of enforced syntactic p. can
hold to one set meaning Hamlet's "To die, to sleep
/ No more and by a sleep to say we end." During
the 19th c., however, the study of the modern
langs. succumbed to the strictures of academic
respectability. Teachers and editors began using
syntactic p. to prescribe their own imagined per-
formances of secular poetry, just as clerics a mil-
lennium earlier had prescribed oral perform-
ances of sacred Lat. prose.

The illuminated works of William Blake provide
striking examples of authorial p. as a guide to
imagined performance, for Blake laboriously en-
graved each plate with letters, visual art, and other
marks, incl. p. In the first stanza of "London,"
nonsyntactic periods that close two lines help ex-
press the narrator's initial, but illusory, sense of
control. Each stanza has progressively lighter p.,
the second spilling with no end mark into the
third, until—as ever more appalling images engulf
the narrator—p. disappears altogether from the
final stanza. The abyss yawns. Despite Blake's ef-
forts, his 20th-c. editor Geoffrey Keynes repunctu-
ated "London" in accord with modern canons of
p. and sense, i.e. in accord with prose syntax, so
that the poem in his edition (though not in oth-
ers) presents a detached narrator calmly catalogu-
ing social problems.

Many standard eds. still impose syntactic prose
p. on poetry. In the Twickenham Ed. of the Works
of Alexander Pope, for example, each editor re-
cords words that differ from the copy-text chosen,
but each modernizes p. at will, despite Pope's
letter telling a printer to "contrive the Capitals &
evry [*sic*] thing exactly to correspond" with an
earlier printing.

How do editors justify changing authorial p.? In
part, they are applying methodologies developed
for Cl. and medieval mss., in which any p. that
appears is based on a local scribal dialect that may
bear little or no relationship to our present stan-
dardized system. In one ms. trad., a virgule (slash,
solidus) might mark poetic caesura, for example;
in another trad. a virgule may mark the shortest
of three pauses, and in yet another the longest of
six divisions into sense units. The slanted line went
nameless until 1837, when Henry Hallam adopted
a zoological term to declare that virgules in
Chaucer mss. always mark caesura—an assertion
which, though dead wrong, was not definitively
disproven until 1982.

In mss., other p. marks also vary from one region
to another, even within the same decade. Medieval
dialects of neumes varied likewise, yet stan-
dardized musical notation is not now expected to
explicate a set meaning for either readers or per-
formers of a score. But editors of Cl. and medieval
poetry began to supply less experienced readers
with syntactic p. suitable to explicative prose.
Nearly all Chaucer eds. since 1835, for example,
have imposed the full range of mod. p. Quotation
marks in particular create demonstrable interpre-

tive problems absent from mss. of Chaucer, wherein a given speech need not be assigned definitely to the narrator or to one or another character. By specifying p. absent from or altering p. present in mss., modern editors continue to prescribe their own silent performances of key poetic passages.

In cultures that have not undergone such a pronounced shift from religious to secular textual education, such as Arabic or Chinese, most p. still signals breath breaks and major new topics. Only occasionally does it indicate change in speaker or the many other vocal intonations commonly prescribed in the West by means of syntactic p. applied—or misapplied—to poetry. See also PERIOD.

P. Simpson, *Shakespearian P.* (1911); W. J. Ong, "Historical Backgrounds of Elizabethan and Jacobean P. Theory," *PMLA* 59 (1944); A. Pope, *The Rape of the Lock and Other Poems*, 3d ed., ed. G. Tillotson (1962), General Note; M. Treip, *Milton's P. and Changing Eng. Usage, 1582-1676* (1970); E. O. Wingo, *Lat. P. in the Cl. Age* (1972); L. D. Reynolds and N. G. Wilson, *Scribes and Scholars*, 2d ed. (1974)—discursive bibl. on current debates re Gr. and Lat. p.; N. Blake, "P. Marks," *Eng. Lang. in Med. Lit.* (1977); G. Killough, "P. and Caesura in Chaucer," *SAC* 4 (1982); B. Bowden, *Chaucer Aloud* (1987), s.v. "p." in index; T. J. Brown, "P.," s.v. "Writing," *New Encyclopedia Britannica: Macropaedia*, 15th ed. (1990); G. Nunberg, *The Linguistics of P.* (1990); J. Lennard, *But I Digress* (1991); M. B. Parkes, *Pause and Effect: The History of P. in the West* (1992). B.BO.

PURE POETRY (Fr. *poésie pure*, Ger. *absolute Dichtung*). This term refers most specifically to "La Poésie pure," a doctrine derived from Edgar Allan Poe by the Fr. symbolist poets—Baudelaire, Mallarmé, and Valéry—and widely discussed in the late 19th and early 20th c. (see SYMBOLISM). In this context, "pure" is equivalent to absolute, on the analogy of absolute music, i.e. structuring of sound without ostensible semantic content. The analogy is significant in that both the theory and practice of the symbolists were influenced by the relations of music and poetry (q.v.).

The doctrine was first enunciated in Poe's essay "The Poetic Principle." For Poe, the essential quality of poetry is a kind of lyricism distinguished by intensity and virtually identical with music in its effects. Since the duration of intensity is limited by psychological conditions, Poe concludes that the long poem is a contradiction in terms and that passages which fail to achieve a high level of intensity should not be included in the category of poetry. Poetry is regarded as being entirely an aesthetic phenomenon, differentiated from and independent of the intellect and the moral sense. The products of the latter faculties, ideas and passions, are more properly relegated to the province of prose, and their presence in a poem is positively detrimental to poetic effect.

In their desire for poetry to attain to the condition of music, the symbolists were wholehearted disciples of Poe; in elaborating his theory, however, they were far more aware of the problem of lang. than Poe had been. The relevance of the doctrine of p. p. to critical theory thus rests almost entirely upon its concern with the symbolic or iconic properties of lang. The impetus toward this line of speculation was given in Baudelaire's rephrasing of Poe: the goal of poetry is of the same nature as its principle, and it should have nothing in view but itself. The aim of the symbolists was to confer autonomy (q.v.) upon poetry by subjecting the semantic properties of lang. to the phonetic properties of words, their sounds, kinship, and connotations.

It would not be accurate, however, to ascribe unity of aim to the whole symbolist movement. For Baudelaire, the autonomy of poetic lang. was incomplete in that meaning involved "correspondances" with an ultimate reality. Poe, in his reference to the "supernal beauty" which p. p. was capable of achieving, had hinted at the possibility of a metaphysical or mystical significance in verbal music. The Abbé Bremond was more explicit in claiming a mystical value for p. p. Mallarmé's conception of p. p. was of a point at which poetry would attain complete linguistic autonomy, the words themselves taking over the initiative and creating the meanings, liberating themselves from the semiotic tyranny of the lang. and the deliberate intentions of the poet. With Mallarmé, subject matter is a function of an intense preoccupation with the medium.

Speculation in this direction reached its limit in Valéry, who eventually found the processes of poetic composition more interesting than the poetry itself. Valéry's contribution to the doctrine of p. p. poetry focused on the most fundamental yet ineluctable aspects of poetic lang., the relation of sound and sense. In his first exposition (prefaced to a volume of verse by Lucien Fabré), Valéry defines p. p. as poetry which is isolated from everything but its essence. Poe's strictures on long poems and on the didactic motive are repeated. The aim of p. p. is to attain from lang. an effect comparable to that produced on the nervous system by music. This essay gave rise to considerable discussion, however, and Valéry was later to deny, without abandoning the doctrine, that he had advocated p. p. in a literal sense. It represented for him a theoretical goal, rarely attainable in view of the nature of lang., wherein sound and meaning form a union as intimate as that of body and soul.

Poe's ideas had little direct influence on Eng.-speaking critics and poets; the idea of p. p. was mainly an importation from France. But the qualities of vagueness and suggestiveness valued by Poe and the symbolists were contrary to the imagist demand (see IMAGISM) for the utmost precision in the rendering of the image (q.v.). In 1924 George Moore brought out an anthol. entitled *P. P.*, but while Moore had absorbed the views of the symbolists, his own conception returns to the earlier, plastic trad. of the Parnassians (q.v.). T. S. Eliot regarded p. p. as the most original devel. in the aesthetic of verse made in the last century, characteristically modern in its emphasis upon the medium of verse and its indifference to content, yet also one which decisively terminated with Valéry. Other critics, however, have continued to find the absolutist, sound-intensive, and antireferential mode in modern poems such as Wallace Stevens' "Sea Surface Full of Clouds," not to mention the more radical experiments which followed the modernist era in Beat poetry, language poetry (qq.v.), "text-sound," intermedia, and "sound poetry" (q.v.). If all poetry does indeed aspire to the condition of music, that aspiration will make itself manifest somewhere in the poetry of every age and culture. See also ABSTRACT POEM; FRENCH POETRY; HERMETICISM; SOUND; SYMBOLISM.

H. Bremond, *La Poésie pure* (1926); F. Porché, *Paul Valéry et la poésie pure* (1926); R. P. Warren, "Pure and Impure Poetry," *KR* 5 (1943); T. S. Eliot, "From Poe to Valéry," *RHR* 2 (1949); F. Scarfe, *The Art of Paul Valéry* (1954); Sr. C. de Ste. M. Dion, *The Idea of "P. P." in Eng. Crit. 1900–1945* (1948); H. W. Decker, *P. P., 1925–1930: Theory and Debate in France* (1962); M. Landmann, *Die absolute Dichtung* (1963); B. Böschenstein, *Studien zur Dichtung der Absoluten* (1968); D. J. Mossop, *P. P.: Studies in Fr. Poetic Theory and Practice 1746 to 1945* (1971); Morier; S. Hart, "Poésie pure in Three Sp. Poets," *FMLS* 20 (1984). S.F.; T.V.F.B.

PUY. See RHYME ROYAL.

PYRRHIC (Gr. "used in the *pyrrichē* or war dance"). In Cl. prosody, a metrical foot of two short syllables. This may be said to have been the shortest metrical foot in Gr. and Lat. verse, although its admissibility was denied by the ancient *rhythmici* such as Aristoxenus, who felt that feet must be of at least three *chronoi* (time elements). In the modern prosodies based on accent, such as Eng., the existence of p. feet is disputed: several important metrists (e.g. Mayor, Bridges, Malof, Wright) have recognized them as legitimate variations or substitutions in iambic verse; others deny them (Schipper, Saintsbury). The dispute between the two camps turns on the issue of whether gradations of stress in the line are to be treated relatively or absolutely. In a line such as Marvell's "To a green Thought in a green Shade," the stress pattern (using Trager-Smith notation of 4 levels of stress numbered 1 through 4, 1 being strongest, 4 weakest) might be said to be 3-4-2-1-3-4-2-1. Since Otto Jespersen's seminal 1903 article "Notes on Metre," many prosodists have accepted his claim that stress is perceived only in relation to its surroundings; and if one asks about each pair of syllables in the Marvell line, 3s outweigh 4s, as 1s do 2s, so that the scansion (q.v.) is properly trochee + iamb + trochee + iamb (see RELATIVE STRESS PRINCIPLE). There are, additionally, some theoretical grounds for thinking that feet composed of homogeneous members should not be recognized; for further discussion of this issue, with bibl., see FOOT and SPONDEE.

Other metrists, however, absolutists, would say that, in the Marvell line, 2s and 1s are both stronger than 3s and 4s, and that readerly distinctions of stressing are made in absolute terms not relative—giving the scansion p. + spondee + p. + spondee. Absolutists thus view the p. as a foot of two weakly stressed syllables; precisely how weak the one syllable is in relation to the other is unimportant. Historically this approach has appealed to Classicizing metrists, and it has a certain direct appeal; Saintsbury is eccentric (here as in so much else) in accepting spondees but not ps. The sequence weaker-weaker stronger-stronger is reasonably common in Eng. iambic pentameter verse; Wright gives many examples from Shakespeare. What one calls it—some Classicizing metrists once liked to call it an ionic (q.v.) foot, while Attridge calls it "stress-final pairing"—is however less important than whether one hears relatively or absolutely.

F. Pyle, "P. and Spondee," *Hermathena* 107 (1968); Crusius; J. Malof, *A Manual of Eng. Meters* (1970); D. Attridge, *The Rhythms of Eng. Poetry* (1982); G. T. Wright, *Shakespeare's Metrical Art* (1988). T.V.F.B; R.J.G.

PYTHIAMBIC. A modern term (*versus pythius* or Pythian verse = dactylic hexameter) for the strophic form of Horace's *Epodes* 14–15 (called First P.: hexameter + iambic dimeter; also found in Archilocus) and *Epode* 16 (Second P.: hexameter + iambic trimeter). There is no ancient authority for the term. See HEXAMETER. J.W.H.

Q

QAṢĪDA. A monorhymed lyric poem common to Arabic, Persian, Turkish, Pashto, and Urdu lit. The rhyme scheme is *aa ba ca*, etc., and some qs. run to over a hundred lines. The Ar. q. generally shows a tripartite structure consisting of an erotic prelude (*nasib*) wherein the poet weeps over the deserted campground of his beloved, an account of a desert journey (*rahil*) which includes a description of his mount, and the panegyric proper (*madih*). It originated among the Arab Bedouin as an oral poem in praise of the tribe or denigration of an enemy, the earliest examples being the seven *muʾallaqat* of pagan Arabia. The q. took its basic form in the early ʾAbbasid period (8th–9th c.), when it became a courtly occasional poem in praise of a patron. Qs. survive in Persian from the 10th c., and under Persian influence the form spread to other lits. At the same time, the subject matter of the q. expanded to include elegies, mystical or philosophical subjects, and satire. The q. gave way to the *ghazal* (q.v.) as the primary lyric form in Persian after the 13th c., and it never rivaled the *ghazal* in Urdu. In the 20th c. the q. lost its relevance and has all but disappeared as a poetic form. In Eng. lit., Tennyson imitates the form in *Locksley Hall*; it was also imitated by the Ger. poet Platen. See also ARABIC POETRY; PERSIAN POETRY; PANEGYRIC; TURKISH POETRY.—E. J. W. Gibb, *Hist. of Ottoman Poetry*, v. 1 (1900); R. Blachère, *Histoire de la litt. arabe* (1952–66); A. J. Arberry, *The Seven Odes* (1957); A. Bausani, *Storia delle letterature del Pakistan* (1958); A. Pagliaro and A. Bausani, *Storia della letteratura persiana* (1960); L. P. Elwell-Sutton, *The Persian Metres* (1976), App. II; *Encyclopaedia of Islam*, 2d ed., s.v. "kasida"; *Cambridge Hist. of Arabic Lit.*, v. 1 (1983). W.L.H.

QINAH. See HEBREW POETRY.

QUANTITATIVE VERSE. See CLASSICAL METERS IN MODERN LANGUAGES; CLASSICAL PROSODY; DURATION; METER; QUANTITY.

QUANTITY.

I. CONCEPTS ANCIENT AND MODERN
II. LINGUISTIC BASIS

I. CONCEPTS ANCIENT AND MODERN. Syllabic "q." or length is the basis of Cl. (Gr. and Lat.) prosody (q.v.), not syllabic accentuation (stress) as in most of the European vernaculars of the Middle Ages and after. Though ancient grammarians recognized the existence of "accent" (q.v.) in the Cl. langs., they always describe it as one of pitch rather than of acoustical intensity or loudness; and the phonological feature used for ordering syllables into regular patterns (i.e. meter) in Cl. verse was neither pitch nor intensity, but rather a long-short contrast based on syllable length (duration), i.e. q. Open syllables—syllables ending in a vowel— are short for metrical purposes if the vowel itself is short; open syllables ending in a long vowel or diphthong are long, as are all closed syllables regardless of the quantity of their vowel. (So most modern metrists, following the lead of ancient authorities like Dionysius of Halicarnassus [1st c. B.C.].) Since the rules for syllabification in Gr. and Lat. require that intervocalic consonants and most consonant groups which can begin a word be taken with the vowel that follows, a syllable will be closed only when its vowel is followed by a group of consonants which *cannot* so appear at the beginning of a word—e.g. the intervocalic groups in *am-bo, an-trum*, and *sanc-tus*, which must be divided as shown. Groups containing *sp* and *cs* [=x], however, even when they begin words, are regularly divided between syllables; and the combination of mute + liquid within a single word may (except in comedy) be divided or not as occasion demands. A single consonant between two vowels is assumed to belong to the syllable containing the second even when it ends a word and is followed by punctuation. Thus in the division of feet within the Lat. hexameter

$$- \cup \cup \quad - \quad \cup \cup - \quad - \quad -- \quad - \cup \cup$$

exsequa|r hanc eti|am, Mae|cena|s, aspice

$$- \ -$$

| partem

the final consonants of the first and fourth words belong respectively to the first syllables of the second and fifth feet. But the occasional retention of the final consonant with the word to which it belongs is at least a mechanical explanation of the not infrequent lengthening in hexameters of short syllables in the first place or "rise" of the feet to which they belong, e.g. "ipse ubi tempus erīt omnis in fonte lavabo."

Some modern metrists (e.g. Allen) prefer to confine the terms "long" and "short" to discussions of *vowel* length, and to speak of *syllables* as, rather, "heavy" and "light." Both distinctions, however, were genuine phonological ones: natural delivery of any text would probably have allowed the ancient ear to classify any syllable it contained as, relatively, long or short. The formal prosodic system erected on the basis of this natural distinction was artificial to the extent that it (1) established a basic time-counting unit (Gr. *sêmos* or *chronos*, Lat. *mora*) and either (2) assigned exact time values to all syllables—one *sêmos* for each short and two for each long—or (3), by a further refinement accepted by some composers and theoreticians (*rhythmici*) but not by others (*metrici*), allowed other artificial lengthenings and shortenings as well. Alongside the "normal," "diseme" long equivalent to two shorts, three other types were recognized: (a) "irrational" (*alogoi*) longs, greater than one *sêmos* and less than two by an indeterminate amount; and (b) "triseme" and (c) "tetraseme" longs, equivalent in length to three and four shorts. The (a) category is assumed to include all long syllables appearing in anceps (q.v.) positions; (b) and (c) are associated with syncopation (q.v.).

Modern metrists, like their ancient counterparts, disagree as to the applicability of the concepts of irrationality and syncopation to actual rhythmical practice. They also disagree on how much the quantitative prosody of Cl. Lat. admitted subsidiary accentual features. Most Am., British, and Ger. metrists, accustomed as they are to stress accent in their own langs., maintain that the Lat. accent was similar, and many have held that coincidences or clashes of ictus (q.v.) and accent were intentional in certain writers (e.g. Plautus and Virgil). But the existence of a pitch accent is arguable from the testimony of the Romans themselves, and Fr. scholars, with the example of their own lang. before them, are convinced that such was the nature of the Lat. accent, at any rate during the literary period. Whichever it was, in Cl. and post-Cl. Lat. it conformed to the "penultimate law," whereby the accent of a disyllabic word fell on its first syllable, while a polysyllabic word was accented on its last syllable but one if this was long, and on the syllable before that if the penultimate was short. For discussion of the modern distinction of tense/lax vowels in relation to q., see DURATION; see also CLASSICAL PROSODY; FOOT.

P. Habermann, "Quantität," *Reallexikon I*, 2.751–54; Maas, sects. 123–34; M. L. West, "A New Approach to Gr. Prosody," *Glotta* 48 (1970)—rejects the long-short contrast in favor of ten lengths; R. A. Zirin, *The Phonological Basis of Lat. Prosody* (1970); I. Lehiste, *Suprasegmentals* (1970); W. S. Allen, *Accent and Rhythm* (1973), esp. ch. 4, *Vox latina*, 2d ed. (1978), *Vox graeca*, 3d ed. (1987); D. Attridge, *Well-Weighed Syllables* (1974), ch. 1; E. Pulgram, *Lat.-Romance Phonology: Prosodics and Metrics* (1975); Snell; West. A.T.C.

II. LINGUISTIC BASIS. The primary task in the analysis of quantitative meters such as those of the Cl. langs. is to determine which of the durational differences of spoken lang. are relevant to the meter. This task is complicated by the fact that absolutely identical speech durations can be metrically distinctive, and very disparate speech durations may be treated as identical for purposes of meter.

Although the terminological difference is not always observed by scholars, it is useful to distinguish duration, q., and syllable weight. Duration is the measured physical time of a speech segment or gesture; q. is a linguistically significant category of vowel or consonant length; and weight is a linguistically significant category of syllable type. Listeners can hear durational differences as small as 10 milliseconds (msec). The average duration of a stressed vowel in Eng. speech is about 130 msec and that of a consonant about 70 msec; low vowels are generally somewhat longer than high vowels and labial consonants longer than dentals and velars. The duration of speech sounds is conditioned by a variety of factors including their position in the word, the nature of adjacent sounds, and the rate of speech: in connected Eng. discourse, vowel duration may vary by as much as ten to one. The fact that speech is intelligible at all despite such massive variation indicates that duration is processed in terms of relative rather than absolute intervals.

In most langs., q. (as defined above) is limited to two categories, long and short; a few langs. have overlong vowels and consonants, notably Estonian. Although syllable weight depends on syllable structure, it is almost never sensitive to the onset (the consonants preceding the vocalic nucleus). Cross-linguistic analysis of stress location reveals a hierarchy of syllable weight which typically reflects differences in the structure of the rhyme (the vocalic nucleus plus the following consonants): the hierarchy is $\breve{V}$ $\breve{V}C$ $\bar{V}$ $\bar{V}C$. This hierarchy is not a straight reflex of duration, since $\breve{V}C$ does not generally have less duration than $\bar{V}$. Most langs. and verse systems do not differentiate all the categories of the hierarchy, but make a binary division into light syllables having one mora (unit of temporal rhythm) and heavy syllables having two morae. Light syllables are those with $\breve{V}$ rhymes (or in some langs., those with $\breve{V}$ or $\breve{V}C$ rhymes), and heavy syllables are those with the remaining rhyme types. Superheavy ($\bar{V}C$) rhymes tend not to be treated as a separate class, though in Japanese they are properly trimoraic, illustrating how syllable weight in speech is controlled by a rhythm generator and is not merely the fortuitous result of stringing together vowels and consonants of different qs.—E. Hermann, *Silbenbildung im Griechischen und in den andern indogermanischen Sprachen* (1923); W. S. Allen (1973 above); A. M. Devine and L. D. Stephens, *Lang. and Metre* (1984), "Stress in Gr.?" *TAPA* 115 (1985). A.M.D.; L.D.S.

QUATORZAIN. Any stanza or poem of 14 lines, including the sonnet (q.v.), though the term is now normally reserved for any 14-line poem other than the classical Petrarchan (It.) or Shakespearean (Eng.) sonnet. The dispersion and success of the sonnet have tended to conceal from view other members of this class of stanzas. The assonantal *laisses* of OF epic poetry are usually qs. (see

LAISSE), as are, in Rus. poetry, the nearly 400 stanzas of Puškin's *Evgenij Onegin* (1830—see ONEGIN STANZA). In Eng. poetry one can point to Capel Lofft's *Laura; or an Anthol. of Sonnets . . . and Elegiac Qs.* (5 v., 1813–14), and in modern Am. poetry qs. have served as the vehicle of the Yuppie verse-novel *The Golden Gate* by Vikram Seth (1986), with the rhyme scheme *ababccddeffegg*.

                                                              T.V.F.B.

QUATRAIN. A stanza of 4 lines, normally rhymed. The q. is, with its many variations, the most common stanza form in European poetry, and very probably in the world. It is for the establishment, in the 3rd c. A.D., of the q. as the meter of the hymn (q.v.), developed from the Lat. iambic dimeter and subsequently to become the great staple meter of the Middle Ages, that C. W. Jones once called Ambrose, Bishop of Milan, "the man who most affected Western verse." Many hymnals still show the variants in a metrical index. This meter—iambic tetrameter (alone or mixed with trimeter) lines, in foot verse—has as its isomer the 4-stress line in stress verse, which is the basis of the several forms of ballad meter (q.v.), another staple (in a lower register) in the Middle Ages and still common in songs today. Hence the irony that when Sternhold and Hopkins, in the middle of the 16th c., sought to find a meter familiar to the masses for their vernacular Psalter, they chose the q. form of ballad meter. The q. is the form of the Sp. *copla*, the Rus. *chastushka*, the Malay *pantun*, the Ger. *Schnaderhüpfel*, and the Sanskrit *sloka*; indeed, most of the Vedic stanzas are qs. It was August Meineke who in 1834 showed that even Horace's *Odes* exhibit q. structure.

Most rhyming qs. fall into one of the following categories: (1) *abab*, alternating or "cross-rhyme" (q.v.), or its variant *xbyb* (in which *x* and *y* represent unrhymed lines), a category which includes ballad meter and the elegiac stanza (q.v.) or "heroic q."; (2) *abba*, "envelope rhyme," hence called the envelope (q.v.) stanza, of which Tennyson's *In Memoriam* stanza (q.v.) is a type; (3) *aabb*, in which an effect of internal balance or antithesis is achieved through the use of opposed couplets, as in Shelley's "The Sensitive Plant"; or (4) the monorhymed q., e.g. Gottfried Keller's "Abendlied," or nearly monorhymed q. such as the Omar Khayyam stanza (q.v.), rhyming *aaxa*. The first two have been the most popular forms in Western poetry since the 12th c. (Meyer 1.314 ff.). In Fr. verse the *abab* scheme is the standard form for qs.; the *abba* pattern is rare: Lamartine and Musset use it precisely once each, and Hugo, the most prolific versifier in the Fr. lang., only once in every ten poems written in qs. Martinon shows that *aabb* qs. are hardly stanzas at all. Stefan George in "Komm in den totgesagten park" tests all the possible forms of the rhymed q.

Qs. interlinked by rhyme are also to be found, as are those displaying such complications as the alternation of masculine and feminine (q.v.) rhyme and the use of heterometric (q.v.) line lengths. In Rus. poetry the q. is by far the most common stanza form, taking the forms *AbAb* or *aBaB* (capitals denote feminine rhymes). The q. has been used in Western poetry primarily as a unit of composition in longer poems, but is also commonly used for the two component parts of the octave (q.v.) of the sonnet. As a complete poem, the q. lends itself to epigrammatic utterance; Landor and Yeats have shown mastery in the composition of such qs. (see EPIGRAM).—P. Martinon, *Les Strophes* (1912).   T.V.F.B.

QUERELLE DES ANCIENS ET DES MODERNES ("Battle of the Ancients and Moderns"). The most serious challenge to the Ren. doctrines of poetic imitation (q.v.) and regularity, the Q., a dispute over the relative superiority of Cl. or modern lit., reflected an anti-authoritarian, rationalistic, progressivist trend dating from Descartes' *Discours de la méthode* (1637) and Pascal's *Traité du vide* (1647) and which reached its height from 1687 to ca. 1719.

In 1687 Charles Perrault asserted (*Le Siècle de Louis le Grand*) that contemp. art outshone the achievements of the Augustan age of Rome. La Fontaine replied for the Ancients in his *Epître à Huet*, followed by La Bruyère in his *Caractères*. Fontenelle took up the Modernist cause in *Digression sur les anciens et les modernes* (1688), and over the next four years, Perrault sharpened his arguments in the *Parallèles des anciens et des modernes* (1688, 1690, 1692). Boileau then defended the Ancients while attacking the Moderns in his *Discours sur l'ode* (1693) and *Réflexions sur Longin* (1694). The opponents reconciled in the same year.

Perrault criticized the Ancients for works he often found tiresome or confused and for physics which had been reduced to absurdity by the telescope and the microscope. Unquestioning admiration of ancient errors could only result, he argued, from a lack of critical spirit; with the advent of modern thought, however, scientists began to study nature itself rather than the writings of Aristotle, Hippocrates, and Ptolemy. Modern artists, too, must reclaim their freedom. Fontenelle, assuming the permanence of human nature, argued that while the Ancients invented everything, equally talented Moderns would have done equally well had they come first. Adding the idea of progress, Perrault in his *Parellèles* likened the arts to the sciences, both of which had advanced in the 17th c.

Mainly practitioners rather than theoreticians, the Ancients advanced arguments strongly influenced by their creative experiences. They first reaffirmed the cult of Greco-Roman lit. La Fontaine did not deny the merits of the Moderns, but reaffirmed Homer and Virgil, among others, as "the gods of Parnassus." Imitation was not to be slavish, however: La Fontaine subsumed it under reason and nature. Boileau emphasized that the rules (q.v.), inferrable from masterpieces, must be used as a *guide* to rather than a blueprint for original composition, as well as a basis for sensible judgment. Boileau also appealed to the test of time: if antiquity is not a title of merit, long standing and constant admiration must be, for the majority of readers do not err over the long term.

The Moderns won the first battle. While in his *Lettre à Charles Perrault* (1694), Boileau denied that the modern writers surpassed all the ancients, he freely admitted that the 17th c. was superior to any similar period of antiquity. Saint-Evremond, taking a more nuanced position in *Sur les poèmes des anciens* (1685), anticipated both evolution and relativism: creative production must accommodate time and place—that is, as religion, government, and manners change, so too must art.

In England, the Q. focused somewhat less on poetry than on the relative merits of scholasticism and its 16th-c. competition—free inquiry and induction as expounded by Bacon, Boyle, and Newton. Debate began with the "Essay on the Ancient and Modern Learning" in Sir William Temple's *Miscellanea* (1690). Temple was as reluctant to defend the Ancients as he was to idolize the Moderns. In 1694 William Wotton countered with *Reflections on Ancient and Modern Learning*, arguing for the artistic superiority of the Ancients and the scientific pre-eminence of the Moderns. The narrowly literary manifestations of the Q. turned on the rules, known through trs. of Rapin and Boileau, among others, and promoted by Thomas Rhymer in a critique of Elizabethan drama, *The Tragedies of the Last Age Considered* (1678). Dryden, a tentative defender of the rules in his *Essay of Dramatick Poesy* (1668), proved inconsistent in his critical views, admiring the Ancients but keenly aware that they and the Moderns inhabited very different worlds. This implies a skeptical posture toward the unthinking and systematic application of inherited frameworks. Independent and antidogmatic, Swift's *Battle of the Books* (1697; pub. 1704) burlesques the Q. without arriving at a definitive conclusion.

The Fr. Q. was reignited in 1714 when Houdard de la Motte published an embellished *Iliad* based on an accurate prose tr. by Mme Dacier (1711). Much that Mme. Dacier had found powerful, harmonious, and majestic in Homer was condemned by La Motte in his *Discours sur Homère* as contemptible and graceless by modern standards. In his celebrated *Lettre à l'Académie*, Fénelon straddled the issue: while modern writers need not idolize their forerunners, neither should they scorn them. The Abbé Du Bos had the last word in his *Réflexions critiques sur la poésie et sur la peinture* (1719). First, he contended, the superiority of modern to ancient science has more to do with the quantity and quality of available fact than with reason, a universal. Second, progress in poetry and

painting depends less on a knowledge of past achievements than on inventive talent or natural genius. Accordingly Du Bos rejected any evaluation of art tied to the history of science. Echoing Boileau, Du Bos argued that the final test is that of time, though he identified sentiment rather than traditional or authority as the decisive factor in aesthetic judgment.

Subsequent attitudes toward the Q. have varied. Like Thomas Macaulay, who dismissed this "most idle and contemptible controversy," Van Tieghem pronounces the issues unimportant and its problems ill-defined. Saisselin finds in the plethora of treatises and broadsides the very germ of major 18th-c. literary theories. While the Q. had no impact on applied poetics, it nevertheless remains a remarkable case study of critical ideas and methods in conflict and change. See also BAROQUE POETICS; CLASSICISM; NEOCLASSICAL POETICS; RENAISSANCE POETICS; RULES; SCIENCE AND POETRY.

H. Gillot, *La Querelle des anciens et des modernes en France* (1914); T. S. Eliot, "Trad. and the Individual Talent" (1917); R. F. Jones, *Ancients and Moderns* (1936); P. Van Tieghem, *Les Grandes Doctrines littéraires en France* (1946); L. Wencelius, "La Querelle des anciens et des modernes et l'humanisme," *Bulletin de la société d'étude du XVII siècle* (1951); Curtius 251 ff.; A. O. Aldridge, "Ancients and Moderns in the 18th C.," *DHI*; G. F. A. Gadoffre, "Le *Discours de la méthode* et la querelle des anciens et des modernes," *Mod. Miscell. Eugène Vinaver*, ed. T. E. Lawrenson et al. (1969); Saisselin; I. O. Wade, *Intellectual Origins of the Fr. Enlightenment* (1971); G. S. Santangelo, *La Querelle des anciens et des modernes nella critica del '900* (1975); Hollier, 364 ff.; J. M. Levine, *The Battle of the Books* (1991).   D.L.R.

QUESTION, EPIC. See EPIC.

QUINTAIN, quintet, cinquain. Any poem or stanza of 5 lines, sometimes isometrical (q.v.) but usually not. Meter and rhyme schemes vary, but the most common schemes are *ababb*, *abaab*, and *abccb*. In all langs. qs. are rarer than quatrains. In Fr. prosody, the term *cinquain* refers more specifically to a form of medieval origin: the earliest extant monument of Fr. poetry, the 11th-c. *Vie de Saint Alexis*, is written in 125 cinquains of decasyllables, and in 1174 it is used by Guernes de Pont-Sainte-Maxence in alexandrines. In the 19th c. it is revived esp. by Victor Hugo, who mixes alexandrines and octosyllables. In Sp., the octosyllabic *quintilla* (q.v.) bears the constraints that there may not be more than two rhymes, nor two consecutive rhymes, nor may the strophe end with a couplet, making only 5 possible rhyme schemes: *ababa*, *abbab*, *abaab*, *aabab*, and *aabba*; the doubled *quintilla* is the *copla real* (see COPLA).

In Eng. there is no common term for stanzas or poems in 5s: Puttenham uses "q." (cf. "quatrain").

"Quintet" is used for prose (e.g. Lawrence Durrell's *Avignon Quintet*) and by some for poetry, perhaps by analogy to "sestet" and "septet" (but not "octet"). Dunbar likes the form; Sidney uses a number of varieties (Psalms 4, 9, 20, 28; *Astrophil*, Song 9; *Old Arcadia*); and others experiment with it, e.g. Donne ("Hymne to God my God"), Carew, Herbert (a number of poems), Waller ("Go, Lovely Rose"), Wordsworth (*Peter Bell, The Idiot Boy*, in tetrameters), Coleridge (*passim* in the *Ancient Mariner*, *abccb* as a variant of ballad meter [q.v.]), Poe ("To Helen"), and Browning. Adelaide Crapsey developed a sharply tailed *cinquain* for her slender *Verse* (1915) in iambic lines of 2, 4, 6, 8, and 2 syllables, respectively, built on analogy to Japanese *tanka* (q.v.) and in effect a stanzaic correlate to rhopalic verse (see PALINDROME). Last— and not least?—there is the limerick (q.v.).— Schipper, v. 2; Lote, v. 2; Scott, 148 ff.   T.V.F.B.

QUINTILLA. The q., a Sp. stanza form formerly considered a type of *redondilla* (q.v.) and so called (Rengifo, *Arte poética española*, 1592), was probably formed by the separation, in the 16th c., of the two parts of the 9- or 10-line *copla de arte menor* when it was embryonic. The q. is a 5-line octosyllabic strophe having the following restrictions: there may not be more than two rhymes or two consecutive rhymes and the strophe may not end with a couplet. The five possible rhyme combinations are therefore: *ababa, abbab, abaab, aabab, aabba.* The last two combinations, which begin with a couplet, are generally avoided in the independent q. but frequently appear as the second half of the *copla real.* The q. probably ranks among the three or four most commonly used octosyllabic strophes in Castilian. N. Fernández de Moratín's (1737–1780) famous *Fiesta de toros en Madrid* is written in qs. employing four of the five possible rhyme schemes.—D. C. Clarke, "Sobre la q.," *RFE* 20 (1933); Navarro.   D.C.C.

R

RAGUSAN POETRY. See YUGOSLAV POETRY.

RASA. See INDIAN POETICS.

RAZOS. See VIDAS AND RAZOS.

READER-RESPONSE CRITICISM. Crit. that focuses on reader or audience and the experiencing of a poem. In general, much more of crit. involves ideas of r.-r. than would appear at first glance. Any poetic theory which makes statements about how we feel as we read a poem, what poetry aims to do, how poetry affects us morally, or how we perceive the world described by the poet (see POETRY, THEORIES OF, *Pragmatic Theories*) is making claims about r.-r. Plato, in banning poets from his *Republic*, and equally those critics who assert against Plato the moral efficacy of poetry, are both making assumptions about r.-r. Aristotle's catharsis (q.v.), Longinus' sublime (q.v.), and modern concepts like Brecht's alienation-effect or the Rus. Formalists' "defamiliarization" all rest on r.-r. claims. One could argue that poetic theory always involves a model of understanding lang., even if the model remains tacit (as often in New Criticism, q.v.).

More specifically, r.-r. crit. refers to a group of critics who explicitly study, not a poem, but readers reading a poem. This critical school emerged in the 1960s and '70s in America and Germany, in work by Fish, Iser, Jauss, and Holland. Important predecessors would include I. A. Richards, who in 1929 analyzed a group of Cambridge undergraduates' misreadings of poems, and Louise Rosenblatt, whose 1937 book insisted on the unique relationship of each reader to aesthetic texts. In opposition, Wimsatt and Beardsley in 1954 attacked the "affective fallacy" (q.v.). To evaluate a poem in terms of its emotional effect, they argued, was to confuse the poem with its result. They thus assumed an "objective" text, separate from its reader but entailing certain appropriate responses. The "affective fallacy" became a theoretical cornerstone of New Criticism, a school that has proved at least as fruitful in the reactions against it as in the practice itself.

One can think of r.-r. crit. as one of those reactions. The r.-r. critic holds exactly the opposite view. A "poem" involves a psychological process in which author and reader interact through a physical text. Therefore one cannot isolate some "objective" poem which exists prior to readers' experience of it. Critics often claim "objectivity," but that is an illusion. In fact, one can only see a poem through our human processes of perception (and they are driven by our sense of the poem's relation to our feelings and values, incl. our ideas of how one ought to read a poem). In r.-r. crit. as in modern physics, the answer one gets depends upon the question one asks.

Within this general position, critics (primarily in Germany and the U.S.) have developed differing versions of r.-r. theory. Some sample the responses of actual readers, while others posit on theoretical grounds a response or (more usually) a reader (the narratee [Prince], the superreader [Riffaterre], the informed reader [Fish 1967], the reader implied or required by this poem [Iser], or simply "the" reader). Among those who consider actual readers, some seek "free" responses (Bleich, Holland), while others use questionnaires that structure response. Thus, some r.-r. critics regard individual differences in response as important, while others prefer to consider response as common to a class or era.

There is a fundamental distinction between those r.-r. critics who envisage a largely uniform response to a poem (with unimportant personal variations) and those who see the reader in control at every point. The former say that which is common to different readers' readings results from the poem, while those who see the reader in control explain that which is common as resulting from common codes and canons for reading which are individually applied by different readers. The most fundamental difference among r.-r. critics is probably, then, between those who regard individual differences among readers' responses as important and those who do not. By and large, Ger. and other Continental critics tend to use generic and theoretical concepts of the reader, Am. critics actual and individual.

For example, Hans Robert Jauss in the landmark paper he gave in 1967 (tr. as "Lit. Hist. as a Challenge to Lit. Theory") defined lit. as a dialectic process of production and reception. In reception, readers have a mental set which Jauss called a horizon of expectations (*Erwartungshorizont*) from which vantage point a reader, at a given moment in hist., reads. Lit. hist. then becomes the charting of these horizons of expectation. Jauss, however, derives this horizon of expectation by reading literary works of the period, thus introducing a circularity in his theory. In subsequent writings he has dealt extensively with the kinds of pleasure we take in lit.

Wolfgang Iser also exemplifies the Ger. tendency to theorize the reader. Drawing on Polish aesthetician Roman Ingarden's idea of *Konkretisa-*

READER-RESPONSE CRITICISM

tion, Iser says a poem is not an object in itself but an effect to be explained. Nevertheless, he brackets the real reader and relies instead on an implied reader, the reader a given poem requires. A poem creates various polarities. Within these, this implied reader, through a "wandering viewpoint," creates expectations, meanings, the appearance of characters and settings, etc. The poem regulates perception, and the reader is active only within limits set by the poem.

Among the Americans, David Bleich pioneered the study of the actual feelings and free associations of actual readers as early as 1967, and he has applied his findings both theoretically, to model the reading process, and practically, to reform the classroom teaching of lit. Bleich has written extensively on particular teaching strategies using readers' responses. His classes generate knowledge by showing how individuals recreate texts individually. Similarly, Walter Slatoff has shown how students' personal responses can provide the basis for critical analyses in the classroom. The journals *Reader, Reading Research Quarterly,* et al., publish articles using r.-r. theory in pedagogy.

In 1967, Stanley Fish provided the first reader-oriented study (*Surprised by Sin*) of a major literary work, *Paradise Lost.* An appendix, "Lit. in the Reader," used "the" reader to examine responses to complex sentences sequentially, word-by-word (like "Nor did they not perceive the evil plight"). Since 1976, however, Fish has emphasized the real differences among real readers, focusing attention on the reading tactics endorsed by different critical schools and by the literary professoriate. *Lycidas* is pastoral for one "interpretive community," a set of themes for another, and fantasy-defense for a third.

In 1968, Norman Holland used psychoanalytic psychology to model the literary work as a core of fantasy formally modified by a defense mechanism into a meaning. Each reader introjects this one ready-made psychological process with individual variations. As Georges Poulet put it, "I am on loan to another," i.e. the author. On examining the responses of real readers, however, Holland found variations too great to fit a core of shared fantasy or defense. One reader found a character in a Hemingway story like a sinister torturer, while another found the same character "warm, hospitable." The first reader perceived texts in terms of threats to his masculinity; the second looked for sources of support. Because of data like this, Holland since 1975 has developed a different model. A personal identity (defined as a theme and variations) *uses* the physical poem and invariable codes (such as the shapes of letters) and variable canons (different critical values, for example). Each reader thus builds a response both like and unlike other responses.

According to both Ger. and Am. r.-r. critics, we are no longer to ask, "What does the poem mean?" but "How do readers make meaning from it?" To some non-readerly critics this seems a profoundly disturbing, topsy-turvy idea of the literary transaction. Many fear an anarchic "subjectivity" in which readers will be free to make the poem mean whatever anyone wants. In r.-r. theory, however, reading is always both subjective and objective. The question is not which it is, but how it is both. Some r.-r. critics answer that question by a doubly active model of reading: the poem controls part of the response and the reader part (Iser, early Fish). Both are active. Others claim the reader controls and the text is only re-active to the reader's activity (later Fish, Kintgen, Holland). In such a reader-active model, readers combine purely personal concerns with professional rules for reading or a transpersonal horizon of expectations and, of course, the text itself.

Particularly the Am. r.-r. critics draw heavily on psychology. From the outset, psychoanalytic psychology has provided critics like Bleich, Holland, and Schwartz with techniques for analyzing the lang. of individual responders. In the 1970s and '80s, cognitive psychology, psycholinguistics, and neuroscience have provided increasingly powerful and detailed models for the way readers read (Rumelhart, Anderson et al., Dillon, Sternberg). In general, psychologists of reading and those who teach illiterates and children to read also concur that readers make meaning (Spiro, Smith, Meek, Crowder). Much late 20th-c. psychology of perception also supports the r.-r. idea that perceivers construct what they perceive. Hence r.-r. crit. can readily be extended to other arts like cinema or painting (as with film theorist David Bordwell or art historian E. H. Gombrich) or to the perception of events (as in the historiography of Hayden White). Similarly, by emphasizing the activity of the critic, r.-r. crit. gives a theoretical justification for the parodies of traditional interp. in deconstruction (q.v.).

Ethically, the r.-r. critic's emphasis on the activity of the reader makes it possible to be precise about the effects of reading, e.g. self-effacement, refining one's moral criteria, learning to heed details, adding to one's knowledge, or discovering new strategies of interp. In this vein, r.-r. critics often share the concerns of feminist critics and critics writing on behalf of gays, minorities, or Third-World peoples. Such readers are likely to arrive at readings of a poem not available to a white, middle-class, Western male reader. Hence r.-r. crit. has led to explorations of "gender and reading" (Flynn and Schweickart).

Socially, because r.-r. critics pay attention to the strategies readers are taught to use, r.-r. critics become concerned with the teaching of reading and lit., with the profession of letters, and with the literary professoriate. What tactics are we teaching, and what do those tactics say about our society and our values?

See also CRITICISM; DECONSTRUCTION; FEMINIST POETICS; INTERPRETATION; POETRY; POETRY,

THEORIES OF, *Recent Developments*; PSYCHOLOGICAL CRITICISM; SEMIOTICS; SPEECH ACT THEORY; THEORY.

OVERVIEWS: A. C. Purves and R. Beach, *Lit. and the Reader* (1972); R. T. Segers, "Readers, Text, and Author," *YCGL* 24 (1975); *The Reader in the Text*, ed. S. R. Suleiman and I. Crosman (1980); *R.-R. Crit.*, ed. J. P. Tompkins (1980); R. C. Holub, *Reception Theory* (1984)—distinguishes between Am. r.-r. crit. and Ger. reception theory.

CRITICAL STUDIES: I. A. Richards, *Practical Crit.* (1929); L. Rosenblatt, *Lit. as Exploration* (1937); W. K. Wimsatt, Jr., and M. Beardsley, "The Affective Fallacy," *The Verbal Icon* (1954); S. Fish, *Surprised by Sin* (1967), *Is There a Text in this Class?* (1980)—collects earlier essays; N. N. Holland, *The Dynamics of Literary Response* (1968, 1989), *Poems in Persons* (1973, 1989), *5 Readers Reading* (1975), "I-ing Film," *CritI* 13 (1986), "The Miller's Wife and the Professors," *NLH* 17 (1986); G. Poulet, "Phenomenology of Reading," *NLH* 1 (1969); H. R. Jauss, *Literaturgesch. als Provokation* (1970), *Aesthetic Experience and Lit. Hermeneutics* (1982), *Toward an Aesthetic of Reception* (1982)—collects earlier essays; W. Slatoff, *With Respect to Readers* (1970); W. Bauer et al., *Text und Rezeption* (1972); W. Iser, *Der Implizite Leser* (1972; tr. as *The Implied Reader*, 1974), *Der Akt des Lesens* (1976; tr. as *The Act of Reading*, 1978); G. Prince, "Intro. à l'étude du narrataire," *Poétique* 14 (1973); D. Bleich, *Readings and Feelings* (1975), *Lit. and Self-Awareness* (1977), *Subjective Crit.* (1978), *The Double Perspective* (1988); M. Schwartz, "Where is Lit.?" *CE* 36 (1975); *Basic Processes in Reading*, ed. D. Laberge and S. J. Samuels (1977); D. E. Rumelhart, *Intro. to Human Information Processing* (1977); *Schooling and the Acquisition of Knowledge*, ed. R. C. Anderson et al. (1977); *The Arts and Cognition*, ed. D. Perkins and B. Leondar (1977); G. L. Dillon, *Lang Processing and the Reading of Lit.* (1978); M. Riffaterre, *Semiotics of Poetry* (1978); *Theoretical Issues in Reading Comprehension*, ed. R. J. Spiro et al. (1980); F. Smith, *Understanding Reading*, 3d ed. (1982); M. Meek, *Learning to Read* (1982), *Achieving Literacy* (1983), ed., *Opening Moves* (1985); R. G. Crowder, *The Psychology of Reading* (1982); *Discovering Reality*, ed. S. Harding and M. B. Hintikka (1983); I. and M. M. Taylor, *The Psychology of Reading* (1983); E. Kintgen, *The Perception of Poetry* (1983); *Human Abilities*, ed. R. J. Sternberg (1985); D. Bordwell, *Narration in the Fiction Film* (1985); *Gender and Reading*, ed. E. A. Flynn and P. P. Schweickart (1986); E. Freund, *Return of the Reader* (1987); A. N. Grant, *Young Readers Reading* (1987); V. B. Leitch, *Am. Lit. Crit. from the Thirties to the Eighties* (1988), ch. 8; S. Noakes, *Timely Reading* (1988); T. Rajan, *The Supplement of Reading* (1990). N.N.H.

REALISM. Following Hegel's *Ästhetik* (1835–38), one may apply the term r. to any literary work that represents a world of social life in which an individual is capable of acting with autonomous motivation. This concept of mimetic narration reveals a strong heritage of speculative idealism, esp. of the kind developed in Schelling's philosophy of identity between subjective consciousness and objective factuality: literary theory is meant to retain the possibility of harmonious order against the experience that the world has become ever more complicated if not chaotic. Art is to be more than a photographic record of surface phenomena; it is to reveal the essential structure of reality in a manner that pleasurably and convincingly repeats and thereby vindicates the processes of sensory cognition.

In France, controversies intensified in the mid 1820s about a style of painting that refused to transfigure the common aspects of life. Its "réalisme" was denounced as a distorting deficiency, a trend that was still vigorous in 1855 when an exhibition of 40 paintings by Courbet (in the pavilion "Le Réalisme" at the Paris World's Fair) initiated a revaluation of critical standards. A theory evolved that sought to balance two principal factors, the subjective perception and expressive individuality of the observer and the objective factualness of empirical reality. Their congruence is to be achieved by a poetic transformation of the real world, by a mimesis that sifts and refines phenomenal diversity through the cognitive filter of subjective inwardness—"the lyrical subject factually *is* the world unified, is the focal point of the world" (F. Th. Vischer).

Consequently, realistic poetry satisfies normal rather than intensified perceptions of reality; it provides plausible rather than imaginative explanations. Its style reinforces rather than contradicts what is generally accepted as truthful and relevant. This means a preference for average characters with modest experiences and simple emotions, a renunciation of rhetorical intensity in favor of controlled naturalness, a suppression of metaphorical fancy in the interest of descriptive verisimilitude. In a general sense, realistic poetry may result from any down-to-earth opposition to what seem artificial rules of versification or arbitrary restrictions on matter or diction.

In historical terms, however, and as a movement, poetic r. is concomitant with the full emergence of bourgeois culture by 1840. In the Ger. countries, this devel. was given a characteristic turn by the fact that the revolutions of 1848 were unsuccessful. They mark a turning-point also for lit. and introduce the new era of "poetischer Realismus" (1848–70).

Suffused with a mood of resignation and informed by a persistent discontent with the practices of *laissez faire* capitalism, with the effects of the Industrial Revolution, and with the stifling of democratic aspirations by authoritarian governments, the lyric poetry of r. eschewed the agitational and satiric temper that had animated the political commitments of *Vormärz* and "Young Ger." verse. Instead, it sought inspiration from folksong and the romantic *Lied* as well as from the trads. of Goethean *Erlebnislyrik*. This inclination exacerbated the polarization of disputes in poetics over the primacy of feeling or thinking. In its wake, a poetry of elegiac and often epigrammatically condensed reflection (*Gedankenlyrik*) emerged, blending nuanced description with contemplation and (occasionally obsessive) analysis of mental states. Its principal representatives were E. Mörike, A. von Droste-Hülshoff, G. Keller, F. Hebbel, and Th. Storm. A renewed interest in the narrative genres of the ballad (q.v.) and of the verse epic (Droste, Th. Fontane) and in the use of dialect (K. Groth) coincided with the popularity of humorous verse as written by W. Busch, a versatile caricaturist of human foibles both in his cartoons and their captions. The concentrated elaboration of one central (and usually allegorical) image in many poems by C. F. Meyer and E. Geibel's immensely popular and genteel versification represent the two complementary goals of the realist search for formal perfection in poetry.

The precepts of r. are often considered inimical to the spirit of lyric poetry, and outside of Germany it is indeed to narrative prose that the term was at first applied almost exclusively. But that changed after about 1870. Even though Fr. lit. produced only a modicum of poetry in the *langue nouvelle* (F. Coppée, S. Prudhomme, members of Zola's *groupe de Médan*, Corbière, Laforgue), the late Victorian Age in England (1870–1900) experienced a remarkable preference for matter-of-fact sobriety over sentimentalism in poems by Browning, Hardy, Kipling, and Synge. And in America, Whitman's democratic fervor and ecstatic praise of the vigorous life left its influence on the work of Sidney Lanier, Hart Crane, E. A. Robinson, and Carl Sandburg.—V. da Sola Pinto, "R. in Eng. Poetry," *E&S* 25 (1939); Auerbach; *Documents of Mod. Literary R.*, ed. G. J. Becker (1963); R. Wellek, "The Concept of R. in Literary Scholarship," *Concepts of Crit.* (1963); H. Schlaffer, *Lyrik im Realismus* (1966); *Realismus und Gründerzeit*, ed. M. Bucher et al. (1975); F. Martini, "Realismus," *Reallexikon*; A. Todorow, "Lyrik und Realismus in der Mitte des 19. Jahrhunderts," *Bürgerlicher Realismus*, ed. K.-D. Müller (1981); L. Völker, "Bürgerlicher Realismus," *Gesch. der deutschen Lyrik*, ed. W. Hinderer (1983); R. C. Cowen, *Der poetische Realismus* (1985); Terras—Rus.; G. Zanker, *R. in Alexandrian Poetry* (1987).   M.W.

RECANTATION. See PALINODE; RECUSATIO.

RECEPTION THEORY. See READER-RESPONSE CRITICISM.

RECESSION OF ACCENT. See ACCENT.

RECIPROCUS VERSUS. See PALINDROME.

RÉCIT. See PLOT.

RECOGNITION. See PLOT.

RECUSATIO (Lat. "refusal"). A term applied by Cl. scholars to a poem in which the speaker implicitly or explicitly "refuses" to write on a certain subject or in a particular style. A type of programmatic poetry, *recusationes* often dramatize the poet's rejection of one kind of poem and choice of another; he or she may claim to have been asked to compose a different kind of poem; he may even pretend to have tried to do so; he may claim to be reacting to crit.; a god may rebuke the poet or give his approval.

Although elements of the form can be found in Sappho, fr. 16 (which implicitly rejects epic martial poetry for lyric love poetry; cf. *Anacreontea* 26, a later imitation which makes the r. explicit), rs. flourish in the Hellenistic period, beginning with the prologue of Callimachus' *Aetia* and the epilogue of his "Hymn to Apollo," in both of which Apollo approves of Callimachus' rejection of grand themes (compared to the sea and the Euphrates river) in favor of highly refined treatment of small subjects (compared to pure drops of water from a spring), thus beginning a long trad. in Lat. poetry that includes Virgil (*Eclogues* 6), Horace (*Odes* 1.6, 2.12, 4.2, 4.15), Propertius (2.1, 3.1, 3.3, 3.9), and Ovid (*Amores* 1.1, 2.1, 3.1 [Wimmel; Clausen; Williams; Nisbet and Hubbard]). In line with Callimachean aesthetics (Cody; Hopkinson), these poets refuse grand-style treatments of epic themes in favor of shorter lyric and elegiac love poetry. Roman satirists such as Horace (*Satires* 2.1), Persius (*Satires* 5), and Juvenal (*Satires* 1) also expressed their poetic programs in rs.

The r. became popular again in the Ren., esp. in anti-Petrarchan sonnets that purport to eschew learned allusions and dense styles for straightforward treatments employing direct lang. Prominent examples in sonnets incl. Du Bellay, *Regrets* 4; Sidney, *Astrophil and Stella* 1, 3, 6, 15, 28, 74; and Daniel, *Delia* 46; also Herbert's two "Jordan" poems. With the exception of Burns' "Epistle to J. Lapraik," the r. was not popular among romantic poets, but beginning with Housman's "Terence, This Is Stupid Stuff," numerous examples appear in the 20th c., incl. Yeats's "A Coat" and "On Being Asked for a War Poem," Stevens' "The Man on the Dump," Auden's "We Too Had Known Golden Hours," J. V. Cunningham's "For My Contemporaries," Czesław Miłosz' "No More," Zbigniew Herbert's "A Knocker," and John Hollander's *Powers of Thirteen*, sonnet 1. See PALINODE.

W. Wimmel, *Kallimachos in Rom* (1960); W. Clausen, "Callimachus and Lat. Poetry," *Greek, Roman, & Byzantine Studies* 5 (1964); G. Williams, *Trad. and Originality in Roman Poetry* (1968); R. G. M. Nisbet and M. Hubbard, *Horace*, Odes *Book I* (1970) and *Book II* (1978); J. V. Cody, *Horace and Callimachean Aesthetics* (1976); G. Davis, "The Disavowal of the Grand (*recusatio*) in Two Poems by

REDERIJKERS

Wallace Stevens," *PCP* 17 (1982); N. Hopkinson, *A Hellenistic Anthol.* (1988); W. H. Race, *Cl. Genres and Eng. Poetry* (1988), ch. 1.　　　　W.H.R.

REDERIJKERS. (Fr. *rhétoriqueurs*.) Members of the *rederijkerskamers* (chambers of rhetoric), which flourished in the Netherlands in the 15th and 16th cs. The chambers, which were organized as guilds, each with its patron, its name, and its distinctive motto and emblem, originated in Flanders and Brabant, almost certainly on the model of analogous Fr. associations, and spread gradually to the north, where they became particularly well established in the province of Holland.

The r. (the term included both practicing poets and students of poetry) tended, like their Ger. counterparts the *Meistersinger* (q.v.), toward a formalistic, almost mechanical concept of art, and some of the forms in which they expressed themselves have a remarkable complexity. Their major interest lay in dramatic and lyric poetry, and their principal forms were: in the drama, the *zinnespel* (allegorical morality play) and the *esbattement* (farce); in the lyric, the *refrein* (q.v.), a strophic poem repeating a one-line refrain at the end of each stanza, and such Fr. forms as the ballade and the rondel (qq.v.).

The r., who were, on the whole, members of the prosperous burgher class, often organized sumptuous drama and poetry competitions, known variously as *landjuwelen, haagspelen,* and *refreinfeesten.* Among the more famous *rederijkerskamers* were *De Heilige Geest* and *De Drie Santinnen* at Bruges, *De Fonteine* at Ghent, *Trou moet Blycken* at Haarlem, and *De Egelantier* and *Het Wit Lavendel* at Amsterdam. The most noted of *rederijker* works are *Elckerlijk* [Everyman], which is probably the source of its Eng. analogue; the anonymous miracle play *Mariken van Nieumeghen,* which contains some proto-Ren. elements lacking in the Eng. version, *Mary of Nimmegen*; Colijn van Rijssele's romantic play *Den Spieghel der Minnen*; the religious *refreinen* of Anna Bijns; and the *esbattements* of Cornelis Everaert.—J. J. Mak, *De r.* (1944); G. J. Steenbergen, *Het landjuweel van de r.* (1950).　　F.J.W.

REDONDILLA. Sp. stanza form. An octosyllabic quatrain rhyming *abba* and sometimes called r. *mayor, cuarteta, cuartilla.* Quatrains having the rhyme *abab* are occasionally called *rs.* but generally use the name *serventesio.* The r. written in lines of fewer than 8 syllables is called *r. menor.* The term formerly included the *quintilla* (q.v.) and was also applied to any octosyllabic strophe in which all verses rhymed. The r. is apparently the result of the breaking in two at the strophic caesura of the *copla de arte menor* (SEE ARTE MENOR). The separation was completed in the 16th c., and the r. has been one of the most commonly used octosyllabic strophes in Castilian ever since. Ezra Pound experimented with the form.—D. C. Clarke, "*R.* and *copla de arte menor,*" *HR* 9 (1941); Le Gentil; Navarro.　　D.C.C.

REFERENCE. See DECONSTRUCTION; IMITATION; INTERTEXTUALITY; MEANING, POETIC; POETRY, THEORIES OF; PSEUDO-STATEMENT; REPRESENTATION AND MIMESIS; SEMANTICS AND POETRY; SEMIOTICS, POETIC; TEXTUALITY.

REFRAIN (Ger. *Kehrreim*). A line, lines, or part of a line repeated verbatim at intervals throughout a poem, usually at regular intervals, and most often at the end of a stanza—a burden, chorus, or repetend (qq.v.). If the repetition is not verbatim, the phenomenon is sometimes called "incremental repetition" (q.v.).

The r. is a conspicuous feature of oral poetry (q.v.), particularly verses sung to the accompaniment of dance or during communal labor, esp. when performed by a group and a leader, the latter taking the stanzas, the former the rs. Rs. occur in the Egyptian *Book of the Dead,* in the Heb. Psalms, in early Gr. lyric poetry, in the Lat. epithalamia of Catullus (61, 64), and in the OE *Deor*; they blossom in medieval poetry, first in Med. Lat. religious hymnody and antiphonal responsion, then in the vernaculars. Their first systematic use in OF verse dates from ca. 1147, but they are equally if not more important in the fixed forms of Occitan poetry (q.v.), as they are also in the medieval ballads. In ME rs. form the *burden* in carols (q.v.) and the tail in tail-rhyme (q.v.), in Occitan and OF the *envoi* (q.v.) in the *ballade* and *virelai* (qq.v.) and the *rentrement* in the *rondeau* (qq.v.), in It. the *ripresa* in the *ballata* (see RITORNELLO), in Sp. the *estribillo* in the *villancico* (qq.v.). In Port. they appear in the *cantiga* (q.v.). In both Ren. lyrics and in romantic poetry their use still results from close association with song (q.v.).

A r. may be as short as a single word or as long as a stanza. Though usually recurring as a regular part of a metrical pattern, it may appear irregularly throughout a poem, in regular form or not, or may even be used in free verse (q.v.). In stanzaic verse it usually occurs at the end of a stanza but may appear at the beginning (the burden in carols) or in the middle (the *stef* in ON skaldic poetry [see DRAPA]). It may be repeated each time with a slight variation of wording appropriate to its immediate context (Rossetti's "Sister Helen"; Tennyson's "Lady of Shalott") or in such a way that its meaning develops from one recurrence to the next. Poe discusses this type of structure in "The Philosophy of Composition." The r. may be a tag or a nonsense phrase seemingly irrelevant to the rest of the poem or relevant only in spirit ("With a hey, and a ho, and a hey nonny-no" [*As You Like It* 5.3.18]), or it may emphasize or reinforce emotion or meaning by catching up, echoing, and elaborating a crucial image or theme. It gives pleasure in its repetition of sound, and it serves to segment and correlate rhythmical units and so unify the poem. The full comparative study of rs. still remains to be written. See also REPETITION.

G. Thurau, *Der R. in der französischen Chanson*

(1901); F. B. Gummere, *The Beginnings of Poetry* (1908); F. G. Ruhrmann, *Studien zur Gesch. und Charakteristik des Rs. in der engl. Lit.* (1927); P. W. Gainer, *The R. in the Eng. and Scottish Popular Ballads* (1933); N. H. J. van den Boogaard, *Rondeaux et rs. du XIIe au début de XIVe siècle* (1969)—useful list of all extant OF rs. ca. 1148–1332; T. Newcombe, "The R. in Troubadour Lyric Poetry," *Nottingham Mediaeval Studies* 19 (1975); C. F. Williamson, "Wyatt's Use of Repetitions and Rs.," *ELR* 12 (1982); J. Hollander, *The Figure of Echo* (1981), *Melodious Guile* (1988), ch. 7; S. M. Johnson, "The Role of the R. in OF Lyric Poetry," *DAI* 44 (1983): 747A; E. Doss-Quinby, *Les Rs. chez les trouvères du XIIe siècle au début du XIVe* (1984). L. Magnus, *The Track of the Repetend: Syntactic and Lexical Repetition in Mod. Poetry* (1989)—use with caution.
T.V.F.B.; L.P.

REFRÁN (Sp., "proverb"). A short, pithy, popular saying in Sp. expressing advice based on wisdom gained through common experience or observation. It may deal with any subject—such as medicine, hygiene, agriculture, morals, or philosophy, to name but a few. It is often composed of two short phrases that rhyme or contain alliteration, or are of parallel structure, or have some other sound-device that makes them appeal to the ear and cling to the memory. The Sp. lang. is exceedingly rich in this sort of expression and collectors have been busy for at least half a millennium gathering them into *refraneros*. The first known collection is the mid-15th-c. *Refranes que dicen las viejas tras el fuego*, generally attributed to the Marqués de Santillana. Many thousands have been gathered by dozens of collectors since then. Some of the important collections are those of Hernán Núñez, Juan de Mal Lara, Gonzalo Correas, F. Rodríguez Marín, and J. Cejador y Frauca.—Le Gentil.
D.C.C.

REFREIN. A poetic form esp. favored by the *rederijkers* (q.v.) in the Netherlands. It consists of four or more stanzas containing the same number of lines and constructed on the same rhyme scheme; the last stanza, however, is often shorter than the rest. All of them end with an identical line, the *stock*, (q.v.). Within the lines the number of syllables is not fixed. The last stanza is usually directed to the "prince" of the chamber of rhetoric or some other person; its initial letters sometimes form an acrostic (q.v.) spelling the name of the poet. In accordance with the highly mannered poetic of the *rederijkers*, great attention is bestowed on rhyme, the intricate use of which makes the r. a difficult form.

A spoken, not a sung, form, the r. derives its name from the Fr. *refrain* and owes its origin largely to the Fr. ballade (q.v.). *Refreinen* are divided into three subgenres: *vroede* (serious, religious, didactic, satiric), *amoureuze*, and *sotte* (comic, jocular, obscene, or nonsensical). *Refreinfeesten* were competitions between various chambers on given questions or *stocks* and with a given number of stanzas and lines. The great age of the r. was ca. 1450–1600; the most notorious examples are those by Anna Bijns and those compiled by Jan van Styevoort, Jan van Doesborch, and Jan de Bruyne.—A. van Elslander, *Het r. in de Nederlanden tot 1600* (1953); J. Coigneau, "Het leugenfefrein bij de rederijkers: Een overzicht," *Studia Germanica Gandensia* (1979), *Refreinen in het zotte bij de rederijkers*, 3 v. (1980–83). R.F.L.

REGULATED VERSE. See CHINESE POETRY.

REIZIANUM. See TELESILLEUM; AEOLIC.

REJET. Part of the Fr. prosodic terminology for *enjambement* (see ENJAMBMENT), but applicable to other verse systems as well. *R.* refers to the word or small group of words "rejeté" by enjambment into a following line, when the larger part of the syntactic unit interrupted by the line-ending occupies the preceding line, e.g. Hugo: "C'est le sceau de l'état. Oui, le grand sceau de cire / *Rouge*" (It is the seal of state. Yes, the great seal of red wax). A r. can also occur line-internally (*r. à l'hémistiche*) when there is syntactic overflow from the first hemistich to the second across the caesura, e.g. Baudelaire: "Pour qui? C'était hier // l'été; voici l'automne!" (For whom? Yesterday it was summer; now the autumn is here!). Correspondingly, *contre-r.* refers to the word or small group of words *initiating* an enjambment when the larger part of the syntactic unit interrupted by the line-ending occupies the following line. *Contre-r.* too has a line-internal equivalent (*contre-r. à l'hémistiche*), where the caesura isolates the smaller part of the syntactic phrase in the first hemistich, e.g. Hugo: "Le Sauveur a veillé pour tous les yeux, *pleuré* / Pour tous les pleurs, *saigné* // pour toutes les blessures" (The Saviour has watched for all eyes, wept / For all tears, bled // for all wounds).—Elwert; Mazaleyrat; H. Golomb, *Enjambment in Poetry* (1979); Morier; Scott. A.G.E.; C.S.

RELATIVE STRESS PRINCIPLE. In a paper given in Denmark in 1900, Otto Jespersen identified the principle which was to become one of the axioms of modern metrics: "the effect of surroundings." Castigating 19th-c. metrists for three fallacies handed down from antiquity—the fallacies of long and short (modern meters employ stress or tone), the foot (an artificial distinction which can only lead to unnatural scansions), and two grades of stress (rather than four)—Jespersen makes the sanguine observation that "our ear does not really perceive stress relations with any degree of certainty except when the syllables concerned are contiguous"; in meter "the only thing required by the ear is an upward and a downward movement, a rise and fall . . . at fixed places" regardless of "how great is the ascent or the descent." Consequently, "the metrical value of a syllable depends on what comes before and what follows after it." (Boundaries such as line-beginning or pauses therefore allow following "inversions" since the effect of a pause is effectually zero stress.) Syllables which would otherwise be stressed appear weaker between very strong syllables, and weaker syllables such as prepositions gain strength between the weakest syllables, such as articles or enclitics.

Subsequent metrists came to see that these two phenomena (later termed demotion and promotion) could be readily employed to bring unusual stress patterns within the rule of a regular iambic meter. So in Pope's line, "On her white Breast, a sparkling Cross she wore" (*Rape of the Lock* 2.7), the first four syllables increase steadily in intensity (W. K. Wimsatt's "crescendo foot"), but since the second is greater than the first, and the fourth greater than the third, these really amount, in relative terms, to two iambs. Jespersen noticed precisely this phenomenon, but he also did not neglect the other significant transition, between syllables two and three, a nexus ignored by traditional foot metrics. In short, Jespersen explicitly rejected the notion of the metrical foot (q.v.). It is an irony that even those of his successors who did not were quick to appropriate his notion that stress values, for scansion purposes, are relative not absolute. Adumbration of the r. s. p. may be found in R. G. Latham's *The Eng. Lang.* (1855). See also PYRRHIC; SPONDEE.—O. Jespersen, "Den psykologiske grund til nogle metriske faenomener," *Oversigt* (1900), tr. in his *Linguistica* (1933). T.V.F.B.

RELIGION AND POETRY.

    I. EARLY EXPRESSIONS OF THE RELATION
   II. RELIGIOUS EPIC
 III. LYRICISM
 IV. POETRY VERSUS RELIGION

I. EARLY EXPRESSIONS OF THE RELATION. In early societies the boundaries between r., myth, and p. are vague. Aristotle (*Poetics* 51b19) equates poetry with the making of *mythos*, tr. as "plot" but related also to "myth" (q.v.). From the point of view of the *Poetics* poems are essentially stories, but the stories on which most early dramatic and narrative poetry (q.v.), incl. drama, is based are myths and legends.

The early drama of a great many cultures derives from religious liturgy or shows the influence of such liturgy. Evidence for this practice includes the use of religious and mythic subjects, of stylized and ritualistic modes of speech, and of lyric choruses, dance, and song. This description is generally accurate, for example, for the early drama of India and for such related dramatic trads. as those of Indonesia and Bali, and also for the Japanese *No* play and for Gr. tragedy (q.v.) and the "Old Comedy" of Aristophanes. Medieval Christian drama separated itself from liturgy in the 10th c., and all early examples are chanted rather than spoken. The Passion plays and Corpus Christi plays of the

14th and 15th cs. use rhymed verseforms and, in England, complex stanzas. It can be added that many apparently nondramatic kinds of poetry evidently originally developed in connection with liturgy and liturgical drama (q.v.). Hymns (q.v.) are an obvious case in point. The "Nine Songs" of China (3rd c. B.C.) are erotic incantations to summon various deities, evidently associated with liturgy and intended to be danced as well as chanted.

In *The Birth of Tragedy* (1872), Friedrich Nietzsche argued that the liturgy of the god Dionysus (Bacchus) was choral and communal and that drama emerged when the leader donned the mask of a legendary hero such as Ajax or Agamemnon, converting liturgy into a form of history play (q.v.). Most Gr. tragedies are based on a few myths and legends such as those associated with the House of Thebes; many of them (e.g. the *Prometheus* of Aeschylus and the *Eumenides* and *Oedipus at Colonus* of Sophocles) treat religious themes, with emphasis on such themes as the apparent cruelty of the gods, human guilt, and the relation of r. to justice. Nietzsche believed that the religious ("Dionysian") element of Gr. tragedy survives with special force in the choral parts, which are chanted and danced, and which refer regularly to the influence of the gods on human affairs. In the tragedies of Euripides the chorus becomes less important, and "Apollonian" and "Socratic" elements become dominant, with religious content increasingly replaced by sophistic argumentation and rhet. The change parallels the devel. of Gr. rationalist philosophy and the decline of religious influences in Gr. culture (see APOLLONIAN AND DIONYSIAN).

Subsequently, the "Cambridge anthropologists," incl. F. M. Cornford and Gilbert Murray, reached conclusions parallel to those of Nietzsche on the basis of comparative anthropology rather than philosophical analysis. They concluded that drama arises in all cultures from primitive religious ceremonies celebrating the birth, death, and rebirth of a "year daimon"—that is, a god representing the annual death and renewal of fertility. Comedy (q.v.) is associated with the birth phase and tragedy with the death phase. Carl Jung understood this idea in relation to the theory of archetypes (q.v.).

Extending these ideas in his *Anatomy of Criticism* (1957), Northrop Frye argues that all of the major genres arise from or are related to primitive religious dramas objectifying the death and rebirth of fertility in nature. As developed by Frye, the theory of the Cambridge Anthropologists explains much, but skeptics have questioned the history on which it is based (see e.g. G. Else, *The Origin of Gr. Tragedy* [1965]), and have also pointed out that even the earliest Gr. tragedies also show concern for political and social issues unrelated to their allegedly archetypal origins.

The notion that poems are divinely inspired has no necessary relation to the theory of the liturgical origins of drama, but it is another instance of the close tie between r. and p. The poets of the Indian Vedas seek inspiration (q.v.) to reveal divine truths and to recall the actions of men. Gr. and Lat. poets invoke the Muses (q.v.), daughters of Zeus and Mnemosyne (Memory). Heb. poets invoke Yahweh, and Christian poets seek inspiration from the Holy Spirit—for example, John Milton begins *Paradise Lost* by invoking a Muse who "from the first / Wast present, and with mighty wings outspread / Dove-like satst brooding o'er the vast Abyss." Allied to the theory of divine inspiration is the idea—advocated with special enthusiasm by Ren. poets such as Torquato Tasso and Sir Philip Sidney—that the making of poems itself is a creative act resembling the far greater creative acts of God.

Inspiration is akin to prophecy, and much early poetry is prophetic, as witness the prophetic books of the OT, the utterances of the Gr. Oracle at Delphi and the Roman Sibyl, runic poetry, and the visions of Celtic bards. The Indian word for poet is *rishi* ("seer"), and the Lat. is *vates* ("prophet"). Obscurity (q.v.) is inherent in prophetic poetry and considered evidence of its divine origin. Religious poetry thus inherits a tolerance—sometimes a positive admiration—for obscurantism. Riddles (q.v.) and enigma poems appear early in many if not all lits. Later poems that invoke the prophetic trad. often use allegory (q.v.) and complex allusive lang. Another common type of religious poem is the charm (q.v.; also "spell" or "incantation"), which attempts to control some aspect of the world or the future by a verbal formula invested with religious or magical power. Charms and spells are usually in verse, and their use in magic and in such quasi-magical activities as divination and alchemy shows their close relation to r.

II. RELIGIOUS EPIC. Long religious poems survive from the early periods of several cultures. They tend to be loosely organized and to absorb much tangential historical, didactic, moral, and philosophical material. The longest poem of this type is undoubtedly the Indian *Mahabharata*, a vast heterogeneous collection of r., mythology, legendary history, and philosophical meditation dating from the 1st millennium B.C. and attributed to the poet Vyasa. The *Ramayana* (1st c. A.D.), attributed to Valmik, is shorter but also draws on religious themes. Analogous poems incl. the Sumerian-Babylonian *Gilgamesh*, the Ger. *Niebelungenlied*, and the Finnish *Kalevala*. The plots of such religious epics tend to be derived from legendary history. In *The Hero With a Thousand Faces*, Joseph Campbell argues that these epics are variations on a single, archetypal plot ("monomyth") about the birth, life, descent into the underworld, return, atonement, and apotheosis of a hero-god.

The heterogeneity of the *Mahabharata* illustrates the limitation of any theory that seeks to reduce early religious epics to a single formula. The *Iliad* and the *Odyssey* illustrate the problem in another way. Although they show the gods interacting with humans and are based on legendary history, the *Iliad* is a deliberately focused art work with emphasis on human rather than divine motivation, while the *Odyssey* wavers between serious narrative and self-conscious romance.

Many early poems with a religious focus are not "epic" at all. The four Indian *Vedas* (some parts from the 2d millennium B.C.) are collections of hymns, though they incl. narrative fragments. The *Upanishads* (9th–5th c. B.C.) are meditations on the nature of the world and of the Brahman. The most famous part of the *Mahabharata*—the *Bhagavad-Gita*—is a verse dialogue between the god Krishna and the warrior Arjuna just before a great battle. At the climax (sect. 11), Krishna reveals he is the terrifying and beautiful god who destroys all even as he has created it.

The Egyptian *Book of the Dead* (15th c. B.C.) is a collection of liturgical texts relating to the journey of the soul to the underworld. The *Mathnavi*, a Persian poem by Jalal al-Din Rumi (13th c. A.D.), describes the soul's search for god. The OT of the Bible is an anthology of narrative, dramatic, and lyric forms so firmly rooted in history that many of its key moments have been independently confirmed by archaeology. Conversely, the *Koran* is a series of 114 chapters (*suras*) containing revelations, rules, and moral exhortations rather than quasi-historical narratives. Like the OT, it is monotheistic: the pantheon of Indian and Gr. r. is replaced by one true God, omnipotent and universal.

Hesiod's *Theogony* (Gr.; 8th c. B.C.) traces the gradual emergence of the world from chaos through the generations of the gods from Uranus (sky) and Gaea (earth) through Chronos (Roman Saturn) and Rhea to Zeus (Jupiter) and Hera (Juno), incl. the wars of the Titans, the begetting of Aphrodite (Venus) from the severed testicles of Chronos, the stealing of fire by Prometheus, and the creation of the human race by Deucalion and Pyrrha. The OT *Genesis* has a similar content, as do many of the early narrative poems mentioned above. Christian poets created equivalent narratives by rewriting the story of the six days (*hexaemera*) of Creation. Among consciously artistic reworkings of the form are Torquato Tasso's *Creation of the World* (late 16th c.), Guillaume Sieur du Bartas's *Divine Weeks*, and Book 7 of Milton's *Paradise Lost* (both 17th c.).

It is tempting to speculate that poetry and r. are coextensive if not identical during the earliest stage of cultural devel. and that only at a later stage does poetry separate itself from r. However, several major cultures seem to lack a rich heritage of early religious poetry. This is true, for example, of Japanese culture, in which religious poetry only becomes an important genre after the introduction of Buddhism and Taoism. Again, prior to the *Koran* (650 A.D.), Muslim culture has little religious poetry. Perhaps such cultures possessed an extensive body of religious poetry in oral form but considered it "primitive" or "pagan" and not worth saving.

In Western culture, r. has been a prime subject of poetry continuously from earliest to most recent times. This is true for both the Graeco-Roman and Hebraic-Christian trads. The heroic poems of Homer, Hesiod, and Virgil illustrate the point for pagan culture. The most striking quasi-heroic Christian poems are Dante Alighieri's *Divina commedia* (14th c.) and Milton's *Paradise Lost*, but entire cycles of medieval poems are based on Christian legends—most obviously, celebrations of the lives of saints and martyrs and of such themes as the quest for the Holy Grail.

III. LYRICISM. For many readers, the relation between r. and p. is closest in the lyric, since the lyric is particularly well suited to expressing the individual's sense of awe and wonder—sometimes bafflement, rage, or shame—in the presence of the divine. The religious lyric impulse expresses itself in poems of mystic encounter, in hymns, in poetic responses to the divine in nature, and in poems of personal experience—e.g. love, devotion, guilt, despair.

Poems of mystic encounter can also be called poems of epiphany or theophany. Sufi mystic poets typically use erotic metaphors to express their epiphanies, as in the poems of Ibn al-Arabi and Ibn al-Farid (both 12th c.). Alternately, mystic poetry can use understatement, as in Henry Vaughan's "Eternity": "I saw Eternity the other night / Like a great Ring of pure and endless light. . . ." Supreme among European mystic poets are two Spaniards—St. Teresa of Avila, who is often intense and playful at the same time, and St. John of the Cross, who uses erotic metaphors as well as figures of negation and paradox drawn from the mystic *via negativa.*

Most hymns have explicit liturgical functions. The "Homeric Hymns" seem to have had such functions even though they mix narrative with lyric passages. The liturgy of the Eastern Orthodox Church is adorned with a series of great hymns (e.g. the *Cheroubikon*, a communion hymn) and also *kontakia*, or poetic homilies, of which the most famous is the 7th-c. *Akathistos* ("Standing") hymn, a passionate expression of devotion to the Blessed Virgin. Catholic hymnody in the West begins with the Ambrosian hymns (4th c.), which are strophic poems in iambic dimeter (e.g. "Deus creator omnium"). Most of the Lat. hymns in the 55 volumes of the *Analecta hymnica* (1886–1922) are to be sung at specific liturgical moments—for example, in the Mass at the transition from the Epistle reading to the Gospel reading (when "sequences" were sung) or during Communion.

Hymns can celebrate God or a saint or martyr; they can be meditations on significant historical moments (e.g. Mary at the foot of the Cross, as in the "Stabat mater"). Often they are didactic, as in the series of hymns expounding the doctrine of transsubstantiation which St. Thomas Aquinas composed for the Feast of Corpus Christi. In general, since Protestant hymns are for congregational singing, they are simple stanzaic poems stressing such common religious experiences as conversion ("Amazing Grace"), trust in God ("A Mighty Fortress is Our God"), or desire for guidance ("Lead Kindly Light").

"Literary hymns" are intended for reading rather than for liturgical use. In the 4th c., Prudentius wrote the *Peristephanon*, 14 hymns celebrating martyrs, and the *Cathemerinon*, 12 hymns for the hours of the day and feasts of the Church year. Literary hymns frequently celebrate personal and idiosyncratic religious views rather than orthodoxies. Edmund Spenser's "Four Hymns" (16th c.), for example, are at least as Neoplatonic as Christian. The "Hymnen an die Nacht" of Novalis (ca. 1800) are romantic meditations on death without specific denominational content, although his "Geistliche Lieder" are more orthodox; two of them are found in Ger. Protestant hymnals. John Donne's *Holy Sonnets* (17th c.) are a sustained meditation on faith. George Herbert's *The Temple* (17th c.) consists of poems on every aspect of a devout Christian life. The great Victorian religious poet Gerard Manley Hopkins wrote lyric celebrations of the divine power immanent in the everyday world ("The Windhover"), and similar themes can be found in Thomas Merton's poems about his spiritual life while a Trappist monk (*Collected Poems*, 1977).

Although Chinese and Japanese poetry tends not to be overtly devotional, Buddhism and Taoism encouraged exquisitely understated lyrics evoking the mutability and fragile beauty of the natural world, as in the *waka* of Priest Saigyo (Japanese, 12th c.). During the romantic period, European poets also celebrated the spiritual aspect of nature. Wordsworth's *Prelude*, for example, is a poetic record of the ways nature shapes the devel. of the poet's mind and moral being. A quasi-religious impulse can also be observed in romantic poems on the brotherhood of man, as in Schiller's "Ode to Joy."

Religious lyrics also seek comfort in the midst of affliction. Many of the Indian *Upanishads* deal with this theme, as does the *Bhagavad-Gita*. The *Book of Job* poses the question of why a loving God permits suffering and concludes that man must accept whatever God ordains. In the tragedies of Aeschylus the gods are often cruel and human destiny controlled by Fate (*Ate*). In the *Eumenides*, however, under the patronage of Athena a tribunal is formed, and the Furies (*Erinyes*) tormenting Orestes for his complicity in the murder of his mother are transformed. In Sophocles' Oedipus trilogy both human and divine agency may be claimed for the catastrophe.

The seven "penitential" psalms of David exemplify the religious lyric expressing the anguish of a guilty conscience. They have often been translated, paraphrased, and imitated by later poets, e.g. Petrarch, Sir Thomas Wyatt. Loss of faith is another common theme of religious poetry, as in James Thompson's "City of Dreadful Night" (19th c.), the late sonnets of G. M. Hopkins, and T. S. Eliot's *The Waste Land* (20th c.). A complementary theme—the search for faith—is exemplified by Eliot's "Ash Wednesday" and *Four Quartets*.

IV. POETRY VERSUS RELIGION. Rational philosophy and science appear to challenge religious belief. The reaction can be a retreat into the hedonism of wine and love (Horace's *carpe diem*), as in the poems of the "Seven Sages of the Bamboo Grove" (Chinese, 3d c. A.D.) and of Catullus (Roman, 1st c. B.C.), or hedonism mixed with philosophical skepticism, as in the *Rubaiyat* of Omar Khayyam (Persian, 12th c.), or religious satire, as in the comic treatment of the pagan gods, with emphasis on their lurid sex lives, by the Roman poet Ovid in his *Metamorphoses* (1st c. A.D.). As religious faith weakens, poems are also written expressing nostalgia for the departed "age of faith"—e.g. Matthew Arnold's "Dover Beach": "The sea of faith / Was once, too, at the full. . . . But now I only hear / Its melancholy, long, withdrawing roar. . . ." It is a theme that also echoes powerfully in the lyrics of Thomas Hardy.

In "The Study of Poetry" (1880), Arnold argues that "Our r. has materialized itself in the fact . . . and now the fact is failing it." Poetry does not depend on fact, and "the strongest part of our r. today is its unconscious poetry." Roughly the same position is taken by the Am. philosopher George Santayana in *Interpretations of Poetry and R.* (1900): poetry at its best "is identical with r. grasped in its inmost truth"—or would be if r. would only "withdraw [its] pretentions to dealing with matters of fact."

The idea that r. is inherently "poetic" and that p. is the appropriate vehicle for religious sentiment is commonplace, but it is untenable historically since many of the finest religious works, incl. most of the NT, St. Augustine's *Confessions, The Cloud of Unknowing*, Jeremy Taylor's *Holy Living and Holy Dying*, and C. S. Lewis's *Screwtape Letters*, are in prose. It does, however, account for the often-encountered argument that p. can be a substitute for r. in modern secular culture.

An Arnoldian preoccupation with the "poetry" of religious texts also underlies much 20th-c. interest in the poetic genres in the Bible—esp. the OT—and in the themes, symbols, and images that are found in the Bible and recur throughout the lit. of Western culture—a position evident, for example, in Northrop Frye's *The Great Code* (1982) and in Kermode and Alter.

At the same time, theologians have frequently and vehemently denied the metaphorical and mythic—and hence the "poetic"—elements of religious texts such as the Bible. In his classic study *The Idea of the Holy* (1923), Rudolf Otto argues that religious experience is an untranslatable but absolutely real encounter with otherness that reveals the superficiality of ordinary experience and hence of all attempts to express it in either myth or poetry. For Michael Novak, this translates into man's need for a redeeming "experience of nothingness" without which "the machines, the mythmakers sink their hands into one's soul."

The central debate on the question of the "poetry" of the Bible is undoubtedly the one initiated by Rudolf Bultmann in his essay on the biblical "proclamation." Bultmann begins by questioning the mythological superstructure of the Bible—precisely that "great code" of symbols so valued by 20th-c. descendents of Arnold and Santayana—and ends with a summary rejection of the very idea of biblical "poetry": "The word of God is not some mysterious oracle, but a sober, factual account of a human life, of Jesus of Nazareth," and "all these assertions are an offense, which will not be removed by philosophical discussion, but only by faith and obedience." This is a hard-line theological point of view, and it contrasts strikingly with Frye's comment in *The Great Code*, which expresses the point of view of the literary critic to whom the "poetry" of r., in the sense of myth and metaphor, is its essential character: "myth is the linguistic vehicle of *kerygma*, and . . . to 'demythologize' any part of the Bible would be the same thing as to obliterate it."

Frye's view of r. rests on a quasi-scientific anthropology, but the trust of 19th-c. philosophy and science in "fact" has been challenged at least as powerfully in the 20th c. as has the faith of Buddhists and Muslims and Christians and animists in their various gods and cosmologies. Paradoxically, the challenge has come from science itself—from relativity, quantum mechanics, and astrophysics—as well as philosophy and r. Increasingly, the structure of the world seems to depend, at least in part, on the way the world is conceptualized. Is there a privileged structure or is structure entirely relative? That would seem to be a religious, not a scientific question.

Rainer Maria Rilke's *Sonnets to Orpheus* (20th c.) objectify the recovery of a mythic—thus religious—view of the world through a series of lyric epiphanies. They are poems in search of the p. of r., and this fact makes them vulnerable to critiques like those of Otto and Bultmann. Wallace Stevens, conversely, remains skeptical and detached. No view of the world is privileged, a point illustrated by his "Thirteen Ways of Looking at a Blackbird." In *Notes Toward a Supreme Fiction*, Stevens calls the orders the mind imposes on the world "necessary fictions" rather than truths of science or of faith. Whether one sides with Otto or Rilke or Stevens or with explicitly religious poets like Eliot and Merton, the idea that poetry can take the place of r. in a world of scientifically established fact has come to seem increasingly problematic. See also BELIEF AND POETRY; HEBREW POETRY; SCIENCE AND POETRY; HYMN; PSALM.

G. Santayana, *Interps. of Poetry and R.* (1900; critical ed., ed. H. J. Saatkamp, Jr., 1990); R. Otto,

The Idea of the Holy, tr. J. Harvey (1923); A. B. Kieth, *A Hist. of Sanskrit Lit.* (1928); R. A. Nicholson, *Lit. Hist. of the Arabs,* 2d ed. (1930); T. S. Eliot, "R. and Lit.," *Essays Ancient and Mod.* (1936); H. N. Fairchild, *Religious Trends in Eng. Poetry,* 6 v. (1939–68); Auerbach; J. Campbell, *The Hero with a Thousand Faces* (1949); Raby, *Christian* and *Secular,* Curtius, ch. 12; *The Indian Heritage,* ed. V. Raghavan (1956)—anthol.; L. Martz, *The Poetry of Meditation* (1954); Frye; M. Eliade, *The Sacred and the Profane* (1959), *Shamanism: Archaic Techniques of Ecstasy* (1964); L. B. Campbell, *Divine Poetry and Drama* (1959); C. I. Glicksberg, *Lit. and R.: A Study in Conflict* (1960); R. May, *Symbolism in R. and Lit.* (1960); F. M. Cornford, *The Origin of Attic Comedy,* ed. T. H. Gaster (1961); R. Bultmann et al., *Kerygma and Myth,* tr. R. H. Fuller (1961); H. Frankfort et al., *Before Philosophy* (1963); *Penguin Book of Religious Verse,* ed. R. S. Thomas (1963); W. J. Reynolds, *A Survey of Christian Hymnody* (1963); C. M. Bowra, *Primitive Song* (1964); O. B. Hardison, Jr., *Christian Rite and Christian Drama in the Middle Ages* (1965); A. S. P. Woodhouse, *The Poet and his Faith* (1965); J. Mascaró, *The Upanishads* (1965); H. Hatzfeld, *Santa Teresa of Avila* (1969); G. Dumezil, *Mythe et épopée,* 2 v. (1968–73); T. Cave, *Devotional Poetry in France c. 1570–1613* (1969); M. Novak, *The Experience of Nothingness* (1970); M. H. Abrams, *Natural Supernaturalism* (1971); N. A. Scott, Jr., *The Wild Prayer of Longing* (1971), *The Poetics of Belief* (1985); D. B. Morris, *The Religious Sublime* (1972); P. Milward, *Shakespeare's Religious Background* (1973); J. A. Ramsaran, *Eng. and Hindi Religious Poetry* (1973); H. Frei, *The Eclipse of Biblical Narrative* (1974); E. S. Shaffer, *"Kubla Khan" and the Fall of Jerusalem: The Mythological School in Biblical Crit. and Secular Lit., 1770–1880* (1975); H. Schneidau, *Sacred Discontent: The Bible and Western Lit.* (1976); G. B. Green, *The Interp. of Otherness: Lit., R., and the Am. Imagination* (1979); *The Critical Study of Sacred Texts,* ed. W. D. O'Flaherty (1979); B. Jordan, *Servants of the Gods: A Study in the R., Hist., and Lit. of 5th-C. Athens* (1979); B. K. Lewalski, *Protestant Poetics and the 17th-C. Religious Lyric* (1979); R. Alter, *The Art of Biblical Narrative* (1981), *The Art of Biblical Poetry* (1985); G. Gunn, "Lit. and R.," *Interrelations of Lit.,* ed. J.-P. Barricelli and J. Gibaldi (1982); *New Oxford Book of Christian Verse,* ed. D. Davie (1982); N. Frye, *The Great Code* (1982); S. A. Handelman, *The Slayers of Moses: The Emergence of Rabbinic Interp. in Mod. Literary Theory* (1982); W. LaFleur, *The Karma of Words: Buddhism and the Literary Arts in Med. Japan* (1983); R. Strier, *Love Known: Theology and Experience in George Herbert's Poetry* (1983); G. Tennyson, *Victorian Devotional Poetry* (1983); D. Daiches, *God and the Poets* (1984); *Penguin Book of Eng. Christian Verse,* ed. P. Levi (1984); M. Sternberg, *The Poetics of Biblical Narrative* (1984); L. M. Poland, *Lit. Crit. and Biblical Hermeneutics* (1985); *The Bhagavad-Gita,* tr. B. S. Miller (1986); S. Prickett, *Words and the Word: Lang., Poetics, and Biblical Interp.* (1986); *Literary Guide to the Bible,* ed. R. Alter and F. Kermode (1987); A. C. Yu, "Lit. and R.," and J. R. Barth et al., "P.," *Encyc. of R.,* ed. M. Eliade, v. 8, 11 (1987)—covers Indian, Chinese, Japanese, Christian, and Islamic religious p.; *Contemp. Religious P.,* ed. P. Ramsey (1987); G. H. Tavard, *Poetry and Contemplation in St. John of the Cross* (1988); T. R. Wright, *Theology and Lit.* (1989); H. Bloom, *Ruin the Sacred Truths* (1989); T. G. Sherwood, *Herbert's Prayerful Art* (1989); F. B. Brown, *Religious Aesthetics* (1989); M. Lichtmann, *The Contemplative Poetry of G. M. Hopkins* (1989); E. J. McNees, *Eucharistic Poetry* (1992). O.B.H.; T.V.F.B.

REMATE. A Sp. metric term denoting a short stanza placed at the end of a poem and serving as a conclusion to the poem. The r. generally repeats the last rhymes of the preceding full-length strophe. It is most commonly used at the end of the *canción* (q.v.). In it the poet addresses himself to the *canción,* giving it a special message to bear to a particular person, "recognizing some flaw in the *canción,* or making an excuse for it, or telling it what it must answer if it should be found wanting in some respect" (Rengifo). It has also been called *vuelta, commiato, despido, envio, ripressa, ritornelo (retornelo),* and *contera.*—Rengifo, *Arte poética española* (1592, ch. 86); E. Segura Covarsí, *La canción petrarquista en la lirica española del siglo de oro* (1949); Navarro. D.C.C.

RENAISSANCE POETICS.

    I. INTRODUCTION
    II. THE DEFENSE OF POETRY
   III. THE LANGUAGE OF POETRY
   IV. THE GENRES OF POETRY
    V. THE PRINCIPLE OF IMITATION
   VI. RHETORIC AND POETIC
  VII. CONCLUSION

I. INTRODUCTION. Lit. crit. was first recognized as an independent form of lit. and the critic first accepted as a new kind of writer in the Ren.; indeed, nearly all modern poetics (q.v.) derives directly from ideas advanced in this period. Ren. crit. began in the struggle to defend imaginative lit. against attacks of immorality and frivolity. In establishing a place for the writing and studying of poetry, the use of the vernacular was debated (and also vindicated); genres were distinguished, each with its own conventions; the humanist movement instituted as the basis of poetics the practice of imitating Cl. texts; and rhetoricians supplied a basic *techne* or set of rules on which poetic art could rely.

II. THE DEFENSE OF POETRY. Boccaccio in his *Genealogiae deorum gentilium* (1360) and in his life of Dante laid down the main lines for defending poetry against clerical and secular charges. He argues that religion and poetry (q.v.) are not opposed; on the contrary, the Bible is poetry and teaches, as all poetry does, by means of allegory (q.v.), i.e. metaphors with fixed and continuing referents. In addition, the poets were the first theologians. Seemingly immoral pagan stories may thus be interpreted in wholly moral ways: "When the ancient poets feigned that Saturn had many children and devoured all but four of them, they wished to have understood from their picture nothing else than that Saturn is time, in which everything is produced, and as everything is produced in time, it likewise is the destroyer of all and reduces all to nothing." For Boccaccio even the story of Leda and the Swan could be viewed allegorically as anticipating (or shadowing) the Virgin and the Dove. Boccaccio also defended poetry against charges of frivolity, arguing that it had always been admired by the people, protected by their leaders and rulers, and supported by wealthy patrons. Moreover, the poet is a creator like God Himself; there is, Boccaccio says, no higher vocation possible for man.

Once these arguments were in place, they were copied, expanded, and developed in nearly all It., Fr., and Eng. defenses of poetry from the 14th through the 16th c. Meanwhile, much technical lore about Cl. poetry was spread abroad through elaborately annotated editions of Horace's *Ars poetica*, most esp. the popular edition by Badius Ascensius first pub. in Paris in 1500. The result was summed up in It. crit. by Marco Girolamo Vida's *De arte poetica* (The Art of Poetry, 1527; tr. R. G. Williams, 1976), a long verse treatise imitating Horace but also incorporating much humanist theory about the moral purpose and genres of poetry, the function of the critic, and the like. As for theory relating specifically to vernacular poetic theory, the most important work of the early 16th c. is Giangiorgio Trissino's *La poetica* (Books 1–4, 1529; Books 5–6, 1563) which is an elaborate analysis of It. versification and verse conventions.

A new factor was introduced into European lit. crit. in 1508 with the publication by Aldus of a reliable Gr. text of Aristotle's *Poetics* and a Lat. tr. by Pazzi in 1536. The *Poetics* was known in the Middle Ages only through a Lat. tr. of a paraphrase by the Arabian philosopher Averroes, and a badly flawed Lat. tr. by Lorenzo Valla that was pub. in the late 15th c. Pazzi's Lat. tr. was an immediate and powerful stimulus to critical thought. Detailed commentaries on the *Poetics* began to appear in the 1540s and continued to be produced in Italy throughout the rest of the century. In the earlier commentaries—e.g. those by Robortelli (1548) and Maggi and Lombardi (1549)—Aristotle mixes exotically with theories derived from rhet. and with didactic theories drawn from the humanist trad. and from Horace. In general, these treatises interpret catharsis (q.v.) as purgation of wicked impulses, and tragedy (q.v.) as a form providing examples of vices to avoid.

The most famous It. Ren. commentary on Aristotle is *Poetica d'Aristotele vulgarizzata e sposta* (The Poetics of Aristotle in the Vulgar Lang.) by Lodovico Castelvetro (1570, 1576; ed. W. Romani, 2 v., 1978; abridged tr. A. Bongiorno, *Castelvetro on the Art of Poetry*, 1984), which insists that tragedy is popular entertainment and that catharsis is insensitivity to suffering created by seeing it in plays. After 1540, most full-blown It. critical essays—e.g. Antonio Minturno's *De poeta* (1559), usually considered a source of Sir Philip Sidney's *Defense of Poesie* (1595)—draw heavily on Aristotle. These texts usually treat lit. as a source of moral instruction through examples of virtue and vice. They regularly combine Aristotelian ideas with the Horatian trad. that poetry should "profit" morally, even as it "delights." More narrowly focused treatises—e.g. Giraldi Cinthio's *Discorsi intorno al comporre dei romanzi, commedie, e tragedie* (Discourses on Composing Romances, Comedies, and Tragedies, 1554; tr. H. L. Snuggs, 1968)—mix Aristotelian ideas with ideas drawn from theories of vernacular versification and trads. about popular vernacular genres like romance.

Whatever the point of view, after 1540 few critical treatises were written in Italy that did not draw on the *Poetics*. That the Sp. followed the It. lead is illustrated by Alonso Pinciano's *Philosophía antigua poética* (1596), a commentary on the *Poetics* treating imitation, verisimilitude, and wonder, among other topics. In northern Europe, conversely, the influence of Aristotle is not felt until the last quarter of the 16th c. Indeed, in northern Europe the most influential critical work was, for many years, the massive but derivative *Poetices libri septem* (Seven Books of Poetics, 1561; ed. A. Bock, 1964) of Julius Caesar Scaliger. Although Aristotle is often cited by northern European critics in the last quarter of the 16th c., not until 1611, with the *De tragoediae constitutione* (On the Nature of Tragedy) of Daniel Heinsius was a study of the *Poetics* produced comparable in scope and sophistication to its It. predecessors. But with Heinsius we begin to move from Ren. to neoclassical poetics (q.v.).

Another critical position, deriving from Aristotle's *Rhet.*, appears in, for example, Baltasar Gracián's *Agudeza y arte de ingenio* (Cleverness and the Art of Wit, 1642) in Spain and Immanuele Tesauro's *Il cannocchiale aristotelico* (Aristotelian Telescope, 1654) in Italy. "Concettismo" (see CULTERANISMO), as it is called, is concerned neither with plot and character nor with moral uplift. Instead, it is concerned with the effect of brilliant imagery, understood for the most part as pleasure and awe.

III. THE LANGUAGE OF POETRY. It. theories about poetic lang. were much influenced by the revival of interest in Cl. poetry that occurred in the 14th c. The humanist movement thus generated spent much of its early years interpreting—and in some cases recovering and perfecting—Gr. and Lat. mss., even though some of the best poets—Dante, Petrarch, Boccaccio—were writing in the vernacular. Humanists assumed that the great texts of the past, in all genres, were best in the Cl.

langs., esp. Lat. The support of vernacular writing was further complicated in Italy because of the many dialects in the separate city-states: the country as yet had no national unification and no national lang. Hence those interested in a vernacular body of work had first to defend a particular dialect for it (see ITALIAN POETRY).

Dante's *De vulgari eloquentia* (Of Eloquence in the Vernacular, ca. 1305; ed. A. Marigo, 1957) is the first and still the best argument for vernacular lit.; it has no worthy successor until Leone Battista Alberti's *Trattato del governo della famiglia* (1438), which contends that the vulgar (or common) tongue would become as polished as Lat. if patriotic writers gave it their attention. In *Prose della volgar lingua* (1524), Pietro Bembo claims the Florentine dialect is as good as Lat., and even superior to it as a lang. for modern subjects. Since Florentine was the one dialect with a strong literary trad., most Italians who wrote in the vernacular used it, yet some opposed it in favor of a truly national literary lang. they termed "Italian" or even "Courtier's Tongue." Il Calmeta and Castiglione (esp. in his *Il cortegiano* [Book of the Courtier]) were foremost among these proponents, although they took most of their arguments from Dante's earlier essay.

Nationalism also aided the cause of vernacular lit. in France. Joachim Du Bellay's *La Deffence et illustration de la langue françoyse* (1549; ed. H. Chamard, 1948) is firmly nationalistic. Du Bellay took many of his arguments from the *Dialogo delle lingue* of Sperone Speroni (1542; ed. and tr. H. Harth, 1975); he claims that the Fr. are as good as the Romans, so that it follows that their lang. is equally good. It is therefore the patriotic duty of all Fr. scholars and poets to write in Fr. and enrich the lang.; translators can also participate by enlarging the Fr. vocabulary with words "captured" from other langs. (see FRENCH POETRY).

The Eng. were, if possible, even more nationalistic than the Fr., yet the widespread taste for Lat. produced by grammar-school education made the battle more difficult than it might otherwise have been. Roger Ascham writes in *Toxophilus* (1545), his defense of the use of the ancient long bow in battle, that "to have written this book either in Lat. or Gr. . . . had been more easier." Indeed, in the 17th c. Bacon had some of his more important scientific works published in Lat. because he feared that "these modern langs. will at one time or other play bankrupt with books." On the other hand, Richard Mulcaster, a prominent educator, thought of Eng. as "the joyful title of our liberty and freedom, the Lat. tongue remembering us of our thraldom and bondage." In this, he undoubtedly spoke for the majority of Englishmen. It should be added that both in England and in northern Europe the cause of national langs. and lits. was enhanced by the growing Reformist and Protestant movements, which insisted that the Scriptures be translated and available for all believers to read for themselves.

But once the cause of vernacular poetry was established, the practice raised problems of its own. The initial problem was meter: how could a vernacular lang. (lacking quantity) imitate the (quantitative) meter natural to the Cl. langs., Gr. and Lat.? Claudio Tolomei in his *Versi et regole de la nuova poesia toscana* (1539) tried to show how It. poetry could be written so as to imitate the prosody of Lat. verse. He was followed in France by Jacques de la Taille, who writes in the preface to his *La Manière de faire des vers en françois, comme en grec et en latin* (1573) that the real issue is the yearnings of "ultraclassicists" to rival Virgil or Homer, and argues for a new Fr. spelling and pronunciation that will permit the lang. to fit Cl. meter. The Eng. were more tolerant still, and many Eng. poets in the later 16th c. came to write an Eng. quantitative verse in imitation of the Gr. and Lat. because the Eng. lang. seemed closer to the Cl. langs., esp. Lat., than it did to It., with its greater percentage of rhyming words, or to Fr., with its more musical accent. For the Eng., meter superseded rhyme, and in *The Scholemaster* (1570) Ascham, associating rhyme with medieval scholastic verse, even calls rhyme "barbarian." See CLASSICAL METERS IN MODERN LANGUAGES.

Later treatises by William Webbe (1586) and (putatively) George Puttenham (1589) provide an additional, Protestant argument by declaring that the past age, when rhyme was employed, was not only "gothic" but papist. Webbe recalls "this tinkerly verse which we call rime" and condemns monks for having invented "brutish Poetry." Puttenham speaks of rhyme (q.v.) as "the idle invention of Monastical men," supporting the superiority of Protestant classicists. Even Edmund Spenser briefly became part of the quantitative movement, and as late as 1602, Thomas Campion in his *Observations* questions "the childish titillation of riming." The positive outcomes of such complaints in Eng. were a notable increase in poetic experimentation and the devel. of a flexible and powerful medium for dramatic poetry (q.v.), namely blank verse (q.v.).

IV. THE GENRES OF POETRY. Ren. concern with Cl. verseforms was matched by interest in Cl. distinctions of genre (q.v.), distinctions first worked out by the commentators on Horace and Aristotle and later codified by such critics as Minturno, Scaliger, and Sidney. In general, the commentators associated each of the major genres with a particular social stratum, with the nobility at the top and peasants and artisans at the bottom.

Epic (q.v.) or "heroic verse" (q.v.) was usually considered the most important and noble of all genres, since its heroes were rulers and military leaders and were meant to represent a nation's best values. In Italy, Ariosto, Trissino, and Tasso attempted major national epics. Their efforts were paralleled by those of Camoës in Portugal, Ronsard in Fr., and Spenser and Milton in Eng. But whether such modern poetic narratives as *Orlando furioso* and *The Faerie Queene* could actually be considered epics was the cause of argument. Ariosto's *Orlando furioso* and Tasso's *Gerusalemme liberata* are popular romances, unlike the more classically oriented *L'Italia liberata dai Goti* of Trissino. Minturno attacks romances for lacking Cl. unity and for appealing to lower tastes, while Cinthio argues for the right of a new age to develop its own forms and to depart from the universal Ren. poetic principle of imitation (q.v.) of the ancients.

Tragedy (q.v.) ranks highest among dramatic genres both because its heroes are rulers and because Aristotle himself ranked tragedy highest in the *Poetics*. Scaliger notes that tragic plots are based on the activities of kings—the affairs of state, fortress, and camp. Cinthio adds that we call the actions of tragedy illustrious not because they are virtuous but because the characters who enact them are of the highest rank. Tragedy calls for elevated style and, in Italy, for magnificent scenery in presentation as well.

Comedy (q.v.) is complementary to tragedy. It treats middle- and lower-class characters, and it concentrates on situations that are amusing or ridiculous rather than pitiable and fearful. In *L'arte poetica* (1563), Minturno suggests that while noble ladies appear in public, middle-class women do not do so until after marriage, and the poet will violate comic decorum if he counters this practice. Castelvetro says that while members of the strong-willed aristocracy constitute a law unto themselves, the middle class will run to magistrates with their difficulties and live under the law. Consequently, the comic plot must not involve vendettas or other inappropriate behavior but instead treat the commonplaces of bourgeois life in which characters speak an everyday lang. Farce (q.v.) concentrates on lower-class characters and situations; here the chief responsibility of the poet is keeping decorum (q.v.), since the action is broad and the speech colloquial.

Most Fr. and Eng. critics followed this threefold generic division, giving almost exactly the same definitions as the It. critics. Pierre de Laudun, for instance, in *L'art poëtique françois* (1597), contends that "The characters of tragedy are grave people of great rank and those of comedy are low and of small position.... The words of Tragedy are grave and those of Comedy are light.... The characters in Tragedy are sumptuously dressed and those of Comedy garbed in an ordinary way." Most Ren. dramatists, incl. Shakespeare, followed these principles or, as in the Prologue to *Henry V*, announce it conspicuously when they do not. In Spain, Lope de Vega explained in *El arte nuevo de hacer comedias* (*The New Art of Making Comedies*, 1609) that while he admires Aristotle's theories, along with those of his Ren. interpreters, he has to make a living, and pleasing the crowd requires violating most of the Cl. rules, incl. those relating to the three unities.

Shakespeare's prologue speaks to the problem of unity—specifically, unity of place—as much as to social decorum, while Ben Jonson in *Sejanus* apologizes for not keeping to a unity of time (one 24-hour period). The unities of place and time were added by Ren. critics to the single unity of action (or plot, q.v.), which Aristotle argues in the *Poetics* is the basis for drama. The three unities were introduced for the first time in England through Sidney's *Defence* (written ca. 1580; pub. 1595). They were never observed rigorously, however, by the Eng. popular dramatists. It was in France that they became critical dogma, and it was principally from France that they were reintroduced into Eng. criticism in the later 17th c.

The theory of genres was complicated by two developing dramatic and narrative forms in the Ren.—tragicomedy and romance (qq.v.). For conservative critics, tragicomedy was by name and definition a "mongrel" form because it mingled kings and clowns, as Sidney puts it. However, Giambattista Guarini, the author of *Il pastor fido* (1590), argued that since the great and the lowly exist side by side in actual life, it is perfectly natural and correct to have both in a single drama. The response came from Jason DeNores (*Apologia*, 1590) when he remarked that comedy instructs citizens how to act, but a mixed genre, since it cannot instruct this way, is without any useful end; moreover, it gives no certain direction to the playwright as to appropriate behavior or lang. Guarini later published an extended reply, *Compendio della poesia tragicomica* (1601), in which he hinted that he writes to please rather than to follow "rules" or to instruct; and he adds that some of his shepherds are noble and some are not, hence his use of both tragedy and comedy. The best playwrights agreed, as we see in Shakespeare's late plays, *Cymbeline, Pericles, The Winter's Tale*, and *The Tempest*, and in Fletcher's prologue to *The Faithful Shepherdess* (1610?): "a God is as lawful in this as in a tragedy, and mean people as in a comedy."

V. THE PRINCIPLE OF IMITATION. The various strands of Ren. *imitatio* began with Plato, who notes in *The Sophist* (219a–c) two kinds of art he calls icastic and fantastic. Icastic or "likeness-making art" occurs "whenever anyone produces the imitation by following the proportions of the original in length, breadth, and depth, and giving, besides, the appropriate colors to each part" (235d)—when the artist records what he sees without any imaginative changes. Icastic art thus copies the original precisely. Fantastic art, on the other hand, either creates that which does not exist—Sidney will suggest the Cyclops as an example—or else gives a disproportioned, inexact representation of the object being imitated—fantastic art thus "produces appearance," according to Plato, "but not likeness" (236c). While both kinds of art share the identical end, representation, their means are opposed: one teaches by exact copying, the other persuades by asking us to accept what seems to be for what is. Since Plato uses sculpture and painting as his examples, his distinction is a distinction in poetics.

Beginning in the 14th c. with Petrarch, another kind of imitation—stylistic imitation of the ancients, esp. Cicero and Virgil—became popular. This theory of imitation persisted throughout the Ren. and overlaps other, more philosophical theories. It was closely associated with Ren. education, since much of the grammar school curriculum involved translating, paraphrasing, and imitating Lat. authors. Questions associated with it incl. whether one should imitate a single author or the best features of many; whether one should use Cl. forms directly or seek vernacular equivalents of them; and how originality (q.v.) and imitation can co-exist. Two treatises that nicely illustrate Ren. understanding of imitation in this sense are the *Ciceronianus* of Erasmus (1528) and the second book of Roger Ascham's *Scholemaster.*

The rediscovery of Aristotle's *Poetics* introduced yet another kind of imitation. Whatever Aristotle may have understood by *mimesis* (see IMITATION; REPRESENTATION AND MIMESIS), most Ren. writers understood it to mean either (a) the direct representation in lang. and dramatic action of the real world, or (b) the representation of typical (or "probable") aspects of the real world. The argument that the *mimesis* should focus on the typical or probable rather than on the specific or topical justified departures in plots from strict historical fact (see CLASSICAL POETICS). A very prominent thrust of the theory was the justification for reshaping history so that it conformed to the requirements of moral instruction. When interpreted in this way the *Poetics* seemed entirely consistent with the traditional theory inherited from Horace that poetry mixes the morally useful with the aesthetically delightful.

Thus in *La poetica* (1536) Bernardino Daniello argues that the poet, unlike the historian, can mingle fiction with fact because he is held not to what is or was but rather to what ought to be. Francisco Robortelli in his commentary on the *Poetics* (1548) likewise argues that the poet can add invented material in imitating reality, citing as exemplars Xenophon's ideal portrait of Cyrus and Cicero's ideal portrait of the orator; moreover, he adds, poets can invent matters which transcend nature so long as they can be logically inferred from what we know in nature: there is even room in the epic, he admits, for the marvelous. Girolamo Fracastoro similarly argues that the poet, in depicting the simple and essential truth of things, should not simply reproduce it but clothe it in beauty—beauty which is formal, ethical, and aesthetic, keeping only to decorum, which is for him suggested by the idea the poet wishes to portray.

Torquato Tasso further complicates the question of imitation in his *Discorsi dell'arte poetica* (Discourses on the Heroic Poem, 1567–70; tr. I. Samuel and M. Cavalchini, 1973) when he attempts to seek some balance between the claims of Christian and allegorical truth and poetic license and adornment: the naked truth, he claims, should be enhanced by novelty and surprise that will increase the sense of wonder. To some critics the requirement that certain kinds of poetry present wonderful and marvelous events and arouse admiration (*admiratio*) as well as teach moral lessons seemed to be compatible with the *Poetics*, but to others it contravened the dictum that the poet should represent the real world (or "nature"). The latter position is taken in the *Della poetica la deca disputata* (1586) of Francesco Patrizi, popularly known as the *Deca ammirabile*. For Patrizi there are two forms of the marvelous: one is a quality of the poem itself, which springs from the divine inspiration or enthusiasm of the poet and suitably combines the credible and incredible, making the work admirable (*mirabile*); the other is the effect produced in the audience, the extrinsic end of poetry (*la maraviglia*).

While the theory of imitation was considerably more advanced in Italy than elsewhere in the 16th c., there was great interest in France, Spain, and England as well. Du Bellay's *Déffence* argues that Fr. poetry can only hope to attain perfection by imitating the classics, and while the true poet is born, only education in the classics will protect his talent from being useless. But Du Bellay does not distinguish one kind of imitation from another; he left that to Jacques Peletier du Mans, who says (not unlike Tasso) in his *L'Art poétique* (1555) that the poet's responsibility is to imitate old things by adding to them something new, something beautiful. Ronsard invokes the fundamental principle of *imitatio* both in his *Abrégé de l'art poëtique françois* (1565) and in the 1572 preface to his incomplete epic. While he urges the use of images that are inspiring (since he sees the end of poetry as moral edification), he rules out images which are fantastic, unnatural, or marvelous. But the sense of morality is strongest in the work of Jean Vauquelin de la Fresnaye, who prefers scriptural themes for poetry. Indeed, he notes in his *Art poétique* (1605) that if the Greeks had been Christian they too would have sung of the life and death of Christ.

VI. RHETORIC AND POETIC. References to ornament and to memory suggest that, for many of the major Ren. critics, Ren. p. also grew directly out of Ren. rhet. Vida's *De arte poetica*, for example, combines a Horatian discussion of the training of the poet and a defense of poetry (in Book I) with rhetorical treatises on invention and disposition (in Book II) and elocution (in Book III). Daniello's *La poetica* expands Horace around the same three rhetorical concerns; and even Minturno's *L'arte poetica* combines Horace and Aristotle's *Poetics* with the rhetorical writings of Cicero and Quintilian. In the 14th c., Salutati had urged in *De nobilitate legum et medicinae* the practice of disputations, or *controversiae*, as a practical means to sharpen the mind, inspire further learning, and engender practical results in the life of early humanist students; in the 15th c., Fracastoro, in the *Naugerius* (1555), argues that the poet can persuade his reader by imitating natural things. Such an art of persuasion was at first the chief purpose not so much of poetry as of rhet., yet poets too needed to persuade readers to the basic truths of their poetry whether it was deliberately verisimilitudinous or not. By the 15th c. in Italy and by the 16th c. in northern Europe, poetics frequently rested on the principles and practices of rhet. because that was the substance of education and, further, because both shared the common end of persuasion.

Extant syllabi and lectures from humanist schools of the 15th and 16th cs. illustrate the close alliance between rhet. and poetics. Humanist students were taught Lat. grammar and syntax followed by orations, imitating historical and imagined speeches; they also practiced fables, biographies, epistles, and descriptions. Regardless of form, such exercises promoted deliberative, judicial, and demonstrative speeches that would discuss an issue, argue a point, or award praise or blame; after this, students would move on to disputations and debates.

Indeed, the rhetorical *techne* taught in the humanist schools provided esp. imaginative ways to think, write, and speak, such as *prosopopoeia* (q.v.), the creation (or feigning, q.v.) of a fictive persona; and *topographia*, the description (or creation) of places. The rhetoric studied in humanist schools also taught the value and practice of *ethos* (q.v.), or the feigned persona of the speaker, and *pathos* (q.v.), the ways in which a speaker (or poet) puts his audience into a particular frame of mind. Such classroom lessons were easily transferred into poetic technique, esp. since Aristotle's chief rhetorical end, probability, was transformed into verisimilitude (q.v.) by Cicero (*De inventione* 1.21.29).

VII. CONCLUSION. One of the important Cl. texts for Ren. p. is Epistle XLV of the Roman philosopher Seneca. According to Seneca, art is best understood as an imitation determined by the four causes of Aristotle's *Prior Analytics*. As Seneca applies them, the first cause is actual matter (such as the bronze of a bronze statue); the second cause is the agent (the artist or workman); the third is the form (the sense of the form and function of a statue); and the fourth is purpose (money, reputation, religious devotion). What became crucial for Ren. p., however, is Seneca's own "fifth cause"— the model or original against which the new creation is made and to which it therefore always, implicitly or explicitly, refers. The theory of models was consonant with the Ren. interest in turning away from the Middle Ages to Gr. and Roman texts for an understanding of form, genres, and *techne*, reinforcing both the understanding and practice of poetry. Cl. models lie behind not only the epics of Ariosto, Tasso, Spenser, and Milton, but the *Praise of Folly* of Erasmus, such plays as Shake-

speare's *Othello* and Ben Jonson's *Volpone*, and such epic fiction as Sidney's *Arcadia* and Cervantes' *Don Quijote*.

The It. Ren. critics and their Sp., Fr., and Eng. successors were the founders of modern European crit. and modern European lit. as well. The Dutch and Ger. critics of the Ren. added little that was new. The theories that were produced by Ren. critics were learned, sophisticated, and detailed, but they were often divorced from the realities of the literary marketplace. This was esp. true of theories of drama. Lope de Vega confessed that, of his 483 comedies, "all except six of them sin grievously against art." In other words, the only way de Vega or anyone else prior to the collapse of the neoclassical spirit could talk about art was in the terms formulated and promulgated by Ren. p., and these terms were for the most part irrelevant to the kind of drama that Lope was writing. See also FICTION; IMAGINATION; IMITATION; INVENTION; RHETORIC AND POETRY; RULES.

BIBLIOGRAPHIES: *For Fr. and Eng.*, see Patterson and Smith below. For It.: R. C. Williams, "It. Crit. Treatises of the 16th C.," *MLN* 35 (1920); W. Bullock, "It. 16th-C. Crit.," *MLN* 41 (1926); Weinberg. *For Sp.*, see Menéndez y Pelayo, *Historia de las ideas estéticas en España*, 9 v. (1883–92), v. 2. *For Eng.*: G. Saintsbury, *Hist. of Crit. and Literary Taste in Europe* (1900–4), v. 2—convenient though inadequate; V. Hall, *Lit. Crit.: Plato to Dryden* (1970).

COLLECTIONS: *English*: Smith—collects the major Ren. prosodists and critics; J. E. Spingarn, *Crit. Essays of the 17th C.*, 3 v. (1907); E. W. Tayler, *Lit. Crit. of 17th-C. England* (1967). *French*: Patterson— a history, but contains copious excerpts from Ren. essays; B. Weinberg, *Crit. Prefaces of the Fr. Ren.* (1950), *Trattati di poetica e retorica del cinquecento*, 4 v. (1970–74); B. Fabian, *Poetiken de Cinquecento*, 25 v. (1967–69); A. Gilbert, *Lit. Crit.* (1940)—a generous selection in tr. *Italian*: the opinions and comments of most of the It. critics are collected in what amounts to a commonplace book of crit. by U. Nisieli (pseud. for B. Fioretti), *Proginnasmi poetici*, 2 v. (Florence, 1639); and see Weinberg (above). *Spanish*: no satisfactory collection.

SECONDARY WORKS: *Books*: K. Borinski, *Die Poetik der Ren.* (1886); F. E. Schelling, *Poetic and Verse Crit. of the Reign of Elizabeth* (1891); W. H. Woodward, *Vittorino da Feltre and Other Humanist Educators* (1897); K. Vossler, *Poetische Theorien in der ital. Frühren.* (1900); F. Padelford, *Select Trs. from Scaliger's Poetics* (1905); I. Scott, *Controversies over Imitation of the Ren. (incl. tr. of Erasmus' "Ciceronianus")* (1910); H. Charlton, *Castelvetro's Theory of Poetry* (1913); *The New Art of Writing Plays, by Lope de Vega*, tr. W. T. Brewster (1914); C. Trabalza, *La critica letteraria nel rinsaciamento* (1915); D. L. Clark, *Rhet. and Poetic in the Ren.* (1922); C. S. Baldwin, *Ren. Literary Theory and Practice* (1939); M. T. Herrick, *The Poetics of Aristotle in England* (1930), *The Fusion of Horatian and Aristotelian Lit. Crit., 1531–1555* (1946), *Comic Theory in the 16th*

C. (1950), *Tragicomedy* (1955); R. J. Clemens, *Crit. Theory and Practice of the Pléiade* (1942); T. W. Baldwin, *William Shakspere's Small Latine & Lesse Greeke*, 2 v. (1944); H. Wilson and C. Forbes, *Gabriel Harvey's Ciceronianus* (1945); V. Hall, Jr., *Ren. Lit. Crit.* (1945), "Scaliger's Defense of Poetry," *PMLA* 63 (1948); W. Lily, *A Shorte Intro. of Grammar and Brevissima Institutio*, 3d ed. (1567), ed. V. J. Flynn (1945); J. W. H. Atkins, *Eng. Lit. Crit.: The Renascence* (1947); J. Burckhardt, *The Civilization of the Ren. in Italy* (1950); J. E. Spingarn, *A Hist. of Lit. Crit. in the Ren.*, 2d ed. (1954); R. R. Bolgar, *The Cl. Heritage and Its Beneficiaries* (1954); W. S. Howell, *Logic and Rhet. in England, 1500–1700* (1956); Weinberg; P. O. Kristeller, *Ren. Thought, I, II* (1961, 1965), with selections in *Ren. Thought and the Arts*, 2d ed. (1990); B. Hathaway, *The Age of Crit.: The Late Ren. in Italy* (1962); O. B. Hardison, Jr., *The Enduring Monument* (1962), *Prosody and Purpose in the Eng. Ren.* (1989); A. Garcia Barrio, *La Formacion de la teoría moderna: La topica Horatiana en Europa* (1963); D. Bush, *Mythology and the Ren. Trad. in Eng. Poetry*, rev. ed. (1963); M. Vitale, *La Questione de la langua* (1967); J.-C. Chevalier, *Histoire de la syntaxe: Naissance de la notion de complément dans la grammaire française (1530–1750)* (1968); J. E. Seigel, *Rhet. and Philosophy in Ren. Humanism* (1968); R. Weiss, *The Ren. Discovery of Cl. Antiquity* (1969); A. Patterson, *Hermogenes and the Ren.* (1970); F. G. Robinson, *The Shape of Things Known: Sidney's* Apology *in Its Philosophical Trad.* (1972); D. Attridge, *Well-Weighed Syllables* (1974); W. J. Kennedy, *Rhet. Norms in Ren. Lit.* (1978); A. Weiner, *Sir Philip Sidney and the Poetics of Protestantism* (1978); R. L. Montgomery, *The Reader's Eye: Studies in Didactic Literary Theory from Dante to Tasso* (1979); C. Greenfield, *Humanist and Scholastic Poetics, 1250–1500* (1981); L. Holtz, *Donat et la trad. de l'enseignement grammatical* (1981); I. Silver, *Ronsard and the Hellenic Ren.*, 2 v. (1981); T. Greene, *The Light in Troy* (1982); M. Donker and G. M. Muldrow, *Dict. of Literary-Rhetorical Conventions of the Eng. Ren.* (1982); W. Trimpi, *Muses of One Mind* (1983); *Jacopo Mazzoni's* On the Defense of the Comedy of Dante, tr. R. L. Montgomery (1983); M. W. Ferguson, *Trials of Desire: Ren. Defenses of Poetry* (1983); J. H. Meter, *The Literary Theories of Daniel Heinsius* (1984); *Englische Literaturtheorie von Sidney bis Johnson*, ed. B. Nugel (1984); V. Kahn, *Rhet., Prudence, and Skepticism in the Ren.* (1985); K. Eden, *Poetic and Legal Fiction in the Aristotelian Trad.* (1986); A. F. Kinney, *Humanist Poetics: Thought, Rhet., and Fiction in 16th-C. England* (1986), *Continental Humanist Poetics* (1989); *Ren. Genres*, ed. B. K. Lewalski (1986); D. K. Shuger, *Sacred Rhet.* (1988); S. K. Heninger, Jr., *Sidney and Spenser: The Poet as Maker* (1989); B. Vickers, *Cl. Rhet. in Eng. Poetry*, 2d ed. (1989).

Articles: See esp. M. W. Bundy, "'Invention' and 'Imagination' in the Ren.," *JEGP* 29 (1930); H. S. Wilson, "Some Meanings of 'Nature' in Ren. Lit. Theory," *JHI* 2 (1941); G. Giovannini, "Historical Realism and the Tragic Emotions in Ren. Crit.," *PQ* 32 (1953); B. Sozzi, "La Poetica del Tasso," *Studi Tassiani* 5 (1955); S. L. Bethell, "The Nature of Metaphysical Wit," *Discussions of John Donne*, ed. F. Kermode (1962); O. B. Hardison, Jr., "The Two Voices of Sidney's *Apology for Poetry*," *ELR* 2 (1972); E. Kushner, "The Concept of Invention and Its Role in Ren. Lit. Theory," *Neohelicon* 8 (1980); N. Struever, "Lorenzo Valla: Humanist Rhet. and the Critique of the Cl. Langs. of Morality," *Ren. Eloquence*, ed. J. J. Murphy (1983);

V.H.; A.F.K.; O.B.H.

RENAISSANCE POETRY. "The Ren." as a historical term is so elastic and so geared to geographical and temporal amplitudes that we will say merely that it occurred in Europe sometime between the completion of Dante's *Divina commedia* in Italy (1307–21) and Milton's *Paradise Lost* in England (1667). In Italy the Ren. is confined to the 1400s, whence it spread to France and almost simultaneously to Spain and Portugal and later to England and Northern Europe. It is sometimes linked to the invention of printing and in art history to the rejection of Byzantine formalism in favor of natural representation, and it has come to be associated with modern ideas such as the supremacy of the individual and the emergence of the modern state, as well as the recovery of Cl. antiquity in its exuberant proclamation of a self rejoicing in its physicality and freed from the shackles of religious bondage. The fact that it began in Italy but that our Eng. name for it derives from the Fr. points to some of the difficulty of definition.

Ren. p. began with the vernacular poetry of Petrarch (1304–74), whose *Canzoniere* and *Trionfi* provided the impetus, the topoi, and the vocabulary of Western lit. for the following two centuries. The question of when the Ren. began and ended can be debated endlessly, but if we start with the poems of the *Canzoniere*, we can make a clear demarcation between Petrarch and the work of Dante in *La vita nuova*, and the *Commedia*, whose achievement Petrarch must have considered complete in its exploitation of the vernacular and the Aristotelian-Thomistic synthesis now considered characteristic of the high Middle Ages. Petrarch turned to the embryo sonnet sequence (q.v.) of *La vita nuova* and exploited the formal devices of lyric form without Dante's prose commentary and without the Aristotelian-Thomistic frame of the *Commedia*. The love ethic is like Dante's, as the progress of the *Trionfi* proclaims, but the elaboration of the symptoms of the love wound and its consequences over 366 poems provided an eloquence that captured the imaginations and imitative faculties of almost every poet for the next 200 years. More than 200 editions of the *Canzoniere*, often with commentaries, were printed during the 15th and 16th cs. Commentaries like that of Pietro Bembo (1470–1547) emphasized the linguistic purity of Petrarch, and the often reprinted commentary of Alessandro Vellutello mapped the occasion and place of many of the poems, turning the *Canzoniere* into the autobiographical confession so dear to the hearts of the 19th and 20th cs. Petrarchan influence (see PETRARCHISM) was the signal that other vernacular lits. had reached what we now call the Ren.; the recognition of Petrarch's poetry characterized a national lit.'s awareness of itself as a contender for the honors paid to the classics.

The endless elaboration of the basic Petrarchan formula of ardent poet-lover pursuing an aloof blonde lady to no avail, either through her good sense or her death, ricocheted across Europe, the Petrarchan sonnet sequences producing the densest mass of love poetry (q.v.) ever produced in the West. No poet of worth avoided the sonnet (q.v.), and most attempted the sonnet sequence, although few had the poetic stamina to carry the plan through to the death of the lady and after, as did Dante and Petrarch. The impulse was so strong that even women established themselves in the mode, such as Vittoria Colonna (1492– 1547) and Gaspara Stampa (ca. 1523–54) in Italy and Louise Labé (?1520–65) in France. In England alone more than 60 sonnet sequences were written between 1580 and 1630, incl. those of Sir Philip Sidney (1554–86), Samuel Daniel (ca. 1562–1619), Michael Drayton (1563–1631), Edmund Spenser (1552–99), Fulke Greville, (1554–1628) and William Shakespeare (1564–1616).

But to concentrate on Petrarch's influence on sonnet lit. alone is to miss the richness of the Petrarchan mode. His fictional amatory involvement with Laura is also the metaphoric pretext for political dreams that included his friends and a desire that the papacy return from its Babylonian captivity in Avignon to its rightful place in Rome. More than ten percent of the poems in the *Canzoniere* are devoted to friends or to the plight of Rome and the corruption of the Papacy, a fact which led Vellutello to sequester those poems in a separate section of his edition. Rome and his friends are very much a part of the matrix and outreach of Petrarch's poems, urging us to see Laura not only as a woman but as a laurel to be won, just as Apollo won his laurel through his pursuit of Daphne, as told by Ovid in the first book of the *Metamorphoses*. The myth literally came true on April 8, 1341, when Petrarch was crowned poet laureate (q.v.) on the very Capitoline hill of Rome celebrated in the Ovidian myth. His coronation proclaimed him through his unfinished Lat. epic, *Africa*, and his widely disseminated polemical and philosophical prose works a political poet as well as a lover, and it is this side of the Petrarchan heritage that influenced even the devel. of the epic (q.v.) in the Ren.

The Middle Ages seemed content to recount endlessly the exploits of three of the Seven Worthies, Charlemagne, Arthur, and Alexander, in works in both Lat. and the vernacular tongues, the most famous now being the OF *Chanson de Roland*, but the heroics of Roland changed radically when, having crossed the Alps, Roland became Orlando. In the late 15th and early 16th c., Orlando was transformed into a Petrarchan lover as well as an epic hero. The transformation was helped along by Aeneas' dalliance with Dido in Virgil's *Aeneid*, with all that liaison's threat to Roman security. City after city in Italy took up the threat of this transformed hero to dynastic security. In Florence Luigi Pulci (1432–87) wrote his rollicking *Morgante maggiore* (1483), in which a roistering giant named Morgante becomes the squire of Orlando after his conversion to Christianity. A few years later a slightly different aspect of the Orlando story was taken up in Ferrara by Matteo Maria Boiardo (1441–94) in *Orlando innamorato* (1495), a work left unfinished at his death. Lodovico Ariosto (1474–1533) took up the unfinished work of Boiardo in his *Orlando furioso* (1532), in which Orlando's love for the fair Angelica finally drives him to madness until his wits are restored to him, literally from an apothecary jar where they are stored in the sphere of the moon. Ariosto's comic genius made his *Orlando* the model of It. epic-romance, and the infinite variety of his invention, linking the love antics of Orlando and dozens of other characters, spliced with the serious claims of the antecedents of the Este dynasty of Ferrara, proclaimed a new and comic version of Virgil's *Aeneid* in which serious political questions were triumphantly celebrated through the mad exploits of a brawny Petrarchan lover. The fact that this epic-romance lover does not resemble the plaintive, grieving lover of the *Canzoniere* is less the fault of Ariosto and his followers than of our deficient sense of the breadth of Petrarchism because Ariosto ransacks the Petrarchan vocabulary and topoi to fill out the story told by Virgil in the fourth book of the *Aeneid*.

The pattern of love-besot heroes and serious political consequences is continued in the *Gerusalemme liberata* (1581) of Torquato Tasso (1544–95), who turned from the exploits of Charlemagne to those of another of the Seven Worthies, Godfrey of Bouillon, in the first Crusade. Here, amidst the serious battles to win back Jerusalem from the Saracens, is the love story of Rinaldo and Armida, a beautiful enemy sorceress, through whose marriage at the end of the poem Tasso intended to give the Este another dynastic genealogy. The dynastic concern of these Ren. epics had enormous influence outside Italy, as evinced by *The Faerie Queene* of Edmund Spenser (1590–96), who made a dynastic genealogy for his sovereign Elizabeth I through the marriage of his heroine Britomart to Arthegall. Even Virgil's *Aeneid* had to partake of the romance impulse when Mapheus Vegius (1407–58) added a 13th book to the poem celebrating Aeneas's marriage to Lavinia as well as his death and stellification, a comic resolution that was printed in most 16th-c.

editions. The Petrarchan love ethic in its concern for political significance extends even to the *Os Lusíadas* (1572) of Luís Vaz do Camões (1524?–80), who redid the Petrarchan love search as Vasco da Gama's discovery of the unknown and fabulous Indies and, like Donne addressing his mistress in Elegy 19, "O my America! my new-found land," rewarded his hero for that victorious voyage with the sensuous celebration of Tethys and her nymphs, in which the dynastic marriage becomes nationalized to reward not merely the hero but the multitude of heroes that characterize Portugal.

Nonetheless, the fate of the epic in the 16th c. was generally incompletion of the epic plan. Spenser finished only six books of his projected 24. Ariosto left the *Cinque canti*, which may or may not have been intended to fit into the 46 cantos of the *Orlando furioso*. Tasso rewrote the *Gerusalemme liberata* as *Gerusalemme conquistata* (1593), in which he excised many of the romantic episodes which today we consider the glory of the poem (Tasso thought his revision was the better poem). Pierre Ronsard (1524–85) struggled endlessly to finish his epic *Franciade*, recounting the struggles of Francus, son of Hector, who bears the same relation to France that Aeneas bears to Rome, but the poem attained to only four books, incl. the love interest of Clymene, Ronsard's revisionary Dido figure. In all these epics the amplification of the love affairs is integrated into the political schemes of dynastic success, and their incompletion echoes Petrarch's incomplete epic, *Africa*. The form in which these epic loves appears may be Virgilian, but the fact that love is a central issue in these Ren. epics is Petrarchan, bolstered by his younger contemporary, Giovanni Boccaccio (1313–75), whose *Teseida* (1340–42) and *Filostrato* (1339–40) developed similar themes in the *ottava rima* stanza that was to become standard in subsequent It. narrative poems in the Ren. In spite of its putative source in the 8-line *strambotto* (q.v.), the ottava rima (q.v.) looks and behaves suspiciously like the octave of a sonnet.

It would be wrong to pretend that Petrarch is responsible for all the forms of poetry that emerged in the Ren., for very often he is only part of an impulse to recapture the classics in the vernacular that would become increasingly apparent in the centuries that followed. Nowhere is this more apparent than in the Ren. outbreak of Ovidian love poems, the erotic epyllion (q.v.), depicting in luxurious detail a seduction, or rape, or failure of some love encounter that metamorphosed the participants, or at least one of them, into something that he or she was not before the encounter. Ovid had been firmly recaptured in the Carolingian Ren. of the 12th c., and Petrarch had helped his friend, the Benedictine Pierre Bersuire (Petrus Berchorius, 1290–1362) with iconographical details for his lengthy and influential commentary on the *Metamorphoses*. Petrarch's *Canzoniere* in all its exfoliations is based on the

Ovidian myth of Apollo's pursuit of Daphne, hence Laura, hence laureation. The form of the epyllion has been traced back to Catullus's poem about the marriage of Peleus and Thetis (64). The genre was unusually popular in England, where Marlowe's *Hero and Leander* (1598) and Shakespeare's *Venus and Adonis* (1593) established the form either in couplets (Marlowe) or in a 6-line *ababcc* stanza (Shakespeare).

Pastoral (q.v.) poetry took a new turn in the Ren., either imitating the harsh, satiric verse of Mantuan or the soft, mellifluous verse of Sannazaro. Although pastoral was early established as a mode in the Hebraic and Cl. trads., it is the most difficult of modes to decipher because its relation to the society that produces it changes constantly. The vehicle of pastoral metaphor is transparently clear—shepherds caring for sheep, lamenting unavailing loves or dead shepherds—but the tenor is always shrouded in the more complicated personal and political actions of the societies that the poet wants to mirror and clarify. The mode brings together "The Lord is my shepherd" of Psalm 23 and Jesus's "I am the good shepherd" with the formal endeavors of the Sicilian Triad (Theocritus, Moschus, and Bion), imitated and brought into the Lat. trad. by Virgil in his *Eclogues*.

Pastoral poetry in the Cl. trad. calls out for the peg of allegory (q.v.), some name, e.g. Edward King in Milton's *Lycidas* or Keats in Shelley's *Adonais*, to accommodate that uneasy delight we take in that mode which Dr. Johnson described as "easy, vulgar, and therefore disgusting." Johnson objected to Milton's imposition of the pastoral mode on the sacred truths of Christianity, and his irritation with Milton poses a major problem of reader response to the mode, thereby ignoring the easy accommodation of Christian pastoral to Cl. mode that led Paschasius Radbertus first to write a Christian lament for his dead bishop in the pastoral mode (9th c.). Attempts to allegorize the figures and actions of Virgil's *Eclogues* have met with equal uneasiness, not because Caesar and the politics of Republican Rome were not intended as part of the meaning by Virgil but because those meanings now seem to get in the way of the verbal excellence, freed from the constraints of historical significance.

Dante, Petrarch, and Boccaccio all wrote formal Lat. pastoral eclogues (q.v.) in imitation of Virgil, and what historical ghosts lurk under the superb Latinity of their verses broach the same problems as Milton's and Virgil's, but in the 15th c. some help came through the division of the pastoral mode into two branches: the "rough" and the "smooth." The rough branch was created by the eclogues of Baptista Spagnuoli Mantuanus (Mantuan, 1448–1516), whose rough diction was used to satirize ecclesiastical or political abuses. The smooth was used for amatory and consolatory eclogues and derived mainly from the *Arcadia* of Jacopo Sannazaro (?1458–1530). The pastoral is to be found everywhere in Ren. p., from Marlowe's simple lyric "Come live with me and be my love" to the more complicated verse structures of Spenser's *Shepheardes Calender* (1579) or the poetic interludes of Sidney's *Arcadia* (1590–93). The pastoral also figured prominently in the re-emergence of drama, beginning with Poliziano's *Favola di Orfeo* (1472). The two most famous Ren. pastoral dramas are Tasso's *Aminta* (1573) and Guarini's *Il pastor fido* (1583), followed by the spate of *bergeries* in France, and culminating in Francis Beaumont's *The Faithful Shepherdess* (1608–09) and Ben Jonson's unfinished *The Sad Shepherd.* Sannazaro introduced the rational innovation of the piscatory eclogue and was imitated in this fishy innovation by Phineas Fletcher, somewhat pre-empted by Milton's "pilot of the Galilean lake."

The proliferation of lyric forms in Ren. p. recaptured many Cl. forms and imitations of authors not pursued during the Middle Ages, e.g. Horace, Catullus, Juvenal, Marital, and the *Greek Anthology.* In Florence alone there were Lorenzo de Medici (1449–92), Angelo Poliziano (1454–94), Pietro Bembo (1470–1547), and Giovanni della Casa (1503–56). In Spain this new Ren. awareness is signaled by the publication of the posthumous works of Juan Boscan (ca. 1490–1542) and Garcilaso de la Vega (1503–36) in *Las obras de Boscan y alqunas de Garcilaso de la Vega* (1543), which created a whole new school of poetry led by Fernando de Herrera (1534–97), and in England by Richard Tottel's *Songs and Sonnets* (1557), a collection that introduced the works of Henry Howard, Earl of Surrey (?1517–47) and Sir Thomas Wyatt (ca. 1503–42) among others. In France there is no sudden posthumous recognition of the new impulses. The work of *les grands rhétoriqueurs* (q.v.) is punctuated by the work of Clement Marot (ca. 1496–1544) and the *Délie* (1544) of Maurice Scève (ca. 1500–60), but the concerted announcement of a deliberate change comes with the work of the Pléiade (q.v.) and its critical manifesto, *La Deffense et illustration de la langue française* (1549) by Joachim Du Bellay (1523–60), second only to Pierre Ronsard (1524–85) in that illustrious poetic group. What the French accomplished through the loose association of the Pléiade is equalled in England by the influence of John Donne (1571–1633) and Ben Jonson (1572–1637) on the Eng. poets of the 17th c., who may be divided into the metaphysical poets (q.v.; followers of Donne) and Cavalier poets (q.v.; neoclassical followers of Jonson).

Emphasis on the new modes and genres in the vernaculars should not make us unmindful that many of the poets mentioned continued to write verse in Lat. (see LATIN POETRY, *Renaissance and Post-Renaissance*) and that neither in Lat. nor in the vernacular did they abandon their essentially Christian outlook on the world. The prevalence of serious religious poetry in the period has been either undervalued or isolated as a special kind of poetry, with as great a gap between "sacred" and "secular" poetry as between Neo-Lat. and vernacular. Most critical attention has been focused on "devotional" poetry—that is, personal, private, and lyric—and numerous studies of St. John of the Cross (1542–91) in Sp. and, in Eng., of Donne, George Herbert (1593–1633), Richard Crashaw (1612–49), Henry Vaughan (1622–95), and Thomas Traherne (1636–74) have explored the artistry of their religious zeal, but seldom has the relationship between the religious and the secular been examined. The motivation of the religious poet has been subjected to the most severe scrutiny, which might equally well have been expended on the reality of the numberless sonnet mistresses who supposedly enlivened the dreary orthodoxy of their poets' daily lives.

We have also established too great a distance poetically between the Protestants and the Roman Catholics, in ways that obscure the basic unity of Christian faith which overrides theological disagreement. It is too easy to set up the undeniable landmarks of conflict such as the Reformation and Counter-Reformation as points of literary discrimination, but to set up either of these historic actions as a guide to literary discriminations leads to a too easy dismissal of the Middle Ages as the necessary matrix of whatever we mean by the Ren. Although the rejection of Lat. liturgy and devotions opened up a great need for vernacular liturgies and hymns (q.v.) and translations of the Bible, one cannot therefore argue that the Reformation is responsible for a new poetics. Petrarch translated the Penitential Psalms into rhythmic Lat. prose not as a rebuff to Jerome's Vulgate but as a spur to the improvement of Latinity. Aretino translated them with a narrative frame of David's remorse over the death of Uriah, a form that Sir Thomas Wyatt adopted into Eng. and for which he was most remembered in 16th-c. England; and neither had the Reformation or politics as an incentive. Sir Philip and Lady Mary Sidney's metrical translations of the entire psalms showed more interest in making the Psalms available in Eng. than in Protestant polemics, although the Reformation made the translation a more pressing issue. Louis Martz showed many years ago that Roman Catholic manuals of meditation provided the logical structure for Protestant poets in 17th-c. England.

The impulse to sing the praises of one's faith took many forms in the Ren., but few critical studies have examined the longer narrative or discursive encounters with religious subjects, such as Sannazaro's *De partu virginis* (1526) or Tasso's *Le sette giornate* (1594) or Du Bartas' *Le premier sepmaine* (1578) or Maurice Scève's *Microcosme* (1562). All of these poems are attempts to make vivid and intellectually apprehensible the truths of a Christian universe in conflict. To ignore them as part of Ren. p. is like the unthinkable critical

RENGA

act of omitting religious painting from a history of art in the Ren.

See also: EPIC; IMAGINATION; IMITATION; INVENTION; LYRIC SEQUENCE; PETRARCHISM; PASTORAL; PLEIADE; RENAISSANCE POETICS; RHETORIC AND POETRY; ROMANCE; SONNET; SONNET SEQUENCE.

Schipper; W. W. Greg, *Pastoral Poetry and Pastoral Drama* (1906); J. M. Berdan, *Early Tudor Poetry* (1920); *The Love Poems of Joannes Secundus*, ed. and tr. F. A. Wright (1930), with valuable essay on Neo-Lat. poetry; A. Scolari, *Ludovico Aristo* (1930); A. Meozzi, *Il Petrarchism europeo: secolo XVI* (1934); Patterson; C. S. Lewis, *The Allegory of Love* (1936), *Eng. Lit. in the 16th C. Excluding Drama* (1954); C. Privitera, *La poesia e l'arte di Torquato Tasso* (1936); L. C. John, *The Elizabethan Sonnet Sequences* (1938); *CBEL*, v. 1; L. Bradner, *Musae Anglicanae: A Hist. of Anglo-Lat. Poetry 1500–1925* (1940); V. L. Rubel, *Poetic Diction in the Eng. Ren.* (1941)—wider scope than title indicates; P. Van Tieghem, *La Lit. lat. de la Ren.* (1944); E. Donadoni, *Torquato Tasso*, 3d ed. (1946); M. Prior, *The Lang. of Tragedy* (1947); R. Tuve, *Elizabethan and Metaphysical Imagery* (1947); *Historia general de las literaturas hispanicas*, ed. G. Diaz-Plaja, 6 v. (1949–68); D. Alonso, *Poesia española* (1950); C. M. Ing, *Elizabethan Lyrics* (1951); H. Smith, *Elizabethan Poetry* (1952); B. Weinberg, *Fr. Poetry of the Ren.* (1954); L. L. Martz, *The Poetry of Meditation* (1954); E. M. W. Tillyard, *The Eng. Epic and its Background* (1954); W. Mönch, *Das Sonett: Gestalt und Gesch.* (1955); *CBFL*, v. 2; G. deF. Lord, *Homeric Ren.: The Odyssey of George Chapman* (1956); H. Weber, *La Création poétique au XVIe siècle*, 2 v. (1956); L. B. Campbell, *Divine Poetry and Drama in 16th-C. England* (1959); A. Kernan, *The Cankered Muse: Satire of the Eng. Ren.* (1959); G. Dickinson, *Du Bellay in Rome* (1960); J. Hollander, *The Untuning of the Sky: Ideas of Music in Eng. Poetry, 1500–1700* (1961); R. Montgomery, *Symmetry and Sense: The Poetry of Sir Philip Sidney* (1961); I. Silver, *Ronsard and the Hellenic Ren. in France*, 2 v. (1961, 1987); J. Thompson, *The Founding of Eng. Metre* (1961); O. B. Hardison, Jr. *The Enduring Monument* (1962), *Prosody and Purpose in the Eng. Ren.* (1989); *Ren. and Baroque Poetry of Spain*, ed. E. Rivers (1964); G. Castor, *Pléiade Poetics: A Study in 16th-C. Thought and Terminology* (1964); P. Thompson, *Sir Thomas Wyatt and his Background* (1964); J. W. Lever, *The Elizabethan Love Sonnet*, 2d ed. (1965); W. L. Grant, *Neo-Lat. Lit. and the Pastoral* (1965); G. Mazzacurati, *Misure del classicismo rinascimentale* (1967); L. Forster, *The Icy Fire: Studies in European Petrarchism* (1969); *New CBEL*, v. 1; R. O. Jones, *Golden Age Prose and Poetry* (1971); P. V. Marinelli, *Pastoral* (1971); S. Fish, *Surprized by Sin* (1971); B. W. Wardropper, *Sp. Poetry of the Golden Age* (1971); D. Attridge, *Well-Weighed Syllables* (1974); I. D. McFarlane, *Ren. France, 1470–1589*, v. 2 of *A Lit. Hist. of France*, ed. P. E. Charvet (1974); Wilkins; J. Nohrnberg, *The Analogy of the Faerie Queene* (1976); D. Javitch, *Poetry and Courtliness in Ren. England* (1978); A. L. Prescott, *Fr. Poets and the Eng. Ren.* (1978); B. K. Lewalski, *Protestant Poetics and the 17th-C. Religious Lyric* (1979), ed., *Ren. Genres* (1986); S. Greenblatt, *Ren. Self-Fashioning* (1980); C. Freer, *The Poetics of Jacobean Drama* (1981); G. Hibbard, *The Making of Shakespeare's Dramatic Poetry* (1981); R. Peterson, *Imitation and Praise in the Poetry of Ben Jonson* (1981); T. Greene, *The Light in Troy* (1982); M. Donker and G. M. Muldrow, *Dict. of Literary-Rhetorical Conventions of the Eng. Ren.* (1982); J. Goldberg, *James I and the Politics of Lit.: Jonson, Shakespeare, Donne, and their Contemporaries* (1983); J. Guillory, *Poetic Authority: Spenser, Milton and Lit. Hist.* (1983); M. Quilligan, *Milton's Spenser: The Poetics of Reading* (1983); D. Quint, *Origin and Originality in Ren. Lit.* (1983); L. Woodbridge, *Women and the Eng. Ren.: Lit. and the Nature of Womankind, 1540–1620* (1984); A. A. Parker, *The Philosophy of Love in Sp. Lit., 1480–1680* (1985); G. Waller and M. Moore, *Sir Philip Sidney and the Interp. of Ren. Culture* (1985); J. E. Howard, "The New Historicism in Ren. Studies," *ELR* 16 (1986); A. Kinney, *Essential Articles for the Study of Sir Philip Sidney* (1986); *Ren. Genres*, ed. B. K. Lewalski (1986); W. Maynard, *Elizabethan Lyric Poetry and its Music* (1986); W. Sessions, *Henry Howard Earl of Surrey* (1986); H. Dubrow, *Captive Victors: Shakespeare's Narrative Poems and Sonnets* (1987); A. Patterson, *Pastoral and Ideology: Virgil to Valery* (1987); G. T. Wright, *Shakespeare's Metrical Art* (1988); T. P. Roche, Jr., *Petrarch and the Eng. Sonnet Sequence* (1989); Hollier; A. R. Jones, *The Currency of Eros: Women's Love L. in Europe, 1540–1620* (1990); R. Greene, *Post-Petrarchism* (1991).

T.P.R.

RENGA. Japanese linked poetry. Although joined poems (*lien-chü*) were composed earlier in China, they did not have the codified nature of r., nor did they develop out of the practice of poetic sequences, as r. did. R. developed from integrated sequences of *waka* (q.v.) in Japanese royal collections and from shorter (esp. 100-poem) sequences modeled on the collections. R. also had ancestry in the capping of one part of a *waka* by one poet with a second part by another: e.g. two lines of 7 + 7 syllables added to three of 5, 7, and 5. In the 12th c., *waka* poets composed r., alternating 3- and 2-line stanzas in a nonserious (*mushin*) fashion. Play led to earnest (*ushin*) r. At first, impressive stanzas were sought. Later, the greatest r. master, Sōgi (1421–1502), emphasized the integrity of sequences along with variety in impressiveness of stanzas and variance in closeness and distance of connection.

A typical r. sequence comprised 100 stanzas composed by about three poets at a single sitting (*za*) of about three hours. A given stanza was therefore composed in less than three minutes. Given the complexities of the r. code, that meant (as the last practitioner of r. put it) that 20 years

- [1034] -

of practice were necessary before it could be discovered whether one had talent.

A *r.* stanza related semantically only to its predecessor and therefore also to its successor: each stanza was like a link in a chain. The sequences were of varying length, the standard being the *hyakuin* (100 stanzas), with its multiples, *senku* (1000) and *manku* (10,000). Shorter units incl. *yoyoshi* (44), *kasen* (36), *hankasen* (18), and *iisute* (a few stanzas—these last three being used mostly in *haikai*, discussed below).

To give the rapid composition of *r.* coherence, other features of its code were developed. Individual stanzas had as topic one of the seasons or were deemed miscellaneous, and numerous subtopics (e.g. love, Buddhism) were classified. Spring, autumn, and love topics should run at least three stanzas, whereas those two sufficed for summer and winter. Some words were governed by suspension: the word for "dream" could not be used more than once in seven stanzas or the word for "insect" more than once in 100 stanzas.

R. (and *haikai*) were written on the fronts and backs of sheets of paper. Each side but the last required a moon stanza, and every sheet a flower stanza. The front side of the first sheet constituted a stately beginning (*jo*) and the back of the last sheet a "fast close" (*kyū*). In between appeared an agitated or broken development (*ha*), a rhythm adapted from court music and bequeathed to *nō* as well as *haikai*. The opening stanza was factual, dealing with the scene and circumstances of the poets as they sat to compose; the remaining stanzas were fictional.

A given sequence would manipulate features of the code. For example, moon and flower stanzas might not appear in the appointed places or might be more numerous than called for. Some sequences were composed by many poets, some by but one and not at a single sitting.

Nonserious *r.* continued to be composed, and from that aberrant practice *haikai* ([no] *r.*) emerged, achieving greatness in the practice of Matsuo Bashō (1644–94), who preferred 36-stanza sequences. Decorum in *haikai* was lower than in *waka* and *r.* It admitted Sinified diction (Japanese versions of Chinese pronunciation of characters rather than the pure Japanese of *waka* and *r.*, somewhat like the Latinate "event" for Eng. "outcome"). *Haikai* introduced other elements, incl. distinct lowerings of tone, quotidian detail, and humor, making it a highly unstable art, difficult to practice well. The emphasis among *haikai* poets on the opening stanzas (*hokku*) led in time to mod. *haiku* (q.v.).

In brief, *r.* (and *haikai*) are distinguished by the authorship of more than one poet composing with great rapidity according to an extremely complex code. The sonnet sequence (q.v.) is sometimes compared to linked poetry, but the comparison is inexact: there is not multiple authorship at a single sitting or anything like the *r.* code, and usually there is plot. The uniqueness of linked poetry has led to debate whether it is narrative or (perhaps most likely) an unusual variety of lyric narrative. For further discussion of *r.*, esp. from the historical perspective, see JAPANESE POETRY.

ANTHOLOGIES AND TRANSLATIONS: *Rengashū* [A Coll. of *R.*], ed. T. Ijichi (1960); *R. Haikai Shū* [A Coll. of *R.* and *Haikai*], ed. K. Kaneko et al. (1974); E. Miner, *Japanese Linked Poetry* (1979); E. Miner and H. Odagiri, *The Monkey's Straw Raincoat and Other Poetry of the Bashō School* (1981).

HISTORY AND CRITICISM: Y. Yamada and S. Hoshika, *R. Hōshiki Kōyō* [Main Elements of *R.* Canons] (1936); Y. Yoshida, *R. Gaisetsu* [A General Explanation of *R.*] (1937); R. Kuriyama, *Haikaishi* [A Hist. of *Haikai*] (1963); J. Konishi, *Sōgi* (1971); S. Kidō, *Rengashi Ronkō* [A Crit. Hist. of *R.*], 2 v. (1973); K. Brazell and L. Cook, "The Art of *R.*," *JJS* 2 (1975)—partial tr. of Konishi; E. Miner (1979 above); Miner and Odagiri (above); Miner et al.
                                                                    E.M.

RENTREMENT. See RONDEAU.

REPETEND. See REPETITION.

REPETITION of sound, syllable, word, phrase, line, strophe, metrical pattern, or syntactic structure lies at the core of any definition of poetry. The notion that too much literal *r.* is tedious, dull, or just plain bad runs counter to the most widely perceived fundamentals of verbal art and its ubiquitous use by poets.

Lat. *versus* derives from the IE etymon meaning "time," "return"; likewise, the Gr. *strophe* (primarily "turning," "revolving") underlies the use of the word "r." in prosody. In the earliest vernacular treatise on It. verse, Dante's *De vulgari eloquentia*, Dante acutely perceives this relationship, as the It. equivalent *volta* ("return") clearly indicates: the recurrence of a formal pattern guides his description of metrical and strophic units: "Cantio est coniugatio stantiarum" (2.9.1). *R.* is a basic unifying device in all poetry. Various aspects of form all involve some kind of recurrence of equivalent elements, differing only in what linguistic elements are repeated. Recurrence of syntactic elements is called parallelism (q.v.); recurrence at the word level in Cl. rhet. is *ploce* and *polyptoton* (qq.v.); recurrence of stress and quantity is called meter (q.v.); and recurrence of vocalic and consonantal sounds is, variously, rhyme, alliteration, assonance, or consonance (qq.v.). The *r.* of signifiers, as above, may be supplemented by *r.* that applies to the signified alone, i.e. synonymy or pleonasm. In all cases, *r.* manifests the projection of the principle of equivalence (q.v.) from the axis of selection to that of combination, resulting in a heightened quotient of self-reference, which Jakobson considers the poetic function (q.v.).

Primitive religious chants (see CHANT) from all cultures show *r.* developing into cadence and song

REPETITION

(q.v.), with parallelism and r. still constituting, most frequently as anaphora (q.v.), an important part of the rhet. of liturgy. When a poem is intended for musical rendition, its structure—both formal and thematic—will tend to be repetitive. Therefore, thematic r. is a structural principle in most song lyrics, and a principle of thematic generation. The resulting paratactic structure can take the form of a list, as in much catalogue verse (q.v.) and in the medieval Occitan genres of the *plazer* and *enueg*, which enumerate pleasant or disagreeable things. One of the most common features of primitive song is the r. of the final line, which underscores its closural force:

> From the country of the Yerewas the
> moon rose;
> It came near; it was very cold;
> I sat down, oh, I sat down,
> I sat down, oh, I sat down.

The term *repetend* usually denotes the irregular recurrence of a word, phrase, or line in a poem (unlike a regular refrain [q.v.]), or a partial rather than complete r. Repetends may be found extensively in the ballad (q.v.) and in such modern poems as Meredith's "Love in the Valley," Poe's "Ulalume" and "The Raven," and Eliot's "Love Song of J. Alfred Prufrock"; an example:

> For a breeze of morning moves,
> And the planet of Love is on high,
> Beginning *to faint in the light* that *she*
> loves
> On a bed of daffodil sky,
> *To faint in the light* of the sun *she loves,*
> *To faint in his light,* and to die.
> (Tennyson, *Maud* 22.7)

The systematic r. of formal elements is a force for continuation (and when emended, for closure) of a poem. Patterns of recurrence set up expectations which are strengthened while they are being fulfilled with each successive instance. When a line, phrase, or even a sound is repeated, the experience of the first occurrence is continuously maintained in the present in each subsequent recurrence.

The poetic effects of patterned expressivity which are conditioned by r. were to Baudelaire a principle of the "organization of the life of the mind" (*Salon de 1859*); he also recognized, further, that a dynamics of pattern must include the fracturing of pattern. The constituents of sound which rhythm (q.v.) exploits consist of four elements: intensity, duration, pitch, and phonemic character. In most systems of versification the primary factor in the creation of rhythm is contained in the intensity or duration of sound, or both, so that the verse relies upon patterns of repeated stress or structured line-lengths or both. Complex phonic patterns are generally secondary rhythmic elements which may coexist with primary ones. Meter (q.v.) is a form of systematic r. most often determined by stress or quantity. In Eng. poetry, since meter is based at least partly on stress, the perception of stress-determined meter depends in turn upon the recognition of thematic elements such as syntax. Nonetheless, meter must be regarded as a formal element, since it patterns a physical property of the sounds. The constant presence of meter in a poem separates it from less highly structured sound, maintaining the distinction between poetic and nonpoetic discourse.

The r. of a complete line within a poem may be related to the envelope (q.v.) stanza pattern, or in other ways, such as at the end of a strophe as a refrain (q.v.). In the OF epics, such as the *Chanson de Roland*, refrains may bind several separate *laisses* (q.v.) into independent larger units. In a multistrophic poem the modification of the refrain may signal closure. A good number of refrains become complex structural elements through minor modification from strophe to strophe (see INCREMENTAL REPETITION). Sometimes thematic alteration collaborates in the sense of an ending, as in this partial quotation of strophe-endings from Wyatt: "But only liff and libertie . . . Lacking my liff and libertie . . . And all for the lack of libertie . . . And loss of liff for libertie . . . Graunt me but liff and libertie . . . My deth, or liff with libertie." The patterns of recurrence have set up expectations strengthened by successive occurrences, and the innovation "deth" bestows integrity upon the reader's experience formally and thematically.

In Heb. poetry (q.v.), biblical semantic parallelism has been described as two cola that express the same meaning using two different sets of words. Yet this traditional definition glosses over the progression and intensification of thought from one colon to another, which can be expressed by the formula, "A; and what's more, B"—e.g. "Do not fret because of evil men / or be envious of those who do wrong" (Kugel). The second colon in these lines from Psalm 37 develops the thought expressed in the first, so that similarity leads to meditation upon the resulting semantic reinforcement. Equivalence, then, always comports a difference of rank. Even the simple fact of temporal discontinuity between repeating elements leads to a difference in their functions, via the accumulation of significance and recontextualization. Therefore pure r. does not exist.

In OE poetry the essence of the poetic artifice lies in structural alliteration. Usually the line is made up of two hemistichs with two stresses each, and the first three stresses of the four alliterate. Synonymically or antithetically related words are thus emphasized in their relationship, so that r. stabilizes important themes, reinforces rhythm, clarifies oral-formulaic aspects of the poems, and enhances periphrase by variation (q.v.).

Any analysis of r. needs to be based on the way in which sound r. interacts with syntactic structure as well as at the level of prosody. Sound patterns often run in parallel with syntactic units, so that the poet stresses the form not only of her verse but also of her syntagms. In traditional metrical verse the meter cannot be effective unless the integrity of the line is frequently reinforced by syntactic integrity. In the final couplet of Shakespeare's Sonnet 18 a complex pattern of alliteration, assonance, paronomasia ("lives . . . life") and syntactic parallelism create a series of mutually reinforcing echoes, including "breathe . . . see," "long . . . live . . . life," and "eyes can see . . . life to thee." Syntactic r. also can aid in the creation of a metaphorical equivalence or the perception of a logical sequence or other correspondences between repeated units, as in Frost's "Nothing Gold Can Stay": "So Eden sank to grief, / So dawn goes down to day." Abetted by verbal r., the alignment of the second line with the first forges the implied relationship "As this . . . so that," an implied logical progression.

In free verse (q.v.), distribution patterns of linguistic features are not only less strictly determined than in metrical verse but also less easily quantifiable. The mere fact of a repeated lineation is itself a form of r. that tells the reader to expect rhythm and to pace the reading of the poem so as to realize, as prominently as possible, the rhythmic parallelism of successive lines: "She owns the fine house by the rise of the bank. / She hides, handsome and richly drest aft the blinds of the window" (Walt Whitman).

Syntactic, grammatical, and thematic parallels can function as significant clues to interp. An author's self-echoes and borrowings often provide material for the analysis of other poems by herself and by others. Milton borrows freely from himself and from others including Lat. poets, often extending the borrowing to entire phrases. The r. of a poetic phrase can have an incantatory effect, as in magic spells, or in the opening three lines of T. S. Eliot's "Ash Wednesday," all of them variants of "Because I do not hope to turn again." The next 28 lines contain no fewer than 11 lines clearly related to these and serve as a unifying factor in a poem otherwise very free in structure. In the following passage from Shakespeare, each noun is picked up in a subsequent line and repeated in some form, with grammatical compression in the third line effecting closure: "And let the kettle to the trumpet speak, / The trumpet to the cannoneer without, / The cannons to the heavens, heaven to earth" (*Hamlet* 5.2.273–75).

In rhymed verse, rhyme determines the spatialized schemes in which rhythmical series are presented and calls attention to the rhythmically important line endings in which meaning has been chiefly concentrated ever since troubadour (q.v.) verse. The r. of similar endings of words or even of identical syllables (*rime riche*, see RICH RHYME) approaches the r. of a whole word, as in identical or equivocal rhyme (qq.v.). Here the accumulation of r. adds meanings and multiplies the possi-

bilities of semantic variation. In the sestina (q.v.), six words repeated identically function to bind together larger units of interstrophic composition transcending the individual strophes. Homonymic equivalence serves to highlight semantic similarity and difference. The use of a single signifier for two signifieds, a form of r., appears in punning (see PUN), where homonymy brings phonetic equivalence relations into play so as to underscore difference of meaning, though not at all necessarily opposed meaning. At times the clash between two associations when brought into an apparently repetitive association challenges the referential stability of lang., substituting a virtual meaning for the anticipated meaning. In paronomasia, a case of r. with variation, near-r. occurs through a slight differentiation of sound which contracts a slight or extreme difference of sense by altering as little as a phoneme. See also VERSE AND PROSE.

E. S. Le Comte, *Yet Once More* (1953)—Miltonic; S. Rimmon-Kinan, "The Paradoxical Status of R.," *PoT* 1 (1960); R. Abernathy, "Rhymes, Non-Rhymes, and Antirhyme," *To Honor Roman Jakobson* (1967); B. H. Smith, *Poetic Closure* (1968); P. Kiparsky, "The Role of Linguistics in a Theory of Poetry," *Daedalus* 102 (1973); E. G. Kintgen, Jr., "Echoic R. in OE Poetry," *NM* 75 (1974); N. B. Smith, *Figures of R. in the Old Prov. Lyric* (1976); J. Lotman, *The Structure of the Artistic Text* (tr. 1977), ch. 6; M. Shapiro, *Hieroglyph of Time* (1980); M. Cornell, "Varieties of R. in OE Poetry," *Neophil* 65 (1981); R. Jakobson, "Linguistics and Poetics," in Jakobson, v. 3; J. L. Kugel, *The Idea of Biblical Poetry* (1981); J. Hollander, *The Figure of Echo* (1981); Morier—long entry; J. H. Miller, *Fiction and R.* (1982)—prose; M. Frédéric, *La R.: Étude linguistique et rhétorique* (1985)—the fullest mod. study; S. Metzidakis, *R. and Semiotics: Interpreting Prose Poems* (1986); G. Chesters, *Baudelaire and the Poetics of Craft* (1988); L. Magnus, *The Track of the Repetend: Syntactic and Lexical R. in Mod. Poetry* (1989)—use with caution. M.S.

REPRESENTATION AND MIMESIS.

  I. REPRESENTATION
 II. MIMESIS
III. CLASSIC AND ROMANTIC
 IV. SAUSSURE AND PEIRCE
  V. THE VERBAL MEDIUM
 VI. TRANSLATION
VII. DESIGN
VIII. THE MASTER TROPE

I. REPRESENTATION. R. is the process by which lang. constructs and conveys meaning. One major component—perhaps the major component—of the process of r. is *reference*: words (texts) refer, or create pointers to, the external world, other words (other texts), themselves, or to the process of referring; Hutcheon (in Whiteside and Issacharoff) identifies these four types or directions of reference as, respectively, extratextual, intertextual, intratextual, and metatextual. Reference concerns the ability of lang. to describe, capture, express, or convey—the verbs have often been interchangeable—the external world in symbols which the mind can manipulate.

R. lies at the very heart of the nature of lang., i.e. speech as a system of communication for encoding information symbolically and transmitting it from speakers to auditors (for diagram, see Jakobson; see also Abrams). R. is one of the most difficult problems in philosophy; the issues are not merely central to aesthetics: they are fundamental to epistemology and metaphysics. Since we are compelled to talk about the nature of lang. in words themselves, the structures and limitations inherent in words presumably already constrain our ability to talk about lang. at all: there is no vantage point from which we can stand outside lang. so as to critique it. But conversely we do not know how severe these constraints are, and we do know that lang. is capable of both creativity and growth so as to convey new concepts. *A priori*, it would seem reasonable to explore the nature of hammers as a construction tool by hammering, and the nature of paint as an aesthetic medium by painting, hence the nature of lang. by engaging in verbal discourse. This is what we have, and, this side of transcendence, much is still possible.

One would think it might be possible to escape r. altogether; and indeed experimental poetries such as *poésie pure* in the 19th c. (see PURE POETRY) and "sound poetry" (q.v.) in the 20th have sought escape from denotation and reference. All art aspires, Mallarmé remarked, to the condition of music. But in fact r. is almost impossible to escape even in nonrealistic or nonreferential art: so Rudolf Arnheim, commenting on abstractionist painting, suggested that "even the simplest patterns point to the meaning of the objects to which they apply," so that ultimately "there is no form without r." Whether abstract or realistic, art largely engages in r.

II. MIMESIS. In general, lang. has two modes for r., one nonmimetic (nonreferential, nonrealistic), the other mimetic. Nonmimetic r. encompasses all abstract art and all r. of imaginary, surreal, and fantastic worlds, worlds other than the quotidian one we inhabit. The second type of r. is m., though the term "m." has been used in two senses, one general, one specific. In the general sense, which is the one canonized by Auerbach, m. amounts to "realistic r.," namely the verbal capturing or conveying of experience in such a way that the mental image or meaning created by the words is judged similar, analogous, or even identical to what we know about the world from sense-data directly. Its structures are symbolic, propositional, and descriptive. Mimetic r. in this sense corresponds to extratextual reference. "Realistic" is of course not much more explanatory, being a very elastic term, but in the general sense of verisimilitude (q.v.) it is clear enough.

M. in the specific sense concerns verbal sequences in which the forms of the words themselves—their sounds, shapes, or sequence—resemble, enact, or reproduce some aspects of that which they refer to. *Resemblance*—i.e. analogy—is the operative term (see section V below). Mimetic lang. is "expressive," "imitative," or iconic. In poetry the medium for mimetic enactment is of course the body of the poem, its corporeal substance, sound (q.v.), and the means are prosodic.

The two senses of m. amount, respectively, to the distinction between mimetic ends and means. Confusion of these is what we may call the Mimetic Fallacy. Critics who infringe the Mimetic Fallacy fail to grasp that artistic means are not to be judged by same criteria as artistic ends. Dickens can describe boring characters without boring us, and Flaubert can depict the shallow intellectual and moral capacities and limited self-knowledge of Emma Bovary without the depiction itself being shallow, naive, or simplistic. On the contrary, it takes great skill to render a shallow character in an incisive and engaging way. Even in realistic art, where the ends are mimetic, the means need not be, though if they are, they compound the effect.

The two functions of lang., referential and mimetic, can be seen in the simple example of how to represent the hue which is a mixture of pink and purple, which we sometimes see through stained-glass windows in the late afternoon. Taking the representational function of lang., by which arbitrary words describe, we could say that the light "has a color blended of pink and purple," or we could say, in a word, "the color was fuchsia." The mimetic function of lang. (in the specific sense) would seek other means: a la Joyce, we might call the color "pinkpurple" (using contiguity to indicate close relation) or "ppuirpnlek" or, better, "PpuIrpNleK" (letting graphic mixture indicate color mixture). Now the graphic signs create an analogy for that which they wish to convey. The analogy is not exact, admittedly—mixing caps and lowercase switches codes—but it works. Note that mimetic forms violate the rules of representational lang.: by calling attention to themselves, they thicken the normal transparency of the sign, forcing us to focus on the signifier itself so as to grasp the meaning. This opacity, which is fundamental to poetry, is what Jakobson termed the "poetic function" (q.v.).

Mimetic processes in lang. are much more extensive than many critics realize, operating not only in phonology but also in morphology and syntax. These processes include not only "sound symbolism" or "phonetic symbolism" (imitative and associative sounds; see SOUND) but also "morphosymbolism" (word-formation and changes in word-shape; see Bolinger) and iconicity in syntax (Haiman). Though mimetic phenomena in poetry such as onomatopoeia (q.v.) have traditionally been disparaged as trivial and mechanical, extensive linguistic evidence shows that these are not mere "poetical" devices: mimetic processes operate on all levels of lang. and in most if not all langs. worldwide. In a seminal essay, Wimsatt focuses directly on the means available in the verbal medium for miming as opposed to its ordinary means for referring. Distinguishing between the *graphemic* and *phonetic* modes of lang., Wimsatt identifies eight types of verbal iconicity, most of which have analogues in poetry. Though Dr. Johnson disparaged "representative meter" in poetry, and though the range of imitative prosodic effects in Pope's *Essay on Crit.* is limited, m. extends much deeper, and the *desire* for it is embedded in the very fabric of poetic lang. It was Ransom who said that poetic lang. aspires to the condition of nature: it "induces the provision of icons among the symbols." In perfected poetic speech, every word would be motivated and wholly natural, appropriate in form to its meaning. When devices such as sound patterning and repetition (q.v.) are used for artistic purposes, the inert categories of ordinary grammar are energized and raised to a higher level of valency where order *is* naturalized: here words *become* natural experience. M. is thus the desire for the motivated sign (for short history, see Essick, ch. 2).

III. CLASSIC AND ROMANTIC. M. was established as a central concept in Western poetics by Plato and Aristotle (see CLASSICAL POETICS). The term "m." derives from Gr. *mimos*, a mime (q.v.) play or actor therein, and seems to have originally meant the mimicking of an animal or person (a mythical hero, a god, or a fabulous creature such as the Minotaur) through facial expression, speech, song, dance, or some amalgam of these. In Eng. it has been customarily translated as "imitation" (q.v.) in the ordinary sense of "copying," though this is very unsatisfactory in several respects (see section VI below).

The Greeks in fact bequeathed to posterity not one conception of poetry but two. The first strain derives from Plato's Theory of Forms; in it the issue of m. as imitation is central. It is the ideality of Forms which made Platonism appealing to Christianity; God is in effect the last Form. Note that the issue of m. is framed explicitly in *visual* terms, as images, shadows, copies. In this theory, which survived until the late 18th c., verbal experience is characterized as secondary and derivative, a *re*-presentation of actual experience, and often only (as in Plato) a poor imitation at that. For Plato, lit. offers only an image of an image, a copy of a copy of the real, so is suspect. By the 18th c., copying "Nature" meant something else (see CONVENTION), but "imitation" was still embraced as sound poetic praxis. In the 19th, Carlyle and Nietzsche's announcements that God Is Dead sealed the fate of this theory forever by removing any possibility of a Being apart from our experience of the world who would validate the accuracy of mimetic rs. In the absence of all such verification, only making remains. All 20th-c. art, there-fore, exists in a postmimetic mode; notice that the chief drive in late-industrial technology is to devise machines of ferocious efficiency at *copying*, at creating facsimiles. Endless repetition becomes the postmodern condition.

The second strain derives from the Gr. conception of *poiesis* as making, the creation of objects from formless matter. This strain eventuated in romantic poetics (q.v.), where form is made over as internal and individual; in organicism (q.v.), every entity has a form which proceeds from a principle that is self-contained, even as the oak tree springs from the acorn. The advent of romanticism effected a fundamental epistemological shift by reformulating lit. not as an *imitative* but as a *constitutive* art, presenting not external reality but a fuller, partly interior version of reality which includes the feeling subject. M. as imitation was thus supplanted in romantic poetics by the concept of creative imagination (q.v.), the faculty by which the poet envisions and creates realities never before seen and not a part of the external world.

The romantic (expressive) strain has roots in antiquity in Aristotle's argument that the poet surpasses the historian because she is not tied to mere fact but provides a more accurate (if less "factual") account of reality. This is the line followed in the Ren. by Scaliger (*Poetices* 1.1) and Sidney: since the poet as seer (see VATES) can envision a higher order of nature than the one known to ordinary mortals, she becomes not a slave to or copier of reality but in effect a creator, a second god. The poet, says Sidney, "doth grow in effect another nature." Since the poet does not make propositional statements about the external world directly ("nothing affirmeth"), the poet is not a fabricator of falsehoods ("never lieth"), as Plato charged. Now the poet models "truth" at a deeper level, where recreating the sense of life as felt experience is largely not a matter of descriptive detail; nor is verisimilitude required in order to persuade a reader of the "reality" of the fiction. It is not required that rs. be "true" to fact: it is only required that they be *meaningful*, i.e. that they persuade us of their sense of reality. "The truest poetry," says Shakespeare's Touchstone, "is the most feigning." The traditional view in the West, after Aristotle, was that art at its deepest was, if fictive, still "true to life."

IV. SAUSSURE AND PEIRCE. The most extensive theories of verbal r. in modern times have been those of Ferdinand Saussure, the publication of whose lecture notes (like Aristotle's) subsequently created an entire school in poetics (see STRUCTURALISM), and Charles Sanders Peirce, whose semiotics has been, if more extensive and philosophically coherent, much less influential in Am. lit. crit. (Sheriff; see SEMIOTICS, POETIC). Both theories place the activity of signification—i.e. symbolization, sign-making and sign-interpreting—at the center of human cognition and interaction with the external world. (For survey and diagrams of the other main theories, see Whiteside and Issacharoff ch. 7, esp. 184–85.)

Saussure followed all Western thought about lang. since Plato in conceiving the nature of linguistic signs to be arbitrary: since the words for the same referent in two different langs. normally differ, there cannot be any innate, natural, or "motivated" relation between the particular sound shape of a word (the signifier) and its referent in the external world (the signified). He departed from such trad., however, in assigning the locus of meaning to the *difference* between such signs and their referents, both between langs. and within a lang. (see SOUND). Since the class of canines is signified by "dog" in Eng. but "chien" in Fr., the meaning "class of canines" must arise not from present phonetic features—which do not coincide at all—but from the differential between them. Since for Saussure the vast majority of words have no motivated form, meaning becomes detached, floating on a sea of contingencies and subjectivities (so Derrida). Meaning arises only in the interplay of signs, hence is polyvalent, unstable, and indeterminate (see INDETERMINACY; TEXTUALITY).

Peirce conceives the world as triadic: his ontology identifies Firstness (any thing which is without relation to any other thing), Secondness (any thing which has its being in relation to any one other thing), and Thirdness (any thing which brings into relation a First and a Second). Thirdness is the realm of signs. For Peirce, all thought is carried on in signs, and hence all r., as thought, is mediate cognition. Things in this triadic world may be either objects, meanings, or signs: a sign mediates between an object and its meaning. Meaning exists *a priori*, apart from human cognition; what remains for us is only to discover and know it in greater or lesser degree. Hence meaning is entirely objective, existing on an ideal plane which Peirce makes clear is essentially Hegelian. Meaning itself, however, is a sign, or interpretant; interpretants too (being perceivers' responses to signs) are triadic in classification, being either thought, action, or emotion, of which only thought is "genuine," the other two being of some lesser reality hence "degenerate."

More generally, the relations of sign to object—i.e. the fundamental modes of r.—possible in Peirce are three: resemblance, producing an *icon* (see ICONICITY); physical contiguity or action, producing an *index*; and thought (cognition), producing a *symbol* or sign. Since all signifying activity is for Peirce mental and even idealist, the first two of these will indicate resemblance or emotive meanings and may express possibilities which might obtain or actualities which do obtain in the world—but not necessary relations which must obtain logically. Such signs are therefore not genuine, though this does not mean they are not important, for in fact their very ambivalences and ambiguities virtually guarantee that they will be used widely and often, and indeed predominate over genuine signs. Genuine signs, incl. lang., exist in the autonomous realm of interpretive thought, which is fundamentally symbolic in character.

The noncongruence of ontological and epistemological assumptions between Peirce and Saussure could hardly be more stark, and hence the ensuing conflicts more inevitable—though often but dimly understood—when structuralism and semiotics came to dominate Am. lit. crit. in the 1960s and 1970s. For Peirce, subjectivity is a minor issue; for Saussure it is fundamental. For Peirce, meaning is always already existent; for Saussure it is local, unstable, and evanescent. It is one of the great ironies of modern crit. that while it was the work of Saussure which exerted the most influence on Am. literary theory of the 1960s and 1970s, Saussure's account of meaning is idiosyncratic and anomalous among the major theories of meaning which have been put forward in the 20th c. (Whiteside and Issacharoff; Sheriff ch. 4). Saussure's account, focusing on the relation signifier–signified, is binary and linear; meaning is endlessly deferred. All the other major philosophical systems are ternary and triangular: all of them—like linguistics, semantics, semiotics, psychology, and cognitive studies—take meaning as a *given*.

Further, Saussure's doctrine of the arbitrariness of the sign is much more limited than is generally recognized. "It has never been contended," says Bolinger, "that complex utterances are arbitrary in the same sense in which *arbitrary* has been applied to morphemes" (234). Even within the word, arbitrariness has limits: the particular form a word takes when coined is heavily determined by the synchronic forces of linguistic evolution, and, once the word exists, it is subject to a further range of diachronic influences from all the other words in the lang.; even "an arbitrary form, once integrated into the system, assumes all the affective and associative privileges enjoyed by the most obvious onomatopoeia" (231). "When we speak of sound-suggestiveness, then, we speak of the entire lang., not just of a few imitative or self-sufficient forms" (234). In general, it would seem reasonable to characterize lang. as a complex mixture of arbitrary forms, mimetic forms, and forms motivated by both the nature of lang. and the nature of cognition, i.e. the mind.

V. THE VERBAL MEDIUM. Lang., the 20th c. realized with a shock, is a modeling system based on a code: everything which is cast into verbal form is *encoded*. Like other systems of expression both natural (gestures) and artificial (ciphers, mathematics), the elements of the system and the rules for combining them are largely arbitrary. Fundamental to all r., therefore—whether mimetic or not—is the nature of the medium. Every r. is a mediation; all rs. are formalizations and symbolizations. It is precisely in the nature of a symbol that it be radically unlike that for which it stands.

All art exploits the imposition of the medium.

It is of the very essence of art that the medium be different from that of its objects. In painting, apples and pears are represented in canvas and paint; in sculpture, flesh is represented in stone. But it is the peculiarity of verbal art that the medium is both physical and symbolic—hence double, and inextricably so. Words, besides having such physical characteristics as shape and length, bear meaning as part of their primary substance. In expository prose the physicality of words is suppressed, whereas in poetry it is foregrounded. If the medium were wholly transparent, the expression would shine straight through and there would be no necessity to have art at all: one needs no pane if one wants the wind to blow through. The *medium* is the *mediation*; lacking it, there is no *translation* of the expression into another form, for all art partakes of the condition of translation (see section VI below). Indeed, we must not think expression itself exempt from this requirement, for expression itself takes place in a medium, and is in this respect aesthetic—i.e. trans-substantial. So lang., like art, is a "secondary modeling system"; and though it is true that lang. is art-full, more deeply, one must say that lang. *is* art in its enabling conditions, processes, and achieved effects. From this perspective, m. looks very different. The notion of imitation in the sense of producing a material simulacrum of an original—a copy—recedes rapidly in favor of the notion of achieving analogous results in a completely different mode.

From the point of view of cognitive science and information theory, one would say that a r. is a type of modeling, and that our recognition that an artwork is an imitation or m. of the external world in some way is one species of pattern recognition. But the re-presentation in every r. is also, more directly, a presentation itself, and in art we must say that this is the more important function. It was Diderot who remarked that in poetry "things are said and represented simultaneously." So every r. is re-present, and re-presents as it represents. It does not stand for what preceded or surrounds it, but extends it into a new modality. The relation of the verbal r. to the original sensory one is not one of imitation (copy) but one of *analogy* or *resemblance*, which is very different. An analogy is a perceived congruity in structural relationships between two sets of phenomena. The subject of analogy is one to which Wallace Stevens devotes two important discussions in *The Necessary Angel* (1951), esp. the first of the "Three Academic Pieces" (1947) and "Effects of Analogy" (1948; see SIMILE). Now the difference in modality is foregrounded, and difference is accepted as an essential part of the process.

One of the recognitions of postmimetic crit. is that r. always does violence to that being represented, in that there is always a gap between the two phenomena; this differential between the representational system and that being represented results from the fact that the medium for r. differs fundamentally. The question is not whether the gap exists, but only about its size. Is it even possible to gauge its size? Many would say no; to judge that would require standing apart from the representing in progress. Such a neutral vantage, Heisenberg showed in physics, we will never have: the presence of the subjective perceiver and the act of looking alter the system and so remove the possibility of objective knowledge irrevocably. Poststructuralist crit. made much of this, but in ordinary lang. use, the size of the gap is not the only or even in some cases the major concern.

Furthermore, in other sign-systems it has certainly proven possible to assess and even decrease the gap between the sign-system and the external world. Chief among such systems is of course mathematics, where, in the Euclidean framework, at least, symbolic rs. are taken to provide information about the external world which is susceptible of verification and which allows prediction; empirical data is in turn fed back into the mathematical model so as to improve the predictive power of the system. Certainly other, nonEuclidean representational systems have been developed; these presumably offer predictions about other universes than our own. Such universes are fictive (not ours) yet may still be "true" (internally coherent). It is important to realize, however, that in mathematics the predictive power of any given equation is dependent not on its individual elements, which are themselves abstract and arbitrary, but rather on their relations and on the construction of the representational system as a whole—its axioms, its rules. It is the same with lang.: single words are meaningless in isolation (so Saussure) but depend on the influences of their neighbors (i.e. the lang. as a whole) for their representational power and accuracy, which is considerable (contra Saussure).

VI. TRANSLATION. From a distance, it is curious that Gr. *m.* should have been translated as Eng. "imitation," for the Gr. denotes a gesturing, a figuring-forth, whereas the translation term approaches the process from the other direction. "Imitation" suggests that the purpose is simply to copy an original; the only question then is how closely the imitation (copy) conforms. But this we cannot judge well, even if it were all that mattered, which it is not (see below). The notion of m. was originally drawn from the mime, who produced stylized gestures *without speech* so that the audience would see in them the characteristic features of the actions of some mythological figure or personality type they already knew. But here the task is simply to match memory to sight, and both elements are of the same system: the mime imitates gesture with gesture. Similarly, drama imitates action and speech with action and speech. But in lang., words are of a altogether different stratum, already charged with meaning.

The nature of verbal r. may become clearer if we consider the case of translation. "Poems may be poorly translated, as they may have been poorly written to begin with," says Willis Barnstone, "but they are not necessarily poorer or better than the original." The quality of the translated version depends rather less on the quality of the original than on "the translator's skill in writing poetry in his own lang." The tr. is not a copy good or bad; it is a *version* enacted in another medium. The nature and quality of the tr. is controlled by the translator's skill, certainly, but greatly too by the resources offered by both the source and the target langs. All tr., that is, is mediation, so that the aim of faithful r. is not to copy the original—which is impossible in any event, every medium (e.g. lang.) being different, and every medium *necessarily* imposing itself at every moment between the knower and the known—but rather to try to do the thing that the original did in its medium as well as that can be done in the new medium, insofar as the doing in the original is understood by the translator.

If the reader grasps the nature of the doing in the tr., then she may perhaps also grasp, *mutatis mutandis*, something of the nature of the doing in the original. But only if she has knowledge of both langs can she judge aright how well the doing in the target lang. compares to how well the original achieved its own end in the source lang., given what the two langs. respectively allow. But this account, which relates one verbal r. to another, can be extended to all r. in art, and indeed to lang. itself as r. All verbal r. *is* tr. by its very nature. A verbal r. is in effect a translation target lang., except that the source lang. is not verbal; it is sensory. To judge the quality of the verbal r., we should not compare it to the original (sensory) r., for that will tell us very little. What we want, rather, is information about what kinds of sensory and cognitive knowledge are and are not possible, as against what the linguistic and literary systems allow. The point is not that direct comparison between the two modes of r. is impossible, but simply that it is confounded by the radical differences between the representational media, which are very different codes. Schematically:

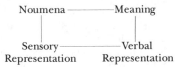

The traditional conception of m. only concerned the SR–VR link. But in the wider field of verbal r., all four relations are important. What we can know about the SR–N link must be derived from psychology, epistemology, physics, and philosophy. We can inspect VR–M directly with discourse about discourse. It is our deepest hope that there is linkage—analogy—between M and N. For some, this is the province of metaphysics; for others, reliable knowledge about the noumenal world comes from religion or transcendent vision. Can

words give us any true knowledge about the noumenal world which lies beyond sense-experience? There have been two views put forward in Western philosophy about the relation of lang. (words) to the noumenal world of "things as they are." The transcendentalist view holds that there is a realm beyond words and even sensation which humans can apprehend, if but dimly or briefly, through words, a realm words can gesture toward or give thought entrance upon when words are ordered aright. The chief modern proponent of this view is the Eliot of *Four Quartets*, who speaks of how "words, after speech, reach / Into the silence." It is a view naturally allied with religious faith. The immanentist view, by contrast, is that noumenal knowledge is forever denied us (so Kant) and that lang. and thought are coextensive. As Hazard Adams puts it, "we can only make a world with a lang., indeed in a lang. There is nothing imaginable independent of a medium to imagine in."

Of course, art always seeks to conceal its own artfulness. One of the monuments of modern thinking about r. is René Magritte's famous image of a smoker's pipe over the caption, *C'eci ne pas une pipe*. Magritte's work addresses precisely our automatic instinct to treat pictorial (and verbal) rs. as is they were the things themselves. If one's child pointed to the picture of the pipe and asked what it is, one would almost never say, "this is a picture of a pipe"; one would instinctively say, "this is a pipe"—thereby subtracting, as a reflex, the distance between the r. of a thing and the thing itself. Of course Magritte's image is not a pipe but rather a r. of a pipe; but when we confront the picture in our ordinary cognitive mode, we attend to the meaning and automatically ignore the fact of the r. itself, i.e. the fact that it is a picture of a thing not a thing. The purpose of Magritte's caption, however, is to force us out of habituated response back into the antecedent recognition of the fact of the r. itself.

VII. DESIGN. Many commentators, esp. of the past two decades, have seemed to think that the verbal r. of experience in lit. does not effect and instantiate any real presence (see Krieger). But it is odd to complain that lit. is of some order of experience secondary to sense experience. We should ask, rather, whether a literary (poetic) artwork represents the same objects, in the same way as, and with the same resulting degree of credibility as sense-experience; if so, how and how much, and if not, why and what instead. Is verbal r. inferior to sensory r.? Plato answers in the affirmative; the romantics answer in the negative. Sense-experience itself is of course a r.; the verbal artefact, however, during the process of reception—reading, hearing, or observing—presents itself directly to cognition, supplanting the external world. It blocks out normal sense-data, replacing it with other data about sensation in a precoded form. "It is hard to write any piece of lit. that corresponds to anything as such, whatever it be," says Victor Šklovskij, because "art is not the shadow of a thing but the thing itself" (*Theory of Prose* [tr. 1990]). The eye sees the words on the page, in prose, only to ignore them: they are transparent. Poetry, by contrast, is translucent if not opaque: meaning is still conveyed, but now in words whose design arrests our attention.

Fundamental to the nature of all art is that it achieves its effects by increase of order, or design. Regardless of authorial intention (q.v.), most artworks show themselves to be supercharged with design. It is traditional in Western poetics to think of the faculty or capacity of imagination (q.v.), i.e. image-making, as central to literary r. This is indeed important, esp. for realistic r. and verisimilitude, but it cannot supplant the making (Gr. *poiesis*), the craft, the shaping of the medium which evokes those images and, as it does so, binds their elements more tightly together by form.

In poetry the shaping is of the sensory medium (sound) and carried out largely at the preverbal (phonological) level (meter, rhyme, sound patterning). In its heightened design, texture, and materiality, poetry does not compete with the external world as a species of r.: it offers additional resources and forms of order which are constitutive, not imitative: they enact a heightened form of r. which creates that heightened mode of consciousness which since antiquity has been called "poetic."

Poetry aims to show that relationships exist among the things of the world which are not otherwise obvious; it accomplishes this by binding words together with the subtler cords of sound and meter. These bindings, like the relations they enact, are formal. It was Fenollosa who observed that "the relations between things are more important than the things which they relate." If m. is to occur at all, therefore—given the differences between the representational media—it must address formal rather than substantial features. As Wittgenstein remarks, "what any picture of whatever form must have in common with reality, in order to be able to depict it . . . is logical form, i.e. the form of reality" (*Tractatus* 2.18). Hence the problem of r. is not so much that of the elements of lang. as, again and ever, the problem of form (see PROSODY).

Even Aristotle supports this view: m. as "imitation" is only part of the account of art given in the *Poetics*. Aristotle certainly views imitation as a central human activity; nevertheless, he makes it clear that the chief criterion for drama is not spectacle, diction, credible character, or even verisimilitude but the making of a strong plot (q.v.), i.e. *structure* (q.v.). As for poetry, the account of the means of imitation given in ch. 1 of the *Poetics* is truncated and somewhat garbled, but several modes are identified, and the manner of the imitation is by no means assumed to be direct or literal. The role attributed to imitation in the *Poetics* has distinct limits: only some arts are imitative. Indeed, Aristotle holds that the order of art need not be—and at least once he holds it must not be—the order of reality (else poetry would be inferior to history). On the whole, Aristotle goes to considerable lengths to differentiate the art object from the reality it imitates, and this almost entirely on account of aesthetic *design*. Both imitative and nonimitative arts share this feature, which suggests that, for Aristotle, it is design itself which distinguishes art from life. Even in realistic and referential art, where design is a signifier for the reality outside the artwork, the signifier is a presentational form. In all art, that is, the artwork itself stands as an icon for signification itself.

VIII. THE MASTER TROPE. There has been much interest in the 20th c. in lang. as it manifests itself in psychology, philosophy, prose fiction, and culture. It was Freud who showed that words are often the keys to dream interp. because lang. itself writes the structure of the unconscious. And while the relation of signifier to signified is central in Saussure, much of Lacan's work explores processes based on links between signifier and signifier. Girard has argued that desire itself derives from m. In philosophy, Heidegger conceived poetic lang. as presentational rather than representational, presenting Being itself, a framework built upon by Gadamer. Reference and r. have been major subjects in the study of narrative fiction. In recent years it has been argued by cultural theorists that the study of r. must focus not only on the code but also on the physical and cultural means of production of that code, since these forces undeniably affect both the nature of the code and the uses speakers put it to. All of these inquiries bear directly and deeply on the fundamental issue of how lang. functions, which is to say, on what is possible in verbal r. All of them take lang. as the master trope for human mind and action.

Some modern critics, charmed by the inscrutabilities of Heidegger, blithely dismiss epistemology with a wave of the hand as tiresome Kantianism; such critics reduce m. to mere lang.-use (so G. Bruns in *Renascence* 37 [1985]). But the consequence of such a reduction is to replace truth with use, and too often use ultimately amounts only to power. Valorizations of Heidegger's thought as the only advance upon Kant must be counterbalanced by the recollection that the Ger. thinker was the would-be darling of National Socialism: any theory is properly to be judged, in part, by the ends it is put to. Certainly some postmodern critics have shown that their real interests lie not in the disinterested pursuit of thought for the benefit of humanity but rather in the exercise of power. Even Marxists can be academic capitalists. Against them stands the lonely ghost of Yvor Winters, whose arguments for the irrefrangibly ethical dimensions of poetry and poetic form (and behind them for civility, reason, and pluralism in critical discourse), while widely ignored, have not diminished in force (Trimpi).

RESOLUTION

See also CRITICISM; EMOTION; EXPRESSION; FICTION, POETRY AS; FIGURATION; ICONICITY; IMAGE; IMITATION; INTERPRETATION; INTERTEXTUALITY; INTUITION; MEANING, POETIC; METER; NATURE; ONOMATOPOEIA; POETICS; POETRY, THEORIES OF (*Mimetic Theories*); RENAISSANCE POETICS; SEMANTICS AND POETRY; SEMIOTICS, POETIC; SPEECH ACT THEORY; SYMBOL; SYMBOLIC ACTION; TEXTUALITY.

PHILOSOPHICAL TEXTS: F. de Saussure, *Cours de linguistique générale* (1916), 5th ed. (1955), crit. ed., ed. R. Engler (1967–74), tr. R. Harris (1983); C. K. Ogden and I. A. Richards, *The Meaning of Meaning* (1923); C. S. Peirce, *Coll. Papers*, ed. C. Hartshorne and P. Weiss, 8 v. (1931–58); C. W. Morris, "Foundations of the Theory of Signs" (1938), *Writings on the Gen. Theory of Signs* (1971); W. V. O. Quine, *Word and Object* (1960); L. Wittgenstein, *Tractatus Logico-philosophicus* (tr. 1961); M. Heidegger, *Poetry, Lang., Thought* (tr. 1971); T. W. Adorno, *Aesthetic Theory* (tr. 1984); H.-G. Gadamer, *Truth and Method*, 2d ed. (tr. 1989).

CRITICAL TEXTS: J. W. Draper, "Aristotelian 'M.' in 18th-C. England," *PMLA* 36 (1926); J. Tate, "'Imitation' in Plato's *Republic*," *ClassQ* 22 (1928), "Plato and 'Imitation,'" *ClassQ* 26 (1932); R. McKeon, "Lit. Crit. and the Concept of Imitation in Antiquity," *MP* 34 (1936); Y. Winters, *In Defense of Reason* (1947); W. J. Verdenius, *M.: Plato's Doctrine of Artistic Imitation* (1949); Auerbach—still essential; Abrams; H. Koller, *Die M. in der Antike* (1954); G. F. Else, "'Imitation' in the 5th C.," *ClassP* 53 (1958), *Plato and Aristotle on Poetry* (1986); R. Jakobson, "Linguistics and Poetics" and "Quest for the Essence of Lang.," both rpt. in Jakobson; R. Bernheimer, *The Nature of R.* (1961); B. Hathaway, *The Age of Crit.* (1962); D. L. Bolinger, *Forms of Eng.* (1965); G. Sorban, *M. and Art: Studies in the Origin and Early Devel. of an Aesthetic Vocabulary* (1966); W. Tatarkiewicz, "M.," *DHI*; E. Schwartz, "M. and the Theory of Signs," *CE* 29 (1968); G. Hermeren, *R. and Meaning in the Visual Arts* (1969); L. Golden, "Plato's Concept of M.," *BJA* 15 (1975); W. K. Wimsatt, Jr., "In Search of Verbal M.," *Day of the Leopards* (1976); N. Goodman, *Langs. of Art*, 2d ed. (1976); D. Savan, *Intro. to Peirce's Semiotics* (1976); G. Genette, *Mimologiques* (1976), excerpted in Eng. tr. in *PMLA* 104 (1989); H. Felperin, *Shakespearean R.* (1977); M. Riffaterre, *Semiotics of Poetry* (1978); K. K. Ruthven, *Critical Assumptions* (1979), ch. 2; M. Krieger, *Poetic Presence and Illusion* (1979), *Ekphrasis* (1991); J. D. Boyd, *The Function of M. and Its Decline*, 2d ed. (1980); N. Wolterstorff, *Works and Worlds of Art* (1980); *M.: From Mirror to Method*, ed. J. D. Lyons and S. G. Nichols, Jr. (1982)—little on m., but see Krieger; J. Campbell, *Grammatical Man* (1982); A. Nehamas, "Plato on Imitation and Poetry in *Republic* 10," *Plato on Beauty, Wisdom, and the Arts*, ed. J. Moravscik and P. Temko (1982); A. D. Nuttall, *A New M.* (1983); *M. in Contemp. Theory*, ed. M. Spariosu, 2 v. (1984); P. Kivy, *Sound and Semblance* (1984)—r. in music; C.-G. Dubois, "Problems of R. in the 16th C.," *PoT* 5 (1984); J. Weinsheimer, *Imitation* (1984); J. L. Mahoney, *The Whole Internal Universe* (1985); T. R. Martland, "When a Poem Refers," *JAAC* 43 (1985); W. Trimpi, "M. as Appropriate R.," *Renascence* 37 (1985); R. Woodfield, "Words and Pictures," *BJA* 26 (1986); C. Prendergast, *The Order of M.* (1986); T. Clark, "Being in Mime," *MLN* 101 (1986); C. J. Brodsky, *The Imposition of Form* (1988); *CHLC*; J. K. Sheriff, *The Fate of Meaning* (1989); R. N. Essick, *William Blake and the Lang. of Adam* (1989), ch. 2; S. K. Heninger, Jr., *Sidney and Spenser* (1989); K. L. Walton, *M. as Make-believe* (1990); O. Avni, *The Resistance of Reference* (1990); W. J. T. Mitchell, "R.," *Critical Terms for Literary Study*, ed. F. Lentricchia and T. McLaughlin (1990)—unsatisfactory; C. Crittenden, *Unreality* (1991); P. Livingston, *Models of Desire* (1992)—on Girard.   T.V.F.B.

RESOLUTION. In Gr. and Lat. metrics, r. refers to the admissibility of two short syllables where the basic pattern of the meter has one *longum*; it is generally distinguished from contraction or substitution (q.v.) of two light syllables for a metrical *breve* or *anceps*. Comparable phenomena can be found in the verse of many langs., such as the classical Somali *gabay* genre and the Prakrit *arya* meter, a fact which suggests that there is a basis for r. in the phonology of ordinary speech. In Gr., r., always excluded from the last foot, is rare in the iambic trimeter and the trochaic tetrameter (qq.v.) of the archaic iambographers, more frequent in tragedy, grows rapidly over the course of Euripides' devel., is more frequent still in satyrplay, and very frequent in comedy. In comedy, substitution in iambic trimeters is very frequent, being excluded from only the last foot; in tragedy, however, it is restricted to the first foot, except for proper names. In general the two light syllables of a r. or substitution cannot be separated or followed by a word boundary.

LINGUISTIC BASIS. When Luganda poems and songs are accompanied on the drums, a single drumbeat is assigned to a light syllable ($\cup$) and two to a heavy syllable ($-$); these drumbeats directly reflect the mora count of linguistic rhythm. The moraic equivalence of two light syllables to one heavy is attested in the linguistic rules of many langs., even those not having long vowels. In Manam, a word ending in a heavy (closed) syllable reduplicates only that last syllable, but a word ending in two light syllables reduplicates both. Moraic equivalence explains why some verse-systems allow a sequence of two light syllables to be mapped onto one rhythmically strong position in the foot (see ARSIS AND THESIS) when that position is preferentially occupied by a heavy syllable.—A. N. Tucker, "The Syllable in Luganda," *Jour. of Af. Langs.* 1 (1962); W. S. Allen, *Accent and Rhythm* (1973), 60, 255; F. Lichtenberk, *A Grammar of Manam* (1983).   A.M.D.; L.D.S.

In Germanic metrics, including OE, OHG, and

ON, where ictus is usually borne by a long syllable, r. applies specifically to a short stressed syllable and the following syllable whether short or long. Metrical r. is not to be confused with phonological elision (q.v.) or contraction (see METRICAL TREATMENT OF SYLLABLES), which depends on certain sonorant patterns (esp. liquids and nasals) such that two syllables are either reduced or have the potential to be reduced to one. In r. the syllables must remain distinct, but they count as one ictus-bearing unit at the metrical level of abstraction (just as, in *Beowulf*, two or more unstressed syllables count as one non-ictus-bearing unit, i.e. a dip)—Sievers.   T.C.

RESPONSION. The relation of equivalence (q.v.) which exists between two or more corresponding (i.e. metrically identical) sections of the same larger rhythmical whole. The term is ordinarily used in reference to the repeated stanzas or strophes of a piece of Gr. choral lyric (see MELIC POETRY; ODE) or to the shorter segments within such a lyric: strophe and antistrophe (qq.v.) in a given poem are then said to be in r. to each other; every syllable in the one either has its responding counterpart in the other, or else belongs to a pair of syllables which has such a counterpart (usually two shorts which respond, through resolution or contraction, to one long, though other possibilities do exist—"anaclastic" r. between – ◡ and ◡ – (see ANACLASIS), for example, or r. between – ◡ and – , found occasionally in the creto-paeonic verse of Gr. Old Comedy). "Exact" or strict r. between single syllables of the same quantity is often contrasted with the "free" r. which exists in pieces which allow anceps resolution, contraction, and the like; and r. between the principal subdivisions of a whole composition (the type to which the term usually refers) is occasionally distinguished, as "external" r., from the "internal" r. of one foot or metron to the next that exists within such subdivisions. Since Maas, the concept of r. has come to seem one of the principal compositional and structural strategies for one kind of strophic verse. See EQUIVALENCE; ISOMETRIC.—Maas, sect. 28 ff.; Dale 62–66, 89–91; E. Wahlström, *Accentual R. in Gr. Strophic Poetry* (1970).   A.T.C.

REST. See PAUSE.

RETROENSA, RETRONCHA. See ROTROUENGE.

REVERDIE. A dance song or poem, popular throughout Europe in the late Middle Ages, which celebrates the coming of spring—the new green of the woods and fields, the singing of the birds, the time of love. By a natural association the r. began to welcome Easter as well as spring; and Ger., OF, Lat., and Occitan poets described how longing for spring leads to longing for heaven and praise of the Blessed Virgin. The form is usually that of the *chanson* of 5 or 6 stanzas without re-frain. A further variation was developed by the Occitan troubadours, who extended their praise to other seasons of the year.—J. Bédier, "Les Fêtes de mai et les commencements de la poésie lyrique au moyen-âge," *Revue des deux mondes* 135 (1896); Jeanroy, *Origines*; P. Diehl, *The Med. European Religious Lyric* (1985).   U.T.H.; R.L.H.

REVERSAL. See PLOT.

REVERSE RHYME, inverse r. In full or true r., the medial vowel and final consonant (or cluster) of the syllable are held constant while the initial consonant is varied. In r. r., the first consonant and the vowel are held constant, the final consonant changed, e.g. Eng. *bat/back, yum/yuck*. This is a rare form in Eng. poetry; indeed, many might deny that it is a r. at all, strictly speaking, since it thwarts the "begin differently, end same" structure that is r. Sometimes the term is also used for a kind of chiasmus (q.v.) in r. where the first and last consonants are switched, e.g. *rap/pair*.   T.V.F.B.

REZEPTIONSÄSTHETIK. See READER-RESPONSE CRITICISM.

RHAPSODE (Gr. "one who stitches songs" or, by false etymology, "one who sings while holding a staff [rhabdos]"). In early Greece, a singer who selected and "stitched together" (partly extemporaneously or partly from memory) his own poetry or that of others, originally a selection or a portion of epic poetry, usually the *Iliad* or *Odyssey*. By the 6th c. B.C., with the establishment of what was regarded as the authentic Homeric texts, the term labelled a class of professional performers who recited the Homeric poems in correct sequence, not merely selected extracts. Rs. are to be distinguished from *citharodes* or *aulodes*, singers of lyric texts to the accompaniment of the cithara or flute. Subsequently, the term "rhapsody" came to denote any highly emotional utterance, a literary work informed by ecstasy and not by rational organization; it is also applied to a literary miscellany or a disconnected sequence of literary works. See GREEK POETRY; cf. GUSLAR; JONGLEUR; MINSTREL; SCOP.—C. M. Bowra, *Trad. and Design in the* Iliad (1930); R. Sealey, "From Phemios to Jon," *REG* 70 (1957); Lord; G. F. Else, *The Origin and Early Form of Gr. Tragedy* (1965); W. Salmen, *Gesch. der Rhapsodie* (1966); Parry; Michaelides; *CHLC*, esp. ch. 3.   R.A.H; T.V.F.B.

RHETORIC AND POETICS. See POETICS; RHETORIC AND POETRY.

RHETORIC AND POETRY.

  I. INTERPRETATION
  II. COMPOSITION

  The art of oratory or public speaking, rhet. has traditionally had two not altogether separable ends: persuasion, which is audience-directed, and eloquence, which is most often form- and style-directed. Three basic genres have been delineated in oratory: deliberative, forensic, and epideictic, with three concomitant types of orations, speeches given before policy-determining bodies, before courts of law, and before occasional assemblies. Rhet. has been a prominent discipline in Western education since antiquity. Indeed, throughout most of the history of Western civilization, p. was written and read by people for whom rhet. was the major craft of composition. At times the similarities of rhet. and p. have been stressed (p. is the "most prevailing eloquence," remarked Ben Jonson in 1641), at times their difference ("eloquence is written to be heard," John Stuart Mill wrote in 1833, "poetry to be overheard"). A distinction revived by Scaliger in the 16th c. that would limit rhet. to *prose* compositions was overwhelmed by a critical commonplace, also inherited from antiquity, that verse itself is no sure sign of p. To the extent that our own time regards p. as having the ends of rhet.—if not exemplary eloquence then persuasive discourse—the two arts remain all but inextricable.

The relationship between rhet. and p. has always extended both to the composition of p. and to the interpretation (q.v.) of it, even on the most elementary levels. Quintilian's uninnovative but highly influential *Institutio oratoria* (1st c. A.D.) offers the traditional attitude: skill in oratory is founded on "speaking correctly" and "interpreting poets" (1.4.2). The inventive processes of rhet. and p. have been differentiated from time to time (see INVENTION), and at least once with revolutionary fervor—"Take Eloquence and wring his neck," Verlaine exclaimed in 1884. These distinctions were usually impelled, like revolutions in interp., by reactions to the intransigence of rhet. and by perceptions of its restrictiveness. Because in our own century the interp. of p. has undergone the more conscious revolution, it will be discussed first in this essay.

I. INTERPRETATION. The rhetorical approach to interp. is, simply, that any discourse should be understood as if it were a public address. Just as a speech act encompasses such extratextual elements as its speaker's delivery and the audience's response, so rhetorical interpreters have insisted that p. too must be understood as something spoken intentionally, at a certain time, by someone to someone (see INTENTION; SPEECH ACT THEORY). Discursive arrangement is a gauge of intention, and forms of thought, *logos*, are only one means of securing that intention. There are at least two other means: *ethos* (q.v.), the audience's perception of the speaker's moral character, and *pathos* (q.v.), the audience's own emotions. Aristotle (*Rhetoric* 1.2) considered these three to be "modes of proof" because they help to establish the speaker's case. The analytical enterprise of rhet. is uniquely a search for identifiable causes of

audience effects, unlike the enterprise of grammar, which is largely a search for the forms of "correctness," or the enterprise of logic (which with grammar and rhet. constituted the Trivium of the ancient liberal-arts curriculum), which is largely a search for the forms of validity. In conducting their search through the three modes of proof, rhetorical interpreters are necessarily historicist and contextual. They conceive of *all* p. as a kind of social act or performance, finding a rhetorical impulse even in that p., such as the symbolist and imagist, which is programmatically non- or even anti-rhetorical (e.g. Gage). They have been attacked in our own time for their prizing of intention and emotion and for their susceptibility to relativist judgment—in the eyes of many, for their failure to view p. *sui generis*.

What p. is, if not rhet., was yet another project of Aristotle, the first critic known to construct a terminology for poetics. Aristotle made *mimesis* (the imitation [q.v.] of human action) the genus of p. and *mythos* (plot—q.v.) its species. Of rhet., by contrast, persuasion was the genus and audience differentiation the species. Aristotle's efforts to distinguish and arrange the arts more or less horizontally form a sharp contrast to Plato's efforts to synthesize the arts and arrange them hierarchically, with dialectic (a mode of disputation more logical than rhetorical) on top. But Aristotle's division was lost sight of for more than a millennium. It was superseded in the Cl. world by Cicero's elevation of rhet. as an art of *eloquence* (to be traced more completely below) and through the Middle Ages by Horace's *Ars poetica*, which gives p. the ends of rhet. The Horatian position, moreover, reaffirmed the Platonic and Ciceronian views that only knowledge should be the basis of persuasion, and mixed those views with the idea that the poet's powers center in his unique ability to delight. To teach, to delight, to move—the subordinate ends of traditional rhet., subsumed alike by persuasion and eloquence—could be effectively achieved by p. Most medieval manuals of poetry were rhetorics and only the sections on versification made any significant distinction between p. and oratory.

When Aristotle's *Poetics* was rediscovered in the 15th c., it brought with it a formalism that increasingly made the ancient symbiosis of rhet. and p. antagonistic. But initially any felt antagonism was muted by the temper of the Ren., for rhet. had again become dominant in the curriculum, restored to something of its centrality after having been displaced for centuries by logic and dialectic. Ren. poetics (q.v.) at first reaffirmed, then surpassed the didactic, rhetorical, Horatian qualities of the Middle Ages: the poem's utility, its proficiency at teaching or moving—argued Minturno (1559), Scaliger (1561), Sidney (1583)—was achieved through its unique capacity for delighting, esp. through "imitative" means. In these and similar apologetics, p. became a superior rhet., and Virgil or Horace the Ciceronian *perfectus orator*, eloquent by virtue of his largely stylistic ability to make wisdom effective. Rhetorical *imitatio*, the composer's exercise of copying the work of others, became in interpretive theory a readerly role of imitating the model behavior represented in a discourse (the poet, Sidney claimed, might "bestow a Cyrus upon the world to make many Cyruses"), a theoretical position ancient as Plato's *Republic* and sanctioned, if negatively, by the Puritan closing of the theaters in 1642. In this way *imitatio* may have initially blunted perceptions of the precise nature of Aristotle's *mimesis* while ostensibly encompassing it. Gradually, however, a new emphasis on form—a poem's organization, a playwright's use of the "unities"—began to sweep crit. Further stimulating this new emphasis was the revival—with Robortelli's edition of Longinus in 1554—of the concept that the sublimity of p. does not simply persuade but more nearly "transports" its audience (see SUBLIME). This concept also revived interest in an "organic" theory of p., compatible with Aristotelianism and echoed in the modern insistence, extending through Coleridge into the 20th c., that p. must be read as if its form (q.v.) and content were fused (see ORGANICISM). Such an insistence controverts the rhetorical view that form is isolable, interchangeable, and strategic, and content, on the other hand, a manageable body of knowledge, truths, or argument.

Although a certain (mainly Aristotelian) formalism was inaugurated in the poetics of the late Eng. Ren., the movement did not reach its apotheosis until our own century, first with Joel Spingarn in 1910 and Benedetto Croce in 1933, both of whom called for a scrapping of all the older, rhetorically infested terminologies, and then with the New Critics (see NEW CRITICISM) of the 1930s and the later "Neo-Aristotelians" (see CHICAGO SCHOOL), with their insistence that a poem constructs its own autonomous universe cut off from the quotidian requirements of ordinary communication. P. speaks a different lang., Richards theorized in 1929. P. does not communicate, Brooks insisted in 1947. Or if it does, Frye argued in 1957, it does so as a kind of "applied lit." Prophetically, Kenneth Burke offered a "counter statement" to this increasingly dominant formalism as early as 1931, calling for the restoration of a rhetorical perspective in which discursive form could again be seen as strategic and in which content could be seen as a complex fusion of speaker, intention, utterance, and audience.

But the subsequent restoration of rhet. to interp. found three main emphases: the author's relation to the text, the role of the reader, and style. The first distinguished two levels of speaking in the poem, the one on which the narrator of the poem is talking to himself or to another person (see VOICE), and the one on which the poet is speaking to us (Olson, Eliot, Booth, Wright; see PERSONA). Increasingly, however, 20th-c. poetics (q.v.) has pursued the second emphasis, focusing on the role of the reader either *of* or *in* the poem— ideal, implied, competent, actual—whose interaction with the text structures it and gives it meaning, or whose presence at least raises questions about the conditions of textuality (q.v.) and communicability (Barthes, Holland, Culler, Iser, Fish, Suleiman and Crossman; see READER-RESPONSE CRITICISM). Whereas formalists, in their "organic" view of p., insist that p. *means* what it *says*, postformalist critics argue that p. means what it *does*. Nonetheless, these first two emphases involve at best a partial or fragmentary use of rhet. and, often, an antagonism toward its ends. But when the reader is a *listener*, as when p. is performed in an oral culture (Errington, Connelly, Sweeney), the role of rhet. becomes much more extensive— at once more traditional and more Burkean, a general heuristic of communicative strategies— and even reaches beyond Western cultural confines (see ORAL POETRY).

For the stylistic analysis of p., rhet. has traditionally supplied detailed taxonomies of figures, schemes, and tropes (see FIGURE, SCHEME, TROPE) ranging from such textural effects as irony (q.v.) to such local effects as alliteration (q.v.). Catalogues burgeoned particularly among medieval and Ren. rhetoricians, for whom an embellished style (q.v.) was the sum total of eloquence (in Peacham [1593] over 350 figures are described). Four tropes—metaphor, metonymy, synecdoche, irony (qq.v.)—were early conceived as master tropes (Fraunce [1588]) because they generate all figurative uses of lang., an idea reiterated by Burke in the 1940s. Jakobson in 1956 found metaphor and metonymy to be attitudes the mind assumes in coping with degrees of similarity or contiguity between matters, and thus began a movement to view tropes as inherent in intellection. Subsequently, the act of interp. itself came to be seen as tropological (Genette; Rice and Schofer): figures, esp. the master tropes, map mental strategies or processes in the reader's work of unraveling the meaning of a text. The figures and tropes have supplied a taxonomy for anthropology, psychology, linguistics, and history; in modern rhet. they serve as indicators of the inherent plasticity of lang. (Quinn). The plasticity and figurality of lang. have also become concerns of modern deconstructionists (Derrida, de Man) in their obliquely rhetorical examination of the often indeterminate gap between what p. *says* and what it ostensibly *does* (see DECONSTRUCTION; INTERTEXTUALITY).

This brief review may suggest that the ultimate choice is to rhetoricize or not to rhetoricize; to consider p. persuasively audience-directed and stylistically eloquence-directed, or to view it as something other than a conventionally communicative act; to restore all of rhet. or only those fragments available in such modern sciences as linguistics and psychology. The alternatives may be further clarified, and some of the gaps in our survey spanned, by shifting our attention to theories of composition—which by offering attitudes toward the use of lang. also offer an implicit hermeneutic.

II. COMPOSITION. Among Western theories of composition, Aristotle's *Rhetoric* is the oldest. His master stroke in the *Rhetoric*—and one which has been too easily overlooked or too readily absorbed within other theories—is his doctrine that rhetorical practice embodies its own unique mode of thought, observable mainly in the orator's efforts to discover the available means of persuading his audience. This practical reasoning, called "invention" (q.v.) in later theories, deals with probable rather than demonstrable matters: the orator weighs alternatives, substantiates his case, and chooses strategies which he believes will sway. To establish the uniqueness of rhetorical invention, Aristotle advanced the *example* and the *enthymeme* as the counterparts, respectively, of logical induction and syllogism—the point being that the orator composes by giving priority not to form but to audience. Compare the enthymeme with the syllogism: whereas the latter has two premises and a conclusion, with very clear canons of formal completeness and validity (*Only* had we world enough and time, this coyness, Lady, were no crime; but we have *not* world enough and time; therefore, this coyness, Lady, *is* a crime), the enthymeme is a syllogism that either draws its major premise from the audience's beliefs or is so loose or incomplete that it compels the audience silently to supply a condition, premise, or the conclusion (hence, while the opening with the addition of "only" is a syllogistic premise, Marvell's entire poem is actually enthymematic). Accordingly, the audience, its knowledge and emotions, has the priority in rhet. that is held by formal validity in logic, by forms of correctness in grammar, and by form itself in poetry.

In one respect, rhetorical invention became poetic invention by default. Aristotle does not describe the latter, and indeed distinguishes the two largely by implication. His *Poetics* is after all not a handbook of composition but a theory of poetry, of its nature and elements, developed in part by comparison with the drama. One of those elements—thought, the power of an agent to say what can be said or what is fitting to be said (in sum, invention)—Aristotle declines to discuss at length (6.16) because he had already treated it in the *Rhetoric*. Poetic invention, where it does not depend upon plot, would seem to arise from a certain natural plasticity (17), the poet's ability to visualize action and assume attitudes—Aristotle's way of avoiding ascribing poetic invention to either inspiration or poetic madness (qq.v.), the two alternatives Plato saw as the poetic counterparts of rhetorical invention. Nonetheless, the Platonic alternatives have certainly had their advocates through the centuries: the divine *furor* usually

associated with Neoplatonism was expressed perfectly by Shakespeare in *A Midsummer Night's Dream* ("The lunatic, the lover, and the poet / Are of imagination all compact") and reached its culmination in the romantic movement of the 19th c. But in the larger historical view, it is rhet., esp. in its developments after Aristotle, which remained the chief discipline whereby writers and speakers learned their craft.

By the time of Cicero, whose Latinity was influential for centuries and whose theories of rhet. were to achieve enormous popularity among Ren. humanists, rhet. had become much more systematized. A unified process of composition implicit in Aristotle became divided into five discrete functions: thought (*inventio*), arrangement (*dispositio*), style (*elocutio*), memory (*memoria*), and delivery (*actio* or *pronuntiato*). Aristotelian rhetorical invention, the search for available means of persuasion, became a pro-and-contra analysis of topics for which forensic oratory was the paradigm. Oratorical arrangement too became more prominent: in forensic oratory, whereas Aristotle had advised only two parts (statement and proof) but allowed four (plus introduction and conclusion), Cicero advised six (exordium, background of the question, statement, proof, refutation, conclusion) and allowed seven (plus a digression). Although Cicero, a poet himself, may have found p. limiting (his persona's famous judgment of p. in *De oratore* 1.70 was exactly reversed by Ben Jonson in *Timber*), nonetheless the two were firmly joined in Cicero's extension of rhet. beyond the end of persuasion, and well beyond the subordinate ends of teaching, pleasing, and moving. Rhet. became the art of *eloquence*, lang. whose artistic force is the formal means whereby its content achieves persuasiveness. As such, rhet. was to cap the statesman's education, and above all be the avenue through which the wisdom of philosophy would be made practical. To accomplish the latter, Cicero rhetoricized philosophy and thereby extended beyond its careful boundaries Aristotle's teachings on rhetorical thought. Rhet., esp. Ciceronian rhet., became a kind of surrogate philosophy which still had great attraction for Ren. humanists fourteen centuries later. In fact, up through the 16th c., Cicero's formalized rhet. and ideal of eloquence were ready tools to fill the practical and apologetic needs of critics and poets—even when his major works were lost.

In the Middle Ages, Cicero's youthful *De inventione* and the pseudo-Ciceronian *Rhetorica ad Herennium* never waned in popularity. Both were only epitomes, offering little more than systematizing. Medieval rhetorics and poetics stressed *dispositio* and *elocutio*, as seen both in St. Augustine's *De doctrina christiana* (426 A.D.) and in Geoffrey of Vinsauf's *Poetria nova* (ca. 1200). The most formalized functions of Ciceronian rhet., functions which directly pertain to the creation of form, seemed to be the critical determinants of eloquence in either art. A concern with rhetorical thought, or any intrusion of *inventio* into systematic philosophy, let alone poetics, was altogether neglected.

But it was precisely that concern with thought which was revived in the Ren. The first published book in Italy was Cicero's masterpiece, *De oratore*, a dialogue in which famous Roman statesmen and lawyers give critical precedence not to arrangement and style, *dispositio* and *elocutio*, but to the strategies of *inventio* in moving others to action. The recovery of Quintilian and the rise to prominence of law as a secular profession gave added impetus to this "new" mode of thought and disputation. Ciceronian legalisms seemed to fire the poets' imaginations as well: *in utramque partem*, the readiness to debate both sides of a question—itself a feature of medieval disputation—becomes a kind of lawyerly embracing of contraries (*controversia*) in the argumentative and ostensibly irresolute fabric of Tudor p. and drama; *qualis sit*, individuating a phenomenon by setting it within a thesis-to-hypothesis (or definite-to-indefinite-question) relationship suffuses Boccaccian fiction and Sidneyan crit.; *ethos* and *ethopoiesis*, the illusion of mind and of behavioral probability, pervade dialogues, mock encomia, and most discussions of courtliness. Schoolroom *imitatio*, including the formal requirements of the forensic oration (esp. the second part, the *narratio* or background of the question), brought fictiveness itself well within rhetorical exercises (see FICTION).

Ultimately, it was Ciceronian *inventio*, including those vestiges within it of Aristotle's distinction between rhetorical and logical modes of thought, which suffered most in the reformations which accompanied the Ren. Rhet. became utterly formalized, far beyond its Ciceronian and even its medieval state. One of the influential books of the early Ren. was *De inventione dialectica* by Rudolphus Agricola (d. 1485). Logic or dialectic, said Agricola, is "to speak in a probable way on any matter"; grammar teaches correctness and clarity, rhet. style. Subsequently the reformers known as Ramists deprived rhet. of *inventio* and *dispositio* (these became solely logical functions) and reduced it to *elocutio* and *actio* (*memoria* was seen as a function of *dispositio*). Though the Ramist reform did not last, rhet. was disintegrated, and it eventually became the subject of such other reformative efforts as Baconian rationalism. Cicero's public mind in search of probabilities was displaced by an isolated, meditative mind totally at odds with traditional *inventio*. Ironically, too, the reform began to undo Cicero's assertion in *Pro archia poeta* (a document whose discovery by Petrarch in 1333 marked a beginning of the Ren.) that a key difference between p. and rhet. lies in their audiences, p. having a general and rhet. a specific one. Sidney restated the argument: only p. has the power to draw children from play and old men from the chimney corner. But by the 17th c., rhetorical *inventio* had become unmoored from

specific audiences, to the further confusion of rhet. and p.

Moreover, as *inventio* declined in prominence, *elocutio* rose, in fashion at least, not only in the new rhetorics of the 16th c. but in the new poetics, the new literary theories of the time. With the rise of the vernacular over Lat. as the lang. of lit., scholarship, and commerce, rhetorical theories burgeoned with discussions of style, suffused with the restored Ciceronian hierarchy (high, middle, and low or plain styles), further cutting across what few boundaries yet remained between rhet. and p. Although Thomas Wilson, who wrote the first Ciceronian rhet. in Eng. (1553), stayed within rhetorical genres for his examples, other traditional stylists such as Sherry, Peacham, and Fraunce treated *elocutio* by drawing virtually all of their examples from vernacular p. Puttenham's *Arte of English Poesie* (1589) devotes much attention to style and is equally a work on rhetorical *elocutio*, involved as both arts are in what Puttenham regards as the courtly requirements of "dissembling."

Puttenham's book, like many of the Continental poetics of the time (Du Bellay, Ronsard, Peletier), divides theory along the lines of the first three offices of traditional rhet.: *inventio, dispositio, elocutio*. But this rhetoricizing of poetics did little to salvage the rapidly disappearing uniqueness of rhetorical thought, including those poetics that had clear bearing on compositional matters. Geoffrey's advice to medieval poets, to invent by thinking of structure first, was seldom superseded. The "inventive" office, Puttenham taught, was to be performed by the "phantasticall part of man," his imagination, and controlled by choice of genre and by decorum (qq.v.). Audience-anchored doctrines of rhetorical *inventio*—whether the Aristotelian search for the means of persuasion via the probable or the Ciceronian pro-and-contra reasoning through a grid of topics toward eloquence—were to all intents and purposes dead. Nor did either of these doctrines play a significant role in the new literary theories fostered by the recovery of Aristotle's *Poetics*, such as those by the 16th-c. humanists Robortelli and Castelvetro, though two terminologies co-existed. Throughout 17th- and 18th-c. poetics, Aristotelian plot ("fable"), character ("manners"), thought ("sentiments"), and diction continued to exist side-by-side with Ciceronian terminology ("passions," "propriety"). *Inventio* remained the creator's first responsibility, but its considerations of audience centered mainly in decorum. Too, whereas in rhet., *inventio* became the unsystematic action of a solitary mind, in poetics it became largely exculpatory (it was, as Dryden put it in 1667, "the first happiness of the poet's imagination"). In the 18th c., the creative processes began to be scrutinized by the new science of psychology and taught through whatever relics of ancient rhet. were refashionable. Among those relics, *elocutio*, or style, retained greater prominence than *inventio*, and for centuries constituted virtually the whole of rhet., only to become the scapegoat of conscious artifice in romantic and postromantic poetics (q.v.), and ultimately to be revived as an important feature of modern interp.

Two remaining offices of rhet. have received comparatively little attention over the centuries. *Actio*, claimed by Demosthenes as the *sine qua non* of persuasion, did achieve some vogue in the 18th and 19th cs. under the name of "elocution." An effort to scientize delivery, which began with John Bulwer in 1644, occupied the attention of 18th-c. lexicographers and actors (Thomas Sheridan, John Mason) in teaching graceful gesture and correct phonation (now called "pronunciation"). With the teachings of Del Sartre in the 19th c., the movement had an impact, through mannered recitations, on Eng. and Am. education, on p. written to be recited, on styles of acting, and on later "modern" dance. *Memoria*, the storehouse of wisdom as it was known in rhet., and the mother of the Muses, was resistant to much theorizing outside medicine, where it was studied as a faculty of the soul (Yates). Rhyme was early considered not only a figure but a mnemonic device; so was the pithy form of eloquence known as *sententia*. When the two were combined (as in Edgar's speech closing *King Lear*, "The oldest hath borne most; we that are young / Shall never see so much, nor live so long"), a *terminus ad quem* was made memorable. The art of memory also became involved with the creation of fantastic images (the more fantastic, Quintilian advised, the easier to remember) and elaborate "memory theaters" for the rapid recall of complex, even encyclopedic knowledge.

In sum, whether one considers the interp. of p. or its composition, a shared interest in persuasion, eloquence, or even simply form and style has always linked rhet. and p. The fragmentation of rhet. and its dispersal through various disciplines and critical approaches were steady developments in Western culture after the Ren., particularly after the rise of science and of formalist crit. Now the uniqueness of p. is arguably more fully understood than that of rhet. On the other hand, modern efforts to reestablish rhetorical *inventio* (e.g. Perelman) may ultimately serve to reauthenticate rhet. too as *sui generis*. See also FIGURE, SCHEME, TROPE; POETICS.   T.O.S.

SOURCES CITED IN TEXT: R. Sherry, *A Treatise of Schemes and Tropes* (1550); T. Wilson, *The Arte of Rhetorique* (1553); S. Minturno, *De poeta* (1559); J. C. Scaliger, *Poetices libri septem* (1561, 1581); P. Sidney, *An Apology for Poetrie* (1583); A. Fraunce, *The Arcadian Rhetorike* (1588); H. Peacham, *The Garden of Eloquence*, 2d ed. (1593); B. Jonson, *Timber* (1641); J. Bulwer, *Chironomia* (1644); J. Dryden, Preface to *Annus mirabilis* (1667); J. Mason, *An Essay on Elocution* (1748); T. Sheridan, *A Course of Lectures on Elocution* (1762); J. S. Mill,

"Thoughts on P. and Its Varieties" [1833], *Dissertations and Discussions* (1859); P. Verlaine, "Art poétique" (1884); J. E. Spingarn, "The New Crit." [1910], *Crit. and America* (1924); I. A. Richards, *Practical Crit.* (1929); K. Burke, *Counter Statement* (1931); B. Croce, *The Defence of P.* (tr. 1933); E. Olson, "Rhet. and the Appreciation of Pope," *MP* 37 (1939); Brooks; T. S. Eliot, *The Three Voices of P.* (1953); R. Jakobson and M. Halle, *Fundamentals of Lang.* (1956); Frye; G. T. Wright, *The Poet in the Poem* (1962); R. Barthes, *S / Z* (1970); N. Holland, *5 Readers Reading* (1975); S. E. Errington, *A Study of Genre* (1975); Culler; Derrida; W. Iser, *The Act of Reading* (1978); S. Fish, *Is There a Text in this Class?* (1980); *The Reader in the Text*, ed. S. R. Suleiman and I. Crossman (1980); J. Gage, *In the Arresting Eye* (1981); W. C. Booth, *The Rhet. of Fiction*, 2d ed. (1983); P. de Man, *The Rhet. of Romanticism* (1984); B. Connelly, *Arab Folk Epic and Identity* (1986); A. Sweeney, *A Full Hearing* (1987).

BIBLIOGRAPHIES: D. Breuer and G. Kopsch, "Rhetorik-Lehrbücher des 16. bis 20. Jahrhunderts," *Rhetorik: Beiträge zu ihrer Gesch. in Deutschland vom 16.–20. Jahrhundert*, ed. H. Schanze (1974); *Historical Rhet.: An Annot. Bibl.*, ed. W. Horner (1980); R. Jamison and J. Dyck, *Rhetorik—Topik—Argumentation: Bibliographie zur Redelehre und Rhetorikforschung im deutschsprachigen Raum 1945 bis 1979/80* (1983); H. F. Plett, *Englische Rhetorik und Poetik, 1479–1660: Eine systematische Bibl.* (1985); J. J. Murphy, *Med. Rhet.: A Select Bibl.*, 2d ed. (1989).

HANDBOOKS AND SURVEYS: R. F. Howes, *Historical Studies of Rhet. and Rhetoricians* (1961); M. H. Nichols, *Rhet. and Crit.* (1962); E. Black, *Rhetorical Crit.* (1965); H. Lausberg, *Elemente der literarischen Rhetorik*, 3d ed. (1967), *Handbuch der literarischen Rhetorik*, 2d ed., 2 v. (1973)—the fullest treatment currently available; L. A. Sonnino, *A Handbook to 16th-C. R.* (1968); P. Dixon, *Rhet.* (1971); W. Jens, "Rhetorik," *Reallexikon* 3.432–56—extensive bibl.; A. J. Quinn, *Figures of Speech* (1982); *Dict. of Literary-Rhetorical Conventions of the Eng. Ren.*, ed. M. Donker and G. M. Muldrow (1982); H. Beristáin, *Diccionario de retórica y poética* (1985); *Methods of Rhetorical Crit.*, ed. B. L. Brock et al., 3d ed. (1989); E. P. J. Corbett, *Cl. Rhet. for the Mod. Student*, 3d ed. (1990); *The Present State of Scholarship in Historical and Contemp. Rhet.*, ed. W. B. Horner, 2d ed. (1990); R. A. Lanham, *A Handlist of Rhetorical Terms*, 2d ed. (1991); *Historisches Wörterbuch der Rhet.*, ed. G. Ueding and W. Jens (forthcoming).

HISTORIES, THEORIES, TEXTS, AND STUDIES: (1) Classical: J. C. G. Ernesti, *Lexicon technologiae graecorum rhetoricae*, 8 v. (1795; rpt 1 v., 1962), *Lexicon technologiae latinorum rhetoricae* (1797; rpt 1 v., 1983)—the fullest mod. sources, though rare; *Rhetores graeci*, ed. C. Walz, 9 v. (1832–36); *Rhetores graeci*, ed. L. Spengel, 3 v. (1856); *Rhetores latini minores*, ed. R. Halm (1863); E. M. Cope, *An Intro. to Aristotle's Rhet.* (1867); R. Volkmann, *Die Rhetorik der Griechen und Römer in systematischer Übersicht*,

2d ed. (1885); C. S. Baldwin, *Ancient Rhet. and Poetic* (1924); W. Rhys Roberts, *Greek Rhet. and Lit. Crit.* (1928); L. S. Hultzén, "Aristotle's *Rhet.* in England to 1600," Diss., Cornell (1932); W. Kroll, "Rhetorik," Pauly-Wissowa, supp., 7.1039–1138; L. Arbusow, *Colores rhetorici* (1948); *Artium Scriptores*, ed. L. Radermacher (1951); M. L. Clarke, *Rhet. at Rome* (1953); D. L. Clark, *Rhet. in Greco-Roman Education* (1957); G. A. Kennedy, *The Art of Persuasion in Greece* (1963)—best Eng. account of Gr. oratory and rhet., *Quintilian* (1969), *The Art of Rhet. in the Roman World, 300* B.C.–A.D. *300* (1972), *Cl. Rhet. and Its Christian and Secular Trad. from Ancient to Mod. Times* (1980), *Gr. Rhet. Under Christian Emperors* (1983); B. Weinberg, "Rhet. After Plato," *DHI*; *Readings in Cl. Rhet.*, ed. T. W. Benson and M. H. Prosser (1969); M. H. McCall, Jr., *Ancient Rhetorical Terms of Similarity and Comparison* (1970); H. Caplan, *Of Eloquence: Studies in Ancient and Med. Rhet.* (1970); A. Scaglione, *The Cl. Theory of Composition from Its Origins to the Present* (1972); *A Synoptic Hist. of Cl. Rhet.*, ed. J. J. Murphy (1972); A. Hellwig, *Untersuchungen zur Theorie der Rhetorik bei Platon und Aristoteles* (1973); G. L. Kustas, *Studies in Byzantine Rhet.* (1973); R. W. Smith, *The Art of Rhet. in Alexandria* (1974); W. Eisenhut, *Einführung in die antike Rhetorik* (1974); J. Martin, *Antike Rhetorik: Technik und Methode* (1974); *Quintilian on the Teaching of Speaking and Writing*, tr. J. J. Murphy (1987); H. L. F. Drijepondt, *Die Antike Theorie der Varietas* (1979); K. Heldmann, *Antike Theorien über Entwicklung und Verfall der Redekunst* (1982); G. Williams, *Figures of Thought in Roman P.* (1980); H. Maguire, *Art and Eloquence in Byzantium* (1981); D. A. Russell, *Crit. in Antiquity* (1981); Norden; M. Fuhrmann, *Die antike Rhetorik* (1984); *CHLC*; *Readings from from Cl. Rhet.*, ed. P. P. Matsen et al. (1990); T. Cole, *The Origins of Rhet. in Ancient Greece* (1991).

(2) *Medieval*: J. M. Manly, "Chaucer and the Rhetoricians," *PBA* 12 (1926); C. S. Baldwin, *Med. Rhet. and Poetic* (1928); A. C. Bartlett, *The Larger Rhetorical Patterns in Anglo-Saxon Poetry* (1935); W. S. Howell, *The Rhet. of Alcuin and Charlemagne* (1941); R. McKeon, "Rhet. in the Middle Ages," *Speculum* 17 (1942); Sr. M. Joseph, *The Trivium*, 3d ed. (1948); H. Kökeritz, "Rhetorical Word-Play in Chaucer," *PMLA* 69 (1954); Curtius, chs. 4, 8; J. J. Murphy, "A New Look at Chaucer and the Rhetoricians," *RES* 15 (1964), *Rhet. in the Middle Ages* (1974), *Med. Rhet.: A Select Bibl.* (above), ed., *Three Med. Rhetorical Arts* (1971); *Readings in Med. Rhet.*, ed. J. M. Miller et al. (1973).

(3) *Renaissance to Modern*: D. L. Clark, *Rhet. and P. in the Eng. Ren.* (1922); I. A. Richards, *Practical Crit.* (1929), *The Philosophy of Rhet.* (1936); M. T. Herrick, *The Poetics of Aristotle in England* (1930), *The Fusion of Horatian and Aristotelian Lit. Crit., 1531–1555* (1946); K. Burke, *Counter Statement* (1931), *A Grammar of Motives* (1944), *A Rhet. of Motives* (1950); C. Winkler, *Elemente der Rede: Gesch. ihrer Theorie 1750–1850* (1931); Patterson;

W. Taylor, *A Dict. of the Tudor Figures of Rhet.* (1937); H. D. Rix, *Rhet. in Spenser's Poetry* (1940); W. G. Crane, *Wit and Rhet. in the Ren.* (1941); V. L. Rubel, *Poetic Diction in the Eng. Ren.* (1941)—wider scope than title indicates; Sr. M. Joseph, *Shakespeare's Use of the Arts of Lang.* (1947); R. Tuve, *Elizabethan and Metaphysical Imagery* (1947); Crane; Abrams; W. S. Howell, *Logic and Rhet. in England, 1500–1700* (1956), *18th-C. British Logic and Rhet.* (1971), *Poetics, Rhet., and Logic* (1975); W. J. Ong, *Ramus, Method, and the Decay of Dialogue* (1958); J. B. Broadbent, "Milton's Rhet.," *MP* 56 (1958–59), *Some Graver Subject* (1960); H.-G. Gadamer, *Wahrheit und Methode* (1960); W. C Booth, *The Rhet. of Fiction* (1961); Weinberg; O. B. Hardison, Jr., *The Enduring Monument* (1962); U. Stötzer, *Deutsche Redekunst in 17. und 18. Jh.* (1962); M.-L. Linn, *Studien zur deutschen Rhetorik und Stilistik im 19. Jahrhundert* (1963); C. Neumeister, *Grundsätze der forensischen Rhetorik* (1964); F. A. Yates, *The Art of Memory* (1966); G. Genette, *Figures I, II, III* (1966, 1969, 1972), selections tr. as *Figures of Literary Discourse* (1982); M. L. Colish, *The Mirror of Lang.* (1968); B. Hathaway, *Marvels and Commonplaces* (1968); E. P. J. Corbett, *Rhetorical Analyses of Literary Works* (1969); E. D. Hirsch, Jr., *Validity in Interp.* (1969); C. Perelman and L. Olbrechts-Tyteca, *The New Rhet.* (tr. 1969); W. Barner, *Barock-Rhetorik* (1970); C. Trinkaus, *In Our Image and Likeness*, 2 v. (1970); J. L. Kinneavy, *A Theory of Discourse* (1971); *The Rhet. of Ren. P. from Wyatt to Milton*, ed. T. O. Sloan and R. B. Waddington (1974); W. Trimpi, *The Quality of Fiction* (1974), *Muses of One Mind* (1983); R. A. Lanham, *The Motives of Eloquence* (1976); Group Mu, *Rhétorique de la poésie* (1977); W. J. Kennedy, *Rhetorical Norms in Ren. Lit.* (1978); M. Fumaroli, *L'Âge d'eloquence: Rhétorique et 'res literaria' de la ren. au seuil de l'epoque classique* (1980); P. Valesio, *Novantiqua: Rhetorics as a Contemp. Theory* (1980); J. J. Murphy, *Ren. Rhet.: A Short-Title Catalog* (1981), ed., *Ren. Eloquence* (1983); Group Mu; J. P. Houston, *The Rhet. of P. in the Ren. and 17th C.* (1983); D. Rice and P. Schofer, *Rhetorical Poetics* (1983); T. O. Sloane, *Donne, Milton, and the End of Humanist Rhet.* (1985); A. F. Kinney, *Humanist Poetics* (1986); K. Meerhoff, *Rhétorique et poétique au XVIe siècle en France* (1986); F. Houlette, *19th-C. Rhet.: An Enumerative Bibl.* (1988); D. K. Shuger, *Sacred Rhet.: The Christian Grand Style in the Eng. Ren.* (1988); R. J. Fogelin, *Figuratively Speaking* (1988); B. Vickers, "Rhet. and Poetics," *Cambridge Hist. of Ren. Philosophy*, ed. C. B. Schmitt (1988), *In Defence of Rhet.* (1988), *Cl. Rhet. in Eng. Poetry*, 2d ed. (1989); R. Barilli, *Rhet.*, tr. G. Menozzi (1989); S. Fish, "Rhet.," *Critical Terms for Literary Study*, ed. F. Lentricchia and T. McLaughlin (1990); *The Rhetorical Trad.: Readings from Cl. Times to the Present*, ed. P. Bizzell and B. Herzberg (1990); *The Rhet. of Blair, Campbell, and Whately*, ed. J. L. Golden and E. P. J. Corbett, rev. ed. (1990); *Richards on Rhet.*, ed. A. E. Berthoff (1990); *The*

Ends of Rhet., ed. J. Bender and D. E. Wellbery (1990); N. Johnson, *19th-C. Rhet. in North America* (1991).

NONWESTERN: G. Jenner, *Die poetischen Figuren der Inder von Bhamaha bis Mammata* (1968); E. Gerow, *A Glossary of Indian Figures of Speech* (1971); S. A. Bonebakker, *Materials for the Hist. of Arabic Rhet. from the Hilyat al-muha-dara of Ha-timi* (1975); M.-C. Porcher, *Figures de style en Sanskrite* (1978); K. S. Y. Kao, "Rhet.," in Nienhauser et al.—Chinese. T.V.F.B.

RHETORICAL ACCENT. See ACCENT.

RHETORICAL CRITICISM. See CRITICISM; DE-CONSTRUCTION; INFLUENCE; TWENTIETH-CEN-TURY POETICS, *American and British*.

RHÉTORIQUEURS, *grands rhétoriqueurs*. Fr. poets of the late 15th and early 16th c., particularly active at the court of Burgundy and, later, at the Parisian court. Their work is characterized by extensive allegory, obscure diction, and intricately experimental meters and stanza forms, and in their technical innovations they performed an important, if usually unacknowledged, service for later Fr. poets. Despite their courtly activity, the r. were generally bourgeois in their antecedents and, in this respect as in their formalism, they are analogous to the German *Meistersinger* and the Dutch *rederijkers* (qq.v.). Their formalism, related to the late medieval confusion of rhetoric and poetics, makes the name by which they are known at least partially appropriate to their work, but it ought to be recognized that they and their contemporaries did not, in all probability, call themselves r., which is a literary-historical designation dating from a much later period.

The first of the r. was Alain Chartier (fl. 1430), and other members of the trad. include J. d'Autun, J. Bouchet, Chastellain, Crétin, Gringore, A. de La Vigne, Lemaire de Belges (considered the best of the group), J. Marot (father of the more famous Clément Marot), Meschinot, Molinet, J. Parmentier, and O. de Saint Gelais. The poetry of the r. was severely criticized by the School of Lyons and by the *Pléiade* (q.v.), a judgment generally maintained up to the mid 20th c., but in recent years a vigorous current of opinion has arisen in their favor. Scholars such as Jodogne, Rigolot, and Zumthor have sought to rehabilitate the r. by establishing texts, by stressing their technical achievements in versification, and by analyzing their contribution in areas such as the *déploration funèbre*, satire, and onomastics. These scholars maintain that the r. are best explained from a sociohistorical and global point of view, that their role in the general devel. of Fr. poetry has been underestimated, and that their work offers a rich area for further study. See also SECONDE RHETO-RIQUE.—*Recueil d'arts de séconde rhétorique*, ed. E. Langlois (1902); Patterson; R. H. Wolf, *Der Stil der*

R. (1939); W. L. Wiley, "Who Named Them R?" *Mediaeval Studies J. D. M. Ford* (1948); H. Liebrecht, *Les Chambres de rhétorique* (1948); *Fleurs de rhétorique*, ed. K. Chesney (1950); F. Simone, *Umanesimo, Rinascimento, Barocco in Francia* (1968); Y. Giraud and M.-R. Jung, *Litt. française*, v. 1: *La Ren.* (1972); P. Jodogne, "R.," *DCLF* 2 (1972); I. D. McFarlane, *Ren. France, 1470–1530* (1974); C. Martineau-Génieys, *Le Thème de la mort dans la poésie française de 1450–1550* (1977); F. Rigolot, *Poétique et onomastique* (1977), *Le Texte de la Ren.* (1983); P. Zumthor, *Le Masque et la lumière* (1978), ed., *Anthologie des grands r.* (1978); *Pre-Pléiade Poetry*, ed. J. Nash (1985); Hollier, 127 ff.
A.PR.; I.J.W.

RHOPALIC VERSE (Gr. "club-like," i.e. thicker toward the end, from *rhopalon*, the club of Hercules). "Wedge verse," in which each word is a syllable longer than the one before it, e.g. *Iliad* 3.182, "o makar Atreide, moiregenes, olbiodaimon," which begins with a monosyllable and closes with a fifth word of 6 syllables, or Virgil's "Ex quibus insignis pulcherrima Deiopeia," or Crashaw's "Wishes to his Supposed Mistress." See OULIPO.— Morier; T. Augarde, *Oxford Guide to Word Games* (1984). T.V.F.B.

RHUPYNT. See AWDL.

RHYME.

    I. DEFINITION
    II. TAXONOMY
    III. TERMINOLOGY
    IV. ANALOGUES
    V. FUNCTIONS
    VI. LANGUAGE AND ART
    VII. DATA
    VIII. ORIGIN AND HISTORY

Sidney calls r. "the chiefe life" of modern versifying, and indeed so it must still seem, despite the advent of the great trad. of Eng. blank verse (q.v.) from Shakespeare to Tennyson and even the advent of the several free-verse prosodies after 1850: the first edition of the *Oxford Book of Eng. Verse* (1900) contains 883 poems, of which only 16 lack r. And what is true of Eng. is even more true of Rus., where the trad. of r. is more extensively developed, and esp. Fr., where r. is truly fundamental to the whole system of versification. R. is, as Oscar Wilde said, "the one chord we have added to the Gr. lyre."

It is often thought that rhyming is one of the most conservative aspects of versecraft. As with every other poetic device, however, it is so only if one chooses to make it so. In periods of intense experimentation, new forms proliferate; in periods of retrenchment, old forms are resuscitated in new contexts. New uses expand the r. lexicon and thereby the scope of poetry: they Make It New. Hence it would be more accurate to say, with

Clark, that "poetry is the growing end of lang., in the matter of r. as in other respects."

R. is also sometimes denigrated on the grounds that it limits semantic possibilities and imposes severe constraints on expression, making of rhymed poetry some kind of artificial, strained, and peculiar lang., some hobbled Pegasus. But complaining that poetic expression is limited or weakened because written in r. misses the point by mistaking convention for nature. It would never occur to anyone to complain that lang. is weaker because carried on in nouns and verbs: these are a given. The question to ask about rhymed verse is not, therefore, whether it would have been better set as blank verse or free: every aesthetic form is presumably adequate to any expressive purpose just as every lang. is presumptively adequate to the expressive needs of its speakers. The only question is what resources this particular form is able to offer, and how effectively they are used.

I. DEFINITION. In the specific sense of the term as used in Eng., r. is the linkage in poetry of two syllables at line end (for internal rhyming see below) which have identical medial vowels and final consonants but differ in initial consonant(s)—syllables which, in short, begin differently and end alike. This is the paradigmatic case for Eng., but in the half-dozen other langs. where r. has been developed as a major poetic device, many other varieties have been developed, resulting in more expansive definitions admitting any one of several kinds of sound echo in verse (see below). More broadly, however, we must say that r. is the phonological correlation (see EQUIVALENCE) of differing semantic units at distinctive points in verse. It is essential that the definition not be framed solely in terms of sound, for that would exclude the cognitive function.

R. calls into prominence simultaneously a complex set of responses based on *identity* and *difference.* On the phonic level, the likeness of the rhyming syllables (at their ends) points up their difference (at their beginnings). The phonic semblance (and difference) then points up semantic semblance or difference: the equivalence of the r. syllables or words on the phonic level implies a relation of likeness or difference on the semantic level. Difference and identity are thus made antinomian in r.: they mutually entail one another. R. in this sense, i.e. "end r.," is the chief form of sound (q.v.) patterning in modern verse, and provides, with meter (q.v.), the two axes—vertical and horizontal—for the schematization of elements (hence meanings) in poetry. R. is not, therefore, a merely sonal phenomenon: it deploys sound similarity as the means to semantic and structural ends.

Crucial to these ends, as with all others in prosody, is segmentation. As with the clausulae of late-antique prose rhythm (q.v.), r. marks the ends of runs of syllables in speech and thereby segments the soundstream into equal or perceived-equal units or sections: this segmentation in turn establishes equivalence, which is essential to repetition (q.v.) and the effects it is capable of. Lotman says that if all equivalences in the poetic line are classed as either positional (rhythmic) or euphonic (sonal), then r. is created at the intersection of the two sets (119).

From the usual sense of the term "r."—i.e. the sound common to two or more words, or a word that echoes another word—other senses derive by synecdoche, i.e. (1) a poem in rhymed verse, or (2) rhymed verse in general; or by metonymy, i.e. (3) any kind of sound echo between words (e.g. alliteration, assonance, consonance [qq.v.]), or (4) more generally, any kind of correspondence, congruence, or accord (cf. James Russell Lowell's "of which he was as unaware as the blue river is of its r. with the blue sky").

The spelling "rhyme" became common in Eng. in the 17th c.; the earlier Ren. and ME spelling, "rime," derives from OF *rime, ritme* < Med Lat. *rithmi* < Lat. *rithmus, rhythmus* < Gr. *rhythmos.* The OF form gave the Occitan, Sp., Cat., Port., and It. cognates *rima* and MHG, ON, and OIcel *rim,* later *rima* "rhymed poem, ballad" (see RIMUR). This form of *rim* is not to be confused with (though it is related, importantly, to) OHG, OE *rim* "number," or with OE, ON *hrim* "hoar-frost," later "rime-frost," which form Coleridge uses for salt-spray in the *Ancient Mariner.* The term *rim* in the modern sense of r. first appears in an Anglo-Norman rhymed sermon of the early 12th c.; it is in the course of this century that r. became a central feature of short-lined lyric poetry in Occitan and came to replace assonance in the *laisses* of the OF *chansons de geste* (q.v.). In Eng. the spelling *rime / ryme* for vernacular, accentual, rhymed verse was preserved to ca. 1560, when Classicizing spelling reform brought in *rithme / rythme* (pronounced to r. with "crime" and spelled *ri'me* by Jonson), current to 1700, after which time *rhythm* became the spelling for that concept in the modern sense. About 1600, however, *rhime/rhyme* appears, presumably to distinguish rhyming from rhythmical/metrical effects; *rhyme* subsequently won out, though the (historically correct) spelling *rime* has never entirely disappeared.

In Med. Lat., *rithmus/rythmus* denotes *versus rithmici,* "rhythmical verse," meaning verse whose meter is based on accent not quantity (*versus metrici*) and which employs end-r. Lat. rhythmical verse appears as early as the 3rd–4th cs. A.D. and reaches its culmination in the 12th c., though verse written on quantitative principles continued to be written throughout the Middle Ages. It is this fact—two metrical systems side by side in Med. Lat.—which is responsible for the modern phrase "without r. or reason," meaning neither *rhythmus* nor *ratio,* i.e. not any kind of verse at all. In short, the word for accentually based and rhymed verse in Med. Lat. vacillated between an -i- and -y- spelling for its vowel; the Ren. distinguished these two criteria and hence terms for them. Ren. spelling reform affected the visual shapes of the words; pronunciation diverged later. "Rhythm" and "r." are thus intimately related not only etymologically but conceptually (see below).

There are two final points about definition. First, the definition of what counts as r. is conventional and cultural: it expands and contracts from one national poetry, age, verse trad., and genre to another. Hence definition must shortly give way to a taxonomy of types (below). Second, there is the issue of positing r. at line end itself (see LINE). Žirmunskij, looking at r. as not only sound echo but also the marker of line end, sees that function as having effect on the rhythmic organization of the line. And indeed it is commonly assumed that r. exerts a metrical function in marking the ends of the lines. But of course r. is not restricted to line end, suggesting that "*any* sound repetition that has an organizing function in the metrical composition of the poem should be included in the concept of r." (1923, 9; italics added). Further, as de Cornulier argues, r. does not exactly reside at line end: its positioning shapes the entire structure of the line, so that we should more accurately say that the r. resides in the entire line. Removing rs. from lines does not merely render them rhymeless; it alters their lexical-semantic structure altogether. End r. is no mere ornament.

II. TAXONOMY. R. correlates syllables by sound. We may describe the structure of the syllable (q.v.) as initial consonant or consonant cluster (the so-called "support" or "prop" consonant [Fr. *consonne d'appui*]; this may be in the zero state, i.e. absent) + medial vowel (or diphthong) + final consonant (or cluster, if present), which we may schematize as CVC. If we ask which elements of a syllable can be repeated in a second syllable in correspondence with the first, letting underlining denote a sound repeated identically, then seven configurations are possible (the eighth possibility is null; these are simply the permutations of a set of three elements), having these forms and Eng. names:

1. C̲V C alliteration (*bad boy*)
2. C V̲ C assonance (*back/rat*)
3. C V C̲ consonance (*back/neck*)
4. C̲V̲ C reverse r. (*back/bat*)
5. C̲V C̲ ([no standard term] frame r., pararhyme (*back/buck*)
6. C V̲ C̲ r. strictly speaking (*back/rack*)
7. C̲V̲ C̲ rich r., *rime riche*, or identical r. (*bat* [wooden cyl-sinder]/*bat* [flying creature].

This schema presumes that both syllables are identical in all other respects, i.e. their phonological and morphological characteristics—for example, that both syllables are stressed monosyllables. But of course this is not usually the case, certainly not for Fr. or It. or Rus., not even for Eng. A more elaborate taxonomy would subsume all such vari-

ants. To date, no such inventory of r. structures has yet been given. When it is, it will explain a number of effects as yet unaccounted for, correlate and clarify relations between forms in the same or different langs. hitherto thought unrelated or remote, and provide a comprehensive and synthetic overview of the structure of the system, showing how r.-processes function *as* an integral system. It will also, presumably, correlate with the schema of rhetorical figures and processes given by Group Mu.

As a preliminary to such a taxonomy, we may distinguish 12 criteria for the analysis and categorization of r. types:

1. By the *number of syllables* involved in the r., i.e.: (a) Single, monosyllabic, or masculine. This is norm or zero state of r., at least in Eng.—two stressed monosyllables, e.g. *Keats/beets* (John Crowe Ransom's examples, here and below). Whether or not this is the norm in any given lang. depends on the morphological and syntactic structure of that lang., i.e. whether it is inflectional or positional or mixed. All other more complex forms of r. are generated by *extension*, either rightward into syllables following the rhyming syllable or leftward to the consonant or syllables preceding the vowel, esp. proclitics and separate words (Ger. *erweiterter Reim*).

(b) Double, disyllabic, or feminine (see MASCULINE AND FEMININE), e.g. *Shelley/jelly*. Two contiguous syllables in each r. word that rhyme. In the paradigmatic case in Eng., both words are disyllables and have a trochaic word shape, and both rhyming syllables (the first in each word) are stressed and stand in the last metrical position (ictus) of the line. The post-rhyming syllables are pronounced but not stressed and are identical; metrically they do not count, they are "extrametrical." (It is also possible for the second syllables themselves also to r., e.g. *soreness/doorless*.) But these conditions do not apply in other langs., and even in Eng., many other complex and variant forms are possible (see below). Indeed, Eng. is probably not a good norm: in It., nearly all rs. are double or triple. Scherr usefully treats syllabic variance after the rhyming syllable in Rus. poetry under the rubric of "heterosyllabic" forms.

(c) Triple (Ger. *gleitender Reim*, "gliding"), also called *compound* and *multiple*, e.g. *Tennyson/venison*. Two extra (identical and extrametrical) syllables after the rhyming syllable. Triple rs. are of course rarer; usually they are mosaic (q.v.), since rhyming of more than two successive syllables is difficult in any lang. The effect in Eng. since Byron has almost always been comic. See TRIPLE RHYME.

2. By the *morphology* of the words which the rhyming syllables inhabit. The zero state is that the rhyming syllables are each monosyllabic words—i.e. that the rs. do not broach a word boundary. In double and triple rs., the words being rhymed are normally di- or polysyllabic, or a series of short words (*stayed with us, played with us*), or

ends of words followed by one or more whole words (be*seech him*/im*peach him*), but it is also possible to r. several short monosyllables with one polysyllable, known as "mosaic" r. in Eng. (*poet, know it*). In Welsh *cywydd* (q.v.) couplets, one of the rs. must be a monosyllable but the other a polysyllable. But if r. depends for its distinctive effects on the morphology of the particular words involved in the r., it also therefore depends on the morphological structure of the lang. itself as the ground against which the pattern becomes visible. Here the inflected Romance langs. will offer differing ground to the more heavily monosyllabic Germanic langs. and esp. hybrid Eng. This may lend credence to Scott's claim that r. does not have the same function in Fr. that it has in Eng. (1988, 11).

Inflectional endings are, as it were, the antithesis or reflex of r., though it is not accurate to say, as did Whitehall, that langs. in which like endings result automatically from inflection will never use r. as a structural device in verse. R. is occasionally to be found, consciously used, in the lit. of the Cl. langs. (see section VIII below). The notion of like endings, Gr. *homoeoteleuton* (q.v.), Lat. *similiter desinens*, is discussed by the ancients—Aristotle (*Rhetoric* 3.9.9–11), Dionysius of Halicarnassus (23), and Quintilian (9.3.77)—under the rubric of "verbal resemblance" or sound correspondence between clauses (*paromoeosis*). Late-antique rhymeprose (q.v.) continues this trad.; the "grammatical r." (q.v.) of the *Grands Rhétoriqueurs* (see RHETORIQUEURS) takes a different slant. But the two systems, case-endings and r., overwrite the same space and so in the main are mutually exclusive. And when, in any lang., rhyming is relatively easy, poets will tend to complicate it by employing forms of rich or identical r. (as in Fr.) or complex stanza forms (as in Occitan and Fr.) or both, or else by eschewing r. completely (as in blank verse). Poets who choose to r. in fact walk a tightrope between ease and difficulty: too easy rhyming or too difficult rhyming eventually produce the same result—the poetic disuse of r.

In some verse systems, the rules in a prosody survive sometimes for centuries after the linguistic facts on which they were originally based have disappeared. One of the chief instances of this process is the mute -e suffix in Fr., which disappeared from pronunciation in the 15th c. but was preserved in a set of elaborate r. rules into the 19th.

Since Eng. dropped nearly all its inflectional suffixes about a thousand years ago, the sets of rhyming words in Eng. are smaller, and different in character as well. How much smaller, however, is an interesting question, for it is often claimed that r. is much more difficult in Eng. than in other langs. But accurate statistical information about the relative "poverty" of r. in one lang. vs. another has yet to be assembled. Owing to the large number of ways in which Eng. words can terminate, the number of words which r. on a sound, on average,

is certainly under three, but the distribution is extremely uneven. The number of words which r. with only one other word is large (*mountain*/*fountain*, *babe*/astro*labe*), and those which cannot be rhymed at all is larger than one might suspect (e.g. *orange, chimney, breadth, circle, desert, monarch, month, virtue, wisdom*). But the rs. on words like "day" are legion.

One other way of approaching this issue, however, is to point out that r. depends less on the structure of the lang. than on the semantic field presently relevant in the poem: only some of the available rs. for a given word are possible candidates for use in a poem on a given subject. What this means, most generally, is that it is dangerous to discuss r. as an abstract entity divorced from the constraints imposed on it in each individual poem. The whole subject of morphology and r. is a large and complex subject which still remains to be mapped out.

3. By the *position of the stress* on the rhyming (and adjacent) syllables. Normally single rs. are ictic and stressed; double rs. add an extra unstressed syllable. Rhyming masculine with feminine words, i.e. a stressed monosyllable with a disyllable the rhyming syllable of which is unstressed (e.g. *sing / loving, free / crazy, afraid / decade*) Tatlock called "hermaphrodite" r. (an odd term, since male mating with female in love would not be thought so). Others have called it "apocopated" or "stressed-unstressed" r.; it was popular in the 16th–17th cs. and is used extensively by Donne and latterly by Pound (*Hugh Selwyn Mauberley*). There is also "unstressed r.," where the rhyming syllables are both unstressed or weak: e.g. *honey*/*motley, mysteries*/*litanies, wretchedness*/*featureless*. But there is some question whether this constitutes r. at all. Scherr calls all such cases in Rus. poetry "heteroaccentual" forms and cites the taxonomy given by Markov.

A related type rhymes a stressed syllable with one bearing only secondary speech stress, which is promoted under metrical ictus, e.g. *sees*/*mysteries*. Many r. pairs of this sort formerly differed in pronunciation and were good rs. in their time, though they are not now; others were not so, then as now. Rs. like *eye*/*harmony, eye*/*symmetry* (Blake), or *flies*/*mysteries* force the critic to call upon the researches of historical phonology.

Perhaps the most interesting case of all is the pair *die*/*poetry*, common in the Ren. There is some evidence (e.g. Alexander Gill) that, for words like "poetry," alternative pronunciations existed as late as the first quarter of the 17th c., one form pronounced as the word is today, to r. with "me," the other to r. with "die." If so, r. pairs like *poetry*/*die*—and others like *majesty*/*eye, crie*/*graciously*, and most others ending in -*ty* or -*ly*—may well have been good rs. for Shakespeare and the Ren. sonneteers, as they were for Milton. But the diphthongal ending apparently lost out, so that sometime after 1650 "poetry" and "die" ceased being a good

r. and became merely conventional. They may well have continued to be used by poets, but only on account of their having precedent. Whether or not poets after 1650 actually altered their pronunciation of "poetry," in reading aloud their verses, so as to r. with "die" is unknown; one may speculate that their acceptance of convention did not extend so far. If so, the reader would be expected to recognize such rs. as poetic convention, a kind of "poetic license" (q.v.) admissible on the grounds that they were so in a former state of the lang. A modern instance appears in Auden's elegy on Yeats: "Let the Irish vessel lie / Emptied of its poetry." But the evidence is very complex and uncertain, and the number of cases where later poets knowingly reproduce such archaic rs. must be few: far more important is the fact that in earlier stages of the lang. they were apparently good rs.

4. By the *lexical category* of the rhyming words. In much verse the rs. are commonly words of the same grammatical category, noun rhyming with noun, verb with verb. The phonic echo highlights semantic differences, certainly, but not functional ones. More striking effects are to be had by extending the differentiation, so that the words not only mean different things but function differently as well. The predominance of substantives for rs. creates a verse of a distinctive texture, whereas the use of function words gives a radically different texture and virtually demands enjambment (q.v.): thus Donne's "Love's not so pure and abstract as they used / To say who have no mistress but their Muse" ("Love's Growth"). Even within substantives, the use of nouns for rs. gives a markedly different texture than the use of verbs, which, as the conveyors of action, energy, state, and change, take on even greater power when highlighted at line end. Wimsatt in his classic 1944 essay discusses the importance of this strategy, but detailed data has only very recently begun to be collected. Cohen, for example, reports that the 17th-c. Fr. Classicists used different-category rs. only 19% of the time, the Romantics 29%, and the Symbolists 31% (1966, 85); one would like to see Eng. data for comparison.

5. By the *degree of closeness of the sound match* in the r. The standard definition for "true" or "perfect" r. (these are the usual Eng. terms; cf. Ger. *reiner Reim*, Rus. *tochnaia rifma*) is relatively narrow, with the result that the other collateral forms, near r. and eye r. (qq.v.), are problematized. But in other verse trads. this is not the case: Rus., for example, admits "inexact r." as part of the standard definition of canonical r. (see Scherr). Welsh poetry (q.v.) recognizes a very large category of "generic r." (q.v.) in which sounds echo closely but not exactly. But it is misleading to frame the analysis in terms of "near" vs. "perfect" to begin with: exactness is not the only or even the most important criterion in some verse systems. As a number of critics (e.g. Burke, Small) have observed,

sounds themselves are related to each other in phonology in categories; within these categories, individual sounds—such as voiced and voiceless fricatives—are interchangeable in some verse trads. To recognize this fact is to recognize that sounds come in "equivalence sets," e.g. nasals (m, n, and ng) or sibilants (s, f, z, sh, zh), which a poet may use to expand the range of rhyming. This approach should neutralize mechanistic attempts to assess the "purity" of rs. (Ger. *Reinheit des reims*). In general it may be said that the strictness of the definition of "true" r. in langs. varies in inverse ratio to the ease of rhyming in that lang., which is itself a function of morphology and syntactic rules: langs. in which rhyming is relatively easy will impose additional constraints, such as the rules constraining the gender of rs. in Fr.; langs. in which it is more difficult will admit wider variation.

6. By the relationship between the sonal figuration created in the r. and the *semantic fields* of the words. R. is a figure of sound, but of course words in poetry as in lang. bear sense, and both levels of information are delivered to the auditor or reader not separately but simultaneously: r. therefore figures meaning. This is how r. is able to increase the amount of information carried in verse, despite the fact that the establishment of a r. scheme (q.v.) leads to expectedness, normally reductive of information load.

Of such semantic figuration there are two possibilities: either sound similarity can imply semantic similarity in words otherwise so unrelated that, in prose, no relation would have ever been noticed; or sound similarity can emphasize contrast in two words that echo. As Lotman puts it, "phonic coincidence only accentuates semantic difference" (123). Gerard Manley Hopkins held that the beauty of r., for the Eng. reader at least, "is lessened by any likeness the words may have beyond that of sound" (*Note-books and Papers*). The "richness" or "sonority" of a r. is therefore not merely a function of the degree of phonic echo but of the semantic aspect as well (Lotman 97).

Wimsatt cites a classic example from Pope's *Rape of the Lock*: "Whether the nymph shall break Diana's law, / Or some frail China jar receive a flaw." Wimsatt remarks that it is the r. which prompts us to ask in what way breaking Diana's law is like marring a valuable vase. The answer we will be led to is that, in Belinda's refined society, losing one's virginity is simply an indiscretion, a clumsiness, equivalent to scarring a Ming porcelain— both signs of poor taste. In this way, study of the semantic effects of the phonic coupling in the r. augments the hermeneutic process, directing us toward a deeper and more powerful interp. Wimsatt calls r., somewhat awkwardly, "alogical" and "counterlogical," by which he means not asemantic but simply bearing semantic import which runs in addition to, and sometimes counter to, the lexico-syntactic, denotative "logic" or sense of the words in the lines. However one chooses to describe it, this sense borne by the rs. is supplemental to the import the words would have borne were they merely set as prose (see VERSE AND PROSE), showing thereby the additional expressive resources of verseform.

At the same time, several poets and critics have remarked that the rs. particularly in a long work come to form a system of their own which is the correlate of an idiolect or, if it be influential, a dialect in natural lang. Clark remarks that "when a poet rs. well" it is "as if he had *invented* a new lang., which has r. as one of its natural characteristics" (176).

R. semantics is a vast subject only beginning to be explored. It was first charted by the Rus. Formalists, esp. Žirmunskij (1923), but his book was not known in the West until the 1960s: in the Anglo-Am. world it was Wimsatt's 1944 essay which paved the way, followed by Lotman's seminal 1970 book (tr. 1977) on the stratification of the artistic text (see also Nemoianu). Shapiro applies the Saussurean paradigm influenced by Peircean semiotics, i.e. markedness theory, under which distinctive features appear in pairs of binary opposites, one present one absent, the present one therefore *marked*: he shows by phonological analysis marked features which seemingly remote rs. have in common.

Study of r. semantics must examine both the semantic fields available in the lang. and those chosen for the poem. As every rhyming poet knows, choice of one word for a r. immediately constrains the range of words available for its mate(s), hence for extension or completion of the sense. In the lang., the sound shape, orthographic form, and semantic fields of each word are determined by the historical interaction of complex sets of both linguistic processes and the accidents of history (wars, migrations, customs). These constraints affect the poem's field of meaning and are in turn affected by choices made by the poet. Some semantic contrasts are already coded into the lang. as rs., e.g. *light / night, Gehalt / Gestalt*. These are pairs that must be actively avoided by serious poets as rs. so outworn that the (semantic) life has gone out of them altogether. Pope satirizes *breeze / trees* in the *Essay on Criticism*, but others—*anguish / languish, length / strength*—are easy to name. The fault in all these is that they seem to let the r. too obviously dictate the sense. A whole semantic field is coded into some r. pairs, e.g. *mad / bad, stranger / danger*.

One other consequence of the preceding is the expectedness or *surprise* of the r.: a common or unprepossessing first r. word followed by a startling or shocking mate from a radically different lexical category is almost certain to be used for either comic or satiric effect. Rs. can also be constructed from nonsense (q.v.) syllables and nonce words, as in Lewis Carroll.

7. By the effects of *further complication of sound patterning* in the r. words themselves. More than one pattern may be figured in the rhyming words: typically assonance or consonance is mounted on top of the r scheme, not as a reduction but as a complication. In Milton's sonnet "On the Late Massacre in Piedmont," for example, the octave rs. are *bones/ cold/ old/ stones/ groans/ fold /rolled/ moans*. The r. scheme is thus *abbaabba*, but the vowel is held constant, assonating *aaaaaaaa*. Milton's "On His Deceased Wife" rhymes *abbaabba cdcdcd* but assonates *aaaaaaaa bbbbbb*. "To the Lord General Cromwell" has for its octave rs. *cloud / rude/ fortitude/ ploughed/ proud/ pursued/ imbued/ loud*, also *abbaabba*, but all 8 lines in consonance on final -d. Yeats achieves the same effect in "Among School Children," reiterating the final consonant of *images/ those/ reveries/ repose/ presences/ knows/ symbolize/ enterprise*. This is r. yet more interwoven and complete.

8. By *participation* of the rs. *in sound patterning nearby*. Part of the perceived effect of the r. also depends on the density of sound patterning in the lines surrounding the r. words. Here we enter the realm of those larger constellations of sound which schematize the entire poetic text, over and above, though not apart from, the r. scheme (see SOUND; SOUND EFFECTS IN POETRY). Like r., these too impose a surplus of design upon the verbal material, binding words together; highlighting salient words; underlining, via phonetic echo, significant semantic parallels between otherwise disparate words; punctuating the seriatim flow of text processing by repetition of significant sounds recently heard and remembered; and marking the text as aesthetic through the increase of attention required—and rewarded—in reading.

9. By the *position in the line* of the rs. Normally r. in presumed to be end r., i.e. sound linkage of lines by marking their ends (it is known that ends of members in series have special cognitive "visibility"), but more complex forms rhyme the word at line end with other words line-internally, or rhyme two line-internal words in the same or successive lines, or both, thus opening up a spectrum of new possibilities for more complex sound figuration; see INTERNAL RHYME; LEONINE RHYME. Further, even the end-r. word itself may be hyphenated or broken over the line end to effect the r.: see BROKEN RHYME.

10. By the *interval* between the rs. Without the space or gap between the r. words, no r. is possible: hence the distance is no less significant than the repetition. In fact, repetition *requires* distance, the absence enabling the presence. The variance of distancing and of repetitions of course yields the patterning of r. in the stanza, i.e. the r. scheme; more interestingly, it also enables the distinction between "non-rs." and "anti-rs." Abernathy points out that it is not sufficient to characterize some types of verse as "unrhymed," for this fails to distinguish between "rhymeless" verse, wherein r. is neither required nor prohibited but merely unspecified, and "anti-rhymed" verse, such as blank

verse, where r. is specifically proscribed. R. schemes reveal intervals not only between rs. but also between unrhymed lines; and in some unrhymed verse, passages of deliberate r. may even appear (T. S. Eliot). It is also worth noting that rs. which are very widely separated *are not rs.* because they are not *perceived* so. There are in fact some hundred-odd rs. in *Paradise Lost*, despite Milton's strictures in his prefatory "Note" against "modern bondage" (his term for r.). But a r. not felt is not a r.

11. By the *order* or sequencing of the rs. The r. architectonics which is schematized in r. schemes binds lines into more complex stanza forms both isometric and heterometric (qq.v.). This is one of the chief pleasures of formal verse (see STANZA). R. schemes also reveal links with identical kinds of order in other domains such as rhet. or meter (Kiparsky, Laferriere). The scheme for the Petrarchan sonnet, for example, is *abbaabba cdecde*, i.e. an octave of two sets of envelope r. followed by a sestet of two tercets whose r. is repeated seriatim. The orders here are envelope (q.v.), a scheme of repetition in reverse, and sequence, repetition in order.

Normally, rhymed stanzas contain rs. which have at least one mate inside the same stanza; other less common but still important elements of order in rhyming are: monorhyme, i.e. iteration of the same r. sound (as in OF assonance, or triplets in couplet verse); lines whose r. is *indeterminate* or optional in the midst of other lines with obligatory participation in the r. scheme (marked with an *x* in the r. scheme); "isolated r." or "thorn rs." (Occitan *rim estramp*, Ger. *Korn*), lines which have a mate only in following stanzas; and rhymeless lines without mates anywhere in the poem (Ger. *Waise*, "orphan" lines; more exploited in Rus.). All these devices structure the aesthetic space either by adding higher levels of order or by opening up spaces within the order for some amount of free play.

12. By *sight versus sound*. In most poetry of all ages and langs., sound is the primary stratum, and rs. are based on sound correspondence; strictly speaking, the spelling of words is irrelevant. Too, spelling can mislead inattentive readers if they respond to the visual shape of the words not the aural. Still, this is a narrow view; and it is undeniable that literate poets of all ages have been aware to some degree of the visual dimension of poetry (Hollander's "poem in the eye"). The relations of sound to orthography in a given lang. are more manifold than is usually supposed, and these must be attended to. The first point is that fundamental processes of sound change in a lang., such as the Great Vowel Shift in Eng., have altered the pronunciation that some words formerly had, but since orthography tends to ossify—to change much more slowly, and via differing laws, than sound—some words that formerly rhymed and were spelled similarly now retain only the orthographic similarity. Some writers have called these

"historical rhymes," but this is only to say that in the original text they were authentic rs. and should be so understood now. Conversely, orthography has itself exerted an influence on pronunciation at times, so that words spelled alike come to be pronounced alike despite former difference: this phenomenon is called "spelling pronunciation."

An important related issue is that of rhyming in dialect poetry (q.v.) and dialect rs. in standard-dialect poetry. Orthography and time conceal some of these rs., such as Keats's Cockney rs., e.g. *thoughts/sorts* (with the -r- suppressed in Cockney slang; see COCKNEY SCHOOL), or the South Ger. dialect rs. of Goethe, Schiller, and others. The scope of such praxis is larger than one might think.

Some poets have exploited the visual forms of words to create visual analogues of aural r.: these maneuvers require rapid shifts in category recognition on the part of the reader to realize the nature of the sleight-of-hand (see EYE RHYME). Finally, the invention of script and then printing has exerted so powerful an influence on modern consciousness that poetry itself is now effectually a bivalent form wherein visuality comes to have, in the modern world, equal legitimacy with sound as the mode of poetic form, leading to the several forms of pattern poetry, concrete poetry, lettrisme, calligrammes, and visual poetry (qq.v.).

III. TERMINOLOGY. The terminologies for r., its varieties, and its analogues in the several Western langs. derive from the 12th c.; they are unsystematic and highly inconsistent. In Med. Lat., r. emerges from the Christian hymn (q.v.) trad. into the elaborate forms of rhyming in the silver-age poetry of the Carolingian Ren. (see Raby); in the vernaculars, rhyming achieves its first flowering in Occitan poetry (q.v.), where the troubadours (q.v.) exhibited, in their verse, perhaps the most sustained interest in r. ever seen in the West, before or since. From Occitan it passed to all the other European vernaculars, with later efflorescence in Northern France in the poetry of the *Rhétoriqueurs* in the late 15th–early 16th cs., influencing even, through Ger., the poetries of the Scandinavian countries. From this thumbnail history one would think that Fr. r. terminology would have dominated all others, incl. Eng. But precise terminology is mainly a critical and scholarly concern, not the poets', and since Eng. prosody developed out of 19th-c. Ger. philology, itself based on Classical Philology, the 20th c. inherited a confused and confusing apparatus.

Further, given the conservatism of traditional prosodists, one would think that r. terminology would be relatively consistent from one lang. to another. But all langs. do not admit the various morphological forms of r. with equal facility and so tend to develop one or another r. form more extensively. The practice of a major poet also has great effect. Thus, simple translation of a term from one lang. to another gives a misleading impression, for the effects of a given structure are not precisely the same in two different langs. This is a significant constraint on building cross-linguistic taxonomies and terminologies. It is not a constraint, however, on the more immediate problems of making the reference of terms clear and precise or of eliminating confusion. To date, no full and systematic analysis of the terminologies in the major Western langs.—Med. Lat, Occitan, OF, OE, ON, ME, MHG, and modern Ger., Fr., Eng., and Rus.—much less in the major Eastern langs., Chinese and Japanese, has yet been given. Since the most influential modern prosodies have been Fr. and Eng., a brief discussion of terminological issues therein will be instructive.   T.V.F.B.

A. *French*. In 19th- and early 20th-c. Fr. prosody, r. classification distinguished between phonemic material following the tonic (rhyming) vowel and phonemic material preceding it, thus:

(a) r. of tonic vowel alone:
rime pauvre or *faible*;
(b) r. of vowel + following consonant(s):
rime suffisante;
(c) r. of vowel + preceding consonant(s):
rime riche;
(d) r. of vowel + preceding syllable(s):
rime léonine.

Under (c), the homophony of the r. words' *consonne d'appui* (the consonant immediately preceding the tonic vowel) was a condition of *rime riche* (see RICH RHYME). The incidence of *rime riche* increased with the Romantic poets and became an important plank in the aesthetic platform of the Parnassians (q.v.): "Without the *consonne d'appui*, there is no r. and, consequently, no poetry" (Banville); but it should not be assumed that this increase in *rime riche* was designed to compensate for the concomitant increase in other metrical freedoms by shoring up the line end (de Cornulier). Among these poets, *rime riche* enriches the rhyming words, investing them with more resonance, color, and dramatic presence. To later 20th-c analysts, however, this 19th-c. system of classification has seemed too crude, particularly in that it allows rs. like *bonté / cité* to be rich, while denser accumulations of phonemes (e.g. *tordre / mordre, arche / marche*) are classed as merely *suffisantes*. Accordingly, a purely numerical approach to r. classification has been preferred, whereby the more identical phonemes there are, in whatever position, the richer the r.:

(1) *rime pauvre* or *faible*:
identity of one element, the tonic vowel
(boss*u* /v*u*);
(2) *rime suffisante*:

identity of two elements, tonic vowel + consonant
(r*oc* /bl*oc*)
or consonant + tonic vowel
(*main* /car*min*);
(3) *rime riche*:
identity of three or more elements in the tonic syllable
(s'ab*rite* /s'eff*rite*, to*rdu* /pe*rdu*; ch*armes* /l*armes*);
(4) *rime léonine*:
identity of two or more syllables, the tonic syllable + one or more syllables preceding it
(ta*mariniers* / *mariniers*, dé*sir, Idées* / des i*ridées*).

But in the assessment of the degree or relative richness of r., other factors also need to be taken into account, e.g. the "amplification" of the r. (identical phonemes in the r. words but not involved in the r. itself, e.g. r*ivage* / *image*; g*alopin* / m*aroquin*) and correspondence of the number of syllables in the r. words or r. measures.   C.S.

B. *English* has never succeeded in codifying its terminology for r. forms. Surveys of usage even in recent works (e.g. Rickert) show very little consistency of treatment. The most common terms for r. in Eng. have been "end r.," "full r.," "perfect r.," and "true r." The first of these simply denotes line position and while unsatisfactory seems least problematic; the second corresponds to Fr. *rime suffisante* and would be useful were that all it were taken to mean, i.e. meeting the minimum criteria for r. The last two, however, imply that the one form of sound echo denominated "r." is somehow the ideal or epitome toward which all other forms strive (and fail), whereas in fact end-r. is but one of several related configurations of sound correspondence (see section II.5 above). The terms "perfect" and "true" should be avoided as prejudicing *a priori* the status of other forms of r., whose own terms ("off r.," "near r.") are also objectionable. See NEAR RHYME.

But again, it is essential to bear in mind that even for r. types directly appropriated from the Romance langs. and for which the Eng. terms are simply direct translations, *the effect is not the same*: r. is a markedly different phenomenon in inflectional langs., where identity of word ending is pervasive and often must be actually avoided, than in positional langs., where inflectional endings are almost entirely absent and sound similarity is more dependent on the historical evolution of the lexicon. Notwithstanding, this does not automatically make the Romance langs. r.-"rich" and the Germanic langs. r.-"poor," as has often been thought: it is not merely the quantity of like endings that is at issue.

IV. ANALOGUES. *Outside poetry* r. is commonly thought of as a "poetical" device, but in fact it is a broadly attested linguistic structure used for marking the ends of important words and phrases to make them memorable. R. is widely used not only for ludic and didactic purposes, as in rhymed and rhythmical calendrical mnemonics (the names of the months do not much co-operate), children's counting-out and jump-rope rs., and jingles for ads; but also for other types of memorable speech such as proverbs, epigrams (qq.v.), inscriptions, mottoes, riddles (q.v.), puns (q.v.), and jokes (Brogan 69, 78). Children seem to be able to manufacture rs. not only spontaneously and happily but more readily than the other six forms cited at the top of section II above, suggesting that the closural or "final-fixed" structure that is r. is somehow more salient for cognitive processing—and more conducive to aesthetic delight. Perhaps the most natural form of rhyming in lang. is seen in mnemonic formulae, catch phrases that r., e.g. *true blue, ill will, fender bender, double trouble, high and dry.* The list of such popular and proverbial phrases is astonishingly long, and the device is also used in poetry (Donne, "Song"; Eliot, *Four Quartets*): see CLOSE RHYME.

In an important study Bolinger has shown that in every lang., words which begin or end alike in sound come to be perceived as related even when they have no etymological connection at all. This sort of paradigmatic or synchronic associativity is even stronger than the historical kinship of words, which is often concealed by spelling and pronunciation changes, and is extended naturally into poetry as r. without any alteration of form or function: r. is *natural*. Rhymelike structure apparently may be found even in nonhuman langs.: whales do it.

Inside poetry there are a number of structures which have rhymelike effects or functions or exceed the domain of r., verging upon repetition, thereby creating superordinate matrices of meaning. The sestina (q.v.), for example, repeats a sequence of whole words rather than r. sounds. The final words in some of Richard Wilbur's poems are so contrived as to offer an elliptical synopsis or ironic commentary on the argument of the poem. Several rhetorical devices generate comparable effects to those of r. even in unrhymed verse: in the 10,000 lines of *Paradise Lost* there are over 100 cases of *antistrophe*, nearly 100 of *anaphora*, 60 of *anadiplosis*, 50 of *epanalepsis*, and 40 of *epizeuxis*, all of them, as Broadbent says, "iterative schemes tending toward the effect of r." Milton also weights words at line end (Broadbent calls this "anti-r."), counterposing semantically heavy and contrastive terms at *PL* 4.561–62, for example: "Tempt not the Lord thy God, he said and stood. / But Satan smitten with amazement fell"—an effect reinforced all the more by reiteration of these two terms via *ploce* ten more times in the following 21 lines, and echoed thereafter at 4.590–91 (cf. 9.832–33).

V. FUNCTIONS. The discussions above should have made clear that the functions of r. are semantic, architectonic, mnemonic, closural, heuristic, and aesthetic. Like meter, and like the clausulae of late-antique prose rhythm (q.v.), r. marks the ends of runs of syllables in speech and thereby segments the soundstream into equal or perceived-equal sections: this segmentation in turn establishes equivalence and allows for the compounding of meaning. Rs. as schemes create an architecture which links lines into larger complexes of pattern and meaning. Within the line, r. exerts an organizing effect: by marking the terminus, it defines the metrical shape of the whole, and by establishing linkages with other sound patterning within the line, it extends the reach and power of the poem's orders. Its effect on auditors and readers both inside and outside poetry is well known: it is a powerful mnemonic device. Shakespeare's regular practice of rhyming a couplet to mark the end of a scene shows its closural function. Nor should r. be thought any impediment to composition: the testimony of poets is clear that the search for a r. opens up new possibilities for shaping lines that would never have been thought of without the pressure of finding a r. From the point of view of psychology, r. may thus seem the object of displaced fixation in consciousness which frees the subconscious mind for more creative wordcraft. Finally, there is the intellectual appreciation of a r., its difficulty, surprise, ingenuity, or wit, as well as the sheer pleasure of its euphony (q.v.).

VI. LANGUAGE AND ART. Every artist's success depends in part on the materials available, but more on the artist's knowledge of those materials and skill at shaping or employing them. Hence a poet's success at rhyming depends in part on what a particular lang. offers: in each lang. the resources are necessarily limited. If, therefore, a poet chooses to write in r., she comes, thereby, to learn *what is possible.* Imitation and study teach much; the rest must always remain the province of experiments and happy discoveri[m]es.

"Love," for example, surely one of the most important words in the Eng. lang., has very few rs.: mainly "dove," and "above," both of which are overworked; and "glove," which is less worn only because its usage is much more limited (one cannot *often* say "like hand in glove"). "Of" is possible but will mainly achieve effects of surprise, from the enjambment. There is "shove," but it seems unlikely one would want to use a phrase like "when push comes to shove" in a love poem. J. V. Cunningham manages something new for this r.: "Jove courted Danae with golden love, / But you're not Danae, and I'm not Jove." But there is some question whether this epigram is a love poem, and in any event the effect hinges on our realizing that the r. is only near: what we are most aware of is the incongruity, the wrenching. That's his point.

VII. DATA. For the student of r., one of the most astonishing discoveries to be made in the course of reading through the secondary lit. is that reliable *facts* about r. are very few and far between.

Part of the explanation for this is the confusion of terminology noted above; part is the general absence of reliable texts before the advent of textual bibliography in the 20th c. Another part is the general drift in late 20th-c. crit. toward "theory" (the cover term for any approach that is anti-New Critical, anti-textual, or anti-empiricist). While theory construction is essential to progress in any intellectual discipline, postmodernist literary theory has priviledged social activism and sought to suppress the kinds of research necessary to generate the detailed facts which would validate critical judgments about texts. But it is facts which are the chief means of validating or disproving any theory at all. The collection of useful data itself requires an astute grasp of theory—i.e. critical intelligence.

To obtain facts, one must first ask questions. Scott opens a major study of r. with a startling barrage of queries: "despite r.'s longevity . . . we know remarkably little about it. . . . Where are the basic statistics, conveniently collected? Where are the histories of changes in characteristic pairings? Where are the r. indexes? And yet it is clear that much could be learned about literary and cultural history if any prominent word were taken, *nature*, say, and the itinerary of its changing partnerships traced; or if a recurrent pair, say *justice/supplice*, were inspected against its changing verse contexts. What do we know about the psychologies and ideologies of r. both as a general phenomenon and as an arsenal of specific lexical pairings? What do we know about the ways different verse forms project r.? What do we know about the way r. relates to different poetic genres, to dramatic structure, to narrative? Do we yet even know how long a r. is, or where r. takes place?" (1988, 1). All these questions are still unanswered.

At present the only extensive collections of data we have on r. are indexes of stanza forms: Frank 1953–57 for Occitan, Schlawe 1972 and Frank 1980 for Ger., Martinon 1912 and Mölk-Wolfzettel 1972 for Fr., and some piecemeal data for Rus., Sp., and It. (see Brogan 1989 for citations); for Eng. we have effectually *nothing at all*. And even such collections as we have do not provide nearly all the information available or wanted on the 12 characteristics of rs. discussed in section II above. Much more information remains to be collected on the types and distributions of r. before we can tender generalizations, map trends, and accurately assess poets' achievements in r. We do not know, for example, what kinds of rs. are used in Eng. folk and oral poetry, or whether these differ significantly from those used in literary verse. In Rus., there is data to suggest that folk and literary rs. are identical in principle (Shapiro 145). The revival of interest in prosody in Russia after 1960 has produced a number of excellent metrical handbooks on specific poets with good data on r.; and several r. dictionaries and concordances for Rus. and Ger. poets have even been published in the West. Nevertheless, the kind of factually detailed overview of the history of Rus. r. that Scherr gives in a dozen pages is still not possible for any of the Western langs.

VIII. ORIGIN AND HISTORY. Many of the older notions about the origin and devel. of r., based on outdated notions of orality and literacy and on very limited information from only a small number of cultures, now seem unsound in the light of better texts and modern linguistics. An accurate and synoptic history of r. does not presently exist and would be a daunting task, esp. since several African poetries are still but dimly understood. Whitehall's attempt at a thumbnail history shows how many difficult and diverse questions require specific answer in order to write any adequate history of the devel. of r., even for the West alone.

There have been two chief views on the origin and devel. of r. The derivationist position is that r. originated in one locus and was disseminated to all others. Turner argued as early as 1808 that r. originated in Ch. or Sanskrit (but not Arabic), whence it spread via the trade routes to Europe. Draper's view is that it originated in Indo-Iranian (the *Avesta*, ca. 1500 B.C.) whence it spread eastward to China and India (since the earliest attested rs. in Chinese date from only ca. 1000 B.C.) and westward to Rome with Persian mystery cults. The alternate view, set forth as early as 1803 by Swift, is that r. does not take its origin exclusively in any one lang. but is a natural linguistic structure which can arise in any lang. having the right set of features. The fact that r. originated once shows that it can originate anytime. It is a simple linguistic fact that the number of sounds available in any lang. is limited, and its many words must therefore be combinations of only a few sounds. There is considerable evidence that children manufacture rs. spontaneously as one basic form of sound permutation; conspicuous too is r. in the chants and charms of many primitive cultures. Systematic rhyming has appeared in such widely separated langs. that its spontaneous devel. in more than one of them seems a reasonable assumption. We should not seek to find the ultimate "origin" of r. in Western poetry by tracing r. forms back through langs. to some common source. Still, it is a thundering fact that most of the world's 4000 langs. lack r. in their poetries altogether (Whitehall).

In the history of the world's poetries, those cultures which have most extensively developed r. have been, in the East, Chinese, and in the West, Arabic, Irish, Occitan, Fr., and Eng. Note that r. is not originally native to any European lang. or even IE. It appears perhaps earliest in Arabic and Chinese, from either or both of which it may have been transmitted to Sanskrit on the Indian subcontinent and to Persian in the Middle East. Regardless of whether r. had one source or several, it is indisputable that, both in ancient and medieval lits., there are several discernible routes of transmission, the tracing of which is neither impossible nor unimportant, merely difficult. It is obvious that specific r. forms, like meters and stanzas, have been imported into langs. via translation or imitation of famous poets and canonical texts in another lang. (Homer, Virgil, Dante, Petrarch, Shakespeare), even where r. was already indigenous (see CANON; INFLUENCE). T.V.F.B.

What can be said reliably at present about the earliest r. trads., Chinese and Arabic, is as follows:

Chinese. R. is an essential element of Ch. versification; it has been largely ignored by Western translators and readers because it cannot be fully reproduced in translation. Because Ch. is a tone lang. not a stress-based lang., and because every Ch. character is pronounced as one syllable, Ch. rhymes more readily than most other langs. (though the distribution of tones may complicate the r. patterns). End r. occurs in all traditional verse, with r. schemes varying according to different forms of poetry. In the open-ended Ancient Style verse (*gushi*), r. generally occurs at the end of each couplet; and the r., either in the level or the oblique tone, may change in the course of the poem. But in a more rigid form such as the 8-line Regulated Verse (*lushi*), the same r. should be used throughout the poem, and is almost always in the level tone. This level-tone r. falls at the end of each couplet, but it is also permissible at the end of the first line of the poem. Compared to Regulated Verse, the *ci* (lyric) is relatively more complex and varied. In composing a song in *ci* style, the poet chooses a tune, out of some 825 tunes, and writes words for it. Each tune pattern determines the tonal category of the end r. and internal rs., as well as the number of lines and the number of syllables per line. For the historical evolution of r. see CHINESE POETRY.—J. Liu, *The Art of Ch. Poetry* (1962); H. Frankel, "Cl. Ch. [Versification]," in Wimsatt. K.S.C.

Arabic and Persian. Until the 20th c., r. (*qāfiya*) was one of two primary features in the Ar. definition of poetry itself; in the famous dictum recorded by Qudāma ibn Jaʿfar (d. after 932), the author of *Kitāb naqd al-shiʿr*, a manual on poetics, poetry is "discourse with r. and meter." The central position accorded r. in Ar. and Persian poetics leads to the devel. of a theoretical science of r. parallel to though separate from that of prosody, with the Basran scholar, al-Khalīl ibn Aḥmad (d. 791), as its alleged founder. In these trads., as indeed in most others, r. is based on sound; there is no visual r. Thus, it may be said that critical writing on r. in Ar. dates from the 8th or 9th c.; r. itself is already present in the first extant exemplars of Ar. poetry (6th c.), its origins lost in the unrecorded beginnings of oral trad. The question of whether r. exists in the Old Iranian *Avesta* is disputed.

In Ar. the essential part of r. is the word-final consonant called *al-rāwī*, which remains constant throughout the poem (this consonant will sometimes be preceded by a further consonant which is also part of the r.). R. in Ar. can be of two sorts:

fettered (*muqayyada*), i.e. ending with a consonant, or loose (*muṭlaqa*), i.e. ending with a vowel. While occasional examples of assonance or near r. are known in Middle Persian poetry, the intricate rules and conventions for r. in Islamic Persian were adapted from Ar. practice. R. in Persian may comprise from one to four syllables, the last ending with the same consonant preceded by the same vowel, e.g. b*ām* / k*ām*; s*ardam* / m*ardam*; rev*āyati* / shek*āyati*; p*āyandagān* / *āyandagān*. Some variation is allowed in the longer rs., but no license.

The majority of cl. *qaṣīda* and *ghazal* (qq.v.) poetry is composed of verses in monorhyme (q.v.), with the r. at the end of the second of two hemistichs (*miṣrāʿ*). More often than not, the r. is called to the attention of the poem's audience by being used at the end of both hemistichs of the first line of the poem, a process called *taṣrīʿ*. A r. word should not be repeated except at distant intervals. A special feature of Persian r. is the *radīf*, a syllable, word, or phrase repeated verbatim following the r., e.g. yār *dāram* / khomār *dāram*, where the r. is *-ār* and the *radīf* is *daram*. Some typical r. schemes are: *qaṣīda* and *ghazal*, *aabaca*; quatrain, *aaaa* or *aaba*; *masnavi* or rhyming couplet, *aabbcc* etc.; *qefʿa*, *bacada*. Strophic forms have more complicated schemes. This can be seen most notably in the Andalusian *muwashshaḥa*, where, within a series of strophes, one section (usually termed *ghuṣn*) will normally have an independent r. for each instance while the other (termed *simṭ* or *qufl*) will retain the r. of the final segment of the poem, the *kharja* (see HISPANO-ARABIC POETRY).

Since the Second World War, r. has lost its formerly privileged position and become but one of a number of features of poetic discourse as poets and critics have abandoned the dictates of cl. Ar. poetics in favor of new (and often imported) genres such as "free verse" and the prose poem. See also RHYME-PROSE.—G. W. Freitag, *Darstellung der Arabischen Verskunst* (1830, rpt. 1968); H. Blochmann, *The Prosody of the Persians according to Saifi, Jami and other writers* (1872, rpt. 1970); W. Wright, *A Grammar of the Arabic Lang.* (1896–98); Shams al-dīn Moḥammad b. Qays al-Rāzī, *Al-Moʿjam fī maʿāyer ashʿār al-ʿajam* (1935); S. Bonebakker, "Kafiya," *Encyclopedia of Islam*, 2d ed. (1954–); Al-Akhfash [d. 793], *Kitāb al-qawāfi* (1970); L. P. Elwell-Sutton, *The Persian Metres* (1976); F. Thiesen, *A Manual of Cl. Persian Prosody* (1982). R.M.A.A.; W.L.H.

In the West, while r. is rare in all Cl. poetry, it is rarer in Gr. than in Lat.: still, it is not unknown in Homer (*Iliad* 2.87–88, 9.236–38) and the Gr. dramatists (*Clouds* 709–15; *Wasps* 133–35; *Acharians* 29–36); Euripides in the *Alcestis* has a drunk Hercules speak in r. (782–86), a passage clearly meant to be comic. R. can be found in the Alexandrian poets and, among Lat. poets, in Ennius and Ovid (a fifth of the lines in the *Tristia* show leonine r.), Virgil (*Aeneid* 1.625–26, 2.124–25, 2.456–57, 3.549, 3.656–57, 4.256–57, 8.620–21, 8.646–47,

9.182–83, 10.804–5), and Horace (*Ars poetica* 99–100).

The emergence of r. in the West had to await the devel. of accent (Clark remarks that "the history of the adoption of r. is almost exactly parallel to, and contemporaneous with, the history of the substitution of accent for quantity"), the shifting of word accent from the root syllable rightward, and, progressively, the transition from inflectional to positional syntax. But since r. obviously appears in inflected langs., we must say that, insofar as it is to be distinguished from homoeoteleuton, it should be seen as arising in response to the decay of the inflectional system, and therefore growing stronger only as like endings disappear (Whitehall). Langs. which retain inflections but use r. (e.g. Fr.) will therefore impose extensive constraints on r. forms so as to differentiate the two systems.

The earliest indigenous r. trad. in Europe was apparently Irish, and elaborate canons of r. have remained a central feature of Celtic prosody (q.v.) up to the 20th c. The Ir. missionaries apparently brought r. with them to the Continent (the older view was that this influence worked in the opposite direction). Assonantal precursors of r. first appear in the Christian Lat. hymns of Hilary of Poitiers, Ambrose, and Augustine (late 3d through 4th cs.). Meyer thought the source for this practice to be Semitic, a view not now followed. In Byzantium, Romanus and Synesius were exploiting its possibilities in hymnology by the 6th c.

Except for the intervention of Med. Lat., the European langs. would have developed their prosodies in opposing directions. The Germanic langs., with fore-stressing of words, developed structural alliteration (q.v.) for their prosody, as in OHG and OE, less ornate than the elaborately interlaced sound patterns of the Celtic poetries, i.e. Irish and Welsh, but more closely linked to meter. The Romance langs., in which word stress was weaker and phrase stress stronger, developed first assonance then r.; the great flowering of short-lined, rhymed stanzas in Occitan poetry (q.v.) by the troubadours (q.v.) directly influenced every other vernacular on the Continent, and even Med. Lat. "goliardic verse" (q.v.). Occitan was itself influenced, perhaps strongly, by Arabic sources, though the nature and extent of this influence is still disputed.

Ger. early fell under the influence of Med. Lat. versification (Otfrid, 7th c.), as Eng. did of Fr. after the Conquest. R. first appears in the Germanic vernaculars in the 9th c. in the work of Otfrid (*Evangelienbuch*, finished 868), directly influenced by Med. Lat. versification. There are also some vestiges of r. in OE as a result of Celtic influence, chiefly the *Rhyming Poem*, which is self-consciously overwrought. Fr. prosody itself was an outgrowth of Med. Lat. principles. Northern Fr. exerted enormous influence on ME from the 12th c. (*The Owl and the Nightingale*, the Harley Lyrics)

through Chaucer (who also knew Boccaccio) into the 15th c. The collapse of the OE inflectional system had left numbers of monosyllabic words in early ME, but the large number of Romance loan-words imported, most of them polysyllabic and oxytonic or paroxytonic, readily encouraged r.: many of them kept their Romance end-stressing in ME and even influenced the stressing of other Eng. words. Chaucer takes advantage of a variable final -e, which was in the process of disappearing during his own lifetime, for both meter and r. After Chaucer, the loss of final -e and the Great Vowel Shift in the 15th c. sounded the end of ME versification; modern Eng. prosody was reinvented by Wyatt and Surrey, though even here on Romance principles of r. and stanza (e.g. the sonnet).

In modern times, the emergence of standardized varieties of the modern langs. has worked to restrict the canons for permissible rhyming in artverse, but three other forces have exerted pressure against this trend: (1) oral trads. and literary imitations of them, esp. folk poetry such as the ballad (q.v.) in the 18th c., have exerted strong influence on artverse, particularly in romanticism (*Lyrical Ballads*) and the 19th-c. Ger. cult of the lit. of the *Volk* (see ORAL POETRY); (2) dialect poetry (q.v.), once extensive and important, as in Scottish, South Ger., and It., has been marginalized from artverse even while it flourishes in oral trad.; and (3) in artverse itself, variant forms of r. such as near and eye r. have been more deliberately pursued in an effort to break out of ossified verseforms, so as to write, and live, at the growing end of lang.   T.V.F.B.

For further discussion of r. structures and effects, see SOUND; SOUND EFFECTS IN POETRY; STANZA. See also ALLITERATION; ANAPHORA; ASSONANCE; BOUTS RIMES; BROKEN RHYME; CELTIC PROSODY; CHAIN RHYME; CLOSE RHYME; COCKNEY SCHOOL; CONSONANCE; COUPLET; CROSS RHYME; CYNGHANEDD; ENJAMBMENT; EYE RHYME; FRENCH PROSODY; GENERIC RHYME; GRAMMATICAL RHYME; HOMOEOTELEUTON; IDENTICAL RHYME; INTERNAL RHYME; ITALIAN PROSODY; LEONINE RHYME; LINE; MASCULINE AND FEMININE; MONORHYME; MOSAIC RHYME; NEAR RHYME; ODL; REVERSE RHYME; RHYME COUNTERPOINT; RHYME-PROSE; RHYME SCHEME; RICH RHYME; SCHUTTELREIM; TAIL RHYME; TRIPLE RHYME; VERSIFICATION.

J. S. Schütze, *Versuch einer Theorie des Reims nach Inhalt und Form* (1802)—Kantian semantic theory; T. Swift, "Essay on the Rise and Progress of Rhime," *Tr. Royal Ir. Acad.* 9 (1803); S. Turner, "An Inquiry Respecting the Early Use of R.," *Archaeologia* 14 (1808); A. Croke, *Essay on the Origin, Progress, and Decline of Rhyming Lat. Verse* (1828); F. Wolf, *Über die Lais, Sequenzen, und Leiche* (1841), 161 ff.—still important; W. Grimm, "Zur Gesch. des Reims" (1852), rpt. in *Kleinere Schriften* (1887)—still the best Ger. survey; W. Masing, *Über Ursprung und Verbreitung des Reims* (1866); T. de Banville, *Petit Traité de poésie française* (1872);

Schipper, 1.1.7, 1.4.1; E. Freymond, "Über den reichen Reim bei altfranzösischen Dichtern," *ZRP* 6 (1882); A. Ehrenfeld, *Studien zur Theorie des Reims*, 2 v. (1897–1904); P. Delaporte, *De la rime française* (1898); G. Mari, *Riassunto e dizionarietto di ritmica italiana* (1901); Kastner, ch. 3; Meyer, v. 1, ch. 2—Med. Lat.; Saintsbury, v. 1, App. 8, and v. 3, App. 4; A. Gabrielson, *R. as a Criterion of the Pronunciation of Spenser, Pope, Byron, and Swinburne* (1909); Schipper, *History* 270 ff.; Thieme, ch. 8 and 376, 379–80—full list of Fr. work to 1914; W. Braune, "Reim und Vers," *Sitzungsb. der Heidelberger Akad. der Wiss., phil.-hist. Klasse* (1916)—etymology; F. Zschech, *Die Kritik des Reims in England* (1917); O. Brik, "Zvukovie povtory," *Poetika* (1919); E. Sapir, "The Heuristic Value of R.," *QQ* 27 (1920); B. de Selincourt, "R. in Eng. Poetry," *E&S* 7 (1921); H. C. Wyld, *Studies in Eng. Rs. from Surrey to Pope* (1923); V. M. Žirmunskij, *Rifma, ee istoriia i teoriia* [R.: Its Theory and Hist.] (1923); W. B. Sedgwick, "The Origin of R.," *RB* 36 (1924); Morris-Jones—Celtic; K. Wesle, *Frühmittelhochdeutsche Reimstudien* (1925); Heusler, pts. 3, 5; P. Habermann, "Reim," etc., *Reallexikon I* 3.25–44; J. W. Rankin, "Rime and Reason," *PMLA* 44 (1929); H. Lanz, *The Physical Basis of R.* (1931); N. Törnqvist, "Zur Gesch. des Wortes Reim," *Humanistika Vetenskapssamfundet i Lund, Årsberättelse* (1934–35), v. 3—Celtic, Germanic, and Romance; Patterson—fullest source for the *Rhétoriqueurs*; K. Stryjewski, *Reimform und Reimfunktion* (1940)—near r. in Eng.; F. W. Ness, *The Use of R. in Shakespeare's Plays* (1941); U. Pretzel, *Frühgesch. des deutschen Reims* (1941); K. Burke, "On Musicality in Verse," *The Philosophy of Literary Form* (1941); A. M. Clark, *Studies in Literary Modes* (1945); Le Gentil, v. 1, bk. 2; A. Oras, "Echoing Verse Endings in *Paradise Lost,*" *South Atlantic Studies S. E. Leavitt* (1953); Raby, *Christian*; W. K. Wimsatt, Jr., "One Relation of R. to Reason," "Rhet. and Poems," *The Verbal Icon* (1954)—classic studies of semantics; J. W. Draper, "The Origin of R.," *RLC* 31 (1957), 39 (1965); Raby, *Secular*; Beare—broad scope for Western; F. G. Ryder, "How Rhymed Is a Poem?" *Word* 19 (1963); M. Masui, *The Structure of Chaucer's Rime Words* (1964); D. L. Bolinger, "Rime, Assonance, and Morpheme Analysis," *Forms of Eng.* (1965); C. A. Owen, Jr., "'Thy Drasty Ryming,'" *SP* 63 (1966)—Chaucer; J. Cohen, *Structure du langage poétique* (1966); R. Abernathy, "Rs., Non-Rs., and Antir.," *To Honor Roman Jakobson*, v. 1 (1967); E. J. Dobson, *Eng. Pronunciation 1500-1700.*, 2d ed., 2 v. (1968); H. Whitehall, "R.: Sources and Diffusion," *Ibadan* 25 (1968); M. Perloff, *R. and Meaning in the Poetry of Yeats* (1970); L. Pszczołowska, *Rym* (1970)—Polish; V. Nemoianu, "Levels of Study in the Semantics of R.," *Style* 5 (1971); E. H. Guggenheimer, *R. Effects and Rhyming Figures* (1972)—Cl.; T. Eekman, *The Realm of R.* (1974)—comparative Slavic; V. F. Markov, "V zaščitu raznoudarnoi rifmy (informativnyi obzor)," *Rus. Poetics*, ed. T. Eekman and D. S. Worth (1975); M. Shapiro, *Asymmetry* (1976), ch. 4; L. P. Elwell-Sutton, *The Persian Metres* (1976), App. 1; *Die Genese der europäischen Endreimdichtung*, ed. U. Ernst and P.-E. Neuser (1977); J. Lotman, *The Structure of the Artistic Text* (tr. 1977); D. S. Worth, "Roman Jakobson and the Study of R.," *Roman Jakobson: Echoes of His Scholarship* (1977); D. W. Taylor, "End-Words in Richard Wilbur's Poems," *PAPA* 4 (1978); W. E. Rickert, "R. Terms," *Style* 12 (1978), "Semantic Consequences of R.," *LPer* 4 (1984); G. Schweikle, "Reim," etc., *Reallexikon* 3.403–31; D. Wesling, *The Chances of R.: Device and Modernity* (1980); Scott; Brogan, 77 ff.—full bibl. for Eng. to 1981, with coverage of other langs. in appendices, extended in *Verseform* (1989); Group Mu; B. de Cornulier, "La rime n'est pas une marque de fin de vers," *Poétique* 46 (1981), "Sur les groupements de vers classiques et la rime," *Cahiers de grammaire* 6 (1983), "Rime 'riche' et fonction de la rime," *Littérature* 59 (1985); Morier; Mazaleyrat; J. Molino and J. Tamine, "Des rimes, et quelques raisons," *Poétique* 52 (1982); D. S. Samoilov, *Kniga o russkoi rifme*, 2d ed. (1982)—fullest study of Rus.; Norden, 2.810 ff.; Navarro—Sp.; F. P. Memmo, *Dizionario di metrica italiana* (1983); *The OE* Riming Poem, ed. O. Macrae-Gibson (1983); R. Birkenhauer, *Reimpoetik am Beispiel Stefan Georges: Phonologischer Algorithmus und Reimwörterbuch* (1983); M. T. Ikegami, *R. and Pronunciation* (1984)—ME; D. Billy, "La nomenclature des rimes," *Poétique* 57 (1984); J. Hollander, "R. and the True Calling of Words," in Hollander; Chambers—Occitan; B. Nagel, *Das Reimproblem in der deutschen Dichtung vom Otfridvers zum freien Vers* (1985); Scherr, ch. 4; W. Harmon, "R. in Eng. Verse: Hist., Structures, Functions," *SP* 84 (1987); L. M. Guinee and K. B. Payne, "R.-Like Repetitions in Songs of Humpback Whales," *Ethology* 79 (1988); C. Scott, *The Riches of R.* (1988); B. M. H. Strang, "Lang., General," *The Spenser Encyc.*, ed. A. C. Hamilton et al. (1990); J. J. Small, *Positive as Sound* (1990); G. Stewart, *Reading Voices* (1990), ch. 2; L. Mugglestone, "The Fallacy of the Cockney R.," *RES* 42 (1991).   T.V.F.B.

RHYME-BREAKING. See BROKEN RHYME.

RHYME COUNTERPOINT. A phenomenon noted by Hayes in the verse of Donne, Vaughan, and esp. Herbert (e.g. "Denial"): the pattern of line-lengths in a heterometric (q.v.) poem is independent of the pattern of the rhymes. For example, a quatrain of lines of 8, 7, 8, and 7 syllables has thereby the metrical pattern *abab*, but the rhyme scheme is *abba*. Normally rhymed verse is of course isometric (q.v.), and even in heterometric verse there is usually some presumption that lines bound together by r. are isosyllabic. But with r. c., meter and rhyme are set in counterpoint, rather than in harmony, giving a distinctive effect that has been seen as formally ambiguous, a trait consonant with others in the poetry of the metaphysical (q.v.) mode.—A. M. Hayes, "C. in Herbert," *SP* 35 (1938).   T.V.F.B.

RHYME-PROSE. I. LATIN. Ancient literary theory in the West posits a gradation from prose to poetry rather than a sharp distinction. The general class of prose which in antiquity was given artfulness by being more heavily figured, phonologically (i.e. by sounds or stressing), than was ordinary prose, Norden's *Kunstprosa* ("art-prose"), includes rhythmical prose (see PROSE RHYTHM; CURSUS) and rhymed prose or r.-p. Such prose is divided into rhythmical units separated by pauses and endmarked by rhyme. The largest units are "periods," full sense units equivalent to modern independent clauses or sentences; the next largest units are "cola," i.e. phrases or subordinate clauses; the smallest are "commas." Prose has "rhythm"; poetry has rhythm and adds "meter" (Aristotle, *Rhetoric* 3.8.1408b30; cf. Augustine, *De musica.*).

The so-called "Gorgian figures" introduced by Gorgias of Leontini (484–375 B.C.) define soundeffects created by control of rhythm through such strategies as parallelism (q.v.; *parisosis*), balance (*isocolon*, q.v.), and antithesis. According to Aristotle (*Rhetoric* 3.1.1404a25), the Gorgian figures were taken from the poets. They are reinforced in antiquity by two devices—terminal rhythms defining natural pauses (see CADENCE), and like sounds created by like endings (*homoeoteleuton* or "case rhyme"). Artprose that makes use of the Gorgian figures and related devices was called *rhetoricus sermo* or *eloquentiae prosa*. Formulas for the period and colon and for types of prose rhythm and *homoeoteleuton* (q.v.) are given in the *Rhetorica ad herennium*, the earliest extant Lat. rhetoric, and in Cicero's *De oratore* and the *Institutio oratoria* of Quintilian. During the Middle Ages, the quantitative terminal rhythms ("cadences") of artprose were expressed in accentual forms (the *cursus*); the Vatican adopted certain of these for Papal correspondence. As the use of prose rhythms became widespread, the use of *homoeoteleuton* was broadened and became full rhyme (q.v.). The convergence of the two resulted in r.-p. Here rhyme is typically used to mark the ends of periods and cola. Much of the rhyme is simple *homoeoteleuton*, but rhymes of two and three syllables are also found. Rhyme pairs, marking the ends of balanced parallel or antithetical elements, are usual, but practice varies, and cross rhyme (*abab*) and bracket rhyme (*abba*) are common. Rhyme is also found within the period or colon, esp. to mark moments of thematic importance or emotional intensity.

R.-p. was cultivated by Christian writers—e.g. Tertullian, Augustine, Lactantius, Fortunatus, and Rabanus Maurus—and flourished most vigorously between the 10th and 14th cs. The significance of r.-p. is disputed. Norden argued that ancient r.-p. coupled with the accentual rhythms of the *cursus* is the source of rhyme in all European vernacular

poetry, but his theory is generally rejected. The more modest position (Polheim) is simply that r.-p. is an important Med. Lat. form (see LATIN POETRY).—Meyer; K. Polheim, *Die lateinische Reimprosa* (1925); G. Schweikle, "Reimprosa," *Reallexikon*; Morier; E. Norden, *Die Antike Kunstprosa*, 9th ed., 2 v. (1983), 2.760 ff.   O.B.H.

II. ARABIC. In Ar., rhyming prose (known as *saj*, literally, "the cooing of a dove") is found from the very beginnings of literary trad. The aphorisms of pre-Islamic soothsayers are couched in this style, in which a sequence of short utterances all end in the same rhyme and also show evidence of stress patterning (with possible implications for the origins of Ar. poetry itself). The text of the Qur'ān itself is predominantly in this style, with a number of the earliest *Suras* (chapters) showing its exclusive use. The most famous literary manifestation of this style occurs in the genre of *maqāmāt*, a combination of verbal virtuosity and picaresque social commentary apparently originated by Badīʿ al-zamān al-Hamadhānī (d. 1008) and exploited with great virtuosity by al-Ḥarīrī (d. 1122).— *Encyc. of Islam* (1913–34), s.v. "Sajʿ"; Anīs al-Maqdisī, *Taṭawwur al-asālīb al-nathariyya* (1968).   R.M.A.A.

III. CHINESE. For discussion of the *Fu*, see CHINESE POETRY, *Classical.*—B. Watson, *Ch. R.-p.* (1971); *Wen xuan, or Selections of Refined Lit.*, ed. and tr. D. Knechtges, 2 v. (1982, 1987); Nienhauser et al., s.v. "Fu."   K.S.C.

RHYME ROYAL. A stanza of seven decasyllabic lines rhyming *ababbcc*, first used in Eng. by Chaucer in *Troilus and Criseyde* (hence its alternate name, "*Troilus* stanza"), *The Parlement of Foules*, and four of the *Canterbury Tales*. It is formed on the model of 7-line stanzas in the lyrics of Machaut and Deschamps, or by dropping the fifth line of the *ottava rima* stanza (*abababcc*, q.v.) as in Boccaccio, or perhaps as a variety of the *chant royal* (q.v.), a festive form of poetry often composed for the *puy*, a guild festival that flourished in France and England from the late 13th c. well into Chaucer's time. The *puy* traditionally elected a "prince" who presided over mock royal feasts and who crowned the *chauncon reale* as the prize-winning poem of the occasion. The r. r. stanza was also used in ceremonies for the entry of royalty into a city. Later examples survive—John Lydgate's civic show in honor of Henry V's return to London in 1432, and the festive entry of Henry VII into York in 1486. Hence, r. r. apparently had its origin in events that honored royalty both real and imaginary, a form it continued to take both directly and as a literary artifice in the poetry of Chaucer, whose *Parlement of Foules* has been widely regarded as an occasional poem in honor of Richard II.

It was long held that the term r. r. was invented to describe the verse of King James I of Scotland, who used the stanza in his *Kingis Quair* (ca. 1425). However, King James himself never used the term;

the earliest use of the term "royal" in association with the stanza appears in John Quixley's tr. (ca. 1400) of Gower's Fr. ballades, which he calls *balades ryale*; and the term *rithme royall* (the terms rhythm and rhyme are synonyms in Med. Lat.) first appears in Gascoigne (*Certayne Notes*, 1575), who uses the term *royal* not with reference to its original use as a form of address but to its gravity of subject, as in Chaucer's *Troilus*.

R. r. in Chaucer is, however, a remarkably flexible form, used as widely and imaginatively as the couplet, in every sort of poetic context. Ample enough for narrative purposes, the stanza is also suited to description, digression, comment, and literary burlesque. It dominated Eng. poetry in the 15th c., being used widely in the poetry of Lydgate, Hoccleve, Dunbar, Henryson, Hawes, and Barclay, as well as in the drama of Skelton and Bale. As late as the second half of the 16th c., r. r. was the chief Eng. stanza for serious verse, as in Spenser's *Foure Hymnes* and Shakespeare's *Rape of Lucrece*. But Michael Drayton's revision of his r. r. narrative *Mortimeriados* into ottava rima (as *The Barron's Wars*) sometime before 1619 signaled the end of r. r. as a great Eng. measure. In modern times it has been essayed by Wordsworth ("Resolution and Independence"), Morris (*Earthly Paradise*), Auden (*Letter to Lord Byron*), and Masefield; Theodore Roethke adapts the rhyme scheme to *ababccc* for "I Knew a Woman."—Schipper; T. Maynard, *The Connection Between the Ballade, Chaucer's Modification of It, Rime Royal, and the Spenserian Stanza* (1934); P. F. Baum, *Chaucer's Verse* (1961); M. Ito, "Gower and R. R.," *John Gower: The Med. Poet* (1976); M. Stevens, "The Royal Stanza in Early Eng. Lit.," *PMLA* 94 (1979); Brogan.

M.STE.; T.V.F.B.

RHYME SCHEME (Ger. *Reimfolge*). The pattern or figure made by the rs. in rhymed strophic verse, usually at the ends of the lines but sometimes also line-internally; and the abstracted, graphic notation of this pattern, the rs. usually indicated by lowercase letters of the alphabet. The s. is the ideal pattern or norm of rhyming to which all instances of the particular form are presumed to conform, or from which they—significantly—vary. The first r.-sound is represented as *a* at its first and every subsequent occurrence, the second *b*, and so on, with *x* (and sometimes *y*, *z*, etc., in sequence) for rhymeless lines. Thus couplets rhyme *aa bb cc dd*, etc.; tercets (and triplets in couplet verse) *aaa bbb ccc*, etc., and terza rima *aba bcb cdc ded*, etc.; quatrains, normally either in cross rhyme, *abab* or *abxb* (e.g. ballad meter), or envelope form, *abba*, or, less commonly, in weaker forms such as *xaya*, as in Coleridge's *Rime of the Ancient Mariner*; rhyme royal *ababbcc*; and the Shakespearean sonnet *abab cdcd efef gg* (see separate entries for all these forms). Other r. ss. may be variable in forms not completely fixed, altered from the traditional form, or never before attempted. As for stanza forms which involve the repetition of entire words (at line-end, or as repetends or tags) or even whole lines (either integrally or as refrains), e.g. the sestina and the villanelle, there is no agreed system for marking these features: common strategies include the use of a capital R or a superscript diacritical mark or number. R. scheming binds lines into larger constellations and complexes of greater and lesser complexity and bond-force (Ger. *Reimzwang*) and is the analogue in sound of figuration in rhet. and meter in prosody (qq.v.). But discovery and notation of r. ss. should never be allowed to obscure the fact that rs. are irrefrangibly semantic devices, so that in noting their figuration, one is pointing up not mere sound echoes but *the patterning of meaning*.   T.V.F.B.

RHYMERS' CLUB. The R. C. consisted of a dozen or so late Victorian poets and men of letters, conventionally characterized as aesthetes and decadents, who met more or less regularly from 1890 to 1894 in a London pub off Fleet Street called The Cheshire Cheese. Its most famous member and co-founder, with Ernest Rhys (1859–1946), was the Ir. poet William Butler Yeats (1865–1939), who is primarily responsible for the impression (in *The Trembling of the Veil*) that membership was limited to a few, and that these few, primarily Ernest Dowson (1867–1900) and Lionel Johnson (1867–1902), in their brilliance and self-destructiveness constituted a "tragic generation." Yeats's critics have until recently perpetuated this view of the Rhymers. In fact, the membership also included John Davidson (1857–1909), Edwin Ellis (1848–1918), George Arthur Greene (1853–1921), Arthur Cecil Hillier (1857–?), Richard Le Gallienne (1866–1947), Victor Plarr (1863–1929), Ernest Radford (1857–1919), T. W. Rolleston (1857–1920), Arthur Symons (1865–1945), and John Todhunter (1839–1916). All the writers named, except for Davidson, contributed to one or both of the verse anthologies produced by the R. C., *The Book of the R. C.* (1892) and *The Second Book of the R. C.* (1894; both rpt. 1977). The work of the Rhymers is significant not only for its aestheticism and decadence (qq.v.), but also for the ways in which this late Victorian poetry anticipated modernism (q.v.) and also coincided with the Ir. Literary Renaissance. T. S. Eliot acknowledged his indebtedness to Davidson's imagery, for instance, and the Ir. Literary Society, also founded in London by Yeats, shared its membership with the R. C. Other famous Victorian writers and artists, such as Francis Thompson (1859–1907) and Oscar Wilde (1854–1900), were associated with the Rhymers on a more casual basis.—N. Alford, *The R. C.* (1980); K. Beckson, "The Legends of the R. C.," *VP* 19 (1981)—rev. art.; B. Gardiner, *The R. C.* (1988); J. Gardner, *Yeats and the R. C.* (1989).

A.BR.

RHYTHM (Gr. *rhythmos*). A cadence, a contour, a

figure of periodicity, any sequence of events or objects perceptible as a distinct pattern capable of repetition and variation. The traditional etymology derives the word from the Gr. verb *rheo* "flow," but Jaeger's alternative derivation, drawn from Archilochus and Aeschylus, suggests "the steady limitation of movement." Plato calls r. "order in movement" (*Laws* 2.665a). R. for the Greeks was flow, movement, but for the Romans it became arithmetical, as number (q.v.; Lat. *numerus*), i.e. counting, and so was confused with measure (q.v.); the difficulties engendered by this millennial semantic shift yet remain. Hauptmann, the 19th-c. music theorist, calls "the constant measure by which the measurement of time is made *Metre*, the kind of motion in that measure *R.*," a distinction still acknowledged as fundamental. Allen calls r. "the pattern assumed at a given moment by a mobile, changing medium" (60). As the principle of organization of temporal events, r. is analogous to symmetry and proportion in spatial arrays; in both planes, r. constitutes the first function of repetition (q.v.). Abstractly speaking, any entity not absolutely unique must be repeated either by itself or among others: if by itself, we speak of *iteration*; if with its opposite or other entities in an ordered design, then we recognize a *pattern*, which is the fundamental principle of all art.

But of course aesthetics is but one domain among many where r. manifests itself; the phenomenon is ubiquitous in natural processes (the diurnal and seasonal cycles of light and weather), in the behavior of plants and animals (the cycles of sleep, growth, and reproduction), and in human physiology (the systolic rs. of heart and breath) and activity (lang., dance, music, song, poetry). Rs. often seem quite simple, but this is an illusion; most of the rs. we are familiar with are astonishingly complex. Rhythmic patterns characteristically display four features: regularity, variation, grouping, and hierarchy.

A. *Regularity*. Rhythmic series are patterns of organization in which markers (such as stress) are deployed at intervals either regular or close enough to reinforce the *expectation* of regularity. Expectation turns out to be a more powerful force in perception than actual stimulus: in reading a text, the mind makes a rapid series of predictions each second about what it ought to see next based on what it has just previously seen (and still holds in short-term memory), and if the expected signal is delayed or missing, the mind often supplies it anyway. In this the mind may seem to sacrifice accuracy for convenience, but in fact some prediction is essential to very rapid processing of large amounts of sense-data. Regularity (spaced repetition) in the data itself is also extremely valuable: there is abundant evidence from experimental psychology, were any needed, that rhythmitization enhances motor behavior, memorization, and learning. In "stress-timed" languages such as Eng., auditors hear stresses at regular intervals regardless of how many syllables actually intervene; this, the much-disputed concept of "isochronism" (q.v.), has led some critics to see Eng. verse as metered by equal timing between beats, as in music.

B. *Variation*. Pure iteration of a whole pattern is usually felt to be monotonous, however, though the exact limen at which pleasurable repetition becomes tedious and the reasons for the shift have only recently begun to be investigated. Being reminded of the sketch or shape of a pattern through its permutations is enjoyable, but exact replication without change (which is in any event rare) is wearying, for adults at least. This phenomenon, called "variation" (q.v.), is conspicuous in perception and cognitive processing. The first law of rhythmicity is consequently that a pattern exists so long as it is perceived as such: any variation which supports the pattern will be perceived as constitutive, while any variation which obscures the pattern or modifies it to the point that it is perceived as another pattern is unrhythmical.

C. *Grouping*. Since a pure continuum of sound would be entirely undifferentiated, segmentation of the soundstream into discrete units seems central to rhythmic perception. Segmentation however requires demarcation, which is the function of stress in Western music and (most) poetic meters; indeed, the very existence of beats themselves seems to entail grouping. The most natural groupings seem to be twos and threes, the prime numbers which can be added together or repeated in various combinations to produce every possible larger group. In grammar these become proclitics and enclitics; in verse, binary and ternary meters; in music, double and triple time. Whether or not weak syllables are perceived as grouped after the stress (musical bars) or before (iambic meter) or both (grammar) is uncertain; experiments show that such perception depends in part on the timing of the pauses around the groups (Woodrow). It almost certainly also depends on which semiotic system the auditor perceives to be operative. In Western music the accent begins the bar, but this is a mere convention not an absolute; the bar-lines themselves did not appear until the 15th c. Of all possible arrangements of beats in a series, simple alternation is by far the most common and most powerful (all meters tend toward this condition), but of the possible groupings, fours (two doubled) are the most conspicuous and perhaps the most stable. Innumerable medieval verses, learned and common, Lat. and vernacular, sacred and profane run in four-beat r. Interestingly, there is some evidence that the largest number of data the mind can assimilate in one group is about seven, give or take two: the regular four-beat line gives eight. Further, grouping seems to allow catalexis (q.v.), a principle whereby final elements can be omitted without disruption, indeed to positive effect: ballad meter, for example, originally ran in eight-beat longline couplets folded into four-stress halfline quatrains, but in the most common form the second and fourth lines of the quatrain (couplet ends) are reduced from four stresses to three, an endclipped form that has been greatly preferred over the centuries.

D. *Hierarchy*. Patterns on lower levels of rhythmic series are frequently repeated across wider spans on higher levels, melding the whole together to yield "a complex action so integrated that it is perceived as simple" (Kramer). In poetry every repetition of sound whether simple (alliteration) or complex (rhyme, meter) is rhythmic; but the clearest example of hierarchical ordering is dipodic verse (q.v.), where stresses follow weak syllables in usual alternation, but the stresses themselves also alternate regularly, strong and very strong, the principle of alternation being preserved as the groupings are doubled on each successively higher level.

E. *R. versus Meter*. The distinction between r. and m. is old, dating to at least the 4th c. B.C. (Aristoxenus, pupil of Aristotle). Since poetry is of course made up of lang., the natural rs. of speech are the threads of which larger rhythmic cadences and meters are woven. It has sometimes been held that the iambic pentameter prevailed in Eng. because Eng. is an iambic lang., but lang. taken as a whole is an enormously varied thing, and the claim has never been proven. The relation of meter to the rs. of lang. (see METER, section IV) is more complex than this. Still, it is evident that the most common syntactic patterns (prepositional phrases, for example) must produce a relatively small inventory of cadences that should appear fairly often. It is these cadences which yield the formulae of literary art-prose known as "prose r." (q.v.). In verse these are meshed with indifferent monosyllables and with special rhetorical emphases and then molded under the pressure of abstract line-patterns to yield regular meters, or else they are iterated systematically via oral-formulaic composition (see ORAL POETRY) or parallelism (q.v.) to achieve other, more expansive rhythmical effects. In metrical verse the stressing a sentence may take is often not identical to its normal "prose r." (Fowler); in accentual verse (q.v.) and in nonmetrical verse, on the other hand, words retain their usual stressing and inflections. See further discussion of the concepts of meter and r. in the entry METER, section III.

The established view is that ultimately meter is simply a subset of r. (Chatman), but this is not exactly true: strictly speaking, meter has no r. Meters provide structure; rs. provide movement within that structure (Weismiller). Without a structure no movement would be possible, but within structure a number of movements may be permissible. In these terms r. certainly appears the more complex and interesting phenomenon of the two.

F. *Problems*. Rhythmic analysis encounters two problems, one ontological, one methodological.

Critics frequently assert that r. is a *felt* phenomenon, a notion that accords with common sense but forces them to treat the poem not as aesthetic object but as aesthetic experience, thus opening the door to all manner of empirical, mechanical, and psychological studies of acoustic perception, psychomotor timing, and reader response. Most early and mid 20th-c. crit. was not receptive to such approaches, in part because of notoriously loose terms (r. is surely the vaguest term in crit.), in part because some conspicuous studies led to eccentric results (at the end of his career E. W. Scripture proudly announced his discovery of compound Gr. feet in Eng. verse). The mind is not some Lockean *tabula rasa*, a passive recipient of impressions; rhythmic perception is very much an *active* organization of sense-data, and when critics turn from the poem as object of perception to studying individual perceivers and their acts of perception, they enter a great wilderness of mostly uncharted terrain. Most of the acoustic and psychological experiments on r. earlier in the century now seem vestigial to poetic analysis on the grounds set forth by the Rus. Formalists: "not the phone but the phoneme as such is utilized as the cornerstone of verse" (Jakobson). It is not the sound as heard but the whole system of structural rapports and differences embedded in the lang. which is the proper object of study.

In theory it should be possible to write general rules of rhythmicity which, *mutatis mutandis*, would then be applicable to each kind of rhythmic phenomenon—lang., music, dance, poetry, perhaps even natural processes. But this remains a so-far unrealized ideal. Historically, theories of r. have nearly always been written in a single field and then extended to other fields which seemed similar. But in practice this has proven to be one of the least productive methods of inquiry. So, for two notable examples, musical rs. have been claimed as (i.e. written over) the rs. of poetry (by Sidney Lanier and his followers, the "musical" metrists), as have linguistic rs. (at the hands of the linguistic metrists), without adequate recognition in either case of the essential differentia between the various domains. Whether poetic rs. are merely a subset of the rs. of the lang. or whether they, like lang. and dance, simply share "family resemblances" (Wittgenstein) under a common genus so far remains an open question. Moreover, modern critics have come to realize that r., like other categories of perception, is very much culture-determined. African drum-music, for example, at first seems completely chaotic to Western ears unused to its extremely rapid shifts of signature and r. And even within one culture researchers have discovered considerable latitude in what auditors recognize as rhythmical.

But this first difficulty entails a corollary problem for critics willing to hazard discussion of poetic r.—analytic precision. In high artverse traditions (the Cl. hexameter, the Romance octo-

RHYTHM

syllable and alexandrine, the Eng. pentameter), meters, being strictly defined, demand and therefore display precision, hence allow minute and exacting analysis. But rhythms, being more diverse and complex, cannot be so accurately described even in stable traditions, much less when a tradition is weak or nonexistent, or when a poet—Whitman is the classic example—revolts against the received prosodic doctrines of the day. Too, r. (unlike meter) may vary widely from one reader to another, one performance to another, even one line to the next. Consequently, critics have tended to view rhythmical variation as too evanescent for exact description. What cannot be described cannot be judged. In this respect poetic analysis has had to wait upon developments in modern linguistics not merely for terms but even for the fundamental concepts themselves necessary so we can talk with any precision about the intricacies of verbal structures.

G. *Progress.* Still, some progress has lately been made toward a revealing analytic of r. La Drière's influential system, with its hierarchical analysis of cadence and grouping (see PROSODY); developments in colonic analysis in Cl. prosody; and the new approach called "grammetrics" (q.v.) developed by Wexler in England and Wesling in America, all focus on the reader's awareness of the grouping of stresses in natural syntactic periods—the word, the phrase, the clause—rather than in the abstract (unsegmented) meter. Traditional prosody treated meter as (and thus limited it to) an organization of phonological elements such as stress or duration. But more recent studies have recognized that verse orders lang. on every available level—phonological, morphological, syntactic—and though these topics were ignored or treated only indirectly in traditional prosody, they are wholly relevant if not fundamental to the common reader's experience of verse. In Eng. poetry the meter patterns the stresses, but all the other linguistic and paralinguistic features such as voice pitch, tempo, pausing, timbre, or special inflection are free to elaborate more expansive cadences. The weighting, pacing, and inflecting of a line of verse (as in the wonderful mimetic examples in Pope's *Essay on Criticism*) are our chief sources of delight in the sensuous medium of sound. In the history of crit. there have been repeated reminders that poetry is too strictly laced if it is to be confined to the metrical, that strictness is not valued by every age, that the expressive power of wider, more varied rs. is not to be disdained—that, after all, to insist wholly on metric is to lose most of Blake, Whitman, the Eng. and Scottish popular ballads, much medieval verse, and a great deal of modern verse as well. See now FOOT; MEASURE; METER; METRICI AND RHYTHMICI; PERFORMANCE; RISING AND FALLING.

PSYCHOLOGY: H. Woodrow, *A Quantitative Study of R.* (1909); J. E. W. Wallin, "Experimental Studies of R. and Time," *Psych. Rev.* 18–19 (1911–12);

C. A. Ruckmich, "A Bibl. of R.," *Am. Jour. of Psych.* 24–35 (1913–24); P. Fraisse, *Les Structures rythmiques* (1956), *Psychologie du rythme* (1974); *Beiträge zur Theorie und Lehre vom Rhythmus*, ed. P. Röthig (1966)—with bibl.; J. G. Martin, "Rhythmic (Hierarchical) Versus Serial Structure in Speech and Other Behavior," *Psych. Rev.* 79 (1972)—important implications.

MUSIC AND MUSICAL METRICS: R. Westphal, *Die Fragmente und der Lehrsätze der griechische Rhythmiker* (1861), *Griechische Rhythmik* (1885), ed., *Aristoxenos von Tarent: Melik und Rhythmik des class. Hellentums*, 2 v. (1883–93)—texts and studies of the Gr. *rhythmikoi;* C. F. A. Williams, *The Aristoxenian Theory of Musical R.* (1911); W. F. J. Knight, *St Augustine's* De Musica: *A Synopsis* (1949); C. Sachs, *R. and Tempo* (1953)—popularizing survey; *Aristoxeni Rhythmica,* ed. G. B. Pighi (1959); G. W. Cooper and L. B. Meyer, *The Rhythmic Structure of Music* (1960); S. D. Winick, *R.: An Annot. Bibl.* (1974); G. Henneberg, *Theorien zur Rhythmik und Metrik* (1974); G. Read, *Mod. Rhythmic Notation* (1978); Michaelides, s.v. "Aristoxenus," "Chronos," "Ethos," "Rhythmos"; W. Dürr and W. Gerstenberg, "Rhythmus, Metrum, Takt," *MGG* 11.383–419; W. Dürr et al., "R.," *New Grove*—excellent survey; *Aristoxenus: Elementa Rhythmica,* ed. L. Pearson (1990)—major new tr.

HISTORY OF THE CONCEPT: Cicero, *Orator* 168–236; Quintilian, *Institutio oratoria* 9.4.45–111; L. Muratori, *Dissertatio de rhythmica veterum poesi* (1740), rpt. Migne, *PL,* 151.755 ff.; W. Brambach, *Rhythmische und metrische Untersuchungen* (1871); Westphal, 175 ff.; E. Graf, *Rhythmus und Metrum: Zur Synonymik* (1891); G. Mari, "Ritmo latino e terminologia ritmica medievale," *Studi di filologia romanza* 8 (1901); O. Schroeder, "Rhythmus," *Hermes* 53 (1918); Meyer, 3.130 ff.; E. Petersen, "Rhythmus," *Abh. der königlichen Gesell. der Wiss. zu Göttingen, philol.-hist. Klasse,* n.s. 16,5 (1917), 1–104; J. W. Rankin, "R. and Rime Before the Norman Conquest," *PMLA* 36 (1921); W. Jaeger, *Paideuma,* 2d ed. (1945), 126, 447; R. Waltz, "RHYTHMOS et numerus," *REL* 26 (1948); Wilamowitz, ch. 3; J. J. Pollitt, *The Ancient View of Gr. Art* (1974).

POETRY: F. B. Gummere, *The Beginnings of Poetry* (1901), ch. 2; G. Seydel, "Rhythmica," Pauly-Wissowa, ser. 2, v. 1A; Meyer, v. 1, ch. 1; E. Landry, *La Théorie du rythme et le rythme du français déclamé* (1911); Thieme, ch. 9 and bibls., 372 ff., 380 ff.—full list of Fr. works to 1914; E. A. Sonnenschein, *What Is R.?* (1925)—very unreliable; I. A. Richards, "R. and Metre," in Richards; P. Habermann, "Takt," *Reallexikon I;* T. Taig, *R. and Metre* (1929)—very much underrated; A. W. De Groot, "Der Rhythmus," *Neophil* 17 (1932), *Algemene Versleer* (1946); D. Seckel, *Hölderlins Sprachrhythmus* (1937)—good bibl.; E. Olson, *General Prosody: Rhythmic, Metric, Harmonics* (1938); H. D. F. Kitto, "R., Metre, and Black Magic," *ClassR* 56 (1942); T. Georgiades, *Der griechischen Rhythmus* (1949); D.

L. Sims, "R. and Meaning," *EIC* 6 (1956); B. Hrushovsky, "On Free Rs. in Mod. Poetry," in Sebeok; G. B. Pace, "The Two Domains: Meter and R.," *PMLA* 76 (1961); N. Frye, *The Well-Tempered Critic* (1963)—typology of speech, prose, and verse rs.; J. Mazaleyrat, *Pour une étude rythmique du vers français moderne* (1963)—excellent bibl. and appraisals; H. Gross, "Prosody as Rhythmic Cognition," *Sound and Form in Mod. Poetry* (1964), "Toward a Phenomenology of R.," *The Structure of Verse* (1979)—the latter recanting the former; J. O. Perry, "The Temporal Analysis of Poems," *BJA* 5 (1965); R. Fowler, "'Prose R.' and Meter," *Essays on Style and Lang*, ed. Fowler (1966)—excellent; A. Cook, "R.," *Prisms* (1967); G. Faure, *Les Éléments du rythme poétique en anglais moderne* (1970); R. Mitchell, "Toward a System of Grammatical Scansion," *Lang&S* 3 (1970); W. S. Allen, *Accent and R.* (1973), ch. 8; P. M. Bertinetto, *Ritmo e modelli ritmici* (1973); A. Dougherty, *A Study of Rhythmic Structure in the Verse of W. B. Yeats* (1973)—La Drière's system; W. Seidel, *Rhythmus: Eine Begriffsbestimmung* (1976); D. W. Harding, *Words Into R.* (1976); D. Laferriere, "The Teleology of R. in Poetry," *PTL* 4 (1979)—Rus. examples; Brogan, ch. 5; Morier, s.v. "Rythme," "Tempo," "Débit"; Attridge, sect. IV; H. Meschonnic, *Critique du rythme* (1982); W. Mohr, "Rhythmus," *Reallexikon*, 3.456–75—comprehensive; A. W. Bernhart, "The Iconic Quality of Poetic R.," *W&I* 2 (1986); Scherr, ch. 5; M. G. Tarlinskaja, "R.—Morphology—Syntax—R.," *Style* 18 (1984), *Shakespeare's Verse* (1987), esp. ch. 7—"rhythmical figures"; T. Clark, "Not Motion, but a Mime of It," *Paragraph* 9 (1987); R. D. Cureton, *Rhythmic Phrasing in Eng. Verse* (1992).   T.V.F.B.

RHYTHMICAL PAUSE. See PAUSE.

RHYTHMICAL PROSE. See PROSE RHYTHM.

RHYTHMICI. See METRICI AND RHYTHMICI.

RICH RHYME. (Fr. *rime riche*, Ger. *reicher Reim*, It. *rima cara*). In true rhyme, the medial vowel and final consonant sounds of the rhyming syllables are held the same while the first consonant (or cluster) is varied, e.g. *cat/rat*. When rhyming is extended leftward, or backward, from the rhyming vowel into the preceding ("prop") consonant or preceding syllables, the r. is said to be "enriched"; this structure is recognized in all Western poetries as one acceptable expansion of r. practice. One may well wonder why this is so, and what relationship obtains between poetic practice and lang. structure, but no data presently exists which might suggest that rich rhyming develops in reaction to, say, excessive sound echoing in syllables after the rhyme syllable as a result of inflectional endings.

In r. r., all three sounds in the rhyming syllables are reiterated, and one of three possibilities obtains. Normally the rhyming syllables are homophones, i.e. they are pronounced alike but differ in spelling and meaning, e.g. Fr. *violence/balance*, or Eng. *night/knight, foul/fowl, stare/stair, to/too/two*. More rarely, they are homographs, i.e. spelled the same but differing in pronunciation and meaning—e.g. Mod. Eng. *read/read* (present tense; past tense), *conflict/conflict* (the noun; the verb)—but these are in fact "eye rhyme" (q.v.) not r. r., since the conditions of rhyme are not met. Finally, they may be homonyms, i.e. both pronounced and spelled alike—this practice is allowed in both Fr. and Eng.—but they *must* differ in meaning, e.g. Fr. *. . . pas à pas/ . . . ne pas, été/été* (summer, been), *nue/nue* (cloud, naked); or Eng. *want/want* (desire; lack), *port/port* (ship haven; kind of wine), *stare/stare* (the bird; to gaze curiously), or *may/May*. Chaucer has many such: e.g. *heere/heere* (here, hear), *herte/herte* (hurt, heart), *seke/seke* (seek, sick). The echo (q.v.) device is one (particularly effective) species of r. r. One step further beyond r. r. is *identical rhyme* (q.v.), where spelling, sound, and sense are all three repeated, i.e. the same part of speech in the same sense; but the precise boundary between r. r. and identical rhyme is, given the nature of polysemy, nearly impossible to draw, and its status as r. is disputed.

R. r. first appears in Fr. poetry in quantity in the 15th c. as one of the devices of the *Rhétoriqueurs* (q.v.; Fabri's *rithme leonine*); the term *rime riche* is first used by Sebillet (1490). The poets of the Pléiade allowed it, both Ronsard and Du Bellay recommending it in moderation, but after 1600 it lapsed until the romantics revived it, making it one of the hallmarks of their metrical style—particularly Hugo. Championed subsequently by Théodore de Banville, it was used even more by the Parnassians (q.v.). In Eng., Chaucer learned the practice of r. r. from Fr., where it was more various, most rhyme words being polysyllabic, but the form was only imperfectly naturalized into Eng., a Germanic lang. Gower, following Chaucer, is its chief exponent. For further discussion of the taxonomy and terminology for rich rhyming in Fr. prosody, see RHYME; then see IDENTICAL RHYME. Ger. *rührende Reim* is a type of mosaic (q.v.) rich or identical (q.v.) rhyme popular in MHG in which one of the rhyming words is a compound of the other, e.g. Ger. *zeigen/erzeigen*, Fr. *aroi/a roi, des cors/descors*, Eng. *mortal/immortal, sickle/icicle*.—T. de Banville, *Petit traité de poésie française* (1872); P. Delaporte, *De la rime française* (1898); Kastner; Schipper, *History* 273; C. von Kraus, "Der rührende Reim im Mittelhochdeutschen," *ZDA* 56 (1918); Patterson; M. Ito, *John Gower The Medieval Poet* (1976)—compares G. to Chaucer; Mazaleyrat; Scott; D. Billy, "La Nomenclature des rimes," *Poétique* 15 (1984); B. de Cornulier, "Rime 'riche' et fonction de la rime," *Litterature* 59 (1985); Scherr; C. Scott, *The Riches of Rhyme* (1988); J. J. Small, *Positive as Sound* (1990), ch. 4.   T.V.F.B.

RIDDLE. An ancient and worldwide form in both

oral lit. (the "folk r.") and written lit. (the "literary r."). Because it embodies fundamental forms of metaphor, word play, and paradox (qq.v.), the r. is also important to poetry and poetics generally. A r. takes the form of a question and answer, i.e. a deceptive question and a "right" answer which pierces some central ambiguity in the question. In a "true r.," the question presents a "description" (in one form, something described in terms of something else) and a "block element" (some contradiction or confusion in the description). For example, the r. "What plows and plows, but no furrow remains?" first appears to describe a plow, then blocks that answer ("no furrow remains"), and finally is resolved by another answer (a ship). Such rs. are essentially metaphors with one term concealed, pointing out both similarities and differences between the terms. Some metaphorical rs. leave the block element implicit: "Back of the village sit those who have donned white kerchiefs" (fence posts, each with a cap of snow). Others replace the single comparison with a series of comparisons, which may conflict with one another: "Open like a barn door, / Shut like a bat. / Guess all your lifetime, / You can't guess that" (umbrella).

Another large class of "true rs." is the punning r., based on lexical or grammatical ambiguity: "What turns without moving?" (milk); "Patch upon patch without any stitches" (cabbage). Other rs. are based on apparent anomalies in the laws of nature: "A fire burns in the middle of the sea" (a lamp); "I tremble at each breath of air, / And yet can heaviest burdens bear" (water); "What is full of holes and holds water?" (sponge). Rs. appear both in verse and prose; often they are "framed" by introductory and closing formulas.

The folk r. usually appears less in casual conversation than in more structured social occasions ranging from children's games to various adult rituals (e.g. courtship in tribal South Africa, funeral wakes in the West Indies). In practice the "true r." is associated with other kinds of enigmatic questions: "biblical rs." (which describe a character in the Bible), joking questions such as "conundrums" ("How is a duck like an icicle?" Both grow down.), "wisdom questions" (for which the answer must be known already, as in a catechism), "charades" (which describe a word syllable-by-syllable), and various parody forms such as the "catch-r." (which tricks the answerer into an embarrassing answer).

The literary r. is essentially an imitation of the folk r. by a sophisticated poet, who may develop the possibilities and expand the limits of the basic form. Literary rs. tend toward longer and more elaborate expression (sonnets, e.g., in Ren. Italy). In contrast to folk rs., they may use abstractions as topics (e.g., creation, humility, death, wisdom), exploit the device of prosopopoeia (q.v.), delight in obscene suggestions, and even give away the answer in the text or title. The literary r. has a long history, appearing in Sanskrit (there are cosmological rs. in the *Rigveda*, parts of which go back to the early first millennium B.C.); in Heb. (a trad. of literary rs. runs from the OT and the Talmud through the Heb. poetry [q.v.] of medieval Spain, which includes the poet Dunash ben Labrat [10th c.], the founder of Sp. Heb. poetry, and the lyric poet Jehuda Halevi [ca. 1085–1140]); in Gr. (esp. in the *Greek Anthology* and in Byzantine lit.); in Arabic (a long trad. of Ar. riddling runs from the 10th c. to the present, the most famous Ar. riddle-master being Al-Hariri, [ca. 1050–1120], whose *Assemblies* includes several chapters of rs. and other enigmatic questions); in Persian (another long trad., extending from the 10th–11th cs. through the 16th, and perhaps best known from the rs. in the epic *Shahnameh* of Firdūsi [b. 940], in which they are used as a test for the hero); and perhaps in Chinese (there is evidence, though no texts, of literary riddling in China in the 12th–13th cs.). A rich medieval tradition began in Europe with 100 Lat. rs. by "Symphosius" (5th c.). In England, Aldhelm (640–709) wrote 100 rs. in Anglo-Lat. hexameters (*Enigmata*), contributing to the genre the "etymological r.," which uses the text of the r. to explore the meaning of the Lat. name of the answer. The 90 or so OE rs. in the Exeter Book are among the glories of early Eng. poetry—in turn vigorous and energetic, sly and wicked, sharply visual and profoundly paradoxical. The Ren. was another productive period for the literary r., particularly in Italy. Later writers attracted to the form incl. Cervantes, Swift, Schiller, and Heine.

The essence of a r., Aristotle noted, "is to express true facts under impossible conditions," a way of thinking deeply related to metaphor (q.v.). Like metaphors, rs. teach us something by engendering thought (*Poetics* 22; *Rhetoric* 3.2, 10). They are meant ultimately to reveal rather than to conceal. Children explore the linguistic and cognitive systems of their culture through r.-contests (McDowell), and in traditional societies adults may use r.-sessions in times of crisis as a model for resolving confusion (Abrahams). Metaphorical rs. teach about reading the unknown in terms of the known, and how the one never quite fits the other; punning rs. teach about the back alleys, short cuts, and dead ends in lang., and of the surprises to be found there; rs. pointing out contradictions in the physical world itself teach about the tentative nature of our categories of reality. See also IMAGERY; KENNING; PUN; WIT.

The Demaundes Joyous (1511; rpt. 1971)—first Mod. Eng. r. book; J. B. Friedreich, *Gesch. des Räthsels* (1860); K. Ohlert, *Rätsel und Gesellschaftsspiel der alten Griechen*, 2d ed. (1886); W. Schultz, "Rätsel," Pauly-Wissowa; W. Schultz, *Rätsel aus dem hellenischen Kulturkreise* (1909–12); *The Rs. of Aldhelm*, tr. J. H. Pitman (1925); M. De Filippis, *The Literary R. in Italy to the End of the 16th C.*, *The Literary R. in Italy in the 17th C.*, *The Literary R. in*

RIDING RHYME

Italy in the 18th C., U. of Cal. Pubs. in Mod. Philol. 34 (1948), 40 (1953), 83 (1967); A. Taylor, *The Literary R. Before 1600* (1948)—good intro., *Eng. Rs. from Oral Trad.* (1951)—comprehensive; V. Hull and A. Taylor, *A Collection of Ir. Rs.* (1955); Frye; J. F. Adams, "The Anglo-Saxon R. as Lyric Mode," *Crit* 7 (1965); C. T. Scott, *Persian and Ar. Rs.* (1965), "On Defining the R.," *Genre* 2 (1969); D. Bhagwat, *The R. in Indian Life, Lore and Lit.* (1965); A. Hacikyan, *A Linguistic and Literary Analysis of OE Rs.* (1966); D. D. Lucas, *Emily Dickinson and R.* (1969); R. Finnegan, *Oral Lit. in Africa* (1970), ch. 15; *Deutsches Rätselbuch*, ed. V. Schupp (1972); R. D. Abrahams, "The Literary Study of the R.," *TSLL* 14 (1972)—misleading title; R. D. Abrahams and A. Dundes, "Rs.," *Folklore and Folklife*, ed. R. M. Dorson (1972); I. Basgöz and A. Tietze, *Bilmece: A Corpus of Turkish Rs.* (1973); J. Lindow, "Rs., Kennings, and the Complexity of Skaldic Poetry," *SS* 47 (1975); *JAF* 89 (1976)—spec. iss. on rs. and riddling; N. Frye, "Charms and Rs.," *Spiritus Mundi* (1976); K. Wagner, "Rätsel," *Reallexikon*; *The OE Rs. of the Exeter Book*, ed. C. Williamson (1977)—OE texts, *A Feast of Creatures* (1982)—tr. of OE rs.; A. Welsh, *Roots of Lyric* (1978); J. H. McDowell, *Children's Riddling* (1979)—sociolinguistic analysis; *Rs. Ancient and Mod.*, ed. M. Bryant (1983)—useful anthol. esp. of literary rs.; W. J. Pepicello and T. A. Green, *The Lang. of Rs.* (1984)—ling. models of punning rs.; A. R. Rieke, "Donne's Rs.," *JEGP* 83 (1984); N. Howe, "Aldhelm's *Enigmata* and Isidorian Etymology," *ASE* 14 (1985); D. Sadovnikov, *Rs. of the Rus. People* (1986). A.W.

RIDING RHYME. See COUPLET.

RIME. See RHYME.

RIME RICHE. See RICH RHYME; IDENTICAL RHYME; RHYME.

RÍMUR. This plural form designates each of the more than one thousand extant narratives—divided because of their length into shorter narrative blocks each called a *ríma*—which, though not always of high quality, were the dominant and most popular form of Icelandic poetry (q.v.) for over five centuries, beginning around 1350. In metrical form they were initially based on foreign models, but reflecting the Icelandic predilection for exacting composition, they developed a large number of intricate stanza forms, usually of four lines (sometimes three). As a rule, except in the oldest ones, no two successive r. in a cycle were in the same metrical form. They were chanted to special tunes called *stemmur* (singular, *stemma*). In subject matter they were not original, being based on written prose narratives, esp. at first the legendary and romantic sagas. Other subjects were added later, such as biblical stories and the Charlemagne cycle, e.g. the cycle of 60 r. on Olgeir danski

(Ogier le danois) composed in 1680 by Guðmundur Bergþórsson.

Bj. K. Þórólfsson, *R. fyrir 1600* (1934)—thorough study of early r.; *Rit rímnafélagsins* (1948)—fullest ed.; *Sýnisbók íslenzkra rímna* [Specimens of Icelandic R.], ed. W. A. Craigie, 3 v. (1952)—useful intros. in Eng.; F. Sigmundsson, *Rímnatal I–II* (1966)—catalogue of all r. and authors; *Íslenzkar miðaldarímur*, ed. Ó. Halldórsson (1973–75)—crit. eds. of early r.; S. F. D. Hughes, "Report on R., 1980," *JEGP* 79 (1980)—surveys work since 1955; V. Ólason, *The Traditional Ballads of Iceland* (1982), 52–82—good recent account of early r. R.CO.

RING COMPOSITION is a structural principle or rhetorical device in which an element or series of elements are repeated at the beginning and at the end of a poem or narrative unit, thus comprising a "ring" framing a nonannular core. Van Otterlo, the pioneer in this branch of literary study, distinguished between simple framing structures, in which a single repeating element encloses the core material in the pattern *a-x-a*, and annular systems, in which the core material is set off by two or more concentric rings, e.g. *a-b-c-x-c-b-a*. The repeating elements in an annular system are chiasmically ordered. Thus, to employ a geometric metaphor, r. c. provides a mechanism for configuring circles into the linearity of the narrational and receptional processes. The terms "ring structure," "envelope pattern" (see ENVELOPE), "framing," and "chiasmus" (q.v.) often refer to the same figure.

R. c. operates on several scales from the microstructural to the macrostructural. Sometimes lexical repetition encapsulates a passage comprising a few lines, a stanza, a fitt, or a short poem; longer episodes or digressions are usually marked off by annular patterns of greater complexity. In their most expanded and intricate forms, ring systems can organize entire epic poems, as Whitman has argued for the *Iliad* and Niles for *Beowulf*. Rings can be made up of repeating material of various sorts—individual words or word roots, themes, images, motifs, or even elaborate narrative sequences. To function successfully as a ring marker, however, the convention of repetition must be sufficiently recognizable within the tradition or the repeating element sufficiently developed within the poem to enable auditors or readers to recognize the recurrence.

R. c. probably arose in response to mnemonic necessity: it provided oral poets with a powerful compositional technique and aural audiences with a means of keeping track of the movement of the story. Structurally, it can function in two ways: (1) to connect the ring-encapsulated passage or episode with the larger story, or (2) to create coherence within such a passage. In either case, it counteracts the paratactic and centrifugal tendencies endemic to oral and oral-derived poetry (Notopoulos). Yet its usefulness can be exaggerated, since the particular pattern that r. c. imposes cannot easily accommodate nonpaired repetitions, linear plot progressions, and other nonsymmetrical movements.

A perspicuous lit. hist. of r. c. cannot yet be written, since its incidence has been assayed in only a few genres and historical periods. The governing scholarly assumption has been that r. c. serves the noetic and stylistic economies of oral-based composition. This assumption has been to a degree validated by the high incidence of the device in the oral or oral-derived poetries (particularly epic and narrative) of the ancient Greeks and Anglo-Saxons. In these two fields, research into r. c. under varying rubrics originated independently during the 1930s and '40s. On the other hand, it had long been known among Celtic scholars that ancient Irish and Welsh poets made extensive use of a ring device called *dúnad(h)*, which requires that a poem begin and end with the same word. In recent decades the device has been documented in other works and traditions arising out of close association with an oral background, such as the OF *chanson de geste* (q.v.), the MHG *Nibelungenlied*, 20th-c. Yugoslav oral epic, Scottish balladry, and even the Gospels. Yet its discovery in Pound's *Cantos* and other modern and highly literate works suggests that r. c. may fill more uses over a broader literary spectrum than has been hitherto suspected. See also CONCATENATION; CORONA.

A. Bartlett, *The Larger Rhetorical Patterns in Anglo-Saxon Poetry* (1935); W. van Otterlo, *De Ringcompositie als Opbouwprincipe in de epische Gedichten van Homerus* (1948); J. Notopoulos, "Continuity and Interconnexion in Homeric Oral Composition," *TAPA* 80 (1949); C. Whitman, *Homer and the Heroic Trad.* (1958); P. L. Henry, "A Celtic-Eng. Prosodic Feature," *ZCP* 29 (1962–64); J. Gaisser, "A Structural Analysis of the Digressions in the *Iliad* and the *Odyssey*," *HSCP* 73 (1969); D. Buchan, *The Ballad and the Folk* (1972); H. W. Tonsfeldt, "Ring Structure in *Beowulf*," *Neophil* 61 (1977); J. D. Niles, Beowulf (1983); K. Davis, *Fugue and Fresco* (1984); B. Fenik, *Homer and the Nibelungenlied* (1986); A. B. Lord, "The Merging of Two Worlds," *Oral Trad. in Lit.*, ed. J. M. Foley (1986); W. Parks, "Ring Structure and Narrative Embedding in Homer and *Beowulf*," *NM* 89 (1988).   W.W.P.

RISING AND FALLING RHYTHM. These terms have traditionally been used in foot-based theories of meter (q.v.) to describe the prevailing rhythm (q.v.) of a line. One would think that r. rhythms would be associated with iambic and anapestic meters, f. with trochaic and dactylic, but this is not so: iambic lines can have a f. rhythm (see below). There is a sense in which iambic feet in succession are felt to give a prevailing "r." effect, perhaps because unstressed syllables in Eng. tend to be enclitics of stresses to their right, the movement being from a syllable of less energy in phonation to one of more. Trochaic meters, however, are more easily felt to be f., for when the heavy ele-

ment comes first, the grouping effect is much stronger. It should be noted that musical theories of meter (see Brogan) find (or produce) a f. rhythm in all verse, even iambic, since stresses always begin bars. Gerard Manley Hopkins ("Author's Preface" to *Poems*) identifies three types of rhythms: r., f., and "rocking" (amphibrachic).

Halpern has argued that iambic meters differ not only from trochaic but also from triple meters and accentual verse (q.v.) as well, for iambic alone is capable of *modulation*, via promotion and demotion based on relativity of stress, while none of the other meters can function so. In iambic meters secondary and occasionally even tertiary stresses may fall under ictus and be acceptable, and stresses outside of ictus may conversely be demoted and treated as weak. But in trochaic and ternary meters the metrical pattern must be marked by primary word-stresses alone. This gives them their heavy, accentual, emphatic character, in comparison with iambic. Many other scholars have assumed that f. is the more "natural" rhythm; and one recollects that it was the trochaic septenarius (q.v.) which the Roman legions used for marching songs. Atkins, however, argues the opposite: it is precisely because trochaic rhythms are *not* natural that they have to be maintained so heavily and overtly, "failing which the natural iambic rhythm inevitably reasserts itself."

The difficulty comes in lines in which no clear rhythm is established or prevails, i.e. in sequences which are rhythmically ambiguous. It used to be held that a r. rhythm could be converted to a f. one by simply deleting a syllable, such as the first syllable of an iambic pentameter line, but this view has been largely abandoned. It should be evident that the perception of r. or f. rhythms is created by the morphological structure of the line, and has nothing to do with metrical foot-boundaries, which typically have little correlation with word boundaries. This means that several words with a trochaic wordshape can give a f. rhythm to an iambic line. Consider, for example, this line from Shakespeare's sonnet 75,

/ x   x / x   / x   / x   / x
Doubting the filching age will steale his treasure

A traditional metrist of the Classicizing school, such as Saintsbury, would would call this a standard iambic pentameter with a "feminine ending," an "initial trochaic substitution," and a f. rhythm. All three of the disyllables in the line have a trochaic wordshape, and both "age will" and "steale his" co-operate in creating a f. rhythm.

Or again, a reader reading Macaulay's accentual imitation of the Saturnian:

x   / x   / x   / x
The queen was in her parlour
  / x   x / x   / x
   eating bread and honey

may not feel that the first 6 syllables exhibit any

strongly f. rhythm; but "parlour," by contrast, does, and certainly the last 6 syllables do: two of the last four words have trochaic shapes, and "bread and" aligns itself with this movement. The result is that, at midline, the movement is felt to shift, decisively. The same effect—sudden transition of rhythm without change of meter—is evident in the often cited quatrain by Sidney's sister, the Countess of Pembroke (see Newton).

Creek's early study concluded that whether a line is viewed as in r. or f. rhythm depends on seven factors: reader expectations, syllable-structure at the beginning of the line, and at the end, and around the caesura, weak endings, phrase structure, and morphology. And some very suggestive experiments done early in the 20th c. by Wallin, Woodrow, Brown, and others (see Brogan, esp. D139, D195–99) showed that alterations in the timing and pausing of the same syllabic sequence changed auditors' perceptions of them from iambic to trochaic decisively. Other researchers have found that in i. and t. verse the distribution of features is asymmetrical: Newton found that initial inversions are four times more prevalent in iambic verse than in trochaic. Hascall found that unmetrical trochaic lines are rare, the meter is fixed at the very outset of the line, and there is "less distance, in trochaic verse, between the metrical line and the poetic line."

The very existence of discussions of r. and f. rhythm is a confirmation of the fact that word-shape and phraseshape patterns matter to our perception of the flow of the line. A number of efforts in the past to distinguish iambic from trochaic meters and r. from f. rhythms (see bibl.) never succeeded in resolving the conceptual and terminological problems; Stewart, drawing on music, decided that *both* distinctions were unwarranted. All these studies, however, should serve as reminders of both the necessary distinction between meter and rhythm (qq.v.) and their deep interrelations. The traditional conception of meter as lang. organization at the phonological level left out of account the very real effects which such organization has on the level of morphology and syntax. See now BINARY AND TERNARY; DURATION; METER; RHYTHM.

H. L. Creek, "R. and F. Rhythms in Eng. Verse," *PMLA* 35 (1920); G. R. Stewart, Jr. "The Iambic-Trochaic Theory in Relation to Musical Notation," *JEGP* 24 (1925); H. G. Atkins, "Holding Down the Trochees," *MLR* 37 (1942); M. Halpern, "On the Two Chief Metrical Modes in Eng.," *PMLA* 77 (1962); D. L. Hascall, "Trochaic Meter," *CE* 33 (1971); R. P. Newton, "Trochaic and Iambic," *Lang&S* 8 (1975); D. Laferrière, "Iambic Versus Trochaic: The Case of Rus.," *IRSL* 4 (1979); Brogan. T.V.F.B.

RISPETTO. An It. stanza of variable length, usually ranging from 6 to 12 lines in hendecasyllables (q.v.), but most commonly an octave rhyming

ababab cc, and for this reason often confused with the Sicilian octave (*abababab*) and *strambotto* (qq.v.). Some variation in the form occurs in the last four verses or *ripresa*, which came to have two rhyming couplets of different rhymes, giving *ababccdd*. Originally a form of Tuscan popular poetry, the r. is now used throughout Italy. The content is generally amorous, hence the name, "respect," i.e. honor paid the beloved woman. In the 15th c., Leonardo Giustinian, Politian, and Lorenzo de' Medici wrote series of *rispetti*; in modern times, Carducci composed many, and Pascoli included a number of them in his *Myricae*. The Fr. *respit* is more peasantlike in feeling.—H. Schuchardt, *Ritornell und Terzine* (1875); G. Lega, *Rispetti antichi pubblicati da un codice magliabechiano* (1905); M. Barbi, *Poesia popolare italiana* (1939); *Rispetti e strambotti del Quattrocento*, ed. R. Spongano (1971); Spongano; Wilkins; Elwert, *Italienische*, sect. 98. L.H.G.; C.K.

RITORNELLO (also *ripresa*). A group of lines (from one to four or more) in a variety of meters (*quinario* through *endecasillabo*) which introduce an It. *ballata* and which are repeated as a refrain at the end of each stanza. The last line (sometimes the last two lines) of each stanza are linked through rhyme to the r., thereby providing a sort of metrical "return" to the refrain. The r. may have begun as a r. *intercalare*, an exclamation from the congregation in response to the priest who was reading a psalm or sequence. In most instances the r. expresses in concise terms either an emotional response to or the essence of the idea or action treated in the stanza or poem as a whole. Since the r. serves as the refrain of a *ballata*, the number of lines in the r. determines the specific name applied to each variety of this lyric form: 1-line r., *ballata piccola*; 2-line r., *ballata minore*; 3-line r., *ballata mezzana*; 4-line r., *ballata grande* (the most common form); 5 (or more)-line r., *ballata estravagante*. See also LAUDA; cf. BURDEN; REFRAN.—H. Schuchardt, *Ritornell und Terzine* (1875); F. Flamini, *Notizia storica dei versi e metri italiani* (1919); L. Castelnuovo, *La metrica italiana* (1979). L.H.G.; C.K.

ROCKING RHYTHM. See RUNNING RHYTHM.

ROCOCO. Taken from art history, "r." is used by literary historians as a collective term for 18th-c. works of which graceful lightness is an outstanding characteristic. Literary r. (fl. 1720–75) includes the mock-heroic poem (Voltaire, Pope, Zachariä), *poésie fugitive* and the fable (Gay, Hagedorn, Gellert, Lessing, Iriarte, Samaniego), Horatian and Anacreontic (q.v.) verse (Günther, E. von Kleist, Gleim, Cadalso, Melendez, Valdés, Bellamy, Bilderdijk, Bellman, Deržavin), the frivolous or lightly ironic tale, the satirically philosophic tale in prose or verse (Voltaire, Cazotte, Wieland, Casti), the humorous novel (Sterne, Wieland),

and satiric and pastoral comedy (Marivaux, Beaumarchais, the early Goethe). At times r. writing is deliberately licentious, but more often it serves to expound gracefully what purports to be the golden mean (Kleist), homely wisdom (the fabulists), or even an enlightened philosophical system (Voltaire, Wieland); always, however, it repudiates, tacitly or explicitly, earnestness as an absolute good, and as exponents of Enlightenment its authors without exception cultivate neoclassical clarity and—except when it is sacrificed to irony—simplicity. Monotony is avoided by brevity or conscious formal variation (use of the *genre mêlé*, verse with irregular rhyme schemes and line lengths; alternation of narrative with dialogue, and of formal tone with colloquialism), while wit is exploited in connection with even the most serious themes, often at the expense of unity of theme or action or of plausible characterization. In tone, r. writing is often frankly jocular; writers cultivate the fiction that they stand in a direct, even personal relationship with their public, at times deliberately interposing themselves between their work and its audience, so that genres and forms inherited from neoclassicism are media for expressing the shared optimistic rationalism and self-confident individualism of 18th-c. middleclass intellectuals.

E. Ermatinger, *Barock und Rokoko in der deutschen Dichtung* (1928); P. Trahard, *Les Maîtres de la sensibilité française au XVIIIe siècle*, 4 v. (1931–33); E. Merker, "Graziendichtung," *Reallexikon*, v. 1; W. Sypher, *R. to Cubism in Art and Lit.* (1960); S. Atkins, "Zeitalter der Aufklärung," *Fischer-Lexicon: Literatur*, v. 2 (1965); A. Anger, *Literarisches R.*, 2d ed. (1968), "Rokokodichtung," *Reallexikon*, v. 3; H. Zeman, *Die deutsche anakreontische Dichtung* (1972); H. Hatzfeld, *The R.: Eroticism, Wit, and Elegance in European Lit.* (1972), "L'Esprit r. dans la poésie du XVIIIe siécle," *Mélanges à la mémoire de Franco Simone*, v. 2 (1981); P. Brady, "R. Style in European Poetry," *Synthesis* 7 (1980).   S.A.

ROMANCE (Sp. ballad). The r. is the simplest and most common fixed form in Sp. poetry. It is usually written in octosyllabic verse in which the even lines assonate alike and the odd-numbered are left free. In the *r. doble*, the odd-numbered lines have one assonance and the even-numbered another. Other variations of the basic form (even some having a periodic refrain) have at times been popular. The learned and the semilearned—and probably even the illiterate—produce these ballads wherever Sp. is spoken, and scholars collect them by the hundreds. They reflect almost every phase of Sp. life.

Since many of them are anonymous and have been transmitted largely in oral form, their origin and complete history cannot be traced. The earliest known written rs. date from the early 15th c. In the early 16th c., *romanceros* (collections devoted exclusively to ballads) began to appear, the first (1545–1550?) being the famous *Cancionero de rs.*—often called the *Cancionero sin año* because it bears no date of publication—by Martin Nucio in Antwerp. The most convenient classification of rs.—that summarized by S. G. Morley and adapted from those of Durán, Wolf and Hofmann, and Milá y Fontanals—covers the period from the 15th through the 17th c. It corresponds, with the exception of the *rs. vulgares*, to three periods of creation—traditional, erudite, and artistic: (1) the anonymous *rs. viejos*, primitive or trad. ballads, usually on historical themes and thought to be among the earliest; (2) the 15th- and early 16th-c. *rs. juglarescos*, minstrel ballads, "longer and more personal, but still supported by trad."; (3) *rs. eruditos*, erudite ballads, written by known authors after 1550 and based on old chronicles; (4) *rs. artisticos*, artistic ballads, usually lyric, on varied themes, and written by known authors from the late 15th c. through the 17th; and (5) the crude *rs. vulgares*, blind beggar ballads, from about 1600 on. Recently, large numbers of orally transmitted rs. have been collected in the Americas and abroad by such scholars as Samuel G. Armistead and Joseph Silverman (Sephardic), Manuel da Costa Fontes (Portuguese), and others. A strong impulse to r. composition was given in the early 20th c. by F. García Lorca, who used the form for expressing multi-emotional (usually dark) subject matter.

The *r. heroico*, also called *r. endecasílabo* or *r. real*, is a r. in Italianate hendecasyllables. A r. in lines of less than eight syllables is called *romancillo*. One variation of the r. is the *corrido* (ballad with guitar accompaniment), esp. popular in Mexico. The *jácara* is a r. in which the activities of ruffians are recounted, usually in a boisterous manner.—E. Mérimée and S. G. Morley, *A Hist. of Sp. Lit.* (1930); E. Honig, *García Lorca* (1944); S. G. Morley, "Chronological List of Early Sp. Ballads," *HR* 13 (1945); Le Gentil; R. Menéndez Pidal, *Romancero hispánico*, 2 v. (1953); *Romancero y poesía oral*, v. 4: *El romancero hoy: Historia, comparatismo, bibliografía crítica*, ed. S. G. Armistead et al. (1979); Navarro; *Sp. Ballads*, tr. R. Wright (1987); F. G. Lorca, *Romancero Gitano*, and *Lorca's* Romancero Gitano: *Eighteen Commentaries*, both ed. H. Ramsden (1988); A. Barea, *Lorca: The Poet and His People* (n.d.).   D.C.C.

ROMANCE, MEDIEVAL OR METRICAL. See MEDIEVAL ROMANCE.

ROMANCE PROSODY. See FRENCH PROSODY; ITALIAN PROSODY; SPANISH PROSODY.

ROMANCE-SIX. See TAIL RHYME.

ROMANIAN POETRY. The earliest surviving texts of R. p. date from the 17th c. In the 17th and 18th cs., R. p. is chiefly of three kinds. The first is religious poetry, esp. verse translations of biblical books.

Thus Dosoftei, a learned Moldavian clergyman, translated the *Psalms* (1673) in rhymed couplets of variable length that indicate equally the influence of R. oral folk verse and of classicist Polish poetry (q.v.). The second is occasional poetry following Western models—elegies, odes, pattern poetry, and epigrams. The most prominent example is by the historian and statesman Miron Costin, whose *Viata lumii* (The World's Life, ca. 1672) is a meditation on the vanity of life and the mutability of fortune, written in rhymed couplets of 12 or 13 syllables in irregular meter. The third kind is represented by a wide variety of historical chronicles in verse that flourished in the 18th c. in the southern principality of Wallachia. These are often polemical, always picturesque, and undoubtedly circulated orally.

The 18th c. also witnessed the culmination of oral folk verse, references to and quotations from which are found already in the 15th and 16th cs. They express in a variety of genres the existential horizon and emotional universe of a stable agrarian society. While steeped in a religiosity that combines a simplified Christianity and a broad pantheistic sacrality, this poetry also preserves some traces of a pre-Roman pagan mythology. Heroic trads. are rendered not in epics but rather in short ballads. The bulk of folk poetry consists of *doinas*, lyrical expressions of love, loneliness, grief, and yearning, or, less often, glee, carousal, or revolt. Broader visions are provided by the myth of master-builder Manole, who sacrificed his and his wife's life to the achievement of a unique building, and particularly by *Miorita*, which is often said to embody a R. folk-philosophy. It tells the story of a migrant shepherd who, upon hearing his companions' plot to murder him, does not defend himself but rather turns the occasion into a grand reconciliation with nature, the stars, and the animals. The popularity of folk poetry declined toward the end of the 19th c., and it had virtually disappeared by the middle of the 20th.

The end of early R. lit. was marked by Anton Pann (1796?–1854), who synthesized the oral, didactic, and mythical-historical modes in a mock-naive style. The decisive turn of R. p. towards Western values and forms occurred in the last two decades of the 18th c. The Wallachian nobleman Ienache Văcărescu (1740?–93) and his two sons wrote gracious and erotic Anacreontic verse on Gr., It., and Fr. models. At almost the same time, in Transylvania, Ion Budai-Deleanu (1760?–1820) wrote a satirical mock-epic of the medieval struggle against the Ottoman empire.

The first half of the 19th c. in R. p. is characterized by the simultaneous assimilation of Enlightenment, neoclassical, romantic, and Biedermeier (qq.v.) forms and ideas, which led to a number of interesting combinations. Dimitrie Bolintineanu (1819–72) and Grigore Alexandrescu (1814–85) wrote historical ballads, satires, fables, and elegies much influenced by Lamartine and Byron. Vasile Alecsandri (1821–90) combined the fervent struggle for democratic reform and national unity common to the generation inspired by the ideals of 1848 radicalism with poetic serenity, a smiling Epicureanism, and a search for classical balance. He excelled in patriotic verse, natural description, poetic drama, and adaptations of the newly recovered oral trad.

The greatest 19th-c. R. poet was Mihai Eminescu (1850–89), who was influenced by the Ger. romantics and by the philosophies of Kant and Schopenhauer. Unfortunate love, social marginality, intense nationalism, mental illness, and early death no less than his towering poetic achievement soon turned Eminescu into a mythic figure. He gave to R. p. the modern form of its poetic lang. Eminescu's poetry (melancholy meditations on history, society, sentimental love, and allegory) is founded on a deeper level of mythical cosmology, irrational vision, and subjective pantheism. Eminescu's unpublished work contains huge fragmentary epics that describe the universe as emerging out of the lamentations of universal or divine self-consciousness; he also evoked the pre-Roman society of the Dacians as a pristine, luxuriant, and crystalline world of which later history is but a series of deformed copies. Eminescu's radical conservatism was the wellspring for all later forms of nationalism in Romania.

For three decades after Eminescu's death, two poetics schools vied for primacy. One was symbolism (q.v.), which appeared largely under Fr. influence; its most important representative was Alexandru Macedonski (1854–1920), a flamboyant artist who believed fervently in aesthetic perfection; his poetry abounds in images of precious stones, fabulous mirages, and morbid obsessions. Ion Minulescu (1881–1944), an able manipulator of grandiloquent images and sentimental intimations, continued the movement. The other school was the populist and idyllic movement mainly advocated by the journal *Semānātorul*. Its proponents emphasized the use of simple lang. and drew their inspiration from national trads. and local themes. The best poets in this trad. were George Cosbuc (1866–1918), who also produced a superb tr. of Dante's *Divine Comedy*; Octavian Goga (1881–1938), whose best verse expresses a kind of primeval suffering; and Stefan O. Iosif (1875–1913).

The unification of all R. provinces following World War I and the beginnings of capitalist democracy favored an unparalleled growth of poetic diversity and power. The R. high modernists strove to combine trad. and innovation; the influence of Ger. expressionism (q.v.) and of Fr. modernists such as Valéry and Mallarmé can often be recognized in them. George Bacovia (1881–1957) expressed a universal hopelessness through his austere and obsessive verse, full of images of rain, mud, illness, and provincial dreariness. His poems, inspired by Moldavian towns, evoked a symbolic universe of humidity and putrefaction. Ion

Barbu (1895–1961), a mathematician, wrote obscure, semantically packed, tightly structured verse exploring philosophical propositions; for him, the formal order of poetry outlined "a purer, secondary game." In other poems Barbu indulged his voluptuous pleasure in the verbal thickness of a lush and lurid Balkan world, with its jesters, whores, and sages. Lucian Blaga (1895–1951), philosopher, diplomat, and professor, inquired poetically into the connections between natural reality and transcendent mystery; he evolved from Dionysian rhapsodic tones to praise of the agrarian order as a suggestion of cosmic harmony. Tudor Arghezi (1880–1967) renewed the discourse of R. p. by mixing metaphysics and realism. He is particularly impressive for his astounding thematic range, from pamphleteering virulence, coarse violence, and sexuality to the worlds of children and of wrestling with religious faith and doubt.

In the same generation there were able traditionalists such as the cultivated neoclassicist Ion Pillat (1891–1945); the natural mystic Vasile Voiculescu (1884–1963); Adrian Maniu (1891–1968), who clothed a decadent weariness in the mock-simplicity of folk iconography; and the late neoromantic Alexandru Philippide (1900–79), whose poems abound in cosmic visions and historical nightmares. Among the many nationalist poets of the age, the most prominent was Aron Cotrus (1891–1957), whose messianic thunderings were couched in rolling free verse and a racy, sonorous vocabulary.

At least as vital and effective was the group of bewildering experimentalists, surrealists, and avant-garde radicals who eventually came to influence even Western European poetry. Best known among them was the founder of dada (q.v.), Tristan Tzara (1896–1963), but of comparable distinction were Benjamin Fondane (1898–1944), Ilarie Voronca (1903–46), and Gherasim Luca (b. 1913), all of whom emigrated to France. Gellu Naum (b. 1915) and Sasa Pană (1902–81) were among the chief animators of poetic anarchism, which they aligned with leftist political attitudes. Camil Baltazar (1902–77) with his fluid and melodious verse and his morbid yearning for paradisal innocence, as well as Ion Vinea (1895–1964) with his jazzy rhythms and strident prose inserts, strove to bring experimental poetry closer to the mainstream and to endow it with more finished forms.

The poets who emerged in the later 1930s and '40s had to suffer the trauma of war and of repeated political upheavals. Some of the early Existentialists, like Vintilă Horia (b. 1915) and Stefan Baciu (b. 1918), chose exile. Others had to accept long periods of silence. They can be roughly grouped into the Bucharest and the Sibiu schools. The former is exemplified by Ion Caraion (1923–86), Geo Dumitrescu (b. 1920), D. Stelaru (1917–71), and Constant Tonegaru (1919–52), all

ironic pessimists who clamored for adventurous vitality and the demolition of philistine prejudices. Among them Caraion is remarkable for the unrelenting and ferocious darkness of his images. The Sibiu group, exemplified by Radu Stanca (1920–62), the abstractionist Ion Negoitescu (b. 1921), and above all Stefan Aug Doinas (b. 1922), eloquently pleaded for the autonomy of culture and the humanizing role of aesthetic production. Doinas is a consummate craftsman in a wide range of genres and forms, an admirable translator of poetry (e.g. *Faust*), a poet of intense metaphoric creativity, and the author of ethical satire and Neoplatonic visionary evocations.

The establishment of a Communist regime in 1947 which suppressed artistic freedoms led to more than a decade of poetic barrenness. Typical of the cliché-ridden and sloganeering versification of the 1950s is Mihai Beniuc (b. 1907). The lyrics of Nina Cassian (b. 1924) often escape banality through their mixture of bantering cynicism, intelligent feminism, and erotic intensity. However, only the more liberal 1960s brought a revival of poetry. Nichita Stănescu (1933–83), a poet with an extraordinary capacity for the transfiguration of everyday reality, became the standard-bearer of a generation devoted to experiment and to a metaphorical version of reality free from ideological interference. Ioan Alexandru's (b. 1941) best verse moved from the cruelty of tragic naturalism toward a kind of religious harmony. Ion Gheorghe (b. 1935) managed to alternate crass primitivism and oracular obscurities with sophisticated lang. games. Mircea Ivănescu (b. 1931) wrote self-analytic elegies in which stream-of-consciousness techniques are applied with lucid irony. Marin Sorescu (b. 1936) dealt in parody and in the jocular debunking of habit. Leonid Dimov (b. 1926) inaugurated an "onereic" movement based on dream imagery and associations of verbal music. Despite adverse political pressures, the feeling that the maintenance of high aesthetic standards is crucial for national survival encouraged the continuation of these efforts, either in the direction of lyrical purity, as in the poems of Sorin Mărculescu (b. 1936) and Ana Blandiana (b. 1942), or in the more open discontent and ethical rage of Ileana Mălăncioiu (b. 1940), Mircea Dinescu (b. 1950), and the dissident Dorin Tudoran (b. 1945). Many of these poets were in the forefront of the 1989 anti-Communist revolution. A new generation emerged soon thereafter, led by the postmodernist Mircea Cartarescu (b. 1955) and the cynical, street-wise Florin Iaru (b. 1955) and Ion Stratan (b. 1954).

Two things should be added. One is that poetic and aesthetic values occupied a much more prominent place in R. culture than in the West: lit. was a respected mode of conveying wisdom and social values. The greater poets and movements were flanked for two centuries by hundreds of minor authors, and only an awareness of these can suggest the thick texture of R. p. The other is that the R. territory was hospitable to lit. written by numerous ethnic groups—Hungarian, Serbian, Saxon Ger., Bukowina Jewish, and others. Important literary figures such as Nikolaus Lenau and Paul Celan, besides others mentioned above, originated here and can thus round off our understanding of the landscape of R. p.

ANTHOLOGIES: *Rumanian Prose and Verse*, ed. E. D. Tappe (1956); *Anthol. of Contemp. R. P.*, ed. R. McGregor-Hastie (1969); *46 R. Poets in Eng.*, ed. S. Avădanei and D. Eulert (1973); *Antologia poeziei românesti*, ed. Z. D. Busulenga (1974); *Petite anthologie de poésie roumaine moderne*, ed. V. Rusu (1975); *Poezia română clasică*, 3 v., ed. A. Piru (1976); *Mod. R. P.*, ed. N. Catanoy (1977); *Poesia romena d'avanguardia: Testi e manifesti da Urmuz a Ion Caraion*, ed. M. Cugno and M. Mincu (1980).

HISTORY AND CRITICISM: E. Lovinescu, *Istoria literaturii romane moderne* (1937); B. Munteano, *Mod. R. Lit.* (1939); G. Călinescu, *Istoria literaturii române* (1940); G. Lupi, *Storia della letteratura romena* (1955); V. Ierunca, "Litt. roumaine," *Histoire des litts.*, ed. R. Queneau, v. 2 (1956); K. H. Schroeder, *Einführung in das Studium des Rumänischen* (1967); C. Ciopraga, *La Personnalité de le litt. roumaine* (1975); *Scriitori români*, ed. M. Zaciu (1978); V. Nemoianu, "The Real R. Revolution," *The World and I* 6 (1991).　　　　V.P.N.

ROMANSH POETRY. See SWISS POETRY.

ROMANTIC AND POSTROMANTIC POETICS.

　I. ROMANTIC POETICS IN THE EIGHTEENTH CENTURY
　　A. *France*
　　B. *Germany*
　　C. *England*
　　D. *Italy*
　　E. *Spain*
　II. NINETEENTH-CENTURY ROMANTICISM AND POSTROMANTICISM
　　A. *Germany*
　　B. *England*
　　C. *America*
　　D. *France*
　　E. *Italy*
　　F. *Russia*
　　G. *Spain*

R. p. is a chronologically shifting category whose conception differs from nation to nation and often, within national trads., from critic to critic. The tendency of r. p. to elude historically fixed and universally valid determination is already apparent in the statement generally regarded as its first outright definition: "R. poetry is a progressive universal poetry" (Friedrich Schlegel, *Athäneums-Fragmente*, 1798). Rather than situate r. p. contextually, Schlegel's statement (discussed below) points to an ahistoric, nongeneric, and nonprescriptive conception of r. poetry, and thus to a r. p.

pertaining, along with its "universal" object, to all places and all times. Unlike the thrust of his inaugural dictum, F. Schlegel (1772–1829) himself was of couse an historically delimited, if not determined, critical thinker, whose recognition of romanticism rose upon a wave of r. poetic theory articulated in the second half of the 18th c.

While the writing of "poetics" in a formulaic or Aristotelian sense had waned by the mid 1700s, a conceptual preoccupation with the nature and role of poetry became a touchstone for the major philosophical and political as well as aesthetic writings of the time. Following the experimental methods advanced in philosophy, natural science, and mathematics by Descartes, Bacon, Pascal, Leibniz, and Newton, speculations on the "natural" rather than divine origin of man's linguistic abilities led to a consideration of the essential part played by poetic lang. in human experience and thinking. Lang., seen as the defining feature of humanity, was historicized in the attempt to identify its source. The view that lang., and thus human reason, were poetic in origin allied poetics with the very possibility of all arts and sciences and located poetry at the starting point of human history

　I. ROMANTIC POETICS IN THE EIGHTEENTH CENTURY. A. In *France*, an early theory of r. p. resulted from the joint investigation of the origins of knowledge and lang. by l'Abée (Etienne Bonnot) de Condillac (1715–80) in the *Essai sur l'origine des connoissances humaines* (1746). Condillac, following Locke in the *Essay Concerning Human Understanding* (1689–90), argued against the Cartesian principle of innate ideas on the grounds that all ideas stem from perceptions and are known through what Locke called "the signs of our ideas," "words." Yet unlike Locke, who maintained a distinction between signs and ideas of things and submitted that one may dispense with signs in contemplating "the reality of things," Condillac argued that signs are "absolutely necessary" to the primary act of reason, the formation of relations between ideas. The relating of ideas (*la liaison des idées*) through imagination and reflection is the "single principle" named in the subtitle of the *Essai* as the source of all understanding, and thus Condillac's inquiry into the origin of human knowledge necessarily became an inquiry into the origin of the linguistic signs by which ideas are related and knowledge is formed. Part Two of the *Essai*, on the "origin and progress of lang.," sketches a history in which "natural signs," or "cries of passion," are slowly replaced by "instituted signs," or "articulate sounds." Music, gesture, and dance all refer back to the natural signs of the passions; metaphor refers forward to articulate sounds in its attempt to "paint" the passions in words. Condillac's poetic theory (v. 2, ch. 8) situates figurative lang. at the origin of articulate sounds and closest to natural sensory expression. All linguistic "style," Condillac hypothesizes, was originally poetic, and poetry and music, articulated in tandem, formed the passionate lang. in which ancient societies first instituted religion and law. The refinement of poetry and music led to their separation, which, along with the increasing diversification of langs. as well as the invention of writing, resulted in the replacement of poetry by prose. Poetry, like music, became an art of pleasing, while prose assumed their original, jointly instructive role. Societies initially created and governed by the employment of poetic expression now developed eloquence as a middle ground between poetry and prose.

The influence of Condillac's speculations on the poetic origin of lang. appear most prominently in the r. p. formulated by Jean-Jacques Rousseau (1712–78) and Denis de Diderot (1713–84). In his *Discours sur l'origine de l'inégalité parmi les hommes* (1754), Rousseau supported Condillac's thesis that the first lang. was one of natural cries and gestures, for which articulate sounds and instituted signs were eventually substituted. The first words, however, are not viewed synesthetically by Rousseau as paintings or copies of gesture and pure sound. Words by nature, Rousseau argued, exist only by common consent, and thus paradoxically would already be necessary to the social process by which they are created. As there can be no development of lang. without lang. and no lang. without social relations, so Rousseau found illogical any diachronically linear solution to the problem of the origin of lang. On this point Rousseau took issue with Condillac, whose historical account of the formation of lang. presupposes a kind of preverbal society from which lang. springs.

The link between social relations, lang., and poetics is also established in the *Essai sur l'origine des langues* (1740s? or 1750s?), in which Rousseau makes the important theoretical distinction between gestures and words. Words are not said, as in the Second Discourse, to replace gestures by a single inexplicable process but to differ from them originally in source and in kind. Gestures are viewed in the *Essai* as the products of physical "needs," while words are considered the offspring of "passions," or "moral needs." Lang. owes its origin not to "reasoning" (based on needs) but "feeling," and the langs. of "the first men" were "the langs. of poets." With this consideration, r. p. achieves one of its first full formulations: poetry does not follow a prior lang. of natural cries and gestures but is itself identical with lang. in its origin. Man's "first expressions were tropes," a "figurative lang." which preceded dispassionate or "proper meanings." In the *Lettre à d'Alembert* (1758) and in the "Préface" to *Julie, ou la Nouvelle Héloïse* (1761), Rousseau's discussions of the deluding effects of artificial literary models also reflect his r. conception of a "natural" poetics, stemming, along with lang., from the impassioned nature of all originary perception.

The r. p. formulated by Diderot also takes root in theory of the origin of lang. before considering questions of natural sentiment and theatricality. In the *Lettre sur les sourds et les muets* (1751), Diderot elaborates an understanding of poetry which remains in evidence throughout the course of his many diverse writings, incl. treatises on the technical and natural sciences (primarily in the *Encyclopédie*, 1751–66), lit. crit., aesthetic crit. and philosophy, and works of drama and fiction. Following Condillac, whom he had praised and debated in his earlier *Lettre sur les aveugles* (1749), Diderot distinguishes between natural and institutional aspects of lang. In order to exemplify a "natural order of ideas" hypothetically correlative with lang. at its origin, Diderot appeals to the gestures employed by deaf mutes. Rather than speculating that gesture preceded articulate sounds, as argued by Condillac and, in part, by Rousseau, Diderot regards such gestures as ongoing evidence of the natural workings of the soul. These he then relates specifically to poetry. Poetry is closer to gesture and the origin of lang. because it combines rather than "decomposes" many simultaneous ideas. His conception of gesture as an "animal lang." lacking any form of subordination leads Diderot to a theory of poetry opposed to the basic successivity of lang. as such. Poetry, he argues, is a fully synchronous medium, fusing movement and simultaneity, and appealing "all at once" (*toute à la fois*) to the senses, to understanding, and to imagination: rather than rendering verbal, it "paints" the "moving tableau" of "the soul." Diderot describes this combination of movement and stasis in poetry as "a tissue of hieroglyphs superimposed upon each other," a form of lang. which is "emblematic" in the visual sense. This understanding of poetry is echoed in the *Encyclopédie* article "Génie" (written by Saint-Lambert, rev. and ed. by Diderot, pub. 1757), in which the "systems" of scientists and philosophers, creations of "imaginations" in a "natural state" of "movement," are compared to "poems"; and in the *Eloge de Richardson* (1762), in which Diderot ranks the Eng. novelist among "the greatest poets" for "putting abstract maxims into action" and "painting" the fleeting "physiognomy" of the passions.

B. In *Germany*, the greatest admirer of Diderot as dramatist was indirectly to write the most significant refutation of his visually oriented poetics. Gotthold Ephraim Lessing (1729–87), while a champion of Diderot's anti-neoclassical dramaturgy, perhaps resembled no other contemp. theorist less with regard to the fundamentals of poetics. His *Laokoon, oder Über die Grenzen der Malerei und Poesie* (1766), a pivotal document in the history of r. p., definitively distinguishes plastic from verbal art by the same criteria that Diderot's conception of poetry had combined, namely, simultaneity and successivity. The pictorial or plastic metaphors used by Diderot in describing poetry—gesture, hieroglyph, painting, emblem, *tableau*—are according to Lessing perfectly appropriate examples of simultaneous media and for that very reason absolutely inappropriate to the discussion of poetry.

Lessing's crucial structural distinction between plastic and verbal art departs from a comment made by Johann Joachim Winckelmann (1717–68), the classical scholar and archaeologist, in his widely influential *Gedanken über die Nachahmung der griechischen Werke in der Malerei und Bildhauerkunst* (1755). Winckelmann had stated with regard to the statue depicting Laocoön being entwined by the serpent, "Laocoön suffers as Sophocles' Philoctetes suffers." Lessing's *Laokoon* argues why, in actual artistic terms, this can never be the case. Winckelmann sees in the statue another instance of the harmony and composure he celebrated in all Gr. artworks, "the noble simplicity and silent greatness" soon to become a catch phrase for the supposed balance and serenity of the Gr. soul. In describing the expression of the statue in terms of the suffering of Philoctetes, however, Winckelmann neglects the fact that the Sophoclean figure does explicitly cry out in pain. Whole lines of the *Philoctetes* are devoted entirely to groans of anguish and screams of outrage. No more stoical than Philoctetes, the doomed Laocoön, Lessing contends, appears noble solely because his plight is carved in marble, and Winckelmann has mistaken the textual reality of Sophocles' *Philoctetes* because he has attributed the aesthetic requirements of the plastic arts to poetics.

These requirements must differ because the "means, or signs" of plastic arts and poetry differ: the media of painters and sculptors are "figures and colors in space" while poetry is composed of "articulate sounds in time." Plastic works of art are synchronic or "coexistent compositions"; poetic works narrate a diachronic series of events. Thus the sculptor or painter must choose for "imitation" the single moment from a narrative sequence which will grant the viewer's "imagination" the greatest "free play" (intimations of Kant). Laocoön is not depicted at the "height" of his agony because that moment above all others "would bind the wings of fantasy," there being "no higher level" (and no equally interesting "lower level") to which the imagination can progress. The "silent greatness" which Winckelmann identifies with Greece is in fact the moment of quiet before the storm: a moment chosen by the artist and recognized by the viewer as "transitory" in that it calls to mind other moments it cannot simultaneously represent, those that came before it or will come after. In *Laokoon*, Lessing's argument is directed not so much against Winckelmann, nor, certainly, antiquity, but the misleading notion commonly underlying aesthetic theory that "painting is mute poetry, and poetry, speaking painting." Effectively refuting the equation of aesthetic media implied in the neoclassical theme of *ut pictora poesis* (q.v.), Lessing's distinction between visual and verbal art in *Laokoon* gives articulate theoretical shape to a fundamental conception of r. p., namely, the unequaled power of poetry to free the mind through "imagination" (q.v.).

Theory of the natural origin of lang. was pursued in the *Abhandlung über den Ursprung der Sprache* (1770) of Johann Gottfried Herder (1744–1803). In a paper to the Berlin Academy of Sciences in 1756, Johann Peter Süssmilch had argued that, due to the fully developed logic evident in lang., man would have first needed lang. in order to invent it (an observation similar to Rousseau's), hence concluding from this circular impasse that lang. was created by God and given to man to increase his power of reason. Herder argues equally against divine and mechanistic views of the origin of lang., asserting that man originally shared the lang. of animals, the inarticulate sounds of pain and passion which, by "natural law," could not be contained within the sufferer: the *Abhandlung*, recalling Lessing, equates the screams of Philoctetes with those of "a suffering animal." But human lang. was formed of man's unique ability for "reflection," already active within his soul even while he was "mute." Herder dismisses Süssmilch's difficulty in establishing a causal and temporal order of occurrence between lang. and reason by directly correlating the two (man had lang. as long as he had reason) and objects to Condillac's derivation of human speech from natural cries since the two are "incommensurate," differing not in "degree" but in "kind."

The *Abhandlung*, however, is heavily indebted to Condillac's original epistemological emphasis upon the function of "reflection" in lang. formation, and, while combatting previous historical accounts of the origin of lang., does not actually offer one of its own. Herder considers lang. tantamount to reason in its ability to make "distinctions," and recommends that, rather than developing "hypotheses" of its genesis, students of lang. would do better to collect linguistic "data" from every age and domain of the human species. This comparative and empirical approach to lang. study is later taken up by Wilhelm von Humboldt (1767–1835), one of the early advocates of comparative linguistics, lit., and anthropology, whose "Einleitung" to *Über die Kawisprache auf der Insel Java* (1836) first proposed what we now call the "Sapir-Whorf" hypothesis, namely that thinking is largely linguistically determined and that individual langs. constitute distinct mental frameworks for thought. In the *Kawi-Einleitung* Humboldt also links poetry to music and hypothesizes that its "free reign of the spirit" probably preceded and provoked the "intellectual" institution of prose.

While he identified linguistic competence with reason rather than passion, Herder's interest in poetic lang. was unequivocally r., a split commonly attributed to his associations with both Immanuel Kant (his professor in Königsberg) and Johann Georg Hamann (his friend and mentor). Under

Hamann's influence he began to formulate a theory of history as progressive revelation (in *Auch eine Philosophie der Geschichte zur Bildung der Menschheit*, 1774, and *Briefe zur Beförderung der Humanität*, 1793–97) which would be developed later by Hegel, and to study the r. literary models he would share with the young Goethe (in Strassburg, 1771), such as the Old Testament, Homer, the purported ballads of the 3d-c. Celtic bard, "Ossian" (Macpherson, pub. 1760–63), folk and popular poetry, and Shakespeare. Like Lessing, he opposed Shakespeare to neoclassical dramatists, praising "the new Sophocles" as an author of "universal nature" whose plays were essentially "historic" rather than generic in conception. His views, pub. in *Shakespear* (1773), exerted a formative influence upon the r. dramas of the *Sturm und Drang* (q.v.) and were reflected in Goethe's enthusiastic *Rede zum Shakespeares-Tag* (1771). Herder's collections of *Volkslieder* (1774; 1778–79), suggested by Percy's *Reliques of Ancient Eng. Poetry* (1765), called for a return to native medieval poetry and contributed to a contemp. revival of the ballad (q.v.), incl. Goethe's and Schiller's later collaborative efforts (1797). His argument for the affinity of Ger. and Eng. lit. (*Über die Ähnlichkeit der mittleren englischen und deutschen Dichtkunst*, 1776) was borne out by the r. p. of these two nations, which shared a preference for poetic simplicity achieved through indigenous forms and themes.

C. In *England*, the single figure to dominate discussion of poetry in the second half of the century was Samuel Johnson (1709–84), whose critical writings, usually developed in an *ad hominem* context, elaborated not so much a specific poetics as the achievements and deficiencies of individual poets. Still, some fundamental criteria remained constants of judgment in Johnson's mind: that all great poetry consists in the new expression of universal or general truths; that these truths are gathered in the observation of "nature" (q.v.) rather than through poetic imitation (q.v.); and (the Horatian dictum) that poetry must provide moral instruction through pleasure—principles Johnson articulated most clearly in Imlac's "Dissertation upon Poetry," ch. 10 of *Rasselas* (1759), in the *Preface to Shakespeare* (1765), and in the *Lives of the Poets* (1779–81). Johnson praised Shakespeare as a "poet of nature," dispelling the importance of the unities (q.v.) and of generic purity in judging the Bard (or any dramatist). His reasons for doing so, however, would not have been shared by Lessing, Herder, or Diderot, and are implied in his conception of dramatic imitation as "a faithful mirror of manners and of life." In viewing a drama, Johnson argued, we never lose "our consciousness of fiction"; thus the adherence to mimetic unities is dramatically beside the point. Any confusion of imitation with reality would destroy our "delight": were staged events believed to be "real they would please no more." Adding a dimension of apperception to the

Cl. topos of *ut pictora poesis*, Johnson compared dramatic "imitations" with "imagination . . . recreated by a painted landscape" in their power not to be "mistaken for realities" but to "bring realities to mind." Because the dramatic "mirror," no matter what its contours, is always recognized as "fiction" by the viewer, the truth of imitations does not lie in their conformity to external rules of verisimilitude (q.v.) but in their reflection of man's general nature.

It is on this basis that Shakespeare is praised and the metaphysicals famously faulted (in the "Life of Cowley"). The metaphysicals, in striving to be original, created a *discordia concors* of unnatural wit; Shakepeare too is censured for occasional "swelling figures" in which "the equality of words to things is very often neglected," as well as for being "more careful to please than to instruct." Milton, on the other hand, sacrifices pleasure to instruction in *Paradise Lost*: the poem, while second only to Homer as epic, lacks "human interest" and is "a duty rather than a pleasure" to read. As for the methodology used for the judgments in the *Lives*, Johnson took into account not only the author's personal history but that of "the age in which he lived." The state of national literacy was weighed along with practical consideration of each author's "opportunities" and "abilities," such as even, in the case of Shakespeare's "neglected" endings, the imputed prospect of soon being paid. Nevertheless, Shakespeare is regarded as a universal poet divested of "the prejudices of his age and his country." In the "Preface" to the *Dictionary* (1755), Johnson, recalling Rousseau, argued there can be no "linguistic constancy" where there is social "inequality." Johnson's concern in the *Dictionary* to make "signs" "permanent" reflects his esteem for "the common intercourse of life" as that "style which never becomes obsolete" (*Preface to Shakespeare*), a theme which achieves prominence in the poetics of Wordsworth and Coleridge.

Edmund Burke (1729–97) differed with Johnson's view of dramatic representation in *A Philosophical Enquiry into the Origin of our Ideas of the Sublime and the Beautiful* (1757), arguing that though tragedy "never approaches to what it represents," its "power" is perfected "the nearer it approaches reality" and "the further it removes us from all idea of fiction" (v. 1, sect. 15). The larger purpose of the *Enquiry* is to examine the psycho-physiological composition of the feelings of the sublime (q.v.) and the beautiful, i.e. which "affections of the mind produce certain emotions of the body," and, reciprocally, what bodily "feelings" produce certain "passions in the mind." The perception of beauty is considered independent of reason and rational proportion; Burke criticizes the formal garden in particular for falsely imposing architectural principles upon nature (and thus turning "trees into pillars, pyramids and obelisks"), thereby pointing to the aesthetic domain first called "r." in England, landscaping. But it is the sublime, in its close association with "ideas of eternity and infinity," that is most closely allied to poetics. In the final part of the *Enquiry*, Burke argues that the effect of words cannot be explained by way of the sensory, physiological model he has hitherto employed: poetic lang. is not "imitative" of nonlinguistic sensations in that there is no "resemblance" between words and "the ideas for which they stand." Burke's *Enquiry* thus develops Locke's principle of the arbitrary relations between signs and ideas into a central problematic of r. p. Hypothesizing (as will Wordsworth) that "unpolished people" are given to more "passionate" or sublime expression, he viewed lang. as a special repository of the sublime because it can join ideas unrelatable by any other medium (citing the example of Milton's "universe of death" as a "union of ideas" "amazing beyond conception," i.e. beyond concrete description). In contrast to the secondary, mimetic status of tragedy maintained at the outset of the *Enquiry*, the words of poetry are argued to affect us "sometimes much more strongly" than "the things they represent." The principle of a necessary equivalence between word and thing which underlies Johnson's criticism of extravagant imagery is superseded in Burke's analysis by the r. consideration of the disproportionate way in which lang. functions and affects us generally.

D. In *Italy*, the functions of lang. are identified with a theory of history in *La scienza nuova* (1725; rev. ed., 1744) of Giambattista Vico (1668–1744). Rather than hypothesizing a historical origin of lang., Vico finds in lang. the origin of history. Uniting poetry and reality in an essentially r. p., *La scienza nuova* attributes to "tropes" and "poetic logic" the beginning and devel. of human history. The "fantastic speech" of man's "first lang." yielded four fundamental tropes, or "corollaries of poetic logic," corresponding to distinct phases in the recurrent history of human consciousness. Metaphor (q.v.) is identified with the divine pagan or poetic phase; metonymy (q.v.), with the aristocratic or (Homeric) heroic; synecdoche (q.v.), with the lawfully democratic or human; irony (q.v.), with the period of reflection leading to the dissolution of civil bodies and reemergence of barbarism (similarly hypothesized in Rousseau's Second Discourse), followed in turn by the divine, heroic, and human phases of Christianity. Poetic lang. is not the "ingenious inventions of writers" but the "common sense of the human race" and key to the structure of "ideal, eternal history." A far more limited view of poetics characterized the transition to romanticism in the field of It. crit. While such critics as Salverio Bettinelli (1718–1808) and Giuseppe Baretti (1719–89) exhorted It. authors to break with cl. norms, the period saw a broad assimilation of diverse literary models in translations of Racine, Corneille, Voltaire, and Pope; the "moderns," Shakespeare, Milton, and Gray; as well as Homer, Aeschylus, Demosthenes,

Virgil, Ovid, and Juvenal. Exemplary of the European cross-currents influencing Italy at the time, Melchiorre Cesarotti (1730–1808), philologist, and philosopher of lang., also translated the r. ballads of Macpherson's "Ossian."

E. In *Spain*, after the Golden Age of Góngora and Calderón, poetics, like poetry, suffered an eclipse throughout the 18th c., as a new wave of Classicism arose in response to mannered imitations of the baroque (q.v.) masters. The major poetic tract of the century was the Aristotelian *Poética* (1737) of Ignacio de Lazán (1702–54).

II. NINETEENTH-CENTURY ROMANTICISM AND POSTROMANTICISM. A. In *Germany*, the rapid devel. of r. p. (more so now than in France and England) and the flowering of postromanticism owed to two enormously influential and not entirely compatible strains of crit.: the critical theory of Friedrich Schlegel (1772–1829) and critical epistemology of Immanuel Kant (1724–1804). Kant's restriction of the field of knowledge to "representations" (q.v.) of experience combatted, on the one hand, the skepticism of Hume, in its exclusive insistence on the random nature of experience, and, on the other, the anti-experiential, dogmatic idealism of Berkeley and Wolff. Kant's critical philosophy, consisting of the *Kritik der reinen Vernunft* (1781), its explanatory summation in the *Prolegomena zu einer jeden künftigen Metaphysik, die als Wissenschaft wird auftreten können* (1783), the *Kritik der praktischen Vernunft* (1788), and the *Kritik der Urteilskraft* (1790), argues, in opposition to idealism, that all knowledge must be related to sensory objects, and, in opposition to skepticism, that our experience of objects is not arbitrary but rather structured *a priori* by mental forms (e.g. time and space) and relational categories (e.g. causality). Our knowledge of experience is thus not of an object as it is "in itself" (as "noumenon"), but of its "representation," the "phenomenon" which our minds construct in the very act of experience. This hypothesis of the phenomenal limits of knowledge in the *First Critique* is countered by the deduction of a necessarily nonphenomenal object of knowledge, the concept of (practical or moral) "freedom," in the *Second Critique*. Moral freedom, the freedom to act without respect to the welfare of one's own phenomenal being, is the one noumenal object of knowledge in Kant's critical system, for without "freedom" all actions would be confined to the causal chain of mentally formed phenomena, and thus no real ground for *moral* action could exist; nor would there be any "real knowledge" which we could lay claim to, not even that of the phenomenal limits of cognitive reason. The "bridge" (*Übergang*) between the real freedom of "practical reason" and the limited phenomenal cognitions of "pure reason" occurs in *aesthetic* judgment; without the mediating power of judgment, Kant stipulates, the entire *Critique* would collapse into two irreconcilable spheres. The unparalleled position

Kant accords aesthetics relates aesthetic judgment both to knowledge and to practical action by way of the separate categories of the beautiful and the sublime. In the first place, the *Third Critique* criticizes the loose identification of aesthetics with personal "taste" in order to prove that aesthetic *judgments*, no less than phenomenal cognitions and moral actions, are based on universal mental operations. Judgments, however, are neither cognitive nor active but contemplative; aesthetic objects please freely because they are "purposive" forms without practical "purpose" (*Zweckmässigkeit ohne Zweck*). In the experience of the beautiful, "imagination and understanding" come together in a state of mutual "free play" (*freies Spiel der Einbildungskraft und des Verstandes*), while the experience of the sublime (q.v.) brings imagination and *reason* into conflict. Such conflict arises when the mind encounters an object of which it can make no adequate sensory image—"absolutely large" objects, for example, or those representing an insuperable "power" in nature—but which reason can nonetheless "think." This freedom of reason evoked by the sublime links aesthetic judgment to moral freedom, and to such nonimageable "ideas" as totality and infinity. Its analysis of the sublime as the unique juncture between moral action and scientific knowledge made the *Kritik der Urteilskraft* the seminal articulation of a r. p. which would find the bridge to the sublime itself within poetry.

Friedrich von Schiller (1759–1805), Kant's first major proponent in the field of poetics, translates Kant's distinction between phenomenon and noumenon into analogous conceptual categories ("matter" and "form," "the physical" and "the moral," etc.) deriving from the opposing "drives" of sensory experience and reason, and mediated, as in Kant, by aesthetic experience. In *Über das Pathetische* (1793), *Über das Erhabene* (ca. 1795), and *Briefe über die ästhetische Erziehung des Menschen* (1793–95), Schiller effectively dispenses with Kant's *Second Critique* by identifying moral freedom wholly with aesthetic experience. "Aesthetic freedom" becomes the locus of moral action for Schiller, who, while indebted to Kant, departs significantly from the *Critique* in defining beauty as the sensory means of making freedom "visible" (*Über das Pathetische*). His *Über Naive und sentimentalische Dichtung* (1795), which names Kant as the source of its theoretical oppositions between "being" and "seeking" nature (the ancients vs. modern admiration for antiquity) and between "feeling" nature and "reflecting" upon feeling (naive vs. sentimental [q.v.]), was credited by Friedrich Schlegel with redirecting his appraisal of modern poetics. While openly disdainful of the systematic nature of Kant's philosophy, it was to the Kantian Schiller and to Kant's devoted follower Johann Gottlieb Fichte (1762–1814) that Schlegel, originally an avatar of classicism (see *Über das Studium der griechischen Poesie*, 1795), owed his conversion

to r. p. In his early writings, Schlegel had opposed the harmony of cl. beauty to the "interesting," irregular, and aesthetically unsatisfying creations of "r. poetry," by which he meant all medieval and modern lit., from chivalric romances through the works of Wieland. Of the moderns, only Shakespeare evoked Schlegel's admiration, at least until his published revaluation of r. p. in no. 116 of the *Athenäums-Fragmente* (1798), beginning, "r. poetry is a progressive universal poetry." In the *Kritische Fragmente* (*Lyceum*, 1797), Schlegel had begun to concentrate on irony (q.v.) as the defining characteristic of poetry both ancient and modern. The form of irony is "paradox" (q.v.), which is "everything simultaneously good and great," and everything which manifests the paradox of "Socratic irony" (no. 108) is r. poetry, incl. and esp. "novels, the Socratic dialogues of our time" (no. 26). "R." is no longer a generic or historical category but the name for poetry perpetually in a "state of becoming" which "no theory can exhaust," while "other kinds of poetry are finished" and can be "fully analyzed" (*Athenäum* no. 116). Criticism of r. poetry would have to be carried out "by way of poetry" (*Lyceum* no. 117), just as "theory of the novel" would have to be itself a novel, the latter defined in *Brief über der Roman* (1799) as "a r. book." What is r. is what is "poetry itself," whether written in verse or prose, whether ancient or modern, and what is poetry is "infinite" by dint of its own eternal self-criticism (*Athenäum* no. 116): the ironic "consciousness of eternal agility" (*Ideen*, 1800) combining the "involuntary" and "completely deliberate" (*Lyceum* no. 108), "instinct and intention," "self-creation and self-destruction" (*Athenäum* no. 51). As Schlegel defines them, the poles of irony informing all r. poetry are recognizable from Fichte's *Wissenschaftslehre* (1794). Intending to "complete" Kant's project, Fichte overreached the essential limits of the *Critique* by identifying the thing-in-itself with a thinking self or ego capable of positing both itself and all that it perceives as not itself, the material world. But whereas Fichte saw the self-positing ego as freely containing contradiction within it (a self which recognizes the not-self must first be itself), Schlegel's conception of *poetic* irony never rests upon a principle of self-certainty. This is made clearest in the essay written for the last issue of the controversial *Athenäum*, "Über die Unverständlichkeit" (1800), in which Schlegel describes "the irony of irony" as a "tiring" of irony from which one nonetheless cannot "disentangle oneself," since to speak about irony either non-ironically *or* ironically is still to be caught in irony, and thus (as in the case of this "essay on incomprehensibility") not to comprehend fully one's own speech.

Schlegel's conception of perpetual self-criticism takes the form of "infinite" textual interp. in the work of Friedrich Schleiermacher (1768–1834), an early friend of Schlegel and the author of *Vertraute Briefe über Schlegels Lucinde* (1800). In his Lectures on Hermeneutics (*Vorlesungen über die Hermeneutik,* 1819; see HERMENEUTICS), Schleiermacher described textual interp. as a properly philosophical endeavor whose endless "task" is to comprehend texts in terms both of the past and of futurity. Hermeneutics attempts "to understand the text as well as and then better than the author" by alternating between two kinds of interp.: the psychological, which investigates how authors influence the lang. they speak, and the grammatical, which investigates how lang. influences "the spirit" of its speakers. As similarly described by Schlegel in *Über Goethes Meister* (1798), the movement back and forth from textual part to whole (cf. Leo Spitzer in the 20th c. on the "hermeneutic circle") is another essential procedure in the infinite process of interp.

Schlegel's views were popularized by his brother August Wilhelm Schlegel (1767–1845), co-founder of *Athenäum* and author of the broadly historical *Vorlesungen über dramatische Kunst und Literatur* (1808), and they were reproduced by such contemporaries as Jean Paul Friedrich Richter (1763–1825), who in his *Vorschule der Ästhetik* (1804) speculates that metaphors preceded denotative expressions in linguistic formation. Karl Solger (1780–1819), in *Erwin: Vier Gespräche über das Schöne und die Kunst* (1815), a work commended by Søren Kierkegaard in his *Concept of Irony* (1841), describes "the true realm of art" as the passing of the idea into the particular, that moment of creation and destruction which "we call irony." Schlegel's and Solger's statements on r. irony are reflected in the critical works of Ludwig Tieck (1773–1853), incl. several volumes devoted to Shakespeare (1811, 1826, 1836, 1920), and the "Fragmente" (*Athenäum,* 1798) and *Dialogen* (1798) of Friedrich von Hardenberg (Novalis; 1772–1801). The self-reflexivity of r. irony is dramatized in supernatural mirrorings of the natural in stories by E. T. A. Hoffmann (1776–1822) and by the absolute absence or absolutely paralyzing presence of self-consciousness in stories and dramas by Heinrich von Kleist (1777–1811).

While the r. p. stemming from Kant and Schlegel are predominantly synchronic in conception—following the "spontaneity" of cognition specified in the *Critique* and the self-cancelling structure of Schlegel's irony—an essentially diachronic understanding of poetry is developed in the poetry and theoretical essays of Friedrich Hölderlin (1770–1843) and in the philosophy and aesthetics of Georg Wilhelm Friedrich Hegel (1770–1831). The concern with antiquity pervading Hölderlin's works owes not to a cl. idealization of the synchronic harmony of Gr. art, but to a conception of the temporal nature of experience exemplified in ancient poetry and mythological history. In early lyrics (1801–03), the dramatic fragments of *Der Tod des Empedokles* (1798–1800), the essays on *Empedokles,* and the essay *Werden im Vergehen* (ca. 1799), Hölderlin focuses on the mo-

ment of passage, of present becoming past, which, fatal for the individual, at once represents the life of the world and is represented in turn by the signs of lang. Poetry both retells this passage in poetic narrative and embodies its occurrence in the creation of poetic lang. until, in Hölderlin's fragments (1803–6), these two linguistic means of representing transience are divided, and signs replace story as the elliptical vehicles of narratives whose own poetic possibility is already past.

The anteriority of art is the overarching theme of Hegel's *Vorlesungen über die Ästhetik* (1820–29; pub. 1835, 1842), in which the famous statement that "in its highest sense, art for us is that which is past," speaks cryptically for Hegel's entire philosophy of the dialectical becoming of spirit over time. In the *Ästhetik* Hegel correlates the epochs of human history with different kinds of art distinguished by their structural relationship of content to form: the dialectical transformation of this relationship signifies the progress of spirit toward its ultimate freedom from all relation at the end of time. The process Hegel outlines moves from "symbolic" art, whose form departs toward the spirit while its (pagan) content assumes a unity of the divine with nature; to "Cl." art, the most "beautiful in history, in that its form is fully pervaded by the content of spirit; to "r." art, which, "higher" than "beautiful appearances" in its signification of a spirit to which no artistic form is adequate, turns the spirit back upon itself and away from any aesthetic objectification. Within the first epoch of symbolic art, Hegel delineates a similar dialectical devel. in three meta-phases: the "unconscious" symbolic, which does not distinguish form from content and thus does not yet conceive of art as "imaged" rather than natural form; the "sublime" symbolic, which (like the larger r. epoch) recognizes the inadequacy of any art form to the spirit; and the symbolic of "comparative art forms," in which form and content are fully separated and art is recognized as art, or "mere images." It is under this last subcategory that Hegel classifies all linguistic images, for "only poetry" can express the mutual "independence" of form and content. In this sense any conscious use of poetic lang. is, for Hegel, postromantic, in that it takes the inadequacy of form to spirit expressed by romanticism for granted, and in this sense, too, art which would embody spirit is, according to Hegel's historical philosophy of spirit, a thing of the past. In keeping with this progressive conception of aesthetics, Schlegel's concept of irony is condemned by Hegel. Departing from Fichte's proposition that all existence is posited by an ego which can also destroy it, Schlegel's irony, Hegel argues, views the artist as a divine genius (q.v.) who can create and annihilate at will, and thus for whom all moral and social relations conducted in reality are also viewed ironically as a "nullity." Hegel praises Solger, whom he distinguishes from Schlegel's followers, for recognizing the negativity of irony as a "dialectical moment of the idea," which, itself negated, reinstates the "general and infinite in the particular." The ironic, Hegel emphasizes, is "only a moment" (in the progress of the idea or spirit), and as such pertains to the diachronic dialectic between human hist. and the universal spirit rather than the Fichtean principle of absolute subjectivity.

Arthur Schopenhauer (1788–1860) rejected Hegel's philosophy of spirit entirely and based his *Welt als Wille und Vorstellung* (1819) on Kant's *Critique*, which he like Fichte claimed to complete. For Schopenhauer the thing-in-itself is not the Fichtean self but the will, represented in all temporally and spatially structured appearances. Reducing Kant's categories to the mechanism of causality, Schopenhauer argues that only disinterested artistic genius is freed from the causal chain of willed representations. The highest forms of art are poetry and music, the latter being a pure reflection, rather than worldly representation, of the will. In *Parerga* (1819), Schopenhauer discusses general aspects of poetics and literary style, observing that good style derives from "having something to say," and that the best authors write "objectively" by employing the "concrete" means of everyday lang., using "common words to say uncommon things." Nonetheless, in their contemplative freedom from the will to live, authors of genius are customarily misjudged in their own lifetime, while their vision is transferred through writing to the life of the "whole species."

Schopenhauer's philosophy of will influenced Friedrich Nietzsche (1844–1900), whose writings effectively transferred romanticism into the 20th c. In *Die Geburt der Tragödie* (1872), Nietzsche rewrites the cl. conception of Gr. antiquity by arguing that combative tendencies underlie the origin of poetry: the Dionysian spirit of music and the Apollonian spirit of imaging (see APOLLONIAN-DIONYSIAN). The Dionysian, which prompts man's "highest symbolic faculties," is likened to a self-transcendent state of intoxication that destroys the individual while simultaneously expressing "the essence of Nature." The Apollonian is compared to an "image world of dreams" whose "beautiful appearances" are delimited by the measure of the individual. Nietzsche commends Schiller, among the Ger. "classicists," for recognizing "the musical mood" which precedes the act of poetic imaging, and analyzes the figure of the tragic hero as an image meant to turn us, through the experience of compassion, from the Dionysian to the individual. Nietzsche does not suggest that poetry is ever entirely Dionysian, i.e. *is* the music from which it originates, but rather that within tragedy the Dionysian and Apollonian are eventually compelled to speak "each other's lang.," and that in this exchange the "highest aim of tragedy and of art in general is reached." The thesis that music is the essential r. art form appears repeatedly in the late *Der Wille zur Macht* (pub. 1901), in

which r. art is also equated with decadent exoticism, "a makeshift substitute for defective 'reality,'" and Flaubert is called a "postromantic" for having transferred the "r. faith in love and the future" into "the desire for nothing." Thus Nietzsche already sees r. *art* as postromantic or self-retrospective (not unlike Hegel), while distinguishing it from *romanticism*, whose "most fundamental form" he identifies as "Ger. philosophy as a whole" (Leibniz through Schopenhauer).

Nietzsche's contemporary Wilhelm Dilthey (1833–1911) pursued the psychological strain in interp. proposed by Schleiermacher, attempting to integrate textual hermeneutics into a larger theory of historical knowledge. In *Das Leben Schleiermachers* (1870), *Die Entstehung der Hermeneutik* (1900), and *Das Erlebnis und die Dichtung* (1905), Dilthey argued that the "reconstruction" of an author's life could proceed by methods as demonstrable as those of the natural sciences. While his grounding of the interpretative "human sciences" in psychology limited his hermeneutics to histories of the individual, Dilthey's attention to the temporality of poetry subsequently proved influential on the philosophy of Martin Heidegger (1889–1976), a characteristic (perhaps the only one) he shared with Nietzsche.

B. In *England*, William Wordsworth (1770–1850) and Samuel Taylor Coleridge (1772–1834) discussed the inclusion of a critical preface to the second edition of their *Lyrical Ballads* (1800): the result, written by Wordsworth, was the *Preface to the Lyrical Ballads* (1800), probably the single most important document in the history of Eng. r. p. The immediate aim of the *Preface* was to explain why the poems constituting the *Lyrical Ballads* were "so materially different" from customary (neoclassical) conceptions of the poetic. The matter in which they differed most, Wordsworth claimed, was their lang.: the *Lyrical Ballads* were written in the "real lang. of men," and they related incidents selected from "common life." Wordsworth's description of the poems tied into a larger argument against the general notions of necessarily ornate "poetic diction" of the exaltation of Poets, and of any "essential difference" between poetry and prose. The presence of meter alone, Wordsworth argues, distinguishes poetry, but meter also enters naturally into the composition of prose. Meter maintains "something regular" in the course of relating situations which most move the passions: those who put it to merely conventional application "greatly under-rate the power of metre in itself." Similarly, figures of speech used as "mechanical devices" for defining poetic style are deadening substitutes for the "metaphors and figures" arising from the passions in "the very lang. of men." Those passions speak most plainly in the unmannered lang. of rustic life, which Wordsworth, recalling Rousseau, regards as a more "permanent" and "philosophical" lang. than that of poets feeding "fickle appetites of their own creation."

Like Rousseau, Wordsworth's emphasis on the passions has led to the misperception of him as a sentimentalist, as has the definition of poetry, which, in its truncated version, is the best known definition in the *Preface*: "all good poetry is the spontaneous overflow of powerful feelings . . ." but which continues, "and though this be true, Poems to which any value can be attached were never produced . . . but by a man who . . . had also thought long and deeply." Other definitions in the *Preface*, such as "Poetry is the first and last of all knowledge"; "Poetry is the most philosophic writing" (following Aristotle) in that its "object" is "general and operative" rather than "individual and local" "truth"; and "the Poet binds together by passion and knowledge the vast empire of human society" clearly indicate a poetics which, instead of substituting feeling for knowledge, finds their only true relation in poetry. Furthermore, Wordworth extends the scope of the poetics described in the *Preface* beyond his own or other contemp. poetry to the "judgment" of "the greatest Poets both ancient and modern." In the "Appendix" to the *Preface*, which elaborates the argument against "poetic diction," Wordsworth re-emphasizes that, with regard to "works of imagination (q.v.) and sentiment," a single lang. is used for both verse and prose. His introduction of the historical argument, familiar from 18th-c. r. p., that the "figurative" lang. of the "earliest poets" was the "lang. of men" animated by "passion," links Wordsworth to Condillac, Vico, Diderot, and Rousseau among others. In the *Essay, Supplementary to the Preface* (1815), Wordsworth discusses historical discrepancies in the reputations of poetic works, citing the Fr. and It. misunderstanding of Shakespeare as well as the regrettable Eng. conception of his "wild irregular genius"; the preference for Macpherson's forgeries over Percy's *Reliques*; and Dr. Johnson's failure, as the arbiter of contemp. taste, to include Chaucer, Spenser, Sidney, and Shakespeare in the *Lives of the Poets*. The term "taste" (q.v.), he argues, metaphorically attributes a passive sense to an act of the intellect; rather, each "original" author, while disappointing prevailing aesthetic expectations, will "create" over time the "taste by which he is to be enjoyed."

Coleridge's *Biographia Literaria* (1817), an idiosyncratic mixture of biographical-critical narrative and philosophical speculation, translation, and summary (esp. of Schelling, Fichte, and Kant), draws a distinction (ch. 12) between imagination, the "shaping or modifying power," and fancy (q.v.), "the aggregative and associative power," thereby disagreeing with Wordsworth, who had held that the imagination shared these latter powers but used them differently to more permanent ends (1815 *Preface*). Coleridge also criticized, somewhat literal-mindedly, Wordsworth's emphasis on the lang. of rustic life, arguing that even among rustics lang. will vary "in every county," whereas whatever is invariable in lang. is

universal and so should not be identified with any particular class (ch. 17). Coleridge further extrapolated a "secondary" from the "primary" imagination, defining it as a recreative "echo" of the latter (ch. 13), and loosely defined poetry as good sense, fancy, and motion pervaded and joined by imagination (ch. 14).

In the *Letters* of John Keats (1795–1821), the identification of truth with beauty (already ambiguous in its context in the "Ode on a Grecian Urn" [1819], for which Keats's poetry is best known) is rendered problematic by formulations relating beauty to the "passions" and truth to their absence in "abstraction," and comparing the truth of imagination to an earthly "dream." Keats's speculations opposing the "delights" of sensation to the desire for truth are complicated by his further consideration that sensations coupled "with knowledge" would be experienced "without fear." This phrase "negative capability" (q.v.), the capacity for "being in uncertainties" attributed in the *Letters* not to himself but to Shakespeare, also contrasts sharply with the either/or constructions and the deep sense of disquiet at uncertainty which frequently dominate Keats's poems. Keats placed Wordsworth above Milton and described the "Wordsworthian or egotistical Sublime" in opposition to "the poetical Character" which, having neither "self" nor "character," is "everything and nothing," and of which "sort" he counted himself a "Member."

Percy Bysshe Shelley (1792–1822), an early admirer of Keats, asserts a poetics which in Keats's view would surely have seemed post-Wordsworthian, in that it admits no enduring rival power to poetry at all. His *Defence of Poetry* (1821), at first distinguishing between the activities of reason and imagination, proceeds to ascribe to imaginative poetic works the ethical character of civilization itself, placing the greatest poets (Dante through Milton) above philosophers (Locke through Rousseau) in their influence upon "the moral nature of man." Shelley provides a sweeping overview of the part played by poetry in the history of civilization in response to Thomas Love Peacock's thesis, in *The Four Ages of Poetry* (1820), that, as civilization develops, poetry must decline. Shelley argues that civilization is, rather, the result of poetry, and that poetry produces man's "moral improvement" not by teaching moral doctrine but by enlarging the power of imagination by which man puts himself "in the place of another." Poetry alone exerts this power over "the internal world," whereas the "external" progress of the empirical sciences incurs man's "enslavement." Like Burke in the *Enquiry*, Shelley considers lang. to be "more plastic" that the plastic arts since it is "arbitrarily produced by the imagination," and so relates "to thoughts alone." Recalling theorists on the Continent, Shelley also equates "lang. itself" with "poetry," asserting that at the beginning of history all authors were poets, and that lang. at its origin resembled "the chaos of a cyclical poem." Because of the propensity for moral speculation stimulated by poetry, poets originally authored not only lang. but all "laws" and "civil society," and remain, the *Defence* concludes, "the unacknowledged legislators of the world." While purposefully all-embracing in its line of argument, the *Defence* illuminates Shelley's own poetry in particular, when it argues that poetry "turns all things to loveliness" both in "strip[ping] the veil of familiarity from the world" *and* by "veiling" earthly "apparitions" in "its own figured carpet." This conception of beauty achieved either by poetic revelation or by concealment is a motive and often self-contradictory force imaged throughout Shelley's poems.

Following the self-romanticizing identification of poetics with personality in the life and poetry of George Gordon Lord Byron (1788–1824), Eng. romanticism yields to a series of postromanticisms attempting to overreach it. Poetic thought after romanticism divides between the doctrinaire, ranging from Classicism to aestheticism (q.v.), and the creatively prosaic, in which works of prose crit. take on a poetic life of their own. Thomas Carlyle (1795–1881), the first major postromantic critic, is probably best known for his *Sartor Resartus* (1833–34), whose subject is the Philosophy of Clothes undertaken by Diogenes Teufelsdröckh, Professor of Things in General at the University of Weissnichtwo ("I-Don't-Know-Where"). The great Teufelsdröckh and his philosophy are at once ludicrous and serious subjects: clothing, it is suggested, is "whatsoever represents Spirit to Spirit," just as the Imagination must "weave Garments" to reveal the otherwise invisible creations of Reason. Carlyle however distinguishes one external form, "lang.," from clothing, stating that lang. is rather "the Body of thought," whose "muscles and tissues" are the old and new "Metaphors" of which all lang. is composed.

A postromantic emphasis on the essentially poetic nature of prose is the theme of John Ruskin (1819–1900) in *Sesame and Lilies* (1865), a series of lectures aimed at answering the question, "Why to read?" Ruskin contrasts the literal act of reading, "syllable by syllable—nay, letter by letter," with all more or less accidental or associative forms of verbal communication. Although primarily a critic of the plastic arts, Ruskin argued that "writing" is "the best" of man (a postromantic theme enlarged upon by Arnold) and outlives him as his "inscription." In *Modern Painters* (2 v., 1846, 1856), Ruskin distinguishes between "Poetical" and "historical Painting," the former being "imaginative," the latter, a relation of "plain facts," and formulates the phrase "pathetic fallacy" (q.v.) to describe self-projecting metaphoric lang. which, while betraying an ungoverned "weakness of character," may nonetheless be true to the emotion expressed.

Matthew Arnold (1822–88), a neo-r. poet who disavowed romanticism in the "Preface" to his collected *Poems* (1853) and the first layman to be made Professor of Poetry at Oxford (1857), reintroduced a Johnsonian strain into crit. Arnold defines the terms "classic, classical" (see CLASSICISM) as meaning of "the class of the very best" (*The Study of Poetry*, 1880) and broadly describes the function of crit. of the classics so defined as "a disinterested endeavour to learn and propagate the best that is known and thought in the world" (*The Function of Crit. at the Present Time*, 1864; Intro. to *Essays in Crit.*, 1865). Crit. which is "disinterested" will "try to know the best that is known" without the interference of any practical consideration (see DISINTERESTEDNESS). Based on an inviolate notion of greatness, Arnold's discussions of crit. and the classics proffer the one in support of the other without further specifying what constitutes great poetry, or, for that matter, poetics generally. His crit. of Shakespeare and praise of stylistic simplicity (q.v.) in the "Preface" recall Johnson, while his exclusion of Chaucer, commended for a "sound representation of things," from the ranks of the classics, owes, Arnold asserts, to that poet's lack of "high seriousness" (*The Study of Poetry*). As a method for recognizing the "best," Arnold suggests the memorization of "touchstone" (q.v.) lines from recognized masters (thereby begging the question of how these masters came to be recognized in the first place), preferring "concrete examples" to any "abstract" or theoretical crit. of what constitutes "a high quality of poetry."

The "Pre-Raphaelite Brotherhood" (q.v.) of William Holman Hunt (1827–1910), Dante Gabriel Rossetti (1828–82), and John Everett Millais (1829–96) proposed a postromantic return to the naturalism of early It. painting, a renewed cooperation between painting and verse, and a rejection of academic rules of composition, conventional since Raphael, in favor of highly detailed representation. As Ruskin wrote in *Lectures on Architecture and Painting* (1853), in medieval art, truth came first and beauty second, while in modern art the reverse order holds sway, a reversal which took place in the course of Raphael's own career and which must devolve from each artist's imagination rather than learned "recipes of composition." In imitation of the medieval allegorical trad., etchings accompanied poems in the Pre-Raphaelite journal *The Gem* (1850), and book illustration and design were given fresh aesthetic status. Whatever their claim to reviving the "sincerity" of the Middle Ages, the self-consciously literary Pre-Raphaelites soon yielded to another movement whose doctrine rapidly became identified with their own: the call for a "return to nature" *after* romanticism yielded not naturalism (q.v.) but aestheticism. The Pre-Raphaelites were adopted by Walter Pater (1839–94) who, in his *Review of Poems* by Morris (1868), famously commended "the love of art for art's sake." Pater's singular emphasis upon beauty as a sensuous experience requiring the possession of "a certain kind of temperament" (*The Renaissance*, 1873) and virtual proscription of any moral or cognitive dimension of art, and thus of crit. *per se*, gave way inevitably to the fetishism of feeling associated with decadence (q.v.).

Reflection upon crit. emerged with a new vigor, however, in the writings of Oscar Wilde (1854–1900). *The Decay of Lying* (1889) revives the problem of the relationship between art and lived experience by provocatively asserting that life imitates art, and that the "ages" of the "human spirit" (by a turn upon Hegel) symbolize aesthetic developments rather than the other way around. Neatly reversing the mimetic principle by arguing that "facts" attempt to "reproduce fiction," Wilde moves beyond the limits of purely sensuous aesthetic criteria by returning, albeit in radically polemical form, to the r. problem of mental perception. Wilde's ultimate conclusion that, like human life, Nature too imitates the lit. which "anticipates" it, is based upon the distinction he draws between mechanically "looking at a thing" and "seeing" it. Nature is only *seen* when its beauty is perceived, and that perception is not immediate but always mediated by "the Arts that have influenced us." Cognition itself is argued to follow from aesthetically mediated perception, for "we do not know anything" about Nature until we have seen it, and we only "see" by way of aesthetic detours. Closely related to perception, in *The Critic as Artist* (1890), is crit. Like the misconceived notion of "unimaginative realism" (exemplified for Wilde by Zola), crit. does not imitate but reveal: it is not aimed at "discovering" the "real intention" of the artist, whose capacity to "judge" is limited by his creative ability. Crit. "leads us" because it generates new creations suggested by the work of art as the critic "sees" it: "new" creations are thus already old with regard to the crit. which foresees them. As if to demonstrate, in the manner Wilde describes, this critical proposition, the poetry of his own age lagged behind his notion of crit. Bombastic neoromantic styles, such as that of Algernon Charles Swinburne (1837–1909), were countered in part by the spare form of the dramatic, periodic monologue (q.v.) developed to great effect by Robert Browning (1812–89), and the recasting of Shakespearean love poetry in the *Sonnets from the Portuguese* (1850) by Elizabeth Barrett Browning (1806–61), whose critically successful "novel-poem," *Aurora Leigh* (1856), influenced by Mme. de Stael's *Corinne* (1807), was praised again in this century by Virginia Woolf (*TLS*, 1931; see NARRATIVE POETRY). The poems of Gerard Manley Hopkins (1844–89), generally regarded as modernist due to their posthumous publication in 1918, combined dense sensuous lang. with the contrapuntal tension of Hopkins' own "sprung rhythm" (q.v.), described in the *Author's Preface* as suggesting "two or more strains of tune going on together." Hopkins argued that Gr., Lat., and OE verse all embodied this rhythmic principle and, recalling a *locus classicus* of r. p., that it best reflected common speech. Closer to romanticism than the ensuing postromanticisms of their time, Hopkins' poems recall the phrase by Wilde which most aptly describes the age: "Life goes faster than realism, but romanticism is always in front of life" (*The Decay of Lying*).

C. In *America*, Ralph Waldo Emerson (1803–82) translated Carlyle's notion of "great men" into "representative men," poets or prophets ("The Poet," 1844) who "transcend" the particular through intense self-absorption. A more democratic version of this apotheosis of the poet is represented in the expansive verse of Walt Whitman (1819–92), whose *Leaves of Grass* (1855), admired early by Emerson, proclaims poetry and the poet to be compounded of all temporal reality, as catalogued in the sweeping rhythms of Whitman's nonmetrical lines. Edgar Allan Poe (1809–49) anticipated Pater's "art for art's sake" credo (see AESTHETICISM) with his antididactic conception of the "poem written solely for the poem's sake," and of poetry as "the rhythmical creation of Beauty" (*The Poetic Principle*, pub. 1850). Through extensive commentary and translation (1856–65) by Baudelaire, and, later, Mallarmé (1888), Poe's emphasis on the analytic craft required to achieve the properly melancholic mood of poetry (*The Philosophy of Composition*, 1846) exerted a singular influence on r. and modernist poetics in France, where it remains central to the heirs of the Parnassian and symbolist movements (qq.v.).

D. In *France*, the nation whose neoclassical poetics became the antithetical *raison d'être* of romanticism in Germany and England, r. p. arrived late and was disputed early and long, causing its displacement into stylistic movements which rapidly fed and replaced each other. Just as the Fr. Revolution was linked intellectually to the romanticism of Rousseau, the ensuing political upheavals in France played a major role in the history of its r. lit. This is most evident in the writings of François René de Chateaubriand (1768–1848), whose r. *Atala* (1801) was followed by *Le Génie du Christianisme* (1802), a work whose assimilation of romanticism to religion won the favor of Napoleon and was expanded into an identification of Christianity with human liberty in *Memoires d'Outre-Tombe* (1848–50). In his *Essai sur la littérature anglaise* (1801), Chateaubriand also criticized Shakespearean drama for its untempered representation of nature. His romanticism thus contrasts sharply with that of another influential novelist and critic, Mme. de Staël (1766–1817), whose writings on Rousseau (1788), the Revolution (1818), and *De la littérature considérée dans ses rapports avec les institutions sociales* (1800) linked the devel. of lit. with political freedom rather than religious belief, and whose *De l'Allemagne*, advocating the importance of Ger. r. philosophy and lit. for France, was suppressed by Napoleon (1811;

pub. in London, 1813). In *Racine et Shakespeare*, Stendhal (Marie Henri Beyle, 1783–1842) argued that any new literary-historical form is "romantic" in its time, thereby refusing to reduce the difference between Classic and r. writing to the then-heated debate between pro-royalist ("ultra") and liberal political tendencies. This debate is most evident in the "Préface de *Cromwell*" (1827) by Victor Hugo (1802–85), whose unequivocal heralding of r. drama identified romanticism with the contemp. liberal movement. Apart from the political factors dividing proponents of Classicism and romanticism in 19th-c. France, a division also developed, unlike any in Germany or England, between practicing poets and critics.

The major critic of the period, Charles Augustin Sainte-Beuve (1804–69), stressed a psychological and personality-oriented approach to authors in his *Portraits littéraires* (1862–64) and *Portraits contemporains* (1869–71), a view expanded into the conception of lit. as a function of documentable social factors by Hippolyte Taine (1828–93), and into the analogy later drawn between literary and empirical scientific methods in the anti-r. writings of Émile Zola (1840–1902). Yet while different forms of historical positivism thus became the methods of literary research advocated critically, nothing could be less positivistic in outlook than the poetry written during this period. The first significant poets of the century, Lamartine (1790–1867), Vigny (1797–1863), Hugo (1802–85), and Musset (1810–57), while differing considerably in style and temperament, were all r. in their turn from conventional Cl. themes and the strict alexandrine (q.v.) meter to the more malleable prosody of emotive verse. Still, the works of the greatest r. lyricist of the century, Charles Baudelaire (1821–67), indicate the endurance of a dialectic between Classicism and romanticism within Fr. poetry. Baudelaire's *Fleurs du mal* (1857, 1861, 1868) focused upon mundane and abstract objects; alternating closely between high themes and low, their cl. severity gave lived reality the quality of dreamed or perpetually receding meaning and identified allegory and myth with the contemp. landscape of the city. The sense of a lucid, nontranscendent irony communicated in Baudelaire's poetry of "modern life" may be compared with the pathos of temporal passage dramatized by Hölderlin's use of antiquity, the death of a courtesan instead of a god now serving to image transience for the poet. Baudelaire's romanticism rejects from the outset any possibility of naturalism; in "Correspondances," his most famous lyric, "nature" is immediately equated with a meaningful construct, "a temple," and "forests" are composed of "symbols." Baudelaire's imagistic precision, graceful versification, and unsurpassed control of Fr. poetic diction made him one of the early Parnassians (q.v.), a group which rejected undisciplined r. effusions for a new classical r. decorum.

Paul Verlaine (1844–96), who, in *Art poétique* (1882), famously advocated "music before everything else," declaring that "everything else" (i.e. all semantic and formal criteria) "is lit." (i.e. contrived artifice), was more a neo-r. than a Parnassian in his emphasis on the suggestive quality of poetry. His views proved influential for a new generation of "free-versifiers," the poets of *vers libre* (q.v.), but were later retracted by Verlaine on the grounds that the new poetry, lacking all rhythm, bordered too closely on prose. Rimbaud, who unlike Verlaine appealed to the visual component of imagination (his "Voyelles" compares vowels with colors and images), described his poetics as a form of self-induced vision, arguing that poets must make themselves *voyants* through a purposeful "disordering of the senses." In this way poetry will no longer relate actions in rhyme but will itself occur "in advance of them," vision thus creating experience. For Rimbaud, all r. poets, but above all Baudelaire, have been *voyants*. Like "critics," he states however, "romantics" themselves have never been able properly to "judge romanticism," from which follows the famous agrammatical dictum, "car Je est un autre" (for *I* is another), by which the self, identified by being "disordered" with what is not the self, acquires the double (creative and reflective) vision of the *voyant*. Rimbaud, who probably wrote his last poetry at the age of 19, exerted tremendous influence upon future poets with the publication of his already repudiated *Illuminations*; his stature at the end of the century was matched only by that of the poet least like him in life, Stéphane Mallarmé (1842–98).

Mallarmé, who was employed as a lycée teacher until retiring at the age of 51, worked at eliminating the visual component from poetic lang., except in the literal sense of the graphic display of letters on the page, as in the late *Un Coup de dés jamais n'abolira le hasard* (1897), the prototype of modernist concrete poetry (q.v.). Mallarmé's verse, grammatical and semantic labyrinths emptied of any distinct imaged dimension, are constructed by means of the manipulation of syntax and the pure sensory properties of sound. This technical control of the composition of poetry whose signification cannot be equally mastered seems to invest lang. with a density outweighing any particular sense made of it. As the opening lines of "Le Tombeau d'Edgar Allan Poe" (1877) indicate that "eternity" alone "changes" "the poet" "into himself," so Mallarmé's compressed poetic lang. seems to acquire inexhaustible substance by severing itself from all worldly service, an extreme version of the negative factor of temporality informing the trad. of r. p. within which it remains.

E. In *Italy*, romanticism appeared late as a distinctly political movement focused on the "revolutionary" figure of Napoleon; the *Ultime lettere di Jacopo Ortis* (1799) of Niccolò Foscolo (1778–1827) added the motive of political disillusion to the suicide of its Wertherian hero. The downfall of Napoleon and the treaty of Vienna

(1815) contributed to a new affiliation of liberalism with romanticism, whose primary literary forum was the journal *Il Conciliatore* (1818–19). The most important poetry of the early 19th c., that of Giacomo Leopardi (1798–1837), involved a r. tension of aspiration and deception distinguished by its apolitical nature. With the achievement of national unity following decades of political struggle, incl. the imprisonment or exile of many authors in the r. movement, It. romanticism began to wane. Giosuè Carducci (1835–1907) wrote lyrics of renewed cl. vigor reflecting an anti-religious, realist spirit most reminiscent of the Fr. *philosophes*. The formulation of a philosophical approach to lit. crit. first appeared in the essays and *Storia della letteratura italiana* (1870–71) of Francesco de Sanctis (1818–83), which aimed at establishing critical practices uninfluenced by particularities of politics, religion, or taste. Gabriele D'Annunzio (1863–1938), poet, novelist, playwright, and the single most significant It. literary figure of the latter 19th c., was also one of the most internationally informed; his literary "decadence" was influenced largely by contemp. postromantic Fr. poetry and Nietzschean philosophy.

Earlier Ger. idealism, by contrast, shaped the *Filosofia dello spirito: estetica come scienza dell'espressione e linguistica generale* (1902) of Benedetto Croce (1866–1952). Croce equated art with instinctive, as opposed to conceptual, knowledge, and subordinated history to aesthetics. He argued that Classicism and romanticism represent not historical categories but rather the views that the artistic symbol (q.v.) is either extrinsic or intrinsic to the content of art. Looking back to the origin-of-lang. debates, Croce suggested that lang. itself is art in a state of "perpetual creation." He viewed Vico as a writer of historical allegory and "precursor of romanticism" but criticized the relationship between "romanticism and metaphysical idealism" as having so "elevated art" as to render it "absolutely useless," a devel. culminating in Hegel's "funeral oration of art." Reaction against Croce's own idealism was soon sounded by the It. futurists (see FUTURISM).

F. In *Russia*, Classicism in the Western European sense had never been a fully integrated literary force, while the new lit. of sensibility of the 18th c. exerted a considerable influence. Romanticism was identified most strongly with Byron and the circle surrounding Alexander Puškin (1799–1837), whose unsentimental portrayal of a jaded Byronic hero in *Eugene Onegin* (1832) used realism to reveal the dramatic insufficiency of high romantic narrative style. A jaded Satan in love with a mortal woman is the doubly alienated Byronic hero of the long poem *The Demon* (1829–40) by Mikhail Yurievich Lermontov (1814–41), whose modern syntax and complex first-person narrative offer a strong contrast to Puškin's classically harmonious verse and mark him as a forerunner of the symbolist movement at the close of the cen-

tury. Influenced by Schopenhauer, Nietzsche, and Rus. mysticism, the symbolists discounted traditional poetics. Foremost among them were Konstantin Balmont (1867–1943), whose crystalline sonnets recall Baudelaire; Valery Bryusov (1873–1924), whose experimental meters and imagery created an exotic effect; Andrey Bely (Boris Bugayev; 1880–1934), known for his devel. of the prose poem (q.v.); and Alexander Blok (1880–1921), whose symbolism was linked to mysticism. The exhaustion of symbolism (q.v.) in Russia was prefigured by the imprisoned Osip Mandelstam (1891–1938), whose lyrics reveal renewed concerns with cl. lit. and with poetic problems of history and temporality. Mandelstam's attention to compositional perfection, characteristic of Rus. acmeism (q.v.), recalls the exactitude sought by the postromantic Parnassians (q.v.).

G. In *Spain*, the return of exiled liberal writers after the death of Ferdinand VII in 1833 led to a belated experimentation with Byronesque romanticism in the works of José de Espronceda (1808–42) and José Zorrilla (1817–93). The most popular r. Sp. drama, *Don Alvaro* (1835) by C. Angel de Saavedra (Duque de Rivas, 1791–1865), echoed the *succès fou* of its Fr. model, Hugo's *Hernani* (1830). The most important pro-r. critical documents were the *Discurso sobre el influyo que ha tenido la crítica moderna en la decadencia del teatro antiguo español* (1828) of C. Augustín Durán (1793–1862), which praised native medieval Sp. lit. as truly r., and the *El clasicismo y romantismo* (1838) of Juan Donoso Cortéo (1809–53). The first Sp. r. poetry devoid of Byronism, the *Rimas* (*El libro de los gorriones*, 1868) of Gustavo Adolfo Bécquer (1836–70), later praised by such critics as Dámaso Alonso as the starting point of all modern Sp. poetry, combined relatively simple poetic lang. with great economy of diction. Bécquer was probably influenced by newly collected Andalusian folk poetry (1836), as Galician folksongs were to influence the *Cantares Gallegos* (1863) of Rosalía Castro (1837–85), who wrote in Galician rather than Castilian. The most important Sp. critic of the 19th c., Marcelino Menéndez y Pelayo (1856–1912), is generally credited with singlehandedly creating a critical and historical framework for the study of cl. Sp. lit. His scholarly renewal of Sp. literary culture, in such works as *Historia de las ideas estéticas en España* (1883–91), *Antología de poetas líricos castellanos* (1890–1908), and *Ensayos de crítica filosófica* (1892), contributed to the liberal and nationally oriented "Generation of '98," which included Miguel de Unamuno (1864– 1937), the individualist philosopher, and José Ortega y Gasset (1883–1955), whose studies in Germany (of Kant in particular) influenced his philosophical work on the relativity of truth and his critique of art (*La deshumanización del arte*, 1925). Finally, Spain's greatest modern poet, Frederico García Lorca (1898–1936), is also its greatest romantic. His *Romancero gitano* (1928), a collection of poems modeled on

Andalusian ballads, elevated native poetic forms to the level of the cl. and baroque masters. In the dramatic trilogy of *Bodas de Sangre* (1933), *Yerma* (1934), and *La Casa de Bernarda Alba* (1936), in elegies such as *Llanto por Ignacio Sanchez Mejías* (1935), and in his short lyrics, García Lorca's impassioned imagery and clear diction may be compared with Wordsworth's *Lyrical Ballads* and Baudelaire's *Fleurs du mal* in the impact they exerted upon an entire national literary trad., already marking this poet as Spain's most significant modern romantic at the time of his murder by a Falangist firing squad during the Sp. Civil War.

See now ENGLISH POETRY; FRENCH POETRY; GERMAN POETRY; ITALIAN POETRY; RUSSIAN POETRY; SPANISH POETRY. See also CRITICISM; FANCY; GENIUS; IMAGINATION; INTENTION; INTUITION; NEOCLASSICAL POETICS; ORIGINALITY; POETICS; POETRY, THEORIES OF; PREROMANTICISM; ROMANTICISM; SPONTANEITY; STURM UND DRANG; THEORY; TWENTIETH-CENTURY POETICS; VISION.

G. Saintsbury, *Hist. of Crit. and Literary Taste in Europe*, 3 v. (1900–4); G. Jacoby, *Herders und Kants Ästhetik* (1907); A. C. Bradley, *Oxford Lectures on Poetry* (1909); B. Croce, *La filosofia di G. Vico* (1911); R. L. Cru, *Diderot and Eng. Thought* (1913); E. Fiesel, *Die Sprachphilosophie der deutschen Romantik* (1927); E. Eggli, *Schiller et le romantisme français*, 2 v. (1927); I. A. Richards, *Coleridge on Imagination* (1935); A. Béguin, *L'Ame romantique et le rêve* (1939); F. Venturi, *Jeunesse de Diderot* (1939); F. O. Nolte, *Lessing's Laokoon* (1940); L. Trilling, *The Liberal Imagination* (1942); M. Kommerell, *Lessing und Aristoteles* (1944); P. Kuehner, *Theories on the Origin and Formation of Lang.* (1944); W. J. Bate, *From Classic to R.* (1946); Brooks; G. Lukács, *Goethe und seine Zeit* (1947); H.-G. Gadamer, "Hölderlin und das Zukünftige," *Beiträge zur geistigen Überlieferung* (1947); A. O. Lovejoy, *Essays in the Hist. of Ideas* (1948); L. Spitzer, *Linguistics and Lit. Hist.* (1948), *Representative Essays* (1988); W. Wimsatt, *Philosophic Words* (1948), *Day of the Leopards* (1974); Abrams; R. Brinkmann, "Romantische Dichtungstheorie in F. Schlegels Frühschriften und Schillers Begriffe der Naiven und Sentimentalischen," *DVJS* 32 (1950); W. Empson, *The Structure of Complex Words* (1954); F. García Lorca, *Conferencia y lecturas*, in *Obras completas* (1954); V. Brombert, *Stendhal et la voie oblique* (1954); Wellek, v. 1–4; H. Friedrich, *Die Struktur der modernen Lyrik* (1956, tr. 1974); B. Markwardt, *Gesch. der deutschen Poetik*, v. 2–3 (1956–58); H. Bloom, *Shelley's Mythmaking* (1959), *The Visionary Company* (1961), ed. *Romanticism and Consciousness* (1970); R. Ayrault, *La Genèse du romantisme allemand*, 4 v. (1961–76); C. M. Bowra, *The R. Imagination*, 2d ed. (1961); J. Starobinski, *L'Oeil vivant* (1961), *J. J. Rousseau, la transparence et l'obstacle* (1971); C. C. Clarke, *The Romantic Paradox: An Essay on the Poetry of Wordsworth* (1962); T. W. Adorno, "Parataxis, Zur Späten Lyrik Hölderlins," *Die Neue Rundschau* 75

(1964); G. H. Hartman, *Wordsworth's Poetry* (1964); H. Dubruck, *Gérard de Nerval and the Ger. Heritage* (1965); K. Burke, *Lang. as Symbolic Action* (1966), *A Grammar of Motives*, 2d ed. (1969); *Historia y antología de la poesía española en la lengua castellana*, ed. F. C. Sainz de Robles, 2 v. (1967); *Europäische Aufklarung*, ed. H. Friedrich and F. Schalk (1967); J. Derrida, *De la grammatologie* (1967), *Marges de la philosophie* (1972), "L'archéologie du frivole," Intro. to Condillac, *Essai sur l'origine des connaissances humaines* (1973, tr. 1987); A. Ferran, *L'Esthétique de Baudelaire* (1968); B. Guetti, "The Double Voice of Nature in Rousseau's *Essai sur l'origine des langues*," *MLN* 84 (1969), "Resisting the Aesthetic," *Diacritics* (1987); R. Chambers, *Gérard de Nerval et la poétique de voyage* (1969); W. Folkierski, *Entre le classicisme et le romantisme* (1969); L. Lipking, *The Ordering of the Arts* (1970); R. D. Miller, *Schiller and the Ideal of Freedom* (1970); O. Barfield, *What Coleridge Thought* (1971); D. J. Mossop, *Pure Poetry: Studies in Fr. Poetic Theory and Practice 1746–1945* (1971); R. J. Onorato, *The Character of the Poet: Wordsworth in the Prelude* (1971); H. Peyre, *Qu'est-ce que le romantisme?* (1971); *Sur l'origine du langage*, ed. R. Grimsley (1971); H. Dieckmann, *Diderot und die Aufklärung* (1972); R. A. Novak, *Wilhelm von Humboldt as a Lit. Critic* (1972); A. G. Bécquer, *Crítica literaria*, in *Obras completas* (1973); H.-D. Weber, *F. Schlegels "Transzendentalpoesie"* (1973); W. Benjamin, *Der Begriff der Kunstkritik in der deutschen Romantik* (1974), *C. Baudelaire: Ein Lyriker im Zeitalter des Hochkapitalismus* (1977); J. Chouillet, *L'Esthétique des lumières* (1974); O. Reboul, *Nietzsche, critique de Kant* (1974); P. Szondi, *Poetik und Geschichtsphilosophie*, 2 v. (1974), *Schriften*, 2 v. (1978); R. B. Harrison, *Hölderlin and Gr. Poetry* (1975); W. Koepsel, *Die Rezeption der Hegelschen Ästhetik im 20. Jahrhundert* (1975); T. Weiskel, *The Romantic Sublime* (1976); R. H. Grimm, *Nietzsche's Theory of Knowledge* (1977); P. Lacoue-Labarthe and J.-L. Nancy, *L'Absolu littéraire: théorie de la litt. du romantisme allemand* (1978, tr. 1988); A. Stender-Petersen, *Gesch. der russischen Literatur* (1978); H. White, *Tropics of Discourse* (1978); P. de Man, *Allegories of Reading* (1979), *Blindness and Insight*, 2d ed. (1983); *The Rhet. of Romanticism* (1984); K. S. Guthke, *G. E. Lessing*, 3d ed. rev. (1979); J. Mehlman, *Cataract: A Study in Diderot* (1979); J. L. Alborg, *Historia de la literatura española*, v. 4, *El Romanticismo* (1980); *Heinrich von Kleist: Aufsätze und Essays*, ed. W. Müller-Seidel (1980); J. P. Houston, *Fr. Symbolism and the Modernist Movement* (1980); V. Erlich, *Rus. Formalism*, 3d ed. (1981); H. Aarsleff, *From Locke to Saussure* (1982), *The Study of Lang. in England, 1780–1860* (1983); H. Vendler, *The Odes of John Keats* (1983); E. Auerbach, *Scenes from the Drama of European Lit.*, 2d ed. (1984); W. Düsing, "Ästhetische Form als Darstellung der Subjektivität," *Schillers Briefe über die ästhetische Erziehung*, ed. J. Bolton (1984); *Das Laokoon-Projekt: Pläne einer semiotischen Ästhetik*, ed. G.

Gebauer (1984); D. E. Wellbery, *Lessing's Laokoon: Semiotics and Aesthetics in the Age of Reason* (1984); *Gesch. der deutschen Literaturkritik (1730–1980)*, ed. P. Hohendahl (1985, tr. 1988); V. A. Rudowski, "Lessing contra Winckelmann," *Lessing and the Enlightenment*, ed. A. Ugrinsky (1986); S. Wolfson, *The Questioning Presence: Wordsworth, Keats, and the Interrogative Mode in Romantic Poetry* (1986); A. Warminski, *Readings in Interp.: Hölderlin, Hegel, Heidegger* (1987); R. Chambers, *Mélancolie et opposition* (1987); T. Pfau, "Critical Intro.," *Friedrich Hölderlin: Essays and Letters on Theory* (1988); D. Flitter, *Sp. Romantic Literary Theory and Crit.* (1992). C.B.L.

ROMANTIC IRONY. See IRONY.

ROMANTICISM. The present essay surveys primarily poetic praxis and cultural shifts in the period 1780–1840 and their consequences in the later 19th and 20th cs.; for fuller discussion of crit. and theory, see NEOCLASSICAL POETICS and ROMANTIC AND POSTROMANTIC POETICS. For wider surveys placing r. in the context of Western poetics, see CRITICISM and POETRY, THEORIES OF.

In most West European langs. the word "romantic" and its cognates came to circulate, in the 17th and 18th cs., as terms referring to the poetic world of medieval romance (q.v.), and by extension to everything bizarre, picturesque, and fantastic; for a while "Gothic" was, in Eng., a near-synonym. Present usage became stabilized, despite multitudes of critical definitions, by the end of the 19th c. The term "r.," however, has remained rather general, since the semantic and temporal boundaries are in dispute; some scholars (e.g. Lovejoy) have even claimed that "r." should be used only in the plural, though others (e.g. Wellek) have argued for a holistic view. However, at least some orientation in the semantic field is possible.

One family of meanings is general and connotes erotic sentiments, spectacular natural scenes, and adventurous action; in this sense r. is a constant or recurring quality of lit. of all times and places. The other family of meanings refers to the poetry (as well as to the art, political history, and intellectual devel.) of Western society as manifested with particular intensity in the period 1780–1840 and, in other cultural expressions in the decades preceding and following this period. The term "r." both serves as a framework of explanation for the events of this period and also designates a conceptual mode and style of art dominant during the time.

Before r. was constituted as a recognizable and coherent mode of vision and imagination (qq.v.), however, a number of changes occurred in European lit. and sensibility which prepared for it. Among these, thematic and emotional extensions in time and space took a leading place. The mountainous reaches of Scotland and Switzerland, the remote North and the exotic Balkans and Near East, and even North America and Polynesia became, in the 18th c., zones accessible to poetic sensibility. Later, mutual exoticism was frequent: the Mediterranean for North Europeans and the North for It., Fr., and Sp. writers became romantic loci. The Middle Ages, early Christianity, the primitive past (see PRIMITIVISM), and a utopian future were also claimed as poetic frameworks. The canon (q.v.) was drastically revised by the inclusion of Shakespeare, the romances of the Middle Ages and Ren., and the recovery of oral poetry (q.v.). Progressively, critics came to admit the role of the sublime (q.v.) and the picturesque as categories completing and correcting the beautiful, while other intellectuals rehabilitated imagination, sensibility (q.v.), instinct, and dream as complements to rationality and virtue. The specific psychologies of early childhood, femininity, old age, morbidity, and even insanity expanded the range of topics available to poets. These modifications, along with the increasing emphasis on spontaneity and subjectivity (qq.v.), sometimes crystallized in movements such as the Gothic novel and *Sturm und Drang* (q.v.) often collectively described as "preromanticism" (q.v.).

Many social, political, and economic devels. favored the growth of a romantic consciousness. Patriarchal and authoritarian structures (monarchy, the feudal, class and clan orders) were breaking down and being replaced by market relations in which transactional behavior and individual autonomy were decisive factors. Wherever these pressures toward more democratic and capitalist frameworks were blocked, revolutionary upheavals ensued, most notably in America and France. The liberation of consciousness was accompanied by idealistic philosophies and political systems promoting expectations of radical social change worldwide. Totalizing philosophical models, radical revolutionary demands, and imaginative visions of all kinds interacted in a variety of forms at the end of the 18th and in the first half of the 19th cs.

The thinking of Rousseau (1712–78), with its emphasis on natural humanity, confessional lit., and social utopia, shaped radically the thinking of the main European romantic writers until after 1800. In Germany, Herder (1744–1803) adapted Rousseau's views by emphasizing the separate identity or personality of historical periods, the common spirit permeating all activities—spiritual and material—of a culture, the literary dignity of small nations, and the value of folk poetry. Hölderlin, Wordsworth, and the Fr. revolutionaries were all in different ways influenced by Rousseau. At least equal in impact was the theorizing on subjectivity by an impressive series of philosophers beginning with Kant and running through Fichte and Schelling to Hegel. They declared the categories of consciousness as the foundation for human knowledge of the external world, and they were therefore widely interpreted as justifying personal understanding as the supreme criterion of truth. Ger. romantic idealism was also considered as providing a common ground for nature, God, and humanity. Indeterminacy (q.v.) and skepticism grew easily from it.

R. proper can be said to have emerged when enough of these separate discourses converged for consciousness to validate its claims of totality. New psychological and social models now emerged. R. was founded upon a desire to regenerate the human being by returning to its original and essential purity (Abrams). This original nature consists precisely in the absence of all those separations and specializations introduced by history in general and by the recent, rationalist ordering of the Enlightenment, of Neoclassicism, and of absolutism and early industrialization in particular. Consciousness and reality are meant to be fused in the romantic version of paradisial recovery; so too are subject and object; reason and imagination; God, nature and the self; opposing social classes; and the past and the future. This central claim of r. expressed itself in lit., in philosophy, and in political action. It was, however, impossible to achieve literally, and thus its explosiveness was coupled with instability, fragmentation, indirection, and absence.

Ger. r. is inextricably interwoven with the Neohumanist and Neoclassical movements occurring almost simultaneously, as well as with the surge of idealistic philosophy in the wake of Kant. A multitude of experiments in poetic form and theoretical fantasy, of which F. G. Klopstock's religious epic *Messias* (1773) and J. G. Hamann's (1744–1803) enthusiastic musings are the most typical, preceded the romantic upsurge. Friedrich Hölderlin (1770–1843), the greatest poet of the age, was not formally connected with groups that called themselves romantic, but his mythologic vision and all-embracing grasp of the cosmos, from the ethereal to the chthonic, as well as his attempt to give existential immediacy to Orphic poetic lang., place him in the neighborhood of Blake, Shelley, and Wordsworth. Johann Wolfgang von Goethe (1749–1832), like Byron, often spoke out publicly against the romantics. However his earliest work is definitely connected with the *Sturm und Drang*, while some of his major works both summarize and transcend r. The most typical is his poetic and philosophical drama *Faust* (1773–1831), a majestic fresco of the evolution of Western culture, and of the possibilities for human creativity. Goethe's friend Friedrich Schiller (1759–1805) underwent a similar evolution, from involvement in *Sturm und Drang* and radicalism as a young man, to the moderate r. of his later verse dramas and philosophical poems, to essays outlining an aesthetic state of humanity in which sensorial, cognitive, aesthetic, social, and moral impulses would be reconciled. The short, gossamer-like *Lieder* of Goethe and the historical ballads and philosophical musings of Schiller provided models for all Ger. and many European romantic poets (see SONG).

In a stricter sense, Ger. r. begins with H. W.

Wackenroder's (1773–98) emotional effusions on religious art and with Ludwig Tieck's (1773–1853) lyrical and fantastic tragicomedies, ironically subjective and Gothic prose, and musical and sentiment-laden verse. The most typical Ger. early romantic poet was Novalis (Friedrich von Hardenberg, 1772–1801), who praised in a series of hymns the nocturnal side of life as the deep and comprehensive, prelinguistic and presocial mode of existence underlying subsequent simplifications and specializations, almost as if life and death formed a unity. The same general drift, with imagination as the guide, the Middle Ages as a model, and intensely shining symbolism, can be recognized in Novalis' one novel and large essay on Western Christendom. The younger Achim von Arnim (1781–1831) and Clemens Brentano (1778–1842) oriented themselves toward the lyricism of dream, fantastic folktale, and an intimate, almost ethereal suggestiveness. Together they engaged (as part of the "Heidelberg group" of Ger. romantics) in the collection and adaptation of folk verse, much like their friends, the Catholic liberal Görres and the brothers Grimm, who brought out highly successful and influential collections of fairy tales.

Idealist philosophers like Fichte, Schelling, and Hegel and essayists like Wilhelm von Humboldt knew the poets closely, influenced them, and in turn articulated views put forward in romantic poetry. Among these, such concepts as organicism (q.v.), the universal subjective consciousness, the world as a system of signs and symbols, history as the unfolding of a universal spirit, and the central role of the aesthetic in human life, played an important part. Among romantic critics the most daring and innovative were the brothers August Wilhelm (1767–1845) and Friedrich (1772–1829) Schlegel. They played a key role in modifying the canon by their attraction to Sanskrit and Hebrew writings and by the elder brother's translations (with Tieck and others) of Shakespeare, Cervantes, and Calderón. Friedrich Schlegel also produced the first influential definition of romantic poetry as one based on universality or cosmopolitanism, on becoming (instead of *stasis*), and on a horizon of infinity. He advocated the mixture of genres (poetry, epic, philosophy) and illustrated it in his *Lucinde* (1799). Perhaps the most seminal of Friedrich Schlegel's theories was the one on irony (q.v.), which he saw as the supreme literary device, managing as it does to make a statement and to contradict it at the same time, thus imitating the functioning of the universe itself, with its basis in equipoised oppositions.

France had preceded other European lits. in preromantic writings and early romantic experimentation. However, in the 1790s and 1800s Fr. poetry was poor in romantic productions. In that period, romantic impulses expressed themselves in the ringing and utopian texts of the Fr. Revolution (Saint-Just is a prime example), as well as in the esoteric visions of Ballanche and Saint-Martin and in the sexual empires of de Sade. The prose of Senancour's *Obermann* (1804) and of Chateaubriand's *Atala* (1801) and *René* (1802) abounded in passionate sentiments, an effusive union with nature, and intense self-centeredness, all in rhythmic cadences. Germaine de Staël (1766–1817), a woman of unparalleled taste and energy, established important rapport between Ger., Fr., and Eng. lit.

In England, r. found full expression in the works of William Blake (1757–1827), who, particularly after 1789, invented a complex personal mythology and symbolism in which he dramatized the interaction of different psychic components and of religious and socio-historical energies. In a lang. inspired by esoteric and mystical authors, Blake castigated rationalism and authority and called prophetically for a new humanity based on imagination, instinct, and creativity. At the same time, and with considerable public attention, William Wordsworth (1770–1850) and S. T. Coleridge (1772–1834) launched their own romantic movement. Their joint volume of *Lyrical Ballads* (1798, 1800, 1802) was accompanied by a preface in which Wordsworth advocated simplicity in lang. and theme, emotive subjectivity ("the spontaneous overflow of powerful feelings"), and a dialectic of nature with consciousness and memory ("recollection in tranquillity"), and of the natural with the supernatural. Wordsworth's central poems in his most productive period (1795–1807)—Tintern Abbey, *Intimations of Immortality*, *The Prelude*—all wrestle with the attempt at capturing a totalizing cosmic vision, its loss, and its memory. Coleridge aimed towards the same redemptive grasp of totality and mused on its elusiveness in a poetic idiom that was often exotic, oneiric, and fantastic. He also theorized on the importance of imagination in poetry and human existence (*Biographia literaria*, 1817), emphasized the centrality of Shakespeare and Milton in Eng. lit., and in his old age composed parts of a huge philosophical framework which he intended to combine Ger. idealism, Christian theology, and romantic vision.

This early romantic Eng. poetry found fuller devel. in some of the poems of Byron (1788–1824) and Keats (1795–1821) and in most of the writings of Shelley (1792–1822). Byron's *Manfred* (1817) and *Cain* (1821), as well as the verse narratives and travelogues he wrote in the preceding decade, reflect on the tension between the potentialities of the individual and the infinity of the universe; a continual wavering between the transcendence of morality and evil, on the one hand, and feelings of guilt and nostalgia on the other is subtly recorded. In Keats' *Endymion* (1817), *Hyperion* (1818), and *The Fall of Hyperion* (1819), large mythological visions enact the passing of ages, the conflict of faculties, and the search for a central poetic self. Even more than his friends, Shelley struggled to evoke an integration between humanity and nature based on pantheism, Platonism, and prophetic revolutionary fervor. Like Keats, he emphasized the union between beauty and truth, arguing passionately in his *Defence of Poetry* (1821) that poets are the "unacknowledged legislators" of the world.

The disappointing and sometimes horrifying consequences of the Fr. Revolution and the displacements of the Napoleonic wars, as well as the sheer instability and unattainability of romantic visions in their pure form, led to serious modifications in romantic praxis after 1815. In England, Byron's *Beppo* (1818) is a smiling and worldly-wise acceptance of human imperfection, and his uncompleted *Don Juan* (1819–24) provides a powerful and convincing variant of the romantic hero in the mode of ironic realism. Keats' six great Odes (1819) engage the reader not in the absolute and the abyss but in the more hopeful and soothing dialectic of dream and reality. Robert Southey (1774–1834), who had always provided a somewhat diluted version of "Lake School" (q.v.) or mainstream r., became poet laureate (q.v.). Meanwhile minor poets like Moore, Campbell, and Hood held the public eye with their quite external assimilation of r. The emergence of the historical novel with Sir Walter Scott provided an exceptionally convenient medium for attenuation of romantic intensities. Talented essayists like Lamb, Hazlitt, and DeQuincey worked hard at providing a version of r. palatable to a moderate middle-class audience and compatible with the Neoclassical trad.

Even more striking were subsequent devels. in Ger. lit., where a poetic middle-class realism often called *Biedermeier* (q.v.) arose. Like Wordsworth and Coleridge, who emphasized religious, patriotic, and conservative themes as they got older, the Ger. romantic poets and essayists, esp. F. Schlegel, Brentano, and Tieck, became conservatives; a sharp turn towards Roman Catholicism can also be noted. While poets like Joseph von Eichendorff (1788–1857), Eduard Mörike (1804–75), and Annette von Droste-Hülshoff (1797–1848) paved the way for pure lyricism with their graceful allusive dreaminess and vibrant passion for details, August von Platen (1796–1835) revived a mannerist, jocular kind of classical elegance. Ludwig Uhland (1787–1862) came to typify a host of writers who reified romantic ideals into localism, idyllism, coarse-grained humor, and historical anecdote. Nikolaus Lenau (1802–50) went from melancholy to pessimism in evoking the strengths and difficulties of individualism.

Heinrich Heine (1797–1856) relativized r. without entirely denying it through his acute social consciousness, lyrically mocking reversals, and masterful poetic technique. The variety of Heine's forms and themes is unparalleled, from Northern to Mediterranean and from satire to melancholy delicacy; perhaps *Atta Troll* (1845), a political, ironic, and fantastic verse epic, best combines these different strains. What they all had in

ROMANTICISM

common, however, was a withdrawal from the revolutionary amplitude of romantic vision to more intimate and specific or more ironic and relative modes, which were also more subjective and individualist. This turn was in keeping with other devels. of Ger. lit. after 1815 such as the growth of poetic tragicomedy, the historical novel and drama, didactic writings, the seeds of aestheticism, armchair travel lit., and cozy sentimentalist prose. The stories and novels of E. T. A. Hoffman are also characteristic of later Ger. r.

Fr. poetic r. flourished in this later phase in consonance with *Biedermeier* diction and themes. Alphonse de Lamartine (1790–1869) dwelt with rhetorical sentimentalism on the melancholies of space, on solitude and on compassion. Alfred de Vigny (1797–1863), Alfred de Musset (1810–57), and the young Victor Hugo (1802–85) showed considerable versatility in evoking remote places and eras, the caprices of the fantasy-filled individual soul, and (Vigny in particular) the right of the strong-willed to ignore social conventions and moral laws. Gerard de Nerval (1808–55) more than his contemporaries gave free rein to his imagination and assigned to lang. the role of reshaping and harmonizing the world. Not only were these romantic poets the contemporaries of a host of other versifiers of the macabre, the bizarre, or the mannerist; they must also be seen in the context of the fantastic and historical fiction written by Balzac, Nodier, Hugo, Musset, Vigny, Nerval, George Sand, Dumas, and others, as well as the fanciful narrative historiography of Michelet or Thierry. Sainte-Beuve (1804–69) was the period's major critic.

The romantic lit. of Southern Europe, Eastern Europe, Scandinavia, and the Americas differs from the lits. mentioned above in two important respects. First, it usually lacks the high romantic ambition of universal vision and total regeneration of the human race. Second, it combines romantic expansions and liberations with practical purposes (national unification and reawakening, social and political reform, structural modernization) as well as with an often simultaneous reception of Neoclassical and Enlightenment values. These features led to highly original and important achievements in virtually all the lits. Thus Ugo Foscolo (1778–1827) evoked the melancholy of night and the grave, while Giacomo Leopardi (1798–1837) expressed the anguish of infinity and explored the dialectics of small things and cosmic feelings. José de Espronceda (1808–42) with his subjective lyrics and G. A. Bécquer (1836–70) with his tortured irony are the chief spokesmen for romantic poetry in Spain. Adam Oehlenschlaeger (1779–1850) in Demark mixed fantasy and irony, while Edgar Allan Poe (1809–49) invoked morbid love and Gothic thrills. Karel Mácha (1810–36) in Czech, Sandor Petöfi (1823–49) in Hungarian, and Mihai Eminescu (1850–89) in Romanian became symbolic for synthesizing the emotional and linguistic values of their national communities at crucial historical moments.

The emerging nations of South and North America found in romantic poetry a similar means of consolidating their identity and validating social and national values. In the United States, New England intellectuals were fascinated by the poetic and ethical potential of a vision in which God, nature, and humanity are in intimate relation or can be even seen as fused. Although movements such as New England Transcendentalism and the Am. Ren. expressed themselves chiefly in prose, the reflective poems of W. C. Bryant (1794–1878) and R. W. Emerson (1803–82) and the fiery imagery and anaphoric cadences of Walt Whitman (1819–92) also worked in the same direction. The Argentines Esteban Echeverría (1809–51) and D. F. Sarmiento (1811–88) succeeded in fusing native scenes (pampas and gauchos) with modern verse vehicles, while J. M. Heredia y Campuzano (1803–39) of Cuba was the first great romantic lyricist of South America.

Later r. was particularly fruitful in Polish and Rus. lits. A. S. Puškin (1799–1837) orchestrated with subtlety the passions of the individual, calls for political freedom, philosophical irony, fantastic imagery, and superb metrical technique to become the greatest Rus. poet of his century. Mikhail Lermontov (1814–41) was more unilateral in his advocacy of the exceptional individual and pure liberties. Adam Mickiewicz (1798–1855), like Puškin, controlled an astonishing range of romantic modes of expression, from apocalyptic and nightmarish to graciously playful. He was closely seconded by Juliusz Słowacki (1809–44), Zygmunt Krasiński (1812–59), and Cyprian Norwid (1812–83), whose sensibility was quickened by their lives in exile at a moment of national disaster.

The literary influence of r. continued into the 20th c. Every literary generation may be said to have had its own neoromanticism and its antiromanticism. Perhaps the most powerful direct influence, on Baudelaire and symbolism (q.v.), put in practice romantic notions of the general correspondence of natural signs, of the secret connections between all parts of the universe, and of the release of imaginative power. Parnassian and Decadent (qq.v.) poets reified romantic views into aesthetic objects, delighting in the imagery of precious stones, mysterious caves, diabolical menaces, and transgressions. A broad stream of idyllic, melodramatic, and sentimental writing in all genres flowed into popular lit., creating a kind of mass r. Swinburne, Yeats, George, Hofmannsthal, de Régnier, and D'Annunzio may all be said to be neoromantic at least at some points in their careers. Realism (q.v.) evolved out of the romantic concern with natural and social detail and based its narrative structures on myths of conflict and reconciliation, as well as on typologies of character originated by the romantics.

The modernist movement, although it often

attacked r., owed much to its impulses and expansions of consciousness; Existentialism borrowed from r. its problematic of the individual; Expressionism (q.v.) derived its frenetic and prophetic dimensions from r.; even postmodernism, with its interest in historical fragment, turns most often to romantic experiments (see MODERNISM AND POSTMODERNISM). Even resolute 20th-c. adversaries of r. like Brunetière, Babbitt, Hulme, and Eliot derive from the romantic mainstream. The historical novel, structurally a romantic invention, continued to prosper as a new and independent genre. Other generic consequences of r. include the flourishing of the prose poem (q.v.), of fragmentary fiction, and of fantastic and lyrical prose. The loosening of generic boundaries, the departure from metrical verse, the interaction of the arts, and the subjectivity of taste (q.v.) are components of the romantic program that remained unchanged well into the 20th c., much as the poetic canon of the 19th and 20th cs. was the one set during the decades of romantic ferment.

Perhaps even vaster was the romantic inheritance in public and intellectual discourse and in ideology and theory from Freudianism, nationalism, and socialism to the philosophies of Nietzsche, Dilthey, Bergson, and Heidegger. Furious opposition to r. used as its vehicles realism (q.v.) in the early 19th c., conservative and traditional ideologies at the end of the 19th c. (particularly in France), colloquial diction (Pound), the cult of machines (Futurism, q.v.), and radical political and philosophical critiques (by the mid 20th c., esp. in Germany). In the 1960s, the world over, a youth culture in popular music and lit. (Jim Morrison, the cult of Hesse and Tolkien, etc.) drew heavily on romantic materials. It is important to note that romantic discourses provided a deepened textual polyvalence, an expansion of ambiguity (q.v.), and an involvement in the nature of textuality (q.v.). Crit. of the 1970s and 1980s, esp. in the work of Paul de Man, foregrounded the deconstructive moment (see DECONSTRUCTION), esp. the uncertainties and skepticism underlying romantic writing: many romantic writers had theorized brilliantly on irony, doubt, and subjectivity and objectivity.

These consequences and ramifications show that r. was far more than one literary movement among others. It came at a key moment in the history of Western culture, of which it was both a product and a shaper. Perhaps more than other literary manifestations, r. is a case when poetry truly incorporates the questionings and values of society as a whole. Western society in the 18th c., first in a few of its parts then over larger areas and at a faster pace, underwent a modernization that had been many centuries in the making and was rapidly coming to a head, bringing with it urbanization, industrialization, demographic explosion, rationalization, ordering and streamlining of social processes, analytical and transactional modes of thinking and behavior, and democratization. Modernization was sometimes revolutionary, but even when it was not it deeply upset the archaic rhythms, the "biological" patterns of traditional behavior. The importance of r. consists in having provided a framework for processing these watershed changes. Inside r., modernization could be denied, approved, qualified, critiqued, and questioned. R. was thus the new idiom for conversing with modernization; it contained human and world models, images and visionary projections that allowed coping with modernity. R. furnished a structure for questioning and interpreting the world.

The capacious systems of Kant and Hegel provided a conceptual vocabulary and theoretical underpinnings that proved indispensable and that are, if at all, becoming obsolescent only at the end of the 20th c. However it was poetic lang. (whether in verse, in prose, or on the stage) that proved the most adequate medium for responding to modernity. It had the kind of variety and indeterminacy, richness and flexibility that could make it a privileged ground for experimenting with human potentialities and responses, redeeming the past, assimilating the present, and projecting the future. These romantic experiments functioned for a long while (and are still being used) as a storehouse for conceptual and imaginative materials. They not only served intellectuals of all kinds but also permeated deeply all levels of discourse and all social classes. They still exert a powerful influence: many of the discourses of racial and gender equality, canonical expansion, global democracy, and multiculturalism prominent at the end of the 20th c. are rooted in romantic categories and experiments. See also COCKNEY SCHOOL; FANCY; IMAGINATION; INFLUENCE; ORIGINALITY; PREROMANTICISM; SATANIC SCHOOL; STURM UND DRANG; VISION; and see the various national poetry surveys.

REFERENCE: D. H. Reiman, *Eng. Romantic Poetry 1800–1835: A Guide to Information Sources* (1979); F. Jordan, *Eng. Romantic Poets: A Rev. of Research and Crit.*, 4th ed. (1985).

ANTHOLOGIES: *R. Reconsidered*, ed. N. Frye (1963); *Eng. Romantic Writers*, ed. D. Perkins (1967); *R. and Consciousness*, ed. H. Bloom (1970); *R.: Points of View*, ed. R. F. Gleckner and G. E. Enscoe, 2d ed. (1970); *The Romantic Period in Germany*, ed. S. Prawer (1970); *Eng. Romantic Poets: Mod. Essays in Crit.*, ed. M. H. Abrams, 2d ed. (1975); *R.*, ed. H. Eichner (1977); *R. and Lang.*, ed. A. Reed (1984); *Ardis Anthol. of Rus. R.*, ed. C. Rydel (1984); *Ger. Aesthetic and Lit. Crit.*, ed. H. B. Nisbet, K. M. Wheeler, and D. Simpson, 3 v. (1984–86); *European R.*, ed. G. Hoffmeister (1990).

STUDIES: I. Babbitt, *Rousseau and R.* (1919); A. O. Lovejoy, "On the Discrimination of Rs.," *PMLA* 39 (1921); O. Walzel, *Deutsche Romantik*, 5th ed. (1923–26); A. Castro, *Les grands romantiques espag-*

RONDEAU

nols (1924); A. Farinelli, *Il romanticismo nel mondo latino*, 3 v. (1927); R. Ullmann and H. Gotthard, *Gesch. der Begriffs Romantisch* (1927); A. Viatte, *Les Sources occultes du r.*, 2 v. (1928); A. Monglond, *Le Préromantisme français*, 2 v. (1930); H. A. Korff, *Geist der Goethezeit*, 5 v. (1940–57), esp. v. 3 (3d ed. 1956) and 4 (2d ed. 1955); A. Béguin, *L'Ame romantique et le rêve* (1946); N. Frye, *Fearful Symmetry* (1947); P. van Tieghem, *Le Romantisme dans la litt. européene* (1948), *Le Romantisme* (1963), *Le romantisme français*, 9th ed. (1969); E. A. Peers, *Short Hist. of the Romantic Movement in Spain* (1949); W. J. Bate, *From Classic to Romantic* (1946); G. Hough, *The Last Romantics* (1949), *The Romantic Poets*, 2d ed. (1957); R. Wellek, "The Concept of 'R.' in Lit. Hist." (1949), and "R. Re-examined," in *Concepts of Crit.* (1963), *Confrontations* (1965); Wellek v. 2; M. Praz, *The Romantic Agony*, 2d ed. (1951); Abrams; Frye; D. Čiževskij, *On R. in Slavic Lit.* (1957); M. Součkova, *The Czech Romantics* (1958); H. Bloom, *The Visionary Company* (1961); R. Haym, *Die romantische Schule*, 6th ed. (1961); F. Strich, *Deutsche Klassik und Romantik*, 5th ed. (1962); W. L. Renwick, *Eng. Lit. 1789–1815* (1963); I. Jack, *Eng. Lit. 1815–1832* (1963); F. Kermode, *Romantic Image*, 2d ed. (1964); F. Schultz and H. J. Lüthi, "Romantik," *Reallexikon* 3.578–94; L. Furst, *R. in Perspective* (1969); M. Peckham, *The Triumph of R.* (1970); M. H. Abrams, *Natural Supernaturalism* (1971), *The Correspondent Breeze* (1984); O. Barfield, *What Coleridge Thought* (1971); *"Romantic" and Its Cognates: The European Hist. of a Word*, ed. H. Eichner (1972); P. Cornea, *Originile romantismului românesc* (1972); *Neues Handbuch der Literaturwiss.*, ed. K. von See (1972–), v. 14–16; Wilkins; B. Zelinsky, *Rus. R.* (1974); A. Vecchio, *Il romanticismo italiano* (1975); F. L. Baumer, "R. (ca. 1780–ca. 1830)," and R. Wellek, "R. in Lit.," *DHI*; G. Hoffmeister, *Deutsche und europäische Romantik* (1978); M. Brown, *The Shape of Ger. R.* (1979); M. Cooke, *Acts of Inclusion* (1979); G. T. Hughes, *Romantic Ger. Lit.* (1979); T. Rajan, *Dark Interpreter* (1980); J. R. de J. Jackson, *Poetry of the Romantic Period* (1980); T. McFarland, *R. and the Forms of Ruin* (1981); M. Butler, *Romantics, Rebels, and Reactionaries* (1981); G. Schulz, *Die deutsche Literatur zwischen französisch Revolution und Restauration* (1983); J. J. McGann, *The Romantic Ideology* (1983); P. de Man, *The Rhet. of R.* (1984); V. Nemoianu, *The Taming of R.* (1984); L. G. Leighton, "R.," in Terras; C. Chase, *Decomposing Figures* (1986); S. Curran, *Poetic Form and British R.* (1986); T. Weiskel, *The Romantic Sublime* (1986); *R. and Contemp. Crit.*, ed. M. Eaves and M. Fischer (1986); L. Chai, *The Romantic Foundations of the Am. Ren.* (1987); *R. and Feminism*, ed. A. K. Mellor (1988); C. H. Siskin, *The Historicity of Romantic Discourse* (1988); P. Lacoue-Labarthe and J.-L. Nancy, *The Literary Absolute* (tr. 1988); C. Jacobs, *Uncontainable R.* (1989); *El Romanticismo*, ed. D. T. Gies (1989); T. Ziolkowski, *Ger. R. and Its Institutions* (1990); H.

Fischer, *Romantic Verse Narrative* (tr. 1991). V.P.N.

ROMANY POETRY. See GYPSY POETRY.

RONDEAU. Originally the generic term for all Fr. fixed forms (r., rondel, triolet [qq.v.]), these being derived from dance-rounds (*rondes* or *rondels*) with singing accompaniment: the refrain was sung by the chorus—the general body of dancers—and the variable section by the leader. The written forbears of the r. are generally thought to be the *rondets* or *rondets de carole* from 13th-c. romances (cf. CAROL). The form by which we know the r. today emerged in the 15th c., and by the beginning of the 16th c. had displaced all competitors. This form, practiced particularly by Clément Marot, consists of 13 lines, octo- or decasyllables, divided into three stanzas of 5, 3, and 5 lines. The whole is constructed on two rhymes only, and the first word (-sound) or words of the first line are used as a *rentrement* (refrain), which occurs at the ninth and fifteenth lines, i.e. at the end of the second and third stanzas, and usually does not rhyme. If we let R. stand for the *rentrement*, the r. has the following scheme: *aabba aabR aabbaR.*

During the course of the 16th c. the r. gradually disappeared. It was restored to fashion at the beginning of the 17th c. by the *précieux* poets, esp. Vincent Voiture, on whose example Théodore de Banville based his 19th-c. revival of the form. Although Musset had experimented with the form earlier in the 19th c., taking some liberties with the rhymes, it was Banville's practice which provided the model for the later 19th-c. explorations of the form. In England, aside from 16th-c. examples (Wyatt in particular), the r., did not really flourish until the end of the 19th c., when under Banville's influence Fr. forms attracted the enthusiasm of poets such as Austin Dobson, Edmund Gosse, W. E. Henley, Ernest Dowson, Thomas Hardy, and Robert Bridges. In Eng. it has, unlike the triolet (q.v.), often been used as a vehicle for serious verse. In Germany, where it has also been called *Ringelgedicht, Ringelreim,* and *Rundreim*, the r. was used by Weckherlin, Götz, Fischart, and later Hartleben.

The management of the *rentrement* is the key to the r.'s expressive capabilities. Banville says that the *rentrement* is "both more and less than a line, for it plays the major role in the r.'s overall design. It is at once the r.'s subject, its *raison d'être* and its means of expression." Fr. poets, wishing to keep the *rentrement* unrhymed yet fatally drawn to rhyme, found a solution in the punning *rentrement*, which rhymes with itself rather than merely repeating itself. Consequently, in the Fr. r. the *rentrement* tends to remain unassimilated, full of wit, buoyancy, and semantic fireworks. The Eng. poets, on the other hand, sought to integrate the *rentrement* more fully, both by frequently allowing it to rhyme with either the *a* or *b* lines, thus pushing the r. in the direction of that exclusively Eng. form,

- [1097] -

the roundel (q.v.), and by exploiting its metrical continuity with the rest of the stanza. The Eng. *rentrement* is also usually longer than the Fr., four syllables rather than one or two. In short, the Eng. r. is altogether graver and more meditative than the Fr., its *rentrement* more clearly a lyric destination, a focus of self-recollection, intimate knowledge, and haunting memory.

As a type of truncated refrain, the *rentrement* probably evolved from copyists' habits of abbreviation, common in the Middle Ages. In Fr. prosody, *rentrements* are usually associated with the r., but whenever the refrains of any poem, in any lang., whether r.-derived or not, are an abbreviated version of the first line either of the poem or of each stanza (e.g. Wyatt, "In *aeternum*," "Forget not yet," "*Quondam* was I"), then the term *rentrement* can be justifiably applied.

The *r. redoublé*, similar in form, is rare even at the time of Marot, who is known to have composed one in 1526. In the 17th c. a few isolated examples occur in the works of Mme. Deshoulières and Jean de La Fontaine; Banville uses the form in the 19th c. Marot's r. r., 24 lines in six quatrains plus the *rentrement*, may be schematized as follows (R signifying the *rentrement* and capitals and primes denoting whole-line refrains): *ABA'B' babA abaB babA' abaB' babaR*. Each line of stanza 1 is employed in turn as the last line of each of the following four stanzas, which thus serve to develop the content of stanza 1; the final stanza then makes a comment or summation. See also RONDEL; ROUNDEL.

T. de Banville, *Petit Traité de poésie française* (1872); J. Gleeson White, *Ballades and Rondeaus* (1887); Kastner; Thieme, 380—lists 10 works 1364–1897; H. L. Cohen, *Lyric Forms from France* (1922); H. Spanke, "Das lateinische R.," *ZFSL* 53 (1929–30); Patterson; M. Françon, "La pratique et la théorie du r. et du rondel chez Théodore de Banville," *MLN* 52 (1937), "Wyatt et le r.," *RQ* 24 (1971); F. Gennrich et al., "R.-Rondo," *MGG* ll.867–84; F. Gennrich, "Deutsche Rondeaux," *BGDSLH* 72 (1950), *Das altfranzösische R. und Virelai im 12. und 13. Jahrhundert* (1963); G. Reaney, "Concerning the Origins of the R., Virelai, and Ballade," *Musica Disciplina* 6 (1952), "The Devel. of the R., Virelai, and Ballade Forms," *Festschrift Karl Fellerer* (1962); M. Rat, "Rondel et r.," *Vie et langage* 14 (1965); N. H. J. van den Boogaard, *Rondeaux et Refrains du XIIe siècle au début du XIVe* (1969)—prints all known rs. ca. 1228–1332, but must be used with caution; F. Deloffre, *Le Vers français* (1969); F. M. Tierney, "An Intro. to the R.," "Origin and Growth of the R. in France," *Inscape* 8 (1970), "The Devel. of the R. in England," "The Causes of the Revival of the R.," *Revue de l'Université d'Ottawa* 41, 43 (1971; 1973); Elwert; C. Scott, "The Revival of the R. in France and England 1860–1920," *RLC* 213 (1980); N. Wilkins, "R.," *New Grove* 16.166–70; Scott; Morier; J. Britnell, "'Clore et rentrer': The Decline of the R.," *FS* 37 (1983). C.S.; T.V.F.B.

RONDEAU REDOUBLÉ. See RONDEAU.

RONDEL. A Fr. fixed form, which has had a long and varied history. Its simplest form: *AB aA ab AB*, reaching back to the 13th c., became known later as the triolet (q.v.). Another early variation was the *r. double*, which had the rhyme scheme *ABBA abBA abba ABBA* (capital letters indicate repeated lines). In the 15th c. the terms "r." and "rondeau" (q.v.) seem to have been used interchangeably: one even finds the phrase "un r., des rondeaux." The r. best known today is a poem of 3 stanzas built on 2 rhymes with the scheme *ABba abAB abbaA(B)*. This is composed of 13 lines in which a 2-line refrain occurs twice in the first 8 lines (1–2 and 7–8), the first line also being repeated as the last line; or it may consist of 14 lines, in which case a 2-line refrain appears thrice in the poem. Henley, Gosse, Dobson, R. L. Stevenson, and others have written Eng. rs.—Kastner; M. Françon, "La pratique et la théorie du rondeau et du r. chez Théodore de Banville," *MLN* 52 (1937); C. Scott, "The Revival of the R. in France and England, 1860–1920," *RLC* 213 (1980). L.B.P.; T.V.F.B.

ROTROUENGE. OF stanza form of uncertain origin (perhaps originally "song of Rotrou") and of indeterminate form. The r. perhaps derived from adaptation to lyric use of the epic *laisse* (q.v.), with its characteristic sequence of isometric lines sung to one repeated musical phrase, but this structure may well have undergone early modification. Adapted into Occitan as *retroensa* or *retroncha*, the term was applied to strophic songs having a 2-line refrain (whence the verb *retronchar*, "to repeat in the manner of a refrain").—F. Gennrich, *Die altfranzösische R.* (1925); Bec; Chambers. J.H.M.

ROUNDEL. In the Middle Ages this term is used simply as a synonym for the rondeau or rondel (qq.v.)—e.g. by Chaucer, *Knight's Tale* 1529. But in its modern sense the term refers to the variant form introduced by Swinburne in his *A Century of Rs.* (1883). Swinburne altered the *rondeau's* 13 lines (plus 2 refrains) in 3 stanzas of 5, 3, and 5 lines rhyming *aabba aabR aabbaR* (R standing for the *rentrement* [refrain; see RONDEAU], which is the first word or phrase in the poem) by shortening the 5-line stanzas to 3 and by moving the *rentrement* forward, giving a 9-line form (plus 2 refrains) in 3 stanzas rhyming *abaR bab abaR*. This still keeps only two rhymes but the effect is now of cross-rhyme (the R is a *b*-rhyme). Swinburne's r. entitled "R." is at once a definition and example of the form (the *rentrement* is "A r. is wrought").—R. Rooksby, "Swinburne in Miniature," *VP* 23 (1985). T.V.F.B.

ROVING OVER. See SPRUNG RHYTHM; BROKEN RHYME.

RUBAI, RUBAIYAT STANZA. See OMAR KHAYYAM QUATRAIN; PERSIAN POETRY.

RULES

RULES. I. HISTORICAL. Formulations of poetic "r." have commonly been founded on the assumption that literary composition is at least partly a matter of conscious "art" (Gr. *techne*; for the Greeks, unlike the moderns, "technique" did not imply "technical") which is carried on on the basis of, hence for which one may construct, a more or less systematic body of principles (Gr. *technologos*; Lat. *ars*). This is an assumption which, when used with wisdom and flexibility, has been the basis of much valuable lit. crit. and theory.

At times, however, as in the 16th and 17th cs., the art of poetry has been viewed as a system of highly detailed and inviolable specifications or precepts for the subject matter, arrangement, presentation, and style of the various poetic genres—e.g. a play must have five acts; only three actors can be on stage at once; the subject matters of the genres cannot be mixed; the pastoral or eclogue (qq.v.) must be written in the low style, about shepherds; tragedy (q.v.) must be in the grand style and about royalty; comedy (q.v.) must be about soldiers, servants, farmers, and prostitutes; the "Aristotelian" unities of time and place must be faithfully observed (see UNITY); and so on. Equally explicit at times have been the r. of versification: the number of syllables in lines must be rigidly controlled by the various forms of elision (q.v.); the metrical pattern must not admit of much variation in stress placement; genres must each have their specific metrical forms, etc.

Most 16th- and 17th-c. collections of such r. were in a large degree codifications of the artistic practices of Cl. antiquity (supported by fragmentary citations of various ancient critics), but they were also quite heavily supported by general theorizing about art, nature (q.v.), the audience, and the poet; and particular r. were frequently defended by different writers on entirely different theoretical grounds. Castelvetro, for example, viewing poetry primarily as designed for a common and ignorant audience, defends the unity of time on the basis of the impossibility—so he reasons—of making such persons "believe that several days and nights have passed when they know through their senses that only a few hours have passed" (*Poetica d'Aristotele* [1570]); Minturno, however, viewing poetry both as the product of natural and artistic faculties and as a collection of separate genres all designed for a more general audience, defends the unity of time as one of the standard intellectual requirements of artistic achievement for a "good" (hence socially useful) dramatic poem, and does not argue that it is demanded by the laws of credibility (*De poeta* [1559]). Indeed, a particular rule could be rejected by one critic on grounds very similar to those on which another defended it; thus Pierre de Laudun argued, in his *Art poétique françois* (1597), that strict adherence to the unity of time is unwise precisely because it tends to force the poet to present impossible and incredible things (see RENAISSANCE POETICS; BA-

ROQUE POETICS).

Notwithstanding the volume of the theorizing in the 16th c., a gradual, general undermining of the so-called "neoclassical" r. began to occur in the 17th c., influenced by trends toward both a more independent, "philosophical" kind of crit. and also a kind of "circumstantial" crit. by which specific r. of the past were rejected as appropriate only to their circumstances. By the middle of the 18th c., esp. in England, most of the more notorious r. associated with the genres and the "unities" had been discredited (cf. Johnson, *Rambler* no. 125 [1751] and *Preface to Shakespeare* [1765]). The concentration particularly on the r. of the established genres gave way first to more flexible definitions of those genres, then to more inclusive lists of legitimate genres (incl., e.g., "heroic plays," comedies of manners, and domestic tragedies), and finally to a shift of interest away from genres to those aspects of nature and art relevant to poetry (see NEOCLASSICAL POETICS).

However, this shift did not effect a general denial of the need for artistic r. Rather, the tendency was to establish new ones, though still based on the ancient principle that the writing of poetry is at least partly an "art," not merely a natural process. Wordsworth, for example, in the Preface to *Lyrical Ballads* (3d ed., 1802), while rejecting the "artificial" practices of most 18th-c. poets, announced the presumably innovative r. of "human" subject matter and diction by which true poetry could be achieved. Nor was the central neoclassical principle of imitation (q.v.)—of guidance by the practices of past masters—ever completely abandoned. Rather, rejection of "ancient" examples was commonly accompanied by endorsement of "modern" ones, esp. of those who departed from the neoclassical r. (see QUERELLE DES ANCIENS ET DES MODERNES). Thus writers as diverse as Lessing, Herder, Voltaire, and Dr. Johnson frequently cited the examples of medieval or "folk" poetry as well as of such nonclassical authors as Shakespeare and Milton. R.M.; T.V.F.B.

II. THEORETICAL. From the foregoing survey it will be seen that many of the changes which occur from time to time in canonical poetic r. seem to result as much from changes in taste (q.v.) toward poetry itself as from changes in critical conceptions of it. But both have had their place in Western poetics. Critics have at one time or another held either (1) that critical r. should be based on the practice of poets, or (2) that poets should base their practice on critical r. Unfortunately, the first sort of r. amount to mere descriptive summaries, constantly vulnerable to radical alteration at the appearance of any new praxis (genre); and if the poet is able to devise any new genre or form she or he wishes, then the poet is responsible to no set of guiding principles at all, only to inspiration, experiment, and accident, and the notion of "r." does not exist. Nor have poets shown themselves conspicuously reliable when reporting on their own poetic principles: Eliot is a notable example of a critic the reality of whose poetic praxis was subtly concealed by the authoritative tone of his own critical pronouncements. Indeed, some theorists would hold that such a situation is not only inevitable but, in psychological terms, necessary.

The second sort of r., by contrast, amount to only prescriptive doctrines, either permitting no new praxis at all, or only at the expense of wholesale poetic revolution, or else pressuring poets to conform to r. devised by critics who may well have much less appreciation for the actual nature and contingencies of poetic creation than do poets. What then of the situation where (1) is followed by (2)? Now critical description of prior praxis becomes normative precept evaluating and regulating subsequent praxis. It is precisely this kind of closed loop, from inductive or descriptive r. to deductive or prescriptive ones, which evoked romantic poetics (q.v.) as a revolt against the felt irrelevance and intransigence of neoclassical r. But in fact even the Augustans had objected that, with r., correctness comes to be preferred over genius, and means become ends. Not this way will poets "snatch a grace beyond the reach of art" (Pope).

The presumption that poetic making is carried on within the framework of a set of principles or procedures, if they be precise and systematic (even if not conscious on the part of the poet), necessarily entails that such principles should be capable of being subsequently discovered and articulated. The issues in dispute are simply how specific the procedures and hence their articulation can be. It is important to bear in mind the flexibility of the critical doctrine of "r." as it was historically understood. As La Drière has remarked, since "a rule is obviously not the principle it formulates," inevitably "all formulation of apprehended principle is imperfect and temporary. Even convention is never perfectly understood or wholly reduced to formula," and "a rule—which indeed once formulated may itself become a convention—may contradict a natural principle, possibly the very principle it is intended to embody."

The emergence of oral-formulaic theory (q.v.) in the 20th c. has given some support to this presumption, which is itself a natural and appealing one. But if the forces of precedent, tradition (q.v.), generic decorum, canonicity, or the strong precursor have usually worked, in the past, to transmute descriptive principles into prescriptive constraints, it has been the work of 20th-c. generative linguistics to alter, fundamentally and irrevocably, our concept of what a "rule" actually is.

Chomsky and his successors specifically called into issue the very concept of a "rule" in the production of lang. and its concomitant, the nature of r. in theoretical analysis. In this account, the r. of a lang. are not merely descriptive but *constitutive:* they are not verbal descriptions but specific processes which determine what will be produced as speech; and all competent native speakers of a lang. know them even if they do not know they know them. Searle used the analogy of games: in chess, if one does not follow the r., one is simply *not playing chess.* Structural linguistics, Chomsky argued, failed because its r. were merely accumulated descriptions or lists: they could not explain *how* or *why* a sentence could be refashioned in certain ways but not others.

After 1965, efforts were made to apply this concept of r. to metrical theory so as to discover r. that would, for example, generate all and only iambic pentameter lines (see GENERATIVE METRICS). This seemed a productive line of inquiry because meters are usually relatively precise. But no definitive set of such r. was ever isolated, nor was it ever shown conclusively that the r. in versification are actually of the same type as those in lang., for aesthetic forms are to a considerable degree conventional, and conventions (q.v.) are to a considerable degree arbitrary. If, then, no r. were forthcoming for the most specifiable part of poetics, how much less likely, it came to seem, would other more sweeping r.—generic or thematic—be? The collapse, in the second half of the 20th c., of traditional genre theory, for example, made exact classification of forms seem more and more of a chimera.

Insofar as the best poetic minds of every age will attempt to articulate and codify praxis, statements both descriptive and exhortatory will continue to be made. But in the modern view these no longer have the status of specifiable r. in the strict sense envisaged in linguistics and science. The difficulty with the very idea of literary "r." is made manifest in the corollary notion of poetic "license" (q.v.)—i.e. permission for poets to violate the r. at will—which is there from the very beginning (Aristotle). All this will suggest that the notion of "r." is simply not a useful conceptual strategy, in comparison with others like "convention," for discussion of the nature and functions of poetic forms.

See also CONVENTION; GENRE; METER; NATURE; POETIC LICENSE; PROSODY.

J. E. Gillet, "The Vogue of Literary Theories in Germany from 1500 to 1730," *MP* 14 (1916); Thieme, 364, 378—lists Fr. works, 17th to 20th c.; R. Bray, *La Formation de la doctrine classique en France* (1931); E. Pound, "Treatise on Metre" (1934); H. T. Swedenberg, "R. and Eng. Critics of the Epic, 1650–1800," *SP* 35 (1938); F. R. Gallaway, *Reason, R., and Revolt in Eng. Classicism* (1940); H. Trowbridge, "The Place of the R. in Dryden's Crit.," *MP* 44 (1946); J. C. Sherwood, "Dryden and the R.," *CL* 2 (1950), *JEGP* 52 (1953), 68 (1969); Abrams; Wellek; N. Chomsky, *Syntactic Structures* (1957); *The Continental Model,* ed. S. Elledge and D. Schier (1960); Weinberg; J. Searle, *Speech Acts* (1969); Saisselin; R. Drux, *Martin Opitz und sein poetisches Regelsystem* (1976); J. Jensen, *The Muses' Concord* (1976), ch. 6; D. Attridge, *The Rhythms of Eng. Poetry* (1982), ch. 6.   T.V.F.B.

RUSSIAN FORMALISM

RUMANIAN POETRY. See ROMANIAN POETRY.

RUNE (or *futhark*, as it is named from the first letters of its series). A character of the Old Germanic alphabet, probably derived partly from Gr. and partly from Lat. characters. From about the 4th c. A.D., rs. were widely used for inscriptions on such objects as weapons, coins, and memorial stones; they also occur in Anglo-Saxon, Icelandic, and Norwegian poems, where the individual letters are to be translated into the body of the verse as common nouns. Certain rs. (e.g. in Eng. the r.-words *wyn, thorn, ethel, dæg*, and *man*) were introduced into native scripts with the advent of Christianity, and served thereafter as regular characters or, more occasionally, as a kind of shorthand. From early times rs. were associated with incantation and magical practices (the word itself meant "whisper, mystery, secret counsel"). The surviving Old Germanic poems which use them as special letters are either gnomic-didactic in character (e.g. the OE *R. Poem*) or else recall more superstitious uses, as when the OE poet Cynewulf signs his works with the rs. for his name woven into the verses so that his readers may pray for him.—H. Arntz, *Bibliographie der Runenkunde* (1937), *Handbuch der Runenkunde*, 2d ed. (1944), "Runenkunde," *Deutsche Philologie im Aufriss*, ed. W. Stammler, v. 3 (1957); R. Dérolez, *Runica Manuscripta* (1954); R. I. Page, *Rs.* (1987); R. W. V. Elliott, *Rs.: An Intro.*, 2d ed. (1989).

J.B.B.; T.V.F.B.

RUNNING RHYTHM (common rhythm). Term coined by Gerard Manley Hopkins to denote the standard rhythm of Eng. accentual-syllabic verse measured, in traditional prosody, by feet of two or three syllables. The rhythm is said to be rising if the stress occurs at the end of the foot (iamb, anapaest), falling if the stress occurs at the beginning of the foot (trochee, dactyl) (see RISING AND FALLING RHYTHM). If the stress occurs between two unstressed or "slack" syllables (amphibrach), however, Hopkins calls it "rocking rhythm." Even though Hopkins describes these distinctions as "real and true to nature," his own rhythmic alternative, sprung rhythm (q.v.), whose feet, for scansional convenience, always take the stress on their first syllable (falling), is equally "the most natural of things," despite appearances.—"Author's Preface," *The Poems of Gerard Manley Hopkins*, ed. W. H. Gardner and N. H. MacKenzie, 4th ed. (1967).

P.F.; C.S.

RUN-ON LINE. See ENJAMBMENT.

RUSSIAN FORMALISM. A school in Rus. literary scholarship which originated in the second decade of the 20th c. and was championed by unorthodox philologists and students of lit. such as Boris Eichenbaum, Roman Jakobson, Viktor Šklovskij, Boris Tomaševskij, and Jurij Tynjanov.

The main strongholds of the Rus. Formalist movement were the Moscow Linguistic Circle, founded in 1915, and the Petrograd "Society for the Study of Poetic Lang." (*Opojaz*), formed in 1916. The initial statement of the Formalist position is found in the symposium *Poetics: Studies in the Theory of Poetic Lang.* (1919) and in *Modern Rus. Poetry* by Jakobson.

The Formalists viewed lit. as a distinct field of human endeavor, as a verbal *art* rather than a reflection of society or a battleground of ideas. They were more interested in the poetry than in the poet, in the actual works than in their alleged roots or effects. Intent upon delimiting literary scholarship from contiguous disciplines such as psychology, sociology, and intellectual history, the Formalist theoreticians focused on the "distinguishing features" of lit., on the artistic devices peculiar to imaginative writing. In Jakobson's words, "the subject of literary scholarship is not lit. in its totality, but *literariness*, i.e. that which makes of a given work a work of lit."

According to the Formalists, imaginative lit. is a unique mode of discourse characterized by an "emphasis on the medium" (Jakobson) or "perceptibility of the mode of expression." In literary art, esp. in poetry, it was argued, lang. is not simply a vehicle of communication. From a mere proxy for an object, the Word becomes here an object in its own right, an autonomous source of pleasure as the multiple devices at the poet's disposal—rhythm, meter, euphony, imagery—converge on the verbal sign in order to dramatize its complex texture.

In defining the locus of "literariness," the Formalists, most notably Šklovskij, took issue with a time-honored theory which proclaimed the use of images as the outstanding characteristic of imaginative lit. It is not in the presence of imagery, urged the *Opoyaz* spokesmen, but in the *use to which it is put* that this differentia should be sought. If in informative or didactic prose a metaphor aims to bring the subject close to the audience, to drive home a point, in literary art it serves the opposite function. Rather than translating the unfamiliar into the terms of the familiar, the poetic image defamiliarizes or "makes strange" the habitual by presenting it in a novel light, by placing it in an unexpected context.

These methodological assumptions were tested in acute studies of rhythm, style, and narrative structure. Probably the most fruitful field of Formalist endeavor was the theory of versification. To the Formalists, verse is not merely a matter of a set of mechanical rules or even of external embellishments, such as meter, rhyme, or alliteration, superimposed upon ordinary speech. It is an integrated type of discourse, qualitatively different from prose, with a hierarchy of elements and internal laws of its own—"a speech organized throughout in its phonic texture." The notion of rhythm as a *Gestaltqualität,* a structural property

- [1101] -

operative at all levels of poetic lang., helped elucidate a crucial problem of poetics—that of the relationship between sound and meaning in verse.

The Formalist approach to lit. was a far cry from that single-minded concern with "social significance" and "message" which dominated so much 19th-c. Rus. lit. crit. Consequently, the Formalist research in the masters of Rus. lit. resulted in dramatic re-examinations. Gogol's famous story "The Overcoat," hailed by its contemporaries as a moving plea for the "little man," became under the pen of Boris Eichenbaum primarily a piece of grotesque stylization. Puškin, viewed this time at the level of style and genre rather than of *Weltanschauung*, appeared as a magnificent culmination of 18th-c. Rus. poetry rather than as the father of Rus. romanticism. And the moral crisis of the young Tolstoy was reinterpreted in largely aesthetic terms as a struggle for a new style, as a challenge to romantic clichés grown stale. In dealing with current literary productions, the Formalist critics favored inventiveness, aesthetic sophistication, a search for new modes of expression. In visual arts they encouraged such trends as constructivism and cubism (qq.v.).

At first the Formalist spokesmen extravagantly overstated their case. In their early studies Jakobson and Šklovskij played down the links between lit. and society and denied the relevance of any "extra-aesthetic" considerations. Eventually, in the face of a concerted attack on the part of Soviet Marxists, they made an effort to combine aesthetic analysis with a sociological approach to lit. But this attempt at synthesis came too late. In 1929–30 the methodological debate in the Soviet Union was rudely discontinued by Stalin. With Soviet crit. being whipped into orthodoxy, Formalism was suppressed as a heresy. Consequently, since 1930 "Formalism" has been in Soviet parlance a term of censure, connoting undue preoccupation with "mere" form, bourgeois "escapism," and like offenses.

If in Russia the Formalist movement was stopped in its tracks, however, during the Thirties its influence was felt in other Slavic countries, esp. Czechoslovakia and Poland. The theorists of so-called Czech structuralism grouped around the Prague Linguistic Circle (see STRUCTURALISM, *Prague School*), Dimitry Cizevsky, Jan J. Mukařovský, René Wellek, and, last but not least, Roman Jakobson, who had lived in Prague since 1920, restated the basic tenets of Rus. F. in more judicious and rigorous terms.

Viewed in a broader perspective, Rus. F. appears as one of the most vigorous manifestations of the modern trend toward structural analysis of lit. and art which made substantial inroads into Eng. and Am. literary study through the 1960s. Formalist doctrine has many points of contact with Am. New Criticism (q.v.), esp. its "organicist" variant, as represented by Cleanth Brooks and Robert Penn Warren. Brooks' emphasis on the organic unity of a poem (see ORGANICISM), with the con-

comitant warning against the "heresy of paraphrase," his keen awareness of the "ambiguity" (q.v.) of poetic idiom and "the conflict-structures" resulting from this ambiguity, such as irony and paradox (qq.v.)—all this is closely akin to the later phase of Formalist theorizing. Perhaps one should add that the affinity between these two schools of thought rests on analytical procedures rather than on criteria of evaluation. While the majority of Anglo-Am. New Critics have worked toward some flexible yet absolute standards applicable to lit. of various ages, the Rus. Formalists frankly espoused critical relativism.

In the last three decades, the influence of Rus. F., esp. in its mature structuralist version, has made itself felt on both sides of the Atlantic. If Prague structuralism was afforded little scope in the postwar period for testing of its hypotheses, one of its chief architects, Roman Jakobson, having settled in the U.S., elaborated a new dimension of structural poetics by exploring the ways in which poetry makes use of grammatical oppositions. In post-Stalinist Russia, a group of scholars based respectively in Moscow and Tartu (Estonia), notably Vsevolod Ivanov, Jurij Lotman, Vladimir Toporov, and B. Uspenskij, have been engaged in a concerted effort to tackle problems of lang., lit., and culture along structuralist-semiotic lines (see STRUCTURALISM, *Moscow-Tartu School*). A somewhat different brand of structuralism came in the 1960s to dominate much of the critical discourse in France (Roland Barthes, Gérard Genette, J. A. Greimas, Tzvetan Todorov), owing in no small measure to the increasing awareness of the Rus. Formalist legacy, an awareness furthered by the anthologizing and interpretive activities of Todorov (see STRUCTURALISM, *French and American Schools*). See also CRITICISM; INTERPRETATION; POETICS; THEORY.

Poetika. Sborniki po teorii poeticheskogo jazyka (1919); V. Šklovskij , *O teorii prozy* (1925); B. Tomaševskij, *O stixe* (1929); R. Jakobson, *Selected Writings*, 7 v. (1962–85), esp. "Linguistics and Poetics" and "Poetry of Grammar and Grammar of Poetry" in v. 3, "Slavic Epic Studies" in v. 4, and "O česškom stixe" in v. 5; K. Pomorska, *Rus. Formalist Theory and Its Poetic Ambiance* (1968); J. Striedter, *Texte der Russischen Formalisten*, 2 v. (1969–72), *Literary Structure, Evolution, and Value* (1989); E. M. Thompson, *Rus. F. and Anglo-Am. New Crit.: A Comparative Study* (1971), "F." in Terras; *Readings in Rus. Poetics: Formalist and Structuralist Views*, ed. L. Matejka and K. Pomorska (1971); F. Jameson, *The Prison-House of Lang.* (1972); *Formalist Theory*, ed. A. Shukman and L. M. O'Toole (1977); R. H. Stacy, *Defamiliarization in Lang. and Lit.* (1977); A. Hansen-Löve, *Der Russische Formalismus* (1978); *F.: History, Comparison, Genre*, ed. A. Shukman (1978); V. Erlich, *Rus. F.: History–Doctrine*, 3d ed. (1981); P. Steiner, *Rus. F.: A Metapoetics* (1984); *Rus. F.: A Retrospective Glance*, ed. R. L. Jackson and S. Rudy (1985).   V.E.

RUSSIAN POETICS. See ROMANTIC AND POSTRO-
MANTIC POETICS; TWENTIETH-CENTURY POETICS.

RUSSIAN POETRY. The birth of Rus. lit. may be
traced to the 11th c., but written texts in verse (i.e.
characterized by rhyme and rhythm) first made
their appearance relatively late, in the 17th c. By
contrast, Rus. folklore, which obviously predated
recorded literary texts, in certain genres had al-
ways been framed in verse. Although relying on
diverse rhythms, Rus. folklore is by and large
tonic, i.e. it has approximately the same number
of stresses in each poetic line (see SLAVIC PROS-
ODY). As a rule, Rus. folklore lacks rhyme, and like
other national folklores was performed to musical
accompaniment, its vocal nature largely determin-
ing its rhythmic structure. Such are the numerous
ceremonial songs (chanted for harvests, weddings,
and divination) which comprise the most poetic
part of Rus. folklore. Historical songs, rooted in
concrete historical events, are a comparatively late
phenomenon. The best-known folklore genre is
the folk epic (bylina, q.v.), which recounts the
exploits of famous warriors (bogatyri) who gath-
ered around the Kievan Prince Vladimir much as
the Knights of the Round Table did around King
Arthur. These heroes regularly sallied forth to
battle enemy invaders and fight dragons, and for
other exploits of quest and adventure.

Elements of rhythmic organization and poetic
lyricism surface in lit. written long before the 17th
c., most notably in one of the earliest works, Slovo
o polku Igoreve (The Lay of Igor's Campaign,
1185). This masterpiece tells of the unsuccessful
campaign of a northern prince, Igor of Novgorod-
Severskij, against nomad tribes, of his captivity,
and his return to his beloved wife. The text consists
of separate, lyrically embellished episodes, e.g. a
description of the battle, the lament of Igor's wife
Jaroslavna, and Igor's flight. A wealth of poetic
devices—epithets, metaphors, similes, repeti-
tion—as well as the rhythmic nature of the prose
in which it is written allies this medieval Rus. text
with poetic rather than prosaic forms. Slovo ex-
erted a broad influence on Rus. art in the 19th and
20th cs., particularly poetry, music, and painting.

From the 13th to the 16th cs., Rus. lit. over-
whelmingly favored prose, with occasional forays
into poetry. To this category belong mainly liturgi-
cal songs as well as folk verse, usually satiric and
farcical (so-called skoromošiny), which also pene-
trated written lit. Epistolary prose of the 16th and
17th cs., which played on readers' emotional re-
sponses, is constructed on the principle of syntac-
tic parallelism, whereby the subject (or the most
significant word) is consistently placed at the be-
ginning or end of every sentence. Such a structure
leads to the creation of a kind of case rhyme based
on inflectional suffixes, a system that generates
root rhymes and approximate rhymes.

These developments prepared the reader for
formal written verse, which emerged in the mid-
dle of the 17th c., transplanted into Russia from
Poland via the Ukraine. This imported system of
versification was called syllabic verse (virši), the
basic features of which are three: (1) isosyllabism
(11- and 13-syllable lines being most widespread);
(2) double (parnaja) rhyme, as a rule feminine,
that resulted from the Polish influence, for in
Polish the stress of each word invariably falls on
the penultimate syllable; and (3) caesura, nor-
mally after the 5th or 6th syllable. The undisputed
master of Rus. syllabic verse was Simeon Polockij
(1629–80), a monk from Byelorussia who sub-
sequently became Tsar Alexis Mikhailovich's clos-
est associate. Paronomasia and unexpected
rhymes mark Polockij's refined and luxuriously
ornate verses. His noteworthy successors in syl-
labic poetry incl. Sylvester Medvedev (1641–91)
and Karion Istomin (mid 17th c. to 1717 or 1722).
A memorable 17th-c. work in syllabic verse is Petr
Buslaev's poema (verse epic) entitled "Umozritel'-
stvo duševnoe . . . o pereselenii v večnuju žizn' . .
. baronessy Stroganovoj" (Spiritual Speculations .
. . About Baroness Stroganova's . . . Removal to
Eternal Life, 1734). Couched in beautiful Rus., it
emanates a palpable sense of sorrow and an in-
spired exaltation in its depiction of Christ. The
syllabic trad. in the 18th c. ends with the works of
Antiox Kantemir (1708–44), who systematized syl-
labic verse and introduced an obligatory caesura;
more important still are his innovations in poetic
lang. and thematics. A proponent of Petrine re-
forms, Kantemir produced satires against such
subjects as ignorance, drunkenness, and court in-
trigue, taking Cl. and contemp. Fr. authors, esp.
Boileau, as models.

The Petrine reforms gave rise to new forms of
cultural life and a rapid if turbulent rapproche-
ment with the West. This process resulted in the
growth of a new, Europeanized lit. that introduced
genres and styles of poetry previously unknown in
Russia. In this area Vasilij Trediakovskij (1703–69)
played a crucial role. His treatise "Novyj i kratkij
sposob k složeniju Rossijskix stixov" (A New and
Short Method of Rus. Versification, 1735) rejected
the syllabic system, replacing it with the principles
of syllabotonic verse, which serve as the founda-
tion of modern Rus. versification (see SLAVIC
PROSODY). Based on the regular alternation of
accented and unaccented syllables, the revised
system clearly took account of and built on the
quintessential nature of the Rus. lang. Trediak-
ovskij, however, did not pursue his notions to their
logical conclusion, confining his reforms to the
trochee and to poems in short lines. Nevertheless,
he created the Rus. hexameter, into which he
translated Fénelon's prose novel, Les Aventures de
Télémaque. The hexameter is used even today for
anthological verse and Cl. trs. In spite of success
in individual enterprises, however, Trediakovskij
lacked the poetic skill to embody his theories in
practice. Neither his contemporaries nor his im-
mediate successors appreciated his brilliant, inno-

RUSSIAN POETRY

vative ideas, and they ridiculed his verses.

It took the great scientist, scholar, and poet Mixail Lomonosov (1711–65) to complete Trediakovskij's reforms, a task he was splendidly equipped to execute. With Trediakovskij's ideas as a point of departure, and adapting the model of Ger. prosody (q.v.), Lomonosov codified an elaborate system of syllabotonic versification (q.v. in Terras). His system provided a theoretical foundation for the inclusion in Rus. prosody of all the meters found to this day: the iamb, the trochee, the dactyl, the amphibrach, and the anapest. Lomonosov also developed the "three styles" system, establishing a generic hierarchy of styles. The degree to which a style was "elevated" depended on the presence in it of archaic, solemn, Church Slavic diction. Such a lexicon became the basic component of the "high style," which was mandatory for odes and heroic epics (*geroičeskie poemy*); in the "middle style," reserved for tragedies, satires, and lyrics, only the Slavonicisms shared by Church Slavic and Rus. and accepted in general use were admissible; the "low style," suitable for comedies and songs, had to limit itself to purely Rus. vocabulary. Although rarely observed *in toto*, this system nonetheless served as the foundation for Rus. classicism. Lomonosov's favorite genre was the ceremonial ode, where he preached enlightened absolutism and in striking, vivid imagery glorified the Rus. Tsars, esp. Peter I, and the greatness of Russia. Probably his highest poetic achievement remain the two "Razmyšlenija o Bož'em Veličestve" (Meditations on the Greatness of God), where the poet and scholar merge to offer a grandiose vision of the universe, the beauty of the northern lights, and the magnificence of the sun. His poetic legacy also includes verse tragedies, an unfinished epic about Peter the Great, and spiritual odes (his versions of the Psalms), the last representing a peak in his creative output.

Lomonosov's literary foe, Aleksandr Sumarokov (1717–69), is the most thoroughgoing classicist in the history of Rus. p. In his bitter polemics against Lomonosov, he accused the latter of excessive grandiosity, over-reliance on metaphor, and the interpolation of improbable imagery in his odes. He himself wrote in a lang. that was clear and simple for the time. Sumarokov created the Rus. verse tragedy, and with justifiable pride called himself the Rus. Racine. His tragedies (*Xorev*, 1747; *Dmitrij Samozvanec* [Dmitry the Pretender], 1771) usually appropriated subjects and plots from Russia's national history, a practice which violated classicist norms. In all other respects, however, Sumarokov strictly observed cl. rules: he abided by the unities, pitted love against duty as the central conflict, had his heroes deliver speeches advocating Enlightenment philosophy, and maintained a purity of style and genre. Unlike Boileau, Sumarokov in his treatise *Epistola o stixotvorstve* (Epistle on Writing Poetry, 1747) stressed the significance of the song in the system

of cl. genres. In transforming the song into a lyric poem that most often described tragic love, Sumarokov became the creator of the Rus. love lyric.

Classicism became firmly established in the works of Sumarokov's successors. In 1779, Mixail Xeraskov published the first complete Rus. epic poem, *Rossiada*, about Ivan the Terrible's conquest of Kazan. The genre of burlesque, which enjoyed special popularity in Russia, is best represented by V. Majkov's epic *Elisej, ili razdražennyj Vax* (Elisei, or Bacchus Enraged, 1771), which parodies the *Aeneid* while depicting the life of Moscow's drunkards. I. Bogdanovič's elegant epic *Dušen'ka* (1783) recounts with sly irony the amorous adventures of Eros and Psyche, who on Rus. soil become Dušen'ka ("soul" in Rus. is *duša*). The fable, a genre demanding the "low style," also thrived during this period, reaching its apogee with Sumarokov, whose fables admittedly sometimes abused colloquial or vulgar lang. Another popular fabulist, Ivan Xemnicer (1745–84), likewise possessed considerable skill, but the fable truly found its master at the beginning of the 19th c., when all the other cl. genres had virtually disappeared, in Ivan Krylov (1768/9–1844). For the first time in Rus. lit., the narrators of his fables spoke a lively colloquial Rus. while embodying typical traits of the Rus. national character.

Soon after consolidating itself in the school of Sumarokov and his followers, Rus. classicism rapidly eroded, losing the clarity and precision characteristic of the movement. This process was accelerated by Gavrila Deržavin (1743–1816), considered by many the supreme poetic genius of the 18th c., whose work already contains elements of preromanticism (q.v.). Although Deržavin called all his poems odes, they altogether lack the majestic grandeur of the genre, its "high" style, and its special lexicon. Boldly mixing lexical levels, Deržavin placed the high and the low side by side. Thus in the famous ode "Felica" (1783), Deržavin describes Catherine II engaged in her official state activities, contrasting her with the nobles engrossed in the most commonplace occupations: drinking coffee, trying on new clothes, searching for fleas in their hair. In his philosophical poems Deržavin meditates on the ineluctability of death and the chilling horror of its approach, as for instance in "Na smert' knjazja Meščerskogo" (On the Death of Prince Meshchersky, 1779), which shows the influence of Edward Young's *Night Thoughts*. The apogee of Deržavin's philosophical verse is the ode "Bog" (God, 1784). Translated into numerous European langs., it envisions man as the center of the universe, the link connecting heaven and earth whose being synthesizes both the spiritual principle and brute matter: "I am a tsar—I am a slave, I am a worm—I am God."

The transition from the 18th c. to the 19th and to new literary tendencies is best represented by Nikolaj Karamzin (1766–1826), the founder of Rus. Sentimentalism and its most ardent spokesman. Although more a prosaist than a poet, Karamzin nonetheless composed verses that played a significant role in the devel. of Rus. lyric. In a lang. free of archaisms, Karamzin's poems sketch the complexity of man's inner world, which his successors and imitators in the early part of the 19th c. explored more thoroughly and with greater intensity.

The first decades of the 19th c., deservedly called "the Golden Age of Rus. lit.," issue in part from the work of Vasilij Žukovskij (1783–1852), one of the best Rus. lyric poets and Karamzin's most inspired successor. Žukovskij's autobiographical, elegiac poetry treats unhappy love, the death of one's beloved, and the hope for a meeting beyond the grave, all in a tone of wistful melancholy. Nature appears in a similarly despondent light in Žukovskij's poems, which repeatedly emphasize evenings, sunsets, mists, and the moon, for Žukovskij strives less to capture surroundings than to share with the reader a mood of doleful, pensive gloom. With Žukovskij, for the first time in Rus. p., the word acquires multiple meanings and shades that are more essential than its basic denotation. In his search for the suggestive, polysemous word, Žukovskij foreshadows the symbolists. The most popular part of his legacy consists of his ballads, the most famous of which is *Svetlana*, a Russified version of Bürger's ballad *Lenore*. Žukovskij's most enduring contribution to Rus. letters remains his innumerable trs. of European and Eastern poets, e.g. Goethe, Schiller, Scott, Byron, Homer's *Odyssey*, *The Mahabharata*, *The Shahname*, and many others.

The other major poet of the Golden Age, Žukovskij's contemporary, Konstantin Batjuškov (1787–1855), lapsed into insanity in 1822 and remained so for the rest of his life. He left behind a small collection of poetry and several prose experiments. Unlike Žukovskij's verse, Batjuškov's is vivid, buoyant, permeated with light, and rather erotic, traits esp. evident in his anthology verse, where Batjuškov strives to depict the color, physicality, and object-studded concreteness of the ancient world he reconstructs. In his efforts to find the precise, expressive poetic word, Batjuškov clearly anticipates the acmeists (see ACMEISM). The fragile hedonism of a fictitious antiquity, however, does not save Batjuškov from a profound pessimism: in his world, fleeting passion, pleasure, and beauty yield to tragedy, evil, and death. Marked by a mellifluous euphony unique in Rus. p., Batjuškov's poems suggest the influence of It. verse, which he knew intimately.

Opposition to the Karamzinian school came from the Archaists, among whom numbered the later Deržavin; Nikolaj Gnedič, the translator of the *Iliad*; and Sergij Širinskij-Šixmatov, the author of two epic poems. They formed a group called The Society of Lovers of the Rus. Word (Beseda liubitelej russkogo slova; 1811–16), at meetings of which they made speeches and read from their works. The Society published a journal containing its members' creative efforts. Karamzin's followers, who included Batjuškov and Žukovskij, founded, in opposition to the Society, a humorous counterpart called Arzamas (q.v.), which disbanded once the Society ceased to exist. The Archaists did not consider smoothness and melodiousness poetic virtues; in their view, the expressiveness of poetic lang. required heavy, awkward rhythms, archaic polysyllables, and complex syntax. These notions were articulated and put into practice in the interesting though ponderous verses of Aleksandr Radiščev (1742–1802), whose predecessors were Trediakovskij and Semën Bobrov (1762–1810), author of philosophical odes and darkly romantic descriptions of nature. Other opposition to and polemics with Žukovskij came from P. Katenin (1792–1853), author of folkloric ballads (*Ol'ga*, *Ubijca* [The Murderer], *Lešij* [The Forest Spirit]), and Wilhelm Kjuxelbeker (1797–1846), a poet, dramatist, and literary critic.

The Golden Age and Rus. p. as a whole reached their apogee in the work of Aleksandr Puškin (1799–1837), who not only deserves the title of genius but belongs in the select company of the four or five geniuses (along with Dante, Shakespeare, and Goethe) who herald the efflorescence of a new European lit. Puškin's oeuvre assimilated the poetic achievements of the 18th and early 19th cs. and set the course for Rus. lit. thereafter. It is not surprising that a bona fide cult of Puškin remains active even in contemp. Rus. cultural life, a cult that surpasses the veneration for Tolstoj and Dostoyevsky. If in his early works Puškin proved to be the heir and pupil of Žukovskij, Batjuškov, and Deržavin, his verses nevertheless showed such mastery and finish that they instantly proclaimed him the foremost poet of his era. His period of apprenticeship culminated in 1820 with the mock heroic poem *Ruslan i Ljudmila* (Ruslan and Liudmila).

Puškin's Southern exile (1820–24), when he was banished from Petersburg for his political verses, coincided with the romantic period of his creativity. His so-called "Southern" or "Byronic" *poemy* portray the romantic hero fleeing civilization for such exotic climes as the Caucasus and a gypsy camp. The structure of these narratives indeed recalls Byron's Oriental tales, but Puškin's romantic hero proves spiritually and morally bankrupt when confronted with the sincere, passionate emotions of representatives of the primitive world (*Kavkazskij plennik* [The Prisoner of the Caucasus], *Cygany* [The Gypsies]). In the later *Poltava* (1828), Puškin synthesized the historical *poema* with a romantic love narrative, while glorifying the achievements of Peter I. The theme of Peter becomes central in Puškin's masterpiece, the epic *Mednyj vsadnik* (The Bronze Horseman, 1833), which dramatizes the Petersburg flood of 1824. Puškin depicts the conflict between the state, symbolized by the statue of Peter I, and the individual—the simple, modest man whose happiness is destroyed at the ruler's command. While acknowledging the claims of the individual and his right to happiness, Puškin's *poema* shows the inevitable conflict between that right and the demands of the state.

During his Southern exile Puškin also embarked on his most ambitious work, which he completed only seven years later (1823–30): his verse-novel *Evgenij Onegin* (Eugene Onegin). At the center of the novel, which charts the tragic fate of the Rus. intelligentsia, stands the disillusioned, skeptical, Byronic hero Onegin, incapable of finding either occupation or happiness. After killing his friend, the young romantic poet Lenskij, in a duel, Onegin travels and finally discovers love, only to have his impassioned declaration spurned, at which juncture the novel breaks off. With the luckless heroine of the novel, Tat'jana, originates the series of pure, strong, young Rus. women whom Turgenev later immortalized. The extremely simple plot of *Eugene Onegin* is amplified by numerous "lyric digressions" which enable the author to participate in the novel both as one of its personae and as commentator. For this work Puškin created the special "Onegin stanza" (q.v.), a quatorzain with a complex rhyme scheme reminiscent of the Eng. sonnet.

As part of his increasing absorption with history, Puškin in 1825 wrote *Boris Godunov*, a tragedy in blank verse assessing the role of the populace in historical cataclysms. A particularly productive period of Puškin's creativity was the autumn of 1830. Forced by cholera quarantine to remain at his estate in Boldino, Puškin completed in an amazingly short span a series of superb works, incl. his "little tragedies": "Mozart and Salieri" ("Mocart i Salieri"), "The Stone Guest" ("Kamennyi gost'"), "The Covetous Knight" ("Skupoj ryear'"), and "The Feast during the Plague" ("Pir vo vremja čumy"). These highly condensed scenes investigate fatal passions such as love, greed, and envy, exploring the tragic, irreconcilable contradictions and polarities of human existence: love and death, inspiration and toil, age and youth. Finally, Puškin bequeathed to Rus. lit. a fund of lyric poetry on a broad range of themes, among them love, nature, and philosophical issues. Each of these masterpieces, which he wrote throughout his life, represents a different psychological situation for the articulation of which Puškin unfailingly finds the single word that perfectly meets the requirements of the moment or scene. That word may belong to any lexical or cultural level, be it colloquial, bookish, archaic, or vulgar. As an entity Puškin's poetry cannot be identified with any poetic system or movement such as romanticism or realism. Always comprehensible to any educated native speaker (hence their ostensible simplicity and accessibility), his poems at the same time defy translation into a foreign lang. precisely on account of the impossibility of locating the perfectly equivalent word, the *only* suitable word, within another linguistic system.

Puškin died prematurely in a duel without having realized many of his plans and, really, his seemingly limitless potential. Around him had clustered a group of gifted poets usually called the Puškin Pleiad, comprising primarily his friends Evgenij Baratynskij, Anton Del'vig, Petr Vjazemskij, Nikolaj Jazykov, and several others. Of these, the most formidable poet was indisputably Baratynskij (1800–44), whose epic *Eda* (1824) implicitly criticized Puškin's brand of romanticism: it replaced exotic gypsies and Circassian damsels with a Finnish peasant girl, and the enigmatic romantic hero with a commonplace officer-seducer. His other well-known *poema, Bal* (The Ball, 1828) has as its heroine a society beauty who poisons herself because of an unfortunate romance. Puškin himself thought highly of Baratynskij's *poemy*, which contrasted dramatically with his own. As a lyric poet, Baratynskij began with meditative elegies that usually mourned irretrievable happiness and juxtaposed the lyric protagonist's past with his melancholy present. Pessimism becomes the dominant note in Baratynskij's mature lyrics, so much so that in "Poslednij poet" (The Last Poet, 1835) he perceives civilization as inimical to beauty; contemp. society leaves the poet no option but to die in disillusioned isolation. Particularly imposing is Baratynskij's tragic masterpiece "Osen'" (Autumn, 1837), which juxtaposes the death of nature in autumn to the autumn of human life. Baratynskij reinforces the dark, morose ponderousness of his reflections with complex syntactic constructions and an intentionally archaic lexicon which contrast sharply with the unusual lightness of Puškin's verse.

Mixail Lermontov (1814–41) essentially also belongs to the Puškin Pleiad, though critical opinion has traditionally assigned Lermontov the role of Puškin's successor and placed him on a par with Puškin in the history of Rus. lit. Lermontov's short and luckless life (military service, Caucasian exile, death by duel at age 26) allowed him little opportunity to realize fully his poetic talent. Although he attained instant fame in 1837 with his poem on Puškin's death, his active literary career lasted only four years, during which he produced the most memorable instances of the quintessential Rus. romantic *poema: Pesnja pro kupca Kalašnikova* (Song of the Merchant Kalashnikov, 1838), which borrows from folklore for its dramatic story of love and death in the time of Ivan the Terrible; *Mcyri* (The Novice, 1840), the final confession of a fugitive novice that in structure and rhythm recalls Byron's *Giaour*; and *Demon* (1829–41), an operatic account of the fatal love of the spirit of evil for the beautiful Tamara. A profound and sweeping disillusionment imbues Lermontov's lyrics—disillusionment with his generation, himself, and life at large (e.g. "Duma" [Ballad], "Poet" [The Poet]). In a world that is "dreary and dismal," bereft of love, populated by a cruel and vicious humanity intent on brutalizing the poet-prophet, death offers the only deliverance. Lermontov's verse is energetic and abrupt, "an iron verse, steeped in bitterness and malice." This energy gains additional force in several poems from the masculine rhymes of Lermontov's iambic tetrameter. Ternary meters, however, occur much more often in his poetry than in Puškin's.

The next important stage in the history of Rus. p. finds its most gifted representative in Fedor Tjutčev (1803–73). A lyric poet of genius as well as a government official and diplomat, a salon wit, and one of the most educated men of his time, Tjutčev wrote very little and published even less: his collected poems, which embody his soul's innermost secrets, his *sancta sanctorum*, fill only a single slender volume. Tjutčev's philosophical poems reveal a Schellingian pantheism which conceives of nature as an organism animated by a spirit incomprehensible and inaccessible to humankind:

> Nature is not what it seems to you,
> It is no blind nor soulless image—
> It has a soul, and freedom too,
> It has love, it has a language.

The boldness of Tjutčev's metaphors stems from his metaphorical perception of the universe. Thus in his "documentary description" of his vision, summer lightning is God's stern pupils shining through his heavy lashes, the Earth's head is crowned with the sun, and its feet are washed by spring waters; the poet sees the gentle smile of fading autumn. Love lyrics which are decidedly tragic in concept and mood occupy a special place in Tjutčev's oeuvre, doubtless owing to the poet's protracted liaison with a much younger mistress who died of consumption. For Tjutčev, love is the manifestation of elemental forces; it dooms human life, unavoidably leading to death—a tragic conception of passion that has affinities with Turgenev's in his fiction. Tjutčev infuses his descriptions of his beloved's last moments and her departure from life with searing, inexpressible pain, and locates that heart-wrenching loss within a general landscape of human suffering. Technically, Tjutčev expanded the traditional rhythmic system of Rus. p., partly through an increased use of the trochee (as opposed to the iambic meters favored by Puškin's school), and esp. through his conscious violation of the rhythmic structure of syllabotonic versification. His unorthodox shifts in rhythm as an artistic device prepared the ground for the *dol'nik* (q.v.), a tonic meter widely used at the beginning of the 20th c.

Although chronologically Tjutčev's poetic output spills over into the 1860s, it nevertheless brings the Golden Age to a close. Interest in verse diminished perceptibly in the 1850s as it was ousted by prose, which rapidly gained dominance as a genre. Both literary theory and crit. of this period enthusiastically embraced the principle of utilitarianism, viewing lit. as a useful means of enlightening the common people and liberating them from social repression. Such a pragmatic approach to lit. esp. characterized the crit. of Nikolaj Černyševskij and Nikolaj Dobroljubov, who derived their ideas from Comte and Feuerbach. Predictably, "ideological" prose fiction could fulfill the utilitarian task better than poetry, which at best was regarded as second-rate material for propaganda. Nikolaj Nekrasov's (1821–78) phrase, "You may not be a poet, / But a citizen you must," became the slogan of this influential literary camp with its leftist political values.

Nekrasov, by birth a member of the landowning class, a brilliant publisher and editor, a successful gambler, and a wealthy snob late in life, was the sole authentically talented poet in this group. At the same time, Nekrasov was a man with a tragic and morbid attitude to life, which found expression in his portrayal of peasant and urban poverty and condignly earned him fame as a popular poet of the people. Given to calling his muse bloody and "horsewhipped," Nekrasov chronicled the sufferings of Rus. peasant women, crushed by hard physical labor in addition to their husbands' drunkenness and beatings ("V doroge" [En Route], 1845; "Trojka," 1846). He immortalized the denizens of city slums exhausted by hunger and cold ("Edu li noč'ju" [Whenever I drive at night], 1847; "Vor" [The Thief], 1850), the forced laborers at their harrowing toil ("Železnaja doroga" [The Railroad], 1864), the unfortunate sick peasants who lacked all rights ("Nesžataja polosa" [An Unharvested Strip], 1854; "Razmyšlenija u paradnogo pod"ezda" [Musings in the Main Driveway], 1856), and the soldier flogged to death by his superiors ("Orina, mat' soldatskaja" [Orina, A Soldier's Mother], 1863). In his huge epic poem *Komu na Rusi žit' xorošo* (Who Is Happy in Russia, 1865–77), Nekrasov attempted a comprehensive canvas of Rus. life in the post-Emancipation 1860s. Several successful sections aside, the poems as a whole failed to cohere and disintegrated into separate units. Nekrasov's poetry tends toward simple rhythms, it favors ternary meters, and it does not aim for metrical variety; consequently, his verses often lapse into a monotonous uniformity of rhythm.

Poets of the 1850s–70s who could legitimately be called members of the "Nekrasov school" include the critic Dobroljubov, who produced poor poetry; the satirist and witty parodist D. Minaev, author of feuilletons in verse; M. Mixajlov, renowned for his revolutionary activities and his civic and political verse, who was the originator of "prison" poetry and left excellent trs. of Heine; the satirical poet V. Kuročkin, who earned a reputation for his trs. of Béranger; the self-taught merchant's son I. Nikitin, who concentrated on peasant life; I. Surikov; and several other lesser figures.

The "art for art's sake" school that stood in opposition to the Utilitarians did not so much defend "pure art" as reject a pragmatic approach to lit. and argue in favor of varied thematics. The most talented and "purest" lyricist among them was Afanasij Fet (1820–92), a follower of Schopenhauer, whose *World as Will and Representation* he translated. According to Fet, the "real" world and the world of poetry and beauty are two utterly unrelated realms. An officer and highly successful landowner in everyday life, Fet, when transported into the sphere of the sublime, became an inspired poet. The poet's task, he maintained, is to perceive the beauty which lies beyond the commonplace purview of the average being and to reveal that beauty to others. Love and nature are the most frequent themes in his lyrics. Fet's nature poems celebrate the alluring, festive beauty of the natural world in its manifold aspects: velvet night, mysterious dawn, dense forest, silver snow, trilling birds, delicate butterflies. Where other poets dwell on the psychological complexity of love relationships, Fet confines himself to the selective mention of a few details from which the reader must deduce the portrait of the beloved or recreate the situation. A momentary impression captured by the poet expands in the reader's mind into a poetic scene which reminds us simultaneously that beauty is transitory and that poetry can only suggest the inaccessible, ideal beauty of a world beyond our reach. Fet's substitution of synecdochic detail for the whole and the musicality of his verse, achieved through systematic alliteration and assonance, make him the first Rus. impressionist poet, whom the symbolists revered as their most important forerunner. Boldly innovative in rhythm, Fet combined diverse meters in a single poem, alternated very long lines with extremely short ones (sometimes consisting of only one word) within a stanza, and followed a stanza in binary meter with one in ternary. All these devices paved the way for the dissolution of syllabotonic versification that took place in Rus. p. at the turn of the century.

Other talented proponents of anti-utilitarian tendencies in the mid 19th c. include Fet's friend Aleksej K. Tolstoj (1817–75), Jakov Polonskij, (1810–97), Apollon Majkov (1821–97), Lev Mej (1822–62), Karolina Pavlova (1807–93), and others. They strove to fuse musicality with reconciliation in their depiction of reality, created beautiful nature and love lyrics, and rediscovered historical and folklore themes. A decisive force in the battle against the utilitarian school was exerted by anthology verse. Characterized by vividness and visual plasticity, anthology verse flourished in the 1850s and 60s, being a genre favored by almost all the poets of the "art for art's sake" movement. It comprised the most significant part of Nikolaj Ščerbina's (1821–69) output.

Despite the decline of interest in poetry in the 1850s at the hands of the utilitarian critics, by the 1860s–70s the "art for art's sake" school had raised poetry to new heights, laying the groundwork for its luxuriant flowering at the turn of the century, when their contributions were reassessed and assimilated. The 1880s, however, witnessed once again a sharp decline in Rus. p. The civic ardor of the utilitarian school ended with the most popular poet of the 1880s, Sëmen Nadson (1862–87), who died from consumption. A sense of doom, a resentment against middle-class satiety and crass vulgarity, and a hatred for "the kingdom of Baal" dominate Nadson's verses, which show talent but suffer from uniformity of both theme and rhythm. Although the "pure art" school as a whole proved more fecund, its representatives in the 1880s paled by comparison with its pioneers. Their ranks included Aleksej Apuxtin (1840–93), with his intimate romances and lyrics in a gypsy vein, Konstantin Slučevskij (1837–1904), and Konstantin Fofanov (1862–1911). These men stood on the threshold of Rus. symbolist poetry, when the brilliant new era of Rus. culture dawned—an era that lasted to 1917 and came to be known as the "Silver Age."

Symbolism, which became the most influential poetic current of this period, found its theoretical underpinnings in the ideas of the Neoplatonic philosopher Vladimir Solov'ëv (1853–1900). At the heart of Solov'ëv's eschatological system rests the idea of the World Soul, the Eternal Feminine, the Feminine Cosmic Source, which can only be attained in the sphere of art. Through the perception of art alone, asserted Solov'ëv, can one come into contact with other worlds. Hence, in the symbolist scheme semantics become unstable and intentionally polysemous (it is no accident that the symbolists cited Žukovskij and Fet among their forerunners).

Considered the founder of symbolism, Valerij Brjusov (1873–1924) willingly fulfilled his role as the movement's theoretician, leader, and publisher. From 1893–95 he pub. three collections entitled *Russkie simvolisty* (Rus. symbolists). His own poetry, which is distinguished by picturesqueness and cold craftsmanship, has a rational, declarative cast and reveals Brjusov's technical adventurousness: he tried his hand at every known poetic genre and all the meters and stanza forms common to world poetry. Two of Brjusov's predecessors who actually realized symbolist ideas were Konstantin Bal'mont (1867–1942), a brilliant master of musical verses and superb rhythms who emigrated in 1920, and Fëdor Sologub (1862–1927), whose pessimistic poems juxtapose the doomed real world of mortality with the beautiful imaginary world of "the Star of Oilay" or "the Star of Mair."

During the second phase of Rus. symbolism, which began ca. 1900, several outstanding poets of various ages joined the by-then-dominant movement. Among the older symbolists one finds Vjačeslav Ivanov (1866–1949), who left the Soviet Union in 1924, and Innokentij Annenskij (1856–1909). The immensely erudite Ivanov became the movement's most outstanding theoretician. His skillfully archaized, allusive verses, which draw attention to their bookishness and the complexity of their rhythmic structure, make considerable demands on their reader. Like Ivanov, Annenskij came to literature relatively late; the majority of his poems were not published in his lifetime. Permeated by unrelieved pessimism, these lyrics repeatedly dwell on death, expressed in images borrowed from the finely perceived details of everyday life. Ancient Greece appears in a guise of equally inconsolable gloom in Annensky's four tragedies, based on motifs from ancient myths. Younger symbolists of the second generation incl. Andrej Belyj (1880–1934) and Aleksandr Blok (1880–1921). A splendid poet and prosodist, Belyj also shone as a prose writer and critic. His major collections of poetry, *Zoloto v lazuri* (Gold in Azure), *Pepel* (Ashes), and *Urna* (The Urn), reflect the abstruse complexity of the symbolist worldview. Both the ideal expanse of the azure and purple sky and the brutal ordinariness of the earth, with its cities and villages, are described in almost Nekrasovian tones (indeed, Belyj dedicated *Pepel* to Nekrasov). The philosophical principles of Baratynskij's and Tjutčev's lyrics find a new meaning and are assimilated into symbolism in Belyj, whose poetry brims with neologisms and shows true originality in stanza construction, whereby an individual word, emphasized through intonation, serves as the basis of a rhythmic pattern and becomes a line of the poetic text. Subsequently, these experiments by Belyj influenced the efforts of Majakovskij and Cvetaeva to break new poetic ground.

A genius whose oeuvre constitutes the summit of poetic achievement in the early 20th c., Aleksandr Blok divided his collected lyrics into three volumes. In the first, which contains the famous collection of "Stixi o Prekrasnoj Dame" (Verses about the Beautiful Lady), true to the philosophy of Solov'ev, Blok exalts the ideal world of beauty, light, and worship of the Deity wherein resides his mystic beloved, the incarnation of the World Soul, the Eternal Feminine. In the second volume, the poet "moves from the divine realm to that of the creatures," abandoning the churches and temples, the poetic *terems* (halls or towers) and azure skies, for the poeticized world of swamps and northern forests populated by evil spirits, phantasmal Petersburg, and winter blizzards. The poet's lyrical devel. culminates in the third volume with a sense of tragic, inconsolable despair that admits of no solution, even in death. Blok was the first poet of the era to write a *poema*, "Dvenadcat'" (The Twelve), about the October Revolution, which he was prepared to accept regardless of the blood, devastation, and terror, for he perceived in the cataclysm a new and purifying beginning. The twelve rebels of his narrative simultaneously appear as twelve apostles, ahead of whom walks the figure of Christ, a symbol of the blessing given to the imminent world. Blok appreciably extended the rhythmic possibilities of Rus. verse, making

extensive use of *dol'niki*. The hallmarks of Blok's poetry are polysemous diction, melodiousness, and expressiveness. One other excellent poet and critic belonging to the youngest generation of symbolists is Vladislav Xodasevič (1886–1939), a substantial part of whose creative activity took place in emigration.

The second decade of the 20th c. witnessed a reaction to the vagueness of symbolist poetry in the emergence of a counter-movement. Mixail Kuzmin (1875–1936), a poet who portrayed scenes (e.g. of the Rus. 18th c.; of Egypt during the Hellenistic era) in extremely vivid and sensual images, called for "beautiful clarity" in poetry. A literary group headed by Nikolaj Gumilëv (1886–1921), later executed for his participation in an anti-Bolshevik plot, answered that summons. Calling themselves "acmeists," the group's members decried the symbolists' neglect of the material world. To acmeism (q.v.) belong two of the greatest 20th-c. Rus poets: Anna Axmatova (1889–1966) and Osip Mandelštam (1891–1938). Both poets observed faithfully acmeism's principles of clarity and plasticity, its pictorial tendencies, and its grounding in material culture. In *Rekviem* (Requiem), pub. in the Soviet Union only in 1987, Axmatova captured in mercilessly clear and expressive verses the horrors of the Stalinist terror of 1937. In one of her last works, *Poema bez geroja* (Poem Without a Hero), she incarnated in masterly rhythms the twilight of the Silver Age on the eve of the October Revolution. Denounced by the Party's Central Committee in 1946, Axmatova became the focus of attacks by politically conservative critics. The course of her poetic devel. ran parallel to Mandelštam's, who perished in Stalin's camps. Both moved thematically from paeans to the beauty of the Ancient and European worlds (esp. the dazzlingly beautiful and cold Petersburg) to the keen-sighted and unsparing depiction of the cruelty, desolation, and vulgar mediocrity of post-Revolutionary Rus. life. One of the last poets "reared on acmeism" was Dmitrij Klenovskij (1893–1976), the majority of whose works were written in emigration. With some reservations, one could include Georgij Ivanov (1894–1958) among the younger acmeists. His fine lyrics matured from *recherché* exoticism to the tragic nostalgia of his later years in emigration.

An essential role in the poetic life of the Silver Age was played by the futurists, who gave prominence to the acoustic aspect of words (see FUTURISM). Rejecting all earlier achievements in Rus. and world poetry, they elaborated the theory of the "self-oriented" (*samovitoe*), i.e. self-significant word, devoid of all semantic associations. On its basis they created a "trans-sense" (*zaumnaja*) poetry: a poetry free of semantic significance, possessing only sound value. Their ideas link the futurists with dada (q.v.) and other avant-garde tendencies not only in poetry but also in the visual arts. The supreme futurist poet and theoretician was Velimir Xlebnikov (1885–1922), a master of experimental verse which richly illustrates his faculty for creating words. One of the most accomplished of the futurist poets was Vladimir Majakovskij (1894–1930), who resembled other futurists insofar as his rejection of the past logically forced him to accept the October Revolution, which he actively supported through his artistic work. Majakovskij's maximalist temperament and hyperbolic tendencies led him to extremes of dedication, so that by the 1920s his poetry became purely propagandistic. His political jingles evinced none of his earlier lyrical powers. After Majakovskij's suicide, Stalin proclaimed him the best poet of the Soviet era, an assessment which still obtains in official Soviet culture. Majakovskij wrote predominantly accentual verse in which the main rhythmic unit becomes the word (a single accent), which itself can comprise a whole line; hence the "ladderlike" effect of Majakovskij's verses on the printed page. To some degree the influence of his rhythms is discernible in contemp. poetry, esp. that of Voznesenskij and Evtušenko.

In contrast to the emphatically urban futurists, their contemporaries Nikolaj Kljuev (1885–1937) and Sergej Esenin (1895–1925) found inspiration almost exclusively in the countryside. Kljuev, who perished in the camps, produced heavily ornamental poetry, dense with imagery derived from the religious beliefs of the Schismatics and patriarchal peasant life. Esenin, whose popularity continues to rise steadily, was Majakovskij's major rival during the 1920s. In melodious verses that suggest Blok's influence, Esenin sang the beauty of nature, peasant life (often in idyllic tones), and Christianity, which he perceived as the peasants' religion. After the Revolution, however, his verses acquired a tragic tone as he mourned the fall of peasant Russia; the degeneration of love into lechery; and the fate of the poet, whose final refuge is the tavern. Sincere despair, which led him to suicide, sounds unmistakably in his last poems, "Moskva kabackaja" (The Moscow of Taverns) and "Černyj čelovek" (The Black Man).

The original and remarkable gifts of Marina Cvetaeva (1892–1941) have their roots in Blok and Axmatova, but the devel. of those gifts was disrupted by the Revolution and Cvetaeva's emigration in 1922. Her energetic poems, packed with inner tension, in broken rhythms of short lines and frequent enjambment, were created in unbearably trying circumstances, amidst poverty, constant travel, and misery exacerbated by Cvetaeva's cheerless temperament. An organic synthesis of Rus. folklore, 18th-c. odic rhetoric, and Deržavin, Puškin, the futurists, Goethe, and Rilke [her favorite poets], her verses won Cvetaeva an enormous audience in Russia in the 1960s. Returning to her homeland in 1939, Cvetaeva could not endure the conditions of her personal life (her daughter's arrest and her husband's execution) and committed suicide.

If poetic life in Russia remained fairly active during the 1920s, that continuation was due largely to inertia. Literary societies and unions arose and disbanded in rapid succession. A partial list of the organizations that proliferated during this period includes Proletcult, devised to forge a proletarian poetry independent of former trads.; LEF (Majakovskij and Aseev), which rejected art in the name of fact; the romantic *Pereval* (Divide) group, with Mixail Svetlov and Eduard Bagrickij; Kuznica (the Smithy), which included M. Gerasimov, V. Kirillov, and S. Rodov, who glorified the proletariat and the "metallic world of machines"; the imagists, incl. Esenin, Vadim Šeršenevič, and Anatolij Mariengof, who in their polemics with futurism emphasized the imagistic nature of the poetic word; and the "Oberjuty," an avant-garde group that founded a theater of the absurd and produced surrealist and expressionist poems. Almost all the members of the group (Daniil Xarms, Nikolaj Olejnikov, Aleksandr Vvedenskij, Nikolaij Zabolockij, and others) were suppressed—and some were shot—in the 1930s. The year 1932 saw the elimination of these and all other groups when, by government decree, the Union of Soviet Writers was established as the sole legitimate writers' association. During the ensuing two decades Rus. p. ground to a standstill. Genuine poets fell silent, wrote "for the drawer" (with no hope of publishing their work), or undertook translation.

Such was the fate of the consummate poet Boris Pasternak (1890– 1960). Although initially allied with the futurists, Pasternak essentially continued the trads. of the Rus. and Ger. philosophical lyric (Tjutčev and Rilke). Laden with profound and complex imagery, his poetry has the intensity of passionate love lyrics. Despite various attempts to engage in postrevolutionary public life (he wrote a *poema* about the 1905 Revolution, for example), Pasternak remained an individualist to the core, and the government never succeeded in wooing him to its side. For a long stretch after the formation of the Writers' Union, Pasternak kept silent, translating Goethe, Schiller, and Shakespeare and working on the novel *Doctor Zhivago*, the last section of which is a verse cycle that draws richly on religious themes and motifs. Pub. in Italy in 1957, the novel earned Pasternak the Nobel Prize the following year. But this unleashed a campaign of vituperative Soviet persecution against Pasternak that eventually pressured him into refusing the award. These events undermined Pasternak's already uncertain health, and he died of cancer in 1960.

The "thaw" ushered in by Stalin's death in 1953 facilitated a renascence in Rus. p. that lasted almost two decades. Young poets entered the literary ranks to form the poetic avant garde of the Sixties. Adrej Voznesenskij (b. 1933) instantly drew readers' attention through his unexpected rhymes, his virtuoso deployment of metaphor, and the boldness and originality of his ideas. In articulating his hatred for despotism (a typical concern after Stalin's death), his poems regularly pitted tyrants against such artists and "masters" as Rus. architects, Goya, Gauguin, Blok, and Rublev. Although as individuals they perished, their art and art in general triumphed, thus achieving a moral victory over tyranny. Voznesenskij's poetry evidences his fascination with constructivism (q.v.) in architecture, with cybernetics, and with modern physics, and juxtaposes the complex rhythms of the modern world with the banality of everyday existence.

The complicated form of Voznesenskij's poems and his attraction to the technocratic tendencies of the West briefly made him the idol of the Rus. intelligentsia. His constant rival, who matched him in popularity and reached a wider audience, was Evgenij Evtušenko (b. 1933). Formally quite primitive (in rhythm, syntax, and imagery), his poems suggest affinities with Majakovskij. Yet his best works not only boast a topicality and dynamic power, but boldly touch on topics forbidden in the Soviet press: Stalinism, anti-Semitism, Party bureaucracy, corruption, bribery, and sex.

The sensational success of Voznesenskij and Evtušenko overshadowed other poets whose talents compared with and perhaps even outstripped that of the two celebrities, for whom public adulation abated at the close of the 1960s. That decade was uncommonly wealthy in talents that emerged suddenly after 30 years of incubation or repression. Of these the most memorable incl. Bella Axmadulina (b. 1937), author of subtle and profound philosophical verse; Aleksandr Kušner (b. 1936); Nikolaj Rubcov (1936–71), who died prematurely, leaving a body of nature lyrics; and Viktor Sosnora (b. 1936), who wrote on Rus. history. Alongside these poets appeared the exponents of a new genre: "bards" who sang their verses to guitar accompaniment. Tape recorders expedited the rapid dissemination of their poems. Of the bards, the most eminent are the subtle lyricist Bulat Okudžava (b. 1924), the keen satirist Aleksandr Galič (1918–77), and the tragic poet and actor Vladimir Vysockij (1938–80). To this group also belongs Novella Matveeva (b. 1934), who composes verses full of philosophical reflection and unexpected romantic imagery.

With the 1970s, the topicality and political subtext that marked the poetry of the previous decade receded into the background. A wholesale rejection of both classical and official Soviet culture now manifested itself in the works of poets belonging to this "barracks" school of poetry, whose spiritual fathers were the futurists and the Oberjuty. Nine large volumes of undigested raw material containing the verse, crit., diaries, and reminiscences of these poets were recently pub. by Konstantin Kuzminskij. Whereas the works of Gennadij Aigi (b. 1934) regularly reveal his debt to the futurist trad., the career of Naum Koržavin (b. 1925), now living in emigration, reflects a definite shift from anti-Stalinist political verse to philo-

sophical musings on the meaning of life and the poet's calling. Among the contemp. poets whose literary powers matured only in emigration, Aleksej Cvetkov (b. 1947) and Baxyt Kenžiev (b. 1950) deserve mention. In the United States they encountered poets working in the cl. mode: Igor' Činnov (b. 1909), Ivan Elagin (1918–87), and Nikolaj Moršen (b. 1917).

In general, poetry jettisoned politics and ideology to reclaim once more the sphere of spiritual values and to explore the immemorial issues of God, truth, and moral fortitude. This devel. resulted in the belated recognition of Arsenij Tarkovskij (b. 1907), whose philosophical poetry, with roots extending to the trad. of Deržavin and Tjutčev, became the reading of choice for the spiritual elite of the 1970s. But the foremost poet of the decade is unquestionably the Nobel Prize winner (1987), Iosif Brodsky (b. 1940), tried and sentenced to exile in 1965 for social parasitism and forced to emigrate in 1972. Brodsky's completely apolitical poetry examines universal problems, to which he seeks solutions partly by drawing analogies between the contemp. world and past cultures, whether biblical Judea, Homeric Greece, ancient China, Cl. Rome, England in the 17th c., or Russia in the 18th.

This submersion in world culture, together with a tangible feel for the past and present, makes Brodsky an heir and successor to the acmeist trad. (Axmatova had a high opinion of his verses). That trad. surfaces also in the works of other poets who are Brodsky's contemporaries and friends. They appropriate from late acmeism not only its preoccupation with concrete objects but also its profoundly religious orientation, as demonstrated in the fine poems of Oleg Oxapkin (b. 1944), Dmitrij Bobyšev (b. 1936), Jurij Kublanovskij (b. 1947), Elena Švarc (b. 1948), Vasilij Betaki (b. 1930), and several others. Calling themselves the poets of "the Bronze Age," they stress their links with Petersburg culture, which passed through a Golden and then a Silver Age. At the same time, the Bronze Age presages in apocalyptic fashion the dawn of the Iron Age, with its subculture and its computers, when, they fear, no room will be left for poetry.

See also ACMEISM; ANAGRAM; ARMENIAN POETRY; BYELORUSSIAN POETRY; GEORGIAN POETRY; FUTURISM; ROMANTIC AND POSTROMANTIC POETICS; TWENTIETH-CENTURY POETICS, *Slavic*; SLAVIC PROSODY; STRUCTURALISM; UKRAINIAN POETRY.

ANTHOLOGIES: *Specimens of the Rus. Poets*, tr. J. Bowring, 2 v. (1821–23); *Russkaja poezija*, ed. S. A. Vengerov, 1–7 (1893–97))—best and most complete anthol. of the 18th c.; *Russkaja poezija XX veka*, ed. I. S. Ezov and E. I. Samurin (1925); *Na Zapade: Antologija russkoj zarubežnoj poezii*, ed. J. P. Ivask (1953)—widest selection of Rus. p. in exile; *12 poetas rusos XIX–XX*, ed. V. Vinogradova (1958); *Anthologie de la poésie russe*, ed. K. Granoff (1961); *The Heritage of Rus. Verse*, ed. D. Obolensky

RUSSIAN PROSODY

(1965)—with literal prose trs.; *Russkie poety: Antologija v četyrex tomax*, ed. D. D. Blagoj et al. (1965–68); *Mod. Rus. P.*, ed. V. Markov and M. Sparks (1966)—with verse trs.; *The New Rus. Poets 1953–1968*, ed. G. Reavey (1968); *Fifty Soviet Poets*, ed. V. Ognev and D. Rottenberg (1969)—in Rus. and Eng.; *Russkaja sillabičeskaja poezija XVII–XVIII vv.*, ed. A. Pančenko (1970); *Ten Rus. Poets* (1970)—in Rus. with biographies and commentaries in Eng.; *The Silver Age of Rus. Culture*, ed. C. and E. Proffer (1971); *Rus. P. Under the Tsars*, ed. R. Burton (1971); *P. from the Rus. Underground*, ed. J. Landland et al. (1973)—bilingual; *The Blue Lagoon*, ed. K. K. Kuzminsky and G. L. Kovalev, v. 1–5 (1980–86); *Third Wave: The New Rus. P.*, ed. K. Johnson and S. M. Ashby (1992).

HISTORY AND CRITICISM: A. N. Sokolov, *Očerki po istorii russkoj poemy 18 v. i pervoj poloviny 19 v.* (1956); *Istorija russkoj poezii*, ed. B. P. Gorodeckij, v. 1–2 (1968–69)—fullest hist. of Rus. p. to 1917; R. Silbajoris, *Rus. Versification* (1968)—studies three 18th-c. theories; V. Žirmunskij, *Teorija stixa* (1968); B. Ejxenbaum, *O poezii* (1969); M. J. Lotman, *Analiz poetičeskogo teksta* (1972, tr. 1976 as *Analysis of the Poetic Text*), *Struktura xudožestvennogo teksta* (1975, tr. 1977 as *The Structure of the Artistic Text*); A. M. Pančenko, *Russkaja stixotvornaja kul'tura XVII veka* (1973)—on the emergence of Rus. p.; L. Ginzburg, *O lirike*, 2d ed. (1974); *Mod. Rus. Poets on Poetry*, ed. C. R. Proffer (1976); E. Etkind, *Materija stixa* (1978); D. Brown, *Soviet Rus. Lit. Since Stalin* (1978); V. Veidle, *Embriologija poezii* (1980); E. J. Brown, *Rus. Lit. Since the Revolution* (1982); *Istorija russkoj sovetskoj poezii, 1917–41; 1941–80*, ed. V. Buzik et al., v. 1–2 (1984)—incomplete and tendentious; G. Struve, *Russkaja literatura v. izgnanii*, 2d ed. (1984); F. Peter, *Poets of Mod. Russia* (1983); G. S. Smith, *Songs to Seven Strings* (1984); M. Altshuller and E. Dryža Kova, *Put' otrečenija: Russkaja literatura 1953–68* (1985)—essays on Rus. p. of the 1950s and '60s; G. A. Gukovskii, *Lomonosov, Sumarokov, and the Sumarokov School*, Soviet Studies in Lit., v. 21,1–2 (1984–85); Terras, esp. s.v. "Bylina," "Poema," "Versification, Historical Survey"; B. P. Scherr,

Rus. P. (1986)—prosody; D. Lowe, *Rus. Writing Since 1953* (1987)—short but valuable survey of contemp. Rus. p.; *Cambridge Hist. of Rus. Lit.*, ed. C. A. Moser (1989); E. Bristol, *Hist. of Rus. P.* (1991); V. Terras, *Hist. of Rus. Lit.* (1992).

WORKS ON INDIVIDUAL WRITERS: B. V. Tomaševskij, *Puškin*, 2 v. (1956, 1961); R. A. Gregg, *Fedor Tiutchev* (1965); R. F. Gustafson, *Imagination of Spring: The Poetry of Afanasy Fet* (1966); S. S. Birkenmeyer, *Nikolaj Nekrasov* (1968); H. Troyat, *Pushkin* (1970); J. West, *Rus. Symbolism: A Study of Vyaceslav Ivanov and the Rus. Symbolist Aesthetic* (1970); A. Cross, *N. M. Karamzin: A Study of his Literary Career (1783–1803)* (1971); B. Dees, *E. A. Baratynsky* (1972); B. M. Žirmunskij, *Tvorčestvo Anny Axmatovoj* (1973); O. R. Hughes, *The Poetic World of Boris Pasternak* (1974); I. Z. Serman, *Konstantin Batyushkov* [in Eng.] (1974); *Mikhail Lomonosov: Life and Poetry* (1988); D. Blagoj, *Mir kak krasota: O "Večernix ognjax" A. Feta* (1975)—the best study of the nature of Fet's lyrics; A. Haight, *Anna Akhmatova: A Poetic Pilgrimage* (1976); G. McVay, *Esenin: A Life* (1976); I. M. Semenko, *Vasily Zhukovsky* [in Eng.] (1976); B. Christa, *The Poetic World of Andrey Belyi* (1977); A. Pyman, *The Life of Aleksandr Blok*, 2 v. (1979–80); E. D. Sampson, *Nikolay Gumilev* (1979); B. M. Eikhenbaum, *Lermontov: A Study in Literary-Historical Evaluation* (1981); *Lermontovskaja enciklopedija*, ed. V. A. Manujlov (1981); V. Terras, *Vladimir Mayakovsky* (1983); J. D. Grossman, *Valery Bryusov and the Riddle of Rus. Decadence* (1985); J. Karabičevskij, *Voskresenie Majakovskogo* (1985)—the only strongly negative study of Majakovskij, which criticizes the Soviet canonization of the poet; S. Karlinsky, *Marina Tsvetaeva* (1985); P. Gromov, *A. Blok, ego predšestvenniki i sovremenniki* (1986); J. G. Harris, *Osip Mandelstam* (1988); V. Xodasevič, *Deržavin* (1988); R. Iezuitova, *Žukovskij i russkaja literatura ego vremeni* (1989); V. Polukhina, *Joseph Brodsky: A Poet of Our Time* (1989). M.G.A.; tr. H.G.

RUSSIAN PROSODY. See SLAVIC PROSODY.

S

SAGA. See EPIC; ICELANDIC POETRY; OLD NORSE POETRY; WELSH POETRY.

SAN FRANCISCO RENAISSANCE. See AMERICAN POETRY; BEAT POETS.

SANSKRIT POETRY. See INDIAN POETRY.

SANSKRIT PROSODY. See INDIAN PROSODY.

SAPPHIC. In early Gr. poetry, an important Aeolic (q.v.) verseform named after Sappho, a Gr. poet from the island of Lesbos of the 7th–6th c. B.C. Prosodically, this form has been of interest to poets throughout most of the history of Western poetry; generically, it has evoked ever-increasing interest in the subjects of gender and love *vis-a-vis* poetry, most recently poetry written by women.

The term "S." refers to both a meter and a stanza form. The S. line, called the "lesser S.," is a hendecasyllable of the pattern $- \cup - x - \cup \cup - \cup -$ $- .$ The S. stanza consists of two Lesser S. lines followed by a 16-syllable line which is an extended form of the other two: $- \cup - x - \cup \cup - \cup - x +$ $- \cup \cup - - .$ This latter has been analyzed in several ways; one traditional account sees the last colon as an Adonic (q.v.) colon, $- \cup \cup - - ,$ and treats it as a separate line, giving the S. stanza 4 lines in all. Sappho's contemporary Alcaeus also used the stanza and may have been its inventor. Catullus (84–54 B.C.?) composed two odes in Ss. (Catullus 11 and 51), the second of which is a tr. and adaptation of Sappho frag. 31 (LP); with these poems he probably introduced the S. into Lat. poetry, but it is not certain. It is Horace (65–8 B.C.), however, who provided the S. model for subsequent Roman and European poets; in his *Odes* he uses the form 27 times, second in frequency only to Alcaics (q.v.). Horace also makes a single use (*Odes* 1.8) of the Greater S. strophe, i.e. an Aristophaneus ($- \cup \cup - \cup - -$) followed by a Greater S. line of 15 syllables ($- \cup - - - | \cup \cup$ $- | - \cup \cup - \cup - -$), which can be analyzed as a S. hendecasyllable with an inserted choriamb. His treatment of the S. as a 4-line stanza canonized that form for posterity. Seneca (4 B.C.–A.D. 65) sometimes uses the separate elements in a different order, e.g. by arranging a continuous series of longer lines with an Adonic clausula.

In the Middle Ages, the S. acquired rhyme and was instrumental in the transition from metrical (quantitative) to rhythmical (accentual) meter (Norberg). After the hexameter and the iambic dimeter quatrain (for hymns) it is the most popular verseform of the medieval period: there are 127 examples in *Analecta hymnica*. In the Ren. and after, accentual versions of the S. became three lines of 11 syllables followed by a fourth line of 5, the whole in trochees and dactyls. The fourth line instances the phenomenon of tailing or end-shortening well attested in other stanza forms (see TAIL RHYME).

The revival of Horatian influence on poetics evoked wide interest in the S. stanza among poets and prosodists in Italy, France, Germany, England, and Spain. Leonardo Dati used it for the first time in It. (1441), followed by Galeotto del Carretto (1455–1530), Claudio Tolomei (1492–1555), and others; in the 19th c., experiments were made by Cavallotti and by Carducci (*Odi barbare*). Estéban de Villegas (1589–1669) is the chief practitioner in Spain. In the 18th-c. Ger. revival of interest in quantitative verse, F. G. Klopstock varied an unrhymed stanza with regular positional changes of the trisyllabic foot in the Lesser S. lines; later, August von Platen and others essayed the strict Horatian form. In Eng., Ss. have been written by Sidney (*Old Arcadia*; *Certain Sonnets* 25), Isaac Watts (*Horae lyricae*), Pope ("Ode on Solitude"), Cowper ("Lines under the Influence of Delirium"), Southey ("The Widow"), Tennyson, Swinburne (*Poems and Ballads*), Hardy (the first poem in *Wessex Poems*), Pound ("Apparuit"), and John Fredrick Nims (*Sappho to Valéry*, 2d ed. [1990]). The S. has been the longest lived of the Cl. lyric strophes in the West. But full studies of its history in several vernaculars still remain to be written. See now CLASSICAL METERS IN MODERN LANGUAGES; LOVE POETRY.

G. Mazzoni, "Per la storia della saffica in Italia," *Atti* dell' Acc. Scienze lett. arti 10 (1894); E. Hjaerne, "Das sapfiska strofen i svensk verskonst," *Sprak och Stil* 13 (1913); Pauly-Wissowa, Supp., 11.1222 ff.; Hardie, pt. 2, ch. 3; Omond; H. Rüdiger, *Gesch. der deutschen Sappho-Übersetzungen* (1934); G. H. Needler, *The Lone Shieling* (1941); D. L. Page, *Sappho and Alcaeus* (1955); Norberg; Bowra; W. Bennett, *Ger. Verse in Cl. Metres* (1963); L. P. Wilkinson, *Golden Lat. Artistry* (1963); Koster; H. Kenner, "The Muse in Tatters," *Agenda* 6 (1968); N. A. Bonavia-Hunt, *Horace the Minstrel* (1969); R. G. M. Nisbet and M. Hubbard, *A Commentary on Horace, Odes Book 1* (1970); R. Paulin, "Six S. Odes 1753–1934," *Seminar* 10 (1974); E. Schäfer, *Deutscher Horaz* (1976); E. Weber, "Prosodie verbale et prosodie musicale: La Strophe sapphique au Moyen Age et à la Ren.," *Le Moyen Français* 5 (1979); Halporn et al.; P. Stotz, *Sonder-*

formen der sapphischen Dichtung (1982); West, 32 ff.; Navarro.　　　　　R.A.S.; T.V.F.B.; J.W.H.

SATANIC SCHOOL. As part of an ongoing feud, Robert Southey, in his preface to *A Vision of Judgement*—the laureate's eulogy on the death of George III—launched a thinly veiled attack on Byron as the head of the "Satanic School" that was polluting Eng. poetry with "monstrous combinations of horrors and mockery, lewdness and impiety." He declared that the evil of these lascivious productions was political as well as moral, constituting one of the worst offenses against society, subverting the very foundations of human virtue. Byron retaliated with his own *Vision of Judgment*, characterizing Southey as a renegade scribbler canonizing and deifying a king who "although no tyrant, . . . shielded tyrants." Of greater importance for European lit. was Byron's creation of a Satanic hero, a cursed rebel who, like Manfred, is his own instrument of damnation. He is the prototype of the *poète maudit* (q.v.) as developed later by Baudelaire and his successors. Some critics have also associated the Satanic hero with the trad. emanating from the Marquis de Sade.—M. Praz, *The Romantic Agony*, 2d ed. (1951). L.MET.

SATIRE, as generally defined, is both a mode of discourse or vision that asserts a polemical or critical outlook ("the satiric"), and also a specific literary genre embodying that mode in either prose or verse, esp. formal verse s. From earliest times s. has tended toward didacticism (see DIDACTIC POETRY). Despite the aesthetic and often comic or witty pleasure associated with much s., their authors incline toward self-promotion as judges of morals and manners, of behavior and thought. The franchise is theirs, they assume, to pass and execute verbal sentence on both individuals and types. Numerous satirists ridicule or berate shortcomings of their own times within a context whose values—ideally—will outlast the occasions or crises of the moment. Whatever they diagnose as corrupt, they confidently venture to "heal"—in Pope's phrase—albeit severely, "with morals what [their s.] hurts with wit" (*Epistle to Augustus* 262). More subtle than most of his predecessors, Pope nonetheless follows in a long trad. of satirists who denied vindictiveness; they insisted, rather, that they were indignant because of social wrongs, and that they aimed to assure human betterment. Such assertions of regard for the social good, however, are mainly formulaic, and have enabled a large body of s. to escape retribution.

This, however, was certainly not the case—nor was it intended to be the case—in the s. of primitive and ancient cultures. Imprecations, threats of reprisal, and invective (q.v.) were in many primitive cultures believed to be imbued with the "magical power" of "word-slaying" (Elliott). Eskimos composed satiric songs to shame individuals and engaged their enemies in satiric duels as a way of settling differences. In Cl. Greece, Archilochus (7th c. B.C.)—arguably the "first" Gr. satirist—was notorious for the "iambic fury" (Ben Jonson's phrase) of his bitterly personal s. With similar vituperative intent, the magic charms of early Ir. bards supposedly could rhyme both rats and men to death. Further parallels exist in the ritualized abuse with which Gr. Old Comedy began and in the practice of the ancient Arab poets, for whom s. was a lethal weapon to be chanted in actual battle; modern analogues exist in the verbal duels of street slang like "the dozens" (see POETIC CONTESTS).

In more sophisticated eras also the satiric voice continues to be heard. The very term *s.* connotes the recognizable structural and topical qualities of a discrete literary genre. But critically charged attributes of s. may also attach themselves to other literary or quasiliterary forms, a usage that occurs in prose and verse (or in mixtures, like the *Satire Ménippée* [1594]). An undercurrent of mockery and parody brightens the chivalric loftiness of Ariosto's 16th-c. *Orlando Furioso.* Following the craft of Theophrastus, 17th-c. authors—e.g. Hall, Overbury, Earle—put forth "character books" as caustic reflections on contemporary manners and persons. Satiric borrowing, similarly, affected the pulpit oratory of a Tillotson or Hoadly, the social condemnation of an Erasmus or Swift, Voltaire or Burke. Both Gay's *Beggar's Opera* and Brecht's 20th-c. adaptation (*Dreigroschenoper*) with gleanings from the 15th-c. Villon show brilliantly how theatrical art and music intermesh for satiric earthiness and imagination. In a related way, the wit of Wilde and Shaw owes much of its effectiveness to an informing satiric intention.

Themes associated with s.—antifeminism, social perversity, duplicity, idiosyncrasy—enrich Aristophanic comedy (4th c. B.C.); comparable themes later served Ren. tragedy as well as neoclassical comedy. For a preeminent example we look to Shakespeare, who even in his tragedies exploited the satiric and comic potential of subjects such as hypocrisy, sycophancy, and feminine wiles. Intolerance and clerical hypocrisy have been set in diverse poetic forms whose tonality ranges from the boisterous and profane to the comic and somber. Toward the end of the 12th c., rowdy "scholar poets," the wandering minstrels of Goliardic verse (q.v.), outraged the European ecclesiastical establishment. One of the most memorable critics of the medieval Church was Jean de Meun (late 13th c.), whose disenchanted perceptions in his portion of the *Roman de la rose* probably suggested to Chaucer traits for his Friar and Pardoner (as well as for the lustily secular Wife of Bath). Comparably adversarial are the 15th-c. "Scottish Chaucerians" (q.v.) and the 16th-c. John Skelton of *Colin Clout.* Related faults of hypocrisy and greed, powerful incentives for satiric rebuke, continued the anticlerical trad. exemplified in Palingenius, Jonson, and Molière.

Fables and beast epics (qq.v.) also contributed

to the medieval proliferation of anticlerical s. Often composed in Lat., they drew upon the durable legacy of Aesop. One of the earliest poets in this mode was Nivard of Ghent (fl. 1150), who told many stories about Isengrim the wolf *qua* monk and Reynard the fox as picaresque trickster. The beast fable enjoyed wide popularity, like the anonymous *Roman de Renart* (ca. 1175–1205), in which the cunning fox shares speaking honors with a lion, wolf, bear, cat, and cock, all of whom comment on a roster of human infirmities and abuses. From the perspective of animals, the social, political, and religious peccadilloes of humanity have been depicted by such major poets as Chaucer, La Fontaine, Dryden, and Swift.

When adapted to other literary modes such as prose, the devices of s. make important textural contributions to their host vehicles. Their ultimate significance, however, inheres in a generic process that evolved from the mythic and superstitious archetypes (q.v.) of primitive culture. *Satura* (also *satira*), a nomenclature of Roman times, connoted both license and obligation to expose every kind of human failure, from wanton malice to mindless folly and vanity. Initially, via misprision of folk etymology, *satura* was confused with *satyr*, the rough and lecherous half-man, halfbeast of Cl. mythology. This mistaken connection persisted for a long time—into the 18th c.—despite Casaubon's rectification in 1605 (*De satyrica graecorum poesi et romanorum satira*). For the better informed, however, *satura*—by analogy with *lanx satura*—meant an abundant mixture (a hodgepodge of public and private issues that warranted severe crit.). This is essentially the subtext of much modern s. When Quintilian (*Institutio oratoria* 10.1.93) boasted that s. emanated from Roman rather than Gr. genius ("s. is all our own"), he contemplated a genre in hexameters, secondary to be sure, and not nearly so definable as others like elegy, lyric, tragedy, comedy, epic (qq.v.). Still, he validated a distinctive poetic mode, the formal verse s. (*sermones*, "conversations") practiced from the time of Lucilius, Horace, Juvenal, and Persius through the 18th c.

Characteristically, such s. "is a quasi-dramatic poem, 'framed' by an encounter between the Satirist [or the transparent *persona* who speaks for him] and an adversarius" (Elliott 110–11; cf. Randolph 372). The latter may be a friendly antagonist who, recruited for the occasion, becomes an acute interlocutor or courtroom lawyer, *amicus curiae*. Thus mandated, he asks provocative questions that invite from the principal speaker assurances of virtue, righteous indignation, resolution, etc. (cf. Pope's *Imitations of Horace*, in which eloquent exchanges between P. [Pope] and F. [Fortescue] parallel those in Horace (*Satire* 2.1] between Horace and the lawyer Trebatius). Alternatively, a compassionate narrator may initiate a dialogue in which an address to a victim of injustice elicits from the latter an often lengthy, passionate complaint (Juvenal's Umbricius, *Satire* 3; Johnson's Thales, *London*).

Barely concealed, the partisan satirist in dialogues like these is never far from the stage. Because the disguises that he wears are as transparent as they are conventional, readers may connect their own realities with a credible satiric fiction. Prominent among the satirist's postures is him speaking in the voice of an apologist, pretending, for example, that he is by nature mildmannered (like Persius, who describes himself as "half a clown") and therefore satirically ineffectual. The irony of the claim is patent in light of the abrasive, often militant temper of the "apologist." But the deferential fiction succeeds if it arouses a sympathetic response to the satirist who appears as a lonely warrior, an honorable man driven by conscience to excoriate wrongdoings, even at some risk to himself. Such is the intended appeal of Churchill in the mid 18th c.: "Lives there a man, who calmly can stand by, / And see his conscience ripp'd with steady eye?" (*The Apology*). In the words of Juvenal, protesting against his failed society, *difficile est saturam non scribere* (*S.* 1.30). Since Cl. times, apology has helped to shape satiric formulae, as much so in France (Régnier, *Satire* 12; Boileau, *Satire* 9) as in England (Scrope, *Defence of Satire*; Pope, *Epistle to Dr. Arbuthnot*; Johnson, *London*).

Linguistically manipulative, satiric poets exploit the ambivalent and loaded terminology of invective, sarcasm, irony, mockery, hyperbole, and understatement. To control a range of tone and substance that may vary from the obvious to the subtle, many have relied upon the structure of Cl. rhet. codified by Aristotle, Quintilian, and Cicero. Rhet. is a more tightly disciplined mode of discourse than s., but the two have enough similarity of persuasive aim that, with modifications, s. may benefit from the organizing prescriptions of rhet. "The truth," says Cicero (*De oratore* 1.15.70), "is that the poet is a very near kinsman of the orator." Dryden must have taken this premise to heart when he composed *Absalom and Achitophel* (1681), a grand defense of the divine right of kingship. A reader can trace the formal rhetorical progression of the argument with little difficulty—as though Dryden were a Cl. debater—through the sequential stages of *exordium, narratio, confirmatio, reprehensio,* and *peroratio.*

Theoretically, satiric intent is humanistic in spirit if notoriously less generous in tone. Much s., to paraphrase Pope, wishes the world well, and, knightlike, its proponents joust as the self-avowed champions of "truth," "justice," and "reformation." Johnson subsequently extended his own definition of s. ("a poem in which wickedness or folly is censured") in declaring: "All truth is valuable, and satirical crit. may be considered as useful when it rectifies errors and improves judgment: he that rectifies the public taste is a public benefactor" (*Life of Pope*). Even Swift, steeped as he was in Juvenalian *saeva indignatio*, claimed benignity, for

"His s. points at no defect, / But what all mortals may correct." (*Verses on the Death of Dr. Swift*).

Not all poets and critics accept the doctrine of *humanitas*, however. For many, the satiric mode destroys, dominated by a "cankered muse" that neither corrects nor reforms, that merely taunts or rejects whatever is gross or absurd. Granted, the fierce energy of Juvenal's s. seems to exude anger, but the underlying incentive is a humane one that should not be mistaken for the pleasure of inflicting pain, which is certainly the impression generated in the 16th c. by Aretino, in his harsh dialogues on tainted It. manners. A similar reaction often accompanies the "hot-blooded rage" of Bishop Hall's *Virgidemia* and Marston's "sharp-fang'd" *Scourge of Villainie*, and, indeed, the threat that they represented to public complacency seemed real enough to the state censors of the time, who responded by having the poems burned at the stake.

As in some of the miscellaneous Restoration *Poems on Affairs of State*, sadism bursts out of Oldham's *Satires upon the Jesuits* (1681), while personal animus—although clever and laughable—hones the slinging matches between Pope and his "furious Sappho," Lady Mary Wortley Montagu. Claims of constructive intent fail to persuade when the tone is palpably strident or venomous. By the 19th c., in Italy, for example, the social and political structure has changed enough to provoke new causes of satiric complaint. But intense anger flourishes still as in Giuseppe Belli, whose dialect sonnets bitterly decry the deficiencies of all Roman institutions—religious, social, and political.

Much of the popular appeal of s. lies in its adaptability of structure and meter to subject, and in its capacity to evoke laughter. The mock epic (q.v.), derived from a serious literary vehicle, inflates a trivial theme with a ludicrous pomposity of style and lang. The device, as timehonored as the ancient Gr. *Batrachomyomachia* (*Battle of the Frogs and Mice*), is perpetuated in Pulci's *Morgante Maggiore*, Tassoni's *La secchia rapita*, Boileau's *Le Lutrin*, and numerous others by Marvell, Dryden, and Pope. Related satiric effects are achieved by additional kinds of incongruous imitation: caricature, travesty, burlesque (q.v.—e.g. diverse poems of Quevedo; Cotton's *Scarronides*; Butler's *Hudibras*; Villiers' *The Rehearsal*); parody (q.v.—e.g. Shelley's version of Wordsworth's *Peter Bell*; Byron's of Southey's *A Vision of Judgment*). The staples of satiric inspiration remain abundant. In Byron, we hear echoes of Pope's intolerance of bad writers and taste, and of man's folly generally. Blake and Browning mock the hypocrisy and worldliness of organized religion; Blake wages war esp. on political dunces and oppressors, while Hugo directs political invective against Napoleon III. Thackeray berates speculators and Eng. courts. From opposed ends of the satiric spectrum, e e cummings praises man's resistance to military tyranny while Roy Campbell belittles "inferior races." Yeats and Eliot find in s. a way to voice disillusion with conflicting values of private spirituality or religion and the public disorder of their times.

Meanwhile, Auden reverts to a surprisingly traditional 18th-c. view: "S. is angry and optimistic; it believes that, once people's attention is drawn to some evil, they will mend their ways" (Foreword to *Sense and Inconsequence*, by A. Stewart [1972]). For him as for earlier generations of poets, s. offers a shared basis of self-examination to individuals with "the normal faculty of conscience" (*The Dyer's Hand*, 1962). See also BURLESQUE; DOZENS; EPIGRAM; FLYTING; INVECTIVE; PARODY; SILLOI; TOAST.

COLLECTIONS: *Poems on Affairs of State*, ed. G. deF. Lord et al, 7 v. (1963–75); *Oxford Book of Satirical Verse*, ed. G. Grigson (1980).

HISTORY AND CRITICISM: Dryden, "A Discourse concerning the Original and Progress of S.," (1693); P. Lejay, "Les Origines et la nature de la s. d'Horace," in his ed. of Horace, *Ss.* (1911); G. L. Hendrickson, "Satura tota nostra est," *CP* 22 (1927); J. W. Duff, *Roman S.* (1936); O. J. Campbell, *Comicall Satyre* (1938); V. Cian, *La satira*, 2 v. (1939); D. Worcester, *The Art of S.* (1940); M. C. Randolph, "The Structural Design of the Formal Verse S.," *PQ* 21 (1942); M. Mack, "The Muse of S.," *YR* 41 (1951); I. Jack, *Augustan S.* (1952); J. D. Peter, *Complaint and S. in Early Eng. Lit.* (1956); Frye; J. Sutherland, *Eng. S.* (1958); A. B. Kernan, *The Cankered Muse* (1959), *The Plot of S.* (1965), "S.," *DHI*; R. C. Elliott, *The Power of S.* (1960); G. Highet, *The Anatomy of S.* (1962); H. Schroeder, *Russische Verssatire im 18. Jahrhundert* (1962); W. S. Anderson, *Anger in Juvenal and Seneca* (1964), *Essays on Roman S.* (1982); *S.: A Critical Anthol.*, ed. J. Russell and A. Brown (1967); M. Hodgart, *S.* (1969); L. Lecocq, *La S. en Angleterre de 1588 à 1603* (1969); H. D. Weinbrot, *The Formal Strain* (1969), *Alexander Pope and the Trads. of Formal Verse S.* (1982), ed., *18th-C. S.* (1988); A. Pollard, *S.* (1970); *S.: Mod. Essays in Crit.*, ed. R. Paulson (1971); C. Sanders, *The Scope of S.* (1971); R. Seldon, "Roughness in S. from Horace to Dryden," *MLR* 66 (1971), *Eng. Verse S. 1590–1767* (1978); P. K. Elkin, *Augustan Defence of S.* (1973); M. Coffey, *Roman S.* (1976); J. Brummack, "S.," *Reallexikon* 3.601–14; E. A. and L. D. Bloom, *S.'s Persuasive Voice* (1979); T. Lockwood, *Post-Augustan S.* (1979); M. Seidel, *Satiric Inheritance* (1979); N. Rudd, *The Ss. of Horace*, 2d ed. (1982); *Die englische S.*, ed. W. Weiss (1982); M. T. Hester, *Kinde Pity and Brave Scorne: John Donne's Satyres* (1982); Fowler; V. Carretta, *The Snarling Muse* (1983); F. A. Nussbaum, *The Brink of All We Hate: Eng. Ss. on Women 1660–1750* (1984); *Eng. S. and the Satiric Trad.*, ed. C. Rawson (1984); A. G. Wood, *Literary S. and Theory* (1984); W. Kupersmith, *Roman Satirists in 17th-C. England* (1985); Terras; C. Rawson, *Order from Confusion Sprung* (1985)—pt. 2; J. S. Baumlin, "Generic Contexts of Elizabethan S.," *Ren. Genres*, ed. B. K. Lewalski (1986); L.

Guilhamet, *S. and the Transformation of Genre* (1987); H. Javadi, *S. in Persian Lit.* (1988); R. E. Pepin, *Lit. of S. in the 12th C.* (1988).   E.A.B.

SATURNIAN. The verseform used in the two earliest Lat. epics, the tr. of the *Odyssey* by Livius Andronicus (ca. 284–204 B.C.) and the *Bellum punicum* of Naevius (ca. 270–190 B.C.), and also of scattered epitaphs, dedications, proverbs, and incantations composed or committed to writing in the 3d and 2d cs. B.C. Fewer than two hundred instances survive; the example of Ennius (239–169 B.C.) turned Lat. prosody to imitating Gr. quantitative meters, with the result that the S. was soon rejected in favor of the hexameter (q.v.) for epic and the elegiac distich (q.v.) and iambic senarius (q.v.) for epitaphs and dedications. Horace's description of the *horridus numerus Saturnius* as an offensive poison ("grave virus") is an example of later taste in regard to it. Structure and origin are accordingly obscure—least so, perhaps, in those verses, roughly a third of the total, which show a 4–3–3–3 grouping of syllables into words or word groups, with a strong central break and parallelism between groups or subgroups, reinforced by frequent alliteration and assonance:

> *virum mihi, camena, insece versutum*
> (Livius);
> im*mortales mortales si foret fasfere*
> (Naevius epitaph).

The regularities here are too numerous and conspicuous to be accidental. Moreover, the structural principle is so unlike anything found in Gr. poetry (q.v.), and so similar to that attested in the balanced alliterative and assonantal dicola and tricola of early Lat. ritual formulae, that the theory espoused by some metrists, both ancient and modern, of direct derivation from Gr. models is highly unlikely. One is left with two possibilities: either (as the name itself ["belonging or pertaining to the reign of Saturn"] would suggest) a native Italic form (perhaps distantly related to the Old Irish heptasyllable), or some early Gr. import domiciled in Italy for several centuries and thereby radically transformed by the time Livius and Naevius tried to give it literary status. Almost everything beyond this is highly problematic. Verses longer than those cited above can always be regarded as resolved versions of the 13-syllable "model," which might suggest the operation of quantitative principles; but there is no one quantitative scheme to which all or even a large majority of extant examples conform, and there exist shorter halflines with 4–2, 3–2 and 2–3 groupings of syllables which are equally hard to reconcile with a quantitative analysis. Explanations which posit the working of two or more different rhythmical principles (quantitative, syllabic, accentual) are, on the whole, more plausible than those which involve a single one. It is possible, for example, that a quadripartite line originally based on grouping of syllables by 4s, 3s, and 2s evolved, under the influence of Gr. models, into a 13-syllable line with the same groupings but a generally iambo-trochaic movement, similar to that found in Macaulay's accentual imitation: "The quéen was ín her párlour, éating bréad and hóney."—F. Leo, *Der Saturnische Vers* (1905); G. Pasquali, *Preistoria della poesia latina* (1936); M. Barchiesi, *Nevio epico* (1962), 310–27; T. Cole, "The S. Verse," *YCS* 21 (1969); J. Starobinski, *Les Mots sous les mots* (1971), 13–36.   A.T.C.

SAUSSUREAN LINGUISTICS. See REPRESENTATION AND MIMESIS; SEMIOTICS, POETIC.

SCALD. See SKALD.

SCANSION. The act of discovery or interp. of the meter (q.v.) of a poem as realized in one of its lines; also the graphic transcription thereof, usually by symbols, numbers, or letters either above the line or alone. S. is a notation system for meter in metrical poetry just as sheet music notates music or writing notates speech.

In Cl. Gr. and Lat. verse (see CLASSICAL PROSODY) and in a very few mod. langs., meter is based on quantity (q.v.); in Med. Lat. rhythmical verse and in virtually all the modern Western vernaculars, it is based on stress (see ACCENT); in several Eastern langs., it is based on tone (see PITCH) and tone change. Hence these are the features to be identified in s. Traditional practice has been to scan quantitative verse with macrons and breves for long and short syllables, respectively, and sometimes *a* or *x* for indeterminate quantity, i.e. *anceps* (q.v.); in stress-based verse, an acute accent mark (x́) or sometimes a virgule is most often used to notate stressed syllables, and neutral symbols such as *x*'s or *o*'s for slacks (unstressed syllables). Mixing symbols (such as using macrons for stressed syllables in modern verse) has unfortunately been common, but such practice only serves to confuse readers. Perhaps the oldest system uses the letters of the alphabet; in the ancient Sanskrit *Chandahsutra* of Pingala, G = long or heavy (*guru*) and L = short or light (*laghu*), and other letters are used to represent combinations of these: M=GGG, N=LLL, R=GLG, etc. Numbers (0 and 1, or 1–4 or higher) have also been used to represent degree or position of stress or level of pitch.

It is also common in s. to mark metrical divisions in the line such as the caesura (q.v.) and the boundaries between feet (see FOOT) or measures: the single vertical bar is often used for the one or the other or both of these; and in some cases where the single bar is used to separate measures, a double bar is used to mark the caesura or hemistich (q.v.). The notation of "metrical pauses" (see PAUSE) is disputed: metrical theories which do not treat meter as a temporal phenomenon cannot take notice of something that is not there, of course; temporal theories, by contrast, make pro-

SCANSION

vision for missing syllables in various ways. Conversely, extrametrical syllables both within the line and at line end are usually notated as optional, though strictly speaking they do not count (see MASCULINE AND FEMININE). Temporal theories of meter have attempted to capture the timing of the line with precision. Musical notation was used by one group of ancient prosodists, the *rhythmici* (see METRICI AND RHYTHMICI), and enjoyed a modern vogue from the early 18th c. (C. Gildon, 1718) through the later 19th c. (S. Lanier, 1880; see Brogan). The difficulty with musical notation, however, is precisely one of overspecification: musical notation in effect describes only one performance. (It also has the unfortunate effect of treating all iambic verse as trochaic, since in music stresses begin bars.)

Unfortunately there is very little agreement on symbols, terms, or concepts: dozens of s. systems have been devised. But such disputes about symbols are by no means trivial; rather, they strike to the heart of fundamental disputes about what meter is and what metrical theory should do. It is for this reason that ss. routinely provoke strong critical disagreements.

Since ancient times, scanning of metrical verse has been carried on *kata stichon*: this procedure presumes and ensures the integrity of the individual line, though at the expense of contiguity and run. In the sprung rhythm (q.v.) of Gerard Manley Hopkins, however, lines are said to be "rove over," so that "the scanning runs on without break from the beginning, say, of a stanza to the end and all the stanza is one long strain, though written in lines asunder" ("Author's Preface" to *Poems*, 1918; 5th ed., ed. N. H. Mackenzie, 1990). S. serves precisely the same function for analysis of poetry that integral calculus serves for calculating the area under a curve: it cuts up motion (*rhythm*, from Gr. "flow") into segments for counting. Counting itself already entails segmentation. The shapes of the segments and the nature of their joints (end to end; dovetailing) are then described. The segments may or may not all be identical.

The elements to be recognized and procedures to be followed in s. must come from formal axioms and definitions in metrical theory. At the outset it would seem reasonable to assume that the best s. system would (1) find the most pattern (2) with the fewest number of elements (3) derived via the fewest rules. In the Cl. langs., the unit of analysis is the foot for some meters and the metron (q.v.) for others, with the colon and period (q.v.) also employed by some metrists. In the medieval Germanic langs. the unit is the hemistich; in the Romance langs., it is the measure (q.v.). In mod. Eng. metrical verse from Chaucer through Browning it is the foot; postmetrical free verse (q.v.) by definition has no regular unit of structure.

Since meter is a system of binary oppositions in which syllables are either marked or unmarked (long or short; stressed or unstressed), a binary code is all that is necessary to transcribe it. But critics and readers have often been frustrated with the narrow and quite specific ends of s. And some prosodists, having realized that two lines with precisely the same s. may not feel at all the same, as in Pope's exhibition of line tempo and weighting in the *Essay on Crit.*, have sought to make their s.-system more complex and detailed, so as to capture more information about the microstructure of the line. Enterprising metrists have devised a number of more complicated s. systems to take note of (1) more degrees of stress than two, (2) pitch and intonation, (3) pausing and timing, or (4) phrasal grouping of syllables. Stewart, for example, identifies four levels of stress and two types of pauses; his ss. also reflect grouping of syllables. Attridge gives 6 symbols for marking linguistic rhythm and 13 for metrical s.

It is natural to want to enrich s. with other kinds of analyses which capture more of the phonological and syntactic structure of the line; Scott speaks of the "real, and indefensible, coarseness" of s. But all such efforts exceed the boundary of strict metrical analysis, moving into description of linguistic rhythm, and thus serve to blur or dissolve the distinction between meter and rhythm. Strictly speaking, s. marks which syllables are metrically prominent—i.e. ictus (q.v.) and nonictus—not how much. Ss. which take account of more levels of metrical degree than two, or intonation, or the timing of syllables are all guilty of overspecification. Such analyses can apply to only one line, and thus obscure what all lines have in common, which is their meter. Metrical s. may well be augmented or flanked by more sophisticated analyses of line rhythm, but these do not supplant or subsume it. There is more to metrical poetry than meter, certainly, and there are more kinds of poetry than metrical, but s. is how we describe meter.

Literary critics were for a long time distracted by excessive claims by some metrists about the "scientific" character of metrical analysis. Many metrists considered their ss. to be facts and attacked rival ss. fiercely. Both these attitudes delayed the recognition that, in the main, ss. are not facts but interpretations, i.e. critical judgments about the meaning of lines, not merely their rhythms. As C. S. Lewis put it, "metrical questions are profitable only if we regard them, not as questions about fact, but as purely practical." Ss., that is, are not normally right or wrong, they are only more or less revealing. In this respect they are no more—or less—privileged than any other critical activity.

Though meter itself determines meanings, by pointing up and by restricting, ss. on the other hand are determined by semantic decisions, not vice versa. To give a s. is to have made interpretive and semantic decisions about what one thinks the line means. Shakespearean actors learn that attention to meter reveals meanings which would otherwise not emerge from paying attention only to sense. Coleridge, in some marginalia on Donne in 1821, remarks that "in poems where the writer *thinks*, and expects the reader to do so, the sense must be understood in order to ascertain the metre."

Despite the devel. of algorithms for computer-assisted s. of electronic texts, fully automated s. is presently impossible. Further, the discovery of the meter of a poem is neither wholly objective nor determinate, nor does it consign prosody irrevocably to a formalist poetics. Since the phonological features relevant to s. are not specified by orthography, and since lines may have identical ss. but otherwise differ greatly, s. is not so much the discovery of a pattern that is "in" the poem as, rather, the reader's construction of a s. that both fits meter and reveals sense. The advantage of s. over other types of interpretive procedures is simply that it is able to tie specific semantic constructions (readings) to specific textual features.

The first requisite in scanning a line of verse is to determine how many syllables it has—i.e. which syllables are (were) pronounced and which not. This is far from obvious: every lang. has been subject to considerable variance in syllabification over the centuries, and hybrids like Eng. more than most; therefore, one must seek the best available evidence from historical phonology concerning elision and hiatus (qq.v.). The classical example in Eng. is the problem of final *-e* in Chaucer. The next procedure is to identify the linguistic structure (e.g. stressing) of the line as if it were prose, i.e. for sense. This has the virtues of recognizing that sense matters and that meter may matter less than everything, but in that it does not allow meter to matter at all, it is only a preliminary. The third is simply to identify the abstract metrical pattern. Normally a reader has some sense of what the meter might be before beginning the poem, but when the meter is not known *a priori*, one may have to test a number of lines to determine it: "the rhythm of the lines must be interpreted by the general rhythm of the piece" (Mayor, 1886). The final procedure mediates between the first two, showing how lang. accommodates itself to meter and meter in turn affects lang. (meaning). In the structuralist account of meter, the processes of metrical *promotion* and *demotion* operate to accomplish the fit. McAuley gives a two-tiered s. above each line, one for the prose rhythm (the first procedure above), one for the resultant s. (the third); knowledge of the abstract meter (the second) is assumed.

S. does not notate the meter of the whole poem; that would be trivial. If we wanted s. to denote the ideal meter underlying every line, all ss. would be the same. If we wanted s. to capture every linguistic detail of a line, no two ss. would ever be identical. Most of the lines in Shakespeare's sonnets and plays are in iambic pentameter, but these pentameters vary slightly from line to line; and it is on these subtle variations that most of Shakespeare's

art depends. What is of interest is precisely *how* meter and lang. are brought into constructive interanimation in a line, and *to what purpose.*

A s. is not a record or scoring of any one particular recitation or performance (q.v.) of a line: its aim is neither to prescribe nor even to describe, fully, any one realization, either internal (silent reading) or external (recitation). Many linguistic or intonational features that must be decided on, either before or while reciting a line of poetry—e.g. pitch patterns, pauses, durations of syllables—as well as many other paralinguistic features—e.g shrillness of voice, laughter, whispers—are left totally unspecified in s., the sole aim of which is to show the metrical pattern. On the other hand, a s. must be one possible realization; it cannot be an impossible one. It cannot flout the rules of the lang.

As for the question of how far the s., once determined, ought to be allowed to influence recitation of a line, opinions vary. Scott suggests that "prosodic definition should, as far as possible, *determine* recitation" (46), but does not draw the line as to what is and is not possible. Must recitation manifest the features noted by a s.? In other words, can one scan one way and perform another, such as by eliding extra syllables in the line in s. but articulating them in performance? Opinions differ sharply. No less a metrist than Bridges argued in the affirmative, though few have followed him. Should performances enact ss. woodenly? Modern opinion is strongly opposed, though such an artificial mode of delivery, which Allen calls "scanning pronunciation," is attested in antiquity, as reported by the grammarian Sacerdos (Keil 6.448). Still, the evidence suggests that the practice of scanning verses one way but reading them another has been more the rule than the exception since antiquity.

The demonstration of systematic patterns proves that they are an element of structure. Whether the poet composed via such elements is not strictly relevant and in most cases can never be known. It would seem reasonable that s. ought not be irrefragably severed from compositional processes, and s. procedures such as those in oral-formulaic theory (q.v.), which are able to show that units of analysis are in fact units of composition, are thereby materially strengthened. But in general the temptation to let analysis follow the pronouncements of poets is great enough a danger to warrant insistence on keeping a distance from compositional models. We have already seen the uses of keeping a distance from performance models. We must confine ourselves to demonstration of structure. Intention there may or may not be; design there certainly is.

See also COUPE; PROSODY; PYRRHIC; RELATIVE STRESS PRINCIPLE; RHYTHM; SPONDEE.

Omond; M. W. Croll, "Report of the Committee on Metrical Notation," *PMLA* 39 (1924); G. R. Stewart, *The Technique of Eng. Verse* (1930); "Eng.

Verse and What It Sounds Like," *KR* 18 (1956); W. K. Wimsatt, Jr., and M. C. Beardsley, "The Concept of Meter," *PMLA* 74 (1959); J. O. Perry, "The Temporal Analysis of Poems," *BJA* 5 (1965); J. McAuley, *Versif.: A Short Intro.* (1966); C. S. Lewis, "Metre," *Sel. Literary Essays* (1969); J. Malof, *Manual of Eng. Meters* (1970); W. S. Allen, *Accent and Rhythm* (1973); R. J. Dilligan and K. Lynn, "Computers and the Hist. of Pros.," *CE* 34 (1973); D. Schaller, "Bauformeln für akzent-rhythmische Verse und Strophen," *MitJ* 14 (1979); Scott; F. Cairns et al., "Textcode," *BALLC* 9 (1981); Brogan; D. Attridge, *The Rhythms of Eng. Poetry* (1982); H. M. Logan, "The Computer and Metrical S.," *ALLCJ* 3 (1982). T.V.F.B.

SCAZON. See CHOLIAMBUS.

SCHEME. See FIGURE, SCHEME, TROPE; RHETORIC AND POETRY.

SCHOOL OF SPENSER. A group of Eng. poets of the earlier 17th c., strongly under the influence of Edmund Spenser (1552–99). Their work is sharply distinguished from the more radical poetic movements of the time, epitomized by the Classicism of Jonson and the "metaphysical" (q.v.) style of Donne. The principal poets of the Spenserian school—Browne of Tavistock, Drayton, Wither, Giles and Phineas Fletcher, and the Scottish poets Drummond of Hawthornden and Sir William Alexander—show the influence of Spenser in their sensuous imagery, smooth meter, archaic diction, and fondness for narrative and pastoral modes of expression. They also owe to Spenser their allegorical and moral tendencies. Such ambitious narrative poems as Giles Fletcher's *Christ's Victory and Triumph* and Phineas Fletcher's *The Apollyonists* suggest Spenser's *Faerie Queene* in their pictorial quality and their stanza forms (modified Spenserian stanzas [q.v.]); they also anticipate Milton, who, occasionally echoing the Fletchers, followed them in the use of Christian material for epic purposes and who himself acknowledged his indebtedness to Spenser, whom he called *master.*—H. E. Cory, *Spenser, the School of the Fletchers, and Milton* (1912); D. Bush, *Eng. Lit. in the Earlier 17th C., 1600–1660*, 2d ed. (1962); *The Eng. Spenserians*, ed. W. B. Hunter, Jr. (1977)—anthol.; J. Grundy, *The Spenserian Poets* (1969); M. Quilligan, *Milton's Spenser* (1987). A.PR.; F.J.W.

SCHÜTTELREIM. In Ger., a rhyme, usually in a single line or couplet, which achieves witty and memorable effect by transposing ("shaking") the initial consonants of two words or syllables. The sudden sound-reversal lends itself peculiarly well to humorous and satirical ends in Ger., though it is also found in proverbs. Some, in couplets or in longer series, have remained popular quotations long after their authors have been forgotten, e.g. "Nicht jeder, der da freite zwo, ward über seine zweite froh," or "Als Gottes Atem leiser ging, schuf er den Grafen Keyserling" (attributed to Friedrich Gundolf). The shortest known S. is "Du bist Buddhist." Regine Mirsky-Tauber (*Schüttelreime*, 1904) and Anton Kippenberg (*Benno Papentrigks Schüttelreime*, 1943) have written whole cycles of light verse (q.v.) in this form. The nearest equivalent in Eng. is the Spoonerism, e.g. "You have hissed my mystery lecture; in fact, you have tasted a whole worm."—M. Hanke, *Die Schüttelreimer* (1968). T.V.F.B.; U.K.G.

SCIENCE AND POETRY.

    I. OVERVIEW
    II. HISTORICAL RELATIONS
    III. THEORETICAL RELATIONS

This article surveys the historical and theoretical relations between Western s. and p. in the post-medieval eras with emphasis on mathematics and on the physical and biological ss.

I. OVERVIEW. We may distinguish between (1) s. in p., (2) p. in s., and (3) analogies between s. and p. The first of these categories has received the most attention.

(1) S. may appear in p. as theme, as underlying worldview, and as a model for poetics. Copernican planetary theory, Darwin's evolution, Einstein's relativity, and other scientific theories have been thematized, popularized, questioned, and satirized by poets. To understand such cases of s. in p. one has to identify the scientific sources, judge the poet's grasp of them, and examine why she or he chose that theory over its competitor. But the p. should not be judged merely on the basis of the poet's understanding of the scientific theory, nor on account of his choice of it, because p. appropriates s. for its own purposes. As Mallarmé said, p. is made of words rather than ideas. Milton (see Svendsen), early 18th-c. Eng. poets (Davie), and Blake (Ault), have (mis)appropriated s. The poet is "a marauder, who ransacks the lang. of his own time and earlier" (Davie 36).

Coleridge's organicism (q.v.), Goethe's "morphological poetics," Novalis's and Valéry's "combinatorial poetics," and Pound's "vorticism" (q.v.) show that s. can offer metaphors for models in poetics.

S. may advance shifts in literary styles and movements; it may also alter the balance among the literary genres. Thus the prominence of the modern novel, for example, is indebted to s. not only because the devel. of printing and the industrial revolution aided the growth of a bourgeois reading public, but also because novels, relying on the modern authority of s., claimed to offer a more scientific way of perceiving and portraying the world. Today, the chief literary genre responding to science is the novel., esp. science-fiction. Conversely, the alternating prominence of the different ss. and scientific theories provides constantly changing inspirations and challenges to p.: Kepler's and Galileo's astronomy preoccupied the poetic imagination of the 17th c., Newton's theory that of the 18th c. The great questions for 19th c. poetry were given by the theory of evolution, for the early 20th c. by the physics of relativity theory and quantum mechanics then linguistics. The changes in the relationship between p. and s. are conditioned by the inner dynamics of each field.

(2) Symmetry and form in scientific theory and scientific creativity have been the traditional examples of p. in s. But recent studies by Anderson, Carlisle, Ghiselin and others have focused on metaphors and other figures, as well as the rhetorical strategies in scientific discourse, showing how s. too is shaped by the medium of its communication. Instead of asking whether the crit. of p. can become scientific, scholars now tend to be interested in the verbal form of s.

(3) Comparative studies of s. and p. must consider the cognitive and social functions of the two fields. P. often claims to convey an intuitive perception of truth, though this has been questioned ever since Plato's *Republic*. In the modern era, esp. since the 18th c., s. has acquired exclusive claims to knowledge, whereas p. has been searching for new, noncognitive foundations and has often come to question the moral and social consequences of s. S. and p. are now often perceived as competing social institutions.

II. HISTORICAL RELATIONS. The line between scientific and "prescientific" forms of knowledge is difficult to draw, and we can perhaps best characterize earlier knowledge if we contrast it with the organization of s. and its function in modern social and intellectual culture. In earlier cultures, incl. non-Western cultures, Cl. Greece, and European medieval culture, knowledge of the natural world was regarded as a subordinate part of a religious worldview, while modern s. strives for (if seldom achieves) autonomy.

Inasmuch as the poetry of earlier cultures expressed a worldview, by necessity it also displayed an interp. of nature. Thus the scientific and technical knowledge of early Greece is implicitly present when Homer describes the making of Achilles' shield or the travels of Odysseus; Vergil's *Georgics* and *Aeneid* portray flora and fauna as well as volcanos. Medieval cosmography is an integral part of Dante's *Divine Comedy*; Chaucer let his characters discuss alchemy (*Canon's Yeoman's Tale*), and he used astrology, astronomy, medicine, and physiognomy to give "greater verisimilitude to the characters in the eyes of his audience" (Curry XVI).

Exposition of a scientific theory in p. was less frequent. In Western culture it appeared first in Lucretius' *De rerum natura* (The Way Things Are), written sometime in the mid 1st c. B.C. Expounding the philosophy of Epicurus, Lucretius described space and the emergence of the material world from the slight swerve of a "rain" of parallel-moving atoms; he also developed ideas on me-teorology, geology, organic life, optics, and many other subjects. Although Lucretius has often been criticized, both for his scientific ideas and his use of p., his poem has nevertheless become a model of didactic p. on s., esp. in the 17th and 18th cs., when Lucretius experienced a veritable revival.

The Ren. introduced conceptually and methodologically new approaches to nature, but the wealth of nature-observations in the 14th and 15th cs. became part of an eclectic worldview with largely traditional concepts and authorities. As Paracelsus (e.g. *Liber paramirum*) exemplifies, Ren. s. aimed at a reading of nature's signs in terms of a universal system of similitudes. Its aim was to bring to light a system of resemblances in which words and things carried the same weight of evidence: "There is no difference between the visible marks that God has stamped upon the surface of the earth . . . and the legible words that the Scriptures, or the sages of Antiquity, have set down in the books preserved for us by trad." (Foucault 33).

The system of analogies that linked the microcosm to the macrocosm, the humors of the body to the four elements, and the Pythagorean cosmos to the harmony of the faculties was incorporated in the great medieval encyclopedias, which became a storehouse of p. until the "breaking of the circle" (Nicolson) in the 17th c. The bookish s. of the Ren. poets (see Schmidt) was still largely indebted to the mixed lore of these compendia. When Ronsard's orphic furor turned to "the secrets of nature and the heavens" ("Hynne de l'éternité," 1556), it sought inspiration from the mythic "demons" inherited from Neoplatonism via Ficino. P. and s. were related because both appeared in the soul as "the work of the demons" (Schmidt 78). Similarly, Maurice Sceve's didactic description of nature in *Microcosme* (1562) is indebted to Pico's Neoplatonism.

The 17th c. witnessed the full impact of the Copernican revolution, Harvey's discovery of the circulation of blood, the invention of the telescope and the microscope (Nicolson), and the appearance of Newton's *Principia*. Descartes, Hobbes, Bacon, and Leibniz gave philosophic formulation to these new scientific conceptions. P. responded with new figures of speech, new themes, new attitudes toward life, and even new conceptions of God (Nicolson, *Imagin.* 2). Thus Abraham Cowley wrote a poem "Upon Dr. Harvey" (1657), a religious apostrophe "To Light," a poetic cycle on plants, and even an ode "To the Royal Society" that praised s. for pressing "the curious Sight" into "the privatest Recess" of nature. The Royal Society welcomed Cowley as well as Denham, Dryden, and Waller among its members, and Cowley's ode accompanied Sprat's history of the Society. Yet Newton considered p. "a kind of ingenius nonsense" that supplied "pleasant pictures and agreeable visions," and Sprat expected no help from p. in scientific inquiry.

Nor were all poets as enthusiastic about s. as Cowley. Donne's "First Anniversaire" (1611) recorded the shock that "'Tis all in peeces, all cohaerence gone," because the new philosophy called "all in doubt." In the new worldview, "The Element of fire is quite put out; / The Sun is lost"; s. was hubris: "Man hath weav'd out a net, and this net throwne / Upon the Heavens, and now they are his owne." Milton's reaction was more complex. His vision of space was indebted to s. (Nicolson, *Imagin.* 93) and he made "spectacular allusions to Galileo" (Svendsen 3). Yet his poetic use of the new cosmology does not seem to have constituted an ideological commitment to it, and much of his s. was culled from outdated popular encyclopedias.

Interaction between s. and p. was most intense in the 18th and early 19th cs., when laymen could still contribute to s., and many poets—among them Mark Akenside, Erasmus Darwin, Samuel Garth, Oliver Goldsmith, Albrecht von Haller, Keats, Novalis, Achim von Arnim, and Chamisso—studied and even practiced s. A handful of scientists, notably the Rus. chemist Michail Lomonossow, wrote p. Buffon's famous Academy speech on "style" and Euler's and d'Alembert's interest in aesthetics indicate the importance of the arts to scientists.

The didactic poetry (q.v.) of the Enlightenment often chose s. as it subject. Cartesian natural philosophy was popularized in Genest's *Principes de Philosophie* (1716) and Polignac's *Antilucretius* (1747), the Leibniz-Wolffian system in Dusch's "Die Wissenschaften" (The Sciences, 1754) and, partly, in the young Wieland's "Die Natur de Dinge" (The Way Things Are, 1750). The physicotheological poems of the early 18th c. (Jones 106–37) sought to demonstrate the Divinity from the glory of nature: Blackmore's *Creation* (1712), Thomson's *Seasons* (1726–30), Smart's "On the Immensity of the Supreme Being" (1751), and the poems of Thomson's Ger. translator, Brockes, repeatedly begin with quasi-scientific descriptions of nature that avoid baroque conceits and personifications (qq.v.) and end with enthusiastic admiration for the divine craftsmanship that s. revealed. A broader category of 18th-c. p. exemplifies Baconian empirical observations of nature.

The status of s. in early 18th-c. p. may be gauged by the praise lavished on Newton. He shines not only in Pope's famous epigram ("Nature and Nature's laws lay hid in night: / God said, Let Newton be! and all was light") but also in Thomson's "Poem Sacred to the Memory of Sir Isaac Newton" (1727), Haller's "Gedanken über Vernunft, Aberglauben und Unglauben" (Thoughts about Reason, Superstition and Disbelief, 1729), Glover's prefatory poem to Pemberton's *View of Sir Isaac Newton's Philosophy* (1735), and the prefatory poems to Algarotti's *Newtonianismo per le dame* (1739). By the time he appears in the *Prelude* as a

moon-bathed statue at the young Wordsworth's Cambridge "with his prism and silent face, / The marble index of a mind for ever / Voyaging through strange seas of Thought, alone" (3.58–63), Blake and Goethe had already begun to disassemble his monument.

We may graphically observe how improvements in the mechanistic model of the physical universe slowly made spiritual forces superfluous by following in Thomson's revisions of the *Seasons* the displacements of references to God's hand by careful descriptions of nature. This growth of the mechanistic worldview, and its social, moral, and religious implications, disturbed several mid-18th-c. poets. For Haller, the most prominent scientist among the poets of the age, only a leap could lead from earth to heaven and from s. to p.: the great poems of his youth ("Die Alpen," "Über den Ursprung des Übels") found no rational resolutions for burning social, theological, and ethical issues, and Haller's poetic vein dried up once he became professor of physiology and a scientific mechanist in Göttingen. In the second half of the century, the poetic genre of s. is no longer the philosophic poem but rather nature poetry, followed by satires against medicine and physicians.

In spite of occasional efforts to versify s. (Erasmus Darwin, *Zoonomia, The Botanic Garden;* Goethe, *Metamorphose der Pflanzen* 1790), p. now became less concerned with the mediation of knowledge. Ironically, Alexander Gottlieb Baumgarten founded aesthetics by claiming that the arts offered knowledge through the senses, but this cognitive function of p. was soon deeply challenged by Kant (*Aesthetica*, 1750–58), who radically severed p. from s., asserting that concepts in art had no cognitive function and that judgments of taste (q.v.) were no s. "Aesthetic ideas" could only *stimulate* thought and harmonize the faculties of the mind. The post-Kantian history of p. and poetics (see ROMANTIC AND POSTROMANTIC POETICS) may be described in terms of two trads.: the first denied cognitive power to p. and conceived of it as an autonomous construct (see AUTONOMY), while the second continued to assign moral and didactic tasks to p., incl. the mediation of s. to society at large.

Romanticism (q.v.) "was a protest on behalf of value" (Whitehead 94), a defense of a "qualitative s., in which nature (q.v.) can be congruent with man against a measuring, numbering s. which alienates the creator of s. from his own creation by total objectification of nature" (Gillispie 199). Indeed, the romantics doubted that facts could be valueless and discourses on nature fully objective. Wordsworth's "The world is too much with us," Keats' "Lamia" (2.229ff.), Poe's "Sonnet to Science," and other romantic poems assert that s. has emptied nature of its mystery, and they plead for a mythopoetic discourse to reanimate nature.

Yet, some romantics could treasure s. for its attachment to nature, and their protest was directed often not against its alienating effect but against its intrusion upon nature. Wordsworth thought that the affections of the scientist dealing with "particular parts of nature" were comparable to those of the poets when "conversing" with "general nature." He believed that if s. produced a "material revolution" in the human condition, poetry would be ready to follow, "carrying sensations into the midst of the objects of the s. itself. The remotest discoveries of the Chemist, the Botanist, or Mineralogist, will be as proper objects of the Poet's art as any upon which it can be employed" (Preface to *Lyrical Ballads*). If he asserted that "Our meddling intellect / Mis-shapes the beauteous forms of things," and that "we murder to dissect" ("The Tables Turned," 1798), he meant by "meddling" both a violation of beauty and a cognitive error caused by our propensity to impose unfitting or destructive schemes upon nature.

This was also Blake's and Goethe's central motivation in attacking Newton and Newtonian mechanism. They argued, albeit from different perspectives, that matter was animated by living forces, hence that abstract ratiocination could not lead to genuine knowledge. For Blake, as Frye and Ault have shown, the Fall meant a displacement of the imagination (q.v.), a hardening and narrowing of the senses, a self-enclosure of man leading to a "Philosophy of Five Senses." Satan was the Prince "of the Wheels of Heaven, to turn the Mills day and night," he was Newton's "Pantocrator," his supreme God "weaving the Woof of Locke" (*Milton*, 4.9–11). Moreover, "if the doors of perception were cleansed every thing would appear to man as it is, infinite" (*Marriage* 14). Regaining a "sweet S." would mean attention to particulars and the abandonment of mechanical causation: "Every Natural Effect has a Spiritual Cause, and Not a Natural; for a Natural Cause only seems" (*Milton* 26). As part of his strategy of liberation, Blake appropriated and transformed such reified Newtonian metaphors as "void," "attraction," and "atom," integrating them into his own mythology (Ault).

Perception of form led Goethe not only to the discovery that human beings also have an intermaxillary bone but also to comparative anatomy, and to the study of metamorphoses in plants, insects, rocks, and clouds. In *Der Versuch als Vermittler von Objekt und Subjekt* (The Experiment as Mediator between Object and Subject, 1792) he cautioned that only patient experimentation could safeguard against the premature reification of abstract thought, and he came to regard Newtonian color theory as an arrogant coercion of nature. Thus Goethe claimed in his *Farbenlehre* (Color Theory, 1810) that Newton's *experimentum crucis*, the kingpin in his demonstration of color, "placed nature on the rack" "in order to force her to confess what he [Newton] had previously already fixed in his mind" (Polemical Part &114). The symbols of s., like those of p., must not be confused with the symbolized: the physicist ought to be

"wary of converting perceptions into concepts and concepts into words, proceeding then by treating these words as if they were objects" (Didactical Part &716). Goethe's use of concepts like polarity, metamorphosis, and enhancement (*Steigerung*) did not always heed this warning, but he has given in the final act of *Faust II* a magnificent image of the moral ambiguities in man's scientific control over nature.

A similar concern with lang. informs all romantic poetry and poetics, revealing an awareness of the figural limitations on knowledge, the ambiguity and opaqueness of linguistic signs, and the resultant gulf between mind and nature. As in the case of Goethe and Wordsworth, holistic and pantheistic visions of unity with nature were consistently undermined by an awareness of separation.

While the figurality of lang. makes precise representation (q.v.) impossible, the irrepressible urge to produce figures suggests that the mind is an *Ideenwebstuhl* or "loom of ideas" (Novalis) that weaves figural tapestries of the world. In this conception, new areas of knowledge are "colonized" by metaphoric transpositions from previous experiences. The "magic wand of analogy," a heritage from the Ren., was the poetic means whereby Novalis wished to construct a counter-book to the scientific encyclopedias of the Enlightenment (Neubauer).

If Shelley regarded poetic lang. as "vitally metaphorical," he did not wish to revive baroque personifications and conceits, which he disdained as much as had the 18th c. Figural lang. was for him not an embellishment but a cognitive force that "marks the before unapprehended relations of things and perpetuates their apprehension." Poetry is "at once the centre and circumference of knowledge; it is that which comprehends all s., and that to which all s. must be referred" because it is the quintessence of figurative lang. (*Defense of Poetry*).

Some romantics found metaphoric lang. in s., but they often imported metaphors from s. to formulate their poetics. Organicism (q.v.) is a biological metaphor they adopted to describe both the working of the imagination and the structure of poems. Following Kant, Coleridge regarded "pleasure, not truth" as poetry's immediate object, and he derived that pleasure from the perception of organization in the poem: p. offers "such delight from the *whole*, as is compatible with a distinct gratification from each component *part*" (*Biographia literaria*, ch. 14). Less known but equally important is the mathematical metaphor, which assumes a double meaning in romantic thought: as a pure construct of the mind and as a Pythagorean metaphor of universal harmony. Wordsworth, for instance, values geometry as a "sense / Of permanent and universal sway" but also as "an independent world, / Created out of pure intelligence" (*Prelude* 6.130–31, 166–67). This dual role turns mathematics into a simile of lang. in Novalis' *Monolog* (1799?): "lang. behaves like mathematical formulas—they form a world of their own, they play only with themselves, express nothing but their own wonderful nature, and for this very reason they are expressive . . . they mirror the strange interplay of objects." On the model of combinatorial mathematics Novalis developed a poetics of verbal combinations (Neubauer). Like organicism, this poetics valorizes the syntactic, "formulaic" patterns of lang. over its semantic-referential function, but it is a figure of mathematical and musical rather than biological patterns.

Throughout much of the 19th c., s. is a theme rather than a metaphoric pattern of p., and the central topics of later 19th-c. p. devolve from the theory of evolution and the consequent crisis of faith. Tennyson's *In Memoriam* (1850) strives to believe "where we cannot prove" (1.4). The initial conjecture that the stars may "blindly run" (3.5) and nature be callously wasteful ("A thousand types are gone: / I care for nothing, all shall go" [56.2–5]) is finally superseded by a pre-Darwinian vision of evolution based on industrial progress and Lyell's *Principles of Geology* (which Tennyson read in 1837). Thomas Hardy, born a generation later, fell into deep pessimism after reading Darwin, but his p. moved toward a final belief in which that pessimism became mitigated by a ray of hope in an "evolutionary meliorism" aided by s. Perhaps the most important impact of 19th-c. s. on p. was indirect, related to the decline of religion and faith brought about by s. As Arnold wrote in "Dover Beach":

The sea of faith
Was once, too, at the full, and round
        earth's shore
Lay like the folds of a bright girdle
        furl'd;
But now I only hear
Its melancholy, long, withdrawing roar.

Like many others, Arnold concluded that the truths of religion and the Bible could not be literal: "The strongest part of our religion today is its unconscious poetry" (Intro. to *The Eng. Poets*, 1880). Conversely, p. assumed for many a quasi-religious significance.

In Whitman's more positive vision, scientists are among "the lawgivers of poets and their construction underlies the structure of every perfect poem" (Preface to *Leaves of Grass*). This echoes Wordsworth and Shelley, though they still considered p. constitutive of s. Poetry's task, according to Matthew Arnold, was to serve as "a criticism of life" (*Wordsworth*), as a mediation "of natural s. to man's instinct for conduct," to emotions and moral action (*Lit. and S.*).

In contrast to this "humanist" thematization of s., we may trace a "formalist" trad. of s. in p. from Novalis through Poe and the symbolists to the modernists. Following Kant, Poe posited "chasmal differences between the truthful and the poetical

modes of inculcation." P. has only "incidental" concerns "with Duty or with Truth," wrote Poe in *The Poetic Principle* (1850); the symbolists, starting with Baudelaire, enthusiastically endorsed his view. Surrendering cognitive claims and a direct rivalry with s., symbolist poetry chose music and mathematics as its models. Mallarmé made actual calculations in his sketches for a prototypical Book, and mathematics is at the heart of his *summa*, the poem "Un coup de dés jamais n'abolira le hasard" (A Dice-Throw Never Will Abolish Chance, 1897). Just as the algebraic formula is never exhausted by any of its arithmetic concretizations, so too the particular word-combination of a poem is only one instantiation of the prosodic skeleton. To flesh out this skeleton is to make semantic choices and to deviate from a conventional syntax that exploits "only a part of the combinations compatible with its rules" (Valéry, *Stéphane Mallarmé*). P. emerges from the realm of the possible by means of "dice-throws," i.e. experiments with permutations: "Syntax, which is calculation, assumed the rank of a muse" (Valéry, *Je disais quelquefois à Stéphane Mallarmé*, 1944).

If writing was, according to Mallarmé's "Le Tombeau d'Edgar Poe" (1875), a purification of "the Words of the tribe," for Valéry it was a cleansing of "the verbal situation," whereby the poet proceeded "like a surgeon who sterilizes his hands and prepares the area to be operated on." Poetry is "a kind of machine for producing the poetic state of mind by means of words" (*Poésie et pensée abstraite*, 1939). Valéry studied s. and mathematics, knew of plans by Lullus, Leibniz, and others for a calculus of ideas, and thought that algebra and geometry would become models for a future lang. (*Avant-propos à la connaissance de la déesse*, 1920). P. was a calculus of words, a *poésie pure* without determinate contents and messages, a verbal geometry animated by figural "substitutions" and "contracted notations." Since figural lang. always exceeds the intentions of the writer, poets move unaware "in an order of possible relations and transformations" (*Questions de Poésie*, 1935).

Valéry's Cartesianism was untypical, yet his views were shared by others: Ortega y Gasset thought that p. "has become the higher algebra of metaphors" (*La deshumanizacion del arte*, 1925), and T. S. Eliot noted that "art may be said to approach the conditions of s." in "depersonalization." The young Pound sought a s. of literary scholarship "which will weigh Theocritus and Mr. Yeats with one balance"; he considered p. as "a sort of inspired mathematics which gives us equations . . . for the human emotions" (*Spirit of Romance*).

Pound's "inspired mathematics" brings together two directions in modernist p. that usually went their separate ways. On the one hand, the modernists tended to valorize "abstraction" over emotional "empathy" (terms from Worringer's essay on art in 1908); they disdained pseudo-romantic inspired madness and took scientific detachment as a model: "The function of an art, is to free the intellect from the tyranny of the affects . . . to strengthen the perceptive faculties and free them from encumbrance"; "what the analytical geometer does for space and form, the poet does for consciousness" (Pound, *The Wisdom of Poetry*). Imagism, vorticism, Rilke's *Dinggedicht* (qq.v.), and Gottfried Benn's *poeisis* all demand hard, clean, exact, and concrete images.

On the other hand, we find in Pound, Eliot, Yeats, Lawrence, Rilke, and other modernists a critique of urban civilization and a hostility to s. and technology that led to explorations of the occult, even to fascination with fascism and war. Interest in s. and modes of irrationalism often existed side by side. Hart Crane, who attempted to synthesize s. and p. in the manner of Whitman, sang of "New verities, new inklings in the velvet hummed / of dynamos" ("Cape Hatteras") but was unable to reconcile the mysticism of Ouspensky with the "organic naturalism" he found in Whitehead. Marinetti and the It. futurists violently rejected the humanistic trad. and advocated an irrational adulation of "geometric and mechanical splendor" (manifesto of March 15, 1914), the beauty of the machines and technology. Vladimir Majakovskij, who was associated with the Rus. futurist movement, admired "this mile of steel" in the Brooklyn Bridge, for "upon it, my visions come to life, erect— / here's a fight for construction instead of style, / an austere disposition of bolts and steel" ("Brooklyn Bridge," 1925). In the Twenties, modernist movements in art and architecture such as Rus. constructivism (q.v.), the Dutch Stijl, and the Ger. Bauhaus, turned to s. and technology and produced a small but significant body of related p.

Concern that poets may remain fixated on a pre-scientific, "Magical View of the World" was at the heart of I. A. Richards' important essay on *S. and P.* in 1926. Richards accepted the neo-positivistic view that the words of a poem constituted "pseudo-statements" (q.v.) whose scientific truth was irrelevant, but went on to suggest that the "experience itself, the tide of impulses sweeping through the mind, is the source and the sanction of the words" (1970: 33), and that these words could reproduce "a similar play of interests" in "suitable readers." This communication of experience and interests was essential because s. had "neutralized nature" and destroyed its magical view. The p. of a scientific age should not hold on to "magical" beliefs like Yeats' spiritualism and Lawrence's "primitive mentality"; the poetic pseudo-statements had to be cut free from belief and put in the service of those interests, which lay beyond the purview of s. Lawrence Durrell, who related relativity theory to modern p. (*A Key to Modern British Poetry*), remarked in a similar vein: "S. is the p. of the intellect and p. the s. of the heart's affections" ("Consequential Data," *Balthazar*).

Richards argued that p. was to deal not with the ideas of s. but with human experience and interests inasmuch as they are affected by s. and technology. Indeed, in the later part of this century s. has most frequently entered p. in terms of its social and ecological effects. Robert Frost, for instance, doubted that s. can assure the survival of the human race ("The Star-Splitter"; "Skeptic") and he asked whether s. will show us "how by rocket we may hope to steer / To some star off there say a half light-year / Through temperature of absolute zero" ("Why Wait for S."). A similar skepticism is often evident in the reaction of poets to man's landing on the moon and to the increasing problems of the environment.

Save notable exceptions, such as Queneau's "Petite cosmogonie portative" (1950), p. rarely assumes the role of popularizing s. today. S. fiction is typically a prose genre. Like John Updike, who wrote his "News from the Underworld" after "blinking" his way through "The Detection of Neutral Weak Currents" in *Scientific American*, the poets of this century are often intimidated by the technical terminology of physics. Nevertheless, poets do respond frequently to the broader philosophical issues raised by s. Robert Duncan and Charles Olson read not only Whitehead but also Norbert Wiener. Cybernetics suggested to Duncan that lang. was a code whose biological analogy was DNA: "When the DNA appeared you'd have thought you'd written it yourself!"

S. and mathematics continues to stimulate the structuring of poetry. Aleatory p., first conceived by Mallarmé and used by Tristan Tzara to write dada (q.v.) poetry, has been systematically explored in the 1960s by the writes and mathematicians in Oulipo (q.v.). More recently, computers have been enlisted for the automated production of poetry (see COMPUTER POETRY).

II. THEORETICAL RELATIONS. Historians, philosophers, and sociologists bring general perspectives to the study of s. and p. and their interrelations. In particular, the philosophical interps. of relativity theory, quantum mechanics, the uncertainty principle, new conceptions of the history and sociology of s., and the growth of literary theory have opened stimulating new possibilities for joint studies of s. and p.

The logical positivism of the early decades of the 20th c. postulated that scientific knowledge was cumulative and ultimately reducible to value-free empirical observations or logical propositions. Newer approaches question these aims and premises by focusing on the psychology, sociology, and history of s.

Karl Popper's *The Logic of Scientific Discovery* (Ger. ed. 1934) was the first to challenge logical positivism by turning from models and postulates to the actual norms used in scientific research. While the logical positivists advocated induction, Popper prefaced his book with two mottos: the first, adopted from Novalis, praises imaginative hypotheses ("theories are nets: only he who casts will catch"); the second, by Lord Acton, encourages scientists to study the history of s., the logic of discovery, the detection of error, and the role of hypotheses. According to Popper, s. proceeds by inventing theories and testing them empirically; s. casts and refines the net of theory to "catch what we call the world: to rationalize, to explain, and to master it" (59). Although both p. and s. start with an invention, s. is "demarcated" from p. because its inventions are subject to efforts to falsify it, whereas poetic inventions cannot be falsified. S. progresses, according to another title by Popper, through *Conjectures and Refutation*—and the second of these terms is as important as the first.

Popper's focus on the progress of s. stimulated more historical theories, foremost among them Thomas Kuhn's *The Structure of Scientific Revolutions* (2d ed., 1970). Kuhn proposed that "mature" ss. normally function within paradigms, which enable researchers to skirt debates about fundamentals and concentrate on the paradigm's "puzzles." At a certain point, however, the paradigm can no longer accommodate the new data and the ensuing revolution will install a new one.

Critics have replied that no paradigm in the history of s. was ever universally accepted and that competition among them is "normal." This implied that the demarcation criterion of s. has to be discarded, for debates about fundamentals are now seen to be as much a feature of s. as of philosophy, history, or the arts. Kuhn himself had already questioned the view that scientific debates are purely rational. The paradigms of normal s., he maintains, are shielded by the community of experts and their institutions (education, textbooks, professional societies, journals); during revolutions the new paradigm is so "incommensurate" with the old that the transition can only be achieved by means of a "gestalt switch" or a "conversion experience" (150). This implies a critique of traditional notions of scientific progress: "normal" s. appears to progress only to those who solve puzzles within the paradigm but not to those that adhere to a competing one, whereas revolutions create the *impression* of progress because "the outcome of revolution must be progress" to the victors (166). Progress is in both cases relative; it "lies simply in the eye of the beholder" (163).

Kuhn's theory has been received skeptically by theorists of s. but enthusiastically by those literary scholars who thought that his notion of scientific change could be applied to the shifts in literary conventions, styles, movements, and modes of crit. Hans Robert Jauss has proposed a rather crude "paradigmatic" history of literary theory, Grant Webster has substituted "Charters" for "paradigms" to write a history of postwar Am. crit., and Stanley Fish has developed an institutional approach to lit. which is in several ways indebted to Kuhn (see READER-RESPONSE CRITICISM). But Kuhn is uneasy about such adaptations (*Essential*

Tension 341), and he sees a contrast between the conservatism of s. as a profession and the value that is placed in the arts on "innovation for innovation's sake" (350). Since p. exists more and more in a multi-paradigmatic state and the ss. develop in Kuhn's model from an "immature" stage of conflicting paradigms to a mature one with a single paradigm, his vision implies that the histories of s. and p. run in contrary directions.

Other contemp. theorists see s. more in terms of its cultural context. According to Feyerabend's "dadaist" view, the shaping power of personal drives, poetry, myth, religion, and magic is a most beneficial antidote to the tendency of "pure" s. toward insularity and aridity. Lepenies suggests that lit. may serve as a pool of scientific ideas, while Serres, whose work is largely on the relation between s. and lit., has repeatedly shown that poetic works (e.g. Lucretius' *De rerum natura*) imply or anticipate scientific theories. Foucault sees the arts and the sciences, their institutionalizations, and their interactions in terms of power relations. Though conflict is thus at the heart of his conception of history, he nevertheless speaks of coherent "epistemes," within which the discourses of s., p., and other cultural manifestations reveal common structures (see HISTORICISM). In contrast to *Geistesgeschichte*, where relations within and between periods are organic, Foucault's history is characterized by recurrent fundamental ruptures.

"Progress," "fact," and "truth," the traditional demarcations of s. from the arts, have all now become problematic. If scientific observations and theorizing are now seen to be "value laden," swayed by psychological, social, and political forces, and therefore less securely objective, s. seems to be closer to p., the arts, and the humanities. The concept of s. seems to have moved from positivistic monism toward a conceptual pluralism that roughly parallels the change within literary theory from positivism via New Criticism (q.v.) toward today's pluralism (q.v.).

The study of s. as well as poetry has refocused attention from the structure of the subject matter to its mode of production, and this has brought new prominence to psychology and sociology. Feyerabend, like Brecht, attributes Galileo's success not to the intrinsic merit of his ideas but to his ambition, drive, cunning, and rhetorical power. James Watson's account of the discovery of DNA (*The Double Helix*, 1986) highlights the role of rivalry with a father-figure and "siblings." Scientific change is perceived today as a process regulated by the conventions (q.v.) of its institutions. Though scientific institutions have an identity of their own, their structure and inner functioning resemble the institutions of lit. and other cultural phenomena, and they too are embedded in the larger institutions of society. Relying on recent sociological approaches to s. and p., future studies could compare their formation and movements;

their forms of patronage; the role that class, race, and gender (see Fox-Keller) play in each; their modes of printing, distributing, and reading; their modes of training; their conventions of crit. and scholarship; and so on. Such studies, all comparative approaches to s. and p., should grant each field its identity. More specifically, recent sociological and poetic approaches to s. must not lead to the conclusion that s. is mere socially negotiated metaphoric lang. A genuine dialogue between students of s. and p. can only come about if it is accepted that s., however metaphoric and socially constructed, has the powers of both prediction and control over nature. See also BELIEF AND POETRY; MEANING, POETIC; THEORY.

BIBLIOGRAPHIES: *The Relations of Lit. and S.: An Annot. Bibl. of Scholarship, 1880–1980*, ed. W. Schatzberg et al. (1987).

HISTORY AND CITICISM: A. N. Whitehead, *S. and the Mod. World* (1925); L. Stevenson, *Darwin Among the Poets* (1932); I. A. Richards, *S. and P.*, 2d ed. (1935), rev. as *Poetries and Sciences* (1970); A. O. Lovejoy, *The Great Chain of Being* (1936); D. G. James, *Scepticism and P.* (1937); A. M. Schmidt, *La Poésie scientifique en France au 16e siècle* (1938); A. Gode, *Natural S. in Ger. Romanticism* (1941); M. H. Nicolson, *Newton Demands the Muse* (1946), *S. and Imagination* (1956), *The Breaking of the Circle*, 2d ed. (1962); F. W. Conner, *Cosmic Optimism: The Interp. of Evolution by Am. Poets from Emerson to Robinson* (1949); N. H. Pearson, "The Am. Poet in Relation to S.," *AQ* 1 (1949); D. Bush, *S. and Eng. P.* (1950), "S. and Lit." *17th-C. S. and the Arts*, ed. H. H. Rhys (1961); H. H. Waggoner, *The Heel of Elohim: S. and Values in Mod. Am. P.* (1950); Abrams, esp. ch. 11; B. Ifor Evans, *Lit. and S.* (1954); K. Svendsen, *Milton and S.* (1956); J. Bronowski, *S. and Human Values* (1956); *Lit. and S.: Proc. of the Triennial Congress of the Internat. Fed. of Mod. Langs. and Lits., 1954* (1956); C. P. Snow, *The Two Cultures and the Scientific Revolution* (1959); K. Popper, *The Logic of Scientific Discovery* (1959); W. Curry, *Chaucer and the Med. Ss.*, rev. ed. (1960); C. C. Gillispie, *The Edge of Objectivity* (1960); P. Ginestier, *The Poet and the Machine*, tr. M. Friedman (1961); F. R. Leavis, "Two Cultures? The Significance of C. P. Snow," *Spectator* 208 (1962); A. Huxley, *Lit. and S.* (1963); D. Davie, *The Lang. of S. and the Lang. of Lit. 1700–1740* (1963); W. P. Jones, *The Rhet. of S.: A Study of Scientific Ideas and Imagery in 18th-C. Eng. P.* (1966); H. R. Jauss, "Paradigmawechsel in der Literaturwissenschaft," *Ling. Berichte* 1 (1969); T. S. Kuhn, *The Structure of Scientific Revolutions*, 2d ed. (1970), *The Essential Tension* (1977); M. Foucault, *The Order of Things* (Eng. tr. 1971); *Mathematik und Dichtung*, ed. H. Kreutzer and R. Gunzenhauser, 4th ed. (1971); K. Richter, *Literatur und Naturwissenschaft* (1972); *Organic Form*, ed. G. S. Rousseau (1972); W. Schatzberg, *S. in the Ger. Enlightenment* (1973); D. D. Ault, *Visionary Physics: Blake's Response to Newton* (1974); P. Feyerabend,

Against Method (1975); M. T. Ghiselin, "Poetic Biology: A Defense and Manifesto," *NLH* 7 (1976); E. Miner, "That Lit. is a Kind of Knowledge," *CI* 2 (1976); M. Serres, *La Naissance de la physique dans le texte de Lucrèce* (1977); G. S. Rousseau, "Lit. and S.: The State of the Field," *Isis* 69 (1978); W. Lepenies, "Der Wissenschaftler als Autor: über konservierende Funktionen der Literatur," *Akzente* 25 (1978); J. Neubauer, *Symbolismus und symbolische Logik* (1978), "Lit. and S.: Their Metaphors and their Metamorphoses," *YCGL* 32 (1983); G. Webster, *The Republic of Letters: A Hist. of Postwar Am. Literary Opinion* (1979); E. F. Carlisle, "Lit., S., and Lang.," *Pre/Text* 1 (1980); *Medicine and Lit.*, ed. E. R. Peschel (1980); E. Proffitt, "S. and Romanticism," *GaR* 34 (1980); W. C. Anderson, "Figurative Lang. and the Scientific Ideal," *Neophil* 65 (1981), "The Rhet. of Scientific Lang.: An Example from Lavoisier," *MLN* 96 (1981); T. Levere, *P. Realized in Nature: Samuel Taylor Coleridge and Early 19th-C. S.* (1981); *Victorian S. and Victorian Values*, ed. J. Paradis and T. Postlewait (1981); I. F. A. Bell, *Critic as Scientist: The Modernist Poetics of Ezra Pound* (1981); H. Eichner, "The Rise of Mod. S. and the Genesis of Romanticism," *PMLA* 97 (1982); G. Slusser and G. Guffey, "Lit. and S.," *Interrelations of Lit.*, ed. J.-P. Barricelli and J. Gibaldi (1982); *S. and Lit.*, spec. iss. *BuR* 27,2 (1983); M. Greenberg, "Blake's 'S,'" *SECC* 12 (1983); W. Koch, *P. and S.* (1983); *Poems of S.*, ed. J. Heath-Stubbs and P. Salman (1984); *Philosophy of S. and Literary Theory*, spec. iss. *NLH* 17, 1 (1985); E. F. Keller, *Reflections on Gender and S.* (1985); *Langs. of Nature: Critical Essays on S. and Lit.*, ed. L. Jordanova (1986)—with bibl.; *S. and the Imagination*, spec. iss. *Annals of Scholarship* 4, 1 (1986); H. Kenner, *The Mechanic Muse* (1987); W. D. Shaw, *The Lucid Veil* (1987); L. M. Steinman, *Made in America: S., Technology, and Am. Modernist Poets* (1987); *Lit. and S.*, spec. iss. *HSL* 19, 1 (1987); W. Paulson, *The Noise of Culture: Literary Texts in a World of Information* (1988); J. P. Russo, *I. A. Richards* (1989). J.N.

SCOP is the OE term, along with "gleeman," for the professional entertainer, a harpist and poet-singer and normally a member of a royal household, who was the shaper and conservator in England of Old Germanic poetic trad. He was of an old and honored class, sharing with his audience a critical interest in his craft; he commanded a mastery of the complex oral-formulaic materials (see ORAL POETRY; ORAL-FORMULAIC THEORY) of Old Germanic prosody (see GERMAN PROSODY; ENGLISH PROSODY). His repertory included more than encomiastic court verse: he was also a folk historian; and his narrative celebrations of heroic boldness and sacrifice, mingled with lyrical reflection and secular or Christian morality, have been preserved in later written forms as a central part of the Anglo-Saxon poetic corpus. There are no extant full-length biographies of OE scops, as there are of some of the Icelandic court poets, for instance; but a fictional biography in verse of one Widsith, together with a quasi-autobiographical lyric by a certain Deor, afford glimpses of the bard's social status and of some of his professional techniques. It is likely, however, that the transmission of verse depended less upon the personality and talent of an individual s. than upon the formulaic materials with which he worked, the cooperative appreciation of his audience, and their common familiarity with traditional themes. It is sometimes hard to distinguish between the art of popular and courtly poetry, between the art of a court gleeman and that perhaps of a chieftain who might take up the harp and recite a lay himself; or that of a warrior-singer whose function as a singer would be incidental to his personal knowledge of a battle; or even that of a humble person like Cædmon (Cædman), described in Bede's *Historia Ecclesiastica* (A.D. 721), who had no training as a singer but who nevertheless developed the art of narrative verse on Christian themes in what must have been, technically, a thoroughly traditional manner.—L. F. Anderson, *The Anglo-Saxon S.* (1903); W. Wissman, "Skop," *Sitzungsberichte der Dt. Akad. der Wiss. zu Berlin* (1935); D. Whitelock, *The Audience of* Beowulf (1951); K. von See, "Skop und Skald," *GRM* 14 (1964); E. Werlich, "Der westgermanische Skop," *ZDP* 86 (1967); J. Opland, *Anglo-Saxon Oral Poetry* (1980).

J.B.B.; T.V.F.B.

SCOTTISH CHAUCERIANS or MAKARS. A name applied to a group of S. poets of the 15th and 16th c. whose work, although the freshest and most original Eng. poetry of the period, shows a common indebtedness to the example of Chaucer. The most important S. C. were King James I of Scotland, Robert Henryson, William Dunbar, Gavin Douglas, and Sir David Lindsay, and of these, Henryson and Dunbar were poets of major importance. Henryson is remembered for *Robene and Makyne*, a superb pastoral, and for *The Testament of Cresseid*, a profound and moving elaboration and continuation of Chaucer's *Troilus and Criseyde*. Dunbar, a poet of wider range, wrote elaborate occasional verse, biting satires, and such memorable short poems as his famous elegiac *Lament for the Makaris*. In formal terms, the S. C. continued the vogue of the 7-line stanza introduced into Eng. poetry by Chaucer; indeed, the name for this form, *rhyme royal* (q.v.), was once thought to have been derived from its use by King James I in his poem *The Kingis Quair*. See SCOTTISH POETRY; see also COURTLY MAKERS.—H. S. Bennett, *Chaucer and the 15th C.* (1947), ch. 6.7; G. G. Smith, "The S. C.," *CHEL*, v. 2 (1949); C. S. Lewis, *Eng. Lit. in the 16th C.* (1954); D. Fox, "The S. C.," *Chaucer and Chaucerians*, ed. D. S. Brewer (1966); A. M. Kinghorn, *Middle Scots Poets* (1970); G. Kratzmann, *Anglo-Scottish Literary Relations, 1430–1550* (1980); W. Scheps and J. A. Looney, *The Middle Scots Poets: A Ref. Guide* (1986); L. A. Ebin, *Illumi-*

nator, Makar, Vates (1988). R.D.T.

SCOTTISH GAELIC POETRY. The origins of S. G. p. are naturally identical with those of Ir. (see IRISH POETRY), since both langs. derive from a common Celtic source. This identity is preserved in classical or "bardic" poetry, which continued to be written without significant regional variation in both countries, up to the 17th c. in Ireland and up to the 18th in Scotland (which held the cultural status of a province vis-á-vis the mother country). This fact, as well as the destruction of mss., has to be considered when noting the comparative paucity of poems of S. provenance or authorship. Nevertheless, there are poems connected with Scotland extant from as early as the 11th or 12th c. Identity is constituted by the same literary dialect, the same expression of "heroic" values, the same metrical forms (although G. is a stressed lang., cl. poetry, based on Med. Lat. verse, observes regularity of syllable count), the same rigorous and complex rules of ornamentation. Not all poems of course conform to this austere standard. Poetry which utilizes an easier, modified technique is fairly common, whether written by members of the hereditary caste of learned men who had undergone the arduous training of the bardic schools or by members of the aristocracy who had not but at least had some facility for composing competent verse. All these features of style are admirably displayed in the earliest and principal compilation of cl. verse to have survived in Scotland, the Book of the Dean of Lismore (ca. 1512–26). It also provides a fair sample of the range and variety of the themes of bardic verse: encomia of court poets for their patrons, satire, religious poetry, "ballads" of Fionn and Oisein, (formally, the G. "ballad," in this context, belongs with the rest of bardic poetry), moral and didactic verse, and poetry in the *amour courtois* trad. This last genre, Continental in origin, mediated by the Anglo-Normans but grafted on a native root, establishes European dimensions of the poetry, as do other kinds influenced directly by Lat. The excellence of bardic verse lies in its highly developed lang., in its sophisticated and allusive style, and above all in the elaborate and subtly modulated music of its intricate metrical patterns. Its limitations, on the other hand, inhere neither in subject matter nor technique but rather in a formalism of conventions inseparable from the office of the professional poet, that of public panegyrist to the great men of his society.

The cl. poets were by definition literate; their counterparts, the vernacular poets, on the whole were not, and with some exceptions their work has been recovered from oral trad. by 18th-c. and later collectors. But too much can be made of this disjunction. Vernacular poets continue to express many of the attitudes of cl. poetry. Irregularly stressed meters, derived from the syllabic versification of literate poets, survived demotically.

Among regularly stressed meters, one of the most interesting, because it is restricted to Scotland and closely associated with vernacular panegyric, is the so-called Strophic meter (minimally, two-stress lines followed by a three-stress line, though extensions and elaborations occur). The two great early practitioners of this form whose work has survived, Mairi Nighean Alasdair Ruaidh (ca. 1615–1707) and Iain Lom (ca. 1620–1710), are not innovators. Although the latter is exercised by national issues, both are clan poets composing in a panegyric trad., and both clearly have the security of established practice behind them—perhaps stretching back to a point anterior to the introduction of Lat. learning. The rhetoric of their verse at its best has a splendidly affirmative quality.

The anthology known as the Fernaig Ms., compiled between 1688 and 1693, contains distinctive examples of poems (religious, political, elegiac, etc.) that help to point the steps, in style and lang., between cl. and vernacular verse, while oral poetry, in many ways the demotic mainstream throughout, has continued to be composed up to the present.

The ballads traditionally attributed to Oisein son of Fionn exist in both literary and oral form. James MacPherson's spurious "translations" of these (pub. 1760–65) are loosely based on, among other sources, collections made from oral recitation, beginning in the early 18th c. The Ossianic Controversy itself stimulated further collections of all kinds of poetry and music. The first phase of this continued into the early 19th c.; thereafter, important collections were made intermittently throughout the 19th and 20th cs.

In the 18th c. a fresh dimension was added to the scope and expressiveness of S. G. p. by Alexander MacDonald (1700–70), the pervervid nationalist and poet of the "Forty-Five," and by Duncan Bán Macintyre (1724–1812), the hunter-poet. A highly educated man drawing on all the resources of G., MacDonald is the outstanding figure of his age. The resonant verse of John MacCodrum (1693–1779) seems more of the 17th c. by comparison, but the controlled, detailed naturalism of Macintyre's *Praise of Ben Dorain* embodies a movement away from clan poetry. These two were completely oral poets, as was Rob Donn (1714–78), the best satirist in vernacular G. The poetry of William Ross (1762–90) manifests a wider sensibility which certainly owes something to his learning in Eng. and in the Cl. langs. Ross's tender, anguished love poems merit a special place in the history of G. lit.

G. verse fell to its nadir in the 19th c. when the breakup of G. society due to Eng. intrusion and forced emigration partially destroyed the G. spirit. Moreover, a good deal of the published work of the time is the product of urbanized Gaels influenced by romanticism and other alien conventions. Yet an appreciable body of vigorous oral poetry continued to be composed, in which the verse of Mary MacPherson of Skye (1821–98) is notable.

The hist. of the Gaels in Scotland has left a profound impression on G. p. Anglicization of the S. dynasty in the 11th c. and the destruction of the Lordship of the Isles in the 15th are two markers in a process of ethnocide which produced a seige mentality. This stimulated the devel. of panegyric praising the caste of aristocratic warrior-hunters who protected and rewarded their people. Organized in sets of conventional images or formulas which work as a semiotic code, panegyric is not only a form but a pervasive style in G. p., particularly ca. 1600 to 1800, but its workings are traceable even in contemp. poetry. G. p. has suffered from being largely excluded from the great innovative movements of post-medieval Europe. Much less important, but equally significant, is the fact that a great deal of G. p. appears to have been sung or chanted. Partly because it was mainly an oral poetry and partly because verse and not prose has always been the primary literary medium of G., a strong, supple, rich lang. has been evolved, capable of immense diversity in form and mood.

This lang. has been triumphantly recharged in the 20th c. Iain Rothach (1889–1918) is the first strong new voice, and Somhairle MacGill-Eain (b. 1911) the doyen: his work marks a revolution in G. writing. George Campbell Hay (1915–84) rehabilitates the subtle movement of the older meters; Ruaraidh MacThomais (b. 1922) introduces and develops *vers libre* (q.v.), a departure of great interest in G. metrics; Domhnall MacAmhlaigh (b. 1930) is a pioneer in the same field. Iain Mac a' Ghobhainn (b. 1928) can be both avant-garde and traditional. Younger poets, e.g. Aonghas MacNeacail (b. 1942), Maoilios Caimbeul (b. 1944), and the sisters Catriona (b. 1947) and Morag (b. 1949) NicGumaraid have made notable contributions. A remarkable devel. is the writing of G. by non-native speakers, among whom William Neill and Fergus MacKinlay are outstanding. All these poets write from a bicultural background with an intense awareness of the 20th-c. universe. In that sense G. p., in the movements of almost a century, has been made modern.

ANTHOLOGIES: *Ortha nan Gaidheal: Carmina Gadelica*, ed. A. Carmichael, 5 v. (1928–54); *G. Songs of Mary MacLeod*, ed. J. C. Watson (1934); *S. Verse from the Book of the Dean of Lismore* (1937), *Bardachd Ghàidhlig: Specimens of G. P. 1550–1900*, 4th ed. (1976), both ed. W. J. Watson; *The Songs of John MacCodrum* (1938), *The Blind Harper: An Clarsair Dall*, both ed. W. Matheson (1970); *Heroic Poetry from the Book of the Dean of Lismore*, ed. N. Ross (1939); *The Songs of Duncan Ban Macintyre*, ed. A. MacLeod (1952); *Orain Iain Luim*, ed. A. MacKenzie (1964); *Hebridean Folksongs*, ed. J. L. Campbell and F. Collinson, 3 v. (1969–81); *Poems and Songs by Sileas MacDonald*, ed. C. Ó Baoill (1972); *Nua-bhardachd Ghàidhlig*, ed. D. Macaulay (1976); *Highland Songs of the Forty-Five*, ed. J. L. Campbell, 2d ed. (1984).

HISTORY AND CRITICISM: D. Thomson, *The G.

SCOTTISH POETRY

Sources of MacPherson's "Ossian" (1952), An Intro. to G. P. (1974), The New Verse in S.G.: A Structural Analysis (1974), The Companion to G. Scotland (1983), "G. Literary Interactions with Scots and Eng. Work," Proc. 1st Internat. Conf. on the Langs. of Scotland (1986); J. MacInnes, "The Oral Trad. in S. G. P.," SS (1968), "The Panegyric Code in G. P. and its Historical Background," Trans. Soc. G. Inverness (1976–78); I. Grimble, The World of Rob Donn (1979); S. Maclean, Ris a' bhruthaich (1985); W. Gillies, "The Cl. Ir. Poetic Trad.," Proc. 7th Internat. Congress of Celtic Studies (1986); Sorley Maclean Critical Essays, ed. R. J. Ross and J. Hendry (1986).　　　　　　　　　　　　　　　J.M.

SCOTTISH POETRY. S. p. has been written in Welsh, Gaelic, Lat., Lallans (Scots), and Eng.; here the concern is for only the last two and their admixture. Because Lallans from Northumbrian Anglian is undeveloped, it has steadily lost ground to Eng. (of the 1200 separate poems submitted to *New Writing Scotland* no. 5 [1987], for example, "a bare sprinkling" is in Lallans); nevertheless, just how much freshness, range, color, and memorability it can still command is clear in *Sterts & Stobies* (1986), the Scots poems of R. Crawford and W. N. Herbert, as well as in the poetic prose of W. L. Lorimer's brilliant tr. of *The New Testament in Scots* (1983).

The Scots poet today, whether always in Eng. (MacCaig) or always in Lallans (Mackie), will reveal himself as a Scotsman when he reads aloud, for many features of pronunciation are common. Like his countrymen he is likely to disclose something of shrewdness, sentiment, common sense, patriotism, piety, and democracy; and he is likely to respect nature, facts, industry, reticence, loyalty, and literacy. For his verse he will favor alliteration, music, obloquy (see FLYTING), nostalgia, the standard Habbie (see BURNS STANZA), the bob and wheel (q.v.), the narrative in octosyllabic couplets, and single malt whisky.

The main sources of early S. p. are three 16th-c. mss.: Asloan, Bannatyne, and Maitland Folio; however, Andrew of Wyntoun's rhymed *Cronykil* (1424) is the source for what is possibly the oldest surviving fragment (ca. 1286)—eight octosyllabic lines rhyming *abababab*, of which the last three have now epitomized Scotland's history for 700 years: "Crist, borne in virgynyte, / Succoure Scotland, and ramede, / That is stade in perplexitie." Several unskilled romances like *Sir Tristrem* ("Thomas the Rhymer's"?) followed these verses before 1374–75, when Barbour composed *The Bruce*, Scotland's first literary achievement. A superb story of freedom narrated with infectious enthusiasm, this "factional" romance, based on the Fr. medieval romance (q.v.), introduces a new subject matter: Scotland. Barbour, the poet-chronicler, seldom slackens his pace through 20 books of octosyllabic couplets; when he does, it may be for such captivating digression as explaining how a warrior's tears differ from a woman's,

but more often it is to show that he is remembered in Scotland because he himself remembers his countrymen's "hardyment," with such lines as "And led thair lyff in gret trawaill, / And oft, in hard stour of bataill, / Wan eycht gret price off chewalry, / And was woydyt off cowardy."

In 1424, Scotland crowned James Stewart after his 18-year imprisonment in London. As James I (1394–1437), he described Chaucer and Gower to his court as "Superlative poetis laureate" and under their influence composed "The Kingis Quair." Here rhyme royal (q.v.), conventional allegory of lover and rose, matter from Boethius, and ME all contend that this James is the first and last "S. Chaucerian" (q.v.). The mid-15th c. claims Sir Richard Holland's *The Buke of the Howlat*, an ingenious beast epic (q.v.) examining Scotland's court life. The late 15th c. claims Blind Harry's extravagant *The Wallace*, an epic romance in heroic couplets extending Barbour's nationalism; *Cockelbie's Sow*, an anonymous country tale with alliterative play in irregular 3- and 5-beat couplets; and the anonymous, amusing *Rauf Coilyear*, a satiric anti-romance on the theme of a king (Charlemagne) among unaware rustics. The 13-line stanza of *Rauf* (nine long and four short lines of black letter) parodies the old alliterative stanza of *Sir Gawain and the Green Knight*. Last, the anonymous descriptive pieces "Christ's Kirk on the Green" and "Peblis to the Play" start a trad. of rustic brawl that finds new life in the 20th-c. merrymaking of Garioch's "Embro to the Ploy." Other poems in this trad. like Fergusson's "Leith Races" and Burns' "Holy Fair" adapt the "Christ's Kirk" stanza of ten lines, 4/3/4/3/4/3/4/3/1/3 rhyming *ababababcd*, the last as refrain.

Nowhere are the post-World War II advances in S. studies more apparent than with respect to S. p. of the 15th c., "The Aureate Age," the high creativity of the "S. Chaucerians" or "makars" (q.v.). Influences upon these superior poets are today known to have been not only Eng. but also directly Fr. and It. as well as native. At the forefront were Henryson and Dunbar.

Robert Henryson (1425?–1506?) drew upon several medieval literary forms (lyric, ballad, pastoral) for his delightful "Robene and Makyne," arguing "The man that will nocht quhen he may, / Sall haif nocht quhen he wald." "The Annunciation" is unusual as religious verse of the Middle Ages in that its appeal is to intellect through paradox; "Orpheus and Eurydice," the most famous of the shorter love poems, masterfully illustrates cl. narration of romance material under Fr. and It. influences. The 13 beast fables after Aesop and Saint Cloude are uncompromisingly Scottish. Skillfully, Henryson reveals personality by gesture and remark; delicately, he controls narrative rhythm in a blend of entertaining story and central moral. Political questions within the allegory (e.g. "The Tale of the Lion and the Mouse") present the poet as a democrat in the line of Lindsay, Fergusson, and Burns. The fable "The Preiching of the Swallow" and *The Testament of Cresseid*, both in rhyme royal, are Henryson's two finest poems, full of his charity, humanity, and high-mindedness. Central to the *Testament* is the question, Why do men made in the image of God become "beistis Irrational"? This beautiful, moving tragedy of sin Henryson develops with the originality of a great mind, permitting him, in contrast to Chaucer, freedom to invent his own ending.

William Dunbar (ca. 1460–ca.1513) was priest and poet at the court of James IV. Strong Fr. and Occitan influences upon a variety of lyric forms are apparent in his 80-odd poems, never long. The temperament is European, the craftsmanship superb in its intricacies, linguistic virtuosity, and harmony of sound and sense, the tone variously personal, witty, exuberant, eccentric, blasphemous, manic-depressive: "Now dansand mery, now like to dee." Dunbar's favorite subjects are himself, his milieu, woman (dame, widow, Madonna), and Catholic Christianity. Some poems, like "The Goldyn Targe," a dream allegory (q.v.), and "Ane Ballat of Our Lady," belong to the poetry of rhetoric and the court; thus they are replete with the favorite phrase "me thocht," internal rhyme, and aureate diction (q.v.); other poems, such as "The Flyting of Dunbar and Kennedie" and "The Tretis of the Twa Mariit Wemen and the Wedo" (the first blank verse in Scots, strongly alliterative), belong to the poetry of ribald speech. Satires of this order are central to Dunbar's work and the truest measure of his restoration of the vernacular.

Bishop Gavin Douglas (1475?–1522) and Sir David Lindsay (1490?–1555?) complete the makars' roll. More learned than either Henryson or Dunbar, Douglas focused his dream vision *The Palace of Honour* on the nature of virtue and honor in educating a young poet and, therewith, acknowledged indebtedness to such It. humanists as Poggio-Braccilini and Petrarch. Douglas' *magnum opus* is his tr. of the *Aeneid*, also in heroic couplets, the first tr. of a classic into Scots and a major source for Surrey's *Aeneid*, the first Eng. blank verse (q.v.). Its prologues, notably that to Book VII, reveal an individual voice, a wealth of lang., and the typical Scots poet's eye for nature. Sir David, Lyon King-at-Arms and promoter of Knox, intellectual revolutionary and early defender of writing for Iok and Thome in the maternal lang., has made his reputation as the most popular Scots poet before Burns primarily on *Ane Pleasant Satire of the Thrie Estaitis*, a morality play or propaganda drama with Lady Sensuality and Flattery as the leads. Blending comedy and common sense, Lindsay gives answer to What is good government? in sophisticated verse-forms: bob and wheel, 8-line stanzas of iambic pentameter in linking rhyme for formal speeches, and exchange of single lines in couplets of stichomythia (q.v.).

With the Wedderburns' *Gude and Godlie Ballatis* and the songs of Alexander Scott, national Scot-

land approached the death of the Eng. queen, Elizabeth I (1603), the Union of the Crowns (James VI of Scotland crowned James I of England), and the loss of court and courtly lang. Such loss, together with the King James *Bible*, the splendor of Spenser and Shakespeare, and the victories of Covenanting Puritans, makes it impossible to name one Scots poet of high distinction during the entire 17th c., not excluding Alexander Montgomerie (1545?–1610?), poet of *The Cherry and the Slae*, dream vision and allegory; any other member of King James' "Castalian band"; or William Drummond of Hawthornden (1585–1649), who showed with some success what a Scotsman could compose in Eng. No longer a court lang., Scots lived on as the vernacular of folk lit.: ballad and song.

S. ballads represent an oral trad. (see Buchan) of anonymous narrative songs arising in the late Middle Ages to flourish in the 16th and 17th cs., and to be collected in the latter 19th c. by Child. Chief subjects are violent history ("Oterborne"), tragic romance ("Clerk Saunders"), and the supernatural ("Tam Lin"). The vernacular is simple and stark, grimly realistic and fatalistic. The vividly dramatic story unfolds through unity of action, characterization, and the relentless pace of the ballad meter (q.v.), but never wholly. Formula, epithet, incremental repetition (q.v.), refrain, alliteration, and question-and-answer advance the plot. Colors are primary; images are violent ("The curse of hell frae me sall ye beir / Mither, mither"), tender ("O waly, waly! but love be bony / A little time, while it is new"), eerie ("The channerin worm doth chide"), and beautiful ("And she has snooded her yellow hair / A little aboon her bree").

Ballads aside, the period from 1603 to World War I produced poets who chose literary Eng. as their medium because they thought it was impossible to use Lallans and be taken seriously. So James Thomson (1700–48), poet of *The Seasons*, Robert Blair, and James Beattie used standard Eng. for their remembered works. Sir Walter Scott (1771–1832) retained the vernacular of the ballads he collected and improved for his *Minstrelsy* but chose Eng. for his long poems (*The Lady of the Lake*) and for the excellent songs in his novels ("Proud Maisie"). Byron and Campbell were Scotsmen, but are better left to Eng. letters. Later poets such as James Thomson (1834–82) and Robert Louis Stevenson again chose Eng. for *The City of Dreadful Night* and *A Child's Garden of Verses*. Poetry in Lallans, however, was alive—just barely—as the 1707 Union of Parliaments reduced Scotland to a "region" of Great Britain.

James Watson's *Choice Collection* in two vols. (1706–09) includes Semple of Beltrees' mock elegy "Epitaph of Habbie Simson" (ca. 1650) in a stanza which gives name to the "standard Habbie," better known as the Burns stanza (q.v.); Hamilton of Gilbertfield's "Bonny Heck" has the same stanza for the last words of a dying greyhound distantly related to Henryson's talking animals and anticipating Burns' "Poor Mailie's Elegy." These poems are in Lallans. So, too, are such works of Allan Ramsay (1685–1758) as his invention of the verse epistle (usually in tetrameters), his burlesque elegy on a church treasurer who could smell out a bawd, his poetic drama *The Gentle Shepherd*, many of the songs in his *The Tea Table Miscellany*, and all of the older Scots poems in his *The Ever Green*. Ramsay's prosody becomes Robert Fergusson's (1750–74); Fergusson's, Burns'. Within a vernacular revival these three poets compose their satires, genre poems, epistles, and comic narratives, principally in six verseforms: common measure (q.v.) with its variant, ballad meter, octosyllabic couplets, heroic couplets, the standard Habbie, "Christ's Kirk," and "Cherrie and the Slee." Among the third of Fergusson's 100-odd poems in Lallans is his masterpiece, "Auld Reekie," realistically describing everyday life in Edinburgh, "Whare couthy chiels at e'ening meet / Their bizzin craigs and mou's to weet."

More and more, except in the S. household where "The Cotter's Saturday Night" and "To a Mouse" hold sway, the measure of Robert Burns' (1759–96) high accomplishment has become the satires like "Holy Willie's Prayer," *The Jolly Beggars*, the narrative "Tam o' Shanter," and the hundreds of songs. The cantata *The Jolly Beggars* has his characteristic merits of description, narration, dramatic effect, metrical diversity, energy, and sensitivity to the beauties inherent in S. words and music. Otherwise, hearing a song like "Scots wha hae" or "Ca' the Yowes," each showing masterful skill at uniting words and music, will unforgettably illustrate this genius. To Burns under the S. Enlightenment we owe the perpetuation of S. folksong. How rich this heritage is has been the further study of those like Sharpe, Duncan, and Greig in the 19th c. and Henderson and others at the School of S. Studies in the 20th. By contrast, literary songs from the 18th c. to the 20th tend toward sentimentalism, whether Jean Elliot's "Flowers o' the Forest," Lady Nairne's "Caller Herrin," or verses by Violet Jacob, Marion Angus, and Helen Cruickshank.

Seldom does 19th-c. S. p. better James Hogg's (1770–1835) "sad stuff." Slavish imitations of Burns strike low, nor rise by the *Whistle-Binkie* (fiddler's seat at merry-makings) anthol. or the couthy sentimentality of Kailyard (a type of fiction from about 1880 of rural life, dialect, and sentiment; see James M. Barries' *A Window in Thrums* or Ian Maclaren's, pseud. for Rev. John Watson's, verse epigraph). Industrialization and the Calvinist ethic of profitability and genteel respectability bring poets to their knees. At century's close, however, Robert Louis Stevenson (1850–94) composes poems like "The Spaewife" in a literary Scots, the precision of which opposes the Kailyard; "blood and guts" John Davidson (1857–1909) experiments in Eng. with new myths, symbols of

science's dethroning religion; and the founder of the S. Ren. grows as a lad in Langholm.

In the 1920s, Christopher Grieve (1892–1978) took the pseudonym "Hugh MacDiarmid" as he abandoned Eng. versifying to become a makar in Scots. Created under the banner "Back to Dunbar!," early lyrics like "Empty Vessel" excel in clarity and power of Scots, intensity of passion, audacity of imagery, and originality of movement and rhythmical pattern. Such verses as the following sing:

> Mars is braw in crammasy,
> Venus in a green silk gown,
> The auld mune her gowden feathers,
> Their starry talk's a wheen o' blethers,
> Nane for thee a thochtie sparin,
> Earth, thou bonnie broukit bairn!
> —But greet, an' in your tears ye'll droun
>   The haill clanjamfrie!
>   (*The Bonnie Broukit Bairn*)

MacDiarmid's masterpiece is *A Drunk Man Looks at the Thistle* (1926), a long sequence of poems in the form of a dramatic monologue. Unity derives from the protagonist, who rhapsodizes on love and death and meditates on Scotland and the world. MacDiarmid's "synthetic" Scots presents difficulties, esp. in longer poems like *To Circumjack Cencrastus*, which become more and more a poetry of fact (statement and argument) and Marxist. Doubtful that Scots is adequate to propagate socialism, MacDiarmid reverts to Eng. as early as 1955.

Others in Eng. and Scots, though not makars, add luster to the S. Ren. extending into the 1960s. "The three skeeliest Lallans makars" around MacDiarmid are Robert Garioch (1908–81), Sydney Goodsir Smith (1915–75), and Alexander Scott (b. 1920). Scott's glitter and glower show in his humorous "Paradise Tint"; Smith's "lemanrie" informs his *Under the Eildon Tree*; and Garioch's full vocabulary marks his scintillating *Sixteen Edinburgh Sonnets* after the Belli *romanesco* originals. Skillful, too, are William Soutar's (1898–1943) "whigmaleeries" (fantasies) and his bairn rhymes *Seeds in the Wind*, with the lyrical "O luely, luely, cam she in." Three poets in Eng. surpass others: Norman MacCaig (b. 1910), who now wears the mantle of Scotland's *eminence grise*; Iain Crichton Smith (b. 1928) within the S. Ren.; and Edwin Muir (1887–1959), without. MacCaig, like G. S. Fraser (1915–80) and T. Scott (b. 1918), begins with the tortured syntax and private imagery of the Apocalypse Movement but develops a romantic-classic stance and Edinburgh Doric for his habitual checking-up on appearance and reality (e.g. "Spraying Sheep"). Closest to him is Alexander Young (1855–1971). Crichton Smith, with roots in Lewis Gaeldom, creates finished verses with recurrent figures of island and old woman on his favorite theme of being alone. Muir's most famous line is "Burns and Scott, sham bards of a sham nation."

SCULPTURE AND POETRY

Scotland's first great metaphysical poet, a symbolist for whose *The Labyrinth* (1949) Kafka, Freud, and Jung are important, Muir "gloriously" (T. S. Eliot) breaks new ground in his mythical romances on the Fall, published as *One Foot in Eden* (1956).

Today some poets experiment: with ON and OE (G. M. Brown [b. 1927]); with Chinese or Japanese forms (Crichton Smith, D. Glen [b. 1933], and K. White [b. 1936]); with surrealism (D. Black [b. 1941]); with psychiatry (K. Morrice [b. 1924]); with feminism (Liz Lochhead [b. 1948] unapologetically in "Laundrette" and Tessa Ransford with a feminist rage in "In the Fishmonger's"); with Euclidian figures (A. Mackie [b. 1925]); with a view to performance (T. Leonard [b. 1944] in the phonetic spellings of Glasgow dialect); with "sound" poetry (G. MacBeth [b. 1932]); and with MacDiarmid's "aggrandized" Scots as flyting (hilariously rendered in R. Crawford [b. 1959] and W. N. Herbert [b. 1961]). Two others experiment with unusual versatility: I. H. Finlay (b. 1925) with the neo-modernism of "poem-prints," "poem-gardens," and "concrete" poetry (e.g. "Star/steer" carved in slate); and E. Morgan (b. 1920) with his "instamatic," "emergent," and "concrete" poems like "Loch Ness Monster's Song." Some poets translate foreign poetry into Scots or Eng. poetry: R. Fulton, some 14 v.; Morgan, from eight foreign langs. into Scots; A. Reid (b. 1926), from Neruda and Borges into Eng. Some poets sing more traditionally: in Eng., the prize-winning D. Dunn (b. 1942) in his narrative elegies (1985); Valerie Gillies (b. 1948) in her animal poems like "The Salmon Loup"; in Scots, A. Mackie in the exceptionally fine *Clytach* (1972); and Sheena Blackhall in "Heelstergowdie" (1986); and C. Rush (b. 1944), in a poem opening in Eng. and closing in Scots, *A Resurrection of A Kind* (1985). See also SCOTTISH-GAELIC POETRY.

ANTHOLOGIES AND TEXTS: *The Scots Musical Museum*, ed. J. Johnson, 6 v. (1786–1803); *Bishop Percy's Folio Ms.*, ed. J. Hales and F. Furnivall, 3 v. (1867–68); *Eng. and S. Popular Ballads*, ed. F. J. Child, 5 v. (1883–98); *The Bruce*, ed. W. W. Skeat, 2 v. (1894); *Scott's Minstrelsy of the S. Border*, ed. T. Henderson, 4 v. (1902); *Works of Sir David Lindsay*, ed. D. Hamer, 4 v. (1931–36); *Works of Gavin Douglas*, ed. D. F. C. Coldwell, 4 v. (1957–64); *Honour'd Shade*, ed. N. MacCaig (1959)—anthol. of mod. S. p.; *Trad. Tunes of the Child Ballads*, ed. B. Bronson, 4 v. (1959–72); *Collected Poems of Edwin Muir* (1965); *Oxford Book of S. Verse*, ed. J. MacQueen and T. Scott (1966); *Poems and Songs of Robert Burns*, ed. J. Kingsley, 3 v. (1968); *Contemp. S. Verse*, ed. N. MacCaig and A. Scott (1970); *Made in Scotland*, ed. R. Garioch (1974); *Coll. Poems of S. G. Smith* (1975)—intro. Hugh MacDiarmid; *Complete Poems of Hugh MacDiarmid 1920–76*, ed. M. Grieve and W. R. Aitken, 2 v. (1978); *Mod. S. Verse 1922–77*, ed. A. Scott (1978); *Poems of William Dunbar*, ed. J. Kinsley (1979); *Poems of Robert Henryson*, ed. D. Fox (1981); *Akros Verse*, ed. D. Glen (1982)—nos. 1–49; *Complete Poetical Works of Robert Garioch*, ed. R. Fulton (1983); R. Crawford and W. N. Herbert, *Sterts & Stobies* (1986); *Twelve More Mod. S. Poets*, ed. C. King and I. C. Smith (1986); *An Anthol. of S. Women Poets*, ed. C. Kerrigan (1991).

HISTORIES AND STUDIES: T. F. Henderson, *S. Vernacular Lit.* (1900); A. Mackenzie, *Historical Survey of S. Lit. to 1714* (1933); J. Speirs, *The Scots Lit. Trad.* (1940); *S. P.*, ed. J. Kingsley (1955); K. Wittig, *The S. Trad. in Lit.* (1958); T. Crawford, *Burns* (1960)—best study of poems; D. Craig, *S. Lit. and the S. People* (1961); K. Buthlay, *Hugh MacDiarmid* (1964); D. Daiches, *The Paradox of S. Culture* (1964), *Lit. and Gentility in Scotland* (1982); T. Scott, *Dunbar* (1966); F. Collinson, *Trad. and National Music of Scotland* (1966); T. C. Smout, *A Hist. of the S. People 1560–1830* (1969), *A Century of the S. People 1830–1950* (1986); H. M. Shire, *Song, Dance and Poetry of the Court of Scotland under King James VI* (1969); A. M. Kinghorn, *Middle Scots Poets* (1970); D. Buchan, *The Ballad and the Folk* (1972); *Hugh MacDiarmid: A Crit. Survey*, ed. D. Glen (1972); R. D. S. Jack, *The It. Influence in S. Lit.* (1972), *S. Lit.'s Debt to Italy* (1986); *Robert Burns*, ed. D. Low (1974); R. Fulton, *Contemp. S. P.* (1974); M. Lindsay, *Hist. of S. Lit.* (1977); R. Knight, *Edwin Muir* (1980)—best study; G. Kratzmann, *Anglo-S. Lit. Relations 1430–1550* (1980); W. R. Aitken, *S. Lit. in Eng. and Scots* (1982)—excellent bibl.; J. MacQueen, *Progress and Poetry 1650–1800* (1982); *Scotch Passion*, ed. A. Scott (1982)—the erotic poetry; *The New Testament in Scots*, tr. W. L. Lorimer (1983); C. Kerrigan, *Whaur Extremes Meet* (1983)—study of MacDiarmid's work; R. Watson, *Lit. of Scotland* (1984); *Concise Scots Dict.*, ed. M. Robinson (1985)—intro. is Aitkins' excellent "A Hist. of Scots"; W. Scheps and J. A. Looney, *The Middle Scots Poets: A Ref. Guide* (1986); *The Hist. of S. Lit.*, ed. C. Craig, 4 v. (1987–); F. Stafford, *The Sublime Savage: James Macpherson and the Poems of Ossian* (1989); D. Glen, *The Poetry of the Scots* (1991). R.D.T.

SCULPTURE AND POETRY. In historical terms, painting has always been the art first addressed by poets when they were given to contemplation of the relation of poetry to the other arts (see EKPHRASIS; DESCRIPTIVE POETRY; VISUAL ARTS AND POETRY). Without resorting to statistics, one may feel confident that poets have written more lines about paintings than about buildings or ss. But ss. have certainly inspired a number of important poems by poets such as Hölderlin, Rimbaud, Rilke, George, Yeats, and others, not to mention critical works such as Lessing's *Laoköon*.

Indeed, the assumed simplicity, unity, and grandeur of free-standing figures and monumental works of human artifice has inspired poets as much as landscape has. There are, for example, Thomas of Britain's description of Tristan's Hall of Images, with the almost-living figure of Ysolt

(12th-c.); the "counterfeits of nature" and the "life-resembling" colored statues and sepulchral effigies in many Ren. dramas and poems; the posings of neoclassical and romantic heroines *à la* Venus de' Medici (most famous of all, Musidora in Thomson's *The Seasons* [1730]) and the comparisons of heroes to some Apollo, Bacchus, or marble Faun, the Elgin Theseus, or even the Torso Belvedere; the Praxitelean shapes by Shelley; and numerous "stationings" of Grecian, Egyptian, Gothic, and Druidic figures by 19th-c. poets. Blake, poet and artist, beheld the records of the Cosmic Memory as "the bright ss. of Los's Halls"— some as linear and relief-like engravings and others as figures in the round, like his Originals of the Gr. Statues (*Jerusalem* 1.16; *Descriptive Catalogue*). Along with mythological, historical, and technical interests in the broken and unbroken marbles of Cl. antiquity, which "went for much" until recently, the poets envied most of all, very likely, the sculptor's reputed ability to represent or re-create human feeling, passion, emotion, and thought in materials more enduring than words. S., they felt, offered significant "moments" made eternal and ever-beautiful—"fair attitudes" in marble (often but not always Parian and white) or "masque-like figures on the dreamy urn."

Poets have also found analogies between poetry and the careful carving, clear design, outline, and relief of the sculptors. Some became "carvers of verbal agates," writing their "ss." and cutting their "gems" of "lapidary verse" after visiting studios and galleries or looking at illustrated volumes, or with their eyes on gems, intaglios, animated or reposeful busts, high or low reliefs, and storied or well-wrought urns. Even at the peak of the interest in "word-painting," the persistent attraction of Alexandrian "metrical carvings" was illustrated, for example, by Stedman and Aldrich's *Cameos Selected from the Works of Walter Savage Landor* (1874). Later, Yeats came to admire the gold metalwork, ivories, and mosaics of Byzantine craftsmen in the age of Justinian, even wishing that he might become, in the artifice of eternity, a work of perfect art, both an object of contemplation and contemplator of Being ("Sailing to Byzantium").

Finally, from the early 19th c., poets and theorists often borrowed critical terms—"statuesque," "sculptural," "sculpturesque"—from the art of s. Individual works and sculptors as well as the technique and principles of the art influenced the Parnassians as well as the poets of Imagism and Objectivism (qq.v.), thereby altering the classic Horatian comparison of painting and poetry, *ut pictura poesis* (q.v.), into a new formulation: *ut sculptura poesis*. There is a history here still to be written. See also EPITAPH.

K. Borinski, *Die Antike in Poetik und Kunsttheorie*, 2 v. (1914–24); S. A. Larrabee, *Eng. Bards and Grecian Marbles* (1943); T. M. Greene, *The Arts and the Art of Crit.* (1940); E. Souriau, *La Correspondance des arts* (1947); Wellek and Warren, ch. 11;

J. H. Hagstrum, *The Sister Arts* (1958); R. W. Ketton-Cremer, "Lapidary Verse," *PBA* 45 (1959); T. Munro, *The Arts and Their Interrelations* (1967); L. Lipking, *The Ordering of the Arts in 18th-C. England* (1970); M. North, *The Final S.: Public Monuments and Mod. Poets* (1985); N. M. Goslee, *Uriel's Eye: Miltonic Stationing and Statuary in Blake, Keats, and Shelley* (1985); W. Adam, "Sehnsuchts-Bilder: Antike Statuen und Monumente in Platens Lyrik," *Euphorion* 80 (1986). S.A.L.; T.V.F.B.

SECONDE RHÉTORIQUE. In late medieval Fr. poetics, a distinction came to be made between the art of persuasion or oratory as applied in prose, i.e. rhet., the figures and tropes, and the art of persuasion in verse, i.e. versification or prosody; the former came to be called "first rhet." and the latter "second." Patterson dates these treatises on the art of verse from 1370 to 1539; they form the middle link between the few Occitan and OF treatises and the *Arts poétiques* of the *Pléiade* (q.v.) in the Ren.

How prosody came to be allied with rhet. is one of the chapters of medieval poetics (q.v.). In Med. Lat., prosody was treated primarily as a branch of grammar, being either included in grammars as a chapter called "Prosodia" or else written as a separate manual, e.g. Bede's *De arte metrica* (both types are collected in Keil). Rhet. took a parallel but distinguishable course except in encyclopedic works like Isidore of Seville's *Etymologiae* (ca. 560–636; prosody and rhet. are the subjects of the first two chapters). Alternatively, some theorists viewed prosody as a branch of music (e.g. Augustine); these two traditions devolve from the *metrici* and *rhythmici* (q.v.) of the ancients. In the 12th and 13th cs. emerged the treatises known as *artes poeticae*, such works, following the inspiration of Horace, treated both rhet. and prosody together. These are instanced in John of Garland's *Parisiana poetria* (much on prosody), Matthew of Vendome's *Ars versificatoria* (virtually nothing), Geoffrey of Vinsauf's *Poetria nova*, Alexander of Ville Dei's *Doctrinale*, and Eberhard the German's *Laborintus* (collected in Faral). Dante's unfinished essay on poetry, *De vulgari eloquentia* (ca. 1303), which treats chiefly diction and prosody, provides the transition to the vernaculars. By the 15th c., in France, manuals distinguish not between rhet. and prosody but prose and verse, and since prosody treats of precisely those devices that are the differentia of verseform, it became a "second rhet."; "pleine rhétoriques" treated both. Langlois collects 7 principal texts by Jacques Le Grand, Baudet Herenc, Jean Molinet, and 4 anonymous authors, but the most influential was Deschamps' *L'Art de dictier* (1392). See also RHETORIQUEURS.—
E. Langlois, *Recueil d'arts de s. r.* (1902)—with long Intro.; Patterson—the fullest account but needs updating; H. Lubienski-Bodenham, "The Origins of the 15th-C. View of Poetry as S. R.," *MLR* 74 (1979); Hollier. T.V.F.B.

SEGUIDILLA. A Sp. poetic form of popular origin. It probably originated as a dance song and was popular, at least in the underworld, early in the 17th c. In the beginning it was probably a 4-line strophe of alternating long (usually 7- or 8-syllable) and short (5- or 6-syllable) lines, the short (even-numbered) lines assonating (called *s. simple* or *s. para cantar*). Later, probably in the 17th c., a second, semi-independent part of 3 lines—short, long, short—was added, the short lines having a new assonance. Eventually the strophe became regularized as a literary form to lines of 7,5,7,5:5,7,5 (the colon denotes a pause in thought), lines 2 and 4 having one assonance, lines 5 and 7 another (called *s. compuesta* or *s. para bailar*), often found in 18th-c. poetry. Sometimes the rhythm only has been used in lines of 7 plus 5 syllables, as by Rubén Darío in his *Elogio de la s.* The s. favors all paroxytonic verses except when 6-syllable oxytones are substituted for the 5-syllable (paroxytonic) lines. The s. sometimes serves as a conclusion (*estribillo*—q.v.) to another song.

The *s. gitana* (Gypsy s.), also called *flamenca* or *playera*, is usually a 5-line strophe of 6,6,5,6,6 syllables, lines 2 and 5 assonating. Lines 3 and 4 may be written together as one line of from 10 to 12 syllables.—F. Hanssen, "La s.," *AUC* 125 (1909); F. Rodríguez Marín, *La copla* (1910); P. Henríquez Ureña, *La versificación irregular en la poesía castellana*, 2d ed. (1933); D. C. Clarke, "The Early S.," *HR* 12 (1944); José Mercado, *La s. gitana* (1982); Navarro.   D.C.C.

SEMANTICS AND POETRY. There are two groups of questions to be addressed here. First: What is s.? What is a semantic theory intended to tell us? What is the current state of the field? Second: What influence has work in s. had on crit. and on theory of poetry? Is there a special s. of poetry?

S. is the study of meaning; the term is derived from the Gr. verb *sēmainein*, to indicate by or to give a sign, and ultimately from the noun *sēma*, a sign or token or omen. Its modern usage derives from Bréal's *Essai de sémantique: science des significations* (1897, tr. 1900).

What is the study (or science) of meaning? During the 19th and early 20th cs., when linguistics was mainly historical and comparative, s. was a relatively important branch of linguistic study. But it was certainly not scientific. Mostly it consisted of anecdotal, *ad hoc* accounts of the ways in which particular words had changed their meanings over time in a given lang. and of the ways in which etymologically related words differed in meaning over a group of related langs. When linguistics shifted its focus, under the influence of Ferdinand de Saussure's *Cours de linguistique générale* (1916), from historical change to the structure of a given lang. system at a particular point in time—from, in Saussure's terms, diachrony to synchrony—s. began to recede in importance.

During the period that saw the rise of structural linguistics in the U.S. and abroad, roughly from the early 1930s to the late 1950s, s. became the domain of analytic philosophers rather than of linguists. The Logical Positivists, a group of Viennese philosophers incl. Moritz Schlick and Rudolf Carnap whose views are (rather oversimply) represented in Eng. by A. J. Ayer's *Lang., Truth and Logic* (1936), proposed the so-called "Verification Principle," according to which the meaning of a sentence is its method of verification. Closely related were the attempts of such behaviorists as Charles W. Morris (*Foundations of the Theory of Signs*, 1938; *Signs, Lang. and Behavior*, 1946) to view the meaning of a sentence as equivalent to the stimulus that causes a speaker to utter it or the response it evokes in a listener or some combination of the two. This was also the view of sentence-meaning put forward in Leonard Bloomfield's influential *Language* (1933), for many years the bible of Am. structural linguistics. Later, more qualified versions of the behaviorist view may be found in W. V. Quine's *Word and Object* (1960) and Paul Ziff's *Semantic Analysis* (1960).

In accounting for word-meaning, most behaviorists attempted to show that the meaning of a word is the object that the word stands for or represents in situations in which it is uttered. Others, such as C. K. Ogden and I. A. Richards in *The Meaning of Meaning* (1923), harked back to the British Empiricist trad. of Locke and Hume, maintaining that the relation between word and object is mediated by some mental entity such as a thought or concept, and that the meaning of a word is the particular mental entity with which it is correlated in the mind of the language-user.

These theories of sentence-and word-meaning are based on the model of true-or-false declarative sentences uttered in face-to-face communication, and assume that all meaningfully used words acquire meaning by being correlated with either physical or mental entities. Both premises were vigorously challenged by the Viennese philosopher Ludwig Wittgenstein, who had had a hand in founding (or at least inspiring) logical positivism (see Waismann), but whose views changed radically during the 1930s.

Wittgenstein begins his *Philosophical Investigations* (written 1945–49, pub. 1953) by calling attention to the enormous variety of types of sentences within any natural lang. and hence to the fallacy of taking the true-or-false declarative sentence as a privileged model. He begins *The Blue Book* (lectures given 1933–34, pub. 1958) by attacking the assumption that a meaningfully used word is necessarily correlated with some entity that we may single out as its meaning. Wittgenstein's challenge to behaviorism was carried on, from a different angle, by the Oxford philosopher J. L. Austin (*Philosophical Papers*, 1961; *How to Do Things With Words*, 1962).

Meanwhile, in linguistics, the transformational-generative grammar formulated by the Am. linguist Noam Chomsky (*Syntactic Structures*, 1957; *Aspects of the Theory of Syntax*, 1965; and other books) undermined the bases of structural linguistics and, by extension, behaviorist accounts of meaning. Chomsky repeatedly stressed the freely creative aspect of lang. learning and lang. use, and their lack of necessary connection with objects or situations in the presence of which sentences and words are actually learned and used.

During the years between the time when Saussure's influence pointed linguistics in the direction of synchrony and the appearance of Chomsky's critique of the resulting structural linguistics, the great strides forward in linguistics were mainly in phonology. With Chomsky, syntax became the primary object of linguistic study. It was only after Chomsky had outlined his syntactic theory in detail that linguists turned their attention to s. The groundbreaking effort was J. J. Katz and J. A. Fodor's "The Structure of a Semantic Theory" (*Language* 39 [1963]), which posited a semantic component that would, together with a phonological and a syntactic component, make up the grammar which systematically reconstructs a speaker's internalized knowledge of his lang. Katz and Fodor broke with behaviorist theories of meaning by eliminating from their investigation external objects, situations, and conditions. Their aim was to draw a sharp distinction between "the speaker's knowledge of his lang. (his linguistic ability) and his knowledge of the world (his beliefs about matters of fact)," and to focus exclusively on the former. Meanings once again became entities, but abstract *sui generis* entities, on a par with phonemes. Katz pursued his inquiries in *The Philosophy of Lang.* (1966) and *Semantic Theory* (1972).

But the work in s. that has been carried on within the framework of transformational grammar has come to very little. Besides providing semantic representations that will capture the conceptual structure of the meanings of the words in a lang., a semantic theory, we are often told, should also provide illuminating explanations of such concepts as word-meaning, sentence-meaning, synonymy, antonymy, ambiguity, anomalousness, contradiction, and entailment. Thus we will be enabled to build up a systematic picture of the semantic structure of a lang. on a par with those provided by phonology and syntax. But this has not worked out in practice.

Over the years, the semantic representations of the meanings of various words that have been offered have turned out to be mere restatements—in technical jargon—of what an ordinary dictionary will tell us, and the same has been true of the characterizations of such concepts as synonymy and ambiguity. We have had interpretive s., generative s., and (most recently) lexical s., but after a quarter-century of vigorous controversy there still seems no way of drawing a clear line between our knowledge of the semantic structure of our lang. and our knowledge of the world. No convincingly systematic knowledge has emerged, and there is at present no agreement among linguists as to even the general form that a semantic theory should take.

What effects do these devels. in semantic theory have for readers, critics, and theorists of poetry? These effects began to be widely felt shortly after, and in direct response to, the first stirrings of logical positivism. From the Verification Principle, it followed that sentences that could not be empirically verified—and hence all modes of discourse mainly composed of such sentences—were, strictly speaking, meaningless. For the positivists these modes included not only traditional metaphysics but also ethics, aesthetics, and imaginative lit. In *Philosophy and Logical Syntax* (1934) Carnap wrote: "Many linguistic utterances are analogous to laughing in that they have only an expressive function, no representative function. Examples of this are cries like 'Oh, Oh,' or, on a higher level, lyrical verses." Critics concerned with justifying the reading and even the very existence of poetry therefore felt impelled to develop an alternative brand of s.

The most frequent strategy was to delineate, and then celebrate, the particular kind of meaning allegedly possessed essentially by poetic lang. and not possessed by the verifiable, factual lang. favored by the positivists. In this, as in so much else, I. A. Richards was ahead of his time. In both *The Meaning of Meaning*, written with C. K. Ogden, and *Principles of Lit. Crit.* (1924), Richards bifurcated the entire field of meaning into the positivists' referential or symbolic meaning and emotive meaning, "the use of words to express or excite feelings and attitudes." Though emotive meaning is "a more simple matter" and "probably more primitive" than referential meaning, it nonetheless has "an equally important and a far more vital function." In his next book, *Science and Poetry* (1926), Richards coined the perhaps unfortunate term "pseudo-statement" (q.v.), which he defined as "a form of words which is justified entirely by its effect in releasing or organizing our impulses and attitudes."

Richards' later books show increasing interest in semantic analysis. But his focus throughout his career was ultimately psychological: he consistently justified the emotive use of lang. by invoking its beneficial psychological effects. Moreover, he often defined a poem as an "experience" or "class of experiences," and he insisted that "critical remarks are merely a branch of psychological remarks." But the critics who wrote under his influence shifted the emphasis toward semantic formalism as they attempted to elaborate Richards' account of the sort of meaning possessed uniquely by poetry—a term they often used broadly to cover all imaginative lit.

In *Seven Types of Ambiguity* (1930), *Some Versions of Pastoral* (1935), and his masterpiece, *The Structure of Complex Words* (1951), Richards' student

William Empson celebrated, with great acuity and wit, poetic polysemy, the capacity of poetry to generate multiple meanings. In his 1942 essay "The Lang. of Paradox," which became the opening chapter of *The Well Wrought Urn* (1947), Cleanth Brooks made nearly the same point about the essential richness of poetry by singling out paradox and irony (qq.v.) as the defining characteristics of poetic lang. Allen Tate, in "Tension in Poetry" (*SoR* 4 [1938]), held that "the meaning of poetry is its 'tension' (q.v.), the full organized body of all the extension and intension that we can find in it," a view supported by Robert Penn Warren in 1943 ("Pure and Impure Poetry," *KR* 5). W. K. Wimsatt, Jr., in "Verbal Style: Logical and Counterlogical" (*PMLA* 65 [1950]), opposed the "one-way transparent intellectual reference" of ordinary discourse, in which "we look right through" the disparity between verbal symbols and the realities they symbolize, to poetry, which "by thickening the medium increases the disparity between itself and its referents."

Other critics were influenced by the psychology of Freud and Jung—e.g. Maud Bodkin (*Archetypal Patterns in Poetry* [1934]; see PSYCHOLOGICAL CRITICISM), the work of cultural anthropologists such as Frazer and Lévy-Bruhl (see MYTH CRITICISM), and the symbol-oriented yet anti-positivist philosophy of Ernst Cassirer and Suzanne K. Langer (Cassirer, *Sprache und Mythos* [1925], tr. Langer as *Lang. and Myth* [1946]; Langer, *Philosophy in a New Key* [1942], *Feeling and Form* [1953]; see EXPRESSION). For these critics, the superior richness and expressiveness of poetic lang. were to be accounted for not only by ferreting out instances of ambiguity, paradox, and irony (qq.v.) on the surface of the poetry but also by discovering deeper connections with the sources of our very humanity. These critics were thus interested not merely in the ways in which poetic lang. is different from ordinary or scientific lang. but also in the ways in which it is similar to the timeless lang. of folktale, ritual, myth, and dream. As practical critics they were therefore concerned not merely with the patterns and structures of meaning created by the poet but also with those the poet inherits, perhaps unconsciously, by virtue of being human. The particular linguistic devices on which this sort of crit. tended to focus were symbol and image (qq.v.).

The writer who most ambitiously combined the quest for an adequate semantic criterion of poetic lang. with the attempt to connect poetic meaning to those deeper levels of ritual and myth was Philip Wheelwright (*The Burning Fountain*, rev. ed. 1968; *Metaphor and Reality*, 1962). Wheelwright proposed the term "plurisignation" as a substitute for Empson's "ambiguity." His way of combatting positivist s. was to rename it "steno-semantics," and to rename the symbols and propositions with which it dealt "steno-signs" and "steno-statements" (the prefix "steno-" derives from Gr. *stenos*, "narrow, confined"). Steno-signs, their meaning estab-

lished by convention and hence invariable, are all very well for "utilitarian" purposes and for attaining "logical exactitude." But "poetic expression, striving more after semantic fullness than after logical exactitude, is hospitable to meanings which do not have definite outlines and which cannot be adequately represented by terms that are strictly defined." Thus poetry deals not in steno-signs but rather in "depth symbols," the most important of which possess archetypal resonances. Wheelwright's aim was to establish a "poeto-semantics" that would "examine the actual character and semantic action of depth symbols in a variety of particular poems" and then to "construct a theory of meaning that does something like adequate justice to these."

During the 1940s and 1950s, professional philosophers responded enthusiastically to the work of both groups of anti-positivist critics in any number of books and articles on such questions as the cognitive content of poetry and the relation of belief and poetry (q.v.). In fact, this attempt to assimilate the concepts and theories of Am. formalism into the framework of traditional aesthetics continues even today.

By the late 1950s, however, as the later work of Wittgenstein became more widely known, some philosophers began to ask whether the effort to establish a s. of poetry might not be misdirected. In *Poetic Discourse* (1958), Isabel C. Hungerland concluded, "first, that the descriptive-emotive dichotomy or any analogous substitute for it is an inadequate instrument for analyzing poetic discourse; and, second, that poetry cannot be characterized in terms of any kind of linguistic meaning or device peculiar to it." As Hungerland and others have shown, all the modes of meaning and functions of lang. found in poetry are also found in ordinary lang.—and vice versa. Both poetry and ordinary lang. are richer and more diverse than either the logical positivists or the New Critics made them out to be.

It is thus impossible to construct the sort of theory of poetic meaning desiderated by Wheelwright and the New Critics. But this in no way hinders the sort of analysis of particular poems that he had in mind and that they practiced so successfully. Aestheticians have traditionally believed that without an all-embracing theory of some sort, specifying the essential characteristics of art in general or of a particular art, crit. of particular works is at best vague or incomplete and at worst meaningless. But as William E. Kennick has argued, this is simply a superstition: "Crit. has in no way been hampered by the absence of generally applicable canons and norms, and where such norms have been proposed they have either, like the notorious Unities in the case of tragedy, been shown to be absurd, or else, like the requirements of balance, harmony, and unity in variety, they have been so general, equivocal, and empty as to be useless in critical practice."

Crit. of the arts is an autonomous and rational activity in no need of justification. The task of critical theory is not to furnish general truths about the nature of art or lit. or music that will stand in the same relation to our particular critical insights and judgments as scientific laws do to our observations of the physical world. Explanations in crit. do not become more adequate as they become more general; they become more adequate as they move toward a fuller and more specific presentation of reasons, gathered from the detail of the work under discussion, that support the description and judgment the critic is offering. Rather than furnishing general truths about art, the task of critical theory is to analyze in detail the way critical arguments work and the logic of the concepts characteristic of crit. Critical theory, that is, should not tell critics what to do but should rather describe what they do (see CRITICISM; METACRITICISM; THEORY).

Much good work has been done in this area; besides the writings of Hungerland and Kennick mentioned above, I think particularly of those of Frank Sibley, Arnold Isenberg, and Paul Ziff. This work has, however, had little discernible effect upon literary theorists working in English and comp. lit. Nor, for that matter, has the recent work done in s. by linguists. Since about 1970, the two dominant trends in literary theory have been structuralism and deconstruction (qq.v.), both of which have their intellectual roots in a world far removed from the one we have been discussing here.

See also CONNOTATION AND DENOTATION; INTERPRETATION; MEANING, POETIC; SIMPLICITY AND COMPLEXITY; SEMIOTICS, POETIC; THEME.

IN LINGUISTICS AND PHILOSOPHY: R. Carnap, *Meaning and Necessity* (1947); M. Black, *Lang. and Philosophy* (1949), *Models and Metaphors* (1962); S. Ullmann, *The Principles of S.* (1951), *S.* (1962); *S. and the Philosophy of Lang.*, ed. L. Linsky (1952); *Logical Positivism*, ed. A. J. Ayer (1959); *The Theory of Meaning*, ed. G. Parkinson (1968); J. R. Searle, *Speech Acts* (1969); W. Chafe, *Meaning and the Structure of Lang.* (1970); H. Putnam, "Is S. Possible?" *Metaphilosophy* 1 (1970); *Studies in Linguistic S.*, ed. C. Fillmore and D. T. Langendoen (1971); *S.*, ed. D. Steinberg and L. Jacobovits (1971); *The S. of Natural Lang.*, ed G. Harman and D. Davidson (1972); *S. and Philosophy*, ed. M. Munitz and P. Unger (1974); *Formal S. of Natural Lang.*, ed. E. Keenan (1975); *Meaning and Truth*, ed. G. Evans and J. MacDowell (1976); J. D. Fodor, *S.* (1977); R. M. Kempson, *Semantic Theory* (1977); J. Lyons, *S.*, 2 v. (1977); F. Waismann, *Ludwig Wittgenstein and the Vienna Circle* (1979); F. R. Palmer, *S.*, 2d ed. (1981); W. T. Gordon, *A Hist. of S.* (1982); *Lexical S. in Review*, ed. S. Levin (1985); R. M. Martin, *The Meaning of Lang.* (1987).

IN POETRY: D. Walsh, "The Cognitive Content of Art," *PhR* 52 (1943); J. Hospers, *Meaning and Truth in the Arts* (1946), "Implied Truths in Lit.," *JAAC* 19 (1960); Brooks; A. Isenberg, "Critical Communication," *PhR* 58 (1949), "The Aesthetic Function of Lang.," *JP* 46 (1949); M. Weitz, *Philosophy of the Arts* (1950); H. D. Aiken, "The Aesthetic Relevance of Belief," *JAAC* 9 (1951); P. Ziff, "The Task of Defining a Work of Art," *PhR* 62 (1953), "Reasons in Art Crit.," *Philosophy and Education*, ed. I. Scheffler (1958); R. S. Crane, *The Langs. of Crit. and the Structure of Poetry* (1953); A. Kaplan, "Referential Meaning in the Arts," *JAAC* 12 (1954); A. Sesonske, "Truth in Art," *JP* 53 (1956); Frye; W. E. Kennick, "Does Traditional Aesthetics Rest on a Mistake?" *Mind* 67 (1958); M. C. Beardsley, *Aesthetics* (1958); *Aesthetics and Lang.*, ed. W. Elton (1959); F. Sibley, "Aesthetic Concepts," *PhR* 68 (1959), "Aesthetic and Nonaesthetic," *PhR* 74 (1965); W. Righter, *Logic and Crit.* (1963); J. Casey, *The Lang. of Crit.* (1966); E. D. Hirsch, *Validity in Interp.* (1967); G. Graff, *Poetic Statement and Critical Dogma* (1970); W. H. Youngren, *S., Linguistics, and Crit.* (1972), "What is Literary Theory?" *HudR* 26 (1973). W.H.Y.

SEMIOTICS, POETIC. The modern usage of the term "s." is attributed to John Locke, who appropriated the Gr. *semeiotiké* to designate the *doctrine of signs*, "the business whereof is to consider the nature of signs the mind makes use *for the understanding of things*, or conveying its knowledge to others." The study of signs, however, has much more ancient roots. In speculating on the origin of lang., the Platonic dialogue *Cratylus* describes the linkage between linguistic sound and meaning as motivated by either nature or convention (*physei* vs. *thesei*), thus establishing one of the basic dichotomies for all subsequent discussions. Aristotle's *On Interp.* and *Rhetoric* and St. Augustine's *On Christian Doctrine* and *The Teacher* are other important ancient treatises on the subject, and various scholastics continued the line of inquiry through the Middle Ages. The major modern figures, besides Locke, are the philosophers and linguists Gottfried Wilhelm Leibniz, Johann Heinrich Lambert, Etienne Bonnot de Condillac, Wilhelm von Humboldt, and Bernhard Bolzano. Contemporary semiotic studies are a combination of several intellectual trads. stemming from the turn of the 20th c. From among them we shall focus here on three schools of thought that stimulated the application of sign theory to poetics: Peircean pragmatism, Husserlian phenomenology, and Saussurian structuralism.

The most comprehensive program for the general science of signs was charted by the Am. philosopher Charles Sanders Peirce. His brilliant work, huge in scope and characterized by ever-multiplying typologies and neologisms, has only recently come under systematic study. According to Peirce, "a sign or *representamen* is something which stands to somebody for something in some respect or capacity." Hence, every sign-process (or *semiosis*) is the correlation of three components:

the sign itself, the object represented, and the interpretant. The relationship between the sign and its object (as the above definition suggests) implies a certain inadequacy between the two. The sign does not stand for the object in its entirety but merely for some of its aspects. Peirce claimed that there are three basic modes in which the sign can represent something else, and hence three types of signs. A sign that resembles its object (such as a model or a map) is an *icon* (see ICONIC-ITY); a sign that is factually linked to its object (such as a weathercock or a pointer) is an *index*; a sign conventionally associated with its object (such as words or traffic signals) is a *symbol*.

The relationship between the sign and the interpretant is determined, Peirce maintains, by the sign's relation to its object, because the interpretant is supposed to stand to the object in the same relation as the sign. In fact, the interpretant of a sign is yet another sign that the original sign has evoked in the interpreter. In short, the process of interp. is nothing but the substitution of certain signs for others. To interpret the word *table* one can resort to an icon (by drawing its picture), an index (by pointing to an actual table), or a symbol (by supplying a synonym). From this perspective, then, thought or knowledge is a web of interconnected signs capable of unlimited self-generation (see DECONSTRUCTION).

In contrast to the Am. pragmatist Peirce, who considered the s. domain in its entirety, Continental thinkers focused above all on lang. as the most important human signifying mechanism. The Ger. phenomenologist Edmund Husserl was concerned with verbal signs as vehicles of logical thought capable of embodying truth. For him, only a repeatable sign that retains its essential self-sameness under all circumstances can fulfill this role. In his quest for a universal s. Husserl divided all signs into two categories: The self-identical *expression* (*Ausdruck*), and the vacillating *indication* (*Anzeichen*) which represents the changeable state of affairs. To explain why expressions can remain unaffected by the context of the significatory act, Husserl analyzed the internal structure of the word (for him an example of the expression par excellence) to isolate a factor resistant to contextual change. "In the case of the name," he wrote, "we distinguish between what it 'shows forth' (i.e. a mental state) and what it means. And again between what it means (the sense or 'content' of its naming presentation) and what it names (the object of that presentation)." Both the "showing forth" and the "naming" are contingent upon empirical reality (whether mental or physical) and thus cannot retain their sameness in repetition. Only the "content of an expression's naming presentation," the "meaning" (*Bedeutung*), is independent of the phenomenal context. It is therefore this lexical meaning inherent in the word prior to its representing other entities that endows the expression with its identity and distinguishes it from the indication.

The nature of verbal signs was also the central concern of another pioneer of modern s., the Swiss linguist Ferdinand de Saussure. "*A science that studies the life of signs with society* is conceivable," Saussure claimed. "I shall call it *semiology* (from the Gr. *sēmeîon* 'sign'). Semiology would show what constitutes signs, what laws govern them. Since this science does not yet exist, no one can say what it would be; but it has a right to existence, a place staked out in advance." Within this general science, then, the study of lang. would be the branch concerned with "the most important . . . system of signs that express ideas."

Since words are the prime example of conventional signs, Saussure focused exclusively on the system of linguistic conventions (*langue*) that makes actual utterances (*parole*) understandable to lang. users. He considered *langue* a purely formal set of relations that (in the absence of other motivations) arbitrarily conjoin the two components of the linguistic *sign*—the sensory *signifier* and the intelligible *signified*. Accordingly, the study of the signifier was to yield a set of oppositions (i.e. the phonological system) that provides sonorous substance (the continuum of the soundstream) with linguistic form by articulating it into a limited inventory of *phonemes*, the minimal sound units capable of differentiating words of unlike meaning in a given lang. (e.g. the voiceless voiced bilabial stops *p* and *b* in *pit* and *bit*, sounds which would be identical except for the one "distinctive feature" of voicing, or vibration of the vocal cords, which feature alone creates, for speakers of Eng., two words, two meanings). The study of the signified, on the other hand, would be concerned with the semantic grid that segments extralinguistic reality into meaningful linguistic units (words). The semantic value of every particular signified would be derived solely from its opposition to other signifieds coexisting within the grid and hence creating a parallel matrix of distinctive oppositions. The Eng. *mutton* differs from Fr. *mouton* precisely because the meaning of the former is circumscribed by the word *sheep*, which has no equivalent in the Fr. vocabulary.

Another set of relations obtains in lang. through the combination of linguistic elements into more complex units. If concatenated into a sequence, the value of each segment is determined both by its juxtaposition to all the actual components in the sequence that precede or follow it, and by the presence or absence of all the potential elements of *langue* in some respect similar to it and capable of taking its place. The first of these, the aspect of the *contiguity* of elements in sequence, which gives lang. its "horizontal" dimension, Saussure termed the *syntagmatic* aspect of lang.; the latter, the "vertical dimension" in which one word which fills a slot in the syntactic string could be replaced, potentially, by others, Saussure termed the *associative* (in later usage, *paradigmatic*) aspect of lang. It remained for Roman Jakobson to give the equation relating the one to the other in verse via *equivalence* (q.v.) as the "poetic principle" (q.v.). As Saussure persuasively argued, these two functions are operative at all three linguistic levels: phonological, morphological, and syntactic. In the example above, the *p* in *pit* is opposed to the *i* that follows it as consonant to vowel, and at the same time it is opposed to the absent *b* that could have been substituted for it (giving *bit*) as voiceless phoneme to voiced. The words *pits, pitted, pitting* and *bits* that combine the same or different stems and affixes illustrate the same dual linkage at the morphological level as, *mutatis mutandis*, the lexical collocations *drilling bit, drilling pit*, and *orchestra pit* do at the syntactic level.

The first systematic attempts to apply the theory of signs to lit. date from the 1920s. The devel. of this critical method has to a large extant been linked to the worldwide interest in the structuralist paradigm over the past 60 years (see STRUCTURALISM). The cultural heterogeneity of this paradigm and its historical diversity has prevented semiotically inclined critics from reaching full agreement about the epistemological underpinnings of their enterprise, its scope and limits, or even common methodologies. What bounds such critics together is merely the general explanatory model that regards lit. as a specific mode of signifying practice governed by conventions that are distinct from all other uses of verbal signs. In the practical application of this model, each school or critic focuses on different facets of literary semiosis, defines in separate terms the conventions governing it, and accounts for its distinctness accordingly.

Though critics have always been aware that the special manipulation of lang. is one of the indispensable properties of poetry, only the anti-mimetic revolt of modernist art at the turn of the 20th c. led them to scrutinize and schematize the ways in which the linguistic medium can be used to achieve poetic effects. Keeping in step with Archibald MacLeish's celebrated slogan that "a poem should not mean / But be," the most radical theorists of the day denied verbal art any referential quality at all, rather identifying its *telos* with the striking orchestration of the linguistic sound devoid of meaning. Semiotic poetics came about as a partial corrective to the one-sidedness of such formalism. Without rejecting the salience of phonic devices for poetry, it attributed to them a value only insofar as they participate in poetic semantics.

This stance was first formulated by Roman Jakobson, perhaps the most seminal figure in this critical trend, in his 1921 booklet on the Rus. futurist poet Velimir Xlebnikov. He based his argument on the two earlier theories of the linguistic sign by Saussure and Husserl. Drawing particularly on the phonological insights of Saussure, Jakobson rejected the possibility of separating sound from meaning in lang. *Phoné*, as the signifier's substance, is always semanticized because its chief function is to distinguish among different signifieds. If poetry were to succeed in voiding the semantic charge of its sonorous substance it would inevitably lose its verbal nature and turn into a kind of vocal music. Moreover, Jakobson made the semiotic orientation of his poetics explicit by anchoring it in Husserl's concept of expression. It is the "set (*Einstellung*) toward expression itself," Jakobson claimed, that designates it "as the only factor essential for poetry." As long as verbal art operates with expressions, meaning will always be present in it.

The phenomenological analysis of the linguistic sign also provided Jakobson with a criterion for distinguishing poetic signs from other locutions. To the three functions of the name—showing forth, naming, and meaning—he attributed three goal-oriented linguistic systems (i.e. functional dialects)—the emotive, the practical, and the poetic. Their respective utterances set the perceiver's attention to three different components of the speech event: respectively, the speaker's mental state, the reality designated, and the sign itself (expression). Jakobson and others (K. Bühler, J. Mukařovský) elaborated and modified this model so that in its final form (Jakobson's "Linguistics and Poetics" in Sebeok, 1960) it appeared as follows:

CONTEXT
(Referential function)

MESSAGE
(Poetic function)

ADDRESSER————————ADDRESSEE
(Emotive function)   (Conative function)

CONTACT
(Phatic function)

CODE
(Metalingual function)

But how is the poetic message structured so as to make the perceiver focus solely on it? According to Jakobson's widely quoted formulation, "the poetic function projects the principle of equivalence from the axis of selection onto the axis of combination." This definition is derived from the Saussurian premise of the dual linkage of every element in an utterance. *Selection* is a process based on the paradigmatic dimension in which a linguistic item is chosen from among a group of items conjoined within the code (Saussure's *langue*) and capable of replacing each other in an actual message on the basis of equivalence. *Combination* is the syntagmatic concatination, the temporal chain of the dissimilar items actually selected, i.e. the sequence of phonemes and morphemes itself.

In utterances dominated by the poetic function, equivalence becomes "the constitutive device of the sequence." All the linguistic elements (from the phonological to the semantic) strive for *repetition* (q.v.) and, in so doing, become equivalent to each other in sequence, i.e. as a matrix of *parallelism* (q.v.). Poetry, in which every element from sound-echo to rhythm to meter to rhyme scheme promotes multiple parallelisms at every level, is the most marked example of this structuring principle, which turns the syntagm into its own paradigm, rendering its linguistic structure a self-generating matrix. It is for this reason that the phenomenon of parallelism came to have an ever-increasing role in Jakobson's thought on verse.

The "set toward the message" has an important consequence for how poetry signifies. It imparts to verbal art what Jakobson called its "thoroughgoing symbolic, multiplex, polysemantic essence." In explaining this phenomenon he drew attention to the associative principles that underlie the two fundamental linguistic operations of selection and combination. Selection substitutes one element for another on the basis of their partial lexical similarity, in the same way as does the rhetorical trope of *metaphor* (q.v.). Combination links elements that are spatially or temporally contiguous, very much as does the trope of *metonymy* (q.v.). The synthetic power of linguistic consciousness stems from its capacity to create an interplay between the metaphoric and metonymic poles. Each concrete utterance strikes its own balance between the two, depending upon the overall function it serves. Since a self-centered poetic message tends to establish as many equations among its constitutive elements as possible, assimilating them into coherent structures of repetition at every level, poetry, in Jakobson's opinion, gravitates clearly toward the metaphoric extreme.

Jakobson's revision of Saussurian *sémiologie* rekindled interest in the most ancient issue of sign theory: how linguistic sound is linked to its meaning. Saussure always insisted that in most instances the relation between the signifier and the signified is wholly conventional, wholly arbitrary. For him, compound words such as *nineteen*, whose signification is motivated through paradigmatic and syntagmatic relations with other words comprised of its constituent morphemes (*nine, -teen*), impose certain limits on this arbitrariness but do not invalidate it. For Jakobson, however, the signification of a poetic sign challenges Saussure's assumption. The meaning of a poem is above all a function of its linguistic texture, and the very make-up of the signifier determines the signified. Hence, their relation is always motivated. In the 1960s, Jakobson turned to the s. of C. S. Peirce to support this claim, and in particular to the concept of the *icon*.

The *icon* can be regarded as a motivated sign, since, according to Peirce, it "stands for something merely because it resembles it." This representational likeness, however, can have a variety of grounds, of which only two are directly relevant to the present discussion. An icon may resemble an object by sharing simple physical qualitites with it (color, shape, etc.), in which case it is what Peirce termed an *image*. Or it might resemble an object by containing within itself the same intelligible relations as the object (the ratio of parts to whole, structural homology, etc.), in which case it is what Peirce called a *diagram*. It is the latter type of iconicity that intrigued Jakobson. Traditional accounts of linguistic mimesis usually neglected this motivation and focused on words whose sound imitates a nonlinguistic sound, i.e. the process traditionally called *onomatopoeia* (q.v.). Given the paucity and marginality of such words in most langs., however, this argument obviously did not carry much weight. In contrast, Jakobson located the iconicity of lang. not in its sonorous matter but in the deep-seated diagrammatic likeness or homology of the signifier to the signified embodied in the sign's phonological, morphological, and syntactic structures. For example, Caesar's dictum, *veni, vidi, vici*, Jakobson insisted, is a motivated sign because the sequence of verbs repeats the sequence of reported events. However, in a nonreferential poetic utterance, the direction of motivation is reversed. Here the relational properties of the signifier, the interactions among its partial signs, create the structure of the signified, the poem's semantic universe.

Jakobson's fusion of previously separate doctrines of the sign into a coherent disciplinary matrix represents a stage in the history of semiotic poetics that reached its apogee in the late 1960s. In subsequent years, however, this theoretical model and the entire structuralist trad. it epitomizes were subjected to thoroughgoing scrutiny. The Fr. philosopher Jacques Derrida and the deconstructionist critics whom he inspired rejected the entire semiotic project *tout court*. It was marred from its inception, they argued, by adherence to "the Western metaphysics of presence," a tendency inimical to the very process of re-presentation because of its drive to obliterate the essential precondition of this process—the radical difference or gap between the sign and what it stands for (see DECONSTRUCTION). Those critics who retained the concept of the sign in their discourse revised it in a number of ways. To schematize their dissent from Jakobsonian s., we may group all these new devels. under three headings, the three charges most commonly leveled against the structuralist heritage: *linguistic imperialism, semantic determinism,* and *monologism*.

Linguistic imperialism is the reduction of poetic (and other) structures to linguistic data. Structuralism might be right in seeing poetry as a purposive manipulation of lang., but not all the patterns which a linguistic analysis discovers in a text need be aesthetically effective, or even perceived. "Stylistic facts," Michael Riffaterre writes, "must have a specific character, since otherwise they could not be distinguished from linguistic facts." In other words, the linguistic code alone is an insufficient tool for reading a poem *qua* poem. It must be supplemented by additional codes, literary conventions that are extra-linguistic. Thus, Jonathan Culler claims, an adequate response to lyric poetry is predicated on the following set of conventional expectations that transcend lang.: (1) distance and deixis (the text is detached from its originator and the speech-situation); (2) coherence (it presents a unified whole); (3) significance (it contains a moment of epiphany); (4) resistance and recuperation (it can be processed despite its surface opacity). The semiotic analysis of poetry, however, need not stop at the subject of literary conventions. Soviet scholars from the Moscow-Tartu school (V. V. Ivanov, J. Lotman, B. Uspenskij—see STRUCTURALISM, sect. 2) conceive of verbal art as a "secondary modeling system," i.e. a code superimposed upon lang. (the "primary system"), yet closely linked with other secondary systems (the arts, science, religion, etc.) within the overarching cultural system of a period. Thus, literary norms are the product of a complex interaction among all the semiotic codes and must be studied in conjunction with them. From this perspective, poetics turns into a branch of the s. of culture, the general discipline concerned with the "collected nonhereditary information accumulated, preserved, and handed on by the various groups of human society."

Semantic determinism: the patterning of the poetic signifier establishes the total range for the constitution of the signified. This assumption has been challenged on a number of grounds. Within the Prague School, a literary historian, Felix Vodička, drew attention to the temporal rupture between the literary sign and the set of conventions against which it is read. This history of literary reception furnishes copious examples of works reconstituted according to codes that did not exist at their inception, thus assuming new and unpredictable semiotic identities. Besides the vicissitudes of history, the very organization of texts can make them resistant to a totalizing interp. Such are, in Umberto Eco's parlance, the "open works" that employ indeterminacy (q.v.) as their structuring principle. Their ambiguity (q.v.) may stem from the fact that they are simultaneously liable to incompatible codes, or that they invite the reader to project them against the exigencies of an uncoded context. Roland Barthes' concept of a "writerly text" celebrates the infinite freeplay of signification in a work that is "a galaxy of signifiers, not a structure of signifieds," because "the codes it mobilizes extend *as far as the eye can reach*" and "are indeterminable (meaning here is never subject to a principle of determination, unless by throwing dice)." Julia Kristeva blames the deterministic tenor of structuralist s. on its neglect of the speaking subject as a psycho-biological being. Poetic lang., she believes, is not just a system-gov-

erned activity but, above all, a system-transgressing creativity corresponding to a subject's capacity for enjoyment (*jouissance*). Rather than the smooth matching of a discrete signified to its proper signifier based on some logical isomorphism, literary discourse is a violent irruption of a subject's semiotic dispositions (e.g. libidinal drives) into preexisting symbolic systems. Hence its liberating force: it has the ability to dissolve the customary linguistic grids and establish new networks of signifying possibilities.

Monologism: the sign is studied only in relation to an abstract system (*langue*), apart from the communicative situation. This issue was raised in the late 1920s by the Rus. scholars around Mikhail Bakhtin (P. N. Medvedev, V. N. Vološinov) but it gained wide currency only some 40 years later. For the Bakhtinians, lang. exists only in communication. In this process, the intersubjective linguistic forms (hypostasized by Saussure as *langue*) serve merely as an auxiliary mechanism for the transmission of contents unique and particular to each interlocutor. Our understanding of the other speaker does not reside in a passive recognition of self-identical signs but in their active appropriation, the translation of an alien word into our own tongue. Accordingly, every lang. use is a dialogue—a response to a word by a word—and the structure of the verbal parcel reflects this. The word is not a static entity with a fixed meaning but a locus of action, a cross-section of different and often clashing points of view. In literary discourse it is the genre of the novel, the Bakhtinians claim, that best embodies this dialogic principle. Bakhtin's insights were subsequently utilized by Kristeva, who coined the term "intertextuality" (q.v.) to designate the polyphonic nature of poetic lang., with its tendency to transpose one system of signs over another; the notion of intertextuality was employed by Riffaterre for his analyses of 19th- and 20th-c. Fr. poetry. According to him, "a word or a phrase is poeticized when it refers to (or if a phrase, patterns itself upon) a preexistent word group." For Riffaterre, poetic texts depend to a considerable extent on what he terms "hypograms"—clichés, quotations, or sayings—the *loci communes* of the given period, and they make sense only if related to the verbal background they engender. The successful interp. of a poem, therefore, requires the discovery of an appropriate hypogram, the semiotic key that locks all the disparate textual elements into a unified whole.

As a general theory of signs, s. extends far beyond the field of poetics, of course. Instrumental for this interdisciplinary diffusion of s. was the rise, in the early 1960s, of structuralism (q.v.), which emphasized the analysis of semiotic codes governing such disparate phenomena as prose narrative (Genette, Segre, Todorov), mythical thought (Lévi-Strauss), the subconscious (Lacan), fashion (Barthes), and film (Lotman, Metz). S. also branched out into various behavioral sci-

SENSIBILITY

ences and new fields of inquiry that began to be charted: *kinesics* (gestures and body movements as conduits of information); *proxemics* (the meaning of spatial organization of the human environment); and animal communication (for which Sebeok coined the label of *zoosemiotics*).

See also ANAGRAM; HISTORICISM; INTERPRETATION; LINGUISTICS AND POETICS; MEANING, POETIC; REPRESENTATION AND MIMESIS; SEMANTICS AND POETRY; SIMPLICITY AND COMPLEXITY; SOUND; STRUCTURALISM; TWENTIETH-CENTURY POETICS.

E. Husserl, *Logische Untersuchungen* (1900); F. de Saussure, *Cours de linguistique générale* (1916), 5th ed. (1955), crit. ed., ed. R. Engler (1967–74), tr. R. Harris (1983); E. Cassirer, *Philosophie der Symbolischen Formen* (1923–29); V. N. Vološinov, *Marksizm i filosofija jazyka* (1929); C. S. Peirce, *Collected Papers*, ed. C. Hartshorne and P. Weiss, 8 v. (1931–58)—esp. v. 2, 8; C. Morris, *Foundations of the Theory of Signs* (1938); J. Mukařovskij, *Kapitoly z české poetiky* (1941); L. Hjelmslev, *Omkring sprogteoriens grundlaeggelse* (1943); Sebeok; M. Bense, *Theorie der Texte* (1962); Jakobson—esp. v. 3; J. Derrida, *De la grammatologie* (1967); U. Eco, *La struttura assente* (1968), *A Theory of S.* (1976); J. M. Lotman, *Struktura chudožestvennogo teksta* (1970); R. Barthes, *S/Z* (1970); *Essais de sémiotique poétique*, ed A. J. Greimas (1972); C. Segre, *Semiotics and Lit. Crit.* (1973); R. Mayenova, *Poetyka teoretyczna* (1974); J. Kristeva, *La Révolution du lang. poétique* (1974); Culler, esp. ch. 3; M. Riffaterre, *S. of Poetry* (1978), *Text Production* (tr. 1983); T. Todorov, *Theories of the Symbol* (tr. 1982); H. Baran, "Structuralism and S.," in Terras; *Encyclopedic Dict. of S.*, ed. T. A. Sebeok (1986); J. Culler, *Ferdinand de Saussure*, 2d ed. (1986); J. K. Sheriff, *The Fate of Meaning* (1989); W. Nöth, *Handbook of S.* (1990).   P.ST.

SENARIUS (Lat. "of 6 each"). The Lat. equivalent of the Gr. iambic trimeter, the s. (x – x – x – x – x – ◡ –) is the common dialogue meter of Roman comedy. This Lat. version is organized by feet rather than metra, as in the Gr., and all odd positions are anceps (q.v.) except the eleventh position, which is always a pure short. "Split anapests" are generally avoided; i.e., a resolved anceps (x – ◡ ◡ –) may not be followed or split in the middle by the end of a word spilling over from the preceding foot. Avoidance of line ends ◡ – | ◡ – and – ◡ – | ◡ – was made so strict in Seneca and Petronius that an iambic word or word end cannot fill the fifth foot in their verses; the ninth position in Seneca's senarii is almost invariably a long even when a four-syllable word fills the last two feet. Though writers from the first century B.C. on adhere to the Gr. practice of allowing short syllables in the 3d and 7th positions, late Lat. archaizing poets, incl. Hilary of Poitiers and Ausonius, return to the s. in its original Lat. form.

See CANTICUM AND DIVERBIUM; SEPTENARIUS.

Hardie, pt. 1, ch. 5; W. M. Lindsay, *Early Lat. Verse* (1922); Norberg; Crusius; C. Questa, *Introduzione alla metrica di Plauto* (1967); Halporn et al.; J. Soubiran, *Essai sur la versif. dramatique des romains: Senaire iambique et septenaire trochaique* (1988).   J.W.H.

SENHAL. A fanciful name ("My Magnet," "Tristan," "Good Hope") used in Occitan poems to address a lady, patron, or friend. A few of the persons so addressed have been identified with some certainty, but for the most part they remain either completely unknown or the objects of more or less probable conjectures.   F.M.C.

SENRYŪ. See JAPANESE POETRY.

SENSIBILITY first became prominent as a literary term in the mid 18th c. to refer to susceptibility to emotional impressions, esp. to tender feelings, a popular quality in the age of Sterne, Goldsmith, and Cowper. The feelings may be one's own or those of others. The person of s. luxuriates not only in pleasant feelings (e.g. love or delight in nature) but also in painful: hence the frequency of such oxymorons as "the luxury of grief" or the "pleasing tear." S. to the feelings of others, if valued, can lead to the claim that s. is not only aesthetically important but also morally praiseworthy, since it releases us from selfishness. This can be—and was—contrasted with Stoic morality, which condemns the useless emotions of pity and grief, and with a stern Christian morality, which insists on the fallen nature of mankind and the consequent untrustworthiness of all natural passions. It can also be attacked by a modern radical critique, which regards the emotions of pity and distress as devices for maintaining the status quo.

The history of the concept is intimately bound up with the history of the word: before the mid 18th c., it is rare and found only in medical or philosophical contexts. Addison (1711) speaks about modesty as an "exquisite s.," but perhaps the first clear-cut instance of its use (without the need for a laudatory adjective) to refer to a praiseworthy emotional susceptibility appears in the periodical *The Prompter* in 1735: the writer is defending that Humanity which "is not satisfied with good-Natured actions alone, but feels the Misery of others with inward Pain. It is then deservedly named S." Thereafter it becomes frequent in lit. crit., as in Warton's remark (1756) that certain beauties "need not be pointed out to any reader of s." It was soon joined by its synonym "sentimentality" (q.v.); the adjective "sentimental" dates from 1749, when it is already referred to as "so much in vogue among the polite." In the course of the 19th c. the two words move apart as "sentimentality" begins to acquire its mod. pejorative connotation. The adjective "sensible" also undergoes a semantic shift in the 19th c., losing its link with s. and retaining only the meaning "endowed with good sense." The nearest thing to an adjective connected with s. then becomes "sensitive," but this has never become a technical term in crit.

S.—and discussion of it—is most prominent in the novel, where it is central to Richardson, Rousseau, and (explicitly so) to Sterne; and Mackenzie's novel *The Man of Feeling* (1771) has long been regarded as a *locus classicus* for most of the cliches of s. But s. has its importance in poetry, too, beginning perhaps with Thomson's celebration of "those whom wisdom and whom nature charm / To steal themselves from the degenerate crowd. . . . And woo lone Quiet in her silent walks" ("Autumn" 964 ff.). Gray and Collins can both be seen as poets of s.: Gray's "Hymn to Adversity" introduces "Pity, dropping soft the sadly-pleasing tear"; and in the "Elegy" we have not only the reference to the distress of dying and our longing to be remembered ("On some fond breast the parting soul relies, / Some pious drops the closing eye requires") but most strikingly—and most conventionally—the concluding picture of the melancholy poet who "gave to mis'ry all he had (a tear)." There are a number of odes to s. from the 1760s on: Goldsmith's *Deserted Village* is a poem of s., with its indulgence in the pleasures of nostalgia; Cowper in *The Task* (esp. Book 6) makes a moral claim for s. and suggests that its opposite is not only insensibility but cruelty.

At first glance, the cult of s. looks like an anticipation of the romantic movement, with its emphasis on the emotional life of the poet and the importance of capturing the true voice of feeling; and such a poem as Wordsworth's "The Brothers" reads very like a conventional 18th-c. poem of s. But there are important differences: it is only with the romantics that the idea of emotion (q.v.) as the source of the ability to write true poetry arises, and there is no longer such emphasis, in Wordsworth, Blake, Shelley, and Keats, on those tender emotions of pity, grief, and nostalgia which give such individuality to the cult of s. Furthermore, there was in the 1790s a marked reaction against s. on moral, political, and aesthetic grounds. Jane Austen is the most famous figure in this, not only in *Sense and S.* but even more directly in *Sanditon*. Coleridge in a sonnet of 1797 mocked at the "doleful egoism" of s.: "And mused me on the wretched ones that pass O'er the bleak heath of sorrow. But alas! Most of myself I thought. . . ."

When the term s. returned to lit. crit. in the 20th c., it was with a much wider meaning, one that drew more clearly on the history of the word as a philosophical term. It can also be seen as a term drawing together a number of ideas that became increasingly important as 20th-c. crit. proceeded. For an important anticipation of these ideas we can turn to Baudelaire, who in his essay on Constantin Guys suggests that the child, the convalescent, and the artist are alike in possessing "the ability to be vividly interested in things, even those that appear most trivial. . . . The child sees every-

thing *afresh*; he is always drunk." We can see here the linking of physical and emotional responsiveness that is the essence of the modern meaning of the term, along with an awareness of flux and a mingling of the senses. The philosophical counterpart to this literary concept is in Bergson and his Eng. disciple T. E. Hulme: reality is a flux of interpenetrated elements unseizable by the intellect. Hulme's tiny fragments of poetry, and the Imagist movement to which they are allied (see IMAGISM), can be seen as deriving from this view.

Of all modern critics, it was T. S. Eliot who did most to draw these ideas together under the term s. For him too the physical element is very strong: "a thought to Donne was an experience: it modified his s." (this must mean that he apprehended it with his five senses—"like the odour of a rose"). For Eliot, however, the term does not indicate one special kind of awareness or yield one particular poetic style: s. is simply a name for the artistic faculty as found in every poet. As a result, he brings the term closer to intellect, incl. in it the ability to offer intellectual resistance to the dangers of generalization. Eliot's famous doctrine of "dissociation of s." (q.v.) refers to a disjunction between the intellect and the senses, and adumbrates a rather simpleminded and nostalgic view of cultural history.

After Eliot, the term s. tended to widen its meaning still further, until the poet's s. came to mean little other than "the sort of person he is." But in the 1980s, s. has almost disappeared as a critical term, as structuralism and post-structuralism have increasingly directed attention away from the creating subject towards factors inherent in the lang. and in codes and discursive practices. S. can be said to have lost its centrality as a critical term not because changing theories of the creative process have proposed other terms, but because crit. has turned to look at different problems. See also NAIVE-SENTIMENTAL; NEOCLASSICAL POETICS; SENTIMENTALITY; SUBLIME.

So distinct are the two uses of "s." that the bibl. which follows is divided into two sections.

18TH-CENTURY USAGE: Addison, *Spectator*, no. 231 (1711), GUARDIAN, no. 19 (1713); V. Woolf, "Mr. Bennett and Mrs. Brown," *The Common Reader* (1925); R. S. Crane, "Suggestions towards a Genealogy of the Man of Feeling," *ELH* 1 (1934); N. Frye, "Towards Defining an Age of S.," *ELH* 23 (1956); A. Sherbo, *Eng. Sentimental Drama* (1957); C. S. Lewis, *Studies in Words* (1960); L. I. Bredvold, *The Natural Hist. of S.* (1962); C. J. Rawson, "Some Remarks on 18th-C. Delicacy," *JEGP* 61 (1962); *From S. to Romanticism*, ed. F. W. Hilles and H. Bloom, (1965), esp. I. Jack, "Gray's Elegy Reconsidered"; G. Dekker, *Coleridge and the Lit. of S.* (1978); J. H. Hagstrum, *Sex and S.* (1980); J. Todd, *S.: An Intro.* (1986); *S. in Transformation*, ed. S. M. Conger (1990).

MODERN USAGE: C. Baudelaire, "Le Peintre de la vie moderne," *L'Art romantique* (1869); H. James, "The Art of Fiction," *Partial Portraits*

(1888); T. E. Hulme, *Speculations* (1924); T. S. Eliot, "The Metaphysical Poets," "Andrew Marvell," in Eliot, *Essays*. L.D.L.

SENSIBILITY, DISSOCIATION OF. See DISSO-CIATION OF SENSIBILITY.

SENTIMENTALITY in poetry: (1) poetic indulgence in the exhibition of pathetic emotions for their own sake; (2) poetic indulgence of more emotion (often self-regarding) than seems warranted by the stimulus; (3) excessively direct poetic expression of pathos (q.v.) without a sufficient artistic correlative. Whether in poet or reader, s., a form of emotional redundancy, and thus a fault of rhet. as well as of ethics and tact, often suggests the presence of self-pity and the absence of mature emotional self-control. The poetic sentimentalist appears to be interested in pathos as an end rather than as an artistic means or as a constituent of broader, less personal experience. The sentimentalist will often be found burdened with an uncritically romantic sensibility: dogs, children, old women, and the deprived are not merely objects of pity, they are objects of reverence and even envy.

S. in poetry tends to register itself in the tags of popular journalism: adjectives are frequently clichés, and emotions remain vague and oversimplified, never becoming transmuted into something more meaningful. (In popular artifacts like souvenirs and domestic bric-a-brac, a similar treatment results in what is known as *Kitsch*). An example of sentimental treatment is the low journalistic habit of using the redundant adjective "little" when referring to an unfortunate child. A similar technique of emotional redundancy appears in the following: "When love meets love, breast urged to breast, / God interposes / An unacknowledged guest, / And leaves a little child among our roses" (T. E. Brown, *When Love Meets Love*).

The quality of self-indulgence in the following parody by Coleridge of the standard late 18th-c. sentimental poem is palpable: the speaker announces, not once but often, that he is experiencing emotion, emotion he does not convey but merely describes: "Pensive at eve on the hard world I mused, / And my poor heart was sad: so at the Moon / I gazed—and sighed and sighed—for ah! how soon / Eve darkens into night" ("Nehemiah Higginbottom"). Here, the feeling, not having located its poetic correlatives (images, symbols), remains naked and untransmuted—and funny. Poetic s. also tends to manifest an unconvincing hyperbole, which often fails because the imagery is trite or vapid: "If I can stop one heart from breaking, / I shall not live in vain; / If I can ease one life the aching, / Or cool one pain, / Or help one fainting robin / Unto his nest again, / I shall not live in vain" (Emily Dickinson).

Historically, s. (at least in the modern sense of the term) seems not to have entered poetry much before the 18th c.; its appearance (e.g. in Cowper,

Gray, Shelley) may be due to a strong current of philosophic optimism popularized by the writings of Shaftesbury and Rousseau. It was in the 18th c. that audiences became fond of sentimental melodramas and comedies such as the plays of Hugh Kelly and Richard Cumberland, which depict characters performing extravagant acts of benevolence. The appearance of s. would also seem to be related to the tendency toward increasing subjectivity (q.v.) in 18th-c. aesthetics. S. is clearly a sign of the gradual attenuation of medieval and Ren. conceptions of the inherent evil of mankind. But it must be emphasized that the presentation of pathos (or of any other strong emotion) is not in itself a poetic vice. S. (and bad poetry) results only when the pathos, for whatever reason, is inadequately registered in the specific means of poetry and thus transformed from emotion into art.—I. A. Richards, *Practical Crit.* (1929); L. Lerner, "A Note on S.," *The Truest Poetry* (1960); L. I. Bredvold, *The Natural Hist. of Sensibility* (1962); G. S. Smith, "Sentimentalism and Preromanticism as Terms and Concepts," *Rus. Lit. in the Age of Catherine the Great*, ed. A. G. Cross (1976); R. O. Allen, "If You Have Tears: Sentimentalism as Soft Romanticism," *Genre* 8 (1977); Terras—Rus.; F. Kaplan, *Sacred Tears: S. in Victorian Lit.* (1987). P.F.

SEPHARDIC POETRY. See JUDEO-SPANISH POETRY.

SEPTENARIUS (Lat. "of 7 each"). The Lat. equivalent of the Gr. trochaic tetrameter catalectic (− x − x − x − x − x − x − ◡ −). The Gr. form is scanned as composed of four metra, but the Lat. version of seven feet and an additional syllable. It is the common recitative meter of Roman comedy. All the even positions except the last are anceps (q.v.) in the s.; the twelfth position is thus always a pure short. Generally there is a diaeresis (q.v.) after the eighth position. "Split dactyls" are generally avoided; i.e., a resolved anceps (− x − ◡ ◡) may not be followed or split in the middle by the end of a word spilling over from the preceding foot. There is the same avoidance of line ends ◡ − | ◡ − and − ◡ − | ◡ − as in the senarius (q.v.). The s. also appears as the *versus quadratus* (see CLASSICAL PROSODY) of soldiers' songs and satires, as well as in Late Lat. and Med. Lat. hymns. Schipper uses the Latinate term "septenary" to refer to the iambic 14-syllable line in ME, based on an assumed derivation of the vernacular line directly from Med. Lat., but this derivation glosses over significant problems of structure and transmission, and as such is but one instance of the appropriation of terminology from one verse-system into another without due consideration of the fundamental differences between the two. See now CANTICUM AND DIVERBIUM; SENARIUS.—Schipper; Hardie, pt. 1, ch. 7; W. M. Lindsay, *Early Lat. Verse* (1922); E. Fraenkel, "Die Vorgesch. des versus quadratus," *Hermes* 62

SEPTET

(1927); Beare; Norberg; Crusius; C. Questa, *Introduzione alla metrica di Plauto* (1967); Halporn et al.; J. Soubiran, *Essai sur la versif. dramatique des romains: Senaire iambique et septenaire trochaique* (1988). J.W.H.; T.V.F.B.

SEPTET (It. *septette*; Fr. *septain*). A 7-line stanza of varying meter and rhyme scheme, usually reserved for lyric poetry. Ss., which first appear in the verse of the troubadours, are most often heterometric (q.v.), as in Shelley's "Mutability." In Eng. the most common form of s. is the 7-line iambic pentameter stanza of rhyme royal (q.v.), a ME form derived from Fr.; rhyme royal with the final line a hexameter—an effect comparable to that of the Spenserian (q.v.)—also occurs often enough to be distinctive, as in Milton. Other 7-line stanzas incl. Donne's pentameter ss. in "The Goodmorrow" (*ababccc*, the final line a hexameter) and "Loves Deitie" (final line tetrameter), his "Loves Exchange" (*aabbccc*, mixed) and "Hymne to Christ" (same scheme, pentameters, the final line a fourteener), and James Thomson's "City of Dreadful Night" (*ababccb* in pentameters, the *c* rhymes feminine).—Schipper, 2.655 ff., 729 ff.; E. F. Kossmann, *Die siebenzeilige Strophe in der deutschen Literatur* (1923); Scott, 144 ff. T.V.F.B.

SEQUENCE, LYRIC. See LYRIC SEQUENCE.

SEQUENCE, SONNET. See SONNET SEQUENCE.

SERBIAN, SERBO-CROATIAN POETRY. See YUGOSLAV POETRY.

SERRANILLA. A Sp. poem composed in any short meter, but esp. in the *arte mayor* (q.v.) half-line, and dealing lightly with the subject of the meeting of a gentleman and a pretty country girl. Sometimes, esp. if it is octosyllabic, it is called *serrana*. The s. was particularly characteristic of the late medieval period. The most famous are those of the Archpriest of Hita (1283?–1350?), and esp. those of the Marqués de Santillana (1398–1458); the latter may have been influenced by the "great volume of Portuguese and Galician *cantigas, serranas,* and *decires*" to which he says he had access in his youth.—Le Gentil; Navarro. D.C.C.

SESTET (It. *sestette, sestetto*; Fr. *septain*). (a) The minor division or last 6 lines of a sonnet (q.v.), preceded by an octave (q.v.). Sometimes the octave states a proposition or situation and the s. a conclusion, but no fast rules for content can be formulated. The rhyme scheme of the s. varies: in an It. sonnet it is usually *cdecde*, in an Eng., *efefgg*, but there are others. (b) Any separable 6-line section of a stanza. "S." is not generally used for an isolable 6-line stanza; Eng. has no modern term for the class, so the older "sexain" (q.v.) is still used. R.O.E.

SESTINA (It. *sestine, sesta rima*). The most complicated of the verseforms initiated by the troubadours (q.v.), the s. is composed of six stanzas of six lines each, followed by an *envoi* (q.v.) of three lines, all of which are unrhymed, and all decasyllabic (Eng.), hendecasyllabic (It.), or alexandrine (Fr.). The function of rhyme (i.e. sound repetition) in the s. is superseded by a recurrent pattern of end-words, i.e. lexical repetition (for discussion of this question see IDENTICAL RHYME). The same six end-words occur in each stanza, but in a shifting order which follows a fixed pattern: each successive stanza takes its pattern from a reversed (bottom up) pairing of the lines of the preceding stanza (i.e. last and first, then next-to-last and second, then third-from-last and third). If we let the numbers 1 through 6 stand for the end-words, we may schematize the pattern as follows:

> stanza 1 : 123456
> stanza 2 : 615243
> stanza 3 : 364125
> stanza 4 : 532614
> stanza 5 : 451362
> stanza 6 : 246531
> envoy : 531 or 135.

More commonly, the envoy, or *tornada* (q.v.), is further complicated by the fact that the remaining three end-words, 246, must also occur in the course of its three lines, so that it gathers up all six together.

The invention of the s. is usually attributed to Arnaut Daniel (fl. 1190), and the form was widely cultivated both by his Occitan followers and by poets in Italy (Dante, Petrarch, Gaspara Stampa), Spain, and Portugal (Camões, Ribeiro). A rhymed version (*abcbca* in the first stanza) was introduced into France by Pontus de Tyard (*Erreurs amoureuses*, 1549), a member of the *Pléiade* (q.v.). Sidney dispenses with rhyme for "Yee Gote-heard Gods," a double s. in the *Old Arcadia* (1590). In Germany, it was the poets of the 17th c. who were attracted to the s. (Opitz, Gryphius, Weckherlin). In France and England the s. enjoyed a revival in the 19th c., thanks to the Comte de Gramont and to Swinburne, both of whom developed rhymed versions, Gramont's all on the same two-rhyme model (*abaabb* in the first stanza), Swinburne's not surprisingly more variable, given that he also composed a double s. of 12 12-line stanzas ("The Complaint of Lisa"). Gramont prefaced his collection with a hist. of the s., in which he describes it as "a reverie in which the same ideas, the same objects, occur to the mind in a succession of different aspects, which nonetheless resemble one another, fluid and changing shape like the clouds in the sky." The s. interested the Fr. and Eng. Parnassians (q.v.) less than the other Romance fixed forms, but has had a certain popularity in the 20th c.; Pound called the s. "a form like a thin sheet of flame, folding and infolding upon itself," and his "S.: Altaforte" and "S. for Isolt," along with

SICILIAN SCHOOL

Auden's "Paysage moralisé" and *Kairos and Logos* cycle, MacNeice's "To Hedli," and Roy Fuller's "S." are distinguished modern examples.—F. de Gramont, *Sestines, précédés de l'histoire de la sextine* (1872); Kastner; F. Davidson, "The Origin of S.," *MLN* 25 (1910); A. Jeanroy, "La 's. doppia' de Dante et les origines de la sestine," *Romania* 42 (1912); H. L. Cohen, *Lyric Forms from France* (1922); L. Fiedler, "Green Thoughts in a Green Shade," *KR* 18 (1956); J. Riesz, *Die Sestine* (1971)—the fullest study; I. Baldelli, "S.," *Enciclopedia Dantesca*, ed. G. Petrocchi et al., 5 v. (1970–78); M. Shapiro, *Hieroglyph of Time: The Petrarchan S.* (1980); Morier; A. Roncaglia, "L'invenzione della sestina," *Metrica* 2 (1981); Elwert, *Italienische*, sect. 82; J. F. Nims, *A Local Habitation* (1985). A.PR.; C.S.

SEXAIN, sixain, sextain, sextet, sestet, hexastich. Names used for various stanza patterns of six lines. The term "sestet" (q.v.) is normally restricted to the final six lines of a sonnet (q.v), esp. an It. sonnet, in distinction to the octave (q.v.) or first 8 lines. The other terms are applied indiscriminately to all 6-line stanzas, only some of which have distinctive names. The best-known varieties of ss. in Eng. poetry are the following: (1) *ababcc*, in iambic pentameter, i.e. a heroic quatrain capped by a couplet, the so-called "Venus and Adonis stanza" (q.v.) from its use by Shakespeare, common for Ren. epyllia and complaints, and one of Arnold's favorite forms; (2) *ababcc*, in iambic tetrameter (e.g. Wordsworth's "I Wandered Lonely as a Cloud"), very popular in Ger. poetry; (3) *tail-rhyme* (q.v.), *aa4b3cc4b3*, sometimes called "Romance-six," which is an extension of ballad meter (q.v.), popular in OF and ME verse, often used by 16th-c. dramatists, found in religious and secular poems up to Herbert, and evidenced as late as Hardy ("The Sigh") and Bridges ("Nightingales"); (4) the Burns stanza (q.v.), *aaa4b2a4b2*, which may go back to Occitan models of the 11th c. and is found also in medieval romances and miracle plays; (5) *xayaza*, e.g. Rossetti's "Blessed Damozel"; and (6) *abcabc*, popular in Eng. poetry since Swinburne, e.g. in Yeats, John Berryman, Dylan Thomas, Richard Wilbur, and Thom Gunn. In Sp., the octosyllabic s. rhyming *aabccb* or *ababcc* is called a *sextilla* (q.v.). One of the earliest extant texts of Fr. verse, the *Vie de Saint Leger*, is set in 129 ss. rhyming in couplets, and the *Rhétoriqueurs* (q.v.) termed a poem of three short-line ss. *plate rime brisée*. The most famous and most spectacular poetic form in ss., the sestina (q.v.), uses elaborate patterns of repeated words. Six-line stanzas occur almost as often as quatrains and couplets (qq.v.) and more frequently than five-line stanzas.— Schipper, *History* 383; Morier, s.v. "Sextine." A.PR.; E.H.

SEXTILLA. A Sp. stanza form of six octosyllabic or shorter lines. In the classic period the usual rhyme schemes were *abbaab, ababba, ababab, abbaba, aabbab*, and *abaabb*; modern definitions often call for *aabccb* or *ababcc* (sometimes this last is called *sestina*) and occasionally stipulate that the *b* lines be oxytones and the others paroxytones. *Ss.* have been pointed out in the prologue to Alfonso the Wise's Galician-Portuguese *Cantigas a Santa Maria* (13th c.) and in the Archpriest of Hita's *Libro de buen amor* (14th c.):

¡Ventura astrosa,
cruel, enojosa,
captiva, mequina!
¿Por qué eres sañosa,
contra mí tan dañosa,
e falsa vesina?

Rengifo, *Arte poética española* (1592); A. de Trueba, *Arte de hacer versos* (1905); Navarro. D.C.C.

SHAPED POETRY. See PATTERN POETRY.

SHI(H). See CHINESE POETRY.

SHIʿR. See ARABIC POETRY.

SHORT. See DURATION; QUANTITY.

SHORT METER, SHORT MEASURE. See BALLAD METER; HYMN.

SIAMESE POETRY. See THAI POETRY.

SICILIAN OCTAVE (*ottava siciliana* or *napoletana*). An 8-line It. stanza rhyming *abababab* and composed of hendecasyllables (q.v.). It was generally used for amorous topics of a popular nature. The origin of this type of octave (q.v.) is still unclear. According to some scholars, it existed early in the 13th c. in Southern Italy and Sicily and influenced the invention of the sonnet (q.v.) by serving as the model for its octave, appearing in Tuscany (*ottava toscana*) only toward the end of that century. Others tend to place its origin in Tuscany and consider it, conversely, a derivation from the octave of the sonnet. The S. o. never had the success that *ottava rima* (q.v.) enjoyed, although it remained in popular use through the 15th c., when it was replaced by the madrigal (q.v.). See also STRAMBOTTO.—Spongano; Wilkins; Elwert, *Italienische*. L.H.G.; C.K.

SICILIAN RHYME. See ITALIAN PROSODY.

SICILIAN SCHOOL. A loosely organized group of poets writing in the vernacular who were active at the court of the Hohenstaufen monarchs in Sicily during the first three quarters of the 13th c. They flourished particularly under Frederick II and his son Manfred. Some 30 poets are associated with the S. s.; the majority of them were Sicilians, but a fair proportion came from the It. mainland, some from as far north as Tuscany. The major importance of the S. poets is that they established It. as a literary lang. They show familiarity with the work of the Occitan troubadours, the Northern Fr. *trouvères*, and with the Ger. *Minnesang* (qq.v.). The primarily amorous content of their work is derived from troubadour models, but unlike their northern It. contemporaries, they abandoned Occitan, the traditional lang. of the love lyric, and wrote in their own tongue. Of almost equal importance is their formal achievement: they invented the sonnet (q.v.), and they developed from Occitan, Fr., and Ger. models the distinctive structure of the *canzone* (q.v.; cf. CANSO), the two most important lyric forms of It. poetry (q.v.). The sonnet of the S. s., as written by its presumed inventor Giacomo da Lentini and others, shows in some instances what will become the characteristic feature of the form, the distinctive separation into octave and sestet. The octave always rhymes *abababab* (see SICILIAN OCTAVE) and the sestet is either *cdecde* or *cdcdcd* (cf. SESTINA).

These first It. poets exerted a powerful effect on all subsequent It. lyric verse through their influence, both formal and thematic, on the Tuscan poets of the 13th and 14th cs., on Guittone d'Arezzo, Guido Guinizelli, Dante, and Petrarch. Indeed, their influence was linguistic as well as literary: the occurrence of typically southern locutions in the Tuscan dialect, which became the standard literary lang. of Italy, may be traced to their example. The best of the S. poets, in addition to Giacomo da Lentini, are Guido delle Colonne, Pier delle Vigne, Giacomino Pugliese, and Rinaldo d'Aquino. See also SONNET.

G. A. Cesareo, *Le origini della poesia lirica e la poesia siciliana sotto gli Svevi*, 2d ed. (1924); V. de Bartholomaeis, *Primordi della lirica d'arte in Italia* (1943); W. T. Elwert, *Per una valutazione stilistica dell'elemento provenzale nel linguaggio della scuola poetica siciliana* (1955); E. Kantorowicz, *Frederick the Second, 1194–1250* (1957); E. H. Wilkins, *The Invention of the Sonnet and Other Studies* (1959); *Poeti del Duecento*, ed. G. Contini, 2 v. (1960); D. Mattalia, "La Scuola siciliana," *I Minori* (1961); *Le Rime della scuola siciliana*, ed. B. Panvini, 2 v. (1962–64); G. Folena, "Cultura e poesia dei siciliani," *Le Origini e il Duecento*, ed. E. Cecchi and N. Sapegno (1965); W. Pagani, *Repertorio tematico della scuola poetica siciliana* (1968); A. Fiorino, *Metri e temi della scuola siciliana* (1969); E. Pasquini and A. E. Quaglio, *Le origini e la scuola siciliana* (1971); T. C. Van Cleve, *The Emperor Frederick II of Hohenstaufen* (1972); Wilkins; M. Marti, "Siciliana, scuola," *Enciclopedia dantesca*, v. 5 (1978); *The Poetry of the S. S.*, ed. and tr. F. Jensen (1986).
A.PR.; C.K.; T.V.F.B.

SIGN, SIGNIFIER, SIGNIFIED. See REPRESENTATION AND MIMESIS; SEMIOTICS, POETIC; SEMANTICS AND POETRY; SYMBOL; DECONSTRUCTION.

SIGNIFICATIO. See PUN.

SIGNIFYING is the dominant satiric form in Afro-Am. verbal expression. It is a rhet. feature which works in implicit and explicit codes, characteristically undergirded by wit, allusion (qq.v.), sarcasm. Even though the s. technique may sometimes be utilized with a complimentary objective, in its basic usage it is doubtful that it can be totally disassociated from sarcasm. The tone of s. may range from harmless teasing to bitter and caustic diatribe. S. was nurtured significantly in Afro-Am. vernacular poetic forms such as toasts (q.v.), sagas, and blues (q.v.). There is a toast tradition known specifically as the s. monkey poems which takes satiric shots at all manner of subjects. Among the sagas, "Titanic Shine" is perhaps the most well known. The blues is replete with s. lines of various contour such as "Ain't a baker in town / Can bake a sweet jelly roll like mine" and "Take this hammer and carry it to my captain: / Tell him I'm gone." Although not restricted at all to poetry, the use of the s. tradition in Afro-Am. writing can be traced back to the earliest poets, such as Jupiter Hammon (b. 1711) on up through Paul Laurence Dunbar (1872–1906), carried mainly by Langston Hughes in the 20th c., then taken to its greatest period of exploration with emerging poets of the 1960s like Haki Madhubuti (don l. lee), Sonia Sanchez, Nikki Giovanni, and June Jordan. Gates has used the s. trad. to formulate a mode of crit. for Afro-Am. lit.—C. Mitchell-Kernan, "S.," *Motherwit from the Laughing Barrel: Readings in the Interp. of Afro-Am. Folklore*, ed. A. Dundes (1973); G. Smitherman, *Talkin and Testifyin* (1977); H. L. Gates, Jr., "The Blackness of Blackness: A Critique on the Sign and the S. Monkey," *Figures In Black* (1987), *The S. Monkey* (1988). E.A.P.

SIJO. See KOREAN POETRY.

SILLOI (Gr. "squint-eyed pieces," i.e. satirical verses). Title of a hexameter poem in three books by Timon of Philus (fl. ca. 250 B.C.) satirizing dogmatic philosophers. Such satirical verse had earlier been written, and perhaps invented, by Xenophanes of Colophon (ca. 570–470 B.C.), the philosopher-poet who founded Eliatic philosophy. By late antiquity five books of *silloi* were credited to him, but only fragments survive. Both poets used to be referred to as *sillographers*. *Silloi* parodied not personalities but the doctrines of philosophers or their schools.—C. Wachsmuth, *Sillographi graeci* (1885); Schmid and Stählin; Pauly-Wissowa; *CHCL*, v. 1. T.V.F.B.

SILVA. A Sp. poem in Italianate hendecasyllables and heptasyllables in which the poet makes strophic divisions at will, usually in unequal lengths, and rhymes most of the lines without set pattern, sometimes leaving a few lines unrhymed. Other meters may be used. The s., introduced in the 16th c., is sometimes considered a form of Italianate *canción* (q.v.) and called *canción libre*.

Morley-Bruerton (*The Chronology of Lope de Vega's Comedias*, 1940, p. 12) distinguishes four types in Lope's ss., which are also the types generally used by other poets: (1) "*s. de consonantes, aAbBcCdD*, etc.*" which "could be called *pareados* [couplets] de 7 y 11"; (2) "sevens and elevens mixed irregularly, no fixed order of length or rime, some unrimed lines"; (3) "all elevens, the majority . . . rimed, not counting the final couplet, no fixed order, mostly pairs, some *ABAB* and *ABBA*. May approximate to *sueltos* [free-riming lines] or *pareados* [couplets] de 11"; (4) "sevens and elevens mixed irregularly, all rimes in pairs."—Navarro.   D.C.C.

SIMILE. A figure of speech most conservatively defined as an explicit comparison using "like" or "as"—e.g. "black, naked women with necks / wound round and round with wire / like the necks of light bulbs" (Elizabeth Bishop). The function of the comparison is to reveal an unexpected likeness between two seemingly disparate things—in this case, the reduction of tribal African women to objects in a certain cultural context, just as light bulbs are objects in the (ironically similar) Am. context. As this s. illustrates, in the hands of a skilled poet, s. is capable of great power and is not merely "a pastime of very low order," as William Carlos Williams once remarked. Moreover, s. is probably the "oldest readily identifiable poetic artifice in European lit." (Holoka), stretching back through Homer and Mycenaean epic poetry to Sumerian, Sanskrit, and Chinese.

Nevertheless, critics and theorists radically disagree as to what distinguishes s. from factual comparisons on the one hand and metaphor (q.v.) on the other. While some theorists argue that factual comparisons ("My eyes are like yours") and ss. (such as Chaucer's "hir eyen greye as glas") differ only in degree, others argue that they differ in kind (a confusion which Wordsworth successfully exploits when he follows the "wreaths of smoke / Sent up, in silence" with "as might seem / Of vagrant dwellers in the houseless woods"). Similarly, some critics adhere to the traditional view that metaphor is a compressed s., distinguishable from s. only in being an implicit rather than an explicit comparison (Miller), whereas others conclude that not all metaphors and ss. are interchangeable—that metaphor is a "use of lang.," whereas comparison itself is a "psychological process" (Ortony). These questions have entered the domain of linguistics, where at least one theorist has argued in favor of a single "deep structure" of comparison, variously realized as either s. or metaphor, which is capable of distinguishing both ss. from factual comparisons and also metaphors from mere copulative equations such as "My car is a Ford" (Mack). The latter solution supports a growing sense that s. may be marked not only by "like" or "as," but also by many other comparative markers, incl. verbs such as "resemble," "echo," and "seem," connectives such as "as if" and "as

though," and phrases such as "the way that" (Darian). From this perspective it seems likely that s. encompasses analogy (q.v.), rather than being a discrete form of comparison. At the very least, the current exploration into the range of s. suggests that it may be a far more pervasive aspect of both lang. and perception than has previously been thought.

One of the most interesting and salient facts about s. is that in Western culture, at least, there has been a traditional prejudice against s. in favor of metaphor. Wheelwright rightly suggests that this trad. begins with Aristotle, who judges s. inferior for two reasons: since it is longer than metaphor, it is "less pleasing"; and since s. "does not affirm that this *is* that, the mind does not inquire into the matter" (*Rhetoric* 3.4.1406b). Yet even Wheelwright, who wishes to rescue us from the "tyranny of grammarians" who have collapsed s. into metaphor from "syntactical, not semantic considerations," still judges metaphor superior to s. by virtue of its "energy-tension" and compression. As Derrida has noted, "there is no more classical theory of metaphor than treating it as an 'economical' way of avoiding 'extended explanations': and, in the first place, of avoiding s." Although this particular prejudice has a long history, the 20th c. has been esp. rigid in privileging metaphor over s. At least prior to poststructuralist crit., many 20th-c. critics and theorists heralded metaphor as a model for understanding lang., thought, and philosophy. Not surprisingly, Frye regards s. as a "displaced" metaphor, which, for him, corresponds to the displacement of mythic identity into naturalism. In essence, following Coleridge's famous passage in the *Biographia literaria*, 20th-c. critics have tended to associate s. with the lower order of "fancy," and metaphor (rather than Coleridge's own term, "symbol") with the higher order of "imagination." Only recently have a few critics begun to regard s. not just as "literary embellishment" but as "a tool for serious thinking, scientific and otherwise" which "transcribes a paradigm of the creative act itself, whether in poetry or physics" (Darian).

Given the long denigration of s. by critics, it is all the more remarkable that s. has been so widely and so consistently used by poets. The earliest recorded Western lit., Sumerian, uses ss. in virtually every genre (Kramer). Among them are ss. that seem uncannily familiar, such as "as wide as the earth" and "as everlasting as the earth," though the second one had far more power in a culture that believed the earth to be "eternally enduring." Ss. are used throughout the *Rig Veda*—e.g. "In the East the brilliant dawns have stood / Like posts set up at sacrifices" (Cook). Certainly Homer uses ss., though his nearly formulaic ones (such as Thetis' rising out of the sea like a mist) hover somewhere between epithet (q.v.) and metaphor; and in this regard it is esp. provocative that Aristotle allies "proportional metaphor, which contains an epithet" with comparions (McCall). As Greene has pointed out, Virgil's "characteristic trope" is the s. Chaucer frequently turns to s., esp. for humor, as when describing "hende Nicholas" as being "as sweete as is the roote / Of lycorys, or any cetewale"; and Shakespeare achieves great irony by negating conventional ss. in "My mistress' eyes are nothing like the sun."

Furthermore, despite the prevailing emphasis in the 19th c. on the symbol (q.v.), Shelley also habitually turns to s. In the "Hymn to Intellectual Beauty," the "unseen Power" visits

> with as inconstant wing
> As summer winds that creep from
> flower to flower,—
> Like moonbeams that behind some
> piny mountain shower,
> It visits with inconstant glance
> Each human heart and countenance;
> Like hues and harmonies of evening,—
> Like clouds in starlight widely
> spread,—
> Like memory of music fled—   (3-10)

Equally curious—given the early 20th-c. bias in favor of imagism (q.v.) that followed Pound's injunction to "use no unnecessary word" (and which encouraged the excision of ss.)—is Wallace Stevens' increasing use of the s. in key passages of his poetry. He concludes his *Collected Poems*, for example, with "It was like / A new knowledge of reality," an especially reverberating s. that calls attention to the problematic relation, even resemblance, between poetry and what it represents. In contrast, ss. are almost nonexistent in Old Icelandic and OE (Ker). *Beowulf* contains only two ss.-the beam that brightens within the mere just as the sun shines from heaven, and the sword that melts like ice when the frost is loosened (1570a–72b, 1607b–11a)—although both stress the hero's final victory in the mere and the concomitant act of creation in restoring order to society.

The most revered form of s. is the epic s., a lengthy comparison between two highly complex objects, actions, or relations. Homer is credited with inaugurating the epic s., there being no known s. before *The Iliad* of such length or sophistication as the following:

> As is the generation of leaves, so is that
> of humanity.
> The wind scatters the leaves on the
> ground, but the live timber
> burgeons with leaves again in the sea-
> son of spring returning.
> So one generation of men will grow
> while another dies.
>   (6.146-49)

While the epic s. may be used by Homer for contrast or digression, as well as for thematic am-

plification, subsequent poets such as Virgil, Dante, Ariosto, Spenser, and Milton have refined the device, making it more integral to the structure of the epic. In part this fact reflects the written trad. within which later poets are composing, versus the oral trad. preceding and perhaps surrounding Homer.

Consequently, it is not surprising that later poets would frequently resuscitate specific Homeric ss. (Holoka), as does Virgil when comparing the "whole crowd" to the "forest leaves that flutter down / at the first autumn frost" (*Aeneid* 6.305-10), or as Milton does when describing Lucifer's "Legions" as "lay[ing] intrans't / Thick as Autumnal Leaves that strow the Brooks / In *Vallombrosa*" (*Paradise Lost* 1.301-3), a s. that continues for ten more lines in a highly complex syntactic and imagistic movement which manages to suggest that both the temporality and mortality implicit in falling leaves are themselves a consequence of Lucifer's insurrection. While many critics agree that the epic s. achieves its highest form in Milton, one critic has even argued that in Milton ss. duplicate, at least in small, "God's primal creative act" (Swift). Such an argument challenges the notion of metaphor or even myth (q.v.) as the primal creative act and reflects the growing seriousness with which this ancient (and contemporary) figure of speech is finally being regarded. See now REPRESENTATION AND MIMESIS.

H. Fränkel, *Die homerischen Gleichnisse* (1921); W. P. Ker, *Form and Style in Poetry* (1928); C. M. Bowra, *Trad. and Design in the* Iliad (1930); J. Whaler, "The Miltonic S.," *PMLA* 46 (1931); I. F. Green, "Observations on the Epic Ss. in the *Faerie Queene*," *PQ* 14 (1935); Frye; K. Widmer, "The Iconography of Renunciation: The Miltonic S.," *ELH* 25 (1958); C. S. Lewis, "Dante's Ss.," *NMS* 9 (1965); P. Wheelwright, *The Burning Fountain*, rev. ed. (1968); M. H. McCall, *Ancient Rhet. Theories of S. and Comparison* (1969); S. N. Kramer, "Sumerian Ss.," *JAOS* 89 (1969); S. G. Darian, "Ss. and the Creative Process," *Lang&S* 6 (1973); D. Mack, "Metaphoring as Speech Act," *Poetics* 4 (1975); J. Derrida, "White Mythology," *NLH* 6 (1975); J. P. Holoka, "'Thick as Autumnal Leaves,'" *MiltonQ* 10 (1976); R. H. Lansing, *From Image to Idea: The Ss. in Dante's Divine Comedy* (1977); G. A. Miller, "Images and Models, Ss. and Metaphors," and A. Ortony, "The Role of Similarity in Ss. and Metaphors," *Metaphor and Thought*, ed. Ortony (1979); J. N. Swift, "Ss. of Disguise and the Reader of *Paradise Lost*," *SAQ* 79 (1980); K. O. Murtaugh, *Ariosto and the Cl. S* (1980); A. Cook, *Figural Choice in Poetry and Art* (1985); J. V. Brogan, *Stevens and S.: A Theory of Lang.* (1986); S. A. Nimis, *Narrative Semiotics in the Epic Trad.: The S.* (1987); S. J. Wolfson, "'Comparing Power': Coleridge and S.," *Coleridge's Theory of Imagination Today*, ed. C. Gallant (1989); W. Prunty, *Fallen from the Symboled World* (1989).   J.V.B.

SIMPLICITY AND COMPLEXITY.

    I. GENERAL
   II. POETIC SIMPLICITY
  III. POETIC COMPLEXITY

S. and c. are terms often encountered in the crit. of poetry but which in fact derive from broader philosophical bases to which we should first attend.

I. GENERAL. Sometimes "simple" and "complex" hold fairly precise denotations, as in the linguist's distinction between simple, compound, and complex sentences, or John Locke's simple and complex ideas, or Aristotle's distinction between simple and complex tragic and epic plots. In the history of philosophy and science, such precision appears particularly in the works of thinkers who use what Richard McKeon has called the "logistic" method: this method commits the investigator to a search for the "simples" (ultimate elements which cannot be analyzed into smaller parts) and for the laws of their combination and change. This trad., however, which is as early as Democritus and as recent as 20th-c. logical positivism, has not produced agreement among theorists. Perhaps there are no irreducible simples, or they cannot be known, or their combination into complex systems may be so intricate that no human mind (even with the help of computers) is yet capable of describing their dynamics. Thus the limits of a logistic analysis are usually determined by the investigator's purpose and the problem being examined.

More frequently, esp. in pretheoretical usage, "s." and "c." are grading terms that point to the degree to which an entity possesses a characteristic that is determined by such factors as its size, scale, or length; the number, diversity, and contrasts of its parts; the intricacy of the interrelations of the parts; and the rate, amount, and kind of change which the entity undergoes. These criteria are of course independent of each other; hence an entity may be simple in one respect and complex in another. Such usage always involves an explicit or implicit comparison. The most easily verifiable judgments of s. or c. state the comparison explicitly, e.g. "*The Eve of St. Agnes* is a more complex poem than the *Ode to Autumn* because it is longer, has a plot with better-developed characters, and contains more figures of speech" or "Pastorals are simpler poems than epics." Or the object being discussed may be compared not to other objects but to some norm of s. and c., established by convention or stipulative definition, which then acts as a dividing line on a scale. If an object falls on one side of the line it is simple, and if on the other, complex. Of course in common usage such norms are seldom precisely given. Furthermore, the norms for s. and c. will be relative to the class of objects being discussed; there will be one set of norms determining the s. and c. of pastorals and a very different set for those of epics. Thus such usage of the terms "s." and "c." is necessarily

vague, sometimes in the extreme. Recent attempts in linguistics, information theory, philosophy of science, and cognitive psychology to formulate more precise norms for s. and c., and to develop a measure for degrees of s. and c., have produced an extensive lit. which, however, shows no sign of a developing agreement.

One final source of vagueness and relativity in the use of "s." and "c." is the inevitable influence of subjectivity. An objectively complex object may be taken as simple through conscious or unconscious bracketing, selective perception, and generalization. Conversely an objectively simple object will be seen as complex when taken as an interrelated part of some larger thing or process. More generally, judgments of s. and c. are dependent on the perceptual skills, intelligence, skill in processing information, maturity, experience, and interest of the person making the judgment.

S. and c. in any of their senses are seldom used as purely descriptive terms. The quality attributed frequently becomes a criterion for supporting a value judgment. Unfortunately human beings have never agreed on whether s. or c. is the more desirable quality, nor have they distinguished the classes of objects in which the one is to be preferred to the other, or determined the means for accurately measuring degrees of these qualities. However, s. and c. are seldom regarded as intrinsic goods, but are rather seen as the means to desirable or undesirable ends. Thus it is claimed that s. produces peace and serenity, economizes time, is a means to clarity and comprehensibility, is a sign of truth. Conversely c. is praised as a means to intellectual stimulation, excitement, heightened consciousness, personal growth, or the joys of infinite variety that age cannot wither nor custom stale. Lovers of one of these qualities frequently condemn the other, esp. when there is no agreement as to the line that distinguishes them. Advocates of plain living and speaking take c. as a sign of ostentation, gaudiness, grandiloquence, grotesqueness, elitism, trickery, wildness, and confusion. Advocates of c. condemn s. for its monotony, sentimentality, or triviality, for its tendency toward stereotypes and clichés, reductionism, and escapism, or for its tendency to standardization, totalitarianism, and intolerance. It is difficult to see how such basic differences can ever be resolved rationally. There will always be those who wish to "drink / Life to the lees" (Ulysses), and there will always be those who advise us to "Simplify, simplify" (Thoreau).

II. POETIC SIMPLICITY. These disagreements as to the definition and value of s. and c. are reflected in poetics and practical crit. from Cl. times to the present, regardless of whether this crit. has focused, at one time or another, on the things imitated in poetry; the attitudes and personality of the poet; the effects of poetry on the reader; or the formal excellences of aesthetic objects. In the *Republic* (397–401), Plato condemns c. and expresses his admiration for s. in the subject matter and formal aspects of poetry and the other arts: "Beauty of style and harmony and grace and good rhythm depend on s.—I mean the true s. of a rightly and nobly ordered mind and character, not that other s. which is only an euphemism for folly" (tr. Jowett). This "true s." is a reflection of the s. of the eternal forms which good poets see in vision and imitate in their work (*Phaedrus* 247). This transcendental epistemology—which speaks of the ascent of the soul from the illusions of this world of appearance and change to union with the undifferentiated One—appears in various formulations in later Neoplatonism (see PLATONISM AND POETRY); in Buddhism and other Eastern religions; in Christian, Muslim, and Heb. mysticism; and in modern versions of what is called the Perennial Philosophy. For Eng. readers, Shelley's *Defence of Poetry* (1821) is perhaps the most eloquent statement of how these systems regard the nature of poets and poetry. The great poets, says Shelley, are "prophets"; they are divinely inspired and participate in "the eternal, the infinite, and the one." Thus the arts must incorporate the universal, abstract, and ideal—all of which qualities depend on s. for their realization.

Western admiration for s. reached its peak in the age of the Enlightenment. In Neoclassical poetics (q.v.) the term "s." was used almost universally to point to one of the highest excellences in the arts. Praise of s. appears in Rapin, Boileau, Addison, Swift, Shaftesbury, Pope, Walpole, Kames, Hume, Johnson, and a host of lesser critics (see the numerous citations in Havens). Poets were advised to imitate the s. of nature and of the Cl. authors. S. was said to be one of the chief virtues of Homer, Virgil, Dante, Shakespeare, Milton, and the Bible. S. was considered an indispensable means to the aesthetic qualities that critics most admired—beauty and sublimity (see SUBLIME); Boileau's dictum that sublimity appears when great thoughts are presented in simple lang. was echoed by many. Of particular concern to Neoclassical critics was s. and "ease" in style; this was a reaction to what they regarded as stylistic extravagance in late 16th- and early 17th-c. Eng. Euphuism and in the conceits (q.v.) of "metaphysical" poetry (q.v.). Of course no critic made s. the sole criterion of value in poetry; the stress on s. was supplemented by other criteria, some associated with c., such as wit, variety, digression, amplification, and ornamentation. Also, most of these critics, like Plato, tried to distinguish "true s." from naive or uncouth rusticity. As the 18th c. wore on, there was increasing interest in primitive cultures (see PRIMITIVISM), in traditional legends and in popular ballads (q.v.) and songs, and in the realistic depiction of nature and the simple life of uneducated and unsophisticated people. This latter interest came to a climax in Wordsworth's early poetry and esp. in his defense, in the Preface to *Lyrical Ballads* (2d ed., 1802), of the use of plain lang. and rural characters in poetry.

III. POETIC COMPLEXITY. Lovejoy, however, interprets romanticism (q.v.) as a move away from s. to the values of c., or from "uniformitarianism" to "diversitarianism." During the Enlightenment, says Lovejoy, the dominant tendency was toward "the simplification and the standardization of thought and life—to their standardization by means of their simplification." The assumption was that in all his activities "man should conform as nearly as possible to a standard conceived as universal, uncomplicated, immutable, uniform for every rational being." Lovejoy then cites German theorists who at the turn of the 19th c. stressed the importance of diversity as "the essence of excellence." This prizing of diversity has remained dominant in Western thought to the present day. Lovejoy lists numerous modern tendencies: "the revulsion against s."; "the cultivation of individual, national, and racial peculiarities"; "the distrust of universal formulas in politics"; "the aesthetic antipathy to standardization"; "the admission of the aesthetic legitimacy of the *genre mixte*"; "the immense multiplication of genres and of verseforms."

C. is certainly a much admired quality in 20th-c. poetics (q.v.). Lovers of c. praise not only diversity but also the other factors making for c., esp. the intricacy of interrelationships of the parts of a poem. C. has been studied as it appears in almost every aspect of the poem: diction, prosody, syntax, imagery, tone, plot, doctrine (qq.v.). But the c. in which 20th-c. critics have shown the greatest interest is linguistic c., esp. semantic "density" or "richness."

One of the principal means by which poets "hypersemanticize" their poems is to incorporate implicit as well as explicit meanings. Readers in earlier ages had looked for multiple levels of meaning in poetry, esp. in allegorical writings (see ALLEGORY), and had puzzled over ironies, symbols, and gnomic verse (qq.v.). But 20th-c. formalist critics went far beyond their predecessors in their "close readings" of poetic texts, to report not only the explicit meanings of the poem's words but also their suggested, latent, and unconscious meanings. These critics isolated a multitude of devices by which implicit meanings are expressed: connotation, association, echo, polysemy, seven types of ambiguity, irony, paradox, symbol, schemes and tropes, allusion, intertextuality, malapropisms, portmanteau words, neologisms, archaisms, foreign idioms, enigmas, fragmentation, nonclosure, seeming incoherence, redundancy.

For I. A. Richards, poetry is "the completest mode of utterance." Factual discourse must limit itself to words with precisely defined referential meanings. But lang. has many other functions, and most words have multiple meanings and many dimensions of meaning. In the "fluid" discourse of poetry, all these modes of meaning are exploited, and through their "interinanimation" a swirl of novel meanings comes into being. Cleanth Brooks, focusing on the use of poetry for conveying attitudes, stresses the effectiveness of modes of indirection; and since attitudes are judged by their maturity (an attitude taken after a full cognizance of a situation and an exploration of a variety of responses), the presence of opposing attitudes is most effectively reflected in irony or paradox. For M. C. Beardsley, verbal c. is one of the principal means for evoking an aesthetic experience in the reader (the other two being unity and intensity of emotional quality).

Subsequent developments in speech-act theory (q.v.) and linguistic pragmatics have shown how much a full and accurate interpretation (q.v.) of an utterance depends on knowing the linguistic and extralinguistic context in which it is made. Ideally an auditor or reader must know the intentions of the speaker, the illocutionary force of the utterance, the constraints of the medium, the requirements of the occasion, and the relation of speaker to audience. In ordinary speech much of this information may be easily inferred from context. But a poem is not an utterance made within a concrete and fully specified context. Parts of the situation may of course be stated explicitly (as in the title) or left to easy inference; but more often, esp. in lyric poetry, the clues may be ambiguous or the poet may simply have left "gaps" in the information provided (see INDETERMINACY). Therefore some critics have held that any interp. of a poem requires an imaginative creation by the reader of the implied context—a creation which may well differ from reader to reader. Many later 20th-c. critics have turned to broader-based procedures—e.g. Marxist, psychoanalytic, deconstructive—to validate their interps. Such critics hold that poems may implicitly deny or qualify what they seem to affirm or may reveal the contents of their authors' unconscious minds or unexpressed ideologies based on class, race, or gender.

Early in the century, T. E. Hulme, following Bergson, said that reality is an "intensive manifold," a Heraclitean flow; the function of poetry is to reproduce by means of its semantic licenses the intuition of a reality as a "flux of interpenetrated elements unseizable by the intellect." But late in the century other critics provided darker pictures of a reality that is full of unresolvable tensions, instability, incoherence, contradiction, and conflict. Consequently there has been a growing tolerance for and even insistence on the validity and desirability of multiple interps. of the text, a trend supported by various metacritical defenses of pluralism (q.v.) in poetics. All of these positions emphasize difference and hence valorize c. See now ANALYSIS; CONCRETE UNIVERSAL; CONTEXTUALISM; FORM; INTERPRETATION; MEANING, POETIC; SEMANTICS AND POETRY; SEMIOTICS, POETIC; STRUCTURE; TENSION.

J. E. Spingarn, ed., "Intro.," *Critical Essays of the 17th C.*, v. 1 (1908); W. Empson, *The Structure of Complex Words* (1951), *Seven Types of Ambiguity*, 3d ed. (1953); A. O. Lovejoy, *The Great Chain of Being* (1936); I. A. Richards, *The Philosophy of Rhet.* (1936); Brooks; R. D. Havens, "S.: A Changing Concept," *JHI* 13 (1953); M. C. Beardsley, *Aesthetics* (1958), "Order and Disorder in Art," *The Concept of Order*, ed. P. G. Kuntz (1968); J. Lyons, *Semantics*, 2 v. (1977); W. Iser, *The Act of Reading* (1978); B. H. Smith, *On the Margins of Discourse* (1978); S. H. Olsen, *The Structure of Literary Understanding* (1978); K. K. Ruthven, *Critical Assumptions* (1979), ch. 3; S. Fish, *Is There a Text in This Class?* (1980); H. R. Pagels, *Dreams of Reason* (1988); G. K. Plochmann, *Richard McKeon* (1990). F.G.

SINCERITY. Derived from Lat. *sincerus* (clean or pure), the word s. entered Eng. in the early 16th c. and briefly retained the meaning of its cognate, so that, for example, "sincere wine" denoted wine that was undiluted. But Shakespeare uses s. exclusively to indicate the absence of duplicity or dissimulation, and by 1600 the term had assumed its modern connotations; it was not until the end of the 18th c. that s. became a valued literary commodity. For Wordsworth and the romantics s. was an indication of literary excellence since it emphasized the necessity of a congruence between the poet's emotion and the poet's utterance. Arnold ambitiously expanded the concept, adding to it a moral dimension, when he claimed that the touchstone (q.v.) of great poetry was "the high seriousness which comes from absolute s."

Much poetry and crit. of the 20th c., however, has questioned the fundamental values implied by the term. Donald Davie has suggested that Yeats's mask, Pound's persona, and Eliot's view of the poem as an impersonal, essentially dramatic structure rendered the question of the poet's s. "impertinent and illegitimate." Roughly contemporaneous with the high modernists, the New Critics in America propounded a methodology that emphasized the analysis of textual features such as imagery, structure, meter, and rhyme. These formal concerns, which foreground the verbal artistry and design of the work, were inimical to a concern with the poet and hence the concept of s.; and during the first half of the 20th c., the term fell into disuse.

Henri Peyre, however, has suggested that s. involves far more than a mere "transposing of autobiographical data," and he accords the longevity of Rousseau's writings, particularly the *Confessions*, to his singleminded devotion to s. Yet even literary cultures less obviously attracted by the ideals of s. are considered by Peyre to have confronted and resolved the issue. For the 16th-c. Fr. poets Du Bellay, Ronsard, Desportes, as well as for the Eng. poets Surrey, Sidney, and Spenser, the critical issue involves not so much whether the poet *achieves* s. as how forcefully the poet, deploying the various conventions of the sonnet sequence, *gives the impression* of s. And Eliot's interest in Donne's verse, which eschewed several ornamentations that had encumbered Elizabethan poetry, resulted simply from the tendency "to read more s. in wit than in pathos, in impudence than in adoration." Much contemp. literary theory, however, has called into question even such an accommodating definition of the term. Deconstructive theories (see DECONSTRUCTION) emphasize the perpetual indeterminacy of textual meaning, in which scheme, s., which depends upon the congruency of feeling and avowal, has no value. Reader-response crit. (q.v.) finds that there is no unity "in the text but in the mind of the reader" (Holland), and that the question of meaning involves analysis of the reading process. For both types of critics, and for much of the linguistically oriented crit. of the late 20th-c., the most pressing engagement available for critical discussion is the one between reader and text, not the one between author and text; and s., which concerns the latter relation, is not a fundamental concern of these methodologies. But there is no reason to assume that crit. might not return to its earlier interest. The recognition of s. depends upon the reader's ability to evaluate the successful fulfillment within the work of the author's intention (q.v.), and E. D. Hirsch's seminal work, *Validity in Interp.*, still represents one of the most formidable attempts in the latter half of the 20th c. to re-establish authorial intention as the guideline for accurate interp.

G. H. Lewes, "The Principle of S.," *The Principles of Success in Lit.* (1865); I. A. Richards, *Practical Crit.* (1929); H. Peyre, *Lit. and S.* (1963); D. Perkins, *Wordsworth and the Poetry of S.* (1964); P. M. Ball, "S.: The Rise and Fall of a Critical Term," *MLR* 59 (1964); E. D. Hirsch, Jr., *Validity in Interp.* (1967); D. Davie, "On S.: From Wordsworth to Ginsberg," *Encounter* (1968); P. M. Spacks, "In Search of S.," *CE* 29 (1968); H. Read, *The Cult of S.* (1969); L. Trilling, *S. and Authenticity* (1972); J. Derrida, "Structure, Sign, and Play in the Discourse of the Human Sciences," *The Structuralist Controversy*, ed. R. Macksey and E. Donato (1972); L. Guilhamet, *The Sincere Ideal* (1974); N. Holland, "Recovering 'The Purloined Letter,'" *The Reader in the Text*, ed. S. Suleiman and I. Crosman (1980); J. P. Russo, *I. A. Richards* (1989), ch. 15.   S.BU.

SINDHI POETRY. See INDIAN POETRY.

SINHALESE POETRY. See SRI LANKAN POETRY.

SIRVENTES. A poem in Occitan which is strophic in form but which is not a love poem. The main themes are personal abuse or (occasionally) praise, literary satire, or moralizing on the evil state of the world, politics and current events, and the crusades (exhortations to go, songs of parting, etc.). The tone is mostly satiric, and gross vituperation is common. In form, the s. came to be re-

garded as a subservient genre, deserving less originality than the *canso* (q.v.). It became a recognized practice to write a s. to the tune of a popular *canso,* and in many cases to adopt the rhyme sounds of the *canso* whose tune was borrowed. This custom was so general that the s. was sometimes defined in these terms, as an imitative poem; but it seems most unlikely that this imitation was ever considered by the poets themselves to be an essential condition of the genre.—E. Köhler, "Die S.-Kanzone," *Mélanges offerts à Rita Lejeune,* v. 1 (1968); A. Adler in *GRMLA,* v. 6.1; K. W. Klein, *The Partisan Voice: A Study of the Political Lyric in France and Germany, 1180–1230* (1971); D. Rieger, *Gattungen und Gattungsbezeichungen der Trobadorlyrik* (1976); S. Thiolier-Méjean, *Les Poésies satiriques et morales des troubadours du XIIe siècle à la fin du XIIIe siècle* (1978); D. Rieger and E. Köhler in *GRLMA,* v. 2.1B.; Chambers.   F.M.C.

SIXAIN. See SEXAIN.

SKALD (ON *skald, skáld* "poet"). Those who composed in the ornate *dróttkvætt* style used the term to refer to themselves, and modern critics have adopted this usage, whence the adjective "skaldic." Approximately 240 ss. are known by name, incl. several women. The oldest s. is tradiionally taken to be Bragi Boddason the Old, who probably lived in the second half of the 9th c. Although most of the earliest ss. were Norwegian, by the end of the 10th c. virtually all were Icelandic. Ss. were frequently attached to royal courts and may have been quasi-professional; the late medieval Icelandic *Skáldatal,* a brief enumeration of ss. and their patrons, assigns specific ss. to Danish, Norwegian, and Eng. kings and leaders from mythic times through ca. 1300. Ss. served their rulers not just by praising them but by offering (judiciously worded) eyewitness accounts of their great moments, usually battles, and these became the foundation of medieval Icelandic historiography. But ss. could blame as well as praise and were powerful in private as well as public matters. Medieval laws regulate their use of love poetry and insult-verse, and they were masters of polemic, satire, innuendo, and *double entendre.* See OLD NORSE POETRY.—R. Frank, *Old Norse Court Poetry* (1978); K. von See, *Skaldendichtung* (1980).   J.L.

SKALDIC POETRY. See OLD NORSE POETRY.

SKELTONIC. A distinctive shortlined meter named after its originator, John Skelton (ca. 1460–1529), priest, tutor, courtier, moralist. Typically the lines carry only 2–3 stresses in 3–6 syllables (though longer lines are not uncommon), and there are frequent short runs of monorhyme (q.v.) called "leashes." It is disputed whether the S. is accentual verse (q.v.) or accentual-syllabic. Parallelism (q.v.) is a major rhetorical device. The S. struck the later Ren. critics and prosodists as doggerel (q.v.), but approving remarks by several of the romantics, esp. Coleridge and Wordsworth, have raised its reputation considerably in the modern mind.

The origins of the S. are similarly disputed: it has been seen as deriving from OE rhyming poems (Guest), as an inspired form of doggerel (Saintsbury), as a form of "tumbling verse" (q.v.; Ker), as an adaptation of Med. Lat. rhythmical verse (Berdan), as an amalgam of the *clausulae* of Med. Lat. prose rhythm (q.v.) with the cadences of rhyme-prose (q.v.; Nelson), as a relative of Lat. and vernacular poems on the "Signs of Death" topos (Kinsman), as learned from the letter-writing Pastons (Norton-Smith), as similar to more medieval poetry than we think (Kendle), as the apt vehicle, "irregular and cascading" (Fish), for "disorder in life rendered by disorder in art" (Lewis); and as a natural rhythmic derivation from liturgical music and responsories, esp. plainsong chant (Kinney). Conflation of several of these is certainly also possible—as is the negation of all of them, Lewis's opinion that "there is nothing really very like Ss. before Skelton." But though we associate the S. with Skelton, the converse is a mistake, for Skelton in his other poems and play employs a greater range of meters than the S. The full and careful study still remains to be done.—*Magnyfycence*, ed. R. L. Ramsay (1908); J. M. Berdan, *Early Tudor Poetry* (1920); W. Nelson, *John Skelton: Laureate* (1939); R. S. Kinsman, "Skelton's 'Uppon a Deedmans Hed': New Light on the Origin of the S.," *SP* 50 (1953); C. S. Lewis, *Eng. Lit. in the 16th C.* (1954); S. B. Kendle, "The Ancestry and Character of the S.," Diss., Univ. of Wisconsin (1961); S. Fish, *John Skelton's Poetry* (1965); J. Norton-Smith, "The Origins of Ss.," *EIC* 23 (1973); Brogan; A. F. Kinney, *John Skelton: Priest as Poet* (1987).
T.V.F.B.

SKOLION. A type of early Gr. lyric poetry, a drinking song. The etymology of the term is uncertain but perhaps derives from Gr. *skolios* "crooked": the guests at a symposium would sing in sequence, each holding a myrtle branch then passing it to another at random—"crookedly." Trad. ascribes its origin to Terpander (fl. mid 7th c. B.C.), who was the first to give it artistic form. Skolia could be purely extemporized pieces, excerpts from lyric poetry, or even selections from Homer. Its stanzas were composed of two Phalaeceans (q.v.), a colon of the form ∪ ∪ – ∪ – – ∪ ∪ – , and another with – ∪ ∪ – ∪ – repeated. The s. was accompanied by the lyre or flute and dealt with historical events, expressed deep personal feeling, or made a trenchant comment on daily life. In the course of the 5th c., it was considerably simplified.—R. Reitzenstein, *Epigramm und S.* (1893); W. Aly, "S.," Pauly-Wissowa, 2.5.558–66; Schmid and Stählin; Maas, sects. 14, 54; A. M. Dale, *Collected Papers* (1969); Michaelides; West, 59.
P.S.C.; T.V.F.B.

SLANT RHYME. See NEAR RHYME.

SLAVIC POETICS. See ROMANTIC AND POSTRO-MANTIC POETICS; TWENTIETH-CENTURY POETICS.

SLAVIC PROSODY.

   I. COMMON SLAVIC
   II. SUBSEQUENT VERSE SYSTEMS
      A. *Polish*
      B. *Czech*
      C. *Slovak*
      D. *Serbo-Croatian*
      E. *Slovenian*
      F. *Russian*

A comparative study of S. pros. has as its aim both the reconstruction of Common S. versification and the description of the individual S. prosodic systems which evolved after the breakdown of S. unity, around the 10th c. A.D. These systems comprise an oral (declamatory or sung) popular trad., which to some extent is the continuation of Common S. pros., and a trad. of written poetry, which is genetically and structurally connected with the former but has been subject to various foreign as well as cross-cultural S. influences. Whatever metrical system exerted an influence on or was adopted by a given S. pros., its needs must be adjusted to the prosodic possibilities of the particular S. lang. implementing it. In recognizing this fact, modern verse theory does not limit itself to an enumeration of ideal metrical schemes but views verse as a structure within which the metrical constants correlate to rhythmic tendencies in differing proportions in different langs.

I. COMMON SLAVIC. Attempts to reconstruct Common S. pros. have so far suggested that Common S. had two types of verse: a spoken asyllabic verse based on syntactic parallelism of the lines, and a syllabic verse based on a fixed number of syllables in each line with a syntactic pause at the end of each. Specimens of the first type are found in S. folklore in the form of wedding-speeches and sayings and in the imparisyllabic lines found in older Western (e.g. 14th-c. Czech epic) and Rus. (17th-c.) poetry. The syllabic type was recitative or sung. Direct descendants of the recitative type are the laments (*tužbalice*, *plači*) and epic songs (*junačke pesme*, *byliny*) preserved among the Balkan Slavs and in Northern Great Russia. The laments consisted of short or long lines with a trochaic rhythm or cadence divided into uniform cola (4 + 4 or 4 + 4 + 4). The epic songs also consisted of long or short lines but were divided into asymmetrical cola: (4 + 6) with a trochaic cadence or (5 + 3 or 3 + 5) with an iambic cadence. The epic verse also had a quantitative clausula. All four types of the recitative verse are very well preserved in the South S. area. In the Northern Rus. area the recitative verse changed its structure considerably after the loss of phonemic length and intonation. The asymmetrical verse of epic songs, both long and short, had lost its syllabic pattern just because of its asymmetry, becoming a purely accentual (tonic) verse with a disyllabic anacrusis and a dactylic clausula (which replaced the quantitative one). The symmetrical verse of the laments preserved its syllabic pattern much better. It also developed a new dactylic clausula owing to an additional syllable. Thus it now consists, as a rule, of 9- or 13-syllable lines with a trochaic cadence.

The oldest learned S. poetry, that of the Old Church Slavonic-Moravian period, was based on isosyllabism without rhyme and owed its origin to Common S. syllabic verse as well as to Byzantine-Gr. forms.

II. SUBSEQUENT VERSE SYSTEMS. The new political, religious, and linguistic devels. which took place around the 10th c. A.D. created the conditions for independent S. poetic trads. and prosodic systems. The formation of separate S. nation-states with their subsequent destinies, the adoption of Christianity, and the Schism (1054) affected the growth and functions of poetry in the various S. countries in different ways. The longest uninterrupted trad. of learned poetry existed among the Western Slavs and, to a lesser degree, in the Catholic Southern S. world, taking its origin during the flowering of the Ren. in this area among Croats and Serbs on the Dalmatian coast. In the Orthodox S. world, learned secular poetry developed much later: among Eastern Slavs in the 17th c. and among Balkan Slavs (Serbs and Bulgarians) in the 18th and 19th c., respectively. As a consequence of the breakdown of Common S., a new word-prosody developed in the various S. langs. (though all preserved phonemic quantity), which can be formulated as follows: in Czech and Slovak, stress has the function only of delimiting word boundaries, being fixed on the initial syllable of a word. In Serbo-Croatian and Slovenian, stress is concomitant with pitch (which is distinctive but metrically irrelevant) or, in the absence of pitch, delimits the word boundary, falling on the first (Serbo-Croatian) or final syllable of a word (Slovenian). In the Eastern S. langs. and in Bulgarian, stress has a distinctive function, whereas in Polish it is bound to the penultimate syllable of a word.

A. *Polish.* Syllabism has been up to now the basis of Pol. versification. In the 14th–15th cs., isosyllabism was merely a tendency, which was pronounced in works influenced by Med. Lat. poetry. The greatest innovator of Pol. syllabic verse was J. Kochanowski (1530–84), who canonized the principle of strict isosyllabism, eliminated parallelism of the lines as a constant, and stabilized the place of the caesura in longer lines. He also introduced a deeper, 1 1/2 rhyme (with a penultimate stress and consonance of the preceding consonant), which was not strictly adhered to by his 17th- and 18th-c. followers. These innovations lent Pol. verse new flexibility, allowing the use of hemistichs and lines of various length and releasing

syntactic phrasing for expressive effects. The consistent adherence to the syllabic principle accounts for the popularity of the longer lines, esp. of 11 (5 + 6) and 13 (7 + 6) syllables, in which the best Pol. lyric and epic poetry has been written. The shorter octosyllable without caesura has generally been used in learned poetry. In popular verse, this line is divided into hemistichs (5 + 3 or 4 + 4), which entails a breakdown of the line into word groups with an equal number of stresses or a strong trochaic tendency.

The rhythmical measures of the folksong enter at first into Pol. romantic poetry as a form of popular stylization. The impulse for a syllabotonic (accentual-syllabic) pros. was, however, provided mainly by the imitation of Cl. quantitative meters and by foreign (Rus.) models. Syllabotonic meters are used by the romantics for lyrics and for sections of dramatic works. The great romantics, who introduced masculine rhyme and iambic and anapestic feet (Mickiewicz, Słowacki), used these meters with moderation. Syllabotonic verse became the norm with the "positivist" poets (Konopnicka, Asnyk), who practiced it with extreme rigor. Modern poets admit frequent deviations from the metrical scheme. The imitation of Cl. meters, esp. the hexameter, actually led to the introduction of purely accentual meters, based on an equal number of stresses in each line. In our times, these meters, as well as free verse, compete successfully with the traditional syllabic verse. See POLISH POETRY.

B. *Czech.* In Cz. the octosyllable formed the backbone of both lyric and epic Old Cz. poetry, with a pronounced trochaic tendency in the former and parallelism nearly a constant in the latter. Dramatic verse, on the other hand, was asyllabic. Syllabotonic meters with trochaic and iambic cadence became popular during the Hussite movement with the flourishing of religious songs. But as a consequence of the frequent discrepancy between music and meter, as well as the general decline of secular poetry, the 15th and 16th cs. saw a return to purely syllabic meters, a devel. which coincided with Pol. syllabic versification and was partly influenced by it. In this system, quantity served only as an element of variation. However, in the poems and songs of the Cz. humanists who imitated Cl. versification (Komenský, Blahoslav), it becomes the metrical principle. At the end of the 18th c., syllabotonic meters, based on the congruence of foot and word boundaries, triumph in Cz. poetry. The poets of the Puchmajer school adhere strictly to the metrical scheme. Later, this rigor is considerably attenuated through the use of quantity, of polysyllabic words, and of heterosyllabic (mainly dactylo-trochaic) feet. The romantics (e.g. Mácha) make very skillful use of iambic feet, which are contrary to the dactylo-trochaic cadence of the Cz. lang. Toward the end of the 19th c., the metrical scheme is again rigorously implemented (by the *Lumírovci*) to finally cede place to the modified syllabotonic meters and to the *vers libre* of the symbolists (Březina). See CZECH POETRY.

C. *Slovak.* In its early, Štúr period, Sl. poetry drew its inspiration from the local folk poetry, which is syllabic. In the last quarter of the 19th c., the Sl. poets (Hviezdoslav, Vajanský) abandoned syllabism for the syllabotonic meters of Cz. origin, which are adhered to strictly near the end of the century. Subsequently the syllabotonic frame became more flexible, marking the transition to free rhythms. See SLOVAK POETRY.

D. *Serbo-Croatian* popular verse shows striking similarities to that of Cz. and Sl., with the difference that quantity sometimes has a metrical function (e.g. the quantitative clausula of the epic decasyllable). Dalmatian poetry of the Ren. owed its verseforms to popular inspiration. The influence of Western (It.) poetry has here been responsible for the introduction of rhyme (and *media rima*), which replaced syntactic parallelism as a constant. Besides the asymmetric (4 + 6) epic and the symmetric (5 + 5) lyric decasyllable, the most common meters are 8- and 12-syllable lines (4 + 4 and 6 + 6) with a pronounced trochaic cadence. Modern poetry also employs 11-syllable lines (5+6). Syllabotonic meters appeared under foreign (Ger. and Rus.) influence during the 19th c. (Radičević, Zmaj, Kostić; Vraz, Preradović, Šenoa, F. Marković). The division into feet depends as in Cz. on word boundaries. Quantity serves mainly as an element of variation, although in some positions it may substitute for stress (esp. in rhymes). See YUGOSLAV POETRY.

E. *Slovenian.* The meters of modern Sloven. poetry, which developed in the 19th c., are syllabotonic. The role of quantity as a rhythmic factor is more restricted here than in Serbo-Croatian. In the poetry of Prešeren, the greatest romantic poet, who used primarily the iambic pentameter (with feminine rhyme), the metrical scheme is still rigorously observed. Modern versification (Aškerc, Župančič), here has, as elsewhere, moved in the direction of relaxing the metrical requirements; it also adopted ternary meters and free verse.

F. *Russian.* Syllabotonic meters became the basis of Rus. pros. in the 1740s, following a period of syllabic verse (the so-called *virshi*), which had reached Russia from Poland via the Ukraine in the 17th c. In contrast to Pol. verse, which had an obligatory penultimate stress before the caesura, Rus. syllabic poetry as practiced by Simeon Polockij, Istomin, and Kantemir developed a pre-caesural stress which oscillated between masculine, feminine, and dactylic to allow for the rhythmic possibilities of the Rus. lang., with its free distribution of stress. The discrepancies between the metrical requirements of the syllabic line and the linguistic use of free stress were resolved by a gradual increase in the regularity of the stresses, a process which led ultimately to the replacement of the syllabic by the syllabotonic line. The transition was accelerated through the influence of Rus. oral poetry and translations of Ger. verse.

The syllabotonic system was originally based on binary meters, esp. trochaic and iambic trimeters, that were cultivated by all major 18th-c. poets (Trediakovskij, Lomonosov, Sumarokov). Imitations of Cl. verse, esp. the trs. of the *Iliad* and *Odyssey* by Gnedič and Žukovskij, introduced the combining of dactylic and trochaic hexameters, and with it the earliest type of accentual verse. By the beginning of the 19th c., the iamb had become established in a variety of genres, with the iambic pentameter prevailing in dramatic verse and the iambic tetrameter in most nondramatic verse (incl. the works of Puškin).

The binary meters were governed by a compulsory stress on the last ictus of the line, with the possibility of omitting the stress on the other ictuses, esp. the even ones, counting back from the last heavy syllable; this is called the "law of regressive dissimilation." The regressive undulatory curve thus obtained is the chief feature of 19th-c. Rus. verse, in contrast to the binary meters of the other S. langs. without phonemic stress, in which the stressed ictuses when graphed form a progressive curve.

Ternary meters made their appearance at the beginning of the 19th c. in Žukovskij's ballads, but became common in the second half of the century in the works of Nekrasov, Fet, and A. Tolstoj. But here the relation of heavy and light syllables was reversed: stress on the heavy syllables became a constant, whereas omission of stress on the light syllables became an element of variation. The excess of constants fostered by these meters gave way in turn to accentual (tonic) verse with a variable number of unstressed syllables (usually 1 to 2) between ictuses (see DOLNIK). This type of verse features in the 20th-c. poetry of the symbolists and acmeists (e.g. Brjusov, Blok, Cvetaeva, Axmatova, and others; see ACMEISM). Throughout the 20th c., the *dol'nik* has been in competition with the "classical" (syllabotonic) meters and with a looser form of accentual verse in which the number of unstressed syllables between the downbeats is not regulated at all. Free verse, introduced by Blok, Kuzmin, and Xlebnikov, has never gained as strong a hold in Rus. as it has in the other S. poetries. The binary meters (esp. the iambic tetrameter and pentameter) and the *dol'nik* remain the dominant forms of contemp. Rus. poetry. See now RUSSIAN POETRY; STRUCTURALISM, *Moscow-Tartu School.*

G. *Bulgarian* and *Ukrainian* learned poetry of the 19th c. (Shevchenko, Botev) is indebted for its verseforms to the popular trad. of the folksong, which shows a strong tendency toward a fixed arrangement of word groups within the short line and a division into hemistichs in the long line. Subsequently both poetries fell under the influence of Rus. syllabotonic versification, which became the prevailing norm, with the exception of

SLAVIC PROSODY

Western Ukrainian poetry, where purely syllabic verse is still written. In the 20th c., the *dol'niki* (Tyčyna, Javorov) and *vers libre* have competed with the syllabotonic meters. See BULGARIAN POETRY; UKRAINIAN POETRY.

BIBLIOGRAPHIES: M. P. Štokmar, *Bibliografija rabot po stixosloženiju* (1933)—for addenda see Scherr (below); K. Taranovsky, "Metrics," *Current Trends in Linguistics I*, ed. T. Sebeok (1963)—discusses work since 1940; G. S. Smith, "A Bibl. of Soviet Publs. on Rus. Versif. since 1958," *RLT* 6 (1973)—lists 311 works with indexes but limited to Soviet authors; I. K. Lilly and B. P. Scherr. "Rus. Verse Theory since 1960: A Commentary and Bibl.," *IJSLP* 22 (1976)—surveys 283 works 1960–73, continued in *IJSLP* 27 (1983)—surveys 398 works 1974–81; I. D. Ral'ko, *Veršaskladanne: Dasledavanni i matèryjaly* (1977), 141–239; S. I. Gindin, "Obščee i russkoe stixovedenie: Sistematičeskij ukazatel' literatury, izdannoj v SSSR na russkom jazyke s 1958 po 1974 gg," in *Issledovanija po teorii stixa* (1978)—lists 1038 works 1958–74 with author and subject indexes, supp. in *Struktura stixotvornoj reči: Sistematičeskij ukazatel' literatury po obščemu i russkomu stixovedeniju, izdannoj v SSSR na russkom jazyke s 1958 g. Čast' II: 1974–1980*, 3 bindings (1982)—extending coverage from 1974 to 1980; *Rus. Verse Theory Newsletter* 1– (Univ. of Auckland, 1983–).

COLLECTIONS: *Poetics, Poetyka, Poetika I*, ed. D. Davie et al. (1961)—62 papers; *Poetics, Poetyka, Poetika II*, ed. R. Jakobson et al. (1966)—18 papers; *Teorie Verše I/Theory of Verse I/Teorija stixa I*, ed. J. Levý (1966)—28 papers; *Teorie Verše II/Theory of Verse II/Teorija stixa II*, ed. J. Levý and K. Palas (1968)—21 papers; *Teorija stixa* and *Issledovanija po teorii stixa*, both ed. V. E. Xolševnikov et al. (1968, 1978); J. Levý, *Paralipomena* (1971)—his coll. essays; *Readings in Rus. Poetics*, ed. L. Matejka and K. Pomorska (1971); *Slavic Poetics*, ed. R. Jakobson et al. (1973); *Problemy stixovedenija*, ed. M. L. Gasparov et al. (1976); *Słowiańska metryka porównawcza*, 3 v. (1978, 1984, 1988); *Metre, Rhythm, Stanza, Rhyme*, ed. and tr. G. S. Smith (1980); *Rus. Poetics*, ed. T. Eekman and D. S. Worth (1983); *Problemy teorii stixa*, ed. V. E. Xolševnikov (1984)—17 essays and 2 bibls.; *Rus. Verse Theory*, ed. B. P. Scherr and D. S. Worth (1989)—28 papers.

GENERAL STUDIES: Jakobson, 8 v. to date, esp. "Linguistics and Poetics" (1960) in v. 3, "S. Epic Verse: Studies in Comp. S. Metrics" (1952) in v. 4, "My Metrical Sketches: A Retrospect" (1979) in v. 5 (*On Verse: Its Masters and Explorers*), and "The Kernel of Comp. S. Lit.," (1953) in v. 6.1; E. Stankiewicz, "S. [Versification]," in Wimsatt; J. Eekman, *The Realm of Rime in the Poetry of the Slavs* (1974).

SPECIALIZED STUDIES: *Polish*: Z. Kopczyńska and M. R. Mayenowa, *Sylabizm* (1956); M. Dłuska, *Sylabotonizm* (1957), *Próba teorii wiersza polskiego* (1962), *Studia i rozprawy*, 3 v. (1972), *Studia z*

historii i teorii wersyfikacji polskiej,. 2d ed., 2 v. (1978); M. R. Mayenowa, *Strofika* (1964), *O sztuce czytania*, 2d ed. (1967); L. Pszczołowska, *Rym* (1970); M. Giergielewicz, *Intro. to Polish Versif.* (1970).

Czech: R. Jakobson, *O češskom stixe* (1923), rpt. with Afterword in Jakobson v. 5, "Old Cz. Verse" (1934), tr. in Jakobson v. 6.2; J. Mukařovskij, "Česky verš: Obecné zásady a vývoj novočeského verše," *Československá Vlastiveda* 3 (1934);

Slovak: M. Bakoš, *Vývin slovenského verša od školy Štúrovej*, 2d ed. (1949); K. Horálek, *Zarys dziejów czeskiego wiersza* (1957)—brief historical survey of Cz. and Sl. verse.

Serbo-Croatian: S. Matić, "Principi umetničke versifikacje srpske," *Godišnica N. Čupica* (1930–32); R. Košutić, *O tonskoj metrici u novoj srpskoj poezji* (1941); K. Taranovski, "Principi srpskohrvatske versifikacije," *Prilozi za književnost* 20 (1954); "The Prosodic Structure of Serbo-Croat Verse," *OSP* 9 (1960).

Slovenian: A. V. Isačenko, *Slovenski verz* (1939).

Byelorussian: A. B. McMillin, "Stanza, Rhyme, and Metre in 19th-C. Byelorussian Verse," *Jour. of Byelorussian Studies* 3 (1974).

Russian: A. Belyj, "Lirika i eksperiment," *Simvolizm* (1910), tr. in *Sel. Essays of Andrey Bely*, ed. S. Cassedy (1985); B. V. Tomaševskij, *Russkoe stixosloženie: Metrika* (1923), *O stixe: Stat'i* (1929); V. M. Žirmunskij, *Rifma: ee istorija i teorija* (1923), *Vvedenie v metriku. Teorija stixa* (1925), the latter tr. C. F. Brown as *Intro. to Metrics: The Theory of Verse* (1966); V. Bryusov, *Osnovy stixovedenija* (1924); J. Tynjanov, *Problema stixotvornogo jazyka* (1924), tr. as *The Problem of Verse Lang.* (1981); O. M. Brik, "Ritm i sintaksis" (1927), tr. in *Two Essays on Poetic Lang.* (1964); K. Taranovski, *Ruski dvodelni ritmovi, 1–2* (1953); R. Burgi, *Hist. of the Rus. Hexameter* (1954); B. O. Unbegaun, *Rus. Versif.* (1956)—useful short intro.; R. Silbajoris *Rus. Versif*, (1968)—tr. of four 18th-c. treatises; V. E. Xolševnikov, *Osnovy stixovedenija: russkoe stixosloženie*, 2d ed. (1972); M. L. Gasparov, *Sovremennyj russkij stix: Metrika i ritmika* (1974), *Očerk istorii russkogo stixa* (1984); R. Lauer, *Gedichtform zwischen Schema und Verfall: Sonett, Rondeau, Madrigal, Ballade, Stanze und Triolett in der russischen Literatur des 18. Jahrhunderts* (1975); J. Bailey, "The Rus. Linguistic-Statistical Method for Studying Poetic Rhythm," *SEEJ* 23 (1979); *Russkoe stixosloženie XIX v.*, ed. M. L. Gasparov (1979); D. S. Samoilov, *Kniga o russkoi rifme*, 2d ed. (1982); *Russkoe stixosloženie*, ed. L. I. Timofeev (1985); G. S. Smith, "The Metrical Repertoire of Rus. Emigré Poetry, 1941–1970," *SEER* 63 (1985); I. K. Lilly, "On Stressed Rus. Rhyme and Nonrhyme Vowels," *SEER* 65 (1987); Scherr.

Bulgarian: A. Balabanov, "Bŭlgarski stix," *Iz edin život* (1934); M. Janakiev, *Bŭlgarsko stixoznanie* (1960).

Ukrainian: V. Jakubs'kyj, *Nauka viršuvannja* (1922).   E.ST.; T.V.F.B.

SLOVAK POETRY

ŚLOKA. See INDIAN PROSODY.

SLOVAK POETRY. Until the 19th c., the Slovaks had virtually no lit. in their own lang.; Lat. and Czech served as written langs., and only sporadic attempts were made to write in S. The 17th c. saw what may be regarded as the beginnings of a national lit. in two great hymnals, the Protestant *Cithara sanctorum* (1636) and the Catholic *Cantus catholici* (1655). The first collection contained mostly Czech hymns, but a few were S. and employed vernacular expressions. The lang. of the *Cantus catholici* represented an attempt by the Jesuits of the University of Trnava to write in Western S. dialects. Throughout the later 17th c. and most of the 18th c., the baroque period in Slovakia, poetry continued to be predominantly religious or didactic.

Neoclassicism dominated S. lit. from the end of the 18th c. up to 1840. A new attempt to standardize S. was made at this time by Anton Bernolák (1762–1813), a Catholic priest; Bernolák's S. was similarly based on Western S. dialects. His follower, Ján Hollý (1785–1849), wrote ponderous epics on patriotic historical subjects, drawing heavily for inspiration on antique poets. The failure of Bernolák's S. to win acceptance, however, doomed Holly's work to oblivion. More successful was Ján Kollár (1793–1852), who wrote in Czech. His great sonnet cycle, *Slávy dcera* (The Daughter of Sláva, 1824), laments the impotence of the Slavic peoples but predicts their future greatness.

Not until the 1840s and the first romantic generation was a standard S. lang. created that would endure. Based on Central S. dialects, and hence more widely acceptable, it was largely the work of two Protestant nationalists, L'udovít Štúr (1815–56) and J. M. Hurban (1817–88). The romantic poets who surrounded Štúr were strongly influenced by the S. folksong; ardent patriots, they largely defined national lit. by its use of popular speech and folk forms. They finally solved the question of prosody; hitherto both quantitative and accentual systems of versification had been employed. Now, on the model of the S. folksong, the romantics adopted accentual verse.

The romantic generation included a number of significant poets. Andrej Sládkovič (pseudonym of Ondrej Braxatoris, 1820–72) created a historical epic, *Detvan* (1853), an idyllic but partly accurate description of S. peasant life. Janko Král' (1822–76), the greatest of the romantics, produced ballads interesting for their use of Oedipal themes. Ján Botto (1829–81) eulogized the famous bandit of the Carpathians who had become a symbol of liberty to the common people in *Smrt' Janošíka* (The Death of Janošík, 1862). Ján Kalinčiak (1812–71) also treated S. historical subjects, but with more realistic detail.

S. hopes for liberty were shattered by the failure of the Revolution of 1848. As the century wore on and Hungarian rule became more severe, a mood of hopelessness set in. Svétozar Hurban Vajansky (1847–1916) and Pavol Országh (1849–1921), who wrote under the pseudonym of Hviezdoslav, were the greatest poets of the era. Hurban Vajanský, the son of J. M. Hurban, was a romantic, but with a vein of irony and satire new to S. lit. Hviezdoslav was a Parnassian poet, whose translations from Shakespeare, Goethe, Puškin, and others provided a new stimulus. In keeping with his cosmopolitanism, he avoided the hitherto dominant tone of the folksong. Hviezdoslav was a lyric, epic, and dramatic poet; his masterpiece is probably the *Krvavé sonety* (Bloody Sonnets, 1919), which mirror the horror of World War I. His late poetry became increasingly disillusioned, though he lived to see Slovakia win freedom.

Symbolism, or *Moderna* as the Slovaks called it, had its chief poet in Ivan Krasko (pseudonym of Ján Botto, 1876–1958), the son of the older Botto. Krasko shares Hviezdoslav's pessimism, but his poetry is more modern in its use of the lexicon and its subtle introspective moods. Janko Jesensky (1874–1945) cultivated a cosmopolitan satire relatively unique in S. p. Among younger writers of the interwar period, Emil B. Lukáč (1900–79) was a complex and contradictory religious poet influenced by Paul Claudel. Ján Smrek (pseudonym of Ján Čietek, 1899–1982) was a vitalist who delighted in sensual descriptions of female beauty. He also flirted with poetism, an indigenous Czechoslovak poetic movement (see CZECH POETRY) which arose in the late 1920s and which contained traits of futurism and dada (qq.v.). Another poetist was Laco Novomesky (1904–76), a Communist journalist noted for his many ideological reversals; he was imprisoned in 1951 for nationalist "deviation" but released in 1956. Ultimately he was rehabilitated, to play the role of the outstanding poet in a period largely without poetry, in which role he is perhaps emblematic of a politically troubled and changing time.

The principal foreign influences on S. p. have been those of Czech, Ger., and Rus. lit. Like Czech, S. has a fixed stress on the first syllable of the word, which facilitates the use of trochaic meters. Still, iambic verse—usually with considerable freedom in the opening foot of the line—is very common, and in fact more popular than trochaic in the second half of the 19th c. Ternary meters are virtually impossible in S. because the stress tends to fall on every odd syllable. Dactylic feet may alternate with trochees, however; such purely tonic rhythms were popular under the influence of classical meters and of native folksongs, both in the romantic era and again in modern times.

The severity of the national problem in Slovakia and the political role played by many S. writers have given S. p. a strongly nationalistic coloring. Those poetic forms are popular in which national ideas can be expressed or implied: narrative poetry, the popular song, and the reflective lyric. Traditionally poetry dominated prose in S. lit., but since World War II this situation has been reversed and prose is now absolutely dominant. For discussion of S. prosody, see SLAVIC PROSODY.

ANTHOLOGIES: *Slovenská poesie XIX. století,* ed. Fr. Frýdecký (1920); *Sborník mladej slovenskej literatúry,* ed. J. Smrek (1924); *Slovenské jaro; ze slovenskej poesie, 1945–1955,* ed. C. Stitnicky (1955); *An Anthol. of S. P.,* tr. I. J. Kramoris (1947)—bilingual; *The Linden Tree,* ed. M. Otruba and Z. Pešat (1963); *Antológia staršej slovenskej literatúry,* ed. J. Mišianik (1964).

HISTORY AND CRITICISM: S. Krčméry, "A Survey of Mod. S. Lit.," *SEER* 6 (1928); M. Bakoš, *Vývin slovenského verša* (1939); A. Mráz, *Die Lit. der Slovaken* (1942), "Dejiny slovenskej literatúry," *Slovenská vlastiveda,* 5 (1948); *Dejiny slovenskej literatúry,* ed. A. Mráz et al., 3 v. (1958–65); J. M. Kirschbaum, *S. Lang. and Lit.* (1975).   W.E.H.

SLOVENE POETRY. See YUGOSLAV POETRY; SLAVIC PROSODY.

SMITHY POETS. A group of early Soviet poets who wrote on themes such as industrialization and proletarian solidarity in the new Soviet society. Formed in 1920, the group (Rus. *Kuznitsa*) included Vladimir Kirillov, Vasilij Kazin, Aleksej Gastev, and others. Their verse, which they strove to make rhythmically free and "modern," was often crude and naive.—G. Z. Patrick, *Popular Poetry in Soviet Russia* (1929); A. Voronskij, "Prozaiki i poèty Kuznicy," *Literarno-kritičeskie stat'i* (1963); Terras.   W.E.H.

SOCIETY AND POETRY.

   I. UNIFIED SOCIETY
  II. DIVIDED SOCIETY
 III. THREATENED SOCIETY
 IV. FRAGMENTED SOCIETY
    A. *Eclecticism*
    B. *Syncretism*
    C. *Mystical Unity*
    D. *Marxism*
    E. *Alienation*
    F. *Imaging the Disorder by Disorder*
    G. *Regionalism*
    H. *Protest Poetry*
    I. *Other Responses*
  V. POETRY AS SOCIAL

The relations of poets and p. to s. are diverse. Pope spat as much as he praised, Yeats cursed, and Shelley fled and prophesied; Shakespeare's and Racine's aristocratically ordered worlds are always threatened by the elemental power of human sin. Homer, Virgil, the Germanic *scops,* and the Heb. prophets spoke in and for their societies, but not with simple acceptance, rather with heroic exaltation, or tragic breadth, or denunciation. Rebels would invigorate change, sometimes justly and productively, sometimes not.

The diversity is not surprising. Neither is the lack of simple relations. No poet can wholly reject his s.; if he accepts it genuinely, he accepts its moral standards and finds, on observing actualities, much cause for lamentation, satire, and fear. Societies do not stand still, nor do poets. Most societies have seen themselves as incomplete against the measure of the divine; those that have not are fragmented, relativistic, pluralistic, and individualistic, like much in modern America; or see themselves as incomplete against the immanent measure of unfolding historical process, like some Marxist regimes, or express strange and unstable combinations of relativism, skepticism, and radical progressivism, like much in modern p. and thought. Therefore poets seldom find their relation to s. simple and secure. Societies assign poets to various roles, high or low; or they ignore p., in which case the alienation of the poet becomes a social issue.

Humans are individuals through and through: they are born alone; they live and decide alone; they die alone, and much of their labor is spent in a never completely successful effort to close down the gap of their separation from their neighbors and God. Humans are social through and through: the conception that gives them existence and the childbirth that brings them into the world (even if there is no midwife or doctor, there are mother and child), are social acts; the food that becomes their physical substance, the lang. with which they think, decide, and perhaps rebel, are socially given. The relations between these counter-truths are deep and complex. As long as this is true, there can be no adequate theory of the relation of the individual to s., and hence no adequate statement of the relation of the poet to s. This general truth, which applies to all, is complicated by the historical complexity of the poet's economic relations to his s. and his various degrees of feeling in or out of, for or against his s.

I. UNIFIED SOCIETY. A s. is unified if it achieves social cohesion, if it is *felt* to be unified by enough relevant members. Primitive societies, Gr. city-states (and Greece in the imagination of later ages), Rome, the Jewish nation, medieval Christendom, and 17th-c. royalist France are examples. The poet is apt to feel an integral part of such a s. rather than a rebel from it, a conveyer of old truth rather than a discoverer of new. The epics of Homer and Virgil convey and dignify the history of a people, the good wars, the gods; they presume the moral dignity of man, the value of civilizing labor, an informed and sympathetic audience. Social wisdom is conveyed by the choruses of Gr. plays. The sufferings of the individual in high station are bound to the s. and even to the fields and harvest by natural, social, and supernatural ties.

A s. may achieve unity—in spite of temporal insecurities and failures—by a dominant and continued purpose. The Jewish nation is one major example. Church is state; the profound agony of the psalmists and the prophets *is* the agony of Israel. The s., its lore, its acts are holy and one, even in exile and separation. The unified s. is apt to have firm belief, and a clear sense of hierarchy. In the Jewish s. of the Old Testament and the early Christian s. of the New, the social hierarchy matters less than the reality of God: the prophets threaten the social structure with sublime derogation. Christian paradox informs the rhet. of much Christian lit. Jesus is a humble carpenter, a titular descendant of David, the Messiah. The homeliest things—sheep, work, bread—are exalted; great things are brought low. But in Cl. Gr. s., hierarchy tends to prevail. The rhet. of Cicero and Quintilian, which exerted a major influence on Western thought about p., divides styles into three: high, middle, and low. These have social connections, esp. between the high style and aristocratic dignity. Theories tend toward a simple propriety of class and function, so that, over 1600 years later, Rymer attacks Shakespeare for making a soldier kindly. Yet standards can make for variety also. Virgil, Ovid, Juvenal, and Horace partake of one firm culture, but Virgil tends to idealize, deepen, and heighten links between past and present, between man, nature, ancestors, and gods. Ovid in *The Art of Love* accepts the standards of a sophisticated s. playfully and cynically, but turns to a strong sense of the past and the lore of his people in the *Metamorphoses*. Juvenal holds high standards of civilized behavior and lashes those who depart from them; Horace's p. offers the vision of the good man in retirement taking a large and sane view of human affairs.

Security—real or apparent—can make for self-conscious elegance, even frivolity, for setting a high value on witty expression and brilliant entertainment. The *précieux* of 17th-c. France have their highly artificial games, but also show, in their elaborate restraints something of the ascetic side of their Catholic trad. In the Eng. Restoration, the complex protocol of seduction in plays is an attempt to systematize, civilize, and justify the debauched morals of a social class. One of the finest of courtly entertainments is the masque (q.v.), esp. in the hands of Jonson and Milton, where aristocrats themselves take part and allegorical figuration of noble ideals blends into the festivity of an evening.

All patriotic p. presumes or seeks the unity of a people. It is easy for 20th-c. readers to forget how much of the world's great p. is profoundly patriotic—Homer, Virgil, David, Dante, Chaucer, Shakespeare, Spenser, Corneille, Wordsworth, Whitman, Frost, Theodore Roethke in his *North American Sequence*, as perhaps most important poets, have all written patriotic p. The power and social value of such p. can be great, even if all of it shares in varying degree the tendency to idealize the nation or people and then defend the actuality by the idealization. When such poetry is war p., as it often is, the enemy is both ennobled—that the victory may be noble—and debased—that the slaughter may be morally admirable.

Those who describe the unified s. as an ideal have been liable (from Plato to Communism) to give p. either its marching orders or a dishonorable discharge. P. must, they insist, transmit social ideals, form social virtues, praise great men, idealize the system. (We should remember that poets have often done these things without being conscripted.) Censorship may be a corollary. Plato in the *Republic* excludes poets from the ideal state because they tell lies, malign the gods, and confuse the unreal and the real. In modern Marxist states, the poet is claimed by historical necessity the servant of the state, yet poets in Russia and elsewhere achieve much greater acclaim than in the West, not for supporting the regime but for offering an expression of unpolitical feeling, shared and thus in a profound sense political.

II. DIVIDED SOCIETY. A s. is divided when there are conspicuously in it distinct sides to be chosen. A s. locked in civil war is the clearest example, but not the only one. A poet in such a s. may firmly choose a side, e.g. Milton in his attack on the Anglican clergy in *Lycidas* or Dryden in his defense of Charles II in *Absalom and Achitophel*. Or he may vacillate, as Venantius Fortunatus who, in the 6th c., wrote both panegyrics of his barbarian patrons and the powerfully liturgical *Vexilla regis*. Christendom has been, in this sense, a divided s. through much of history, given the choice between the worldly and the holy, a fact that provides for the medieval literary genre of the debate between body and soul. Or the poet (or his culture) may reconcile, as in the Christianization of the Classics by allegory (so that such an unpalatable story as that of Saturn eating his children comes to mean merely Time bearing all his sons away; or the *Aeneid* becomes a pilgrim's progress), or as in the continuation and re-creation of Cl. ideas and literary forms (as Aquinas is to Aristotelian philosophy, so is Milton to the Virgilian epic).

III. THREATENED SOCIETY. The threat may come from God's wrath, plague or famine, military force, a potent new system of thought and feeling, or internal social decay. The essential condition is that men face changes they intensely fear. All tragedy and all apocalyptic p. envisions s. as fearfully unstable, and such fears may be felt even at the time of greatest unity and achievement. The plague underwrites Chaucer's *Pardoner's Tale* and Thomas Nashe's "Adieu, farewell earth's bliss"; the theme of the Last Judgment figures in poems as diverse as the *Dies irae*, the close of Dryden's *Song for St. Cecilia's Day*, Michael Wigglesworth's popular *The Day of Doom*, and Dylan Thomas' "And death shall have no dominion." Shakespeare, in *King Lear* and *Hamlet* and, expressly in the famous "degree" speech in *Troilus and Cressida*, sees the overturn of social hierarchy echoed in nature, adumbrating apocalypse. The 16th- and 17th-c. debate whether nature (and hence s.) has decayed, which issues on the one hand into Baconian optimism, also provides pessimistic motifs for p., as in Donne's *Anniversaries*. Racine's *Phédre* images the underworld of sinful human passion as an explosive and mysterious social force. So does Baudelaire in such poems as *Les Sept Vieillards*. Both works focus on an agonized individual consciousness, but the social consequences are plainer in Racine. Phédre is a queen, Baudelaire's *persona* an *alienated* poet. The close of Pope's *Dunciad* rises to pessimistic grandeur, telling and foretelling how men fall away from great norms of thought and conduct.

Poets have responded in many other ways to threatened, or present, or imagined social cataclysm. A poet may turn from the cataclysm to the universal in common experience, as did Hardy in "In Time of Breaking of Nations," or Herrick in most of his poems. A poet may express violent reversal of feeling and commitment, like Coleridge in "France: An Ode." He may, like Yeats, adopt dozens of variant, persuasively expressed attitudes, then attempt to unify them into a contemplative whole. He may simply call for a greater allegiance to the common cause: Donald Stauffer, writing as a Marine captain in World War II, invented a memorable phrase—"Get thee behind me, Buddha." He may call for vindication of the oppressed, like Hugo in "L'Enfant," and many Black poets; or he may triumphantly express, among greater things, the vindication of a nation (the final chorus of Milton's *Samson Agonistes*). He may indict deity like Voltaire in his poem on Lisbon, or call men back to God like Johnson in the peroration of "The Vanity of Human Wishes," or achieve pessimistic universality like Juvenal in his 10th Satire or de Vigny in "La Mort du loup."

IV. FRAGMENTED SOCIETY. Such a s. is ours, in many ways: individualistic, pluralistic, uncertain of its values, certainly in the literary domain, at least. There have been several major responses to this fragmentation.

A. *Eclecticism.* The poet imaginatively and temporarily appropriates values from various cultures to express in his p. Karl Shapiro has stated that he writes as a Jew one day, a Christian the next. Yeats, Eliot, Auden, Stevens, Pound, Valéry, all share something of the quality that Yvor Winters castigated in Pound when he called him, in a memorably savage phrase, "a barbarian on the loose in a museum."

B. *Syncretism.* No sharp line is fixed between the eclectic and the syncretic. It depends on how much is *joined*. A successful syncretism in modern p. is yet to come. Yeats's *A Vision* is the boldest attempt (though in prose, it is a system for p.), though it is not surprising that he spoke of it ambiguously; and his p.—great in its power and beauty and in its deep cultural awareness—is more various than unified.

C. *Mystical Unity.* A long way from traditional mysticism, this is the solution of Walt Whitman, Hart Crane, and (at times) Emerson. Relativism and pluralism may themselves be praised, but a cultural unity assumed: Whitman assumes a cultural unity in Am. democratic brotherhood, feels (perhaps more deeply) a unity of life with death. Crane tries to achieve such unity by his powerful, many-stranded image of the bridge.

D. *Marxism.* This cultural force, tremendously powerful until its collapse in 1989, has not had much place in 20th-c. p., though it has had its say in lit. crit. (see MARXIST CRITICISM) and has revolutionary forebears of the stature of Shelley. Stephen Spender's sentimental and unconvincing "Death is another milestone on the way" is an example. This judgment holds for America and Britain, though the reputation of Pablo Neruda and some others may reach beyond a time of partisanship: the extreme bitterness of Neruda's late p. is worth our thought.

E. *Alienation* of the individual from s., himself, the past, or God. This is one of the favorite themes of modern p., intensified by doubts of the conceptual validity of the unified self. Romanticism taught the primacy of the self and of self-expression; postromanticism is in severe doubt whether there be any self: the fragments writhe in some odd ways. Yet that sort of divisiveness is hardly a postmodern invention: it is George Herbert who writes, "He is some twentie sev'rall men at least / Each sev'rall houre," and "My bent thoughts, like a brittle bow, / Did flie asunder." Such p. takes varied forms. It is nostalgic, pathetic, yet dignified in the best of MacLeish's earlier work, powerfully complex and tragic in Tate's *Ode to the Confederate Dead,* multifariously and pretentiously sly in Stevens' *The Comedian as the Letter C,* modest and precise in several of Donald Justice's poems, arrogantly stoic in Robinson Jeffers, ragingly bitter in the later Yeats. It flavors, or occasions, several of the other responses.

F. *Imaging the Disorder by Disorder.* Disorder as expressive of social disorder, recommended by Henry Adams, is a major feature of Eliot's *The Waste Land* and Pound's *Cantos*, and of many shorter poems by such writers as e e cummings, Wallace Stevens, and Dylan Thomas, reaching its extremes in dada and surrealism (qq.v.) and in imitators of such schools. Outside of Eliot—perhaps not even excluding his work—the most powerful writing of this kind is that of Robert Lowell, notably in "The Quaker Graveyard in Nantucket" and "New Year's Day."

G. *Regionalism.* The most important exemplars of this "strategy" (a word they have significantly liked) are the Southern traditionalists, particularly John Crowe Ransom, Allen Tate, and Robert Penn Warren. They look to the past to judge the present, the region to judge the nation, but do not accept simple nostalgia, idealization, or patriotism as adequate responses. Rather, they express division and tragic inconclusiveness and deal with their subject with irony and ambiguity. Their criticism of the America of their day had a surprising amount in common with Marxist approaches, and the insistence on ironic uncertainty prefigures the more extreme skepticism of deconstruction.

H. *Protest Poetry. Lycidas* is great protest p.—it protests in agony the blank cruelty of nature and the sea; so is *Absalom and Achitophel*: it protests injustice and misrepresentation and the left-wing propaganda of its day. All p. is in a deep sense—perhaps the deepest—either panegyric or satire; p. must by its nature celebrate or blame. To blame is to protest, and implies some standard by which to judge. Biblical prophecy is often protest p. and is emulated as such by later poets (as in the Black spiritual "Let my people go"). Such p. has many occasions and takes many forms and tones: the dignity of biblical prophecy, the hysterical stridency of some p. of the Am. 1960s, the quiet but telling wit of Sarah Cleghorne: "The golflinks lie so near the mill / That almost every day / The laboring children may look out / And see the men at play."

I. *Other Responses.* Poets turn to the personal life (Delmore Schwartz, e e cummings, Edwin Arlington Robinson among others), whether lyrically or unhappily. Others turn to the permanent and universal in human experience and by an act of will appropriate and continue the major trad. of Western ethics (Yvor Winters). There are various, not very bold modern versions of Art for Art's Sake, taking such forms as the focus on physical detail in the work of Marianne Moore and William Carlos Williams, the playful variety of synaesthetic and vocal effects in Edith Sitwell, the mannered, graceful, and apologetic elegance of some of Richard Wilbur; and Confusion for Confusion's Sake, art as flat or odd conversation expressing the trivially (or rawly and bitterly, or fragmentedly) personal in casual and casually divided prose. But such clutter of the journals of our day shall pass.

V. POETRY AS SOCIAL. Lang. itself is social. P. is refined speech, hence is always (1) communicative and (2) invented. Sir Philip Sidney said that p. asserts nothing, hence cannot be accused of lying. I. A. Richards held, at least for part of his career, a similar doctrine (see PSEUDO-STATEMENT), and Suzanne Langer holds that p. is never "about" s., since it is always pure invention. Without maintaining such paradoxes, one can clearly see that the s. in p. is always, in a sense, invented rather than actual. Further, all p. is about invented s., since—even in the most abstractly didactic or personally expressive of poems—the fundamental invention of each poem is a persona or a voice (qq.v.), a someone speaking to someone. There is, Wittgenstein argues cogently, no private lang., though some poets give it a good try. Still, one needs to distinguish between the s. of voice and listener, the invented s. within the poem, and the actual s. imitated. And p. does offer various

invented societies that have their manifold bearings on our experience: the world of pastoral, the world of folk belief, the world of the *Faerie Queene*, the world of medieval dream visions. There are many degrees of re-creation of s. Herrick's country people and scenes are less realistic than Goldsmith's, Goldsmith's less than Crabbe's. But there is always re-creation *and* imitation, however mixed. P., then, is always social in its instrument, its chief purpose, its subject, and its invention. It also constitutes a unified s., an atemporal order of its own. Its great themes and great continuities of form are one of the real strands of unity in our history, across nations, across bitter religious and political differences, across centuries. The ideal of literary emulation is one of the greatest Western ideals and of immeasurable social utility.

But if p. is social, it is not only social. The individual towers above s. in the very act of naming it; poets universalize as well as express their times; they see s. in change, limited by hist. and apocalypse; they imagine individuals alienated from s. in exile and fear (as we always to some degree are). They can also see s. in relation to permanent standards and realities that transcend civilization and indeed make it possible. See also ANTHROPOLOGY AND POETRY; CULTURAL CRITICISM; SYMBOLIC ACTION.

V. F. Calverton, *The Newer Spirit: A Sociological Crit. of Lit.* (1925); M. W. Bundy, *The Theory of Imagination in Cl. and Med. Thought* (1927); H. N. Fairchild, *The Noble Savage* (1928); L. I. Bredvold, *The Intellectual Milieu of John Dryden* (1934); T. R. Henn, *Longinus and Eng. Crit.* (1934); Lewis; A. O. Lovejoy, *The Great Chain of Being* (1936); D. Daiches, *Lit. and S.* (1938), "Sociology and Lit.," *Critical Approaches to Lit.*, 2d ed. (1981); J. C. Ransom, *The New Crit.* (1941); T. Spencer, *Shakespeare and the Nature of Man* (1942); E. M. W. Tillyard, *The Elizabethan World Picture* (1943); Auerbach; L. C. Knights, *Explorations* (1947); Y. Winters, *In Defense of Reason* (1947); T. S. Eliot, *Notes Toward the Definition of Culture* (1948); A. Beljame, *Men of Letters and the Eng. Public in the 18th C.* (1948); J. F. Danby, *Shakespeare's Doctrine of Nature* (1949); C. Dawson, *Religion and the Rise of Western Culture* (1950); R. C. Wallerstein, *Studies in 17th-C. Poetic* (1950); Crane; I. Jack, *Augustan Satire* (1952); H. D. Duncan, *Lang. and Lit. in S.* (1953); A. Tate, *The Forlorn Demon* (1953); G. Whicher, *P. and Civilization* (1955); Wellek and Warren, ch. 9; M. Krieger, *The New Apologists for Poetry* (1956); Frye; H. Levin, *Contexts of Crit.* (1957); A. Salomon, "Sociology and the Literary Artist," *Spiritual Problems in Contemp. Lit.*, ed. S. R. Hopper, 2d ed. (1957); W. J. Ong, "Voice as Summons for Belief," *Thought* 33 (1958); R. N. Wilson, *Man Made Plain: The Poet in Contemp. S.* (1958); K. Burke, *Attitudes Toward Hist.* (1961); P. Ginestier, *The Poet and the Machine,* tr. M. B. Friedman (l961); B. Snell, *P. and S.* (1961); G. Lichtheim, *Marxism,* 2d ed. (1964);

SOCIETY VERSE

G. Lukács, *Studies in European Realism* (1972); *Lit. Crit. and Sociology*, ed. J. Strelka (1973); *The Lit. of Fact*, ed. A. Fletcher (1976); W. K. Wimsatt, Jr., *The Day of the Leopards* (1976); R. Williams, *Marxism and Lit.* (1977); E. Goodheart, "Eng. Social Crit. and the Spirit of Reformation," *The Failure of Crit.* (1978); L. Wittgenstein, *Culture and Value*, tr. P. Wolff (1980); F. Lentricchia, *Crit. and Social Change* (1983); A. MacIntyre, *After Virtue*, rev. ed. (1983); P. Ramsey, *The Truth of Value* (1985); A. Bewell, *Wordsworth and the Enlightenment* (1989).
P.R.

SOCIETY VERSE. See LIGHT VERSE.

SOLILOQUY. See MONOLOGUE.

SOMALI POETRY. Somalia has been called a nation of poets because of the extensive use of verse in social intercourse by these East African people. S. poetic trad. employs poetry for discussing politics, expressing love, sending secret messages, conducting family and clan business, and bantering between the sexes. Until the mid 1950s, S. p. was totally oral. Even after 1972, when a Roman script was introduced, most poetry continued to be composed and performed orally. Printed poetry is rare, to be found only in a few books published by government agencies and daily newspapers. Some religious poetry is written in Arabic, and one S. poet in the Négritude trad., Wm. J. F. Syad, has emerged.

The S. poetic trad. ranges from verbatim memorization of complex forms to formulaic and improvised composition (simultaneous composition and recitation) of simpler forms. Specific poems in complex genres are attributed to named poets, and the roles of poet and reciter/memorizer, though overlapping, are separate. Some reciter/memorizers, like Ḥussein Dhiqle, have gained prestige in their own right. Ḥussein was the spokesperson for Sayid Maḥammad 'Abdille Ḥassan, called the "Mad Mullah" by his British enemies. This S. national hero, religious leader, and warrior was a brilliant poet of classical verse, which aided his 20-year holy war against foreign colonials early in the 20th c.

Generic differentiation in S. p. is accomplished by a combination of scansion rules, function, topic, and musical setting. The genre of highest prestige is the *gabay*, which functions in political discourse, social debate, religion, and philosophical contemplation. Next in prestige are the *jiifto* and *geeraar*, which deal with similar subjects but have different scansions and recitation melodies. These three genres are used by men; the *buraambur* is used by women for many of the same functions. These four genres are practiced and disseminated with an attempt at verbatim memorization and are composed of irregular strophaic stanzas recognizable by prolonged notes at the end of the last word in each strophe.

Work songs are less complex and include an element of formulaic composition. Each defined type of work among the nomads (ca. 44% of the population) has its own genre and range of topics. Camels are watered two times per trip to the wells, and two genres of *hees geel* accompany these tasks. Different genres of *hees maqal* are associated with the separate tasks of taking baby sheep and goats to wells and herding them from one campsite to another. Separate genres of *hees adhi* are employed for the same two tasks associated with adult sheep and goats. Women weave three varieties of mats, and different genres are recited during each task (*hees harrar, hees alool, hees kebed*). The pounding of grains (*hees mooye*) and the churning of milk (*hees haan*) also have specific genres. These poems set rhythm and work pace and function socially as indirect modes of communication between the sexes. In one *hees adhi*, for example, a woman sings to her ram admonishing him for choosing the wrong husband for his kid. Metaphorically she is admonishing her own husband for arranging the marriage of their daughter to a man of whom she does not approve.

While work genres of the same meter are widespread throughout Somalia, recreational genres are regional and tend to be composed via improvisation. Many genres are employed for dancing when young men and women are permitted to mix. A popular genre in the North is the *dhaanto*, where the *hirwo, wiglo*, and *belwo* were popular in the past. Having the same function, all four genres scan identically; they are differentiated by their melodies. Over 15 other dance genres have been identified; these are employed as media for dance gestures and modes of expression by creative poets who gain considerable prestige if they prove skillful.

In contrast to the quantitative scansion of classical S. poetry, the *heello* has gained prestige since the 1950s and is recited by both men and women. Modeled first on Indian, then European song modes, it is lyric in nature and accompanied by European musical instruments. Topics are similar to those assigned to the *gabay*, along with many others considered too frivolous for classical verse. The *heello* is complex in structure; hence its composition tends to be similar to that of the *gabay*. Diffusion is accomplished by means of radio and tape recorder as well as oral memory.

Memorization of S. p. is made possible by strict rules of prosody. Scansion patterns, the text of the poem, and musical accompaniment minimize the effects of faulty memory. Minor variation sometimes occurs from one reciter/memorizer to another, but changes are made so the text will scan properly. Classical poetry scans with a quantitative system involving a relationship between syllables and vowel length. The smallest units are short vowels which have the temporal equivalence of one *mora*; long vowels, as in words like *gabadh* (girl) and *koob* (cup), have two morae. *Ilaah* (God) has three, and *daanyeer* (monkey) has four. Morae

SONG

fit into metric slots called *semes*. *Monosemes* hold short vowels, but *disemes* hold either two short vowels or one long unless a genre rule requires a long vowel. Monosemic or disemic boundaries may not be crossed by long vowels. The configuration of semic patterns in part defines the genre. Syllables also play a role, and three different relationships can be isolated. Open set moro-syllabic relationships allow as many syllables as morae on a line. Closed sets allow only one syllable per seme. Semi-closed sets designate specific numbers of morae and syllables but allow too many disemes, so short vowels are forced into some disemes while long vowels are forced into others.

The scansion pattern of the *gabay* will illustrate the intricacies of classical poetry. The following line is from *Jiinley* (Poem Alliterating in "J"), by Sayid Maḥammad 'Abdille Ḥassan:

∪‖⊥|⊥ | ∪‖⊥ | ∪|∪| ∪‖⊥
Ḥuseenow jikraar lama hadlee,
 ⊥ | ∪ ‖ ⊥ | ∪|∪ |∪‖
jaalkay baad tahay e.

O Ḥussein, do not speak with obstinance,
for you are my comrade.

The *gabay* is a tetrameter. Feet are demarcated by double bars, semes by single bars, and open and semi-closed moro-syllabic relationships by broken bars. Anacrusis is allowed (the breve before the first double bar). The pattern within each foot is diseme + diseme + monoseme, and a caesura falls between the first and second disemes in the third foot. An open set moro-syllabic relationship occurs in the first hemistich, where any diseme may hold one long vowel or two shorts. In the second hemistich the relationship is semi-closed, specifying eight morae and six syllables. Since there are three disemes, one must hold two short vowels, but the poet may chose which diseme to so treat. Throughout the entire poem only one alliteration is allowed, at least one instance of which must occur in each hemistich. The manipulation of semic configurations and moro-syllabic relationships constitutes the manner Somalis use to expand their generic repertoires. When these patterns are rearranged, new genres are created.

Published collections of S. p. feature mostly verse of the nomads, but poetic activity among those who work the land is equally common. Research is carried out in the National Academy of Sciences and Arts and at the S. National University, where investigation of unclassified genres is conducted.

B. W. Andrzejewski and I. M. Lewis, *S. P.* (1964); B. W. Andrzejewski, "Poetry in S. Society," *Sociolinguistics*, ed. J. B. Pride and J. Holmes (1972), "The Poem as Message: Verbatim Memorization in S. Oral P.," *Memory and Poetic Structure*, ed. P. Ryan (1981); J. W. Johnson, "The Family of Miniature Genres in S. Oral P.," *Folklore Forum* 5 (1972), *Heellooy Heelleellooy: The Devel. of the Genre Heello in*

Mod. S. P. (1974), "S. Prosodic Systems," *Horn of Africa* 2 (1979), "Recent Researches into the Scansion of S. Oral P.," *Proc. of the 2d Internat. Congress of S. Studies*, ed. T. Labahn (1984), "Set Theory in S. Poetics," *Proc. of the 3d Internat. Congress of S. Studies*, ed. A. Puglielli (1988); Jaamac Cumar Ciise, *Diwaanka gabayadii Sayid Maxamed Cabdulle Xasan* (1974); Abdillahi Derie Guled, "The Scansion of S. P.," *Somali and the World*, ed. Hussein Mohamed Adam (1980); Said Sheikh Samatar, *Oral P. and S. Nationalism* (1982); *Lit. in Af. Langs.*, ed. B. W. Andrzejewski et al. (1985); F. Antinucci and Axmed Faarax Cali, "Idaajaa," "Poesia orale somala: storia di una nazione," *Studi Somali* 7 (1986).   J.W.JO.

SONG (Lat. *carmen*, Fr. *chanson*, Ger. *Lied*). A term used broadly to refer to verbal utterance that is musically expressive of emotion; hence more narrowly, the combined effect of music and poetry (q.v.) or, by extension, any poem that is suitable for combination with music or is expressive in ways that might be construed as musical; also occasionally used to designated a strictly musical composition without text, deemed "poetic" in its expressivity or featuring markedly "vocal" melodic writing for instruments. From the musical standpoint, "s." has been restricted almost exclusively to musical settings of verse; experiments in setting prose have been very limited. Further, "s." has usually meant compositions for solo voice or a small group of voices (typically one or two voices to a part) rather than a full choir, and for voice(s) alone or in combination with only one or two instruments rather than a full orchestra. Hence, the resulting balance, favoring the audibility of the text and thus appreciation of the nuances of its combination with music, is a defining characteristic of the genre; for literary purposes, these characteristics have also fostered perception of s. as personal utterance projecting a limited emotional stance experienced by a single persona (q.v.).

As a literary term, "s." is related to "lyric" (q.v.), originally the single event consisting of a poem sung to the lyre, and eventually used in lit. in divergent senses to refer on the one hand to any poem actually set or intended to be set to music (ditty), and on the other to any poem focusing on the arousal of emotion—the latter taking its derivation from the kind of poem typically sung to the lyre (or to any other musical accompaniment) as s. "Lyric," however, has attained much wider currency than has "s." "Lyric" is the commonly accepted term today for both these meanings, whereas "s.," as a literary term, means an utterance partaking in some way of the condition of music.

For poetry, "s." has been applied in numerous ways corresponding to the nature of the implied relationship with music. The principal categories for treating the setting of poetry in s. are two: formal (including metrical, linear, strophic representation) and semantic (including verbal representation—rendering the meaning of individual words—and expressive—the rendering of a musical simulacrum of the tone or mood of the poem). They need not, of course, exclude each other, and indeed it is frequently difficult if not impossible to separate what may be a metrical rendering from its verbal or expressive function. The categories are useful, however, as some ss. favor one or the other, in turn influencing what are considered "s.-like" elements or effects in poetry.

The association of poetry with music in the ss. of the late Eng. Ren. provides prototypes of almost every meaning of s. In some (as in Thomas Campion, who wrote both words and music for his ss.), the rendering of the formal dimensions of poetry is precise: musical meter is aligned with poetic meter (q.v.), lines of verse are of uniform length and set to musical phrases of the same length (words are not repeated or extended by musical means), and the strophic repetition (q.v.) of the poem is rendered through repetition of music (as in traditional hymn singing). Poetry that lends itself to settings of this sort is typically predictable in all of these dimensions; hence, such a poem may be designated "s." In the madrigal (q.v.) and in some lute ss., by contrast, such formal properties are likely to be ignored and musical devices instead correlated with individual words to enhance meaning. This might mean repetition of words of special poignancy ("weep, weep") or highlighting of such words through exaggerated duration or unusually high or low pitch; frequently such representation is accomplished through a technique called word-painting, which aligns individual words with musical figures that can be said to depict their meaning (a descending scale for the word "down"; a dissonance for the word "grief"). Inevitably such practices also lead to predictability, in this case in diction. In the poetic miscellanies of the period, "s." and "sonnet" (q.v.) sometimes seem to be used interchangeably and often refer to poems with one or more of these characteristics. At worst they are poems filled with cliche and cloyingly regular in formal properties; at best they achieve a delicate balance between the demands of successful musical rendition and fresh invention.

Ss. featuring more general expressivity of mood or tone in music appear less frequently in this period, although the lutenist-composer John Dowland achieved some remarkable successes in this mode. Perhaps most famous is his "Lachrimae," which existed as an instrumental composition before being provided with its now-famous text, "Flow, my tears." The pervasively doleful mood of the piece is created musically in the accompaniment through its preponderance of descending melodic lines, its minor harmonies, its low register, and the slow, deliberate pace of its phrasing; the poem seems, in effect, to make verbal what the musical rhet. of emotion has already manifested.

The role of music, then, in this type of s. is less specifically text-dependent than in other types, and the required balance between music and poetry depends to a greater extent upon the availability of appropriate instrumental resources to combine with the voice.

The *Lied* of 19th-c. Ger. lit. best exemplifies the fully developed expressive setting. In the hands of Franz Schubert, and to a great extent of those who followed him (Schumann, Brahms, Wolf), the role of the accompanying instrument was enhanced to create a highly emotional s. evocative of the overall tone or mood of the poem. Many give credit to the devel. of the modern grand piano for the success of the *Lied*; certainly the notion of expressive setting was not new, as the role of the instrumental accompaniment in Monteverdi's "Combattimento di Tancredi e Clorinda" demonstrates. Such pieces, however, violated the required intimacy of voice and single instrument characteristic of s., and it was not until the devel. of a single instrument with the expressive range of the piano that this mode of s. could flourish. The genre also depended upon—and stimulated—a poetry that provided the appropriate moods, expressed in terms that could be adequately mimicked by music. This is found in the poetry of Ger. romanticism, with its frequent evocation of nature or of ordinary human activity as the locus of emotion. For Schubert, the presence in the poem of a running brook or a woman spinning wool as the background to an emotion-filled reverie provided a means for music to enhance, significantly, what the poem could only suggest. In this context, poetry can be said to be songlike if it presents an intense, sustained, clear emotional stance, called forth by an activity that takes place in time. Typically such poems feature only one such stance or a decided shift from one to another; striking ambiguity or paradox (qq.v.) is less songlike insofar as these conditions are less readily imitated in music.

Curiously, poems that depend extensively on the so-called musicality of words (e.g. Edith Sitwell's "abstract poetry" [see ABSTRACT POEM] and the later experiments in sound poetry [q.v.]) are not necessarily songlike, because the sounds of the words draw attention to themselves and thereby detract from the poem's ability to evoke an emotional state. John Hollander's "Philomela" does call forth an emotional state through the association of its sounds with the images they portray, but this work was created for a specific composer and performer and thus may be thought a small libretto rather than a s. in the literary sense.

The most extended use of "s." to refer to a kind of poetry takes the connection well beyond any mechanical representation or concurrence to questions of intent or of the relation to strains of creativity. Thus Jacques Maritain uses "s." to designate the entire genre of lyric poetry, as distinct from narrative or dramatic, referring to "the Poem or the S. as *the poetry of internal music* . . . the immediate expression of creative intuition, the meaning whose intentional content is purely a recess of the subjectivity awakened to itself and things—perceived through an obscure, simple, and totally nonconceptual apperception" (394). Such conceptions of the nature of s. center on the ability of music to tap some source of understanding or sympathy that is not touched by lang. Lawrence Kramer speaks of "the mythical union of a lower reality embodied in lang. and a higher one embodied in music," stating that "through s., usually the s. of a disincarnate voice or of a figure touched by divinity, lang. is represented as broaching the ineffable" (2); it is this sense that is implied in the use of music to evoke the supernatural, whether through strictly instrumental means or through charms (q.v.), as is common in drama. Music has traditionally been associated with magic and, of course, with religious experience (despite the objections at various times of both Catholic and Puritan), and it has throughout known history been thought of as the lang. of love. The fusion, therefore, of music and poetry in s. has been thought to bring about the most perfect communication possible, combining the ineffable expressivity of music with the rational capabilities of words. And by derivation, poems that are perceived as visionary, conjuring some understanding beyond the normal capacities of words, may be called ss. Spenser's "Epithalamion" and "Prothalamion," Blake's *Ss. of Innocence and Experience*, and Whitman's "S. of Myself" come to mind.

It should be noted that "s." has come to designate certain purely musical compositions too, presumably those, like poems called s., that partake in some measure of the shared experience of music and poetry. Most frequent in this usage are such 19th-c. compositions as Mendelssohn's "Ss. without Words" for piano—short, expressive pieces, typically with a striking, singable melody and the sense that one could describe in words a suitable emotional frame of reference. Their proximity to the *Lied* is probably not coincidence; s., or *Lied*, in that context *means* once again that combination of words and music producing a compressed and intense expression of the rhet. of emotion, and if words are merely implied, the effect is nevertheless present and the composition known as s.

Several specialized types of s., established by use, have similarly given their names to poetic types, esp. elegy, lament, hymn, lay or *lai*, ballad, carol, rondeau (qq.v.), and canzonet. See also AIR; ALBA; BALLAD; CACOPHONY; CANSO; CARMEN; CHANT; CHARM; DESCORT; DITTY; EUPHONY; GESELLSCHAFTSLIED; LYRIC; METER; MUSIC AND POETRY; RHYTHM; SOUND; SOUND EFFECTS IN POETRY; SPIRITUALS; TAGELIED.

F. Gennrich, *Grundriss einer Formenlehre des mittelalterlichen Liedes* (1932); T. S. Eliot, "The Music of Poetry" (1942); W. R. Bowden, *The Eng. Dramatic Lyric, 1603–42* (1951); J. Maritain, *Creative Intuition in Art and Poetry* (1953); R. Lebèque,

"Ronsard et la musique," *Musique et poésie au XVI siècle* (1954); G. Müller and G. Reichert, "Lied," *Reallexikon* 2.42–62; D. Cooke, *The Lang. of Music* (1959); J. Hollander, *The Untuning of the Sky: Ideas of Music in Eng. Poetry, 1500–1700* (1961); A. Sydow, *Das Lied* (1962); C. M. Bowra, *Primitive S.* (1962); R. H. Thomas, *Poetry and S. in the Ger. Baroque* (1963); *Penguin Book of Lieder*, ed. S. S. Prawer (1964); P. J. Seng, *The Vocal Ss. in the Plays of Shakespeare* (1967); R. Taylor, *The Art of the Minnesinger* (1968); B. H. Bronson, *The Ballad as S.* (1969); D. Ivey, *S.: Anatomy, Imagery, and Styles* (1970)—on musical setting of Eng., Fr., Ger., and It. poetry, 17th to 20th cs.; J. M. Stein, *Poem and Music in the Ger. Lied* (1971); E. Brody and R. A. Fowkes, *The Ger. Lied and Its Poetry* (1971); M. C. Beardsley, "Verse and Music," in Wimsatt; E. Garke, *The Use of Ss. in Elizabethan Prose Fiction* (1972); J. H. Long, *Shakespeare's Use of Music* (1972); H. van der Werf, *The Chansons of the Troubadours and Trouvères* (1972); D. Fischer-Dieskau, *Schubert's Ss.: A Biographical Study* (1977); C. Ericson-Roos, *The Ss. of Robert Burns* (1977); *Med. Eng. Ss.*, ed. E. J. Dobson and F. Ll. Harrison (1979); B. H. Fairchild, *Such Holy S.: Music as Idea, Form, and Image in the Poetry of William Blake* (1980); "S." and "Lied" in *New Grove*; M. Booth, *The Experience of Ss.* (1981); R. C. Friedberg, *Am. Art S. and Am. Poetry*, 2 v. (1981); S. Ratcliffe, *Campion: On S.* (1981); J. A. Winn, *Unsuspected Eloquence: A Hist. of the Relations between Poetry and Music* (1981); W. R. Johnson, *The Idea of Lyric* (1982); E. B. Jorgens, *The Well-Tun'd Word: Musical Interps. of Eng. Poetry, 1597–1651* (1982), ed., *Eng. S., 1600–1675*, 12 v. (1986–89), esp. v. 12, *The Texts of the Ss.*; L. Kramer, *M. and P.: The 19th C. and After* (1984); L. Schleiner, *The Living Lyre in Eng. Verse from Elizabeth through the Restoration* (1984); S. Banfield, *Sensibility and Eng. S.: Critical Studies of the Early 20th C.*, 2 v. (1985); Hollander; M. M. Stoljar, *Poetry and S. in Late 18th-C. Germany* (1985); E. Doughtie, *Eng. Ren. S.* (1986); W. Maynard, *Elizabethan Lyric Poetry and Its Music* (1986); J. Stevens, *Words and Music in the Middle Ages* (1986); D. Seaton, *The Art S.: A Research and Information Guide* (1987)—esp. "Aesthetics, Analysis, Crit."; J. W. Smeed, *Ger. S. and Its Poetry, 1740–1900* (1987); D. M. Hertz, *The Tuning of the Word* (1988); E. H. Winkler, *The Function of S. in Contemp. British Drama* (1990); *Lyrics of the Middle Ages*, ed. J. J. Wilhelm (1990).

E.B.J.

SONNET (from It. *sonetto*, a little sound or song). A 14-line line poem normally in hendecasyllables (in It.), iambic pentameter (in Eng.), or alexandrines (in Fr.) whose rhyme scheme has, in practice, varied widely despite the traditional assumption that the s. is a fixed form. The three most widely recognized versions of the s., with their traditional rhyme schemes, are the It. or Petrarchan (octave: *abbaabba*; sestet: *cdecde* or *cdcdcd* or a similar combination that avoids the closing couplet), the Spenserian (*abab bcbc cdcd ee*), and the Eng. or Shakespearean (*abab cdcd efef gg*). Weeks (1910) showed in a sample of just under 6000 Eng. ss. that 60% used the *abba abba* pattern for the octaves, and 22% *abab cdcd*.

With respect to the It. pattern (by far the most widely used of the three), it will be observed that a two-part division of thought is invited, and that the octave offers an admirably unified pattern and leads to the *volta* (q.v.) or "turn" of thought in the more varied sestet. The *abbaabba* octave is actually a blend of 3 brace-rhyme quatrains, since the middle four lines, whose sounds overlap the others, reiterate the identical envelope pattern but with the sounds reversed, i.e. *baab*. Normally, too, a definite pause is made in thought development at the end of the eighth line, serving to increase the independent unity of an octave that has already progressed with the greatest economy in rhyme sounds. Certainly it would be difficult to conceive a more artistically compact and phonologically effective pattern. The sestet, on the other hand, with its element of unpredictability, its usually more intense rhyme activity (three rhymes in six lines coming after two in eight) and the structural interdependence of the tercets, implies an acceleration in thought and feeling, a mood more urgent and animated.

The Spenserian and Shakespearean patterns, on the other hand, offer some relief to the greater difficulty of rhyming in Eng. and invite a division of thought into 3 quatrains and a closing or summarizing couplet; and even though such arbitrary divisions are frequently ignored by the poet, the more open rhyme schemes tend to impress the fourfold structure on the reader's ear and to suggest a stepped progression toward the closing couplet. Such matters of relationship between form and content are, however, susceptible of considerable control in the hands of a skilled poet, and the ultimate solution in any given instance may override theoretical considerations in the interests of artistic integrity.

Most deviations from the foregoing patterns have resulted from liberties taken in rhyming, but there have been a few innovations in use of the s., among them the following: *alternating*, where the tercets alternate with the quatrains (Mendès); *caudate* (q.v.), with "tails" of added lines (Hopkins, Samain, Rilke); *chained* or *linked*, each line beginning with the last word of the previous line; *continuous*, *iterating*, or *monorhymed* on one or two rhyme sounds throughout (Giacomo da Lentini, Mallarmé, Gosse); *corona* (q.v.), a series joined together by theme (It.) or rhyme or repeated lines (Sp., Eng.) for panegyric; *curtal* (q.v.), a s. of ten lines with a halfline tailpiece, divided 6 + 4 1/2 (Hopkins); *dialogue*, a s. distributed between two speakers and usually pastoral in inspiration (Cecco Angiolieri, Dobson); *double*, a s. of 28 lines (Monte Andrea); *enclosed*, in which the tercets are sandwiched between the quatrains (Baudelaire,

Rambosson); *interwoven*, with medial as well as end rhyme; *retrograde*, reading the same backward as forward; *reversed* (also called *sonettessa*), in which the sestet precedes the octave (Baudelaire, Verlaine, Huch)—for a reversed Shakespearean s., see Brooke's "Sonnet Reversed"; *rinterzato*, a s. with eight short lines interspersed, making a whole of 22 lines (Guittone d'Arezzo); *terza rima* (q.v.), with the linked-tercets *aba bcb* rhyme scheme; *unrhymed*, where the division into quatrains and tercets is still observed, but the lines are blank (Du Bellay, Becher). In Eng. the most conspicuous variant, the 16-line poems of George Meredith's sequence *Modern Love* (1862), is clearly related to the s. in its themes and *abba cddc effe ghhg* rhyme scheme. In the 20th c., John Hollander has devised a cycle of 169 13-line poems in 13-syllable unrhymed lines (*Powers of Thirteen*, 1983).

Historically, the s. began as some variant of the It. pattern; it is probable that the form resulted either from the addition of a double refrain of six lines (two tercets) to the 2-quatrain Sicilian *strambotto* (q.v.) or from conscious modeling on the form of the *canzone* (q.v.). In any event (for the origins remain uncertain), the earliest antecedents of the "true" It. s. are credited to Giacomo da Lentini (fl. 1215–33), whose hendecasyllables usually rhymed *abababab cdecde*. Although others of Lentini's contemporaries (the Abbot of Tivoli, Jacopo Mostacci, Piero delle Vigne, Rinaldo d'Aquino) used the form and established the octave-sestet divisions (with quatrain-tercet subdivisions), it remained for Guittone d'Arezzo (1230–94) to invent the *abbaabba* octave, which became traditional through its use by Dante (*Vita nuova; Rime*) and Petrarch (*Canzoniere*). Antonio da Tempo, in his *Summa artis rithmici* (1332), is the first to enunciate theoretical discussion of the s. as a type. The ss. of Dante to Beatrice, and of Petrarch to Laura ("spells which unseal the inmost enchanted fountains of the delight which is the grief of love"—Shelley) normally opened with a strong statement which was then developed; but they were not unmarked by the artificiality of treatment that stemmed from variations on the Platonic love themes, an artificiality that was to be exported with the form in the 15th–16th cs. as the s. made its way to Spain, Portugal, France, the Netherlands, Poland, and England, Germany, Scandinavia, and Russia, until its use was pan-European and the number of poets not attempting it negligible (see PETRARCHISM). Following Petrarch there was in Italy some diminution of dignity in use of the form (as in Serafino dall'Aquila [1466–1500]), but with the work of Michelangelo, Bembo, Castiglione, and Tasso, the s. was reaffirmed as a structure admirably suited to the expression of emotion in lyrical mood, adaptable to a wide range of subject matter (e.g. love, politics, religion), and employed with skill by many writers in the centuries to follow (Alfieri, Foscolo, Carducci, D'Annunzio).

It was the Marquis de Santillana (1398–1458) who introduced the s. form (in hendecasyllables, even) to Spain, although it was not established there until the time of Juan Boscán (1490–1552) and, esp., Garcilaso de la Vega (1503–36) and Lope de Vega (1562–1635) and other dramatists of the *siglo de oro*. Sá de Miranda (1485–1558) and his disciple, Antonio Ferreira, brought the s. to Portugal, where it is better known in the *Rimas* of Camões (1524–80) and, more recently, in the exquisite work of Anthero de Quental (1842–91). Clément Marot (1496–1544) and Mellin de Saint Gelais (1491–1558) introduced it to France, but it was Joachim du Bellay (1522–60) who was most active, writing (in the Petrarchan pattern) the first non-Italian cycle, *L'Olive*, as well as *Les Regrets* and *Les Antiquités de Rome* (tr. by Spenser as *The Ruins of Rome*, an important source for Shakespeare's ss.). Ronsard (1524–85), who experimented with the form in alexandrines, and Philippe Desportes (1546–1606) wrote many ss. and were instrumental in stimulating interest both at home and in England; while Malherbe (1555–1628) put the weight of his authority behind the *abbaabba ccdede* pattern in alexandrines, which became the accepted line length. After a period of decline (general throughout Europe) in the 18th c., Gautier (1811–72), Nerval (1808–55), and Baudelaire (1821–67) revived the form, which soon reached new heights in the work of Verlaine, Mallarmé, Rimbaud, Heredia, and Valéry. Germany received the form relatively late, in the writings of G. R. Weckherlin (1584–1653) and, esp. insofar as creative achievement is concerned, Andreas Gryphius (1616–64). There followed a period of disuse until Gottfried Bürger (1747–94) revived the form and anticipated its use by Schlegel, Eichendorff, Tieck, and other romantic writers. The ss. of August Graf von Platen (1796–1835), *Sonette aus Venedig*, rank among the best in modern times, while in more recent years the mystical sequence, *Sonette an Orpheus* (1923), of Rilke and the writings of R. A. Schröder have brought the Ger. s. to another high point.

In England the s. has had a fruitful history. Wyatt (1503–42) brought the form from Italy but showed an immediate preference (possibly influenced by the work of minor writers while he was abroad) for a closing couplet in the sestet. Wyatt did, however, adhere to the Petrarchan octave; it was Surrey (1517–47) who established the scheme *abab cdcd efef gg*, a pattern more congenial to the comparatively rhyme-poor Eng. lang. in that it filled the 14 lines by 7 rhymes not 5. This pattern was used extensively in the Ren. but by no means exclusively, for there was wide variation in rhyme schemes and line lengths. It was brought to its finest representation by Shakespeare. A rhyme scheme more attractive to Spenser (and in its first 9 lines paralleling his Spenserian stanza [q.v.]) was *abab bcbc cdcd ee*, in effect a compromise be-

tween the more rigid It. and the less rigid Eng. patterns. The period also saw many s. sequences (q.v.), beginning with Sidney's *Astrophil and Stella* (1580) and continuing in the sequences of Daniel (*Delia*), Drayton (*Idea*), Spenser (*Amoretti*), and Shakespeare, with a shift to religious themes shortly thereafter in Donne's *Holy Ss.* It remained for Milton to introduce the true It. pattern, to break from sequences to occasional ss., to give greater unity to the form by frequently permitting octave to run into sestet (the "Miltonic" s., but anticipated by the Elizabethans), and a greater richness to the texture by employing his principle of "apt numbers, fit quantity of syllables, and the sense variously drawn out from one verse into another," as in his blank verse. And s.-like structures of 14 lines have even been discerned in the stichic verse of *Paradise Lost*, a practice later echoed by Wordsworth and Hardy (Johnson). Milton's was the strongest influence when, after a century of disuse, the s. was revived in the late 18th c. by Gray, Thomas Warton, Cowper, and Bowles; and reestablished in the early 19th by Wordsworth (also under Milton's influence but easing rhyme demands by use of an *abbaacca* octave in nearly half of his more than 500 ss.) and by Keats, whose frequent use of the Shakespearean pattern did much to reaffirm it as a worthy companion to the generally favored Miltonic-Italian. By this time the scope of s. themes had broadened widely; in Leigh Hunt and Keats it even embraced an unaccustomed humor. S. theory was also developing tentatively during this period (as in Hunt's "Essay on the S."), to eventuate in an unrealistic extreme of purism in T. W. H. Crosland's *The Eng. S.* (1917) before it was more temperately approached by later writers. Since the impetus of the romantic revival, the form has had a continuing and at times distinguished use, as in D. G. Rossetti (*The House of Life*), Christina Rossetti, E. B. Browning (*Ss. from the Portuguese*), and Swinburne. Few writers in the present century (W. H. Auden and Dylan Thomas might be named) have matched the consistent level of production found in the earlier work, although an occasional single s., such as Yeats's "Leda and the Swan," has rare beauty.

The s. did not appear in America until the last quarter of the 18th c., in the work of Colonel David Humphreys, but once introduced, the form spread rapidly if not distinctively until Longfellow (1807–82), using the It. pattern, lifted it in dignity and lyric tone (esp. in the *Divina Commedia* sequence) to a level easily equal to its counterpart in England. Following him there was wide variety in form and theme, with commendable work from such writers as Lowell, George Henry Boker, and Paul Hamilton Hayne. Of the later writers E. A. Robinson, Edna St. Vincent Millay, Merrill Moore, Allen Tate, and e e cummings (who wrote a considerable number) hold a recognized place, although, space permitting, many others might be named who stand well above what Robinson called

. . . these little sonnet men
Who fashion, in a shrewd mechanic
way,
Songs without souls, that flicker for a
day,
To vanish in irrevocable night.

During the past century, s. themes in both
Europe and America have broadened to include
almost any subject and mood, even though the
main line of development has remained remark-
ably⁻stable. Structurally, even within the tradi-
tional patterns, the s. has reflected the principal
influences evident in modern poetry as a whole:
the sprung rhythm (q.v.) of Hopkins and free-
verse (q.v.) innovations have frequently led to less
metronomic movement within the iambic norm;
alternatives to exact rhymes have replenished the
stock of rhyme-pairs and have sophisticated acous-
tic relationships; and a more natural idiom has
removed much of the artificiality that had long
been a burden. This adaptability within a tradition
of eight centuries' standing suggests that there
will be no diminution of interest in and use of the
form in the foreseeable future, and that the inher-
ent difficulties that have kept the numbers of truly
fine ss. to an extremely small percentage of those
written will deter neither versifier nor genius from
testing for her- or himself the challenge of what
Rossetti called "a moment's monument,— / Me-
morial from the Soul's eternity / To one dead
deathless hour." See also COLLECTIONS, POETIC;
ITALIAN PROSODY; LYRIC SEQUENCE; ONEGIN
STANZA; QUATORZAIN; SONNET SEQUENCE.

H. Welti, *Gesch. des Sonettes in der deutschen Dich-
tung* (1884); Schipper, 2.835 ff.; L. Biadene, *Mor-
fologia del sonetto nei secoli XIII e XIV* (1889); M.
Jasinski, *Histoire du s. en France* (1903); L. T.
Weeks, "The Order of Rimes of the Eng. S.," *MLN*
25 (1910): 176–80, 231—data; Thieme, 381 ff.—
lists 17 Fr. works, 1548–1903; F. Villey, "Marot et
le premier s. français," *RHL* 20 (1920); R. D.
Havens, *The Influence of Milton on Eng. Poetry*
(1922)—surveys 18th- and 19th-c. Eng. ss.; W. L.
Bullock, "The Genesis of the Eng. S. Form," *PMLA*
38 (1923); L. G. Sterner, *The S. in Am. Lit.* (1930);
E. Oliphant, "S. Structure: An Analysis," *PQ* 11
(1932); L. C. John, *The Elizabethan S. Sequences*
(1938); L. Zillman, *John Keats and the S. Trad.*
(1939); H. Smith, *Elizabethan Poetry* (1952); W.
Mönch, *Das Sonett: Gestalt und Gesch.* (1955)—the
most comprehensive study to date, with extended
bibl.; E. Rivers, "Certain Formal Characteristics of
the Primitive Love S.," *Speculum* 33 (1958); E. H.
Wilkins, *The Invention of the S. and Other Studies in
It. Lit.* (1959); F. T. Prince, "The S. from Wyatt to
Shakespeare," *Elizabethan Poetry*, ed. J. R. Brown
and B. Harris (1960); J. W. Lever, *The Elizabethan
Love S.*, 2d ed. (1965); E. Núñez Mata, *Historia y
origen del soneto* (1967); S. Booth, *An Essay on
Shakespeare's Ss.* (1969); B. Stirling, *The Shakespeare
S. Order: Poems and Groups* (1969); *Das deutsche
Sonett: Dichtungen, Gattungspoetik, Dokumente*, ed.
J. U. Fechner (1969); J. Levý, "The Devel. of
Rhyme-Scheme and of Syntactic Pattern in the
Eng. Ren. S.," "On the Relations of Lang. and
Stanza Pattern in the Eng. S.," rpt. in his
Paralipomena (1971)—difficult to obtain but valu-
able; M. Françon, "L'Introduction du s. en
France," *RPh* 26 (1972); J. Fuller, *The S.* (1972);
L. M. Johnson, *Wordsworth and the S.* (1973); F. Jost,
"The S. in its European Context," *Intro. to Comp.
Lit.* (1974); Wilkins; R. L. Colie, *Shakespeare's Liv-
ing Art* (1974); C. Scott, "The Limits of the S.,"
RLC 50 (1976); F. Kimmich, "Ss. Before Opitz,"
GQ 49 (1976); D. H. Scott, *S. Theory and Practice
in 19th-C. France* (1977); H.-J. Schlütter, *Sonett*
(1979); S. Hornsby and J. R. Bennett, "The S.: An
Annot. Bibl. from 1940 to the Present," *Style* 13
(1979); J. Geninasca, "Forme fixe et forme discur-
sive dans quelques ss. de Baudelaire," *CAIEF* 32
(1980); Brogan, 455 ff.; Morier; L. M. Johnson,
Wordsworth's Metaphysical Verse (1972)—blank
verse ss.; *Penguin Book of Ss.*, ed. C. Withers
(1979); W. L. Stull, "'Why Are Not Ss. Made of
Thee?'" *MP* 80 (1982)—the religious s. trad.; H.
S. Donow, *The S. in Eng. and Am.: A Bibl. of Crit.*
(1982); Fowler; *Russkij sonet*, ed. B. Romanov, and
Russkij sonet, ed. V. S. Sovalin (both 1983)—an-
thols.; A. D. Ferry, *The "Inward" Lang.* (1983); F.
Rigolot, "Qu'est-ce qu'un s.?" *RHL* 84 (1984);
Elwert, *Italienische*, sect. 83; C. Kleinhenz, *The
Early It. S.: The First Century (1220–1321)* (1986);
Hollier; P. Oppenheimer, *The Birth of the Mod.
Mind* (1989); G. Warkentin, "S., S. Sequence," *The
Spenser Encyc.*, ed. A. C. Hamilton et al. (1990); A.
L. Martin, *Cervantes and the Burlesque S.* (1991);
Six Masters of the Sp. S., ed. and tr. W. Barnstone
(1992).   T.V.F.B.; L.J.Z.; C.S.

SONNET CYCLE. See SONNET SEQUENCE.

SONNET SEQUENCE or cycle. A subset of the
lyric sequence (q.v.) consisting of a series of son-
nets, of any number, that may be organized ac-
cording to some fictional or intellectual order.
The sequence made entirely of sonnets is rarer
than readers often suppose, and seldom holds an
author's or a culture's attention for long before
deliberate variations emerge. The rise of the s. s.
in most European langs. coincides with that of
Petrarchism (q.v.): because Petrarch's late 14th-c.
Canzoniere is made largely but not exclusively of
sonnets (317 of 366 poems), many of its imitators
and adapters in Fr., Eng., Port., and Sp. saw their
roles as involving the domestication of his sonnet-
form; hence the first Petrarchans in the vernacu-
lars (e.g. Wyatt and Surrey in Eng.) are often the
first sonneteers in their langs. as well (e.g. Du
Bellay and Ronsard in Fr., Sá de Miranda and
Camões in Port., Boscán and Garcilaso in Sp.).
The most extreme vogue for s. ss. was that of Eng.
poets in the later 16th c.: examples include Wat-
son's *Hekatompathia* of 18-line sonnets (1582), Sid-

ney's *Astrophil and Stella* (written early 1580s, pub. 1591), Spenser's *Ruins of Rome* (1591—an adaptation of Du Bellay's *Antiquitez de Rome* [1558] and drawn upon by Shakespeare) and *Amoretti* (with its completing *Epithalamion* [1595]), Constable's *Diana* (1592), Daniel's *Delia* (1592), Drayton's much-revised *Idea* (1593), and Shakespeare's *Sonnets* (written 1590s, pub. 1609). In the 17th c., while poets such as the Spaniard Francisco de Quevedo, Sidney's niece Mary Wroth, and the Mexican nun Sor Juana Inés de la Cruz continue to extend the reach of the amatory and philosophical s. s., the orientation of the s. s. at large (like that of the lyric sequence) turns toward devotional writing. Aside from Quevedo and John Donne, notable religious sonneteers incl. the Ger. Andreas Gryphius, the It. Tommaso Campanella, the Dutchman Constantijn Huygens, and the Frenchman Jean de la Ceppède.

In the early modern period generally, the s. s. is often thought to have a special, almost automatic claim to overall integrity—whether topical (as in Du Bellay's *Les Regrets* [1558]), meditative (as in the "corona" [q.v.] used by Donne and others), or vaguely chronological (as in the common usage of the Eng. word "century" for 100 sonnets). As scholars such as Fumerton and Jones have recently demonstrated, the s. s. can be as much a cultural as a literary construction—a canvas for the working-out of collective interests, a ritual experience, a type of public space—with potential analogues in painting, religion, and architecture, among other disciplines. The job of cultural mediation enacted by the s. s. perhaps indicates why poetic amateurs of note—such as the It. sculptor and painter Michelangelo Buonarroti in the 1530s and 1540s, the Eng. Puritan polemicist Henry Lok in the 1590s, or the Am. philosopher George Santayana in the 1890s—are drawn to this form as a uniquely deprivileged space: it enables them to think through emotional, philosophical, or religious issues in a formally determined, publicly accessible medium. In fact, the first s. s. in Eng.—Ann Lok's *Meditation of a Penitent Sinner* (1560), inspired by the Scottish Puritan John Knox—is the ideologically charged work of a poetic amateur, intervening in contemporary religious debates in the mode of a deeply personal meditation (Roche).

Like the lyric sequence, the s. s. seems to have had few important instances in the 18th c., but became a major romantic and postromantic vehicle. Notable examples incl. Wordworth's several s. ss.; E. B. Browning's *Sonnets from the Portuguese* (1850); Meredith's narrative *Modern Love* (1862), in which the "sonnets" have 16 lines; D. G. Rossetti's *House of Life* (1881); Darío's "sonetos" and "medallones" in *Azul . . .* (1888), a book that impelled Sp.-Am. *modernismo* (q.v.), which had a recurrent fascination with the sonnet in loosely organized collocations; Pessoa's *35 Sonnets* in Eng. (1918); Rilke's *Sonette an Orpheus* (1923); and cummings' several s. ss. in his early volumes *Tulips*

and Chimneys (1923), *&* (1925), and *XLI Poems* (1925). With the 20th-c. modernisms came another hiatus, followed by a renewed sense of the s. s.'s potential for organizing experience, esp. love, though in the later 20th c. it is perhaps impossible for the s. s. to occur without formal irony, cultural critique, or anachronistic pathos. Thus Nicolás Guillén's political volumes are founded on his early experiments as a sonneteer, a role to which he returns for ironic effect (as in "El abuelo" in *West Indies, Ltd.* [1934]); John Berryman's adulterous *Sonnets* (written 1940s, pub. 1968) seek out a self-conscious Petrarchism (esp. no. 15, an adaptation of *Canzoniere* 189). Robert Lowell became all but exclusively a sonneteer in late career: his experiments in recasting the s. s. *Notebook 1967–68* as *Notebook* (1970), *History* (1973), and *For Lizzie and Harriet* (1973) might be considered the climax of his work, culminating in *The Dolphin* (1973) and *Day by Day* (1977). Among more recent adaptations in Eng. are Seamus Heaney's ten "Glanmore Sonnets" (in *Field Work*, 1979) and his 8-sonnet elegy "Clearances" (in *The Haw Lantern*, 1987); Tony Harrison's dissonant rewriting of the formal trad. in *Continuous: 50 Sonnets from the School of Eloquence* (1982); Marilyn Hacker's amatory *Love, Death, and the Changing of the Seasons* (1986), incl. an updated crown of sonnets; and Bill Knott's cultural polemic in *Outremer* (1989).

See also COLLECTIONS, POETIC; CORONA; RENGA; SONNET.

Elizabethan Sonnet-Cycles, ed. M. F. Crow (1896); L. C. John, *The Eng. S. Ss.* (1938); W. Mönch, *Das Sonett: Gestalt und Gesch.* (1955); A. Gryphius, *Lyrische Gedichte*, ed. H. Palm, v. 3 of *Werke* (1961); *European Metaphysical Poetry*, ed. F. J. Warnke (1961); D. Stone, *Ronsard's Sonnet Cycles* (1966); B. Stirling, *The Shakespeare Sonnet Order* (1968); S. Booth, *An Essay on Shakespeare's Sonnets* (1969); T. Cave, *Devotional Poetry in France 1570–1613* (1969), *The Cornucopian Text* (1979); essays on Ronsard, Scève, and Du Bellay in *YFS* 47 (1972); P. E. Blank, Jr., *Lyric Forms in the S. Ss. of Barnabe Barnes* (1974); J. de la Ceppède, *From the Theorems*, tr. K. Bosley (1983); R. A. Katz, *The Ordered Text* (1985)—Du Bellay's s. ss.; J. Fineman, *Shakespeare's Perjured Eye* (1986); Scherr 235; P. Fumerton, "'Secret' Arts: Elizabethan Miniatures and Sonnets," *Representing the Eng. Ren.*, ed. S. Greenblatt (1988); Hollier; T. P. Roche, Jr., *Petrarch and the Eng. S. Ss.* (1989); G. Warkentin, "S. S.," *The Spenser Encyc.*, ed. A. C. Hamilton et al. (1990); W. C. Johnson, *Spenser's Amoretti* (1990); A. R. Jones, *The Currency of Eros* (1990).   R.GR.

SONS OF BEN. See CAVALIER POETS.

SORITES. See AUXESIS; CLIMAX.

SOTADEAN. In Cl. poetry, a type of stichic verse usually analyzed as a succession of three complete major ionic metra ($--\smile\smile$) followed by a doubly shortened ("brachycatalectic") concluding one (−−). Resolution and contraction are possible in any metron but the last, as is the substitution of −◡−◡ or, in freer forms of composition, certain other tetrasyllabic variants. The meter was associated with obscene or satiric verse. Most examples are from the late Hellenistic or Imperial period, the earliest Gr. ones being by Sotades himself, an Alexandrian poet (3d c. B.C.). The S. was introduced to Lat. by Ennius, but though it can be found in Plautus, Accius, Varro (*Menippean Satires*), Petronius (twice), and Martial (3.29), it was never extensively used in Lat. poetry.—F. Koch, *Ionicorum a maiore historia* (1926); Crusius; Halporn et al; West.   A.T.C.

SOUND. This article treats the general and theoretical issues raised by the nature of s. and its use in poetry. For more extended discussion of the theory of verse as based on the structuring of s., see PROSODY. For more specific discussion of poetic s. effects, see SOUND EFFECTS IN POETRY.

    I. THEORETICAL STATUS
   II. ARTICULATION, ACOUSTICS, AUDITION
  III. DECONSTRUCTION
  IV. PATTERN
   V. EXPRESSIVENESS
  VI. AESTHESIS
 VII. MUSICALITY
VIII. ANALYSIS
  IX. FULLNESS

I. THEORETICAL STATUS. Teachers of poetry for centuries have exhorted students to ignore the poem on the page and pay attention, rather, to the words in the lines as sounded aloud. This is still salubrious advice. It does not mean, however, that spoken s. is the ontological locus of "the poem." It only means that—for poems written in traditional, aural pros., at least—students of poetic form must not be distracted by the visual or graphic format, since writing is a very inexact representation of sounded speech.

In Western poetics, there have been three views about the status of s. in poetry. (1) The traditional literary view, and the presently reigning view in linguistics, is that poetry (lang.) is s., and the written or printed text is a derivative phenomenon merely meant to represent s., hence of only secondary interest. (2) The reverse view, namely that the written form is primary, the s. form secondary, is the point of view of deconstruction (q.v.) and, interestingly, most Ren. grammarians, who treated Lat. grammar and pros. as a set of rules applying to a *written* lang. (3) The more radically diremptive (but also synthetic) view of poetry (and lang.) is that the aural and written modes are equivalent but simply differ, both deriving from the ontologically prior nature of lang. itself. The first of these views holds that s. exists only in performance (q.v.) and in time, and that the words on the page are a mere notation or score, as in music. The

second holds that lang. has behind it no self-certifying voice and that important aspects of poetry follow from purely visual features of textuality.

The third point of view, which is that taken in the present account, holds that poetry (the Word) is an ontologically bivalent entity. On this account, lang. is a set of structured formal relations which may be manifested in either or both of two physical media, one sonic the other graphic, neither of which has any particular logical or ontological priority despite the fact that the aural mode happened to appear first. Poetry, in short, is a structure or system of s., just as lang. is not the physical ss. of speech but the set of rules which makes the speaking possible. Even s. itself is only a form, not a thing with an independent existence: it is merely an organization of the air. Unlike light, which seems to be an entity unto itself because it can flow through a vacuum, s. would not exist without a carrier medium. S. is realized in a medium, so is composed of that medium, of course, but in itself is wholly form.

Modern readers are accustomed first to seeing a poem on a page, then to reading it silently, and only rarely to hearing it read aloud. Prior to the invention of writing and printing and the spread of literacy, however, the situation was quite the reverse: orality was the condition of poetry. This contrariety should lead us to ask the deeper question about the ontological status or site of poetry, i.e. the question of where a poem exists. Few would want to hold that a poem exists on the page, for then someone could burn the page and claim that "the poem" was thereby destroyed. We might then point out that there are other copies of the poem. Suppose our incendiary then burnt all known texts of the poem—is "the poem" then gone? So long as humans exist who remember the text of the poem exactly and can reproduce it, the poem is not lost. If all who remember the poem should die, then presumably the poem indeed ceases to exist. Barring that, most would be uncomfortable saying that poems exist only in our minds, a view which echoes Croce's theory that "real" artworks exist only in their creator's conception, the physical manifestation being but a poor secondhand version. No, we want to insist that artworks, like people, have both a physical and a social existence.

The analogy with music is instructive: presumably few would hold that sheet music is "music." The musical score is only a set of marks on paper which via a set of known conventions are intended as directions for performance. Many would naturally say that music therefore exists only when it is being played and heard. But of course each performance varies in greater or lesser degree; each is music, but not "the music." All performances are however related by the set of invariant features (formal relations) notated on the score which, despite innumerable minute variations, are constant through all accurate performances and thus

SOUND

constitute "the music."

For theoretical purposes, therefore, the term "s." does not refer, literally and most directly, to the s. of the poem actually heard in performance, for in the recitation of verse, speakers produce any number of linguistic and even paralinguistic features which are optional and variable and may well be unique to each performance, and so cannot be a part of that system of invariants common to all performances because they are cued by the text. It is this latter set of features which constitutes the s. system of the poem. We are interested, as Jakobson said, not in the phone but in the phoneme, in ss. as coded into categories by the phonological structure of the lang. and so treated at an abstract level, as a *system* of signs. Poetic s. responds to the lang. system but is further constituted (coded) on a different principle in verse.

A number of prosodic conventions do *not* treat s. as heard: both correct scansion (q.v.) of a meter and correct recognition of a rhyme (q.v.), for example, depend on knowing which letters in the printed text of a poem were sounded in the poem's historical context, not which are sounded now. Several metrical rules in fact take account of syllable ss. regardless of whether they exist or not. In Fr. prosody (q.v.), there is a rule forbidding a masculine–feminine rhyme: feminine rhymes (all words which end in mute -e) must mate with feminine, and masculine (words ending in any other vowel or a consonant) with masculine, regardless of the fact that the mute ending has not been sounded since the 15th c. And in It. prosody (q.v.), lines are treated in scansion as having 11 syllables even if they have only 9 or 10. "Sound" therefore is as much a conventional and theoretical construct as any other literary concept, varying in definition from lang. to lang. and subject to further constraints by verse systems.

The distinctive feature of poetry is that it is set in lines, i.e. articulated into segments. This segmentation is however of a different nature than the visual format of the poem might suggest; the visual text is determined in part simply by the exigencies of the codex page. As s., however, in the air, "the poem" is pure soundstream, continuous except for being punctuated at various points by pauses (see SYNAPHEIA). The poem is thus one long string of ss.; the only reason it is not set as one string of characters on the page is that the page is not wide enough. Similarly, a paragraph in a file on a computer disk is actually stored as one continuous string of characters. This chain is wrapped between margins on the screen only for reading convenience. (The right-margin "soft carriage return" characters which are saved in the file but invisible on screen are in effect invisible rhymes.) This analogy suggests that characteristics specific to the display format are not constitutive of the poem but rather derivative. What is constitutive is the segmentation of the soundstream, i.e. its articulation, the fissures breaking and binding together its features.

II. ARTICULATION, ACOUSTICS, AUDITION. Vocal s. is a very different phenomenon depending on whether one asks about how it is produced (its place and manner of production), how it is structured (its inherent characteristics), and how it is received (processed in cognition). These three sets of phenomena are not congruent. At various times, many prosodists have claimed that one or another of these is relevant to the study of poetry. Here it is important that objective acoustic and linguistic facts be distinguished from subjective perceptions by speakers and auditors (though such perceptions themselves also constitute facts).

Articulation. Any modern introductory linguistics or phonetics textbook will reproduce the trapezoid describing the articulation points of the vowels in the mouth, classed from high to low and front to back, and also the standard chart of consonant groups also based on place and manner of articulation, esp. voicing. Distinctive-feature analysis (q.v.) has been applied to poetic s. to see if patterning can be discovered on that basis. One type of onomatopoeia (q.v.) or expressive s., called kinesthetic (see below), is based on the presumption that the mouth and facial gestures involved in s. production contribute to meaning.

Acoustics. In simplified form, the acoustic facts about the nature of s., as we presently understand them, are as follows. S. is a waveform which passes through (organizes) air (or any medium) from a source to a receiver. Its acoustic dimensions or characteristics are: *frequency, amplitude,* and *intensity*; and one must consider also *duration* and *quality*. Its shape can be visualized as the sine waves one sees on an oscilloscope. One wave (from crest to crest) = one cycle; cycles/sec. = *frequency*, measured in Hertz (Hz). The human voice ranges from ca. 100–200 Hz; middle C is 264 Hz. The human ear can hear ss. in the range from ca. 20 to 20,000 Hz. Frequency correlates (complexly) with perceived pitch (q.v.): the higher the frequency (the more waves per second), the higher the perceived pitch. Conversely, higher frequency of waves per sec. entails shorter wavelength. The *amplitude* of the wave (the height of its peaks and depth of its valleys) correlates (complexly) with perceived loudness. The human ear is not good at discriminating loudness: a s. must increase in intensity by a factor of 10 to be perceived as twice as loud. *Intensity* (i.e. stress) has to do with the overall power of the s. and is measured in decibels (dB). *Duration* ("length," sometimes "quantity" [q.v.]) concerns how long a s. is prolonged or held in speech production: some langs. organize this aspect systematically in phonology, and most of these schematize it in verse as quantitative meter. The *quality* ("timbre," "tone-color") of a s. concerns not the nature of the s. itself but of the source making it: the same note played on a flute sounds differently to us than it does from an oboe or guitar or human voice: quality is thus paralinguistic not linguistic, so it is not clear that it is relevant to the analysis of poetry (see TIMBRE). Verse systems normally select one of the three features—pitch, stress, or duration—and pattern it systematically as meter (q.v.); other s. patterning is secondary and compounds the degree of order in the text.

Audition. There have been several significant developments in the study of the audition and mental processing (cognition) of s. which may bear on poetry. The most important concerns the hemispheric specialization of functions in the brain, which leads to the brain's differentiation of modes of s., a phenomenon called "dichotic listening." Lateralization of cerebral functions is by now well established. Acoustic signals are received by the brain and processed according to whether they are linguistic or nonlinguistic, the latter including both ambient environmental ss. and music. The analysis and interp. of lang. ss. is (in right-handed people) a left-brain activity, the same hemisphere responsible for cognition, motor activity, and rational thought. At the same time, musical ss. are interpreted in the right brain (see Jaynes). Complex aural stimuli such as vocal song, where words and music are delivered simultaneously, are processed on double tracks. Poetry, too, which is coded into sonal patterns which are both lexical-semantic as well as prosodic (e.g. meter, rhyme, assonance), is processed by both hemispheres simultaneously, the former ss. being interpreted by one side of the brain as linguistic and the latter ss. by the other as aesthetic. In short, rhythm in lang. is left-brain but pattern recognition is right-brain. As verse is heard, speech pros. is handled and sense extracted—or created, depending on one's epistemology—by the left brain, while verse-art pros. is handled and aesthetic pattern recognized by the right brain. Both sides of the brain are listening to poetry simultaneously but differently. (Tsur gives a different account of this process, postulating a third, "poetic" mode of speech perception.) It is probable that not all elements in the double code are recognized on only one pass, a fact which legitimizes the close prosodic analysis of poetry as training for heightened response in subsequent readings.

A number of researchers in several disciplines have pursued this concept of differential processing of auditory information. Schaeffer, interested in musical timbre, distinguished two modes of hearing: in ordinary listening, ss. are perceived mainly by identifying their source; the s. itself is only secondarily of interest. But in "reduced hearing" we ignore the source and respond to the inherent properties of the s. itself, as a "s. object" (*objet sonore*). In psychoacoustics, Liberman and his colleagues distinguished "speech mode" from "nonspeech mode": in the former, acoustic signals are reduced to phonological categories, while in the latter, they are not, but some acoustic features can cue both, and in general the coding of acoustic signals is very complex.

III. DECONSTRUCTION. But if s. has been a central interest of modern psychoacoustics and cognitive studies, it has been consciously excluded from mainstream critical thinking in America over the past three decades due to the influence of deconstruction and poststructuralist crit.

Deconstruction is grounded in the work of the Swiss linguist Ferdinand de Saussure, who reminded the 20th c. that the form of the words in any given lang. is purely arbitrary: words have no *natural* or motivated connection to things in the external world. The Eng. word for canines is "dog," but in Fr. it is "chien": this *difference* between langs. shows that the form of any word is determined differentially by each lang. Further, *difference* is also operative within a lang.: in Eng., minimal pairs such as *bit* and *bat* refer to two quite different things by virtue of the fact they differ in one phoneme. Saussure concluded that it is the differential itself which creates and constitutes the meaning of two words, not, as here, their identities (in *b* and *t*), and that it is therefore not the *presence* of features in the words of a lang. but the systematic differentials between them that makes meaning possible at all. Readers of Nietzsche will remember his argument that if presence is a reality, absence is too. Derrida later used this reasoning to attack the notion of *logocentrism*, i.e. that lang. is grounded in anything outside itself which would authorize meaning; for him, there is nothing outside of the text. By this he meant to dismantle any metaphysics of presence underpinning all Western thought.

It was a mistake, however, for Saussure to focus on the differential features of lang. to the exclusion of features of presence. Rather, one wants an account in which both presence and absence are held in tension as antinomies, as opposites which require each other in order to exist at all, and in the absence of one of which the other cannot function. Further, one must also recognize that the particular forms of *bit* and *bat* were derived not out of the blue but by historical process, via the regular laws of etymological development and s. change at work in lang., e.g. Grimm's Law. Words, like people, have a historical life: they change their shape over time in response to both internal and cultural forces, and they beget progeny recognizably theirs.

It is indubitable that the word *bat* has no necessary connection to cylindrical wooden objects made by the Louisville Slugger Company for the purpose of hitting balls to left field; any other word would do so long as we agreed by convention to use it. What we should conclude from this, however, is not that there is *no* attachment between our words and the world, nor even that we make the world, i.e. that we live in a self-composed set of fictions, for in fact we know that words do in some sense generate constructions that do at times accurately reflect the external world as humans experience it. At times they do not—but at times they do. This is true for words in exactly the same sense that, in other representational systems, such as mathematics, one can construct equations that lead to predictions that turn out to be correct. Such equations do in fact describe aspects of reality as we know it. It is certainly possible to construct other sets of equations that do not describe this reality but rather some other realities. All well and good. But the more salient fact is simply that some equations *can* be constructed that are indisputably accurate representations of *this* reality.

Unfortunately, however, we cannot say that a sentence in lang. is precisely equivalent to an equation in mathematics in any easy or obvious way, and it is agreed that the shapes of words do not represent things in any directly reliable way. The reliability we sense in lang. is therefore constitutive not of any single word or even string of words but rather at the level of the system. The "fit," insofar as there ever is a fit between words and the world, must be a homology between the two systems taken as wholes, not between any specific elements of the systems. It is idle, on this account, to fault a net for having holes. "Since lang. is form and not substance," says Culler, "its elements have only contrastive and combinatorial properties" (*Saussure* 49). It was the former of these that Derrida chose to emphasize. But in so doing he ignored the latter, and one might well counter that lang. does not after all function like an anchor or rivet gun to the world, but rather like a net, in which the holes are indeed large and many—but not the means by which it does its work.

Moreover, lang. is not solely a representational system; it is a communication system having a variety of functions such as the expression of emotion or the certification of social process. In ordinary speech, the representational function is often primary, but in poetry, that function is both reduced by the heightened level of phonological patterning and of s. effects unusual to speech and prose, and also augmented by other functions, producing a more comprehensive and synthetic mode of speech. The referential function of lang. is capitalist: it exploits the usefulness of words only to discard them. The poetic function (q.v.) of words however grants them their being; foregrounds their nature, their *quidditas*; and cherishes their quirky uniqueness, their *haecceitas*.

In the course of his attempt to show the impossibility of our ever standing outside of lang. so as to validate any intention or determinate meaning, Derrida denied the primacy of speech over writing in lang. This Derridean emphasis on *l'écriture* (writing) over *lecture* (speech) reversed the traditional and Saussurean identification of s. as primary in lang. For more than a decade after the pub. of the Eng. tr. of *Of Grammatology* in 1976, poststructuralist critics focused on writing and textuality (q.v.), acting as if s. did not exist, at least in

theory. Stewart claims of Derrida that there is "an emphasis on the phoneme more prevalent in his practice than in his theory." Perhaps so. In any case, Derrida, reacting to formalist notions of expressive lang. and intentional meaning, nevertheless went too far in the other direction. If all is lang., then all is certainly text. But phonemic patterning still remains in the structure of the text even when authorizing voice is subtracted, and it is easy to show, as Stewart does (see esp. 103–6), that it is s. alone which is responsible for many of the playful, homophonic textual effects so dear to poststructuralist critics like de Man.

What should be of interest to literary critics is therefore not the question of whether or how words attach to the world but what they are capable of in consort—i.e. what effects they have on each other and, more importantly still, what effects they are capable of when these mutual interanimations are complicated, enriched, compounded, heightened, and made manifest by pattern—in short, when lang. is made over into poetry. The casting of ordinary lang. into poetic form generates meanings and effects *not otherwise possible* absent from them; these are the whole reason for having poetry at all. Hence we should view poetry not as an imitative or mimetic art but as a *constitutive* one (see PROSODY).

IV. PATTERN. We are left, then, with the fact—not under erasure—of pattern, of design. S. patterning in poetry covers a wide range of important functions ranging from the aural "tagging" of syllables in semantically important words in the line, to the tagging of thematically important words in the poem, to even more extensive and formalized structures. Alliteration (q.v.) in particular is simply the most conspicuous manifestation of a broad-scale process of semantic underlining. S. patterning often highlights a sequence of key terms central to the thematic progression of the poem. In Shakespeare's sonnet 129, for example, sonal repetition binds and points up the series "purpose, pursuit, possession, proof, proved, proposed" as a metonymic litany of the evils of "lust in action," itself already marked fivefold as "hated . . . bait . . . laid to make the taker" mad. Lynch found that, in some poems, key components of s. patterns important throughout the poem, like the one above, were even brought together in a thematically "summative word."

In Old Germanic and OE poetry, alliteration patterning of halflines is even made part of the meter, vestiges of which lingered for centuries in ME alliterative verse, Ren. artverse, and post-Ren. popular verse and song (see ALLITERATIVE VERSE IN MODERN LANGUAGES). Correlate structures appear in several other verse-systems, incl. Welsh *cynghanedd* (q.v.), where a sequence of consonants in the first hemistich is repeated in the second; and the binary and ternary forms of the Fr. alexandrine (q.v.), whose metrical structures may be confirmed and enhanced by s. patterning. S. patterns within the line may coincide with (also contradict) metrical stress, link halflines, heighten the symmetry of the line, and augment or complicate other metrical patterning (Chesters).

It is not required that a s. pattern be consciously perceived for it to have effect, nor is it required that the words even make sense, as one can see in both nonsense verse (q.v.) and Gerard Manley Hopkins. Pattern organizes, highlights, and intensifies meaning in all verbal strings. This suggests that it is necessary, even essential, to study pattern, and dangerous to study it in isolation from meaning for very long. Despite some very elaborate taxonomies of s. patterning set forth in the past by scholars such as Masson, no taxonomy which is complex has yet achieved wide acceptance. It seems more profitable to identify only a few relatively simple processes with broad application on a variety of levels of the text. These would presumably include processes such as *sequence* (ABC > ABC), *chiasmus* (ABC > CBA; q.v.), *alternation* (ABAB), *envelope* (ABBA; q.v.), and all the secondary mixtures and complications of these simple or primary forms: a pattern expanded, a pattern contracted, a pattern inserted into another pattern, two patterns alternated, two or more patterns interlaced in more complex ways, and patterns with subpatterns which become motifs to be repeated, varied, and embellished. Masson in 1953 identified two archetypal s. patterns, sequence and chiasmus, and in 1960 suggested that strength or intensity of patterning could be quantified in terms of "bond density." Laferrière in 1974 explored some of the processes listed above.

Study of s. patterning infringes neither the deconstructive critique of authorizing "voice" in lang. nor the formalist "intentional fallacy" (q.v.). Intention there may or may not be, but design there certainly is, and design inevitably has an effect different from no-design. We may not always be able to specify what that effect is, and the effect may not be identical from one reader/auditor to another, but effects there are, and at least some demonstrably result from textual and performative cues. Stability of response to heightened textual organization is not to be wished away. We must attend to both cues and effects if we wish to say anything accurate about how readers read poetry and what happens when they do.

V. EXPRESSIVENESS. The issue of whether ss. bear meaning directly, over and apart from lexical meaning, is disputed. Traditionally, prosodists pointed to onomatopoeia (q.v.), often derided by other critics, but after Peirce, the concept of iconicity (q.v.) has been taken seriously in semiotics. There is good cross-cultural evidence in linguistics that mimetic processes in lang.—phonological, morphological, and even syntactic—are more diverse and extensive than was previously thought. But a number of modern critics have reacted against the older view that ss. could in themselves be "expressive" of meaning, esp. since lexical

meaning is never absent to begin with. I. A. Richards constructed a "dummy" of stanza XV of Milton's Nativity Ode to show that ss. really only reinforce meaning, not create it; and John Crowe Ransom parodied Tennyson's "The murmuring of innumerable bees" as "The murdering of innumerable beeves" to show that even when the overall s. pattern is changed only very slightly, the meaning of the words is changed radically and the "mimetic" effect nearly obliterated (see REPRESENTATION AND MIMESIS).

On the whole, one surmises, mimetic effects in poetry most often reinforce lexical sense, so that the strong presumption will remain that when critics assign expressive values to a s. or s. pattern, they are usually responding more immediately to effects that are lexically induced. In short, the s. pattern discovered is made to fit the interp. rather than the reverse. But a more constructive approach is certainly possible: one can view such effects as providing not the same kind of sense as lexical, but rather a different kind on a different level. In Frost's "Desert Places," for example, where the scene is winter and the first two words are "Snow falling," 16 of the 40 syllables in the first stanza contain sibilants. These, as anyone who knows winter knows, are the ss. that snow makes. The poem is talking about snow, certainly, but at the same time it is *making* snow ss. "Mimetic" ss. are not, therefore, representational but presentational: they add to lexical meaning the enactment of that meaning. Poetic s. always focuses attention on itself even as it delivers meaning, and in this respect, it increases the palpability of the sign and so widens the division between signs and objects (Jakobson), making poetic lang. in fact not more representational, in the simplest sense, but less.

But the range of expressiveness of ss. includes not only imitative ss. but also the further range of associative phenomena, wherein the mind generates meanings by making associations between ss. as objects with other objects, or between ss. as one kind of sensation with other kinds of sensory experience or other mental phenomena (memory, desire, images, ideas). Association probably counts for a great deal in all cognition. One may object that associations are transient, creative, and unpredictable, but they are no less real or important for that, and there is evidence to suggest that they are considerably less idiosyncratic than is usually thought. On the breath, s. is a physical entity and has, like every other real entity, dimensionality: size, length, shape. Dante even classes words as "combed out," "shaggy," "glossy," and "rumpled." It is a demonstrable fact that auditors perceive ss. to have aspects of physical shape which they correlate with those of other physical objects. These correlations are associative.

If many expressive ss. are not imitative but associative, then there is no *necessary* connection between the nature of the s. and the terms used to describe it; this follows from the Saussurean doctrine of the arbitrariness of the sign. On the other hand, empirical testing reveals a good deal of common response across cultures to certain types of associations. Some of this stability of association appears to be built into the structure of lang., and may be—since all speakers worldwide have essentially the same articulatory mechanism in the throat—lang.-independent. Other aspects are lang.-specific, however, for langs. of course differ in the size and variety of their phonetic inventories. Yet other associative processes occur not in speakers' cognitive processing but in lang. itself: both Bolinger and Malkiel have shown that words have not only rich and complex diachronic lines of affiliation but equally extensive relationships synchronically, so that at any point in time, some words are exerting a gravitational pull on others, influencing them lexically (semantically), in s. shape, and even orthographically. Malkiel calls this process, aptly, "morphosymbolism."

To describe and to articulate difference between the ss. we hear, we seem all but forced to choose descriptive adjectives—e.g. light, dark, velvety, red—from the other senses. The literary form of this phenomenon is known as synaesthesia (q.v.). Such cross-sensory description is far from being merely metaphorical: there is some evidence that the neural centers in the brain which process sensory stimuli may share information. It is certain that memory combines such information. The operation of this process in poetry is akin to "s. painting" in music, when ss. or their patterns evoke sensory impressions of geography or topography, e.g. thin, steep, high, low, sunken, vast, open, broad, dark, gloomy. Romantic and symbolist poets of the 19th c. in England, France, Germany, and Russia took a keen interest in the associative and expressive values of s. and in synaesthesia. Both A. W. Schlegel and Rimbaud associated vowels with colors. This interest infected newly-emergent psychology, producing a barrage of works in the late 19th and early 20th c. Later scholars such as Delbouille, however, have sharply criticized much of this work as fanciful, arbitrary, and of dubious linguistic accuracy.

One final type of expressive s. is kinesthetic. Here the feel of the s. in the vocal tract or mouth, or the shape of the mouth, or the facial expression produced in making the s. evokes or is associated with an emotion or meaning suggested by the words. Plosives and sibilants, for example, can evoke actual spitting and hissing in relevant contexts, as when Adam turns on Satan in *Paradise Lost*: "Out of my sight, thou Serpent, that name best / Befits thee with him leagu'd, thy self as false / And hateful."

VI. AESTHESIS. The aesthetic function of poetic s. for the auditor or reader evokes the instinctive pleasure of articulating or hearing ss., or of perceiving s. patterns, or of the repetition of s. This is a pleasure of the mouth and ear, and of the right brain, the intuitive side. Soundplay arises natu-

rally from ordinary lang., where it is prominent in children's games, nonsense verse, lullabies, college cheers, advertising jingles, magical charms, chants, and of course song. In prose, it appears in Attic and baroque rhythmical and rhymed prose (see PROSE RHYTHM; RHYME-PROSE) and in such movements as euphuism and mannerism (q.v.). In artverse, however, literary critics have often taken the view that s. patterning which is not closely tied to sense, or which outstrips sense where sense is stale or thin, or which seems cultivated at the expense of sense is the mark of an inferior poet (e.g. Poe, Swinburne, Dylan Thomas). Such critics often associate excessive s. repetition with the soundplay of childhood, with mental derangement (Smart, Hölderlin) or altered states of consciousness, or with literary attempts to imitate either or both (Blake). Nevertheless, in every age there have been movements in poetry toward the condition of music, i.e. pure patterning of s. without regard for meaning (see PURE POETRY), just as there have been opposed movements toward poetries of clear and direct sense—narrative, descriptive, dramatic. The persistence of all such movements testifies to the fact that poetry is both sense and s., and that artistic and critical fashions will oscillate perennially between the two.

VII. MUSICALITY. Discussions of poetic s. as "musical" have a pedigree in the history of crit. which has been productive in inverse relation to its length. Since s. structuring is systematized in music, and since the relations of music to poetry are as old as accompanied song, the use of musical terminology and even sigla to describe poetic s. has seemed natural and appropriate. Critics who have taken an interest in poetic s. have usually followed the ancient practice of construing s. phenomena on the analogy of music, i.e. as some version of "harmony," "mellifluousness," "melodiousness," "euphony" (q.v.), or their opposites (see CACOPHONY; DISSONANCE; see also COUNTERPOINT). This has not been a productive approach, however, for the kinds of structuring of s. characteristic of music are not, as Northrop Frye pointed out, those of verse, precisely. Further, even music itself is a very complex system of structuration of s. (see MUSIC AND POETRY). S. in lang. is very different from s. in music, not to mention their mixed forms: recited verse is one thing, sung verse quite another, and verse recited to the accompaniment of music yet another. It was Wimsatt who remarked that "the music of spoken words in itself is meager"; "the art of words is an intellectual art, and the emotions of poetry are simultaneous with conceptions and largely induced through the medium of conceptions." Like much in Wimsatt, this is too severe, but it aims in the right direction.

VIII. ANALYSIS. Discussion of s. is an important topic among the ancients. The arbitrariness of lang. was of course a concern of Plato in the *Cratylus*; other important ancient commentators on s. and poetry incl. Aristotle (*Rhet.* 3.9.9–11);

Demetrius (*On Style*), who uses "parhomoeosis" as the generic for all types of s. correspondence and who discusses such topics as imitative effects, cacophony in Homer, and distinctions between "smooth" and "rough" words; and Dionysius of Halicarnassus (*On Literary Composition*, chs. 14–16, 23; tr. Roberts), who discusses aspects of word choice, esp. s., incl. such phenomena as sigmatism and imitative words. Many theories of poetic s. in antiquity attempt some kind of calculus of euphony, some mechanism whereby s. combinations are ranked on a scale. In Cl. rhet., figures were traditionally divided into the schemes and tropes; the former were said to be arrangements or figures of s., the latter of sense. So alliteration, a scheme, is a s.-pattern, while metaphor, a trope, is a relation of idea or thought. This dichotomy, however, which itself varied greatly over time, is too simple: schemes also schematize meaning, and tropes rarely appear in poetry without additionally schematized s. Both Cicero and Quintilian (*Institutio oratoria* 9.3.75–80, 9.4) treat s. under the rubric of prose rhythm (q.v.). Expressive s. is as significant a topic for Dante (*De vulgari eloquentia*) as it is for Baudelaire.

In the 20th c., empirical studies of poetic s. patterning have appealed to some scholars, and in general it is undeniable that extensive inventories of accurate data on such s. phenomena as rhyme and alliteration simply do not exist at present (see RHYME; METER). But statistical data in isolation is of little use without interp. Empirical and statistical work—i.e. quantitative analysis via computer—yields only narrow results, and must be interpreted with care, for a great deal of the specific data thus generated is trivial—the background noise of the channel. And s. patterns themselves must always be correlated with meaning, a process which must always require the application of critical judgment. It would seem that, for most purposes, inventories of s. figuration treated in isolation from meaning are not very revealing. Certainly the most fruitful modern studies of rhyme, at least (Wimsatt, Jakobson), have seen that phenomenon as irrefrangibly sonal and semantic. Analyses attempting to integrate s. and meaning on several levels of sonal architecture have been few; only recently have some theorists (e.g. Lotman) begun to integrate s. patterning into a larger, unified field theory of poetic structure (see PROSODY).

Some empirical researchers have made the mistake of assuming that counting justifies itself, hence that empirical work is theory-free. Not so: no work at all is possible without theory, for counting presupposes deciding what is to be counted, and what is to be counted is thereby already reified: those decisions constitute theory. Data itself is never theory-free. Nor is it of use without consideration of reader response. Frequency counts and phoneme inventories can reveal which s. patterns exist, certainly, but not which ones are perceived, i.e. *salient*. Some s. patterns either go unnoticed or count for little if they are separated by too great a distance. Some "rhymes" in *Paradise Lost*, for example, are so far apart that most readers are not aware they exist. It must always remain to be shown that a statistically significant pattern is perceived or contributes to meaning. Here one would want to say that it is precisely training in the analysis of poetry which heightens readers' abilities to recognize and respond, more fully, to s. patterning in versified texts.

All analysis must be based on accurate diachronic linguistics, as verified by available evidence from historical phonology; the rhymes in dialect poetry (q.v.), for example. cannot be understood at all without linguistic study of that dialect. But linguistics alone cannot tell us all we need to know about poetic form, for even such seemingly obvious s. patterns as rhyme or alliteration vary in definition from one lang. to another and, within one lang., from one metrical system to another. What constitutes a particular form of poetic s. is conventional and changes from age to age and poetry to poetry.

Each lang. differs in the phonological resources it offers for aesthetic design. The Germanic langs. (incl. Eng.) are dense in consonant clusters and tend to forestressing, hence consonants have less weight there than the same ones would in the Romance langs., where stress is distributed more evenly and vowels more important. A full frequency analysis of the distributional patterns for a large number of langs. would be of value, though it must be remembered that artverse only selects from a narrow register of the lexicon in any lang. Further, within any single poem, a given pattern only has its effect against the ground provided by the local environment of one line and its neighbors, where much is possible. In general, poetic s. effects must be felt, and assessed, against the whole phonology of a lang., the principles of the verse system, the particular verseform presently in play, and the semantic structure of the specific and adjoining lines. That is, the nature and effect of any given structure are constrained in poetry not by fewer systems of conventions but by more.

IX. FULLNESS. Poetry teaches us that verbal experience is fundamentally double. On the most direct level, there is meaning, but underneath there is s. In ordinary speech, we listen only for the meaning: the s. of words is wholly transparent—we listen straight through it. Most of the time, that is, we live, in languaging, on the level of meaning. The ss. of words are ignored by the meaning-making mind when processing s. as lang. Poetic lang. of course bears meanings also. But in poetry, s. has a life of its own, purely on the level of s., structuring meanings, shading and nuancing meanings, and organizing the temporal experience of reading via patterned repetition. These are not epiphenomena, but full components of cognition; lang. without them is not merely less but *other*.

Not to attend to s. in poetry is therefore not to understand poetry at all. But it is important at the same time that we not conceive the concept of "s." too narrowly, and certainly not merely within whatever framework the currently reigning version of linguistics happens to valorize. Note that Ger. distinguishes between *Klang*, the total sonal impression produced by a piece of lang., and *Laut* or *Tön*, each specific s.: the former would approximate Eng. "intonational pattern," i.e. the amalgam of accent, pitch, speed, timbre, and rhythm—s. taken at the full. Mallarmé remarks in "Crise de vers" that "le vers qui de plusieurs vocables refait un mot total, neuf, étranger à la langue et comme incantatoire, achève cet isolement de la parole: niant, d'un trait souverain, le hasard demeuré aux termes malgré artifice de leur retrempe alternée en le sens et la sonorité, et vous cause cette surprise de n'avoir oui jamais tel fragment ordinaire d'élocution, en même temps que la réminiscence de l'objet nommé baigne dans une neuve atmosphère." That clarified space may recall to us what T. S. Eliot once called the "auditory imagination," that fully sentient consciousness which responds to the ss. of poetry in the richest sense, finding them more fully articulate in their joint effect and interanimations, so that the saying is accomplished more fully.

When Wallace Stevens said, in his 1941 lecture on "The Noble Rider and the S. of Words," that "a poet's words are of things that do not exist without the words," he was saying that words are not secondary to our experience of the world, they are primary. The words in poetry are words not because they express meaning—they do that in prose—but because they are also s., because they take their life in s. It is as s. that they teach us what words are.

See also ALLITERATION; ANAGRAM; ASSONANCE; CACOPHONY; CHANT; CONSONANCE; COUNTERPOINT; CYNGHANEDD; DISSONANCE; DISTINCTIVE-FEATURE ANALYSIS; ECHO; EUPHONY; INCANTATION; MELOPOEIA, PHANOPOEIA, LOGOPOEIA; MUSIC AND POETRY; ONOMATOPOEIA; PHONES-THEME; PROSODY; REPETITION; RHYME; STANZA; STRUCTURE; SYNAESTHESIA; TEXTURE; TIMBRE; VERSE AND PROSE.

BIBLIOGRAPHIES: No full comparative bibl. exists. Thieme 372—full bibl. for Fr. to 1916; Brogan, esp. pp. 53–108—comparative survey of studies to 1981, supp. in *Verseform* (1989).

STUDIES: I. A. Richards, *Practical Crit.* (1929); C. P. Smith, *Pattern and Variation in Poetry* (1932); Patterson; S. Bonneau, *L'Univers poétique d'Alexandre Blok* (1946); A. Spire, *Plaisir poétique et plaisir musculaire* (1949); D. T. Mace, "The Doctrine of S. and Sense in Augustan Poetic Theory," *RES* 2 (1951); D. I. Masson, "Patterns of Vowel and Consonant in a Rilkean Sonnet," *MLR* 46 (1951), "Vowel and Consonant Patterns in Poetry," *JAAC* 12 (1953), "Word and S. in Yeats's 'Byzantium,'" *ELH* 20 (1953), "Free Phonetic Patterns in Shakespeare's Sonnets," *Neophil* 38 (1954), "Wilfred Owen's Free Phonetic Patterns," *JAAC* 13 (1955), "Thematic Analysis of S. in Poetry," *PLPLS-LHS* 9, pt. 4 (1960), "S. Repetition Terms," *Poetics—Poetyka—Poetika*, ed. D. Davie et al. (1961), "Poetic S.-Patterning Reconsidered," *PLPLS-LHS* 16 (1976)—this last a survey of 8 national lits.; A. Oras, "Surrey's Technique of Phonetic Echoes," *JEGP* 50 (1951), "Echoing Verse Endings in *Paradise Lost*," *So. Atlantic Studies* S. E. Leavitt (1953), "Intensified Rhyme Links in *The Faerie Queene*," *JEGP* 54 (1955); S. S. Prawer, *Ger. Lyric Poetry* (1952); J. J. Lynch, "The Tonality of Lyric Poetry," *Word* 9 (1953); A. Stein, "Structures of S. in Milton's Verse," *KR* 15 (1953); H. Kökeritz, *Shakespeare's Pronunciation* (1953); H. W. Belmore, *Rilke's Craftsmanship* (1954); F. Scarfe, *The Art of Paul Valéry* (1954); W. K. Wimsatt, Jr., "One Relation of Rhyme to Reason," *The Verbal Icon* (1954); Wellek and Warren, ch. 13; J. Hollander, "The Music of Poetry," *JAAC* 15 (1956), *The Figure of Echo* (1981); Frye; K. Burke, "On Musicality in Verse," *Philosophy of Literary Form* (1957); S. Chatman, "Linguistics, Poetics, and Interp.," *QJS* 43 (1957); *S. and Poetry*, ed. N. Frye (1957), esp. A. Oras, "Spenser and Milton: Some Parallels and Contrasts in the Handling of S."; D. Hymes, "Phonological Aspects of Style," in Sebeok; N. I. Herescu, *La Poésie latine: Étude des structures phoniques* (1960); P. Delbouille, *Poésie et sonorités*, 2 v. (1961, 1984); I. Fónagy, "Communication in Poetry," *Word* 17 (1961), *Die Metaphern in der Phonetik* (1963), "The Functions of Vocal Style," *Literary Style: A Symposium*, ed. S. Chatman (1971), *La vive voix: Essais de psychophonétique* (1983); L. P. Wilkinson, *Golden Lat. Artistry* (1963); D. Bolinger, *Forms of Eng.* (1965)—morphosemantic effects; J. Levý, "The Meanings of Form and the Forms of Meaning," *Poetics—Poetyka—Poetika*, ed. R. Jakobson et al. (1966); W. B. Stanford, *The S. of Gr.* (1967); A. M. Liberman et al., "Perception of the Speech Code," *Psych Rev.* 74 (1967); P. Schaeffer, *Traité des objets musicaux* (1968); E. J. Dobson, *Eng. Pronunciation, 1500–1700*, 2d ed., 2 v. (1968); B. Hrushovski, [Do Sounds Have Meaning? The Problem of Expressiveness of Sound-Patterns in Poetry], *Ha-Sifrut* 1 (1968), "The Meaning of S. Patterns in Poetry," *PoT* 2 (1980); A. A. Hill, "A Phonological Description of Poetic Ornaments," *Lang&S* 2 (1969); R. W. Bailey, "Statistics and the Ss. of Poetry," *Poetics* 1 (1971); N. Geschwind, "Lang. and the Brain," *Scientific Am.* 226 (1972); P. Ostwald, *The Semiotics of Human S.* (1973); E. D. Polivanov, "The General Phonetic Principle of Any Poetic Technique," *Sel. Works*, ed. A. A. Leontev (1974); D. Laferrière, "Automorphic Structures in the Poem's Grammatical Space," *Semiotica* 10 (1974); F. W. Leakey, *S. and Sense in Fr. Poetry* (1975); J. Jaynes, *The Origin of Consciousness in the Breakdown of the Bicameral Mind* (1976); C. L. van den Berghe, *La Phonostylistique du français* (1976); Derrida; J. Lotman, *The Structure of the Artistic Text* (tr. 1977), esp. 106 ff., 178 ff.; M. Kaimio, *Characterization of S. in Early Gr. Lit.* (1977); Y. Malkiel, "From Phonosymbolism to Morphosymbolism," *Fourth LACUS Forum,* ed. M. Paradis (1978); R. Jakobson and L. Waugh, "The Spell of Speech Ss.," *The S. Shape of Lang.* (1979), rpt. in Jakobson v. 8; V. Erlich, *Rus. Formalism: History–Doctrine,* 3d ed. (1981); R. P. Newton, *Vowel Undersong* (1981); L. O. Bishop, *In Search of Style* (1982); R. Lewis, *On Reading Fr. Verse* (1982), esp. chs. 4, 7; R. Chapman, *The Treatment of Ss. in Lang. and Lit.* (1984); J. C. Ransom, "Positive and Near-Positive Aesthetics," in Ransom; Hollander, esp. chs. 1, 4; B. Scherr, "Instrumentation," in Terras; C. Scott, *The Riches of Rhyme* (1988); G. Chesters, *Baudelaire and the Poetics of Craft* (1988); G. Stewart, *Reading Voices* (1990); R. Tsur, *What Makes S. Patterns Expressive?* (1992). T.V.F.B.

SOUND COLOR. See TIMBRE.

SOUND EFFECTS IN POETRY. From the emergence of the vernaculars as vehicles of poetry in the West, poets have looked upon rhyme (q.v.) as the chief form of s. patterning in verse. They developed rhyme, however, not apart from but in close conjunction with the various other forms of s. patterning, perceiving that the effects to be obtained were almost endlessly variable and subtle. In what follows we will look first at certain s. effects most conspicuous in rhyme, then at other effects in s. patterning conceived more broadly.

In the first place, rhyme links words otherwise than as syntax connects them, producing associations, correlations, equations we must take note of without losing our sense of what is being said syntactically. When the linkages are used primarily to delineate, or confirm, a metrical pattern, the occurrence of the linked words at spaced intervals, i.e. their identification with an abstract, quasi-mathematical pattern, will normally minimize the degree to which the reader will seek illumination of meaning in the connections between one word and another made through s. alone. Nonmetrical patterns of s. are, nonetheless, often associated with metrical patterns, and are most audible in verse and therefore most appreciable when they occur in stressed syllables, the occurrences of which are in some manner ordered. S. patterning and metrical patterning are thus (in metered verse) seldom independent of one another. Because the words connected by s. patterning do have meaning, however, the figuration may be used in any circumstances to enhance meaning.

Expectation and Surprise. When Pope says, in the *Epistle to Bathurst* (97), "But thousands die without or this or that," we know the next line will be rhymed—crisply, doubtless, but hardly portentously, for what depths of meaning can be found in "that"? But Pope knows how to satisfy expectation and deflect it, wonderfully, at the same time: "Die, and endow"—good, good—"a College,"—

oh, very good—"or a Cat." And the whole swiftly built, elegant structure collapses in our own laughter, upon our own heads. The rhyme is there, and it is flawless. But focus has shifted to the last two nouns—equated through alliteration, their weights of meaning so unequal that the right-hand scale-pan flies up and the scale tips over. Well, but anonymous "thousands" have minds, have purposes no steadier, no better balanced. And we? Only Pope says it more swiftly, cleanly, unforgettably.

When Patience reminds the blind Milton, in lines 9–12 of Sonnet 19, that

> . . . God doth not need
> Either man's work or his own gifts, who
> best
> Bear his mild yoak, they serve him
> best, his State
> Is Kingly,

three simple words are posed at line-ends, set into the mosaic of the verse, which we (knowing the It. sonnet, the sestet) expect will be rhymed: probably in the same order, *abc*, but perhaps *cba* or *bac*. And the verse continues, satisfyingly but unremarkably,

> Thousands at his bidding speed
> And post o're Land and Ocean without
> rest,

leaving one full line to complete the poem, a line of which we know, now, that it will rhyme with "State." How could we imagine that the poem is to be exploded in our minds through that *c* rhyme?:

> They also serve who only *st*and and
> w*aite.*

So for man the elements of God's *State* are divided between two humble words, the first also descended from Lat. *stare,* "stand," but the connection is made and then apparently abandoned—to circle back and complete itself in the simple rhyme word *waite,* the meaning of the whole phrase acceptant, submissive even, emptied of that storm of thought that had roiled through the sonnet's first lines. In our divided way, however, we have in those last words achieved a totally unlooked-for right connection with God, a kind of unsentimentalized identification, even, with Him and with the order of His universe. The two rhymes preceding are merely sufficient, are there in the service of the form, where they should be. If all s. patterning were used to point up meaning, we perceive, the device would lose force, would become oppressive.

Emergent Patterning. Mention has been made of expectation; and it is clear that once we as readers of or listeners to verse detect in it what is evidently a continuing pattern of s. repetition, we come to expect repetition of a certain kind at a certain place or places in the line, and a part of our response is to the fulfillment of that expectation. It is otherwise with what may be called emergent s. patterning. Look, for instance, at the opening lines of Edwin Muir's "The Rider Victory":

The rider Victory reins his horse
Midway across the empty bridge
As if head-tall he had met a wall.
Yet there was nothing there at all.

The reader notes that "horse" and "bridge" do not rhyme with one another, and may therefore be rhymed *ab* (or *xa*) with lines 3 and 4; the patterns of rhyme and line length in every stanzaic poem are in general "emergent" in the first stanza, expected thereafter. Nothing in the first two lines prepares us for the internal rhyme in the third line; still less are we likely to expect that the fourth line will end with a repetition of this already insistent, shocking *c* rhyme. In the Pope couplet, the occurrence of "that" at the end of an odd-numbered line makes us certain that the next line will end on -*at*, but in the Muir lines we recognize the rhyme only when we have it. "Wall" yanks us back to "tall," stops our forward movement as sharply as the movement of the horse is stopped. Again s. participates in the delivery of meaning. "All" is further disconcerting—though now we expect rhyme, and have learned to accommodate ourselves to surprise. Doubtless the completion of every s. pattern sends some part of our attention back to identify or acknowledge the word with which it began; this act is probably closer to consciousness, less submerged in our response to denotation, when the pattern identified was not expected.

Position and Pattern. But the nature and quality of our response to s. patterning is affected by many other considerations as well. One is the position of the sound(s) repeated—in the syllable or word, in the phrase or sentence, in the line. Alliteration (q.v.) of stressed syllables is immediately striking, but the syllables involved must always end with unlike ss.; by the time word meanings are established, the concord has dissolved. Simple assonance (q.v.) too is a unison we perceive in syllables changing away from it, and destined to end in divergent ss. that are in all probability not patterned. Assonant vowels may of course rhyme if no consonants follow: "low," "grow." Ordinarily, however, rhyme is the repetition of the two final elements of the syllable: "loan," "grown." Because, in rhyme, the stressed vowel and everything following it in the word ("owning," "groaning")—sometimes in the phrase ("own it," "thrown it")—are repeated, rhyme is a device unusually well suited to marking the *ends* of metrical and syntactical units; it is strongest when it ends both together. Power must not, of course, be squandered: Milton suspends the marked noun in "his State / Is Kingly" both to keep us thinking about it and to give the final line of the sonnet its greatest possible effect, from all sources.

All s. patterning claims our attention most when the elements repeated are relatively close together. Full rhyme can probably be heard at a greater distance than alliteration or assonance, and the distance can be extended if the ss. that make up the rhyme are unusual, or are themselves repeated (internally or at line end, and perhaps at regularly spaced intervals) along the way, but there are no rules here. It is an unanswered question whether s. patterning of which we are not specifically aware may have a subliminal effect, may add somehow to the harmony of verse even if its presence can be demonstrated but still not—on another reading—heard.

Just as the ss. that make up a word may be separated and repeated in separation, so ss. which first occur apart from one another may be combined into words—and the pattern left complete, or unraveled again: "All *p*a*th* of *M*a*n* or *B*ea*st* that *past* that way" (*PL* 4.177), "*Hesperus* that *led* / The *starrie Host*, r*ode* brighte*st*" (*PL* 4.605–6). In these lines the effect is generally musical, it would seem; the meaning is enhanced, if at all, complexly, or obscurely. In neither example does the completion of the s. pattern coincide with phrase- or line- or sentence-end, so that one is not permitted to dwell for long on the figuration. The intermixture of pattern with pattern, as in the second example, complicates and enriches our response, but we do not, in all probability, find it arresting. The unexpected internal rhyme in line 3 of "The Rider Victory" is the more startling because it occurs in lines otherwise empty of s. patterning.

Meaning. When Gerard Manley Hopkins writes, in "The Leaden Echo and the Golden Echo" (1–2),

How to keep—is there ány any, is there
   none such,
  nowhere known some, bow or
  brooch or braid or
  brace, láce, latch or catch or key to
  keep
Back beauty, keep it, beauty, beauty,
  beauty, . . .
  from vanishing away?

the extraordinary brocading of the lines with s. patterns does not, then, startle, though we are intensely aware of it. Here, however, s. repetition is very directly a part of meaning. The words that name the possible-impossible holds on beauty grasp at and cling to one another, lose one hold to clutch at another, unevenly, uselessly, for beauty's evasion of them, its vanishing, is foretold in the pouring out of increasingly unchecked s. in the second line. The lines, we note, are not of a measured length, and have no end rhyme; we may imagine that an elaborate patterning of s. line-internally would weaken the effect of end rhyme, and vice versa. Again, however, there are no rules. Shelley's "Ozymandias" is a superb example of the two kinds of s. patterning—one defining and reinforcing meter, the other irregularly yet persistently emergent—being used together, to dazzling effect. It is an astonishing poem, its form probably far less regular, or less conventionally regular, than most readers suppose.

Finally, we should perhaps remind ourselves that ss. are themselves physical objects and hence have recognizable qualities—such terms as "liquid" and "plosive" affirm this—and that the patterning of one kind of s. will have a different effect from the patterning of another. The point can be taken too far; ss. do not in themselves have meaning, nor even, perhaps, a latent tendency to be used to communicate certain classes of meaning: compare "ax" and "flax," "war" and "warm," "hell" and "heal," "struggle" and "strawberry." Nonetheless the effectiveness of Pope's rhyme above depends in part on the fact that /æ/ is a short front vowel, /t/ a stop. Some ss. are difficult to articulate, others less so; some "take time" to say. In Arnold's lines "on the French coast the light / Gleams and is gone" ("Dover Beach" 3–4), the s. of "Gleams"—the length of the vowel, the continuant nature of the consonants following—is a carefully designed part of the meaning, a part of the reader's actual experience of the poem.

It is meaning, of course, for which we read—meaning in its fullest sense, beyond mere denotation, though meaning begins with the obvious elements of denotation. And while the syntactic ties that relate concept to concept do not result in a communication of meaning that is ever simply or necessarily straightforward, we tend to know where we are in sentences. In general, the movement of thought is forward, toward completions, partial or culminative, which we (all but) require.

Sound patterning complicates this movement: slows it, often; changes sentence rhythms, prose emphases; makes us dwell on words we should otherwise, perhaps, attend to less; multiplies our awarenesses, our kinds of awareness. Structures of s. the existence and force of which we register in the words that complete them coexist with syntactic structures, and all these relate to one another, affect one another, orchestrate the flow of thought. As readers of verse we must learn how to listen, how to receive fully, how to move susceptive through the landscapes of thought and feeling and on the ways the great poets have laid down for us. Because art is not science, and because we are many, not one, we will not all apprehend precisely in the same way. But art does involve the use of various kinds of artifice to which we can train ourselves to respond in accurate and appropriate ways; and the more we do this, the more meanings we shall find to share. See also PROSODY; REPETITION; RHYME; VERSIFICATION.   E.R.W.

SOUND POETRY is the performance intermedium in which verbal and sound art are not just mixed, as in a song, but are actually fused. While any poetic text, when read aloud, employs sound elements to reinforce lexical sense, when sound for its own sake becomes the principal expressive medium, sometimes even at the expense of lexical sense, then it becomes meaningful to describe a work as s. p.

Many traditional forms of oral poetry (q.v.) have used incantations (q.v.), sometimes even nonsense syllables, which function similarly to s. p., as in the "heigh nonnie no" refrains of many Eng. folksongs, though more commonly they function onomatopoetically, as in the healing chants of some Am. Indian tribes. This is also true of early poetic passages such as the famous "brekk kekk kekk kekk koax koax" chorus in Aristophanes' *The Frogs* (4th c. B.C.). The artistic potential for s. p. was recognized in antiquity; the early Lat. poet Quintus Ennius (239–169 B.C.) wrote the earliest known passage, a tautogram: "O Tite tute, Tati tibi tanta tyranne tulisti." This sort of alliteration run wild reaches its zenith (or nadir) with the 9th-c. Benedictine, Hugobald, who wrote a poem of 146 hexameters for Charles the Bald praising baldness, the *Ecloga de Calvis*, every word of which begins with a C.

The few 19th-c. pieces of s. p. are almost always light verse (q.v.; see also NONSENSE VERSE), such as Robert Southey's "The Cataract of Lodore." Early in the 20th c., futurists such as F. T. Marinetti and F. Cangiullo (see FUTURISM), dada poets such as Raoul Hausmann (see DADA), Rus. constructivists such as V. Xlebnikov (see CONSTRUCTIVISM), and, above all, the independent Ger. artist K. Schwitters (1887–1948) in works such as the *Ursonata* (1925–27) made s. p. a medium for major works.

While phonograph records were made of some early modern s. p. experiments, the expansion of the field came only with the advent of wire and tape recorders in the years following World War II. Until then almost all s. p. had distinguished performances from text, the text serving the function of a musical score for the performer to follow. Works employing this distinction (and many are still being composed) are now known as "text-sound" works (see Kostelanetz).

But in the 1950s a second variety of s. p. became possible, one in which recorded sound, primarily but not exclusively verbal, is manipulated. The final result is not a performable, written notation or text, but a recording, either intended to be played alone or with another performance occurring over it. Such pieces are now known as "audio poems" (Chopin's term). In the 1950s and 1960s many new s. poets emerged, such as H. Chopin (b. 1922), B. Heidsieck (b. 1928) and F. Dufrêne (1930–85) in France, B. Cobbing (b. 1920) in England, F. Mon (b. 1926) in West Germany, G. Rühm (b. 1930) in Austria, and A. Lora-Totino (b. 1928) in Italy, to name only a few. Also, many concrete poets (see CONCRETE POETRY), musical composers, and visual artists have done important work in s. p., and younger poets continue to be attracted to the genre: a complete global listing of serious s. poets would run to hundreds of names. Since the late 1960s, major festivals of s. p. have developed the audience for it in a dozen countries.

Mention should also be made of the interaction of s. p. with the *hörspiel*, which was originally the ordinary Ger. word for "radio play." However, in several European countries, particularly West Germany, and esp. at Westdeutscher Rundfunk in Cologne, several works are commissioned and broadcast each year which are *neues Hörspiel*—sustained audio-acoustical poems written not just by Germans but by artists of other nationalities as well, such as the Am. composer John Cage (b. 1912), whose four *hörspielen* are among several dozen by Americans which have been broadcast and recorded, but for which there is as yet no available public medium in the USA. See also ABSTRACT POEM; LANGUAGE POETRY; PURE POETRY; SOUND.

STUDIES: E. Jolas, "From 'Jabberwocky' to 'Letterism,'" *Transition* 48 (1948); A. Liede, *Dichtung als Spiel*, 2 v. (1963); "Internat. Electronic Music Catalog," *Electronic Music Rev.* 2–3 (1967)—lists all known audio poems to 1967; *Neues Hörspiel*, ed. K. Schöning (1969); K. Schwitters, *Das literarische Werk*, ed. F. Lach, 6 v. (1973–82); *S. P.: A Catalog*, ed. S. McCaffery and B. Nichol (1978); *Text-Sound Texts* (1980), and Spec. Issue on s. p., *Precisely* 10 (1981), both ed. R. Kostelanetz; H. Chopin, *Poésie Sonore Internationale* (1981)—book with accompanying cassette (new ed. will have expanded bibl. and discography); J. Cage, *Roaratorio: ein irischer Circus über* Finnegans Wake (1982)—book and cassette; J. Rothenberg, *Technicians of the Sacred*, 2d ed. (1985); D. Higgins, *Pattern Poetry* (1987)—sect. on s. p. before 1900; R. Döhl, *Das Neue Hörspiel* (1988). Periodicals devoted primarily to s. p. were *Ou*, ed. H. Chopin (1963–68), and *Stereo Headphones*, ed. N. Zurbrugg (1972–)—most issues incl. records.

DISCOGRAPHY: L. Greenham, *Internationale Sprachexperimente der 50/60er Jahre* (1970)—shows how concrete poetry converges with s. p.; *Futura: Poesia Sonora*, ed. A. Lora-Totino, Cramps 5206–301 to 307 (1978)—six-record internat. anthol. with book incl. notations and other information; *Text Sound Compositions*, RELP 1049, 1054, 1072–74, 1102–03 (1968–70)—seven records of the Stockholm festivals of s. p. There are also cassette series of s. p., notably the "New Wilderness Audiographics" series (1975–). D.H.

SOUND SYMBOLISM. See ICONICITY; ONOMATO-POEIA; PHONESTHEME; SOUND.

SOUTH AFRICAN POETRY.

I. IN AFRIKAANS. With the exception of a few sporadic examples in the late 18th and first half of the 19th c., the first Afrikaans poetry in South Africa dates from the last quarter of the 19th c., when the first real attempts were made to raise Afrikaans—which up to that time had been the lang. of conversation at the Cape of Good Hope for more than a century, developing out of 17th-c. Dutch—to the level of a written lang. The themes of this early Afrikaans poetry were limited by the close bonds with the South Af. fatherland in general and the Afrikaner in particular and dealt with the life of ordinary Afrikaans burghers and their folklore. The poets aimed at encouraging the people to fight for their rights and at inspiring, teaching, and entertaining them. The poems are very often oratorical and programmatic in nature and make use of a labored style. In effect, the literary products of this period are based principally on a subculture, given the writers' isolation from foreign influence, although there are imitations of Scottish examples (Burns) and early 19th-c. Dutch poetry (q.v.).

After the Anglo-Boer War (1899–1902), during which time very little attention was paid to lit., a number of younger writers saw it as their task to develop Afrikaans as an instrument through which the deepest emotions of the individual and of the people could be expressed. The Anglo-Boer War, South Af. landscape, and religious experience—all exemplified in the work of Jan F. E. Celliers (1865–1940), Totius (pseudonym of J. D. du Toit, 1877–1953), and C. Louis Leipoldt (1880–1947)—were important stimuli to poetry immediately after 1900. Apart from strictly metrical poetry there were experiments with free verse, and apart from poems written in stanzas and the sonnet, the dramatic monologue was practiced. The poets of this generation were influenced by Dutch, Ger., Eng., and Fr. models, but the influence is neither significant nor conclusive and was very seldom contemporary.

The poets of the third generation, with Toon van den Heever (1894–1956) as the most important, do not, on the whole, achieve the standard of the previous generation, although there is greater individualism present in their writings, and love and eroticism are introduced as themes. Two older poets who produced their best work at this time are Eugène N. Marais (1871–1936) and A. G. Visser (1878–1929).

Around 1930 a new generation of poets, who display a far greater professionalism than their predecessors, began to publish. The new artists—of whom N. P. van Wyk Louw (1906–70), Uys Krige (1910–87), W. E. G. Louw (1913–80), and Elisabeth Eybers (b. 1915) are the most important—perceive poetry as a conscious task and, unlike their predecessors, claim the right to explore all areas of human life. Initially their poetry was focused on the inner life and was self-analytic and confessional, but the danger of an exaggerated withdrawal from the outside world was counteracted by devel. toward a more oblique poetry, although Krige's work shows a greater receptiveness to external stimuli from the beginning. This movement toward objectification found its strongest expression in Van Wyk Louw, who, in addition to a new type of psychological ballad and dramatic monologue, wrote the modern epic *Raka* (1941), which explores the tension between two contrasting characters. Later he produced one of the most important volumes of Afrikaans poetry, *Tristia* (1962). In Eybers' work, the world of the woman and the bond between her and her family is explored. Her later poetry, written in the Netherlands, is stripped of every external embellishment and has a new vital quality. In contrast to the poets who wrote after the Anglo-Boer War, the "Dertigers" (the Afrikaans poets of the Thirties) are more receptive to Dutch, Ger., and Eng. poetry.

In the Forties, a fifth generation of poets, initially influenced strongly by the "Dertigers," made their debut. From the beginning, however, the war, the city, and a new social consciousness were more strongly present in their poetry, qualities which gave rise to a harsher and sharper-edged verse. Of these poets, the work of Ernst van Heerden (b. 1916) catches the reader's attention as the struggle of a sensitive and defenseless person against the modern world, whereas G. A. Watermeyer (1917–72) practiced a new type of melodious verse; and compassion for the Jew and the Colored appears in the works of Olga Kirsch (b. 1924) and S. V. Petersen (b. 1914). The most important poet of this generation is D. J. Opperman (1914–85), who explores the world with a virtually mystic urge to identify with all earthly things. His poetry has a concentrated verbal economy which finds expression in the compact metaphor and the short-circuited image. He writes a cryptic type of poem with successive layers of meaning; he uses the sonnet, quatrain, cycle, soliloquy, and epic (*Joernaal van Jorik*, 1949) with great expertise. He achieves an intricate unity in volumes such as *Blom en baaierd* (Flower and Void, 1956) and *Komas uit 'n bamboesstok* (Comas from a Bamboo Stick, 1979).

Since the mid 1950s, several important poets have made their appearance. Peter Blum (b. 1925) initiated this renewal with poetry in which rhythmical abandon, startling imagery, and an anti-sentimental, demasking tone catch the reader's attention. Adam Small (b. 1936) writes strongly satirical, derisive, and sometimes bitter political poetry. In her best work, Ingrid Jonker (1933–65) prefers a free verse similar to that of Éluard and the Dutch experimentalists of the Fifties. The most important new talent is that of Breyten Breytenbach (b. 1939), who shows his mastery of Afrikaans in his originality and in his amazing power to convey images through a daring exploitation of the face value of words. After Breytenbach, the most important poet is Wilma

Stockenström (b. 1933), with her meaningful exploration of the dry, harsh Af. landscape, written in tersely figurative and barbed lang. A reaction to the too-amorphous free verse of the Sixties also appears in a number of poets who received their grounding in the art of poetry from Opperman (e.g. Antjie Krog, Lina Spies, Fanie Olivier, Marlene van Niekerk) or who built on his trad. through wordplay and linguistic legerdemain (J. C. Steyn, T. T. Cloete), whereas Sheila Cussons, whose poetry has a mystical element, is the most important exponent of Roman Catholicism in Afrikaans.

ANTHOLOGIES: *Afrikaans Poems with Eng. Trs.*, ed. A. P. Grové and C. J. D. Harvey (1962); *Penguin Book of South Af. Verse*, ed. J. Cope and U. Krige (1968), ed. S. Gray (1989); *Groot verseboek*, ed. D. J. Opperman, 9th ed. (1983).

HISTORY AND CRITICISM: R. Antonissen, *Die Afrikaanse letterkunde van aanvang tot hede*, 3d ed. (1965); R. Antonissen et al., "Afrikaans Lit.," *Standard Encyc. of Southern Africa*, v. 1 (1970); G. Dekker, *Afrikaanse literatuurgeskiedenis*, 12th ed. (1972); J. C. Kannemeyer, *Geskiedenis van die Afrikaanse literatuur*, 2 v. (1978–83), *Die Afrikaanse literatuur, 1652–1987* (1988); *Perspektief en profiel*, ed. P. J. Nienaber, 5th ed. (1982).   J.C.K.

II. IN ENGLISH. South Africa first appears in Eng. poetry in the work of Donne, Milton, and Dryden, in the wake of the Port. Luis de Camões, who mentions the Cape of Good Hope as a passage to be rounded on the sailing route to the East. Anonymous British visitors there, wintering from service in India, brought occasional poetasting to its shores, which in 1820 became substantially colonized by Eng. speakers. The first South Af. Eng. poet as such, Thomas Pringle (1789–1834), emigrated from Scotland to the Eastern Frontier and adapted Scottish border ballads and the Wordsworthian reverie for lyrics such as "Afar in the Desert," which still opens many anthologies today. Pringle also established *The South Af. Literary Journal* in 1824.

The semi-permanent warfare between Dutch speakers, indigenous blacks, and the British in 19th-c. South Africa gave rise to an alternate popular trad. of anti-emancipationist verse in the person of Andrew Geddes Bain (1797–1863), who in the Victorian era used his polyglot resources for humorous purposes. His successor, Albert Brodrick (1830–1908), wrote of the diamond fields and gold fields and of the early process of industrialization.

The Anglo-Boer War of 1899–1902, which became a media event (incl. the first newsreels), was also the first round of a poet's battleground that extended into World War I. Rudyard Kipling (1865–1936) on the jingo side advocated Imperial progress, while South Af.-born poets like Beatrice Hastings (1879–1943) in *The New Age* defended home rule. Black poets, particularly in multilingual newspapers, began a trad. of protest against deprivation of human rights which persists to the present day.

After the Union of the Southern Af. states in 1910, Natal produced two major poets whose careers developed around the cultural magazine *Voorslag* in the 1920s: Roy Campbell (1901–57) and William Plomer (1903–73). Both eventually settled in Europe to pursue right-wing and left-wing politics, respectively. Campbell's early *The Flaming Terrapin* (1924) combined imagist and symbolist influences to assert a futuristic Af. life-force, while Plomer's successive volumes from 1927 maintained a democratic, satirical view of the segregated south.

After World War II many returning soldier-poets, such as Anthony Delius (b. 1916) and Guy Butler (b. 1918), asserted a "stranger to Europe" view of their local culture with a white Af. sense of belonging in the subcontinent. This in turn produced the journals, societies, and academic discipline which now make South Af. Eng. poetry an independent channel of the British mainstream.

With the accession to power of the Afrikaner apartheid government in 1948, Eng. as a cultural medium moved into an oppositional role which has produced a lit. of resistance written by blacks and whites alike. The banning or forcing into exile of many poets in the 1960s, such as Dennis Brutus (b. 1924) and Mazisi Kunene (b. 1930), further fragmented the poetry into an international diaspora whose links to the internal scene are increasingly tenuous. But in 1971, with the publication of *Sounds of a Cowhide Drum* by Mbuyiseni Mtshali (b. 1940), a period of intense internal publication commenced, notably in the work of Sipho Sepamla (b. 1932) and Mongane Serote (b. 1944), sometimes known (after the June 1976 uprising) as "Soweto poets."

During the 1980s, South Af. Eng. poetry has remained a central literary activity in journals as diverse as *Contrast* and *Staffrider*, incl. many non-native Eng. lang. poets. More general and specialist anthologies have appeared in this decade than in all previous South Af. history combined, and the secondary lit. too is now sophisticated.

The leading poet of the present, Douglas Livingstone (b. 1932), who published his first slim volume (*Sjambok*) in 1964, produced his *Selected Poems* in 1984. With its metaphysical style, his work displayed an openness to British and Am. poetic developments while being regional in its documentary range and subject matter. Other poets with substantial oeuvres incl. Lionel Abrahams (b. 1928), Stephen Gray (b. 1941), Jeni Couzyn (b. 1942), and Christopher Hope (b. 1944). Jeremy Cronin (b. 1949), following the less linguistically purist direction of a Bain, has brought the freedom songs of a romantic like Pringle into a new synthesis.

At one end of the spectrum, poetry serves as a protesting and educational instrument for black liberation, while at the other, Eng. is seen as a continuous medium of aesthetic conciliation and negotiation among the many other lang. experiences of Southern Africa.

ANTHOLOGIES: *Centenary Book of South Af. Verse*, ed. F. C. Slater, 2d ed. (1945); *A Book of South Af. Verse*, ed. G. Butler (1959); *Penguin Book of South Af. Verse*, ed. J. Cope and U. Krige (1968); *Return of the Amasi Bird: Black South Af. P. (1891–1981)*, ed. T. Couzens and E. Patel (1982); *Mod. South Af. P.* (1984), *Penguin Book of Southern Af. Verse* (1988), both ed. S. Gray; *Paperbook of South Af. Eng. P.*, ed. M. Chapman (1986).

HISTORY AND CRITICISM: G. M. Miller and H. Sergeant, *A Critical Survey of South Af. P. in Eng.* (1957); M. van Wyk Smith, *Drummer Hodge: The Poetry of the Anglo-Boer War* (1978); M. Chapman, *South Af. Eng. P.: A Mod. Perspective* (1984); *Companion to South Af. Eng. Lit.*, ed. D. Adey et al. (1986); M. Van Wyk Smith, *Grounds of Contest: A Survey of South Af. Eng. Lit.* (1989). S.G.

III. INDIGENOUS. Poetry in the indigenous Af. langs. of southern Africa is conveniently classified into an *oral* and a *written* (i.e. modern) component.

A. *Praise poetry* is an acclaimed mode of expression in the oral trad. In the Xhosa and Zulu languages (Republic of South Africa) such poetry is known as *izibongo*, in Southern Sotho (Lesotho and Republic of South Africa) as *dithoko*, in Setswana (Botswana and Republic of South Africa) as *maboko*, and in Northern Sotho (Republic of South Africa) as *direto*. In the langs. of the northern parts, however, such as Shona (Zimbabwe), and Tsonga and Venda (Republic of South Africa), heroic praise poetry does not exist as extensively. It is a poetry of celebration of kings, national leaders, and war heroes. Basically eulogistic, the poems are broadly comparable to the panegyric (q.v.) in other trads., though with more laudatory than narrative objectives. The poems are composed on the spur of the moment by the heroes themselves or recited by personal or national bards. The occasion of recitation varies from just after personal feats and victorious battles to national gatherings of various kinds.

Also in existence are *clan praises*. These occur fairly extensively, though not exclusively, in the langs. of the northern parts of the region. In Shona they are known as *nhétémbo dzorúdzi*, in Venda as *zwikhodo*, and in Tsonga as *swiphato*. In Xhosa they are called *isiduko*, in Zulu *izithakazelo*, and in Southern Sotho *diboko*. These are praises of specific clans or their branches, but may also incl. praises of other subjects such as clan initiates, animals, Af. beer, and divining bones.

Another oral type was developed after the discovery of minerals, when thousands of Af. laborers went to the South Africa mines. In Southern Sotho this is called *difela tsa ditsamayanaha* (songs of the "country travelers"), and in Xhosa *izibongo zasezimayini* (mine praises). A mixtures of nostalgia, aggression, and satire, this type relates the experiences of the novice migrant worker finding himself in foreign circumstances.

B. *Modern poetry* shows various generic and technical features of the oral trad. along with other influences of the same kind from foreign, mainly Eng., lit. Although these genres have been developing since the early 20th c., most are still transitional. Experimentation with imported devices such as end rhyme was less successful than the adaptation of devices carried over from the oral trad. such as repetition, parallelism (qq.v.), enumeration, and a wide register of imagery. In later years a kind of free verse developed, the potential and direction of which are still being explored. The output of modern poetry in most lits. is impressive, with the literary poets venturing on a variety of types, such as modern praises, shorter epics, ballads, elegies, sonnets, and satires. In Xhosa these poets incl. Mqhayi, Jolobe, Burns-Ncamashe, Yali-Manisi, and Qangule (who also writes verse drama); in Southern Sotho, Ntsane, the Khaketlas, Mokhomo, Mohapeloa, Lesoro, Maphalla, and Masiea (who also writes verse drama); in Zulu, Vilakazi, the Ntuli brothers, Msimang, Khumalo, and Dlamini; in Northern Sotho, Mamogobo, Matsepe, Matlala (who also writes verse drama), and Lentsoane; in Setswana, Seboni, the Kitchin brothers, Magoleng, and Shole Shole; in Tsonga, Masebenza, Nkondo, Marhanele, and Magaisa; and in Venda, Tsindane, Nemukovhani, and Sigwavhulimu. Mod. poetry in Swati (Swaziland and Republic of South Africa) started to emerge in the 1980s, with Mkhatshwa (verse drama), Zwane, and Luphoko the pioneers.

Most of the taxonomy sketched here also applies to the poetry of neighboring states such as Lesotho, Swaziland, Botswana, Zimbabwe, and even beyond.

Praise Poems of Tswana Chiefs, ed. I. Schapera (1965); *Izibongo: Zulu Praise Poems*, ed. T. Cope (1968); D. P. Kunene, *Heroic Poetry of the Basotho* (1971); *Lithoko: Sotho Praise-Poems*, ed. M. Damane and P. B. Sanders (1974); *Shona Praise Poetry*, ed. A. C. Hodza and G. Fortune (1979); P. S. Groenewald, "Die pryslied, prysgedig, prysdig, prysvers," *Studies in Bantoetale* 7 (1980); C. T. Msimang, "Imagery in Zulu Praise-Poetry," *Limi* 9 (1981); M. I. P. Mokitimi, *A Literary Analysis of Lifela tsa litsamaya-naha Poetry* (1982); A. S. Gérard, *Comp. Lit. and Af. Lits.* (1983); J. Opland, *Xhosa Oral Poetry: Aspects of a Black South Af. Trad.* (1983); C. F. Swanepoel, *Sotho Dithoko tsa Marena: Perspectives on Composition and Genre* (1983); J. M. Lenake, *The Poetry of K. E. Ntsane* (1984); D. B. Z. Ntuli, *The Poetry of B. W. Vilakazi* (1984); L. Vail and L. White, *Power and the Praise Poem* (1991); *Musho: Zulu Popular Praises*, ed. and tr. L. Gunner and M. Gwala (1992). C.F.S.

SOUTH AMERICAN POETRY. See BRAZILIAN POETRY; GAUCHO POETRY; SPANISH AMERICAN POETRY.

SPACE, POETIC. See GENEVA SCHOOL.

SPANISH AMERICAN POETRY. This entry covers poetries written in Sp., the lang. of those areas in the Western hemisphere which, after their independence from Spain in the first half of the 19th c., came to be known as nation-states—i.e. Argentina, Chile, Colombia, Cuba, Ecuador, Guatemala, Peru, Uruguay, and Venezuela. For a survey of the indigenous poetries of this area see AMERICAN INDIAN POETRY. The poetry of the Portuguese-speaking part of South America is treated s.v. PORTUGUESE POETRY and BRAZILIAN POETRY.

Sp. Am. p. shall be described here as a powerful stream in a constant process of changes, actions, and reactions, revealing, as well, essential constants that, considered from the proper perspective, suggest a fundamental unity. This stream had its origins in the cl. trad. of the Sp. and It. Ren. At first it was written by Spaniards for Spaniards. The Am. setting appeared only as an exotic world to captivate the fancy of Europeans. As some of the soldier-poets stayed in America, however, a strange sense of attachment and loyalty to the New World developed in their writings. Soon they began to express the saga of the Am. Conquest with a social consciousness which was not entirely European, but rather the result of humanism tested under the forces of war and death. These soldier-poets, of whom Alonso de Ercilla (1533–94) is the most eminent example, could not bring themselves to follow the fashion of It. epic poetry. They had no need to make up adventures in America. The poet had hardly anything to invent. He was fighting not only Indians but his own allies as well, and quite often he wrote his poems to secure royal favor, to promote the cause of a kind patron, or to thwart a personal enemy. Male protagonists were real, indeed, but heroines were a luxury with which he could dispense; romance was used sparingly and only to break the monotony of narrative. Touched by the self-sacrificing attitude of the Indian people and by the un-Christian exploitation of which they were victims, these poets glorified the Indians, presenting them to the European readers of the 16th and 17th cs. as pure and noble creatures driven to desperation by the evil ambitions of Western civilization. The Black Legend thus was born and the foundations laid for the idealization of primitivism (q.v.) to be expounded by the philosophers of the 18th c.

Sp. Am. epic poetry of the 16th and 17th cs. thus differed somewhat from the epic poetry of the European Ren. Indeed, one could say that a poet such as Ercilla actually developed an original form of epic which might be described as follows: his poem has no individual hero, since the poet sings the birth of a nation, exalting the people both of Spain and of America; Ercilla devotes a great deal of space to the narrative of his own adventures; and the intention is more political and social than purely artistic. From a literary viewpoint, Ercilla's epic blends the direct realism of primitive poetry and the artistic flair of the It. *Romanzi.* Ercilla's masterpiece, *La Araucana* (Araucana), is divided into three parts which appeared separately in 1569, 1578, and 1589. He had a school of imitators; among them, one is still remembered by critics: Pedro de Oña (1570–1643?), a Chilean, whose poem *Arauco domado* (Arauco Subdued) appeared in 1596 but who is more appreciated now for the lyric quality of *El Vasauro* (The Golden Vase).

There was another kind of soldier in the Sp. conquest of America, just as fearless and determined as the heavily armored Conquistador: the missionary. Between the cross and the sword the Am. Indian found his way into the literary world of Western civilization. Since the priest-poet could not deal directly with contemp. wars, he wrote sacred verse on subjects taken from the Middle Ages and ancient history.

The best examples of this type of epic produced in Sp. America are: *La Cristiada* (Cristíada) by Fray Diego de Hojeda (1570–1615), an Andalusian by birth who lived and died in Peru; and *La grandeza mexicana* (The Greatness of Mexico, 1604) by Bernardo de Balbuena (1561–1627), a contemporary of Góngora, who lived in Mexico. Balbuena praised the splendor of the Mexican vice-royalty in cl. tercets, thus providing the basis for Sp. Am. baroque poetry. Relegated to obscurity by the popular success of Ercilla, the priest-poets increasingly withdrew into the learned isolation of their monasteries to engage in rhetorical contests. They opened their hearts and minds to the intellectual pyrotechnics of the great Góngora, the Sp. master of euphuism, vying with each other in expressing deep concepts in a syntax laden with Gr. and Lat. complexities. Testimony to these contests is Carlos de Siguenza y Góngora's (1645–1700) *Triunfo parténico* (Athenian Triumph), and proof of Góngora's predominance among the Sp. Am. baroque poets is the *Apologético en favor de don Luis de Góngora* (Apology for Góngora, 1662) by the Peruvian Juan de Espinosa Medrano (1632–88). It is obvious that these and other poets of the period did have an inkling of what Góngora was attempting: they knew that in his rhetorical labyrinth he was creating a poetic lang. of his own and, with it, a world of fantasy that stood defiantly against the logic of cl. realism. But in general his disciples failed him.

One alone approached him in depth of thought and poetic power: Sor Juana Inés de la Cruz (1648–95), the Mexican nun who excelled in every literary genre she attempted. She produced comedies, dramas, and religious plays; she wrote an autobiographical essay, *Respuesta a Sor Filotea de la Cruz* (Reply to Sor Filotea de la Cruz, 1691), that stands even today as a model of independent thinking and brilliant argumentation; she wrote graceful *villancicos* (q.v.) in a popular vein; she emulated the great euphuistic poets of Spain, Góngora and Calderón (see AUTO SACRAMENTAL)

in *Primero sueño* (First Dream), and produced a highly sophisticated interp. of a subconscious world built into a complex poetic structure; she wrote of love with an insight and a profound understanding which have made her critics wonder if real passion might not have been the reason for her religious seclusion. One example may give the reader an idea of the excellence of her love sonnets, which the critics have compared to those of Lope de Vega and Shakespeare:

> Love, at first, is fashioned of agitation,
> Ardors, anxiety, and wakeful hours;
> By danger, risk, and fear it spreads its
>   power,
> And feeds on weeping and on supplication.
>
> It learns from coolness and indifference,
> Preserves its life beneath faithless veneers,
> Until, with jealousy or with offense,
> It extinguishes its fire in its tears.
>
> Love's beginning, middle, and its end
>   are these:
> Then why, Alcino, does it so displease
> That Celia, who once loved you, now
>   should leave you?
>
> Is that a cause for sorrow and remorse?
> Alcino mine, no, love did not deceive
>   you:
> It merely ran its customary course.
>   (tr. S. G. Morley)

Colonial Sp. Am. baroque poetry was a hothouse flower, nursed by artifice and killed by artifice. Far away from the literary academies and the solitude of the cloisters, a new poetry was slowly coming into being: a rough, impetuous song of mountains, pampas, rivers, and seas. This poetry was the Am. descendant of the Sp. *Romancero* (see ROMANCE). Old Sp. ballads were on the lips of the Conquistadors and, used as they were in the manner of proverbs, served to illustrate many a decision and to give a historical twist to local incidents. Hernán Cortés was quick to quote an old ballad, if we are to believe his historian, Bernal Díaz del Castillo. Perpetuated by oral trad., these ballads underwent colorful modifications and eventually came to express the Am. spirit that was treasuring them. From the great variety of subjects in the Sp. *Romancero*, Sp. Am. people chose those that esp. appealed to their imagination and worked on them with exuberance. They made and remade the adventures of Charlemagne, El Cid, Los Infantes de Lara, Conde Alarcos, and Juan de Austria. They memorized the deeds of famous bandits and invented new outlaws, romantically brave, full of vengeance against the Sp. masters and the wealthy creoles. This was the birth of the so-called Gaucho poetry (q.v.), which reached its peak in the second half of the 19th c. and produced at least one masterpiece: José Hernández' (1834–86) *Martín Fierro* (1872, 1879).

The young scions of wealthy Sp. Am. families, who had the fortune to study in France, Spain, and England, absorbed the political and literary effervescence created by the romantic movement. They were joined by the exiles in Paris and London who plotted the overthrow of the Sp. rulers in America. Shortly after, Napoleon's invasion of Spain brought about the political independence of Sp. America, and as the new republics were coming into existence, the political and literary expatriates started their journey home.

Romanticism took root in Sp. America without the structure of a movement. Poets wrote romantic poems without realizing they were doing so. A Cuban, José María Heredia (1803–39), brought up in the best neoclassical trad., wrote *En el Teocalli de Cholula* (On the Ancient Temple of Cholula, 1820) ten years before the romantic movement was launched in Spain. His themes were idealization of the Mexican landscape, decadence, and death. Heredia searches for the expression of ideal beauty, but his words are only approximations lost among mysterious echoes in an atmosphere of melancholy and disillusionment. *Niagara* is generally recognized as his best poem: Heredia's description of the waterfall, eloquent and impassioned, his masterly blending of landscape and mood—solitude, homesickness, an invocation to God—make this poem a true example of the best Sp. Am. romanticism.

Two other poets also contributed to the introduction of romanticism to Sp. America: José Joaquín Olmedo (1780–1847), born in Ecuador and author of *A la victoria de Junín: canto a Bolívar* (To the Victory at Junín), and Andrés Bello (1781–1865), the eminent Venezuelan humanist whose poem *Silva a la agricultura de la zona tórrida* (The Agriculture of the Torrid Zone), though of dubious artistic merit, is truly Am. in subject matter and intent. The expression of both these poets is strictly bound to classical norms, but the love for their homeland, their deep lyrical feeling for the beauties of the Am. landscape, their exaltation of Am. heroes, their use of Am. Indian diction, transcend rhetorical limitations to give their compositions an undeniable romantic meaning.

Sp. Am. romanticism blossomed in the second half of the 19th c. Its success as a school was strengthened by the presence of a number of distinguished Sp. poets who had come to America seeking wealth and honor. Among these, two should be remembered for the influence they had on their contemporaries: José Joaquín de Mora (1783–1864), who settled down as a teacher in Chile and traveled extensively in America before returning to Spain, and the famous José Zorrilla, who spent some time in Mexico. Soon, Sp. Am. poets realized that romanticism as a school was a thing of the past in Europe. They knew that Fr.

poetry was already undergoing a transformation which would soon crystallize in Parnassianism and symbolism (qq.v.). The reluctance of some writers to recognize the romantic nature of their poetry produced an odd situation: Bello and the Argentine Domingo Faustino Sarmiento urged the creation of a truly Am. literary style; Bello was identified as a classicist and Sarmiento as a defender of romanticism. But Bello had been a powerful factor in the establishment of romanticism not only as a poet but as a translator as well, and Sarmiento had savagely ridiculed romanticism in his newspaper articles. In fact, both were arguing for the same thing, only from different viewpoints: they wanted a lit. that would reflect the genius of the New World, a forceful expression which would inspire its people to create their own civilization. Bello had an eclectic mind and wished to benefit from the classical heritage as well as from modern achievements; above all, he had complete faith in the genius of Spain. Sarmiento, on the other hand, believed that Spain had run its course and that Sp. Americans should sever all ties with her and open their minds to the fresh and invigorating influence of France.

The younger poets, whether following Bello or Sarmiento, emulated models which sang in a surprisingly similar key: Zorrilla or Espronceda, Chateaubriand or Lamartine or Hugo. Sp. Am. poets suddenly discovered themselves at odds with bourgeois society; they fought tyranny, went into exile, longed for the homeland, felt bitter and rejected, sang the glories of Greece, Poland, and Mexico in their struggles for independence, and even evoked the Middle Ages, although historical interest led them more often to a colorful Indian past; they took the ocean as a symbol, twilight as the emblem of their melancholy; they wrote legends and historical plays—in a word, they produced romanticism. They are too numerous to list; few are remembered today as good poets, but among them one should mention the Cubans Gabriel de la Concepción Valdés (1809–44) and Gertrudis Gómez de Avellaneda (1814–73); the Argentines Estéban Echeverría (1805–51), José Mármol (1817–71), Olegario Andrade (1839–82), and Rafael Obligado (1851–1920); the Peruvian Manuel González Prada (1848–1918); the Mexican Manuel Acuña (1849–73); and the Uruguayan Juan Zorrilla de San Martin (1855–1931). Of these, some are regarded with particular interest: Echeverría, for example, the author of *Elvira o la novia del Plata* (Elvira or the Argentine Bride, 1832), an early romantic poem; Gómez de Avellaneda, who won literary fame in Spain as the author of passionate poems such as "Al partir" (Departing); González Prada, a revolutionary poet and forceful polemicist; and Zorrilla de San Martin, whose poem *Tabaré* (1888) is one of the landmarks of Sp. Am. romanticism. One cannot neglect the work of two major Colombian poets: José Eusebio Caro (1817–53), a masterful painter of landscapes, a philosopher and moralist of pungent originality; and Gregorio Gutiérrez González (1826–72), the author of a bold regionalist poem, *Memoria sobre el cultivo del maíz en Antioquia* (Memoir on the Cultivation of Corn in Antioquia, 1866), whose delicate sentimentalism has been compared to that of Bécquer.

Gradually the romantic fever subsided, and the poets who began to write in the last third of the 19th c. showed a growing concern for refinement and sophistication. Eloquence is toned down. The desire to escape reality becomes a search for the exotic and the decadent. No longer do the expatriates weep for a distant homeland; they enjoy the foreign places they visit and write about them with elegance and a sort of playful irresponsibility. They are still romantic, of course, and many refuse to go the way of damnation singing its praises. Instead, they pine away in touching *nocturnos*. Two of them are good poets in a dated sort of way: Julián del Casal (1863–93), a Cuban, and José Asunción Silva (1865–96), a Colombian. What makes these poets different from their romantic predecessors is only the sophistication of the symbolism they borrowed from Fr. lit. They wrote short bits of melancholy amorousness, whereas their predecessors wrote vast cascades of passionate lamentations. They show little concern for historical events, except that they condescend sometimes to attack the United States for its budding imperialism in Sp. America. If they feel at odds with society, they do not confront it but escape from it, sometimes literarily and sometimes literally by committing suicide, as in the case of Silva. The most socially conscious of them, the Cuban José Marti (1853–95), is the least modernistic and, at the same time, the most universal. Better than most of his contemporaries, Marti represents the Am. effort to establish the image of a new man and a new society in Western lit. His poetry, *Ismaelillo* (1882), is innovative in a popular manner, eloquent without being emphatic, and profoundly individualistic. In contrast, the Mexican Salvador Díaz Mirón (1853–1928) continues to be romantic in his love poems and neoclassical in his descriptions of nature. Much of his poetry is still rooted in the Libertarian trad. so much admired by Rubén Darío. *Lascas* (Rock Chippings, 1901) is considered his best book, a fine example of refinement in form and subdued sentimentalism. Some important critics believe that another Mexican, Manuel Gutiérrez Nájera (1859–95) played an essential role in introducing the main features of *modernismo* into Sp. Am. p. Musicality, a power to suggest the hidden meanings in everyday life, a natural sense of mystery, and predestination add substance to his poetry.

By the end of the 19th c., a new poetic movement was developing in Sp. America. Its leader was the Nicaraguan Rubén Darío (1867– 1916). At a very young age he left his native land, lived for a while in Guatemala and El Salvador, and settled for a few years in Santiago, Chile. Here he came into contact with writers who introduced him to the work of Fr. symbolists. Under strong Fr. influence he published a book of poems and short stories, *Azul* (Azure, 1888), which immediately garnered him an international reputation. At the turn of the century, his books—*Prosas profanas* (Lay Hymns, 1896), *Cantos de vida y esperanza* (Songs of Life and Hope, 1905), *El canto errante* (The Wandering Song, 1907)—became the Bible of the new poets, and his name was revered. Critics and historians of Sp. Am. lit. have written scores of books dealing with *modernismo* (q.v.—Sp. modernism). This poetic trend, which lasted to about 1920, could be described as the Sp. Am. expression of Fr. *Parnasse* and *Symbolisme*. In the beginning it represented an escape from reality (exoticism was then one of its main features), and later it turned its attention to America, influenced somewhat by Walt Whitman. From Parnassianism it inherited a fastidious concern for beauty of form; from symbolism it learned to subdue emotions, replacing exclamation by suggestion, and also it inherited a liking for pure fantasy and an interest in the aesthetic of decadence (q.v.). From Gongorism, which Darío revived in all its splendor (see NEOGONGORISM), *modernismo* took a fondness for intricate and brilliant imagery. Putting all this together was the fascinating miracle wrought by Darío. He made people think that a "new civilization" was being born, but today one realizes that with Darío an old historical fact found its affirmation in the work of art: Sp. Am. "new civilization" was the blossoming of European culture, mainly Fr. and Sp., in the midst of a continent whose natural forces and soul were still unknown entities. Darío awakened many a dream in the minds of Sp. Am. intellectuals. His magic touch sent his disciples away with the dangerous notion that they too were demigods. After his disappearance, *modernismo* faded in the winds of our materialistic age like a cloud of golden dust.

A number of poets who achieved distinction following in the steps of the Nicaraguan master include the Argentine Leopoldo Lugones (1874–1938), an eloquent, rather overpowering poet in whose works—*Las montañas del oro* (The Golden Mountains, 1897), *Los crepúsculos del jardín* (Twilights of the Garden, 1905), *Lunario sentimental* (Sentimental Lunar Poems, 1909), and *Poemas solariegos* (Poems of the Homestead, 1928)—one finds an amazing blend of all the major literary currents of the 19th c. and strong anticipations of avant-garde schools such as Ultraism (q.v.); Amado Nervo (1870–1919), the refined, gently religious, amiable Mexican, a genuine romantic, author of *Serenidad* (Serenity, 1914), *Elevación* (Elation, 1917), and *Plenitud* (Plenitude, 1918); Luis G. Urbina (1868–1934), also a Mexican, sentimental, ironic, surprisingly original in his treatment of subjects considered prosaic in his own time (*Lámparas en agonía* [Lamps in Agony], 1914;

El glosario de la vida vulgar [Glossary of Everyday Life], 1916); Rufino Blanco Fombona (1874–1944), Venezuelan, a brilliant, colorful poet too strongly bound by the likings of his epoch (*Pequeña ópera lírica* [Small Lyrical Works], 1904; *Cancionero del amor infeliz* [Songbook of Unhappy Love], 1918); Julio Herrera y Reissig (1875–1910), Uruguayan, undoubtedly the greatest poet of modernism after Darío, a true representative of contemp. Sp. Am. baroque, deeply preoccupied with the creation of a poetic lang. that would combine the best elements of Gongorism, symbolism, and Parnassianism—he is the real link between the poetry of the 19th and 20th cs. in Sp. Am. and a forerunner of Huidobro's creationism (q.v.); Ricardo Jaimes Freyre (1868–1933), Bolivian, exquisite in his already outmoded exoticism, a true master of versification (*Castalia bárbara* [Barbarian Castaly], 1899; *Los sueños son vida* [Dreams are Life], 1917); Guillermo Valencia (1872–1943), Colombian, a poet of profound pictorial sense whose classical aloofness, in the midst of a period when color and brilliance were used with naive profuseness, is proving to be the reason for his survival among the most respected literary figures of his country (*Ritos* [Rites], 1898; enl., 1914); José Santos Chocano (1875–1934), Peruvian, a bombastic versifier and self-styled interpreter of the Am. world (*La selva vírgen* [The Virgin Jungle], 1901; *Alma América* [Soul-America], 1906); José María Eguren (1874–1942), another Peruvian, who made his reputation as a poet by being subtle and subdued in contrast to Chocanos's grandiloquence; and the Chileans Manuel Magallanes Moure (1878–1924) and Carlos Pezoa Véliz (1879–1908). Today it seems obvious that the Mexican Enrique González Martínez (1871–1952) was the outstanding figure among this group. One of the poems in his book *Los senderos ocultos* (The Hidden Paths, 1911)—"Tuércele el cuello al cisne" (Wring the Swan's Neck)—sounded the death knell for *modernismo*.

Some poets, too young to accompany Darío as disciples but too old to overtake the avant-garde forces, found themselves stranded with the remnants of modernism. A few of them became excellent poets, but as a group they represent a lost generation. The best known among them are: the Uruguayan Carlos Sabat Ercasty (1887–1982), the Chileans Angel Cruchaga Santa María (1893–1964) and Juan Guzmán Cruchaga (1895–1979), the Mexicans Ramón López Velarde (1888–1921) and Juan José Tablada (1871–1945), the Colombian Porfirio Barba Jacob (1883–1942), and the Puerto Rican L. Lloréns Torres (1878–1944). Cruchaga Santa María and López Velarde deserve special mention; each in his own way established an important link with the baroque poetry of midcentury Lat. America: Cruchaga as a sensuous mystic very close to the early Neruda, and López Velarde, the author of "Suave patria" (Soft Motherland), as the forerunner of a conversational type

of lyric poetry which would reach its climax with César Vallejo and Nicanor Parra.

In a place by themselves one should mention four women poets who transformed the lit. of Lat. America: Gabriela Mistral, Delmira Agustini, Alfonsina Storni, and Juana de Ibarbourou. These women helped to bring about a social revolution of far-reaching effect; they fought for the social and psychological emancipation of Sp. Am. women. The Chilean Gabriela Mistral (1889–1957), who won the Nobel Prize in 1945, became the living banner of a movement for child welfare, for women's rights, and for social laws to protect the Indians. It has been said that the Nobel Prize may have been given to her as a reward for an entire life devoted to defending the poor and the outcast, and that her glorification of motherhood convinced the Swedish Academy of the true universality of her poetry. To the students of Sp. Am. lit. her greatness reaches beyond the limits of mere philanthropy: in her three most important books, *Desolación* (Desolation, 1922), *Tala* (Land Clearing, 1938), and *Lagar* (Grape-Crushing Vat, 1954), Mistral created a style solidly realistic, direct, and forceful, deeply religious in a biblical sense, and oddly rural in its vocabulary; her lang. offered a sharp contrast to the decadent elegance of modernism. The Uruguayan Delmira Agustini (1886–1914) began writing before she was 17 years old. Her prescience of a violent death—she was killed when she was 28—her yearning for an all-satisfying love, her passionate descriptions of masculine beauty, her direct and voluptuous allusions to the sexual act, were taken by the critics as the daring but innocent poetic exercises of a gifted adolescent. But when her poems appeared in book form—*El libro blanco* (The White Book, 1907)—Darío and his disciples recognized that a major new poet had arrived. Not a shade of artifice mars the pathos of her sensuous pleas. Touched by the sublime emotion of a real artist, the crude reality of her naked figures assumes classical aloofness. In the Argentine poet Alfonsina Storni (1892–1938), the tragic story of Delmira Agustini is repeated. After a nightmarish life of loneliness and economic strain, she committed suicide. Sex flashes violently in her metaphors (*Ocre* [Ocher], 1925). But she lacks the natural refinement of Agustini and her poetry, after pounding on the emotions of the reader who senses the coming unhappy climax, falls to earth in a mixture of bewilderment and anguished, almost cynical defeat: *El mundo de siete pozos* (The World of Seven Wells, 1934), *Mascarilla y trébol* (Mask and Clover, 1938). The Uruguayan Juana de Ibarbourou (1895–1979), on the other hand, devotes her wholesome life to singing of motherhood and youth, of maturity and the strain of a vanishing existence (*Las lenguas de diamante* [The Diamond Tongues], 1919; *Raíz salvaje* [Savage Root], 1920; *La rosa de los vientos* [Sextant], 1930). With her the revolutionary period of women's poetry in Sp. Am. comes to an end. Mention of these women brings one to the threshold of contemp. Sp. Am. p. However, their turbulence remains. With the rhetoric of passion drastically diminished, and finally eliminated, this poetry goes on changing directions, finding existentialism on the way, baring the roots of its linguistic search, coming to rest in a form of conversational expression of love, loneliness, and sadness. In Uruguay one senses a reaction against the serenity of Ibarbourou; new voices arise, avoiding emphasis through the use of an oral lang., in the poetry of Idea Vilariño (b. 1920), Ida Vitale (b. 1923), and Circe Maia (b. 1932). Vilariño's books—*La suplicante* (The Suppliant, 1945), *Cielo, cielo* (Heaven, Heaven, 1947), *Por aire sucio* (Through Dirty Air, 1950), *Poemas de amor* (Love Poems, 1957), and *No* (1980)—reach a surprisingly wide audience. Vitale's best known works are: *Oidor andante* (Walking Listener, 1972) and *Jardín de Sílice* (Silicon Garden, 1980); among Maia's books one should mention: *En el tiempo* (Within Time, 1958) and *Presencia diaria* (Daily Presence, 1974).

The poetry by women of other Lat. Am. countries shows a similar tendency to deemphasize the rhetoric of sentimentalism. A few names have gained international recognition: the Mexican Rosario Castellanos (1925–74), author of *Al pie de la letra* (To the Letter, 1959), *Lívida luz* (Livid Light, 1960); the Salvadorean Claribel Alegría (b. 1924), with books such as *Vigilias* (Vigils, 1953), *Acuario* (Aquarium, 1955), *Aprendizaje* (Apprenticeship, 1970), and *Sobrevivo* (Surviving, 1978); and the Argentine Olga Orozco (b. 1922), with *Desde lejos* (From Afar, 1946), *Las muertes* (Deaths, 1952), *Los juegos peligrosos* (Dangerous Games, 1962), and *Cantos a Berenice* (Songs for Berenice, 1977).

In the maturing of the new schools that came after Darío, France again played an important role, for it was the spirit of dada (q.v.) that killed the nostalgic decadence of Darío's late disciples, and it was surrealism and creationism (qq.v.) that provided the aesthetic ideas which brought Lat. Am. poets closer to Spain's Generation of 1927 (see SPANISH POETRY) and to Ultraism (q.v.). Contemp. Sp. Am. p. seems to have come into its own through the combined action of four main factors: the work of Mistral, Agustini, Storni, and Ibarbourou mentioned above; the reaction against Darío; a critical examination and revision of poetic lang.; and the search for mythical forms of realism led by Pablo Neruda and César Vallejo.

The reaction against Darío's *preciosité* came around 1920. Mexican *Estridentismo*, the Whitmanism of Armando Vasseur and Sabat Ercasty, the sensual pessimism of Barba Jacob, and the metaphorical values of ancestral regionalism led the movement against a "modernist" revolution which in less than 30 years had already become reactionary. These poets abandoned the objective or "representational" approach to nature; they gave up rhyme and, briefly, even punctuation. They cre-

ated a new form of exoticism: the escape into abstraction. The most brilliant of these poets was the Chilean Vicente Huidobro (1893–1948). In his country he was followed by a gifted group of poets, among them: Rosamel del Valle (1901–63), Humberto Díaz Casanueva (b. 1908), Juvencio Valle (b. 1906), and Eduardo Anguita (b. 1914). Huidobro involved himself in a dramatic search for a creative lang., claiming that the poet should not imitate nature but should assume instead the role of a true creator, whence the name for his brand of poetics, *Creationism* (q.v.). As a poetic speaker he was a king of metaphors. His readers could not fail to detect irony in his efforts. This irony and his playfulness in proposing his theories hurt his literary reputation. At the end, far away from the fireworks of the avant-garde, Huidobro wrote deep, meditative poetry about the mysterious symbols of the ocean and of the passing of time—*El cuidadano del olvido* (Citizen of Forgetfulness, 1941) and *Ultimos poemas* (Last Poems, 1948); his most famous work continues to be *Altazor* (Altazor, 1931).

In the early 1930s, another Chilean directed a rebellion against abstract poetry: Pablo Neruda (1904–73), whose poetry evolved from the melodious symbolism of *Veinte poemas de amor y una canción desesperada* (20 Poems of Love and a Song of Despair, 1924) to an astonishing glorification of the most prosaic elements of reality. Slowly and deliberately he proceeded to destroy all that Sp. modernism considered sacred. In conceiving the monumental chaos which constitutes the essence of *Residencia en la tierra* (Residence on Earth, 1925–35), Neruda has expressed, as no one had done before, the metaphysical anguish of the Sp. Am. man, his terrors, his superstitions, his sense of guilt imposed on him by religious teachings and the broken trad. of his Indian forefathers, his loneliness in the midst of a strange civilization that he does not understand and cannot appreciate, his consternation before nature that crushes him with its untamed jungles, oceans, and mountains, his decadence coming as the result of exploitation, malnutrition, alcoholism, poverty, and disease. *Residencia en la tierra* is an expression of the psychological and social drama affecting great numbers of Sp. Am. people today. From this surrealistic statement of the decadence of the Western world, Neruda moved towards a politically committed poetry, beginning with *España en el corazón* (Spain in My Heart, 1937), a book inspired by the Sp. Civil War, followed by *Las furias y las penas* (The Furies and the Sorrows, 1939), *Nuevo canto de amor a Stalingrado* (New Song of Love for Stalingrad, 1943), and *Canto general* (General Song, 1950).

Neruda strongly believed in identifying his personal life with his creative work. After the Sp. Civil War he joined the Chilean Communist Party and was elected senator. Toward the end of his life he became a candidate for the presidency of Chile. However, he was never a strictly political poet;

Canto general, a masterpiece of surrealistic mythology, contains anecdotal material together with some of the most profound lyrical poetry ever written by Neruda ("Alturas de Macchu Picchu" [Heights of Macchu Picchu], "El gran océano" [The Great Ocean]). All during his most active political life Neruda never ceased writing great love poetry (*Cien sonetos de amor* [A Hundred Sonnets of Love], 1959) and delicate, ingenious miniatures such as his *Odas elementales* (Elementary Odes), 1954. After winning the Nobel Prize (1971) and serving as Chilean Ambassador to France, Neruda returned to Chile in 1972. He died the following year during the bloody military coup in which President Salvador Allende was killed. Neruda left several books that were published posthumously; in them one finds remarkable expressions of Neruda's materialistic philosophy of life and death together with touching autobiographical remembrances.

When César Vallejo (1892–1938), the great Peruvian poet, began to publish his mature work, Darío's modernism was dead. Vallejo's formal break with modernism, however, did not mean a direct return to reality, but a move from Darío's abstractions to another kind of abstraction, a world of violent myths, sometimes oneiric, sometimes the result of furious sadness. Perhaps one could describe Vallejo's poetic vision as a particularized counterpart of Neruda's apocalyptic imagination in *Residencia en la tierra*. Vallejo, like Neruda, had avoided the *Ultraísta* movement. His Neosymbolism, erotic and regionalistic, gained in solitude a moribund, existential sediment. This explains why Vallejo is so different from the boisterous playfulness of the Peninsular and Lat. Am. avant-garde poets of the 1920s. This approach to mythology, so characteristic of Andean pathos, is accomplished by Vallejo not by losing, but rather by improving his conversational, eccentric attitude in the face of poetic fact. His colloquial phrases in *Los heraldos negros* (The Black Harbingers, 1918), *Trilce* (Trilce, 1922), and *Poemas humanos* (Human Poems, 1939) are given the suggestive power of *leitmotif*; they work as magical formulae. Numbers, at random, do likewise. This is Vallejo's road toward an essential reality, toward a unifying image of man facing the processes of life and death: Vallejo equates opposite terms. To do this he uses several devices, two of which are fundamental in his poetry: the false passage of time, and the nostalgic feeling for persons and things from the standpoint of a living death. To understand man, he is saying, we must detect the skull behind the smile. Life, thinks Vallejo, is a great death, great because of the size of the deceit involved. In spite of this pessimism, Vallejo's poetry has been interpreted as an expression of Christian faith, and even as a form of socialistic humanism. Young poets of the second half of the 20th c. particularly venerate Vallejo.

At the present time, Jorge Luis Borges (1899–1986) might be more famous as a writer of short-stories and essays than as a poet; however, it is entirely possible that in the years to come he will be remembered for his poetry. Works such as *Fervor de Buenos Aires* (Fervor for Buenos Aires, 1923), *Luna de enfrente* (Moon Across the Street, 1926), and *Cuaderno San Martín* (San Martin's Notebook, 1929) are being rediscovered as if miraculously untouched by time. Borges describes reality in terms of essential existence, bordering on metaphysical truth. Yet he works with humble objects and artifacts—an old house, a backyard, a guitar, knives, flowers, portraits—in which he uncovers myths, ancestral roots, unmovable and perennial. He asserts the unreality of time—"Poema conjectural" (Conjectural Poem)—as he perceives the reality of death. Things and beings revolve around this sense of duality. For Borges, poetry is an instrument of knowledge and understanding; it is not magic, nor historical prophecy. The poet discovers his cadences as he enters daily life wisely unaware of the mysteries that surround him. Borges avoids all traces of artificiality, having early in his career abandoned his sophisticated attempts at *ultraísmo*. For many years he pruned his early works in order to destroy every possible link with the avant-garde. At the end, almost completely blind, he dictated his poems, usually impeccable sonnets, full of wisdom, simple charm, and a sort of courtly, innocent love. Buenos Aires, the city of his birth, shines in his poems: Borges describes it as "my home, its familiar neighborhoods, and, along with them, what I experienced of love, of suffering, and of misgivings." In "Casas como ángeles" ("Houses like Angels") he writes:

> I think of the pale arms that make eve-
>   ning glimmer
> and of the blackness of braids: I think
>   of the grave delight
> of being mirrored in their deep eyes,
>   like arbors of the night.
>
> I will push the gate of iron entering
>   the dooryard
> and there will be a fair girl, already
>   mine, in the room.
> And the two of us will hush, trembling
>   like flames,
> and the present joy will grow quiet in
>   that passed.
>
> (tr. Robert Fitzgerald)

This devotion to themes of nostalgia in the heart of the overpowering city, not far from the Argentine plains full of passionate history, was also characteristic of a group of Borges' contemporaries: Ricardo Molinari (b. 1898), Eduardo González Lanusa (b. 1900), Francisco Luis Bernárdez (1900–79), Leopoldo Marechal (1900–70), and Raúl González Tuñón (1905–74). The subtleties of creationist abstraction were maintained by Enrique Molina (b. 1910).

Mexican poetry during this period was untouched by the portentous events of the Mexican Revolution, which had deep effects on the novel, on painting, and on music. The leading poets were suspicious of foreign influences and extremely reluctant to allow themselves any enthusiasm for lately arrived *isms*. Curiously loyal to Sp. trad. and cl. form, poets experimented, however, with subjects of varied and profound significance. Carlos Pellicer (1899–1977; *Material poético* [Poetic Materials], 1962) encompassed a world of music and color in highly stylized form. José Gorostiza (1901–73) explored in depth the metaphysical projections of Mexican culture (*Muerte sin fin* [Death Without End], 1939), and Xavier Villaurrutia (1903–50) made of his love poetry the epitome of exquisite sophistication (*Nocturnos* [Nocturns], 1933; *Décima muerte* [Tenth Death], 1941). Salvador Novo (1904–74) played with grandiose themes of Mexican history (he was the official *cronista* of Mexico City), but his poetry also reveals tenderness and pathos (*Poesía* [Poetry], 1961). See also CHICANO POETRY.

The last brilliant flashes of the Sp. Am. avantgarde are to be found in the poetry of Jorge Carrera Andrade (Ecuador, 1902–76), Luis Cardoza y Aragón (Guatemala, b. 1904), Emilio Adolfo Westphalen (Perú, b. 1911), Vicente Gerbasi (Venezuela, b. 1913), José Lezama Lima (Cuba, 1910–76), and Efraín Huerta (Mexico, 1914–82).

At this point the historian might feel tempted to include Nicolás Guillén (b. 1902) among the poets reacting against the elitism of *Ultraísmo*. That would be only partly right. Guillén was above the polemics of the avant garde. He created a powerful poetic movement that became characteristic of the Caribbean world. With Guillén, black poetry ceased to be an exotic pastime to become the expression of an oppressed people struggling for social liberation. Guillén's poetry is not just "political"; it is great art that combines the refined intricacies of old Sp. ballads with the fascinating rhythms and cadences of African music and dance. Some of his books (*Motivos de son* [Motifs for Cuban "Sones"], 1930; *Cóngoro Cosongo* [Congoro Cosongo], 1931; *El son entero* [Complete "Sones"], 1947) are already classics in Sp. Am. p. To the acknowledgment of the baroque poet and novelist Lezama Lima, we should add the names of Eliseo Diego (b. 1920) and Cintio Vitier (b. 1921), who represent the link between pre- and post-revolutionary poetry in Cuba. Both appeared at a time when philosophical and even religious currents dominated the literary world in Havana. After the revolution in 1959, they remained in Cuba and now are looked upon as leaders by a younger generation.

When Octavio Paz (b. 1914) assumed the leadership of his generation in Mexico, the whole poetry of Sp. America once again underwent rebellion and change. But this time the main issue was *language*: prose writers and poets felt the urgency of doing away with the dated rhetoric of the avant garde. Short-story writer Julio Cortázar, novelists such as Juan Rulfo, Gabriel García Márquez, Elena Garro, and Enrique Molina, and poets like Nicanor Parra (b. 1914), Alfredo Cardona Peña, Germán Belli, Alí Chumacero, Mario Benedetti, Olga Orozco, Jaime Sabines, Homero Aridjis, Ernesto Cardenal, Enrique Lihn, Jorge Tellier, and others sound the alarm and engage in a passionately critical consideration of literary lang. The return to vernacular, unrhetorical, direct lang. is thoroughly established. Anti-poetry is born, led by Parra's outrageously funny and merciless attack against the capitalist establishment in *Poemas y antipoemas* (Poems and Antipoems, 1954). His conversational, ironic discourse serves as a cover for a bitter condemnation of society and, more recently, of nature's destruction by man. Parra absorbed a tone of controlled desperation in his careful readings of British poetry, particularly T. S. Eliot. He owes some of his surrealistic populism to earlier Sp. Am. poets, such as Pablo de Rokha (1894–1968), a Chilean, author of *Gran temperatura* (Great Temperature, 1937) and *Canto del macho anciano* (Song of an Ancient Male, 1965) among many books, and León de Greif (1895–1976), one of the leading figures in contemp. Colombian poetry (*Obras completas* [Complete Works], 1960). Parra's counterpart in Chilean poetry is Gonzalo Rojas (b. 1917), whose expression of profound existentialist density has gained in importance and projection in recent years (*Oscuro* [Dark], 1977; *Del relámpago* [On Lightening], 1981).

Paz stands at the opposite extreme of Parra. His poetic discourse is surrealistic in form but philosophical in content. His preoccupation with the soul and the fate of his people lends an almost tragic tone to his poetry. Paz's impact on Sp. Am. p. has grown steadily. His roots are in Fr. surrealism (*Libertad bajo palabra* [Freedom on My Own Word], 1935–57; *Salamandra* [Salamander], 1958–61); but philosophically he has delved deeply into Oriental trads., as if he were slowly tracing a path from ancient religions through pre-Colombian cosmogonies toward modern existentialism. Following in Paz's footsteps, José Emilio Pacheco (b. 1939) has gained a solid reputation as a poet, essayist, and translator (*Los elementos de la noche* [Night Elements], 1963; *Islas a la deriva* [Aimless Islands], 1976; *Desde entonces* [Since Then], 1980).

As we approach the end of the 20th c., Sp. Am. p. reflects a movement from surrealism and conversationalism toward an explicit discourse of philosophical desperation, sometimes attributed to national conditions of ruin and pessimism, sometimes to struggles of social liberation, but most often to individual anguish. Neruda's voice continues to be heard, but young poets close their ears to his cosmic clamor; they are drawn to more strong, direct, down-to-earth statements. Their discourse seems rough in its directness but is filled with loneliness and tenderness as well. Some of these new voices are already rising above the chorus of small presses and little magazines, establishing a solid international reputation: in Central America, the Salvadorean Roque Dalton (1933–75; *Taberna y otros lugares* [Tavern and Other Places], 1969); in Peru, Antonio Cisneros (b. 1942; *Canto ceremonial contra un oso hormiguero* [Ceremonial Song Against an Anteater], 1968; *Crónica del Niño Jesús de Chilca* [Chronicle of the Chilca Child Jesus], 1981); in Chile, Jaime Quezada (b. 1942; *Las palabras del fabulador* [The Fabulist's Words], 1968; *Huerfanías* [Orphan Themes], 1985), and Raúl Zurita (b. 1951; *Purgatorio* [Purgatory], 1979; *Anteparaíso* [Ante Paradise], 1982).

Looking back over the second half of the 20th c. the reader knows that she has seen the rise and end of a rich and splendid trad. of baroque poetry. In the twilight of this period, a few names became firmly established in Western lit. The move now is back to fundamental poetic statements in the midst of decisive social changes. See also PORTUGUESE POETRY; BRAZILIAN POETRY; SPANISH POETRY; CHICANO POETRY.

ANTHOLOGIES: *Antol. de poetas hispanoamericanos*, ed. M. Menéndez y Pelayo, 4 v. (1893–95)—mostly 19th c.; *Antol. de la poesía española e hispanoamericana*, ed. F. de Onís (1934); *La poesía chilena nueva*, ed. E. Anguita and V. Teitelboin (1935); *Indice de la poesía uruguaya contemporánea*, ed. A. Zum Felde (1935); *Indice de la poesía argentina contemporánea*, ed. J. González Carballo (1937); *Indice de la poesía ecuatoriana contemporánea*, ed. B. Carrión (1937); *Orbita de la poesía afrocubana*, ed. R. Guirao (1938); *Indice de la poesía peruana contemporánea*, ed. L. A. Sánchez (1938); *Nuevos poetas venezolanos*, ed. R. Olivares Figueroa (1938); *Anthol. of Contemp. Lat. Am. P.*, ed. D. Fitts (1942)—Sp. and Eng. texts; *Twelve Sp. Am. Poets*, ed. H. R. Hays (1943)—Sp. and Eng. texts; *Indice de la poesía paraguaya*, ed. S. Buzó Gómez (1943); *La poesía mexicana moderna*, ed. A. Castro Leal (1953); *Cien años de poesía en Panamá*, ed. R. Miró (1953); *Antol. de la poesía hispanoamericana*, ed. G. de Albareda and F. Garfias, 10 v. (1957–); *Anthol. of Mexican Poetry*, ed. O. Paz, tr. S. Beckett (1958); *Antol. de la poesía chilena contemporánea*, ed. R. E. Scarpa and H. Montes (1968); *Con Cuba: An Anthol. of Cuban Poetry of the Last 60 Years*, ed. N. Tarn (1969); *New Poetry of Mexico*, ed. O. Paz and M. Strand (1970); *Antol. de la poesía hispanoamericana contemporánea: 1914–1970* (1971), *Antol. crítica de la poesía modernista hispanoamericana* (1985), both ed. J. O. Jiménez; *Penguin Book of Lat. Am. Verse*, ed. E. Caracciolo-Trejo (1971); S. Yurkievich, *Fundadores de la nueva poesía latinoamericana* (1971); *Lat. Am. Revolutionary Poetry: a Bilingual Anthol.*, ed. R. Marquez (1974); *Antol. crítica de la poesía tradicional chilena*, ed. I. Dolz Blackburn (1979); *Poesía peruana, antol. general*, ed. A. Romualdo et

al, 3 v. (1984); *Woman Who Has Sprouted Wings: Poems by Contemp. Lat. Am. Women Poets*, ed. M. Crow (1984); *Muestra de poesía hispanoamericana del siglo 20*, ed. J. A. Escalona-Escalona, 2 v. (1985); *Antol. de la nueva poesía femenina chilena*, ed. J. Villegas (1985); *Poets of Chile: A Bilingual Anthol., 1965–1985*, ed. and tr. S. F. White and J. A. Epple (1986); *Three Women Poets: Louise Labe, Gaspara Stampa, and Sor Juana Ines de la Cruz*, ed. F. J. Warnke (1987); *A Sor Juana Anthol.*, tr. A. S. Trueblood (1988)—intro. by O. Paz.

HISTORY AND CRITICISM: A. Torres-Ríoseco, *Rubén Darío: casticismo y americanismo* (1931); J. E. Englekirk, *Edgar Allan Poe in Hispanic Lit.* (1934); A. Alonso, *Poesía y estilo de Pablo Neruda*, 2d ed. (1951); S. Rosenbaum, *Mod. Women Poets of Sp. America* (1945)—excellent bibl.; P. Henríquez Ureña, *Literary Currents in Hispanic America* (1945); M. del Carmen Millán, *El paisaje en la poesía mexicana* (1952)—esp. 19th c.; F. Alegría, *Walt Whitman en Hispanoamérica* (1954), *La poesía chilena* (1954); M. Henríquez Ureña, *Breve historia del modernismo* (1954); E. Anguita, *Antol. de Vicente Huidobro* (1954)—fine critical intro.; R. Fernández Retamar, *La poesía contemporánea en Cuba* (1954); F. Dauster, *Breve historia de la poesía mexicana* (1956); Unión Panamericana, *Diccionario de la lit. latinoamericana* (1958–); A. Rama, *Rubén Darío y el Modernismo* (1970); C. Fernández Moreno, *América Latina en su lit.* (1972); *A Woman of Genius: The Intellectual Autobiography of Sor Juana de la Cruz*, tr. M. S. Peden (1982); J. A. Escalona, *Muestra de poesía hispanoamericana del Siglo XX*, 2 v. (1985); F. Schopf, *Del Vanguardismo a la Antipoesía* (1986); O. Paz, *Sor Juana*, tr. M. S. Peden (1988); G. Kirkpatrick, *The Dissonant Legacy of "Modernismo"* (1989); F. W. Murray, *The Aesthetics of Contemp. Sp.-Am. Social Protest Poetry* (1990).

F.A.

SPANISH POETICS. See BAROQUE POETICS; NEOCLASSICAL POETICS; ROMANTIC AND POSTROMANTIC POETICS; TWENTIETH-CENTURY POETICS.

SPANISH POETRY. (This article treats primarily Sp. p. in Castilian, the lang. of the central region of the Iberian peninsula; for the poetries of the western and eastern langs., see GALICIAN POETRY and CATALAN POETRY.)

SPANISH POETRY

I. THE EARLIEST LYRICS. Sp. p. originated, no doubt, simultaneously with the Sp. lang. itself or, more precisely, with those Romance dialects which developed on the Iberian peninsula during the Middle Ages (see SPANISH PROSODY). The dialects began, of course, not as written but as spoken langs.; hence the first Sp. p. was, naturally, oral poetry. Only almost indecipherable fragments of this poetry have been preserved, transcribed in Ar. or Heb. letters, as refrains (*kharjas*) appended to longer, more learned poems (*muwashshahana*) written as early as the 11th c. by Moorish or Jewish poets of southern Spain (see HISPANO-ARABIC PROSODY; HEBREW POETRY). The dialect of the *kharjas*, known as Mozarabic, reflects the earliest stage of a recognizably Sp. lang. These *kharjas*, which antedate even the lyric poems of the Occitan troubadours, are predominantly love songs, snatches of lamentation in which girls bewail the absence of their lovers; the poetic intensity of these fragments, tremulously chaste in the Heb. poems, more sensual in the Ar. ones, can still be felt by the Sp. reader, despite one or two archaic words of Semitic origin:

My heart is leaving me.
Oh God, I wonder whether it will re-
    turn?
My grief for my beloved is so great!
He is sick: when will he be well?

Such fragments are the only survivors of a body of oral poetry which must have been common to most communities of the Iberian peninsula. The first Sp. p. recorded in the Lat. alphabet, that of the 13th-c. Galician-Portuguese *cancioneiros* or collections of songs (see CANCION), includes *cantigas de amigo* (see CANTIGA) which are quite similar to the *kharjas* in theme; in the traditional folk poetry of Castile, as well, the *villancicos* (q.v.) or refrain carols, deriving from the Hispano-Ar. *zéjel* (q.v.), are frequently *Frauenlieder* of a similar sort.

II. THE MEDIEVAL EPIC. The oldest monument of Sp. lit. is the anonymous *Poema del Cid* or *Cantar de Mío Cid*; written about 1140, it is the best surviving example of the Sp. medieval epic. Like the Fr. *chansons de geste* (q.v.), the *Poema del Cid* reflects feudal customs of Germanic origin which may be traced back to the Visigothic period; it also shows signs of the direct influence of Fr. literary models and, perhaps, of certain Ar. sources as well. The word "cid" itself is of Ar. origin and means feudal lord, which is the title of the poem's hero, Rodrigo Díaz de Vivar, a well-documented historical personage who, exiled by Alfonso VI of Castile and Leon between 1079 and 1099, took the city of Valencia from the Moors in 1089. Given a degree of historicity and of geographical precision which clearly distinguishes this poem's level of realism from the fantasy of Fr. epics such as the *Chanson de Roland*, the *Poema del Cid* is essentially the dramatic depiction of a relatively restrained and modest type of feudal hero.

Written in lines of variable length (14-syllable lines predominate) divided into hemistichs, with assonance (q.v.) at the ends of the lines, the poem was evidently composed for dramatic oral recitation by a *jongleur* (q.v.) or professional court entertainer. It begins with the pathos of the hero's unjust exile. But Rodrigo Díaz is always a faithful vassal to the king, sending him booty from each of the battles that he wins in Moslem land. After taking Valencia, he is restored to the good graces of the king, who honors him by sponsoring his daughters' marriages to two Leonese noblemen. But the sons-in-law turn out to be as decadent and cowardly as they are proud. When they beat and abandon their wives, the Cid does not take vengeance into his own hands, but appeals to the king for justice to be administered in accordance with law. His second vindication is even more glorious than his first.

The sober understatement of this epic poem's style reflects the orderly, measured character of its hero. Thus, the first major work in the history of Sp. p. has none of the baroque exuberance or picaresque cynicism which are often considered typical of Sp. lit.; it is, in fact, quite classically subtle in its balanced avoidance of all extremes.

Other Sp. medieval epics certainly existed which can be reconstructed from later chronicles and ballads, but the original versions are for the most part lost. Among the surviving texts are a 13th-c. clerkly reworking of an epic on Fernán González and the much later *Mocedades de Rodrigo*, in which the Cid is depicted, not as an austere feudal vassal but as an arrogant, fiery youth. It is this later, more romantic Cid who was to become famous in ballads and plays.

III. MONASTIC POETRY. In the 13th c., the scholarly poet of the cloister begins to compete with the *jongleur* of the feudal court. He replaces the militaristic Romanesque virtues of feudal society with the Gothic virtues of devotion to Our Lady, the saints, and the Mass. His sources are not recent Sp. history or oral legends but Lat. manuscripts: the Bible, the lives and miracles of the saints, even legends of Cl. antiquity. And he uses not a loose oral meter but a fixed stanzaic form known as *cuaderna vía* (q.v.): four 14-syllable lines (*alejandrinos*; cf. *alexandrine*, q.v.), all ending in a single true rhyme.

Gonzalo de Berceo (ca. 1200–65) is the best representative of this poetic school. A secular priest and confessor of La Rioja, he was closely associated with the important monasteries of San Millán de la Cogolla and Santo Domingo de Silos. His works deal exclusively with religious subjects: lives of saints, theology, the Virgin Mary. His *Milagros de Nuestra Señora* (Miracles of Our Lady), for example, consist of 25 brief stories, each telling of a miracle wrought by the Virgin's intercession. These stories are almost all adapted from standard Lat. sources common to most of medieval Europe.

Berceo's poetic achievement was to popularize and humanize these legends by retelling them in Castilian, the local lang. of the people. His style is simple and clear to the point of being almost prosaic, but his attitude of childlike faith and his rustic images are often charming and occasionally quite lyrical. A spirit of Christian egalitarianism and a sense of humor contributed to a 20th-c. revival of Berceo's popularity as a poet.

Somewhat different, though of the same metric genre and period (the first half of the 13th c.), is the *Libro de Alexandre,* doubtfully attributed to a Leonese cleric, Juan Lorenzo "Segura" de Astorga. Following Lat. and Fr. sources, it reveals Alexander the Great in the medieval guise of a legendary hero. It is encyclopedic in scope, combining Cl. reminiscences, exotic fantasies, mythology, evocations of the springtime garden of love, and moral didacticism. It is definitely more sophisticated than Berceo's works, and more formally polished in style. Other poems of this school are the *Libro de Apolonio,* the *Poema de Yusuf* (the story of Joseph based on the Koran rather than on the Old Testament and written in Ar. rather than Lat.), and the *Vida de Santa María Egipcíaca.*

IV. POETRY OF THE 14TH CENTURY. It is significant that Spain's greatest medieval poet lived south of the Guadarrama Mountains, that is, not in the more soberly European Old Castile of Burgos and the Cid but in the Mozarabic New Castile of Toledo. Juan Ruiz (ca. 1283–1350), probably born in Alcalé de Henares, no doubt studied at the episcopal seminary of Toledo; here the archbishop, primate of Spain, maintained a strongly clerical center of studies in the midst of a peculiarly Sp. goliardic (q.v.) atmosphere of taverns and Moorish dancing girls. Though ordained and made Archpriest of Hita, Juan Ruiz conveys in his poetry this Mozarabic atmosphere as he assimilates to it his readings in the Med. Lat. lit. of Europe, ranging from the Bible and the Breviary to preachers' moral fables and aphorisms to goliardic love songs and Ovid's erotic poems.

Though his great poem, the *Libro de buen amor* (The Book of Good Love), is written chiefly in the same *cuaderna vía* stanzas that Berceo had used in the previous century, it really belongs to a different genre altogether. It is, in fact, *sui generis* so far as European lit. is concerned; its peculiar autobiographical and didactic form has been related by María Rosa Lida to the Semitic *maqamat,* a genre cultivated by various Hispano-Hebraic authors preceding Juan Ruiz. In a general way its picaresque tone and content might remind the Eng. reader most of the contemporary Chaucerian *Wife of Bath's Tale.* Its essentially equivocal nature allows the author to play constantly between poles which are usually considered to be mutually exclusive: personal experiences and adaptations from Lat. sources, moral didacticism and irrepressible humor, ascetic fervor and erotic fever. The author seems simultaneously to be a priest and a sidewalk *jongleur.*

When one analyzes more literally the objective content of the *Libro de buen amor,* one can distinguish from the basic plot, which is a series of erotic adventures told in the first person, several elements which are more or less loosely attached: moral fables, adaptations of Ovid's *Ars amandi* and of the 12th-c. Lat. comedy *Pamphilus,* burlesque allegories associated with Lent and Easter, assorted satires, and a few lyric poems, mostly devoted to the Virgin. The work is, in sum, Spain's poetic synthesis of Gothic culture, a crudely human comedy worthy of comparison with Dante's refined divine one, full of the joy and pathos of life under the shadow of death, and permeated by a deeply ironic humor and childlike sense of playfulness.

There is only one poem worthy of note in the second half of the 14th c.: The *Rimado de palacio* by the solemn Basque Chancellor Pero López de Ayala (1332–1407). This "palace rhyme" is primarily political in its emphasis; it is austerely, severely moralistic as it fiercely satirizes contemporary decadence of church and state.

V. THE REIGN OF JUAN II. Lyric poetry as an independent genre developed much later in Castilian than in Galician-Portuguese or Catalan, the western and eastern languages of the peninsula. Early Catalan poetry (q.v.) is, in fact, part of the history of the troubadour (q.v.) lyric, the linguistic difference between Occitan and Catalan being relatively slight. In the west, lyric poetry written in the Galician-Portuguese dialect included both the *cantigas de amigo,* related to the folk poetry in the early Mozarabic *kharjas,* and more sophisticated love poems stemming from the direct influence of the Occitan troubadours. Thus the cult of courtly love (q.v.) entered Sp. lit.; even poets who spoke Castilian as their native dialect used Galician for writing lyric poetry during the 13th and most of the 14th cs. The scholarly Alfonso X of Castile (1221–84) wrote his 430 *Cantigas de Santa María* in Galician, evincing a wide range of metrical virtuosity *à la provençale.* But between 1350 and 1450 the center of Sp. lyric poetry shifts from Galician to Castilian; the first collection of Castilian lyrics, the *Cancionero de Baena,* is dated 1445. In this collection the troubadour style predominates, but the allegorical and philosophical influence of It. poetry, particularly Dante, is also apparent.

The two major prehumanistic poets of Juan II's reign are Íñigo López de Mendoza, first Marquis of Santillana (1398–1458), and Juan de Mena. Santillana was a leading figure of the northern Castilian nobility, involved militarily in the civil wars of Juan II's reign. His youthful lyrics include witty *dezires,* courtly *canciones,* and pseudo-rustic *serranillas* (*pastourelles*); the latter, based on the encounter of traveling knight with mountain lass, are delightfully sophisticated variations of a popular genre. More ambitious is his *Comedieta de Ponça* (1436), an elaborate allegorical narrative in the

It. trad. An interesting product of Santillana's final 20 years are 42 sonnets, the first to be written in any lang. other than It.; they reveal the influence of the "dolce stil nuovo" (q.v.) and of Petrarch. A final category of poetry includes mature works treating of moral, political, and religious themes; typical is *Bias contra Fortuna* (ca. 1450), in which the semilegendary philosopher-statesman of ancient Greece engages in Stoic debate with an arbitrary and tyrannical Fortune.

Juan de Mena (1411–56), born in Cordova the son of a leading family of converts from Judaism, is the typically scholarly humanist of southern Spain; he studied at the University of Salamanca and at Rome and was named Lat. Secretary at the court of Juan II. His poetry is of two types: troubadour love poetry as it had developed in Spain, marked by scholastic "wit," psychological subtleties, and a strong tendency to use pseudoreligious hyperbole; and politico-moral poetry such as *La coronación*, a difficult allegory in which literary personages are presented as though either in Hell or in Paradise, with the Marquis of Santillana crowned as perfect knight in both arms and letters. Mena's most ambitious poem is the *Laberinto de Fortuna*, consisting of almost 300 *arte mayor* (q.v.) stanzas. In it the poet visits the crystal palace of Fortune; allegorical wheels and planetary circles lead to the culminating vision of Jupiter and Saturn, representing Juan II and his minister Don Álvaro de Luna, prophesying the achievement of national unity. His rhet. grandiloquence, Latinized vocabulary, aesthetic use of Cl. allusion, and emphatic nationalism make of Juan de Mena the most significant herald of the Ren. in 15th-c. Sp. p.

One other poem of this period deserves special mention: the *Coplas por la muerte de su padre* of Jorge Manrique. This elegy for the death of his father is one of the most perfectly controlled poems in Sp. lit.; its classical flow of simple lang. makes it a perennial favorite of the Sp.-speaking world. Its themes are late medieval commonplaces: the transience of earthly life (the "Ubi sunt" theme) and a compensating Christian faith in eternal life. But at the hands of Jorge Manrique they receive a molding of verbal expression that is inimitable:

> ... how swiftly pleasure leaves us; how,
> when we recall it, it grieves us; how, in
> our opinion, any time past was better
> than now.

VI. THE REIGN OF FERDINAND AND ISABELLA. With the marriage of Ferdinand of Aragon and Isabella of Castile, the political unity of the peninsula (except for Portugal) was achieved; religious unity was achieved in 1492 by the expulsion of all unconverted Jews and by the capture of Granada, the sole remaining Moslem kingdom on Sp. soil. The Middle Ages were receding; in art and in education the It. Ren. was clearly arriving. But in poetry it was still a transitional period. The His-

panized troubadour lyric continued without great change. Religious poetry took on a more sentimental coloration in the works of the popular Franciscan poets Íñigo de Mendoza and Ambrosio Montesino. The most important devel. was a new interest on the part of literate poets in the folk trad.; *villancicos* (refrain-carols) and *romances* (ballads) were now collected, elaborated upon, and published. All of the above elements may be observed in the great folio *Cancionero general*, first published by Hernando del Castillo in 1511 and revised several times during the 16th c. This late medieval corpus of poetry continued to exert an influence upon Ren. poets of succeeding generations, even into the 17th c.

The ballads or *romances* (q.v.) are especially interesting and important in the history of Sp. lit. The semilyrical fragments deriving from national epics such as the *Poema del Cid* maintained an epic meter: 16-syllable lines divided into 8-syllable hemistichs with continuous assonance at the ends of the lines. (In modern editions the hemistichs are usually printed as complete octosyllabic lines, and the assonance thus appears only at the ends of the even-numbered lines.) Similar ballads grew out of Carolingian, Arthurian, Moorish, and other romantic or popular stories. They were published first in small groups as broadsides; these were gradually collected and reprinted as small volumes; finally, in 1600, a voluminous *Romancero general* was published. Famous Golden Age plays were based upon the more popular cycles; everyone seems to have been familiar with the *romances*, for they were constantly cited and alluded to. The ballad (q.v.) genre has been familiar to every generation, from the Golden Age to the romantics and the neopopularists of Lorca's generation; and the oral trad. has lived on into the 20th c. among the more isolated communities of Spain, the Sephardic Balkans and North Africa, and Sp. America.

VII. RENAISSANCE POETRY (16TH CENTURY). In 1526, at the court of Charles V in Granada, the Venetian ambassador Andrea Navagero suggested to the courtier-poet Juan Boscán (ca. 1490–1542) that he try his hand at writing sonnets and other It. forms in Sp. With the encouragement and collaboration of his friend Garcilaso de la Vega (1503–36), Boscán's experiment was successful; a new type of poetry eventually took root in Spain, marking a distinct shift in poetic sensibility. The success of this revolution was due largely to the superior aesthetic gifts of Garcilaso, who not only assimilated It. metric forms (the hendecasyllabic line in sonnets, *canzoni, terza rima, ottava rima, rima al mezzo,* and blank verse), but also captured an essential part of the It. Ren. spirit in his poetry: a sensuous, metaphoric flow of bucolic, erotic, and mythological themes expressing a new sense of beauty in grief and in idealized Cl. scenes and landscapes. Despite his many stylistic debts to Virgil and Sannazaro, to Petrarch and Ovid, Garcilaso's Sp. p. (he also wrote Lat. odes) strikes a new note which belongs to him alone.

> Near the Tagus River in sweet solitude
> there is a thicket of green willows
> all covered over and filled with ivy
> which climbs the trunk to the top
> and so weaves and enchains it up there
> that the sun cannot penetrate the ver-
>   dure;
> the water bathes the greensward with
>   sound,
> making joyful the grass and the human
>   ear.

The poetry of Boscán and Garcilaso was published posthumously in a single volume in 1543 and was republished many times during the 16th c. Garcilaso's poetry was first published separately in 1570; it was treated as a humanistic classic by being annotated by a professor at the University of Salamanca in 1574 and by the scholar-poet Fernando de Herrera of Seville in 1580. Thus Garcilaso's 35 sonnets, five odes, two elegies, one epistle, and three eclogues became the foundation of a Ren. trad. of poetry in Spain. Very little poetry has been written in Sp. since the 16th c. that has not been influenced to some extent by that of Garcilaso de la Vega. We could list innumerable 16th-c. poets belonging to Garcilaso's new school: Diego Hurtado de Mendoza (1503–75), Hernando de Acuña (1520?–80), Baltasar del Alcázar (1590–1606), Francisco de Figueroa (1536–1617?), Francisco de Aldana (1537–78), Gutierre de Cetina (1520–57?), et al. There was a more or less serious movement of nationalistic resistance against the new It. meters, headed by Cristóbal de Castillejo (1490?–1550); even his own poetry, however, while avoiding the new meters, frequently reflects the Ren. spirit much more than it does the spirit of the Sp. 15th c.

Christianity and the Ren. join forces in the poetry of the Augustinian friar Luis de León (1527–91) and of the reformed Carmelite monk San Juan de la Cruz (1542–91). Luis de León was a biblical scholar and professor at the University of Salamanca. In his vigorously classical odes he manages to fuse the satirical rusticity of Horace with a soaring Neoplatonic Christianity which at times approaches true mysticism. Because of its explicit philosophical content, his poetry often receives more serious attention than does that of Garcilaso; it seems to reconcile the Greco-Roman and the Hebraic-Christian trads. and certainly reaches more than once the heights of truly great Cl. poetry. Much more ethereally mystical is the even smaller body of lyrics by San Juan de la Cruz. His major poem, the *Cántico espiritual*, draws directly upon the Song of Solomon and indirectly upon Garcilaso's eclogues; the resultant imagery, tremulously sensual, lends itself to an extended allegory of the soul's mystic love for God. Nowhere else in Western poetry is erotic intensity so essen-

tial to the expression of an overwhelming religious experience; St. John of the Cross is without doubt one of the few great mystic poets. Just after a climactic moment, he writes these lines:

> I stayed there forgetting myself,
> I leaned my face over the Beloved;
> everything stopped and I let myself go,
> leaving my cares
> forgotten among the lilies.

At the same time, on a lower plane, poets continue to use the traditional Sp. meters, esp. the octosyllable (q.v.). Scholastic wit of a 15th-c. sort is revived for religious purposes in the *Conceptos espirituales* (1600) of Alonso de Ledesma (1562–1623).

The most serious attempt to continue Garcilaso's trad. was that of his annotator Fernando de Herrera (1534–97), the central figure of a school of poets developing in Andalusia, principally in Seville. His voluminous notes to Garcilaso's works are, in fact, a poetic manifesto of a Neoplatonic sort. Herrera declares that erudition is necessary for great poetry, that the Sp. lang. is as richly expressive as the It., and that the poetic genius expresses divine reality. His Cl. learning is inexhaustible; in his notes he writes veritable histories of the poetic genres and uses a large Gr. vocabulary in making rhetorical analyses. Thus his *Anotaciones* (1580) are a major contribution to Ren. poetics (q.v.), second in Spain only to the Aristotelian *Filosofía antigua poética* (1596) of A. López Pinciano.

Having taken minor orders, Herrera devoted his entire life to scholarship and poetry. He wrote several heroic odes or hymns on national themes; their grandiloquent echoes of the Old Testament define Herrera's organ voice. But the social center of his life was the literary *tertulia*, or salon, of the Count and Countess of Gelves; here Herrera found it natural to focus his poetry, in the manner of Petrarch, upon the lovely young countess. These sonnets, odes, and elegies, in which he exquisitely suffers and delights, reflect primarily a literary experience within an aristocratic, scholarly setting; they won for him among his contemporaries the title of "the Divine," when in 1582, a year after the countess's death, he published them with the modest title of *Algunas obras de Fernando de Herrera*. Other members of this Andalusian school of poets are Luis Barahona de Soto (1548–95), Pedro de Espinosa (1578–1650), Francisco de Rioja (1583–1659), and Francisco de Medrano (1570–1607).

Mention should here be made of Ren. epic poetry. Spain has nothing to compare with Portugal's *Lusiadas* (1572), but the epic of the conquest of Chile, *La Araucana* (1569–90) by Alonso de Ercilla (1533–96?), can still be read with interest and pleasure. Worthy of note is the literary treatment of the Indian chieftain Caupolicán as a "noble savage."

VIII. BAROQUE POETRY (17TH CENTURY). From

among the dozens of considerable poets of 17th-c. Spain, we can select for special attention the three who are generally considered greatest: Luis de Góngora (1561–1627), Lope de Vega (1562–1635), and Francisco de Quevedo (1580–1645). Among them they represent the main trends of Sp. lyric poetry during the second half of the Golden Age. Góngora, like Juan de Mena, was born in Cordova and, like Herrera, took minor orders entitling him to an ecclesiastical benefice; in Cl. erudition and aristocratic intellect he was second to neither of his Andalusian predecessors, rivaling Garcilaso himself as a major creative figure of Sp. p. In a sense he continues and elaborates upon Garcilaso's trad., carrying each of his stylistic traits to its ultimate poetic consequences, achieving an aesthetic purity almost devoid of any quotidian human emotion deriving from such common themes as love, religion, or politics.

Like Lope and Quevedo, Góngora cultivated poetry not only of the Ren. trad. in Italianate meters, but also of the more med. folkloric trad. in octosyllables and other short lines. His *romances* and *villancicos* (or *letrillas*) show a thorough familiarity with the more popular themes and meters; Góngora characteristically polishes and elaborates upon them, however, in such a way that we could never mistake his exquisite poems for those of the anonymous trad. His burlesque and satirical poems are equally polished. And his sonnets achieve a final formal perfection, whether heroic, funereal, erotic, or burlesque in theme. His most ambitious Cl. poems are quite difficult to read, both because of their unusual syntax and because of the intellectual complexity of their metaphors, conceits, and mythological allusions. His masterpieces in this style are baroque pastorals: the *Fábula de Polifemo y Galatea,* based on Ovid's Polyphemus, and the *Soledades,* the plot of which is more original, though hardly a line is without Cl. allusions. This style of his, traditionally labeled *culteranismo* (q.v.) or *cultismo,* though widely imitated in Spain and Sp. America, has never been surpassed:

> Sicily in its mountains never armed a beast with such ferocity nor shod it with such wind that it might either fiercely or swiftly save its many-colored skin: it is already a jacket, that former mortal terror of the woods, for him who with slow step brought back the oxen to his shelter, treading the doubtful light of day [i.e. twilight].

The world of Góngora's major poems is a material world of solid substances and glittering colors in which the poet, using words, attempts to rival the artificiality of nature, of *Natura Artifex,* herself. It is no accident that a taste for this poetry has been revived in the 20th c. by Spain's most sophisticated modern poets (SEE NEOGONGORISM).

Lope de Vega, the creator of Spain's lyrical Golden Age theater, was also a very productive poet; his sonnets alone number 1600 or more. He also wrote many long narrative poems, of which his Tassoesque *Jerusalén conquistada* is perhaps the most noteworthy. Between 1604 and 1637 five important collections of his lyric poems were published; they are not so polished as those of Góngora, but they are full of variety, spontaneity, and flowing grace. His odes, eclogues, elegies, and sonnets belong to Garcilaso's Cl. trad., with light baroque elaborations of all sorts; he occasionally attempts to rival even Góngora. His poems actually do surpass Góngora's in personal emotion, if not in erudition and technical skill. At the other pole, Lope's folkloric lyrics are unexcelled; unlike Góngora's, they are often indistinguishable from those of the anonymous trad. And his ability to fuse these two trads., the learned and the popular, is similarly unsurpassed. No other poet could compete with Lope de Vega's facile abundance; he was indeed a veritable phenomenon, "Nature's monster."

Finally, Francisco de Quevedo, though his poetry too is extremely various, represents chiefly a severe moralistic trend, an awareness of universal human corruption, in Spain's baroque poetry. An incisive satirical wit characterizes most of Quevedo's poetry, which at times is quite obscene; his colloquial puns and other witticisms are often very funny in a grim sort of way. His profoundest lyrical note is struck when he faces death with Stoic desperation:

> Now fearfully within the heart
> resounds the final day;
> and the last hour, black and cold,
> draws near, filled with terrible shad-
> ows. . . .

The literary power of Quevedo's love poetry has been rediscovered in recent years. To the worn courtly and Petrarchan conventions he added a new dimension of existential anguish deriving from his awareness of time and death, epitomized in his masterpiece, a sonnet entitled "Love Constant Beyond Death":

> My eyes may be closed by the final
> shadow which will take away from me
> the bright day, and this soul of mine
> may be freed by an hour indulgent to
> its anxious longing; but it will not, on
> the further shore, leave the memory in
> which it used to burn; my flame is able
> to swim across the cold water and dis-
> obey a harsh law. A soul which has
> been imprisoned by no less than a god,
> the veins which have supplied the
> moisture to so great a fire, the marrow
> which has gloriously burned: it will
> leave its body, not its [loving] anguish;
> they will be ash, but it will have feel-
> ings; they will be dust, but dust which
> is in love.

The element of fire (love, suffering, life) engages in a desperate battle for survival against water (extinction, oblivion, death); despite all evidence the poet-lover asserts the invincibility of his passionate will, even when buried in the element of earth (ashes, dust, the dead body). The octet affirms in general terms what the sestet repeats in psychological and physiological detail, ending emphatically with the word "enamorado." This sonnet belongs to a cycle of 64 sonnets dedicated "A Lisi," a high point in the neo-Petrarchan trad. of Sp. love poetry.

It is traditional, though inaccurate, to list Spain's 17th-c. poets either as *cultista* followers of Góngora (Jáuregui, Bocángel, Espinosa, Soto de Rojas, Villamediana, Polo de Medina, et al.) or as *conceptistas* like Quevedo (the Argensola brothers, Esquilache, the anonymous author of the *Epistola moral a Fabio*). As a matter of fact, Cl. erudition and mythological allusions, the trademarks of *culteranismo,* were almost universal in 17th-c. poetry; and few poets completely avoided indulging in puns, conceits (qq.v.), and other forms of baroque wit. The question is, with regard to each poet, how he developed an individual style as he made use of the available popular devices. The modern critic can usefully study the poetics of the period: the *Libro de erudición poética* (1611) by L. Carrillo y Sotomayor; the *Discurso poético* (1623) by J. de Jáuregui; and, above all, the *Agudeza y arte de ingenio* (1642), in which the great Jesuit *conceptista* Baltasar Gracián (1601–58) cites Góngora far more than any other poet. Among 17th-c. epic poems, perhaps two are worthy of mention here: *La Christiada* (1611), based on Christ's Passion, by Diego de Hojeda (1571?–1615), and *El Bernardo* (1624), on a national epic hero, by Bernardo de Balbuena (1568–1627).

IX. NEOCLASSICAL POETRY (18TH CENTURY). With the Bourbon dynasty replacing the Hapsburgs in the 18th c., the Fr. neoclassical standards of Ignacio de Luzán's *Poética* (1737) rejected the baroque poetry of Góngora and Quevedo, advocating a return to the cl. "good taste" of Garcilaso. But there seemed to be few new creative poets. Nicolás Fernández de Moratín (1737–80) emphasized moral, social, and political utilitarianism in his verse, while continuing to imitate Cl. models in his metrical experiments. A more personal preromantic note appears in José Cadalso (1741–82), whose *Ocios de mi juventud* is somewhat influenced by Edward Young. Juan Meléndez Valdés (1754–1817) was the best representative of a new enlightened lyricism in which modern science and social utility entered the Platonic universe of cl. poetry, with a special emphasis on music and sensuousness. His poetry had a strong influence on the following generation of N. Alvarez de Cienfuegos (1764–1809) and Manuel José Quintana (1772–1857).

X. ROMANTIC AND POSTROMANTIC POETRY (19TH CENTURY). The romantic movement, like neoclassicism, came into Spain from outside; it was the Germans and the Eng. who helped Spaniards to rediscover and appreciate anew their own *romances* or ballads and Golden Age lyrics. This leads eventually to the publication of the *Romances históricos* (1841), new poems by the Duke of Rivas (1791–1865), in which national legends and atmospheres are nostalgically evoked in colorful pictures. More passionately romantic and lyrical was José de Espronceda (1808–42), an active Byronic personality rife with political and amorous escapades. His *Poesías líricas* (1840) are filled with emotions which are violent, if not profound, and with the sound and rhythm of a renovated poetic lang.; his erotic and libertarian impulses are often colored with a rebellious, nihilistic Satanism. The best example of this is his Don Juanesque *Estudiante de Salamanca,* full of vitality and technical virtuosity. Greatly influenced by Rivas and Espronceda was José Zorrilla (1817–93), whose romantic stage version of the Don Juan story is full of similar poetry and is still played annually. With Zorrilla the romantic movement put roots deep into Sp. history. Zorrilla wrote verse facilely and in tremendous quantities; by the time he died, he had become himself a national monument to romanticism, a 19th-c. Lope de Vega.

The only Sp. poet of the 19th c. whose works can still be read without condescension in the 20th is Gustavo Adolfo Bécquer (1836–70). Bécquer combines the clear ideas and ineffable sentiments of a late romantic Platonism with a mathematical rigor of stanzaic form; his characteristic figure is anaphora (q.v.), emphasizing an inexorable parallelism leading up to a climactic conclusion. Whereas modernist and postmodernist poets scorned as formless sentimentalists or dead rhetoricians other romantic and bourgeois poets of the 19th c., they looked back to Bécquer as a founding father, the first truly modern poet of Spain. His 76 short *Rimas* (1871) are marked by a simplicity and musicality of lang. reminiscent of folksong; their inner dream-world of sentiment is, however, more ethereal, sophisticated, deliberately artistic. A constant theme is the ineffability of love, despair, memories, and all profound emotional values.

> Can it be true that when sleep touches
> our eyes with its rose-colored fingers,
> our spirit flees the prison it inhabits
> and soars away in haste?

Perhaps two non-Castilian poets, writing in dialects revived literarily by romantic regionalists, are remotely comparable in quality to Bécquer: Rosalía de Castro (1837–85), writing in Galician, and Jacinto Verdaguer (1845–1902), writing in Catalan. Rosalía de Castro, along with Bécquer, because of her clear sense of form and feeling, and her metrical experiments, has been one of the few 19th-c. poets to be praised and imitated by modernist and postmodernist poets. More widely read than any of these, however, were two postromantic, solidly bourgeois poets, the prosaic humorist Ramón de Campoamor (1817–1901) and the rhetorical idealist Gaspar Núñez de Arce (1832–1903); with these two, Sp. lyricism reached a nadir from which it was to rise only under the impulse of Ruben Darío's *modernismo* (q.v.).

XI. THE 20TH CENTURY. Ruben Darío (1867–1916) was born in Nicaragua, but his poetic innovations reached every corner of the Sp.-speaking world. His cult of beauty, evinced in his metrical experiments, in his Parnassian sensuousness, and even in his Verlainean religiosity, amounted to a stylistic revolution hardly less important than that of the 16th c. Yet Spain's first great poet in the 20th c. was not a modernist; in fact, Antonio Machado (1875–1939) seems to illustrate, as an Andalusian living in somber Castile, a reaction against all that was showy and external in Darío, a deliberate turning within, a searching for his own unknown God. His style is simple, apparently almost prosaic at times; yet there are always deep inner resonances. Even his landscapes have their true existence, not in the world of geography, but upon the contours of the soul. His most typical symbolic scene is that of a fountain trickling in a deserted square at sunset:

> The embers of a purple twilight
> smoke behind the dark cypress grove.
> In the shadowy arbor is the fountain
> with its winged nude Cupid of stone
> silently dreaming. In the marble basin
> reposes the still water.

His first volume of poems, entitled *Soledades* (1903), was written between 1899 and 1902, a period dominated by the impressive *Prosas profanas* (1896) of Rubén Darío. Anticipating in some ways the latter's *Cantos de vida y esperanza* (1905), Machado in his *Soledades* was less concerned with the direct representation of sound, color, and other physical sensations; he sought a poetry of subtle inner responses to the images of an outer world. In this respect he represents the introspection of the peninsular Generation of 1898, as opposed to the spectacular sensuousness of Rubén Darío's internationally important *modernismo*. More directly related to Darío is the poet of transition who stands between modernism and Lorca's generation, Juan Ramón Jiménez (1881–1958). A perfectionist like Valéry, Jiménez spent his life working on his poetry, stripping it of all nonessentials, seeking forms of expression to reflect as precisely as possible the subtle shadings of his emotional world. In 1956 he received the Nobel Prize both for his own work and, vicariously, for that of two Sp. poets no longer living at that time, Antonio Machado and Federico García Lorca.

Lorca (1899–1936) is the most widely known member of the major constellation of 20th-c Sp. poets who reached maturity during the 1920s. With Alberti (b. 1902) he represents primarily the Andalusian, folkloric tendency: a popular intuitive genius of great lyrical power, fusing in his poetry elements drawn from many currents within the Sp. cultural heritage, ranging from childlike ingenuousness to the sophistication of a Góngora. Lorca's anguished poems on urban dehumanization and the loss of myth make of his *Poeta en Nueva York* (1940) a cultural monument for all Hispanic exiles in the United States. More cosmopolitan and intellectual members of the same group are the Castilians Pedro Salinas (1892–1952) and Jorge Guillén (1893–1985). Salinas was above all a love poet, reducing his whole world to an intense relationship of dialogue between an I and a Thou: "In order to live I have no need / of islands, palaces, towers. / What an immense joy it is / to live in our pronouns!"

Guillén's perfectionism is reminiscent of Juan Ramón Jiménez. He owes something no doubt to Rimbaud and other Fr. poets, but his poetry as contained in *Cántico* (definitive ed., 1950) is his own creation, an attitude of boundless joy and wonder at existence in this world—though in his later years his poetry took on a somewhat more anguished, less exuberant tone. Two other important members of Lorca's generation have continued to write influential poetry in Spain since the Civil War: Dámaso Alonso (b. 1898) and Vicente Aleixandre (1900–85). Aleixandre released the Freudian subconscious in mythic images of love and violence climaxing in *Sombra del paraíso* (1944); he returned to everyday life in *Historia del corazón* (1954). In Franco Spain he encouraged many younger poets with his support. Alonso, Spain's leading philologist and analyst of poetry, initiated a distinctly existentialist movement in Sp. p. with his *Hijos de la ira* (1944), which, with its God-forsaken anguish at human suffering and social injustice, echoes in modern terms certain notes of the Heb. Psalms.

During and after the Civil War, many new poets have found readers in Spain; poetry in fact was less stunted by the Fascist Franco regime than either drama or fiction. One very promising poet, Miguel Hernández (1910–42), died in prison; a country boy with very little formal education, he read Sp. baroque poetry for himself and wrote some highly original verse. He was a link between Lorca's generation, Quevedo's and Neruda's poetry, and the socially committed poets of the Franco era.

Given the large number of good Sp. poets who have been writing since the Civil War, it is convenient to group them in terms of influential magazines, series of editions, and anthologies. A relatively conservative group of poets who had participated actively in the Civil War published in the postwar review *Escorial*: Luis Felipe Vivanco (b. 1907), Leopoldo Panero (b. 1909), Luis Rosales (b. 1910), Dionisio Ridruejo (b. 1912). The younger poets tended to gravitate toward two poles. The more neoclassical and orthodox ones, following the lead of the *Escorial* poets, incl. José García Nicto (b. 1914), Rafael Morales (b. 1919),

José María Valverde (b. 1926), and others, entitled their review *Garcilaso* A more baroquely existentialist group looked rather to Quevedo and *Hijos de la ira* for guidance, gravitating around the review *Espadaña*: Gabriel Celaya (b. 1911), Blas de Otero (b. 1916), Leopoldo de Luis (b. 1918), Vicente Gaos (b. 1919), Carlos Bousoño (b. 1923), Eugenio de Nora (1923). In the younger generation as a whole there is a definite reaction against the aestheticism of Juan Ramón Jiménez and the Lorca generation; their poetry is often directly concerned with questions of social justice.

In 1943, José Luis Cano (b. 1912), himself a poet, established the Adonais series of monthly poets, with annual prizes and occasional anthols. (1953, 1962); for 20 years this was the major center for current Sp. p. More recently, other series, esp. Visor editions, have become more important. Critical moments in the history of postwar Sp. p. were marked by the publication of certain anthols., particularly the one based on a survey by Ribes (1952), three controversial collections edited by Castellet (1962, 1966, 1970), and those of Batlló (1968, 1974), José Olivio Jiménez (1972), and Jiménez Martos (1972). Buenaventura's anthol. of Sp. women poets appeared in 1985.

The Andalusian Luis Rosales, who had published a collection of sonnets (*Abril*, 1935) before the Civil War, created a highly personal love poetry in *La casa encendida* (1949), combining lyric and narrative modes with free verse, colloquial lang., and surrealist images. A voice fully representative of an antithetic poetry of social anguish and realism was that of the prolific Basque Gabriel Celaya (born Rafael Múgica), bursting with indignation and disgust in *Tranquilamente hablando* (1947) and *Las cosas como son* (1949). Blas de Otero (1916–79) moved from religious anguish in the trad. of Unamuno and Alonso toward a similar social and political poetry in *Pido la paz y la palabra* (1955), a veritable Sp. Communist Manifesto in moving verse. Carlos Bousoño, a distinguished literary critic who worked with Alonso and analyzed Aleixandre's poetry in his doctoral dissertation, began as a poet with *Subida al amor* (1945) and has remained faithful to a metaphysical ideal. José María Valverde, on the other hand, moved from neoclassical and religious to socially committed poetry with *La conquista de este mundo* (1960) and *Años inciertos* (1961).

Major poets who began to publish somewhat later, in the 1950s, incl. Gloria Fuertes (1918–81), Ángel González (b. 1925), Carlos Barral (b. 1928), Jaime Gil de Biedma (b. 1929), José Ángel Valente (b. 1929), Francisco Brines (b. 1932), and Claudio Rodríguez (b. 1934). Among these there was for over 20 years a strong cosmopolitan group centered in Barcelona and writing in Castilian, with the support of the critic Castellet and important publishers. Carlos Barral with his *Metropolitano* (1957) and Jaime Gil de Biedma with *Moralidades* (1966) were perhaps the most representative and important members of this group. Ángel González, from Oviedo, cultivated an ironic detachment culminating in *Procedimientos narrativos* (1972). Brines, from Valencia, published in 1984 a retrospective collection of his own work entitled *Ensayo de una despedida (1960-1977)*, in which meditation on everyday scenes leads to impassioned imagery.

The following constitute a later and even more heterogeneous group: Félix Grande (b. 1937), Carlos Sahagún (b. 1938), Pedro Gimferrer (b. 1945), Antonio Colinas (b. 1946), Guillermo Carnero (b. 1947), Antonio de Villena (b. 1951). Gimferrer, a bilingual Catalan-Castilian poet and critic, achieved a notable and influential success in Castilian with his *Arde el mar* (1966), reflecting his absorption of readings from Lorca to Eliot. Carnero, from Valencia, writes only in Castilian; he has moved from baroque imagery to an exemplary sober discipline in *El azar objetivo* (1975).

A 15-year gap, 1961–76, divides the poetic oeuvre of María Victoria Atencia (Málaga) into two parts. In his prologue to her *Ex libris* (1984) Carnero has testified to the literary maturity of her second period, beginning with *Marta & María* (1976). In the new post-Franco Spain, the poetic voices of women, long absent, are beginning to be heard.

See now BASQUE POETRY; CATALAN POETRY; CHICANO POETRY; GALICIAN POETRY; HEBREW POETRY; HISPANO-ARABIC POETRY; PORTUGUESE POETRY; ROMANTIC AND POSTROMANTIC POETICS; SPANISH AMERICAN POETRY; SPANISH PROSODY; TWENTIETH-CENTURY POETICS, *Spanish*.

ANTHOLOGIES: *Contemp. Sp. P.* (1945), *Ten Centuries of Sp. P.* (1955), both ed. E. L. Turnbull; *The Heroic Poem of the Sp. Golden Age*, ed. F. Pierce (1947); *Antologia de la poesía lírica española*, ed. E. Moreno Báez (1952); *Antología consultada de la joven poesía española*, ed. F. Ribes (1952); *Sp. Lyrics of the Golden Age*, ed. P. D. Tettenborn (1952); *Penguin Book of Sp. Verse*, ed. J. M. Cohen (1956); *Floresta lírica española*, ed. J. M. Blecua (1957); *Poesía española*, ed. D. Marín (1958); *Veinte años de poesía española (1939–1959)* (1962), *Un cuarto de siglo de poesía española (1939–1964)* (1966), *Nueve novísimos* (1970), all ed. J. M. Castellet; *Ren. and Baroque Poetry of Spain*, ed. E. L. Rivers (1964); *Antología de la nueva poesía española* (1968), *Poetas españoles poscontemporáneos* (1974), ed. J. Batlló; *Diez años de poesía española (1960–1970)*, ed. J. O. Jiménez (1972); *La generación poética de 1936*, ed. L. Jiménez Martos (1972); *Textos medievales españoles*, ed. R. Menéndez-Pidal (1976); *Antología de la poesía española (1900–1980)*, ed. G. Correa (1980); *Las diosas blancas: antología de la joven poesía española escrita por mujeres*, ed. R. Buenaventura (1985).

HISTORY AND CRITICISM: A. Coster, *Fernando de Herrera* (1908); H. A. Rennert and A. Castro, *Vida de Lope de Vega* (1919); A. F. G. Bell, *Luis de León* (1925); J. Cano, *La poética de Luzán* (1928); K.

SPANISH PROSODY

Vossler, *Lope de Vega und seine Zeit* (1930); J. Baruzi, *St. Jean de la Croix* (1930); A. Valbuena Prat, *La poesía española contemporánea* (1930); E. Joiner Gates, *The Metaphors of Luis de Góngora* (1933); F. Lecoy, *Recherches sur le Libro de buen amor* (1938); R. Menéndez Pidal, *La España del Cid* (1939), *Le epopeya castellana a través de la literatura española* (1946), *Los orígenes de las literaturas románicas* (1951); E. A. Peers, *A Hist. of the Romantic Movement in Spain* (1940); W. E. Colford, *Juan Meléndez Valdéss* (1942); A. del Río, *Pedro Salinas* (1942); J. Guillén, "La poética de Bécquer," *Revista Hispanica Moderna* 8 (1942); E. Honig, *García Lorca* (1944); M. Menéndez y Pelayo, *Antología de poetas líricos castellanos* (1945); J. Casalduero, *Jorge Guillén: Cántico* (1946); P. Salinas, *Jorge Manrique, o tradición y originalidad* (1947); G. Díaz-Plaja, *Historia de la poesía lírica española* (1948); R. Lapesa, *La trayectoria poética de Garcilaso* (1948); M. R. Lida de Malkiel, *Juan de Mena, poeta del prerrenacimiento español* (1950), *Two Sp. Masterpieces: The Book of Good Love and The Celestina* (1961); G. Brenan, *Lit. of the Sp. People* (1951); D. Alonso, *Poesía española* (1952), *Poetas españoles contemporáneos* (1952), *Estudios y ensayos gongorinos* (1955), *De los siglos oscuros al de oro* (1958); A. Castro, *La realidad histórica esp.* (1954); F. Cantera, *La canción mozárabe* (1957); E. Asensio, *Poética y realidad en el cancionero peninsular de la edad media* (1957); R. Lapesa, *La obra literaria del marqués de Santillana* (1957); C. D. Ley, *Sp. P. Since 1939* (1962); O. H. Green, *Spain and the Western Trad.* (1963–); J. E. Keller, "Med. Sp. Lit.," in Fisher; J. Lechner, *El compromiso en la poesía española del siglo XX*, 2 v. (1968–75); F. Grande, *Apuntes sobre poesía española de posguerra* (1970); V. García de la Concha, *La poesía española de posguerra* (1973); J. L. Cano, *Lírica española de hoy* (1974); F. Rubio, *Las revistas poéticas españolas (1939–1975)* (1976); M. E. Simmons, "The Sp. Epic," *Heroic Epic and Saga*, ed. F. J. Oinas (1978); *Historia y crítica de la literatura española*, ed. F. Rico, 8 v. (1980); A. L. Geist, *La poética de la generación del 27* (1980); A. Carreño, *La dialéctica de la identidad* (1982); A. P. Debicki, *Poetry of Discovery* (1982); S. Daydí-Tolson, *The Post-Civil War Sp. Social Poets* (1983); Navarro; M. H. Persin, *Recent Sp. P. and the Role of the Reader* (1987); *After the War*, ed. J. Wilcox (1988). E.L.R.

SPANISH PROSODY. Until the advent of free verse (q.v.), and aside from time-measured song form (*verso lírico medieval*) and the chanted epic verse (*verso épico, mester de juglaría*), Sp. verse measure was based on syllable count, involving the principles of hiatus, synaloepha, synaeresis, and dieresis (see METRICAL TREATMENT OF SYLLABLES). Syllables per line are counted to the last stressed syllable, plus one count. In the earliest period, hiatus was obligatory in syllable counting, but by the late 14th c., synaloepha in court poetry prevailed. Hemistichs are metrically independent

(see KHARJA).

One of the earliest and most lasting of Sp. verseforms is the octosyllable (q.v.) or *romance* (q.v.—Sp. ballad) meter. The earliest strophe is probably the couplet (*pareado*—see SEXTILLA). Medieval two-part verse of the *mester de juglaría* (minstrel verse) dating from or before the 12th c. is the earliest known long-form measure, found primarily in the *cantar de gesta* (popular epic—see CANTAR). The hemistichal lines vary in length from about 10 to 20 syllables. The more sophisticated *mester de clerecía* (clerical verse) poems composed in *cuaderna vía* (q.v.) stanzas, whose 7 + 7-syllable *alejandrino* lines were probably in imitation of the Fr. alexandrine (q.v.), date from ca. 1200 (see COPLA; SERRANILLA, ZEJEL). The all-purpose *copla de arte menor*, a stanza of any moderate length in octosyllabic or shorter verse, and its variation, the *copla de pie quebrado* (see COPLA), became popular. In verse, the favored long lines, all with caesuras creating metrically independent hemistichs, were 12, 14, or 16 syllables in length, each with its optional *quebrado*.

While these forms, along with other less prominent strophic arrangements (e.g. *villancico* [q.v.]), were being developed for both didactic purpose and popular entertainment, the courtly and learned poets of the 14th and 15th cs. were often composing in Galician-Portuguese, which had been used in the 13th c. by King Alfonso X, e.g. in his *Cantigas de Santa María*, and was still lingering in the early 15th c., when most poets were favoring Castilian. The couplet (*pareado, pareja*), the tercet (*terceto*) in any rhyme scheme, various types of *eco* (see ECHO), and some experimental forms are found. Poetic license was tolerated, e.g. accent shift in a word, syncope, haplology, disregard of the penult of a proparoxytone, and acoustic equivalence for true rhyme (see ARTE MAYOR, ARTE MENOR, COPLA, DECIMA, ENDECHA, ESTRIBILLO, FINIDA, GAITA GALLEGA, GLOSA, LETRILLA, MOTE, PREGUNTA, REFRAN, REMATE).

The 16th and 17th cs. in Spain, a period of perfecting the old and borrowing or creating the new, firmly established Italianate verse and stanza forms. The *sáfico* (see SAPPHIC) soon appeared. Old forms were regularized (e.g. the *alejandrino*, the *seguidilla*). The *pentasílabo* (pentasyllable) served occasionally as hemistich of the hendecasyllable and was also used with the *adónico* (pentasyllabic paroxytonic verse) to form the *sáfico adónico* strophe (three *sáficos* plus one *adónico*), a.k.a. *oda sáfica*. Italianate importations incl. the *soneto, terza rima* (q.v.), *octava rima* or *heroico* or *real* octave (see OTTAVA RIMA), *verso suelto* (unrhymed verse, usually hendecasyllabic, sometimes combined with 7- or 5-syllable verse—cf. VERSI SCIOLTI). The hendecasyllabic *romance heroico* (or *endecasílabo* or *real*), the *lira* (q.v.) variations, and the *silva* (q.v.) are among the new. The *redondilla, quintilla*, and *seguidilla* (qq.v.), and their relatives became popular, as did irregular meters and such minor stanza forms as the *ensalada, espinela,* and *folía* (qq.v.).

Publication of Luzán's *Poética* (1737) coincides approximately with the beginning of Sp. neoclassicism, when poets resurrected, restored, and regularized the old and borrowed (mainly from Fr.) or created new variations on old verse- and stanza forms. Experimentation was common. From the *alejandrino* and *verso de arte mayor* to the *trisílabo* (3-syllable verse), every verse length, often with set rhythmic pattern, can be found. Decasyllabic patterns included (1) ‿ ‿ − ‿ ‿ − ‿ ‿ − (‿), (2) − ‿ ‿ − ‿ | − ‿ ‿ − (‿), (3) ‿ − ‿ − ‿ | ‿ − ‿ ‿ − (‿), (4) the double adonic (*adónico doblado* or *asclepiadeo*), and (5) the *libre,* without fixed pattern. The 9-syllable line includes the *eneasílabo iriartino* (predominantly ‿ ‿ − ‿ ‿ − ‿ − [‿]), the *esproncedaico* (‿ − ‿ ‿ − ‿ ‿ − [‿]), the *eneasílabo de canción* (‿ ‿ ‿ − ‿ ‿ − [‿]), the *eneasílabo laverdaico* or *brachycatalecto* (‿ − ‿ ‿ ‿ − ‿ − [‿]), and the *eneasílabo libre* or *polirrítmico* (no set pattern). Occasionally an octosyllabic poem has stress consistently on the third syllable, simulating *pie quebrado.* A fixed rhythm, esp. iambic, sometimes appears in heptasyllabic compositions; the *hexasílabo,* usually with fluctuating inner stress patterns, is occasionally trochaic. The seldom independent pentasyllabic *adónico,* generally in combination with the hendecasyllabic *sáfico,* may have fluctuating inner stress.

Romantic nostalgia is reflected in the use of the *verso de arte mayor,* the *alejandrino,* and their *quebrados* but did not slow the process of innovation: the *alcaico* (5 + 5 syllable line), the 9-syllable *laverdaico,* and the anapestic 13-syllable were added to the repertory. Within a poem random assonance could replace true rhyme, and rhythm-mixing served a purpose. Essentially *ad hoc* strophes were common; free verse was in the offing. In the modern period, poets continued reaching for the new while clinging to the old, further loosening the rules without releasing them completely. The major advance was the full acceptance of *verso libre,* a natural outgrowth of centuries of change. Metric structure no longer dominates or restricts verse but serves it flexibly as the background instrumental accompaniment to the words. See also CATALAN POETRY; GALICIAN POETRY; SPANISH POETRY.

J. Vicuña Cifuentes, *Estudios de métrica española* (1929); P. Henríquez Ureña, *Versificación irregular en la poesía castellana,* 2d ed. (1933); D. C. Clarke, *Una bibliografía de versificación española* (1937), *Chronological Sketch of Castilian Versification* (1952); E. Díez Echarri, *Teorías métricas del siglo de oro* (1949); Navarro; J. Domínguez Caparrós, *Diccionario de métrica española* (1985); A. Quilis, *Métrica española,* 3d ed. (1986). D.C.C.

SPASMODIC SCHOOL. A derisive term first applied in 1853 by Kingsley and more strikingly in 1854 by Aytoun to a group of neoromantic poets then popular. Influenced by Goethe's *Faust,* Byron, and Shelley, they produced long, formless works, usually modern in subject matter, in which the hero, often himself a morbidly self-conscious poet, mingles cosmic yearnings for human betterment with dubious practical morality. A profusion of images was their hallmark. They were made ridiculous by Aytoun's parody, *Firmilian: A S. Tragedy,* whose hero, yearning "to paint the mental spasms that tortured Cain," realizes that in order to feel Cain's remorse he must commit Cain's crime. Unfortunately, after multiple murders he feels nothing. Charter members of the school were P. J. Bailey (*Festus*), S. Dobell (*Balder*), and Alexander Smith (*A Life-Drama*). Lesser lights to whom the name has been applied incl. J. S. Bigg, J. W. Marston, Ebenezer Jones, G. Massey, R. H. Horne, W. B. Scott, and George Gilfillan, the critic of the group. Arnold's Preface of 1853 was directed partly against the Spasmodics. Elizabeth Barrett Browning's *Aurora Leigh,* Tennyson's *Maud,* and Longfellow's *Golden Legend* were thought by contemp. critics to show "spasmodic" traits.—"T. Percy Jones" [W. E. Aytoun], hoax review of *Firmilian, Blackwood's* 75 (1854); *OED*; J. H. Buckley, *The Victorian Temper* (1951); M. A. Weinstein, *W. E. Aytoun and the S. Controversy* (1968). A.D.C.

SPEAKER. See PERSONA.

SPEECH ACT THEORY. A pragmatic theory of lang. compatible in many respects with the philosophy of the later Wittgenstein, first articulated by J. L. Austin (1911–60) and elaborated by H. P. Grice and John Searle. S. a. t. defines lang. in terms not of formal structures but of use. When people speak, they are assuming a complex system of rules that give meanings to particular utterances according to the context in which they are performed. The minimal linguistic unit is therefore not the symbol, word, or sentence but "the production or issuance of the symbol or word or sentence in the performance of the s. a." (Searle 1969).

This understanding of lang. led Austin to identify a previously overlooked component of speech which he called *illocutionary action.* A s. a. is not merely an assertion of truth or falsehood (i.e. a propositional or *locutionary* act); in uttering propositions, a speaker also communicates a relationship or commitment to the utterance. Searle classifies illocutionary acts into five categories: representatives (e.g. claiming, predicting, suggesting); directives (e.g. requesting, commanding, inviting); commissives (e.g. promising, threatening, vowing); expressives (e.g. congratulating, thanking, welcoming); and declarations (e.g. blessing, baptizing, firing). While all illocutionary acts are "performative" in the sense that they function as social action, a declaration actually brings about the state of affairs it predicates.

Austin calls an illocution "felicitous" when it

successfully evokes the conditions that communicators conventionally assume for the performance of that particular s. a. In ordinary circumstances, "I hate your dress" would not constitute a compliment, and "I marry you" would be "infelicitous" if the speaker were already married. This means that intention (q.v.) resides not in a psychological or moral state but in the proper evocation of conventions, incl. a convention of sincerity. An illocutionary act properly accomplished should have what Austin calls "perlocutionary effects": for example, the act of urging will conventionally persuade; a firing will cause an employee to assume she or he has been dismissed.

Since illocutionary action relies on complex rules and assumptions about sociocultural behavior and lang. use, the meaning of an illocutionary act depends less on its precise verbal form than on the conventions of its performance. "That stove is hot" might be an assertion, a warning, a complaint, or even a compliment. Conversely, a warning about the stove might be expressed in any number of sentences. Therefore auditors understand lang. not only by decoding signs but by drawing on contextual assumptions to make inferences. For example, the utterance "I have an aspirin," in response to "I have a headache" can be said to constitute an offer even though no explicit words of offering have been uttered. S. a. t. thus suggests that matters of context limit the potentiality of lang. for ambiguity and "free play." However, rules of inference assume a shared linguistic context between speaker and listener that may or may not be operating in a given s. a.—a particular problem in written discourse, since writing is usually detached from its origins.

S. a. t. asks readers to consider aspects of discourse that formal analysis tends to overlook. The most direct avenue s. a. t. opens for lit. is the study of the speech acts of textual speakers and characters, as for example in Fish's reading of the double banishment in *Coriolanus* and Altieri's analysis of Williams' "This is Just to Say." But in defining speech acts Austin made a distinction between "ordinary circumstances" and literary ones that complicates the application of s. a. t. to lit. and certain other forms of discourse. In lang. now notorious, Austin spoke of speech acts as "hollow or void if said by an actor on the stage, or if introduced in a poem, or spoken in soliloquy," considering such uses to be "not serious" and "parasitic." On this basis he excluded fictional speech acts from his enterprise.

Proponents of s. a. t. have suggested alterations in the theory in order to accommodate the uses of lang. that occur in fictional contexts. This issue, as well as concerns about s. a. t.'s concepts of the subject and of the operations of lang., have generated between s. a. theorists and poststructuralists a continuing debate begun as an exchange between Searle and Jacques Derrida in *Glyph* 1 (1977). However, because s. a. t. and Derridean deconstruction (q.v.) share certain understandings, there has also been fruitful dialogue between the two theories—e.g. in Felman's analysis of the seductive false promises of Don Juan. There has been similar dialogue between s. a. theorists and social critics who share s. a. t.'s commitment to the contextualization of lang. but who object to its abstracting of both the subject and the conventions of speech from cultural and political circumstances.

S. a. theorists attempt to show that lit. is itself a context rather than an independence from context. Searle, W. Iser, R. Ohmann, and M. Pratt have all argued that fictional speech acts carry a particular kind of illocutionary force and that lit., and even individual genres, constitute particular speech situations with rules and conventions of their own. Using Grice's work on "implicature," which postulates certain maxims by which people speak in ordinary conversation, Pratt evolves maxims for the specific speech situations of lit. Searle has suggested s. a. theories of such "literary" tropes as irony and metaphor. The field is thus in the process of defining its own terms even as applications of s. a. t. proceed.—J. L. Austin, *How To Do Things With Words* (1962); J. Searle, *Speech Acts* (1969), *Expression and Meaning* (1979); R. Ohmann, "Lit. as Act," *Approaches to Poetics*, ed. S. Chatman (1973); H. P. Grice, "Logic and Conversation," *Syntax and Semantics*, ed. P. Cole and J. Morgan, v. 3 (1975), *Studies in the Way of Words* (1989); *Glyph* 1 (1977); M. Pratt, *Toward a S. A. T. of Literary Discourse* (1977); W. Iser, *The Act of Reading* (1978); S. Fish, *Is There a Text in This Class?* (1980); C. Altieri, *Act and Quality* (1981); S. Lanser, *The Narrative Act* (1981); S. Felman, *The Literary S. A.* (1983); D. Sperber and D. Wilson, *Relevence* (1986); "S. A. T. and Biblical Crit.," special issue of *Semeia* 41, ed. H. White (1988), S. Petrey, *Speech Acts and Literary Theory* (1990).

S.S.L.

SPELL. See CHARM.

SPENSERIAN STANZA. The stanza invented by Edmund Spenser for his *The Faerie Queene* (1589–96; 6 Books completed), composed of 9 iambic lines, the first 8 being pentameter and the 9th a hexameter or alexandrine, rhyming *ababbcbcc*. The S. s. bears some similarity to It. *ottava rima* and the Occitan-Fr. *ballade* (qq.v.), and also owes some debt to *rhyme royal* (q.v.) as used by Chaucer, but in Spenser's hands it becomes distinctive, and one of the most original metrical innovations in the history of Eng. verse. The stanza is perfectly suited to the nature of Spenser's poem—at once dreamlike and intellectual, by turns vividly narrative and lushly descriptive—for it is short enough to contain sharply etched vignettes of action and yet ample enough to lend itself to digression, description, and comment. The cross rhyming interlocked by the medial *bb* couplet gives the stanza unity, and the final alexandrine lends its greater weight to effects of closure (q.v.), which Spenser counterbalances however with concatenation (q.v.), linking otherwise integral stanzas into a longer sequence.

The S. s. fell into disuse in the 17th c., although variants of it occur in the work of Giles and Phineas Fletcher, and, later in the largely forgotten allegorical narratives of the philosopher Henry More. Some 18th-c. poets revived the stanza, chiefly William Shenstone (*The Schoolmistress*, 1742), James Thomson (*The Castle of Indolence*, 1748), James Beattie (*The Minstrel*, 1771–74), and Robert Burns (*The Cotter's Saturday Night*, 1785). But it is the Eng. romantics who made the stanza once again a major vehicle. Wordsworth has 6 poems in the S. s., including "Guilt and Sorrow," but it remained for the younger romantics to produce verse in Spenserians comparable to *The Faerie Queene*. Byron divides the stanza often so as to achieve frequent shifts in tone in *Childe Harold's Pilgrimage* (1812, 1816). Shelley's *Revolt of Islam* (1818) and *Adonais* (1821) show their author to be the greatest master of the form since its creator. Keats in *The Eve of St. Agnes* (1820) revives the rich sensuousness associated with Spenser's whole art. After Keats the S. s. was little used except by Tennyson for "The Lotos-Eaters" and by William Cullen Bryant for "The Ages" (1821), praised by Poe. For further discussion, see STANZA.—Schipper; H. Reschke, *Die Spenserstanze* (1918); T. Maynard, *The Connection Between the Ballade, Chaucer's Modification of It, Rime Royal, and the S. S.* (1934); Empson 33–34; P. Alpers, *The Poetry of* The Faerie Queene (1967), ch. 2; E. Häublein, *The Stanza* (1978), 31-33; Brogan 453–55 for other citations; W. Blissett, "Stanza, S.," and B. M. H. Strang, "Lang., Gen.," *The Spenser Encyc.*, ed. A. C. Hamilton et al. (1990).   A.P.; T.V.F.B.

SPIRITUALS. Although blues singers say, "All of our music came out of the church," the s. and the blues (q.v.) are quite different. Originating probably in the 18th c., the s. are powerful religious folksongs, originally called jubilees, which are centered in the daily lives and concerns of the slaves and driven by the Protestant revivals of the 18th and 19th cs. Arna Bontemps pointed out the earthiness of the blues in contrast to the heavenly aspirations of the s. In addition, the s. are communal and choral rather than individualistic like the blues. The simplest form of the s. is a line repeated three times, but there are many variations. This formal elasticity is due in part to a tendency toward improvisation common to much of black music. Dena J. Epstein and John Lovell discuss the process in historical perspective and cite the reactions of contemp. observers. One contrasts this practice with the later rise of the "arranged" s. made popular by Negro college choirs in the trad. established by the Fisk University Jubilee Singers. Tribute to the deeply moving music may be found

in accounts by James Weldon Johnson, W. E. B. DuBois, Thomas W. Higginson, and others. In his account, Higginson repeatedly refers to the texts of the songs as poetry, a word frequently used by others who heard the music. This evaluation became a focal point of debate for many decades as prejudiced scholars attempted to attribute all the verbal beauty and transcendent vision of the s. to the white hymns on which they were based. Sterling A. Brown summarized the argument and concluded that there are no significant analogues in camp meeting hymns for the best of the songs, which, in J. W. Johnson's words, "sang a race from wood and stone to Christ."—W. E. B. DuBois, *The Souls of Black Folks* (1903); J. W. and J. R. Johnson, *The Books of Am. Negro S.* (1940); J. Lovell, Jr., *Black Song* (1974); D. J. Epstein, *Sinful Tunes and S.* (1977); E. Peters, "The Poetics of the Afro-Am. S.," *BALF* 23 (1989), *Lyrics of the Afro-Am. S.* (1991).   S.E.H.

SPLIT LINES, shared lines; rarely, "amphibious," "broken." In dramatic poetry (q.v.), a means for accommodating at once both the importance of rapid change of speakers, at times, and the necessity of making verse lines that are metrical wholes, by splitting one line between two or among three or more speakers. Whole-line exchanges between characters do not sufficiently allow for the rapid give-and-take of emotional or energetic scenes. Shakespeare shows steadily increasing use of s. l. over his career—the late plays show incidences of from 15 to almost 20%, peaking in *Antony and Cleopatra* and *Coriolanus*—and, concomitantly, the point of break in the line steadily moves to the right. Shakespeare certainly knew the Cl. device of stichomythia (q.v.), which is common in Gr. comedy (but not tragedy), but may also have learned the technique of short and s. l. from Virgil, whose use of broken lines and hemistichs was well known in the Ren. In the theater the effect of s. l. is increase of speed and liveliness without yet disrupting the rhythmic flow.—M. G. Tarlinskaja, *Shakespeare's Verse* (1987), ch. 4; G. T. Wright, *Shakespeare's Metrical Art* (1988), ch. 8.
                     T.V.F.B.

SPLIT RHYME. See BROKEN RHYME.

SPONDAIC VERSE. See HEXAMETER.

SPONDEE (Gr. "used at a libation," i.e. poured to the accompaniment of the 2 long notes). In Cl. prosody (q.v.), a metrical unit consisting of two long syllables; in the modern accentually based prosodies, a foot of two stressed syllables. Cl. meters entirely composed of spondees—*versus spondaicus*, "spondaic verse"—are rare but do occur (West 55–56). But normally, as in the dactylic hexameter, the s. is an optional substitution for a dactyl in the first five feet and obligatory in the last (metrical marking of closure is a widely attested phenomenon). Allen therefore thinks the s. "can hardly be termed a 'foot' in its own right," since it does not manifest internal opposition or contrast of members, and cites Pohlsander, who holds that the s. "has no real existence of its own . . . but must always be considered the contracted form of some other metrical unit" (123).

In the prosodies of the modern Germanic langs., which have been traditionally scanned in feet, the existence of spondaic feet is disputed. Several knowledgeable and sensible modern metrists (Mayor, Saintsbury, Pyle, Scott, Wright) have long held that the foot of two heavy syllables is a legitimate variation in iambic verse: they point to examples such as the last two syllables of the following lines: "The dove pursues the griffon, the mild hind" (Shakespeare, *MND* 2.1.232), or "The long day wanes, the slow moon climbs" (Tennyson, *Ulysses*), or "Silence, ye troubl'd waves, and thou Deep, peace" (Milton, *PL* 7.216); or the third and fourth syllables of "That in one speech two Negatives affirme" (Pope). These metrists, absolutists, hold that if two contiguous odd-even stresses in a line are both strong—perhaps not perfectly equal in strength (though that is certainly possible), but nearly so—then they should both be counted as strong, and the foot is thus a s. That is, if both stresses are, on a Trager-Smith scale of four degrees of stress (1 strongest, 4 weakest), 1s or 2s (i.e. either the sequence 1–2 or 2–1)—then scansion should reflect the fact that these levels are both above 3 and 4. As in the examples from Tennyson and Milton, such alleged instances of ss. are often made possible by two adjacent monosyllables or, more clearly, by a major syntactic juncture within the foot.

Other modern metrists (e.g. Guest, Skeat, Schipper, Attridge), esp. those who base their theories on linguistics, deny the existence of the s. and pyrrhic (q.v.) in modern verse, either on the basis of their definition of the foot (q.v.) itself as an element of metrical theory, or else on the basis of Jespersen's Relative Stress Principle (q.v.), which explicitly prohibits absolute weighting of stress (hence two heavy syllables within one foot). Jespersen's relativity principle assumed the existence of metrical feet and amounted to the claim that stress only matters in relation to immediately contiguous syllables, esp. the one syllable preceding. Hence for him the sequence "and thou Deep, peace" amounts to two iambs—unequal ones, perhaps, but iambs. The RSP yielded, for many metrists, elegant and subtle scansions which preserved both extensive metrical conformity (it allowed only iambs and trochees, in effect) and expressive readings. But it did this at the expense of variety in feet and of, some felt, due recognition of weighting in the line. Pyle rightly identifies the underlying issue at stake as being the question of "how far does the metre actually influence our rendering of stress as we read?" Readers and metrists who grant a strong influence will deny the

existence of ss. (McAuley, Malof), those a weak influence, affirm (Pyle). Relativist scansion more accurately tracks the shape of line movement; absolutist scansion more accurately takes account of which syllables are heavy and which not.

It is evident that in certain contexts where full syllable realization is granted every syllable, spondaic words can occur (Fussell gives the example of "Amen"), but these may represent an unusual performance mode and so be exceptions. In any event, the normal processes of stress alternation and reduction operate so systematically in Eng. phonology that in compound words or in phrases of any length, ss. are difficult at best. Still, absolutists in scansion (q.v.) can produce strong examples, as Wright does from Shakespeare. Of course, modern imitations of Cl. meters such as the hexameter attempt to reproduce ss. either accentually or by some theory of quantities (see CLASSICAL METERS IN MODERN LANGUAGES). For further discussion of the underlying issues, see FOOT; PYRRHIC.—J. McAuley, *Versification* (1966); F. Pyle, "Pyrrhic and S.," *Hermathena* 107 (1968); W. S. Allen, *Accent and Rhythm* (1973); West; Scott; G. T. Wright, *Shakespeare's Metrical Art* (1988). T.V.F.B.

SPONTANEITY is a key term in the poetics of romanticism although in one form or another it has had a long history in literary theory. In its fullest sense it is at one end of the perennial debate over whether craft or inspiration (q.v.) is the source of great art. As early as Horace's *Ars poetica*, some room is left for invention (q.v.), although it must be harmonious and tempered by caution and practice. The good poem is the product of both nature and conscious art. Sidney writes of the poet being "lifted up with the vigour of his own inventions," but his ultimate concern is with the didactic. British empirical philosophy, notably in Hobbes and Locke, stresses the power of wit (q.v.), of invention, and the need to control that power by judgment. S. was not especially prized in 18th-c. neoclassical poetry and poetics; witness the poetry of Pope and Johnson. Yet there are notable exceptions—Addison on the creativity of the imagination (q.v.), Burke on the sublime (q.v.), Young on originality (q.v.), and the poetry of Thomson, Macpherson, the Wartons, and Burns.

The Eng. romantics provide the strongest and most eloquent statements. Wordsworth speaks of poetry as the "spontaneous overflow of powerful feelings" ("Preface" to *Lyrical Ballads*, 1800). Shelley distinguishes poetry from reasoning, "a power to be exerted according to the determination of the will" and insists that "A man cannot say 'I will compose poetry.'" Keats, in a famous letter, remarks that "if Poetry comes not as naturally as the Leaves to a tree it had better not come at all" (27 February, 1818). Carlyle and Emerson stress the prophetic nature of the poet's sentiments, Emerson counseling, "Doubt not, O poet, but persist. Say 'It is in me, and shall out'" (*The Poet*,

1844). Baudelaire and the Fr. symbolists regard symbol as a vehicle for catching the feelings of the poet immediately and concretely. Manifestations of s. in the 20th c. can be seen in surrealism (q.v.), the expression of imagination and emotion without deliberate control. In America, esp. after World War II, the confessional poetry of Robert Lowell and the work of the Beat poets (q.v.), with its rebellious spirit, loose structures, and eccentric diction, furnish other good examples.

S. is an ambivalent term, and it is important to distinguish what one regards as genuine s. from the kind of carefully contrived *appearance* of s. found in, for example, Petrarch's expression of an unfulfilled passion for Laura in sonnets of tight form and refined lang., or in Rousseau's deliberate statement at the opening of his *Confessions* (1781): "My purpose is to display to my kind a portrait in every way true to nature, and the man I portray shall be myself." See also INTENTION.—S. Monk, *The Sublime* (1935); W. J. Bate, *From Classic to Romantic* (1946), *The Burden of the Past and the Eng. Poet* (1970); G. McKenzie, *Critical Responsiveness* (1949); Abrams; E. Tuveson, *The Imagination as a Means of Grace* (1960); W. Jackson, *Immediacy: The Devel. of a Critical Concept* (1973); J. Engell, *The Creative Imagination* (1981); W. Fox, *Immediacy: A Poetic Stance from the Romantics to the Contemporaries, DAI* 42 (1981): 2674A. J.L.M.

SPRUCHDICHTUNG. A body of didactic lyrics produced in Ger.-speaking areas from the 12th through the 14th c. S., like the poems of the *Minnesang* (q.v.) with which it is transmitted, was intended to be sung and is therefore also known as *Sangspruchdichtung*. It is distinct from a type of gnomic verse in 4-beat couplets intended for recitation (*Sprechspruch*) and more closely akin to the didactic treatise and moral tale in verse. The term S., and the distinction between *Spruch* and *Lied*, is modern; medieval authors tend to use the two latter terms interchangeably. S. treats religious and biblical subject matter; rules of conduct and wise counsel, eulogy and lament, and complaints of poverty and pleas to patrons; political themes first appear in Walther von der Vogelweide. There is a general similarity between S. and the Med. Lat. and Romance didactic and political lyric, but no direct Lat. or Romance influence.

The first recorded examples of S., ascribed to Spervogel, probably represent the work of two 12th-c. poets, the more archaic using a stanza made up predominantly of four-beat couplets with assonating beside pure rhymes, the later poet a polymetric stanza with mainly pure couplet rhyme. The stanzas in the first form are loosely grouped in thematic units of five or three, whereas those in the second form are all independent. These two basic types of structural organization persist in later S. At the end of the 12th c., Walther introduced into S. tripartite stanza structure and variety of metrical pattern, already established in the *Minnesang*, but the forms of S. tend to greater weight in length and number of lines. The S. of Walther consists of groups of 3–19 stanzas, each group in a distinctive metrical form, the longer series often uniting relatively disparate subject matter, e.g. specific reference to contemporary events with general didactic themes.

There is a considerable proliferation of S. in the 13th c., which runs parallel to a general increase in didactic lit. Most authors of S. appear to be nonaristocratic; some are known only as didactic poets, whereas others, such as Walther, Konrad von Würzburg, or Der Marner, also cultivate the *Minnesang*. There are also crossings between the two areas of the lyric, in particular the intrusion of themes pertaining to love into S.

The main body of S. illustrates the two types of structural organization evident in the earliest examples, either the use of one metrical form for an unlimited number of independent stanzas (in the extreme case, Reinmar von Zweter—229 stanzas in the same form) or, as in Walther, the use of distinctive forms for series of varying length, in which there may be both self-contained units and groups of closely or loosely linked stanzas. Rearrangements in the mss. indicate the continuing relative independence of the single stanza and the probability that different selections were made for individual performances. It is, above all, these two structural principles which distinguish S. from the *Minnesang* and from the didactic lyric in Med. Lat. and Romance, which is not formally distinct from the love lyric. The metrical forms of S. are mostly unique, which permitted them to be given distinctive titles and used again for new subject matter by poets of the *Meistersang* (q.v.). See also GERMAN PROSODY, *Middle High German*.

EDITIONS: *Die Jenaer Liederhandschrift*, ed. G. Holz et al., 2 v. (1901); *Die Jenaer Liederhandschrift in Abbildung*, ed. H. Tervooren and U. Müller (1972); *Politische Lyrik des deutschen Mittelalters*, ed. U. Müller, 2 v. (1972–74); *Liederdichter des 13. Jahrhunderts*, ed. C. von Kraus, 2d ed. (1978).

GENERAL: W. Nickel, *Sirventes und S.* (1907); K. W. Klein, *The Partisan Voice* (1971); F. Maurer, *Die politische Dichtung Walthers von der Vogelweide*, 3d ed. (1972); *Mhd. S.*, ed. H. Moser (1972); B. Wachinger, *Sängerkrieg* (1973); K. Franz, *Studien zur Soziologie des Spruchdichters in Deutschland im späten 13. Jahrhundert* (1974); U. Müller, *Untersuchungen zur politischen Lyrik des deutschen Mittelalters* (1974); H. Brunner, *Die alten Meister* (1975); R. Ehnert, *Möglichkeiten politischer Lyrik im Hochmittelalter* (1976); H. Tervooren, "S.," and K. Kanzog, "Spruch," *Reallexikon*; Sayce, ch. 10.

O.L.S.

SPRUNG RHYTHM. Term coined by Gerard Manley Hopkins to describe what he thought to be his most important metrical discovery: "S. R. . . . is measured by feet of from one to four syllables, regularly, and for particular effects any number of weak or slack syllables may be used. It has one stress, which falls on the only syllable, if there is only one, or, if there are more, then scanning as above, on the first, and so gives rise to four sorts of feet, a monosyllable and the so-called accentual Trochee, Dactyl, and the First Paeon [/ x x x]. . . . S. R. cannot be counterpointed." S. r. is achieved by "springing" loose the more common "running rhythm" (q.v.) into a plane of higher stressing where the fundamental principle of Eng. accentual-syllabic metrics—prohibition of frequent contiguous stresses by alternation or spacing of stress—is dissolved, permitting lines dense in stress yet nevertheless (via Hopkins's stipulative principles) susceptible to scansion.

It is odd that Hopkins should have retained the foot (q.v.) at all in his new prosody. To judge from his correspondence, he envisaged s. r. as a pure-stress meter—"To speak shortly, [the new rhythm] consists in scanning by accents or stresses alone" (letter to R. W. Dixon, Oct. 6, 1878)—whose stresses are sense-stresses rather than metrical ones, expressive rather than purely rhythmic. S. r. also shares with OE verse a cultivation of alliteration, though not raised to a metrical principle, and other echoic patterns (assonance, internal rhyme); these patterns help to compress the verse into word-clusters in which stress tends to be compacted and unstressed material only minimally perceived. But efforts to show genuine affiliation of s. r. with OE prosody are misguided, being based on naive conceptions of the sophisticated metrical system of cl. OE poetry.

Why then is the foot necessary for Hopkins, despite his speaking of it as a mere analytic convenience? He needed the foot for promotional reasons, to convince his contemporaries that s. r. was an extension of standard poetic rhythm, via counterpoint rhythm (q.v.), rather than a revived primitive meter which bypassed the Eng. post-Ren. accentual-syllabic tradition. He needed the foot (as equivalent of the musical bar) to establish his principle of isochrony and stress-compensation: "in S. R. . . . the feet are assumed to be equally long or strong and their seeming inequality is made up by pause or stressing" ("Author's Preface" to *Poems* [ed. MacKenzie, 5th ed., 1990, 115 ff.]). He also needed the foot to account for, if not necessitate, three further metrical innovations: "outrides" or "hangers," "roving over," and hovering stress.

"Hangers" or "outrides" (marked, in Hopkins's notation, by a loop underneath them) are extrametrical weak syllables added to a foot but not counting in scansion; according to Hopkins, "they are so called because they seem to hang below the line or ride forward or backward from it in another dimension than the line itself": the stress of an outriding foot is noticeably stronger than others and the outride itself is followed by a pause. "Roving over" is a process whereby scansion continues directly from one line to the next without interruption; this kind of metrical enjambment is made necessary by Hopkins's adoption of an exclusively falling rhythm for s. r., as a way of admitting unstressed syllables at the beginning of a line. In hovering stress, "the mark ⌐ over two neighbouring syllables means that, though one has and the other has not the metrical stress, in the recitation-stress they are to be about equal" (note on "To what serves Mortal Beauty?"), e.g. "gashed flesh," "galled shield" ("In honour of St. Alphonsus Rodriguez"). This looks like metrical sleight-of-hand: hovering stress presents the reader with two stressed syllables, requiring her, for metrical purposes, to stress only one, while allowing her in reading to stress both.

Hopkins's innovations seem to have had the following objectives in view: to create a meter which allows the reader to "recite" more stresses than the meter itself makes available; to increase the intensity of stress; to drive the reader on from stress to stress, slurring slack syllables, so that compression and stress-density result; to intimate that the verse-line operates in several "dimensions." These objectives would square with Hopkins's pursuit of "inscape," the apprehension of an object or creature's irreducible haecceity, and of the "instress" (stress) which actualizes "inscape" and embodies the force exerted by "inscape" on the mind of the perceiver. After all, stress is "the making of a thing more, or making it markedly, what it already is; it is the bringing out its nature" (to C. Patmore, Nov. 7, 1883). According to Hopkins, s. r. is at once the most natural of rhythms (being the rhythm of common speech, prose, and nursery rhymes) and the most marked—the least forced and the most emphatic. See also COUNTERPOINT RHYTHM; INSCAPE AND INSTRESS; RUNNING RHYTHM.—H. Whitehall, "S. R.," in The Kenyon Critics, *G. M. H.* (1945); M. M. Holloway, *The Prosodic Theory of G. M. H.* (1947); W. H. Gardner, *G. M. H. (1844–1889)*, 2 v. (1948–49); W. Ong, "Hopkins' S. R. and the Life of Eng. Poetry," *Immortal Diamond*, ed. N. Weyand (1949); E. Schneider, *The Dragon in the Gate* (1968); H.-W. Ludwig, *Barbarous in Beauty* (1972); C. Scott, *A Question of Syllables* (1986), ch. 5; E. A. Stephenson, *What S. R. Really Is* (1987); P. Kiparsky, "S. R.," *Rhythm and Meter*, ed. P. Kiparsky and G. Youmans (1989); N. MacKenzie, "Metrical Marks," etc., *Poetical Works of G. M. H.*, 5th ed. (1990).

C.S.; T.V.F.B.

SRI LANKAN POETRY covers work in three langs.: Sinhala poetry, which dates to the 1st c. A.D.; Tamil poetry, which developed a distinctly S. L. identity in the 20th c.; and English poetry, of which a small but significant body of work now exists dating mainly from the mid 20th c.

SRI LANKAN POETRY

I. SINHALA POETRY. A. *The Ancient Period* (1st–9th cs. A.D.). A few rock inscriptions of unrhymed couplets and a more substantial body of graffiti poems from Sigiriya are all that survive. The graffiti are short lyrics in a variety of metrical forms expressing the varied responses of visitors to the magnificent rock fortress of Sigiriya.

B. *The Classical Period* (10th–19th cs.). The earliest extant complete poems are from this period. The *Siyabaslakara*, a 10th-c. treatise on rhet., the *Sasadāvata* (Birth Story of the Hare, 12th c.), the *Muvadevdāvata*, (Birth Story of the Deer), and the *Kavsilumina* (Diadem of Poetry, 13th c. A.D.) are the major works. They are in unrhymed couplets or *gī* (lyric) verse and are strongly influenced by classical Sanskrit theories of poetics (see INDIAN POETICS).

By the mid 14th c., a literary form known as the *sandēsa* (message poem), in four-lined, end-rhymed stanzas, becomes popular. The author sends a message, usually through a bird, to a god or religious dignitary asking blessings. The form allows the poet to describe the towns, villages, landscape, shrines, rituals, and festivals encountered en route and the poems are thus of considerable literary and sociological interest. The *Mayura* (Peacock), the *Tisara* (Goose), and the *Sëlalihini* (Mynah) *Sandēsas* are 15th-c. works. The *Kāvyasēkara*, the *Guttila Kāvya*, the *Buduguṇālaṃkāraya* and *Lōvādasaṃgrahaya* are other Buddhist works of this period.

From the 16th c. onward, the Portuguese, Dutch, and British in turn gained increasing control of the island. Literary activity declined. Although the poets of the Mātara School (late 18th c.) kept the trad. nominally alive, nothing of significance appears until the 20th c.

C. *The Modern Period* (20th c.). Nationalistic movements around the turn of the century stimulated literary activity again, much of it Buddhist, classicist, revivalist, and didactic. The 20th c. also saw the growth of a secular poetry, nationalist in theme and traditional in form. By the Thirties, Munidāsa Kumāranatunge had begun a movement for lang. reform, termed *Hela*, to rid Sinhala of Sanskrit influences. Kumāranatunge's critical writings had considerable impact, and his poems for children introduced a new simplicity into Sinhala poetry.

The major breakthrough came with the introduction of free verse (*nisandäs kavi*). G. B. Senanayake had experimented with unrhymed verseforms as early as 1945 in his poems in *Paligänīma* (Revenge). However, it was Siri Gunasinghe in *Mas Lē Näti Äta* (Bones Without Flesh or Blood, 1956), *Abhiṇikmana* (Renunciation, 1958), and *Ratu Käkulu* (Red Buds, 1962) who established and popularized the form. Gunasinghe together with others such as Gunadasa Amerasekera and Wimal Dissanayake, who were part of the literary world of the University of Peradeniya in the Fifties, became known as the Peradeniya poets. Influ-

enced by the literary theories of Am. New Criticism (q.v.), they were at first criticized as Westernized ivory tower aesthetes, but their work soon gained acceptance. Their writings gave a new vitality and flexibility to the lang. Ediriweera Sarachcharanda, the foremost critic and theorist for the group, also revolutionized the theater with his poetic dramas *Manamē* (1956) and *Siṃhabāhu* (1958).

The Seventies saw a fresh burst of poetic activity by writers whose works reflect a strong social concern. However, their evocative use of lang. and the control and confidence with which they draw on classical and folk as well as foreign literatures, give their work an energy that overrides the didacticism. Mahagama Sekera's *Heṭa Irak Pāyayi* (Tomorrow a Sun Will Rise, 1971), *Nomiyami* (I Will Not Die, 1973), and *Prabuddha* (1976); Parakrama Kodituwakku's *Akīkaru Putrayakugē Lōkayak* (The World of a Disobedient Son, 1974) and *Aluṭ Minihek Äviṭ* (A New Man Has Come, 1976); and Monica Ruwanpathirana's *Tahanam Dēsayakin* (From a Forbidden World, 1972) and *Obē Yeheliya Äya Gähäniya* (Your Friend, She is Woman, 1975) are some of the important works of this group.

The dynamic energy of the Seventies slackens perceptibly by the Eighties. The civil war, disturbing and demoralizing but strangely distant because fought in the North, leaves hardly any mark on the poetry. The creative impetus seems to shift away from poetry to drama.   R.O.

II. TAMIL POETRY. While the Tamil presence in Sri Lanka goes back to very early times, Tamil lit. gained a distinct Sri Lankan identity only much later. The earliest reference to a S. L. Tamil poet is in the *Sangam* lit. of the 3d c. A.D., where verses attributed to Putatēvanar with the prefix *Elathu* (Lanka) appear. In 1310 A.D., *Caracotimalai* by Pōcaraca Panditār was presented in the court of the Sinhala king Parākramabāhu III at Dambadeniya. These are the only references for the early period.

The flourishing Tamil kingdom in the Jaffna peninsula (14th–17th cs.) gave rise to several poetical works. The best known was *Rakuvamcam* by Aracakēcari, the poet laureate. Under colonial rule the proselytizing activities of Christian missionaries spawned a genre of religious poetry which was given further impetus by the introduction of printing.

Early S. L. Tamil poetry had traditionally been seen merely as an extension of Indian Tamil writing, but by the 1940s a renaissance occurred, when many young poets began to emphasize their S. L. identity. A distinctly different Tamil poetry soon evolved. Nantāran, Kantacami, and Mahakavi are important poets of this period. An emphasis on simplicity, colloquial meters, and concrete visual images is the hallmark of this Lankan Tamil poetry.

When Sinhala was made the official lang. in 1956, a new political consciousness evolved among the Tamils. Three schools of poetry emerged. The first was nationalist, in support of a Tamil Federal state. The second group called themselves "Progressives," were influenced by left-wing ideologies, and advocated a radical transformation of S. L. society, both Sinhala and Tamil. The third refused to be identified with either group and wrote a very individualized poetry. Modern forms such as free verse were introduced, and poets and poetry proliferated.

By the 1970s, Tamil political aspirations for a separate state led to guerilla war. Thereafter, the experience for S. L. Tamil poets was blood, tears, violence, battle, exile, death, and life amidst death. The new "war poetry" reflected these realities. S. L. Tamil poetry now charts its own course and is totally different from Indian Tamil writing unexposed to such experiences. The major poets of the 1980s are Jeyapālan, Cēran, Celyan, Yēcuraca, Vicayēntran, and Vilvaratinam.

Love and war had been the basic themes of early Sangam lit. Once Tamil military exploits ceased after colonial conquest, war poetry died out. The trad. has been revived in the past decade. However, new political developments after the Indo-Lankan peace accord may evoke yet other changes in S. L. Tamil writing.   D.B.S.J.

III. ENGLISH POETRY in Sri Lanka develops its own identity in the mid 20th c. The poetry of the past two decades clearly reflects a growing confidence and maturity. Lakkdasa Wikkramasinghe in his pioneering work boldly experimented with the rhythms of Lankan Eng. *Lustre Poems* (1965) has a dynamic energy, while later works such as *The Grasshopper Gleaming* (1976) show his growing control of his medium. Patrick Fernando's *Selected Poems* (1984) is more formal in style. He is an accomplished poet at ease in the Eng. lang. Yasmine Gooneratne's *Word, Bird and Motif* (1971) and *Lizard's Cry* (1972) reveal her flair for the satiric mode, where her control of tone and sensitivity to the nuances of words have full play. Anne Ranasinghe's *Poems* (1971) and *Plead Mercy* (1975) provide sharp insights into a range of personal experiences that bridge two worlds. Basil Fernando in *A New Era to Emerge* (1973) and Jean Arasanayagam in *Apocalypse* (1983) and *A Colonial Inheritance* (1985) write movingly of the current realities of S. L. life. The readership for Eng. poetry in Sri Lanka is small but influential. It also has the potential of an international readership.
                                                    R.O.
  GENERAL: M. Wickramasinghe, *Mod. Sinhalese Lit.*, tr. E. R. Sarachchandra (1949); C. E. Godakumbura, *Sinhalese Lit.* (1955); K. S. Sivakumaran, *Tamil Writing in Sri Lanka* (1964); R. Obeyesekere, *Sinhalese Writing and the New Critics* (1974); K. Sivathamby, *Tamil Lit. in Eelam* (1978).
  ANTHOLOGIES: *Poetry from the Sinhalese*, tr. G. Keyt (1939); *Sigiri Graffiti*, ed. and tr. S. Paranavitarne (1955); *An Anthol. of Cl. Sinhalese Lit.*, ed. C. Reynolds (1970); *Poetry of Sri Lanka*, ed. Y. Gooneratne, *JSAL* v. 12 (1976); *Mod. Writing in Sinhala*,

ed. R. Obeyesekere and C. Fernando (1978); *Marantul Valvōm [We live amidst Death]: A Collection of Tamil War Poetry 1977–1985* (1985); *Sinhala and Tamil Writing from Sri Lanka*, ed. R. Obeyesekere, *JSAL* v. 22 (1987).   R.O.; D.B.S.J.

STANCES. Fr. verseform which is, on the one hand, synonymous with the *strophes* of the ode (q.v.) and, on the other hand, often confused with *strophes*, from which s. appear to differ by their restriction to lyrical themes and, in conformity with the etymology (Lat. *stantia*, "pause"; It. *stanze*, "stopping places"), by a more definite pause at the end of each division. Introduced into France from Italy in the second half of the 16th c., s. continued in use until well into the 19th c. (e.g. Musset, Sully Prudhomme). In early 17th-c. theater, esp. tragedy, they were used as highly organized lyric monologues: their thematic density, varied meters, and complex rhyme schemes contrasted vividly with the alexandrine couplets of dialogue. About 1600, s. were banished from the theater in the name of verisimilitude: that characters should possess such poetic skill when in the throes of violent emotion was no longer considered logical.—P. Martinon, *Les Strophes* (1912), App. 2; J. Scherer, *La Dramaturgie classique en France* (1950), pt. 2, ch. 6; D. Janik, *Gesch. der Ode und der "S." vom Ronsard bis Boileau* (1968).   A.E.E.; C.K.

STANZA. The notion of end rhyme (see RHYME) and the notion of s. are all but reciprocal: the vowel and final consonant of the rhymed words are repeated, and the repetition not merely identifies line ends clearly but also produces a sound structure, a relationship among lines. The rhyming of adjacent lines produces couplet; larger structures are made possible by the intermixture of further rhymes in complex patterns. Ss. may be isometric (q.v.), i.e. made up of lines of the same length, or heterometric (q.v.), i.e. made up of lines of differing lengths. The relationship of syntax (q.v.) to line (q.v.) may vary, within limits, as much in s. as in blank verse (q.v.). Syntactic variation, i.e. changing the grammatical structure of lines so that differing syntactic elements are linked by rhyme, is one of the poet's chief means of achieving variety of effect within and between ss.

Once established, the metrical structure of the s., including the rhyme pattern, tends to be repeated exactly in subsequent ss. (see RESPONSION). Indeed, if we are uncertain of the metrical structure of a line in the first s. of a poem written before the 20th c.—as we might well be of the opening line of Donne's "Twicknam Garden," for example, or the third line of Blake's "Ah! Sunflower"—we can ordinarily resolve the problem by looking at the corresponding line of a later s. Failures of correspondence occur, of course, even in traditional verse; usually they serve some expressive purpose. Most exceptionally, rhyme can be used throughout a poem in emergent and constantly varying (i.e. irregular) patterns, as in *Lycidas* or "Dover Beach," or, more nearly regularly, as in Herbert's "Man."

Much 20th-c. verse is quasi-stanzaic; that is, it looks on the page as though it were composed of groups of lines (approximately) equal in number, the corresponding lines in each group roughly equal in length. There may be a rhyme pattern, strictly or loosely maintained; or the line ends may be marked by lighter sound repetitions. On the other hand, all forms of rhyme may be avoided. In traditional s., a complete lack of rhyme would be all but unthinkable, esp. if the lines in the s. were heterometric, as is often the case: the lines of such a s. may be defined syntactically, but unless we exaggerate the definition in the reading, unrhymed lines of differing lengths tend to blur in form, to shift toward the cadences of prose.

Verse without end rhyme could in theory be divided syntactically into precisely equal groups, equal pulses of two (or any number of) lines of the *same* length. But whether the ear could hear even these equalities without the added signal of rhyme is uncertain; this is the charge laid against Milton by Dr. Johnson. A part of our deepest sense of blank verse (q.v.) is that it is nonstanzaic: in the drama, the brevity or amplitude appropriate to the individual speech determines the speech's length, while in nondramatic blank verse the unit next larger than the line is the verse paragraph (q.v.), its length also determined by something other than metrical requirement.

In isometric ss., the principal source of formal effect lies in the patterning of rhyme and in the relation between rhyme and syntax. Couplet rhyme completes its pattern promptly and concisely; the closed couplet, in which the sense and the rhyme structures are completed together, has this effect more fully, of course, than does the open couplet. Of slightly larger structures, *terza rima* (q.v.) is progressive, unfolding continuously via concatenation (q.v.) until it is closed off. Alternating rhyme (see CROSS RHYME) has a somewhat similar effect, though our sense of the symmetries of three and of four is not the same. *Abba*, the envelope (q.v.) s., circles back to close as it began. Because rhyme in the envelope s. returns to its beginnings, there is a sharper hiatus between, say, *abba* and *cddc* than between *abab* and *cdcd*; the s. must be used appropriately. A longer s., like that of Hardy's "According to the Mighty Working," may appear to propose other patterns, then end by describing a figure comparable to the envelope: in the *abcbca* of that s. we have first three unrhymed lines, then what seems an *xaxa* quatrain, then *xabab*, and finally the addition that reveals the true and full rhyme structure by pairing the last line with the first.

In a s. rhymed *abba*, the second and third lines will have only the slightest effect of couplet unless the quatrain is punctuated heavily (period, semicolon, colon) at the end of lines 1 and 3; but even

then, the fact that the *b* lines are even- and odd-numbered, not odd- and even-, will skew the effect. In longer ss.—*ababb, ababcc, ababbcc* (rhyme royal [q.v.]), *ababacc* (*ottava rima* [q.v.])—one can see how the patterns relate, and it is easy to imagine what differing effects might be achieved by breaking up the lines syntactically into varying symmetrical or asymmetrical groups. For discussion of the bipartite-tripartite AA/B pattern of stanza construction, see CANZONE.

One of the most fascinating ss. to study, for the (perhaps unexpected) variety it affords, is the Spenserian (q.v.) s., $ababbcbc_5c_6$. Assuming for the moment that the lines are so constructed as to terminate with the ends of phrases, clauses, or sentences, consider how different in effect the following are likely to be: *ab.ab.bc.bc.c*; *abab.bcbc.c*; *ab.abb.cb.cc*; *aba.bb.cbc.c*; *ababb.cbcc*; *aba.bbc.bcc*. One can find examples of all these in *The Faerie Queene*. One can also find extraordinary ss. in which a full stop line-internally strands an important phrase at the end of a sentence, without giving us the sense of completion normally conferred by rhyme (e.g. *FQ* 1.1.11.7). The effect, once we have accustomed ourselves to rhyme, can be strangely disorienting until we are reassured by the resumption of rhyming (cf. *Lycidas* 76).

The Spenserian s. gives us a glimpse of what may be done in even minimally heterometric ss. Characteristically the longer final line brings a sense of amplitude, of fuller utterance, to its conclusion: the "more" of the longer line is a metaphor ready to attach itself to any appropriate signification. S. movement can also be from longer to shorter lines, from more to less: see Henry Vaughan's "The World," or John Crowe Ransom's "Blue Girls." The "less" of the shorter line may also seem a metaphor, its effect that of an arresting brevity, of concision—or perhaps of humbleness, smallness, or fragility.

The 12-syllable line with which the Spenserian ends is susceptible of perfect balance if it breaks 6–6 or 4–4–4, or of what may seem an uneasy imbalance if it breaks 7–5, or 5–7, or 3–4–5. The balance possible in lines containing an even number of 2-syllable groups is also a potential metaphor ready to confer a special sense of order, of harmony, where the lines' denotation encourages this. The "Hymn" s. of Milton's *Nativity Ode* is from this point of view (as from many others) a magnificent invention: rhymed $aa_3b_5cc_3b_5d_4d_6$, it begins with two 3-line pulses, in each of which the last line is ampler than (though proportionate to) the first and second, reaches what seems a preliminary closure at the end of line 6—but proceeds almost unexpectedly to parallel the rising 3–5 progression with a fuller and more perfectly proportioned 4–6, closing, as does the Spenserian, on a long and potentially balanced line. The last line is prefigured by lines 1–2 and 4–5, and the pentameter lines tend to break syntactically 2–3; the last two lines double these proportions, 2–2 and 3–3. Just as lines of the same length produce equalities in verse, or the sense of equality, so proportionality of one line to another is a potentially meaningful characteristic to which the ear, and the mind, accustoms itself in s. It is a characteristic which, once expected, makes failure of proportion, or the breaking of proportion, the more notable. Again and again in the "Hymn" s., simplicities are compounded into triumphant symmetries. Against this, contrast the—equally meaningful—disproportion (or unresolved proportion) between the lengths of the last two lines of "Dover Beach."

The parallel between a repeatable melody in music and a series of line clusters identical in metrical pattern in poetry is clear, and it is tempting to think of s. as originating in song (q.v.). Stanzaic verse can indeed be written specifically to be sung to a pre-existing melody. But words to ancient melodies survived where the music to which they had been sung or chanted did not, and lyric stanzaic verse as a literary form, valued apart from a possible relationship to music, goes back a very long way (see MUSIC AND POETRY). The two traditions continue, naturally, to intertwine. Ultimately we may expect a greater complexity of thought and feeling in verse written to be read than in verse meant, rather, to be sung; in the latter there is also relatively less place for intricate patterning of sound (q.v.) than we find in verse which is its own music.

S. is artificial; no sensible person would deny that. Rhyme itself is artificial: its occurrence at measured intervals is the more so. And whatever metrical pattern is chosen for a given s., this will, as in nonstanzaic verse, impose limits on the rhythms available to the individual line. The shorter the line, generally, the stricter the limits. But syntactic structures have their rhythms too, and while these may be modified in many ways, the fitting together of the two kinds of rhythm, within relatively small spaces, and in lang. that seems unconstrained, requires much skill.

In stanzaic verse, line-end tends to coincide with phrase-, clause-, or sentence-end; rhyme and enjambment (q.v.), closure (q.v.) and the avoidance of it, are at odds, and can be played against one another only temporarily. Ss. themselves are not often enjambed: that is, s.-end and sentence-end normally arrive together. Long ss. would seem to permit greater internal variety of syntactic construction than short ss., and to a degree this is so. But rhythmic constraints on the individual line remain. And it is no more natural to have ideas expressed in repeated units of (say) 92 syllables than of 40, or 28, or 20. Blank verse, the sense it carries "variously drawn out from one verse into another," may therefore seem more "natural" than stanzaic verse, having available—despite constraints—some syntactic freedom. In conversation we do not speak in rhyme; we would not when we speak be chained to the symmetries of s. But in the hands of a skillful poet, the limits ss. impose

are transformed into devices and resources, tools for creating meanings, and beauties, not otherwise attainable. See also ALLAEOSTROPHA; LINE; ODE; STANCE; STICHOS; STROPHE; TAIL RHYME. E.R.W.

STUDIES AND SURVEYS: *General*: Thieme, 382—lists Fr. studies; E. Häublein, *The S.* (1978)—best modern study, though brief; Scott, ch. 5; Brogan, sect. G—bibl.; L. Turco, *The New Book of Forms* (1986)—very eclectic. *Classical*: Wilamowitz, chs. 15–16; Maas, sects. 61–72; Koster, ch. 14; Dale, ch. 12, and "Stichos and S.," *Collected Papers* (1969); West.

STANZA INDEXES: *French*: P. Martinon, *Les Strophes* (1912); I. Frank, *Répertoire métrique de la poésie des troubadours*, 2 v. (1953, 1957); W. Pfrommer, *Grundzüge der Strophenentwicklung Baudelaire au Apollinaire* (1963); U. Mölk and F. Wolfzettel, *Répertoire métrique de la poésie française des origines à 1350* (1972).

German: F. Schlawe, *Die deutsche Strophenformen 1600-1950* (1972); A. H. Touber, *Deutsche Strophenformen des Mittelalters* (1975); S. Ranawake, *Höfische Strophenkunst* (1976); H. J. Frank, *Handbuch der deutsche Strophenformen* (1980); W. Suppan, "Strophe," *Reallexikon* 4.245–56.

English: Schipper; Schipper, *History*; J. L. Cutler, "A Manual of ME Stanzaic Patterns," 2 v., Diss., Ohio State Univ. (1949); M. C. Honour, "The Metrical Derivations of the Med. Eng. Lyric," 2 v., Diss., Yale Univ. (1949); E. Häublein, *Strophe und Struktur in der Lyrik Sir Phillip Sidneys* (1971), and Häublein (above); B. O'Donnell, *Numerous Verse* (1989).

Spanish, Galician, and Portuguese: G. Tavani, *Repertorio metrico della lirica galego-portoghese* (1967); T. Navarro, *Repertorio de estrofas españolas* (1968). *Italian*: F. P. Memmo, *Dizionario di metrica italiana* (1983); A. Solimena, *Repertorio metrico dello Stil novo* (1980). *Russian*: G. S. Smith, "The Stanza Typology of Rus. Poetry 1735-1816: A General Survey," *Rus. Lit.* 13 (1983); Scherr. T.V.F.B.

STANZA LINKING. See CONCATENATION.

STASIMON (Gr. "stationary song"). In Gr. drama, an ode sung by the Gr. chorus after it has taken its position in the orchestra. Aristotle distinguishes the s. from the *parodos*, the entrance-ode of the chorus (in anapaestic meter) as it marches into the orchestra, and defines it as "a song of the chorus without anapaests or trochees" (*Poetics* 1452b20 ff.). The *stasima* alternate with the episodes, the dialogue passages delivered by the actors; their number in tragedy varies between three and five. Originally, and during the greater part of the 5th c. B.C., the *stasima* were intimately connected with the subject matter of the episodes. However, this connection gradually became tenuous until finally Agathon (ca. 447–400 B.C.) replaced them by the *embolima*, intercalary pieces, mere choral interludes which could be introduced into any play (*Poetics* 1456a29–30).—W. Aly, "S.,"

STATEMENT

Pauly-Wissowa, ser. 2, 3 (1926), 2156–66; W. Kranz, S. (1933); W. J. W. Koster, "De metris stasimi I and II Electrae Euripidis," *Mélanges Emile Boisacq*, v. 3 (1938); A. M. Dale, *Collected Papers* (1969), ch. 3; Michaelides. P.S.C.

STATEMENT. See MEANING, POETIC; PSEUDO-STATEMENT.

STAVE (a back formation from the plural *staves*, of *staff*). (1) The old term for a group of lines or a stanza of a poem or song, particularly a hymn or drinking song, both of which often use refrains. The term was perhaps derived from the musical *staff* and once was restricted to poems intended to be sung. (2) The initial alliteration (sound) in a line of Old Germanic or OE verse (see GERMAN PROSODY; ENGLISH PROSODY). This sense of the term comes from Ger. *Stab* ("staff"), hence the Ger. terms *Stabreim* for alliteration and *stabreimender Vers* or *Stabreimvers* for alliterative verse. R.O.E.

STICHOMYTHIA (Gr. "line-speech"). First named by Pollux, a 2d c. A.D. grammarian, s. refers specifically to line-by-line conversation between two characters in Gr. and Lat. drama but is usually broadened to include exchanges of distichs and repartee in split lines (q.v.; Gr. *antilabé*), which join to form one metrically correct line, thereby preserving the meter amid rapid dialogue (Gross). Gr. dramatists used s. in situations such as simple dialogue, question and answer, and prayer, but its most impressive function is to render intense debate (e.g. Sophocles, *Antigone* 508-23) or interrogation (e.g. Sophocles, *Oedipus Rex* 1141-77). Seneca's effective use of s. and *antilabé* for keen repartee subsequently influenced Elizabethan dramatists. Shakespeare uses s. (e.g. *Richard III* 4.4 and *Hamlet* 3.4), as does Molière, esp. in *Les Femmes Savantes* (Hancock). Adaptations of s. in other genres include Socratic question and answer in Platonic dialogues and amoebean verses in pastoral (q.v.) poetry (e.g. Theocritus, *Idyll* 5, and Milton, *Comus*).—A. Gross, *Die Stichomythie in der griechischen Tragödie und Komödie* (1905); J. L. Hancock, *Studies in S.* (1917); J. Myres, *The Structure of S. in Attic Tragedy* (1950); W. Jens, *Die Stichomythie in der frühen griechischen Tragödie* (1955); E.-R. Schwinge, *Die Verwendung der Stichomythie in den Dramen des Euripides* (1968); B. Seidensticker, *Die Gesprächsverdichtung in den Tragödien Senecas* (1968), and "Die Stichomythie," *Die Bauformen der griechischen Tragödie*, ed. W. Jens (1971); S. Ireland, "S. in Aeschylus," *Hermes* 102 (1974). W.H.R.

STICHOS (Gr. "row," "line"), pl. *stichoi*. In Cl. prosody (q.v.), the term for a line of verse. A single line (or a poem 1 line long) is therefore called a monostich (q.v.), a couplet a distich (q.v.), a halfline a hemistich (q.v.), etc. Outside of Cl. prosody, the noun form now used is "line," though

the adjectival "stichic" is still common. Stichic verse—e.g. narrative verse (q.v.)—is that which is written *kata stichon*, i.e. in a continuous run of isometric (q.v.) lines, whereas in stanzaic verse—e.g. the lyric (q.v.)—a small number of lines or cola (usually less than 10, but often 4 or multiples of 4) are grouped together by structures such as rhyme (q.v.) into integral units. Stichic arrangement is the norm for recited verse—in antiquity, the dactylic hexameter for epic and the iambic trimeter for drama—whereas song verse (incl. the lyric) is normally stanzaic. It is not exactly true, as Maas points out, that verseforms are either stichic or strophic: there are some intermediary or transitional forms, and some of the same principles of construction apply to both types. See now ALLAEOSTROPHA; LINE; MONOSTICH; STANZA; STROPHE.—J. W. White, *The Verse of Gr. Comedy* (1912); Maas, sects. 15–17, 61–72; A. M. Dale, "S. and Stanza," *Collected Papers* (1969). T.V.F.B.; R.J.G.

STILFORSCHUNG. See STYLISTICS.

STILNOVISMO, STIL NOVO. See DOLCE STIL NUOVO.

STOCK (also called *sto(c)kreg(h)el*, *reg(h)el*, *sluutvers*). The identical refrain line which concludes each stanza of the Dutch poetic form *refrein* (q.v.) practiced by the *rederijkers* (q.v.). It expresses the theme or leading thought of the poem and is borrowed from the Fr. ballade (q.v.). Occasionally the s. may consist of two or one and a half lines, or even of a half-line. See DUTCH POETRY.—A. Borguet, "De 'stok' van het Referein," *Revue des langues vivantes* 12 (1946); A. van Elslander, *Het refrein in de Nederlanden tot 1600* (1953). R.F.L.

STORNELLO (sometimes called *fiore*). A short It. folk verseform whose name (from Occitan *estorn*, "struggle") suggests the manner in which it was sung—responsively—as well as the sort of popular poetic contests (q.v.) which measure the improvisational talents of the competitors. While the earliest examples date from the 15th c., the s. flourished in Tuscany in the 17th c. and from there spread throughout central and southern Italy. The s. has three principal forms: (1) a rhymed couplet, the oldest form and a type now common in Sicily, which may trace its origin to rhymed proverbs; (2) a tercet of hendecasyllables (q.v.), the first and third rhyming and the second in assonance or consonance with them; and (3) a couplet of hendecasyllables prefixed by a *quinario* or a *settenario* which often consists of an invocation to a flower or plant (hence the alternate name, *fiore*) or an exclamatory or vocative phrase.—V. Santoli, *I Canti popolari italiani* (1940); Spongano; L. Castelnuovo, *La metrica italiana* (1979); Elwert, *Italienische*, sect. 99. J.G.F.; C.K.

STORY-PATTERN. See FORMULA.

STRAMBOTTO. A monostrophic It. composition of either 8 or 6 hendecasyllables (q.v.). One of the oldest of It. verseforms, the s. has uncertain but surely popular origins. The term derives from Fr. *estrabot* (Occitan *estribot*), but whereas the Fr. used it to apply to satirical compositions, the Italians have restricted it to rhymes that are sentimental and amorous in content. The number of its verses and the characteristic rhyme scheme vary from region to region: the so-called Sicilian s. (see SICILIAN OCTAVE), and the Tuscan s. has several: *ababccdd* (preferred; see RISPETTO), *ababababcc, aabbccdd, ababcc, ababab*, and *aabbcc*. In its Sicilian form, the s. may have influenced the development of the sonnet (q.v.) by serving as the model for the octave. The s. has been employed by numerous poets over the centuries, from the 15th c. (Leonardo Giustinian, Politian, Francesco Galeota) to the 19th (Carducci, Pascoli). See also OTTAVA RIMA.—H. R. Lang, "The Sp. *estribote, estrambote* and Related Poetic Forms," *Romania* 45 (1918–19); E. Li Giotti, "Precisazioni sullo s.," *Convivium* (1949); G. D'Aronco, *Guida bibliografica allo studio dello s.* (1951); Spongano; Wilkins; L. Castelnuovo, *La metrica italiana* (1979); Elwert, *Italienische*, sect. 98.   J.G.F.; C.K.

STREET BALLAD. See BROADSIDE BALLAD.

STRESS. See ACCENT.

STRESS MAXIMUM. See GENERATIVE METRICS.

STRESS TIMED. See ISOCHRONISM.

STRICT METERS. See WELSH POETRY.

STRONG LINES. See METAPHYSICAL POETRY.

STROPHE (Gr. "turn"). Originally, the initial section of a choral ode, as in Cl. Gr. drama, where the chorus chanted the s. while turning toward the altar (turn), followed by the antistrophe (q.v.) of identical metrical structure chanted in accompaniment to a reverse movement (counter-turn), concluded by the epode (q.v.) of different metrical structure, chanted as the chorus stood still (stand). The Eng. terms (in parentheses in the sentence above) are used in Ben Jonson's Cary-Morison Ode and in Theodore Roethke's "I Knew a Woman." Later the term "s." was extended to mean a structural division of a poem containing stanzas (q.v.) of varying line-length, esp. odés (q.v.). Hence in poems divided into identical or similar units (such as long narrative or epic poems, or ballads) the term "strophic" is essentially synonymous with "stanzaic"; but poems which comprise only one stanza of a distinct metrical form, such as the sonnet, would normally be called "strophic" but not "stanzaic," the latter term implying response (q.v.), i.e. division into a series of repeated units. In modern poetry the term is occasionally applied to units of free verse and verse paragraphs (qq.v.), probably because the original Cl. s. was free concerning length or meter, but such usage is loose at best. See ALLAEOSTROPHA; STANZA, with bibliography; STICHOS.

                                         E.H.; T.V.F.B.

STRUCTURALISM.

   I. PRAGUE SCHOOL
  II. MOSCOW-TARTU SCHOOL
 III. FRENCH AND AMERICAN SCHOOLS

I. PRAGUE SCHOOL (hereafter P. S.). The P. S. is an established label for the international group of scholars in linguistics, lit., theater, folklore, and general aesthetics which organized as the Prague Linguistic Circle from 1926 to 1948. In its origins, the P. S. was in part indebted to Rus. Formalism (q.v.), esp. its Moscow branch, the Moscow Linguistic Circle (see below), whose institutional name it echoed, sharing both some of its members (Pĕtr Bogatyrĕv, Roman Jakobson) and also the concept of lit. as the art of lang. At the same time, the P. S. borrowed from the Czech trad. of 19th-c. Herbartian formalism (Josef Durdík, Otakar Hostinský), which conceived of the artistic work as a set of formal relations, and also certain post-Herbartian developments in poetics and theater (Otakar Zich). Among other schools of thought, the P. S. was influenced by Saussurian linguistics, Husserl's phenomenology, and Gestalt psychology. Such intellectual affinities were welcomed by the members of the P. S., since they perceived their enterprise as the crystallization of a new scholarly paradigm for the humanities and social sciences, which in 1929 they christened *structuralism* (hereafter, s.)—the term was coined by Jakobson.

The history of the P. S. can be conveniently divided into three periods. The first begins with the establishment of the Circle in 1926 and continues until 1934. During this period, the research of the Prague structuralists focused on the internal organization of poetic works, esp. their sound stratum. Roman Jakobson and Jan Mukařovský's histories of old and modern Czech metrics are the most representative works of this phase. The subsequent period, 1934 to 1938, opens with Mukařovský's study of a little-known Czech poet of the early 19th c., Milota Zdirad Polák, and ends with the Circle's collective volume devoted to the leading Czech romantic, Karel Hynek Mácha. In this period the P. S. transcended its orientation toward lit. hist. and began to study verbal art in relation to other social phenomena. The earlier preoccupation with poetic sound was supplemented with a concern for how literary works signify extra-linguistic reality. The last period, dating roughly from 1938 to 1948, is delimited by external interventions. The Ger. invasion forced some members of the P. S. (Bogatyrĕv, Jakobson, René Wellek) to

STRUCTURALISM

leave Czechoslovakia; the Communist takeover ten years later effectively banned the structuralist study of art and eventually led to the disbanding of the Circle. During this final period, the research of the P. S. shifted to study of the human dimension of the artistic process, both author and perceivers. Felix Vodička's systematic attempt at elaborating the hist. of literary reception belongs among the most promising developments of this period.

In the postwar years, the intellectual heritage of the P. S. was disseminated throughout the world by those members who left Prague. The structuralist revolution of the 1960s in France and the United States (see below) was to a considerable degree stimulated by Roman Jakobson, who in the 1940s helped to establish the Linguistic Circle of New York, of which the Fr. anthropologist Claude Lévi-Strauss was a member. Pětr Bogatyrěv, who returned to his native land after the outbreak of the War, performed a similar role in the Soviet Union. A group of young literary scholars (Miroslav Červenka, Lubomír Doležel, Mojmír Grygar, Milan Jankovič) attempted to resurrect the P. S. in Czechoslovakia in the 1960s, but the Soviet invasion of 1968 dealt a final blow to s. in that country.

For the P. S., s. was a dialectical synthesis of the two global paradigms dominating European thought in the 19th c., romanticism and positivism. Whereas the former sacrificed empirical data to universal philosophical schemes, the latter, in its blatant inductivism, tipped the scales in the opposite direction. S., the Prague scholars argued, would avoid the onesidedness of both its predecessors by being neither a philosophical system nor a concrete science, but an *epistemological stance* incessantly negotiating between the general and the particular. What characterizes the Prague version of s. in particular is a conceptual frame of reference formed by the interplay of three complementary notions—structure, function, and sign.

The concept of *structure*, which gave the paradigm its name, requires special attention. In the parlance of the P. S., it referred to what might be seen as two distinct entities. On the one hand, it denoted the holistic organization of a single work as a hierarchical system of dominant and subordinate elements. But in the same way as Ferdinand de Saussure recognized that every concrete utterance (*parole*) is meaningful only against the background of the collectively shared linguistic code (*langue*), the Prague scholars saw every individual artwork as an implementation of a particular aesthetic code—the set of artistic norms. These they also termed a structure. In contrast to Saussure, however, the P. S. did not believe that any code (whether ling. or aesthetic) exists in and of itself. Rather, these individual sets of norms together comprise a higher structure (a structure of structures)—the cultural system valid for a given society at a particular stage in its historical development.

The second key concept, *function*, was the trademark of Prague s. It served the Circle's members as a criterion for differentiating among individual cultural codes. Functionally speaking, such codes are nothing but hierarchies of norms regulating the attainment of socially sanctioned values. The dominance of the symbolic function, for example, distinguishes the symbolic code from the aesthetic and theoretical codes. Individual artifacts, then, embody these immaterial structures, and their material organization implements the hierarchy of functions they serve. However, artifacts not only carry out their functions, they also signify them. Hence the importance of the third element of the P. S. frame of reference, the *sign*. As a conjunction of the material vehicle and immaterial meaning, the sign reiterates in different terms the dual nature of the concept of structure—its mental, socially shared existence and its physical embodiment in individual artifacts. From the semiotic point of view, culture appears as a complex interaction of signs mediating among the members of a given collectivity (see SEMIOTICS, POETIC).

In the field of poetics, the P. S. pioneered the linguistic approach to verbal art. Its members conceived of lit. as a particular mode of utilizing lang.: a functional dialect. In contrast to other such dialects (e.g. the emotive, the practical), which focus on the extra-linguistic components of the speech-act (the speaker, the referent), poetic lang. foregrounds the very medium of discourse, the linguistic sign itself. This "set toward the message" has important consequences for the structure of poetic signs and the way they signify. The sound stratum of poetic lang. is organized according to the code peculiar to this dialect. Consequently, the P. S. investigated closely the problems of sound orchestration, intonation, and prosody (q.v.) in poetic compositions. The distinctive feature of these inquiries was their phonological basis. That is, for the P. structuralists only those phonic elements of lang. capable of differentiating cognitive meanings could be exploited poetically. By the same token, the P. S. regarded the sound configurations permeating the poetic work not as mere formal constructs but as partial semantic structures comprising the overall meaning of the text. The unusual arrangement of poetic sounds in the literary sign disrupts the conventional link between the signifier and the signified, and the meaning of the work becomes a function of its internal organization rather than of the reality outside it. Hence, the designation "poetic" refers only obliquely, and its truth-value cannot be tested. By problematizing the process of verbal representation, poetic lang., according to the P. S., performs a signal role in the linguistic system. Whereas other functional dialects stress the adequacy of signs to what they stand for, attempting to obliterate their difference, poetic lang. underscores the reciprocal inadequacy of the two, their deep-seated nonidentity. In this way the poetic function (q.v.) promulgates linguistic self-awareness, enabling us to renew our semiotic grasp of reality and revealing lang. as the most versatile tool of human cognition and communication.

Jakobson, esp. v. 3, 5, 6; *A P. S. Reader on Esthetics, Literary Structure, and Style*, ed. P. L. Garvin (1964); J. Vachek, *The Ling. School of Prague* (1966); *Semiotics of Art: The P. S. Contribution*, ed. I. R. Titunik and L. Matejka (1976); S. Rudy, "Jakobson's Inquiry into Verse and the Emergence of Structural Poetics," *Sound, Sign, and Meaning*, ed. L. Matejka (1976); J. Mukařovský, *Structure, Sign, and Function* (tr. 1977), *The Word and Verbal Art* (tr. 1978); *The P. S.: Selected Writings, 1929–1948*, ed. P. Steiner (1982); H. Baran, "S. and Semiotics," in Terras; F. W. Galan, *Historic Structures: The P. S. Project, 1928–1946* (1985); J. Striedter, *Literary Structure, Evolution, and Value* (1989). P.ST.

II. MOSCOW-TARTU SCHOOL (hereafter M.-T. S.). This term designates a broad research effort in semiotics and such related disciplines as structural poetics, verse theory, cultural theory, folklore, and mythology which has been carried on since 1960 by a number of Soviet scholars principally at the Academy of Sciences in Moscow (Vjačeslav Ivanov, Vladimir Toporov, Mikhail Gasparov, Eliazar Meletinskij) and at Tartu University in Estonia (Jurij Lotman, Zara Minc, Igor' Černov). The M.-T. S. originated in the relatively liberal atmosphere of the Khrushchev period and represented both a rejection of official Marxist-Leninist scholarship and a return to the strong Rus. philological trad. of the early 20th c. Initially, it drew on the critical heritage of Rus. Formalism (q.v.) and Prague School structuralism (see above), esp. the work of Jurij Tynjanov and Roman Jakobson. This theoretical legacy was enriched by perspectives offered by general linguistics, semiotics, information theory, and cybernetics; by comparative IE and Oriental studies; by the study of versification, reconstituted in the late 1950s after lying in abeyance for decades; and by the intellectual heritage of a number of major Rus. thinkers, some of them reclaimed from obscurity by the efforts of the M.-T. S.: e.g. Mikhail Bakhtin, Ol'ga Frejdenberg, Pavel Florenskij, Gustav Špet, Vladimir Propp, and Pëtr Bogatyrev. As important as the many publications of the M.-T. S., esp. the celebrated Tartu series *Trudy po znakovym sistemam* (Works on Semiotics; 23 issues to date) were its summer schools (which ended in the mid-1970s), noted for their effervescent and interdisciplinary atmosphere.

During the 1970s and early '80s, several key figures of the M.-T. S. emigrated to the West (Aleksandr Pjatigorskij, Boris Ogibenin, Boris Gasparov, Dmitrij Segal), yet the movement remained the focus of intensive scholarly and cultural activity by younger scholars. During the tumultuous Gorbachev period, the M.-T. S. was affected by conflicting forces. On the one hand, several of its leading participants, previously under ideological

pressure in the Soviet Union, won significant recognition within official Soviet scholarly circles as semiotics, once attacked by ideological conservatives, was fully legitimated. At the same time, death, emigration, appointments at Western universities, and the strained political relations between Estonia and the fast-crumbling Soviet Union in the late 1980s raised the question of the future of the movement.

The work of the M.-T. S. has been distinguished by (1) its emphasis on concrete facts, esp. analysis of previously unstudied literary works and of cultural phenomena, by (2) its pragmatism and methodological openness (several conceptions of poetics and literary theory were represented within its ranks), and by (3) the evolution of its theoretical framework. In its early phase (until the mid-1970s), the methodology of the M.-T. S. based primarily on the model provided by structural linguistics (esp. Saussure, Trubetzkoy, Jakobson), the central concepts of which—e.g. *langue / parole* (*code / message*), *synchrony / diachrony*, and *marked / unmarked*—were broadly applied. Lit., folklore, myth, film, and other fields of human cultural activity where *signs* play a central role were described as *secondary modeling systems* or *languages*: these were regarded as built up on the basis of natural lang., hence analyzable in similar terms.

Thus for each system, one could establish both a *lexicon* (a set of signs and their associated meanings) and a *grammar* (combinatorial rules). A number of studies from this period offer descriptions of simple semiotic systems such as the system of road signs, the rules for cartomancy, or the paremiological genres in folklore (Grigorij Permjakov, *Ot pogovorki do skazki* [1970] and other works): behind these efforts lay a broad assumption that describing more complex objects, such as the novel or lit. as a whole, would be a more difficult yet fundamentally similar task—one sure to be tackled in the future with the devel. of a rigorous yet sophisticated *metalanguage*. The initial optimism faded in the 1970s, however, when the methodology of much of the M.-T. S. work shifted away from the linguistic model. While their terminology has remained the same, many of the scholars have focused on the *text* rather than the *code*, turning from simple systems describable by means of formalized metalanguages towards complex semiotic objects, each of which involved far more than an implementation of a particular set of rules. Culture, regarded as a complex mechanism of interrelated, often conflicting codes, became the principal focus of the M.-T. S., while the role of neurolinguistic and sociological factors in its creation, preservation, and transformation received special attention.

Poetry and poetics have always been areas of major interest for the M.-T. S., due to the influence of the Rus. trad. of the linguistic study of the poetic text (Lev Ščerba, Jakobson), the role of verse theory in formalist and early structuralist endeavors, and the special situation of post-Stalinist Russia, where entire layers of early 20th-c. culture, esp. lit., had to be brought out of the oblivion to which they had been officially consigned. The latter factor has been of special importance in the activities of the M.-T. S., which has played a cultural role in Soviet society unmatched by structuralist movements elsewhere. The heritage of acmeism (q.v.; e.g. Nikolaj Gumilev, Anna Axmatova, Osip Mandel'štam) has been a special focus of a number of scholars (Toporov, Segal, Jurij Levin, Tat'jana Civ'jan, Roman Timenčik, Gavriil Levinton). At the same time, under the leadership of Zara Minc (d. 1990), the M.-T. S. has devoted much effort to research on the symbolist movement, esp. the writings of Aleksandr Blok and Andrej Belyj, as well as the Silver Age in general (many studies appearing in the Tartu series *Blokovskie sborniki* [Blok volumes]).

In poetics, two main research trends have characterized the activities of the M.-T. S. The first, structuralist in the traditional sense, has involved the study of the individual text, regarded as a hierarchy of levels (phonic, rhythmical, grammatical) that may be studied individually or as a totality. This approach, discussed extensively in Lotman's early monographs (*Analysis of the Poetic Text* [tr. 1976], *Structure of the Artistic Text* [tr. 1977]) and at the core of his structuralist poetics, owes much to Jakobson, esp. his classic article "Linguistics and Poetics" (1960) and his many studies of the "grammar of poetry," as well as to Tynjanov's classic work on poetic semantics (tr. M. Sosa and B. Harvey as *The Problem of Verse Lang.* [1981]). Lotman emphasizes the notion that the poetic function (q.v.) establishes hierarchically organized networks of equivalence (parallelisms) throughout the poetic work, and he traces the effect of such relationships (absent in ordinary discourse) on both the *paradigmatic* and the *syntagmatic* planes, seeking to identify the underlying semantic opposition(s) from which the work as a whole may be seen as deriving. In addition to studying the semantic effects resulting from lang. operating within the horizontal (intralinear) and vertical (interlinear, interstrophic) dimensions of the poem, Lotman and his colleagues have focused on the structural role of extratextual factors, esp. on the aesthetic results of the poem's relationship to various contexts (a poetic cycle, a collection [q.v.], an author's oeuvre, the work of a poetic school); here, they have relied on a semiotic conception of the text which emphasizes the flexibility of its boundaries and its mutually reinforcing relationship with different cultural codes. Ivanov, Toporov, M. Gasparov, Levin, and other scholars have analyzed with great success 19th- and 20th-c. poems (by Batjuškov, Puškin, Tjutčev, Mandel'štam, Axmatova, Xlebnikov, Majakovskij, Cvetaeva): in the best studies, rigorous analysis of the lower levels of a text, supplemented by a sophisticated analysis of relevant literary, cultural, and historical factors, leads to an interpretation (q.v.) of its meaning (q.v.). A variant of this "monographic" method is found in the writings of A. Žolkovskij and Ju. Ščeglov, creators of the "Theme-Text" model of the literary work, in which a highly formalized metalanguage is used to describe the connections between the content-plane and the expression-plane of a literary work (see, for example, A. Žolkovskij, *Themes and Texts: Towards a Poetics of Expressiveness* [1984]; Yu. Ščeglov and A. Žolkovskij, *Poetics of Expressiveness: A Theory and Applications* [1987]). This was an important approach in the early work of the M.-T. S., though not favored by other researchers in the group.

The other trend in M.-T. S. poetics has involved research on three broad classes of phenomena:

(1) *Verse Rhythm*, studied by means of the linguo-statistical model developed by Tomaševskij, expanded by Kiril Taranovsky in the 1950s, and reformulated by the mathematician Andrej Kolmogorov and his students. The principal figure in this area—which developed independently of broad semiotic formulations but was closely linked with the structural-semiotic movement in the Soviet Union—has been Mikhail Gasparov, whose work on 20th-c. systems of versification in Rus. poetry has charted this previously unexplored area and provided a unified approach to the variety of metrical and rhythmical forms found in modern poetry. Major work, in some cases applying newer linguistic methodologies to problems of versification (e.g. generative theory), has also been carried out by such scholars as P. Rudnev, V. Baevskij, and M. Ju. Lotman (son). Subsequently, major interest turned to the history of Rus. verse, including mapping the metrical repertoires of individual poets and poetic movements. Two major monographs by Gasparov (*Očerk istorii russkogo stixa: metrika, ritmika, rifma, strofika* [1984], *Očerk istorii evropejskogo stixa* [1989]) are exemplary of this current trend. Gasparov and others also have been increasingly drawn to the relationship between metrical forms and semantics, i.e. towards the history of associations between certain meters and specific themes—a complex, difficult, yet promising area of investigation.

(2) *Poetic Lexicon*, the study of which attracted a number of scholars in the early period of the M.-T. S. Establishing the specific vocabulary used by a poet in a single work, a collection, a period, or an oeuvre, has been seen as a way of objectively analyzing the shifts lang. undergoes in the process of poetic creation, and of pinpointing the difficult, often highly displaced meanings of images and motifs in the work of modern poets. Collections by Blok, Axmatova, Mandel'štam, and other poets have been subjected to this type of study.

(3) *Intertextual Relations*, which came into the purview of the Soviet structuralists in the early 1970s in connection with their research into acmeism. Soon, the poetics of this school was

shown to be fundamentally oriented toward preceding literary trads.: in an acmeist poem, discovering subtexts and elucidating their relationship to the work is often indispensable to comprehending its semantics. Study of acmeist subtexts by Toporov, Levinton, Timenčik, and others was strengthened by parallel research in the U. S. by Taranovsky and his school (see G. A. Levinton and R. D. Timenčik, "Kniga K. F. Taranovskogo o poèzii O. È. Mandel'štama," *Rus. Lit.* 6 [1978]; R. D. Timenčik, "Tekst v tekste u akmeistov," *TZS* 14 [1981]). Much research also has been devoted to intertextual elements of works by symbolist authors, esp. Blok, Belyj, and Sologub, and by other major Silver-Age figures (Mixail Kuzmin, Aleksej Remizov). Zara Minc is the author of the conception of the *polygenetic* nature of symbolist (modernist) subtexts: in many cases, a cited element may derive from several different sources, which themselves may enter into complex, potentially conflicting relationships with each other (see her "Funkcija reminiscencij v poetike A. Bloka," *TZS* 6 [1973]). This approach to intertextuality (q.v.), taken up by other scholars, has proved highly fruitful, yielding a sophisticated theoretical model and vastly enriching our understanding of Rus. modernism. The shift towards the text as a principal focus of M.-T. S. research has increased the emphasis on intertextuality, with the concept being extended to other areas of semiotic activity such as film. See also ANAGRAM; SLAVIC PROSODY.

BIBLIOGRAPHIES: K. Eimermacher and S. Shishkoff, *Subject Bibl. of Soviet Semiotics: The M.-T. S.* (1977).

ANTHOLOGIES: *Texte des sowjetischen literaturwissenschaftlichen Strukturalismus,* ed. K. Eimermacher (1971); *Semiotics and Structuralism: Readings from the Soviet Union,* ed. H. Baran (1976); *Soviet Semiotics: An Anthol.,* ed. and tr. D. P. Lucid (1977); *Readings in Soviet Semiotics,* ed. L. Matejka et al. (1977); *Rus. Poetics in Tr.,* v. 1'–10, ed. L. M. O'Toole and A. Shukman (1975–83).

HISTORY AND CRITICISM: E. M. Meletinskii and D. M. Segal, "Structuralism and Semiotics in the USSR," *Diogenes* 73 (1971); D. M. Segal, *Aspects of Structuralism in Soviet Philology* (1974); V. V. Ivanov, *Očerki po istorii semiotiki v SSSR* (1976); A. Shukman, *Literature and Semiotics: A Study of the Writings of Ju. M. Lotman* (1977); H. Baran, "Structuralism and Semiotics," in Terras, and "Ob itoga x i problemax semiotičeskix issledovanij," *Trudy po znakovym sistemam* 20 (1987); E. Bojtár, *Slavic Structuralism* (tr. 1985); S. Rudy, "Semiotics in the USSR," *The Semiotic Sphere,* ed. T. Sebeok and J. Umiker-Sebeok (1986); B. A. Uspenskij, "K probleme geneziza tartusko-moskovskoj semiotičeskoj školy," *TZS* 20 (1987); P. A. Rudnev, *Vvedenie v nauku u russkom stixe. Vyp. 1* (1989); B. M. Gasparov, "Tartuskaja škola 1960-x godov kak semiotičeskij fenomen," *Wiener Slawistischer Almanach* 29 (1989).   H.B.

III. FRENCH AND AMERICAN SCHOOLS. Inspired by developments in structural linguistics and structural anthropology (see MYTH CRITICISM), s. as a method of analysis and a theory of lit. reached its height in France in the 1960s, in the work of Roland Barthes, Gérard Genette, A. J. Greimas, Roman Jakobson, and Tzvetan Todorov, whence it was transported to Am. crit. S. is difficult to delimit because interesting structuralist work swiftly became assimilated to so-called post-s. (see DECONSTRUCTION), a movement often defined in opposition to a caricature of s. but which in fact carried on many of its projects. There are continuities between s. and post-s. in the work of Barthes, Julia Kristeva, and Jacques Derrida, for example. Outside the literary field the most eminent structuralist thinkers are Claude Lévi-Strauss, Michel Foucault, and Jacques Lacan.

In general terms, s. can be opposed to all atomistic theories which attempt to explain phenomena individually. F. de Saussure (1857– 1913), the founder of modern linguistics, distinguishes concrete speech acts (*parole*) from the underlying system of the lang. (*langue*), a formal entity whose elements have no positive or inherent qualities but are defined solely in relational terms. *Synchronic* study, treating lang. as a formal system of interrelated elements functioning at a particular time, takes precedence over *diachronic* study tracing the history of individual elements. Lévi-Strauss, the central figure of s., adopted this perspective in anthropology and rejected attempts to explain social and cultural phenomena in piecemeal fashion, treating them instead as manifestations of underlying formal systems. His studies of primitive logic, totemism, and myth reconstruct a "logic of the concrete," the conceptual systems which enable people to think about and organize the world. The codes by which myths operate are sets of binary oppositions drawn from different areas of experience which can be used to express a variety of contrasts; they thus bear striking resemblance to those operative in poetic discourse. For example, in the sonnet "Two loves I have of comfort and despair," Shakespeare takes the opposition good/evil and explores it through a variety of codes: the religious (angel/devil, saint/fiend), the moral (purity/pride), and the physical (fair/colored ill).

Structuralist analysis of this logic of the concrete is related to semiology (see SEMIOTICS), the study of sign systems. The two fundamental insights on which s. is based are (1) that social and cultural phenomena do not have essences but are defined both by their internal structures and by their place in the structures of the relevant social and cultural systems, and (2) that social and cultural phenomena are signs: not physical events only, but events with meaning. One may try to separate the structural from the semiological—the study of patterns from the study of signs—but the most successful structural analyses isolate those structures which permit phenomena to function as signs.

S. in lit. crit. began as a revolt against the particular types of erudition—lit. hist. and biographical crit.—which dominated the Fr. university orthodoxy. S. sought to return to the text, but unlike Anglo-Am. New Criticism (q.v.), it assumed that one could not study a text without preconceptions, that naive empiricism was an impossible critical position, and that in order to discover structures one required a methodological model. The goal of s. was not the interp. of texts but the elaboration, through encounters with particular texts, of an account of the modes of literary discourse and their operation. Barthes distinguished *criticism* (q.v.), which places the text in a particular context and assigns it meaning, from a science of lit. or *poetics* (q.v.), which studies the conditions of meaning, the formal structures that organize a text and make possible a range of meanings (see MEANING, POETIC). Tr. of the Rus. Formalists (see RUSSIAN FORMALISM) in the late 1960s gave structuralists analogues to their own work and stimulated the study of lit. as an autonomous institution with its own modes of self-transcendence, but the principal model was linguistic. Two versions of s. can be distinguished by their different uses of linguistics: as a technique applied directly to the description of the lang. of texts, or as the model for a poetics which would stand to lit. as linguistics stands to lang. (see LINGUISTICS AND POETICS)

The first strain involves study of the patterns formed by the distribution in the text of elements defined by phonological and syntactic theory. Jakobson's characterization of the poetic function (q.v.) of lang. as "the projection of the principle of equivalence [q.v.] from the axis of selection into the axis of combination" led to study of the ways in which items that are paradigmatically equivalent (related by membership of a grammatical, lexical, or phonological class) are distributed in linguistic sequences (on the axis of combination). Jakobson's analyses of poems focus on symmetrical and asymmetrical patterns of distribution which unify the text and throw certain elements into relief. It has been claimed that many patterns he discovers are irrelevant to the reader's experience and thus to the meaning of the poem, but the issue is a difficult one, since appeal to the reader's experience is scarcely decisive—patterns may work subliminally—and formal patterns need not contribute to meaning in order to have a unifying effect. Other critics, such as Nicolas Ruwet and Jacques Geninasca, working with Jakobson's theories and techniques, have preferred to concentrate on ways in which linguistic patterning supports semantic effects. This version of s., though it has revealed the intricacy of the formal organization of verse, tends to separate the structural from the semiological and should be distinguished from the attempt to develop a poetics modeled on linguistics.

Structuralist poetics is founded on the presumption that while lit. uses lang., it is also itself *like* a lang. in that its meanings are made possible by systems of convention (q.v.) which serve readers as models for interp. Analyzing a lit. is analogous to analyzing a lang., and one must develop a series of concepts designed to account for the operation of lit. as a system. The work of Genette, Riffaterre, and esp. Barthes has contributed to a metalanguage that serves both as a theory of lit. and as the outline of an analytical method.

Lit. is not just sentences but sentences made signs in a second-order literary system. A given sentence will have different meanings, depending on whether it is used in a lyric poem or in a newspaper report. Within the literary system, linguistic signs become second-order signifiers whose signifieds are their special meaning in the literary discourse. The conventions that give sentences additional meanings and functions are those of what Barthes calls an *écriture*: a particular mode of writing involving an implicit contract between author and reader. The system or institution of lit. is made up of a series of *écritures* which constitute its historical or generic moments. In reading a sentence in a lyric differently from a sentence in a newspaper report, one is implicitly recognizing and employing the conventions of a particular lyric *écriture*.

Cultures tend to *naturalize* their signs, to motivate the connection between signifier and signified so that meanings seem natural and not the result of convention; lit. may therefore be described according to the ways in which it resists or complies with this process. Interp. is itself a mode of *naturalization* or *recuperation*, the attempt to bring the text within a logical discursive order by making it the expression of a meaning. We read texts in accordance with a series of *codes* which provide, on the one hand, models of human behavior (coherence and incoherence of personality, plausible and implausible relations between action and motive, logical and illogical chains of events), and, on the other hand, models of literary intelligibility (coherence and incoherence, plausible and implausible symbolic extrapolations, significance and insignificance) that enable us to make sense of texts by organizing their elements into coherent series. These codes are models of the *vraisemblable*, in the broad sense in which structuralists use the term—models of the natural and intelligible; and a work which lends itself to this process of recuperation is *lisible* (readable), whereas one that is unintelligible in terms of our traditional models is *scriptible* (writable): it can be written but not read, except in a kind of vicarious writing. A structuralist analysis of a work aims less at interpreting and thereby recuperating it than at examining the ways in which it responds to the reader's attempts to make it unified and coherent. The critic does not discover its structure so much as explore possibilities of *structuration*. The critic therefore attends to a play of signifiers which defer meaning by offering materials that exceed meanings that can be assigned them—e.g. meter, rhyme, and sound patterns in poetry, all instances of the surplus of the signifier. The play of the signifier is the productivity of the text because it forces the reader to become not the passive consumer of an intelligibility to be recognized but the active producer of meaning and participant in the exploration of possible modes of order.

This series of concepts leads to a critique of the representational aesthetic (which locates values in what is represented) and to a stress on the text as linguistic surface. The play of lang. is valued for the ways in which it leads to a questioning of the relationship between lang. and experience; and hence critics attend to effects of *intertextuality* (q.v.): the interaction within a text of various modes of discourse or of langs. drawn from other literary texts and from other discourse about the world. Whereas the Rus. Formalists saw the text as a way of "making strange" ordinary objects or activities, structuralists emphasize the "making strange" of discourses which order the world and which the work puts on display. The value of lit. is thus related to its foregrounding of rhetorical processes: undermining culture's attempts to make meanings natural, it asserts its own status as artifice and produces in the reader a self-conscious exploration of ways of ordering experience.

Although structuralist crit. has focused primarily on the novel, there is a body of work on poetry which may be grouped under several headings. (1) The reconstruction of poetic codes or systems: Gérard Genette has described baroque imagery as a system of interrelated items defined less by individual connotation than by oppositions, and has analyzed images of day and night as a poetic code; Paul Zumthor has reconstructed the codes of medieval poetry, from the generic types of discourse to systems of *topoi* (see TOPOS), rhythmical formulae, descriptive schemata, and conventionalized knowledge. (2) The correlation of particular structures with the interpretive operations they require: Michael Riffaterre has analyzed a variety of poetic devices, from the revitalized cliché to the extended metaphor of surrealist poetry, and describes lyrics as periphrastic transformations of clichés or prior literary formulae; S. Levin's theory of "couplings" shows how phonological or grammatical equivalence affects semantic interp.; A. J. Greimas and his followers have attempted to show how a level of coherence or *isotopie* is attained in the interp. of poetic sequences. (3) The rehabilitation of rhet.: Genette, Group Mu, and others have redefined rhetorical figures in linguistic terms and opened the way to a theory which would treat the figures as instructions for symbolic reading, as sets of conventional operations which readers may perform on poetic texts. (4) The reinvention of poetic artifice: Kristeva and poets of the *Tel Quel* school (Marcelin Pleynet, Denis Roche) have undertaken readings of poets designed to show how they undermine by their formal invention the traditional operations of the sign and have emphasized the need for contemp. poets to question and write against the codes and implicit contracts of poetry; Veronica Forrest-Thomson stresses the constructive rather than destructive aspect of this project, arguing that only the invention of new conventions and explicit artifice can enable poetry to play its traditional role of investigating and criticizing our unexamined ordering of experience and assumptions about the relationship between lang. and the world.

Generally, the structuralist study of poetry investigates the implicit conventions that enable poetry to be read and understood and focuses on the unsettled relationship between these conventions, always threatened by naturalization, and poetic texts. In the late 1970s and 1980s, s. was often opposed to post-s., which represented s. as a scientific attempt to reduce lang. and lit. to codes and identified itself as an exploration of the ways texts outplay the codes or undermine the oppositions on which they depend. But the structuralist investigation of codes was always linked to an interest in their disruption by literary experimentation. See also CRITICISM; CULTURAL CRITICISM; DECONSTRUCTION; HISTORICISM; INFLUENCE; INTERPRETATION; INTERTEXTUALITY; STRUCTURE; TEXTUALITY; THEORY; TWENTIETH-CENTURY POETICS.

BIBLIOGRAPHIES: J. Harari, *Structuralists and Structuralisms* (1971); Culler; J. M. Miller, *Fr. S.: A Multidisciplinary Bibl.* (1981); S. Freedman and C. Taylor, *Roland Barthes* (1983).

HISTORY AND CRITICISM: F. de Saussure, *Cours de linguistique générale* (1916), 5th ed. (1955), crit. ed., ed. R. Engler (1967–74), tr. R. Harris (1983); R. Barthes, *Le Degré zéro de l'écriture* (1953), *Essais critiques* (1964), *Critique et vérité* (1966), "Intro. á l'analyse structurale des récits," *Communications* 8 (1966); *S/Z* (1970); C. Lévi-Strauss, *La Pensée sauvage* (1962), *Le Cru et le cuit* (1964); S. Levin, *Ling. Structures in Poetry* (1962); M. Pleynet, *Comme* (1965); G. Genette, *Figures* (1966), *Figures II* (1969), *Figures III* (1972); A. J. Greimas, *Sémantique structurale* (1966), *Du Sens* (1970), *Maupassant* (1976), *Du Sens II* (1983); "S.," *YFS* 36–37 (1966); M. Foucault, *Les Mots et les choses* (1966); J. Derrida, *L'Écriture et la différence* (1967), *La Dissémination* (1972); "S.: Idéologie et méthode," *Esprit* 35 (1967); U. Eco, *La struttura assente* (1968); D. Roche, *Eros énergumène* (1968); P. Sollers, *Logiques* (1968); *Qu'est-ce que le structuralisme?* ed. F. Wahl (1968); J. Kristeva, *Semeiotikè* (1969); S. Booth, *An Essay on Shakespeare's Sonnets* (1969); G. Deleuze, *Proust et les signes* (1970); Group Mu, *Rhétorique de la poésie* (1977); *The Structuralist Controversy*, ed. R. Macksey and E. Donato (1972); T. Todorov, *La Lit. fantastique* (1970); J. Geninasca, *Analyse structurale des Chiméres de Nerval* (1971); *Essais de sémiotique poétique*, ed. A. J. Greimas (1971); M. Riffaterre, *Essais de stylistique structurale* (1971), *Semiotics of Poetry* (1978), *La Production du texte* (1979); F. Jameson, *The Prison-House of Lang.* (1972); N. Ruwet, *Lang., musique, poésie* (1972); P. Zumthor, *Essai de poétique médiévale* (1972); R. Jakobson, *Questions de poétique* (1973), *Selected Writings,* esp. v. 3, 5 (1981), *Lang. in Lit.* (1987); Culler; R. Scholes, *S. in Lit.* (1974); J. Broekman, *S.: Moscow, Prague, Paris* (1974); P. Caws, "S.," *DHI*; E. Stankiewicz, "Structural Poetics and Linguistics," *Current Trends in Linguistics, XII,* ed. T. A. Sebeok (1974); *Sound, Sign and Meaning,* ed. L. Matejka (1976); T. Hawkes, *S. and Semiotics* (1977); V. Forrest-Thomson, *Poetic Artifice* (1978); K. Silverman, *The Subject of Semiotics* (1983); J. Culler, *Roland Barthes* (1983), *Ferdinand de Saussure,* 2d ed. (1986); D. Rice and P. Schofer, *Rhetorical Poetics* (1983); J. Fekete, *The Structural Allegory* (1984); M. Titzmann, "Struktur, Strukturalismus," and G. Martens, "Text," *Reallexikon* 4.256–78, 403–17; J. G. Merquior, *From Prague to Paris* (1986); R. Harland, *Superstructuralism* (1987); P. Caws, *S.: The Art of the Intelligible* (1988); V. B. Leitch, *Am. Lit. Crit. from the Thirties to the Eighties* (1988), ch. 9; T. G. Pavel, *The Feud of Lang.* (1989); D. Holdcroft, *Saussure* (1991). J.C.

STRUCTURE (Ger. *Aufbau*). S. is an important interpretive and methodological concept for critics who are more interested in the internal dynamics of a literary work (the interrelationships which comprise a literary system) than in its relation to external phenomena, its thematic content, or its genetic origins. Emphasis on s. allows the literary work to be conceived as an autonomous object (see AUTONOMY) and to be characterized in terms of its s. or internal relations, whence the importance of s. in all formalist approaches to poetry. This view of s. recalls Aristotle's *Poetics*, which could be said to attempt an analysis of poetic ss. For the new theoretical formulation revives that Cl. idea of form which underlies Aristotle's systematic mapping of genres—epic and lyric poetry, tragedy, and comedy. Thus Aristotle's focus on "poetry in itself and of its various kinds" has certain affinities with important 20th-c. conceptions of s. (though the Aristotelian analysis tends to relegate the formal character of poetic s. to the periphery of investigation in favor of such psychological issues as *catharsis*—q.v.).

Some of the most crucial aspects of the concept of s. may be seen in the divergence between two dominant theoretical models: the generic and the organic. Genre crit. (see GENRE) stresses the relationship between the whole (the overall generic code which articulates the structural rules, formal characteristics, or subcategories of the class) and the part (the particular poem which deviates merely in details). This formulation of the relationship of part to whole is radically unlike that which is given in organic theories of poetry (see ORGANICISM), which assume that each individual poem, each individual poetic s., is unique. In the organic model, the s. of the poem has priority over

generic rules, and the identification of that s. (i.e. the s. of its logical argument or its image patterns) becomes the privileged object of study.

The distinction between the internal s. of the poem and its extra-literary or contextual references is set forth most clearly in New Criticism (q.v.), and most particularly informs Cleanth Brooks' influential study *The Well Wrought Urn* (1947), subtitled *Studies in the S. of Poetry*. Brooks is not concerned with a conventional analysis of content; rather, he endeavors to work out a systematic theory of poetic s. In Brooks' conception, what is essential is the inner, *paradoxical* s. of the poem, with its tensions (q.v.), stresses, and contradictions. As he writes, the structural "principle is not one which involves the arrangement of the various elements into homogeneous groupings, pairing like with like. It unites the like with the unlike." More than anything else, it is these inner tensions and paradoxes uniting "like with unlike" that define poetic s. Far from seeking to establish some homogeneous grouping (common themes, period styles, recurring images), Brooks seeks to isolate the "pattern of resolved stresses" which comprises the completed s. of the poem. Thus he is able to show that the inner coherence of poetic s. is constituted by balanced tensions, harmonized meanings, and dramatized resolutions.

John Crowe Ransom, too, directs the critic's attention away from extra-linguistic references toward the inner form and verbal autonomy of the poetic s. itself. But he differs from Brooks in that the logical s. of the poem—its paraphrasable core—is bound up with its local texture (q.v.). Nothing illustrates Ransom's distinction between s. and texture so well as his architectural metaphor: poetic s. corresponds to the walls, beams, and supports of a house, texture to the paint, wallpaper, and surface decoration. Whereas Brooks emphasizes s., for Ransom s. gives added importance to texture. This conceptual reversal accentuates the sensuous immediacy and vital concreteness of the poem.

It is worth noting that Ransom's distinction was taken up by Monroe C. Beardsley (*Aesthetics,* 1958), who extended it to the plastic arts, music, and narrative. Nevertheless, it should be observed that the systematic investigation of the internal s. of the poem has been called into question by critics of formalism. New-Historicist critics, for example, take as their purpose to demonstrate that the poem comprises something more than its organized ss. There is a shift from consideration solely of the inner s. of a poem to consideration of its historical context or situation. To put it another way, the inner articulation of poetic s. becomes better understood when the poem is relocated within its sociohistorical context.

The separation of the formal poetic s. from the object of reference is to be found not only in Am. New Criticism, however, but also in much Slavic and Fr. structuralist thought as well—a significant parallel. However, in structuralism (q.v.) the still too organic model is discarded for a new linguistic paradigm. In contrast to the usage of the term in New Criticism, s. in structuralism denotes the domain of the signifier as such (the sounds or letters that are meaningful in a given lang. system). What is important in structuralism is the primacy of the signifier itself. This displacement brackets and suspends the object of reference; it detaches the signifier from what is signified. As a result, the fundamental locus becomes the complex differential relationships of the signifiers within the boundaries of the linguistic system, not the relation of the signifier to the external world. The dominant model is that of the Swiss linguist Ferdinand de Saussure (1857–1913) with his seminal distinction between *langue* (the linguistic possibilities which make up a total lang. system) and *parole* (the local and contingent speech acts which are performed by individuals). On a theoretical level, structuralism as a whole owes very much to this initial assumption. Thus defined, the analytic methods of structuralism always involve a deliberate effort to restore to the object of study the hidden and unarticulated rules of its synchronic functioning (or disfunctioning). As Roland Barthes notes, "s. is therefore actually a *simulacrum* of the object, but a directed, *interested* simulacrum, since the imitated object makes something appear which remained invisible or, if one prefers, unintelligible in the natural object" ("The Structuralist Activity").

Such a construct of a synchronic system allows Roman Jakobson and Claude Lévi-Strauss to delineate a basic poetic s. in Baudelaire's "Les Chats." In particular, the emphasis on synchronic s. makes visible the tensions between two sets of symmetrical/asymmetrical relations. This decoding device foregrounds "a division of the poem into two sestets separated by a distich whose s. contrast[s] vigorously with the rest." The frame is provided by a system of oppositions in dynamic progression which moves via the distich from the first sestet to the second. Jakobson and Lévi-Strauss reconstruct the superimposed formal levels (phonetic, phonological, syntactical, and semantic) of the two sestets. In the first, real cats occupy an important place; in the second, an unexpected reversal opens up an imaginary space beyond the factual and physical world where surreal cats stand out. From a structuralist point of view, these intentional ambiguities combine to produce a new utterance: the sensual and exterior world of the first sestet is maintained at the same time that it is transferred to the intellectual and interior world of the second. Through this example the two critics are able to explore a series of oppositions (fact/myth, constriction/dilation, exteriority/interiority) which are reconciled in the poem in various combinatory forms of linguistic organization. There is no doubt that Lévi-Strauss and Jakobson's reading of "Les Chats" is a paradigmatic example of structuralist method. Yet it should be remarked that other critics have contested their decipherment of the formal features in question. Michael Riffaterre, for example, suggests that the s. of the sonnet is "a sequence of synonymous images, all of them variations on the symbolism of the cat as representative of the contemplative life."

The same application of a linguistic or synchronic model to poetry is to be found in the poetics of Tzvetan Todorov, where the task of the critic is the discovery and description of an overall "s. of significations whose relations can be apprehended." For Todorov, like Jakobson and Lévi-Strauss, the speech act is reconstituted as a signifying system or set of linguistic relations so that the content of a poem becomes lang. itself (rather than the referential object). For example, the *Odyssey* is more appropriately described as a poem about the formal ss. of lang. than as an epic narration of Odysseus' adventures. Seen in this way, all referential aspects of the poem (the speeches, the song of the Sirens, and esp. prophecies) assume the character of a linguistic s.—that is to say, an event of lang. As Todorov puts it: "every nondiscursive event is merely the incarnation of a discourse."

The conception of formal gaps or breaks in Gérard Genette's *Figures of Literary Discourse* provides yet another definition of the nature and function of poetic s. It is characteristic of Genette's theory of figures that his readings emphasize the spaces and gaps inscribed within the poetic text. This distinguishes Genette's microscopic analyses of poetic s. from Todorov's more general theoretical propositions about poetic lang. According to Genette, "poetry finds its place and its function *where lang. falls short*, in precisely those shortcomings that constitute it." For Genette, poetic s. is the particular space that disconnects two or more forms. Yet poetic s. is also a negation of the gap, for it projects a utopia of lang. in which the gap between signifier and signified would be effaced. Poetry, Genette writes, is "gap from the gap, negation, rejection, oblivion, effacement of the gap, of the gap that *makes* lang.; illusion, dream, the necessary and absurd utopia of a lang. without gap, without hiatus—without shortcomings." At the same time, it should be noted that Genette's theory of poetics is unmistakably linked with that of Todorov, in that both critics attempt to define the formal properties of poetic ss.

Saussure's fundamental analysis of the signifier is also explicitly taken up in the recent works of Jacques Derrida and other theorists (most notably the *Tel Quel* group and, in particular, Julia Kristeva). But in this group of writers a new conception emerges which distinguishes them from the contributions of structuralism. This is the deconstruction (q.v.) of those hypostases of s. which fix it conceptually as a centered s. or transcendental signified. Such hypostasized ss.—Derrida sees them as metaphysical substances or mythical plenitudes—derive from a nostalgia for origins, a longing for a metaphysic of absolute presence. Derrida attempts to escape the closure of such a centered s. by emphasizing the free play of the signifier. This indeterminacy (q.v.) of the heterogeneous text is intimately connected with what he has called *différance*, a term which implies both difference and deferral: an interminable temporal movement of signification that cannot be arrested in an absolute presence or closure of "meaning." However, it must be recognized that Derrida's ultimate emphasis on the free play of the signifier is still tied to the way the question of s. is posed within the linguistic premises and traditional logic of Western metaphysics. The decoding of poetic script, the textual decipherment of poetry's specific ss., can be achieved in the first place only in terms of the older modes of lang. and thought which Derrida sets out to deconstruct—that is to say, in terms of what he calls the "always-already-written" (the *trace*). This suggests that his deconstructionist readings and analyses remain somehow structural, in spite of Derrida's effort to avoid the metaphysical closure of centered s. or absolute presence. For further discussion of modes of form and s. in poetry, see ORGANICISM and UNITY; see also SIMPLICITY AND COMPLEXITY.

Brooks; Crane—important critique of Brooks; W. Emrich, "Die Struktur der moderne Dichtung," *WW* (1952–53); R. S. Crane, *The Langs. of Crit. and the S. of Poetry* (1953); S. Fishman, "Meaning and S. in Poetry," *JAAC* 14 (1956); M. C. Beardsley, *Aesthetics* (1958); *Sens et usage du terme s.*, ed. R. Bastide (1962); R. Wellek, "Concepts of Form and S. in 20th-C. Crit.," *Concepts of Crit.* (1963); H. Meyer, "Über der Begriff Struktur in der Dichtung," *NDH* 10 (1963); J. Lotman, *The S. of the Artistic Text* (1971; tr. 1977); R. Barthes, "The Structuralist Activity," *Critical Essays*, tr. R. Howard (1972); T. Hawkes, *Structuralism and Semiotics* (1977); R. Jakobson and C. Lévi-Stauss, "Charles Baudelaire's 'Les Chats,'" *The Structuralists*, ed. R. and F. DeGeorge (1972); M. Riffaterre, "Describing Poetic Ss.," *Structuralism*, ed. J. Ehrmann (1970); D. Wunderlich, "Terminologie des Strukturbegriffs," *Literaturwiss. und Linguistik*, ed. J. Ihwe, v. 1 (1972); F. Jameson, *The Prison-House of Lang.* (1972)—excellent analysis; F. Martinez-Bonati, "Die logische Struktur der Dichtung," *DVJ* 47 (1973); Culler; T. Todorov, *The Poetics of Prose*, tr. R. Howard (1977); T. D. Young, "Ransom's Critical Theories: S. and Texture," *MissQ* 30 (1977); J. Derrida, "S., Sign and Play," *Writing and Difference*, tr. A. Bass (1978), "Living on: *Border Lines*," *Deconstruction and Crit.* (1979); G. Genette, *Figures of Literary Discourse*, tr. A. Sheridan (1982); R. Williams, "Structural," *Keywords* (1983); J. Kristeva, *Revolution in Poetic Lang.*, tr. M. Waller (1984); J. C. Ransom, "Crit. as Pure Speculation" (1941), in Ransom; J. C. Rowe, "S.," *Critical Terms for Literary Study*, ed. F. Lentricchia and T.

McLaughlin (1990).   P.M.; T.V.F.B.

STURM UND DRANG (Storm and Stress). The second title of a wildly bombastic play (1776) by F. M. Klinger, and a hendiadys (q.v.) for the impulse to give violent expression to one's individuality, S. u. D. is the name most commonly given a revolutionary literary movement that flourished in Germany from the late 1760s to the early 1780s. Because most of its representatives ("Originalgenies"—hence "Geniezeit" as an earlier term for S. u. D.) ceased to be radicals with advancing years, the term frequently denotes a brief period of youthful exuberance or maladjustment.

Hostile to neoclassicism as exemplified in Fr. lit., and hence often deliberately indecorous in theme and lang., S. u. D. was greatly influenced by Fr. and Eng. preromanticism (q.v.), the latter esp. important in that, since the 1740s, Eng. lit. had been regarded as particularly congenial to the Ger. national character (Bodmer, Breitinger, Klopstock, Lessing). A general repudiation of normative aesthetics based itself on: (1) the new sense of historical relativism and the importance attributed to environmental differences (Montesquieu, Herder); (2) the revaluation of the primitive and of early national lit. and art (Rousseau; Macpherson and Ossian; popular balladry; the Gothic revival; Homer as interpreted by Young, and Pindar, the Bible, and Shakespeare by Herder); and (3) the cult of original genius (Shaftesbury; Young as author of *Conjectures on Original Composition*, 1759; see GENIUS), which Herder, like Adam Ferguson, conceived as dynamic (because of the importance Herder attached to dynamism—Ger. *Kraft*—he and his followers were soon labeled, usually ironically, "Kraftgenies").

S. u. D. developed as the optimism of 18th-c. rationalists began to seem unwarranted in light of what the Enlightenment had actually achieved. Herder and his theologically less liberal teacher Hamann were both centrally concerned with religious issues, and many S. u. D. writers subscribed to a Herderian pantheism in which elements of Spinoza and Leibniz were sometimes fused with pietistic subjectivism. With nature felt to be a demonic force not entirely accessible to reason, a deliberate cult of the irrational—and of myth as opposed to allegory (qq.v.)—became widespread.

For the drama, Shakespeare, as formally unconventional, and Diderot and Mercier, as socially realistic, were inspirations and models (Goethe, Lenz, H. L. Wagner, F. Müller, the early Schiller). The lyric was permanently enriched with folksong elements (new structural freedom, simpler and more direct lang.) and forceful Pindaric directness (Goethe), although the ode in Klopstock's manner was still cultivated, esp. by members of the Göttingen Dichterbund. Yet despite new, almost expressionistic technical experiments in drama and lyric, the movement was abortive. Its primary interests being private rather than social—repudiation of despotic absolutism was perhaps the only sociopolitical attitude shared by all S. u. D. writers, whose apparent concern with contemporary social issues often reflects only the choice of unconventionally naturalistic themes—it could not realize in a complex and sophisticated age its vision of a broadly popular national lit. such as Homer and Shakespeare were held once to have exemplified. S. u. D. exerted a direct contemporary influence on Swedish and, more feebly, on Eng. lit.; analogous features have been discerned in some other 18th-c. lits., but only in Germany was S. u. D. a self-conscious movement. Though S. u. D. was strongly secular and limitedly cosmopolitan, by radically undermining traditional conceptions of poetry it undoubtedly hastened the first flowering of a conscious romanticism (q.v.), that of Germany in the 1790s.

ANTHOLOGIES: *S. u. D.: Kritische Schriften*, ed. E. Loewenthal (1949); *S. u. D.: Dramatische Schriften*, ed. E. Loewenthal, 2 v. (1959); *S. u. D.*, ed. R. Strasser, 3 v. (1966); *S. u. D.: Dichtungen und theoretische Texte*, ed. H. Nicolai, 2 v. (1971); *S. u. D. und Empfindsamkeit*, ed. U. Karthaus (1978); *S. u. D.: Weltanschauliche und ästhetische Schriften*, ed. P. Müller, 2 v. (1978).

HISTORY AND CRITICISM: K. Wais, *Das antiphilosophische Weltbild des französischen S. u. D.* (1934); E. A. Runge, *Primitivism and Related Ideas in S. u. D. Lit.* (1946); F. S. Schneider, *Die deutsche Dichtung der Geniezeit* (1952); H. B. Garland, *Storm and Stress* (1952); R. Pascal, *The Ger. S. u. D.* (1953); Wellek, v. 1.9; E. Blackall, "The Lang. of S. u. D.," *Stil- und Formprobleme in der Literatur*, ed. P. Böckmann (1959); S. Atkins, "Zeitalter der Aufklärung," *Fischer-Lexikon; Literatur*, v. 2 (1965); W. Kliess, *S. u. D.* (1966); H. A. Korff, *Geist der Goethezeit*, 8th ed., v. 2 (1966); A. Heuyssen, *Drama des S. u. D.* (1980); H. Thomke, "S. u. D.," *Reallexikon* 4.278–96; Kollektiv für Literaturgeschichte, *S. u. D.*, 6th ed. (1983); B. Kieffer, *The Storm and Stress of Lang.* (1986). S.A.

STYLE. How are we to distinguish between what a poem says and the lang. in which it says it? On the one hand, there is no such thing as a "content" utterly separable from words; on the other hand, something can be said about the words which does not refer directly to the content. The relation between the two has been described metaphorically, and looking at these metaphors we discover two kinds. The first suggests (focusing on the creation of the poem) that the relation is mechanical or rhetorical, that s. is something added, more or less at the writer's discretion. On the other hand, if we alter the perspective to focus upon the text, i.e. on s. as the relationships of the lang. in a poem, we find an organic metaphor.

The first kind is common in Ren. and Neoclassical crit., which derives from Cl. rhet. (Aristotle, Cicero): the Eng. term *rhetoric* derives from Gr. *rhetorike*, elliptical for the art of the orator. One part of rhet. was *elocutio*, the selection and placement of words. Longinus in sections 16–43 of *On the Sublime* (1st c. A.D.?) cites the three rhetorical sources of the sublime (q.v.) as figures, diction, and syntax (qq.v.). Puttenham (1589) compares "ornament" (q.v.) to flowers, jewels, and embroidery, but the term had a wider meaning then than now, embracing virtually all the strategies of lang. in a piece of writing. Common too is the comparison of s. to a garment: "lang. is but the apparel of Poesy," says Sir William Alexander (1634).

The organic view begins to be expressed most insistently in the 19th c. (see ORGANICISM). One formulation of the concept is biographical, the other textual. Coleridge states both. Images, he says in the *Biographia literaria*, "become proofs of original genius only as far as they are modified by a predominant passion; or by associated thoughts or images awakened by that passion." Among the ancient critics only Longinus (sect. 17) had expressed such a view. After Coleridge, many critics use or imply the organic metaphor. For Pater, successful s. is, instead of a constructed house, a body "informed." To John Henry Newman, s. is a "thinking out into lang." Middleton Murry considers s. "organic—not the clothes a man wears, but the flesh and bone of his body." In Leo Spitzer's account of the "philological circle," the details of a linguistic structure and its postulated cause or "inner significance" are inextricable.

S., then, has been considered something added, or the parts of a whole, or an extension of mind and character. But this riddle may be more apparent than real, since choice is fundamental to rhet. (persuasion), unity, and authorship. As Spitzer believes, the details of art are not inchoate, chance aggregation, but rather parts of a deliberately related whole. The distinction mechanic / organic may be resolved by treating these as two perspectives on the creative process, as a matter not of opposed formulations but of consideration of the appropriate expressive level or category. The relationship of individual parts and their association in a text to the authorial selection and arrangement of those parts is clarified by the concept of synonymity and by information theory. According to the argument for synonymity, different linguistic forms can produce identical meanings. Differences in expression are then differences in emphasis and not necessarily differences in meaning (Hirsch). According to information theory, natural langs. are inherently redundant. Redundancy makes it possible to convey a message in more than one form, according to the preference or disposition of the individual writer, in contrast to a nonredundant code like telephone messages (Milic, "S."). Thus one can understand designed cohesion (emphasis and correlation) without the mystification of prejudicial metaphors. Choice and text are not inextricably intertwined, but related in the creative process of a writer's choices and a text's coherence.

On the one hand, observation of any text (or discourse: see Kinneavy), but esp. of a closely woven "aesthetic" text, reveals how the meaning of words depends upon the contexts created by the other words in the text. Meaning entails correlation, every word bearing the pressure of all the other words. Hence Riffaterre believes that "the unity of meaning peculiar to poetry" is "the entity of the text," a traditional formalist argument.

On the other hand, study of the strategies and devices of composition reveals the innumerable linguistic techniques by which one can "ornament" thought. Cl. rhetoricians divided such techniques into tropes and schemes, words and syntax (see FIGURE, SCHEME, TROPE). More than 200 figures of speech were recognized by the Tudor rhetoricians. But rhet. was never limited to simile, synecdoche, anaphora, and asyndeton (qq.v.). From its origins in Aristotle and earlier it embraced the process of creation (*inventio*: finding topics) as well as larger expanses of discourse— *dispositio* (organization), logic, point of view, and ethical and emotional appeals (see ETHOS; PATHOS). Indeed, textual strategies continue to be created and discovered—for example, graphicology (typographical, visual, and multimedia devices), or a text's deliberate incompleteness, its gaps (Iser).

But s. involves more than the author's production of a text, more than choices and wholes (or lack thereof). S. is also habitual, which is of two kinds: (1) lang. habits shared by a group of people, and (2) lang. habits unique to an individual writer. Group habits can be further divided into three kinds: period, nation, and genre. People share modes of expression over a period of time; nations share certain linguistic and literary habits; and certain specific modes of expression become established by convention (q.v.) as genres (q.v.). Because of the magnitude of the data, national ss. are least understood, but reliable studies are increasing. Period s. is often international in scope, e.g. futurism (q.v.).

Author s. is also now being studied with increasing thoroughness. We recognize in this orientation the familiar theory that s. reflects the individual author, or "Le s. est l'homme meme" (Buffon). According to Puttenham, writers choose their subjects "according to the metal of their minds." Over the past half-century, stylistics (q.v.) has been accumulating statistical data of extensive scope and detail on authors' s. in full-length studies of individual authors (e.g. Milic, Cluett). Following romanticism (q.v.), and esp. since Freud, this idea has been extended to unconscious expression. Recent studies have also examined the relationships between authors and their ages, nations, and genres—the interaction of writers and the lang. available to them. To Ohmann, s. is "epistemic"—it reflects the epistemological assumptions of each author. Auerbach argues that s. is a reflection of the tension between the force of an author's individuality and the pressure of social forces, in which society is the more powerful force of the two. Cruttwell believes that only one or two ss. are possible at any given time. Eventually we may have a reliable base of information about the history of s. through the comparison of thorough studies of individual writers in their age. But the problem is complicated by the dynamic reality of writing, which often evolves; hence the lang. of an author must be studied chronologically. Improved methods of quantitative analysis using mathematics and computers (Abercrombie, Oakman) have made possible the gathering of the enormous data necessary for accurate stylistic description of authors and groups. Such data bring us closer to the truly comparative approach to s. advocated by Spencer and Gregory, Enkvist, and Dressler.

They also greatly clarify attempts to trace the history of s. in terms of register, or patterns derived from class. The issue of the appropriateness of lang. to situation and subject was familiar to Cl. rhetoricians and was systematized in the Ren. doctrine of the three ss., high, middle, and low. According to Richard Sherry in 1550, "there hath bene marked inespecially thre kindes of endigh tynge: The Greate, the smal, the meane." Writers should fit their lang. to their subject, a lofty s. for an eloquent subject, as in tragedy and epic; middle for elegies; low for satire (Puttenham; see STYLE). This is the doctrine of stylistic decorum (q.v.). The grand s. has received particular attention in the past, esp. in Neoclassical crit.

Related to the problem of stylistic levels of decorum is the parallel issue of the kinds of s., particularly plain vs. ornate. Quintilian believed the three ss. were suited to each of the three functions of rhet. and assigned the plain s. to instruction. These categories have always been notoriously imprecise, but linguistic studies are making them clearer. Adolph, for example, compares two translations of the same passages to conclude that Elizabethan writers tend toward unusual collocations and syntax, while Restoration writers tend toward normal. This history is both vexed and benefitted by the recognition of the existence of varieties not yet systematically studied—Ciceronian and antiCiceronian, curt and loose, Puritan antirhetorical, scientific plain, periodic, pointed, utilitarian, and so on, with description being complicated by 20th-c. innovations such as Joyce's sentence in progress (Bennett, *Prose*).

Extraordinarily diverse and complex, s. has been studied intensively during the last 30 years by literary critics, linguists, and sociologists searching for a comprehensive, disciplined understanding. Emergent from these studies is a view of s. as text features in context—as the material of dialogue both within a text (referentiality and reflexivity) and between those dynamic features and readers in their cultural conditions—of nation, period, and genre. See now STYLISTICS, with additional bibliography; see also POETIC LICENSE; RULES.

STYLISTICS

W. Pater, "S.," *Appreciations* (1889); G. L. Hendrickson, "The Origin and Meaning of the Ancient Characters of S.," *AJP* 26 (1905); J. M. Murry, *The Problem of S.* (1925); Sr. M. Joseph, *Shakespeare's Use of the Arts of Lang.* (1947); L. Spitzer, *Linguistics and Lit. Hist.* (1948); Auerbach; Curtius; M. C. Bradbrook, "50 Years of Crit. of Shakespeare's S.," *ShS* 7 (1954); P. Cruttwell, *The Shakespearean Moment* (1954); Wellek and Warren, ch. 14; W. Staton, "The Characters of S. in Elizabethan Prose," *JEGP* 57 (1958); W. Nowottny, *The Lang.* (1962); W. Trimpi, *Ben Jonson's Poems* (1962)—on the plain s.; C. Ricks, *Milton's Grand S.* (1963); N. Enkvist, "On Defining S.," *Linguistics and S.*, ed. N. Enkvist et al. (1964); S. Ullmann, *Lang. and S.* (1964); L. T. Milic, *S. and Stylistics* (1967), *A Quantitative Approach to the S. of Jonathan Swift* (1967), "S., Literary," *Encyc. of Communication* (1987); D. L. Peterson, *The Eng. Lyric from Wyatt to Donne* (1967)—on the plain s.; R. Adolph, *The Rise of Mod. Prose Style* (1968); R. A. Sayce, "S. in Lit.," *DHI*; G. Hough, *S. and Stylistics* (1969); A. M. Patterson, *Hermogenes and the Ren.: Seven Ideas of S.* (1970); *Patterns of Literary S.*, ed. J. Strelka (1971); J. Kinneavy, *A Theory of Discourse* (1971); J. R. Bennett, *Prose S.* (1971); N. Goodman, "The Status of S.," *CritI* 1 (1975); E. D. Hirsch, Jr., "Stylistics and Synonymity," *CritI* 1 (1975); R. Cluett, *Prose S. and Critical Reading* (1976); *Current Trends in Textlinguistics*, ed. W. Dressler (1978); W. Iser, *The Act of Reading* (1978); I. Fairley, "Experimental Approaches to Lang. in Lit.," *Style* 13 (1979); R. Oakman, *Computer Methods for Literary Research* (1980); D. A. Russell, "Theories of S.," *Crit. in Antiquity* (1981); Fowler; M. Riffaterre, *Text Production* (1983); L. Urdang and F. Abate, *Literary, Rhetorical, and Linguistic Terms Index* (1983); S. Levinson, *Pragmatics* (1983); H. Seidler, "Stil," *Reallexikon* 4.199–213; J. Abercrombie, *Computer Programs for Literary Analysis* (1984); W. Keach, *Shelley's S.* (1984); *The Concept of S.*, ed. B. Lang, rev. ed. (1987); D. K. Shuger, *Sacred Rhet.: The Christian Grand Style in the Eng. Ren.* (1988).

J.R.B.

STYLISTICS, the systematic study of texts with the aid of concepts and tools borrowed from linguistics, has its roots in ancient rhet., in Fr. *stylistique* and Ger. *Stilforschung*, and, in the 20th c., in Anglo-Am. New Criticism and Rus. Formalism (qq.v.). Fr. *stylistique* has had a long trad. from Buffon to Barthes. Famous authors of manuals of rhet. from the 17th to the 19th c. were Bary, Lamy, Du Marsais, Crevier, Domayron, and Fontanier. By the 20th c., therefore, France had a well-developed trad. of Cl.-philological s. applied to Fr. lit. But this trad. lapsed as the 20th c. began, with different modes of analysis being advocated by Bally, Bruneau, J. Marouzeau, Cressot, Y. Le Hir, G. Antoine, and, more recently, M. Riffaterre, R. Barthes, T. Todorov, and G. Genette. For example, Marouzeau conceived of s. as the science of expressivity. Antoine showed special interest in statistics and problems of structure. Riffaterre treats texts as encoded by their author so as to be decoded by their readers. The term *stylistique* has been replaced by such terms as textual or literary semiotics, poetics (q.v.), and structuralism (q.v.), and study has concentrated in Paris with the École pratique des hautes études, the Université de Paris 8 (Vincennes), and the Centre national de la recherche scientifique.

Ger. scholars under the rubrics of *Stilforschung* and *Motiv und Wort* have a long trad. of analyzing literary texts as expressive of the philosophical or psychological attitudes of their authors. (In recent years, R. Ohmann [on epistemic choice] and others have pursued more rigorous investigations of habitual usage.) In his *Goethe* (1915), F. Gundolf traced connections between the lang. of the poet's poems and his conception of nature. Leo Spitzer explored the relationships between the repetitions of Péguy and his Bergsonianism (1924). Spitzer also investigated how style reflected the psychological traits of an author, e.g. Rabelais' play with word roots (1910). Many of these ingenious studies distorted their evidence, however, leading Wellek and Warren to urge readers to treat Ger. *Stilforschung* "with considerable caution" (184). In recent years, Ger. s. has participated actively in the international effort to create a literary science (Riesel and Schendels; Sandig).

Following Aristotle and Cicero, many analysts of texts conceive of effective communication (*elocutio*, in the terms of Cl. rhet.) as a process of inventing content (see INVENTION) and then of choosing and arranging the lang. best suited to the purpose. Many modern rhetoricians, also accepting this approach to *elocutio*, have therefore sought to ground their work in the modern science of linguistics. During the 1920s, the Prague-School structuralists, and from the 1920s to the 1950s, British and Am. formalists focused attention on lang.— e.g. on imagistic and tropic patterns employed for text unity or as revealing period tendencies. By the 1960s this work had provided a substantial repertory of the expressive devices constituting literary texts.

But structuralist and formalist research, while innovative in many respects over 19th-c. philology, was not, by and large, based on systematic theoretical foundations. During the 1960s (some date the beginning from the Indiana Conference on Style in 1958 [see Sebeok]), efforts intensified to apply linguistic theories and methods and to articulate carefully defined and delimited theoretical models homologous with linguistics (see LINGUISTICS AND POETICS). Models proposed derived from both structural and generative grammar. It was assumed that native-speaker linguistic competence could be translated into analytic techniques for the better understanding of texts, particularly literary ones (see Ching et al., intro.). Stylistic analysis would then be the coordination of shared linguistic knowledge with the individual experience of texts (Kintgen, Fairley) and, more generally, the recognition of the systemic nature of everyday utterances (Saussure's *langue*) and of the lang. of lit. S. after 1960 thus became first and foremost technical and descriptive, and only subsequently interpretive, by correlating linguistic phenomena with responses elicited from readers (Bennett, sects. 5.0 and 6.0). The syntactic and semantic features of a text, for example, might be correlated with the nonlinguistic perception of symmetry in a passage, in the pursuit of a more precise and verifiable meaning (Austin, ch. 3; Levin).

As the bibliographies show, there rapidly developed a worldwide effort to make the description of lit. scientific, i.e. to provide rigorous theory, method, and technique, and to apply this new descriptive, systematic, and therefore progressive knowledge to the interp. of texts, authors, genres, nations, and periods. Significant theoretical foundations were laid, with the provision not only of comprehensive paradigms but of the concept and process of specific modes of signification—systematic studies of diction, imagery, sound, syntax, rhythm, and figures (qq.v.). The taxonomic study of these modes led to renewed interest in how the constituents of a text cohere and function to communicate meaning. But this more familiar (New Critical) s. was matched by the growth of authorial studies also based upon principled procedures, particularly when backed by empirical, statistical data made possible by the advent of computers (Oakman, Abercrombie). The program of s. included the concerted effort to develop reliable ways to describe an author's characteristic features (Cluett, Milic) and to interpret their roles in the expression of meanings (Bennett, sect. 4.0). A similar endeavor, also crucially supported by new and more accurate methods of quantification, inspired the study of styles as generic (e.g. Hemingway's novels), national (Hemingway as an Am. novelist), and period (Hemingway as a 20th-c. novelist). The importance of an awareness of these contexts to a full and satisfying reading of a text has become increasingly plain (Bennett, sect. 3.0). For example, narratology (theory of narrative) has become a major field (e.g. Prince, Chatman).

In recent years s. has also developed in reaction to the skepticism regarding meaning emphasized in poststructuralist crit. In the 1970s and '80s the validity of major literary concepts such as text, genre, and author came under attack from such schools as deconstruction, hermeneutics, and reader-response criticism (qq.v.), which undermined determinate signification in texts by emphasizing play, event, and interaction. The reaction from s. was both an increased acknowledgement of complex subjectivity and a renewed commitment to rigor and system. Austin's theory of poetic syntax (q.v.), for example, specifically addresses deconstruction and reader response. The rhetori-

cal trad., which supported the set of communicational bridges from culture to author to text to reader, itself challenged by the radically subjective and skeptical character of deconstruction, responded with a new, empirical subdiscipline of s. Sometimes called "pragmatics," and including analysis of locutionary functions based on speech-act theory (q.v.), this new approach began to study systematically the conventional relationships between linguistic constructions and the users and uses of lang. (see Pagnini on drama). Perhaps to be labeled "reader s." in line with the designations of the other subdisciplines (theoretical s., period s., national s., genre s., author s., text s.), pragmatics concentrates upon the systematic study of responses to texts with the aid of linguistics. Another kind of response to poststructuralism is labelled "social semiotics" by the linguists Hodge and Kress, who stress the primacy of the social dimension and ideology, esp. the relations of power, in understanding lang. structures and processes.

The epistemological challenge to s. is not the only reason why its methods and domain have been enlarged in recent years. Once preoccupied with small linguistic textual details and with the patterns of words in a unified text, s. is also widening methodologically in line with the growing critical concern over the relations of lit. to society, politics, and power. S. in these areas is joining forces with sociolinguistics, and some critics (e.g. Fowler) employ the terms interchangeably. A significant reflection of this trend is the shift away from the concept of lit. to the recognition of the diversity of discourses, of which *belles lettres* constitute but one part. A linguistics-based rhet. encompassing both the traditional author-text-reader relationship and the study of reader, reading event, and culture (genre, period, nation) would seem to be the path of the future for s. But as the conventions for making sense of a particular discourse are multiplied, the problem for stylisticians of maintaining rigor, explicitness, clarity, comprehensiveness, and systematicity—fundamentally, of what will be linguistic—intensifies.

See now FIGURE, SCHEME, TROPE; GENRE; INTERPRETATION; MEANING, POETIC; POETICS; READER-RESPONSE CRITICISM; RHETORIC AND POETRY; RULES; SEMANTICS, POETIC; SPEECH ACT THEORY; STRUCTURALISM; STYLE.

BIBLIOGRAPHIES: H. Hatzfeld, *A Critical Bibl. of the New S. Applied to the Romance Lits., 1900–1952* (1953), *Supplement* [1953–1965] (1966); H. Hatzfeld and Y. Le Hir, *Essai de bibliographie critique de stylistique française et romane, 1955–1960* (1961); L. Milic, *Style and S.* (1967); R. W. Bailey and D. Burton, *Eng. S.* (1968); J. R. Bennett, *Bibl. of S. and Related Crit., 1967–83* (1986).

ANTHOLOGIES: Sebeok; *Essays on Style and Lang.*, *Style and Structure in Lit.*, both ed. R. Fowler (1966, 1975); *Essays on the Lang. of Lit.*, ed. S. Chatman and S. R. Levin (1967); *Mathematik und Poetik*, ed. H. Kreuzer and R. Gunzenhäuser, 2d ed. (1967);

Linguistics and Literary Style, Essays in Mod. S., both ed. D. C. Freeman (1970, 1981); *Literary Style*, ed. S. Chatman (1971); *The Computer and Literary Studies*, ed. A. J. Aitken et al. (1973); *Style and Text*, ed. H. Ringbom (1975); *Linguistic Perspectives on Lit.*, ed. M. K. L. Ching et al. (1980); *Lang. and Lit.*, ed. R. Carter (1982); *Literary Text and Lang. Study*, ed. R. Carter and D. Burton (1982); *Methoden der Stilanalyse*, ed. B. Spillner (1984); *Linguistics and the Study of Lit.*, ed. T. D'haen (1986); *Functions of Style*, ed. D. Birch and M. O'Toole (1988).

STUDIES: L. Spitzer, *Linguistics and Lit. Hist.* (1948), *Representative Essays* (1988); Auerbach; H. Seidler, *Allgemeine Stilistik* (1953); P. Guiraud, *La Stilistique* (1954); Wellek and Warren, ch. 14; Jakobson, esp. v. 2, 5; R. Jakobson and C. Lévi-Strauss, "'Les Chats' de Charles Baudelaire," *L'Homme* 2 (1962), reply by M. Riffaterre, "Describing Poetic Structures," *YFS* 36–37 (1966); S. R. Levin, *Linguistic Structures in Poetry* (1962); L. Doležel and R. Bailey, *Statistics and Style* (1969); G. Leech, *A Linguistic Guide to Eng. Poetry* (1969); R. Ohmann, *Shaw: The Style and the Man* (1969); R. Fowler, *The Langs. of Lit.* (1971), *Lit. as Social Discourse* (1982), *Linguistic Crit.* (1986); T. Eaton, *Theoretical Semics* (1972); N. Enkvist, *Linguistic S.* (1973); G. W. Turner, *S.* (1973); A. Cluysenaar, *Aspects of Literary S.* (1975); E. Riesel and E. Schendels, *Deutsche Stilistik* (1975); R. Cluett, *Prose Style and Critical Reading* (1976); S. Chatman, *Story and Discourse* (1978), *The Rhet. of Narrative in Fiction and Film* (1990); G. Dillon, *Lang. Processing and the Reading of Lit.* (1978); M. Riffaterre, *Semiotics of Poetry* (1978); I. Fairley, "Experimental Approaches to Lang. in Lit.," *Style* 13 (1979); D. Burton, *Dialogue and Discourse* (1980); R. Oakman, *Computer Methods for Literary Research* (1980); S. Fish, "What is S. and Why Are They Saying Such Terrible Things About It?" *Is There a Text In This Class?* (1980); T. J. Taylor, *Linguistic Theory and Structural S.* (1980); E. Traugott and M. Pratt, *Linguistics for Students of Lit.* (1980); Group Mu; Brogan, passim; T. Van Dijk, *Studies in the Pragmatics of Discourse* (1981), *Handbook of Discourse Analysis* (1985); D. Attridge, *The Rhythms of Eng. Poetry* (1982); A. Banfield, *Unspeakable Sentences* (1982); M. Cummins and R. Simmons, *The Lang. of Lit.* (1983); C. C. Hollis, *Lang. and Style in* Leaves of Grass (1983); S. Levinson, *Pragmatics* (1983); B. Sandig, *Stilistik* (1983); "Literariness and Linguistics," ed. V. Herman and P. Dodd, spec. iss. of *Prose Studies* 6.2 (1983); J. Abercrombie, *Computer Programs for Literary Analysis* (1984); T. R. Austin, *Lang. Crafted* (1984); R. Chapman, *The Treatment of Sounds in Lang. and Lit.* (1984); R. Jakobson, *Verbal Art, Verbal Sign, Verbal Time* (1984); E. Kintgen, *The Perception of Poetry* (1984); M. Halliday, *Lang., Context, Text* (1985); R. Carter and W. Nash, *Styles of Eng. Writing* (1987); G. Prince, *A Dict. of Narratology* (1987); R. Hodge and G. Kress, *Social Semiotics* (1988); M. Pagnini, *The Pragmatics of Lit.* (1988). J.R.B.

SUBJECTIVE CRITICISM. See CRITICISM; GENEVA SCHOOL; INTUITION; POETICS; READER-RESPONSE CRITICISM; THEORY.

SUBJECTIVITY AND OBJECTIVITY are terms which apply to both poetic praxis and crit. In praxis the distinction is reasonably well established, but in crit. it has been strenuously disputed in the 20th c. S. is generally used to describe writing of strong personal feeling directly expressed and dominated by the mind's shaping power. It also refers to the activity of the reader when she or he is less a passive recipient than an active participant in the act of reading. O. describes a more restrained or detached writing which, while it may still reveal the feelings of the writer, reveals also an awareness of the attitudes of others, or of lang. as having a denotative meaning apart from any individual reader. Wimsatt and Beardsley (*The Affective Fallacy*, 1949) attack the evaluation of a poem on the basis of the reader's emotional response and posit an "objective" text separate from its reader but entailing certain appropriate responses (see AUTONOMY). Norman Holland sees reader-response crit. (q.v.) as a reaction to this objectivist and formalist position. For him "a 'poem' involves a psychological process in which author and reader interact through a physical text."

Up to the 18th c., crit. was dominated by the classical—what would come to be called objective or mimetic—and neoclassical—what would be called pragmatic—concepts of the poem. Aristotle's conception in the *Poetics* of imitation of "men in action," of a reality outside the mind, held sway. Much Ren. poetic theory—e.g. Sidney's *Apology for Poetry*—saw the poet as maker and the poem as "speaking picture," a rhetorical vehicle for conveying religious and moral values. 17th-c. rationalism, notably the work of Descartes, Hobbes, and Locke, established the philosophical premises of a distinction (indeed, dualism) between subject and object, reason and feeling, mind and body. The impact of such rationalism can be seen in much Enlightenment lit., with its more rigid generic categories and its poetry more didactic in manner, more denotative in lang.

Still, the roots of s. can be seen in Locke's warning about the dangers of imagination, and the 18th c. saw a great concern with the subjective, the individual, the expression of emotion, a concern which brought about the gradual introduction of new terminology. Kant is at the heart of Ger. romanticism with his ringing assertion that we can never know "things in themselves" (*noumena*), but only as they are touched by our perceptions (*phenomena—Critique of Judgment* [1790]). Witness esp. his distinction between the beautiful and the sublime (q.v.). The Schlegels articulate its premises, distinguishing classic and romantic, decorum and freedom, order and process. Taking issue with Pope and Johnson, A. W. Schlegel admires Shakespeare "for his exhibition of passion, taking this word in its widest signification" (*Lectures on Dramatic Art and Lit.*, 1809–11).

In England, emerging from the psychology of Locke was a new interest in the workings of the imagination (q.v.) from the standpoint of both poet and reader. A large body of poetry loosely classified as preromantic and including Thomson, Collins, Akenside, Burns, Cowper, and others took its place beside that of the major writers, this group stressing the vitality of nature, including humankind, and the strong expression of personal feeling.

This romantic revolution in poetic stance is most dramatic in the highly subjective poetry of Blake, esp. in the lyrical *Songs of Innocence and Experience* (1789–93) and the intensely personal mythology of the *Prophecies*, and continues in poems like Wordsworth's *Tintern Abbey* and Coleridge's *Frost at Midnight*, where the speakers half perceive and half create the natural settings of the poems. The great monument is Wordsworth's *Prelude*, a full-blown epic of the poet's inner life. Shelley's *Ode to the West Wind* and *To a Skylark* dramatize an intensely passionate speaker in search of transcendence. The central critical text is Coleridge's *Biographia literaria*, ch. 12. J. J. Rousseau's *Confessions* (1781), with its opening promise to portray "Simply myself," and Goethe's *The Sorrows of Young Werther* (1774), which offers the intensely personal letters of a young man recounting a tragic love affair, were major Continental exemplars of romantic s. In the Victorian period, Tennyson issues the call for a strongly personal poetic voice, while Arnold cautions against extreme s.

In the 20th c., T. S. Eliot elaborates a new criterion of o., a response to what he regarded as the excessive self-expression and abstraction of Eng. poetry since the 17th c. In *Trad. and the Individual Talent* (1917) he contends, "No poet, no artist of any art, has his complete meaning alone." In *Hamlet and His Problems* (1919), arguing that a poet has not so much a "personality" to express but a "medium," he offers the notion of the "objective correlative" (q.v.) as "the only way of expressing emotion in the form of art"—"a set of objects, a situation, a chain of events which shall be the formula of that particular emotion." Along with T. E. Hulme, Eliot exerted a strong influence on Am. New Crit. (q.v.) which laid clear emphasis on the poem as autonomous object, a view repeatedly emphasized by W. K. Wimsatt, Jr. I. A. Richards, by contrast, held to psychological theories whereby the poem balances opposing emotions. Post-New Critical theory, esp. deconstruction (q.v.), by foregrounding the ineradicable gap between signifier and signified, undercuts the subject-object distinction of Cartesian dualism and so poses the issues—or the very possibility of the issues—at a deeper level. See also CRITICISM; GENEVA SCHOOL; INTENTION; INTUITION; POETICS; READER-RESPONSE CRITICISM; THEORY.—W. J.

Bate, *From Classic to Romantic* (1946); Abrams, 235–44; Wimsatt and Brooks; W. Tatarkiewicz, "O. and S. in the Hist. of Aesthetics," *PPR* 24 (1963–64); D. Bleitch, *Subjective Crit.* (1978); H. Gnüg, *Entstehung und Krise lyrischer Subjektivitat* (1983); W. Cain, *The Crisis in Crit.* (1984); R. Selden, *Crit. and O.* (1984); J. Mahoney, *The Whole Internal Universe* (1985); R. M. Strozier, *Saussure, Derrida, and the Metaphysics of S.* (1988); R. Shusterman, *T. S. Eliot and the Philosophy of Crit.* (1988); S. Kay, *S. in Troubadour Poetry* (1990); K. G. Butler, *The Concept of O.* (1991); *S. and Lit. from the Romantics to the Present Day*, ed. P. Shaw et al. (1991).   J.L.M.

SUBLIME.

    I. CLASSICAL
    II. ENLIGHTENMENT TO MODERN

I. CLASSICAL. "S.," a Lat.-derived word meaning literally "(on) high, lofty, elevated," owes its currency as a critical and aesthetic term to the anonymous Gr. treatise *Peri hypsous* (*hypsos*, "height, elevation") once ascribed to the rhetorician Cassius Longinus of the 3d c. A.D. but now generally agreed to belong to the 1st c., perhaps around 50 A.D. Whatever his name and origin, its author was certainly a rhetorician and a teacher of the art, but one of uncommon mold. His essay, with its intimacy of tone (it is addressed to a favorite pupil, a young Roman) and breadth of spirit, stands more or less isolated in its own time, but has had a recurrent fascination for the modern mind since the 17th c.

The idea of sublimity had its roots in the rhetorical distinction, well established before "Longinus," of three levels of style (q.v.), high, middle, and low. His achievement was to draw it out of the technical sphere, where it had to do primarily with style, and to associate it with the general phenomenon of greatness in lit., prose and poetry alike. "Longinus" regards sublimity above all as a thing of the spirit, a spark that leaps from the soul of the writer to the soul of his reader, and only secondarily as a matter of technique and expression. "Sublimity is the echo of greatness of spirit." Being of the soul, it may pervade a whole work (speech, history, or poem: "Longinus" pays little attention to genre distinctions); or it may flash out at particular moments. "Father Zeus, kill us if thou wilt, but kill us in the light." "God said, 'Let there be light,' and there was light." In such quotations as these, "Longinus" shows among other things his sharp eye for the particular passage and his capacity for empathy (q.v.) with the actual work, qualities which are in fact rare in ancient crit. and which presage the modern spirit.

The distinguishing mark of sublimity for "Longinus" is a certain quality of feeling. But he will not allow it to be identified simply with emotion (q.v.), for not all emotions are true or noble. Only art can guard against exaggerated or misplaced feeling. Nevertheless, art plays second fiddle to genius (q.v.) in his thinking. He enumerates five sources of the s.: great thoughts, noble feeling, lofty figures, diction, and arrangement. The first two, the crucial ones, are the gift of nature, not art. "Longinus" even prefers the faults of a great spirit, a Homer, a Plato, or a Demosthenes, to the faultless mediocrity that is achieved by following rules (q.v.).

In later antiquity and the Middle Ages, the treatise remained unknown, or at least exercised little influence. In the Ren., it was first published by Robortelli in 1554, then tr. into Lat. in 1572 and into Eng. in 1652 (by John Hall). But it made no great impression until the late 17th c. Paradoxically enough, it was Boileau, the high priest of Fr. neoclassicism, who launched the *Peri hypsous* on its great modern career and thus helped to prepare the ultimate downfall of Classicism (q.v.). His tr. (1672) had immense reverberation, esp. in England. The Eng., always restive under the "Fr. rules," instinctively welcomed "Longinus" as an ally. As neoclassicism advanced and subjectivity became increasingly central to Eng. thinking, not only about lit. but about art in general, the s. became a key concept in the rise of romanticism (q.v.) in poetry and the concurrent establishment of aesthetics as a new, separate branch of philosophy. See also BATHOS; JE NE SAIS QUOI; NEOCLASSICAL POETICS.   G.F.E.; T.V.F.B.

II. ENLIGHTENMENT TO MODERN. In the 18th c., the s. represented merely one type of experience that could be described under the general philosophical rubric of sensationism (see NEOCLASSICAL POETICS). For a host of writers producing everything from aesthetic treatises to Gothic novels, it was synonymous with irresistible forces that produced overwhelming sensations. In the 18th and 19th cs., the s. came increasingly to be a term of aesthetic approbation, as attested by the interest in both s. landscapes and paintings of s. landscape. In the popular view, the term amounted to a description: it represented primarily a subject matter, the wild and desolate natural scene (see NATURE) or the natural force that dwarfed the individual human figure. Its effect was simultaneously to make one conscious of one's own comparative weakness in the face of natural might and to produce a sense of the strength of one's own faculties. As John Baillie put it in his *Essay on the S.* (1747), "Vast Objects occasion vast Sensations, and vast Sensations give the Mind a higher Idea of her own Powers."

Along with the increasing currency of the term in the 18th c., two particularly strong arguments about the place of the s. and s. nature emerged: Edmund Burke's *Philosophical Enquiry into the Origin of Our Ideas of the S. and Beautiful* (1757) and Immanuel Kant's *Critique of Judgement* (1790; commonly referred to as his Third Critique, after the *Critique of Pure Reason* [1781] and *Critique of Practical Reason* [1788]). In the history of what we now call aesthetics, these two works were esp. impor-

tant for according significance to pleasure in objects that were not, strictly speaking, beautiful. Burke developed the sensationist position into an affectivism that continually connected the s. with the issue of an individual's relationship to society (q.v.), and Kant made his discussion of the s. a cornerstone of a formalist account of aesthetics (see INTUITION).

Burke's *Enquiry* sets out the affectivist position on the s. in an argument that emphasizes the power of experience. In the "Intro. on Taste" added to the 2d ed. (1759), Burke made two claims for the importance of taste (q.v.). First, his emphasis on the regular operation of the senses makes taste as meaningful and as generalizable as reason: "as the conformation of their organs are nearly, or altogether the same in all men, so the manner of perceiving external objects is in all men the same, or with little difference." Second, his emphasis on the origin of the passions treats taste as a field of determinate knowledge in which the "remembrance of the original natural causes of pleasure" can be distinguished from the acquired tastes that fashion and habit promote. People, he observes, are not likely to be mistaken in their reactions to sensation even though they may often be confused in their reasoning about them.

Burke traced the attractions of the beautiful and the s. to human impulses that are ultimately utilitarian. The beautiful he saw as a manifestation of the human instinct towards sociability, with sociability in turn serving the purpose of the continuation of the species. The s. he treated as a manifestation of the instinct for self-preservation, the response of terror that "anticipates our reasonings, and hurries us on by an irresistible force." The beautiful represents what we love (and love specifically for submitting to us and flattering our sense of our own power); the s. represents all that we fear for being greater and more powerful than we are.

If the notion of sympathy (see EMPATHY AND SYMPATHY) had for writers like Adam Smith suggested how persons might identify with the interests of others, Burke's discussion of the s. and the beautiful emphasizes relationships between individuals and objects far more than intersubjective relationships. Yet Burke nonetheless argues for the social utility of our feelings of the s. and beautiful. He increasingly aligns the beautiful not merely with the sociable and pleasing but also with a relaxation of the bodily functions that eventually becomes disabling. The s., by contrast, presents difficulties that require "exercise or labour" to be overcome. Although the s. feelings of astonishment or awe may resemble pain, the excitation and exertion that they produce yield a very real pleasure—a consciousness of one's own powers and even a physical exercise that keeps the various organs of sensation in tone. Burke's account may be empiricist in suggesting that objects have regular and predictable operations on the senses, but it ultimately de-emphasizes knowledge of the external world and stresses instead the uses of objects in gratifying and challenging the individual human organism.

Kant, in his *Critical Observations on the Feeling of the Beautiful and S.* (1784), does not depart strikingly from the Burkean position. He identifies the beautiful and the s. as terms under which contrasting kinds of objects of experience might be subsumed; and he sees the enjoyment or displeasure in these objects as having essentially a psychological dimension. In this, his remarks are consistent with the familiar critical view that shifted discussions of pleasure in art and nature from an emphasis on production—what the artist must do to achieve certain effects—to an emphasis on reception—how the response to certain objects raises questions of a viewer's or reader's psychology.

With the Third Critique, however, Kant reoriented aesthetic discussion. Burke and other writers (including the Kant of the *Observations*) had described the s. and the beautiful in terms of both natural and manmade objects; Homeric and Miltonic poetry could serve as examples of sublimity as well as the seemingly infinite expanse of the ocean or a powerful animal in whom "the terrible and s. blaze out together." Kant reduced the metaphorical reach of the term "s." and identified it exclusively with natural objects. The net effect of this reduction was to enable him to argue that the s. is not—or not particularly—important for establishing human inferiority relative to natural might. Rather, the pleasure that one takes in s. nature reveals a pleasure in judging objects that are not the vehicles of a message and not expressions of anyone's intentions. If a poem or a statue cannot exist without the intentional action of its maker, natural sublimity appeals to human viewers in a fashion that stands outside of such communication of intention (q.v.).

Kant's claim for s. intentionlessness obviously opposes itself to the "argument from design," which reads the book of nature as revealing divine intention. Its primary significance, however, is not so much to argue against belief in divinity as to identify aesthetic judgment as a faculty which is, in interesting ways, unable to ground itself in claims about the prior value of external objects. The s. becomes the primary vehicle for the Kantian argument about the importance of "purposiveness without purpose" in aesthetic objects. While natural beauty might appear to have been formed by design (echoing Addison's sense of the mutually enhancing relationship of art and nature to one another), the s., lacking the form of beautiful nature, bespeaks pleasure in an object that is without bounds not merely in appearing infinite but in having no form. The aesthetic judgment, that is, does not respond to the intrinsic beauty of an object in appreciating natural sublimity, but neither does it merely provide a screen on which individual psychology is projected. Rather, the s.

in its intentionlessness and formlessness, makes visible the judgment's role as a form-giving faculty.

Most recently, the s. has gained prominence in deconstruction (q.v.) and rhetorical crit. In the work of Jacques Derrida, for instance, it has figured prominently in his challenge to Kantian formalism. Indeed, for many critics it has come to represent something like an inversion of the Kantian claim about it: namely, the view that the s. represents an "excess" in lang. that keeps it from ever assuming any fixed form or meaning. F.F.

See also DESCRIPTIVE POETRY; IMAGINATION; ROMANTIC AND POSTROMANTIC POETICS; for discussion of the Hebraic trad. of the s., see HEBRAISM.

PRIMARY WORKS: *Longinus on the S.*, ed. and tr. W. Rhys Roberts, 2d ed. (1907)—best and fullest ed.; *Anonimo del S.*, ed. and tr. A. Rostagni (1947). Tr.: W. H. Fyfe (1927; Loeb ed.); B. Einarson (1945); G. M. A. Grube (1958); D. A. Russell (1965; text and commentary, 1964).

SECONDARY WORKS: T. R. Henn, *Longinus and Eng. Crit.* (1934); S. T. Monk, *The S.: A Study of Crit. Theories in 18th-C. England* (1935); B. Weinberg, "Trs. and Commentaries on Longinus to 1600, A Bibl.," *MP* 47 (1949–50); F. Wehrli, "Der erhabene und der schlichte Stil in der poetisch-rhetorischen Theorie der Antike," *Phylobolia für P. von der Mühll* (1946); E. Olson, "The Argument of Longinus' *On the S.*," in Crane; Wimsatt and Brooks, esp. chs. 6, 14; W. J. Hipple, *The Beautiful, The S., and the Picturesque* (1957); J. Brody, *Boileau and Longinus* (1958); M. H. Nicolson, *Mountain Gloom and Mountain Glory* (1959), "S. in External Nature," *DHI*; E. Tuveson, *The Imagination as a Means of Grace* (1960); M. Price, "The S. Poem," *Yale Rev.* 58 (1969); Saisselin; A. Litman, *Le S. en France, 1666–1714* (1971); T. E. B. Wood, *The Word "S." and Its Context, 1650–17600* (1972); D. B. Morris, *The Religious S.* (1972); A. O. Wlecke, *Wordsworth and the S.* (1973); W. P. Albrecht, *The S. Pleasures of Tragedy* (1975); J. Derrida, "Economimesis," *Mimesis: Des Articulations* (1975), *La Verité en peinture* (1983), tr. as *The Truth in Painting* (1987); T. Weiskel, *The Romantic S.* (1976); S. A. Ende, *Keats and the S.* (1976); P. H. Fry, *The Reach of Crit.* (1983); P. de Man, "Hegel on the S.," *Displacement*, ed. M. Krupnick (1983); J.-L. Nancy, "L'Offrande s.," *Po&sie [Poesie]* 30 (1984); F. Ferguson, "The Nuclear S.," *Diacritics* (1984), *Solitude and the S.* (1992); A. Leighton, *Shelley and the S.* (1984); "The S. and the Beautiful: Reconsiderations," spec. iss. of *NLH* 16 (1985); N. Hertz, *The End of the Line* (1985); E. Escoubas, "Kant ou la simplicité du s.," *Po&sie* 32 (1985); J.-F. Lyotard, "Le S., à present," *Po&sie* 34 (1985); S. Knapp, *Personification and the S., Milton to Coleridge* (1985); P. Lacoue-Labarthe, "La Verité s.," *Po&sie* 38 (1986); L. W. Marvick, *Mallarmé and the S.* (1986); *The Am. S.*, ed. M. Arensberg (1986); *La Via al S.*, ed. M. Brown et al. (1987); T. M. Kelley, *Wordsworth's Revisionary Aesthetics* (1988); P. Crowther,

SUMERIAN POETRY

The Kantian S. (1989); P. Boitani, *The Tragic and the S. in Med. Lit.* (1989); *Das Erhabene*, ed. C. Pries (1989); G. L. Stonum, *The Dickinson S.* (1989 1990); S. Guerlac, *The Impersonal S.* (1990); R. Wilson, *Am. S.* (1991); J. F. Diehl, *Women Poets and the Am. S.* (1991); V. A. De Luca, *Words of Eternity: Blake and the Poetics of the S.* (1991).

T.V.F.B.; G.F.E.; F.F.

SUBSTITUTION. In Cl. prosody (q.v.), the doctrine that, in most Gr. and Lat. meters, one component of a metrical foot may under certain conditions be substituted for another. In general, all replacements rely on the fundamental equivalence (q.v.) of two shorts to one long. The replacement of one long by two shorts is called resolution (q.v.); its opposite, the replacement of two shorts by one long (West says, "more accurately, one long syllable is treated as simultaneously filling two short positions"), is variously called contraction or s. The enabling conditions for these two processes are, however, not the same, suggesting they are not one process and its reverse but two different ones. For the ancient metrists, these replacements created units of different names, so that the spondee (q.v.), for example, could be regarded as a s. for a dactyl (q.v.) in the epic hexameter. Maas coined the term "biceps" for "a long equivalent to two shorts, or two shorts equivalent to a long," but West says "it is important to keep resolution and contraction distinct, and not to speak of a general equivalence between ‿ ‿ and —" (35).

The concept of s. was transferred in simplified form (i.e. s. of one type of foot for another, not elements within the foot) to the modern vernacular prosodies by Classically minded prosodists of the late 19th and early 20th cs.—of whom Saintsbury is the most conspicuous and notorious—as a means of accounting for metrical variation, i.e. irregularity. Thus it was claimed that the pattern /xx/ in the first four syllables of the Eng. iambic pentameter was an "initial trochaic s." foll. by an iamb; extra syllables in iambic lines were accounted for as "trisyllabic ss." Opponents of footmetrics and s. tried to remove extra syllables via elision (q.v.) and explained initial trochaic ss. by more desperate stratagems such as a "monosyllabic foot" followed by an anapest (see FOOT). In the modern langs., the difficulty with the doctrine of s. is that it unnecessarily adds categories (e.g. trochees) to account for metrical patterns that exist: it is unable to offer a generative principle which explains *why* trochees occur in first feet of the pentameter far more often than, say, fifth. The doctrine of s. posits alternatives within the definition of meter itself; some other theorists have sought to posit them at the level of linguistic rhythm (syllables are often elided in speech, for example). See EQUIVALENCE.

T.V.F.B.

SUBTEXT. See TEXTUALITY.

SUMERIAN POETRY. Written in cuneiform script, S. texts of an undeniably poetic nature first appear around 2600 B.C. S. lit. is preserved in a large number of clay tablets, most of them school exercises, since the training of administrative scribes included learning traditional poetry. Most of the preserved texts date from the 18th c. B.C. or shortly before, although some of them are copies of poems attested in tablets dating from the Ur III dynasty (2112–2004 B.C.) or even earlier. Tablets written after the 18th c., when S. had become an extinct lang., are mostly compilations of excerpts of earlier texts or imitations of them and were used in liturgical services in Mesopotamian temples until the 2d c. B.C.

Copious native lexical compilations allow the meaning of S. words to be determined with a precision unusual in ancient langs., but our present knowledge of S. phonology lacks the precision necessary to determine metrical patterns with confidence. In particular, vowel quality and quantity, as well as the accentual system, remain largely unknown. Attempts to find metrical patterns based on vowel length and stress should therefore be viewed with skepticism. The number of syllables, however, presents definite regularities. Large portions of poems (rarely entire ones) are written in lines of 8+5 syllables, but other types of verse are also known; fillers and alterations of the normal morphological forms keep the syllable count within the intended limit. Alliteration and assonantal rhyme are known, but sparingly used. A strophic type common in laudatory hymns consists of two identical sections, the first preceded by a descriptive epithet or by nothing, the second by the name of the praised one. From a song to the Moon god, patron of dairies:

> en šu sikil-la dug.šakir-e hé du₇
> níg šu-dug₄-ga-zu an-ra ᵈen-líl-ra
> ša-mu-un-ne-sag₉
> ᵈnanna en šu sikil-la dug.šakir-e hé du₇
> níg šu-dug₄-ga-zu an-ra ᵈen-líl-ra
> ša-mu-un-ne-sag₉

> Oh Lord, you made the butter churn
>   fit the pure hands,
> you made your foods a delight for
>   Heaven and for [the god] Enlil.
> Oh Moon, oh Lord, you made (etc.).

A favorite form of strophe consists of a fixed frame with slots filled by members of a lexical set (e.g. parts of a sacred boat or plants grazed by sheep) accompanied by descriptive or laudatory phrases. Some copies of hymns contain rubrics of uncertain meaning, but they are probably musical since several start with the word for "chord" or "string." Very late copies of liturgical poems occasionally include notations that may be intended to guide the recitation or singing of the text. Several native designations identify the various poetic genres. In most cases they seem to refer to the performance of the poem or its function rather than its formal structure (note, however, *šìr-gíd-da*, "long song").

S. poetic lang. is characterized by various types of parallelism, refrains, repetitions, and figurative speech. Stereotyped images, formulaic passages, and traditional expressions are among its major components. Internal analysis, confirmed by textual history, indicates that S. p. existed primarily as oral trad. With very rare exceptions, the poems are anonymous. A compilation of songs in praise of the shrines of the major cities is attributed to Enheduanna, daughter of king Sargon (2334–2279 B.C.), and some self-laudatory songs are said to have been composed by the kings themselves. No term for "poet" is known. The texts were intended for public recitation by the *nar*, "musician," or, in the case of cultic songs, by the *gala*, "cantor," rather than for private reading.

The most extensive poems are narrative. Some deal with legendary heroes from the city of Uruk; five belong to the epic cycle of Gilgamesh (episodes from them were later included in the Akkadian Gilgamesh epic) and three to the cycle of Lugalbanda and Enmerkar. Others are mythological texts about divine beings (e.g. "Inanna's Descent into Hades," "Dumuzi's Dream," "Birth of the Moon God"). Poems that should be considered court lit. include royal hymns—known for practically all kings of the Ur III, Isin, and Larsa dynasties (21st to 18th c. B.C.)—and contests (*a-da-mìn*) between personifications of natural entities (e.g. "Winter and Summer," "Tree and Reed," "Silver and Copper"). Songs in praise of deities or temples are particularly numerous. The goddess Inanna is the central figure in many of the narratives. Political events inspired laments over the destruction of cities; the oldest refers to the destruction of Nippur by Naram-Sin, ca. 2230 B.C., the most recent to a similar event during Ishme-Dagan's reign, ca. 1940 B.C. After the 16th c. B.C., liturgical laments over the destruction of shrines are the dominant form of lit. Other types of texts include agricultural songs, a lullaby from the end of the 3d millennium B.C., dirges for individuals, poetic letters, and love songs. It is difficult at times to decide if a text, e.g. a didactic one, should be considered poetry or prose. The average length of a poem is 300–400 lines; but epic texts can be longer and there are much shorter poems, esp. among hymns and songs. What contributes to making S. p. interesting, besides its early date, is the presence in it of forms and themes (e.g. the Flood) that are echoed in the Bible.

ANTHOLOGIES IN TRANSLATION: S. N. Kramer, *Ancient Near Eastern Texts*, ed. J. B. Pritchard (1969); M. Cohen, *S. Hymnology* (1981); D. Wolkstein and S. N. Kramer, *Inanna Queen of Heaven and Earth* (1983); T. Jacobsen, *The Harps that Once* (1987).

STUDIES: M. Bielitz, "Melismen," and W. Heimpel, "Observations on Rhythmical Structure," *Ori-*

entalia 39 (1970); H. Sauren, "Zur poetischen Struktur," *Ugaritische Forschungen* 3 (1971); H. Limet, "Essai de poétique," *Alter Orient und Altes Testament* 25 (1976); C. Wilcke, "Formale Gesichtspunkte," *Assyriological Studies* 20 (1976); M. Civil, "Feeding Dumuzi's Sheep," *Am. Oriental Series* 67 (1987).　　　　　　　　　　　　　　　　M.C.

SURREALISM.

  I. DEFINITION
  II. HISTORY
  III. PROBLEMATICS

I. DEFINITION. One of the chief channels of 20th-c. modernism, s. was headed by André Breton (1896–1966), who gave two definitions in his first *Manifesto* (1924), one concerning modes of expression, the other relating to the dimensions of reality. Both announced a fundamental break with existing modes of communication and the conventional manner in which one perceives and accepts the exterior world. The first promotes the practice of psychic automatism to manifest orally, in written form ("automatic writing"), or by other means the repressed activities of the mind. If thought is liberated from the dictates of reason and from moral and aesthetic strictures, it may achieve a form of expression beyond the domains of hitherto recognized artistic expression. Surrealist rebellion and the recuperation of the imagination involved all the institutions and aspects of social behavior, which a small group of young writers and artists, returning to Paris from service in World War I, found under the yoke of a regimentation comparable to that of the military.

The second definition, called "encyclopedic" by Breton, casts s. as an awareness of certain forms of associations previously neglected, but particularly immanent in the dream state, in sexual attractions, and in the free play of thought, creating heightened sensory perceptions that could open new vistas for the arts and help "solve the principal problems of life." Lit. in this context becomes a means and not an end: "Lyricism is the development of a protest," declared Breton and his colleague Paul Éluard (1895–1952) in *Notes sur la poésie* (1936). In a *Second Manifesto* (1929), Breton determined the perspective of s. as the level of reality where "life and death, the real and the imaginary, the past and the future, the communicable and the incommunicable, the high and the low cease to be perceived as contradictory."

Lang. is an essential vehicle for the creation of the surrealist state because of its capacity to suggest the dream and to express the irrational by effecting a synthesis out of opposite meanings, by freeing the signifiers congealed in stereotyped relationships with signifieds, by searching for "words without wrinkles." But if experimentation was first to occur on the linguistic plane, it had to be accompanied by efforts to restore the eye to its pristine condition, to see and associate objects and phenomena without preconceived interferences; then it could be given expression in any of the arts. The surrealists found that primitive societies gave ample examples of this primal vision. Beyond automatic writing, the surrealists explored aleatory opportunities to capture the benefits of random chance and to fulfill the high measure of desire (see FOUND POETRY).

II. HISTORY. Situated between World Wars I and II, s. should be viewed in four stages. As a philosophical current, its roots go back to Baudelaire and Nerval, and, curiously enough, to prose *écriture* rather than to verse. Baudelaire started the "great modern tradition" by converting the well-known romantic metaphor of the *voyage* into a metaphysical journey into the "unknown," going beyond the boundaries of good (*ciel*) and evil (*enfer*) by exploration of the disorientations of sensuality. In his essays on his own experiences with opium and hashish he developed a new vocabulary relating the *seer* ("voyant," with the connotation of the illuminists or drug users of ancient cults). The word was appropriated and its meaning developed by Arthur Rimbaud (1854–91) in his "alchemy of the Word," and became subsequently the basis of surrealist poetic theory.

Nerval, in his narrative *Aurélia*, had ventured into the nether spaces between sanity and insanity, the subconscious and the conscious. He became the model for Breton's autobiographical prose, *Nadja* (1928), in which he narrates his encounter in the streets of Paris with a young woman who treads the fringes of insanity, and of his efforts to communicate with her on a common basis of visionary transformation of habitual sites. The surrealists also found support in the nocturnal Ger. romantics such as Novalis, Achim von Arnim, Jean-Paul, and E. T. A. Hoffman, who had probed the abyss to find beyond the antitheses of light and dark or the real and the fantastic a monistic unification of vision *hic et nunc*.

The second stage of s. revolved around Rimbaud and Comte de Lautréamont (Isidore Ducasse, 1846–70), whose experimental writings were both subversive responses to standard theology and to rationalism at the end of the 19th c. In search of a new ontology that distorted the notion of the beautiful were Lautréamont's frightening metaphors; and through the use of alchemistic lang. Rimbaud expressed his "illuminations," redefining the function of the poet in a letter to his teacher, Paul Demeny, published posthumously in 1912 in time to reach the first generation of the surrealists. Its basic message, to achieve the poetic stage through "the reasoned disorder of all the senses," was identified with the notion of a perilous reality. In search of the creative function of the metaphor, they also focused on Mallarmé, Saint-Pol-Roux, Reverdy, and Apollinaire. Mallarmé and Apollinaire were models in the practice of the polyvalent and calligrammatic poem (see CALLIGRAMME), and Apollinaire's initiative was also followed in forging close ties between painters and poets (see CUBISM). All these "precursors" changed the orientation of the arts from the aesthetic to the epistemological, from the search for beauty to the acquisition of knowledge and insight, still following in the direction of Apollinaire, who in his last poem, "Collines," had described the new poet as being "more pure, more alive, and more learned."

Apollinaire himself had used the word "surréaliste" to qualify his satirical play, *Les Mamelles de Tirésias*. These young iconoclasts appropriated the word "surréaliste" but gave it quite a different meaning as they encountered the anarchists who had gathered under the banner of dada (q.v.). With the arrival of Tristan Tzara (1892–1963) from Zurich in 1919, they shared their contempt for bourgeois mores and united in their demonstrations against all forms of standardization, voicing their subversive feelings in the magazine *Littérature* and in the dada pamphlets. But a literary movement occurs only when there is a concerted consciousness of a constituency pursuing principles that lead from the destructive to the constructive, from theory to practice. The separation of dada and s. occurred not at the time of the first surrealist text in automatic writing, *Les Champs magnétiques* (1919), a collaboration between Breton and Philippe Soupault (b. 1897), but in 1924, when s.'s links with dada were severed both physically and ideologically.

The surrealist coalition thus formed consisted of both poets and painters, incl., along with Breton and Soupault, a number of other young poets: Louis Aragon, Antonin Artaud, René Crevel, Robert Desnos, Éluard, Michel Leiris, Benjamin Péret, and eventually a rehabilitated Tzara. Some non-Fr. poets and painters joined forces with them—Max Ernst, Salvador Dali, Juan Miro, René Magritte, E. L. T. Mesens, and Paul Nougé—along with some Fr. artists, Yves Tanguy and André Masson, and a burgeoning network from around the world. Under the leadership of Breton there emerged a laboratory atmosphere probing human relationships, lang., objects, and sites in the contexts of psychology, alchemy, mathematics, the laws of probability, and linguistics. The application of the methodologies of psychiatry to the stimulation of the poetic imagination occurred because the leading surrealists had become versed partly in the writings of Freud, but more directly with those of his predecessors, Jean Martin Charcot and Pierre Janet. With scientific methods they aimed to liberate the imagination from the overwhelming forces of scientific positivism. The group's membership fluctuated constantly because of ideological disagreements and personality clashes. But the fundamental result of their adherences, even for limited time spans, had an inalterable impact on the manner of viewing and practicing the arts as a channel of self-knowledge and comprehension of the relative nature of reality.

SURREALISM

The resources of occultism were tapped to explore the fermentation of analogical patterns and abolish antinomies. In the plastic arts, analogical thinking produces the dislocation of objects from their expected positions and alteration of their habitual functions. This deviation was symptomatic of "the crisis of the object." The general tendency to amalgamate subject with object was a revision of the external world without recourse to a fantastic or artificial one. S. was a search for the "marvelous" *within* reality. The poet and the artist, perturbed by what was perceived to be an inherent randomness in the universe, adjusted the art of representation to capture this convulsive and unpredictable nature of the cosmic environment. Such were the preoccupations of s. works of art between 1924 and 1939, called its "heroic years." Much of the theoretical writings, the poetry, the so-called "surrealist texts," the accounts of experiments, and the surrealist games appeared in a series of journals starting with *Révolution surréaliste* (1924–29), followed by *Le Surréalisme au service de la révolution* (1930–33), *Minotaure* (1933–39), and other shorter-lived reviews. A second generation of surrealists included René Char, Aimé Césaire, Leopold Senghor, A. Pieyre de Mandriargue, Julien Gracq, Jean Mayoux, Georges Shéhadé, and David Gascogne.

The last and most enduring stage of s. starts after World War II, when diluted forms of the theories and altered assemblages of techniques invade all the arts, particularly poetry, and particularly in Latin America and in the European countries previously under authoritarian regimes. Among neosurrealists may be cited Cesar Moro, Octavio Paz, Aldo Pellegrinn, Braulio Arenas, Enrique Molina, Enrique Gomez-Correa, the Sp. playwright Arabal, and the Egyptian Joyce Mansour, and among painters Toyen, Alexander Calder, Archile Gorky, Matta, Wifredo Lam, Dorothea Tanning, Léonor Fini, and Leonora Carrington. The distinguishing features that hold them together are the prevailing intimacy between poetry and painting, and the hallucinatory image of "the one in the other" (simulacrum) or, in Dali's terminology, "paranoiacritique," the juxtaposition of distant realities, but *distant* only insofar as the interrelationships fail to be manifest to the outside beholder. The correspondences established between the convulsive character of erotic encounters and those of natural phenomena such as earthquakes, geysers, and torrents, are, in short, the cultivation of the chthonian imagination supported by a monistic philosophy which redefines the "sacred" within the limits of the material world.

The innovations in prosody earlier manifested in most poetry of the Western world held no great significance for the surrealists because for them the hypnotically evocative power of words and the capacity for representation were independent of the rules of versification or rhet.; inner resonances rather than rhythms, psychic priorities rather than practical necessities of logical communication dictated the structure of the poem. Yet unlike dada, surrealist poetry held to strict observance of syntax and to a linguistic structure striving toward unity rather than fragmentation.

Automatism is the primary feature that has been associated with s., but there is another ingredient just as significant: the need for vigilance in the organization of the psychic data culled through dreams, automatic writing, and self-induced hallucination. Encounter of objects, encounter of persons (particularly of man with woman), and encounter of the words are the basis of the poetic composition which adapts the physical world to the poet's ability to see connections. The poem is generally located in a perpetual present, the immediacy of life cast in the present tense. The power of magnetism joins nature and man/woman in unexpected analogies; Breton: "Your flesh, splashed with the flight of a thousand birds of paradise / Is a high flame lying in the snow." The analogy's literary frame of reference lies largely in the emblems and symbols of hermeticism (q.v.) such as the four elements of fire, water, earth, and air, the vase, the philosopher's stone, and biological amalgams such as the mandragora, the minotaur, the nymph, and the salamander.

Among the most representative surrealist poetry between the two World Wars can be cited Éluard's collection, *Capitale de la douleur* (1926), Breton's *Le Revolver à cheveux blancs* (1932), Desnos's *Corps et Biens* (1930), and Péret's *De Derrières les fagots* (1935). Breton's last poetic prose, *Arcane 17* (1945), pointed up by a three-level structure of autobiography, hermeticism (the legend of Melusine), and nature (the Percé Rock on the Gaspé peninsula), the tripartite surrealist pursuit of liberty, love, and poetry. *Fata Morgana* (1941) and *Les Etats-Généraux* (1943), followed by *Ode à Charles Fourier* (1947), are the last poems of Breton, epic in dimensions but cast in noncircumstantial surrealist *écriture*.

III. PROBLEMATICS. Since World War II many avatars have emerged in the forms of representation derivative of s. There have been identifications with black humor, the fantastic, and the pornographic. Mannerist uses of surrealist techniques have been deprived of their philosophical interface. In *S. and Painting* Breton emphasized that s. was to be found in the real, not in the fictitious. And although he created an anthology of black humor, he did not equate all black humor with s., which deals as much with sublimation as with derision. The powerful sexual attraction between male and female, expressed both verbally and visually by s., respected the human form and expressed a sacred element in the physical union, prohibitive of the contempt and fragmentation evident in pornographic eroticism. Surrealist works show need of the critical discrimination which has been applied to previous literary movements. But in its global impact s. can be considered the major

SWAHILI POETRY

poetic and artistic current of the 20th c.

Since 1965, there has been intense research on s., particularly in France and the U.S. Much scholarly documentation has been collected in research forums such as the *Centre de Recherche Surréaliste* (CAR) in France, a branch of *Centre National de Recherche Scientifique* (CNRS), and disseminated in its journal, *Mélusine,* and many bibliographical bulletins. In the U.S. there are centers of research, besides the long-standing collection of the Museum of Modern Art in New York, at the Universities of Texas (Austin), Iowa, and Michigan, and the Weingrow collection at Hofstra. The Am. journal *Dada/Surrealism* circulates widely. See also DADA; FRENCH POETRY; LETTRISME.

M. Raymond, *De Baudelaire au S.* (1933); D. Gascogne, *A Short Survey of S.* (1935); G. Lemaître, *From Cubism to S. in Fr. Lit.* (1941); M. Nadeau, *Histoire du S.* (1945), *Documents surréalistes* (1946); A. Balakian, *Literary Origins of S.* (1947), *S.: The Road to the Absolute* (1986), *André Breton: Magus of S.* (1971); J. Gracq, *André Breton* (1948); C. Mauriac, *André Breton* (1949); M. Carrouges, *André Breton et les données fondamentales du s.* (1950, tr. 1974); W. Fowlie, *Age of S.* (1950); A. Bosquet, *Surréalismus* (1950); A. Kyrou, *Le S. au Cinéma* (1952); F. Alquié, *Philosophie du s.* (1955, tr. 1965); J. Hardré, "Present State of Studies on Literary S.," *YCGL* 9 (1960); *YFS* 31 (1964); *Le Siècle éclaté* 3 (1965); J. H. Matthews, *Intro. to S.* (1965), *S. and Film* (1971), *The Custom-House of Desire* (1975), *Toward the Poetics of S.* (1976), *S., Insanity, and Poetry* (1982), *Langs. of S.* (1986); R. Short, "The Politics of S.," *The Left-Wing Intellectuals Between the Wars, 1919–1939,* ed. W. Laqueur and G. Mosse (1966); R. Champigny, *Pour une esthétique de l'essai: "Une Définition du S."* (1967); *Europe* 46 (1968); P. Ilie, *The S. Mode in Sp. Lit.* (1968); M. A. Caws, *The Poetry of Dada and S.* (1970), *André Breton* (1971), *A Metapoetics of the Passage* (1981); X. Gautier, *S. et sexualité* (1971); P. Ray, *The S. Movement in England* (1971); M. Foucault, *Ceci n'est pas une pipe* (1972, tr. 1983); M. Riffaterre, "Semantic Incompatibilities in Automatic Writing," *About Fr. Poetry,* ed. M. A. Caws (1974); *The Poetry of S.,* ed. M. Benedikt (1974); H. Gershman, *The S. Revolution in France* (1974); S. Alexandrian, *Le S. et le rêve* (1974); L. Binni, *Il movimiento surrealista* (1975); G. Legrand, *Breton en son temps* (1976), *Breton* (1978); M. Bonnet, *André Breton: Naissance de l'aventure surréaliste* (1975); *Le S. dans le texte* (1978); H. Finkelstein, *S. and the Crisis of the Object* (1979); *Tracts surréalistes et déclarations collective (1922–1969),* ed. J. Pierre (1980); D. Desanti, *Les Clés d'Elsa* (1983); J. Chénieux, *Le Roman surréaliste* (1983); J. Pierre, *Surréalisme et le Anarchie* (1983); *Le S. portugais,* ed. L. de Moura Sobral (1984); *Les Avant-gardes litts. au XXe siècle,* ed. J. Weisgerber (1985); Terras—Rus.; P. Mourier-Casile, *De La Chimère à la merveille* (1986); R. Riese, *S. and the Book* (1987); *André Breton Today,* ed. A. Balakian and R. E. Knenzli (1989).   A.B.

SWAHILI POETRY. S. p., traceable to Ar. models of Islamic verse, developed as an African poetic form in 19th-c. coastal East Africa. Earlier S. mss. go back to the early 18th c., with the earliest, *al-Hamziya,* a S. version of the Ar. poem *Umm al-Qura* (Mother of Villages [Medina]), in *takhmis* (long-measure verse) form, actually presented as a S. interlinear tr. of the Ar. version. *Takhmis,* a term derived from the Ar. "to make five," denotes 3-line stanzas with 2 original hemistichs added, rhyming *aaab.* Sheikh Saiyid Abdallah bin Nasir (ca. 1720–1820), a Saiyid (Muslim) from Hadramawt as was the author of *al-Hamziya,* used the *takhmis* form in the renowned story of the legendary hero Liyongo. This S. poetic form later gave rise to quatrain (*shairi*) and serenade- or praise-song (*t'umbuizi*) forms. The most important prosodic features of S. p. are rhyme and fixed patterns of syllabic measure. The earliest extant *t'umbuizi* are in indeterminate long measure of at least 15 syllables.

Another early S. poetic form, *tendi,* has lines of four short hemistichs; the first three rhyme together and the fourth carries a rhyme repeated as the terminal rhyme of each stanza. *Tendi* (singular form *utendi*) are long narrative poems embodying oral trad. and circumstantial accounts of historical and contemp. events. For the S. people, the vehicle of hist. is poetry. Early S. p. was written in Ar. script, accommodating Swahili's extra vowels and non-Ar. consonants by adding diacritics to the Ar. characters. Other versions of the exploits of Liyongo have been done in this form which in modern times has been used to document, for example, the struggles for independence in Kenya and Tanzania, and the Maji-Maji rebellion of 1905.

The most popular S. verseform for short themes of topical interest is *shairi,* originally chanted on the island of Lamu in the context of traditional *gungu* dances. Akin to the quatrain in form, *shairi* contrasts with the indigenous *mavugo,* celebration songs without patterned rhyme or meter. *Shairi* are sung at the "great national dances of the Mombasi S.," such as the procession to the groom's house on the eve of a wedding, the celebration of the S. new year in Mombasa, and at the *gungu* marriage dance itself. *Shairi* may be as short as one line or as long as 19. Each line is self-contained in such a way that longer poems ingeniously reiterate the same theme through riddles, wordplay, and homonymy. The *shairi* form is most often associated with the poet Muyaka bin Haji al-Ghassaniy (1776–1840) of Mombasa, who is credited with extending S. p. to commentary on contemp. events, i.e. with secularizing the genre.

Perhaps the S. poet most widely known in the West is Shaaban Robert (1909–62). Ironically, though his poetry is conventional and adheres to traditional forms, he extended the range of S. lit. by borrowing Western forms such as the essay, novella, and autobiography. 20th-c. S. p. continues to be conservative; some is still written in Ar. script. Julius Nyerere, while President of Tanzania, brought poetry into the political arena by encouraging poets such as Mathias Mnyampala (1919–69) to stage public performances of S. song p. (*ngonjera*), hoping that such poetry would teach "good conduct, indigenous culture, and national politics."

As a poet himself, Nyerere brought innovative practices to S. p, introducing enjambment and modes of free verse that had been frowned upon by traditional S. poets, who saw free verse (*guni*) as defective. More recent poets eschew the negative aspects of such creativity and, like Nyerere, admit unconventional rhyme schemes and odd numbers of syllables, departing from the conventionalized norms of the 19th c. In the late 1960s, a new breed of poet began to emerge, exemplified by Mnyampala, who began to incorporate foreign terms in his works even within traditional forms—to the extent of producing *shairi* of three Eng. lines and a fourth in broken Ar.

S. song p. of the nationalist public type of *ngonjera* exists alongside poetry chanted in S. musical clubs, which is topical, deeply allusive, and close to oral trad. The female singer Siti binti Saad (1880–1950) was widely known for her singing and compositional abilities in that mode.

Ahmad Nassir bin Juma Bhalo (1937–) of Mombasa is a S. poet whose poetry is within the traditional mode, yet its performance and composition on the radio is contemporary. His works are chanted by a professional singer to a melodic pattern based on Ar. modal scales. The verses are gnomic, the poet's responsibility oratorical. Bhalo may be seen to be influenced by both Muyaka and Shaaban Robert, yet his works were written to be read and sung. Notable among the modern poets who, with Mnyampala, have departed from the strictures of Muyaka's *shairi* form are E. Kezilahabi and Ibrahim Hussein, who present their own themes, personal sentiments, and philosophies.

One other form of S. p. is the *wimbo* (sonnet, ballad, lyric, hymn). Such lyric S. p. may be in *shairi* meter or use 12-syllable lines with a caesura occurring after either the 4th or (most commonly) the 6th syllable. (Some *wimbo* have 16-syllable lines.) *Wimbo* are *never* written. They may preserve oral trads. or be composed for contemp. events (e.g. the *mavugo* wedding songs), but in either case they represent a form of oral S. p., while the more classical forms were written to be sung. According to Allen (1971), "the composer thought in the tune and the sense follows the tune," while at the same time the music of the poetry is secondary to the form and content. The musical demands on S. p. are thus less than those of text. Music is used to heighten the effect of the poetry—indeed, *tendi* are often thought of as heightened speech—which is frequently sung by an unaccompanied soloist using a nasal tone and a narrow range of pitches. A single melody can be used for many *tendi*.

One fact often overlooked about S. p. is the importance of women in most S. verse. One of the most revered poems is that by Mwana Kupona (d. ca. 1860), written by a woman for her daughter and intended to be read by women as a guide to proper behavior. Women scholars have also been instrumental in preserving classical S. p. mss., since when such mss. exist they are held by the women of the house. Most oral trad. is in the heads of women, and it is the women who are acclaimed for the best recitations (Allen).

Permeating all forms of S. p. is the notion that recitation is appropriate when a suitable occasion arises. Poetry is an impromptu part of S. life, not dependent on formal settings yet appropriate to them (as in celebratory contexts). Features of S. p. such as rhyme extend to jokes and riddles as well as *wimbo*. S. p. is also an instrument used to comment upon society's problems. It may be composed by anyone, and most people can and do so when they need to. It is common to see *shairi* in the daily papers, submitted in the trad. of "letters to the editor" as 4-line stanzas beginning with phrases such as "Give me a space in your daily, editor" (*unipe nafasi mwako gazetini mhariri*). The noted political scientist Ali Mazrui, commenting on the integral role of poetry in S. daily life, tells of letters he received from people who had heard that two of his sons had gone blind: these letters were in the form of topical *shairi*. He responded appropriately by composing his "Ode to the Optic Nerve."

The recent signs of S. p. adapting in form, content, and lang. to modern modes of presentation (e.g. newspaper and radio) indicate that the genre remains vital. Tightly constrained cl. verseforms seem to be giving way to more flexible ones. The now-common use of Roman script is conducive to the introduction of words from Eng. and other langs. As both Kenya and Tanzania evolve their national cultures, it is likely that S. p. will continue to be a prime mode of literary expression by coastal people. The incorporation of *tendi* within genres such as drama, where aspects such as dialogue make it natural, may be expected to increase. Indeed, S. p. may be expected to be incorporated increasingly in the other literary forms to which S. writers are now turning their attention.

COLLECTIONS: Muyaka bin Haji, *Diwani ya*, ed. W. Hichens (1940)—collected works; A. Nassir, *Poems from Kenya*, ed. L. Harries (1966); *Waimbaji wa Juzi* [Singers of Yesteryear], ed. A. A. Jahadhmy et al. (1966); J. W. T. Allen, *Diwani ya Shaaban*, ed., (1968), *Tendi*—6 examples of cl. S. verseforms with tr. and notes (1971); M. Shabaan et al., *Malenga wa Mvita*, ed. S. Chiraghdin (1971); *Islamic Poetry*, ed. and tr. J. Knappert (1971), *An Anthol. of S. Love Poetry* (1972); *Muyaka*, ed. M. H. Abdulaziz (1979)—19th-c. popular S. p; *Johari za Kiswahili* (1960)—series of edited *tenzi* pub. by the East African Lit. Bureau.

HISTORY AND CRITICISM: L. Harries, *S. P.* (1962), "S. Lit. in the National Context," *RNL* 11

SWEDISH POETRY

(1971); J. Knappert, *Traditional S. P.* (1967); *Uchambuzi wa Maandishi ya Kiswahili* [Analysis of S. Writings], ed. F. Topan (1971); "Intro." to Spec. Iss. on S. Verbal Arts, ed. C. M. Eastman, *RAL* (1986).   C.M.E.

SWEDISH POETRY. Very little is known about the earliest S. p., since none has been recorded. Rune (q.v.) inscriptions show, however, that *fornyrðislag* (q.v.), the Edda stanza, was known, and possibly also *dróttkvætt* (q.v.), the cl. skaldic verseform. An extensive oral poetry existed, comprising pagan hymns and mythological verse. There may be traces of Sweden's heroic poetry in *Beowulf* and in the skaldic poem *Ynglingatal.*

The chief monuments of medieval S. p. are the folk ballads, at their height in the 13th and 14th cs. The S. ballad approximates the Scottish in spirit and structure. The versified chronicles, from *Erikskrönikan* (Eric's Chronicle, 1320–21) to *Stora rimkrönikan* (The Great Rhymed Chronicle, ca. 1500), are important productions in *knittelvers* (q.v.). Of the known poets, Tomas af Strängnäs (d. 1443) adumbrated a national trad. with his patriotic lyrics, like *Frihetsvisan* (The Song of Freedom). The 16th c. (1511–1611) produced mostly didactic poetry, typified by the first S. attempt at drama, the biblical play *Tobiae comedia* (ca. 1550) ascribed to Olavus Petri (1493–1552).

In the 17th c. (1611–1718), S. poets aimed to create a vernacular lit. matching the achievements of antiquity. With his epoch-making allegorical-didactic epic *Hercules* (1648; pub. 1658), Georg Stiernhielm (1598–1672) demonstrated the aptness of S. for hexameter verse. Stiernhielm nationalized the Greco-Roman gods and introduced vivid personified abstractions, thereby avoiding excessive artificiality. The resultant merging of Classicism and Gothicism—S. nationalism—was to remain a shaping force in S. p. until the end of the 19th c. Stiernhielm's art was broadly realistic, a trait that may derive from his acquaintance with Dutch poets, esp. Jacob Cats. He also introduced the sonnet (q.v.), composed in alexandrines, a practice abandoned only by the romantics. Samuel Columbus (1642–79), who with Urban Hiärne (1641–1724) and others made up the first S. literary coterie, was Stiernhielm's chief follower, but his lyric verse, such as *Odae Sveticae* (1674), is more melodious. Intimately personal as well as national was the inspiration of Lars Wivallius (1605–69), first in a fairly continuous line of unschooled singers whose popular lyrics have enriched S. p. He was followed by Lars Johansson, or Lucidor (1638–74), whose forte was the convivial song, where he provides a link between Wivallius and Bellman, the 18th-c. virtuoso of the genre.

Baroque poetry found a practitioner in Gunno Eurelius Dahlstierna (1661–1709), whose allegorical epic *Kunga Skald* (The King's Poem, 1697) introduced ottava rima (q.v.) into S. p., also characteristically in alexandrines. The poem, however,

lacks narrative unity, and the uneven marinistic style fails to sustain the mood. Later, Samuel Triewald (1688–1743) advocated Fr. neoclassicism, while the Finn Jacob Frese (1691–1729) became Sweden's first significant subjective poet. Frese's Christian epic *Passionstankar* (Thoughts on the Passion, 1728) expresses profound religious feeling. As transformed by the romantics, Frese's introspective lyricism became an enduring trad. in S. p. Johan Runius (1679–1713) was a virtuoso rhymer celebrating bourgeois jocundity. Triewald, Frese, and Runius represent the chief styles of the upcoming century: Fr. neoclassicism, sentimental romanticism, and S.-Carolinian poetic realism.

In the 18th c., neoclassic principles were *de rigueur* both in epic, with its obligatory alexandrines, and in drama. Olof von Dalin (1708–63) produced both a tragedy and an epic in the prescribed style, but modern readers prefer his ballads and epigrammatic satires. In the 1750s Hedvig Charlotta Nordenflycht (1718–63) established a literary *salon* in order to further refine the poetic standards of Dalin. Its principal habitués were Finnish-born Gustaf Filip Creutz (1731–85) and Gustaf Fredrik Gyllenborg (1731–1808). Creutz's *Atis och Camilla* (1761) is a lovely pastoral poem. Gyllenborg was more didactic; his best work, *Människans elände* (The Misery of Man, 1761), shows traces of Rousseau. The poetry of Carl Michael Bellman (1740–1809) is peculiarly individual as well as national. It exhibits a wide gamut of moods, from burlesque humor to dark melancholy; but Bellman is best known, and loved, for his *joie de vivre.* He was also a superb narrator and created an unforgettable gallery of comic types.

The Gustavian Age (1772–1802) was *par excellence* the age of Enlightenment and of Fr. artistic taste, enforced by such literary societies as *Utile Dulci* and *Svenska akademien* (The S. Academy, est. 1786). But a preromantic movement inspired by Rousseau, Eng. preromantics, Klopstock, and *Sturm und Drang* (q.v.) acquired considerable influence. The satirist Johan Henrik Kellgren (1751–95), initially an advocate of neoclassicism, with *Den nya skapelsen* (The New Creation, 1789) expressed a profound idealism foreshadowing the romantic age. By contrast, Anna Maria Lenngren (1755–1817) was the voice of common sense, treating everyday subjects in a simple style that makes her verse readable even today. Among preromantic Gustavians, Bengt Lidner (1757–93) demonstrated an impressive formal virtuosity in *Grevinnan Spastaras död* (The Death of Countess Spastara, 1783), and the Finn Frans Michael Franzén (1772–1847) developed an imaginative, musical poetic idiom, which he used in *Människans anlete* (The Human Countenance, 1793) as the vehicle of an aesthetic-religious idealism.

The 19th c. initiated a great period in S. p. Ger. romanticism and philosophical idealism were the dominant influences. Through Germany, S. poets became acquainted with Shakespeare and Ren. Fr.

and It. authors. Accordingly, the new poetry was exceedingly varied in form. The first group of romantics belonged to *Auroraförbundet* (The Aurora League), founded at Uppsala in 1807. Its members came to be called Phosphorists, from the name of their periodical, *Phosphoros* (1810–13). Per Daniel Amadeus Atterbom (1790–1855), who was inspired by the Jena school of romanticism, emerged with *Blommorna* (The Flowers, 1812–37) as the chief Phosphorist poet. His most ambitious work, *Lycksalighetens ö* (The Isle of Bliss, 1824–27), is an allegorical fairytale play which embodies the confict between aestheticism and an ethical ideal. With its imaginative fervor and cl. form, the poetry of Erik Johan Stagnelius (1793–1823), one of the most gifted S. poets, is related to Phosphorism. The lyric cycle *Liljor i Saron* (Lilies of Sharon, 1821–23) alternates between worldweary mysticism and erotic passion. His greatest work, *Bacchanterna* (The Bacchae, 1822), treats the fate of Orpheus in Cl. Gr. style, dramatizing the contrast between spiritual rapture and sensual intoxication. Known for his ability to convey intense feeling and to concretize abstractions, Stagnelius—who epitomizes the subjective mode in S. p.—has been very influential.

The second group of S. romantics were associated with *Götiska förbundet* (The Gothic League), which called for a national literary revival. Its head, Erik Gustaf Geijer (1783–1847), treated regional subjects in a simple style. It was Esaias Tegnér (1782–1846), one of the foremost S. poets, who came closest to realizing the Gothicist program. Drawing upon the Heidelberg school of romanticism and Ger. classicism, Tegnér achieved a new national poetry. His most important works are *Nattvardsbarnen* (The Children of the Lord's Supper, 1820), a religious-didactic narrative in hexameter verse influenced by Goethe's *Hermann und Dorothea*, and *Frithiofs saga* (1825), his greatest achievement. Despite a lack of historical verisimilitude, the virile, courtly character of Frithiof became an instant idol. The poem is a free rendering of an Old Icelandic saga. Its form, a cycle of 24 romances in various meters, is modeled on Oehlenschläger's *Helge*. Tegnér shows remarkable skill at evoking the changing moods of the story by varying the stanzaic forms and metrical patterns. In his masterful handling of Homeric hexameter, he was a worthy heir to Stiernhielm. The 1830s and 1840s produced only one original romantic, Carl Johan Love Almquist (1793–1866), a bizarre and exotic writer inspired by Byron whose poems are notable for their free-verse qualities and emotional wizardry. His chief work, *Törnrosens bok* (The Book of the Briar Rose, 1832–51), contains lyric, narrative, and dramatic pieces—and prose. His *Songes*, with their artless form, suggestive music, and gripping tone, link Almquist with Stagnelius, both forerunners of poetic modernism in Sweden.

In the sensibility of the great Finnish poet Johan Ludvig Runeberg (1804–77), realism and romanticism go hand in hand. Of his narrative poems may be mentioned *Elgskyttarne* (The Elkhunters, 1832), in hexameters, and the somber *Kung Fjalar* (1844), his best work, in which influences from Nordic myth, Ossian, and Cl. antiquity are merged. But the verseforms, modeled on Nordic meters, are his own creation. Runeberg is best known for his immortal *Fänrik Ståls sägner* (The Tales of Ensign Stål, 1848–60), a narrative-lyric cycle. *Idyll och epigram* (1830–33), with its laconic verses in trochaic meter, contains strikingly original lyrics.

After two relatively barren decades, in the 1870s Carl Snoilsky and Viktor Rydberg ushered in a period of new creativity. Snoilsky (1841– 1903) belonged to *Namnlösa Sällskapet* (The Nameless Society, est. 1860), whose realistic poetic program was inspired by Runeberg and contemp. Norwegian poetry (q.v.). His *Dikter* (Poems, 1869) demonstrates great versatility and a joyous love of life and freedom. But his later poetry is richer, combining, as in "Afrodite och Sliparen" (Aphrodite and the Knife-Grinder, 1883), social awareness with personal moods. Through his blend of romantic idealism, Cl. form, and national inspiration, Rydberg (1828–95) became a successor to Stiernhielm and Tegnér. With *Dikter* (1882, 1891), however, his reflective poetry acquired a distinctly modern note. "Den nya Grottesången" (The New Song of Grotti, 1891), launching fiery imprecations against industrial slavery, typifies his later work.

The best poet of the 1880s was August Strindberg (1849–1912), who had a first-rate lyrical talent. By its flair for actuality and its free, careless rhythms, Strindberg's poetry effected a break with the late romantic style. His bold imagery was to be much emulated in the 1890s. *Dikter på vers och prosa* (Poems in Verse and Prose, 1883) and *Ordalek och småkonst* (Word-Play and Minor Art, 1902–05) contain a world of impressions, moods, and visions. Urban scenes coexist with family idylls, while poems like "Chrysaëtos" and "Holländarn" (The Dutchman, 1902) resonate with chords of passion. With its irregular rhythm and scientific imagery, his hymn to the female body in "The Dutchman" was significant for the future. Like Stagnelius and Almquist, Strindberg helped pave the way for the poetic modernism of the postwar period. Of other poets of the 1880s, Ola Hansson (1860–1925) renounced realism in an attempt, inspired by Poe, Nietzsche, and Mallarmé, to penetrate beneath appearances. This endeavor was facilitated by a superb sense of rhythm.

In the 1890s, S. p. experienced a veritable renascence. Though the new poets adhered to the minute observation and psychological analysis of the naturalists, the renascence was decidedly neoromantic: beauty, imagination, and self were apotheosized. Moreover, the decade evinced, by its interest in regional poetry and historical subjects, a desire to rediscover its roots and redefine the nation's identity. The poets practiced a variety of forms and, in romantic fashion, aimed to create a

SWEDISH POETRY

grand style.

Four figures—Heidenstam, Levertin, Karlfeldt, and Fröding—were the vehicles of this poetic renewal. With his first collection, *Vallfart och vandringsår* (Pilgrimage and Wander-Years, 1888), Verner von Heidenstam (1859–1940), originally a painter, created an epoch in S. p. Its impressionistic, richly visual style replete with baroque images and daring coinings—Heidenstam later called it "imaginative naturalism"—would have been impossible without the example of Strindberg. In *Dikter* (1895)—supported critically in *Renässans* (Renascence, 1889) and *Pepitas bröllop* (Pepita's Wedding, 1890), both of which repudiated "shoemaker realism"—his central themes appeared: the glories of the imagination, of his native region, and of his country. These were also the basis of *Ett folk* (One People, 1920), a narrative cycle celebrating a S. ideal of chivalry and heroism. Oscar Levertin (1862–1906) was the most romantic of the new poets. The main themes of his work, love and death, are treated in a richly textured style influenced by the Eng. Pre-Raphaelites. Erik Axel Karlfeldt (1864–1931) was the voice of his native region, Dalecarlia, whose landscape, people, and customs he presented in *Fridolins visor* (Fridolin's Songs, 1898) and *Fridolins lustgård* (Fridolin's Pleasure Garden, 1901).

Gustaf Fröding (1860–1911) is one of the greatest lyric poets of Sweden. Already *Guitarr och dragharmonika* (Guitar and Concertina, 1891), critically prepared for by his essay *Om humor* (On Humor, 1890), evidenced a mature talent. It was precisely its brilliant and contagious humor that made this collection stand out. *Nya dikter* (New Poems, 1894) also contained serious, even somber poems, such as "Bibliska fantasier" (Biblical Fantasies), with their dark *Weltschmerz*. But only in *Stänk och flikar* (Splashes and Rags, 1896) and *Nytt och gammalt* (New and Old Pieces, 1897) does Fröding lay bare his soul—in Nietzschean visions, paeans to pagan beauty, and intimate confessions like "Narkissos." Here also, in "Sagan om Gral" (The Story of the Grail), he makes his first attempt at a catharsis of life's paradoxes by means of metaphysical humor. Fröding is the last great figure in the S. trad. of spontaneous realistic verse which originated in Wivallius. His broad appeal is chiefly due to his naked intensity and the innate skill with which he exploits the lyric potentialities of the S. lang. This lang., with its undulating rhythm, rich modulation, and great variety of expressive vowel sounds, is admirably suited for lyric poetry, and not surprisingly the strength of S. p. lies precisely in this genre. S. is esp. effective for expressing moods of passion and grotesque humor, and Bellman and Fröding demonstrate a prodigious aptitude for both. The latter could produce the subtlest nuance of melody, tone, and mood by conjuring with rhyme, rhythm, and sound effects.

The writers who appeared after 1900 inherited the realism of the 1880s along with neoromanti-cism, but they worked out their own forms of expression. Bo Bergman (1869–1967) created a new style marked by clarity, a colloquial idiom, and simple rhythms. With *Marionetterna* (The Puppets, 1903) he initiated an urban poetry in the modern manner. Vilhelm Ekelund (1880–1949) showed a preference for unrhymed verse and free rhythms à la Pindar, Hölderlin, and Strindberg in his reflective verse. Anders Österling (1884–1981) adopted in *Idyllernas bok* (The Book of Idylls, 1917) a moderate poetic realism inspired by the Eng. Georgians.

World War I imbued S. p. with pessimism and religious questing. In *Ångest* (Anguish, 1916), Pär Lagerkvist (1891–1975) expressed moods of anxiety in an unadorned, unrhythmical verse of striking novelty. His manifesto *Ordkonst och bildkonst* (Verbal and Pictorial Art, 1913) had announced a radical modernism related to Ekelund's experiments and to expressionism in painting. Anticipating the Swedo-Finnish Modernists (q.v.), Lagerkvist inaugurated the modernist movement in S. p. The evolutionary humanism of Erik Blomberg (1894–1965), whose Faustian lyric confession *Den fångne guden* (The Captive God, 1927) inspired younger writers, became an important rallying-point for poets in an age of religious skepticism. During the 1920s the melancholy idyll, related to Österling's poetry, was the dominant genre. In the work of Erik Lindorm (1889–1941), a proletarian poet of city life, the bourgeois idyll was dissolved. Birger Sjöberg (1885–1929), a troubadour of disillusion, introduced a new spirit and style. Sjöberg's *Kriser och kransar* (Crises and Laurel Wreaths, 1926) expressed postwar anxiety in an idiom using slang and jargon in discordant counterpoint with more conventional diction.

The definite breakthrough of modernism—the devel. of which constitutes a central movement in 20th-c. S. p.—came with the appearance in 1929 of the anthol. *Fem unga* (Five Young Poets), two of whose contributors, Harry Martinson (1904–78) and Artur Lundkvist (b. 1906), should be noted. These writers, whose program found a nonliterary complement in a primitivism inspired by D. H. Lawrence and Freudian psychology, reinforced Lagerkvist's emphasis on immediacy of poetic expression by demanding the use of objective visual imagery, a doctrine derived from the Am. imagists. The poetry of Karin Boye (1900–41), while spiritually akin to primitivist modernism, is fraught with idealism and an uncompromising ethos. Gunnar Ekelöf (1907–68), who started as a surrealist, further elaborated the modernist technique by employing musical principles of poetic structure, nonlogical syntax, and verbal telescoping à la James Joyce. Three other important poets, known for their militant humanism during the 1930s, were Hjalmar Gullberg (1898–1961), Johannes Edfelt (b. 1904), and Bertil Malmberg (1889–1958). Though none was a programmatic modernist, both Gullberg and Edfelt practiced

Sjöberg's disturbing reversals in rhythm and idiom; and when drawing upon the cl. trad., they used it in a characteristically modern manner, namely to reinforce their somber probings of the contemp. psyche and political scene through ironic contrast.

During the 1940s the modernist movement, headed by Erik Lindegren (1910–68) and Karl Vennberg (b. 1910), advanced on a broad front. It encompassed the programs and techniques of both the "pure" and the "engaged" poets of the 1930s. The pressure of the war situation and impulses from Kafka, Eliot, and Rilke combined to produce a poetry marked by dissonance and anguished pessimism—in Lindegren's words, a "catharsis of impotence." The poets' disillusionment and skepticism are illustrated by what Vennberg termed a choice "between the indifferent and the impossible." Epochal was Lindegren's *Mannen utan väg* ("The Man Without a Way," 1942; Eng. tr. 1969), a cycle of sonnets broken up into couplets in which the disorder of the war years is expressed in explosive images. Of *fyrtiotalisterna* (q.v.; "The Poets of the Forties"), one may mention Werner Aspenström (b. 1918), Sven Alfons (b. 1918), Bernt Erikson (b. 1921), Ragnar Thoursie (b. 1919), and Stig Carlson (1920–71). The tortured individualism and existentialist questionings of these poets were expressed in experimental modes that evoked charges of obscurity from the general public.

The generation of poets emerging after the war returned to a more concrete reality, with everyone seeking a new point of departure. The result was a poetry of great diversity. One trend was toward either the idyllic-romantic, as in the work of Bo Setterlind (b. 1923), or toward nature description, as in the early work of Folke Isaksson (b. 1927). Linguistic sophistication and semantic irony predominated in the meta-poetry of Göran Printz-Påhlsson (b. 1931) and Majken Johansson (b. 1930), members of a group of poets at the University of Lund who excelled in the cultivation of unusual forms such as the sonnet and the villanelle. The irony and bitter pessimism of Sandro Key-Åberg (b. 1923) and the posturings of Lars Forssell (b. 1928) as jester or clown concealed a search for commitment and ideological identification. The theatricality of Forssell's poetry sharpened the satire, and in his cabaret songs, patterned after Fr. *chansons*, he found an effective vehicle for his political engagement. Östen Sjöstrand (b. 1925) emerged as a religious mystic whose poetry is often couched in the idiom of the natural sciences; with Lindegren's later work, it shares a striving toward the condition of music, an attempt to express the absolute. The unobtrusive formal perfection of the poetry of Tomas Tranströmer (b. 1931) and his sure instinct for the liberating metaphor placed him in the forefront of the new generation of poets when he made his appearance in 1954. Subsequent works, such as the collections

Hemligheter på vägen (Secrets on the Way, 1958), *Mörkerseende* (Night Vision, 1970; Eng. tr. 1971), and *Östersjöar* (Baltics, 1974; Eng. tr. 1975), confirmed his position as one of the most significant, and most translated, of modern S. poets.

In the years following mid-century a number of well-established poets presented some of their most important works. Pär Lagerkvist crowned his long poetic career with *Aftonland* (Evening Land, 1953; Eng. tr. 1974), a summation of familiar themes—childhood memories and metaphysical probings—from the writings of this self-styled "religious atheist." Harry Martinson had already earned a unique position in S. lit. by his unsurpassed nature poetry and his sweeping vision encompassing microcosm and macrocosm at one glance. In 1956 he published the space epic *Aniara* (Eng. tr. 1963), in which the poet saw himself as "a medium and reporter from his own time." Science fiction and allegory in one, the poem offers a chilling vision of a technological future gone astray and a nostalgic celebration of the earth, with an implied warning against its potential destruction at the hands of man. Hjalmar Gullberg presented a whittled-down verse of stark simplicity in his last collection of poetry, *Ögon, läppar* (Eyes, Lips, 1960).

Gunnar Ekelöf's stature as the central figure in Scandinavian poetry became indisputable with the publication of *En Mölna-elegi* (A Mölna Elegy, 1960; Eng. tr. 1985) and his last three collections, which form a "Byzantine triptych": *Diwan över Fursten av Emgión* (Diwan on the Prince of Emgion, 1965), *Sagan om Fatumeh* (The Tale of Fatumeh, 1966), and *Vägvisare till underjorden* (Guide to the Underworld, 1967; Eng. tr. 1980). By means of avatars and archetypes, the poet offers in these works a learned summation of the human experience, a simultaneous view of humanity's past and present, of myth and history. Like Martinson's *Aniara*, Ekelöf's poetry abounds in literary allusions. Thanks to the efforts of such poets as Ekelöf and Forssell, official recognition was given to the poetic genius of the popular troubadour Evert Taube (1890–1976), whose songs extolling love, the S. summer, and seafaring adventures made him a worthy successor to Bellman.

The poets of the 1960s placed a strong emphasis on communication, with a growing demand for reader participation in "creating" a poem. The period was characterized by a distrust for established social and linguistic structures and a questioning of the ability of traditional poetic lang. to break through these structures. Anti-symbolic, non-metaphoric "concretism" even enlisted electronics and cybernetics to create a new lang. The parallels with pictorial pop art were obvious, as shown in the work of the poet and painter Carl Fredrik Reutersvärd (b. 1934). Göran Palm (b. 1931) advocated a "new simplicity," making poetry an instrument for exploring a tangible socio-political reality locally as well as globally. Sonja Åkesson

SWISS POETRY

(1926–77) offered a woman's perspective on everyday life, viewing its trivialities and absurdities with humor and irony. The new political awareness was a dominant aspect of the works of Åke Hodell (b. 1919), Erik Beckman (b. 1935), and Björn Håkanson (b. 1937). It found its emblematic expression in the poem *Om kriget i Vietnam* (About the War in Vietnam, 1965) by Göran Sonnevi (b. 1939). Sonnevi's poetry is typical of the period in its blend of concrete observation and abstract theory, of radical activism and acute linguistic awareness.

Whereas the common political concerns of the 1960s offered a somewhat misleading appearance of unity to the poetry of that decade, the 1970s and 1980s present a picture of great diversity. The nakedly reductive poetry of Lars Norén (b. 1944) and the verbal experiments of Bengt Emil Johnson (b. 1936) in his extensive poetry of the four seasons represent conspicuously different approaches. A tentative distinction could be made between two temperaments, both of which find a voice in the most recent S. p.: romantic, musical, and verbally opulent in the works of Tobias Berggren (b. 1940) and Niklas Rådström (b. 1953); intellectual, learned, and reflective in those of Lars Gustafsson (b. 1936), highly theoretical and conscious of critical fashions in those of the "postmodernist" Ulf Eriksson (b. 1958). Traditionally, poetry is the S. literary genre *par excellence*. There is every indication that it will continue to be so.

ANTHOLOGIES: *Oxford Book of Scandinavian Verse*, ed. E. W. Gosse and W. A. Craigie (1925); *Anthol. of S. Lyrics from 1750–1925*, ed. C. W. Stork (1930); *Mod. S. P.*, ed. C. D. Locock (1936); *S. Songs and Ballads*, ed. M. S. Allwood (1950); *Lyrikboken*, ed. T. Nilsson (1951)—illustrated; *40-talslyrik*, ed. B. Holmqvist (1951); *Masterpieces of S. P.*, ed. F. Ahlberg (1952); *50-talslyrik*, ed. B. Holmqvist and F. Isaksson (1955); *Barocklyrik* (1962), *Rokokolyrik*, both ed. B. Julén (1962); *Eight S. Poets*, ed. and tr. F. Fleisher (1969); *Friends, You Drank Some Darkness*, ed. and tr. R. Bly (1975)—poems by Martinson, Ekelöf, and Tranströmer; *Svensk dikt från trollformler till Lars Norén*, ed. L. Gustafsson (1978)—comprehensive; *Mod. S. P. in Tr.*, ed. G. Harding and A. Anselm Hollo (1979); *Contemp. S. P.*, ed. and tr. J. Matthias and G. Printz-Påhlsson (1980).

HISTORY AND CRITICISM: E. W. Gosse, *Northern Studies* (1890); H. Schück, *Hist. de la litt. suédoise* (1923); O. Sylwan, *Den svenska versen från 1600-talets början*, 3 v. (1925–34), *Svensk verskonst från Wivallius till Karlfeldt* (1934)—versification; L. Maury, *Panorama de la litt. suédoise contemporaine* (1940); C. A. D. Fehrman, *Kyrkogårdsromantik: Studier i engelsk och svensk 1700-talsdiktning* (1954)—comparative study, summarized in Eng.; I. Holm and M. von Platen, *La litt. suédoise* (1957); A. Gustafson, *A Hist. of S. Lit.* (1961); R. B. Vowles, "Post-War S. P.," *WHR* 15 (1961); G. C. Schoolfield, "The Recent Scandinavian Lyric," *BA* 36

(1962); E. N. Tigerstedt et al., *Ny illustrerad svensk litteraturh.*, 5 v. (1967)—standard lit. hist. with annotated bibl; G. Brandell and J. Stenkvist, *Svensk litt. 1870–1970*, 3 v. (1974–75); L. Gustafsson, *Forays into S. P.* (1978); S. H. Rossel, *A Hist. of Scandinavian Lit, 1870–1980* (1982); B. Olsson and I. Algulin, *Litteraturens Historia i Sverige* (1987). S.LY.; L.G.W.

SWEDO-FINNISH MODERNISTS. A group of significant poets in Finland writing in Swedish during and shortly after World War I. Among the chief members were Edith Södergran (1892–1923), Hagar Olsson (1893–1978), Elmer Diktonius (1896–1961), Gunnar Björling (1887–1960), Rabbe Enckell (1903–74), and Henry Parland (1908–30). They were influenced by Ger. expressionism, Rus. futurism, and Anglo-Am. imagism (qq.v.) as well as by various other European movements in poetry, painting, and music, but cannot be defined as a separate "school." Nor were they imitators: their work was a unique creation—a response to a turbulent period in Finnish history and culture—whose form varied according to their individual talents. Their poetic program, presented in two avant-garde periodicals, *Ultra* (1922) and *Quosego* (1928–29), indicates that these poets and critics were ahead of the Scandinavian and Finnish lit. of the time. Its revolutionary aesthetic defines poetry as a dynamic process whose forms, changing with time, give direct expression to instinctual and subconscious life while reflecting historically determined shifts in sensibility, intellectual and moral values, and sexual attitudes. Their work included many new poetic techniques (q.v.), such as *vers libre*, unrhymed lines with free rhythms, a strong emphasis on associative imagery, and startling, spontaneous lang. They expanded the topics of poetry, dealing with the inner life of the individual as well as with contemp. society. Their influence can be seen in Sweden, particularly in the leading poetic modernist Gunnar Ekelöf, and in the *fyrtiotalisterna* (q.v.), "The Poets of the Forties." They also influenced the Finnish modernist poets, the "Fire-bearers." See FINNISH POETRY.—B. Holmqvist, *Mod. finlandssvensk litteratur* (1951); B. Carpelan, *Studier i Gunnar Björlings diktning* (1960); J. Wrede, *Tidskriften Ultra* (1970); E. Södergran, *Complete Poems*, tr. D. McDuff (1983). S.LY.; K.K.S.

SWISS POETRY.

    I. OVERVIEW
    II. IN GERMAN
    III. IN FRENCH
    IV. IN ITALIAN
    V. IN RHAETO-ROMANSH

I. OVERVIEW. Contrary to an old and popular cliché employed in books on the hist. of S. lit., the production of poetry in this small country has been extremely prolific and diverse, particularly in the 19th and 20th cs. Thus we arrive at the not very original conclusion that even within such a spatially and temporally limited area encyclopedic "completeness" is an utopian notion and that, therefore, we have to content ourselves with giving mostly positions and developments or, as Werner Weber says, with looking for "indications of the whole in individual phenomena." As to the existence of a specifically "Swiss" p., this question cannot be answered here. In the S. Confederacy, with its four langs., the types of relationships between culture and lit. are quite different from one another, and some authors (for example, the "globe-trotter" Blaise Cendrars) may more aptly fit into international categories than into those applying to a small country.

Chronologically, the evolution runs from the medieval Minnesingers in the Ger.- and Fr.-speaking parts of Switzerland (Rudolf von Fenis, Johannes Hadlaub, Steinmar, Oton de Grandson) to the poetry of "the children of Marx and Coca-Cola," a phrase echoing Jean-Luc Godard which was used by Daniel Walter (b. 1953) as the title of one of his texts. The poets themselves perceive an arc extending from metaphysical meditations via the wordplays of *lettrisme* (q.v.) to couplets expressing *engagé* criticisms of established society. Philippe Jaccottet (b. 1925) likens the labor of a poet to the night watch of a herdsman ("Le Travail du poète" in *L'Ignorant*, 1958):

> The task of a look becoming weaker by
>   the hour
> is not to go on dreaming or shedding
>   tears,
> but to be on the watch like a shepherd
>   and to summon
> all those who risk getting lost by falling
>   asleep.
>
> (tr. P. Spycher)

The "house poet of Basel," Berthold Redlich, is considerably less ambitious; for a commission he produces rhymed love letters, speeches, and advertisements, and he recommends himself like this: "Sensible people dial his number / For it frees you from a poet's worries!" There is room for opposites and, moreover, for absurdities in a "postmodern" society that regards itself as pluri-cultural and that lives by the rules of consumerism. To the extent that the functions of poetry are (still?) separate ones, "high poetry" can be characterized as the concern of a specific, linguistically and intellectually educated reading public which constitutes a small share of the public targeted by advertising- and everyday-poetry. A connection between both of them is established, among other things, by "concrete poetry" (q.v.), whose protagonist Eugen Gomringer (b. 1925 in Zurich), perhaps the internationally best known representative of more recent S. p., writes in his "23 Points about the Problem of 'Lit. and Society'" (1958; in his collection *Worte sind Schatten*, 1969): "no longer

being adequate for our changing times, classic-humanistic organicism has been superseded by what Max Bense has called 'synthetic rationality.'" Logically enough, Gomringer defines the "new poem" as an "object for use." It is true that "concrete poetry" takes an extreme position (some people have thought they recognized something typically Swiss in its mechanically puzzled-out quality). But the question of just how shopworn that which we designate here as "classical-humanistic organicism" was and has a general relevance, the more so since this cultural trad. put its firm stamp on the style and thematics of "bourgeois" poetry between ca. 1850 and 1950. In 1950, the year in which he died, Werner Zemp, a poet writing in this Classical-romantic trad., deplored what he perceived as the new antagonism of the technological mind with the soul: "Day after day we have to watch precious things getting irretrievably lost!" (Letter of April 3, 1959, in Zemp's *Das lyrische Werk, Aufsätze, Briefe*, 1967). Zemp was a *poeta doctus*, combining lyrical production with critical reflection, a combination that is represented throughout Switzerland by important writer-critics (Max Rychner [1897–1965] embodies it perfectly; below, in the Fr.-speaking section, see Georges Nicole and Pierre-Louis Matthey [1893–1970]; in the It.-speaking section, see Giorgio Orelli [b. 1921] and Adolfo Jenni [b. 1911]; in the Rhaeto-Romansh-speaking section, see Andri Peer [1921–85]). Only rarely does this inclination find expression in poetological programs, or, even less likely, in manifestoes; the distinctly preferred form is that of essays about other writers. One can say that the lyrical production of Switzerland is unprogrammatic, but also that the poets are keenly aware of the universality of poetry. A fairly unique case is that of the adoptive Genevan George Haldas (b. 1917); his literary output, beginning with the essay *Les Poètes malades de la peste* (1954), is accompanied by a steadily increasing diaristic one in which poetological reflection plays a significant role.

The break with cultural trad. in the course of the 1950s, notably in the Ger.-speaking part of Switzerland (considerably less so in the Fr.-speaking part, where writers continue cultivating a kind of inwardness that derives from romantic sources, among them Ger. ones), manifested itself not only in a new conception of form, which was influenced by the West European and Am. modernism and by the West Ger. "Kahlschlag" (forest-clearing) lit., but also in the abandonment of the traditional S. themes of the poetry of the Alps and of idyllic nature. The transformation of a centuries-old rural society into a modern, urbanized, service-job society has had a revolutionary effect on the writers' views of life. It would be wrong, however, to regard this transformation as a total one and thus to overlook (modernized) re-establishments of relationships with the poetry of earlier generations. The roots of a specifically S. modernity have been discovered in the works of Robert Walser (1878–1956), Hans Morgenthaler (1890–1928), and Adrien Turel (1890–1957); in the recently edited texts of the outsider, the ostracized "sick man" and "naive" painter Adolf Wölfli (1864–1930), an overwhelming wealth of linguistic "picture puzzles" has come to light. And the often radical social engagement of many contemp. poets is, in the last analysis, part of a S. trad. of political poetry that can be traced back through Gottfried Keller and Juste Olivier to the folk- and war-songs of the late Middle Ages.

Lyrical speech means participation in a global lang.; at the same time, poetry is the lang. of subjectivity and thus, at least potentially, of marginality. The consensus of a certain kind of elitist poetry, but also that of a certain kind of stereotyped patriotic poetry, could deceive the reader about its subjectivity and marginality. Contemp. poetry rejects this consensus and takes up the counter-rhetoric of both its own lit. and foreign lits. It has never completely escaped the threat of a new conformity (which frequently was a thematic, but also, given its adoption of fashionable lyrical understatement and discontinuity, a formal one). The freedom for poetic production and the freedom of the critically selective reader have never been as great as they are now. Reflecting this new freedom is "Jenseits von heute," by Hans Schuhmacher (b. 1910) in his *Meridiane* (1959):

It's lovely today.
A lot lies in ruins
And new things
Are not yet in use.
Anything may happen.

ANTHOLOGIES AND COLLECTIONS: *Lesebuch schweizerischer Dichtung*, ed. S. Lang (1938); *Bestand und Versuch: Schweizer Schrifttum der Gegenwart*, ed. B. Mariacher and F. Witz (1964); *Textbuch der Gruppe Olten I, II* (1975, 1976); *Schweizer Lyrik des zwanzigsten Jahrhunderts*, ed. B. Jentzsch (1979); *Neue Schweizer Literatur* (1980); *Anthol. of Mod. S. Lit.*, ed. H. M. Waidson (1984).

HISTORY AND CRITICISM: G. de Reynold, *Histoire littéraire de la Suisse au XVIIIe siècle*, v. 1, 2 (1909, 1912); E. Jenny and V. Rossel, *Gesch. der schweizerischen Literatur* (1910), *Histoire de la litt. suisse* (1910); F. Ernst, *Die Schweiz als geistige Mittlerin von Muralt bis Jacob Burckhardt* (1932), *Gibt es eine schweizerische Nationalliteratur?* (1955); C. Clerc et al., *Panorama des littératures contemporaines de Suisse* (1938); T. Greiner, *Der literarische Verkehr zwischen der deutschen und welschen Schweiz seit 1848* (1940); G. Locarnini, *Die literarischen Beziehungen zwischen der italienischen und der deutschen Schweiz* (1946); K. Schmid, "Versuch über die schweizerische Nationalität," *Aufsätze und Reden* (1957); G. Calgari, *Storia delle quattro letterature della Svizzera* (1959), *Die vier Literaturen der Schweiz* (1966); F. Jost, "Y a-t-il une litt. suisse?," *Essais de litt. comparée I: Helvetica* (1964); K. Marti, *Die Schweiz und ihre*

Schriftsteller—die Schriftsteller und ihre Schweiz (1966); D. de Rougemont, *La Suisse ou l'histoire d'un peuple heureux* (1969); P. Nizon, *Diskurs in der Enge* (1970); *Der Schriftsteller in unserer Zeit*, ed. P. A. Bloch and E. Hubacher (1972); M. Gsteiger, "Litt. et nation en Suisse romande et en Suisse alémanique," *RLC* 216 (1980), ed., *Die zeitgenössischen Literaturen der Schweiz* (1980); A. Muschg, "Gibt es eine schweizerische Nationalliteratur?" *Ich hab im Traum die Schweiz gesehn*, ed. J. Jung (1980); *Die Viersprachige Schweiz*, ed. J. C. Arquint et al. (1982); G. Steiner, "What is 'S.'?" *TLS* 7 (1984); *Mod. S. Lit.: Unity and Diversity*, ed. J. L. Flood (1985).

II. IN GERMAN. If we disregard the Med. Lat. sequences (Notker Balbulus of St. Gall died in 912) and the Minnesingers (see MINNESANG) of the 12th–13th cs., mentioned earlier (the *Manessische Liederhandschrift*, created in the 14th c., probably compiled in Zurich, is the most famous specimen of its genre in the Ger.-lang. territory), the origins of Ger.-S. p., i.e. the poetry written in the Ger.-speaking part of Switzerland, are to be found in the mostly anonymous political and ecclesiastic poems of the late Middle Ages (*Das Sempacherlied*, end of the 14th c.; *Das Tellenlied*, ca. 1474; the spiritual poetry of Heinrich von Laufenberg, 15th c.); but it was not until the 18th c. that a theoretically underpinned, genuinely "S." p. emerged (J. J. Breitinger's *Critische Dichtkunst* [1740] with a foreword by J. J. Bodmer, put forth fundamental theories guided by models of Eng. lit.). Yet Albrecht von Haller's *Versuch schweizerischer Gedichte* (1732), containing "Die Alpen," had already won European fame for the "land of the herdsmen," partly due to V. B. von Tscharner's Fr. tr. This, along with the prose poems of Salomon Gessner (1730–88, *Idyllen*, 1756), disseminated throughout the Continent the image of a mythic rural society and of an alternately heroic and idyllic Nature. The *Schweizerlieder* (1767) of the theologian and physiognomist J. C. Lavater (1741–1801) were intended to reactivate the legacy of the national history in the style of preromantic ballads, while the *Gedichte* (1793) of J. G. von Salis-Seewis discreetly transposed the elegiac lyricism of the Ancien Régime to a Helvetic mode. Political poetry, represented by Niklaus Manuel (1484–1530), and satire, represented by Pamphilus Gengenbach (1480–1525) and Johannes Grob (1643–97), recede into the background during the time of upheaval between revolution, restoration, and regeneration. Not until young Gottfried Keller (1819–90) began to write did political poetry re-awaken, influenced by the political age 1815–48; Keller, creator of nature poems, festive and patriotic poems ("O mein Heimatland!") came to be viewed as an exemplary S. national writer, yet next to, or in, his rhetorical faith in progress, overtones of sorrow and hopelessness are not to be ignored. His fellow S. and contemporary, Conrad Ferdinand Meyer (1825–98), is the creator of an original variant of European symbolism, of a poetry of escapism and isolation, turning to hist., nature, and the world of ballads for his subjects. Heinrich Leuthold (1827–79) was a remarkable translator and was close to the Munich Circle of Writers; his poetry was also one of escapism and isolation.

Carl Spitteler (1845–1924), whose *Olympischer Frühling* (1900– 10) is the fruit of his anachronistic attempt to write verse epics about a somewhat modernized mythical world, and Josef Victor Widmann (1842–1911), author of idyllic poetry, point forward to the 20th c.—that is, to a tension between the trad. of *l'art pour l'art* and what the expressionistic S. poet Karl Stamm (1890–1914) called "the start of the heart's journey," and between bourgeois life and marginality. Werner Zemp (1906–59), Siegfried Lang (1887–1971), and Urs Martin Strub (b. 1910) belong to the former tendency; Albin Zollinger (1895–1941), Albert Ehrismann (b. 1908), and Max Pulver (1889–1952) to the latter. The period after the Second World War saw a revitalization of the production of poetry running from the *lied*-like melodies of Silja Walter (b. 1919) to the pointed modernism of Alexander Gwerder (1923–52) and the wordplay of Eugen Gomringer (mentioned above). Rainer Brambach (1917–86), Gerhard Meier (b. 1917), Walter Gross (b. 1924), and Erika Burkart (b. 1922) among many have striven for, and achieved, a synthesis.

Dialect poetry does not simply exist face to face with poetry in standard Ger.; in most cases the former complements the latter. Whereas the earlier authors of dialect poetry, e.g. Gottlieb Jakob Kuhn (1775–1849), Meinrad Lienert (1865–1933), Alfred Huggenberger (1867–1960), and Josef Reinhart (1875-1957), prefer subjects taken from the peasant homeland, the "modern dialect" movement has articulated modern changes in lang. and society in a new form of dialect poetry (Kurt Marti [b. 1921], Ernst Eggimann [b. 1936], and others). The poetry of the cabaretists and the folksingers (Max Werner Lenz [1887–1973], Alfred Rasser [1907–77], Mani Matter [1936–72]), who often combine dialect with standard lang., warrants special mention.

ANTHOLOGIES AND COLLECTIONS: *Schwyzer Meie: Die schönsten schweizerdeutschen Gedichte*, ed. G. Thürer and A. Guggenbühl (1938); *Gut zum Druck: Literatur der deutschen Schweiz seit 1964* (1972), *Mach keini Schprüch: Schweizer Mundartlyrik des 20. Jahrhunderts*, both ed. D. Fringeli (1972); *Kurzwaren: Schweizer Lyrik*, ed. Zytglogge-Verlag, 5 v. (1975–88); *Fortschreiben: 98 Autoren der deutschen Schweiz*, ed. D. Bachmann (1977); *Belege: Gedichte aus der deutschen Schweiz seit 1900*, ed. W. Weber (1978); *Gegengewichte: Lyrik unserer Tage aus dem deutschsprachigen Raum der Schweiz*, ed. H. Schaub (1978).

HISTORY AND CRITICISM: J. Baechtold, *Gesch. der deutschen Literatur in der Schweiz* (1892); J. Nadler, *Literaturgesch. der deutschen Schweiz* (1932); E. Ermatinger, *Dichtung und Geistesleben der deutschen*

Schweiz (1933); M. Blöchlinger, *La Poésie lyrique contemporaine en Suisse allemande* (1947); A. Bettex, *Die Literatur der deutschen Schweiz von heute* (1950); A. Zäch, *Die Dichtung der deutschen Schweiz* (1951); M. Wehrli, "Gegenwartsdichtung der deutschen Schweiz," *Deutsche Literatur in unserer Zeit*, ed. W. Kayser et al. (1959); W. Günther, *Dichter der neueren Schweiz*, 3 v. (1963–87); *Schweizer Schriftsteller im Gespräch*, ed. W. Bucher and G. Ammann (1970–71); *Der Schriftsteller und sein Verhältnis zur Sprache dargestellt am Problem der Tempuswahl*, ed. P. A. Bloch (1971); E. Pulver, "Die deutschsprachige Literatur der Schweiz seit 1945," *Die zeitgenössischen Literaturen der Schweiz*, ed. M. Gsteiger (1980); *Helvetische Steckbriefe: 47 Schriftsteller aus der deutschen Schweiz seit 1800*, ed. W. Weber et al. (1981).

III. IN FRENCH. From the Minnesingers to Haller and Lavater to Frisch and Dürrenmatt (of the two world-famous contemporaries, only Dürrenmatt has written some poetry on very rare occasions), the lit. of the Alemanic part of Switzerland has moved forward in a fairly close symbiosis with "cultural" Germany. Conditions in the *Romandie*, the Fr.-speaking part of Switzerland, however, are distinctly different. On the one hand, the Romandie has made outstanding contributions to Fr. lit. (e.g. Rousseau), and its consciousness of belonging to a larger linguistic and cultural realm has always been keen—indeed, at times too keen (which may, in part, explain the almost total disappearance of its original Franco-Provençal dialects)—but the relationship between the "motherland" and the small "cultural provinces," which have clung to their political autonomy and to their preponderantly Protestant orientation, has only recently become more relaxed. For a long time, Fr.-lang. S. lit. has existed as a mere footnote to Fr. lit. Apart from the examples of folk poetry (cf. the famous "Ranz des vaches," written in dialect) and from Oton de Grandson (mentioned earlier), no attempts at poetry were made until the 18th c., when Fr. idyllic poetry was adopted (*La Vue d'Anet* by the Bernese writer S.-L. von Lerber, 1723–83), or when contemp. Ger.-S. "national lit." was emulated (*Poésies helvétiennes* by the Vaudois Philippe-Sirice Bridel, 1757–1845). Romantic poetry, which was nonexistent in the Ger.-speaking part, was cultivated in the Romandie; its (none too original) practitioners, Jacques Imbert-Galloix (1807–28), Frédéric Monneron (1813–37), and Etienne Eggis (1830–67), show not only the continuing influence of the Ger. romantic mind in the 20th c. (the distinguished critic Albert Béguin confirmed this influence in his book *L'Ame romantique et le rêve*, 1937) but also the tragic isolation and introversion which has frequently been branded as the "original sin" of the Romandie lit. In the works of Louis Duchosal (1862–1901), Edmond-Henri Crisinel (1897–1948), and of the superior master of forms Pierre-Louis Matthey (1893–1970), the search for poetic expression has its quasi-religious correlate in the search for the meaning of isolation and loneliness, and, conversely, the feeling of being existentially threatened turns into devotion to pure art. Edouard Tavan (1842–1919) carries this devotion most skillfully to an extreme; Alice Chambrier (1861–82) pours it into rather sentimental molds; Henry Spiess (1876–1940) translates the contrast between the intellect and the senses into melodious cadences. All of these poets are close or distant literary brothers and sisters or descendants of Henri-Frédéric Amiel (1821–81), the gifted poet and translator and author of the unique *Journal intime* (first ed. in part, 1923; ed. complete, 1976ss.): being wedged between grace and nausea, between exaltation and world-weariness, they write their verses in order to convert their individual destiny to myth. There is no dearth of patriotic subjects, of realistically drawn nature images, and, above all, of examples of traditional poetry about the Alps in the 19th and early 20th c.—for example, in the poetry of Juste Olivier (1807–76) and Henry Warnery (1859–1902); paradoxically, the outsider Amiel is also the author of "Chant de guerre helvétique," which is a celebration of the patriotic uprising of 1857.

Calvin's legacy, Rousseau's love for nature, the experience of a tragic sense of life, and the cult of form remain powerful influences on the poetry of the "Renaissance des lettres romandes," which emerged at the time of the First World War, although these influences assume new dimensions. The novelist C.-F. Ramuz (1870–1947) wrote only a few poems (*Le petit village*, 1903), and Gonzague de Reynold (1880–1970) does not venture beyond patriotic rhetoric; but in the lyrical work of Gustave Roud (1897–1976), metaphysical inquiry crystallizes into structures of perfect linguistic unity. The title of his late volume of poetry, *Campagne perdue* (1972), signals a change in the traditional picture of poetry in the Romandie; yet as much as ever, regional and cantonal subjects retain their place (Geneva, Vaud, Neuchâtel, Valais, Fribourg); and in an exemplary way, Alexandre Voisard (b. 1930) contributed to the debate on the desirable size and shape of the new canton of Jura through his long poem *Liberté à l'aube* (1967). The Jura also appears in the works of Werner Renfer (1898–1936), tragically broken in those of Francis Giauque (1934– 65), and in the manner of balladry in those of Jean Cuttat (b. 1916). Corinna Bille (1912–79) and Maurice Chappaz (b. 1916) depict a time of change in their Valais when it was still partly archaic and idyllic, partly drawn into technological progress; Georges Haldas (b. 1917) and Vahé Godel (b. 1931) represent urban poetry and the cosmopolitan scene of Geneva. Anne Perrier (b. 1922), Jacques Chessex (b. 1934), and Jean Pache (b. 1933) combine a sense of trad. with the avantgardism typical of the Vaudois; the most prominent of them is Philippe Jaccottet (b. 1925), who lives in France. Finally, we should take note of cosmopolitan S. such as Nicolas Bouvier (b. 1929), one of the distant disciples of the Franco-Swiss writer Blaise Cendrars (1887–1961). These examples illustrate the richness and the multidimensionality of the poetry of a so-called "small" lit. which is by no means small.

ANTHOLOGIES AND COLLECTIONS: *Chants du Pays: Recueil poétique de la Suisse romande*, ed. A. Imer-Cuneo (1883); *Anthol. des poètes de la Suisse romande*, ed. E. de Boccard (1946); *Ecrivains de Suisse française*, ed. C. Guyot (1961); *Anthol. jurassienne*, ed. P.-O. Walzer, v. 1–2 (1964); *Anthol. romande de la litt. alpestre*, ed. E. Pidoux (1973); *A Contre temps: Huitante textes vaudois de 1980 à 1380* (1980); *Rencontres poétiques internationales en Suisse romande, Yverdon-les-Bains*, ed. L. and R.-L. Junod (1984); "Anthol. lyrique de poche," *La Litt. de la Suisse romande expliquée en un quart d'heure*, ed. B. Galland (1986)—incl. hist. and crit.; "Poèsie aujourd'hui," *Ecriture* 30 (1988).

HISTORY AND CRITICISM: P. Godet, *Histoire littéraire de la Suisse française* (1890–95); V. Rossel, *Histoire littéraire de la Suisse romande des origines à nos jours* (1903); P. Kohler, "La litt. de la Suisse romande," *Histoire de la litt. française*, ed. P. Kohler et al., v. 3 (1949); M. Weber-Perret, *Ecrivains romands 1900–1950* (1951); A. Berchtold, *La Suisse romande au cap de XXe siècle: Portrait littéraire et moral* (1964); *Pourquoi j'écris*, ed. F. Jotterand (1971); J. Chessex, *Les Saintes Ecritures* (1972); M. Gsteiger, *La Nouvelle litt. romande* (1978); J.-P. Monnier, *Ecrire en Suisse romande entre le ciel et la nuit* (1979); J.-C. Potterat, *L'Ombre ab souk, études sur la poèsie romande* (1989).

IV. IN ITALIAN. One of the topoi of historians of S. lit. is that of prefacing any discussion about the It.-speaking part of Switzerland with a reference to the precarious state of this third national lang. As a matter of fact, the influx of (primarily Ger.-speaking, incl. S.) "foreigners" into southern Switzerland constitutes a serious cultural problem. It is all the more surprising to see how interesting and diverse the poetry of a minority (about 300,000 inhabitants in the canton of Ticino and in the It.-lang. valleys of the Grisons) actually is, esp. in the second half of the 20th c. Up until Francesco Chiesa (1871–1973), the founding father of the more recent lit. of the Ticino, who was a classicist in his poetry (*Calliope*, 1907), there had been only a few memorable poets: Francesco Soave (1743–1806), the translator of Gessner and Young; Giampiero Riva (1696–1785); and Angelo Nessi (1873–1932), who resided in Milan for the better part of his life (the ties of southern Switzerland with the It. province of Lombardy are close). Giuseppe Zoppi (1890–1952) wrote traditionally helvetic lyrical prose about the Alps; Valerio Abbondio (1891–1958) was an author of elegies. It is the "post-Chiesa generation" that has brought about a real flowering of poetry; this generation has received support from small literary publishing houses, periodicals, and the radio and television networks of southern Switzerland, but also, increasingly, recognition from Italy. Its best-known member is Giorgio Orelli (b. 1921); an adherent of Italy's school of hermetic poetry, he has distinguished himself as a translator of Goethe, and in his search for precise poetic ciphers, he manages to build the dissonances of modern life into his depictions of nature in his homeland (*Sinopie*, 1977). The It.-speaking Grisonian Remo Fasani (b. 1922), a *poeta doctus*, addresses the phenomenon of the destruction of nature by civilization, particularly forcefully in his recent works (e.g. *Pian San Giacomo*, 1983). Generally, we can say that the It.-lang. poetry of modern times has changed from an idyllic genre to one of mundane life and social criticism. Angelo Casè (b. 1936), Alberto Nessi (b. 1940), Amleto Pedroli (b. 1922), Aurelio Buletti (b. 1946), and contemp. dialect poets like Ugo Canonica (b. 1918) and Sergio Maspoli (b. 1920) fit into this pattern, whereas Adolfo Jenni (b. 1911), Federico Hindermann (b. 1921), and Grytzko Mascioni (b. 1936) are more interested in artistic matters.

ANTHOLOGIES AND COLLECTIONS: *Scrittori della Svizzera italiana*, 2 v. (1936); *Scrittori ticinesi dal Rinascimento a oggi*, ed. G. Zoppi (1936); *C'è un solo villaggio nostro: Scrittori della Svizzera italiana*, ed. P. R. Frigeri (1972); *Südwind: Zeitgenössische Prosa, Lyrik und Essays aus der italienischen Schweiz*, ed. C. Castelli and A. Vollenweider (1976); *Rabbia di vento: Un ritratto della Svizzera italiana attraverso scritti e testimonianze*, ed. A. Nessi (1986); *Svizzera italiana*, ed. G. Orelli (1986).

HISTORY AND CRITICISM: P. Fontana, "L'ultima generazione di Scrittori della Svizzera italiana e l'eredità di F. Chiesa," *Il Veltro* 11 (1967); A. Vollenweider, "Die italienischsprachige Literatur der Schweiz seit 1945," *Die zeitgenössischen Literaturen der Schweiz*, ed. M. Gsteiger (1980); R. Fasani, *La Svizzera plurilingue* (1982); "Litt. de Suisse italienne: Recueil d'articles," *Études des lettres* 4 (1984); G. Orelli, "Scrivere nella Svizzera italiana," *Versants* 6 (1984); D. Janack-Meyer, "Aspetti culturali di una minoranza linguistica," *Quaderni Grigionitaliani* (1987); *Lingua e letteratura italiana in Svizzera: Actes du Colloque de Lausanne*, ed. A. Stäuble (1987).

V. IN RHAETO-ROMANSH. The position of Rhaeto-Romansh or Grisons-Romansh, the fourth national lang. of Switzerland (linguistically related to the Romansh of the It. Dolomites and Friuli, but geographically and culturally separate and confined to parts of the canton of Grisons) is in several respects a singular one: Romansh is the lang. of a small minority (about 50,000 people). Almost without exception this minority speaks Ger. as a second lang.; it does not have a common written lang., but is split into a number of regional groups (Ladin, Surselva, Central Grisons)—it was only a short time ago that apparently successful efforts were made towards the creation of a unifying idiom, which was to be called *Rumantsch Grischun*.

This lang. of an archaic-Alpine peasant culture is seriously threatened with extinction but nevertheless possesses a strong vitality in the midst of an industrial and postindustrial society. Therefore, a hist. of Rhaeto-Romansh lit. (incl. poetry) can never really be completely detached from the struggle for linguistic survival and cultural identity.

In early times, the epic *Chanzun da la Guera dal Chastè da Müsch* (Song of the War of Müss) by Giav Travers (1483–1563) and a rich body of oral lit., from which the *Canzun da Sontga Margriata* (Song of St. Margareta) have to be singled out; in the age of the Reformation and the Counter-Reformation, there were primarily religious texts, e.g. the Psalm translations by Johann Grass (1683) and the church hymns by Balzar Alig (1674). In the 19th c., the epoch of the "renaissance of Rhaeto-Romansh," a partly folksong-like, partly elegiac poetry, arises because of Gian Battista Sandri (1787–1857), Conradin de Flugi (1787–1874), Chasper Po (1856–1936), and others. Gion Antoni Huonder (1824–67) wrote "Pur suveran" (The Sovereign Peasant), Gudench Barblan (1860–1916) a poem about his mother tongue ("Chara lingua de la mama" [Dear Lang. of My Mama]), Zaccaria Pallioppi (1820–73) philosophical poetry, and Giachen Hasper Muoth (1844–1906) historical ballads. Folklore and Alpine nature remain chief subjects in the poetry of Gion Cadieli (1876–1957) and Rudolf Lanz (1854–1927) among others. Caspar Decurtins (1855–1916) gathered together the literary legacy in a bulky anthology.

The revival of Rhaeto-Romansh lit. was initiated by three eminent writers: Peider Lansel (1863–1943), Alexander Lozza (1880–1953), and Gian Fontana (1897–1935). Lansel, the most original of them, strongly advocated reading older poetry, too. In the 20th c., the traditionalists are Chasper Ans Grass (1900–63), Artur Caflisch (1893–1967), Giatgen Michél Uffer (1883–1965), Sep Modest Nay (1892–1945), Duri Gaudenz (b. 1929), and others. The satirist Men Rauch (1888–1958), Curo Mani (b. 1918), Tista Murk (b. 1915) have turned to the modern forms of the universal lang. of poetry; even more daring are Flurin Darms (b. 1918) and Hendri Spescha (1928–83), but the true model is the poetry of Andri Peer (1921–85), who also wrote essays on the problems of being a contemp. writer. Ranging from the pedagogical ethos of Gion Deplazes (b. 1918) to the aggressive criticism of progress by Theo Candinas (b. 1929) and Armon Planta (b. 1917), these poets express their awareness of living in a world of radical change. A formal correspondence to this awareness is furnished on the one hand by poets such as Felix Giger (b. 1946), with his broad brushstrokes, and on the other Leta Semadeni (b. 1946) with his concise notation. Hardly anybody, however, has equaled the utterly unpretentious, perfect modernity of the Engadinian Luisa Famos (1930–74).

ANTHOLOGIES AND COLLECTIONS: *Rätoromanis-*

che Chrestomathie, ed. C. Decurtins, 12 v. (1896–1919); *Musa Rumantscha: Anthol. poetica moderna*, ed. P. Lansel (1950); *The Curly-Horned Cow: Anthol. of Swiss-Romansh Lit.*, ed. R. R. Bezzola (1971); *Rumantscheia: Eine. Anthol. rätoromanischer Schriftsteller der Gegenwart*, ed. Quarta Lingua (1979). HISTORY AND CRITICISM: J. Pult, "Die rätoromanische Literatur," *Romanische Philologie*, ed. G. Rohlfs, v. 2 (1952); G. Mützenberg, *Destin de la langue et de la litt. rhétoromanes* (1974); I. Camartin, *Rätoromanische Gegenwartsliteratur in Graubünden* (1976); R. R. Bezzola, *Literatura dals Rumauntschs e Ladins* (1979); L. Uffer, "Die rätoromanische Literatur der Schweiz: Ein Ueberblick bis heute," *Die zeitgenössischen Literaturen der Schweiz*, ed. M. Gsteiger (1980).   M.GS.; tr. P.SP.

SYLLABA ANCEPS. See ANCEPS.

SYLLABIC VERSE. In the conventional taxonomy of the verseforms of modern poetry (see Brogan 319), meters are measured out by constraining number of syllables or number of stresses or both. Accentual-syllabic or syllabotonic verse regulates both; free verse neither, accentual verse (q.v.) only stresses, and s. v. only syllable-count. But it is very doubtful that verse lines regulated by nothing more than identity of numbers of syllables would be perceived by auditors as verse, for there would be nothing to mark them as such except for end-of-line pauses in performance, if that (though see Beum). Further, absent the whole notion of meter as *pattern*, one may question whether s. v. is "metrical" at all. And, if not metrical, and not free, one may question whether "verse" at all. The examples usually given are Robert Bridges and Marianne Moore, though other examples occur in Elizabeth Daryush, Kenneth Rexroth, and Dylan Thomas. Bridges wrote nearly five thousand lines of s. alexandrines, esp. for *New Verse* (1925) and *The Testament of Beauty* (1929), the longest s.-v. poem in the lang. Moore's s. v. in fact employs a number of other structural and ornamental devices of verbal figuration, which may work to minimize sole reliance on syllable count and bring her lines closer to free verse, where lines often have rhythmic shape; it is of interest Moore first worked in free verse. Fuller suggests that Moore thus brought into poetry the resources of prose; this suggests that the form of s. v. should be conceived more properly alongside those of the verset (q.v.) and the prose poem (q.v.). The term "s. v." used in relation to Irish and Welsh prosody means "syllable-counting."

R. Bridges, *"New Verse*: Explanation of the Pros. of My Late S. 'Free Verse,'" *Coll. Essays*, v. 2 (1933); E. C. Wright, *Metaphor, Sound and Meaning in Bridges'* Testament of Beauty (1951); R. Beum, "S. V. in Eng.," *Prairie Schooner* 31 (1957); R. Beloof, "Prosody and Tone," *KR* 20 (1958); Sr. M. G. Berg, *The Prosodic Structure of Robert Bridges' "Neo-Miltonic Syllabics"* (1962); R. Fuller, "An Artifice of Versification," *Owls and Artificers* (1971). T.V.F.B.

SYLLABLE. The s. is at once both a traditional element of grammatical analysis handed down in the West since antiquity and also one of the most elusive concepts of 20th-c. linguistics. The soundstream that is speech is segmented by junctures (pauses) into sentences, sentences into phrases, and phrases into words. These can be identified with electronic instrumentation. But the analysis of words into ss. cannot, or at least not easily. The rules for syllabification of words in a lang., such as Eng., are far from consistent or exact (which explains why hyphenation is still difficult for typists to learn).

From the point of view of articulatory phonetics, the s. has been conceived as (1) one separate respiratory movement (Stetson's "chest pulse"), (2) one opening and closing of the vocal tract aperture (Saussure), (3) one peak of sonority in the soundstream (Jespersen), and (4) simply a fiction (Scripture), but no one phonetic criterion or definition has proven sufficient; and in any event, the definition must be posed at the phonemic level, not the phonetic, since rules of syllabification are, in part, conventional and lang.-specific. Thus a speaker of Tamil may hear a certain sound sequence as one s. while a speaker of Eng. will hear it as two; this follows from differences in the phonemic structure of the two langs.

In general, however, it is possible to develop a structure that will describe the s. in most langs. Specific terms vary, but the s. can be said to have three parts, "onset," "nucleus" or "peak," and "coda." The nucleus most often corresponds to a vowel; the onset and coda are consonants and consonant clusters. The s. is thus commonly schematized as consonant + vowel + consonant, or CVC. Ss. are also differentiated as to whether "closed" or "open" (the coda may be absent); the rules of syllabic quantity (q.v.) in Gr. and Lat. prosody depend on whether the vowel is long and whether the syllable is closed. This CVC schema also proves remarkably useful for analyzing varieties of sound patterning in poetry such as alliteration and rhyme (qq.v.).

When lang. is submitted to the system of phonological organization in poetry that is meter, the s. is made equivalent to the metrical "position," normally one syllable but under some conditions two. Thus the iambic pentameter meter has ten positions, and the normal line of such verse will have ten ss. The relation of s. to position can only take three forms: one to one, many to one, or one to many; metrical theory specifies which forms are allowed and then gives "correspondence rules" for the mapping of ss. onto positions in the line. These vary somewhat from age to age as usage and conventions for pronunciation (and spelling) change, and our ability to read earlier poetry correctly thus depends on evidence obtained from research in historical phonology. For further discussion of the handling of syllabification in metrics, see METRICAL TREATMENT OF SYLLABLES and ELISION.

In linguistics, the problem of s. boundaries is an issue: this becomes a question of whether the s. is to be taken as running from onset to onset or peak to peak. This makes a difference, but can be by-passed in the phonemic model; the only suggestion has been that statistical probabilities of the various consonant combinations permitted in a given lang. should determine structure. Early in the 20th c., a good deal of effort was invested in trying to apply research in acoustics directly to metrics (for references see Brogan 226 ff.), incl. the quesiton of s. boundaries. But since Jakobson, sound in poetry has been treated as phonemic not phonetic, so the issue of boundaries is, at least according to present thinking, not a problem in metrics, where ss. for modern words are essentially taken as the ones given in any ordinary dictionary. What is most important for metrics is, more simply, the issue of how many syllables there are in a line, i.e. whether or not syllables were elided in contemporaneous pronunciation or pronounced in full. In some periods syllabification is fairly carefully coded into orthography ("heav'n" is monosyllabic, while "heaven" is disyllabic), in others not. There is a presumption that scansion (q.v.) and possibly also performance (q.v.) should conform to the usage of the time.

E. Hermann, *Silbenbildung im Griechischen und in den anderen indogermanischen Sprachen* (1923); K. L. Pike, *Phonemics* (1947); E. Haugen, "The S. in Linguistic Description," *For Roman Jakobson* (1956); B. Hala, "La syllabe, sa nature, son origine et ses transformations," *Orbis* 9 (1961)—full review of the older theories; S. Chatman, *A Theory of Meter* (1965), ch. 3; R. A. Zirin, *The Phonological Basis of Lat. Prosody* (1970), ch. 1; E. Pulgram, *S., Word, Nexus, Cursus* (1970); W. S. Allen, *Accent and Rhythm* (1973), esp. ch. 3; E. O. Selkirk, "The S.," *The Structure of Phonological Representations II*, ed. H. van der Hulst and N. Smith (1978), *Phonology and Syntax* (1984), 22 ff.; *Ss. and Segments*, ed. A. Bell and J. B. Hooper (1978); Scott; Morier, s.v. "Syllabe"; Brogan; J. A. Goldsmith, *Autosegmental and Metrical Phonology* (1990), esp. 103 ff.
T.V.F.B.

SYLLABLE TIMED. See ISOCHRONISM.

SYLLABOTONIC. See METER.

SYLLEPSIS (Gr. "taking together"). A figure closely related to and probably one species of zeugma (q.v.), i.e. constructions in which one word serves two others (typically a verb and a compound object); in zeugma the "yoking" word agrees grammatically or semantically with both its objects or subjects, but in s. it agrees with only one. (Since both grammar and sense are involved, technically one could make a fourfold distinction.)

The one word, then, bears two differing senses, the first one asserted, the second one, however, only implied—hence the surprise. Herodian, the Gr. rhetorician of the 2d c. A.D., gives an example from Homer (*Iliad* 9.5): "The north wind and the west wind that blow from Thrace" (true only of the north wind; the verb is the predicate of a compound subject). And Virgil (*Aeneid* 5.508) has: "alta petens, pariterque oculos telumque tetendit" (he looked up [at the target, a pigeon] with gaze and arrow alike extended). It is rare in the It. and Fr. sonneteers, but Shakespeare, to whom all senses of a word occurred at once when it entered his mind, makes of it a major verbal device for double entendre both witty and serious, as at *Othello* 4.1.34 ff., where Iago plays on the senses of "lie," lie with vs. lie on, i.e. sleep with vs. tell lies about, in order to inflame Othello, and all by implication. Pope uses s. frequently: "Here thou, great Anna! whom three realms obey, / Dost sometimes counsel take—and sometimes Tea"; "Or stain her Honour, or her new Brocade"; "Or lose her Heart, or Necklace, at a Ball" (*Rape of the Lock*). All three of these instances agree grammatically but not semantically (brocade being stained literally, but honor abstractly). The effect, which is striking, depends on the sudden reinterpretation of the sentence as the reader recodes the shift in meaning. As such s. seems one form of paronomasia or pun (q.v.); some have also seen it as an effect of ambiguity (q.v.), though there it would seem that an element of doubt is introduced which the Pope examples do not evince. Riffaterre, following Derrida, who uses s. in the sense of pun to point to the binding together of opposite senses in a word, even as one coin has two sides, distinguishes three roles for s. and hence three types of intertextuality (q.v.); he sees the two ways we understand the word as its "contextual meaning" vs. its "intertextual meaning" and thus views s. as "the literary sign par excellence." For further bibliography see ZEUGMA.—M. Riffaterre, "S.," *CritI* 6 (1980).
T.V.F.B.

SYMBOL.

   I. IN LARGER CONTEXTS
  II. IN POETRY
     A. *Identification*
     B. *Interpretation*

The word "s." derives from the Gr. verb *symballein*, "to put together," and the related noun *symbolon*, "mark," "token," or "sign," referring to the half-coin carried away as a pledge by each of the two parties to an agreement. Hence it means basically a joining or combination and, consequently, something once so joined or combined that stands for or represents, when seen alone, the entire complex. Since almost anything can be seen as standing for something else, the term has, and has engendered, a broad range of applications and interpretations. In the study of lang., for example, words are symbols of what they stand for, but the more common linguistic terminology after Saussure (see STRUCTURALISM) is "signifier" and "signified." A related distinction is that between "sign" and "s.," where the former refers to a relatively specific representation of one thing by another—a red traffic light, for example, means "stop"—while the latter refers to a more polysemous representation of one thing by another—as when the sea, for example, is used to stand for such different feelings as the danger of being overwhelmed (by analogy with drowning), or the excitement and anxiety of making a transition (as in a journey), or the power and fulfillment of strength (as in mighty), and so on.

For the present purpose, however, the meanings and uses of symbolism can be analyzed in terms of two main categories: on the one hand is the study of the s. in such larger contexts as lang. and the interp. of lang. (philology, rhet., linguistics, semantics, semiotics, hermeneutics), of philosophy (metaphysics, epistemology, aesthetics), of social science (sociology, anthropology, psychology—see Bryson's anthols., and Duncan), and of history and religion; on the other hand is the study of the s. in its more specific contexts as an aspect of art, of literary theory and crit., and of lit. (see Wimsatt [1965] and Hayes).

I. IN LARGER CONTEXTS. Historically as well as logically the larger field comes first. Where people once tended habitually to see the physical world in terms of emotional and spiritual values, they now tend to separate their values from the world. It has become one of the clichés of modern crit. that, partly due to the anti-imagistic crusade of the Protestant Reformation (see IMAGERY), partly to the growth of science and its search for "objective" knowledge, partly to the changes in focus from sacred to secular gradually effected in school curricula, and partly to the mere passage of time, not only have many traditional ss. been rendered meaningless to poets and readers alike, but also the very power of seeing the physical world in terms of values has diminished. Thus symbolism has been called in the 20th c. the "lost" or "forgotten" lang. (Bayley, Fromm).

It may be said, then, that the evolution of symbolism began with the evolution of primitive humanity. It was not until the med. period, however, that ss. and the interp. of ss. became a specific branch of learning. The patristic trad. of biblical exegesis, heavily under the influence of the Platonic and Neoplatonic schools of thought, developed standards and procedures for the doctrinal interp. of Holy Writ according to four levels of meaning—literal, allegorical, moral and tropological, and anagogic (see INTERPRETATION, FOURFOLD METHOD). The purpose was twofold: to reconcile the Old Testament with the New, and to reconcile various difficult portions of each with Catholic teaching. Thus, for example, while "The Song of Solomon" is a mildly erotic wedding poem on the literal level, its true meaning on the allegorical level is the "marriage" of Christ and the Church.

This exegetical trad. evolved during the 16th c. into Ren. nature philosophy and, under the influence of the mysticism of the German, Jakob Boehme (1575–1624), and the Swede, Emanuel Swedenborg (1688–1772), into the doctrine of correspondences, which viewed the external world as a system of ss. revealing the spiritual world in material form. By the romantic period, the view that nature is the visual lang. of God or Spirit became established as one of the mainstays of poetry, but two fundamental shifts had occurred: the material and spiritual worlds were seen as merged rather than related simply as representation to thing represented; and, as a result, the meaning of ss. became less fixed and more ambiguous (see Seward, Sewall, Hirst, Wimsatt, Todorov, and Adams).

Out of this romantic trad. has grown a large and influential 20th-c. movement which has tried to reunite what the Reformation and science ostensibly had sundered. Following the lead of such writers as Urban, Cassirer, Langer, and Wheelwright, modern philosophers and critics have developed a set of concepts whereby the lang. of ss. can be regarded as having as much epistemological status as—if not more than—the lang. of fact and reason. The question therefore is: If the latter refers to the "real" or "objective" world, and is subject to test and verification, what does the former refer to, and does it too have analogous evaluative procedures?

The answers range along a spectrum: at the one extreme are the positivists, who say that the lang. of fact and science is the only true lang., and therefore that all other langs. are nonsense; at the other end are the mystics, who claim that the lang. of fact and science is trivial, and that the only true lang. is that of symbols. Northrop Frye, however, falls off the spectrum altogether: neither world for him, at least as literary critic, exists. He has simply postulated that there is an "order" of lit., that this order has an objective existence in the totality of literary texts, and that it is based upon the fundamental seasonal monomyth of Death and Rebirth (see IMAGERY, ARCHETYPE).

Closer to the center are two other positions which seek either to balance this subject-object split or to reconcile it. The first is exemplified by I. A. Richards, who accepted the distinction between scientific and poetic lang. but then proceeded to accord to the latter a status and value of its own. Thus he distinguished between "referential" lang., the lang. of fact and science, and "emotive" lang., the lang. of poetry. The status and value of the latter were found in its ability to arouse and organize our emotions, thus giving poetry some sort of psychological and therapeutic if not metaphysical "truth." The New Critics (see NEW CRITICISM), not entirely satisfied with this distinction, claimed further that poetry gives us another and "higher" kind of truth, a truth of human existence which is more complex and profound than that of mere fact and science.

The reconcilers, exemplified chiefly by Cassirer and Langer and their followers, claim that *all* langs., whether of science or poetry, or of any in between, are various ways in which the human mind constructs reality for itself, and therefore that all our knowledges give *pictures* of reality rather than reality *itself*. For this school, humanity has not "lost" or "forgotten" the lang. of ss.; it has merely come to prefer one kind of symbolic lang. to another.

Such is the process of history, however, that this ambitious theory itself has been turned inside out, and later movements have claimed that, since all our langs. are equally symbolic, they are all equally meaningless—at least insofar as the quest for "objective" truth is concerned. Thus we find the theory of "paradigms" in the philosophy of science (Kuhn, Rorty—see SCIENCE AND POETRY), which says that scientific hypotheses are merely arbitrary constructs which may appear true in one era but are supplanted by other hypotheses in another era—"truth" being more a matter of cultural convenience, mental set, and consensus than of objective verifiability. And we find the theory of "deconstruction" (q.v.) in ling. and lit. theory and crit. (see Culler), which claims that, since the relation between signifier and signified is arbitrary, lang. itself cannot be made to carry determinate meanings.

Another and somewhat more "rational" approach, represented by Wimsatt (1954), Kermode, and Fingesten, and anticipated by Whitehead, is that ss., since they come between ourselves and reality, can be the agents of distortion and error as well as of knowledge and insight. Thus they urge that the subjective be balanced by the objective (see SUBJECTIVITY AND OBJECTIVITY).

II. IN POETRY. To the hapless reader confronting the problem of how to recognize, understand, and interpret ss. in poetry, these philosophical disputes may seem not only bewildering but also irrelevant. The fact is, however, that one's practical approach to ss. will be governed in large part by one's theory, for a critic's use of any given term is determined by the assumptions she or he makes about lit., lang., and reality, and by the kind of knowledge sought.

Olson (in Crane), for example, as a neo-Aristotelian, is primarily concerned with literary works in their aspect as artistic wholes of certain kinds, and he therefore regards symbolism as a device which is sometimes used in the service of the work's artistic effect—to aid in the expression of remote ideas, to vivify what otherwise would be faint, to aid in framing the reader's emotional reactions, and the like. Yeats, by contrast, is primarily interested in the suggestive powers of poetry, and so he extends his definition of symbolism to include not only images, metaphors, and myths, but also all the "musical relations" of a poem—rhythm, diction, rhyme, sound. Or again, Wheelwright, Langer, Cassirer, and Urban, as anti-positivists, are concerned to defend poetry as having epistemological status, so they stress symbolism's powers of bodying forth nondiscursive meaning (see CONNOTATION AND DENOTATION), truth, or vision. Kenneth Burke, as a student of lang. in terms of human motives, deduces the form of a literary work from speculations as to how it functions in relation to the poet's inner life, and so he emphasizes the way in which various elements of that work symbolize an enactment of the poet's psychological tensions.

But the simplest way to begin interpretation is to regard ss., although they may derive from literal or figurative images or both, as a kind of figurative lang. in which what is shown (normally referring to something material) means, by virtue of some sort of resemblance, suggestion, or association, something *more* or something else (normally immaterial).

A. *Identification.* When interpreting ss. in a poem, it is helpful to begin by identifying its imagery (q.v.) and analyzing the source of that imagery in experience, whether from the natural world, the human body, human-made artifacts, and so on. We then proceed to ask whether the imagery in question is literal or figurative. If it is literal, it may belong to any aspect or combination of aspects in the work, whether plot, character, setting, point of view, and the like, and we are to interpret it on this literal level. If we find that such a reading seems in some way incomplete, that we are not fully doing justice to what the work ultimately seems to be about, then we are to go further and look for the following clues: (1) the connection between image and s. is made explicit, as when the speaker in Arnold's "Dover Beach," after describing the actual seashore scene, goes on to talk about the "Sea of Faith"; (2) the work accumulates additional meanings in context by means of suggestion and association, as in Marvell's "The Garden," where it develops that the speaker is responding to this particular garden with the Garden of Paradise in mind; (3) the literal action portrayed in the poem is embedded within the larger contexts of lit. and myth, as in Tennyson's "Ulysses," where the speaker is presented as an actual person but can only be truly understood within the larger contexts of Homer and Dante.

If the imagery, on the other hand, is not literal, it may be of two sorts: (1) it is presented as if it were literal, but as it develops we see that it is, rather, a dream, a vision, a fantasy, or an imaginary action, and hence must be understood entirely on a symbolic level, as is the case in Yeats's "Sailing to Byzantium," where the speaker talks about crossing the sea and coming to the holy city, which seems literally improbable; (2) there is a literal action and situation, but certain metaphors and similes are also presented in relation to one another and to the literal action so as to produce an additional level of meaning—by way of expanded, recurring, or clustered figures (see Burke and Brower).

Thus, symbolism resembles figures of speech in having a basic doubleness of meaning between what is meant and what is said (tenor and vehicle, q.v.), but it differs in that what is said is *also* what is meant. The "vehicle" is also a "tenor," and so a s. may be said to be a metaphor in reverse, where the vehicle has been expanded and put in place of the tenor, while the tenor has been left to implication (cf. Bartel). And this applies even to recurring figures within a literal action, because such figures are embedded in a context of more complex relationships within the work as a whole rather than occurring simply as figures *per se*.

Similarly, symbolism resembles allegory (q.v.). Technically, allegory refers to the use of personified abstractions in a literary work. Spenser's *The Faerie Queene* is a standard example: the Redcross Knight represents the Christian soul, Duessa the duplicity of temptation, Una the true Church, and so on. Not only the characters may be allegorical, however; the setting and actions may also follow suit. Thus the work as a whole may be allegorical. The difference between this form and symbolic works is that allegory begins with the tenor, the vehicle being constructed to fit, while s. begins with the vehicle and the tenor is discovered, elicited, or evoked from it. Beginning with Goethe and Coleridge, this distinction was turned into a value judgment, with allegory being condemned as didactic and artificial and s. being praised as natural and organic. This judgment became a commonplace of romantic and modern crit., until a line of defense was established for allegory by more recent critics such as Honig, Fletcher, Hayes, de Man (in Singleton), Brett, Bloomfield, Todorov, and Adams.

B. *Interpretation*. Once we know an image is symbolic, we need to see how it became so and therefore what it means. As a final practical suggestion, we will inquire into the various ways in which links may be established between image and idea to form a s.

(1) The connection, as in metaphor and simile, may be based on resemblance, as mentioned above. A great many natural and universal ss. arise in this way: accomplishing something is like climbing a mountain, making a transition in life is like a journey to a new land, etc. Examples are to be found everywhere in poetry (Bevan, Kimpel, Frye, Douglas, Embler) as well as in everyday usage.

(2) The link may evolve into an associative connection by virtue of repetition, as when a metaphor or simile is repeated so often, either in the work of a single author or in literary trad., that the vehicle can be used alone to summon up the tenor to which it was usually attached, somewhat in the manner of a code. An interesting example is found by comparing Mallarmé's swan imagery in "Le Vierge, le vivace et le bel aujourd'hui" with Yeats's in "Leda and the Swan" and "Among School Children."

(3) The connection may be based on the internal relationships which obtain among the elements of a given work, whereby one thing becomes associated with another by virtue of structural emphasis, arrangement, position, or devel. (which is, of course, true to some degree in all works containing ss.). Examples are the wall as division between the primitive and civilized in Frost, the guitar and the color blue as the aesthetic imagination in Stevens, and the island as complacency and the sea as courage in Auden.

(4) The connection may be based on primitive and magical associations, as when the loss of a man's hair symbolizes the loss of strength (Samson) or the rejection of worldly desires (monastic and ascetic practice), not because of any resemblance between them but rather because a mythic and ritualistic relationship has been established between secondary sex characteristics, virility, and desire. The underlying sterility/fertility symbolism in Eliot's *The Waste Land* is a conspicuous example.

(5) The connection may be derived from a particular historical convention, such as the transmutation of lead to gold as redemption, the lily as chastity and the rose as passion, or the fish as Christ (see Hirst). A noted poetic instance is Yeats's use of the Rosy Cross, derived from Rosicrucianism, to symbolize the joining of flesh and spirit.

(6) The connection may derive from some private system invented by the poet—for example, the phases of the moon as the cycles of history combined with the psychology of individuals in Yeats, or embalmment as an obstacle that cannot be overcome in the attempt to resurrect the spirit in Dylan Thomas (see Olson 1954).

Critics rightly warn that symbolic associations of imagery should be neither too explicit nor too fixed, for implications of this sort are better felt than explained, and they vary from work to work depending on the individual context (see, for example, Carlson, Mischel, Cary, Wimsatt [1965], and Todorov). See also FIGURATION; SEMIOTICS, POETIC.

W. B. Yeats, "The Symbolism of Poetry," *Ideas of Good and Evil* (1903); H. Bayley, *The Lost Lang. of Symbolism*, 2 v. (1912); I. A. Richards, *Science and Poetry* (1926); D. A. Mackenzie, *The Migration of Ss.* (1926); A. N. Whitehead, *Symbolism* (1927); H. F. Dunbar, *Symbolism in Med. Thought* (1929); E. Bevan, *Symbolism and Belief* (1938); W. M. Urban, *Lang. and Reality* (1939); K. Burke, *The Philosophy of Literary Form* (1941), *Lang. as Symbolic Action* (1966); S. K. Langer, *Philosophy in a New Key* (1942), *Problems of Art* (1957); C. M. Bowra, *The Heritage of Symbolism* (1943); E. Cassirer, *An Essay on Man* (1944), *Lang. and Myth* (1946), *The Philosophy of Symbolic Forms*, 3 v. (1953–57); E. W. Carlson, "The Range of Symbolism in Poetry," *SAQ* 48 (1949); R. Hertz, *Chance and S.* (1949); M. Foss, *S. and Metaphor in Human Experience* (1949); E.

Fromm, *The Forgotten Lang.* (1951); R. A. Brower, *The Fields of Light* (1951); T. Mischel, "The Meanings of 'S.' in Lit.," *ArQ* 8 (1952); E. Olson, "A Dialogue on Symbolism," in Crane, and *The Poetry of Dylan Thomas* (1954); Special Issue on Symbolism, *YFS* 9 (1952–53); Special Issue on Symbolism, *JAAC* 12 (1953); H. D. Duncan, *Lang. and Lit. in Society* (1953), *Ss. and Social Theory* (1969); C. Feidelson, Jr., *Symbolism in Am. Lit.* (1953); B. Kimpel, *The Ss. of Religious Faith* (1954); W. K. Wimsatt, Jr., *The Verbal Icon* (1954), *Hateful Contraries* (1965); P. Wheelwright, *The Burning Fountain* (1954), *Metaphor and Reality* (1962); *Ss. and Values* (1954), *Ss. and Society* (1955), both ed. L. Bryson et al.; F. F. Nesbit, *Lang., Meaning and Reality* (1955); W. Y. Tindall, *The Literary S.* (1955); Wellek and Warren, ch. 15; Frye; F. Kermode, *Romantic Image* (1957); J. Cary, *Art and Reality* (1958); E. Honig, *Dark Conceit* (1959); J. W. Beach, *Obsessive Images* (1960); *Literary Symbolism*, ed. M. Beebe (1960); *Metaphor and S.*, ed. L. C. Knights and B. Cottle (1960); B. Seward, *The Symbolic Rose* (1960); *Symbolism in Religion and Lit.*, ed. R. May (1960); E. Sewell, *The Orphic Voice* (1961), *The Human Metaphor* (1964); H. Musurillo, *S. and Myth in Ancient Poetry* (1961); *Truth, Myth, and S.*, ed. T. J. J. Altizer et al. (1962); T. J. Kuhn, *The Structure of Scientific Revolutions* (1962); R. Ross, *Ss. and Civilization* (1962); *Myth and S.*, ed. B. Slote (1963); A. Fletcher, *Allegory* (1964); D. Hirst, *Hidden Riches* (1964); *Literary Symbolism*, ed. H. Rehder (1965); G. Hough, *An Essay on Crit.* (1966); W. Embler, *Metaphor and Meaning* (1966); N. Goodman, *Langs. of Art* (1968); *Perspectives on Literary Symbolism* (1968), *Lit. Crit. and Myth* (1980), both ed. J. P. Strelka; R. Wellek, "S. and Symbolism in Lit.," *DHI*; C. Hayes, "S. and Allegory," *GR* 44 (1969); *Interp.*, ed. C. S. Singleton (1969); R. L. Brett, *Fancy and Imagination* (1969); M. Douglas, *Natural Ss.* (1970); P. Fingesten, *The Eclipse of Symbolism* (1970); C. Chadwick, *Symbolism* (1971); J. R. Barth, *The Symbolic Imagination* (1977); *S., Myth, and Culture*, ed. D. P. Verene (1979); R. Rorty, *Philosophy and the Mirror of Nature* (1979); *Allegory, Myth, and S.*, ed. M. Bloomfield (1981); Morier; J. D. Culler, *On Deconstruction* (1982); T. Todorov, *Theories of the S., Symbolism and Interp.* (1982); H. Adams, *Philosophy of the Literary Symbolic* (1983); R. Bartel, *Metaphors and Ss.* (1983).   N.F.

SYMBOLIC ACTION is a term used by Kenneth Burke to signify that poetry is different from practical action but parallel to it, a notion which stands at the center of his crit. The practical act is the physical or social act, the poem an imitation (q.v.) or representation of such an act. Burke acknowledges that "there is a difference between building a house and writing a poem about building a house . . . there are *practical* acts and there are symbolic acts," even though practical acts have a "symbolic ingredient," as when someone buys a commodity not only for use but for testifying to social level (*Philosophy of Literary Form* 8). That overlap bothers Burke some. Is value superimposed and unreal? He suspects so, though he discerns much of what is valuable in poetry and human life.

S. a. is crucial to Burke because of his basic view that "man is the symbol-using (symbol-making, symbol-misusing) animal, inventor of the negative (or moralized by the negative)" (*Lang. As S. A.* 7). He adds that mankind is "separated from his natural condition by instruments of his own making." Moralizing is something that man illegitimately, if inescapably, imposes on nature. Such a suspicion is implied in or at least hinted at in his question, "which motives derive from man's animality, which from his symbolicity, and which from the combination of the two?" (*LSA* 7).

Our lang. makes us, then, yet is also a sort of freak or epiphenomenon, unaccountable; at times Burke comes very close to the deepest despairs of modern scepticism: "but can we bring ourselves to realize just what that formula [man as symbol-using animal] implies, just how overwhelmingly much of what we mean by 'reality' has been built up for us through nothing but our symbol systems? . . . To meditate on this fact until one sees its full implications is much like peering over the edge of things into an ultimate abyss. And doubtless that's one reason why, though man is typically the symbol-using animal, he clings to a kind of naive verbal realism that refuses to realize the full extent of the role played by symbolicity in his notions of reality" (*LSA* 5).

Yet Burke's doubts and fears do not rule his crit., partly because he has a nice gift for qualifying his allegiances or presumptions. Thus in *Terms for Order* he sees the transforming power of lyric as essential to what s. a. in good poetry should be, yet fairly and thoughtfully adds, "the short lyric is the *most difficult* form to explain" because of its "urgent need to establish intense unity of mood" (148). At other times he qualifies or ignores his assumptions. He achieves more strength than vacillation or despair.

Burke finds s. a. to be the "dancing of an attitude" (*PSF* 9), and since all practical arts whatsoever require attitudes (motives), the distinction between practical and symbolic tends to mean a distinction more of style than matter, but a style of substance and consequence. "Eloquence," says Burke, "is simply the end of art, and thus its essence"; eloquence is not "showiness" but rather "that desire in the artist to make a work perfect by adapting it in every minute detail to the . . . [human] appetites" (*Counter-Statement* 4). To fit the human appetites is to make a persuasive and developed work *and* to show understanding of what motivates human beings.

Poetry is, for Burke, a way of acting out tensions and symbolically resolving irresolutions in the poet and in society. Burke, that is, by his concept of s.

a., seeks social healing and poetic power and unity and self-being. Such a theory has its own ways of resolving or trying to resolve the irresolutions which it itself engenders.

Burke began working as a critic when the New Criticism (q.v.) was in the ascendancy. Following the romantic notion of organicism (q.v.) in form, the New Criticism insisted on intense and transformed unity (q.v.) and on the autonomy of the poetic work from propaganda, autobiography, and sociology. Burke was sympathetic to that, both because of the immediate literary climate and his manifest love of lit., but he was also profoundly concerned about the conditions of industrial society, and he felt the influence of the strong social bent of much Am. crit. and lit. The result is not so much a compromise or a series of vacillations, though those happen, as an impressive and often unifying accommodation. The poem symbolically resolves irresolutions in the poet *and* the society, gives warning or wisdom, and has its own unity, eloquence, and power. As Davis puts it, for Burke "lit. is the most complex mode of rhetorical activity. The purpose of lit. is to communicate a coherent framework of attitudes and motives to an audience by involving them in a s. a. The artist begins with a disruptive conflict within the social order and proceeds to transform the situation by dramatizing it. Our participation in that action engenders in us a new order of attitudes and motives" (36).

Burke wants poetry to be, and loves the best poetry for being, very much what it is, and not another kind of thing; but what poetry is is not only eloquent form but, as eloquent form and *in* the eloquence of the forming, "equipment to live by" (*PLF* 61). The poetry which is only self-concerned fails in its nature as poetry; it must be, as Aristotle saw and many since Aristotle have seen, morally, humanly serious. In traditional crit., the aesthetic and ethical and social intertwine, and s. a. seeks its accordings. For example, Burke discusses in *Counter-Statement* how the notion of amorality (unmorality) in art is used to protect Flaubert and others from censorship. "But 'unmorality' was in the end a much greater danger to the prestige of art than 'immorality' could ever have been, since it implied once again the ineffectiveness of art" (66). Here, as often, he comes startlingly close to Yvor Winters' theory of poetry as moral understanding exactingly and feelingly expressed, even though Winters treats Burke's theory with disdain, simplifying it to do so, as when Winters overstates and then attacks Burke's reliance on qualitative progression.

Burke combines Aristotle, plot (q.v.), the devel. of action via motives and frustrations to success or failure, and the notions of organic form and imaginative unity. The poem is a mimesis of an act, and the action of performing that mimesis (see IMITATION). Poems such as the "Ode on a Grecian Urn" achieve a dialectical and "dramatistic" devel. to a unity between passion and thought, presence and

transcendence, truth and beauty, *through* a series of changes. One of Burke's fundamental critical tropes is poetry as drama. The poet forms a role and then transforms it, symbolic death and rebirth being a primary pattern.

At times (*PLF* 36–37), Burke speaks of three levels of s. a.—biological, familistic, and abstract—but more typically he deals with "act, scene, agent, agency, purpose" as the best modes for understanding lit. and philosophy. Polar oppositions (e.g. sublime–ridiculous) and image clusters (often elaborately interpreted) are important to his method, and synecdoche (q.v.) is to him the basic literary device. The resemblance to Freudian crit. is evident, but he carefully avoids the Freudian metaphysical reduction of all levels of meaning and motive to the sexual, attempting instead to interpret motive more charitably than Freudian crit. generally does (see PSYCHOLOGICAL CRITICISM).

Burke does not deal rigorously with his problems, and much of his crit. is, as Davis complains, "pretty casual and suggestive." Knox sees Burke as a "failed poet," more concerned with lively rhet. than with precision of truth, even though, as Knox would admit, Burke is not an entirely failed poet: his imagination and lang. sometimes serve him well. In the s. a. is poetic and social strength, an interweaving of the aesthetic and the didactic. In *Counter-Statement*, he writes that "truth in art is not the discovery of facts. . . . It is, rather, the exercise of human propriety, the formulation of symbols which rigidify our sense of poise and rhythm. Artistic truth is the externalization of taste" (42). That sounds like pure, if rich, aestheticism, but Burke takes as a supreme example of sound eloquence St. Ambrose's writing "'of night-birds; esp. of the nightingale which hatches her eggs by song; of the cock at cock-crow; in what wise these may apply to the guidance of our habits,' and in the sheer rightness of that program there is the truth of art." The truth of art is taste, poise, rhythm, emotional and rhetorical power, and *thereby* "guidance of our habits" or equipment for living.

S. Freud, *Psychopathology of Everyday Life* (1901), ch. 9; K. Burke, *Counter-Statement* (1931), "Symbol and Assoc.," *HR* 9 (1956), *Lang. as S. A.: Essays* (1966), *Philosophy of Literary Form: Studies in S. A.*, 2d ed. (1967), "(Nonsymbolic) Motion/(Symbolic) Action," *CritI* 4 (1978), "Poetry as S. A.," *What Is a Poet?*, ed. H. Lazer (1987); Y. Winters, *In Defense of Reason* (1947); G. Knox, *Critical Moments: Kenneth Burke's Categories and Critiques* (1957); *Critical Responses to Kenneth Burke 1924–1966*, ed. W. H. Rueckert (1969); E. A. Watson, "Kenneth Burke: S. A. and a Theory of Forms," *DAI* 29 (1969): 3161A; W. A. Davis, *The Act of Interp.* (1978); F. R. Jameson, "The Symbolic Inference: Kenneth Burke and Ideological Analysis," *CritI* 4 (1978): 507 ff., reply and rejoinder, *CritI* 5 (1978): 401–22; W. H. Rueckert, *Kenneth Burke and the Drama of Human Relations*, 2d ed. (1982);

SYMBOLISM

Representing Kenneth Burke, ed. H. White and M. Brose (1982); Wellek, v. 6, ch. 14; V. B. Leitch, *Am. Lit. Crit. from the Thirties to the Eighties* (1988), 40 ff.; G. E. Henderson, *Kenneth Burke: Lit. and Lang. as S. A.* (1988); P.R.; T.V.F.B.

SYMBOLISM.

    I. DEFINITION
   II. HISTORY AND EVOLUTION
  III. CRITICISM

A major literary movement of the 19th c., based in Paris, s. is often associated with other labels—decadence, aestheticism (qq.v.), neoromanticism, hermeticism (q.v.), modernismo, and imagism (qq.v.). It is also connected with impressionism (q.v.) in painting. S. contains elements of all these currents, but it is distinct in its aesthetics and mystique. It had wide repercussions through the early decades of the 20th c.

    I. DEFINITION. S. can be defined as the refinement of the art of ambiguity to express the indeterminate in human sensibilities and in natural phenomena. Its "symbol" must be distinguished from the religious, anthropological, psychological, and semiotic uses of the word. Its immediate referent is the Swedenborgian terminology from which Charles Baudelaire (1821–67) borrowed the notions of "correspondences" and "the forest of symbols," which were crystallized in his sonnet, "Correspondances." But he modified the Swedenborgian allegorical relationships between the material world and the supernatural, between physical characteristics of objects and landscapes and moral qualities. He used the vertical correspondence indirectly in linking the visible with the invisible, and horizontally he connected the various sense perceptions through images that suggested synaesthesic analogies. In his essays he called upon the "evocative bewitchment" of words to make the symbol open-ended in its power to signify and polyvalent in its reception. He also replaced romantic inspiration with deliberate craftsmanship in the spirit of Edgar Allan Poe's *The Philosophy of Composition* and *The Poetic Principle.*

    The most famous of all the symbols in European lit. after Baudelaire was the *swan,* a code word with shifting frames of reference representing pure beauty and the poet's alienation from his surroundings. In association with the myth of Leda it came to suggest the instillation of the divine spirit in the mortal work of art; in Hispanic poetry it acquired overtones of political invasion; and in Yeats's politico-historical system, "Leda and the Swan" demonstrated the far-reaching consequences of a momentary act in a lang. of suggestive metonymies.

    If Baudelaire was the unwitting intermediary between romanticism and s., Stephane Mallarmé (1842–95) became the theoretician of the movement after having written his major poems,

"L'Après-midi d'un faune" and "Hérodiade," and a number of elliptical sonnets which served as models for his theories. He observed that the creation of the symbol occurs in two ways: a haunting object permeates little by little the consciousness of the poet and is associated with a state of being of which the poet was not initially aware. (Cf. "Le Vierge, le vivace et le bel aujourd'hui".) The other direction of the image/mood association is from the inside outward: a state of being or an unnamable feeling is projected onto an exterior world, targeting an object or landscape which gives it embodiment. In Paul Verlaine's "Clair de lune," the quality of the soul of the beloved becomes metaphorically a landscape "that bergamasks have charmed," singing a happy tune in a minor mode. In either case, an ambivalence prevails, much in the manner in which music affects us as an immanent experience, a sensual reception impossible to identify with any particular emotion or idea, transfigurative in its effect on the receiver and very precise in its form. Applying the structure and evocative power of music to literary composition, Mallarmé characterized the new poetry as "architectural and premeditated."

    II. HISTORY AND EVOLUTION. The poets who surrounded Mallarmé in a *cénacle* and met regularly on Tuesday evenings at his home between 1885 and 1895 adopted Richard Wagner as their patron saint because he had promoted the coalition first between music and poetry and then among all the arts. In his honor the first symbolist journal was called *La Revue Wagnerienne* (1885–88). Other late 19th- and early 20th-c. journals in which symbolist poems and theoretical statements appeared included *La Vogue, La Revue Blanche, La Wallonie, La Plume, Vers et prose,* and *La Décadance.* Contributors came from all over the world but used Fr. as their common lang.

    The relation between music and poetry had been conceived philosophically by Baudelaire and Mallarmé; for other members of the coterie it had simpler, more technical implications. Paul Verlaine (1844–96) insisted on the nature of poetry as "Music above all else" in his "Art poétique," moving poetry from its visual base toward phonemic and tonal structures. His "Chanson grise" catalyzed a wide range of poetry simulating musical instruments: from his violins to the flute or "syrinx" in Mallarmé, on to harps, bugles, bells, and guitars, each with its particular timbre. Other repeated images formed a code as recognizable as a scale in music: grey skies; a variety of birds ranging from seagulls to crows; flying creatures such as fireflies and bees; a topography of wastelands, glaciers, stagnant pools, frozen parks, fossilized and shining stones, and sterile and melancholy landscapes, all suggestive of an end-of-the-world lassitude; a notion of festering beauty; and a general sense of mortality and the daily tragic character of life. Some, like René Ghil (1862–1925) in his theoretical essay *Le Traité du verbe,* aimed at a scientific basis for the correlation between instrumental sound and sound combinations in poetic lang., identifiable with discrete human characteristics. Others, like Gustave Kahn (1859–1936), concentrated on versification, aiming to liberate Fr. prosody from the control of four centuries of the alexandrine (see VERS LIBRE).

Also included in the Fr. coterie were two Americans writing in Fr., Stuart Merrill and François Viélé-Griffin. Important Belgians expanding the range of symbolist *écriture* were Maurice Maeterlinck, Emile Verhaeren, Georges Rodenbach, and Albert Mockel. Another category of symbolists acted as intermediaries between the Paris group and their own national lits., adapting s. to their own langs. and cultures. Among these, Ruben Darío, the Nicaraguan, touched base with the Fr. and went on to Spain to elaborate Hispanic modernism (see MODERNISMO) in liberated verse, incorporating many conventional symbolist symbols. Among the first Spaniards who went to Paris and returned home to adapt s. to Sp. poetry were the Machado brothers, Antonio and Manuel. From Germany came Stefan George, whose *Algabal* created a recognizably arid symbolist landscape; he also widely translated Fr. symbolist poetry. The Austrian Hugo von Hofmannsthal, impressed primarily by Maeterlinck's poetic theater, effected in dramatic format a stylized projection of inner character conveying dark mood and holding audiences spellbound—as did Yeats and Synge in Ireland. The critical interpreters of s. in England were George Moore, Edmund Gosse, and Arthur Symons. In Eastern Europe, those who were influenced by s. used local folklore in the symbolist manner of myth-transformation and turned the cult of self into a more universal Ego of the collective psyche; notably among these are Endré Ady from Hungary and Alexander Blok and Andrej Belij from Russia.

By 1895 s. had come to the crossroads. On the one hand, there had emerged a convention of symbols and forms of lyrical verse simulating music, a poetic communication intimate and suggestive of a dialogue soul to soul; on the other hand, a more intricate, private poetry followed Mallarmé's notion that the "symbol" was the mind's closest opportunity to create mystery. The poet, performing as a priest in a temple, causing the trembling of the veil between the known and the unknown, produced a sacred enigma. The work of art aimed to surpass the work of nature. In an era of grave agnosticism, Mallarmé had declared the arts to be a form of compensation, the only possibility for human survival over physical death, and at that without guarantee.

But if such thoughts were also expressed by the decadents and Aesthetes in the waning years of the century, symbolist poems, by contrast, avoided direct philosophical discourse and adhered with varying degrees of success to concrete representation through several systematic maneuvers which Mallarmé called "its fictions." These became the basic techniques of the art of suggestion beyond the obvious one of a vague lexicon: misnaming of objects, substitution of signifieds for each other, deviations from accepted connotations to return to forgotten denotations, or acceptance of contrary signifieds simultaneously. Mallarmé warned against narrative, which relied on logical sequence: the rejection of chronological time perception allowed the image to create a time-free ontology in defiance of the ravages that time exercises on human existence.

In an effort to avoid the heavy subjectivity of the romantic voice, the symbolist immersed his "I" in the object of his creation. Mallarmé's elimination of elocutionary rhetoric was expressed in *Crise de vers*: the "pure work" implies the elocutionary disappearance of the poet "in surrendering the initiative to words according to the mobilization of their unequal stresses." Jules Laforgue (1860–87), who was not a member of the symbolist *cénacle* but worked along parallel lines, is particularly associable with the movement in terms of his practice of the rhetorical figure *litotes* in reaction to romantic hyperbole. T. S. Eliot as a neo-symbolist was to declare Laforgue his chief precursor among the symbolists. There is another rhetorical evolution to be noted in passing from romanticism to s.: the metaphor as symbol is often replaced by metonymy (q.v.) and finally by the single word considered as a prism which assumes an analogical function through its many inherently interrelated significations. For instance, the generic "flower" has concrete meaning, but distilled to its essence it conjures a plurality of images: Mallarmé's flower "absent from all bouquets" is not an abstraction but a nonrestrictive presence. (Cf. the *Avant-dire au Traité du verbe* of Ghil by Mallarmé.) The prismatic function of words turned into symbols finds its most striking instance in Mallarmé's final poetic partita, *Un Coup de dés jamais n'abolira le hasard*.

When, around 1900, there seemed to be a waning of the symbolist signature in France, it had a strong resurgence in the world at large, including in its transformed version some of the major poets of the Western world: Yeats, Eliot, Rilke, Guillen, Jimenez, Quasimodo, Lorca, and Stevens, as well as the direct Fr. heirs, Valéry and Claudel. One of the great differences that becomes evident in symbolist aesthetics of the 20th c. is the changed role of the reader. Particularly under the influence of Eliot, an increasing number of readers were invited to tackle the enigma of the poem, which, no longer suggestive of an indescribable condition of life, became a source of imaginative speculation—an obscure artifice, but resulting from a conscious strategy, hence eventually decipherable. In France a more pristine adherence to the s. process led to "pure poetry" (q.v.; cf. L'Abbé Brémond) or to sheer silence; Eliot, recognizing a greater need for communication between writer and reader, admitted that sense was necessary to buoy up the poem while it made its deeper impact on the reader.

The image in itself lost its omnipotence as Eliot reopened the gates of narration and description, thus clarifying sense but weakening inevitably the indirect and multidimensional character of the image. With the "objective correlative" (q.v.)—which modified the notion of *correspondences*—the demon of allegory reappeared, as well as the practice of philosophical verse. As, earlier, the lexicon had become more conventionalized through excessive usage, so in a later generation the mythical allusions began to take on philosophically precise meanings: Byzantium came to mean the fragility of power (since historically the Byzantine empire fell at its peak), combining the notions of beauty and fragility, an illustration of Mallarmé's "la faute idéale de rose." Other emblems whose meanings congealed with time were artifices wrought in metal such as George's "spange" or Yeats's golden bird, exemplifying the superiority of human craftsmanship over nature's. Ambiguous mythical figures were identifiable with the artist's agnostic representations of superhuman forces at work to transform nature into his artificial universe. Of these angels, ephebes, druids, and other figures, the most important and universally recognizable was Orpheus. Whereas Hamlet, a favorite figure of the early symbolists, represented "the bourne from which no traveler returns," the Orpheus-poet was challenged, in Mallarmé's *Igitur* (1870), Rilke's *Sonnets to Orpheus* (1922), and in many analogous poems, to return indeed and express his vision of the invisible in visible terms.

In view of the struggle between the aesthetics and the mystique of s., between verbal alchemy and versified philosophy, the more successful in the symbolist sense were those poems which found conciliation between image and concept and integrated the mystique with the poetics of composition to permit the image its full share of sense and sensuality, sewing together the concrete and the abstract in such a way as not to show the seams.

III. CRITICISM. Fr. critics consider the label "symbolist" applicable to poets in the 15-year period of 1885–1900. Non-Fr. critics go back to Baudelaire, Verlaine, Mallarmé, and Rimbaud. Although Rimbaud co-existed with the symbolists and his sonnet "Les Voyelles" constitutes the most explicit use of synaesthetic imagery, his theories about the poet as "seer" emerged in his *Voyant* letter (see SURREALISM) published posthumously in 1912. Although J. K. Huysmans's (1848–1907) protagonist, Des Esseintes, in *À rebours* (1884), and the neo-romantic Axel of Villiers de l'Isle-Adam (1838–89) in a poetic play of that name became identified as the archetypes of the symbolist poet in the eyes of the general public, these works had little connection with symbolist *écriture*. Villiers' character provided the title for Edmund Wilson's *Axel's Castle*, a book of critical essays which publicized most widely in America the symbolist movement. A similar popularization occurred in Eng-

land via Arthur Symons' *The Symbolist Movement in Lit.* Both works were more expansive of the scope of the movement than later assessments. In America, Amy Lowell, Alan Tate, and John Crowe Ransom were most prominent in bringing to light the works of the symbolists, although in their own works as imagists they avoided the alchemical and mystical interface of the symbolists. Misunderstandings about symbolist aesthetics have occurred in part because of its Swedenborgian nomenclature, which makes s. appear to be the tail-end of romanticism, a view strongly supported by the It. critic Mario Praz, who included it in his century-length history of *The Romantic Agony*. But this view ignores the fact that s. is the poetic response to the fundamental question of the *fin de siècle*, "where do I come from, where am I going?" in offering an in-between world of artifice as an alternate existence.

See now DECADENCE; FRENCH POETRY; IMAGERY; POETE MAUDIT; PURE POETRY; ROMANTIC AND POSTROMANTIC POETICS; SURREALISM; SYMBOL; SYNAESTHESIA; TWENTIETH-CENTURY POETICS.

BIBLIOGRAPHIES: H. Krawitz, *A Post-Symbolist Bibl.* (1973); D. L. Anderson, *S. as an International Movement* (1975).

CRITICAL STUDIES: A. Symons, *The Symbolist Movement in Lit.* (1899); W. B. Yeats, "The S. of Poetry," *Ideas of Good and Evil*, 2d ed. (1903); A. Barre, *Le Symbolisme* (1911); M. Nordau, *Degeneration* (tr. 1912); E. Mapes, *L'Influence française dans l'oeuvre de Ruben Darío* (1925); J. Charpentier, *Le Symbolisme* (1927); R. Taupin, *L'Influence du symbolisme français sur la poésie américaine (de 1910 à 1920)* (1929), rev., tr., and ed. W. Pratt (1985); E. Wilson, *Axel's Castle* (1931); M. Raymond, *De Baudelaire au surréalisme* (1933); E. L. Duthie, *L'Influence du symbolisme français dans le renouveau poétique de l'Allemagne* (1933); E. Raynaud, *En Marge de la mêlée symboliste*, 2d ed. (1936); P. Valéry, "Existence du symbolisme," *Oeuvres* (1938); S. Johansen, *Le Symbolisme* (1945); L. Cazamian, *Symbolisme et poésie: l'exemple anglais* (1947); G. Michaud, *Message poétique du symbolisme*, 3 v. (1947), *Documents* (1947); T. S. Eliot, *From Poe to Valéry* (1948); A. G. Lehman, *The Symbolist Aesthetic in France (1885–95)* (1950); K. Cornell, *The Symbolist Movement* (1951), *The Post-Symbolist Period* (1958); O. A. Maslenikov, *The Frenzied Poets: Andrey Bely and the Rus. Symbolists* (1952); R. Z. Temple, *The Critic's Alchemy* (1953); *Index du vocabulaire du symbolisme*, ed. P. Guiraud (1953–60); *Romanic Review* 46, 3 (1955); L. J. Austin, *L'Univers poétique de Baudelaire: Symbolisme et symbolique* (1956), *Poetic principles and practice* (1987); B. Gicovate, *Julio Herrera y Reissig and the Symbolists* (1957); O. Ragusa, *Mallarmé in Italy* (1957); C.F. MacIntyre, *Fr. Symbolist Poetry* (1958); G. Donchin, *The Infl. of Fr. S. on Rus. Poetry* (1958); M. Décaudin, *La Crise des valeurs symbolistes* (1960); N. Richard, *À l'aube du symbolisme* (1961); H. M. Block, *Mallarmé and the*

Symbolist Drama (1963); A. Bertocci, *From Symbolism to Baudelaire* (1964); P. Ricoeur, "Le Symbolisme et l'explication structurale," *Cahiers Internationaux du Symbolisme* 4 (1964); B. Weinberg, *The Limits of Symbolisme* (1966); A. Balakian, *The Symbolist Movement: a Crit. Appraisal* (1967); J. R. Lawler, *The Lang. of Fr. S.* (1969); R. Wellek, "The Term and Concept of S. in Lit. Hist.," *Discriminations* (1970); J. West, *Rus. S.* (1970); C. Chadwick, *S.* (1971); J. H. Boon, *From S. to Structuralism* (1972); H. Peyre, *Qu'est-ce que le symbolisme?* (1974); D. O'Connell, *The Opposition Critics* (1974); T. Todorov, *Théories du symbole* (1977); *Waiting for Pegasus*, ed. W. Risley (1979); J. P. Houston, *Fr. S. and the Modernist Movement* (1980); *An Anthol. of Fr. Symbolist Poetry*, ed. J. P. Houston and M. T. Houston (1980); *The Symbolist Movement in the Lit. of European Langs.*, ed. A. Balakian (1982); B. Stimpson, *Paul Valéry and Music* (1984); Terras; P. Florence, *Mallarmé, Manet and Rodin: Visual and Aural Signs and the Generation of Meaning* (1986); *Andrey Bely: Spirit of S.*, ed. J. E. Malmstad (1987); D. M. Hertz, *The Tuning of the Word* (1987); Hollier.   A.B.

SYMPATHY. See EMPATHY AND SYMPATHY.

SYMPLOCE. See ANAPHORA.

SYNAERESIS (Gr. "drawing together"). The coalescing of two contiguous vowels within a word, usually for metrical purposes, e.g. *theoi* for *thĕoĭ* (*Iliad* 1.18) or *Thĕudŏsĭŭs* for *Thĕŏdŏsĭŭs*. Strictly speaking, s. in Gr. denotes coalescing, where the second vowel is *iota* or *upsilon*, in order to form a diphthong. This is indicated in Gr. by the cornois mark (equivalent to smooth breathing). The term is often confused with or synonymous with synizesis, syncope, and synaloepha (qq.v.). An Eng. example would be "seest" for "seëst." In the opening line of *Paradise Lost*, "Of Man's First Disobedience, and the Fruit," the "ie" in "Disobedience" changes to what is called a "y-glide," reducing the word from five syllables to four. But to some degree s. is simply a normal linguistic process carried on in ordinary speech all the time, of which the poet simply takes advantage for writing verse with regulated syllable count: a number of words have syllabically alternative forms, e.g. "heaven" as both disyllable and monosyllable. Coalescing of vowels across a word boundary (end of one word, beginning of next) is *synaloepha* (q.v.). See ELISION; METRICAL TREATMENT OF SYLLABLES.—W. S. Allen, *Accent and Rhythm* (1973); Morier; West.   T.V.F.B.; R.A.H.; J.W.H.

SYNAESTHESIA. The phenomenon wherein one sense modality is felt, perceived, or described in terms of another, e.g. describing a voice as velvety, warm, heavy, or sweet, or a trumpet-blast as scarlet ("To the bugle," says Emily Dickinson, "every color is red"). Evidence for s. in lit. is ancient and cross-cultural, but critical conceptualization of it in the West dates only from the 18th c., and a specific term for it only appeared in 1891 (*Century Dict.*); in the literary sense it seems to have been first employed by Jules Millet in 1892. S. was popularized by two sonnets, Baudelaire's "Correspondances" (1857) and Rimbaud's "Voyelles" (1871), and by Huysmans' novel *A rebours* (1884), and from these sources became one of the central tenets of symbolism (q.v.); but the device had been widely employed earlier in Ger. and Eng. romantic poetry, and it also can be found in some of the earliest lit. of the West (in *Iliad* 3.152, the voices of the old Trojans are likened to the "lily-like" voices of cicalas; in *Iliad* 3.222, Odysseus' words fall like winter snowflakes; and in *Odyssey* 12.187, in the "honey-voice" of the Sirens). In Aeschylus' *Persians* (395), "the trumpet set all the shores ablaze with its sound." In the Bible, Hebrews 6.5 and Revelations 1.12 refer to "tasting" the word of God and "seeing" a voice. Dante refers to a place "where the sun is silent" (*Inferno* 1.60). Donne mentions a "loud perfume," Crashaw a "sparkling noyse." Shelley refers to the fragrance of the hyacinth as "music," Heine to words "sweet as moonlight and delicate as the scent of the rose."

S. as the expression of intersense analogues has been exploited in lit. for a variety of effects, particularly increase of textural richness, complication, and unification. It is evident that metaphor (q.v.), esp. in the tenor and vehicle (q.v.) model, and simile (q.v.) too can approximate the same kinds of suggestion, albeit in looser and more taxonomic forms. Shelley, apparently the first Eng. poet to use s. extensively, uses it particularly in connection with visionary and mystical states of transcendental union ("Alastor," "Epipsychidion," "The Triumph of Life"); here s. suggests not only a greater "refinement and complexity of sensuous experience" but also a "harmony or synthesis of all sensations" and kind of "supersensuous unity" (O'Malley). Cf. Baudelaire's "métamorphose mystique / De tous mes sens fondus en un" ("Toute Entière").

One important species of s. is *audition colorée*, in which sound (or even silence) is described in terms of colors. Silence is "perfumed" (Rimbaud), "black" (Pindar), "dark" (Macpherson, *Ossian*), "green" (Carducci), "silver" (Wilde), "blue" (D'Annunzio), "chill" (Edith Sitwell), "green water" (Louis Aragon). This phenomenon is common in lit., the most famous example being Rimbaud's sonnet "Voyelles" (Vowels) beginning: "A noir, E blanc, I rouge, U vert, O bleu, voyelles." Such terms as "golden voice," *coloratura soprano*, "chromatic scale," Ger. *Klangfarbe* ("sound-color"; see TIMBRE) show the assimilation of *audition colorée* into both common and scholarly usage. More important still is the "light–dark" opposition in vowels first demonstrated by Wolfgang Köhler in 1910 and subsequently shown to exist in many of the world's langs.: Köhler argued that this opposition is not merely metaphorical but in fact a feature of all the senses resulting from some "central physiological perceptual correlate."

The related term *synaesthesis* appears in the late 19th c. in the course of evolving psychological theories of beauty to mean a wholeness in perception, or anti-atomism in epistemology. I. A. Richards takes this term into his psychological theory of crit. as part of his neurologically derived account of literary value (*Principles*): he too uses it in the sense of "wholeness" to refer to the synergistic nature of sense-experience, wherein wholes, "sensation-complexes," are greater than the sum of their parts. Cf. UNITY.

J. Millet, *Audition colorée* (1892); V. Ségalen, "Les synesthésies et l'école symboliste," *MdF* 42 (1902); I. Babbitt, *The New Laokoon* (1910), ch. 6—attacks s. as decadent; W. Köhler, "Akustische Untersuchungen," *Zeitschrift für Psychologie* 54–72 (1910–15); E. von Erhardt-Siebold, "Synästhesien in der englischen Dichtung des 19. Jahrhunderts," *Englische Studien* 53 (1919–20), "Harmony of the Senses in Eng., Ger., and Fr. Romanticism," *PMLA* 47 (1932); A. Wellek, "Das Doppelempfinden im abendländischen Altertum und Mittelalter," "Zur Gesch. und Kritik des Synästhesie-Forschung," *Archiv für die gesamte Psychologie* 79–80 (1931); W. D. Stanford, *Gr. Metaphor* (1936); S. de Ullmann, "Romanticism and S.," *PMLA* 60 (1945); A. G. Engstrom, "In Defense of S. in Lit.," *PQ* 25 (1946); E. Noulet, *Le premier visage de Rimbaud* (1953); M. Chastaing, "Audition colorée," *Vie et langage* 105, 112 (1960, 1961); G. O'Malley, *Shelley and S.* (1964); R. Étiemble, *Le Sonnet des voyelles* (1968); L. Schrader, *Sinne und Sinnesverknüpfungen* (1969)—s. in It., Sp., and Fr., incl. bibl.; G. Cambon, "S. in the *Divine Comedy*," *DSARDS* 88 (1970); P. Ostwald, *The Semiotics of Human Sound* (1973); L. Vinge, *The Five Senses* (1975); L. E. Marks, *The Unity of the Senses: Interrelatins among the Modalities* (1978); Morier, s.v. "Correspondances"; D. Johnson, "The Role of S. in Jakobson's Theory of Lang.," *IJSLP* 25–26 (1982); N. Ruddick, "S. in Emily Dickinson's Poetry," *PoT* 5 (1984); J. H. Ryalls, "S.," *Semiotica* 58 (1986); J. P. Russo, *I. A. Richards* (1989).　　　　T.V.F.B.; A.G.E.

SYNALOEPHA, synalepha, synalephe (Gr. "coalescing"). In Cl. prosody (q.v.), s. is the term for all forms of elision (q.v.) in which two syllables are reduced to one. In modern usage it tends to be restricted to the coalescing of a vowel at the end of one word with one which begins the next word. *Crasis* (Gr. "mixture," "combination") is a synonymous term sometimes used for the fusion of a vowel or diphthong with another which follows, e.g. *haner* for *ho aner*, *kago* for *kai ego*, *onax* for *o anax*, and *mentan* for *mentoi an*. S. in not allowed in Fr. prosody—a final mute *e* followed by a vowel is simply elided—but is used liberally in It., at times almost to excess. In Sp. it is used moderately and generally unobtrusively. In Eng., it is a con-

spicuous feature of 17th- and 18th-c. prosody, e.g. Milton and Pope, where it is used to maintain the syllabic conformity of lines. In metrical theory, therefore, s. is the important mechanism affecting situations where the relation of metrical position to syllable is one to many, acting to reduce excess number of syllables. By contrast, *diaeresis* (q.v.) affects the situation position : syllable = many : one. Coalescing of contiguous vowels within a word is *synaeresis* (q.v.); see also ELISION; METRICAL TREATMENT OF SYLLABLES.—Koster; W. S. Allen *Accent and Rhythm* (1973); West.

　　　　T.V.F.B.; R.J.G.

SYNAPHEIA (Gr. "fastening together"). In Cl. prosody (q.v.), (metrical) continuity between any two syllables or syllable sequences that follow each other in delivery without interruption, as part of the same flow of sound. As a general rule, s. was felt to exist between all contiguous syllables which did not belong to two separate, independent rhythmical units such as line or stanza. Even sequences in contrasting rhythms—the components of most asynartete verses (see ASYNARTETON), for example—could be "in s.," provided it was felt that neither one, taken by itself, constituted an autonomous rhythmical whole. Break in s. involved some sort of pause in delivery—a pause long enough to allow contiguous vowels to stand in apparent "hiatus" (q.v.) with each other, and to lengthen a preceding syllable, even if it would have been short under other circumstances (*brevis in longo*; see ANCEPS). The occurrence of either hiatus or *brevis in longo* in a poetic text is thus an indication that s. has been broken. Their absence, however, need not indicate that s. has been maintained: break may simply have occurred at a point where there are no short syllables or contiguous vowels to reveal its presence. Hence some of the uncertainties which plague modern editors of Gr. lyric texts: in the absence of identifiable breaks in s., it can be difficult to know where one major rhythmical unit ends and another begins. See also PERIOD.—Hardie, 266; Dale; L.E. Rossi, "La sinafia," *Studi in onore di Anthos Ardizzoni* (1978); West.　　　　A.T.C.

SYNCHRONY. See STRUCTURALISM.

SYNCOPATION. In modern discussions of Cl. prosody, s. is a common way of referring to what musicians would call a "hold" or "rest" (see PAUSE), namely the suppression (syncope) of one syllable in a metrical pattern and the filling of its time value either by a rest (usually notated by a dot or caret) or by the protraction of an adjoining long syllable so that it becomes equivalent in length to three or four shorts rather than two. These two phenomena are, respectively, the "empty time length" (*kenòs chrónos*) and "trisemic"/"tetrasemic" longs of ancient metrical theory. Both have been regarded on occasion as

SYNECDOCHE

peculiar to a late—i.e. Hellenistic or post-Hellenistic—stage of Gr. versification, but their occurrence in the lyrics of Gr. drama—frequently where the rhythm is iambic or trochaic, sporadically elsewhere—is now fairly generally accepted. In modern discussions of prosody, the term s. is only used by those who hold that time, and particularly musical time, is the basis of metrical organization, but these theories have not been widely accepted through most of the 20th c.—J. D. Denniston, "Lyric Iambics in Gr. Drama," *Gr. Poetry and Life* (1936); Koster, 87–88; Dale, 72–74; W. S. Allen, *Accent and Rhythm* (1973), 111; West.

A.T.C.; T.V.F.B.

SYNCOPE (Gr. "a cutting up"). Omission of a syllable or sound from the middle of a word. In Gr. poetry, the compression of a rhythmical unit such as a trochee or dactyl into one syllable which is then felt to be exceptionally long. Lat. poetry appears not to do this. In modern verse, the syllable cut out is normally unstressed, as in Goldsmith's line, "Ill fares the land, to hastening ills a prey" (*The Deserted Village*, 51), where "hastening," normally trisyllabic, is reduced by s. to a disyllable. Other examples: "prob'ly" for "probably," "prosp'rous" for "prosperous," "o'er," "e'er," "med'cine" for "medicine," "necess'ry" for "necessary." See ELISION; METRICAL TREATMENT OF SYLLABLES.—Morier.

T.V.F.B.; R.A.H.

SYNCRISIS. See ANTITHESIS.

SYNECDOCHE (Gr. "act of taking together," "understanding one thing with another"). A rhetorical figure in which part is substituted for whole (hired "hands" for hired men), species for genus (live by the "sword" for weapons) or vice versa; or individual for group (the "Roman" won for the Roman army). Lausberg and Group Mu would limit s. to these types, characterizing the figure as a change of quantity, or of a word's semantic features or "semes"—particularizing or generalizing, material or conceptual. But in the trad. of Cl. rhet., s. also includes material for the object made of it ("steel" for sword) and abstract quality for its possessor ("pride" for the person displaying it); the figure of *antonomasia* (q.v.) substitutes a proper name for a common one so as to capture its associations.

In 20th-c. attempts to reduce the varied figures inherited from Cl. rhet. to an intelligible order, one group of critics has followed Ramus and Vico, arguing that there are four basic tropes—metaphor, metonymy, s., and irony (qq.v.). Others, following Jakobson, have claimed that there are only two—metaphor and metonymy. In the latter classification, s. is treated as a subclass of metonymy; in both, there is an evident connection, conceptual or physical, between the figurative word and what it designates, whereas no such connection exists in the case of metaphor.

Todorov and Group Mu reawakened interest in s. with their claim that it is the fundamental figure—based on an increase or decrease of a word's semes (lexical features)—from which metaphor and metonymy are derived (see METAPHOR, IV.A). Attempting to draw a clear distinction between metonymy and s., Sato and others suggest that s. be limited to semantic or conceptual relations, with all material connections, such as part–whole, being assigned to metonymy. Meyer (1985) would limit the latter to contextual or accidental connections, s. being a more abstract relation. Others see s. as a figure of integration, metonymy being then one of fragmentation or reduction.

Reacting against such generalizations, Ruwet and Le Guern argue that most examples of s. are not in fact figurative: they are either fully lexicalized (i.e. part of ordinary usage) or can be understood literally. Expressions such as "give me a hand" and "all hands on deck" no longer strike us as figurative. The use of "tree" or "oak" for oak tree, or "weapon" for pistol, need not be considered s., since the generic name can be applied literally to the species. Linguists find that purported instances of s. often result from deletion of a phrase that, if included, would result in redundancy. "A herd of thirty head" does not require "of cattle." Here modern critics reveal why Cl. and Medieval rhetoricians found it difficult to distinguish tropes (nonliteral uses of lang.) from figures of thought (varied modes of literal expresssion—see FIGURE, SCHEME, TROPE). "Thirty head" can be understood as ellipsis, while "the animal that laughs" (man) and "the gods of blood and salt" (Mars and Neptune) are better classified as periphrasis (q.v.) than as s. plus qualification. Thus s. can be viewed as a stylistic phenomenon, its effect being dependent on whether or not it is expected in its context (Klinkenberg).

Exhaustively studied in linguistics and rhet., s. has attracted less attention in poetics. The former disciplines seldom analyze examples other than nouns, nor do they consider the (hypothetical) genus–species and species–species substitutions that, according to Aristotle, are esp. important in naming that-for-which-no-word-exists. Frost's line "The *shattered* water made a misty din" and his reference to "the *crumpled* water" pushed by a swimming buck are examples. In Pound, the "night sea *churning* shingle" illustrates a precise species-for-species substitution; we lack a generic word for the motion. In some cases, one feels that a s. creates an *ad hoc* genus, as in Williams' description of the falls in *Paterson*: the river "*crashes* from the edge of the gorge / in a *recoil* of spray." If others disagree with the classifications here proposed for these examples, they thereby confirm Klinkenberg's assertion that the identification of s. is often a matter of perception if not of critical rationalization.—K. Burke, "Four Master Tropes," *A Grammar of Motives* (1945); T. Todorov, "Synecdoques," *Communications* 16 (1970); Lausberg; M.

SYNIZESIS

Le Guern, *Sémantique de la métaphore et de la métonymie* (1973); H. White, *Metahistory* (1973); N. Ruwet, "Synecdoques et métonymies," *Poétique* 6 (1975); N. Sato, "Synecdoque, un trope suspect," *Revue d'esthétique* 1 (1979); B. Meyer, "Synecdoques du genre?" *Poétique* 57 (1980); Group Mu; J.-M. Klinkenberg, D. Bouverot, B. Meyer, G. Silingardi, J.-P. Schmitz in *Le Français moderne* 51 (1983); B. Meyer, "La synecdoque d'espèce," *Langues et Littératures* 3 (1983), "Sous les pavés, la plage: Autour de la synecdoque du tout," *Poétique* 62 (1985).   W.M.

SYNIZESIS. See ELISION.

SYNTAX, POETIC. All human lang. derives its expressive power in part from s., the placement of words in arbitrary but conventional sequences. More than most other lang. users, poets exploit this potential when they write. Other properties of the linguistic medium such as its rhythmic and phonetic form are, of course, equally adaptable and have been more commonly subjected to systematic study by scholars. Nonetheless, poetic s. merits close analysis whether as an isolated feature or in interaction with other linguistic dimensions of poetic form such as lexis, meter, or rhyme.

Increasingly explicit descriptions of the syntactic norms of nonpoetic lang. use have stimulated study of poets' reliance on or disregard of them when composing verse. Consider a single syntactic factor: the word-class membership (the "part of speech") of the words a poet employs. At the simplest level, frequent recourse to words from any one category, even if perfectly acceptable according to the syntactic norms of the lang involved, may still yield a texture that is usually "nominal" or "verbal." An approach to the characterization of syntactic style along these lines has shown that successive literary periods have favored different proportional mixes of nouns, adjectives, and verbs (Miles). Other poets, though, challenge readers' expectations about lexical selection more directly—for example by using words assigned to one syntactic class as if they were members of another (the rhetorical figure known as *anthimeria*). Thus "did" acts as a noun in e e cummings' line "he danced his did," and "grief" becomes a temporal expression in Dylan Thomas's "a grief ago."

Diversity also characterizes poets' deployment of phrasal and clausal structures. On the one hand, repeated use of even the commonest syntactic template may lead to its stylistic dominance in that particular context: the linguistic conciseness so valued in the Augustan heroic couplet, for example, derives in large part from the frequent elision of material from one of two adjacent clauses whenever the reader can infer it from the other (Davie). Thus Dryden, writing "Concurrent Heathens prove the Story True: / The Doctrine, Miracles; which must convince" (*Religio Laici* 147-48), relies on his readers to supply the full form of the second clause, "Miracles prove the Doctrine True."

Other poets, by contrast, employ syntactic structures alien to nonpoetic contexts. At one extreme we find a relatively small inventory of syntactic licenses, e.g. inversion, which poets from many periods have drawn on freely (Dillon). Tennyson's title line "Fair is her cottage in its place" inverts the predicate adjective "fair" with the sentence's subject, "her cottage." Tennyson is fond of such permutations; cf. "Hateful is the dark-blue sky" ("The Lotos-Eaters" 84) and "Calm is the morn without a sound" (*In Memoriam* 11.1). But other instances are common, e.g. in Chaucer ("Short was his gowne" [*Gen. Prol.* 93]), Lovelace ("Thus richer than untempted kings are we" ["The Grasshopper" 37]), Milton ("But peaceful was the night" [Nativity Ode 61]), and Ransom ("Tawny are the leaves turned" ["Antique Harvesters" 1]). See HYPERBATON.

At the other extreme, some poets may delete or permute material, or may so construct whole sentences that readers must struggle to parse them at all (see OBSCURITY). Although usually associated with the style of 20th-c. poets such as cummings (Cureton, Fairley), extreme syntactic complexity may also be found in the works of Shelley and even of Pope, where perhaps we would least expect it (Austin). Pope writes in his "Pastorals," "Now leaves the trees, and flow'rs adorn the ground," ("Spring" 43), eliding the verb from the first clause in violation of the norms of Eng., while Shelley's *Adonais* includes the almost impenetrable sentence:

> Thy extreme hope, the loveliest and
>   the last,
> The bloom, whose petals nipped be-
>   fore they blew
> Died on the promise of the fruit, is
>   waste (51-53).

Naturally, it is important not to confuse mere verbal repetition (q.v.)—even in a poem composed in a fixed form—with genuine syntactic patterning. The refrain line "Do not go gentle into that good night" recurs, as the form demands it should, four times in Thomas's villanelle (q.v.) of the same name. Yet Thomas avoids monotony by denying readers the strict syntactic parallelism they might otherwise expect: lines 1 and 18 constitute self-contained imperative clauses, but lines 6 and 12 are enjambed completions of indicative sentences begun in the preceding lines.

Some poems depend heavily on syntactic patterning as a structural device. Chidiock Tichborne's "Elegy," for example, encapsulates its striking sequence of metaphorical paradoxes in a series of syntactically congruent one-line clauses. Nor need dependence on this particular aspect of syntactic style be confined to individual works; in the Heb. poetry of the Old Testament, parallelism (q.v.) constitutes the basis for an entire poetic

- [1262] -

trad. (see HEBREW PROSODY). Both parallel structures and the subtler, less extensive device of using concentric or mirror-image patterning (see CHIASMUS; RING COMPOSITION) figure prominently in Augustan syntactic practice. Thus Matthew Prior writes in "To A Lady," "Deeper to wound, she shuns the fight: / She drops her arms, to gain the field." In texts from other literary periods, however, syntactic patterning may be less blatantly, less conventionally displayed. As a result it may achieve a highlighting or foregrounding effect, throwing into relief the passage in which it occurs.

Poets' motives for selecting particular syntactic forms range from the deliberately iconoclastic to the imitative. R. D. Havens has exhaustively documented the way in which Milton influenced the syntactic style of poets for more than two centuries after his death. Both in that instance and, indeed, in the attention paid by Milton himself (among many others) to the techniques of Lat. poets, we must concede the considerable degree to which poets' syntactic choices may be attributable to *tradition* (q.v), whether openly acknowledged or silently deferred to.

Syntactic patterns of all kinds, and even the absence of a pattern where one might otherwise be expected, may also function in contextually appropriate ways. Attributing such "mimetic" or "iconic" force to poetic s. has generated considerable controversy since about 1960 (see Brogan for citations). In part, this is due to the fact that its advocates have tended to apply what is an essentially critical method in an unnecessarily mechanistic, pseudo-scientific way (Fish). Nevertheless, lively debate on this question seems likely to continue.

The technically and functionally diverse ways in which poets have turned to use the syntactic raw material of lang. should not be regarded as existing in isolation, however. Enjambment (q.v.) occurs where syntactic form fails to conform with an independently determined metrical line boundary; similar factors determine the strength of a caesura (q.v.) within a line. The rhymes of Hudibrastic verse (q.v.) derive their impact from linking phonetically similar but syntactically contrasted constructions. Semantically, s. may play a crucial role in creating or sustaining poetic ambiguity (Empson). The prominence of poetic s. relative to such other features with which it may interact cannot be predicted out of context. Where a sonnet adheres strictly to the metrical and rhyme conventions of that form, the poem's s. may contribute little to its impact; but when, esp. as in late 19th and 20th c. poetry, such formal constraints weaken, poetic s. may assume an increasingly significant role.

For further discussion of syntactic deletion and compression see ELLIPSIS; see also GRAMMETRICS; HYPERBATON; LEXIS; LINGUISTICS AND POETICS; MEANING, POETIC; PARATAXIS AND HYPOTAXIS; POETIC LICENSE.

E. A. Abbott, *A Shakespearean Grammar* (1879); W. Franz, *Die Sprache Shakespeares*, 4th ed. (1939); Empson; D. Davie, *Articulate Energy* (1955); J. Miles, *Eras and Modes in Eng. Poetry* (1957); F. Berry, *Poet's Grammar* (1958); Sebeok; C. Ricks, *Milton's Grand Style* (1963); S. R. Levin, "Internal and External Deviation in Poetry," *Word* 21 (1965); *Essays on the Lang. of Lit.*, ed. S. Chatman and S. Levin (1967), sect. 3; A. Scaglione, *The Cl. Theory of Composition from its Origins to the Present* (1972); G. Dillon, "Inversions and Deletions in Eng. Poetry," *Lang&S* 8 (1975); I. Fairley, *E. E. Cummings and Ungrammar* (1975); S. Fish, *Is There A Text In This Class?* (1980); R. Cureton, "The Aesthetic Use of S.," *DAI* 41, 11A (1980), 4698; Brogan, sect. F; R. Jakobson, *Poetry of Grammar and Grammar of Poetry*, v. 3 of Jakobson; G. Roscow, *S. and Style in Chaucer's Poetry* (1981); T. R. Austin, *Lang. Crafted* (1984); V. Bers, *Gr. Poetic S. in the Cl. Age* (1984); B. Mitchell, *OE S.*, 2 v. (1985), *Critical Bibl. of OE S.* (1990); F. C. Robinson, *Beowulf and the Appositive Style* (1985); C. Miller, *Emily Dickinson: A Poet's Grammar* (1987); D. Donoghue, *Style in OE Poetry* (1988); J. P. Houston, *Shakespearean Sentences* (1988). T.R.A.

SYNTHESIS. See ANALYSIS.

SYSTEM (Gr. *systema*). In Gr. metrics a period (q.v.) composed of a sequence of either similar cola "so dovetailed that it is impossible to make a break until the end is reached" (Lindsay) or identical metra (whether or not grouped in cola). In this (modern) sense a s. is a special kind of period; ancient metrists tended to restrict its meaning still further, to periods of this type when they exceed a certain length and when metra, if present, are easily grouped into cola. When no such groupings are apparent, the more usual term is *hypermeter*. This latter term is coined on the analogy of trimeter, tetrameter, hexameter, etc., to designate a structure that differs from them only in that it goes over [*hyper*] the customary limit on the maximum number of metra a single line may contain. See COLON; METRON; PERIOD.—Koster 17; West 93, 200. A.T.C.

SYSTEM, FORMULAIC. See FORMULA.

SYSTEM, LITERARY. See POETICS; STRUCTURALISM.

SYZYGY (Gr. *syzygos*, "yoked together"). In Cl. prosody, an older term for fusion, combination: so the hexameter is by some metrists said to be s. of two (hemistichic) metrical cola. In the 19th c., "phonetic s." is a term coined apparently by Sylvester and adopted by Sidney Lanier to describe types of sound patterns and elision (q.v.), but this usage is eccentric and never found acceptance.—J. J. Sylvester, *Laws of Verse* (1870); S. Lanier, *The Science of Eng. Verse* (1880). T.V.F.B.

T

TACHTIGERS. ('80ers, the generation of the 1880s). A group of young Dutch poets and prose writers who, in the last two decades of the 19th c., revived their country's lit. from a lethargy of almost 200 years and restored it to a respectable position in European letters. In reaction against the then-dominant sentimentalism, didacticism, and domesticity of Dutch poetry, the poets Kloos, Verwey, and van Eeden organized *De Nieuwe Gids* (The New Guide), a publication in which their doctrines of individualism, aestheticism, and realism were preached by precept and example. In addition to the *Nieuwe Gids* group, which also included the poet Herman Gorter, the short-lived Jacques Perk (1859–81) deserves mention as a T. The T. were sensitive to a variety of foreign influences, chiefly Eng. romanticism, contemporaneous Fr. symbolism and naturalism, and the Ger. *Kunst für die Kunst* movement. The very diversity of T. ideals prophesied the instability of any formal school of T.; the major figures of the movement developed in different directions after 1890. Though their metrical and lexical innovations had no lasting influence, the T. represent a high point in the history of Dutch poetry (q.v.).—F. Coenen, *Studiën van de T. Beweging* (1924); A. Donker, *De episode van de vernieuwing onzer poëzie* (1929); G. Stuiveling, *Versbouw en ritme in de tijd van '80* (1934); G. Colmjon, *De oorsprong van de renaissance der litteratuur in Nederland in het laatste kwart der negentiende eeuw* (1947). F.J.W.

TAGELIED. Ger. dawn song: a lyric of narrative type (MHG *tageliet, tagewīse*), usually containing dialogue, describing the parting of lovers at dawn, cultivated in Ger.-speaking areas from the 13th through the 16th cs. Music survives for some of the later examples by named poets. The dawn song appears to enshrine archetypal situations widely attested in world lit. (see Hatto), but the specific characteristics of the Ger. T. leave no doubt that it has been influenced by, and probably derived from, its Romance counterpart (see *alba*). It is in any case noteworthy that most examples of the T. date from the 13th c. onwards, after the onset of a second wave of Romance influence.

Heinrich von Morungen and Wolfram von Eschenbach are the first major poets to show knowledge of the T., the first in his fusion of motifs and a type of refrain characteristic of the Prov. *alba* with the native *Wechsel* (see MINNESANG), the second in dramatic dawn songs proper and an anti-dawn song celebrating marriage. The T. is cultivated by a number of 13th-c. poets and in the 14th

and 15th cs. by Hugo von Montfort, Der Mönch von Salzburg, Oswald von Wolkenstein, and Hans Folz. There are also many anonymous examples preserved in 15th- and 16th-c. songbooks (see GESELLSCHAFTSLIED).

There are two types of metrical structure characteristic of the T.: a relatively plain stanza of normal length, or a long stanza with a proliferation of internal and other rhyme. Some examples of the T. have refrains, sometimes containing the word *tac*, on the pattern of the occurrence of *alba* in Prov. refrains; and *tac* or its derivative *tagen*, "to dawn," is common in rhyme and at the end of a stanza or poem.

The wide currency of the T. is evidenced in frequent allusions to its conventions and structural features in other types of lyric and elsewhere, by parodies, and by didactic and religious contrafacta. A classic example of the transference of dawn-song motifs to another genre is found in *Romeo and Juliet* 3.5. Twentieth-c. Ger. poets occasionally treat the theme, e.g. Rilke, "T.," and H. M. Enzensberger, "Utopia." See also GERMAN PROSODY, *Middle High German*; LOVE POETRY.

T. Kochs, *Das deutsche geistliche T.* (1927); A. T. Hatto, "Das T. in der Weltliteratur," *DVLG* 36 (1962); *Eos*, ed. A. T. Hatto (1965)—comprehensive anthol.; U. Knoop, *Das mittelhochdeutsche T.* (1976); A. Wolf, *Variation und Integration* (1979); *Owe, do tagte ez, Tagelieder und motivverwandte Texte*, ed. R. Hausner, v. 1 (1983); *Deutsche Tagelieder*, ed. S. Freund (1983); U. Müller, "T.," *Reallexikon*, "Ovid 'Amores'—alba—tageliet," *Der deutsche Minnesang*, ed. H. Fromm, v. 2 (1985). O.L.S.

TAIL RHYME (Med. Lat. *versus tripertiti caudati*, Fr. *rime couée*, ME *rime couwee*, Ger. *Schweifreim*; rarely, caudate rhyme). A popular medieval verse-form usually of 6 or 12 lines (or multiples) in which a rhyming couplet is followed by a t. line, the rhyme of which unites the stanza, i.e. *aabccb* or *aabaab*, or *aabccbddbeeb* or *aabaabaabaab*. T. r. appears in Med. Lat. and OF verse, from the one or other or both of which it was transmitted to ME, where it flourished in the 14th c. It is well established by the 12th c., with examples perhaps as early as the 10th. The older view was that t. r. devolved from the medieval sequence, but the generally accepted view now (Guest, Jeanroy, Stengel, Meyer) is that it was created by sectioning of the Med. Lat. long line, most likely the trochaic or iambic tetrameter (the ME equivalent being the fifteener of the *Ormulum*) via internal or leonine rhyme (q.v.).

TANKA

In Med. Lat., t. r. is used almost exclusively for religious lyric (not at all for narrative verse), the most common form being of 6 lines rhyming $a_8a_8b_7a_8a_8b_7$ (8 + 7 syllables; *aaabaaab* is also common), the premier example being the *Stabat mater*. Most Eng. prosodists have assumed that the ME form derived from Fr., but the distribution of genres makes this seem unlikely, though it was popular in AN. Moreover, true t. r. must not be confused with the Fr. *douzaine* (*aabaabbbabba* in octosyllables). In the Fr. forms the *b* line is of the same length as the *a*s, whereas in both Med. Lat. and ME the t. line is shorter: this is distinctive of the form. In ME the 6-line form (Saintsbury's "Romance Sixes": $a_4a_4b_3c_4c_4b_3$, counting stresses) is still used for lyric, but the 12-line form became dominant for romance; half of the 70 extant metrical romances use this form, which enjoyed a vogue in East Anglia in the 14th c. (Trounce). The fact that Chaucer parodies t. r. in the *Sir Thopas* also certifies its popularity.

After 1500 t. r. disappears as a common form, though there are many later examples in sixains or mutations, e.g. Drayton's "Nymphidia" and Tennyson's "The Lady of Shalott." Burns revived it (see BURNS STANZA), and Wordsworth uses it more often than any other stanzaic form save ballad meter (14 poems). The more general point is that many other arrangements of longer and shorter lines exhibit the phenomenon of tailing—conspicuously, the Sapphic (q.v.)—regardless of whether or not the t. line is used as a refrain (q.v.). See also BOB AND WHEEL; CAUDA; CAUDATE SONNET.—Schipper; Meyer, v. 1; C. Strong, "Hist. and Relations of the T. R. Strophe in Lat., Fr., and Eng.," *PMLA* 22 (1907); A. McI. Trounce, "The Eng. T.-R. Romances," *MÆ* 1–3 (1932–34); U. Dürmüller, *Narrative Possibilities of the T. R. Romances* (1975); A. T. Gaylord, "Chaucer's Dainty 'Dogerel,'" *SAC* 1 (1979). T.V.F.B.

TALK POEM. See SOUND POETRY; PERFORMANCE.

TAMIL POETRY. See INDIAN POETRY; SRI LANKAN POETRY.

TANKA (also called *waka* or *uta*). A Japanese form originating in the 7th c. which consists of 31 morae (conventionally construed as syllables) in lines of 5, 7, 5, 7, and 7. Hypersyllabic but not hyposyllabic lines are allowed. The 3 "upper lines" (*kami no ku*) and 2 "lower lines" (*shimo no ku*) are distinguished in some poems, and a distinction is sometimes made between a dominant 5–7 or 7–5 rhythm (*go-shichi, shichi-gocho*). Although used singly or multiply as envoys (*hanka, kaeshiuta*) to "long poems" (*chōka*, q.v.), these "short poems" have been the premier Japanese form for centuries.

Their brevity has raised some question as to how seriously Western readers should take t. In practice, t. composition is, however, multiple or contextual. From early times they were considered parts of ordered and often integrated collections (*kashū*), units in a series (as of a hundred, *hyakushuuta*, or a less formal series, *rensaku*).

T. and prose narrative contexts have proved extraordinarily congenial. Given the assumption that poetry grows from moving experience and the device of using headnotes in lieu of titles to identify the experience, the prose introductions to poems could also become stories of poems. And given the use of poetry in social intercourse at court, accounts of court life naturally included poems exchanged. Such conditions led to ready combination of t. with prose narrative of factual, fictional, and mixed kinds. Among the prose kinds hospitable to t. there are tales of poems (*uta-monogatari*), of which the *Ise Monogatari* (*Tales of Ise*) is the most famous; poetic diaries (*utanikki*), of which the *Tosa Nikki* (*Tosa Diary* [ca. 935]) is the first; and fictional stories, of which the *Genji Monogatari* (*Tale of Genji*) is the greatest.

After experimentation with various methods of classification, incl. some ultimately of Chinese origin, t. were arranged in collections giving pride of place to poems on the seasons and on love. Travel, laments, and complaints were among other hardy topics. Some other topics disappeared, and yet others achieved later popularity, e.g. religious (both Shinto and Buddhist) and miscellaneous, in which no single topic predominated.

In the 14th c., t. declines in quality, if not prestige, in favor of linked poetry (*renga*, q.v.). Until modern times, cl. diction and even topics were thought unnecessary, and as a result the necessary refinement led to serious attenuation arrested only now and again by originality. The modern decline of linked poetry (*haikai* as well as of *renga*) and the popularity of *haiku* (q.v.) were matched by a revival of t. invigorated with new subject matter and lang. T. societies exist throughout Japan, and the royal household maintains the custom of a New Year's poetry contest on announced topics. The form was revived to greatness by Yosano Akiko (1878–1942); among other modern t. poets of note are Masaoka Shiki (1867–1902), Saitō Mokichi, Kitahara Hakushū (1885–1942), Kubota Utsubo (1877–1967), and Maeda Yūgure (1889–1951). Premodern poets of t. are too numerous to mention and are usually considered *waka* poets.

Although t. has excited intermittent interest in Western writers, for whatever reason, t. has never had the influence of *nō* or *haiku*. All the same, it is the definitive literary form in Japanese poetry (q.v.)—which cannot be understood without knowledge of the assumptions, criteria, and achievements of t.

Ishikawa Takuboku, *A Handful of Sand*, tr. S. Sakanishi (1934); E. Miner, *The Japanese Trad. in British and Am. Lit.* (1958); R. H. Brower and E. Miner, *Japanese Court Poetry* (1961); Yosano Akiko, *Tangled Hair*, tr. S. Goldstein and S. Shinoda (1971); D. Keene, *World within Walls* (1976), *Dawn to the West* (1984); Nobuyuki Yuasa, *The Zen Poems of Ryōkan* (1981); H. Sato and B. Watson, *From the Country of Eight Islands* (1981): M. Ueda, *Mod. Japanese Poetry and the Nature of Lit.* (1983); A. V. Heinrich, *Fragments of Rainbows* (1983)—poetry of Saitō Mokichi; J. Konishi, *A Hist. of Japanese Lit.*, 5 v. (1984–); S. Kodama, *Am. Poetry and Japanese Culture* (1984); H. C. McCullough, *Kokin Wakashū* (1985); Saitō Mokichi, *Red Lights*, tr. S. Shinoda and S. Goldstein (1989)—selected *t.* sequences.

E.M.

TARTU SCHOOL. See STRUCTURALISM.

TASTE. When used in an aesthetic context, the term "t." may refer to (1) a person's capacity to perceive and discriminate aesthetic qualities or (2) a person's aesthetic preferences or likings. Both the capacity and the preferences may be treated factually: we have histories that describe national ts. or changes in t. from epoch to epoch; we have psychological studies of the nature of the capacity and sociological studies of the genetic, cultural, and economic forces that determine the preferences of both individuals and groups. However, the term "t." is also frequently used normatively; it then becomes a synonym for "good t." or "correct t." Thus "X has t." may mean "X has the capacity for perceiving and appreciating the truly excellent in art and can be depended upon to make valid aesthetic judgments."

Historically, the term "t." has been most closely associated with aesthetic theories that define their subject as the investigation of such qualities as beauty and sublimity, whether in nature or the fine arts, and of the aesthetic responses that these qualities arouse. The term first became important in European crit. in the late 17th c. Addison in his 1712 *Spectator* papers on t. and on the pleasures of the imagination (nos. 409, 411–21) nicely formulated the main topics discussed by critics belonging to the "School of T." (Spingarn's term). Addison defines t. as "that faculty of the soul which discerns the beauties of an author with pleasure, and the imperfections with dislike." He points out that the term is a metaphor, found in most langs., based on a likeness of "mental t." to the "sensitive t. which gives us a relish of every different flavor that affects the palate." The chief signs of a well-developed state of this faculty are an ability to discriminate differences and to take pleasure in excellencies. Though t. is a natural faculty, it can be improved by reading the authors whose works have stood the test of time, by conversation with persons of refined t., and by a familiarity with the views of the best critics ancient and modern. The critic whom Addison singles out for particular praise is "Longinus." "Longinus" is almost the only critic who has described a class of excellencies that are "more essential to the art" than the excellencies produced by adherence to "mechanical rules which a man of very little t. may discourse

upon." The excellencies that Addison is particularly interested in are aesthetic qualities, which in his papers on the pleasures of the imagination he enumerates as novelty, beauty, and grandeur (sublimity).

An important line of 18th-c. critics (chiefly Hutcheson, Hume, Gerard, Burke, Kames, Blair, Reynolds, and Alison) explored in detail this new approach to aesthetic problems. All of these critics were concerned, at least in part, with aesthetic qualities (to those listed by Addison a number of others were added, e.g. the picturesque, the witty, the humorous, the pathetic) and the nature of the faculty (t.) that perceives and enjoys them. Some of the questions concerning t. that these critics tried to answer were the following: Is t. a natural or acquired faculty? What is its relation to genius (q.v.)? Is it an independent faculty, a special internal sense, or is it derivative from man's other faculties? Is it a single faculty or a combination of simpler faculties? What is the relation of t. to reason, emotion, and morality? What is the relation of t. to the rules (q.v.)? To what extent can t. be changed or corrected and by what methods? Is there a standard that determines the correctness of t.? If there is such a standard, how can it be validated? How are divergencies in t. to be explained?

Eng. and Fr. 18th-c. critics, most of whom were empiricists, gave a bewildering variety of answers to these questions. The variety became even more bewildering when Ger. transcendental philosophers and their followers in other countries began to speculate on beauty, sublimity, and other aesthetic qualities. The complex meaning of Kant's explanation of beauty ("purposiveness without a purpose") or Hegel's ("the sensuous appearance of the Idea") can be understood only in the light of each philosopher's transcendental assumptions. The transcendentalists also discovered faculties in the human mind undreamed of in empirical philosophy, and t. achieved a dignity that it never had before. Coleridge, for example, echoing Kant, defines "t." as "the intermediate faculty which connects the active with the passive powers of our nature, the intellect with the senses; and its appointed function is to elevate the *images* of the latter, while it realizes the *ideas* of the former"; t. is "a sense, and a regulative principle, which may indeed be stifled and latent in some, and be perverted and denaturalized in others, yet is nevertheless universal in a given state of intellectual and moral culture; which is independent of local and temporary circumstances, and dependent only on the degree in which the faculties of the mind are developed" ("On the Principles of Genial Crit.," 1814).

T. remained an important concept for later beauty theorists, particularly for those who, like Poe and Pater, defended an "art for art's sake" position. But toward the end of the 19th c., Tolstoy severely attacked the philosophies of beauty and

t. that had dominated 18th- and 19th-c. aesthetics, and in the 20th c., I. A. Richards rejected the "phantom aesthetic state" (*Principles of Lit. Crit.* [1924], ch. 2). Perhaps the most vigorous opposition to the principles of the School of T. has come from certain postmodernist theorists who wish to reestablish a relationship between lit. and other aspects of human experience. For such critics the assumptions that the aesthetic is an autonomous realm and that it should be appreciated and judged by the "disinterested contemplation" of cultivated t. are associated with elitism, aristocratic exclusiveness, aestheticism, a withdrawal from life, and a commitment to an ordained canon of literary works which, when analyzed, can be shown to reflect and reinforce a set of power relations involving social, political, and economic factors no longer consonant with the most enlightened ethical ideals of modern times. In spite of such attacks t. is still widely used to refer to the faculty by which a person perceives aesthetic qualities; but following the work of Frank Sibley and his commentators, t. is no longer confined to the perception of beauty and a few other qualities. The number of qualities considered "aesthetic"— e.g. unified, balanced, grotesque, serene, delicate, elegant, garish, ugly, gaudy, exquisite—has increased tremendously. The enumeration, classification, and analysis of such concepts offer fresh challenges to aestheticians.

Throughout the history of crit. a perennial problem has been the relation of t. (in the sense of preference or liking) to evaluation (q.v.). It is proverbial that there is no disputing about ts. (*de gustibus non est disputandum*), and theorists have enumerated a great variety of determinants of aesthetic preferences—the temperament and experience of the individual, cultural institutions, and conscious or unconscious assumptions about the nature and value of the arts. The diversity of preferences seems to imply a relativism in t. which calls into question the 18th-c. hope for the discovery of a standard of correct t. based on a consensus of the ages as to which works of lit. should rank as masterpieces, or on the uniformity of a natural faculty present universally in human nature. Lit. has many different values, and different species of lit. have different values. As long as each theorist insists on building a system that prescribes a class of values that lit. "ought" to have and excludes all other possible values, a universally acceptable definition of "good t." cannot be formulated. A commitment to some form of critical pluralism would seem a much more sensible solution; at least it would avoid creating confusion, conflict among dogmatisms, and skepticism in observers. (For discussion of relativism vs. pluralism in crit., see Booth; see also PLURALISM.)

Critical Essays of the 17th C., ed. J. E. Spingarn, v. 1 (1908), Intro.; A. F. B. Clark, *Boileau and the Fr. Cl. Critics in England, 1660–1830* (1925); F. P. Chambers, *Cycles of T.* (1928), *The Hist. of T.* (1932); E. E. Kellett, *The Whirligig of T.* (1929), *Fashion in Lit.* (1931); E. N. Hooker, "The Discussion of T. from 1750 to 1770 and the New Trend in Lit. Crit.," *PMLA* 49 (1934); L. Venturi, *Hist. of Art Crit.*, tr. C. Marriott (1936); J. Steegmann, *The Rule of T.* (1936); J. Evans, *T. and Temperament* (1939); H. H. Creed, "Coleridge on 'T.,'" *ELH* 13 (1946); G. Boas, *Wingless Pegasus* (1950); F. L. Lucas, *Lit. and Psychology* (1951); H. A. Needham, *T. and Crit. in the 18th C.* (1952); A. Bosker, *Lit. Crit. in the Age of Johnson*, 2d ed. (1953); T. Munro, *Toward Science in Aesthetics* (1956); W. J. Hipple, *The Beautiful, the Sublime and the Picturesque in 18th-C. British Aesthetic Theory* (1957); B. Markwardt, "Geschmack," *Reallexikon*, v. 1—with extended bibl.; B. Jessup, "T. and Judgment in Aesthetic Experience," *JAAC* 19 (1960); F. Sibley, "Aesthetic Concepts," *Philosophy Looks at the Arts*, ed. J. Margolis (1962); R. Saisselin, *T. in 18th-C. France* (1965), and "T.," in Saisselin; G. Tonelli, "T. in the Hist. of Aesthetics from the Ren. to 1770," *DHI*; W. C. Booth, *Critical Understanding* (1979); P. Bourdieu, *Distinction: A Social Critique of the Judgment of T.* (1984); B. H. Smith, *Contingencies of Value* (1988); M. Moriarty, *T. and Ideology in 17th-C. France* (1988).   F.GU.

TECHNIQUE. See VERSIFICATION.

TECHNOPAIGNEIA. See PATTERN POETRY.

TELESILLEUM, Telesillean. In Cl. prosody, the technical term for the metrical sequence x – ◡ ◡ – ◡ – , which is one of the Aeolic (q.v.) cola (an acephalous glyconic [q.v.]), though its use is not confined to the Aeolic poets. It is named after Telesilla, a poetess of Argos of the early 5th c. B.C., who used it for stichic verse. It also occurs in Gr. choral lyric and in the choruses of Gr. drama. The catalectic form of the T., i.e. the sequence x – ◡ ◡ – – , is sometimes called the Reizianum, so named by the early 19th-c. Cl. scholar Hermann after his teacher Reiz (1733–90). In Lat. the R. has a slightly different form and occurs both as a colon (in Plautus it has the form x – x – –) and as part of an asynarteton (q.v.), i.e. a verse composed of two differing cola, known as the *versus Reizianus* and having the pattern x – x – ◡ – | x – x – – . See AEOLIC.—L. Havet, "Le Distique (dit 'vers') de Reiz," *REL* 19 (1941); Dale; J. W. Halporn, "Reizianum (2)," *Lexikon der alten Welt* (1965), 2572; Koster; Snell; West.   J.W.H.

TELESTICH. See ACROSTIC.

TELIAMBOS. See MEIURUS.

TELUGU POETRY. See INDIAN POETRY.

TENOR AND VEHICLE. Because he was dissatisfied with the traditional grammatical and rhetorical account of metaphor, which he believed emphasized its merely decorative and embellishing powers, I. A. Richards reintroduced this pair of terms—already reflected, as Engell points out, in the 18th c. in Dr. Johnson's *Dictionary* (1755) and used by such later Augustan rhetoricians as George Campbell and Hugh Blair—in 1936 with the notion of "a borrowing between and intercourse of thoughts" (*Philosophy of Rhet.*). Since any metaphor at its simplest gives us two parts, the thing meant and the thing said, Richards used "t." to refer to thing meant—purport, underlying meaning, or main subject of the metaphor—and "v." to mean thing said—that which serves to carry or embody the t. as the analogy brought to the subject.

But Richards intended more than simply to reintroduce this terminology for existing concepts; rather, he intended to develop a modern concept not just of metaphor but of the nature of poetry itself. Having traced out t. and v. as the essential ingredients of metaphor, he (and the critics who followed him) went on to distinguish between *poetic* metaphor and other kinds. In attempting to show that true poetic metaphor is never merely decorative, logical, explanatory, or illustrative, he claimed that the "transaction" it establishes between t. and v. "results in a meaning (to be clearly distinguished from the t.) which is not attainable without their interaction"—which is, in effect, not attainable by direct and literal prose statement. The v., he continued, "is not normally mere embellishment of a t. which is otherwise unchanged by it but . . . v. and t. in cooperation give a meaning of more varied powers than can be ascribed to either."

These special powers of poetic metaphor he credited to the way the v. brings with it, because it derives from an aspect of experience outside of or different from the literal experience in the poem, a host of implicit associations which, although circumscribed by the t., are never quite shut out entirely. This unsuppressible range of connotations closely resembles what John Crowe Ransom later called "irrelevant texture,," which he (and other modern critics) valued as the very essence of poetry. Such an approach to poetry presumed special qualities for poetic lang.—richness, ambiguity, irony, paradox, and so on—which found their cause in the tension set up between the t. in a poetic metaphor and the emotional, sensory, or conceptual connotations brought into the poem by the v. This approach goes beyond simply attributing emotional and imaginative powers to metaphor to claim for it special cognitive powers as well (see also ARCHETYPE; SYMBOL; IMAGERY; NEW CRITICISM). Thus, for example, Hawkes sees metaphor as embodying in little the larger relation between lang. and reality: there is the world (t.), and there are the terms in which we see it (v.); Ricoeur finds an interesting similarity between metaphor and the psychoanalytic concept of transference, where an adult tends to see the world of the present (t.) via the habits of mind he or she learned from the parents as a child (v.).

Other critics, however, have found the t. and v. distinction unclear, inconsistent, or inaccurate. Black went on to develop the boundaries of four distinct theories of metaphor—the comparison, integration, interaction, and substitution theories—as a way of placing Richards' concept in a fuller context. While most critics (Wimsatt, Shibles, and Gerhart and Russell) agree that the tension of difference and interaction between t. and v. is central, Empson and Brooke-Rose, for example, emphasize the presence of the necessary basic similarity and fusion. Still others, such as Wheelwright, have tried to coin new definitions for t. and v.

However this may be, two main points should be kept in mind. The first is that metaphor depends, as Aristotle said, on the perception of the similarity in dissimilars. It is true that the v. must be logically different from the t., but it is also true that the basic effect depends upon seeing the similarities between two things which at first appear to be different. It is true, moreover, that a third and new meaning is created between t. and v. which is not the same as the t., but this effect depends not so much upon the "irrelevancies" or differences imported by the v. as upon the surprising fullness of appropriate meanings it brings to the t. There are thus two additional parts to a metaphor: the point or points of contact or similarity between t. and v., and the role played by the consequent differences. The second and related point is that the interpretation must be limited and controlled by the poetic context.

In the well-known "stiff twin compasses" figure in Donne's "A Valediction: Forbidding Mourning," the t. (two lovers about to part) and the v. (a piece of mechanical drawing equipment) seem particularly remote, even incongruous. But closer inspection will reveal the similarity or point of contact: the lovers will remain connected in separation even as the legs of the compass remain attached at the top when pushed apart at the bottom. And there are the obvious differences, esp. if we consider the range of connotations: compasses are a scientific measuring device, are cold and impersonal, are stiff and unbending, while the lovers are passionate, yearning, and fearful. Interpretation could emphasize difference by pointing up the complexity of the speaker's mind, uniting thought and feeling, aware of the subtle contradictions of love, or it could remain within the poem's context and show how the analogy is appropriate to the speaker's effort to console his lady about their impending separation: he is trying to cool their passion, arguing that a separation will not be a threat to their love. The "irrelevant texture" is relevant after all, and the third and new meaning, which arises out of the interaction between "lovers parting and needing to be consoled" as t. and "compasses which remain connected at the top even when their feet are separated" as v., is that there is a strong and precise mental and spiritual bond between true lovers which unites them when they must part physically. The meanings brought into the t. by the v. have mainly to do paradoxically with making "material" the bond which is on its deepest level mental and spiritual: the compasses, that is, while denoting unity in separation, connote the qualities of accuracy and firmness, and they do this in terms of a sharp and clear image. These meanings and their interplay create a complex of meanings which could not be conveyed by direct and literal prose statement—exemplified by the present interpretation of "A Valediction"—because a large part of what is being conveyed is thought-and-feeling-in-situation. This contextual reality could be "explained" in prose, but it could not very well be *felt*, and that is the function of poetic metaphor.

H. W. Wells, *Poetic Imagery* (1924); K. Burke, *Permanence and Change* (1935); I. A. Richards, *The Philosophy of Rhet.* (1936); C. Brooks, *Mod. Poetry and the Trad.* (1939); J. C. Ransom, *The New Crit.* (1941); W. Empson, *The Structure of Complex Words* (1951); W. K. Wimsatt, Jr., *The Verbal Icon* (1954); Wellek and Warren; C. Brooke-Rose, *The Grammar of Metaphor* (1958); M. Black, *Models and Metaphors* (1962); M. Peckham, "Metaphor," *The Triumph of Romanticism* (1970); P. Wheelwright, *Metaphor and Reality* (1962); W. Embler, *Metaphor and Meaning* (1966); K. K. Ruthven, *The Conceit* (1969); W. A. Shibles, *An Analysis of Metaphor in the Light of W. M. Urban's Theories* (1971); M. C. Beardsley, "The Metaphorical Twist," *Essays on Metaphor*, ed. W. A. Shibles (1972); T. Hawkes, *Metaphor* (1972); P. Ricoeur, *The Rule of Metaphor* (1977); D. Lodge, *The Modes of Mod. Writing* (1977); *Metaphor*, ed. D. S. Miall (1982); M. Gerhart and A. M. Russell, *Metaphoric Process* (1984); E. R. MacCormac, *A Cognitive Theory of Metaphor* (1985); D. E. Cooper, *Metaphor* (1986); R. J. Fogelin, *Figuratively Speaking* (1986); J. Engell, "The New Rhetoricians," *Psych. and Lit. in the 18th C.*, ed. C. Fox (1987). N.F.

TENSION is a term that has been used by many 20th-c. critics to refer to elements of opposition, resistance, strain, and antinomy that may appear in a poem. By 1958 the concept had become so popular that W. K. Wimsatt proposed a "tensional" or "dramatic" poetics as an alternative to traditional genetic, affective, didactic, and formalist critical orientations. Usually when critics speak of t. they have in mind a quality or relation that may appear in a poem, but such poetic t. may also be taken as reflecting t. in the personality of the author, creating t. in the mind of the reader, or paralleling tensional elements in nature or human affairs.

A special concern of formalist literary theory in the 20th c., esp. the New Criticism (q.v.), has been to isolate the phonetic and semantic characteristics which make the lang. of poetry a unique linguistic system. T. has been helpful for making such an analysis. Thus when Allen Tate spoke of t. in poetry, he meant that a poem is a "configuration of meaning" in which both the extensional (denotative) and intensional (connotative) meanings of words are exploited to the limit. Philip Wheelwright developed a far more sophisticated semantics of the "tensive" or "depth" lang. of poetry; for him, tensive lang., unlike the literal, precise lang. of science and practical life, has characteristics like iconicity, plurisignation, suggestiveness, and "soft focus"; its special devices are paradox, oxymoron, symbol, and metaphor (qq.v.). Wheelwright gave these devices an extended tensional analysis, particularly metaphor, the essence of which "consists in a semantic t. which subsists among the heterogeneous elements brought together in some striking image or expression." A variety of tensional analyses of metaphor appeared in many other critics, from I. A. Richards to Murray Krieger.

T. appears not only in the lang. a poet uses but also in other aspects of verse as well. Thus in analyzing a poem a reader may find strain and conflict reflected in the opposing or uncertain beliefs, impulses, attitudes, or loyalties of a character; in the interaction of that character with other characters or with the world; in the ambiguous attitudes of the narrator toward the materials presented; or in the opposition between the meanings explicitly stated and those suggested by other elements such as imagery. Finally, tensional analysis can be used to illuminate the structure (q.v.) of a poem. For Brooks and Warren a poem has a "dramatic" structure in which oppositions generating t. are resolved into some state of final equilibrium. The universal form of all poems is "motion toward a point of rest," but this motion should be a "resisted motion," building a t. and conflict whose resolution is the conclusion of the poem.

Critics have also used t. for evaluating poems. T. is a quality that contributes to an important aesthetic value—complexity (see SIMPLICITY AND COMPLEXITY). Thus Brooks regards poems with little or no t. (those in which a single idea or attitude finds expression) as uninteresting and simple; such poems may have unity (q.v.), but it is a thin repetition of homogeneous elements. A satisfying aesthetic unity must incorporate complexity; it must be one in which heterogeneous elements have been brought into an organic relationship (see ORGANICISM). Complexity generated by t. also contributes to the cognitive value of lit. Tensional critics frequently speak of lit. as developing "awareness" in the reader. The content of this awareness is dictated by the critic's metaphysical and epistemological commitments. For the New Critics, a "truthful" poetry is simply a reflection of the complexities and ironies of human experience and the ts. they arouse. The poet is expected to try to resolve the ts. and to "make sense" of this experience so that the poem will convey "knowledge of a value-structured world." In the case of Wheelwright, the most important part of reality—the What Is—that tensive lang. brings to human awareness is a glimpse of the spiritual reality that lies beyond the threshold of ordinary human experience.

Historically, the concept of t. has played a key role in systems of thought which seek to understand phenomena (whether cosmological, political, historical, religious, or artistic) as an interaction between opposing forces. Such dualistic or polar thinking is found in both Eastern and Western philosophy and religious thought from Cl. times to the present. Coleridge gives credit to Heraclitus for first promulgating "the universal Law of Polarity or essential Dualism" which he found developed in Ger. idealist philosophy; he used the Law to theorize about biological organisms, politics, religion, metaphysics, and aesthetics. His description of the operation of the imagination as the "balance or reconciliation of opposite or discordant qualities" is cited by most tensional critics.

A good survey of polar thinking appears in the crit. of Murray Krieger, in which oppositions (presence and illusion, identity and difference, spatiality and temporality, aesthetic and thematic, closure and openness, unique and generic, form and chaos) are pervasive. In his view each set of opposites is "a sustained tensional polarity: both sides, each defined by the other, always paradoxically there, at once sustaining and negating one another." Thus in metaphor (q.v.) the poles—the tenor and vehicle—are "at once opposite, reversible, identical." Unresolvable tensional opposition is thus a characteristic feature of Krieger's crit., and he carefully distinguishes his views from rival formulations of dualistic method (as in Platonism, Manichaeism, or Hegelianism) and from the tensional poetics of the New Critics.—Richards; A. Tate, "T. in Poetry," *Reason in Madness* (1941); W. V. O'Connor, "T. and Structure of Poetry," *SR* 51 (1943); Brooks; Wimsatt and Brooks; W. K. Wimsatt, Jr., "Horses of Wrath," *Hateful Contraries* (1965); P. Wheelwright, *Metaphor and Reality* (1962), *The Burning Fountain*, rev. ed. (1968); M. Krieger, *The Play and Place of Crit.* (1967), *The Classic Vision* (1971), *Theory of Crit.* (1976), *Poetic Presence and Illusion* (1979), "Both Sides Now," *Murray Krieger and Contemp. Critical Theory*, ed. B. Henricksen (1986); C. Brooks, "I. A. Richards and the Concept of T.," *I. A. Richards*, ed. R. Brower et al. (1973); F. Lentricchia, *After the New Crit.* (1980); J. P. Russo, *I. A. Richards* (1989). F.GU.

TENSO (Occitan, also *tençon*; It. *tenzone*). An amoebean type of poetic composition which matured in Provence early in the 12th c. It consists of a verbal exchange largely in the form of invective (q.v.) expressed through the medium of *sirventes* or *coblas* (qq.v.). The earliest example seems to be by Cercamon and Guilhelmi. Later it developed

into the *partimen* (q.v.) or *joc partit*, an exchange minus the personal element, and was applied to moral, literary, and political problems. In many cases the subject matter is imaginary, and often the original argument and the exchange are by the same person. The wandering troubadours carried the device into Italy, where we find Lanzia Marques and Alberto Malaspina making use of it in Occitan compositions. In Sicily the feigned *t.* in *canzone*-form called *contrasto* was quite popular (e.g. Cielo d'Alcamo, Giacomino Pugliese). In Italy, however, a *t.* generally assumes the form of an exchange of sonnets (q.v.) among two or more poets on a specific topic. One *t.* of the Sicilian School (q.v.) treats of the nature of love and contains sonnets by Jacopo Mostacci, Pier della Vigna, and Giacomo da Lentini. In Tuscany the example of Guittone d'Arezzo was extremely influential in making it common among the *guittoniani* and the poets of the *dolce stil nuovo* (q.v.), incl. Dante and Cino da Pistoia.—P. E. Guarnerio, *Manuale di versificazione italiana* (1893); H. Stiefel, *Die italienische Tenzone des XII Jahrhunderts und ihr Verhältnis zur provenzalischen T.* (1914); S. Santangelo, *Le tenzoni poetiche nella letteratura italiana delle origini* (1928); D. J. Jones, *La Tenson prov.* (1934); E. Köhler in *GRLMA*, v. 2.1.B.3 (1979); Elwert, *Italienische.* J.G.F.; C.K.

TENZI. See SWAHILI POETRY.

TENZONE. See TENSO.

TERCET. A verse unit of 3 lines, usually rhymed, most often employed as a stanzaic form. It was first developed systematically in It. poetry (*terzina*): Dante chose the t. with interlocking rhymes (*terza rima* [q.v.]) for the stanza of the *Divine Comedy*, whence it spread to the other vernacular poetries. In those versions of the sonnet (q.v.) derived from It., the sestet (q.v.) is made up of two ts. rhyming (often) *cde cde*. Eng. users of ts. or terza rima incl. Wyatt, Donne, Herrick ("Whenas in Silks my Julia Goes"), and Shelley ("Ode to the West Wind," "The Triumph of Life"). The t. became the major form of the mature Wallace Stevens: fully half of the poems in his last three books of poetry use it, incl. nearly all of the major poems ("Notes toward a Supreme Fiction," "Auroras of Autumn," "Sea Surface Full of Clouds"). William Carlos Williams uses a variant "triadic stanza" as his staple form. Monorhymed ts. in stichic verse are *triplets* (see TRIPLET). Though 3-line stanzas are less common in the poetries of the world than quatrain, still, they are important: the Fr. *villanelle* (q.v.) comprises 5 ts. and a quatrain, and two forms of Welsh *englynion* are in ts., incl. most of the work of Llywarch Hen (6th c.; see ENGLYN). Western trs. of the Japanese *haiku* (q.v.) normally set it as a t. of 5-, 7-, and 5-syllable lines, unrhymed.—E. Berry, "W. C. Williams' Triadic-Line Verse," *TCL* 35 (1989). T.V.F.B.

TERNARY METERS. See BINARY AND TERNARY.

TERZA RIMA (Ger. *Terzine*). It. verseform consisting of interlinked tercets, in which the second line of each tercet rhymes with the first and third lines of the one following, *aba bcb cdc*, etc. The series of tercets formed in this way may be of any length, and is brought to a conclusion by a single final line which rhymes with the second line of the tercet preceding it, *yzy z*. T. r. has a powerful forward momentum, while the concatenated rhymes provide a reassuring structure of continuity, though they may on occasion imprison the poet in a movement of mindless flux (Vigny, "Les Destinées"; Hofmannsthal, "Ballade des äusseren Lebens"). T. r. may equally represent permanence in change. In all its realizations, however, t. r. suggests processes without beginning or end, a *perpetuum mobile* in which linkage and continuation are seamlessly articulated.

T. r. (in hendecasyllables) was introduced by Dante as an appropriate stanza form for his *Divina Commedia*. The symbolic reference to the Holy Trinity is obvious, and the overtones of tireless quest and of the interconnectedness of things to be found in t. r. were particularly apposite. Most probably Dante developed t. r. from the tercets of the *sirventes* (q.v.), but whatever the origin of the form, it found immediate popularity with Boccaccio, who used it in his *Amorosa visione*, and with Petrarch (*I Trionfi*). After Dante, t. r. became the preferred meter for allegorical and didactic poems such as Fazio degli Uberti's *Dittamondo* and Federico Frezzi's *Quadriregio*. Some later poems are written in a variety of t. r. called *capitolo ternario* (see CAPITOLO). The implicit difficulty of t. r. discouraged its widespread use after the 14th c., although Monti in the late 18th c. and Foscolo in the early 19th c. wrote noteworthy poems in t. r.

In France, t. r. first appeared in the work of Jean Lemaire de Belges ("Le Temple d'honneur et de vertus," 1503; "La Concorde des deux langages," 1511) and was taken up by poets of the *Pléiade* (q.v.)—Pontus de Tyard, Jodelle, Baïf. The decasyllable (q.v.) almost invariably used by these 16th-c. poets yielded to the alexandrine (q.v.) in the 19th-c. revival of t. r., a revival subscribed to by Parnassians (Gautier, Banville, Leconte de Lisle, Richepin) and symbolists (Verlaine, Ephraim Mikhaël, Pierre Quillard) alike.

The form makes even greater demands on poets who write in a lang. less rich in rhymes than It. or Fr. Chaucer first experimented with t. r. in Eng. for parts of his early "Complaint to his Lady," but its first significant use is by Wyatt, followed by Sidney, Daniel, and Milton. The romantics experimented with it, Byron for "The Prophecy of Dante" and Shelley for "Prince Athanase" and "The Triumph of Life." Shelley's "Ode to the West Wind" is composed of five sections, each rhyming *aba bcb cdc ded ee* (see TERZA RIMA SONNET). Since the romantics, t. r. has been used, usually with variation of line-length and looser rhymes, by Browning, Hardy, Yeats, Eliot, Auden ("The Sea and the Mirror"), Roy Fuller ("Centaurs"; "To my Brother"), and Archibald MacLeish ("Conquistador"). Other European poets of the 19th and 20th cs. who employed t. r. include the Dutch poets Potgieter and van Eeden and the Germans A. W. Schlegel, Chamisso, Liliencron, Heyse, George, and Hofmannsthal. See ITALIAN PROSODY.

H. Schuchardt, *Ritornell und Terzine* (1875); Schipper, *History* 381; L. E. Kastner, "Hist. of the T. R. in France," *ZFSL* 26 (1904); P. Habermann, "Terzine," *Reallexikon I*; J. S. P. Tatlock, "Dante's *T. R.*," *PMLA* 51 (1936); T. Spoerri, "Wie Dantes Vers enstand," *Vox romanica* 2 (1937); L. Binyon, "T. R. in Eng. Poetry," *English* 3 (1940); J. Wain, "T. R.," *RLMC* 1 (1950); R. Bernheim, *Die Terzine in der deutsche Dichtung* (1954); M. Fubini, "La Terzina della *Commedia*," *DDJ* 43 (1965); P. Boyde, *Dante's Style in his Lyric Poetry* (1971); I. Baldelli, "Terzina," *Enciclopedia Dantesca*, ed. G. Petrocchi et al., v. 5 (1978); Wilkins; J. D. Bone, "On Influence and on Byron and Shelley's Use of T. R. in 1819," *KSMB* 32 (1982); J. Freccero, "The Significance of T. R.," *Dante, Petrarch, Boccaccio*, ed. A. S. Bernardo and A. L. Pellegrini (1983). L.J.Z.; C.S.

TERZA RIMA SONNET. A term sometimes used to describe a quatorzain whose rhyme scheme makes use of the interweaving pattern characteristic of t. r. (*aba bcb cdc*, etc.). It has sometimes been thought that the pattern *aba bcb cdc ded ee*, the form of each section of Shelley's *Ode to the West Wind*, resembles the Spenserian sonnet with its couplet ending (*abab bcbc cdcd ee*). But the connection is tenuous: the quatrains of the Spenserian sonnet are a sequence of alternating rhyme-pairs rather than a series of interlinked tercets; the Spenserian sonnet allows little room for the forward momentum of t. r.; and its final couplet does not function as a refrain or invocation as those in Shelley's cycle do. On the other hand, it should be noted that the Sicilian sonnet has been suggested as the source of t. r. In any event, the idea of this hybrid form has not been lost from sight: Frost's "Acquainted with the Night" (in an envelope [q.v.] pattern) is a splendid modern example.
C.S.; T.V.F.B.

TETRALOGY. See TRILOGY.

TETRAMETER. (Gr. "of four measures"). I. CLASSICAL. In Gr. and Lat., the basic meter for recitation forms is the trochaic t. catalectic, i.e. four trochaic metra ($- \cup - x$, where x = *anceps* [q.v.]) with truncation (catalexis) of the final *anceps*. There is a diaeresis after the second *anceps*, which in comedy is sometimes replaced by a caesura before it or, more rarely, the third *breve*. In Gr. drama this meter is often associated with scenes of excitement. Several prosodic phenomena, such as (1) the occasional response of $- \cup \cup \cup$ with a trochaic metron in Aristophanes; (2) the fact that even in the strict versification of Solon, Havet's bridge (see BRIDGE) in his ts. is slightly less stringent than Porson's bridge in his trimeters; and (3) the lower rate of the substitution of ⌣ ⌣ for ⌣ or x as compared to the trimeter (q.v.) suggest that the trochaic t. was less constrained in its access to the rhythms of Gr. speech than some other meters. Ancient trad. (e.g. Aristotle, *Rhetoric* 1407; Marius Victorinus 4.44)˙considered the trochaic t. a faster meter than the iambic trimeter. At any rate, the greater speed of the t. is probably more than a matter of conventional performance tempo and may reflect a universal feature of falling rhythm in ordinary speech (see RISING AND FALLING). The trochaic t. catalectic was employed by the archaic iambographers; Aristotle (*Poetics* 1449a2) states that it was used in tragedy before the iambic trimeter, but in extant drama it is much less frequent than the latter.

Besides its use in trochaic, the t. length was also used in antiquity with anapaestic and iambic metra. The anapaestic t. catalectic is used in comic dialogue. It is characterized by metron diaeresis (q.v.) as well as regular median diaeresis, frequent contraction of all but the last pair of *brevia*, and resolution of *longa*. The iambic t. catalectic was used by Hipponax and is fairly frequent in comedy for the entrance and exits of choruses and for contest scenes. Diaeresis after the second metron is preferred but caesura after the third *anceps* is common; resolution and substitution are frequent. The acatalectic iambic t. is used only by Sophocles in the *Ichneutai* and in Ion's satyr-play *Omphale*.

The Lat. adaptation of the Gr. trochaic t. catalectic is the trochaic *septenarius* (q.v.), used commonly for comic dialogue and favored by Plautus. It stands in the same relation to its Gr. model as does the *senarius* (q.v.), showing the same regard for linguistic stress. The absence of polysyllabic oxytones and infrequency of proparoxytones in Lat. means that the frequent trochaic closes of paroxytonic words will effect a prevailingly trochaic rhythm. As a popular form it is known as the *versus quadratus*. Beare summarizes the long-held view that it was this meter, widely used for popular verseforms such as the marching songs of Caesar's legions, and common in late antiquity, which became the basis for much of Med. Lat. versification. It is the meter of the *Pervigilium veneris* and a number of Christian hymns, notably Venantius Fortunatus' *Pange lingua* (see HYMN), and was surpassed only by the iambic dimeter hymn quatrain (itself octosyllabic when regular) and the sequence as the most popular meter of the Middle Ages.—J. Rumpel, "Der trochäische T. bei den griechischen Lyrikern und Dramatikern," *Philologus* 28 (1869); H. J. Kanz, *De tetrametro trochaico* (1913); Beare; Crusius; F. Perusino, *Il tetrametro giambico catalettico nella commedia greca* (1968); A. M. Devine and L. D. Stephens, *Lang. and Metre* (1984); West.   A.M.D.; L.D.S.

II. MODERN. The t. in the prosodies of the modern vernaculars is based on feet rather than metra, hence is but half as long as the Cl. type, typically eight syllables for the iambic and trochaic t., the two commonest forms. Anapestic t. is always experimental, as in Byron's "The Destruction of Sennacherib." The t. strictly speaking shows regularity of metrical patterning (stress-alternation); with freer metrical patterning, it is simply an octosyllable (q.v.), as in Fr. and Sp. versification, or else accentual verse (q.v.), as in ballad meter (q.v.) and hymn meter. The Fr. *tétramètre* (q.v.) is however a four-sectioned alexandrine (q.v.). The t. in both iambic and trochaic forms has retained closer ties with popular verse (it is common for songs, as in Shakespeare) and with orality than the longer line forms, the decasyllable (q.v.) and the dodecasyllable. It is almost always rhymed: in a famous footnote to his 1933 Leslie Stephen lecture, A. E. Housman singles out as one of the mysteries of versification "why, while blank verse can be written in lines of ten or six syllables, a series of octosyllables ceases to be verse if they are not rhymed." In Eng. poetry it appears in couplets through Wordsworth; with Tennyson, it begins to be used in quatrains. Well-known Eng. examples of iambic ts. incl.: one (only) of Shakespeare's sonnets (145), Donne's "The Extasie," Marvell's "To His Coy Mistress," Coleridge's "The Pains of Sleep," Keats' "Eve of St. Mark," Tennyson's *In Memoriam*, Browning's "Porphyria's Lover," and Arnold's "Resignation."

But it is in Rus. prosody that the iambic t. has achieved its greatest realization: Puškin wrote nearly 22,000 ts., over half his entire output, for *The Bronze Horseman* (1833) and *Evgenij Onegin* (1825–31). In Rus. it is a "solid, polished, disciplined thing," says Nabokov, who sees the Eng. form as a "hesitating, loose, capricious" line, always in danger of having its head chopped off, "maimed for life" in the 17th c. by Hudibrastic verse (q.v.), and ever after emasculated as a serious meter by light verse, mock heroics, didactic verse, and the hymns (54). Statistical profiling of the filling of metrical ictuses with stresses shows that in Rus. there have been three subforms of the t.: in the 18th-c. variant, ictuses 1 and 4 are filled with stresses the most frequently, with 2 heavier than 3; in the mid 19th-c. variant, 2 and 4 are heaviest and nearly equal, with 1 nearly as heavy and 3 very weak; in Belij's 20th-c. variant, 1 and 4 are again heaviest, but 3 is heavier than 2. In Eng., Jonson and Pope write a line in which ictuses 2 and 4 are much stronger than 1 and 3, while in Milton the weights rise steadily through the line (Bailey).

In Eng., trochaic ts. are almost as common as iambic, a fact of interest because trochaic pentameters, for example, are almost nonexistent. One of the more notorious instances of modern trochaic t., Longfellow's *Hiawatha*, is however less wooden metrically than many of its detractors have claimed, and was in any case meant to imitate the meter of the Finnish folk-epic, the *Kalevala*. Catalexis is also remarkably common—as much so in the vernaculars as in Lat.—so that one finds, almost as often as runs of 8s, runs of 7s (Carew, "A Prayer to the Wind"; Shakespeare, *MV* 2.7.65–73) and distinctive mixtures of 8s and 7s in both trochaic (Shakespeare, *Passionate Pilgrim* 21) and iambo-trochaic (Milton, *L'Allegro* and *Il Penseroso*; Shelley, "Lines Written among the Euganean Hills"). The introduction of trochees into iambic ts. is common in Eng., but wholly alien to Rus. prosody. See RISING AND FALLING; see also OCTOSYLLABLE.—Schipper; P. Habermann, "T.," *Reallexikon I*; V. Nabokov, *Notes on Prosody* (1964); J. Bailey, *Toward a Statistical Analysis of Eng. Verse* (1975); Morier.   T.V.F.B.

TÉTRAMÈTRE. A term used to denote the metrical structure of the regular 12-syllable Fr. alexandrine (q.v.) and so distinguish it sharply from the less-common *trimètre* structure (q.v., and below). Strictly speaking, the regular alexandrine has only two *fixed* accents, on the sixth and twelfth syllables, i.e. at the caesura and line-end, marking off each hemistich. It is usual, however, for the alexandrine to have two further "secondary" accents, of no fixed position, one in each hemistich, making a total of four in the line—hence *t*. Racine's *Phèdre* (1.3.306) affords a famous example: "C'est Vénus / tout entière // à sa proie / attachée."

A regular *t*. may therefore contain two accents only, e.g. Baudelaire: "Elle se développe // avec indifférence" (6+6); or three, e.g. Apollinaire: "Une chanson d'amour // et d'infidélité" (4+2+6); or four, e.g. Vigny: "La Nature t'attend // dans un silence austère" (3+3+4+2); but four is the conventional number. The optionality and mobility of the two secondary accents furnish the *t*. with 36 different rhythmic configurations. The *trimètre*, by contrast, which has three measures and no caesura, is indelibly ternary in structure; even when the *t*. has three accents, its medial caesura still preserves its essentially binary character. The *t*., whose roots go back at least to *Le Pèlerinage de Charlemagne* (12th c.), was shaped in the Cl. age by the strict rules of Malherbe into the form championed by Boileau and brought to perfection in the tragedies of Corneille and Racine.—Kastner; Elwert; Mazaleyrat; Scott; C. Scott, *A Question of Syllables* (1986).
                                    A.G.E.; C.S.

TEXT. See TEXTUAL CRITICISM; TEXTUALITY; INTERTEXTUALITY; CRITICISM; THEORY; SOUND; POETRY; POETICS.

TEXT PRODUCTION. See VERSIFICATION; ORAL-FORMULAIC THEORY; POET; RHETORIC AND POETRY.

TEXT-SOUND. See SOUND POETRY.

TEXTUAL CRITICISM is the term traditionally used to refer to the scholarly activity of analyzing the relationships among the surviving texts of a work so as to assess their relative authority and accuracy. It is also often taken, more broadly, to encompass the activity of scholarly editing, in which the conclusions drawn from such examination are embodied in the text or annotation (or both) of a new edition. T. crit. is a historical undertaking, for its aim is to elucidate the textual history of individual works and to attempt to reconstruct the precise forms taken by the texts of those works at particular moments in the past. Like all efforts to recover the past, it depends on judgment at every turn, and the word "criticism" is therefore an appropriate element in the standard term for this activity. Nevertheless, there has been a widespread misconception of t. crit. as somehow mechanical or objective, and one often encounters the view that t. crit. precedes lit. crit., i.e. that the textual critic merely establishes the text for the literary critic to interpret. But in fact the text produced or advocated by a textual critic is inevitably a product of lit. crit., for a textual critic's decisions (about what words and marks of punctuation should constitute the text of a given work) will reflect, whether consciously or not, some point of view toward lit. in general, some assumptions about the nature of poetic production, and some interp. of the work in question and its constituent passages. It is consequently as inappropriate to call a scholarly edition containing a critically edited text "definitive" as it is to apply that adjective to a critical essay. Conceivably the apparatus in such an ed. can be definitive, if it accurately reports all known relevant evidence; but the text itself can never be, for the conclusions it embodies cannot be declared the only reasonable ones that can ever emerge from an assessment of that evidence.

T. crit. and lit. crit. are therefore not separable activities: questioning the make-up of the text is an essential element in the act of reading, and any conclusions about it reflect a critical predisposition. Paradoxically, however, literary critics in recent years have increasingly been using terms like "textual analysis" or t. crit. to refer to their activities without having this point in mind. Those responsible for this shift of terminology have generally been led into it by their use of "text" and "work" as synonyms. Distinguishing texts from works, however, is fundamental to all discussion of lit. (or any other verbal communication) and goes to the heart of why t. crit. is necessary. A text is a particular arrangement of words and marks of punctuation; a literary work, a verbal construct, consists of a text (or succession of texts), but its text cannot be assumed to coincide with any written or printed text purporting to be the text of that work. The medium of lit. is lang., which is abstract, not paper and ink, which merely serve as one vehicle for transmitting lang. Therefore works of lit. do not exist on paper, and the texts that appear there are only the texts of physical documents, which may be relatively successful or unsuccessful in representing the texts of works.

Just how successful any one of them is will forever be a matter of discussion. We can never know when we have in fact recreated the text of a work; but if we are interested in works rather than documents, all we can do is continually to attempt the recreation of works by critically assessing the evidences of those works that we find in the extant printed or ms. texts at our disposal. Most readers recognize that typographical errors and slips of the pen can occur, and many readers occasionally detect and correct such errors. But few seem to be aware that by this elementary action they are recognizing a basic truth about the nature of lit.— that the effort to read the texts of literary works requires a questioning of the texts of the documents that attempt to convey those works. This problem is equally central in poetry and in prose, in the texts of medieval mss. or of modern printed books: it is the unavoidable consequence of the intangibility of the medium of lit. Similar points could be made about oral texts (see ORAL-FORMU-LAIC THEORY) or the texts of other arts, such as music, that employ intangible media.

There is thus no such thing as a literary work that does not pose a textual problem, if "work" is taken to mean a communication from the past. Readers may of course choose not to approach lit. historically, and there are various schools of lit. crit. founded on that premise. For such readers and critics, texts are not links to the past but found objects existing in the present. Any text they encounter can serve as an object for analysis, and t. crit. is therefore largely irrelevant to their concerns—unless they make historical connections between texts, such as saying that two texts are from the same period or represent works by the same author. Even if all surviving texts of a work were to be found identical, the historical scholar would still examine that single text critically with a view to detecting errors in it. But texts of a work usually differ, and not only because of scribes' or printers' errors (which, however, are almost inevitable whenever a text is copied or reset in type). Some authors revise their works—some repeatedly—and textual variants may reflect shifting authorial intentions at different points in an author's life. Other variants may result from alterations made by other persons involved in bringing a work to the public, as when a publishing-house editor imposes a house style or tones down an expression of opinion that might give offense. Readers who wish to approach a work as a communication from the past need to know the variants that have appeared in its documentary texts, and the errors that former readers have postulated, so that they are not at the mercy of the idiosyncrasies of individual documents.

Investigating the textual history of a work involves the identification and examination of the documents (both ms. and printed) containing texts of it, along with any relevant associated documents such as letters, diaries, notebooks, books that served as the author's sources, and publishers' records. Just which of the documentary texts of a work are relevant depends on one's historical focus: if one is interested in the author's intentions (whether early or late), for example, the group of documents to be considered might be different from those that would be relevant if one's concern were with the texts that were available to readers at a given time. Once the potentially relevant documentary texts are located, they must be collated (compared word by word, punctuation mark by punctuation mark—perhaps with the assistance of mechanical aids, such as collating machines for copies of the same edition, scanners with optical character recognition for copies of different editions, and infra-red light sources for manuscript readings that have been marked out) and any variances between them recorded. The variant readings are then analyzed in an effort to determine the relationships among the texts, identifying which are direct ancestors or descendants of others, which represent collateral lines of descent, and which result from conflation of different lines. Several methods have been advanced over the years for performing this analysis. The classic "genealogical method" (displayed by Lachmann in his eds. of the New Testament in 1831 and Lucretius in 1850, and codified by Maas in 1927) assumes that texts with errors in common have a common ancestor and classifies texts into families on this basis. Recognition of some of the limitations of this approach has led to a series of 20th-c. attempts at quasi-mathematical methods (e.g. Quentin, Greg [1927], Hill, Hrubý, Dearing). All these efforts strive for objectivity, but each reaches a point where critical judgment is required. The problem of determining relationships among the extant texts of a work is most acute for ancient writings, which are generally represented by mss.—sometimes in great number—produced long after the authors' deaths. But the problem also exists for later writings, published during their authors' lifetimes in printed eds., because the text of each successive ed. is not always based on that of the immediately preceding ed. It is a fundamental truth of t. crit. that the chronology of mss. and printed eds. (if it can be established) does not necessarily coincide with the genealogy of the texts contained in those documents. (Nevertheless, the analysis of the physical evidence present in documents is essential for understanding how the production history of documents affects the texts they contain, and much work of this kind on printed material has been accomplished in the 20th c., as in the writings of McKerrow [1927], Hinman, and Bowers [1964]. Some of the necessary background in printing history for this kind of work has been provided by Gaskell [1972]).

What use editors make of the postulated genealogy of the texts of a work depends principally on their view of two questions, the first of which is the role of judgment in historical inquiry. One position on this matter is that editorial judgment should be kept to a minimum and that the most valuable editorial activity is the accurate transcription or reprinting of individual documents. Judgment is involved here, of course, in deciding (in the light of the genealogy) which document to focus on and—in the case of handwritten material—deciphering the script; but, beyond that, the editor's judgment is not allowed to operate. (Those who produce such eds. of ms. texts should be aware of the need to supplement transcriptions with photographic facsimiles and verbal descriptions, which together can partially report the associated physical evidence; those who prepare facsimiles of printed texts—of any period—should recognize the necessity of appending to each of them a record of the variants found in other copies of the same ed., since photographs of a single copy cannot adequately represent an ed. as a whole without such information.) In contrast, one may believe that the textual accidents embodied in individual documents make the texts of those documents a less reliable guide to past intentions than eclectic texts, which aim—through editorial choices among variant readings ("recension" in classical t. crit.) and editorial emendations of perceived errors ("emendatio")—to restore texts to the states that existed or were intended at particular times in the past. Thus every text presented by an editor is either *critical,* embodying critical judgments as to whether or not to emend a copy-text with variant readings and other corrections, or *noncritical* ("diplomatic"), attempting to reproduce without alteration what appears in a particular document.

The other major influence on editors' approaches to their task is their assumptions about the nature of literary works—indeed, of all works made of words—and their consequent preference for one stage rather than another in the history of individual works. Even a facsimile ed. is affected by the critical predisposition of its editor: for example, editors who believe that literary works are essentially the products of writers working alone might choose an author's final ms. for reproduction rather than the published ed. based on it, whereas editors who feel that literary works are social products, resulting from the interaction of authors and other persons involved in the publishing process, would be inclined to choose the printed ed. Most discussion of this issue, however, has occurred in connection with critical eds., and over the centuries most of the thinking about such eds. has assumed that the aim of making alterations in documentary texts is to bring them closer to what their authors intended (see INTENTION). This aim has not necessarily meant that authors were regarded as having had single intentions: in some cases, such as Wordsworth's *The Prelude* or Whitman's *Leaves of Grass,* an author's differing

intentions at different times have been recognized as producing discrete versions that are deserving of separate editions. Even those who have felt that all they can attempt to reconstruct is the common ancestor of the surviving texts have nevertheless thought that the process was worth pursuing because it brought them closer to the author's intended text. The history of t. crit. is largely the story of shifting attitudes concerning how to define the role that editors' critical judgment should play in attempting to attain this goal.

In the early 20th c., two influential eds. made the case for minimizing such judgment by adopting a "best text" and correcting only the obvious slips in it: McKerrow's ed. of Nashe (1904) and Bédier's second ed. of Renart's *Le Lai de l'ombre* (1913). At about the same time, however, Housman (in his 1903 ed. of Manilius) ridiculed the idea that a "best" text was correct at points where it was not obviously in need of emendation, and he called for eclectic texts that relied more heavily on critical insight. It was not until 1950, when W. W. Greg published his seminal article "The Rationale of Copy-Text," that the editing of modern lits. began moving in the same general direction that Housman had recommended for classicists 50 years earlier. Greg argued, on the basis of his experience with Eng. Ren. drama, that an editor should normally adopt as a copy-text the text that is closest to the author's final ms. because it will reflect more fully than later texts the author's practices in spelling and punctuation ("accidentals," as he called them); the editor should then emend that text with any variants from other texts, particularly variants in words ("substantives"), that can be convincingly argued to be authorial, as well as with any other alterations deemed necessary. This procedure, he believed, would maximize one's chances of producing a text that represents, insofar as surviving evidence permits, the author's final intention.

Greg's approach, esp. as extended by Fredson Bowers to works of other periods, has unquestionably been the most influential rationale of editorial procedure among scholars of Eng. and Am. lit. in the second half of the 20th c., though it has by no means been universally accepted. Questions have been raised about its applicability to periods in which printing and publishing practices were different from those of the Ren. and to situations in which mss. and proofs survive (as well as printed eds.) or in which different versions reflect different "final" intentions (as with Auden, or with Wordsworth and Whitman as noted above). But in fact Greg's general principles are easily adaptable to these cases; the more significant questions concern the appropriateness of authorial final intention itself as the goal of textual reconstruction. Such questionings, which have received increasing attention in the late decades of the 20th c., run the gamut from Parker's belief that sometimes an author's own revisions should not be accepted (if they come after an intense period of creativity is over, for they then shatter the coherence of the work) to McGann's view that lit. is a social product (requiring attention to the result of the collaborative efforts of the author, the author's advisers, the publisher, and others) and to McKenzie's concept of the "sociology of the text" (in which, for instance, the physical features of textual presentation, such as typography and layout, are part of the social context that influences readers' responses). Arguments for each of these approaches have frequently been offered as if their acceptance entails the rejection of other approaches; but there is no exclusively valid approach to the past. An interest in authors' intentions (whether original, intermediate, or final) and an interest in the texts that were made available to readers do not invalidate one another: each focuses on a different aspect of textual history, and each therefore tells one part of a larger story. T. crit., like other forms of history, can never tell the whole story, nor can it reconstruct any part of it with certainty; but we must make the attempt to uncover the story whenever we wish to read works as communications from the past.

INTRODUCTORY SURVEYS AND GUIDES: F. Bowers, *T. and Lit. Crit.* (1959), "T. Crit.," *The Aims and Methods of Scholarship in Mod. Langs. and Lits.*, ed. J. Thorpe, 2d ed. (1970); B. M. Metzger, *The Text of the New Testament*, 2d ed. (1968); L. D. Reynolds and N. G. Wilson, *Scribes and Scholars: A Guide to the Transmission of Gr. and Lat. Lit.*, 2d ed. (1974); E. J. Kenney, *The Cl. Text* (1974); G. T. Tanselle, "T. Scholarship," *Intro. to Scholarship in Mod. Langs. and Lits.*, ed. J. Gibaldi (1981), *T. Crit. Since Greg* (1987), *A Rationale of T. Crit.* (1989), "Cl., Biblical, and Med. T. Crit. and Mod. Editing" (in Tanselle [1990] below), "T. Crit. and Literary Sociology," *SB* 44 (1991); W. P. Williams and C. S. Abbott, *An Intro. to Bibliographical and T. Studies* (1985).

ANTHOLOGIES: *Bibl. and T. Crit.*, ed. O. M. Brack and W. Barnes (1969); *Art and Error*, ed. R. Gottesman and S. Bennett (1970); *Med. Mss. and T. Crit.*, ed. C. Kleinhenz (1976); *Editing Poetry from Spenser to Dryden*, ed. A. H. de Quehen (1980); *Texts and Transmission*, ed. L. D. Reynolds (1983); *Play-Texts in Old Spelling*, ed. G. B. Shand and R. C. Shady (1984); *T. Crit. and Lit. Interp.*, ed. J. J. McGann (1985); *Manuscripts and Texts: Editorial Problems in Later ME Lit.*, ed. D. Pearsall (1987); *Editing and Editors: A Retrospect*, ed. R. Landon (1988); *New Directions in Textual Studies*, ed. D. Oliphant and R. Bradford (1990); *Editing in Australia*, ed. P. Eggert (1990); *Devils and Angels: Textual Editing and Literary Theory*, ed. P. Cohen (1990); *Representing Modernist Texts: Editing as Interp.*, ed. G. Bornstein (1991).

STUDIES: K. Lachmann, ed. of New Testament (1831) and Lucretius (1850); B. F. Westcott and F. J. A. Hort, intro. to New Testament (1881); A. E. Housman, pref. to ed. of Manilius, *Astronomicon* (1903), "The Application of Thought to T. Crit.,"

Coll. Poems and Selected Prose, ed. C. Ricks (1988); R. B. McKerrow, ed. of Th. Nashe (1904), *An Intro. to Bibl. for Literary Students* (1927), *Prolegomena for the Oxford Shakespeare* (1939); J. Bédier, intro. to ed. of J. Renart, *Le Lai de l'ombre*, 2d ed. (1913); H. Quentin, *Mémoire sur l'établissement du texte de la Vulgate* (1922); W. W. Greg, *The Calculus of Variants* (1927), "The Rationale of Copy-Text," *Coll. Papers*, ed. J. C. Maxwell (1966); A. A. Hill, "Some Postulates for Distributional Study of Texts," *SB* 3 (1950-51); G. Pasquali, *Storia della tradizione e critica del testo*, 2d ed. (1952); P. Maas, *T. Crit.*, tr. B. Flower (1958); C. Hinman, *The Printing and Proof-Reading of the First Folio of Shakespeare* (1963); F. Bowers, *Bibl. and T. Crit.* (1964), "Multiple Authority," *Essays in Bibl., Text, and Editing* (1975), "Greg's 'Rationale of Copy-Text' Revisited," *SB* 31 (1978); A. Hrubý, "A Quantitative Solution of the Ambiguity of Three Texts," *SB* 18 (1965); E. C. Colwell, *Studies in Methodology in T. Crit. of the New Testament* (1969); F. P. Wilson, *Shakespeare and the New Bibl.*, ed. H. Gardner (1970); J. Thorpe, *Principles of T. Crit.* (1972); M. L. West, *T. Crit. and Editorial Techniques Applicable to Gr. and Lat. Texts* (1973); V. Dearing, *Principles and Practice of T. Analysis* (1974); M. D. Feld, "The Early Evolution of the Authoritative Text," *HLB* 26 (1978); P. Gaskell, *A New Intro. to Bibl.* (1972), *From Writer to Reader* (1978); A. Foulet and M. B. Speer, *On Editing OF Texts* (1979); G. T. Tanselle, *Selected Studies in Bibl.* (1979), *T. Crit. and Scholarly Editing* (1990); J. J. McGann, *A Critique of Mod. T. Crit.* (1983), "Textual Studies and Practical Crit.," *The Beauty of Inflections* (1985); H. Parker, *Flawed Texts and Verbal Icons* (1984); D. F. McKenzie, *Bibl. and the Sociology of Texts* (1986); P. L. Shillingsburg, *Scholarly Editing in the Computer Age* (1986); D. H. Reiman, *Romantic Texts and Contexts* (1987).

G.T.T.

TEXTUALITY, a key concept in poststructuralism, signals a new way of understanding writing, reading, and the relations between them. It stands in opposition to the idea of the "work," its unity, and its humanistic underpinnings, and thus underwrites an attack on the metaphysical presuppositions of the traditional conception of lit. in the West.

The concept of the "work" (see POETICS; TEXTUAL CRITICISM) entails meaning, unity, and the authority of a transcendent source. A work is complete, it exists in space, it is wrought by the creative power of the artist, and its meaning is stable across time and culture. A text, on the other hand, inhabits and is inhabited by lang., without a privileged outside—an origin or source—to guarantee or authorize its meaning. The source of each text is always another text, but there is always another text before that. No text lies outside the endless play of lang., and no text is complete: each exhibits traces or "sediments" of some other text in an endless repetition of originary lack. To humanistic ("logocentric") assertions of a transcendent referent (the transcendental signified) that organizes human experience and renders lang. meaningful, t. opposes the notion that at the origin there is "always already" lang., writing, a trace of some other text. The terms "trace," "supplement," and "writing" indicate an absence in the text, its impossibility of self-presence. Each text is haunted by this absence, which opens it up to an entangled web of relations with every other text and which permits the articulation of a "subtext." The subtext is not what is "meant" or "expressed," but rather that which tends to "dissimulate or forbid" and which it nonetheless makes evident at certain points of stress or conflict. The subtext functions as a text's unconscious—what it does not know it knows—and indicates a reading against the grain.

The subtext was not always conceived as a strategic dismantling of the text. In the work of the Rus. Formalists (see RUSSIAN FORMALISM), and in the early stages of structuralism (q.v.), the subtext was one of the visible components of the text, one of the parts that fitted into the whole. The stable linguistics that gave rise to structuralism perceived the subtext as a partially hidden segment of the text, elucidation of which would provide a synchronic view of the whole. Later views of t., which perceived the text diachronically rather than synchronically, in terms of what is missing or absent rather than merely hidden from view, think of the subtext as a destabilizing element in the play of significations. The subtext is not assimilable to the text; it works against and undermines a text's potential meaning.

T. is thus fraught with dissonance. Each text is a locus of conflict which cannot be decided without repression. More recently, t. has become associated with questions of power: not only the power play between text and subtext, but of the competing claims and ideologies which make themselves evident in a text. The major effect of t. is to problematize the question of knowledge—the relation between *what* we know and *how* we know. T. assumes the impossibility of thought without lang., thus effectively subsuming knowledge within lang. itself. Disciplinary knowledge, like the work, also lacks a transcendental signified and is not authorized by any epistemological high ground. Each discipline constitutes itself as a discipline by repressing its linguistic, rhetorical nature, but t. disrupts this movement of repression, highlights it, and focuses on what a field of knowledge tends to "dissimulate" or "forbid." T. assumes the "t." of all disciplines and thus the tropological (rhetorical) nature of all knowledge. Texts read and write one another and translate one another without regard for primacy, secondariness, or disciplinary borderlines. T. transforms the relations between reading and writing and even the very nature of academic institutions: in the world of the work, knowledge is transmitted; in the world of t., knowledge is produced, and that production is always open to question. Barthes' claim that

"there is no father-author" and Derrida's statement that "writing is an orphan" (themselves descriptive of the condition of t.) open texts and disciplines to an indeterminacy (q.v.) that infects disciplines with a rhetorical self-consciousness and disrupts the borderlines that made possible their self-definition. In affirming that there is no outside to t. ("il n'y a pas de hors-texte"), t. generates a problematizing of knowledge and the conditions of power which knowledge authorizes. See also ALLUSION; DECONSTRUCTION; ORGANICISM; INTERTEXTUALITY.

J. Derrida, *De la grammatologie* (1967, tr. 1976)— with essential preface by G. Spivak, and "Signature, Event, Context," *Marges de la philosophie* (1972); M. Foucault, *The Archaeology of Knowledge and the Discourse on Lang.* (tr. 1972), *Power/Knowledge* (tr. 1980); R. Barthes, *Le plaisir du texte* (1973), "De l'oeuvre au texte," *Revue d'esthétique* (1974); E. Said, "Abecedarium Culturae," *Beginnings* (1975), "The Problem of T.: Two Exemplary Positions," *CritI* 4 (1978); *Textual Strategies*, ed. J. Harari (1979)—excellent intro., bibl.; M. Riffaterre, *La production du texte* (1979, tr. 1983); S. Stewart, "Some Riddles and Proverbs of T.," *Criticism* 21 (1979); *Untying the Text*, ed. R. Young (1981); J. Culler, *On Deconstruction* (1982); *The Question of T.*, ed. W. Spanos and P. Bové (1982); J. MacCannell, "The Temporality of T.: Bakhtin and Derrida," *MLN* 100 (1985); H. Baran, "Subtext," in *Terras*; *Textual Analysis*, ed. M. A. Caws (1986); *Unnam'd Forms: Blake and T.*, ed. N. Hilton and T. A. Vogler (1986); S. Weber, *Demarcating the Disciplines*, (1986), ed., *Institution and Interp.* (1987); G. Harpham, *The Ascetic Imperative in Culture and Crit.* (1987); C. Norris, *Derrida* (1987); G. Jay, "Paul de Man: Being in Question," *America the Scrivener* (1990).   H.R.E.

TEXTURE. T. signifies the palpable, tangible details inscribed in the poetic text. It refers to the distinguishing elements in a poem which are separate and independent of its structure (q.v.), the elements that persist when the argument (q.v.) of a poem has been rendered into a prose paraphrase (q.v.). The term has close affinities with the concept of surface detail in painting and sculpture. Such a conception is designed to solve the difficulties posed by schematic and over-generalized theories of poetics. A poem has t. to the degree to which the phonetic and linguistic characteristics of its surface promote stylistic density. At one level t. involves the familiar poetic techniques of assonance and alliteration (qq.v.); at another level it assumes the form of sensory intensities and tactile associations (e.g. harshness or softness—cf. EUPHONY). It is to these surface qualities that t. corresponds and is made more complex by metrical patterns.

John Crowe Ransom's theory of poetry, in particular, with its stress on the dense t. of meanings in poetry, privileges the notion of t. For Ransom the t. of the poem is specifically related to "a sense of the real density and contingency of the world." By definition, then, t. is intended to correct the exaggerations of "logic" in poetry that cause the colorful local details to disappear into the grayness of systematized abstraction. Thus, in his formulation, poetic t. is characterized by its "sensuous richness," by its "fullness of presentation," by its "immediacy," and by its "concreteness" (see CONCRETE AND ABSTRACT). This is quite distinct from what Ransom saw as Cleanth Brooks' exclusive reliance on poetic structure. In Ransom's crit., the function of the concrete detail is not to authorize the abstract generality of structure (as, for example, in Brooks' claim that paradoxical structure underpins all poetry from the *Odyssey* to *The Waste Land*). Rather, the detail becomes formally and explicitly disjoined from the structure when the poet chooses her words, metaphors, images, and other devices. Thus Ransom's idea of poetic t., his transformation of it into a specific grounding for a theory of poetics, reverses the relationship between structure and detail in Brooks' model. This reversal serves to reimmerse poetics in the immediate and sensory experience of a contingent reality (something he felt Brooks' paradoxically abstract poetics could not do). Now the filled density of the discrete detail guarantees an experience which exceeds structure as it comes nearer to the physical body of the poem.

However, it would be an exaggeration to say that the new emphasis on t. encourages a blanket repudiation of structure. The poem, Ransom says, always retains a logical structure—what he calls the "substance"—which coincides with its prose paraphrase: "the poem actually continues to contain its ostensible substance which is not fatally diminished from its prose state: that is its logical core or paraphrase." What is significant for him is the close relationship between this logical structure of the poem and its accompanying local t.: both must be present within the poem. This is the ultimate meaning and importance which Ransom gives to t. in his metaphysic of particularity (though he does speak elsewhere of the "almost incessant tendency of poetry to *over-particularization*").

In general usage, textural detail is "irrelevant" to structure, being discovered or selected in the act of composition at a level independent of organization. From such a viewpoint it follows that one important function of detail is precisely to *impede* the argument of the poem. The poet's accommodation of the details to the demands of meter and euphony affords new and quite unexpected insights which then become themselves the most prominent feature of t.; t. thus generates a set of unforeseen and unique meanings out of the reach of structure. On the whole, these specifically poetic meanings are what formalist crit. has made its main object of study.—J. C. Ransom, *The World's Body* (1932), "The Inorganic Muses," *KR* 5 (1943), "Crit. as Pure Speculation," and

"Wanted: An Ontological Critic," both in Ransom; Brooks; Wimsatt and Brooks; M. C. Beardsley, *Aesthetics* (1958); J. E. Magner, *John Crowe Ransom: Critical Principles and Preoccupations* (1971); T. D. Young, "Ransom's Critical Theories: Structure and T.," *MissQ* 30 (1977). P.M.

THAI POETRY. Poetry dominated T. lit. until the early 20th c., when prose also became widespread. Noted for rhyme and sound play, T. p. is written in syllabic meters in five major verseforms: *rāi*, *khlōng*, *kāp*, *chan*, and *klọn*. The T. (Siamese) lang. presently has five tones which also form part of the metrical requirements. The king and court poets used these forms nearly exclusively until 1932, though in many cases the works are anonymous.

The earliest verse appeared during the Sukhothai period (ca. 1240–1438). Sukhothai reached a high level of civilization, but extant poems are few; the only significant extant text is *Suphāsit phra ruang*, a series of moral maxims written in *rāi* and credited to King Ramkhamhaeng (ca. 1279–98). These stanzas have an indefinite number of 5-syllable lines linked by rhyme. Melodious and concise phrases, suggestive of poetry, also appear in inscriptions from the period.

The Ayutthaya period (1351–1767) saw the rise of classics in *rāi*, *khlōng*, *kāp*, and *chan*. *Khlōng*, like *rāi*, originally appeared when T. had only three tones. *Khlōng* consists of 5-syllable lines grouped into stanzas of two lines (*khlōng sọng*), three (*khlōng sām*), and four (*khlōng sī*). The *kāp* stanzas, probably borrowed from Khmer, include *yānī* with two 11-syllable lines, *surāngkhanāng* with seven 4-syllable lines, and *chabang* with one 4-syllable line between two 6-syllable lines. Indic in origin, the *chan* meters were adapted from meters found in Sanskrit and Pali (see INDIAN PROSODY) during this period.

One of the earliest and most difficult Ayutthayan works is *Ōngkān chāēng nam* (The Water Oath), a composition used by officials to reaffirm their loyalty to the king. Throughout the era, Buddhist themes dominate many compositions. In 1482, King Traylokkhanat (1448–88) commissioned a royal version of the *Vessantara Jataka*, the Buddha's life prior to his last birth on earth. In this version, the *Mahāchāt kham luang*, consists of passages in Pali followed by T. translations into *rāi*, *khlōng*, and *chan*. Important compositions with historical themes began with *Lilit yuan phāi* (ca. 1475). Written in *lilit*, a combination of *rāi* and *khlōng*, this poem describes the victories of King Traylokkhanat. The popular *nirāt* genre, in which the poet compares his lover's features to the beauties of nature, also developed about this time. During the reign of King Narai (1656–88), the court became a major center of poetry production, and the era came to be known as the Golden Age of T. lit. Probably the most famous of Narai's court poets was Sri Prat. In and out of favor with the king because of his sharp wit, he composed the famous *Kamsuan sī prāt*, a *nirāt* describing his journey to his place in exile. The *chan* meters gained prominence with the adaptation of Buddhist birth stories into verse such as the *Samutthakhōt kham chan* and *Sua khō kham chan*. Probably the most famous work from this period, although some scholars date it in the reign of King Traylokkhanat, is the *lilit* classic *Phra lọ*, the tragic romance of Prince Phra Lọ and two princesses from a neighboring kingdom. Literary output declined after Narai, however, due to war and internal strife. Notable works from the end of the Ayutthaya period incl. a collection of boating songs in *kāp*, *Kāp hāē rua*, and a description in *chan* of the king's journey to a Buddhist shrine, *Bunnōwāt kham chan*. In 1767 the Burmese destroyed Ayutthaya.

The establishment of the new capital at Bangkok revived literary production at court, this time primarily in *klọn*, which probably first appeared during the Thonburi period (1767–82). Since then it has been the favored T. verseform, with two types used regularly: *klọn hok* with six syllables per line and *klọn pāēt* with eight. The 4-line *klọn* stanzas are famous for rhyme schemes and rhyme links that often continue for thousands of stanzas. Hoping to recreate lost works, Rama I, Phra Phutthayotfa (1782–1809), the first king at Bangkok, organized a royal composition committee that produced the *Rāmakian* (the T. version of the Indian classic, the *Rāmāyana*) and parts of *Inau* and *Dālang* (romances based on the Javanese Panji cycle introduced through Malaysia). Rama II, Phra Phutthaloetla (1809–24) continued the literary revival with another version of the *Rāmakian* and a complete version of *Inau*, much of which, it is thought, he composed himself. Sunthorn Phu (1786–1856), arguably Thailand's greatest poet, used *klọn* for many *nirāt* poems and for the long imaginative romance *Phra aphaimanī*. Prince Paramanuchit (1790–1853), monk, poet, and Indic classicist, contributed textbooks on the *chan* meters, the final part of *Samutthakhōt kham chan*, and *Lilit talēng phāi*, a glorification of the battles of King Naresuan. Khun Phum (1815–80), the leading woman poet of the 19th c., produced satirical poems of biting wit in her famous literary salons. Traditional narrative poetry continued into the 20th c. in compositions by Prince Bidyalongkarana (1876–1945); one of his most noted works is *Sām krung*, a history of the three T. capital cities, Ayutthaya, Thonburi, and Bangkok.

The 1932 revolution gave Thailand a constitutional monarchy; and court-dominated poetry thereafter ceased. Post-1932 poetry differed from classical works in its brevity, its lyricism, and its emphasis upon crit. and instruction. Many of these changes resulted from the efforts of Chao Phraya Thammasakdimontri, known as Khru Thep (1876–1943), a journalist-poet. Later, in the 1940s and '50s, Assani Phonlachan (b. 1918) sought to de-emphasize the importance of rhyme and sound in T.

p. At the same time, Chit Phumisak (1932–65), a political idealist, helped launch the "Art for Life's Sake" movement, which attacked individuals and even whole political systems; Phumisak criticized cl. T. p. for not meeting the needs of the people. Other poets such as Prakin Xumsai, writing as Ujjeni (b. 1919), and later Naowarat Pongpaiboon (b. 1940) emphasized nature, love, and emotion along with social crit. The 1960s saw much experimentation with verseforms, incl. free verse (*klọn plāū*). During this time the poet-painter Angkarn Kalayanapongse (b. 1926), probably the most respected of contemp. poets, developed his themes and style. Often described as a nature poet, he finds expressions of universal messages in nature, art, and the past. The fluid political climate of the early 1970s revived protest and socialist themes. The student uprising of October 14, 1973, the return to democracy, and the subsequent suppression on October 6, 1976, have provided the themes for much of T. p. up to the present. Naowarat Pongpaiboon has emerged as the most eloquent chronicler of these events ("Mere Movement," "The Day that Killed the Dove," "From Sunday to Monday: October 14, 1973"). Political and social crit. continue to serve as major themes of T. p. today, and poets continue to use both cl. and a variety of experimental verseforms.

ANTHOLOGIES AND TRANSLATIONS: *Magic Lotus, a Romantic Fantasy* (1949), *The Story of Phra Abhai Mani* (1952), *The Story of Khun Chang and Khun Phan* (1955), all ed. and tr. P. Chaya; *Khun Chang, Khun Phèn: La Femme, le héros et le vilain*, tr. J. K. Sibunruang (1960); P. na Nakhōn, *Prawat wannakhadī T.* (1964); R. Jones and R. Mendiones, *Intro. to T. Lit.* (1970); *Sang Thong*, tr. F. S. Ingersoll (1973); *Ramakien*, tr. J. M. Cadet (1982); *Mere Movement*, tr. N. Pongpaiboon (1984); *A Premier Book of Contemp. T. Verse*, ed. M. Umavigani et al. (1985); *Phādāēng Nāng Ai: A Thai-Isan Folk Epic in Verse*, tr. W. Tossa (1990).

HISTORY AND CRITICISM: H. H. Prince Bidyalankarana, "The Pastime of Rhyme-making and Singing in Rural Siam," *Jour. of the Siam Soc.* 20 (1926), "Sebha Recitation and the Story of Khun Chang Khun Phan," *Jour. of the Siam Soc.* 33 (1941); P. Schweisguth, *Étude sur la litt. siamoise* (1951); P. Anuman Rajadhon, *T. Lit. and Swasdi Raksa* (1953); P. Purachatra, "Thailand and Her Lit.," *Diliman Rev.* 6 (1958); J. N. Mosel, *A Survey of Cl. T. P.* (1959), *Trends and Structure in Contemp. T. P.* (1961); K. Wenk, *Die Metrik in der Thailändischen Dichtung* (1961), *Sunthọn Phū—ein T. Literat* (1985); T. H. Bofman, *The Poetics of the Ramakian* (1984); T. J. Hudak, "Poetic Conventions in T. *chan* Meters," *JAOS* 105 (1985), "The T. Corpus of *chan* Meters," *JAOS* 106 (1986), *The Indigenization of Pali Meters in T. P.* (1990). T.J.H.

THEMATICS. The modern study of themes (see THEME) and motifs (1965–) received its original impetus (1913–) from folklorists and scholars who based their concepts on the practice of Ger. *Stoffgeschichte*, the investigation of either prominent literary figures (Judith, Caesar, Elizabeth) or typical situations (father-son conflict) that recur throughout the centuries. They advanced working hypotheses (Aarne, Petersen, Thompson 1961); identified motifs as basic building blocks of lit. and classified them as textual units that could be anticipatory, referential (internal and external, central or core), ornamental, filler, situational, descriptive, or dynamic (Christensen, Petersen, Krogmann, Frenzel 1966, Lüthi); and published indexes and reference works (Raasch, Thompson, Bouty, Frenzel, Schmitt). Many studies traced the origin, recurrence, development, and variation of specific themes or motifs through centuries of Western lit. The outlook of these scholars was and remains historically oriented (Beller, Levin), since they stress the significance of the textual unit for the literary trad. and the history of ideas. As can be seen from the material collected in Daemmrich and Daemmrich (1987), the direction of research was influenced both by the often conflicting definitions proposed by leading scholars in the field and by the advances made in the numerous detailed analyses of specific themes or motifs in a given work, author, or period.

Changing practices in modern crit. (*explication de texte, werkimmanente Methode*, formalism, New Criticism, and sociological and psychoanalytic crit.) led to a greater awareness by thematologists of unique stylistic patterns and of the impact of sociopolitical forces on the transformation of literary themes or motifs. In the United States, several scholars provided systematic studies aimed toward a general theory of t. Zholkovsky demonstrated that all generic themes are rendered invariable through structural patterns and established that thematic analysis furnishes essential information for any structural model. Ziolkowski (1972, 1983) delineated the congruence of thematic textual organization during specific historical periods. Daemmrich and Daemmrich (1987) substantiated the reciprocal relationship between themes, figures, motifs, and motif sequences in the organization of texts; showed that themes are central organizational units; and confirmed the existence of schematized action sequences or basic strategies in texts which are aligned with long-established themes.

Thematic analysis has therefore (1) traced important stylistic patterns from specific childhood incidents and encounters in the lives of authors (Richard); (2) disclosed connections between individual psychic reality and cultural hist. (Feder); (3) identified similarities in metaphoric correlates in works not grouped together by literary historians (Petriconi, Falk, Fontaine, Wais, Ziolkowski); (4) established new information about period codes (Musschoot, Poulet); (5) showed that many thematic variations are possible even though a situation (e.g. a son's homecoming) and

event (murder) determine the textual situation (Frauenrath); (6) demonstrated that changing historical perspectives guide thematic preferences even though the figure can retain certain clearly identifiable features (Trousson 1964); (7) revealed the dynamic interaction between individual and collective consciousness (Todorov); and (8) established basic structural relationships between texts that are widely scattered throughout Western lit. (Trousson, Klotz). Beller and Falk have shown that themes recurring over long periods of time may retain their basic quality and frequently remain associated with identical images or motif clusters and analogous descriptive details. Yet most scholars recognize that the continuous redistribution and creative transformation of themes will lead to significant variations. The most ardent supporters of t. (Bachelard, Beller, Petriconi, Poulet, Trousson, Wais) consider the study of themes or motifs the central domain of lit. hist. By concentrating on the literary heritage gradually built up by the repetition and devel. of a theme or motif instead of biographical data, social conditions, or historical events, their studies focus on the impulses an author receives from the trad., point to the choices made, and develop a comparative literary typology that transcends national lits.

Since poets have linked heterogeneous themes with their appraisal of historical forces (Pound, *The Cantos* [1914–64]; T. S. Eliot, *The Waste Land* [1922]; Karl Krolow, *Herodot oder der Beginn von Geschichte* [1983]), have explored in individual poems such diverse themes as the awakening of spring, the joyous affirmation of life, death, madness, power, and war, and have articulated the emotions evoked by visions of the blue flower and shipwreck, it is apparent that poetry incorporates a great range of themes. However, the close reading of poetry originally encouraged the unwarranted transference of topical thematic analysis. For instance, an urn, a lamp, Napoleon, or a ship are not themes. The perception that beauty is enduring and may give direction to life (Keats, "Ode on a Grecian Urn" [1819]; Eduard Mörike, "Auf eine Lampe" [1846]) can be developed thematically. The extraordinary exertion of the will of an admired statesman (Hugo, "Bonaparte" [1822], "Ode à la colonne" [1827]), but also the collective resistance of the oppressed (Erkmann-Chatrain, "Le conscrit de 1813," "Waterloo" [1846]) can form the basis for themes. The helmsman facing the elements and contemplating either shipwreck or safe return may become the focal point for the thematic exploration of self-realization or failure in life (Goethe, "Seefahrt" [1776]; Alfred de Vigny, "La bouteille à la mer" [1854]; Tennyson, "The Voyage" [1864]). Detailed motif studies of poetry over the last several decades document that descriptive details and images serve as basic building blocks for motifs and themes which in turn determine structural patterns (Blumenberg, Daemmrich, Bänzinger,

Langford, Elliot, Reynolds).

There is growing critical awareness that themes may occur scattered over time, can be concentrated in a given epoch, and are also resurrected after long periods of disuse when an author's perception of changing institutions prompts their revaluation. In addition, t. increasingly recognizes that the effectiveness of motifs depends far more on their position and repetition, and on the relations they establish, than on any detail or feature from which they originate. T., then, can show true literary constants, significant motif transformations, and similarities as well as characteristic differences in works by authors far removed from each other in time and place. See THEME.

A. Aarne, *Leitfaden der vergleichenden Märchenforschung* (1913); A. Christensen, "Motif et thème," *Finnish Folklore Communications* 59 (1925); J. Petersen, "Das Motiv in der Dichtung," *Dichtung und Volkstum* 38 (1937); G. Bachelard, *L'Eau et les rêves* (1942); J.-P. Richard, *Littérature et sensation* (1954); S. Thompson, *Motif-Index of Folk Lit.* (1955–58); W. Krogmann, "Motiv," *Reallexikon*; A. Aarne and S. Thompson, *The Types of the Folktale* (1961); G. Poulet, *Les métamorphoses du cercle* (1961); J.-P. Weber, *Domaines thématiques* (1963); R. Trousson, *Un problème de littérature comparée* (1965), *Thèmes et mythes* (1981); E. Frenzel, *Stoff-, Motiv- und Symbolforschung* (1966), *Motive der Weltliteratur* (1976), *Stoffe der Weltliteratur* (1983)—thematological lexicon; E. Falk, *Types of Thematic Structure* (1969); V. Klotz, *Die erzählte Stadt* (1969); M. Beller, *Jupiter Tonans* (1979), "Thematologie," *Vergleichende Literaturwissenschaft*, ed. M. Schmeling (1981); *Thèmes et variations dans la poésie française*, ed. A. Raasch (1970); T. Todorov, *Introduction à la litt. fantastique* (1970); H. Petriconi, *Metamorphosen der Träume* (1971); M. Bouty, *Dictionnaire des oeuvres et des thèmes de la litt. française* (1972); H. Levin, "Thematics and Crit.," *Grounds for Comparison* (1972); T. Ziolkowski, *Fictional Transfigurations of Jesus* (1972), *Disenchanted Images* (1977), *Varieties of Literary T.* (1983); M.-M. Fontaine, *L'homme et la machine* (1973); M. Frauenrath, *Le fils assassiné* (1974); H. S. Daemmrich and I. Daemmrich, *Wiederholte Spiegelungen* (1978), *Themes and Motifs in Western Lit.: A Handbook* (1987), *Themen und Motive in der Literatur* (1987)—expanded ver. of the preceding; H. Blumenberg, *Schiffbruch mit Zuschauer* (1979); L. Feder, *Madness in Lit.* (1980); M. Lüthi, "Motiv, Zug, Thema," *Elemente der Lit.*, ed. A. J. Bisanz and R. Trousson (1980); H. Bänzinger, *Schloss, Haus, Bau* (1983); M. Langford, *La Poétique de l'animal* (1983); K. Wais, *Europäische Literatur im Vergleich* (1983); A. Elliot, "Isis Kuanon," *Paideuma* 13 (1984); A. Zholkovsky, *Themes and Texts* (1984); D. S. Reynolds, *Beneath the Am. Ren.* (1988).   H.S.D.

THEME. In common usage "t." refers simply to the subject or topic treated in a discourse or a part of it. Thus to speak of the t. of a poem may be only to give a brief answer to the question, "What is this poem about?" The t. of a poem may be trees, a Grecian urn, liberty, the growth of a poet's mind, the vanity of human wishes. But in literary studies, t. is also used in a number of more specialized senses, esp. as a recurrent element (or particular type of recurrent element) in literary works, and as the doctrinal content of a literary work. The first of these specialized senses is treated in the article THEMATICS.

Critics who use "t." in the second sense assume that all (good) literary works have a doctrinal content. In fables, apologues, parables, moralities, meditations, allegories, and many lyrics and dramatic monologues, this doctrinal content may receive explicit statement; in mimetic or representational genres it may be present only implicitly. In either case it is claimed that the doctrinal content is the true subject of the poem and is the element that deepens and gives significance to the experience of reading the poem. Further, the "central t." (a poem may reflect a number of related ts.) may be regarded as a formal principle—it governs the author's selection and ordering of all of the other components of the work (the concrete particulars of the poem operate as exemplars or symbols of the thematic content—see CONCRETE UNIVERSAL). A critic might point to a poem's t. by using a word or phrase, but for greater fullness and precision she will try to summarize a poem's doctrinal content in a sentence—a general proposition, an expression of attitude or evaluation, or a precept.

This conception of t. has appeared in crit. under a variety of names: "moral," "message," "precept," "thesis," "meaning," "interpretation," "sentence," "idea," "comment," etc. Over the history of crit., one or another of these terms has formed part of the vocabulary of most critics who assign a primary position to the extrinsic values of poetry. Much medieval, Ren., and neoclassical crit. was didactically oriented (see DIDACTICISM). Medieval literary theory, for example, conceived of poetry as an adjunct to religion and philosophy. The aim of the poet, like that of a preacher, should be to present persuasively a valid moral precept; his means is the use of attractive parable, allegory, or exemplum. The moral precept is the "t.," "nucleus," "sentence," "fruit," or "grain" of the poem.

Ren. didactic crit., of which Sidney's *Apologie for Poetrie* (1595) is a good example, was similar to the medieval position. The aim of human life, says Sidney, is virtuous action, and poetry is a discipline worthy of man's most serious attention because it is more effective than any other human learning in molding human behavior morally. Neoclassical crit., following Horace, identified pleasure and instruction as the double aims of poetry. This position resulted in a continued stress on the instrumental values of poetry, and the terms "moral" and "t." were used to point to the final cause of a poem and to its principle of unity (q.v.). Thus

Dryden: "The first rule which Bossu prescribes to the writer of an Heroic Poem, and which holds too by the same reason in all Dramatic Poetry, is to make the moral of the work: that is, to lay down to yourself what that precept of morality shall be, which you would insinuate into the people.... 'Tis the moral that directs the whole action of the play to one centre; and that action or fable is the example built upon the moral, which confirms the truth of it to our experience" ("The Grounds of Crit. in Tragedy" [1679]).

Modern critics identified with the New Criticism (q.v.) regard with suspicion expressions such as the "moral" or the "message" of a poem. But they do talk of poetry as a kind of knowledge, and, when induced to speak of the uses of poetry, they speak of its cognitive and moral values. As a consequence, they have found the term "t." (or "meaning," "significance," "interpretation") indispensable for pointing to the values and principle of unity in a poem. However, they warn that the poem, or at least the good poem, is not a mere rhetorical device for ornamenting a prosaic t. (see PARAPHRASE, HERESY OF) or making it more persuasive. The good poem does not assert its t. (see PSEUDO-STATEMENT). Rather, the poem should be regarded as fictive discourse (see FICTION) which dramatizes a human situation or moral problem. The purpose of the good poet is to explore the problem or situation in a particularized context. The net result may be simply a detailed diagnosis of the nature and complexities of the problem, though more often the poet comes up with a moral judgment or evaluation which is a possible solution to the problem. Such tentative solutions may also be called "ts."; however, these are only hypotheses which the good poem clarifies, tests, qualifies, and subjects to the fires of irony (q.v.). In this process of testing, the original t. may be so qualified that no general or paraphrastic statement of it will represent it accurately.

The assumption of traditional doctrinal thematism—that all good poems must have an explicit or implicit moral, religious, or philosophical t. as their unifying principle—has been attacked by a variety of other theorists. Proponents of aestheticism (q.v.), which by now has had a history of over 200 years, have argued that the function of poetry is not to provide an interpretation of life but to generate an aesthetic experience (thematic elements may of course contribute to the intensity of this experience and may have independent cognitive value as well). Also, critics of the Chicago School (q.v.) vigorously condemned the monism of thematic crit., which, they argued, reduces all the varied forms of lit. to a single type.

Modern nihilism has produced absurdism and a variety of other schools of poetry whose manifestoes and practice show little respect for the assumptions of doctrinal thematism. Perloff analyzes many of the strategies used by these poets to frustrate a reader's attempts to discover a thematic unity in their poems—foregrounding, for example, the qualities of the medium rather than content, the part rather than the whole, the concrete detail rather than the concept, vagueness and uncontrolled suggestiveness rather than explicitness and precision, obscurity (q.v.) and mystification rather than intelligibility, and incoherence (through omissions, inconsistencies, discontinuities) rather than unity and closure. The result is an indeterminate text. Some of its effects are mystery, bewilderment, promise of a meaning which is never fulfilled (unless, paradoxically, meaninglessness is itself considered a meaning). Indeterminacy (q.v.), undecidability, unreadableness are also key concepts in much poststructuralist crit. (see DECONSTRUCTION). But while Perloff studies the poetics of a group of poets who deliberately created indeterminate texts, other theorists have argued that the lessons of modern epistemology, semiotics, and the psychology of the reading process are that all texts are indeterminate. A text may *appear* to be centered—to present a coherent thematic development—but a close reading will always reveal ambiguities, irrelevancies, contradictory implications, and obscurities that deconstruct the surface coherence and send the reader wandering down the paths of a labyrinth from which, she soon discovers, there is no exit. The search for a determinate thematic synthesis of a text is futile; interpretations cannot be verified or falsified; the reader should give up her demand for significance and simply enjoy the linguistic play for which a polysemous text provides the opportunity. If she must have significance, some deconstructionists suggest, she may regard all texts as allegories of the reading process with undecidability or indeterminacy as the explicit or implicit central t. of every text. See also INTERPRETATION; SEMANTICS AND POETRY; SEMIOTICS, POETIC.

R. S. Crane, *The Langs. of Crit. and the Structure of Poetry* (1953); Frye; M. C. Beardsley, *Aesthetics* (1958); M. Krieger, *The Tragic Vision* (1960); S. Sacks, *Fiction and the Shape of Belief* (1964); G. Graff, *Poetic Statement and Critical Dogma* (1970); C. Brooks, *A Shaping Joy* (1971); Culler; R. Levin, *New Readings vs. Old Plays* (1979); M. Perloff, *The Poetics of Indeterminacy: Rimbaud to Cage* (1981); J. Culler, *On Deconstruction* (1982); C. Norris, *The Deconstructive Turn* (1983).   F.GU.

THEME (ORAL-FORMULAIC). See FORMULA.

THEORETICAL CRITICISM. See THEORY.

THEORY.

    I. SCOPE
    II. DEVELOPMENT
    III. MAJOR ISSUES
        A. *Relation of Literary Text to Historical Context*
        B. *Content and Function of Literary Texts*

THEORY

I. SCOPE. Th. of crit. may reasonably be said to include any reflection upon or analysis of general issues which arise in the crit. or study of lit., e.g. questions of the nature and function of lit. and its relation to other aspects of a culture; of the purposes, procedures and validity of crit.; of the relation of literary texts to their authors and historical contexts; of the meaning and value of literary texts (see TEXTUALITY); of the nature and importance of genres (see GENRE); and many others.

There are two modes of theoretical work: the one is advocative or assertive, the other analytical. In the former mode, new general views of some aspect of crit. or lit. are proposed: a th. is advocated. In the latter mode, theories, new and old, are examined and analyzed (see ANALYSIS). The two modes are not entirely separable (new ideas are likely to originate from at least a rudimentary new analysis of a problem, while on the other hand deeper analysis of old ideas may result in new theoretical suggestions), but in particular instances and even at particular times one mode or the other may predominate. Whenever a sense has arisen that the practice of crit. must change and that critical efforts should be redirected in important ways, th. becomes more advocative and prescriptive in tone; but after the initial impetus of a movement for change has been spent, th. generally returns to its analytic mode.

Thus in the early period of the New Criticism (q.v.), "th." was in practice understood to refer to the proposals for change in the priorities of crit. that had been advanced by the New Critics, but with time this identification gradually weakened. Similarly, when the deconstructionist Paul de Man subsequently complained of the "resistance to th.," what he meant was the resistance to his own preferred viewpoint in crit., namely deconstruction (q.v.); conversely, th. is often attacked because it is confused with a given critical agenda favored by particular theorists. Because of this recurring tendency to confuse th. with one of its latest manifestations, it is probably best to regard th. as an activity which is primarily analytical in character. Seen in this way, th. is as much a part of the field of lit. crit. as of any other field of inquiry; analysis and evaluation of the concepts and practices of crit. are necessary parts of the critic's intelligence. The identification of th. primarily with analysis has the further advantage of allowing us to see that its value for literary studies lies in the quality and depth of the analysis, and in the increased understanding which results, rather than in commitment to any particular critical position. Moreover, when commitment looms too large (as is commonly the case with, for example, crit. linked to political or social activism), the quality of analysis and with it the usefulness of th. often suffers as it degenerates into mere case-making for a partisan purpose.

As against the view taken here that th. in the field of crit. functions in much the same way as it does in other fields—i.e. to analyze the concepts and procedures of the field and thereby possibly to modify or replace them—attitudes are sometimes expressed and even claims made to the effect that th. of crit. is categorically dissimilar from th. in other fields. At its most extreme, th. of crit. is regarded and judged as a species of imaginative lit. Thus Sircello has argued ("The Poetry of Th.," *JAAC* [1984])—albeit mainly on the basis of a single (yet by no means untypical) example—that literary th. is in general defective as th. in that it generates ideas without the analysis and argument needed to support and explicate them. Excesses and inadequacies of this kind have occasionally led to the blanket claim that th. of crit. is not a useful activity (see Mitchell 1985). A more limited version of this rejection of th. is embodied in some forms of pluralism (q.v.) which advocate eclectic acceptance of a plurality of ideas rather than attempting to analyze their relative strengths and weaknesses. None of these attitudes or claims succeeds in establishing a separate status for th. in the field of crit. Immediate or temporary deficiencies of literary th. should not be allowed to define its scope, nor should the occasional failure to distinguish the function of imaginative lit. from that of theoretical analysis prevent us from differentiating these quite different functions; and the scope, usefulness, and possible results of theoretical analysis can never be prejudged or restricted a priori before its results have been examined in each particular instance of its use. Finally, the questions arising in th. of crit. are sometimes also discussed under the rubric of "metacriticism" (q.v.); it would be difficult, however, to demarcate reliably a separate set of issues specific to metacrit.

Because literary texts touch on virtually every facet of human existence, th. of crit. is inextricably connected to broad theoretical issues in a number of other disciplines. For example, the questions to what degree knowledge can be objective, or how evaluation relates to description, take th. of crit. into areas explored more typically by philosophers; questions of style and meaning take it into linguistic th.; questions of human behavior, both of authors and fictional characters, take it into the realms of psychology and ethics (see ETHICS AND CRITICISM); and questions of the structure of the societies portrayed in lit. take critical th. into the territory of political philosophy, sociology, and even historiography. Understandably, then, references to theorists in other fields abound in th. of crit., and some of those theorists (most notably Freud and Marx) have even become the major determinants of particular theories of crit.

There is, however, both a gain and a loss for crit. in this cross-disciplinary appropriation. The positive results are easily stated: through being able to draw on the results of theoretical reflection in so many fields, literary th. gains in diversity and complexity, finds ready-made many useful ideas developed in other contexts, and may in fact contribute to the consolidation of thought. Yet in practice these potential gains are frequently turned into liabilities because of the difficulty of mastering the full context and meaning of ideas in so many different fields; the consequence has often been an amateurish misuse of borrowed concepts. Instances of such misappropriation in the 1960s, '70s, and '80s have included the widespread garbling of the ideas of the linguist Ferdinand de Saussure and misguided polemics against outdated notions of objective truth in knowledge. It has also proved too easy for literary scholars to overlook the obsolescence of the ideas they borrow. A case in point is the heightened interest in Marxism (see MARXIST CRITICISM) among literary scholars at a time when its importance as a political and economic philosophy declined precipitously, after a seemingly decisive test of its viability in a number of nations.

II. DEVELOPMENT. Three stages can be distinguished in the devel. of th. of crit. In the first stage, general reflections on the nature of lit. and of crit. are in the main sporadic by-products of the literary scene, often arising from the manifestoes of particular authors and literary groups or from contemporary commentary upon them. Examples occur from the earliest times, Aristotle's *Poetics* and Horace's *Ars poetica* being the most notable Western examples; even Herder's still influential th. of cultural relativism originated in the launching of the Ger. Sturm und Drang (q.v.) movement.

A new stage is reached when, in the early 20th c., th. of crit. begins to be a more self-conscious activity, one now more independent of the creative writing of the day. The first organized group of theorists for whom the devel. of a conceptual framework for the understanding of lit. became an issue formed the school which came to be known as Rus. Formalism (q.v.). The dispersal of this group (due to the increasing hostility of the Bolshevik regime) led to the founding of the Prague Linguistic Circle, a group later known as the Prague School (see STRUCTURALISM), which took a similar view of the goals of critical th. This more systematic attitude to th. spread to Germany, where a spate of theoretical works appeared in the Twenties as a result of the example of Oskar Walzel, to England, where I. A. Richards was active, and then to America, where former members of the pioneer groups of Eastern Europe such as Roman Jakobson and René Wellek were influential. With the publication in 1947 of *Th. of Lit.* by Wellek and Austin Warren, it became clear that the systematic analysis of theoretical issues had reached a sophisticated level. Yet th. of crit. was still very much a minority interest; most Am. critics at this time were indifferent or even mildly hostile to what they viewed as abstract theorizing.

A distinct third phase is reached in the 1970s, when th. of crit. in America and elsewhere came under the influence of Fr. poststructuralist theories, esp. deconstruction. France had traditionally been the most conservative of the major European nations in literary study, at first scarcely taking any part in the 20th-c. theoretical devel., until a sudden outburst of theoretical speculation produced a series of influential thinkers in Claude Lévi-Strauss, Roland Barthes, Jacques Derrida, Jacques Lacan, and Michel Foucault. Derrida, a philosopher, was particularly influential in Am. lit. crit. and th., though his impact both in his own field and in Fr. crit. was comparatively minor. This new influx of energy into the theoretical scene proved infectious, in part because elsewhere th. had become stagnant; the momentum of the second phase of critical th. had for some time seemed spent. The most important consequence of this new energy was that th. for the first time became accepted as an indispensable part of the knowledge and outlook of any critic, a state of affairs which the theorists of the prior phase had not been able to achieve. A second major consequence of this new influence was a change in the terms of the debate; the vocabulary of th. was now heavily influenced by Fr. sources.

In this transition from the second to the third phase of th. there are gains and losses too. The influx of new ideas from France certainly revitalized a stagnant field, but the adoption of large amounts of new vocabulary also made for a damaging discontinuity in the devel. of theoretical understanding. A widespread sense of beginning afresh with new terminology allowed much important work of the second phase to be forgotten. To take one example: the newer idea of the "death of the author" was crude compared to the earlier, more complex, and better developed debate over the "Intentional Fallacy" (see INTENTION). And while th. in its third phase achieved far wider currency than it had ever achieved before, this gain has to be weighed against the loss in depth of analysis that comes with undue commitment to whatever vogues happen to be current in crit.

III. MAJOR ISSUES. Though the scope of th. of crit. is broad, a small group of basic issues continue to be the focus of attention. What follows is a brief statement of those issues and an outline of some of the more important positions taken with respect to them.

A. *Relation of Literary Text to Historical Context.* The most significant and far-reaching division of opinion among theorists is found here; ramifications extend to virtually every other aspect of literary th. One group of theorists views the literary text strictly in relation to the social and historical context in which it arose, interpreting the text mainly or even solely within that context as something which speaks to the events and concerns of its time. In the opposing view, the fact that literary texts rise above their own time to speak in a vital way to future ages makes their relevant context the broader one of a whole culture—and possibly all of civilization—rather than any particular historical moment. On this view, the local, transitory concerns of the historical moment would give too restrictive an account of a text's meaning, one that could not account for the vivid interest of readers long after other contemporaneous texts and concerns had been forgotten.

Within the former group, an older, more general stance can be distinguished from a newer one which focuses on very specific issues in the context. Critics committed to the older stance used historical information to elucidate the text without having fixed assumptions about the particular kinds of information that would be useful or relevant. This approach originated in Herder's cultural relativism (see CULTURAL CRITICISM) and developed into the literary-historical orthodoxy of the 19th and early 20th cs. Critics committed to the newer stance differ from the older in two important respects. Instead of accepting an eclectic, undefined use of history, these critics focus on clearly defined historical factors relevant to a particular political ideology; and instead of working from context to text with the aim of elucidating the text, they reverse the direction so that the text is used to illuminate the workings of the social context. For example, in both Marxist and feminist (see FEMINIST POETICS) versions of this view, texts illustrate the assumptions on class or gender of their time and the resulting contradictions and strains in society, or else they show attempts by their authors to overcome them.

Each of these positions has been subject to crit. A major weakness of the older historicism (q.v.) has been seen as its lack of focus and inability to account for the continuing relevance of great writers to future ages. Conversely, its antihistoricist opponents themselves have difficulty in dealing with matters of lang., taste, tone, and setting, features which seem to require reference to the era in which the text was written. The newer versions of historicist crit. encounter different problems: particularly difficult are the complaints that the content of very diverse texts is arbitrarily restricted to a narrow set of political issues (see section B. below) and that the distinctive difference between literary texts and other texts, as well as other kinds of historical evidence, is ignored. The more general human as opposed to merely historical interest of literary texts is as problematic for one version of historicism as for the other.

B. *Content and Function of Literary Texts.* These two issues cannot be separated: a view of one entails a view of the other. The oldest approach is based on the simple observation that we both enjoy literary texts to a high degree, and that we also seem to learn something about human life from them. The essential basis of this th. can already be seen in classical and neoclassical poet-ics (qq.v.): in the Horatian formula, poetry delights and instructs. This has been a very durable view, and if its two key terms are formulated somewhat more broadly, it is still viable. We can expand the verb "to delight" to include other aspects of a strong and immediate response to poetry: to involve, intrigue, move, fascinate. Similarly, by "instruct" we can also understand "cause to reflect," or even "afford greater insight into human life." The advantage of this approach is its avoidance of any restriction of focus; there is no aspect of human existence that may not be the subject of a literary text and the occasion for both involvement and reflection. By contrast, the chief logical difficulty with other views of the content and function of lit. lies in their departure from this level of generality and in the problems which they encounter in finding adequate justification for the narrowing of focus they require.

Most theories which attempt a more specific and delimited statement of the content and function of literary texts (and thus of the pre-eminent concerns of lit. crit.) generally take some aspect of political or social content as their chosen theme. Within the broad group of such approaches, some distinctions can be made. A focus on lit. as reflection of or response to social divisions and political conditions is characteristic of Marxist crit.; lit. as a means of social control and maintenance of the established order is the focus both of many feminist critics and of totalitarian governments, the former deploring, the latter valuing lit. which functions in this way. The "New Historicism" recommends a primary focus on lit. as an expression of power relations in historical situations.

The diversity of literary texts presents difficulties for theories which narrow the essential content of literary texts to a single factor. While some texts may reinforce aspects of the status quo of a particular culture or era, great writers have more usually had strained relations with the reigning moralities and power structures of their time. Plato went so far as to say that poetry was always disruptive of the social order, but this too is a single-factor analysis that misrepresented a more diverse reality. The classic argument for the primacy of the single factor is that given by critics with political interests or commitments: "everything is political." But arguments of this kind confuse generality and priority. The fact that any text or action has a political dimension and thus political consequences does not entail the quite different conclusion that political considerations take precedence over all others. Many other kinds of considerations are equally general—there are psychological, economic, ecological, and many other dimensions to every act.

In short, power relations are the only issue in lit. crit. only to those whose only concern they are; literary texts have many other concerns, and it is difficult to justify a decision taken in advance of looking at the particular text that a given concern must predominate. In fact, this analysis is paradigmatic for all theories which attempt to narrow the essential content and function of lit. to specific factors; it is as relevant to Freudian crit. (see PSYCHOLOGICAL CRITICISM) as it is to the obsession of some New Critics with paradox and ambiguity (qq.v.). It seems best to regard lit. as a kind of catholic forum for presentation of, absorption in, and reflection on any of life's issues and problems. Such may be its function. If so, its content must be as diverse as humanity itself, and a critic who becomes fixated a priori on any single factor does violence to this diversity.

C. *Definition of Literature*. The question "What is lit.?" has been a perennial concern of th. To the extent that it asks for information about a category the existence of which is assumed, it is only the same question as that immediately preceding. A quite distinct issue arises if the question is understood as one of definition: what is it that sets lit. apart from other texts? Early attempts to define lit. assumed that a definition should focus on those features common to all members of a category; these features would then be the criteria for deciding whether a given text is or is not lit. This approach breaks down because no aspect of either form or content can be found which is common to all literary texts and only to them. Attempts to specify certain literary kinds of form and organization as the criteria have sometimes seemed plausible—versification, for example, seems an obvious example in the case of verse—but only at the expense of being too vague to permit a clear test. The most extreme such case was the Rus. Formalist notion of "literariness," but this suggested criterion is clearly circular.

Two reactions to this impasse accept the general approach to definition from which it results, but argue that "lit." represents a special case. The first is that of W. B. Gallie, who called concepts like this one "essentially contested concepts," concepts whose purpose is to be argued about ("Art as an Essentially Contested Concept," *Philosophical Q.* 6 [1956]). This solution is ingenious but has the drawback of being intuitively wrong: mention of the word "lit." is met with a ready comprehension that does not inevitably provoke an intellectual squabble. The second, more recent, consists in the view that "lit." is not really a category at all, for literary texts are not separable from other texts. This view is congenial to those groups of critics whose orientation is political. For their purposes, the difference between lit. and other historical documents may not matter, since one kind of evidence of political forces at play in a culture is in principle as good as another. The drawback to this view is that its inability to distinguish between Shakespeare and an Elizabethan cookbook erodes its legitimacy as having any claim to the name of lit. crit. The fact that two things are equally relevant for the purposes of a political analysis does not mean that there are no other categorical differences between them.

The problem would lose much of its logical difficulty if we recognized that the basis of categorization is as often a matter of the common purposes of things that are grouped together as it is of their common properties. A common pattern of use is defining in the case of many everyday categories, e.g. clothes, tables, or vegetables; individual examples share only our expectations of them. The definition of literary texts should therefore focus on a common pattern of use (Ellis 1974). Our ordinary use of lang. is directly related to the immediate context of our lives, and is governed by the purposes of that daily context; having achieved its local purpose, a piece of lang. is rarely recalled except when that context itself is studied in retrospect. By contrast, the pattern of use characteristic of literary texts consists in recurrent attention without any necessary concern for the local, practical give-and-take of their original context; this indicates a more general reflection on their human content and meaning. The category "Fr. lit.," in this view, is simply the group of texts around which a consensus develops on the part of readers that they can and should be used as lit. A consequence of this view would be that the problem of definition is closely related to that of evaluation.

D. *Intention and Biography*. One of the most characteristic features of the second phase of literary th. was an intensive debate over the relevance for literary interpretation (q.v.) of the author's intention. W. K. Wimsatt and Monroe Beardsley's seminal article "The Intentional Fallacy" (1946; rpt. in Wimsatt's *The Verbal Icon* [1954]) is one of the most celebrated essays in all th. of lit. Wimsatt and Beardsley argued that the intention of the author was neither available nor desirable as a standard by which to interpret and judge a literary text. Two major claims supported their argument. First, the author is not necessarily the best judge of what she or he has done; the author's inside knowledge may be outweighed by the outsider's greater perspective. Second, the text communicates its meaning through the conventions of lang., and those conventions are public not personal in nature. A text means what it actually says, not what its author later thinks she or he meant to say but perhaps did not.

The main arguments against this view have been that we normally seek to resolve ambiguities or uncertainties in lang. by asking the speaker for clarification, and that we generally interpret what is said in the light of what we think the speaker intends. The nature of the dispute was obscured, however, by a practical matter which had no necessary relationship to the logic of these arguments. Biographically oriented critics often used quite brief, undeveloped statements by authors as the key to a literary text. But the discrepancy between a short, simple authorial statement and the longer and more extensively developed literary text (itself also the author's lang.) would have made much intentional crit. seem reductive and primitive regardless of the validity of the theoretical arguments about intention. That the fullest and most explicit evidence of intent is the lang. of the text itself might have been obvious to both sides in the dispute, but in practice intentionalists did not give this fact due weight; anti-intentionalist th. was thus motivated in large measure by a practical rather than a theoretical concern.

The proper focus of the theoretical issue here is the special status of literary texts. Ordinary uses of lang. have no fixed boundaries, which means that it is always possible to seek amplification or clarification of any given verbal sequence by looking more broadly at what came before and after it. The question then becomes to what extent it can be said that literary texts have firm boundaries (say, the first and last lines of a poem) which do not permit a reader to add more text or information (whatever its source) at her or his wish. The logic of the intentionalist case requires one answer, that of the anti-intentionalist another.

After the long and productive exploration of the logic of both sides of this question in the second phase of literary th., discussion in the third has been rather less useful. The issue is often framed or articulated dramatically, but its content is generally limited to the question of whether the text has a stable and delimitable meaning, understood as authorial meaning (see MEANING, POETIC; SEMANTICS AND POETRY). In effect, the matter of intention is confused with the quite separate issue of the nature of critical knowledge (discussed in section *E*. below). Recent feminist th. has taken both sides of the question. One view holds that to take a text in the context of its author's intent is to be committed to a patriarchal notion of authority, while the opposing view insists that to ignore author is to ignore gender. Both appear to be equally arbitrary, and here the damage done by the lack of continuity between the second and third phases of literary th. is at its most apparent: in neither case is any contact made with the analysis of intention already well developed in crit. before 1965.

E. *Criticism as a Form of Knowledge.* Much has been written about the status of lit. crit. and history: does it give us knowledge in the same sense as the kinds of knowledge we expect in other fields of study, or does it give us something else, and if so, what? The most persistent opinion has been and still is that typified by Harry Levin's assertion (*Why Lit. Crit. is not an Exact Science* [1967]) that literary crit. is not an exact science; nevertheless, from time to time, groups of critics have arisen whose instinct has been to put crit. on a more systematic basis. These two basic positions have alternated as action and reaction throughout Western poetics. The most recent phase of this cycle has evoked some strident denunciations of the delusions of objectivity in past crit., but this is only a reprise of the majority view of the past (see

SUBJECTIVITY AND OBJECTIVITY).

The orthodoxy of the 19th c. was a kind of synthesis of both poles. Lit. hist. and biography afforded genuine knowledge, but crit., in the sense of a critic's writing about the meaning and impact of a literary text, was inherently an impressionistic and subjective matter. It was precisely this defeatism which made the literary historian cling to biographical and historical fact. With the turn of the 20th c., the orthodox synthesis began to break up, but two quite different tendencies emerged. In Germany, critics began to question the assumed quasi-scientific objectivity of lit. hist. Reacting against what had become a rigidly positivist climate, Wilhelm Dilthey (*Einleitung in die Geisteswissenschaft* [1883]) argued that lit. hist. was unlike science in that it demanded empathy and imagination (qq.v.) if the spirit of an age was to be grasped.

But elsewhere the challenge was mostly to the other half of the older synthesis, namely the notion that crit. was irredeemably subjective. A major thrust of the New Criticism, for example, was a rejection of defeatism about knowledge of the text. This reaction manifested itself in intense attention to "close reading" of texts, in the devel. of a vocabulary of technical terms for crit., and in a refusal to rely on biography—in part because that reliance was the result of assuming that text-oriented crit. could only be impressionistic. Another notable article by Wimsatt and Beardsley, "The Affective Fallacy" (1949; also in Wimsatt 1954), argued that the qualities of the text, not the response of the reader, were the central concern of crit. (see AFFECTIVE FALLACY). The culmination of Anglo-Am. New Criticism's search for a more systematic study of lit. is Northrop Frye's *Anatomy of Crit.* (1957), an ambitious attempt to develop a taxonomy of literary forms, now more admired for its ambition than its accomplishment.

Even before the New Critics, the Rus. Formalists had also sought to make literary study systematic, and when, many decades later, a reaction against 19th-c. literary historicism finally appeared in France, it took a similar form, beginning with Claude Lévi-Strauss' attempt to analyze the basic patterns of narratives (*Anthropologie structurale* [1958]). The analogy here was clearly that of empirical science: Lévi-Strauss was looking for the basic building-blocks, the atomic structure, of narrative. Doubts about Lévi-Strauss' system soon arose, however, as his choice of underlying patterns came to seem arbitrary; some details of the plot of a narrative were declared essential while others were discarded to make them fit a common pattern, but it was hard to justify radically divergent treatment of elements which did not inherently seem very different.

In the late 1960s, a sharp reaction set in against the over-ambitious, systematizing tendencies of Frye and of Fr. structuralism. The new mood soon became one of disparaging the possibility of objective knowledge and even of determining what a literary text means (see INDETERMINACY). So strong was this reaction that even social activist critics joined in the denunciation of certainty and objectivity, even though this made their positions contradictory; any determined pursuit of a social goal requires a firm conviction that that goal is correct and (in this case) that the "oppression" to be overcome is a fact. A further manifestation of this radical change was the rise of a school of crit. (see READER-RESPONSE CRITICISM) devoted to the idea that literary texts are indeterminate and that it is the creative role of the reader rather than the text which supplies meaning. This trend was reinforced by some aspects of deconstruction, but in its essentials it was a return to the view of the relation of text to reader found in 19th-c. lit. hist.; and the criticisms of Wimsatt and Beardsley are still just as difficult for it to answer. Another strand of deconstructive crit. suggested a somewhat different goal for crit. It assumed that we grasp what is important only when we have penetrated to that concealed level at which all texts undermine and embrace the reverse of what they appear to say on the surface. But it is not clear that such a rigid prescription must be appropriate to all lang. and hence all texts, and only this uniformity prevents its being subsumed under the more general notion that we should always make the effort to respond to all that is there in a text. The considerable vogue achieved by deconstructive crit. after its introduction to Am. crit. in 1967 began to decline in the 1980s and was effectively at an end with the publication of critiques by Ellis (1989) and Lehman (1991).

In general, the question of crit. as a possible form of knowledge remains one that has not been well explored. Much more visible than serious analysis of the issues have been the mood swings and fashions of the field, ranging from an attraction to the controlled methods and empirical verification of the physical and social sciences to an equally extreme distaste for and rejection of them. Throughout, discussion has been hampered by both unrealistic notions of the mechanical quality of scientific procedure which do not allow for the role of imagination and conceptualizing in the devel. of hypotheses, and equally unrealistic notions of crit. as an imaginative activity which ignore the role of disciplined, controlled thought, without which the imagination would wander aimlessly.

The most sober attempt to develop a careful view of the procedure of lit. crit. is still that of Leo Spitzer (*Linguistics and Lit. Hist.* [1948]). Spitzer suggested that the procedure of crit., unlike that of science, was circular: we proceed from general impressions of the text to careful inspection of specific features of it, which then leads to amended and improved general ideas, which in turn lead us to look again at other parts of the text. Spitzer called this the "hermeneutic circle" (see TWENTIETH-CENTURY POETICS). This view of criti-

cal procedure is a sophisticated one, and it shows very well the weakness of a reader-response crit. which makes the reader's response a dead end. What Spitzer did not see was that he had described the typical method of the sciences—hypothesis and experiment—though to be sure in terms which were far superior to the misconceptions about scientific method that have been predominant in th. of crit.

F. *Evaluation.* Predominant attitudes toward evaluation (q.v.) in crit. are markedly different in the three phases of the history of literary th. In the first phase, evaluation of works of art is assumed to be central to crit.; there is strong interest both in the nature of concepts which represent the value of works of art (e.g. beauty, the aesthetic experience), and in normative theories of poetry (e.g. how should a tragedy be constructed?). In the second phase, skepticism arises about the justification for value judgments and normative poetics; now crit. becomes more descriptive in character. In the most recent phase, evaluation becomes a politicized idea, and interest turns to the canon (q.v.) of great works as the repository of evaluations reflecting the attitudes of dominant social groups.

The archetype of normative crit. is Aristotle's *Poetics*, which sets out the basis for composing and thus also for evaluating tragedy. Similar normative treatises are found throughout the early phase of th., usually accompanying each new literary movement. While intended evaluatively, they are actually descriptions of the practice of a particular school, each new manifesto demonstrating the arbitrariness of its predecessor while concealing its own. Interest in theories of beauty and of an aesthetic experience distinguishable from other kinds of experiences begins in the 18th c. (see NEOCLASSICAL POETICS). The most interesting of such theories is that of Schiller, whose *Briefe über die ästhetische Erziehung des Menschen* (Letters on the Aesthetic Education of Man, 1793–95) is a bold and intriguing attempt to relate aesthetic experience (and thus the value of art) both to cognition and to the moral sense through the interplay of the two. The 20th c., however, has witnessed a collapse in critical receptivity to both beauty as an aesthetic ideal and the idea of a distinct aesthetic state.

The temper of the second period in this regard is best exemplified by Northrop Frye, for whom serious crit. is a form of knowledge and thus descriptive, while evaluative crit. is the province of journalists. Frye granted that evaluation was presupposed by a critic's choosing to give attention to this text rather than that, but masterpieces had already been separated from mediocrities by the test of time before the arrival of the modern critic on the scene. Frye's priorities are clearly parallel to those of early analytic philosophy; in A. J. Ayer's exposition of logical positivism, for example, descriptive statements are the basic form of lang.,

THEORY

while evaluative statements are mere expressions of emotive response without cognitive content (*Lang., Truth, and Logic* [1936]). For Ayer as for Frye, therefore, evaluative lang. is something of an indulgence and thus too close to subjectivism (see TASTE). Later analytic work sought to rescue evaluative statements from this low status by distinguishing different uses of lang., one of which was appraisive. While more respectful toward evaluation, this view still denied that it had cognitive content, and thus seemed unable to account for our intuitive belief that some writers really are better than others. This puzzle led many theorists to try to reduce evaluative statements to descriptive ones by finding descriptive "criteria" of value, but none have been generally convincing because the criteria themselves (e.g. "complexity") were covertly evaluative (see SIMPLICITY AND COMPLEXITY).

Elsewhere this writer has suggested that evaluation becomes such a puzzling issue only because of a misconception about the status of general value judgments such as "X is good" (1974). The unspoken assumption in aesthetics and critical th. has often been that general value judgments constitute a higher order of statement than more specific ones, which deal with the value of particular aspect of a particular thing for a certain purpose. But this is not the case: the more general the evaluative statement, the more it functions as a kind of brief reduction and summary of a complex situation that would need more specific information to do it justice. The hierarchy would then be reversed: brief summary accounts are cognitively inferior to the fuller account that they summarize. They are well suited only to certain practical purposes, such as the decision to buy this novel rather than that to read on vacation, or to include this book rather than that in a syllabus. They are, however, not well suited at all to more precise thought about literary value, for while they do have cognitive content, that content is too imprecise for serious purposes. The mistake of past th. has been to confuse the practical usefulness of summary evaluations with their cognitive usefulness. If we treat summary judgments as vague and indistinct starting points that are quickly left behind rather than grandiose conclusions up to which everything must lead, their mystery vanishes. The unbridgeable gap between descriptive and evaluative statements then resolves into a scale whose points differ only in specificity or generality, and all description becomes part of evaluation. In the same way the separation of "aesthetic" and more material judgments can be broken down, for this too depends on overemphasizing the distinctness and priority of judgments of the most general form.

Th. near the end of the 20th c. has seen a revival of the importance of evaluation, but this has been accompanied by a serious restriction in the concept of value. Now the value of literary texts is seen largely in terms of relevance to certain social and political goals. A major focus of attention has been the traditional "canon" of great works, often seen as both embodying and perpetuating the anti-egalitarian values of politically dominant groups (e.g. the upper class, esp. the educated university elite; the white population of Western societies; men rather than women). This attitude rests on claims about the world of experience rather than on any new theoretical or conceptual analysis of the nature of lit., and as a result it stands or falls on the factual accuracy of those claims. Many of them can be questioned. For example, governments have more often viewed writers and artists as troublesome subversives than willing propagandists for the social order; racism and male dominance are more blatant in non-Western than in Western cultures; and in general the spread of egalitarian values has been a consequence of the Enlightenment, in which educated elite groups played a leading role. The view that lit. has been an agent of harmful social control misses the point. The value of lit. lies rather in the fact that it does not impose a controlling uniformity of outlook on us, but instead through its sheer diversity challenges our imagination; in this it provokes and moves us in unexpected ways which broaden our intellectual, emotional, aesthetic, and moral horizons.

See now AUTONOMY; CRITICISM; CULTURAL CRITICISM; DECONSTRUCTION; ETHICS AND CRITICISM; EXPLICATION; METACRITICISM; PLURALISM; POETICS; POETRY, THEORIES OF; ROMANTIC AND POSTROMANTIC POETICS; TWENTIETH-CENTURY POETICS.

Richards; O. Walzel, *Das Wortkunstwerk* (1926); W. Kayser, *Das sprachliche Kunstwerk* (1948); S. Hyman, *The Armed Vision* (1948); F. R. Leavis, *The Common Pursuit* (1952); Crane; Empson; W. K. Wimsatt, Jr., *The Verbal Icon* (1954); Wellek; Wellek and Warren; Frye; M. C. Beardsley, *Aesthetics* (1958); R. Wellek, *Concepts of Crit.* (1963); *Critical Th. Since Plato*, ed. H. Adams (1971); J. M. Ellis, *The Th. of Lit. Crit.: A Logical Analysis* (1974), *Against Deconstruction* (1989); W. Iser, *The Implied Reader* (tr. 1974); *Structuralism and Since*, ed. J. Sturrock (1979); *The Reader in the Text*, ed. I. Crosman and S. Suleiman (1980); V. Erlich, *Rus. Formalism*, 3d ed. (1981); *What Is Crit.?* ed. P. Hernadi (1981); T. Todorov, *Fr. Literary Th. Today* (tr. 1982); J. Culler, *On Deconstruction* (1982); T. Eagleton, *Literary Th.: An Intro.* (1983)—Marxist; *Against Th.*, ed. W. J. T. Mitchell (1985); *Making a Difference: Feminist Lit. Crit.*, ed. G. Greene and C. Kahn (1985); *The New Feminist Crit.*, ed. E. Showalter (1985); *Critical Th. Since 1965*, ed. H. Adams and L. Searle (1986); F. Crews, *Skeptical Engagements* (1986); *The Current in Crit.*, ed. C. Koelb and V. Lokke (1987); *20th-C. Literary Th.: An Introd. Anthol.*, ed. V. Lambropoulos and D. Miller (1987); W. C. Booth, *The Company We Keep* (1988); *Théorie littéraire*, ed. M. Angenot et al. (1989); *The*

THEORY OF VERSE

New Historicism, ed. A. H. Veeser (1989); Literary Th. Today, ed. P. Collier and H. Geyer-Ryan (1990); G. S. Morson and C. Emerson, Mikhail Bakhtin (1990); D. Lehman, Signs of the Times: Deconstruction and the Fall of Paul de Man (1991).
J.M.E.

THEORY OF VERSE. See PROSODY.

THESIS. See ARSIS AND THESIS.

THODDAID. See AWDL.

THRENODY. See DIRGE.

TIBETAN POETRY. The T. term for poetry is snyan-ngag (Sanskrit kāvya), "ornamental lang.," and for poet is snyan-ngag-mkhan (Sanskrit kavi). Snyan-ngag is characterized by the use of rhetorical ornament (don-rgyan, Skt. arthālaṃkāra) and phonetic ornament (sgra-rgyan, Skt. śabdālaṃkāra). It may be in either verse or prose, and there is little deliberate use of rhyme. Colloquially, however, Tibetans speak of rtsom (literally "composition") to refer to poetic verse in particular. T. verse typically consists of quatrains, with lines of 5 to 15 syllables, and in very ornate verse sometimes more. Shorter lines are characteristic of archaic and folk poetry, while translations of Sanskrit poetry and poetry influenced by Sanskrit models use lines of 7 or more syllables. The lines are most often metrically regular and generally trochaic, with a final syllable added when the line contains an odd number of syllables. Parallel syntax is often employed, one or more syllables being repeated at the beginning, middle, or end of each line, or the same syllable within a single line. Tropes include various sorts of simile (dpe-rgyan) and metaphor (gzugs-rgyan), and the use of stylized literary synonyms (mngon-brjod).

The indigenous T. poetic genres, little influenced by translated lit., include folksongs (glu, songs of varied meter, and gzhas, dance-songs of four 6-syllable lines), epic and bardic verse (sgrung-glu), and versified folk oratory (tshig-dpe/mol-ba). These are generally unwritten but have informed T. lit. in several respects. The inspiration of folksong, for instance, permeates the poems of the Sixth Dalai Bla-ma (1683–1706), as in this example, in the characteristic trochaic trimeter of the dance-song:

If I follow my girl friend's heart,
Life's religious wealth will run out;
If I adhere to single retreat,
I'll be running against my girl's heart.

The subject matter of T. folksong may include love, politics, grief, nature, or activities such as grazing, sowing and harvesting, or construction work. Literary redactions of Tibet's epic and bardic trads. are represented by manuscript and printed versions of the popular tales of King Gesar

(ge-sar sgrung). Folk oratory, on the other hand, has seldom been recorded, though its colorful rhet. occasionally punctuates T. yogic songs and biographies.

The T. script and literary lang. developed in the 7th c. A.D., early literary effort being primarily devoted to tr., particularly of Indian Buddhist lit. During the 13th c. this translated lit. was canonized in the form of two great collections, the Kanjur (bka'-'gyur, "translated pronouncements") in roughly 100 volumes, consisting of the discourses attributed to the Buddha, and the Tanjur (bstan-'gyur, "translated treatises") in roughly 200 volumes, consisting of the writings of later Indian scholars and sages. These incl. much verse, providing enduring examples for T. writers. The latter collection also includes trs. of Sanskrit treatises on the "lang. sciences" (sgra-rig, śabdavidyā)—grammar, synonymy, poetics (above all the Mirror of Poetics, Kāvyādarśa, by Daṇḍin), metrics, dramaturgy—the basis for all later T. literary education.

As in India, verse was often the vehicle for works on philosophy and doctrine (lta-ba/grub-mtha'). While highly technical works were versified for mnemonic reasons, poetic elaboration of Buddhist doctrine employed scriptural figures of speech, as in this example from the work of Klong-chen Rab-'byams-pa (1308–63):

Life is impermanent like clouds of
   autumn,
Youth is impermanent like flowers of
   spring,
The body is impermanent like bor-
   rowed property,
Wealth is impermanent like dew on the
   grass.

Many of Tibet's major religious writers composed outstanding doctrinal verse, incl. Tsong-kha-pa (1357–1419), 'Jigs-med Gling-pa (1729–98), and Shar-rdza Bkra-shis rgyal-mtshan (1859–1935).

Gnomic verses (legs-bshad) modeled on aphorisms from Indian books of polity (nītiśāstra) found their greatest exponent in Sa-skya Paṇḍita (1182–1251), whose Treasury of Aphoristic Gems (legs-bshad rin-po-che'i gter) is cited proverbially. Other famed aphoristic collections are those of Paṇ-chen Bsod-nams grags-pa (1478–1554) and Mi-pham rnam-rgyal (1846–1912). Ethical and spiritual instructions (zhal-gdams) may adhere closely to doctrinal models, or to the conventions of gnomic verse; but they may also make powerful use of colloquialisms and elements of folksong, as do the Hundred Admonitions to the People of Ding-ri (ding-ri brgya-rtsa) of Pha-dam-pa Sangs-rgyas (12th c.), by origin an Indian yogin, and the Thirty-seven Skills of the Bodhisattva (rgyal-sras lag-len so-bdun-ma) by Rgyal-sras Thogs-med bzang-po (1295–1369).

The complex ritualization of T. religion has encouraged the devel. of ritual and devotional verse (cho-ga, gsol-'debs). Accomplished academic

TIMBRE

poets, such as Pan-chen Blo-bzang chos-rgyan (1570–1662), author of a popular *Worship of the Guru (Bla-ma mchod-pa)*, have contributed here, as have inspired "treasure-discoverers" (*gter-ston*), whose revelatory verses are chanted daily by devout Buddhists throughout Tibet.

Verse narratives (*rtogs-brjod*) may be fables or legends, histories or hagiographies (*rnam-thar*). Such works are sometimes reminiscent of Indian Purānic texts, as is the *Testament of Padmasambhava (Padma bka'-thang)*, redacted by O-rgyan Gling-pa (b. 1323), or may be modeled on exceedingly ornate Sanskrit *kāvya*, as are the *Narrative of the Lord of Men (Mi-dbang rtogs-brjod)* and other writings by Mdo-mkhar Tshe-ring dbang-rgyal (1697–1763).

Drawing thematic inspiration from the Apabhramśa songs of the Indian Buddhist tantric masters, and imagistic and metrical resources from indigenous bardic and popular verse, the Buddhist yogins of Tibet created an entirely distinctive family of verseforms collectively known as *mgur*, yogic songs. The greatest author of *mgur* was the inspired sage Mi-la-ras-pa (1040–1123), famed as Tibet's national poet. Here he sings of his foremost disciple, Ras-chung (b. 1084):

> He's gone off riding a fine steed:
> Others' steeds are skittish,
> But Ras-chung's steed doesn't shy.
> On the stallion of thought's vital wind,
> My son Ras-chung, he's gone riding off.

The poetry anthol. was not a well-developed form in Tibet, perhaps owing to the emphasis on the collected works of individual authors and yogins; commentaries on Buddhist doctrine often make such extensive use of quotations that they amount to anthologies in any case. Nonetheless, mention must be made of the extraordinary *Ocean of Songs of the Bka'-brgyud School (bka'-brgyud mgur-mtsho)*, originally compiled by the eighth Karma-pa hierarch, Mi-bskyod rdo-rje (1507–54), an anthol. of masterpieces of the *mgur* genre.

Indian erotic lore was known primarily through Buddhist tantric lit., and frankly erotic imagery is often used symbolically in religious verse, less frequently in secular verse. A modern author, Dge-'dun chos-'phel (1894–1951), has composed an original and highly amusing *Treatise on Love ('dod-pa'i bstan-bcos)*, inspired by the *Kāma Sūtra*, but in some respects also reminiscent of Ovid's *Art of Love*.

Owing to the stability of the T. cl. literary lang., the form and lexicon of T. poetic composition as represented in the most recent authors differ little from models dating back a millennium. The secularizing and colloquializing tendencies of contemp. T. journalism have gradually begun to influence T. literary activity in other spheres, so that we do see some evidence of very recent poetic experimentation. Any attempt to assess such devels. at present, however, would be premature.

FOLK VERSE AND BARDIC TRADITIONS: R. A. Stein, *L'épopée tibétaine de Gesar dans sa version lamaïque de Ling* (1955), *Recherches sur l'épopée et le barde au Tibet* (1959); G. Tucci, *T. Folk Songs*, 2d ed. (1966); N. N. Dewang, "Musical Trad. of the T. People: Songs in Dance Measure," *Orientalia Romana: Essays and Lectures*, v. 2 (1967); M. Helffer, *Les Chants dans l'épopée tibétaine de Ge-sar d'après le livre de la Course de cheval* (1978); B. Nimri Aziz, "On Translating Oral Trads.: Ceremonial Wedding Poetry from Dingri," *Soundings in T. Civilization*, ed. B. N. Aziz and M. Kapstein (1982).

TRANSLATIONS: J. Bacot, *Three T. Mysteries* (1924); G.-C. Toussaint, *Le Dict de Padma* (1933); E. Conze, *The Buddha's Law Among the Birds* (1955); *The Hundred Thousand Songs of Milarepa*, tr. G. C. C. Chang, 2 v. (1962); J. Bosson, *A Treasury of Aphoristic Jewels* (1969); R. A. Stein, *Vie et chants de 'Brug-pa Kun-legs le Yogin* (1972); S. Beyer, *The Cult of Tārā* (1973); Longchenpa, *Kindly Bent to Ease Us*, tr. H. Guenther, 3 v. (1975–76); *The Rain of Wisdom*, tr. Nālandā Tr. Committee (1980); K. Dhondup, *Songs of the Sixth Dalai Lama* (1981); L. G. Wangyal, *The Prince Who Became a Cuckoo* (1982).

HISTORY AND CRITICISM: P. Poucha, "Le vers tibétain," *ArO* (Prague) 18 (1950), 22 (1954); J. Vekerdi, "Some Remarks on T. Prosody," *AODNS* 2 (1952); K. Chang, "On T. P.," *CAsJ* 2 (1956); E. G. Smith, Intros. to *Encyclopedia Tibetica*, v. 3–5 (1969); R. A. Stein, *T. Civilization* (1972), ch. 5.
T.T.; M.T.K.

TIMBRE, tone-color, sound color (Ger. *Klangfarbe*); there is no generally accepted term. "T." derives from Low Lat., then Fr. terms for a drum, a bell, the sound of a bell. T. now denotes the sonorous quality of a sound, as opposed to its length (duration) or loudness or pitch or accent. (Note that the quality of a color, its tint or shade, is called its *tone*.) Technically, t. is changed by increasing the intensity of one or another set of harmonics or formants comprising the sound. Formants may be roughly defined as pitch zones in which voice overtones are strengthened, owing to the voice-cavity configuration. In music and speech, t. is the characteristic auditory quality of a musical instrument or voice producing a sound, and, by extension, the kinesthetic "feel" of the sound to the listener.

In the early 20th c., Arnold Schoenberg, who experimented with organizing music via t. rather than pitch in his 1909 *Five Pieces for Orchestra*, wrote, "the evaluaiton of tone color, the second dimension of tone, is in a much less cultivated, much less organized state than is the aesthetic evaluation of [pitch]. Nevertheless we go right on boldly connecting sounds with one another, contrasting them with one another, simply by feeling; and it has never yet occurred to anyone to require of a theory that it should determine laws by which one may do that sort of thing." And "if it is possible

- [1291] -

TMESIS

to create patterns out of pitch," i.e. melody, "then it must also be possible to make progressions out of . . . 'tone color,' progressions whose relations with one another work with a kind of logic entirely equivalent to that logic which satisfies us in the melody of pitches" (*Theory of Harmony* [1911, tr. 1978]). But Schoenberg's theories and experiments found few followers for the next half century.

It is an open question whether, and how, t. might be applied to the organization of sound in poetry, for the nature of sonal organization differs fundamentally in music and in lang. Every listener instinctively recognizes the differences between sounds of the same pitch produced by different instruments—for example, a clarinet vs. a saxophone, or oboe, or flute, or violin or guitar or bagpipe, or the vocal cords. Articulating these differences verbally, however, is neither instinctive nor easy: one almost automatically turns to descriptive adjectives, and these almost inevitably seem to arise from and hence invoke the other sense modalities. Common adjectives for the description of sound derived from sight, touch, and taste include heavy, light, dark, soft, rough, crisp, salty, sweet, sharp, dim, long, shallow, and blunt: these are the province of the phenomenon known in Eng. as synaesthesia (q.v.).

Beyond synaesthesia, how might t. be identified in poetry? Not, one might think, by source: in music the sounds are made by different instruments, but in poetry all the sounds are made by the human voice (q.v.), whether actual or virtual. However, at least one view holds that the voice is in effect a different instrument for each vowel, since the vocal cords change shape. And in Slawson's theory, t. is a function of the filter not the source of a sound.

And not, one would think, simply by pitch. Two other possibilities suggest themselves: (1) *place of articulation* and (2) *distinctive features*. It is necessary first to distinguish between articulatory phenomena (manner and place of production of the sound), acoustic phenomena (the inherent characteristics of the sound itself, as measured with instruments in acoustics experiments), and auditory (perceptual) phenomena (the way sounds are classed by hearers). It is a fact of psychoacoustics that these three sets of phenomena are not congruent. And beyond this triad, there is the further, third range of associative phenomena, whereby the mind makes associations between sounds, other kinds of sense experience, and other mental pehnomena (memory, desire, ideas). Concerning place of articulation—i.e. high–mid–low and front–mid–back on the standard phonetic chart of articulatory points in the mouth cavity—there is evidence that auditors make category distinctions between groups of sounds, e.g. all vowels that are high vs. low, or front vs. back. This could be subject to patterning in poetry, as could the several sets of binary pairs of distinctive acoustic features of

sounds, as classified by modern linguists such as Halle and Jakobson (for bibl., and application to metrics, see DISTINCTIVE-FEATURE ANALYSIS). Whether or not the sounds of poems have in fact been patterned on the basis of such features, and have been recognized by auditors or readers, even if unconsciously, remains to be shown—as do, indeed, the full relations of this class of human sound response to the other two major classes, mimesis (see ONOMATOPOEIA) and association (see SYNAESTHESIA). See also SOUND.

S. Lanier, *The Science of Eng. Verse* (1880)—unsound; K. Bühler, *Sprachtheorie* (1934); K. Hevner, "An Experimental Study of the Affective Value of Sounds in Poetry," *Am. Jour. Psych.* 49 (1937); H. Lützeler, "Die Lautgestaltung in der Lyrik," *Zeitschrift für Aesth.* 29 (1935); W. Schneider, "Über die Lautbedeutsamkeit," *ZDP* 63 (1938); M. M. Macdermott, *Vowel Sounds in Poetry* (1940); P. Delattre, "The Physiological Interp. of Sound Spectrograms," *PMLA* 66 (1951); F. Lockemann, *Das Gedicht und seine Klanggestalt* (1952); P. Delbouille, *Poésie et sonorités*, 2 v. (1961, 1984); R. Cogan, "Tone Color," *Sonus* 1 (1980); W. Slawson, *Sound Color* (1985). T.V.F.B.

TMESIS (Gr. "a cutting"); also *diacope*. Insertion of a word within another word or phrase. Addition of a mere syllable (sometimes for metrical purposes) is *epenthesis*. Modern rhetoricians (Group Mu, 81) define t. so as to include "all the cases where two morphemes or syntagms that grammatical usage ties together strictly are separated by the insertion of additional elements." Earlier rhetoricians traditionally separated such syntactical permutations into two forms of t. according to whether a single word or a sentence is divided by an intercalated element. In Gr. syntax, t. means the separation of a preposition from its verb to which, in postepic lang., it was completely joined. In Attic Gr. poetry the two elements were separated by unimportant words for the sake of emphasis. Lat. poetry does the same thing, e.g. *seque gregari* for *segregarique*. Eng. allows the breaking up of any compound word, e.g. "that Man—how dearly ever parted" (*Troilus and Cressida* 3.3.96); "See his wind—lilycocks—laced" (Gerard Manley Hopkins, "Harry Ploughman"). By far the most extensive modern practitioner of t. in poetry is e e cummings, who makes it virtually a constitutive principle of poetic form in his verse. Modern linguistics describes one form of this process in colloquial speech as "expletive insertion," commonly scissoring words such as "outstanding" by a profanity for a sarcasm. An example of syntagmatic interpolation: "Lay your sleeping head, my love, / Human on my faithless arm" (W. H. Auden, "Lullaby").—Lausberg; F. Amory, "T. in Med. Lat., ON, and OIr Poetry," *Arkiv för Nordisk Filologi* 94 (1979); Morier; Group Mu. R.A.H.; A.W.H.; T.V.F.B.

TOAST. A long poetic tale or saga of salute or tribute (hence the term), a form of street and prison poetry found in the Afro-Am. community. The t., like the dozens (q.v.), is characteristically a performed poetry generally created and performed by males. The origin of the form dates to the second half of the 19th c. in celebrations of bad men, bandits, and tricksters, and possibly back to the praise poem trad. which is pervasive in Africa. Some ts. are related to and derived from the narrative trad. of the Wild West. The oral form has been appropriated into written lit. by writers such as Nikki Giovanni and Julius Lester. The raconteur may open or close the performance with a tribute or salute to the celebrant, e.g. "Here's to Shine!" or "Here's to the Signifyin Monkey!" The subject of the t. is generally secular and its lang. witty, satiric, bawdy, and profane, told mostly in couplets or in ballad meter (*abcb* in alternating 4- and 3-stress lines). There may be internal rhyme, off-rhyme, and triplet rhymes as well. Through its adventurous narrative, the t. may provide astute commentary on any number of subjects from human vanity to politics. It is episodic, lengthy, and detailed. Because it is improvised, the t. requires of its composer tremendous verbal ingenuity and dexterity for creating wit and excitement, for controlling the rhyme or off-rhyme and frequently irregular rhythm, and for maintaining a high level of spontaneity. The dominant tone of the t. is braggadocio. Typical of the disposition of the speaker are the lines: "I've got a tombstone disposition, graveyard mind, / I know I'm a bad motherfucker, that's why I don't mind dying" (Levine 413). See now DOZENS; INVECTIVE; POETIC CONTESTS.—R. D. Abrahams, *Deep Down in the Jungle* (1970); B. Jackson, *Get Your Ass in the Water and Swim Like Me* (1974); D. Wepman et al, *The Life: The Lore and Folk Poetry of the Black Hustler* (1976); L. W. Levine, *Black Culture and Black Consciousness* (1977); G. Smitherman, *Talkin and Testifyin* (1977). E.A.P.

TONE. (1) In the general sense, "t." denotes an intangible quality which is metaphorically predicated of a literary work or of some part of it such as its style, and often felt to pervade and "color" the whole, like a mood in a human being, so that the t. becomes its pervading "spirit," "atmosphere," or "aura." To describe the t., critics usually choose adjectives, such as serious, witty, ironic, dignified, sincere, refined, apologetic, playful, vigorous, majestic, quaint, delicate, passionate, leisurely, tranquil, tender, gay, savage, melancholy, grim, playful; more complex descriptors, which attempt to map onto the text larger blocks of a given version of lit. hist., are such attributives as "sentimental," "classical," and "romantic." This usage attributes to the text what other theorists regard as either (a) a projection of the fictive speaker's attitude toward his audience—which is the sense of "t." given it for modern crit. by I. A.

Richards—as manifested by markers within the text, or (b) the poet's intention (q.v.) in writing the poem, which may or may not be identical to (a). In either case some degree of intentionality on some level is presumed and, as a corollary, some conception of the poem as an expressive or affective instrument—i.e. a piece of rhet., meant to move its audience. From the rhetorical point of view, successful management of t., on which the effectiveness of a discourse largely depends, consists primarily in the tactful selection of content and in the adjustment of style to influence a particular audience. Other critics have held that any stylistic feature of a text—word choice, syntax, imagery, metaphors, or other figurative devices—can contribute to t. as expressing the attitude of the speaker. This sense of the term "t." is closely related to that of voice (q.v.). But one must keep distinct the t. of the poem's speaker and that of the poem itself.

(2) More specifically, "t." means t. of voice, i.e. the inflections given to words by speakers in normal discourse and heard by auditors. It is possible to utter any simple sentence, such as "I never said I loved you," with any one of a number of different intonational contours and thereby mean quite different things (one of which is "But I do love you"). The t. of a speaker's voice thus reveals information about her attitudes, beliefs, feelings, or intent, or, barring that, at least about the real meaning of the utterance. T. may add to, qualify, or even reverse the meaning of what is said. Sarcasm, for example, repudiates the plain lexical sense of the words with a contrary intonational pattern—speakers almost always give preference to intonation over denotation in deciding what an utterance means. These inflections—stress patterns, pitch changes, pauses, and extensions of duration for emphasis—are natural and perspicuous to auditors in oral speech, but written speech (and thereby lit.) has but few orthographic markers for conveying inflections (which in structural linguistics were called "suprasegmentals"), so t. has to be inferred from the context by attentive readers, reasoned out or argued for as a plausible interp. (q.v.) of the statement. It is by virtue of the fact that written speech but poorly captures inflection that opportunity is created for richness of ambiguity and irony (qq.v.).

Some poets have very keen powers of exhibiting the t. of the utterances of their poetic personas (q.v.) and of shifting those ts. rapidly. In Eng. one thinks most immediately of Donne, who in a poem like "The Indifferent" can rapidly shift tonal structures, creating effects of paradox (q.v.), irony, humor, and satire (q.v.). Most of the *Songs and Sonets* develop this suppleness of tonal fingering, which is one prominent characteristic of the metaphysical (q.v.) style. Some valuable modern research has been carried out to determine the phonological and syntactic mechanisms of these shifts, which seem to be effected in large part by concluding either a series of parallel members (phrases or clauses) or a main clause with its associated subordinate clauses at points of closure or transition, such as at the volta (q.v.) in the sonnet (Rich).

(3) In a more restricted sense of (2), "t." may mean simply pitch (q.v.), as when Chinese, for example, is referred to as a t.-lang., the poetry of which has a tonal prosody, a versification based on pitch (see CHINESE POETRY). This is an extension of the meaning of "t." in music. In short, t. as a characterization of most or all of a discourse derives from t. of voice in the linguistic sense, intonation, which derives from t. as pitch. See also CONNOTATION AND DENOTATION.—I. A. Richards, *Practical Crit.* (1929); J. S. Bastiaenen, *The Moral T. of Jacobean Drama* (1930); I. C. Hungerland, *Poetic Discourse* (1958); L. A. Marre, "Spenser's Control of T.," Diss., Univ. of Notre Dame (1971); M. D. Rich, *The Dynamics of Tonal Shift in the Sonnet* (1975). T.V.F.B.; F.GU.

TONE COLOR. See TIMBRE.

TOPOGRAPHICAL POEM. See DESCRIPTIVE POETRY; VISUAL ARTS AND POETRY.

TOPOS (Gr., literally, "place, region"; pl. *topoi*). A conventionalized expression or passage in a text which comes to be used as a resource for the composition of subsequent texts. The term is first used in a technical sense in Cl. rhet., where it is treated under invention (q.v.) and refers to a standard line of argument based on generally accepted logical probabilities such as "possible or impossible" or "greater or lesser" or "post hoc ergo propter hoc" or "a fortiori," as when it is argued, for example, that since Achilles gave in to wrath, it is not surprising that ordinary citizens sometimes do so too. T. can be specific to a certain type of discourse—demonstrative, legal, or epideictic—or common to all types. The former are *eide*; the latter are *koinoi topoi* (Lat. *loci communi*), which translates literally as "commonplaces." This calls attention to the enlargement of meaning of the term to include standard metaphors and "topics" such as the invocation of the Muse or the description of the ideal "pleasant place" (*locus amoenus*)— e.g. Eden—by poets and writers of narrative. Originally *topoi* were presumably not formulas but spontaneous creations, and even in their schematized form they are activated out of a distinct aesthetic feeling.

T. in the sense of standard topics is central to the approach to lit. taken by E. R. Curtius (*European Lit. and the Lat. Middle Ages*, tr. 1953). In his system, *topoi* are established schemes of thought, extended metaphors, standardized passages of description, and the like that recur in the lit. of Western Europe from Homer to the modern age, most strikingly during the Lat. Middle Ages and the Ren. T. constitutes a principle unifying element in this lit. Among the examples described by

Curtius are the "inexpressability" t., in which the poet describes his inability to do his subject justice (see ADYNATON); the "world upside-down" t. (*mundus inversus*), in which the world's disorder is shown by fish in trees, children ruling parents, and the like; and set pieces like the *locus amoenus* t. The opposite of the *locus amoenus* t. is the wasteland t., which was adapted from medieval sources by T. S. Eliot for *The Waste Land.* Among metaphors considered *topoi* by followers of Curtius are "the world as a stage," "the Book of Nature," and the "cosmic dance." Generalized in this way, the use of *topoi* is closely related to imitation (q.v.), and there is a legitimate sense in which most of the standard motifs of the Petrarchan sonnet sequence (see PETRARCHISM) can be called *topoi*.

Although certain kinds of *topoi* are related to certain literary forms or genres, the forms and genres are not themselves *topoi*, since the term refers to a standardized content rather than a structure or regular sequence of events. Thus the literary consolation (*consolatio*) has a definite shape created by its use of a selection from among a number of consolatory *topoi* (for example, "all must die," "he is gone to a better world," "his memory will be eternal," "his example will lead many to virtue") but is not, itself, a t. A perfect example of a poem that is almost a collage of such *topoi* plus many others from different trads. such as pastoral (q.v.) is John Milton's lament for the death of his friend Edward King, *Lycidas.* The remarkable vitality of *topoi* over centuries is illustrated by independent use of many of the same ones found in *Lycidas* over two centuries later by Matthew Arnold in "Thyrsis" and by Walt Whitman in "When Lilacs Last in the Dooryard Bloomed."

Later critics (e.g. Gadamer, Adorno) have taken Curtius as a point of departure for a critique of ideas of cultural unity and continuous trad. Others (e.g. Garcia-Berrio) have pointed out that the very existence of a well defined set of *topoi* and conventions such as those found in the Petrarchan sonnet gives the poet a means of expressing individuality by variations on expected norms.

Curtius; J. M. Lechner, *Ren. Conceptions of the Commonplaces* (1962); B. Emrich, "Topik und Topoi," *Deutschunterricht* 18 (1966); A. R. Evans, Jr., "E. R. Curtius," *Four Mod. Humanists*, ed. A. R. Evans, Jr. (1970); *T.-Forschung: Eine Dokumentation*, ed. P. Jehn (1972); *T.-Forschung*, ed. M. L. Baeumer (1973); *Topik: Beiträge zur interdisziplinären Diskussion*, ed. D. Breuer and H. Schanze (1981); F. J. D'Angelo, "The Evolution of the Analytic Topoi: A Speculative Inquiry," *Cl. Rhet. and Mod. Discourse*, ed. R. J. Connors et al. (1984); L. Bornscheuer, "Topik," *Reallexikon*, v. 4; R. Wellek, "Ernst Robert Curtius als Literarkritik," *Französische Literatur des zwanzigsten Jahrhunderts* (1986); R. J. Goebel, "Curtius, Gadamer, Adorno: Probleme literarische Trad.," *Monatshefte* (1986); E. P. J. Corbett, "The Topoi Revisited," *Rhet. and Praxis*, ed. J. D. Moss (1986). O.B.H.; E.H.B.

TORNADA. A final short stanza, comparable to the Fr. *envoi* (q.v.), added to many Occitan poems as a kind of dedication to a patron or friend. In form, the t. usually reproduces the metrical structure and the rhymes of the last part of the preceding stanza. Some poems have 2 or even 3 *ts.*, addressed to different persons. See also FINIDA; OCCITAN POETRY.—U. Mölk, "Deux remarques sur la tornade," *Metrica* 3 (1982); Chambers.

F.M.C.

TOUCHSTONES. Matthew Arnold's term for "short passages, even single lines" of classic poetry that serve the critic as an "infallible" resource "for detecting the presence or absence of high poetic quality, and also the degree of this quality, in all other poetry which we may place beside them." The examples of t. Arnold gave in "The Study of Poetry" (pub. 1880, rpt. 1888 in Arnold's *Essays in Crit.*, 2d ser.) were 11 lines, 3 each from Homer, Dante, and Milton, and 2 from Shakespeare. Chaucer ("not one of the great classics") was—famously—excluded. These lines, Arnold held, have in common a "diction" and "movement" that convey and match their "truth and seriousness." Arnold's idea of "high seriousness" borders on the melancholy, though one touchstone from Dante expresses joy in resignation: "In Thy will is our peace."

The critic's reference to touchstone passages, according to Arnold, permits a "real estimate" rather than a "historic" or a "personal estimate" of poetic value. By this claim he defends the established canon (q.v.) against historicist and impressionist contemporaries for whom all terms of excellence were relative, and the canon therefore malleable. Arnold feared that democracy and the free market would encourage, as "a vast and profitable industry," the production of a "charlatan" lit.—his t. were to solve that dilemma by making excellence accessible in anthols. The Am. institution of "Great Books" courses owes something of its rationale for an ahistorical approach to Arnold's argument.

The method of commenting on "beauties and faults" in individual lines of poetry is ancient (Longinus) and was in vogue in the 18th c. (Diderot, Addison, Dennis, Joseph Warton). Arnold's method has also been compared with that of Chinese "poetry-talk" crit. (*shih-hua tz'u-hua*), in which, beginning in the 11th c., lines were selected for appreciation out of context.—T. S. Eliot, *The Use of Poetry and the Use of Crit.* (1933), ch. 6; L. Trilling, *Matthew Arnold* (1939); Abrams, ch. 6; J. Eels, Jr., *The Ts. of Matthew Arnold* (1955); Wellek, v. 4, ch. 7; W. Wong, "Selection of Lines in Chinese Poetry-talk Crit.," *New Asia Academic Bull.* (1978); G. Graff, *Professing Lit.* (1987).   J.M.P.

TRACE. See DECONSTRUCTION; TEXTUALITY.

TRADITION. I. LITERARY OR WRITTEN. T. is a term used routinely to name a line of literary works

falling under a particular description, which may be generic ("the epic t."), historical ("the Augustan t."), thematic ("the modern t."), or composed of any combination of features ("the t. of 19th-c. black women's autobiography"). More generally, "t." has been defined as "the body of texts and interps. current among a group of writers at a given time and place" (J. V. Cunningham)—a definition suggestive of the high degree of contingency most contemp. critics tend to ascribe to the idea of t. These usages seem neutral and commonsensical enough, but "t." is a concept implicated in almost every aspect of the crit. of poetry, and it has acquired in the 20th c. a good deal of ideological baggage as well.

An emphasis on the traditional character of successful poetry has been a feature of crit. since Aristotle's *Poetics*. This emphasis reflects the view that lit. is a highly traditional activity, and that new writers continue to develop, differently but not necessarily "progressively," the forms and themes of their predecessors (see GENRE). We learn to understand and to evaluate a poem by placing it first in the context of the "t.," meaning the whole of the lit. we know, and then in the more restricted context of the t. or ts. (e.g. "epic," "romantic") to which we judge it to belong. This contextualization may produce analyses that are structural, emphasizing formal similarities and differences, or genetic, emphasizing sources and influences, or both. Flagrantly antitraditional—avant-garde or experimental—writing is, on this view, still writing that can be understood only in terms of the t. from which it deviates; and such writing itself once widely practiced will then be regarded as constituting a t. of its own.

How the individual poem fits into the t., which t. or ts. it is best understood in the context of, whether its mix of conformity and difference constitutes a "strong" or a "weak" response to the t.—these questions are clearly at the heart of much crit. of poetry, both scholarly and evaluative. And it is easy to see how they bear as well on the consideration of a number of central literary values, issues, and techniques such as imitation, influence, originality, textuality (qq.v.), authority, belatedness, allusion (q.v.), appropriation, and intentionality (see INTENTION).

In 20th-c. crit., the term "t." is most strongly associated with modernism, and particularly with the writing of Yeats, Pound, and Eliot, who make prominent mention of "the" t., referring sometimes to the whole of the literary past, but more often to a single line of poetry (and other, sometimes nonliterary, writing) which the poet regards as central to the culture, and within which his own work is designed to fit. Eliot's "T. and the Individual Talent" (1919) remains the classic theoretical expression of the modernist idea of t.: the new work takes its significance from the pre-existing t. and at the same time alters the t. The argument was designed in part to justify modernist formal innovation as "traditional" in the true sense, and to condemn apparently traditional writing, e.g. the poetry of the British Georgians, as merely conventional.

That the appropriation of the term by poets who seemed to many contemp. observers to be *breaking* with t. was a tactical coup was made clear by essays like Eliot's "The Metaphysical Poets" (1921), which championed 17th-c. metaphysical poetry (q.v.) by arguing that it belonged to "the direct current of Eng. poetry," with the implication that most Eng. poetry of the 19th c. did not. The defense of modernist poetry in the name of a continuity that leapfrogged a century or more of Eng. lit. became standard among modernism's academic champions, notably Cleanth Brooks and F. R. Leavis. Moving from these literary judgments to an attack on modern culture as a whole was a simple matter, and in the later crit. of Eliot and of Southern New Critics such as Allen Tate, "t." and its synonyms became the names for the homogeneous culture of Western Christendom that liberalism and secularism were accused of destroying.

Even when "t." is intended in a neutral descriptive sense, the connotations of orthodoxy and exclusivity are difficult to avoid, and since the 1950s, the idea of "the t." has become clouded by the suspicion that, as Northrop Frye argued, the criteria for inclusion always involve extraliterary values. The responses to this problematizing of the term have taken two general forms, both explicitly reactive against the crit. of Eliot and his followers. The first entails an overt engagement with the politics of literary tradition-making (or, more commonly, "canon-formation"—see CANON). The received t., it is argued, reflects the interests of the dominant culture, which formulates ostensibly literary criteria to exclude minority or dissenting voices—hence the construction by some critics of alternative canons, defined sometimes as cohesive in their own right, sometimes as echoing and subverting the dominant t. The interest in lit. by women as a discrete category of writing is only the most prominent instance of this widespread trend. Motivated by different concerns, Harold Bloom has proposed a theoretical model of the relations between t. and the individual talent designed to replace Eliot's. Bloom's account stresses the efforts of the new poet to escape the oppressive influence of his precursors—by, among other, rhetorical strategies, misreading their work to make his own possible (see INFLUENCE). This theory supports a romantic t. composed principally of writers written out of the modernist and New Critical canon.

The second postmodernist devel. is the attack on the hypostasization of the t., and the assertion of its provisional, historical character. The effort to arrive at a theoretical description of the relations between what is new and what is already there in the culture has been influenced most significantly by the hermeneutic philosophy of Hans-Georg Gadamer, which emphasizes the impossibility of stepping outside the interpretive matrix of one's own t.; but the general issue has absorbed the attention of critics from a variety of philosophical persuasions.　　　　　　　　　　L.ME.

II. ORAL. The 20th c. has also witnessed the rediscovery of oral poetic trads., both defunct and continuing, in cultures all over the world. With the classicist Milman Parry, his co-worker Albert Lord, and the advent of the oral-formulaic theory (q.v.), scholars became aware of the oral traditional roots of Homer and dozens of other trads. This school of "literary anthropology" has shown how oral poets eschew the original in favor of the traditional and how they use not only a repertoire of repeated "formulas" (q.v.) to compose metrical lines in performance but also an array of stock narrative patterns ("themes") to move the story forward. Trad. in this sense is the sum total of all the oral performances by all the poets who practice in the culture, and thus comes also to refer both to what lies behind the texts that are written down and to the transitional poems that derive from oral trads. (see ORAL POETRY).　　J.M.F.

T. S. Eliot, "T. and the Individual Talent" (1919) and "The Metaphysical Poets" (1921) in *Essays*; G. Murray, *The Cl. T. in Poetry* (1927); J. L. Lowes, *Convention and Revolt* (1930); F. R. Leavis, *Revaluations* (1936); C. Brooks, *Mod. Poetry and the T.* (1939); A. Tate, *Reason in Madness* (1941); G. Highet, *The Cl. Trad.* (1949); Frye; H. Rosenberg, *The T. of the New* (1959); J. V. Cunningham, *T. and Poetic Structure* (1960); Lord; H. Bloom, *The Visionary Company* (1961), *The Anxiety of Influence* (1973), *The Breaking of the Vessels* (1982); E. M. W. Tillyard, *The Eng. Epic T.* (1969); W. J. Bate, *The Burden of the Past and the Eng. Poet* (1970); H.-G. Gadamer, *Truth and Method* (tr. 1975); R. K. Martin, *The Homosexual T. in Am. Poetry* (1979); Parry; J. Foley, *Oral Formulaic Theory and Research* (1985), *The Theory of Oral Composition* (1988); L. Menand, *Discovering Modernism* (1987); P. Meisel, *The Myth of the Mod.* (1987); S. Gilbert and S. Gubar, *No Man's Land*, 2 v. (1987–89); L. Keller, *Remaking It New: Contemp. Am. Poetry and the Modernist T.* (1987); R. Shusterman, *T. S. Eliot and the Philosophy of Crit.* (1988). *Oral Trad.* 1– (1986—)—journal.　　L.ME.; J.M.F.

TRADUCTIO. See POLYPTOTON.

TRAGEDY.

    I. HISTORY OF THE CONCEPT
   II. HISTORY OF PERFORMANCE

I. HISTORY OF THE CONCEPT. T. is a particular form of Western drama originating in or around Athens in the second half of the 6th c. B.C. Various authors from Aristotle to René Girard, via Nietzsche and Gilbert Murray, have speculated on its derivation from a "tragico-lyrical" chorus of some kind, i.e. the dithyramb (q.v.) or even some earlier form of ritual violence or sacrifice (the Gr. root of the term for t. refers to goats). Such rites have been understood variously—by Murray as symbolizing the passage of spring and a regenerative cycle; by Nietzsche as marking a rupture between some "Dionysiac" involvement of humans with the natural world and their "Apollonian" rational distancing from it (see APOLLONIAN-DIONYSIAN); by Girard as marking some pathway from inhuman and asocial violence toward organized society and culture. The tragic protagonist is a scapegoat, *pharmakos*, whose death or ejection from the social group somehow cleanses, rejuvenates, or indeed creates ordered society. Such speculations are interesting, but they tend to be tautological (since the evidence comes from the ts. themselves) and slightly reactionary, in that their tendency has been to view the rationality ascribed to t. as a kind of fall from the grace of the sacred irrationality that preceded it. Let us simply say, with the preponderance of the critical trad., that ts. act out the failures of human effort, however grand, before some process (call it "fate," "the gods," etc.) of which humans are, by definition, supposed ignorant—although the very existence of ts. itself proposes some kind of knowledge, for they could not otherwise have been composed.

The earliest reasonably assured historical fact is that Thespis, an Athenian, performed some kind of t. at the City (or Greater) Dionysia between 536 and 533 B.C. The subsequent devel. of t. suggests that this performance was probably a kind of duet or dialogue (q.v.) between the poet himself, playing the protagonist, and a chorus (q.v.). Aristotle informs us that Thespis also invented the tragic mask, at first simply face paint, then cloth, and later perhaps of clay. Arion of Corinth is said to have developed the dithyramb. Cleisthenes, tyrant of Sicyon at war with Argos, gave to Dionysus the "tragic choruses" that had honored the Argive hero Adrastos. At Phleius, a little later, it is believed that Pratinas composed the first satyr plays. It also seems clear that, from the first, authors of ts. were competing with one another; reports of several contests are extant.

This paucity of information about the origins of t. should constrain speculation. In fact, matters are even worse. Although some information has come to us from papyri and occasional remarks (e.g. by Herodotus), our main informant remains Aristotle, who wrote his *Poetics* a century and a half later, in the mid 4th c. B.C. And that work is not entirely reliable. Although his stated purpose was to analyze t.'s structure and function, comparing it on the one hand to epic (q.v.) and on the other to comedy (q.v.)—the section on comedy has been lost—there is evidence that he distorted his account of t.'s history for political and ideological ends (Jones). Not unnaturally, he also emphasized his own favorites among the large corpus of plays to which he had access; one of his choices conspicuously retains pride of place: *Oedipus Rex*. In

his view, this t. exemplified the genre: narrating a serious, complete, and unique human action (howbeit introduced *in medias res* [q.v.]), revealing both its typicality and its limitation, involving people of high estate and issues central to the *polis* as a whole, depicting characters neither wholly good nor entirely bad, and passing through change(s) of fortune, recognition, and catastrophe. The play illustrated precisely, he found, the six essential parts of t.: plot (q.v.), character, diction (poetic style and order), thought, spectacle, and music (see discussion below; see also CLASSICAL POETICS).

It is not in the least surprising, however, that Aristotle's 4th c. B.C. *Poetics* should have had political goals. Throughout the 5th c. B.C., Athens (and Greece as a whole) was in a state of political and social uncertainty, constantly fraught with conflict. Both ts. and their authors were centrally involved in these affairs, almost before the reforms of Athenian "democracy" in 510. In 500 the revolt of the Ionian cities of Asia Minor provoked the Persian Wars. The revolt ended in 494 with the fall of Miletos, but the wars dragged on until 449, though the city-states were free of serious threat after 480–79. But then other wars broke out.

Both Aeschylus and Sophocles took part in these events. Aeschylus fought at both Marathon and Salamis; Sophocles was *strategos* with Pericles in the Samian war of 441–39, and apparently again in 428, was frequently employed as an ambassador, and was a member of the ruling council after 413. Clearly, political and military events cannot be irrelevant to the devel. of tragic drama: they provide the context essential to any understanding of t.'s role in Athenian society. For ts. quickly became a profoundly serious forum for dealing with political and religious issues. In 472, for example, Aeschylus' *Persians* concerned Greece's war, as had Phrynichos' *Capture of Miletos* (performed 493–92, just a year after the fall of that city). Again, one of the common interps. of Aeschylus' *Oresteia* (the only extant trilogy [q.v.]) has been that it shows the passage from a society dominated by divine justice to one relying on human justice within a city the authority for whose status nonetheless remains divine. (It is the goddess Athena who finally exonerates Orestes as she simultaneously institutes the new governing order.) No one, we may suppose, doubted the political significance of ts.

There are other obstacles as well to generalizations we may wish to propose, not least of which is the dearth of extant plays. Of the enormous output of 5th- and 4th-c. ts., only the merest handful survive in full—7 each by Aeschylus and Sophocles, and 18 by Euripides. One of the earliest authors, Phrynichos, like Choirilos, was reputed to have composed some 160 ts.; and from the 4th c., Astydamas II was reputed to have composed some 240 plays. Both Aeschylus and Euripides composed between 70–90 plays, Sophocles between 120–30, and they were but three among many. Some 60 authors are known from the Hellenistic period, and records survive of competition late into the 1st c. B.C. For the 5th and 4th cs. alone, this implies several hundred plays at minimum. The surviving corpus thus represents a minuscule proportion of the whole. Worse, perhaps, their survival was due to much later Alexandrian anthologizers, whose purposes were not what we might now consider "literary" but rather philological, grammatical, or rhetorical.

We must thus exercise extreme care in drawing any sweeping or universal conclusions about the nature of Gr. t. The material hazards of transmission, the nondramatic purposes of anthology composition, and the importance of one critic's predilections alone would guarantee that such could not be the case. Yet another barrier to comprehension has been revealed by recent scholarly work which shows that the post-Ren. and Enlightenment emphasis on individual character and psychological "self-understanding" falsified both the plays and the ancient idea of t. in particular, and of personhood and its place in society in general (Belsey; Reiss; Vernant and Vidal-Nacquet). We cannot but conclude, then, that for practical reasons (survival of the corpus), for contextual reasons (e.g. Aristotle's preferences and their consequences for that survival), and for conceptual reasons (our unfamiliarity with Gr. beliefs about humanity, society, and the world), we need to understand Gr. t. not as some generalizable artistic form but as something particular which it requires an effort to comprehend in something like its own terms.

One would say, therefore, that Christopher Leech is quite right to tell us bluntly to beware of overly grand pronouncements about t. It is simply "a concept that we deduce from the contemplation of a heap of ts." (24). Moreover, if this be so, and even had the concept as such existed for antiquity (which it did not), it would have been different from any notion we may now have, because it would derive from different examples. How much such a (false) abstract concept may affect not only our judgment but even our contemplation of *facts* has been amply demonstrated by George Steiner, who argues for a view of t. that is quite un-Gr. (though using it to assert the subsequent "death" of t.). In his words, "any realistic notion of tragic drama must start from the fact of catastrophe. Ts. end badly" (8). From the early Ren. to the present, many others have maintained the same view. But for the Greeks catastrophe was a technical device that did not have to conclude a t., as we can see in the plays themselves (e.g. *Eumenides, Oedipus at Colonus,* or *Helen*) and can learn by reading Aristotle, who preferred a more fortunate ending. To accept such a concept as defining t. would mean "we must either exclude a very large part of extant Gr. t. or redefine *t.* or *badly*" (Reiss 13). Nor does the caveat apply only to Gr. t. Was Corneille's *Le Cid* a t.? Or his *Horace*?

What of Racine's *Bérénice* or Tate's *King Lear?* Certainly the first two *contain* catastrophe, but it would be a nice critic who could define their conclusions as unambiguous in that regard. As for *Bérénice*, does it even contain a catastrophe? (For that matter, does the *Alcestis* of Euripides?) And while we may think Tate's *Lear* simply an absurd botching of a glorious predecessor, neither late 17th- nor 18th-c. audiences thought so.

We ought therefore to be careful before adopting any universal concept of t. or of the tragic. Aristotle's *critical* text did establish a trad., but modern philology, fresh discoveries, greater contextual awareness, all advise us to examine it with care. We should first give their separate due to authors and audiences of the Gr. 5th c. B.C., of the Sp., Fr., and Eng. 16th–17th cs., and of the Ger. and Scandinavian 19th c. We may add, too, those of a 20th c. that has seen a line stretching from Büchner to Hauptmann to Brecht. At the same time, such a list itself implies that despite the differences of history, society, and culture, something has nonetheless enabled people to believe, if not in the identity of t. through time and place, certainly in at least *some* similarity of function or meaning. But we can explore that similarity precisely by emphasizing those very historical and cultural differences. Indeed, only by so doing can we obtain some clear notion of what t. has actually *done*, of what has been the cultural *function* of ts. in the environments in which they have really existed. For it is manifestly the case that a dramatic form called "t." has persistently recurred at moments in the Western trad. since the Greeks.

The customary critical claim has been that the trad. was continuous and essentially homogeneous. Scholars, critics, and dramatists have all asserted that t. derived the rules for its comprehension from Aristotle, and for actual practice and production from the Greeks and Seneca. From Aristotle to Scaliger, from Heinsius to Hume, and from Hegel to Croce, they affirmed that its purpose was that of *katharsis* (see CATHARSIS), understood variously (and often vaguely) as some "purging" of the spectators' emotions of pity and terror, as a kind of "medical" reduction of their force, or as a "religious" emotional purification which made the spectators wiser and more tolerant. (Modern critics tend to see these claims as a response to Plato's argument that far from calming human emotions, mimetic art roused them to greater violence.) Also from Aristotle come the ideas that t. functioned by means of *mimesis* or representation (see IMITATION; REPRESENTATION AND MIMESIS); that its ordering structure was that of a linear "plot" (q.v.) or *mythos*, leading the spectator from a beginning *in medias res* (q.v.) through a middle involving some confusions and at least one "change of fortune" (*peripeteia*) to an end which embodied a "recognition" (*anagnorisis*) of previous ignorance and a new understanding; and that its main protagonist (a person of high estate, and neither wholly "good" nor "bad") underwent this experience because of some "tragic flaw" (*hamartia*).

Part of the difficulty with all this has been subsequent critics' inability to agree on the meaning of even these fundamental terms. *Katharsis* has been the single most disputed term, yet occurs only once in Aristotle's *Poetics*. (Most commentators have agreed, however, that it refers to the spectators, not the actors.) *Mimesis* has posed similar problems, though it is now generally agreed that it does not mean representational copying, but rather some depiction of what is essential to human action, enabling any particular instance to be generalized as in some way typical. *Mythos* denotes the form taken by such depiction.

Hamartia has also proved provocative. From the Ren. until quite recently, *hamartia* was interpreted as something close to *hubris*, a kind of overweening pride, whose exemplary Ren. figures were Marlowe's Tamburlaine and Faustus: indeed, such an interp. works well when applied to the growing individualism depicted in late Ren. and Enlightenment t. The term was traditionally interpreted, then, in a fundamentally ethical sense: i.e. it was a moral failure for which the protagonist was personally responsible. More recently, this has been shown not to work for Gr. drama, with its entirely different view of subject and character, and to be an erroneous interp. of Aristotle (Vernant and Vidal-Nacquet). Closer analysis of the *Poetics* has shown that the term is connected not so much with the sense of a lack of will (though it *can* imply that) as with that of "unwittingness." Indeed, Halliwell has shown that it ranges from willful evil (but is *that* then a "failure"?) to simple lack of knowledge (215–30). We can then perhaps say that *hamartia*, the so-called "tragic flaw," simply named the apparent single cause of *any* failure by the protagonist to act or to know, presented as such to the spectators' understanding. We will soon see the importance of such audience understanding.

Much disputation may be avoided if we understand that these descriptive terms had their origin in Aristotle's effort to comprehend how t. functioned in his own time and place. The way that Ren. and then Enlightenment critics took them over may tell us a lot about what *they* wanted, but it tells us very little about antiquity. To understand t., therefore, we might cease looking first at Aristotle's terms and begin instead with the historical contexts of the works in question. And here we can see immediately something rather notable about t.'s appearances. Apart from "t." itself, only two things are common to its several appearances in Western societies.

First, t. has occurred at moments of precarious social and political consolidation, which quickly proved to be moments of transition from one form of society to another. In Greece, for example, the heyday of Aeschylus, Sophocles, and Euripides fell precisely between the Persian and the Peloponnesian Wars. The first war signaled a passage from archaic Gr. society toward the consolidation of the city-states, while the latter marked the decay of those conflict-prone states before the consolidation of the Macedonian hegemony and the coming of the "Hellenistic world." Similarly, in the European 16th and 17th cs., the great age of t. was also an age of warfare, incl. the revolts against the Hapsburgs of Spain and Empire, the religious wars in France, the Thirty Years War, the Eng. Civil War, and finally the Frondes. It was a period that marked a transition between the death throes of feudalism and the birth of capitalism. In Germany, the period between the mid 18th and mid 19th cs. (from Lessing, Schiller, and Goethe to Kleist, Hölderlin, and Grillparzer) shows the beginning of a transformation from the feuding principalities of the 18th c. to the Prussian Customs Union of 1830, toward eventual unification and empire under Bismarck.

Second, t. has *in every case* been followed by the consolidation of a political theory of extraordinary power: Plato and Aristotle, Hobbes and Locke, Hegel and Marx. It is as if t. had discovered in its confused environment, and then related, some new conceptual and discursive process enabling certain doubts to be overcome, clearing up the incomprehensions inherent in earlier social and political decay and dissolution, and facilitating the establishment of a new order of rationality. Many recent commentators have observed at length just how much Gr. t. focused upon "lack of security and misplaced certainty in and about lang." (Goldhill; cf. Segal). The same can be said of Ren. t. (Reiss) and has been shown for the Ger. romantics (Benjamin).

Within those limits, what links ts. is their presentation of a protagonist whose powerful wish to achieve some goal seems inevitably to come up against limits against which she or he is powerless. The limits may be self-created, or imposed from without (by people or by some impersonal force), or they may even represent an inability to establish any precise sense of what may be at issue (this is common in the Ren. ts. of Buchanan, for instance). The result is an impasse for the protagonist—defeat, humiliation, often death. Whatever particular interp. we may make of this, in general such drama is itself the sign of the transitional moment after the collapse of a stable order and the re-establishment of another.

II. HISTORY OF PERFORMANCE. To assess either the nature of tragic performance or the playing space in 5th-c. Athens with precision or in detail is difficult. Trad. indicates that performances originally took place in the *agora* (marketplace), which we have no reason to doubt, and all the less so, perhaps, because we know how the ts. of Lope de Vega, Calderón, Tirso de Molina, or Rojas Zorilla were played in the innyards of Golden Age Spain, and how those of Marlowe, Shakespeare, Middleton, Webster, and Beaumont and Fletcher were performed in open-air theaters in England. By the early 5th c., the performances of the Dionysia took place in a wooden structure erected on stone foundations at the foot of the south cliff of the Acropolis. This and other impermanent structures have left almost no trace. The first stone structure dates from the late 4th c. B.C.; the theater of Dionysus visible in our own time is a much later structure on a site that has seen many buildings. Vase paintings may provide some additional evidence, but we need to be wary of drawing conclusions from an artform with its own conventions. The plays themselves, of course, provide most evidence.

The chorus seems to have performed in front of a slightly raised stage, accompanied by a musician (*auletes*) playing on a double pipe. (Later, the stage was raised much higher.) The chorus was composed of citizens drawn from a single *deme*, while the actors themselves were semiprofessional. No women performed. Thespis is thought to have invented the mask; Aeschylus introduced a second actor, Sophocles a third. The former is also credited with being the first to compose a tetralogy (q.v.) on a single theme.

Throughout the 5th c., as explained in Part I, t. had remained deeply caught up in issues involving both the internal political order of an Athens whose form of government and power relations were a constant matter of debate and conflict, and also external relations whose instability reached a climax in the war with Sparta in 431. Final defeat came in 404. But the whole period was one of political and military struggle against which the Athenians had mounted various offensives. Among these t. was one. Contrary to what has all too often been claimed, t. has not been a demonstration of human incapacity in the face of some powerful or incomprehensible event. It has rather been a means of explaining what might otherwise be incomprehensible, a way to show just why a given group or individual failed or was defeated by some set of circumstances. The Athenians sought to create a new, trustworthy political and epistemological order. To do that, in addition to actual practice, they had to create some ordered conceptual process able to "enclose" whatever might escape such knowledge and such order (since no conceptual or political process can in fact function save by selection and exclusion), and to place it outside their new system. To do that, they had to find a means either of indicating that nothing escaped such order, or else of asserting it could explain and therefore understand such events as did escape it. T. was one of those means, and the audience had so to understand it. It performed order in a theater where semi-professional actors, the representative chorus of the *deme*, and the citizen body gathered together on the slopes of the Acropolis within shouting distance of the Pnyx, the everyday arena of political debate (Else 1965).

As Athens approached its final loss of stability

in the late 5th c. B.C. (a process that culminated in Euripides' *Bacchae*, where the order of state finally cedes to a dissolution created by Dionysus himself), t. became increasingly ambiguous. Both the *Bacchae* and *Oedipus at Colonus* were performed posthumously, precisely around the period of the Athenians' final defeat. Both represent the end of the great days of Gr. t. The "classics" started to be performed once again after 385, but in this period of "revival," theater was a matter for traveling professional troupes and was no longer central to the city's political and cultural fabric. Never again in antiquity was it to recover such a role. Perhaps such lack of cultural centrality explains why the 500 years between 5th-c. Athens and Nero's Rome are represented by little more than fragments and titles of ts. and the names of their authors.

T. was "rediscovered" by the European Ren.—by Italy, and then by France, England, the Netherlands, and Spain. Seneca was far and away the single most important influence, esp. as to his bombastic style, but Sophocles and Euripides both had some mild impact. Initially a school exercise in rhetorical composition and performance, a means to improve the vernaculars, and a way to communicate the political and ethical commonplaces of the ancients, the humanist t. of the Ren. rapidly took on an aura of national political commentary. It also helped create vernaculars able to compete in quality of expression with both Gr. and Lat., and provided a means for writers to elaborate an elite literary genre the perfection of which would contribute to establishing equality between the new European cultures and those of antiquity (see RENAISSANCE POETRY). At the same time, esp. in France, ts. became tools in genuine political battles: Protestant and Catholic confrontations occurred on stage as well as on the battlefield. Bèze's *Abraham sacrifiant* of 1550, for instance, was "answered" by Jodelle's *Cléopâtre captive* of 1552, which praised Henri II and equated him with Octavian. In Spain the ts. of honor written by dramatists such as Lope de Vega and Calderón reflected both the glory of imperial Spain and the ambiguities brought on by growing internal instability and external threats. In England, the hubristic individualist ts. of a Marlowe, and Shakespearian ts. that seem to place their protagonists up against conflicts they cannot resolve, gave way to the darkening tones and violence of Jacobean revenge t. (see ENGLISH POETRY), as though in preparation for the political and military struggles to come. In France, humanist t. was replaced by the generation of the elder Corneille: Mairet, Scudéry, Du Ryer, Tristan l'Hermite, and particularly Rotrou. In Corneille, esp., one can follow that era's confrontations between feudal nobility and central monarchical authority, between conspiratorial conflict and State stability. That trad. was continued (albeit in his own way) by Racine, whose ts. may readily be interpreted as a set of "experiments" performed upon different political situations and conditions. At the same time, these plays show how individuals and circumstances threatening to social stability were overcome and removed.

It is probably fair to pick out five or six playwrights from this era who are considered generally, or within their own country, to epitomize the genre. Shakespeare is no doubt premier among them. Writing in blank verse (q.v.), using subjects drawn from history or legend, he presents characters ranged against obstacles frequently not simply of their own choosing, but even of their own making: *Hamlet* and *Macbeth* introduce supernatural elements, to be sure, but these do not gravely effect the instance of choice. Richard II glories in his eloquent railing, but fails through mistaking his place in a now altered divine order. *King Lear* is possibly the most terrifying of all tragedies, in that Lear himself seems responsible for setting the heavens against him, and brings disaster on innocent and culpable victims alike in a general collapse of the kingdom. In France, the debate was always between the elder Corneille and Racine, between the opulent and Rubenesque Corneille and the clean-cut, ascetic, and Vermeerlike Racine, whose clarity of diction, paucity of display, and tautness of alexandrine (q.v.), were all quite unique. All three playwrights created the modern psychological tragic figure, as the Schlegels and other Ger. romantic critics claimed Lope de Vega and Calderon did in Spain (though recent work suggests otherwise) and, less familiarly, Joost van den Vondel in Holland, whose 1556 *Lucifer* was a source of Milton's epic and a possible precursor of Goethe's *Faust*. Vondel's vigorous diction, vehement sense of place, feeling for the ancient and modern theater, and above all creation of powerful characters allow the Dutch to call him their "Shakespeare."

T. in 18th-c. Europe tended to be a rather dry attempt to recapture that earlier active t., and tended therefore to be but a pale reflection of the political and conceptual order in whose creation earlier t. had participated. Such work was represented in Italy, for example, by Alfieri, in France by Crebillon and Voltaire, and in England by Addison (*Cato*) and Lillo (*The London Merchant*). These plays present a kind of moralistic support for what was by then the accepted order of Enlightenment rationality and political organization. Only in Germany from the mid 18th c. on do we find t. achieving the kind of constructive process seen in 5th-c. Athens or in late Ren. Italy, England, Spain, Holland, and France. Lessing was the first to launch this creative t., and the process culminated, brilliantly, in Schiller, Goethe, Kleist, and the (failed) efforts of Hölderlin.

After 1850, Ibsen and Strindberg are doubtless the most likely candidates for consideration as writers of t. Yet even here the characters do not really *compose* a realm of knowledge and action as they did in the great periods of t. Rather do they deal with systematic truths that pre-exist their activities—much as did the protagonists of the 18th c. Whether the same may be asserted of O'Neill and Miller, of Beckett and Pinter, or of Lorca and other modern authors is a question not perhaps to be answered here. One may suggest, however, that in Bertolt Brecht the questions haunting the great ages of t. *do* once again become "constitutive." In his theatrical practice he rediscovers t. as an effort to create a new systematic process in a period marked by the overthrow of cultural and political order. Coming after Büchner, Hauptmann, and Piscator, Brecht shows his protagonists striving to understand a historical movement they themselves create even as they are created by it. History in Brecht becomes fundamentally ambiguous, for the characters themselves have to make it meaningful. History and social action, that is, create one another simultaneously. Once again in Brecht's hands drama becomes creative of a new order and of a new understanding of the social and political practice enabled by such order. See also CATHARSIS; COMEDY; DRAMATIC POETRY; GENRE; GREEK POETRY; TRAGICOMEDY.

G. Freytag, *Die Technik des Dramas* (1863), 6th ed. tr. as *Technique of the Drama* (1898)—"Freytag's Pyramid"; F. Nietzsche, "The Birth of T." (1872), rpt. *Complete Works*, v. 1 (1924); A. C. Bradley, *Shakespearian T.* (1904); W. B. Yeats, "Tragic Theatre," *Essays* (1924); A. Pickard-Cambridge, *Dithyramb, T. and Comedy* (1927); H. C. Lancaster, *Fr. T. in the Time of Louis XV and Voltaire*, 2 v. (1950); J. V. Cunningham, *Woe or Wonder* (1951); Wimsatt and Brooks, chs. 3, 25; K. Muir, *Shakespeare and the Tragic Pattern* (1958); G. F. Else, *Aristotle's Poetics: The Argument* (1959), *The Origin and Early Form of Gr. T.* (1965), *Plato and Aristotle on Poetry* (1986); I. Ribner, *Patterns in Shakespearian T.* (1960), *Jacobean T.* (1962); H. D. F. Kitto, *Gr. T.*, 3d ed. (1961); G. Steiner, *The Death of T.* (1961); E. Olson, *T. and the Theory of Drama* (1961); E. A. Havelock, *Preface to Plato* (1962); J. H. F. Jones, *On Aristotle and Gr. T.* (1962); W. Benjamin, *Ursprung des deutschen Trauerspiels* (1963, tr. J. Osborne as *The Origin of Ger. Tragic Drama*, 1977); *T.: Mod. Essays in Crit.*, ed. L. Michel and R. B. Sewall (1963); M. T. Herrick, *It. T. in the Ren.* (1965); A. Lesky, *Gr. T.* (1965), *Gr. Tragic Poetry*, tr. M. Dillon (1983); R. Williams, *Mod. T.* (1966); B. M. Knox, *The Heroic Temper: Studies in Sophoclean T.* (1966), *Word and Action* (1979); N. Frye, *Fools of Time: Studies in Shakespearean T.* (1967); J. M. R. Margeson, *Origins of Eng. T.* (1967); G. M. Sifakis, *Studies in the Hist. of Hellenistic Drama* (1967); E. G. Ballard, "Tragic, Sense of the," *DHI*; C. Leech, *T.* (1969); J. M. Bremer, *Hamartia* (1969); L. Michel, *The Thing Contained: Theory of the Tragic* (1970); R. Girard, *La Violence et le sacré* (1972); B. Vickers, *Towards Gr. T.* (1973); F. R. Adrastos, *Festival, Comedy and T.: The Gr. Origins of Theatre,* tr. C. Holmes (1975); R. B. Sewall, *The Vision of T.*, 2d ed. (1980); T. J. Reiss, *T. and Truth* (1980); M. C. Bradbrook, *Themes and Conventions in Elizabethan T.*, 2d ed. (1980); Trypanis, chs. 3, 9; *T., Vision and Form*, ed. R. W. Corrigan, 2d ed. (1981); J. Orr, *Tragic Drama and Mod. Society* (1981); M. S. Silk and J. P. Stern, *Nietzsche on T.* (1981); C. Segal, *T. and Civilization* (1981), *Dionysiac Poetics and Euripides' Bacchae* (1982), *Interpreting Gr. T.* (1986); J. P. Vernant and P. Vidal-Naquet, *T. and Myth in Ancient Gr.*, tr. J. Lloyd (1981), *Gr. T. and Political Theory* (1986); Fowler; O. Mandel, *A Definition of T.* (1982); S. Booth, *King Lear, Macbeth, Indefinition, and T.* (1983); W. B. Stanford, *Gr. T. and the Emotions* (1983); E. Faas, *T. and After: Euripides, Shakespeare, Goethe* (1984); J. Dollimore, *Radical T.* (1984); C. Belsey, *The Subject of T.* (1985); S. L. Cole, *The Absent One: Mourning Ritual, T., and the Performance of Ambivalence* (1985); H. P. Foley, *Ritual Irony: Poetry and Sacrifice in Euripedes* (1985); J. Herington, *Poetry into Drama* (1985); G. Braden, *Ren. T. and the Senecan Trad.* (1985); *CHCL*, v. 1; *Gr. T. and Political Theory*, ed J. P. Euben (1986); S. Goldhill, *Reading Gr. T.* (1986); S. Halliwell, *Aristotle's Poetics* (1986); M. C. Nussbaum, *The Fragility of Goodness* (1986); M. Heath, *The Poetics of Gr. T.* (1987); N. Loraux, *Tragic Ways of Killing a Woman* (1987); A. Poole, *T.: Shakespeare and the Gr. Example* (1987); M. Gellrich, *T. and Theory: The Problem of Conflict since Aristotle* (1988); E. Hall, *Inventing the Barbarian* (1989); M. J. Smethurst, *The Artistry of Aeschylus and Zeami: A Comparative Study of Gr. T. and Nō* (1989); *Nothing to Do with Dionysos: Athenian Drama in Its Social Context*, ed. J. J. Winkler and F. I. Zeitlin (1989); B. Zimmermann, *Gr. T.: An Intro.*, tr. T. Marier (1990); J. P. Euben, *The T. of Political Theory* (1990); T. C. W. Stinton, *Coll. Papers on Gr. T.* (1990); J. Gregory, *Euripides and the Instruction of the Athenians* (1991).   T.J.R.

TRAGIC IRONY. See IRONY.

TRAGICOMEDY is a term that refers to tragedies, melodrama, and ironic drama which contain comic scenes or characters. The earliest plays mixing such elements are those of Euripides (480–400 B.C.), e.g. *Alcestis*; Aristotle remarks on a public taste for plays in which bad characters came to a bad end and good characters survived happily (*Poetics* 13). Plautus (d. 184 B.C.) coined the term t., applying it to his *Amphytrion*, a play anomalous in its time for mixing noble and humble characters as well as serious and comic action. However, Plautus established no clear generic form (Herrick), and the forms of liturgical drama (q.v.) in the Middle Ages precluded t. It begins to emerge only in the Ren. when both Neo-Lat. and vernacular plays adapt Cl. Lat. comic forms to the dramatization of biblical narrative. A number of them, such as Gascoigne's *Glass of Government*, mix melancholy material with endings that avoid catastrophe and include explicit moral lessons.

Secular t. becomes firmly established in Italy in the plays of Giraldi Cinthio (1504–73), though he is careful to avoid commitment to the idea of a separate genre. His essay *His Discourse on the Composition of Romances, Comedies, and Tragedies* (1554) identifies two kinds of tragedy, one ending in sorrow, the other in happiness. Cinthio prefers the second: "Plots that are terrible because they end unhappily (if it appears the spirits of the spectators abhor them) can serve for closet dramas; those that end happily, for the stage" (Gilbert; Herrick).

What Cinthio calls a type of tragedy, Giovanni Battista Guarini (1538–1612), the most important Ren. partisan, openly and extensively defends as t. In his *Compendio*, his argument, like that of Cinthio, places its main theoretical emphasis on audience response, but more than a happy ending is involved. He regards tragedy, as Aristotle defines it, as less likely to settle the troubled passions of the audience than t. He proposes therefore to retain compassion and forego horror. Hence his definition of t. as a mean between affective extremes: "the mingling of tragic and comic pleasure, which does not allow hearers to fall into excessive tragic melancholy or comic relaxation" (Gilbert).

Guarini's aim is to produce a balanced and harmonized state in the soul of the spectator by means of tightly plotted comic intrigues moving from potential disaster to a happy conclusion. Guarini would retain elevated or distinguished protagonists but situate them in private, domestic experience. More important perhaps is the paradigm he establishes for character development: in his *Pastor Fido* (The Faithful Shepherd) he employs for his protagonist Silvio the topos of inner transformation from scorning to acceptance of love, "a natural metaphor for his conception of t. as a genre which functions as a medicine to purge the human temperament of excesses and so bring men, like Silvio, to a happier balance" (Cope).

One of the chief inheritors of both the romantic plots of Cinthio and the pattern of inner change formulated by Guarini was Shakespeare, though with the exception of *The Tempest* he inclined to a much greater looseness of plot and everywhere mingled levels of character and incongruous subjects in successful defiance of neoclassical principles of decorum. An indifference to rules of structure or decorum is standard in Eng. Ren. drama, and the habit of mixing the serious and the farcical, even in plays nominally identified as tragic, such as *Dr. Faustus* or *King Lear*, seriously undermines neoclassical concepts of genre. In Shakespeare's later plays and in some of the work of Beaumont and Fletcher the presence of t. is evident in the encouragement of paradoxical responses through the mixture of fantastic event and moral redemption. In *A Winter's Tale* there is repeated stress on artifice, as in Hermione's long survival as a statue, where adherence to the rules would require verisimilitude (q.v.).

Fr. theater of the 17th c. tended to a more rigorous observance of imposed standards and hence to less theoretical tolerance of t., though Corneille's *Le Cid* is a tragedy with a happy ending, and his self-justifying "Discourse on Tragedy" (1660) argues, as Guarinni had, that the catastrophic ending was not the best kind. Hence his tragedies can be viewed as t. under a different name and *Le Cid* as "the supreme flowering of neoclassical tragicomic romance" (Hirst; see Lancaster for discussion of t. as a dominant genre in 16th- and early 17th-c. France). There are elements of t. in the work of Molière as well, as in *Le Misanthrope*. In Eng., the 17th and early 18th c. witnessed radically opposed opinions on t. Milton decries the "error of intermixing Comic stuff with Tragic sadness and gravity" (preface to *Samson Agonistes*), a view echoed by Addison (*Spectator* 40). But Dryden in his "Essay of Dramatick Poesy" approves of t. as more natural and indeed wrote several plays in that mode. Johnson's judgment is prophetic of more recent views: "Is it not certain that the tragic and comic affections have been moved alternately with equal force and that no plays have oftener filled the eye with tears and the breast with palpitation than those which are variegated with interludes of mirth?" (*Rambler* 156).

With the decline of verse drama and the relaxing of firm generic standards, t. becomes associated with 19th-c. popular melodrama and the more cerebral plays of Shaw and Chekhov (Hirst). Two formal patterns can be identified in the 19th c.: one largely involves the rescue of sympathetic victims at the last minute, continuing the emphasis on careful and suspenseful plotting established by Guarini; the other is more a matter of tone, a mixing of attitudes toward character and event that tends towards a drama of ironies. Thus the critical and theoretical terms for discussion of t. emphasize audience response over formal or generic contexts or patterns of character change. Twentieth-century drama ignores such considerations as the social status of characters, consistency in levels of lang., and decorum in subject matter, deliberately mixing tragic and comic elements without any attempt at the harmony and balance advocated by Guarini. As in Eliot's *Murder in the Cathedral*, the audience may be encouraged simultaneously to tragic empathy and comic detachment, and complexity of tone and hence of response become common features of modern dramas as diverse as those by Shaw and Chekhov and the writers of the Theater of the Absurd (see Hernadi; Guthke; Hirst).

See also DRAMATIC POETRY; GENRE.

H. C. Lancaster, *The Fr. T.* (1907); H. Corbach, "Tragikomödie," *Reallexikon I*, v. 4; P. Corneille, "Discourse on Tragedy," rpt. in *Dramatic Essays of the Neoclassic Age*, ed. H. Adams and B. Hathaway (1947); K. S. Guthke, *Gesch. und Poetik der deut-*schen *Tragikomödie* (1961); M. Esslin, *Theatre of the Absurd* (1962); M. T. Herrick, *T.* (1962); G. Guarini, *The Compendium of Tragicomic Poetry*, excerpted in *Lit. Crit. Plato to Dryden*, ed. A. Gilbert (1962), *The Faithful Shepherd*, tr. R. Fanshawe (1964); J. L. Styan, *The Dark Comedy* (1962); C. Hoy, *The Hyacinth Room* (1964); K. Guthke, *Mod. T.* (1966); J. Hartwig, *Shakespeare's Tragicomic Vision* (1972); J. Cope, *The Theater and the Dream* (1973); B. J. Bond, *Literary Transvaluation from Vergilian Epic to Shakespearean T.* (1984); M. Carlson, *Theories of the Theatre* (1984); D. L. Hirst, *T.* (1984); P. Hernadi, *Interpreting Events* (1985); R. Dutton, *Mod. T. and the British Trad.* (1986); J. Orr, *T. and Contemp. Culture* (1990).   R.L.M.

TRANSCENDENTALISTS. See AMERICAN POETRY.

TRANSGRESSIO. See HYPERBATON.

TRANSLATION. Significantly, most langs. have more than one word for this somewhat mysterious and poorly understood process. Indonesian uses *terjemahan*, *pertalan*, and *penjalinan*, the latter from the root meaning to bear a child or to change one's clothes; Ger. employs *übertragen*, meaning transference or negotiation, or *übersetzen*, meaning crossing or jumping over; even Fr., which like Eng. derives its word for tr. from the Lat. (*translatio*, with the primary sense of carrying or transporting), uses both *traduction* and *version*, as does Sp. (*tradución*, *versión*); It. uses *traduzione* and *transferimento*. The present discussion will necessarily concern itself with literary tr. of poetry from other langs. into Eng.; it will focus on the actual process of tr. in the Eng.-speaking world.

Although approaches to tr. vary from culture to culture and from one period to another, worldwide there have been three basic stances. (1) The text in the original lang. is seen as all-controlling: form, prosody, and lexicon in the host lang. must be as "faithful" as possible. (2) Literary values are viewed as less important than content, and in any case unattainable in tr.; consequently, full tr. in sense (1) should not be attempted: all poetic texts should be rendered in plain prose. (3) The literary *effectiveness* of the translated text is considered primary: form, prosody, and lexicon must be adapted to the requirements of the new lang. and culture: the tr. must be as much like an original work as possible. Most of those who have commented on tr. do not distinguish between renderings of poetry and renderings of prose; until very recent times, the same standards tended to be applied to both. Approach (1) sees tr. as the rendering of *words*, approach (2) as the rendering of *information* and *ideas*, approach (3) as the rendering of *spirit* and *style*.

A translator's relationship to current literary values in the lang. into which he is translating is frequently what determines the approach taken.

Tradition-minded writers and some academics favor approach (1); most academics favor approach (2); and those friendly to current literary values favor approach (3). Although it remains true that over the centuries tr. practice has varied enormously, approach (3) has deeper and more universal roots both in the West and in the East. This is usually understood as a matter of practicality rather than anything idealistic or romantic: as Feng Yuan-Chun explains, "good writing encourages us to advance, while bad writing drags us back." Chinese, Indian, and other Eastern translators have felt that the texts they produced had to be primarily successful as literary equivalents of their distinguished originals. So too St. Jerome, in the preface to his tr. of Eusebius, declares forthrightly that "I have at once translated and written a new work." *Non verbum e verbo, sed sensum exprimere de sensu*, was his rule: "Not word for word, but sense for sense."

Tr. in Eng. certainly does not begin with King Alfred (ca. 880 A.D.), but his determination to "translate certain books which are most necessary for all men to know, into the lang. that we can all understand" is perhaps the clearest surviving evidence from the OE period of tr.'s cultural importance. Alfred was of course thinking primarily in religious terms, but Chaucer's many trs. (Boethius, *Le Roman de la rose*, Boccaccio, Machaut, Deschamps)) range from philosophy to lit. to science. Wyatt translated widely from the It.; Surrey's *Aeneid* is a milestone in the regularization of Eng. prosody. Sidney, Donne, Herrick, Milton, Pope, Wordsworth, Coleridge, Shelley, Byron, Rossetti, Yeats—even Tennyson—translated; and Dryden, of course, is one of tr.'s theoretical as well as practical pillars. The basic approach of these poets is Dryden's: "A good poet is no more like himself in a dull tr., than his carcass would be to his living body. . . . He who excels all other poets in his own lang., were it possible to do him right, must appear above them in our tongue." As for "faithfulness," Dryden insisted that "There are a sort of blundering, half-witted people who make a great deal of noise about a verbal slip. . . . True judgment . . . takes a view of the whole together, whether it be good or not; and where the beauties are more than the faults, concludes for the poet against the little judge" (Preface to *Sylvae* [1685]).

In 20th-c. verse tr. the single largest figure is Ezra Pound. This or that of Pound's trs. can be faulted in one or another respect. He was neither programmatic nor consistent, merely amatory— and as gifted as he was energetic. No translator of Heinrich Heine into Eng. has ever so elegantly, movingly, and *accurately* captured the very essence of that wry, yearning German-Jewish poet:

I dreamt that I was God Himself
  Whom heavenly joy immerses,
  And all the angels sat about
  And praised my verses.

("Trs. and Adaptations from Heine")

And no one has ever pierced so brilliantly, even achingly into the very core of the vast and splendid poetry of China:

By the gate now, the moss is grown, the
  different mosses,
Too deep to clear them away!
The leaves fall early this autumn, in
  wind.
("The River-Merchant's Wife: A Letter")

Understanding the fundamental truth that each age, having its own needs and approaches, needs to remake trs. in its own image, Pound serves not so much as a model, and certainly not as a formulator of theories or rules, but as an inspirational beacon. The mark of his influence lies on virtually all important poetic tr. in this century; if ours is, as has often been claimed, a great age of tr., Pound more than any other figure is responsible.

In more specific terms, what Pound seems instinctively to have understood is that the tr. of poetry is an art, but at its best only a partial and inevitably a somewhat derivative art. He saw that we not only do not but cannot translate *words*, if living poetry is the desired result. Pedantic notions of "faithfulness" and "fidelity" seemed to him, as they did to Dryden, irrelevant. He understood that *ideas* are completely secondary to poetry, if even of that much importance. His own magnificent version of the OE poem, "The Seafarer," barely translates the words and completely skews the content—and yet no other tr. so successfully captures the vitality and drive of OE verse. And what he grasped most completely, accordingly, was that the positive side of tr.'s intrinsic and inevitable imperfection is that it allows the translator to focus on whatever aspects of the original seem most worth reproducing—in short, to concentrate on and recreate the original's *spirit* and *style*. Since the basic, ineluctable truth is that no tr. can ever be the original, Pound saw that, no matter how imperfectly, each poetically valid tr. could thus capture and transmit at least a significant degree of the original's central nature.

In linguistic terms, Pound intuited that the essence of the tr. process was not a single-stage transposition, original into tr., with the focus on either words or on information and ideas, but rather a complex, organic, and multi-stage procedure in which, first, the original is disassembled and then, often more or less laboriously, reassembled—but reassembled within the constraints of the host lang. and the conventions of its poetic culture. There can be many levels within this complex procedure; the translator can push against the limitations of the host lang. or its poetic culture. But no fundamental breakage of those boundaries is possible. Indonesian, for example, has no long vowels, virtually no tense structure, and an agglutinative syntax. The translator into a lang. like Eng. can at best suggest aspects of these linguistic features: he cannot hope to reproduce them straightforwardly, since Eng. exhibits regular alternations in vowel length, relatively elaborate tense structures, and an analytic syntax. Linguistic features like the Indonesian reduplicative plural simply cannot be carried over into Eng., where they are totally alien and unknown. Rather than focus on what he cannot hope to accomplish, and without ever doubting that tr. is both possible and worthwhile (no matter how inevitably imperfect), the translator of an Indonesian poem must therefore concentrate on discovering what aspects of the original the host lang., and his personal skill, will allow him to transmit.

In short, what Pound learned (his stiff and sometimes graceless early trs. show that he acquired the knowledge fairly slowly and over a long time) was that the poetic translator must at the end of his labors finally and definitively turn his back on the original and stress the poetic achievements of the tr. A necessary corollary is that the translator of poetry must be a competent poet; another fundamental corollary is that the tr. of a poem must itself be a poem. Tr. into prose abandons too much. To surrender the original's rhyme scheme, or even its rhyme entirely, is of course a loss, but the poem can survive such deprivations. To turn a poem into prose, however, is to surrender its existence as a poem.

Less important corollaries, but equally poorly understood by nontranslators and most academics, are that the translator's knowledge of and poetic competency in the host lang. count for very much more than his knowledge of and poetic competency in the lang. of the original. Indeed, as Pound himself proved when he began to translate Chinese poems, knowing not a word of Chinese and wholly dependent on notes left by the art critic and historian, Ernest Fenellosa (whose own primary interest was Japan rather than China), a poet-translator can turn out viable versions of poems he cannot himself read, while a trained scholar with a superb and extensive grasp of the original lang. and culture will more often than not turn out inert, inutile versions. Another corollary, consequently, is that poet-translators can work with native informants, or in combined linguistic and literary teams, and produce first-rate trs. Not accidentally, there has been more such activity in the years since Pound than in all of prior recorded history.

Another way of viewing Pound's tr. revolution is to understand that its central figure is in fact neither the original poet nor the translator but the general reader. To translate poems for those who have a significant but imperfect knowledge of the original lang. and culture is perfectly appropriate. However, that sort of tr., which focuses on words, is better thought of as a crib or pony—a kind of linguistic aid. Similarly, to translate only the information and ideas of the original poem, abandoning all literary values in favor of a supposedly "faithful" prose, is in truth not to translate at all, but merely to *paraphrase*. Again, there is an audience for paraphrase (q.v.)—but it is not the same as the audience for true tr.

Ideally, to be sure, the translator should not only be a poet in the host lang., but should be completely fluent in the lang. of the original, deeply versed in its culture (poetic and social), and fully informed of all relevant historical, geographic, and other contextual matters bearing on the poem. Such standards are not always appropriate for our entirely unideal world. As Pound and those who have learned from him understand, we must strive for attainable goals. It remains true that, to understand properly and fully a Cl. Gr. poet, one must know Cl. Greece and its culture. But *no* trs. of Cl. Gr. poems are ever made for people thus fully equipped. Most such trs. are made for readers who do not know Gr. but who want and need to savor and, as far as possible, understand the spirit and style of Cl. Gr. poetry; they do not need to achieve (though they may long for) the fuller appreciation and comprehension available to more learned readers.

"Western Europe," writes Louis Kelly, "owes its civilization to translators." To a considerable extent, we all owe what civilization we ourselves embody to translators. We need to understand what tr. can give us, but also what it cannot. Just as every age has its prototypical writers, so too every age has its prototypical trs.—and both change from age to age. Pope's *Iliad* is now a magnificent 18th-c. poem, as Dryden's *Aeneid* belongs to 17th-c. poetry.   B.R.

J. Dryden, Pref. to *Ovid's Epistles Tr. by Several Hands* (1680), Ded. to *The Works of Virgil* (1697); W. Dillon, Earl of Roscommon, *An Essay on Tr. Verse* (1684); A. Pope, Pref. to *The Iliad of Homer* (1715); T. Parnell, Preface to *Homer's Battle of the Frogs and Mice* (1717); J. Spence, *An Essay on Mr. Pope's Odyssey* (1726–27); W. Benson, *Letters Concerning Poetical Trs.* (1739); M. Arnold, *Last Words On Translating Homer* (1862); J. Conington, "Eng. Translators of Virgil," *QR* 110 (1861); C. Whibley, "Translators," *CHEL.*, v. 4 (1909), "Tudor Translators," in his *Lit. Studies* (1919); F. R. Amos, *Early Theories of Tr.* (1920); J. W. Draper, "The Theory of Tr. in the 18th C.," *Neophil* 6 (1920); D. Bush, "Eng. Translators of Homer," *PMLA* 41 (1926); R. C. Whitford, "Juvenal in England, 1750–1802," *PQ* 7 (1928); F. O. Mathiessen, *T.: An Elizabethan Art* (1931); H. J. C. Grierson, *Verse Tr.* (1949); E. Pound, *The Trs. of Ezra Pound* (1953); W. Frost, *Dryden and the Art of Tr.* (1955); *On Tr.*, ed. R. A. Brower (1959); *The Craft and Context of Tr.*, ed. W. Arrowsmith and R. Shattuck (1961); J. C. Catford, *A Linguistic Theory of Tr.* (1965); *The Nature of Tr.*, ed. J. S. Holmes (1970); B. Raffel, *The Forked Tongue: A Study of the Tr. Process* (1971), *The Art of Translating Poetry* (1988); *The World of Tr.* (P.E.N.) (1971); R. M. Adams, *Proteus, His Lies, His Truth*

(1973); R. Brower, *Mirror on Mirror* (1974); A. Lefevere, *Translating Poetry* (1975); E. A. Nida, *Lang. Structure and Tr.* (1975); G. Steiner, *After Babel* (1975); L. Kelly, *The True Interpreter: A Hist. of Tr. Theory and Practice in the West* (1979); J. Felstiner, *Translating Neruda* (1980); R. Kloepfer, "Übersetzung," *Reallexikon*, v. 4; R. Apter, *Digging for the Treasure: Tr. After Pound* (1984); *Tr.: Literary, Linguistic, and Philosophical Perspectives*, ed. W. Frawley (1984); *The Craft of Tr.*, ed. J. Biguenet and R. Schulte (1989); *The Med. Translator*, ed. R. Ellis (1989); A. Benjamin, *Tr. and the Nature of Philosophy* (1989); D. Robinson, *The Translator's Turn* (1990); *Theories of Tr.*, ed. R. Schulte and J. Biguenet (1992); W. Barnstone, *The Poetics of Tr.* (1993).   T.V.F.B.

TRANSUMPTION. See METALEPSIS.

TRIBE OF BEN. See CAVALIER POETS.

TRIBRACH. In Gr. and Lat. verse, a sequence of three short syllables, almost always a resolved iamb or trochee rather than an independent foot (see RESOLUTION). The ictus falls on the second syllable if it replaces an iamb and on the first if it replaces a trochee.—Koster; West.   P.S.C.

TRIHEMIMERAL. See CAESURA.

TRILOGY. In Gr. drama, a group of three tragedies that treat a single myth. At the annual Great Dionysia in Athens, three poets competed, each offering three tragedies plus a satyr play, a humorous parody of the tragic form which employed a chorus of satyrs; if this satyr play also deals with the same myth, then the whole is called a *tetralogy*. The origin of the custom requiring three tragedies is unknown; the addition of the satyr play occurred around 500 B.C. Aeschylus is believed to have been the first playwright to connect the plays in one year's offering into a t. or tetralogy. In the *Oresteia*, the only extant t., Aeschylus traces the problem of blood-guilt through successive generations of Agamemnon's family; *Seven against Thebes*, the final tragedy in a t. on the House of Laius, exhibits a similar concern with a family curse. Yet the outcomes are very different: the Theban t. ends in the ruin of the royal house, while *Eumenides*, which concludes the *Oresteia*, dramatizes a resolution of the guilt and the foundation of a new order of justice. The Danaid t., of which the first play, *Suppliant Women*, survives, evidently climaxed in a similar celebration of the sanctity of marriage. Yet this t. differs in that its three tragedies dramatized a single, tightly-knit event spanning only a few days rather than events separated by many years. The fragmentary evidence of other Aeschylean ts. suggest that such unity of plot was not uncommon. After Aeschylus, the t. as a form fell into disuse. Sophocles abandoned it (the composition of his three Theban plays spanned 40 years, so that one refers to the Oedipus cycle as a t. only in a loose

sense), and Euripides apparently only once offered three tragedies connected in subject matter: his *Trojan Women* is the third play in a series on the Trojan War. The terms "t." and "tetralogy" were not current in 5th-c. Athens, nor does Aristotle use them; they first appear in Alexandrian commentaries. A modern sequence of plays consciously based on the ancient model is the trilogy by Eugene O'Neill, *Mourning Becomes Electra*.

It was uncommon in the Ren. to link tragedies, but sequences of two plays were written occasionally, e.g. Marlowe's *Tamburlaine* (parts 1 and 2), Shakespeare's *Henry IV* (parts 1 and 2), and Chapman's *Bussy D'Ambois* and *The Revenge of Bussy D'Ambois*. Shakespeare's *Henry VI* is in three parts, and he wrote two series of four history plays which modern scholars (but no Elizabethans) sometimes call "tetralogies." These are the four plays extending from *Henry VI, Part 1*, to *Richard III* (the first historical "tetralogy" to be written, though the later of the two tetralogies chronologically) and the four plays extending from *Richard II* to *Henry V*. In modern usage the terms simply refer to dramatic or literary works written in three or four parts.—G. F. Else, *The Origin and Early Form of Gr. Tragedy* (1967); A. Lesky, *Die tragischen Dichtung der Hellenen*, 3d ed. (1972); A. Pickard-Cambridge, *The Dramatic Festivals of Athens*, 2d ed. rev. and corr. (1989).   V.P.; O.B.H.

TRIMETER (Gr. "of three measures"). Aristotle (*Poetics* 1449a24, *Rhetoric* 1408b33) regards the iambic t. as the most speechlike of Gr. meters (see IAMBIC). It is first employed mixed with dactylic hexameters in the *Margites* ascribed to Homer, though some scholars regard the first line of the "Nestor's cup" inscription, ca. 750–700 B.C., as a t. Despite ancient trad. (e.g. Pseudo-Plutarch, *De musica* 28), Archilochus (fl. 650 B.C.) is not its inventor, although he was the first to use the word "iamb" and developed the t. as a medium for personal invective (q.v.), a practice in which he was followed by Semonides. The Athenian lawgiver Solon used it for political poetry. The t. is the basic dialogue meter of Gr. tragedy, satyr-play, and comedy. It consists of three iambic metra (x represents *anceps*): x – ᴗ – | x – ᴗ – | x – ᴗ –. The penthemimeral caesura (after the fifth position [second *anceps*]) is much more frequent than the hephthemimeral (after the seventh position [second *breve*]); median diaeresis (q.v.) is permitted occasionally in tragedy, though in Euripides only when accompanied by elision. Resolution (q.v.) of a *longum* is permitted at differing rates in all feet but the last. On substitution of – for *breve* or *anceps*, see RESOLUTION. The final element may be short (*brevis in longo*). Most of these departures from the basic iambic pattern are subject to a complex of finely graded phonological, lexical, and syntactic constraints which form a hierarchy of strictness which decreases from the archaic iambographers through early tragedy and later

Euripides to satyr-play and finally comedy. The t. is subject to a number of bridges (see BRIDGE), the strictness of which follows the same generic and stylistic hierarchy.

The Lat. adaptation of the Gr. t. is the *senarius* (q.v.), first used by Livius Andronicus, a common dialogue meter of early Lat. drama and frequent in funerary inscriptions. This version of the meter, however, is organized as six feet rather than three metra. The most striking departure from the Gr. t. is the permissibility of spondees in the second and fourth feet. This variation and many differing constraints on word boundaries are motivated by the differing nature of the Lat. stress accent. Iambic-shaped words, even those of the type not regularly subject to iambic shortening (q.v.), are severely restricted in the interior of the line, since otherwise they would produce conflict of accent with metrical ictus. Spondee-shaped (or – ending) words, however, could be permitted in trochaic segments of the verse, since their stress pattern would preserve the iambic rhythm. In contrast to the *senarius*, the Lat. lyric poets, such as Catullus and Horace, and Seneca in his dramas, follow the pattern of the Gr. t. more closely, excluding spondees in even feet, restricting resolution and substitution, and not admitting iambic shortening (q.v.).

The prosodies of the modern vernaculars followed the Lat. metrical practice of scanning in feet rather than metra, so that the t. of the Germanic langs. (incl. Eng.) of the later Middle Ages, Ren., and modern period is most often a very short line of three binary feet or six syllables—too short to be capable of sustained effects in narrative or dramatic verse, but very suitable for song. Literary examples incl. a dozen songs by Wyatt ("I will and yet I may not," "Me list no more to sing") and Surrey, Jonson's "Dedication of the King's New Cellar" (with feminine rhymes), Elizabeth Barrett Browning's "The Mourning Mother," and a dozen poems by Shelley, one of them, "To a Skylark," trochaic t. with an alexandrine close. In Fr. prosody, the line now called the *trimètre* (q.v.) is not a t. in this sense: it is an alexandrine (q.v.) of 12 syllables divided into three rhythmical phrases, and made its appearance only with the advent of romanticism.

Schipper; F. Lang, *Platen's T.* (1924); J. Descroix, *Le Trimètre iambique* (1931); G. Rosenthal, *Der T. als deutsche Versmasse* (1934); P. W. Harsh, *Iambic Words and Regard for Accent in Plautus* (1949); Maas, sects. 101–16; D. S. Raven, *Lat. Metre* (1965); C. Questa, *Introduzione alla metrica di Plauto* (1967); W. S. Allen, *Accent and Rhythm* (1973); West; S. L. Schein, *The Iambic T. in Aeschylus and Sophocles* (1979); A. M. Devine and L. D. Stephens, *Lang. and Metre* (1984).

A.M.D.; L.D.S.; T.V.F.B.

TRIMÈTRE. In Fr. pros., a variation on the *tétramètre* (q.v.); an alexandrine (q.v.) of three

measures rather than four. It is an extension of the rhythmic and expressive range of the *tétramètre*, not an alternative form, since no poems have been written exclusively in *t.* Examples of *t.* are to be found in the freer alexandrines of the *Pléiade* (q.v.) poets and in the less punctilious genres of the 17th and 18th cs. (comedy, fable). It was with the romantics, and with Hugo in particular, that it achieved an ideological status and a subversive intention, hence another of its names, the *alexandrin romantique* (it is also called the *alexandrin ternaire*). Care should be taken to distinguish between different degrees of *t.* The romantics, and the poets who preceded them, maintained the possibility of an accent on the sixth syllable, even though, in the event, it was not accented; in other words, the caesura still enjoyed a spectral existence despite being effaced by the greater syntactic and rhythmic claims of ternary structure; the romantic *t.* is thus quite easy to envisage as a *tétramètre* with enjambment (q.v.) at the caesura, e.g. Hugo: "Nous demandons, vivants // douteux qu'un linceul couvre" (4 + 4 + 4). The romantic *t.* usually has this regular 4 + 4 + 4 pattern, though it may occasionally explore other combinations, e.g. 3 + 5 + 4. The Parnassians and symbolists developed more extreme forms of the *t.* by frequently erasing the caesura completely, e.g. Banville: "Où je filais pensivement la blanche laine" (4 + 4 + 4), and by multiplying asymmetrical combinations of measures, e.g. Mallarmé: "Une ruine, par mille écumes bénie" (4 + 5 + 3). It is in these more radical forms that the *t.* became a central feature of *vers libéré* (q.v.).—Kastner; G. Aae, *Le T. de Victor Hugo* (1909); Elwert; J. Mazaleyrat, "Élan verbal et rythme ternaire dans l'alexandrin," *FM* 40 (1972); Mazaleyrat; Scott. C.S.

TRIOLET. A Fr. fixed form composed of eight lines and using only two rhymes, disposed in the following scheme: ABaAabAB (a capital letter indicates a repeated line), e.g. W. E. Henley:

> Easy is the triolet,
> If you really learn to make it!
> Once a neat refrain you get,
> Easy is the triolet.
> As you see!—I pay my debt
> With another rhyme. Deuce take it,
> Easy is the triolet,
> If you really learn to make it!

The challenge of the form lies in managing the intricate repetition so that it seems natural and inevitable, and in achieving in the repetitions variety of meaning or, at least, a shift in emphasis.

The word "t." is not found until 1486, but the form as we know it is much older, the *Urform* in fact of the whole rondeau (q.v.) family. It can be traced back to the 13th c., e.g. in the *Cléomadès* of Adenet-le-Roi, and was subsequently cultivated by such medieval poets as Eustache Deschamps and Jean Froissart. After lapsing from favor, it was revived in the 17th c. by Vincent Voiture and La Fontaine, and again in the latter half of the 19th c. as part of Théodore de Banville's general promotion of the Romance fixed forms. It challenged the skills of poets such as Daudet, Mallarmé, Rimbaud, Robert Bridges, Austin Dobson, Edmund Gosse, W. E. Henley, Andrew Lang, Hardy, and Arthur Symons.

Banville overstates the case when he writes of the satirical capabilities of the t.; it is too playful a form to achieve anything more than benign kinds of ridicule. The frequency of dialogue, particularly in the Eng. t., is also dispersive of any satirical intent. Gosse's summary of the t. is more accurate: "nothing can be more ingeniously mischievous, more playfully sly, than this tiny trill of epigrammatic melody, turning so simply on its own innocent axis." The refrain of the t. may express, among other things, a cocky superiority, or a lively defense of a *status quo*; it may achieve a certain lyric intensity in the fourth line. The fifth and sixth lines both support the refrain and resist it; they support it structurally by re-establishing some formal stability after the irregularities of the third and fourth lines and thus providing a platform for the final appearance of the refrain; they resist it by allowing a temporary release from its apparent stranglehold, usually accompanied by an expansion of the subject-matter. The Eng. poets create out of the t. a structure of some complexity involving variations both of line-length and meter; the Fr. poets are less adventurous, sticking to octosyllables and often finding it easier to work with sequences of t.-stanzas than with single units. T.-stanzas must find a delicate balance between formal autonomy and formal interdependence.—T. de Banville, *Petit Traité de poésie française* (1872); E. Gosse, "A Plea for Certain Exotic Forms of Verse," *Cornhill Magazine* 36 (1877); J. Gleeson White, *Ballades and Rondeaus* (1887); Kastner; H. L. Cohen, *Lyric Forms from France* (1922); P. Champion, *Histoire poétique du XVe siècle*, 2 v. (1923); L. Spitzer, "T.," *RR* 39 (1948); P. J. Marcotte, "An Intro. to the T.," "More Late Victorian T. Makers," "A Trio of T. Turners," *Inscape* 5-6 (1966–68); C. Scott, "The 19th-C. T.: Fr. and Eng.," *Orbis Litterarum* 35 (1980); Morier. A.PR.; C.S.

TRIPLE METERS. See BINARY AND TERNARY.

TRIPLE RHYME, three consecutive syllables at the end of two or more lines that rhyme. Rhyming more than two syllables in sequence is difficult in Eng., hence relatively rare. In Eng. Ren. verse, double and t. rs. are more common than is usually supposed, however. These are almost always the result of deliberate imitation of It. models; since *sdrucciolo* (proparoxytonic) endings on words are more frequent in It. than in the other Romance langs., compound rs. of 2, 3, or more syllables are an important component of It. versification. Sidney mentions t. r. in the *Defence of Poesie* and has

virtuoso examples of it in the *Arcadia*. Since Byron (*Don Juan*, "Beppo," etc.), however, most examples have been comic and deliberately exhibitionist: thus Byron has *gymnastical/ecclesiastical* ("Beppo") and *intellectual/ hen-peck'd you all* (virtually quadruple, if -*te*- in *intellectual* is elided; cf. *meticulous / ridiculous*). In the 20th c., good examples are to be found in Ogden Nash.

In the most common form of t. r., only the first syllable of the three is stressed, the other two being extrametrical—e.g. *glaringly/sparingly*. The word-shape is dactylic, which is sometimes used as an alternate term for t. r., as is "double feminine." But all three syllables might be metrical if the third syllable bears secondary stress (cretic word-shape) and falls under the final ictus in the line. Since in Eng. it is more difficult to rhyme two polysyllabic words than a phrase of monosyllables, most t. rs. (e.g. the second Byron example) are mosaic (q.v.)— i.e. several short words rhyming with one long one. T. r. is to be distinguished from the tercet (q.v.), a rhymed stanza of three lines, and the triplet (q.v.), a run of three rhymes in couplet verse. No careful or full study of t. r. has yet been made. See RHYME.
T.V.F.B.

TRIPLET (Ger. *Dreireim*). In Eng. Restoration and 18th-c. verse written in heroic couplets (q.v.), a run of three lines rhymed together. Often these are marked visually as well by a brace in the margin. Dryden says he employs them "frequently" because "they bound the sense"; he makes the third line an alexandrine (Dedication to *Aeneis*). Ts. are familiar in Dryden and (less so) in Pope; Donne wrote most of his verse epistles in monorhymed iambic ts. Schipper shows other examples in the fourteeners and pentameters of Chapman, Hall, and Browning. Keats follows Dryden for their use in *Lamia*.—Schipper; C. A. Balliet, "The Hist. and Rhet. of the T.," *PMLA* 80 (1965). T.V.F.B.

TRIVIUM. See RHETORIC AND POETRY.

TROBAR CLUS, TROBAR LEU. Controversy between troubadours defending the t. c. ("enclosed, hermetic poetry") and those extolling the t. l. ("light" or "easy poetry") is found ca. 1160–1210, with later echoes, and seems to have centered on some poets' desire to write for a select audience of connoisseurs. The *clus* manner is characteristically allusive, oblique, and recherché in vocabulary and rhymes (e.g. Raimbaut d'Orange), though similar features occur in earlier troubadours (q.v.) who make no claim to be *clus* (e.g. Marcabru). Though the t. l. ultimately prevailed, the t. c. influenced a manner often called *trobar ric* ("rich," i.e. "elaborate" poetry) involving verbal and metrical acrobatics without much of the profundity of thought claimed by *clus* poets. All three categories concerned poetic aims rather than specific stylistic traits and were never mutually exclusive: Guiraut de Bornelh, notably, claimed to excel in t. c. and t. l. alike. The terminology itself was far from fixed: *t. car* ("dear") and *t. prim* ("delicate, subtle") seem to refer to much the same manner as *t. ric*, while *t. plan* ("smooth") is a synonym of *t. leu*.—U. Mölk, *T. c., t. l.* (1968); A. Roncaglia, "T. c.: discussione aperta," *CN* 29 (1969); L. M. Paterson, *Troubadours and Eloquence* (1975).   J.H.M.

TROCHAIC (Gr. *trochee, choree*, respectively "running," "belonging to the dance"). A term used for both metrical units and whole meters having the rhythm "marked—unmarked" in series. In the modern accentual meters, a trochee is a foot (q.v.) comprising a stressed syllable followed by a unstressed; in the quantitative meters of the Cl. langs., however, the elements were long and short. In Lat. the t. foot comprised one long syllable followed by one short, whereas in Gr., the unit was the t. metron (q.v.), $- \cup - x$ (x denotes *anceps*). T. measures were used in archaic Gr. poetry at least from the time of Archilochus; and in Gr. tragedy and comedy, they appear in both choral lyric and spoken dialogue. In Lat. comedy, the t. seems to have lent itself esp. well to rapid movement and dancing; the most common meter of Plautus and Terence is the t. tetrameter catalectic or septenarius (q.v.), a meter also used by Caesar's legions for marching songs (Beare). In all these registers it seems to maintain close ties with popular speech and song.

In modern verse, t. meter used for entire poems is far less common than iambic (hereafter i.) and does not appear until the Ren.: the first clearly accentual ts. in Eng. are by Sidney (*Certain Sonnets* 7, 26, 27), followed by Nicholas Breton; From Sidney's example, they became more popular in the 1590s, though still mainly in tetrameters. Lear's "Never, never, never, never, never" is an exception meant to reaffirm the i. rule. On the other hand, t. meters are quite common in many songs, chants, and nursery rhymes; in idioms, formulaic expressions, proverbs, riddles, slogans, jingles, and college cheers; and in much popular and folk verse. In short, t. verse is rare in literary verse but common in popular. The most obvious explanation for this differential would be that most of these forms have some close relation to song (q.v.). They are either sung to music, recited in a singsong chant, or originally derived from song (q.v.). In music, t. rhythm is structural since a stress begins every bar. Presumably the use of t. meters for text simplifies the fitting of the words to music.

Some metrists (e.g. Tomaševskij, Xolševnikov) have denied there is any difference between i. and t. meters except for the first syllable (see ANACRUSIS). But in fact the poets make it very clear that they perceive a radical distinction between the two meters. Whole poems in t. meter are relatively rare in any modern verse trad. (Saintsbury 3.529; Gasparov 1974, 50–62), and t. meter is clearly associated with only certain kinds of genres, sub-

jects, and rhythmic movements. The distribution of line forms is also quite different: t. pentameter is almost unheard of, while t. tetrameters are as common as i. if not more so. Poems where metrical code-switching between i. and t. is systematic are rare (Maria Cvetaeva in Rus.; the verse known as "8s and 7s" in Eng.—see below). And internal line-dynamics differ radically: first-foot stress reversals are 4 times more common in i. verse (12%) than in t. (3%) in Eng. and 30 times more common in Rus. There is a widespread perception among poets and prosodists that t. meters are in some way more rigid, more brittle, "more difficult to maintain" (Hascall) than i. ones.

In Eng. there is a mixed iambo-t. form known as 8s and 7s, instanced most famously in Milton's *L'Allegro* and *Il Penseroso*, which seems to mix i. and t. lines seamlessly, or else to mix normal i. lines with acephalous (q.v.) ones which only *seem* to be t. (see ANACRUSIS; RISING AND FALLING). This problem points up the importance of distinguishing between t. *meters* and t. *rhythms* in i. meters. Traditional Eng. metrics would say that an i. pentameter line such as "And quickly jumping backward, raised his shield," while in i. meter, has a "falling rhythm" which is the result of t. wordshapes. While meter organizes lang. on the phonological level, it nevertheless affects, and is affected by, morphology as well (see IAMBIC).

There is some evidence that t. rhythms predominate in certain speech contexts, esp. children's speech, and that t. rhythms are easier both to produce and to perceive (see IAMBIC). But it is disputed whether Eng. as a lang. is essentially i. or t. in character. Comprehensive data on wordshapes in the lexicon (i.e. how many are monosyllabic, disyllabic i., disyllabic t., trisyllabic, polysyllabic) and the frequencies of these words in ordinary speech vs. poetry (many words in the dictionary will never appear in poetry), along with comparable data on the shapes of Eng. phrases and their frequencies, are difficult to come by, even for one lang. Gil makes a global distinction between i. and trochaic langs.: i. "are characterized by SVO word order, simple syllable structures, high consonant-vowel ratios, and the absence of phonemic tones," while trochaic have SOV, complex syllable structures, low C-V ratios, and phonemic tone.

Several efforts have been made to analyze the frequency of word types both in i. vs. t. verse and in these as set against the norm of the lang., in order to try to discover significant statistical deviations (e.g. Jones; Tarlinskaja, following Gasparov). Some striking statistics have emerged. But the very idea of a linguistic "norm" against which poetic lang. "deviates" is an approach now viewed as suspect. Lexical selection is not the only or even perhaps the central issue; certainly poets think in terms of significant words, but more generally these must be woven into the fabric of the verse in syntactically predetermined ways. Analyzing wordshape rhythms in relation to line rhythms misses the crucial point that lines are not formed by stringing words together but rather (mainly) by putting phrases together: most words come in prepackaged phrasal containers of relatively fixed rhythmic shape—prepositional phrases, noun phrases, compound verbs. And once a poet selects a word in a line, the range of relevant words for that or even following lines is constrained by the chosen semantic field. It is precisely the power of i. verse, for example, that an i. line may comprise two monosyllables and four t. words. T. verse, by contrast, requires t. words. Wordshapes are the elements, and certainly these vary in significant ways, but it is the stitching which counts.

See now BINARY AND TERNARY; METER; PYRRHIC; SENARIUS; SEPTENARIUS; SPONDEE; TETRAMETER.

Schipper 2.375–98 and *History*, chs. 13, 14.2; W. Brown, *Time in Eng. Verse Rhythm* (1908); H. Woodrow, *A Quantitative Study of Rhythm* (1909); J. E. W. Wallin, "Experimental Studies of Rhythm and Time," *Psych. Rev.* 18 (1911), 19 (1912); J. W. White, *The Verse of Gr. Comedy* (1912); Wilamowitz, pt. 2, ch. 5; K. Taranovski, *Ruski dvodelni ritmovi* (1953); P. Fraisse, *Les Structures rythmiques* (1956), *The Psychology of Time* (tr. 1963), *Psychologie du rythme* (1974); Beare; Norberg, 73 ff.; C. L. Drage, "T. Metres in Early Rus. Syllabo-Tonic Poetry," *SEER* 38 (1960); Koster, ch. 6; C. Questa, *Introduzione alla metrica di Plauto* (1967); Dale, ch. 5; G. Faure, *Les Éléments du rythme poétique en anglaise moderne* (1970); D. L. Hascall, "T. Meter," *CE* 33 (1971); M. L. Gasparov, *Sovremennyj russkij stix* (1974); R. P. Newton, "T. and I.," *Lang&S* 8 (1975); M. G. Tarlinskaja, *Eng. Verse: Theory and History* (1976); D. Laferrière, "I. Versus T.: The Case of Rus.," *IRSL* 4 (1979); R. G. Jones, "Linguistic and Metrical Constraints in Verse," *Ling. and Lit. Studies A. A. Hill*, v. 4 (1979); Halporn et al.; Snell; West; D. Gil, "A Prosodic Typology of Lang.," *Folia Linguistica* 20 (1986); *CHCL*, v. 1, ch. 5; G. T. Wright, *Shakespeare's Metrical Art* (1988), ch. 13; B. Bjorklund, "I. and T. Verse," *Rhythm and Meter*, ed. P. Kiparsky and G. Youmans (1989).　　T.V.F.B.

TROCHEE. See TROCHAIC.

TROPE, TROPOLOGICAL, TROPOLOGY. See ALLEGORY; FIGURE, SCHEME, TROPE; INTERPRETATION, FOURFOLD METHOD OF; TEXTUALITY.

TROUBADOUR. Medieval Occitan lyric poet. The term expresses the agent of the verb *trobar* "to find, invent, compose verse"; the etymon of *trobar* may have been hypothetical Med. Lat. *tropare* "to compose a trope" (a liturgical embellishment, Gr. *tropos*) or hypothetical Sp. Arabic *trob* "song" (cl. Arabic *ṭarab* "to sing") or Lat. *turbare* "to disturb, stir up." These proposed etyma correspond to theories of the origin of courtly love (q.v.) in Arabic or in Cl. or Med. Lat.

Extant t. production dates from ca. 1100 to ca. 1300 A.D., beginning with William IX, Duke of Aquitaine and Count of Poïtiers (1071–1127), alternately bawdy and courtly, and continuing with Jaufre Rudel (fl. 1125–48), whose distant love tantalizingly blends secular and religious qualities; the biting moralist Marcabru (fl. 1130–49); the love-poet Bernart de Ventadorn (fl. 1147–70?); the witty Peire Vidal (fl. 1183–1204), who travelled as far as Hungary; the political satirist and war poet Bertran de Born (ca. 1150–1215); and the jolly, worldly Monk of Montaudon (fl. 1193–1210). Composition in a difficult style or *trobar clus* (q.v.) is associated with the names of Peire d'Alvernhe (fl. 1149–68), Raimbaut d'Aurenga (d. 1173), and Arnaut Daniel (fl. 1180–95); Giraut de Bornelh (fl. 1162–99), "the master of the ts.," practiced both *trobar clus* and *trobar leu*, or the easy style. In the early 13th c. appear two *trobairitz* or women troubadours, the moody Castelloza and the more vivacious Comtessa de Dia, who left several songs apiece. Peire Cardenal (fl. 1205–72) followed the satirical trad. of Marcabru and Bertran de Born but was more concerned with religious issues in the period of the Albigensian Crusade; late in the century, Guiraut Riquier (fl. 1254–82) lamented that he was among the last of the ts. In all we know some 450 ts. by name. In the 14th–15th cs., Occitan poetry became an academic prolongation of the earlier trad.; those who wrote it are not called ts., but poets.

Though we have the melodies of only one-tenth of them, it is assumed that virtually all t. poems were set to music. The t. wrote both text and melody, which were performed by the joglar (see JONGLEUR), who served as the messenger for a particular t. by singing his song before its addressee. We have circumstantial information about 101 individual ts. in the prose *vidas* and *razos* (see VIDAS AND RAZOS) which accompany the poems in some mss. This information is considered reliable in objective matters, such as the t.'s place of birth, place of death, and social class, but unreliable in regard to his amorous adventures, which were largely invented by the prose-writers on the basis of what they read in the poems. The outstanding example of such imaginative biography is the *vida* of Jaufre Rudel, which has him perish of love in the arms of the countess of Tripoli.

The ts. exerted influence in both form and content on the Fr. *trouvères* (q.v.) as early as the 12th c., and in the 13th c. on poets writing in Galician-Portuguese and in German. In Italy their influence was felt in the Sicilian school (q.v.) presided over by Frederick II Hohenstaufen, and then by Dante and his friends who created the *dolce stil nuovo* (q.v.). Through Petrarch, who acknowledged his debt, they affected the development of poetry of the Ren. and beyond. See OCCITAN POETRY for further bibl. on ts.—M. R. Menocal, "The Etymology of Old Prov. *trobar, trobador*: A Return to the 'Third Solution,'" *RPh* 36 (1982).　　W.D.P.

TROUVÈRE. Medieval lyric poet of Northern France. The term corresponds to Occitan *troubadour* (q.v.), and since the troubadours composed mostly lyric poetry, t. is commonly applied only to lyric poets and not to the authors of OF narrative. We know over 200 ts. by name, and over 400 troubadours. Troubadour lyrics were written ca. 1100–1300; extant t. production began later, ca. 1190–1300, and was much influenced by the troubadours in form and content. The lyric corpus in the two langs. is comparable in size (about 2500 songs); the ts. cultivated esp. the genres of the courtly *chanson* or love song; religious verse; and the *pastourelle* (q.v.), while avoiding the *sirventes* (q.v.) or satire; genres in the popular style, better preserved in Fr. than in Occitan, incl. the *mal mariée* (q.v.), the *chanson de toile*, and dance-songs such as the *rondet de carole*, the *ballette*, and the *estampie* (q.v.). We have the melodies for about three-quarters of t. lyrics, but for only one-tenth of those of the troubadours. See also OCCITAN POETRY; FRENCH POETRY.

ANTHOLOGIES: *Lirica francese del medio evo*, ed. C. Cremonesi (1955); *Poètes et romanciers du moyen âge*, ed. A. Pauphilet (1958); *Penguin Book of Fr. Verse, v. 1: To the 15th C.*, ed. B. Woledge (1961); *La Poésie lyrique d'oïl*, ed. I.-M. Cluzel and L. Pressouyre (1969); *Lyrics of the Troubadours and Ts.*, ed. F. Goldin (1973); *Lirica cortese d'oïl*, ed. G. Toja, 2d ed. (1976); *Chanter m'estuet*, ed. S. N. Rosenberg (1981); *A Med. Songbook*, ed. F. Collins, Jr. (1982); *Poèmes d'amour des 12e et 13e siècles*, ed. E. Baumgartner (1983); *Mittelalterliche Lyrik Frankreichs, II: Lieder der Ts.*, ed. D. Rieger (1983); *The Med. Lyric*, ed. M. Switten et al., 3 v. (1987–88).

HISTORY AND CRITICISM: J. Frappier, *La Poésie lyrique française aux XIIe et XIIIe siècles* (1954); R. Dragonetti, *La Technique poétique des ts. dans la chanson courtoise* (1960); G. Lavis, *L'Expression de l'affectivité dans la poésie lyrique française du moyen âge* (1972); H. van der Werf, *The Chansons of the Troubadours and Ts.* (1972)—music; P. Zumthor, *Essai de poétique médiévale* (1972); Bec—study with texts; G. Zaganelli, *Aimer, soffrir, joir* (1982).
W.D.P.

TRUE RHYME. See RHYME.

TRUNCATION. See CATALEXIS.

TRUTH. See CRITICISM; DECONSTRUCTION; FICTION, POETRY AS; MEANING, POETIC; POETRY, THEORIES OF; REPRESENTATION AND MIMESIS; SCIENCE AND POETRY; SEMANTICS AND POETRY; SEMIOTICS, POETIC.

TUMBLING VERSE. A phrase used by King James VI of Scotland in his *Reulis and Cautelis* for making Scottish verse (1584) to characterize lines which in modern terminology we would say are loosely anapestic, or else in falling rhythm and 4-stress accentual verse (q.v.). James distinguishes "t." v.

from "flowing" (text in Smith, 1.218–19, 223, 407n); the latter clearly means "regular," so the former may simply mean doggerel (q.v.), i.e. irregular, rough. He also terms it "rouncefallis" (*OED*, s.v. "rouncival") and associates it with flyting (q.v.). In Eng. poetry the example of t. v. usually pointed to is Thomas Tusser's very popular *Five Hundred Points of Good Husbandry* (1557 et seq.), which is in anapests and other meters (see C. S. Lewis, *Eng. Lit. in the 16th C.* [1954], 262–64). Schipper thought that t. v. was the descendant of the ME alliterative line, a view now abandoned. Ker relates it to the 4-stress lines of popular song, ballad meter, and Sp. *arte mayor* (qq.v.). "T. v." seems more likely crude terminology than any distinct species of verse.—Schipper 2.223–25, *History* 89–90; G. Saintsbury, *Hist. of Eng. Prosody* (1906–10), 1.326–28, 408; W. P. Ker, *Form & Style in Poetry* (1928).
T.V.F.B.

TURKISH POETRY.

I. EARLY TURKISH POETRY
II. DIVAN (CLASSICAL) POETRY
III. RELIGIOUS OR TEKKE POETRY
IV. INDIGENOUS FOLK POETRY
V. EUROPEANIZATION OF TURKISH POETRY

I. EARLY TURKISH POETRY. Some early lyrics (found in Chinese tr.) and vestiges of oral epics seem to lend credence to the speculation that poetic sensibility among the Turks of Central Asia probably dawned before the birth of Christ. However, the actual beginnings of the T. poetic trad. lie in the period between the late 9th and mid 11th c. A.D., when T. tribes moved into and settled parts of Anatolia, which was under the influence of Islam and of Arab and Persian cultures. These *Oğuz* Turks brought with them a dialect already rich in expressive resources and a developed popular lit. By the end of the 11th c., however, the Turks had converted to Islam in huge numbers and embraced its prevalent culture, incl. its philosophy and lit. Out of this assimilation came the first poetic work of stature that clearly bears the imprint of the new literary orientation, *Kutadgu Bilig* (Wisdom of Royal Glory, ca. 1069–70) by Yusuf Khass Hajib. Composed in *aruz* (Arabic-Persian quantitative prosody), this mirror for princes, consisting of about 6500 couplets, is a vast philosophical treatise on government, justice, and ethics. Written about the same time, Kasgarlı Mahmut's *Divan ü Lügat-it Türk* is a lexicon and compendium of the T. lang. and its major dialects which includes many specimens (some fragmentary) of pre-Islamic and early Islamic T. p.

From the end of the 13th c., when the Ottoman state came into being, through the mid 19th c., three main trads. of T. p. evolved: (1) Persian-influenced *Divan* (classical) poetry, (2) religious or *Tekke* poetry, and (3) indigenous folk poetry. From the mid 19th c. up to the present day, T. p. has undergone an extensive European orientation.

TURKISH POETRY

II. DIVAN (CLASSICAL) POETRY. *Divan* poetry (also called Court poetry), whose course ran almost parallel to the glories and decline of the Ottoman Empire, spanned more than six centuries. Composed by and for an intellectual elite mostly affiliated with the Court, its main vehicle of expression was the Anatolian T. dialect. From beginning to end, cl. T. p. remained under the dominance of Persian and Arabic poetry. It tried to emulate the meters, stanzaic forms, and mythology used by Persian and Arab poets, as well as a substantial portion of their vocabulary. To suit the metric requirements of *aruz*, *Divan* poets often deliberately distorted T. vowels or employed words of Arabic and Persian origin which lent themselves better to *aruz*. *Divan* poetry also used the major verseforms of Persian and Arabic lit., e.g. *ghazal* and *qaṣīda*, *maṣnavi* (qq.v.), *rubâi*, *tuyuğ*, *Şarkı* (originally *murabba*), *musammat*, and *tarih* (chronogram).

Form reigned supreme over *Divan* poetry. Content, most *Divan* poets felt, was the autonomous substance of a literary trad. whose concepts and values were not to be questioned, let alone renovated. They considered originality fortuitous at best, and preferred to achieve perfection in craftsmanship. Despite the tyranny of form, prominent *Divan* poets often attained a profound spirituality, a trenchant sensitivity, an overflowing eroticism. Perhaps no *Divan* poet can be said to show a broad range of poetic sensibilities. Tradition sanctioned not range, but depth. Between the given extremes of the continuum of subject matter, the masters, i.e. Fuzulî, Baki, Şeyh Galip, and others, achieved an impressive profundity of passion expressed with gripping power—from self-glorification to self-abnegation, from agony to ebullient joy, from fanatic continence to uninhibited hedonism. Islamic mysticism, as the soul's passionate yearning to merge with God, formed the superstructure of this poetry. In the hands of the first-rate poets, the *Divan* trad. produced a corpus of exquisite lyric and mystic poetry which has steadily retained its impressive literary significance.

Early *Divan* masters were Seyhî (d. ca. 1431), Ahmedî (1334–1413), Ahmet Paşa (d. 1497), Ahmed-i Dâî (15th c.), and Necati (d. 1509). Many of the Sultans were accomplished poets, incl. Mehmed, who crushed Byzantium, and Selim II (d. 1574). The most prolific among them was Süleyman the Magnificent (d. 1566) who composed close to 3000 verses. The greatest figures of the *Divan* trad. emerged in the period of the Ottoman Empire's grandeur. Fuzulî (1494–1556) stands as the most impressive creative artist of cl. T. lit. He composed three *Divans* (major collections of poems), one in T., one in Arabic, and one in Persian, in addition to several *mesnevîs* (verse narratives). His masterpiece *Leylâ vü Mecnun* is a *mesnevî* of close to 4000 couplets in which Fuzulî made a philosophical and dramatic exploration into worldly and mystic love. Perhaps no other poet exerted as much influence on the *Divan* poetry of the following centuries. Among his most memorable lines: "I wish I had a thousand lives in this broken heart of mine / So that I could sacrifice myself for you once with each life." Fuzulî chose to write his T. poems in the *Azerî* dialect in the manner of Nesimî (d. 1404). Baki (1526–99) achieved wide fame for the aesthetic perfection of his secular *ghazals* and *qaṣīdas* in lines and couplets which often have an epigrammatic concentration; his best-known line has become a proverb among Turks: "What endures in this dome is but a pleasant sound." Hayalî (d. 1557) and Taşlıcalı Yahya Bey (d. 1582) attained renown for their craftsmanship and sensitive lyricism. Rûhi-i Bağdadi (d. 1605) composed a *Terkib-i Bend*, which still stands as a masterpiece of social and philosophical satire with a strong moral concern. The supreme satirist of the *Divan* trad., however, was Nef'i (1582–1635), who, in his masterful *qaṣīdas*, courageously lampooned hypocrisy and affectation. Şeyhülislâm Yahya (1552–1644) produced refined *ghazals*, while Nailî (d. ca. 1666) won renown for his delicately elegant lyrics. Intellectual exploration and social commentary abounded in the poetry of Nâbi (1642–1712). Nedim (d. 1730) sang the joys of living and the beauties of nature (particularly in the city of Istanbul). He contributed to *Divan* poetry a lilting, entrancing style derived mainly from the colloquial Istanbul T. of his day. The last master of *Divan* poetry was Şeyh Galip (1757–99), who, in addition to a superb *Divan,* produced *Hüsn ü Aşk* (Beauty and Love), an allegorical work of passionate mysticism. Although the cl. trad. continued until the early part of the 20th c., after Şeyh Galip it produced no figure or work of significance.

III. RELIGIOUS OR TEKKE POETRY. Religious poetry flourished among the mystics, Muslim clergy, and the adherents of various doctrines. Members of the *tekkes* (theological centers) were particularly prolific in such poetry, which drew upon and overlapped both *Divan* and folk trads. Ahmet Yesevî (d. 1166) and Ahmet Fakih (d. ca. 1250) were early masters. Perhaps the greatest figure of religious lit. was the poet-saint Mevlânâ Celâleddin-i Rumi (1207–73), who wrote a six-volume Persian *mesnevî* of nearly 26,000 couplets about the ways of mysticism. In the late 13th and early 14th c., Sultan Veled (Mevlânâ's son), Âşık Paşa, and Gülş ehrî achieved distinction. The most renowned T. masterpiece to come out of the religious trad. was *Mevlid-i Şerif* (1409), composed by Süleyman Çelebi (d. 1422). An adulation of the Prophet Mahomet, this poem is chanted as a requiem among Muslim-Turks. Two folk poets, Kaygusuz Abdal (15th c.) and Pir Sultan Abdal (16th c.), have made substantial contributions to T. religious poetry. Their poetry represents the Alevî-Bektaşi movement (long considered heretical) and is a deviation from and reaction against some of the tenets of traditional Islam.

IV. INDIGENOUS FOLK POETRY. Parallel to *Divan* poetry, T. folk poetry has run its own evolutionary course. Its roots lie in the pre-Islamic epic trads. of the peripatetic T. tribes. Although most of these epic poems were lost in whole or part, one major epic entitled *Oğuznâme* reveals that Turks had a developed poetic faculty long before they fell under the influence of the Persian and Arab cultures. The *Dede Korkut Tales* of the Oğuz tribes contain poems in rather free renditions which also stand at the source of the folk trad. Folk poetry has been created and kept alive to our day by the *ozans, saz şairleri* (poet-musicians), and *âşıks*. It has voiced, in its spontaneous, sincere, and often matter-of-fact fashion, the poetic sensibilities of the uneducated classes, in contrast to cl. poetry, which was composed and read by the intellectual elite. In indigenous verseforms, e.g. *türkü, koşma, mani, destan, semai*, and *varsaği*, mostly extemporized and sung to music, replete with assonances and inexact rhymes, and composed in simple syllabic meters, folk poetry gave voice to the themes of love, heroism, the beauties of nature, and, at times, Islamic mysticism. Unsophisticated and unpretentious, it evolved a serene realism, an earthy humor, and a mellifluous lyric quality. The trad. still remains alive in Turkey's rural areas, as well as among urban devotees of lit., and has exerted an appreciable influence on the T. p. of modern times. In fact, many versifiers of the late 19th and 20th c. have adopted the vivid rhythms and much of the vocabulary and idiom of folk poetry.

A genius who emerged in the 13th c. came to dominate folk verse: Yunus Emre (d. ca. 1321). Employing both folk prosody and *aruz* meters, he created an impressive corpus of poems (some now lost) rich in philosophical content, intensely mystical, steeped in the best folk idiom, melodious, and full of vivid imagery and fresh metaphor. Later centuries witnessed the first-rate works of Karacaoğlan (ca. 1606–80), a poet of love and pastoral beauty, Âşık Ömer (d. 1707), Gevheri (d. ca. 1740), Dadaloğlu (1785–1868), Dertli (1772–1845), Bayburtlu Zihni (d. 1859), Erzurumlu Emrah (d. 1860), and Seyrani (1807–66).

V. EUROPEANIZATION OF TURKISH POETRY. The decline of the Ottoman Empire reached a critical point by the middle of the 19th c. Younger T. intellectuals started seeking the Empire's salvation in technological devel., political reform, and cultural progress fashioned after European models. The so-called *Tanzimat* (Transformations) of the 1840s aimed at realizing some of these far-reaching changes. A new orientation toward Europe (France, in particular) brought the younger poets into contact with the aesthetic theories and verseforms of Fr. poetry. While *aruz* was not abandoned, T. poets experimented with forms, rhythms, and styles. A reaction set in against words of Arabic and Persian origin. Poetry acquired a social awareness and a political function in the hands of some poets who endeavored to gain

independence from external political domination. Ziya Paşa (1825–80), Şinasi (1826–71), and Namik Kemal (1840–88) emerged as champions of nationalism. Recaizade Ekrem (1847–1914) and Abdülhak Hâmit Tarhan (1852–1937) echoed the Fr. romantics. The latter, a prolific poet and author of numerous verse dramas, gained stature as a ceaseless renovator. His poetry, which covered a wide range of topics, had a philosophic bent as well as dramatic impact.

In the late 19th and early 20th c., under Sultan Abdülhamit's suppression, most T. poets retreated into a fantasy world of innocent, picturesque beauty where, in a mood of meek sentimentality and lackadaisical affection, they attempted to forge the aesthetics of the simple, the pure, and the delectable. Their lyric transformation of reality abounded in new rhythms and imaginative metaphors expressed by dint of a predominantly Arabic-Persian vocabulary and an appreciably relaxed *aruz*. A Fr.-oriented group of poets referred to as *Servet-i Fünun*, after the literary magazine they published, became prominent on the literary scene. Its leader Tevfik Fikret (1867–1915) also wrote angry political poems against the Sultan's despotism and the Empire's crumbling institutions. His poetry represented a new direction for the formal and conceptual progress of T. p.

During the same period, *Divan* poetry was continued by a few minor poets. Folk poetry maintained much of its vigor and exerted considerable influence on many younger poets striving to create a pervasive national consciousness and purify the T. lang. by eliminating Arabic and Persian loanwords. Ziya Gökalp (1875–1924), social philosopher and poet, wrote poems expounding the ideals and aspirations of T. nationalism. Mehmet Emin Yurdakul (1869–1944) and Rıza Tevfik Bölükbaşi (1869–1949) used folk meters and forms as well as an unadorned colloquial lang. in their poems. Mehmet Âkif Ersoy (1873–1936), a meticulous craftsman and a deft master of *aruz*, wrote mainly of T. glory and of Islam's *sumnum bonum*. Eşref (1846–1912) emerged as Turkey's best satirical poet of the past hundred years. The *Fecr-i Âti* movement contributed in some measure toward the creation of a poetry that Turks could claim as their own.

The T. Republic came into being in 1923. It consolidated national unity and moved swiftly to eliminate Islamic elements from T. life. Emphasis was placed on Westernization, including the introduction of the Lat. alphabet. In the early part of the Republican era, poetry served primarily as a vehicle for the propagation of nationalism. Younger poets branded *Divan* forms and meters as anathema. Native verseforms and syllabic meters gained popularity. Intense efforts were undertaken toward a systematic purification of the lang. The group *Beş Hececiler* (Five Syllabic Poets)— Faruk Nafiz Çamlibel (1898–1973), who was equally adept at *aruz*, Orhan Seyfi Orhon (1890–

1972), Enis Behiç Koryürek (1898–1949), Halit Fahri Ozansoy (1891–1971), and Yusuf Ziya Ortaç (1896–1967)—produced simple, unadorned poems celebrating love, the beauties of nature, and the glories of the T. nation. Other poets, however, shied away from chauvinism and evolved individualistic worldviews and styles. Symbolism attained success in the consummate poetry of Ahmet Hâşim (1884–1933), who employed *aruz* freely. Neoclassicism gained considerable popularity under the aegis of Yahya Kemal Beyatlı (1884–1958). A supreme craftsman, Beyatlı wrote of love, nostalgia for the Ottoman past, the beauties of Istanbul, and the metaphysics of life and death in poems memorable for their refined lang. and melodiousness. Necip Fazıl Kısakürek (1905–83) engaged in teleological explorations into modern man's agony. Ahmet Muhip Dıranas (1909–80) and Ahmet Hamdi Tanpınar (1901–61) wrote some of the most refined lyric poems to come out of their generation.

From the 1920s onward, modern poetry was dominated by Nazım Hikmet (he sometimes used Ran as his last name; 1902–63), who was an exponent of the Communist ideology. It was Hikmet who introduced free verse as adapted from Majakovskij. Thanks to the extensive translation of his love lyrics and revolutionary poems, he became the most famous T. poet in the world. His profound influence on his disciples in Turkey remains potent decades after his death.

In the years following World War II, poets furthered their earlier innovations, incl. *vers libre* (q.v.) imported from France. After surrealism (q.v.) cast a brief spell on the literary scene, a new school emerged setting forth what may be defined as poetic realism. Introduced by Orhan Veli Kanık (1914–50), Oktay Rifat (1914–88), and Melih Cevdet Anday (b. 1915), and subscribed to by others, incl. Bedri Rahmi Eyuboğlu (1913–75) and Cahit Külebi (b. 1917), this doctrine placed the poet in the center of society and made poetry's function utilitarian. In the late 1940s, most T. poets served as standard-bearers of the social problems of their day. Poetry became a vehicle for the expression less of subjective experience than of objective truth. Written in free verse (occasionally in folk forms and meters), postwar poems drew on all that was alive, vivid, and colorful in the T. idiom. The critic Nurullah Ataç (1898–1957) played a major role in setting the directions of modern poetry in the 1940s and 1950s. In the same period, Cahit Sıtkı Tarancı (1910–56) produced impeccable lyrics. Fazıl Hüsnü Dağlarca (b. 1914) emerged as a superior poet of impressive range. His is the poetry of philosophical quest, and it displays a wealth of metaphor and a sonority almost unequalled in 20th-c. T. p. Behçet Necatigil (1916–79) writes poems rich in intellectual substance, while Salâh Birsel (b. 1919) interfuses ingenious verbal patterns and sonic capers.

The abstract movement (sometimes referred to as "meaningless poetry") which held sway from the mid 1950s onward sought to mobilize the imaginative resources of the T. lang. and created a new obscurantism. While İlhan Berk (b. 1916), Attilâ İlhan (b. 1925), Turgut Uyar (1926–85), Edip Cansever (1928–86), and Cemal Süreya (b. 1931) expanded the horizons of metaphor and melody in their highly complex poems, the social realists, during various spurts of freedom from the early 1960s on, took up the battlecries of social justice. Because Turkey's literary establishment is enamored of its own cultural legacy as well as the aesthetics of other nations, contemp. T. p. stands as a remarkably rich synthesis which embraces aspects of the *Divan* and folk trads., the prevalent themes of world poetry, and the myths and values of diverse civilizations. It is both authentically national and self-assuredly universal.

ANTHOLOGIES AND SELECTIONS: E. J. W. Gibb, *Ottoman Lit.: The Poets and Poetry of Turkey* (1901)—awkward trs.; *The Star and the Crescent,* ed. D. Patmore (1946); F. H. Dağlarca, *Selected Poems* (1969); O. V. Kanık, *I am Listening to Istanbul* (1971), *The Book of Dede Korkut* (1972); *Penguin Book of T. Verse,* ed. N. Menemencioğlu (1978)—excellent selections; *Yunus Emre and His Mystical Poetry* (1981), *Contemp. T. Lit.* (1982), both ed. T. S. Halman; Yusuf Khass Hajib, *Wisdom of Royal Glory,* ed. and tr. R. Dankoff (1983); N. Hikmet, *Sel. Poems* (1987); *Süleyman the Magnificent-Poet,* ed. and tr. T. S. Halman (1987).

HISTORY AND CRITICISM: E. J. W. Gibb, *A Hist. of Ottoman Poetry,* 6 v. (1900–1909)—the classic study; F. Köprülü, "Ottoman T. Lit.," *Encyclopaedia of Islam,* v. 4 (1934); A. Bombaci, *Storia della letteratura turca* (1956)—excellent general survey; T. S. Halman, "Poetry and Society: The T. Experience," *Mod. Near East: Lit. and Society,* ed. C. M. Kortepeter (1971); W. G. Andrews, *An Intro. to Ottoman Poetry* (1976), *Poetry's Voice, Society's Song: Ottoman Lyric Poetry* (1985); I. Basgöz, "The Epic Trad. among Turkic Peoples," *Heroic Epic and Saga,* ed. F. J. Oinas (1978).   T.S.H.

TWENTIETH-CENTURY POETICS.

I. AMERICAN AND BRITISH
II. FRENCH AND GERMAN
III. ITALIAN
IV. SPANISH
V. SLAVIC

I. AMERICAN AND BRITISH. Poetics (q.v.; hereafter p.) in this century has not been a neutral, uncontroversial activity, if ever it was. Even without regard to specific theses about the nature of lit., about its production and reception, about the nature and scope of textuality (q.v.), about meaning and the possibility of interpretation (q.v.), the very construction of a pure p. itself rests upon assumptions far from self-evident. Of these assumptions two are fundamental. First, lit. can be neither reduced to more fundamental constituents (e.g. lang.) nor dissolved in any larger whole to which it might be conceived to belong (e.g. culture); second, there exists a systematic whole of lit. which takes precedence over any historical instance of it. Without assuming the specificity of lit., literary study results not in p. but in politics or rhet., and without assuming the primacy of system over history, the totality of lit. over individual works, the result is not p. but interpretation (q.v.) or judgment. Yet 20th-c. Anglo-Am. p. has made substantial contributions to the field not although but indeed because its own legitimacy has been subject to scrutiny and debate.

T. S. Eliot's "Trad. and the Individual Talent" (1919), arguably the most influential essay in the first half of the 20th c., had among its most significant effects the creation of a founding object for a p., namely trad. (q.v.). Like Shelley before him and Frye after, Eliot suggested that literary trad. be conceived as the "ideal order of existing monuments"; and just as Coleridge had located organic form in each successful poem, Eliot located it in the one great book of trad., "the living whole of all the poetry that has ever been written." Though "living" (that is, open to augmentation by talented individuals and therefore possessing a history), trad. nevertheless constitutes an "ideal order" amenable to systematic description. Thus Eliot's vision of the ideal whole provided a positive foundation for p., and on it Northrop Frye based his own guiding conception of p. as "a theory (q.v.) of crit. (q.v.) whose principles apply to the whole of lit."

However, just as deconstruction (q.v.) subsequently raised doubts about the unity of individual works, so also feminism called into question the ideal wholeness of literary trad., as well as the wholeness of humanity underlying it (see FEMINIST POETICS). Unless we can assume "that man exists and that his fundamental oneness transcends the innumerable differences," Wimsatt and Brooks suggested, we must "necessarily abandon any concept of an aesthetics of poetry." But from a feminist perspective, the idea that "*man* exists" becomes highly problematic. Generalizing from women's writing, Donovan, Showalter, and du Plessis have characterized feminist p. in terms of non-linear plotting, subjectivity, impermanence, and undistanciated intimacy between author and reader. But more fundamental than these specifics is that the project of feminist p. is founded on a constitutive distrust of spurious universalization, esp. the spurious universalization of a literary canon almost exclusively by, for, and about men. If, as Donovan writes, women form "a separate community, a separate culture, with its own customs, its own epistemology, and, once articulated, its own aesthetics," then even a hypothetical "androgynist p." (which criticized masculinist "universals" for not being universal enough) would be debilitated by its failure to realize that a universal gender-neutral p. has no object. For the separatist wing of feminism, at least, it is not man that exists but only

men and women, and men's and women's lits.

In this respect feminism parallels the Marxist critique of universals (see MARXIST CRITICISM). "It is a central proposition of Marxism," remarks Raymond Williams, that no writing speaks for the whole. Rather it is always partial and interested, "always aligned; that is to say, it variously expresses ... specifically selected experience from a specific point of view." So also Jameson expresses the Marxist suspicion of p. when he describes Marxist analysis as penetration of the "apparently systematic and intellectually coherent, self-contained surface" of the work and the discovery that it is "an ideological product" with a "functional and strategic value as a weapon of a determinate kind in a concrete and local struggle." In confining itself to the general and systematizable rather than the local and the irremediably differentiated, p. either minimizes the particular or mistakes it for the universal. Moreover in confining itself to the literary, p. aggrandizes and falsifies lit. by ignoring the fact that, as Williams puts it, "literary theory cannot be separated from cultural theory." Not only aligned but politically committed, feminist theory disavows pure p. and merges instead into cultural criticism (q.v.) precisely in order to do justice to its object. Since writing by women has often been denigrated as "popular" or "low," feminism charges traditional p. not only with chauvinism but also with generalizing on the narrow, class-specific basis of "high" art alone, whereas it ought to integrate "high" and "low," literary and folk art, with the larger realm of cultural studies. Similarly, insofar as "the 'female aesthetic' is simply a version of that aesthetic position that can be articulated by any nonhegemonic group" (du Plessis), it is bound to view a purely literary p. that tries to position itself outside the cultural as naive at best and complicit with oppression at worst. This is not to say that feminist or Marxist (anti)p. must necessarily ignore the specificity of lit. within its larger context (though Williams does note the "naive reduction, in much Marxist thinking, of consciousness, imagination, art, and ideas to 'reflections,' 'echoes,' 'phantoms,' and 'sublimates'"). To consign lit. to the superstructure, to the merely reflective, is to reaffirm the schism of individual mental life from material social life which was the target of Marxist critique in the first place.

In another respect, Eliot's influence, too, worked against the devel. of p., not because it reduced lit. to culture but rather because it subordinated general p. to particular analysis (q.v.). Eliot's own critical practice was more judicial than theoretical; and critical judgment evaluates the individual work, or at most a poet's oeuvre. It patently cannot take as its object the "whole of all the poetry that has ever been written" (thus Frye rejected judgment as the business of p.). Eliot did most to promote interpretive crit. when he divided "the man who suffers" from "the mind which creates," concluding that "honest crit. and sensitive appreciation are directed not upon the poet but upon the poetry." This redirection of critical attention toward the *medium* and away from the author tended both to devalue biographical crit. and to make formal explication (q.v.) the primary task of literary study. Even though (or perhaps precisely because) symbolist and imagist p. emphasized the unfathomable richness of the symbol (q.v.) and the undissociable complexity of the image (q.v.), crit. which concentrated on the poetry (q.v.) rather than the poet (q.v.) sought to fathom that richness and unpack that complexity in exegesis. The practical crit. that Richards considered an experiment became the norm (see NEW CRITICISM). Certainly this almost exclusive focus on the individual work did not preclude p. entirely, but it limited its scope to providing the theoretical foundations for interpretive practice.

Most important among these foundations was the principle of the work's self-containment or autonomy (q.v.) and the corollary metaphor of an inside and outside of that enclosure. In *Theory of Lit.*, Wellek and Warren categorized crit. as "intrinsic" or "extrinsic," depending on whether it emphasized the individuality of the work or its place in a larger, extra-poetic realm. So too Wimsatt and Beardsley objectified the "poem itself" by prescinding it from its genesis and effect; both authorial intention and readerly affect, they argued, lie outside the object domain of "specifically critical judgment." Within that domain—that is, within the "work itself"—the emphasis fell on heterogeneity. What Coleridge had called the reconciliation of opposites came to be called *paradox* or *irony* (qq.v.—Brooks) or *impurity* (Robert Penn Warren), and this quality was taken not only to discriminate greater poems from lesser but also to characterize poetry as such. Even as Kant had demonstrated the autonomy of the aesthetic, mid 20th-c. theoreticians defended the irreducible specificity of lit. which is a condition of pure p.; but, perhaps influenced by Croce, many tended to deny the priority of the whole of lit. over the individual work that p. must no less necessarily affirm.

The specific character of lit. qua lit. is more forcefully maintained by appealing to its differentia than to its species, by negative rather than positive definition. Among the most fundamental tasks of Anglo-Am. p. was to say what poetry was *not*. Eliot rejected Arnold's suggestion that poetry offers a substitute for religion; Brooks refused to measure poems "against a philosophical yardstick"; and whereas Pound could say, "the arts, lit., poesy, are a science, just as chemistry is a science," for Richards, Ransom, and Tate "poetry is in its essence opposed to science" (see SCIENCE AND POETRY). The frequency and vigor of such warnings against confusing poetry with what is alien to it register the strength of the impetus to find in poetry some authentic truth, as well as the vehemence of the denial that it has any truth to offer at all (see MEANING, POETIC). Richards formulated this denial in his thesis (reminiscent of De-Quincey's distinction between the lits. of knowledge and power) that poetry consists of "pseudo-statements" (q.v.) with exclusively therapeutic value: "the statements which appear in the poetry are there for the sake of their effects upon the feelings, not for their own sake. Hence to challenge their truth, or to question whether they deserve serious attention as statements claiming truth, is to mistake their function."

But the most proximate Other against which p. sought to define lit. was not philosophy, theology, or science *per se* but lit. crit. "I have assumed as axiomatic," Eliot wrote, "that a creation, a work of art, is autotelic; and that crit. by definition, is about something other than itself." One effect of this dichotomy was to restate the opposition between poetry and science as an opposition between poetry and crit. Lit. and literary study are two distinct activities, Wellek and Warren begin: "one is creative, an art; the other, if not precisely a science, is a species of knowledge." So also Ransom urges that "crit. must become more scientific," and in *Anatomy of Crit.* Frye offers a full-scale p. defined as "a coherent and comprehensive theory of lit., logically and scientifically organized, [that will] assimilate its work into a unified structure of knowledge, as other sciences do." A second consequence of taking crit. as the defining Other and lit. as autotelic is that its "prime and chief function is fidelity to its own nature" (Wellek and Warren); the aim of lit. is to produce "a structure of words for its own sake" (Frye). In one respect, the autotelic character of lit. implies that, unlike crit., lit. is not about anything: it has no reference or meaning—Eliot remarked that meaning is the bone a burglar throws the dog to keep it quiet. The emphasis on literary autonomy thus produced a formalist, anti-mimetic p. (see NEW CRITICISM; CONTEXTUALISM). The denial of meaning did not preclude interpretation (q.v.), however; it only prescribed its results. If crit. can only intend something other than itself, then lit. conversely must mean nothing other than itself. Significantly, in *The Well Wrought Urn* Brooks chose poems (e.g. Wordsworth's Intimations Ode) that are more or less explicitly self-referential: they are about the nature of poetry and reflexively about themselves. The consequence, ironically, is that these poems about themselves cannot be categorically distinguished from Brooks' crit. about them—indeed, poems about poetry in general (notably Mac-Leish's "Ars Poetica") came to merge with p.

Only implicit in Brooks, what Hartman termed the "fading distinction between primary and secondary texts" later became explicit. Bloom described *The Anxiety of Influence* as "a theory of poetry that presents itself as a severe poem." So also in *Blindness and Insight* de Man wrote, "the usual distinctions between expository writing *on* lit. and the "purely" literary lang. *of* poetry or fiction have been deliberately blurred." The consequence of this blurring was not necessarily the loss of literary specificity (de Man, as we will see below, was in fact "concerned with the distinctive quality" of lit.); however it did mean that p. could no longer be content with defining lit. by contrasting it to crit.

The reaction against interp. gave p. renewed vigor. Typical of the symbolists, Eliot held a suspicion of meaning that made him dubious about the process of interp. "Instead of insight," he complained, "you get a fiction"—though it does not appear that he ever claimed authorial privilege in pronouncing definitive interps. of his own work. As the ideal of interp., Richards could postulate the recovery of the "whole state of mind which shaped the poem originally," and by 1970 Hillis Miller (under the influence of Poulet) embraced a "crit. of identification" in which understanding was conceived as entering the consciousness of the author (see GENEVA SCHOOL). Nevertheless, after the "intentional fallacy" (q.v.) became dogma, few theorists (other than Hirsch) would claim that interp. ceases when it arrives at what the author meant, and interpreters were left only with what Wimsatt and Beardsley called "the linguistic fact" to delimit semantic proliferation. But for reasons which Hirsch elaborated in "Stylistics and Synonymity," the words on the page cannot of themselves effect interpretive closure. As Richards remarked, "No one can say, 'There is only this and this in the poem and nothing more.'" Richards' four types of meaning soon became Empson's seven types of ambiguity (q.v.), and though in the 1930s and '40s this ambiguity could be celebrated as proof of symbolic richness, by the '60s the richness faded to mere embarrassment, and interp. suffered a consequent loss of prestige. Sontag stigmatized it as "the revenge of intellect against art," and Hartman labeled exegesis "our Whore of Babylon."

Once it was generally recognized, as Frye remarked, that "any great work can carry an infinite amount of commentary," comment was perceived to be futile. But "things become more hopeful," he went on, "as soon as there is a feeling, however dim, that crit. has an end in the structure of lit. as a total form, as well as a beginning in the text studied." For Frye, interp. ends in archetypal crit. (see ARCHETYPE; MYTH CRITICISM). But it can be argued that, instead of constructing a p., Frye merely replaced one type of interp. with another, and while sidestepping the morass of interpreting myth (q.v.) allegorically, he falls into interpreting lit. as the allegory of myth. Jameson denounced the "system of allegorical interp. in which the data of one narrative line are radically impoverished by their rewriting according to the paradigm of another narrative, which is taken as the former's master code or Ur-narrative and proposed as the ultimate hidden or unconscious meaning of the first one." Both Marxist and Freudian interp., at least in their common forms, fall under this indict-ment; and in taking history as the determining and terminal meaning of lit., Jameson avoids being hoist on his own petard only by arguing that "history is *not* a text, not a narrative, but an absent cause."

Structuralism (q.v.) too can be accused of being merely another form of interp., one that makes lang. itself the master code; in this respect it confirms the imagist creed of Hulme, Pound, Eliot, and Mallarmé that poems are made out of ideas but words. But equally importantly, structuralism fulfilled, probably more satisfactorily than Frye, the aim of constructing a p. that would be more than the theoretical arm of exegesis. Based on Saussurean semiology, its aim was not to discover meanings, even ultimate meanings, but rather to show how meaning *per se* is possible. Structuralism promoted the cause of p. insofar as it explained the possibility of meaning by appealing to the lang. system (*langue*), postulated as prior to any personal act of utterance (*parole*), just as Marxism had asserted the priority of the social system to individual acts of will and knowledge; but because structuralism abstracted beyond the whole of lit. to the whole of lang., it had difficulty in distinguishing between p. and semiotics (q.v.): the specificity of literary lang. became lost in the undifferentiated totality of lang., just as, for Marxism, lit. tended to dissolve into sociopolitical history. But in Anglo-Am. theory, structuralist p. was more often explicated (most ably by Culler) than applied or amplified, which explains why, as primarily a Continental movement, it receives only cursory treatment here. But the very proliferation of explications of structuralism and other theories indicates that the repressed drive to interpret lit. returned as the no less powerful drive to interpret literary theory; and whereas for the formalists, poems about poetry began to seem like crit., for those who had moved "beyond formalism," crit. that hitherto had been about something else came to be primarily about itself.

Whereas Wellek and Warren wrote a "theory of lit.," Frye called his p. an "anatomy" not of lit. but of "crit.," and this title is symptomatic of a general shift in emphasis. Raymond Williams has observed that "it is difficult to prevent any attempt at literary theory from being turned, almost *a priori*, into critical theory." That *p.* is now largely synonymous with *theory of crit.* in Anglo-Am. parlance indicates not just that lit. and crit. have reached an equilibrium of interest but, more pointedly, that the critical act has been accorded priority over the creative. One index of this critical self-regard (in both senses) is that, in the view of many, the reader has displaced both the author and the objectified text as the locus of meaning and interest. Eliot, and later Wellek and Warren, placed "the poem's existence somewhere between the writer and the reader," arguing that the "poem is not just either what the poet 'planned' or what the reader conceives." But whereas rhetorical critics such as

Burke assumed a passive reader as the register of rhetorical effect, "reader-response critics" conceive of the reader as active creator of meaning (see READER-RESPONSE CRITICISM). Fish states this position most bluntly: "the meaning of an utterance is its experience." What Wimsatt and Beardsley termed "the affective fallacy" (q.v.) becomes for Fish not an error to be avoided but the principle of explanation itself, and it explains not only how meaning is possible but also how meanings multiply in the many experiences of many readers. Neither "the linguistic fact" nor authorial intention can limit this proliferation; only the limitations of particular interpretive communities can. The concept of unity (q.v.) too has undergone redefinition in terms of readers. "Every poem must necessarily be a perfect unity," Blake wrote; but Frye understood this to be "not a statement of fact about all existing poems, but a statement of the hypothesis which every reader adopts in first trying to comprehend even the most chaotic poem." Similarly, genre (q.v.), previously considered a characteristic of the work (indeed the most important one in Aristotelian p., followed by Crane and the Chicago School [q.v.]), is reinterpreted under the dominion of the reader as a convention of expectation or an interpretive competence.

In *Blindness and Insight*, de Man, like many formalists, proposes to locate the distinctive quality of literary lang. But like the reader-response theorists, he writes that "prior to theorizing about literary lang., one has to become aware of the complexities of reading." The danger is that, just as philosophers who put epistemology before metaphysics never seem to get to metaphysics at all, so also systematic attention to the process of reading can easily preclude attention to the text being read—and reflexive crit., already preoccupied with itself, then becomes wholly autotelic. De Man protests that "the study of critical texts can never be an end in itself and has value only as a preliminary to the understanding of lit. in general." But the preliminary becomes the terminal, for it is in crit., he argues, rather than in novels or poems, that the "complexities of reading" are most clearly displayed, and thus it is from crit. that he derives his "understanding of lit. in general." As we have noted above, de Man blurs the distinction between crit. and lit., so that basing his p. on the rhetoric of critical lang. is less dubious than would first appear. Yet it is not without striking interpretive consequences. Though de Man did not interpret works of lit. as allegories of existential ideals or myths, or of the sexual or political unconscious, nevertheless by giving precedence to reading, he was led to interpret them as "allegories of reading."

Just as Frye recognized that any literary text can support infinite commentary, so de Man conceived "the act of reading as an endless process," but he also went on to portray it (borrowing from Heidegger) as a process "in which truth and falsehood are inextricably intertwined." The primary reason for this inextricability is that, as structural linguistics had shown, lang. (incl. the lang. of interp.) is constituted by the arbitrary relation between signifier and signified, and thus by a discrepancy between sign and meaning. This conclusion throws the very possibility of interp. into doubt, and de Man warned that "the possibility of reading can never be taken for granted." Richards too had viewed "correct understanding as a triumph against odds. We must cease to regard misinterp. as a mere unlucky accident. We must treat it as the normal and probable event." De Man radicalized this doubt and proposed to explain how misinterp. is not probable but inevitable. Insofar as interpretive lang. signifies (i.e. is discrepant from) the meaning of lit., "interp. is nothing but the possibility of error," and critics are "doomed to say something quite different from what they meant to say." Via a different route, Harold Bloom comes to the similar conclusion that "there are no interps. but only misinterps." Unless an interp. differs from what it interprets, it is not an interp. but a copy; and yet the very difference, on which the existence of the interp. depends, insures that it is in error. On the other hand, unless interp. possesses a sameness to what it interprets, it is not interp. but merely a new and unrelated piece of writing, and this sameness (no less necessary to its being an interp.) insures that interp. possesses truth. Thus truth and error, blindness and insight, are inextricably intertwined in the act of interp.

This raises the question, basic to p., of whether literary lang. constitutes an exception—that is, whether it has some special quality that would distinguish it from everyday forms of lang. Structuralism granted lit. no privilege in terms of unity and truth, and no freedom from the arbitrariness of the sign. With this demystification de Man concurred, in that he too posited literary plenitude or self-presence that would heal what Hartman calls "the wound in the word," the gap on which representation (q.v.) depends and in which it founders. Indeed, de Man wrote that "lit. does not fulfill a plenitude but originates in a void that separates intent from reality."

But its specific difference is that "poetic lang. names this void." Beginning with the conventional identification of literary lang. with figural and rhetorical lang., de Man first characterized the literary as that lang. which invites the confusion of figural and literal; more generally, it invites "the archetypal error: the recurrent confusion of sign and substance." Second, he suggested that literary lang. does not merely employ rhetoric but self-reflexively calls attention to its own rhetoricity, and thus it "knows and asserts that it will be misunderstood." Drawing on Wallace Stevens, Kermode had in similar fashion distinguished myths from fictions in that the latter are "consciously held to be fictive." But de Man attributed no saving power to self-consciousness: "the cognitive function resides in the lang. and not in the subject." Rather than in authors or readers, the awareness that sign and meaning can never coincide is to be found in the literary text itself—that is, in "any text that implicitly or explicitly signifies its own rhetorical mode and prefigures its own misunderstanding." Poetic writing, de Man concluded, "may differ from critical or discursive writing in the economy of its articulation, but not in kind," for crit. and philosophy too may be reflexively rhetorical and thus show not how understanding and meaning are possible (as was the project of structuralism) but how they are impossible. "Poetic writing," we discover, is only "the most advanced and refined mode of deconstruction" (q.v.). Literary writing is the allegory of, in particular, deconstructive reading. "The reading is not 'our' reading," de Man protests; "the deconstruction is not something we have added to the text but it constituted the text in the first place." But this immanence is just what the most innocent reader would claim, and one can only assume that de Man's lang. here is figurative.

This brief survey must end with deconstructive p., and in a sense fittingly so. For in the very breadth and rigor of its skepticism de Man's work epitomizes the ambition, intense self-scrutiny, and theoretical refinement characteristic of Anglo-Am. p. throughout this century.

See now CRITICISM; CULTURAL CRITICISM; DECONSTRUCTION; FEMINIST POETICS; INTERPRETATION; MARXIST CRITICISM; POETICS; POETRY, THEORIES OF; PSYCHOLOGICAL CRITICISM; READER-RESPONSE CRITICISM; ROMANTIC AND POSTROMANTIC POETICS; SEMIOTICS, POETIC; SPEECH ACT THEORY; STRUCTURALISM; THEORY.

T. E. Hulme, *Speculations*, ed. H. Read (1924); I. A. Richards, *Principles of Lit. Crit.* (1923), *Practical Crit.* (1929); C. Caudwell, *Illusion and Reality* (1937); J. C. Ransom, *The World's Body* (1938); K. Burke, *The Philosophy of Literary Form* (1941); R. P. Warren, "Pure and Impure Poetry," *KR* 5 (1943); Brooks; Y. Winters, *In Defense of Reason* (1947); T. S. Eliot, "The Use of Poetry and the Use of Crit," in Eliot, *Essays; Literary Opinion in America*, ed. M. D. Zabel, rev. ed. (1951); W. V. O'Connor, *An Age of Crit.: 1900-1950* (1952); E. Pound, *Literary Essays*, ed. T. S. Eliot (1954); Crane; W. K. Wimsatt, *The Verbal Icon* (1954); A. Tate, *The Man of Letters in the Mod. World* (1955); M. Krieger, *The New Apologists for Poetry* (1956); Wellek and Warren; Wimsatt and Brooks; F. Kermode, *Romantic Image* (1957), *The Sense of an Ending* (1967); Frye; J. H. Miller, *Poets of Reality* (1965); *Fiction and Repetition* (1982); E. D. Hirsch, Jr., *Validity in Interp.* (1967), *The Aims of Interp.* (1976); N. Holland, *The Dynamics of Literary Response* (1968); G. Hartman, *Beyond Formalism* (1970), *Crit. in the Wilderness* (1980), *Saving the Text* (1981); F. Jameson, *Marxism and Form* (1971), *The Political Unconscious* (1981); H. Bloom, *The Anxiety of Influence* (1973); *Feminist Lit. Crit.*, ed. J. Donovan (1975); Culler; R. Williams,

Marxism and Lit. (1977); E. Showalter, "Towards a Feminist Poetics," *Women Writing and Writing about Women*, ed. M. Jacobus (1979); P. de Man, *Allegories of Reading* (1979), *Critical Writings, 1953-1978*, ed. L. Waters (1989); S. Fish, *Is There a Text in this Class?* (1980); *The Future of Difference*, ed. H. Eisenstein and A. Jardine (1980); F. Lentricchia, *After the New Crit.* (1980); J. Culler, *On Deconstruction* (1982); de Man; T. Eagleton, *Literary Theory* (1983); J. Donovan, "Towards a Women's Poetics," *Tulsa Studies in Women's Lit.* 3 (1984); K. Ruthven, *Feminist Literary Studies* (1984); Ransom; Wellek, v. 5, 6.
J.W.

II. FRENCH AND GERMAN. Continental p. remain remarkably autonomous and isolated within their national trads. A few major figures extend their influence beyond national borders, and there are instances of fruitful cooperation between writers from different nationalities, but on the whole there is less contact between, for instance, Fr., Ger., and It. poetic theorists than there is between the actual poets of these countries.

A. In *France*, concerns with literary theory were displaced by the pedagogical purposes of *explication de texte* (see EXPLICATION), an interpretive method not primarily focused on questions of p. Until recently, *explication de texte* aimed at the correct reading of literary works and was positivist rather than critical in perspective. From Hippolyte Taine (1828–93) it inherited an interest in the extrinsic forces that act upon lit.: social, intellectual, and political hist. played a large part in the works of its most eminent representative, Gustave Lanson (1857–1934). Because of the particular structure of Fr. lit. hist., with its high period in the cl. 17th and 18th cs., the techniques of explication were devised to deal with authors of that period, hence the emphasis on rhetoric in the neoclassical sense developed in conformity with Aristotelian prescriptions. Orthodox explication is much less at home with 19th-c. romantic and (esp.) symbolist poets, whose figurative practices were avowedly antirhetorical in purpose (see ROMANTICISM; SYMBOLISM). In the 20th c., the gap between live poetry, which continued to develop in the wake of symbolism, and the methods taught in the schools continued to widen, and a reaction was bound to occur.

Among the main initiators of this reaction, both Henri Bergson (1859–1941) and Paul Valéry (1871–1945) translated the heritage of symbolism into poetic theory. Valéry continued the trad. of a poetry characterized, since Baudelaire (1821–67) and Mallarmé (1842–90), by an acute awareness of the theoretical problems created by its own existence. Valéry's numerous and widely influential essays, advocating the study of poetic creation independent of historical and critical considerations, contributed to reawakening an interest in theoretical p. as such. It was primarily the self-reflective, hyper-conscious aspect of symbolism (esp. in Mallarmé) that interested Valéry, who, while viewing the poetic work as a "by-product" rather than primary expression of the human spirit, described poetry as "a constructive science" of precise verbal combinations which diminished the "arbitrary" element of content prevalent in other forms of lit. Poetry achieves this precision by recognizing and, insofar as possible, symbolizing its struggle with contingency, a view of p. articulated most influentially in Mallarmé's visual poem, "Un coup de dés jamais n'abolira le hasard" (see VISUAL POETRY). In his critique of naive conceptions of "inspiration" and his emphasis on the calculated aspect of poetic composition, Valéry reestablished the relationship, in 20th-c. p., between the workings of the poetic and the rational mind. Extending this conception of mental work to the reception of poetry, he identified the "true subject" of lit. hist. with the "formation and fluctuations" of the "quality" of attention paid in "reading."

Although he was not primarily concerned with p. and did not write systematically on the subject, Bergson exercised a profound influence on early modern Fr. poetic theory. His constant emphasis on the presence, in human consciousness, of subjective elements pertaining to memory, imagination, and intuition, next to—though sharply separated from—elements that possess objective reality, recalls in many respects the epistemologically oriented p. of Giambattista Vico (1668–1744), Étienne de Condillac (1715–80), Jean-Jacques Rousseau (1712–78), and others, and amounts, as in the works of those early romantic theorists, to a poetization of human experience. Arguing against mechanical notions of mental association, he described imaged cognition as a creative movement between diverse remembered moments. So understood, the poetic image becomes a close verbal approximation to what perception and sensation are actually like—much closer, at any rate, than the purely intellectual representation of reality found in the scientific concept. The entire area of man's contact with the external world becomes similar to the experience found in works of art and lit. As the formal unity of a symbolist work always resides in the internal relationships of its images, so Bergson is concerned with the imaging process as the unifying activity of human consciousness.

Following Bergson, Gaston Bachelard (1884–1962), a philosopher of science, devoted a series of studies to what he calls "material imagination," which, apprehending matter according to unconscious archetypes rather than through rational mediation, resembles a "dreaming about matter" more than an act of cognition (see ARCHETYPE). Bachelard's attempted typology of the poetic imagination, cataloguing images according to their dominant material elements (fire, water, earth, air), referred poetic experience to the experience of *concrete* reality, a reference already implicit in Bergson's philosophy, and exerted a considerable impact on Fr. crit. His *Poétique de l'espace* (1957), written after the elemental studies, appeals instead to a phenomenology of consciousness to describe the pre-psychological impact of images on the mind and equates poetry, whose "creativity" indicates an originary rather than archetypal imaginative consciousness, with the "phenomenology of the soul" (see GENEVA SCHOOL).

Although often critical of Bergson, Jean-Paul Sartre (1905–80) is close to him in his contributions to poetic theory. His study of the imagination insists upon the radical distinction between perception and imagination, a thesis which figures prominently in Bergson's early *Matière et mémoire* (1900). The method of existential psychoanalysis which Sartre advocates in *L'Être et le néant* (1943) involves an interpenetration between matter and consciousness which, despite important differences of emphasis, remains Bergsonian. In later writings, such as *Qu'est-ce que la littérature?* (1948), Sartre draws a sharp distinction between literary prose and poetry while defining writing in general as the only artistic medium formally capable of signification and thus of political engagement. Stipulating that author and reader, in individual liberty while in need of each other, "share responsibility" for the injustices "revealed" in writing and (re)"created" in the "concrete" act of reading, Sartre reintroduced interpersonal ethical considerations into the evaluation of lit. In so doing he abandoned the pursuit of theoretical p. indicated at least potentially in *Situations* (1947–49) and in his early literary studies in the *Nouvelle Revue Française*, in which important analyses of such modern authors as Faulkner, Dos Passos, Camus, Blanchot, Bataille, and Ponge marked a significant juncture between critical philosophy and crit. of lit.

The p. of Bachelard and Sartre are attempts at a phenomenology of poetic consciousness. They differ from each other with regard to the original situation which each takes as a starting-point: in Bachelard it is man's relationship to the textual and spatial dimensions of matter; in Sartre it is the existential situation. Another writer who belongs in the same group, Georges Poulet (b. 1902), starts from the poet's intuitions of time and space and shows how these mark his poetic style. The interest of this approach stems from the link it suggests between phenomenological analysis and stylistics (q.v.), yet the metaphoric style of Poulet's own interpretive descriptions (e.g. "Goethe-centre" and "Goethe-périphérique," in a work describing consciousness according to a center-circumference model, *Les Métamorphoses du cercle*, 1961) conveys the sense of texts as objects extended in space and of interpretation as topological or directional maps (see GENEVA SCHOOL).

Poulet's approach has been carried out by Jean Pierre Richard (b. 1922) in studies of the novel and of symbolist poetry (*Poésie et profondeur*, 1955). Richard's phenomenological conception of poetry is shared to a certain extent by the phenomenalization of truth and fiction (as transparent immediacy and socially mediated opacity) in Jean Starobinski's (b. 1920) influential analyses of Rousseau (*J.-J. Rousseau: la transparence et l'obstacle*, 1957; *L'Oeil vivant*, 1961). The writer who has perhaps gone furthest in the formulation of an ontology of the poetic act is Maurice Blanchot, who, turning from phenomenological to linguistic dimensions of consciousness, shows how literary works by definition gravitate toward the ontological question, and how individual authors try and fail always again to define human existence by means of poetic lang., concerns already evidenced, albeit as negative givens, in the tormented meditations of Georges Bataille (1897–1962).

Such theories of poetry, primarily centered on 19th-c. lit., modified the traditional picture of Fr. lit. hist. as dominated by 17th-c. Classicism (see NEOCLASSICAL POETICS) and led to the success of historical studies founded on romantic and symbolist p., such as Albert Béguin's *L'Ame romantique et le rêve* (1937) and Marcel Raymond's *De Baudelaire au surréalisme* (rev. ed., 1952). At the same time, the trad. of *explication de texte* took on transformed vitality in the work of Fr. structuralist and semiotic theorists, who about 1950 began to formulate a new notion of text based on the systematic insights of Ferdinand de Saussure's *Cours de linguistique générale* (1916) and the technical-critical methods of the Rus. Formalist school (see RUSSIAN FORMALISM) and the Prague Linguistic Circle (see STRUCTURALISM). Influenced by Vladimir Propp's *Morphology of the Folktale* (1928), Claude Lévi-Strauss (b. 1908) used the formalist method, in studies of myths and customs gathered during his tenure in Brazil (*Tristes tropiques*, 1955; *Anthropologie structurale*, 1958; *La Pensée sauvage*, 1962), to redefine both the conceptual object and analytic practices of contemp. cultural anthropology. His structural model, describing the perception and resolution of binary oppositions as the operative motives of narrative myths, indicated the crucial role played by mediation in the cognitive activity of the "primitive mind." This observation was applied to narrative theory ("narratology"; see PLOT) by A. J. Greimas (b. 1917), whose semiotic studies translated Lévi-Strauss' one-to-one binary structures onto the double axis of the *carré sémiotique* ("semiotic rectangle") or *combinatoire*, a chiastic paradigm for the oppositions informing all narrative logic.

The theoretical affinity between structuralism and semiotics (q.v.) was revealed in Roland Barthes' (1915–80) *Mythologies* (1957), analyses of Western cultural myths ranging from advertisements, cult images, and quotidian objects to intellectual stereotypes (see MYTH; MYTH CRITICISM). Barthes' early *Le Degré zéro de l'écriture* (1953) had hypothesized a nonliterary and nonideological "white writing," whereas *Mythologies* revealed the rhetorical nature of apparently "transparent" cultural signs, explaining the structure of mythologizing semantics as a production of meaning to the

second degree, "a second-order semiological system." According to Barthes' model of the signifying system of myth, the sensory component or signifier (*signifiant*) of the mythic sign is not related arbitrarily, as in Saussure, to its conceptual component, the signified (*signifié*), but derives from a preceding signified, thereby constituting an already motivated or connotative, instead of arbitrary and denotative, form of meaning. Neutral or natural in appearance, the signification of myth is always a meaning "in excess," i.e. a message which, constructed upon the sense of the already "known" (ideology, *idées reçues*, or *doxa*), supplants the cognitive process of interpretive reading by confusing overdetermination with unambiguous truth. The theorist of myth reveals or "demystifies" that overdetermination by attending to the semiotic *form* through which it is produced, an analytic activity Barthes identified with "the structuralist activity" generally in the essay of the same name (1964). Barthes' semiological insights, based at first on an equation of all "literary" works with ideology, opposing ideology to the impermeable lang. of poetry at the close of *Mythologies*, and positing lit. as the transgressive "third term" of the oppositional signifying structures outlined in *Eléments de sémiologie* (1964), gave way to a polysemous approach to lit. in *S/Z* (1970), in which the semiological analysis of a "readerly" or "classical" text, Balzac's *Sarrasine*, carried out by way of five hypostatized "codes," reveals literary "realism" to share the same ongoing process of "production" defining Barthes' heuristic notion of the ideal "writerly text." Barthes' later works, abandoning the ideo-semiological critique of representation (identified in the mid-1960s with the vanguard journal *Tel Quel*), maintained a conception of lit. as a production of form in perpetual departure from mythologizing signifying systems. The enduring tension, in Barthes' writings, between the transgressive structure of lit. and the inherently overdetermined structure of myth is perhaps best represented in the next-to-last work published before his death, *Roland Barthes* (1975). *Roland Barthes*, written for the canonical "Ecrivains de toujours" series, literalized the myth of factual and interpretive transparency conveyed by the series slogan, "par lui-même," in being authored for the first time on actual rather than rhetorical authority, i.e. "par [Roland Barthes] lui-même." By a second turn of signification, however, *Roland Barthes* is granted the meaning of nonfiction, and its author the distinction of representing "himself," on the basis of the popular opinion (or *doxa*) which had already mythologized Barthes in life. In the text *Roland Barthes*, Barthes realizes and reveals representational authority *as* fiction, whether referential (i.e. biographical) or critical in intent, by writing an autobiography *in theory* (incl. passages of representational "fiction" written by the "real" autobiographical author). Thus "the structuralist man" is transformed into the object of "structural activity" through the written production of his own representation as now lit., now myth.

As reflected in Barthes' crit., the linguistic orientation of structuralism and semiotics extended notions of p. to the study of narrative lit.: prose fiction, rather than poetry, became the new object of a technical analysis which focused, on the one hand, on regular grammatical and syntactic patterns and, on the other, on grammatically constituted narrative tropes. Watershed studies by such linguists as Roman Jakobson (1896–1982; "Two Aspects of Lang. and Two Types of Aphasic Disturbances," 1956; "Linguistics and P.," 1960) and Émile Benveniste (*Problèmes de linguistique générale*, 1966) located the formal bases for a p. of narrative in grammatical rather than lexical figures (such as metonymy as opposed to metaphor [qq.v.]) and in the essentially grammatical function of narrative subjectivity. Their influence upon such "narratologists" as Tzvetan Todorov (*La grammaire du Décameron*, 1969; *La Poétique de la prose*, 1971) and Gérard Genette (*Figures*, 1966; *Figures II*, 1969; *Figures III*, 1972; tr. 1982) was enormous, if ephemeral, since both those critics rejected or retreated from internal formal analysis in their subsequent work (Todorov, *Critique de la critique littéraire* [1986]; Genette, *Mimologiques* [1976], *Palimpsestes* [1982], *Seuils* [1987]).

"Poststructuralism," the collective name for a wide range of individually articulated critical positions, shares the interdisciplinary thrust of structuralist and semiotic theories while subverting the synchronic and symmetrical bases of their methods (see DECONSTRUCTION; MODERNISM AND POSTMODERNISM; POETRY, THEORIES OF). If any single characteristic can be ascribed generally to poststructuralist tendencies, it is their rejection, or refutation, of systematicity. Rather than the attempt to constitute itself as a cognitive "science" through the elaboration of internally coherent methodologies, the questioning of coherence as a criterion for knowledge, and of the objectivity of the theoretical system, frequently provides the critical point of departure for poststructuralist thinking. Thus, even when not explicitly focused upon problems of p., poststructuralism may be seen to view all the human sciences through the prism of poetic theory: the poetic is not an external object of theoretical reflection but the defining angle of all reflection, whether in critical writing or in verse.

In France, this perception owes primarily to the renewed interfusion of the discourses of philosophy and aesthetics in the writings of Jacques Derrida (b. 1930) and, to a lesser degree, to Michel Foucault's (1926–86) influential conception of history as cognitive archaeology (see HISTORICISM). In Foucault's account, the shape of human institutions at any historical moment is determined by an organizing representation of knowledge, itself a mode of maintaining relations of power. History thus consists of strata of conceptual representations, individual synchronic "fields" defined and delimited by a dominant cognitive form or *épistémè*. The succession of one self-enclosed stratum by another is generated by the noncausal or discontinuous occurrence of an epistemological "break" (*Les Mots et les choses*, 1966; *L'Archéologie du savoir*, 1969). Derrida's pivotal conception of *différance*, identical in pronunciation to the Saussurian and structuralist notion of *différence* (i.e. lang. as a negatively differentiating system without positive features), differs from its acoustic double by combining two verbs for effecting distinctions, the synchronic, "to differ," and diachronic, "to defer." The significance of this half neologism, at once a poetic and critical creation, rests upon a wordplay perceivable only in its graphic form, and is thus directly related to Derrida's codeterminant notion of *écriture*.

For Derrida, "writing" indicates the inherently temporal constitution of lang.; the necessary endurance of the linguistic sign beyond any given context, its actual physical iterability, renders it irreducible to the self-identity of any phenomenological moment or present of consciousness in a speaker. By stressing the presence of "writing" (i.e. a presence marking a phenomenal absence) in lang., while embracing lang. for that very reason as the only possible currency of knowledge, Derrida evokes the involvement of that which is neither knowledge nor nonknowledge within knowledge: the indispensable "supplement" to intelligibility which must precede all statements of being but never "is" in "itself," the graphic sign. Derrida's interpretation of Western metaphysics as the effacement *and* rewriting of "writing" as *différance*, his reflection on the indelible mark of lang. within the thinking of experience, brings into relief the relation of speculative philosophy to the consciously self-"differing" composition of lit. While not directly concerned with textual p., the psychoanalytic theory of Jacques Lacan (1901–80) describes the workings of the unconscious according to a linguistic model of perpetually deferred signification in some respects similar to the notion of "writing" developed by Derrida.

B. *Germany*. While Fr. *explication de texte* originally derived its methods from the natural sciences, Ger. literary studies of the same era seem to have been esp. eager to emulate contemporary practices of the social sciences. Various forms of organic historicism appear as the dominant characteristic of several works. Sometimes, as in H. A. Korff's *Geist der Goethezeit* (5 v., 1925–27), the concept of history is triadic and Hegelian; in others, such as Walzel (1864–1944) or Hans Werner Richter (b. 1908), it is derived from the visual arts—in this case Heinrich Wölfflin's (1864–1945) theories of "open" and "closed" form. Others continue to search for historical continuity in specific literary trads. and *topoi* (Ernst Curtius), in recurrent themes and attitudes (Unger, Rehm), in archetypal patterns (Kerenyi), or in philosophical or aesthetic attitudes (Cassirer, Auerbach). In all these instances, the problem is essentially one of historical continuity: a certain theory of history is shown to bring order and coherence to the apparently erratic devel. of lit. Some of these authors produced works of lasting value which went far in revealing the workings of the poetic mind. But since they all start from the literary work as an unquestionable empirical fact, they do not claim to be writing on p. It is partly in reaction against the considerable authority of much philological and historical *Literaturwissenschaft* that a new concern with p. developed, not unlike that in France.

The disciples of the poet Stefan George, for example, set themselves up as deliberate opponents of the prevalent methods of literary study. Although George claimed that "from him, no road led to science," several of his later followers taught in universities and exercised a great deal of influence. Their approach was antiphilological in the extreme (no footnotes or bibliographies), but their merit lies rather in their respect for the autonomy of the poetic mind than in their attacks on traditional methods. George's disciples renewed the established image of Goethe, and they were instrumental in the discovery of Hölderlin. As disciples, however, they also emphasized the messianic role of the poet as an almost superhuman figure to be dealt with in a lang. closer to that of myth or religion than science. That such an approach is not always incompatible with true learning is clear from Gundolf's books on Shakespeare and Goethe; still the insistence on the messianic element tended to overshadow the formal element of poetry altogether. For George himself, the tangible expression of the transcendental value of poetry was to be found in the perfection of the form: it was by the act of extreme formal discipline, a kind of *askesis* of the form, that the poet earned the right to statements of prophetic weight. If this formal discipline is taken away, the messianic attitude becomes dangerously arbitrary. Significantly, it is after he had left the George Circle that Max Kommerell (1902–44), one of the most gifted of its members, wrote studies that show real insight into poetic motivation and its relation to formal structure. Kommerell's influence appears most prominent in the work of Hugo Friedrich, whose landmark study of European lyric poetry since Baudelaire (*Die Struktur der modernen Lyrik*, 1956) owes much to Kommerell's insistence on poetic form.

Another challenge offered to Ger. philology emanated from the philosopher Martin Heidegger (1889–1976). In 1937 Heidegger began the publication of commentaries on the poetry of Hölderlin, and in subsequent works he gave increased importance to the poetic as a part of his philosophy, with occasional excursions into the practical field of exegesis. Heidegger's conception of the poetic is part of his attempt to reach beyond what he considers the limitations of the Western metaphysical trad., a concern shared by Derrida in France, where confrontation with Heidegger was largely delayed by the influence of existentialism (the first official Fr. tr. of *Sein und Zeit* appeared only in 1986). Because of their greater proximity to lang., poets, for Heidegger, reflect the fundamental tensions of human existence more faithfully than even the greatest among the metaphysicians. And the purest of them all, Hölderlin, the poet who, according to Heidegger, has been able to name the very essence of poetry, offers therefore an insight into Being which is without antecedent in the history of human thought. Whoever is able, with the assistance of the commentary, to listen to Hölderlin will stand in the presence of the poetic itself and discover that it is the unmediated lang. of Being. For Heidegger, poetic lang. has eschatological power and is to be interpreted, not by means of a critical analysis which assumes a common frame of reference, but as a kind of revelation which, at best, we can only hope to perceive but never to grasp critically.

The eclipse of critical poetic thinking signified by Heidegger's equation of poetry with the voice of Being is indicated, in tentative and deferential terms, by two critics with whom he corresponded, Kommerell and Emil Staiger. Although sympathetic with (or, in Staiger's case, explicitly indebted to) Heidegger's philosophy, both critics recognized that his apotheosis of poetry disturbingly precluded any interrogation of what constitutes the poetic: i.e., for Staiger, the question of "how" an individual poem is formed; and for Kommerell, what "specifies" a poetic (as distinct from a philosophical) statement. Both critics suggest that, in uniting poetry with ontology, Heidegger also renders p. superfluous: the pure lang. of Being is not the lang. of reading, in any sense of the effort to understand which attends the term. By contrast, Derrida maintains a critical distance between Being and lang. in the being of *writing*, thereby departing from Heidegger, whose concept of temporal *Differenz* prepared the way for Derrida's formulation of *différance*.

If Heidegger's commentaries are an extreme example of a p. identified with revelatory "creation," Ger. scholars have also made important contributions to a p. founded on the analysis of style. Stylistic research (*Stilforschung*) may be the most international among the trends we have mentioned. It originated out of an encounter between Ger. philology and the philosophy of the It. aesthetician Benedetto Croce (1866–1952), and was influenced by the close friendship between Croce and the Ger. philologist Karl Vossler (1872–1949), leader of the Munich school of stylistic crit. to which Leo Spitzer (1887–1960) belongs. Both Croce and Vossler criticized the scientific positivism of the 19th c. in the name of Hegelian idealism; the title of Vossler's first work is, revealingly,

Positivismus und Idealismus in der Sprachwissenschaft (1904). Vossler's later work is mainly a study of the dominant stylistic traits of literary lang. as a key, not only to the personality of an author but even, as in his book on France (*Frankreichs Kultur und Sprache*, 1929), to the spirit of a nation. In the posthumously published *Dichtungsformen der Romanen* (1951), the principle of versification is importantly rejected as a poetic criterion. Arguing that no general prescriptions could ever account for each "individual verseform," and that much of "true poetry" is in fact written in "prose," Vossler proposes that only "the concept of lang." can essentially "define" poetic form; that "human lang.," rather than any specific "Urform," is the practical origin of all *Dichtungsformen*.

Spitzer's stylistic analyses, using more intricate and refined techniques, focused upon distinctive features of style as a means of penetrating and illuminating the entire composition of a poetic world; the study of one crucial passage in *Phèdre*, or of the structure of the periodic sentence in *À la recherche du temps perdu*, leads to general interpretations of Racine and Proust. This kind of stylistic analysis, differing sharply from positivistic stylistics in that it assumes the work to be an autonomous aesthetic object, refined the tools of literary analysis and interp. while extending the notion of the "hermeneutic circle" to the methods of *explication de texte*. Vossler, who enjoyed a high reputation in Spain, established a link between Ger., It., and Sp. literary studies; the extensive critical works of Dámaso Alonso (b. 1898) were perhaps the most accomplished to come out of this school.

Partly in reaction against the monistic and psychological aspects of Vossler's method, another trend in stylistic study originated in Zürich around Emil Staiger (b. 1908) and the review *Trivium*. Staiger's techniques are still those of stylistic analysis, but his ultimate purpose is to reveal the metapersonal attitude of the poet toward the fundamental categories of existence, esp. temporality. While Heideggerian in philosophical orientation, his work thus recalls trends in phenomenological p. in France. Departing from Husserl rather than Heidegger, the Hungarian critic Roman Ingarden (1893–1970) attempted to ground phenomenological interp. in a schematic ontology of the act of reading literary works (*Das literarische Kunstwerk*, 1931).

Another parallel between Fr. and Ger. p. arises in the theory of *Kulturkritik* developed by T. W. Adorno (1903–69) and Max Horkheimer (1895–1973), the leaders of the Frankfurt School of social crit. (see MARXIST CRITICISM). Whereas Barthes' crit. of cultural myth employed semiotic techniques developed specifically in France, Adorno and Horkheimer's critique of cultural phenomena, initiated in the 1930s under the aegis of the Institute for Social Research, stemmed from the trad. of Ger. metaphysics and epistemology. Adorno's aesthetic theory combined Hegelian dialectics with the insights of Marx and Freud into social and psychic formations; his "negative dialectics" diverged from Hegel in rejecting any point of synthesis as idealist reification, and criticized all philosophical systematization as the conceptual counterpart to commodity fetishism. While Adorno did not isolate poetry from other aspects of culture, he emphasized the "representational" dimension of philosophical discourse, proposing that crit. "save," rather than attempt to eradicate, "the rhetorical moment" within its own thinking as the negative moment in which philosophy constitutes itself dialectically.

Associated with Adorno and the Institute for Social Research was Walter Benjamin (1892–1940), the critical writer whose hardships in all matters of literary and literal survival may be matched only by the intensity and diversity of interest his largely posthumous publications have evoked since their first partial collection (*Schriften*, ed. Adorno, 1955). An essayist of tremendously varied subjects and instinctively disinclined toward identifiable method, Benjamin, who considered himself first a literary critic, has gained with delayed recognition a heterogeneous range of adherents. Criticized by Adorno during his lifetime for substituting "magical positivism" for dialectical materialism, he was also considered a literary mind without equal by his close intellectual companion, Bertolt Brecht, and is widely admired by contemp. Marxist critics.

Claimed by his friend Gershom Scholem for the cause of messianic gnosticism, Benjamin has since become a central figure in the essentially anti-messianic aesthetics of postmodernism. As literary critic, however, Benjamin wrote his two most comprehensive finished works, the long essay "Goethes *Wahlverwandtschaften*" (1924), and *Ursprung des deutschen Trauerspiels* (his *Habilitationsschrift*, completed and rejected in 1925), in which, either implicitly or explicitly, a single poetic figure is key: allegory (q.v.). The concept of allegory is also central to Benjamin's extensive (uncompleted) study of Baudelaire, as is Baudelaire to his uncompleted (and uncompletable) study of 19th-c. Paris, the monumental and fragmentary *Passagen-werk*. In Benjamin's writing, poetic allegory, conceived as the objective "ruins" of "thought," characterizes the relation between human lang. and actual creation. A writer of translations (of Baudelaire and Proust) and on translation ("Die Aufgabe des Übersetzers") who identified translatability with literary trad., Benjamin revealed the historical, nonsubjective life of literary forms—as of cities—by retranslating them into allegorical objects. Just as poetry, the true art of translation, takes the form of allegory with regard to its own posterity, so p., for Benjamin, is what remains of, and engenders, thinking. The intensely allegorical nature of his own critical thought may explain the deeply and differently committed commentary it has attracted, for Benjamin shapes a p. which, like the objects it translates, does not reveal itself.

While Benjamin's allegorical understanding of poetry maintains a strikingly anomalous position within modern Ger. p., the theory of the aesthetics of reception, formulated by Hans Robert Jauss and Wolfgang Iser, colleagues at the University of Constanz, has developed into a school of interp. influential both in Germany and abroad (see READER-RESPONSE CRITICISM). According to Jauss, who follows in the Ger. hermeneutic trad., *Rezeptionsästhetik* indicates the way in which a literary work both corresponds to and points beyond an ideally hypothesized reader's horizon of expectation, thereby grounding the course of lit. hist. in the p. of the reading experience. As in France, the study of p. in Ger. has returned to Enlightenment and romantic lit. and theory for its basic texts; the writings of Peter Szondi, in which scholarly interpretations of developments in 19th-c. p. benefit from a thorough knowledge of the philosophy of the same period, are exemplary of this trend. See also INTERPRETATION.

FRANCE: H. Bergson, *Matière et mémoire* (1900), *Essai sur les donnés immédiates de la conscience*, 4th ed. (1904), *Le Rire* (1908); F. de Saussure, *Cours de linguistique générale* (1916); G. Lanson, "Quelques mots sur l'explication de textes," *Methodes de l'histoire littéraire* (1925); V. Propp, *Morphology of the Folktale* (1928); R. Vigneron, *L'Explication de texte* (1928); A. Béguin, *L'Ame romantique et le rêve* (1937); G.'Bachelard, *La Psychanalyse du feu* (1940), *L'Eau et les rêves* (1942), *L'Air et le songes* (1943), *La Terre et les rêveries du repos* (1948), *La Poétique de l'espace* (1957); J.-P. Sartre, *L'Imaginaire* (1940), *Situations*, 3 v. (1947–49), *Qu'est-ce que la littérature?* (1948); M. Blanchot, *Faux Pas* (1943), *L'Espace littéraire* (1955); G. Poulet, *Études sur le temps humain* (1949), *Les Métamorphoses du cercle* (1961), *L'Espace proustien* (1966); M. Raymond, *De Baudelaire au surréalisme*, 2d ed. (1952); R. Barthes, *Le Degré zéro de l'écriture* (1953), *Mythologies* (1957), *Eléments de sémiologie* (1964), *S/Z* (1970), *Roland Barthes* (1975), *Poétique du récit* (1977); J. Hytier, *La Poétique de Paul Valéry* (1953); J. P. Richard, *Littérature et sensation* (1954), *Proust et le monde sensible* (1974); C. Lévi-Strauss, *Tristes tropiques* (1955), *Anthropologie structurale* (1958), *La Pensée sauvage* (1962); R. Jakobson, "Two Aspects of Lang. and Two Types of Aphasic Disturbance" (1956) and "Linguistics and P." (1960) in Jakobson; P. Valéry, *Variétés, Dialogues, Cahiers, Oeuvres* (1957–74); M. Merleau-Ponty, "Le Langage indirect et les voix du silence," *Signes* (1960); J. Starobinski, *L'Oeil vivant* (1961), *J.-J. Rousseau: la transparence et l'obstacle*, 2d ed. (1970); J. Rousset, *Forme et signification* (1962); M. Foucault, *Naissance de la clinique* (1963), *Les Mots et les choses* (1966), *L'Archéologie du savoir* (1969); E. Benveniste, *Problèmes de linguistique générale*, 2 v. (1966–74); G. Genette, *Figures* (1966), *Figures II* (1969), *Figures III* (1972), selections tr. as *Figures of Literary Discourse* (1982); A. J. Greimas, *Séman-*

tique structurale (1966), *Du Sens* (1970), *Maupassant* (1976); J. Lacan, *Écrits* (1966); J. Derrida, *La Voix et le phénomène* (1967), *L'Écriture et la différance* (1967), *De la grammatologie* (1967), *Positions* (1972), *Glas* (1974), *Mémoires: Trois lectures pour Paul de Man* (1986), *Psyché* (1987), *De l'esprit* (1987, tr. 1989), *Acts of Lit.*, ed. D. Attridge (tr. 1992); J. Kristeva, *Sèméiôtiké* (1969); T. Todorov, *La Grammaire du Décameron* (1969), *La Poétique de la prose* (1971); *The Structuralist Controvery*, ed. R. Macksey and E. Donato (1972); P. de Man, *Blindness and Insight* (1971), *Allegories of Reading* (1979), *The Resistance to Theory* (1986); F. Jameson, *The Prison-House of Lang.* (1972), "Imaginary and Symbolic in Lacan," *YFS* 55/56 (1977); S. Heath, *Vertige du déplacement* (1974); J. D. Culler, *Structuralist Poetics* (1975); M. Riffaterre, *Semiotics of Poetry* (1978), *La Production du texte* (1979); C. Norris, *The Contest of Faculties* (1987), *Derrida* (1987); S. Weber, *Return to Freud* (tr. 1991).

GERMANY: K. Vossler, *Positivismus und Idealismus in der Sprachwissenschaft* (1904), *Frankreichs Kultur und Sprache* (1929), *Dichtungsformen der Romanen* (1951); F. Gundolf, *Shakespeare und der deutsche Geist* (1911), *Goethe* (1916), *George* (1920); O. Walzel, *Gehalt und Gestalt im Kunstwerk des Dichters* (1923); R. Unger, *Aufsätze zur Prinzipienlehre der Literaturgesch.*, 2 v. (1923), *Herder, Novalis, Kleist* (1923); E. Cassirer, *Philosophie der symbolischen Formen* (1924); H. Pongs, *Das Wortkunstwerk* (1926); M. Kommerell, *Der Dichter als Führer in der deutschen Klassik* (1928), *Geist und Buchstabe der Dichtung* (1944), *Die Kunst Calderóns* (1946); W. Rehm, *Der Todesgedanke in der deutschen Dichtung* (1928); L. Spitzer, *Stilstudien*, 2 v. (1928), *Romanische Stil und Literaturstudien* (1931), *Linguistics and Lit. Hist.* (1948), *Essays on Eng. and Am. Lit.* (1962), *Representative Essays*, ed. A. K. Forcione et al. (1988); E. Staiger, *Die Zeit als Einbildungskraft des Dichters* (1939), *Grundbegriffe der Poetik* (1946, tr. J. C. Hudson and L. T. Frank as *Basic Concepts of Poetics* [1991]), *Die Kunst der Interp.* (1955), *Stilwandel* (1963); M. Heidegger, *Erläuterungen zu Hölderlins Dichtung* (1944), "Der Ursprung des Kunstwerkes," "Wozu Dichter . . . ," *Holzwege* (1950), " . . . dichterisch wohnet der Mensch," *Vorträge und Aufsätze* (1954), *Identität und Differenz* (1957); F. Strich, *Deutsche Klassik und Romantik*, 4th ed. (1949), *Carteggio Croce-Vossler 1899–1949* (1951); M. Wehrli, *Allgemeine Literaturwiss.* (1951); E. Buddeberg, "Heidegger und die Dichtung," *DVLG* 26 (1952); Auerbach; Curtius; H. Friedrich, *Die Struktur der modernen Lyrik* (1956); B. Alleman, *Hölderlin und Heidegger*, 2d ed. (1957); F. Martini, "Poetik," *Deutsche Philologie im Aufriss*, ed. W. Stammler, 2d ed., v. 1 (1958); H. G. Gadamer, *Wahrheit und Methode* (1960); R. Ingarden, *Das literarische Kunstwerk*, 2d ed. (1960); G. Lukács, *Die Eigenart des Ästhetischen*, 2 v., sect. 1 of *Ästhetik* (1963); T. W. Adorno, *Eingriffe. Neun kritische Modelle* (1963), *Stichworte. Kritische Modelle 2* (1965), *Negative Dialektik* (1966), *Prismen* (1967),

Ästhetische Theorie (1970); M. Durzak, "Walter Benjamin und die Literaturwiss.," *Monatshefte* 58 (1966); B. Markwardt, *Gesch. der deutschen Poetik*, v. 5 (1967); H. Arendt, Intro. to W. Benjamin, *Illuminations* (1968); R. Bubner et al., *Hermeneutik und Dialektik* (1970); F. Jameson, *Marxism and Form* (1971); W. Benjamin, *Gesammelte Schriften*, 6 v. (1974–); H. R. Jauss, *Ästhetische Erfahrung und literarische Hermeneutik* (1974, tr. 1982); P. Szondi, *Poetik und Geschichtsphilosophie* (1974), *Schriften*, 2 v. (1978); S. Buck-Morss, *The Origin of Negative Dialectics: T. W. Adorno, W. Benjamin and the Frankfurt School* (1977), *The Dialectics of Seeing: Walter Benjamin and the Arcades Project* (1989); P. Demetz, Intro. to W. Benjamin, *Reflections* (1978); H. Stern, *Gegenbild, Reihenfolge, Sprung: An Essay on Related Figures of Argument in Walter Benjamin* (1982); P. de Man, *The Rhet. of Romanticism* (1986); M. Jennings, *Dialectical Images: Walter Benjamin's Theory of Lit. Crit.* (1987); H. Kaulen, *Rettung and Destruktion: Untersuchungen zur Hermeneutik Walter Benjamins* (1987); A. Warminski, *Readings in Interp.: Hölderlin, Hegel, Heidegger* (1987).

P.DE M.; C.B.L.

III. ITALIAN. Poetic theory in 20th-c. Italy has been dominated by the overwhelming personality of Benedetto Croce (1866–1952), whose *Estetica come scienza dell'espressione e linguistica generale* (tr. D. Ainslie, 1922) appeared in 1902. In polemical reaction to late 19th-c. positivism, and in the trad. of G. Vico and F. De Sanctis, Croce, an idealist philosopher of the Hegelian school, held that art is the first of the four forms of spiritual activity (art seeking the beautiful, philosophy the true, ethics the good, economy the useful), and can be defined as expression (q.v.) of intuition (q.v.), whereas philosophy consists of logical thinking. Art materializes through several media and in different degrees, but is ultimately one, and poetry (or lyric) is only the name of its pure form in the literary medium, whether in verse or not. It is not the technique of a particular medium which gives origin to art, but vice versa: the naive, free imagination ("fantasia") creates its own medium and technique; hence, lang. is expression, originally poetic, and the particular use of lang. (i.e. style) cannot be separated from the individual experience or intuition it expresses. Image is the poetic nucleus of the work of art, the concrete manifestation of the intuition, and the word is the sensorial sign of the image (see IMAGERY). A collective lang. is originally made of images. The distinction between poetry and nonpoetry (or plain "literature") is basic to Croce's thought and to his method of lit. crit. and is brought to a focus in his definitive book of theory, *La Poesia* (1936; tr. G. Gullace, *Poetry and Lit.*, 1981).

Croce's position was challenged by Giovanni Gentile (1875–1944), a "pure idealist" and the authoritative founder of *attualismo*. Gentile objected to Croce's emphasis on distinctions, which he countered with an emphasis on the basic unity of spiritual life (*La filosofia dell'arte*, 1931). For him, the poet, the logician, and the critic are essentially one in that the faculties which preside over their respective activities can be distinguished only from the outside, in techniques and methods, not from the inside—the inner "taste" (q.v.) that guides them all. Ultimately they all are pure modes of existence of the spirit, "pure acts."

Gentile has had a very limited influence on practical crit. but a more noticeable one on cultural historiography (e.g. in the field of the Ren.); Croce's impact in Italy has been pervasive both on theory and practice. The metaphysical foundations of his system have by now been challenged from several quarters, but the basic methodology of his aesthetics has left deep roots in all segments of It. culture, e.g. his disqualification, in the field of art, of "raw" sentiment (the source-material of art, not the actual content), of intellectualism (ideas are not found in art *qua* art), and of moralism and utilitarianism (the rapport between the work of art and both prevailing ethical standards and its practical functionality is irrelevant to aesthetic judgment). After mid-century an articulate reaction to Croce has loomed ever larger, even though he has overshadowed all other It. theorists. Nevertheless, all modern critical currents have been actively represented in Italy, from G. Pascoli's postromantic doctrine of the poet as a perennial child (the *fanciullino*), to G. D'Annunzio's decadent view of poetry as the verbal triumph of the "superman," A. Tilgher's concept of art as *amor vitae* and representation of the impossible (see his *Estetica* and *Studi di poetica* [both 1931]), Enzo Paci's and Nicola Abbagnano's existentialism, and Guido Rensi's relativistic scepticism. An early student of existentialism, Luigi Pareyson has continued his philosophical career as a major theorist of aesthetics (*Estetica, teoria della formatività*, 1954). Another major philosopher departing from the idealistic main current was Ugo Spirito (*La vita come arte*, 1948).

All the trends that have been prevailing internationally are represented in Italy, the sociological and the structuralist being the strongest, but always with a continuing concern for the historical dimension, and with a growing awareness of the semiotic perspective in more recent years. For a critical presentation of the case for sociological crit. and the Marxist point of view, see Cesare Cases, *Marxismo e neopositivismo* (1958), while the most authoritative representative of Marxist crit. (q.v.) and historiography is Antonio Gramsci (*Letteratura e vita nazionale* [1950]). Armando Plebe (*Processo all'estetica*, 1959) and Rosario Assunto (*Teoremi e problemi di estetica contemporanea*, 1960) have explored the critical predicament of current aesthetics. Stylistics (q.v.), stemming from the Geneva linguist Charles Bally, Renato Serra, the Ger. critic Karl Vossler, the Austrian Leo Spitzer, and Giuseppe De Robertis, is best represented by Gianfranco Contini (*Varianti e altra linguistica*,

1970), while Giacomo Devoto (*Studi di stilistica*, 1950; *Nuovi studi di stilistica*, 1962), Benvenuto Terracini, and Antonino Pagliaro (*Nuovi saggi di critica semantica*, 1956) display a more strictly linguistic orientation. Spitzer, a Neo-Humboldtian who felt close to Croce and to Vossler, besides Walzel, has remained a major inspiration in Italy to this day (*Stilstudien*, 1928; *Romanische Stil- und Literaturstudien*, 1931). For a broader application of basically stylistic approaches, see Mario Fubini's *Critica e poesia* (1956). It is difficult to configure the precise borderlines of an orientation which is strongly represented in Italy—namely, the aesthetic of symbolic forms, bordering on anthropology, mythography, and psychology. Though the major contributions in this area remain Anglo-American, It. contributions incl. works by Gillo Dorfles (*Simbolo comunicazione consumo*, 1962; *Nuovi riti, nuovi miti*, 1965; *L'estetica del mito*, 1967). Mario Praz is a well-known master of comparative interdisciplinary cultural history. Formalist crit. is also well represented (e.g. Ezio Raimondi, *Techniche della critica letteraria*, 1967). Maria Corti and Cesare Segre (*I metodi attuali della critica in Italia*, 1970) and Gabriele Catalano (*Teoria della critica contemporanea*. *Dalla stilistica allo strutturalismo*, 1974) give good overviews of the recent decades, while detailed analyses and presentations of methods and critics are available in the series *Orientamenti culturali: Letteratura italiana: I critici* (5 v., 1969). Enrico Falqui in *Bibliografia e iconografia del Futurismo* (1959) and Luciano De Maria in *Marinetti e il Futurismo* (1973) give up-to-date information and evaluations of futurism (q.v.), while the theoretical implications of hermeticism (q.v.) are expertly explored in Silvio Ramat's *L'ermetismo* (1969) and Ferdinando Giannessi's *Gli ermetici* (1951, 1963).

All in all, the traditional strength of the historical approach among It. scholars makes it natural for them to bend the critical methods of the last half century—esp. Rus. Formalism, structuralism, and semiotics (qq.v.)—into union with a keen historical concern, so that synchrony is seldom divorced from diachrony: see, for example, Galvano della Volpe, *Critica del gusto* (1960, 1966); Luciano Anceschi, *Progetto di una sistematica dell'arte* (1983); Marcello Pagnini, *Struttura letteraria e metodo critico* (1967); Emilio Garroni, *Semiotica ed estetica* (1968); and, best known of all, with original interps. of the application of semiotics to lit., Umberto Eco's several works, e.g. *Trattato di semiotica generale* (1975) and *Semiotics and the Philosophy of Lang.* (1984). Among the journals, *Strumenti Critici* is one that shows unrivalled interest in theoretical explorations. Its regular contributors include philologists and theorists of the caliber of Maria Corti (*Principi della comunicazione letteraria*, 1976), d'Arco Silvio Avalle (*L'analisi letteraria in Italia: formalismo—strutturalismo—semiologia*, 1970), and Cesare Segre (*I segni e la critica*, 1969; *Semiotica filologica: Testo e modelli culturali*, 1979), all of them

applying philological, linguistic, structuralist, and semiotic methods within a historicizing context. For a detailed survey of the whole field, see *Momenti e problemi di storia dell'estetica*, 4 v. (1961). See also INTERPRETATION.

G. Bertoni, *Lingua e poesia: Saggi di critica letteraria* (1937); M. Apollonio, *Ermetismo* (1945); L. Russo, *La critica letteraria contemporanea*, 2d ed., 3 v. (1953); G. N. G. Orsini, *B. Croce, Philosopher of Art and Lit. Crit.* (1961); A. Borlenghi, *La critica letteraria postdesanctisiana* (1972); M. P. Musitelli, *La critica e i suoi metodi* (1979); M. E. Moss, *B. Croce Reconsidered* (1987), ed. and tr., *B. Croce: Essays on Lit. and Lit. Crit.* (1990). A.SC.

IV. SPANISH. The 20th-c. renaissance of poetry in Spain is accompanied by few major treatises on poetics, but through the years there has been a steady flow of commentary, written and oral, in a wide variety of public and private organs, concerning the status of the lyric. Thus, to speak of 20th-c. Sp. poetics means primarily to speak of these ongoing deliberations which are identified most extensively with the poets themselves, but also with at least one major thinker, José Ortega y Gasset, with various additional critics, incl. the philologist-critics Amado Alonso and Dámaso Alonso, and, in the postwar period, with a disciple of the latter, Carlos Bousoño, author of the most ambitious "theory of poetic expression" of the century. For discussion of 19th-c. Sp. poetics, see ROMANTIC AND POSTROMANTIC POETICS.

At the beginning of the century there was a heightened awareness of poetry as an art form, with the primary incentives, ideas, and models coming from Sp.-Am. modernism (see MODERNISMO), but also from the Fr. symbolist poets (see SYMBOLISM); from two key 19th-c. Sp. figures as much "modern" as romantic, G. A. Bécquer and Rosalía de Castro; and from Spain's own Golden Age poets and their rich folkloric trads. Sp. modernism at one level was a complex of new styles and themes, and at another, beyond the early wave of elegance and cosmopolitanism, a long-range phenomenon too subtle for hasty characterization, a durable attitude protective of individuality and artistic integrity. Introduced into Spain along with *modernismo* were the plastic beauty of the Parnassians (q.v.), the cult of suggestivity, the musicality of the symbolists, new metric forms, exotic themes ranging from Hellenic to Oriental, novel artistic styles such as primitivism (q.v.) and art nouveau, a much enriched poetic vocabulary, poetic prose, and, implicitly, certain new principles, among them one which had been propounded by Poe and the modern Fr. poets—that the true domain of poetry was not truth or morality but beauty. Such outstanding writers as Ramón del Valle-Inclán, Manuel Machado, and Juan Ramón Jiménez reflect a positive absorption of certain of modernism's innovations, although the martial ring, the swans, the azure, the Versaillesque gardens, and other decorative elements associated with Rubén

Darío are not long enduring. Others, however, most notably Miguel de Unamuno and Antonio Machado, voice doubts early and persistently about the possible dominance of an art-for-art's-sake movement. Thus is born an artistic dichotomy—very loosely, the aesthetic vs. the "human"—which becomes inseparable from theoretical conceptions of poetry throughout much of the century. Early in the century this dichotomy was narrowly viewed as a struggle between modernism and the Generation of '98 (the all-pervading "preoccupation about Spain" had as its most immediate inducement the War of 1898). But the limited, if not fallacious, nature of this presumed polarity is discernible in the numerous common elements found among writers of allegedly divergent directions, and even more significantly, in the communal support for a spiritual regeneration in opposition to what were seen by all as the materialistic and prosaic trends of the later 19th c.

Two dominant poets of the century, A. Machado and J. R. Jiménez, not only illustrate these and other directions over a series of decades, but also have been functional in shaping the modern hist. of the Sp. lyric, both through their own poetry and through their abundant writings on poetics. In 1917, the former still questioning modernism's emphasis on sensory effects, identified poetry as "a deep trembling of the spirit" which at its best would be a "shadow of ourselves." His most important contribution to 20th-c. Sp. poetics, an existential and Bergsonian position, was his theory of poetry as "the essential word within time," a temporal art to reflect man's temporal condition. Jiménez was known from the start for his painterly and musical qualities, which included synesthesia, but he practiced what Bécquer had aspired to do, join "sighs and smiles, colors and notes," with no more renunciation of the underlying romantic vein than in Machado. Within his own Platonic system, Jiménez also saw poetry as a paradoxical union of time with the absolute.

Whereas Machado was essentially monolithic in adhering to his belief in a single "true" poetry, Jiménez not only evolved constantly but left a chronicle of the rationale behind his evolution. Both poets demanded selectivity, but that of Machado refers to the experience of inspiration in which the "voices" must be distinguished from the "echoes," whereas Jiménez, in a famous metapoem of 1917, symptomatic of a decisive new direction in his work, asks: "Intelligence, give me / the exact name of things," a shift in focus from experience to the poetic word, specifically the act of naming, a lesson derived from both Mallarmé and the imagist credo. But the change does not represent a fully anti-mimetic negation of "external" reality ("things"), as in the nearly contemporaneous plea for pure creation by Vicente Huidobro (see CREATIONISM). The self-referential posture seen in Jiménez here will abound in future poets. Pedro Salinas, in *Todo más claro* (1949),

credits his own poetic word with transforming the world and thereby creating it anew. The stress on formal perfection and purification which accompanies Jiménez's aspiration to attain an ultimate beauty is a direction continued by Jorge Guillén, a poet who has invited comparison with Paul Valéry, and who allowed for "'poesía bastante pura,' *ma non troppo*" (somewhat pure poetry, though not excessively), and whose *Cántico* (1928) again illustrates formalist perfectionism in harmony with a "human" basis, here one of sustained exultation.

Toward 1920, countering the effete remnants of *modernismo*, the only carefully orchestrated vanguardist movement in Spain, *ultraísmo* (see ULTRAISM) erupts with a fervor for renovation and liberation, proclaiming the essential autonomy of poetry, defending novelty—"adventure" in the term of its major critic, Guillermo de Torre—as the basis of poetic creation, and exalting metaphor (q.v.) as the device which would open the door to new worlds. The way had been prepared particularly by Ramón Gómez de la Serna, inventor of the metaphorical whimsy which he called the "greguería," and theoretical support was contributed by Huidobro and Jorge Luis Borges. As in the debates about "pure poetry" (q.v.) in France, this movement sought the elimination of nonpoetic elements, among which de Torre listed "the anecdotal, narrative theme, [and] erotic effusion."

The major figures among the Generation of 1927 (e.g. Federico García Lorca, Guillén, Salinas, Rafael Alberti, Vicente Aleixandre, Luis Cernuda) were somewhat reluctant to allow *ultraísta* prescriptions to impinge on their original conception of poetry (Juan Larrea and Gerardo Diego were major exceptions), although their verbal experiments and ludic spirit owe much to the movement. In a culminating moment for this group, the reassessment of Góngora in 1927 vindicated this baroque poet of the charge of obscurity and brought to light his potential "modernity" (see NEOGONGORISM): his was a poetry of beautiful lang., decipherable to the point of "transparency," according to D. Alonso, implicitly defending the principle that poetry is not to be judged for what it says but for what it does. In his famous essay of 1925 on the "Dehumanization of Art," Ortega y Gasset characterized the poets of his age as inclined toward the cultivation of metaphor as an end in itself. Underlying this view is a first principle of Orteguian aesthetics, the definitive opposition between art and reality, but the diagnosis was extreme insofar as none of the members of the group of '27 can accurately be termed "dehumanized." By the 1930s a new brand of obscurity co-exists with the intellectual, Gongoristic type—the irrational imagery usually associated with surrealism (q.v.), later portrayed by Bousoño as the line of demarcation between tradition and modernity.

Working independently of the mainstream of poetic production, two philologists of the Menéndez-Pidal school, A. Alonso (d. 1952) and D. Alonso, refined stylistic studies by bringing an awareness of linguistic theory and a background in textual analysis to their investigations of both cl. and modern poets. The first serious critical works on the poetic lang. of Góngora (by D. Alonso) and of Pablo Neruda (by A. Alonso) have probably been read as much for their value as methodological models as for information about the two figures under examination. Amado has left us what are still basic works on poetic prose; Dámaso's voluminous legacy combines linguistic analyses with the critical intuition of a poet with faith in the "mystery of poetry."

After the Civil War (1936–39), Spain becomes the scene of a poetics of survival and recovery, reflecting a "rehumanization" imposed largely by pressures extrinsic to lit. The reaction had already begun before the war, as may be seen in Aleixandre's words to G. Diego in 1932, in which he attacks the "almost obscene savoring of verbal mastery" and asserts, "no, poetry is not a matter of words." The appeal by Neruda, while in Spain, for a "poetry without purity" overshadows the rejoinder of Jiménez, whose once great influence has waned. In the wake of the disaster, the country's principal poets have been lost to death or exile. A brief neoclassical revival, and then a religious and existential outpouring (which includes the *poesía desarraigada* [uprooted poetry] described by D. Alonso) are followed by the most powerful collective phenomenon in the poetry of the postwar period, the "social poetry" of the Fifties. The majority voice now decries escapism and aestheticism, defends realism in subject matter and vocabulary, and advocates commitment and communication. The chief mentor of the time, Aleixandre, describes the major theme of this group as "human life in its historical dimension," i.e. poetry of the here and now. He himself shifts his basic concept of poetry from one of pantheistic fusion of poet with cosmos to one of solidarity, a merging of man with man. Blas de Otero invokes "the immense majority," countering Jiménez's dedications to the "minority," and he defends social themes so long as they are felt as poetry. Gabriel Celaya describes poetry as an "instrument . . . with which to transform the world." On the other hand, a preoccupation with the danger of perverting the genre is found in many, including the outstanding poet and theorist, José Hierro, who sees himself and his fellow poets condemned by the age to a simple, honest "testimonial poetry," but who in 1952 described poetry as a "gift from God" and set forth a meticulous theory of poetic inspiration as musical in nature.

The therapeutic resurgence of the Fifties was a force difficult to avoid for many excellent young poets, no less vocal about their poetics than their predecessors. The mood of the Sixties was no less bitter, but critical statements were now metamorphosed into an intense irony (Quevedo was now

appropriately evoked). While social poetry could still find sound theoretical defense in the 1960s (e.g. that of Angel González), many rejected it as facile or exhausted and turned toward the word itself. "Might the word itself *be* reality?" is a question posed explicitly in the work of José María Valverde. José Ángel Valente, too, portrays the act of writing as itself a means for discovering reality rather than responding to it. In the following decade, the *novísimos* (the "very new" poets, born since the War) were characterized on the one hand (by a major new critic, J. M. Castellet) as "campy," a pop-culture manifestation, but on the other hand, they point toward a new intellectualism which extends into the 1980s, in which such figures as Eliot, Rilke, and Hölderlin replace other models, signaling an all-out search for new values. See also INTERPRETATION; SPANISH POETRY; SPANISH-AMERICAN POETRY.

G. de Torre, *Literaturas europeas de vanguardia* (1925), *Historia de las literaturas de vanguardia* (1965); J. Ortega y Gasset, *La deshumanización del arte* (1925); *Poesía española contemporánea (1901–1934)*, ed. G. Diego, 2d ed. (1934)—anthol. with *poéticas*; A. Alonso, *Poesía y estilo de Pablo Neruda* (1940), *Materia y forma en poesía* (1955); P. Salinas, *Literatura española: Siglo XX* (1941); D. Alonso, *Obras completas*, 8 v. (1972–85)—esp. v. 2–8; *Antología de la joven poesía española* (1952), *Poesía última* (1963), both ed. F. Ribes—with *poéticas*; C. Bousoño, *Teoría de la expresión poética* (1952), *El irracionalismo poético (El símbolo)* (1977), *Surrealismo y simbolización* (1978); V. Aleixandre, *Algunos caracteres de la nueva poesía española* (1955); *Veinte años de poesía española (1939–1959)*, ed. J. M. Castellet (1960)—anthol. with seminal intro.; J. Guillén, *Lang. and Poetry* (1961); R. Gullón, *Una poética para Antonio Machado* (1964), ed., *El modernismo visto por los modernistas* (1964); B. Ciplijauskaite, *El poeta y la poesía* (1966); J. O. Jiménez, "Poética y poesía de la joven generación española," *Hispania* 2 (1966); *La generación poética de 1927*, ed. J. González Muela and J. M. Rozas (1966)—anthol. with documents; G. Siebenman, *Los estilos poéticos en España desde 1900* (1973); J. R. Jiménez, *Política poética* (1982); A. Geist, *La poética de la generación del 27 y las revistas literarias* (1980); A. Debicki, *Poetry of Discovery* (1982).

D.M.R.

V. SLAVIC. Slavic p. is as varied as the cultures and ideologies of the several Slavic peoples. Nevertheless, it shows common themes, and it has contributed signally to the dominant trends of 20th-c. thought not only in lit. crit. but also in philosophy, linguistics, and cultural studies. A historical survey of Slavic p. must include not only poetic theory as promulgated in manifestoes but also the role of that theory in practice. In the Slavic countries, avant-garde movements formed around emergent theories, e.g. (in Russia) symbolism and its heirs, incl. futurism, surrealism, acmeism, constructivism, and imagism (qq.v.); (in

Czechoslovakia) poetism; and (in Poland) the theories of such authors as S. I. Witkiewicz and W. Gombrowicz.

In all its varieties, Slavic p. has emphasized two basic concerns: (1) the problem of the literary work itself, and (2) its social and ideological function. (1) As for the work itself, it was seen as the expression of an autonomous human activity, as a verbal act with specific artistic qualities. Philosophically this theoretical emphasis found a significant resource in phenomenology (see GENEVA SCHOOL), which both criticized traditional interps. (historical, psychological, or sociological) and addressed the specifically aesthetic dimension of verbal activity. From this theoretical standpoint came not value judgments but descriptive analyses of literary works, as well as a decided view of the ultimate source of poetic activity. This theoretical standpoint found specific realization in the formalist and structuralist modes of analysis and in the phenomenological approach to p. (see STRUCTURALISM). (2) As for the social and ideological function of the literary work, this tendency sprang from strong sociological trads. but was indelibly marked by Marxist interps., as seen primarily in Russia, both prerevolutionary and Soviet. To trace the devel. of these two trends, it is well to divide the century in half. The end of World War II represents not a simple chronological terminus, but a change that shaped the ensuing hist. of the Slavic countries, and so affected poetic theory and practice as well.

A. *Formalism and Structuralism.* The poetic theories that most influenced 20th-c. studies began either with Rus. Formalism or structuralism (qq.v.), a further devel. of formalism that was advanced by the Prague School. These theories were concerned with the literary work as a specific type of discourse. Thus they highlighted p., and for them the foundation of p. was linguistics, which offered them a model of the stratification inherent in the verbal utterance. In the first half of the century, symbolism (q.v.) and other modernist movements stressed the verbal act and linked literary production with literary theory (as in the works of Andrej Belij and Osip Mandelštam in Russia, and V. Nezval in Czechoslovakia). This new concern shifted the traditional conception of p. from *descriptive* or *normative* classification of means, devices, styles, and genres toward the *act*— the process of communication, and the potential of *langue* as a system of signs.

The younger generation of Rus. scholars who founded the school of theory known as Rus. Formalism focused on the problems of poetic lang. and poetic devices, i.e. stylistic and thematic phenomena. As Boris Eichenbaum wrote, "The material of p. is the word; the basis of a systematic organization of p. must be the classification of linguistics facts." R. Jakobson assigned to p. the study of "literariness" and of "devices." The essential aim of Rus. Formalism was the "poeticity" of

literary works, or "what makes the verbal message a work of art" (Jakobson); it was further concerned with the dichotomy between poetry and prose. This stress on poeticity evoked a response among some Rus. scholars (Viktor Žirmunskij, V. Vinogradov, Vladimir Propp, and others) who focused even more closely on the theory of the verbal act, in relation to other studies of the European langs. (Wölfflin, Walzel, the Neo-Kantians, Vossler, Spitzer) but did not agree entirely with the whole program of the Rus. Formalists. These scholars helped to broaden the reach of p. into the areas of history, stylistics, and theory of genre and narrative. They also helped to overcome the reductionism inherent in the study of a text's dominant aspects and to resist its segmentation into what Šklovskij called "the sum of its devices."

This focus on the literary work brought theoretical p. closer to lit. crit. Theorists studied the functioning of poetic lang. and devices, but few attempted to synthesize a general theory. The best known exceptions are Žirmunskij's *Zadači poètiki* (Problems of Poetics, 1919) and Boris Tomaševskij's *Teorija literatury (Poètika)* (Theory of Lit. [Poetics], 1925). Typically, Tomaševskij denied that this latter was a scholarly work, and added, "our task is to open up problems, not to put facts into boxes." Tomaševskij's book divides the subject into Stylistics, Comparative Metrics, and Thematics, a division that also included a theory of genres based on "motivations" and on "arrangement of devices." Žirmunskij's is both a programmatic essay and a crit. of some Formalist concepts. Like Tomaševskij, Žirmunskij defines Stylistics (q.v.) as the study of poetic lang.; his other categories are Thematics (q.v.) and Composition, under which he handles genres as realizations of specific compositional intentions analogous to musical forms.

Formalism and its respondents pursued further researches in Czechoslovakia and Poland. In Czechoslovakia, Jakobson brought the formalist ideas to a domestic trad. based on Herbartian formalism and trends in modern crit. and art. He developed them in his contacts with scholars of linguistics and aesthetics in the Prague Linguistic Circle, and later at a second center of learning in the Slovak capitol, Bratislava. The Prague School's contribution to p. was summarized in 1937 when Jan Mukařovskij, in the Czechoslovakian encyclopedia *Ottuv Slovník naučny nové doby,* defined p. as "the aesthetics and theory of poetry." Its goals are "the analysis of poetic structure," "the study of semantic aspects of poetry" [the expressive means and the exploitations of themes], and "the examination of the basic noetic problems of poetry, e.g. time and space, subject, function, and aesthetic and extra-aesthetic values and norms."

In the 1930s and '40s, these concerns turned to historical p. and the question of intertextuality (q.v.), and steps were made toward a semiotics of lit. and art, chiefly by Jakobson, Mukařovskij, P. Bogatyrev, F. Vodička, and J. Veltrusky and pub. in

Travaux du Cercle Linguistique de Prague and in the journal *Slovo a slovesnost*. This work showed two fundamental trends. One was oriented toward the linguistic dimension of literary discourse (Jakobson and his successors); the other took its cue from structural linguistics, which offered a model and a vocabulary for structural p., but expanded it into the historical, social, and, most importantly, aesthetic dimension of literary discourse (Mukařovskij and his followers).

In other Slavic countries, the systematic study of theoretical p. was not developed, and the formalist-structuralist trend penetrated only in the work of individual scholars, such as the South Slavic prosodic studies of K. Taranovsky and A. Isačenko (see SLAVIC PROSODY). In Poland, on the other hand, the new p. coming from Russia and Czechoslovakia was affected by an earlier trad. inspired by K. Wóycicki. Rus. Formalism was introduced and evaluated in M. Kridl's *Wstpep do badań nad dziełem literackiem* (Intro. to Literary Studies, 1936). During the 1930s, Polish scholars employed Prague-School structuralist theories in studies of verse (F. Siedlecki) and in studies of stylistics (K. Budzyk and J. D. Hopensztand).

B. *The Phenomenological Trend*, by contrast, advanced markedly in Poland, where scholars stressed the literary text but approached it as an object of intentional operation by its author and recipient. Their dominant concern was not with linguistics, as in Czech p., but with philosophy and aesthetics. Z. Łempicki, for example, was concerned with "pure poetics" (a term that echoes Husserl's "pure logic"), and his aim was to achieve a new mode of description for literary works. Following the Ger. scholars W. Conrad and M. Geiger, Łempicki asserted the difference between artifact and aesthetic object, and between p. and aesthetics. His theory stressed the difference between common and artistic lang., anticipating modern semiotic and hermeneutic studies.

Systematic theoretical studies were carried out by Husserl's pupil Roman Ingarden (*Das literarische Kunstwerk* [The Literary Work of Art], 1931, tr. 1973; *O poznawaniu dzieła literackiego* [The Cognition of the Literary Work of Art], 1937, tr. 1973). Ingarden conceived of p. as "the general theory of the essential structures, properties, or connections actually existing in the literary work." In his view, p. was the central discipline in the theory of lit., its sister disciplines being the philosophy of lit., the science of lit., and lit. crit. He did not live to finish his *Poetics*. In connection with the cognition of the literary work, Ingarden invoked the dichotomy between the work of art and the aesthetic object which was the outcome of an individual "concretization." In the work itself he discerned two dimensions, vertical and horizontal. The vertical consists of four strata: verbal sounds, semantic units, "schematized aspects" (in which various objects portrayed in the work come to appearance), and "the objectivities portrayed in

the intentional states of affairs projected by the sentences." The vertical strata comprise the basic structure of the work, while the horizontal dimension refers to its composition. The published draft of Ingarden's unfinished *Poetics* shows that he planned to encompass the problems of genres, style, the relationship of content and form, problems of judgment, and the sociology of lit.

C. *Marxism*. In the Slavic countries, the roots of Marxist p. lie in a trad. of historical and sociological concerns. In Russia, p. took shape as thinkers both before and after the Revolution evaluated the cultural and ideological functions of lit. and called for new ways to define lit. The long search for a "socialist p." (B. M. Friče, P. M. Medvedev) took place in the context of a variety of theories—psychological, sociological, aesthetic, even religious. That search and the resulting debates continued until the 1920s. Even dedicated revolutionaries disagreed about whether lit. could be autonomous and nonpolitical. The Rus. Formalists drew the attention of Marxist theoreticians, among them L. Trocky and A. Lunačarsky. There were even attempts at a synthesis of Formalism and socialism, called "Socioformism" (B. Arvatov, A. G. Cejtlin). M. Bakhtin's circle gave serious, although critical, attention to Formalist theories, as is evident from the first edition of P. M. Medvedev's *Formal' nyi metod v literaturovedenii* (The Formal Method in Literary Scholarship, 1928). But the pluralism of approaches ceased in the 1930s, when the Stalinist regime enforced uniformity. The concepts of p. issued now from socialist and ideological dogma. Literary discourse was determined primarily by the principles of a national or "people's" lit.; by "party-mindedness" in terms of the author's political and ideological identification with the party's program; by "typicalness"; and by "truthfulness" in terms of social realism. The leading concept of poetic imagination was based on Lenin's "theory of reflection" of reality. Along these lines, p. changed into a descriptive and normative discipline and lost its creativity both in poetic activity and lit. crit. Thus demoted, p. gave way to models found in the "national classical literary heritage," official formulations of which were published by L. Timofeev and I. A. Vinogradov.

D. *The Contemporary Situation*. During the last decades, p. in the Slavic countries has been stimulated by international developments. The older Formalist, structuralist, and phenomenological theories spread to the U. S., France, West Germany, and Italy; there they met both further elaboration and criticism. The credit for this spread goes to Roman Jakobson, René Wellek, Roman Ingarden, and their followers. Jakobson contributed signally with his "Linguistics and P." (1958) and "The Poetry of Grammar and the Grammar of Poetry" (1968), two essays in a voluminous output.

In the Slavic countries, p. (like other disciplines) felt the yoke of politics. The Marxist worldview, the official doctrine, governed both ideology and public life. Theories such as structuralism and phenomenology were restricted or banned in lit., art, and science. Traditional Soviet concepts of p. were exported to the Slavic countries to serve as models. During the late 1950s this dogmatism gradually abated but never disappeared entirely. Here and there arose new initiatives in literary life; even p. appeared again as a focus of intensive studies. Such developments sprang both from contacts with other contemp. trends and from the re-evaluation of domestic trads. in the rediscovery of an officially banned heritage, as in the U.S.S.R. when formalism, structuralism, and the works of Bakhtin and his circle achieved prominence.

Beginning in the late 1950s, interest grew in "structural p.," a term developed by a group of scholars centered mainly in Moscow and Tartu (see STRUCTURALISM, *Moscow-Tartu School*). These groups approached the subject from two directions, linguistic studies and literary theory; and they did not neglect lit. hist. They found their theoretical and methodological basis in a variety of disciplines: structural and generative linguistics, structuralist literary theory, folklore studies, semiotics, machine translation, mathematical linguistics, information theory, and cybernetics. They analyzed both literary and folk texts. Boris Uspensky approached lit. from a general theory of art in his *Poetics of Composition* (1970). The most elaborate attempt to summarize the problems of theoretical p. with regard to Soviet Marxism was Jurij Lotman's *Lekcii po struktural' noj poètike* (Lectures on Structural Poetics, 1964) and *Struktura xudožestvennogo teksta* (The Structure of the Artistic Text, 1970). The leading tendency here is the approach to p. on the one hand from the structure of the text itself, but on the other hand within the concept of art as semiotic system and of lit. as a "secondary modeling system." This view conceives p. as part of higher systems (culminating in the highest system, culture) and explores the relationship between text and extratextual context.

With the tendency toward typological studies came a renewed concern for historical p. (Lotman, Uspensky, Ivanov, Toporov). The heritage of the 1920s and '30s was renewed and critically examined in works such as those by Bakhtin and his circle, esp. P. N. Medvedev and V. N. Vološinov. Bakhtin's work continued into the 1970s, concerning itself with the specificity of the literary text and the autonomy of lit. and art, with the result that the role of p. was reactivated in the Slavic world. Bakhtin pointed to further categories of p. by his stress on intertextuality and on the epistemological, historical, and aesthetic context of poetic activity, as reflected in his concepts of the "dialogical principle," the "chronotope," and the "carnivalesque." His concern for the categories of time and space in connection with the theory of genre pointed to ways of bringing historical and synchronic poetics closer together. Bakhtin's work has been extraordinarily influential for contemp. studies in Soviet Russia and abroad, esp. for the confrontation with the formalist-structuralist heritage.

In Poland, after political limitations lifted somewhat, structuralism, phenomenology, and Marxism again delimited the field decisively. Marxist studies treated the problems of p. within the broader framework of the theory of lit. (S. Żółkiewski, M. Janion, H. Markiewicz, S. Morawski), but the primary work lay in structuralist and phenomenological studies. Continuity with this trad. was represented by M. Dłuska and S. Furmanik (prosody); S. Skwarczyńska (general p.; genre theory); and M. R. Mayenowa, whose structural studies of p. included contemp. theories of linguistic p. and led to a synthesis entitled *Poetyka teoretyczna (Zagadnienia języka)* (Theoretical Poetics [Problems of Lang.], 1972). The younger generation of scholars (e.g. M. Głowiński, J. Sławiński, J. Pelc, E. Czaplejewicz) responded to contemp. topics such as narratology, genre, themes, style, and versification, as well as methodological problems, transmission of poetic texts, and "mathematical p." Several publications highlight this interest, esp. the series *Poetics: An Encyclopedic Outline* and the two collections of conference proceedings, *Poetics—Poetyka—Poetika* (ed. D. Davie et al., 1961; ed. R. Jakobson et al., 1966).

In Czechoslovakia in the 1960s, new conditions led to a revival of p. Theoretical studies gained momentum: structuralist studies at home were paralleled in similar work by Czechs and Slovaks living abroad. Structuralism resumed where it had left off before World War II, reintroducing its principles into the contemp. context. P. moved from descriptive analysis to a focus on the author's creative act, the p. of reception, and the process of communication (F. Vodička, M. Červenka, O. Čepan, F. Miko, A. Popovič). Vodička took a leading role in exploring both these issue and questions of periodization, i.e. the p. of historical periods, which he characterized as multileveled vertical structures of different types of works. Thus he proposed a coordination of synchronic and diachronic aspects, as well as of the p. of poetry and prose. Concern with reception and with lit. hist. turned attention to historical p. (F. Vodička, M. Bakoš). The linguistic orientation of poetics has also made use of generative linguistics, but at the same time indicated that the solution of specific literary aesthetic problems lie beyond the borders of linguistics. Along these lines, traditional topics such as versification, style, narrative modes, genre, semantics, and semiotics continued to make p. the central discipline in studies of texts and of the creative act (J. Levý, L. Doležel, K. Hausenblas, J. Hrabák, K. Horálek, N. Krausová, V. Kochol, J. Veltruský, P. Steiner). J. Levý tried to demonstrate exact methods in p. by adapting communication theory and mathematics.

The South Slavic countries during the second half of the 20th c. lacked a trad. of systematic p.;

here it was the Marxist concept of lit. that directed theoretical studies. In Bulgaria, the main stream was fed from the U.S.S.R., while impulses from Rus. Formalism, Slavic structuralism, and other trends were restricted to small groups or individuals (M. Janakiev, *Bŭlgarsko stixoznanie* [Bulgarian Versology], 1960, and articles in *Literaturna misŭl* and *Literaturen front*). Two Bulgarian scholars, Tzvetan Todorov and Julia Kristeva, could invoke this trad. in the context of Fr. structuralism.

As early as the 1950s, Yugoslavia creatively confronted contemp. trends in p., esp. the Marxist orientation, at the same time witnessing energetic new poetic activity. Both processes occurred, however, not in synthetic works but in articles dedicated to specific problems of p. and the interp. of literary texts. Scholars (A. Flaker, Z. Škreb, S. Petrović, M. Flašar, V. Žmegač) published in magazines such as *Rad, Umjetnost riječi, Delo, Književna reč*, and the publications of *Matica srpska*. The phenomenological trad. also received significant stress (Z. Konstantinović).

By these routes the Slavic countries advanced from the concept of p. as an inner system of modes of realization of literary discourse to newer conceptions nourished both by the crit. of theories formed early in the century and by evolution within these theories. They developed along two lines: (1) from the structural analysis of individual texts to inclusion of the role of the author or reader and of the social phenomena involved in poetic creation and reception; and (2) from concentration on the expressive means and devices of poetic lang. to the study of the semantics of the poetic text and of its truth value and reference, based on the dichotomy between sign and object, i.e. between the autoreferential and referential aspects of the verbal message.

See also CRITICISM; DECONSTRUCTION; FEMINIST POETICS; INTERPRETATION; POETRY, THEORIES OF; PSYCHOLOGICAL CRITICISM; READER-RESPONSE CRITICISM; ROMANTIC AND POSTROMANTIC POETICS; SEMIOTICS, POETIC; SPEECH ACT THEORY; STRUCTURALISM.

ANTHOLOGIES: *Slavic Poetics*, ed. R. Jakobson et al. (1973); *Structure of Texts and Semiotics of Culture*, ed. J. van der Eng and M. Grygar (1973); *Zur Kritik literaturwiss. Methodologie*, ed. V. Žmegač und Z. Škreb (1973); *The Structure of the Literary Process*, ed. P. Steiner et al. (1982); *Lang. and Literary Theory*, ed. B. A. Stolz et al. (1984); *Semiosis: Semiotics and the Hist. of Culture*, ed. M. Halle et al. (1984).

HISTORY AND CRITICISM: A. Bely, *Simvolizm* (1910); F. Vodička, *Počátky krásné prózy novočeské* (1948); J. Mukařovskij, *Kapitoly z české poetiky*, 3 v. (1948), *Structure, Sign, and Function* (tr. 1977), *The Word and Verbal Art* (tr. 1977); Wellek; J. Lotman, *Lectures on Structural P.* (1964), *The Structure of the Artistic Text* (1970, tr. 1977), *Analysis of the Poetic Text* (1972, tr. 1976); B. Tomaševskij, "Thematics," tr. in *Rus. Formalist Crit.: Four Essays* (1965), *Theorie der Literatur, Poetik* (tr. 1985); Z. Łempicki, *Wybór pism* (1966); R. Ingarden, "O poetyce," *Studia z estetyki I* (1966); E. Meletinsky and D. Segal, "Structuralism and Semiotics in the USSR," *Diogène*, v. 73 (1971); M. M. Bakhtin, *Problems of Dostoevsky's P.* (tr. 1973); B. Uspensky, *P. of Composition* (tr. 1973); G. G. Grabowicz, "Translator's Intro.," R. Ingarden, *The Literary Work of Art* (1931, tr. 1973); J. Striedter, intro. F. Vodička, *Die Struktur der lit. Entwicklung* (1976); M. Červenka, *Der Bedeutungsbau des lit. Werkes* (1978); M. M. Bakhtin and P. N. Medvedev, *The Formal Method in Literary Scholarship* (tr. 1978); Jakobson; M. Kaiser, "P. N. Medvedev's 'The Collapse of Formalism,'" *Lang. and Literary Theory* (above); K. Clark and M. Holquist, *Mikhail Bakhtin* (1984); K. Pomorska, "P. of Prose," in R. Jakobson, *Verbal Art, Verbal Sign, Verbal Time* (1985); *Rečnik književnih termina* (1986). F.SV.

TYPOGRAPHY. See LETTRISME; VISUAL POETRY.

TYPOLOGY, TYPOLOGICAL INTERPRETATION. See ALLEGORY; FIGURATION; INTERPRETATION, FOURFOLD METHOD OF.

TZU. See CHINESE POETRY.

U

UGARITIC POETRY. See HEBREW POETRY.

UKRAINIAN POETRY. The history of U. p. can be divided into three major periods, made all the more distinct by sharp discontinuities between them. Underlying and producing these discontinuities are profound shifts in U. society; not only do basic political and social structures disappear, to be replaced by entirely new ones, but, at least until the modern period, U. literary and historical consciousness does not succeed in bridging these changes.

The first period, from the beginnings in the 10th–11th c. to roughly the 14th c., coincides largely with the lit. of Kievan Rus', which by general consensus is taken as the common patrimony of the East Slavs—the Ukrainians, Byelorussians, and Russians. The second, middle period, from the late 16th to the late 18th cs., reflects primarily the poetics of the baroque and witnesses a flowering of U. lit. and culture, even though later the bookish and church-dominated character of this lit. came to be seen as a fatal flaw, given 19th-c. U. sociopolitical development, and the entire period underestimated or even dismissed from the canon. The third period, from the beginning of the 19th c. to the present, coincides with the birth of the modern U. nation and the emergence of contemp. literary U. based on the vernacular. Because of the strong populist current underlying this political and cultural revival, the idea and content of "U. lit." was often identified, throughout the 19th and even into the 20th c., with this third period alone.

In the course of the early modern (17th–18th cs.) and modern periods poetry has consistently played a dominant role. However, the privileged place of poetry in the system of genres of U. lit. must be seen as reflecting the concrete circumstances and limitations within which it existed; through much of the 18th and 19th cs., for example, U. lit. survived practically without institutions (publishing houses, a press, the theater) and without a social consensus as to its validity, to its "right to life" alongside the Imperial Rus. lit., and indeed for some decades in the face of official proscription. While such strictures were highly deleterious for prose and drama, however, poetry not only survived but grew, establishing trads. and a certain hegemony.

The question of the role of poetry in old U. (Kievan) lit. is made particularly complex by the characteristic diffuseness and interpenetration of genres in that lit. In general, from this period there are no extant works that point to distinct poetic genres, let alone to theories of poetics, histories of or commentaries on poetry, and so on. This absence is striking in view of the fact that Byzantine lit., which served as a primary if not always immediate model for the old Kievan lit., had a rich gamut of poetic genres. We can, however, speak of poetry in Old U. lit. in terms of (1) the oral trad., (2) translated and "borrowed" lit., and (3) verse elements in the original lit. The first of these, with which histories of U. and Rus. lit. traditionally begin, is complex and surrounded by much confusion. The major misconception is that Old U. oral lit. is to be identified with folklore, with the creativity of the folk; in fact, as in various other analogous situations, this lit., while oral, was most probably a product of a court or "high" trad. which only over the centuries "sank" into the repertoire of folklore. The actual evidence for this oral poetry, moreover, is only indirect. Whether as the epic cycle of *byliny* (U. *staryny*) which depict the Kievan context and setting, but which were preserved only in the northern Rus. territories, or as the broad gamut of ritual poetry related to the agricultural cycle and various pagan rites, the actual texts date only from the 18th–19th cs., so that conclusions about the range and function of oral lit. in this earliest period must remain speculative.

Verse as such is found in the various translations and adaptations of Byzantine liturgical lit., particularly hymnography (see BYZANTINE POETRY). These hymns influenced contemp. Kievan texts and even had an impact on the bookish versification of the 16th–18th cs. By general consensus the major poetic work of this period is the *Igor Tale* (*Slovo o polku Igoreve*) describing a relatively minor and unsuccessful military campaign of 1185. Putatively written sometime in the early 13th c., it was discovered and published at the turn of the 19th c. Although some doubts remain, its authenticity has been argued on both linguistic and historical grounds. Its syncretic form, mixing military and cautionary tale, lyrical moments with dynastic programme (which some, ahistorically, prefer to read as "patriotic" fervor) is also taken as proof of its authenticity. Its sonorous, vivid lang. and imagery, its deft many-stranded narrative of rhythmic prose, have made of the *Slovo* for all the modern East Slavic lits. the quintessential poetic correlative of Kievan Rus'.

The period of the 14th to the late 16th c. is remarkable and still puzzling for its dearth of cultural and literary texts; the ravages of the Mongol invasion, the Tartar raids, the peculiar cultural stasis during the Lithuanian domination of the U. lands, and the movement of Orthodox churchmen and sees north of Muscovy only partially explain this lacuna. A major exception to this bleak picture is the emergence sometime in the 16th c. of a new form of oral poetry, the *duma* (pl. *dumy*), which supplanted the older *staryny* and was to have a strong impact on much of subsequent U. p. Though oral (the *dumy* were sung by wandering, often blind singers), this was not a narrowly folkloric genre—its perspective encompassed all of U. society. The *dumy*, reflecting elements of heroic epic, ballad, and elegy, are above all "sacred songs" conveying profound social and historical experiences. The latter are highlighted in cycles of *dumy* dealing with wars with the Turks and Tartars, and then later with the 17th-c. wars of liberation from Poland. Apart from introducing a vibrant new form, the *dumy* also establish the pattern of a popular poetry that can lay claim to being more "authentic," closer to the national experience, than any bookish form.

At the end of the 16th c., U. society and culture undergo a remarkable revitalization, which culminates in the mid 17th c. with an autonomous Cossack state that, with changing fortunes, was to last more than a century. Under the impact first of Ren. ideas, but soon thereafter of the still more pervasive baroque, U. p. proceeds to expand its repertoire of genres, and with the establishment of ever more centers of learning, esp. the Mohyla Academy in Kiev (founded in 1632), it finds a self-confidence that allows it to compete with the highly developed and sophisticated Polish poetry of the time. Nevertheless, a characteristic feature of Middle U. lit. is its bilingualism: throughout the 17th and early 18th cs., it is written in U. or in Polish, depending on theme or genre or projected audience. By the mid 18th c. this bilingualism—again reflecting a concrete social and political reality—becomes U.-Rus. In both cases the choice of the other lang. reflects not a hedging of the writer's U. identity but rather the conventions of the literary system.

The earliest poetry of this period, beginning from the 1580s and '90s, is syllabic in meter, in genre emblematic and heraldic. Throughout the first part of the 17th c., U. p. is represented mainly by panegyric, historical, and didactic verse. The poetry of praise in particular reflects the emergence of new cultural centers and leaders, such as Jelisej Pletenec'kyj, archimandrite of the Caves Monastery in Kiev (e.g. *The Image of Virtue*, 1618), or the metropolitan Petro Mohyla (e.g. the *Eucharisterion*, 1632, or the *Euphonia*, 1633), who establishes an Academy that is not only the mainstay of the cultural efflorescence of 17th-c. U. but the major center of learning in the Slavic Orthodox world. The genre system at this time is still not crystallized, with historic narrative often merged with lament or polemic (e.g. *The Lament of Ostrog*, 1636), or the didactic with the lyrical (e.g. Kyryl

Trankvilion Stavrovec'kyj's *The Much-Valued Pearl*, 1646). The panegyric mode itself may be infused with dramatic elements, as in Kasjan Sakovyč's eulogy of Hetman Sahajdačnyj (1622).

By the second half of the 17th c. U. p. shows a relatively broad range of forms and a differentiation into "high" genres (reflecting baroque poetics) and popular genres. In the former, such important poets as Lazar Baranovyč and esp. Ioan Velyčkovs'kyj, while writing in both bookish U. and Polish, and while still predominantly reflecting religious themes, give a new depth to national self-expression. The popular genres in turn—fables, satires, and Christmas and Easter verse—are mostly anonymous and close to the vernacular. At times, as in the poetry of the wandering monk Klymentij Zinovijev, with its encyclopedic overview of U. life and customs (incl. a large collection of proverbs), they are an invaluable mirror to a whole epoch.

The early 18th c. witnesses the maturation of U. school drama—in the works of Feofan Prokopovyč, Lavrentij Horka, Manujil Kozačyns'kyj, and Mytrofan Dovholevs'kyj. Prokopovyč's tragicomedy *Vladymir* (1705), the best known of these, exemplifies the didactic poetics of this genre, as the historical theme—the Christianization of Kievan Rus'—becomes a vehicle for political satire and for the apotheosis of the U. hetman, Mazepa. After the defeat of Mazepa in 1709, Prokopovyč became the prime ideologue of the new Rus. state founded by Peter I; his departure for St. Petersburg epitomizes the massive movement of U. scholars, clergyman, and writers to Russia at the beginning of the 18th c. In broad historical terms the growth and centralization of the Rus. empire signal in the course of the 18th c. the ever-greater provincialization of Ukraine. In poetry two significant developments accompany this. On the one hand, there is an ever more conservative and hidebound reliance in books of poetics on the norms and conventions of the baroque (which in Russia is quickly abandoned—beginning with Prokopovyč himself—for neoclassicism). On the other hand, as a function of the new laws promulgated by Peter I prohibiting the publication of books in U., U. lit. was forced to go underground, to exist only in ms. form. Various genres did, however, survive: lyric poetry, puppet plays, burlesque verses, dialogues and verse satires. Paradoxically, at the end of the 18th c. there appears the most significant talent of premodern U. lit.—the peripatetic mystic philosopher and poet Hryhorij Skovoroda (1722–94). His book of devotional poetry, *The Garden of Divine Songs*, synthesizing Cl. and biblical, mystical and folk elements, remains the highpoint of 18th-c. U. p.

Modern U. p. is traditionally dated with the appearance of Ivan Kotljarevs'kyj's *Enejida* of 1798, a travesty of Virgil's *Aeneid*. Finding its analogue to the fall of Troy in the destruction of the last Cossack stronghold (the Zaporozhian Sitch), marking the end of U. autonomy in the 18th c., the *Enejida* focuses on the wanderings of a band of Cossacks, and in the course of its six cantos provides an encyclopedic and loving account of U. provincial life and customs. Mixing an energetic optimism, satire, nostalgia for the past, and above all broad humor, the poem became a rallying point for a new U. lit. in the vernacular. Although he abandoned the old syllabic versification in favor of the iambic tetrameter that was then ascendant in Rus. poetry, Kotljarevs'kyj did draw on a broad range of comic and burlesque devices characteristic of 18th-c. U. p. In fact, his example was almost too successful, in that for over three decades U. p. came to be dominated by the burlesque mode.

In this period even talented poets like Petro Hulak-Artemovs'kyj (1790–1865) paid their dues to this trad. (popularly called "Kotljarevščyna")—in his case by writing travesties of Horace's Odes. Beginning with the 1820s, however, U. romantic (or more precisely, preromantic) poets, like Lev Borovykovs'kyj, Amvrozij Metlyns'kyj, and Mykola Kostomarov (1817–85—who later became a major U. and Rus. historian and spokesman for the U. cause), introduced an entirely new poetics: in conjunction with the ethnographic historical and antiquarian work of such scholars as I. Sreznevskij, M. Bodjans'kyj, and M. Maksymovyč, the focus of this poetry fell on the turbulent Cossack past and on the wealth of U. folklore.

A similar literary and cultural revival was initiated in the mid 1830s in western Ukraine, then under Austria-Hungary. Led by such young clergymen-poets as Markian Šaškevyč (1811–43), Ivan Vahylevyč (1811–66), and Jakiv Holovac'kyj (1814–88), the so-called Ruthenian Trinity, it sought to legitimize the vernacular lang., to rediscover historical and ethnic roots, and to advance cultural and national autonomy.

A sea change in the range and depth—and status—of U. p. was effected by the first true romantic, Taras Shevchenko (1814–61). Born a serf and freed only at the age of 24, Shevchenko virtually at once came to be lionized by both U. and Rus. society as a uniquely powerful and inspired poet. Arrested in 1847 in connection with the secret *Brotherhood of Saints Cyril and Methodius* and exiled for ten years, he returned in ill health but with poetic powers unimpaired. Seen as a martyr and bard even in his lifetime, Shevchenko became upon his death the animating spirit of the U. national movement, and indeed the object of a popular cult to this day. Shevchenko's poetry, traditionally called the *Kobzar* (the Minstrel) after his first slim collection of 1840, divides along the lines of intimate lyric poetry (with a range of folkloric stylizations); political poetry, with powerful excoriations of social and national oppression, particularly by Tsarist authority; and narrative poems, incl. historical poems and ballads. All of these modes are unified and guided by structures of mythical thought which basically project a movement from the present state of victimization—personal as well as collective—to a redeemed and purified humanity, where "on the renewed earth / there will be no enemy, no tempter, / but there will be a son and a mother, / and there will be people on this earth."

Pantelejmon Kuliš (1819–97), friend and critic, exegete and rival of Shevchenko, also significantly broadened the range of U. p.—by new historical themes, expanded formal concerns, and, not least, translations of Shakespeare and the Bible, of Byron and other Western poets. Many of Shevchenko's successors tended to be overshadowed however, and their voice distorted by his Muse. This was particularly true of the fine western U. poet Jurij Fed'kovyč (1834–88). Of those who resisted the pull of Shevchenko's model the most important were two poets on the borderline of romanticism and realism, Stepan Rudans'kyj (1834–73) and Jakiv Ščoholiv (1823–98).

Generally, poetry in the latter half of the 19th c. was strained by the weight of perceived realist obligations and, more concretely, by official Rus. edicts of 1863 and 1876 banning the publication and importation of U. books. A poet who exemplifies both the call of national, civic duty and the thrust of an authentic, personal poetry is the western U. Ivan Franko (1856–1916). A man of indefatigable energy, prose writer and dramatist, critic, translator and scholar as well as poet, Franko too became the conscience of his people. His poetry covers a broad gamut—exhortatory, historical, satiric, lyrical, and confessional, this last is by far the most successful.

The period of modernism, generally from the 1890s to World War I, witnessed the differentiation of the U. literary marketplace and the emergence of poetry for a more select public. One of the first to turn to European and universal historical and philosophical themes was Larysa Kosač-Kvitka (pen name, Lesja Ukrajinka; 1872–1913); her drama (much more than her lyric poetry) serves to establish these concerns in U. p. Her masterpiece, *The Forest Song*, draws its inspiration from folklore and psychological introspection.

On the eve of World War I there appeared the symbolist poetry of Oleksandr Oles' (1878–1944), Mykola Voronyj (1871–1942), and Mykola Filjans'kyj (1873–1938), an anticipation of the outstanding poet of the 20th c.—Pavlo Tychyna (1891–1967). At first a symbolist and spirited supporter of the U. national revolution, and at the end of his life an orthodox spokesman for the Soviet system, Tychyna underwent a complex evolution, but in his early and mature poetry, at least, remains the most innovative and influential poetic voice of his time.

In the 1920s, with the establishment of Soviet rule in Ukraine and esp. the official policy of "Ukrainization," U. lit. for the first time since the 17th c. enjoyed the support of a state; its growth and energy were spectacular, as manifested in the proliferation of separate movements, particularly the neoclassicists, with such outstanding poets as Maxym Ryl's'kyj (1895–1969), Mykola Zerov (1890–1930?); and the futurists (see FUTURISM), with Myxajl Semenko (1892–1930?), the theorist and impresario of the movement, and Mykola Bažan (1904–83), who began as a futurist but quickly outgrew it to become, by virtue of his intellectualism and historicism, the second most important U. Soviet poet of the century. Adding to the variety, ferment, and sheer breadth of expression of U. p. in the 1920s and early '30s were the constructivists (e.g. Valerjan Polishchuk), neoromantics (e.g. Oleksa Vlyz'ko), and others who belonged to no formal organization or movement—such as Jevhen Pluzhnyk or esp. Volodymyr Svidzins'kyj (1885–1941), master of lyrical, almost mystical introspection.

But by the 1930s the Stalinist terror had crushed the national and cultural revival, and hundreds of writers perished in camps and purges. With Soviet U. p. reduced to silence or the empty rhet. of paeans to Stalin and the Party (most poignant when written by such as Tychyna, or indeed Ryl's'ky and Bažan), the poetic scene shifted to western Ukraine, then under Poland, or to Poland itself, and Czechoslovakia, where various poets and writers had emigrated, fleeing the Bolsheviks. Though in the inter-war period the literary climate there was often obscured by nationalist fervor, such poets as Jevhen Malanjuk, Oleksa Stefanovyč, Oksana Ljaturyns'ka, and others did make distinct contributions, the greatest being that of Bohdan Ihor Antonych (1909–37). Beginning with formal experimentation and a fascination with the rich imagination of his native Carpathian (Lemko) region, he attains in his mature poetry an expressive power and metaphysical and symbolic complexity that put him in the forefront of 20th-c. European poetry.

Immediately after World War II, U. p. had a short period of intense activity in the emigration, beginning with the Displaced Person camps in Germany, where long-repressed energies came to fruition in a multitude of publications. Outstanding among a range of poets of the middle generation were Oleh Zujewskyj and Vasyl Barka. Each, in rejecting the rhet. of the earlier emigré generation, tended toward a hermetic difficulty, Zujewskyj by searching for a pure poetry without emotional and even semantic signposts, and Barka by a baroque lang. and religiosity. The highpoint of U. emigré poetry, however, was the informal "New York Group" that arose in the late 1950s and lasted to the early 1970s. Emma Andijevs'ka, Jurij Tarnawsky, Bohdan Boychuk, and Bohdan Rubchak, all of them born between the wars, but very much attuned to the West, gave to U. p. a new and valuable avant-garde cast.

Even though decimated in the 1930s and then long repressed, Soviet U. p. remained in the mainstream. A major revival occurred in the early and mid 1960s with the appearance of such significant young poets as Vasyl' Symonenko, Lina Kostenko, Mykola Vinhranovs'kyj, Dmytro Pavlychko, and the most talented of them, Ivan Drach. Their common concern for authenticity and lyric intensity was amplified by historical and ethical concerns. In contrast to the rather traditional poetics of his contemporaries, the poetry of Vasyl Holoborod'ko moved toward the surreal and fantastic; for this very reason it was largely not published and had only a limited impact. This is all the more true of such dissident poets as Vasyl' Stus and Ihor Kalynets. Most significantly, however, the liberalization of Soviet society then political collapse of the Soviet Union in the 1980s had a profound and positive effect on the general climate of U. p.—in its rehabilitation of victims of repression and of historical memory as such, in its galvanization of various established poets, in its reassertion of the social and historical role of U. p., and above all in its facilitation of the emergence of a new generation of poets in the U. republic.

See now SLAVIC PROSODY.

ANTHOLOGIES: *The U. Poets*, ed. and tr. C. H. Andrusyshen and W. Kirkconnell (1963); *Xrestomatija davn'oji ukrajins'koji literatury*, ed. O. I. Bilec'kyj (1967); *Koordynaty*, ed. B. Boychuk and B. T. Rubchak (1969); *Antolohija ukrajins'koji liryky*, ed. O. Zilyns'kyj (1978); *Ukraijins'ka literature XVIII st.*, ed. O. V. Myšanyč (1983); *Antolohija ukrajins'koji poezii*, ed. M. P. Bažan et al. (1984).

HISTORY AND CRITICISM: G. Luckyj, *Literary Politics in the Soviet Ukraine 1917–1933* (1956); *Istorija ukrajins'koji literatury*, ed. J. P. Kyryljuk et al. (1967–71); D. Čyževs'kyj, *A Hist. of U. Lit.* (1975); G. Grabowicz, *Toward a Hist. of U. Lit.* (1981); Terras. G.G.G.

ULTRAISM. A Sp. iconoclastic movement which first appeared in 1919 and had virtually disappeared by 1923. Spain's answer to the European avant garde, U. proposed to merge advanced contemporary artistic tendencies. Jorge Luis Borges, who was in Spain in 1918, contributed to the origins of U. and carried its theories back to Buenos Aires in 1921. A founder and major theoretician of the group was the critic Guillermo de Torre, author of the *Manifiesto Vertical*. Rafael Cansinos-Assens, writer and intellectual figure of the postwar period, also had much to do with the promotion of the new aesthetics; and Ramón Gómez de la Serna too deserves his place as a significant antecedent. Both led important *tertulias*, the latter being the first to publish Marinetti's futurist manifesto in Sp. (see FUTURISM). U. was a youthful revolt against outworn, secondhand modernism; it fiercely opposed routine and inertia. The Ultraists welcomed modern life and were nurtured by subversive postwar attitudes. Above all, they sought to rehabilitate the poem by daring imagery; their most characteristic poems were generally formed by a series of unconnected images, the more original the better. The poets of

UNDERSTATEMENT

U. rejected narrative and anecdotal matter as well as sentimentality and rhetorical effusion, preferring to cultivate a humor and playfulness reminiscent of futurism. They advocated free verse and the elimination of rhyme and punctuation, and they strove to give visual form to their images by typographical techniques.

Creationism (q.v.) and U. were not only simultaneous movements but also very similar in form and intent, although the former was more restrictive in dogma and perhaps more rigorous or serious in its composition. The presence of the Chilean poet Vicente Huidobro in Madrid in 1918, after having been associated with Pierre Reverdy in Paris, planted seeds for this new adventure in irrationality. It has been said that U. had no great poet, nor did it produce lasting works; hence, to some extent it has been disregarded by literary historians. Yet many journals of the time published Ultraist poems by such known writers as Gerardo Diego and Juan Larrea. Diego's *Manual de espumas* is usually cited as the best Ultraist book, while images modeled on the same aesthetic precepts can be found in a number of poets. Moreover, U. did promote creative freedom and experimentation concomitant with what was taking place in other countries, and it also opened up new avenues for the future. U. is a movement which must be taken into account if what followed in 20th-c. Sp. poetry is to be fully understood. See also MODERNISMO; SPANISH POETRY; TWENTIETH-CENTURY POETICS, *Spanish.*—M. de la Peña, *El ultraísmo en España* (1925); G. de Torre, *Literaturas europeas de vanguardia* (1925), *Historia de las literaturas de vanguardia* (1965); R. Cansinos-Assens, *La nueva literatura* (1927); G. Videla, *El ultraísmo* (1963); J. G. Manrique de Lara, *Gerardo Diego* (1970); M. Scrimaglo, *Literatura argentina de vanguardia (1920–1930)* (1974); *Los vanguardismos en la América Latina*, ed. O. Collazos (1977); J. Cano Ballesta, *Literatura y tecnología. Las letras españolas ante la revolución industrial: 1900–1933* (1981); W. Bohn, *The Aesthetics of Visual Poetry 1914–1928* (1986).
A.W.P.; K.N.M.

UNDERSTATEMENT. See LITOTES; MEIOSIS.

UNITY is a fundamental—quite possibly *the* fundamental—aesthetic criterion, akin to harmony, integrity, and coherence. In the *Phaedrus* Plato holds that an oration should have u. analogous to the organic u. of a living creature; in the *Symposium* he suggests, in connection with the musical scale, that u. is a reconciliation of opposites or discords. The first full-blown Western theory of dramatic u. emerges in Aristotle's *Poetics*. U. of plot is dramatic in that it expresses u. of action (the only u. Aristotle actually sponsors). Tragedy is held to be superior to epic because of its tighter internal relations (5.23–24). The ideal tragedy is an imitation of a unified action, large enough to be perspicuous while small enough to be comprehensible. Aristotle's conception of u. is closely related to his artistic requirements of probability and necessity (see FICTION) as they constitute the criteria for the connection of parts (6–9).

Aristotle is concerned only with dramatic u.; Horace has a looser but broader conception of u. which refers not only to action but, even more, to diction. He thinks of it as an effect of harmony obtained by skillful "order and arrangement," analogous either to music or, more significantly, to the blending of colors, light, and shadow in painting ("ut pictura poesis," q.v.). *On the Sublime,* the late-Cl. text long ascribed to Longinus, includes an analysis of an ode by Sappho in which intensity of feeling is seen to produce an organic u. which manifests itself as a reconciliation of opposing elements, a view which has obvious affinities to both Plato and Horace.

With the rediscovery of the text of Aristotle's *Poetics* and its tr. and commentary by Castelvetro in the Ren. (*Poetica d'Aristotele vulgarizzata e sposta,* 1570; abridged tr. A. Bongiorno, *Castelvetro on the Art of Poetry,* 1984), Aristotle's argument for u. of action gradually became doctrine, then ossified into a prescription, one of the poetic "rules" (q.v.) of Fr. Classicism, the "Three Unities"—of action, time, and place. Aristotle had remarked that tragedies confined themselves to the events of a single day, but it was J. C. Scaliger who first established the tendency to identify the duration of the action represented with the duration of the representation. This was done in the name of verisimilitude (q.v.); Sidney thought it was common reason (i.e. concern for verisimilitude) as well as Aristotle's precept that the stage should always represent but one place and the events of one day. Yet as formal criteria the three unities rather challenge the artist to concentrate on the autonomy of his work. In the heyday of the unities, in the drama of 17th-c. Fr. Classicism, Racine clearly drew strength from them, whereas Corneille strained against them—his play *Le Cid* occasioned a great controversy over the unities (see CLASSICISM; RULES).

The three unities were never fully adopted in England, and Dryden assessed the reasons in the *Essay of Dramatic Poesy* (1668, 1684), justifying the Eng. preference for subplot. Dr. Johnson's "Preface to Shakespeare" (1765) showed, with great humor, how such mistaken scruples as to verisimilitude were given the lie by the very nature of dramatic illusion. The audience manages a shift of scene from Rome to Alexandria with the same ease they accepted the original setting as Rome. At the same time, the artifice of strictly observing the unities enhances the dramatic illusion wherever the concentration is psychologically compelling. Eng. critics since Dryden, and particularly Dennis, had gone back to Aristotle for a deeper grasp of the principle of dramatic u. in its interdependence with probability and necessity as felt by the audience. The three unities were thus not central to the more general concern with dramatic u. but merely a subset of it.

From antiquity up to the mid 18th c., theories of u. had been mainly theories of dramatic u. But 18th-c. theories of u. dealt with other genres besides drama, as Le Bossu's *Traité du Poëme épique* (1675) and Addison's *Spectator* papers on *Paradise Lost* show. And the rise of psychological aesthetics in the 18th c. opened the way to more adequate ideas of the role of u. in lyric poetry as well. New and enlarged conceptions of the creative imagination (q.v.) and the shift from a mechanistic to a vitalist worldview led to the romantic emphasis on organic u. (see ORGANICISM). This appeared variously as u. of feeling, u. as an imitation of the poet's mind in the act of creation, and imaginative u., with the imagination being the shaping, unifying ("esemplastic"), and reconciling power (Coleridge, *Biographia literaria*, ch. 14).

The conception of poetic u. fostered by the New Criticism (q.v.) of the mid 20th c. was directed against romanticism but remained romantic nonetheless. Organic u. was also a mainstay of the subsequent schools of formalist, psychological, and myth crit. (qq.v.), both as a standard of judgment and as a method of exposition. Thus, even beyond the explicitly Aristotelian emphasis of the Chicago school (q.v.), poetic u. was also explained by I. A. Richards as a reconciliation of impulses; by Cleanth Brooks as a reconciliation of thought and feeling manifested in the interaction of theme with lang. and metaphor; by the surrealists as a unifying of the total mind through freeing of the unconscious; by the Freudians through poetic analogues of the "dream-work" following associations of symbols; and by the Jungians in the replication of archetypal motifs.

At the same time, the principle of u. was variously questioned and even made problematic by some of these same movements, just as some romantics had developed an aesthetic of the fragment. Indeed, such a reversal may be implicit in the interiorization of the sense of u. which drew it away from formal constraints. The structuralist and poststructuralist tendencies which followed in the wake of New Crit. may outwardly have resembled it in its attention to the complexities and tensions which articulate a given work as a whole, but in effect they showed its u. to be contingent, relative, and superficial. The text is a meeting place for myriad relations that have no common objective form; real u. is either that of the underlying systems or an illusion, the lure held out by the surface of the work. The poetic gesture of imposing or inducing u. is just a jar in Tennessee, as poetry itself turns against that pretension. Yet the will to form may always have to express itself in art by breaking with accustomed modes of u., and one sort of crit. will find its task in showing that, where a work is experienced as art, some manner of u. has been created and communicated. For further discussion of modes of u. and the postmodernist reaction thereto, see ORGANICISM.—H. Breitinger, *Les Unités d'Aristote avant le Cid de Corneille* (1895); H. B. Charlton, *Castelvetro's Theory of Poetry* (1913); Richards; J. W. H. Atkins, *Lit. Crit. in Antiquity* (1934); M. Bodkin, *Archetypal Patterns in Poetry* (1934); Brooks; Crane; Abrams; Wellek; Wellek and Warren; Wimsatt and Brooks; G. F. Else, *Aristotle's Poetics* (1957); Frye; G. M. A. Grube, *The Gr. and Roman Critics* (1965); Culler; G. J. H. van Gelder, *Beyond the Line* (1982)—Arabic poetry; de Man; M. F. Heath, *U. in Gr. Poetics* (1989).   R.H.F.; J.B.

UPAJĀTI. See INDIAN PROSODY.

URDU POETRY. See GHAZAL; INDIAN POETRY.

URUGUAYAN POETRY. See SPANISH AMERICAN POETRY.

UT PICTURA POESIS. Few expressions of aesthetic crit. have led to more comment over a period of several centuries than *u. p. p.*, "as is painting so is poetry" (Horace, *Ars poetica* 361). Since Horace mentions the subject thrice (362–65, 1–47, 343–45), we may assume he had some particular interest in it, though investigations of Horatian dicta *vis à vis* contemporaneous Roman painting mostly still remain to be made. Suggestions of the similitude of poetry and painting were certainly made before Horace, who almost certainly knew—even if he may not have assumed that his audience would recall—the more explicit earlier statement of Simonides of Keos (first attested in the *Auctor ad Herrennium* [4.39] and recorded by Plutarch as a commonplace [*De gloria Atheniensium* 3.347a] more than a century after *Ars poetica*): "poetry is a speaking picture, painting a silent [mute] poetry."

The views of Aristotle—esp. that poetry and painting as arts of imitation (q.v.) should use the same principal element of composition (structure), namely, *plot* (q.v.) in tragedy and *design* (outline) in painting (see *Poetics* 6.19–21)—furnished additional authority for Ren. and later attempts to measure the degree and the nature of the kinship of the arts (the "parallel" of the arts) and to determine the order of precedence among them (the "paragone" of the arts). Moreover, as Lee observes in his analysis of the humanistic doctrine of painting, for which the Horatian dictum served as a kind of final sanction, "writers on art expected one to read [*u. p. p.*] 'as is poetry so is painting.'"

The Horatian simile, however interpreted, asserted the likeness, if not the identity, of painting and poetry; and from so small a kernel came an extensive body of aesthetic speculation and, in particular, an impressive theory of art which prevailed in the 16th, 17th, and most of the 18th c. (see NEOCLASSICAL POETICS). While a few poets assented to the proposition that painting surpasses poetry in imitating human nature in action as well as in showing a Neoplatonic Ideal Beauty above nature, more of them raided the province of painting for the greater glory of poetry and announced that the pre-eminent painters are the poets. Both Cicero (*Tusc. Disp.* 5.114) and Lucian (who praises Homer as painter [*Eikones* 8]) gave ancient authority for that view, which Petrarch and others reinforced. Among the poets described as master-painters have been Theocritus, Virgil, Tasso, Ariosto, Spenser, Shakespeare, and Milton, not to mention numerous later landscapists in descriptive poetry (q.v.), the Pre-Raphaelites, and the Parnassians (qq.v.). Painter and critic, Reynolds instanced Michelangelo as the prime witness to "the poetical part of our art" of painting (*Discourse* 15, 1790). Thus a "poetical" or highly imaginative painter could be compared with the "painting" poets.

U. p. p. offered a formula—the success of which "one can hardly deny," Wellek has remarked—for analyzing the relationship of poetry and painting (and other arts). However successful, the Horatian formula proved useful—at least was used—on many occasions as a precept to guide artistic endeavor, as an incitement to aesthetic argument, and as a basic element in several theories of poetry and the arts. Alone and with many accretions, modifications, and transformations, *u. p. p.* inspired a number of meaningful comments about the arts and poetry and even contributed to the theory and praxis of several painters, most notably "learned Poussin." Moreover, like other commonplaces of crit., the Horatian formula stimulated and attracted to itself a variety of views of poetry and painting that are hard to relate to the original statement.

The Horatian simile has of course evoked opposition. Plutarch himself questions its validity (*Mor.* 748A). In *Plastics* (1712), Shaftesbury warned, "Comparisons and parallel[s] ∴. . between painting and poetry . . . [are] almost ever absurd and at best constrained, lame and defective." The chief counterattack came in *Laokoön* (1766), where Lessing contended that the theories of art associated with *u. p. p.* had been the principal, if not the only, begetter of the confusion of the arts which he deplored in the artistic practice and theory of the time. In this he was anticipated by Da Vinci, who raises these issues in his *Notebooks* (*Literary Works*, ed. J. P. Richter [1970], 1.48–68, 79–81). Saisselin has shown clearly that the "relations between the sister arts . . . were more complex than a reading of Lessing might lead one to believe." Since then similar charges have been raised by other critics, e.g. Babbitt.

On the other hand, since the late 19th c. the kinship of poetry and painting has appeared in a more favorable light in connection with the arts of the East—particularly in generalizations about the "poetic feeling" of Oriental painting and the pictorial characteristics of Chinese and Japanese poetry (qq.v.) and, with the ever-increasing knowledge of Eastern art, in historical and critical studies setting forth the close relationships between Oriental poetry and painting. In China, poets were often painters; and critics, particularly in the 11th and 12th cs., stated the parallelism of poetry and painting in lang. close to that of Simonides and Horace. According to Chou Sun, "Painting and writing are one and the same art." Writing implied calligraphy, which linked painting with poetry. Thus, a poet might "paint poetry" and a painter write "soundless poems." These Eastern views led a number of Occidental poets to follow Japanese rules for poems and Chinese canons of painting in their poems—"images" directly presented to the eye, "free" impressions in a few strokes of syllables and lines, evocations of mood, lyrical epigrams, and abstractionist representations (see IMAGISM). Still, these poems reflecting the Eastern tendency to regard poetry and painting as "two sides of the same thing" were experimental and specialized works tapping but a few of the resources of the two arts. Moreover, the critical analysis of "the same thing," with its "two sides" remains at least as difficult as the explanation of the Horatian observation, "as is painting so is poetry."

See also VISUAL ARTS AND POETRY.

W. G. Howard, "*U. p. p.*," *PMLA* 24 (1909), ed., *Laokoön: Lessing, Herder, Goethe* (1910); I. Babbitt, *The New Laokoön* (1910); E. Manwaring, *It. Landscape in 18th-C. England* (1925); E. Panofsky, *Idea* (1929, tr. 1968); C. Davies, "*U. p. p.*," *MLR* 30 (1935); R. W. Lee, "*U. p. p.*," *Art Bull.* 22 (1940), "*U. p. p.*," *Dict. of World Lit.*, ed. J. T. Shipley, rev. ed. (1953); C. M. Dawson, *Romano-Campanian Mythological Landscape Painting* (1944); K. Schefold, *Pompejanische Malerei* (1952, Fr. tr. 1972)—Roman poetics vs. pictorial styles; P. W. Lehmann, *Roman Wall Paintings* (1953); Wellek and Warren, ch. 11; H. H. Frankel, "Poetry and Painting: Chinese and Western Views," *CL* 9 (1957); J. R. Spencer, "*Ut pictura rhetorica*," *JWCI* 20 (1957)—rel. to the rhetorical trad.; Wimsatt and Brooks, ch. 13; J. H. Hagstrum, *The Sister Arts* (1958); R. G. Saisselin, "*U. p. p.*: DuBos to Diderot," *JAAC* 20 (1961); P. H. v. Blanckenhagen, *The Paintings from Boscotrecase* (1962); H. D. Goldstein, "U. p. p.: Reynolds on Imitation and Imagination," *ECS* 1 (1967–68); R. Park, "*U. p. p.*: The 19th-C. Aftermath," *JAAC* 28 (1969); D. T. Mace, "*U. p. p.*," *Encounters*, ed. J. D. Hunt (1971); H.-C. Buch, "*U. p. p.*": Die Beschreibungsliteratur und ihre Kritik von Lessing bis Lukács* (1972); "U. P. P.: A Bibl.," *BB* 29 (1972); W. Trimpi, "The Meaning of Horace's U. p. p.," *JWCI* 36 (1973), "Horace's 'U. p. p.': The Argument for Stylistic Decorum," *Traditio* 34 (1978); J. Graham, "*U. p. p.*," *DHI*; C. D. Reverand, "*U. p. p.* and Pope's *Satire* II.i," *ECS* 9 (1975–76); W. K. Wimsatt, Jr., "Laokoön: An Oracle Reconsulted," *Day of the Leopards* (1976); E. H. Gombrich, *Art and Illusion*, 5th ed. (1977); E. Gilman, *The Curious Perspective* (1978); R. A. Goodrich,

"Plato on Poetry and Painting," *BJA* 22 (1982); J.-M. Croisille, *Poésie et art figuré de Néron aux Flaviens* (1982), and rev. in *JRS* 73 (1983); A. Dolders, "*U. p. p.*: A Sel. Annot. Bibl. of Books and Articles Pub. 1900–1980," *YCGL* 32 (1983); H.

Markiewicz, "U. p. p.: A Hist. of the Topos and the Problem," *NLH* 18 (1987). S.A.L.; T.V.F.B.; W.T.

UTA. See TANKA; JAPANESE POETRY.

V

VAGANTENSTROPHE. See GOLIARDIC VERSE.

VALUE. See EVALUATION.

VARIABLE FOOT. A term coined by William Carlos Williams which he first associated with the triadic stanzas of his *Paterson* 2.3 (1948), later reprinted separately as "The Descent." Claiming that the concept of the foot had to be altered to suit a newly relativistic world, Williams insisted that the v. f. allowed both order and variability in so-called free verse (q.v.), which he maintained never could be truly free. The v. f., he asserted, supplanted the fixed foot of traditional Eng. prosody in order to represent more accurately the speech rhythms of the modern Am. idiom. Attempting to demonstrate his measurement of the v. f., Williams explained that he counted "a single beat" for each line of his three-line stanzas so as to regulate the "musical pace" of his verse, though in fact his lines contain varying numbers of stresses and syllables. But, as his nine-poem sequence "Some Simple Measures in the Am. Idiom and the V. F." (1959) shows, Williams did not consistently identify the v. f. with the triadic stanza form. Because his own explanations of the device often lack precision and consistency, subsequent critics have questioned sharply the legitimacy of the concept of the v. f., one remarking that the v. f. in verse is as impossible as a variable inch on a yardstick; a more promising approach to Williams' prosody lies in treating it as visual. Edgar Allan Poe had earlier used the term to describe the caesura; for Poe, the caesura was "a perfect foot" the length of which would vary in accordance with the time it takes to pronounce other feet in the line. Williams read Poe's essays on prosody, which apparently influenced his conception of verse structure.—E. A. Poe, "The Rationale of Verse," *Complete Works*, ed. J. A. Harrison, v. 14 (1902); W. C. Williams, Letter to R. Eberhart (May 23, 1954), *Sel. Letters*, (1957), *I Wanted to Write a Poem*, ed. E. Heal (1958), "The Am. Idiom," *Interviews with W. C. Williams*, ed. L. Wagner (1976); H. M. Sayre, *The Visual Text of W. C. Williams* (1983); S. Cushman, *W. C. Williams and the Meanings of Measure* (1985). S.C.

VARIATION is used in three senses in the study of poetry. (1) In OE, the term refers to a technique of poetic composition by which the metrical pattern of half-lines, itself partially formulaic, is deliberately not repeated from the first half-line to the second. Since the number of half-line types is deliberately kept low (only about half a dozen), and since these types may well have been recognizable to or even identified for auditors in performance (e.g. by accompanying harp notes), v. seems to have been a deliberate attempt to avoid monotony in line-construction. (2) Metrical v. is often cited as an explanation for the fact that most actual lines of poetry do not entirely match the pattern of the meter they are said to be written in; see METER. (3) More generally, v. is often held to be a desirable characteristic of structure which sustains reader interest. Critics who see literary works as developing, exploring, or asserting "themes" (q.v.) sometimes adapt the analogy of "theme and v." from music, as in the construction of a symphony, where v. is recognized as one of only a few compositional strategies open to any composer. Auditor and reader recognition of a v. as in some respects different from but in others conforming to a prior theme is simply one form of pattern recognition, a fundamental cognitive process applicable across media.—C. P. Smith, *Pattern and V. in Poetry* (1932); W. K. Wimsatt, Jr., "When Is V. 'Elegant?'" *The Verbal Icon* (1954); C. S. Brown, "Theme and Vs. as a Literary Form," *YCGL* 27 (1978); S. L. Tarán, *The Art of V. in the Hellenistic Epigram* (1979); F. C. Robinson, *Beowulf and the Appositive Style* (1985); E. R. Sisman, *Haydn and the Cl. V.* (1993). T.V.F.B.

VATES. Two concepts of the poet, as craftsman (maker) and as inspired seer or quasi-priest, are already established in early Gr. lit. In Pindar they coexist, but Plato (notably in the *Ion*) exaggerates the notion of poetic "mania" (*furor poeticus*; see POETIC MADNESS) in order to devalue the poet's claim to rational knowledge of truth. Lat. lit. adopted the Gr. term *poeta* in the sense of craftsman, and accordingly Ennius, followed by Lucretius, attacked the native *v.*, soothsayer and oracle-monger, as uncouth and ignorant. But under the influence of the Stoic philosopher Posidonius and of Varro Reatinus, the Augustans revived the term *v.*, suitable to their notion of the genuinely Roman poet voicing the moral reforms inspired by the new regime. This vatic ideal is esp. advanced in Horace's *Ars poetica* (391–407), where Orpheus is hailed as the original *v.*, though poets are also exhorted to tireless improvement of their lines by the "labor of the file." Virgil claimed to be a *v.* (*Aeneid* 7.41), but after his death in 19 B.C., enthusiasm for the *v.* waned even in Horace; and Ovid pokes open fun at his claims. But later poets like Manilius and Lucan are more respectful, and even in Tacitus' *Dialogus* some memory of the Augustan status of the poet as seer persists. Eventually, in Pseudo-Longinus' treatise *On the Sublime*, the concept of the inspired poet took on fresh and influential life. See now INSPIRATION; LATIN POETRY; CLASSICAL POETICS.—T. Carlyle, *Heroes and Hero-Worship* (1841), lecture 3; J. K. Newman, *The Concept of V. in Augustan Poetry* (1967); C. O. Brink, *Horace on Poetry, The* Ars poetica (1971).   J.K.N.

VEDIC POETRY. See INDIAN POETRY.

VEDIC PROSODY. See INDIAN PROSODY.

VEHICLE. See TENOR AND VEHICLE.

VENEZUELAN POETRY. See SPANISH AMERICAN POETRY.

VENUS AND ADONIS STANZA. The most popular sexain (q.v.), consisting of a heroic quatrain and couplet rhyming *ababcc* in iambic pentameter. Its name derives from Shakespeare's verse epic *Venus and Adonis*, although it was used before Shakespeare by Surrey, Sidney, Spenser (January and December eclogues of the *Shepheardes Calender*), Donne ("The Expiration"), and other Ren. poets for solemn lyrics as well as for shorter amorous and longer narrative poems: it is particularly common for complaints and epyllia. Shakespeare used it again in *Romeo and Juliet, Love's Labour's Lost,* and other plays. Many 18-line poems of the 16th c. contain three V. a. A. stanzas; some of them (many of the 100 sonnet-related poems in Thomas Watson's *Hekatompathia*; Sidney's *Old Arcadia* 46, *Certain Sonnets* 19; Lodge's *Scillaes Metamorphoses*) seem to be larger structural imitations of the stanza form itself: two corresponding or analogous stanzas are followed by a third departing from the analogy and concluding the poem succinctly. This AA/B pattern is descended from the *canzone* and *canso* (qq.v.). The Shakespearian sonnet clearly resembles such poems in that it ends with a couplet having the same closural function. The V. a. A. stanza has been one of the most popular and superbly handled forms in Eng. and Am. poetry up to our time (7 poems by Wordsworth; John Wain, "Time Was"; Theodore Roethke, "Four for John Davies"; Thom Gunn, "Mirror for Poets"; Robert Lowell, "April Birthday at Sea").

E.H.; T.V.F.B.

VERBAL IRONY. See IRONY.

VERISIMILITUDE. The doctrine that poetry should be "probable" or "likely" or "lifelike." Much of Western critical theory has in some measure accepted the idea of v., though differences in strictness of interp. are major. The primary source is the concept of *tó eikós* (the probable, the verisimilar) in Aristotle's *Poetics*, which is closely related to his fundamental notion of the imitation of nature. If a poem is not lifelike (at least in some sense), it can hardly be called an imitation (q.v.). Aristotle's account is perceptive but brief, and thus leaves a good bit to the judgment of later critics. He says that the poet describes not historical actions but "the kind of thing that might happen" (ch. 9). Historical occurrences may or may not be probable in this sense, and in tragedy the marvelous or astonishing must and the supernatural may be included. In ch. 15 he gives some scope (though not very much) to propriety of character, as he allows "consistent inconsistency"; in ch. 25 he allows a great deal of scope to the impossible so long as it is "convincing," and even some allowance that improbable events will happen. And the writer may depart from representation of common reality in depicting the ideal or in following common opinion. In all of this, what Aristotle insists on is universality and the apparent moral and psychological consequentiality of actions. After Aristotle, Cicero, Quintilian, Plutarch, and Horace accept the idea, but tend to restrict it somewhat more than did Aristotle in the direction of the ordinary and the commonly probable.

In the Ren., theorists from Scaliger through the "querelle du Cid," and later, take the concept seriously and debate its range and meaning. Propriety of character, where Aristotle himself gave little enough freedom, is interpreted so strictly that stock characters tend to become the exclusive ideal (notoriously in Thomas Rymer's animadversions against Shakespeare), though in one notable instance, Dryden defends the character of Caliban on strict grounds of propriety and v. (*Essays*, ed. Ker, 1.219). Somewhat more freedom is allowed in the handling of the marvelous (Christian critics being hardly willing to deny the supernatural a place in serious lit.), though there is great disagreement here. Castelvetro, Maggio, Chapelain, and d'Aubignac discriminate between ordinary and extraordinary v. Rymer, and later—rather surprisingly—Johnson, take a conservative view on this point, Dryden and Rapin take moderate positions, and Chapelain (who wants a more Christian poetry) a radical one. It was on grounds of *vraisemblance* that the Fr. Academy censured *The Cid* of Corneille. Corneille and Racine accepted the principle of *vraisemblance* v. quite genuinely, and the struggle in each of them between the abstracted rules (q.v.) and the pressures of their artistic habits and desires was, for both, fruitful.

Though the term has had much less use in the last two centuries, the idea, as a perennial and inescapable demand, persists in various, often implicit, forms: Wordsworth's turning to the common realities and the "lang. of men"; Coleridge's frequent appeals to "good sense"; Arnold's "crit. of life"; the New Critics' concern for paradox, irony, and "toughness" as giving an adequate, which is to say verisimilar, image of our experience; and deconstructive views that the preferable texts should be "about" their own non-aboutness, i.e. should reiterate, self-referentially, the *aporia* and collapse which all texts, as all discourse, mean. What gives the reader "infinite" "play" gives the reader no freedom whatever to interpret, since there can be no interp. on evidence, no reason to choose one reading against another. Romantic freedom once more, as in the determinism and progressivism of Shelley's "Ode to the West Wind" and in various forms of volitionism from Schopenhauer through Nietzsche and after, becomes a psychological trap—the will is free to will whatever it wills but with no grounds whatever to do so. What is vital and lively and beautiful remains to console, and to triumph. See also FICTION, POETRY AS; IMITATION; REALISM; REPRESENTATION AND MIMESIS.—R. M. Alden, "The Doctrine of V.," *Matzke Memorial Volume* (1911); R. Bray, *La Formation de la doctrine classique en France* (1931); Y. Winters, *In Defense of Reason* (1947); Tuve, esp. ch. 9; Weinberg; *New Essays on Plato and Aristotle*, ed. R. Bambrough (1965), esp. essays by Bambrough and Owen; Saisselin, s.v. "Truth and V."; R. Barthes, *Le Plaisir du texte* (1973); G. Graff, *Lit. Against Itself* (1979); P. Ramsey, *The Truth of Value* (1985). P.R.

VERS. (1) In Occitan, a term used by the early troubadours to designate any song, including the love-song, later called *canso* (q.v.) or *chanso*. The term derives from Med. Lat. *versus*. Distinctions between *chanso* and *v*. were discussed by some troubadours ca. 1200, when it was becoming an outmoded term. During the 13th c., it was revived to denote songs on moral, political, or satirical subjects (see SIRVENTES) rather than amatory ones. The *v*. is apt to have short and uncomplicated stanzas. (2) In modern Fr., the principal term for both the individual line of verse and verse taken generically, as a form or mode of expression.—Jeanroy, v. 2; J. Chailley, "Les Premiers Troubadours et le *versus* de l'école d'Aquitaine," *Romania* 76 (1955); J. H. Marshall, "Le V. au XIIe siècle: genre poétique?" *Revue de langue et litt. d'Oc* 12-13 (1965); Chambers; E. Köhler, "'V.' und Kanzone," *GRLMA*, v. 2.1.3 (1987).

F.M.C.; J.H.M.; C.S.

VERS DE SOCIÉTÉ. See LIGHT VERSE.

VERS IMPAIR, *vers imparisyllabique*. In Fr. pros., a distinctively unusual phenomenon—a line of verse with an odd number of syllables. Although the v. i. is to be found throughout the history of Fr. verse (e.g. in *Aucassin et Nicolette*, the 16th-c. ode,

Malherbe, La Fontaine, Marceline Desbordes-Valmore, Hugo), it is particularly associated with the *vers libéré* (q.v.) of the proto-symbolists (Verlaine, Rimbaud, Mallarmé) and their successors, because in their work it is exploited more systematically and more polemically—Leconte de Lisle, leader of the Parnassians (q.v.), was of the opinion that "Fr. verse thrives on equilibrium; it dies if its parisyllabic nature is tampered with." Because it is slightly "out of true," a kind of *vers faux*, and because of its lack of self-assured equilibrium, the v. i. can be seen as intrinsically anti-oratorical, and particularly suited to the depiction of moods that are unstable, nervous, indeterminate (see IMPRESSIONISM), or ironic and mischievous. At the same time, however, by increasing the reader's alertness to syllabic values, it can achieve modal and tonal effects of great subtlety. Verlaine's *Art poétique*, in lines of nine syllables, advocates the v. i. in these terms:

De la musique avant toute chose,
Et pour cela préfère l'Impair
Plus vague et plus soluble dans l'air
Sans rien en lui qui pèse ou qui pose

(Above all else be musical,
And therefore prefer the v. i.
Vaguer and more evanescent,
Weightless and volatile.)

M. Grammont, *Le Vers français*, rev. ed. (1961), *Petit Traité de versification française*, 10th ed. (1982); F. Deloffre, *Le Vers français* (1969); Elwert; M. Deguy, "Notes sur le rythme ou comment faire un i.," *Langue française* 56 (1982); L. Victor, "À propos de vers," *FM* 53 (1985). C.S.

VERS IRRÉGULIERS. See VERS LIBRES CLASSIQUES.

VERS LIBÉRÉ. Not to be confused with either *vers libre* (q.v.), 19th-c. Fr. free verse proper, or with the *vers libres classiques* (q.v.) of the 17th and 18th cs., that is, regular lines irregularly disposed, v. l. is Fr. verse "liberated" from many of the traditional rules concerning meter, caesura, and endstopping, but still observing the principles of isosyllabism and regularly patterned rhyme. The beginnings of liberation are to be found among the romantic poets, who resorted to enjambment and use of the *trimètre* (qq.v.) with less inhibition than their forbears. These two devices were pushed to extremes in the latter half of the 19th c., the line-terminal word often being no more than a particle, the *trimètre* assuming ever more asymmetrical configurations (5+3+4, 3+6+3, 4+3+5, etc.) often involving the erasure not merely of the caesura, but of its very position, e.g. Verlaine: "Du bout fin de la quenotte de ton souris" (3+4+5). The poets of v. l. also cultivated the *vers impair* (q.v.) and the expressive, but rhythmically disruptive, effects of the *coupe lyrique* (see COUPE). All these developments contributed to the rhythmic destabilization of the line and undermined its cl. integrity; rhythms lost their firm contours and consequently their aptitude for eloquent and oratorical utterance; instead, they acquired a certain looseness, fluidity, and indeterminacy which favored the intimate, the prosaic, the impromptu, the *fantaisiste*. Verlaine's fondness for poems in exclusively feminine rhymes seems to serve the same purpose, allowing the line to fade or dissolve rather than come to an unequivocal end. But this device was simply part of a wider tendency to disregard the rule of the alternation of masculine and feminine rhymes, a tendency whose origins lie in Baudelaire's "Ciel brouillé" and "À une mendiante rousse" (1857) and Banville's "Erinna" and "L'Enamourée" (1866; SEE MASCULINE AND FEMININE). Other rules of rhyming were also infringed: masculine words rhyme with feminine ones (Banville's "Élégie," 1846; Verlaine's "Ariettes oubliées VI," 1874), singulars with plurals (Laforgue). Thus, even though rhyme was still felt to be indispensable to Fr. verse, poets sought to reduce its privileged status, both by treating it "carelessly" and by scumbling the line-ending. Some poets, however—Mallarmé in particular—worked with inordinately rich rhymes, not only to subvert rhyme by excess, but also to activate larger acoustic fields. The step from v. l. to *vers libre* (q.v.) was a short one; it was a step taken by Rimbaud ("Marine" and "Mouvement," 1873) and by Laforgue (*Derniers Vers*, 1890); but Rimbaud also developed in a more radical prosodic direction (the prose poem), as did Mallarmé, whose *Un Coup de dés* in 1897 already exploits most of the resources of visual poetry (q.v.).—L. Guichard, *Jules Laforgue et ses poésies* (1950); M. Grammont, *Le Vers français*, rev. ed. (1961); C. Cuénot, *Le Style de Paul Verlaine* (1962); Elwert; Mazaleyrat; B. de Cornulier, *Théorie du vers* (1982); C. Scott, *Vers libre* (1990), ch. 2.   C.S.

VERS LIBRE. Because of its prosodic relatedness to *vers libres classiques* and *vers libéré* (qq.v.), this term is best reserved for 19th-c. Fr. free verse and those modernist free-verse prosodies (see FREE VERSE) that acknowledge a debt to it (e.g. the It. futurists, the Anglo-Am. *vers-libristes*, Pound, Eliot, and the imagists). The directions mapped out by the *vers-libristes* of the late 19th c. have been variously explored and adapted by 20th-c. practitioners such as Apollinaire, Blaise Cendrars, Pierre-Jean Jouve, Pierre Reverdy, Éluard, Robert Desnos, René Char, Yves Bonnefoy, and Michel Deguy.

The emergence of v. l. is specifically datable to 1886, the year in which the review *La Vogue*, edited by Gustave Kahn, published, in rapid succession, Rimbaud's free-verse *Illuminations*, "Marine," and "Mouvement" (possibly written in May, 1873), translations of some of Whitman's *Leaves of Grass* by Jules Laforgue, Kahn's series of poems entitled

"Intermède" (to become part of his *Les Palais nomades*, 1887), ten of Laforgue's own free-verse poems (later collected in his *Derniers Vers*, 1890) and further examples by Paul Adam and Jean Moréas. To this list of initiators, Jean Ajalbert, Édouard Dujardin, Albert Mockel, Francis Vielé-Griffin, Émile Verhaeren, Adolphe Retté, Maurice Maeterlinck, Camille Mauclair, and Stuart Merrill added their names in the years immediately following.

One might believe that the relative freedoms of *vers libres classiques* combined with those of *vers libéré* would produce the absolute freedom of v. l., but this is not quite so. V. l. indeed indulges in heterometricity and free-rhyming, and its lines are rhythmically unstable; but it goes further still: it rejects the indispensability of rhyme with its line-demarcative function and instead relates lineation not to number of syllables but to the coincidence of units of meaning and units of rhythm, or to integral impulses of utterance, or else simply to the optimal expressive disposition of its textual raw materials. And indeed, the *vers-libristes* seek to abandon the principle of syllabism itself, by making the number of syllables in a line either irrelevant or indeterminable or both. The undermining of the syllabic system is facilitated by the ambiguous syllabic status of the *e atone* (mute *-e*)—should it be counted when unelided?—and by doubts about the syllabic value of contiguous vowels. Laforgue summarizes the *tabula rasa* of v. l. in a letter to Kahn of July 1886: "I forget to rhyme, I forget about the number of syllables, I forget about stanzaic structure."

Paradoxically, though, syllabic amorphousness produces rhythmic polymorphousness, and polysemy; in other words, a single line of v. l. is potentially several lines, each with its own inherited modalities. In addition, because of its heterometricity, v. l. can maximize rhythmic shifts between lines, creating a verse-texture of multiplied tonalities. Within this paradox lies another fruitful contradiction. One of the original justifications for v. l. was its inimitability, its resistance to abstraction and systemization; thus it could theoretically mold itself to the uniqueness of a personality, a psyche, a mood. Again Kahn: "For a long time I had been seeking to discover in myself a personal rhythm capable of communicating my lyric impulses with the cadence and music which I judged indispensable to them" (Preface to *Premiers Poèmes*, 1897). And yet, v. l. equally proposes a range of rhythmic possibilities which the reader is left to resolve into any one of a number of specific recitations. Given the significance of typographical arrangement in v. l., this contradiction might be reformulated as a polarization of the visual and the oral, of the linguistic and the paralinguistic, of the text as text, demanding to be read on its own terms, and the text as script, a set of incomplete instructions to the reader's voice. One further contradiction might be mentioned: for all v. l.'s ambiguation of syllabic number, with its transference of focus from syllable to accent, from number of syllables to number of measures, many free-verse poems are constructed on a "constante rythmique" (rhythmic constant), an intermittently recurrent measure which can only be defined syllabically.

Two broad currents of development can be distinguished in v. l.: one derives its rhythmic purchase from its varying approximation to, and distance from, recognizably regular lines and often cultivates ironic modes of utterance; the other seeks to undermine the primacy of the line by promoting rhythmic units larger than the line—the *verset* (q.v.) or the stanza—or smaller than the line—the individual measure; this latter strain is often informed by a rhapsodic voice. But in both currents, the line's role as guardian of metrical authority and guarantor of verse as ritual and self-transcendence is removed.

In both currents, too, the stanza finds itself without pedigree, infinitely elastic, insuring no structural continuity. The stanza of v. l. ends not in conformity with some visible structural imperative—though who may say what invisible imperatives operate—but because a movement of utterance comes to an end, and because only by ending can a sequence of lines define its own field of structural and prosodic activity. The stanzas of v. l. are a pursuit of unique kinds of formality constantly renewed, not the repeated confirmation of a certain stanzaic blueprint.

V. l. can claim, with some justification, to have "psychologized" verse-structure, to have made the act of writing apparently simultaneous with the changing movements of mind: "A poem is not a feeling communicated just as it was conceived before the act of writing. Let us acknowledge the small felicities of rhyme, and the deviations caused by the chances of invention, the whole unforeseen symphony which comes to accompany the subject" (Laforge, *Mélanges posthumes*). By allowing the aleatory and the improvised to inhabit verse, by exploiting the psychological layering produced by variable rhyme-interval and variable margin, by locating verse at the intersection of multiplied coordinates (rhyme, rhymelessness, repetition, the metrical, the nonmetrical), by using linguistic structures to attract and activate paralinguistic features (tempo, pause, tone, accentual variation, emotional coloring), v. l. establishes its affinities with the stream of consciousness of contemporary fiction and proffers a stream of consciousness of poetic reading.

G. Kahn, "Préface," *Premiers Poèmes* (1897); F. Marinetti, *Enquête internationale sur le v. l. et manifeste du futurisme* (1909); Thieme, 386; T. S. Eliot, "Reflections on V. L.," *New Statesman* (1917), rpt. in *To Criticize the Critic* (1965); M. Dondo, *V. L., a Logical Devel. of Fr. Verse* (1922); E. Dujardin, *Les Premiers Poètes du v. l.* (1922); J. Hytier, *Les Techniques modernes du vers français* (1923); Patterson; L.-P. Thomas, *Le Vers moderne: ses moyens d'expres-*sion, son esthétique (1943); H. Morier, *Le Rythme du v. l. symboliste,* 3 v. (1944); P. M. Jones, *The Background of Mod. Fr. Poetry* (1951), Part 2; Z. Czerny, "Le V. l. français et son art structural," *Poetics, Poetyka, Poetika,* ed. D. Davie et al. (1961); *Le Vers français au 20e siècle,* ed. M. Parent (1967); F. Carmody, "La Doctrine du v. l. de Gustave Kahn," *CAIEF* 21 (1969); J. Mazaleyrat, "Problèmes de scansion du v. l.," *Philologische Studien für Joseph M. Piel* (1969); Mazaleyrat; J. Filliolet, "Problématique du v. l.," in *Poétique du vers français,* ed. H. Meschonnic (1974); Elwert; Scott; Morier; D. Grojnowski, "Poétique du v. l.: *Derniers Vers* de Jules Laforgue (1886)," *RHLF* 84 (1984); C. Scott, *A Question of Syllables* (1986), ch.6, *V. l.: The Emergence of Free Verse in France* (1990). C.S.

VERS LIBRES CLASSIQUES (*vers mêlés, vers irréguliers*). These terms describe the kind of verse used in minor or hybrid genres of the 17th and 18th cs. in France, in which lines of different lengths, though regular in internal construction, are irregularly and unpredictably combined. In other words, v. l. c. replace both isosyllabism with heterosyllabism, and also the single, repeated rhyme scheme of stanzaic verse with free-rhyming stichic or strophic structures—still subject, however, to the rule of the alternation of masculine and feminine rhymes. V. l. c. became current in France from the 1640s and are to be associated particularly with *préciosité* and the baroque (qq.v.). They are to be found in burlesque poetry, the madrigal, the verse-epistle, the epigram, the idyll, the elegy (qq.v.), even in some religious verse (e.g. Corneille, *Les Louanges de la sainte Vierge,* 1665), and also in much narrative verse, esp. the fable (q.v.: La Fontaine; Florian). In the theater, v. l. c. were exploited in the *pièce à machines* (e.g. Corneille, *Andromède,* 1650), in semi-burlesque mythological comedy (Molière, *Amphitryon,* 1668), and in tragicomedy and opera libretti (Quinault; La Fontaine). The attraction of v. l. c. lay not only in their improvised, volatile, even acrobatic quality, but also in their apparently unlaboured and flexible naturalness. In the Preface to his first Fables, La Fontaine wrote: "The author wanted to test which form was most appropriate for setting stories in verse. It was his belief that irregular verse, which has a character very close to that of prose, might seem the most natural and, consequently, the best." See HETEROMETRIC.—R. Bray, "L'Introduction des *vers mêlés* sur la scène classique," *PMLA* 66 (1951); W. Elwert, "La Vogue des vers mêlés dans la poésie du 17e siècle," *XVIIe Siècle* 88 (1970); C. Scott, *Vers libre* (1990), ch. 2. C.S.

VERS MÊLÉS. See VERS LIBRES CLASSIQUES.

VERS MESURÉS *à l'antique.* Imitations of the quantitative meters of Cl. pros. in Fr. verse mainly of the 16th c. Given the emphasis, during the

Ren., on the imitation of Cl. models, it is not at all surprising that poets of the *Pléiade* (q.v.), i.e. Ronsard, Baïf, and Jodelle, and their contemporaries (Pasquier and Jacques de la Taille) would want to transfer to poetry in the vernacular the metrical principles which had given rise to the august canon of Cl. poetry: how attain similar ends but by similar means? The impulse was particularly strong where direct translation was involved. These attempts usually entailed a rigid and quite arbitrary specification of quantitative values (long or short) for Fr. syllables, from which any functional distinction between long and short vowels had all but disappeared. Of the 16th-c. quantitative poets, Baïf was perhaps the most celebrated and most prolific (e.g. *Étrènes de poézie fransoèze au vers mesurés*, 1574, which contains hexameters, iambic trimeters, Sapphics, Alcaics, and other Cl. meters). Even though reactions to Baïf's experiments were at best skeptical and at worst mockingly incredulous, others followed in his footsteps, notably Nicholas Rapin (ca. 1540–1608) and Agrippa d'Aubigné (1550–1630). After a prolonged absence, v. m. reappeared in the 18th c., championed by l'Abbé d'Olivet and Turgot. V. m. work best when supported by rhyme—a most unclassical device, but long perceived as an essential rhythmic *point de repère* for the Fr. ear—and when patterns of accented and unaccented vowels are made to correspond to Cl. patterns of long and short (i.e. accentual imitations of quantitative verse). But even where this latter equivalence is practiced, the gradual weakening of the Fr. accent, with its consequent shift from word to word-group, has left fewer accents at the Fr. poet's disposal than there are long syllables in the Cl. meter being imitated. The greater frequency of accents in Eng. and Ger. is one reason why verse based on Cl. meters has had a longer history in these two poetries. See CLASSICAL METERS IN MODERN LANGUAGES.—L. Bellanger, *Études historiques et philologiques sur la rime française* (1876); Kastner; Patterson; Elwert; F. Deloffre, *Le Vers français* (1969); B. Stäblein, "V. M.," *MGG*, v. 13; H. M. Brown, "V. M.," *New Grove*, v. 19.　　C.S.

VERSE AND PROSE.

   I. DISTINCTIONS
  II. ESSENCE AND FORM
 III. INTERANIMATIONS
    A. *Speech Forms*
    B. *Prose Forms*
    C. *Verse Forms*
 IV. HISTORY

I. DISTINCTIONS. V. and pr. are two of the three terms central to any discussion of, and distinctions about, the nature and modes of verbal art. The third is "poetry" (q.v.), which is the most difficult—and crucial—concept of the three. Northrop Frye once remarked that establishing a viable distinction between v. and pr. would allow us to write "page two" of the "elementary textbook expounding the fundamental principles" of crit. (*Anatomy* 13). Page one, insofar as it is possible, would answer the question, "What is lit.?" For Frye, the v.–pr. distinction seemed "the most far-reaching of literary facts"; nevertheless, he said in 1957, page two still remained blank. It does not seem so now.

The chief functions of pr. in the modern world are the written representation and communication of information about events, processes, and facts that obtain in the external world. Many readers also implicitly believe that lit. itself, even poetry, makes truth-claims about the world despite the fact that on the surface it is a "fiction" (q.v.): if they believed it didn't, they would find it little worth reading no matter how great its entertainment value. Many poets, e.g. Auden, have assented strongly to this view. Most modern critics, however, would not assent to such a view, or at least not directly: I. A. Richards, for example, held that propositions asserted in poetry are only "pseudo-statements" (q.v.), and most of the New Critics followed Richards in insisting on an absolute distinction between the langs. of science and poetry (q.v.). Frye himself maintained that lit. "makes no real statements of fact" and is judged not on its truth or falsehood but on its "imaginative consistency" (see MEANING, POETIC).

Apart from judgments about truth-value, however, both common readers and critics recognize a distinction between v. and pr. Most speakers use "poem" as a synonym for "composition in v.": they expect poetry to be cast in verse. Yet the attributive term "poetic" is often applied as well to works not in v., works which readers feel are of greater insight, intensity (q.v.), or depth of meaning than ordinary writing. And everyone knows that pr., as Eliot once remarked, is written in pr. Such confusing usage raises the logical questions of whether all v. is poetry, or whether all poetry is in v. If the former is true, the latter, its converse, is not, necessarily. The contrapositive, however, "if X is not poetry, then it is not in v.," will be true if the proposition is true. Put another way, the questions are, to begin with, is verseform necessary for "poetry"? And second, is it sufficient?

We must first recognize that the two modes, v. and pr., intersect the concept "poetry" and its opposite, nonpoetry. Crossing these yields four categories, which Eng. usage does not capture at all well. Intensified or heightened lang. in verseform, i.e. "v. poetry," represents what most people automatically think of as "poetry"; quotidian lang. in verseform is "v. nonpoetry," sometimes accepted as poetry but considered doggerel (q.v.), sometimes denied to be poetry at all. Heightened lang. not in v. is sometimes called "poetry" or, better, "poetic," and if it has rhythmic or sound patterning at all, sometimes "prose poetry" (see below); quotidian lang. not in v. is, for lack of a term, just "pr." To define "poetry" as "a collective term for all poems" (Hynes) simply begs the question. Some readers find the differentia of poetry in heightened lexis and syntax (qq.v.); some find it in versification (q.v.). Either or both will lead to heightened emotion and compressed meaning. If the figuring of lexis and syntax is accomplished via strategies of repetition that are regular enough to be rhythmic, however, the two modes converge toward the middle and merge, producing intermedia.

II. ESSENCE AND FORM. Since antiquity there have been two positions taken on the distinction between v. and pr.; for convenience we may call these the *essentialist* and the *formalist* positions.

Essentialists—"affectivists" might be a better term—do not consider verseform essential to the definition of poetry and view poets as more and sometimes other than versifiers. For centuries, from Quintilian (1st c. A.D.) to romanticism, it was a critical commonplace that Lucan was a rhetorician or historian who wrote in v. and that Plato, Xenophon (*Cyropaedia*), and Heliodorus (*Ethiopian History*) were poets. The major Western proponents of this view incl. Plato, Aristotle, Cicero, Horace, Sidney, Wordsworth, Shelley, Arnold, and Croce.

Aristotle himself argues at the outset of the *Poetics* that metrical form is not a sufficient criterion for "poetry"; for him, the fact that the works of philosophers and historians are in hexameters does not make them poetry. Form does not supersede function in the Aristotelian view. Admittedly, it is difficult to see what Aristotle's conception of poetry is, fully, because the *Poetics* concerns itself mainly with dramatic and secondarily with narrative lit., giving only scant attention to what we would now call lyric; and the very sketchy taxonomy of types of poetry and music given in ch. 1 of the *Poetics* is both confusing and incomplete, either deliberately (Aristotle rightly points out that some forms do not have names) or by virtue of corruption of the text. Aristotle of course grounds his theory on the human instinct or drive for imitation (q.v.), an assumption which would seem to lead naturally to a referential philosophy of lang. (see POETICS) and a mimetic theory of lit. (see REPRESENTATION AND MIMESIS).

Nevertheless, it is clear that Aristotle makes plot structure (see PLOT) or fictiveness (see FICTION) the crucial criterion of literariness, as Horace does grandiloquence of lang. and sublimity (see SUBLIME). Sidney considers verseform neither a necessary nor a sufficient cause: "It is not ryming and versing that maketh Poesie. One may bee a Poet without versing and a versifier without Poetry"; verseform is "but an ornament and no cause of Poetry" (Smith 1.159). For Shelley, "the popular division into pr. and v. is inadmissible in accurate philosophy." From the essentialist point of view, if the criterion of verseform as the differentia of poetry is abandoned, readers will turn to heightening of diction and figuration (q.v.) of syntax as the criteria. There is, after all, little else.

Formalists consider verseform to be either necessary or sufficient—mainly the former—for the achievement of precisely those effects of heightened intensity, compression, or figured speech which are commonly considered the hallmark of "poetry." They believe that the resources of verseform are not available to pr., or only minimally so. The difference may seem merely a difference of degree, since of course rhythmical structure and sound patterning can be accomplished in pr. But whereas in pr. the constitutive principle is syntax, and through that, sense, in v. the constitutive device of the sequence (so Jakobson) is design itself, design manifested in sound and rhythm and leading to sense and order, i.e. the organization of readerly experience in the processing of the text. Consequently, the difference in degree of formal structure between v. and pr. raises v. onto another plane and creates a difference in kind.

The chief Western formalists incl. Gorgias, Scaliger, Coleridge (*Biographia literaria* ch. 14, perhaps the central text), Hegel, Richards, and Ransom, along with the Rus. Formalists, the New Critics, and Jakobson. Central to their position is the denial of any naive distinction between form and content; they do not consider verseform supererogatory. It is well known that several major Eng. poets, incl. Jonson, Pope, and Whitman, used as a compositional technique the practice of first making a pr. paraphrase (q.v.) of the argument, then casting that into v. But this should not be taken to mean that verseform is merely rearrangement of the words or some superadded wrapper, as Wordsworth seemed to think. Rather, we must see that poets who versify pr. texts, their own or others', or who translate pr. texts into v., are remaking one verbal mode into an altogether different one. For Coleridge, the very act of introducing meter and rhyme into a discourse fundamentally alters the nature of the expression, not merely the form: all relations between words (hence all meanings) are changed by a change in their principle of selection. The eye altering alters all.

Thoughts do not come into being independent of verbal mode, and consequently change of mode entails change of thought. As Masson put it, meaning "is conditioned beforehand by the form of the expression selected." This is the antithesis of Croce's thesis that the aesthetic idea precedes its externalization in a medium. Rather, the physical medium—its limitations, its possibilities, its strategies for formulating concepts, its orders—is an indispensable part of cognition, hence of the creative results of cognition. The New Critical insistence on the irrefrangibility of form and meaning, which is based on Richards and Coleridge and fundamental to formalist method, still seems necessary and valid, though not perhaps sufficient.

At a deeper level, however, it would appear that the formalist and the essentialist perspectives on the problem of poetic form are not two answers to the same question but answers to two different questions about the same issue. The formalist answer concerns itself with the poem as artifact, the essentialist with the poem as experience. "Verse," we may recall, etymologically means "turn," namely the turn at the end of the line (q.v.): v. is therefore lang. (1) given rhythmic order and (2) set into lines. But this does not mean that all v. is metrical, for meter is but one form of v. prosody among several, and even metrical v. has several subtypes varying in strictness. Consequently it is a mistake to say that what is not metrical is not poetry or even not v. The point is that v., pr., and poetry are not mutually exclusive or even correlate categories: v. and pr. are modes, while poetry, like drama and fiction, is, for lack of a better word, a genre. Any of the three literary genres may be written in either of the modes *or any mixture thereof.* The "modes," however, are not merely forms of writing, but rather forms of structure, since rhythm manifests itself in a linguistic sequence regardless of whether spoken or read. The distinction between v. and pr. is not one between media and essences, precisely, but between structures and effects. Can the formal devices of v. produce effects not obtainable in pr.? The preservation of the distinction demands that the answer be yes.

Lines of v. as manifested on the page are, after all, rhythmic entities before they are graphic entities: if the graphic lines do not show at least some kind of equivalence (q.v.) at the level of sound, they might as well be set as pr., whereas if lines which do show patterning are reset as pr. paragraphs, the meter or rhythmic structure can still be discerned, the line-divisions rediscovered, and the discourse reset as lineated v. This shows that the rhythmic structuring that we associate with v. is inherent in the syntactic strings regardless of presentational mode and would be left intact if print did not exist at all. One of the most interesting and revealing exercises in the study of poetry is to select passages and read them aloud, or else unlineate them and present them as pr., asking auditors or readers to judge whether they are pr. or v.; this was a salon game in the 18th c. Finally, it is worth recalling that much ancient and medieval v. was transcribed without lines, sometimes even without spacing, in order to save costly parchment—written by default, as it were, in pr.

III. INTERANIMATIONS. But making a simple binary distinction between v. and pr. has two shortcomings. First, it may give the misleading impression that what constitutes "v." or "pr." is merely a fact to be discovered rather than a cultural and aesthetic convention which varies from one lang. or v. system to another and, even within one lang., from one age to another. Second, it obscures all the more complex and more interesting mixtures, blends, and intermedia which result from each literary mode influencing the other, not to mention the interesting effects of speech forms. Indeed, all the varieties of spoken and written verbal art, pure and mixed, may be schematized as a constellation of types generated from the three gravitational centers, speech forms, pr. forms, and v. forms.

A. *Speech Forms* invade both v. and pr. in drama. In v. drama, esp. in blank v. (q.v.), speech is so rapid that the audience usually cannot discriminate ends of v. lines and has little sense of overt meter; as Wright suggests, there is only the more general sense of a rhythmical current. This does not make blank v. "v. only to the eye," as Dr. Johnson complained, for there is no evidence that auditors of poetry recognize even stricter verseforms (e.g. sonnets) quickly. It does suggest, however, that the visual form of a poem, its textuality (q.v.) or manifestation in print mode, is an undeniable part of its nature. It also confirms that rhythm itself, which is a phenomenon independent of presentational mode, is a necessary condition of v. In plays where verbal modes are used systematically by a playwright to differentiate characters or the social rank of characters—the paradigm case is Shakespeare's *Midsummer Night's Dream*, where the nobles usually speak blank v., the fairies couplets, and the mechanicals pr.—it is only that subtle but essential "rhythmical current" which enables auditors to distinguish versified speeches from pr. speeches at all. Note, however, that plays cast entirely in v., even heroic couplets, are no more "artificial" than plays written in pr. because all literary artworks naturalize their verbal mode, automatize them, so that auditors or readers take the mode as a given. It is only a question then of what effects v. mode may offer which pr. mode cannot, or vice versa. Failure to grasp this point occasioned much critical confusion in the controversies over blank v. and rhyme in the 17th c.

It would seem, then, that blank v. obtains such power precisely because it strikes a balance between rhythmic current and syntactic sense. That is the secret of its success. In Shakespeare's late plays, where the blank v. achieves more complex and less definable rhythms, the balanced play of phrase against line (Wright) becomes harder to hear, and all clear distinctions between v. and pr. verge on dissolution.

Speech forms invade strict verseforms to produce not a balance or fusion but contrast and tension. Heavy rhyming in short-lined v. with brisk, colloquial, and racy lexis produces the striking comic effects of light v. and satire (qq.v.), as for example in Butler's *Hudibras* (see HUDIBRASTIC VERSE), Byron's *Don Juan*, and Ogden Nash, and sometimes in Housman ("Terence, This Is Stupid Stuff"). The weight of expectation in the verseform is countered by the lexical surprise of the rhymes: sense springs open at these appointed places. But the ring of natural speech is quite possible in unrhymed lines as well, of course, e.g. Shakespeare's "I never saw my father in my life" (*Comedy of Errors*).

Pr. too contains representations of speech, such as dialogue and monologue (qq.v.); these are two keys to the success of the novel. Closely allied is what used to be called "stream of consciousness" pr., the staple of Joyce's *Ulysses*. These representations have the clear ring of speech and are fundamentally distinct from the nearly voiceless character of discursive pr., which has altogether different rhythms, lexis, and syntax from ordinary speech. Few speakers, for example, produce sentences beginning with conjunctive adverbs or absolutes, or sentences with extensive subordination. Pr. is not speech; it is speech more logically and elaborately wrought, an accomplishment made possible by a medium where reflection and rereading are encouraged and where the receiver-reader rather than the speaker controls the pace of the delivery of information.

The other conspicuous manifestation of speech forms in literary art concerns sound patterning. Increase in sound patterning, apart from purely rhythmic effects, appears in speech for a variety of effects. Among the first of these is the mnemonic one, for it is as certain as it is unexplained that sound figuration in short speech forms such as aphorisms, epigrams, and proverbs greatly enhances memorization. Longer forms include (apart from speech disorders) both conscious and unconscious patterning, as in echolalia and glossolalia. Most auditors do not perceive aphorisms or proverbs as pr. and probably would not classify the longer forms so either, though they do recognize them as verbally artful.

In lit., sound patterning is used almost automatically for passages of visionary or prophetic passages, from the Old Testament to Blake, and also for literary imitations (often comic) of the speech of illiterate people (e.g. Mistress Quickly in Shakespeare), drunks (Falstaff), and insane persons (some of Tom o' Bedlam's speeches in *King Lear*). It also appears prominently, of course, in the works of poets who themselves have been thought to have been insane (Christopher Smart, Hölderlin). In pr., the great modern masters are Sterne, Stein, and Joyce. In v., as sound patterning increases, apart from structural sound such as alliteration (q.v.) in OE or rhyme in modern Eng., meaning density is both increased and counterbalanced by pure pattern and the nonsemantic perception thereof. But critics routinely condemn poets such as Swinburne and Dylan Thomas in whose work sound-patterning far outstrips sense, a fact which suggests that matter—meaning, import, "prosaic" sense—is, in mainstream critical judgment, superordinate as a criterion to versecraft. The poets most valorized in our own time, such as Gerard Manley Hopkins, have pressed against convention in both directions.

B. *Prose Forms.* We must remember that modern notions of "pr." are localized and conventional, formed largely by the invention of printing, the shape of the codex page, and (esp.) the devel. of the novel. In the ancient and medieval worlds, the kinds of expository texts now automatically cast into pr. were often cast in v., incl. works on botany, zoology, astronomy, physics, history, genealogy, law, medicine, philosophy, mathematics, rhetoric, and grammar. So were fictional texts. All the literary genres were once versified; now only some are.

Further, pr. itself must not be thought of as the neutral ground or zero degree against which v. deviates; pr. of whatever form, literary or quotidian, is already an artificial and stylized form, heavily influenced by the conditions of writing and by the rhythms of discursive thought. And deviation is not finally the most productive means for distinguishing v. from pr. or for conceptualizing either of them, for both modes are already deviations from speech, and both contain an enormous range of variation within their domains. Even speech itself varies greatly with context. Ordinary conversational speech is mainly fragmentary and discontinuous in character, highly elliptical, often paratactic, sometimes repetitive and other times extensively reliant on tacit conventions of mutual assumption and implication. But there are many contexts in which speech is highly stylized and figured, such as sermons or political oratory, where gifted or trained speakers can compose figured discourse extemporaneously. The strategies for such figuration are the figures codified in Cl. rhetoric. Stylization, therefore, may be applied to speech, to pr., and to v.; it is degree of figuration or stylization that matters for heightening lang., not the presentational mode.

It is for these reasons that Frye and others have held that meter is in fact closer to speech than pr., in being a less complex form of stylization, and have used this claim to explain why pr. does not develop in some cultures, whereas v. has been developed in every known culture, and why, even when pr. does develop, it is "normally a late and sophisticated devel. in the history of a lit."

Pr. rhet. written into v. produces forms such as the neoclassical closed or heroic couplet (q.v.). In the couplets of Pope, the fitting of sentence structure with meter is so finely wrought as to seem all but inevitable, *sprezzatura* executed nearly to perfection. Here metrical structure and rhyme-binding are close and tight, and syntax structural and rhetorical, while lexis (pure word choice) is, by contrast, altogether natural. This *discordia concors* is what led Matthew Arnold to call Pope one of the masters of Eng. pr. That remark happens to apply more accurately to the enjambed or open couplet than the closed; in any event, it clarifies the more important point that quotidian diction and syntax inside any verseform always *pose the threat* of pr. Conversely, elevated diction or convoluted syntax heighten the impression of poetry even in simple or conventionalized verseforms like the sonnet— as in the sonnets of Hopkins.

C. *Verse Forms* also influence or overwrite pr.: in some cultures, such as Chinese and Arabic, rhythmical pr. (see PROSE RHYTHM) and even rhymeprose have been extensively cultivated. The chief effect of using rhetorical devices in pr. is simply to impose lexical and syntactic structure. Increased rhetorical patterning leads to parallelism, balance, symmetry, contrast, and "point" in phrases and clauses. If the patterning is extended down to the level of syllables and sound, pr. achieves effects which are rhythmical if not metrical, precisely as in v. Such effects are conspicuous in Ciceronian pr., with its clausulae, in the medieval *cursus* (see PROSE RHYTHM), in 16th-c. euphuism (incl. elaborate sound-patterning), in 17th-c. mannerist and baroque (qq.v.) pr., and in all religious and meditative pr. deriving from the penitential and sermon traditions and so influenced by the parallelistic structure of the Hebrew prosody of the Old Testament, such as Sir Thomas Browne's *Urn Burial* or Jeremy Taylor's *Holy Dying*.

Western poets have also experimented with v. novels; indeed, the line between such v. novels as E. B. Browning's *Aurora Leigh* or Nabokov's *Pale Fire* and narrative poems such as Puškin's *Evgenij Onegin* is, if one ignores page lineation, indeterminate (for discussion of both, see NARRATIVE PO-ETRY). Subtler manifestations of v. influence also appear: the two paragraphs printed as pr. in Fitzgerald's *This Side of Paradise* which are in fact Spenserian stanzas (q.v.) remind one of the sonnets embedded in *Romeo and Juliet*, and there is blank verse in Dickens' *The Old Curiosity Shop*.

IV. HISTORY. In the Middle Ages, intermingling of modes and genres was more pervasive than at any other time in the history of Western letters and not seriously rivaled again until the late 19th c. The importance of the processes of translation, imitation, adaptation, and paraphrase in rhet. insured that the boundaries between v. and pr. would be fluid. Translations and paraphrases were made sometimes by the same writer, other times at a distance of several centuries. Particularly conspicuous are the metrical saints' lives, the medieval equivalent of the modern popular novel: pr. versions abound throughout the Middle Ages. Several writers explored the *opus geminatum*, a work written in two versions, one v., one pr., typically for two different audiences (learned and lay); examples incl. Aldhelm's *De virginitate* and Bede's life of St. Cuthbert. These have their poetic parallel in works of metrical (quantitative) poetry adapted to rhythmical (accentual) form for the illiterate masses. Writers of metrical texts might also place a pr. paraphrase in a facing column, as Hrabanus Maurus does in the *De laudibus sanctae crucis*. School training in Cl. rhet. included standard exercises in translation and paraphrase, the *copia*, back and forth from Lat. to vernacular and from v. to pr., in both directions and modes: the young Shakespeare endured these exercises at school as did the young Augustine before him. Rhet. and poetic, later distinct, were mutually permeable in the Middle Ages.

In addition to works written in alternative v. and pr. modes, a variety of mixtures and blends were explored, some of which developed into important genres with long lives. Chief among the mixtures is the prosimetrum (q.v.), , a pr. text with lyric insets in a variety of meters, inspired in Med. Lat. by the example of Boethius' *Consolation of Philosophy* and extended to vernacular forms such as the OF *chante-fable* (q.v.), a performance sung and spoken by two minstrels in alternation. From such medieval exemplars, as well as the model of the *canticum and diverbia* (accompanied song and spoken dialogue—q.v.) of Lat. drama (Plautus), medieval drama developed the practices of (1) using v. and pr. modes to differentiate characters and (2) intercalating lyric insets or songs in texts whether v. or pr. Both practices were carried into Ren. drama, where even subtler transitions are possible: a character shifting from loftier to more mundane thoughts may shift from one mode to the other; or, under the pressure of shattering emotion, a character may (as more than once in Marlowe) run from v. into pr. in mid-sentence.

It is of interest that pr. was not developed extensively in drama until late: despite the appearance of early works such as Gascoigne's *Supposes* and later comedies, the success of Shakespearean blank v. and the 17th-c. heroic couplet was such that the first Eng. tragedy in pr., George Lillo's *The London Merchant*, did not appear until 1731; and pr. was not the staple mode of drama until the 19th c., a result of the novel. Ren. drama, following medieval precedent, first developed rhymed verseforms (esp. the fourteener [q.v.]), some of them very elaborate, and ornate rhetorical diction. Thereafter it moved (esp. in the hands of Shakespeare) mainly in the direction of natural speech; pr. was used mainly for contrastive functions in versified plays, and became the medium of choice only after dramatists had become more conscious of the page than of the theater.

In addition to mixtures were medieval blends: v. rhythm and rhyme influenced pr. to produce rhymed pr. (Norden) and the rhythmical pr. of ecclesiastical correspondence known as the *cursus*. Both of the two principal outlets for pr. in the Middle Ages, letter-writing (*ars dictaminis*) and preaching (*ars praedicandi*), tended to be rhythmical. Pr. also influenced v.: *prosa* was the standard technical term for the medieval sequence, on account of the wording of its close (see Curtius).

In the modern age, the two chief blended forms have both been movements from v. toward pr. First is "free v." (q.v.), which is the awkward and misleading modern term for a heterogeneous group of nonmetrical but still rhythmical or (at the very least) lineated verbal sequences. Many reactionary critics of the late 19th and early 20th cs. (e.g. Saintsbury) objected to free v. as scarcely v. at all, since it lacked the badge of meter, which would certify strict control of the medium, strict rules making for strong order in a rigidly hierarchical world view. Free v. is obviously literary and minimally v. by the simple criterion of being set in (graphic) lines even if it has no other rhythmical structure, heightened diction, or figured syntax, though many varieties have sought at least some kind of rhythm (see PROJECTIVE VERSE; VARIABLE FOOT). That fact, however, is only a fact and not a value judgment; absence of metrical structure may be deemed a pejorative by critics hostile to sweeping changes in the cultural conditions which valorized meter, or an approbative by avant-garde critics who welcome those changes. The blurring of the line (!) between v. and pr. is simply one literary index of an age which prefers to avoid sharp distinctions, or at least distinctions as traditionally drawn, and to prefer overlapping forms, blended forms, boundary conditions, and all more complex or more fluid composites.

Second is the prose poem (q.v.), developed in France in the late 19th c. and cultivated intensively again in America in the deluge after the Sixties. As with the rhythmical pr. which developed in antiquity, it is difficult to tell whether the modern prose poem developed from the direction of pr. or v. Since it has been cultivated mainly by poets, it would seem the latter. If so, then prose poets refuse v. lineation and the regularity of v. rhythm yet nevertheless write rhythmical or rhetorical figuration back onto pr. in an effort to attain a level of incantatory speech and incandescent consciousness which ratiocinative pr. cannot achieve, because it has not the means.

See now LINE; NARRATIVE POETRY; POLYPHONIC PROSE; PROSE POEM; PROSE RHYTHM; PROSIMETRUM; PROSODY; RHYME-PROSE; VERSET; VERSIFICATION.

D. Masson, "Pr. and V.," *Essays Biographical and Critical* (1856); R. L. Stevenson, "On Style in Lit.," *Contemp. Rev.* 47 (1885); D. Winter, "V. and Pr.," *JEGP* 5 (1903–5); J. W. Mackail, "The Definition of Poetry," *Lectures on Poetry* (1911); B. Petermann, *Der Streit um Vers und Prosa in der französischen Literatur des 18. Jhs.* (1913); Thieme, 374–75—lists Fr. works 1548–1912; T. S. Eliot, "Pr. and V.," *The Chapbook* 22 (1921); P. J. Hartog, *On the Relation of Poetry to V.* (1926); W. P. Ker, *Form and Style in Poetry* (1928), ch. 10; A. M. Clark, "Poetry and V.," *Studies in Literary Modes* (1946); M. C. Costello, *Between Fixity and Flux* (1947); Curtius, ch. 8; Frye; S. Hynes, "Poetry, Poetic, Poem," *CE* 19 (1958); N. Frye, *The Well-Tempered Critic* (1963); P. Klopsch, "Prosa und Vers in der mittellateinischen Literatur," *MitJ* 3 (1966); T. McFarland, "Poetry and the Poem," *Literary Theory and Structure*, ed. F. Brady et al. (1973); I. A. Richards, *V. versus Pr.* (1978); Norden; P. Habermann and K. Kanzog, "Vers, Verslehre, Vers und Prosa," *Reallexikon*; M. Perloff, *The Futurist Moment* (1986), ch. 5; W. Godzich and J. Kittay, *The Emergence of Pr.* (1987); T. Steele, *Missing Measures* (1990), ch. 3.   T.V.F.B.

VERSE-ART, VERSECRAFT. See VERSIFICATION.

VERSE DESIGN. See METER.

VERSE DRAMA. See DRAMATIC POETRY.

VERSE EPISTLE (Gr. *epistole*, Lat. *epistula*). A poem addressed to a friend, lover, or patron, written in a familiar style and in hexameters (Cl.) or their modern equivalents. Two types of v. es. exist: the one on moral and philosophical subjects, which stems from Horace's *Es.*, and the other on romantic and sentimental subjects, which stems from Ovid's *Heroides*. Though the v. e. may be found as early as 146 B.C. (L. Mummius Achaicus' letters from Corinth and some of the satires of Lucullus), Horace perfected the form, employing common diction, personal details, and a plain style to lend familiarity to his philosophical subjects. His letters to the Lucius Calpurnius Piso and his sons (ca. 10 B.C.) on the art of poetry, known since Quintillian as the *Ars poetica*, became a standard genre of the Middle Ages and after. Ovid used the same style for his *Tristia* and *Ex Ponto* but developed the sentimental e. in his *Heroides*, which are fictional letters from the legendary women of antiquity—e.g. Helen, Medea, Dido—to their lovers (tr. D. Iiine, 1991). Throughout the Middle Ages, the latter seems to have been the more popular type, for it had an influence on the poets of courtly love (q.v.) and subsequently inspired Samuel Daniel to introduce the form into Eng., e.g. his *Letter from Octavia to Marcus Antonius.* Such also was the source for Donne's large body of memorable v. es. ("Sir, more than Kisses, letters mingle souls") and Pope's *Eloisa to Abelard.*

But it was the Horatian e. which had the greater effect on Ren. and modern poetry. Petrarch, the first humanist to know Horace, wrote his influential *Epistulae metricae* in Lat. Subsequently, Ariosto's *Satires* in terza rima employed the form in vernacular It. In all these epistles Christian sentiment made itself felt. In Spain, Garcilaso's *Epístola a Boscán* (1543) in blank verse and the *Epístola moral a Fabio* in terza rima introduced and perfected the form. Fr. writers esp. cultivated it for its "graceful precision and dignified familiarity"; Boileau's 12 es. in couplets (1668–95) are considered the finest examples. Ben Jonson began the Eng. use of the Horatian form (*Forest*, 1616) and was followed by others, e.g. Vaughan, Dryden, and Congreve. But the finest examples in Eng. are Pope's *Moral Essays* and the *Epistle to Dr. Arbuthnot* in heroic couplets. The romantics did not value the v. e., though Shelley, Keats, and Landor on occasion wrote them. Examples in the 20th c. incl. W. H. Auden's *New Year Letter* and Louis MacNeice's *Letters from Iceland.*

H. Peter, *Der Brief in der römische Lit.* (1901); J. Vianey, *Les Epîtres de Marot* (1935); W. Grenzmann, "Briefgedicht," *Reallexikon*; J. A. Levine, "The Status of the V. E. Before Pope," *SP* 59 (1962); W. Trimpi, *Ben Jonson's Poems* (1962); J. Norton-Smith, "Chaucer's Epistolary Style," *Essays on Style and Lang.*, ed. R. Fowler (1966); *John Donne: The Satires, Epigrams and V. Letters*, ed. W. Milgate

VERSE LETTER

(1967); N. C. de Nagy, *Michael Drayton's* England's Heroical Es. (1968); R. S. Matteson, "Eng. V. Es., 1660–1758," *DAI* 28 (1968): 5023A; D. J. Palmer, "The V. E.," *Metaphysical Poetry*, ed. M. Bradbury and D. Palmer (1970); C. Levine, "The V. E. in Sp. Poetry of the Golden Age," *DAI* 35 (1974): 3690A; M. Motsch, *Die poetische Epistel* (1974); A. B. Cameron, "Donne's Deliberative V. Es.," *ELR* 6 (1976); C. C. Koppel, "Of Poets and Poesy: The Eng. V. E., 1595–1640," *DAI* 39 (1978): 2292A; M. R. Sperberg-McQueen, "Martin Opitz and the Trad. of the Ren. Poetic E.," *Daphnis* 11 (1982); J. E. Brown, "The V. Es. of A. S. Pushkin," *DAI* 45 (1984): 201A; C. Guillén, "Notes toward the Study of the Ren. Letter," *Ren. Genres*, ed. B. K. Lewalski (1986); M. Camargo, *The ME Verse Love E.* (1991); W. C. Dowling, *The Epistolary Moment* (1991)—on the 18th c.   R.A.H.; T.V.F.B.

VERSE LETTER. See VERSE EPISTLE.

VERSE NOVEL. See NARRATIVE POETRY.

VERSE PARAGRAPH. If a p. is defined as one or more sentences unified by a dominant mood or thought, then poetry, like prose, can be seen as moving forward in units which could be called ps. Many lyrics might be described as single v. ps., the sonnet as one or, if the *volta* (q.v.) be sufficiently marked, two. Further, because for centuries stanza was syntactically (as well as metrically) defined, the sense in elaborate stanzaic forms like the Spenserian and *ottava rima* (qq.v.) tends to assume p. form. However, most traditional stanzas are isometrical or isomorphic—i.e. identical in number of lines, meter, and rhyme scheme—and variety of effect is difficult to achieve in such poems. The result, esp. in long works by inferior poets, can be a numbing monotony of effect.

A distinctive characteristic of the p. in prose is of course that it does not have a settled length, that each individual p. may take the form most appropriate to the thought requiring expression. In poetry such freedom can best be achieved in narrative and descriptive poetry (qq.v.), where the ps. are often indicated by indentation of or spacing between lines. They are most prominent, however, in blank verse. (Rhymed v. ps. do occur—e.g. the irregular *canzoni* of Milton's *Lycidas* or the indented sections of varying numbers of couplets within the subdivisions of Pope's *Essay on Man*.) But it is in nondramatic blank verse that the v. p. as we customarily think of it reaches its fullest devel. Lacking the somewhat arbitrary organization provided by an established rhyme scheme, blank verse must provide units supporting the organization of idea such that the narration, description, or exposition unfolds in a series of stages felt as justly proportioned. In this sense the v. p. is a syntactic period, frequently a complex or periodic sentence, deployed in enjambed stichic verse so that the beginnings and ends of the syntactic frames conspicuously do not coincide with those of the metrical frames (the lines), with the result that meter and syntax are in counterpoint or tension.

The v. p. is a common feature of Old Germanic heroic poetry and is an important element in Eng. poetry as early as *Beowulf*, where sentences often begin at the caesura. But by general consent the greatest master of the v. p. is John Milton. Many of the most characteristic effects of *Paradise Lost*—its majesty, its epic sweep, its rich counterpoint of line and sentence rhythms—are produced or enhanced by Milton's v. ps. To sustain his ps., Milton employed enjambment (q.v.), interruption, inversion, and suspension, the device of the periodic sentence whereby the completion of the thought is delayed until the end of the period. The average sentence in Milton covers 17 lines, but often may cover 25 to 30. So powerful was Milton's influence on later poets that his voice, his distinctive rhythms, even his vocabulary and syntactic strategies can be recognized in much Eng. metrical verse of the 18th and 19th cs. (Havens). Whitman too, and the subsequent free verse (q.v.) for which he provided one model, makes much use of the v. p. (e.g. the first 22 lines of "Out of the Cradle Endlessly Rocking"). Thus far, however, no one distinctive free-verse p. has been devised—since free verse lacks the background of the constant meter against which the v. p. can be perceived to play, it is doubtful one could be—and when the v. p. is spoken of, one is still likely to think automatically of Milton.—G. Hübner, *Die stilistische Spannung in Milton's P.L.* (1913); R. D. Havens, *The Influence of Milton on Eng. Poetry* (1922); J. Whaler, *Counterpoint and Symbol* (1956); E. Weismiller, "Blank Verse," *A Milton Encyc.*, ed. W. B. Hunter, Jr., et al. (1978); W. H. Beale, "Rhet. in the OE V. P.," *NM* 80 (1979); J. Hollander, "'Sense Variously Drawn Out,'" in Hollander.   A.PR.; E.R.W.; T.V.F.B.

VERSE THEORY. See PROSODY.

VERSET This term is derived from the short "verses" of the Bible (cf. *versicle*) and etymologically refers to short lines (Occitan and OF); in Eng. it has been so used, esp. to refer to the lines of Hebraic and biblical verse translations, but in Fr. it refers to lines longer than standard meters in the later 19th-c. symbolist prosodies of poets such as Claudel. In this latter sense it denotes a Blakean or Whitmanesque line of variable but most often long length, neither rhymed nor metrical but organized by rhythmic and phrasal cadences. The presence of Whitman in late 19th- and early 20th-c. Fr. verse ensured that the Fr. v. was rhythmically oriented more toward verse than prose, however multiform its realizations. In Claudel's *Cinq grandes odes* (1910), the *v. claudélien* becomes a hybrid; now "line" and "paragraph" are indistinguishable except that the v. is clearly a rhythmic whole. The movement between degrees of rhythmicity allows an ascension from rhapsodic involvement with the

VERSIFICATION

world's primary elements, from a cataloguing "connaissance," to a less differentiated realm of omniscient "conscience." And even where, as in Péguy's verse (*Les Mystères*, 1910–13), the v. emerges from prose, lineation provides those variations in accentual prominence, length of measure, and markedness of juncture which bespeak the modalities of inspiration and response: prose is transcended by the poised and expanded consciousness of verse. In Saint-John Perse's work (*Anabase*, 1924), the v. confronts the reader with challenging decisions about segmentation and association: the v. is a journey punctuated by a variety of rhythmic thresholds and boundaries. If accounts of the structure of v. veer between ones which find in it a larger agglomeration of recognizably traditional rhythmic/metrical units, and ones which locate its rhythm in the movements of enunciation in a periodicity founded upon acoustic echoing and syntactic patterning, it is perhaps because the form is inclusive enough to tolerate their coexistence. See also POLYPHONIC PROSE; VERSE AND PROSE.—P. Fort, "Préface," *Le Roman de Louis XI* (1898); L. Spitzer, "Zu Charles Péguys Stil," *Stilstudien*, 2 v. (1928); P. Claudel, "Réflexions et propositions sur le vers français," *Positions et propositions*, 2 v. (1928); Y. Bozon-Scalzitti, "Le V. claudélien," *ALM* (1965): P. van Rutten, *Le Langage poétique de St.-John Perse* (1975); F. Moreau, *Six études de métrique* (1987); C. Scott, *Vers libre* (1990).
T.V.F.B.; C.S.

VERSI SCIOLTI (*versi sciolti da rima*, "verse freed from rhyme"). In It. prosody, verses (generally hendecasyllables [q.v.], i.e. *endecasillabi sciolti*) not bound together by rhyme or grouped in regular strophes. V. s. appear late in the 13th c. in the anonymous satire the *Mare amoroso* but were first cultivated during the Ren. as the It. equivalent of the Cl. epic meter the hexameter (q.v.). Trissino used them in his tragedy *Sofonisba* (1515; cf. his treatise *La poetica*, 1529) and in his epic *L'Italia liberata dai Goti* (begun 1528; pub. 1547), as did Tasso in his *Le sette giornate del mondo creato*. They quickly became the preferred meter for It. trs. of Cl. epics (e.g. A. Caro's *Eneide*, 1581). Despite Trissino's lack of success, however, a controversy arose between the advocates of cl. austerity and the advocates of rhyme (q.v.). In the 16th c., rhyme won the day, but in the 18th c. and thereafter, v. s. were used with great success, particularly by Parini (*Il giorno*), Foscolo (*I sepolcri*), Leopardi (some of *I canti*), and Manzoni (*Urania*). Alfieri almost singlehanded made them the standard meter for tragedy. In more recent times, the dramatist Sem Benelli used them for several dramas, and Pascoli adopted them for all but the last of his *Poemi Conviviali*. Endecasillabi sciolti are equivalent to blank verse (q.v.) and were an important influence on the devel. of that form in Eng. See also ITALIAN PROSODY.—J. M. Steadman, "Verse Without Rime: 16th-C. Defenses of V. S.," *Italica* 41

(1964); Wimsatt; F. Caliri, *Tecnica e poesia* (1974); L. Castelnuovo, *La metrica italiana* (1979); Elwert, *Italienische*, sect. 72, 57, 119; O. B. Hardison, Jr., *Prosody and Purpose in the Eng. Ren.* (1989).
L.H.G.; C.K.

VERSIFICATION.

I. ETYMOLOGY
II. COMPOSITION AS PRAXIS
III. TECHNIQUE

V. has traditionally been considered the art or craft of writing verse, as distinguished from prosody (q.v.), the branch of poetics devoted to the theory and analysis of the structures of verse. Verseforms look quite different from the poet's point of view than from the theorist's: the poet learns to recognize doubleness (difference) as the very nature of the word's two bodies (soundshape, sightshape), to think in rhythmical patterns, to know the chances (and dangers) of a rhyme, to discover the freedoms of constraint within a stanza, perhaps to feel the weight of formal trad. or even the freedom of invention, and so by these to find her way of proceeding. The theorist asks how a meter is related to its lang. medium, what happens to a verseform when transplanted into another lang., what a form is capable of, and whether there exist metrical universals. These would seem quite distinct spheres of interest, the one of "technique," the other "technical" (see below). But in fact it is impossible to draw any clear line between v. and prosody: even the poet herself, when explaining her work, must choose concepts and terms with which to describe technique, and those terms inexorably imply a theory. Poetic praxis always entails theory, even if unconsciously, for performance in a skilled craft implies competence, and competence implies an internalized system of procedures which govern the making and which result in demonstrable regularities of structure in the text (see PROSODY). The prosodist's rules (q.v.) are simply graphical representations of these processes. Theory and praxis are, in much of their middle ground, indistinguishable.

Such mutual implicature is natural and appropriate. Still, it is sometimes essential to recognize the differences between the processes of making and knowing. Unfortunately the lit. of prosody is of little help here, for critics have used the terms "v." and "prosody" with virtually no consistency. The final ed. of Robert Bridges' seminal *Milton's Prosody* (1921) is subtitled "An Examination of the Rules of the Blank Verse in Milton's Later Poems," but an earlier ed. added "With An Account of the V. of Samson Agonistes"; George Saintsbury's three-volume study of the practice of the Eng. poets is entitled *A Hist. of Eng. Prosody* (1906–10), but T. V. F. Brogan's critical survey of prosodic studies is entitled *Eng. V.* (1981). To the critics and theorists, evidently, an account of praxis *is* the praxis. Still, there are discernible routes of refer-

- [1353] -

ence which, when traced, will lead to valuable distinctions.

I. ETYMOLOGY. In its primary sense of "composing verse," v. descends to us from Lat. *versificatio* (noun) < *versifico* (verb) = *versus* + *facio*, as in Quintilian. *Versus* itself is "a turning," particularly the turning of the plow at the end of the furrow (cf. Auden, elegizing Yeats, extolling "the farming of a verse"): significantly, it is the ending of the furrow that creates, by demarcation, the furrow itself, and not vice versa. So the poet becomes a turner of lines (see LINE). Words for the making of the thing (*fersian* "to versify" is a regular OE verb, with descendants in *Piers Plowman* and *The Monk's Prologue*) and the thing accomplished (the *OED* gives as a secondary sense of v. "verse-form or -structure; meter") are old, but the noun of action is apparently recent: the first certain citation of "v." in Eng. is 1603. Late and unstable, the word seems quaint even in the Ren., and in the late 19th c., in the reaction to the numbing excesses of Ger. Philology, it took on the pejorative connotation of "pseudo-scientific," a coloring that still lingers a century later.

"Prosody" derives from Lat. *prosodia*, "the accent on a syllable," which is of interest because Cl. Lat. verse was quantitative, though the confusion of accent and quantity was literally millennial. In Ren. Eng., *prosodie* denoted "the Art of accenting, or the rule of pronouncing wordes truely long or short" (Henry Cockeram, *The Eng. Dictionarie*, 1623). Early Eng. grammars, following their Med. Lat. models, ordinarily treated sounds, letters, syllables, spelling, punctuation, and syntax, followed by a concluding section (commonly called the "Prosodia" or "Prosody") treating pronunciation (accent) and usually also verse (misconstrued as "quantity"). Verse was treated under this rubric because the grammarians conceived verse as spoken, hence subject to the rules of pronunciation, and because verse was considered the most important of all uses of lang. "Prosody" therefore came to treat the inflections of speech not marked by orthography and their organization in verse. Though "prosody" originally referred to only the former of these subjects, the term soon came (since the "Prosodia" contained both) to be used for both, as evidenced by Dr. Johnson's definition in the *Dictionary*: "Prosody comprises orthoëpy, or the rules of pronunciation, and orthometry, or the rules of v." Unfortunately, the word has been preserved in both senses even to the present day—for the prosody of speech, a linguistic phenomenon, and for prosody as analysis of verse-structure, i.e. verse theory. The conflation of the distinction, which arose historically as a mere textbook convenience, has led to some eccentric results in modern times, such as Jakobson's claim that the study of poetry lies entirely within the pale of linguistics. The view taken here and in the entry PROSODY (q.v.) is that while lang. is the material out of which poetry is made, the laws of rhythmical organization evidenced in verse are not merely laws of linguistic structure but rather one manifestation—like others in music and dance—of higher laws of rhythmicity as a perceptual frame and cognitive skill which humans use to organize the experience of any event or text wherein repetition is made systematic.

II. COMPOSITION AS PRAXIS. It is worth trying to assess what can be said about poetic praxis as performance in a skilled craft, here the craft of words. This is an important subject because praxis is a vast subject only dimly understood and because both poets and critics have at times objected to its study, albeit for very different reasons. For many critics in the 20th c., the study of compositional praxis has been derailed by the successive critical repudiations of biographical crit., the intentional fallacy (q.v.), the several versions of psychological crit. (q.v.), and the notions of authorial presence and voice (q.v.). Nor have studies of poetic performance (q.v.) been mainly interested in craft. In our time, only oral-formulaic theory (q.v.) has been willing to investigate, carefully, modes of poetic creation where composition and performance coincide. It has also been the only critical mode able to produce substantial results at correlating compositional processes, including their presumed motivations (e.g. speed of oral composition, fluency in fitting phrases together), with the structural features of recorded texts (i.e. the formula).

Many other critics, recollecting the excesses of both mechanism (so Schipper) and impressionism (so Saintsbury) in prosody ca. 1880 to 1930, have disparaged the study of versecraft as too "technical." These critics find the study of craft inimical to whatever ethos of insight or intensity (q.v.) or expressiveness or memorableness that the age defines as "poetry." For them, the poet's knowledge about forms and meanings is personal and intuitive, the kind of hand-knowledge accrued by any worker in a skilled craft such as woodworking or painting, knowledge which, once acquired, becomes a habit of action, not pieces of verbal information stored in the brain. But this is to misunderstand the nature of *techne* in art.

Finally, many believe, quite reasonably, that fitting words to any pattern is a process which is capable of infinite products, so that even superficially similar instances (say, any two villanelles) are profoundly different. Every instance Makes It New. Wright has made a strong case that nearly all the effects that are of interest in poetry are local and semantic. If so, abstract prosodic forms such as rhyme schemes and metrical patterns are only of limited interest; since they are invested with radically different meaning in every specific case, every case is unique. This is the empiricist view of poetry, the argument from organicism (q.v.). On this account, a comprehensive register or index of poetic forms would be mainly useless if it were even possible.

This may be true for the fitting of words into

lines, but at the larger level of text organization, versecraft can teach poets—and critics—what types of narrative, thematic, or structural developments are facilitated or even made possible by a given form, such as the tripartite logic encouraged by the quatrain-quatrain-couplet structure of the Shakespearean sonnet. And (computerized) analyses of forms can have any number of productive uses in providing illuminating comparisons between poets. Poets vary widely in the range of their formal interests. Some try many forms. Victor Hugo, for example, arguably "the most creative versifier in the history of Fr. poetry" (Grimaud), wrote 146 stanza forms in 153,000 lines of verse—but only 7 sonnets. Thomas Hardy, he of the most fertile formal invention in Eng. poetry, tried 170 different forms. Some try only a few. Some develop only a few forms extensively, exploring their expressive limits; others experiment. Some seek distinction by showing superior mastery of forms already handled by the great masters of the past; others repudiate these forms as worn out, preferring to seek out modes as yet unknown (so W. C. Williams). But we cannot know all this without taking stock.

III. TECHNIQUE. But we must realize that technique need have little to do with the genesis of composition. Hence study of v. does not infringe the "intentional fallacy." As for the two general theories that have so far been advanced about the nature of composition—that the poem is the result of inspiration (q.v.), or that it occurs only by dint of hard work (revision)—the artist will not see these as mutually exclusive. Intention (q.v.) there may or may not be in a work, but design there certainly is, and the study of design and its effects is the study of the transactions between a text and a reader. Regardless of how ideas or felicitous phrasings come into the mind—in a trance, reverie, or waking dream, read in the newspaper or overheard in a restaurant—the poet must work them into the fabric, stitching until the seams are rendered invisible, hidden artfully in the design. In "Adam's Curse," Yeats says,

A line will take us hours maybe;
Yet if it does not seem a moment's
   thought,
Our stitching and unstitching has been
   nought.

This is as much as to say that the processes of writing and of reading are, if bound together, inverse. It is therefore the task of any student of technique to study most carefully the kinds of fabrics and the types of stitchings that were used in the work so as to see how mere fabric became design, or order, hence art.

As an antidote to our instinctive modern aversion to whatever is "technical," an aversion which, let us note, comes from technology, it is worth remembering that Eng. *art* comes from Lat. *ars*, Gr. *techne*, i.e. "the knowledge of how to make something." Art therefore arises, literally, from *technique*, skill at making. Technique is therefore the antithesis of the technical. As one critic puts it,

> Discovering the secrets of a *techne*, particularly as employed by a great artist, is first and foremost a passage into delight. And since artists tend to work by taking apart the whole of reality and then reassembling it according to the techniques of their art, purely technical considerations may be the surest threads to their labyrinths.
>
> (Mullen 5)

Insofar as one comes to perceive technique, one comes to be able to understand how a poet managed her craft, how well she controlled the medium and turned it to her ends. This is the sense in which one can say that one develops an informed critical judgment, for it is not true of judgment as it is of taste (q.v.), to each her own: judgment surpasses mere taste in recognizing *skill* and accomplishment. Technique is not all of art. But absent accident, discovery, *furor poeticus* or the divine afflatus, it is the one compositional strategy left, and indeed the only one among them all which presumes the possibilities of learning artistic means and accruing skill over time.

Poets may learn technique consciously, by imitation of models, or by study of prosodic manuals, or by discovery and invention; and poets may very well manifest technique in their work without consciously knowing or even being able to articulate what they do: this is quite common. Making and knowing, even knowing and articulating, are distinct. Consequently, when the critic studies v., she must inspect not what poets say they are doing but what they actually do. What a poet says or even thinks she is doing may be quite different from what she can be shown to have actually done, a fact sometimes made manifest by poets who reflect on their own art (Coleridge's marginalia; Hardy's notebooks; Bridges' letters), who write mimetic examples of technical effects (e.g. ll. 337–83 of Pope's *Essay on Crit.*; Hollander's *Rhyme or Reason*), or who write critical essays on poetry (Dryden, Coleridge, Housman, Valéry, Eliot). What they say usually reveals much more about who they are and how they conceive their craft than about what in fact they did.

To study a poet's v., then, is to recognize which forms were chosen and whence they were learned, to try to assess the scope of the poet's formal invention (how many forms tried, old or new, in what modes, and of what difficulty), and to gauge how the chosen forms activated meaning. In the course of such work, the critic may well make use of statistical data, but her chief aim is to discover not so much what the instruments were—though that is an essential preliminary—as what the poet did with her instruments, i.e. what she did with what she had.

W. K. Wimsatt, Jr., "One Relation of Rhyme to

Reason," *MLQ* 5 (1944), rpt in *The Verbal Icon* (1954); R. Jakobson, "Linguistics and Poetics," in Sebeok, rpt. in Jakobson; W. Mullen, *Choreia* (1982); G. Chesters, *Baudelaire and the Poetics of Craft* (1988); G. T. Wright, *Shakespeare's Metrical Art* (1988).   T.V.F.B.

VERSO PIANO. In It. prosody, any line that has the principal accent on the penultimate syllable, making the line ending paroxytonic; It. line forms are named on this basis. Thus an *endecasillabo piano* is a line of 11 syllables with the principal accent on the tenth (e.g. Dante, *Inferno* 1.1: "Nel mezzo del cammin di nostra vìta"); a *settenario piano* is a line of 7 syllables with the principal accent on the sixth (e.g. Petrarch, *Canzoniere* 126.1: "Chiare, fresche e dolci àcque"). V. p. is the most common line form in It. See now ITALIAN PROSODY; VERSO TRONCO; VERSO SDRUCCIOLO.— Wimsatt; Elwert, *Italienische*.   L.H.G.; C.K.

VERSO SDRUCCIOLO. In It. prosody, any line that ends in a *parola sdrucciola*, a word with the principal accent on the antepenultimate syllable, making the line ending proparoxytonic. Thus an *endecasillabo sdrucciolo* of 12 syllables has the principal accent on the tenth (e.g. Dante, *Inferno* 15.1: "Ora cen porta l'un de' duri màrgini"). A *settenario sdrucciolo* has 8 syllables, retaining the principal accent on the sixth (e.g. Cielo d'Alcamo: "Rosa fresca aulentìssima"). The *endecasillabo sdrucciolo* was cultivated in the 16th c. instead of the Lat. iambic trimeter: Ariosto used it in his Comedies to imitate that meter in the theater of Plautus and Terence; Monti used it later in the *Canto d'Apollo* and in his *Prometeo*; Carducci used it still later in his *Canto di Marzo*, wherein he tried to reproduce even the accents and pauses of the iambic trimeter. See now ITALIAN PROSODY; VERSO PIANO; VERSO TRONCO; HENDEÇASYLLABLE.—Wimsatt; Spongano; Elwert, *Italienische*.   L.H.G.; C.K.

VERSO TRONCO. In It. prosody, any line ending with an accented syllable, i.e. oxytonic. In particular, an *endecasillabo tronco* is a line with the principal accent on the tenth, because the final unstressed syllable has been dropped (*tronco*, from *troncato*, "cut off"), giving the line 10 rather than the usual 11 syllables (e.g. Dante, *Inferno* 4.60: "E con Rachele, per cui tanto fé"). In the generation after Dante, Antonio Pucci began a sonnet with a v. t. ("Caro sonetto mio, con gran pietà") and used *versi tronchi* throughout the octave of another ("Maestro mio, deh non mi mandar più"). The *caccia* (q.v.) frequently presents examples of v. t. Later poets occasionally employed such lines for special metrical effects (Manzoni, Palazzeschi). See now ITALIAN PROSODY.—Wimsatt; Elwert, *Italienische*.   L.H.G.; C.K.

VERSUS PYTHIUS. See HEXAMETER.

VERSUS QUADRATUS. See CLASSICAL PROSODY; SEPTENARIUS; TETRAMETER.

VIDAS and RAZOS. In some mss. of troubadour (q.v.) songs, the work of each poet is preceded by a brief prose biography. These *v.* commonly mention a poet's social and geographical origin, name his patrons and (real or supposed) lady loves, and briefly characterize him and his work. Composed, like the *v.*, in the 13th c., mainly in Italy, a *razo* ("reason, explanation") relates the circumstances (actual or imagined) in which an individual song had been composed and may originally have prefaced a performance of the song. Both *v.* and *r.*, though extrapolating details from songs, also contain valuable independent information.—*Biographies des troubadours*, ed. J. Boutière and A. H. Schutz, 2d ed. (1964); *The V. of the Troubadours*, tr. M. Egan (1984); E. A. Poe, *From Poetry to Prose in Old Prov.* (1984).   J.H.M.

VIDEO POETRY. See VISUAL POETRY.

VIETNAMESE POETRY. Early V. p. developed on the basis of both cl. poems by Buddhist monks and Confucian scholars and numerous folk verses sung by minstrels and peasants at rural festivals. The genre used most often in popular verse is the six-eight (*lục-bát*) couplet form, a V. innovation in which a line of six monosyllabic works is followed by a line of eight. This form can comprise a number of tonal iambs or anapests, with both final and medial rhyme, as shown in the first four lines of *The Tale of Kiêu*, with *o* representing either of the two flat or even tones, *x* one of the four sharp or oblique tones, and *R* a rhyme:

o   o   o   x   o   oR1
Trăm năm trong cõi nguòi ta
   x   o   x   x   x   oR1 x   oR2
Chu tài chu mênh khéo là ghét nhau
   x   o   x   x   x   oR1
Trai qua môt cuôc bê dâu
   x   o   o   x   o   oR2 x   oR3
Nhung þièu trông thây mà þau þón lòng

A hundred years—in this life span on earth
Talent and destiny are apt to feud
You must go through a play of ebb and flow
And watch such things as make you sick at heart

Such couplets are found in proverbs and sayings, work songs, love songs, children's songs, lullabies, and riddles. But the alternation of hexasyllables and octosyllables can continue almost without limit, the number of lines reaching several thousand in the case of such long narratives as *The Tale of Kiêu* by Nguyen Du, *The Story of Phan Trân* by Dô Cân, and *Lục Vân Tiên* by the blind poet Nguyên Ð'inh Chiêu. A variation of the six-eight meter is preceded by two lines of seven words, thus engendering the "double-seven six eight" (*song-thât lục-bát*) meter, used in elegies and ballads and typified by Phan Huy Ich's or Đoàn Thị Điêm's tr. of *The Song of a Soldier's Wife* (a poem first written in cl. Chinese by Đăng Trân Côn), or Marquis Ôn-nhu's *The Plaint of an Odalisque*. All those moving pieces, first meant to be chanted, later became limited blockprint editions circulated among friends and connoisseurs and printed in *chu nôm*, the demotic script which in the 11th c. assimilated Ch. characters to transcribe individual V. words.

The same gentry scholars who created such popular stories in vernacular V. verse, several of whom remained anonymous, often authored prodigious poetic compositions well crafted in Ch. itself. Whichever lang. they used, their clear preference was for the 8-line stanza (*bát cú*), sometimes reduced to a quatrain called *tú tuyêt*, with each line containing either 7 words (*thât ngôn*) or 5 (*ngu ngôn*) and obeying the rules of Ch. prosody (see CHINESE POETRY). The 254 poems left by Nguyên Trãi in the 15th c., the collection composed by Emperor Lê Thánh-tông and the court ministers who clustered around him as the "28 constellations" in his Tao-þàn Academy, and the pastorals of Nguyên Binh Khiêm all reveal features of V. culture in a distinctly native rhythm—the caesura falling after the third syllable of the seven in the line rather than after the fourth, as in T'ang poems—as well as native imagery, allusions, and metaphors.

With the ascendancy of the Roman script (*quôc-ngu*), invented in the 17th c. by Western missionaries, both Ch. and "southern" characters lost their hold on V. education and culture. By 1918, the year the old-style literary examinations were abolished, the new romanization designed to facilitate assimilation of Fr. culture and the newborn press rapidly stimulated literary output among Fr.-trained writers. Thê Lu, Luu Trọng Lu, Chê Lan Viên, Huy-Thông, Xuân-Diêu, and Huy-Cân began to write "new poetry," an innovative genre launched by Phan Khôi in 1932, turning away from Ch. versification with its rigid rules for tonal harmony and parallelism, and utilizing new rhythms (e.g. 8-word lines) and new rhymes, as well as alliterative and assonantal reduplication and sound symbolism. Poets in and around the literary group Self-Reliance (*Tự-lục*) exhorted love, individual freedom, and the beauty of Nature in stanzas that were first printed in the group's magazines *Phong-hoá* and *Ngày nay* before appearing in book form.

Romanticism and lyricism took full advantage of the musicality of the lang. in poems by the original Nguyên Khăc Hiêu, who experimented with verse in 3-word and 5-word lines; by Trân Tuân Khai, who succeeded in combining the old and the new; and by Quách Tân, who sounded like a Nguyên Khuyên, a Trân Tê Xuong, or a Đông-hô, who exuded love of the countryside. This trad. of modern poetry couched in plebeian terms was quickly followed by such talented writers as Nguyên Bính,

Đinh-Hùng, Vu Hoàng-Chuong, and Bàng Bá Lân, who overnight became the idols of a city youth attuned to their newly expressed sensibilities. Whereas Buddhist, Confucian, and Taoist themes still dominated a segment of 20th c. V. p., new ideals of liberty and happiness crowded compositions by a new generation who, north of the 17th Parallel, concentrated on anticolonial and socialist topics or who, south of the demarcation line, lamented the moral decay, broken families, and disrupted careers that they readily blamed on the war years. Women, who figure prominently in the literary scene, inherited the trad. begun by female poets such as Đoàn Thị Điêm, Hô Xuân-Huong (well-known for her erotic imagery through clever double entendre) or Nguyên Thị Hinh (known as "Lady Thanh-quan" and noted for her sober and elegant cl. verse).

In content dependent on the social context and expressing a painful conflict between traditional (i.e. Sino-Vietnamese) and foreign (i.e. Western) elements, and in form rising above the old constraints to ingenious inventiveness, modern V. p. steadily increases its riches, whether inebriated with "achievements" of socialism inside the country or, since 1975, despondent over the travail of the emigrés' separation from the motherland, writers who yet express their nostalgia in prolific creations in expatriate publications around the world.

ANTHOLOGIES: Vietnam P.E.N. Center, *Poems and Short Stories* (1966); *Anthologie de la poésie vietnamienne*, ed. Chê Lan Viên (1969); *The War Wife: V. P.*, tr. K. Bosley (1972); *A Thousand Years of V. P.*, ed. and tr. Nguyên Ngọc Bích (1975); *The Heritage of V. P.*, ed. and tr. Huynh Sanh Thông (1979); *Le Chant vietnamien: Dix Siècles de poésie*, ed. Nguyên Khắc Viên (1981); *Fleurs de pamplemoussier: Femmes et poésie au Vietnam*, ed. Huu Ngọc and Françoise Corrèze (1984).

HISTORY AND CRITICISM: Trân Trọng Kim, *Viêt-thi* (1956); Duong Đình Khuê, *Les Chefs d'oeuvre de la littérature vietnamienne* (1966); Xuân-Diêu, "V. p. over the past 30 years," *Lotus* 26 (1975); Duong Þình Khuê and Nicole Louis-Hénard, "Aperçu sur la poésie vietnamienne de la décade prérevolutionnaire," *BEFEO* 65 (1978); Nguyên Tiên Lãng, "Panorama de la poésie contemporaine vietnamienne," *Littératures contemporaines de l'asie du sud-est*, ed. Lafont and Lombard (1984); M. Durand and Nguyên-Trân Huân, *Intro. to V. Lit.* (1985); Công-huyên-tôn-nu Nha-Trang, "The Role of Fr. Romanticism in the New Poetry Movement in Vietnam," *Borrowings and Adaptations in V. Culture*, ed. Truong Buu Lâm (1987).   D.-H.N.

VILLANCICO. The v. is a Sp. poem, often on a religious or popular theme, and usually composed in a short meter, to be sung as a carol (q.v.). The introductory stanza (*cabeza, estribillo, repetición,* or *retornelo*), typically brief, sets forth the theme to be glossed in the body of the poem, and frequently serves, in whole or in part, as the refrain

VILLANELLE

(*estribillo*). The body (*pies*) of the poem, composed of a few (usually about six) strophes, each of about six lines plus the chorus, develops the theme, often repeating verbatim phrases or lines from the introduction.—Rengifo, *Arte poética española* (1592); P. Henríquez Ureña, *Versificación irregular en la poesía castellana*, 2d ed. (1933); Le Gentil; P. Le Gentil, *Le Virelai et le v.: Le Problème des origines arabes* (1954); A. Sanchez Romeralo, *El V.* (1969); Navarro.   D.C.C.

VILLANELLE (from It. *villanella*, a rustic song or dance, *villano*, a peasant). Introduced into France in the 16th c. (Grévin, Du Bellay, Desportes), the v. first had as its only distinguishing features a pastoral subject and use of a refrain; in other respects it was without rule, although a sequence of four 8-line stanzas with a refrain of one or two lines repeated at the end of each stanza was a popular option. The form only became standardized in the 17th c., when prosodists such as Richelet based their definition on "J'ay perdu ma tourterelle" by Jean Passerat (1534–1602), a poem in tercets on only two rhymes, in which the first and third line of the first tercet are repeated alternately as the third line of the following tercets, and appear together at the end of the final stanza, thus creating a quatrain. Passerat's v. is of 19 lines and can be schematized thus: $A_1bA_2\ abA_1\ abA_2\ abA_1\ abA_2\ abA_1A_2$ (A_1 and A_2 denote different [rhyming] refrain lines). Obviously the v. is essentially stanzaic in nature, and this is how Fr. poets have treated it, extending it and contracting it at will; in his presentation of the form, Théodore de Banville quotes a v. of Philoxène Boyer "La Marquise Aurore," which has 25 lines, while "L'Ornière," one of Maurice Rollinat's large output of vs., has as many as 85 lines; Leconte de Lisle, on the other hand, uses only 13 lines in his "V." and 18 in "Dans l'air léger," which omits the final A_2 and takes other liberties with the final stanza's rhyme scheme.

While the Fr. poets who revived the v. in the later 19th c. treated it as a stanza type, their Eng. counterparts, however, invested it with the status of a fixed form. Although Austin Dobson tried to present the v. to the Eng. as he found it in Banville, declaring "there is no restriction as to the number of stanzas," his compatriots stuck rigidly to the 19-line Passerat model popularized by Joseph Boulmier (*Vs.*, 1878). Enthusiasts for the form were legion (Edmund Gosse, Dobson, Andrew Lang, W. E. Henley, Ernest Dowson, Hardy, Wilde, E. A. Robinson). While the v. continued to attract pastoral subjects (Dowson, Wilde), it also became a vehicle for *vers de société* (see LIGHT VERSE) and, in a small way, part of the attempt to find an equivalent for the Horatian ode in the Romance fixed forms (e.g. Dobson, *Tu ne quaesieris*, Odes 1, 11). Lang remarked: "There is a foreign grace and a little technical difficulty overcome in the Eng. *ballade* and *v.*, as in the Horatian sapphics and alcaics."

Surprisingly, perhaps, the fortunes of the v. have prospered in the 20th c. Following Leconte de Lisle, Auden ("If I Could Tell You," "Miranda's Song"), Dylan Thomas ("Do not go Gentle into that Good Night") and Roy Fuller ("The Fifties," "Magic") among others (Empson, Roethke, Plath) have explored the v.'s capacity to deal with serious, even metaphysical subjects while adhering to the strict 19-line model. A more recent tendency, deriving in part perhaps from Pound's free-verse "V.: The Psychological Hour," has sought to introduce greater flexibility into the traditional form by exploiting enjambment, metrical variation, and half-rhymes (James Merrill, Richard Hugo). There have even been efforts at a prose v., 19 sentences matching the pattern in repetition but not rhyme.

Banville describes the v. as "a plait of gold and silver threads into which is woven a third, rose-colored thread." The *A* refrains certainly have a metallic, unyielding character. Of Dowson's vs. Pound writes: "the refrains are an emotional fact which the intellect, in the various gyrations of the poem, tries in vain and in vain to escape." Banville's rose-colored thread, on the other hand, is to be found in the *b* lines, which attempt to withstand the conspiracy of the refrains and assert change and mortality, and for that reason have a peculiar poignancy and vulnerability.—T. de Banville, *Petit Traité de poésie française* (1872); E. Gosse, "A Plea for Certain Exotic Forms of Verse," *Cornhill Magazine* 36 (1877); A. Dobson, "A Note on Some Foreign Forms of Verse," *Latter Day Lyrics*, ed. W. Davenport Adams (1878); J. Gleeson White, *Ballades and Rondeaus* (1887); Schipper; Kastner; H. L. Cohen, *Lyric Forms from France* (1922); Scott; Morier; R. E. McFarland, "Victorian Vs.," *VP* 20 (1982), "The Revival of the V.," *RR* 73 (1982), "The Contemporary V." *MPS* 11 (1982); M. Pfister, "Die V. in der englischen moderne," *Anglia* 219 (1982).   C.S.

VIRELAI (also called *chanson baladée* and *vireli*). Originally a variant of the common dance song with refrain, of which the rondeau (q.v.) is the most prominent type, this medieval Fr. lyric form developed in the 13th c. and at first may have been performed by one or more leading voices and a chorus. It begins with a refrain, followed by a stanza of four lines, of which the first two have a musical line (repeated) different from that of the refrain. The last two lines of the stanza return to the music of the refrain. The opening refrain, words and music, is then sung again. The v. usually continues with two more stanzas presented in this same way. A v. with only one stanza would be a *bergerette*. In Italy the 13th-c. *laude*, and in Spain the *cantigas*, follow the same form. The syllables *vireli* and *virelai* were probably nonsense refrains, originally, which later came to designate the type.

The large number of variations and optional elements both in the *lai* (q.v.) and in the v. (as practiced by Guillaume de Machaut and Jean

VISION

Froissart, Christine de Pisan, and Eustache Deschamps) has produced much uncertainty among 20th-c. Fr. prosodists about how both forms should be defined, so that one must approach any modern definition with great caution. Most recent commentators follow Théodore de Banville (1872), who, relying on the authority of the 17th-c. prosodist le Père Mourgues (*Traité de la poésie française*, (1685), tried to settle matters once and for all by defining the *lai* as a poem in which each stanza is a combination of 3-line groups, two longer lines followed by a shorter one, with the longer lines sharing one rhyme-sound and the shorter lines another (*aabaabaab ccdccdccd*, etc.). Then, calling upon a false etymology of v.—from *virer* (to turn) and *lai*—he defined the v. as a *lai* (q.v.) in which the rhyme-sounds are "turned" from stanza to stanza; that is, the rhyme of the shorter lines becomes the rhyme of the longer lines in the following stanza (*aabaabaab, bbcbbcbbc*, etc.). Calling the v. thus defined the *v. ancien*, Banville goes on to describe the *v. nouveau*, which bears no relation to the *v. ancien* and is, if anything, more akin to the villanelle (q.v.). The *v. nouveau* opens with a refrain, whose two lines then recur separately and alternately as the refrains of the stanzas following, reappearing together again only at the end of the final stanza, but with their order reversed. The stanzas of the *v. nouveau* may be of any length and employ any rhyme scheme, but the poem is limited to two rhyme-sounds only. Here again, Banville merely follows le Père Mourgues, whose "Le Rimeur rebuté" is used as an illustration. John Payne's "Spring Sadness" (*v. ancien*) and Austin Dobson's "July" (*v. nouveau*) are the only evidence that these two forms have excited any interest.

T. de Banville, *Petit Traité de poésie française* (1872); E. Gosse, "A Plea for Certain Exotic Forms of Verse," *Cornhill Magazine* 36 (1877); J. Gleeson White, *Ballades and Rondeaus* (1887); Kastner; H. L. Cohen, *Lyric Forms from France* (1922); Le Gentil; P. Le Gentil, *Le V. et le villancico* (1954); M. Françon, "On the Nature of the V.," *Symposium* 9 (1955); G. Reaney, "The Devel. of the Rondeau, V., and Ballade," *Festschrift Karl Fellerer* (1962); F. Gennrich, *Das altfranzösische Rondeau und V. im 12. und 13. Jahrhundert* (1963); F. Gennrich and G. Reaney, "V.," *MGG* 13.1802–11; N. Wilkins, "V.," *New Grove*; Morier.   U.T.H.; C.S.

VIRGULE. See PUNCTUATION.

VISION may refer simply to the capacity of the bodily eye to see, under normal conditions, the qualities that constitute the appearance of corporeal objects. But the term and its derivative "visionary" are also used to refer to perceptions generated by means other than ordinary sight. Such perceptions may range from the images produced in the mind by memory, fancy, imagination, intuition (qq.v.), dream, foresight, or the reading of lit.

to the insights into spiritual reality claimed by the mystic in trance or ecstasy.

Psychological, epistemological, and religious questions are involved in theoretical discussions of v. There is no widely accepted general theory of v. and no agreement on the grounds that determine the authenticity, truth, validity, or usefulness of various categories of visionary experience. Clearly, positivist, Freudian, Neoplatonist, Christian, and Buddhist thinkers will differ strikingly in their definitions, explanations, and evaluations of vs. What one theorist may regard as perception of a supernatural being (angel or devil), revelation of mysteries behind the veil, prophecy of a New Heaven or New Earth, or the glory of the Beatific V., another theorist will regard as fantasy, illusion, or hallucination engendered in a mind conforming to culturally determined expectations, pervaded by fear, hope, or love, stimulated by drugs, or suffering from mental disease.

The numerous senses, literal and analogical, in which the terms "see," "sight," and "perception" are used make "v." a polysemous term in discussion of poetry. A poem may be considered as a report of a visionary experience or as a means for inducing such an experience in the reader. But the poet may be reporting what she (or one of her characters) has seen with the physical eye, the imaginative eye, or the spiritual eye. Thus v. may refer simply to a poet's use of visual images (see IMAGE; IMAGERY) as these appear in descriptive passages or figures of speech (Zimmermann). But more often v. suggests a content beyond those perceptions that can be explained by the normal operation of the physical eye. In cultures in which people believe in the possibility of interaction between the human and the supernatural, the v. of the spiritual eye is inevitably placed at the top of the hierarchy of visionary experience. To be great, the poet, like the prophet, must be inspired from on high (see INSPIRATION; POETIC MADNESS; VATES). The poet's function is to reveal God's will to others and evaluate their progress on God's "way." In the West, this view of poetry was common in the Middle Ages, esp. in devotional lit., in confessions of the mystics, and in the popular dream allegories (see DREAM VISION); it received its most exalted expression in Dante's *Divine Comedy*.

Recent scholarship (e.g. Wittreich, Kerrigan, Lieb) has stressed the influence of the Book of Revelation and OT apocalyptic prophecy in the devel. of a Christian trad. of "visionary poetics" which began with St. Augustine and received its definitive formulation in the Ren. in the work of Spenser and Milton. After the Age of Enlightenment, the influence of Milton reappeared in the work of the principal Ger., Am., and Eng. romantic poets and philosophers. Powerfully moved by the revolutionary spirit of their times, these authors, like Milton, regarded themselves as seers; they belonged to the "visionary company" (Bloom) whose mission was to convey an apocalyptic v. of a lost Golden Age, the present misery and crisis, a sudden conflagration destroying the corrupt modern world, and a paradise thereby regained. However, the epistemologies of the members of this visionary company differed strikingly; no unitary theory of seership emerged. And, after the failure of the Fr. Revolution to establish a New Earth, they tended to allegorize apocalyptic plot design and imagery (Abrams).

Following the model of another long trad. of biblical exegesis, they internalized the apocalyptic pattern, stressing the growth, tension, alienation, and renewal of the individual soul: the New Earth is to come now through inner transformation rather than political change. The means to this transformation is to learn to "see" differently. V. becomes imaginative perception, and poetry the most important means by which consciousness is expanded, deepened, or raised. Poets are gifted seers in the sense that they have already achieved this renovated mode of consciousness, though the claim to divine inspiration in the biblical sense remains as an overtone (see MEANING, POETIC; BELIEF AND POETRY). Thus, according to Abrams, v. was "naturalized," and he distinguishes three principal kinds of transforming perception claimed by the romantics: to see the wonder of the old and familiar (to return to the freshness of sensation of the child); to experience an epiphany in which an ordinary object or event is suddenly charged with a mysterious significance (Wordsworth's "spots of time"); and to perceive objects as invested with values different from those custom has accorded them (the sublimity of the lowly and humble). Abrams traces the continuation in the later 19th and 20th cs. of this concern with transformed ways of seeing in such diverse authors as the Am. Transcendentalists, Fr. Symbolists, Gerard Manley Hopkins, James Joyce, Wallace Stevens, and the Beat writers. Despite the influence of modern scientific positivism, the mystic modes of visionary perception never totally disappeared. The claim of transcendence appears particularly in the work of authors such as W. B. Yeats who were attracted to the occult or to Eastern religions.

In 20th-c. crit., one very common use of "v." is to refer to the worldview reflected in an individual literary work, the works of a particular author, or the typical literary works of an age. This worldview consists of ideas, attitudes, feelings, and valuations about God, nature, and humanity. Theorists have claimed that this "perspective," "ideology," or "v." is a precious wisdom, whether the author acquired it by supernatural inspiration or simply from life's experiences. Earlier 20th-c. critics gave a good deal of attention to formulating interpretive procedures for discovering and clarifying this v. which frequently was only implied in an author's works. Success in the pursuit of this goal was made more difficult, if not rendered futile, by the discovery in most literary works of hidden meanings, ironies,

ambiguities, and contradictory implications of which the author may or may not have been conscious but which form a subtext that often subverts the surface meaning of a work (see TEXTUALITY). Thus the formulation of a consistent v. embodied in a particular poem or in the works of a particular author or age has come to seem more and more an impossibility (unless the wreckage of deconstructed texts and the splintered hopes of their authors for communication with others can itself be called a "v."). At midcentury Northrop Frye was arguing that lit. is the dream of man, an imaginative projection of man's desires and fears; literary works, taken together, express a total v. ("the v. of the end of social effort, the innocent world of fulfilled desires, the free human society"). At century's end, alas, the total v. of lit. seems to be nihilism; lit., some now claim, reveals a human condition which is a meaningless chaos of human desires controlled at best by whatever power relations obtain at a particular time.

G. Hartman, *The Unmediated V.* (1954); Frye; E. Sewell, *The Orphic Voice* (1960); M. Krieger, *The Tragic V.* (1960), *The Classic V.* (1971), *Poetic Presence and Illusion* (1979); H. Bloom, *The Visionary Company* (1961); P. Wheelwright, *Metaphor and Reality* (1962), *The Burning Fountain*, 2d ed. (1968); N. Frye, *Fables of Identity* (1963); G. Bays, *The Orphic V.: Seer Poets from Novalis to Rimbaud* (1964); P. M. Spacks, *The Poetry of V.* (1967); S. Lawall, *Critics of Consciousness* (1968); E. Zimmermann, "'V.' in Poetry," *The Disciplines of Crit.*, ed. P. Demetz (1968); M. H. Abrams, *Natural Supernaturalism* (1971); W. Kerrigan, *The Prophetic Milton* (1974); P. Portugés, *The Visionary Poetics of Allen Ginsberg* (1978); J. A. Wittreich, *Visionary Poetics: Milton's Trad. and His Legacy* (1979); M. Lieb, *Poetics of the Holy* (1981); H. H. Waggoner, *Am. Visionary Poetry* (1982); *The Apocalypse in Eng. Ren. Thought and Lit.*, ed. C. A. Patrides and J. Wittreich (1984); D. T. O'Hara, *The Romance of Interp.: Visionary Crit. from Pater to de Man* (1985); J. Welburn, *The Truth of Imagination: Intro. to Visionary Poetry* (1990).   F.GU.

VISUAL ARTS AND POETRY. The parallels that have traditionally been drawn between the v. a. (painting in particular) and p. are based on Western conceptions of mimetic representation (see REPRESENTATION AND MIMESIS; IMITATION). Both painting and poetry have long been thought to be imitative arts, devoted to the depiction of human life and the external world. It is with this mimetic function clearly in view that Aristotle groups the various arts together in the opening of the *Poetics*; in a similar vein, Horace suggests in the *Ars poetica* (361) that "as a painting, so also a poem" (see UT PICTURA POESIS). Perhaps the most explicit comparison, however, is a remark attributed by Plutarch to Simonides of Ceos, who is said to have called poetry a "speaking picture" and painting a "silent [mute] poem." This intriguing epigram—

both parallel and distinction—emphasizes the representational force of both arts while also calling attention to their essential dissimilarities. It remained for Lessing to point out, in *Laokoön*, that poetry is fundamentally a temporal art, whereas the primary attribute of painting is spatial. Lessing and a host of subsequent theorists have warned of the dire effects of disregarding these crucial distinctions, but writers and painters have always been fascinated by the relations that serve to join words and images.

The most tangible relation between the v. a. and p. occurs when words and images are combined or when words themselves also constitute a visual image (see VISUAL POETRY). Pattern poetry (q.v.) such as George Herbert's "Easter Wings" or John Hollander's *Types of Shape* might be thought of as doubly representational, with visual shape and poetic argument simultaneously reinforcing each other. Concrete poetry (q.v.), moreover, normally privileges the "visibility" above the "readability" of the verbal image. In both shaped and concrete poetry, however, the text has become more fully iconic (in the semiotic sense) because it substantially replicates the object it represents.

Despite Suzanne Langer's observation that "There are no happy marriages in art—only successful rape," poets, painters, and engravers have managed to combine their work in a variety of interesting ways. The rarest occurrence—and also one of the most complex—is composite art, a fusion of writing and visual images from the hand of the same artist. William Blake, generally agreed to be the greatest poet-painter, created a startlingly wide range of compositions that vary from engraved poems with little illustrative accompaniment to ambitious visual images with minimal verbal reinforcement. Even when word and image are closely intertwined (as in some of the more successful *Songs of Innocence and Songs of Experience*), the precise function of this composite form is not necessarily consistent. The illustration may reinforce the meaning of the poem, or it may complicate or undermine it (as in many states of "The Tyger"); it is also possible that the poem will make little sense without the visual images that penetrate and frame it. In their interdependence of word and image, Blake's designs represent a provocative reworking of the traditional emblem (q.v.), in which motto, verse, and engraving all serve to illuminate the same idea.

Blake illustrated the texts of other poets as well as his own, and invariably his contribution must be seen as a powerful reinterpretation of Dante or Milton or Gray or Young. The visual illustration of poetry is normally not this ambitious, of course; even when the poet and engraver agree to appear in print together, the result—as in the early illustrations of Pope's *Rape of the Lock*—can be flat and insipid. Mutual illumination, as in Richard Bentley's witty and urbane designs for six poems by Thomas Gray, is much harder to find, but when it

does occur it reinforces our sense of a shared taste, sensibility, or ideological conviction that can find expression in either artistic form.

Poets who paint and painters who write do not necessarily combine word and image in a single text; it is more likely, in fact, that they will produce separate works, incl. works that are difficult to compare or reconcile with each other. This is certainly the case with e e cummings, whose large body of work on canvas seems unusually conventional when compared with his experiments in verse. But even where these relations are tenuous, the entangled careers of these "double agents" are often worth examining. It is useful to know, for example, that Pope studied with Charles Jervas, that Turner and Michelangelo were poets, that D. H. Lawrence—so often considered within the trad. of the novel alone—was, like Dante Gabriel Rossetti, an accomplished painter *and* poet.

Moreover, the v. a. serve as a topic for p., even when the author is not a poet-painter nor even closely connected with the world of art (as Ariosto and Aretino were with Titian, for example). Poetry can take the form of a treatise on art, as in Du Fresnoy's *De arte graphica*, translated by Dryden. A poet such as Marvell may structure his satire in the guise of "Last Instructions to a Painter"—an esp. popular genre within the 17th c.—or as a tour through a portrait gallery (as in Pope's "Epistle to a Lady" or Browning's "My Last Duchess"). Just as prevalent as satires are encomiastic poems in which the writer attempts to judge and praise the skills of the painter. One of the shrewdest is Lovelace's poem on Lely's double portrait of Charles I and his son, the Duke of York, in which he is able to gauge movement toward more naturalistic representation in portraits of the mid 17th c. In similar (if less discriminating) ways Waller would address himself to Van Dyck, Dryden to Kneller and Anne Killigrew, Pope to Jervas, Gray to Bentley, and Wordsworth to Reynolds. Baudelaire, himself a distinguished critic of art, devoted sections of *Les Phares* to eight painters and sculptors, and Browning—in "Andrea del Sarto" and "Fra Lippo Lippi"—provided his own imaginative and provocative reassessment of early Ren. painting.

Poems or parts of poems that describe specific paintings are traditionally said to partake of *ekphrasis* (q.v.). Ekphrastic poems (literally) speak to, for, or about a work of art; they are verbal representations of visual representations. The paintings (or other objects) they describe may be actual or fictive. Sometimes these ekphrastic fragments provide the only depiction we have of lost objects, thus voicing a pre-emptive verbal presence in place of an absent visual source. More often they are figurative encounters between words and image: encounters, as Mitchell has argued, that are not necessarily innocent of masculine, verbal assaults on a silent (or muted) object of desire or terror (Keats's still unravished bride of quietness; Shelley's Medusa). The relationship between the verbal and visual representation may or may not be clear. William Carlos Williams's "Portrait of a Lady" appears to be inspired by, or indebted to, Fragonard's *The Swing*. "Your thighs are appletrees / whose blossoms touch the sky," it begins, but the speaker's answer to "Which sky?" is, problematically, "The sky / where Watteau hung a lady's / slipper." Even when the connection is clear, the image that serves as the nominal starting point for the poem may quickly disappear as the poet pursues his or her own line of argument. In "Walker Skating" (the title alone suggests the paradoxes to follow), Brian Morris contemplates a handsome but chilly portrait sometimes attributed to Raeburn:

A grave liver if ever I saw one:
His speech would be more stately than
   his suit.
With folded arms and peremptory hat
The Reverend Robert Walker walks on
   water.
Ineffable superiority.

Morris focuses on how external representation (dress, paint) reveals the qualities that lurk within; he attempts to open up the painting, to envision the "sharp teeth, sea-snakes, / And the cold eye of the treacherous eel" that lie beneath the scored ice, baleful reminders of "How frail a foundation, laird of the kirk, / Is laid for your assurance. . . ."

Ekphrastic poetry is necessarily limited to a description (or verbal bodying forth) of a specific visual object; as Krieger has noted, "the poem must convert the transparency of its verbal medium into the physical solidity of the medium of the spatial arts." In so doing, ekphrastic poetry must have recourse to descriptive vividness and particularity, the corporeality of words, and the patterning of verbal artifices, all of which are essential to the much broader category of literary pictorialism. According to Hagstrum, in order to be called pictorial a description or image "must be, in its essentials, capable of translation into painting or some other visual art." It need not resemble a particular painting or school of painting, but "its leading details and their manner and order of presentation must be imaginable as a painting or sculpture." Visual detail constitutes the pictorial, but these details must also be ordered in a picturable way. The pictorial, moreover, necessarily "involves the reduction of motion to stasis or something suggesting such a reduction." It also implies some "limitation of meaning": meaning must seem to arise from the *visibilia* that are present in the poetical context.

Pictorialism therefore places stringent demands upon its readers; it requires us to develop the ability to *see* what the poet describes, to develop (in Pope's famous phrase) "quick poetic eyes." Pictorial poetry sometimes evokes the paintings (or *kinds* of paintings) that lie behind the verbal icon, as in the Claudes and Salvatore Rosas that are evoked in the shadowy texts of Collins' odes (Swinburne called Collins the "perfect painter of still life or starlit vision"). Or the pictorial poet may focus on the discrete image (q.v.), as Joseph Warton did in an unpublished passage in his Winchester College gathering book:

The Solemn Silence of the Pyramids.
   The Dark
gloomy Scenes in Mines. The Fall of
   the Nile.
Distant Noises. Indian Brachmins wan-
   dering by
their Rivers. Medea's nightly Spells.
   Meteors
in the Night. Griping of a Serpent or a
   Crocodile.
A Lamp in a lone Tow'r . . . . The Fall
   of the River
Niagara. Oedipus and his Daughters in
   the *Storm* a fine
Subject for a Picture. Woman with
   Child meeting a
devouring serpent in a Desart.

The relationship between these pictorial scenes and poetry is clear from Warton's titles: the images were suitable both as "Subjects for a Picture" and as "Similes" to be used in poems ("Loathsom as the twining of a Serpent round one's Body"). As Warton argued in his essay on Pope, "The use, the force, and the excellence of lang. certainly consists in raising *clear, complete*, and *circumstantial* images, and in turning *readers* into *spectators*."

Implicit in the practice of pictorialism is the belief that poetry and painting may both address themselves to the same issues (allegorical subjects, for example), depict the same scenes (often landscapes), or elicit similar emotional or aesthetic responses in the reader-turned-spectator or spectator-turned-reader (this is particularly noticeable in 17th- and 18th-c. experiments to depict "the passions" in poetry, music, painting, and drama). It is important for students of poetry to recognize, moreover, that these common elements—which are so often crucial to the rhetorical energy and vividness of verbal texts—have also played an instrumental role in legitimizing painting's claim to be a liberal art (Lee). If pictorialism serves as an index of the ways in which poetry has been influenced by or aspires to be translated into some aspect of the v. a., we must also recall how frequently poetry has directly inspired work in painting or the graphic arts, and not merely in book illustration alone. (The Shakespeare and Milton galleries of the late 18th c. are perhaps the best-known examples of how painters and engravers have attempted to recreate—sometimes slavishly, but often not—the imaginative world of their articulate precursors.) Recent analyses of paintings, moreover, have increasingly turned to semiotics (q.v.) and "visual poetcs" as they attempt to interpret the role of time and narrative in the visual arts (*Style*; Steiner).

It is precisely on this common ground, however—similar subject matter or aesthetic response—that more speculative attempts to link the v. a. and p. have so often faltered. Even attempts (such as Mario Praz's) to draw parallels between poetry and painting based on their contemporaneity have encountered serious opposition. Wellek and Warren caution that "the arts did not evolve with the same speed at the same time," and—like Steiner—they seriously question the usefulness of translating Wölfflin's famous characterizations of "closed" and "open" forms in Ren. and baroque painting into the vocabulary of literary analysis. More recent theory has therefore attempted to confront both similarity and difference in interartistic comparisons in a much more rigorous way. One influential theory, first proposed by Frank, draws attention to "spatial form" (or at least the thwarted temporality and consecutiveness) of modern lit., incl. the poetry of Eliot and Pound. Frank argues that, in their disjunctiveness and breach of narrative, modernist poems mirror the instability, the loss of control over meaning and purpose that we experience in an increasingly scientific and technological world.

This thesis has been radically broadened by Mitchell, who argues that "far from being a unique phenomenon of some modern lit., and far from being restricted to the features which Frank identifies in those works (simultaneity and discontinuity), spatial form is a crucial aspect of the experience and interp. of lit. in all ages and cultures." Mitchell's task is to convince us that temporality and spatiality are not necessarily at odds with each other, that we shall in fact encounter interpretive difficulties whenever we attempt to analyze the function of one without considering the role of the other. In *Iconology*, esp., he attempts to expose the ideological assumptions on which interartistic difference is based. He proposes that "there is no *essential* difference between poetry and painting, no difference, that is, that is given for all time by the inherent natures of the media, the objects they represent, or the laws of the human mind." Each culture will simply sort out the distinctive qualities of its mimetic symbols according to the various differences that are in effect at the time. The *paragone* "or debate of poetry and painting is never just a contest between two kinds of signs, but a struggle between body and soul, world and mind, nature and culture," a critique that he applies to the aesthetic treatises of Lessing and Burke (see ICONICITY; ICONOLOGY).

A quite different approach lies in the analysis of artistic structures. Wellek and Warren conceded at least this to the historical comparison of the arts, that it might be profitable to examine "how the norms of art are tied to specific social classes and thus subject to uniform changes, or how aesthetic values change with social revolutions." But they held out more hope for what they called "the most central approach to a comparison of the arts," which would be based on "an analysis of the actual objects of art, and thus of their structural relationships." When Steiner analyzes an ekphrastic poem by Williams within the context of the Brueghel painting on which it is based, for example, she eschews history in order to study the "ever-changing set of correlations by painters and writers, who are free to stress different elements of the structures of their art in order to achieve" a correspondence. An interartistic parallel, she argues, "is not dictated by the pre-existent structures of the arts involved; instead, it is an exploration of how these two structures can be aligned." Semiotics (q.v.), she claims, having defined the terms in which we examine different sign systems, has made the analogy between lit. and painting a more interesting area of investigation.

A more historical approach has been offered by Abel, who has deftly shown how the 18th-c. concern with thematic subject matter gave way to quite different values during the romantic period: "As the study of iconography is appropriate to the relationship between two arts in which content is primary, and the emphasis on different signs is appropriate to arts in which the nature of the sign is considered to be primary, the study of relationships among the signs themselves is appropriate to arts in which the power of imagination (q.v.) is held the primary feature." The similarity between Baudelaire's poems and Delacroix's paintings does not derive from their subjects or from the actual pattern of their signs but "from their common emphasis on establishing interrelationships achieved in the different ways dictated by their different signs." Two works may be alike as wholes but not in their individual features; despite their stylistic differences, "the functions of these different methods are the same in both the arts: to balance form and movement in an interrelated whole."

A final, more empirical approach—combining reader-response crit. (q.v.) and the theory of spatial form with a common-sense appraisal of what has worked best in earlier scholarship—has been proposed by Gilman, who isolates three areas of discourse that, when combined, he believes will form a workable comparative method. These are "the study of cultural concerns that influence expression in the various artistic media; the construction of likely analogies (with proper regard for the limitations of the analogical relationship); and the testing of the fruitfulness of such analogies in the experience of the witness" (the reader and viewer). If the analogy is worth making, he argues, "the sister arts should strike sparks whose light is only visible from an interdisciplinary point of view." See also CUBISM; DADA; DESCRIPTIVE POETRY; EKPHRASIS; ENARGEIA; FUTURISM; IMAGE; MINIMALISM; NATURE; SURREALISM; cf. MUSIC AND POETRY; SCULPTURE AND POETRY.

VISUAL POETRY

J. Dryden, *A Parallel of P. and Painting* (1695); G. Lessing, *Laokoön* (1766); I. Babbitt, *The New Laokoön* (1910); K. Borinski, *Die Antike in Poetik und Kunsttheorie*, 2 v. (1914–24); C. B. Tinker, *Painter and Poet* (1938); T. M. Greene, *The Arts and the Art of Crit.* (1940); R. W. Lee, *"Ut Pictura Poesis"* (1940); J. Frank, "Spatial Form in Mod. Lit." (1945), rpt. in *The Widening Gyre* (1963); E. Souriau, *La Correspondance des arts* (1947); W. Stevens, *The Necessary Angel* (1951); H. A. Hatzfeld, *Lit. through Art* (1952); Curtius; S. Langer, *Feeling and Form* (1953), "Deceptive Analogies: Specious and Real Relationships Among the Arts," *Problems of Art* (1957); Wellek and Warren, ch. 11; Wimsatt and Brooks, ch. 13; J. H. Hagstrum, *The Sister Arts* (1958); G. Bebermeyer, "Literatur und bildende Kunst," *Reallexikon* 2.82–103; I. Jack, *Keats and the Mirror of Art* (1967); M. Krieger, "The Ekphrastic Principle," *The Play and Place of Crit.* (1967); T. Munro, *The Arts and their Interrelations* (1967); *A Bibl. on the Relations of Lit. and the Other Arts 1952–1967* (1968); L. Lipking, *The Ordering of the Arts in 18th-C. England* (1970), "Quick Poetic Eyes: Another Look at Literary Pictorialism," *Articulate Images*, ed. R. Wendorf (1983)—substantial bibl.; M. R. Pointon, *Milton and Eng. Art* (1970); M. Praz, *Mnemosyne* (1970); I. Tayler, *Blake's Illustration to the Poems of Gray* (1971); D. Rosand, "*Ut Pictor Poeta*: Meaning in Titian's *Poesie*," *NLH* 3 (1972); J. D. Hunt, *The Figure in the Landscape* (1976); M. R. Brownell, *Alexander Pope and the Arts of Georgian England* (1978); *The Relationship of Painting and Lit.: A Guide to Information Sources*, ed. E. L Huddleston and D. A. Noverr (1978); W. J. T. Mitchell, *Blake's Composite Art* (1978), *Iconology* (1986); E. B. Gilman, *The Curious Perspective* (1978); E. Abel, "Redefining the Sister Arts," and W. J. T. Mitchell, "Spatial Form in Lit.: Toward a General Theory," *The Lang. of Images* (1980); R. Halsband, "*The Rape of the Lock*" and its Illustrations, 1714–1896 (1980); *Ezra Pound and the V. A.*, ed. H. Zinnes (1980); M. A. Caws, *The Eye in the Text* (1981); L. Gent, *Picture and Poetry 1560–1620* (1981); W. Steiner, *The Colors of Rhet.* (1982), *Pictures of Romance* (1988); J. M. Croisille, *Poésie et art figuré de Néron aux Flaviens* (1982); R. A. Goodrich, "Plato on P. and Painting," *BJA* 22 (1982); W. Marling, *W. C. Williams and the Painters 1909–1923* (1982); U. Weisstein, "Lit. and the V. A.," *Interrelations of Lit.*, ed. J.-P. Barricelli and J. Gibaldi (1982)—with bibl.; W. Trimpi, *Muses of One Mind* (1983); H. M. Sayre, *The Visual Text of W. C. Williams* (1983); W. S. Heckscher, *Art and Lit.: Studies in Relationship* (1985); E. B. Loizeaux; *Yeats and the V. A.* (1986); C. Pace, "'Delineated lives': Themes and Variations in 17th-c. Poems about Portraits," *Word & Image* 2 (1986); M. Roston, *Ren. Perspectives in Lit. and the V. A.* (1987), *Changing Perspectives in Lit. and the V. A.* (1990); D. Scott, *Picturalist Poetics* (1987); M. A. Cohen, *Poet and Painter* (1987); *Style* 22, 2 (1988); *Poets on Painters*, ed. J. D. McClatchy (1988); *Teaching Lit. and Other Arts*, ed. J.-P. Barricelli et al.

(1990); C. Hulse, *The Rule of Art* (1990); T. J. Hines, *Collaborative Form* (1991).   R.W.

VISUAL POETRY.

  I. FUNCTIONS
  II. DEVELOPMENT
  III. FREE VERSE
  IV. VIDEO POETRY

V. p. is poetry composed for the eye as well as, or more than, for the ear. All printed poetry is v. p. in a broad sense, in that when we read the poem the v. form affects how we read it and so contributes to our experience of its sound, movement, and meaning. In traditional verse, however, the written text serves mainly a notational role, and its v. aspects are subordinate to the oral form they represent. In v. p. in the strict sense, on the other hand, the v. form of the text becomes an object for apprehension in its own terms. As Mooij points out, "written poetry allows for devices of foregrounding not available to oral poetry." Among the devices for creating v. form that written lang. furnishes the poet are lineation, line-length, line-grouping, indentation, intra- and interlinear white space, punctuation (q.v.), capitalization, and size and style of type.

In general, the v. form of a poem may be figurative or nonfigurative; if figurative, it may be mimetic or abstract. The v. form of most poems is nonfigurative: such poems are isometrical or heterometrical, hence consist of regular or irregular blocks of long or short lines. Open arrangements of lines on the page space are usually also nonfigurative. This is not to say that such poems are not v. p., however; their v. form may still be important. In the case of short poems, the shape of the whole poem is apprehended immediately as open or dense, balanced or imbalanced, even or uneven, simple or intricate. It is worth remembering that the overwhelming majority of lyric poems are meant to fit on a codex page, hence to meet the reader's eye as a simultaneously apprehensible whole. In stanzaic poems, the regular partitioning of the text may convey a sense of order and control and generate an expectation of regular closure. Further, the individual stanzas themselves are apprehensible v. units. Stanzas in symmetrical shapes may suggest stability or stillness, while asymmetrical shapes may suggest instability or movement in a direction. Stanzas of complex shape may convey a sense of elaborate artifice. For the reader steeped in poetry, the v. forms of stanzas also carry resonances and echoes from trad.: they recall antecedent poems written in stanzas of similar shape. The basic shape of the Sapphic (q.v.) stanza, for example, is recognizable even in extreme variations. Printing stanzas with lines of different lengths or rhymes indented different amounts enhances the sense of their order and pattern, as in John Donne's *Songs and Sonnets*.

In Cl. and Ren. pattern poetry (q.v.) we find

examples of figurative v. form that is mimetic: the printed text takes the shape of objects, such as altars or wings; there are also 20th-c. examples of mimetic v. form, among them Apollinaire's calligrammes (q.v.) and some concrete poetry (q.v.). Poems in the shape of geometric figures such as circles and lozenges, another kind of pattern poetry, realize the possibility of figurative v. form that is abstract: in the Ren., 15 such forms are enumerated by Puttenham. Less rigidly geometric forms are not uncommon in conventional poetry (Ranta).

I. FUNCTIONS. The viability of v. p. as a literary mode depends directly on the functions that can be served by v. form. These fall into two classes: (a) those which reinforce the sense of the poem's unity and autonomy (qq.v.), and (b) those which tend to be disintegrative and intertextual. In group (a) we can enumerate six functions: (1) to lend prominence to phonological, syntactic, or rhetorical structures in the text (this would include scoring for performance and the use of white space to express emotion, invite contemplation, or signal closure); (2) to indicate juxtapositions of images and ideas; (3) to signal shifts in topic, tone, or perspective; (4) to render iconically the subject of the poem or an object referred to in it (incl. the use of white space as an icon of space, whiteness, distance, void, or duration); (5) to present the reader with an abstract shape of energy; and (6) to help foreground the text as an aesthetic object. In group (b) we can discriminate a further six functions: (1) to signal a general or particular relation to poetic trad.; (2) to allude to various other genres of printed texts; (3) to engage and sustain reader attention by creating interest and texture; (4) to cross-cut other textual structures, producing counterpoint between two or more structures occupying the same words; (5) to heighten the reader's awareness of the reading process; and (6) to draw attention to particular features of the text and, more generally, to defamiliarize aspects of lang., writing, and textuality (q.v.). The v. form of a poem can of course realize several different functions, even inconsistent ones, at once.

II. DEVELOPMENT. Historically, "all poetry is originally oral, and the earliest inscriptions of it were clearly ways of preserving material after the trad. of recitation had changed or been lost" (Hollander). Subsequently, "the development has been from . . . v. organization of phonological data . . . to a v. organization that carries meaning without reference to the phonological" (Cummings and Simmons). Finally, "once the inscribed text was firmly established as a standard . . . end-product of literary art and typical object of literary appreciation, it was only natural that the literary artist would exploit the rich aesthetic possibilities offered by the inscribed medium" (Shusterman). V. effects have been exploited at least from ca. 300 B.C. in various modes of v. p. and in mixed-media works.

Perhaps the best known of the modes of v. p. is pattern poetry; *versus intexti*, first composed in the 4th c. and reaching their fullest devel. in the work of Hrabanus Maurus (9th c), constitute a lesser known subgenre of pattern poetry. Such poems were composed on a grid, 35 squares by 35, each square containing a letter, with type size and, later, color and outlining used to distinguish v. images from the background of the rest of the text. In the Ren. flourished the mixed-media genre of the emblem (q.v.), which typically comprised a short motto, a picture, and an explanatory, moralizing poem. An ancient v. genre, the acrostic (q.v.), subverts the convention of reading from left to right and from top to bottom. Inscriptions, originally cut in stone with no regard for the appearance of the text, acquired beautiful lettering in Roman monumental art, which was reproduced and imitated in the Ren. In the 16th and 17th cs., esp. in northern Italy, they flourished briefly as a literary genre in printed books (Sparrow). The form, used mainly for religious and political eulogy, was really lineated prose—prose composed and printed in centered lines of uneven lengths, with the line-divisions supporting the sense.

The 20th c. has seen an abundance of highly v. works. These were heralded, just before the turn of the century, by Stéphane Mallarmé's late work "Un coup de dés jamais n'abolira le hasard," a v. composition in two-page spreads employing various type sizes and abundant white space. Early in the 20th c. appeared the calligrammes of Apollinaire, in which lettering (often handwriting) of different sizes typically sketches the shape of an object (e.g. a smoking cigar). The typographical experiments of futurism and dada (qq.v.), the typewriter compositions of the Am. poet e e cummings, and concrete poetry all use v. form to overcome the transparency of the medium, to make written lang. palpable and the poem thing-like.

III. FREE VERSE. V. form plays a more important role in the prosody of free verse (q.v.) than in that of metrical verse. One recognized function in free verse is scoring the text for performance. Charles Olson in his 1950 essay "Projective Verse" (q.v.) claimed that there should be a direct relationship between the amount of white space and the length of pause; different marks of punctuation could also be used to signal different lengths of pause. But regardless of whether it signals pause, intra- or interlinear white space can fulfill such mimetic, expressive, and rhetorical functions as (1) iconically rendering space, distance, length of time, void, silence, or whiteness; (2) signaling emotion too great for words; and (3) inviting the reader to take time for contemplation of the preceding text, signaling closure. Many free-verse poets exploit these possibilities through arrangement of text in the page space, as does Denise Levertov in this passage from "The Five-Day Rain":

Sequence broken, tension
  of sunlight broken.
    So light a rain

fine shreds
pending above the rigid leaves.

In other free-verse poems, esp. many of the experiments of e e cummings, white space and unconventional typography have the effect of defamiliarizing split or isolated textual elements. Lineation is often used to juxtapose images, as in Ezra Pound's famous imagist poem "In a Station of the Metro." In short-line free verse with normative strong enjambment (q.v.), lineation sets up a counterpoint to the syntactic structure of the text, i.e. to the phrasing with which it would normally be spoken. Much modernist free verse tends to eschew line-initial capitals, which otherwise give v. prominence to the line as a unit. In long-line free verse, when capitals are used only at the beginnings of sentences, lineation tends to be submerged in syntax.

Free-verse poets, notably W. C. Williams, sometimes arrange their lines in "sight-stanzas." Whereas traditional stanzas can be described in terms of meter and rhyme scheme, such couplets, tercets, and quatrains (qq.v.) are perceptible as stanzas only by virtue of their having equal numbers of lines and creating iterated v. patterns. In verse arranged in sight-stanzas, tight syntactic and semantic connections typically extend across stanza boundaries, while major syntactic and semantic boundaries occur with stanzas. The separation of v. from other semantic aspects of the text's form liberates a previously subservient (pattern-marking) element from previously privileged (pattern-making) elements, while the v. order may compensate for considerable looseness of syntax or argument.

IV. VIDEO POETRY. The computer has introduced a new medium of text production and display, one which opens new possibilities for v. p. Besides facilitating the creation of spatial form, the integration of graphic elements with text, the automated generation of text (see COMPUTER POETRY), and the use of color, the computer, by putting the pace of appearance and disappearance of segments of text under control of the poet, allows temporal rhythms to be realized visually. In such electronic texts, temporality, hitherto a primary aspect of the prosody of oral poetry, becomes central to v. p. See also CONCRETE POETRY; LETTRISME.

G. Puttenham, *The Arte of Eng. Poesie* (1589), rpt. in Smith; J. Sparrow, *Visible Words* (1969); R. Massin, *La Lettre et l'image,* 2d ed. (1973); *Speaking Pictures,* ed. M. Klonsky (1975)—anthol.; J. J. A. Mooij, "On the 'Foregrounding' of Graphic Elements in Poetry," *Comparative Poetics,* ed. D. W. Fokkema et al. (1976); J. Ranta, "Geometry, Vision, and Poetic Form," *CE* 39 (1978); *V. Lit. Crit.,* ed. R. Kostelanetz (1979); R. Kostelanetz, *The Old Poetries and the New* (1981); Morier, s.v. "Blanchissement," "Vide"; R. Shusterman, "Aesthetic Blindness to Textual Visuality," *JAAC* 41 (1982); H. M.

Sayre, *The V. Text of W. C. Williams* (1983); M. Cummings and R. Simmons, "Graphology," *The Lang. of Lit* (1983); C. Taylor, *A Poetics of Seeing* (1985); S. Cushman, *W. C. Williams and the Meanings of Measure* (1985), ch. 2; Hollander; W. Bohn, *The Aesthetics of V. P., 1914–1928* (1986); R. Cureton, "V. Form in e e cummings' *No Thanks,*" *Word & Image* 2 (1986); *The Line in Postmodern Poetry,* ed. R. Frank and H. Sayre (1988). E.B.

VISUAL PROSODY. See VISUAL POETRY.

VISUAL RHYME. See EYE RHYME.

VOICE. To stress v. in discussions of poetry may be simply a reminder of the large extent to which poetry depends on sound. The qualities of vocal sounds enter directly into the aesthetic experience of performance, of poetry readings, but no less do those sounds resonate in the "inner ear" of a fully attentive silent reading. T. S. Eliot felt that one may hear at least three voices of poetry: that of the poet in silent meditation, that of the poet addressing an audience, and that of a dramatic character or persona (q.v.) created by the poet. Implicit in Eliot's division is the notion that behind these various vs. lies one original v.—or what Aristotle called *ethos*—that expresses the poet's intentions (q.v.) and organizes the various personae.

Within romantic theories of poetry, v. plays a significant role as the embodiment of the author's expression (q.v.). Whether the poet speaks in Wordsworth's "lang. of men" or through Blake's prophecies, v. is the vehicle through which private vision is translated to the world. This romantic spirit has been revived by more recent poets for whom the oral trad. represents a positive model of poetry's unmediated access to an audience. At the same time, contemp. theories of "projective verse" (q.v.) have stressed the role of v. and breath in the construction of the poetic line.

The expressive view of v. has been qualified by much modern theory, beginning with New Criticism (q.v.) and its prohibitions against biographical crit. and the "intentional fallacy." More recent caveats have been offered by reader-response (q.v.) and reception theories, which view v. less as the product of a speaking subject than as the site of multiple narrative positions. In his influential *Rhetoric of Fiction* (1961), Wayne C. Booth uses the phrase "implied author" to describe the constructed or fictive nature of intentional acts. Authorial v. in this view is an idealized projection of the historical author, a figure to whom the reader must give tacit approval if verisimilitude (q.v.) is to be maintained. In an "Afterword" to the 2d ed. (1983), Booth distinguishes five senses of "author," and therefore five senses of authorial "v."

A more complex discussion of literary v. has been offered by structuralist analyses of narrative. For Tzvetan Todorov and Gérard Genette, most treatments of v. have been conducted under the rather vague concept of "point of view," which tends to equate narrator with author, i.e. the perspective through which the story is being told with the one who tells it. Genette uses the term v. to describe relations established between narrator and audience, relations that define "the way in which the narrating itself is implicated in the narrative." By using the term v., Genette foregrounds the role that grammar plays in creating person. When a character uses the passive rather than the active v. or when the verb tense changes from present to past, a new level of narration is introduced for which traditional notions of point of view are inadequate.

Structuralist narratology deals with v. as a construction within a specifically aesthetic frame. For Marxist philologists and linguists such as V. N. Volosinov and Mikhail Bakhtin, v. and speech are social in origin and exist as exchanges between specific historical individuals. Whereas structuralist thinkers such as Ferdinand de Saussure had mapped the terrain of lang. as a neutral system of phonemic differences (*la langue*), Volosinov (*Marxism and the Philosophy of Lang.* [1973]) argued that utterances are choices made in response to specific social and ideological conditions. Speech does not occur within a closed system of signifiers, as Saussure maintained, but within a constantly shifting ideological landscape. Bakhtin extended (some feel invented) Volosinov's historical definition of lang. and applied it to the novel (*The Dialogic Imagination* [tr. 1981]).

Implicit in both Marxist and structuralist analyses of literary texts is the idea that lang. constitutes subjects rather than serving as the instrument through which an original subject speaks. The philosophical ramifications of this fact are worked out within the poststructural thought of Jacques Derrida. Like Volosinov and Bakhtin, Derrida builds his critique on Saussure's linguistics, but instead of faulting an ahistorical definition of lang., he argues against Saussure's metaphysical privileging of speech over writing. In *Of Grammatology* (1973) and other essays, Derrida studies the way that Western thought since Plato has taken for granted the ontological priority of speech and presence, even (as in Heidegger) when that very presence is being called into question. Derrida attacks the assumption that v. or speech is directly linked to some metaphysical essence or quality that precedes its textual inscription. Any system of thought based on such a presupposition recapitulates the entire history of metaphysical thought and thus fails to recognize the radical difference that structures all discourse. Since difference is visible in the printed word but inaudible in the spoken, writing (*écriture*) becomes Derrida's preferred model for lang. as a system of signs in which presence is bracketed.

Although neither Marxist, structuralist, nor poststructuralist views relate directly to the specific use of v. in poetry, these forms of crit. theorize

the intentional nature of literary lang. insofar as it expresses what a specific author "wants" to say. It remains a paradoxical fact of postwar literary life that the revival of romantic theories of poetry with their strong emphasis on orality and presence has coincided with a theoretical critique of those very assumptions. See also DECONSTRUCTION; ETHOS; INFLUENCE; PERFORMANCE; SOUND.

T. S. Eliot, "The Three Vs. of Poetry," *On Poetry and Poets* (1957); C. Olson, "Projective Verse," *Selected Writings* (1960); W. J. Ong, *The Barbarian Within* (1962); F. Berry, *Poetry and the Physical V.* (1962); A. D. Ferry, *Milton's Epic V.* (1963); R. Delasanta, *The Epic V.* (1967); J. Derrida, *Of Grammatology* (tr. 1976); T. Todorov, *The Poetics of Prose* (1977); G. Genette, *Narrative Discourse* (1980); M. M. Bakhtin, *The Dialogic Imagination* (tr. 1981); *Lyric Poetry: Beyond New Crit.*, ed. C. Hošek and P. Parker (1985); P. Zumthor, *La Poésie et la voix dans la civilisation médiévale* (1987); R. O. A. M. Lyne, *Further Voices in Virgil's Aeneid* (1987); E. Griffiths, *The Printed V. of Victorian Poetry* (1989); D. Appelbaum, *V.* (1990). F.GU.; M.D.

VOLTA, volte (It. "turn"). A musical and prosodic term for a turn, particularly the transition point between the octave and sestet (q.v.) of the sonnet (q.v.), which in its It. form usually rhymes *ab-baabba cdecde*. The v. is significant because both the particular rhymes unifying the two quatrains of the octave and also the envelope (q.v.) scheme are abandoned simultaneously, regardless of whether this break is further reinforced syntactically by a full stop at the end of the octave (though usually it is), creating a decisive "turn in thought." By extension the term is applied to the gap or break at line 9 of any sonnet type, though in the Shakespearean form, for example, the type of rhyming (cross rhyme) is not abandoned at that point. From the point of view of print culture, the turn is effected in white space, i.e. in the gap between stanzas. One can hardly imagine any stronger v. than that between the octave and sestet of Donne's Holy Sonnet VII. which marks a momentous shift from the imagined scene of Judgment Day, cosmic in scale, to the quiet immediacy of the here and now, the narrator deep in thought. T.V.F.B.

VORTICISM. Though essentially a movement in the visual arts, v. is related directly to modern poetry through Ezra Pound's involvement in it when he abandoned imagism (q.v.). Founded by Wyndham Lewis in 1914, v. was a short-lived reaction to the romantic and Vitalist theories of futurism (q.v.) and stood most positively and clearly for all that is abstract and nonrepresentational in art, qualities which reflected the energies of the new machine age. Energy was the crucial quality that the imagists lacked, according to Pound, and he invented the term *vorticism* to suggest the greater energy of the poetic image as the vorticist used it.

In v., the image is not a picture but a force. In the first issue of the journal *BLAST* (1914), Pound declared that the vorticists use the "primary pigment" of their art: "Every concept, every emotion presents itself to the vivid consciousness in some primary form. . . . If sound, to music; if formed words, to literature; the image, to poetry . . . colour in position to painting." Poetry that goes beyond a static representation of the image to expressing "a world of moving energies" is vorticist, as in the lines from H. D.'s "Oread":

Whirl up, sea—
whirl your pointed pines,
splash your great pines
on our rocks,
hurl your green over us,
cover us with your pools of fir.

V.'s ambition to create form that is still and yet moving reflects a paradox that is central to modern poetics, from Hulme's "analogy" to the formalist theories of the New Criticism; and its insistence on a nonmimetic poetry and the links it forged with the other arts anticipates the devel. of subsequent poetry and crit.

BLAST 1–2 (1914–15); E. Pound, *Gaudier–Brzeska: A Memoir* (1916); W. Lewis, *Wyndham Lewis on Art*, ed. W. Michel and C. J. Fox (1969); H. Kenner, *The Pound Era* (1971); W. C. Wees, *V. and the Eng. Avant-Garde* (1972); R. Cork, *V. and Abstract Art in the First Machine Age*, 2 v. (1976); T. Materer, *Vortex: Pound, Eliot, Lewis* (1976); R. W. Dasenbrock, *The Literary V. of E. Pound and W. Lewis* (1985); M. Perloff, *The Futurist Moment* (1987). T.M.; S.K.C.

W

WAKA. See JAPANESE POETRY.

WAR POETRY. See POLITICS AND POETRY.

WEDGE VERSE. See RHOPALIC VERSE.

WELSH POETRY has a history spanning 14 centuries, from the odes of Taliesin and Aneirin in the 6th c. to the odes of the poets who now compete for the chair every year at the Royal National Eisteddfodau of Wales (see EISTEDDFOD). We deduce from Gildas' diatribe on the bards of Maelgwn, King of Gwynedd (d. ca. A.D. 547) that theirs was a trad. which, derived through the Celts from Indo-European peoples, accorded bards a special role on account of the magical powers attributed to them—in relation to their rulers. They were expected to call into being and to praise in those rulers the qualities most needed to fulfill their functions, esp. prowess and valor in battle. In short, bards were assigned a sacral role in the life of their people.

During the early period of its history W. p. was composed and handed down orally. Most of the extant poetry written before the death of the last W. princes in 1282–83 is preserved in the *Black Book of Carmarthen*, *The Book of Aneirin*, *The Book of Taliesin*, *The Book of Hendregadredd*, and the *Red Book of Hergest*, ms. volumes the first of which was written ca. 1260, the last toward the end of the 14th c. The oldest poetry, that composed from the beginning of the W. lang. to the end of the 11th c. (although more has been preserved from the earliest century than the later ones) is usually called *Yr Hengerdd* (the Old Song), and its composers are called *Y Cynfeirdd* (the Early Bards).

The Book of Taliesin, written in the first half of the 14th c., purports to contain the poems of Taliesin, but it is obvious that there are two Taliesins, one historical and the other legendary. Most of the twelve poems, mainly panegyrics, which can be attributed to the historical Taliesin are addressed to Urien, who ruled ca. 575 over Rheged, a realm including parts of modern Galloway and Cumbria.

The Book of Aneirin (second half of the 13th c.) opens with the statement in W., "This is the Gododdin. Aneirin sang it." The Gododdin, originally the name of a people in northeast England and southeast Scotland, is a long poem celebrating the bravery of a war-band sent to recapture a stronghold from the English about the year 600 A.D., although the date lacks any archaeological backing. They fought almost to a man, gloriously but unsuccessfully. Aneirin eulogizes them for the most part individually, so that the poem comprises a series of elegies. More importantly, though, the poem contains evidence that the Britons of southern Scotland had poets who practiced the same poetic art to celebrate the heroic deeds of the dead and the quick as that of the Britons of Wales or the W., so that we have here the reason why the poetry of Taliesin and Aneirin was appropriated as traditionally their own by the poets of Wales. Further, there is very little linguistically to distinguish the earliest poetry produced in Wales from that of ancient northern England and southern Scotland. It was sung to exalt the rulers on whose heroic qualities the survival of the people depended, and it used the same poetic embellishments, end-rhyme to link lines and, within the line, the repetition of the same consonant or vowel sounds, i.e.

WELSH POETRY

incipient *cynghanedd* (q.v.).

By the middle of the 9th c., Powys, the kingdom adjoining Gwynedd in north Wales, was hard pressed by the Eng. Its struggle is reflected in the work of a bard or school of bards who composed a series of dramatic stories woven round the 6th-c. figure of Llywarch Hen (Llywarch the Old), his kin, and the 7th-c. prince of Powys, Cynddylan, although the stories reflect the emotions aroused by contemporary events on the borders of Powys. At one point in the saga, Llywarch Hen urges his son Gwên to go into battle against the Eng. invaders. Gwên goes and, like his brothers before him, is killed on the dyke. There follows a magnificent elegy in which the father mourns the last and the best of his sons. Whether there was once a prose framework to these poems, composed of monologues and dialogues, is still disputed, but it seems reasonable to assume its existence, and to assume also that the W., like the Irish in the West and the Hindus in the East, followed a practice, dating from Indo-European times, of using prose for ordinary narrative and verse for the expression of strong emotion and moments of heightened tension. On the other hand, W. lit., like Irish, has no early verse epics.

The W. kingdoms found themselves in a state of endemic warfare not only against the Eng. but among themselves. Since they were slow to accept primogeniture inheritance, internecine dynastic feuds were frequent, and W. bards could not fail to be propagandists. Some of them claimed powers of vision and prognostication; in times of dire distress, these donned the role of prophesying victory against the Eng. foe. The most remarkable W. prophetic poem, *Armes Prydain*, (The Prophecy of Britain), composed about 930 A.D., foretold that the W. would be joined by the Cornishmen, the Bretons, the Britons of Strathclyde and the Irish, incl. the men of Dublin (the Danes), to overthrow the Eng. and banish them across the sea whence they had come. Although in the W. trad. the legendary Taliesin and the equally legendary Myrddin (Merlin) were the seers *par excellence*, and as such were credited with many anonymous prophecies, internal evidence suggests that *Armes Prydain* was composed by a monk in one of the religious houses of south Wales. Vaticinatory poems appear throughout the Middle Ages and were esp. numerous in the form of *cywyddau* (plural of *cywydd*, q.v.; sometimes referred to as *cywyddau brud*, prophetic *cywyddau*) during the Wars of the Roses.

At one time it appeared that the Normans would conquer Wales as easily as they had conquered England, but the W. rallied and preserved their independence more or less intact until 1282–83. The national revival, which secured the survival of the W. under their princes, manifested itself also in a fresh flowering of poetry. The poets of the princes, sometimes called the *Gogynfeirdd* (the "not so early" bards, to distinguish them from their predecessors the *Cynfeirdd*), sang in much

the same way Taliesin had sung, but they were not content simply to imitate their predecessors; they developed a much more complex poetic style and a more sophisticated system of *cynghanedd*, sometimes called *cynghanedd rydd*, ("free" *cynghanedd*, to distinguish it from *cynghanedd gaeth* or "strict" *cynghanedd*, which the bards of the nobility later evolved). Their poetry indicates that they formed a kind of order in which the *pencerdd*, the master craftsman who had won his position in competition, taught one or more apprentices in a school of *ars poetica*. According to some accounts, the function of the *pencerdd* was to sing the praise of God and the king. Next in order of rank stood the *bardd teulu*, originally the bard of the king's household-troops; apparently he was expected to sing to these troops before they set off for battle, but he could also be called to sing to the queen in her chamber.

Among the foremost of these *Gogynfeirdd* were Gwalchmai (ca. 1140–80), Cynddelw (ca. 1155–1200), Llywarch ap Llywelyn (ca. 1173–1220), and Dafydd Benfras (ca. 1220–57). Their range of themes was not large, and their poetry dazzles by the intricacies of its *cynghanedd*, the superb command of lang., and the wealth of literary and historical references rather than by any individuality of thought. If the *Gogynfeirdd* borrowed their themes and much of their technique from the *Cynfeirdd*, they succeeded by their ingenuity in elaborating the former and refining the latter, in producing poems remarkable for originality of expression. After the defeat of the W. princes their patrons, they were saved from extinction partly by the resilience of their guild, though mostly by patronage from the newly emergent nobility. It is thus appropriate that they should now be called "Poets of the Nobility," *Beirdd yr Uchelwyr.*

In the reorganization following 1282, W. society finally had to shed its heroic-age features: no wars were allowed, and martial prowess and valor ceased to have their old value. The poets as well as the nobility had to reassess their function, the former becoming more of a craft guild than an order. The *cywydd* (*deuair hirion*) superseded the *awdl* as the favorite meter, "strict" *cynghanedd* took the place of "free" *cynghanedd*, and entertaining the nobility became more important than exalting it. The effects of foreign influences were mediated mainly by the new religious orders and by a few *clerici curiales*, esp. Einion Offeiriad, whose "bardic grammar" sought not only to impose order on the practice of the poets but also to give it a new intellectual framework. Einion's is the earliest extant attempt at a metrical analysis of W. p. His division of "meters" into the three categories of *awdl*, *cywydd*, and *englyn* (qq.v.), subject to the modifications by Dafydd ab Edmwnd in 1450 (who arranged the "24 meters" into these three classes) became the accepted forms of "strict-meter" poetry and has remained so to this day.

Dafydd ap Gwilym (fl. 1320–70) perhaps owes

a great deal of his indisputable brilliance as a poet to the fact that he had inherited the poetic craft of the *Gogynfeirdd* and was able to adapt it to popularize the *stil nuovo*. He wrote *awdlau* in the old style, but by grafting the embellishments associated with them, *cynghanedd*, on the lower-order verseform, the *traethodl*, he made the resulting *cywydd deuair hirion* into a meter which the new poets of the nobility took pride and delight in using and which won the favor and patronage of the nobility. Dafydd addressed *cywyddau* to his patron Ifor ap Llywelyn (fl. 1340–60), celebrating his generosity so much that he became renowned as "Ifor the Generous," henceforth the exemplar of all bardic patrons. But Dafydd's fame rests ultimately on his *cywyddau* to women and his masterly expression in them of his love of women and of nature. He must have recited or sung these *cywyddau* to small audiences for their entertainment. One of his favorite strategies is to picture himself in a false or undignified situation, making himself the butt of his audience's laughter. Thus he describes in a *cywydd* how one night in an inn he tried to make his way in the dark to the bed of a girl whose favour he had bought in advance by wining and dining her, only to strike his leg against a stool and his head against a trestle table, knocking over a huge brass pan in the process, and creating such a din that the household woke up and began to search for him as an intruder. It was only through the grace of the Lord Jesus and the intercession of the saints, he tells us, presumably with tongue in cheek, that he escaped detection, and he begs God for His forgiveness. But he describes such situations with such wit, invention, verbal dexterity, and technical skill that one must conclude that the audience's enjoyment of the theme was secondary to its enjoyment of the expression, and that the poet's extensive use of *dyfalu* (q.v.), etc., presumes a high degree of literary appreciation on the part of his listeners.

It was inevitable that Dafydd ap Gwilym should set the stamp of his poetry on that of his younger contemporaries and immediate successors, and that, once the shock of his originality and exuberance had been absorbed, the trad. should reassert itself, albeit in modified form. The poets retained their guild organization, their way of transmitting knowledge of the poetic craft, and sundry privileges. But they and their patrons had become aware of the world outside Wales—the influences of the Hundred Years War must not be underestimated—and some at least had become conscious that the eulogies that bound poet and patron could be interpreted as sycophancy. A poet of strong conscience, such as Siôn Cent in the first quarter of the 15th c., could not fail to feel this tension, and his vivid pessimism and gloomy *Weltanschauung* made him condemn the traditional W. Muse as deceitful and proclaim his own as the "true" or Christian Muse. But Siôn Cent had few followers. The bardic institution was strong enough to withstand his influence, as well as the disastrous effects of the Owain Glyndwr Rebellion and the Black Death. Indeed, there is evidence that, contrary to expectation, Wales shared, albeit to a lesser extent, the prosperity which England enjoyed in the 15th c.—the Black Death seems to have put greater wealth in the hands of fewer people—and the poets shared in the prosperity of their patrons. The result is that the century 1435–1535, the *grand siècle* of W. p., is remarkable not only for its large number of poets but also for the very high standard achieved by many of them. The poets were sufficiently self-confident to assemble in *eisteddfodau*—first in Carmarthen (about 1450) and then in Caerwys (1523)—to make improvements in their metrical and *cynghanedd* systems. Dafydd ab Edmwnd is the poet esp. associated with the first *eisteddfod*, and Tudur Aled with the second, but other great names are not lacking: Dafydd Nanmor, Guto'r Glyn, Lewis Glyn Cothi, and Gutun Owain. Such poets (and the work of many has survived) broadened the themes of praise to include the more domestic and civilized: dynastic marriages, well-built mansions with gardens, excellent tablefare, and material as well as cultural wealth.

After 1282 perhaps the most important date for W. p. is 1485, the year Henry VII acceded to the throne of England, though the implications of that event became apparent only gradually. The most immediate result was that the W. nobility found even greater opportunities for advancement in England, so that many of them abandoned their role as patrons of the W. Muse. And there were a number of others whose contact with the Reformation and the Ren. made them eager to bring their native culture into line with that of England and the Continent. This meant that W. poets should abandon their guild organization, make the secrets of their craft accessible to the general public, and, more important still, assimilate the new learning proffered by the recently invented printing press, esp. knowledge of the art of rhetoric. Above all, a purpose other than praise, esp. unwarranted praise, had to be found for the W. Muse. Most of these points were raised in the famous debate of 1580–87 between Archdeacon Edmwnd Prys and the poet Wiliam Cynwal, and in the open letter which Siôn Dafydd Rhys addressed to the poets in 1597. Some efforts were indeed made to help the W. poets adjust to the new circumstances: descriptions of the W. poetic art and handbooks of rhetoric were published. Of special interest is the description of the poetic art published by Dr. Gruffydd Robert of Milan, a Roman Catholic in exile: he advocated a relaxing of the rules of "strict" *cynghanedd* and the adoption of the "free" accentual meters for epic poetry.

But it was extremely difficult to abandon a poetic trad. and practice that had endured for a thousand years, and very few W. poets found it possible to take up the new learning. Deprived of patrons, the poets found themselves devoid of incentive either to teach or to learn the art which hitherto had been handed down from generation to generation. Grufydd Phylip of Ardudwy, who died in 1666, was the last of the "old" or professional poets. Henceforth their art was to be kept alive by amateurs drawn from the clergy or the ranks of the gentry. Edmwnd Prys showed what could be achieved, but by the end of the first quarter of the 18th c., the old trad. seemed dead.

In some mss. written after 1550, poems in the free accentual meters began to appear side by side with poems in the strict meters. There is no reason to suppose that the free accentual meters had not been previously used; they would not have been considered worthy enough to be copied into ms. collections with the more professional strict-meter poems. Their presence in increasing numbers in the mss. implies that they were becoming more esteemed. It is usual to distinguish two kinds of free accentual meters, one old and native, the other new and borrowed, although some of the embellishments of the strict meters were added to both. The newly borrowed accentual meters were based on those of Eng. songs set to popular airs. There is, for instance, a W. ballad dated 1571 to be sung to the tune "Adew my pretty pussie." The practice of composing W. lyrics to musical airs, native and borrowed, continued throughout the 18th and 19th cs. and persists to this day.

Wales experienced two revivals in the 18th c. The religious or Methodist revival is important in the history of W. p., indirectly because it helped to extend literacy among the people and directly because it gave an impetus to the composition of hymns and hence to other kinds of poetry as well. William Williams, "Pantycelyn" (1717–91), wrote a long poem, "Theomemphus," in which he describes the spiritual experiences of a soul caught up in the Methodist revival, as well as hundreds of hymns. "Pantycelyn" has every right to be regarded as the father of the modern W. lyric. A later hymn-writer, Ann Griffiths (1776–1805), rivals him only in the emotional intensity of her expression.

The literary revival is associated with the "Morrisian" circle, whose leading members—Lewis Morris (1701–65), Goronwy Owen (1723–69), and Evan Evans ("Ieuan Fardd," 1731–88)—were not only poets but also scholars, and as such drew much of their inspiration from the contemporary Eng. literary scene. The Ossianic productions of the Scot Macpherson had stimulated general interest in the ancient popular lits., and the "Morrisian" circle were anxious to demonstrate the antiquity of the W. poetic trad. Evans, their finest scholar, searched for material in the libraries of the landed gentry. Though most of the material he collected remained unpublished, his *Specimens of the Poetry of the Antient W. Bards* marked an important milestone in the rediscovery of the W. poetic trad. It also anticipated the publication of the *Myvyrian Archaiology of Wales* in 3 v., of which v. 1 (1801) was until modern times the only printed source for the texts of the work of the *Cynfeirdd* and the *Gogynfeirdd*.

Goronwy Owen, the "Morrisian" circle's most accomplished poet, was so enamored of the W. strict-meter trad. that he could not bring himself to call anything else poetry. He was prepared to accord every praise to Milton's compositions, but since they were not written in *cynghanedd* he could not call them poetry. Yet at the same time he was too much of a classical scholar not to accept that the most significant poetic genre was the heroic epic. Much to his disappointment, the W. poetic trad. could not boast a heroic epic in strict meter. This deficiency he attempted to supply by writing *Cywydd y Farn Fawr* (The *Cywydd* of the Great Judgment); he also left a legacy of critical ideas, esp. the principles that poetry should follow strict rules of composition and that it could be judged according to criteria derived therefrom.

Later *eisteddfodau* were, in the early 19th c., meetings at which small groups of poets delivered themselves of impromptu verses to test their skill and to entertain a few bystanders. The *eisteddfod* has since developed in several ways. The range of the competitions held has been extended to include music and the other arts, but one feature has remained constant: the highest honor is still accorded to the poet who can produce the best long poem in strict meters. When it could no longer be maintained, following Goronwy Owen, that poetry without strict meters was impossible, the second highest honor was accorded to the poet who could produce the best long poem in the free accentual meters or even in free verse. The presupposition for all these poetic competitions remained Owen's tenet, that poetry is composed according to certain rules, so that success in following these rules can be measured and judged. On the whole, poems in the strict meters lent themselves better than those in the free accentual meters to this kind of competition: indeed, the two categories invited different kinds of criticism. Still, both sorts of poems tended to have common characteristics: they are predominantly objective, impersonal, descriptive, formal in structure, and stylized in diction.

Although W. literary culture in the 19th c. had remarkable achievements to its credit, incl. the work of Evan Evans ("Ieuan Glan Geirionydd," 1795–1855), John Blackwell ("Alun," 1707–1840), and Robert Williams ("Robert ap Gwilym Ddu," 1766–1850), it had no firm base in a well-established educational system. Schooling did not become compulsory until the end of the century, and even then only scant attention was paid to the W. lang. One of the results was a curious lack of self-confidence shown even by the most talented poets, an inability to recognize what they could do best and a failure to persevere and develop it when they achieved success. This is true of Ebenezer

Thomas ("Eben Fardd," 1802–63), who wrote the best *eisteddfodic awdl* of the century in strict meter, *Dinystr Jerusalem* (The Fall of Jerusalem), for the Welshpool *Eisteddfod* of 1824 and then, dissatisfied with his success in the strict meters, wrote a long mediocre poem on the Resurrection (*Yr Adgyfodiad*) in the free accentual meters.

As a poet, critic, and editor, William Thomas ("Islwyn," 1832–78) concentrated in his mature years on poetry in the strict meters, but his major contribution to W. p. was made as a young man, when he wrote two long poems entitled *Yr Ystorm* (The Storm). They show a young man struggling to express thoughts and emotions vaguely understood in words only rarely adequate, but they leave the reader with a feeling that in better circumstances and with more persistence he could have developed into a finer poet. Islwyn was claimed as the "Father" of a group of poets calling themselves the "New Poets." They believed that they were breathing new life into the W. poetic trad. by eschewing the strict meters in favor of the free accentual meters for long philosophical poems. But the nebulous nature of their thought is betrayed in their equally nebulous lang., which is often extremely bombastic.

John Morris-Jones (1864–1929) had a clearer vision than the "New Poets" of what was needed. He undertook the task of restoring the literary standards of classical W. On the one hand, he was able to standardize the orthography, to restore the syntax, and to purify the idiom of the lang. On the other, by emphasizing the entire span of the W. poetic trad. from its beginnings, he was able to reveal its greatness and to uncover some of the forgotten secrets of the prosody underlying that greatness. As a professor and author of both the standard grammar of the lang. and the definitive description of its prosody, his authority was unassailable, but he was also a successful poet in both strict and free meters, and hence a constant adjudicator at the national *eisteddfodau* of his time. He took the W. nation to school. And he was fortunate in his brilliant disciples, some even more generously gifted at poetry than he. His influence is most obvious in the work of T. Gwynn Jones, W. J. Gruffydd, and R. Williams Parry. The next generation of poets—T. H. Parry-Williams, D. Gwenallt Jones, Waldo Williams, Saunders Lewis—also benefited from his work on the lang. but developed their own ideas of poetic diction and form. Although many mastered the art of the strict meters, their most outstanding contributions have been in the free accentual meters. Some, notably Euros Bowen, have developed *vers libre* in which a form of *cynghanedd* is almost essential. Euros Bowen, Bobi Jones (R. M. Jones), and Gwyn Thomas are the most prolific, most diverse, and most significant poets of their generation.

There has recently been a remarkable increase in the popularity of the strict meters among the youngest generation of W. poets, foremost of whom is Alan Llwyd. This is perhaps because television and radio have provided a platform for poetry as entertainment, esp. poetry in the strict meters. Teams drawn from the W. counties compete with each other in composing poems in the strict meters, the *cywydd* (q.v.), the *englyn* (q.v.), as well as lyrics in the free accentual meters; their meetings are recorded for broadcasting, and successful teams compete again at the *National Eisteddfod* in *Y Babell Lên*, the Literary Pavilion. Such has been the success of these meetings that a Strict Meter Society (*Cymdeithas Cerdd Dafod*) has been established with more than a thousand members, publishing a monthly periodical called *Barddas* and several volumes of poetry and criticism each year.

See also BRETON POETRY; CELTIC PROSODY; HEN BENILLION; IRISH POETRY; ODL.

BIBLIOGRAPHIES: G. O. Watts, "Llyfryddiaeth Llenyddiaeth Gymraeg," *BBCS* 30 (1983); C. Donahue, "Med. Celtic Lit.," in Fisher; R. Bromwich, *Med. Celtic Lit.: A Select Bibl.* (1974); *Llyfryddiaeth Llenyddiaeth Gymraeg*, ed. T. Parry and M. Morgan (1976).

ANTHOLOGIES: *Poems from the W.* (1913), *W. Poems of the 20th C.* (1925), both ed. H. I. Bell and C. C. Bell; *The Burning Tree* (1956), *Presenting W. P.* (1959), both ed. G. Williams; *Oxford Book of W. P.*, ed. T. Parry (1962); *Med. W. Lyrics* (1965), *The Earliest W. P.* (1970), *20th-C. W. Poems* (1983), all ed. J. P. Clancy; *The Gododdin*, ed. K. Hurlstone Jackson (1969); *The Poetry of Llywarch Hen*, tr. P. K. Ford (1974); *Dafydd ap Gwilym: A Selection of Poems*, ed. R. Bromwich (1982); *Dafydd ap Gwilym*, tr. R. M. Loomis (1982); *W. Verse*, ed. T. Conran, 2d ed. (1986)—long intro. and useful appendices; *Early W. Saga P.*, ed. J. Rowland (1990).

HISTORY AND CRITICISM: H. I. Bell, *The Devel. of W. P.* (1936); G. Williams, *An Intro. to W. P.* (1953); Parry, *History*; Jarman and Hughes, esp. the articles by Bromwich, Lewis, and Rowlands; Stephens; B. Jones and G. Thomas, *The Dragon's Pen* (1986); R. Bromwich, *Aspects of the Poetry of Dafydd ap Gwilym* (1986).

PROSODY: J. Loth, *La Métrique galloise*, 2 v. (1900–2), but see the rev. by Morris-Jones in *ZCP* 4 (1903), 106–42; Morris-Jones—still useful, indexed by G. Bowen, *Mynegai i Cerdd Dafod* (1947); R. M. Jones, "Mesurau'r canu rhydd cynnar," *BBCS* 28 (1979); A. T. E. Matonis, "The W. Bardic Grammars and the Western Grammatical Trad.," *MP* 79 (1981); "Appendix on Metres" in Conran (above).
J.E.C.W.

WELSH PROSODY. See CELTIC PROSODY.

WEST INDIAN POETRY refers to poetry written in the Eng. which has evolved as the lang. of the formerly British possessions in the Caribbean area. This poetry is essentially a 20th-c. phenomenon. Most of the verse written in the West Indies before 1900 is minor British poetry using the tropical landscape only as a different setting for epic and pastoral or as a new source of the picturesque. The people in this exotic garden, the slaves, were either ignored or marginalized by British poets. Indeed, little was done to give formal education to the slaves before Emancipation in 1834. By the early 20th c., however, post-Emancipation efforts to provide universal elementary education had begun to produce literates from all races and classes. These island-born writers regarded the landscape as more than just a setting; nascent nationalisms in all the islands began to affect the form and esp. the content of literary productions.

The first important W. I. poet, Claude McKay (Jamaica, 1890–1948) was a cultural nationalist. He wrote in dialect as well as in Standard Jamaican, drawing upon country life and folk trads. (*Songs of Jamaica*, 1912), and his experience of the city where he served as a policeman (*Constab Ballads*, 1912). McKay's emigration to the United States in 1912 enhanced his literary achievement and he continued writing as a W. I. poet, but at home he had no influence during his lifetime. So the visible shapes of W. I. p. came from the practice of more conventional authors who had little use for dialect or the folk heritage. The efforts of the early 20th-c. practitioners have been preserved in four period anthologies (McFarlane 1929 and 1949, Cameron 1931, and Clarke 1943).

These pioneers produced a dependent colonial poetry that looked loyally to the Mother Country ("For England is England, who mothers my soul") and saw no conflict between that and loving the "little green island far over the sea." They took their support and models from the Victorians, from the romantics, and from the Victorian watering down of the romantics. They turned out stiff imitations of accepted models, favoring the sonnet, blank verse, and, esp. in Jamaica, the doubly imported villanelle (qq.v.). Like most Eng. poets of the time they wrote in fixed forms, and they believed that certain subjects were poetic and others not, even certain words were inherently poetic, while others (e.g. dialect) were not fit for expressing "Great Thoughts." They saw their "landscape" but they wrote about "Nature."

By the late 1930s, the artificial poetry of what has been variously called "the Caribbean pastoral trad." and "poetry for recitation" was coming to an end. The trad. begun by Edward Cordle (*Overheard*, 1903), enlarged by the emigré Claude McKay, and kept ebullient and alive by Louise Bennett (see *Selected Poems*, 1982) would soon animate W. I. writing.

On the social scene, responses to the Depression of the Thirties were colored by racial and cultural ideologies derived from movements like Pan-Africanism, Garveyism, the Rus. Revolution, and the Harlem Renaissance (q.v.); the whole process was to be accentuated by the harsh experience of World War II. In writing (incl. the calypso), there was a definite turning away from Nature to social issues. Landscape was rediscovered and used to reflect the human struggle. There was a departure from conventional forms and poetic diction, an exuberant indulgence in dialect, and a reckless plunge into declamation and a free verse so free it sometimes became only angry prose. The new subject matter included history, historical processes, and a wide range of folk material not hitherto considered literary. This period of social protest and racial affirmation embraced the use of the lang. of the streets, forced a rapprochement between writing and the speaking voice, and instituted a free trade between poetry, dialect verse, folksong, and calypso. The calypso is a highly rhythmic secular song on topical matters which developed among the slaves and has flourished in the 20th c., esp. in Trinidad and Tobago, as a medium for social commentary, satire, and lyricism. Dance and music are integral to its performance by a bardic figure and chorus who usually generate enthusiastic audience participation.

The 1940s and early '50s saw the establishment and flourishing of important periodicals: in Jamaica, *Focus*; in Barbados, *Bim*; in Guyana, *Kyk-Over-Al*; in Trinidad, *The Beacon*. These periodicals, the BBC's radio magazine *Caribbean Voices* (Figueroa 1970), and two anthologies (1954, 1958) are the key sources for the poetry of the 1940s and 1950s. There were many fine poems in this period, but few authoritative and lasting voices. This was as much a result of the plain fact that there was no outstanding talent as that there was no audience, and no particular value placed on W. I. p. except by the practitioners themselves ("the unknown, the abortive poets") and a small reading circle. Of the poets writing in this period, George Campbell (b. 1918; *First Poems*, 1945), Una Marson (1905–65; *Heights and Depths*, 1932), M. G. Smith (b. 1921), H. A. Vaughan (b. 1901), Frank Collymore (1893–1980; *Selected Poems*, 1971), A. J. Seymour (b. 1914; *Selected Poems*, 1965), E. McG. Keane (b. 1927; *L'Oubli*, 1950), and Wilson Harris (b. 1921; *Eternity to Season*, 1954) were considerable and are still very much in the trad.

Three others achieved greater heights. Eric Roach (1915–74) was born in Tobago; his work is immersed in the peasant life and history, incl. the Af. connection. His experiments with dialect and the speaking voice were controlled by a careful concern with craft. A. L. Hendricks (b. 1922; *On This Mountain*, 1964, and other volumes) is another poet of substance; Hendricks' wit, elegance and lyricism have not been duly appreciated, and the smooth surface of his verse is muscled (not bulgingly enough for some) by a deeply native inspiration. Hendricks is one of the few Jamaicans to show the sea-consciousness that seems to characterize the southern Caribbean writers. But the most outstanding poet of the period was the Guyanese, Martin Carter (b. 1927; see *Poems of Succession*, 1977). Carter's involvement in social and metaphysical issues, his apparently instinctive control of free verse, and his ability to retain the dialect tone (its harshness as well as its lyricism) combine to make his compressed epic, "University of Hunger," perhaps the best single poem ever written by a W. I.

At last, in the 1960s W. I. p. came of age with the establishment of the international reputations of the Barbadian, Edward Brathwaite (*The Arrivants*, 1973), and the St. Lucian, Derek Walcott (*Selected Poems*, 1964), both born in 1930. Brathwaite's great subject is Africa and the Af. heritage. His world is made up of all the places where the Af. has set foot and laboring hand. His rhythmic poetry draws inventively upon folk and urban experience, and he makes brilliant use of the wide range of forms to be found not only among New World descendants of Africans, but also in Africa itself. Walcott, playing a more subdued music, is the W. I. poet of landscape and the sea. His themes are personal—love, death, loss—and his sociocultural vision is of the meeting of cultures which engendered the newness of the New World:

> I'm just a red nigger who love the sea,
> I had a sound colonial education,
> I have Dutch, nigger and English in me,
> and either I'm nobody, or I'm a nation.
> ("The *Schooner* Flight," from *The Star-Apple Kingdom* [1979])

In the works of Walcott and Brathwaite the formalist attitude of the early practitioners fuses at last with the dialect line introduced by Cordle and McKay. The fallout has been widespread. At last there were native masters who belonged to and were defining a trad. Poetry in the West Indies, now shown to be a possible profession, suddenly became popular. The new generation, represented by Mervyn Morris (b. 1937; *The Pond*, 1973 and other volumes), Dennis Scott (b. 1939; *Uncle Time*, 1973 and other volumes), Anthony McNeill (b. 1941; *Reel from "The Life Movie,"* 1972), and Wayne Brown (b. 1944; *On the Coast*, 1972), is alive to social, political, and cultural issues but feels no necessity to proclaim or advertise its West Indianness. Still, these poets write in the shadow of Walcott (*Another Life*, 1973) and Brathwaite (*Mother Poem*, 1977; *Sun Poem*, 1982), who continue strongly as contemporaries.

But while the dialect trad. and the formalist attitude have been fusing (there are stunning experiments by Walcott and Brathwaite), there has also emerged a trend toward a more democratic and instant performance poetry sometimes referred to as "rapso" or "dub." Some of this is akin to those combinations of music, drumming, and poetry that are by now reasonably familiar. But the new trend unites elements of traditional orality (which uniquely are alive in Caribbean societies) with the new or secondary orality opened up by the devel. and spread of electronic media (Smith 1987). This phenomenon draws upon the popular calypso and reggae music and marks an important area of collaboration between the recent island poetry and the Black British poetry now being written by descendants of West Indians in the U.K. (Johnson 1978).

This account of a rich and diverse poetic scene would be incomplete without noticing the recent upsurge in women's poetry. In Jamaica, women's poetry can be traced back to the troubled Arabella Moulton-Barrett, Una Marson, and Barbara Ferland (b. 1919), and it would be possible to find similar figures in the other territories. But regardless of whether or not we can so construct a trad., the work of Dionne Brand (*Fore Day Morning*, 1978), Claire Harris (*From the Women's Quarters*, 1984), Judy Miles (b. 1942), and Grace Nicholls (*I is a Long-Memoried Woman*, 1983), to mention only a few, suggests that W. I. p. is once more about to transform itself.

ANTHOLOGIES: *Voices from Summerland*, ed. J. McFarlane (1929); *Guianese Poetry 1831–1931*, ed. N. E. Cameron (privately pub. in Guyana, 1931); *Best Poems of Trinidad*, ed. A. M. Clarke (1943); *A Treasury of Jamaican Poetry*, ed. J. McFarlane (1949); *Anthol. of Guianese Poetry*, ed. A. J. Seymour (1954); *Anthol. of W. I. P.*, Federation Commemoration Issue of *Caribbean Quart.* 15,2 (1958); *Caribbean Voices*, ed. O. R. Dathorne (1967); *Breaklight*, ed. A. Salkey (1971); *Caribbean Voices*, ed. J. Figueroa (1971); *Jamaica Woman*, ed. P. Mordecai and M. Morris (1971); *Seven Jamaican Poets*, ed. M. Morris (1971); *Caribbean Poetry Now*, ed. S. Brown (1984); *Penguin Book of Caribbean Verse in Eng.*, ed. P. Burnett (1986); *The New Brit. Poetry*, ed. Allnutt et al. (1988); *W. I. P.*, ed. K. Ramchand and C. Gray (1989).

HISTORY AND CRITICISM: E. Baugh, *W. I. P. 1900–1970* (1971); G. Rohlehr, "W. I. P.: Some Problems of Assessment," *Bim* (1976); L. Brown, *W. I. P.* (1978); K. Ramchand, "Parades Parades: Modern W. I. P.," *SR* (1979).   K.R.

WHEEL. See BOB AND WHEEL.

WIT. In Plato's *Republic* and in Aristotle's *Poetics* the word *euphuia* occurs in senses ranging from "shapeliness" to "cleverness." In Cicero and Quintilian the Lat. equivalent is *ingenium* in senses that would seem to generate the whole historical range of the meanings of w. in Eng. Its equivalents in other langs. also undergo historical semantic change: *esprit* (or *bel esprit*) in Fr., *agudeza* and *gracia* in Sp., *ingegno*, *acutezza*, and *argutezza* in It., *Witz* and *Schärfe* in Ger., and *um* and *ostroumie* in Rus. All these terms have different histories, yet in the 17th and 18th cs. a fairly close correspondence of meaning develops among them. By this time, perhaps under the influence of Quintilian (10.1.130), w. (*ingenium*) is contrasted with *judgment* (*iudicium*): w. (or fantasy and its congeners) must be controlled by the discipline of judgment to produce proper works of art. The later, specialized senses of w. as risible sparkle or mere levity have

WIT

parallels in other langs., and have no great artistic interest other than our own currently felt meaning.

In its heyday as a critical term, w. referred to the inventive or imaginative faculty and, in particular, to the ability to see similarity in disparates (cf. Aristotle, *Poetics* 1459a). Indeed, w. could be prized for its ability to discover brilliant, paradoxical, or far-fetched images and figures, esp. metaphor, metonymy, irony, paradox, pun, or antithesis (qq.v.), notably as propounded by Baltasar Gracián in *Agudeza y arte de ingenio* (1642; expanded 1648) and Emmanuele Tesauro in *Il cannocchiale aristotelico* (1654). Their contemporary Thomas Hobbes in his *Leviathan* (1651) asserted in a general psychological vein that "*Naturall W.* consisteth in two things: *Celerity of Imagining* (that is, swift succession of one thought to another) and *steddy direction* to some approved end." This use of w. shows historical continuity from early times when both ingenuity and judgment could be encompassed in the same term, as also in the use of *esprit* by Descartes and Pascal. For imaginative lit., however, Eng. *w.* and its parallel terms in other tongues retained into the late 18th c. the specialized meaning of ingeniousness: it is this meaning which is the most fruitful to trace.

A prime text in Eng. is Pope's "Essay on Crit." (1711): "*True W. is Nature to Advantage drest, / What oft was Thought, but ne'er so well Exprest.*" It sums up in its context the central sense of w. to be found in poet-critics from Dryden to Johnson and indicates a rejection of the "false w." or mere cleverness of the previous as well as the current age. Yet Pope, as others elsewhere, granted license to "Great Wits" who could "*snatch a grace* beyond the Reach of Art." Empson counts 46 occurrences of the word "w." in the "Essay on Crit." and sorts out at least six different meanings. Such polysemy is not unusual, nor is it distracting so long as we recognize the use of *w.* in a technical aesthetic sense to mean the imaginative or striking figure, the flash of verbal intuition, the marmoreal phrase, the pointed dictum. While Pope constitutes a norm or middle point, however, the history of the literary sense of w. in Britain begins with Shakespeare and the metaphysical poets (cf. esp. T. Carew's "Elegie upon the Death of . . . Dr. John Donne" [1640] and A. Cowley's "Of W." [1656]), continues through Dryden (e.g. "Preface to *Annus mirabilis*, 1666), Addison's *Spectator* papers on w. (e.g. 58–61), and Dr. Johnson to the romantics, who transformed its meaning.

In Fr. the word *esprit* is polyvalent in many of the same ways; indeed Boileau's *Art poétique* (1674) was clearly a prime model for Pope. *Esprit* was a more unstable or modish word than *w.* (a symptomatic text is the anonymous *Entretiens galants* [1681]), yet it survived in its focused meaning at least through Voltaire. In Italy *acutezza* or *argutezza* and *arguzia* and in Spain *agudeza* were generally treated as the rhetorical ornament enhancing the thought (*concetto, concepto*). In belated Rus. lit. the

most famous use of the parallel term *um* occurs in Griboedov's comedy *Gore ot uma* (Woe from W., 1824). The key words in It., Sp., and Rus. have survived in contemp. speech, though bereft of their literary specificity, while Eng. "w." entered quite a new realm of meaning parallel to that other historically complex word "humor" (see Lewis).

The early Ger. romantics, in their profound originality, gave new life to traditional terms such as *Witz*. Jean Paul Richter (*Vorschule der Ästhetik*, 1804) and Friedrich Schlegel (in his three sets of *Fragmente* or *Aphorismen*, 1789–1802) used *Witz* not merely in its rhetorical sense but, more significantly, to denote a whole world view of creativity in such a way as to vie even with *Phantasie* and *Ironie*. Schiller's *Spieltrieb* ("play drive") and Solgar's *Ironie* are also important in the romantic overthrow of neoclassical orthodoxy (Wellek, v. 2).

A whole new constellation of literary terminology was forming in the earlier 19th c. of which we are the heirs. *Imagination* (q.v.) came to take on the sense of discovery and invention formerly embraced by *w.*, leading to a reduction in the sense of the latter (and its cognates in other langs.) to mere humor, a tendency which became widespread. In the course of the 20th c., notions related to the older meaning of w. have come to the fore, e.g. Freud's psychoanalytic concept of *Witz*, T. S. Eliot's revaluation of "metaphysical" w., C. Brooks' emphasis on irony and paradox (qq.v.) as the principal devices of literary complexity and structure, and a persistent strain of parody (q.v.) as a means to what might be called intertextual w., as in Joyce's *Ulysses* and Mann's *Doktor Faustus*. Thus the meaning of w., though it may not have come full circle, has in the 20th c. regained some critical force and, through its literarily serious connection with irony and parody, begun to approach again its old kinship with imagination. See also BAROQUE POETICS; GENIUS; GONGORISM; MARINISM; METAPHYSICAL POETRY; PRECIOSITE.

S. Freud, *Jokes and their Relation to the Unconscious* (1905; tr. 1960); *Critical Essays of the 17th C.*, ed. J. E. Spingarn, v. 1 (1908)—see Intro.; M. A. Grant, *The Ancient Rhetorical Theories of the Laughable* (1924); W. G. Crane, *W. and Rhet. in the Ren.* (1937); C. Brooks, *Mod. Poetry and the Trad.* (1939); S. H. Monk, "A Grace Beyond the Reach of Art," *JHI* 5 (1944); E. B. O. Borgerhoff, *The Freedom of Fr. Classicism* (1950); T. S. Eliot, "The Metaphysical Poets" and "Andrew Marvell" in *Essays*; W. Empson, *The Structure of Complex Words* (1951); J. E. Spingarn, *A Hist. of Lit. Crit. in the Ren.*, 2d ed. (1954); Wellek, v. 1–2; Wimsatt and Brooks, ch. 12; C. S. Lewis, *Studies in Words* (1960)—comprehensive sketch of the semantic hist.; A. Stein, "On Elizabethan W.," *SEL* 1 (1961); G. Williamson, *The Proper W. of Poetry* (1961); S. L. Bethell, "The Nature of Metaphysical W.," *Discussions of John Donne*, ed. F. Kermode (1962); T. N. Marsh, "Elizabethan W. in Metaphor and Conceit," *EM* 13 (1962); J. A. Mazzeo, *Ren. and 17th-C.*

Studies (1964); *The Idea of Comedy*, ed. W. K. Wimsatt, Jr. (1969); *Historisches Wörterbuch der Philosophie*, ed. J. Ritter and K. Gründer (1971), s.v. "Ingenium"; M. C. Wanamaker, *Discordia Concors* (1975); E. B. Gilman, *The Curious Perspective* (1978); A. J. Smith, *Metaphysical W.* (1992); J. Sitter, *Arguments of Augustan W.* (1992).
W.V.O'C.; L.NE.

WORD ACCENT. See ACCENT.

WORD CHOICE. See ARCHAISM; AUREATE DICTION; CONCRETE AND ABSTRACT; CONNOTATION AND DENOTATION; EPITHET; KENNING; LEXIS.

WORK. See TEXTUALITY; POETICS.

WRENCHED ACCENT. See ACCENT.

WRITING. See SOUND; TEXTUALITY; INTERTEXTUALITY.

X

XHOSA POETRY. See AFRICAN POETRY; SOUTH AFRICAN POETRY.

Y

YIDDISH POETRY.

    I. PRE-19TH CENTURY VERSE
    II. THE 19TH CENTURY
    III. THE TWENTIETH CENTURY

Y. is the lang. of Eastern European Jewry and that culture's offshoots the world over. It is commonly believed to date back at least a thousand years, with its roots in Western Europe. Modern Y. p. exhibits every subject and technique known in the lits. of Europe and America and derives an extra measure of cosmopolitanism from a readership distributed over five continents. But out of its combined prehistory and history of nearly a millennium, only two or three generations have witnessed this unrestricted flourishing. In traditional Ashkenazic culture, it was rather study—the continuous interp. of basic Talmudic law in the light of changing conditions of life—that absorbed the creative passions of the society. Literary expression in the Western sense was unimportant, and Jewish poetry of the premodern period (both Y. and Heb.) is marked, for all its diversity, by a generally ancillary character.

Then, with the revolutionary upheavals in East European Jewry in the late 19th and 20th c.—urbanization, industrialization, internal migration and emigration, political organization and eventual civic emancipation, attended by widespread secularization and "Europeanization" of Jewish culture—Jewish poetry in both langs. was lifted to the very top of the cultural values of Judaism. It attracted a body of talent which in previous centu-

ries would have been otherwise engaged, and, in accordance with the increased receptivity of its writers and readers to outside influences, it quickly managed to catch up with common European accomplishments. Y. p. "in one grand leap landed in the general 20th c." (Harshav). Even in its treatment of specifically Jewish themes in an imagery full of traditional allusions, Y. p. became avowedly and factually part and parcel of modern European and Am. poetic culture.

I. PRE-19TH CENTURY VERSE. The origins of Y. lit. have been lost, but early contemp. references to it as well as the developed poetic technique of the oldest dated works so far discovered (A.D. 1382) indicate a prehistory antedating the extant evidence. Prior to the 19th c., Y. lit., the bulk of which is in verse, was written in an idiom based predominantly on Western Y. dialects, a standardized lang. which was preserved without interruption in Western Europe until about 1800, then superseded by a rapidly evolving new standard on an East European interdialectal base. The influence of medieval Ger. poetic trads. and a stylistic irradiation from intentionally literal translations of the Bible caused literary Y. to be highly stylized, and only a weak reflection of contemp. colloquial speech.

Scholars originally theorized that much of this verse was meant for oral performance by professional minstrels or laymen, esp. since, even after the introduction of printing, the tune was often specified at the beginning or end of a work. More recently, however, convincing arguments have been advanced against the so-called *shpilman* theory. Epic poems both of the general European repertoire (King Arthur, Gudrun, etc., with specifically Christian references deleted) and on Old Testament themes (e.g. Samuel or the Sacrifice of Isaac) are extant in 14th- and 15th-c. recensions which show relatively strict meters and, generally, "long-line" stanza-structure of the type *xaxa xbxb.* There is now reason to believe that the European epics are translations or transcriptions of Ger. originals and that the works based on Jewish themes were written by scribes or other well-educated writers (Shmeruk).

Two verse novels by Elye Bokher (E. Levita, 1469–1549) strikingly bridge the gap between original Jewish works and borrowed secular ones. Using It. sources, Bokher created his own versions in which Jewish elements are freely integrated with the primary material. In addition, he introduced ottava rima (q.v.) into Y. well over a century before it was attempted in Ger. poetry. Elye Bokher also seems to have been the first to use accentual iambs in any European poetry.

The metrical structures of epic poetry were not carried forth elsewhere in Y. verse. This is evident in collections of 16th- and 17th-c. popular songs (which reflect a convergence of traditional with current Ger. models), in religious lyrics, in the many verse chronicles and dirges describing historical events, and also in satirical or moralizing occasional pieces, where the meters decrease in regularity until the number of syllables per measure of music varies widely and sometimes grows quite high. Y. p. of early modern times thus corresponds in its free-accentual basis to most contemp. Ger. verse. Drawing on the Heb. liturgical trad., Y. verse sometimes made use of the acrostic (q.v.) and ornamental extravagances such as making all lines of a reasonably long poem end in the same syllable.

II. THE 19TH CENTURY. Through most of the 19th c. the folksong flourished, and the recitative improvisation, narrative (on biblical subjects), and moralizing poem remained productive genres. Meanwhile Y. lit. made a new beginning, centered this time in Eastern Europe and carried by the emigrations toward the end of the century to England, the United States, and the far corners of the earth. The new writers were stimulated mostly by the *Haskalah* (Enlightenment) movement, which encouraged familiarity with European (esp. Ger. and Rus.) lit. and made Jewish writers increasingly self-conscious about the underdeveloped state of their langs., Y. and Heb., for the purposes of social crit., philosophy, and secular education.

While Heb. lit. toyed with a biblical manner, Y. writers explored the cultural framework offered by the folksong, which was noticed at last after a "submerged" existence spanning centuries, during which it was neither recorded nor reflected in lit. The Y. folksong favored an *xaxa* stanza and a free-accentual meter (usually 4 stresses per line) in which, compared with Ger. folksong, the use of unstressed syllables to fill the musical measures

was increased, probably as a result of the Slavicized prosodic structure of the lang. However, more European standards of song construction and phrasing introduced more elaborate rhyme schemes (*abab* and *aabccb* became widespread), and strict syllabotonic meters became *de rigueur* in the theater and in quasi-theatrical songs. The rising labor movement furnished a new public for song verse, but also for declamatory verse—an additional factor conducive to regular syllabotonic meters.

In the 1890s Y. p. hit its stride at last. Though it lagged noticeably behind the development of prose—particularly the shorter forms—it now became the vehicle of truly lyrical expression, as exemplified by S. Frug (1860–1916), I. L. Peretz (1852?–1915), and M. Rosenfeld (1862–1923). These authors, who had all complained about the lexical and stylistic inadequacy of Y., now laid the foundations of modern Y. p. by efforts to master a lyrical viewpoint and experiments with a variety of imagery and structural patterns.

IV. THE 20TH CENTURY. The existence of a new intelligentsia with secular education, some of it acquired in Y.-lang. schools, cast Y. p. in this period of its culmination into the mainstream of contemp. world trends. Y. lit. now showed itself more sensitive than ever to developments in other lits. with which it was in contact. There were the interest and the formal means to attempt modernism along Am., Ger., and Rus. lines. At the same time, in the Y. poetic culture there appeared genuine internal responses to innovation. The group *Di Yunge* (Young Ones) in America (M.-L. Halpern [1886–1932], Mani Leyb [1883–1953], Z. Landau [1889–1937], and others) early in the century reacted to the political tendentiousness and rhetoric of the labor poets by trying to write poetry that would be "more poetic" in diction and subject matter and more individuated in its sentiments.

Dedicated to "art for art's sake," the poets of *Di Yunge* emphasized the expression of aesthetic experience even while supporting themselves as laborers: "thank goodness I'm not a cobbler who writes poems, / But a poet who makes shoes" (Mani Leyb). *Di Yunge* cherished a vision of Y. lit. in which a monolingual reader could be a well-educated world citizen. To this end, they turned some of their energies to translation and to introducing "exotic" themes, such as Christianity and sexuality, into Y. p.

Di Yunge called forth the protest of *In zikh* (The Introspectivists), a group (A. Leyeles [1889–1966], J. Glatstein [1896–1971], and N. B. Minkoff [1893–1958], among others) which, avowedly inspired by Yehoyosh (1872–1927) and influenced by contemp. Eng. and Am. poetry, denied in principle a distinction between the intellectual and the emotional and opened wide the door of its poetry to all themes, all words, all rhythms, no matter how free or regular, so long as they embodied the personal experience of the poet. As expressed in its manifesto of 1920, the *In zikh* poets saw no theoretical reason to identify themselves as Jewish artists other than that they were Jews and wrote Y. Moreover, although they accepted syllabotonic meters as a possibility, they were in fact convinced that free rhythms were the surest vehicle for achieving poetic truth. Finally, they had no fear of exposing their deepest psychic realities, embracing free association as their chief poetic method.

As the cumulative effect of a growing corpus of poetry made itself felt, the demands for originality pushed Y. poets onto new paths. Assonance as a substitute for rhyme was explored (e.g. by P. Markish [1895–1952] and other Soviet poets). Sonnet sequences and works in the more difficult Romance fixed forms were successfully created (e.g. L. Naydus [1890–1918]). Syntactic parallelism, etymological figures, and consonance were mobilized to recreate biblical Heb. effects in a new Jewish medium. Epic poems, verse novels, and verse drama (esp. by H. Leivick [1888–1962]) were produced and acclaimed. Interest in Old Y. p. was awakened, and several writers attempted new works in 16th-c. lang. The poems of S. Etinger (1800–56), a forgotten modernist, were published posthumously. The folksong reappeared, but this time in subtly stylized forms (e.g. by Halpern and I. Manger [b. 1901]).

Post-World War I regional constellations such as the expressionist group *Di Khaliastre* (the Gang) in Warsaw (U. Z. Greenberg [d. 1896–1981], Melech Ravitch [d. 1976], and others) and *Yung-Vilne* (Young Vilna) in Vilna (notably Chaim Grade [1910–82] and A. Sutzkever [b. 1913]) set themselves specialized tasks against a common literary background. The sweet awareness of a poetic trad. being formed was reflected in poetic allusions to well-known poems. A standardized literary lang. came into use in which dialectal rhymes and expressions grew ever rarer.

In this period, the "discovery of the mother tongue," now emancipated in its functions, was completed. Poets by the scores, following the major writers of the late 19th c., learned to use the Y. lang. to its full extent. Y. prosodic structure, Germanic but remodeled presumably along Slavic lines, was employed to create easy triple and even paeonic meters. The refreshing syntax of conversational folk Y. was channeled into poetry (notably by E. Shteynbarg [1880–1932]). The pernicious etymologizing approach of the past was dead: words were used according to their precise Y. phonology and semantics, without reference to—and sometimes in defiance of—their form and meaning in the stock langs. Sound frequencies typical of a particular component of Y. were forged into a new poetic device, making it possible, for instance, to suggest "Slavicness," and hence village earthiness, by an accumulation of *z* and *c* sounds (thus M. Kulbak [1896–1940]), or "Germanness" by emphasizing *a* and final *e* sounds (e.g. Glatstein).

At the same time, the idiom of traditional Jewish study was annexed to the modern literary lang.; it found use not only when required by the subject (as in the poetry of M. Boraisho [1888–1949], A. Zeitlin [1899–1974], or Grade), but also in thematically unspecialized writing, where it functions simply as a flexible abstract vocabulary. Above all, the many derivational patterns of Y. grammar were exploited for the enrichment of the lang. New coinages abounded, and some, like *umkum* (violent death) and *vogl* (restless wandering), have become common elements of the lang. The poetry of Glatstein and Sutzkever is particularly rich in novel derivations.

With the genocide of six million Jews by Germany and her Axis collaborators, Jewish cultural life in most of Eastern Europe was virtually destroyed; what was left received a second devastating blow through Stalin's ban of Y. culture and the elimination of Y. writers in the USSR after 1949, culminating in the August 12, 1952 murder of the Y. poets Markish, D. Hofshteyn (b. 1889), L. Kvitkob (b. ca. 1890), and I. Fefer (b. 1900), among others. The Holocaust of the war years naturally became the central theme of Y. lit. not only in the Nazi-made ghettos, but globally. However, after 1948, the rebirth of a Jewish state in Israel opened new subjects, descriptive, psychological, and ethical, to Y. p.; there an active Y. cultural life rapidly developed, incl. publication of *Di goldene keyt* (The Golden Chain), the premier Y. literary journal.

The technical brilliance of Y. p. did not diminish in the postwar period. In its rhythmic features, however, postwar writing seems to have retreated from the experimentation of the previous period. As Leyeles put it: "When there are no bounds to suffering, create, through pain, a ritual fence [i.e. a preventive measure] of rigorously restrained patterning."

What might be called the second generation since the catastrophic events of the Holocaust and Stalinism reveals a shift in the balance of Y. verse. Whereas actual poetic output is shrinking, scholarship has reached new levels of sophistication and intensity. This phenomenon is directly related to the decimation of the Y.-speaking community and hence the number of native speakers of Y. Those poets who remain, such as Sutzkever, B. Heller (b. 1908), and G. Preil (b. 1910), must contend with the problem of creating in a lang. whose future is, at best, uncertain: "During daytime a funeral, at night a concert / And inevitably, I go to both" (Sutzkever). Scholarly research, by contrast, has been increasingly active, and undertaken more and more by those who are not native speakers of Y. Their work, encompassing a wide variety of perspectives, e.g. historical, social, feminist, psychoanalytic, and comparative, highlights the tremendous vitality of the poetic corpus, even if the number of poets living today is small. One major outcome of recent studies and anthologies is the greater recognition and appreciation of Y. women poets. See also HEBREW POETRY.

YUGOSLAV POETRY

ANTHOLOGIES: *Antologye: finf hundert yor yidishe poezye*, ed. M. Bassin, 2 v. (1917); *Yidishe dikhterins: antologye*, ed. E. Korman (1928); *Naye yidishe dikhtung*, ed. Y. Paner and E. Frenkl (1946); *Dos lid iz geblibn*, ed. B. Heller (1951); *Mivhar Shirei Y.*, tr. into Heb. by M. Basuk (1963); *A shpigl af a shteyn*, ed. Kh. Shmeruk (1964)—focuses on murdered Soviet writers; *A Treasury of Y. P.*, ed. I. Howe and E. Greenberg (1969); *Selected Poems of Jacob Glatstein*, tr. R. Whitman (1972); M.-L. Halpern, *In New York: A Selection*, ed. and tr. K. Hellerstein (1982); *Am. Y. P.: A Bilingual Anthol.*, ed. B. and B. Harshav [Hrushovski] (1986); *Penguin Book of Mod. Y. Verse*, ed. I. Howe et al. (1987)—Y. and Eng.

HISTORY AND CRITICISM: L. Wiener, *Hist. of Y. Lit. in the 19th C.* (1899); M. Weinreich, *Bilder fun der yidisher literatur-geshikhte* (1928); D. Hofshteyn and F. Shames, *Literatur-kentenish (poetik)*, 2 v. (1927–28); M. Erik, *Di geshikhte fun der yidisher lit.* (1928); Z. Reyzen, *Leksikon fun der yidisher lit.*, 4 v. (1928); Y. Tsinberg, *Di geshikhte fun der lit. bay yidn*, v. 6 (1935); N. B. Minkoff, *Yidishe klasiker poetn*, 2d ed. (1939), *Pyonern fun yidisher poezye in amerike*, 3 v. (1956); Y. Mark, "Y. Lit.," *The Jews*, ed. L. Finkelstein, v. 2 (1949); N. B. Minkoff and J. A. Joffe, "Old Y. Lit.," and S. Niger, "Y. Lit. of the Past 200 Years," *The Jewish People Past and Present*, v. 3 (1952); B. Hrushovski [Harshav], "On Free Rhythms in Mod. Y. P.," *The Field of Y.*, ed. U. Weinreich, v. 1 (1954), "The Creation of Accentual Iambs," *For Max Weinreich on his 70th Birthday* (1964), *The Meaning of Y.* (1990); *Leksikon fun der nayer yidisher literatur*, 8 v. (1956–); U. Weinreich, "On the Cultural Hist. of Y. Rime," *Essays on Jewish Life and Thought*, ed. J. L. Blau (1959); S. Liptzin, *The Flowering of Y. Lit.* (1964), *The Maturing of Y. Lit.* (1970); I. Howe, *World of Our Fathers* (1976), ch. 13; J. Hadda, *Yankev Glatshteyn* (1980); Kh. Shmeruk, *Prokim fun der yidisher literatur-geshikhte* (1988); R. Wisse, *A Little Love in Big Manhattan* (1988); F. W. Aaron, *Bearing the Unbearable: Y. and Polish P. in the Ghettos and Concentration Camps* (1990). U.W.; J.H.

YORUBA POETRY. See AFRICAN POETRY.

YUEH-FU. See CHINESE POETRY.

YUGOSLAV POETRY. (This article surveys the poetries written in the regions of Ragusa, Dalmatia, Serbia, Slovenia, Croatia, and Macedonia in the former country known as Yugoslavia. For discussion of Serbian, Croatian, and Slovene prosody, see SLAVIC PROSODY.)

The natural aptitude of the Y. peoples for poetic invention throughout their history is demonstrated by the wealth and beauty of their folk poetry. This poetry is of two kinds, "heroic" or epic, and lyric. The lyric poems, in lines of varying lengths and meters, express every emotion and every aspect of the life of the people. There are ritual and ceremonial songs, dirges, love songs, work songs, and songs sung to accompany dancing or various celebrations. The majority of the epic (heroic) songs relate events from the country's past. Mythological or semi-legendary themes occur in those of earlier origin: the more recent the ballad the more authentic its subject. The ballads with historical subjects deal for the most part with the struggles against the Turks. The cycle describing incidents connected with the disastrous battle of Kosovo in 1389 has the greatest aesthetic value and is the most moving. Metrically, a regular line in the majority of the epic ballads is decasyllabic, with a caesura after the fourth syllable and a clear tendency toward trochaic distribution of stresses and with a quantitative close: ∪ ∪ – ∪ . (When stressed, the ninth syllable is usually long, and the eighth and seventh are short.) The basis of Y. epic meter is thus both stress and quantity and has been a matter of detailed study. There is little or no rhyme.

Y. folk poetry was virtually unknown outside of the country until the field studies in Yugoslavia of Milman Parry and Albert B. Lord in the 1930s and 1950s and the publication of the results of their findings. Parry and Lord (after Parry's death, Lord and David E. Bynum) recorded many oral folksongs, on the basis of which they formulated their theories about the characteristics, structure, and formulas of South Slavic folksongs. They applied their theories about the formulaic idioms to other ancient and medieval epics, which, in turn, has led to a continuing discussion about the basic nature of folk poetry, becoming an indispensable part of the genre's study today.

As regards written verse, the earliest consisted principally of 13th- and 14th-c. translations of hymns and other poems of an ecclesiastical nature. The liturgical verse of the Orthodox Church, influenced by Byzantium, was mostly translated from Gr. and was written in Serbian recensions of Old Church Slavonic in the Cyrillic alphabet. That of the Roman Catholic Church, in the Glagolitic alphabet, was similar in character, but Catholic religious verse not purely liturgical was also written in the vernacular. The earliest extant records of this poetry date from the 15th c.

When the cultural development of the peoples of the interior was suppressed under foreign domination, conditions were favorable for the cultivation of lit. only in the free republic of Dubrovnik (Ragusa) and elsewhere in Dalmatia. Here poetry began to flourish in the 15th c. under the influence of the It. Ren. The Petrarchan lyric was imitated in Dubrovnik first by the "troubadour" poets Šiško Menčetić (1457–1527) and Džore Držić (1461–1501), of whom the latter was less imitative and more sincere. These poets favored a slightly modified form of the *strambotto* (q.v.) as well as the Petrarchan sonnet. The conceits (q.v.) employed by the It. lyricists were introduced with ingenuity into this poetry, which yet retained some indigenous elements and certain reminiscences of folk ballads. Love is the predominant motive, but other themes such as patriotism and religion occur. The meter is usually a dodecasyllabic line with internal rhyme, but an octosyllabic line is also employed by certain subsequent poets. Songs of a similar character, sung by shepherds, were introduced into the "pastoral novel" *Planine* (The Mountains) by Petar Zoranić (b. 1508?) of Zadar. Another aspect of It. influence is seen in imitations of Florentine carnival poetry. Of these, *Jedjupka* (The Gypsy) by Mikša Pelegrinović (1500?–26) of Hvar, has the greatest charm and originality. The earliest epic was *Judita* (1501) by Marko Marulić (1450–1524) of Split. Using the dodecasyllabic line, and in verse in which fashionable adornments are not absent, he relates the biblical story of Judith, suggesting an analogy between its background and his own country's perils. Other notable poetic works of the 16th c., in the same meter, are *Robinja* (The Slave-girl) by Hanibal Lucić (1485?–1553) of Hvar, the earliest secular dramatic work in Croatian lit., though a narrative poem in dialogue form rather than a drama; and *Ribanje i ribarsko prigovaranje* (Fishing and Fishermen's Talk) by Petar Hektorović (1487–1572), also of Hvar. Although this poem, describing a fishing expedition, is to some extent reminiscent of It. piscatorial eclogues, it is one of the most original and realistic works of the period. Folk-epic songs sung by fishermen in the poem represent the earliest written record of Y. traditional poetry. The lyrical, contemplative, and epic poetry of Mavro Vetranović (1482–1576), often with a moralizing purpose, was relatively free from foreign influences but generally of little aesthetic value. New metrical forms, imitated or adapted from It. lyrics, were introduced to Ragusan poetry by Dinko Ranjina (1536–1607) and Dinko Zlatarić (1558?–1613?), whose work as translators of Gr. and Lat. verse also reflects the Ren. revival of interest in Cl. lit. in Italy.

With the work of Ivan Gundulić (1589–1638), Ragusan lit. is generally considered to have reached its "Golden Age." The influence of the Ren. had given way to that of the Counter-Reformation; national consciousness, a moral purpose, religious feeling, and philosophical meditations—elements found scattered among the works of most of his predecessors—are supreme in those of Gundulić. His *Suze sina razmetnoga* (The Tears of the Prodigal Son), in 3 cantos, is a confession of sin and a meditation on the transitoriness of earthly things. In his greatest work, the epic *Osman*, a poem inspired by his faith in the Slavs and in Christianity, Gundulić weaves a complex pattern of incidents around his central theme—an event in the contemporary war between the Poles and Turks. The epic is akin to those of Tasso and Ariosto, with stylistic traits of Marinism (q.v.). It is composed in quatrains of octosyllables rhyming *abab*.

The Ragusan love lyric continued to flourish in the verse—with characteristics of Marinism—of Stijepo Djurdjević (1579–1632), best known for his satirical *Derviš*, describing the emotions of an elderly dervish in love; and in the exquisite, concise, and erotic poems of Ivan Bunić (1591–1658?). Both Bunić and the last great Ragusan lyricist, Ignjat Djurdjević (1675–1737), in whose work the baroque influence predominates, also treated the subject of the repentant Mary Magdalene in longer works inspired by Gundulić.

As lit. slowly revived elsewhere in the Y. lands, verse was at first put to practical uses. Employing the convenient decasyllabic line of the epic folk-ballads, Andrija Kačić-Miošić (1704–60), of central Dalmatia, wrote a chronicle of the South Slavs, and Matija Reljković (1732–98), a Slavonian, composed his admonitory poem *Satir* (The Satyr). The Serb Jovan Rajić (1726–1801) composed, among other works, an allegorical-historical epic *Boj zmaja s orlovi* (The Battle of the Dragon with the Eagles) in the artificial *rusko-slovenski* lang. cultivated by Serbian writers of his period. The didactic element, characteristic of the lit. of this time, is present in the pseudo-classical lyric poetry of the Serb Lukijan Mušicki (1777–1837). Meanwhile the foundations of Slovene poetry were laid by Valentin Vodnik (1758–1819), the first Slovene poet to write in the vernacular.

With the romantic movement came the revival of poetic composition as an art and the inspiration derived from the indigenous folk poetry, vast collections of which were made in the first half of the 19th c. by Vuk Karadžić (1787–1864), to whom future Serbian and Croatian writers were also indebted for his linguistic reforms. The folk-poetry element is a characteristic of the work of Sima Milutinović (1791–1847), whose epic and lyric poetry glorifying the Serbs is a mixture of realism and fantasy. It is also a characteristic of the work of the great Serbian poet, Petar Petrović Njegoš (1813–51), Prince-Bishop of Montenegro. Njegoš's lyric and epic poetry, composed in intellectual isolation, expresses his intense patriotism and his groping for a solution to the philosophical problems which tormented him. His *Luča mikrokozma* (The Torch of the Microcosm) treats a subject similar to that of Milton's *Paradise Lost*; his greatest work, *Gorski vijenac* (The Mountain Wreath), is an epic in dramatic form and a synthesis of aspects of Montenegrin life. The epic *Smrt Smail-Age Čengica*, by the Croat Ivan Mažuranić (1814–90), also in the style of the epic songs, graphically and powerfully depicts the sufferings of Montenegrins under Turkish oppression. The sonnet was introduced to the Croatian lit. of the period by Stanko Vraz (1810–51), who wrote also in the style of the folk ballads. Both he and Petar Preradović (1818–72) composed moving love lyrics at a time when poetry in Croatia comprised mainly patriotic verse.

New inspiration was brought to Serbian poetry by the fresh, spontaneous lyrics of Branko Radičević (1824–53). The meter is again often

YUGOSLAV POETRY

that of the folk ballads, but the themes are very diverse. Lyric poetry became the principal literary product of young Serbian writers after the middle of the century: Jovan Jovanović Zmaj (1833–1904) wrote simple and moving personal lyrics, later pouring out verses commenting on contemp. events; Djura Jakšić (1832–78) composed patriotic verse whose stridency contrasts with the melancholy tone of his emotional poems, e.g. his poignant *Na Liparu* (In the Lime-grove). The last of the great Serbian romantic poets was Laza Kostić (1841–1910), a translator of Shakespeare and composer of Shakespearean verse dramas and of lyric poetry.

The work of Slovenia's greatest poet, France Prešeren (1800–49) showed for the first time the potentialities of Slovene as a literary lang. His sonnets, sincere expressions of emotion, are examples of perfect harmony of form and theme. The cultivation of lyric poetry in various forms continued in Slovenia. That of Fran Levstik (1831–87) is sincere and expressive; Josip Stritar (1836–1923) skillfully experimented with various meters and poetic forms. This concern with form is seen also in the lyrics of Simon Gregorčič (1844–1906), expressing his love of nature and his longing to promote tolerance. The influence of folk poetry is evident in the lyrics of Simon Jenko (1835–69), a poet of patriotism, nature, and love; and the historical ballads which Anton Aškerc (1856–1912), nationalist and social critic, made the vehicle for expression of his principles were sometimes composed in the decasyllabic line; but no one meter can from this period onward be considered characteristic of Y. verse.

In Croatia, Silvije Strahimir Kranjčević (1865–1908) wrote with great violence or pathos, his work reflecting his nationalistic, socialistic, and anti-clerical views, and his pessimism and bitterness. Meanwhile the Croatian critic A. G. Matoš (1873–1914), himself a poet, demanded complete freedom of expression in poetry, which should be untrammelled by any tendentious elements and in which aesthetic value should be of supreme importance. To his teaching were added lessons in form and technique derived from the Parnassians (q.v.). Prominent among Matoš's contemporaries, the Croatian "modernists," were the poets Dragutin Domjanić (1875–1933), Vladimir Vidrić (1875–1909), and Milan Begović (1876–1948). Ljubo Wiesner (1885–1951) and Nikola Polić (1890–1960) were among those who continued the trad. of the subjective, aesthetic lyric, and an outstanding Croatian lyricist, Tin Ujević (1891–1955), with verse of great diversity of subject, emotion, expression, and form, may be counted as a disciple of Matoš. The eminent Croat Vladimir Nazor (1876–1949), optimistic and exuberant, expressed an intense love of all forms of life and nature in lyric verse and in epics with legendary or historical themes.

In Serbia, Vojislav Ilić (1860–94), a pure lyricist,

provided examples of poetic technique for future poets. The works of a trio of lyric poets, Aleksa Šantić (1868–1924), a writer of patriotic and emotional verse; Jovan Dučić (1871–1943), whose lyrics, exquisite in phrasing and form, show the influence of the Parnassians, and Milan Raki'c (1876–1938), equally a perfectionist but a poet of profounder ideas and emotions, represent some of the best and purest in Serbian poetry of the next decades. Meanwhile there appeared a great Serbian lyricist of another school, Vladislav Petković-Dis (1880–1917), a poet of dreams and despair, to whom the sincere expression of emotions was of more importance than a studied perfection of form. Characteristics of the decadent movement in Serbian poetry before the First World War are found also in the melancholy verse of Sima Pandurović (1883–1960); Veljko Petrovič (1884–1967) wrote verse of sympathy for the victims of social injustices as well as vigorous patriotic verse. Pessimism is characteristic of the lyrics of Dušan Vasiljev (1900–24), the poet of revolt. One of the most prominent 20th-c. Serbian poets, Miloš Crnjanski (1893–1977), expresses his emotions and disillusionment in verses of great originality of both form and theme. The poetry of Rade Drainac (1899–1943) and of the poetess Desanka Maksimović (b. 1898) is also intimate, subjective, and emotional; but while that of the former may be bitter in tone, that of the latter is sensitive and delicate, and notable for its beauty and purity of expression. Oskar Davičo (b. 1909), a consummate craftsman, began as a surrealist in the late 1920s and has remained vitally present ever since. In postwar Serbian poetry, the most prominent poets are Vasko Popa (b. 1922) and Miodrag Pavlović (b. 1928). In his cyclical poetry Popa combines traditionalism and new myths, offering a new vision of man and universe. Pavlović also creates new myths out of old Serbian legends in contemplative, erudite, and stunningly crafted poems. Stevan Raičković (b. 1928) is down-to-earth and nature-bound, a pure lyricist, while Ivan V. Lalić (b. 1931) writes intellectual, neoclassical, masterfully refined poems. Branko Miljković (1934–61) created an influential body of poetry of intense contemplation and heightened lyricism. Of the younger generation, Ljubomir Simović (b. 1935), Borislav Radović (b. 1935), and Matija Bećković (b. 1939) epitomize a large group of gifted poets.

Miroslav Krleža (1893–1981), the dominant figure in contemp. Croatian lit., has composed ballads and lyrics, many of which are indictments of social injustice, most of them vigorous and intense. Of other Croats, Ivan Goran Kovačić (1913–43) will be remembered chiefly as a poet of the Second World War for his impressive cycle *Jama* (The Pit). Gustav Krklec (1899–1980), Dobriša Cesarić (1902–77), Nikola Šop (1904–82), and Dragutin Tadijanović (b. 1905) contribute to the wealth of 20th-c. Croatian lyric poetry, remarkable for its variety, spontaneity, and originality. The work of Krklec has been described as a "lyrical monologue" reflecting the varying emotions of the poet's life; Cesarić, without striving after unconventional forms of expression, has written works of great aesthetic value; Šop, earlier known for his sensitive religious lyrics, has now turned his attention to longer philosophical works inspired by poetic visions of space; the spontaneous and sincere lyrics of Tadijanović express his dreams and emotions, his love of nature, and his nostalgia for the simple life. In the postwar generation, the works of Jure Kaštelan (b. 1919)—whose style has been compared with that of Walt Whitman—and of Vesna Parun (b. 1922), while still subjective, are concerned with more general human problems. Of other important postwar Croatian poets, Zvonimir Golob (b. 1927) is an image-maker influenced by Sp. and South Am. poets; Slavko Mihalić (b. 1928) meditates on the fate of the individual in a modern society, blending simplicity, precision, and lyrical fluency; and Milivoj Slaviček (b. 1929) poeticizes a running dialogue with his fellow man and with himself about the basic questions of existence. In the next generation, Ivan Slamnig (b. 1930), a diligent experimenter, blends black humor, seriousness, and strong intellectualism. Vlado Gotovac (b. 1930) writes a terse, hermetic, yet authentically lyrical poetry of ideas, while Antun Šoljan (b. 1932), influenced, like Slamnig, by Eng. and Am. poetry, creates clear images and parables, revealing an intense inner life. Daniel Dragojević (b. 1934), also a creator of parables and images with philosophical, religious, and visual-artistic undertones, leads a welter of promising young poets.

Oton Župančič (1878–1949), the greatest Slovene poet of the 20th c., turned from the early influence of the symbolists to the composition of lyrics which are striking in their originality and variety in form and phrasing. His influence is seen in the work of Alojz Gradnik (1882–1967). Between the wars, social criticism was the concern not only of Slovene prose writers but of poets; outstanding among the latter were Anton Podbevšek (b. 1898) and Mile Klopčič (b. 1905). Župančič and the poet-dramatist Matej Bor (b. 1913) composed verse inspired by World War II. Other prominent Slovene poets are Srečko Kosovel (1904–26), Edvard Kocbek (1904–81), and Miran Jarc (1900–42), one of the foremost exponents of expressionism. Of the younger generation, Ciril Zlobec (b. 1925), Tone Pavček (b. 1928), Dane Zajc (b. 1929), Gregor Strniša (1930–87), and Kajetan Kovič (b. 1931) have established themselves as the leading poets. Zlobec mixes lyrical sensitivity with a concern for prosaic problems. Zajc depicts the loneliness and alienation of modern man beset with fear of the futility of existence. Strniša created highly articulate allegories, metaphors, and dream sequences. Kovič combines sensitive contemplation, intellectual vigor, and radical experimentation. More recently, Veno Taufer (b. 1933), influenced by modern Eng. poetry, exhibits surrealist and neo-expressionist traits, while Tomaž Šalamun (b. 1941), the most vocal and iconoclastic among younger poets, writes associative poetry, using its seeming chaos as a freeing agent to drive his points home.

The youngest of Y. lits., Macedonian, has existed underground for centuries but came into full bloom only after World War II. Among pioneers, Kosta Racin (1908–43) deserves a place of honor for his sincere and emotional poems about the fate of his countrymen. The three founders of contemp. Macedonian poetry are Slavko Janevski (b. 1920), Blaže Koneski (b. 1921), and Aco Šopov (1923–83). The picturesque and boldly imaginative poetry of Janevski is complemented by Koneski's direct, intimate, and meditative poetry and by Šopov's subtle lyricism and intense sensitivity. The next generation, represented by Mateja Matevski (b. 1929) and Gane Todorovski (b. 1929), extends the horizons, as do Radovan Pavlovski (b. 1934) and Bogomil Djuzel (b. 1939), two of the many promising younger poets. In a time of bitter ethnic and regional warfare, contemp. Y. p. nevertheless continues to be characterized by unabating vitality, modern idiom, freedom of expression, variety, experimentation, and openness to world poetry.

ANTHOLOGIES: *Heroic Ballads of Serbia*, tr. G. R. Noyes and L. R. Bacon (1913); *Serbian Songs and Poems*, tr. J. W. Wiles (1917); *Kossovo: Heroic Songs of the Serbs*, tr. H. Rootham (1920); *Ballads of Marko Kraljevic*, tr. D. H. Low (1922); *Antologija novije hrvatske lirike*, ed. M. Kombol (1934); *Anthologie de la poésie yougoslave des XIXe et XXe siècle*, tr. and ed. M. and S. Ibrovac (1935); *The Revolt of the Serbs against the Turks, 1804–1813*, tr. W. A. Morison (1942); *Srpske narodne pjesme*, ed. Vuk Karadžić, 1–4 (1953–58); *Antologija novije srpske lirike*, ed. B. Popović, 9th ed. (1953); *The Parnassus of a Small Nation, An Anthol. of Slovene Lyrics*, tr. and ed. W. K. Matthews and A. Slodnjak (1957); *Antologija dubrovačke lirike*, ed. D. Pavlović (1960); *An Anthol. of Mod. Y. P.*, ed. J. Lavrin (1962); *Novija jugoslavenska poezija*, ed. V. Popović (1962); *Antologija srpskog pesništva*, ed. M. Pavlović (1964); *Contemp. Y. P.*, ed. V. D. Mihailovich (1977); *Marko the Prince: Serbo-Croat Heroic Songs*, ed. and tr. A. Pennington and P. Levi (1984); *Serbian P. from the Beginnings to the Present*, ed. M. Holton and V. D. Mihailovich (1988).

HISTORY AND CRITICISM: J. Torbarina, *It. Influence on the Poets of the Ragusan Republic* (1931); D. Subotić, *Y. Popular Ballads* (1932); A. Slodnjak, *Geschichte der slowenischen Literatur* (1958); A. Kadić, *Contemp. Croatian Lit.* (1960), *Contemp. Serbian Lit.* (1964); M. P. Coote, "Serbocroatian Heroic Songs," *Heroic Epic and Saga*, ed. F. J. Oinas (1978); S. Koljević, *The Epic in the Making* (1980).
V.J.; V.D.M.

Z

ZÉJEL (Ar. *zajal;* Fr. *zadjal*). A Sp. poem consisting of an introductory strophe (known as the *cabeza*), presenting the theme to be developed and followed by strophes each patterned as follows: a monorhymed tercet, called the *mudanza,* followed by the *vuelta* (repetition) of one. line or more rhyming with the introductory stanza. The simplest form of this strophe is the quatrain rhyming *aaab cccb* and so on, the *b* rhyme remaining constant throughout the poem. Multiple variations of this basic form are found. The octosyllable is a frequent line length, though others are also used. The problem of the z.'s origins is the subject of scholarly debate: colloquial Hispano-Romance, Med. Lat., and Hispano-Ar. poetry each have their advocates. See HISPANO-ARABIC POETRY.—P. Le Gentil, "A propos de la 'strophe zéjelesque,'" *RLR* 70 (1949), *Le Virelai et le villancico* (1954); M. Frenk, *Estudios sobre lírica antigua* (1978), 309–26; E. C. Minkareh, "The Z. in 15th-c. Castile," *FCS* 6 (1983); Navarro; V. Beltrán Pepió, "De zéjeles y *dansas*: Orígenes y formación de la estrofa con vuelta," *RFE* 64 (1984); J. T. Monroe, "Poetic Quotation in the Muwaššaha and Its Implications: Andalusian Strophic Poetry as Song," *La Corónica* 14 (1986). D.C.C.

ZEUGMA (Gr. "means of binding"; cf. Gr. *zeugos,* "yoke"). (1) In Cl. rhet., the use of a single verb with a compound object. Quintilian (*Institutio oratoria* 9.3.62) calls this construction *synezeugmenon;* in his examples, however, the subject or object or both may be compound, and later rhetoricians extend the definition to the "yoking" together of any two parts of speech by means of any other, both of which it agrees with grammatically and semantically. Puttenham (Bk 3, ch. 12) and other Ren. rhetoricians (e.g. Johannes Susenbrotus, *Epitome troporum ac schematum* [1541]) distinguish three varieties of z. according to whether the "yoking" word precedes the words it "yokes" (*prozeugma*); stands between them (*mesozeugma,* e.g. "Much he the place admired, the person more"—Milton, *Paradise Lost* 9.444); or follows them (*hypozeugma*). But this placement schema sometimes confuses the grammatical construction.

In *syllepsis* (q.v.) the "yoking" word agrees grammatically with only one of the "yoked," giving the effect of a semantic sleight-of-hand, the verb now having two senses. Puttenham calls z. "the single supply" and syllepsis "the double supply," treating z. as one form of ellipsis (q.v.), i.e. the class of figures that "work by defect." Since no double meaning is involved, z. is a merely "auricular" figure, "reaching no higher then th'eare and forcing the mynde little or nothing." Much confusion has been generated through the failure to distinguish the species (syllepsis) from the genus (z.), and even today agreement on definitions in the rhetorical handbooks is virtually nil. Syllepsis seems by far the more interesting and forceful figure.

(2) In Cl. prosody, z. (Lat. *iunctura*) refers to restrictions on the position of word-boundaries in verse, i.e. *bridge* (q.v.).—C. Walz, *Rhetores graeci,* 9 v. (1832–36), 8.474, 686, 709; Sr. M. Joseph, *Shakespeare's Use of the Arts of Lang.* (1947), 58, 166, 296; L. A. Sonnino, *Handbook to 16th-C. Rhet.* (1968), 22, 50; Lausberg, sect. 702–7; Group Mu, 70, 75; Morier; A. Quinn, *Figures of Speech* (1982), 29–31; B. Vickers, *Cl. Rhet. in Eng. Poetry,* 2d ed. (1989); Corbett, 448. T.V.F.B.

ZULU POETRY. See AFRICAN POETRY.

Books by Stephen W. Sears

THE CENTURY COLLECTION OF CIVIL WAR ART

HOMETOWN U.S.A.

THE AUTOMOBILE IN AMERICA

LANDSCAPE TURNED RED
THE BATTLE OF ANTIETAM

GEORGE B. McCLELLAN
THE YOUNG NAPOLEON

THE CIVIL WAR PAPERS OF GEORGE B. McCLELLAN
SELECTED CORRESPONDENCE, 1860–1865

MAJOR GENERAL GEORGE B. MCCLELLAN,
photographed by Mathew Brady

HARVARD COLLEGE LIBRARY

WITHDRAWP

THE CIVIL WAR PAPERS OF
GEORGE B. McCLELLAN,

SELECTED CORRESPONDENCE, 1860–1865

973.73
M132c

EDITED BY

STEPHEN W. SEARS

LIBRARY ST. MARY'S COLLEGE

TICKNOR & FIELDS
NEW YORK
1989

178361

Copyright © 1989 by Stephen W. Sears

ALL RIGHTS RESERVED

For information about permission to reproduce selections
from this book, write to Permissions, Ticknor & Fields,
52 Vanderbilt Avenue, New York, New York 10017.

Library of Congress Cataloging-in-Publication Data

McClellan, George Brinton, 1826–1885.
[Correspondence. Selections]
The Civil War Papers of George B. McClellan : selected
correspondence, 1860–1865 / edited by Stephen W. Sears.
p. cm.
Includes indexes.
ISBN 0-89919-337-4
1. McClellan, George Brinton, 1826–1885 — Correspondence.
2. United States — History — Civil War, 1861–1865 — Campaigns.
3. Generals — United States — Correspondence. I. Sears, Stephen W.
II. Title.
E467.1.M2A4 1989 88-29447
973.7'82'0924 — dc19 CIP

Printed in the United States of America

V 10 9 8 7 6 5 4 3 2 1

$32.55 Acq 4-10-90 (J.R.B.)

CONTENTS

July 22, 1861 -
- Took control of Army
of the Potomac

April 23, 1861 - Appt'd
Major General of volunteers
May 14, 1861 - Major Gen. of
Union Army

Nov 11, 1862 - Final relief
of command

INTRODUCTION

THIS COLLECTION of General George B. McClellan's Civil War correspondence presents him in a wide variety of wartime roles — army commander, theater commander, general-in-chief, grand strategist, battlefield tactician, military executive, political partisan, presidential candidate. Among Union commanders, only Grant and Halleck matched McClellan's range of military positions; overall, his combination of roles made him unique in the war years.

General McClellan served on active duty for something over eighteen months, from late April 1861 to early November 1862. He was in the upper echelons of command from the very beginning. When he was appointed major general of volunteers on April 23, 1861, and then major general in the regular army on May 14, it ranked him second only to Winfield Scott, the general-in-chief. After directing operations in the western theater as head of the Department of the Ohio and campaigning in western Virginia, he was summoned to Washington following the Bull Run debacle to organize and train the Army of the Potomac — the task he always regarded as his greatest wartime accomplishment. During the same period, in the winter of 1861–1862, he served for four months as general-in-chief of all the Union armies. His Peninsula campaign in the spring and summer of 1862 was one of the major operations of the war. In the Second Bull Run campaign his role was peripheral but highly controversial. His operations in Maryland that fall witnessed, at Antietam, what is still the bloodiest single day of battle in the nation's history. When he was relieved of command seven weeks after Antietam, he was the army's senior general.

Until the emergence of Grant and Sherman, McClellan was unquestionably the best-known military figure in the North, and he stands alongside those two generals in the importance of his impact on the war. No one came close to matching him as a center of controversy. In the election of 1864 some 1.8 million of his fellow citizens voted for him as the Democratic nominee for president, and if on Election Day he lost to Lincoln by a full ten percentage points, his vote count nonetheless represented a sizable constituency. By any measure, George McClellan was a figure to be reckoned with in the Civil War years.

This first collection of his wartime papers includes a surprising number of previously unpublished military letters and dispatches, many of them of considerable historical importance. Very little of his personal correspondence has been published, or published as he wrote it, until now. Of the 813 pieces of correspondence selected for this volume, 260, nearly a third, have not been in print before, and another 192 — his letters to his wife — appear here uncensored for the first time.

Although McClellan military correspondence may be found in greater or lesser amounts scattered through some twenty volumes of the *Official Records* of the Civil War armies — and in volumes of the *Official Records* of the navies as well — the compilers of these war records had by no means the entire body of McClellan's military documents from which to choose. Hundreds of his dispatches remained unseen in his personal papers.

When he took final leave of the Army of the Potomac at Warrenton Junction, Virginia, on November 11, 1862, McClellan carried away with him virtually all the army's headquarters papers. The new commander, Ambrose Burnside, can have inherited little more than current paperwork. That winter and into the spring of 1863 McClellan and his staff, stationed in New York City, worked through this mass of records in the course of preparing the final report of his tenure as commander of the Potomac army. This book-length work, when it was published in 1864, contained page after page of the general's letters and telegrams selected to document — and to rationalize — his actions. As delivered to the War Department, the manuscript of McClellan's *Report on the Organization of the Army of the Potomac, and of Its Campaigns in Virginia and Maryland* was accompanied by numerous maps and 263 reports by subordinates, but nothing more of the army's records was returned to the government.

McClellan regarded what remained in his hands — copies of his dispatches and dispatches received from others, unofficial and informal communications to and from him, drafts and memorandums and planning papers, intra-army battlefield messages and communications of every kind and in great number — as his property; only the contents of his *Report* and what related directly to it (such as the reports of his subordinates) were by his description public documents belonging to the government. On one occasion, at the request of the War Records Office, he supplied copies of a few papers bearing on his western Virginia campaign, but on the whole he contributed almost nothing to the *Official Records* project in the postwar years. In 1896, eleven years after McClellan's death, his son, New York congressman George B. McClellan, Jr., loaned a few of his father's dispatch books to the War Records compilers, and the considerable number of dispatches they utilized from them in the supplementary volumes of the *Official Records* suggests how much more complete the official historical record of the war for the years 1861 and 1862 might have been had the McClellan Papers in their entirety been made available from the first.

In selecting the contents of this volume, only McClellan's letters, telegrams, memorandums, and certain documents such as proclamations and addresses to his army have been considered, and only what is signed or unmistakably written by him. Correspondence signed by others "by command of General McClellan" is not included unless found in manuscript in his hand. Due to their length, his official campaign reports have also been excluded; they are few in number in any event, and readily available in the *Official Records* or, in the case of his *Report,* in separate book form as well. Other types of material excluded are matters of everyday military routine, orders and endorsements of little significance, multiple drafts, and, in private correspondence, perfunctory acknowledgments. To avoid repetition, when McClellan wrote several accounts of an event, the most complete and intrinsically valuable has been selected. When all else was equal, the unpublished was given precedence over the published.

All of McClellan's strategic papers and campaign plans are included here, as well as everything of significance bearing on his tactical decisions. In matters of military administration, as many representative examples of his actions as possible have been chosen. Virtually everything he wrote, officially and privately, bearing on the issues, policies, and politics of the war, and his roles in it, has been included. The purpose is to present, as nearly as the material allows, a comprehensive narration of events as General McClellan wrote it at the time.

By the nature of his elevated rank and service, the bulk of his official correspondence was with top officials of the government and the high command of the army — President Lincoln; Secretary of War Simon Cameron and his successor, Edwin M. Stanton; and the general-in-chief, first Winfield Scott and later Henry W. Halleck. McClellan wrote his first letter to Lincoln hardly a month after taking up his command in Ohio; the final dispatches he wrote as head of the Army of the Potomac were to the president. As a consequence, most military topics of significance in the years 1861 and 1862 are touched on here, often at the highest levels of decision-making.

McClellan wrote a remarkably large share of his military correspondence himself, and almost everything that relates to matters he regarded as important can be found in his handwriting. Seventy percent of this collection is in his autograph. While the military letters he sent were often in his hand, he not infrequently drafted letters to be copied for sending by an aide or clerk, keeping the draft for his files, and these autograph drafts, rather than the addressees' copies, are utilized here. Much the same is true of his military telegrams. It was McClellan's usual habit to write out dispatches for his telegrapher, who then copied and enciphered them for sending, a process repeated in reverse by the receiving operator. When found, these originals have been used instead of any later copies made during the telegraphic process. He less often retained copies of his personal correspondence, however, and many letters survive solely in the recipient's papers. For correspondence surviving only in the form of copies, the earliest version has been used.

A few excerpts from his private correspondence appeared in William Starr Myers's 1934 biography, *General George Brinton McClellan: A Study in Personality,* but among his personal writings certainly the best known are the excerpts from the wartime letters to his wife that appeared in his posthumous memoirs, *McClellan's Own Story,* published in 1887. McClellan had married Mary Ellen Marcy (called Ellen, or Nell or Nelly in these letters) in May 1860, eleven months before he took command of Ohio's volunteer troops. During their separations he tried to write her every day, and whenever possible he sent her a daily telegram as well. She followed a similar regimen in her replies. In his letters he told her everything of his emotions and opinions and motives; she was, he assured her, his alter ego, "you, who share all my thoughts. . . ." Nothing else he wrote was so revealing of himself. Periodically during his life McClellan had kept a diary, and these letters to his wife, in their frequency and content, have very much the flavor of a daily diary. They give a special quality of immediacy to his accounting of events, and from the historian's perspective there is regret that on occasion their separations ended. This is particularly true for most of the period when McClellan was general-in-chief, in the winter of 1861–1862, and Mrs. McClellan joined him in Washington.

In his biography of Lincoln, the historian J. G. Randall termed these home letters "a kind of unstudied release, not to be taken too seriously," but this judgment was based on only slight familiarity with the larger body of the general's correspondence, especially his personal correspondence. In fact McClellan's actions frequently followed the patterns he spelled out to his wife. While in these letters he did indeed vent his feelings in outspoken opinions about Lincoln and his administration and its policies and the people in it, there was nothing unstudied (or even necessarily private) about this. He repeated the same views, sometimes in even more forceful terms, to prominent leaders of the Democratic opposition, and he assuredly intended them to be taken seriously.

In the mid-1870s, while assembling material for his memoirs, McClellan had copied portions of a large number of these letters in a notebook under the heading, "Extracts from letters written to my wife during the war of the Rebellion." From the content and uninhibited frankness of these extracts it is clear enough that he had no thought of their publication but simply intended them as reminders to himself, while writing his memoirs, of his wartime attitudes toward events. On the evidence of what he included, it seems equally clear that what he left out of these copies — which he indicated by ellipsis marks — was nothing more than personal matter. The several surviving original letters written to his wife in 1863 and 1864 that are printed in their entirety here suggest the often personal content, such as professions of his love, that he would logically have deleted in making the copies.

Following the general's death in 1885 his literary executor, William C. Prime, found the notebook among his papers and made the decision to print these extracts as part of *McClellan's Own Story*, which he was then assembling for publication. Feeling that his friend's personal qualities were not fully enough represented in these extracts, Prime persuaded the McClellans' daughter, May, to comb the original letters for more personal and private matter. Her copies, made in 1886, mark the last time these original letters McClellan wrote while on active service can be accounted for. (Similarly, only a handful of his wife's letters to him, and a few of her telegrams, are known to have survived.) Editor Prime combined the two sets of copies, had them transcribed (with less than scrupulous concern for accuracy), put them in what he took to be chronological order, severely censored them through cutting and alteration, and let them serve as eleven of the book's forty chapters.

In preparing the letters for publication in this volume, the editorial license practiced by Prime has been revoked. The copies by McClellan and his daughter have been retranscribed in their entirety and dates corrected or supplied. Where May McClellan copied more of a particular letter than her father had included, the letter has been reassembled based on content and on McClellan's usual pattern of writing. The daily telegrams to his wife that are of interest are included, but not the many simply stating the condition of his health and that of her father, Chief of Staff Randolph B. Marcy.

While on campaign he addressed by far the largest share of his private correspondence to his wife — his sole relaxation, he once told her, was "reading your letters & writing to you" — but occasionally he found time to write to other members of his family and to those he regarded as his supporters on the home front. Next to his wife the personal correspondent he wrote to most frequently in the years 1860–1865 was Samuel L. M. Barlow, an old friend and prominent New York Democrat who in 1864 became his unofficial political manager. These letters to Barlow, thirty-seven of which are included here, present perhaps the clearest picture of McClellan's views on major political issues and on his place in Civil War politics.

EDITORIAL PROCEDURES

General McClellan wrote rapidly in a distinctive and well-formed hand, with an innate concern for spelling and syntax, and his correspondence has required no editorial alterations to be easily readable. His abbreviations and sometimes minimal punctuation create no ambiguity. The letters and dispatches appear here exactly as he wrote them, except that the positioning of headings, salutations, and signatures is made uniform. Any necessary correction or clarification, most often in matters of date and place of writing, is placed within brackets or in the annotations. The ellipses McClellan indicated in his copies of letters to his wife are retained.

The arrangement is in chapters conforming to the major phases of his wartime career and intermixes military and personal documents in chronological order. The context and circumstances of their writing is noted in the chapter introductions. A fuller account of events and McClellan's role in them will be found in Stephen W. Sears, *George B. McClellan: The Young Napoleon* (New York: Ticknor & Fields, 1988). McClellan sometimes added to a private letter through the course of a day or even over two days, and in such cases it is placed according to the earliest date or time mentioned. Where the chronology is not explicit or obvious, placement is based on McClellan's writing habits. He did office work in the morning, for example, and often ended his day with a letter to his wife.

Routine, minor editing or correcting done by McClellan has been incorporated here without notice, as has any necessary decoding from cipher messages. However, where there is crossed-out material of substance or interest, it has been indicated and restored within brackets. For example, the original content of his telegram written to General Halleck during the Battle of Antietam, which he altered before sending, reveals something of his true feeling in the midst of that great battle. A long passage that on second thought he decided to cut from a letter of December 5, 1862, to General Charles P. Stone gives (for another example) new details on that officer's arrest for alleged disloyalty.

Following each document is its description by manuscript type and its source. Citation to the McClellan Papers in the Manuscript Division of the Library of Congress includes the collection volume number followed by the microfilm reel number. Citation to the Civil War records in the National Archives is by the record group (RG) and number, followed by the microfilm series and reel number, or by the entry number. Citation is also made to previous printing in *The War of the Rebellion: A Compilation of the Official Records of the Union and Confederate Armies* or the *Official Records of the Union and Confederate Navies in the War of the Rebellion,* using the abbreviations *OR* and *NOR,* respectively. Addressees and other persons mentioned are identified the first time they appear but not subsequently unless there is a significant change in status or position; the index serves as a guide to these identifications. Where relevant, the communication to which McClellan was responding, and the answer he received, are summarized in the annotations.

The following manuscript abbreviations are used:

AD	Autograph Document
ADS	Autograph Document Signed
ADf	Autograph Draft
ADfS	Autograph Draft Signed
AL	Autograph Letter or Telegram
AL copy	Autograph Letter or Telegram copy by McClellan
AL copy ; copy	In reference to McClellan's letters to his wife, a copy in part by McClellan and in part by his daughter
ALS	Autograph Letter or Telegram Signed
Copy	Copy not made by McClellan
D	Document
Df	Draft
DP	Document Printed
DS	Document Signed
LS	Letter or Telegram Signed

THE CIVIL WAR PAPERS OF
GEORGE B. McClellan

ONE

COMMAND IN THE WESTERN THEATER

DECEMBER 27, 1860–JULY 22, 1861

AT THE OUTBREAK of war in April 1861, George McClellan was living in Cincinnati and serving as preside it of the eastern division of the Ohio and Mississippi Railroad. He had resigned from the army in 1857 to enter the railroad business, first with the Illinois Central and then, in August 1860, with the Ohio and Mississippi. As the first letters here suggest, he had followed the course of the secession crisis closely and hoped that compromise might settle the sectional conflict, but he was not optimistic. The decision for war did not surprise him.

At the time of his resignation, Captain McClellan had been considered one of the most promising young officers in the service. Graduating from West Point second in class in 1846, he was commissioned in the Corps of Engineers and served capably in the Mexican War. A wide range of increasingly important peacetime assignments followed. He was best known for his year-long service as an observer in the Crimean War and an analyst of the organization of European armies. When President Lincoln called for troops to put down the rebellion, the North's three most populous states all sought the thirty-four-year-old McClellan to command their forces.

The offers from Ohio and Pennsylvania may be traced here; New York's bid, not mentioned in McClellan's correspondence, reached him (like Pennsylvania's) after he had taken the position of major general of Ohio's volunteer troops. It is clear that his first preference had been for a high command with the Pennsylvania forces, and that it was more by chance — a misdirected telegram — than by any other cause that he went to war in the western theater. There is every likelihood that had he headed the Pennsylvania Reserves in the eastern army rather than the Department of the Ohio the course of his Civil War career — or at least the early phases of it — would have been very different.

McClellan's letter of April 27 to Winfield Scott, composed just four days after he took up his military duties, is noteworthy for being the first strategic plan by a Union general for carrying on the war on a large scale. It was a seriously flawed plan, as General Scott pointed out, but it inspired Scott in his reply to formulate a strategy of his own, the Anaconda Plan, which featured a blockade of Southern ports and an advance on the line of the Mississippi River. The correspondence here with and about Scott, some of it previously unpublished, reveals the roots of McClellan's conflict with the general-in-chief, which would grow and worsen in the coming months.

When McClellan was named to head the Department of the Ohio on May 3, his command initially consisted of the states of Ohio, Indiana, and Illinois; subsequently it included western Pennsylvania and western Virginia and (on June 6) the state of Missouri. He would play only a minor role in operations in the Mississippi Valley before a new Western Department was formed on July 3. He made his headquarters in Cincinnati and for the most part focused his attention as department commander on the Ohio River line, and specifically on Kentucky and western Virginia.

In dealing with Kentucky's proclaimed neutrality and with the threat of a Confederate occupation of strategically important western Virginia, McClellan first displayed the combining of military and political objectives that would mark the entire course of his wartime service. In his proclamation to the people of western Virginia (May 26) and in his letter to General Scott on Union policy toward Kentucky (June 5), for example, he made clear his belief that slavery must not become an issue in the war. He emphasized as well a benevolent attitude toward Southern civilians in the war zone. "All private property whether of secessionists or others must be strictly respected," he ordered (July 14), "and no one is to be molested merely because of political opinions."

From June 21 onward, General McClellan was in the field in a month-long campaign in western Virginia that involved him in a single action, at Rich Mountain on July 12. This first experience of field command is described in revealing detail in his dispatches to his subordinates and to Washington, and in his letters to his wife. In operations marked more by maneuver than by pitched battle, the Union forces in the region were everywhere victorious. "Our success is complete & secession is killed in this country," McClellan telegraphed Washington on July 14.

It was the first important Northern success of the war, and McClellan's role in it, as both military administrator and field commander, took on added significance when the Federal army in the eastern theater was defeated a week later at Bull Run. On July 22, 1861, General McClellan was ordered to Washington to take command of what he was to christen the Army of the Potomac.

To Samuel L. M. Barlow

Private

My dear S L M   Cincinnati Dec 27 [1860]

We arrived here two or three days ago & found our house desolate — my wife's mother & sister having been suddenly called off to St Jo by the serious illness of Maj Marcy[1] — to day we hear that he is out of danger, so we are merry again after our sad Christmas.

I find very little *excitement* here, but a great deal of quiet determination. In a conversation with a very intelligent Republican, from Indiana, this morning I put to him the direct question whether he & his friends are willing to run the Missouri Compromise line to the Pacific & to repeal the Personal Liberty Bills — he replied that they would *Pro-* gladly do the first & more than the second — that they were perfectly *Slavery* willing that when a fugitive slave was rescued, or impediments thrown in the way of his arrest & return, that the *county* should pay his full value. I am sure that this is the feeling of the Republican party in the West. More than this — the feeling of *all* people here is that the North West will do justice to the South if they will give us time — but that if they go off half cocked & listen to nothing but the Republican politicians at Washington (who, from the nature of the case, cannot represent the *present* feeling of the North) we will meet the consequences unitedly, let it be war or peace — but the general opinion is that it will be *war*.

Most men here acknowledge that the South has much to ask that the North ought to & would grant — at the same time we think that in many things the South is in the wrong. Great Scott! I did not intend to preach politics — of which you must be sick enough — so I will ask pardon & change the subject. Some little affairs have turned up here which make it important that I should know *confidentially* what Bacon's[2] movements will probably be. Does he intend leaving the road, &, if so, when? I have been told here that he was about to engage in some business which would take him away from St Louis. Please let the question & answer be between ourselves.

My wife desires her kindest remembrances to Mrs B & yourself, not forgetting Miss Carrie — we were very sorry not to see Mrs B again — on the whole I don't know that I regret it, for I really began to be jealous of her — my better half was so much fascinated by her.

It is becoming so dark that I must close.

Your sincere friend
Geo B McClellan

S L M B Esq

ALS, Barlow Papers, Huntington Library. Barlow was a New York lawyer, railroad executive, and Democratic party leader.

1. Maj. Randolph B. Marcy, GBM's father-in-law. 2. Henry D. Bacon, an executive with the Ohio and Mississippi Railroad.

To Thomas C. English

My dear Thomas   Cincinnati Feb. 7 1861

You will probably be surprised to hear from me, & in truth I have not a great deal to say — but it struck me that I would write before the mails are entirely stopped. I presume that you are in the midst of a great deal of excitement — there is little or none here in the cold blood of the North. I have yet strong hopes that the existing difficulties will be satisfactorily arranged. The feeling among the *people* in this vicinity is strongly in favor of doing justice to the South & leaving out the ultra men in certain limited districts, I think that feeling is prevalent in the North. I do believe that the border states will be satisfied, & that being accomplished, I think the further steps of satisfying all the other slave states save South Carolina will not be difficult.

I was very, very sorry to miss you in Phila. — had I had the slightest idea that you were coming on so soon I would have strained a point & waited for you. Nelly was very anxious to see you, & she begs me to say that when you next come north you *must* pass through Cincinnati if it is a possible thing for you to do it. We have taken a house here for three years. I hope the disturbances in the country may not make it necessary for me to change my plans as to living here. I suppose you will make no change in regard to the children — no state of affairs between the sections can make it unpleasant for them to be in Phila. while going to school — tho there may be considerations at home which would affect it.

Nelly sends her love.

Yours affectionately
Geo B McClellan

Mr. T. C. English

Copy, McClellan Papers (A-11:5), Library of Congress. English, GBM's brother-in-law, lived in Mt. Pleasant, Ala.

To Fitz John Porter

Ohio & Mississippi Railroad Company,
Eastern Division   President's Office
My dear old Fitz   Cincinnati, April 18, 1861

Your welcome note has just reached me.[1]

I have already received an intimation that I have been proposed as the Comdr of the Penna Reserves, & asked if I would accept — replied yes! If Genl Scott would say a word to Gov Curtin in my behalf I think the matter could be easily arranged.[2]

Say to the Genl that I am ready as ever to serve under his command; I trust I need not assure him that he can count on my loyalty to him & the dear old flag he has so long upheld.

I throw to one side now all questions as to the past — political parties etc — the Govt is in danger, our flag insulted & we must stand by it. Tho' I am told I can have a position with the Ohio troops I much prefer the Penna service — I hope to hear something definite from them today & will let you know at once. Help me as far as you can.

Ever yours

McC

My wife is on a trip to Fort Randolph with her father & mother. Very pressing business here requires my presence for a few days.

ALS, Nicholson Collection, Huntington Library. Maj. Porter was stationed in the Adjutant General's Office in Washington.

1. Porter wrote GBM on Apr. 15 urging him to take a high command in the Pennsylvania or Ohio volunteers. McClellan Papers (A-11:5), Library of Congress. 2. General-in-Chief Winfield Scott; Andrew G. Curtin, governor of Pennsylvania.

To Robert Patterson

Ohio & Mississippi Railroad Company,
Eastern Division   President's Office
Cincinnati, April 18 1861

Maj Genl Patterson
General

Your telegram of today is received. I at once replied "what rank & when do you want me." I have some very important business on hand here that will necessarily detain me a few days — it is not private business, but that of my employers, so that I feel bound to attend to it. One cannot in a day break off from such a business as that entrusted to me.

On every account — yours, mine, & the good of the service — I think the rank of Chf Engineer ought to be that of a Brig Genl — I could be of much more use to you in that than in a lower grade. I hope to hear from you by letter tomorrow, when I can at once determine.

I expect two of the principal owners of the Road here tonight — & feel that it is only proper to inform them before taking so decided a step.

Trusting that you will understand the nature of my delay, & that I shall have the pleasure of serving once more under your orders[1]

I am, General, your sincere friend

Geo B McClellan

The reason for my enquiring about the rank is that before receiving your telegram I have received intimations that a high command would be tendered me.

ALS, Miscellaneous Collections, Huntington Library. Maj. Gen. Patterson commanded Pennsylvania's three-month volunteers.

1. GBM had served under Patterson during the Mexican War.

To William Dennison

Private

His Excellency W Dennison

My dear Sir   Cincinnati April 18/61

Your telegram of yesterday is received. In mine to Gen Bates[1] I had reference to the policy of retaining in Cincinnati, for its defence, a large portion of the organized Volunteer Companies belonging here.

It is clear that Cincinnati is the most important strategical point in the valley of the Ohio, both from its position & the resources it will furnish to the party holding it.

Should the Confederate States operate west of the Alleghenies, Cincinnati will doubtless be their objective point.

If it is left defenceless it would afford too great a temptation to lawless men, who by a sudden incursion might do a great deal of mischief.

I suggest that immediate steps should be taken to guard effectually against the latter evil & that means should secretly be proposed to pave the way for meeting the more formidable attempt first alluded to.

It appears to me that no time should be lost in arming & rendering efficient several regiments of Volunteers in this city for home service — I would send no men away from here until a sufficient well armed & organized force is raised to protect the city fully from insult. I would offer inducements & all facilities for gaining this end.

I think the "Home Guard" movement now in progress here is an ill advised one, tho' prompted by good motives; they will prove to be inefficient from the fact that they have no common head. It would be far better to organize regiments under the Militia Law, with the distinct understanding, if necessary, that they are not liable to be drafted for foreign service. The entire armed forces of all kinds in Cinc. should be in every respect under the orders of the militia officer comdg the District.

I understand that there is not a single powder magazine on this side of the River! Of arms there are next to none, especially of heavy guns. Both of these fatal defects should be remedied at once with regard to the first mentioned contingency. I think that the ground around Cincinnati should be carefully studied (especially on the south bank of the river), so that a plan of defence could be drawn up, all ready to be acted upon when the necessity for it arises. The most important thing to be done, in this connection, is to select the points on the Covington side to be occupied by field works, should it become necessary to do so, in order to cover the city on that side; the plans of the works should be carefully studied & arranged, the necessary form fixed upon, intrenching tools, & artillery provided so that no time would be lost when the emergency arises. It may well be that the necessity for all this will not occur, but there is only one safe rule in war — i.e. to decide what is the very worst thing that can happen to you, & prepare to meet it.

By proper precautions I think that this city can be rendered secure, & the available power of the state left free to act in other quarters.

Should my views strike you as correct I will gladly communicate with you more in detail if you care about my doing so. I hope that you will regard this letter as strictly confidential.

AL retained copy, McClellan Papers (A-11:5), Library of Congress. Dennison was governor of Ohio.

1. Brig. Gen. Joshua H. Bates, Ohio militia.

To Winfield Scott

Lt Genl Winfield Scott
Comdg U.S. Army   Head Quarters Ohio Volunteers
General: Columbus Ohio April 23 1861

I have the honor to inform you that I have been appointed by the Governor of Ohio as the Major General Commanding all the Ohio troops called into the service of the Genl Govt, & to report for duty accordingly.

I wish to lay before you as full a statement as is now in my power of the condition of my command & its necessities.

There are four full Regts at Cincinnati, ready to be mustered into the service, some 3500 men encamped near this city, and about 600 at Cleveland; large numbers are now en route here, more than enough to complete the requisition — this state will supply 50,000 if desired.[1]

I have seen the men at Cincinnati & this city — I have never seen so fine a body of men collected together — the material is superb, but has no organization or discipline.

Capt Granger has probably mustered into service the Cleveland detachment today; Gov Dennison has telegraphed him to proceed at once to Cincinnati to muster in four Regts tomorrow; Major Burbank will commence mustering in the troops at this place tomorrow.[2]

Of the troops at Cincinnati two Regts have been encamped for four days, a third Regt goes into camp tomorrow. The Legislature will tomorrow authorize the Gov. to accept the services of eight Regts in addition to the 13 already called for.

None of these troops have any camp equipage, except some 100 state tents here, & about 20 at Cincinnati; we will probably be able to hut them.

I may say that we have no arms nor ammunition — for there are only some 480 muskets at Cincinnati & some 1400 here, many of the latter being rifles (without bayonets) & altered flint locks; we have in the state about 900 Rifled Muskets. I propose using these, & such of the Rifles as I can provide with bayonets in forming picked Battalions of Riflemen.

The Gov. received information today that 10,000 percussion muskets had been ordered here from Watervliet, & that the accouterments will be sent from Pittsburg as soon as manufactured, also that 200,000 cartridges would be forwarded. We have 19 6 pdr guns at Cincinnati, a battery of 6 guns (with fairly drilled cannoneers) at Marietta, & 6 indifferent guns here.

I cannot urge too strongly the absolute necessity of our receiving at once at least 10,000 stand of arms in addition to those now ordered here, & that as many as possible of these be of the new pattern Rifled-Musket; — cannot the St Louis, or the Dearborn Arsenal supply us? We will need the corresponding accouterments, & should have at least 5,000,000 cartridges, as I am anxious to perfect the men in target practice.

The state has thus far been very unsuccessful in its efforts to purchase arms in the East. Of camp equipage we need a full supply for 20,000 men; we require knapsacks, clothing, some means of transportation etc.

I find myself, General, in the position of a Comdg Officer with nothing but men — no arms or supplies.

I would respectfully request that Maj Fitz John Porter may be assigned to the position of Adjt Genl of the Ohio troops, to report to me at Cincinnati; Capt Jno H Dickerson as Qtr Mr Genl; Maj R B Marcy as Paymaster;[3] a Comsy of Subsistance. I also think it very necessary that I should have at least one officer of Engrs, of Topographical Engrs, & if possible two of Ordnance. The state is willing to undertake the manufacture of some iron field guns & guns of position for the defence of the Ohio River frontier; to carry out the project it is necessary that we should have an experienced officer of the Ordnance Corps, while another will be required to superintend the issue, care, & repairs of arms & ammunition. Whenever the necessities of defence at Washington etc will justify it I would be glad to have McCook's & Wilson's Regts (1st & 2nd Ohio, now at Lancaster or Harrisburg) ordered back here, if you intend that my command shall operate on the Ohio line.[4]

I propose, until receiving orders from you, to establish my command in a Camp of Instruction at some point near Cincinnati, where I will get them into shape as soon as possible. Until I hear from you I will consider it my duty to take all possible measures for the protection of Cincinnati & the line of the Ohio, from the Great Miami to Wheeling; I will obtain all the information possible in regard to ground opposite Cincinnati on the Ky side, & without attracting attention take all the steps necessary to occupy the heights when the moment arrives.[5] I will take steps by the use of secret service money to obtain early information as to any hostile movements from the south.

A few heavy guns & howitzers would be very desirable at Cincinnti in case it should become necessary to occupy heights on the Ky side, or to return the fire of hostile batteries.[6] We ought to have *at least* one light battery, & I will do what I can to organize one or more while awaiting your further orders.

A force of cavalry will also be very necessary for patrol duty. I make these suggestions in the supposition that it will be, for the present at least, my duty to provide for the defence of the frontier.

It would be well that I should have some understanding with the Comdt of the Indiana troops, by which a movement on Louisville could be made, should it become necessary in order to relieve a pressure upon Cincinnati.

If I am correct in supposing that for the present my command is to be kept together & charged with the defence of the Ohio, or a movement in advance should political events require it, I would recommend that it be formed into a Corps d'Armee & furnished with suitable batteries, & a cavalry force — a battalion of regulars would be of great assistance. I would urge the immediate dispatch of the staff officers I have asked for — you can imagine the condition in which I am, without a single instructed officer to assist me.[7]

I will take steps to secure the safety of the Railways in Ohio, & will make such arrangements with the Railway Managers as to enable me to control their entire resources.

> I am Genl very respectfully yr obdt svt
> Geo B McClellan
> Maj Genl O.V.M.

12	24 pdrs
6	8″ howitzers
6	12 pdrs
2	8″ mortars
2	10″ ″
2	8″ Columbiads

ALS retained copy, McClellan Papers (A-11:5), Library of Congress. *OR,* Ser. 1, LI, Part 1, pp. 333–34. This transcription combines two drafts written by GBM. The copy sent to Washington included the variations noted below.

1. Ohio's share of the president's call for 75,000 militia was thirteen regiments, or about 10,000 men. 2. Mustering officers Capt. Gordon Granger, Mounted Rifles, and Maj. Sidney Burbank, 1st U.S. Infantry. 3. Maj. Porter, Capt. John H. Dickerson, and Maj. Marcy were staff officers in the Adjutant General's Office, Quartermaster's Office, and Paymaster General's Office, respectively. 4. These three-month regiments had been ordered to Washington. 5. The copy sent to Washington included at this point the sentence: "I will be careful to do nothing that can compromise the Government in any way with the inhabitants of Kentucky." 6. The list of requested ordnance in the postscript (except the last item)

appeared here in the letter as sent. 7. Gen. Scott's adjutant, Lt. Col. E. D. Townsend, replied on Apr. 30: "The general very much regrets it will not be possible to place at your disposal the officers for whom you ask, except Major Marcy.... The very large number of resignations just in an emergency,... sufficiently explains the necessity for asking you to do as well as you can with the talent and zeal you can find in your command." *OR*, Ser. 1, LI, Part 1, pp. 342–43.

To Joseph W. Alsop

The State of Ohio, Executive Department
My dear Mr Alsop   Columbus, April 24, 1861

They have passed the law allowing the Govr to appoint the Maj Genl Comdg — I receive my commission this morning, & am to have the command of all the Ohio troops called into the service of the Genl. Govt., together with the defence of the State.[1] I am already overwhelmed with business — up till late in the morning. Sent off last night long dispatch to Genl Scott reporting in full.[2]

Hope to return to Cincinnati to night. Feel in my own element.

Truly yours
Geo B. McClellan

My regards to Mr Bartlett[3]

ALS, Alsop Family Papers, Yale University Library. Alsop was president of the Ohio and Mississippi Railroad.

1. On Apr. 23 the Ohio legislature passed a special bill for GBM's benefit, permitting the governor to apppoint any Ohio resident a major general rather than only a member of the state militia. 2. GBM to Scott, Apr. 23, *supra*. 3. Edwin Bartlett, an officer of the Ohio and Mississippi Railroad.

To Andrew G. Curtin   [TELEGRAM]

[Columbus] Apl 24 [1861]

Your telegram to Chicago never reached me.[1] Before I heard from you that you wanted me in any position I had accepted the command of the Ohio forces. They need my services & I am bound in honor to stand by them. I regret that I cannot command the Penna troops, and thank you for the offer.

G. B. McClellan

Gov Curtin
Harrisburg

ALS (telegram sent), McClellan Papers, Illinois State Historical Library.

1. Gov. Curtin's misdirected telegram offered GBM command of the Pennsylvania Reserves.

To Allan Pinkerton

Allan Pinkerton, Esq.

Dear Sir : —   Columbus, Ohio, April 24, 1861.

I wish to see you with the least possible delay, to make arrangements with you of an important nature. I will be either here or in Cincinnati for the next few days — here to-morrow — Cincinnati next day. In this city you will find me at the Capitol, at Cincinnati at my residence.

If you telegraph me, better use your first name alone. Let no one know that you come to see me, and keep as quiet as possible.

Very truly yours,

Geo. B. McClellan

Maj. Gen'l Comd'g Ohio Vols.

Allan Pinkerton, *The Spy of the Rebellion* (New York, 1883), pp. 140–41. Pinkerton, a Chicago private detective, became head of GBM's intelligence-gathering operations.

To Ohio Volunteer Militia

General Order,   Head Quarters, Ohio Volunteer Militia,

No. 1.   [Columbus] April 25th, 1861

By the direction of the Governor of Ohio, the undersigned hereby assumes command of the Ohio Volunteer Militia mustered into the service of the United States.

In doing so, he desires to call the attention of the officers and men to the fact, that discipline and instruction are of as much importance in war as mere courage. He asks for and expects the cheerful co-operation of the entire command in his efforts to establish discipline and efficiency, the surest guarantees of success.

Until the organization is perfected, many inconveniences must be endured, for the sudden exigency, which has made it necessary to call so largely upon your patriotism, has rendered it impossible for the authorities to make, in an instant, the requisite preparation.

We do not enter upon this war as a pastime, but with the stern determination to repel the insults offered to our flag, and uphold the honor and integrity of our Union.

In the coming struggle, we have not only battles to fight, but hardships and privations to endure, fatigue to encounter.

The General Commanding does not doubt, that the spirit which has prompted you to leave your homes and those most dear to you, will support you firmly in the future.

He asks your willing obedience and full confidence — having obtained that, he feels sure that he can conduct you to glory, and to victories that will ensure safety to your homes and lasting repose to the country.

Geo. B. McClellan,

Major General O.V.M.

DP, McClellan Papers (A-11:5), Library of Congress.

To Winfield Scott

Lieut Genl Winfield Scott
Comdg U.S. Army   Head Quarters O.V.M.
General: Columbus Ohio April 27 1861

Communications with Washington being so difficult, I beg to lay before you some views relative to this region of country, & to propose for your consideration a plan of operations intended to relieve the pressure upon Washington, & tending to bring the war to a speedy close.

The region North of the Ohio, and between the Mississippi and the Alleghenies, forms one grand strategic field in which all operations must be under the control of one head, whether acting offensively or on the defensive.

I assume it as the final result that hostilities will break out on the line of the Ohio.

For two reasons it is necessary to delay this result, by all political means, for a certain period of time.

1st   To enable the North West to make the requisite preparations now very incomplete.

2nd   That a strong diversion may be made in aid of the defense of Washington, & the Eastern line of operations.

First urging that the General Govt. should leave no means untried to arm & equip the Western States, I submit the following views.

Cairo should be occupied by a small force, say 2 Battalions, strongly entrenched, & provided with heavy guns, & a gun boat to control the river.

A force of some 8 battalions to be in observation at Sandoval (the junction of the Ohio & Miss, & the Illinois Central Railways) to observe St Louis, sustain the garrison of Cairo, & if necessary to reinforce Cincinnati.

A few Companies should observe the Wabash below Vincennes.

A Division of about 4000 men at Seymour, to observe Louisville, & be ready to support Cincinnati or Cairo.

A Division of 5000 men at or near Cincinnati.

Two Battalions at or near Chillicothe.

Could we be provided with arms, the North West has ample resources to furnish 80,000 men for active operations, after providing somewhat more than the troops mentioned above for the protection of the frontier.

With the active army of operations it is proposed to cross the Ohio at, or in the vicinity of Gallipolis, & move up the valley of the Great Kanawha on Richmond; in combination with this Cumberland [Md.] should be seized, and a few thousand men left, at Ironton or Gallipolis, to cover the rear & right flank of the main column — the presence of this detachment & a prompt movement on Louisville, or the heights opposite Cincinnati would effectually prevent any interference on the part of Kentucky. The movement on Richmond should be conducted with the utmost promptness, & could not fail to relieve Washington, as well as to secure the destruction of the Southern Army if aided by a decided advance on the Eastern line.

I know that there could be difficulties in crossing the mountains, but would go prepared to meet them.

Another plan could be, in the event of Kentucky assuming a hostile position, to cross the Ohio at Cincinnati or Louisville with 80,000 men, march straight on Nashville, & thence act according to circumstances.

Were a battle gained before reaching Nashville, so that the strength of Kentucky & Tennessee were effectually broken, a movement on Montgomery, aided by a vigorous [offensive] on the Eastern line, towards Charleston & Augusta, should not be delayed. The ulterior movements of the combined armies might be on Pensacola, Mobile & New Orleans.

It seems clear that the forces of the North West should not remain quietly on the defensive, & that under present circumstances, if the supply of arms is such as to render it absolutely impossible to bring into the field the numbers indicated above their offensive movements would be most effective on the line first indicated; but if so liberal supply can be obtained as to enable us to dispose of 80,000 troops for the active army, then the 2nd line of operations could be the most decisive.

To enable us to carry out either of these plans, it is absolutely necessary that the Genl Govt should strain every nerve to supply the West with arms, ammunition & equipments.

Even to maintain the defensive we must be largely assisted.

I beg to urge upon you that we are very badly supplied at present, & that a vast population, eager to fight, are rendered powerless by the want of arms — the nation being thus deprived of their aid.[1]

I have the honor to be, General, very respectfully yours

Geo B McClellan

Maj. Genl. Comdg O.V.

ALS, Records of the Adjutant General's Office, RG 94 (M-619:41), National Archives. *OR*, Ser. 1, LI, Part 1, pp. 338–39.

1. Gen. Scott's May 2 endorsement on this letter reads in part: "As at the date of this letter Genl. Mc. knew nothing of the intended call for two years' volunteers, he must have had the idea of composing his enormous columns of three months' men ..., that is, of men whose term of service would expire by the time he had collected & organized them.... 2. A march upon Richmond from the Ohio would probably insure the revolt of Western Virginia.... 3. The general eschews water transportation by the Ohio & Mississippi, in favor of long, tedious & *break-down* (of men, horses & wagons) marches. 4. His plan is to subdue the seceded states, by piecemeal, instead of enveloping them all (nearly) at once,

by a cordon of posts on the Mississippi to its mouth, . . . & by blockading ships of war on the sea-board. . . .'

To Lorenzo Thomas

Col L. Thomas
Adjt General U.S.A.   Head Quarters OVM
Colonel: Columbus Ohio April 27 1861

I have the honor to request that Capt G. Granger, Regt Mounted Rifles, may be assigned to duty as Division Inspector of my Division. The Captain is now engaged in mustering in troops at Cincinnati & will be available for duty in a few days.

I have also to request that Lt O M Poe, Topl Engrs, now stationed at Detroit may be assigned to duty on my staff.

I hope that my request to have Major Fitz John Porter, & Capt Dickerson assigned to duty with my Division may be at once complied with. You will see that in organizing a force of 30,000 men it is very necessary that I should have such officers.

I found Lt McCleary, 6th Infty, on leave of absence & have taken him temporarily on my staff. I hope he may be allowed to remain there, as I shall probably in a few days ask to have him as one of my Aides-de-Camp.[1] I shall commence tomorrow moving the men into a camp of instruction on the Little Miami Railroad 17 miles from Cincinnati, a fine turnpike 12m in length also leads from it to Cincinnati.

From this position I can move the command rapidly to any point where it may be required.

In three days I shall have 7 Regts at Camp Dennison (the permanent camp), & 4 Regts at Camp Harrison 6 miles from Cincinnati.

By the end of the week the Cleveland & Columbus camps will be abandoned, & there will be some 17 Regts at Camp Dennison.

By the end of two weeks there will be 24 Regts in that camp, unless I find it necessary in the mean time to detach some Regts toward Marietta. My desire is to concentrate the whole command in this camp, & to thoroughly organize, discipline & drill them. By the end of six weeks I hope they will be in condition to act efficiently in any direction where they may be required.

I hope that my wish can be carried out, & that I may not be required to take my men under fire until they are reduced to some order & discipline.

Should they be required to act together I would desire to organize some batteries & cavalry.

Some squadrons of regular cavalry & regular batteries would be desirable.

We are very deficient in small arms, guns, ammunition & equipment — I have been doing all in my power to overcome these deficiencies, & most earnestly urge upon the consideration of the General in Chief the necessity of furnishing me with these supplies at once. Give me these & I will provide the men.)

Money & a Subsistence officer should be sent at once — we have no U.S. money, & I am working with money furnished by the State.

The state will call 30 Regts (in all) into service, all of which they place under my command; 13 are now called out. 75 can be furnished by this state alone if you can arm us.

In hopes that you will find it in your power to comply at once with my requests

I am, Colonel, very respectfully your obedient servant

Geo B McClellan

Major Genl

In a few days I will probably move my Head Quarters to Cincinnati or Camp Dennison; there is a good deal of excitement in Cincinnati.

ALS, Records of the Adjutant General's Office, RG 94 (M-619:37), National Archives. *OR*, Ser. 1, LI, Part 1, pp. 339–40. Col. (later Brig. Gen.) Thomas was the army's adjutant general.

1. Of the officers mentioned — Capt. Granger, Lt. Orlando M. Poe, Maj. Porter, Capt. Dickerson, and Lt. John McCleary — only Poe and Dickerson were assigned to GBM's command.

To Robert Patterson ⚹ procrastination

Maj Genl Robt Patterson
Comdg Dept
General

Head Quarters OVM
Cincinnati, April 29 1861

Your dispatch is received. I have not a single Regiment in condition to take the field or perform efficient service.

There has been great delay in mustering in the troops & no supplies arms or money have been received from Washington — not even orders.

I have urged the Head Quarters for supplies, & am obliged to use the money of the State & act altogether on my own responsibility.

I am moving the troops into a Camp of Instruction where I propose organizing, equipping, & arming them — & will get them ready for service in the shortest possible time.

We have no arms yet & none of my Regts ought to be sent away from here in their present condition.

I have written to the Genl in Chief proposing a plan of operations which would keep the Ohio, Indiana & Illinois contingents west of the Alleghenies.

I am, General, very truly yours
Geo B McClellan
Maj Genl

ALS retained copy, McClellan Papers (A-11:5), Library of Congress.

To Winfield Scott

Lt. Genl Winfield Scott
Comdg the Army   Head Quarters OVM
General   Cincinnati May 7 1861

I have the honor to acknowledge the receipt of your confidential letter of the 3rd.[1] From certain remarks in an order transmitted to me by Col Townsend I learn that it has been decided to place me in command of a new Dept.[2]

I beg to thank you, General, for this mark of your confidence, & to assure you that you may rest satisfied that I will leave nothing undone to assist in carrying out your plans.

When I have time to think over the matter carefully I hope you will permit me to make such suggestions as to details as my intimate knowledge of the country may cause to occur to me.

I will do all I can, General, to reconcile public feeling here to the necessary delay. You are entirely correct in supposing this to be the greatest difficulty we have to encounter.

I fully appreciate the wisdom of your intentions & recognize the propriety of all your military dispositions, & will quietly urge the necessity of preparation.

Even if I did not agree with you I have that implicit confidence in the General under whom I first learned the art of war that would free me thereby to carry out his views.

I am respectfully very truly yours
Geo B McClellan

ALS retained copy, McClellan Papers (C-3:62), Library of Congress.

1. Gen. Scott's letter of May 3 outlined his so-called Anaconda Plan, the main features of which were a blockade of the Southern coasts and an advance down the Mississippi River to New Orleans. *OR*, Ser. 1, LI, Part 1, pp. 369–70. 2. On May 3 GBM was named to the command of the Department of the Ohio.

To Winfield Scott

Personal
Lieut General Winfield Scott
Commanding U.S. Army   Head Quarters O.V.M.
General.   Cincinnati Ohio May 9th 1861

I feel assured that you not only will not misunderstand me, but that you will patiently bear with me while I make an appeal to you that involves the entire interests of my command and of the West.

I assumed control of an unorganized mass of men, with neither arms, clothing, equipments, supplies, discipline, instruction, nor money. I had no staff, not one single instructed Officer to assist me, no orders, no authority to do anything.

I knew that it must be your intention that the troops should be rendered efficient in the shortest possible time, and that economy should be introduced. I felt that from the very many instances of official and personal kindness I have received from you, I could implicitly rely upon your support in any reasonable measures, that might be taken by me. Please remember too, that for several days we were entirely cut off from all communication with Washington[1] and that it was but fair to suppose that it might at any moment prove necessary for me to move to the assistance of the General under whom I learned my first lessons in War, and whom I have been and ever shall be ready to support to the bitter end.

Under these circumstances I, for many days, performed in person the duties of all the Staff Depts, imperfectly it is true, but perhaps as fully as one man could. Knowing that Capt. Dickerson was unemployed I wrote to Gen Harney begging him to lend me the Captain, in his absence Major McKinstry[2] was kind enough to send the Capt to me, and I at once put him at work. Capt Burns[3] providentially made his appearance with no duty on his hands — I took the opportunity and kept him until I could obtain your approval. These Officers have done themselves infinite credit; they have introduced system and economy — every thing is going on in the regular order, and they have saved many thousands of dollars for the General Government.

I learn that the corresponding departments in Illinois and Indiana are totally disorganized, and I counted upon these Officers to introduce among the Volunteers from those States a system as good as that now existing in Ohio. I cannot supply their places — there are no men in these states competent to perform the duty.

If you will give me these two Officers, General, I will undertake that they shall perform the whole duty of their Dept's in the district to the command of which I may be assigned — without them I feel that there is no possibility of organizing the service. I would also urge that I may be allowed to retain Captain Granger, whose Regt. is in New Mexico. He knows now most of the Volunteers from this State, and is really indispensable to assist me in my efforts to instruct the Officers & introduce discipline.

Next to maintaining the honor of my country, General, the first aim of my life is to justify the good opinion you have expressed concerning me, and to prove that the great soldier of our country can not only command armies himself but teach others to do so. I do not expect your mantle to fall on my shoulders, for no man is worthy to wear it, but I hope that it may be said hereafter that I was no unworthy disciple of your school. I cannot make an army to carry out your views, unless I have the assistance of instructed soldiers. There are multitudes of brave men in the West, but no soldiers. I frankly and most earnestly call upon you to supply the want. I need, not only the Officers I have named, but a first rate Adjutant General and two good Aides de Camps. Major Porter is my preference as Adjt. General — if I cannot have him, I would be glad to have Capt. Williams.[4] Webb of the 5th Infantry and young Kingsbury just graduating would suit me well as Aides.[5]

The condition of things out here really makes an Ordnance Officer necessary — Capt Reno[6] would be glad to serve with me and I would be very glad to have him.

ASKS to have assistance

I have written frankly to you, General, for I am sure you will understand me and will not misinterpret my motives, the good of the service is what I seek. I cannot work without tools — I cannot be every where and do every thing myself. Give me the means and I will answer for it that I will take care of the rest.[7]

I have urgent demand for heavy guns, none are yet within my reach, notwithstanding your orders. It is absolutely necessary that a competent Officer should at once go to Cairo, and give directions, as to its defence — I have none at my disposal, and have not the authority to go myself.

Not one dollar have I yet received from the Genl. Gov. not any expression of opinion as to the steps I have taken. Excuse General, the length of this, the matter is urgent and I cannot well place it in a smaller compass. I ask your personal attention to it, and whatever the decision may be I will cheerfully acquiesce, and take my measures accordingly.

> I am very respectfully your obt svt
> Geo B McClellan
> Maj Genl

LS, McClellan Papers, New-York Historical Society. *OR,* Ser. 1, LI, Part 1, pp. 373–74.

1. Maryland secessionists had cut Washington's rail and telegraph lines. 2. Brig. Gen. William S. Harney, commander of the Department of the West, at St. Louis; Maj. Justus McKinstry, of his staff. 3. Capt. William W. Burns, Commissary General's Office. 4. Capt. Seth Williams, Adjutant General's Office. 5. 1st Lt. William A. Webb, 5th U.S. Infantry; 2nd Lt. Henry W. Kingsbury, West Point 1861. 6. Capt. Jesse L. Reno, Ordnance Office. 7. Of the officers mentioned, Dickerson, Burns, and Williams were assigned to GBM's staff.

To William Dennison

Gov Wm Dennison
Columbus   Head Quarters Dept of the Ohio
Governor   Cincinnati May 13 1861

My reasons for advising that there should be no haste in sending the State Troops to the frontier, unless political reasons demanded it, are that I am in daily expectation of hearing from Washington the policy of the Govt, & that most of the information I obtain from the frontier indicates that the moral effect of troops directly on the frontier would not be very good, at least until Western Virginia has decided for herself what she will do. You no doubt are better posted than I am, & if it is clear that the Union men will be strengthened by the movement of course it will be made.

For military reasons I would prefer awaiting Lt Poe's return before selecting the points to be occupied — he should be here in a day or two, & we can then act understandingly.[1] I am pressed by Gov Morton[2] for troops & heavy guns along his frontier. Yates[3] wants all the troops at East St Louis & a battery of heavy guns there. Guns are also wanted at Cairo. With no means of supplying these demands it is sometimes a little difficult to satisfy them.

[margin notes: Procrast / Pressure from Gov't]

The apathy in Washington is very singular & very discouraging. The order placing me in command of the Dept was issued on May 3 — I have not yet received it! I can get no answers except now & then a decided refusal of some request or other — perhaps that is a little exaggerated, but the upshot of it is that they are entirely too slow for such an emergency, & I almost regret having entered upon my present duty.

No money has yet arrived.

I drew today on the Treasury of the State for $1250 on account, of next session — some $4000 or $5000 more should be placed to my credit in the Commercial Bank before the close of the week — the beginning of the session will be the most expensive.

I fear I shall have to go to Cairo in the morning — dare not leave here now until I hear from Harney & see Benham & Bell[4] — will go to you at the earliest moment.

Very truly yours
Geo B McClellan
Maj Genl

ALS retained copy, McClellan Papers (C-3:62), Library of Congress.

1. Lt. Poe of GBM's staff had been sent into Kentucky and western Virginia to gather intelligence. 2. Oliver P. Morton, governor of Indiana. 3. Richard Yates, governor of Illinois. 4. Capt. Henry W. Benham, Corps of Engineers; Maj. William H. Bell, Ordnance Office.

To E. D. Townsend

To Col E D Townsend
A.A.G.   Head Quarters Dept of the Ohio
Colonel   Cincinnati May 17 1861

The intelligence I have from Western Virginia is not encouraging. The Union men there lack courage, I fear. From a long conversation with a well informed & reliable person this morning I have gathered some facts that may serve to corroborate information in your possession. The gist of the information was about as follows — viz: Harper's Ferry held by not over 2500 men, including those at Point of Rocks & the outposts; their arms, discipline etc. bad; no entrenchments erected on either side of the river; no guard at Shepherd's Town, where there is a good ford, & roads leading to Charlestown & Keys Ford. I would suggest a movement in that direction as the readiest method of driving the rebels from Harper's Ferry.

You are aware that the structures of the B & O RR most liable to injury are west of Cumberland. I beg to call to the attention of the Genl in Chief the importance of occupying Cumberland without delay — I learn that the population there, at Piedmont, Grafton etc are loyal — the importance of occupying Cumberland cannot be overestimated. In connection with that movement I propose moving one Regt of State troops to a point near Bellaire, another to a point in the vicinity of Marietta, another to Athens, another to Jackson on the Portsmouth RR. I wish to keep these away from the frontier, but near enough to produce a certain moral effect.

If Cumberland & Hancockstown can be occupied by the Maryland Troops now called out, it would probably be the best arrangement; if this cannot be done troops might be moved down from Pittsburg, if there are any there disposable.

Is it true as stated in the papers that Western Penna & Western Virginia have been added to my Dept? I have received no notification to that effect.[1]

The Union men of Kentucky express a firm determination to fight it out — yesterday Garret Davis[2] told me "we will remain in the Union by voting if we can, by fighting if we must, & if we cannot hold our own we will call on the General Govt to aid us." He asked me what I would do if they called on me for assistance & convinced me that the majority were in danger of being overpowered by a better armed minority.

I replied that if there were time enough I would refer to General Scott for orders — if there was not time, that I would cross the Ohio with 20,000 men, if that were not enough with 30,000, & if necessary with 40,000, but that I would not stand by & see the loyal Union men of Kentucky crushed. I have strong hopes that Kentucky will remain in the Union, & the most favorable feature of the whole matter is that the Union men are now ready to abandon the position of "armed neutrality," & to enter heart & soul into this contest on our side. I hope yet to pay a visit to the Hon Jefferson Davis at Montgomery.

I expect the three Randall Companies[3] tomorrow — will place them at Camp Dennison for the present. I hope to receive permission to mount more than one battery — I do not like the idea of being without regular batteries.

Is it possible for me to get the 1st Cavalry & the remaining Companies of 2nd Infantry? We shall need them very much.

With the hope that Cumberland may be promptly occupied

I am, Colonel, with great respect very truly yours

Geo B McClellan

Major Genl Comdg

ALS retained copy, McClellan Papers (C-3:62), Library of Congress. *OR*, Ser. 1, LI, Part 1, pp. 380–81.

1. These areas were made part of the Department of the Ohio on May 9. 2. Garrett Davis was a Unionist leader in Kentucky. 3. Fort Randall, Nebraska Territory, was a station of the 4th U.S. Artillery.

To John Rodgers

Comdr. John Rodgers
U.S. Navy   Head Quarters Dept. of the Ohio
Captain   Cincinnati Ohio May 19, 1861

I am not yet in possession of the views of the administration, with respect to ulterior offensive operations, sufficiently to express my opinion as to the extent and nature of the naval means of attack and transportation that we will finally require. As to the defense of Cairo, however, and the necessity for a strict blockade in that vicinity my mind is very clear.

Measures have been taken to place Cairo in a position to repel any attack that is likely to be made upon it; these measures consist in the erection of heavy batteries, so strengthened as to be able to resist an assault.

In connection with these defenses, I propose a system of active defense by means of gun boats and fast dispatch boats.

It seems desirable to have, as soon as possible, at least three gun boats, capable of carrying, say ten heavy guns each, and with steam power sufficient to enable them to fight their way back if met by superior force. If the boats used for this purpose are not possessed of great speed, we should have light and very fast tenders that can cooperate with them, and carry intelligence with great rapidity.

These tenders should be armed with one or two light guns, and they, as well as the gun boats, should be arranged so as to render an attempt to carry them by boarding very difficult, to say the least. With such boats in our possession, the garrison of Cairo can be materially reduced.

I would be glad to have you proceed to Cairo at your earliest comvenience, and examine the boats belonging to the Wrecking Company; if you find them adapted to the purpose, please close the purchase on such terms as you think the interests of the Government require.

I would also be glad to have you purchase proper tenders, if the Wrecking Company's boats have not the requisite speed. Should these boats not answer, I would be pleased to have you find others that will meet the purpose, and let me know, at once, the terms on which they can be had.

While at Cairo, Mound City, St Louis &c, it would be well to obtain all possible information as to the construction of gun boats, floating batteries &c.

Evansville has also been mentioned as a point affording many facilities for construction. I have, however, no personal knowledge of it. I would be glad to place you in communication with Mr. W. D. Field, who was sent out by the Secretary of War in relation to floating batteries, and Capt. W. J. Kountz, (an experienced steam boat Captain) also sent out to me by the Secretary of War as a proper person to assist in buying boats &c &c.[1]

I shall be glad, Captain, to place in your hands all matters pertaining to fighting on the rivers, giving you from time to time my views and wishes, and leaving the details to your superior knowledge.[2]

So far as the necessities of the service will permit, I would like to have you establish your self at my Head Quarters, that we may consult freely. In conclusion, allow me to express gratification that an Officer of your reputation and ability has been assigned to this duty. I have received so many marks of kindness from Officers of your branch of the service, and have so often witnessed their adaptability, skill and courage, that it will afford me the greatest pleasure and satisfaction to cooperate with you and I am sure that our intercourse will be mutually profitable and agreeable.

I am, Captain, very truly yours
Geo. B. McClellan
Maj. Genl.

Copy, Rare Book Collection (RB 37810 v. 1 p. 60a), Huntington Library. Comdr. Rodgers had been sent west by the Navy Department to report to GBM and under his direction devise a fleet of river warships.

1. GBM put William J. Kountz, owner of a fleet of steamboats, in charge of river transportation in his department. 2. On June 9 Rodgers wrote GBM that he had purchased the sidewheel steamers *Tyler, Lexington,* and *Conestoga* and was converting them into gunboats. McClellan Papers (A-13:6), Library of Congress.

To Simon Cameron   [TELEGRAM]

[Cincinnati] May 20/61

Important to occupy Cumberland at once. Advices indicate movement through it to Western Virginia to influence election.[1] Occupation of Cumberland will stop the movement. I hope Ohio contingent will not be limited to nine regiments, but be brought up to twenty.[2] I have as yet received neither instructions nor authority. My hands tied until I have one or the other. Every day of importance.[3]

G B McClellan
Maj Genl

Hon Simon Cameron
Secy of War Washington D C

ALS (telegram sent), McClellan Papers (C-3:62), Library of Congress. *OR*, Ser. 1, II, p. 642. Cameron was secretary of war.

1. A referendum on Virginia's ordinance of secession was scheduled for May 23. 2. Ohio was called on for nine regiments of three-year volunteers to supplant the thirteen regiments of three-month men. 3. Winfield Scott replied on May 21 that he was "surprised at your complaint to the Secretary of War against me that you are without instructions or authority and with your hands tied." He reviewed his communications to GBM on the subject, and added: "It is not conceived what other instructions could have been needed by you." *OR*, Ser. 1, LI, Part 1, pp. 386–87.

To E. D. Townsend

Col E D Townsend AAG   Head Quarters Dept of the Ohio
Colonel   Cincinnati May 21 1861

Gov Dennison has sent to me copies of his telegraphic communication of yesterday to the Lieut Genl comdg, with the Genl's reply.[1] A movement into Western Virginia may become necessary any day — so, also, it may at any moment become imperative to move into Kentucky, in order to save the loyal men of that state. With my present force it would be very dangerous to make these movements, particularly in view of the condition of the troops & the administrative branches. If we are to carry on this war in earnest, & in a manner to insure success, there should be at least 40,000 troops available for active operations in this Department, & the means of transportation should be provided, as well as clothing & equipment. Not less than 20, & if possible 30, Regts should be called for from this state.

I was extremely sorry a few moments since to receive a dispatch from the Adjt General stating that no recruits can be allowed for companies from Randall — there are between 400 & 500 recruits at Newport Barracks,[2] & plenty can be had by opening rendezvous on this side of the river.

I am very respectfully yr obdt svt
Geo B McClellan
Maj Genl USA

ALS retained copy, McClellan Papers (C-3:62), Library of Congress. *OR*, Ser. 1, LI, Part 1, p. 383.

1. Gov. Dennison's telegram of May 20 reported intelligence that Confederate troops were advancing on Grafton and Clarksburg in western Virginia. Scott replied that the matter was "within the competency of Gen McClellan to whom please refer." McClellan Papers (B-7:46). 2. Newport Barracks was a recruiting depot at Newport, Ky.

To Lorenzo Thomas

Genl L Thomas
Adjt Genl U.S.A.   Head Qtrs Dept of the Ohio
General   Cincinnati May 21 1861

I have the honor to acknowledge the receipt of your communication of the 14th inst, enclosing my appointment as a Major General in the U.S. Army.

I accept the appointment & herewith return my oath of allegiance to the U.S. duly executed.

I beg, General, that you will convey to the Presdt, the Secretary of War, and the Lieut General Commanding, my most sincere & heartfelt thanks for this distinguished honor.

I confess it is with great diffidence that I enter upon the discharge of the momentous duties pertaining to my office, and with a grave sense of their magnitude & responsibility. I hope, however, that by bringing to the task a firm determination to devote my best abilities to the service of my country, I may succeed in justifying the exalted opinion of those to whom I am indebted for the post.

I am, General, very respectfully yours
Geo B McClellan
Maj Genl U.S. Army

ALS, Records of the Adjutant General's Office, RG 94 (M-619:37), National Archives.

To Winfield Scott   [TELEGRAM]

To Gen. Winfield Scott   Morris Ind [May 24, 1861]

Will do what you want. Make it clean sweep if you say so. Answer Cincinnati.[1]

G. B. McClellan

Received copy, Records of the Office of the Secretary of War, RG 107 (M-504:9),National Archives.

1. Sent by GBM when he was attending a military conference in Indiana, this telegram was in reply to Scott's of the same date, calling on him to counteract the Confederate advance on Grafton in western Virginia. *OR*, Ser. 1, II, p. 648.

To William Dennison   [TELEGRAM]

To/Gov Wm Dennison
Columbus Ohio   [Cincinnati] May 25/61

Genl. Scott is as you are aware eminently sensitive, and does not at all times take suggestions kindly from military subordinates especially when they conflict with his own preconceived notions.

In view of this, and of the importance of his hearty cooperation in future military operations in this Department, I beg to suggest that you request Gov. Yates by telegraph in carrying out the objects of his mission at Washington not to use my name in such a way as to disturb the sensitive complexion of the General's mind.[1]

criticism of Gen. Scott

Retained copy, McClellan Papers (A-12:5), Library of Congress.

1. Gov. Yates of Illinois was to deliver a "memorial" on military policy in the western theater to Gen. Scott. *OR*, Ser. 1, LII, Part 1, pp. 146–47.

To the Troops of the Department of the Ohio

                                       Hd Qtrs Dept of the Ohio
Soldiers   Cincinnati May 26 1861

You are ordered to cross the frontier & enter upon the soil of Virginia.

Your mission is to restore peace & confidence, to protect the majesty of the law, & to rescue our brethren from the grasp of armed traitors. You are to act in concert with Virginia troops,[1] & to support their advance.

I place under the safeguard of your honor the persons & property of the Virginians — I know that you will respect their feelings & all their rights.

Preserve the strictest discipline — remember that each one of you holds in his keeping the honor of Ohio & of the Union.

If you are called upon to overcome armed opposition, I know that your courage is equal to the task — but remember that your only foes are the armed traitors — & show mercy even to them when they are in your power, for many of them are misguided.

When under your protection the loyal men of Western Virginia have been enabled to organize & arm they can protect themselves, & you can then return to your homes with the proud satisfaction of having preserved a gallant people from destruction.

                                       G B McClellan

ADS, McClellan Papers (A-12:5), Library of Congress. *OR*, Ser. 1, II, p. 49.

1. The 1st Virginia (Union).

To the Union Men of Western Virginia

Virginians!   [Cincinnati, May 26, 1861]

The General Govt has long enough endured the machinations of a few factious rebels in your midst. Armed traitors have in vain endeavored to deter you from expressing your loyalty at the polls;[1] having failed in this infamous attempt to deprive you of the exercise of your dearest rights, they now seek to inaugurate a reign of terror & thus force you to yield to their schemes & submit to the yoke of the traitorous conspiracy dignified by the name of the Southern Confederacy. They are destroying the property of the citizens of your state, & ruining your magnificent railways. The Genl Govt has heretofore carefully abstained from sending troops across the Ohio, or even from posting them along its banks, although frequently urged by many of your prominent citizens to do so. It determined to await the result of the late election, desirous that no one might be able to say that the slightest effort had been made from this side to influence the free expression of your opinion, although the many agencies brought to bear upon you by the rebels were well known. You have now shown, under the most adverse circumstances, that the great mass of the people of Western Virginia are true & loyal to that beneficent Govt under which we & our fathers have lived so long. As soon as the result of the election was known the traitors commenced their work of destruction.

The Genl Govt cannot close its ears to the demand you have made for assistance. I have ordered troops to cross the river. They come as your friends & brothers — as enemies only to the armed rebels who are preying upon you.

Your homes, your families & your property are safe under our protection. All your rights shall be religiously respected. Notwithstanding all that has been said by the traitors to induce you to believe that our advent among you will be signalized by interference with your slaves, understand one thing clearly — not only will we abstain from all such interference but we will on the contrary with an iron hand, crush any attempt at insurrection on their part.

Now that we are in your midst I call upon you to fly to arms & support the Genl Govt.

Sever the connection that binds you to traitors — proclaim to the world that the faith & loyalty so long boasted by the Old Dominion are still preserved in Western Virginia, & that you remain true to the Stars & Stripes.

AD, McClellan Papers (A-12:5), Library of Congress. *OR*, Ser. 1, II, pp. 48–49.

1. The far western counties had opposed the Virginia ordinance of secession in the May 23 referendum.

To E. D. Townsend

Lt Col E D Townsend   A.A.G.   Head Qtrs Dept of the Ohio
Colonel   Cincinnati May 30 1861

Feels
success

I have the honor to report the successful occupation of Grafton without the loss of a single life. My previous dispatches have informed you of the circumstances under which the movement was undertaken & the orders given for carrying it into effect.[1]

The movement was greatly delayed by the necessity of repairing the burned bridges — I constantly advised Col Kelly[2] to use great caution & I am happy to say that he has been able to combine it with unusual energy.

He promptly arrived at the burned bridge; at once set a working party at preparing timber for repairs, moved an advanced guard forward to the very important bridge over the Monongahela at Fairmont, & seized all the secessionists he could find.

At 11 o'clock this a.m. he moved forward & reached Grafton at 2.30 p.m.

The secessionists had evacuated the place before his arrival.

The Colonel will pursue them on the Beverly Road in the morning, & endeavor to capture at least some arms that they sent away before they started. I cannot commend too highly the prudence & energy displayed by Col Kelly in this movement — he has in every instance carried out his instructions, & has displayed very high military qualities — I beg to recommend to the Genl that he may be made a Brig Genl of the Va Volunteers.[3]

*Stresses
no lives
lost*

It is a source of very great satisfaction to me that we have occupied Grafton without the sacrifice of a single life. Col Stedman's[4] advance from Parkersburg has not been so prompt as that of Col Kelly — he has met with many difficulties on his route. I am happy to say that the movement has caused a very great increase of the Union feeling. I am now organizing a movement on the valley of the Great Kanawha — will go there in person & endeavor to capture the occupants of the secession camp at Buffalo, & return in time to direct such movements in Ky or Tenna as may become necessary.

Victory

I will make a more detailed report when I receive Col Kelly's full report.

I am very respectfully yr obd svt
Geo B McC
Maj Genl USA

ALS retained copy, McClellan Papers (A-12:5), Library of Congress. *OR*, Ser. 1, II, pp. 49–50.

1. These dispatches and instructions are in *OR*, Ser. 1, II, pp. 44–48. 2. Col. Benjamin F. Kelley, 1st Virginia. 3. Kelley was so commissioned, to date from May 17. 4. Col. James B. Steedman, 14th Ohio.

To Abraham Lincoln

Unofficial
His Excellency Abraham Lincoln
Presdt of the US   Head Quarters Dept of the Ohio
Sir   Cincinnati May 30 1861

I avail myself of the return of Lieut Nelson[1] to inform you briefly of
what has been said to me by some of the leading Union men of Kentucky
in regard to the recent distribution of arms among them. They uniformly
represent that the effect has been extremely beneficial, not only in giving
strength to the Union party & discouraging the secessionists, but that it
has proved to the minds of all reasonable men that the Genl Govt has
confidence in their loyalty & entertains no intention of subjugating them.
I am confidently assured that very considerable numbers of volunteers
can be raised in Western Virginia as well as in Ky, & I would most
respectfully urge that an ample supply of arms be placed at my disposal
to arm such regiments — we shall need in addition equipment, money, &
clothing. The issue of the arms to Kentuckians is regarded by the staunch
men as a masterpiece of policy on your part, & has — if I may be per-
mitted to say so — very much strengthened your position among them.

A very delicate question is arising as to Western Ky — that portion
west of the Tenna River; Lieut Nelson will explain to you that a con-
vention is now being held at Mayfield which may declare the "Jackson
Purchase"[2] separate from Ky, its annexation to Tenna, & that this will
be followed by an advance of Tenna troops upon Columbus & Paducah.
The Union men say that immediately upon this being done they will call
upon Gov Magoffin[3] to drive out the invaders, & that, should he fail to
do so, they will at once call upon me to aid them. I will respond to this
call without delay — & should they delay in making it, will endeavor to
find means to cause Genl Pillow to repeat his Cerro Gordo movement
without violating the soil of Ky. I am informed that my proclamation
to the Western Virginians[5] has produced the happiest effect in Ken-
tucky — it not being possible for me to refer the matter to Washington,
I prepared it in great haste & on such a basis as my knowledge of your
Excellency's previous course & opinions assured me would express your
views — I am confident that I have not erred in this very important
matter — if I have, a terrible mistake has been made, for the proclamation
is regarded as expressing the views of the Presdt, & I have not intimated
that it was prepared without authority.

I received the information that two bridges on the B & O RR had been
burned, at a late hour on Sunday P.M. [May 26] & at once made all my
arrangements by telegraph — in the hurry I could only endeavor to ex-
press your views & shall be very much gratified to learn that you approve
of what I have done.

I am preparing to seize the valley of the Great Kanawha, there are some 1200 secessionists encamped there — I shall go there in person with from three to four rgts & endeavor to capture them — then to occupy the Gauley Bridge, & return here in time for any necessary movement on Ky. By occupying Grafton & Gauley Bridge we hold the passes thro' the mountains between Eastern & Western Va. It is also possible that I may occupy Guyandotte — a small hot bed of secession. By that means I hope to secure Western Virginia to the Union.

Rest assured that I will exert all my energies to carry out what I suppose to be your policy, & that I will be glad to be informed if I have misconstrued your views.

Should it not be in the power of the Govt to send Lt Nelson back to distribute arms, I would be glad to have him attached to my staff, on account of his intimate relations with the Union men of Ky.

I am very respectfully your obd svt & friend
Geo B McClellan
Maj Genl USA

ALS, Lincoln Papers, Library of Congress.

1. Lt. William Nelson, USN. 2. So named for Andrew Jackson, who played a leading role in its purchase from the Chickasaw Indians in 1818. 3. Beriah Magoffin, governor of Kentucky. 4. Maj. Gen. Gideon Pillow, Tennessee militia. GBM served under him in Mexico at the Battle of Cerro Gordo, which was an American victory despite Pillow's blundering. 5. GBM to the Union Men of Western Virginia, May 26, *supra*.

To Abraham Lincoln

His Excellency Abram Lincoln
Presdt of the U.S.   Head Qtrs Dept of the Ohio
Sir   Cincinnati June 1 1861

I take the liberty of asking your favorable consideration of a request that involves not only the efficiency of my command, but to a certain extent my personal feelings.

I wish to ask of you the appointment of Inspector General (in the place of Col Mansfield,[1] promoted) for Maj R B Marcy of the Pay Department, with the earnest request that he may be assigned to my command as the Chief of my staff.[2]

I need not advert to the eminent services rendered to the Govt by this admirable soldier — they are known to all who have kept themselves informed of the operations of our active army in the West — his numerous explorations, his trying & successful march over the mountains, in the dead of winter, from Camp Bridger to New Mexico, are familiar to all.[3] I may be permitted to add that my intimate personal & official relations with him show him to be possessed of precisely those qualities that I need in my advisor & chief of staff.

You will double my efficiency if you can find it possible to place Major Marcy in the position I refer to.

I have a large & unorganized command — requiring only instruction, discipline, & organization to make it the best Army in the world — to effect this I must have the necessary staff, & my first wish is to have Major Marcy in the place I have referred to.

I feel very deeply that the honor of the West is to a great extent in my keeping — I know that your excellency will share my wish to raise the reputation of the Western troops to the highest point — & I feel sure that you will grant my urgent request. If Maj M cannot be made Inspector Genl I hope that he may command a Brigade of Regulars under me.[4] I am, sir, very respectfully

> your obedient servant
> Geo B McClellan
> Maj Genl USA

ALS, Records of the Office of the Secretary of War, RG 107 (M-492:10), National Archives.

1. Brig. Gen. Joseph K. F. Mansfield, promoted to command of the Department of Washington. 2. Maj. Marcy, GBM's father-in-law, was then serving as inspector general in the Department of the Ohio. 3. This march was made in the winter of 1857–58, during the Mormon War. 4. Secretary of War Cameron replied on June 8 that the post had been filled. RG 107 (M-492:10), National Archives. Marcy was appointed inspector general in the regular army on Aug. 9, 1861, and served as GBM's chief of staff with the rank of brigadier general.

To Winfield Scott

Lt Genl Winfield Scott
Head Quarters Army
Washington D.C.   Head Quarters Dept of the Ohio
General   Cincinnati June 5 [1861]

Your telegram in relation to Mr Rousseau was received.[1] I am informed that Mr. R. is a perfectly reliable Union man but that he is too impolitic for the present moment. I have watched the Kentucky movement with far more than ordinary care &, I think, understand it. It is my firm belief that the Union party is gaining strength every day, & that with care & great tact the State may be saved to the Union.

You are aware that there are two elections yet to take place in that state — one on June 20th for members of Congress. Another Aug. 4th for the State Legislature. The Union men are sure that they can carry both of these, if no undue elements of excitement are introduced into the canvass. You are also aware that the present legislature elected long since, is nearly secession & does not truly represent the feeling of the people.

Bearing in mind that the Kentuckians desire to remain in the Union *without a revolution, under all the forms of law & by their own action,* you will see, General, how important it is that they should be treated with the utmost delicacy until the elections are over.

To carry out this policy I urge that no troops be sent into Kentucky (except in an emergency, to which I will presently refer), that no comdr be appointed to the Dept of Kentucky, at least until he has some troops to command, & above all things that the comdg genl be either a Kentuckian or a man particularly acceptable to the Kentuckians.

If Tenna troops invade the state of Ky then we should act promptly and send reinforcements to drive them out — but let the first invasion take place from the South; not from here. It is my opinion that arms, equipment and funds should at once be placed at my disposal to arm my troops. I expect before I send this letter to see gentlemen from the other side on this subject, & am informed that we can have a thousand real Kentuckians in Covington & its vicinity, and at least ten thousand in Louisville, who will march anywhere and fight anybody. But it would be vain to muster these men before we can provide for them, & I think that instant action should be taken.

I send to-night a thoroughly reliable gentleman, a Kentuckian by birth, & a man of standing and intellect, to confer with leading Kentuckians; I ask as a great favor that all action may be deferred until I can report the result of his visit. I trust, General, that my action in the Grafton matter will show you that I am not given to procrastination but I feel so keenly the vital importance of keeping Kentucky in the Union that I must urge delay until we know exactly what we are doing.

I am convinced that it would be disastrous in the extreme to send either Col. Guthrie or his command to Ky. Were they real Kentuckians, as I at first believed, the case might be very different.[2]

I do not think that too much importance can be attached to the necessity of allowing the elections to proceed quietly, & I hope that no one will be detailed to command the Dept of Kentucky until Col. Anderson's health will permit him to enter upon the duty.

I think the advantage to be gained by delay, will far more than counterbalance the disadvantage arising from the shipment of provisions from Louisville for a short time.

> I am very respectfully yr obdt svt
> Geo B McClellan
> Maj Genl USA

LS retained copy, McClellan Papers (C-3:62), Library of Congress.

1. Gen. Scott's telegram of June 4 proposed Lovell H. Rousseau of Louisville as commander of the newly established Department of Kentucky in place of the ailing Col. Robert Anderson. *OR*, Ser. 1, LII, Part 1, p. 157. 2. Col. James B. Guthrie, an earlier candidate for the Department of Kentucky post, was opposed by GBM on the grounds that he was not a native Kentuckian, and that his regiment contained more Ohioans and Indianians than Kentuckians. *OR*, Ser. 1, LII, Part 1, pp. 156–57.

To Thomas A. Morris   [TELEGRAM]

[Cincinnati, June 20, 1861][1]

I will move from Parkersburg on the flank & rear of your opponents. My force will be sufficient to fight a battle. I leave to you the care of Cheat River, which you will strongly reinforce & hold at all hazards.

Concentrate on Grafton if you cannot certainly hold Phillipi. I trust to you entirely the defence of Phillipi, Grafton & Fairmont. I will recall towards Parkersburg when I move, the troops on that road, leave a sufficient garrison there & advance prepared to fight whatever I meet. Be prudent but do not give one inch that you can avoid. Have urged Genl Scott to send a strong column by Cumberland on Romney to cut off retreat of the rebels.[2] Be cool & firm & we will gain the first brilliant success.

G B McClellan
Maj Genl USA

Genl T A Morris

ALS (telegram sent), McClellan Papers (B-41:61), Library of Congress. Brig. Gen. Morris commanded the force that on June 3 had routed the Confederates at Philippi, Va.

1. Date supplied from a draft of this telegram. McClellan Papers (B-13:6). 2. GBM's June 19 telegram called for this column to be furnished by Maj. Gen. Patterson, commanding the Department of Pennsylvania. *OR*, Ser. 1, II, p. 706.

To Mary Ellen McClellan

Marietta June 21/61

I must snatch a few moments to write you. We got off about 11 1/2 yesterday morning & had a continual ovation all along the road.[1] At every station where we stopped, crowds had assembled to see the "Young General." Gray-headed old men & women; mothers holding up their children to take my hand, girls, boys, all sorts, cheering and crying, God bless you! I never went thro' such a scene in my life & never expect to go thro' such another one. You would have been surprised at the excitement. At Chillicothe the ladies had prepared a dinner & I had to be trotted through. They gave me about 20 beautiful bouquets, & almost killed me with kindness. The trouble will be to fill their expectations, they seem to be so high. I could hear them say, "He is our own general"; "Look at him, how young he is"; "*He* will thrash them"; "He'll do," &c, &c ad infinitum.

We reached here about 3 in the morning, & at once went on board the boat, where I got about 3 hours sleep until we reached Parkersburg. I have been hard at work all day for I found everything in great confusion. Came up here in the boat alone an hour ago & shall go back to Parkersburg in 2 or 3 hours. . . .

We start from Parkersburg at 6 in the morning. With me go McCook's rgt (9th Ohio), Mack's Company (4th US Artillery), the Sturgess Rifle Co., a battery of 6 guns (Loomis) & 1 company of Cavalry (Barker's Illinois).[2]

Two Indiana rgts leave in the morning just after us. I shall have 5 additional rgts at Grafton tomorrow afternoon. I shall have some 18 rgts, 2 batteries, 2 co's of cavalry at my disposal — enough to thrash anything I find. I think the danger has been greatly exaggerated & anticipate little or no chance of winning laurels. . . .

A terrible storm is passing over us now — thunder & lightning terrible in the extreme. . . .

AL copy; copy, McClellan Papers (C-7:63/D-10:72), Library of Congress. Mrs. McClellan would remain in Cincinnati until December 1861, when she joined GBM in Washington.

1. GBM left Cincinnati by train on June 20 to take command of the campaign in western Virginia. 2. These were units of the headquarters escort.

To E. D. Townsend

Col E D Townsend
A.A.G.   Head Qtrs Dept of the Ohio
Colonel   Parkersburg June 22 1861

I reached here yesterday morning, hoping to move forward during the day, but was delayed by want of wagons & the disorganization to be expected on the part of new troops moving for the first time into the field. In a few minutes (now 7 am) I shall move with the advance to Clarksburg — taking one regiment Infty, 2 detached co's (1 of regulars), 1 battery, & a company of cavalry. 2 Indiana regts will follow during the morning, two Ohio regts tomorrow. Two other Ohio regts will reach Grafton via Bellair today. Reports from the front are somewhat contradictory, but agree in representing the enemy in strong force near Piedmont & Beverly. Notwithstanding that Genl Morris & others seem sure that we have a large force to contend with, I now am inclined to doubt it. I will without delay beat them up in their quarters & endeavor to put an end to their attempts in this direction.

I have, I think, force enough to fight them wherever I find them. Genl McCall[1] telegraphs that Cumberland will be reinforced on Monday [June 24] — if that is accomplished we should be able to cut off the force near Piedmont.

As I cannot learn yet the quality of their troops (there are reports that there are some regiments of the regular Confederate troops), I shall be cautious in my movements.

I feel very much the absolute necessity of more Commsy & Qtr Mr officers — also of cavalry. I hope the Lt Genl will find it in his power to let me have the companies of 1st Cavalry now at Leavenworth.

I received on the *18th* inst. the order adding Missouri to my Dept[2] —
my arrangements for coming here to take command were so far advanced
that it was not possible for me to go to Missouri. I shall go there im-
mediately on my return from this state.

I move hence on Clarksburg & will act thence according to the infor-
mation I receive — either move in force on the rear of the enemy at
Beverly, or go on to Piedmont.

Excuse, Colonel, the hurried nature of this.

> Very respectfully your obdt svt
> Geo B McClellan
> Maj Genl USA

ALS, Richards Collection, Boston University Library. *OR,* Ser. 1, II, p. 194.

1. Brig. Gen. George A. McCall, Pennsylvania Rerserves. 2. This order was dated June 6.

To Mary Ellen McClellan

Grafton Sunday June 23/61

... We did not reach here until about 2 in the morning & I was tired
out....

Today I have been so busy that I did not know until 10 mins. ago that
it is Sunday & cannot yet realize the fact. Everything here needs the
hand of the master & is getting it fast. I shall hardly be able to move
from here for a couple of days — so difficult is it to get these Mohawks[1]
in working trim....

The weather is delightful here — we are well up in the hills & have
the mountain air....

AL copy, McClellan Papers (C-7:63), Library of Congress.

1. A pejorative term for volunteers in the Mexican War.

To the Inhabitants of Western Virginia

To the Inhabitants of	Head-Quarters, Department of the Ohio.
Western Virginia:	Grafton, Va., June 23d, 1861.

The army of this Department, headed by Virginia troops, is rapidly
occupying all Western Virginia. This is done in co-operation with and
in support of such civil authorities of the State as are faithful to the
Constitution and laws of the United States. The proclamation issued by
me, under date of May 26th, 1861,[1] will be strictly maintained. Your
houses, families, property, and all your rights, will be religiously re-
spected. We are enemies to none but armed rebels, and those voluntarily

giving them aid. All officers of this army will be held responsible for the most prompt and vigorous action in repressing disorder, and punishing aggression by those under their command.

To my great regret, I find that enemies of the United States continue to carry on a system of hostilities prohibited by the laws of war among belligerent nations, and of course far more wicked and intolerable when directed against loyal citizens engaged in the defense of the common Government of all. Individuals and marauding parties are pursuing a guerilla warfare; firing upon sentinels and pickets; burning bridges; insulting, injuring, and even killing citizens because of their Union sentiments, and committing many kindred acts.

I do now, therefore, make proclamation, and warn all persons, that individuals or parties engaged in this species of warfare — irregular in every view which can be taken of it — thus attacking sentries, pickets or other soldiers; destroying public or private property, committing injuries against any of the inhabitants because of Union sentiments or conduct, will be dealt with in their persons and property according to the severest rules of military law.

All persons giving information or aid to the public enemies, will be arrested and kept in close custody; and all persons found bearing arms, unless of known loyalty, will be arrested and held for examination.

> Geo. B. McClellan
> Maj. Gen. U.S. Army,
> Commanding Department

DP, McClellan Papers (B-7:46), Library of Congress. *OR*, Ser. 1, II, p. 196.

1. To the Union Men of Western Virginia, May 26, *supra.*

To the Army of the West

To the Soldiers of the Army of the West:	Head-Quarters, Dep't of the Ohio Grafton, Va., June 25th, 1861.

You are here to support the Government of your country and to protect the lives and liberties of your brethren, threatened by a rebellious and traitorous foe. No higher and nobler duty could devolve upon you, and I expect you to bring to its performance, the highest and noblest qualities of soldiers — discipline, courage and mercy. I call upon the officers, of every grade to enforce the strictest discipline, and I know that those of all grades, privates and officers, will display in battle cool heroic courage, and will know how to show mercy to a disarmed enemy.

[Bear in mind that you are in the country of friends, not of enemies; that you are here to protect, not to destroy.] Take nothing, destroy nothing, unless you are ordered to do so by your General officers. Remember that I have pledged my word to the people of Western Virginia, that their rights in person and property shall be respected. I ask every one of you to make good this promise in its broadest sense. We come here to save, not to upturn. I do not appeal to the fear of punishment, but to your appreciation of the sacredness of the cause in which we are engaged. Carry with you into battle the conviction that you are right, and that God is on your side.

Your enemies have violated every moral law — neither God nor man can sustain them. They have without cause rebelled against a mild and paternal Government; they have seized upon public and private property; they have outraged the persons of Northern men merely because they came from the North, and of Southern Union men merely because they loved the Union; they have placed themselves beneath contempt, unless they can retrieve some honor on the field of battle. You will pursue a different course. You will be honest, brave, and merciful; you will respect the right of private opinion; you will punish no man for opinion's sake. Show to the world that you differ from our enemies in the points of honor, honesty and respect for private opinion, and that we inaugurate no reign of terror where we go.

Soldiers! I have heard that there was danger here. I fear now but one thing — that you will not find foemen worthy of your steel. I know that I can rely upon you.

Geo. B. McClellan
Major Gen'l Commanding

DP, McClellan Papers (B-7:46), Library of Congress. *OR*, Ser. 1, II, pp. 196–97.

To Salmon P. Chase

Hon S P Chase
Washington
My dear Sir   Grafton Va June 26 1861

I take pleasure in acknowledging the receipt of your letters of the 19 & 20 which reached me here yesterday. I will send the necessary instructions in reference to the Regiments which Mr Gurley[1] is interested in.

Gov Dennison has in no way interfered with my control of the troops mustered into the U.S. service, all that he has had to do with them was to carry into effect the War Dept orders in regard to changing the 3 mos into 3 year regiments, & on this subject he received instructions from the War Dept I think. In addition to this Gov D. has exerted himself to the fullest extent in providing equipment for the troops — if Ohio has not equipped her contingent quite so rapidly as some other states it is mainly due to the fact that her force was very large. There has been in no respect any conflict between Gov Dennison & myself.

I will take the earliest possible steps to have the necessary pay rolls etc made out — now that I have so large a portion of the active force in front of the enemy I do not think the question of pay will come up for some little time. It may be necessary for me to retain the 3 mos Indiana men in the field beyond the term of their enlistment — I am sure that I can count upon their patriotism. I have 5 of the 3 mos Indiana troops here — well provided in every respect; 5 rgts of 3 years Ohio Vols, 8 rgts Ohio State troops, about 2 Va Regts, 1 Regular Battery, 1 Battery Michigan 3 yrs vols., 1 Ohio State Battery, 1 company Ohio State cavalry, 1 co. Illinois 3 years cavalry, 1 company Regular Artillery serving as Infty, 1 company Illinois Rifles.

These troops are generally well armed & well equipped — I am delayed by non arrival of rations & transportation, but we are adding to the efficiency every day & supplying small deficiencies.

The men are in most excellent spirits & require only careful handling. They will render a good account of themselves, or I am much mistaken. I think we can show that one Southerner is not equal to *more* than 3 Northern men! We have the most magnificent material for an army that was ever brought together — give me three months in a camp of instruction after this little campaign is over & I would not hesitate to put these men at the best of European troops. The officers are not so good as the men, & I beg, Governor, that you will use your influence in giving us educated soldiers for the General Officers & those of the staff.

The Union feeling is strengthening where we are, & I think will grow as we proceed. I find that my proclamations have produced a happy effect. I take the liberty of enclosing a copy of my last, together with my address to the soldiers.

I have fully instructed Capt Rodgers as to the gun boats[2] — my chief difficulty heretofore has been to obtain reliable plans — I have driven some men away in great disgust with my slowness merely because I was not willing to authorize them to go to work until I could ascertain what they intended to do. I feared the loss of time that would be caused by a failure far more than the loss of money. There is pretty good reason to believe that we have Georgia, So Car, & Tenna troops in front of us. Their main force is at the Laurel Mountain between Phillipi & Beverly — I shall move the main column rapidly from Clarksburg on Buckhannon & Beverly to turn that position while the force now at Phillipi slowly advances to distract their attention. I hardly hope that they will be foolish enough to fall into the trap — whether they do so or not I shall then advance on Huttonsville & drive them into & across the mountains. Having accomplished that I will sweep the Kanawha & overrun the country with small columns & assure the Union men.

Begging that you will excuse the length of this, I am respectfully

ALS retained copy, McClellan Papers (A-15 :7), Library of Congress. Chase was secretary of the treasury and a former Ohio governor and senator.

1. John A. Gurley, congressman from Ohio. 2. See GBM to Rodgers, May 19, *supra*.

To Winfield Scott   [TELEGRAM]

To Lt. Gen. W. Scott   Received June 26 1861 From Grafton Va

A letter of Genl Buckner to Gov Magoffin dated Louisville June tenth (10th) has just reached me through the newspapers.[1] It fills me with astonishment. I can scarcely believe what he wrote. It is an entire misconception & is incorrect throughout. The arrangement & stipulations spoken of by him were got within my authority or my imagination.[2] The interview was purely personal solicited by him several times & granted by me mainly in the hope of reclaiming to the cause of the Union an old & intimate friend.[3] My views of the political relations between the General Government & the state of Kentucky were radically different from these attributed to me in his letter. The whole interview was to me inconclusive & unsatisfactory & the only thing in the nature of a stipulation made between us was his voluntary proffer to attack & drive out any secession troops which might enter Kentucky. May I ask that you will explain this fully to the President & cabinet. I write more fully.

G. B. McClellan
Maj Genl

Received copy, Lincoln Papers, Library of Congress.

1. This letter by Maj. Gen. Simon B. Buckner, head of Kentucky's home guard, reported on his meeting with GBM in Cincinnati on the night of June 7–8. Buckner wrote Gov. Magoffin that certain "stipulations" had been agreed to, seemingly guaranteeing Kentucky's neutrality. Frank Moore, ed., *The Rebellion Record* (New York, 1862), II, Documents, p. 163. GBM reported to Col. E. D. Townsend on June 11: "General Buckner came to see me on Friday last. We sat up all night, talking about matters of common interest. Buckner gave me his word that should any Tennessee troops cross the frontier of Kentucky he would use all the force at his disposal to drive them out, and, failing in that, would call on me for assistance." *OR,* Ser. 1, II, p. 674. 2. This garbled passage was presumably meant to read: "... were got without my authority or my instigation." 3. Buckner, a Kentuckian, had known GBM since their cadet days at West Point. He joined the Confederate service in September.

To Winfield Scott

Lt Genl Winfield Scott   Head Qtrs Dept of the Ohio
General   Grafton Va June 26 1861

Since my last letter in regard to the Buckner matter[1] I telegraphed to a friend who was present at a second interview I had with Buckner at Cairo on the 13th & have just received a reply.

I had gone to Cairo on a tour of inspection & while there Buckner arrived with three citizens of Kentucky. The object of his visit was to confer with Genl Prentiss[2] or myself in relation to the cutting down of a secession flag at Columbus by one of our armed boats, & the landing of an armed party into Ky a few days before by Genl P.

Mr. J. M. Douglass[3] of Chicago, well known to the President, was present with me during the whole interview, & the line of conversation pursued was nearly the same (it was shorter) than in the interview of June 8th — the main difference was in the fact that I told these gentlemen that if secession flags were hoisted on the river bank our people would cut them down & I would authorize them to do so, also, that if they did not prevent the outrages committed on Union men our men could not & would not be restrained from aiding them.

I this morning telegraphed Mr. Douglass asking the question whether anything in the Cairo interview justified or confirmed Buckner's letter.

His reply is as follows — "At the Cairo interview etc — [*omitted:* no word was uttered by you bearing the construction published relative to previous interview at Cincinnati — no allusion made to previous treaty or agreements. I was amazed to read the published correspondence touching an agreement which was not of importance enough to mention at Cairo. You distinctly disclaimed any authority to act except as you might be ordered by the government.]"[4]

I submit this to you with the request that you will ask the President his opinion of the intelligence & reliability of Mr. Douglass — then give his reply, General, the weight you think it worth.

Judge Key,[5] who is intimately acquainted with my entire views & action in regard to Ky has written a letter to Secy Chase, which embodies the facts of the case in such a clear form that I cannot do better than to ask you to read it & give it full credence.[6]

This transaction has surprised me beyond expression — my chief fear has been that you, whom I regard as my strongest friend in Washington, might have supposed me to be guilty of the extreme of folly. My personal relations with Buckner, & my high regard for his character, have led me to be more chary perhaps in my expressions than my own interests would warrant — I know that you will appreciate & respect the feeling which has dictated this course.[7] I shall be fully satisfied if I hear from you that you are not displeased with me, & I trust to my actions of the coming week to show to the people that you have not made a mistake in placing me in the position I now occupy.

I am General whatever the result may be your obliged, sincere & respectful friend

Geo B McClellan

ALS retained copy, McClellan Papers (A-15:7), Library of Congress. *OR*, Ser. 1, LII, Part 1, pp. 182–83.

1. Written earlier in the day, the letter elaborated the account of the Buckner interview outlined in GBM's telegram of this date, *supra. OR*, Ser. 1, LII, Part 1, pp. 183–84. 2. Brig. Gen. Benjamin M. Prentiss, in command at Cairo, Ill. 3. John M. Douglas, a lawyer

with the Illinois Central Railroad. 4. In Douglas to GBM, June 26, McClellan Papers (A-15:7). 5. Col. Thomas M. Key of GBM's staff, a former Cincinnati commercial court judge. 6. Key wrote Chase on June 26: "Not one word was said by Gen. McC of any arrangement, stipulation or conclusion whatever...." Key suggested that Buckner's letter to Gov. Magoffin was published to "set a trap for McClellan." Chase Papers, Library of Congress. 7. A witness to the Cincinnati interview, Samuel Gill, in a telegram to GBM, implied that a somewhat broader understanding was reached with Buckner than GBM suggests in this letter: "I didn't consider ... that you were stipulating for the Government, but that for the present you would act in accordance with the general views expressed by Simon." Gill to GBM, June 27, McClellan Papers (A-15:7).

To Mary Ellen McClellan

Grafton June 29 [1861]

... I am bothered half to death by delays in getting up supplies — unless where I am in person everything seems to go wrong. ...

I expect in the course of an hour or two to get to Clarksburg — will probably march 12 mi thence today — with Howe's Battery, Mack's & the Chicago Co's., & 1 Co. of cavalry.

I shall have a telegraph line built to follow us up. Look at the maps & find Buckhannon & Beverly — that is the direction of my march. I hope to thrash the infamous scamps before a week is over — all I fear is that I can't catch them. ...

What a strange performance that of Buckner's was! Fortunately I have secured the testimony of Gill, & Douglass (present at the Cairo interview) that Buckner has entirely misrepresented me. It has annoyed me much, but I hope to do such work here as will set criticism at defiance. ...

AL copy, McClellan Papers (C-7:63), Library of Congress.

To Mary Ellen McClellan

Clarksburg June 30 [1861]

... Again great delays here — will certainly get off by 4 am. tomorrow & make a long march probably 28 mi. After the next march I shall have a large tent, borrowed from the Chicago Rifles; your Father & I will take that, make it reception room, sleeping apartment, mess room &c. ...

One thing takes up a great deal of time, yet I cannot avoid it — crowds of the country people who have heard of me & read my proclamations come in from all directions to thank me, shake me by the hand, & look at their "liberator, the General"! Of course I have to see them & talk to them. Well, it is a proud & glorious thing to see a whole people here, simple & unsophisticated, looking up to me as their deliverer from tyranny.

AL copy; copy, McClellan Papers (C-7:63/D-10:72), Library of Congress.

To Mary Ellen McClellan

Camp 14 mi south of Clarksburg July 2 [1861]

... We start in a few moments to Buckhannon. I have with me 3 Rgts — a battery — 2 cavalry co's — 3 detached co's. Had several heavy rains yesterday. Rosecranz[1] is at Buckhannon, very meek now after a very severe rapping I gave him a few days since.[2] I doubt whether the rebels will fight — it is possible they may, but I begin to think that my successes will be due to manoeuvres, & that I shall have no brilliant victories to record. I would be glad to clear them out of West Virginia & liberate the country without bloodshed if possible. The people are rejoiced to see us.

AL copy, McClellan Papers (C-7:63), Library of Congress.

1. Brig. Gen. William S. Rosecrans, in command of a brigade. GBM frequently misspelled his name. 2. Rosecrans was reprimanded for allowing some of his troops to camp too far in advance, possibly alerting the enemy to GBM's intentions. *McClellan's Own Story*, draft, McClellan Papers (D-9:71).

To Jacob D. Cox

[Buckhannon, July 2, 1861]

On receipt of this you will at once assume command of the 1st & 2nd Kentucky regiments & the 12th Ohio. Call upon Governor Dennison to supply you with one company of cavalry and six guns. Captain Kingsbury[1] probably has state guns enough to give you.

You will expedite the equipment of those regiments & move them at once to Gallipolis via Hamden & Portland — hiring teams for the supplies of the troops between Portland & Gallipolis, sending Qtr Mst in advance to have teams ready. With the regiment first ready to move proceed to Gallipolis & assume command of the 21st. Cross the river & occupy Point Pleasant; with the regt that next arrives occupy Letart's Falls, & then move the other two regiments to the mouth of ten mile creek, or the point near there where the road from Letart's Falls intersects Kanawha river. Place the last regiment arriving in reserve at Pt Pleasant or any proper point in rear of your line of defence. Entrench two guns at Letart's, four at your advanced position on the Kanawha. Remain on the defensive & endeavor to keep the rebels near Charleston until I can cut off their retreat by movement from Beverly. Should you receive certain intelligence that I am hard pressed seek to relieve me by a rapid advance on Charleston, but place no credit in rumors, for I shall be successful. Use your cavalry as pickets, not exposing them. Punish Ripley if you can. Repress any outbreaks that may occur at Guyandotte or Barboursville.

Remember, my plan is to cut them off, and do all you can to assist that object.[2] Always keep two or three boats on hand. Call on Capt. W.

J. Kountz, at Marietta or Ripley, to supply boats from his fleet. If the two companies of Seventeenth Ohio are still at Ravenswood when you reach Gallipolis, order them to rejoin their regiment, via Parkersburg or Webster. Communicate frequently. A telegraph line follows me out.

Very respectfully, yours,

Geo. B. McClellan

Major General, Commanding

ADf, McClellan Papers (A-17:8), Library of Congress; *OR*, Ser. 1, II, p. 197. Brig. Gen. Cox, Ohio volunteers, was formerly an officer in the state militia. Only the first page of this draft has been found. The last third of the letter is taken from the *Official Records*.

1. Capt. Charles P. Kingsbury, chief of ordnance, Department of the Ohio. 2. Cox stated that this sentence was incomplete as it appeared in the *Official Records*. In his copy it read: "Remember that my present plan is to cut them off by a rapid march from Beverly after driving those in front of me across the mountains, and do all you can to favor that by avoiding offensive movements." Cox, *Military Reminiscences of the Civil War* (New York, 1900), I, p. 60n.

To Thomas A. Morris

Genl T A Morris
Phillipi   Head Qtrs Dept of the Ohio
General   Buckhannon Va July 3 1861

Yours of the 2nd has reached me.[1] After questioning your messenger & hearing his full story I confess that I do not share your apprehensions, & that I am not a little surprised that you feel the defence of Phillipi so hazardous & dangerous an operation. If four thousand (nearly) of our men, in a position selected & fortified in advance — with ample time to examine the ground carefully & provide against any possible plan of attack — are not enough to hold the place against any force these people can bring against it, I think we had better all go home at once. If we cannot fight in position I am much mistaken as to our men.[2]

I have, however, in deference to your views, ordered the 6th Ohio on temporary duty with you, until the crisis has past — although I believe they can be employed to more advantage at other points.

This is all the reinforcement I can now spare — as to the one or two squadrons of efficient cavalry asked for by Captain Benham[3] it seems hardly necessary for me to repeat that I have only one & a half companies — such as they are — & that more important duty is for them here.

You have only to defend a strong position, or at most to follow a retreating enemy. I fear you do not share the confidence I feel in our men, & that you regard their cavalry as more dangerous than I do — I feel that these men of ours can be worked up to any deed of daring, that their leaders can make them cool under fire, & that a couple of good companies of Infantry can drive off all their cavalry in this mountainous country.

I propose taking the really difficult & dangerous part of this work on my own hands — I will not ask you to do anything that I would not be willing to do myself. But let us understand each other, I can give you no more reinforcements — I cannot consent to weaken any further the really active & important column which is to decide the fate of the campaign — if you cannot undertake the defence of Phillipi with the force now under your control I must find some one who will — I have *Contradiction* ordered up Latham's company, all of Key's Cavalry that are fit to take the field, & the 6th Ohio — do not ask for further reinforcements — if you do I shall take it as a request to be relieved from your command & to return to Indiana. I have spoken plainly — I speak officially — the crisis is a grave one, & I must have Generals under me who are willing to risk as much as I am, & to be content to risk their lives & reputation with such means as I can give them. Let this be the last of it — give me full details as to the information you obtain — not mere rumors, but facts — & leave it to my judgment to determine what force you need. I wish action now, & determination.

AL retained copy, McClellan Papers (B-7:46), Library of Congress. *OR*, Ser. 1, II, pp. 208–209.

1. Morris wrote that a scouting report "impresses us all here with the fact that there exists a much larger force at Laurel Hill than we have heretofore thought possible. . . . I confess I feel apprehensive unless our force could equal theirs. . . ." McClellan Papers (B-7:46). 2. In fact, the plan of campaign called for Morris to advance to Laurel Hill and occupy the attention of the enemy force there by threatening an attack. See GBM to Salmon P. Chase, June 26, *supra*. 3. Capt. Benham was chief engineer.

To Mary Ellen McClellan

Buckhannon July 3 [1861]

. . . We had a pleasant march of 16 mi yesterday, through a beautiful mountain region — magnificent timber, lovely valleys running up from the main valley — the people all out, waving their hdcfs & giving me plenty of bouquets & kind words. . . .

We nearly froze to death last night. I retired, as I thought, at about midnight, intending to have a good night's sleep. About half an hour after I shut up my tent, a colonel in command of a detachment, some 15 miles distant, came to report, so I received him in bed, & fell asleep about six times during the three hours I was talking with him. Finally however he left, & I alternately slept & froze until seven o'clock. This morning I sent Bates[1] on an expedition & raked up a couple of horse blankets, by the aid of which, I hope hereafter to be reasonably comfortable.

I hope to get the trains up tomorrow & make a final start during the day. We have a good many of the scamps to deal with, but my men have the greatest confidence in me & I in most of them. I ordered the Guthrie Grays[2] to Philippi this pm. — to resist a stampede attack that Genl Morris feared. I have not a Brig Genl worth his salt — Morris is a timid old woman — Rosecranz a silly fussy goose — Schleich[3] knows nothing. . . .

I have made your father Inspector Genl of this Army. . . .

AL copy; copy, McClellan Papers (C-7:63/D-10:72), Library of Congress.

1. Bates was GBM's personal servant. 2. 6th Ohio infantry. 3. Brig. Gen. Newton Schleich.

To E. D. Townsend

Col E D Townsend
A.A.G.   Hd Qtrs Dept of the Ohio
Col   Buckhannon Va July 5 1861

You will probably feel as much regret as I do in finding that I am still here — the cause is the difficulty of getting up supplies & arranging transportation. I hope that today's arrivals will enable me to move in the morning. While waiting here I have endeavored to employ our time to advantage.

You will observe that this is the important strategical position in this region — from it I can cover our base of operations & supplies, & move readily by good roads in any desired direction. I have directed the positions on Cheat River, at Grafton, Webster, Clarksburg & Parkersburg to be intrenched, that the necessary garrisons may be reduced as much as possible. The bridges, tunnels etc on the two branches of the RR are now well guarded. The Cheat River (covering the left of our base is guarded by 11 Companies), Grafton by a regiment, Clarksburg some 8 Cos. besides Va recruits, Parkersburg 6 Cos, 2 regts Indiana troops to arrive there today & to be disposable as a reserve where needed. Two other Indiana 3 yrs regts are en route to Bellaire to be sent wherever needed. 6 Cos occupy Wirt County C.H. where Union men have suffered much. 4 Cos at Ravenswood repulsed O. J. Wise[1] night before last; I hope that he determined to renew the attempt, as in that case he will have been cut off by a column of 1200 men, under Col Norton, that were to reach Ripley from Letart at 2 pm. yesterday. I shall not be surprised to learn before this letter is closed that he is captured.[2] In consequence of the threatening aspect of affairs in the Great Kanawha Valley I have ordered 4 Regts there, as explained in my instructions to Genl J D Coxe, a copy of which has been forwarded to you.[3]

Of the troops composing the active army 51 companies & 1 battery are at Phillipi, amusing the enemy who is strongly intrenched with artillery on the Laurel Mountain between that place & Beverly. I have with me here 6 entire regts of Infty, 6 detached Cos, 2 batteries, 2 Cos. of cavalry — two more regiments & some 5 or 6 detached companies of infantry will reach here by tomorrow night. The 7th Ohio occupied Weston some three days since & 4 cos. of the 17th reached Glenville from Parkersburg yesterday — I ordered strong detachments from these commands to move last night on Bull Town & break up a large force of armed rebels congregating there — I can if necessary have them all back with me by tomorrow night. I have sent out frequent small parties to break up the collections of rebels — we have them pretty well under now. One of our parties of 40 last night broke up 200!

The morale of our men is excellent — could not be better. It is difficult to get perfectly accurate information, but we are improving in that respect every day. The feeling of the people here is most excellent — we are acclaimed wherever our men go. It is wonderful to see how rapidly the minds of many of the people become enlightened when they find we can protect them! Fear & ignorance combined have made most of the converts to secession — the reverse process is now going on with great rapidity.

I expect to find the enemy in position on Rich Mountain, just this side of Beverly. I shall if possible turn the position to the south, & then occupy the Beverly road in his rear — if possible I will repeat the manoeuvre of Cerro Gordo.[4]

Assure the General that no prospect of a brilliant victory shall induce me to depart from my intention of gaining success by manoeuvring rather than by fighting; I will not throw these men of mine into the teeth of artillery & intrenchments, if it is possible to avoid it.

Say to the General too that I am trying to follow a lesson long ago learned from him — i.e. — not to move until I know that everything is ready, & then to move with the utmost rapidity & energy. The delays that I have met with have been irksome to me in the extreme — but I felt that it would be exceedingly foolish to give way to impatience & advance before everything was prepared. I think the troops are improving decidedly in their performance of guard & outpost duty & that we are losing nothing in efficiency by the halt at this place. From all that I learn the enemy is still uncertain as to where the main attack is to be made, & is committing the error of dividing his army in presence of superior forces.

If he abandons the position on Laurel Mountain, the troops at Phillipi will press him closely. I shall know tonight with certainty what he has in the pass near Huttonsville. I am told that he has moved all his troops thence towards Beverly. By our present positions we have cut off all his supplies of provisions from this region — so that he must depend almost entirely on Staunton — a long haul over a rough mountain road.

G.B. McClellan
Maj Genl U.S.A.
Comdg Dept

ALS retained copy, McClellan Papers (A-17:8), Library of Congress. *OR,* Ser. 1, II, pp. 198–99.

1. Capt. O. Jennings Wise, CSA. 2. The attempt by Col. Jesse S. Norton's Ohio militia to capture Wise failed, so GBM telegraphed Townsend on July 6, ''in consequence of the rapidity with which the rebels fled at the first news of the approach of danger.'' *OR,* Ser. 1, II, p. 199. 3. GBM to Cox, July 2, *supra.* 4. Winfield Scott's victory at Cerro Gordo, in the Mexican War, was gained by a turning movement.

To Mary Ellen McClellan

Buckhannon July 5 1861

Yesterday was a very busy day with me — reviewing troops all the morning & giving orders all day & pretty much all night. . . .

I realize now the dreadful responsibility on me — the lives of my men — the reputation of the country & the success of our cause. The enemy are in front & I shall probably move forward tomorrow — but not come in contact with them until about the next day. I shall feel my way & be very cautious, for I recognize the fact that everything requires success in my first operations. You need not be at all alarmed as to the result — God is on our side.

This is a beautiful country in which we now are — a lovely valley surrounded by mountains — well cultivated. The people hail our parties as deliverers wherever they go, & we meet with perfect ovations. Yesterday was very hot, & my head almost roasted as I stood bareheaded while the troops passed by in review. We have a nice little camp of our own here — Mack's & Steele's Co's — Howe's Battery next — 2 Co's of cavalry — & 2 well behaved Virginia Co's. When we next go into camp we shall have the German Regt (9th Ohio) with us in camp. I intend having a picked Brigade with me all the time. Lytle's rgt is on the march up from Clarksburg, they signalized their advance into the country by breaking into & robbing a grocery store at Webster![1] The Guthrie Grays are at Philippi; they leave there today & will be here tomorrow night — following us up in reserve, or perhaps overtaking us before we meet the enemy. . . .

AL copy, McClellan Papers (C-7:63), Library of Congress.

1. Col. William H. Lytle commanded the 10th Ohio.

To William Dennison

His Excellency Wm Dennison
Governor of Ohio
Sir:

Hd. Qrs. Dept. of the Ohio,
Buckhannon Va July 6th 1861

I enclose herewith to you copies of Genl. Order No. 19 & of the report of a Court of Inquiry, and of a communication from Brig. Gen'l Rosecrans all relating to Co. C. 19th Regt. O.V.M.[1]

I know that your excellency will deeply regret that a Co. of Ohio Volunteers should be the subject of a proceeding so painful yet I feel assured that your judgment will sustain its propriety and necessity, and that I shall receive your support in maintaining that good order, discipline and regard for private rights, in which I am happy to say the Ohio troops of the Army have been as a body worthy of much commendation.

The protection of the persons, homes, families and property of all peaceful citizens has been by me guaranteed to the people of Western Virginia by the most solomn pledges, and I rejoice to say that since I have entered the State these pledges have been substantially observed by this Army. The beneficial effect of this course has been everywhere apparent. Persons entertaining secession sentiments continually and generally state that they had been deceived and misled as to the purposes of the Government and its course of military action, and the revulsion of feeling and sentiment seems to be very great. I regard such peaceful conquests as very important.

Upon the most mature reflection I have become satisfied that the rule laid down in my general order "holding officers and their commands liable to be ordered home upon the occurrence of such acts as indicate an insubordinate condition of companies or regiments" is the most efficient and practicable method of preserving good order and necessary control.

In the case of Co. C. there appears to prevail among its members very erroneous notions of the purposes of the Government and the duties of soldiers. I therefore advise that the company on its arrival at Columbus be disbanded.

Very Resply yr obt servt
Geo B McClellan
Maj Gen'l Comdg.

Retained copy, McClellan Papers (A-18:8), Library of Congress.

1. Members of Company C, 19th Ohio, were charged with robbing the house of a Virginia secessionist. The case was finally disposed of by the punishment and dismissal of an officer and seven privates of the company. Documents in McClellan Papers (A-17:8, A-18:8).

To Nathaniel Lyon

Genl N Lyon, Missouri   Head Qtrs Dept of the Ohio
General   Buckhannon Va July 6 1861

Yours of the 22d reached me only a few hours ago. In view of the information sent to me by Capt Harding, some days since, of apprehended danger in S.E. Missouri,[1] I directed that three or four of the Illinois Regts should hold themselves in readiness to obey a call from Genl Prentiss, & instructed him (if the report was verified) to move a respectable force from Birds Point upon the place where the rebels were said to be congregating — to enable him to do this I directed Maj McKinstry to provide the requisite wagons & teams. In compliance with other requests from you & your Adjt Genl I have placed two of the Quincy & one Caseyville Regt at your disposal. I have today instructed Genl Pope,[2] comdg at Alton, to place himself & 3 regts at your disposal, for the operation you suggest — the necessity for which I fully recognize.[3] This makes 6 Illinois Regts for service in Missouri in addition to those liable at any moment to move from Cairo.

The exigencies of the service in which I am now personally engaged render it impossible to spare any Indiana or Ohio troops for service in Missouri — in addition to the operations in Western Virginia it is necessary to hold some troops in reserve ready to act in Kentucky when occasion demands — as I believe will be the case before very long. Unless the effect of decisive operations on your part in Missouri, & on mine in Western Virginia, is to intimidate the secession party in Kentucky, it seems to me that there must finally be a collision between the two parties, in Ky, & that we must throw our weight into the scale.

Distant as I am from Missouri — I can only say, General, that so long as it remains attached to my Dept, you may confidently rely upon my giving you all the support in my power.

I do not know what the intention of the Dept was in regard to the Dept of the West, as I have received no instructions beyond the General Order attaching Missouri to the Dept of the Ohio. I presume that the command of the Dept of the West now devolves on Col Alexander.[4]

With my warmest wishes for your continued success

I am General very truly yours
Geo B McClellan
Maj Genl USA Comdg Dept

ALS retained copy, McClellan Papers (A-18:8), Library of Congress. Brig. Gen. Lyon commanded Federal forces in Missouri.

1. Lyon's telegram of June 21 (as it was dated) called on GBM for strong reinforcements. Capt. Chester Harding, Lyon's adjutant, telegraphed on June 27 that Confederate troops were moving into southeastern Missouri "in large numbers.... No force here sufficient to meet them.... Will you take the matter in hand." McClellan Papers (A-14:6, A-15:7). 2.

Brig. Gen. John Pope. 3. Lyon planned an advance on Springfield, Mo. 4. It is not known to whom GBM was referring. Command of the newly formed Western Department went to Maj. Gen. John Charles Frémont.

To E. D. Townsend   [TELEGRAM]

Col. E. D. Townsend   A.A.G.   Head Quarters Department of the Ohio,
Washington D.C.   Buckhannon Va. July 6th 1861[1]

Newspaper reports say that my department is to be broken up. I hope the General will leave under my control, both the operations on the Mississippi and in Western Virginia. If he cannot do so, the Indiana and Ohio troops are necessary to my success. With these means at my disposal and such resources as I can command in Virginia if the Government will give me ten thousand arms for distribution in Eastern Tennessee I think I can break the backbone of Secession. Please instruct whether to move on Staunton or on Wytheville.[2] I thank the General for his commendation, and hope to deserve it rather in the future than in the past.[3] Please enforce the occupation of Cumberland and Piedmont. The condition of things in that vicinity renders it absolutely necessary to occupy both these points and you will remember that my command does not extend that far. I cannot too strongly impress upon you the necessity of holding these points. The Pennsylvania State troops now in the vicinity of Cumberland will answer the purpose perfectly well.

G. B. McClellan
Major General U.S.A.
Commanding Department

Retained copy, McClellan Papers (C-9:63), Library of Congress. *OR*, Ser. 1, II, p. 201.

1. The *Official Records* dates this July 7, probably the date it was received. 2. Townsend replied on July 7: "The General concedes that you are the best judge of your means and the importance of the objects to be gained; but when you speak of extending your operations to Staunton, and even to Wytheville, he fears your line will be too long without intermediate supports. He wishes you to weigh well these points before deciding." *OR*, Ser. 1, II, pp. 201–202. 3. Townsend had telegraphed GBM on July 6: "General Scott is charmed with your activity, enterprise and success." Records of the Headquarters of the Army, RG 108 (M-857:6), National Archives.

To Mary Ellen McClellan

Buckhannon July 7 [1861]

I have been obliged to inflict some severe punishments & I presume the Abolition papers of the Western Reserve will be hard down on me for disgracing some of their friends guilty of the small crime of burglary.[1] I believe the Army is beginning to comprehend that they have a master over them who is stern in punishing & means what he says. I fear I shall have to have some of them shot or hung; that may convince some of the particular individuals concerned that they are not in the right track exactly....

I have not told you about our camp at this place. It is in a large grass field on a hill a little out of town; a beautiful grove near by. Your Father & I share the same tent, a very large round one, pitched under a tree. Seth has one near by as an office. Lawrence Williams another as office & mess tent. Marcy, the two Williamses, Judge Key & Lander mess with me; Poe & the rest of the youngsters are in tents near by.[2] ...

I had a very complimentary despatch from Genl Scott last night, he said he was "Charmed with my energy, movements & success." Pretty well for the old man! I hope to deserve more of him in the future.

Move at 6 tomorrow morning to overtake adv gd, which consists of 3 rgts, a battery & 1 co cavalry. I take up hd qtrs escort (Mack, Steele, Loomis' battery, Barker's cav, 2 co's. Va infty) & 4 rgts infty — 3 more follow next day. The large supply train up & ready to move. Rob Garnett in command of enemy.[3]

AL copy; copy, McClellan Papers (C-7:63/D-10:72), Library of Congress.

1. See GBM to William Dennison, July 6, *supra*. The case involved the 19th Ohio, a three-month regiment raised in Cleveland. 2. The staff members mentioned are Maj. Marcy, Maj. Seth Williams, Capt. Lawrence A. Williams, Col. Thomas M. Key, Brig. Gen. Frederick W. Lander, and Lt. Orlando M. Poe. 3. Brig. Gen. Robert S. Garnett, CSA.

To Mary Ellen McClellan

Roaring Creek July 10 [1861]

We have occupied the important position on this line without loss. The enemy are in sight & I am about sending out a strong armed reconnaissance to feel him & see what he is. I have been looking at the camps with my glass — they are strongly entrenched, but I think I can come the Cerro Gordo over them.

AL copy, McClellan Papers (C-7:63), Library of Congress.

To Salmon P. Chase   [TELEGRAM]

[Roaring Creek, c. July 10, 1861]

Your letter of 7th just received.[1] The movement you suggest meets with my full concurrence. I regard it as the most important that can be undertaken. I have been engaged in maturing its details in my mind & intended preparing for it as soon as through with Western Virginia.

G B. McClellan
Maj Genl USA

Hon S P Chase
Secty of Treasury   Washington DC

ALS (telegram sent), McClellan Papers (A-23:11), Library of Congress.

1. In his letter of July 7, Chase described efforts to enlist troops in Kentucky and Tennessee. "You can very materially forward these preparations by your counsel and cooperation: and just as soon as circumstances will allow, you can yourself take the open command of the regiments, and, with your Ohio and Indiana men, march down through the mountain-region, deliver the whole of it, including the mountain districts of North Carolina, Georgia, and Alabama, from the insurrection, and then reach the Gulf at Mobile and New Orleans, thus cutting the rebellion in two." Jacob S. Schuckers, *The Life and Public Service of Salmon Portland Chase* (New York, 1874), pp. 427–28.

To Thomas A. Morris

Hd Qtrs Dept of the Ohio
[Beverly] July 12 1861

Have just gained the enemy's position[1] & occupy the road to Beverly. Rosecrans turned the works by a march of some 7 miles through the mountains. Defeated a large party at Hart's House, taking guns. We now have their intrenchments, all their guns, baggage & some prisoners. Have not lost over 10 men in whole operation. Will send details by another messenger. I move the column to Beverly at once. Do not attack until further orders.[2] I learn that fugitives have retreated towards Laurel Hill.

G B McClellan

Genl T A Morris

ALS copy, in GBM to Ezra A. Carman, Feb. 25, 1880. Civil War Collection, Huntington Library.

1. At Rich Mountain. 2. Morris's brigade faced the main Confederate force under Gen. Garnett at Laurel Hill.

To E. D. Townsend   [TELEGRAM]

Col. E. D. Townsend   Beverly Va. [July 12] 1861

Success of today is all that I could desire. We captured six brass cannon of which one rifled, all their camp equipage & transportation even to his tents. The number of tents will probably reach two hundred and more than sixty wagons. Their killed & wounded will amount to fully hundred & fifty. At least one hundred prisoners & more coming in constantly. I know already of ten officers killed & prisoners. Their retreat complete. Occupied Beverly by a rapid march. Garnett abandoned his camp early this morning, leaving much of his equipage. He came within a few miles of Beverly but our rapid march turned him back in great confusion and he is now retreating on the road to St George. I have ordered Gen Morris to follow him up closely. I have telegraphed for the two Penna Regts at Cumberland to join Genl Hill[1] at Rowlesburg. The Genl is concentrating all his troops at Rowlesburg [to] cut off Garnett's retreat near West Union or if possible St George. I may say that we have driven out some ten thousand troops strongly entrenched with the loss of eleven killed & thirty five wounded. Provision returns found here show Garnett's force to have been ten thousand men.[2] They were eastern Virginians, Georgians, Tennesseans and I think Carolinians. To-morrow I can give full details as to prisoners &c. Will move on Huttonsville tomorrow and endeavor to seize the Cheat mountain pass where there are now but few troops. I hope that Genl Cox has by this time driven Wise out of the Kanawha Valley.[3] In that case I shall have accomplished the object of liberating Western Virginia. I hope the General will approve my operations.

Geo. B. McClellan
Maj Genl Comdg Dept of Ohio

Received copy, Lincoln Papers, Library of Congress. *OR*, Ser. 1, II, pp. 203–204.

1. Brig. Gen. Charles W. Hill, Ohio militia. 2. GBM included in this figure four regiments intended to reinforce Garnett but which never reached the scene. Garnett's total force was about 5,300 men. 3. Brig. Gen. Henry A. Wise commanded the Confederate forces in the Kanawha Valley.

To Charles W. Hill   [TELEGRAM]

Genl C W Hill — Grafton   Huttonsville July 13 [1861]

Your dispatch received.[1] I presume mine of last night directing concentration on St George or West Union had not reached you. But a small force now necessary at Clarksburg since depot to be changed to Webster for this column. You can safely diminish garrisons along the line & give Stanley[2] a chance. Look out for Garnett at West Union & try to head him off. Endeavor to get messenger to the rgts at Cumberland so that if they cannot unite with you one of them may at least occupy Piedmont. Do not regard Department lines in cases of emergency. I am at Huttonsville. The advanced guard just moving into the Pass.

Pegram[3] with entire rgt surrendered this morning. Morris was 6 miles in rear of Garrett at last account. Never mind bridges if you can catch Garnett.

G B McClellan
Maj Genl

ALS (telegram sent), McClellan Papers (A-19:9), Library of Congress. Brig. Gen. Hill was charged with the defense of the Baltimore and Ohio Railroad.

1. Dated July 12, Hill's dispatch reported that Confederate cavalry was burning bridges on the railroad to the east. McClellan Papers (A-19:9). 2. Col. T. R. Stanley, 18th Ohio, commanding at Clarksburg. 3. Lt. Col. John Pegram, who had commanded the Confederate detachment at Rich Mountain.

To Mary Ellen McClellan

Huttonsville July 13 [1861]

Since you last heard from me I received from Pegram a proposition to surrender which I granted. L Williams went out with an escort of cavalry & received him — he surrendered with another Col, some 25 offs. and 560 men. . . .

I do not think the enemy in front of us in the Cheat Mtn pass, but that they have fallen back in hot haste — if they are here I will drive them out tomorrow & occupy the pass. . . .

It now appears we killed nearly 200 — took almost 900.

The valley in which we are is one of the most beautiful I ever saw & I am more than ever inclined to make my Head Quarters at Beverly & have you with me. Beverly is a quiet, old fashioned town in a lovely valley; a beautiful stream running by it. A perfectly pastoral scene such as the old painters dreamed of, but never realized. I half think I should be King of it. I find that the prisoners are beyond measure astonished at my humanity towards them. The bearer of the flag from Pegram reached me about 5 this morning. He had been two days without food. I at once gave him some breakfast, & shortly after gave him a drink of whiskey; as he drank it said "I thank you, General — I drink that I may never again be in rebellion against the general government."

AL copy; copy, McClellan Papers (C-7:63/D-10:72), Library of Congress.

To Jacob Beyers

Jacob Beyers   Camp near Huttonsville
Granville   Monongalia Co Va   July 14 [1861]

Your letter of the 8th inst has been received.[1] No one has any authority to make arrests unless commissioned in the Army of the US or acting under my immediate orders or having such authority from the State Government at Wheeling. It is not intended that such power shall be delegated to private persons by order of officers under my command. Almost all arrests hitherto made have been injudicious and wrong and have operated injuriously to the Union cause. No persons must be arrested except those who are or have been in arms against the US Govt, or have given actual aid or information to armed enemies, or who are especially dangerous as inciting others to take arms, or who attack the persons or property of Union men as such. The arrest of persons not in arms should be very cautiously conducted, but few of these yet made being warranted. All private property whether of secessionists or others must be strictly respected, and no one is to be molested merely because of political opinions.

Yours
G. B. McClellan
Maj Genl Comdg

Retained copy, McClellan Papers (A-19:9), Library of Congress. Beyers was a mustering agent for militia being raised by the newly formed Unionist government of western Virginia.

1. Beyers wrote: "Gen Morris gave me an order to capture or arrest any person in the region of Morgantown who had violated the laws of the United States or in any way aided or abeted the secession army...." He asked if this authority was valid. McClellan Papers (A-18:8).

To Mary Ellen McClellan

July 14 [1861] *Sunday* Huttonsville

Started this morning with a strong advanced guard, supported by 2 rgts to test the question as to whether the rebels were really fortified in the Cheat Mtn pass. I went prepared for another fight — but found that they had scampered. We picked up some of their plunder — but they have undoubtedly gone at least to Staunton. The pass was considerably strong & they might have given us an immense deal of trouble. I went with a few men to Cheat River — the other side of the mtn....

I have made a very clean sweep of it — never was more complete success gained with smaller sacrifice of life — our prisoners will exceed 1000!

On my return I found a telegram from Genl Scott, sent before he had received information as to the full results of my victory. It was "The General in Chief, & what is more the Cabinet, including the Presdt, are charmed with your activity, valour, & consequent success. We do not doubt, that you will in due time, sweep the rebels from West Va, but do not mean to precipitate you, as you are fast enough. Winfield Scott."[1]

I released today on parole, a Dr Walke, on account of his having a sick wife &c. He turned out to have been a student of Father's, knows John very well.[2] He has Father's likeness in his parlor &c. Poor fellow, he felt horribly, & I must confess, that my heart bleeds for these poor misguided men....

Our ride today was truly magnificent, some of the most splendid Mt. views I ever beheld. The Mt we crossed is fully 3000 ft above its base, & the lovely little valleys, the cleared farms, the long ranges of Mountain in the distance all made a varied scene that I cannot describe to you. At the Mt. top was a pretty little farm, neat as neat could be. A very old couple lived there, the old lady, as rosy & cheerful as a cricket. It is sad that war should visit even such sequestered spots as that.

Monday morning [July 15]. After closing my letter last night a courier arrived with the news that the troops I had sent in pursuit of Garnett had caught him, routed his army, captured his baggage, one gun, taken several prisoners — & that Garnett himself lay dead on the field of battle!!![3] Such is the fate of traitors — one of their comdrs a prisoner, the other killed! Their armies annihilated — their cause crushed in this region. . . .

You ask what my plans are — why, you little witch, don't you know that my movements depend much on those of Mons. l'ennemi? I expect to hear in a few hours of the final extermination of the remnants of Garnett's army. Then I am almost hourly awaiting news of Coxe's success in the Kanawha. Should Coxe not be prompt enough I will go down there myself & bring the matter to a close.

West Va being cleared of the enemy I have then to organize & consolidate the army — the time of the 3 mos men is about expiring & they form so large a portion of my force that some delay will ensue. . . .

AL copy; copy, McClellan Papers (C-7:63/D-10:72), Library of Congress.

1. Scott's telegram was dated July 13. *OR,* Ser. 1, II, p. 204. 2. Maj. J. Wistar Walke, surgeon of the 20th Virginia. GBM's father, Dr. George McClellan, had been a founder of Jefferson Medical College in Philadelphia. GBM's brother John H. B. McClellan was also a doctor. 3. Garnett was mortally wounded on July 13 in a rear-guard skirmish against Morris's pursuing Federals.

To Charles W. Hill [TELEGRAM]

Huttonsville, July 14, 1861

Garnetts army completely routed yesterday (13) at 2 p.m. on Cheat River on St George road — baggage captured one gun taken — Garnett killed — his forces demoralized. I charge you to complete our operations by the capture of the remainder of his force. If you have but one regiment attack & check them until others arrive. You may never have such an opportunity again — do not throw it away. Conduct this movement in person & follow them à l'outrance.

G B McClellan
Maj Genl USA

Brig Genl C W Hill
Grafton Va.

ALS (telegram sent), McClellan Papers (A-19:9), Library of Congress. *OR,* Ser. 1, II, p. 227.

To Jacob D. Cox [TELEGRAM]

Huttonsville July 14 1861

In addition to previous success we have routed Garnett's army, captured his baggage & one gun. Garnett killed, his army entirely demoralized. Secession crushed in this direction. Win your spurs by capturing

Wise & occupying Gauley Bridge. I impatiently wait to hear from you that my expectations are justified. Do not fail me but push straight on & complete the first act of our drama.

G B McClellan
Maj Genl USA

Brig Genl J D Coxe
Care Col Smith, Parkersburg

ALS (telegram sent), McClellan Papers (A-19:9), Library of Congress.

To E. D. Townsend   [TELEGRAM]

[Huttonsville, July 14, 1861]

Garnett's forces routed — his baggage & one gun taken, his army demoralized — Garnett killed. We have annihilated the enemy in Western Virginia & have lost 13 killed & not more than 40 wounded. We have in all killed at least 200 of the enemy & their prisoners will amount to at least one thousand — have taken 7 guns in all. I still look for the capture of the remnant of Garnett's army by Genl Hill. The troops defeated are the crack regiments of Eastern Virginia, aided by Georgians, Tennesseans & Carolinians. Our success is complete & secession is killed in this country.

G B McClellan
Maj Genl USA

Col E D Townsend
AAG Washington D.C.

ALS (telegram sent), McClellan Papers (A-19:9), Library of Congress. *OR*, Ser. 1, II, p. 204.

To Henry R. Jackson

To the Comdg Officer of the Forces   Hd Qtrs Dept of the Ohio
near Staunton[1]   Camp near Huttonsville Va
Sir: July 15 1861

I have today received orders from the Comdr in Chief of the U.S. Army respecting the disposition to be made of the prisoners of war now in my hands.[2] These orders are substantially that the non comd officers & privates shall be permitted to return to their homes provided they willingly subscribe an oath or affirmation binding them not to bear arms or serve in any military capacity against the United States, until released from this obligation according to the ordinary usages of war.

The officers to be permitted to return to their homes upon giving a similar parole of honor; from this privilege, however, are excepted such officers as may have recently left the U.S. service with the intention of taking arms against the U.S. Such officers will for the present be sent to Fort McHenry, where they will without doubt be kindly treated.

There are at Beverly some 33 officers, 5 surgeons, & almost 600 non comd offs & privates — there are others at Laurel Hill etc the numbers of whom I do not yet accurately know; with the wounded the number will probably amount to at least 800 men besides officers.

It is my desire to arrange with you for the return to their homes of such of these as may accept the terms offered them.

I would be glad to know what transportation etc you can furnish for them & at what point I may expect it. If no other arrangement will be convenient to you I will provide wagons & tents, as well as rations & cooking utensils for the party, with the understanding that the proper authorities shall undertake to return them to me. The wagons & tents will probably be of those captured at Camp Garnett.[3] Please inform me how many days rations it will be necessary to furnish to the party. I will be glad also to arrange for the return of the wounded as soon as their condition will pemit it — in the mean time their friends may rest assured that every attention will be paid to them.

You will ere this have been informed no doubt of the unhappy fate of Genl Garnett, who fell while acting the part of a gallant soldier — his remains are now at Grafton, preserved in ice, where they will await the instructions of his relations should they desire to remove them to his home.

While I am determined to play my part in this unhappy contest to the utmost of my energy & ability, permit me to assure you of my desire to do all in my power to alleviate its miseries, & to confine its effects to those who constitute the organized armies & meet in battle. It is my intention to cause the persons & property of private citizens to be respected, & to render the condition of prisoners & wounded as little oppressive & miserable as possible.

I trust that I shall be met in the same spirit, & that this contest may remain free from the usual horrible features of civil war.[4]

I am, sir, very respectfully your obedient servant

Geo B McClellan

Maj Genl USA

Comdg Dept of the Ohio

I send this by Lieut R. J. Lipper [Lipford] of the 44th Regt Va Vols who chances to be the captured officer most convenient. I have not yet taken his final parole, but have given him a special one for the purpose of carrying this letter & bringing back an immediate reply. After his return he will be accorded the same parole as the others. For obvious reasons I request that your reply may be transmitted by Lt Lipper.

I will proceed with as little delay as possible to the release of the prisoners, & if ready to forward any before your reply reaches me will take it for granted that you accede to my proposals in regard to the return of the property sent with them.

ALS retained copy, McClellan Papers (A-20:9), Library of Congress. *OR*, Ser. 1, II, pp. 250–51.

1. Brig. Gen. Jackson assumed command of Garnett's forces after that general's death. 2. Dated July 14. *OR*, Ser. 2, III, pp. 9–10. 3. The captured Confederate encampment at Rich Mountain. 4. Jackson replied on July 17 that these arrangements would be satisfactory. In response to GBM's assurances that the wounded would be well cared for, he wrote: "Permit me to add that your well known character as a man had rendered those assurances a matter of supererogation." *OR*, Ser. 1, II, pp. 251–52.

To Mary Ellen McClellan

[Huttonsville] July 15 [1861]

... Nothing from the Kanawha tonight — I fear Coxe is slow. If my generals had obeyed my orders I should before this have captured every rebel in this region but unfortunately I have not a single Brig who is worth his salt.

AL copy, McClellan Papers (C-7:63), Library of Congress.

To Charles W. Hill   [TELEGRAM]

Beverly July 16/61

I have just learned of your movement of last night. I think you should have attacked the enemy on Sunday [July 14] when so near their rear guard and that you then allowed the favorable opportunity to pass.[1] I can see no good result likely to follow from your present movement which seems likely to become too extended and is not in the spirit of your instructions which were to cut off the enemy's retreat, not to go into the heart of Virginia unless you are directly on the enemy's track and you are sure to cut him off at once. You will please on receipt of this abandon the pursuit to avoid the possibility of disaster.

G B McC

To Genl Hill

ALS (telegram sent), McClellan Papers (B-20:9), Library of Congress.

1. Hill had taken position at West Union as ordered — see GBM to Hill, July 13, *supra* — but the Confederate column slipped away by another road.

To the Army of the West

	Head Quarters
Soldiers of the Army	Army of Occupation, Western Virginia,
of the West!	Beverly, Va., July 16th, 1861

I am more than satisfied with you.

You have annihilated two armies, commanded by educated and experienced soldiers, and entrenched in mountain fastnesses fortified at their leisure. You have taken five guns, twelve colors, fifteen hundred stand of arms, one thousand prisoners, including more than forty officers — one of the two commanders of the rebels is a prisoner, the other lost his life on the field of battle. You have killed more than two hundred and fifty of the enemy, who has lost all his baggage and camp equipage. All this has been accomplished with the loss of twenty brave men killed, and sixty wounded on your part.

You have proved that Union men, fighting for the preservation of our Government, are more than a match for our misguided and erring brethren; more than this, you have shown mercy to the vanquished. You have made long and arduous marches, often with insufficient food, frequently exposed to the inclemency of the weather. I have not hesitated to demand this of you, feeling that I could rely on your endurance, patriotism and courage.

In the future, I may have still greater demands to make upon you, still greater sacrifices for you to offer; it shall be my care to provide for you to the extent of my ability; but I know now, that by your valor and endurance, you will accomplish all that is asked.

Soldiers! I have confidence in you, and I trust you have learned to confide in me. Remember that discipline and subordination, are qualities of equal value with courage.

I am proud to say that you have gained the highest reward that American troops can receive — the thanks of Congress, and the applause of your fellow citizens.

Geo. B. McClellan
Major General U.S.A.,
Commanding

DP, McClellan Papers (B-8:47), Library of Congress. *OR*, Ser. 1, II, p. 236.

To Winfield Scott   [TELEGRAM]

[Beverly, July 17, 1861]

Will a movement of mine on Staunton facilitate your plans. If so I can probably take that position. I do not know your plan of operations but can move on Staunton if you desire. Please reply at once.[1]

G B McClellan
Maj Genl

Lt Genl Winfield Scott
Washington D.C.

ALS (telegram sent), McClellan Papers (A-23:11), Library of Congress. *OR*, Ser. 1. II, p. 743.

1. On July 16 Brig. Gen. Irvin McDowell's army had advanced from Washington. Scott replied on July 18: "Your suggestions in respect to Staunton would be admirable, like your other conceptions and acts, with support.... If you come to Staunton, and McDowell's

victory at the [Manassas] Junction be complete, he may, with Patterson, give you a hand about Winchester." *OR*, Ser. 1, II, p. 743.

To Mary Ellen McClellan   [TELEGRAM]

[Beverly, c. July 18, 1861]

Still here awaiting developments. All goes well. Do go to the Springs & remain there until I tell you when & where to meet me.[1] No possible chance of further fighting here at present — no one left to fight with.

I will soon be with you. I hear that I have received the thanks of Congress — the highest honor I could aspire to.[2]

G B McClellan
Maj Genl

Mrs. M E McClellan
Cincinnati

ALS (telegram sent), McClellan Papers, New Jersey Historical Society.

1. Mrs. McClellan, in the seventh month of pregnancy with her first child, would spend much of this summer at the mineral baths at Yellow Springs, near Cincinnati. 2. The Thanks of Congress to GBM and his command was adopted unanimously by joint resolution on July 16.

To Winfield Scott

Unofficial   Head Qtrs Dept of the Ohio
General   Beverly Va July 18 1861

I have received your telegraphic dispatches including that of today.[1]

Knowing how completely your time is occupied, I merely wish to say to you, that I value the commendation, you have been kind enough to bestow upon me, more highly than any reward I can receive from any other source.

All that I know of war I have learned from you, & in all that I have done I have endeavored to conform to your manner of conducting a campaign, as I understand the history of your achievements.

It is my ambition to merit your praise & never to deserve your censure.

Thanking you for your kind expressions

I am, General, truly & respectfully your friend & obdt svt
Geo B McClellan

ALS retained copy, McClellan Papers (A-21:10), Library of Congress.

1. See GBM to Scott, July 17, note 1, *supra*.

To Mary Ellen McClellan

[Beverly] July 19, 1861

I enclose "Bulletin No 5" printed with our portable press.[1] You see we have carried civilization with us in the shape of the printing press &

the telegraph; institutions decidedly neglected in this part of the world heretofore & I hear not likely to be paying institutions in this vicinity after we go. The good people here can read but little & have but few ideas & I don't regard them as the most brilliant people in the world. Genl Scott is decidedly flattering to me. I received from him yesterday a despatch beginning "Your suggestion in respect to Staunton would be admirable like your other conceptions & acts." I value that old man's praise very highly & wrote him a short note last night telling him so.[2] I enclose some scraps clipped off a dirty rebel flag captured at Rich Mountain.

Am engaged now in arranging to march home the 3 mos. men to be reorganized & in clearing up matters generally. . . .

I suppose McDowell drove the enemy from Manassas Junction yesterday — if so the way will be pretty well cleared for the present. If any decided movement is made towards Richmond I shall feel sure that they cannot intend to trouble my people here.

AL copy; copy, McClellan Papers (C-7:63/D-10:72), Library of Congress.

1. Probably his address to the Army of the West, July 16, *supra*. 2. See Scott to GBM, July 18, *OR*, Ser. 1, II, p. 743, and GBM to Scott, July 18, *supra*.

To E. D. Townsend   [TELEGRAM]

[Beverly, July 19, 1861]

Cox checked on the Kanawha. Has fought something between a victory & a defeat. A wounded Col of ours taken prisoner & a possibility of having lost two Colonels & a Lt Colonel who amused themselves by a reconnaissance beyond the pickets.[1] Have ordered him to remain where *Criticism* he is & will start as soon as possible to cut Wise's rear & relieve our credit. In heaven's name give me some General Officers who understand their profession. I give orders & find some who cannot execute them unless I stand by them. Unless I command every picket & lead every column I cannot be sure of success. Give me such men as Marcy, Stoneman, Sackett, Lander etc & I will answer for it with my life that I meet with no disaster.[2] Had my orders been executed from the beginning our success would have been brief & final.

G B McClellan
Maj Genl

Col E D Townsend
AAG Washington D.C.

ALS (telegram sent), McClellan Papers (A-21:10), Library of Congress. *OR*, Ser. 1, II, p. 288.

1. The wounded officer was Col. Jesse S. Norton, 21st Ohio. The others were Col. Charles A. De Villiers, 11th Ohio, and Col. William E. Woodruff and Lt. Col. George W. Neff,

2nd Kentucky. The skirmish was at Scarey Creek on July 17. 2. Maj. Marcy, Maj. George Stoneman, Lt. Col. Delos B. Sacket, Brig. Gen. Frederick W. Lander.

To Jacob D. Cox   [TELEGRAM]

Brig Genl J D Cox
Mouth of Poca via Pomeroy   [Beverly, July 19, 1861]

I am entirely disappointed with the result of your operations. You have in front of you but twenty five hundred men badly armed, disciplined and commanded and disaffected to their cause. You should have advanced to the Gauley Bridge without a check. Your Army is nearly as numerous as that which has achieved brilliant results on this line. I see that your Army is demoralized.[1] Encourage your men by telling them that I myself will move upon the enemy's rear and accomplish what ought to have been done without my personal presence. In the mean time hold your own and at least save me the disgrace of a detachment of my Army being routed. In future keep your officers within the line of pickets and impress upon your men that as soon as the long and difficult march before me can be accomplished they will find the road opened for them. The officers taken prisoners are justly punished for their folly and deserve no consideration. I hope it will serve as a useful lesson for the rest.

Geo B McClellan
Maj Genl Comdg

Retained copy, McClellan Papers (A-23:11), Library of Congress.

1. This appraisal of Cox's operations was based on second-hand and inaccurate reports. Cox would presently outflank Henry A. Wise and take both Charleston and Gauley Bridge.

To James Barnett

Col Barnett   Head Quarters Army of Occupation
Col,   Camp near Beverly July 19, 1861

I am aware that the term of service of your command expires in a few days, yet I feel obliged to call upon the patriotism of your officers & men for a short extension of their service. I find it necessary to make one more movement to accomplish the full results we have conferred to ourselves. That movement will probably involve some more fighting & I wish to have your battery in my command.

I feel sure that men who have served their country so gallantly & effectively in the past will not hesitate at the sacrifice of at most 2 or 3 weeks more of their lives but that they will gladly accompany me to the front & avail themselves of the opportunity afforded to add to the reputation they have already gained.[1]

I have to request that you will move your battery to this place tomorrow where you will receive further instructions.

I am respectfully your obd servant

Geo. B. McClellan

Maj Genl Comdg

ALS retained copy, McClellan Papers (A-21:10), Library of Congress. Col. Barnett commanded an Ohio battery of three-month volunteers.

1. Barnett's battery was mustered out on July 27. Other appeals to three-month units by GBM were similarly unavailing.

To Francis H. Peirpoint

F H Peirpoint
Wheeling Va   Head Qtrs Army of Occupation West Va
Your Excellency   Camp near Beverly July 20 1861

I trust you will pardon me for venturing upon a few suggestions in regard to matters in which we both have the deepest & most direct interest. I allude to the military & political reorganization of Western Virginia. I do not regard the purpose of my presence here as being merely the military conquest & occupation of this region — it is to drive out the intruding army, which consisted of troops from Eastern Virginia & from other states, & to afford to the loyal citizens that protection due to them from the Federal Govt while engaged in the task of reorganizing their political affairs, & in the formation of an armed force sufficient to guarantee their safety & independence.

The troops under my command are of course at the service of the people you represent, but in view of the probability of a large portion of them being eventually required in other localities, & of the favorable moral effect that would be produced upon your own people by the consciousness of their possessing the means to protect themselves, I would respectfully urge upon your excellency the propriety, necessity I might say, of prompt & energetic measures being taken to raise troops among the population as we pass through & protect them. Such measures should be well organized & nothing should be left undone to rouse the enthusiasm of the people, who are a race of farmers, of simple habits, not prone to adopt the profession of arms & who seem to need strong urging to induce them to act in their own defence. I think they are somewhat apathetic, & I see no strong disposition manifested to take up arms. Would it not be well that leading & influential citizens should make it their business to traverse the country, address the people, & rouse them to action; this should be followed, on the part of the authorities by vigorous measures to raise regiments for the service. I confess that I am much disappointed by the extreme slowness with which recruiting goes on — cannot something be done at once to expedite matters. Before I left Grafton I made requisitions for arms clothing etc for 10,000 Virginia troops — I begin to fear that my estimate was much too large.

Of no less importance — it may be more — is the vital necessity of establishing the civil authority of the Govt in the counties protected by my troops. I would suggest in regard to this that steps be at once taken to hold elections for minor offices, the opening of the courts, reestablishment of postal facilities, & in fact the placing in operation the whole machinery of Govt.

Is it not important to send to every place occupied by the troops, or covered by their presence, commissioners with authority to enforce the recognition of your Govt by all officials, with power to remove or suspend such as refuse to give the required assurances? I should be pleased to have at my Head Quarters any Commissioner you may deem fit to send, provided he be a gentleman of marked energy & character. Trusting you will appreciate my motives in making these suggestions

I am, Governor, with high respect your obt svt

Geo B McClellan
Maj Genl USA

ALS retained copy, McClellan Papers (A-21:10), Library of Congress. On June 19 a convention meeting in Wheeling had named Peirpoint provisional governor of Unionist Virginia.

To Randolph B. Marcy   [TELEGRAM]

Maj R B Marcy
Willard's Hotel Washington D.C.[1]   [Beverly, c. July 21, 1861]

I have taken steps to order home all the three months Regts. Cox has been checked on the Kanawha which renders it necessary for me to move there at once with all my available force — so that the Stanton[2] movement is impossible for the present unless I am largely reinforced. Please state this to the Genl in Chief in explanation of my apparent inaction and inform him that the cause of my delay has been the uncertainty of affairs on the Kanawha. Say to him that when I have driven Wise out of the Kanawha I will be ready to execute his final orders — but that I think a movement through Kentucky, Western Tennessee and Northern Alabama would be decisive of the war.

Geo B McClellan
Maj Genl Comdg

Retained copy, McClellan Papers (A-23:11), Library of Congress.

1. Marcy reached Washington on July 18, carrying GBM's report of his western Virginia operations for delivery to Gen. Scott. 2. Staunton, in the Shenandoah Valley.

To Mary Ellen McClellan

Beverly July 21 [1861]

... Were you satisfied with the result? 9 guns taken 12 colors — lots of prisoners — & all this done with so little loss on our side! We found yesterday some more guns abandoned by Garnett — bringing the number taken up to *9.* ...

Genl Cox has been badly checked in the Kanawha — one wounded Col (Norton) taken prisoner — two others & a Lt Col (Neff) captured while amusing themselves by an insane expedition in advance of the pickets — served them right. Cox lost more men in getting a detachment thrashed than I did in routing two armies. The consequence is I shall move down with a heavy column to take Mr. Wise in rear & hope either to drive him out without a battle or to catch him with his whole force. It is absolutely necessary for me to go in person. I have no one to whom I can entrust the operation. More than that I don't feel sure that the men will fight very well under anyone but myself. They have the utmost confidence in me & will do anything I put them at. I lose about 14 rgts now whose term of service is about expiring & am sorry to say that I have as yet found but few whose patriotism is sufficient to induce them to remain beyond their time.

I expect to get away from here by day after tomorrow at latest. The march to the Kanawha will require about 7 days — I hope to be able to start for Cincinnati in about 2 weeks from tomorrow. I expect the Guthrie Grays here today & will take them with me to the Kanawha.

AL copy, McClellan Papers (C-7:63), Library of Congress.

To Winfield Scott   [TELEGRAM]

Beverly 11 p.m. July 21/61

Your telegram of 8 p.m. rec'd.[1] I am much pained at its contents. My 3 months men are homesick & discontented with their officers & determined to return at once. When I suggested the Staunton movement I expected these regiments to unite in it. I should be compelled to fight the enemy now ascertained to be in force at Monterey & should reach Staunton without men enough to accomplish much. McDowell's check would greatly increase my difficulties & render numerous detachments necessary to keep open my communications & protect my flank.

How would it meet your views were I to leave say 4 regts at Huttonsville and in the strong position of Cheat Mountain, 1 at Beverly, send two or three & a better general to reenforce Cox, leaving 1 at Bulltown. Then move with the rest by Railroad to New Creek on B & O R.R., & effect a junction with Patterson near Jamesburg on the road from New Creek to Charlestown?

With this force in addition to such state troops as Penna can furnish we should be able either to defeat Johnston or to separate him from Beauregard & in connection with McDowell fight them in detail.[2]

I shall know early tomorrow the exact condition of the 3 years regiments now in Ohio & Indiana. Depending on that information I can join Patterson with probably 15,000 men besides what Penna can furnish. The time required would be about 7 days, perhaps 6, from the day on which I receive your orders until the junction with Patterson at Jamesburg. This tho' not so brilliant a plan as a movement on Staunton in force, appears to be the sounder & safer one.

Whatever your instructions may be, I will cheerfully do my best to carry them out. I will suspend all further preparations for my projected movement on the Kanawha until I hear from you. Please reply by telegraph at once.

G B McClellan
Maj Genl USA

Lt Genl Winfield Scott

ALS (telegram sent), McClellan Papers (A-22:10), Library of Congress. *OR*, Ser. 1, II, p. 752.

1. Scott's telegram read: "McDowell has been checked. Come down to the Shenandoah Valley with such troops as can be spared from Western Virginia, and make head against the enemy in that quarter...." *OR*, Ser. 1, II, p. 749. 2. GBM was unaware that Brig. Gen. Joseph E. Johnston had evaded Patterson in the Shenandoah Valley and had joined Brig. Gen. P. G. T. Beauregard at Manassas for the battle against McDowell.

To Lorenzo Thomas   [TELEGRAM]

To Gen. L. Thomas   Head Quarters Department
Adjt General of U.S.A.   of the Ohio
Washington D.C.   Beverly Va. July 22 1861

Your dispatch of this date has been received.[1] I will make the necessary arrangements for the security of W. Va. & proceed without delay to Washington & report in person at the War Dept. I will take with me three or four Western Regiments.[2]

G B McClellan
Maj Genl U.S.A.

Retained copy, McClellan Papers (A-22:10), Library of Congress.

1. Thomas's telegram read: "Circumstances make your presence here necessary. Charge Rosecrans or some other general with your present department and come hither without delay." *OR*, Ser. 1, II, p. 753. 2. Gen. Scott's reply of this date instructed GBM to bring no troops with him. *OR*, Ser. 1, II, p. 755.

To Jacob D. Cox   [TELEGRAM]

Brig Genl J D Cox
via Gallipolis   [Beverly, July 22, 1861]

Your telegram of 22nd received.[1] Retain the 21st until you have completed the occupation of the Kanawha Valley. Follow up the retreating enemy. Concentrate all your troops and drive them beyond the Gauley Bridge. I have been ordered to Washington and have turned over command of the department to Genl Rosecrantz who is about to repair to the Kanawha to retrieve your want of success. As his presence is very necessary elsewhere I hope that you will by the vigor of your movements render it unnecessary for him to come to your assistance. I had more confidence in you than in any of my Brig Genls. It is not too late for you to justify my first impression of you. Our Army in the East has met with a great disaster. You must if possible drive Wise beyond the Gauley Bridge. It is no longer possible to take him in rear as I proposed. Communicate with Rosecrantz or myself by way of Parkersburg at least twice a day. Two regts are ordered to Bull Town to feel the enemy in that direction.

Geo B McClellan
Maj Genl USA

Retained copy, McClellan Papers (A-22:10), Library of Congress.

1. Cox reported that the 21st Ohio three-month regiment was agitating to go home. McClellan Papers (A-22:10).

To Mary Ellen McClellan   [TELEGRAM]

[Beverly, July 22, 1861]

I am ordered to Washington. Get Larz Anderson[1] to bring you at once to Wheeling at the Machum House. I expect to be there on Wednesday morning [July 24]. Be ready to go with me at least to Philadelphia if your health will permit. It may be that I will reach Wheeling tomorrow. Answer at once.

G B McClellan
Maj Genl

Mrs. M E McClellan
Cincinnati, Ohio

ALS (telegram sent), McClellan Collection, New Jersey Historical Society.

1. Larz Anderson, brother of Robert Anderson, the defender of Fort Sumter, was a friend of the McClellans in Cincinnati.

TWO

THE ARMY OF THE POTOMAC
JULY 27–OCTOBER 31, 1861

THE LARGEST SHARE of General McClellan's correspondence in this three-month period deals with matters of special significance to his wartime career — the organization and training of the Army of the Potomac, and the formulation of a mental picture of the enemy that would stay fixed in his mind for as long as he remained in command. A third major feature of these months was McClellan's struggle against what he regarded as Winfield Scott's baneful influence on the Northern war effort, a struggle that finally concluded on October 31, 1861, when he learned that he would replace Scott as general-in-chief of the Union armies the next day. These themes are revealed with particular clarity in McClellan's letters to his wife, which make up nearly half of the sixty-seven letters and dispatches included here.

Mrs. McClellan, who was expecting their first child, did not accompany the general when he was called to Washington in July but remained instead in Cincinnati, and his frequent letters to her disclose a growing obsession with his enemies, real and imagined, both in the field and on the home front. Editor Prime was at particular pains to censor those he printed in *McClellan's Own Story*. In the case of one especially angry letter, written probably on October 11, in which McClellan savagely characterized the president and most of the Cabinet, Prime eliminated everything of the diatribe but its opening phrase — "I can't tell you how disgusted I am becoming with these wretched politicians...."

The long memorandum of August 2 to President Lincoln, which McClellan characterized for his wife that day as his plan to conduct the war " 'En grand' & crush the rebels in one campaign," represented a considerable change in his strategic thinking as first described in his April 27 letter to General Scott. The emphasis was now on making a single major campaign in the eastern theater with a Napoleonic grand army of over a quarter of a million men. By thoroughly defeating the Confederate forces in the field, he wrote, ''and pursuing a rigidly protective policy as to private property and unarmed persons, and a lenient course as to common soldiers, we may well hope for the permanent restoration of peaceful Union. . . . ''

Less than a week after submitting this plan, McClellan raised the alarm with Scott (August 8) that Washington was in danger of attack by an army of 100,000 men, twice the size of his own forces. Succeeding letters depict the Confederate menace growing ever larger as he worked desperately to ready the Army of the Potomac for the decisive battle. The danger was greatest, by McClellan's reckoning, on September 13, when he warned Secretary of War Simon Cameron, in a letter previously unpublished, that he would be unable to bring more than 60,000 or 80,000 soldiers to the battlefield, while ''The enemy probably have 170,000!'' In fact, the peak strength of the Confederate field army facing Washington in these months was less than 45,000.

With his August 8 letter to Scott, McClellan invented a crisis and created the delusion of an all-powerful enemy which was only later abetted by the imaginative reports of his intelligence chief, Allan Pinkerton. The letters to Mrs. McClellan clearly demonstrate the strength of the delusion and how desperate he believed his plight to be. At the same time, they demonstrate the strength of his Calvinistic belief in predestination. He was certain he had been called upon by God to save the Union. On October 31, for example, he wrote her, ''God will support me & bear me out — he could not have placed me here for nothing,'' and in that belief he took both comfort and refuge.

In his war against General Scott and others in the government who refused to recognize the gravity of the crisis, McClellan initially had an ally in Edwin M. Stanton, a fellow Democrat and former member of President Buchanan's Cabinet. The draft of McClellan's major strategy paper of October 31 to Cameron reveals that it was written in part by Stanton, at whose Washington house McClellan concealed himself that day (as he told his wife) ''To dodge all enemies in shape of 'browsing' Presdt etc.'' The paper set his conditions for making a campaign before winter against an enemy army facing him ''on the Potomac not less than 150 000 strong well drilled & equipped, ably commanded & strongly intrenched.'' If the Army of the Potomac was raised to parity with the enemy by calling up reinforcements from other theaters and if he was put in overall command, he wrote, he would take the offensive within a month.

To Mary Ellen McClellan

July 27/61 Washington D.C. Saturday

I have been assigned to the command of a Division — composed of Depts of N.E. Va (that under McDowell) & that of Washington (now under Mansfield)[1] — neither of them like it much — especially Mansfield, but I think they must ere long become accustomed to it, as there is no help for it. . . .

I find myself in a new & strange position here — Presdt, Cabinet, Genl Scott & all deferring to me — by some strange operation of magic I seem to have become *the* power of the land. I almost think that were I to win some small success now I could become Dictator or anything else that might please me — but nothing of that kind would please me — *therefore* I *won't* be Dictator. Admirable self denial! I see already the main causes of our recent failure — I am *sure* that I can remedy these & am confident that I can lead these armies of men to victory once more. I start tomorrow very early on a tour through the lines on the other side of the river —it will occupy me all day long & a rather fatiguing ride it will be — but I will be able to make up my mind as to the state of things. Refused invitations to dine today from Genl Scott & four Secy's — had too many things to attend to. . . .

I will endeavor to enclose with this the "thanks of Congress" which please preserve. I feel very proud of it. Genl Scott objected to it on the ground that it ought to be accompanied by a gold medal. I cheerfully acquiesce in the Thanks by themselves, hoping to win the medal by some other action, & the sword by some other fait d'éclat.

AL copy; copy, McClellan Papers (C-7:63/D-10:72), Library of Congress.

1. GBM headed the Division of the Potomac, with Brig. Gens. Irvin McDowell and Joseph K. F. Mansfield serving under him, McDowell in command of a division, Mansfield in command of the District of Columbia.

To Allan Pinkerton   [TELEGRAM]

To E. J. Allen, Esq.[1]
Cincinnati, Ohio   Washington July 30/61

Join me in Washington as soon as possible. Come prepared to stay and bring with you two or three of your best men.[2] Answer by telegraph.

Geo. B. McClellan
Major General

Retained copy, Records of the Office of the Secretary of War, RG 107 (M-504:9), National Archives.

1. Pinkerton customarily employed the nom de guerre E. J. Allen. 2. GBM put Pinkerton in charge of military intelligence-gathering for the Army of the Potomac.

To Mary Ellen McClellan

July 30/61 Washington

... Had to work until nearly 3 this morning. ...

I am getting my ideas pretty well arranged in regard to the strength of my army — it will be a large one. I have been employed in trying to get the right kind of Genl officers. ...

Have been working this morning at a bill allowing me to appoint as many Aides as I please from civil life & from the army.[1]

I went to the Senate to get it through (the bill increasing number of Aides) & was quite overwhelmed by the congratulations I received & the respect with which I was treated. I suppose half a dozen of the oldest made the remark I am becoming so much used to. "Why how young you look — & yet an old soldier!!" It seems to strike everybody that I am very young. They give me my way in everything, full swing & unbounded confidence. All tell me that I am held responsible for the fate of the Nation & that all its resources shall be placed at my disposal. It is an immense task that I have on my hands, but I believe I can accomplish it. ...

When I was in the Senate Chamber today & found those old men flocking around me; when I afterwards stood in the library looking over the Capital of our great Nation, & saw the crowd gathering around to stare at me, I began to feel how great the task committed to me. Oh! how sincerely I pray to God that I may be endowed with the wisdom & courage necessary to accomplish the work. Who would have thought when we were married, that I should so soon be called upon to save my country? I learn that before I came on they said in Richmond, that there was only one man they feared & that was McClellan.

AL copy; copy, McClellan Papers (C-7:63/D-10:72), Library of Congress.

1. A bill for the stated purpose was passed by Congress and on Aug. 5 signed into law by the president.

To Abraham Lincoln

Memorandum for the Consideration
of His Excellency the President,
submitted at his request.   [Washington, August 2, 1861][1]

The object of the present war differs from those in which nations are usually engaged, mainly in this; that the purpose of ordinary war is to conquer a peace and make a treaty on advantageous terms; in this contest it has become necessary to crush a population sufficiently numerous, intelligent and warlike to constitute a nation; we have not only to defeat their armed and organized forces in the field but to display such an

LIBRARY ST. MARY'S COLLEGE

overwhelming strength, as will convince all our antagonists, especially those of the governing aristocratic class, of the utter impossibility of resistance. Our late reverses make this course imperative; had we been successful in the recent battle it is possible that we might have been spared the labor and expense of a great effort; now we have no alternative; their success will enable the political leaders of the rebels to convince the mass of their people that we are inferior to them in force and courage, and to command all their resources. The contest began with a class; now it is with a people. Our military success can alone restore the former issue. By thoroughly defeating their armies, taking their strong places, and pursuing a rigidly protective policy as to private property and unarmed persons, and a lenient course as to common soldiers, we may well hope for the permanent restoration of peaceful Union; but in the first instance the authority of the Government must be supported by overwhelming physical force. Our foreign relations and financial credit also imperatively demand that the military action of the Government should be prompt and irresistible.

The rebels have chosen Virginia as their battle-field — and it seems proper for us to make the first great struggle there; but while thus directing our main efforts, it is necessary to diminish the resistance there offered us, by movements on other points, both by land and water. Without entering at present into details, I would advise that a strong movement be made on the Mississippi, and that the rebels be driven out of Missouri. As soon as it becomes perfectly clear that Kentucky is cordially united with us, I would advise a movement through that state into Eastern Tennessee, for the purpose of assisting the Union men of that region, and of seizing the Railroads leading from Memphis to the East. The possession of those roads by us, in connection with the movement on the Mississippi, would go far towards determining the evacuation of Virginia by the rebels. In the mean time all the passes into Western Virginia from the East should be securely guarded; but I would make no movement from that quarter towards Richmond unless the political condition of Kentucky renders it impossible or inexpedient for us to make the movement upon Eastern Tennessee through that state; every effort should however be made to organize, equip, and arm as many troops as possible in Western Virginia, in order to render the Ohio and Indiana regiments available for other operations.

At as early a day as practicable it would be well to protect and reopen the Baltimore & Ohio Railroad. Baltimore & Fort Monroe should be occupied by *garrisons* sufficient to retain them in our possession.

The importance of Harper's Ferry and the line of the Potomac in the direction of Leesburg will be very materially diminished as soon as our force in this vicinity becomes organized, strong and efficient; because no capable general will cross the river north of this city, when we have a strong army here ready to cut off his retreat.

To revert to the West. It is probable that no very large additions to the troops now in Missouri will be necessary to secure that state. I presume that the force required for the movement down the Mississippi will be determined by its commander and the President.

If Kentucky assumes the right position, not more than 20,000 troops will be needed, together with those that can be raised in that state and Eastern Tennessee, to secure the latter region and its railroads; as well as ultimately to occupy Nashville. The Western Virginia troops with not more than from 5 to 10,000 from Ohio and Indiana should under proper management, suffice for its protection. When we have reorganized our main army here, 10,000 men ought to be enough to protect the Balt. & Ohio R.R. and the Potomac — 5000 will *garrison* Baltimore — 3000 Fort Monroe; and not more than 20,000 will be necessary, at the utmost, for the defence of Washington.

For the main Army of Operations I urge the following composition.

250 Regt's Infantry — say	225,000 men
100 Field Batteries — 600 guns	15,000 "
28 Regts. Cavalry	25,500 "
5 " Engineer troops	7,500 "
Total	273,000 "

This force must be supplied with the necessary engineer and ponton trains, and with transportation for everything save tents. Its general line of operations should be directed that water transportation can be availed of from point to point, by means of the ocean and the rivers emptying into it.

An essential feature of the plan of operations will be the employment of a strong naval force, to protect the movement of a fleet of transports, intended to convoy a considerable body of troops from point to point of the enemy's seacoast; thus either creating diversions and rendering it necessary for them to detach largely from their main body in order to protect such of their cities as may be threatened; or else landing and forming establishments on their coast at any favorable places that opportunity might offer. This naval force should also cooperate with the main army in its efforts to seize the important seaboard towns of the rebels.

It cannot be ignored that the construction of railroads has introduced a new and very important element into war, by the great facilities thus given for concentrating at particular positions large masses of troops from remote sections, and by creating new strategic points and lines of operations. It is intended to overcome this difficulty by the partial operations suggested, and such others as the particular case may require;

we must endeavor to seize places on the railways in the rear of the enemy's points of concentration; and we must threaten their seaboard cities in order that each state may be forced by the necessity of its own defence to diminish its contingent to the Confederate Army.

The proposed movement down the Mississippi will produce important results in this connection. That advance and the progress of the main army at the East will materially assist each other by diminishing the resistance to be encountered by each. The tendency of the Mississippi movement upon all questions connected with cotton are too well understood by the President and Cabinet to need any illustration from me.

There is another independent movement which has often been suggested and which has always recommended itself to my judgment. I refer to a movement from Kansas and Nebraska through the Indian Territory upon Red river and Western Texas, for the purpose of protecting and developing the latent Union and free state sentiment well known to predominate in Western Texas, and which like a similar sentiment in Western Virginia, will, if protected, ultimately organize that section into a free state. How far it will be possible to support this movement by an advance through New Mexico from California is a matter which I have not sufficiently examined to be able to express a decided opinion; if at all practicable, it is eminently desirable as bringing into play the resources and warlike qualities of the Pacific States, as well as identifying them with our cause and cementing the bond of Union between them and the General Government. If it is not departing too far from my province I will venture to suggest the policy of an intimate alliance and cordial understanding with Mexico; their sympathies and interests are with us; their antipathies exclusively against our enemies and their institutions. I think it would not be difficult to obtain from the Mexican Government the right to use, at least during the present contest, the road from Guaymas to New Mexico; this concession would very materially reduce the obstacles of the column moving from the Pacific; a similar permission to use their territory for the passage of troops between the Panuco and the Rio Grande would enable us to throw a column by a good road from Tampico or some of the small harbors north of it upon and across the Rio Grande into the country of our friends, and without risk, and scarcely firing a shot. To what extent if any it would be desirable to take into service, and employ Mexican soldiers is a question entirely political, on which I do not venture to offer any opinion.

The force I have recommended is large — the expense is great. It is possible that a smaller force might accomplish the object in view, but I understand it to be the purpose of this great Nation to reestablish the power of the Government, and to restore peace to its citizens, in the shortest possible time. The question to be decided is simply this; shall we crush the rebellion at one blow, terminate the war in one campaign, or shall we leave it as a legacy for our descendants? When the extent of the possible line of operations is considered, the force asked for, for the main army under my command, cannot be regarded as unduly large. Every mile we advance carries us further from our base of operations and renders detachments necessary to cover our communications; while the enemy will be constantly concentrating as he falls back. I propose with the force which I have requested, not only to drive the enemy out of Virginia and occupy Richmond, but to occupy Charleston, Savannah, Montgomery, Pensacola, Mobile, and New Orleans; in other words to move into the heart of the enemy's country, and crush out this rebellion in its very heart. By seizing and repairing the railroads as we advance, the difficulties of transportation will be materially diminished.

It is perhaps unnecessary to state that in addition to the forces named in this memorandum strong reserves should be formed, ready to supply any losses that may occur. In conclusion, I would submit that the exigencies of the treasury may be lessened by making only partial payments to our troops when in the enemy's country and by giving the obligations of the United States for such supplies as may there be obtainable.

Geo B McClellan
Maj Genl USA

Washington D.C. Aug 2 1861

DS, Lincoln Papers, Library of Congress. *OR*, Ser. 1, V, pp. 6–8.

1. The retained copy of this memorandum bears the endorsement that it was delivered personally to the president by GBM on Aug. 2, and that GBM read it to the Cabinet at 10:00 A.M. the next day. McClellan Papers (A-23:11), Library of Congress.

To Mary Ellen McClellan

[Washington] Aug 2nd/61

Rode over the river, looked at some of the works & inspected 3 or 4 rgts — worked at organizing Brigades — just got thro' with that. I handed to the Presdt tonight a carefully considered plan for conducting the war on a large scale....

I shall carry this thing on "En grand" & crush the rebels in one campaign — I flatter myself that Beauregard has gained his last victory — we need success & must have it — I will leave nothing undone to gain it. Genl Scott has been trying to work a traverse to have Emory made Inspector Genl of *my* army & of *the* army[1] — I respectfully declined the favor & perhaps disgusted the old man, who by the by, is fast becoming very slow & very old. He cannot long retain command I think — when he retires I am sure to succeed him, unless in the mean time I lose a battle — which I do not expect to do....

I have Washn perfectly quiet now — you would not know that there was a regiment here. I have restored order very completely already.

I have on the staff Seth Williams as Adjt Genl, Barnard as Chief Engineer, Van Vliet, Chief Qt Master, H. F. Clarke, Chief Commissary, Barry, Chief of Artillery — Meade will be senior Topog — Dr. Tripler Medical Director.[2] I have applied for Kingsbury as Chief of Ordnance, & for Armstrong & Sweitzer as aides de camp.[3] I dine with the Presdt tomorrow, where I presume I shall meet Prince Napoleon.[4] . . .

You would laugh if you could see the scores of queer letters I receive in these days. I am sorry to say I do not answer any of them, I do no writing myself, except to you. . . .

I was in the saddle nearly 12 hours yesterday. I broke down your Father & sent Seth home half an hour since, neither of them having been out all today.

AL copy; copy, McClellan Papers (C-7:63/D-10:72), Library of Congress.

1. Lt. Col. William H. Emory was not appointed to either position. 2. Majors Seth Williams, John G. Barnard, Stewart Van Vliet, Henry F. Clarke, William F. Barry, Capt. George G. Meade, Maj. Charles S. Tripler. All assumed the posts mentioned except Meade, who would command an infantry brigade. 3. Capts. Charles P. Kingsbury and N. B. Sweitzer were appointed to these positions. The identity of Armstrong is unknown. 4. Napoleon Joseph Charles Paul Bonaparte, cousin of France's Emperor Napoleon III.

To General Officers, Division of the Potomac

[Washington, c. August 4, 1861][1]
Instructions to General Officers

The basis of organization is in the Brigades, & to the Brig Genls the Genl Comdg looks for the instruction, discipline & efficiency of the troops. The Brig Genls will at once establish schools of instruction. They will personally instruct & drill all the field officers, & as many of the Capts & Lts as possible, at least one hour every day. They will require these officers to recite to them in the tactics, regulations, duties of outpost guards & sentinels, forms of parade, inspection, guard mounting, reviews etc; they will instruct them thoroughly as to the various reports & customs required by existing regulations; drill them in the school of the soldier; occasionally drill the companies & battalions, always enforcing the instructions given by their subordinates, & paying especial attention to the drill for skirmishers, that with the bayonet, & target practice. Whenever the Colonels or other regimental officers are already competent the Brig Genls will establish subordinate schools of instruction, always taking care that the company officers & n.c. offs[2] are theoretically instructed every day.

Particular attention is enjoined to the duties of sentinels & the various forms of ceremony etc prescribed by the regulations.

In view of the fact that the greater part of the General Officers are instructed soldiers, the Genl Comdg does not deem it necessary to dwell further upon points of detail, trusting to their soldierly spirit to carry out his wishes, & to perfect the strict discipline & instruction of the troops.

There are, however, some general points to which it is desired to call their attention — i.e.

1. Guards, outposts & sentinels —

The Grand guards will always be posted — their number & position to be determined by circumstances. The outposts & sentinels must be so placed as to render it impossible for any one to pass the lines without being observed, & so as to give ample notice to the grand guards & main body of the approach of the enemy. Sentinels must be obliged to walk their posts constantly & always to be on the alert — in presence of the enemy they will in preference be posted in pairs.

Patrols of infantry & cavalry will be constantly kept out to the front. Sentinels must know that the punishment of death for sleeping, abandoning their arms, or neglecting their duty will be inexorably inflicted.

[2.] *Marches* Frequent military marches will be made for the purpose of instruction, sometimes at night. The trains will accompany the columns, knapsacks will be carried, & all military precautions observed with regard to advanced guards, flankers, rear guard etc. Every place in which an enemy could be concealed will be carefully searched by skirmishers before the main body passes the point, defiles & villages will be searched before & occupied while the main body passes. Every precaution will be taken to render a surprise impossible & to gain intelligence of the position & strength of the enemy in ample time to enable the main body to act as circumstances may require. The composition of the advanced guard will depend upon circumstances — if the country is open cavalry will lead, supported by infantry ; if the ground is broken & wooded infantry should lead with only cavalry enough to carry intelligence to the rear. A halt of 15 minutes will be made half an hour after the march is commenced, & one of 10 minutes during every hour, besides a noon halt of at least an hour when circumstances permit. Halts will be made in preference where water & shade can be obtained. Arms will be stacked, not more than one fourth of the men permitted to leave the immediate vicinity of the stacks at the same time, sentinels placed over private houses & gardens, as well as outposts thrown out to prevent a surprise. In no case will the men be allowed to enter houses & gardens, except to obtain water when they cannot obtain it otherwise. The sentinels will always prevent the destruction of property. In marching straggling will be strictly prohibited & the rear guard will have positive orders not to allow any soldier or camp follower to lag behind it. The rear guard will be provided a suitable number of ambulances & a surgeon, who will decide what stragglers should ride — the others will be forced to march in advance of the rear guard.

The men will carry in their knapsacks only a change of underclothing, an extra pair of shoes, towel soap etc. The blanket & shelter tent will form the rest of their load. In winter they will wear the overcoat.

Forty rounds will always be carried in the cartridge boxes. Punctuality in the hour of starting will be always required.

3. *Battles* In regard to *battles* & *affairs* the Genl Officers will receive such specific instructions as the peculiar circumstances may require, the Comdg Genl now desires only to call attention to some general principles which must always be observed.

The orders must be strictly conformed to; no excuse can be received for bringing on an action against or without his instructions, & every Genl Officer, of whatever rank, will be held accountable that the directions given to him are carried out both in the spirit & letter. The Genl Officers must understand that success can only be obtained by carefully observing the orders they receive, & will in no case allow their impulses or individual judgment to induce them to depart from their instructions.

Infantry may act on any kind of ground; in an open country, preferably in column or line; in a broken or wooded country skirmishers should precede, supported by columns — the habitual employment of skirmishers to open the way is advised. Artillery should never be left without a support of both infantry & cavalry, if the ground will permit the employment of the latter, nor should it ever be brought (except in extreme cases) within rifle range of woods or other cover occupied by the enemy; it should always if possible have a clear space of at least 500 or 600 yards in front of it.

Cavalry must be used entirely in an open country, unless its flanks are covered by infantry as it advances; in no case should it be required to act in woods, or along a road skirted by timber.

As a general rule an engagement should be opened by the fire of all the artillery that can be concentrated on the decisive point, when the requisite effect is produced the infantry should advance, supported by the cavalry held ready to follow up their success.

AD, McClellan Papers (A-16:7), Library of Congress

1. This probable date is assigned from the contents of the memorandum, and from an entry of Aug. 4 in the headquarters journal that called all brigade commanders to headquarters "for instructions regarding the duties of their Brigades when formed." McClellan Papers (A-23:11). 2. Noncommissioned officers.

To Mary Ellen McClellan

[Washington] August 4 1861

I dined at the Presdt's yesterday. I suppose some 40 were present — Prince Napoleon & his staff, French Minister, English ditto, Cabinet, some Senators, Genl Scott & myself. Mrs. Lincoln doesn't shine particularly as a hostess. The dinner was not especially interesting; rather long, & rather tedious as such things generally are. I was placed between Col. Pisani,[1] one of the Prince's aides, who spoke no English, & a member of the Legation who laboured under the delusion that he spoke our native tongue with fluency. I had some long talks with the Prince, who speaks English very much as the Frenchmen do in the old English comedies. He is an intelligent man, but not prepossessing. . . .

My horse has at last arrived.[2] I hear there is another one on the way for me, a present from Chicago, I wish some other people would give me two or three more. . . .

It made me feel a little strangely last evening when I went in to the Presdt's with the old General leaning on me — the old veteran (Scott) & his young successor; I could see that many marked the contrast.

Copy, McClellan Papers (D-10:72), Library of Congress.

1. Lt. Col. Camille Ferri Pisani. 2. Presumably Dan Webster, a gift from what GBM called his "railroad friends" in Cincinnati.

To Nathaniel P. Banks [TELEGRAM]

Maj. Genl. N. P. Banks
Comdg in Camp

Head Quarters, Army of the Potomac
Washington, Aug 4 1861 2.30 p.m.

Information has been received which goes to show that the enemy may attack us within the next forty eight hours. Please direct all your guards to exercise the utmost vigilance and hold your command ready to move at the shortest notice, with cooked rations for two days ready.[1] Telegraph to me at least four times each day.

Geo B McClellan
Maj Genl Comdg

Retained copy, McClellan Papers (A-23:11), Library of Congress. Maj. Gen. Banks commanded the Department of the Shenandoah, with headquarters at Sandy Hook, Md., on the upper Potomac.

1. The same alert was sent to all brigade commanders. On Aug. 6 the alert was renewed. *OR*, Ser. 1, V, p. 553.

To Winfield Scott

Lieut. Gen'l Winfield Scott
Comdg U. S. Army
General:

Head Quarters Division of the Potomac
Washington Aug. 8th 1861

Information from various sources, reaching me to-day, through spies, letters and telegrams confirm my impressions derived from previous advices, that the enemy intend attacking our positions on the other side of the river, as well as to cross the Potomac north of us. I have also to-day received a telegram from a reliable agent just from Knoxville Tenn. that large reinforcements are still passing through there to Richmond. I am induced to believe that the enemy has at least 100,000 men in our front. Were I in Beauregard's place, with that force at my disposal, I would attack the positions on the other side of the Potomac and at the same time cross the river above the city in force.

I feel confident that our present army in this vicinity is entirely insufficient for the emergency, and it is deficient in all the arms of the service — Infantry, Artillery, and Cavalry. I therefore respectfully and most earnestly urge that the garrisons of all places in our rear be reduced at once to the minimum absolutely necessary to hold them, and that all the troops thus made available be forthwith forwarded to this city; that every company of regular artillery within reach be immediately ordered here to be mounted; that every possible means be used to expedite the forwarding of new regiments of volunteers to this Capital, without one hour's delay. I urge that nothing be left undone to bring up our force for the defence of this city to 100,000 men before attending to any other point. I advise that at least 8 or 10 good Ohio and Indiana Regiments may be telegraphed for from Western Virginia; their places to be filled at once by the new troops from the same states, who will be at least reliable to fight behind the entrenchments which have been constructed there. The vital importance of rendering Washington perfectly secure, and its *imminent danger,* impel me to urge these requests with the utmost earnestness, and that not an hour be lost in carrying them into execution.[1]

A sense of duty which I cannot resist, compels me to state that in my opinion military necessity demands that the departments of N. E. Viginia, Washington, the Shenandoah, Pennsylvania including Baltimore, and the one including Fort Monroe should be merged into one Department under the immediate control of the Commander of the main army of operations, and which should be known and designated as such.

> Very Respty Your obdt servt.
> Geo B McClellan
> Maj Gen'l Comdg.

"The original of which the foregoing is a copy was delivered to Genl Scott on the day of its date in the usual course of official communications, and a copy of same was on the same day delivered to the President of the United States personally by Thomas M Key — volunteer aid of Genl McClellan."(Attest T M Key)[2]

Retained copy, McClellan Papers (A-24:11), Library of Congress. *OR,* Ser. 1, XI, Part 3, pp. 3–4.

1. Scott responded, to Secretary of War Cameron, on Aug. 9: "I am confident in the opposite opinion; . . . I have not the slightest apprehension for the safety of the Government here." Suffering the infirmities of age and long service, and considering himself undercut by GBM, he asked to be put on the retired list. *OR,* Ser. 1, XI, Part 3, p. 4. 2. With the copy for the president GBM sent a covering letter expressing the hope that Lincoln would

see Key ''at once & read attentively the copy of my letter to Genl Scott which he will hand you.'' William Henry Seward Papers, Rush Rhees Library, University of Rochester.

To Mary Ellen McClellan

[Washington] Aug 8 [1861]

... Rose early today (having retired at 3 am) & was pestered to death with Senators etc & a row with Genl Scott until about 4 o'clock, then crossed the river & rode beyond & along the line of pickets for some distance — came back & had a long interview with Seward[1] about my ''pronunciamento'' against Genl Scott's policy. . . .[2]

How does he think that I can save this country when stopped by Genl Scott — I do not know whether he is a *dotard* or a *traitor!* I can't tell which. He *cannot* or *will* not comprehend the condition in which we are placed & is entirely unequal to the emergency. If he cannot be taken out of my path I will not retain my position, but will resign & let the admn take care of itself. I have hardly slept one moment for the last three nights, knowing well that the enemy intend some movement & fully recognizing our own weakness. If Beauregard does not attack tonight I shall look upon it as a dispensation of Providence — he *ought* to do it. Every day strengthens me — I am leaving nothing undone to increase our force — but that confounded old Genl always comes in the way — he is a perfect imbecile. He understands nothing, appreciates nothing & is ever in my way.

AL copy, McClellan Papers (C-7:63), Library of Congress.

1. Secretary of State William H. Seward. 2. GBM to Scott, Aug. 8, *supra.*

To Mary Ellen McClellan

Washington Aug 9 [10] 1861 1 am.

I have had a busy day — started from here at 7 in the morning & was in the saddle until about 9 this evening [August 9] — rode over the advanced positions on the other side of the river, was soundly drenched in a hard rain & have been busy ever since my return. Things are improving daily — I received 3 new rgts today — fitted out one new battery yesterday, another today — two tomorrow — about five day after. Within four days I hope to have at least 21 batteries — say 124 field guns — 18 co's. of cavalry & some 70 rgts of infantry. Genl Scott is the great obstacle — he will not comprehend the danger & is either a traitor or an incompetent. I have to fight my way against him & have thrown a bombshell that has created a perfect stampede in the Cabinet — tomorrow [August 10] the question will probably be decided by giving me absolute control independently of him. I suppose it will result in a mortal enmity on his part against me, but I have no choice — the people call upon me ↘

to save the country — I *must* save it & cannot respect anything that is in the way.

I receive letter after letter — have conversation after conversation calling on me to save the nation — alluding to the Presidency, Dictatorship &c. As I hope one day to be united with you forever in heaven, I have no such aspirations — I will never accept the Presidency — I will cheerfully take the Dictatorship & agree to lay down my life when the country is saved. I am *not* spoiled by my unexpected & new position — I feel sure that God will give me the strength & wisdom to preserve this great nation — but I tell *you,* who share all my thoughts, that I have no selfish feeling in the matter. I feel that God has placed a great work in my hands — I have not sought it — I know how weak I am — but I know that I mean to do right & I believe that God will help me & give me the wisdom I do not possess. Pray for me, darling, that I may be able to accomplish my task — the greatest, perhaps, that any poor weak mortal ever had to do....

God grant that I may bring this war to an end & be permitted to spend the rest of my days quietly with you....

I met the Prince [Napoleon] at Alexandria today & came up with him.[1] He says that Beauregard's head is turned & that he acts like a fool. That Joe Johnston is quiet & sad, & that he spoke to him in very kind terms of me.

AL copy, McClellan Papers (C-7:63), Library of Congress.

1. On Aug. 8–9 Prince Napoleon and his suite visited the Confederate command at Manassas and toured the Bull Run battlefield.

To Abraham Lincoln

To/ The President   Head Quarters, Division of the Potomac
Sir: Washington, August 10th 1861

The letter addressed by me under the date of the 8th inst. to Lieutenant General Scott, commanding the United States Army, was designed to be a plain and respectful expression of my views of the measures demanded for the safety of the Government in the imminent peril that besets it at the present hour. Every moment's reflection and every fact transpiring convinces me of the urgent necessity of the measures there indicated, and I felt it my duty to him and to the country to communicate them frankly. It is therefore with great pain that I have learned from you this morning, that my views do not meet with the approbation of the Lieutenant General, and that my letter is unfavorably regarded by him. The command with which I am entrusted, was not sought by me, and has only been accepted from an earnest and humble desire to serve my country in the moment of the most extreme peril. With these views I am willing to do and suffer whatever may be required for that service. Nothing could be further from my wishes than to seek any command or urge any measures not required for the exigency of the occasion, and above all I would abstain from any word or act that could give offense to General Scott or embarrass the President or any Department of the Government.

Influenced by these considerations, I yield to your request, and withdraw the letter referred to. The Government and my superior officer being appraised of what I conceive to be necessary and proper of the defence of the National Capital, I shall strive faithfully and zealously to employ the means that may be placed in my power for that purpose, dismissing every personal feeling or consideration, and praying only the blessing of Divine Providence on my efforts. I will only add that as you requested my authority to withdraw the letter, that authority is hereby given, with the most profound assurances of respect for General Scott and yourself.[1]

> Very respectfully your Obd't Serv't
> G B McClellan
> Maj Gen'l Comdg.

LS, Lincoln Papers, Library of Congress. *OR*, Ser. 1, XI, Part 3, pp. 4–5.

1. Seeking to reconcile his two generals, the president showed this letter to Scott, with the request that he in turn withdraw his letter of resignation sent to Secretary Cameron. Scott, although respecting Lincoln's "patriotic purpose of healing differences," refused, citing the disrespect and neglect of his "ambitious junior" and GBM's dealings with members of the Cabinet "without resort to or consultation with me, the nominal General-in-Chief of the Army." Aug. 12, *OR*, Ser. 1, XI, Part 3, pp. 5–6.

To Gideon Welles

Hon. Gideon Welles
Sec'y U. S. Navy   Head Quarters Division of the Potomac
Sir: Washington Aug. 12th 1861

I have to day received additional information which convinces me that it is more than probable that the enemy will within a very short time, attempt to throw a respectable force from the mouth of Aquia Creek into Maryland. This attempt will probably be preceded by the erection of batteries at Mathias & White House[1] points. Such a movement on the part of the enemy in connection with others probably designed would place Washington in great jeopardy. I most earnestly urge that the strongest possible naval force be at once concentrated near the mouth of Aquia Creek and that the most vigilant watch be maintained day and night, so as to render such passage of the river absolutely impossible. I recommend that the Minnesota and any other vessels available from Hampton Roads be at once ordered up there,[2] and that a quantity of coal be sent to that vicinity sufficient for several weeks supply. At least one strong war vessel should be kept at Alexandria, and I again urge the concentration of a strong naval force in the Potomac without delay. If the naval Dep't will render it absolutely impossible for the enemy to cross the river below Washington, the security of the Capital will be greatly increased. I cannot too earnestly urge an immediate compliance with these requests.

> I am, Sir, very respectfully Your Obdt Servt.
> Geo. B. McClellan
> Maj. Gen'l Comdg.

"The original of which the foregoing is a copy was upon the day of the date delivered to the Secretary of the Navy by Thomas M Key, volunteer aid of Genl McClellan."(Attest T M Key)

Retained copy, McClellan Papers (A-24:11), Library of Congress. *OR*, Ser. 1, V, p. 47. Welles was secretary of the navy.

1. Presumably GBM meant Whitestone Point, on the lower Potomac upstream from Aquia Creek; Mathias Point is downstream from the creek. 2. The steam frigate *Minnesota* was on blockade duty in Hampton Roads.

To Mary Ellen McClellan

[Washington] Aug 13 [1861]

I am living in Com. Wilkes's house, the N. W. corner of Jackson Square, close to where you used to visit Secy Marcy's family.[1] It is a very nice house. I occupy the three front rooms on the 2nd story, Van Vliet the room in rear of mine, Judge Key behind him, Colburn the story above. I receive the staff every morning until ten & every evening at nine. Quite a levee it makes, & a rather fine looking set they are. Kingsbury arrived last night. Did I tell you that Hudson is one of my regular aides?[2]

Copy, McClellan Papers (D-10:72), Library of Congress.

1. Capt. Charles Wilkes, USN; William L. Marcy, secretary of state under Franklin Pierce and a cousin of Randolph B. Marcy. 2. For GBM's staff, see GBM to Army of the Potomac, Aug. 20, *infra*.

To Mary Ellen McClellan

[Washington] August 15th [14, 1861] midnight

...I am almost tired out. I cannot get one minute's rest during the day — & sleep with one eye open at night — looking out sharply for Beauregard, who I think has some notion of making a dash in this direction. Genl Scott is the most dangerous antagonist I have — either he or I must leave here — our ideas are so widely different that it is impossible for us to work together much longer — tant pour cela![1]

My day has been spent much as usual....

Rose at 6 1/2, did any reasonable amount of business — among which may be classed quelling a couple of mutinies among the patriotic volunteers — started on my usual ride at 4 1/2, came home at 9, have been hard at work ever since. As to my mutinous friends — I have ordered 63 of the 2nd Maine rgt to be sent as prisoners to the Dry Tortugas, there to serve out the rest of the war as prisoners at hard labor. I reduced the other gentlemen (79th N.Y.) by sending out a battalion, battery & squadron of regulars to take care of them. The gentlemen at once laid down their arms & I have the ringleaders in irons — they will be tried & probably shot tomorrow — an example is necessary to bring these people up to the mark, & if they will not fight & do their duty from honorable motives, I intend to coerce them & let them see what they have to expect if they pretend to rebel.[2] I deprived the 79th of their colors & have them down stairs — not to be returned to them until they have earned them again by good behavior. The great trouble is the utter worthlessness of the officers of these rgts — we have good material, but no officers.

AL copy, McClellan Papers (C-7:63), Library of Congress.

1."So much for that." 2. No executions were carried out. The mutinies involved mainly a dispute over whether the regiments' term of service was for three months or three years.

To Elizabeth B. McClellan

My dearest Mother   Washington DC Aug 16 [1861]

I enclose some photographs of your wandering son which the artist insisted upon taking by main force & violence. Please give one to Maria, one to Mary, keep one & give the others to Annie Phillips & the "Coxe girls" with my love.[1] I have a weary time here in exile — a load of cares & anxiety on my mind sufficient to crush any one — difficulties to contend against that you cannot imagine. "The Young General" has no bed of roses on which to recline. I try to do my best & trust in God to assist me for I feel full well that I can do nothing in this great crisis without *His* aid.

                    With my truest love to all ever your affectionate son
                                        Geo McClellan

ALS, McClellan Papers (B-8:47), Library of Congress. GBM's widowed mother lived in Philadelphia.

1. Maria Eldredge McClellan was the wife of GBM's older brother, John H. B. McClellan. Mary McClellan was GBM's younger sister. The Phillips and Coxe families were maternal relations.

To Mary Ellen McClellan

                            [Washington, August] 16th [1861]

... I am here in a terrible place — the enemy have from 3 to 4 times my force — the Presdt is an idiot, the old General in his dotage — they cannot or will not see the true state of affairs. Most of my troops are demoralized by the defeat at Bull Run, some rgts even mutinous — I have probably stopped that — but you see my position is not pleasant. . . .

I have, I believe, made the best possible disposition of the few men under my command — will quietly await events & if the enemy attacks will try to make my movements as rapid & desperate as may be — if my men will only fight I think I can thrash him notwithstanding the disparity of numbers. As it is I trust to God to give success to our arms — tho' he is not wont to aid those who refuse to aid themselves. . . .

I am weary of all this. I have no ambition in the present affairs — only wish to save my country — & find the incapables around me will not permit it! They sit on the verge of the precipice & cannot realize what they see — their reply to everything is "Impossible! Impossible!" They think nothing possible which is against their wishes.

6 p.m. — . . . Gen. Scott is at last opening his eyes to the fact that I am right & that we are in imminent danger. Providence is aiding me by heavy rains, which are swelling the Potomac, which may be impassable for a week — if so we are saved. If Beauregard comes down upon us soon I have everything ready to make a manoeuvre which will be decisive. Give me two weeks & I will defy Beauregard — in a week the chances will be at least even.

AL copy, McClellan Papers (C-7:63), Library of Congress.

To Charles P. Stone

Letter No. 1   Head Quarters Division of the Potomac
                                 Washington Aug. 18th 1861

Your letter of Aug 17th 1861 10 pm has been received.[1] Information received from Gen Banks today confirms the belief that the enemy intend crossing the Potomac in your vicinity & move on Baltimore or Washington. There are also strong indications of their intention of attempting the passage of the Potomac south of this city near Aquia Creek (where they are erecting strong batteries), or at some other point. I will recommend to you the utmost vigilance and that you continually bear in mind the necessity of securing your retreat towards Rockville whenever you are unable to prevent the passage of the enemy. Gen Banks will be instructed to move up to your support in case of necessity & will also be instructed to effect his retreat in the same direction in conjunction with you should it become necessary. It is still my wish that the enemies passage of the river & subsequent advance should be opposed & retarded to the utmost of your ability to give me time to make my arrangements & come up to your assistance. A general order has been issued merging the departments of N.E. Va, Shenandoah & Balt. into the Dept of the Potomac under my immediate command.[2] Steps have been taken which will secure us a large reinforcement during the coming week. Give me by next courier the exact strength & disposition of your troops.

Hereafter number your letters in series as they are sent & acknowledge the numbers of those received so that I can be sure you receive all sent.

Very Respt yr obdt servt

G B McClellan

Maj Genl

U.S. Army Brig Gen C. P. Stone

Retained copy, McClellan Papers (A-24:11), Library of Congress. *OR*, Ser. 1, V, pp. 567–68. Brig. Gen. Stone commanded a brigade on the upper Potomac, with headquarters at Poolesville, Md.

1. Stone's dispatch reported his arrival at Poolesville, and that he was "unable as yet to discover the presence of any large force opposite." *OR*, Ser. 1, V, p. 567. 2. Aug. 17, 1861, *OR*, Ser. 1, V, p. 567.

To Mary Ellen McClellan

[Washington, August] 19th [1861]

... Beauregard probably has 150,000 men — I cannot count more than 55,000! If this week passes without a battle & reinforcements come in I shall feel sure that a dangerous point is turned.

6 pm. I have been inspecting the defenses over the river & find them quite strong — if they give us a week we shall be so strong on that side that they cannot attack us — or if they do they will be fearfully cut up. We are becoming stronger in our position every day, & I hope for large reinforcements this week.

AL copy, McClellan Papers (C-7:63), Library of Congress.

To the Army of the Potomac

GENERAL ORDERS,   HEADQUARTERS ARMY OF THE POTOMAC,
No. 1.   *Washington, August 20, 1861.*

In accordance with General Order, No. 15, of August 17th, 1861, from the Headquarters of the Army, I hereby assume command of the Army of the Potomac, comprising the troops serving in the former Departments of Washington and Northeastern Virginia, in the valley of the Shenandoah, and in the States of Maryland and Delaware.

The organization of the command into divisions and brigades will be announced hereafter.

The following named officers are attached to the Staff of the Army of the Potomac:

Major S. Williams, Assistant Adjutant General.

Captain A. V. Colburn, Assistant Adjutant General.

Colonel R. B. Marcy, Inspector General.

Col. T. M. Key, Aid-de-camp.

Captain N. B. Sweitzer, 1st Cavalry, Aid-de-camp.

Captain Edward McK. Hudson, 14th Infantry, Aid-de-camp.

Captain Lawrence A. Williams, 10th Infantry, Aid-de-camp.

Major A. J. Meyer, Signal Officer.

Major Stewart Van Vliet, Chief Quartermaster.

Major H. F. Clarke, Chief Commissary.

Surgeon C. S. Tripler, Medical Director.

Major J. G. Barnard, Chief Engineer.

Major J. N. Macomb, Chief Topographical Engineer.

Captain C. P. Kingsbury, Chief of Ordnance.

Brigadier General Geo. Stoneman, Volunteer service,
    Chief of Cavalry.

Brigadier General W. F. Barry, Volunteer service, Chief of Artillery.

GEO. B. MCCLELLAN,
Major General U. S. Army

DP, McClellan Papers (D-12:74), Library of Congress. *OR*, Ser. 1, V, p. 575.

To Abraham Lincoln

His Excellency
Abraham Lincoln   Presdt
Sir   Washington D.C. Aug 20 [1861]

I have just received the enclosed dispatch in cypher. Col Marcy knows what he says, & is of the coolest judgment.[1]

I recommend that the Secty of War ascertain at once by telegram how the enlistment proceeds in N.Y. & elsewhere, & that if it is not proceeding with great rapidity drafts be made at once. We must have men without delay.

Very respectfully your obdt svt
Geo B McClellan
Maj Genl USA

ALS, Lincoln Papers, Library of Congress.

1. Marcy's telegram, sent from New York that day, read: "I urge you to instantly make a positive and unconditional demand for an immediate draft of the additional troops you require. Men will not volunteer now, & drafting is the only successful plan. The people will applaud such a course, rely upon it." Lincoln Papers.

To Mary Ellen McClellan

[Washington, August] 20th [1861]

... If Beauregard does not attack this week he is foolish — he has given me infinite advantages & you may be sure I have not neglected the opportunity. Every day adds to the strength of my defenses, to the perfection of the organization & some little to our forces. I have now about 80 field guns (there were but 49 at Bull Run) & by Saturday [August 24] will have 112. There were only some 400 cavalry at Bull Run — I now have about 1200, & by the close of the week will have some 3000. I am gaining rapidly in every way — I can now defend Washington with almost perfect certainty. When I came here it could have been taken with the utmost ease. In a week I ought to be perfectly safe & be prepared to defend all Maryland — in another week to advance our positions.

The men were very enthusiastic & looked well. My old State will come out handsomely....

I appeared today for the first time in full tog, chapeau, epaulettes etc — & flattered myself "we" did it well — at least Barry & Kingsbury told me they were quite jealous about what their wives said. I have been much vexed tonight by sundry troublesome things, & fear that I have been very cross; the only comfort has been your Father's arrival, which is a great relief to me — I like to see that cool steady head near me.

AL copy; copy, McClellan Papers (C-7:63/D-10:72), Library of Congress.

To Mary Ellen McClellan

[Washington, August] 23rd [1861]

... Yesterday I rode to Alexandria & reviewed 4 Brigades, that is 17 rgts ...

Beauregard has missed his chance, & I have gained what I most needed — time! ...

I do not *live* at all. Merely exist, worked & worried half to death. I have no privacy, no leisure, no relaxation, except in reading your letters & writing to you. We take our meals at Wormley's, a "colored gentleman" who keeps a restaurant just around the corner in "I" Street. I take breakfast there pretty regularly; sometimes have it sent over here. As to dinner, it takes its chances, & generally gets no chance at all, as it is often ten o'clock when I get back from my ride & have nothing to eat all day....

Glad to hear that McCook is looking so well. I will try to have his Brigade ordered on here.[1]

AL copy; copy, McClellan Papers (C-7:63/D-10:72), Library of Congress.

1. Probably either Robert L. McCook or his brother, Alexander McD. McCook. Both remained in the western theater.

To Simon Cameron

Head Qtrs Army of the Potomac
[Washington] Aug 24 1861

Respectfully referred to the Hon Secty of War with the recommendation that the request of Gov Andrews be at once granted.[1] I do not think it possible to employ our Army officers to more advantage than in comdg Divisions, Brigades & Regts of new troops, particularly when it is remembered that we have almost *none* of the old troops at our disposal.

Geo B McClellan
Maj Genl USA comdg

ALS, Records of the Adjutant General's Office, RG 94 (M-619:38), National Archives, *OR*, Ser. 3, 1, pp. 444–45.

1. This endorsement is on a letter dated Aug. 22 that GBM received from Gov. John A. Andrew of Massachusetts. Andrew sought the appointment of a regular army officer, Capt. Thomas J. C. Amory, 7th U. S. Infantry, to command the newly formed 17th Massachusetts. The appointment was made.

To Simon Cameron

Head Quarters, Army of the Potomac,
Sir: Washington, August 25th, 1861

I would respectfully suggest that a circular be sent from your Department to the Governors of the several States from which Volunteers have been accepted, requesting that *no* regiments hereafter to be received, whether raised under the authority of the Governors or of the Department, may be uniformed in gray, that being the color generally worn by the enemy.[1]

Very respectfully, your mo. obt. servt.
Geo B McClellan
Major General U.S.A.

Hon. Simon Cameron
Secretary of War.

LS, Records of the Office of the Secretary of War, RG 107 (M-221:193), National Archives. *OR*, Ser. 3, I, p. 453.

1. GBM had made a similar request, following the western Virginia campaign, of the governor of Indiana. GBM to Oliver P. Morton, July 21, McClellan Papers (A-22:10), Library of Congress.

To Mary Ellen McClellan

[Washington] Aug 25 [1861]

Yesterday started at 9 am — rode over Long Bridge & reviewed Richardson's Brigade — then went 3 miles further & at 12 reviewed Blenker's Brigade at Roach's Mills — then rode some 10 miles looking for a position in which to fight a battle to cover Alexandria should it be attacked. I found one which satisfies me entirely, & where I can surely beat M de Beauregard should he arrive to pay his respects. I then returned to Fort Runyon near the head of Long Bridge & reviewed the 21st N.Y. — after which reviewed 4 Batteries of Light Artillery....

This morning telegram from other side announcing enemy advancing in force. Started off Aides & put the wires at work — when fairly started alarm found false....

Friend Beauregard has allowed the chance to escape him. I have now some 65,000 effective men — will have 75,000 by end of week. Last week he certainly had double our force. I feel sure that the dangerous moment has passed.

AL copy, McClellan Papers (C-7:63), Library of Congress.

To William S. Harney

Brig Gen W S Harney
US Army   Head Quarters Army of the Potomac
General   Washington Aug 30th 1861

I was much surprised and grieved when I received a few moments since, your telegram of to-night. I had understood from several officers that you desired to enter again upon active service, and that it was your wish to serve in the East rather than in the West.[1]

It is probably my misfortune that chance has placed me in command of the main army of the U.S. — supposing that you wished to serve in the field I embraced the earliest opportunity to offer you the highest position in my gift, and took no little trouble to accomplish this purpose.

I did all this in a manner that I thought to be eminently respectful towards you, and having fully in mind the difference between your experience and mine. I wish to say that I was guided by the kindest possible feelings towards you — and that it was my desire to place you in the position I thought you eminently qualified to fill. You have chosen to pursue a very extraordinary course — your telegraphic message is, to say the least of it, difficult to explain.

I have too much respect for your age and rank to comment upon it — & have only to add that I do not feel that you have any longer any claim upon me as a fellow soldier — though I was this morning very anxious to see you.[2]

Very respectfully your obdt servt,
[George B. McClellan]
Maj. Gen'l U.S.A.

Retained copy, Records of U.S. Army Continental Commands, RG 393 (3964: Army of the Potomac), National Archives.

1. Brig. Gen. Harney, third-ranking Federal general at the beginning of the war, had been relieved of command of the Department of the West on May 29. On Aug. 30 GBM wired him an offer of a division in the Army of the Potomac: "I feel sure that in the present emergency you will waive all considerations of previous rank & will cheerfully give to this army the prestige of your name & presence." Harney replied: "Your telegraph is just received. I consider your conduct to say the least of it exceedingly impertinent." McClellan Papers (A-25:11), Library of Congress. 2. Harney played no further role in the war.

To Mary Ellen McClellan

[Washington] Aug 31 [1861]

Drove out yesterday as far as McCall's camp & today down over the river for several hours — have not yet ventured on horseback again — may try it tomorrow.[1] . . .

Our defenses are becoming very strong now & the army is increasing in efficiency & numbers quite rapidly. I think Beauregard has abandoned the idea of crossing the river above us & I learned today again that my movements had entirely disconcerted their plans & that they did not know what to do. They are suffering much from sickness, & I fancy are not in the best possible condition. If they venture to attack us here they will have an awful time of it — I do not think they will dare to attack — we are now ready for them altho' I would much like another week to complete my arrangements. The news from every quarter tonight is favorable — all goes well.

AL copy, McClellan Papers (C-7:63), Library of Congress.

1. GBM had been ill for nearly a week.

To Simon Cameron

Hon Simon Cameron
Secty of War   Head Quarters Army of the Potomac
Sir   Washington Sept. 6, 1861

I have the honor to suggest the following proposition with the request that the necessary authority be at once given me to carry it out: to organize a force of two brigades of five regiments each of New England men, for the general service, but particularly adapted to coast service. The officers and men to be sufficiently conversant with boat service to manage steamers, sailing vessels, launches, barges, surf boats, floating batteries &c. To charter or buy for the command a sufficient number of propellers, or tugboats for transportation of men and supplies, the machinery of which should be amply protected by timber; the vessels to have permanent experienced officers from the merchant service, but to be manned by details from the command. A naval officer to be attached to the staff of the commanding officer. The flank companies of each regiment to be armed with Dahlgren boat guns, and carbines with water proof cartridges; the other companies to have such arms as I may hereafter designate, to be uniformed and equipped as the Rhode Island regiments are. Launches and floating batteries with timber parapets of sufficient capacity to land or bring into action the entire force.

The entire management and organization of the force to be under my control, and to form an integral part of the Army of the Potomac.

The immediate object of this force is for operations in the inlets of Chesapeake Bay and the Potomac; by enabling me to thus put and land troops at points where they are needed; this force can also be used in conjunction with a naval force operating against points on the sea coast. This Coast Division to be commanded by a general officer of my selection. The regiments to be organized as other land forces. The disbursements for vessels &c to be made by the proper departments of the Army upon the requisitions of the general commanding the Division with my approval.

I think the entire force can be organized in thirty days, and by no means the least of the advantages of this proposition is the fact that it will call into the service a class of men who would not otherwise enter the Army. You will immediately perceive that the object of this force is to follow along the Coast, and up the inlets and rivers, the movement of the Main Army when it advances.[1]

> I am very respectfully your obt servant
> G B McClellan
> Maj Genl Comdg

Copy, McClellan Papers (D-7:69), Library of Congress. *OR,* Ser. 1, V, pp. 586–87.

1. This proposition eventually took the form of the Burnside expedition to the North Carolina coast in February 1862.

To General Officers, Army of the Potomac

Head Quarters, Army of the Potomac,
Genl Orders No [7]   Washington, Sept 6, 1861

The Major Genl Comdg desires & requests that in future there may be a more perfect respect for the Sabbath on the part of his command. We are fighting in a holy cause, & should endeavor to deserve the benign favor of the Creator. Unless in the case of an attack by the enemy, or some other extreme military necessity, it is commended to Comdg officers that all work shall be suspended on the Sabbath, that no unnecessary movements shall be made on that day, that the men shall as far as possible be permitted to rest from their labors, that they shall attend divine service

after the customary Sunday morning inspection, & that officers & men
shall alike use their influence to ensure the utmost decorum & quiet on
that day. The Genl Comdg regards this as no idle form — one day's rest
in seven is necessary to men & animals; — more than this — we owe at
least this small tribute of respect to the God of Mercy & of Battles whom
we believe to be on our side.[1]

Geo B McClellan
Maj Genl Comdg

ADfS, McClellan Papers (A-26:12), Library of Congress. OR, Ser. 1, LI, Part 1, pp. 472–
73.

1. This concluding passage was altered to read (as printed in the *Official Records*), "More
than this, the observance of the holy day of the God of Mercy and of Battles is our sacred
duty."

To Abraham Lincoln

Confidential
His Excellency
Abraham Lincoln   Head Quarters, Army of the Potomac,
Sir: Washington, Sept 6, 1861

I sincerely doubt whether the officer you alluded to is exactly the right
man for the particular place, although he is invaluable in the duty to
which I have assigned him.[1] You well know, Mr. President, that every
man has a peculiar fitness for some particular duty — such is the case in
this instance. It would *very* seriously impair the efficiency of this army
were he to be removed from it. I would suggest for your consideration
the name of Genl E. A. Hitchcock, late of the Army (Chief of Genl
Scott's staff during the Mexican war), & now a resident of St Louis as
probably eminently adapted for the duty in question. I understand that
Genl H. has offered his services to the Govt. I think this will be a happy
solution of the difficulty. Genl Scott can tell you all about Genl H.[2]

I am sure you will appreciate my motives in being so anxious to retain
the services of such officers as Genls Buell,[3] Stoneman etc whose appoint-
ment I asked for with special reference to service in this army — on the
efficiency of which depends the fate of the nation.

Very respectfully & truly yours
Geo B McClellan
Maj Genl USA

ALS, Lincoln Papers, Library of Congress.

1. Gen. Scott had proposed Brig. Gen. George Stoneman, GBM's chief of cavalry, as chief
of staff to Gen. Frémont in the Western Department. Scott to Lincoln, Sept. 5, Lincoln
Papers. 2. The post was not filled, and Frémont was relieved on Nov. 2. Ethan Allen
Hitchcock was appointed a major general in Feb. 1862. 3. Brig. Gen. Don Carlos Buell
was slated to command a division in the Army of the Potomac.

To Mary Ellen McClellan

[Washington, September] 6th/61

I *must* ride much every day for my army covers much space, & unfortunately I have no one on my staff to whom I can entrust the safety of affairs — it is necessary for me to see as much as I can every day, & more than that to let the men see me & gain confidence in me. . . .

I started out about 3 this afternoon & returned at 10 — rode down to the vicinity of Alexandria & on my return (en route) received a dispatch to the effect that the rebels at 6 1/2 this morning were breaking up their camp at Manassas — whether to attack or retreat I do not yet know.[1] If they attack they will in all probability be beaten, & the attack ought to take place tomorrow. I have made every possible preparation & feel ready for them. . . .

AL copy, McClellan Papers (C-7:63), Library of Congress.

1. Randolph Marcy telegraphed GBM on this date: "I am informed that the enemy at Manassas struck their tents and packed their wagons at seven this morning. I send the informer to meet you. . . ." McClellan Papers (A-26:12).

To Mary Ellen McClellan

[Washington, c. September 7, 1861]

. . . Do not expect Beauregard to attack — will not be ready to advance (ourselves) before November. . . .

AL copy, McClellan Papers (C-7:63), Library of Congress.

To Simon Cameron

Hon Simon Cameron
Secy of War   Head Quarters, Army of the Potomac
Sir.   Washington, September 8th 1861.

Your note of yesterday is received.[1] I concur in your views as to the exigency of the present occasion. I appreciate and cordially thank you for your offers of support and will avail myself of them to the fullest extent demanded by the interests of the Country.

The force of all our arms within the immediate vicinity of Washington is nearly eighty five thousand men. The effective portion of this force is more than sufficient to resist with certain success any attack on our works upon the other side of the river. By calling in the commands of Genls Banks and Stone it will probably be sufficient to defend the City of Washington, from whatever direction it may be assailed. It is well understood that although the ultimate design of the enemy is to possess himself of the City of Washington, his first efforts will probably be directed towards Baltimore, with the intention of cutting our line of communications and supplies as well as to arouse an insurrection in Maryland. To accomplish this, he will no doubt show a certain portion of his force in front of our positions on the other side of the Potomac, in order to engage our attention there and induce us to leave a large portion of our force for the defence of those positions. He will probably also make demonstrations in the vicinity of Aquia Creek, Mathias Point and Occoquan, in order still further to induce us to disseminate our forces. His main and real movement will doubtless be, to cross the Potomac between Washington and Point of Rocks, probably not far from Seneca Falls, and most likely at more points than one. His hope will be so to engage our attention by the diversions already named, as to enable him to move with a large force direct and unopposed on Baltimore. I see no reason to doubt the possibility of his attempting this with a column of at least one hundred thousand effective troops; if he has only one hundred and thirty thousand under arms, he can make all the diversions I have mentioned with his raw and badly armed troops, leaving one hundred thousand effective men for his real movement. As I am now situated, I can by no possibility bring to bear against this column more than seventy thousand and probably not over sixty thousand effective troops.

In regard to the composition of our Active Army, it must be borne in mind, that the very important arms of Cavalry and Artillery had been almost entirely neglected until I assumed command of this Army, and that consequently the troops of these arms, although greatly increased in numbers, are comparatively raw and inexperienced, most of the Cavalry not being yet armed or equipped.

In making the foregoing estimate of numbers I have reduced the enemy's force below what is regarded by the War Department and other official circles as its real strength, and have taken the reverse course as to our own. Our situation then is simply this. If the Commander in Chief of the enemy follows the simplest dictates of the military art, we must meet him with greatly inferior forces. To render success possible, the Divisions of our Army must be more ably led and commanded, than those of the enemy. The fate of the nation and the success of the cause in which we are engaged, must be mainly decided by the issue of the next battle, to be fought by the Army now under my command. I therefore feel, that the interests of the nation demand that the ablest soldiers in the Service should be on duty with the Army of the Potomac, and that contenting ourselves with remaining on the defensive for the present at all other points, this Army should be reinforced at once, by all the disposable troops that the East and West and North can furnish.[2] To ensure present success, the portions of the Army available for active operations should be at least equal to any force which it may be called to encounter. To accomplish this, it is necessary that it should be at once and very largely reinforced. For ulterior results and to bring this war to a speedy close, it will be necessary that our Active Army shall be much superior to the enemy in numbers, so as to make it reasonably certain, that we shall win every battle which we fight and at the same time be able to cover our communications as we advance. I would also urgently recommend, that the whole of the regular army — old and new — be at once ordered to report here, excepting the mounted batteries actually serving in other departments, and the minimum number of companies of Artillery actually necessary to form the nucleus of the garrisons of our most important permanent works. There should be no delay in carrying out this measure. Scattered as the regulars now are, they are nowhere strong enough to produce a marked effect; united in one body, they will ensure the success of this Army.

In organizing the Army of the Potomac, I have selected General and Staff Officers with distinct reference to their fitness for the important duties that may devolve upon them. Any change or disposition of such officers, without consulting the Commanding General, may fatally impair the efficiency of this Army and the success of its operations. I therefore earnestly request, that in future every General Officer appointed upon my recommendation shall be assigned to this Army; that I shall have full control of the officers and troops within this Department; and that no orders shall be given respecting my command, without my being first consulted. It is evident that I can not otherwise be responsible for the success of our arms. In this connection I respectfully insist that Brigadier Generals Don Carlos Buell and J F Reynolds, both appointed upon my recommendation and for the purpose of serving with me, be at once so assigned.[3]

In obedience to your request I have thus frankly stated "in what manner you can at present aid me in the performance of the great duty committed to my charge," and I shall continue to communicate with you in the same spirit.

> Very respectfully Your Obt Servt
> Geo B McClellan
> Maj Genl Comdg

Retained copy, Records of the Adjutant General's Office, RG 94 (M-619:41), National Archives, *OR*, Ser. 1, V, pp. 587–89.

1. Cameron wrote, on Sept. 7: "It is evident that we are on the eve of a great battle — one that may decide the fate of the country. Its success must depend on you, and the means that may be placed at your disposal. Impressed with this belief, and anxious to aid you with all the powers of my Department, I will be glad if you will inform me how I can do so." McClellan Papers (A-26:12), Library of Congress. 2. In a draft for this letter, GBM was more specific: "In view of these facts I respectfully urge that all the available troops in Ohio, Indiana, Michigan, Wisconsin and at least ten thousand Illinois troops (there being fifteen thousand there unarmed) and all those of the Eastern and Northern states be at once directed to report to me for duty. I beg leave to repeat the opinion I have

heretofore expressed that the Army of the Potomac should number not less than three
hundred thousand men in order to insure complete success and an early termination of the
war.'' McClellan Papers (A-26:12). **3.** Buell would soon command a division, and John F.
Reynolds a brigade, in the Army of the Potomac.

To Mary Ellen McClellan

[Washington] Sept [11, 1861]

I started early in the day to be present at the presentation of colors
to McCall's division by Gov. Curtin.[1] It was long & fatiguing. I then rode
over the Chain Bridge & back by Fort Corcoran. When I returned I had
a great deal of tedious work to do & fell asleep in the midst of it. This
morning I have had a siege with the Sanitary Committee[2] & don't think
I will ride out today. How did you learn that Buckner & Smith have
joined the rebel army? I can hardly believe it.[3]

You have no idea how the men brighten up now, when I go among
them — I can see every eye glisten. Yesterday they nearly pulled me to
pieces in one regt. You never heard such yelling. I did not think the
Presdt liked it much. Did I tell you that Lawrence Williams has been
promoted & leaves my staff? I do not in the least doubt his loyalty.[4] I
enclose a card just received from ''A. Lincoln'' — it shows too much
deference to be seen outside.[5]

Copy, McClellan Papers (D-10:72), Library of Congress.

1. This review of the Pennsylvania Reserves, on Sept. 10, was attended by President Lincoln
and Secretary of War Cameron as well as Pennsylvania's Gov. Curtin. 2. A committee of
the U.S. Sanitary Commission, a civilian group organized to promote the welfare of the
troops. 3. Simon B. Buckner and Gustavus W. Smith, close army friends of GBM's, had
recently entered the Confederate service. 4. Lawrence A. Williams was appointed major
of the 6th U.S. Cavalry on Sept. 7. His Virginia background had caused him to be suspected
of disloyalty. 5. Probably an undated note from Lincoln reading: ''May I not now appoint
[Isaac I.] Stevens a Brig. Genl? I wish to do it.'' McClellan Papers (A-27:12).

To Winfield Scott   [TELEGRAM]

To Gen'l W Scott   Smiths Qrs near Chain Bridge
President Lincoln and Secy War   Sep 11 1861

Gen'l Smith[1] made reconnaissance with two thousand men to Lewins-
ville, remained several hours & completed examination of the ground.
When work was completed & the command had started back the enemy
opened fire with shell, killing two men & wounding three.

Griffin's battery silenced the enemy's battery.

Our men then came back in perfect order & excellent spirits. They
behaved most admirably under fire.

We shall have no more *Bull Run* affairs.

Geo. B. McClellan
Maj Gen'l USA

Received copy, Records of the Office of the Secretary of War, RG 107 (M-504:9), National Archives. *OR*, Ser. 1, V, pp. 167–68.

1. Brig. Gen. William F. Smith.

To Nathaniel P. Banks

Headquarters Army of the Potomac
Washington Sept. 12, 1861

Genl: After full consultation with the President, Secretaries of State, War &c. it has been decided to effect the operation proposed for the 17th.[1]

Arrangements have been made to have a Govt. steamer at Annapolis to receive the prisoners & carry them to their destination.

Some 4 or 5 of the chief men in the affair are to be arrested to-day.[2] When they meet on the 17th you will please have everything prepared to arrest the whole party, and be sure that none escape.

It is understood that you arranged with Genl Dix & Gov. Seward[3] the *modus operandi*. It has been intimated to me that the meeting might take place on the 14th. Please be prepared. I would be glad to have you advise me frequently of your arrangement in regard to this very important matter.

If it is successfully carried out it will go far toward breaking the backbone of the rebellion. It would probably be well to have a special train quietly prepared to take prisoners to Annapolis.

I leave this exceedingly important affair to your tact & discretion & have but one thing to impress upon you — the absolute necessity of secrecy & success.[4]

With the highest regard, I am my dear Genl. your sincere friend
Geo B. Mc.
Maj Genl U.S.A.

Retained copy, McClellan Papers (B-26:12), Library of Congress. The contents indicate Banks as the addressee.

1. On Sept. 11 Banks was notified by Secretary of War Cameron that it was believed that the Maryland legislature, meeting in Frederick, would secretly pass an ordinance of secession. "If necessary all or any part of the members must be arrested," Cameron wrote. *OR*, Ser. 2, I, pp. 678–79. 2. On orders drafted by GBM, these arrests were carried out in Baltimore under the direction of Allan Pinkerton. *OR*, Ser. 2, I, pp. 678, 688. 3. Maj. Gen. John A. Dix, in command at Baltimore; Secretary of State William H. Seward. 4. Banks carried out arrests on Sept. 17. *OR*, Ser. 2, I, pp. 684–85. See also GBM to Samuel S. Cox, Feb. 12, 1864, *infra*.

To Simon Cameron

Hon Simon Cameron
Secy of War.   Head Quarters, Army of the Potomac,
Sir   Washington, September 13th, 1861 12 PM.

The movement of the enemy so far as discovered by us and information reaching us from many directions and sources all indicate that the enemy intend at a very early day to advance; even that he has already commenced the movement. It is also more than probable that he has been and is now concentrating all his forces in front of us — and that for this purpose he has called to his aid a large portion of the troops formerly operating in Missouri and on the line of the Mississippi — if this be true it is evident that the decisive battle of the War is soon to be fought in this vicinity — it is therefore clear that we must follow the enemy's example and reinforce the Army of the Potomac by all our available troops. I am told that Genl Fremont has some fifty thousand troops in the vicinity of St Louis; if this is the case the safety of the nation requires that twenty five thousand of them be sent here without one day's delay; and that the orders already given for other troops to be sent from the West and East to this Army should be repeated and steps taken to insure immediate compliance with them. Unless the force of the enemy is greatly overrated and all the information I have received concerning it be erroneous it will be found when we meet in the field, that their Active Army outnumbers ours by nearly two to one.

very respectfully your obt servt
Geo B McClellan
Maj Genl USA

[enclosure]

Total present for duty in Army of Potomac	122,072
Deduct Genl Dix at Baltimore	7,323
Present on line of Potomac	114,749
deduct Banks & Stone[1]	21,523
Present in vicinity of Washington	93,226
Deduct T. W. Sherman's rgts[2]	8,000
Present at Washington belonging there	84,226[3]
deduct garrison — say	25,000
Leaving here available for active movements	59,226[4]
Add Banks & Stone if rebels cross only to north	21,523
	80,749[5]

The enemy probably have 170,000!

LS (enclosure AD), Cameron Papers, Library of Congress.

1. The commands of Banks and Stone were stationed on the upper Potomac. 2. Brig. Gen. Thomas W. Sherman's expedition was scheduled to attack Port Royal, S.C. 3. This figure should be 85,226. 4. This figure should be 60,226. 5. This total should be 81,749.

To Nathaniel P. Banks

Maj Genl N P Banks   Head Quarters Army of Potomac
Genl,   Washington Sep 16 1861

Your letter of the 15 to the Secy of State has been sent to me. I think you misapprehend the state of affairs.

By General Order No 15 you are, as the Comdr of a division of Vols. entitled to two Aides & one Asst Adjt. Genl. — the Aides to be selected from the company officers of your division, the Adjt. Genl. to be appointed by the President who will no doubt appoint any one you may select. I do not believe it will be possible to give you one of the Regular Adjts. Genls. You have an officer of Topographical Engrs. & a regular Qr. Mr.

No idea has been entertained by me of taking Bests battery from you. On the contrary I had directed that the suggestion be made to you to fill its ranks by details from the volunteers.

As to the regular Cavalry — I have directed all of it to be concentrated in one mass that the numbers in each company may be increased & that I may have a reliable & efficient body on which to depend in a battle.

For all present duty of Cavalry in the upper Potomac volunteers will suffice as they will have nothing to do but carry messages & act as videttes.

Arms will be sent for them as soon as obtained.

Clothing will soon be ready & will be sent at the earliest possible moment. Shoes, socks, underclothing, drawers etc will be sent you at once.

I will send you 800 rifled arms with the supply of stores etc.

I think General that you forget that the present duty of your division is simply to support the division of Genl Stone in opposing any attempt of the enemy to cross the River & that if such an attempt bids fair to succeed I am ready to move up with my large reinforcements & assume command myself.

So long as the purposes of the enemy are uncertain it is necessary for me to hold the mass of the Army concentrated in such a position that it can readily move wherever required.

It may be well for me to state that these measures are taken in consequence of what passed at our interview of Saturday [September 14][1] & are not brought about by your letter to the Hon Secty of State.

If you will fully communicate your wants direct to me through the proper military channel you will find that they will meet the most prompt attention possible, as I feel the same interest in the efficiency of your division that I do in any other portion of the Army under my command

& fully realize that its advanced position renders it necessary that it should in every respect be efficient.

I am General very truly yours
Geo B McClellan
Maj Genl USA

LS, William Henry Seward Papers, Rush Rhees Library, University of Rochester.

1. GBM had met with a number of his field commanders at Rockville, Md., on Sept. 14.

To Simon Cameron

Hd Qtrs Army of the Potomac
Washington Sept 16 1861

I cannot recommend the appointment of General Cadwallader, I do not think it would promote the interests of the country. If he be appointed from any political considerations — which I do not think are proper to be considered in the present exigency — I would respectfully request that he may not be assigned to duty with the Army under my command.[1]

Very respectfully your obt svt
Geo B McClellan
Maj Genl USA

ALS, Cameron Papers, Library of Congress.

1. This is written on the back of a sheet of letters recommending George Cadwalader, a brigadier general of volunteers in the Mexican War and a prominent Philadelphia Democrat, for appointment as a general officer. The president endorsed his approval, and Cameron's endorsement read: "I will be very glad to act in this matter as General McClellan will advise." Cadwalader was not commissioned a major general until April 1862.

To Mary Ellen McClellan

[Washington, c. September 18, 1861]

... The enemy keeps very quiet & do not seem disposed to move just now — the arrest of the Maryland Legislature has no doubt taken them by surprise & defeated their calculations. ...

AL copy, McClellan Papers (C-7:63), Library of Congress.

To William B. Sprague

Rev W B Sprague
Albany   Head Quarters Army of the Potomac
My dear Sir   Washington Sept 27 1861

Dr Thompson has been kind enough to send me your letter to him of the 14 inst.[1]

I confess that I do not appreciate the importance & interest you attach to the autograph of one whose future is so entirely beyond his own control as mine is.

I do not yet realize or comprehend how I am placed in my present position, & — without affectation — I full realize that the future is not in my hands, but in that of the Diety, to whom we all sincerely pray that he may be pleased to give success to our cause, which to us seems righteous.

While I implicitly believe that the good God can cause the weak to overcome the strong, I still feel that it is our duty to avail ourselves of all the mundane advantages we may happen to possess — therefore I have done all in my power to increase the strength, as well as to improve the discipline & morale of the Army that I have the honor to command — & I am sure that you will be pleased to learn that the Army of the Potomac is rapidly becoming a magnificent Army. It is not only becoming organized, disciplined & well instructed — but, more than all, I feel sure that the moral tone of the men is improving.

We have a splendid body of men — their impulses & feelings are just & honorable — I have not been able to detect among them that profanity & irreligion of which they have been often accused — I think that, as a mass, our Army is composed of the best men who ever formed an army.

I ask only for the delay necessary to make a real army of them — that public opinion shall not urge us to premature action — & I feel confident that, with God's blessing, we have seen our last defeat.

If you could witness the enthusiasm of the troops, their subordination, their confidence & desire to meet the enemy — I am sure that you would agree with me in feeling confident of success.

Thanking you for your kind expressions

I am, my dear sir, truly your friend
Geo B McClellan
Maj Genl USA Comdg

ALS, Houghton Library, Harvard University.

1. In a letter dated Sept. 11, Rev. L. S. Thompson, an acquaintance of GBM's from Cincinnati, asked for a signed document of some sort for his friend Rev. William B. Sprague, "a famous autograph collector." GBM probably misstated the date of Sprague's letter to Thompson. McClellan Papers (B-8:47), Library of Congress.

To Mary Ellen McClellan

[Washington] Sept 27 1861

He (the Presdt) sent a carriage for me to meet him & the Cabinet at Genl Scott's office. Before we got through the General "raised a row with me." I kept cool, looked him square in the face, & *rather* I think I got the advantage of him. In the course of the conversation he very strongly intimated that we were no longer friends. I said nothing, merely looked at him, & bowed assent. He tried to avoid me when we left, but I walked square up to him, looked him fully in the eye, extended my hand & said "Good Morning, General Scott." He had to take my hand, & so we parted. As he threw down the glove & I took it up, I presume war is declared — so be it. I do not fear him. I have one strong point; that I do not care one iota for my present position.[1]

Copy, McClellan Papers (D-10:72), Library of Congress.

1. In what Gideon Welles in his diary recalled as an "unpleasant interview," Gen. Scott made objection that he could get no information on the numbers and condition of the Army of the Potomac, and implied that GBM was instead informing members of the Cabinet. *Diary of Gideon Welles*, ed. Howard K. Beale (New York, 1960), I, pp. 241–42.

To Mary Ellen McClellan

[Washington, September 29, 1861]

A most unhappy thing occurred last night, among some of W. F. Smith's raw rgts. They three times mistook each other for the enemy & fired into each other. At least 6 were killed, & several wounded, besides two horses killed.[1] It is dangerous to make night marches on that account, but Smith's march was delayed by causes I could not foresee, & it was necessary to advance at all hazards. The manoeuvring in advance by our flanks alarmed the enemy whose centre at Munson's & Upton's was much advanced.[2] As soon as our pickets informed me that he had fallen back I rushed forward & seized those very important points. We now hold them in strength & have at once proceeded to fortify them. The moral effect of this advance will be great & it will have a bad influence on the troops of the enemy. They can no longer say that they are flaunting their dirty little flag in my face, & I hope they have taken their last look at Washn . . .

Copy, McClellan Papers (D-10:72), Library of Congress.

1. The *National Intelligencer* for Sept. 30 reported the casualties in Brig. Gen. William F. Smith's division as nine killed and twenty-one wounded. 2. Munson's Hill and Upton's Hill, near Falls Church, Va., were Confederate outposts.

To Simon Cameron

The Hon Simon Cameron
Sect of War   Head Quarters, Army of the Potomac
Sir   Washington, Sept 30th, 1861.

I submit for your perusal a report of a reconnaissance made by Genl J. G. Barnard Corps of Engineers as far as Mathias Point.[1] I beg to say that I fully concur in his views.

I have made all the necessary arrangements to send tonight a strong party (4000 men) under Brig Genl D. C. Buell to cut away the timber on Mathias Point. If this meets your views the expedition will be carried out, unless something turns up during the day to make it necessary to move this command in a different direction.[2] Either this same party or a command to be detached by Genl Franklin will do the same thing at White House Point.[3]

Will you be kind enough to signify your approval or disapproval of the measures I have taken.[4]

> I am Sir very Respectfully your Obt Servt.
> Geo B McClellan
> Maj Genl USA

LS, Cameron Papers, Library of Congress.

1. The report of Sept. 28 by Brig. Gen. John G. Barnard, GBM's chief engineer, dealt with a threatened blockade of the lower Potomac by Confederate batteries. *OR*, Ser. 1, V, pp. 606–608. 2. Neither this expedition nor one scheduled subsequently were carried out, and the Confederate blockade was established without opposition. Gustavus V. Fox testimony, *Report of the Joint Committee on the Conduct of the War*, I (1863), pp. 240–41. 3. Brig. Gen. William B. Franklin; no attack was made on Whitestone Point. 4. Cameron replied on this date: ''The measures you have taken . . . meet my entire approval.'' Cameron Papers.

To Mary Ellen McClellan

[Washington] Oct. 2nd [1861]

. . . Genl Gibson's funeral takes place this morning.[1] I have to go, though I can ill afford the time. . . .

I am becoming daily more disgusted with this administration — perfectly sick of it. If I could with honor resign I would quit the whole concern tomorrow; but so long as I can be of any real use to the nation in its trouble I will make the sacrifice. No one seems able to comprehend my real feeling — that I have no ambitious feelings to gratify, & only want to serve my country in its trouble, & when this weary war is over to return to my wife. . . .

AL copy, McClellan Papers (C-7:63), Library of Congress.

1. Maj. Gen. George Gibson died Sept. 29.

To Mary Ellen McClellan

[Washington] Oct 6 [1861]

. . . I am quite sure that we will spend some time together after your recovery — preparations are slow & I have an infinite deal to do before my army is really ready to fight a great battle. Washington may now be looked upon as quite safe — they cannot attack in front. My flanks are also safe, or soon will be. Then I shall take my own time to make an army that will be sure of success . . .

Genl Scott did try to send some of my troops to Kentucky, but did not succeed — he has become my inveterate enemy! They shall not take any from here if I can help it. The real fighting must be here — that in Ky will be a mere bagatelle — you need not be at all alarmed by any apprehensions you hear expressed. The trouble with Genl Scott has simply arisen from his eternal jealousy of all who acquire any distinction. I have endeavored to treat him with the utmost respect, but it is of no avail; let him do what he chooses. . . .

I do not expect to fight a battle near Washington — probably none will be fought until I advance, & that I will not do until I am fully ready. My plans depend upon circumstances — so soon as I feel that my army is well organized & well disciplined & strong enough, I will advance & force the rebels to a battle on a field of my own selection. A long time must yet elapse before I can do this, & I expect all the newspapers to abuse me for delay — but I will not mind that.

AL copy, McClellan Papers (C-7:63), Library of Congress.

To Mary Ellen McClellan

[Washington] Oct 10 [1861]

I have just time to write a very few lines before starting out. Yesterday I threw forward our right some four miles, but the enemy were not accommodating enough to give me a chance at them, so I took up a new position there & reinforced it by sending McCall over to that side. I am now going over again to satisfy myself as to the state of affairs, & perhaps edge up another mile or so — according to circumstances. When I returned yesterday after a long ride I was obliged to attend a meeting of the Cabinet at 8 pm. & was bored & annoyed. There are some of the greatest geese in the Cabinet I have ever seen — enough to tax the patience of Job. . . .

AL copy, McClellan Papers (C-7:63), Library of Congress.

To Mary Ellen McClellan

[Washington] Friday [c. October 11, 1861]

Yesterday rode to Chain Bridge, thence to Upton's Hill & did not get back until after dark.

I can't tell you how disgusted I am becoming with these wretched politicians — they are a most dispicable set of men & I think Seward is the meanest of them all — a meddling, officious, incompetent little puppy — he has done more than any other one man to bring all this misery upon the country & is one of the least competent to get us out of the scrape. The Presdt is nothing more than a well meaning baboon. Welles is weaker than the most garrulous old woman you were ever annoyed by. Bates[1] is a good inoffensive old man — so it goes — only keep these complimentary opinions to yourself, or you may get me into premature trouble. I believe I have choked off Seward already — & have strong hopes that he will keep himself to his own business hereafter. . . .

AL copy, McClellan Papers (C-7:63), Library of Congress.

1. Attorney General Edward Bates.

To Mary Ellen McClellan   [TELEGRAM]

Mrs. Geo McClellan   [Lewinsville, Va.] Oct 12 1861

I thank God you are safe.[1] I am this moment looking after the enemy.[2] Will be in the saddle all day. Telegraph me frequently. All goes well here.

Geo B McClellan

Received copy, McClellan Papers (B-8:47), Library of Congress.

1. Mrs. McClellan gave birth to a daughter, Mary (or May, as she would be called), that morning. Mary M. Marcy telegram to GBM, Oct. 12, McClellan Papers (B-8:47). 2. It was believed (wrongly) that the Confederates were readying an attack.

To Mary Ellen McClellan

[Washington] Oct 13th [1861]

I am firmly determined to force the issue with Genl Scott — a very few days will determine whether his policy or mine is to prevail — *he* is for inaction & the defensive, he endeavors to cripple me in every way — yet I see that the newspapers begin to accuse me of want of energy. He has even complained to the War Dept of my making the advance of the last few days. Hereafter the truth will be shown & he will be displayed in his true light. On the 12th while at Porter's camp I heard that the enemy was advancing in force. Spent last night in W F Smith's camp expecting an attack at daylight.

AL copy, McClellan Papers (C-7:63), Library of Congress.

To Mary Ellen McClellan

[Washington] Oct. 16 1861

I have just been interrupted here by the Presdt & Secty Seward who had nothing very particular to say, except some stories to tell, which were as usual very pertinent & some pretty good. I never in my life met anyone so full of anecdote as our friend Abraham — he is never at a loss for a story apropos of any known subject or incident.

Copy, McClellan Papers (D-10:72), Library of Congress.

To Thomas A. Scott   [TELEGRAM]

Hon. Thos. A. Scott,
Asst. Sec. of War.   Camp Griffin [Lewinsville] Oct. 17, 1861

I gave Genl Sherman all the Regts he asked for.[1] At least two of those originally intended for him and promised to me, have been diverted from me. The Artillery promised me to replace Hamilton's Battery has not been given to me. I will not consent to one other man being detached from this Army for that expedition. I need far more than I now have to save this Country and cannot spare any disciplined Regt.

Instead of diminishing this Army true policy would dictate its immediate increase to a large extent. It is the task of the Army of the Potomac to decide the question at issue. No outside expedition can affect the result. I hope that I will not again be asked to detach any body.[2]

                                        Geo. B. McClellan
                                        Maj. Gen. Comd'g.

Received copy, Records of the Office of the Secretary of War, RG 107 (M-473:97), National Archives. *OR*, Ser. 1, VI, p. 179. Scott was assistant secretary of war.

1. Scott telegraphed GBM on this date to ask for the 79th New York regiment for Brig. Gen. Thomas W. Sherman's expedition against Port Royal. *OR*, Ser. 1, VI, p. 179. 2. The 79th New York was in fact assigned to the Port Royal expedition.

To Gideon Welles

                                Headquarters, Army of the Potomac,
Sir: [Lewinsville] October 18, 1861.

I have this minute received your letter of this date[1] with reference to the navigation of the Potomac, and in reply have the honor to inform you that a command comprised of infantry and cavalry started this morning for different points below here on the Potomac River, accompanied by a staff officer, with orders to examine the country thoroughly to ascertain whether or not it is necessary to erect heavy batteries for the protection of navigation and to accomplish the object asked for in your letter.

            I am, sir, very respectfully, your obedient servant,
                                        Geo. B. McClellan,
                                        Major-General

Hon. Gideon Welles,
Secretary of the Navy.

NOR, Ser. 1, IV, p. 727.

1. In his letter Secretary Welles reported that navigation on the lower Potomac was daily and hourly becoming "more dangerous." If the enemy erected batteries to block navigation, he added, the navy would require the army's help to keep the river open. *NOR*, Ser. 1, IV, pp. 726–27.

To Mary Ellen McClellan

[Lewinsville] Oct 19th [1861]

It seems to be pretty well settled that I will be Comdr in Chf within a week. Genl Scott proposes to retire in favor of Halleck. The Presdt & Cabinet have determined to accept his retirement, but *not* in favor of Halleck.[1] The old —— 's antiquity is wonderful & lasting. . . .

The enemy have fallen back on Manassas — probably to draw me into the old error. I hope to make them abandon Leesburg tomorrow.

AL copy, McClellan Papers (C-7:63), Library of Congress.

1. GBM had learned of the decision taken at a Cabinet meeting on Oct. 18 to accept Gen. Scott's resignation. Scott hoped that Maj. Gen. Henry W. Halleck would be named to succeed him as general-in-chief.

To Charles P. Stone [TELEGRAM]

Brig. Gen. C. P. Stone   McClellan's Headquarters
Edwards Ferry   [Washington] October 21, 1861

Is the force of the enemy now engaged with your troops opposite Harrison's Island large?[1] If so, and you require more support than your division affords, call upon General Banks, who has been directed to respond. What force, in your opinion, would it require to carry Leesburg?[2] Answer at once, as I may require you to take it to-day; and, if so, I will support you on the other side of the river from Darnestown.[3]

Geo. B. McClellan
Major General, Commanding

OR, Ser. 1, LI, Part 1, p. 499.

1. The site of the fighting was Ball's Bluff, on the Virginia shore of the Potomac near Leesburg. 2. GBM informed Stone on Oct. 20 that McCall's division had occupied Dranesville, Va., which he hoped would force the Confederates to give up Leesburg, and added: "Perhaps a slight demonstration on your part would have the effect to move them." A. V. Colburn to Stone, *OR*, Ser. 1, V, p. 32. 3. Stone took this ambiguous statement to mean that additional support was available to him from McCall at Dranesville, across the river from Darnestown, Md., the headquarters of Banks's division. Without notifying Stone, however, GBM had already ordered McCall back to the Washington lines. Stone testimony, *Report of the Joint Committee on the Conduct of the War*, II (1863), pp. 488–89.

To Charles P. Stone [TELEGRAM]

[Washington, October 21, 1861]

Call on Banks for whatever aid you need. Shall I push up a Division or two on other side of river. Take Leesburg.

McClellan
Maj Genl

Genl C P Stone

ALS (telegram sent), Records of the Office of the Secretary of War, RG 107 (M-504:65), National Archives. *OR*, Ser. 1, LI, Part 1, p. 500.

To Charles P. Stone   [TELEGRAM]

General C. P. Stone   Hd Qrs Army of the Potomac
Edwards Ferry   [Washington] Oct 21, 1861 [10 P.M.]

Hold your position on the Virginia side the Potomac at all hazzards.[1] General Banks will support you with one Brigade at Harrisons Island and the other two at Seneca. Lander[2] will be with you at daylight.

Geo B McClellan
Maj Genl Comdg

Change the disposition of Genl. Banks Division if you think it necessary so as to send two brigades to Harrisons Island instead of one.

Retained copy, McClellan Papers (A-28:12), Library of Congress. *OR*, Ser.. 1, LI, Part 1, p. 500.

1. Stone had two contingents across the river, at Ball's Bluff and at Edwards Ferry, four miles downstream. The fighting was confined to Ball's Bluff. 2. Brig. Gen. Frederick W. Lander commanded a brigade in Stone's division.

To Nathaniel P. Banks   [TELEGRAM]

Head Qrs Army of Potomac

To General N. P. Banks   [Washington] Oct 21 [1861] 10.45 p.m.

Push forward your command as rapidly as possible and put as many men over the river to reinforce Genl. Stone as you can before daylight. Genl. Stone is directed to hold his command on the Virginia side the Potomac at all hazzards and informed that you will support him. You will assume command when you join General Stone.

Geo B McClellan
Maj Genl Comdg

Retained copy, McClellan Papers (A-28:12), Library of Congress.

To Abraham Lincoln   [TELEGRAM]

Received Oct 22d 1861

To President Lincoln   From Poolesville 5.30 pm

From what I learn here the affair of yesterday was a more serious disaster than I had supposed. Our loss in prisoners & killed was severe. I leave at once for Edwards Ferry.

G B McClellan
Maj Genl USA

Received copy, Lincoln Papers, Library of Congress.

To Division Commanders, Army of the Potomac [TELEGRAM]

[Poolesville, October 24, 1861]

The affair in front of Leesburg on Monday last [October 21] resulted in serious loss to us, but was a most gallant fight on the part of our men, who displayed the utmost coolness & courage. It has given me the utmost confidence in them.

The disaster was caused by errors committed by the immediate Commander[1] — *not* Genl Stone. I have withdrawn all the troops from the other side, since they went there without my orders & nothing was to be gained by retaining them there.

G B McClellan
Maj Genl

Genls McDowell F. J. Porter W. F. Smith Franklin Buell
Heintzelman Blenker McCall

ALS (telegram sent), Records of the Office of the Secretary of War, RG 107 (M-504:66), National Archives. *OR*, Ser. 1, V, p. 626.

1. Col. Edward D. Baker, in command at Ball's Bluff. He was killed in the fighting.

To Mary Ellen McClellan

[Washington] Oct 25 [1861]

... How weary I am of all this business — case after case — blunder after blunder — trick upon trick — I am well nigh tired of the world, & were it not for you would be fully so.

That affair of Leesburg on Monday last [October 21] was a terrible butchery — the men fought nobly, but were penned up by a vastly superior force in a place where they had no retreat. The whole thing took place some 40 miles from here without my orders or knowledge — it was entirely unauthorized by me & I am in no manner responsible for it.

The man *directly* to blame for the affair was Col Baker who was killed — he was in command, disregarded entirely the instructions he had received from Stone, & violated all military rules & precautions. Instead of meeting the enemy with double their force & a good ferry behind him, he was outnumbered three to one, & had no means of retreat. Cogswell is a prisoner — he behaved very handsomely. Raymond Lee is also taken.[1] We lost 79 killed, 141 wounded & probably 400 wounded & prisoners — stragglers are constantly coming in however, so that the number of missing is gradually being decreased & may not go beyond 300.[2] I found things in great confusion when I arrived there — Genl Banks having assumed command & having done *nothing*. In a very short time order & confidence were restored. During the night I withdrew everything & everybody to this side of the river — which in truth they should never have left.

AL copy, McClellan Papers (C-7:63), Library of Congress.

1. Cols. Milton Cogswell, 42nd New York, and Raymond Lee, 20th Massachusetts. 2. The final casualty list was 49 killed, 158 wounded, and 714 missing, a total of 921. *OR*, Ser. 1, V, p. 308.

To Mary Ellen McClellan

[Washington] Oct 26 [1861]

For the last 3 hours I have been at Montgomery Blair's talking with Senators Wade, Trumbull & Chandler about war matters[1] — they will make a desperate effort tomorrow to have Genl Scott retired at once. Until that is accomplished I can effect but little good — he is ever in my way & I am sure does not desire effective action — I want to get thro' with the war as rapidly as possible. . . .

I go out soon after bkft to review Porter's Divn, about 5 miles from here.

AL copy, McClellan Papers (C-7:63), Library of Congress.

1. Montgomery Blair was postmaster general. The three senators — Benjamin Wade of Ohio, Lyman Trumbull of Illinois, and Zachariah Chandler of Michigan — were Republican radicals.

To Mary Ellen McClellan

[Washington, Oct. 30, 1861]

. . . You remember my wounded friend Col Kelley, whom we met at Wheeling? He has just done a very pretty thing at Romney — thrashed the enemy severely, taken all their guns etc.[1] I am very glad to hear it. You may have heard from the papers etc of the small row that is going on just now between Genl Scott & myself — in which the vox populi is coming out strongly on my side. The affair had got among the soldiers, & I hear that offs & men all declare that they will fight under no one but "our George," as the scamps have taken it into their heads to call me. I ought to take good care of these men, for I believe they love me from the bottom of their hearts. I can see it in their faces when I pass among them. I presume the Scott war will culminate this week — & as it is now very clear that the people will not permit me to be passed over it seems easy to predict the result.

Whatever it may be I will try to do my duty to the army & to the country — with God's help & a single eye to the right I hope that I may succeed. I appreciate all the difficulties in my path — the impatience of the people, the venality & bad faith of the politicians, the gross neglect that has occurred in obtaining arms clothing etc — & also I feel in my innermost soul how small is my ability in comparison with the gigantic dimensions of the task, & that, even if I had the greatest intellect that was ever given to man, the result remains in the hands of God. I do not

feel that I am an instrument worthy of the great task, but I *do* feel that ⤙
I did not seek it — it was thrust upon me. I was called to it, my previous
life seems to have been unwittingly directed to this great end, & I know
that God can accomplish the greatest results with the weakest instru-
ments — therein lies my hope. I feel too that, much as we in the North
have erred, the rebels have been far worse than we — they seem to have
deserted from the great cardinal virtues.

AL copy, McClellan Papers (C-7:63), Library of Congress.

1. Brig. Gen. Benjamin F. Kelley took Romney, in western Virginia, on Oct. 26.

To Abraham Lincoln

Head-Quarters, Army of the Potomac,
Your Excellency   Washington, Oct 31, 1861

May I ask you to do me the favor to see Col Kingsbury Chf of Ordnance
of my staff, in regard to the purchase of arms.

The matter is of the first importance & unless you interfere in person
I see no reason to expect any more arms.

Please accept my apology for not calling in person as I am very hard
at work upon the paper I referred to yesterday.[1]

Very respectfully yr obt svt
Geo B McClellan
Maj Genl

Presdt Lincoln

ALS, Lincoln Papers, Library of Congress.

1. See GBM to Simon Cameron, Oct. 31, *infra*.

To Mary Ellen McClellan

[Washington, October 31, 1861]

... I have been at work all day nearly on a letter to the Secy of War
in regard to future military operations.

I have not been home for some 3 hrs, but am "concealed" at Stanton's[1]
to dodge all enemies in shape of "browsing" Presdt etc....

I have been very busy today writing & am pretty thoroughly tired out.
The paper is a very important one — as it is intended to place on record
the fact that I have left nothing undone to make this army what it ought
to be & that the necessity for delay has not been my fault. I have a set
of scamps to deal with — unscrupulous & false — if possible they will
throw whatever blame there is on my shoulders, & I do not intend to be ⨯
sacrificed by such people. It is perfectly sickening to have to work with
such people & to see the fate of the nation in such hands. I still trust
that the all wise Creator does not intend our destruction, & that in his

own good time he will free the nation from the imbeciles who curse it & will restore us to his favor. I know that as a nation we have grieviously sinned, but I trust that there is a limit to his wrath & that ere long we will begin to experience his mercy. But it is terrible to stand by & see the cowardice of the Presdt, the vileness of Seward, & the rascality of[1] Cameron — Welles is an old woman — Bates an old fool. The only man of courage & sense in the Cabinet is Blair, & I do not altogether fancy him!

I cannot guess at my movements for they are not within my own control. I cannot move without more means & I do not possess the power to control those means. The people think me all powerful. Never was there a greater mistake — I am thwarted & deceived by these incapables at every turn. I am doing all I can to get ready to move before winter sets in — but it now begins to look as if we are condemned to a winter of inactivity. If it is so the fault will not be mine — there will be that consolation for my conscience, even if the world at large never knows it. . . .

I have one great comfort in all this — that is that I did not seek this position, as you well know, & I still trust that God will support me & bear me out — he could not have placed me here for nothing. . . .

1 am [November 1]. I have just returned from a ride over the river where I went pretty late, to seek refuge in Fitz Porter's camp. You would have laughed if you could have seen me dodge off. I quietly told the little duke (Chartres)[2] to get our horses saddled, & then we slipped off without escort or orderlies & trotted away for Fitz John's camp where we had a quiet talk over the camp fire.

I saw yesterday Genl Scott's letter asking to be placed on the Retired List & saying nothing about Halleck. The offer was to be accepted last night & they propose to make me at once Commander in Chief of the Army. I cannot get up any especial feeling about it — I feel the vast responsibility it imposes upon [me]. I feel a sense of relief at the prospect of having my own way untrammelled, but I cannot discover in my own heart one symptom of gratified vanity or ambition.

AL copy; copy, McClellan Papers (C-7:63/D-10:72), Library of Congress.

1. Edwin M. Stanton. 2. The Duc de Chartres, of the House of Orléans, one of GBM's aides.

To Simon Cameron

To/   The Secretary of War
Sir   [Washington, October 31, 1861][1]

In conformity with a personal understanding with the President yesterday I have the honor to submit the following statement of the condition of the Army under my command and the measures required for the preservation of the government and the suppression of the Rebellion.

It will be remembered that in a memorial I had the honor to address to the President soon after my arrival at Washington, and in my communication addressed to Lieutenant General Scott under date of the 8th of August, in my letter to the President authorizing him at his request to withdraw the letter written by me to General Scott and in my letter of the 8th of September answering your note of enquiry of that date my views on the same subject are frankly & fully expressed.[2] In these several communications[3] I have stated the force I regarded as necessary to enable this Army to advance with a reasonable certainty of success, at the same time leaving the Capital & the line of the Potomac sufficiently guarded not only to secure the retreat of the main army in the event of disaster, but to render it out of the enemy's power to attempt a diversion in Maryland.

So much time has passed & the winter is approaching so rapidly that but two courses are left to the Government, viz: Either to go into winter quarters, or to assume the offensive with forces greatly inferior in numbers to the army I regarded as desirable & necessary.

If political considerations render the first course inadvisable the second alone remains. While I regret that it has not been deemed expedient or perhaps possible to concentrate the resources of the nation in this vicinity (remaining on the defensive elsewhere), keeping the attention & efforts of the Govt fixed upon this as the vital point where the issue of the great contest is to be decided, it may still be that by introducing unity of action & design among the various armies of the land, by determining the course to be pursued by the various commanders under one general plan, transferring from the other armies the superfluous strength not required for the purpose in view, & thus reenforcing this main army whose destiny it is to decide the controversy — we may yet be able to move with a reasonable prospect of success before the winter is fairly upon us. The nation feels, & I share that feeling, that the Army of the Potomac holds the fate of the country in its hands. The stake is so vast, the issue so momentous, & the effect of the next battle will be so important throughout the future as well as the present, that I continue to urge, as I have ever done since I entered upon the command of this army, upon the Govt to devote its energies & its available resources towards increasing the numbers & efficiency of the Army on which its salvation depends.

A statement, carefully prepared by the Chiefs of Engineers & Artillery of this Army, gives as the necessary garrison of this city & its fortifications 33,795 men — say 35,000.

The present garrison of Baltimore & its dependencies is about 10,000 — I have sent the Chief of my Staff to make a careful examination into the condition of these troops & to obtain the information requisite to enable me to decide whether this number can be diminished or the reverse.

At least 5000 men will be required to watch the river hence to Harpers Ferry & its vicinity; probably 8000 to guard the lower Potomac.

As you are aware all the information we have from spies, prisoners &c agrees in showing that the enemy have a force on the Potomac not less than 150 000 strong well drilled & equipped, ably commanded & strongly intrenched.[4] It is plain therefore that to ensure success, or to render it reasonably certain, the active army should not number less than 150,000 efficient troops, with 400 guns, unless some material change occurs in the force in front of us, or an aggregate of present & absent of about 240,000 men should the losses by sickness etc not rise to a higher % than at present.

The requisite force for an advance movement by the Army of the Potomac may be thus estimated.

		guns
Column of active operations	150 000	400
Garrison of the City of Washington	35 000	40
To guard the Potomac to Harpers Ferry	5 000	12
To guard the Lower Potomac	8 000	24
Garrison for Baltimore & Annapolis	10 000	12
Total effective force required	208 000	488[5]

Having stated what I regard as the requisite force to enable this Army to advance, I now proceed to give the actual strength of the Army of the Potomac.

The aggregate strength of the Army of the Potomac by the official report on the morning of the 27th inst. was 168,318 officers & men of all grades & arms; this includes the troops at Baltimore, Annapolis, on the upper & lower Potomac, the sick, absent etc. The force present for *duty* was 147,695. Of this number 4268 Cavalry were completely unarmed, 3163 Cavalry only partially armed, 5979 Infantry unequipped making 13410 unfit for the field (irrespective of those not yet sufficiently drilled), & reducing the effective force to 134,285, & the number disposable for an advance to 76,285.[6] The Infantry regiments are to a considerable extent armed with unserviceable weapons.

Quite a large number of good arms which had been intended for this army were ordered elsewhere, leaving the Army of the Potomac insufficiently & in several cases badly armed.

On the 30th October there were with this army 228 field guns ready for the field, so far as arms & equipment are concerned; — some of the batteries are still quite raw & unfit to go into action.

I have intelligence that 8 New York batteries are en route hither, two others are being formed here; when these are ready for the field I will still (if the N.Y. batteries have 6 guns each) be 112 guns short of the number required for the active column, saying nothing for the present of those necessary for the garrisons and corps on the Potomac, which would make a total deficiency of 200 guns.

I have thus briefly stated our present condition & wants; it remains to suggest the means of supplying the deficiencies.

First: That *all* the cavalry & infantry arms as fast as procured, whether manufactured in this country, or purchased abroad, be sent to this army until it is fully prepared for the field.

Second. That the two companies of the 4th Artillery now understood to be en route from Fort Randall to Fort Monroe be ordered to this army to be mounted at once; also that the companies of 3rd Artillery en route from California be sent here. Had not the order for Smead's battery to come here from Harrisburg, to replace the battery I gave Genl Sherman, been so often countermanded I would again ask for it.[7]

Third. That a more effective regulation may be made authorizing the transfer of men from the Volunteers to the regular batteries, infantry & cavalry; that we may make the best possible use of the invaluable regular "skeletons."

Fourth. I have no official information as to the United States forces elsewhere but from the best information I can obtain from the War Department & other sources I am led to believe that the United States troops

in Western Virginia are about	30 000
in Kentucky about	40 000
in Missouri about	80 000
in Fortress Monroe about	11 000
Total	161 000

Besides these I am informed that more than 100,000 are in process of organization in other Northern & Western States.

I would therefore recommend that not interfering with Kentucky there should be retained in Western Virginia and Missouri sufficient force for defensive purposes & that the surplus troops be sent to the Army of the Potomac to enable it to assume the offensive; that the same course be pursued in respect to Fortress Monroe & that no further outside expeditions be attempted until we have fought the great battle in front of us.[8]

Fifth. That every nerve be strained to hasten the enrollment, & organization & armament of new batteries & regiments of Infantry.

Sixth. That all the battalions now raised for the new rgts of regular Infantry be at once ordered to this Army, & that the old Infty & Cavalry en route from California be ordered to this army immediately on their arrival in N.Y.

I have thus indicated in a general manner the objects to be accomplished & the means by which we may gain our ends.

A vigorous employment of these means will in my opinion enable the Army of the Potomac to assume successfully this season the offensive operations which ever since entering upon the command it has been my anxious desire & diligent effort to prepare for and prosecute.[9]

The advance should not be postponed beyond the 25th Nov if possible to avoid it.

Unity in councils, the utmost vigor & energy in action are indispensable. The entire military field should be grasped as a whole not in detached parts; one plan should be agreed upon & pursued; a single will should direct & carry out these plans.

The great object to be accomplished — the crushing defeat of the rebel army at Manassas — should never for one instant be lost sight of; but all the intellect & means & men of the government poured upon that one point. The loyal States possess ample force to effect all this, & more. The rebels have displayed energy unanimity & wisdom worthy of the most desperate days of the French Revolution — should we do less?

The unity of this nation, the preservation of our institutions are so dear to me that I have willingly sacrificed my private happiness with the single object of doing my duty to my country — when the task is accomplished I shall be glad to return to the obscurity from which events have drawn me. Whatever the determination of the Govt may be I will do the best I can with the Army of the Potomac, & will share its fate whatever may be the task imposed upon it.

Permit me to add that on this occasion as heretofore it has been my aim neither to exaggerate nor underrate the power of the enemy nor fail to express clearly the means by which in my judgment that power may be broken; urging the energy of preparation & action which has ever been my choice, but with the fixed purpose by no act of mine to expose this government to hazard by premature movement.[10]

Requesting that this communication may be laid before the President.

ADf (in part in the handwriting of Edwin M. Stanton), McClellan Papers (A-29:13), Library of Congress. *OR*, Ser. 1, V, pp. 9–11.

1. Although this manuscript is undated, Oct. 31 is the only date that fits its contents and the circumstances of its writing as mentioned in the two previous letters. 2. These letters were dated, respectively, Aug. 2, 8, 10, and Sept. 8, 1861, *supra*. 3. The handwriting to this point is that of Edwin M. Stanton, and elaborated GBM's brief original opening: "In various papers submitted to the Presdt & War Dept I have stated ...." 4. This sentence is by Stanton, edited by GBM. The Confederate strength figure of 150,000 came from intelligence reports by Allan Pinkerton dated Oct. 28 and by Brig. Gen. Winfield S. Hancock dated Oct. 30. McClellan Papers (A-29:13). 5. Stanton here put figures from GBM's draft into tabular form. 6. This figure was arrived at by subtracting garrison forces of 58,000, as tabulated above, from the effective force of 134,285. The return of "the 27th inst." is that of Oct. 27, 1861. *McClellan's Own Story*, p. 78. 7. The battery of Capt. John R. Smead, 5th U.S. Artillery, in reference to Gen. Thomas Sherman's Port Royal expedition. 8. This point four by Stanton replaced the following phrasing by GBM: "Fourth. That from 6000

to 10 000 good troops be ordered here from Western Va & that the Army there, as well as that in Missouri be reduced as soon as possible to the defensive, that their surplus troops may be sent here without delay to enable us to assume the offensive. That the same principle be applied to the garrison at Fort Monroe. . . .'' 9. This paragraph is by Stanton. 10. Stanton rewrote the concluding paragraph from this GBM draft: ''But I wish to have again on record the fact that I have neither underestimated the force of the enemy nor failed to perceive the means by which that force may be broken. I urge as the only means of salvation the energetic course which has ever been my choice. No time is to be lost — we have lost too much already — every consideration requires us to prepare at once, but not to move until we are ready.''

THREE

GENERAL-IN-CHIEF
NOVEMBER 1, 1861–MARCH 11, 1862

THIS SECTION most clearly portrays George McClellan's wartime role as a military executive in detailing the somewhat more than four months he served as both general-in-chief and commander of the Army of the Potomac. New generals were appointed and new initiatives taken. He named Don Carlos Buell to head the Department of the Ohio and Henry W. Halleck to the Department of Missouri. Operations were started, or continued, and plans made to tighten the blockade of the Confederacy's Atlantic coast and to operate against New Orleans from the Gulf of Mexico. At the same time, General-in-Chief McClellan abandoned any previous thought (or promise) of advancing with the Army of the Potomac before the spring of 1862.

The strategy he evolved in this period, described in his letters of instruction, called for forces in every theater of war to act in concert with the Potomac army, still the grand army of his plans. In the western theater, for example, his goal was to seize the Confederates' only direct east-west railroad to prevent them from bringing reinforcements from the west to oppose his spring offensive. Ambrose Burnside's operations on the North Carolina coast were designed to block other reinforcements from reaching the Rebel army in Virginia by cutting the railroads south of Richmond. Once he defeated the enemy in Virginia, it was McClellan's intention to personally command the movement against New Orleans. As for his Potomac army, he devised a new strategy, a turning movement by way of Chesapeake Bay, that was to outflank the Confederates at Manassas near Washington and force them to battle on ground of his own choosing near Richmond. He spelled out his plan in a long letter to the new secretary of war, Edwin Stanton, on February 3, 1862, the most important strategy paper of his Civil War career.

For much of this time, due to the absence of letters to his wife, McClellan's correspondence offers fewer clues than usual to his thoughts and motives. On October 12, 1861, Ellen McClellan had given birth to a daughter, and early in December she and the child joined the general in Washington. They would remain together until he embarked on the Peninsula campaign, and he only wrote her twice, during brief excursions away from Washington. Among the previously unpublished letters that appear here, however, are several that present unique glimpses of his actions, including one offering the Washington command to General John A. Dix (January 14), one to Secretary Stanton (January 26) outlining a plan for shifting the main Federal offensive to Kentucky, and a letter to Chief of Staff Marcy (January 29) confirming McClellan's unusual scheme for gaining the support of the nation's largest newspaper, the *New York Herald*.

Militarily, the most important Union gains of the period were made in Tennessee, in February 1862, when Forts Henry and Donelson were captured and Nashville occupied. McClellan's dispatches illustrate his efforts to coordinate the movements of the forces under Generals Halleck and Buell, his one major venture in operational direction during his time as general-in-chief.

He was meanwhile becoming increasingly bound by controversy, due primarily to his failure to make good with even the smallest operation of the Army of the Potomac. Throughout the winter of 1861–1862 Washington remained virtually blockaded by Confederate forces on the upper and lower Potomac, leaving the capital linked to the rest of the North by only a single rail line, while General McClellan (so his detractors said) did nothing but hold grand reviews of his army. His one effort to break the blockade, at Harper's Ferry in late February, ended in ignominious failure.

His refusal to inform the president of his plans or to take him into his confidence created further problems, and led to what he regarded as interference in operations by the commander-in-chief. McClellan's correspondence demonstrates his ambiguous attitude toward Lincoln. He might describe the president to his wife as "the *original gorrilla*" and unworthy of his office (November 17), yet on the death of young Willie Lincoln of typhoid fever, write him an affecting and apparently heartfelt letter of condolence (February 22). At the beginning of his tenure as general-in-chief McClellan felt confident in his relations with the administration; at the end of it his alienation was almost complete. "If I can get out of this scrape you will never catch me in the power of such a set again," he wrote his wife on his last day in the post.

General Orders No. 19

                                        Head-Quarters, Army of the U.S.
Genl Order No [19]   Washington: Nov 1, 1861

In accordance with Genl Order No [94] from the War Dept, I hereby assume command of the Armies of the United States. In the midst of the difficulties which encompass & divide the nation, hesitation & self distrust may well accompany the assumption of so vast a responsibility; but confiding as I do in the loyalty, discipline & courage of our troops, & believing as I do that Providence will favor ours as the just cause, I cannot doubt that success will crown our efforts & sacrifices.

The Army will unite with me in the feeling of regret that the weight of many years & the effect of increasing infirmities, contracted & intensified in his country's service, should just now remove from our head the great soldier of our nation — the hero who in his youth raised high the reputation of his country on the fields of Canada, which he watered with his blood; who in more mature years proved to the world that American skill & valor could repeat, if not eclipse, the exploits of Cortes in the land of the Montezumas; whose whole life has been directed to the service of his country; whose whole efforts have been directed to uphold our honor at the smallest sacrifice of life; a warrior who scorned the selfish glories of the battle field when his great qualities as a statesman could be employed more profitably for his country; a citizen, who in his declining years has given to the world the most shining instance of loyalty in disregarding all ties of birth, & clinging still to the cause of truth & honor. Such has been the career, such the character of Winfield Scott — whom it has long been the delight of the nation to honor both as a man and a soldier. While we regret his loss there is one thing we cannot regret — the bright example he has left for our emulation.

Let us all hope & pray that his declining years may be passed in peace & happiness, and that they may be cheered by the success of the country & the cause he has fought for & loved so well. Beyond all that — let us do nothing that can cause him to blush for us; let no defeat of the Army he has so long commanded embitter his last years — but let our victories illuminate the close of a life so grand.

                                        Geo B McClellan
                                        Maj Genl Comdg USA

ADS, Simon Gratz Autograph Collection, Historical Society of Pennsylvania. *OR*, Ser. 3, I, pp. 613–14.

To John C. Frémont   [TELEGRAM]

Hd Qtrs of the Army Wash.
November 1st 1861

I have assumed command of the Armies of the U.S. Please report by telegram in cipher the numbers, position & condition of your troops. Build a telegraph line as your main column advances.[1] State your situation & intentions — the same with regard to the enemy. Report at least once each day by telegram, & by letter. Send me by letter a full account of the state of affairs in your command.[2]

Geo B McClellan
Maj Genl Comdg USA

Maj Genl J C Fremont
Dept of the West

ALS (telegram sent), McClellan Papers, New-York Historical Society. Maj. Gen. Frémont would be relieved of command of the Western Department on Nov. 2.

1. Frémont had advanced to Springfield, Mo. 2. In this period GBM telegraphed all departmental commanders in a similar vein.

To Mary Ellen McClellan

[Washington] November 2/61 1 1/2 am.

I have been at work with scarcely one minute's rest ever since I arose yesterday morning — nearly 18 hours. I find the "Army" just about as much disorganized as was the Army of the Potomac when I assumed command — everything at sixes & sevens — no system, no order — perfect chaos. I *can* & *will* reduce it to order — I *will* soon have it working smoothly.

AL copy, McClellan Papers (C-7:63), Library of Congress.

To Mary Ellen McClellan

[Washington] Nov 3 [November 2, 1861]

I have already been up once this morning — that was at 4 o'clock to escort Genl Scott to the depot — it was pitch dark & pouring rain — but with most of the staff & a squadron of cavalry I saw the old man off. He was very polite to me — sent various kind messages to you & the baby — so we parted. The old man said that his sensations were very peculiar in leaving Washn & active life — I can easily understand them — & it may be that at some distant day I too shall totter away from Washn — a worn out soldier, with naught to do but make my peace with God. The sight of this morning was a lesson to me which I hope not soon to forget. I saw there the end of a long, active & ambitious life — the end of the career of the first soldier of his nation — & it was a feeble old man scarce able to walk — hardly any one there to see him off but his successor. Should I ever become vainglorious & ambitious remind me of that spectacle. I pray every night & every morning that I may become neither vain nor ambitious — that I may be neither depressed by disaster nor elated by success — & that I may keep one single object in view, the good of my country. At last I am the "Maj Genl Comdg the Army" — I do not feel in the least elated, for I *do* feel the responsibility of the position — & I feel the need for some support. I trust that God will aid me.

AL copy, McClellan Papers (C-7:63), Library of Congress.

To Mary Ellen McClellan

[Washington] Nov 3 1861

. . . After that I came back & received quite a number of congratulatory calls — then went to dine with Andrew Porter,[1] where I had a very pleasant time; Andrew & his wife; her brother; her sister in law, Seth & myself. After dinner Seth & I went to look at some houses; the only one that suited was one formerly occupied by Senator Gwin & once by Senator Aiken, corner of 19th & I — quite an army neighborhood. I think we can make up our minds to residing in Washington for some years.

. . . In the evening a small deputation of 30 waited on me & presented me with that long talked of sword from the city of Phila — it is certainly a very fine one. I listened meekly to a long set speech & replied in my usual way i.e. in very few words. I then had a collation — I abominate the word, it is so *steamboaty*, in the back parlor. Wormley did himself credit on the occasion & got it up very well indeed. The Presdt came in during the proceedings — after I got through with him I was obliged to undergo a "boring operation" from the —— who talked me almost to death. . . .

Copy, McClellan Papers (D-10:72), Library of Congress.

1. Brig. Gen. Andrew Porter was provost marshal of the Army of the Potomac.

To Thomas A. Scott

Thos A Scott Esq   Head Quarters of the Army
Asst Sect of War   [Washington] Nov 7th 1861

I respectfully request that no more Cavalry regiments be authorized in any part of the country. Those already authorized cannot be armed and equipped for several months & they will be all that will be required this winter.[1]

Very Respectfully Your Obt Srvt
G B McClellan
Maj Gen Comg USA

Retained copy, Records of the Headquarters of the Army, RG 108 (M-857:6), National Archives. *OR*, Ser. 3, I, p. 622.

1. In a report to Secretary of War Edwin M. Stanton on Jan. 29, 1862, GBM sought to reduce further the number of cavalry regiments through disbanding and consolidation. *OR*, Ser. 3, I, p. 873.

To Don Carlos Buell

Brig. Gen. D. C. Buell   Head Quarters of the Army
General.   Washn. Nov. 7 1861

In giving you instructions for your guidance in command of the Department of the Ohio, I do not design to fetter you.[1] I merely wish to express plainly the general ideas which occur to me in relation to the conduct of operations there. That portion of Kentucky west of the Cumberland River is by its position so closely related to the States of Illinois & Missouri that it has seemed best to attach it to the Department of Missouri. Your operations, then, in Kentucky will be confined to that portion of the State east of the Cumberland River. I trust I need not repeat to you that I regard the importance of the territory committed to your care as second only to that occupied by the army under my immediate command. It is absolutely necessary that we shall hold all the State of Kentucky; not only that, but that the majority of its inhabitants shall be warmly in favor of our cause, it being that which best subserves their interests. It is possible that the conduct of our political affairs in Kentucky is more important than that of our military operations. I certainly cannot overestimate the importance of the former. You will please constantly bear in mind the precise issue for which we are fighting, — that issue is the preservation of the Union and the restoration of the full authority of the General Government over all portions of our territory. We shall most readily suppress this rebellion and restore the authority of the Government by religiously respecting the Constitutional rights of all. I know that I express the feelings and opinion of the President when I say that we are fighting only to preserve the integrity of the Union and the Constitutional authority of the General Government.

The inhabitants of Kentucky may rely upon it that their domestic institutions will in no manner be interfered with, and that they will receive at our hands every Constitutional protection. I have only to repeat that you will in all respects carefully regard the local institutions of the region in which you command, allowing nothing but the dictates of military necessity to cause you to depart from the spirit of these instructions.

So much in regard to political considerations. The military problem would be a simple one could it be entirely separated from political influence; — such is not the case. Were the population among which you are to operate wholly or generally hostile, it is probable that Nashville should be your first & principal objective point. It so happens that a large majority of the inhabitants of Eastern Tennessee are in favor of the Union; it therefore seems proper that you should remain on the defensive on the line from Louisville to Nashville, while you throw the mass of your forces by rapid marches, by Cumberland Gap or Walker's Gap on Knoxville, in order to occupy the railroad at that point, & thus enable the loyal citizens of Eastern Tennessee to rise, while you at the same time cut off the railway communication between Eastern Virginia and the Mississippi. It will be prudent to fortify the Pass before leaving it in your rear.

Copy, McClellan Papers (D-7:69), Library of Congress. *OR*, Ser. 1, IV, p. 342.

1. Buell was officially appointed to command the Department of the Ohio on Nov. 9. This letter of instructions may not have been issued, although possibly it was the basis for conversations between the two men that are mentioned in GBM to Buell, Nov. 12, *infra*. In a later report, Buell mentioned receiving only the Nov. 12 instructions. *OR*, Ser. 1, XVI, Part 1, p. 23.

To Samuel R. Curtis   [TELEGRAM]

For Gen Curtis   Washington Nov. 7, 1861

Arrest the paymaster alluded to in your telegram of today if you find there are grounds for your suspicions, and if you find it necessary to accomplish the object, arrest Fremont. Seize the funds.[1]

Geo B McClellan
Maj Gen

Retained copy, Records of the Office of the Secretary of War, RG 107 (M-504:9), National Archives. Brig. Gen. Curtis commanded the garrison at St. Louis.

1. Curtis's telegram, not found, apparently dealt with suspected fraud by Gen. Frémont's paymaster. Curtis recovered the pay chest without exercising GBM's authorization to arrest Frémont. *OR*, Ser. 1, III, pp. 566–67.

To Mary Ellen McClellan

[Washington] Nov 7 [1861]

I am glad to learn that my order (the military obituary)[1] changed Genl Scott's feelings entirely, & that he now says I am the best man & the best General that ever existed! Such is human nature — the order *was* a little rhetorical — but I wrote it *at* him — for a particular market! It seems to have accomplished the object.

AL copy, McClellan Papers (C-7:63), Library of Congress.

1. General Orders No. 19, Nov. 1, *supra*.

To William T. Sherman   [TELEGRAM]

[Washington, November 8, 1861][1]

Your request will be complied with by sending Genl Buell to take command in Kentucky.[2]

G B McClellan
Maj Genl Comdg USA

Brig Genl W T Sherman
Louisville Ky

ALS (telegram sent), Records of the Office of the Secretary of War, RG 107 (M-504:9), National Archives. Brig. Gen. Sherman headed the Department of the Cumberland, with headquarters at Louisville.

1. Dated from an encoded copy. 2. Sherman had telegraphed GBM on Nov. 4: "The publication of Adjutant General Thomas's report impairs my influence. I insist upon being relieved to your army, my old brigade." McClellan Papers (A-30:13), Library of Congress. Lorenzo Thomas's report of Oct. 21 detailed Secretary of War Cameron's interview with Sherman in Louisville five days earlier. Sherman's pessimistic view of events, and his estimate that 200,000 troops would be needed in the western theater, reached the newspapers through a reporter present at the meeting. *OR*, Ser. 1, IV, pp. 313–14. Sherman was assigned a subordinate position in the Department of Missouri.

To Samuel L. M. Barlow

My dear Samuel L. F. X. Q. Q.[1]   Washington Nov 8 1861

Better late than never is a pretty good adage — & never better applied in this instance. I am pretty well fagged out, for it is 1 am, & as I have still more work to do, it suggested itself to me that I would refresh myself by an interlude in the way of a few words to an old friend whom I have treated shamefully. First let me thank you for that "carpet bag" which has been the companion of my woes in Western Va & here — I never shave without thinking of you, & religiously determining to write to you before the close of the day — you can therefore judge how little my promises are to be relied upon! Next let me say that that fine blanket you sent me by Van Vliet[2] (our revered & venerable friend) shall comfort me when we advance. Speaking of an advance let me beg of you not to be impatient (I do not know that you are) — do you & all your friends trust implicitly in me — I am more anxious to advance than any other person in this country — there is no one whose interests would be so much subserved by prompt success as myself.

I feel however that the issue of this struggle is to be decided by the next great battle, & that I owe it to my country & myself not to advance until I have reasonable chances in my favor. The strength of the Army of the Potomac has been vastly overrated in the public opinion. It is now strong enough & well disciplined enough to hold Washington against *any* attack — I care not in what numbers. But, leaving the necessary garrisons here, at Baltimore etc — I cannot yet move in force equal to that which the enemy probably has in my front. We are rapidly increasing in numbers & efficiency. My intention is simply this — I will pay no attention to popular clamor — quietly, & quickly as possible, make this Army strong enough & effective enough to give me a reasonable certainty that, if I am able to handle the form, I will win the first battle. I expect to fight a terrible battle — I know full well the capacity of the Generals opposed to me, for by a singular chance they were once my most intimate friends[3] — tho' we can never meet except as mortal foes hereafter — I appreciate too the courage & discipline of the rebel troops — I believe I know the obstacles in our path. I will first be sure that I have an Army strong enough & well enough instructed to fight with reasonable chances of success — I do not ask for perfect certainty. When I am ready I will move without regard to season or weather — I can overcome *these* difficulties. I think that the interests of the country demand the "festina lente"[4] policy. But of one thing you can rest assured — when the blow *is* struck it will be heavy, rapid, & decisive. Help me to dodge the nigger — we want nothing to do with him. *I* am fighting to preserve the integrity of the Union & the power of the Govt — on no other issue. To gain that end we cannot afford to raise up the negro question — it must be incidental & subsidiary. The Presdt is perfectly honest & is really sound on the nigger question — I will answer for it now that things go right with him. As far as you can, keep the papers & the politicians from running over me — that speech that some rascal made the other day that I did *not dare* to advance, & had said so, was a lie — I have always said, when it was necessary to say anything, that I was not yet strong enough — but, did the public service require it, I would *dare* to advance with 10,000 men & throw my life in the balance.

I have said enough for tonight — & must go back to my work. I hope some time next week to have a review of from 30,000 to 50,000 good troops — can you not bring Madame on to it? If you come alone I can certainly accommodate you in my new house (that once occupied by Bayard Smith, corner of H & 15th) — I *think* I will have my ménage so arranged within two days that I shall be glad to have *her* come too. Telegraph me whether she can accompany you, & I will frankly reply whether my *cook* is ready — I *think* I can have everything ready for it. Do write to me often, & don't get mad if I delay replies — for I am rather busy.

Ever your sincere friend
Geo B McClellan

All this is confidential.

I think that it is now best to resign the Presidency of the O & M — Qu'en pensez vous?[5] Do come on here & see me.

ALS, Barlow Papers, Huntington Library.

1. A jape at Barlow's use of initials. 2. Brig. Gen. Stewart Van Vliet was chief quartermaster of the Army of the Potomac. 3. Joseph E. Johnston, P. G. T. Beauregard, Gustavus W. Smith. 4. "Make haste slowly." 5. "What do you think of that?" GBM was still president of the Eastern Division of the Ohio and Mississippi Railroad. See GBM to Barlow, Jan. 18, 1862, *infra.*

To Elizabeth B. McClellan

My dear Mother   Washington Nov 9 [1861] 2 am

I enclose with this a copy of the order assigning me to duty as Comdg Genl of the USA, & my own order on assuming command.[1] I have but one thing more that I desire to send to you in the military line — a report of our next victory!

Nell is improving rapidly — she rode out today. I hope she will be able to join me here in less than a month. I have taken a very good house here, & you *must* come on to see us as soon as your new grand daughter is fairly established. Marcy & Arthur are for the present living with me.[2] Arthur is doing very well & will make an excellent soldier. Let me repeat, my own dear Mother, that just as soon as Nell is well & established here you & Mary[3] *must* come on to pay us a visit — I have plenty of room here for you — & I *rather* think that you will enjoy services etc as much as anyone else.

In great haste your affectionate son
Geo McClellan

My best love to Mary — John, Maria & the *other* grand children.[4]

ALS, McClellan Papers (B-9:47), Library of Congress.

1. General Orders No. 19, Nov. 1, *supra.* 2. Chief of Staff Marcy; GBM's brother Arthur, a captain on his personal staff. 3. GBM's sister. 4. GBM's brother John H. B. McClellan and his family.

To Ulysses S. Grant   [TELEGRAM]

Washington [November 10, 1861] 10 am

Inform me fully of the number & condition of your command. Tell me your wants & wishes. Give positions numbers & condition of enemy. Your means of transportation by land and water. Size and armament of gun boats. Communicate fully & often.

G B McClellan
Maj Genl Comdg USA

Brig Genl U.S. Grant
Cairo Illinois

ALS (telegram sent), Nicholson Collection, Huntington Library. *OR*, Ser. 1, LIII, p. 507. Brig. Gen. Grant commanded the Military District of Cairo.

To Henry W. Halleck

Maj. Gen. H. W. Halleck, U.S.A.
Comd'g Dept of Missouri   Head Quarters of the Army
General.   Washington, D.C. Nov. 11 1861

In assigning you to the command of the Department of Missouri,[1] it is probably unnecessary for me to state that I have entrusted to you a duty which requires the utmost tact and decision.

You have not merely the ordinary duties of a Military Commander to perform; but the far more difficult task of reducing chaos to order, of changing probably the majority of the personnel of the Staff of the Department, and of reducing to a point of economy consistent with the interests & necessities of the State, a system of reckless expenditure and fraud perhaps unheard of before in the history of the world.

You will find in your Department many General & Staff officers holding illegal commissions & appointments — not recognized or approved by the President or Secretary of War. You will please at once inform these gentlemen of the nullity of their appointment, and see that no pay or allowances are issued to them until such time as commissions may be authorized by the President or Secretary of War.

If any of them give the slightest trouble, you will at once arrest them and send them, under guard, out of the limits of your Department, informing them that if they return they will be placed in close confinement. You will please examine into the legality of the organization of the troops serving in the Department. When you find any illegal, unusual, or improper organizations you will give to the officers and men an opportunity to enter the legal military establishment under general laws & orders from the War Department; reporting in full to these Head Quarters any officer or organization that may decline.

You will please cause competent and reliable Staff Officers to examine all existing contracts immediately, and suspend all payments upon them until you receive the report in each case. Where there is the slightest doubt as to the propriety of the contract, you will be good enough to refer the matter, with full explanation, to these Head Quarters, stating in each case what would be a fair compensation for the services or materials rendered under the contract. Discontinue at once the reception of material or services under any doubtful contract. Arrest and bring to prompt trial all officers who have in any way violated their duty to the Government. In regard to the political conduct of affairs, you will please labor to impress upon the inhabitants of Missouri and the adjacent States, that we are fighting solely for the integrity of the Union, to uphold the power of our National Government, and to restore to the nation the blessings of peace and good order.

With respect to military operations, it is probable, from the best information in my possession, that the interests of the Government will be best served by fortifying and holding in considerable strength Rolla, Sedalia and other interior points; keeping strong patrols constantly moving from the terminal stations; and concentrating the mass of the troops on or near the Mississippi, prepared for such ulterior operations as the public interests may demand.

I would be glad to have you make as soon as possible a personal inspection of all the important points in your Department, and report the result to me. I cannot too strongly impress upon you the absolute necessity of keeping me constantly advised of the strength, condition, and location of your troops, together with all facts that will enable me to maintain the general direction of the Armies of the United States which it is my purpose to exercise. I trust to you to maintain thorough organization, discipline and economy throughout your Department. Please inform me as soon as possible of everything relating to the gunboats now in process of construction, as well as those completed.

The militia force authorized to be raised by the State of Missouri for its defence, will be under your orders.

I am, General, &c, &c.

Geo. B. McClellan

Maj. Gen. Comd'g U.S.A.

Copy, McClellan Papers (D-7:69), Library of Congress. *OR*, Ser. 1, III, pp. 568–69.

1. Halleck was officially appointed to command the Department of Missouri on Nov. 9, in a reorganization superceding Frémont's Western Department.

To Don Carlos Buell

Brig. Gen. D. C. Buell
Comd'g Dept. of the Ohio.   Head Quarters of the Army
General.   Washn. Nov. 12 1861.

Upon assuming command of the Department, I will be glad to have you make as soon as possible a careful report of the condition & situation of your troops, and of the military and political condition of your command. The main point to which I desire to call your attention is the necessity of entering Eastern Tennessee as soon as it can be done with reasonable chances of success, & I hope that you will with the least possible delay organize a column for that purpose, sufficiently guarding at the same time the main avenues by which the rebels might invade Kentucky. Our conversations on the subject of military operations have been so full, and my confidence in your judgment is so great, that I will not dwell further upon the necessity of keeping me fully informed as to the state of affairs, both military and political, & your movements. In regard to political matters, bear in mind that we are fighting only to preserve the integrity of the Union and to uphold the power of the General Government; as far as military necessity will permit religiously respect the constitutional rights of all. Preserve the strictest discipline, among the troops, and while employing the utmost energy in military movements, be careful so to treat the unarmed inhabitants as to contract, not widen, the breach existing between us & the rebels. I mean by this that it is the desire of the Government to avoid unnecessary irritation by causeless arrests & persecution of individuals. Where there is good reason to believe that persons are actually giving aid, comfort, or information to the enemy, it is of course necessary to arrest them; but I have always found that it is the tendency of subordinates to make vexatious arrests on mere suspicion. You will find it well to direct that no arrest shall be made except by your order or that of your Generals, unless in extraordinary cases, always holding the party making the arrest responsible for the propriety of his course. It should be our constant aim to make it apparent to all that their property, their comfort, and their personal safety will be best preserved by adhering to the cause of the Union. If the military suggestions I have made in this letter prove to have been founded on erroneous data, you are of course perfectly free to change the plan of operations.

Copy, McClellan Papers (D-7:69), Library of Congress. *OR*, Ser. 1, IV, pp. 355–56.

To Mary Ellen McClellan

[Washington] November [c. 14] 61

You will have heard the glorious news from Port Royal — our Navy has covered itself with glory & cannot receive too much credit. The thing was superbly done & the chivalry well thrashed — they left in such haste that officers forgot even to carry away their swords. It was true that but one white man was found in Beaufort — & he drunk![1] The negroes came flocking down to the river with their bundles in their hands ready to take passage! There is something inexpressibly mournful to me in that — those poor helpless ignorant beings — with the wide world & its uncertainties before them — the poor serf with his little bundle ready to launch his boat on the wide ocean of life he knows so little of. When I think of some of the features of slavery I cannot help shuddering. Just think for one moment & try to realize that at the will of some brutal master you & I might be separated for ever! It is horrible, & when the day of adjustment comes I will, if successful, throw my sword into the scale to force an improvement in the condition of those poor blacks. I will never be an abolitionist, but I do think that some of the rights of humanity ought to be secured to the negroes — there should be no power to separate families & the right of marriage ought to be secured to them. ...

I will not fight for the abolitionists. ...

Early next week I will have a grand review of some 7 divns — say 70,000 men.

AL copy, McClellan Papers (C-7:63), Library of Congress.

1. The engagement in Port Royal Sound, S.C., took place on Nov. 7. Beaufort was occupied on Nov. 9. Accounts of these victories appeared in Northern newspapers on Nov. 14.

To Simon Cameron

Sir   [Washington, c. November 15, 1861]

The command of the Army has devolved upon me so recently that I feel scarcely able to make this report as full as it ought to be, & must ask your indulgence for confining myself to general suggestions.[1]

It is not in observance of a mere form or custom that I express my deep regret that circumstances made it necessary for Lt Genl Scott to retire from active service. Many years spent in the service of his country had so worn down his body that it was no longer equal to the vigor of his mind or to the devotion of his heart every pulsation of which was for the nation. No one could regret more than he that it was no longer possible to give to our sacred cause the benefit of so great an intellect & such varied experience. When the hour arrives for me, in my turn, to commit to other hands the military destinies of this nation, I shall be well contented if my successor looks upon me or my memory with the filial reverence & affection, the deep professional admiration that I feel for Winfield Scott.

I shall be more than contented if he feels as fully as I do the contrast between the experience & reputation of his predecessor & his own.

I feel in the depths of my heart the magnitude of the task committed to me — yet, so great is my confidence in the justice of our cause, &, more than all, in the great mercy of the Creator — that I entertain no doubt as to the result, & have no doubt that I shall be one of the humble instruments employed in the suppression of this unnatural rebellion, & the maintenance of the Union.

During the eventful period that has elapsed since the last annual Report of the Comdg General the rebellion has culminated in open hostilities; skirmishes & battles have been fought with varied results. The most important affair, that of Bull's Run, was a serious reverse for us — this result was plainly due to the fact that our army, raw, unorganized & inexperienced, attacked the enemy in his chosen position — had the case been reversed we should have been successful. The general result of all the affairs that have occurred has been to show that our troops are fully equal, & I am sure, superior to the rebels in courage. The policy of the rebels has been as a general rule to remain on the defensive & receive our attacks in their positions chosen & fortified beforehand. I am glad to advert to the operations in Western Virginia as proving that even behind intrenchments they can readily be beaten if the clear relative proportion of force is maintained to compensate for the advantages of position. Discipline & instruction — mutual confidence between Generals & soldiers — all are necessary to secure success in attacking an enemy strongly intrenched. There is a vast difference between the degree of preparation required to resist an attack successfully, & that needed to assault intrenched positions.

I need not remind you of the fact that since the day when I assumed command of the Army of the Potomac everything had to be created, still less need I call your attention to the rapidity with which the admirable General Officers under my command have accomplished this task.

I ask at the hands of the Administration & the country confidence & patience. So long as I retain my present position I must claim to be the best judge of the time to strike — I repeat, what you already know, that no one is more anxious to terminate speedily this fratricidal war than I am.

One of our chief difficulties consists in the scarcity of instructed staff officers — a want that can only be supplied from the Military Academy. I would therefore urge that the number of Cadets be immediately increased to 400, that being the number for which accommodations can at once be provided; I would also recommend that measures be taken for the prospective increase of the Corps to from 700 to 800.[2]

In the mean time it is absolutely necessary to make some prompt provision to supply the wants of the Staff Depts — it is simply impossible to improvise staff officers — mere intelligence & courage will not answer — a good military education is absolutely necessary. Two plans suggest themselves to me — the one is to modify temporarily the course of instruction at West Point; the other to establish a temporary school independent of the Alma Mater.

ADf, McClellan Papers (A-32:14), Library of Congress.

1. In a calendar of his papers for this period, GBM described this as a "rough draft of report as Genl in Chief." McClellan Papers (A-106:42). He elected not to submit such a report. 2. In another draft, GBM elaborated on this point: "By appointing some 200 additional Cadets & devoting their time to strictly military studies, probably 100 good Infantry officers could be turned out at the end of two months, the other 100 would be fair Artillery & Cavalry officers at the end of four months, & the places of the first one hundred having been at once supplied there would be another 100 ready at the end of the first four months. . . . The standard of the preliminary examination for these additional Cadets should be very high, & none admitted less than 18 or 19 years of age while the maximum limit might be 25 years. Either Lts of Volunteers should be eligible to these classes, upon the recommendation of the Genls of Brigades, or there should be established a distinct school for volunteer officers of all grades." A bill to enlarge the cadet enrollment at West Point was defeated in Congress in January 1862.

To Mary Ellen McClellan

[Washington] Nov 17 [1861]

... I find that today is not to be a day of rest for me. This unfortunate affair of Mason & Slidell has come up, & I shall be obliged to devote the day to endeavoring to get our Govt to take the only prompt & honorable course of avoiding a war with England & France.[1] Our Govt has done wrong in seizing these men on a neutral ship: — the only manly way of getting out of the scrape is a prompt release with a frank avowal of the wrong — before a demand for reparations is made. After our recent successes we can afford to be generous & frank. It is sickening in the extreme & makes me feel heavy at heart when I see the weakness & unfitness of the poor beings who control the destinies of this great country. How I wish that God had permitted me to live quietly & unknown with you — but his will be done!

I will do my best — try to preserve an honest mind — to do my duty as best I may — & will ever, I hope, continue to pray that He will give me that wisdom courage & truth that are so necessary to me now, & so little of which I possess. The outside world may envy me no doubt — they do not know the weight of care that presses on me....

I will try again to write a few lines before I go to Stanton's to ascertain what the Law of Nations is on this Slidell & Mason seizure....

I am very glad you liked the Scott order.[2] I feared you might think it too rhetorical....

I have just returned from Stanton's where I have had a long discussion on the law points of the M & S capture. I am surprised to find that our Govt is fully justified by all the rules of International Law & all the decisions in the highest courts which bear upon the case — so it matters but little whether the English Govt & people make a fuss about it or not, for as we are manifestly & undoubtedly in the right it makes little difference to us, as we can afford to fight in a just cause....

I went to the White House shortly after tea where I found "the *original gorrilla*,"[3] about as intelligent as ever. What a specimen to be at the head of our affairs now! I then went to the Prince de Joinville's[4] — we went up stairs & had a long confidential talk upon politics etc. He showed me some letters from his mother, & his brothers d'Aumale & Nemours, which gave me important information as to the relations of France & England. He, the Prince, is a noble character — one whom I shall be glad to have you know well — he bears adversity so well & so uncomplainingly. I admire him more than almost any one I have ever met with — he is true as steel — like all deaf men very reflective — says but little & that always to the point....

After I left the Prince's I went to Seward's, where I found the "Gorilla" again, & was of course much edified by his anecdotes — ever apropos, & ever unworthy of one holding his high position. I spent some time there & *almost* organized a little quarrel with that poor little varlet Seward by giving him the information I had received from the Prince (without telling the source) — he said he *knew* it was not so. I said I thought I was right — he again contradicted me & I told him that the future would prove the correctness of my story. It is a terrible dispensation of Providence that so weak & cowardly a thing as that should now control our foreign relations — unhappily the Presdt is not much better, except that he is honest & means well. I suppose our country has richly merited some great punishment, else we should not now have such wretched triflers at the head of affairs. . . .

As I parted from the Presdt on Seward's steps he said that it had been suggested to him that it was no more safe for me than for him to walk out at night without some attendants; I told him that I felt no fear, that no one would take the trouble to interfere with me, on which he deigned to remark that they would probably give more for my scalp at Richmond than for his. . . .

AL copy, McClellan Papers (C-7:63), Library of Congress.

1. On Nov. 8 Confederate envoys James M. Mason and John Slidell were taken from the British mail packet *Trent* off Cuba by Capt. Charles Wilkes of the U.S.S. *San Jacinto*. 2. General Orders, No. 19, Nov. 1, *supra*. 3. An epithet for President Lincoln, which GBM had apparently adopted from Edwin M. Stanton. *McClellan's Own Story*, p. 152. 4. Prince de Joinville, of the exiled House of Orléans, was acting as guardian for his nephews, the Duc de Chartres and the Comte de Paris, pretender to the French throne, who were members of GBM's staff.

To Mary Ellen McClellan

[Washington] Nov 18, 1861

I had Genl Sumner & Raymond[1] to dinner — then the Gorrilla came in. Then I tried to take a nap & was *quietly* interrupted by a deputation of twelve ladies & twelve gentlemen (there was *one* very good looking young female in the party) who came on a visit of ceremony, headed by the Governor of Massachusetts.[2] I was as polite as I know how to be; (cross as could be all the time); said something that was intended to be pleasant to all, (especially to the good looking young female — you had better come on soon at that rate), & was delighted to bow them out. Then I had a long interview with David Porter of the Navy, about future plans & operations;[3] then I had to see Mr Astor[4] of N.Y. & appointed him a vol. aide; then I had a long confab with the inevitable McDowell, who left just before I commenced this scrawl & during which interview your Papa as well as Arthur skulked off ignominiously leaving me to bear the brunt of the bathery.

Copy, McClellan Papers (D-10:72), Library of Congress.

1. Brig. Gen. Edwin V. Sumner; Capt. Edward A. Raymond, of GBM's staff. 2. Gov. John A. Andrew. 3. Comdr. David D. Porter. Their discussion concerned an operation against New Orleans. 4. John Jacob Astor, Jr.

To Mary Ellen McClellan

[Washington] Wednesday [November 20, 1861] 8 1/2 pm.

The Grand Review went off splendidly — there were nearly 65,000 men on the ground — not a mistake made, not a hitch. I never saw so large a Review in Europe so well done — I was completely satisfied & delighted beyond expression.

AL copy, McClellan Papers (C-7:63), Library of Congress.

To Mary Ellen McClellan

[Washington] Nov. 21 [1861]

... Herr Hermann, "a great Magician" volunteered to give us a private entertainment, so I invited all the staff etc [to] it. The most striking feature of the performance was that the Magician asked the Presdt for his handkerchief — upon which that dignitary replied promptly "You've got me now, I ain't got any"!!!!

AL copy, McClellan Papers (C-7:63), Library of Congress.

To Charles P. Stone   [TELEGRAM]

[Washington] Nov 29 [1861]

Please inform Genl Hill[1] that I have no wish to protect robbers & that I will cordially unite in any proper effort to repress marauding. If he will turn these men over to me with the evidence necessary to convict them before a commission they shall be tried & punished in good faith.

Say to him that I have no plea to interpose for men who have disobeyed my orders by stealing, except to recommend the utmost care and reflection in the infliction of a punishment which, although just, may lead to reprisals beyond my power to control & may lend to this contest a degree of ferocity which I desire to avoid.[2]

G B McClellan
Maj Genl Comdg USA

Brig Genl C P Stone
Comdg at Poolesville

ALS (telegram sent), Records of the Office of the Secretary of War, RG 107 (M-504:9), National Archives. *OR*, Ser. 1, V, p. 669.

1. Brig. Gen. D. H. Hill, CSA, stationed at Leesburg, Va. 2. At issue were certain Federal prisoners in Hill's hands. On Dec. 16 Hill received instructions in the matter from Gen.

Joseph E. Johnston: "Let General Hill try and hang our own traitors for murder, robbery, and treason, but the Northern soldiers cannot be dealt with thus summarily." *OR*, Ser. 1, V, pp. 999–1000.

To the Children's Aid Association of Trenton

My dear Children   Washington Nov 29 1861

Your very welcome present & your still kinder note reached me today.[1]

I feel encouraged & strengthened in the performance of the task imposed upon me when even the children of the land wish me "God speed." Your mothers have taught you that no work can succeed without God's blessing, and our Saviour himself has taught us all not to dispair, but to cherish the purity & innocence of childhood. Of all the unmerited tributes of praise it has fallen to my lot to receive, I assure you, my dear children, your simple prayer has touched me most — I am sure that it comes from your hearts.

I hope & pray that you may preserve through life your present innocence, & that when in years to come you hear that I have passed to another world, you may still be able to wish me "God speed" from the depths of your hearts.

I will do my best ever to deserve your prayers & blessing; do *your* best, dear children, to preserve the right to pray for a soldier who has devoted his honor & life to his country in its greatest need.

I am, dear little ones, your sincere friend
Geo B McClellan
Maj Genl Comdg USA

ALS retained copy, McClellan Papers (B-9:47), Library of Congress.

1. The undated letter, signed with seventeen names, reads: "Will you please accept this small offering from the 'Children's Aid Association of Trenton'? We wish you 'God speed.'" The offering has not been found. McClellan Papers (B-13:49).

To Don Carlos Buell

Brig. Genl. D. C. Buell,
Louisville   Washington, Monday night.
My dear Buell: [December 2, 1861]

Your welcome letter of the 27th, reached me this evening.[1] I have just telegraphed you expressing my satisfaction at its contents. I now feel sure I have a "lieutenant" in whom I can fully rely. Your views are right. You have seized the true strategic base and from Lebanon can move where you will. Keep up the hearts of the Tennesseans, make them feel that far from any intention of deserting them, that all will be done to sustain them. Be sure to maintain their ardor, for it will avail you much in the future. I am not as a general rule, at all disposed to scatter troops. I believe in attacks by concentrated masses, but it seems to me, with the little local knowledge I possess, that you *might* attempt two movements, one on Eastern Tenn., say with 15,000 men, and a strong attack on Nashville as you propose with say 50,000 men.

I think we owe it to our Union friends in Eastern Tenn. to protect them at all hazards. First secure that, *then*, if you possess the means, carry Nashville.

If I can ever get the account of the small arms in our possession I can tell you what you may expect, but with the present Chief of Ordnance[2] I scarcely hope for so simple a result. You can count on one thing, viz: that you shall have all I can give you. You have already been informed that 12 regiments have been ordered to you from W. Va. I have also ordered thence to you one regular and one *excellent* volunteer battery. These with the Randall companies will give you 5 batteries equivalent to regulars. Give each of these Captains 3 other batteries and you will soon have your light artillery in good order. I am informed that large supplies of cavalry arms will arrive this week. Telegraph me what you need and I will *try* to supply you. Give me by telegraph and letter the statement of your command by regiments and batteries as soon as possible. I have telegraphed to-day to Halleck for information as to his gun-boats. You shall have a sufficient number of them to perform the operations you suggest. I will place C. F. Smith[3] under your orders and replace his command by other troops.

Inform me some little time before you are ready to move, so that we may move simultaneously. I have also other heavy blows to strike at the same time. I doubt whether all the movements can be arranged so that the grand blows shall be struck in less than a month or six weeks from the present time.

Make the best use of your time in organizing and drilling your command. Unless circumstances render it necessary do not strike until I too am ready. Should I be delayed I will not ask you to wait for me. I will at once take the necessary steps to carry out your views as to the rivers.

In haste truly yours,

Geo B McClellan

Maj Genl

ALS (typewritten copy), Buell Papers, Woodson Research Center, Rice University Library. *OR*, Ser. 1, VII, pp. 457–58 (misdated).

1. Buell's letter described the condition and position of his command, and proposed three possible courses of action: an advance either on Nashville or on East Tennessee, or a simultaneous advance on both. In conjunction with whatever plan was selected he called for two "flotilla columns" to move up the Tennessee and Cumberland rivers. *OR*, Ser. 1, VII, pp. 450–52. 2. Brig. Gen. James W. Ripley. 3. Brig Gen. Charles F. Smith.

To Don Carlos Buell

Brig. Genl. D. C. Buell, Louisville   Washington,
My dear Buell: December 3d, 1861.

I enclose two letters which were referred to me by the Presdt. and were intended for your eye.[1] I do so feeling sure that you sympathize with me in my *intense* regard for the noble Union men of Eastern Tenn., that you will overlook all mere matters of form, and that you will devote all your energies towards the salvation of men so eminently deserving our protection. I understand your movements and fully concur in their propriety, but I must still urge the occupation of Eastern Tenn. as a *duty* we owe to our gallant friends there who have not hesitated to espouse our cause.

Please send there with the least possible delay troops enough to protect these men. I still feel sure that the best strategical move in this case will be that dictated by the simple feelings of humanity. We *must* preserve these noble fellows from harm. Everything urges us to do that — faith, interest and loyalty. For the sake of these Eastern Tennesseans who have taken part with us I would gladly sacrifice mere military advantages. They deserve our protection, and at all hazards they must have it. I know that your nature is noble enough to forget any slurs they may cast upon you. Protect the true men and you have everything to look forward to. In no event allow them to be crushed out.

I have ordered one regular and one *excellent* volunteer battery to join you. To-day I ordered 10,000 excellent arms to be sent to you at Louisville. I have directed all your requisitions to be filled at once. You may fully rely on my full support in the movement I have so much at heart — the liberation of Eastern Tennessee.

Write to me often, fully and confidentially. If you gain and retain possession of Eastern Tennessee you will have won brighter laurels than any I hope to gain.

With the utmost confidence and firmest friendship, I am truly yours,
Geo B McClellan
Maj Genl Comdg USA

P.S. This letter has been dictated by no doubt as to your movements and intentions, but only by my feelings for the Union men of Eastern Tenn.

McC

ALS (typewritten copy), Buell Papers, Woodson Research Center, Rice University Library. *OR*, Ser. 1, VII, p. 468.

1. These letters, dated Nov. 21 and 25, were written to Tennessee congressman Horace Maynard by Lt. Samuel P. Carter, USN, detailed to the War Department to recruit Tennessee troops for the Union. Carter called for an immediate advance into East Tennessee.

Both letters bore the president's endorsement, ''Please read and consider this letter.'' *OR*, Ser. 1, VII, pp. 468–69.

To Don Carlos Buell

Private   Washington —
My dear Buell   [December] 5th [1861][1]

I have only time before the mail closes to acknowledge yours of the 30th.[2] Give me at once in detail your views as to the number & armament of gun boats necessary for the water movement — the necessary land forces etc. Would not C F Smith be a good man to command that part of the expedition. When should they move?[3]

Pray do not abandon the Pikeville region. I consider it important to hold that line — your supplies can go by water to Prestonburg. I will also reinforce the Guyandotte region at once.[4] Let me again urge the necessity of sending something into East Tenna as promptly as possible — our friends there have thrown their all into the scale & we must not desert them. I tell the East Tenna men here to rest quiet — that you will take care of them & will never desert them. I ordered today two fully armed regts of cavalry to join you from Dennison[5] — will send you some more inftry from the North West in a day or two.

I will try to write more fully tonight — by all means hold Somerset & London — better entrench both — still better the crossing of the river nearest those points.

In haste truly your friend
McClellan

Genl D. C. Buell

ALS, Buell Papers, Woodson Research Center, Rice University Library. *OR*, Ser. 1, VII, pp. 473–74, 583.

1. As printed in the *Official Records* this letter is tentatively dated Dec. 5, 1861, but a note is inserted changing the date to Feb. 5, 1862. The Dec. 5 date is correct. 2. Buell's letter of Nov. 30 called for ''some concert between Halleck's action and mine'' and stressed the importance of the advance up the Tennessee and Cumberland rivers that he had proposed. McClellan Papers (B-9:47), Library of Congress. 3. Buell replied on Dec. 10 that 10,000 men would be needed for each of the river movements, but that more information was needed on the enemy posts at Forts Henry and Donelson. He expressed reservations about Charles F. Smith as commander. *OR*, Ser. 1, VII, pp. 487–88. 4. GBM refers here to eastern Kentucky and western Virginia. 5. Camp Dennison, near Cincinnati.

To Henry W. Halleck   [TELEGRAM]

For Gen Halleck
St Louis   Washington Dec 5, 1861

Please inform me at once the exact number, condition, and armament of the gunboats. If necessary, to complete the crews, detail an unarmed regiment of good men for the purpose. How many troops can you spare from Missouri for an important operation. On receipt of your reply by telegraph I will give you details.[1]

Geo B Mc Clellan
Maj Gen

Retained copy, Records of the Office of the Secretary of War, RG 107 (M-504 :9), National Archives.

1. Halleck telegraphed on Dec. 6 that his forces were untrained and disorganized. "We are not prepared for any important expedition out of the State ; it would imperil the safety of Missouri. Wait till we are ready." *OR*, Ser. 1, VIII, p. 408.

To Simon Cameron

Hon Simon Cameron
Secty of War   Hd Qtrs of the Army
Sir   Washington Dec 9 1861

I have the honor to enclose herewith a copy of the N.Y. Times of Dec 4 1861, containing as you will see a map of our works on the other side of the Potomac, & a statement of the composition of the Divisions in that same locality.

This is clearly giving aid comfort & information to the enemy, & is evidently a case of treasonable action as clear [as] any that can be found. You will remember that this same paper did its best to aid the rebels by publishing full details as to Genl Sherman's expedition before it sailed.[1] I have therefore to represent that the interests of our arms require the suppression of this treasonable sheet, & urgently recommend that the necessary steps to suppress the paper may be taken at once.[2]

Very respectfully yr obdt svt
Geo B McClellan
Maj Genl Comdg USA

ALS retained copy, Records of the Headquarters of the Army, RG 108 (M-857 :6), National Archives.

1. The *New York Times* had published the composition — but not the target — of the Port Royal expedition. J. Cutler Andrews, *The North Reports the Civil War* (Pittsburgh, 1955), p. 143. 2. The *Times* was not suppressed. Editor Henry J. Raymond wrote Cameron on Dec. 13 that both the map and the divisional listing were taken from information released to the press by army headquarters. Raymond Papers, Rare Books and Manuscripts Division, New York Public Library.

To Abraham Lincoln

Confidential

Your Excellency   Washington Dec 10 [1861]

I enclose the paper you left with me — filled as you requested. In arriving at the numbers given I have left the minimum number in garrison & observation.[1]

Information received recently leads me to believe that the enemy could meet us in front with equal forces *nearly* — & I have now my mind actively turned towards another plan of campaign that I do not think at all anticipated by the enemy nor by many of our own people.

Very respectfully your obdt svt
Geo B McClellan
Maj Genl

His Ex the President

ALS, Lincoln Papers, Library of Congress. *OR*, Ser. 1, XI, Part 3, p. 6.

1. Lincoln's memorandum, written about Dec. 1, proposed an immediate advance by the Army of the Potomac to the area of the Occoquan River, to cut the railroad supply line of the Confederate Army at Manassas Junction. In annotating the memorandum, in response to the president's questions, GBM estimated that the movement might take place between Dec. 15 and Dec. 25, with forces totaling 104,000 men. *The Collected Works of Abraham Lincoln*, ed. Roy P. Basler (New Brunswick, N.J., 1953–55), V, pp. 34–35.

To Henry W. Halleck

Maj. Gen. H. W. Halleck,   Headquarters of the Army
Commanding Department of Missouri: Washington,
General: December 10, 1861.

Yours of the 6th has this moment reached me.[1] I am obliged to you for the spirit of frankness in which it is written. Let me begin by replying to the last part of your letter.

You will probably remember that soon after General Hunter assumed command of the department he ordered two divisions from Western Missouri to Saint Louis, regarding them as available for other service.[2] My dispatch was predicated on that, and if you had informed me that you had any available troops I intended to propose to you a movement in concert with Buell. His project, though very important, must either be deferred or be carried out in some other way.[3] I have no intention of stripping you of troops when you cannot spare them. I to-day directed General Thomas to telegraph to you that Major Ketchum[4] might remain with you and that I would recommend him as a brigadier-general. I had already determined to try to secure his appointment. I do not understand your statement that four or five of the regular officers you now have are ordered away, but will look into it in the morning. There is some mistake about it, unless you allude to the paroled officers, who cannot under their parole be of any service to you. You are also misinformed as to the number of regular officers on my personal staff. I have two regular aides, instead of the authorized number of three, and one chief of staff; the others apparently are my personal staff, and are really doing their appropriate duties in the line and their respective corps. Even my personal aides are on duty constantly as inspectors.

I am sorry to learn the very disorganized condition of the troops. I appreciate the difficulty of the task before you, and you may rest assured that I will support you to the full extent of my ability. Do not hesitate to use force with the refractory. Can you yet form any idea of the time necessary to prepare an expedition against Columbus or one up the Cumberland and Tennessee rivers, in connection with Buell's movements? I shall send troops to Hunter,[5] to enable him to move into the Indian Territory west of Arkansas and upon Northern Texas. That movement should relieve you very materially. It will require some little time to prepare Hunter, but when he moves you might act in concert with him.

> In haste, very truly, yours,
> Geo. B. McClellan,
> Major-General, Commanding
> U.S. Army

OR, Ser. 1, VIII, p. 419.

1. Halleck's letter of Dec. 6 detailed the fraud, corruption, and disorganization of the command he inherited from Frémont, and his lack of troops and instructed officers. *OR*, Ser. 1, VIII, pp. 408–410. 2. Maj. Gen. David Hunter had temporarily commanded the Western Department in place of Frémont. 3. See GBM to Buell, Dec. 2, *supra*. 4. Maj. W. Scott Ketchum, inspector general, Department of Missouri. 5. See GBM to Hunter, Dec. 11, *supra*.

To David Hunter

Unofficial   Head Quarters of the Army
General,   Washington Decem 11, 1861

Your telegram to General Thomas surprised me exceedingly.[1] Realizing as I do the very trying nature of the circumstances in which you are placed, I have attributed it to momentary irritation which your cooler judgment will at least lead you to regard as unnecessary.

In regard to placing General Halleck in Command of the Department of Missouri, that step was taken from the evident necessity of placing some one there who was in no manner connected, for or against, with the unfortunate state of affairs previously existing in that Department. Immediately after you were assigned to your present Department I requested the Adjutant General to inform you that it was deemed expedient to organize an expedition under your Command to secure the Indian Territory west of Arkansas, as well as to make a descent upon Northern Texas, in connection with one to strike at Western Texas from the Gulf. The General was to invite your prompt attention to this subject, and to ask you to indicate the necessary force and means for the undertaking.

I would again call your attention to this very important subject stating the necessary force shall be placed at your disposal. Three regiments of Wisconsin Infantry have been ordered to report to you, also a battery and two Companies of Cavalry from Minnesota. This is intended only as a commencement and will be followed up by other troops as rapidly as your wants are known and circumstances will permit.

Requesting your early attention to this subject,[2]

Very respectfully yr obt svt
Geo B McClellan
Maj Genl Comdg

LS, Miscellaneous Collections, Huntington Library. *OR*, Ser. 1, VIII, pp. 428–29. Maj. Gen. Hunter was named to the Department of Kansas on Nov. 20.

1. In his dispatch of this date to Lorenzo Thomas, Hunter stated that he was outnumbered ten to one and would be fortunate to keep possession of Kansas. He added that dividing the Western Department into the departments of Missouri and Kansas "was not for the good of the service." *OR*, Ser. 1, VIII, p. 428. 2. Hunter replied on Dec. 19 that at least 20,000 additional troops and a substantial wagon train would be required. *OR*, Ser. 1, VIII, pp. 450–51. See GBM to Edwin M. Stanton, c. Jan. 25, 1862, *infra*.

To Abraham Lincoln

[Washington, c. December 18, 1861]

I would recommend that fifty of the "Coffee Mill" guns be furnished at 20% advance on cost price, which cost may be ascertained by competent Ordnance officers — I think $1200 entirely too high.[1]

Geo. B. McClellan
Maj. Genl. Comg.

Copy, Lincoln Papers, Library of Congress.

1. This copy is in Lincoln's handwriting. GBM apparently wrote the note to the president in response to a letter sent him on Dec. 12 by J. D. Mills, the representative of the maker of this early machine gun. On Dec. 19 Lincoln sent GBM's recommendation to Gen. Ripley, the army's chief of ordnance, with his endorsement: "Let the fifty guns be ordered on the terms above recommended by Gen. McClellan & not otherwise." *Collected Works of Lincoln*, V, p. 75; *Supplement*, p. 115.

To John A. Andrew

His Excellency John A. Andrew,
Governor of Massachusetts   Headquarters Army of the Potomac
Sir: Washington, December 20, 1861.

A letter addressed to Lieutenant-Colonel Palfrey, commanding Twen-
tieth Regiment Massachusetts Volunteers, signed by Thomas Drew, as-
sistant military secretary, and purporting to have been written by your
excellency's authority has just been brought to my notice.[1] In this letter
Lieutenant-Colonel Palfrey is directed to convey censure and reprimand
to an officer of his regiment for acts performed in the line of his military
duty. If the officer referred to had been guilty of any infraction of
military law or regulation the law itself points out the method and manner
for its own vindication and the channel through which the punishment
shall come. Any departure from this rule strikes immediately at the root
of all discipline and subordination. The volunteer regiments from the
different States of the Union when accepted and mustered into the service
of the United States became a portion of the Federal Army and are as
entirely removed from the authority of the governors of the several States
as are the troops of the regular regiments. As discipline in the service
can only be maintained by the strictest observance of military subordi-
nation nothing could be more detrimental than that any interference
should be allowed outside the constituted authorities.[2]

Trusting that these considerations will commend themselves to your
excellency's judgment,

I remain, very respectfully, your obedient servant,

Retained copy, Records of U.S. Army Continental Commands, RG 393 (3964: Army of the
Potomac), National Archives. *OR*, Ser. 2, I, pp. 790–91.

1. This letter, dated Dec. 9 and addressed to Lt. Col. Francis W. Palfrey, charged one of
Palfrey's officers with ''discreditable conduct'' in returning fugitive slaves to their Mary-
land owners ''without any observance of even the forms of law, either civil or military.''
The letter was forwarded to GBM by Charles P. Stone, Palfrey's division commander, who
termed it an ''unwarranted and dangerous interference'' with his command. *OR*, Ser. 2,
I, pp. 786–88. 2. While Gov. Andrew and GBM continued to argue the issue of state versus
federal authority over volunteer troops (*OR*, Ser. 2, I, pp. 791–93, 796–97), public debate
centered on Stone's handling of fugitive slaves, a debate intensified by the investigation of
the Joint Committee on the Conduct of the War into Stone's part in the Ball's Bluff defeat.

To Henry W. Halleck

Maj. Gen. H. W. Halleck,
Commanding Department of Missouri: Headquarters of the Army
General: Washington, January 3, 1862.

It is of the greatest importance that the rebel troops in Western Ken-
tucky be prevented from moving to the support of the force in front of

General Buell. To accomplish this an expedition should be sent up the Cumberland River, to act in concert with General Buell's command of sufficient strength to defeat any force that may be brought against it. The gunboats should be supported by at least one and perhaps two divisions of your best infantry, taken from Paducah and other points from which they can best be spared. At the same time such a demonstration should be made on Columbus as will prevent the removal of any troops from that place; and, if a sufficient number have already been withdrawn, the place should be taken. It may be well also to make a feint on the Tennessee River, with a command sufficient to prevent disaster under any circumstances.

As our success in Kentucky depends in a great measure on our preventing re-enforcements from joining Buckner and Johnston,[1] not a moment's time should be lost in preparing these expeditions.

I desire that you give me at once your views in full as to the best method of accomplishing our object, at the same time stating the nature and strength of the force that you can use for the purpose and the time necessary to prepare.

Very respectfully,
Geo. B. McClellan
Major-General, Commanding.

OR, Ser. 1, VII, pp. 527–28.

1. Brig. Gen. Buckner in Kentucky served under Gen. Albert Sidney Johnston, Confederate commander in the western theater.

To Don Carlos Buell

Confidential
Brig. Gen. D. C. Buell,
Louisville, Ky.:

My dear General: Washington, Monday, January 6, 1862.

You will have learned ere this that Colonel Cross has been ordered to relieve Colonel Swords,[1] and that two or three active young quartermasters from the Regular Army have been ordered to report to you. Two hundred wagons from Philadelphia have been ordered to you, and Meigs[2] is stirring up the country generally to procure means of transportation for you. There are few things I have more at heart than the prompt movement of a strong column into Eastern Tennessee. The political consequences of the delay of this movement will be much more serious than you seem to anticipate. If relief is not soon afforded those people we shall lose them entirely, and with them the power of inflicting the most severe blow upon the secession cause.

I was extremely sorry to learn from your telegram to the President that you had *from the beginning attached little or no importance* to a movement in East Tennessee.[3] I had not so understood your views, and it develops a radical difference between your views and my own, which I deeply regret.

My own general plans for the prosecution of the war make the speedy occupation of East Tennessee and its lines of railway matters of absolute necessity. Bowling Green and Nashville are in that connection of very secondary importance at the present moment. My own advance cannot, according to my present view, be made until your troops are solidly established in the eastern portion of Tennessee. If that is not possible, a complete and prejudicial change in my own plans at once becomes necessary.

Interesting as Nashville may be to the Louisville interests, it strikes me that its possession is of very secondary importance in comparison with the immense results that would arise from the adherence to our cause of the masses in East Tennessee, West North Carolina, South Carolina, North Georgia, and Alabama, results that I feel assured would ere long flow from the movement I allude to.

Halleck, from his own account, will not soon be in a condition to support properly a movement up the Cumberland. Why not make the movement independently of and without waiting for that?

I regret that I have not strength enough to write a fuller and more intelligible letter, but this is my very first effort at writing for somewhat more than two weeks.[4]

> In haste, my dear general, very truly, yours,
> Geo. B. McClellan,
> Major-General, Commanding.

OR, Ser. 1, VII, p. 531.

1. Maj. Osborn Cross, Col. Thomas Swords. 2. Brig. Gen. Montgomery C. Meigs, the army's quartermaster general. 3. Buell's telegram of Jan. 5 to Lincoln read, in part: "I will confess to your excellency that I have been bound to it [the East Tennessee operation] more by my sympathy for the people of East Tennessee and the anxiety with which you and the General-in-Chief have desired it than by my opinion of its wisdom as an unconditional measure. As earnestly as I wish to accomplish it, my judgment has from the first been decidedly against it...." *OR*, Ser. 1, VII, pp. 530–31. 4. GBM had fallen ill with typhoid fever on Dec. 23, 1861.

To Ambrose E. Burnside

Brig Genl A E Burnside
Comdg Expedn   Hd Qtrs of the Army
Genl   Washington Jany 7 1862

In accordance with verbal instructions heretofore given you, you will after uniting with Flag Officer Goldsborough[1] at Fort Monroe, proceed under his convoy to Hatteras Inlet, when you will in connection with him take the most prompt measures for crossing the Fleet over the "Bulk-head" into the waters of the Sound. Under the accompanying General Order constituting the Dept of North Carolina you will assume the command of the garrison at Hatteras Inlet & make such dispositions in regard to that place as your ulterior operations may render necessary — always being careful to provide for the safety of that very important station in any contingency.

Your first point of attack will be Roanoke Island & its dependencies.

It is presumed that the Navy can reduce the batteries in the marshes & cover the landing of your troops on the main Island, by which — in connection with a rapid movement of the gun boats to the northern extremity as soon as the marsh battery is reduced — it may be hoped to capture the entire garrison of the place.

Having occupied the Island & its dependencies you will at once proceed to the erection of the batteries & defences necessary to hold the position with a small force.

Should the Flag Officer require any assistance in seizing or holding the debouches of the canals from Norfolk, you will please afford it to him.

The Commodore & yourself having completed your arrangements in regard to Roanoke Island & the waters north of it, you will please at once make a descent upon Newbern, having gained possession of which & the RR passing through it, you will at once throw a sufficient force upon Beaufort & take the steps necessary to reduce Fort Macon & open that Port. When you seize Newbern you will endeavor to seize the RR as far west as Goldsboro' should circumstances favor such a movement — the temper of the people, the rebel force at hand will go far towards determining the question as to how far west the RR can be safely occupied & held.

Should circumstances render it advisable to seize & hold Raleigh the main north & south line of RR passing through Goldsboro' should be so effectually destroyed for considerable distances north & south of that point as to render it impossible for the rebels to use it to your disadvantage. A great point would be gained, in any event, by the effectual destruction of the Wilmington & Weldon R.R.

I would advise great caution in moving so far into the interior as upon Raleigh. Having accomplished the objects mentioned the next point of interest would probably be Wilmington, the reduction of which may require that additional means shall be afforded you.

I would urge great caution in regard to proclamations — in no case would I go beyond a moderate joint proclamation with the Naval Comdr, which should say as little as possible about politics or the negro — merely state that the true issue for which we are fighting is the preservation of the Union & upholding the laws of the Genl Govt, & stating that all who conduct themselves properly will as far as possible be protected in their persons & property.

You will please report your operations as often as an opportunity offers itself.

With my best wishes for your success

I am, General, sincerely your friend
Geo B McClellan
Maj Genl Comdr in Chief

P.S. Any prisoners you take should be sent to the most convenient northern post — you can however exchange any of them for any of your own men who may be taken.

Geo B McC

ALS, Records of the Adjutant General's Office, RG 94 (159: Burnside Papers), National Archives. *OR*, Ser. 1, IX, pp. 352–53. Brig. Gen. Burnside had been assigned command of the Roanoke Island expedition, with headquarters at Annapolis, Md., on Oct. 23, 1861.

1. Flag Officer Louis M. Goldsborough, commander of the North Atlantic Blockading Squadron.

To Nathaniel P. Banks   [TELEGRAM]

[Washington, January 7, 1862]

Say to Genl Lander[1] that I might comment very severely on the tone of his dispatches but abstain. Give him positive orders to repair at once to Romney & carry out the instructions I have sent already to fall back on the Railway.

It would be folly to cross the river at Hancock under present circumstances, except with a small corps of observation, but not to follow up the enemy.

Genl Lander is too suggestive & critical.[2]

G B McClellan
Maj Genl Comdg

Maj Genl N P Banks
Frederick

ALS (telegram sent), McClellan Papers (A-35:15), Library of Congress.

1. Brig. Gen. Lander commanded a division under Banks in the upper Potomac area. 2. Presumably GBM referred to Lander's dispatches of Jan. 6 to Banks that called for a prompt crossing of the Potomac to attack the Confederates under Maj. Gen. Thomas J. Jackson, who were raiding such targets as the Baltimore and Ohio Railroad; and of Jan. 7 to Banks that read: "I now demand direct orders" to cross the river. McClellan Papers (A-35:15, B-10:47).

To Alexander D. Bache

Prof A D Bache
Supt Coast Survey   Hd Qtrs of the Army
My dear Sir   Washington Jany 10 1862

I regret to learn that the House of Reps. have decided to suspend work in the Coast Survey during the war.

This decision has caused me great concern, & not knowing whom else to address I have determined to write to you, asking you to make any use you can of my views.

With the exception of the results of the Govt Expeditions on the Plains etc the only reliable topographical information we have of our country is derived from the Coast Survey.

Without the Coast Survey maps it would certainly have been very difficult, if not impossible, to have arranged & carried out most of our military operations. The only maps of any value that we possess of the country on the other side of the Potomac is the result of the labors of the Coast Survey.

Far from suspending the operations of the Coast Survey, I would strongly urge that military necessity demands that its work be pushed with the greatest vigor, & that its field of work be extended as far inland as possible.

The money expended upon the Coast Survey will be repaid an hundred fold in our time of need.[1]

I am very truly & respectfully your obdt svt
Geo B McClellan
Maj Genl Comdg USA

ALS, Rhees Collection, Huntington Library. Bache was superintendent of the United States Coast Survey.

1. Bache replied on the same date that no one "would doubt the terrible blow your letter will deal to the enemies of the Coast Survey." He wrote again on Jan. 16 that GBM's letter "will I feel certain determine Congress against the suspension of the Coast Survey." The Survey's operations did not cease during the war. McClellan Papers (B-9:47, B-10:47), Library of Congress.

To Don Carlos Buell

Brig. Gen. D. C. Buell,   Headquarters of the Army,
Commanding Department of the Ohio: Washington,
My dear General: January 13, 1862.

Your telegram asking for six more batteries is received. I have taken measures to have them ordered to you at once, and will endeavor to order two more to you to-morrow. I hope you will ere long receive the two regular companies from Fort Randall.

You have no idea of the pressure brought to bear here upon the Government for a forward movement. It is so strong that it seems absolutely necessary to make the advance on Eastern Tennessee at once. I incline to this as a first step for many reasons. Your possession of the railroad there will surely prevent the main army in my front from being reenforced and may force Johnston[1] to detach. Its political effect will be very great. Halleck is not yet in condition to afford you the support you need when you undertake the movement on Bowling Green. Meigs has sent to you the 400 wagons for which requisition was made. Should the supply of Government wagons be insufficient, I would recommend hiring private teams. If the people will not freely give them, why then, seize them. It is no time now to stand on trifles. I think Ohio can now give you five or six new regiments, that can at least guard your communications, and are probably about as good as the mass of the troops opposed to you.

I am now quite well again, only somewhat weak. Hope to be in the saddle in a very few days.

> In haste, truly, yours,
> Geo B. McClellan
> Major-General, Commanding.

OR, Ser. 1, VII, p. 547.

1. Albert Sidney Johnston, commanding the western Confederate army.

To Abraham Lincoln

> Washington Tuesday [January 14, 1862]

I enclose for your Excellency's perusal copies of letters from Genl Halleck which will explain themselves.[1]

I have replied to him in regard to my letter of the 3rd that he had not read it carefully.[2] In it I told him what I wanted done & asked his views, as well as the number of troops he could spare for the purpose.

Will your Excellency be good enough to return me the enclosed when you have got through with them. All goes well. I worked until after midnight yesterday, & that with a good deal of work today has fatigued me so much that I will hardly be able to call upon you today.

> Very respectfully & truly
> Geo B McClellan

I am rapidly getting matters in hand again & will carry out the promise I made to you yesterday.[3]

ALS, Lincoln Papers, Library of Congress.

1. Probably Halleck's dispatches to GBM of Jan. 9 and 10. OR, Ser. 1, VII, pp. 539–40, 543. 2. GBM to Halleck, Jan. 3, *supra*. Halleck had replied on Jan. 9: "If a sufficient

number of troops are to be withdrawn from Missouri at the present time to constitute an expedition up the Cumberland . . . , we must seriously peril the loss of this State." 3. At a military conference at the White House on Jan. 13, GBM refused to reveal his plans for the Army of the Potomac, but agreed (in Lincoln's words) to "press the advance in Kentucky." Montgomery C. Meigs, "General M. C. Meigs on the Conduct of the Civil War," *American Historical Review*, 26 :2 (Jan. 1921), p. 293.

To John A. Dix

Confidential   Hd Qtrs of the Army
My dear General   Washington Jany 14 1862

It will soon become necessary for me to make a movement in advance with the main army; when the advance takes place the safety of the Capital becomes a matter of vital interest & must be confided to sure hands.

Circumstances which I will explain to you when we meet will render the task doubly interesting.

After full consideration I have determined to ask you to take upon yourself this very delicate & responsible position.

I write to you thus early to invite your attention to the choice of your successor in the immediate command at Baltimore (which will remain under your control) as well as to enable you quietly to make your arrangements for the change in your station.

Very soon after I am able to get into the saddle again I shall ask you to come here to go over all the ground with me, that we may have a complete understanding, & that you may know the purpose of all I have done in the last few months. The plan of campaign I shall probably follow will be such as to make your position doubly responsible.[1]

Begging that this communication may be regarded as most strictly confidential & asking your views as to the proper person to command at Baltimore

I am sincerely & respectfully your friend
Geo B McClellan
Maj Genl

Maj Genl J A Dix
Comdg at Baltimore

ALS, Dix Papers, Rare Book and Manuscript Library, Columbia University. Maj. Gen. Dix commanded the garrison at Baltimore.

1. Dix did not assume the Washington command. He was appointed to head the Department of Virginia, with headquarters at Fort Monroe, on June 1.

To Abraham Lincoln

Your Excellency

Head-Quarters, Army of the Potomac,
Washington, Jany 15 1862

I am so much better this morning that I am going before the Joint Committee. If I escape alive I will report when I get through.[1]

I think Halleck is a little premature but that Buell will check his feint until the proper time arrives.[2] It is singular that H. has not received the 11,000 arms.

Very truly & respectfully
Geo B McClellan
Maj Genl

His Ex the Presdt

ALS, Lincoln Papers, Library of Congress.

1. The Joint Committee on the Conduct of War. GBM told a newspaperman the next day that the session went well, and that the committee was fully satisfied with his testimony. Malcolm Ives to Frederic Hudson, Jan. 16, 1862, James Gordon Bennett Papers, Library of Congress. Senator Zachariah Chandler, however, reported that committee members were blunt in questioning the Army of the Potomac's inactivity. Detroit Post and Tribune, *Zachariah Chandler: An Outline Sketch of His Life and Public Services* (Detroit, 1880), pp. 224–26. 2. Halleck had ordered a demonstration toward Columbus, Ky., to divert attention from Buell's proposed advance on East Tennessee. *OR*, Ser. 1, VII, pp. 539–40.

To Samuel L. M. Barlow

My dear Barlow   Washington Jany 18 [1862]

I owe you replies to about a dozen notes & thanks for at least the same number of acts of kindness, not forgetting *these* boots! Let me thank you in a lump & assure you that my thanks are none the less sincere for being crowded together in this style. I am quite well now but still weak — the trouble is that they don't give me time to recover — but allow me not one minute of rest when I need it most. If I *could* pass a day or two at 229[1] I *know* I should recover — but I shall not see N.Y. until either I have thrashed Joe Johnston or he has whipped me — should the latter unhappily prove to be the case I don't think I will care to show my face in N.Y.!!

I sent my resignation direct to Alsop the other day — so I am no longer a RR man[2] — but strongly suspect that I will go back to some occupation in civil life when this rebellion is over.

Stanton's appointment was a most unexpected piece of good fortune, & I hope it will produce a good effect in the North.[3]

There is somebody after me! So I must close.

My wife sends her kindest regards to Mrs. B & yourself — present mine also.

In haste ever your friend
Geo B McClellan

S L M Barlow Esq

ALS, Barlow Papers, Huntington Library.

1. 229 Fifth Avenue, Barlow's New York residence. 2. GBM's resignation as president of the Eastern Division of the Ohio and Mississippi Railroad was dated Jan. 9. 3. Edwin M. Stanton was confirmed as secretary of war on Jan. 15.

To Mary M. Marcy

[Washington] Thursday evng
[January 23, 1862]

My dear Grandmama

Prince[1] & I have been looking into our domestic affairs this evng & find part of the family in a sad condition. Poor Nell wanted to go out to a party this evng & found that she was absolutely in the condition of Miss Flora McFlimsey! Nell talks about economy — but that is nonsense.

So please get her *at least one* very handsome silk for an evening dress — some color that will become her — red (not brick dust) is my favorite, but she has one already — get her a *very* handsome one.

If you think she ought to have two now, please get them. I don't know whether there ought to be any flowers for the hair to go with silk dresses — if yes get them also.

Please get the young woman also a *wreath* of *rose color* to match the white (trimmed with pink) dress she had made here — she says you will know the color & had better go to Haldimans unless you can happen in upon some smart auction store where partially injured articles are going cheap.

Get me also a wreath of roses for myself — I think I'll come out in a new way. Please send *Nell's* rose colored wreath by Adams Express — I'm not in so great a hurry for mine.

The baby is splendid — laughs inordinately & so loudly that it is almost a nuisance — converses intelligently in 3 languages — & when missed day before yesterday was found strolling around Willard's Hotel after a search of an hour or two.

Nell has behaved very well considering! She patronizes the "thing" [*illegible*] extensively, & I manage to pass a peaceable & quiet time in the day time by staying at the office from breakfast time until 6 o'clock. Poor Nell — bears her disappointment tonight like a young angel. Nothing new here — except that the mud is almost two feet deeper than when you left.

Tell Fan[2] to pay particular attention to spelling at school — it does not look well for a young lady of 16 (?) to write, or spell, "Highdrew-foebiah" "Dearexshun" "Miss Dar Meaner" eatsetthera eatsetthera. Tell her I wish to impress upon her the fact that spelling is equally important with callisthenics. Tell her that if she will wash her face regularly, not drink too much coffee, & whistle occasionally she will be happy.

My paper is out — like your patience. Love to miserable Grandpapa & tell him to festina lente[3] — love also to Fanny. All well here except Prince who is disgusted this evng.

> With much love to all from Nell & myself
> Your affectionate son
> G B McC

Give love to all the family. Tell the Dr that I braved to their faces about a dozen alopaths in the Sanitary Comm today![4] Say to Emma that I learn that Raymond only uses words beginning with *D*. Whether they end with a vowel or consonant I have not yet learned.

ALS, McClellan Papers (B-40:60), Library of Congress. Mrs. Marcy, GBM's mother-in-law, was in New York with Randolph Marcy during his recuperation from typhoid fever.

1. The McClellans' dog. 2. Fanny Marcy, GBM's sister-in-law. 3. Make haste slowly. 4. Dr. Erastus E. Marcy, a homeopathic physician who was caring for his brother Randolph Marcy, had also treated GBM for his typhoid. A contingent from the U.S. Sanitary Commission, including practitioners of more conventional allopathic medicine, called on GBM that day to seek reform of the army's medical service. *The Diary of George Templeton Strong: The Civil War, 1860–1865*, eds. Allan Nevins and Milton H. Thomas (New York, 1952), p. 203.

To Edwin M. Stanton

Hon E. M. Stanton
Secretary of War   Head Quarters of the Army
Sir.   Washington January 24, 1862.

Many complaints have reached me through Division commanders and otherwise as to the manner in which vacancies among the Officers of Volunteer Regiments are filled by the Governors of States in many instances. Instead of promoting meritorious Officers non-commissioned Officers and Soldiers who have shown a fitness for their position and have acquired a certain amount of experience and confidence, it is too often the case that such persons are passed over and superceded by men entirely raw and untried appointed from political or personal considerations, and altogether unfit for their duties.

I would respectfully beg leave to invite your attention to this great evil and to suggest for your consideration the propriety of asking from Congress the passage of a law regulating the system of promotion and supplying vacancies in the Volunteer Regiments.

I think also that when a vacancy occurs it should be filled by the next in rank, if fit for the position and that the lower grades should to a great extent be filled by capable non-commissioned Officers. I would also suggest that the troops of each State should be considered as a unit for the purpose of promotion, viz. if the Colonel of a New York Regiment dies then the senior Lieutentant Colonel of the State of New York would, if competent, be promoted to the place.

Some system of this kind would, I am sure, remedy many evils now existing.[1]

I enclose herewith the project of an order from the War Department in regard to inscribing on the Colors of Regiments &c the names of Battles. I spoke to the Secretary about this and submit the order for his consideration.[2]

There are cases of Regiments raised under the direct authority of the War Department, independently of the State authorities — difficulties exist still in regard to some of these. I would suggest that, if the consolidation of the troops from each State, for purposes of promotion, be favorably considered, these independent Regiments be merged in the organization of *some* State, for there are cases where a Regiment is composed of companies from various States.[3]

I am, Sir, very respectfully Your Obdt Servant

Retained copy, Records of the Headquarters of the Army, RG 108 (M-857:6), National Archives.

1. Congress did not act on this proposal. 2. This order was issued on Feb. 22, 1862. *OR*, Ser. 3, I, p. 898. 3. An order to this effect was issued on Feb. 21, 1862. *OR*, Ser. 3, I, p. 898.

To Edwin M. Stanton

[Washington, c. January 25, 1862]

I think that no expedition of 30,000 men, as proposed, is either practicable or advisable at present. From recent information it seems certain that forage cannot be found between Ft Leavenworth & Fort Scott even for the force proposed by Genl Lane.[1] It would be next to impossible & very expensive to transport it from Illinois etc. The true line of supply would seem to be by the Pacific RR &c, keeping north of the Osage, direct to Fort Scott.

I recommend that the expedition in question be at least kept within the numbers asked for by Genl Lane; that the Qtr Mr Gl be instructed to ascertain if it is practicable to send the necessary supplies, & the cavalry asked for, over the route I suggest, at a reasonable cost in the present season; and that the movement of all troops now under orders or en route for Leavenworth be at once suspended until either supplies have been sent in advance or the possibility of obtaining forage in the country is demonstrated. If the expedition asked for by Genl Hunter is necessary, or if it proves to be the case that forage must be transported for the smaller force asked by Genl Lane, I would advise that the expedition be at least deferred until the season is so far advanced that the grass is up.[2]

Very respectfully
Geo B McClellan
Maj Genl Comdg USA

Hon E M Stanton
Secty of War

ALS, Records of the Adjutant General's Office, RG 94 (M-619:36), National Archives. This endorsement by GBM appears on Montgomery C. Meigs to Stanton, Jan. 24.

1. Quartermaster Meigs analyzed the supply needs of two alternative proposals: that of Maj. Gen. Hunter for 30,000 men carrying all their own supplies, and that of Brig. Gen. James H. Lane for 20,000 men living largely off the country. The expedition was to march southwest from Fort Leavenworth through Kansas and Indian Territory toward northern Texas. See GBM to Hunter, Dec. 11, 1861, *supra.* 2. On Jan. 31 Lincoln wrote to Stanton of this expedition: "I have not intended, and do not now intend that it shall be *a great exhausting affair*; but a snug, sober column of 10,000 or 15,000." *Collected Works of Lincoln,* V, pp. 115–16. The expedition was not undertaken.

To Edwin M. Stanton

Confidential

My dear Stanton   [Washington] Sunday — [January 26, 1862]

Have you anything from Scott as to the means we can command in the way of moving troops westward by rail & water.[1] My mind is more & more tending in that direction, tho' not fully committed to it. But there should be no delay in ascertaining precisely *what we can do* should it prove advisable to move in that direction.

Please put the machinery in motion to ascertain exactly how many troops we can move per diem hence to Kentucky, how many days the transit would occupy etc.[2] Should we change the line I would wish to take about 70,000 infantry, 250 guns, 2500 cavalry — at least 3 bridge trains.[3]

truly yours
Geo B McClellan

ALS, Stanton Papers, Library of Congress.

1. Assistant Secretary of War Thomas A. Scott was then making a study of army transportation. Scott to Stanton, Jan. 23, 1862, *OR*, Ser. 3, I, pp. 807–808. 2. Acting on Stanton's instructions dated Jan. 29, Scott was sent to the Midwest to examine this question, and on Feb. 1 sent his first report to Stanton on shifting troops from the Army of the Potomac to Kentucky. Stanton Papers. 3. This suggests that GBM intended to command personally any shift of the main advance to the western theater. Neither he nor any troops from the Army of the Potomac went to Kentucky, however. See GBM to Scott, Feb. 20, *infra.*

To Henry W. Halleck

Maj. Gen. H. W. Halleck, Saint Louis
My dear General: Washington, January 29, 1862.

I have recommended A. J. Smith for brigadier-general, as you requested, and when his name is acted upon will assign him to duty with you. I have also recommended General Hitchcock, as you desire.[1] Your welcome letter in regard to future operations is received.[2] I will reply in full in a day or two. In the mean time get your force in hand and study the ground. I will try to-day to send you some more infantry arms. Cavalry arms are terribly scarce. I have had to take to lances here to supply deficiencies. I like your views as to the future. They fully agree with my own ideas from the beginning, which has ever been against a movement in force down the Mississippi itself. The news from the Burnside expedition is by no means so unfavorable as the telegram reports. He had terrible gales while crowded in a small harbor. The only real evil of consequence is the delay.

I will try to devote this afternoon to you and Buell, to give you my views and intentions in full.

Can you spare Stanley to Buell as chief of cavalry, or shall I look elsewhere to get him one? He (Buell) has not asked for him, but I know him to be a first-rate officer.[3]

While I think of it, do you not think it would be well to try one of those mortar floats thoroughly with 50 or 100 discharges before arming them all? Je m'en doute un peu.[4] It is very desirable to move all along the line by the 22d February, if possible.[5]

In haste, sincerely, your friend,
Geo. B. McClellan

OR, Ser. 1, VII, pp. 930–31.

1. Col. A. J. Smith, Halleck's chief of cavalry, was named brigadier general on Mar. 17. Ethan Allan Hitchcock was named major general on Feb. 10. 2. Written Jan. 20, Halleck's letter proposed an end to a scattered "pepper-box strategy" in favor of a concentrated operation of 60,000 men along the line of the Cumberland and Tennessee rivers. The Mississippi, he wrote, "is not a proper line of operations...." OR, Ser. 1, VIII, pp. 508–511. 3. Brig. Gen. David S. Stanley became a division commander under Gen. Pope. 4."I have my doubts about them." 5. On Jan. 27 President Lincoln had issued his General War Order No. 1, calling for "a general movement" by land and naval forces on Feb. 22. *Collected Works of Lincoln*, V, pp. 111–12.

To Don Carlos Buell   [TELEGRAM]

[Washington, January 29, 1862]

A deserter just in from the rebels says that Beauregard had not left Centreville four days ago but that as he was going on picket he heard officers say that Beauregard was under orders to go to Kentucky with 15 regts from the Army of Potomac.[1]

G B McClellan
Maj Genl

Brig Genl D. C. Buell
Louisville Ky

ALS (telegram sent), Records of the Office of the Secretary of War, RG 107 (M-473:10), National Archives. *OR*, Ser. 1, VII, p. 571. The same telegram was sent to Halleck.

1. Beauregard left Centreville, Va., for Kentucky on Feb. 2 to be second-in-command to Albert Sidney Johnston. He took no troops with him from the Confederate Army of the Potomac, but acting largely on the strength of this telegram Halleck approved Gen. Grant's plan to attack Fort Henry, on the Tennessee River, before it could be reinforced. *OR*, Ser. 1, VII, p. 572.

To Randolph B. Marcy

[Washington] Wednesday (Evening)
My dear Marcy   [January 29, 1862]

I am glad to hear that you are improving — do not hurry back until you are perfectly restored[1] — the weather has been so bad here that you would have faired illy had you been here.

I am getting on very well — Stanton's appointment has helped me infinitely thus far, & will still more in the future.

I wish you would see Mr Bennett or Hudson (the former if possible) & ask him which (*if either*) is his *confidential agent* Dr Ives or Hanscom![2] The Secty & myself are both puzzled a little to know "t'other from which" — Ives intimates that Hanscom is not the "confidential" man, & H intimates that Ives is not.[3]

I would like to know which one Mr B. wishes me to communicate fully & unreservedly with — I am anxious to keep Mr B. well posted & wish to do it fully — ask how far I can go in communicating important matters to either.[4]

Roads horrid — I think I can arrange my pleasure party very satisfactorily.[5]

Love to Grandma & Fanny — Nell will add a line.

Yours affectionately
Geo B McC

My kindest regards to the Dr & family.

ALS, McClellan Papers (A-106:42), Library of Congress.

1. Chief of Staff Marcy was still in New York recuperating from typhoid fever. 2. James Gordon Bennett, owner of the *New York Herald*; Frederic Hudson, his managing editor; Malcolm Ives and Simon P. Hanscom, *Herald* reporters. 3. On Jan. 28 Hanscom told Stanton that Ives was not the newspaper's accredited Washington correspondent. Ives to Bennett, Jan. 29, Bennett Papers, Library of Congress. 4. Ives wrote Bennett on Jan. 15 that Stanton

had introduced him to GBM the previous evening. GBM told him, according to Ives: "... I am now going to convey through you to Mr Bennett and *Mr Hudson*; I am going to give you *all* the knowledge I possess myself, with no reserve...." Bennett Papers. GBM continued to brief the reporter, but Ives soon ran afoul of Stanton and was imprisoned for some three months for violating censorship regulations. Andrews, *The North Reports the Civil War*, pp. 57–58. 5. Presumably his plan for a flanking movement against the Confederates by water. See GBM to Stanton, [Feb. 3], *infra*.

To John M. Brannan

Brig. Gen. John M. Brannan: Headquarters of the Army,
General: Washington, January 30, 1862.

So soon as arrangements have been perfected for the necessary supplies and ordnance you will please proceed at once to your destination, and on your arrival assume command of the Department of [Key West]. Your first and most important duty will be to place Forts Jefferson and Taylor on the war footing and in a thorough condition for defense, assigning the troops and distributing the guns and material at your disposal between the forts to the bes of your judgment, and constructing such temporary batteries and defenses as, upon consultation with the engineer officer, may seem advisable. Cause your men to be well instructed in the service of heavy guns. Preserve the strictest vigilance as to the admission of vessels of all kinds into the harbors, and allow no persons to visit the forts, except those in Government employ, without a pass from the commanding officer. Repress all disunion movements in Key West, arresting any citizens whose presence is manifestly dangerous to the Government or who may give aid and comfort to the rebels, if necessary sending them under guard to the North. In fine, exercise all the vigilance and precaution usual in time of war, bearing in mind that your greatest danger is from surprise, and that you are not likely to receive warning of the breaking out of hostilities. You will please afford such protection as may be in your power to the Light-House Board in re-establishing and maintaining the lights most necessary for navigation in those waters, and cover the operations of the Coast Survey so far as may be done without risk. Should the commanders of Forts Pickens and Ship Island call upon you in an emergency you will lend them such assistance as you can without risk to the security of your own posts. Should the state of affairs render it advisable to occupy Tampa for the purpose of procuring supplies of fresh beef for the army and navy forces in the Gulf, you are authorized to seize and hold it, calling upon the naval commander in the vicinity for the necessary assistance. I hope to send you at an early day at least one steamer and one or more schooners. When you have transportation you must use your discretion as to any movements upon Cedar Keys or Apalachicola. No movement on the former would be necessary, unless for a mere foray, except in case of the occupation of Fernandina by Sherman;[1] on the latter, advisable only to seize cotton and prevent contraband trade. You are authorized to occupy such land as may be necessary for the erection of batteries and defenses or for the encampment of your troops, and to take possession of any buildings which may be required for the preservation and security of public stores. As your command might suffer from the want of fresh water before the requisite condensers can be furnished, you are also authorized, in case of emergency, to take such supplies of it as may have been collected for sale to naval and other vessels.

I am, &c.

Geo. B. McClellan,
Major-General, U.S. Army,
Commanding.

OR, Ser. 1, LIII, pp. 74–75. Brig. Gen. Brannan was named head of the Department of Key West on Jan. 11.

1. Brig. Gen. Thomas W. Sherman, commander of the Port Royal expedition.

To Frederick W. Lander   [TELEGRAM]

| | Head Quarters, Army of the Potomac, |
| General F. W. Lander | Washington, Feb. 2 1862 |

Ohio regiments & battery ordered temporarily to New Creek. In attacking Romney you must use your discretion & be certain that the enemy is not reinforced from Winchester. Do not advance beyond Romney. Banks needs time to prepare to cooperate & you would be in danger East of Romney if he were not in position to distract enemy.[1]

If you gain Romney look out for return of Jackson, whom I know to be a man of vigor & nerve, as well as a good soldier.

Geo. B. McClellan
Maj General Comdg

Retained copy, Records of the Office of the Secretary of War, RG 107 (M-473 :11), National Archives. OR, Ser. 1, LI, Part 1, p. 523.

1. Confederate Thomas J. "Stonewall" Jackson had occupied Romney, Va., on Jan. 10. He would withdraw to Winchester, Va., on Feb. 7.

To Edwin M. Stanton

Hon E M Stanton
Secty of War   Head Quarters of the Army
Sir: Washington January 31st [February 3] 1862[1]

I ask you indulgence for the following paper, rendered necessary by circumstances.

I assumed command of the troops in the vicinity of Washington on Saturday July 27 1861, 6 days after the battle of Bull Run.

I found no army to command, a mere collection of regiments cowering on the banks of the Potomac, some perfectly raw, others dispirited by their recent defeat.

Nothing of any consequence had then been done to secure the southern approaches to the Capital by means of defensive works; nothing whatever had been undertaken to defend the avenues to the city on the northern side of the Potomac.

The troops were not only undisciplined, undrilled & dispirited — they were not even placed in military positions — the city was almost in a condition to have been taken by a dash of a single regiment of cavalry.

Without one day's delay I undertook the difficult task assigned to me — the task the Hon Secty knows was given to me without my solicitation or foreknowledge. How far I have accomplished it will best be shown by the past & present. The Capital is secure against attack — the extensive fortifications erected by the labor of our troops enable a small garrison to hold it against a numerous army; the enemy have been held in check; the State of Maryland is securely in our possession; the detached counties of Virginia are again within the pale of our laws, & all apprehension of trouble in Delaware is at an end; the enemy are confined to the positions they occupied before 21 July; — more than all this, I have now under my command a well drilled & reliable Army to which the destinies of the country may be confidently committed. This Army is young, & untried in battle, but it is animated by the highest spirit, & is capable of great deeds. That so much has been accomplished, & such an Army created in so short a time from nothing will hereafter be regarded as one of the highest glories of the Administration & the nation.

Many weeks, I may say many months, ago this Army of the Potomac was fully in condition to repel any attack; — but there is a vast difference between that & the efficiency required to enable troops to attack successfully an Army elated by victory, and entrenched in a position long since selected, studied, & fortified. In the earliest papers I submitted to the Presdt I asked for an effective movable force far exceeding the aggregate now on the banks of the Potomac — I have not the force I asked for. Even when in a subordinate position I always looked beyond the operations of the Army of the Potomac; I was never satisfied in my own mind with a barren victory, but looked to combined & decisive operations.

When I was placed in command of the Armies of the U.S. I immediately turned my attention to the whole field of operations — regarding the Army of the Potomac as only *one*, while the most important, of the masses under my command.

I confess that I did not then appreciate the absence of a general plan which had before existed, nor did I know that utter disorganization & want of preparation pervaded the western armies. I took it for granted that they were nearly, if not quite, in condition to move towards the fulfillment of my plans — I acknowledge that I made a great mistake.

I sent at once, with the approval of the Executive, officers I considered competent to command in Kentucky & Missouri — their instructions looked to prompt movements. I soon found that the labor of creation & organization had to be performed there — transportation, arms, clothing, artillery, discipline — all were wanting; these things required time to procure them; the Generals in command have done their work most creditably — but we are still delayed. I had hoped that a general advance could be made during the good weather of December — I was mistaken.

My wish was to gain possession of the Eastern Tennessee Railroads as a preliminary movement, — then to follow it up immediately by an attack on Nashville & Richmond as nearly at the same time as possible.

I have ever regarded our true policy as being that of fully preparing ourselves & then seeking for the most decisive results; — I do not wish to waste life in useless battles, but prefer to strike at the heart.

Two bases of operations seem to present themselves for the advance of the Army of the Potomac. —

I. That of Washington — its present position — involving a direct attack upon the enemy's entrenched positions at Centreville, Manassas etc, or else a movement to turn one or both flanks of those positions, or a combination of the two plans.

The relative force of the two Armies will not justify an attack on both flanks.

An attack on his left flank alone involves a long line of wagon communication & cannot prevent him from collecting for the decisive battle all the detachments now on his extreme right & left.

Should we attack his right by the line of the Occoquan & a crossing of the Potomac below the Occoquan & near his batteries, we could perhaps prevent the junction of the enemy's extreme right with his centre (we *might* destroy the former), we would remove the obstructions to the navigation of the Potomac, reduce the length of wagon transportation by establishing new depots at the nearest points of the Potomac, & strike more directly his main railway communication.

The fords of the Occoquan below the mouth of Bull Run are watched by the rebels, batteries are said to be placed on the heights in rear (concealed by the woods), & the arrangement of his troops is such that he can oppose some considerable resistance to a passage of the stream. Information has just been received to the effect that the enemy are entrenching a line of heights extending from the vicinity of Sangster's (Union Mills?) towards Evansport. Early in Jany. Sprigg's ford was occupied by Genl Rhodes with 3600 men & 8 guns; there are strong reasons for believing that Davis' Ford is occupied.[2]

These circumstances indicate, or prove, that the enemy anticipate the movement in question & are prepared to resist it.

Assuming for the present that this operation is determined upon, it may be well to examine briefly its probable progress.

In the present state of affairs our columns (for the movement of so large a force must be made in several columns, at least 5 or 6) can reach the Accotinck without danger; during the march thence to the Occoquan our right flank becomes exposed to an attack from Fairfax Station, Sangster's & Union Mills; — this danger must be met by occupying in some force either the two first named places, or, better, the point of junction of the roads leading thence to the village of Occoquan — this occupation must be continued so long as we continue to draw supplies by the roads from this city, or until a battle is won.

The crossing of the Occoquan should be made at all the fords from Wolf's Run to the mouth, the points of crossing not being necessarily confined to the fords themselves.

Should the enemy occupy this line in force we must, with what assistance the flotilla can afford, endeavor to force the passage near the mouth, thus forcing the enemy to abandon the whole line or be taken in flank himself.

Having gained the line of the Occoquan, it would be necesary to throw a column by the shortest route to Dumfries, partly to force the enemy to abandon his batteries on the Potomac, partly to cover our left flank against an attack from the direction of Acquia, & lastly to establish our communication with the river by the best roads, & thus give us new depots.

The enemy would by this time have occupied the line of the Occoquan above Bulls Run, holding Brentsville in force & perhaps extending his lines somewhat further to the S.W.

Our next step would be to prevent the enemy from crossing the Occoquan between Bull Run & Broad Run, to fall upon our right flank while moving on Brentsville; this might be effected by occupying Baconrace Church & the cross roads near the mouth of Bull Run, or still more effectually by moving to the fords themselves & preventing him from debouching on our side. These operations would probably be resisted, & would require some time to effect them. As nearly at the same time as possible we should gain the fords necessary to our purposes above Broad Run.

Having secured our right flank it would become necessary to carry Brentsville at any cost, for we could not leave it between our right flank & main body. The final movement on the Railroad must be determined by circumstances existing at the time.

This brief sketch brings out in bold relief the great advantage possessed by the enemy in the strong central position he occupies, with roads diverging in every direction, & a strong line of defence enabling him to remain on the defensive with a small force on one flank, while he concentrates everything on the other for a decisive action. Should we place a portion of our force in front of Centreville while the rest crosses the Occoquan we commit the error of dividing our Army by a very difficult obstacle & by a distance too great to enable the two portions to support each other, should either be attacked by the masses of the enemy while the other is held in check.

I should perhaps have dwelled more decidedly on the fact that the force left near Sangster's must be allowed to remain somewhere on that side of the Occoquan, until the decisive battle is over, to cover our retreat in the event of disaster, unless it should be decided to select & entrench a new base somewhere near Dumfries — a proceeding involving much time.

After the passage of the Occoquan by the main Army, this covering force could be drawn in to a more central & less exposed position, say Brimstone Hill or nearer the Occoquan.

In this latitude the weather will for a considerable period be very uncertain, & a movement commenced in force on roads in tolerably firm condition will be liable, almost certain, to be much delayed by rains & snow. It will therefore be next to impossible to surprise the enemy, or take him at a disadvantage by rapid manoeuvres; — our slow progress will enable him to divine our purposes & take his measures accordingly.

The probability is, from the best information we possess, that he has improved the roads leading to his lines of defence, while we must work as we advance.

Bearing in mind what has been said, & the present unprecedented & impassable condition of the roads, it will be evident that no precise period can be fixed upon for the movement on this line, nor can its duration be closely calculated; it seems certain that many weeks *may* elapse before it is possible to commence the march.

Assuming the success of this operation & the defeat of the enemy as certain, the question at once arises as to the importance of the results gained.

I think these results would be confined to the possession of the field of battle, the evacuation of the line of the upper Potomac by the enemy, & the moral effect of the victory — important results it is true, but not decisive of the war, nor securing the destruction of the enemy's main Army; for he could fall back upon other positions, & fight us again & again, should the condition of his troops permit.

If he is in no condition to fight us again out of range of the entrenchments at Richmond we would find it a very difficult & tedious matter to follow him up there — for he would destroy the railroad bridges & otherwise impede our progress through a region where the roads are as bad as they well can be; & we would probably find ourselves forced at last to change the entire theatre of war, or to seek a shorter land route to Richmond with a smaller available force & at an expenditure of much more time than were we to adopt the short line at once.

We would also have forced the enemy to concentrate his forces & perfect his defensive measures at the very points where it is desirable to strike him where least prepared.

II. The second base of operations available for the Army of the Potomac is that of the lower Chesapeake Bay, which affords the shortest possible land routes to Richmond, & strikes directly at the heart of the enemy's power in the East.

The roads in that region are passable at all seasons of the year.

The country now alluded to is much more favorable for offensive operations than that in front of Washington (which is *very* unfavorable) — much more level — more cleared land — the woods less dense — soil more sandy — the spring some two or three weeks earlier.

A movement in force on that line obliges the enemy to abandon his entrenched position at Manassas, in order to hasten to cover Richmond & Norfolk.

He *must* do this, for should he permit us to occupy Richmond his destruction can be averted only by entirely defeating us in a battle in which he must be the assailant.

This movement if successful gives us the Capital, the communications, the supplies of the rebels; Norfolk would fall; all the waters of the Chesapeake would be ours; all Virginia would be in our power; & the enemy forced to abandon Tennessee & North Carolina.

The alternatives presented to the enemy would be to beat us in a position selected by ourselves; disperse; — or pass beneath the Caudine Forks.[3] Should we be beaten in a battle, we have a perfectly secure retreat down the Peninsula upon Fort Monroe, with our flanks perfectly secured by the fleet. During the whole movement our left flank is covered by the water, our right is secure for the reason that the enemy is too distant to reach us in time — he can only oppose us in front; we bring our fleet into full play.

After a successful battle our position would be — Burnside forming our left, Norfolk held securely, our centre connecting Burnside with Buell, both by Raleigh & Lynchburg, Buell in Eastern Tennessee & Northern Alabama, Halleck at Nashville & Memphis.

The next movement would be to connect with Sherman on the left, by reducing Wilmington & Charleston; to advance our centre into South

Carolina & Georgia; to push Buell either towards Montgomery, or to unite with the main army in Georgia; to throw Halleck southward to meet the Naval Expedition at New Orleans.

We should then be in a condition to reduce at our leisure all the southern seaports; to occupy all the avenues of communication; to use the great outlet of the Mississippi; to reestablish our Govt & arms in Arkansas, Louisiana & Texas; to force the slaves to labor for our subsistence instead of that of the rebels; — to bid defiance to all foreign interference.

Such is the object I have ever had in view; this is the general plan which I have hoped to accomplish. For many long months I have labored to prepare the Army of the Potomac to play its part in the programme; from the day when I was placed in command of all our armies, I have exerted myself to place all the other armies in such a condition that they too could perform their allotted duties. Should it be determined to operate from the lower Chesapeake, the point of landing which promises the most brilliant results is Urbana on the lower Rappahannock.

This point is easily reached by vessels of heavy draught, it is neither occupied nor observed by the enemy; it is but one long march from West Point, the key to that region, & thence but two marches to Richmond.

A rapid movement from Urbana would probably cut off Magruder[4] in the *Peninsula,* & enable us to occupy Richmond before it could be strongly reinforced. Should we fail in that we could, with the cooperation of the Navy, cross the James & throw ourselves in rear of Richmond, thus forcing the enemy to come out & attack us — for his position would be untenable, with us on the southern bank of the river.

Should circumstances render it not advisable to land at Urbana we can use Mob Jack Bay, — or — the worst coming to the worst — we can take Fort Monroe as a base, & operate with complete security, altho' with less celerity & brilliancy of results, up the Peninsula.

To reach whatever point may be selected as the base, a large amount of cheap water transportation must be collected — consisting mainly of canal boats, barges, wood boats, schooners etc towed by small steamers — all of a very different character from those required for all previous expeditions. This can certainly be accomplished within 30 days from the time the order is given.

I propose, as the best possible plan that can, in my judgment, be adopted, to select Urbana as the landing place of the first detachments. To transport by water four (4) Divisions of Infantry, with their batteries, the Regular Infty, a few wagons, one bridge train & a few squadrons of Cavalry — making the vicinity of Hooker's position the place of embarkation for as many as possible.[5] To move the Regular Cavalry, & Reserve Artillery, the remaining bridge trains, & wagons to a point somewhere near Cape Lookout, then ferry them over the river by means of North River ferry boats, march them over to the Rappahannock (covering the movement by an Infantry force placed near Heathsville), cross the Rappahannock in a similar way.

The expense & difficulty of the movement will thus be much diminished (a saving of transportation of about 10,000 horses!), & the result none the less certain.

The concentration of the Cavalry etc in the lower counties of Maryland can be effected without exciting suspicion, & the movement made without delay from that cause.

This movement, if adopted, will not at all expose the city of Washington to danger.

The total force to be thrown upon the new line would be (according to circumstances) from 110,000 to 140,000. I hope to use the latter number, by bringing fresh troops into Washington, & still leaving it quite safe.

I fully realize that, in all projects offered, time is probably the most valuable consideration — it is my decided opinion that in that point of view the 2nd plan should be adopted. It is possible, nay highly probable, that the weather & state of the roads may be such as to delay the direct movement from Washington, with its unsatisfactory results & great risks, far beyond the time required to complete the second plan. *In the first case*, we can fix no definite time for an advance — the roads have gone from bad to worse — nothing like their present condition has ever been known here before — they are impassable at present, we are entirely at the mercy of the weather. In the second plan, we can calculate almost to a day, & with but little regard to the season.

If at the expense of 30 days delay we can gain a decisive victory which will probably end the war, it is far cheaper than to gain a battle tomorrow that produces no final results, & may require years of warfare & expenditure to follow up.

Such, I think, is precisely the difference between the two plans discussed in this long letter. A battle gained at Manassas will result merely in the possession of the field of combat — at best we can follow it up but slowly, unless we do what I now propose, viz: — change the line of operations.

On the Manassas line the rebels can, if well enough disciplined (& we have every reason to suppose that to be the case) dispute our advance, over bad roads, from position to position.

When we have gained the battle, if we do gain it, the question will at once arise — "What are we to do next?" —

It is by no means certain that we can beat them at Manassas.

On the other line I regard success as certain by all the chances of war.

We demoralize the enemy, by forcing him to abandon his prepared position for one which we have chosen, in which all is in our favor, & where success must produce immense results. My judgment as a General is clearly in favor of this project.

Nothing is *certain* in war — but all the chances are in favor of this movement.

So much am I in favor of the southern line of operations, that I would prefer the move from Fort Monroe as a base, as a certain, tho' less brilliant movement than that from Urbana, to an attack on Manassas.

I know that his Excellency the President, you & I all agree in our wishes — & that our desire is to bring this war to as prompt a close as the means in our possession will permit. I believe that the mass of the people have entire confidence in us — I am sure of it — let us then look only to the great result to be accomplished, & disregard everything else.

In conclusion I would respectfully, but firmly, advise that I may be authorized to undertake at once the movement by Urbana.

I believe that it can be carried into execution so nearly simultaneously with the final advance of Buell & Halleck that the columns will support each other.

I will stake my life, my reputation on the result — more than that, I will stake upon it the success of our cause.

I hope but little from the attack on Manassas; — my judgment is against it. Foreign complications may entirely change the state of affairs, & render very different plans necessary. In that event I will be ready to submit them.

I am very respectfully your obedient servant

Geo B McClellan

Maj Genl Comdg USA

ALS, Lincoln Papers, Library of Congress. *OR*, Ser. 1, V, pp. 42–45.

1. The dating of this letter requires clarification. As printed in GBM's *Report on the Organization of the Army of the Potomac* (Washington, 1864) and reprinted in the *Official Records*, it is dated Feb. 3, and several paragraphs near the end in the original manuscript are omitted. According to GBM's *Report* (pp. 42–43), it was prepared in response to the President's Special War Order No. 1 of Jan. 31, which called for the Army of the Potomac to advance in the area of the Occoquan River against the communications of the Confederate army at Manassas Junction. After receiving this order, GBM wrote, he went to the president with his objections and obtained permission to present his case in writing. On Feb. 3 he submitted his letter to Secretary of War Stanton, but before Stanton forwarded it to the president GBM received Lincoln's own thoughts on the issue, dated Feb. 3. Lincoln contrasted his Occoquan plan with GBM's Urbanna plan by means of a series of questions:

"1st. Does not your plan involve a greatly larger expenditure of *time,* and *money* than mine?

"2nd. Wherein is a victory *more certain* by your plan than mine?

"3rd. Wherein is a victory *more valuable* by your plan than mine?

"4th. In fact, would it not be *less* valuable, in this, that it would break no great line of the enemie's communications, while mine would?

"5th. In case of disaster, would not a safe retreat be more difficult by your plan than by mine." *Collected Works of Lincoln,* V, pp. 115, 118–19.

GBM assumed these questions were "substantially answered" by his letter to Stanton — possibly the letter was forwarded to Lincoln at his request — and he made no further reply.

Portions of a draft of GBM's letter preserved in the McClellan Papers (A-39:16), Library of Congress, suggest the letter originated somewhat differently. Marked-out phrases indicate that it was originally intended for Lincoln and was drafted in response to an earlier meeting with the president, probably about the third week in January, at which at Stanton's suggestion he presented his Urbanna plan verbally (*Report*, p. 42). At one point the draft reads: "Such I think is precisely the difference between the two plans discussed this morning"; "this morning" is crossed out and replaced by "in this long letter." An undated Lincoln memorandum on his Occoquan plan is almost certainly related to this conference (*Collected Works*, V, p. 119).

After receiving Lincoln's War Order No. 1 on Friday, Jan. 31, and obtaining permission to respond, GBM spent the weekend revising and expanding the draft he had prepared earlier. As indicated in note 2 below, one change involved incorporating new intelligence information that was only received on Feb. 1. He then copied the revised draft, making further changes and rearranging material, and submitted it to Stanton on Monday, Feb. 3, without making a fair copy for his files.

Why he dated it Jan. 31 is unclear. Perhaps he intended it to be a direct response to the president's war order of that date; perhaps he had started the first pages of the finished copy that day. From its contents, however, it is certain that much of it was written on or after Feb. 1. As a whole, the letter responds more directly to Lincoln's earlier Jan. memorandum than to the Feb. 3 questions, but in any event the questions are answered, if only indirectly.

When GBM's *Report* was being prepared a year or so later, the copyist apparently found only the draft of this letter to work from. The paragraphs omitted from the *Report* printing are in fact in the draft, but in a different place and marked for repositioning, a process the copyist may not have understood. This would explain the omissions in the printed versions. 2. A telegram dated Feb. 1 from Gen. McDowell noted that according to an informant "the enemy are fortifying a range of hills from Sangsters to Evansport." A second intelligence report supplying data current "until February 1st" gave the size and armament of Brig. Gen. Robert Rodes's command. McClellan Papers (A-39:16). 3. The narrow defile in Italy where a Roman army was captured by the Samnites in 321 B.C. and forced to pass under a yoke of crossed spears. 4. Maj. Gen. John B. Magruder, commanding the Confederate Department of the Peninsula. 5. Brig. Gen. Joseph Hooker was posted in lower Maryland on the Potomac.

To Henry W. Halleck

Private
My dear General

Head Quarters, Army of the Potomac,
Washington, Feby 6, 1862

I received your letters in regard to Siegel & at once showed them to Secty Stanton who requests me to say to you from him that *you can rely upon his full & cordial support*.[1] He thinks that the power of the Germans by no means equals their wishes, & that you will find means to keep order. You may rely upon it that you have the confidence of all here — I need not repeat to you that you have mine.

The roads being impassable between Buell & his opponents it now becomes a question whether we cannot throw all our available force by

the two rivers[2] upon Nashville — can we move there *now* in that manner?
I will try tonight to write you my views more fully.

In great haste truly yours
Geo B McClellan

Maj Genl H W Halleck

ALS, Civil War Collection, Huntington Library. *OR,* Ser. 1, VII, p. 937.

1. Halleck's letter of Feb. 2, enclosing intelligence reports, outlined an alleged plot by German-born officers and German-language newspapers in St. Louis to displace Halleck with Brig. Gen. Franz Sigel, paving the way for a return to power of Frémont and his abolitionist supporters. *OR,* Ser. 1, VIII, pp. 828–29. 2. The Cumberland and Tennessee rivers.

To Don Carlos Buell   [TELEGRAM]

[Washington, February 6, 1862, 7 P.M.]

Halleck telegraphs that Fort Henry largely reinforced from Columbus & Bowling Green.[1] If roads so bad in front had we not better throw all available force on Fort Henry & Fort Donelson? What think you of making that the main line of operations? Answer quick.[2]

G B McClellan
Maj Genl

Brig Genl D. C. Buell
Louisville Ky

ALS (telegram sent), Records of the Office of the Secretary of War, RG 107 (M-473:11), National Archives. *OR,* Ser. 1, VII, p. 587.

1. Halleck warned on this date that the Fort Henry garrison might become too strong for Grant's troops and Flag Officer Andrew H. Foote's gunboats. *OR,* Ser. 1, VII, pp. 586–87. 2. Buell replied at midnight that he agreed, although the operation would be hazardous. *OR,* Ser. 1, VII, pp. 587–88.

To Henry W. Halleck   [TELEGRAM]

Maj. Gen. H. W. Halleck   Headquarters Army [Washington],
Saint Louis, Mo.:   February 7, 1862 — 7.15 p.m.

Dispatch received.[1] I congratulate you upon the result of your operations. They have caused the utmost satisfaction here. I would not undertake a dash at Columbus now. Better devote everything towards turning it; first collecting a sufficient force near Forts Henry and Donelson to make success sure.

Either Buell or yourself should soon go to the scene of operations. Why not have Buell take the line of Tennessee and operate on Nashville, while your troops turn Columbus? Those two points gained, a combined movement on Memphis will be next in order. The bridges at Tuscumbia and Decatur should at all hazards be destroyed at once.[2]

Please number telegraphic dispatches and give hour of transmittal. Thank Grant, Foote, and their commands for me.

Geo. B. McClellan

Major General, Commanding

OR, Ser. 1, VII, p. 591.

1. Halleck telegraphed that day : "Fort Henry is ours. The flag of the Union is re-established on the soil of Tennessee. It will never be removed." *OR*, Ser. 1, VII, p. 590. 2. Railroad bridges over the Tennessee River in northern Alabama.

To Andrew Porter

Brig Genl Andrew Porter

Provost Marshall   Hd Quarters of the Army

General   Washn Feby 8th 1862

You will please at once arrest Brig Genl Chas P Stone U.S. Volunteers & retain him in close custody, sending him under suitable escort by the first train to Fort Lafayette[1] there to be placed under charge of the comdg officer [*crossed out:* to await trial]. See that he has [no] communication with any one from the time of his arrest.[2]

Very respectfully yours

Geo B McClellan

Maj Genl

[verso]

Comdg officer Fort Lafayette

Sir

This will be handed to you by the officer sent in charge of Brig Genl Chas P Stone who is under close arrest.

You will please confine Genl Stone in Fort Lafayette, allowing him the comforts due his rank, & allowing him no communication with any one by letter or otherwise except under the usual inspection.

ALS retained copy, McClellan Papers (A-40:16), Library of Congress. *OR*, Ser. 1, V, pp. 341–42.

1. A fort in New York Harbor used as a military prison. 2. GBM was acting under instructions from Secretary of War Stanton dated Jan. 28. *OR*, Ser. 1, V, p. 341. In its investigation of the Ball's Bluff defeat, the Joint Committee on the Conduct of the War heard testimony impugning Gen. Stone's loyalty. He would be neither tried nor formally charged, however, and after 189 days' imprisonment was released. See GBM to Stone, Dec. 5, 1862, *infra*.

To Albert S. White

Hon Albert White   Hd Qtrs of the Army
Dear Sir   Washn Feby 8 1862

　　Your letter of the 7th is received.

　　The last arrest of Mr Dickins was made very reluctantly on my part, & after a most careful examination of the evidence against him.[1]

　　That evidence was to the effect that he was in the habit of communicating with the rebels; rendering them aid & comfort; giving them information of our movements, of the position of our pickets etc.

　　There is no one for whose patriotism & feelings I have more regard than yourself, so that I could not bring myself to ordering the arrest of your brother in law, until I could give my personal attention to the evidence against him.

　　I transmitted the case to the Secty of War before deciding upon his arrest.

　　I am compelled to believe that the presence of Mr F. A. Dickins between our lines & those of the enemy is very dangerous to our cause, & that it is absolutely necessary that he should be held in custody until he can no longer do injury to our cause.

　　　　　　　　　　　　　　I am very truly yours
　　　　　　　　　　　　　　Geo B McClellan
　　　　　　　　　　　　　　Maj Genl Comdg USA

ALS, Francis A. Dickins Papers, Southern Historical Collection, University of North Carolina Library. White was a congressman from Indiana.

1. Francis A. Dickins of Annandale, Va., was arrested as a spy on Jan. 14 on the testimony of his slave and of neighbors, and was confined to Old Capitol Prison in Washington. He was paroled on Mar. 28. Allan Pinkerton to GBM, Jan. 28, 1862, McClellan Papers (A-38:16), Library of Congress; *OR*, Ser. 2, II, pp. 238, 277.

To Abraham Lincoln

His Excellency the President   [Washington] Saturday evng
Dear Sir   [February 8, 1862]

　　Your note was received by me very late this evening.[1]

　　I had a long conversation with Genl Hooker about the roads etc in the region we were speaking of, & would beg until Monday morning [February 10] to give a final opinion.

　　I have not yet heard from the canal boats above.

　　The experiment of arranging the two will be completed on Monday, when I can make the necessary calculations with exactness.[2]

I have nothing new from Halleck or Buell tonight. Apologizing for the delay

> I am most respectfully & truly yours
> Geo B McClellan
> Maj Genl

ALS, Lincoln Papers, Library of Congress.

1. In his note of this date Lincoln called for news "from the West" and "from the Canalboats," and asked: "Have you determined, as yet, upon the contemplated movement we have talked of?" *Collected Works of Lincoln*, V, p. 130. 2. GBM refers here to a plan he had discussed with Lincoln to attack the Confederate batteries on the Potomac from Gen. Hooker's position across the river at Liverpool Point in lower Maryland. It was proposed to use canal boats as troop carriers, linked in pairs by timber platforms to increase their capacity. The idea was abandoned. Hooker to Seth Williams, Feb. 17, *OR*, Ser. 1, V, pp. 723–24.

To Ambrose E. Burnside

Private

My dear old Burn　　　　　　　　　　　　Washn Feby 10 1862

Your dispatches of 29th Jan & 3d Feby received yesterday — together with your private notes.[1] I feel for you in your troubles — but you have borne yourself nobly in difficulties more trying than any that remain to you to encounter — & the same energy & pluck that has carried you through up to the present will take you through to the end.

We hear various rumors today about firing at Roanoke Island — I hope to hear tomorrow that you have taken it. In any event I shall feel sure that you have done all that a gallant & skilful soldier can accomplish. We are in status quo here — have gained a great point in Tenna by the capture of Fort Henry — which opens the road to us into Tenna.

Everything is bright — except the roads. Madame, Marcy & his wife all send their kindest. God bless you old fellow & give you success.

> Ever yours
> Geo B McClellan

Genl A E Burnside

ALS, Records of U.S. Army Continental Commands, RG 393 (3964: Army of the Potomac), National Archives. *OR*, Ser. I, IX, p. 360.

1. Burnside detailed the obstacles he faced in getting his expedition into Pamlico Sound and in condition to attack Roanoke Island. *OR*, Ser. 1, IX, pp. 356–57, 358–59. In a private note dated Jan. 31 he wrote of "elements of a decided failure looking me square in the face. . . . I think you have overestimated my ability, but shall try not to disappoint you." McClellan Papers (B-40:60), Library of Congress.

To William H. Seward

Hon W H Seward
Secty of State   Hd Qtrs of the Army
Dear Sir: Washn Feby 11 1861 [1862]

I have had an interview with Col Cluseret, late of the Italian Army, introduced to me by Capt Mohain of the suite of the Prince de Joinville. Col C. also brought me a letter of introduction from Genl Garibaldi. Col C, whose "etat de service" is good, informs me that he resigned his commission as Col in the Italian Army upon the instance of Mr Marsh, who had corresponded with the late Secty of War & yourself upon the subject. That he resigned after receiving what he regarded as a promise that he should have the grade of General of Brigade in our service.[1]

He seems to be a gentleman & good soldier. He has been waiting here many weeks, so that his slender means have become exhausted. May I ask you to inform me whether your records throw any light on the case & whether the good faith of the Govt is pledged to this officer.[2]

The Secty of War being absent from his office it seemed better to address you direct without delay as Col C has been waiting a long time.

Very truly & respectfully
Geo B McClellan
Maj Genl Comdg USA

ALS, William Henry Seward Papers, Rush Rhees Library, University of Rochester.

1. French soldier of fortune Gustave Paul Cluseret had supported Orléanist rule in 1848 and fought in the Crimea before casting his lot with Garibaldi. He was recruited for American service by George P. Marsh, envoy to Sardinia, with the apparent approval of Secretaries Cameron and Seward. 2. Seward replied the next day that in order to conciliate European opinion it would be "good policy" to accommodate Cluseret. Seward Papers. In his memoirs GBM recalled Cluseret less favorably. "I did not like his appearance and declined his services," he wrote, adding that even after Secretary Stanton appointed him a staff colonel in the Army of the Potomac, "I still declined to have anything to do with him...." *McClellan's Own Story*, p. 143. Cluseret allied himself with Gen. Frémont and led a checkered Civil War career before resigning in 1863.

To Edwin M. Stanton

Hon E. M. Stanton
Secretary of War   Head Quarters of the Army
Sir.   Washington Feby 11, 1862

I would respectfully submit to you the following extracts taken from the Report of Major A. Baird, Assistant Inspector General, U.S. Army on the inspection of the Kansas troops, viz.

"If the practice of seizing and confiscating the private property of rebels which is now extensively carried on by the troops known as "Lanes

Brigade'' is to be continued, How may it be managed so as to prevent the troops being demoralized and the Government defrauded?

This practice has become so fixed and general that I am convinced that orders arresting it would not be obeyed and that the only way of putting a stop to it would be to remove the Kansas troops to some other field of action.''[1]

The fact that the property of Citizens is seized and confiscated by the troops engaged in the service of the U.S. is substantiated by both official and reliable private evidence, and from the frequent repetition of these acts the Commanding Officers in Kansas appear to have assumed its legality. The authority under which it is done is unknown to me further than such destruction of private property as is unavoidable from a state of war conducted according to the established usages of civilized nations. I would therefore request the policy of the Government for my guidance in dealing with questions of this nature.[2]

To what extent can the right of confiscation legally be carried? And by what tribunal civil or military are the questions that will naturally arise, to be decided, that the innocent will not suffer while punishing the guilty and that the dignity and justice of the Government may not be at the mercy of individuals governed by cupidity or revenge? This question has assumed such proportions that it will require vigorous means and well defined authority to suppress or direct its applications.

I am Sir very respectfully Your obt Servant

[George B. McClellan]

Maj Genl Commdg U.S.A.

Retained copy, Records of the Headquarters of the Army, RG 108 (M-857:6), National Archives. *OR*, Ser. 1, VIII, pp. 552–53.

1. Maj. Absalom Baird's inspection was undertaken in connection with the so-called Lane expedition. See GBM to Stanton, c. Jan. 25, *supra*. 2. The brigade raised by Kansas senator James H. Lane was notorious. ''Their principal occupation for the last six months,'' Halleck wrote Stanton on Mar. 25, ''seems to have been the stealing of negroes, the robbing of houses, and the burning of barns, grain, and forage. The evidence of their crimes is unquestionable.'' *OR*, Ser. 1, VIII, p. 642. At GBM's direction, the Kansas forces, including the units in Lane's brigade, were reorganized. *OR*, Ser. 1, VIII, pp. 615–17.

To Ambrose E. Burnside

Brig Genl A E Burnside
Comdg Dept of North Carolina   Hd Qtrs of the Army
General   Washn Feby 12 1862

We are all rejoiced to hear, through rebel sources, the gallant capture of Roanoke Island & the rebel gun boats[1] — I hope to receive your account of it in a day or two, & take it for granted that your success has been at least as decisive & brilliant as indicated & assured by the rebel accounts.

I am glad to see that Comdr Goldsborough & yourself have pushed the enemy so rapidly & so far — I hope that the effect has been produced of drawing the attention of the rebels towards Norfolk &c, so that, after having fully secured what you have gained, you will by a rapid countermovement be enabled to make the second attack with every chance of success.[2] I still hope that you will be able to seize & hold Goldsboro, as well as gaining possession of the seaport in view.

You will have heard of our marked success in Tennessee — the capture of Fort Henry & the trip of our gun boats into Alabama.

Everything goes well with us but your success seems to be the most brilliant yet — I expect still more from you. While in the Sound please gain all possible information as to the possibility of attacking Norfolk from the south — that *may* prove to be the best blow to be struck. Although as I am not yet quite prepared to secure it as it should be, it may be our best policy to defer that until you have accomplished all the original objects of the expedition, when, with suitable reinforcements you may attack Norfolk to great advantage.

I regret that the special messenger is waiting & that I must close this.

> Very truly yours
> Geo B McClellan
> Maj Genl Comdg USA

ALS, Records of U.S. Army Continental Commands, RG 393 (3964: Army of the Potomac), National Archives. *OR*, Ser. 1, IX, pp. 362–63.

1. These actions were fought on Feb. 7–8. 2. Burnside's objectives were New Bern and Beaufort, to the south.

To Thomas W. Sherman

Brig. Gen. T. W. Sherman
Comd'g at Port Royal, &c   Head Qrs of the Army
General.   Washington, Feb. 14 1862

Your despatches in regard to the occupation of Dafuskie Island[1] &c. were received to-day. I saw also to-day for the first time your requisition for a siege train for Savannah.

After giving the subject all the consideration in my power, I am forced to the conclusion that, under present circumstances, the siege and capture of Savannah do not promise results commensurate with the sacrifices necessary. When I learned that it was possible for the gunboats to reach the Savannah River above Fort Pulaski, two operations suggested themselves to my mind as its immediate result. *First;* — the capture of Savannah by a "coup de main," — the result of an instantaneous advance and attack by the Army & Navy. The time for this has passed, & your letter indicates that you are not accountable for the failure to seize the propitious moment, but that, on the contrary, you perceived its advantages.[2] *Second;* — to isolate Fort Pulaski, cut off its supplies, and at least facilitate its reduction by a bombardment. Although we have a long delay to deplore, the second course still remains open to us; and I strongly advise the close blockade of Pulaski, and its bombardment as soon as the 13 in. mortars and heavy guns reach you. I am confident you can thus reduce it. With Pulaski, you gain all that is really essential. You obtain complete control of the harbor, you relieve the blockading fleet, and render the main body of your force disposable for other operations.[3]

I do not consider the possession of Savannah worth a siege after Pulaski is in our hands. But the possession of Pulaski is of the first importance. The expedition to Fernandina is well, and I shall be glad to learn that it is ours.

But, after all, the greatest moral effect would be produced by the reduction of Charleston and its defences. There the rebellion had its birth; — there the unnatural hatred of our Government is most intense; there is the centre of the boasted power and courage of the rebels. To gain Fort Sumter and hold Charleston is a task well worthy of our greatest efforts, and considerable sacrifices. That is the problem I would be glad to have you study. Some time must elapse before we can be in all respects ready to accomplish that purpose. Fleets are en route and armies in motion which have certain preliminary objects to accomplish, before we are ready to take Charleston in hand. But the time will before long arrive when I shall be prepared to make that movement.[4] In the meantime, it is my advice and wish that no attempt be made upon Savannah, unless it can be carried with certainty by a "coup de main."

Please concentrate your attention and forces upon Pulaski and Fernandina. St. Augustine might as well be taken by way of an interlude, while awaiting the preparations for Charleston. Success attends us everywhere at present.

Very truly yours

Geo. B. McClellan

Maj. Gen. Comdg. U.S.A.

Copy, McClellan Papers (D-7:69), Library of Congress. *OR,* Ser. 1, VI, p. 225.

1. Daufuskie Island is at the mouth of the Savannah River. 2. In a Feb. 5 dispatch Sherman attributed this delay to the navy. *OR,* Ser. 1, VI, p. 221. 3. Fort Pulaski would be bombarded into surrender on Apr. 11. 4. Sherman replied on Mar. 8 that he believed Charleston "can be carried with much more ease than I anticipated...." He would not play a role in the extended operations against Charleston, however. *OR,* Ser. 1, VI, p. 240.

To Henry W. Halleck

Maj Genl H. W. Halleck
Commdg Dept of Missouri   Head Quarters of the Army
General.   Washington Feby 14, 1862.

I have just received your gratifying dispatch that our forces occupy Springfield[1] and are in hourly expectation of having similar news in regard to Fort Donelson.

Your proposition in regard to the formation of a Western Division has one fatal obstacle, viz. that the proposed Commander of the new Department of Missouri ranks you![2] I would be glad to hear from you in detail as to the troops from your Department now on the Tennessee and Cumberland rivers.

Do you learn anything as to Beauregard's whereabouts and what troops (if any) he took with him?

What disposition do you intend to make of Hitchcock?[3] If you do not go in person to the Tennessee & Cumberland I shall probably write Buell to take the line of the Tennessee so far as Nashville is concerned — if his advance on Bowling Green must be done, it may well be necessary to throw a large portion of his troops up the Tennessee in which case he is entitled to their command.

Burnside has been very successful. All seems to be well.

Very truly yours
[George B. McClellan]
Maj Genl Commdg U.S.A.

Retained copy, Records of the Headquarters of the Army, RG 108 (M-857:6), National Archives. *OR,* Ser. 1, VII, p. 614.

1. Federal forces occupied Springfield, Mo., on Feb. 13. 2. Halleck wrote GBM on Feb. 8 proposing himself for overall command in a reorganized Western Division, with Buell, Ethan Allen Hitchcock, and David Hunter as his departmental lieutenants. Hunter's commission as a major general of volunteers predated Halleck's as a major general in the regular army by six days. *OR,* Ser. 1, VII, p. 595. In his reply on Feb. 19 Halleck wrote: "It was decided in the Mexican war that regulars ranked volunteers, without regard to dates. This decision, if sustained, makes everything right for the Western Division." *OR,* Ser. 1, VII, p. 636. 3. Hitchcock declined the appointment.

To Frederick W. Lander   [TELEGRAM]

[Washington] 10 p.m. Feby 14 [1862]

Telegram received. Your conduct is just like you. Don't talk about resigning. If your health makes it necessary for you to be relieved of course you shall be.[1] I advise, in view of probable movements, that you quietly rest at Cumberland & endeavor to recruit your health before making another move. If you can recover more rapidly here I will arrange to relieve you & give you other work as soon as you are well enough.[2] Give my thanks to the gallant officers & men under your command, & accept my own yourself.

G B McClellan
Maj Genl Comdg USA

Brig Genl F W Lander
Paw Paw etc

ALS (telegram sent), Records of the Office of the Secretary of War, RG 107 (M-473:11), National Archives. *OR,* Ser. 1, LI, Part 1, p. 531.

1. Lander reported on this date that he had personally led a successful assault on a "rebel nest" at Bloomery Gap in western Virginia. Suffering the aftereffects of a wound received at Ball's Bluff, he asked to be relieved. *OR,* Ser. 1, V, pp. 405–406. 2. Lander was stricken with pneumonia and died on Mar. 2.

To Ulysses S. Grant [TELEGRAM]

[Washington] Saturday [February] 15 [1862] 10 p.m.

Telegraph in full the state of affairs with you.[1]

G B McClellan
Maj Genl

Brig Genl U S Grant
Fort Henry

ALS (telegram sent), Records of the Office of the Secretary of War, RG 107 (M-473:11), National Archives. *OR,* Ser. 1, LII, Part 1, p. 212.

1. This telegram was not received until March 3. Grant, *Personal Memoirs* (New York, 1885), I, p. 326.

To Henry W. Halleck [TELEGRAM]

For Halleck [Washington] Feby 15/62 [11 P.M.]

Yours of 8 pm received. Your idea is in some respects good but if Buell can rapidly advance on Nashville he will take it and cut off the enemy who are near Fort Donelson if they do not retreat immediately.[1] His advance in force beyond Bowling Green will at once relieve Grant. His orders are to reinforce Grant if he cannot reach Nashville in time. The immediate possession of Nashville is very important. It can best be gained by the movement I have directed. The possession of Decatur will not necessarily cause the rebels to evacuate Nashville. You must also threaten to occupy Stevenson to accomplish that.[2] I do not see that Buell's movement is bad strategy for it will relieve the pressure upon Grant and leads to the results of first importance. If the destruction of the railroad is so extensive as to make the operation impracticable or very difficult and slow I have provided for the alternative in my instructions to Buell.[3]

Enable Grant to hold his own and I will see that Buell relieves him. The Decatur movement and the one on Memphis are the next steps in my programme. I am arranging to talk with Buell and yourself over the wires tomorrow morning and would be glad to have you at the telegraph office when all is ready. Buell will also be in Louisville office and we can come to a full understanding.

McClellan

Retained copy, Records of the Office of the Secretary of War, RG 107 (M-473:11), National Archives. *OR,* Ser. 1, VII, pp. 617–18.

1. In a dispatch of this date Halleck described an advance on Nashville by Buell as "bad strategy," arguing instead that Buell should assist Grant's operations against Fort Donelson and then advance on Decatur, Ala., to cut the Memphis and Charleston Railroad. "Nashville would then be abandoned, precisely as Bowling Green has been, without a blow." *OR,* Ser. 1, VII, p. 617. 2. Stevenson, Ala., marked the junction of the second of the two railroads linking Nashville with the Memphis and Charleston line. 3. In a dispatch of this date, GBM instructed Buell to send a column beyond Bowling Green. "If Nashville is open the men could carry their small rations and bread, driving meat on the hoof." *OR,* Ser. 1, VII, p. 626.

To Edwin M. Stanton

Dear Stanton   [Washington, February 16, 1862]

I enclose copy of dispatch to Navy Dept which speaks for itself. I shall be able to *talk* over the crisis with Buell and Halleck some time today & arrange all things. We have a brilliant chance to bag Nashville. I have no fears for the ultimate fall of Donelson notwithstanding Foote's drubbing.[1] As soon as I know the exact state of things I will inform you.

I have taken such steps as will make Grant safe & I think force the evacuation of Donelson or its surrender.

Truly yours
McClellan

ALS, Records of the Office of the Secretary of War, RG 107 (M-473:96), National Archives.

1. Flag Officer Foote's gunboats were repulsed by the Fort Donelson batteries on Feb. 14.

To Elizabeth B. McClellan

My dear Mother   Washn Feby 16 [1862]

It is so long since we have heard from any of you at home that I am half inclined to think you must have "seceded" & gone over to the enemy — but I know you are not fond of stage riding & am sure that I have not signed any passport for you, so that unless you & Mary[1] have assumed the name of Jones or Brown, you are probably still in the peaceful city of Phila. I am so glad to know that Mary has recovered from her illness as I was sorry to hear of her attack.

We have good news again today in the shape of the taking of a portion of Fort Donelson — the rest will soon come — it seems to be merely a matter of time now.

My friend Burnside has so far done splendidly, & I am sure will continue in the same path. In truth the rebellion has received some hard blows of late, & we can hope that it will have some harder cracks yet before long. Nelly sends her best love & wishes to know whether you ever received a letter from her some time ago asking you & Mary to come on & pay us a visit as soon as Mary had recovered sufficiently.

I cannot see much of you when you do come for I have but little spare time on my hands — but we would both be very glad if you would come on before I start South. We have a room ready for you at all times.

So one of the juvenile Coxes has taken unto himself a wife — he began early, did he not? Is it not almost time for Brinton & the girls? I presume Eckley is still in Europe — deep down in mines, occasionally refreshing himself by revisiting the upper air & sitting on a coal heap. Give my kindest love to all the Coxes — from the Judge down. If the Phillips are yet in the land of the Union give our love to them too — is it true that Annie has grown thin as Holmes & wears blue spectacles? I did not believe it when I heard it, & attribute it to the malicious abolitionists.[2] The last I heard from Maria[3] was that she had 4 Latin, 6 arithmetic, 3 spelling, & one whipping lesson to give when she called on some friend of hers in Phila. What does Mary do in these days? — keep her usual early hours? Please let us know when to expect you on here. With kindest love to Mary, John, Maria & the children we are your affectionate children

The McCs

Arthur[4] is well except a plaster on one side of his face. The baby has got so far as to have her photograph taken & very pretty.

ALS, McClellan Papers (B-41:61), Library of Congress.

1. GBM's younger sister. 2. References are to members of the Coxe and Phillips families, relations of Mrs. McClellan's in Philadelphia. 3. GBM's sister-in-law. 4. GBM's younger brother.

To the Army of the Potomac

General Orders, No.[1]

Head Quarters, Army of the Potomac, Washington, Feby 17 1862

Soldiers of the Army of the Potomac!

I announce to you glorious victories gained by our fellow soldiers in the west & south. The names of Mill Spring, Roanoke, Fort Henry & Fort

Donelson will hereafter be the pride of all true Americans, & will cause the hearts of all loyal men to throb with joy. None can rejoice in these successes, my comrades, more than we do; but, if I judge aright by taking my feelings as yours — and I know that one common impulse actuates us — there is awakened in your minds another sentiment, — the desire to eclipse these noble deeds of our brethren.

You wish to strike *your* blow, & to show that the Army of the Potomac strikes hard & true, & that it is equal to the great hopes reposed in it by the nation.

I have long held you back my comrades, at first that from a mass of brave but undisciplined citizens I might cement you into an Army — equal to any task that might be imposed upon you. I have restrained you for another reason also. I wished you to strike when the time arrived to give the death blow to this accursed rebellion.

The task of discipline is completed — I am satisfied with you. The time has well nigh arrived when your mission is to be accomplished.

When I place you in front of the rebels remember that the great God of Battles ever favors the just cause, remember that you are fighting for all that men hold dearest. You have battles to win, fatigues to endure, sufferings to encounter, but remember that they will conduct you to a goal from which you will return, covered with glory, to your homes, & that each one of you will bear through life the proud honor of being one of the men who crushed the most wicked rebellion that ever threatened free institutions & a beneficent government.

AD, McClellan Papers (A-41:17), Library of Congress.

1. This address was not issued. See GBM's address to the Army of the Potomac, Mar. 14, 1862, *infra*.

To Henry W. Halleck   [TELEGRAM]

Washn. Feby 18 1862 1.30 pm

I am directed by the Secty of War to instruct you that no arrangements either by equivalents or otherwise will be made for the exchange of the rebel Generals Johnson Buckner, Pillow & Tillman, nor for that of prisoners who had served in our regular army without special orders from these Head Quarters.[1]

G B McClellan
Maj Genl Comdg USA

General Halleck

ALS (telegram sent), Records of the Office of the Secretary of War, RG 107 (M-473:11), National Archives. *OR,* Ser. 2, III, p. 275. The same telegram was sent to Generals Buell, Rosecrans, and John E. Wool.

1. Of the Confederate generals named — Bushrod Johnson, Simon B. Buckner, Gideon Pillow, and Lloyd Tilghman — only Buckner and Tilghman were in fact captured at Forts Henry and Donelson. When prisoner exchange was later agreed to, Confederate officers and men formerly in U.S. service were included, and both generals were exchanged.

To Thomas A. Scott [TELEGRAM]

T A Scott [Washington, February 20, 1862]

Telegram received.[1] Increase rolling stock on Nashville Railway. At present no troops will move from East. Ample occupation for them here. Rebels hold firm at Manassas Junction.

McClellan

ALS (telegram sent), Records of the Office of the Secretary of War, RG 107 (M-473:12), National Archives. *OR*, Ser. 1, VII, p. 641.

1. Assistant Secretary of War Scott telegraphed GBM from Louisville on Feb. 19: "Buell immediately needs re-enforcements. Will they come?" *OR*, Ser. 1, VII, p. 635.

To Don Carlos Buell [TELEGRAM]

Buell [Washington, February 20, 1862]

Halleck says Columbus reinforced from New Orleans & steam up on their boats ready for move probably on Cairo. Wishes to withdraw some troops from Donelson.[1] I tell him improbable that rebels reinforced from New Orleans or attack Cairo. Think will abandon Columbus. What force have you in Bowling Green what in advance of it and where today. How soon can you be in front of Nashville & in what force. What news of the rebels. If the force in West can take Nashville or even hold its own for the present I hope to have Richmond and Norfolk in from three to four weeks. Answer fully.

McClellan

ALS (telegram sent), Records of the Office of the Secretary of War, RG 107 (M-473:11), National Archives. *OR*, Ser. 1, VII, p. 640.

1. In his telegram of Feb. 19, Halleck also called for reinforcements from Buell, who he predicted would be unable to advance on Nashville "for two or three weeks." *OR*, Ser. 1, VII, pp. 636–37.

To Don Carlos Buell [TELEGRAM]

Head-Quarters, Army of the Potomac,
Washington, Feby 21, 1862 1 am

Telegraph me at least once every day the position of your own troops — that of the rebels & the state of affairs. Unless I have this detailed information I cannot tell whether it is necessary or not to suspend or abandon my own plans here. Neither Halleck nor yourself give me as much detailed information as is necessary for me. This is the critical period & I must be constantly informed of the condition of your affairs.

G B McClellan
Maj Genl

Brig Genl D. C. Buell
Louisville or Bowling Green

ALS (telegram sent), Records of the Office of the Secretary of War, RG 107 (M-473:12), National Archives. *OR*, Ser. 1, VII, p. 645. A similar dispatch was sent on this date to Halleck.

To Henry W. Halleck [TELEGRAM]

Head Quarters Army of the Potomac

Halleck   St. Louis   Washington, D.C. Feb. 21 1862

Buell at Bowling Green knows more of the state of affairs than you at St. Louis. Until I hear from him I cannot see necessity of giving you entire command.

I expect to hear from Buell in a few minutes. I do not yet see that Buell cannot control his own line. I shall not lay your request before the Secretary until I hear definitely from Buell.[1]

McClellan

Retained copy, Records of the Office of the Secretary of War, RG 107 (M-473:12), National Archives. *OR*, Ser. 1, VII, p. 645.

1. Halleck had telegraphed on Feb. 20: "I must have command of the armies in the West. Hesitation and delay are losing us the golden opportunity. Lay this before the President and Secretary of War. May I assume the command? Answer quickly." *OR*, Ser. 1, VII, p. 641.

To John E. Wool [TELEGRAM]

Gen J E Wool
Fortress Monroe   [Washington] Feb 21 '62 [4 P.M.]

The iron clad steamer Monitor and a large frigate will be at Hampton Roads within the time you specify.[1] Do you need troops to replace those intended for Genl Butler?[2] If so how many? With the cooperation of the navy how many additional troops do you need to take Yorktown, and how many by a subsequent operation to take Norfolk? Send me your best map of Norfolk and vicinity. Please communicate fully. Let me hear from you every day. Can you take the Sewells Point battery?[3] If so do it and spike the guns.

G B McClellan
Major Genl Comdg USA

Retained copy, Records of the Office of the Secretary of War, RG 107 (M-473 :12), National Archives. *OR,* Ser. 1, IX, pp. 15–16. Maj. Gen. Wool commanded the Department of Virginia, with headquarters at Fort Monroe.

1. In a Feb. 21 dispatch to GBM, Wool reported the intelligence that the *Merrimack,* a steam frigate captured at Norfolk by the Confederates and converted into an ironclad, would lead an attack on Newport News within five days. *Confidential Correspondence of Gustavus Vasa Fox,* eds. Robert M. Thompson and Richard Wainwright (New York, 1920), I, p. 428. The new Federal ironclad *Monitor* was then undergoing trials at New York. 2. These troops at Fort Monroe were slated for operations against New Orleans. See GBM to Benjamin F. Butler, Feb. 23, *infra.* 3. The Sewell's Point battery guarded the approach to Norfolk.

To Abraham Lincoln

Private

My dear Sir   Washn Feby 22 1862

I have not felt authorized to intrude upon you personally in the midst of the deep distress I know you feel in the sad calamity that has befallen you & your family — yet I cannot refrain from expressing to you the sincere & deep sympathy I feel for you.[1]

You have been a kind true friend to me in the midst of the great cares & difficulties by which we have been surrounded during the past few months — your confidence has upheld me when I should otherwise have felt weak. I wish now only to assure you & your family that I have felt the deepest sympathy in your affliction.

I am pushing to prompt completion the measures of which we have spoken, & I beg that you will not allow military affairs to give you one moment's trouble — but that you will rest assured that nothing shall be left undone to follow up the successes that have been such an auspicious commencement of our new campaign.

I am very sincerely & respectfully your friend & obt svt

Geo B McClellan

His Excellency Abraham Lincoln
Presdt, US.

ALS, Lincoln Papers, Library of Congress.

1. The president's eleven-year-old son, Willie, had died of typhoid fever on Feb. 20.

To Benjamin F. Butler

Maj Genl B. F. Butler
U.S. Army   Head Quarters of the Army
General   [Washington] February 23d 1862

You are assigned to the command of the land forces destined to co-operate with the Navy in the attack upon New Orleans.[1] You will use every means to keep your destination a profound secret, even from your staff officers, with the exception of your chief of staff, and Lt Weitzel[2] of the Engineers.

The force at your disposal will consist of the first thirteen regiments named in your memorandum handed to me in person,[3] the 21st Indiana, 4th Wisconsin & 6th Michigan (old and good regiments from Baltimore) ; these three regiments will await your orders at Fort Monroe. Two companies of the 21st Indiana are well drilled at heavy artillery. The Cavalry force already en route for Ship Island, will be sufficient for your purposes. After full consultation with officers well acquainted with the country in which it is proposed to operate I have arrived at the conclusion that 3 light batteries fully equipped and one without horses will be all that are necessary.

This will make your force about 14,400 Infantry, 275 Cavalry, 580 Artillery — total 15,255 men.

The Comdg Genl of the Dept of Key West is authorized to loan you temporarily, 2 regiments. Fort Pickens can probably give you another, which will bring your force to nearly 18,000. The object of your expedition is one of vital importance — the capture of New Orleans. The route selected, is up the Mississippi River & the first obstacle to be encountered (perhaps the only one) is in the resistance offered by Forts St Philip & Jackson. It is expected that the Navy can reduce the works, in that case you will after their capture leave a sufficient garrison in them to render them perfectly secure, & it is recommended that on the upward passage a few heavy guns, and some troops be left at the Pilot Station (at the forks of the river) to cover a retreat in the case of a disaster (the troops and guns will of course be removed as soon as the Forts are captured).

Should the Navy fail to reduce the works, you will land your forces, & siege train, and endeavor to breach the works, silence their fire, and carry them by assault.

The next resistance will be near the English bend, where there are some earthen batteries; here it may be necessary for you to land your troops to cooperate with the naval attack, altho' it is more than probable that the Navy unassisted can accomplish the result. If these works are taken the city of New Orleans necessarily falls.

In that event it will probably be best to occupy Algiers with the mass of your troops. Also the Eastern bank of the river above the city — it may be necessary to place some troops *in* the city to preserve order tho' if there appears sufficient Union sentiment to control the city it may be best for purposes of discipline to keep your men out of the city.

After obtaining possession of New Orleans, it will be necessary to reduce all the works guarding its approaches from the East, and particularly to gain the Manchac Pass.

Baton Rouge, Berwick Bay & Fort Livingston will next claim your attention.

A feint on Galveston may facilitate the objects we have in view. I need not call your attention to the necessity of gaining possession of all the rolling stock you can, on the different railways, and of obtaining control of the roads themselves. The occupation of Baton Rouge by a combined naval and land force should be accomplished as soon as possible after you have gained New Orleans. Then endeavor to open your communication with the Northern column of the Mississippi, always bearing in mind the necessity of occupying Jackson Miss. as soon as you can safely do so, either after or before you have effected the junction. Allow nothing to divert you from obtaining full possession of *all* the approaches to New Orleans. When that object is accomplished to its fullest extent, it will be necessary to make a combined attack on Mobile, in order to gain possession of the harbor and works, as well as to control the railway terminus at the city. In regard to this I will send more detailed instructions as the operations of the Northern column develop themselves. I may simply state that the general objects of the expedition are *first* the reduction of New Orleans and all its approaches, then Mobile and all its defenses, then Pensacola, Galveston etc. It is probable that by the time New Orleans is reduced it will be in the power of the Government to reinforce the land forces sufficiently to accomplish all these objects; in the mean time you will please give all the assistance in your power to the Army and Navy commanders in your vicinity, never losing sight of the fact that the great object to be achieved is the capture and firm retention of New Orleans.

> Very Respectfully Your Obt Sevt
> Geo B McClellan
> Maj Genl Comdg USA

LS, Butler Papers, Library of Congress. *OR,* Ser. 1, VI, pp. 694–95. Maj. Gen. Butler was appointed to command of the Department of the Gulf on this date.

1. On Jan. 25 GBM had recommended that the proposed army-navy operation against New Orleans, which he suggested would require 30,000 to 50,000 troops, be suspended. *OR,* Ser. 1, VI, pp. 677–78. At that time he anticipated commanding any such expedition himself. Malcolm Ives to James Gordon Bennett, Jan. 15, 1862, Bennett Papers, Library of Congress. 2. Lt. Godfrey Weitzel, Corps of Engineers. 3. Probably a memorandum dated Feb. 12. *OR,* Ser. 1, VI, p. 687.

To Joseph Hooker   [TELEGRAM]

Washn Feb 23 [1862]

We can count upon the assistance of the iron clad steamer Erricson, armed with 2 eleven inch guns during the present week.[1] Will it in your judgment be better to wait for her or to adopt the original plan?[2] It seems to me that the safest plan is to use the Erricson, supported by the whole flotilla & a heavy force prepared to land. I can furnish here the means of landing at any point from 10,000 to 15,000 men in addition to your command. Answer by telegram.[3]

G B McClellan
Maj Genl Comdg

Brig Genl J Hooker
Budd's Ferry

ALS (telegram sent), Records of the Office of the Secretary of War, RG 107 (M-473:12), National Archives. *OR,* Ser. 1, LI, Part 1, p. 536.

1. The *Monitor,* designed by John Ericsson. She did not reach Hampton Roads until Mar. 8. 2. The plan for assaulting the Confederate batteries on the lower Potomac from Maryland. 3. Hooker replied on this date that he was ready to proceed without waiting for the *Monitor,* and recommended expanding the operation to include the seizure of Fredericksburg. *OR,* Ser. 1, V, pp. 726–27.

To Henry W. Halleck   [TELEGRAM]

Head Quarters Army of the Potomac,
Halleck, St. Louis   Washington, D.C. Feb. 24th 1862

Cullum telegram in regard to reconnaissance of Columbus received.[1] Buell will be in front of Nashville tomorrow evening. Best cooperate with him to the full extent of your power, to secure Nashville beyond a doubt. Then by a combined movement of troops and gun boats seize Decatur. Buell will be directed to occupy and hold in force the railroad junctions in vicinity of Chattanooga and to reestablish the railroads from Nashville to Decatur and Stevenson. This will very nearly isolate A. S. Johnston from Richmond.

The next move should be either a direct march in force upon the rear of Memphis or else first upon the communications and rear of Columbus, depending entirely on the strength and movements of the Rebels. In the mean time it would be well to amuse the garrison of Columbus with our mortar boats as soon as a sufficient number of them can be spared with gun boats from the Tennessee and Cumberland rivers.

The early possession of Humboldt in force is of importance, but should not be undertaken until Nashville is securely ours.

The possession of Grand Junction will complete the isolation of the rebels. It may be better to occupy Corinth instead of Decatur after Chattanooga is firmly in our possession. Please communicate fully and frequently.

McClellan

Retained copy, Records of the Office of the Secretary of War, RG 107 (M-473:12), National Archives. *OR,* Ser. 1, VII, p. 661.

1. Brig. Gen. George W. Cullum, Halleck's chief of staff, reported on Feb. 23 that Columbus, Ky., was still held by the enemy. *OR*, Ser. 1, VII, p. 658.

To Edwin M. Stanton [TELEGRAM]

Hon E M Stanton [Sandy Hook, Md.] Feb. 26 [1862, 10:20 P.M.]

The bridge was splendidly thrown by Captain Duane, assisted by Lieutenants Babcock, Reese, and Cross.[1] It was one of the most difficult operations of the kind ever performed. I recommend Captain Duane to be made a major by brevet for his energy and skill in this matter, also Lieutenants Babcock, Reese, and Cross, all of the Corps of Engineers, to be captains by brevet. We have 8500 infantry, eighteen guns, and two squadrons of cavalry on the Virginia side. I have examined the ground and seen that the troops are in proper positions and are ready to resist any attack. Loudon and Bolivar Heights as well as Maryland Heights are occupied by us. Burns' brigade will be here in a couple of hours and will cross at day break. Four more squadrons of cavalry and several more guns pass here. Reports that G W Smith[2] with fifteen thousand men is expected at Winchester.

Colonel Geary[3] deserves praise for the manner in which he occupied Virginia and crossed after the construction of the bridge. We will attempt the canal boat bridge tomorrow. The spirit of the troops is most excellent. They are in the mood to fight anything. It is raining hard but most of the troops are in houses.

G B McClellan

Retained copy, Records of the Office of the Secretary of War, RG 107 (M-473:12), National Archives. *OR*, Ser. 1, V, p. 727.

1. Capt. James C. Duane, Lts. Orville E. Babcock, Chauncey B. Reese, Charles E. Cross. For the plan of operations, see GBM to War Department, c. Mar. 1, *infra*. 2. Maj. Gen. Gustavus W. Smith, CSA. 3. Col. John W. Geary, 28th Pennsylvania.

To Mary Ellen McClellan

Sandy Hook near Harper's Ferry
Thursday am Feby 27 1862

... Here I still am — I crossed the river as soon as the bridge was finished & watched the troops pass. It was a magnificent spectacle — one of the grandest I ever saw. As soon as my horse & escort got over I rode out to the line of pickets & saw for myself that everything was right & ready for an attack. The position is a superb one.

I got over about 12 guns & 8000 infty before dark — also a squadron of cavalry. I heard in the p.m. a rumor that G. W. Smith was expected at Winchester with 15,000 men — altho' I did not fully credit it I nevertheless took all the military precautions necessary & felt perfectly secure during the night. The enemy are not now in sight, but I have sent out cavalry patrols that may bring in intelligence of value. It was after dark & raining hard when I recrossed the bridge. The narrow road was so completely blocked up that it was a very difficult matter to make one's way among the wagons.

It rained hard & was very cold during the night. . . .

The rest of us slept in a car — I was up most of the night, telegraphing etc. This morning it is blowing a hurricane, but the bridge stands well thus far. Burns' Brigade came up during the night. I left them in the cars & crossed them this morning early. The wagons have gone over, a regt of cavalry is now crossing, another battery will follow, & I will have everything well cleared up before the arrival of Abercrombie's Brigade, which should be here by 2 o'clock. I will get it over before dark, also the heavy artillery & regular cavalry if it arrives. I hope to be able to occupy Charleston tomorrow & get Lander to Martinsburg. It will then require but a short time to finish matters here. The roads on the other side are good — the country more open than near Washn. You have no idea how the wind is blowing now — a perfect tornado — it makes the crossing of the river very difficult & interferes with everything. I am anxious about our bridge. . . .

AL copy, McClellan Papers (C-7:63), Library of Congress.

To Edwin M. Stanton   [TELEGRAM]

Hon. E. M. Stanton
Secretary of War   Sandy Hook 3 1/2 p.m. Feby 27th 1862

The lift lock is too small to permit the canal boats to enter the river so that it is impossible to construct the permanent bridge as I intended.[1] I shall probably be obliged to fall back upon the safe and slow plan of merely covering the reconstruction of the Railroad. This will be done at once but will be tedious. I cannot as things now are be sure of my supplies for the force necessary to seize Winchester which is probably reinforced from Manassas. The wiser plan is to rebuild the Railroad Bridge as rapidly as possible and then act according to the state of affairs.

G. B. McClellan
Maj Gen'l

Received copy, Records of the Office of the Secretary of War, RG 107 (M-473:98), National Archives. *OR*, Ser. 1, V, p. 728.

1. These canal boats, intended as piers for the bridge, had been floated to the site in the Chesapeake and Ohio Canal paralleling the Potomac.

To Randolph B. Marcy   [TELEGRAM]

Gen R B Marcy   Sandy Hook [February 27, 1862] 8 pm

Revoke Hooker's authority in accordance with Barnard's opinion.[1] Immediately on my return we will take the· other plan and push on vigorously.[2]

G B McClellan

Received copy, Records of the Office of the Secretary of War, RG 107 (M-504:9), National Archives. *OR*, Ser. 1, V, p. 728.

1. In a Feb. 27 telegram Brig. Gen. John G. Barnard, chief engineer of the Army of the Potomac, expressed opposition to Hooker's plan for attacking the batteries on the lower Potomac from Maryland. *OR*, Ser. 1, LI, Part 1, p. 542. 2. The "other plan" was an advance on the Virginia side of the Potomac against the batteries.

To Abraham Lincoln   [TELEGRAM]

For A Lincoln, President   [Sandy Hook, February 28, 1862]

It is impossible for many days to do more than supply the troops now here & at Charlestown. We could not supply and move to Winchester for many days, & had I moved more troops here they would have been at a loss for food on the Virginia side. I know that I have acted wisely & that you will cheerfully agree with me when I explain. I have arranged to establish depots on that side so we can do what we please. I have secured opening of the road.

G B McClellan
Maj Genl Comdg

ALS (telegram sent), McClellan Papers (C-10:63), Library of Congress. *OR*, Ser. 1, V, p. 730.

To the War Department

[Washington, c. March 1, 1862][1]

When I started for Harper's Ferry I plainly stated to the Presdt & the Secty of War that the chief object of the operation would be to open the Baltimore & Ohio Railroad, by crossing the river in force at Harper's Ferry. That I had collected the material for making a permanent bridge by means of canal boats, that from the nature of the river it was doubtful whether such a bridge could be constructed, that if it could not I would at least occupy the ground in front of Harper's Ferry, in order to cover the rebuilding of the R.R. bridge, & finally when the communications were perfectly secure move on Winchester.

When I arrived at the place I found the Bateau Bridge nearly completed — the holding ground proved better than had been anticipated — the weather was favorable, there being no wind. I at once crossed over the two brigades which had arrived, & took steps to hurry up the other two, belonging respectively to Banks' & Sedgwick's Divisions. The difficulty of crossing supplies had not then become apparent. That night I telegraphed for a regt of regular cavalry & four batteries of heavy artillery to come up the next day (Thursday) [February 27]; besides directing Keyes Division of Infantry to be moved up on Friday.

Next morning the attempt was made to pass the canal boats through the lift lock in order to commence at once the construction of a permanent bridge — it was then found for the first time that the lock was too small to permit the passage of the boats, it having been built for a class of boats running on the Shenandoah Canal, & too narrow by some 4 or 6 inches for the canal boats. The lift locks above & below are all large enough for the ordinary boats — I had seen that at Edward's Ferry thus used — it had always been represented to the Engineers by the railway employees & others that the lock *was* large enough, & the difference being too small to be detected by the eye, no one had thought of measuring it, or suspecting any difficulty. I thus suddenly found myself unable to build the permanent bridge; — a violent gale had arisen which threatened the safety of our only means of communication; — the narrow approach to the bridge was so crowded & clogged with wagons that it was very clear that under existing circumstances nothing more could be done than to cross over the baggage & supplies of the four brigades; of these instead of being able to cross both during the morning, the last arrived only in time to go over just before dark. It was evident that the troops under orders would only be in the way should they arrive, & that it would not be possible to subsist them for a rapid march on Winchester. It was therefore deemed necessary to countermand the order, content ourselves with covering the reopening of the R.R. for the present, & in the mean time use every exertion to establish as promptly as possible depots of forage & subsistence on the Virginia side to supply the troops & enable them to move on Winchester independently of the bridge. The next day — Friday — I sent a strong reconnaissance to Charleston, & under its protection went there myself. I then determined to hold that place, & to move the troops composing Lander's & Williams' commands at once on Martinsburg & Bunker Hill — thus effectually covering the reconstruction of the R.R.

Having done this, & taken all the steps in my power to ensure the rapid transmittal of supplies over the river I returned to this City well satisfied with what had been accomplished. While up the river I learned that the Presdt was dissatisfied with the state of affairs, but on my return have understood from the Secty of War that upon learning the whole state of the case the Presdt was fully satisfied. I contented myself therefore with giving to the Secty a brief statement, about as I have written it here — he did not even require that much of me. He was busy — I troubled him as little as possible, & immediately went to work at other important affairs.[2]

AD copy, McClellan Papers (A-43:17), Library of Congress. *OR*, Ser. 1, V, pp. 48–49.

1. Although this manuscript bears a later endorsement, not by GBM, describing it as a "copy of letter to the War Department written somewhere about Feb 1862 on the movement at Harper's Ferry," its contents indicate that it was written no earlier than Mar. 1, the day GBM returned to Washington. The original has not been found. The concluding sentences further suggest that it might better be described as a memorandum or notes based on the original. 2. GBM wrote in his memoirs that in fact Stanton "deceived" him and never showed the statement to the president. *McClellan's Own Story*, p. 195.

Memorandum on Potomac Batteries

[Washington, March 1, 1862]

Barnard, McDowell, Franklin, Hooker & Heintzelman to meet say tomorrow to prepare & propose a plan for opening the lower Potomac batteries on the following basis —

To occupy Dumfries (some 9 miles from Colchester) in sufficient force to draw off the enemy in the vicinity & thus enable detachments to move down to the batteries and thoroughly destroy them. A part of this plan will be to occupy Fairfax C.H., Vienna (?), Drainsville (?), Fairfax or perhaps still better Sangster's Station & strongly secure Wolf Run shoals, while a sufficient force crosses at Occoquan & Colchester, throwing out parties to the right to cover its flank & secure the retreat. The landing of a Division[1] near Freestone Point would materially facilitate the passage of the Occoquan & might form the advance guard on the march to Dumfries. The cooperation of the flotilla including the Erricson[2] will form a necessary part of the plan.[3]

AD, McClellan Papers (A-88:35), Library of Congress.

1. Hooker's division, from lower Maryland. 2. The *Monitor*. 3. Attached calculations by GBM specified a force of over 118,000 men for the proposed operation.

To Henry W. Halleck

Private & strictly confidential

My dear Halleck   Washington March 3 1862

Yours of the 24th arrived while I was up the river.[1]

I went there to superintend the passage of the river & decide as to the ulterior movements of the troops. The passage was a *very* difficult one, but the Engineer Troops under Duane did wonders. I found it impossible to supply a large body of troops without first establishing depots on the Virginia side — which we are rapidly doing. So I contented myself for the present with occupying Charleston etc in order to cover the reopening of the B & O RR. I have also occupied Martinsburg & will tomorrow throw out a strong force to Bunker Hill. We are thus in position to attack Winchester as soon as our supplies are collected.

I hope to open the Potomac this week — provided the weather permits — it will require a movement of the whole Army in order to keep "Manassas" off my back — I cannot count upon any effective cooperation on the part of the Navy. As soon as I have cleared the Potomac I shall bring here the water transportation now ready (at least it will be in four or five days) & then move by detachments of about 55,000 men for the region of sandy roads & short land transportation. When you have asked me for 50,000 men from here, my dear fellow, you have made one of two mistakes — either you have much overrated my force or you have thought that I intended to remain inactive here.[2]

I expect to fight a desperate battle somewhere near Richmond — the most desperate of the war — for I am well assured that the army of Manassas remains intact & that it is composed of the best armed & best disciplined troops that the rebels have — with the prestige of Bull's Run in their favor. I have, or expect to have, one great advantage over you, as the result of my long & tedious labors — troops that will be demoralized neither by success nor disaster. I feel that I can count upon this Army of mine, & shall gladly venture my life in the scale.

If you had been as long in command you would have had as good, or perhaps a better, army than this of which I feel very proud — but that has been your bad luck & my good fortune. You have done all that could have been done with the means at your disposal — the fate of war is yet to decide whether I shall prove as skilful as you have been — I am sure that I have your good wishes & prayers.

I hardly know what to say as to your proposition about new grades. Why change the European order in the military hierarchy & make a "General" junior to a "Lieut General"? I see no especial reason for it.

I had determined to bide my time — content with my present rank for the present, & hoping that Congress would give another grade after marked success. I have ever felt that higher grades than that of Maj Genl are necessary in so large an Army as that we now have — but I have felt great delicacy in alluding to it. But very few weeks will elapse before the questio vexata will be decided — suppose we let it wait until then & then say what we think? I am willing however to defer to your judgment in the matter & will do all I can to carry out the plan. I don't think *I* can do anything now — I have but few friends in Congress — the abolitionists are doing their best to displace me & I shall be content if I can keep my head above water until I am ready to strike the final blow. You have no idea of the undying hate with which they pressure me — but I take no notice of them, & try to keep Warren Hasting's motto in mind — mens aequa in arduis![3] I sometimes become quite angry, but generally contrive to keep my temper. Do write me fully your views as to future movements in the West — I think the first thing to be done is to separate Johnson[4] from Memphis by seizing Decatur — Buell must then force Chattanooga & you can then with perfect safety operate on Memphis etc & open your communications with the combined expedition which ought to gain New Orleans within three weeks from this date. Butler will have about 16,000 men — the naval fleet is tremendous in power. Nothing new from Sherman — he & Dupont are not on good terms — they neutralize each other.[5]

Burnside is doing well.

> Very sincerely your friend
> . Geo B McClellan

Maj Genl H W Halleck
St Louis

ALS, James S. Schoff Collection, William L. Clements Library, University of Michigan. *OR*, Ser. 1, XI, Part 3, pp. 7–8.

1. Halleck's letter of Feb. 24 proposed a plan to frustrate the "abolition party" from promoting its favorites over GBM by creating "the rank of *General* between the Major Genl & Lieut Genl, and leave the latter as it now is, for brevet only." Only he and GBM would be named to the new rank. "Of course you will get the Brevet Lt Genlship as soon as Richmond is taken, and . . . I will try to come in for a Brevet at the close of the war." He noted "attempts of the abolition press to create jealousies between us. . . . I have too high a regard for your character & military skill to permit any thing of that kind." McClellan Papers (A-42:17), Library of Congress. 2. In an interview with Assistant Secretary of War Scott, Halleck had called for 50,000 reinforcements from the Army of the Potomac. Scott to Stanton, Feb. 17, 1862, Stanton Papers, Library of Congress. 3. Warren Hastings, governor-general of India, advised an even temper in adversity as the lesson of his acquittal in 1795 after a seven-year impeachment trial. 4. Gen. Albert Sidney Johnston. 5. Flag Officer Samuel F. Du Pont was Gen. Thomas Sherman's naval counterpart in the Port Royal expedition.

To Henry W. Halleck   [TELEGRAM]

Washn March 3/62 6 pm

Your dispatch of last evening received.[1]

The future success of our cause demands that proceedings such as Grant's should at once be checked. Generals must observe discipline as well as private soldiers. Do not hesitate to arrest him at once if the good of service requires it, & place C F Smith in command. You are at liberty to regard this as a positive order if it will smooth your way. I appreciate the difficulties you have to encounter & will be glad to relieve you from troubles as far as possible.[2]

> G B McClellan
> Maj Genl Comdg USA

Maj Genl H W Halleck
St Louis

ALS (telegram sent), Records of the Office of the Secretary of War, RG 107 (M-473:50), National Archives. *OR,* Ser. 1, VII, p. 680. This dispatch is endorsed "Approved Edwin M. Stanton Sec of War."

1. Halleck telegraphed that he had received no word from Grant in more than a week, and that he "richly deserves" censure for "this neglect and inefficiency." *OR,* Ser. 1, VII, pp. 679–80. 2. The difficulty was resolved — it was later traced to a communications breakdown — and Grant was not arrested.

To John A. Dix   [TELEGRAM]

Wash Sunday March 9 [1862] 11 am

Merrimac sank the Cumberland, the Congress surrendered. Minnesota & St. Lawrence ran aground in approaching scene of contest. At half past eight last night Merrimac had retired to Craney Island. Please be fully on alert. See that Fort Carroll[1] is placed in a condition for defense as rapidly as possible in case Merrimac should run by Fort Monroe. Until further orders stop passage of army transports passing from Phila to Annapolis & Perryville by Canal.[2] What is condition of Fort Carroll.

G B McClellan
Maj Genl Comdg USA

Maj Genl J A Dix
Baltimore Md

ALS (telegram sent), Records of the Office of the Secretary of War, RG 107 (M-473:50), National Archives. *OR,* Ser. 1, LI, Part 1, p. 549. GBM sent similar warnings to fort commanders at Philadelphia, New York, Newport, New London, Boston, and Portland. *OR,* Ser. 1, IX, p. 19.

1. Fort Carroll guarded the Patapsco River approach to Baltimore. 2. The canal linking the Delaware River with Chesapeake Bay.

To John E. Wool   [TELEGRAM]

[Washington] March 9 [1862] 1 p.m.

If the rebels obtain full command of the water it would seem impossible for you to hold Newport News. You are therefore authorized to evacuate that place, drawing the garrison in upon Fort Monroe which I need not say to so brave an officer is to be held at all hazards, as I will risk everything to sustain you should you be attacked by superior forces. From indications here I suspect an intention of the enemy to fall back nearer to Richmond that they may better concentrate their forces. An attack upon you is not improbable. If the fifteen inch gun is at Newport News I would suggest its immediate removal to either Fort Monroe or Fort Calhoun, unless it will enable you to retain possession of Newport News.

By authorizing you to withdraw from Newport News I do not mean to give you the order to do so, but to relieve you from that grave sense of responsibility which every good officer feels in such a case — I would only evacuate Newport News when it became clear that the rebels would certainly obtain complete control of the water & render it untenable. Do not run the risk of placing its garrison under the necessity of surrendering. You will also please inform me fully of your views & wishes — the practicality & necessity of reinforcing you &c. The performances of the Merrimac place a new aspect upon everything, & may very probably change my whole plan of campaign, just on the eve of execution.[1]

G B McClellan
Maj Genl Comdg

Maj Genl John E Wool
Fort Monroe

ALS (telegram sent), Records of the Office of the Secretary of War, RG 107 (M-473:50), National Archives. *OR*, Ser. 1, IX, p. 23.

1. Wool replied on Mar. 10: "If I can get the number of men and batteries asked for, I think I will be able to keep Newport News, that is, if no accident happens to the *Monitor.*" *NOR*, Ser. 1, VII, p. 84.

To Edwin M. Stanton

Private Head-Quarters, Army of the Potomac,
My dear Sir Washington [March 9, 1862]

The preparation of the boats etc to be sunken in the Potomac is being carried out. As fast as enough are prepared for one tug boat they will go down to Wyman.[1]

Very truly yours
Geo B McClellan

Hon E M Stanton
Secty of War

I think we will find the danger less as we learn more, & am less & less inclined to apprehend that the Merrimac will venture out — nevertheless we must take it for granted that the worst will happen.

McC

ALS, McClellan Papers, New-York Historical Society.

1. Stanton had ordered scows loaded with stone in preparation for blocking the channel should the *Merrimack* venture up the Potomac toward Washington. Lt. Robert H. Wyman commanded the Potomac flotilla. The plan was soon canceled.

To Abraham Lincoln, Edwin M. Stanton   [TELEGRAM]

[Hall's Hill, Va., March 9, 1862]

We have Sangster's Station & Fairfax Court House. I am arranging to move forward to push the retreat of rebels as far as possible.[1] I have ordered railway & telegraph repairs to be pushed tomorrow. I shall return late tonight & start out early in morning.

G B McClellan
Maj Genl

A Lincoln   Presdt
E M Stanton   Secty of War

ALS (telegram sent), McClellan Papers (A-50:20), Library of Congress.

1. It was reported on this date that the Confederates had withdrawn from Manassas Junction and Centreville.

To Edwin M. Stanton   [TELEGRAM]

[Hall's Hill, March 10, 1862, 1 A.M.]

You have entirely misunderstood me, & the idea I intended to convey was simply that I could not under the pressure of the new aspect of affairs immediately carry out the Presdt's order as to the formation of Army Corps.[1] It is absolutely necessary that I should at once move Divisions as they stand — if you require me to suspend movements until Army Corps can be formed I will do so, but I regard it as a military necessity that the Divisions should move to the front at once without waiting for the formation of Army Corps. If it is your order to wait until the Corps can be formed I will of course wait. I will comply with the Presdt's order as soon as possible. I intended to do so tomorrow, but circumstances have changed. If you desire it I will at once countermand all the orders I have given for an advance until the formation of Army Corps is completed. I have only to add that the orders I have given tonight to advance early tomorrow morning were dictated solely by the present position of affairs.

If the leave to suspend the order be granted there will be no unreasonable delay in the formation of Army Corps. I await your reply here, that I may countermand my orders at once. Please reply at once.[2]

G. B. McClellan
Maj Genl Comdg

ALS (telegram sent), McClellan Papers (A-52:20), Library of Congress. *OR*, Ser. 1, V, pp. 740–41.

1. In his General War Order No. 2 of Mar. 8, the president ordered the divisions of the Army of the Potomac to be grouped into army corps, under Generals Irvin McDowell,

Edwin V. Sumner, Samuel P. Heintzelman, Erasmus D. Keyes, and Nathaniel P. Banks. On Mar. 9 GBM requested the order be suspended until his movement toward Manassas was made. Stanton responded that "it is the duty of every officer to obey the President's orders." *OR*, Ser. 1, V, pp. 18, 739. 2. Stanton replied on this date: "Move just as you think best now, and let the other matter stand until it can be done without impeding movements." *OR*, Ser. 1, V, p. 741.

To Edwin M. Stanton [TELEGRAM]

Head-Quarters of the Army,
Fairfax C.H. March 11, 1862 8.30 p.m.

I have just returned from a ride of more than forty miles. Have examined Centreville, Union Mills, Blackburns ford, Manassas, the battle field etc. The rebels have left all their positions & from the information obtained during our ride today I am satisfied that they have fallen behind the Rapidan holding Fredericksburg & Gordonsville. Their movement from here was very sudden — they left many wagons, some caissons, clothing, ammunition, personal baggage, etc. Their winter quarters were admirably constructed, many not yet quite finished. The works at Centreville are formidable — more so than Manassas.

Except the turnpikes the roads are horrible — the country entirely stripped of forage & provisions. Having fully consulted with Genl McDowell I propose occupying Manassas by a portion of Banks's command, & then at once throwing all the forces I can concentrate upon the line agreed upon last week.[1] The Monitor justifies this course. I telegraphed this morning to have the transports brought to Washington to start from there — I presume you will approve this course. Circumstances may keep me out here some little time longer.

Geo B McClellan
Maj Genl Comdg USA

Hon E M Stanton
Secty of War Washington

ALS (telegram sent), Records of the Office of the Secretary of War, RG 107 (M-504:66), National Archives. *OR*, Ser. 1, V, p. 742.

1. A council of war meeting on Mar. 8 had approved an advance on Richmond by way of the lower Chesapeake.

To Randolph B. Marcy [TELEGRAM]

Fairfax CH [March 11, 1862] 9 pm

Dispatch received.[1] It is impossible for me to come in tonight — I am completely tired out. Besides I think the less I see of Washington the better. Be careful to have copies of all my dispatches of any importance sent to Secty & President. See Secty about ordering transports to Washington.

G B McClellan
Maj Genl

Genl R B Marcy
Washington

ALS (telegram sent), Records of the Office of the Secretary of War, RG 107 (M-504:66), National Archives. *OR,* Ser. 1, LI, Part 1, p. 550.

1. Marcy telegraphed on this date that he had seen former Ohio governor William Dennison, and urged GBM to inform the administration "what you propose to do & are now doing. Come to Washn tonight. . . . Dennison desires to see you before you see any one else." McClellan Papers (B-10:47), Library of Congress. Dennison had been delegated to explain to GBM the decision taken that day to remove him as general-in-chief and limit him to the command of the Army of the Potomac while it was on campaign.

To Mary Ellen McClellan

Fairfax C.H. March 11 1862

. . . None of our wagons came up until after I rode out this morning, so we got along as best we could last night. Some one lent me some blankets, & somebody else a cot, so I was very well off — tonight I have my own bed. I started at about 9 this morning, & rode first to Centreville. We found there quite a formidable series of works, which would have been somewhat uncomfortable for new troops to carry by storm. Thence I rode over horrid roads to the celebrated Manassas, which we found also abandoned. Thence to the battle field of last July, & over pretty much the whole of it. Thence home via Stone Bridge & Centreville reaching here about 8 1/2. I rode Kentuck today & as the rascal was fretful he fatigued me very much — so that it is impossible for me to go to Washn tonight, notwithstanding your father's pressing telegram.

I regret that the rascals are after me again. I had been foolish enough to hope that when I went into the field they would give me some rest, but it seems otherwise — perhaps I should have expected it. If I can get out of this scrape you will never catch me in the power of such a set again — the idea of persecuting a man behind his back. I suppose they are now relieved from the pressure of their fears by the retreat of the enemy & that they will increase in virulence. Well — enough of that — it is bad enough for me to be bothered in that without annoying you with it.

The country thru' which we passed today was very desolate. I think Manassas is the most desolate & forbidding spot I ever beheld. They have not destroyed many of their winter quarters, which are very well built & comfortable — far more so than I expected to see them. From the great number of camps scattered about it is evident that they had a very large force here. They must have left in a great hurry, for they abandoned a great deal of baggage, tents, stores, ammunition, caissons, wagons etc.

It seems that the order was given very suddenly — they left on Sunday [March 9], except a rear guard. It is said by *"intelligent contrabands"* & others that the men were very much disgusted & disheartened. . . .

AL copy, McClellan Papers (C-7 :63), Library of Congress.

FOUR

THE PENINSULA CAMPAIGN
MARCH 12–MAY 30, 1862

O N MARCH 12, 1862, General McClellan made the decision to base his grand campaign against Richmond at Fort Monroe, the Union-held position at the tip of the peninsula between the James and York rivers, seventy-five miles southeast of the Confederate capital. Fort Monroe had been the "worst coming to the worst" option in his February 3 plan of operations for the Army of the Potomac; now it was forced on him by the sudden actions of the enemy.

On March 8 the Rebel ironclad *Merrimack* had steamed into Hampton Roads from Norfolk and decimated the Federal blockading squadron. Although the Union's *Monitor* fought her to a draw the next day, the *Merrimack* remained a threat to McClellan's supply line in the Chesapeake and also blocked any Federal advance on Richmond by way of the James. At the same time, General Joseph E. Johnston withdrew his army from Manassas to a position behind the Rappahannock River. His move frustrated McClellan's long-matured plan for a surprise landing at Urbanna on the Rappahannock and any hope he might have had for getting between Johnston's army and Richmond. Operating from Fort Monroe was now his only alternative to an overland advance on Richmond from Washington. Once he was assured that the *Monitor* could at least hold the *Merrimack* in check, he put the scheme to a vote of his corps commanders, who approved it unanimously, and on March 17 the first contingents sailed for Fort Monroe. The correspondence reproduced here covers planning for the movement and the first two months of the Peninsula campaign, taking McClellan to the eve of the final battle for Richmond.

On the evidence of such letters as that of March 28 to General Totten of the engineers, it is obvious that he went to the Peninsula predisposed to siege operations. His first experience in war had been at the siege of

Vera Cruz in the Mexican War, and he had made a close study of the siege lines at Sevastopol when he was in the Crimea in 1855. It was a form of warfare he felt he had mastered, and his decision to put Yorktown under siege was made more decisively than most of his military actions. By contrast, at Williamsburg on May 5 he waited nearly the entire day to be called to the field despite the continuing sound of heavy firing indicating that a pitched battle was in progress.

These letters and dispatches demonstrate an increasing remoteness from factual reality. Running through McClellan's correspondence in these months, for example, is the positive and recurring assertion that he was greatly outnumbered by the enemy. He telegraphed Secretary Stanton on April 7 from Yorktown that within a matter of days he expected to be facing 100,000 Rebel troops. On May 14 he warned President Lincoln that with his 80,000 men he would have to attack an enemy entrenched in numbers double his own; "I beg that you will cause this Army to be reinforced without delay by all the disposable troops of the Government."

The logic of these calculations seemed to General McClellan obvious. An opponent who had confronted him at Washington in August of 1861 with 100,000 men (as he himself had estimated) and then raised that count to 150,000 by the end of October would hardly make the final defense of his capital with a lesser number. In truth, on his arrival before Yorktown on April 5 and for some days afterward he was bluffed by a force about one-fifth the size of his own. When he insisted to the president on May 14 that he was confronting some 160,000 enemy soldiers, General Johnston could muster but 62,500 to contest his advance. From first to last, McClellan's military decisions on the Peninsula were based on his belief in a phantom Confederate army.

A second important thread running through the correspondence here is his conviction that the administration in Washington was failing to support him, and was in fact acting deliberately to insure his defeat. "History will present a sad record of these traitors who are willing to sacrifice the country & its army for personal spite & personal aims," he wrote his wife on April 11. This belief was as illusory as his picture of the enemy. The truth of the matter is that when he was finally ready to make his final advance on Richmond, the government had put more troops at his disposal than his plans had called for.

To Mary Ellen McClellan   [TELEGRAM]

For Mrs. Genl McClellan   *Fairfax C.H. March 12/62*

Do not be at all worried by what has occurred & say nothing about it.
I have meant well for my country — & God will not desert me.[1] Am very
well today.

G B McClellan
Maj Genl

Retained copy, McClellan Papers (C-11:63), Library of Congress.

1. Marcy had telegraphed GBM that an order relieving him as general-in-chief was printed
in the *National Intelligencer* that morning. McClellan Papers (A-45:18).

To Gustavus V. Fox   [TELEGRAM]

For G V Fox Fort Monroe   Fairfax CH Mar 12 '62

Can I rely on the Monitor to keep the Merrimac in check so that I can
take Fort Monroe as a base of operations.[1]

Geo. B. McClellan
Maj Genl

Please answer at once.

Retained copy, McClellan Papers (C-11:63), Library of Congress. *OR,* Ser. 1, IX, p. 27.
Fox was assistant secretary of the navy.

1. Fox replied on Mar. 13: "The Monitor may, and I think will, destroy the Merrimac in
the next fight; but this is hope, not certainty." *OR,* Ser. 1, IX, p. 27.

To Gustavus V. Fox   [TELEGRAM]

Received March 12, 1862
To Secy Fox Ft Monroe   From Fairfax Court House

Is it possible to block up the channel from Hampton roads to Norfolk
some where between Sewalls Point and Craney Island by sinking hulks
loaded with stone so that the Merrimac cannot get out if so how soon can
it be done using every exertion. Please let me know at the earliest possible
moment.[1]

G B McClellan

Received copy, Lincoln Papers, Library of Congress.

1. Gen. Wool replied to Secretary of War Stanton on Mar. 13 that to block the mouth of
the Elizabeth River as GBM proposed would require the *Monitor* to reduce the enemy
batteries on Sewall's Point and Craney Island. Both he and Flag Officer Goldsborough
opposed this "lest she should become crippled. She is our only hope against the Merrimac."
OR, Ser. 1, IX, p. 30.

To Abraham Lincoln

Unofficial
His Excellency Abraham Lincoln
President   Head-Quarters Army of Potomac
My dear Sir: Fairfax C.H. March 12 1862

I have just seen Gov. Dennison who has detailed to me the conversations he held with you yesterday & today.

I beg to say to you that I cordially endorse all he has said to you in my behalf, and that I thank you most sincerely for the official confidence & kind personal feelings you entertain for me. I believe I said to you some weeks since, in connection with some western matters, that no feeling of self interest or ambition should ever prevent me from devoting myself to your service — I am glad to have the opportunity to prove it, & you will find that under present circumstances I shall work just as cheerfully as ever before, & that no consideration of self will in any manner interfere with the discharge of my public duties.[1]

Again thanking you for the official & personal kindness you have so often evinced towards me

I am most sincerely & respectfully your friend
Geo B McClellan

ALS, Lincoln Papers, Library of Congress.

1. On Mar. 14 Dennison wrote GBM: "Have just left the President. He is very much gratified with your letter and says my construction of the order as I gave it to you is exactly correct. You command the Army of the Potomac wherever it may go. Everything is right — move quick as possible." McClellan Papers (A-46:18), Library of Congress.

To Edwin M. Stanton   [TELEGRAM]

Head-Quarters, Army of the Potomac,
Hon Sect of War   Flint Hill 6.15 pm March 13th 1862

Your dispatch was received at 6.10 pm at this place, about three miles from Fairfax CH where I am reviewing a Division. The members of the council together with myself were unanimous in favoring the plan which was presented to you by Gen McDowell.[1]

Steps have already been taken so that if the plan meets your approval the movement can commence early tomorrow morning. I will communicate more fully as soon as I return to my camp. Your speedy action will facilitate the movement.[2]

G B McClellan
Maj Genl

Retained copy, McClellan Papers (A-46:18), Library of Congress.

1. Stanton's dispatch sought clarification of the plan approved that day by a council of corps commanders for an advance on Richmond via the Virginia Peninsula. *OR*, Ser. 1, V, pp. 55–56, 750. 2. Stanton telegraphed that evening that the president approved the plan provided that Washington and Manassas Junction were strongly garrisoned, and that the advance be made ''at once'' to Fort Monroe ''or anywhere between here and there....'' *OR*, Ser. 1, V, p. 56.

To Lorenzo Thomas   [TELEGRAM]

Head-Quarters of the Army,
Fairfax C.H. March 13 1862 8.30 pm

In the uncertainty as to General Burnside's position & how far he may now be engaged in his final operations it is difficult to give him very precise orders at present.[1] I think it would be well that he should not engage himself further inland than at Newbern & should at once reduce Beaufort. Leaving there a sufficient garrison in Fort Macon he should at once return to Roanoke Island ready to cooperate with all his available force either by way of Winton or by way of Fort Monroe as circumstances may render necessary. I advise this on the supposition that Capt Fox is correct in his opinion that Burnside will have Newbern this week.[2] If he has become fairly engaged in the movement I would not stop him.

G B McClellan
Maj Genl

L Thomas
Adjt Genl

ALS (telegram sent), Records of the Office of the Secretary of War, RG 107 (M-504:66), National Archives. *OR*, Ser. 1, V, p. 751.

1. Thomas had been instructed by Stanton to ascertain GBM's plans for cooperating with Burnside's Roanoke Island expedition. War Board minutes, Mar. 14, Stanton Papers, Library of Congress. 2. Gustavus V. Fox to GBM, Mar. 13, *OR*, Ser. 1, IX, p. 27.

To Edwin M. Stanton   [TELEGRAM]

Fairfax C.H. March 13 [1862] 9.40 pm

I would respectfully suggest that the Secretary of the Navy be requested to order to Fort Monroe whatever force Dupont can now spare, as well as any available force that Goldsborough can send up as soon as his present operations are completed.[1]

G B McClellan
Maj Genl

Hon E M Stanton
Secty of War

ALS (telegram sent), Records of the Office of the Secretary of War, RG 107 (M-504:66), National Archives. *OR*, Ser. 1, V, p. 751.

1. Flag Officers Du Pont and Goldsborough commanded, respectively, naval forces with the Port Royal and Roanoke Island expeditions. Gideon Welles wrote Stanton on Mar. 14 that the navy would gladly cooperate in capturing Norfolk — "always a favorite measure of this Department" — but he was otherwise reluctant to weaken his blockading squadrons. *OR,* Ser. 1, V, pp 758–59.

To Gustavus V. Fox

Private   Head-Quarters of the Army,
My dear Fox   Fairfax C.H. March 14 1 A.M. 1862.

From all accounts received I have such a lively faith in the gallant little Monitor that I feel that we can trust her — so I have determined on the Fort Monroe movement. A part of this programme will be the reduction of Yorktown & Gloucester — to effect this rapidly we shall need your help. Can you not under present circumstances bring up some of Dupont's force, as well as some of Goldsborough's gunboats? I shall probably commence embarking today, & by tomorrow be under full headway, so no time is to be lost & I hope you will be able to give us powerful aid.

If you will pardon me for talking about a matter may I venture to repeat a suggestion made to me by the Prince de Joinville this afternoon — probably nothing new — viz that the Monitor should take a long cable (hemp) in tow & by running around the Merrimac endeavor to foul her propeller! To a landsman it seems a good idea. Can't we do something in the way of blocking up the Channel to Norfolk?[1]

Congratulating you on Worden's gallant action[2]

I am ever your friend
Geo B McClellan

P.S. How soon will the Mystic iron clad ship be finished?[3]

ALS, Fox Papers, New-York Historical Society.

1. Fox replied on this date that Joinville's idea was a good one, "but too much risk to the Monitor should she back herself." The Norfolk channel could be blocked, he added, only after the batteries guarding it were taken. McClellan Papers (A-46:18), Library of Congress. 2. Lt. John L. Worden had commanded the *Monitor* against the *Merrimack.* 3. The *Galena,* an ironclad under construction in Mystic, Conn. Fox reported that she "will not be ready in time."

To Edwin M. Stanton

Hon E. M. Stanton
Secretary of War.   Head-Quarters, Army of the Potomac,
My Dear Sir.   Fairfax Court House March 14th 1862

The situation of the Army of the Potomac at present is about as follows: Keyes' Division in reserve at Prospect Hill, with a Regiment of Cavalry

(Rush) in advance; McCall at Hunter's Mills; Smith at Flint Hill; Porter & Franklin at this place; McDowell in advance towards Centreville; Blenker near the Railroad, in advance of Burke's Station; Cooke's Cavalry Brigade between Blenker & Fairfax Station; Sumner at Union Mills & Manassas, with one regiment thrown forward to guard Stoneman's forage train, — General Stoneman being en route to the Rappahannock with ten squadrons of Cavalry.

The orders of Gen. Stoneman are to capture or drive in any force he may find on this side of the Rappahannock, and to reconnoitre that river. Heintzelman in reserve near Alexandria. One of Banks's Divisions is ordered to move at once to Centreville, — the majority of another to follow it. I propose placing the mass of Banks's Army Corps near Manassas (to cover the approaches to Washington) leaving detachments adequate to guard the Manassas Gap Railway, Strasburg and Winchester. I think the result of Gen. Stoneman's advance will be the destruction (by the rebels) of the railway bridge over the Rappahannock, thus making Manassas safe. I propose giving General Banks a large Cavalry force to enable him to scour the country completely in front of Manassas, & in the valley of the Shenandoah. From all the information I have received, I have no doubt that the mass of the rebels have retired to Gordonsville, leaving a force on the Rappahannock. I am well assured of the fact that the true reasons for their evacuation of their works were twofold — 1st My advance from Harper's Ferry — 2nd The intimation that I intended to turn their right flank. Most accounts substantially agree in this, & my information is very full. They have expended a very large amount of labor upon their works at Centreville and Manassas. I would be glad if you could find it convenient to visit these places yourself. You would then be sure that it would have been a desperate affair to have attacked Centreville.

The slaves are being taken South as rapidly as possible. A levy of 80,000 men seems to have been ordered in this State, & I shall be much mistaken if we have not a severe battle to fight before reaching Richmond. Of the result of this, however, I feel very sure, for I have the utmost confidence in the spirit & discipline of our men.

I have been arranging the multitude of details necessary to take up the new line, and anxiously await certain information as to the transports.

I shall have the Army well in hand & ready for anything that occurs.

I am Very Respectfully & Truly
Geo B McClellan
Maj Genl USA

LS, Lincoln Papers, Library of Congress.

To the Army of the Potomac

SOLDIERS OF THE ARMY   Headquarters Army of the Potomac,
OF THE POTOMAC!   *Fairfax Court House, Va., March 14, 1862.*

For a long time I have kept you inactive, but not without a purpose: you were to be disciplined, armed and instructed; the formidable artillery you now have, had to be created; other armies were to move and accomplish certain results. I have held you back that you might give the death-blow to the rebellion that has distracted our once happy country. The patience you have shown, and your confidence in your General, are worth a dozen victories. These preliminary results are now accomplished. I feel that the patient labors of many months have produced their fruit; the Army of the Potomac is now a real Army, — magnificent in material, admirable in discipline and instruction, excellently equipped and armed; — your commanders are all that I could wish. The moment for action has arrived, and I know that I can trust in you to save our country. As I ride through your ranks, I see in your faces the sure presage of victory; I feel that you will do whatever I ask of you. The period of inaction has passed. I will bring you now face to face with the rebels, and only pray that God may defend the right. In whatever direction you may move, however strange my actions may appear to you, ever bear in mind that my fate is linked with yours, and that all I do is to bring you, where I know you wish to be, — on the decisive battlefield. It is my business to place you there. I am to watch over you as a parent over his children; and you know that your General loves you from the depths of his heart. It shall be my care, as it has ever been, to gain success with the least possible loss; but I know that, if it is necessary, you will willingly follow me to our graves, for our righteous cause. God smiles upon us, victory attends us, yet I would not have you think that our aim is to be attained without a manly struggle. I will not disguise it from you: you have brave foes to encounter, foemen well worthy of the steel that you will use so well. I shall demand of you great, heroic exertions, rapid and long marches, desperate combats, privations, perhaps. We will share all these together; and when this sad war is over we will all return to our homes, and feel that we can ask no higher honor than the proud consciousness that we belonged to the ARMY OF THE POTOMAC.

GEO. B. MCCLELLAN
Major General Commanding

DP, McClellan Papers (A-46:18), Library of Congress.

To Nathaniel P. Banks

[Washington, March 16, 1862]

Genl Banks to post his command in the vicinity of Manassas — to entrench himself there and to throw his cavalry pickets well out to the front. His first care to be the rebuilding of the railway from Washington to Manassas & Strasburg in order to open his communications with the valley of the Shenandoah.

As soon as the Manassas Gap RR is in order Genl B. to entrench a brigade of Infantry (say 4 regiments) with a couple of batteries at or near the point where the M.G. RR crosses the Shenandoah. Something like 2 regts of cavalry should be left in that vicinity to occupy Winchester & thoroughly scout the country south of the R.R. & up the Shenandoah valley — as well as through Chester (?) Gap which might perhaps be advantageously occupied by a detachment of Infty well entrenched. Blockhouses to be built at the RR bridges.

Warrenton Junction, or the *place* (Warrenton) itself to be occupied — also some still more advanced point on the O & A RR by a Grand Guard as soon as the RR bridges repaired. Great activity to be observed by the Cavalry — besides the two regts at Manassas. Another regt of Cavalry will be at the Genl's disposition to scout towards the Occoquan & probably a 4th towards Leesburg.

The important points are —

1st A strong force well entrenched in the vicinity Manassas — perhaps even Centreville — another force (a brigade) near Strasburg — also well entrenched.

2nd Block houses at RR bridges.

3rd Constant employment of Cavalry well to the front.

4th Grand guards at Warrenton & in advance as far as Rappahannock if possible.

5th Great care to obtain full & early information as to enemy.

6th General object to cover line of Potomac & Washington.

ADf, McClellan Papers (A-50:20), Library of Congress. *OR*, Ser. 1, V, p. 56. This draft order is in GBM's handwriting. As issued it was signed by his adjutant, Seth Williams.

To Edwin M. Stanton

Hon E M Stanton
Secty of War   Hd Qtrs Army of Potomac
Sir: Washn March 16 1862

In order to carry out the proposed object of this Army it has now become necessary that its Commander should have the entire control of affairs around Fort Monroe. I would respectfully suggest that the simplest method of effecting this would be to merge the Dept of Virginia into that of the Potomac, the name of which might properly be changed to that of the Dept of the Chesapeake; in carrying this into effect I would respectfully suggest that the present Comdr of the Dept Virginia be assigned to some other command.[1] Genl Mansfield can take temporary charge of Fort Monroe & its dependencies until the Army arrives there.

I am very respectfully yr obt svt

Geo B McClellan

Maj Genl USA

ALS, Lincoln Papers, Library of Congress. *OR*, Ser. 1, XI, Part 3, pp. 8–9.

1. The presence of John E. Wool at the head of the Department of Virginia created a touchy command situation. The seventy-eight-year-old Wool, a major general by brevet since the Mexican War, considered himself GBM's superior. On Mar. 18, however, he agreed to Stanton's proposal "to waive the exercise of your authority temporarily in his [GBM's] favor." Wool was transferred to the command of the Middle Department on June 1. *OR*, Ser. 1, IX, p. 29; XI, Part 3, pp. 14, 207.

To Samuel L. M. Barlow

My dear Barlow   Washington March 16 1862

I am here for a few hours only, my Hd Qtrs being on the other side of the river.

I came back last night from Fairfax C.H. — en route for the decisive battle. My movements gave us Manassas with the loss of one life — a gallant cavalry officer — history will, when I am in my grave, record it as the brightest passage of my life that I accomplished so much at so small a cost. It will appear in the future that my advance from Harper's Ferry, & the preparation for turning their right flank have induced them to give up what Halleck & the newspapers would call "the rebel stronghold of the East."

I shall soon leave here on the wing for Richmond — which you may be sure I will take. The Army is in magnificent spirits, & I think are half glad that I now belong to them alone.

Mrs McC joins me in kindest regards to Mrs B & yourself. Do not mind the abolitionists — all I ask of the papers is that they should defend me from the most malicious attacks — tho' to speak frankly I do not care to pay much attention to my enemies.

My wife received your note & desires her thanks for it.

The President is all right — he is my strongest friend.

In haste sincerely yours

Geo B McClellan

S L M Barlow Esq

ALS, Barlow Papers, Huntington Library.

To Edmund C. Stedman

My dear Sir   Hd Qtrs Seminary [Alexandria] March 17 1862

I cordially thank you for your kind letter & your efforts in my behalf.[1] Kind words are so seldom heard by me of late that I do indeed appreciate them. I know now fully the value of true & disinterested friends.

I believe that we are now on the eve of the success for which we have been so long preparing — yet I have felt for several days that there was a strong probability that I should be denied the satisfaction of leading the Army of the Potomac to victory & of sharing the fruit of the work of many months. I now begin to hope for better things. If permitted to retain command of this Army I feel assured of the result, & trust that end will justify the great confidence that you & so many other friends have placed in me. Again thanking you for your friendship

I am very truly yours
Geo B McClellan

E C Stedman Esq.
Washington

ALS retained copy, McClellan Papers (B-10:48), Library of Congress. Stedman was the Washington correspondent for the *New York World.*

1. With his letter of this date Stedman enclosed a clipping, from the previous day's *World,* of an article he wrote in support of GBM, and assured him : "We have watched and sustained your efforts from the first and . . . shall continue to counteract your detractors as best we may." McClellan Papers (B-10:48).

To Edwin M. Stanton   [TELEGRAM]

Hon E M Stanton,
Secy of War   Alexandria 1.15 pm March 18th [1862]

Please have McCallum[1] provide Engines and Cars sufficient to transport supplies only for an army of one hundred and thirty thousand men, including twenty thousand horses over the West Point and Richmond Railway.[2] The road is about twenty eight miles long. The only trouble at present is in regard to horse transports. If shall arrive promptly, we shall have rapid & glorious results.

G. B. McClellan
Maj Gen

Received copy, Records of the Office of the Secretary of War, RG 107 (M-473:98), National Archives. *OR,* Ser. 1, XI, Part 3, pp. 15–16.

1. Col. Daniel C. McCallum, director of military railroads. 2. The Richmond and York River Railroad, connecting Richmond with West Point, where the Mattapony and Pamunkey rivers join to form the York.

To Edwin M. Stanton

Hon E. M. Stanton
Secty of War   Head Quarters Army of the Potomac
Sir   Theological Seminary Va. March 19 1862

I have the honor to submit the following notes on the proposed operations of the active portion of the Army of the Potomac.

The proposed plan of campaign is to assume Fort Monroe as the first base of operations taking the line by Yorktown and West Point upon Richmond as the line of operations, Richmond being the objective point. It is assumed that the fall of Richmond involves that of Norfolk and the whole of Virginia; also that we shall fight a decisive battle between West Point and Richmond, to give which battle the rebels will concentrate all their available forces, understanding as they will that it involves the fate of their cause. It therefore follows —

1st. That we should collect all our available forces, and operate upon adjacent lines, maintaining perfect communications between our columns.

2d. That no time should be lost in reaching the field of battle.

The advantages of the Peninsula between the York and James Rivers are too obvious to need explanation. It is also clear that West Point should as soon as possible be reached and used as our main depot, that we may have the shortest line of land transportation for our supplies, and the use of the York River.

There are two methods of reaching this point —

1st. By moving directly from Fort Monroe as a base and trusting to the roads for our supplies, at the same time landing a strong corps as near Yorktown as possible in order to turn the rebel lines of defence south of Yorktown. Then to reduce Yorktown and Gloucester by a siege in all probability, involving a delay of weeks perhaps.

2d. To make a combined naval and land attack upon Yorktown, the first object of the campaign. This leads to the most rapid and decisive results. To accomplish this the Navy should at once concentrate upon the York River all their available and most powerful batteries. Its reduction should not in that case require many hours: a strong corps would be pushed up the York under cover of the Navy directly upon West Point immediately upon the fall of Yorktown and we could at once establish a new base of operations at a distance of some twenty five miles from Richmond — with every facility for developing and bringing into play the whole of our available force on either or both banks of the James.

It is impossible to urge too strongly the absolute necessity of the full cooperation of the Navy, as a part of this programme. Without it the operations may be prolonged for many weeks and we may be forced to carry in front several strong positions which by their aid could be turned without serious loss of either time or men.

It is also of first importance to bear in mind the fact already alluded to, that the capture of Richmond necessarily involves the prompt fall of Norfolk — while an operation against Norfolk if successful at the beginning of the campaign facilitates the reduction of Richmond merely by the demoralization of the rebel troops involved, and that after the fall of Norfolk we should be obliged to undertake the capture of Richmond, by the same means which would have accomplished it in the beginning having mean while afforded the rebels ample time to perfect their defensive arrangements — for they would well know from the moment the Army of the Potomac changed its base to Fort Monroe that Richmond must be its ultimate object.

It may be summed up in few words that for the prompt success of this campaign it is absolutely necessary that the Navy should at once throw its whole available force, its most powerful vessels, against Yorktown. There is the most important point — there the knot to be cut. An immediate decision upon the subject matter of this communication is highly desirable, and seems called for by the exigencies of the occasion.

> I am, Sir, Very Respectfully Your Obt Servant
> Geo B McClellan
> Maj Gen'l

Copy, McClellan Papers (D-7:69), Library of Congress. *OR,* Ser. 1, V, pp. 57–58.

To Randolph B. Marcy

Confidential — Memorandum[1]   [Alexandria, March 22, 1862]

For operations against Yorktown, Richmond &c where we will probably find exterior earthworks heavily garrisoned, we shall require the means of overwhelming them by a vertical fire of shells.

I should therefore be glad to have disposable at Fort Monroe —

I.	1st	20 10″ mortars complete
	2nd	20 8″ ″ ″
II.		20 8″ siege howitzers
III.		20 (?) 4 1/2″ wrought iron siege guns
IV.		40 20 pdr Parrotts
V.		__ 24 pdr siege guns

The 20 pdr Parrotts with the batteries will of course be counted as available.

I do not know number of 4 1/2 guns available, if not so many as I have indicated, something else should be substituted.

I wish Genl Barry and Col Kingsbury to consult with Genl Marcy, to make such suggestions as occur to them, and ascertain at once to what extent this memorandum can be filled.

It is possible we cannot count upon the Navy to reduce Yorktown by their independent efforts, we must therefore be prepared to do it by our own means.[2]

There are said to be at Yorktown from 27 to 32 heavy guns, at Gloucester 14 Columbiads. The probable armament of Yorktown, when exterior guns are drawn in, will be from 40 to 50 heavy guns, from 24 pdrs to 8″ and perhaps 10″ Columbiads.

Copy, McClellan Papers (A-48:19), Library of Congress.

1. This memorandum was sent to Chief of Staff Marcy on Mar. 22 with the notation: "The matter is an important one and should be attended to without delay." 2. Marcy replied on this date that eighteen siege pieces were then aboard ship, and an additional fifty-six had been ordered from various military arsenals. McClellan Papers (A-48:19).

To Nathaniel P. Banks [TELEGRAM]

Head Quarters, Army of the Potomac,
Seminary March 24 11 am 1862

Dispatch received.[1] Your course was right. As soon as you are strong enough push Jackson hard & drive him well beyond Strasburg pursuing at least as far as Woodstock & if possible with Cavalry to Mount Jackson. Strasburg should then be held in force & the repairs of the Railway bridge over the Shenandoah pushed forward as rapidly as possible. The very moment the thorough defeat of Jackson will permit it, resume the movement on Manassas, always leaving the whole of Shields' command at or near Strasburg & Winchester until Manassas Gap Railway is fully repaired. Call on Sedgwick for aid if you require it — but not unless necessary. Communicate fully & frequently & act vigorously.

G B McClellan
Maj Genl

Maj Genl N P Banks
Comdg 5th Corps Winchester

ALS (telegram sent), Records of the Office of the Secretary of War, RG 107 (M-504:66), National Archives. *OR*, Ser. 1, XII, Part 3, p. 16.

1. Banks telegraphed on this date that Brig. Gen. John Sedgwick's division was standing by in the wake of Stonewall Jackson's repulse at Kernstown the previous day by Brig. Gen. James Shields's command. *OR*, Ser. 1, XII, Part 3, p. 16.

LIBRARY ST. MARY'S COLLEGE

To Joseph G. Totten

Unofficial & Private   Hd Qtrs Army of Potomac
My dear General[1]   Seminary March 28 1862

I learn that you are very anxious to get two Engineers from this Army for service on Permanent Fortifications; I fully appreciate your anxiety & necessities but would beg to lay before you a few considerations which will I hope induce you to allow the matter to lay over for a few weeks.

You know that the Army is being embarked as rapidly as possible for Fort Monroe — the first operation will be the capture of Yorktown & Gloucester, this *may* involve a siege (at least I go prepared for one) in case the Navy is not able to afford the means for destroying the rebel batteries at these points. Again it is probable that we may have some siege operations to undertake against Richmond, & perhaps finally, against Norfolk. I do not expect to go through *all* the regular operations of a siege against all these places, but *do* expect to be obliged to establish batteries & perhaps open some trenches — operations which will require the services of a number of Engineer officers. I would therefore ask you to endeavor to postpone your call for two more Engineer officers until these operations are accomplished — which cannot involve a delay of more than a very few weeks. If I can even keep them until the question of Yorktown is disposed of I shall feel better satisfied.[2]

I feel sure that the good of the service & the Corps will be best served by the course I propose — asking your views in reply to this

I remain very sincerely your friend
Geo B McClellan
Maj Genl Comdg

ALS, Pierpont Morgan Library. Brig. Gen. Totten headed the Corps of Engineers.

1. Although the addressee is not named, this letter is clearly in response to a request by Totten for engineers to work on the fortifications of Northern coastal cities. War Board minutes, Mar. 18, 19, 1862, Stanton Papers, Library of Congress. 2. The Army of the Potomac retained these engineers.

To Samuel P. Heintzelman   [TELEGRAM]

Bg Gen S P Heintzelman   Hd Qrs Seminary
Comdg 3d Corps — Ft Monroe   Mch 28/62 [11:45 A.M.]

Your telegram of yesterday morning received only last night.[1] I hope the movement on Big Bethel was well considered in view of my wish not to prematurely develop our plans to the enemy. If the destruction of their batteries and your subsequent return confirms the idea that we are after Norfolk all is well except the mere fact of falling back. If this reaches you in time it would be well to hold the position of Big Bethel if its reoccupation by the enemy can give us any trouble. You on the ground can best judge of this.

G. B. McClellan
Maj Gen Comdg

Retained copy, McClellan Papers (C-10:63), Library of Congress. *OR*, Ser. 1, XI, Part 3, p. 43.

1. Heintzelman's telegram of Mar. 27 reported on reconnaissances sent out that day from Fort Monroe. *OR*, Ser. 1, XI, Part 3, p. 42.

To Edwin M. Stanton [TELEGRAM]

Seminary [March 28, 1862] 9.30 pm

I have instructed Genl Williams to telegraph Mr. Morley[1] to procure at Baltimore the lumber requisite to rebuild the Manassas Railway bridge over the Shenandoah. I would advise that Mr McCallum at once look into the practicability of connecting Winchester with Strasburg by a railway. If this can be done within a reasonable time it will be of immense advantage to us in a military point of view.

The repairs of the Manassas Gap Railway being completed & this new road built we would have easy control of that entire region.[2]

I would ask immediate attention to this very important matter.

G B McClellan
Maj Genl

Hon E M Stanton
Secty of War

ALS (telegram sent), Records of the Office of the Secretary of War, RG 107 (M-504:66), National Archives. *OR*, Ser. 1, XII, Part 3, p. 26.

1. Capt. R. F. Morley, general manager of military railroads. 2. GBM proposed to complete a railroad line running the length of the Shenandoah Valley by linking the Manassas Gap and Winchester and Potomac railroads. The proposal was not carried out.

To Abraham Lincoln

Private

My dear Sir   Washington March 31/62

Your note in regard to Genl Blenker's Division has reached me just as I am on the point of leaving for Alexandria.[1]

I need not say that I regret the loss of Blenker's Division first because they are excellent troops — second — because I know they are warmly attached to me.

I fully appreciate, however, the circumstances of the case, & hasten to assure you that I cheerfully acquiesce in your decision without any mental reservation.

Recognizing implicitly as I ever do the plenitude of your power as Commander in Chief, I cannot but regard the tone of your note as in the highest degree complimentary to me, & as adding one more to the many proofs of personal regard you have so often honored me with.

I shall do my best to use all the more activity to make up for the loss of this Division, & beg again to assure you that I will ever do my very best to carry out your views & support your interests in the same frank spirit you have always shown towards me.

I am very respectfully and sincerely your friend

Geo B McClellan

His Excellency Abraham Lincoln
Presdt

ALS, Lincoln Papers, Library of Congress.

1. The president wrote on this date: "This morning I felt constrained to order Blenker's Division to Fremont; and I write this to assure you that I did so with great pain, understanding that you would wish it otherwise. If you could know the full pressure of the case, I am confident you would justify it — even beyond a mere acknowledgment that the Commander-in-chief, may order what he pleases." *Collected Works of Lincoln*, V, pp. 175–76. Brig. Gen. Louis Blenker's division was sent as reinforcement to Frémont's Mountain Department, in western Virginia.

To Nathaniel P. Banks

Maj. Gen. N. P. Banks   Hd. Qtrs. Army of the Potomac.
Comdg. 5th Corps   Onboard the Commodore [Alexandria],
General,   April 1/62

The change in affairs in the valley of the Shenandoah has rendered necessary a corresponding departure — temporarily at least — from the plan we some days since agreed upon.[1] In my arrangements I assume that you have with you a force amply sufficient to drive Jackson before you, provided he is not re-inforced largely. I also assume that you may find it impossible to detach anything towards Manassas for some days, probably not until the operations of the main Army have drawn all the rebel forces towards Richmond.

You are aware that Genl. Sumner has for some days been at Warrenton Junction, with two Divisions of Infantry, 6 batteries, & two Regts. of Cavalry; & that a reconnaissance to the Rappahannock forced the enemy to destroy the railway bridge at Rappahannock station on the Orange & Alexandria R.R. Since that time our Cavalry have found nothing on this side of the Rappahannock in that direction, and it seems clear that we have no reason to fear any return of the rebels in that quarter. Their movements near Fredericksburg also indicate a final abandonment of that neighborhood. I doubt whether Johnston will now re-inforce Jackson with a view to offensive operations, — the time has probably passed when he could have gained anything by doing so. I have ordered in one of

Sumner's Divisions (that of Richardson,[2] late Sumner's) to Alexandria for embarkation; Blenker's has been detached from the Army of the Potomac, & ordered to report to Genl. Fremont.

Abercrombie is probably at Warrenton Junction today, — Geary at White Plains.[3]

Two regts. of Cavalry have been ordered out & are now on the way to relieve the two regts. of Sumner.

Four thousand infantry & one battery leave Washington at once for Manassas, some 3000 more will move in one or two days, & soon after some 3000 additional.

I will order Blenker to march on Strasburg, & to report to you for temporary duty, so that should you find a large force in your front, you can avail yourself of his aid. As soon as possible please direct him on Winchester, thence to report to the Adjt. Genl. of the Army for orders — but keep him until you are sure what you have in front.

In regard to your own movements — the most important thing at present is to throw Jackson well back & then to assume such a position as to enable you to prevent his return. As soon as the railway communications are re-established it will be probably important & advisable to move on Staunton, but this would require secure communications, & a force of from 25,000 to 30,000 for active operations. It should also be nearly coincident with my own move on Richmond, — at all events not so long before it as to enable the rebels to concentrate on you & then return on me. I fear that you cannot be ready in time, — altho' it may come in very well, with a force less than that I have mentioned, after the main battle near Richmond.

When Genl. Sumner leaves Warrenton Junction, Genl. Abercrombie will be placed in immediate command of Manassas & Warrenton Junction, under your general orders.

Please inform me frequently by telegraph and otherwise as to the state of things in your front.

I am very truly yours

Geo B McClellan

Maj. Gen. Comdg.

P.S. From what I have just learned, it would seem that the two Regts of Cavalry intended for Warrenton Junction have gone to Harper's Ferry. Of the four additional regts. placed under your orders, two should as promptly as possible move by the shortest route on Warrenton Junction.

I am respectfully your obdt. servt.

G. B. McClellan

Maj. Genl. Comdg.

Retained copy, McClellan Papers (A-50:20), Library of Congress. *OR*, Ser. 1, V, pp. 59–60.

1. See GBM to Banks, Mar. 16, *supra*. 2. Brig. Gen. Israel B. Richardson. 3. Brig. Gen. John J. Abercrombie, Col. John W. Geary.

To Lorenzo Thomas

Brigadier General L. Thomas
Adjutant General U.S. Army   Head-Quarters, Army of the Potomac,
General: Steamer Commodore, April 1, 1862

I have to request that you will lay the following communication before the Hon. Secretary of War.

The approximate numbers and positions of the troops left near and in the rear on the Potomac are about as follows.

Genl. Dix has, after guarding the railroads under his charge, sufficient troops to give him 5000 for the defence of Baltimore, and 1988 available for the Eastern shore, Annapolis &c. Fort Delaware is very well garrisoned by about 400 men.

The garrisons of the forts around Washington amount to 10,600 men; other disposable troops now with Genl. Wadsworth[1] being about 11,400 men.

The troops employed in guarding the various railways in Maryland amount to some 3359 men. These it is designed to relieve, being old regiments, by dismounted Cavalry, and to send forward to Manassas.

Gen. Abercrombie occupies Warrenton with a force, which including Col. Geary at White Plains and the Cavalry to be at his disposal, will amount to some 7780 men, with 12 pieces of Artillery. I have the honor to request that all the troops organized for service in Pennsylvania & New York, and in any of the Eastern States, may be ordered to Washington. I learn from Governor Curtin that there are some 3500 men now ready in Pennsylvania. This force I should be glad to have sent at once to Manassas. Four thousand men from Genl. Wadsworth I desire to be ordered to Manassas. The troops with the railroad guards above alluded to will make up a force under the command of Genl. Abercrombie to something like 18,639 men.

It is my design to push Genl. Blenker's division from Warrenton upon Strasburg. He should remain at Strasburg long enough to allow matters to assume a definite form in that region before proceeding to his ultimate destination.

The troops in the valley of the Shenandoah will thus, — including Blenker's Division, 10,028 strong with 24 pieces of Artillery, Banks' 5th Corps which embraces the command of Genl. Shields, 19,687 strong with 41 guns, some 3652 disposable Cavalry, and the Railroad guards, about 2100 men, — amount to about 35,467 men.

It is designed to relieve General Hooker by one regiment, say 850 men; leaving with some 500 Cavalry, 1350 men on the Lower Potomac.

To recapitulate, — at Warrenton there is to be,   7,780 men
        at Manassas, say   10,859 "
        In the valley of the Shenandoah   35,467 "
        On the lower Potomac,   1,350 "
                              In all,   55,456 men

There would thus be left for the garrisons, and the front of Washington under Genl. Wadsworth, some 18,000 men — exclusive of the batteries under construction.

The troops organizing or ready for service in New York, I learn will probably number more than four thousand. These should be assembled at Washington subject to disposition where their services may be most needed.

                  I am very Respectfully your obedient servant
                  Geo. B. McClellan
                  Maj. Genl. Comdg.

Copy, Lincoln Papers, Library of Congress. *OR*, Ser. 1, V, pp. 60–61.

1. Brig. Gen. James S. Wadsworth commanded the Washington defenses.

To Mary Ellen McClellan

                  Steamer Commodore April 1 1862 Potomac River
   4.15 pm. As soon as possible after reaching Alexandria I got the Commodore under weigh & "put off" — I did not feel safe until I could fairly see Alexandria behind us. I have brought a tug with us to take back dispatches from Budd's Ferry, where I shall stop a few hours for the purpose of winding up everything. I feared that if I remained at Alexandria I would be annoyed very much & perhaps be sent for from Washn. Officially speaking, I feel very glad to get away from that sink of iniquity....

   8 pm. I have just returned from a trip in one of the naval vessels with Capt Wyman to take a look at the rebel batteries (recently abandoned) at Shipping Point etc. They were pretty formidable & it would have given us no little trouble to have taken possession of them had they held firm. It makes only the more evident the propriety of my movements by which Manassas was forced to be evacuated & their batteries with it. The trip was quite interesting....

AL copy, McClellan Papers (C-7:63), Library of Congress.

To Ambrose E. Burnside

Maj. Gen. Ambrose E. Burnside,
Commanding Department of North Carolina:
General:

Headquarters Army
of the Potomac
Steamer Commodore,
April 2, 1862.

I expect to reach Fort Monroe to-day, to take control of active operations from that point. The line of operations will be up the Peninsula, resting our line on the York River and making Richmond the objective point. In the course of events it may become necessary for us to cross the James below Richmond and move on Petersburg. It has now become of the first importance that there should be frequent communication between us, and that I should be informed of the exact state of things with you and in your front. Four additional regiments should have reached you by this time.

I am entirely in the dark as to the condition of your operations against Beaufort, the force of the enemy there and at Goldsborough. Will you please at once inform me fully, stating how soon you expect to be in possession of Fort Macon,[1] what available troops you will then have for operating on Goldsborough, what can, in your opinion, be affected there in the way of taking possession of it, of neutralizing a strong force of the enemy there, and of doing something toward preventing the enemy's retreat from Richmond. On the other hand, please inform me what you can do in the way of a demonstration at Winton on Suffolk.

You will readily understand that if I succeed in driving the enemy out of Richmond I will at once throw a strong force on Raleigh and open the communication with you via Goldsborough; after which I hope to confide to you no unimportant part of subsequent operations.

Taking all things into consideration, it appears probable that a movement in the direction of Goldsborough would be the best thing for you to undertake, as you can make it in larger force than that on Winton, for as soon as you have possession of Fort Macon nearly all your force will be available. Great caution will, however, be necessary, as the enemy might throw large forces in that direction. The main object of the movement would be to accomplish that, but it would not do for you to be caught. We cannot afford any reverse at present. I wish your opinion in regard to the whole affair.

Very truly, yours,
Geo. B. McClellan

OR, Ser. 1, IX, p. 374.

1. Fort Macon guarded the approach to Beaufort.

To Mary Ellen McClellan [TELEGRAM]

Fort Monroe April 2 11 1/2 pm /62

Have arrived here all well. Navy fully prepared to sink the Merrimac. I only hope she may appear tomorrow. The grass will not grow under my feet.

G B McClellan

Mrs. McClellan
Washington

ALS (telegram sent), Records of the Office of the Secretary of War, RG 107 (M-504:66), National Archives.

To Mary Ellen McClellan

Steamer Commodore April 3 [1862] Hampton Roads 1 1/2 pm.

... I have been up to my eyes in business since my arrival. We reached here about 4 yesterday pm. — ran in to the wharf & unloaded the horses, then went out & anchored. Marcy & . at once took a tug & ran out to the flag ship Minnesota to see Goldsborough where we remained until about 9, taking tea with him.

On our return we found Genl. Heintzelman — soon followed by Porter & Smith — all of whom remained here all night. I sat up very late arranging movements, & had my hands full. I have been hard at work all the morning & not yet been on shore. Dine with Genl Wool today at 4 — & go thence to our camp. We move tomorrow a.m. Three Divisions take the direct road to Yorktown, & will encamp at Howard's Bridge. Two take the James River road & go to Young's Mills. The Reserve goes to Big Bethel, where my Hd Qtrs will be tomorrow night. My great trouble is the want of wagons — a terrible drawback — but I cannot wait for them. I hope to get possession before tomorrow night of a new landing place some 7 or 8 miles from Yorktown, which will help us very much. It is probable that we shall have some fighting tomorrow — not serious — but we may have the opportunity of drubbing Magruder. You need not be at all anxious about me — I shall be in reserve as tomorrow will be merely an affair of advanced guards. The harbor here is very crowded — facilities for landing are bad — Van Vliet (as usual) has not arrived — ever late when most needed. I hope to get possession of Yorktown day after tomorrow. Shall then arrange to make the York River my line of supplies. The eclat of taking Yorktown will cover a delay of the few days necessary to get everything in hand & ready for action. The great battle will be (I think) near Richmond as I have always hoped & thought. I see my way very clearly — & with my trains once ready will move rapidly. ...

AL copy, McClellan Papers (C-7:63), Library of Congress.

To Louis M. Goldsborough

Flag Officer Goldsborough
Comdg Squadron   Head-Quarters of the Army of Potomac
Dear Sir   Hampton Roads April 3 1862.

I find that I have wagons sufficient to move the greater part of the force now here & have accordingly concluded to advance towards York tomorrow morning.

Unless delayed by an obstinate resistance on the part of the enemy our advanced guard ought to be in rear of the Ship's Point Battery at about 2 o'clock tomorrow afternoon, & in possession of it by from 3 to 3 1/2 o'clock.

I propose on the next day (5th) to invest Yorktown, throwing a sufficient force above it to prevent the escape of the Garrison by land, unless they abandon the place on our approach. So many days would elapse before I could collect the transports necessary to land a force on the Gloucester side, that I have thought it more prudent to advance upon Yorktown without waiting for the movement on the other side. I would now respectfully ask for such assistance in the way of gun boats as you can properly afford.

A couple (or more of) gun boats) tomorrow *afternoon* near Ship's Point battery would be of great use to us.

If you can send all your available force — after providing for the other objects you have in view — so as to reach the vicinity of Yorktown day after tomorrow, I think we can make short work of it.

If we can arrange matters so that I can get in rear of Yorktown before you open fire we ought very soon to get the place.

I shall have troops at Howards Bridge tomorrow by midday, & we might arrange to communicate there; but I expect to have the telegraph completed to my Hd Quarters tomorrow evening & can then tell you the exact state of affairs, & the time when I shall probably reach the rear of Yorktown. If at all possible I will come out to see you this evening, but in the mean time let me ask the favor that you will inform me what I can probably count upon at Ships's Point & Yorktown in the way of Naval assistance.

very truly yours
Geo B McClellan
Maj Genl Comdg

ALS, Office of Naval Records and Library, RG 45 (M-625:85), National Archives. *NOR*, Ser. 1, VII, pp. 195–96.

To Edwin M. Stanton   [TELEGRAM]

Head-Quarters,
Hon. E. M. Stanton   Army of the Potomac,
Secretary of War   Washington D.C.   Fort Monroe April 3, 1862

I expect to move from here tomorrow morning on Yorktown, where a force of some fifteen thousand of the rebels are in intrenched position, and I think it quite probable they will attempt to resist us.

No appearance of the Merrimac as yet.

Commodore Goldsborough is quite confident he can sink her when she comes out.

Geo. B. McClellan
Maj Genl Comdg

Retained copy, McClellan Papers (C-10:63), Library of Congress. *OR*, Ser. 1, XI, Part 3, p. 64. The same telegram was sent to Gen. Sumner.

To Irvin McDowell

Maj. Gen. I. McDowell,
Commanding First Corps: Headquarters Army of the Potomac,
General: Fort Monroe, April 4, 1862.

The information I have obtained here has induced me to move forward the troops for whom I have wagons, in order to invest Yorktown.

I still think that it will be advisable for you to land at least one division on the Severn, in order to insure the fall of Gloucester. I have therefore telegraphed to Franklin and Rucker[1] to get your First Division embarked as soon as possible (supposing you will be here by this morning) to make this movement.

I hope to turn the battery at Ship Point this afternoon or early to-morrow morning and to get in rear of Yorktown to-morrow. I can therefore tell to-morrow what is the best disposition to make of your corps. It will probably be best to land one division on the Severn and to hold the others ready to move up the York River immediately upon the fall of Yorktown. My headquarters will be at Big Bethel to-night.

I had a full conversation with Flag-Officer Goldsborough and Captain Missroon[2] last evening, and would be glad if you will see them also.

You know that we are substantially weakened to the extent of two divisions; first, by the loss of Blenker; next, by the rescinding of the order placing this fort and its dependencies under my command.[3]

If you can get up to Big Bethel I can take care of you to-night and make you comfortable. Should I miss you, I will write fully, as events develop themselves.

> Very truly, yours
> Geo. B. McClellan
> Major-General

OR, Ser. 1, XI, Part 3, p. 68.

1. Col. Daniel H. Rucker, quartermaster's department. 2. Comdr. John S. Missroon headed the naval force at Hampton Roads assigned to cooperate with GBM. 3. On Apr. 4 Gen. Wool wrote Stanton: "I will with my force occupy the stations abandoned by the rebels as the general advances. This will protect . . . his rear and left flank, which was suggested by myself, which the general readily assented to. . . ." *OR,* Ser. 1, XI, Part 3, p. 66.

To Mary Ellen McClellan

Big Bethel April 4 [1862] 8 1/2 pm.

. . . Everything has worked well today — I have gained some strong positions without fighting & shall try some more manoeuvring tomorrow. . . .

I shall try to invest Yorktown tomorrow & may have a fight.

AL copy, McClellan Papers (C-7:63), Library of Congress.

To Abraham Lincoln   [TELEGRAM]

Hon A. Lincoln, President   Near Yorktown, [April 5, 1862] 7.30 p.m.

The Enemy are in large force along our front and, apparently, intend making a determined resistance. A reconnaissance just made by Genl. Barnard, shows that their line of works extends across the entire Peninsula from Yorktown and Warwick river. Many of these are formidable. Deserters say that they are being reinforced daily from Richmond, and from Norfolk.

Under these circumstances I beg that you will reconsider the order detaching the first Corps from my Command.[1] In my deliberate judgment the success of our cause will be imperilled[2] when it is actually under the fire of the enemy, and active operations have commenced. Two or three of my Divisions have been under fire of Artillery most of the day. I am now of the opinion that I shall have to fight all of the available force of the Rebels not far from here. Do not force me to do so with diminished numbers. But whatever your decision may be, I will leave nothing undone to obtain success. If you cannot leave me the whole of the first Corps, I urgently ask that I may not lose Franklin and his Division.

> G B McClellan
> Maj General

Received copy, Lincoln Papers, Library of Congress. *OR*, Ser. 1, XI, Part 3, p. 71.

1. Announced by a telegram sent on Apr. 4 but just received. In a letter of Apr. 4 Adj. Gen. Thomas wrote GBM : "The President, deeming the force to be left in front of Washington insufficient to insure its safety, has directed that McDowell's army corps should be detached from the forces operating under your immediate direction." *OR*, Ser. 1, XI, Part 1, p. 10, Part 3, p. 66. 2. At this point the phrase "by so greatly reducing my force" was omitted, apparently inadvertently, from the copy of the telegram given to the president.

To Louis M. Goldsborough

Head-Quarters of the Army of Potomac
My dear Flag Officer   5 miles from Yorktown April 5 1862 10.30 PM

The rebels are close in my front & we have had sharp cannonading most of the afternoon — with but little loss on our side — some 8 or 10 killed. Our neighbors are in a very strong position, their left at Yorktown (strongly entrenched, with numerous guns), thence extending along the line of the Warwick River to its mouth. This river is some seven feet deep to a point near Lee's Mills, banks marshy & almost impassable; from point to point they have batteries. The roads are infamous & I have had great difficulty in moving. Tomorrow I shall spend in making reconnaissances, in repairing the roads, getting up supplies, & establishing my depots at Ship Point. I cannot turn Yorktown without a *battle*, in which I must use heavy artillery & go through the preliminary operations of a siege. The reconnaissances of tomorrow will enable me to form a pretty correct judgment of what I have to meet & the best way of overcoming the difficulties before me. Naval cooperation seems to me more essential than ever, I can best give you my ideas by tomorrow night. I learn that the Mystic[1] has reached you — will you be able to put her at the Yorktown batteries if I find it necessary?

If I find the position as strong as I now anticipate I will probably propose to you that I shall put my siege guns & mortars in battery to open simultaneously with the action of such naval vessels as you can spare.

Reinforcements are said to be arriving from Richmond & Norfolk.

I fear our Severn expedition may be impracticable — I received this evening a dispatch from the Adjt General informing me that McDowell's Corps (some 35,000 men) has been withdrawn from my command. I need not tell you that nothing could have astonished me more — I received the dispatch while listening to the rebels guns, & when well assured that I required all the force I had counted upon. I shall send this through Missroon & ask him to read it.

Do let me hear from you occasionally — as often as your duties will permit.[2]

I can tell you better tomorrow evening about the Severn & will ask Missroon to come & see me tomorrow.

> Ever your friend
> Geo B McClellan
> Maj Genl Comdg

Flag Officer Goldsborough
Comdg Squadron

ALS, Office of Naval Records and Library, RG 45 (M-625:85), National Archives. *NOR*, Ser. 1, VII, pp. 205–206.

1. The ironclad *Galena*. 2. Goldsborough replied on Apr. 6 that he did not expect the *Galena* "for some time to come. Until the guns on Gloucester Point be turned by the movement up the Severn it will be wholly impracticable, in my judgment, for the small naval force I can now detail to assist you to attack the forts at Yorktown and Gloucester with any prospect of success.... I dare not leave the Merrimac and consorts unguarded." *OR*, Ser. 1, XI, Part 3, p. 80.

To Mary Ellen McClellan

Near Yorktown April 6 [1862] 1 am.

... I find the enemy in strong force & in a very strong position but will drive him out. Fitz John is in the advance on the right, Baldy on the left[1] — they are doing splendidly. Their Divisions have been under fire all the afternoon [April 5] — have lost only about 5 killed in each & have punished secesh badly. Thus far it has been altogether an artillery affair. While listening this pm. to the sound of the guns, I received the order detaching McDowell's Corps from my command — it is the most infamous thing that history has recorded. I have made such representations as will probably induce a revocation of the order — or at least save Franklin to me. The idea of depriving a General of 35,000 troops when actually under fire! Tomorrow night I can tell you exactly what I intend doing.

We have no baggage tonight — our wagons being detained by the bad roads. Have taken possession of a *hut* in a deserted secesh camp — found a table therein — & sleep on a horse blanket if I find time to "retire." Colburn is copying a long letter — Seth, standing by the fire, looking *very* sleepy![2] He wakes up & sends his kindest regards, in which Colburn asks to participate — I am sorry to say that your Father is snoring loudly in a corner.

AL copy; copy, McClellan Papers (C-7:63/D-10:72), Library of Congress.

1. Brig. Gens. Fitz John Porter and William F. Smith. 2. Lt. Col. A. V. Colburn and Brig. Gen. Williams, of GBM's staff.

To Abraham Lincoln   [TELEGRAM]

Head Quarters Army of the Potomac

A. Lincoln Presdt   [Before Yorktown] April 6th 1862 [11 A.M.]

⌈ The order forming new Departments, if rigidly enforced deprives me of the power of ordering up wagons and troops absolutely necessary to enable me to advance to Richmond.[1] I have by no means the transportation I must have to move my army even a few miles.⌉ I respectfully request I may not be placed in this position, but that my orders for wagons — trains, ammunition and other material that I have prepared & necessarily left behind, as well as Woodbury's brigade,[2] may at once be complied with. The Enemy is strong in my front, & I have a most serious task before me, in the fulfillment of which I need all the aid the Government can give me.[3] I again repeat the urgent request that Genl Franklin & his division may be restored to my command.

G. B. McClellan Maj Genl

Received copy, Records of the Office of the Secretary of War, RG 107 (M- 473 :99), National Archives. *OR*, Ser. 1, XI, Part 3, pp. 73–74.

1. This order, of Apr. 4, created the Department of the Shenandoah, under Banks, and the Department of the Rappahannock, under McDowell. *OR*, Ser. 1, XI, Part 3, pp. 67–68. 2. Brig. Gen. Daniel P. Woodbury commanded a brigade of engineering troops. 3. Lincoln replied by telegraph on this date: "Sec. of War informs me that the forwarding of transportation, amunition, & Woodburys, brigade, under your orders, is not, and will not be interfered with." *Collected Works of Lincoln*, V, p. 182.

To William B. Franklin   [TELEGRAM]

Near Yorktown Apr 6th 1862

I have twice urgently telegraphed the Presdt requesting that you & your Division might be restored to my command.

Do all you can to accomplish it. Heaven knows I need you here.[1]

McClellan

Gen W B Franklin
Alexandria

ALS (telegram sent), McClellan Papers (A-50 :20), Library of Congress.

1. On Apr. 7 Franklin replied: "I was so entirely taken by surprise, and so entirely powerless in the matter that I was unable to do anything to stave the thing off. . . . McDowell told me that it was intended as a blow at you. That Stanton had said that you intended to work by strategy, and not by fighting, that all of the opponents of the policy of the administration centred around you — in other words that you had political aspirations." McClellan Papers (A-50 :20).

To Edwin M. Stanton   [TELEGRAM]

Head-Quarters, Army of the Potomac,
In front of Yorktown April 7 7 pm 1862

Your telegram of yesterday[1] arrived here while I was absent examining the enemy's right which I did pretty closely.

The whole line of the Warwick which really heads within a mile of Yorktown is strongly defended by detached redoubts & other fortifications armed with heavy & light guns. The approaches except at Yorktown are covered by the Warwick over which there is but one or at most two passages, both of which are covered by strong batteries. It will be necessary to resort to the use of heavy guns & some siege operations before we can assault. All the prisoners state that Gen J. E. Johnston arrived in Yorktown yesterday with strong reinforcements. It seems clear that I shall have the whole force of the enemy on my hands, probably not less than one hundred thousand (100,000) men & possibly more. In consequence of the loss of Blenkers Division & the First Corps my force is possibly less than that of the enemy, while they have all the advantage of position.

I am under great obligation to you for the offer that the whole force and material of the Govt. will be as fully and speedily under my command as heretofore, or as if the new departments had not been created.

Since my arrangements were made for this campaign at least fifty thousand (50,000) men have been taken from my command.

Since my dispatch of the 5th Inst.[2] five divisions have been in close observation of the enemy and frequently exchanging shots.

When my present command all joins I shall have about eighty five thousand 85,000 men for duty, from which a large force must be taken for guards, escorts &c. With this Army I could assault the enemys works and perhaps carry them — but were I in possession of their entrenchments and assailed by double my numbers I should have no fears as to the result.

Under the circumstances that have been developed since we arrived here I feel fully impressed with the conviction that here is to be fought the great battle that is to decide the existing contest. I shall of course commence the attack as soon as I can get up my siege train and shall do all in my power to carry the enemys works but to do this with a reasonable degree of certainty requires in my judgment that I should if possible have at least the whole of the 1st Army Corps to land upon the Severn River and attack Gloucester in the rear. My present strength will not admit of a detachment sufficient for this purpose without materially impairing the efficiency of this column.

Flag Officer Goldsborough thinks the works too strong for his available vessels unless I can turn Gloucester. I send by mail copies of his letter and one of the commander of the gun boats here.[3]

Geo. B. McClellan
Maj Genl

AL (in part) retained copy, McClellan Papers (A-50:20), Library of Congress. *OR*, Ser. 1, XI, Part 1, pp. 11–12. Only the first third of this dispatch is in GBM's handwriting.

1. Stanton explained that the "force under Banks and Wadsworth was deemed ... much less than had been fixed by your corps commanders as necessary to secure Washington. ... Your advance on Yorktown gratified me very much, and I hope you will press forward and carry the enemy's works and soon be at Richmond." *OR*, Ser. 1, XI, Part 3, p. 73. 2. GBM to Lincoln, Apr. 5, *supra*. 3. Letters from Goldsborough and Missroon to GBM, Apr. 6, *OR*, Ser. 1, XI, Part 3, pp. 80, 81–82.

To Abraham Lincoln [TELEGRAM]

To the President   Head-Quarters of the Army of the Potomac
Washington   [Before Yorktown] April 7 1862 [11 P.M.]

Your telegram of yesterday received.[1] In reply I have the honor to state that my entire force for duty only amounts to about eighty five thousand (85,000) men. General Wool's command as you will observe from the accompanying order has been taken out of my control, although he has most cheerfully cooperated with me.

The only use that can be made of his command is to protect my communications in rear of this point. At this time only fifty three thousand (53,000) men have joined me, but they are coming up as rapidly as my means of transportation will permit.

Please refer to my dispatch to the Secretary of War of tonight for the details of our present situation.[2]

G. B. McClellan
Maj. Genl.

[*verso*]

Return of March 31st 1862 shows men for duty —		171,602
Deduct — 1st Corps Inft & Arty	32,119	
Blenker	8,616	
Banks	21,759	
Wadsworth	19,308	
Cavalry of 1st Corps — say	1,600	
" Blenker	800	
Van Alen & Wyndham	1,600	
	85,792[3]	85,792
For duty —		85,810[4]
Officers about	3,900	
Total absent from whole command	23,796	

Retained copy (verso AD), McClellan Papers (A-50:20), Library of Congress. *OR*, Ser. 1, XI, Part 1, p. 11.

1. Lincoln telegraphed, in part: "You now have over one hundred thousand troops, with you independent of Gen. Wool's command. I think you better break the enemies' line from York-town to Warwick River, at once. They will probably use *time*, as advantageously as you can." *Collected Works of Lincoln*, V, p. 182. 2. GBM to Stanton, Apr. 7, *supra*. The president responded on Apr. 9: "Your despatches complaining that you are not properly sustained, while they do not offend me, do pain me very much. . . . I think it is the precise time for you to strike a blow. By delay the enemy will relatively gain upon you — that is, he will gain faster, by *fortifications* and *re-inforcements*, than you can by re-inforcements alone. And, once more let me tell you, it is indispensable to *you* that you strike a blow. *I* am powerless to help this. . . . The country will not fail to note — is now noting — that the present hesitation to move upon an intrenched enemy, is but the story of Manassas repeated. I beg to assure you that I have never written you, or spoken to you, in greater kindness of feeling than now, nor with a fuller purpose to sustain you. . . . *But you must act.*" *Collected Works of Lincoln*, V, pp. 184–85. 3. This figure should be 85,802. 4. This figure should be 85,800.

To Mary Ellen McClellan

[Before Yorktown] April 8 [1862] 8 am.

Raining hard all night & still continues to do so. Am now encamped about 5 mi from Yorktown — have been here 2 or 3 days. Have now visited both the right & left, & in spite of the heavy rain must ride to Ship Point & our right immediately after breakfast & all I care for about the rain is the health & comfort of the men. They are more fond of me than ever — more enthusiastic than I deserve — wherever I go it seems to inspire the fullest confidence. . . .

I have raised an awful row about McDowell's Corps — & have I think rather scared the authorities that be. The Presdt very coolly telegraphed me yesterday that he thought I had better break the enemy's lines at once! I was much tempted to reply that he had better come & do it himself.

AL copy, McClellan Papers (C-7:63), Library of Congress.

To Edwin M. Stanton   [TELEGRAM]

Head Quarters, Army of the Potomac,
Near Yorktown April 11 12.30 am 1862

The reconnaissances of today [April 10] prove that it is necessary to invest & attack Gloucester Point. Give me Franklin's & McCall's Divisions under command of Franklin & I will at once undertake it.

If circumstances of which I am not aware make it impossible for you to send me two Divisions to carry out the final plan of campaign I will run the risk & hold myself responsible for the results if you will give me

Franklin's Division. If you still confide in my judgment I entreat that you will grant this request — the fate of our cause depends upon it.

Although willing under the pressure of necessity to carry this through with Franklin alone, I wish it to be distinctly understood that I think two Divisions necessary. Franklin & his Division are indispensable to me. Genl Barnard concurs in this view. I have determined upon the point of attack & am at this moment engaged in fixing the position of the batteries.

G B McClellan

Maj Genl

Hon E M Stanton

Secty of War

ALS (telegram sent), McClellan Papers (A-51:20), Library of Congress. *OR*, Ser. 1, XI, Part 3, p. 86.

To Mary Ellen McClellan

[Before Yorktown] April 11 [1862] 8 am.

I am just recovering from a terrible scare. Early this morning I was awakened by a dispatch from Fitz John's Hd Qtrs, stating that Fitz had made an ascension in the balloon this morning, & that the balloon had broken away & come to the ground some 3 miles S.W. — which would be within the enemy's lines! You can imagine how I felt! I at once sent off to the various pickets to find out what they knew, & try to do something to save him — but the order had no sooner gone, than in walks Mr. Fitz just as cool as usual — he had luckily come down near my own camp, after actually passing over that of the enemy!! You may rest assured of one thing: you won't catch me in the confounded balloon nor will I allow any other Generals to go up in it!...[1]

Dont worry about the wretches — they have done nearly their worst & can't do much more. I am sure that I will win in the end, in spite of all their rascality.

History will present a sad record of these traitors who are willing to sacrifice the country & its army for personal spite & personal aims. The people will soon understand the whole matter & then woe betide the guilty ones.

AL copy; copy, McClellan Papers (C-7:63/D-10:72), Library of Congress.

1. Thaddeus S. C. Lowe, the army's chief aeronaut, remarked of Porter's experience: "I found it difficult for a time to restore confidence among the officers as to the safety of this means of observation on account of this accident...." *OR*, Ser. 3, III, p. 274.

To Winfield Scott

Dear General;

Head-Quarters, Army of the Potomac,
Camp Winfield Scott April 11 1862

I find myself with a siege before me, and as I entertain strong hopes that the result of the operations now impending will be decisive of the present contest, I have taken the liberty to give to this Camp the name of the General under whom I first learned the art of war and whom I have ever regarded as my sincere friend. I hope, General, that the operations emanating from this Camp will not be unworthy of the approbation of the great General whose name it now bears.

When I moved from Fort Monroe, I was deceived by the maps laid before me and supposed that Yorktown could be turned and its garrison cut off by two rapid marches. I therefore moved the Divisions F. J. Porter and Hamilton by the road from Hampton and Big Bethel to Howard's Bridge, throwing a strong advance guard far enough to the front to force the evacuation of Ship Point; at the same time, I moved the Divisions Smith (W. F.) and Couch from Newport News on Young's Mill; with Sedgwick's Division, the regular Infantry and Cavalry and the Artillery Reserve, I moved to Big Bethel. The orders for the next day's march were for the left column to move rapidly to "Halfway House" — 6 miles from Yorktown on the Williamsburg road, in order to cut the communications of the garrison of York; the right column to move upon York and invest it. I moved the reserves to a point 5 miles from Yorktown, whence I could direct it to the support of either column, supposing that the left would most require its aid.

It proved, however, to be the case that the topography of the country was very different from what had been supposed and that the enemy had occupied and strongly entrenched the right bank of the Warwick River, which heads about one-half a mile from Yorktown. The works are formidable, the Artillery pretty heavy. The bed of the Warwick is next to impassable owing to its marshy nature and numerous inundations. The defences of Yorktown itself and of Gloucester are truly formidable. The water batteries are so heavy as to deter the gun-boats from attacking them. The roads have been infamous — we are working energetically upon them — are landing our siege guns, and leaving nothing undone.

We are forced to the use of mortars and heavy guns, although I do not expect, at present, to be obliged to resort to the tedious operations of a formal siege. Franklin's Division has just been restored to me. With it, I shall attack Gloucester Point.

The "Mystic," iron-clad, has been promised me. I shall try to have her run through the passage between York and Gloucester, in order to cut off the supplies and reinforcements constantly received by the rebels by way of York River, and at the same time take their water batteries in reverse.

You are probably aware, General, that, since I commenced this movement, my Army has been weakened by detachments to the extent of nearly 50,000 men. Of these, Franklin's Division (say 11,000) has today been restored to me.

Excuse me, General, for troubling you with this long and hasty letter; but I feel assured that you entertain a strong interest in the movements of this Army; so much so, that I will take the liberty of occasionally writing to you, if it is not disagreeable to you.

I send, with this, a map which will give you a general idea of the position. Tomorrow, I can send you a clear and good one. Only two or three of the enemy's numerous batteries are marked on this.

I am General your sincere & attached friend,
Geo. B. McClellan
Major General

Lt. Genl. Winfield Scott,
U.S. Army

Copy, McClellan Papers (A-51:20), Library of Congress.

To Edwin M. Stanton [TELEGRAM]

[Camp Winfield Scott, April 12, 1862, noon]

Your telegram received. I thank you most sincerely for the reinforcements sent to me.[1]

Franklin will attack on the other side. The moment I hear from Missroon I will state point of rendesvous. I am confident as to results now.

G B McClellan
Maj Genl Comdg

Hon E M Stanton
Secty of War

ALS (telegram sent), McClellan Papers (A-51:20), Library of Congress. *OR*, Ser. 1, XI, Part 3, p. 92.

1. Stanton telegraphed Apr. 11: "Franklin's division is marching to Alexandria to embark. McCall's will be sent if the safety of this city will permit." *OR*, Ser. 1, XI, Part 3, p. 90.

To Gustavus V. Fox

Private   Head-Quarters, Army of the Potomac,
My dear Fox   Camp Winfield Scott April 14, 1862.

Wyman[1] is here & I will send this by him. I fear friend Missroon is not the man for the place exactly, he is a little too careful of his vessels, & has as yet done us no good — not even annoyed the enemy.

Can't you possibly arrange the matter so as to put Wyman or some one like him in command? It would of course be a great advantage that the Army & Navy Comdrs should know each other & understand each other, so as to secure perfect cooperation — put Wyman in command & I feel perfectly sure that the thing will work out right. I received this morning a dispatch from Missroon as follows — ''The enemy are increasing troops in rear of picket station abreast the ships today'' — I replied ''Won't you shell them out?'' — Have received no reply, but have heard no shells. I have an indistinct idea that it would not be disagreeable to Missroon to go on Ordnance duty — a duty of great importance in these times. Do give me Wyman if you can — I like him & feel by instinct that he is a first rate officer for the work.[2]

Effective naval cooperation will shorten this affair by weeks. Don't forget to let me have the Mystic. I shall soon open trenches.

The work before us is rum but I can see the way to gain new and brilliant success.

Give my kindest regards to Judge Blair & say to him that I received his letter & will not fail to act upon his suggestions.[3]

If Wyman comes here can you not send the Anacosta & Badger with him?[4]

In haste very truly your friend
Geo B McClellan

Hon G V Fox
Asst Secty

ALS, Fox Papers, New-York Historical Society.

1. Commander of the Potomac flotilla. 2. On Apr. 30 Missroon was replaced by Comdr. William Smith. 3. Montgomery Blair, Fox's brother-in-law, wrote GBM on Apr. 9: ''Whilst a bloody battle & a dear bought victory will not place you higher in the estimation of men of professional skills, it will perhaps do more to raise you in the estimation of people generally than successes achieved by strategy merely.... I hope for your own sake & that of the country that you now feel that it is both necessary & proper to fight at once.'' McClellan Papers (A-50:20), Library of Congress. 4. The gunboat *Anacostia*, commanded by Lt. Oscar C. Badger.

To Abraham Lincoln [TELEGRAM]

Head Quarters, Army of the Potomac,
Camp Winfield Scott April 14 8.40 pm 1862

I have seen General Franklin & beg to thank you for your kindness & consideration. I now understand the matter, which I did not before.[1]

Our field guns annoyed the enemy considerably to day. Roads & bridges now progressing rapidly — siege guns & ammunition coming up very satisfactorily — shall have nearly all up tomorrow. The tranquility of Yorktown is nearly at an end.

G B McClellan
Maj Genl Comdg

A Lincoln
President   Washington

ALS (telegram sent), McClellan Papers (A-51:20), Library of Congress. *OR*, Ser. 1, XI, Part 3, p. 98.

1. Franklin had been summoned to the White House and told (so Gen. McDowell learned from the president) "to acquaint General McClellan with the reasons, which were purely of a public character," for retaining McDowell's corps at Washington. *OR*, Ser. 1, XII, Part 1, p. 277.

To Mary Ellen McClellan

Camp Winfield Scott April 14 [1862] 11 p.m.

... I believe I now know who instigated the attack upon me & the country.[1] ...

So Fox told you all about our troubles[2] — they *were* severe for some time, but we are pretty well over the worst of them. . . .

I do not expect to lose many men, but to do the work mainly with artillery, & so avoid much loss of life. Several brave fellows have already gone to their long home, but not a large number.

I can't tell you how soon I will attack, as it will depend upon the rapidity with which certain preliminary work can be done & the heavy guns brought up. I do not fear a repulse — I shall not quit this camp until I do so to continue the march on Richmond. If I am repulsed once, will try it again & keep at it until we succeed — but I do not anticipate a repulse — am confident of success. . . .

I received today a very kind letter from old Mr. Blair, which I enclose for you to keep for me.[3] . . .

Remained at home this morning doing office work, but rode out all the p.m., rode to the front & took another look at secesh. . . .

AL copy, McClellan Papers (C-7:63), Library of Congress.

1. GBM had just talked with Gen. Franklin, who was persuaded of Stanton's perfidy, and this is perhaps a reference to the secretary of war. See GBM to Franklin, Apr. 6, *supra*,

note 1. 2. Assistant Navy Secretary Fox had visited GBM on Apr. 9. 3. Francis P. Blair
wrote GBM on Apr. 12: "If you can accomplish your object of reaching Richmond by a
slower process than storming redoubts & batteries in earth works, the country will applaud
the achievement which gives success to its arms, with greatest parsimony of the blood of
its children." McClellan Papers (A-51:20).

To Mary Ellen McClellan

[Camp Winfield Scott] April 18th [1862] 1.15 am.

... About 1/2 hr ago the accustomed intermittent sound of artillery
was varied in its monotony by a very heavy & continued rattle of musketry
with the accompaniment of a very respectable firing of artillery. I started
at once for the telegraph office & endeavored in vain for some ten or
fifteen minutes to arouse the operators at the stations in the direction of
the firing. So I ordered twenty of the escort to saddle up, & started off
Hudson, Sweitzer & the Duc de Chartres to learn the state of the case.
The firing has ceased now for some minutes & I am still ignorant as to
its whereabouts & cause. Of course I must remain up, until I know what
it is. I had had Arthur, Wright, Hammerstein, Radowitz & the Count de
Paris as well as Colburn also up, with some of the escort ready to move
or carry orders, as the case may be, but just now told them to lie down
until I sent for them.[1] It is a beautiful moonlight night clear & pleasant,
almost too much so for sleeping. . . .

Have not ridden out today [April 17], but have found plenty of work
at home. Have arranged tonight for the commencement of 5 batteries
tomorrow — mounting 41 guns — this is a mere preliminary & as soon
as I get the roads & bridges finished I will commence several more. . . .

Poor Wagner of the Topogs, lost an arm this afternoon by the bursting
of a shell — he is doing well however. Merrill was severely, but not dan-
gerously wounded in the arm yesterday.[2]

In Smith's affair yesterday [April 16] we lost I fear nearly 200 killed
& wounded.[3] The object I proposed had been fully accomplished with the
loss of about 20 — when after I left the ground a movement was made
in direct violation of my orders, by which the remainder of the loss was
uselessly incurred. I do not yet know the details nor who is responsible.
We have a severe task before us, but we will gain a brilliant success. . . .

The great trouble I have is in the want of good staff officers — Colburn
is my stand by — so true & faithful. Many of my aides are excellent but
the trouble is in the Chfs of Depts whose lack of experience I am obliged
to supply by personal labor. No Genl ever labored under greater disad-
vantages, but I will carry it through in spite of everything. I hope Frank-
lin will be here tomorrow or next day. I will then invest Gloucester &
attack it at the same time I do York. When the Galena arrives I will

cause it to pass the batteries, take them in reverse & cut off the enemy's communications by York River. As I write I hear our guns constantly sounding, & the bursting of shells in Secessia.

9 am.   The firing of last night was caused by the attempt of a part of the enemy to cross the stream in Smith's front. They were repulsed at once; tried it later & were again driven back.

AL copy; copy, McClellan Papers (C-7:63/D-10:72), Library of Congress.

1. All members of GBM's staff: Edward McK. Hudson, N. B. Sweitzer, Arthur McClellan, Edward H. Wright, Herbert Hammerstein, Paul Von Radowitz, A. V. Colburn, and the two young Frenchmen, the Duc de Chartres and the Comte de Paris. 2. Lts. Orlando G. Wagner, Topographical Engineers, and William E. Merrill, Corps of Engineers. Wagner's wound was mortal. 3. A sortie involving the division of Brig. Gen. William F. Smith.

To Edwin M. Stanton   [TELEGRAM]

Head-Quarters, Army of the Potomac,
Camp Winfield Scott April 18 1862 10 pm.

Dispatch received.[1] I cannot hope such good fortune as that the enemy will take the offensive. I am perfectly prepared for any attack the enemy may make. He will do nothing more than sorties. I beg that the Presdt will be satisfied that the enemy cannot gain anything by attacking me — the more he does attack the better I shall be contented.

All is well. I am glad to hear of Banks good fortune.

G B McClellan
Maj Genl

Hon E M Stanton
Secty of War

ALS (telegram sent), McClellan Papers (A-52:20), Library of Congress. *OR*, Ser. 1, XI, Part 3, p. 108.

1. Stanton telegraphed on this date that the president "directed me to ask you whether the indications do not show that the enemy are inclined to take the offensive." *OR*, Ser. 1, XI, Part 3, p. 107.

To Abraham Lincoln   [TELEGRAM]

Confidential & in cipher	Head Quarters, Army of the Potomac, Camp Winfield Scott April 18 11.30 pm 1862

If compatible with your impressions as to the security of the Capital & not interfering with operations of which I am ignorant I would be glad to have McCall's Division so as to be enabled to make a strong attack upon West Point to turn position of the enemy. After all that I have heard of things which have occurred since I left Washington & before I would prefer that Genl McDowell should not again be assigned to duty with me. [*crossed out:* Better that some other field of action should be given him.]

G B McClellan
Maj Genl Comdg

His Excellency A Lincoln
Presdt

ALS (telegram sent), McClellan Papers (A-52:20), Library of Congress. *OR*, Ser. 1, LI, Part 1, p. 578.

To Ambrose E. Burnside

Private   Head-Quarters, Army of the Potomac,
My dear Burn   Camp Winfield Scott April 19 1862

Your welcome letter of the 17th has just reached me, together with your dispatch.[1]

You are too modest in regard to your report — I do not find too many men in these days who *will* tell the truth — but I will not bore you by expressing my thanks again — I can never forget the debt I owe you for your manly truth. I feel, Burn, as you an implicit trust that God will carry me through — at all events that he will order things for the best. Now that such vast responsibility is upon me — the lives of thousands — the happiness of tens of thousands — the honor & salvation of a Govt, I more than ever feel the necessity of the aid of God — I pray that we may have his arm on our side.

I think you are making the best use of your time & hope to hear soon that Macon is in your hands — I will suggest to the Secty the propriety of sending to you some of the siege material rendered disposable by the fall of Pulaski.[2] I will do all in my power to get for you the regiment of cavalry & the two batteries you ask for — you should have them.

As soon as Macon falls you can undertake some forward movement — but whether that should be in the direction of Goldsborough or Winton must depend upon the state of affairs here at the time.

I find myself brought up all standing by a formidable line of earth works with a marshy river in front — I am building siege batteries & shall attack the town itself in spite of its strength. I have had great difficulties arising from the weather & the roads — most of them are now overcome & we are fairly started with the preparations for opening fire. The batteries I am now building are mostly concealed from view — about the time they are armed I will commence the first parallel & exposed batteries — we will have lively times here & have difficulties to overcome but I feel confident of success.

Barnard has just come in to discuss tomorrow's operations so I must stop.

Remember me most kindly to Parke, Foster & Reno — *how* handsomely they have acted! Give my regards also to Williamson & any other of my friends that are with you.[3]

McC

I have just telegraphed to the Secty of War requesting that the Rhode Island Cavalry & two good batteries 1st N.Y. Artillery under Lt Col Turner be sent to you at once.

McC

ALS, Records of the Adjutant General's Office, RG 94 (159: Burnside Papers), National Archives.

1. Burnside's letter of Apr. 17 detailed operations against Fort Macon. *OR*, Ser. 1, IX, pp. 377–78. 2. Fort Pulaski, at Savannah, was captured Apr. 11. 3. Brig. Gens. John G. Parke, John G. Foster, and Jesse L. Reno, brigade commanders under Burnside; and Capt. Robert S. Williamson, Topographical Engineers.

To Mary Ellen McClellan

[Camp Winfield Scott] April 19 [1862] 10 1/2 pm.

... Today it has been very quiet — our batteries have merely fired enough to keep the enemy entirely silent at his works in front of Smith & at Wynn's Mill. Last night we commenced a Battery at Farenholdt's house for 5 100 pdr Parrotts & 1 200 pdr Parrott — also one for 15 heavy guns about 2000 yds from the enemy's main defenses, another for 6 & one for 5 close by. Another for 6 was armed today, & kept down the enemy's fire at Wynn's Mill. Tomorrow morning we commence batteries for 13″ mortars. About Monday night [April 21] we will construct the first parallel & several other batteries in exposed positions, leaving those already commenced to cover the work & render it more safe. We shall soon be raining down a terrible tempest on this devoted place. Today the enemy sent a flag of truce to Smith, asking a suspension of hostilities to bury the killed of the 16th. The officer who met Sweitzer acknowledged that their loss was very severe & the bearing of our men admirable. I recd today a letter from Burnside which I enclose....

Franklin arrived yesterday & spent the night in my tent — he is at Ship Point tonight — I expect his Divn tomorrow....

Don't be at all discouraged — all is going well — the more there are in Yorktown the more decisive will the results be. I know exactly what I am about & am quite confident that with God's blessing I shall utterly defeat them. I can't go "*with a rush*" over strong posts. I must use heavy guns & silence their fire — all that takes much time & I have not been longer than the usual time for such things — much less than the usual in truth....

I can't tell you when Yorktown is to be attacked, for it depends on circumstances that I cannot control. It shall be attacked the first moment I can do so successfully — but I don't intend to hurry it — I cannot afford to fail. I have a little over 100,000 effective men including Franklin's Division....

I may have the opportunity of carrying the place next week — or may be delayed a couple of weeks — much of course depends on the rapidity with which the heavy guns & ammunition arrive. Never mind what such people as Wade[1] say — they are beneath contempt. I telegraphed the Presdt last night requesting that McDowell might *not* again be assigned to duty with me.[2]

I will put in a leaf of holly from the bower some of the men have made in front of my tent today; they have made quite an artistic thing of it — holly & pine — it adds much too, to my comfort, as it renders the tent more private & cool.

AL copy; copy, McClellan Papers (C-7:63/D-10:72), Library of Congress.

1. Senator Benjamin F. Wade, chairman of the Joint Committee on the Conduct of the War. 2. GBM to Lincoln, Apr. 18, *supra*.

To Abraham Lincoln

Private

His Excellency The President   Head-Quarters, Army of the Potomac,
My dear Sir   Camp Winfield Scott April 20 1862

I enclose herewith a copy of the first reliable map we have prepared of this vicinity — it will give you a good general idea of positions. In a day or two we will have one on a larger scale which will be more satisfactory to you. I will soon send you one of the immediate front of Yorktown on which I will mark the batteries now being entrenched & send such information as will enable you to put down the new works as they progress.

We are now actually at work, & nearly through, with 6 batteries for guns, have commenced a series for 10 13" mortars, & commence tomorrow morning another gun battery. As soon as these are armed we will open the first parallel & other batteries for 8" & 10" mortars & some heavy guns. Everything is going on admirably & we shall soon open with a terrific fire. I hope to hear hourly of the arrival of Franklin's Division, & shall lose no time in placing him in position. I hope the Galena will be here to assist us very soon.

Genl Robt Lee is in command in our front — Johnston is *under him*![1] I learn that there has been quite a struggle on the subject between Davis & his Congress, Davis insisting upon Johnston. I prefer Lee to Johnston — the former is *too* cautious & weak under grave responsibility — personally brave & energetic to a fault, he yet is wanting in moral firmness when pressed by heavy responsibility & is likely to be timid & irresolute in action.

The difficulties of our position are considerable, that is the enemy is in a very strong position — but I never expected to get to Richmond without a hard fought battle, & am just as willing to fight it here as elsewhere — I am confident of success, not only of success but of brilliant success. I think that a defeat here substantially breaks up the rebel cause.

They are making great efforts — enforcing the conscription with the utmost vigor, & now have their regiments full — whether the infusion of raw & perhaps unwilling men will benefit them remains to be seen. I doubt whether it is a disadvantage to us.

I am, Sir, most respectfully and sincerely your friend
Geo B McClellan

ALS, Lincoln Papers, Library of Congress.

1. On Mar. 13 Gen. Robert E. Lee was called to Richmond and, "under the direction of the President, . . . charged with the conduct of military operations in the armies of the Confederacy," a position that in effect made him chief of staff of the Confederate army. *OR*, Ser. 1, V, p. 1099.

To Mary Ellen McClellan

[Camp Winfield Scott] April 23 [1862] 11 1/2 pm.

. . . Have been working hard all day, but not in the saddle — it has been head work in my tent today. I am getting on splendidly with my *slow* preparations — the Prince[1] is delighted & thinks my work gigantic — I *do* believe that I am avoiding the faults of the Allies at Sebastopol & quietly preparing the way for a great success. I have brought *40* heavy guns in battery — tomorrow night I hope to have 12 more guns & 5 to 10 heavy mortars in battery.

I begin in the morning the redoubts to cover the flank of the 1st Parallel which will be constructed tomorrow night. I will not open fire unless the enemy annoys us — hoping to get all the guns in battery & the trenches well advanced before meeting with serious opposition. We have done much more than they suspect. Have ordered a forced reconnaissance of a dangerous point in the morning — it may cost several lives, but I have taken all possible precautions & hope to gain the information necessary with but little loss — there is no other choice than to run the risk. I think I see the way clear to success & that at no distant day. . . .

Everything is as quiet now as if there were no enemy within a hundred miles of us. The Galena, under Rodgers,[2] will be here the day after tomorrow — in a day or two after she arrives you will hear of a blow struck that will surprise secesh & delight the country — I *may* delay it for a few days if I meet with any delays in my preparations, but it will soon come in a way secesh does not expect.

AL copy, McClellan Papers (C-7:63), Library of Congress.

1. Prince de Joinville. 2. Comdr. John Rodgers.

To Abraham Lincoln

Head-Quarters, Army of the Potomac,
Private & confidential   [Camp Winfield Scott]
Your Excellency: April 23 midnight 1862

I am well aware of the firm friendship & confidence you have evinced for me, & instead of again thanking you for it will endeavor to assure you that it is not misplaced.

Do not misunderstand the apparent inaction here — not a day, not an hour has been lost, works have been constructed that may almost be called gigantic — roads built through swamps & difficult ravines, material brought up, batteries built. I have tonight in battery & ready for action 5 100 pdr Parrott guns, 10 4 1/2″ Ordnance guns, 18 20 pdr Parrotts, 6 Napoleon guns & 6 10 pdr Parrotts — this not counting the batteries in front of Smith & on his left — 45 guns. I will add to it tomorrow night 5 30 pdr Parrotts, 6 20 pdr Parrotts, from 5 to 10 13″ mortars, & (if it arrives in time) 1 200 pdr Parrott. Before sundown tomorrow I will essentially complete the redoubts necessary to strengthen the left of the 1st Parallel; & will construct that Parallel as far as Wormley's Creek from the left, & probably all the way to York River tomorrow night. I will then be secure against sorties. It has become necessary to make tomorrow morning early a "forced reconnaissance" to gain some information as to the ground on the left flank of the proposed 1st Parallel — this ground is strongly held by the enemy's pickets, is swampy & covered with thick brush & timber — I cannot now tell what facilities they possess for crossing the stream in force — to gain this information I have ordered Col Gove[1] to move with his Regt, the 22nd Massachusetts, early in the morning — I have taken all possible precautions, so that the object *may* be gained without loss — yet it is possible that many lives *may* be lost — there is no other way of accomplishing the object, & I merely wish to state beforehand what the purpose is, in order that the result may be understood. I do not propose to open fire at present unless the enemy attempt to interfere with the construction of the 1st Parallel & the new batteries which will be commenced at once. If he will permit it I will at once build a battery at close range for 5 more 100 pdrs & another 200 pdr rifle, batteries for the 10 & 8 inch mortars, 8″ howitzers, & additional 30 & 20 pounder Parrotts, in the mean time pushing the approaches forward as rapidly as possible. I still hope that we will not be seriously interfered with until I can open an overwhelming fire & give the assault from a reasonable distance under its cover. My course must necessarily depend to a great extent upon that of the enemy — but I see the way clear to success & hope to make it brilliant, although with but little loss of life. I expect great aid from the Galena — Franklin will probably land as soon as she arrives — his preparations ought to be completed tomorrow.

> I am most respectfully & truly your friend
> Geo B McClellan

His Excellency the President

ALS, Lincoln Papers, Library of Congress.

1. Col. Jesse A. Gove.

To Edwin M. Stanton

Hon E.M.S.   Head Quarters, Army of the Potomac,
Sir   Before Yorktown [c. April 27, 1862]

I received today a note from Asst Secty Watson enclosing an extract from a letter the author of which is not mentioned.[1] I send a copy of the extract with this.

I hope that a copy has also been sent to Genl McDowell, whom it concerns more nearly perhaps than it does me.

At the risk of being thought obtrusive I will venture upon some remarks which perhaps my position does not justify me in making, but which I beg to assure you are induced solely by my intense desire for the success of the Govt in this struggle.

You will, I hope, pardon me if I allude to the past, not in a captious spirit, but merely so far as may be necessary to explain my own course & my views as to the future.

From the beginning I had intended, so far as I might have the power to carry out my own views, to abandon the line of Manassas as the line of advance — I ever regarded it as an improper one; my wish was to adopt a new line, based upon the waters of the lower Chesapeake. I always expected to meet with strong opposition on this line, the strongest that the rebels could offer, but I was well aware that after overcoming this opposition the result would be decisive, & pregnant with great results.

Circumstances, among which I will now only mention the uncertainty as to the power of the Merrimac, have compelled me to adopt the present line, as probably safer, tho' far less brilliant than that by Urbana. When the movement was commenced I counted upon an active & disposable force of nearly 150,000 men, & intended to throw a strong column upon West Point either by York River, or, if that proved to be impracticable, by a march from the mouth of the Severn — expecting to turn in that manner all the defences of the Peninsula. Circumstances have proved that I was right & that my intended movements would have produced the desired results.

After the transfer of troops had commenced from Alexandria to Fort Monroe, but before I started in person, the Division Blenker was detached from my command — a loss of near 10,000 men.

As soon as the mass of my troops were fairly started I embarked myself. Upon reaching Fort Monroe I learned that the rebels were being rapidly reinforced from Norfolk & Richmond — I therefore determined to lose no time in making the effort to invest Yorktown, without waiting for the arrival of the Divisions Hooker, Richardson & the 1st Corps; intending to employ the 1st Corps in mass to move upon West Point, reinforcing it as circumstances might render necessary.

The advance was made on the morning of the second day after I reached Fort Monroe. When the troops reached the immediate vicinity of Yorktown the true nature of the enemy's position was for the first time developed — while my men were under fire I learned that the 1st Corps was removed from my command — no warning had been given me of this, nor was any reason then assigned. I should also have mentioned that the evening before I left Fort Monroe I received a telegraphic dispatch from the War Dept informing me that the order placing Fort Monroe & its dependent troops under my command was rescinded, no reason was given for this, nor has it been to this day — I confess that I have no right to know the reason.

This order deprived me of the support of another Division which I had been authorized to form for active operations from among the troops near Fort Monroe. Thus when I came under fire, I found myself weaker by five Divisions (near 50,000 men) than I had expected when the movement commenced. It is more than probable that no General ever was placed in such a position before. Finding myself thus unexpectedly weakened & with a powerful enemy strongly entrenched in my front I was compelled to change my plans & become cautious. Could I have retained my original force I confidently believe that I would now have been in front of Richmond instead of where I now am — the probability is that that city would now have been in our possession.

But the question now is in regard to the present & the future rather than the past.

The enemy, by the destruction of the bridges of the Rappahannock has deprived himself of the means of a rapid advance on Washington. Lee will never venture upon a bold movement on a large scale.

The troops I left for the defence of Washington, as I fully explained to you in the letter I wrote the day I sailed,[2] are ample for its protection.

Our true policy is to concentrate our troops on the fewest possible lines of attack — we have now too many, & an enterprising enemy could strike us a severe blow. I have every reason to believe that the main portion of the rebel forces are in my front — they are *not* "drawing off" their troops from Yorktown.

Give me McCall's Division & I will undertake a movement on West Point which will shake them out of Yorktown. As it is I will win — but I must not be blamed if success is delayed — I do not feel that I am answerable for the delay of victory.

I do not feel authorized to venture upon any suggestions as to the disposition of the troops in other Depts, but content myself with stating the least that I regard as essential to prompt success here — If circumstances render it impossible to give what I ask, I still feel sure of success — but more time will be required to achieve the result.

AL retained copy, McClellan Papers (A-88:35), Library of Congress.

1. This extract, enclosed with Assistant Secretary of War Peter H. Watson's letter of Apr. 25, suggested that Jefferson Davis was successfully detaining GBM at Yorktown while drawing off troops from there to fall on McDowell's forces at Fredericksburg. *OR*, Ser. 1, XI, Part 3, p. 121. 2. GBM to Lorenzo Thomas, Apr. 1, *supra*.

To Mary Ellen McClellan

[Camp Winfield Scott] April 27 [1862] midnight

... Was engaged with Barnard, Porter etc until about one, when I rode to the trenches. Then of course had to walk — a good deal was muddy so it was tiresome. Went over the whole extent & saw everything with care. The enemy have fired a good deal today, but the men are now so well covered that no one has been hurt today. Commenced today batteries for 15 10″ mortars, & tonight another battery for heavy guns — another for 10 mortars tomorrow morning — an extension of the parallel on the left commenced tonight. By tomorrow night the parallel should be finished in all its details, as well as the two covering redoubts on the left. Some time day after tomorrow I hope to have 35 mortars in battery. Tomorrow night will open a boyau in advance leading to a new gun battery — fast getting ready to blow secesh up & he will have a bad time of it after we open. Think he will find Yorktown very uncomfortable. Have news this evening via Richmond that New Orleans is in our possession. I presume it is true — so the work goes bravely on. . . .

Yesterday [April 27] made Fitz Porter "Director of the Siege" — a novel title but made necessary by the circumstances of the case. I give all my orders relating to the siege through him — making him at the same time comdt of the siege operations & a chief of staff for that portion of the work. It not being *M*'s[1] specialty he cannot assist me in siege operations. This new arrangement will save me much trouble, relieve my mind greatly & save much time. In going over the line of trenches yesterday I found so many blunders committed that I was very thankful to put Porter on duty at once. . . .

Be careful to say not one word about Stanton, McDowell or any of my enemies, let us present a contrast with those people & show by no word or act that we care what they say or do.

The good fellow (Colburn) never leaves me — wherever I ride, he sticks close after me. He is one of the very best men I ever knew; so thoroughly honest & reliable. His judgment is excellent & he is perfectly untiring. Day and night are about the same to him & he will start out on a long ride at midnight in a pitch dark or rainy night with as much good humour as at midday. Kentuck is still at Fort Monroe sick, will rejoin in a few days I hope — Marsh is with him, & I am sometimes half wicked enough to suspect that Marsh finds Fort Monroe more comfortable than camp would be.

AL copy; copy, McClellan Papers (C-7:63/D-10:72), Library of Congress.

1. Chief of Staff Marcy.

To Mary Ellen McClellan

[Camp Winfield Scott] April 30th [1862] am.

Had a quiet night — very little firing — drove them out of an orchard where they had been annoying us, & pushed them still further in towards their works. A good deal of firing on their part yesterday — did very little harm — killing some 3 & wounding 4 or 5 of our people. Scarcely a gun fired today as yet — we are working like horses & will soon be ready to open. It will be a tremendous affair when we do begin & will I hope make short work of it. . . .

Have put the Regulars in the exposed portions of the work — they work so much better. A raw disagreeable day — I fear it will rain — unless it snows — wind from east. . . .

10.30 p.m.   After I got thro' my morning work went down to see the opening of Battery No. 1 — it worked handsomely — drove all the rebel schooners away from the wharf & made a general scatteration. The effect was excellent. Shall not open the general fire for some *four* days.

Next morning. Another wet drizzly uncomfortable sort of a day. Good deal of firing during the night. I shall be very glad when we are really ready to open fire & then finish this confounded affair. I am tired of public life — & even now when doing the best I can for my country in the field I know that my enemies are pursuing me more remorselessly than ever, & "kind *friends*" are constantly making themselves agreeable by informing me of the pleasant predicament in which I am — the rebels on one side, & the abolitionists & other scoundrels on the other — I believe in my heart & conscience, however, that I am walking on the ridge between the two gulfs, & that all I have to do is to try to keep the path of honor & truth & that God will bring me safely through — at all events I am willing to leave the matter in his hands & will be content with the decision of the Almighty.

AL copy, McClellan Papers (C-7:63), Library of Congress.

To Abraham Lincoln   [TELEGRAM]

Head Quarters, Army of the Potomac,
Camp Winfield Scott May 1 1862 9.30 pm

I asked for the Parrott guns from Washington for the reason that some expected had been two weeks nearly on the way & could not be heard from.[1] They arrived last night. My arrangements had been made for them & I thought time might be saved by getting others from Washington. My object was to hasten not procrastinate. All is being done that human labor can accomplish.

G B McClellan
Maj Genl

His Excellency the President
Washington D C

ALS (telegram sent), McClellan Papers (A-55:22), Library of Congress. *OR*, Ser. 1, LI, Part 1, p. 589.

1. The president telegraphed on this date: ''Your call for Parrott guns from Washington alarms me — chiefly because it argues indefinite procrastination. Is anything to be done?'' *Collected Works of Lincoln*, V, p. 203.

To Louis M. Goldsborough   [TELEGRAM]

Head Quarters, Army of the Potomac,
Confidential   Camp Winfield Scott May 2 [1862] 9.30 pm

It is probable that I will be able to open a very heavy fire on Monday morning [May 5], certainly by Tuesday morning. I think the gun boats can pass the batteries any dark night — they certainly can after a day's firing on our part. I have proposed to Capt Smith that he shall run by the night after we open. Rogers will I suppose be available for the same purpose.[1] I think the effect of such a movement will be to enable me to gain possession of Yorktown on the 2d or 3d day. Can you spare for this decisive attack some more vessels? It is all important to make this blow a sure one.

G B McClellan
Maj Genl

Flag Officer L M Goldsborough
Hampton Roads

ALS (telegram sent), McClellan Papers (A-55:22), Library of Congress. *OR*, Ser. 1, LI, Part 1, p. 591.

1. Comdr. William Smith, of the gunboat flotilla; Comdr. Rodgers, of the ironclad *Galena*.

To Mary Ellen McClellan

[Camp Winfield Scott] May 3 [1862] 12.30 am.

After the hot firing of today [May 2] everything is so unusually still that I am a little suspicious that our friends may intend a sortie — so I have taken all the steps necessary to be ready for them & am sitting up for a while to await developments. I feel much better satisfied when they are firing than when they are silent — today they have wasted almost a thousand rounds & have done us no harm worth speaking of — except (Irish) bursting one of their own guns. We are now nearly ready to open — shall begin I think on Monday morning [May 5], certainly by Tuesday. If all works well it is not impossible that we shall have Yorktown by Wednesday or Thursday. The task is a difficult one, yet I am sure we have taken the right way to accomplish our purpose & that we will soon win. I fear that we are to have another storm tonight — we want no more rain, but will make the best of it if it comes. Had plenty of work to do at home all the morning, & in the afternoon rode down to "Shield's House" to meet the new comdr. of the flotilla — Capt Smith — he is a great improvement on Mr. Missroon & will do something I hope. . . .

I don't half like the perfect quietness which reigns now — I have given orders to take advantage of it & push our approaches as far forward as possible — it don't seem natural — it looks like a sortie or an evacuation — if either I hope it may be the former. I do not want these rascals to get away from me without a sound drubbing, which they richly deserve & which they will be sure to get if they remain. . . .

I need rest — my brain is taxed to the extreme — I feel that the fate of a nation depends upon me, & I feel that I have not one single friend at the seat of Govt — any day may bring an order relieving me from command — if such a thing should be done our cause is lost. If they will simply let me alone I feel sure of success — but, will they do it?

Saturday [May 3] am. All quiet — nothing unusual has occurred — no more at present.

AL copy, McClellan Papers (C-7:63), Library of Congress.

To Edwin M. Stanton [TELEGRAM]

Head Quarters, Army of the Potomac,
Camp Winfield Scott May 4 1862

Yorktown is in our possession.

G B McClellan
Maj Genl

Hon E M Stanton
Secty of War

ALS (telegram sent), McClellan Papers (C-13:64), Library of Congress. *OR*, Ser. 1, XI, Part 3, p. 133.

To Edwin M. Stanton [TELEGRAM]

Headquarters, Army of the Potomac,
Camp Winfield Scott May 4 1862 9 am

We have the enemy's heavy guns ammunition camp equipage etc — hold the entire line of his works which the Engineers report as being very strong. I have thrown all my cavalry & horse artillery in pursuit, supported by Infantry.

I move Franklin & as much more as I can transport by water up to West Point today. No time shall be lost. Gun boats have gone up York River. I omitted to state that Gloucester is also in our possession. I shall push the enemy to the wall.

G B McClellan
Maj Genl

Hon E M Stanton
Secty of War

ALS (telegram sent), McClellan Papers (A-55:22), Library of Congress. *OR*, Ser. 1, XI, Part 3, p. 134.

To Winfield Scott [TELEGRAM]

Lieut. Genl. Winfield Scott   Head-Quarters, Army of the Potomac,
Brevort House   New York   Yorktown Va May 4 1862

The enemy abandoned Yorktown last night in great haste. Our parallels were pushed within eleven hundred yards of their strong-hold. They abandoned eighty heavy guns, with a large amount of ammunition, their tents, camp equipage &c &c. I am pushing forward to overtake them and one of our columns has come up with their rear.

I am also sending a large force on transports up York River to cut off the retreat.

Their works here were very formidable and could not have been carried without shelling which I was today prepared to commence.

The rebel forces are represented by deserters to be greatly demoralised. Their numbers are stated to be from 100,000 to 120,000, with large light artillery force.

Geo. B. McClellan
Maj. Genl.

Retained copy, McClellan Papers (A-55:22), Library of Congress.

To Edwin M. Stanton   [TELEGRAM]

Head Quarters, Army of the Potomac,
Yorktown May 4 — 7 pm. 1862

Our cavalry & horse artillery came up with enemy's rear guard in their entrenchments about (2) two miles this side of Williamsburg. A brisk fight ensued. Just as my aide left Smith's Division of Infantry arrived on the ground & I presume carried the works tho' I have not yet heard. The enemy's rear guard is strong but I have force enough up there to answer all purposes.

We have thus far (82) eighty two heavy guns, large amounts of tents, ammunition etc all along the line.

Their works prove to have been most formidable & I am now fully satisfied of the correctness of the course I have pursued. Our success is brilliant & you may rest assured that its effects will be of the greatest importance.

There shall be no delay in following up the rebels.

The rebels have been guilty of the most murderous & barbarous conduct in placing torpedoes *within* the abandoned works, near wells & springs, near flag staffs, magazines, telegraph offices, in carpet bags, barrels of flour etc. Fortunately we have not lost many men in this manner — some 4 or 5 killed & perhaps a dozen wounded.

I shall make the prisoners remove them at their own peril.

G B McClellan
Maj Genl Comdg

Hon E M Stanton
Secty of War

ALS (telegram sent), McClellan Papers (A-55:22), Library of Congress. *OR,* Ser. 1, XI, Part 3, pp. 134–35.

To Mary Ellen McClellan   [TELEGRAM]

Head Quarters, Army of the Potomac,
Yorktown May 4 — 7 pm 1862

Dear Nell. Results glorious — (82) eighty two heavy guns and large amounts of stores taken.

Stoneman[1] brought their rear guard to bay in their works within two (2) miles of Williamsburg, & I expect every moment to hear that Smith has carried the works.

All well & in splendid spirits. The enemy's works of very great strength. He must have been badly scared to have abandoned them in such a hurry.

G B McClellan
Maj Genl

Mrs. G B McClellan
5th Avenue Hotel N.Y. City[2]

ALS (telegram sent), McClellan Papers (C-13:64), Library of Congress.

1. Brig. Gen. George Stoneman commanded the advance guard. 2. Mrs. McClellan had left Washington in April and would stay for varying periods, over the next five months, in New York City; North Orange, N.J.; and Hartford, New London, and Middletown, Conn.

To Edwin M. Stanton   [TELEGRAM]

Head-Quarters, Army of the Potomac,
Yorktown May 5 9 am 1862

Raining hard now & most of the night — roads consequently infamous. Enemy still at Williamsburg — heavy firing now going on. The weather has delayed Franklin — I hope to overcome all obstacles today & throw a sufficient force up the York to cut the enemy's line of retreat. Several of our batteries are actually stuck fast in the mud. The men have done all that could be done.

No signs of cessation of rain.

G B McClellan
Maj Genl

Hon E M Stanton
Secty of War

ALS (telegram sent), McClellan Papers (A-56:22), Library of Congress. *OR*, Ser. 1, XI, Part 3, p. 139.

To Mary Ellen McClellan

[Before Yorktown] May 5 [1862] 9 1/2 am.

... You will have learned ere this that Yorktown is ours — it is a place of immense strength & was very heavily armed — it so happened however that our preparations for the attack were equally formidable, so that Lee, Johnston & Davis confessed that they could not hold the place — they evacuated it in a great hurry, leaving their heavy guns, baggage etc. I sent the cavalry after them at once — & our advance is now engaged with them at Wmsburg. The weather is infamous — it has been raining all night & is still raining heavily — no signs of stopping — roads awful. I hope to get to West Point today — altho' the weather has delayed us terribly — it could not well be worse — but we will get through nevertheless. The villains (secesh) have scattered torpedoes everywhere — by springs, wells etc etc — it is the most murderous & barbarous thing I ever heard of.

AL copy, McClellan Papers (C-7:63), Library of Congress.

To Edwin M. Stanton   [TELEGRAM]

Hon E M Stanton   In front of Williamsburg
Secy of War, Washington   [May 5] 1862 [10 P.M.]

   After arranging for movement up York River I was urgently sent for here. I find Joe Johnston in front of me in strong force, probably greater a good deal than my own & very strongly entrenched. Hancock has taken two redoubts & repulsed Early's Brigade[1] in a real charge with the bayonet taking one color & one hundred & fifty prisoners, killing at least two Colonels & as many Lieut Colonels and many privates. His conduct was brilliant in the extreme. I do not know our exact loss but fear Hooker has lost considerably on our left. I learn from prisoners that they intend disputing every step to Richmond. I shall run the risk of at least holding them in check here while I resume the original plan. My entire force is undoubtedly considerably inferior to that of the Rebels, who still fight well, but I will do all I can with the force at my disposal.

                                         Geo B McClellan
                                         Maj Genl Comdg

Received copy, Stanton Papers, Library of Congress. *OR*, Ser. 1, XI, Part 1, pp. 448–49.

1. Brig. Gen. Winfield S. Hancock, Brig. Gen. Jubal A. Early, CSA.

To Mary Ellen McClellan   [TELEGRAM]

                         Williamsburg May 6/62 11 pm. [A.M.]
   The battle of Wmsburg has proved a brilliant victory. We have the enemy's strong works, the town & all sick & wounded of the enemy etc. None of your friends injured though our loss considerable. That of the enemy severe. The Quaker Army is doing very well. Hancock was superb

yesterday. I am in Joe Johnston's Hd Qtrs of yesterday. This is a beautiful little town & quite old & picturesque.

G B McC

ALS copy (telegram sent), McClellan Papers (C-7:63), Library of Congress.

To Mary Ellen McClellan

Williamsburg May 6 1862

I telegraphed you this morning that we had gained a battle — every hour its importance is proved to be greater. On Sunday [May 4] I sent Stoneman in pursuit, with the cavalry & 4 batteries of Horse Artillery; he was supported by the Divisions Hooker, Smith, Couch, Casey & Kearny[1] — most of which arrived on the ground only yesterday. Unfortunately I did not go with the advance myself — being obliged to remain to get Franklin & Sedgwick started up the River for West Point.

Yesterday I received pressing private messages from Smith & others begging me to go to the front. I started with half a dozen aides & some 15 orderlies & found things in a bad state. Sumner had proved that he was even a greater fool than I had supposed & had come within an ace of having us defeated. Hancock was engaged with a vastly superior force some 2 miles from any support. Hooker fought nearly all day without assistance, & the mass of the troops were crowded together where they were useless. I found everybody discouraged — officers & men — our troops in wrong positions, on the wrong side of the woods — no system, no cooperation, no orders given, roads blocked up etc. As soon as I came upon the field the men cheered like fiends & I saw at once that I could save the day. I immediately reinforced Hancock, & arranged to support Hooker — advanced the whole line across the woods — filled up the gaps & got everything in hand for whatever might occur. The result was that the enemy saw that he was gone if he remained in his position & scampered during the night.

His works were very strong — but his loss was very heavy. The roads are in such condition that it is impossible to pursue except with a few cavalry — it is with the utmost difficulty that I can feed the men, many of whom have had nothing to eat for 24 hours & more. I had no dinner yesterday, no supper, a cracker for breakfast & no dinner yet.

I have no baggage — was out in the rain all day & until late at night — still in my clothes & boots, & could not even wash my face & hands. I, however, expect my ambulance up pretty soon, when I hope for better things. I have been through the hospitals, where are many of our own men & of the rebels. One Virginian sent for me this morning & told me that I was the only General from whom they expected any humanity etc. I corrected his mistake. This is a beautiful little town — several very old houses & churches, pretty gardens etc. I have taken possession of a very fine house which Jo Johnston occupied as his Hd Qts — it has a lovely flower garden & conservatory — if you were here I would be much inclined to spend some weeks here. *G.W.* was one of the whipped community — also Jo Johnston, Cadmus Wilcox, A. P. Hill, D. H. Hill, Longstreet, Jeb Stuart, Early (badly wounded) & many others that we know.[2] We have *all* their wounded, 8 guns so far — in short we have given them a tremendous thrashing — & I am not at all ashamed of the conduct of the Army of the Potomac. Had I been on the field five hours earlier I think we would have taken 20,000 prisoners — but the utter stupidity & worthlessness of the Corps Comdrs came near making it a defeat. Heaven alone can help a General with such commanders under him. . . .

AL copy, McClellan Papers (C-7:63), Library of Congress.

1. Brig. Gens. Joseph Hooker, William F. Smith, Darius N. Couch, Silas Casey, and Philip Kearny. 2. Williamsburg was defended by the division of Maj. Gen. James Longstreet, supported by Maj. Gen. Daniel H. Hill's division. The brigades of Brig. Gens. Cadmus M. Wilcox, Ambrose P. Hill, Jubal A. Early, and J. E. B. Stuart (cavalry) were engaged. Maj. Gen. G. W. Smith was not on the field.

To Edwin M. Stanton   [TELEGRAM]

Hon E M Stanton
Secy War   Williamsburg May [8] 1862

I respectfully ask permission to [reorganize] the Army Corps. I am not willing to be held responsible for the present arrangement experience having proved it to be very bad & it having very nearly resulted in a most disastrous defeat. I wish either to return to the organization by Divisions or else be authorized to relieve incompetent Commanders of Army Corps. Had I been one half hour later on the field on the fifth we would have been routed & would have lost everything.

Notwithstanding my positive orders I was informed of nothing that had occurred & I went to the field of Battle myself upon unofficial information that my presence was needed to avoid defeat. I found there the utmost confusion & incompetency, the utmost discouragement on the part of the men. At least a thousand lives were really sacrificed by the organization into Corps. I have too much regard for the lives of my comrades & too deep an interest in the success of our cause to hesitate for a moment. I learn that you are equally in earnest & I therefore again request full & complete authority to relieve from duty with this army Commanders of Corps or Divisions who prove themselves incompetent.[1]

G B McClellan
Maj Genl Comdg

Received copy, Stanton Papers, Library of Congress. *OR*, Ser. 1, XI, Part 3, pp. 153–54.

1. Lincoln's reply on May 9 (sent over Stanton's name) gave GBM permission to suspend the corps organization ''in the Army now under your immediate command, and adopt any you see fit until further orders.'' The president wrote him privately on May 9: ''I now think it indispensable for you to know how your struggle against it [the corps organization] is received in quarters which we cannot entirely disregard. It is looked upon as merely an effort to pamper one or two pets, and to persecute and degrade their supposed rivals. . . . I am constantly told . . . that you consult and communicate with nobody but General Fitz John Porter, and perhaps General Franklin. . . . But . . . are you strong enough, even with my help — to set your foot upon the necks of Sumner, Heintzelman, and Keyes all at once? This is a practical and very serious question for you.'' *Collected Works of Lincoln,* V, pp. 207–209. GBM retained the corps organization, but added two additional corps, under Porter and Franklin, on May 18.

To Edwin M. Stanton   [TELEGRAM]

Head-Quarters, Army of the Potomac,
Williamsburg May 8 12.30 pm 1862

Your two telegrams received.[1] I have sent cavalry to Jamestown to endeavor to communicate with Rogers. Genl Stoneman is some fourteen or fifteen miles in advance, & may be able to communicate with Franklin tonight. I shall start Smith's Division this afternoon, & I hope three others tomorrow morning. The difficulties arising from the roads are very great but I will manage to surmount them. If I can effect the junction with Franklin I shall consider our next step gained — it is a delicate matter but can be done. I think that the time has arrived to bring all the troops in Eastern Virginia into perfect cooperation. I expect to fight another and very severe battle before reaching Richmond & with all the troops the Confederates can bring together, & therefore should have all the reinforcements that can be given me. It is of course possible that the enemy may abandon Richmond without a battle but we have no right to take that for granted. All the troops on the Rappahannock, & if possible those in the Shenandoah should take part in the approaching battle. We ought immediately to concentrate everything, & not run the risk of engaging a desperate enemy with inferior numbers. All minor considerations should be thrown to one side & all our energies & means directed towards the defeat of Johnston's Army in front of Richmond.

G B McClellan
Maj Genl Comdg

Hon E M Stanton
Secty of War

ALS (telegram sent), McClellan Papers (A-56:22), Library of Congress. *OR,* Ser. 1, XI, Part 3, pp. 150–51.

1. Stanton's telegrams of May 7 dealt with a naval expedition on the James River, led by Comdr. Rodgers in the *Galena,* and reports that Norfolk would soon be abandoned. *OR,* Ser. 1, XI, Part 3, pp. 147, 148.

To Mary Ellen McClellan

[Williamsburg] Thursday [May 8, 1862] 1 pm.

... I hope to get Smith's Divn off this afternoon — followed by others in the morning. Stoneman is some 15 miles in advance & will I hope communicate with Franklin tonight — although I am not yet sure that the enemy may not still be between the two. I shall start tomorrow morning & overtake Smith.

I have ordered up Hd Qtrs '& the accompanying paraphernalia at once — so I hope to get within a few miles of my tooth brush in a day or two — it is not very pleasant — this going entirely without baggage — but it could not be helped. I find that the results of my operations are beginning to be apparent — the rebels are evacuating Norfolk I learn. Your two letters of Sunday & Monday reached me last night. I do not think you overmuch rejoiced at the results I gained. I really thought that you would appreciate a great result gained by pure skill & at little cost more highly than you seem to.

It would have been easy for me to have sacrificed 10,000 lives in taking Yorktown, & I presume the world would have thought it more brilliant — I am content with what I have done, & history will give me credit for it. I am sorry that you do not exactly sympathize with me in the matter. The battle of Williamsburg was more bloody — had I reached the field three hours earlier I could have gained far greater results & have saved a thousand lives — it is perhaps well as it is, for the officers & men feel that I saved the day....

I don't know when the next battle will occur. I presume on the line of the Chickahominy — or it may be tomorrow in effecting a junction with Franklin. It may suit the views of the masses better as being more bloody — *I* hope not, & will make it as little so as possible....

AL copy, McClellan Papers (C-7:63), Library of Congress.

To Edwin M. Stanton   [TELEGRAM]

Hon. E. M. Stanton   Ewells Farm May 10 1862
Secretary of War   3 miles from Williamsburg 5 A.M.

From the information reaching me from every source, I regard it as certain that the enemy will meet us with all his force, on, or near the Chickahominy. They can concentrate many more men than I have, and are collecting troops from all quarters, especially, well disciplined troops from the South. Casualties, sickness, garrisons and guards have much reduced our numbers, and will continue to do so. I shall fight the Rebel army, with whatever force I may have, but duty requires me to urge that every effort be made to reinforce me, without delay, with all the disposable troops in Eastern Virginia, and that we concentrate all our forces, as far as possible to fight the great battle now impending, and to make it decisive.

It is possible that the enemy may abandon Richmond without a serious struggle, but I do not believe he will, and it would be unwise to count upon anything but a stubborn and desperate defense, — a life and death contest. I see no other hope for him than to fight this battle, — and we must win it. I shall fight them, whatever their force may be; but I ask for every man that the Department can send me. No troops now should be left unemployed. Those who entertain the opinion that the Rebels will abandon Richmond without a struggle, are, in my judgment, badly advised, and do not comprehend their situation, which is one requiring desperate measures.

I beg that the President and Secretary will maturely weigh what I say, and leave nothing undone to comply with my request. If I am not reinforced, it is probable that I will be obliged to fight nearly double my numbers, stronger entrenched. I do not think it will be at all possible for me to bring more than seventy thousand men upon the field of battle.

> George B. McClellan
> Major General

Received copy, Stanton Papers, Library of Congress. *OR,* Ser. 1, XI, Part 1, p. 26.

To Edwin M. Stanton [TELEGRAM]

Head Quarters, Army of the Potomac,
Camp 19 miles from Williamsburg May 10 — 5 pm. 1862

I have fully established my connection with the troops near West Point & the dangerous moment has passed. The West Point Railway is not very much injured — materials for repairs, such as rails etc, cars & engines may now be sent to me. Should Norfolk be taken & the Merrimac destroyed I can change my line to the James River & dispense with the Railroad.

I shall probably occupy New Kent in force tomorrow, & then make my final preparations for battle. As it is my troops are in advance of their supplies & I must so arrange my depots that I can follow up success.

When at New Kent I will be in position to make a thorough examination of the country so as to act understandingly.

Genl Johnston cannot well be in front of Fremont for two reasons — first he has no business there — second, I know that I fought him on Monday [May 5] & that he is now on the Chickahominy.[1] I have used his vacated Head Quarters from day to day. He is certainly in command here with all the troops he can gather. Two or three more of the cavalry

regiments I left on the Potomac would be very acceptable — I am over-
working what I have.

> G B McClellan
> Maj Genl Comdg

Hon E M Stanton
Fort Monroe

ALS (telegram sent), McClellan Papers (A-57:22), Library of Congress. *OR*, Ser. 1, XI,
Part 3, pp. 160–61.

1. Stanton telegraphed on this date: "Frémont thinks that Johnston with a large force is
in front of him." *OR*, Ser. 1, XI, Part 3, p. 160. The general in question was Brig. Gen.
Edward Johnson, of Jackson's command.

To Mary Ellen McClellan

> May 10 [1862] Saturday 11.45 pm.
> Camp 19 miles from Williamsburg

... Am encamped now at an old wooden church, & in easy communi-
cation with Franklin, Porter &c. Fitz came over to see me this afternoon
& I go over to see him & Franklin tomorrow. Tomorrow being Sunday I
give the men a rest — merely closing up some of the troops in rear. I
begin to find some Union sentiment in this country....

I expect to fight a very severe battle on the Chickahominy, but feel no
doubt as to the result. All my officers & men have unlimited confidence
in me — I saw the effect of my presence the other day in front of
Wmsburg — & the men all felt the change — they behaved superbly &
will do better if possible next time. Tomorrow I will get up supplies —
reorganize — arrange details & get ready for the great fight — feeling
that I shall lose nothing by respecting Sunday as far as I can. Secesh is
gathering all he can in front of me — so much the better — I will finish
the matter by one desperate blow. I have implicit confidence in my men
& they in me! What more can I ask....

Sunday [May 11] 8 am.   As I told you last night I am giving my men
some rest today — they need it much — for they have for some time been
living on long marches, short rations & rainy bivouacs....

My cavalry were within 6 miles of the upper Chickahominy yesterday.
Norfolk is in our possession, the result of my movements....

Monday [May 12] pm.   While I write the 2nd Dragoon band is ser-
enading & about 50 others are playing tattoo at various distances — a
grand sound this lovely moonlight night. My camp is at an old frame
church in a grove — I differ from most of the Generals in preferring a
tent to a house — I hope not to sleep in a house again until I see you....

Are you satisfied now with my bloodless victories? Even the abolitionists seem to be coming around — judging at least from the very handsome Resolution offered by Mr. Lovejoy in the House.[1] I look upon that Resolution as one of the most complimentary I know of — & that too offered by my bitterest prosecutors — but the union of civic merit with military success is what pleases me most — to have it recognized that I have saved the lives of my men & won success by my own efforts is to me the height of glory. I hope that the result in front of Richmond will cause still greater satisfaction to the country. I still hope that the God who has been so good to me will continue to smile upon our cause, and enable me to bring this war to a speedy close, so that I may at last have the rest I want so much....

I do need rest — you know I have had but little in my life. But the will of God be done — what is given me to do I will try to do with all my might....

I think one more battle here will finish the work. I expect a great one, but feel that confidence in my men & that trust in God which makes me very sanguine as to the result. They will fight me in front of Richmond I am confident — defeat there is certain destruction to them & I think will prove the ruin of their wretched cause. They are concentrating everything for the last death struggle — my government, alas, is not giving me any aid! But I will do the best I can with what I have & trust to God's mercy & the courage of my men for the result....

We march in the morning for Cumberland — gradually drawing nearer to Richmond.

AL copy, McClellan Papers (C-7:63), Library of Congress.

1. Owen Lovejoy, an abolitionist congressman from Illinois. The House resolution, adopted May 9, tendered thanks "to Major-General George B. McClellan, for the display of those high military qualities which secure important results with but little sacrifice of human life."

To Edwin M. Stanton   [TELEGRAM]

Camp 19 m from Williamsburg May 11 — 9 am [1862]

I congratulate you from the bottom of my heart upon the destruction of the Merrimac.[1] I would now most earnestly urge that our gun boats & the iron clad boats be sent as far as possible up the James River without delay. This will enable me to make our movements much more decisive.

G B McClellan
Maj Genl Comdg

Hon E M Stanton
Secty of War   Fort Monroe

ALS (telegram sent), McClellan Papers (A-57:22), Library of Congress, *OR*, Ser. 1, XI, Part 3, p. 164.

1. Drawing too much water to reach Richmond, the *Merrimack* was destroyed by her crew on this date.

To Salmon P. Chase

Hon. S. P. Chase   Hd. Qtrs Army of the Potomac
Secretary of the Treasury   Camp at Cumberland [Landing],
Washington   New Kent Co. Va. May 14, 1862

I beg to call your attention to the subject of opening trade with this Peninsula and its adjacent waters as rapidly as our land & naval forces establish our flag. The country is very destitute of all the necessaries of life, and many of its families are suffering for food. An order authorizing commerce under such restrictions as you may deem proper, would serve of humanity, promote our political interests, and even contribute to the comfort of some of our own forces, especially sick & wounded men.[1]

Very Resp. Your obt servt.
Geo. B. McClellan
Maj. Genl. Comdg.

Copy, McClellan Papers (A-57:22), Library of Congress.

1. Chase responded by telegraph on May 16: "Whatever the law allows to be done will be done as promptly as possible to give effect to your suggestions." McClellan Papers (A-57:22).

To Abraham Lincoln   [TELEGRAM]

His Excellency Abraham Lincoln   Camp at Cumberland,
President of the United States   May 14th [1862]

I have more than twice telegraphed to the Secretary of War,[1] stating that, in my opinion, the enemy were concentrating all their available force to fight this army in front of Richmond, and that such ought to be their policy. I have received no reply whatever to any of these telegraphs. I beg leave to repeat their substance to your Excellency and to ask that kind consideration which you have ever accorded to my representations and views. All my information from every source accessible to me, establishes the fixed purpose of the rebels to defend Richmond against this Army by offering us battle with all the troops they can collect from East, West, and South, and my own opinion is confirmed by that of all my commanders whom I have been able to consult.

Casualties, sickness, garrisons, and guards have much weakened my force and will continue to do so. I cannot bring into actual battle against the enemy more than eighty thousand men at the utmost, and with them I must attack in position, probably entrenched, a much larger force, perhaps double my numbers. It is possible that Richmond may be abandoned without a serious struggle but the enemy are actually in great strength between here and there and it would be unwise and even insane for me to calculate upon anything except a stubborn and desperate resistance. If they should abandon Richmond it may well be that it is done with the purpose of making the stand at some place in Virginia south or west of there, and we should be in condition to press them without delay. The Confederate leaders must employ their utmost efforts against this Army in Virginia, and they will be supported by the whole body of their military officers, among whom there may be said to be no Union feeling, as there is also very little among the higher class of citizens in the seceding states. I have found no fighting men left in this Peninsula. All are in the ranks of the opposing foe. Even if more troops than I now have should prove unnecessary for the purposes of military occupation our greatest display of imposing force in the Capital of the Rebel Government will have the best moral effect. I most respectfully and earnestly urge upon your Excellency that the opportunity has come for striking a fatal blow at the enemies of the Constitution and I beg that you will cause this Army to be reinforced without delay by all the disposable troops of the Government. I ask for every man that the War Department can send me. Sent by water, they will soon reach me. Any commander of the reinforcements whom your Excellency may designate will be acceptable to me, whatever expression I may have heretofore addressed to you on the subject.[2] I will fight the enemy, whatever their force may be, with whatever force I may have, and I firmly believe that we shall beat them, but our triumph should be made decisive and complete. The soldiers of this Army love their Government and will fight well in its support. You may rely upon them. They have confidence in me as their General and in you as their President. Strong reinforcements will at least save the lives of many of them. The greater the force, the more perfect will be our combinations and the less our loss.

For obvious reasons, I beg you to give immediate consideration to this communication and to inform me fully, at the earliest moment, of your final determination.[3]

Geo. B. McClellan
Major General Comdg

Retained copy, McClellan Papers (A-57:22), Library of Congress. *OR,* Ser. 1, XI, Part 1, pp. 26–27.

1. See GBM to Stanton, May 8, 10, *supra.* 2. See GBM to Lincoln, Apr. 18, *supra.* 3. Lincoln telegraphed on May 15: "Have done, and shall do, all I could and can to sustain you. . . . I am still unwilling to take all our force off the direct line between Richmond and here." *Collected Works of Lincoln,* V, p. 216. On May 17 McDowell's First Corps was ordered to join the Army of the Potomac by the overland route.

To Henry Wilson, Francis P. Blair, Jr.

Hon H. Wilson, Chairman Mil. Com. U.S. Senate.   Camp near
Hon. F. P. Blair,   "   "   "   " H.R.   Cumberland, Va.
Gentlemen,   May 15, 1862

The legislation in relation to the corps of Engineers and Topographical Engineers, which I requested last winter as a measure required by the good of the service, I have greatly felt the need of during the siege of Yorktown. These officers, with very insufficient numbers, have performed laborious and highly important duties, which have resulted in the bloodless reduction of the place, — bloodless, so far as the Army in general is concerned, but costly enough for them. Each corps has lost a valuable officer, — one killed, and the other dangerously wounded — and this from a total of only seventeen. They have fairly earned the favorable consideration of Congress.

Legislation is greatly needed to effect three practical objects immediately :

1st   To unite the Corps of Engineers and Topographical Engineers, and thus to do away with a complicated and faulty organization.

2nd   To provide a proper means for filling the numerous and increasing vacancies, — a matter which is becoming embarrassing. My Engineer officers have been greatly overworked, and in fact crippled, from the want of the young officers, who, if the bill submitted last winter had become a law, would now be actively engaged. These vacancies (about thirty) cannot be properly filled without legislation.

3d   To give the rank — at least temporary — which is demanded by every principle of equity and expediency.

I have a battalion of three companies of regular Engineer troops. It is commanded by a *captain,* an officer of fourteen years' invaluable experience, who may well feel aggrieved at not having even the rank to which his actual command would entitle him in any regiment of the line. Each of these companies is commanded by a lieutenant, upon whom the same relative injustice is inflicted. This is all the more galling to the officers of these two corps, because they are habitually and necessarily refused permission to accept the command of volunteer regiments, on the ground that their professional services cannot be spared.

I therefore earnestly hope that a bill providing for these three needs of the service may very speedily become a law. The necessity for it is injuriously felt every day. The bill submitted by these corps last winter, had and still has, my full approval ; but if Congress is unwilling to increase so largely the permanent rank, the provisions for temporary rank during the war, added as an amendment to the bill reported by the

Military Committee of the Senate, will provide for the immediate and pressing needs of the service.[1]

Geo. B. McClellan
Maj. Gen. Comdg.

Copy, Miscellaneous Manuscripts Collection, American Antiquarian Society. Sen. Wilson of Massachusetts and Rep. Blair of Missouri were chairmen, respectively, of the Senate and House military affairs committees.

1. Legislation merging the Topographical Engineers into the Corps of Engineers was enacted on Mar. 3, 1863.

To Mary Ellen McClellan

Cumberland May 15 [1862] 2.30 pm.

Another wet horrid day! It rained a little yesterday morning, more in the afternoon, much during the night & has been amusing itself in the same manner very persistently all day. I had expected to move Hd Qtrs to White House today — but this weather has put the roads in such condition that I cannot do more than get Franklin & Porter there today. Hd Qtrs cavalry & Hunt[1] will move there tomorrow — perhaps one or two other Divisions as well. We had quite a visitation yesterday, in the shape of Secy Seward, Gideon Welles, Mr. Bates, Fred Seward, Dahlgren, Mrs. Goldsborough & one of her daughters, Mrs. Fred Seward & some other ladies whose names I did not catch.[2] I went on board their boat — then had some ambulances harnessed up & took them around camp — was very glad when I got thro' with them — such visits are always a nuisance.

We are just about 25 miles from Richmond here — the advance considerably nearer. I don't yet know what to make of the rebels — I do not see how they can possibly abandon Virginia & Richmond without a battle — nor do I understand why they abandoned & destroyed Norfolk & the Merrimac unless they also intended to abandon all of Virginia! There is a puzzle there somewhere which will soon be solved....

I am heartily tired of this life I am leading — always some little absurd thing being done by those gentry in Washington. I am every day more & more tired of public life & earnestly pray that I may soon be able to throw down my sword & live once more as a private gentleman....

I confess I find it difficult to judge whether the war will soon be at an end or not — I think that the blows the rebels are now receiving & have lately received ought to crush them up — but one can do no more than speculate. Yes I *can* imagine peace & quietness reigning once more in this land of ours — it is just what I am fighting for!...

Still raining hard & dismally — an awful time for the men — the only comfort is that they all have plenty to eat.

9 pm. ... Have received today the official copy of the Resols of the House.[3] I learn that the abolitionists begin to think that I am not such a wretch after all, or else that it is best to say so.

It was all a humbug about my being struck by a piece of a shell at Wmsburg. That reminds me of a joke some of the youngsters played upon Billy Palmer[4] at Yorktown. They sent him to see an immense "shell" that had fallen in our Head Qtrs camp. He found it, but it proved to be a large *oyster* shell. ...

I send you a photograph which I have just received from Genl Blume Chief of Artillery in the Prussian Army. I knew him abroad, & the old gentleman writes to me occasionally.

AL copy; copy, McClellan Papers (C-7:63/D-10:72), Library of Congress.

1. Col. Henry J. Hunt, artillery reserve. 2. Secretary of State Seward, Secretary of the Navy Welles, Attorney General Bates, Secretary Seward's son Frederick and his wife, Capt. John A. Dahlgren of the Washington Navy Yard, and the wife and daughter of Flag Officer Goldsborough. 3. See GBM to his wife, May 10, *supra*. 4. Capt. William R. Palmer, Topographical Engineers.

To Edwin M. Stanton   [TELEGRAM]

Head Quarters, Army of the Potomac,
White House May 17 [1862] — 10.45 pm

After a careful consideration of the meager accounts I have received of the gun boat operations on the James River I am inclined to think that we ought not to be discouraged.[1] They were caught in very adverse circumstances & I think their repulse will prove to be due to the fact that they were subjected to a close musketry fire they could not reply to.

I would urge the necessity of perfect cooperation between all the Army & Navy forces in Eastern Virginia. I have not one word of official information as to the objects to be attained by any of them.

G B McClellan
Maj Genl

Hon E M Stanton

ALS (telegram sent), McClellan Papers (A-57:22), Library of Congress. *OR*, Ser. 1, XI, Part 3, p. 177.

1. On May 15 a Federal flotilla, including the *Monitor*, was defeated by batteries at Drewry's Bluff, eight miles short of Richmond.

To Mary Ellen McClellan

White House May 18th [1862] Sunday 6 pm.

... We leave here in the morning — Porter & Franklin march at 4 & 8 am — Hd Qtrs at 7. We will go to Tunstall's, or perhaps a little beyond it, & will now soon close up on the Chickahominy & find out what secesh is doing. I think he will fight us there, or in between that & Richmond — & if he is badly thrashed (as I trust he will be) incline to believe that he will begin to cry peccavi & say that he has enough of it — especially if Halleck beats him at Corinth.

Midnight ... I start early in the morning....

Those hounds in Washington are after me again. Stanton is without exception the vilest man I ever knew or heard of.

AL copy, McClellan Papers (C-7:63), Library of Congress.

To Ambrose E. Burnside

Maj. Gen. Ambrose E. Burnside,
Commanding Department
of North Carolina: Headquarters of the Army
My dear Burn: Tunstall's Station, May 21, 1862

Your dispatch and kind letter received. I have instructed Seth to reply to the official letter[1] and now acknowledge the kind private note. It always does me good, in the midst of my cares and perplexities, to see your wretched old scrawling. I have terrible troubles to contend with, but have met them with a good heart, like your good old self, and have thus far struggled through successfully. Our progress has been slow, but that is due to ignorance of the country (we have to feel our way everywhere; the maps are worthless), the narrowness, small number, and condition of the roads, which become impassable for trains after a day's rain, of which we have had a great deal.

I feel very proud of Yorktown; it and Manassas will be my brightest chaplets in history; for I know that I accomplished everything in both places by pure military skill. I am very proud and grateful to God that he allowed me to purchase such great success at so trifling a loss of life. We came near being badly beaten at Williamsburg. I arrived on the field at 5 p.m. and found that all thought we were whipped and in for a disaster. You would have been glad to see, old fellow, how the men cheered and brightened up when they saw me. In five minutes after I reached the ground a possible defeat was changed into certain victory. The greatest moral courage I ever exercised was that night, when, in the face of urgent demands from almost all quarters for re-enforcements to hold our own, I quietly *sent back* the troops I had ordered up before I reached the field. I was sure that Johnston would leave during the night if he understood his business, or that I could be able to thrash him in the morning by a proper use of the force I had. It turned out that Jo. left! Hancock conducted himself magnificently; his charge was elegant!

I expect to fight a desperate battle in front of Richmond, and against

superior numbers, somewhat intrenched. The Government have delib-
erately placed me in this position. If I win, the greater the glory. If I
lose, they will be damned forever, both by God and men.

Well, I have bored you long enough, old fellow. I will merely add that
my light troops have crossed the Chickahominy at Bottom's Bridge this
morning, 10 miles from Richmond, and that the advanced guard, under
Stoneman, has driven in everything upon New Bridge (on my right), 6
miles from Richmond. The crisis cannot long be deferred. I pray for
God's blessing on our arms, and rely far more on his goodness than I do
on my own poor intellect. I sometimes think now that I can almost realize
that Mahomet was sincere. When I see the hand of God guarding one so
weak as myself, I can almost think myself a chosen instrument to carry
out his schemes. Would that a better man had been selected. . . .

If I thrash these rascals we will soon be in direct communication, and
I shall then wish to give you a command from this army to add to the
noble men you now have.

Good-by, and God bless you, Burn. With the sincere hope that we may
soon shake hands,

I am, as ever, your sincere friend,
McClellan

OR, Ser. 1, IX, p. 392.

1. Seth Williams's reply of this date to Burnside's May 17 request for instructions was
based on a GBM memorandum reading in part: "I would therefore think that cautious
yet bold advance on Goldsboro as soon as transportation arrives would produce a better
effect than anything else that can be done and would have the effect to neutralize a larger
portion of the enemys force." McClellan Papers (A-108:43), Library of Congress; *OR*,
Ser. 1, IX, pp. 389, 393.

To Abraham Lincoln   [TELEGRAM]

Hd Qurs. Army of the Potomac
His Excellency Abraham Lincoln   Camp near Tunstall's Station Va.
President of the United States.   May 21, 1862 11 p.m.

Your dispatch of yesterday respecting our situation and the batteries
at Fort Darling was rec'd while I was absent with the advance, where I
have also been all this day.[1] I have communicated personally with Capt.
Goldsborough & by letter with Capt. Smith. The vessels can do nothing
without cooperation on land, which I will not be in position to afford
for several days. Circumstances must determine the propriety of a land
attack.

It rained again last night, and rain on this soil soon makes the roads
incredibly bad for army transportation. I personally crossed the Chick-
ahominy today at Bottom's bridge ford and went a mile beyond, the
enemy being about half a mile in front. I have three Regts on the other

bank guarding the rebuilding of the bridge. Keyes' Corps is on the New Kent road, near Bottom's bridge. Heintzelman is on the same road, within supporting distance. Sumner is on the R.R. connecting right with left. Stoneman with advanced guard is within one mile of New bridge. Franklin with two Divisions is about two miles this side of Stoneman. Porter's Division with the Reserve of Infantry & Artillery is within supporting distance. Head Quarters will probably be at Coal [Cold] Harbor tomorrow, one mile this side of Franklin. All the bridges over the Chickahominy are destroyed.

The enemy are in force on every road leading to Richmond, within a mile or two west of the stream. Their main body is on the road from New bridge encamped along it for four or five miles, spreading over the open ground on both sides. Johnston's Head Quarters are about two miles beyond the bridge.

All accounts report their numbers as greatly exceeding our own. The position of the rebel forces, the declarations of the Confederate authorities, the resolutions of the Virginia legislature, the action of the City Govt., the conduct of the citizens, and all other sources of information accessible to me, give positive assurance that our approach to Richmond, involves a desperate battle between the opposing armies.

All our Divisions are moving towards the foe. I shall advance steadily & carefully & attack them according to my best judgment, and in such manner as to employ my greatest force.

I regret the state of things as to Genl. McDowell's command. We must beat the enemy in front of Richmond. One Division added to this Army for that effort would do more to protect Washington than his whole force can possibly do anywhere else in the field. The rebels are concentrating from all points for the two battles at Richmond & Corinth. I would still most respectfully suggest the policy of our concentrating here by movements on water. I have heard nothing as to the probabilities of the contemplated junction of McDowell's force with mine. I have no idea when he can start, what are his means of transportation, or when he may be expected to reach this vicinity. I fear there is little hope that he can join me overland in time for the coming battle. Delays on my part will be dangerous. I fear sickness & demoralization. This region is unhealthy for northern men, and unless kept moving I fear that our soldiers may become discouraged. At present our numbers are weakening from disease, but the men remain in good heart.

I regret also the configuration of the Department of the Rappahannock. It includes a portion even of the City of Richmond. I think that my own Department should embrace the entire field of active military operations designed for the capture of that city.

Again, I agree with your Excellency that one bad General is better than two good ones. I am not sure that I fully comprehend your orders of the 17th inst. addressed to myself & Genl McDowell.[2] If a junction is effected before we occupy Richmond, it must necessarily be east of the RR to Fredericksburg, & within my Department. This fact, my superior rank, & the express language of the 62d Article of War will place his command under my orders unless it is otherwise specially directed by your Excellency. I consider that he will be under my command except that I am not to detach any portion of his forces, or give any order which can put him out of position to cover Washington. If I err in my construction I desire to be at once set right. Frankness compels me to say, anxious as I am for an increase of force, that the march of McDowell's column upon Richmond by the shortest route, will in my opinion uncover Washington as to any interposition by it, as completely as its movement by water. The enemy cannot advance by Fredericksburg on Washington. Should they attempt a movement, which to me seems utterly improbable, their route would be by Gordonsville & Manassas. I desire that the extent of my authority over Genl. McDowell may be clearly defined, lest misunderstandings & conflicting views may produce some of those injurious results which a divided command has so often caused. I would respectfully suggest that this danger can only be surely guarded against by explicitly placing Genl. McDowell under my orders in the ordinary way, & holding me strictly responsible for the closest observance of your instructions. I hope, Mr. President, that it is not necessary for me to assure you that your directions would be observed in the utmost good faith, & that I have no personal feelings which could influence me to disregard them in any particular.[3]

I believe that there is a great struggle before this Army, but I am neither dismayed nor discouraged. I wish to strengthen its force as much as I can, but in any event I shall fight it with all the skill, caution, & determination that I possess, & I trust that the result may either obtain for me the permanent confidence of my Government, or that it may close my career.

Geo B McClellan
Maj Genl Comdg

Retained copy, McClellan Papers (A-58:23), Library of Congress. OR, Ser. 1, XI, Part 1, pp. 28–29.

1. Lincoln's telegram asked if any action could be taken against the Fort Darling batteries at Drewry's Bluff. Collected Works of Lincoln, V, p. 224. 2. A copy of Stanton's May 17 instructions to McDowell, "By order of the President," was sent to GBM, and read in part: "While seeking to establish as soon as possible a communication between your left wing and the right wing of General McClellan, you will hold yourself always in such position as to cover the capital of the nation against a sudden dash of any large body of the rebel forces." OR, Ser. 1, XI, Part 1, p. 28. 3. The president replied on this date: "You will have just such control of Gen. McDowell and his force as you therein indicate.... By land he can reach you in five days after starting, whereas by water he would not reach you in two weeks, judging by past experience." Collected Works of Lincoln, V, p. 226.

To Abraham Lincoln [TELEGRAM]

Head Quarters A of P
Coal Harbor,[1] May 22 —
His Excellency A Lincoln *Presdt*   12.30 p.m. 1862

Your dispatch just rec'd.[2] The discipline of the army will not permit the restoration of General Hamilton to his division. Since the matter is pressed as it is I feel obliged to state what I did not care to before viz. that Gen. Hamilton is not fit to command a division. The task before me is too serious to permit me to hesitate when called upon to express an opinion. The cause of his removal from this army was ample to justify me in the course I pursued. You cannot do anything better calculated to injure my army and diminish the probabilities of success in the approaching battle now imminent than to restore Gen Hamilton to his Division. I earnestly protest against any such action and I trust that after this statement you will not think of sending Gen Hamilton back to this army.[3]

G. B. McClellan
Maj Genl Comdg

Retained copy, Records of the Office of the Secretary of War, RG 107 (M-504:66), National Archives. *OR*, Ser. 1, XI, Part 3, pp. 185–86.

1. Cold Harbor. 2. In his telegram of May 21, Lincoln reported receiving a petition signed by twenty-three senators and eighty-four representatives calling for the reinstatement of Brig. Gen. Charles S. Hamilton, relieved from duty during the Yorktown siege. *Collected Works of Lincoln*, V, p. 227. 3. Hamilton did not again serve with the Army of the Potomac.

To Mary Ellen McClellan

May 22 [1862] 6 1/2 pm.
Camp near Chickahominy

I can't tell you how often I have thought of you today, & how often my thoughts have reached to two years ago. At *two* exactly I wrote a dispatch to you which you will understand.[1] I have just returned from a ride to the front where I have taken a good look at the rebel lines. I suppose I must have ridden some 30 miles today. Some one just brought me a bouquet of wild white flowers — a negro at that — I clutched it most eagerly, as reminding me of one, who two years ago became my wife. It is on the table in front of me as I write; in a tin tumbler, to be sure, but none the less pure & white.

[May] 23rd pm. Soon after I finished the last page I was taken quite sick & continued so most of the night. I have remained in my tent all day feeling quite miserable — but will be all right & able to ride out in the morning. . . .

The occurrences of the next few days are quite uncertain. I have secured one passage of the Chickahominy & hope to get two more tomorrow. I have been within 6 miles of the rebel capital, & our balloonists have been watching it all day. The intentions of the enemy are still doubtful. I go on prepared to fight a hard battle, but I confess that the indications are not now that he will fight. Unless he has some deep laid scheme that I do not fathom, he is giving up great advantage in not opposing me on the line of the Chickahominy — he could give me a great deal of trouble & make it cost me hundreds or thousands of lives. If he fights now he must do so in the very outskirts of Richmond, which must in that event suffer terribly, & perhaps be destroyed. I do not know that I can control fully this army of volunteers if they enter the city on the heels of the enemy after an assault. I will do my best to prevent outrage & pillage, but there are bad men in all armies & I hope that I shall not be forced to witness the sack of Richmond. God knows I am sick of this civil war — altho' no feeling of the kind unsteadies my hand or ever makes me hesitate or waver — it is a cruel necessity. I am very glad that the Presdt has come out as he did about Hunter's order — I feared he would not have the moral courage to do so. I can't think how Hunter could have done such a thing without authority from some one.[2] ...

If I succeed in getting the two additional passages of the River tomorrow I will move next day — in fact I hope to have a strong advanced guard within a couple of miles of Richmond tomorrow evening. Then I shall be able to examine the enemy's positions & arrange for the battle. I will not fight on Sunday if I can help it. If I am obliged to do so I will have faith that God will defend the right, & trust that we have the right on our side. How freely I shall breathe when my long task of months is over & Richmond is ours! I know the uncertainty of all human events — I know that God may even now deem best to crush all the high hopes of the nation & this army — I will do the best I can to insure success & will do my best to be contented with whatever result God sees fit to terminate our efforts. I have long prayed that I might neither be elated by success nor unduly cast down by defeat. I hope my prayers may be granted. I am here on the eve of one of the great historic battles of the world — one of those crises in a nation's life that occurs but seldom — far more than my fate is involved in the issue. I have done the best I could. I have tried to serve my country honestly & faithfully — all I can now do is to commit myself to the hands of God & pray that the country may not be punished for my sins & shortcomings.

11 pm.   ... Have had some skirmishes & cannonading today — successful in all.

AL copy; copy, McClellan Papers (C-7:63/D-10:72), Library of Congress.

1. May 22 was the McClellans' wedding anniversary. His telegram read: "I send this only to show you that I remember about occurrences exactly two years ago. The most fortunate moment of my life. I cannot celebrate it in Richmond but hope soon to be there...." Records of the Office of the Secretary of War, RG 107 (M-504:66), National Archives. 2.

On May 19 the president disavowed an order issued by Maj. Gen. David Hunter that abolished slavery in South Carolina, Georgia, and Florida.

To Abraham Lincoln   [TELEGRAM]

Head-Quarters, Army of the Potomac,
Coal Harbor May 24 [1862] 8.30 pm

Telegram of four PM received.[1] I will make my calculations accordingly.

G B McClellan
Maj Genl Comdg

The President   Washington D.C.

ALS (telegram sent), McClellan Papers (A-58:23), Library of Congress. *OR*, Ser. 1, XI, Part 3, p. 190.

1.The president's telegram read: "In consequence of Gen. Banks' critical position I have been compelled to suspend Gen. McDowell's movement to join you. The enemy are making a desperate push upon Harper's Ferry, and we are trying to throw Fremont's force & part of McDowell's in their rear." *Collected Works of Lincoln*, V, p. 232.

To Mary Ellen McClellan

May 25 [1862] Sunday 3 1/2 pm. Coal Harbor

... Have been rather under the weather the last three days — had to ride out in the rain yesterday & was kept up very late last night — so I was not so well as I might have been this morning. ...

It cleared off about sunset yesterday, & today has been bright & pleasant — drying up the roads rapidly — they have been so cut & bad as to prevent any movements in force or with rapidity — fortunately the ground dries rapidly here & will soon be in such condition that we can move anywhere. I have this moment received a dispatch from the Presdt who is terribly scared about Washington — & talks about the necessity of my returning in order to save it![1] Heaven save a country governed by such counsels! I must reply to his telegram & finish this by & by!

5 pm.   Have just finished my reply to his Excellency![2] It is perfectly sickening to deal with such people & you may rest assured that I will lose as little time as possible in breaking off all connection with them — I get more sick of them every day — for every day brings with it only additional proofs of their hypocrisy, knavery & folly — well, well, I ought not to write in this way, for they may be right & I entirely wrong, so I will drop the subject. ...

I feel much better this afternoon, quite myself again. ...

If I should find Washn life as bad after the war as it was when I was there I don't think I could be induced to remain in the army after peace.

10 pm.   ... It seems from some later dispatches I have received that

Banks has been soundly thrashed & that they are terribly alarmed in Washn. A scare will do them good, & may bring them to their senses. . . .

I have a fire in my tent tonight.

AL copy, McClellan Papers (C-7:63), Library of Congress.

1. The president telegraphed on this date that the enemy was advancing in the Shenandoah Valley "in sufficient force to drive Banks before him. . . . I think the movement is a general and concerted one, such as could not be if he was acting upon the purpose of a very desperate defence of Richmond. I think the time is near when you must either attack Richmond or give up the job and come to the defence of Washington." *Collected Works of Lincoln,* V, pp. 235–36. 2. GBM to Lincoln, May 25, *infra.*

To Abraham Lincoln   [TELEGRAM]

Head-Quarters, Army of the Potomac
Coal Harbor May 25 [1862] 5 p.m.

Telegram received. Independently of it the time is very near when I shall attack Richmond. The object of enemy's movement is probably to prevent reinforcements being sent to me. All the information obtained from balloons, deserters prisoners & contrabands agrees in the statement that the mass of rebel troops are still in immediate vicinity of Richmond ready to defend it.

I have no knowledge of Banks's position & force, nor what there is at Manassas, therefore cannot form a definite opinion as to force against him. I have two Corps across Chickahominy within six miles of Richmond — the others on this side at other crossings within same distance & ready to cross when bridges completed.

G B McClellan
Maj Genl Comdg

His Excellency A. Lincoln
Presdt

ALS (telegram sent), McClellan Papers (A-58:23), Library of Congress. *OR*, Ser. 1, XI, Part 1, p. 32.

To Mary Ellen McClellan   [TELEGRAM]

Head Quarters, Army of the Potomac,
Camp near New Bridge May 26 1862 1.30 pm

Have reached my new Camp. All quite well although it is raining again. The net is quietly closing & some fish will soon be caught.

G B McClellan
Maj Genl Comdg

Mrs G B McClellan
Care N Shipman Esq
Hartford Connecticut

ALS (telegram sent), McClellan Papers (C-13:64), Library of Congress.

To Abraham Lincoln   [TELEGRAM]

Head-Quarters, Army of the Potomac,
Camp near New Bridge May 26 [1862] 7.30 pm

Have arranged to carry out your last orders.[1] We are quietly closing in upon the enemy preparatory to the last struggle. Situated as I am I feel forced to take every possible precaution against disaster & to secure my flanks against the probably superior force in front of me. My arrangements for tomorrow are very important, & if successful will leave me free to strike on the return of the force detached.

G B McClellan
Maj Genl Comdg

His Excellency A Lincoln
Presdt

ALS (telegram sent), McClellan Papers (A-58:23), Library of Congress. *OR*, Ser. 1, XI, Part 1, p. 33.

1. These orders presumably referred to cutting railroads north of Richmond.

To Mary Ellen McClellan

May 26 [1862] 8 pm. Camp near New Bridge.

... We broke up the last camp about 2 & moved to this place which is quite on the banks of the Chickahominy & very near New Bridge. It *of course* commenced raining about an hour after we started — but as it was not a very heavy rain we got on very well. ...

I have been troubled by the old Mexican complaint, brought on I suppose by exposure to the wet etc, but I am really substantially well again.[1] ...

Fitz starts off in the morning on a trip that will take a day to go & one to return — the object being to cut off & disperse a force of the enemy threatening my right & rear — also to destroy the RR bridges — when this is done I will feel very comfortable in that direction & shall be quite ready to attack. My men are in such excellent condition & such good spirits that I cannot doubt the result. I feel that we must beat the rebels & I hope end the war — from all that I can learn the gaining of this battle will insure the return of Virginia to her allegiance — the people here have not much Union feeling but are becoming heartily tired of the war — especially as they now feel its evils in their midst — a fate from which I pray that God may deliver our own Northern states.

My camp is about 4 1/2 to 5 miles from Richmond. I fancy secesh is becoming rather disturbed — he don't know exactly what I am about. I could not help laughing this afternoon when I received from the Secy of War a copy of a dispatch from McDowell which proves them all to have been a precious lot of fools & that I have been right all the time.[2] Had the instructions I left for Banks & Wadsworth been complied with we should have been spared the shame of Banks' stampede. It will prove that Banks ran away from a small force & needlessly evacuated the part of Va. in possession of which I placed him. Some of the Presdt's dispatches for the last two days have been amazing in the extreme. I cannot do justice to them so I shall not attempt to describe them. I feared last night that I would be ordered back for the defense of Washington! You can imagine the course I had determined to pursue in such a contingency.

AL copy, McClellan Papers (C-7:63), Library of Congress.

1. GBM's "old Mexican complaint" was malaria, contracted during the Mexican War. 2. McDowell's dispatch, dated May 25, reported intelligence that Confederate forces were ordered "back to Richmond to take part in the great battle now about to take place there." *OR*, Ser. 1, XII, Part 3, p. 233.

To Edwin M. Stanton   [TELEGRAM]

New Bridge May 27 1862 2.30 pm

Very severe storm last night & this morning has converted everything into mud again & raised Chickahominy. Richmond papers urge Johnston to attack now he has us away from gun boats. I think he is too able for that. I communicated with gun boats yesterday by a small party. Am not yet ready to cooperate with them. Every day is making our result more sure & I am wasting no time. Rather heavy firing in direction of Porter from whom I expect good news in a few hours. What about Banks? Will answer in a few minutes about arms. Am obliged for the promised reinforcements.[1]

G B McClellan
Maj Genl Comdg

Hon E M Stanton
Secty of War

ALS (telegram sent), McClellan Papers (A-58:23), Library of Congress, *OR*, Ser. 1, XI, Part 3, p. 193.

1. Stanton telegraphed on this date that two regiments of infantry and one of artillery would be sent for garrison duty. *OR*, Ser. 1, XI, Part 3, p. 193.

To Edwin M. Stanton   [TELEGRAM]

Hon E. M. Stanton
Secy of war   McClellans May 27, 1862 8.30 p.m.

I find some of the newspapers publish letters from their Correspondents with this Army, giving important information concerning our movements, positions of troops &c. in positive violation of your orders. As it is impossible for me to ascertain with certainty who these anonymous writers are I beg to suggest that another order be published holding the Editors responsible for its infraction.[1]

G. B. McClellan
Maj Genl.

Retained copy, Records of the Office of the Secretary of War, RG 107 (M-504:65), National Archives. *OR*, Ser. 1, XI, Part 3, p. 194.

1. In a second telegram on this subject, sent three hours later, GBM wrote: "Notwithstanding the trouble, I would be glad to have them required to submit all letters as well as telegraphs to these headquarters." *OR*, Ser. 1, XI, Part 3, p. 194.

To Edwin M. Stanton   [TELEGRAM]

Hanover CH May 28 [1862] 4 pm

Porter's action of yesterday was truly a glorious victory — too much credit cannot be given to his magnificent Division & its accomplished leader. The rout of the rebels was complete — not a defeat but a complete rout. Prisoners are constantly coming in — two companies have this moment arrived with excellent arms.

There is no doubt that the enemy are concentrating everything on Richmond. I will do my best to cut off Jackson, but am doubtful whether I can.

It is the policy & duty of the Govt to send me by water all the well drilled troops available. I am confident that Washington is in no danger.

Engines & cars in large numbers have been sent up to bring down Jackson's command. I may not be able to cut them, but will try. We have cut all but the F & R RR.[1] The real issue is in the battle about to be fought in front of Richmond — all our available troops should be collected here, not raw regiments but the well drilled troops. It cannot be ignored that a desperate battle is before us — if any regiments of good troops remain unemployed it will be an irreparable fault committed.

G B McClellan
Maj Genl Comdg

Hon E M Stanton
Secty of War

P.S. our total loss in the battle of Hanover C.H. is 397 (three hundred & ninety-seven) killed, wounded & missing, of which (53) fifty three killed. The loss of enemy at least (1000) one thousand & totally disorganized.

ALS (telegram sent), McClellan Papers (A-59:23), Library of Congress. *OR*, Ser. 1, XI, Part 1, p. 35.

1. The Richmond, Fredericksburg and Potomac Railroad.

To Mary Ellen McClellan   [TELEGRAM]

Mrs. G. B. McClellan   Hanover CH
Care N Shipman Hartford Conn   [May] 28 [1862] 4.15 pm

I am on Fitz field of battle. His success of yesterday was a glorious victory. The old rascal has done all that I could ask. The rebels are completely routed. It is a fair presage of the great victory which awaits us at Richmond. God bless you.

                                        G B McClellan
                                        Maj Genl

Received copy (War Dept.), Records of the Office of the Secretary of War, RG 107 (M-504:65), National Archives.

To Edwin M. Stanton   [TELEGRAM]

                                New Bridge May 30 [1862] — am

From tone of your dispatches & President's I do not think that you at all appreciate the value & magnitude of Porter's victory.[1] It has entirely relieved my right flank which was seriously threatened, routed & demoralized a considerable portion of the rebel force, taken over 750 (seven hundred & fifty) prisoners, killed & wounded large numbers, one gun, many small arms & much baggage taken. It was one of the handsomest things of the war both in itself & its results. Porter has returned & my Army is again well in hand. Another day will make the probable field of battle passable for artillery. It is quite certain that there is nothing in front of Genl McDowell (Fredericksburg). I regard the burning of S Anna bridges as least important result of Porter's movement.

                                        G B McClellan
                                        Maj Genl Comdg

Hon E M Stanton
Secty of War

ALS (telegram sent), McClellan Papers (A-59:23), Library of Congress. *OR*, Ser. 1, XI, Part 1, p. 37.

1. In response to incomplete information sent to Washington, Lincoln telegraphed on May 28 to express puzzlement that a key railroad bridge over the South Anna River was not destroyed by Porter. The bridge was subsequently burned. *Collected Works of Lincoln*, V, pp. 244–45.

To Edwin M. Stanton   [TELEGRAM]

Head-Quarters, Army of the Potomac,
New Bridge May 30 [1862] 9.30 pm

A contraband reports that Beauregard arrived in Richmond day before yesterday, with troops & amid great excitement.

I cannot vouch for the truth of this but give it for what it may be worth in connection with evacuation of Corinth.

Terrible storm this afternoon & tonight — roads again frightful. Need more ambulances.

G B McClellan
Maj Genl

Hon E M Stanton
Secty of War

ALS (telegram sent), McClellan Papers (A-59:23), Library of Congress. *OR*, Ser. 1, XI, Part 3, p. 201.

FIVE

THE BATTLE FOR RICHMOND
MAY 31–JULY 2, 1862

THE BATTLE OF Fair Oaks, on May 31 and June 1, 1862, and the Seven Days' battles that opened on June 25 severely tested General McClellan as a battlefield commander. How he met the test is revealed with unusual clarity in the letters and dispatches that follow, especially in the considerable number — thirty-six of the total of seventy-eight — that appear here for the first time or (in the case of those to his wife) for the first time as they were originally written.

During the month following the Yorktown siege, McClellan had edged his army up to the Chickahominy River and crossed his left wing — Heintzelman's Third Corps and Keyes's Fourth — to the south bank of that stream and to within six miles of Richmond. When Joe Johnston struck at this wing at Fair Oaks on May 31, McClellan was lying ill at his headquarters north of the river with what he termed his "Mexican disease," a recurrent malarial fever he had first contracted during the Mexican War. He was able to do little beyond ordering up reinforcements, and only reached the battlefield on June 1 when the fighting was over. His men beat off the uncoordinated Rebel attacks, leaving the two sides about where they were when the battle began.

General Johnston was badly wounded at Fair Oaks, and on June 1 Robert E. Lee took command of the Army of Northern Virginia. In his letter of April 20 to the president McClellan had written that as a commander General Lee was "likely to be timid & irresolute in action," a judgment that proved signally unprophetic. Although Lee succeeded in massing some 85,000 men to defend Richmond, the largest army he would ever command, it was a count far short of the 200,000 McClellan credited him with on the eve of the Seven Days. Thinking himself outnumbered by two to one, his intended tactic against this host, described in his letter of June 15 to Mrs. McClellan, was to use his advantage in artillery to make Richmond and its defenders hostage to his heavy siege guns.

When the armies moved up the Peninsula, the Confederates were forced to destroy the *Merrimack*, which drew too much water to fall back to Richmond, but McClellan did not take advantage of this to shift his line to the James. Instead he continued to make his line of communications the York and Pamunkey rivers to White House, from where the 600 tons of supplies he needed daily, and his siege guns, could be carried directly to the front over the York River Railroad. Lee determined to strike at this supply line, and Fitz John Porter's Fifth Corps guarding it, with a turning movement. He was taking a calculated risk, leaving fewer than 30,000 men to defend Richmond against the four Federal corps south of the Chickahominy should McClellan counterattack.

[margin note: Did not Take advantage of situations]

On the evidence of his June 26 telegram to his wife, McClellan at first gave thought to exactly that tactic — "I give you my word that I believe we will surely win & that the enemy is falling into a trap," he told her — but then failed to act on the opportunity. He surrendered the initiative to his opponent, and when Lee's series of assaults on Porter finally succeeded at Gaines's Mill on June 27, he admitted defeat and put his army in retreat toward the James, where it could be protected by the navy's gunboats.

In the month spent on the Chickahominy line the Federals had linked their positions by field telegraph, and consequently there is a remarkably full telegraphic record of the first days of the Seven Days' fighting, before the Army of the Potomac retreated. The telegrams McClellan wrote during the Gaines's Mill battle, for example, reveal his belief that he was under attack that day south of the Chickahominy as well as north of it, a measure of how successfully the Richmond defenders stage-managed their operation while Lee was carrying out his offensive.

These telegrams form the background for McClellan's aberrant dispatch of June 28 to Secretary of War Stanton, in which he insisted he had been defeated "because my force was too small" and accused the administration of deliberately attempting to sacrifice his army. Unaware that the dispatch was censored by the supervisor of military telegrams in Washington before it was shown to Stanton, McClellan took the secretary's failure to respond to his charge of treason as a silent admission of guilt. That he made the accusation intentionally is evident from his letter of June 29 to General Dix, in which he repeated the charge and called on Dix, should the campaign claim his life, to make the letter public.

The record here of the fighting during the retreat to the James is less full, primarily because McClellan played only a limited role in it. During the critical action at Glendale on June 30 he was aboard a gunboat in the James. He only witnessed the next day's fighting at Malvern Hill from a distance, and directed none of it. Having already elected to continue the retreat to Harrison's Landing, he gave no thought to taking advantage of the incisive Federal victory at Malvern Hill with a counteroffensive of his own.

To Samuel P. Heintzelman   [TELEGRAM]

General Heintzelman,   Headquarters Army of the Potomac,
Commanding Left Wing: New Bridge, May 31, 1862 — 5 p.m.

You have done what I expected of you in retrieving the disaster of
Casey.[1] With the remaining five divisions you should hold your own. I
will post everything during the night, so as to be able to cross at New
Bridge to-morrow. Tell Kearny, Hooker, and [Couch] that I expect them
to hold firm and repulse every and any attack. Recapture, if possible,
any guns taken. Keep me fully informed of all that passes. Let me send
to Washington as soon as possible the news that all is right.

> Geo. B. McClellan
> Major-General

OR, Ser. 1, XI, Part 3, p. 203.

1. The Battle of Fair Oaks opened with an attack on Gen. Casey's division.

To Randolph B. Marcy   [TELEGRAM]

Genl R B Marcy   Head Quarters, Army of the Potomac
Chief of Staff   [Tyler House] 31st of May 1862 9.20 p.m.

Have rations cooked & ammunition issued to all the commands tonight
& have the men ready for action tomorrow without fatiguing them too
much tonight. Have the works & approaches to all possible bridges pushed
to the utmost tonight, so that as many as possible may be practicable in
the morning. Have the Trains ready to park. I have sent to Heintzelman
and Keyes & will communicate with you. Select carefully the positions
for parking the Trains & have Stoneman & the command at Mechanicsville
well in hand.

If the Engineers cannot build the bridges tonight, commit the work to
Porter & Franklin. I am sure Duane can do it. If they cannot, the sooner
we get rid of the Corps of Engineers the better — communicate this to
Barnard. It is absolutely necessary that several bridges be practicable
for Artillery in the morning.

> G B McClellan
> Maj Genl

ALS (telegram sent), McClellan Papers, New-York Historical Society. *OR*, Ser. 1, LI, Part
1, p. 647.

To Edwin M. Stanton   [TELEGRAM]

Headquarters Army of the Potomac
June 1 [1862] 12 M — Field of Battle

We have had a desperate battle in which the Corps of Sumner, Heintzelman & Keyes have been engaged against greatly superior numbers. Yesterday at one the enemy taking advantage of a terrible storm which had flooded the valley of the Chickahominy attacked our troops on the right bank of that river. Casey's Division which was in first line gave way unaccountably & discreditably. This caused a temporary confusion during which some guns & baggage were lost. But Heintzelman & Kearny most gallantly brought up their troops, which checked the enemy.

At the same time Sumner succeeded by great exertions in bringing across Sedgwick's & Richardson's Divisions, who drove back the enemy at the point of the bayonet, covering the ground with his dead. This morning the enemy attempted to renew the conflict but was every where repulsed. We have taken many prisoners, among whom Genl Pettigrew and Col. Long.[1] Our loss is heavy, but that of the enemy must be enormous. With the exception of Casey's Division our men have behaved splendidly — several fine bayonet charges have been made. The Second Excelsior[2] made two today.

G B McClellan
Maj Genl

Hon E M Stanton
Secty of War — Washington

ALS (telegram sent), McClellan Papers, New-York Historical Society. *OR*, Ser. 1, XI, Part 1, p. 749.

1. Brig. Gen. J. Johnston Pettigrew, Lt. Col. John O. Long. 2. The 71st New York regiment.

To Edwin M. Stanton   [TELEGRAM]

Head Quarters, Army of the Potomac,
New Bridge June 2 1862 12.30 pm

I am delighted to hear of Halleck's success.[1] I have sent to learn numbers of killed, wounded & prisoners — it will take some time to ascertain details. The attack was a sudden one by the enemy in large force on Casey on Saturday [May 31]. Casey's pickets rushed in without attempting a stand & the camp was carried by the enemy. Heintzelman moved up at once with Kearny's Divn & checked the enemy. A portion of Hooker's arrived about dark. As soon as informed of the state of affairs I ordered Sumner across the Chickahominy. He displayed the utmost energy in bringing his troops into action, & handled them with the utmost courage in action. He repulsed every attack of the enemy, & drove him wherever he could get at him.

The enemy attacked in force & with great spirit yesterday morning, but were everywhere most signally repulsed with great loss. Our troops charged frequently on both days & uniformly broke the enemy.

The result is that our left is now within four (4) miles of Richmond. I only wait for the river to fall to cross with the rest of the force & make a general attack. Should I find them holding firm in a very strong position I may wait for what troops I can bring up from Fort Monroe — but the morale of my troops is now such that I can venture much & do not care for odds against me. The victory is complete & all credit is due to the gallantry of our officers & men.

G B McClellan
Maj Genl

Hon E M Stanton

ALS (telegram sent), McClellan Papers (C-13:64), Library of Congress. *OR*, Ser. 1, XI, Part 1, pp. 749–50.

1. Stanton telegraphed on this date: "Dispatches from General Halleck represent the rebel army from Corinth retreating in great disorder to Okolona. General Pope is pursuing and harassing them with 50,000 men. . . . " *OR*, Ser. 1, XI, Part 3, p. 209.

To the Army of the Potomac

SOLDIERS OF THE ARMY   Head-Quarters, Army of the Potomac,
OF THE POTOMAC!   *Camp near New Bridge, Va., June 2d, 1862.*

I have fulfilled at least a part of my promise to you: you are now face to face with the rebels, who are at bay in front of their Capital. The final and decisive battle is at hand. Unless you belie your past history, the result cannot be for a moment doubtful. If the troops who labored so patiently, and fought so gallantly at Yorktown, and who so bravely won the hard fights at Williamsburg, West Point, Hanover Court House and Fair Oaks, now prove worthy of their antecedents, the victory is surely ours. The events of every day prove your superiority; wherever you have met the enemy you have beaten him; wherever you have used the bayonet he has given way in panic and disorder. I ask of you now one last crowning effort. The enemy has staked his all on the issue of the coming battle. Let us meet and crush him here in the very centre of the rebellion.

Soldiers! I will be with you in this battle, and share its dangers with you. Our confidence in each other is now founded upon the past. Let us strike the blow which is to restore peace and union to this distracted land. Upon your valor, discipline and mutual confidence that result depends.

Geo. B. McClellan,
Major General Commanding

DP, McClellan Papers (D-12:74), Library of Congress. *OR*, Ser. 1, XI, Part 3, p. 210.

To Mary Ellen McClellan   [TELEGRAM]

Mrs. G B McClellan   McClellan's [June] 2 [1862]
Care N Shipman Hartford Conn   6.30 [P.M.]

Your two dispatches received. I said that none of your acquaintances killed & none that I know of wounded. Battle desperate & loss heavy but success complete. One more & we will have Richmond & I shall be there with Gods blessing this week. It is possible that yesterday's victory will open Richmond to us without further fighting. The result is very glorious for my gallant troops. I am quite well. Sleeve buttons not yet rec'd. Have not had time to write.

G B McClellan

Received copy (War Dept.), Records of the Office of the Secretary of War, RG 107 (M-504:66), National Archives.

To Mary Ellen McClellan

June 2 [1862] 8 pm. New Bridge

It has been impossible for me to write to you for the last two or three days. I was quite sick on Friday [May 30] & Saturday — on the last day rose from my bed & went to the field of battle — remained on horseback most of the time until Sunday evening. I came back perfectly worn out & exhausted — laid down at once & tho' I could not sleep much I got some rest. I think tonight will bring me quite up again — as I am not anxious.[1]

The Chickahominy is now falling & I hope we can complete the bridges tomorrow. I can do nothing more until that is accomplished. The enemy attacked on Saturday & Sunday with great ferocity & determination — their first attack alone was successful — Casey's Division broke & ran — losing most of their guns & their camp. As the other Divisions came up they checked the enemy & we gradually got the better of him — he was badly handled before night. On Sunday morning he renewed the attack & was everywhere repulsed in disorder & with heavy loss. We had regained all the ground lost & more last night — today we are considerably in advance of the field of battle. It is certain that we have gained a glorious victory. I only regret that the rascals were smart enough to attack when the condition of the Chickahominy was such that I could not throw over the rest of the troops to follow up the success — but the weather now seems settled & I hope the river will be low enough tomorrow to enable me to cross. I expect to fight another battle, but trust it will be a decisive one. I feel sure of success — so good is the spirit of my men & so great their ardor. But I am tired of the sickening sight of the battlefield, with its mangled corpses & poor suffering wounded! Victory has no charms for me when purchased at such cost. I shall be only too glad when all is over, & I can return where I best love to be. . . .

I think the Richmond question will be settled this week. . . .

Your Father is quite well — so are all the Staff. I don't think any of your friends were hurt in the battle — several colonels killed & some wounded.

AL copy, McClellan Papers (C-7:63), Library of Congress.

1. GBM was suffering from malaria.

To Edwin M. Stanton   [TELEGRAM]

Head Quarters, Army of the Potomac,
New Bridge June 3 6 pm 1862

Some firing today — nothing serious. Hard at work upon the bridges, removing wounded etc.

I expect at White House tonight six regiments ordered up from Fort Monroe.[1] These will at once be distributed among the old Brigades. The next leap will be the last one.

G B McClellan
Maj Genl Comdg

Hon E M Stanton
Secty of War   Washington

ALS (telegram sent), McClellan Papers (A-60:24), Library of Congress. OR, Ser. 1, XI, Part 3, p. 212.

1. On June 1 the Fort Monroe garrison was put under GBM's control. OR, Ser. 1, XI, Part 3, p. 207.

To Abraham Lincoln   [TELEGRAM]

Head Quarters, Army of the Potomac,
New Bridge June 4 [1862] 1 p.m.

Terrible rain storm during the night & morning — not yet cleared off. Chickahominy flooded, bridges in bad condition — are still hard at work at them. I have taken every possible step to insure the security of the Corps on the right bank, but I cannot reinforce them from here until my bridges are all safe as my force is too small to insure my right & rear should the enemy attack in that direction, as they may probably attempt. I have to be very cautious now. Our loss in the late battle will probably exceed (5000) five thousand. I have not yet full returns. On account of the effect it might have on our own men & the enemy I request that you will regard this information as confidential for a few days. I am satisfied that the loss of the enemy was very considerably greater — they were terribly punished.

I mention these facts now merely to show you that the Army of the Potomac has had serious work & that no child's play is before it. You must make your calculations on the supposition that I have been correct from the beginning in asserting that the serious opposition was to be here.

G B McClellan
Maj Genl Comdg

A Lincoln   President

ALS (telegram sent), McClellan Papers (A-61:24), Library of Congress. *OR*, Ser. 1, XI, Part 1, p. 45.

To Abraham Lincoln   [TELEGRAM]

Head Quarters, Army of the Potomac,
New Bridge June 5 1862 [4 P.M.]

May I again invite your Excellency's attention to the great importance of occupying Chattanooga & Dalton by our western forces. The evacuation of Corinth would appear to render this very easy — the importance of this move in force cannot be exaggerated.[1]

G B McClellan
Maj Genl Comdg

His Excellency A Lincoln
Presdt   Washington

ALS (telegram sent), McClellan Papers (C-13:64), Library of Congress. *OR*, Ser. 1, XI, Part 3, p. 215.

1. The president forwarded this dispatch to Halleck, who replied on June 7 that he was already advancing toward Chattanooga. *OR*, Ser. 1, X, Part 1, p. 670.

To Mary Ellen McClellan

[New Bridge] June 6th [1862] 10 pm.

... Have been as usual very quiet today — lying down almost all the time & leaving my tent scarcely at all. . . .

It has at last cleared up, & for some days I think. . . .

It is now quite certain that Joe Johnston was severely wounded last Saturday [May 31] — now said to be in the shoulder by a rifle ball — I think there is little doubt but that it is so. That places Smith G. W. in command.[1] I have drawn 9 rgts from Fort Monroe — the first use I made of the command given me of that place[2] — the last of them will be up tomorrow; these will go far towards filling our ranks. The losses in the late battle were almost 5500 — of course we have lost many by disease. I am promised either McCall's or King's Division in a very few days. If I hear tomorrow that they will surely be here in three or four days I will wait for them, as it would make the result certain & less bloody. I can't afford to have any more men killed than can be avoided. . . .

June 7 8.30 am.   . . . The sun is struggling very hard this morning with the clouds — thus far the latter have rather the better of him, but I hope the old fellow will persevere & beat them out in an hour or two. I presume the mystery of the two telegraphic messages has been cleared up before this. I said that *none* of your acquaintances were killed. The operator must have been unmanned by excitement, for my official dispatch was terribly bungled in many ways. One of the two similar dispatches must have been sent on the operator's own account. I think I sent you but two altogether that day. Did not that solution occur to you?

AL copy, McClellan Papers (C-7:63), Library of Congress.

1. G. W. Smith led the army for a matter of hours. Gen. Lee took command of the Army of Northern Virginia on June 1. 2. When the Department of Virginia was put under GBM on June 1, Gen. Dix replaced Gen. Wool at Fort Monroe.

To Edwin M. Stanton   [TELEGRAM]

Hon. E M Stanton
Secy War   McClellan's [June] 7 [1862] 1 pm

Your dispatch of twelve thirty pm today recd & I must confess that its contents have not only struck me with astonishment but have given me much pain.[1] The care of our sick & wounded has tasked the unremitted energies of the whole medical corps in this army as well as occupied a great share of my attention from other important duties & I feel conscious that everything has been done for their comfort that human efforts could accomplish. The White House of the rebel Gen Lee referred to is a small frame building of six rooms worth probably fifteen hundred dollars & the medical director states that it would not accommodate more than 30 patients. He has tents where the patients are comfortable & he has therefore never conceived it necessary to call for the use of the house as a hospital. As to the story about thirsty wounded suffering soldiers having to buy a glass of water its only foundation probably originated in the fact that some civilian who was too indolent to go for the water himself may have paid a negro for bringing it to him. The following extract from a dispatch just recd from Col R Ingalls[2] the chief Q M in charge at White House will give you some light upon this subject & perhaps satisfy you as to the motive of the individuals who make the urgent complaints in question. "No one here has ever had cause to suffer for water unless he was too drunk or sick to drink it. We have water in unnecessary abundance. The springs are numerous the water is very fine & no prohibition has ever been placed on the free & unlimited use of it. The author of any report to the contrary of this statement must be a simpleton or a malicious knave." I have given special directions to protect the property of the White House from any unnecessary injury or destruction because it was once the property of Gen Washington & I cannot believe that you will regard this a cause for rebuke or censure. I protect no house against use when they are needed for sick or wounded soldiers. Persons who endeavor to impose upon you such malicious & unfounded reports as those alluded to are not only enemies of this army but the cause in which we are now fighting.[3]

Geo B McClellan
Maj Gen

Received copy, Records of the Office of the Secretary of War, RG 107 (M-473 :102), National Archives.

1. Stanton telegraphed: "Very urgent complaints are being made from various quarters respecting the protection afforded to the Rebel General Lee's property, called the 'White House,' instead of using it as a hospital for the care of wounded soldiers. It is represented that they have even to purchase a glass of water.... " Stanton Papers, Library of Congress. 2. Lt. Col. Rufus Ingalls. 3. Stanton replied the next day: "I am glad that your explanation will enable me to correct this misapprehension. Neither you nor I can hope to correct all such stories, but so far as it is in my power I shall labor to do so." Stanton Papers. See GBM to Barlow, June 23, *infra.*

To Edwin M. Stanton [TELEGRAM]

Hon Edwin M. Stanton
Secy of War   McClellan's June 7th 4.40 pm 1862

In reply to your dispatch of two pm today[1] I have the honor to state that the Chickahominy River has risen so as to flood the entire bottoms to the depth of three & four feet. I am pushing forward the bridges in spite of this and the men are working night and day up to their waists in water to complete them. The whole face of the country is a perfect bog entirely impassable for artillery or even cavalry except directly in the narrow roads which renders any general movement either of this or the rebel army utterly out of the question at present until we have more favorable weather. I am glad to learn that you are pressing forward reinforcements so vigorously. I shall be in perfect readiness to move forward to take Richmond the moment that McCall reaches here & the ground will admit the passage of artillery. I have advanced my pickets about a mile today driving off the rebel pickets and securing a very advantageous position. The rebels have several batteries established com-

manding the debouches from two of our bridges & fire upon our working
parties continually but as yet they have killed but very few of our men.

                                        G B McClellan

Received copy, Records of the Office of the Secretary of War, RG 107 (M-473:102), National
Archives. *OR*, Ser. 1, XI, Part 1, p. 46.

1. Stanton telegraphed that McCall's division plus seven regiments would be sent as re-
inforcements. "Please state whether you will feel sufficiently strong for your final move-
ment when McCall reaches you." *OR*, Ser. 1, XI, Part 3, p. 219.

To Robert E. Lee

                                     Head Quarters Army of the Potomac
General.   [New Bridge]June 8th 1862

   I have the honor to acknowledge the receipt of Major General A. P.
Hill's letter of to day[1] and to express my thanks for the prompt com-
pliance with my request in regard to Lieut Perkins. I would beg to
apologize for failing to send Lieut Throneburg or Bohannon with this,
they were sent to Fort Monroe inadvertently. I have directed that one
be returned at once, and have no doubt that he can be delivered to you
by day after to-morrow morning. I fully agree that a general exchange
or cartel would be preferable and should it be agreeable to you, would
be very glad to designate a General or Staff Officer to meet one to be
selected by you for the purpose of endeavoring to arrange the cartel.
   It has reached me that circumstances have rendered it inconvenient
for you to supply our wounded with all the necessary stores; while thank-
ing you for the kind treatment which has been extended to wounded and
prisoners taken from the Army under my command since it entered the
Peninsula, may I ask permission to send such supplies as may be re-
quired by men in your possession, in such manner as may be designated
by you.
   A reply to this would reach me most conveniently by way of Meadow
Bridge, where the officer commanding my picket will be instructed to
receive it.[2]

                          I am Sir Very Respectfully Your Obt Servant
                              [George B. McClellan]
                              Maj General Comdg
To the Officer Commanding the Army of Northern Virginia[3]
Richmond, Va.

Copy, Records of U.S. Army Continental Commands, RG 393 (3964: Army of the Potomac),
National Archives. *OR*, Ser. 2, III, p. 663.

1. Gen. Hill's letter dealt with prisoner exchange. *OR*, Ser. 2, III, p. 662. 2. Lee replied
on June 11 that he had designated Brig. Gen. Howell Cobb to arrange for a general exchange
of prisoners, and added: "I am not aware that your wounded in our hospitals are suffering

for the want of medical stores, but can assure you that they will receive the same attention as our own." *OR*, Ser. 2, III, pp. 674–75. See GBM to Stanton, June 15, *infra*. 3. The following letter shows that GBM believed G. W. Smith commanded the Army of Northern Virginia.

To Mary Ellen McClellan

[New Bridge, June 9, 1862] Monday morning

... A large dose of Spaniards yesterday — Genl Prim[1] & staff arrived & are quartered on us — some seven in all — a rather inconvenient addition to the mess. On the other hand, however, they are very gentlemanly & a very nice set of people. Genl Prim speaks only French & Spanish — he is a dark-faced, black-haired, bright, young looking man of 45 — I like him much. His Chief of Staff — Genl Milans — is a perfect old trump who speaks English & looks for all the world like a French Marquis of the stage. His hair & beard iron gray — his moustache of the most approved pattern of the Spanish Cavaliers of old — a cane suspended to his button hole — red pants tucked in high boots — a loose green coat covered with silver embroidery — the funniest little hat imaginable — on the whole a most peculiar picture; such as I never saw before. They are delighted with what they have seen (I hear the funny little fellow's voice now — "Gd mornin Sir — 'Hope yr well") fully appreciate the great difficulties under which we have been laboring & will do much I think towards giving a just idea in Europe of the difficulties we have to contest against in this most singular of all campaigns....

I had a telegram from your friend McDowell last evening stating that he was ordered down here with his command & assuring me that he received the order with great satisfaction!![2] I have not replied to it, nor shall I — the animal probably sees that the tide is changing & that I am not entirely without friends in the world. The Secy & Presdt are also becoming quite amiable of late — I am afraid that I am a little cross to them & that I do not quite appreciate their sincerity & good feeling — "Timeo Danaos et dona ferentes." How glad I will be to get rid of the whole lot. I had another letter from our friend *A.P.H.* yesterday in reply to mine to Jo Johnston — so I am now confident that Jo is badly wounded. In my reply sent this morning I ignore Hill entirely & address mine to the "Comdg Genl etc." So G.W. will have to come out this time. I hope to arrange for a general exchange of prisoners & thus relieve our poor fellows who have been so long confined. I must do secesh the justice to say that they now treat our wounded & prisoners as well as they can....

AL copy, McClellan Papers (C-7:63), Library of Congress.

1. Gen. Juan Prim y Prats. 2. In his telegram of June 8 McDowell wrote: "In view of the remarks made with reference to my leaving you and my not joining you before by your

friends, and of something I have heard as coming from you on that subject, I wish to say that I go with the greatest satisfaction, and hope to arrive with my main body in time to be of service." *OR*, Ser. 1, XI, Part 3, pp. 220–21.

To Maria E. McClellan

My dear Maria   Camp near New Bridge June 9th 1862

I have time only to write a line or two to thank you for your kind letter of Wednesday. I am very glad to hear that you are all well and that John is so busy. Wistar,[1] who is still here, told me that John had been away from home for some days cutting off some unhappy man's leg. There have been only too many surgical cases among these poor fellows of mine of late, & I fear that there are to be a good many more before Richmond is reached. They have determined to give one more battle I am confident. Perhaps it is best that they should be made to suffer still more that the war may the sooner be over.

We are tolerably quiet here — waiting for the Chickahominy to become practicable & the ground to dry enough for artillery to pass over it. A little musketry firing & the occasional exchange of artillery shots relieve the monotony — some artillery firing is going on now as I write.

You are mistaken about Nelly & the baby holding levees in Hartford[2] — they are there to rest & are resting most quietly. I have Genl Prim & his staff on my hands just now — a good set, but it is rather a bore to take care of so many at such a time.

My breakfast is ready so I will stop. With love to all

Your affectionate brother
Geo B McClellan

Mrs J H B McC

ALS, McClellan Papers (B-11 :48), Library of Congress. Maria Eldredge McClellan, GBM's sister-in-law, was the wife of John H. B. McClellan.

1. Caspar Wistar, a family friend from Philadelphia. 2. Mrs. McClellan and daughter May were then staying with friends in Hartford, Conn.

To Mary Ellen McClellan

[New Bridge] June 10 [1862] 7 1/2 am.

It is again raining hard & has been for several hours! I feel almost discouraged — that is I would do so did I not feel that it must all be for the best, & that God has some just purpose in view through all this. It is certain that there has not been for years & years such a season — it does not come by chance. I am quite checked by it — first the Chicka- hominy is so swollen & the valley so covered with water that I cannot establish safe communication over it — then again the ground is so muddy that we cannot use our artillery — the guns sink up to their axle trees.

I regret all this extremely — but take comfort from the thought that God will not leave so great a struggle as this to mere chance — if he ever interferes with the destinies of men & nations this would seem to be a fit occasion for it.

Whenever I feel discouraged by adverse circumstances, I do my best to fall back on this great source of confidence & almost always find that it gives me strength to bear up against anything that may occur. I do not see how anyone can fill such a position as I do without being constantly forced to think of higher things & the Supreme Being. The great responsibility — the feeling of personal weakness & incompetency — of entire dependence on the will of God — the thousand circumstances entirely beyond our control that may defeat our best laid plans — the sight of poor human suffering — all these things *will* force the mind to seek rest above....

I feel quite well today — by far better than at any time before — I think that if I can stand the test of this rainy day all must be right. I will not go out while it rains if I can help it....

The Spaniards are still here, & I fear will remain some time unless this rain drives them off. Prim is very well, but it is a nuisance to be obliged to be polite when one's head is full of more important things....

Still raining very hard — I don't know what *will* become of us!

AL copy; copy, McClellan Papers (C-7:63/D-10:73), Library of Congress.

To Edwin M. Stanton [TELEGRAM]

[New Bridge] June 10 [1862] 3.30 pm

I have again information that Beauregard has arrived & that some of his troops are to follow him. No great reliance, perhaps none whatever, can be attached to this, but it is possible & ought to be their policy.

I am completely checked by the weather.

The roads and fields are literally impassable for Artillery, almost so for Infantry. The Chickahominy is in a dreadful state — we have another rain storm on our hands. I shall attack as soon as the weather & ground permit, but there will be a delay — the extent of which no one can foresee, for the season is altogether abnormal.

In view of these circumstances I present for your consideration the propriety of detaching largely from Halleck's Army to strengthen this, for it would seem that Halleck has now no large organized force in front of him, while we have.

If this cannot be done, or even in connection with it, allow me to suggest the movement of a heavy column from Dalton upon Atlanta. If but the one can be done it would better conform to military principles to strengthen this army; & even although the reinforcements might not arrive in season to take part in the attack upon Richmond the moral effect would be great, & they would furnish valuable assistance in ulterior movements.[1]

I wish it to be distinctly understood that whenever the weather permits I will attack with whatever force I may have, although a larger force would enable me to gain much more decisive results. I would be glad to have McCall's Infantry sent forward by water at once without waiting for his Artillery & Cavalry.

If Genl Prim returns via Washington please converse with him as to the condition of affairs here.

G B McClellan
Maj Genl Comdg

Hon E M Stanton
Secty of War

ALS (telegram sent), McClellan Papers (A-62:24), Library of Congress. *OR*, Ser. 1, XI, Part 1, pp. 46–47.

1. Stanton forwarded this proposal to Halleck, who replied on June 12 rejecting "the supposition that Beauregard or any considerable part of his force has gone to Richmond." He added, on June 16: "Should our forces be too much weakened here by detachment I have no doubt Beauregard would immediately march back and attack us." *OR*, Ser. 1, XVI, Part 2, pp. 8, 14, 26.

To Mary Ellen McClellan

June 11 [1862] New Bridge   am.

... Am very well today & the weather is good & will start in half an hour or so for the other side of the river — it threatens rain again, so that I do not believe I can make the entire tour — probably only on Smith & Sumner — do the rest tomorrow. Besides I do not care to ride too far today — as I have not been on horseback before since the day of the battle. I must be careful for it would be utter destruction to the army were I to be disabled so as not to be able to take command — Sumner would ruin things in about two days....

Burnside left yesterday, thinks there is a great deal of Union feeling in North Carolina & that our gaining possession of Richmond will at once bring N.C. back into the Union....

I half doubt whether there is much Union feeling south of N.C....

McCall's Division has commenced arriving — some of them reached the White House last night. This relieves me very much.

AL copy, McClellan Papers (C-7:63), Library of Congress.

To Mary Ellen McClellan

June 12 [1862] 8 am.   New Bridge

... Am about to break up this camp & move over the Chickahominy to Dr Trent's house — to its vicinity at least, for I abominate houses when in the field. In addition have to take a farewell ride some 7 or 8 miles up this side of the river to look again at the ground & give the last instructions to Porter & Franklin for their guidance on this side of the river. I took quite a ride yesterday — the first since the battle & got through with it nicely. I am about as nearly well now as I expect to be in this climate — bright & strong enough to fight a much better battle than any yet. I had a wonderful telegram from the Secy of War last night — he declares that he is & ever has been my best friend![1] By the way did you ever criticize Stanton, McDowell or any of that tribe in talking with Sturgis?[2] I don't believe you ever did say much to such people & denied it strongly. But do be very careful what you say — I apprehend Sturgis is a Jesuit. The fact is that you & I cannot be too careful how we talk — but perhaps it don't make much difference, because people put words in our mouths. I think we will have good weather now — it *seems* to have changed for the better.

AL copy, McClellan Papers (C-7:63), Library of Congress.

1. Stanton had telegraphed on June 11 : "Be assured, general, that there never has been a moment when my desire has been otherwise than to aid you with my whole heart, mind, and strength since the hour we first met; and whatever others may say for their own purposes, you have never had, and never can have, any one more truly your friend, or more anxious to support you...." *OR*, Ser. 1, XI, Part 1, p. 47. 2. Brig. Gen. Samuel E. Sturgis held a command in the Washington defenses.

To Edwin M. Stanton   [TELEGRAM]

Hon E M Stanton   Head-Quarters, Army of the Potomac,
Secy of War   [Camp Lincoln] June 12 1862

In your telegram respecting reinforcements you inform me that Genl McDowell with the residue of his command will proceed overland to join me before Richmond.[1] I beg leave to suggest that the destruction of the RR bridges by flood & fire cannot probably be remedied in under 4 weeks, that an attempt to employ wagon transportation must involve great delay and may be found very difficult of accomplishment. An extension of my right wing to meet him may involve serious hazard to my flank and my line of communications and may not suffice to rescue him from any peril in which a strong movement of the enemy may involve him. I would advise that his forces be sent by water. Even a portion thus sent would by reason of greater expedition and security and less complications of my movements probably be more servicable in the operations before Richmond. The roads throughout the region between the Rappahannock and the James can not be relied upon and may become execrable even should they be in their best condition. The junction of his force with the extension of my right flank can not be made without derangement of my plans and if my recent experience in moving troops be indicative of the difficulties incident to McDowell's march the exigencies of my present position will not admit of the delay. I have ordered back all the transports used in bringing McCall's Division, that they may be ready for service if you deem it best to employ water transportation. I have to day moved my Head Quarters across the Chickahominy to a central position so that I can readily reach any point of attack or advance. The enemy are massing their troops near our front, throwing up earthworks on all the approaches to Richmond and giving every indication of fight.

                                             Geo B. McClellan
                                             Maj Genl

Retained copy, McClellan Papers (A-62:25), Library of Congress. *OR*, Ser. 1, XI, Part 3, p. 225.

1. Stanton's telegram was dated June 11. *OR*, Ser. 1, XI, Part 1, p. 47.

To Edwin M. Stanton   [TELEGRAM]

Hon E. M. Stanton   Head-Quarters, Army of the Potomac,
Sec. of War   [Camp Lincoln] June 14, 11 a.m. 1862

A rebel force of Cavalry and Artillery variously estimated at from one to five thousand came around our right flank last evening, attacked and drove in a picket guard of two squadrons of Cavalry stationed at Old Church. Thence they proceeded to a landing three miles above White House where they burned two forage schooners and destroyed some wagons. Thence they struck the Rail Road at Tunstalls station — fired into a train of cars killing some five or six.

Then they met a force of Infantry which I sent down to meet them, where they ran off.

I have several Cavalry detachments out after them and hope to punish them. No damage has been done to the Rail Road.[1]

                                             Geo. B. McClellan
                                             Major General

Retained copy, McClellan Papers (A-63:25), Library of Congress. *OR*, Ser. 1, XI, Part 1, p. 1005.

1. Brig. Gen. J. E. B. Stuart's cavalry force completed its circuit of the Federal army on June 16.

To Edwin M. Stanton   [TELEGRAM]

Head-Quarters, Army of the Potomac,
Camp Lincoln June 14 [1862] midnight

All quiet in every direction. The stampede of last night has passed away.

Weather now very favorable. I hope two days more will make the ground practicable.

I shall advance as soon as the bridges are completed & the ground fit for artillery to move. At the same time I would be glad to have whatever troops can be sent to me — I can use several raw regiments to advantage.

It ought to be distinctly understood that McDowell & his troops are completely under my control. I received a telegram from him requesting that McCall's Division might be placed so as to join him immediately upon his arrival.[1] That request does not breathe the proper spirit — whatever troops come to me must be disposed of so as to do the most good. I do not feel that in such circumstances as those in which I am now placed Genl McD should wish the general interests to be sacrificed for the purpose of increasing his command. If I cannot fully control all his troops I want none of them, but would prefer to fight the battle with what I have & let others be responsible for the results. The Department lines should not be allowed to interfere with me, but Genl McD & all troops sent to me should be placed completely at my disposal to do with them as I think best. In no other way can they be of assistance to me.

[*Crossed out*: I doubt whether he will ever reach me by land & I shall not count upon his aid, but if he does come] I therefore request that I may have entire & full control of all the troops that are sent to me. The stake at issue is too vast to allow personal considerations to be entertained — you know that I have none.

G B McClellan
Maj Genl Comdg

Hon E M Stanton
Secty of War

The indications are from our balloon reconnaissances & from all other sources that the enemy are entrenching, daily increasing in force & determination to fight desperately.

McC

ALS (telegram sent), McClellan Papers (A-63:25), Library of Congress, *OR*, Ser. 1, XI, Part 1, pp. 47–48.

1. McDowell telegraphed on June 12: "My third division McCalls has embarked and is now on the way. Please do me the favor to so place it that it may be in position to join the others as they come down from Fredericksburg." McClellan Papers (A-62:25).

To Edwin M. Stanton   [TELEGRAM]

Hon E. M. Stanton   Head Quarters Army of the Potomac
Secy of War   [Camp Lincoln] June 15 7.40 pm. 1862

Another rain set in about 3 p.m. today and has continued up to the present time. This will retard our operations somewhat, as a little rain causes the ground in this section to become soft and boggy rendering it impossible to move Artillery except directly in the travelled roads. In this arm especially consists our great superiority over the enemy, and as we will have to cut out several roads through new ground for the Army to advance on, it is absolutely necessary that we should have some few days of dry weather to make the ground firm enough to sustain horses & guns.

Our bridges are progressing rapidly and we shall very soon be ready to strike the final blow.

Colonel Key has had an interesting interview with Howell Cobb today, the particulars of which I will explain to you by letter.[1] It proves among other things most conclusively that they will defend Richmond to the last extremity. The interview was arranged for the purpose of bringing about an exchange of prisoners, but in the course of the conversation other matters were introduced and discussed.

Six prisoners just captured from the 1st N. Carolina state troops say their Regt. arrived in Richmond a few days ago from Goldsborough with the 3rd N. Carolina, 30th Virginia, 44th & 49th Georgia troops.

I think it important in view of this to hurry on transportation to Burnside.

Geo. B. McClellan
Maj Genl

Retained copy, McClellan Papers (A-64:25), Library of Congress. *OR*, Ser. 1, XI, Part 3, pp. 229–30.

1. GBM forwarded Col. Key's report on June 17. His conversation with Gen. Cobb ranged into political affairs, and Key gave his impressions: "That the rebels are in great force at Richmond, and mean to fight a general battle in defense of it;... that there is little hope of reconstruction so long as the rebels have a large army in the field anywhere; that it may be found necessary in particular States, if not in all, to destroy the class which has created this rebellion, by destroying the institution which has created them." *OR*, Ser. 1, XI, Part 1, pp. 1052–56.

To Mary Ellen McClellan

June 15 [1862] 10.15 p.m. Camp Lincoln

...We have had several skirmishes — the rebels have attacked our pickets on several points, but were everywhere beaten back with the loss of several killed & respectable number of prisoners....

The worst interruption of all, was a "party" of ladies & gentlemen that Van Vliet had no more sense than to insist upon coming up here. Senator [Harris][1] & a lot of others. All of whom I was really glad to see, although this was no place for them. I am sorry to say that when I heard of their arrival, I *swore* a little *internally* & sent Russell[2] flying out of my tent, declaring that I would not see any of them. But soon afterwards Senator [Harris] came here & he was so kind & friendly that I was at once mollified. I talked to him some time & he went back to Van Vliet's tent. I then gave to Averell[3] my orders for a "surprise party" tomorrow, to repay Secesh for his raid of day before yesterday. Then went over to call on Mrs. ——— . Then I *was* in for it. I was presented to all the ladies, listened to Mrs. [Ricketts's][4] version of her trip to Richmond, & very rapidly beat a retreat, giving business as an excuse. Charles got up a lunch for the party, a rainstorm coming on in the meanwhile. When they were nearly through, I took Averell over & talked with them for a while. Then we adjourned to my tent, where I was *rather* victimized. The two dear old Mesdames were just as good & *fat* as they could be; can I say more? When they left, they asked me to give them sprigs from the bower in front of my tent, so I send you one too.

Of one thing you may rest assured — I will do all that is in my power to bring us together again. There is no happiness or contentedness for me when away from you. I fear that I do not yet fully appreciate our dear little baby, for she is always a secondary consideration. I do love her — bless her sweet little self! But I am free to say that she does not yet rival her Mother.

I do not think our rain of today will do much harm. The chances now are that I will make the first advance on Tuesday [June 17] or Wednesday. By that time I think the ground will be fit for the movements of artillery & that all our bridges will be completed. I think the rebels will make a desperate fight, but I feel sure that we will gain our point. Look on the maps I sent you a day or two ago & find "Old Tavern" on the road from New Bridge to Richmond — it is in that vicinity that the next battle will be fought. If we gain that the game is up for Secesh — I will then have them in the hollow of my hand. I think they see it in that light & that they are fully prepared to make a desperate resistance. I shall make the first battle mainly an artillery contest — I think I can bring some 200 guns to bear & sweep everything before us. As soon as I gain possession of the "Old Tavern" I will push them in upon Richmond & behind their works — then I will bring up my heavy guns — shell the city & carry it by assault. I speak very confidently but if you could see the faces of the troops as I ride among them you would share my confidence. They will do anything I tell them to do.

I could not help laughing when on the day of the last battle I was riding along in front of Keyes Corps, *with Keyes* (!) a man jumped out in an interval of the cheering & addressed me quite familiarly, saying "Hallo George — how are you? You are the only one of the whole crowd of Genls that is worth a ——." I won't fill up the last word, but will only say that the whole command shouted "that's so!"

... I think there is scarcely a man in this whole army who would not give his life for me & willingly do whatever I ask. I have tried them more than once & whenever I am near they never fail me. The next battle will doubtless be a very desperate one, but I think that I can so use our artillery as to make the loss of life on our side comparatively small. ...

AL copy; copy, McClellan Papers (C-7:63/D-10:72), Library of Congress.

1. In copying this paragraph, GBM's daughter left this name and others blank. Mrs. McClellan's father wrote her on this date that a party headed by New York Senator Ira Harris visited army headquarters, and Gen. Heintzelman also mentioned the party in his diary. Randolph B. Marcy to Mary Ellen McClellan, McClellan Papers (B-10:48); Samuel P. Heintzelman diary, June 15, 1862, Library of Congress. 2. Maj. W. W. Russell, of GBM's staff. 3. Col. William W. Averell, 3rd Pennsylvania cavalry. 4. Mrs. James B. Ricketts, the wife of an officer wounded and captured at First Bull Run, had nursed her husband during his imprisonment in Richmond.

To Edwin M. Stanton   [TELEGRAM]

Hon E M Stanton   Head-Quarters, Army of the Potomac,
Secy of War   Camp Lincoln June 15, 1862 11 pm.

In the battle of Fair Oaks the division of Gen Casey was broken in such manner as to show that its commander had failed to infuse proper morale into his troops. In the action he behaved with personal gallantry but he does not command the confidence of his soldiers. He is a most excellent tactician of infantry, having written a manual on the subject and would be very useful in the camp of instruction of Annapolis. I suggest that he be at once assigned to duty there; but in such manner not to convey reproach.[1]

G. B. McClellan
Maj Genl

Retained copy, McClellan Papers (A-64:25), Library of Congress.

1. Stanton replied on June 19 that new troops "will have to go into the field as fast as they can be raised so that there can be no occasion for the general's services in the way you propose." McClellan Papers (A-65:26). On June 23 Casey was assigned to command the supply base at White House, and later transferred to a training command.

To Abraham Lincoln   [TELEGRAM]

His Excellency Abraham Lincoln   Camp Lincoln June 18th 62

I have the honor to acknowledge the receipt of your dispatch of today.[1] Our army is well over the Chickahominy except the very considerable forces necessary to protect our flanks and communications. Our whole line of pickets in front runs within six miles of Richmond. The rebel line runs within musket range of ours. Each has heavy supports at hand. A general engagement may take place any hour. Any advance by us involves a battle more or less decisive. The enemy exhibit at every point a readiness to meet us. They certainly have great numbers and extensive works. If ten or fifteen thousand men have left Richmond to reinforce Jackson it illustrates their strength and confidence . After tomorrow we shall fight the rebel army as soon as Providence will permit. We shall await only a favorable condition of the earth and sky & the completion of some necessary preliminaries.

Geo. B. McClellan
Maj Genl Comdg

Retained copy, McClellan Papers (C-10:63), Library of Congress. *OR*, Ser. 1, XI, Part 3, p. 233.

1. In response to reports from GBM and elsewhere that 10,000 to 15,000 reinforcements were going to Jackson in the Shenandoah Valley, Lincoln wrote: "If this is true, it is as good as a re-inforcement to you of an equal force. I could better dispose of things if I could know about what day you can attack Richmond. . . . " *Collected Works of Lincoln*, V, p. 276.

To Ambrose E. Burnside [TELEGRAM]

General A. Burnside   Head-Quarters, Army of the Potomac,
New Berne N.C.   [Camp Lincoln] June 20 1862 12.30 pm

How many troops could you bring to White House and leave everything secure in your present position and what time would it require to get the disposable troops to Fort Monroe.

What is the earliest moment you can move with your present transportation on Goldsborough.

Answer at once.[1]

Geo. B. McClellan
Major General

Care of General J. A. Dix Fort Monroe to be sent forward without delay.

Geo B. McClellan
Maj. Genl.

Retained copy, McClellan Papers (A-66:26), Library of Congress. *OR*, Ser. 1, XI, Part 3, p. 237.

1. Burnside replied on June 23 that within five days he could land 7,000 men at Norfolk, or advance that many against Petersburg from the south, or in two and a half days move against Goldsboro, N.C., with 10,000 men. McClellan Papers (C-11:63).

To Abraham Lincoln [TELEGRAM]

Head Quarters, Army of the Potomac,
Camp Lincoln June 20 1862 2 pm

Your Excellency's dispatch of 11 am received also that of Genl Sigel.[1] I have no doubt that Jackson has been reinforced from here. There is reason to believe that Genl R S Ripley has recently joined Lee's Army with a Brigade or Division from Charleston. Troops have arrived recently from Goldsboro'.

There is not the slightest reason to suppose that the enemy intends evacuating Richmond; he is daily increasing his defenses.

I find him everywhere in force & every reconnaissance costs many lives. Yet I am obliged to feel my way foot by foot at whatever cost — so great are the difficulties of the country. By tomorrow night the defensive works covering our position on this side of the Chickahominy should be completed. I am forced to this by my inferiority in numbers so that I may bring the greatest possible numbers into action & secure the Army against the consequences of unforeseen disaster. I would be glad to have permission to lay before your Excellency by letter or telegram my views as to the present state of military affairs throughout the whole country. In the mean time I would be pleased to learn the dispositions as to numbers & position of the troops not under my command in Virginia and elsewhere.[2]

G B McClellan
Maj Genl Comdg

His Ex A Lincoln
Presdt

ALS (telegram sent), McClellan Papers (C-13:64), Library of Congress. *OR*, Ser. 1, XI, Part 1, p. 48.

1. Lincoln's telegram, and Gen. Sigel's of June 19 from the Shenandoah Valley, dealt with "the proposition that Jackson is being re-inforced from Richmond. This may be reality, and yet may only be contrivance for deception; and to determine which, is perplexing." *Collected Works of Lincoln*, V, pp. 277–78; *OR*, Ser. 1, XII, Part 3, p. 411. 2. The president replied on June 21 that he was concerned about security in sending such correspondence, and on June 22 GBM telegraphed that he would postpone the matter. *Collected Works of Lincoln*, V, p. 279; *OR*, Ser. 1, XI, Part 1, p. 48. See GBM to Lincoln, July 7, 1862, *infra*.

To Mary Ellen McClellan

[Camp Lincoln] June 22 [1862] Sunday 3 pm.

I had no letter from you this morning, & no telegram yesterday or today!! I have telegraphed you every day & fear the dispatches don't go well to Orange.[1] . . .

The only pleasant thing I look forward to, is our reunion. All that I care to live for is to be with you & our sweet child. It is too bad that I should lose so much of you both. . . .

I almost envy you the rest & quiet you must be now enjoying & am very anxious to have you tell me how the place looks; what the surroundings are, & what the house.

By an arrival from Washn today (Allen)[2] I learn that Stanton & Chase have fallen out; that McDowell has deserted his friend C & taken to S!! That Seward & Blair stand firmly by me — that Honest A has again fallen into the hands of my enemies & is no longer a cordial friend of mine! Chase is evidently desirous of coming over to my side! Alas poor country that should have such rulers. I tremble for my country when I think of these things, but still can trust that God in his infinite wisdom will not punish us as we deserve, but will in his own good time bring order out of chaos & restore peace to his unhappy country. His will be done — whatever it may be. I am as anxious as any human being can be to finish this war, yet when I see such insane folly behind me I feel that the final salvation of the country demands the utmost prudence on my part & that I must not run the slightest risk of disaster, for if anything happened to this army our cause would be lost. I feel too that I must not unnecessarily risk my life — for the fate of my army depends upon me & they all know it. . . .

I got up some heavy guns today & hope to give secesh a preliminary pounding tomorrow & to make one good step next day. The rascals are very strong & outnumber me very considerably — they are well intrenched also & have all the advantages of position — so I must be prudent — but I will yet succeed notwithstanding all they do & leave undone in Washington to prevent it. I would not have on my conscience what those men have for all the world. I am sorry to say that I shall lose the dear old Prince de Joinville in a few days — he is obliged to return to Europe. Genl Prim has sent me his photograph. . . .

It is quite hot this afternoon. . . .

It is almost time for our evening skirmish — secesh has been very quiet today — scarcely fired a shot. I am very glad of it as it enabled me to give my men a good quiet rest for Sunday. It is stated that GW[3] has again been afflicted with a paralytic stroke. . . .

AL copy; copy, McClellan Papers (C-7:63/D-10:72), Library of Congress.

1. Mrs. McClellan was staying with her uncle, Dr. Erastus E. Marcy, in North Orange, N.J. 2. Allan Pinkerton, employing the nom de guerre E. J. Allen. 3. Maj. Gen. G. W. Smith, CSA.

To Samuel L. M. Barlow

Head-Quarters, Army of the Potomac,
My dear Barlow   [Camp Lincoln] June 23 1862

I have only time to thank you for your kind letter of the 17th,[1] as well for the great kindness Mrs B & you have shown to my wife.

By a recent arrival from Washington I hear that Chase & Stanton have parted company, & that McDowell has attached himself to Stanton!

They have got themselves into a nice scrape with their White House business — I have written to Frank Blair requesting him to call for my letter to the Secty on the topic.[2]

Never was there a more groundless slander & never a malicious lie more thoroughly exposed than this will be when all is known about it. The worst of it is that Stanton knew the facts *before* the subject was agitated in Congress & did not choose to explain — my letter has incorporated in it what had passed between S & myself & will expose his treachery most completely!

We are making slow progress here — but I dare not risk this Army on which I feel the fate of the nation depends. I will succeed, but for the sake of the cause must make a sure thing of it.

Considerable skirmishing this afternoon — even as I write — must break off to look after it.

In great haste, & with my kindest regards to Mrs. Barlow
Sincerely your friend
Geo B. McClellan

S L M Barlow Esq
N.Y.

ALS, Barlow Papers, Huntington Library.

1. "Supposing ... that the final struggle is now close at hand," Barlow wrote, "I cannot refrain from telling you how hearty & unanimous the whole people are in your favor & if the War Dept. does its duty I am sure of your success. I was in Washington last week. Saw Blair. He is your friend. He said among other things, 'If Chase & the others don't let McClellan alone, they will make him president.' I told him that I thought no one had less political ambition than yourself." McClellan Papers (A-65:26), Library of Congress. 2. See GBM to Stanton, June 7, *supra*. GBM's letter to Francis P. Blair, Jr., has not been found, but his correspondence relating to the White House affair was laid before Congress on July 8.

To Mary Ellen McClellan

Hd Qtrs Trent's House June 23 [1862] 10 1/2 pm.

... You may be sure that no man in this army is so anxious as its General to finish the campaign — every poor fellow that is killed or wounded almost haunts me! My only consolation is that I have honestly done my best to save as many lives as possible & that many others might have done less towards it.

I have had a rather anxious day — the movements of the enemy being mysterious — but I have gained something, & am ready for any eventuality I think. I have a kind of presentiment that tomorrow will bring forth *something* — *what* I do not know — we will see when the time arrives. I expect to be able to take a decisive step in advance day after tomorrow, & if I succeed will gain a couple of miles towards Richmond. It now looks to me as if the operations would resolve themselves into a series of partial attacks, rather than a general battle.

[June] 24th 10 am. I was interrupted just here by some stampede telegrams that kept me up until 1 1/2 or 2 this morning — in the mean time a terrible storm came up, & blew this unhappy sheet into the mud & rain. I send it as it is however, as a slight specimen of the "sacred soil." Also because I am about starting out on a ride from which I am not likely to return before the mail leaves camp. Nothing of any interest this morning — all quiet — weather cloudy & may rain today again. If it rains hard I will come home early. I think nothing will be done today on either side of the river — so we will probably be quiet.

AL copy, McClellan Papers (C-7:63), Library of Congress.

To John Rodgers

[TELEGRAM]

Head Quarters, Army of the Potomac,
Camp Lincoln June 24 6 pm 1862

Dispatch received. If you can effectually destroy the bridge in question the sooner it is done the better.[1] They cannot replace a bridge of that length for many weeks & I am about to commence decisive measures. Circumstances force me to begin my attack at some distance from the James River — in a few days I hope to gain such a position as to enable me to place a force above Ball's & Drewry's Bluffs, so that we can remove the obstructions & place ourselves in communication with you so that you can cooperate in the final attack. In the mean time please keep some gun boats as near Drewry's Bluff as prudence will permit. Within the next two or three days I hope to be within range of Richmond.

By that time I hope to see you in person to arrange our movements. I will inform you fully how I progress.

G B McClellan
Maj Genl

Comdr Jno Rodgers
U.S. Steamer Galena off Jamestown

ALS (telegram sent), McClellan Papers (C-13:64), Library of Congress. *OR*, Ser. 1, XI, Part 3, p. 250.

1. Rodger's dispatch of this date described a plan to burn the Swift Creek bridge, on the railroad between Petersburg and Richmond. The attempt, on June 29, failed. *OR*, Ser. 1, XI, Part 3, p. 250; *NOR*, Ser. 1, VII, p. 524.

To Samuel P. Heintzelman   [TELEGRAM]

Head Quarters, Army of the Potomac,
Camp Lincoln 6.30 pm [June] 24th 1862

Dispatch of 6 pm received. If it is a possible thing take advantage of the weakness of the enemy & push your pickets at least to the edge of the next clearing. Please give your personal attention to this & arrange with Genl Sumner so that he may maintain constant connection.

I have been all over the right today & will open with heavy guns tomorrow. Tomorrow night I hope to gain possession of the Garnett field, & by another day of the Old Tavern & some ground in advance. It will be chiefly an Artillery & Engineering affair. Keep your command as fresh as possible, ready for another battle — I cannot afford to be without Heintzelman, Kearny & Hooker in the next effort. I have satisfactory communications from the gun boat fleet in James River.

The enemy have done an immense amount of work on our right but seem to be deceived as to our intentions. All looks well.

G B McClellan
Maj Genl

Genl S P Heintzelman
Comdg 3rd Corps

ALS (telegram sent), McClellan Papers (C-13:64), Library of Congress. *OR*, Ser. 1, XI, Part 3, pp. 250–51.

To Edwin M. Stanton   [TELEGRAM]

Head-Quarters, Army of the Potomac
[Camp Lincoln] June 24 12 pm 1862

A very peculiar case of desertion has just occurred from the enemy. The party states that he left Jackson, Whiting & Ewell[1] fifteen Brigades at Gordonsville on the 21st. That they were moving to Frederickshall & that it was intended to attack my rear on the 28th.

I would be glad to learn at your earliest convenience the most exact information you have as to the position and movements of Jackson as well as the sources from which your information is derived that I may better compare it with what I have.[2]

G B McClellan
Maj Genl

Hon E M Stanton
Secty of War

ALS (telegram sent), McClellan Papers (A-67:27), Library of Congress. *OR*, Ser. 1, XI, Part 1, p. 49.

1. Brig. Gen. W. H. C. Whiting and Maj. Gen. Richard S. Ewell commanded divisions under Jackson. 2. "We have no definite information as to the numbers or position of Jackson's force," Stanton telegraphed on June 25. After reviewing the conflicting intelligence, he concluded: "I think, therefore, that while the warning of the deserter to you may also be a blind, it could not safely be disregarded." *OR*, Ser. 1, XI, Part 1, p. 49.

To Edwin M. Stanton   [TELEGRAM]

Headquarters Army of the Potomac
Redoubt No 3 June 25 [1862] 3.15 pm

Enemy are making desperate resistance to advance of picket lines. Kearny & one half of Hooker's are where I want them. Have this moment reinforced Hooker's right with a Brigade & a couple of guns & hope in a few minutes to finish the work intended for to day. Our men are behaving splendidly — the enemy fighting well also. This is not a battle merely an affair of Heintzelman's Corps supported by Keyes. Thus far all goes well & we hold every foot we have gained. If we succeed in what we have undertaken it will be a very important advantage gained. Loss not large thus far. The fighting up to this time done by Hooker's division which has behaved as usual — that is most handsomely.[1] On our right Porter has silenced the enemy's batteries in his front.

G B McClellan
Maj Genl Comdg

Hon E M Stanton
Secty of War

ALS (telegram sent), McClellan Papers, New-York Historical Society. *OR*, Ser. 1, XI, Part 1, p. 50.

1. This action at Oak Grove was the first of the Seven Days' battles.

To Edwin M. Stanton   [TELEGRAM]

Camp Lincoln June 25 [1862] 6.15 pm

I have just returned from the field and find your dispatch in regard to Jackson.[1]

Several contrabands just in give information confirming supposition that Jackson's advance is at or near Hanover CH & that Beauregard arrived with strong reinforcements in Richmond yesterday. I incline to think that Jackson will attack my right & rear. The rebel force is stated at (200,000) two hundred thousand including Jackson & Beauregard. I shall have to contend against vastly superior odds if these reports be true. But this Army will do all in the power of men to hold their position & repulse any attack.

I regret my great inferiority in numbers but feel that I am in no way responsible for it as I have not failed to represent repeatedly the necessity of reinforcements, that this was the decisive point, & that all the available means of the Govt should be concentrated here. I will do all that a General can do with the splendid Army I have the honor to command & if it is destroyed by overwhelming numbers can at least die with it & share its fate.

But if the result of the action which will probably occur tomorrow or within a short time is a disaster the responsibility cannot be thrown on my shoulders — it must rest where it belongs.

Since I commenced this I have received additional intelligence confirming the supposition in regard to Jackson's movements & Beauregard's arrival. I shall probably be attacked tomorrow — & now go to the other side of the Chickahominy to arrange for the defense on that side.

I feel that there is no use in my again asking for reinforcements.[2]

G B McClellan
Maj Genl

Hon E M Stanton
Secty of War

ALS (telegram sent), McClellan Papers (A-68:27), Library of Congress. *OR*, Ser. 1, XI, Part 1, p. 51.

1. See GBM to Stanton, June 24, note 2, *supra*. 2. Lincoln replied on June 26 that this dispatch "suggesting the probability of your being overwhelmed by 200,000, and talking of where the responsibility will belong, pains me very much. I give you all I can, and act on the presumption that you will do the best you can with what you have, while you continue, ungenerously I think, to assume that I could give you more if I would. I have omitted and shall omit no opportunity to send you re-enforcements whenever I possibly can." *OR*, Ser. 1, XI, Part 3, p. 259.

To Ambrose E. Burnside   [TELEGRAM]

To Maj Gen A. E. Burnside

[Camp Lincoln] Head Qrs
June 25 [1862, 7 P.M.]

Reports from contrabands and deserters today make it probable that Jackson's forces are coming to Richmond and that a part of Beauregard's force have arrived at Richmond. You will please advance on Goldsborough with all your available forces, at the earliest practicable moment. I wish you to understand that every minute in this crisis is of great importance. You will therefore reach Goldsborough as soon as possible destroying all the RR communications in the direction of Richmond in your power. If possible destroy some of the bridges on the Raleigh & Gaston RR and threaten Raleigh.[1]

G. B. McClellan

Copy, Records of the Office of the Secretary of War, RG 107 (M-473:103), National Archives. *OR*, Ser. 1, XI, Part 3, pp. 252–53.

1. The Goldsboro operation was abandoned in favor of reinforcing the Army of the Potomac. See GBM to John A. Dix, June 28, *infra*.

To Randolph B. Marcy   [TELEGRAM]

Porter's Hd Qtrs June 25 [1862] 10 pm.

Urge Sumner & Heintzelman to cut as much timber as possible in front of their positions tonight & in the morning. Be sure to have the (8) eight inch howitzers all in position & well supplied with ammunition before morning. Also the four (4) Napoleon guns intended for the redoubts. Impress upon Sumner & especially Heintzelman that if an attack is made in force it must be awaited in the line of entrenchments — that the pickets are only to give warning & should be supported only sufficiently to prevent them from being driven in by a small force. If attacked by a large force they must at once fall back on the entrenchments, taking care to leave full play for the Artillery & as far as possible for the musketry as they retire. Sumner should occupy the rifle pits between Naglee's right & Hooker just before daylight by a sufficient force to hold against first attacks. The different parts of the line should be occupied so as to leave near one half the force disposable as reserves to strengthen the parts most vigorously attacked. I think that the mass of Birney's & Palmer's Brigades, as well as De Russy's two guns should at once be drawn behind the entrenchments if Heintzelman is confident that the enemy will attack in force in the morning — leaving merely the picket lines with rather more than the usual supports to hold the ground against any new attack by skirmishers & to observe the enemy.[1]

You cannot too strongly impress upon the Generals the fact that I wish to fight behind the lines if attacked in force, & that the force in front should be only sufficient to watch & resist heavy skirmishers.

Be sure that the timber is cut as much as possible tonight. Get a specific reply to this & be sure they understand it.

                                        Geo B McClellan
                                        Maj Genl Comdg

Genl R B Marcy
Chief of Staff

ALS (telegram sent), McClellan Papers (A-68:27), Library of Congress.

1. GBM had four army corps — those of Keyes, Heintzelman, Sumner, and Franklin — on the south, or Richmond, side of the Chickahominy, leaving only Porter's corps north of the river.

To Edwin M. Stanton   [TELEGRAM]

Porter's Hd Qtrs [June 25, 1862] 10.40 pm

The information I receive on this side tends to confirm impression that
Jackson will soon attack our right & rear. Every possible precaution is
being taken. If I had another good Division I could laugh at Jackson.
The task is difficult but this Army will do its best & will never disgrace
the country. Nothing but overwhelming forces can defeat us. Indications
are of attack on our front tomorrow. Have made all possible arrange-
ments.

G B McClellan
Maj Genl

Hon E M Stanton
Secty of War

ALS (telegram sent), McClellan Papers (A-68:27), Library of Congress. *OR*, Ser. 1, XI,
Part 3, p. 254.

To Stewart Van Vliet   [TELEGRAM]

Camp Lincoln June 25 [1862] 10.45 pm[1]

Please be sure to push up all the provisions, grain & ammunition you
can tonight & tomorrow.

We need much more ammunition for the (4 1/2) four & a half inch —
say (600) six hundred rounds each & as much for Parrott (30) thirty
pounders.

Leave nothing undone to accomplish this. Tell Kingsbury[2] to arrange
to have a good supply of assorted ammunition afloat on James River with
the provisions & forage.

G B McClellan
Maj Genl

Genl S Van Vliet
Chf Qtr Mr   Head Qtrs

ALS (telegram sent), McClellan Papers (A-68:27), Library of Congress.

1. This telegram was actually sent from Gen. Porter's headquarters north of the Chicka-
hominy River. 2. Col. Charles P. Kingsbury, chief of ordnance.

To Edwin M. Stanton   [TELEGRAM]

Head Quarters, Army of the Potomac,
Camp Lincoln June 26 — 12m 1862

I have just heard that our advanced cavalry pickets on left bank of
Chickahominy are being driven in — it is probably Jackson's advanced

guard. If this be true you may not hear from me for some days as my communications will probably be cut off. The case is perhaps a difficult one but I shall resort to desperate measures & will do my best to out manoeuvre & outwit & outfight the enemy. Do not believe reports of disaster & do not be discouraged if you learn that my communications are cut & even Yorktown in possession of the enemy. Hope for the best & I will not deceive the hopes you formerly placed in me.

G B McClellan
Maj Genl

Hon E M Stanton
Secty of War

ALS (telegram sent), McClellan Papers (C-13:64), Library of Congress. *OR*, Ser. 1, XI, Part 1, pp. 51–52.

To Mary Ellen McClellan

June 26 [1862] 2 pm. Trent's

If you knew how tired I am you would not blame me if I did not write, but I cannot rest contented until I do write, if only a few lines. I telegraphed you yesterday twice & today.

We had quite a little affair yesterday. I wished to advance our picket line & met with a good deal of opposition. We succeeded fully however & gained the point with but little loss. The enemy fought pretty hard but our men did better. I was out there all day taking a personal direction of affairs & remained until about 5 1/2 pm. when I returned to camp, & met on my way the news that Stonewall Jackson was on his way to attack my right & rear. I rode over to Porter's soon after I reached camp & returned about 2 1/2 am. At 3 I started off again & went to the front where an attack was expected by some — finding all quiet I rode all along the line & returned here. You may imagine that I am *rather* tired out. I think that Jackson is en route to take us in rear — have just received the positive information that Jackson is en route to take us in rear — you probably will not hear for some days but do not be at all worried. . . .

AL copy; copy, McClellan Papers (C-7:63/D-10:72), Library of Congress.

To Louis M. Goldsborough   [TELEGRAM]

Head-Quarters,
Department Army of Potomac

Flag Officer L. M. Goldsborough   [Camp Lincoln] June 26th 1862.

Dispatch received. I take it for granted that Commander Rodgers will execute the service you alluded to before he visits me. On my return from the field yesterday I saw your reply to Genl Van Vliet. I regret your completely misunderstanding of the meaning of Genl Van Vliet's telegram & cannot understand how you could possibly draw from it the inference you did. I did send copies to Secretaries of Navy & War with the request that orders may be given to you that will insure a prompt complyance with such reasonable requests as I may make. The case of the Provision Transports in James River is a matter of vital importance to the safety of this Army & you will please pardon me for saying that I do not think this is a time for searching for points of etiquette & that the tone of your dispatch surprises me exceedingly — it has ever been my endeavor to treat you with the utmost deference & politeness, but my situation is at present too serious to permit me to stand on trifles.[1] I again request that the request made in my name by Genl Van Vliet in regard to transports in James River may be complied with. It is a matter of vital importance & may involve the existence of this Army.

Very Respy

Geo B McClellan

Maj Genl Comdg

Received copy, Office of Naval Records and Library, RG 45 (M-625:86), National Archives. *NOR*, Ser. 1, VII, p. 510.

1. This contretemps grew out of Flag Officer Goldsborough's offense at the tone of a dispatch addressed to him by Quartermaster Van Vliet on June 23. While pledging his full cooperation with the army, Goldsborough wrote Secretary of the Navy Welles on June 27 that he hoped GBM might be enjoined on "the propriety of inculcating better official manners of addressing me as his equal in rank; and ... not permitting an officer under his command to address me as a subordinate and refuse to confer upon me the denomination given me by law." *NOR*, Ser. 1, VII, pp. 500, 511–12.

To Fitz John Porter   [TELEGRAM]

Camp Lincoln June 26 [1862] 3.15 pm

From all the information you give me it would seem best to hold your position at least until after dark.

I will hold everything in readiness here to move all available troops to your support when needed. We must save all baggage & guns. Keep me constantly informed & instruct your pickets etc to give you constant information. Let me know where Stoneman[1] is & in what direction he will retreat so that I may at once give the necessary orders to the troops at Tunstalls & White House. Give me your views in full & all you know as to the force of enemy now about to attack you. Tell me whether position of affairs is such that an attack on Old Tavern by Franklin would aid you.[2] Be prepared to throw everything over the Chickahominy if possible — better send your heavy baggage over as soon as possible. What is appearance of things near Mrs Prices' etc.

G B McClellan
Maj Genl Comdg

Genl F J Porter
Comdg 5th Corps

ALS (telegram sent), McClellan Papers (A-69:27), Library of Congress.

1. Gen. Stoneman commanded the cavalry screening Porter's position. 2. A position south of the Chickahominy in the Confederate lines defending Richmond.

To Mary Ellen McClellan   [TELEGRAM]

To Mrs. McClellan,   Camp Lincoln June 26 [1862]
North Orange New Jersey   4.30 pm

Dear Nell. I may not be able to telegraph or write to you for some days. There will be great stampedes but do not be alarmed. I think the enemy are making a great mistake, if so they will be terribly punished. There will be severe fighting in a day or two but you may be sure that your husband will not disgrace you and I am confident that God will smile upon my efforts & give our arms success. You will hear that we are cut off, annihilated etc. Do not believe it but trust that success will crown our efforts. I tell you this darling only to guard against the agony you would feel if you trusted the newspaper reports. I give you my word that I believe we will surely win & that the enemy is falling into a trap. I shall allow the enemy to cut off our communications in order to ensure success.

G. B. McC

Eckert: Send to her in cipher if cant send it some way privately & regard strictly confidential. Answer.[1]

Retained copy, McClellan Papers (C-10:63), Library of Congress.

1. Maj. Thomas T. Eckert, supervisor of military telegrams, replied that evening: "I will forward your message to Mrs. McClellan confidentially & from time to time send her such information as I know would receive your sanction. She shall not suffer for want of news in your temporary exile...." McClellan Papers (A-107:42).

To Edwin M. Stanton   [TELEGRAM]

Head Quarters, Army of the Potomac,
Porters Hd Qtrs June 26 1862 7.40 pm

A very heavy engagement in progress just in front of me. McCall & (2) two Brigades of Morell are fighting gallantly against superior numbers so far with marked success.[1] There is no longer any doubt as to the strength of attack on this (left) bank of Chickahominy. My men are behaving superbly. But you must not expect them to contest too long against great odds. The engagement is very serious & is just below Mechanicsville.[2] You may rely upon this Army doing all that men can do. I still keep communication with White House but it may be cut any moment & I cannot prevent it.

G B McClellan
Maj Genl

Hon E M Stanton

ALS (telegram sent), McClellan Papers (A-69:27), Library of Congress. *OR*, Ser. 1, XI, Part 3, p. 259.

1. Brig. Gens. George A. McCall and George W. Morell commanded two of Porter's divisions.
2. The fighting this day would be termed the Battle of Mechanicsville.

To Edwin M. Stanton   [TELEGRAM]

Hon E M Stanton
Sec of War   Porter's June 26 8 pm 1862

Engagement still continues with great vigor. The enemy have not gained a foot & McCall is doing splendidly. He is showing that his Division is equal to the veterans of the Army of Potomac. Rebel forces very large but our position good & our men as brave as can be. The stragglers are all to the front. Not one to the rear. Morell's men just as McCall's. Dispatch as to reinforcements this moment read.[1] I thank you for them. I am rejoiced that the troops in front of Washington are to be placed under one command. Keep at that & all will be well. I will answer for it that this Army will do all that the Country expects of it.

G B McClellan
Maj. Genl.

Retained copy, McClellan Papers (A-69:27), Library of Congress. *OR*, Ser. 1, XI, Part 3, p. 260.

1. Stanton's telegram of this date promised 5,000 reinforcements. "They will be followed by more, if needed. McDowell's, Banks', and Fremont's force will be consolidated as the Army of Virginia, and will operate promptly in your aid by land." *OR*, Ser. 1, XI, Part 1, p. 52.

To Mary Ellen McClellan [TELEGRAM]

Head Quarters, Army of the Potomac,
[Porter's Headquarters] June 26 8.15 pm. 1862

We have again whipped secesh badly. McCall & Morell are the heroes of the day. Stonewall Jackson is the victim this time.

G B McClellan
Maj Genl

Mrs. G B McClellan
Care Dr E E Marcy North Orange New Jersey

ALS (telegram sent), McClellan Papers (A-69:27), Library of Congress.

To Randolph B. Marcy [TELEGRAM]

Head Quarters, Army of the Potomac,
Porters 9 pm [June 26] 1862

We have completely gained the day — not lost a single foot of ground. McCall has done splendidly as well as Morell.

Tell our men on your side that they are put to their trumps & that with such men disaster is impossible.

Geo B McClellan

Genl R B Marcy
Chf Staff

ALS (telegram sent), McClellan Papers (A-69:27), Library of Congress.

To Edwin M. Stanton [TELEGRAM]

Head Quarters, Army of the Potomac,
Porter's Bivouac June 26 1862 9 pm

The firing has nearly ceased. I have nearly everything in the way of impediments on the other side of Chickahominy & hope to be ready for anything tomorrow. Please see that Goldsborough complies promptly with my requests. Victory of today complete & against great odds. I almost begin to think we are invincible.

G B McClellan
Maj Genl

Hon E M Stanton
Secty of War

ALS (telegram sent), McClellan Papers (A-69:27), Library of Congress. *OR*, Ser. 1, XI, Part 3, p. 260.

To Edwin M. Stanton   [TELEGRAM]

Head-Quarters, Army of the Potomac,
Camp Lincoln [June] 27 10 am 1862

The night passed quietly. During it we brought all wagons, heavy guns etc to this side and at day break drew in McCall's Division about three miles. This change of position was beautifully executed under a sharp fire with but little loss.

The troops on the other side are now well in hand & the whole Army so concentrated that it can take advantage of the first mistake made by the enemy.

White House as yet undisturbed. Success of yesterday complete.

G B McClellan
Maj Genl

Hon E M Stanton
Secty of War

ALS (telegram sent), McClellan Papers (A-70:28), Library of Congress. *OR*, Ser. 1, XI, Part 3, p. 264.

To Edwin M. Stanton   [TELEGRAM]

Camp Lincoln June 27 [1862] 12m

My change of position on other side just in time. Heavy attack now being made by Jackson & two other Divisions.[1] Expect attacks also on this side.

G B McClellan
Maj Genl

Hon E M Stanton
Secty of War

ALS (telegram sent), McClellan Papers (A-70:28), Library of Congress, *OR*, Ser. 1, XI, Part 3, p. 264.

1. The fighting on June 27 would be called the Battle of Gaines's Mill.

To Mary Ellen McClellan   [TELEGRAM]

Mrs. G B McClellan   [Camp Lincoln, June 27, 1862]
Care Dr E E Marcy North Orange NJ   1:15 pm

Dispatch rec'd. Heavy firing in all directions. So far we have repulsed them everywhere. I expect wire to be cut every moment. All well & very busy. Cannot write today.

G B McClellan

Received copy (War Dept.), Records of the Office of the Secretary of War, RG 107 (M-504:66), National Archives.

To Edwin M. Stanton [TELEGRAM]

Head-Quarters, Army of the Potomac,
[Camp Lincoln] June 27 1 pm 1862

Your dispatch of noon received. I thank you for it.

We are contending at several points against superior numbers. The enemy evince much desperation but as we have no choice but to win you may be sure that we will do all that can be expected. Thus far we have been successful but I think the most severe struggle is to come. The enemy neglects White House thus far & bestows his whole attention on us. If I am forced to concentrate between the Chickahominy & James I will at once endeavor to open communications with you. All reinforcements should for the present go to Fort Monroe to which point I will send orders. It is absolutely certain that Jackson, Ewell & Whiting are here. As this may be the last dispatch I send you for some time I will beg that you put some one General in command of the Shenandoah & of all the troops in front of Washington. For the sake of the country secure unity of action & bring the best men forward. Good bye & present my respects to the President.

G B McClellan
Maj Genl

Hon E M Stanton
Secty of War

ALS (telegram sent), McClellan Papers (A-70:28), Library of Congress, *OR,* Ser. 1, XI, Part 3, pp. 264–65.

To William B. Franklin [TELEGRAM]

Brig. Gen W B Franklin [Camp Lincoln] June 27th 1862

If you see a chance to go over the Duane bridge and take the enemy in flank please do it. I will support you with something.[1]

G B McClellan
Maj Genl

Retained copy, McClellan Papers (A-70:28), Library of Congress.

1. Franklin replied that crossing the Chickahominy for a flank attack was impossible, for he had destroyed the bridge when the enemy threatened to capture it. McClellan Papers (A-70:28).

To Fitz John Porter [TELEGRAM]

To Genl F J Porter Camp Lincoln [June 27, 1862] 3.25 pm

Slocum is now crossing Alexander's Bridge with his whole command. Enemy have commenced on Infantry attack on Smith's left.[1] I have ordered down Sumner & Heintzelmans reserves & you can count on the whole of Slocum. Go on as you have begun.

G B McClellan
Maj Genl

ALS (telegram sent), McClellan Papers (A-48:19), Library of Congress. *OR*, Ser. 1, XI, Part 1, p. 58.

1. Brig. Gen. Henry W. Slocum commanded a division in Franklin's corps. Franklin's other division, under Brig. Gen. William F. Smith, remained south of the Chickahominy.

To Fitz John Porter   [TELEGRAM]

To Brig Genl F J Porter   [Camp Lincoln] June 27th 1862

Gen Slocum's Division has gone over to support you. If the enemy are retiring and you are a chasseur, pitch in.[1]

G B McClellan
Maj Genl

Retained copy, McClellan Papers (A-70:28), Library of Congress.

1. This may have been sent in response to a report from Capt. George A. Custer that there was a pause in the attack on Porter and the enemy appeared to be retiring. GBM to Franklin, McClellan Papers (A-70:28).

To Fitz John Porter   [TELEGRAM]

General Fitz John Porter,
Commanding Fifth Corps: Camp Lincoln, June 27, 1862 — 4.30 p.m.

Your dispatch of 4.10 received.[1] Send word to all your troops that their general thanks them for their heroism, and says to them that he is now sure that nothing can resist them. Their conduct and your own has been magnificent, and another name is added to their banners. Give my regulars a good chance. I look upon to-day as decisive of the war. Try to drive the rascals and take some prisoners and guns. What more assistance do you require?

Ever yours
McClellan

OR, Ser. 1, XI, Part 3, p. 265.

1. Probably Porter's message that he had "just returned from the whole front and found everything most satisfactory.... Our men have behaved nobly and driven back the enemy many times, cheering them as they retired...." McClellan Papers (A-69:27), Library of Congress.

To Fitz John Porter   [TELEGRAM]

To Genl F J Porter   Camp Lincoln 5.30 pm [June 27] 1862

Hold your own.¹ Eight regts from Sumner move at once to your support. Probably a Brigade from Smith, & certainly one from Couch. You must beat them if I move the whole Army to do it & transfer all on this side.

G B McClellan
Maj Genl

ALS (telegram sent), McClellan Papers (A-69:27), Library of Congress.

1. About 5:00 P.M. Porter telegraphed: "I am pressed hard, very hard. About every Regiment I have has been in action," and added that without assistance "I am afraid I shall be driven from my position." McClellan Papers (A-69:27).

To Edwin M. Stanton   [TELEGRAM]

Camp Lincoln June 27 8 p.m. 1862

Have had a terrible contest — attacked by greatly superior numbers in all directions. On this side we still hold our own, though a very heavy fire is still kept up.

On the left bank of Chickahominy the odds have been immense. We hold our own very nearly. I may be forced to give up my position during the night, but will not if it is possible to avoid it. Had I (20,000) twenty thousand fresh & good troops we would be sure of a splendid victory tomorrow. My men have fought magnificently.

G B McClellan
Maj Genl

Hon E M Stanton
Secty of War

ALS (telegram sent), McClellan Papers (A-70:28), Library of Congress. *OR*, Ser. 1, XI, Part 3, p. 266.

To Mary Ellen McClellan   [TELEGRAM]

Mrs. McClellan   Camp Lincoln 8 pm June 27th [1862]

Have had a terrible fight against vastly superior numbers. Have generally held our own & we may thank God that the Army of the Potomac has not lost its honor. It is impossible as yet to tell what the result is. I am well but tired out. No sleep for two nights & none tonight. God bless you.

G. B. McC

Retained copy, McClellan Papers (C-10:63), Library of Congress.

To Samuel P. Heintzelman   [TELEGRAM]

To Brig Genl S P Heintzelman   [Camp Lincoln] June 27 1862

On the other side of the Chickahominy the day is lost. You must hold your position at all cost.

> G B McClellan
> Maj Genl Comdg

Retained copy, McClellan Papers (A-70:28), Library of Congress.

To Louis M. Goldsborough   [TELEGRAM]

Flag Officer Goldsborough   Head Quarters, Army of the Potomac,
Norfolk   [Camp Lincoln] June [27] 1862 10.30 pm

I desire you will send some light draft gun boats at once up the Chickahominy as far as possible, and also that you will forthwith instruct the gun boats on the James River to cover the left flank of this Army. I should be glad to have the gun boats proceed as far up the river as may be practicable, & hope they may get in as far as the vicinity of Newmarket.

We have met a severe repulse to day having been attacked by vastly superior numbers, and I am obliged to fall back between the Chickahominy and the James River.

I look to you to give me all the support you can, in covering my flanks as well as in giving protection to my supplies afloat in James River.[1]

> G. B. McClellan
> Maj Gen

Retained copy, McClellan Papers (A-71:28), Library of Congress. *OR*, Ser. 1, XI, Part 3, p. 267.

1. Goldsborough replied at 1:00 A.M. on June 28: "Without a moment's delay instructions shall be communicated to Commander Rodgers to comply immediately with all you desire." *OR*, Ser. 1, XI, Part 3, pp. 268–69.

To Edwin M. Stanton   [TELEGRAM]

Savage Station June 28 [1862] 12.20 am

I now know the full history of the day [June 27]. On this side of the river — the right bank — we repulsed several very strong attacks. On the left bank our men did all that men could do, all that soldiers could accomplish — but they were overwhelmed by vastly superior numbers even after I brought my last reserves into action. The loss on both sides is terrible — I believe it will prove to be the most desperate battle of the war. The sad remnants of my men behave as men — those battalions who fought most bravely & suffered most are still in the best order. My regulars were superb & I count upon what are left to turn another battle in company with their gallant comrades of the Volunteers. Had I (20,000) twenty thousand or even (10,000) ten thousand fresh troops to use tomorrow I could take Richmond, but I have not a man in reserve & shall be glad to cover my retreat & save the material & personnel of the Army.

If we have lost the day we have yet preserved our honor & no one need blush for the Army of the Potomac. I have lost this battle because my force was too small. I again repeat that I am not responsible for this & I say it with the earnestness of a General who feels in his heart the loss of every brave man who has been needlessly sacrificed today. I still hope to retrieve our fortunes, but to do this the Govt must view the matter in the same earnest light that I do — you must send me very large reinforcements, & send them at once.

I shall draw back to this side of the Chickahominy & think I can withdraw all our material. Please understand that in this battle we have lost nothing but men & those the best we have.

In addition to what I have already said I only wish to say to the Presdt that I think he is wrong, in regarding me as ungenerous when I said that my force was too weak.[1] I merely reiterated a truth which today has been too plainly proved. I should have gained this battle with (10,000) ten thousand fresh men. If at this instant I could dispose of (10,000) ten thousand fresh men I could gain the victory tomorrow.

I know that a few thousand men more would have changed this battle from a defeat to a victory — as it is the Govt must not & cannot hold me responsible for the result.

I feel too earnestly tonight — I have seen too many dead & wounded comrades to feel otherwise than that the Govt has not sustained this Army. If you do not do so now the game is lost.

If I save this Army now I tell you plainly that I owe no thanks to you or any other persons in Washington — you have done your best to sacrifice this Army.[2]

G B McClellan

Hon E M Stanton

ALS (telegram sent), McClellan Papers (A-71:28), Library of Congress. *OR*, Ser. 1, XI, Part 1, p. 61.

1. See GBM to Stanton, June 25, 6:15 P.M., note 2, *supra*. 2. Shocked by this concluding paragraph, Edward S. Sanford, head of the War Department's telegraphic office, had the deciphered telegram recopied without the offending sentence before delivering it to Stanton. David H. Bates, *Lincoln in the Telegraph Office* (New York, 1907), pp. 108–109. The president replied on this date: "Save your Army at all events. Will send re-inforcements as fast as we can.... I have not said you were ungenerous for saying you needed reinforcement. I thought you were ungenerous in assuming that I did not send them as fast as I could. I feel any misfortune to you and your Army quite as keenly as you feel it yourself. If you have had a drawn battle, or a repulse, it is the price we pay for the enemy not being in Washington. We protected Washington, and the enemy concentrated on you...." *Collected Works of Lincoln*, V, pp. 289–90.

To Mary Ellen McClellan   [TELEGRAM]

Mrs. McClellan   [Savage's Station] June 28 '62

Dear Nell. We are well tonight. I fear your uncle has been seriously hurt in the terrible battle of yesterday. They have outnumbered us every where but we have not lost our honor. The Army has acted magnificently. I thank my friends in Washn for our repulse. Clitz is badly wounded.[1]

Geo. B. McClellan

Retained copy, McClellan Papers (C-10:63), Library of Congress.

1. Maj. Henry B. Clitz, 12th U.S. Infantry.

To John A. Dix   [TELEGRAM]

Gen. J. A. Dix   Fort Monroe   [Savage's Station, June 28, 1862]

Please send a message to Gen. Burnside not to move on Goldsboro' but to have everything ready to move to Fort Monroe. Col. Ingalls Q.M. and Cap. Bell[1] Commissary will go to Fort Monroe. Please direct them to push up supplies to the gun boats on James River.

Geo. B. McClellan
Maj. Gen.

Copy, Fitz John Porter Papers, Library of Congress. Gen. Dix took command at Fort Monroe on June 3.

1. Capt. George Bell.

To John A. Dix

Head Quarters, Army of the Potomac,
In field June 29 1862, 2 o'clock PM

This will be sent by Genl Keyes who is on our left. Please send up to the front he occupies a large number of entrenching tools — viz axes, shovels & picks. Send up also whatever reinforcements arrive.

We have had desperate work & a most terrible battle, but I hope by tonight to have my line based on James River. Thus far I have saved all the heavy guns & hope to save all my wagons. I need all the reinforcements that can be sent. Pray take good care of Yorktown — that must be made perfectly secure at once. If necessary abandon Williamsburg & let the troops now there fall back on Yorktown. This army has behaved nobly. We are all worn out & tired to death but retain strength enough to take Richmond. May God forgive the men who have caused the loss this army has experienced.

It is now clear beyond a doubt that 20,000 more men would have given us a glorious victory. I for one can never forget nor forgive the selfish men who have caused the lives of so many gallant men to be sacrificed. I have at least one proud consolation & that is that the Army of the Potomac has preserved its honor. We may not yet be safe & the whole of this army may be sacrificed — but I have at least the satisfaction of a clear conscience.

If we get through this it will be better for you to keep this to yourself as confidential — if I lose my life make such use of it as you deem best.

> Ever your friend,
> McClellan
> Maj Genl

Genl J A Dix

ALS, Dix Papers, Rare Book and Manuscript Library, Columbia University.

To Mary Ellen McClellan

Head Quarters, Army of the Potomac
My own dear Nelly   In the field June 29 [1862] 3 pm.

I send you only this line to say that I still think God is with us. We have fought a terrible battle against overwhelming numbers. We held our own & history will know that I have done all that man can do. Your uncle is killed.[1] I fear my telegraph about that has not reached you.

Please break the news to Frank & Maria as gently as you can & say to them that you & I will stand in the place of their father & husband. Poor fellow, he died gallantly & like a true soldier. I feel now that I will still retrieve our fortunes & that God will smile upon me. We will trust him.

> Your loving husband,
> Geo

ALS, McClellan Papers (B-11:48), Library of Congress.

1. Maj. Nathan B. Rossell, U.S. 3rd Infantry.

To Randolph B. Marcy

June 30, 1862
Haxall's house Turkey Island[1]

Please bring Hd Qrs down here. The wagons have been down towards Harrison's bar — 6 miles below here. Navy men say we must occupy a point below City Pt in order to enable us to use transports. Let all the Engineers & Topo Engrs go to work to examine the point on which we must take up our new position. The probability is we must take up a new line parallel to that we now hold and come down the River below City Point. Send back to Smith and ascertain how much more of the train is yet to move. Also ascertain what roads exist leading from our present position e.g. from White Oak bridge to Long Bridge & Jones Bridge.

G B McClellan

Maj Genl

ALS, McClellan Papers (A-71:28), Library of Congress.

1. On the James River, behind Malvern Hill.

To Edwin M. Stanton   [TELEGRAM]

Hon Edwin M. Stanton   Turkey Bridge June 30th [1862] 7 pm[1]

Another day of desperate fighting.[2] We are hard pressed by superior numbers. I fear I shall be forced to abandon my material to save my men under cover of the Gun Boats. You must send us very large reinforcements by way of Fort Monroe and they must come very promptly. My Army has behaved superbly and have done all that men could do. If none of us escape we shall at least have done honor to the country. I shall do my best to save the Army. Send more Gun Boats.[3]

G. B. McClellan

Maj Genl Commanding

Received copy, Lincoln Papers, Library of Congress. OR, Ser. 1, XI, Part 3, p. 280.

1. Telegrams from this period were delivered by navy vessels for sending over the Fort Monroe line. 2. The fighting on June 30 took place at Glendale. 3. President Lincoln replied on July 1: "It is impossible to re-inforce you for your present emergency. If we had a million of men we could not get them to you in time. . . . Maintain your ground if you can; but save the Army at all events, even if you fall back to Fortress-Monroe. We still have strength enough in the country, and will bring it out." Collected Works of Lincoln, V, p. 298.

To Mary Ellen McClellan   [TELEGRAM]

Headquarters Army of the Potomac

Turkey Bridge 7 pm. June 30 [1862]

I am well but worn out — no sleep for many days. We have been fighting for many days & are still at it. I still hope to save the army.

None of our especial friends lost except your poor uncle who was killed on Friday [June 27] in the battle of Gaines Mill. We have fought every day for five days. Good bye dear Nell & God bless you.

G B. McClellan

Maj Genl

Mrs G B McClellan

Care Dr E E Marcy

South Orange New Jersey

ALS (telegram sent), McClellan Papers (B-11:48), Library of Congress.

To Lorenzo Thomas [TELEGRAM]

Turkey Island July 1st [1862] 2.40
L. Thomas, Adjt Genl Tuesday morning[1]

Another desperate combat today [June 30]. Our reinforcements repulsed the enemy. I was sending orders to renew the combat tomorrow [July 1], fearing the consequences of further retreat in the exhausted condition of the reinforcements, & being as willing to stake the last chance of battle in that position as any other under the circumstances, when I learned that the right had fallen back, after dark, & that the centre was following. I have taken steps to adopt a new line, the left resting on Turkey Island, & thence along a ridge parallel to James River as far as I have the force to hold it. Rodgers will do all that can be done to cover my flanks. I will probably be obliged to change the line in a few days, when I have rested the men, for one lower down & extending from the Chickahominy to the James River. If it is the intention of the Government to reinforce me largely, it should be done promptly, and in mass. I need fifty thousand *50,000* more men, and with them I will retrieve our fortunes. More would be well, but that number sent at once, will, I think enable me to assume the offensive. I cannot too strongly urge the necessity of prompt action in this matter. Even a few thousand fresh men within the next twenty four or forty eight hours, will do much towards relieving & encouraging this wearied army, which has been engaged in constant combat for the last five or six days. I must apologize for the incoherency of this letter. I am exhausted by want of sleep and constant anxiety for many days.[2]

Very Respcty Yours
Geo B McClellan
Maj Genl

Received copy, Records of the Office of the Secretary of War, RG 107 (M-473 :50), National Archives. *OR,* Ser. 1, XI, Part 3, p. 281.

1. This dispatch was written on Malvern Hill about midnight on June 30, and later marked for sending from army headquarters on the James. 2. On July 2 Lincoln replied, in part: "Allow me to reason with you a moment. When you ask for fifty thousand men to be promptly sent you, you surely labor under some gross mistake of fact.... All of Fremont in the valley, all of Banks, all of McDowell, not with you, and all in Washington, taken together do not exceed, if they reach sixty thousand.... Thus, the idea of sending you fifty thousand, or any other considerable force promptly, is simply absurd.... If you think you are not strong enough to take Richmond just now, I do not ask you to try just now. Save the Army, material and personal; and I will strengthen it for the offensive again, as fast as I can." *Collected Works of Lincoln,* V, p. 301.

To Mary Ellen McClellan

July 1 [1862] Haxall's Plantation

... The whole army is here — worn out & war worn — after a week of daily battles. I have still very great confidence in them & they in me — the dear fellows cheer me as of old as they march to certain death & I feel prouder of them than ever.

I am completely exhausted — no sleep for days — my mind almost worn out — yet I *must* go through it. I still trust that God will give me success & I cheerfully entrust to his will. . . .

AL copy, McClellan Papers (C-7:63), Library of Congress.

To Lorenzo Thomas   [TELEGRAM]

Brig Genl L Thomas
Adjt Genl USA   Hd Qtrs Army of Potomac
Genl   Haxall's Plantation July 1/62

My whole army is here with all its guns & material. The battle of yesterday was very severe — but the enemy were repulsed & severely punished. After dark the troops retired to this position. My men are completely exhausted & I dread the result if we are attacked today by fresh troops. If possible I shall retire tonight to Harrison's Bar where the gun boats can render more aid in covering our positions. Permit me to urge that not an hour should be lost in sending me fresh troops. More gun boats are much needed. I hope that the enemy was so severely handled yesterday as to render him careful in his movements today — I now pray for time. My men have proved themselves the equals of any troops in the world — but they are worn out. Our losses have been very great. I doubt whether more severe battles have ever been fought — we have failed to win only because overpowered by superior numbers.

Very truly yours
Geo B McClellan
Maj Genl

ALS, James S. Schoff Collection, William L. Clements Library, University of Michigan. *OR*, Ser. 1, XI, Part 3, p. 282.

To John A. Dix

Genl J A Dix
Comdg at Fort Monroe   Hd Qtrs Army Potomac
My dear General   Haxhall's Plantation July 1/62

Will you do me the favor to urge forward with the utmost rapidity whatever reinforcements arrive for this Army — we need them much, &

the arrival of even a thousand fresh men would do much towards reviving the worn out men under my command. They have fought every day for a week — are exhausted by want of food & sleep — & long marches.

Urge Casey & all others who command reinforcements to bring them up to Harrison's Bar at once.

My whole command is here — we have preserved our material & guns — but my men are in no condition to fight without 24 hours rest — I pray that the enemy may not be in condition to disturb us today. If left quiet I will move tonight to Harrison's Bar where the gun boats can render more efficient aid.

> Very truly your friend
> Geo B McClellan
> Maj Genl

ALS, Dix Papers, Rare Book and Manuscript Library, Columbia University.

To Abraham Lincoln [TELEGRAM]

Berkeley, Harrison's Bar
Hon A Lincoln President US   July 2nd [1862] 5.30 pm

I have succeeded in getting this Army to this place on the banks of the James River. I have lost but one gun which had to be abandoned last night because it broke down. An hour and a half ago the rear of the wagon train was within a mile of Camp and only one wagon abandoned. As usual we had a severe battle yesterday and beat the Enemy badly, the men fighting even better than before.[1] We fell back to this position during the night and morning. Officers and men thoroughly worn out by fighting every day and working every night for a week. They are in good spirits and after a little rest will fight better than ever. If not attacked during this day I will have the men ready to repulse the Enemy tomorrow. General Ferry is here.[2] Our losses have been very heavy for we have fought every day since last Tuesday. I have not yielded an inch of ground unnecessarily but have retired to prevent the superior force of the Enemy from cutting me off — and to take a different base of operations.

I thank you for the reinforcements. Every thousand men you send at once will help me much.[3]

> G B McClellan
> Maj Genl

Received copy, Lincoln Papers, Library of Congress. *OR*, Ser. 1, XI, Part 3, pp. 287–88.

1. The Battle of Malvern Hill. 2. Brig. Gen. Orris S. Ferry brought 5,000 reinforcements from Alexandria, the vanguard of Gen. Shields's division from the Shenandoah Valley. 3. Lincoln replied on July 3: "I am satisfied that yourself, officers and men have done the best you could. All accounts say better fighting was never done. Ten thousand thanks for

it.... We hope you will have help from him [Burnside] soon. To day we have ordered Gen. Hunter to send you all he can spare. At last advices Halleck thinks he can not send reinforcements, without endangering all he has gained." *Collected Works of Lincoln*, V, p. 303.

To Mary Ellen McClellan

July 2 [1862] 11 pm. Steamer Ariel

... I will now take a few moments from the rest which I really need & write at least a few words....

We have had a terrible time. On Wednesday [June 25] the serious work commenced. I commenced driving the enemy on our left & by hard fighting gained my point. Before that affair was over I received news that Jackson was probably about to attack my right. I galloped back to camp, took a fresh horse & went over to Porter's camp where I remained all night making the best arrangements I could, & returned about daybreak to look out for the left. On Thursday afternoon Jackson began his attack on McCall, who was supported by Porter. Jackson being repulsed, I went over there in the afternoon & remained until 2 or 3 am. I was satisfied that Jackson would have force enough next morning to turn Porter's right, so I removed all the wagons, heavy guns etc during the night & caused Porter to fall back to a point nearer the force on the other side of the Chickahominy. This was most handsomely effected — all our material being saved. The next day Porter was attacked in his new position by the whole force of Jackson, Longstreet, Ewell, Hill & Whiting. I sent what supports I could — but was at the same time attacked on my own front & could only spare 7 Brigades. With these we held our own at all points after most desperate fighting. It was on this day that your poor uncle was gallantly leading his rgt — he was struck in the breast & died in a few hours. Clitz fell that day also.

John Reynolds[1] was taken prisoner. I was forced that night to withdraw Porter's force to my side of the Chickahominy & therefore to make a very dangerous & difficult movement to reach the James River. I *must* say good night now, for I am very tired, & may require all my energies tomorrow.

AL copy, McClellan Papers (C-7:63), Library of Congress.

1. Brig. Gen. John F. Reynolds, a brigade commander in McCall's division.

SIX

HARRISON'S LANDING
JULY 3–AUGUST 23, 1862

DURING THE seven weeks that followed the Army of the Potomac's arrival at Harrison's Landing, the Federal war effort in the East remained stalled on dead center. These were weeks of waiting and frustration for McClellan. He spent his time trying to restore the morale and strength of his army and debating with the government the proper strategy for pressing the war. In numerous private letters — thirty-four of the seventy-seven pieces of correspondence in this section — he excused the failure of his Peninsula campaign and, in increasingly vitriolic terms, laid blame for the failure on the administration in Washington.

Since reducing McClellan to the command of only the Army of the Potomac, President Lincoln and Secretary of War Stanton had attempted to manage the war without a general-in-chief. In the wake of the defeat before Richmond they found themselves in need of professional military advice, and on July 11 Lincoln named Henry Halleck to be general-in-chief. When he assumed the position on July 23, Halleck found a situation he regarded as highly dangerous.

General John Pope's Army of Virginia, newly assembled from the various forces that fought unsuccessfully against Stonewall Jackson in the Shenandoah Valley earlier in the year, was posted in northern Virginia with responsibility for guarding Washington. McClellan's army on the James, some twenty-five miles from Richmond, was well beyond supporting distance of Pope. Between them was Lee's Army of Northern Virginia, its strength appraised by McClellan at 200,000 men. Foreseeing that with a force that great Lee could strike at first one and then the other of the two widely separated Federal armies, Halleck ordered McClellan to evacuate the Peninsula and combine his army with Pope's. A primary reason for his decision was McClellan's letter to him of July 26, which in its demand for 50,000 to 55,000 reinforcements more than doubled the number McClellan had agreed at their Harrison's Landing meeting would meet his needs.

In his anger and disgust at the situation, General McClellan expressed his views of men and events with more candor and force than at probably any other time during the war. His famous Harrison's Landing letter to Lincoln (July 7) gave an exposition of his political stance on war issues that was outspoken enough to become a widely distributed campaign document during his 1864 presidential bid. Letters to Samuel Barlow, the New York Democratic leader, were unsparing in their attacks on the Lincoln administration. Letters to his wife were filled with equally unsparing opinions of Secretary Stanton and of Generals Pope and Halleck.

A recurring theme in the letters to Mrs. McClellan that summer was his frequent musing on the will of God. To George McClellan, all fortune, whether ill or good, was an expression of God's will. His reverses on the battlefield and the slurs he suffered at the hands of his enemies on the home front must have, he believed, some ultimately wise purpose, and it led him to conclude (July 10), "If I had succeeded in taking Richmond now the fanatics of the North might have been too powerful & reunion impossible. However that may be I am sure that it is all for the best." He did admit (August 22) that with so many contrary events taking place, "it is often difficult to understand the ways of Providence. . . ."

The pace at which the Army of the Potomac evacuated the Peninsula would become a matter of heated controversy. The underlying but unstated element in the correspondence between McClellan and Halleck on the subject is the differing perspectives of the two men. Halleck, expecting an attack on Pope at any moment, wanted an immediate and steady flow of reinforcements from the Army of the Potomac. McClellan, expecting the Rebels' attack to fall on him if he made the least slip during his retreat down the Peninsula, hoarded his forces for defense throughout his preparations. He then withdrew virtually the entire army from Harrison's Landing in one movement, with consequent delays in shipping the troops northward. It was yet one more result of his belief in overwhelming Confederate numbers.

To Edwin M. Stanton

Hon E M Stanton
Secty of War
Sir:

Head Quarters Army of Potomac
Harrison's Bar July 3 1862

In order to ensure a perfect understanding of the exact condition of this Army I have directed my Chief of Staff, Genl R B Marcy, to repair to Washington & give you full explanations of the events of last few weeks.

A simple summary is that this Army has fought every day for a week against superior numbers, holding its own, at least, often repulsing the enemy by day, then retiring at night. Our light & heavy guns are saved, with the exception of one; all the wagons are now within the line of pickets — & I hope will all be saved. The Army is thoroughly worn out & requires rest & very heavy reinforcements.

Our losses have been very great — for the fighting has been desperate, & officers and men have behaved heroically.

I am in hopes that the enemy is as completely worn out as we are; he was certainly very severely punished in the last battle; the roads are now very bad — for these reasons I hope that we shall [have] enough breathing space to reorganize & rest the men, & get them into position before the enemy can attack again. I have ordered Burnside to bring up all his available force, & leave to your judgment the question of evacuating Newbern & its dependencies so as to bring every available man to reinforce this Army. It is of course impossible to estimate as yet our losses — but I doubt whether there are today more than 50,000 men with their colors.

To accomplish the great task of capturing Richmond & putting an end to this rebellion reinforcements should be sent to me rather much over than much less than 100,000 men.

I beg that you will be fully impressed by the magnitude of the crisis in which we are placed — we require action on a gigantic scale — one commensurate with the view I expressed in a memorandum to the Presdt submitted early last August[1] — when first ordered to command the Army of the Potomac. The safety of the country & the preservation of its honor demand the utmost energy & intelligence.[2]

I am very respectfully your obdt svt
Geo B McClellan
Maj Genl Comdg

ALS, Houghton Library, Harvard University. *OR*, Ser. 1, XI, Part 3, pp. 291–92.

1. GBM to Lincoln, Aug. 2, 1861, *supra*. 2. The president wrote GBM on July 4: "I understand your position as stated in your letter, and by Gen. Marcy. To reinforce you so as to enable you to resume the offensive within a month, or even six weeks, is impossible. . . . Under these circumstances the defensive, for the present, must be your only care.

Save the Army — first, where you are, if you *can;* and secondly, by removal, if you must. . . . P.S.
If, at any time, you feel able to take the offensive, you are not restrained from doing so."
Collected Works of Lincoln, V, pp. 305–306.

To Randolph B. Marcy   [TELEGRAM]

Head-Quarters Berkeley July 4 62

After I left you I went at once to the front & found chaos. I rode in
advance of the troops halted everything — selected the positions for my-
self. Moved Smith at double quick to seize the key point & rapidly got
the troops in position. The positions are now occupied by three Corps,
two in reserve — the ground is in advance of Barnard's line & is partly
on the dangerous hills beyond Herring Creek. I am now ready to fight.
In twenty hours more shall be secure. Troops in splendid spirits. All now
goes well. Had a long telegram from the Presdt[1] which quite discourages
me as it shows a fatal want of appreciation of the glorious achievements
of this Army, & of the circumstances of the case, as well as of the causes
which led to it. I will save this Army & lead it to victory in spite of all
enemies in all directions.

G B. McClellan

Brig Genl R B Marcy Washington
Care Stager or Eckert[2]

ALS (telegram sent), McClellan Papers (A-72:29), Library of Congress.

1. See GBM to Lorenzo Thomas, July 1, 1862, note 2, *supra,* 2. Anson Stager and Thomas
T. Eckert, of the military telegraph office.

To Mary Ellen McClellan

July 4 [1862] Berkeley's

. . . You will understand before this reaches you the glorious yet fearful
events which have prevented me from writing. . . .

We have fine weather today, which is drying the ground rapidly. I was
quite stampeded yesterday just before your Father left — a report came
to me that the enemy were advancing in overwhelming numbers, & that
none of my orders for placing the troops in position & reorganizing them
had been carried out. I at once rode through the troops, clear in front
of them — to let them see there was no danger — they began to cheer as
usual, & called out that they were all right & would fall to the last man
"for little Mac"! I saw at once where the trouble was — halted all the
commands — looked at the ground, & made up my mind what the true
position was — started Smith at a double quick to seize the key point,
followed by a Battery of Horse Artillery at a gallop — they went up
most beautifully — opened on the enemy, drove him off after 18 rounds
& finally held the place. I pushed Slocum's Divn up in support — hurried

off Heintzelman's Corps to take its position on Franklin's left, supported by Keyes still further to the left, & came back to camp a little before dark with a light heart for the first time in many days. I am ready for an attack now — give me 24 hours even & I will defy all Secessia — if they will let my men rest 3 days I will begin to press them. The movement has been a magnificent one — I have saved all our material, have fought every day for a week & marched every night.

You can't tell how nervous I became — everything seemed the opening of artillery, & I had no rest, no peace except when in front with my men. The duties of my position are such as often to make it necessary for me to remain in the rear — it is an awful thing.

I believe now we are all right. I have reinstituted the playing of bands, beating the calls etc by way of keeping the men in good spirits, & have ordered the national salutes to be fired today at noon from the camp of each corps. I have some more official letters to write, so I must close this & must soon start to ride around the lines.

AL copy, McClellan Papers (C-7:63), Library of Congress.

To John A. Dix

Head Qrs dept of Virginia
July 4, 1862

My dear General:

I beg to acknowledge the receipt of your letter of yesterday. The necessity of maintaining Fortress Monroe and Yorktown is a primary consideration. I think myself sufficiently strong here; and if the enemy will abstain from attack for twenty four hours more, I shall be able to maintain myself against any force that the enemy can bring against me. Even now, I have no fears as to the issue of an attack. I do not advise therefore that you further strip yourself of troops to send to me. I have ordered to Genl. Burnside to join me with all his disposable force. It would be well to hold Suffolk if possible — and if indispensable to the defence the railroad bridges there might be destroyed. But I hope no such necessity will arise, inasmuch as our line of advance may be on that side.

The result of the affair of the 27th ulto which was so serious in its consequences to the army is already known to you. Superior bodies of the enemy overwhelmed my right wing which was only saved from destruction by the good conduct and obstinate resistance of the troops. Cut off from my base at the White House, I had to take Richmond or find another base on the James River. With a marked success on the 27th, I could have, by crossing the right wing, concentrated my forces, and on the succeeding day been in Richmond. As it was, the only course was to concentrate and change my base to this point. Having decided upon the movement I threw bridges across the White Oak Swamp, brought the right wing across the Chickahominy the night after the battle, withdrew the left and the right through the Swamp; and after sustaining a battle and winning it with the centre, withdrew it also through the Swamp, on the night of the 29th ulto.

On the 30th ulto, the whole army marched to the James River at Turkey Island, being engaged on the flanks and in rear, during the day, in battles each of which from the numbers engaged and the fierceness of the conflicts will have its separate place in our military annals. We repulsed the enemy at each attack. The day succeeding we sustained a combined attack of the pursuing columns of the enemy, and drove them off with great loss.

Turkey Island not having however the requisites for security as a base and the safety of the army now so reduced rendering it imperative to retire to this place, the army moved hither with celerity and entire success on the night of the 2nd inst, bringing with us our artillery and trains.

Nothing of consequence, in all this important movement, fell into the hands of the enemy, subsistance for some few days, and a quantity of reserve ammunition having been destroyed.

The operations of this army have not unfortunately been such as to produce the results so anxiously hoped for by my countrymen — though happily the end is not frustrated, and I have been able to extricate my army from difficulties sudden, unanticipated and almost overwhelming. In a military point of view, neither the country nor the profession to which we belong, have any cause for complaint of this army or its leader.

I tender you, my dear General, my grateful acknowledgments for the patriotic and self sacrificing spirit which you have evinced in responding to my calls for troops &c. It has been potent in sustaining me.

> I am very truly your friend
> Geo B McClellan
> Maj Genl

Maj Gen J. A. Dix
Comdg Ft. Monroe

12 M. *July 4.* The national salute is firing — bands are playing. The troops are in fine spirits.

LS, Dix Papers, Rare Book and Manuscript Library, Columbia University.

To Abraham Lincoln   [TELEGRAM]

Head-Quarters, Army of the Potomac,
To the President   Harrison's Bar, James River. July 4th 1862 [noon]

I have the honor to acknowledge the receipt of your dispatch of the 2d inst.[1] I shall make a stand at this place and endeavor to give my men the repose they so much require.

After sending my communication on Tuesday [July 1], the enemy attacked the left of our lines and a fierce battle ensued lasting until night — they were repulsed with great slaughter. Had *their* attack succeeded the consequence would have been disastrous in the extreme. This closed the hard fighting which had continued from the afternoon of the 26th ult. in a daily series of engagements wholly unparalleled on this continent for determination and slaughter on both sides. The mutual loss in killed and wounded is enormous ; that of the enemy certainly greatest. On Tuesday evening — the 1st — our Army commenced its movement from Haxall's to this point, our line of defence there being too extended to be maintained by our weakened forces. Our train was immense, and about 4 am on the 2d a heavy storm of rain began which continued during the entire day and until the forenoon of yesterday. The roads became horrible. Troops, Artillery and wagons moved on steadily and our whole Army, men and material, was finally brought safe into this camp. The last of the wagons reaching here at noon yesterday. The exhaustion was very great but the Army preserved its morale, and would have repelled any attack which the enemy was in condition to make.

We now occupy a line of heights about two miles from the James, a plain extending from there to the river. Our front is about three miles long. These heights command our whole position and must be maintained. The gun boats can render valuable support upon both flanks. If the enemy attack us in front, we must hold our ground as we best may and at whatever cost [*crossed out*: because the loss of the heights involves the total destruction of the Army]. Our positions can be carried only by overwhelming numbers. The spirit of the Army is excellent. Stragglers [*crossed out*: of whom there was a vast number] are finding their regiments, and the soldiers exhibit the best results of discipline. Our position is by no means impregnable, especially as a morass extends on this side of the high ground, from our center to the James on our right. The enemy may attack in vast numbers and if so, our front will be the scene of a desperate battle which if lost will be decisive. Our Army is fearfully weakened by killed, wounded & prisoners. I can not now approximate to any statement of our losses, but we were not beaten in any conflict. The enemy was unable to by their utmost efforts, to drive us from any field. Never did such a change of base, involving a retrograde movement, and under incessant attacks from a most determined and vastly more numerous foe, partake so little of [*crossed out*: the character of a rout or result in so] disorder. We have lost no guns except 25 in the field of battle — 21 of which were lost by the giving way of McCall's Division under the onset of superior numbers.

Our communications by the James river are not secure. There are points where the enemy can establish themselves with cannon or musketry and command the river and where it is not certain that our gun boats can drive them out. In case of this or in case our front is broken I will still make every effort to preserve at least the personnel of the Army and the events of the last few days leave no question that the troops will do all that their country can ask. Send such reinforcements as you can. I will do what I can.

We are shipping our wounded and sick — and landing supplies. The Navy department should cooperate with us to the extent of its resources. Capt Rodgers is doing all in his power, in the kindest and most efficient manner.

When all the circumstances of the case are known, it will be acknowledged by all competent judges that the movement just completed by this Army is unparalleled in the annals of war. Under the most difficult circumstances we have preserved our trains, our guns, our material — & above all our honor.

Geo. B. McClellan
Maj Genl

AL (in part) retained copy, McClellan Papers (A-72:29), Library of Congress. *OR*, Ser. 1, XI, Part 1, pp. 71–72.

1. See GBM to Lorenzo Thomas, July 1, 1862, note 2, *supra*.

To Abraham Lincoln   [TELEGRAM]

Hd Qrs Army of Potomac

The President   Harrisons Bar James River July 4 [1862] 1 pm

I have the honor to acknowledge the receipt of your dispatch of yesterday afternoon.[1] I thank you for your expression of satisfaction with the conduct of this army & myself. On yesterday I ordered Genl Burnside to send me such reinforcements as he could afford. I thank you for the order to Genl Hunter to send me all the troops he can spare. I regret that Genl Halleck considers all his force necessary to maintain position. I do not wish to endanger in any way the secure occupation of what has been gained in the southwest. I will do the best I can with such force as I have & such aid as you can give me. I think that the Army of Virginia should keep out strong cavalry reconnaissances in the direction of Richmond less the enemy should prefer an advance to Washn to attacking this Army. I wish to be advised fully of all matters in front of that Army. If the Capital should be threatened I will move this Army at whatever hazard in such direction as will best divert the enemy. Our whole Army is now drawn up for review in its positions, bands playing, salutes being fired & all things looking bright.[2]

Geo B McClellan
Maj Genl Comdg

Received copy, Lincoln Papers, Library of Congress, *OR* Ser. 1, XI, Part 3, p. 294.

1. See GBM to Lincoln, July 2, 1862, note 3, *supra*. 2. Lincoln telegraphed on July 5: "A thousand thanks for the relief your two despatches of 12 & 1 P.M. yesterday — give me. Be assured the heroism and skill of yourself, officers, and men, are, and forever will be appreciated. If you can hold your present position, we shall '*hive*' the enemy yet." *Collected Works of Lincoln*, V, p. 307.

To the Army of the Potomac

Soldiers of the Army of the Potomac!

Head-Quarters, Army of the Potomac,
Camp near Harrison's Landing, Va.,
July 4th, 1862.

Your achievements of the last ten days have illustrated the valor and endurance of the American Soldier! Attacked by vastly superior forces, and without hope of reinforcements, you have succeeded in changing your base of operations by a flank movement, always regarded as the most hazardous of military expedients. You have saved all your material, all your trains, and all your guns, except a few lost in battle, taking in return guns and colors from the enemy. Upon your march you have been assailed day after day with desperate fury by men of the same race and nation, skillfully massed and led; and under every disadvantage of numbers, and necessarily of position also, you have in every conflict beaten back your foes with enormous slaughter. Your conduct ranks you among the celebrated armies of history. No one will now question that each of you may always say with pride: "I belonged to the Army of the Potomac!" You have reached this new base, complete in organization and unimpaired in spirit. The enemy may at any moment attack you. We are prepared to receive them. I have personally established your lines. Let them come, and we will convert their repulse into a final defeat. Your Government is strengthening you with the resources of a great people. On this our Nation's Birthday we declare to our foes, who are rebels against the best interests of mankind, that this Army shall enter the Capital of their so-called Confederacy; that our National Constitution shall prevail; and that the Union which can alone insure internal peace and external security to each State must and shall be preserved, cost what it may in time, treasure and blood.

Geo. B. McClellan
Major-General Commanding

DP, McClellan Papers (B-11:48), Library of Congress. *OR*, Ser. 1, XI, Part 3, p. 299.

To Mary Ellen McClellan   [TELEGRAM]

Head-Quarters, Army of the Potomac,
Berkeley's July 5 3.30 pm 1862

Dear Nelly. All is bright. The Army is safe & we will soon be after secesh. I hope they may attack — it will be their ruin if they do. I am very well & not so much fatigued for my mind is at rest.

G B McClellan
Maj Genl

Mrs G B McClellan
Care Dr E E Marcy   North Orange New Jersey

ALS (telegram sent), Records of the Office of the Secretary of War, RG 107 (M-504:65), National Archives.

To Mary Ellen McClellan

[Berkeley] July 6 [1862] Sunday morning 2.15

Early in the evening [July 5] I received the intelligence that secesh was in full force in front of me. I have just completed my arrangements to meet him & believe that with God's blessing we will defeat him terribly. I go into this battle with the full conviction that our honor makes it necessary for me to share the fate of my army. My men are confident & I have no doubt as to our success unless the Creator orders otherwise. I believe we will give them a tremendous thrashing & I still hope that from my universal anxieties I will yet find repose — may God grant it thus! Whatever the result may be I am sure that you will never have cause to blush for me — therefore my conscience is quite clear — God has done far more for me than I had any right to expect — I trust, most humbly, that unworthy as I am he will not desert me now. I yet believe that there is in store for us the supreme happiness of being together once more. If this cannot be in this world, I trust I may be forgiven for my many faults & sins & be permitted to rejoin in Heaven the one who has made my life so happy. . . .

Tomorrow [July 6] will probably determine the fate of the country — I expect to be attacked by greatly superior numbers & hope to beat them.[1]

AL copy; copy, McClellan Papers (C-7:63/D-10:72), Library of Congress.

1. No enemy attack was made that day.

To Mary Ellen McClellan

[Berkeley] Monday [July 7, 1862] 7.30 am.

I had a good refreshing night's sleep. . . .

We are to have another *very* hot day — it is already apparent — I am writing in my shirt sleeves, with tent walls raised etc. . . .

Our army has not been repulsed — we fought every day against greatly superior numbers & were obliged to retire at night to new positions that we could hold against fresh troops. The army behaved magnificently — nothing could have been finer than its conduct....

You need not be ashamed of your husband or his army — we have accomplished one of the grandest operations of Military History....

I don't think the enemy will now attack us here — we are strengthening our position very rapidly & will with God's help surely beat them if they do attack.

AL copy, McClellan Papers (C-7:63), Library of Congress.

To Abraham Lincoln [TELEGRAM]

Headquarters, Army of the Potomac,
Berkeley, July 7 [1862] 8.30 am

As boat is waiting I have only time to acknowledge receipt of dispatches by Genl Marcy. Enemy have not attacked — my position is very strong & daily becoming more so — if not attacked today I shall laugh at them.

I *have* been anxious about my communications.[1] Had long consultation about it with Flag Officer Goldsborough last night — he is confident he can keep river open. He should have all gun boats possible. Will see him again this morning. My men in splendid spirits & anxious to try it again.

Annoy yourself as little as possible about me & don't lose confidence in this army.

G B McClellan
Maj Genl

A Lincoln Presdt.

ALS (telegram sent), Records of the Office of the Secretary of War, RG 107 (M-473:50), National Archives. *OR*, Ser. 1, XI, Part 1, p. 73.

1. In his letter of July 4, the president gave it as his opinion that the Army of the Potomac could hold its position "provided, and so long as, you can keep the James River open below you. If you are not tolerably confident you can keep the James River open, you had better remove as soon as possible." *Collected Works of Lincoln*, V, p. 306.

To Edwin M. Stanton

To the Hon Edwin M Stanton   Head Quarters Army of the Potomac
Sec'y of War   Camp near Harrison's Landing,
Sir.   July 7th 1862.

The energy, ability, gallantry and good conduct displayed throughout the eventful period of this campaign through which we have just passed by Brig Genl F. J. Porter, desires the marked notice of the Executive and the nation.

From the very commencement his unwearied assiduity in his various duties, his intelligent and efficacious assistance which he has rendered me under all circumstances, his skilful management of his command on the march, in the siege and on the field of battle and his chivalric and soldierly bearing under fire, have combined to render him conspicuous among the many faithful and gallant spirits of this Army.

I respectfully therefore recommend that Brig Genl Fitz-John Porter receive the brevet of Brigadier General in the regular Army for Hanover Court House and the brevet of Major General in the regular Army for the battle of Gaines Mills.

If there were another grade to add I would ask for it for the battle of Malvern. The latter eclipses in its results any other engagement in the campaign, and too much credit cannot be given to Genl Porter for his skill, gallantry, and conduct on the occasion.

If there be any vacancy among the General Officers in the regular Army I ask one for him. I saw myself the dispositions he made and the gallantry he displayed. I do not speak from hearsay, but from personal observation; would that the country had more General Officers like him.[1]

I have the honor to be, Sir, very respectfully your obt servant
Geo B McClellan
Maj Genl Commanding

LS retained copy, McClellan Papers (C-6:63), Library of Congress. *OR*, Ser. 1, XII, Part 2 supplement, p. 1111.

1. Porter was named a brigadier general by brevet in the regular army, to date from June 27, and major general of volunteers, to date from July 4.

To John Pope

Major General John Pope   Head Quarters Army of the Potomac
Comd'g Army of Virginia   Camp near Harrison's Bar, Va.
General   July 7th 1862

I have to acknowledge the receipt of your letter of the 4th instant and to thank you for your offers of co-operation and assistance.[1] I cordially approve your project of concentrating your troops. The departure from this wise principle has been the cause of all our troubles in front of Washington. I cannot too strongly represent to you the pressing necessity there is for the rapid concentration of your forces, for it is not yet determined which policy the enemy intend to pursue, whether to attack Washington or to bestow his entire attention upon this Army. I am in a very strong natural position, rendered stronger every day by the labor of the troops and which in a few days will be impregnable. I hope in the course of tomorrow to seize a position on the right bank of the James which will enable me to use either bank of that river at will. I am pushing up supplies as rapidly as possible in order to be perfectly independent of the navigation of the river until strong reinforcements can reach me. The Army is in admirable spirits and discipline. It would fight better tomorrow than it ever did before. I shall carefully watch for any fault committed by the enemy and take advantage of it. As soon as Burnside arrives, I will feel the force of the enemy and ascertain his exact position. If I learn that he has moved upon you I will move upon Richmond, do my best to take it and endeavor to cut off his retreat.

If you are not molested I would urge that you lose not a day in the concentration of your troops and at least push your cavalry so far forward as to partially divert the attention of the enemy from this Army. The Army of the Potomac has lost heavily in killed and wounded during the series of desperate battles which it has given during the past two weeks but I repeat it is in no way disheartened. Its morale, discipline and desire to fight are not only unimpaired but increased. Although to insure success it is absolutely necessary that we promptly receive heavy reinforcements, the spirit of this Army is such that I feel unable to restrain it from speedily resuming the offensive unless reconnaissances should develop so overwhelming a force of the enemy in front as to render it out of the question. Even in that event we will endeavor to find some weak point in the enemy's lines which we will attack in order to break it.

I would be glad to be in daily communication with you both by telegraph and by letter.

I may say in conclusion that so far as my position is concerned, I feel abundantly able to repulse any attack. I feel only for the other side of the river and for my communications. To preserve the morale of my men I must maintain my present position as long as it is possible. Therefore I shall not fall back unless absolutely forced to do so.

Again thanking you for your cordial offer of support

I am, very sincerely yours,

Geo. B. McClellan

Maj Genl Comdg

Retained copy, McClellan Papers (C-6:63), Library of Congress. *OR,* Ser. 1, XI, Part 3, p. 306. Maj. Gen. John Pope commanded the newly formed Army of Virginia.

1. Pope's letter detailed the strength, location, and condition of his forces. It was his general design, he wrote, "to cut off any force which may penetrate into the valley of the Shenandoah from the direction of Richmond, and at the same time be able to concentrate my whole force with little delay in front of Washington in case of necessity." *OR,* Ser. 1, XI, Part 3, pp. 295–97.

To Abraham Lincoln

(Confidential)   Head Quarters, Army of the Potomac
Mr President   Camp near Harrison's Landing, Va. July 7th 1862[1]

You have been fully informed, that the Rebel army is in our front, with the purpose of overwhelming us by attacking our positions or reducing us by blocking our river communications. I can not but regard our condition as critical and I earnestly desire, in view of possible contingencies, to lay before your Excellency, for your private consideration, my general views concerning the existing state of the rebellion; although they do not strictly relate to the situation of this Army or strictly come within the scope of my official duties. These views amount to convictions and are deeply impressed upon my mind and heart.

Our cause must never be abandoned; it is the cause of free institutions and self government. The Constitution and the Union must be preserved, whatever may be the cost in time, treasure and blood. If secession is successful, other dissolutions are clearly to be seen in the future. Let neither military disaster, political faction or foreign war shake your settled purpose to enforce the equal operation of the laws of the United States upon the people of every state.

The time has come when the Government must determine upon a civil and military policy, covering the whole ground of our national trouble. The responsibility of determining, declaring and supporting such civil and military policy and of directing the whole course of national affairs in regard to the rebellion, must now be assumed and exercised by you or our cause will be lost. The Constitution gives you power sufficient even for the present terrible exigency.

This rebellion has assumed the character of a War; as such it should be regarded; and it should be conducted upon the highest principles known to Christian Civilization. It should not be a War looking to the subjugation of the people of any state, in any event. It should not be, at all, a War upon population; but against armed forces and political organizations. Neither confiscation of property, political executions of persons, territorial organization of states or forcible abolition of slavery should be contemplated for a moment. In prosecuting the War, all private property and unarmed persons should be strictly protected; subject only to the necessities of military operations. All private property taken for military use should be paid or receipted for; pillage and waste should be treated as high crimes; all unnecessary trespass sternly prohibited; and offensive demeanor by the military towards citizens promptly rebuked. Military arrests should not be tolerated, except in places where active hostilities exist; and oaths not required by enactments — Constitutionally made — should be neither demanded nor received. Military government should be confined to the preservation of public order and the protection of political rights.

Military power should not be allowed to interfere with the relations of servitude, either by supporting or impairing the authority of the master; except for repressing disorder as in other cases. Slaves contraband under the Act of Congress, seeking military protection, should receive it. The right of the Government to appropriate permanently to its own service claims to slave labor should be asserted and the right of the owner to compensation therefor should be recognized. This principle might be extended upon grounds of military necessity and security to all the slaves within a particular state; thus working manumission in such state — and in Missouri, perhaps in Western Virginia also and possibly even in Maryland the expediency of such a military measure is only a question of time. A system of policy thus constitutional and conservative, and pervaded by the influences of Christianity and freedom, would receive the support of almost all truly loyal men, would deeply impress the rebel masses and all foreign nations, and it might be humbly hoped that it would commend itself to the favor of the Almighty. Unless the principles governing the further conduct of our struggle shall be made known and approved, the effort to obtain requisite forces will be almost hopeless. A declaration of radical views, especially upon slavery, will rapidly disintegrate our present Armies.

The policy of the Government must be supported by concentrations of military power. The national forces should not be dispersed in expeditions, posts of occupation and numerous Armies; but should be mainly collected into masses and brought to bear upon the Armies of the Confederate States; those Armies thoroughly defeated, the political structure which they support would soon cease to exist.

In carrying out any system of policy which you may form, you will require a Commander in Chief of the Army; one who possesses your confidence, understands your views and who is competent to execute your orders by directing the military forces of the Nation to the accomplishment of the objects by you proposed. I do not ask that place for myself. I am willing to serve you in such position as you may assign me and I will do so as faithfully as ever subordinate served superior.

I may be on the brink of eternity and as I hope forgiveness from my maker I have written this letter with sincerity towards you and from love for my country.

Very respectfully your obdt svt
Geo B McClellan
Maj Genl Comdg

His Excellency A Lincoln
Presdt U.S.

LS, Lincoln Papers, Library of Congress. *OR*, Ser. 1, XI, Part 1, pp. 73–74.

1. GBM handed this letter to the president upon his arrival at Harrison's Landing on July 8. It is probable, however, that he had drafted it, at least in general outline, as early as June 20. See GBM to Lincoln, June 20, 1862, *supra*.

To Mary Ellen McClellan

[Berkeley] July 8 [1862]

I have only time before your father starts on his return to Washington to say two words to you. It is terribly hot & has been so for the last two days — almost overpowering — but we manage to worry through it. There is nothing new here — we are strengthening our position daily — the enemy waiting for something or other a few miles off. I hardly know what they will try next — probably to cut off our supplies — but I have quite a large amount here now & I do not think they can trouble us much in that way....

The day is insufferably hot — intense — so much so that I have suspended all work on the part of the men. I have written a strong frank letter to the Presdt, which I send by your father[1] — if he acts upon it the country will be saved. I will send you a copy tomorrow, as well as of other important letters which I wish you to keep as my record. They will show, with the others you have, that I was true to my country, that I understood the state of affairs long ago, & that had my advice been followed we should not have been in our present difficulties....

My conscience is clear — I have done the best I could — God has disposed of events as to him seemed best. I submit to his decrees with perfect cheerfulness, & as sure as he rules I believe that all will yet be for the best....

How I have longed to see you in the midst of my troubles. The thought of you has been an immense consolation & support to me. How perfectly happy I shall be if God sees fit to permit me to be with you once more. I will never leave you again if it is in the power of humanity to avoid it. No rank, nor wealth, nor honors can reconcile me to absence from you.

AL copy; copy, McClellan Papers (C-7:63/D-10:72), Library of Congress.

1. GBM to Lincoln, July 7, *supra*. Lincoln's arrival at Harrison's Landing later this day made it unnecessary to send the letter to Washington by Gen. Marcy.

To Edwin M. Stanton

Head Quarters, Army of the Potomac
Dear Sir　　　　　　　Camp near Harrison's Landing, Va. July 8th 1862

Your letter of the 5th instant by General Marcy has made a deep impression on my mind.[1] Let me in the first place express my sympathy with you in the sickness of your child, which I trust may not prove fatal.

I shall be better understood by you and our friendly relations will become more fixed if I am permitted to recur briefly to the past.

When you were appointed Secretary of War I considered you my intimate friend and confidential adviser; of all men in the nation you were my choice for that position. It was the unquestionable prerogative of the President to determine the military policy of the administration and to select the commanders who should carry out the measures of the government. To any action of this nature I could of course take no personal exception. But from the time you took office, your official conduct towards me as commander in chief of the Army of the U.S. and afterwards as commander of the Army of the Potomac was marked by repeated acts done in such manner as to be deeply offensive to my feelings and calculated to affect me injuriously in public estimation. After commencing the present campaign your concurrence in the withholding of a large portion of my force, so essential to the success of my plans, led me to believe that your mind was warped by a bitter personal prejudice against me. Your letter compels me to believe that I have been mistaken in regard to your real feelings and opinions and that your conduct so unaccountable to my own fallible judgment, must have proceeded from views and motives which I did not understand.

I have made this frank statement, because I thought that it would best accord with the spirit of your communication.

It is with a feeling of great relief that I now say to you that I shall at once resume on my part the same cordial confidence which once characterized our intercourse. You have more than once told me that together we could save this country, it is yet not too late to do so.

To accomplish this, there must be between us the most entire harmony of thought and action and such I offer you. The crisis through which we are passing is a terrible one. I have briefly given in a confidential letter to the President my views (Please ask to see it.) as to the policy which ought to govern this contest on our part.[2] You and I during last Summer so often talked over the whole subject that I have only expressed the opinions then agreed upon between us. The nation will support no other policy. None other will call forth its energies in time to save our cause, for none other will our Armies continue to fight. I have been perfectly frank with you. Let no cloud hereafter arise between us.

Very respectfully your obdt sevt

Geo B McClellan

Maj Genl Comdg

Hon E M Stanton
Secty of War

LS retained copy, McClellan Papers (A-72:29), Library of Congress.

1. Stanton's letter read, in part: "There is no cause in my heart or conduct for the cloud that wicked men have raised between us for their own base and selfish purposes. No man had ever a truer friend than I have been to you and shall continue to be. You are seldom absent from my thoughts and I am ready to make any sacrifice to aid you." McClellan Papers (A-72:29). 2. GBM to Lincoln, July 7, *supra*.

To Mary Ellen McClellan

July 9 [1862] 9 1/2 pm. Berkeley

I telegraphed you briefly this afternoon that I thought secesh had retired — this opinion seems to be fully confirmed — at least to the extent of his having fallen back a certain distance — he is not within 6 or 7 miles of us even with his cavalry & considerably further with his infantry. I am not sorry on the whole that he has gone, for the reason that it will enable my men to rest tranquilly — just what they need. I do not expect to receive many reinforcements for some time — even Burnside's men are halted at Ft Monroe by order of the Presdt! His Excellency was here yesterday & left this morning. He found the army anything but demoralized or dispirited — in excellent spirits. I do not know to what extent he has profited by his visit — not much I fear, for he really seems quite incapable of rising to the height of the merits of the question & the magnitude of the crisis. I will enclose with this a copy of a letter I handed him, which I would be glad to have you preserve carefully as a very important record.

I thank you a thousand times for your kind & loving sympathy you have evinced for me in my trials. I can't tell you what a comfort it is to have your sweet sympathy. I do feel that God has ordered all these later events for some wise purpose. I am sure of it.

My camp is now immediately on the bank of the James River, in the woods....

AL copy; copy, McClellan Papers (C-7:63/D-10:72), Library of Congress.

To Mary Ellen McClellan

[Berkeley, July] 10th [1862] 7 am.

Rose a little before six etc....

I do not know what paltry trick the administration will play next — I did not like the Presdt's manner — it seemed that of a man about to do something of which he was much ashamed. A few days will however show, & I do not much care what the result will be. I feel that I have already done enough to prove in history that I am a General, & that the causes of my want of success are so apparent that no one except the Chandler tribe can blame me hereafter.[1] My conscience is clear at least to *this* extent — viz: that I have honestly done the best *I* could; I shall leave it to others to decide whether that was the best that *could* have been done — & if they find any who can do better am perfectly willing to step aside & give way. I would not for worlds go through that horrid work again — when with my heart full of care I had to meet everyone with a cheerful smile & look as light hearted as tho' nothing were at stake! . . .

9.30 pm. . . . I have not done splendidly at all — I have only tried to do my duty & God has helped me, or rather he has helped my army & our country — & we are safe. I think I begin to see his wise purpose in all this & that the events of the next few days will prove it. If I had succeeded in taking Richmond now the fanatics of the North might have been too powerful & reunion impossible. However that may be I am sure that it is all for the best.

AL copy, McClellan Papers (C-7:63), Library of Congress.

1. Zachariah Chandler of Michigan delivered a strong attack on GBM in the Senate on July 7.

To Randolph B. Marcy   [TELEGRAM]

[Berkeley] July 10th 1862

Enemy has fallen back. I shall get fuller information today & know what I can do if Burnside joins me. Use your judgment about Keyes etc. I must modify some staff departments to ensure success. If Barry & Kingsbury can be placed on other duty I can get on better. Same for Barnard.[1] All quite well. Note received & in every respect attended to.

G B McClellan
Maj Genl

Brig Genl R B Marcy
Chief of Staff   Washington D.C.

ALS (telegram sent), McClellan Papers (A-72:29), Library of Congress.

1. Gen. Keyes retained his corps command, but did not serve again under GBM in the field. Artillerists William F. Barry and Charles P. Kingsbury were appointed to other duties. Gen. Bernard was put in command of the Washington fortifications.

To Lorenzo Thomas   [TELEGRAM]

Brig. General L. Thomas
Adjutant General USA   Head Quarters Army of the Potomac
General   Berkeleys Landing July 10th 1862

I would beg leave to call your attention most urgently to the necessity of taking immediate measures for filling up to the regulation standard all the regiments and batteries of the regulars and volunteers composing this Army. This system is by far preferable, in every respect to that of raising new regiments and batteries.

If it can be done in no other way I would suggest consolidating the old regiments into a small number of companies for each, and receiving the number of entire companies necessary to raise the regiments to the maximum standard. If it be possible to fill up the existing skeleton companies it would be preferable, but it is probable that much valuable time would be gained by following the course first suggested.

I do not believe that any *general* system of recruiting for volunteers will succeed. It must be attempted for particular regiments and companies in the localities where they originated. Recruits scattered among the veteran regiments would soon become efficient; while a long time would be required to render raw recruits reliable. The regular batteries (I may say the same of the volunteer) are very deficient in men.

Commending this subject to the immediate attention of the department, I am

> very respectfully your obedient servant
> G. B. McClellan
> Maj Gen Comdg

Retained copy, McClellan Papers (C-6:63), Library of Congress. *OR*, Ser. 1, XI, Part 3, p. 310.

To Edwin M. Stanton

> Hd Qtrs Army of Potomac
> Berkeley July 10 1862[1]

Desiring to obtain all possible information in regard to rifled guns, I sent, in December last, one of my aides (Col Hudson)[2] who is an excellent Artillery officer to witness experiments made with the *new* James projectile & guns. The result was about as follows —

The batteries withdrawn from service by Genl Barry were old six pounders rifled — the new gun is of a different model, though the same calibre.

The projectile (James) used before these guns (old batteries) were withdrawn was very objectionable — the new projectile is entirely different & free from the defects which rendered the other useless. With the new projectile the old guns would doubtless be available, tho' probably inferior to the new model.

Col H. did not see the steel guns, but they were represented by Mr James as superior to the others which Col H. regarded as superior to any others in use.

I have that opinion of Col H's judgment in such matters that induces me to attach weight to his opinions. I *know* from personal observation that the projectiles furnished by the Ordnance Dept for the 20 & 30 pdr

Parrotts, & the 3″ gun, as well as some of those for the 10 pdr Parrott are worthless, & have not infrequently killed our own men.

The Schenkl is far better — the best so far — but I am decidedly in favor of trying anything which promises to be better than the wretched ammunition which has so often been furnished this Army by the Ordnance Dept. I would also add that no reliance could be placed on the 4 1/2″ guns until we found the Schenkl ammunition.

It is full time to throw prejudice to one side & seek only the true interests of the service.[3]

Very respectfully
Geo B McClellan
Maj Genl Comdg

Hon E M Stanton
Secty of War Washington

ALS, Houghton Library, Harvard University.

1. This letter is written on the back of Brig. Gen. James W. Ripley's letter of July 7 to GBM, in which Ripley, chief of the Ordnance Department, objected on the basis of earlier trials to purchasing three batteries of bronze and steel guns from Charles T. James. 2. Lt. Col. Edward McK. Hudson. 3. A limited number of James guns saw service with the Army of the Potomac.

To Mary Ellen McClellan

[Berkeley] Friday [July] 11th [1862] 7 am.

Am a little belated for it has been raining all the morning & most of the night, so that I rather overslept myself. . . .

There is now strong reason to believe that Clitz is not dead — I hope for the best for the gallant fellow.[1] . . .

You have no idea of the number of general officers applying to go off on sick leave — nearly 20 — more than that including those who have already gone! I do not interpose many obstacles — for I want none but willing ones. . . .

I have commenced receiving letters from the North urging me to march on Washington & assume the Govt!! . . .

AL copy, McClellan Papers (C-7:63), Library of Congress.

1. Maj. Henry B. Clitz had been wounded and captured at the Battle of Gaines's Mill on June 27.

To Abraham Lincoln   [TELEGRAM]

Berkeley July 11th [1862] 8 am

The enemy have certainly retreated — but it has been in good order & with a fair amount of wagons. Our Cavalry follow their rear guard closely & have taken a few prisoners but have made no decided impression.

None of the enemy appear to have crossed the Long Bridge — but all to have gone in direction of Richmond — some crossing White Oak Swamp. None towards mouth of Chickahominy now. Considerable force of enemy at Haxalls yesterday — probably Cavalry almost entirely.

Stonewall Jackson not dead. Prisoners all state that I had (200,000) two hundred thousand enemy to fight — a good deal more than two to one, & they knowing the ground.

G B McClellan
Maj Genl Comdg

A Lincoln
Presdt

ALS (telegram sent), McClellan Papers (A-72:29), Library of Congress. *OR*, Ser. 1, XI, Part 3, p. 315.

To Hill Carter

Hill Carter, Esqr
Shirley   Head Quarters, Army of the Potomac
My dear Sir   July 11/62

Your letter of yesterday is received. Allow me to express my thanks to you for the humane and Christian conduct you and your family have displayed towards my helpless sick & wounded; my attention had already been called to this subject.

Without pausing to inquire or desiring to learn whether you are friend or foe to the cause I have the honor to serve, it was my intention to do all in my power to alleviate in your case the sufferings caused by the inevitable exigencies of this unhappy war.

Permit me here to state that it ever has been, and ever shall be, my constant effort to confine the effects of this contest to the armed masses and political organization directly concerned in carrying it on. I have done my best to secure protection to private property, but I confess that circumstances beyond my control have often defeated my purposes. I have not come here to wage war upon the defenseless, upon non-combatants, upon private property, nor upon the domestic institutions of the land. I and the Army I command are fighting to secure the Union & to maintain its Constitution & laws — for no other purpose.

I regret the losses you have suffered, & the inconveniences you have endured.

I send this by a confidential officer of my Staff who is instructed to ascertain from you what kind of a safeguard will best secure your person and property, how I can best indemnify you for your losses, & in what manner the other requests you make can best be carried out.

Again expressing my thanks for the noble spirit of humanity you have shown towards men whom you probably regard as bitter foes

I am sir, with the highest respect your obedient servant
Geo B McClellan
Maj Genl USA Comdg

Copy, McClellan Papers (B-11:48), Library of Congress. *OR*, Ser. 1, XI, Part 3, p. 316.
Carter was the proprietor of the James River plantation Shirley.

To Abraham Lincoln [TELEGRAM]

Berkeley July 12 [1862] 7.15 am

Hill and Longstreet crossed into New Kent County via Long Bridge.
I am still ignorant what road they afterwards took but will know shortly.
Nothing else of interest since last dispatch.

Rain ceased & everything quiet. Men resting well, but beginning to be
impatient for another fight.

I am more & more convinced that this Army ought not to be withdrawn
from here — but promptly reinforced & thrown again upon Richmond.
If we have a little more than half a chance we can take it. I dread the
effects of any retreat upon the mor.le of the men.

G B McClellan
Maj Genl Comdg

A Lincoln
Presdt

ALS (telegram sent), McClellan Papers (A-72:29), Library of Congress. *OR*, Ser. 1, XI,
Part 1, pp. 74–75.

To Ira Harris

Head Quarters Army of the Potomac
My Dear Sir. Berkeley, Va. July 12th 1862

I perceive by the newspaper reports of congressional proceedings that
there has been considerable discussion on the subject of requiring Mili-
tary Commanders to receive Negroes seeking protection in their camps
and to employ them in suitable labor connected with Military Service.
It may be well for the fact to be made known that all Negroes, male and
female, who have come into the camps of the Army of the Potomac on
this peninsula, have been protected and set to work at wages, in per-
forming offices which would otherwise have devolved upon our soldiers.
The supply of these operatives has thus far been insufficient for our
wants.

I am my dear Senator Very truly your friend
Geo B McClellan
Maj Genl Commanding

Hon Ira Harris
N.Y. Senator

Retained copy, McClellan Papers (C-6:63), Library of Congress. Harris was a senator from New York.

To Mary Ellen McClellan

[Berkeley, July] 13th [1862] Sunday 7.45 am.

It is a little hard that I cannot see my own baby or her dear Mother, but I trust it is all for the best, & how happy we will be when we do meet. I am so glad little May is such a comfort to you. God was good when he gave you the dear little thing. How lonely you would be without her in my absence. I wish indeed I could see her, & *some body else too.*

I hope to get rid of Barnard in a few days — he has nearly exhausted my troops. I have ordered all labor suspended today, to give the men a chance to think of what they have gone through. We are to have service today by the chaplain of Gregg's rgt Penna cavalry. Next Sunday I think I will invite Mr. Neal to preach for us, provided there is any attendance today.

I enclose this in an envelope with some others I send you. One from Bishop McIlvaine, which will gratify you, I know; another from some poor fellow in Indiana, who has named his child after me. If you choose to send out some little present for it, well and good.

1:30 pm. ...Had service this morning by the chaplain of Gregg's rgt, the Rev. Mr. Egan, an Episc. clergyman of Phila....

There never was such an army, but there have been plenty of better generals. When I spoke about being repulsed, I meant our failure to take Richmond — in no *battle* were we *repulsed.* We always at least held our own on the field if we did not beat them....

I still hope to get to Richmond this summer — unless the Govt commits some *extraordinarily* idiotic act — but I have no faith in the administration & shall cut loose from public life the very moment my country can dispense with my services. Don't be alarmed about the climate — it is not at all bad yet & we are resting splendidly — the men look better every day. So you want to know how I feel about Stanton, & what I think of him now? I will tell you with the most perfect frankness. I think that he is the most unmitigated scoundrel I ever knew, heard or read of; I think that (& I do not wish to be irreverent) had he lived in the time of the Saviour, Judas Iscariot would have remained a respected member of the fraternity of the Apostles, & that the magnificent treachery & rascality of E. M. Stanton would have caused Judas to have raised his arms in holy horror & unaffected wonder — he would certainly have claimed & exercised the right to have been the Betrayer of his Lord & Master, by virtue of the same merit that raised Satan to his "bad eminence." I *may* do the man injustice — God grant that I may be wrong — for I hate to think that humanity *can* sink so low — but my opinion is just as I have told you. He has deceived me once — he never will again. Are you satisfied now — lady mine? I ever will, hereafter, trust your judgment about men — your woman's tact & your pure heart make you a better judge than my dull apprehension. I remember what you thought of Stanton when you first saw him — I thought you were wrong — I now know you were right. Enough of the creature — it makes me sick to think of him! Faugh!!

Since I reached here I have received about 8500 or 9000 fresh troops — my losses in the battles will not be over 12,000. Burnside has 8000 (about) at Ft Monroe, where he was detained by order of the Presdt — he has been in Washn & will probably be here *himself* tonight when I will know the views of the Presdt. The probability is that I will attack again very soon — as soon as some losses are supplied — such as canteens & some small things necessary for the comfort of the men. I also must first get off all the sick & wounded. I'll give them a hard fight this time.

11 1/2 pm.   Have just been at work dictating my report of the recent operations — got as far as bringing Porter back across the Chickahominy & quit in disgust. . . .

Please reply to Mr —— & say that I thank him & feel deeply grateful for his trust & kind feeling, & that I am glad to say that there is no reason for despondency on account of my present position. I flatter myself that this army is a greater thorn in the side of the rebellion than ever & I most certainly (with God's blessing) intend to take Richmond with it. . . .

I trust that we have passed through our darkest time & that God will smile upon us & give us victory. . . .

I do not want to be Secy of War — but of course will do anything that will be useful to my country. I am glad to know that my countrymen still love me — *I* have honestly done my best to save my country & I trust will yet save it.

I would give up most cheerfully all the reputation I have gained, or may yet acquire, all the hold I have upon the love of the people; everything would I gladly give up just to be with you & our little child. I don't think I would ever want to see anybody else, or talk to anybody else. You are all I care for in the wide world, yet I am deprived of the society of those I cherish most. Well, well, we must not complain. I presume it is all for the best & I hope that in after years we will look upon these dreary months of separation as the foundation of our true happiness. I must say good bye now & finish some blessed official letters. You must take this note as lubie[1] & not look upon it as a letter. Love to all. Kiss my little May a dozen times for me.

AL copy; copy, McClellan Papers (C-7:63/D-10:72), Library of Congress.

1. An odd or whimsical notion.

To Randolph B. Marcy   [TELEGRAM]

Head-Quarters, Army of the Potomac,
Berkeley July 13 1862 [8 A.M.]

Dispatch received. Am sorry you are not well. This is no place to recuperate so do not return until you are strong. Nothing new, except that Lee is giving me my wounded and sick. All is going on well & quietly. I am better than for months & ready for any work. Watch my new friend — I fear he is in collusion with that vile fellow Chandler, at least I am so informed.[1]

G B McClellan
Maj Genl Comdg

Genl R B Marcy
Washington D.C.

ALS (telegram sent), McClellan Papers (A-72:29), Library of Congress.

1. This is apparently a reference to Gen. Pope. Marcy replied that day: "Your new friend is all right and not in cahoots with the member from Michigan, so wise ones believe." McClellan Papers (A-73:29).

To Robert E. Lee

Head-Quarters, Army of the Potomac,
General,   July 13th 1862

I have the honor to inform you that I have received official information that the Secretary of War has invested Major General John A Dix with authority "to negotiate for a general exchange of all prisoners taken and held on both sides. The exchange to be on the principles of the Cartel between the United States and Great Britain in the last war with that power." If your views on this subject remain as heretofore expressed it is presumed that there will be little difficulty in bringing the negotiation to a satisfactory conclusion. General Dix is under my command and will meet any representative whom you may appoint at such place in the vicinity and not within our lines as you may designate. It will be necessary for you to give me 36 hours notice of the time and place that General Dix may be enabled to meet the appointment.[1] I have the honor to be, General

Very Respectfully, Your obt svt
Geo B McClellan
Maj Genl Commanding

General R E Lee
Comdg Army of Northern Va.

Retained copy, John A. Dix Papers, Rare Book and Manuscript Library, Columbia University. *OR*, Ser. 2, IV, pp. 189–90.

1. Gen. Lee designated Maj. Gen. D. H. Hill to negotiate with Dix, and an agreement on prisoner exchange was signed on July 22. *OR,* Ser. 2, VI, pp. 210, 266–68.

To Abraham Lincoln   [TELEGRAM]

Head Quarters, Army of the Potomac,

To the President,   [Berkeley] July 14th 1862

Your telegram of yesterday has been received.[1] The difference between the effective force of troops and that expressed in returns is considerable in every army. All commanders find the actual strength less than strength represented on paper. I have not my own returns for the trimonthly periods since arriving at Fortress Monroe, at hand at this moment, but even on paper I will not, I am confident, be found to have received 160,000 officers and men present — although present and absent my returns will be accountable for that number.

You can arrive at the number of absentees, however, better by my returns of July 10, which will be ready to send shortly. I find from official reports that I have present for duty,

Officers 3215. Enlisted men 85,450. In all present for duty, 88,665. Absent by authority 34,472; without authority 3778. Present and absent 144,407.[2]

The number of officers and men present sick is 16,619.

The Medical Director will fully explain the cause of the amount of sickness, which I hope will begin to decrease shortly.

Thus the number of men really absent is 38,250. Unquestionably of the number reported present, some are absent, say 40,000 will cover the absentees.

I quite agree with you that more than one half these men are probably fit for duty to day.

I have frequently called the attention lately of the War Department to the evil of absenteeism.

I think that the exciting of the public press to persistent attacks upon officers and soldiers absent from the Army; the employment of deputy marshals to arrest and send back deserters; summary dismissals of officers whose names are reported for being absent without leave and the publication of those names will exhaust the remedies applicable by the War Department. It is to be remembered that many of those absent by authority and those who have got off either sick or wounded or under pretense of sickness or wounds, and having originally pretext of authority, are still so reported absent by authority. If I could receive back the absentees, could get my sick men up I would need but small reinforcements to enable me to take Richmond.

After the battle of Williamsburg, Fair Oaks, &c &c most of these men got off. Well men got on board hospital boats taking care of sick etc, etc. There is always confusion and haste in shipping and taking care of wounded after a battle. There is no time for nice examination of permits to pass here or there.

I can now control people getting away better, for the natural opportunities are better. Leakages by desertion occur in every Army — and will occur here of course but I do not at all, however, anticipate anything like a recurrence of what has taken place.[3]

Geo B McClellan
Maj Genl Comdg

Retained copy, McClellan Papers (C-12:64), Library of Congress. *OR*, Ser. 1, XI, Part 3, pp. 321–22.

1. The president had been told, he wrote on July 13, that over 160,000 men were in the Army of the Potomac on the Peninsula, yet by his calculations he found "45,000 of your Army still alive, and not with it. I believe half, or two thirds of them are fit for duty to-day.... If I am right, and you had these men with you, you could go into Richmond in the next three days. How can they be got to you? and how can they be prevented from getting away in such numbers for the future?" *Collected Works of Lincoln*, V, p. 322. 2. Included in this total, but unlisted by GBM, are the Fort Monroe garrison and the quartermaster guard. *OR*, Ser. 1, XI, Part 3, p. 312. 3. See also GBM to Lorenzo Thomas, Sept. 28, 1862, *infra*.

To Mary Ellen McClellan

[Berkeley] July 15 [1862] 7.30 am.

... I was amused at a couple of telegrams yesterday urging me to the offensive as if I were unwilling to take it myself!! It is so easy for people to give advice — it costs nothing! But it is a little more difficult for poor me to create men & means, & to wipe out by mere wishes the forces of the enemy. I confess that I sometimes become provoked. I have *16,600* men sick in camp!!! and but 85,000 for duty. I could not bring 70,000, at most 75,000, into battle — & it *is so easy to attack* from 150,000 to 170,000 brave men entrenched with that number!!

I had quite an adventure in a small way last night, that was rather ludicrous. I yesterday sent a flag of truce after some wounded men, Sweitzer going on the boat. Well, it appears that he & the doctor on board, between them, allowed a young English nobleman to come down with them, and Raymond was discreet enough to bring him up to Hd Qtrs & was apparently quite proud of his prize — wished me to see him &c. Upon inquiry, I found that he came from Richmond, had no papers or passports, save a pass from the secesh Secy of War & acknowledged that he had surreptitiously slipped into Richmond a couple of weeks ago. This was a pretty kettle of fish! I did not like to hang the young rascal for a spy, for fear of getting up a row with England — I determined he *should not* go through & so I this morning sent him back to Secessia & told him to try it again at his peril. The young man was exceedingly disgusted & has, I presume, by this time, come to the conclusion that the fact of being an Englishman is not everywhere a sufficient passport.

AL copy; copy, McClellan Papers (C-7:63/D-10:72), Library of Congress.

To Randolph B. Marcy [TELEGRAM]

[Berkeley] July 15 8 am 1862

Your proposition is easily enunciated but not so readily carried out.[1] You may rest assured that it is not necessary to urge me from a distance — I on the spot am quite as anxious to finish this agreeable game as any of my disinterested friends away from here. I get neither men nor a policy. I doubt my new friend.

G B McClellan
Maj Genl

Genl R B Marcy
Washington D.C.

ALS (telegram sent), McClellan Papers (A-73:29), Library of Congress.

1. Marcy telegraphed on July 13: "It is very generally thought that an advance on Richmond at an early period would be received with more enthusiasm now than at any time since the war commenced. The people seem to demand it...." McClellan Papers (A-73:29).

To Nathaniel S. Berry

His Excellency, the Governor of New Hampshire,
Concord
Sir, Berkeley, July 15th 1862.

I am sure that in the present emergency you will pardon me for venturing upon a few suggestions as to the most useful manner of increasing the strength of this Army.

The greatest benefit that can be conferred upon it would be to fill to the maximum the old regiments which have so nobly sustained the honor of the Union and their State; I would prefer 50,000 recruits for my old regiments to 100,000 men organized into new regiments, and I cannot too earnestly urge the imperative necessity of following this system.

By far the best arrangements would be to fill up all the old companies; if that cannot be done, the next best thing is to consolidate the old companies and add new ones to each regiment. We have here the material for making excellent officers in the regiments; these men, tried and proved in many hard fought battles, all infinitely to be preferred to any new appointments. More than that they have won their promotion; policy and gratitude alike demand that their claims should be recognized.

With the old regiments thus filled up the whole Army would in a very few weeks be ready for any service. New regiments would require several months to fit them for service, and they would be brought into action with untried, and in many cases unfit officers.

Again, I would earnestly impress upon you the great mistake of bringing men into the field for a less period than three years or the War; the contact of such troops with those enlisted for three years would soon breed dissatisfaction among the latter, while the term of service of the former would expire about the time they became valuable to the service. I would also urge the propriety, necessity rather, of sending recruits to their regiments as rapidly as enlisted. They will become Soldiers here in one tenth of the time they could in the home depots, and would have all the advantages of contact with the veterans who now compose this Army.

I have also to ask your attention to the many officers and men who are now in the north on sick leave, etc. Many thousands of these are fit for duty, and should at once be made to join their regiments. May I ask the earnest efforts of your excellency to secure this very important end. I would also request that no officer who has resigned from this Army be commissioned in another regiment unless furnished with a special recommendation to that effect from the Commander of his Division or Army Corps. I regret to say that many officers have resigned to avoid the consequence of cowardly conduct, inefficiency etc — it is a melancholy fact, that, while many noble exceptions are to be found, the officers of Volunteers are as a mass (perhaps I should say, were, for the worst are sifted out) greatly inferior to the men they command.

Trusting that you will pardon me for the liberty I have taken in making these suggestions and that you will be good enough to give them your careful consideration,

I have the honor to be Sir Most Respectfully, your obdt servant
Geo B McClellan
Maj Genl Comdg

LS, Houghton Library, Harvard University. The same letter was sent to other Northern governors.

To Samuel L. M. Barlow

Head-Quarters, Army of the Potomac,
My dear Barlow   July 15 Berkeley 1862

Your kind letter of the 6th reached me a day or two since — but I have been too busy to reply to it, & now can only scrawl off a few brief lines. There was truly propriety in your mingled feelings "of sadness & joy" upon receiving the news of recent events here — joy that the Army behaved with such heroism, so worthily of its country — sadness that so many brave & good men have fallen victims to the stupidity & wickedness at Washington which have done their best to sacrifice as noble an Army as ever marched to battle. I cannot express to you my admiration of the superb conduct of my men — their heroic gallantry, extreme patience, great endurance & excellent discipline. You will have learned ere this that Clitz is *not* dead — but that we may soon hope to have him again among us. He was severely but not dangerously wounded. I do not care if they *do* remove [me] from this Army — except on account of the Army itself. I have lost all regard & respect for the majority of the Administration, & doubt the propriety of my brave men's blood being spilled to further the designs of such a set of heartless villains.

I do not believe that Stanton will go out of office — he will not willingly, & the Presdt has not the nerve to turn him out — at least so I think. Stanton has written me a most abject letter — declaring that he has ever been my best friend etc etc!![1] Well, burn this up when you have read it. Give my kindest regards to the Madame & believe me truly your friend

Geo B McClellan

S L M Barlow Esq

I will write you fully in a day or two — we are doing well here — waiting!

ALS, Barlow Papers, Huntington Library.

1. See GBM to Stanton, July 8, note 1, *supra*.

To Abraham Lincoln   [TELEGRAM]

Head-Quarters, Army of the Potomac,
Berkeley July 17 — 8 am 1862

I have consulted fully with Genl Burnside & would commend to your favorable consideration the General's plan for bringing (7) seven additional regiments from North Carolina by leaving Newburn to the care of the gun boats.

It appears manifestly to be our policy to concentrate here everything we can possibly spare from less important points to make sure of crushing the enemy at Richmond, which seems clearly to be the most important point in rebeldom. Nothing should be left to chance here. I would recommend that Genl Burnside with all his troops be ordered to this Army to enable it to assume the offensive as soon as possible.[1]

Very respectfully
G B McClellan
Maj Genl Comdg

A Lincoln
Presdt

ALS (telegram sent), McClellan Papers (A-73:29), Library of Congress. *OR*, Ser. 1, XI, Part 1, p. 75.

1. On July 15 Burnside wrote GBM from Fort Monroe: "I've much to say to you.... The President has ordered me to remain here for the present.... I dont know what it means; but I do know my dear Mac that you have lots of enemies, but you must keep cool; dont allow them to provoke you into a quarrel...." McClellan Papers (A-73:29).

To Mary Ellen McClellan

[Berkeley] July 17 [1862] am.

Genl Dix & Burnside are both here....

Burnside is very well & if the Presdt permits will bring me large (respectably) reinforcements....

Am quite well today — a little disgusted at the stupidity of people in Washington. You need not be at all alarmed as to my being deceived by them. I *know* that they are ready to sacrifice me at any moment & are only restrained by fear of the people. I shall not be at all surprised to have some other Genl made Comdr of the whole army, or even to be superseded here — & to tell you the truth I don't care how soon they do it. I have lost confidence in the Govt, & would be glad to be out of the scrape — keep this to yourself....

7 pm. ... You ask me when I expect to reach Richmond & whether I shall act on the offensive this summer. I am at the mercy of the Govt — after the first 9000 or 10,000 men sent to me they have withheld all further reinforcements. Burnside is halted at Ft Monroe — with his own troops & those of Hunter he can bring me some 20,000 troops — but I have no idea of the intentions of the Govt — if I am reinforced to that extent I will try again, with the least possible delay — I am not at all in favor of baking on the banks of this river, but am anxious to bring matters to an issue. I agree with you that a certain eminent individual *is* "an old stick" — & of pretty poor timber at that.[1] I confess that I do not at all appreciate his style of friendship. The army did *not* give him an enthusiastic reception — I *had to order* the men to cheer & they did it very feebly — this you can keep to yourself, it is a "jurer mon secret." You need not be at all alarmed lest any of these people *flatter* me into the belief that they are my friends — it's mighty little flattery or comfort I get out of any of them in these days, I assure you....

Don't think much about the war. I think the crisis will soon be upon us. If the adm conducts the war on right principles it will soon be over — if it adopts those radical & inhuman views to which it seems inclined, & which will prolong the struggle over a great length of time, I cannot well in conscience serve the Govt any longer....

So you like my letter to the Presdt?[2] I feel that I did my duty in writing it tho' I apprehend it will do no good whatever — but it clears my conscience to have spoken plainly at such a time. You do not feel one bit more bitterly towards those people than I do; I do not say much about it — but I fear they have done all that cowardice, folly & rascality can do to ruin our poor country — & the blind people seem not to see it, but to submit like serfs to the lash. It makes my blood boil when I think of it. I cannot resign so long as the fate of the Army of the Potomac is entrusted to my care — I owe a great duty to this noble set of men — & that is the only feeling that sustains me. I fear that my day of usefulness to the country is past — at least under this administ — I have no respect for any member of it & *our* opinions do not differ in the slightest. I hope & trust that God *will* watch over guide & protect me — I accept most resignedly all the adversity he has brought upon me — perhaps I have really brought it on myself, for while striving conscientiously to do my best, it may well be that I have made great mistakes, that my vanity does not permit me to perceive — when I see so much self blindness around me, I cannot arrogate to myself greater clearness of vision & self examination. I *did* have a terrible time during that week — for I stood alone, without *anyone* to help me — I felt that on me rested everything & I felt how weak a thing poor mortal erring man is! I felt it sincerely & shall never I trust forget the lesson — it will last me to my dying day. . . .

I *am* very well now — perfectly well & ready for any amount of fatigue that can be imagined.

AL copy, McClellan Papers (C-7 :63), Library of Congress.

1. The reference is to President Lincoln. 2. GBM to Lincoln, July 7, *supra.*

To Abraham Lincoln   [TELEGRAM]

Head Quarters, Army of the Potomac,
Berkeley July 18 8 am 1862

No change worth reporting in the state of affairs. Some (20,000) twenty to (25,000) twenty five thousand of enemy at Petersburg, & others thence to Richmond. Those at Petersburg say they are part of Beauregard's Army. New troops arriving via Petersburg. Am anxious to learn determination of Govt that no time may be lost in preparing for it. Hours are very precious now, & perfect unity of action necessary.

G B McClellan
Maj Genl Comdg

A Lincoln
Presdt

ALS (telegram sent), McClellan Papers (C-15 :64), Library of Congress. *OR*, Ser. 1, XI, Part 1, p. 75.

To Mary Ellen McClellan

July 18 [1862] Berkeley Friday 9 pm.

... I have my head half occupied with the idea of making another last appeal to the Presdt to endeavor to beat some sense into his head....

I am inclined now to think that the Presdt will make Halleck comdr of the Army[1] & that the first pretext will be seized to supersede me in command of this army — their game seems to be to withold reinforcements & then to relieve me for not advancing — well knowing that I have not the means to do so. If they supersede me in command of the Army of the Potomac I will resign my commission at once; if they appoint Halleck Comg Genl I will remain in command of this army as long as they will allow me to, provided the army is in danger & likely to play an active part. I cannot remain as a subordinate in the army I once commanded any longer than the interests of my own Army of the Potomac require. I owe no gratitude to any but my own soldiers here — none to the Govt or to the country. I have done my best for my country — I expect nothing in return — they are my debtors, not I theirs....

My letter to Stanton was fairly "diplomatic" & if you read it carefully you will see that it is bitter enough — politely expressed, but containing much more than is on the surface.[2] ...

If things come to pass as I anticipate I shall leave the service with a sad heart for my country, but a light one for myself. I am tired of being dependent on men I despise from the bottom of my heart. I cannot express to you the infinite contempt I feel for these people; but one thing keeps me at my work — love for my country & my army. Surely no General had ever better cause to love his men than I have to love mine. Unhappily the men are too often better than their officers.

Smith W. F. went off today. I don't think he intends returning, & don't think he was as sick as many who remained — he had not even the decency to bid me good bye after all I have done for him! Such is gratitude — I no longer expect such a feeling. I don't care to have him come back.

AL copy, McClellan Papers (C-7:63), Library of Congress.

1. GBM's surmise was correct. On July 11 Halleck was ordered to the post of general-in-chief. The appointment was reported in the press on July 20, and he assumed command on July 23. 2. GBM to Stanton, July 8, *supra*.

To Randolph B. Marcy   [TELEGRAM]

Head-Quarters, Army of the Potomac,
Berkeley July 19 — 8 am 1862

Dispatch of (17) seventeenth received.[1] No change whatever. Not a man since you left. Not a word from Gomorrah. Burn[2] not under my orders and do not know whether he will be. The event cannot occur without stupid insanity on my part until I have tools to work with & I am surprised that it is alluded to under the circumstances. You need not hurry. Will inform you the moment I receive any help or know anything. I do not know what to expect.

G B McClellan
Maj Genl

Brig Genl R B Marcy
North Orange New Jersey

ALS (telegram sent), McClellan Papers (A-73:29), Library of Congress.

1. This dispatch, not found, presumably dealt with an advance by the Army of the Potomac.
2. Gen. Burnside.

To William H. Aspinwall

Confidential　　　　　　　Head-Quarters, Army of the Potomac,
My dear Mr Aspinwall　　　　 Berkeley July 19th 1862

I again find myself in a position such that I may ere long have to tax your friendship.

I have reason to believe that Genl Halleck is to be made Comdr in Chief of the Army, &, if I am not mistaken, I think I detect the premonitory symptoms of still further changes.

I can get no replies from Washington to any of my dispatches — Burnside and his troops are taken out of my hands — I receive no reinforcements & no hope of them is held out to me ; — the game apparently is to deprive me of the means of moving, & then to cut my head off for not advancing — in other words it is my opinion that I will be removed from the command of this Army in a short time. The present policy is, I think, merely a continuation of the inveterate persecution that has pursued me since I landed on the Peninsula — weakening my command so as to render it inadequate to accomplish the end in view, & then to hold me responsible for the results. I am quite weary of this.

If I am superseded in the command of the Army of the Potomac I shall resign my commission in the service — feeling that I can no longer be of use — on the contrary only in the way.

Looking forward to that event, my main object in writing to you is to ask you to be kind enough to cast your eyes about you to see whether there is anything I can do in New York to earn a respectable support for my family — I have no exaggerated ideas or expectations, all I wish is some comparatively quiet pursuit — for I really need rest. Pretty much everything I had has been sacrificed in consequence of my reentering the service, & when I leave it I must commence anew & work for my support — that I am quite willing to do.

I *know* that I need not apologize for troubling you in regard to this matter.

Please regard this as confidential except with Mr Alsop & Mr Bartlett.[1]

I am, my dear sir, most sincerely your friend

Geo B McClellan

Wm H Aspinwall Esq
New York City

ALS retained copy, McClellan Papers (A-73:29), Library of Congress. Aspinwall, a New York buinessman and financier, had hired GBM for the Ohio and Mississippi Railroad in 1860.

1. Joseph W. Alsop and Edwin Bartlett, executives with the Ohio and Mississippi. Alsop wrote GBM on July 24: "Dont think of resigning. The Country will follow you. In the end *Truth* will be made manifest and those in power will be unable to make you bear the burthen of their inequities." On the same day, Aspinwall wrote: "Your sphere whilst the war lasts, is the army — you have no right to entertain any idea of a return to civil life just now... weigh well the political bearing of advice which may be given you to the contrary." McClellan Papers (A-73:29).

To Abraham Lincoln   [TELEGRAM]

Head-Quarters, Army of the Potomac,
Berkeley July 20 1.30 pm   1862

I have again heard from returned prisoners that Jackson's troops commenced leaving Richmond about one week ago by rail either towards Gordonsville or Fredericksburg, & that the movement continued for some three (3) days by night & day. This comes through so many sources that I feel obliged to call your close attention to it.

I also learn that large numbers of conscripts are constantly arriving in Richmond from the south. My cavalry scouts are today amusing themselves with the enemy at Malvern Hill.

Jackson's movement may be against Buell — the fact of his taking the Gordonsville route would in that case be accounted for by the necessity of their keeping the Petersburg & Danville roads free for the transit of wounded, recruits and supplies. In any event I beg to urge concentration of the masses of troops in front of Washington, & the sending of cavalry far to the front. If I am to have Burnside's troops I would be glad to avail myself of at least a portion of them to occupy a point on the south bank of James River.

Health of the command improving a little. I should be glad to hear daily from Pope's outposts — it is important that I should do so.

G B McClellan
Maj Genl Comdg

A Lincoln
Presdt

ALS (telegram sent), McClellan Papers (A-73:29), Library of Congress. *OR*, Ser. 1, XI, Part 3, pp. 328–29.

To Mary Ellen McClellan

[Berkeley] July 20 [1862] pm.

... Which dispatch of mine to Stanton did you allude to — the telegraphic one in which I told him that if I saved the army I owed no thanks to anyone in Washn, & that he had done his best to sacrifice my army?[1] It was pretty frank & quite true. Of course they will never forgive me for that — I knew it when I wrote it, but as I thought it possible that it might be the last I ever wrote it seemed better to have it exactly true. The Presdt was entirely too smart to give my correspondence to the public — it would have ruined him & Stanton forever. Of course he has not replied to my letter, & never will — he *cannot*.[2] His reply may be, however, to avail himself of the first opportunity to cut my head off.

I see it reported in this evening's papers that Halleck is to be the new Genl in Chief. Now let them take the next step & relieve me & I shall once more be a free man....

Later   ... I believe it is now certain that Halleck is comdr in chief — I have information this evening from Washn from private sources which seems to render it quite certain — so you will have to cease directing your letters to me as Comdg US Army & let the address be ''Comdg the Army of the Potomac'' — quite as proud a title as the other, at all events. I shall have to remove the three stars from my shoulders & put up with two — Eh bien — it is all for the best I doubt not. I hope Halleck will have a more pleasant time in his new position than I did when I held it. This of course fixes the future for us — I cannot remain permanently in the army after this slight. I must of course stick to this army so long as I am necessary to it, or until the Govt adopts a policy in regard to the war that I cannot conscientiously affirm — the moment either of these events comes to pass I shall leave the service....

No position in the gift of the country can ever tempt me into public life again — my experience in it has been sad enough, but I have learned a useful lesson. I have tried to do my best, honestly & faithfully, for my country — that I have to a certain extent failed I do not believe to be my fault — tho' my self conceit probably blinds me to many errors that others see. But one useful lesson I have learned — to despise earthly honors & popular favor as vanities — I am content — I have not disgraced my name, nor will my child be ashamed of her father — thank God for that. I shall try to get something to do which will make you comfortable & it will be most pleasant & in the best taste for me that we should lead hereafter a rather quiet & retired life — it will not do to parade the tattered remnants of my departed honors to the gaze of the world. Let us try to live for each other & our child, & to prepare for the great change that sooner or later must overtake us all. I have enough of earthly honors & place — I have drained the goblet nearly to the dregs, & found it poison. I believe I can give up all, & retire to privacy once more, a better man than when we gave up our dear little home with wild ideas of serving the country — I feel that I have paid all that I owe her — I am sick & weary of this business — I am tired of serving fools & knaves. God help my country — he alone can save it.

It *is* grating to have to serve under the orders of a man whom I know by experience to be my inferior — but so let it be — God's will be done. My conscience is clear & all will turn out for the best. My trust *is* in God & I cheerfully submit to his will. . . .

AL copy, McClellan Papers (C-7:63), Library of Congress.

1. GBM to Stanton, June 28, 1862, *supra*. 2. This is probably a reference to GBM's Harrison's Landing letter to Lincoln of July 7, *supra*.

To Mary Ellen McClellan

[Berkeley] July 22 [1862] 7 1/2 am.

. . . While I think of it be very careful what you telegraph & tell your father the same thing. *I have the proof that the Secy reads all my private telegrams.* If he has read my private letters to you also his ears must have tingled somewhat. I am more & more convinced that he is the most depraved hypocrite & villain that I have ever had the bad fortune to meet with. . . .

I am about doing a thing today which will I suppose cause the abolitionists & my other *friends* to drive the last nail in my official coffin! You know that our sick & wounded in Richmond are suffering terribly for want of proper food, medicines, hospital supplies etc — well — I have ordered a boat load of all such things (lemons, tea, sugar, brandy, underclothing, lint, bandages, chloroform, quinine, ice etc etc) to be sent up to Genl Lee today to be used at his discretion for the sick & wounded of *both* armies. I know he would not, & could not, receive them for our men alone, therefore I can only do it in the way I propose, & trust to his honor to apply them properly — half & half.[1] I presume I will be accused now of double dyed treason — giving aid & comfort to the enemy etc. What do *you* think of it? Am I right or wrong? . . .

I see that the Pope bubble is likely to be suddenly collapsed — Stonewall Jackson is after him, & the paltry young man who wanted to teach me the art of war will in less than a week either be in full retreat or badly whipped. He will begin to learn the value of "*entrenchments, lines of communication & of retreat, bases of supply etc*" — they will learn bye & bye.[2]

Pm.   It is a lovely afternoon, bright & sunny, a pleasant breeze blow-
ing, & everything charming to the eye. The old river looks beautiful
today — as bright as when John Smith, Esq, & my dusky ancestress
Madame Pocahontas Rolfe neé Powhatan paddled her canoe & children
somewhere in this vicinity. If it were not for the accompaniments &
present surroundings it would delight me beyond measure to have you
here, to see the scenery & some of the fine old residences, which stud its
banks. The old rascals of two or three generations ago, must have lived
in great state & comfort here, when abolitionists were not dreamed of &
pestiferous wooden nutmeg, psalm singing yankees were animals as rare
as camelopards & black swans. I suspect they had a pretty good time,
interrupted only by the chills & fever, bad luck in gambling & horse
racing & the trouble of providing for their woolly headed dependents.

6 pm.   ...I see that the fickle press (& I presume the people) are
beginning to turn & worship Halleck as the rising star — as soon as
Stanton & the Presdt feel that they can safely do so they will either
supersede me or do something to put me out of service. I shall surely
take care not to let them put me in the wrong....

I do not like the political turn that affairs are taking....

AL copy; copy, McClellan Papers (C-7:63/D-10:72), Library of Congress.

1. On July 23 Gen. Lee replied to GBM that these supplies were unnecessary, in view of
the prisoner exchange agreement made the previous day. *OR*, Ser. 2, IV, p. 269. 2. On July
14, in an address to his Army of Virginia, Gen. Pope announced: "I have come to you
from the West, where we have always seen the backs of our enemies.... I desire you to
dismiss from your minds certain phrases, which I am sorry to find so much in vogue amongst
you. I hear constantly of 'taking strong positions and holding them,' of 'lines of retreat,'
and of 'bases of supplies.' Let us discard such ideas...." *OR*, Ser. 1, XII, Part 3, pp. 473–74.

To Samuel L. M. Barlow

My dear Barlow   Berkeley Wednesday [July] 23 [1862]

Your two kind letters received, the last this evening.[1]

I will briefly reply to both at once. I have *not* been in any manner
consulted as to Halleck's appointment & it is intended as "a slap in the
face." I do not think it best to reply to the lies of such a fellow as
Chandler — he is beneath my notice, & if the people are so foolish as to
believe aught he says I am content to lose their favor & to wait for history
to do me justice. I am in my own mind satisfied that I will be relieved
from the command of this Army, & shall then leave the service.

I am weary, very weary, of submitting to the whims of such *"things"*
as those now over me — I have suffered as much for my country as most
men have endured, & shall be inexpressibly happy to be free once more.

If relieved from command of this Army I shall ask Halleck for a leave
of absence for a month or so to give me time to think — will go with my

wife & child to some very quiet place where not a human being knows me & try to rest — for I need repose.

Stanton's statement that I outnumbered the rebels is simply false — they had more than two to one against me. I could *not* have gone into Richmond with my left.

However I will not discuss these things now.

From a remark in your last letter I infer that you think that Burnside's troops are under my control — they are *not,* he having been withdrawn from my control by the order of the Presdt — I have several times asked for him but cannot get him.

I have not received 10,000 fresh troops since I reached this place — have had none for a long time, am receiving none, & see no chance of getting any except Burnside's. When the Presdt was here he asked for no explanations, expressed no dissatisfaction — treated me with no confidence, & did not ask my opinion except in *three* questions —

1st. "How many troops have you left?"

2nd. "How many did you lose in the late actions?"

3rd. "Can you move this Army still further in retreat?"

You see pretty well how the case stands. If I go north I may possibly see you for a few moments altho' I shall avoid N.Y. & all crowded places.

With my kindest regards to Madame

> Ever your friend
> McClellan

S L M Barlow Esq

My regards to Meagher.[2] Excuse the brevity of this but I am pressed for time.

ALS, Barlow Papers, Huntington Library.

1. Barlow's letter of July 18 read, in part: "When the history of this war is written, the fault will be thrown upon Stanton and I think upon no one else.... I think I do him no injustice when I say that no intelligent man knows Stanton without knowing that he is the greatest hypocrite alive.... I hope this change [Halleck's appointment] has been made with your knowledge & sanction. If not, if it totally intercedes as a slap in the face, I still hope that you will not resign.... I have always believed that through you we may win this war & restore our government & that it is your duty under almost all circumstances to stand by the country." He suggested that if GBM would "give the facts in a paper" his friends would "say all that is necessary" to counter the attacks of Senator Chandler. Barlow Papers. 2. Brig. Gen. Thomas F. Meagher, on leave in New York.

To Mary Ellen McClellan

[Berkeley] July 24 [1862]

... Your Father arrived this evening....

Took a long ride in the sun today. Our men look better than ever — like real veterans now — tough, brown & fearless....

I have nothing yet from Washn, & must confess that I am as indifferent as possible to what they do. If they reinforce me I am ready to fight harder than ever & will give secesh a sharp rub for his capital. If they make it necessary for me to resign I am quite ready to do so. . .

I presume I shall learn something tomorrow about the destination of Burnside — I can then enable you to guess how matters will go — I am yet in complete ignorance — being no longer taken into the confidence of the "powers that be." . . .

You ask me whether my self respect will permit me to remain longer in the service after Halleck's appt?[1] It will permit me to remain only so long as the welfare of the Army of the Potomac demands — no longer. Don't mind these things — I have done the best I could, history will justify me — I bide my time. Whatever God sends me, be it defeat & loss of rank — or be it success & honor — I will cheerfully submit to & try neither to be unduly depressed by the one, or too much elated by the other — may God help me in this.

I do not see whither events are tending, & the poor country does seem to be under a terrible cloud — but God's will be done — he will in his own good time bring all this to the best termination. . . .

I presume I shall hear something today from that council of military pundits who have been about in Washn — there is not a handful of brains among them all & a nice mess they will make of it.

AL copy, McClellan Papers (C-7:63), Library of Congress.

1. Mrs. McClellan had written, on July 22: "To have a man put over you without even *consulting* with you is rather more than I can endure — & if you do not resign I will!!... You know there was a consultation of Cabinet & *General* officers & probably Pope. McD[owell] & Wadsworth were the Officers. I am *indignant*. What *is* this country coming to, darling? We are certainly under a terrible cloud." McClellan Papers (B-11:48).

To Joseph W. Alsop

Head Quarters Army of the Potomac

My dear Mr Alsop   Berkeley July 26 1862

Your kind note of the 24th as well as that of Mr Aspinwall reached me this morning.[1] I do not (nor have I for a moment) considered Halleck's appointment as a reason for resigning. My fate is linked with that of the Army of the Potomac, and so long as I can be useful with it I must remain with it. I have seen Halleck and believe that he will act with me in good faith.[2] . . .

Your sincere friend
Geo B McClellan

J. W. Alsop Esq
New York

Copy, McClellan Papers (A-73:29), Library of Congress.

1. See GBM to Aspinwall, July 19, note 1, *supra*. 2. Gen. Halleck conferred with GBM at Harrison's Landing on July 25–26.

To Henry W. Halleck

Maj Genl H W Halleck
Comdg U.S. Army   Head Quarters Army of the Potomac
General   Berkeley July 26th 1862

I have seen to day nearly a thousand of our sick & wounded just returned from Richmond; some refugees have also arrived, & a number of surgeons and chaplains taken prisoners at Bull Run. All of these who have enjoyed any opportunities of observation unite in stating, that reinforcements are pouring into Richmond from the South.

Dr L H Stone (U.S.A.) saw at Charlotte from 7000 to 8000 troops en route to Richmond; he & others unite in stating that it is quite positive that the troops on James Island (Charleston) have arrived in Richmond, & that the Southern States are being drained of their garrisons to reinforce the Army in my front. It is said that the troops of Beauregards old Army are also en route hither — this last is not positive, & I hope to learn the truth in regard to it tomorrow.

3 rgts (1 So Ca, 1 No Ca, 1 Georgia) reached Richmond yesterday; supplies are being rapidly pushed in by all routes.

It would appear that Longstreet is in front of Richmond, on this side of the James; D. H. Hill at Fort Darling & vicinity.

Our cavalry pickets on Charles City Road were driven in today by a heavy force of cavalry & some artillery — Averell started after them with a sufficient force — I have not yet heard the result.

Allow me to urge most strongly that *all* the troops of Burnside & Hunter[1] — together with all that can possibly be spared from other points — be sent to me at once. I am sure that you will agree with me that the true defence of Washington consists in a rapid & heavy blow given by this Army upon Richmond.

Can you not *possibly* draw 15,000 or 20,000 men from the West to reinforce me temporarily? They can return the moment we gain Richmond. Please give weight to this suggestion — I am sure it merits it.

I have to be, General, very respectfully Your obedient Svt
Geo B McClellan
Maj Genl USA

ALS, Records of the Adjutant General's Office, RG 94 (159: Halleck Papers), National Archives. *OR*, Ser. 1, XI, Part 3, pp. 333–34.

1. The troops in these two commands totaled some 35,000.

To Lorenzo Thomas   [TELEGRAM]

Brig Gen L Thomas   Head-Quarters, Army of the Potomac,
Adjt Genl USA   [Berkeley] July 27 1862

I respectfully apply for permission to send an officer from each regiment to the place where it was raised, with authority to bring on every officer and man he can find fit for duty whether on leave of absence or not, no matter from what source the leave may be granted. I have official assurance that the number of people absent on leave is having an injurious effect on the recruiting service. Absentees tell such exaggerated stories of the hardships and sufferings of campaign life and of the carnage of the battle field that they deter recruits from enlisting. The leaves might be revoked by an order from the Adjt's Genl's office, except where the case is that of bona fide sick and wounded unable to join.

The officers I propose to send from each regiment should report at your office; and receive orders (such is my application) to visit all hospitals and places where soldiers may be detained, whether on extra duty or otherwise, no matter by what order or whose authority and bring them here to their regiments. The recruiting service or important duty of course will be excepted. I am satisfied that the most fertile source of increase to the diminished ranks of the regiments is to get back the absentees from the army. There are two well men absent to one really sick man.[1]

G B McClellan
Maj Genl Cmdg

LS (telegram sent), McClellan Papers, New-York Historical Society. *OR*, Ser. 1, XI, Part 3, p. 338.

1. General Orders No. 92, issued July 31 by Stanton, addressed the problem of absentees, relying on civil authorities for enforcement. *OR*, Ser. 3, II, pp. 286–87.

To Mary Ellen McClellan

[Berkeley] July 27 [1862] Sunday

When the mail came, & my package of letters was handed me, my heart sank way down to the toes of my slippers, was rapidly wearing a hole through one of them, for there was no letter from you. In about twenty minutes, Seth[1] gladdened my heart, saved my slippers & put me generally in a good humour with the whole world by handing me your glorious & splendid five pager. I tell you, I took the first chance to read it, & have just finished it. "Tired of it"? You knew when you wrote it, that you were acting on Mr. Weller's[2] principle & stopped short to make me "wish there was more of it"; its brevity was the only thing that disgusted me....

We feel alike about these trials. I do feel that God does what is right

& that my interests, my troubles are & ought to be nothing in comparison with the general good. I will do my best to continue to act unselfishly & solely with an honest heart & am sure that if we do not find peace & happiness in this world we *will* be rewarded in the great eternity. My prayer to God is, that he will permit us to be together in the next world, & that we may pass through eternity hand in hand, heart joined to heart, looking back with a smile to the ephemeral troubles on this poor sinful earth.

I can't tell you how glad I am that I went to see all those poor wounded men yesterday. Another batch will come tonight, & I will if possible go to see all of them tomorrow morning. I regard it as a duty I owe the poor fellows — rather a hard one to perform, but still one that cannot be neglected. I am sorry that no other General officer does the same — it would do the men good....

You ask me whether I advised the Presdt to appoint Halleck — the letter of which I sent you a copy[3] is all that ever passed on the subject, either directly or indirectly — not another word than is there written. We never conversed on the subject — I was never informed of his views or intentions, & even now have not been officially informed of the appt. I only know it through the newspapers. In all these things the Presdt & those around him have acted so as to make the matter as offensive as possible — he has not shown the slightest gentlemanly or friendly feeling & I cannot regard him as in any respect my friend — I am confident that he would relieve me tomorrow if he dared do so. His cowardice alone prevents it. I can never regard him with other feelings than those of thorough contempt — for his mind, heart & morality. I can assure you that my regard for the A of P is the only feeling that induces me to remain in the service....

I can't say that I think that the Presdt is very fortunate in his military advisers. I hope Halleck will scatter them to the four winds. McDowell is morally dead — he has no longer one particle of influence & is despised by all alike....

Fitz Porter has, on the contrary, stuck through it all most nobly — he is all that I thought him & more. Nothing has depressed him; he is always cheerful, active & ready, & is much more efficient than all put together....

AL copy; copy, McClellan Papers (C-7:63/D-10:72), Library of Congress.

1. Seth Williams, of GBM's staff. 2. Samuel Weller, in Dickens's *The Pickwick Papers*. 3. GBM to Lincoln, July 7, *supra*.

To Henry W. Halleck   [TELEGRAM]

Head-Quarters, Army of the Potomac,
Berkeley July 28 8 am 1862

Nothing especially new except corroboration of reports that reinforcements reaching Richmond from South. It is not confirmed that any of Bragg's troops are yet here.[1] My opinion is more & more firm that here is the defence of Washington & that I should be at once reinforced by all available troops to enable me to advance.

Retreat would be disastrous to the Army & the cause — I am confident of that.

G B McClellan
Maj Genl

Maj Genl H W Halleck
Comdg US Army Washington D.C.

ALS (telegram sent), McClellan Papers (A-73:29), Library of Congress. *OR*, Ser. 1, XI, Part 1, p. 75.

1. Braxton Bragg had replaced Beauregard in command of the Confederate Army of Tennessee.

To Mary Ellen McClellan

[Berkeley] July 29 [1862]

. . . I have nothing as yet from Washn, & begin to believe that they intend & hope that I & my army may melt away under the hot sun — if they leave me here neglected much longer I shall feel like taking my rather large military family to Washn to seek an explanation of their course — I fancy that under such circumstances I should be treated with rather more politeness than I have been of late. . . .

Secesh is very quiet of late — scarcely even a cavalry skirmish — he is almost too quiet for good & must be after some mischief — may be we *will* have a visit from monster Merrimac No 2![1] What a row it would create among the transports — such a scampering. I am in hopes that I will receive orders of *some kind* from Washn this evening — I am getting dreadfully tired of sucking my thumbs & doing nothing. I begin to feel the want of a little quiet excitement. I could rest at home away from my men — but the idea of remaining quietly in camp, with an army about me, & an active enemy at some mischief or other, is a very very different thing.

10 1/2 pm   . . . Nothing tonight from Washn, so that I am yet completely in the dark as to the intentions of our benign Govt.

AL copy, McClellan Papers (C-7:63), Library of Congress.

1. The Confederate ironclad *Richmond*. She was not completed before the Army of the Potomac evacuated the Peninsula.

To Henry W. Halleck

Maj Genl H W Halleck
Cmdg US Army   Head-Quarters, Army of the Potomac,
General   Berkeley July 30 1862

There is nothing new of any interest to give you. The Cavalry scouts are daily extending their beats, & meet with less resistance during the last few days. The enemy still at Malvern, its vicinity rather, in small force — probably a brigade with a battery. Nothing seems to be doing on the other side of the James — if I had even a part of Burnside's command I could beat them up on that bank of the James, as well as stir them up at Malvern. I am very weak in Cavalry — not more than 3800 for duty — could not Williams' Regt from Port Royal, & Mix' from Newbern both be ordered up here. A large part of my Cavalry was taken from me when I left Washington for Fort Monroe — I feel the want of it very much.

It is not true (my information goes) that either of the Hills or Longstreet are with Jackson near Gordonsville — nor does it seem probable that J's force is more than 30,000 to 35,000 — altho' it is possible that I may be deceived about the latter point. Heavy reinforcements have arrived in Richmond and are still coming.

I still feel that our true policy is to reinforce this Army by every available means & throw it again upon Richmond.

Should it be determined to withdraw it I shall look upon our cause as lost, & the demoralization of this Army certain — I sincerely hope that *some* decision may be promptly arrived at, & that it may be in accordance with the views I have so frequently expressed.

I am very respectfully your obdt svt
Geo B McClellan
Maj Genl Cmdg

ALS, Records of the Adjutant General's Office, RG 94 (159: Halleck Papers), National Archives. *OR*, Ser. 1, XI, Part 3, p. 342.

To Samuel L. M. Barlow

My dear Barlow   Berkeley July 30 1862

Yours of the 26 received. You are right *to this extent at least* — it has only been the fear of the effect upon my men, & partly perhaps of public opinion, that has prevented my being removed from the command of the Army of the Potomac. The command was for two days persistently pressed upon a General Officer, who happened to be a true friend of mine, & declined the offer.[1] I *know* that the rascals will get rid of me as soon as they dare — they all know my opinion of them. They are aware that I have seen through their villainous schemes, & that if I succeed my foot will be on their necks.

I do not believe there is one honest man among them — & I know what I say — I fear none of them wish to save the Union — they prefer ruling a separate Northern Confederacy — God will yet foil their abominable designs & mete out to them the terrible punishment they deserve.

Don't trust *McD*,[2] or anything he says or writes — he is wily & specious — but is not true.

Halleck remained but a few minutes (comparatively) here & saw *nothing* of the Army — departed just as wise as he came.

I get no reinforcements & no information — until Halleck came I had no word from Washington, since he left I have received nothing. I know nothing, absolutely nothing as to the plans & intentions of the Govt — but I have strong reason to believe that they literally have *no* plans, but are halting in a wretched state of indecision — trembling at the storm they themselves have conjured & not knowing how to quiet it.

Much obliged to you for the copy of Meagher's speech — give him my regards & tell him that I am very anxious for his success — we want many more "wild Irishmen."

If this Army is retired from here I abandon all hope — our cause will be lost. It ought *not* to yield an inch — here is the true defense of Washington.

If I hear anything today or tomorrow I will let you know.

In the mean time, with my kindest regards to Mrs Barlow,

believe me sincerely your friend
Geo B McClellan

S L M Barlow Esq
N.Y.

ALS, Barlow Papers, Huntington Library.

1. Gen. Burnside. 2. Gen. McDowell.

To Mary Ellen McClellan

[Berkeley] July 30 [1862] 10.15 pm.

... Another day elapsed & nothing from Washn. I have positive information today that the command of this army was pressed upon Burnside & that he peremptorily refused it. I learn that Meigs is very anxious for it — much good may it do him. I still think from all that comes to me that the chances are at least even that I will be superseded. ...

We were relieved today by a little excitement — the gun boats reported that 6 rebel gun boats (including Mr. Merrimac No 2) were on the way down — so we were for some hours considerably brightened up by the prospect of seeing a shindy — but it turned out to be a false report. ...

I see among other lies, that the papers say that the enemy drove off 500 of our beef cattle the other day — a lie cut of whole cloth. . . .

I am sorry to say that I hear that too much faith must not be rested in Halleck — I hope it is not so — but will be very careful how far I trust him, or any other man in these days. He has done me *no good yet*. As a counterpart to what you say Alsop said of H's conversation in the cars (that McC was the ablest soldier in the world)[1] he told some one else (that is *H*. did) that *I* was too dilatory. The adm. have proclaimed a policy that I will not carry out. As soon as I receive the official copy of the Presdt's Proclamation I shall issue orders directly opposite to Pope's — then there will be a furious row![2]

AL copy, McClellan Papers (C-7:63), Library of Congress.

1. Mrs. McClellan had recently visited Joseph W. Alsop and his wife in New York. Alsop had related the same story to GBM in his letter of July 24: "Mr. Lord (of the Illinois C.) is here. . . . He said to me this (which I immediately noted down) that in a conversation had with Genl Halleck on Monday last [July 21] in the cars, he (the General) said *that McClellan was the ablest military man in the world*. This delighted me." McClellan Papers (A-73:29). 2. The president's proclamation of July 25 promulgated the recently enacted Second Confiscation Act. *Collected Works of Lincoln*, V, p. 341. GBM's response was to issue General Orders No. 154 on Aug. 9, which read, in part: "The general commanding takes this occasion to remind the officers and soldiers of this army . . . that we are not engaged in a war of rapine, revenge, or subjugation; that this is not a contest against populations, but against armed forces and political organizations; that it . . . should be conducted by us upon the highest principles known to Christian civilization." *OR*, Ser. 1, XI, Part 3, pp. 362–64.

To Mary Ellen McClellan

[Berkeley] July 31 [1862]

. . . This morning I visited the Genl Hospital not far from here, & went through it all — finding the patients comfortable & all improving in health. They are nearly all in hospital tents & are well provided for — in truth they are about as well off as they could be away from home, & many of them doubtless better off than they would be there. I find the men more contented than the officers — the truth is that if the officers were in their sphere one tenth as good as the men in theirs we should have the finest army in the world. I confess that the men enlist my sympathies much more warmly than the officers — they are so patient & devoted — they have generally entered the service too from higher & more unselfish motives. Poor fellows — I can never willingly break the link that unites me to them & shall always be very proud of them & of their love for me — even if it is not decreed by Providence that I am to lead them to Richmond. After the long time that has elapsed without my hearing anything from Washn I can hardly hope to learn anything by today's mail — but I assure you that we are all becoming very impatient at the long delay here, so unnecessary as it seems to us.

I commenced turning over a new leaf today — that is neither writing or telegraphing to Washn & have about determined to draw back into my shell until the oracle deigns to speak. I have said all I well can — I have told them about all I think & know — have pointed out to them what I regard as the genl effects of the course I fear they are likely to adopt — words can no further go — by saying more & repeating what has already said I should only render myself ridiculous & a bore — so I will be silent & if they send me the order I dread (that of withdrawing this army) I will make one last desperate appeal before obeying it & then let matters take their course — confident that I have honestly endeavored to do the best I could, altho' I may not have done as well as others could. There is a great consolation in feeling that one has tried to do right, & not been actuated by selfish motives — of the last I *know* that I am free, & would say so were I even on my death bed....

To tell the truth (which it will not be necessary for you to repeat to ——) I have quite enough civilians on my staff — they are of little or no use to me, & are a great deal more trouble than they are worth. I manage to employ those I have in writing & in carrying unimportant orders — but the really serious work, especially under fire, has to be done by Colburn, Sweitzer, Hudson, Radowitz, Hammerstein, Wright (who has picked up a good deal), Lowell & some youngsters I have caught. The most useless thing imaginable is one of these "highly educated" civilians — it takes them a long time to learn the fact that they know nothing & they are very apt to give offense by their assumption of manner etc. I have raked mine down so that they are now pretty regulated, but I would not for the world have any new ones....

I told you the result of the interview with Halleck — thus far practically nothing — not a word have I heard from Washn since his return there. I shall not write or telegraph another word until I hear from them, unless something of great importance occurs. I shall stand on what is left of my dignity now!!...

I cannot feel that I have any intentional error to reproach myself with, & I feel prepared to meet with a brave heart, firm will & clear brain anything that may occur.

1 am. [August 1] As I was just about comfortably asleep about 3/4 of an hour ago I was awakened by a tremendous shelling — the rascals (not you — but secesh) opened on us with field guns from the other side of the river & kept up a tremendous fire. It is now pretty much over, but still going on — no shells have burst nearer than 300 or 400 yds to my camp so I am quite indifferent. It took me about 5 minutes to wake Marcy — he did not hear a single shot....

Still some firing — now heavy again — gun boats at work — they were very slow in getting ready. A queer thing this writing a letter to my wife at this time of night to the music of shells — I fear they must have done some harm. Now they are quiet again — there goes a *whopper* from the gun boats! Queer times these!

1 1/2 [A.M.]   Pretty quiet now — only an occasional shot, apparently from the gun boats — there goes one! Now another! Marcy & I have just been discussing (another) people in Washn & conclude that they are "a mighty trifling set" — indeed it is very criminal to leave me thus without one word of information as to their plans & purposes. If any lives have been lost tonight the guilt (another shot) is on their shoulders — for I told them that I desired to occupy with Burnside's troops the very point where this firing has come tonight — another shot — but I begin to believe that they wish this army to be destroyed — the wretches! How sick & tired I am of serving such a set of incompetent knaves — I do not believe that any nation was ever accursed with such a set of people as those who now rule in Washn.

2.45 [A.M.]   Tired of waiting for Hammerstein's return with the news of the damage done. . . .

Well! He has just returned — it was so dark that no one could tell what the damage was — one man at Fitz Porter's Hd Qtrs had his leg shot off — no vessels set on fire — the camps all quiet.

8 am.   All quiet & comfortable — no harm done by all that firing except the one poor fellow hit in the leg. . . .

AL copy, McClellan Papers (C-7:63), Library of Congress.

To Henry W. Halleck

Confidential and unofficial   Head-Quarters, Army of the Potomac,
My dear General;   Berkeley August 1st 1862

Your kind and very welcome letter of the 30th reached me this morning.[1]

My own experience enables me to appreciate most fully the difficulties and unpleasant features of your position. I have passed through it all and most cordially sympathize with you; for I regard your place, under present circumstances as one of the most unpleasant under the Government.

Of one thing, however, you may be sure, and that is of my full and cordial support in all things. Had I been consulted as to who was to take my place, I would have advised your appointment. So far as you are concerned, I feel towards you, and shall act, precisely as if I had urged you for the place you hold. There is not one particle of feeling or jealousy in my heart towards you. Set your mind perfectly at rest on that score. No one of your old and tried friends will work with you more cordially and more honestly than I shall.

If we are permitted to do so, I believe that together we can save this unhappy country and bring this war to a comparatively early termination; the doubt in my mind is whether the selfish politicians will allow us to do so. I fear the results of the *civil* policy inaugurated by recent Acts of Congress and practically enunciated by General Pope in his series of orders to the Army of Virginia.[2]

It is my opinion that this contest should be conducted by us as a *War,* and as a War between civilized nations; that our efforts should be directed towards crushing the armed masses of the rebels, not against the people; but that the latter should, as far as military necessities permit, be protected in their constitutional, civil, and personal rights.

I think that the question of slavery should enter into this war solely as a *military* one; that while we do our best to prevent the rebels from making military uses of their slaves, we should avoid any proclamations of general emancipation, and should protect inoffensive citizens in the possession of that, as well as of other kinds of property. If we do not actively *protect* them in this respect, we should at least, avoid taking an active part on the other side and let the negro take care of himself.

The people of the South should understand that we are not making war upon the institution of slavery, but that if they submit to the Constitution and Laws of the Union they will be protected in their constitutional rights of every nature. I think that pillaging and outrages to persons ought not to be tolerated; that private persons and property should enjoy all the protection we can afford them, compatible with the necessities of our position. I would have the conduct of the Union troops present a strong contrast with that of the rebel Armies and prove by our action, that the Government is, as we profess it to be, benign and beneficent; that, wherever its power extends, protection and security exist for all who do not take an active part against us.

Peculiar circumstances may force us to depart from these principles in exceptional cases, but I would have these departures the exceptions, not the rule.

I and the Army under my command are fighting to restore the Union and the supremacy of its laws, not for revenge; I therefore deprecate, and view with infinite dread, any policy which tends to render impossible the reconstruction of the Union and to make this contest simply a useless effusion of blood.

We need more men: the old regiments of this Army should be promptly filled — by immediate drafting, if necessary. We should present such an overwhelming force as to render success certain, be able to follow it up, and to convince the *people* of the South that resistance is useless.

I know that our ideas as to the concentration of forces agree perfectly. I believe that the principles I have expressed in this letter accord with your own views. I sincerely hope that we do not differ widely. You see I have met you in your own spirit of frankness, and I would be glad to have your views on these points, that I may know what I am doing. We *must* have a full understanding on all points, and I regard the civil or political question as inseparable from the military, in this contest.

It is unnecessary for me to repeat my objections to the idea of withdrawing this Army from its present position. Every day's reflection but serves to strengthen my conviction that the true policy is to reinforce this Army, at the earliest possible moment, by every available man, and to allow it to resume the offensive with the least possible delay.

I am, General, your sincere friend,
Geo. B. McClellan

Major General H. W. Halleck,
Commanding U.S. Army

Retained copy, McClellan Papers (A-73:29), Library of Congress. *OR*, Ser. 1, XI, Part 3, pp. 345–46.

1. Halleck wrote on July 30: "I have always had strong personal objections to mingling in the politico-military affairs of Washington.... There seemed to be a disposition in the public press to cry down any one who attempted to serve the country instead of party. This was particularly the case with you, as I understand.... There was no one in the Army under whom I could serve with greater pleasure, and I now ask from you that same support and co-operation and that same free interchange of opinions as in former days." *OR*, Ser. 1, XI, Part 3, p. 343. 2. In addition to the Second Confiscation Act, GBM refers to a series of harsh orders issued by Gen. Pope relating to Southern civilians living in the war zone. *OR*, Ser. 1, XII, Part 2, pp. 50–52.

To Mary Ellen McClellan

[Berkeley] Aug 2 [1862]

... Circumstances have made it unavoidable for me to send out two important expeditions & a large working party, altho' it is Sunday [August 3]. One of the expeditions goes to Malvern, the other on the other side of the James River....

I had quite an interesting visit on the other side today — the place we burned up yesterday was a very handsome one — it was a rather hard case to be obliged to do it, but it could not be avoided.[1] ...

I had (as usual) not a single word from Washn today from any one, nor anything from Burnside. If the latter is really under orders for the Rappahannock there is something very strange in his failure to communicate with me — not even giving me the slightest hint of it; therefore I am disposed to discredit Com. Wilkes' report[2] & to think that he must be mistaken in regard to it — for I *know* Burnside to be true to me — there can be no doubt about *that*. If he *is* ordered to the Rappahannock I believe that this army will be withdrawn from here, & then the cup of misery of this country will be full indeed....

When you contrast the policy I urge in my letter to the Presdt[3] with that of Congress & Mr. Pope you can readily agree with me that there can be little mutual confidence between the Govt & myself — we are the antipodes of each other & it is more than probable that they will take the earliest opportunity to relieve me from command & get me out of sight. I shall endeavor to pursue the plain path of duty — as I have often told you my mind is prepared to endure anything that a man of honor can — but I shall consult my own sense of right & my own judgment — not deferring to that of others when my own convictions are strong. There are *some* things to which I cannot submit & to which nothing can induce me to yield. . . .

7.30 am. Aug. 3rd   . . . One of my expeditions of last night failed[4] — had to come back because the guides lost the way — will try again tonight or tomorrow. The other one not yet heard from, but has I hope met with better luck than the first. . . .

Everything quiet during the night — no firing & no stampede of any kind. . . .

AL copy, McClellan Papers (C-7:63), Library of Congress.

1. The place from which Confederate field guns had shelled the Harrison's Landing camp on the night of July 31–Aug. 1. 2. Commodore Charles Wilkes had replaced John Rodgers in command of the James River flotilla. Burnside's command was ordered to the Rappahannock on Aug. 1. 3. GBM to Lincoln, July 7, *supra*. 4. To Malvern Hill.

To Henry W. Halleck   [TELEGRAM]

Head-Quarters, Army of the Potomac,
Berkeley August 4 12m 1862

Your telegram of last evening is received.[1] I must confess that it has caused me the greatest pain I ever experienced, for I am convinced that the order to withdraw this Army to Acquia Creek will prove disastrous in the extreme to our cause — I fear it will be a fatal blow.

Several days are necessary to complete the preparations for so important a movement as this & while they are in progress I beg that careful consideration may be given to my statements.

This Army is now in excellent discipline & condition; we hold a debouche on both banks of the James River, so that we are free to act in any direction, & with the assistance of the gun boats I consider our communications as now secure. We are (25) twenty five miles from Richmond & are not likely to meet the enemy in force sufficient to fight a battle until we have marched (15) fifteen to (18) eighteen miles, which brings us practically within (10) ten miles of Richmond. Our longest line of land transportation would be from this point, (25) twenty five miles; but with the aid of the gun boats we can supply the Army by water, during its advance, certainly to within (12) twelve miles of Richmond. At Acquia Creek we would be (75) seventy five miles from Richmond, with land transportation all the way.

From here to Fort Monroe is a march of about (70) seventy miles, for I regard it as impracticable to withdraw this Army and its material except by land.

The result of the movement would thus be to march (145) one hundred and forty five miles to reach a point now only (25) twenty five miles distant, & to deprive ourselves entirely of the powerful aids of the gun boats & water transportation.

Add to this the certain demoralization of this Army which would ensue, the terribly depressing effect upon the people of the North, & the strong probability that it would influence foreign Powers to recognize our adversaries, & these appear to me sufficient reasons to make it my imperative duty to urge in the strongest terms afforded by our language that this order may be rescinded, & that far from recalling this Army it be promptly reinforced to enable it to resume the offensive.

It may be said that there are no reinforcements available — I point to Burnside's force, to that of Pope not necessary to maintain a strict defensive in front of Washington & Harper's Ferry, to those portions of the Army of the West not required for a strict defensive there. Here, directly in front of this Army, is the heart of the rebellion; it is here that all our resources should be collected to strike the blow which will determine the fate of this nation.

All points of secondary importance elsewhere should be abandoned & every available man brought here — a decided victory here and the military strength of the rebellion is crushed — it matters not what partial reverses we may meet with elsewhere. Here is the true defence of Washington, it is here on the banks of the James that the fate of the Union should be decided.

Clear in my conviction of right, strong in the consciousness that I have ever been and still am actuated solely by love for my country, knowing that no ambitious or selfish motives have influenced me from the commencement of this war — I do now what I never did in my life before — I entreat that this order may be rescinded.

If my counsel does not prevail I will, with a sad heart, obey your orders to the utmost of my power, directing to the movement, which I clearly foresee will be one of the utmost delicacy & difficulty, whatever skill I may possess.

Whatever the result may be, and may God grant that I am mistaken in my forebodings, I shall at least have the internal satisfaction that I have written & spoken frankly, & have sought to do the best in my power to avert disaster from my country.[2]

> G B McClellan
> Maj Genl Comdg

Maj Genl H W Halleck
Comdg US Army

ALS (telegram sent), McClellan Papers (A-74:29), Library of Congress. *OR,* Ser. 1, XI, Part 1, pp. 81–82.

1. Halleck telegraphed on Aug. 3: "It is determined to withdraw your army from the Peninsula to Aquia Creek. You will take immediate measures to effect this, covering the movement the best you can." *OR,* Ser. 1, XI, Part 1, pp. 80–81. **2.** In Halleck's reply on Aug. 6 he wrote, in part: "You, general, certainly could not have been more pained at receiving my order than I was at the necessity of issuing it." He referred to GBM's estimate that Lee had 200,000 men at Richmond, while Pope had 40,000 and the Army of the Potomac 90,000. "You are 30 miles from Richmond and General Pope 80 or 90, with the enemy directly between you, ready to fall with his superior numbers upon one or the other, as he may elect. Neither can re-enforce the other in case of such an attack.... If you or any one else had presented a better [plan] I certainly should have adopted it, but all of your plans require re-enforcements, which it is impossible to give you." *OR,* Ser. 1, XII, Part 2, pp. 9–11.

To Mary Ellen McClellan

Berkeley Aug 4 [1862] 6 1/2 pm

... I was off on the other side of the river all day yesterday — where I had a hot & fatiguing tramp on foot, besides getting a little damp in the rain. Our enterprise on that side of the river was quite successful. I found a splendid position to cover that bank, so as to enable us to cross the army if necessary as well as to prevent any more midnight serenades like that of last week. I now hold the other shore with a sufficient number of troops to prevent a surprise. Averell went out with 3 squadrons, met & thrashed an entire regiment, drove them to & through their camp, which he captured & leisurely destroyed — thus making the 13th Va Cavalry exceedingly uncomfortable last night, for all their tents, provisions, cooking utensils & baggage were effectually burned up! He got some prisoners & sabred a respectable number — having only two wounded himself — the 5th Regular Cavalry & the 3rd Penna Cavalry did the work....

11 1/2 pm. I had a note from Burnside this evening — he has been ordered to the Rappahannock & has I presume started — not one word have I heard on that subject from Wash. Halleck has begun to show the cloven foot already — he will kill himself in less than two weeks....

So Genl Scott told Aspinwall that he had not lost confidence in me! I am quite sure that I owe Halleck's appointment to him!!¹ ...

I have a large expedition out tonight — a couple of Divns of Infty & some 2000 Cavalry to try to catch the secesh who are at Malvern Hill. Shall not hear from them before tomorrow noon. Colburn has gone with them....

7 am [August 5]. Pretty sharp cannonading has been going on in my front this morning — Hooker's command at Malvern — they are still

cracking away pretty sharply — have not heard details, but will ride out in that direction as soon as I get my bkfst. . . .

AL copy, McClellan Papers (C-7:63), Library of Congress.

1. On July 31 Mrs. McClellan wrote GBM: "Genl Scott told Mr. Aspinwall that his confidence in you was *undiminished* & Mr. Alsop seemed to think every thing is going on well & that all these little trials & annoyances will only redound to your good in the end. . . . " McClellan Papers (B-11:48).

To Randolph B. Marcy

Aug 5 [1862] — Malvern Hill 1 pm

. . . Hooker has been entirely successful in driving off the enemy — took about 100 prisoners, killed & wounded several. The mass escaped under cover of a thick fog. Hooker's dispositions were admirable & nothing but the fog prevented complete success. We have lost 3 killed & 11 wounded — among the latter 2 officers. I shall retain the command here tonight. Keep all things ready to move out should we be attacked. I shall not return before dark & may remain all night — will send in for my blankets & ambulance if I stay. I am now starting to look over the ground. I have sent a party to communicate with Averell — directing him to take post tonight near Nelson's farm. Will send in again as soon as I return from my ride.

Excuse the illegibility of this, as it is written on horseback & the flies trouble Dan. The enemy in strong force at New Market. Better send a special dispatch to Halleck & tell him that I hate to give up this position. Secesh is under cover, & tho' he is in strong force I can beat him if they will give me reinforcements.[1] Send this to Nell if I do not get back in time for mail.

AL copy, McClellan Papers (C-7:63), Library of Congress.

1. Marcy's dispatch of this date to Halleck, sent over GBM's name, read, in part: "This is a very advantageous position to cover an advance on Richmond and only 14 3/4 miles distant, and I feel confident that with re-enforcements I could march this army there in five days." *OR*, Ser. 1, XI, Part 1, pp. 77–78.

To Joseph Hooker

Hd Quarters Army of Potomac
My dear General   Berkeley Aug 6 [1862] 10 pm

I find it will not be possible to get the whole Army in position before some time tomorrow afternoon, which will be too late to support you & hold the entire position should the enemy attack in large force at day break, which there is strong reason to suppose he intends doing. Should we fight a general battle at Malvern it will be necessary to abandon the whole of our works here & run the risk of getting back here should the enemy prove too strong for us.

Under advices I have received from Washington I think it necessary for you to abandon the position tonight, getting everything away before day light.[1]

Please leave cavalry pickets at Malvern with orders to destroy the Turkey Creek Bridge when they are forced back.

The roads leading in to Haxall's from the right should be strongly watched & Haxall's, at least, held by strong cavalry force & some light batteries as long as possible.

I leave the manner of the withdrawal entirely to your discretion.

Please signal to the fleet when the withdrawal is almost completed.

Report frequently to these Head Quarters. Genl Sumner was ordered up to support you, but will halt when this passes him & will inform you where he is.

Truly yours
Geo B McClellan
Maj Genl

Genl. J. Hooker
Comdg at Malvern Hill

ALS, McClellan Papers (A-74:29), Library of Congress. *OR*, Ser. 1, XI, Part 1, p. 79.

1. Before Halleck's letter of Aug. 6 reached him (see GBM to Halleck, Aug. 4, note 2, *supra*), GBM received a telegram from the general-in-chief on Aug. 5 informing him that the order to withdraw from the Peninsula would not be rescinded. At 3 A.M. on Aug. 6 Halleck telegraphed: "I have no re-enforcements to send you." *OR*, Ser. 1, XI, Part 1, pp. 82, 78.

To Mary Ellen McClellan

Aug 8 [1862] Saturday [Friday] Berkeley

I can't convey an idea of the heat today — it has been intense — not a breath of air stirring. I got through with the ordinary business of receiving Generals, decided on papers &c about 12. Then took the ambulance & drove down to see Fitz about some business matters, remained there until three when I came home, made an attempt to take a nap, but it was so terribly hot, that I was lamentably unsuccessful & pretty soon got up in disgust; went out under the trees in light costume, & smoked cigarettes until dark, when we dined. Then, I had quite a host of visitors; first a naval officer on duty; then Allen just back from Washington; then, Ingalls, Brooks, Sykes, Porter & Franklin[1] — the latter having returned tonight. After they had all gone I had a long talk with Allen, who gave me the last news & present state of affairs in Washington. Then I had a talk with Marcy & dictated an order to Key. Then, I read the defense of my course in the N.Y. World of yesterday;[2] then received some reports from Pleasonton[3] that the enemy were pressing him hard near Malvern Hill, & gave the necessary orders. . . .

I am in strong hopes that the enemy will be foolish enough to drive Pleasonton in & attack me in this position — I have ordered P. to draw them on if possible, & if they come in sight will try to keep my men concealed & do my best to induce them to attack me. Should they be so foolish as to do that I will surely beat them & follow them up to Richmond but I fear they are too smart for that. I can hardly hope for so much good luck — if it is a possible thing to humbug them into an attack I will do it.

I will issue tomorrow an order giving *my* comments on Mr. Jno Pope[4] — I will strike square in the teeth of all his infamous orders & give directly the reverse instructions to my army — forbid all pillaging & stealing & take the highest Christian ground for the conduct of the war — let the Govt gainsay it if they dare. I am willing to fall in such a cause. I will not permit this army to degenerate into a mob of thieves, nor will I return these men of mine to their families as a set of wicked & demoralized robbers — I will not have that sin on my conscience. . . .

I have received my orders from Halleck — I cannot *tell* you what they are, but if you will bear in mind what I have already written to you, you can readily guess them when I say that they are as bad as they can be, & that I regard them as almost fatal to our cause. I have remonstrated as warmly as I know how to do — but to no avail. My only hope now is that I can induce the enemy to attack me. I shall of course obey the orders unless the enemy gives me a very good opening — which I should at once avail myself of. I hear thru private sources that they have not yet determined how to dispose of me — personally. Their game is to force me to resign — mine will be to force them to place me on leave of absence, so that when they begin to reap the whirlwind that they have sown I may still be in position to do something to save my country. With all their faults I *do* love my countrymen & if I can save them I will yet do so. . . .

I had another letter from Halleck tonight — I strongly suspect him of being a "scallawag."[5]

AL copy; copy, McClellan Papers (C-7:63/D-10:72), Library of Congress.

1. Allan Pinkerton, Rufus Ingalls, W. T. H. Brooks, George Sykes, Fitz John Porter, William B. Franklin. 2. In an editorial published Aug. 7, editor Manton Marble of the *New York World* wrote, in part: "The failure of this campaign, the profitless expenditure of hundreds of millions of treasure, and of tens of thousands of lives, were due, not to any want of capacity, nor courage, nor energy, nor forethought of Gen. McClellan; . . . but . . . were the direct, natural and necessary result of the suicidal policy which deprived the general-in-chief of a part of his command, and transferred the control of our armies, and conduct of the war, to an irresponsible committee [the Joint Committee on the

Conduct of the War] and an incompetent civilian [Secretary of War Stanton]." 3. Brig. Gen. Alfred Pleasonton had commanded the cavalry in the Malvern Hill expedition. 4. General Orders No. 154, Aug. 9. See GBM to his wife, July 30, note 2, *supra*. 5. Probably Halleck's letter of Aug. 6. See GBM to Halleck, Aug. 4, note 2, *supra*.

To Mary Ellen McClellan

[Berkeley] Aug 10 [1862] 8 am

... Halleck is turning out just like the rest of the herd — the affair is rapidly developing itself, & I see more clearly every day their settled purpose to force me to resign. I am trying to keep my temper & force *them* to relieve me or dismiss me from the service. I have no idea that I will be with this army more than two or three weeks longer & should not be surprised any day or hour to get my "walking papers." I have a strong idea that Pope will be thrashed during the coming week — & very badly whipped he will be & ought to be — such a villain as he is ought to bring defeat upon any cause that employs him. ...

4 pm.   ... I am inclined to believe that Pope will catch his Tartar within a couple of days & be disposed of. The absurdity of Halleck's course in ordering the army away from here is that it cannot possibly reach Washn in time to do any good, but will necessarily be too late — I am sorry to say that I am forced to the conclusion that H. is very dull & very incompetent — alas poor country! I hope to be ready tomorrow afternoon to move forward in the direction of Richmond — I will try to catch or thrash Longstreet & then if the chance offers follow in to Richmond while they are lamming away at Pope. It is in some respects a desperate step, but it is the best I can do for the nation just now & I would rather even be defeated than retreat without an effort to relieve Washn in the only way at all possible. If I fail — why well & good. I will fall back. If I win I shall have saved my country & will then gratefully retire to private life. ...

I am getting the sick away quite rapidly now — but they are in large numbers & it is at best a slow process. The heavy baggage is all being stored on board ships so that in whatever direction we move it will be comparatively unencumbered. I shall send off all that I have except a carpet bag & pair of blankets — change my large tent for a "wall tent" & go about as light as any of them. I half apprehend that they will be too quick for me in Washn & relieve me before I have the chance of making the dash. If so — well & good. I am satisfied that the dolts in Washn are bent on my destruction if it is possible for them to accomplish it — but I believe that Providence is just enough to bring their own sins upon their heads & that they will before they get through taste the dregs of the cup of bitterness. The more I hear of their wickedness the more am I surprised that such a wretched set are permitted to *live* much less to occupy the positions they do. It is no doubt all for the best & Providence has some wise purpose to fulfil thro' them. . . .

The next few days will probably be decisive. If I succeed in my coup everything will be changed in this country so far as we are concerned & my enemies will be at my feet. It may go hard with some of them in that event, for I look upon them as the enemies of the country & of the human race. . . .

Midnight.   I received a very harsh & unjust telegram from Halleck this evening & a very *friendly private* letter from the same individual — blows hot & cold.[1] I replied to his telegram — closing by quietly remarking "The present moment is probably not the proper one for me to refer to the unnecessarily harsh & unjust tone of your telegrams of late. It will however make no difference in my official action."[2] Under the circumstances I feel compelled to give up the idea of my intended attack upon Richmond & must *retrace my steps*. Halleck *writes* that all the forces in Virginia including Pope, Burnside etc are to be placed under my command — I doubt it, but will accept no less place. They are committing a fatal error in withdrawing me from here — & the future will show it. I believe that I could take Richmond were I to advance tomorrow. I think the result of their machinations will be that Pope will be badly thrashed within two days & that they will be very glad to turn over the redemption of their affairs to me. I won't undertake it unless I have full & entire control. . . .

AL copy, McClellan Papers (C-7:63), Library of Congress.

1. In his letter of Aug. 7, Halleck wrote: "I fully agree with you in regard to the manner in which the war should be conducted, and I believe the present policy of the President to be conservative. . . . I deeply regret that you cannot agree with me as to the necessity of reuniting the old Army of the Potomac. I, however, have taken the responsibility of doing so, and am to risk my reputation on it. As I told you when at your camp, it is my intention that you shall command all the troops in Virginia as soon as we can get them together; and with the army thus concentrated I am certain that you can take Richmond. I must beg of you, general, to hurry along this movement. . . . " His telegram of Aug. 10 read: "The enemy is crossing the Rapidan in large force. . . . There must be no further delay in your movements. That which has already occurred was entirely unexpected, and must be satisfactorily explained." *OR*, Ser. 1, XI, Part 3, pp. 359–60, Part 1, p. 86. 2. GBM to Halleck, Aug. 10, *OR*, Ser. 1, XI, Part 1, p. 86.

To Henry W. Halleck   [TELEGRAM]

Genl Halleck   Berkeley Aug 12 [1862] 4 pm

Information from various sources received within a few days past goes to corroborate the evidence you have rec'd that the rebel army at Richmond has been much weakened by detachments sent to Gordonsville & that the remaining forces have been so much dispersed between Richmond & this place on both sides James River as to render it doubtful if they can be concentrated again rapidly. D. H. Hill with a division or more is in the vicinity of Petersburg, others are along the south bank of James River back of Fort Darling & I am quite certain that Longstreet with about eighteen thousand men now occupies an intrenched position which can probably be turned & is about three miles above Malvern Hill. I can in forty eight hours advance on him & either drive him into the works around Richmond or defeat & capture his forces. Should I succeed in accomplishing the latter I see but little difficulty if my information is correct in pushing rapidly forward into Richmond. This would involve the cooperation of all my available forces but the question would soon be decided & if successful I should require reinforcements to maintain my communications. This effort would it seems to me have the effect to draw back the forces now before Genl Pope & thus relieve Washington from all danger. One of my general officers who for five days past has held a position near Malvern Hill in a letter just received says The enemy before us is weak. From all I can learn there is not thirty six thousand men between this & Richmond nor do I believe they can get more before we can whip them. I have good guides etc.[1] Genl Barnard, Chief of my Engineers, is decidedly in favor of this movement at this time. Under these circumstances I consider it my duty to present the foregoing information & for your consideration, as under existing orders I do not feel authorized to make the movement. I shall continue to forward reinforcements & sick as rapidly as transports arrive & have given the necessary instructions to insure no delay in moving the army.

Geo. B. McClellan

Maj Genl Comdg

Retained copy, McClellan Papers (C-10:63), Library of Congress. *OR*, Ser. 1, XI, Part 3, pp. 372–73.

1. Quoted from a dispatch by Gen. Pleasonton to Gen. Marcy, Aug. 11. *OR*, Ser. 1, XI, Part 3, p. 369.

To Henry W. Halleck [TELEGRAM]

Berkeley August 12 [1862] 11 pm

Your dispatch of noon today received.[1] It is positively the fact that no more men could have embarked hence than have gone & that no unnecessary delay has occurred. Before your orders were received Col Ingalls directed all available vessels to come from Monroe. Officers have been sent to take personal direction. Have heard nothing here of Burnside fleet. There are some vessels at Monroe such as Atlantic & Illinois which draw too much to come here. Hospital accommodations exhausted this side New York.

Propose filling Atlantic & Illinois with serious cases for New York &

to encamp slight cases for the present at Monroe. In this way can probably get off the (3400) thirty four hundred sick still on hand by day after tomorrow night. I am sure that you have been misinformed as to availability of vessels on hand. We cannot use heavily loaded supply vessels for troops or animals & such constitute the mass of those here which have been represented to you as capable of transporting this Army.

I fear you will find very great delay in embarking troops & material at Yorktown & Monroe both from want of vessels & of facilities for embarkation. At least two additional wharves should at once be built at each place — I ordered two at the latter some (2) two weeks ago, but you countermanded the order.

I learn that wharf accommodations at Acquia are altogether inadequate for landing troops & supplies to any large extent — not an hour should be lost in remedying this. Great delays will ensue there from shallow water.

You will find a vast deficiency in horse transports. We had nearly (200) two hundred when we came here. I learn of only (20) twenty provided now. They carry about (50) fifty horses each.

More hospital accommodations should be provided. We are much impeded here because our wharves are used night & day to land current supplies. At Monroe a similar difficulty will occur. With all the facilities at Alexandria & Washington (6) six weeks about were occupied in embarking this Army & its material. Burnside's troops are not a fair criteria for rate of embarkation — all his means were in hand, his outfit specially prepared for the purpose & his men habituated to the movement. There shall be no unnecessary delay — but I cannot manufacture vessels.

I state these difficulties from experience & because it appears to me that we have lately been working at cross purposes because you have not been properly informed by those around you who ought to know the inherent difficulties of such an undertaking. It is not possible for any one to place this Army where you wish it ready to move in less than a month. If Washington is in danger now this Army can scarcely arrive in time to save it — it is in much better position to do so from here than from Acquia.

Our material can only be saved by using the whole Army to cover it if we are pressed.

If seriously weakened by detachments the result might be the loss of much material & many men.

I will be at the telegraph office tomorrow morning to talk with you.[2]

G B McClellan
Maj Genl

Maj Genl H W Halleck
Washn DC

ALS (telegram sent), McClellan Papers (A-74:29), Library of Congress. *OR*, Ser. 1, XI, Part 1, pp. 87–88.

1. Halleck telegraphed: "The Quartermaster-General informs me that nearly every available steam vessel in the country is now under your control.... Burnside moved nearly 13,000 troops to Aquia Creek in less than two days, and his transports were immediately sent back to you. All vessels in the James River and the Chesapeake Bay were placed at your disposal, and it was supposed that 8,000 or 10,000 of your men could be transported daily.... The bulk of your material on shore it was thought could be sent to Fort Monroe, covered by that part of the army which could not get water transportation...." *OR*, Ser. 1, XI, Part 1, p. 87. 2. In reply to GBM's two telegrams of this date, Halleck replied, on Aug. 14: "There is no change of plans. You will send up your troops as rapidly as possible. There is no difficulty in landing them. According to your own accounts, there is now no difficulty in withdrawing your forces." *OR*, Ser. 1, XI, Part 1, p. 89.

To Henry W. Halleck [TELEGRAM]

Head Quarters, Army of the Potomac,
Berkeley Aug 14 11 pm 1862

Movement has commenced by land & water. All sick will be away by tomorrow night.

Everything being done to carry out your orders. I don't like Jackson's movements — he will suddenly appear when least expected. Will telegraph fully & understandingly in the morning.

G B McClellan
Maj Genl

Maj Genl H W Halleck
Washington DC

ALS (telegram sent), McClellan Papers (C-15:64), Library of Congress. *OR*, Ser. 1, XI, Part 1, p. 89.

To Fitz John Porter [TELEGRAM]

Barrett's Ferry Aug 17 [1862] 12.30 pm

Your dispatches of last evening & 8.20 this morning just received. You were misinformed as to Franklin having arrived here, no troops of consequence have yet arrived since your own left. As things are it is probably well that you have moved on, but the consequences might be very serious should the enemy attack in force. I do not think we shall be troubled but will not feel entirely safe until all the wagons are over the bridge. My wish was to have had everything in hand until getting the wagons past Williamsburg. As it is now you could not return in time & had better continue the movement. If there are transports at Monroe embark your command at once & proceed to Acquia Creek, leaving some suitable officer to bring up the wagons as soon as transportation is ready.[1]

> G B McClellan
> Maj Genl Comdg

Maj Genl F J Porter
Comdg 5th Corps   Williamsburg Va

ALS (telegram sent), McClellan Papers (A-74:29), Library of Congress.

1. See GBM to Porter, Dec. 19, 1862, *infra*.

To Henry W. Halleck

Private

General   Barrett's Ferry Chickahominy Aug 17 2.30 pm / 62

I have had this morning a full conversation with General Burnside. To be perfectly frank with you I must say that I did think from some of your recent telegrams that you were not disposed to treat me in a candid or friendly manner — this was the more grating to me because I was conscious that although I differed from you in opinion I had done so with entire frankness & loyalty, and that I had not delayed one moment in preparing to carry out your orders [*crossed out:* while I availed myself of the unavoidable delay to urge upon you my own view of the case]. I am glad to say that Burnside has satisfied me that you are still my friend — in return I think he can satisfy you that I have loyally carried out your instructions, altho' my own judgment was not in accordance with yours.

Let the past take care of itself — so long as I remain in command of this Army I will faithfully carry out the new progamme [*crossed out:* but I will make no more suggestions unless you ask for them]. I feel quite confident that I will have everything across the Chickahominy by daylight. If all is then quiet I will regard my command as reasonably safe & feel justified in moving it solely with reference to its speedy embarkation.[1]

> Very respectfully yours
> Geo B McClellan
> Maj Genl Comdg

Maj Genl H W Halleck
Comdg US Army Washn D.C.

ALS retained copy, McClellan Papers (A-74:29), Library of Congress. *OR*, Ser. 1, XI, Part 3, p. 378.

1. Halleck replied on Aug. 20: "When I felt that the safety of Washington depended on the prompt and rapid transfer of your army it is very probable that my messages to you were more urgent and pressing than guarded in their language. I certainly meant nothing harsh, but I did feel that you did not act as promptly as I thought the circumstances

required. . . . That Lee is moving on Pope with his main army I have no doubt. . . . Under these circumstances you must pardon the extreme anxiety (and perhaps a little impatience) which I feel. Every moment seems to me as important as an ordinary hour." *OR*, Ser. 1, XI, Part 3, pp. 379–80.

To Mary Ellen McClellan

Aug 17 [1862] 3 pm. Barrett's Ferry, Chickahominy

. . . I have the greater part of the army over now, & if we are not disturbed for six hours more all will be well. I have abandoned neither men nor material, & the *"retreat"* has been conducted in the most orderly manner, & is a perfect success so far as so disgusting an operation can be. I learn that all the troops in Va. are to be placed under my command. Burnside came down to assure me from Halleck that he (H.) is really my friend — qu'il soit! I begin to think that I may still be master of the situation. . . .

I hope to get everything over tonight & will be at my old Hd Qtrs at Williamsburg tomorrow evening. Next day at Yorktown. If all is then quiet I will go thence by water to Ft. Monroe & complete the arrangements for embarking. . . .

I took a savage satisfaction in being the last to leave my camp at Berkeley yesterday! . . .

AL copy, McClellan Papers (C-7:63), Library of Congress.

To Mary Ellen McClellan

Aug 18 [1862] pm. Williamsburg

. . . Am pretty well tired out, for I have been much in the saddle lately & have been very anxious — besides having slept very little. . . .

I crossed the Chickahominy yesterday & remained there today until all the troops had crossed & moved several miles in advance. When I left the Bridge was taken up & nothing but a few worthless stragglers left behind — they will all be brought over tonight I think — tho' so far as they are concerned individually I would much prefer that secesh should capture them all. I have made a remarkably successful retreat — left absolutely *nothing* behind — secesh can't find one dollar's worth of property if he hunts a year for it. I have not seen the enemy since we started, & I rather doubt whether he knows where we are now. Shall go to Yorktown in the morning — remain there one or two days, then go to Ft. Monroe. . . .

It will take a long time to embark this army & have it ready for action on the banks of the Potomac. . . .

The men all know that I am not responsible — I have remained constantly with the rear guard — was the very last one to leave our camp at Berkeley, remained on the Chickahominy until the bridge was removed & still have the proud satisfaction of hearing the cheers of the men as I pass, seeing their faces brighten up....

Strange as it may seem the rascals have not I think lost one particle of confidence in me & love me just as much as ever.

I am glad to inform you that your friend Pleasonton has done *splendidly*. I placed him in command of the rear guard. The little fellow (Pleasonton) brightened up very much this morning when he came to report. I looked very sternly at him & told him that I had a very serious complaint to make against him. He looked rather wild, injured, & disgusted, & wished to know what it was. I replied that he had entirely disappointed me, that he had not created a single stampede, nor called for any reinforcements. That such heinous conduct was something I did not at all look for, & that if it was persisted in, I must send him to Pope. The little fellow began to grin & was well pleased. He *is* a most excellent soldier & has performed a very important duty most admirably.

I have felt every moment that I was conducting a false movement, & which was altogether against my own judgment & that of the army. I have done it without demoralizing the army....

AL copy; copy, McClellan Papers (C-7:63/D-10:72), Library of Congress.

To Henry W. Halleck   [TELEGRAM]

Head-Quarters, Army of the Potomac,
[Williamsburg] August 18, 11 pm. 1862

Please say a kind word to my Army that I can repeat to them in Genl Orders in regard to their conduct at Yorktown, Williamsburg, West Point, Hanover C.H. & on the Chickahominy — as well as in regard to the (7) seven days, & the recent retreat. No one has ever said anything to cheer them but myself. Say nothing about me — merely give my men & officers credit for what they have done. It will do you much good & will strengthen you much with them if you issue a handsome order to them in regard to what they have accomplished — they deserve it.[1]

G B McClellan
Maj Genl

Maj Genl Halleck
Comdg USA Washington D.C.

ALS (telegram sent), McClellan Papers (A-74:30), Library of Congress. *OR*, Ser. 1, XI, Part 1, pp. 91–92.

1. Halleck made no reply to this telegram.

To Ambrose E. Burnside

Confidential
Maj. Gen. Ambrose E. Burnside: Fort Monroe, Va.,
My dear Burn: August 20, 1862.

You will have learned ere this that our movement in retreat was most successfully accomplished, without loss and without abandoning any property.

Since my arrival here I have received a couple of telegrams from Halleck, indicating that Pope was in danger, and urging that re-enforcements be sent on as rapidly as possible.

I am pushing everything; not a moment is being lost, and it shall not be my fault if the troops do not arrive in time.

Yesterday and to-day I have received intelligence from confidential sources leading me to think it probable that Halleck either will not or cannot carry out his intentions in regard to my position, as expressed to you. This shall make no difference with me. I shall push on everything just as if I were to remain in command. Please keep me posted as to all you know.

I shall remain here until the whole or the mass of this army is embarked, unless I receive orders to the contrary in the mean time.

I send this by a special messenger.

Ever your friend,
Geo. B. McClellan,
Major-General

OR, Ser. 1, XII, Part 3, p. 605.

To Mary Ellen McClellan

Aug 21 [1862] 8 pm. Fort Monroe (camp) *Sent to Pope*

I believe I have triumphed!! Just received a telegram from Halleck stating that Pope & Burnside are very hard pressed — urging me to push forward reinforcements, & to *come myself as soon as I possibly can*[1] I am going to the Fortress now to hurry on my arrangements — shall put Hd Qtrs on board a vessel tomorrow morning & probably go myself in a fast boat tomorrow afternoon. Now they are in trouble they seem to want the "Quaker," the "procrastinator," the "coward" & the "traitor"! Bien — my ambulance is ready & I must go. I will write more when I come back.

AL copy, McClellan Papers (C-7:63), Library of Congress.

1. Telegram of this date. *OR*, Ser. 1, XI, Part 1, p. 92.

To Henry W. Halleck   [TELEGRAM]

Head Quarters, Army of the Potomac,
Fort Monroe Aug 21 10.25 pm 1862

I have ample supplies of ammunition for Infantry & Artillery & will have it up in time.

I can supply any deficiencies that may exist in Genl Pope's Army.

Quite a number of rifled field guns are on hand here. The forage is the only question for you to attend to — please have that ready for me at Acquia. I want many more schooners for cavalry horses — they should have water on board when they come here.

If you have leisure & there is no objection please communicate to me fully the state of affairs & your plans — I will then be enabled to arrange details understandingly.

G B McClellan
Maj Genl

Maj Genl Halleck
Washington

ALS (telegram sent), McClellan Papers (C-15:64), Library of Congress. *OR*, Ser. 1, XI, Part 1, p. 92.

To Fitz John Porter   [TELEGRAM]

Head Quarters, Army of the Potomac,
Fort Monroe Aug 21 10.40 pm 1862

Tell your men & those of Heintzelman when they arrive that I will leave here tomorrow & will be with them when they are engaged. I am pushing everything forward.

Franklin is here & embarking tonight. Sumner arrives in the morning. I am forwarding ample supplies of everything except forage for which I have called on Washington. Whatever occurs hold out until I arrive.[1]

G B McClellan
Maj Genl

Maj Genl F J Porter
Acquia Creek

ALS (telegram sent), McClellan Papers (C-15:64), Library of Congress. *OR*, Ser. 1, XII, Part 3, pp. 615–16.

1. Porter replied on Aug. 22: "I guess we shall have no trouble to hold out for five or six days." Lincoln Papers, Library of Congress.

To Mary Ellen McClellan

[Fort Monroe] Aug 22 [1862] 10 am.

... I did not get back from the Fort until sometime after midnight & too tired to write....

I shall go to the Fort pretty soon & as soon as the tents are dry move everything on board the vessels so that I shall be ready to start at a moment's notice. I have two Corps off & away.

Franklin ought to have been off nearly by this time, but he & Smith have so little energy that I fear they will be very slow about it. They have disappointed me terribly — I do not at all doubt Franklin's loyalty now, but his efficiency is very little — I am very sorry that it has turned out so. The main, perhaps the only cause is that he has been & still is sick — & one ought not to judge harshly of a person in that condition. I presume I ought also to make a great deal of allowance for Smith also on the same account — so will try to be as charitable as we can under all these circumstances. I think they are pretty well scared in Washn & probably with good reason. I am confident that the disposition to be made of me will depend entirely upon the state of their nerves in Washn. If they feel safe there I will no doubt be shelved — perhaps placed in command here vice Genl Dix. I don't care what they do — would not object to being kept here for a while — because I could soon get things in such condition that I could have you here with me. . . .

Their sending for me to go to Washn only indicates a temporary alarm — if they are at all reassured you will see that they will soon get rid of me. I shall be only too happy to get back to quiet life again — for I am truly & heartily sick of the troubles I have had & am not fond of being a target for the abuse & slander of all the rascals in the country. Well, we will continue to trust in God & feel certain that all is for the best — it is often difficult to understand the ways of Providence — but I have faith enough to believe that nothing is done without some great purpose. But enough of my troubles! . . .

I feel so sick & tired of human nature that I am already wary of being brought in contact with it. To think that a man whom I so sincerely admired, trusted & liked as I did Stanton turning against *me* as he has — & that without any cause that I am aware of! Pah — it is too bad! . . .

AL copy, McClellan Papers (C-7:63), Library of Congress.

To Mary Ellen McClellan

Aug 23 [1862] 3 pm. Steamer City of Hudson

I am off at last & on the way to Acquia. . . .

9 1/2 pm. We are pounding along up the Potomac now, & as the boat is a fast one are passing anything we find. . . .

We will reach Acquia sometime after midnight. Early in the morning I will telegraph to Halleck informing him of my arrival & asking for orders. I have no idea what they will be, nor do I know what has been happening on the Rappahannock yesterday & today. I take it for granted

that my orders will be as disagreeable as it is possible to make them —
unless Pope is beaten, in which case they may want me to save Washn
again. Nothing but their fear will induce them to give me any command
of importance or to treat me otherwise than with discourtesy. Bah! We
will know tomorrow what it is to be — in the mean time I am perfectly
cool & not in the slightest degree excited. . . .

AL copy, McClellan Papers (C-7:63), Library of Congress.

SEVEN

SECOND BULL RUN
AUGUST 24–SEPTEMBER 4, 1862

DURING THE twelve-day period covered here, the tone of General McClellan's correspondence ranges between extremes as varied as his fortunes. On arriving at Aquia Landing on August 24 from the Peninsula, he anticipated being "master of the situation" (as he told his wife) and in command of both the Army of the Potomac and the Army of Virginia. Moving his headquarters to Alexandria, he witnessed instead his troops taken away unit by unit to be fed into General Pope's Second Bull Run operations until he, the highest ranked general in the Federal service, commanded no more than a few staff officers and orderlies. Finally, called to Washington in the first days of September to salvage the wreck of yet another Union defeat, he had not only his own army returned to him but Pope's as well. "A terrible & thankless task...," he wrote his wife on September 2. "I only consent to take it for my country's sake & with the humble hope that God has called me to it...."

At the first evidence of the Army of the Potomac's withdrawal from the Peninsula, General Lee had shifted his forces northward to strike at Pope's Army of Virginia before McClellan's forces could combine with it. When he was unable to bring the Federals to battle on the line of the Rappahannock, Lee sent a column under Stonewall Jackson on a long flanking march to cut Pope's communications by striking at his main supply depot at Manassas Junction. Jackson's vanguard seized the depot on the night of August 26, just as McClellan reached Alexandria. The raiders also cut Pope's telegraphic link with Washington, and many of the dispatches McClellan exchanged with General-in-Chief Halleck in the days following reveal their uncertainty as to what was happening at the front.

As Pope called in his scattered commands and turned back to search out the raiders, Jackson took position on the old Bull Run battlefield of 1861. On August 28 he revealed his location by assaulting one of Pope's passing columns. The next day Pope opened the Second Bull Run fighting with an attack on Jackson. His dispatch written on the morning of August 30, his first to reach Washington in four days, predicted victory. That afternoon, however, with his army again united, Lee counterattacked and drove Pope from the field. The campaign ended at Chantilly on September 1, when Lee's attempt to turn the flank of the retreating Federals fell short.

The majority of McClellan's dispatches written during this time dealt with the disposition of the two Army of the Potomac corps — Sumner's Second and Franklin's Sixth, 25,000 men in all — that were under his direct control at Alexandria. In common with the Harrison's Landing withdrawal, he and General Halleck viewed the issue from very different perspectives. Halleck saw Franklin's and Sumner's troops as essential reinforcements for Pope, and he telegraphed on August 28 that they must reach the front without delay, "ready or not ready. If we delay too long to get ready there will be no necessity to go at all, for Pope will either be defeated or be victorious without our aid."

Considering Pope incompetent and anticipating his defeat, McClellan viewed the case as throwing good money after bad, and exposing Washington to capture if its defenders were weakened by the smallest amount. He urged that Pope be ordered not to give battle but instead fall back to the Washington lines. As he telegraphed the president on August 29, using a particularly unfortunate turn of phrase, the course he obviously favored was "To leave Pope to get out of his scrape & at once use all our means to make the Capital perfectly safe."

Acting on this conviction, McClellan held back the two corps for as long as possible in the face of Halleck's orders. Sufficient artillery had finally arrived from the Peninsula to enable both Franklin and Sumner to have reached the field in time to take part in the second day's fighting at Bull Run, but in fact they arrived only in time to cover Pope's retreat. McClellan argued that the enemy was present in such force as to endanger the reinforcements on their way to the front. "Reports numerous from various sources," he warned Halleck on August 28, indicated that the entire Army of Northern Virginia, 120,000 strong, was on the scene. This figure, more than twice the actual size of Lee's army and based on rumor rather than credible evidence, was another reflection of the illusory picture of the enemy that General McClellan had carried in his mind for more than a year.

The president's decision to place him in charge of Washington's defenses and then in command of the combined armies, described in McClellan's letters to his wife on September 2, was based on two realities of the situation — McClellan's known skills as an organizer and administrator, and the concern that in the crisis the demoralized troops would fight for no other general. Lincoln was candid in admitting to his cabinet that McClellan suffered from the "slows" and was "good for nothing for an onward movement," yet for defending the capital at that moment he was the best available.

To Mary Ellen McClellan

Aug 24 [1862] Sunday 9.30 am. Acquia Creek

We reached here during the night — sent a dispatch about 6 to Halleck informing him that I had arrived here & awaited orders; also sent one to Burnside. . . .

I have no reply as yet to my dispatches & am not at all impatient. I learn that all my troops are ordered to Alexandria for embarkation — so I presume they will be merged in Pope's army. If that is the case I will (if I find it proper) try for a leave of absence! . . .

I learn nothing whatever of the state of affairs — not even whether Pope is still falling back, or whether there has been any fighting — so I suppose it is all right. I fancy that Pope is in retreat — tho' this is only a guess of mine without anything to base it on. I don't see how I can remain in the service if placed under Pope — it would be too great a disgrace, & I can hardly think that Halleck would permit it to be offered me. . . .

I am glad you like the last order — it seems to have knocked Mr. Pope & the administration.[1] . . .

I expect Porter & Burnside here in a few minutes & then will know something of the state of affairs I hope. This is a wretched place — utterly unfit for the landing & supplying of a large body of troops — they have at last found it out, tho' *H.* insisted upon it that there were ample facilities here for all purposes. . . .

12.15 pm.   I have seen Burnside & Porter & gained some information from them. Pope ran away from the Rappahannock last night, shamefully abandoning Porter & Burnside without giving them one word of warning. They only found it out this morning by sending a cavalry patrol there, who found everything deserted. It was most infamous conduct & he deserves hanging for it. They will extricate themselves however. I have not one word yet from Washn & am quietly waiting here for something to turn up. I presume they are discussing me now — to see whether they can get along without me. . . .

They will suffer a terrible defeat if the present state of affairs continues. I *know* that with God's help I can save them. . . .

AL copy, McClellan Papers (C-7:63), Library of Congress.

1. General Orders No. 154, Aug. 9. See GBM to his wife, July 30, 1862, note 2, *supra.*

To Henry W. Halleck   [TELEGRAM]

Head Quarters, Army of the Potomac,
Acquia Creek Aug. 24 2 pm 1862

Your telegram received.[1] Morrell's scouts report Rappahannock station burned & abandoned by Pope without any notice to Morrell or Sykes. This was telegraphed you some hours ago. Reynolds Reno & Stevens are supposed to be with Pope as nothing can be heard of them today.[2] Morrell & Sykes are near Morrisville Post Office watching the lower fords of Rappahannock with no troops between them & Rappahannock station which is reported abandoned by Pope. Please inform me immediately exactly where Pope is & what doing. Until I know that I cannot expedite Porter's movements; he is much exposed now & decided measures should be taken at once. Until I know what my command & position are to be, & whether you still intend to place me in the command indicated in your first letter to me, & orally through Genl Burnside at the Chickahominy I cannot decide where I can be of most use. If your determination is unchanged I ought to go to Alexandria at once. Please define my position & duties.[3]

G B McClellan
Maj Genl

Maj Genl H W Halleck
Comdg USA   Washington DC

ALS (telegram sent), McClellan Papers, New-York Historical Society. *OR,* Ser. 1, XI, Part 1, pp. 93–94.

1. Halleck telegraphed at 12:30 P.M. on this date: "Porter and Reno should hold the line of the Rappahannock below Pope, subject for the present to his orders. I hope by to-morrow to be able to give some more definite directions. You know my main object, and will act accordingly." *OR,* Ser. 1, XII, Part 3, p. 645. 2. Maj. Gen. George Morell, Brig. Gen. George Sykes, and Brig. Gen. John F. Reynolds commanded divisions in Porter's Fifth Corps. Maj. Gens. Jesse L. Reno and Isaac I. Stevens commanded divisions in Burnside's Ninth Corps. 3. Halleck replied that night: "You ask me for information which I cannot give. I do not know either where General Pope is or where the enemy in force is. These are matters which I have all day been most anxious to ascertain." *OR,* Ser. 1, XI, Part 1, p. 94.

To Henry W. Halleck   [TELEGRAM]

Maj Genl H W Halleck   Falmouth Va. 12.45 am Aug 25 '62

The only additional information I hear from Pope is from a multitude of his stragglers who say that he abandoned Rappahannock Station & retreated towards Warrenton Station carrying off the Artillery from the lower fords to some unknown point. You have no doubt taken all possible means to ascertain the exact position of Pope and I hope you will soon be able to give me definite information. All the means possible to gain it on this line have been used. In the meantime you may be sure of my hearty cooperation.

Geo B McClellan

Maj Genl

Received copy, Records of the Office of the Secretary of War, RG 107 (M-473 :50), National Archives. *OR*, Ser. 1, XII, Part 3, p. 659.

To Mary Ellen McClellan

Aug 27 [1862] am. Alexandria

We arrived here last night — rose early — reported to Washn that I had arrived & am waiting for something to turn up. It seems that some 500 of the enemy's cavalry made a dash last night & burned the Bull Run RR bridge. I fear this will cause much inconvenience as the troops in front are mainly dependent on the RR for supplies. My troops are getting pretty well into position — Porter between Fredericksburg & Rappahannock Station — Heintzelman at Rappk Sta. — Franklin near this place — Sumner landing at Acquia Creek. I have heard nothing new today & don't know what is going on in front — am terribly ignorant of the state of affairs & therefore somewhat anxious to know. . . .

I find all going on well enough here. Davis[1] has just returned from selecting a camp for Hd Qtrs — he has picked out a place between the Seminary (*our* old camp) & the river, about 1/2 or 3/4 mile from the Seminary. I shall go into my tent this time & not trouble a house. With the exception of the 2 or 3 days I passed at Wmsburg on our upward march & one night at Ft. Monroe I have not slept in a house since I left you. I know nothing definite yet in regard to my fate. . . .

10.30 [A.M.] Have been again interrupted by telegrams requiring replies. Halleck is in a disagreeable situation — can get no information from the front either as to our own troops or the enemy. I shall do all I can to help him loyally & will trouble him as little as possible, but render all the assistance in my power without regard to myself or my own position. . . .

Our affairs here now much tangled up & I opine that in a day or two your old husband will be called upon to unsnarl them. In the mean time I shall be very patient — do to the best of my ability whatever I am called upon to do & wait my time. I hope to have my part of the work pretty well straightened out today — in that case I shall move up to Washn this evening. . . .

Have just heard that it is probable that a general engagement will be fought today or tomorrow near Warrenton. . . .

AL copy, McClellan Papers (C-7 :63), Library of Congress.

1. Maj. Nelson H. Davis, of GBM's staff.

To Henry W. Halleck   [TELEGRAM]

Head-Quarters, Army of the Potomac,
Alexandria Aug 27 10.20 am 1862

Telegram this moment received.[1] I have sent orders to Franklin to prepare to march with his Corps at once, & to repair here in person to inform me as to his means of transportation.

Kearny was yesterday at Rappahannock Station — Porter at Bealeton, Kelly's, Barnett's etc. Sumner will commence reaching Falmouth to day. Williams' Massachusetts cavalry will be mostly at Falmouth today. I loaned Burnside my personal escort — (1) one squadron (4th) fourth regulars to scout down Rappahannock. I have sent for Couch's Division to come at once.

As fast as I gain any information I will forward it altho' you may already have it.[2]

G B McClellan
Maj Genl

Maj Genl H W Halleck
Washington D.C.

ALS (telegram sent), Records of the Office of the Secretary of War, RG 107 (M-504:65), National Archives. *OR*, Ser. 1, XI, Part 1, p. 95.

1. Halleck telegraphed at 10:00 A.M.: "I can get no satisfactory information from the front.... There seems to have been great neglect and carelessness about Manassas. Franklin's corps should march in that direction as soon as possible." *OR*, Ser. 1, XI, Part 1, p. 95. 2. Halleck replied: "Take entire direction of the sending out of the troops from Alexandria. Determine questions of priority in transportation, and the places they shall occupy." *OR*, Ser. 1, XI, Part 1, p. 95.

To Henry W. Halleck   [TELEGRAM]

Head-Quarters, Army of the Potomac,
Alexandria Aug 27 11.20 am 1862

In view of Burnside's dispatch[1] just received would it not be advisable to throw the mass of Sumner's Corps here to move out with Franklin to Centreville or vicinity?

If a decisive battle is fought at Warrenton a disaster would leave any troops on lower Rappahannock in a dangerous position — they would do better service in front of Washington.[2]

G B McClellan
Maj Genl

Maj Genl Halleck
Washington D.C.

ALS (telegram sent), Records of the Office of the Secretary of War, RG 107 (M-504:65), National Archives. *OR*, Ser. 1, XII, Part 3, p. 689.

1. Burnside's telegram of this date included dispatches from Porter announcing that a battle was imminent. *OR*, Ser. 1, XII, Part 3, p. 701. 2. Halleck telegraphed at 1:50 P.M. that he approved bringing Sumner's corps to Alexandria. *OR*, Ser. 1, XII, Part 3, p. 691.

To Henry W. Halleck [TELEGRAM]

Head-Quarters, Army of the Potomac,
Alexandria Aug 27 12M 1862

I have just learned through Genl Woodbury[1] that it was stated in your office last night that it was very strange that with (20,000) twenty thousand men here I did not prevent the raid upon Manassas. This induces me to ask whether your remark in your telegram today that there had been great neglect about Manassas was intended to apply to me.[2] I cannot suppose it was, knowing as you do that I arrived here without information & with no instructions beyond pushing the landing of my troops. The bridge was burned before my arrival, I knew nothing of it till this morning. I ask as a matter of justice that you will prevent your staff from making statements which do me such gross injustice at a time when the most cordial cooperation is required.[3]

G B McClellan
Maj Genl

Maj Genl H W Halleck
Washington D.C.

ALS (telegram sent), Records of the Office of the Secretary of War, RG 107 (M-504:65), National Archives. *OR*, Ser. 1, XII, Part 3, p. 690.

1. Brig. Gen. Daniel P. Woodbury, engineer brigade. 2. See GBM to Halleck, Aug. 27, 10:20 A.M., note 1, *supra*. 3. Halleck replied on this date that no censure of GBM was intended. "Indeed, I did not blame any particular person, but merely said there must have been neglect somewhere." *OR*, Ser. 1, XII, Part 3, p. 690.

To Henry W. Halleck [TELEGRAM]

Head Quarters, Army of the Potomac,
Alexandria Aug 27 1.15 pm 1862

Franklin's Artillery have no horses except for (4) four guns without caissons.[1] I can pick up no cavalry. In view of these facts will it not be well to push Sumner's Corps here by water as rapidly as possible. To make immediate arrangements for placing the works in front of Washington in an efficient condition of defense. I have no means of knowing the enemy's force between Pope & ourselves. Can Franklin without his Artillery or Cavalry effect any useful purpose in front. Should not Burnside at once take steps to evacuate Falmouth & Acquia at the same time covering the retreat of any of Pope's troops who may fall back in that direction. I do not see that we have force enough in hand to form a connection with Pope whose exact position we do not know. Are we safe in the direction of the valley?

G B McClellan
Maj Genl

Maj Genl Halleck
Washington

ALS (telegram sent), McClellan Papers (C-15:64), Library of Congress. *OR,* Ser. 1, XI, Part 1, p. 96.

1. In a telegram sent at noon, Halleck gave the positions of units of the Army of Virginia. "Porter reports a general battle imminent. Franklin's troops should move out by forced marches, carrying three or four days' provisions, and to be supplied as far as possible by railroad." *OR,* Ser. 1, XI, Part 1, p. 94.

To Henry W. Halleck [TELEGRAM]

Head Quarters, Army of the Potomac,
Alexandria Aug 27 1.35 pm 1862

I learn that Taylor's Brigade[1] sent this morning to Bulls Run Bridge is either cut to pieces or captured. That the force against them had many guns & about (5000) five thousand Infantry — receiving reinforcements every moment. Also that Gainesville is in possession of enemy. Please send some Cavalry out towards Dranesville via Chain Bridge to watch Lewinsville & Dranesville & go as far as they can. If you can give me even one squadron of good Cavalry here I will ascertain state of case. I think our policy now is to make these works perfectly safe, & mobilize a couple of Corps as soon as possible, but not to advance them until they can have their Artillery & Cavalry. I have sent for Col Tyler[2] to place his artillery men in the works.

Is fort Marcy securely held?

McClellan

Genl Halleck

Some of Cox's troops were also engaged with another force of enemy.[3]

ALS (telegram sent), McClellan Papers (C-15:64), Library of Congress. *OR,* Ser. 1, XII, Part 3, p. 690.

1. Brig. Gen. George W. Taylor's brigade of the Sixth Corps. 2. Col. Robert O. Tyler commanded the Army of the Potomac's siege train. 3. Brig. Gen. Jacob D. Cox commanded four regiments of the Kanawha Division, newly arrived from western Virginia.

To Henry W. Halleck [TELEGRAM]

Maj Genl H. W. Halleck   Alexandria, August 27, 1862. 2.30 pm.

Sumner has been ordered to send here all of his Corps that are within reach. Orders have been sent to Couch to come here from Yorktown with the least possible delay. But one squadron of my cavalry has arrived, that will be disembarked at once and sent to the front. If there is any cavalry in Washington it should be ordered to report to me at once.

I still think that we should first provide for the immediate defence of Washington on both sides of the Potomac. I am not responsible for the past and cannot be for the future, unless I receive authority to dispose of the available troops according to my judgment. Please inform me at once what my position is. I do not wish to act in the dark.[1]

G. B. McClellan
Maj Genl

Retained copy, McClellan Papers (A-75:30), Library of Congress. *OR*, Ser. 1, XI, Part 1, pp. 96–97.

1. Halleck replied that afternoon: "From your knowledge of the whole country about here you can best act.... As you must be aware, more than three-quarters of my time is taken up with the raising of new troops and matters in the West. I have no time for details. You will therefore, as ranking general in the field direct as you deem best...." *OR*, Ser. 1, XII, Part 3, p. 691.

To Henry W. Halleck   [TELEGRAM]

Maj. Genl. H W Halleck
Comdr. in Chief U.S.A.   Head Quarters, Army of the Potomac,
Washington D.C.   Alexandria August 27 1862 6 p.m.

I have just received the copy of a dispatch from Genl. Pope to you dated 10 a.m. this morning in which he says: All forces now sent forward should be sent to my right at Gainesville.[1]

I now have at my disposal here about ten thousand (10,000) men of Franklin's Corps, about twenty eight hundred (2800) of Genl Tyler's Brigade, and Col. Tyler's[2] 1st Conn. Artillery, which I recommend should be held in hand for the defence of Washington.

If you wish me to order any part of this force to the front it is in readiness to march at a moments notice to any point you may indicate.

In view of the existing state of things in our front I have deemed it best to order Genl. Casey[3] to hold his men for Yorktown in readiness to move but not to send them off till further orders.

Geo. B. McClellan
Maj Genl

Retained copy, McClellan Papers (C-15:64), Library of Congress. *OR*, Ser. 1, XI, Part 1, p. 97.

1. *OR*, Ser. 1, XII, Part 3, p. 684. 2. Brig. Gen. E. B. Tyler, Col. Robert O. Tyler. 3. Gen. Casey headed a training command for new troops.

To Mary Ellen McClellan

Aug 28th [1862] 9 1/2 am. Steamer Ariel

I am just about starting back for Alexandria. I came up here (Washington) last night — reached Halleck's house about midnight & remained talking with him until 3. . . .

I have a great deal of hard work before me now but will do my best to perform it. I find Halleck well disposed, he has had much to contend against. I shall keep as clear as possible of the Presdt & Cabinet — endeavor to do what must be done with Halleck alone — so I shall get on better. Pope is in a bad way — his communications with Washn cut off & I have not yet the force at hand to relieve him. He has nearly all the troops of my army that have arrived. I hope to hear better news when I reach Alexdra.

AL copy, McClellan Papers (C-7:63), Library of Congress.

To Amiel W. Whipple   [TELEGRAM]

Alexandria Aug 28 [1862] 2.30 pm

I think you had better send the guns & artillerists to Fort Buffalo & Ramsay at once. Can you send enough reliable infantry to complete the garrisons? As soon as I know whether I must move my men to the front or not I can decide as to sending a division or two to the point in question. I think they should be held in force. Please reply.

G B McClellan
Maj Genl

Brig Genl Whipple
Arlington

ALS (telegram sent), Records of the Office of the Secretary of War, RG 107 (M-504:65), National Archives. Brig. Gen. Whipple commanded Washington's defenses on the Virginia side of the Potomac.

To Henry W. Halleck   [TELEGRAM]

Maj Genl H. W. Halleck
Genl in Chief   Alexandria Va Aug 28th 1862

From a full conversation with Col Scammon[1] I am satisfied that the enemy is in large force between us & Pope. One of his surgeons who was taken & released saw Jackson, A. P. Hill & three other Generals. At about five p.m. yesterday there was heavy cannonading in direction of Manassas. It is my opinion that any movement made from here must be in force with Cavalry & Artillery or we shall be beaten in detail. Can you find a squadron to go to Vienna via Lewinsville & ascertain whether enemy there. The right of our line of works on this side the river should be most carefully watched & pickets well out on all roads. Videttes should extend at least to Lewinsville & Prospect Hill. If possible to Meridian Hill & on the ridge thence to Dranesville. It is of vital importance to know what there is near Vienna at once. The impressions I receive from Scammon are corroborated from other sources. I dont see how McDowell can well be at Gainesville. Have this moment received intelligence from a prisoner captured the other night & just escaped that he saw Jackson, Stewart & Minke[2] — that enemy were 30,000 strong in vicinity of Manassas & being reinforced constantly. I suggest that you take into consideration the propriety of Pope's falling back via Davis, Spriggs & Bradleys fords etc between the Occoquan & Potomac & rejoining via Wolfs run Shoals, Occoquan etc. Our best troops here advancing say tomorrow morning or tonight if ready so far as Fairfax, Brimstone Hill & Wolfs run Shoals to cover the movement. I do not think it now worthwhile to attempt to preserve the Railway. The great object is to collect the whole Army in Washington ready to defend the works & act upon the flank of any force crossing the upper Potomac. If Pope makes this movement steps must be taken at once to build Pontoon Bridges over the Occoquan.

Geo. B. McClellan
Maj Genl Comdg

Received copy, Records of the Office of the Secretary of War, RG 107 (M-473:50), National Archives. *OR*, Ser. 1, XII, Part 3, p. 708.

1. Col. E. P. Scammon had made a reconnaissance along the Orange and Alexandria Railroad to Bull Run. 2. Stonewall Jackson and J. E. B. Stuart; "Minke" is no doubt a telegrapher's error for Richard S. Ewell.

To Henry W. Halleck   [TELEGRAM]

Head-Quarters, Army of the Potomac,
Hd Qtrs Camp near Alexandria Aug 28 4.10 pm 1862

General Franklin is with me here. I will know in a few minutes the condition of Artillery & Cavalry. We are not yet in condition to move.[1] May be by tomorrow morning. Pope must cut through today or adopt the plan I suggested. I have ordered troops to garrison the works at Upton's Hill. They must be held at any cost. As soon as I can see the way to spare them I will send a Corps of good troops there. It is the key to Washington, which cannot be seriously menaced as long as it is held.

G B McClellan
Maj Genl

Maj Genl Halleck
Washn D.C.

ALS (telegram sent), Records of the Office of the Secretary of War, RG 107 (M-504:65), National Archives. *OR*, Ser. 1, XI, Part 1, p. 97.

Disobey orders

1. At 12:40 P.M. on this date Halleck had ordered Franklin by telegraph "to move with your corps to-day toward Manassas Junction, to drive the enemy from the railroad." At 1:00 P.M. GBM replied: "The moment Franklin can be started with a reasonable amount of artillery he shall go." *OR,* Ser. 1, XII, Part 3, pp. 707, 708.

To Henry W. Halleck   [TELEGRAM]

Camp near Alexandria Aug 28 [1862] 4.45 p.m.

Your dispatch received.[1] Neither Franklin's nor Sumner's Corps are now in condition to move & fight a battle — it would be a sacrifice to send them out now. I have sent aides to ascertain the condition of the Commands of Cox & Tyler,[2] but I still think that a premature movement in small force will accomplish nothing but the destruction of the troops sent out. I repeat that I will lose no time in preparing the troops now here for the field, & that whatever orders you give after hearing what I have to say will be carried out.

G B McClellan
Maj Genl

Maj Genl Halleck
Washington

ALS (telegram sent), Records of the Office of the Secretary of War, RG 107 (M-504:65), National Archives. *OR,* Ser. 1, XII, Part 3, p. 709.

1. At 3:30 P.M. Halleck had telegraphed: "Not a moment must be lost in pushing as large a force as possible toward Manassas, so as to communicate with Pope before the enemy is re-enforced." *OR,* Ser. 1, XII, Part 3, p. 709. 2. Brig. Gens. Cox and E. B. Tyler.

To Henry W. Halleck   [TELEGRAM]

Genl H W Halleck
Genl in Chief U.S.A.   Head-Quarters, Army of the Potomac,
Washington D.C.   Alexandria Aug. 29 [28] 1862.   10 pm.

Your dispatch received.[1]

Franklin's Corps has been ordered to march at 6 o'clock tomorrow morning.

Sumner has about fourteen thousand Infantry without Cavalry or Artillery here.

Cox's Brigade of four Regiments is here with two batteries of Artillery. Men of two Regts much fatigued — came in today. Tyler's Brigade of three new regiments but little drilled is also here.

All these troops will be ordered to hold themselves ready to march tomorrow morning — and all except Franklin's to await further orders.

If you wish any of them to move toward Manassas please inform me.

Colonel Wagner[2] 2d N. York Vol. Artillery has just come in from the front. He reports strong Infantry & Cavalry force of rebels near Fairfax Ct. House.

Reports numerous from various sources, that Lee & Stuart with large forces are at Manassas. That the enemy with 120,000 men intend advancing on the forts near Arlington and Chain Bridge, with a view of attacking Washington & Baltimore.

Genl. Barnard[3] telegraphs me tonight that the length of the line of fortifications on this side of the Potomac requires 2000 additional Artillery men, and additional troops to defend intervals, according to circumstances. At all events he says an old regiment should be added to the force at the Chain Bridge, and a few Regts distributed along the lines to give confidence to our new troops.

I agree with him fully and think our fortifications along the upper part of our line on this side the river very unsafe with their present garrisons — and the movements of the enemy seems to indicate an attack upon those works.

Geo. B. McClellan
Maj Genl

Retained copy, McClellan Papers (A-75:30), Library of Congress. *OR*, Ser. 1, XII, Part 3, p. 710.

1. At 7:40 P.M. Halleck had telegraphed: "There must be no further delay in moving Franklin's corps toward Manassas. They must go to-morrow morning, ready or not ready. If we delay too long to get ready there will be no necessity to go at all, for Pope will either be defeated or be victorious without our aid." *OR*, Ser. 1, XII, Part 3, p. 710. 2. Col. Gustav Waagner. 3. Gen. Barnard now commanded the Washington defenses.

To John G. Barnard   [TELEGRAM]

Genl J. G. Barnard   Head-Quarters, Army of the Potomac,
Washington D.C.   Alexandria Aug. [29] 1862 2 a.m.

Your dispatch received.[1]

I have ordered two Regiments and a Battery to proceed at once up this side of the river to the Chain Bridge, and I have told the officer who sends them (Genl. Sumner) that you would have an officer there to post them.

I would advise you to hold the works as long as you can with safety and at the same time be prepared to destroy the Bridge at short notice.

Geo. B. McClellan
Maj Genl

Retained copy, Records of the Office of the Secretary of War, RG 107 (M-504:65), National Archives. *OR*, Ser. 1, XII, Part 3, p. 725.

1. In his telegram, sent forty minutes earlier, Barnard called for reinforcements at the Chain Bridge, on the Potomac some three miles upstream of the city. At about the same time Halleck telegraphed: "I think you had better place Sumner's corps as it arrives near the fortifications, and particularly at the Chain Bridge. The principal thing to be feared now is a cavalry raid into this city...." *OR*, Ser. 1, XII, Part 3, p. 725, XI, Part 1, p. 97.

To Henry W. Halleck   [TELEGRAM]

Camp near Alexandria Aug 29 10.30 am 1862

Franklin's Corps is in motion — started about (6) six am. I can give him but two squadrons of cavalry. I propose moving Genl Cox to Upton's Hill to hold that important point with its works & to push cavalry scouts to Vienna via Freedom hill & Hunter's Lane. Cox has (2) two squadrons cavalry. Please answer at once whether this meets your approval. I have directed Woodbury with the Engineer Brigade to hold Fort Lyon. Sumner detached last night two regiments to vicinity of Forts Ethan Allen & Marcy. Meagher's brigade is still at Acquia. If he moves in support of Franklin it leaves us without any reliable troops in & near Washington, yet Franklin is too weak alone.[1] What shall be done? No more cavalry arrived — have but (3) three squadrons. Franklin has but (40) forty rounds of ammunition & no wagons to move more. I do not think Franklin is in condition to accomplish much if he meets with serious resistance. I should not have moved him but for your pressing order of last night. What have you from Vienna & Dranesville?[2]

G B McClellan
Maj Genl

Maj Genl Halleck
Washington DC

ALS (telegram sent), Records of the Office of the Secretary of War, RG 107 (M-504:65), National Archives. *OR*, Ser. 1, XI, Part 1, pp. 97–98.

1. Presumably GBM refers here to Sumner's Second Corps, of which Gen. Meagher's brigade was a part. 2. Halleck replied at noon: "Upton's Hill arrangements all right. We must send wagons and ammunition to Franklin as fast as they arrive. Meagher's brigade ordered up yesterday.... I have nothing from Dranesville." *OR*, Ser. 1, XI, Part 1, p. 98.

To Henry W. Halleck   [TELEGRAM]

Head-Quarters, Army of the Potomac
Camp near Alexandria Aug 29 1 pm 1862

I anxiously await reply to my last dispatch in regard to Sumner.[1] Wish to give the orders at once. Please authorize me to attach new regiments permanently to my old Brigades. I can do much good to old & new troops in that way.

I shall endeavor to hold a line in advance of Forts Allen & Marcy at least with strong advanced guards. I wish to hold the line through Prospect Hill, Mackall's, Minor's & Hall's Hills. This will give us timely warning. Shall I do as seems best to me with all the troops in this vicinity, including Franklin who I really think ought not under present circumstances to advance beyond Annandale.[2]

G B McClellan
Maj Genl

Genl Halleck

ALS (telegram sent), Records of the Office of the Secretary of War, RG 107 (M-504:65), National Archives. *OR*, Ser. 1, XI, Part 1, p. 99.

1. GBM had telegraphed at noon, proposing to post Sumner's corps to cover the approaches to Washington. *OR*, Ser. 1, XI, Part 1, p. 99. 2. Halleck replied at 3:00 P.M.: "Dispose of all troops as you deem best. I want Franklin's corps to go far enough to find out something about the enemy. Perhaps he may get such information at Annandale as to prevent his going farther; otherwise he will push on toward Fairfax. Try to get something from the direction of Manassas.... Our people must move more actively and find out where the enemy is. I am tired of guesses." *OR*, Ser. 1, XII, Part 3, p. 722.

To Abraham Lincoln   [TELEGRAM]

Head Quarters, Army of the Potomac,
Camp near Alexandria Aug 29, 2.45 pm 1862

The last news I received from the direction of Manassas was from stragglers to the effect that the enemy were evacuating Centreville & retiring towards Thorofare Gap.[1] This by no means reliable. I am clear that one of two courses should be adopted — 1st To concentrate all our available forces to open communication with Pope — 2nd To leave Pope to get out of his scrape & at once use all our means to make the Capital perfectly safe. No middle course will now answer. Tell me what you wish me to do & I will do all in my power to accomplish it. I wish to know what my orders & authority are — I ask for nothing, but will obey whatever orders you give.

I only ask a prompt decision that I may at once give the necessary orders. It will not do to delay longer.[2]

G B McClellan
Maj Genl

A Lincoln Presdt
& copy to Genl Halleck

ALS (telegram sent), McClellan Papers (C-15:64), Library of Congress. *OR*, Ser. 1, XI, Part 1, p. 98.

1. At 2:30 P.M. the president had telegraphed: "What news from direction of Mannassas Junction? What generally?" *Collected Works of Lincoln*, V, p. 399. 2. The president replied at 4:10 P.M.: "I think your first alternative to wit 'To concentrate all our available forces to open communication with Pope' is the right one but I wish not to control. That I now leave to Genl Halleck aided by your counsels." McClellan Papers (A-30:75).

To Mary Ellen McClellan

[Alexandria] Aug 29 [1862] 3 pm.

... I was awake all last night & have not had one moment until now to write to you. I have a terrible task on my hands now — perfect imbecility to correct. No means to act with, no authority — yet determined if possible to save the country & the Capital. I find the soldiers all clinging to me — yet I am not permitted to go to the post of danger! Two of my Corps will either save that fool Pope or be sacrificed for the country. I do not know whether I will be permitted to save the Capital or not — I have just telegraphed very plainly to the Presdt & Halleck what I think ought to be done — I expect merely a contemptuous silence....

I am heart sick with the folly & ignorance I see around me — God grant that I may never pass through such a scene again....

AL copy, McClellan Papers (C-7:63), Library of Congress.

To Henry W. Halleck   [TELEGRAM]

Maj Genl H W Halleck   Head-Quarters, Army of the Potomac,
Comdg US Army   [Alexandria] August 29th 1862 5.25 p.m.

Before receiving the President's message[1] I had put Sumner's Corps in motion towards Arlington and the Chain Bridge, not having received any reply from you. The movement is still under your control in either direction though now under progress as stated.

                                        G B McClellan
                                        Maj Genl

I think that one of the two alternatives should be fully carried out.

Retained copy, Records of the Office of the Secretary of War, RG 107 (M-504:65), National Archives. *OR*, Ser. 1, XII, Part 3, p. 723.

1. See GBM to Lincoln, Aug. 29, note 2, *supra*.

To Henry W. Halleck   [TELEGRAM]

Head Quarters, Army of the Potomac,
Camp near Alexandria 8 pm Aug 29 1862

By referring to my telegrams of 10.30 am, 12 m, 1 pm together with your reply of 2.48 you will see why Franklin's Corps halted at Annandale.[1] His small cavalry force, all I had to give him was ordered to push on as far as possible towards Manassas. It was not safe for Franklin to move beyond Annandale under the circumstances until we knew what was at Vienna. Genl Franklin remained here until about 1 pm endeavouring to arrange for supplies for his command. I am responsible for both these circumstances & do not see that either was in disobedience to your orders. Please give distinct orders in reference to Franklin's movements of tomorrow. I have sent to Col Haupt[2] to push out construction & supply trains as soon as possible — Genl Tyler to furnish the necessary guards.

I have directed Genl Banks' supply trains to start out to night at least as far as Annandale, with an escort from Genl Tyler.

In regard to tomorrow's movements I desire definite instructions as it is not agreeable to me to be accused of disobeying orders when I have simply exercised the discretion you committed to me.

G B McClellan
Maj Genl

Maj Genl Halleck
Washington D.C.

ALS (telegram sent), McClellan Papers (C-15:64), Library of Congress. *OR*, Ser. 1, XI, Part 1, pp. 99–100.

1. At 7:50 P.M. Halleck had telegraphed: "I have just been told that Franklin's corps stopped at Annandale.... This is all contrary to my orders; investigate and report the facts of this disobedience. That corps must push forward, as I directed...." *OR*, Ser. 1, XII, Part 3, p. 723. See GBM's telegrams of this date, 10:30 A.M. and 1:00 P.M., *supra;* his telegram of noon dealt with allocating forces for the defense of Washington: *OR*, Ser. 1, XI, Part 1, p. 99. Halleck's "reply of 2.48" is probably his 3:00 P.M. telegram; see GBM to Halleck, Aug. 29, 1:00 P.M., note 2, *supra*. 2. Col. Herman Haupt was the Army of Virginia's chief of construction and transportation.

To Mary Ellen McClellan

[Alexandria] Aug 29 [1862] 9 1/2 pm.

I have been terribly busy since reaching here — not a moment have I had to myself. I found everything in the most terrible confusion — apparently inextricably so, but affairs are now better. The works on this side the river are in condition for defense....

I see the evening paper states that I have been placed in command of all the troops in Va. — this is not so — I have no command at present — that is to say I have none of the Army of the Potomac with me & have merely "turned in" on my own account to straighten out whatever I catch hold of. By tomorrow evening I hope to have the works etc in fair condition of defense....

Pope has been in a tight place, but from the news received this evening I think the danger is pretty much over. Tomorrow will tell the story.

I am terribly crippled by the want of cavalry. None of mine have arrived except 3 small squadrons. I hope for more tonight. There was a terrible scare in Washn last night. A rumor got out that Lee was advancing rapidly on the Chain Bridge with 150,000 men — & such a stampede! I did not get 5 minutes consecutive sleep all night — so thick were the telegrams!...

I have seen neither the Presdt nor the Secy since I arrived here — have been only once to Washn & hope to see very little of the place — I abominate it terribly....

I have no faith in anyone here & expect to be turned loose the moment their alarm is over. I expect I got into a row with Halleck tonight — he sent me a telegram I did not like & I told him so very plainly. He is not a refined person at all, & probably says rough things when he don't mean them....

AL copy, McClellan Papers (C-7:63), Library of Congress.

To Mary Ellen McClellan

Aug 30 [1862] 8 am Camp near Alexandria

... Was awakened last night by a few scattering shots that no doubt came from some of those *very* raw troops that are about here. Shall start soon after bkfst & ride to Upton's Hill — thence to the Chain bridge & along the line of Forts. I want to see all on this side of the river today if I can. No one in Washington appears to know the condition of matters, & I have a fancy for finding them out for myself. If I once get matters reasonably straight I shall not trouble myself much more. What I am doing now is rather a volunteer affair — not exactly my business, but you know that I have a way of attending to most other things than my own affairs.

I had a very funny letter yesterday from the Duc de Chartres which I will enclose with this, as it may amuse you — the *English* is *superb*!

1 1/2 pm. ...I expected to start out on a long ride, but have thus far been detained by various matters which have kept me very busy....

There has been heavy firing going on all day long somewhere beyond Bull Run. I have sent up every man I have, pushed everything, & am left here on the flat of my back without any command whatever. It is dreadful to listen to the cannonading & not be able to take any part in it — but such is my fate....

I must close now for I have some more orders to give.

9.15 pm. ...I feel too blue & disgusted to write any more now, so I will smoke a cigar & try to get into a better humor. They have taken *all* my troops from me — I have even sent off all my personal escort & camp guard & am here with a few orderlies & the aides. I have been listening to the distant sound of a great battle in the distance — my men engaged in it & I away! I never felt worse in my life.

AL copy; copy, McClellan Papers (C-7:63/D-10:72), Library of Congress.

To Ambrose E. Burnside   [TELEGRAM]

Head-Quarters, Army of the Potomac,
Camp near Alexandria Aug 30 1862 8.20 am

Telegram of midnight received.[1] Use your discretion about the cavalry — I have only three squadrons two of which with Franklin — I expect some today. Do not strip yourself of anything. Your information about Pope substantially confirmed from this side. His troops are at Centreville. Supplies have gone to him by rail & by wagon. Secesh has missed his first coup. We will soon see what his second is to be.

G B McClellan
Maj Genl

Maj Genl Burnside
Falmouth

ALS (telegram sent), Records of the Office of the Secretary of War, RG 107 (M-504:65), National Archives. *OR*, Ser. 1, XII, Part 3, p. 758.

1. Burnside's telegram reported on the situation at Falmouth and the disposition of his forces. *OR*, Ser. 1, XII, Part 3, pp. 757–58.

To Henry W. Halleck

Major General H. W. Halleck
General in Chief U.S.A.,
Washington D.C.   Head Quarters Army of the Potomac,
General: [Alexandria] August 30, 1862 [11:30 A.M.][1]

Ever since General Franklin received notice that he was to march from Alexandria he has been using every effort to get transportation for his extra ammunition, but he was uniformly told by the Quarter Masters here that there was none disposable and his command marched without wagons.[2] After the departure of his Corps at 6 A.M. yesterday, he procured twenty wagons to carry a portion of his ammunition by unloading some of General Banks' supply train for that purpose.

General Sumner was one entire day in endeavoring by application upon Quarter Masters and others to get a sufficient number of wagons to transport his reserve ammunition but without success, and was obliged to march without it.

I have this morning sent all my Head Quarters train that is landed to be at once loaded with ammunition for Sumner and Franklin, but they will not go far toward supplying the deficiency.

Eighty-five wagons were got together by the Quarter Master last night, loaded with subsistence, and sent forward, under an escort at 1 A.M. via Annandale.

Every effort has been made to carry out your instructions promptly.

The difficulty seems to consist in the fact that the greater part of the transportation on hand at Alexandria and Washington has been needed for current supplies of the garrisons. At all events such is the state of the case as represented to me by the Quarter Masters, and it appears to be true.

I take it for granted that this has not been properly explained to you.

I am very respectfully your obt servt
Geo B McClellan
Maj Genl USA

LS, Records of the Adjutant General's Office, RG 94 (159: Halleck Papers), National Archives. *OR*, Ser. 1, XII, Part 3, pp. 744–45.

1. A retained copy of this communication indicates it was originally intended to be a telegram. McClellan Papers (A-75:30), Library of Congress. 2. Halleck had telegraphed at 9:40 A.M.: "I am by no means satisfied with General Franklin's march of yesterday. Considering the circumstances of the case, he was very wrong in stopping at Annandale. Moreover, I learned last night that the Quartermaster's Department could have given him plenty of transportation, if he had applied for it, any time since his arrival at Alexandria. He knew the importance of opening communication with General Pope's army, and should have acted more promptly." *OR*, Ser. 1, XII, Part 3, p. 744.

To Henry W. Halleck

[TELEGRAM]

Maj Genl H W Halleck
Comdg USA

Head Qtrs Army Potomac
[Alexandria] August 30th 1862

Sumners command was fully in motion by 2 1/2 pm & Franklins was past Fairfax at 10 am. All moving forward as rapidly as possible.[1] I have sent the last cavalry man I have to the front. Also every other soldier in my Command except a small camp guard.

G B McClellan
Maj Genl

The firing in front has been extremely heavy for the past hour.

Retained copy, Records of the Office of the Secretary of War, RG 107 (M-504:65), National Archives. *OR*, Ser. 1, XII, Part 3, pp. 747–48.

1. Halleck had telegraphed at 2:10 P.M.: "Franklin's and all of Sumner's corps should be pushed forward with all possible dispatch. They must use their legs and make forced marches. Time now is everything. . . ." *OR*, Ser. 1, XII, Part 3, p. 747.

To Henry W. Halleck

[TELEGRAM]

Head Quarters, Army of the Potomac,
Camp near Alexandria Aug 30 10.30 pm 1862

I have sent to the front all my troops with the exception of Couch's Division & have given the orders necessary to ensure its being disposed of as you directed.[1] I hourly expect the return of one of my aides who will give authentic news from the field of battle. I cannot express to you the pain & mortification I have experienced today in listening to the distant sound of the firing of my men. As I can be of no further use here I respectfully ask that if there is a probability of the conflict being renewed tomorrow I may be permitted to go to the scene of battle with my staff — merely to be with my own men if nothing more — they will fight none the worse for my being with them.

If it is not deemed best to entrust me with the command even of my own Army I simply ask to be permitted to share their fate on the field of battle. Please reply to this to night.[2]

I have been engaged for the last few hours in doing what I can to make arrangements for the wounded. I have started out all the ambulances now landed.

G B McClellan
Maj Genl

Maj Genl Halleck
Comdg USA Washington

As I have sent my escort to the front I would be glad to take some of Gregg's Cavalry with me if allowed to go.

ALS (telegram sent), Records of the Office of the Secretary of War, RG 107 (M-504:65), National Archives. OR, Ser. 1, XI, Part 1, pp. 101–102.

1. Halleck had telegraphed at 12:20 P.M.: "I think Couch should land at Alexandria and be immediately pushed out to Pope. Send the troops where the fighting is." OR, Ser. 1, XII, Part 3, pp. 747–48. 2. Halleck replied the next morning: "I cannot answer without seeing the President, as General Pope is in command, by his orders, of the department." OR, Ser. 1, XI, Part 1, p. 102.

To Henry W. Halleck   [TELEGRAM]

Head Quarters, Army of the Potomac,
Camp near Alexandria Aug 31 3.30 am 1862

My aide just in. He reports our army as badly beaten. Our losses very heavy. Troops arriving at Centreville. Have probably lost several batteries. Some of the Corps entirely broken up into stragglers. Shall Couch continue his movement to the front?[1] We have no other tried troops in Washington. Sumner between Fairfax & Centreville. Franklin now at Centreville — having fallen back from Bull's Run. Enemy has probably suffered severely. Hammerstein is a cool head & old soldier.

G B McClellan
Maj Genl

Maj Genl Halleck
Washington

ALS (telegram sent), McClellan Papers (C-15:64), Library of Congress. *OR*, Ser. 1, XII, Part 3, pp. 771–72.

1. Halleck replied: "I think Couch's division should go forward as rapidly as possible and find the battlefield." *OR*, Ser. 1, XI, Part 1, p. 102.

To Mary Ellen McClellan

[Alexandria] Sunday [August] 31st [1862] 9.30 am.

... There was a severe battle yesterday, almost exactly on the old Bull Run battle ground. Pope sent in accounts during the day that he was getting on splendidly, driving the enemy all day, gaining a glorious victory etc etc. About 3 this morning Hammerstein returned from the field (where I had sent him to procure information) & told me that we were badly whipped. McDowell & Sigel's Corps broken — the troops of my own army that were present (Porter & Heintzelman) badly cut up, but in perfect order. Banks was not engaged. Franklin had arrived & was in position at Centreville. Sumner must have got up by this time. Couch's Division is about starting. It is probable that the enemy are too much fatigued to renew the attack this morning, perhaps not at all today. So that time may be given to our people to make such arrangements as will enable them to hold their own. I telegraphed last evening asking permission to be with my troops, received a reply about half an hour ago from Halleck that he would have to consult the Presdt first!! If they refuse to let me go out I think I shall feel obliged to insist upon a leave or something of the kind the moment the question of the existing battle is settled. I feel like a fool here — sucking my thumbs & doing nothing but what ought to be done by junior officers. I leave it all in the hands of the Almighty — I will try to do my best in the position that may be assigned to me & be as patient as I can....

10.45 [A.M.] ... I feel in that state of excitement & anxiety that I can hardly keep still for a moment. I learn from Hammerstein that the men in front are all very anxious for me to be with them — it is *too* cruel!

12 1/2 pm. A short time since I saw the order defining commands etc[1] — mine is that part of the Army of the Potomac *not* sent to Pope — as all is sent there I am left in command of *nothing* — a command I feel fully competent to exercise, & to which I can do full justice. I am going to write a quiet moderate letter to Mr. Aspinwall presently, explaining to him the exact state of the case, without comment, so that my friends in New York may know all....

Everything is too uncertain & unsafe around Washington at present for you to dream of going there. As a matter of self respect I cannot go there....

I do not regard Washn as safe against the rebels. If I can quietly slip over there I will send your silver off.[2] There is an order forbidding anyone going there without permission from the War Dept, & I do not care to ask them even for so slight a favor as that. . . .

AL copy, McClellan Papers (C-7:63), Library of Congress.

1. Adj. Gen.'s Office, Special Order 89, Aug. 30, 1862, read, in part: "General McClellan commands that portion of the Army of the Potomac that has not been sent forward to General Pope's command." *OR*, Ser. 1, XI, Part 1, p. 103. 2. Mrs. McClellan had expressed concern over their possessions in Washington. She wrote on Aug. 30, for example: "I don't like to trouble you . . . but I really do feel a little nervous about the silver & dont know what had better be done about it. It is in a trunk at Corcoran & Riggs Bank. . . ." McClellan Papers (B-11:48)

To Henry W. Halleck [TELEGRAM]

Head-Quarters, Army of the Potomac,
Camp near Alexandria Aug 31 1862 2.30 pm

Maj Haller[1] is at Fairfax Station with my Provost & Head Quarters Guards & other troops. I have requested (4) four more companies to be sent at once & the precautions you direct to be taken.[2]

Under the War Department order of yesterday[3] I have no control over anything except my staff some one hundred men in my camp here & the few remaining near Fort Monroe. I have no control over the new regiments, do not know where they are or anything about them except some of those near here. Their commanding officers & those of the works are not under me. When I have seen evils existing under my eye I have corrected them. I think it is the business of Genl Casey to prepare the new regiments for the field & a matter between him & Genl Barnard to order others to vicinity of Chain Bridge. Neither of them is under my command & by the War Dept order I have no right to give them orders.

G B McClellan

Genl Halleck
Washington

ALS (telegram sent), Records of the Office of the Secretary of War, RG 107 (M-504:65), National Archives. *OR*, Ser. 1, XI, Part 1, p. 102.

1. Maj. G. O. Haller, 7th U.S. Infantry. 2. At 12:45 P.M. Halleck had telegraphed: "The Subsistence Department are making Fairfax Station their principal depot. It should be well guarded . . . As many as possible of the new regiments should be prepared to take the field. Perhaps some more should be sent to the vicinity of Chain Bridge." *OR*, Ser. 1, XI, Part 1, p. 102. 3. See GBM to his wife, Aug. 31, note 1, *supra*.

To Henry W. Halleck [TELEGRAM]

Camp near Alexandria Aug 31 [1862] 7.30 pm

Having been informed that there were some (20,000) twenty thousand stragglers from Popes army between this & Centreville all of Gregg's cavalry have been sent to endeavor to drive them back to their regiments.

Two hundred of 8th Illinois Cavalry will be ready in the morning, and two hundred & fifty (250) more as soon as disembarked. The armament of Forts Buffalo & Ramsay is very incomplete.

G B McClellan
Maj Genl

Maj Genl Halleck
Washington D.C.

ALS (telegram sent), Records of the Office of the Secretary of War, RG 107 (M-504:65), National Archives. *OR*, Ser. 1, XII, Part 3, p. 773.

To Henry W. Halleck [TELEGRAM]

Head Quarters, Army of the Potomac,
Camp near Alexandria Aug 31 10.25 pm 1862

I am ready to afford you every assistance in my power, but you will readily perceive how difficult an undefined position such as I now hold must be.[1]

At what hour in the morning can I see you alone, either at your own house or the office?

G B McClellan
Maj Genl

Maj Genl Halleck
Washington D.C.

ALS (telegram sent), McClellan Papers (C-15:64), Library of Congress. *OR*, Ser. 1, XII, Part 3, p. 773.

1. Halleck had telegraphed at 10:07 P.M.: "You will retain the command of everything in this vicinity not temporarily belonging to Pope's army in the field. I beg of you to assist me in this crisis with your ability and experience. I am utterly tired out." *OR*, Ser. 1, XI, Part 1, pp. 102–103.

To Henry W. Halleck [TELEGRAM]

Camp near Alexandria Aug 31 [1862] 11 1/2 pm

The squadron of 2nd regular Cavalry that I sent with General Sumner was captured today about 2 pm some 3 miles from Fairfax CH beyond it on the Little River Pike by Fitzhugh Lee[1] with (3,000) Cavalry & three (3) light batteries. I have conversed with the 1st Sergeant who says that when he last saw them they were within a mile of Fairfax. Pope has no troops on that road, this squadron getting there by mistake. There is nothing of ours on the right of Centreville but Sumner's Corps. There was much Artillery firing during the day. A rebel Major told the sergeant that the rebels had driven in our center & left today. He says the road is filled with wagons & stragglers coming towards Alexandria. It is clear from the Sergeant's account that we were badly beaten yesterday & that Pope's right is entirely exposed.

I recommend that no more of Couch's Division be sent to the front, that Burnside be brought here as soon as practicable, & that everything available this side of Fairfax be drawn in at once including the mass of the troops on the Railroad. I apprehend that the enemy will, or have by this time, occupied Fairfax CH & cut off Pope entirely unless he falls back tonight via Sangster's & Fairfax Station.

I think these orders should be sent at once — I have no confidence in the dispositions made as I gather them — to speak frankly, & the occasion requires it, there appears to be a total absence of brains & I fear the total destruction of the Army. I have some Cavalry here that can carry out any orders you may have to send.

The occasion is grave & demands grave measures. The question is the salvation of the country.

I learn that our loss yesterday amounted to (15,000) fifteen thousand — we cannot afford such losses without an object. It is my deliberate opinion that the interests of the nation demand that Pope should fall back tonight if possible and not one moment is to be lost.

I will use all the Cavalry I have to watch our right. Please answer at once.[2] I feel confident that you can rely upon the information I give you — I shall be up all night & ready to obey any orders you give me.

> G B McClellan
> Maj Genl

Genl Halleck
Washington

ALS (telegram sent), Records of the Office of the Secretary of War, RG 107 (M-504:65), National Archives. *OR*, Ser. 1, XI, Part 1, p. 103.

1. Brig. Gen. Fitzhugh Lee, commanding a brigade of Stuart's cavalry division. 2. Halleck replied at 1:30 A.M. on Sept. 1: "I must wait for more definitive information before I can order a retreat, as the falling back on the line of works must necessarily be directed in case of a serious disaster.... I am fully aware of the gravity of the crisis and have been for weeks." *OR*, Ser. 1, XII, Part 3, p. 786.

To Mary Ellen McClellan

Sept 1 [1862] Washington 2 pm.

I have only' time to tell you that I have been placed in command of Washn & all the garrison etc in the vicinity — to do the best I can with it. The decisive battle will be fought today near Fairfax C.H. My Hd Qtrs are to be in town. If the squall passes over & Washn is a safe place you shall come on to see me if I can't get off to see you. . . .

AL copy, McClellan Papers (C-7:63), Library of Congress.

To Fitz John Porter   [TELEGRAM]

Head-Quarters of the Army,
[September 1] 1862 [5:30 P.M.]

I ask of you for my sake that of the country & of the old Army of the Potomac that you and all my friends will lend the fullest & most cordial cooperation to Genl Pope in all the operations now going on. The destinies of our country the honor of our arms are at stake, & all depends now upon the cheerful cooperation of all in the field. This week is the crisis of our fate. Say the same thing to my friends in the Army of the Potomac & that the last request I have to make of them is that for their country's sake they will extend to Genl Pope the same support they ever have to me.[1]

I am in charge of the defenses of Washington & am doing all I can to render your retreat safe should that become necessary.[2] [*crossed out:* I am now sure that the President & the Genl in Chief neither wish nor intend that the Army shall remain in its present position one moment after its safety becomes jeopardized. It is desirable that it should retain its present position if it is reasonably safe to do so but it will never be sacrificed.][3]

G B McClellan

ALS (telegram sent), McClellan Papers (A-76:30), Library of Congress. *OR*, Ser. 1, XII, Part 3, pp. 787–88.

1. This appeal was made at Lincoln's urging after Gen. Pope telegraphed Halleck on this date to report "the unsoldierly and dangerous conduct of many brigade and some division commanders of the forces sent here from the Peninsula. Every word and act and intention is discouraging, and calculated to break down the spirits of the men and produce disaster." *OR*, Ser. 1, XII, Part 2, pp. 82–83. 2. Gen. Porter replied on Sept. 2: "You may rest assured that all your friends, as well as every lover of his country, will ever give, as they have given, to General Pope their cordial co-operation and constant support. . . ." *OR*, Ser. 1, XII, Part 3, p. 798. 3. Apparently GBM intended this as a response to Porter's dispatch of Aug. 31 that read, in part, "I do not wish to see the army back . . . ; but I fear it may be kept here at the will of the enemy, to cripple it so that when it does get back it will be so crippled that it cannot defend the forts . . . ," but then thought better of it. *OR*, Ser. 1, XII, Part 3, pp. 768–69 (misdated).

To Mary Ellen McClellan

[Washington] Sept 2 [1862] 1 am.

... Last night [August 31] I had just finished a very severe application for a leave of absence when I received a dispatch from Halleck begging me to help him out of the scrape & take command here[1] — of course I could not refuse, so I came over this morning [September 1], mad as a March hare, & had a pretty plain talk with him & Abe — a still plainer one this evening. The result is that I have reluctantly consented to take command here & try to save the Capital — I don't know whether I can do it or not, for things are far gone — I hope I shall succeed....

I will not work so hard again as I used to — for the next few days I must be at it day & night — once the pressure is over I will make the staff do the work. If when the whole army returns here (if it ever does) I am not placed in command of all I will either insist upon a long leave of absence or resign....

AL copy, McClellan Papers (C-7:63), Library of Congress.

1. See GBM to Halleck, Aug. 31, 10:25 P.M., note 1, *supra.*

To Mary Ellen McClellan

[Washington] Sept 2 [1862] 12.30 pm.

I was surprised this morning when at bkft by a visit from the Presdt & Halleck — in which the former expressed the opinion that the troubles now impending could be overcome better by me than anyone else. Pope is ordered to fall back upon Washn & as he reenters everything is to come under my command again! A terrible & thankless task — yet I will do my best with God's blessing to perform it. God knows that I need his help. I am too busy to write any more now — Pray that God will help me in the great task now imposed upon me — I assume it reluctantly — with a full knowledge of all its difficulties & of the immensity of the responsibility. I only consent to take it for my country's sake & with the humble hope that God has called me to it — how I pray that he may support me!...

Don't be worried — my conscience is clear & I can trust in God.

AL copy, McClellan Papers (C-7:63), Library of Congress.

To Abraham Lincoln

Unofficial

Your Excellency   Washington Sept 2 [1862] 12.30 pm

I have by telegraph & through my Aides placed all the garrisons on the alert, ready to cover the reentrance of the Army — have placed guards upon all the roads to collect stragglers & arranged to have them fed at once. Cavalry are out hastening in Genl Pope's trains so as to clear the roads as rapidly as possible & get everything out of the way of the troops. The wagons are being placed in secure spots where they will not interfere with the free movement of troops in the event of an action. A brigade of Couch's Division (Abercrombie's) is ordered to Chain Bridge. Col Kelton[1] informed me that he saw no stragglers this side of Fairfax. I shall be on the ground before any stragglers of moment or any troops arrive — in the mean time I have been & am busily engaged in transmitting the necessary orders & obtaining the requisite information. If Pope retires promptly & in good order all will yet go well. I have telegraphed to Burnside to learn the state of affairs with him.

You may rest certain that nothing I can think of shall be left undone.

Most respectfully your obdt svt
Geo B. McClellan
Maj Genl Comdg

His Excellency the President

ALS, Lincoln Papers, Library of Congress.

1. Col. John C. Kelton, Halleck's assistant adjutant general.

To John Pope

Maj. Gen. John Pope
Commanding Army of Virginia: Headquarters,
General: Washington, September 2, 1862.

General Halleck instructed me to repeat to you the order he sent this morning to withdraw your army to Washington without unnecessary delay.[1] He feared that his message might miss you, and desired to take this double precaution.

In order to bring troops upon ground with which they are already familiar, it would be best to move Porter's corps upon Upton's Hill, that it may occupy Hall's Hill, &c.; McDowell's to Upton's Hill; Franklin's to the works in front of Alexandria; Heintzelman's to the same vicinity; Couch to Fort Corcoran, or, if practicable, to the Chain Bridge; Sumner either to Fort Albany or to Alexandria, as may be most convenient.

In haste, general, very truly, yours
Geo. B. McClellan
Major-General, U.S. Army.

OR, Ser. 1, XIX, Part 1, p. 38.

1. Halleck's dispatch to Pope read, in part: "You will bring your forces as best you can within or near the line of fortification. General McClellan has charge of all the defenses,

and you will consider any direction, as to disposition of the troops as they arrive, given by him as coming from me." *OR*, Ser. 1, XII, Part 3, p. 797.

To Henry W. Halleck

Major-General Halleck:

My dear Halleck: [Washington] September 2 [1862] 1.20 p.m.

My ordnance officer (Lieutenant Porter)[1] informs me that General Ripley says that he has just received an order from the Secretary of War to ship everything from this arsenal to New York.

I had sent to General Ripley to learn what small arms were here, so that I might be prepared to arm stragglers, &c. I do not think this order ought to be carried out so promptly. I do not despair of saving the capital. Better destroy all there is there at the eleventh hour than to send them off now. Will you not say something as to this?[2]

In haste, truly, yours,

Geo. B. McClellan

I am pushing things through and shall soon have everything we have in readiness.

McC

OR, Ser. 1, XII, Part 3, p. 802.

1. Lt. Horace Porter, the Army of the Potomac's chief ordnance officer. 2. Halleck replied on this date: "At least 50,000 or 60,000 arms will be left and a large number of pieces of artillery." *OR*, Ser. 1, XII, Part 3, p. 805.

To Abraham Lincoln

Unofficial

Your Excellency   [Washington] Sept 2 [1862] 3 pm

Several excellent batteries of field Artillery have arrived, also some more Cavalry & are all rapidly disembarking.

I now have members of my staff examining everything except the works south (*east*) of the East Branch, with distinct instructions as to what is to be done in every work in case of attack, & of the disposition to be made of the troops outside of the works. I have nothing yet from Burnside. I hope to be able to inform you by 8 tonight that everything I have in hand is prepared for action.

It is right that Pope should now fall back with the utmost rapidity consistent with good order. In my view we must now prepare at once to cover the Chain Bridge, & be ready to attack the enemy in flank should they venture to cross the upper Potomac. As it is *possible* I do not say *probable* that our Railway communication with Baltimore may be cut off, I would respectfully suggest that the *mass* of Comm. Wilkes' James River Flotilla be ordered to the Potomac to ensure our water communication.[1] If orders can be given to the Commodore to bring to the Potomac whatever he thinks necessary I am sure that there will be no trouble on that score — for he has ever evinced the strongest disposition to assist the Army, instead of waiting to be called upon for aid, he *volunteers* it — he can arrange the matter with me in a few minutes. I am about riding to the front & as I am anxious about the Chain Bridge will return that way — & will endeavor to pass by the Soldiers Home to report to you the state of affairs unless called elsewhere. I am still confident, altho' I fully appreciate the magnitude of the task committed to me.

With the highest respect I am your Excellency's obd svt

Geo B McClellan

His Excellency the President
Executive Mansion

ALS, Lincoln Papers, Library of Congress.

1. This action had already been taken, beginning with Wilkes's appointment to command the Potomac flotilla on Aug. 29, *NOR*, Ser. 1, VII, pp. 687–88.

To Mary Ellen McClellan

[Alexandria] Sept 3 [1862] 11.30 am.

. . . I am now about to jump into the saddle & will be off all day. I did not return from my ride last night until after midnight — I rode out to meet the troops & place them in position. Colburn & I rode out several miles to the front. All is quiet today, & I think the Capital is safe. Just as I was starting off yesterday to gather up the army, supposing that I would find it savagely followed up by the rebels & that I might have dangerous work before me I commenced the enclosed scrawl on a scrap of paper as a good bye — could not even finish it. It may amuse you now that the danger is over.

[*enclosure*]

Sept 2 4 pm.   I am just about starting out to pick up the Army of the Potomac. Don't know whether I will get back — but can't resist saying one last word to you before I start. . . .

AL copy, McClellan Papers (C-7:63), Library of Congress.

To Henry W. Halleck

Head Quarters, Washington

General   Sept 4 [1862] 12 1/2 pm

Banks' Corps is on the march for Rockville, Poolesville etc to watch & check the enemy should he attempt to cross the Potomac below the

Point of Rocks. Sumner is in position near Tennallytown — Couch's division is probably by this time concentrated at Chain Bridge.

Have ordered more cavalry & a battery to Edwards Ferry. The troops are being rested & refitted as well as circumstances will permit — no time has been lost in doing this. I am not quite well enough to ride out today, except in case of necessity, but have sent my aides in all directions. The shelling of the canal boats is an old amusement of the rebels — it is probably a pretty strong proof that they do not intend to cross at Edwards' Ferry.[1]

Very respectfully yours
Geo B McClellan
Maj Genl

Maj Genl H W Halleck
Comdr in Chief

ALS, Records of the Adjutant General's Office, RG 94 (159: Halleck Papers), National Archives. *OR*, Ser. 1, XIX, Part 2, pp. 174–75.

1. Halleck forwarded a report on this date that the enemy was firing on boats in the Chesapeake and Ohio Canal. *OR*, Ser. 1, XIX, Part 2, p. 175.

EIGHT

THE MARYLAND CAMPAIGN AND ANTIETAM

SEPTEMBER 5–19, 1862

THE MARYLAND CAMPAIGN was the climax of George McClellan's military career and Antietam his greatest and most important battle. His description of Antietam for his wife as "the most terrible battle of the age" was a fair enough statement for 1862, and its cost — combined casualties in the two armies of nearly 23,000 men — has never been surpassed on any single day of warfare in the nation's history. Lee's first invasion of the North was turned back and (so McClellan told General Halleck) "Maryland & Penna. are now safe."

Lacking the weaponry and manpower to besiege Washington after Second Bull Run, General Lee had elected to cross the Potomac into Maryland to shift the theater of war to what he called the Confederacy's northern frontier. He did so to retain the strategic initiative and to provision his men and forage his animals on Northern soil, but primarily he went north to force a battle he believed would be decisive for the South's independence. He intended to draw McClellan far from his Washington base and fight him on a battleground of his own choosing somewhere in the Cumberland Valley of Maryland and Pennsylvania. McClellan followed slowly into Maryland, guarding Washington and Baltimore against attack and reorganizing his army and his command system.

In the first days of the campaign McClellan's letters to his wife reveal him to be confident of his prospects, but this tone is soon replaced by the more familiar litany of the daunting odds that faced him. Although his intelligence came now from Alfred Pleasonton's cavalry and from civilian informants, its counts of the enemy were as grossly inflated as anything Allan Pinkerton had produced on the Peninsula — and General McClellan was as predisposed as ever to accept them. The figure of 120,000 he settled on for Lee's army and reported to Washington on September

10 came to him from a church elder who had heard it from talkative Rebels. It was three times Lee's actual strength.

The campaign, and Lee's plan for it, was abruptly and fundamentally altered by the Lost Order. The copy of his operational plan lost by a Confederate courier and found on September 13 by a Union soldier revealed to McClellan that Lee had divided his army to surround and capture the Federal garrison at Harper's Ferry, and gave the location of each of the widely scattered commands. As McClellan himself phrased it, the Lost Order presented him with the unique opportunity ''to cut the enemy in two & beat him in detail.'' His dispatches on September 13 reveal his reaction to the find, and also the hedging in his report to General Halleck as to when he learned of it and what it contained. Indeed, many of his dispatches on this and the next few days are notable for their distortions and their exaggeration of the speed of his movements and the magnitude of what he accomplished.

The five days beginning on September 13 witnessed the discovery of the Lost Order, the fighting at South Mountain, the surrender of Harper's Ferry, the movement to Sharpsburg, and the great battle there on the seventeenth; yet during this momentous period McClellan wrote comparatively few dispatches and they are less revealing than those written (for example) during the Seven Days. His sole description of a tactical plan is his letter of September 13 to General Franklin, outlining his intentions for breaking through South Mountain the following day. His failure in those days to write down anything of how he planned to fight the Battle of Antietam leaves the largest single gap in his contemporaneous military record. The telegram he sent to General Halleck during the fighting on the seventeenth gives only a very brief description of actions already taken.

The scarcity of battlefield communications in the Maryland fighting is due in part to the nature of the operations there. While movements on the Peninsula had been deliberate enough to allow time to link the various commands by field telegraph, there was no similar opportunity at South Mountain and Antietam. Flag signals and couriers took the place of the telegraph. Rather than writing out orders and messages himself, in these actions McClellan seems to have communicated almost entirely through oral commands and directions to his aides. In that event, his actions at Antietam spoke louder than his words.

To Mary Ellen McClellan

[Washington] Sept 5 [1862] 11 am.

... Again I have been called upon to save the country — the case is desperate, but with God's help I will try unselfishly to do my best & if he wills it accomplish the salvation of the nation.[1] My men are true & will stand by me to the last. I still hope for success & will leave nothing undone to gain it....

How weary I am of this struggle against adversity. But one thing sustains me — & that is my trust in God — I know that the interests at stake are so great as to justify his interference — not for me, but for the innocent thousands, millions rather, who have been plunged in misery by no fault of theirs. It is probable that our communications will be cut off in a day or two — but don't be worried. You may rest assured that I am doing all I can for my country & that no shame shall rest upon you willfully brought upon you by me....

My hands are full, so is my heart....

4 pm. ... It makes my heart bleed to see the poor shattered remnants of my noble Army of the Potomac, poor fellows! and to see how they love me even now. I hear them calling out to me as I ride among them — "George — don't leave us again!" "They *shan't* take you away from us again" etc etc. I can hardly restrain myself when I see how fearfully they are reduced in numbers & realize how many of them lie unburied on the field of battle where their lives were uselessly sacrificed. It is the most terrible trial I ever experienced — Truly God is trying me in the fire....

AL copy, McClellan Papers (C-7:63), Library of Congress.

1. Earlier that morning President Lincoln directed GBM to take command in the field against the Confederate invaders in Maryland.

To Abraham Lincoln

Your Excellency   Washington Sept 5 [1862]

I have ordered a portion of the Provost Guard of the Army of the Potomac to take post at the Soldiers' Home for the purpose of guarding your Excellency's residence.[1]

The officer in command is instructed to deliver this note & receive your orders.

> Very respectfully yr obdt svt
> Geo B McClellan
> Maj Genl

His Excellency the President

ALS, Lincoln Papers, Library of Congress.

1. During the summer months the president often stayed in a cottage on the grounds of the Soldiers' Home, on the northern outskirts of Washington.

To Henry W. Halleck

General

Head-Quarters, Army of the Potomac, [Washington] Sept 6 1862

Genl Sumner reports the enemy moving towards Rockville. It will save a great deal of trouble & invaluable time if you will suspend the operation of the order in regard to Franklin & Porter until I can see my way out of this difficulty. I wish to move Franklin's Corps to the front at once. To prevent a change in Burnside's command while on the march I would urgently recommend that Hooker be assigned to McDowell's Corps.[1]

The Secty[2] told me he would cheerfully agree to anything of this kind that met your approval, & I really feel it necessary for me to ask for these things at once.

Very truly yours
Geo B McClellan
Maj Genl

Maj Genl Halleck

ALS, Records of the Adjutant General's Office, RG 94 (159: Halleck Papers), National Archives. *OR*, Ser. 1, XIX, Part 2, pp. 189–90.

1. In Army Hd. Qtrs., Special Orders 223 (Sept. 5) and 224 (Sept. 6), Porter and Franklin and Brig. Gen. Charles Griffin were relieved from duty while charges against them stemming from the Second Bull Run battle were investigated, Hooker was assigned command of Porter's corps, and Jesse L. Reno relieved McDowell as a corps commander. *OR*, Ser. 1, XIX, Part 2, pp. 188, 197. The orders were suspended, and Hooker was put in command of McDowell's corps. 2. Secretary of War Stanton.

To Abraham Lincoln

Confidential
Your Excellency

Head-Quarters, Army of the Potomac, [Washington] Sept 6 1862

I venture to say a few words in regard to a note I have just written to Genl Halleck[1] asking that Genl Hooker may be assigned to the command of McDowell's Corps instead of Genl Reno — I ask this altho' an intimate friend & an admirer of Genl Reno. Hooker has more experience with troops & is *perfectly* disposable — to take Reno now is to break up Burnside's Corps the temporary command of which will fall to Reno the moment I have placed Burnside *in command of a wing.* I also asked that the order removing Porter, Franklin & Griffin from their commands may be suspended until I have got through with the present crisis. I would not ask these things did I not feel that they were necessary in the present crisis. The Secretary of War (with whom I had a very pleasant interview) promised me that he would cheerfully agree to anything of this kind that I regarded as necessary.

Asking, with all due respect, a prompt decision on these important points[2]

I am respectfully your obt svt
Geo B McClellan
Maj Genl

ALS, McClellan Papers (A-77:31), Library of Congress.

1. GBM to Halleck, Sept. 6, *supra*. 2. The president returned this letter to GBM with the endorsement: "With entire respect, I must repeat that Gen. Halleck must control these questions."

To Edwin M. Stanton

Headquarters Army of the Potomac,
[Washington], September 7, 1862.

Sir:

I have been applied to by General Stone for permission to serve with the Army during the impending movements, even if only as a spectator.

I have no doubt as to the loyalty and devotion of General Stone, but am unwilling to use his services unless I know that it meets the approval of the Government.

I not only have no objection to his employment in this army, but, more than that, would be glad to avail myself of his services as soon as circumstances permit.[1]

Very truly, yours,
Geo. B. McClellan,
Major-General

Hon. E. M. Stanton, Secretary of War.

OR, Ser. 1, V, p. 342.

1. Gen. Stone, who had been released from imprisonment on Aug. 16, did not serve in the Army of the Potomac during the Maryland campaign. For the circumstances of his arrest, see GBM to Andrew Porter, Feb. 8, 1862, note 2, *supra*, and GBM to Stone, Dec. 5, 1862, *infra*.

To Mary Ellen McClellan

[Washington] Sept. 7th [1862] 2.30 pm. Sunday

... I leave in a couple of hours to take command of the army in the field. I shall go to Rockville tonight & start out after the rebels tomorrow. I shall have nearly 100,000 men, old & new, & hope with God's blessing to gain a decisive victory. I think we shall win for the men are now in good spirits — confident in their General & all united in sentiment. Pope & McDowell have morally killed themselves — & are relieved from command — a signal instance of retributive justice. I have done nothing towards this — it has done itself. I have now the entire confidence of the Govt & the love of the army — my enemies are crushed, silent & disarmed — if I defeat the rebels I shall be master of the situation. . . .

AL copy, McClellan Papers (C-7:63), Library of Congress.

To Mary Ellen McClellan   [TELEGRAM]

Washington Sept 7/62 2.50 pm.

We are all well & the entire army is now united, cheerful & confident. You need not fear the result for I believe that God will give us the victory. I leave here this afternoon to take command of the troops in the field. The feeling of the Govt towards me, I am sure, is kind & trusting. I hope with God's blessing, to justify the great confidence they now repose in me, & will bury the past in oblivion. A victory now & we will soon be together. I send short letter today. God bless & reward your trust in him & all will be well.

G. B. McC

AL copy, McClellan Papers (C-7:63), Library of Congress.

To Henry W. Halleck   [TELEGRAM]

Head Quarters, Army of the Potomac,
Camp near Rockville Sept 8 8 pm 1862

Nothing new to report except that I have heard from the cavalry at Mechanicsville who report railroad destroyed by rebels from Monrovia to the Monocacy & that a force of about (7000) seven thousand reached Frederick yesterday, they being a part of Jackson's force. The cavalry skirmishes today near the Monocacy were quite successful so far as heard from. I have ordered reconnaissances in all directions tomorrow including one well to the north & north west. I think that we are now in position to prevent any attacks in force on Baltimore, while we cover Washington on this side. I am rather weak in cavalry on the right but am hourly expecting more of Averell's Brigade. We are prepared to attack anything that crosses the Potomac this side of the Monocacy. I am by no means satisfied yet that the enemy have crossed the river in very large force — our information is still entirely too indefinite to justify definite action. I am ready to push in any direction & hope very soon to have the supplies & transportation so regulated that we can safely move farther from Washn & clear Maryland of the rebels.[1] The time occupied in ascertaining their position, strength & intentions will enable me to place the Army in fair condition. I do not feel sure that there is no force in front of Washington. I think I can now answer for it that they shall not cross the river this side of Monocacy & that they shall not take Baltimore without defeating this Army — I am also in position to hasten to the assistance of Washington if necessary. As soon as I find out where to strike I will be after them without an hour's delay.

G B McClellan
Maj Genl

Maj Genl Halleck
Washington D.C.

ALS (telegram sent), McClellan Papers (C-15:64), Library of Congress. *OR*, Ser. 1, XIX, Part 2, p. 211.

1. At 1:05 P.M. Halleck had telegraphed that the Confederates were reported at Leesburg. ''If so, it seems to me that a sufficient number of your forces to meet the enemy should move rapidly forward, leaving a reserve in reach of you and Washington at the same time.'' *OR*, Ser. 1, XIX, Part 2, p. 210.

To Andrew G. Curtin   [TELEGRAM]

To His Excy Gov Curtin   Hd Qrs Army Potomac
Harrisburg   Rockville Md Sept 8 1862 9 pm

My information about the enemy comes from unreliable sources & is vague & conflicting. This army is in position to move against the Rebels whatever their plan may be. If they intend an advance towards your state I shall act with all possible vigor. I can scarcely believe that such is their purpose. I shall use every effort to ascertain the actual state of the fact & trust that you will do whatever you can in the same direction & that you will keep me advised of whatever you may learn. It would be well for you to push your investigations towards Frederick as far as possible.[1]

Geo B. McClellan
M.G. Comdg.

Retained copy, Records of the Office of the Secretary of War, RG 107 (M-504:66), National Archives. *OR*, Ser. 1, XIX, Part 2, p. 216.

1. At 3:15 A.M. on Sept. 9 Gov. Curtin replied, in part: ''No doubt appears to exist as to the intention of the enemy to invade our state & are now probably now on or over our border. I will telegraph you all reliable information received by me....'' McClellan Papers (A-78:31), Library of Congress.

To Mary Ellen McClellan

Sept 8 [September 9, 1862] Camp near Rockville[1]

In coming to Rockville, we reached there somewhere about midnight [September 7] & had no baggage. Sacket[2] & I found a room together in the house of a Miss Beall, an old maid of strong Union sentiment, who refused to receive any pay &c. Yesterday we came out to this camp which is about half a mile from the town, & in a pleasant situation in a clover field, on a hill where we have all the air that is stirring.

You don't know what a task has been imposed upon me! I have been obliged to do the best I could with the broken & discouraged fragments of two armies defeated by no fault of mine — nothing but a desire to do my duty could have induced me to accept the command under such circumstances — not feeling at all sure that I could do anything I felt that under the circumstances no one else *could* save the country, & I have not shrunk from the terrible task. Pope has subsided into oblivion with the contempt of all — he has proved to be a perfect failure & all acknowledge it. McDowell had to flee for his life — his own men would have killed him had he made his appearance among them — even his staff did not dare to go among his men. Did you ever hear of a more striking instance of retributive justice — the man who wickedly turned against me when I had done all I could to aid him has now no friends left — utterly despised, entirely lost, *he* has also been consigned to oblivion — I can afford to forgive & forget him. I saw Pope & McD for a few moments at Upton's Hill when I rode out to meet the troops & assume command — I have not seen them since — I hope never to lay eyes on them again — between them they are responsible for the lives of many of my best & bravest men — they have done all they could (unintentionally I hope) to ruin & destroy the country — I can never forgive them for that. Pope has been foolish enough to try to throw the blame of his defeat on the Army of the Potomac — the resulting inquiry will beyond a doubt be most disastrous to him & nail him as an incompetent General. He would have been wiser to have accepted his defeat without complaint. I will probably move some 4 or 5 miles further to the front tomorrow [September 9] — as I have ordered the whole army forward. I expect to fight a great battle & to do my best at it — I do not think secesh will catch me very badly — the men & officers have complete confidence in me & I pray to God that he will justify their trust.

AL copy; copy, McClellan Papers (C-7:63/D-10:72), Library of Congress.

1. It appears that this letter was written in the early hours of the morning, shortly after midnight. 2. Col. Delos B. Sacket, GBM's inspector general.

To Henry W. Halleck   [TELEGRAM]

Maj Gen H. W. Halleck   Camp near Rockville Md
Gen in Chief   Sept. 9th [1862] 7.30 am

Rebel scouts last night at Lisbon. In the Cavalry skirmish at Poolesville yesterday the Rebels lost one Captain & fifteen men killed & wounded besides six prisoners. 3rd Ind Cavalry one squadron did the work very handsomely on our side. Last reports that the Rebels were not in sight near Poolesville & Hyattstown. Our Cavalry are pushing forward in all directions while the Army will at least occupy the line of the Seneca today. Pleasonton's report of last night that there were 100,000 Rebels on this side of the river was derived from the notorious Capt White; it is not fully reliable.[1] We shall know better today. I will keep you fully informed.

G. B. McClellan

Maj Genl

Received copy, Records of the Office of the Secretary of War, RG 107 (M-473:50), National Archives. *OR*, Ser. 1, XIX, Part 2, pp. 218–19.

1. Pleasonton's dispatch read, in part: "Most reliable information has been obtained that the enemy has crossed the River in force over 100,000 strong. They are to march to *Frederick* thence to *Gettysburg* thence to *York* & thence to *Baltimore*." Capt. Elijah V. White acted as a guide for the Confederates. McClellan Papers (A-78:31), Library of Congress.

To Mary Ellen McClellan

[Rockville] Tuesday morning [September 9, 1862] 8 1/2 am.

... I hope to learn this morning something definite as to the movements of secesh to be enabled to regulate my own. I hardly expect to equal the genius of Mr. Pope but I hope to waste fewer lives & to accomplish something more than lame defeat. I have ordered a general advance of a few miles today — which will bring us on the line of the Seneca & near enough to secesh to find out what he is doing & take measures accordingly. I shall follow him wherever he goes & do my best to beat him — if I accomplish that it is all over with him & the campaign will be ended.

9.30 [A.M.] ... The fact is that commanding such an army as this — picked up after a defeat, is no very easy thing — it does take a great deal of time & infinite labor. In coming to Rockville we arrived about midnight. Yesterday we came out to this camp, which is about 1/2 a mile from the town. I am still uncertain whether I shall move Hd Qtrs today, or on which road, as that depends on the information I receive as to the enemy. I probably won't go more than four or five miles in a central direction. ...

It is something of a triumph that my enemies have been put down so completely, & if to that I can add the defeat of secesh I think I ought to be entitled to fall back into private life. ...

AL copy, McClellan Papers (C-7:63), Library of Congress.

To Henry W. Halleck

[TELEGRAM]

Head Quarters, Army of the Potomac,

Camp near Rockville Sept 9 3.30 pm 1862

At noon today all the troops ordered forward were in motion for their new positions. The latest information from the front indicates the enemy in large force near Frederick. Our cavalry have taken several prisoners

& the standard of a rebel regiment of cavalry today. From the parties now out I hope to know soon something definite as to the strength, position & intentions of the enemy. They talk of going to Gettysburg & York. I do not think they have yet left Frederick in any force. I am anxious for the prompt arrival of the rest of my cavalry from Fort Monroe. When the prisoners get in I shall learn something of them. Thus far my cavalry have gained the advantage.

G B McClellan
Maj Genl

Maj Genl Halleck
Washington D.C.

ALS (telegram sent), McClellan Papers (C-15:64), Library of Congress. *OR*, Ser. 1, XIX, Part 2, p. 219.

To Mary Ellen McClellan

Sept 9 [1862] Camp near Rockville 5 pm.

... Am going out in a few minutes to ride over to the camp of the Regulars, whom I have not been to see for a long time, & who welcomed me so cordially the other night — brave fellows that they are.

It is hard to get accurate news from the front — the last reports from Pleasonton are that the enemy have 110,000 on this side of the river.[1] I have not so many, so I must watch them closely & try to catch them in some mistake, which I hope to do. My people are mostly in front of here — some 6 to 10 miles — moved forward today. They are I think well placed to be concentrated wherever it may be necessary & I want now a little breathing time to get them rested & in good order for fighting. Most of them will do well now — a few days will compose them still further, increase my cavalry force & put me in better condition generally. I think my present positions will check their advance into Penna & give me time to get some reinforcements that I need very much. ...

I have this moment learned that in addition to the force on this side of the river the enemy have *also* a large force near Leesburg — so McC has a difficult game to play, but will do his best & try to do his duty.

AL copy, McClellan Papers (C-7:63), Library of Congress.

1. Pleasonton's dispatch to this effect was sent at 3:15 P.M. GBM forwarded the estimate to Gen. Halleck at 6:00 P.M. McClellan Papers (A-78:31); *OR*, Ser. 1, XIX, Part 2, p. 219.

To Fitz John Porter [TELEGRAM]

Maj Genl F. J. Porter
Arlington   Rockville 8.40 pm Sept 9 1862

Dispatch rec'd.[1] Our Cavalry have had some handsome affairs today fully maintaining the morale they gained in the Peninsula. We have regained Barnsville & Sugar Loaf Mt. The Army is tonight well posted to act in any direction the moment the enemy develops his movements. I am now in condition to watch him closely & he will find it hard to escape me if he commits a blunder. We shall do our best & I think that will suffice.

G B McClellan
MG

Retained copy, Records of the Office of the Secretary of War, RG 107 (M-504:66), National Archives. *OR*, Ser. 1, XIX, Part 2, p. 221.

1. Porter's telegram of this date reported on the condition of his forces in the Washington lines. *OR*, Ser. 1, XIX, Part 2, p. 220.

To Abraham Lincoln [TELEGRAM]

Head Quarters,
Army of the Potomac,
Camp near Rockville

His Excellency the President   Sept. 10th 12m 1862

In reply to your dispatch of this morning[1] I have the honor to state that Genl Pleasonton at Barnesville reports that a movement of the enemy last night is said to have been made across the Potomac from this side to the other side. We shall know the truth of this rumor soon. Pleasonton is watching all the fords as high as Conrad's Ferry & has pickets out to the mouth of the Monocacy. He has sent out this morning to occupy Sugar Loaf Mt. from which a large extent of country can be seen in all directions. Genl Burnside had his scouts out last night at Ridgeville & within (3) three miles of Newmarket. No enemy seen with the exception of a few pickets. They were told that Stuart's cavalry (5000) five thousand in number occupied Newmarket, & that the main Rebel forces under Jackson were still at Frederick. Burnside has sent a strong reconnaissance today to the mountain pass at Ridgeville. I propose if the information I have rec'd proves reliable regarding the natural strength of this position, to occupy it with a sufficient force to resist an advance of the enemy in that direction. I have scouts and spies pushed forward in every direction and shall soon be in possession of reliable & definite information. The statements I get regarding the enemy's forces that have crossed to this side range from eighty (80) to one hundred & fifty (150) thousand. I am perfectly certain that none of the enemy's troops have crossed the Potomac within the last twenty four hours below the mouth of the Monocacy. I was informed last night by Genl Pleasonton that his information rendered it probable that Jackson's force had advanced to Newmarket with Stuart's cavalry at Urbanna.[2] In view of this I ordered the Army forward this morning to the line along the high ridge from Ridgeville, thro' Damascus, Clarksburg &c. But the information subsequently obtained from Genl Burnside's scouts that the mass of the enemy was still at Frederick induced to suspend the movement of the right wing until I could verify the truth of the reports by means of Burnside's reconnaissances in force today.[3] My extreme left advances to Poolesville this morning. The work of re-organization & refitting is progressing very satisfactorily under the new heads of Staff Departments. Despatch this instant rec'd from Genl Pleasonton dated Barnesville 10.30 a.m. says "my scouts occupy the ferry at the mouth of the Monocacy. They found no enemy except a few pickets on the other side of the Monocacy. At Licksville about (3) three miles from that stream it was reported there was a force of six thousand (6000) men."

Geo B McClellan

Maj Genl Comdg

LS (telegram sent), McClellan Papers (C-16:65), Library of Congress. *OR*, Ser. 1, XIX, Part 2, p. 233.

1. The president telegraphed: "How does it look now?" *OR*, Ser. 1, XIX, Part 2, p. 232. 2. Pleasonton's dispatch to this effect was sent at 7:30 P.M. on Sept. 9. McClellan Papers (A-78:31). 3. Burnside's dispatch of this date read, in part: "A large force is reported at Frederick under Lee & Jackson but all the reports are indefinite, am trying to get more definite information through citizens." McClellan Papers (A-78:31).

To Henry W. Halleck

Maj. Genl. H. W. Halleck,
General-in-Chief.   Hd. Qtrs. Camp near Rockville,
General: Septr. 11th [September 10] 1862.[1]

At the time this army moved from Washington, it was not known what the intentions of the Rebels were in placing their forces on this side of the Potomac. It might have been a feint to draw away our troops from Washington, for the purpose of throwing their main army into the city as soon as we were out of the way, or it might have been supposed to be precisely what they are now doing. In view of this uncertain condition of things, I left what I conceived to be a sufficient force to defend the city against any army they could bring against it from the Virginia side of the Potomac.

This uncertainty, in my judgment, exists no longer. All the evidence that has accumulated from various sources since we left Washington goes to prove most conclusively that almost the entire Rebel army in Virginia, amounting to not less than 120,000 men, is in the vicinity of Frederick City.

These troops, for the most part, consist of their oldest regiments, and are commanded by their best Generals. Several brigades joined them yesterday direct from Richmond, two deserters from which say that they saw no other troops between Richmond and Leesburg. Every thing seems to indicate that they intend to hazard all upon the issue of the coming battle. They are probably aware that their forces are numerically superior to ours by at least twenty-five per cent. This, with the prestige of their recent successes, will, without doubt, inspire them with a confidence which will cause them to fight well. The momentous consequences involved in the struggle of the next few days impel me, at the risk of being considered slow and overcautious, to most earnestly recommend that every available man be at once added to this army.

I believe this army fully appreciates the importance of a victory at this time, and will fight well. But the result of a general battle, with such odds as the enemy now appears to have against us, might, to say the least, be doubtful; and if we should be defeated, the consequences to the country would be disastrous in the extreme. Under these circumstances, I would recommend that one or two of the three army corps now on the Potomac, opposite Washington, be at once withdrawn and sent to reinforce this army. I would also advise that the force of Colonel Miles,[2] at Harper's Ferry, where it can be of but little use and is continually exposed to be cut off by the enemy, be immediately ordered here. This would add about twenty-five thousand old troops to our present force, and would greatly strengthen us.

If there are any Rebel forces remaining on the other side of the Potomac, they must be so few that the troops left in the forts, after the two corps shall have been withdrawn, will be sufficient to check them; and with the large cavalry force now on that side kept well out in front to give warning of the distant approach of any very large army, a part of this army might be sent back within the entrenchments to assist in repelling an attack. But even if Washington should be taken while these armies are confronting each other, this would not, in my judgment, bear comparison with the ruin and disasters which would follow a signal defeat of this Army. If we should be successful in conquering the gigantic rebel army before us, we would have no difficulty in recovering it. On the other hand, should their force prove sufficiently powerful to defeat us, would all the forces now around Washington be sufficient to prevent such a victorious army from carrying the works on this side the Potomac, after they are uncovered by our Army? I think not.

From the moment the rebels commenced the policy of concentrating their forces, with their large masses of troops operating against our scattered forces, they have been successful. They are undoubtedly pursuing the same policy now, and are prepared to take advantage of any division of our troops in future.

I therefore most respectfully, but strenuously urge upon you the absolute necessity, at this critical juncture, of uniting all our disposable forces. Every other consideration should yield to this; and if we defeat the army now arrayed before us, the rebellion is crushed; for I do not believe they can organize another army. But if we should be so unfortunate as to meet with defeat, our country is at their mercy.[3]

> Very respectfully, Your obt. svt.
> Geo B McClellan
> Maj. Genl.

Copy, Stanton Papers, Library of Congress. *OR*, Ser. 1, XIX, Part 2, pp. 254–55.

1. Although this War Dept. copy is dated Sept. 11 (and so appears in the *Official Records*), a copy by Gen. Marcy is dated Sept. 10, and in his reply Halleck refers to "your letter of the 10th." McClellan Papers (A-80:32), Library of Congress; *OR*, Ser. 1, XIX, Part 2, p. 280. Furthermore, it is logical that GBM's telegraphed calls for the troops at Harper's Ferry and for specific reinforcements from Washington (*infra*) would follow the writing of this letter rather than precede it. 2. Col. Dixon S. Miles. 3. In his reply on Sept. 13, Halleck wrote: "You attach too little importance to the capital. I assure you that you are wrong. The capture of this place will throw us back six months, if it should not destroy us." *OR*, Ser. 1, XIX, Part 2, pp. 280–81.

To Andrew G. Curtin   [TELEGRAM]

Andrew G. Curtin
Governor of Pennsylvania:

Headquarters Army of the Potomac,
[Brookeville, Md.]
September 10, 1862 — 10.30 p.m.

Everything that we can learn induces me to believe that the information you have received is substantially correct.[1] I think the enemy are checked in the directions of Baltimore and Gettysburg. You should concentrate all the troops you can in the vicinity of Chambersburg, not entirely neglecting Gettysburg. I will follow them up as rapidly as possible, and do all I can to check their movements into Pennsylvania. Call out the militia, especially mounted men, and do everything in your power to impede the enemy by the action of light troops; attack them in flank, destroying their trains and any property which must inevitably come into their possession. You may be sure that I will follow them as closely as I can, and fight them whenever I can find them. It is as much my interest as yours to preserve the soil of Pennsylvania from invasion, or, failing in that, to destroy any army that may have the temerity to attempt it.

> Geo. B. McClellan
> Major-General

OR, Ser. 1, XIX, Part 2, pp. 248–49.

1. Curtin's telegram of 10:00 A.M. on this date reported intelligence that the Confederate force "around Frederick is not less than 120,000 men. . . . From all we can learn, the enemy has selected his ground and massed his force near Frederick, to give you battle, the result of which will probably decide the future of our country." *OR*, Ser. 1, XIX, Part 2, p. 248.

To Henry W. Halleck   [TELEGRAM]

Maj Gen Halleck   Brookeville Sept 10th [1862] 11.55 pm

I have ordered a general advance tomorrow. Send me up all the troops you can spare.

Geo B McClellan
Maj Genl

Received copy, Records of the Office of the Secretary of War, RG 107 (M-473:50), National Archives. *OR*, Ser. 1, XIX, Part 2, p. 234.

To Henry W. Halleck   [TELEGRAM]

Major General Halleck   Head Quarters, Army of the Potomac,
Washington   Camp near Rockville Sept. 11, 1862 9.45 am

Colonel Miles is at or near Harper's Ferry, I understand with nine thousand troops. He can do nothing where he is, but could be of great service if ordered to join me. I suggest that he be ordered at once to join me by the most practicable route.

Geo. B. McClellan
Maj. Gen. Comdg.

Retained copy, McClellan Papers (C-18:65), Library of Congress. *OR*, Ser. 1, XIX, Part 1, p. 758.

1. Halleck replied at 2:00 P.M.: "There is no way for Colonel Miles to join you at present. His only chance is to defend his works till you can open communication with him. When you do so he will be subject to your orders." *OR*, Ser. 1, XIX, Part 1, p. 758.

To Henry W. Halleck   [TELEGRAM]

Major Gen Halleck
General in Chief,   Head Quarters, Army of the Potomac,
Washington   Camp near Rockville Sept 11 1862 3.45 pm

Please send forward all the troops you can spare from Washington, particularly Porter, Heintzelman, Sigel and all other old troops.[1] Please send them to Brookville via Leesboro, as soon as possible. General Banks reports seventy two thousand five hundred troops in and about Washington.[2] If the enemy has left for Pennsylvania, I will follow him rapidly. I move my head quarters to Middlebrook immediately.

Geo. B. McClellan
Maj Genl Comdg

Retained copy, McClellan Papers (C-18:65), Library of Congress. *OR*, Ser. 1, XIX, Part 2, p. 253.

1. The three field corps left at Washington were commanded by Porter, Heintzelman, and Maj. Gen. Franz Sigel, formerly of the Army of Virginia. 2. The president telegraphed at 6:00 P.M. that Porter "is ordered to-night to join you as quick as possible. I am for sending you all that can be spared, & I hope others can follow Porter very soon." *Collected Works of Lincoln*, V, p. 415.

To Henry W. Halleck   [TELEGRAM]

	Head Quarters, Army of the Potomac,
Major General Halleck	Middleburg [Middlebrook]
Genl in Chief, Washington	Sept. 11, 1862 11.30 pm

My signals have today been established on Sugar Loaf Mountain. At last advices Burnside's troops were within two miles of New Market. I have ordered him tomorrow to advance if possible to Frederick and occupy it. Sumner and Franklin to advance early in the morning to Urbana. Couch following the movement after leaving a force to guard the fords below the Monocacy. I am much obliged to you for sending me Porter's Corps and should like the remainder of Keyes' Corps as soon as possible. I shall follow up the rebels as rapidly as possible.

Geo. B. McClellan
Maj Genl Comdg

Retained copy, McClellan papers (C-16:65), Library of Congress. *OR*, Ser. 1, XIX, Part 2, p. 255.

To Henry W. Halleck   [TELEGRAM]

Gen H W Halleck   Hd Qrs A.P. Clarksburg Sept 12, 1862 10 am

My columns are pushing on rapidly to Frederick. I feel perfectly confident that the enemy has abandoned Frederick moving in two directions. Viz. on the Hagerstown & Harpers Ferry roads.

Fitz Lee with 4 Regts of Cavalry & 6 pieces Artillery left New Market yesterday for Liberty. They are being followed by Burnside's Cavalry.

G B McClellan
MGC

Received copy, Records of the Office of the Secretary of War, RG 107 (M-473:50), National Archives. *OR*, Ser. 1, XIX, Part 2, pp. 270–71.

To Mary Ellen McClellan

Sept 12 [1862] 3 pm. Camp near Urbana

As our wagons are not yet up & won't be for a couple of hours or more I avail myself of the "advantages of the situation" to scrawl a few lines to you. I am sitting on a saddle blanket, under a tree — tore this paper from the back of a dispatch sent to me this morning, & am using my "Album" (the Photograph Gallery you gave me) as a writing desk. I stopped half an hour this morning at a little place called Clarksburg. Some Union people invited me into the house, when presently one of the young ladies, brought me with great pride a large photograph album & showed me that the first picture in the book was one of those we had taken together. They were all so anxious to know whether it resembled you, that I showed them some of those in *my* collection, which *happened* to be in my pocket at the time — don't you think it was a lucky *accident* that brought it there. The place selected for our camp tonight is where I am writing, in a beautiful grove on the summit of a hill; one of the prettiest camps we have yet had. We are travelling now thro' one of the most lovely regions I have ever seen — quite broken with lovely valleys in all directions, & some fine mountains in the distance.

From all I can gather secesh is skedadelling & I don't think I can catch him unless he is really moving into Penna — in that case I shall catch him before he has made much headway towards the interior. I begin to think that he is making off to get out of the scrape by recrossing the river at Williamsport — in which case my only chance of bagging him will be to cross lower down & cut into his communications near Winchester. He evidently don't want to fight me — for some reason or other....

The doctrines enunciated by Mr. Mahan[1] are very excellent, but I don't see the application to myself in respect of McDowell. I have never injured McD — therefore I am not called upon to make any advances to him as the Prof. seems to think I ought. I bear no hatred to the man — I simply regard him as a scoundrel a liar & a fool who in seeking to injure me has killed himself — I have the most thorough contempt for him — nothing more. All I ask is that I may never set eyes on him again — as for ever having any friendly relations with him it is simply absurd....

7 1/2 pm.   My tent has been pitched some time. I have given all the orders necessary for tomorrow & they have all gone to the various corps....

I believe that I have done all in my power & that the arrangement of the troops is good. I learned an hour or two ago thro' the signal that our troops were entering Frederic. We certainly ought to be there in respectable force by this time — my only apprehension now is that secesh will manage to get back across the Potomac at Wmsport before I can catch him. If he goes to Penna I think I must overhaul him before long & give him a good lesson. If he does go to Penna I feel quite confident that I

can so arrange things that the chances will be that he will never return —
but I presume he is smart enough to know that & to act accordingly....

Interrupted here by the news that we really have Frederic — Burnside
& Pleasonton both there. The next trouble is to save the garrison of
Harper's Ferry, which is I fear in danger of being captured by the rebels.
They were not placed under my orders until this afternoon, altho' before
I left Washn I strongly urged that they should be withdrawn at once as
I feared they would be captured. But other counsels prevailed & I am
rather anxious as to the result. If they are not taken by this time I think
I can save them — at all events nothing in my power shall be left undone
to accomplish this result. I feel sure of one thing now, & that is that my
men will fight well. The only doubtful ones are McD's old troops, who
are in bad condition as to discipline & everything else. Hooker will how-
ever soon bring them out of the kinks, & will make them fight if anyone
can. The moment I hear that Harper's Ferry is safe I shall feel quite
sure of the result....

I learn that the people cheered the troops tremendously when they
entered Frederic. I have thus far found the Union sentiment much stronger
in this region than I had expected — people are disposed to be very kind
& polite to me — invite me into their houses, offer me dinner & various
other acts of kindness that were quite unknown in the Peninsula.

AL copy; copy, McClellan Papers (C-7:63/D-10:72), Library of Congress.

1. Dennis Hart Mahan, of the West Point faculty. Apparently he had written to Mrs.
McClellan.

To Henry W. Halleck   [TELEGRAM]

                                            Head Qrs Army Potomac,
Maj Gen Halleck   Near Urbana Sept. 12 [1862] 5.30 pm

I have just learned by signal from Sugar Loaf that our troops are
entering Frederick. The remainder of Burnside's troops are between
Frederick & New Market. Sumner is near Urbana with an advanced guard
thrown out to the Monocacy, Williams on his right, Franklin on his left,
Couch at Barnesville. Cavalry has been sent towards Point of Rocks to
ascertain whether there is any force of the enemy in that direction.
Burnside has cavalry in pursuit of Fitz Hugh Lee towards Westminster.
Should the enemy go towards Penna I shall follow him. Should he attempt
to recross the Potomac I shall endeavor to cut off his retreat. My move-
ments tomorrow will be dependent upon information to be received dur-
ing the night. The troops have marched today as far as was possible and
proper for them to move.

                                            Geo. B. McClellan
                                            Maj Gen Comdg

P.S. I have ordered Banks to send eight new Regts to relieve parts of Couch's command I left at Offutts' cross roads, Seneca and Conrads & Edwards Ferries. How soon may I expect these troops. Their presence at the points indicated are very necessary.[1]

G B McClellan

Received copy, Records of the Office of the Secretary of War, RG 107 (M-473 :50), National Archives. *OR*, Ser. 1, XIX, Part 2, p. 271.

1. Halleck replied on Sept. 13 that Gen. Banks, in command of Washington's defenses, "cannot safely spare eight new regiments from here.... Until you know more certainly the enemy's force south of the Potomac, you are wrong in thus uncovering the capital. I am of opinion that the enemy will send a small column toward Pennsylvania, so as to draw your forces in that direction; then suddenly move on Washington...." *OR*, Ser. 1, XIX, Part 2, pp. 280–81.

To Henry W. Halleck [TELEGRAM]

Hd Qrs Army Potomac

Maj Gen Halleck   Near Urbana Sept 12 [1862] 6 pm

I learn nothing reliable as to the enemy south of Potomac.[1] I this morning ordered Cavalry to endeavor to open communication with Harper's Ferry and in my orders of movement for tomorrow have arranged so that I go or send to his[2] relief if necessary. I have heard no firing in that direction & if he resists at all I think cannot only relieve him but place the rebels who attack him in great danger of being cut off. Everything moves at daylight tomorrow. Your message to him this moment received. Will forward by first opportunity.[3]

G B McClellan
Maj Genl Comdg

Received copy, Records of the Office of the Secretary of War, RG 107 (M-473 :50), National Archives. *OR*, Ser. 1, XIX, Part 2, pp. 271–72.

1. Halleck had telegraphed at 1 :45 P.M. : "Have you any reliable information of enemy's force south of the Potomac ? Is it not possible to open communication with Harper's Ferry, so that Colonel Miles' forces can co-operate with you ?" *OR*, Ser. 1, XIX, Part 2, p. 271. 2. Col. Miles. 3. Halleck's dispatch of this date to Miles read : "You will obey such orders as General McClellan may give you. You will endeavor to open communication with him and unite your forces to his at the earliest possible moment." *OR*, Ser. 1, XIX, Part 1, p. 758.

To Abraham Lincoln [TELEGRAM]

Head Quarters, Army of the Potomac,
Camp near Urbana Sept 12 1862 9 pm

You will have learned by my telegrams to Genl Halleck that we hold Frederick & the line of the Monocacy.[1]

I have taken all possible means to communicate with Harper's Ferry so that I may send to its relief if necessary. Cavalry are in pursuit of the Westminster party with orders to catch them at all hazards. The main body of my cavalry & horse artillery are ordered after the enemy's main column with orders to check its march as much as possible that I may overtake it. If Harper's Ferry is still in our possession I think I can save the garrison if they fight at all. If the rebels are really moving into Penna I shall soon be up with them. My apprehension is that they may make for Williamsport & get across the river before I can catch them.

G B McClellan
Maj Genl

His Excellency the President

ALS (telegram sent), McClellan Papers (C-15:64), Library of Congress. *OR*, Ser. 1, XIX, Part 2, p. 272.

1. The president had telegraphed at 5:45 P.M. that information received "corroborates the idea that the enemy is recrossing the Potomac. Please do not let him get off without being hurt." *Collected Works of Lincoln*, V, p. 418.

To Lorenzo Thomas

Brigadier General L. Thomas
Adjutant General, U.S. Army   Head Quarters Army of the Potomac,
General: [Frederick] September 13th 1862.

There is no more important arm of the military service than the regular artillery, and none which during the existing war has achieved more and upon which, hope for the future success during the contest, is to rely. It is of the greatest consequence to maintain it in a condition of efficiency. For this end it must be recruited. Out of the twenty six regular batteries in this army, ten are now but four gun batteries, when it is of great importance that they should be of six guns, and this for want of can-noneers and drivers. The volunteers serving with the batteries in many cases have demanded to be returned to their regiments and I have been compelled since they have a sort of right to it to return them. During the present month and the fall months, the terms of service of many men will expire. Thus the condition of the regular artillery is precarious, unless some stimulus is given to the recruiting service. I view it of the highest importance to the country and the service, that the six gun bat-teries should be increased to eight gun batteries. We would thus need fewer volunteer batteries; would have a more manageable artillery force at less expense than we have now, and would have one vastly more reliable.

To carry the ten, four gun batteries up to eight gun batteries would require one hundred men each, say one thousand men. To carry the sixteen six gun batteries up to eight gun batteries, would require sixty men each, say nine hundred sixty men.

To fill up the twenty six batteries, to full batteries of six guns each, with the proper complement of men, would require from one thousand to twelve hundred men.

I earnestly invite the serious attention of the Adjutant General and the War Department to the subject of filling up the Artillery; and I ask that every means be exhausted to procure two thousand men for the Artillery.

I also enclose a memorandum of the number of recruits needed for the regular Infantry.[1] The regular Infantry regiments, are the most reliable foot troops that we have. Their existence is threatened by the paucity and continual diminution of their numbers. I earnestly request, that if the resources of the War Department can control the matter, that they be used to their utmost to reinforce the thinned ranks of these regiments.[2]

> I am Very Respectfully Your obedient Servant,
> [George B. McClellan]
> Major General Commanding

Retained copy, Records of U.S. Army Continental Commands, RG 393 (3946: Army of the Potomac), National Archives. *OR*, Ser. 1, XIX, Part 2, pp. 282–83.

1. Not found. 2. For efforts to recruit for the regular army from the ranks of the volunteers, see Adj. Gen.'s Office, General Order 154, Oct. 9, 1862, *OR*, Ser. 3, II, p. 654.

To Abraham Lincoln   [TELEGRAM]

2.35 AM[1]

To the President   Hd Qrs Frederick Sept 13th [1862] 12 M

I have the whole Rebel force in front of me but am confident and no time shall be lost. I have a difficult task to perform but with Gods blessing will accomplish it. I think Lee has made a gross mistake and that he will be severely punished for it. The Army is in motion as rapidly as possible. I hope for a great success if the plans of the Rebels remain unchanged. We have possession of Cotocktane.[2] I have all the plans of the Rebels[3] and will catch them in their own trap if my men are equal to the emergency. I now feel that I can count on them as of old. All forces of Pennsylvania should be placed to cooperate at Chambersburg. My respects to Mrs Lincoln.

Received most enthusiastically by the ladies.[4] Will send you trophies. All well and with Gods Blessing will accomplish it.

> Geo B. McClellan

Received copy, Records of the Office of the Secretary of War, RG 107 (M-473:50), National Archives. *OR*, Ser. 1, XIX, Part 2, p. 281.

1. Telegraphic communication was not yet re-established between Frederick and Washington, and this dispatch, written at noon (12 M, or meridian) on Sept. 13, was relayed by courier or flag signal to an intermediate telegraph station and received in Washington at 2:35 A.M. on Sept. 14. 2. The Catoctin range, west of Frederick. 3. The so-called Lost Order, a copy of Gen. Lee's Special Orders No. 191 found that morning near Frederick by a Federal soldier. 4. A reference to GBM's welcome in Frederick.

To William B. Franklin

Maj. Genl. W. B. Franklin   Head Quarters, Army of the Potomac, Camp near Frederick
Comdg. 6th Corps   Sept. 13 1862 6.20 pm

Genl: I have now full information as to the movements & intentions of the enemy.

Jackson has crossed the Upper Potomac to capture the garrison at Martinsburg & cut off Miles' retreat towards the west. A division on the south side of the Potomac was to carry Loudoun Heights & cut off his retreat in that direction. McLaws with his own command & the division of R. H. Anderson[1] was to move by Boonsboro & Rohrersville to carry the Maryland Heights. The signal officers inform me that he is now in Pleasant Valley. The firing shows that Miles still holds out.

Longstreet was to move to Boonsboro & there halt with the reserve trains, D. H. Hill to form the rear guard, Stuart's cavalry to bring up stragglers etc. We have cleared out all the cavalry this side of the mountains & north of us. The last I heard from Pleasonton he occupied Middletown after several sharp skirmishes. A division of Burnside's command started several hours ago to support him. The whole of Burnside's command, including Hooker's Corps march this evening & early tomorrow morning followed by the Corps of Sumner & Banks & Sykes' Divn upon Boonsboro to carry that position. Couch has been ordered to concentrate his divn & join you as rapidly as possible. Without waiting for the whole of that divn to join you, you will move at daybreak in the morning by Jefferson & Burkittsville upon the road to Rohrersville. I have reliable information that the mountain pass by this road[2] is practicable for artillery & wagons. If this pass is not occupied by the enemy in force seize it as soon as practicable & debouch upon Rohrersville in order to cut off the retreat or destroy McLaws' command. If you find the pass held by the enemy in large force make all your dispositions for the attack & commence it about half an hour after you hear severe firing at the pass on the Hagerstown pike,[3] where the main column will attack. Having gained the pass your duty will be first to cut off, destroy or capture McLaws' command & relieve Col Miles. If you effect this you will order him to join you at once with all his disposable troops, first destroying the bridges over the Potomac if not already done & leaving a sufficient garrison to prevent the enemy from passing the ford. You will then return by Rohrersville on the direct road to Boonsboro, if the main column has not succeeded in its attack. If it has succeeded take the road from Rohrersville to Sharpsburg & Williamsport in order either to cut off the retreat of Hill & Longstreet towards the Potomac, or to prevent the repassage of Jackson. My general idea is to cut the enemy in two & beat him in detail. I believe I have sufficiently explained my intentions. I ask of you at this important moment all your intellect & the utmost activity that a general can exercise. Knowing my views & intentions you are fully authorized to change any of the details of this order as circumstances may change, provided the purpose is carried out — that purpose being to attack the enemy in detail & beat him.

Genl Smith's dispatch of 4 p.m. with your comments is received.[4] If with a full knowledge of all the circumstances you consider it preferable to crush the enemy at Petersville before undertaking the movement I have directed, you are at liberty to do so, but you will readily perceive that no slight advantage should for a moment interfere with the decisive results I propose to gain. I cannot too strongly impress upon you the absolute necessity of informing me every hour during the day of your movements & frequently during the night. Force your Colonels to prevent straggling & bring every available man into action.

I think the force you have is, with good management, sufficient for the end in view. If you differ widely from me & being on the spot you know better than I do the circumstances of the case, inform me at once & I will do my best to reinforce you. Inform me at the same time how many more troops you think you should have.

Until 5 a.m. tomorrow Genl Hd Qtrs will be at this place. At that hour they will move upon the main road to Hagerstown.[5]

I am, Genl, very respt yr obt svt

Geo B McClellan

Maj Genl Comdg

LS retained copy, McClellan Papers (C-16:65), Library of Congress. *OR*, Ser. 1, XIX, Part 1, pp. 45–46, LI, Part 1, pp. 826–27.

1. Maj. Gens. Lafayette McLaws and Richard H. Anderson. 2. Crampton's Gap, in South Mountain. 3. Turner's Gap. 4. Maj. Gen. William F. Smith's message to Franklin reported strong enemy forces at Petersville, and proposed an attack on the rear of those besieging Harper's Ferry from Pleasant Valley. McClellan Papers (A-79:31). 5. Franklin replied at 10:00 P.M.: "I have rec'd your orders . . . , understand them, and will do my best to carry them out. My command will commence its movement at 5 1/2 A.M." McClellan Papers (A-79:31).

To Henry W. Halleck   [TELEGRAM]

Maj. Gen. H. W. Halleck   Head Quarters, Army of the Potomac,
Genl in Chief, Washington   Frederick, Sept. 13, 1862 8.45 pm

We occupy Middletown and Jefferson. The whole force of the enemy
in front. They are not retreating into Virginia. Look well to Chambers-
burg. Shall lose no time. Will soon have decisive battle.[1]

G. B. McClellan
Maj. Gen. Comdg.

Retained copy, McClellan Papers (C-18:65), Library of Congress. *OR*, Ser. 1, XIX, Part
2, p. 288 (misdated).

1. Halleck replied on Sept. 14: "Scouts report a large force still on Virginia side of the
Potomac, near Leesburg. If so, I fear you are exposing your left flank, and that the enemy
can cross in your rear.... I do not understand what you mean by asking me to look out
for Chambersburg. I have no troops to send there." *OR*, Ser. 1, XIX, Part 2, p. 289.

To Henry W. Halleck   [TELEGRAM]

Head-Quarters, Army of the Potomac,
Frederick City Sept. 13, 11 p.m. 1862

An order of Genl. R. E. Lee addressed to Genl. D. H. Hill which has
accidentally come into my hands this evening the authenticity of which
is unquestionable discloses some of the plans of the enemy and shows
most conclusively that the main rebel army is now before us including
Longstreet's, Jackson's, the two Hill's, McLaws', Walker's, R. H. An-
derson's & Hood's commands.[1] That army was ordered to march on the
10th and to attack and capture our forces at Harper's Ferry and Mar-
tinsburg yesterday, by surrounding them with such a heavy force that
they conceived it impossible they could escape. They were also ordered
to take possession of the B. & O. Railroad & afterward to concentrate
again at Boonsboro or Hagerstown. That this was the plan of campaign
on the 9th is confirmed by the fact that heavy firing has been heard in
the direction of Harper's Ferry this afternoon and that the columns took
the roads specified in the order.

It may therefore in my judgment be regarded as certain that this rebel
army which I have good reason for believing amounts to 120,000 men or
more and known to be commanded by Lee in person intended to attempt
penetrating Pennsylvania. The Officers told their friends here that they
were going to Harrisburg and Philadelphia. My advance has pushed
forward to day and overtaken the enemy on the Middletown and Harper's
Ferry roads and several slight engagements have taken place in which
our troops have driven the enemy from their positions. A train of wagons
about 3/4 of a mile long was destroyed today by the rebels in their flight.
We took over fifty prisoners.

This Army marches forward early tomorrow morning and will make forced marches to endeavor to relieve Col. Miles, but I fear unless he makes a stout resistance we may be too late. A report came in just this moment that Miles was attacked today and repulsed the enemy but I do not know what credit to attach to the statement.[2] I shall do everything in my power to save Miles if he still holds out.

Portions of Burnside's and Franklin's Corps moved forward this evening. I have received your dispatch of 10 am today.[3] You will perceive from what I have stated that there is but little probability of the enemy being in much force south of the Potomac. I do not by any means wish to be understood as undervaluing the importance of holding Washington. It is of great consequence, but upon the success of this Army the fate of the nation depends.

It was for this reason that I said everything else should be made subordinate to placing this Army in a proper condition to meet the large rebel force in our front.

Unless Genl Lee has changed his plans I expect a severe general engagement tomorrow. I feel confident that there is now no rebel force immediately threatening Washington or Baltimore but that I have the mass of their troops to contend with & they outnumber me when united.

Geo B McClellan
Maj Genl

Genl H. W. Halleck
Genl in Chief Washington

Retained copy, McClellan Papers (A-79:31), Library of Congress. *OR*, Ser. 1, XIX, Part 2, pp. 281–82.

1. Longstreet and Jackson were in fact corps commanders. The Confederate infantry divisions were led by D. H. Hill, A. P. Hill, Lafayette McLaws, John G. Walker, John B. Hood, David R. Jones, John R. Jones, and Alexander R. Lawton. 2. In a dispatch sent at 6:15 P.M. Pleasonton wrote: "Report from Harper's Ferry says Longstreet attacked them today & was repulsed, & started up the river with his wagons. A man from Harper's Ferry brought this news." McClellan Papers (A-79:31). 3. See GBM to Halleck, Sept. 11 [Sept. 10], note 3, *supra*.

To Henry W. Halleck [TELEGRAM]

Genl H. W. Halleck   Head Quarters, Army of the Potomac,
Genl in Chief, Washington   Near Frederick Sept. 14th 1862 [9 A.M.]

Courier from Col Miles who left in the night has just arrived and says Col Miles is surrounded by a large force of the enemy but thinks he can hold out two days. Genl White[1] has joined him with his command from Martinsburg.

Miles is in possession of Harper's Ferry & Loudoun Heights. If he holds out today I can probably save him. The whole Army is moving as rapidly as possible. The enemy is in possession of Maryland Heights.

Geo. B. McClellan
Maj Genl

Retained copy, McClellan Papers (C-16:65), Library of Congress. *OR*, Ser. 1, XIX, Part 1, p. 758.

1. Brig. Gen. Julius White.

To Mary Ellen McClellan

Sept 14th [1862] Frederick am.

I have only time to say good morning this bright sunny Sunday & then start to the front to try to relieve Harper's Ferry, which is sorely pressed by secesh. It is probable that we shall have a serious engagement today & perhaps a general battle — if we have one at all during this operation it ought to be today or tomorrow. I feel as reasonably confident of success as any one well can who trusts in a higher power & does not know what its decision will be. I can't describe to you for want of time the enthusiastic reception we met with yesterday at Frederic — I was nearly overwhelmed & pulled to pieces. I enclose with this a little flag that some enthusiastic lady thrust into or upon Dan's bridle. As to flowers!! — they came in crowds! In truth I was seldom more affected than by the scenes I saw yesterday & the reception I met with — it would have gratified you very much. . . .

AL copy, McClellan Papers (C-7:63), Library of Congress.

To William B. Franklin

Maj Gen Franklin   Head Quarters, Army of the Potomac.
General.   Middletown, Sept. 14, 11.45 am 1862

The enemy occupies the main pass in front of Middletown with infantry and artillery. Pleasonton has silenced one battery, and our infantry are now endeavoring to turn the pass by our left. I have just been informed that the enemy have about 1500 cavalry and some artillery at Burkheadsville[1] and that they are in considerable force in vicinity of Boonsboro. I learned this morning by a messenger direct from Colonel Miles that he had abandoned the Maryland Heights yesterday afternoon and occupied the Loudon and Bolivar Heights and that the garrison of Martinsburg had joined him. Reno's Corps is partially engaged in front of here, and Hooker is arriving rapidly. Please lose no time in driving the rebel cavalry out of Burkheadsville, and occupying the pass. Have Saunders[2] keep the communication open between us and keep me informed of everything transpiring at the pass before you. Let me know first whether the enemy occupies the pass and if so the strength of their force there.

Continue to bear in mind the necessity of relieving Colonel Miles if possible.

I am, General very respectfully your ob't servt

Geo B. McClellan

Maj Genl Comdg

LS retained copy, McClellan Papers (C-18:65), Library of Congress. *OR*, Ser. 1, LI, Part 1, p. 833.

1. Burkittsville. The report was from Pleasonton. *OR*, XIX, Part 2, p. 290. 2. Capt. William P. Sanders, 6th U.S. Cavalry.

To Dixon S. Miles

Triplicates sent by Maj. Allen's men.[1]

Col D S Miles   Head Quarters, Army of the Potomac,
Col   Middletown 1 pm Sept 14 1862

The Army is being rapidly concentrated here. We are now attacking the pass in the Hagerstown Road over the Blue Ridge.[2] A column is about attacking the Burkittsville and Boonsboro pass.[3] You may count on our making every effort to relieve you. You may count upon my accomplishing that object. Hold out to the last extremity. If it is possible reoccupy the Maryland Heights with your whole force. If you can do that, I will certainly be able to relieve you. As the Catoctin Valley is in our possession, you can safely cross at Berlin or its vicinity so far as opposition on this side of the river is concerned. Hold out to the last.

Geo B. McClellan

Maj Gen Comdg

LS retained copy, McClellan Papers (C-18:65), Library of Congress. *OR*, Ser. 1, XIX, Part 1, p. 45.

1. Civilians employed by Allan Pinkerton. None of them reached Col. Miles. 2. Turner's Gap in South Mountain. 3. Crampton's Gap.

To William B. Franklin

Head Quarters, Army of the Potomac

Maj. Gen. Franklin   Frederic [Middletown] Sept 14 2 pm 1862

Your dispatch of 12.30 just received.[1] Send back to hurry up Couch. Mass your troops and carry Burkittsville at any cost. We shall have strong opposition at both passes. As fast as the troops come up, I will hold a reserve in readiness to support you. If you find the enemy in very great force at the pass let me know at once, and amuse them as best you can so as to retain them there. In that event I will probably throw the mass of the Army on the pass in front of here. If I carry that it will clear the way for you, and you must then follow the enemy as rapidly as possible.[2]

> Geo B McClellan
> Maj Genl Comdg

LS retained copy, McClellan Papers (C-18:65), Library of Congress. *OR*, Ser. 1, XIX, Part 1, p. 46.

1. Franklin reported that the enemy on his front was reinforced by artillery. "I think from appearances that we may have a heavy fight to get the pass." McClellan Papers (A-79:31). 2. In his reply of 5:20 P.M., Franklin wrote: "I report that I have been severely engaged with the enemy for the last hour. . . . The force of the enemy is too great for us to take the pass to night I am afraid. I shall await further orders here & shall attack again in the morning without further orders." McClellan Papers (A-81:32).

To Henry W. Halleck   [TELEGRAM]

> Headquarters Army of the Potomac
> Sept 14 4 pm 1862 In front of Middletown

We are forcing the passage of the Blue Ridge. Have possession of the heights on left of Hagerstown pike & are now attacking on the right. Franklin is attacking the Rohrersville pass through same range. Thus far all goes well. Have taken about a hundred (100) prisoners already. I have the troops well in hand & they are very confident. Hope to have full possession of the passes by dark. Firing near Harper's Ferry within last hour.

> G B. McClellan
> Maj Genl

Maj Genl Halleck
Washington DC

ALS (telegram sent), Chicago Historical Society. *OR*, Ser. 1, XIX, Part 2, p. 289.

To Joseph Hooker

> Head Qrs Army of Potomac
Maj. Gen. Hooker   [Bolivar, Md.] Sept 14, 1862 9 p.m.

General Reno has succeeded in carrying the heights on the left of the main pike.

Please hold your present position at all hazards. General Richardson has been placed under your orders.[1] Let me know at daybreak tomorrow morning the state of affairs in your vicinity, and whether you will need further reinforcements. I presume, however, that Richardson's division is all that will be required by you.

Franklin has had a severe contest with the enemy at pass in front of Jefferson, the result of which is not yet known to me.

G B McClellan
Maj Genl Comdg

LS, Hooker Papers, Huntington Library. *OR*, Ser. 1, LI, Part 1, p. 831.

1. Brig. Gen. Richardson commanded a division in Sumner's Second Corps.

To Henry W. Halleck [TELEGRAM]

Maj Genl Halleck   Head Quarters Army of the Potomac
Genl in Chief   Beyond Middletown Sept 14th [1862] 9.40 pm

After a very severe engagement the Corps of Hooker and Reno have carried the heights commanding the Hagerstown road.

The troops behaved magnificently. They never fought better. Franklin has been hotly engaged on the extreme left. I do not yet know the result except that firing indicated progress on his part. The action continued until after dark and terminated leaving us in possession of the entire crest.

It has been a glorious victory; I cannot yet tell whether the enemy will retreat during the night or appear in increased force in the morning. I am hurrying up everything from the rear to be prepared for any eventuality.

I regret to add that the gallant and able Genl Reno is killed.

G B McClellan

Received copy, Records of the Office of the Secretary of War, RG 107 (M-473:50), National Archives. *OR*, Ser. 1, XIX, Part 2, p. 289.

To Mary Ellen McClellan [TELEGRAM]

Mrs. McClellan   Hd Qrs Army of the Potomac
New London Conn.   Bolivar [September] 14 1862 9.40 pm

We have carried the Heights near here after a hard engagement & gained a glorious victory. All your particular friends well.

G B McClellan
Maj Genl USA

Received copy (War Dept.), Records of the Office of the Secretary of War, RG 107 (M-504:66), National Archives.

To Henry W. Halleck [TELEGRAM]

Maj Genl H. W. Halleck   Head Quarters, Army of the Potomac,
Genl in Chief, Washn   Hd Qtrs Bolivar Sept 15th 8 am 1862

I am happy to inform you that Franklin's success on the left was as complete as that in the center & right & resulted in his getting possession of the Burkittsville Gap after a severe engagement. On all parts of the line the troops, old & new, behaved with the utmost steadiness & gallantry, carrying with but little assistance from our own artillery, very strong positions defended by artillery & infantry. I do not think our loss very severe. The Corps of D. H. Hill & Longstreet were engaged with our right. We have taken a considerable number of prisoners. The enemy disappeared during the night. Our troops are now advancing in pursuit of them. I do not yet know where he will next be found. The morale of our own men is now restored.

Geo B McClellan
Maj Genl Comdg

LS (telegram sent), McClellan Papers (C-16:65), Library of Congress. *OR*, Ser. 1, XIX, Part 2, p. 294.

To Henry W. Halleck   [TELEGRAM]

Maj Genl H. W. Halleck   Head Quarters, Army of the Potomac,
Comdr in Chief   Bolivar, Sept. 15 8.30 am 1862

I have just learned from Genl Hooker in the advance, who states that the information is perfectly reliable, that the enemy is making for Shepherdstown in a perfect panic, & that Genl Lee last night stated publicly that he must admit they had been shockingly whipped.[1]

I am hurrying everything forward to endeavor to press their retreat to the utmost.

Geo B McClellan
Maj Genl Comdg

LS (telegram sent), McClellan Papers (C-16:65), Library of Congress. *OR*, Ser. 1, XIX, Part 2, p. 294.

1. GBM is quoting from Hooker's dispatch, sent about 8:00 A.M., the source of which was "some citizens from Boonsboro." McClellan Papers (A-79:31).

To Nathaniel P. Banks   [TELEGRAM]

                                Head Quarters, Army of the Potomac,
Maj. Gen. Banks   Bolivar — three miles beyond Middletown
Washington   Sept. 15, 1862 9 am

I think that under present circumstances it will be well for you to move the greater part of your command to the south side of the Potomac. I do not consider that any danger to Washington is now to be feared from the north side of the river.[1]

Geo. B. McClellan
Maj. Genl. Commandg

Retained copy, McClellan Papers (C-18:65), Library of Congress. *OR*, Ser. 1, XIX, Part 2, p. 294.

1. Banks replied at 2:00 P.M. that forces would be sent from Washington to cover the Potomac crossings downstream from Harper's Ferry, and that he would "carry out your instructions as far as practicable." *OR*, Ser. 1, XIX, Part 2, pp. 298–99.

To Mary Ellen McClellan

Sept 15 [1862] Monday 9.30 am. Bolivar

... Just sent you a telegram[1] informing you that we yesterday gained a glorious & complete victory : every moment adds to its importance. R E Lee wounded, Hill D H reported killed — Lee is *reported* to state his loss at 15,000 yesterday.[2] I am pushing everything after them with the greatest rapidity & expect to gain great results. I thank God most humbly for his great mercy. How glad I am for my country that it is delivered from immediate peril. I am about starting with the pursuit & must close this. ...

If I can believe one tenth of what is reported, God has seldom given an army a greater victory than this. ...

AL copy, McClellan Papers (C-7:63), Library of Congress.

1. His telegram, sent at 9:00 A.M., read: "Have just learned that the enemy are retreating in a panic & that our victory is complete. We are pushing everything after them." Records of the Office of the Secretary of War, RG 107 (M-504:66), National Archives. 2. This is taken from a dispatch sent from the front by Capt. George A. Custer of GBM's staff. Gen. Lee had injured his hands in a fall several days before. Gen. Hill was unhurt in the previous day's fighting. McClellan Papers (A-79:31).

To Henry W. Halleck   [TELEGRAM]

Maj. Gen. H. W. Halleck   Head Quarters, Army of the Potomac,
Comdr in Chief, Washington   Bolivar Sept. 15th 10 am 1862

There are already about seven hundred rebel prisoners at Frederick, under very insufficient guard, and shall probably send in a larger number today. It would be well to have them either paroled or other wise disposed of as Frederick is an inconvenient place for them. Information this moment rec'd completely confirms the rout & demoralization of the rebel Army. Genl. Lee is reported wounded & Garland killed.[1] Hooker alone has over a thousand more prisoners. It is stated that Lee gives his loss as fifteen thousand. We are following as rapidly as the men can move.[2]

Geo B McClellan
Maj Genl Comdg

LS (telegram sent), McClellan Papers (C-16:65), Library of Congress. *OR*, Ser. 1, XIX, Part 2, pp. 294–95.

1. Brig. Gen. Samuel Garland was killed at Fox's Gap. 2. That afternoon President Lincoln telegraphed: "Your dispatches of to-day received. God bless you, and all with you. Destroy the rebel army, if possible." *Collected Works of Lincoln*, V, p. 426.

To Winfield Scott   [TELEGRAM]

Lieut Gen Winfield Scott
West Point   Camp near Boonsboro Md Sept 15th 1862

We attacked a large force of the enemy yesterday occupying a strong mountain pass four miles west of Middletown. Our troops old and new regiments behaved most valiantly & gained a signal victory. R E Lee in command. The Rebels routed and retreating in disorder this morning. We are pursuing closely and taking many prisoners.[1]

Geo. B. McClellan
Major General

Copy, Records of the Office of the Secretary of War, RG 107 (M-473:50), National Archives. *OR*, Ser. 1, XIX, Part 2, p. 295.

1. Gen. Scott replied on Sept. 16: "Bravo my Dear General — twice more & its done." McClellan Papers (A-80:32), Library of Congress.

To William B. Franklin

Headquarters Army of the Potomac
[Boonsboro, September 15, 1862, 1:20 P.M.]

Burnside's Corps & Sykes' Division are moving on Porterstown & Sharpsburg by the road almost 1 mile south of Hagerstown Pike with orders to turn & attack a force of the enemy supposed to be at Centreville.[1] I will instruct them to communicate with you at Rohrersville & if necessary reinforce you. It is important to drive in the enemy in your front but be cautious in doing it until you have some idea of his force.[2]

The Corps of Sumner, Hooker & Banks[3] are moving to Boonsboro on the main pike. At least one Division has already passed down towards Centreville. I will direct a portion to turn to the left at the first road beyond the mountain (west) so as to be in position to reinforce you or to move on Portersville. Sykes will be at the Boonsboro & Rohrersville road in about 1 1/2 hours Burnside following close. Thus far our success is complete but let us follow up closely but warily. Attack whenever you see a fair chance of success. Lose no time in communicating with Sykes & Burnside.[4]

McC

To Franklin

ALS retained copy, McClellan Papers (A-79:31), Library of Congress. *OR*, Ser. 1, LI, Part 1, p. 836.

1. At the time more commonly known as Keedysville. 2. Franklin had reported at 8:50 A.M. that the Confederates on his front were drawn up in line of battle across Pleasant Valley. "If Harper's Ferry has fallen — and the cessation of firing makes me fear that it has — it is my opinion that I should be strongly re-enforced." *OR*, Ser. 1, XIX, Part 1, p.

47. 3. The Twelfth Corps was formerly Banks's Second Corps of the Army of Virginia.
Maj. Gen. Joseph K. F. Mansfield took command that day. 4. Franklin replied at 3 :00 P.M.
that the enemy was withdrawing swiftly down Pleasant Valley toward Harper's Ferry.
"Under your last orders, I do not feel justified in putting my whole command in motion
toward the front, but shall act according to the dictates of my judgment, as circumstances
may occur." *OR*, Ser. 1, XIX, Part 2, p. 296.

To Ambrose E. Burnside

Major Genl Burnside   Head Quarters, Army of the Potomac,
General   [Boonsboro] Sept. 15, 1862 3.45 pm

The last news received is that the enemy is drawn up in line of battle
about two miles beyond Centreville, which will bring them on the west
and behind Antietam Creek. They are represented to be in considerable
force under Longstreet.[1] Our troops are rapidly moving up. If not too
late I think you had better move on Rohresville communicating meantime
with Franklin. If with your assistance, he can defeat the enemy in front
of him, join him at once. If however he can hold his own, march direct
on Sharpsburg & cooperate with us unless that place should be evacuated
by the enemy. In that case, move at once to cooperate with Franklin.
Porter of course will continue on his march to Sharpsburg.

                         Very Resp'y Yr ob't Servt
                         G B McC

Retained copy, McClellan Papers (C-18 :65), Library of Congress. *OR*, Ser. 1, LI, Part 1,
pp. 837–38.

1. Capt. Custer had reported : "The enemy is drawn up in line of battle on a ridge about
two miles beyond [Keedysville]. They are in full view. Their line is a perfect one about a
mile and a half long. . . . Longstreet is in command and has forty cannon that we know
of." McClellan Papers (A-80 :32).

To Henry W. Halleck

                                      [TELEGRAM]

                Head Quarters, Army of the Potomac,
Maj Gen H. W. Halleck   Bivouac near Sharpsburg
Comdr in Chief, Washington   Sept. 16th 7 am 1862

The enemy yesterday held a position just in front of Sharpsburg. When
our troops arrived in sufficient force it was too late in the day to attack.
This morning a heavy fog has thus far prevented our doing more than
to ascertain that some of the enemy are still there. Do not yet know in
what force. Will attack as soon as situation of the enemy is developed. I
hear that Miles surrendered at 8 a.m. yesterday unconditionally. I fear
his resistance was not as stubborn as it ought to have been. Had he held
the Maryland Heights he would inevitably have been saved.

The time lost on account of the fog is being occupied in getting up supplies for the want of which many of our men are suffering.[1]

Geo B McClellan
Maj Genl Comdg

LS (telegram sent), McClellan Papers (C-16:65), Library of Congress. *OR*, Ser. 1, XIX, Part 2, pp. 307–308.

1. Halleck replied on this date, in part: "I think ... you will find that the whole force of the enemy in your front has crossed the river. I fear now more than ever that they will recross at Harper's Ferry or below, and turn your left, thus cutting you off from Washington. This has appeared to me to be a part of their plan, and hence my anxiety on the subject." *OR*, Ser. 1, XIX, Part 1, p. 41.

To Mary Ellen McClellan   [TELEGRAM]

Mrs. McClellan
Care J W Alsop   Hd Qrs AP [September] 16th [1862] 7 am
Middletown Conn   Near Sharpsburg

Have reached thus far & have no doubt delivered Penna & Maryland. All well & in excellent spirits.

G B McClellan

Received copy (War Dept.), Records of the Office of the Secretary of War, RG 107 (M-504:66), National Archives.

To William B. Franklin

Major Genl Franklin   Head Quarters, Army of the Potomac,
General   Centreville Sept 16, 1862 7.45 am

The man O'Sullivan[1] who passed through your lines yesterday as a bearer of dispatches to Colonel Miles has returned, and informs me that Miles surrendered unconditionally at 8 o'clock yesterday morning — and that the rebels on this side of the river were rapidly recrossing to the Virginia side by our pontoon bridge at Harper's Ferry. He did not see this with his own eyes, but was so informed by persons in whom he has implicit confidence. I think the enemy has abandoned the position in front of us, but the fog is so dense that I have not yet been enabled to determine. If the enemy is in force here, I shall attack him this morning. The instant I know whether he is still here or not I shall inform you. I would again caution you to watch Knoxville and Berlin with a small cavalry force, so that no enemy can get in your rear.

Very Resp'y Yr. obt Servt.
Geo B McClellan
Maj Genl Comdg

LS retained copy, McClellan Papers (C-18:65), Library of Congress. *OR*, Ser. 1, LI, Part 1, p. 839.

1. Probably T. O'Sullivan, one of Pinkerton's men.

To Alfred Pleasonton

Genl Pleasonton　　　　[Before Sharpsburg] Sept 17 [1862] 11:45 am

Do not expose your batteries without necessity unless they are inflicting on the enemy a loss commensurate with what we suffer. How goes it with you.

G B McClellan

P.S. Can you do any good by a cavalry charge?[1]

ALS, Private Collection.

1. Gen. Pleasonton's cavalry and horse artillery were posted at the center of the Federal line.

To Henry W. Halleck　　　　　　　　　　　[TELEGRAM]

Headquarters Army of the Potomac
[Before Sharpsburg] Sept 17 [1862] 1.25 pm

Please take military possession of the Chambersburg & Hagerstown rail road that our ammunition & supplies may be hurried up without delay.[1]

We are in the midst of the most terrible battle of the war, perhaps of history — thus far it looks well but I have great odds against me. Hurry up all the troops possible. Our loss has been terrific, but we have gained much ground. I have thrown the mass of the Army on their left flank. Burnside is now attacking their right & I hold my small reserve consisting of Porters (5th Corps) ready to attack the center as soon as the flank movements are developed. [*Crossed out:* It will be either a great defeat or a most glorious victory. I think & hope that God will give us the latter.] I hope that God will give us a glorious victory.

G B McClellan
Maj Genl

Maj Genl Halleck
Genl in Chief　Washn

ALS (telegram sent), McClellan Papers (A-80:32), Library of Congress. *OR*, Ser. 1, XIX, Part 2, p. 312.

1. Halleck telegraphed that evening to Gen. Wool, in command at Baltimore, to send all possible reinforcements to GBM. "Also, see that all ammunition and other supplies are

forwarded as expeditiously as possible. If necessary, take military possession of the railroads for that purpose." *OR*, Ser. 1, XIX, Part 2, p. 319.

To Mary Ellen McClellan　　　　　　　　　　[TELEGRAM]

Mrs. McClellan　　　　　　　　　　　　　Hd Qrs A.P. near Sharpsburg
Care J. W. Alsop　Middletown Ct　　　1.45 p.m. [September] 17 [1862]

We are in the midst of the most terrible battle of the age.

So far God has given us success but with many variations during the day. The battle is not yet over & I write this in the midst of it.

I trust that God will smile upon our cause. I am well. None of your immediate friends killed that I hear of. Your father with me quite safe.

　　　　　　　　　　　　　　　　　　　　G B. McClellan
　　　　　　　　　　　　　　　　　　　　M.G.C.

Received copy (War Dept.), Records of the Office of the Secretary of War, RG 107 (M-504:66), National Archives.

To James W. Ripley　　　　　　　　　　　[TELEGRAM]

Brig Gen Ripley　　　　　　　　　　　Hd Qrs A.P. [near Sharpsburg]
Chf Ordn　　　　　　　　　　　　　　Via Hagerstown Sept 17th 1862

If you can possibly do it force some 20 pdr Parrott ammunition through tonight via Hagerstown & Chambersburg to us near Sharpsburg Md.

　　　　　　　　　　　　　　　　　　　　G B McClellan
　　　　　　　　　　　　　　　　　　　　Maj Genl Comdg

Received copy, Records of the Office of the Secretary of War, RG 107 (M-473:50), National Archives. *OR*, Ser. 1, XIX, Part 2, p. 312.

1. This telegram was endorsed in the Ordnance Office: "Attended to at once, September 17 — 11 p.m."

To Henry W. Halleck　　　　　　　　　　[TELEGRAM]

Major General Halleck　　　　　　Head Quarters, Army of the Potomac,
General-in-Chief, Washington　　Keedysville Sept. 18, 1862 8 am

The battle of yesterday continued for fourteen hours, and until after dark. We held all we gained except a portion of the extreme left that was obliged to abandon a part of what it had gained. Our losses very heavy, especially in General officers. The battle will probably be renewed today. Send all the troops you can by the most expeditious route.

　　　　　　　　　　　　　　　　　　　　G. B. McClellan
　　　　　　　　　　　　　　　　　　　　Maj. Genl. Comdg.

Retained copy, McClellan Papers (C-18:65), Library of Congress. *OR*, Ser. 1, XIX, Part 2, p. 322.

To Mary Ellen McClellan   [TELEGRAM]

Headquarters Army of the Potomac
[Keedysville] Sept 18 [1862] 8 am

The battle of yesterday a desperate one. We hold all we gained. The contest will probably be renewed today. Your father & I well.

G. B. McClellan
Maj Genl

Mrs McClellan
Care J W Alsop Esq Middletown Conn

ALS (telegram sent), McClellan Papers (A-80:32), Library of Congress.

To Mary Ellen McClellan

Sept 18 [1862] 8 am. Camp near Sharpsburg

... We fought yesterday a terrible battle against the entire rebel army. The battle continued *14* hours & was terrific — the fighting on both sides was superb. The general result was in our favor, that is to say we gained a great deal of ground & held it. It was a success, but whether a decided victory depends upon what occurs today. I hope that God has given us a great success. It is all in his hands, where I am content to leave it. The spectacle yesterday was the grandest I could conceive of — nothing could be more sublime. Those in whose judgment I rely tell me that I fought the battle splendidly & that it was a masterpiece of art. I am well nigh tired out by anxiety & want of sleep....

God has been good in sparing the lives of all my staff. Genls Hooker, Sedgwick, Dana, Richardson & Hartsuff & several other general officers wounded. Mansfield is dead I fear, but am not certain — I just learn that he is not mortally wounded[1] ...

AL copy, McClellan Papers (C-7:63), Library of Congress.

1. For a later count of officer casualties, see GBM to his wife, Sept. 20, 1862, note 1, *infra*.

To Mary Ellen McClellan   [TELEGRAM]

Mrs McClellan   Hd Qrs near Sharpsburg
Care J. W. Alsop   Middletown Ct   8 am [September] 19 [1862]

Our victory complete. Enemy has left his dead & wounded on the field. Our people now in pursuit. Your father and I are well.

G. B. McClellan

Retained copy, Records of the Office of the Secretary of War, RG 107 (M-504:66), National Archives.

To Henry W. Halleck   [TELEGRAM]

Headquarters Army of the Potomac
Near Sharpsburg Sept. 19 [1862] 8.30 am

But little occurred yesterday except skirmishing, we being fully oc-
cupied in replenishing ammunition, taking care of wounded, etc. Last
night the enemy abandoned his position leaving his dead & wounded on
the field. We are again in pursuit. I do not yet know whether he is falling
back to an interior position or crossing the river. We may safely claim
a complete victory.

G B. McClellan
Maj Gen

Maj Genl Halleck
Comdr in Chief

ALS (telegram sent), McClellan Papers (A-80:32), Library of Congress. *OR*, Ser. 1, XIX,
Part 2, p. 330.

To Henry W. Halleck   [TELEGRAM]

Headquarters Army of the Potomac
[Near Sharpsburg] Sept 19 10.30 am 1862

Pleasonton is driving the enemy across the river. Our victory was
complete. The enemy is driven back into Virginia. Maryland & Penna.
are now safe.

G B McClellan
Maj Genl

Genl H W Halleck
Comdr in chief

ALS (telegram sent), McClellan Papers (A-80:32), Library of Congress. *OR*, Ser. 1, XIX,
Part 2, p. 330.

To Henry W. Halleck   [TELEGRAM]

Maj. Gen. H. W. Halleck   Head Quarters, Army of the Potomac,
Comdg in Chief   Sharpsburg, Sept. 19 1.30 pm 1862

I have the honor to report that Maryland is entirely freed from the
presence of the enemy, who has been driven across the Potomac. No fears
need now be entertained for the safety of Pennsylvania. I shall at once
reoccupy Harper's Ferry.

G. B. McClellan
Maj. Genl. Comdg.

Retained copy, McClellan Papers (C-18:65), Library of Congress. *OR*, Ser. 1, XIX, Part
1, p. 68.

NINE

AN END TO ACTIVE SERVICE
SEPTEMBER 20–NOVEMBER 10, 1862

THERE IS NOTHING in General McClellan's correspondence following the Battle of Antietam to indicate he recognized the unique opportunity he had missed for a decisive victory on that field. Instead he was gratified simply to have saved his army from defeat and the North from invasion. What he witnessed on the Maryland battlefields caused no change in his mental picture of the Confederate army. "In the last battles the enemy was undoubtedly greatly superior to us in number, and it was only by very hard fighting that we gained the advantage we did . . . ," he assured General Halleck on September 27. Nor is there any suggestion here that in his final weeks of command of the Army of the Potomac he understood anything closer to the truth about his foe than in his first weeks.

Indeed, as he wrote Mrs. McClellan on September 20, he measured the results of Antietam as entitling him to insist on the removal of his immediate superiors, General-in-Chief Halleck and Secretary of War Stanton. He expected to accomplish this through the intervention of Northern state governors and of "certain friends of mine . . . ," and to regain for himself the post of general-in-chief. In reality, the far greater pressure exerted on President Lincoln was for the removal of General McClellan.

The president's preliminary Emancipation Proclamation and his suspension of the privilege of habeas corpus soon afterward were deeply shocking to McClellan. In the interval between his angry initial reaction, as reflected in letters to his wife and to William H. Aspinwall (September 25 and 26), and the general order he issued on October 7 advising his army of its duty to support these actions by the chief executive, he was repeatedly advised by friends and political supporters not to publicly oppose the government on these issues. Afterward, however, his letters suggest a growing reluctance to serve the Lincoln administration any further. (For part of this period his views on matters are stated less explicitly than usual due to the absence for some two weeks of letters to his wife, who during this time was with him at his camp in Pleasant Valley, near Harper's Ferry.)

Throughout the correspondence in this section McClellan was unwavering in his opposition to taking the Army of the Potomac on campaign once more. He insisted that his troops were unprepared in numbers, organization, morale, supplies, and equipment to renew the contest against Lee anytime soon, and he stubbornly resisted the president's urgings and then his direct order to begin an advance. ''These people don't know what an army requires & therefore act stupidly,'' he told his wife on October 2. On October 30, finally crossing the Potomac into Virginia to begin what proved to be his last march as army commander, he telegraphed Lincoln a listing of reasons he opposed the advance, and added, ''I write this only to place the responsibility where it belongs....''

The course he advocated instead was first to secure the line of the Potomac and the Shenandoah Valley against further Confederate incursions, a process requiring extensive bridge-building and railroad construction and fortification, and then (as he told Halleck on October 7) ''to adopt a new & decisive line of operations which shall strike at the heart of the rebellion.'' Behind this generalized objective was his unstated desire to return his army to the Peninsula, in the spring of 1863, to repeat his advance on Richmond.

The president's basic reason for relieving McClellan of command — and for seeking his replacement at least twice before — was the general's reluctance to fight. Lincoln had urged him to cross the Potomac and march rapidly (as rapidly as the Confederates customarily marched, he told him) so as to threaten Lee's communications with Richmond and bring him to battle at the earliest opportunity. Privately he made that the test: if McClellan allowed the Rebels to get ahead of him and block his path he would be dismissed. In the event, McClellan moved with his usual deliberation, requiring nine days just to cross the Potomac, and on November 4 it was reported to Washington that the enemy was at Culpeper Court House, on the Federals' line of advance. That day also saw the last of the midterm elections in the Northern states, another important factor in the timing of the president's decision. General McClellan had let himself be made the most visible symbol of political opposition to the administration, and that fact, when added to his military shortcomings, made his dismissal inevitable — and would be a decisive factor, over the next two years, in preventing his reinstatement.

To Mary Ellen McClellan

Sept 20 [1862] 8 am. Camp near Sharpsburg

... Yesterday the enemy completed his evacuation of Maryland — completely beaten — we got many prisoners, muskets, colors, cannon etc — his loss in killed & wounded was very great — so was ours, unfortunately.

Genl Mansfield was killed (or rather died of his wounds) — Genls Sedgwick, Richardson, Dana, Brooks, Hooker, Weber, Rodman — & two others whose names I cannot recall were wounded on Wednesday. Poor Henry Kingsbury died of his wounds the day after the battle.[1]

The battle lasted 14 hours & was without doubt the most severe ever fought on this continent, & few more desperate were ever fought anywhere.

9 am. ... Am glad to say that I am much better today — for to tell you the truth I have been under the weather since the battle — the want of rest & anxiety brought on my old disease. The battle of Wednesday *was* a terrible one. I presume the loss will prove not less than 10,000 on each side.[2] Our victory was complete & the disorganized rebel army has rapidly returned to Virginia — its dreams of "invading Penna" dissipated for ever. I feel some little pride in having with a beaten and demoralized army defeated Lee so utterly, & saved the North so completely. Well — one of these days history will I trust do me justice in deciding that it was not my fault that the campaign of the Peninsula was not successful. An opportunity has presented itself through the Governors of some of the states to enable me to take my stand — I have insisted that Stanton shall be removed & that Halleck shall give way to me as Comdr in Chief.[3] I will *not* serve under him — for he is an incompetent fool — in no way fit for the important place he holds. Since I left Washn Stanton has again asserted that *I* not *Pope* lost the battle of Manassas No 2! The only safety for the country & for me is to get rid of both of them — no success is possible with them. I am tired of fighting against such disadvantages & feel that it is now time for the country to come to my help, & remove these difficulties from my path. If my countrymen will not open their eyes & assert themselves they must pardon me if I decline longer to pursue the thankless avocation of serving them....

Thank Heaven for one thing — my military reputation is cleared — I have shown that I can fight battles & *win* them! I think my enemies are pretty effectively killed by this time! May they remain so!!

AL copy, McClellan Papers (C-7:63), Library of Congress.

1. Maj. Gens. Joseph K. F. Mansfield, John Sedgwick, Israel B. Richardson, Joseph Hooker; Brig. Gens. N. J. T. Dana, W. T. H. Brooks, Max Weber, Isaac P. Rodman; Col. Henry W. Kingsbury, 11th Connecticut. Brig. Gens. George L. Hartsuff and Samuel W. Crawford were the two others wounded. The wounds of Richardson and Rodman were mortal. 2.

Losses at Antietam would be later calculated as 12,401 Federal, 10,318 Confederate. 3. GBM refers here to a conference of Northern governors scheduled for Sept. 24 at Altoona, Pa. The tenor of the meeting proved strongly anti-McClellan, however, with only Andrew G. Curtin of Pennsylvania, David Tod of Ohio, and Augustus W. Bradford of Maryland opposing demands for his removal. *New York Herald,* Sept. 26, 1862.

To Joseph Hooker

Maj. Gen. Joseph Hooker
Commanding Corps   Headquarters Army of the Potomac
My dear Hooker: Sharpsburg, September 20, 1862.

I have been very sick the last few days, and just able to go where my presence was absolutely necessary, so I could not come to see you and thank you for what you did the other day, and express my intense regret and sympathy for your unfortunate wound. Had you not been wounded and when you were, I believe the result of the battle would have been the entire destruction of the rebel army, for I *know* that, with you at its head, your corps would have kept on until it gained the main road. As a slight expression of what I think you merit, I have requested that the brigadier-general's commission rendered vacant by Mansfield's death may be given to you. I will this evening write a private note to the President on the subject, and I am glad to assure you that, so far as I can learn, it is the universal feeling of the army that you are the most deserving in it.

With the sincere hope that your health may soon be restored, so that you may again be with us in the field,

I am, my dear general, your sincere friend,
Geo. B. McClellan
Major-General

OR, Ser. 1, XIX, Part 1, p. 219.

To Abraham Lincoln

Head-Quarters, Army of the Potomac,
Your Excellency   [Sharpsburg, September 20] 1862

I would most respectfully ask that the commission of Brig Genl in the regular army rendered vacant by the death of Brig Genl Mansfield may be conferred upon Maj Genl J Hooker US Vols.

The able & gallant services of this most excellent officer upon many a hard-fought field render him eminently deserving of it; no one has rendered greater service to his country & I am confident that I but express the general feeling of the army when I ask this appointment for him —

it cannot be better disposed of, nor to a more deserving, able & gallant officer.[1]

I am very respectfully your obdt svt

AL retained copy, Records of the U.S. Army Continental Commands, RG 393 (3964: Army of the Potomac), National Archives.

1. GBM had telegraphed Gen. Halleck to the same effect on Sept. 19. *OR,* Ser. 1, XIX, Part 1, p. 182. The appointment was made, effective on this date.

To Henry W. Halleck [TELEGRAM]

Major General Halleck Head Quarters, Army of the Potomac,
General-in-Chief, Washington Near Sharpsburg, Sept 20, 1862 8 pm

Your telegram of to day is received.[1] I telegraphed you yesterday all I knew, and had nothing more to inform you of until this evening. Williams' Corps (Banks') occupied Maryland Heights at 1 p.m. to day. The rest of the Army is near here, except Couch's division which is at this moment engaged with the enemy in front of Williamsport. The enemy is retiring via Charlestown and Martinsburg on Winchester. He last night reoccupied Williamsport by a small force, but will be out of it by morning. I think he has a force of infantry near Shepherdstown.

I regret that you find it necessary to couch every dispatch I have the honor to receive from you, in a spirit of fault finding, and that you have not yet found leisure to say one word in commendation of the recent achievements of this Army, or even to allude to them. I have abstained from giving the number of guns, colors, small arms, prisoners, etc. captured, until I could do so with some accuracy. I hope by tomorrow evening to be able to give at least an approximate statement.[2].

G. B. McClellan
Maj. Gen. Comdg.

Retained copy, McClellan Papers (C-18:65), Library of Congress. *OR,* Ser. 1, XIX, Part 1, pp. 68–69.

1. Halleck's telegram of this date read: "We are still left entirely in the dark in regard to your own movements and those of the enemy. This should not be so. You should keep me advised of both, so far as you know them." *OR,* Ser. 1, XIX, Part 1, p. 68. 2. Halleck replied on Sept. 21, in part: "The Government has been most anxious for the last two days to obtain the information given in yours of yesterday . . . , and you have entirely misconstrued the urgency of my request for it. Except your short dispatch, in regard to Pleasonton's pursuit [Sept. 19, 1862, 10:30 A.M., *supra*], I had no official information of what had taken place since the battle of the 17th." *OR,* Ser. 1, XIX, Part 2, p. 339.

To Mary Ellen McClellan

Sept 20 [1862] 9 pm. Camp near Sharpsburg

... I hope that my future will be determined this week. Thro' certain friends of mine I have taken the stand that Stanton must leave & that Halleck must restore my old place to me. Unless these two conditions are fulfilled I will leave the service. I feel that I have done all that can be asked in twice saving the country. If I continue in its service I have at least the right to demand a guarantee that I shall not be interfered with — I know I cannot have that assurance so long as Stanton continues in the position of Secy of War & Halleck as Genl in Chief. You will understand that it is a matter of indifference to me whether they come to terms or not.

I now feel that my military reputation is safe & that I can retire from the service for sufficient reasons without leaving any stain upon my reputation. I feel now that this last short campaign is a sufficient legacy for our child, so far as honor is concerned....

You should see my soldiers *now*! You never saw anything like their enthusiasm — it surpasses anything you ever imagined, & I don't believe that Napoleon even ever possessed the love & confidence of his men more fully than I do of mine....

My tent is filled quite to overflowing with trophies in the way of captured rebel battle flags. We have more than have been taken in all battles put together — & all sorts of inscriptions on them....

AL copy, McClellan Papers (C–7:63), Library of Congress.

To Henry B. Whipple

Head Quarters, Army of the Potomac
My dear Bishop,   Camp near Sharpsburg Sept. 21, 1862

Will you do me the favor to perform Divine service in my Camp this evening. If you can give me a couple of hours notice I would be glad of it that I may be able to inform the Corps in the vicinity. After the great success that God has vouchsafed us, I feel that we cannot do less than avail ourselves of the first opportunity, to render to Him the thanks due to Him alone. I for one feel that the great result is the result of His great mercy, and would be glad that you should be the medium to offer the thanks which I feel due from the Army and from the Country. Earnestly hoping that you will accede to my request[1]

I am very Respectfully your humble servant,
[George B. McClellan]
Maj Genl Comdg

Retained copy, McClellan Papers (B-12:48), Library of Congress. Whipple was Episcopal bishop of Minnesota.

1. Bishop Whipple was then visiting the army's wounded. He wrote GBM on Sept. 23: "I . . . cannot close without telling you how sweet is the remembrance of the pleasant service held in your Camp, nor to assure you, that it is a pleasure every day to ask God to bless you." Society Collection, Historical Society of Pennsylvania.

To Mary Ellen McClellan

[Sharpsburg] Sept 21st [1862] Sunday am.

. . . Do you know that I have not had one word from Halleck, the Presdt nor the Secy of War about the last great battle! All, except fault finding, that I have had since leaving Washn was one from *Abe* about the Sunday battle [South Mountain] in which he says "God bless you & all with you"—that is all I have—but plenty from Halleck couched in almost insulting language & prophesying disaster! I telegraphed him last night that I regretted the uniformly fault finding tone of his dispatches & that he had not as yet found leisure to notice the recent achievements of my army. . . .

AL copy, McClellan Papers (C-7:63), Library of Congress.

To Mary Ellen McClellan

[Sharpsburg] Sept 22 [1862] 9 am.

. . . I rode out on the battle field yesterday — the burial of the dead is by this time completed & a terrible work it has been — for the slain counted by thousands on each side. . . .

I look upon the campaign as substantially ended & my present intention is to seize Harper's Ferry & hold it with a strong force. Then go to work to reorganize the army ready for another campaign. . . .

I shall not go to Washn if I can help it, but will try to reorganize the army somewhere near Harper's Ferry or Frederic. . . .

It may be that now that the Govt is pretty well over their scare they will begin again with their persecutions & throw me overboard again. I don't care if they do. I have the satisfaction of knowing that God has in his mercy a second time made me the instrument for saving the nation & am content with the honor that has fallen to my lot. I feel that the short campaign just terminated will vindicate my professional honor & I have seen enough of public life. No motive of ambition can now retain me in the service — the only thing that *can* keep me there will be the conviction that my country needs my services & that circumstances make it necessary for me to render them. I am confident that the poison still rankles in the veins of my enemies at Washn & that so long as they live it will remain there. . . .

I have received no papers containing the news of the last battle & do not know the effect it has produced on the Northern mind. I trust it has been a good one & that I am reestablished in the confidence of the best people of the nation. . . .

Everything quiet today — not a shot fired as yet — I am moving troops down to Harper's Ferry & hope to occupy it tomorrow — then I will have the Potomac clear. . . .

AL copy, McClellan Papers (C-7:63), Library of Congress.

To Henry W. Halleck   [TELEGRAM]

Head Quarters,
Army of the Potomac,
Camp near the Potomac
Sept. 22d 1862 [noon]

Maj. Gen. H. W. Halleck
Commander in Chief, Washington

When I was assigned to the command of the Army in Washington it was suffering under the disheartening influences of defeat, it had been greatly reduced by casualties in Genl Pope's campaign, and its efficiency had been much impaired.

The sanguinary battles fought by these troops at South Mountain and Antietam Creek have resulted in a loss to us of ten General officers & many regimental and Company officers, besides a large number of enlisted men. Two Army Corps have been sadly cut up and scattered by the overwhelming numbers brought against them in the battle of the 17th inst, and the entire Army has been greatly exhausted by unavoidable overwork, hunger, & want of sleep & rest. When the enemy recrossed the Potomac the means of transportation at my disposal was inadequate to furnish a single day's supply of subsistence in advance. Under these circumstances I did not feel authorized to cross the river in pursuit of the retreating enemy, & thereby place that stream, which is liable at any time to rise above a fording stage, between this Army & its base of supply.

As soon as the exigencies of the service will admit of it, this Army should be re-organized. It is absolutely necessary to secure its efficiency that the old skeleton regiments should be filled up at once, & officers appointed to supply the numerous existing vacancies. There are instances where Captains are commanding Regiments & Companies are without a single commissioned officer.

Franklin's Corps marched to Wmsport yesterday morning to reinforce Couch. They now occupy that place, the enemy having retreated on their approach.

Williams' (Banks') Corps occupies Maryland Heights. Sumner's Corps is en route for the same point, & Meade's (Hooker's) Corps will probably follow it soon. I propose as soon as the pontoon bridge can be relaid (it is expected to arrive there today) to cross these troops and occupy Harper's Ferry & Charlestown, with a view of pushing them out into the Shenandoah Valley as soon as practicable. Burnside's & Porter's Corps are here. The enemy still continues to show his pickets along the river & with a large force drove back the last reconnaissance that was attempted on the other side. A large body of the enemy was reported last night as moving from Charlestown towards Bunker Hill, and I am of opinion that the mass of their Army is retreating in that direction. I am sending out scouts in every direction, and will keep you advised of all I learn of the movements of the enemy.

Geo B McClellan
Maj Gen Comdg

LS (telegram sent), McClellan Papers (C-16:65), Library of Congress. *OR*, Ser. 1, XIX, Part 2, pp. 342–43.

To Henry W. Halleck　　　　　　　　　　　　　　　　[TELEGRAM]

	Head Quarters, Army of the Potomac,
Major General Halleck	Near Shepherdstown,
General in Chief Washington	Sept 23, 1862 9.30 am

From several different sources I learn that Gen. R E Lee is still opposite to my position at Leestown, between Shepherdstown and Martinsburg, and that General Jackson is on the Opequon Creek about three miles above its mouth, both with large forces. There are also indications of heavy reinforcements moving towards them from Winchester and Charlestown. I have therefore ordered Gen Franklin to take position with his Corps at the crossroads about one mile northwest of Bakersville on the Bakersville and Williamsport road, and Gen Couch to establish his division near Downsville, leaving sufficient force at Williamsport to watch and guard the ford at that place. The fact of the enemy's remaining so long in our front, and the indications of an advance of reinforcements seem to indicate that he will give us another battle, with all his available force. As I mentioned to you before our Army has been very much reduced by casualties in the recent battles, and in my judgment all the reinforcements of old troops that can possibly be dispensed with around Washington and other places should be instantly pushed forward by rail to this Army via Harper's Ferry and Hagerstown. A defeat at this juncture would be ruinous to our cause. I cannot think it possible that the enemy will bring any forces to bear upon Washington till after the question is decided here; — but if he should troops can soon be sent back from this Army by rail to reinforce the garrison there.[1]

The evidence I have that reinforcements are coming to the rebel army consists in the fact that long columns of dust extending from Winchester to Charlestown and from Charlestown in this direction and also troops moving this way were seen last evening. This is corroborated by the statements of citizens.

G. B. McClellan
Maj. Genl. Comdg.

P.S. Gen. Sumner with his Corps & Williams (Banks) occupies Harper's Ferry and the surrounding heights. I think he will be able to hold his position till reinforcements arrive.

G. B. McC.

Retained copy, McClellan Papers (C-18:65), Library of Congress. *OR*, Ser. 1, XIX, Part 1, p. 70.

1. Halleck telegraphed on Sept. 24, in part: "Sigel's corps is the only old one here. . . . On what point would you prefer it to move?" *OR*, Ser. 1, XIX, Part 2, p. 353.

To Henry W. Halleck   [TELEGRAM]

Major General Halleck
General in Chief Washington

Head Quarters, Army of the Potomac,
Near Shepherdstown
Sept. 24, 1862 11 am

The enemy's pickets occupy the Virginia side of the river near Shepherdstown, and he is still said to be in position with large forces between Shepherdstown and Martinsburg. It has been raining for several hours. If the storm continues the river will probably be raised above a fording stage. Should this occur, I propose to concentrate the greater portion of the Army in the vicinity of Harper's Ferry, ready to act against the enemy in the direction of Winchester. The pontoon bridge arrived at Harper's Ferry last evening and is probably laid by this time.

A reconnaissance made from Harper's Ferry yesterday found the enemy's artillery, infantry and cavalry in force drawn up in line near Charlestown.

G. B. McClellan
Maj. Genl. Comdg.

Retained copy, McClellan Papers (C-18:65), Library of Congress. *OR*, Ser. 1, XIX, Part 2, p. 353.

To Henry W. Halleck   [TELEGRAM]

Maj Gen Halleck
Gen-in-Chief Washington

Head Quarters, Army of the Potomac,
[Sharpsburg] Sept 24, 1862 10 pm

It is necessary to build a permanent double track wagon bridge over the Potomac at Harper's Ferry — also a wagon bridge over the Shenandoah at the same place on the piers now standing. The Potomac bridge must probably be built on crib piers filled with stone and will be about nine hundred feet in length, the Shenandoah bridge about four hundred feet long. I have to request that Colonel D. C. McCallum may be placed in charge of this work, and instructed to report to me at Harper's Ferry without delay. He should take steps before leaving Washington to organize the gangs of workmen and to procure all the material possible. I cannot too strongly urge the importance of expedition in this matter. Until this or the rail road bridge is finished it is scarcely possible to advance from Harper's Ferry in force, and as that is clearly our true line of operations, I need not urge upon you the necessity of completing our communications there.[1]

G. B. McClellan

Maj. Genl. Comdg.

Retained copy, McClellan Papers (C-18:65), Library of Congress. *OR*, Ser. 1, XIX, Part 2, pp. 354–55.

1. In his reply on Sept. 26, Halleck wrote th it there must be agreement on a general plan of operations before bridge-building was und :rtaken. "I had hoped that, instead of crossing at Harper's Ferry ..., you would be able to cross lower down the Potomac, so as to cover Washington.... It seems to me that Washington is the real base of operations, and that it should not under any circumstances be exposed." *OR*, Ser. 1, XIX, Part 2, p. 360.

To Mary Ellen McClellan

[Sharpsburg] Sept 25 [1862] 7.30 am.

... We are so near the mountains that it is quite cold at night....

I think the health of our men is improving much — they look a great deal better than they did on the Peninsula — eyes look brighter — & faces better....

My plans are easily given — for I really do not know whether I am to do as I choose or not. I shall keep on doing what seems best until brought up with a round turn — *then* I'll kick up *my* heels. My own judgment is to watch the line of the Potomac until the water rises, then to concentrate everything near Harper's Ferry — reorganize the army as promptly as possible & then if secesh remains near Winchester to attack him — if he retires to follow him up & attack him near Richmond....

It is very doubtful whether I shall remain in the service after the rebels have left this vicinity. The Presdt's late Proclamation,[1] the continuation of Stanton & Halleck in office render it almost impossible for me to retain my commission & self respect at the same time. I cannot make up my mind to fight for such an accursed doctrine as that of a servile insurrection — it is too infamous. Stanton is as great a villain as ever & Halleck as great a fool — he has no brains whatever!...

It *is* a mercy of God that none of my staff have been hit considering how much they have been exposed to danger — they have had plenty of horses killed, sabres hit, clothes cut etc — but have thus far escaped unhurt. Am going on a visit to Harper's Ferry this morning....

AL copy, McClellan Papers (C-7:63), Library of Congress.

1. The preliminary Emancipation Proclamation, issued Sept. 22. *Collected Works of Lincoln*, V, pp. 433–36.

To William H. Aspinwall

Head-Quarters Army of the Potomac,
My dear Sir   Sharpsburg Sept 26, 1862

I am very anxious to know how you and men like you regard the recent Proclamations of the Presdt inaugurating servile war, emancipating the slaves, & at one stroke of the pen changing our free institutions into a despotism — for such I regard as the natural effect of the last Proclamation suspending the Habeas Corpus throughout the land.[1]

I shall probably be in this vicinity for some days &, if you regard the matter as gravely as I do, would be glad to communicate with you.[2]

In haste I am sincerely yours
Geo B McClellan

Wm H Aspinwall esq
New York City

ALS, Civil War Collection, Huntington Library.

1. GBM refers to the preliminary Emancipation Proclamation and to the president's proclamation of Sept. 24 suspending the writ of habeas corpus as it applied to persons accused of "discouraging volunteer enlistments, resisting militia drafts, or guilty of any disloyal practice, affording aid and comfort to Rebels...." *Collected Works of Lincoln*, V, pp. 436–37. 2. Aspinwall visited GBM at his camp a short time later. See GBM to his wife, Oct. 5, 1862, *infra*.

To Henry W. Halleck   [TELEGRAM]

Maj. Gen. Halleck   Head Quarters, Army of the Potomac,
Genl in Chief Washington   [Sharpsburg] Sept. 27, 1862 10 am

All the information in my possession goes to prove that the main body of the enemy is concentrated not far from Martinsburg with some troops at Charlestown — not many in Winchester.[1] Their movements of late have been an extension towards our right and beyond it. They are receiving reinforcements in Winchester, mainly I think of conscripts, perhaps entirely so. This Army is not now in condition to undertake another campaign nor to bring on another battle, unless great advantages are offered by some mistake of the enemy or pressing military exigencies render it necessary. We are greatly deficient in officers. Many of the old regiments are reduced to mere skeletons, the new regiments need instruction. Not a day should be lost in filling the old regiments, our main dependence, and in supplying vacancies among the officers by promotion. My present purpose is to hold the Army about as it now is, rendering Harper's Ferry secure and watching the river closely, intending to attack the enemy should he attempt to cross to this side.

Our possession of Harper's Ferry gives us the great advantage of a secure debouche; but we cannot avail ourselves of it until the railroad bridge is finished, because we cannot otherwise supply a greater number of troops than we now have on the Virginia side at that point. When the river rises so that the enemy cannot cross in force, I propose concentrating the Army somewhere near Harper's Ferry and then acting according to circumstances viz, moving on Winchester if from the position and attitude of the enemy we are likely to gain a great advantage by doing so; or else devoting a reasonable time to the organization of the Army and instruction of the new troops preparatory to an advance on whatever line may be determined. In any event I regard it as absolutely necessary to send new regiments at once to the old Corps for purposes of instruction, and that the old regiments be filled at once.

I have no fear as to an attack on Washington by the line of Manassas; holding Harper's Ferry as I do, they will not run the risk of an attack on their flank and rear while they have the garrison of Washington in their front. I rather apprehend a renewal of the attempt in Maryland, should the river remain low for a great length of time and should they receive considerable addition to their force. I would be glad to have Peck's division as soon as possible.[2] I am surprised that Sigel's men have been sent to Western Virginia without my knowledge. The last I heard from you on the subject was that they were at my disposition.

In the last battles the enemy was undoubtedly greatly superior to us in number, and it was only by very hard fighting that we gained the advantage we did; as it was, the result was at one period very doubtful and we had all we could do to win the day. If the enemy receives considerable reinforcements and we none, it is possible that I may have too much on my hands in the next battle.

My own view of the proper policy to be pursued is to retain in Washington merely the force necessary to garrison it and to send everything else available to reinforce this Army. The railways give us the means of promptly reinforcing Washington should it become necessary. If I am reinforced as I ask, and am allowed to take my own course, I will hold myself responsible for the safety of Washington.

Several persons recently from Richmond say that there are no troops there except conscripts and they few in number.

I hope to be able to give you details as to the late battles by this evening.[3] I am about starting again for Harper's Ferry.

G. B. McClellan

Maj. Genl. Comdg.

Retained copy, McClellan Papers (C-18:65), Library of Congress. *OR*, Ser. 1, XIX, Part 1, pp. 70–71.

1. Halleck had telegraphed on Sept. 26, in part: "Before more troops are moved from here into the field, we ought to have a full understanding in respect to your future operations. As I now understand, you propose to cross the Potomac at or above Harper's Ferry, and move up the valley. Will not this line again expose Washington, and compel us to keep a large force here? The enemy is repairing bridges on the Rapidan and Rappahannock, preparatory to throwing a force on Washington. . . . Cannot your army move, so as to cover Washington, by keeping between it and the enemy? I particularly wish your views on this subject." *OR*, Ser. 1, XIX, Part 2, pp. 359–60. 2. Maj. Gen. John J. Peck's division was at Yorktown. 3. See GBM to Halleck, Sept. 29, 1862, *OR*, Ser. 1, XIX, Part 1, p. 181.

To Lorenzo Thomas

To Brig Genl L Thomas,

Adjt. Genl. U.S. Army   Head Quarters Army of the Potomac

General: [Sharpsburg] September 28th 1862.

The reduced condition of the old regiments, and the futility of dependence upon the recruiting service for the replenishing of their ranks, points to the necessity of earnest endeavor to collect all the absent officers and men belonging to these organizations. I am aware that this subject has already occupied the attention of the War Department, but I am now more especially alluding to the class of absentees employed on extra duty in the hospital and other staff departments of the Army, who are the most valuable of the absentees (for many absent men are runaways) and who can be sent to their regiments now without difficulty, inasmuch as their places can be readily supplied from new troops.

I am now getting together stragglers and convalescents from hospitals, and if I could get extra duty men also, a very considerable addition would be made to the diminished ranks of the old regiments.

In order to carry this into effect, I respectfully suggest than an order be issued fixing a time, say the 15th of October, when all hospital attendants and other extra duty men shall be relieved and sent to the Convalescent Camp at Alexandria in depot, from which they can be drawn and sent to their regiments as soon as a sufficient number have accumulated to justify the sending for them. The order should prohibit any officer retaining a soldier of the old regiments without the consent of the War Department or of the Commander of the Army or Department to which the soldier belongs. I suggest that every hospital and staff office be inspected within the month of October, by, if necessary, scores of officers detailed for the purpose, to ferret out the old soldiers hidden away therein. Such an inspection would produce more fruit in one week, than the recruiting service can in three months.

And finally I suggest to the War Department the employment of the deputy provost marshals throughout the north more particularly in the arrest of deserters. Convalescent soldiers leave hospitals and have done so for the past year and return home, habitually. It is the experience of every Army Commander, that not more than a tenth of the soldiers who are left behind sick, ever rejoin. A regiment here, which has been employed pretty much during the whole year as depot guard &c., has had in the course of the year some five hundred sick sent to hospitals in the rear. Of these, it has received back some fifteen or twenty. The stragglers too, are numerous in every division of the Army; many of these desert. The States of the North are flooded with deserters, absentees, &c. One Corps of this Army has 13,000 and odd men present and 15,000 and odd absent. Of this 15,000, 8,000 probably are at work at home, deserters. They can be secured and returned — and I beg that the fullest exercise of the power of the government may be devoted if necessary to the accomplishment of this end. It will have the happiest result in swelling the ranks of the old regiments and in preventing their future reduction.[1]

> I am General Very Respectfully, Your obedient servant,
> [George B. McClellan]
> Major General Commanding

P.S. Since writing the above G.O. No. 140 of Sept. 24 1862 has come to my notice. The Department has therefore anticipated my suggestions with regard to the employment of Deputy Provost Marshals.[2]

Retained copy, Records of the U.S. Army Continental Commands, RG 393 (3964: Army of the Potomac), National Archives. *OR,* Ser. 1, XIX, Part 2, p. 365.

1. On Oct. 7 Halleck replied that every effort was being made to collect the absentees. He urged GBM to take stronger measures against straggling and to increase the army's mobility. "The country is becoming very impatient at the want of activity of your army, and we must push it on.... If we compare the average distances marched per month by our troops for the last year with that of the rebels, or with European armies in the field, we will see why our troops march no better. They are not sufficiently exercised to make them good and efficient soldiers." *OR,* Ser. 1, XIX, Part 2, pp. 394–95. 2. Issued by the Adjutant General's Office: *OR,* Ser. 3, II, p. 586.

To Mary Ellen McClellan

Sept 29 [1862] Sharpsburg am.

... I think secesh has gone to Winchester — the last I heard last night was to that effect. If he has gone there I will be able to arrange my troops more with a view to comfort & if it will only rain a little so as to raise the river will feel quite justified in asking for a short leave....

We are having fine weather. . . .

I don't know what will be done about Stanton etc. I only feel that I cannot in justice to myself remain in the service if he continues in office. Not yet even have I a word from anyone in Washn about the battle of the Antietam & nothing in regard to South Mountain except from the Presdt in the following *beautiful* language. "Your dispatch received. God bless you & all with you. Can't you beat them some more before they get off?"!!![1] I don't look for any thanks at their hands & believe that they scarcely pretend to conceal their malevolence. I still hope that the indignant people will punish them as they deserve. I fully agree with you that forbearance is no longer a virtue. I shall make it only a matter of interest. If by pushing a little the people will take the matter in hand that will be the best solution.

11 pm. . . . I have been hard at work all day upon a mere preliminary report of the recent battles & find that in order to arrive at anything like the truth, I must tomorrow take all my aides to the ground and talk with them there. I would really prefer *fighting three* battles to *writing* the report of one. You can hardly imagine the difficulties of such a task. You are necessarily combating the amour propre, the vanity of every officer concerned when you say one word in commendation of anybody else. Each one is firmly convinced of the fact that no one *but* he had anything to do with the result, every commander of a brigade even becomes firmly convinced that he fought the whole battle & that he arranged the general plan, of which he knew simply nothing.

I *ought* to rap Burnside *very* severely & probably will — yet I hate to do it. He is very slow & is not fit to command more than a regiment. If I rap him as he deserves he will be my mortal enemy hereafter — if I do not praise him as he thinks he deserves & as I know he does *not,* he will be at least a very lukewarm friend. I mention this merely as an instance that you will comprehend. . . .

AL copy; copy, McClellan Papers (C-7 :63/D-10 :72), Library of Congress.

1. See GBM to Halleck, Sept. 15, 1862, 10 :00 A.M., note 2, *supra.*

To Henry W. Halleck   [TELEGRAM]

General H. W. Halleck   Head Quarters, Army of the Potomac,
General in Chief   [Sharpsburg] Sept. 30 10 am 1862

From all the information I can obtain I am satisfied that the mass of the Rebel Army has left Martinsburg and marched for Winchester where it is said they will make a stand and await our approach.

They have been forcing every man they could find capable of bearing arms into their ranks. They have compelled the farmers to bring their grain to their Army and they have thereby caused great dissatisfaction among the people of Northern Virginia.

Geo. B. McClellan
Maj Genl

Retained copy, McClellan Papers (C-16:65), Library of Congress. *OR,* Ser. 1, XIX, Part 2, p. 371.

To Mary Ellen McClellan

[Sharpsburg] Oct 1 [1862] 7.30 am.

... A cloudy day. If it does not rain I think I will go to Wmsport & Hagerstown today — to see that part of the country, for there is no telling but that I might have to fight a battle there one of these days & it is very convenient to know the ground. In this last battle the rebels ̇possessed an immense advantage in knowing every part of the ground, while I knew only what I could see from a distance....

I rode all over the battle field again yesterday — so as to be sure that I understand it all before writing my report. I was but the more impressed with the great difficulties of the undertaking & the magnitude of the success. Did I tell you that our losses at South Mt & Antietam amounted to within one or two hundred of 15,000, that we took some 6000 prisoners, 39 colors, 14 guns, 14,500 small arms etc etc. Pretty fair trophies after a battle so stubbornly contested....

Yesterday I received at last a telegram from Halleck about the battle of Antietam[1]....

I don't know where we are drifting but do not like the looks of things — time will show....

I do not yet know what are the military plans of the gigantic intellects at the head of the Govt!...

AL copy, McClellan Papers (C-7:63), Library of Congress.

1. Halleck telegraphed on Sept. 30: "Your report of yesterday giving the results of the battles of South Mountain and Antietam has been received and submitted to the president. These were hard fought battles but well earned and decided victories. The valor and endurance of your army in the several conflicts ... are creditable alike to the troops & to the officers who commanded them. A grateful country while mourning the lamented dead will not be unmindful of the honors due the living." McClellan Papers (A-81:32).

To Henry W. Halleck   [TELEGRAM]

Maj. Gen. Halleck   Head Quarters, Army of the Potomac,
General in Chief, Washington   [Sharpsburg] October 1 1862 11 a.m.

I take it for granted that we will hereafter hold Harper's Ferry as a permanent arrangement, whatever line of operations may be adopted for the main Army. In this event a permanent and reliable bridge is needed there across the Shenandoah. Mr. Roebling[1] can build a double track suspension bridge on the existing piers in three or four weeks. The wire is now in possession of government and the cost will be some five thousand dollars ($5000) besides the wire. No pontoon nor trestle bridge can be made to resist the freshets. I ask authority to have this work undertaken at once. I would also renew the recommendation that a permanent wagon bridge be made across the Potomac at Harper's Ferry.[2] This without reference to the future operations of the main Army, but simply as a necessity for the proper defence of Harper's Ferry itself.[3]

G B McClellan
Major Genl Comdg

Retained copy, McClellan Papers (C-18:65), Library of Congress. *OR*, Ser. 1, XIX, Part 1, p. 10.

1. Bridge builder John A. Roebling. 2. See GBM to Halleck, Sept. 24, 10:00 P.M., *supra*. 3. Halleck replied on this date that "the Government does not contemplate the delay in your movements for the length of time required to build permanent bridges." He repeated his view that the army should cross downstream from Harper's Ferry "and compel the enemy to fall back or to give you battle," an operation that should be started at once. *OR*, Ser. 1, XIX, Part 1, p. 10.

To Mary Ellen McClellan

[Sharpsburg] Oct 2 [1862] am.

... I do think that man Halleck is the most stupid idiot I ever heard of — either that or he drinks hard — for he cannot even comprehend the English language.[1] ...

I found the Presdt at Genl Sumner's qtrs at Harper's Ferry — none of the Cabinet were with him, merely some Western officers such as McClernand & others.[2] His ostensible purpose is to see the troops & the battle fields. I incline to think that the real purpose of his visit is to push me into a premature advance into Virginia. I may be mistaken, but think not. The real truth is that my army is not fit to advance — the old rgts are reduced to mere skeletons & are completely tired out — they need rest and filling up. The new rgts are not fit for the field. The remains of Pope's army are pretty well broken up & ought not to be made to fight for some little time yet. Cavalry & artillery horses are broken down — so it goes.

These people don't know what an army requires & therefore act stupidly. ...

AL copy, McClellan Papers (C-7:63), Library of Congress.

1. Presumably this refers to the exchange of telegrams with Halleck the previous day. 2. On Oct. 1–4 President Lincoln visited the Army of the Potomac. Brig. Gen. John A. McClernand was among those in his party.

To Israel Washburn

To His Excellency the Governor of the State of Maine: Sir,

Headquarters Army of the Potomac, Camp near Sharpsburg, Md., October 4, 1862.

In view of the reduced and shattered condition of the Seventh Regiment of Maine Volunteers, the result of arduous service and exposure during the campaigns on the Peninsula and in Maryland, I made on the 2d inst. a special application to the War Department that the regiment should be sent to report to you in Maine, that it might be recruited and reorganized under your personal supervision.[1] I yesterday received the necessary authority, as you will observe by the copy of Special Order No. 271 from these headquarters, inclosed herein. I send the regiment to you for the purpose indicated. I beg that when this purpose shall have been accomplished, that the regiment may be ordered to report to me with all practical dispatch.

In returning this gallant remnant of a noble body of men, whose bravery has been exhibited on every field almost in the campaigns cited, to the State whose pride it is to have sent them forth, I feel happy that it has been in my power to signify, even in this insufficient manner, my appreciation of their services and of their value to this army, and I will venture on the latter account to ask your Excellency's best endeavors to fill at once their diminished ranks, that I may again see their standard in the Army of the Potomac.[2] I am, with much respect,

Your obedient sevant,
Geo. B. McClellan
Major-General, U.S.A.

Thomas W. Hyde, *Following the Greek Cross or, Memories of the Sixth Army Corps* (Boston, 1895), pp. 110–11.

1. In his telegram to Adj. Gen. Thomas on Oct. 2, GBM noted that the 7th Maine was reduced to sixty-five men. McClellan Papers (A-82:33), Library of Congress. 2. The regiment returned to the Army of the Potomac in February 1863.

To Mary Ellen McClellan

[Sharpsburg] Oct 5th [1862] Sunday 7.30 am

... The Presdt left us about 11 yesterday morning. I went with him as far as over the battle field of South Mtn & on my way thither was quite surprised to meet Mr. Aspinwall en route to my camp....

The Presdt was very kind personally — told me he was convinced I was the best general in the country etc etc. He was very affable & I really think he does feel very kindly towards me personally. I showed him the battle fields & am sure he departed with a more vivid idea of the great difficulty of the task we had accomplished. Mr. Aspinwall is decidedly of the opinion that it is my duty to submit to the Presdt's proclamation & quietly continue doing my duty as a soldier. I presume he is right & am at least sure that he is honest in his opinion. I shall surely give his views full consideration. He is of the opinion that the nation cannot stand the burdens of the war much longer & that a speedy solution is necessary — in this he is no doubt correct — & I hope sincerely that another successful battle may conclude my part of the work. I will try to find time to think over the whole affair today & tonight, & do my best to hit upon some plan of campaign that will enable me to drive the rebels entirely away from this part of the country forever.

AL copy, McClellan Papers (C-7:63), Library of Congress.

To William H. Aspinwall

Head-Quarters Army of the Potomac,
My dear Sir   Camp near Sharpsburg Oct 5 1862

Will you allow me to present to you the accompanying piece of the color staff of the flag of a Texas Regt of Hood's Brigade. The color & staff were captured by the U.S. Army of the Potomac at the battle of the Antietam Sept 17 1862. The staff was broken by a ball — the colors are deposited at Washington.

Please accept this staff as a slight token of my personal friendship for you & as a memento of our trip over the field of Antietam today.

Very truly & sincerely your friend
Geo B. McClellan
Maj Genl Comdg

W H Aspinwall Esq
New York

ALS, Miscellaneous Collections, Huntington Library.

To Robert E. Lee

General R. E. Lee,
Commanding Army
of Northern Virginia: Headquarters Army of the Potomac,
General: [Sharpsburg] October 5, 1862.

I have the honor to acknowledge the receipt of your letter of the 4th instant, inclosing a letter to Mrs. Philip Kearny, and, at the same time, committing to my care the sword, horse, and saddle of Major-General

Kearny, to the end that, in accordance with the expressed wish of Mrs. Kearny, they may be placed in her keeping.[1] The articles have been received, and, with the letter, will be forwarded to Mrs. Kearny by the earliest opportunity. I beg you to accept my thanks for your courteous and humane attention to the request of the widow of this lamented officer. I shall be happy to reciprocate the courtesy when circumstances shall place it in my power to do so.

> Very respectfully, your obedient servant,
> Geo. B. McClellan
> Major-General, Commanding.

OR, Ser. 1, XIX, Part 2, p. 384.

1. Lee to McClellan, Oct. 4, *OR,* Ser. 1, XIX, Part 2, p. 381. Gen. Kearny was killed on Sept. 1 at the Battle of Chantilly. His body had been returned earlier.

To Henry W. Halleck   [TELEGRAM]

Genl H. W. Halleck   Head-Quarters, Army of the Potomac,
Genl. in Chief   [Sharpsburg] Oct. 6, 4.30 pm 1862

Your telegram ordering Cox's division to Clarksburg was received before the one directing the movement across the Potomac.[1] Is it still intended that Cox shall march at once.

It is important in making my decision regarding the route to be taken by the Army that I should know 1st what description of troops I am to be reinforced with upon the Shenandoah route, and also upon the other route between the enemy & Washington, whether they are to be old or new troops or what proportion of each. If possible I should be glad to have Pecks division sent to me if it can be got here within a reasonable time.

2d Will you inform me what the present condition of the Alexandria and Leesburg Rail Road is, also the Manassas Gap Rail Road, and what time it would require to put them in working order.

It is believed that the Harpers Ferry & Winchester Rail Road is not materially injured.[2]

> Geo. B. McClellan
> Maj Genl

Retained copy, McClellan Papers (A-82:33), Library of Congress. *OR,* Ser. 1, XIX, Part 2, p. 387.

1. Halleck's telegram of this date ordered the Kanawha Division to western Virginia. *OR,* Ser. 1, XIX, Part 2, p. 387. Also on Oct. 6 Halleck telegraphed, in part: "The President directs that you cross the Potomac and give battle to the enemy or drive him south. Your army must move now while the roads are good. If you cross the river between the enemy and Washington, and cover the latter by your operations, you can be ·re-enforced with 30,000 men. If you move up the Valley of the Shenandoah, not more than 12,000 or 15,000

can be sent to you. The President advises the interior line, between Washington and the enemy, but does not order it.... I am directed to add that the Secretary of War and the General-in-Chief fully concur with the President...." *OR*, Ser. 1, XIX, Part 1, p. 72. 2. Halleck replied on Oct. 7: "Cox's division must go west at once. [Peck's] division is at Yorktown and Suffolk. The Manassas Gap road can be repaired in a few days. The Leesburg road is much more injured. Your army can reach the former in less time than would be required to repair the latter. The troops to be sent you will be partly new and partly old — mostly new." *OR*, Ser. 1, XIX, Part 2, p. 393.

To Mary Ellen McClellan

[Sharpsburg] Oct 7 [1862] 8 am.

... I yesterday afternoon received orders to advance & attack the enemy or drive him south (this is confidential). I can't go far for the reason that I cannot carry many supplies. So far as I can see the little campaign can't last many days for when it is once fought some other line of operations will have to be taken as the one up here leads to no final result.

AL copy, McClellan Papers (C-7:63), Library of Congress.

To Henry W. Halleck   [TELEGRAM]

[Sharpsburg, October 7, 1862, 1 P.M.]

After a full consultation with the Corps Commanders in my vicinity I have determined to adopt the line of the Shenandoah for immediate operations against the enemy now near Winchester. On no other line north of Washn can the Army be supplied nor can it on any other cover Maryland and Penna. Were we to cross the river below the mouth of the Shenandoah we would leave it in the power of the enemy to recross into Maryland & thus check the movement. In the same case we would voluntarily give him the advantage of the strong line of the Shenandoah no point of which could be reached by us in advance of him. I see no objective point of strategical value to be gained or sought for by a movement between the Shenandoah & Washn. I wish to state distinctly that I do not regard the line of the Shenandoah valley as important for ulterior objects — it is important only so long as the enemy remains near Winchester & we cannot follow that line far beyond that point simply because the country is destitute of supplies & we have not sufficient means of transportation to enable us to advance more than 20 or 25 miles beyond a railway or canal terminus. If the enemy abandons Winchester & falls back upon Staunton it will be impossible for us to pursue him by that route, & we must then take a new line of operations based upon water or railway communication. The only possible object to be gained by an advance from this vicinity is to fight the enemy near Winchester — if they retreat we have nothing to gain by pursuing them, & in fact cannot do so to any great distance. The objects I propose to myself are to fight the enemy if they remain near Winchester, or failing in that to force them to abandon the valley of the Shenandoah — then to adopt a new & decisive line of operations which shall strike at the heart of the rebellion.

I have taken all possible measures to insure the most prompt equipment of the troops, but from all that I can learn it will be at least three days before the 1st, 5th & 6th Corps are in condition to move from their present camps — they need shoes & other indispensible articles of clothing, as well as shelter tents &c. I beg to assure you that not an hour shall be lost in carrying your instructions into effect.

Please send the reinforcements to Harper's Ferry — I would prefer that the new regts be sent as regts — not brigaded — unless already done so with old troops. I would again ask for Peck's Div & if possible Heintzelman's Corps. If the enemy give battle near Winchester it will be a desperate affair, requiring all our resources.

I hope that no time will be lost in sending forward the reinforcements, that I may get them in hand as soon as possible.

G B McC

Maj Genl H W Halleck
Washn

ALS (telegram sent), McClellan Papers (A-83:33), Library of Congress. *OR*, Ser. 1, XIX, Part 1, pp. 11–12.

To Abraham Lincoln [TELEGRAM]

Hd Quarters Army Potomac
The President, U.S. [Sharpsburg, October] 7th [1862, 11:35 P.M.]

I have issued the following order on your proclamation.

"Hd Quarters Army Potomac Camp near Sharpsburg Md Oct 7th 1862 Genl Order No. 163. The attention of the officers & soldiers of the Army of the Potomac is called to Genl Order No. 139 War Dept Sept 24th 1862, publishing to the Army the Presidents proclamation of Sept 22d.[1]

A proclamation of such grave moment to the Nation officially communicated to the Army affords to the Genl Commanding an opportunity of defining specifically to the officers & soldiers under his Command the relation borne by all persons in the Military service of the U.S. towards the Civil Authorities of the Government. The Constitution confides to the Civil Authorities legislative judicial and executive, the power and duty of making expounding & executing the federal laws. Armed forces are raised & supported simply to sustain the Civil Authorities and are to be held in strict subordination thereto in all respects. This fundamental rule of our political system is essential to the security of our Republican Institutions & should be thoroughly understood & observed by every soldier. The principle upon which & the objects for which Armies shall be employed in suppressing Rebellion must be determined & declared by the Civil Authorities and the Chief Executive, who is charged with the administration of the National affairs, is the proper & only source through which the views & orders of the Government can be made known to the Armies of the Nation. Discussions by officers & soldiers concerning public measures determined upon and declared by the Government when carried at all beyond temperate and respectful expressions of opinion tend greatly to impair & destroy the discipline & efficiency of troops by substituting the spirit of political faction for that firm steady & earnest support of the Authority of the Government which is the highest duty of the American soldier. The remedy for political error if any are committed is to be found only in the action of the people at the polls. In thus calling the attention of this Army to the true relation between the soldiers and the Government the Genl Commanding merely adverts to an evil against which it has been thought advisable during our whole history to guard the Armies of the Republic & in so doing he will [not] be considered by any right minded person as casting any reflection upon that loyalty & good conduct which has been so fully illustrated upon so many battle fields. In carrying out all measures of public policy this Army will of course be guided by the same rules of mercy and Christianity that have ever controlled its conduct toward the defenceless.

By Command of Maj Genl McClellan. James Hardie Lt Col Aide de Camp Acting Ajt. A Genl.''

Geo B McClellan
M.G. Comdg

Received copy, Lincoln Papers, Library of Congress. *OR,* Ser. 1, XIX, Part 2, p. 395.

1. The preliminary Emancipation Proclamation.

To Henry W. Halleck   [TELEGRAM]

Major Genl Halleck   Head Quarters, Army of the Potomac,
General in Chief Washington   [Knoxville, Md.] Oct 10, 1862, 10 pm

Every disposition has been made to cut off the retreat of the enemy's cavalry that today made the raid into Maryland and Pennsylvania.

G. B. McClellan
Maj Genl Comdg

Retained copy, McClellan Papers (C-18:65), Library of Congress. *OR,* Ser. 1, XIX, Part 2, p. 59.

To Henry W. Halleck [TELEGRAM]

Genl H. W. Halleck   Head Quarters, Army of the Potomac,
Genl-in-Chief   [Knoxville] October 11 9 am 1862

An engine has been sent from Hagerstown towards Chambersburg this morning and I shall probably hear from there in a short time. I have made such disposition of troops along the river that I think we will intercept the rebels on their return. All of my available Cavalry was ordered in pursuit last night but as yet nothing has been heard from it.

Cox's division is loaded in cars at Hancock with Cavalry well out towards the Penna. line, and if the rebels attempt to return above Hancock that division will be certain to intercept them. If they attempt to cross below Hancock I have infantry at or near all the different fords.

I have six Regiments of Cavalry now up the river between Hancock and Cumberland. All of these troops have been ordered to keep a sharp lookout for the return of the rebels.

The force which crossed the river I learn from several different sources consists of four Regiments of Cavalry with four guns (about 2500 men). I have given every order necessary to insure the capture or destruction of these forces, and I hope we may be able to teach them a lesson they will not soon forget. The great difficulty we labor under is the want of Cavalry, as many of our horses are overworked and unserviceable.

We have been making every effort to get supplies of clothing for this Army, and Colonel Ingalls[1] has received advices that it has been forwarded by rail road. But owing to bad management on the Roads or from some other cause it comes in very slowly and it will take a much longer time than was anticipated to get articles that are absolutely indispensable to the Army unless the Rail Road managers forward supplies more rapidly.

> Geo. B. McClellan
> Maj Genl

Retained copy, McClellan Papers (C-16:65), Library of Congress. *OR*, Ser. 1, XIX, Part 2, p. 66.

1. Lt. Col. Rufus Ingalls, chief quartermaster of the Army of the Potomac.

To Henry W. Halleck [TELEGRAM]

Maj Gen H. W. Halleck   Head Quarters, Army of the Potomac,
Com in Chief, Washington   [Knoxville] Oct. 11th 1862 [3:30 P.M.]

I am compelled again to call your attention to the great deficiency of shoes & other indispensable articles of clothing that still exists in some of the Corps of this Army. Upon the assurances of the Chf Qtr Master who based his calculations upon information rec'd from Washington that clothing would be forwarded at certain times, Corps commanders sent their wagons to Hagerstown & Harper's Ferry for it. It did not arrive as promised & has not yet arrived. Unless some measures are taken to insure the prompt forwarding of these supplies there will necessarily be a corresponding delay in getting the Army ready to move, as the men cannot march without shoes. Everything has been done that can be done at these Head Qtrs to accomplish the desired result.

> G. B. McClellan
> Maj Genl Comdg

LS (telegram sent), McClellan Papers (C-16:65), Library of Congress. *OR,* Ser. 1, XIX, Part 1, p. 12.

To Henry W. Halleck   [TELEGRAM]

Major General Halleck   Head Quarters, Army of the Potomac,
General in Chief   [Knoxville] October 12, 1862 12.45 pm

It is absolutely necessary that some energetic means be taken to supply the cavalry of this Army with remount horses. The present rate of supply is (1050) ten hundred and fifty per week,[1] for the entire Army here and in front of Washington. From this number the Artillery draw for their batteries.[2]

> Geo. B. McClellan
> Maj. Genl. Comdg.

Retained copy, McClellan Papers (C-16:65), Library of Congress. *OR,* Ser. 1, XIX, Part 1, p. 13.

1. As the telegram was received at the War Dept., due to a telegrapher's error this figure was written as 150. Records of the Office of the Secretary of War, RG 107 (M-473:50), National Archives. 2. Halleck replied on Oct. 14: "I have caused the matters complained of in your telegrams of the 11th and 12th to be investigated. I am now informed by the Quartermaster-General that every requisition from you for shoes and clothing had been filled and the articles forwarded as directed...." He enclosed a report from Quartermaster General Meigs that an average of 1,459 horses had been supplied in each of the previous six weeks, and that the total number of animals with GBM's army was 31,000. "It is believed that your present proportion of cavalry and of animals is much larger than that of any other of our armies," Halleck wrote. *OR,* Ser. 1, XIX, Part 1, p. 15.

To Henry W. Halleck   [TELEGRAM]

General H. W. Halleck   Head Quarters, Army of the Potomac,
Genl in Chief   [Knoxville] October 12 5 pm 1862

The Rebel Cavalry under Stuart which left Chambersburg yesterday morning in the direction of Gettysburg reached the Potomac near the mouth of the Monocacy at about 9 a.m. today having marched about one

hundred miles in twenty four hours. General Stoneman who was at Pools-
ville near where they passed was ordered by telegraph at 1 o'clock p.m.
yesterday to keep his cavalry well out on all the different approaches
from the direction of Frederick so as to give him time to mass his forces
to resist their re-crossing into Virginia.[1]

As you will see from the dispatch of Genl Pleasonton just received
and herewith transmitted it does not appear that he complied with this
order.[2] He will be called upon for an explanation of this matter.[3] It would
seem that Pleasonton's forces although within a short distance of Pools-
ville received but little assistance from Stoneman.

Geo. B. McClellan
Maj. Genl.

Retained copy, McClellan Papers (C-16:65), Library of Congress. *OR*, Ser. 1, XIX, Part
2, p. 30.

1. Marcy to Stoneman, Oct. 11, *OR*, Ser. 1, XIX, Part 2, pp. 76–77. Brig. Gen. George
Stoneman commanded a division of the Third Corps. 2. Pleasonton reported at 1:30 P.M.
on this date that he had skirmished with the enemy cavalry but could not prevent them
recrossing the Potomac. "There was no artillery at this point, and, with the exception of
a few infantry companies, I had no assistance." *OR*, Ser. 1, XIX, Part 2, p. 30. 3. Marcy
to Stoneman, Oct. 12, *OR*, Ser. 1, LI, Part 1, pp. 881–82. Stoneman replied on Oct. 13 that
with thirty miles of the Potomac to cover he considered his dispositions judicious, but they
were "rendered nugatory by the rapidity and uncertainty of the enemy's movements."
OR, Ser. 1, XIX, Part 2, pp. 42–44.

To Henry W. Halleck [TELEGRAM]

Gen H W Halleck   Hd Qrs Army of Potomac
Gen in Chief   [Knoxville] Oct. 13 [1862] 7.30 p.m.

The recent raid of Stuart who in spite of all the precautions I could
take with the means at my disposal went entirely around this Army has
shown most conclusively how greatly the service suffers from our defi-
ciency in the Cavalry Arm. The great extent of the River line from Washn
to Cumberland the major portion of which in the present stage of water
is fordable at almost every point renders it necessary to scatter our
Cavalry for a very great distance in order to watch the numerous cross-
ings. At the time Stuart crossed it so happened that the greater part of
our Cavalry was absent near Cumberland in pursuit of another Rebel
Cavalry force which had made its appearance at the Little Cacapon and
other points on the upper Potomac destroying RR bridges etc. I had
pickets at McCoy's Ferry where Stuart crossed but they were captured
by his men and in consequence of this I did not learn of the crossing for
some hours afterwards. All the Cavalry that could be collected to pursue
Stuart only amounted to less than one thousand men. With these Plea-
sonton marched seventy eight miles in twenty four hours with a horse

battery but only came up with Stuart at the Potomac after he had marched over ninety miles during the same time with change of horses.

The track of the Rebels was entirely outside of our Infantry until he came near Gen Stoneman at Poolesville who has not as yet explained why he did not mass his troops and engage him as he was ordered. The rapid movement of the rebel Cavalry precluded the possibility of marching our Infantry from any point of our lines with a probability of intercepting them. Cavalry is the only description of force that can prevent these raids. Our Cavalry has been constantly occupied in scouting and reconnaissances and this severe labor has worked down the horses and rendered many of them unserviceable so that at this time no more than one half of our Cavalry are fit for active service in the field. The enemy is well provided with Cavalry while our Cavalry force even with every man well mounted would be inadequate to the requirement of the service and to the large Infantry force with the Army. I therefore again most strenuously urge upon the Dept the imperative necessity of at once supplying this Army including the command of Gen Banks with a sufficient number of horses to remount every dismounted Cavalry soldier within the shortest possible time. If this is not done we shall be constantly exposed to Rebel Cavalry raids.[1]

> Geo B McClellan
> Maj Genl

Received copy, Records of the Office of the Secretary of War, RG 107 (M-473:50), National Archives. *OR*, Ser. 1, XIX, Part 2, p. 417.

1. Halleck replied on Oct. 14 that "the Government has been, and is, making every possible effort to increase the cavalry force.... The President has read your telegram, and directs me to suggest that, if the enemy had more occupation south of the river, his cavalry would not be so likely to make raids north of it." *OR*, Ser. 1, XIX, Part 2, p. 421.

To Henry W. Halleck   [TELEGRAM]

Genl. H. W. Halleck   Head Quarters, Army of the Potomac,
Genl-in-Chief   [Knoxville] October 14 7 pm 1862

Your dispatch of today received.[1] The only force that could operate to the least advantage against such a force as has been reported near Leesburg is Cavalry. At the present time I have but one regiment available in addition to the one with Genl. Stoneman, and that one is needed in front of Harper's Ferry where I have but two weak squadrons. Moreover if I had a regiment or two more they would only be exposed to capture if they were sent across the river in the face of such a force as was reported to be there. Stoneman has been instructed to watch all the fords as high as the mouth of the Monocacy. I would suggest that a sufficient guard of Infantry & Artillery be sent from Washington to hold the fords from Great Falls to the Seneca Creek. This would enable Stoneman to concentrate his forces more upon his line.

With my small Cavalry force it is impossible for me to watch the line of the Potomac properly or even make the reconnaissances that are necessary for our movements. This makes it necessary for me to weaken my line very much by extending the infantry to guard the innumerable fords. This will continue until the river rises and it will be next to impossible to prevent the rebel Cavalry raids. My Cavalry force as I urged this morning should be largely & immediately increased under any hypothesis — whether to guard the river or advance on the enemy or both.

Geo. B. McClellan

Maj Genl

Retained copy, McClellan Papers (C-16 :65), Library of Congress. *OR*, Ser. 1, XIX, Part 2, pp. 421–22.

1. See GBM to Halleck, Oct. 13, note 1, *supra*.

To Abraham Lincoln

His Excellency the President   Head-Quarters Army Potomac,
Sir   Camp in Pleasant Valley Oct 17 1862

Your letter of the 13th inst reached me yesterday morning by the hands of Col Perkins.[1]

I had sent out strong reconnaissances early in the morning in the direction of Charlestown Leetown etc, & as sharp artillery firing was heard I felt it incumbent to go to the front. I did not leave Charlestown until dark so that I have been unable to give to your Excellency's letter that full & respectful consideration which it merits at my hands.

I do not wish to detain Col Perkins beyond this morning's train, I therefore think it best to send him back with this simple acknowledgment of the receipt of your Excellency's letter. I am not wedded to any particular plan of operations — I hope to have today reliable information as to the position of the enemy, whom I still believe to be between Bunker Hill and Winchester. I promise you that I will give to your views the fullest & most unprejudiced consideration, & that it is my intention to advance the moment my men are shod & my cavalry are sufficiently remounted to be serviceable.

Your Excellency may be assured that I will not adopt a course which differs at all from your views without first fully explaining my reasons & giving you time to issue such instructions as may seem best to you.

I am Sir very respectfully your obdt Servant

Geo B McClellan

Maj Gen USA

ALS, Lincoln Papers, Library of Congress. *OR*, Ser. 1, XIX, Part 1, p. 16.

1. In a long and carefully reasoned letter dated Oct. 13, delivered to GBM by Col. Delavan D. Perkins, Lincoln outlined his views on the Army of the Potomac's future operations. "You remember my speaking to you of what I called your over-cautiousness," he wrote. "Are you not over-cautious when you assume that you can not do what the enemy is constantly doing? Should you not claim to be at least his equal in prowess, and act upon the claim?" If the Confederate army in the Shenandoah Valley could subsist far from a railhead, he asked, why could not GBM advance beyond his own rail supply line? To wait for railroad construction "ignores the question of *time,* which can not, and must not be ignored." He proposed that the Army of the Potomac advance swiftly on a line east of the Blue Ridge, by which it should reach Richmond before the enemy. "His route is the arc of a circle, while yours is the chord." Should Lee instead cross the Potomac and march on Pennsylvania, GBM would be squarely on his supply line, "and you have nothing to do but to follow, and ruin him...." If Lee moved toward Richmond to protect his communications, the president wrote, "I would press closely to him, fight him if a favorable opportunity should present, and, at least, try to beat him to Richmond on the inside track. I say 'try'; if we never try, we shall never succeed." After reviewing in detail the advantages of the route he suggested, he concluded by saying, "It is all easy if our troops march as well as the enemy; and it is unmanly to say they can not do it. This letter is in no sense an order." *Collected Works of Lincoln,* V, pp. 460–61.

To Henry W. Halleck   [TELEGRAM]

	Head Quarters,
Maj. Gen. H. W. Halleck	Army of the Potomac,
Commander in Chief, Washington	[Pleasant Valley] Oct 17th 1862

As the draft is now in progress in some of the States I beg to recall to your attention the necessity of filling up the old regiments at the earliest possible moment, and to urge that the first results of the draft be at once applied towards accomplishing this object, which will so greatly and so rapidly increase the efficiency of this Army.[1]

                                          Geo B McClellan
                                          Maj Gen Comdg

LS (telegram sent), McClellan Papers (C-16:65), Library of Congress. *OR*, Ser. 1, XIX, Part 2, p. 439.

1. These were drafts of militia to meet any shortfall in a state's quota of volunteers.

To Samuel L. M. Barlow

| | Head-Quarters Army of the Potomac, |
| My dear Barlow | [Pleasant Valley] Oct 17 1862 |

Your letter of the 14th has just reached me — I cry peccavi & bow down submissively under the weight of your righteous indignation — hit me again & I won't murmur — except a confession that I have been very wrong in so long neglecting to write to so good a friend as you are. The cause of the omission has by no means been that I have forgotten you — but the truth is that I have very little time or inclination to write. When I manage to write to my wife I feel that a great feat has been accomplished, & I am in these days even too lazy to telegraph except by proxy.

I am much obliged to you for Van Buren's speech — which one of these days I hope to have leisure to read.[1] I am *rather* glad to hear this morning that the democrats have carried Penna[2] — the only trouble about their carrying N.Y. also may be in the rather ultra tone of Seymour's first speech. If N.Y. goes democratic some of our dear friends in Washn will feel a little crest fallen. I must confess a double motive for desiring the defeat of Wadsworth — I have so thorough a contempt for the man & regard him as such a vile traitorous miscreant that I do not wish to see the great state of N.Y. disgraced by having such a thing at its head.[3]

I should have been glad to have seen *that* meeting incognito — no doubt it was very exciting.

My wife is with me here — in a quiet old fashioned little farm house near my camp — Mrs Marcy is also here & we are having a very quiet & pleasant time all by ourselves.

Lee is still near Winchester & will probably remain there until I am prepared to move upon him — I am badly in need of two things now, besides men — viz: horses & shoes for the men — I hope for still further success when I next advance.

Now don't wait for answers from me — write when you feel in the humor, & I will try to be a better correspondent in the future — in any event never doubt my sincere friendship for you, & don't get any absurd notions in your head because I seldom write. Why, man alive, I have not written to my own Mother for nearly a year! — I haven't written to my wife for more than a week. With my kindest regards to the Madame in which my wife & Mrs M join

> I am sincerely your friend
> Geo B McClellan

S L M B. Q. A. D. X. K. Barlow Esq[4]
New York City

ALS, Barlow Papers, Huntington Library.

1. No doubt the speech of New York Democratic state chairman John Van Buren, delivered to a meeting on Oct. 13 that ratified the party's nominees for the state elections. 2. The Pennsylvania election for congressional seats and state offices was held on Oct. 14. 3. In New York's gubernatorial election Democrat Horatio Seymour was opposed by Republican James S. Wadsworth. Wadsworth had served in the Army of the Potomac and as military governor in Washington. The election, on Nov. 4, went to Seymour. 4. GBM often teased Barlow on his use of initials.

To Henry W. Halleck

> Head Qrs Army of the Potomac
> October 18th 1862

General,

Your letter of the 14th inst, enclosing a copy of one to you of the same date from the Quarter Master General, has been received.[1]

LIBRARY ST. MARY'S COLLEGE

In this letter you say you are informed by the Quarter Master General that every requisition from me for Shoes and Clothing has been filled, and the articles forwarded as directed. General Meigs may have ordered these articles to be forwarded, but they have not yet reached our Depots; and unless greater effort to insure prompt transmission is made by the Department of which General Meigs is the head, they might as well remain in New York or Philadelphia so far as this Army is concerned.

I am officially informed by one Corps Commander that there is a deficiency of five thousand pairs of Shoes in the amount he called for; and other commanders are continually making similar complaints. The soldiers of this Army have for some time past been suffering for Clothing, and I am constrained to believe it in a great degree owing to the want of proper action on the part of the Quarter Master's Department.

Genl Meigs states further that the Army of the Potomac has, since the battles in front of Washington, received 9254 horses to replace losses; and in this connection inquires most seriously if there is an instance of record of such drain and destruction of horses.

When I marched this Army from Washington on the 8th day of September, it was greatly deficient in Cavalry horses, — the hard service to which they had been subjected in front of Washington having rendered about one half of them unserviceable. Nearly all the horses that this Army has received since then have been to replace those that were broken down at that time; but there have not been anything like the number named by the Quarter Master General. The following statement furnished at my order by Lt Col Myers, Asst Chf Qr Master, gives the actual number of horses received by this Army since September 8th 1862 —

By Capt. J. C. Crane, A.Q.M. Frederick	
Horses from Frederick	732
By Capt. Weeks, A.Q.M. Hagerstown	
Horses from Hagerstown	134
By Capt. Pitkin, A.Q.M. Harpers Ferry	
Horses from Washington	201
By Capt. Bliss, A.Q.M. Harpers Ferry	
Horses from Washington	498
By Capt. J. B. Howard, A.Q.M. Hd Qr	
Horses from Washington	399
Total Rec'd Horses	1964
So stated by Quarter Mas. Genl	9254
Difference	7290

From this statement it will be seen that the total number of horses received by this Army since the commencement of the present campaign is only 1964 — 7290 less than the number given by the Quarter Master General. Of those delivered, very many were totally unfitted for the service, and should never have been received. General Pleasonton Comdg a Cavalry Division, says in a report made yesterday. — "The horses now purchased for Cavalry service are much inferior to those first obtained, and are not suitable for the hard service of Cavalry Horses."[2]

> I am very respectfully your obt servt
> Geo B McClellan
> Maj Genl U.S.A.

Major Genl Halleck

LS, Records of the Adjutant General's Office, RG 94 (159: Halleck Papers), National Archives. *OR*, Ser. 1, XIX, Part 1, pp. 16–17.

1. See GBM to Halleck, Oct. 12, 12:45 P.M., note 2, *supra*. 2. Gen. Meigs reported at length to Halleck on Oct. 21, and by telegram to GBM on Oct. 22, that inefficient transportation and the failure to unload supplies at the army's depots were the primary causes of the delays. As to the supplying of horses, he said that by order they had only been issued under GBM's authorization, and the "missing" horses must have gone to the forces at Washington. "Had you so ordered, not less than 10,000 so distributed to troops under your command would have been sent to Harper's Ferry or Frederick." *OR*, Ser. 1, XIX, Part 1, pp. 17–20, Part 2, pp. 464–65.

To Augustus W. Bradford

	Head Quarters
To His Excellency A. W. Bradford,	Army of the Potomac
Governor of Maryland	Pleasant Valley Md.
Governor:	October 18th 1862

I have the honor to acknowledge the receipt of your Excellency's Order of September 29th,[1] in which you advert in such flattering terms to the conduct of this Army in the recent battles fought upon the soil of your State.

It was with the utmost pride and gratification that I received this most prompt acknowledgement of the skill of the Officers and the gallantry of the men of the Army of the Potomac; we felt it all the more deeply because it emanated from the Executive of the State whose inhabitants had witnessed our efforts, and whose fields were rescued from the invader.

Your praise will stimulate this Army to renewed efforts in the sacred cause of the Union.

Permit me, Governor, in the name of the Army of the Potomac, to thank you for your appreciation of its victories.

With the sincere hope and belief that no Rebel Army shall again pollute the loyal State of Maryland, and committing to you as a sacred trust, the remains of our gallant comrades who now rest beneath its soil

> I am, Governor, with high respect Your obedient Servant
> Geo. B. McClellan
> Maj. Genl. U.S.A.

Copy, Bradford Papers, Maryland Historical Society Library.

1. McClellan Papers (A-81:32), Library of Congress.

To Henry W. Halleck   [TELEGRAM]

Maj. Gen. H. W. Halleck   Head Quarters, Army of the Potomac,
Comdr in Chief, Washington   [Pleasant Valley] Oct. 21st 1862

Since the receipt of the President's order to move on the enemy I have been making every exertion to get this Army supplied with clothing absolutely necessary for marching. This I am happy to say is now nearly accomplished. I have also during the same time repeatedly urged upon you the importance of supplying Cavalry and Artillery horses to replace those broken down by hard service, and steps have been taken to insure a prompt delivery. Our Cavalry even when well supplied with horses is much inferior in numbers to that of the enemy, but in efficiency has proved itself superior. So forcibly has this been impressed upon our old Cavalry Regts by repeated successes that the men are fully persuaded that they are equal to twice their number of rebel Cavalry.

Exclusive of the Cavalry force now engaged in picketing the river, I have not at present over about one thousand (1000) horses for service. Officers have been sent in various directions to purchase horses, & I expect them soon. Without more Cavalry horses our communications from the moment we march would be at the mercy of the large Cavalry forces of the enemy, and it would not be possible for us to cover our flanks properly or to obtain the necessary information of the position & movements of the enemy in such a way as to insure success. My experience has shown the necessity of a large & efficient Cavalry force. Under the foregoing circumstances I beg leave to ask whether the President desires me to march on the enemy at once, or to await the reception of the new horses, every possible step having been taken to insure their prompt arrival.[1]

Geo B McClellan
Maj Genl Comdg

LS (telegram sent), McClellan Papers (C-16:65), Library of Congress. *OR*, Ser. 1, XIX, Part 1, p. 81.

1. Halleck replied at 3:00 P.M. that the president "directs me to say that he has no change to make in his order of the 6th instant. If you have not been and are not now in condition to obey it, you will be able to show such want of ability. The President does not expect impossibilities, but he is very anxious that all this good weather should not be wasted in inactivity." *OR*, Ser. 1, XIX, Part 1, p. 81.

To Montgomery C. Meigs   [TELEGRAM]

Brig. Genl. M. C. Meigs
Qtr Mastr Genl U.S.A.   Head Qtrs Army Potomac
Washington DC   [Pleasant Valley] Oct 22d 1862

Your dispatch of this date received.[1] I have never intended in any letter or dispatch to make any accusation against yourself or your department for not furnishing or forwarding clothing as rapidly as it was possible for you to do. I believe that everything has been done that could be done in this respect both by yourself and the Dept. The idea that I have tried to convey was that certain portions of the command were without clothing and the Army could not move until it was supplied.

G B McClellan
Maj Genl Comdg

Retained copy, McClellan Papers (A-85:34), Library of Congress. *OR*, Ser. 1, XIX, Part 1, pp. 9–10.

1. See GBM to Halleck, Oct. 18, note 2, *supra*.

To Henry W. Halleck   [TELEGRAM]

Head Quarters, Army of the Potomac,
Pleasant Valley Oct 22 1862 [2:30 P.M.]

Your dispatch of the 22nd (twenty second) [October 21] is received.[1] After full consultation I have decided to move upon the line indicated by the Presdt in his letter of the 13th inst[2] and have accordingly taken steps to execute the movement. I will inform you from time to time of the occupation of Leesburg, Hillsboro', Snickersville etc. I shall need all the cavalry & other reinforcements you can send me from Washington.

G B McClellan
Maj Genl

Maj Genl Halleck
Genl in Chief Washington D.C.

ALS (telegram sent), McClellan Papers (C-15:64), Library of Congress. *OR*, Ser. 1, XIX, Part 2, p. 464.

1. See GBM to Halleck, Oct. 21, note 1, *supra*. 2. See GBM to Lincoln, Oct. 17, note 1, *supra*.

To Henry W. Halleck   [TELEGRAM]

Head Quarters, Army of the Potomac,
Pleasant Valley Oct 24th 1862 [3:30 P.M.]

Referring to your telegram of 3.30 pm yesterday I understand the (20,000) twenty thousand reinforcements to be made up of Heintzelman

& Sigel's Corps.[1]Am I right in this or do you intend giving me (20,000) twenty thousand men in addition to these two Corps?[2]

If some of Bayard's Cavalry could join me by way of Leesburg it would expedite my movement considerably.[3] The trouble will be with the cavalry. I expect large numbers of horses early in the week. Of course I shall not wait for a complete remount.

G B McClellan
Maj Genl

Maj Genl Halleck
Genl in Chief Washington DC

ALS (telegram sent), McClellan Papers (C-15:64), Library of Congress. *OR*, Ser. 1, XIX, Part 2, p. 476.

1. Halleck had proposed in an Oct. 23 telegram to reinforce GBM with the corps of Heintzelman and Sigel from Washington, to join him by way of the Manassas Gap Railroad at Thoroughfare Gap in the Bull Run Mountains. *OR*, Ser. 1, XIX, Part 2, p. 470. 2. Halleck replied the next day that the figure of 20,000 men represented the two corps. *OR*, Ser. 1, XIX, Part 2, p. 483. 3. Brig. Gen. George D. Bayard commanded a cavalry brigade in the Third Corps.

To Henry W. Halleck

Brig Genl H W Halleck
Genl in Chief USA   Head-Quarters Army of the Potomac,
General   Pleasant Valley Oct 24 1862

Your letter of the 20th reached me only this morning.[1] As I stated in my dispatch of last evening[2] I had not contemplated the erection of other than field works in the vicinity of Harper's Ferry. On the heights there is little or no earth & the only recourse is to build blockhouses of dry or loose stone & timber. I have advocated the defence of Harper's Ferry on account of its importance in covering the line of the Potomac & not as a base of operations.

I hope that the boats will all be in position today for the construction of a bridge at Berlin. As soon as the bridge is finished I will place Stoneman at Leesburg, & occupy Waterford & Hillsboro. I will thus be in position, as soon as my cavalry is in reasonably good condition, to bring down the three Corps now near Sharpsburg & to effect rapidly the junction with Genls Heintzelman & Sigel as you propose. I think the occupation of Thorofare Gap a wise measure.

This will be handed to you by my aide de camp Lt Col Colburn who can explain to you the general state of affairs here, & who will receive your views as to the troops to be left in garrison at Harper's Ferry.

AL retained copy, McClellan Papers (A-85:34), Library of Congress.

1. In his letter of Oct. 20 Halleck rejected the idea of anything more elaborate than field works for the defense of Harper's Ferry. "Harper's Ferry is not, in my opinion, a proper

base of military operations, and it would be an error to expend time and money there for such an object." *OR*, Ser. 1, XIX, Part 2, p. 451. 2. GBM to Halleck, Oct. 23, *OR*, Ser. 1, XIX, Part 2, p. 469.

To Mary Ellen McClellan

[Pleasant Valley] Oct 25 [1862] am.

I hope my bridge at Berlin is finished & if so I can cross some troops today & shall be all ready to march the moment the cavalry is ready, which will be shortly. I don't think Lee will fight me nearer than Richmond — I expect no fight in this vicinity....

My report is at last finished & will I presume be copied today....

I see that there is much impatience throughout the country for a move — I am just as anxious as anyone, but am crippled by want of horses....

I sent Bishop McIlvaine[1] over to Harper's Ferry in my ambulance. He is accompanied by the Rev. Mr. Clements.

AL copy, McClellan Papers (C-7:63), Library of Congress.

1. Charles P. McIlvaine, Episcopal bishop of Ohio.

To Alexander S. Webb

Head-Quarters Army of the Potomac

My dear Webb   [Pleasant Valley] Oct 25 1862

I return herewith your Father's[1] letter which you were kind enough to send me. When you write to him tell him that I am most highly gratified by the kind feelings he entertains towards me, & that in the midst of the abuse with which I have been so roundly & frequently pursued it is indeed a comfort to find that I possess the good opinion of such a person as he is — it more than counterbalances the abuse.

I am sincerely your friend
Geo B McClellan

Col A S Webb

ALS, Alexander Stewart Webb Papers, Yale University Library. Lt. Col. Webb was chief of staff of the Fifth Corps.

1. James Watson Webb, minister to Brazil and former owner of the *New York Courier and Enquirer*.

To Albert V. Colburn   [TELEGRAM]

[Pleasant Valley, October 25, 1862]

Remain as you propose. Explain to Genl Halleck exactly the condition of our cavalry & what measures have been taken to obtain horses promptly. Also that it is yet impossible for me to fix the exact time when I will be at the points agreed upon. I hope by Monday [October 27] to be able to fix the day.[1]

G B McClellan
Maj Genl

Lt Col A V Colburn
Washington DC

ALS (telegram sent), McClellan Papers (A-86:34), Library of Congress. Lt. Col. Colburn was GBM's assistant adjutant general.

1. Colburn replied on this date that he had just seen Halleck. "There was no use of trying to explain matters to him because he would not listen to anything. When I spoke to him about the cavalry horses he said that that was the Quarter Masters business & he had nothing to do with it. I will try again but think it no use." McClellan Papers (A-86:34).

To Abraham Lincoln [TELEGRAM]

Head Qrs Army of Potomac

His Excellency the President　　[Pleasant Valley] Oct. 25 6 pm 1862

In reply to your telegram of this date,[1] I have the honor to state that from the time this Army left Washington on the 7th of Sept my Cavalry has been constantly employed in making reconnaissances, scouting and picketing. Since the battle of Antietam six Regiments have made one trip of two hundred miles, marching fifty five miles in one day while endeavoring to reach Stewart's[2] Cavalry. General Pleasonton in his official report, states that he with the remainder of our available Cavalry while on Stewart's track marched seventy eight miles in twenty four hours. Besides these two remarkable expeditions our Cavalry has been engaged in picketing and scouting one hundred and fifty miles of river front, ever since the battle of Antietam, and has made repeated reconnaissances since that time, engaging the enemy on every occasion. Indeed it has performed harder service since the battle than before. I beg you will also consider that this same Cavalry was brought from the Peninsula where it encountered most laborious service, and was at the commencement of this campaign in low condition and from that time to the present it has had no time to recruit.

If any instance can be found where overworked Cavalry has performed more labor than mine since the battle of Antietam I am not conscious of it.[3]

Geo. B. McClellan
Maj. Genl.

Retained copy, McClellan Papers (A-86:34), Library of Congress. *OR,* Ser. 1, XIX, Part 2, p. 485.

1. The president had seen a cavalry officer's report, forwarded by GBM, which stated that his horses were "absolutely broken down with fatigue and want of flesh," and he tele-

graphed, ''Will you pardon me for asking what the horses of your army have done since the battle of Antietam that fatigue anything?'' *OR*, Ser. 1, XIX, Part 2, pp. 484–85; *Collected Works of Lincoln*, V, p. 474. **2.** Maj. Gen. J. E. B. Stuart. **3.** On Oct. 26 GBM sent Lincoln a lengthy chronicle of the cavalry's record, and concluded, ''I feel confident you will concur with me that our Cavalry is equally as efficient as that of the rebels.'' *OR*, Ser. 1, XIX, Part 2, pp. 490–91.

To Henry W. Halleck   [TELEGRAM]

Maj General Halleck
General in Chief Washington

Head Quarters, Army of the Potomac,
[Pleasant Valley] October 25, 1862
10.45 pm

As the moment is at hand for the advance of this Army a question arises for the decision of the General in Chief, which although perhaps implicitly decided by the President in his letter of the 13th should be clearly presented by me as I do not regard it as in my province to determine it. This question is the extent to which the line of the Potomac should be guarded after this Army leaves, in order to cover Maryland and Pennsylvania from invasion by large or small parties of the enemy. It will always be somewhat difficult to guard the immediate line of the river, owing to its great extent and the numerous passages which exist. It has long appeared to me that the best way of covering this line would be occupying Front Royal, Strasburg, Wardensville and Moorefield at the debouches of the several vallies in which they are situated. These points, or suitable places in their vicinity, should be strongly intrenched and permanently held. One great advantage of this arrangement would be the covering of the Baltimore and Ohio Railroad, and an essential part of the system would be the construction of the link of railway from Winchester to Strasburg, and the rebuilding of the Manassas Gap Railway bridge over the Shenandoah. The intrenchment of Manassas Junction would complete the system for the defence of the approaches to Washington and the Upper Potomac. Many months ago I recommended this arrangement, in fact gave orders for it to be carried into effect.[1] I still regard it as essential under all circumstances.

The views of the Chief Engineer of this Army in regard to the defences and garrisons of Harper's Ferry and its dependencies are in your possession.[2] The only troops under my command outside of the organization of the Army of the Potomac are the Maryland Brigade under Gen. Kenly, the 54 Pennsylvania, Col. Voss' 12th Illinois Cavalry, Col Davis' 8th New York Cavalry — total 2894 Infantry, one battery and about 900 cavalrymen. There are also two of my regiments of Cavalry (about 750 men) guarding the Balto. and Ohio R. Road between Hancock and Cumberland.

As I have no Department and command simply an active Army in the field, my responsibility for the safety of the line of the Potomac and the states north of it must terminate the moment I advance so far beyond that line as to adopt another for my base of operations. The question for the General in Chief to decide and which I regard as beyond my province is this:

1st Shall the safety of Harper's Ferry and the line of the Potomac be regarded as assured by the advance of the Army south of the Blue Ridge and the line left to take care of itself?

2nd If it is deemed necessary to hold the line, or that herein before indicated in advance of it, how many troops shall be placed there, at what points, (and in what numbers and of what composition at each), and where shall they be supplied; i.e. from this Army or from other sources?

Omitting the detached troops mentioned above and the small garrisons of Boonsboro and Frederick, the last returns show the strength of this Army for duty to be about 116,000 officers and men. This includes the divisions of Stoneman and Whipple, but does not include Heintzelman, Sigel and Bayard.

If Harper's Ferry and the river above are rendered fully secure it is possible that the active army, if it supplies the garrisons may be reduced so much as to be inadequate to the purposes contemplated; if it is preserved intact Maryland, Pennsylvania and the Balto. & Ohio R. Road may be unduly exposed. I leave the decision of these grave questions to the General in Chief. I know nothing of the number of troops at Baltimore, etcetera.

An important element in the solution of this problem is the fact that a great portion of Bragg's Army is probably now at liberty to unite itself with Lee's command.

I commence crossing the river at Berlin in the morning, and must ask a prompt decision of the questions proposed herein.[3]

G. B. McClellan
Maj Genl Comdg

Retained copy, McClellan Papers (C-19:66), Library of Congress. *OR*, Ser. 1, XIX, Part 1, p. 84.

1. See GBM to Nathaniel P. Banks, Mar. 16, 1862, *supra*. 2. GBM to Halleck, with enclosures, Oct. 18, *OR*, Ser. 1, XIX, Part 2, pp. 441–42. 3. Halleck replied on Oct. 26, in part: "The Government has intrusted you with defeating and driving back the rebel army in your front. . . . You are informed of my views, but the President has left you at liberty to adopt them or not, as you may deem best. You will also exercise your own discretion in regard to what points on the Potomac and the Baltimore and Ohio Railroad are to be occupied or fortified. . . . I think it will be time enough to decide upon fortifying Front Royal, Strasburg, Wardensville, and Moorefield when the enemy is driven south of them and they come into our possession. I do not think that we need have any immediate fear of Bragg's army. You are within 20 miles of Lee's, while Bragg is distant about 400 miles." *OR*, Ser. 1, XIX, Part 1, pp. 84–85.

To Mary Ellen McClellan

[Pleasant Valley] Oct 26th [1862] am

... I move a respectable number of troops across the Potomac today — the beginning of the general movement, which will however require several days to accomplish — for the cavalry is still terribly off. I was mad as a "march hare" yesterday at a telegram received from the Presdt asking what my "cavalry had done since the battle of Antietam to fatigue anything" — it was one of those dirty little flings that I can't get used to when they are not merited.

AL copy, McClellan Papers (C-7:63), Library of Congress.

To Herman Haupt

[TELEGRAM]

Brigadier General Herman Haupt
Superintendant Mil. Railways
Washington

Head Quarters, Army of
Potomac [Pleasant Valley]
October 26th 1862 10.45 am

I have the honor to request you to ascertain how far the Leesburg R. Road is practicable.

I have also to request you to be ready to supply this Army via Orange and Alexandria and Manassas Gap Railroads; to take steps at once to reestablish the wharves etc. at Acquia, and to be prepared to rebuild the Railroad bridge over the Rappahannock at Fredericksburg, and to supply that road with rolling stock.[1]

Geo. B. McClellan
Maj. Gen. Comdg.

Retained copy, McClellan Papers (C-19:66), Library of Congress. *OR,* Ser. 1, XIX, Part 2, p. 494.

1. Haupt replied that afternoon that rebuilding the railroad from Washington to Leesburg was impracticable for any present campaign, but that he was prepared to repair the Orange and Alexandria and Manassas Gap railroads. Federal troops had destroyed the line between Aquia Creek and Fredericksburg and four months would be needed to rebuild the wharves and facilities at Aquia Landing. Considering the great effort involved, he requested instructions "as to the relative military importance of these roads & the order of priority in which they should be prepared for service." McClellan Papers (A-86:34).

To Abraham Lincoln

[TELEGRAM]

Head Quarters Army of Potomac
His Excellency the President   [Pleasant Valley] October 27 1862 3 pm

Your Excellency is aware of the very great reduction of numbers that has taken place in most of the old regiments of this command, and how necessary it is to fill up these skeletons before taking them again into action.

I have the honor therefore to request that the order to fill up the old regiments with drafted men may at once be issued.[1]

Geo. B. McClellan
Maj Genl Comdg

Retained copy, McClellan Papers (C-19:66), Library of Congress. *OR,* Ser. 1, XIX, Part 2, p. 496.

1. Lincoln replied on this date that the request "would be complied with as far as practicable. And now I ask a distinct answer to the question, Is it your purpose not to go into action again until the men now being drafted in the States are incorporated into the old regiments?" *OR,* Ser. 1, XIX, Part 2, p. 497.

To Abraham Lincoln

[TELEGRAM]

His Excellency the President   Head Qrs Army of Potomac
Washington   [Pleasant Valley] Oct 27 1862 7.15 pm

I have the honor to acknowledge the receipt of your dispatch of 5.10 pm today. Feeling deeply impressed with the importance of filling up the old regiments at the earliest practicable moment, I have upon several different occasions urged this measure upon the War Dept as well as upon Your Excellency, as the most speedy and effectual method of giving us effective troops for future operations. Some time ago an agent of the Governor of Pennsylvania informed me that an order from the War Dept was necessary to authorize the transfer of drafted men to the old regiments. On the 17 inst I requested Gen Halleck to have the necessary order given.[1] I received no reply to this, and learned this afternoon that no such order had been issued. In the press of business I then called an aide and telling him that I had conversed with you upon this subject, I directed him to write for me a dispatch asking Your Excellency to have the necessary order given. I regret to say that this officer after writing the dispatch, finding me still engaged, sent it to the telegraph office without first submitting it to me, under the impression that he had communicated my views. He however unfortunately added "before taking them into action again." This phrase was not authorized or intended by me. It has conveyed altogether an erroneous impression as to my plans and intentions.

To Your Excellency's question I answer distinctly that I have not and have not had any idea of postponing the advance until the old regiments are filled by drafted men.

I commenced crossing the Army into Virginia yesterday and shall push forward as rapidly as possible to endeavor to meet the enemy. Burnside's Corps and part of Slocum's have been crossing yesterday and today, and Reynolds' Corps is ready to follow. Pleasonton with the cavalry is at Purcellville this evening. The crossing will be continued as rapidly as the means at hand will permit. Nothing but the physical difficulties of the operation shall delay it.

Geo. B. McClellan
Maj. Genl Comdg.

Retained copy, McClellan Papers (C-19 :66), Library of Congress. *OR*, Ser. 1, XIX, Part 2, pp. 497–98.

1. GBM to Halleck, Oct. 17, *supra*.

To Herman Haupt [TELEGRAM]

Brigadier Gen Haupt
Supt Military Railways   Head Quarters Army of Potomac
Washington   [Pleasant Valley] Oct 27 1862   10 pm

Please take immediate steps to enable you to forward supplies via Orange & Alexandria & Manassas Gap Railroads for this Army, at the rate of seven hundred (700) tons per day. Also be prepared to repair the Orange and Alexandria Railroad beyond Manassas Junction, wherever it may be damaged. Please communicate to the General in Chief the information you gave me yesterday[1] in regard to the Fredericksburg Railroad and consult with him as to the possibility of repairing that road in season to use it for the purposes of this campaign.

Geo. B. McClellan
Maj Genl Comdg

Retained copy, McClellan Papers (C-19 :66), Library of Congress. *OR*, Ser. 1, XIX, Part 2, p. 498.

1. See GBM to Haupt, Oct. 26, note 1, *supra*.

To Henry W. Halleck [TELEGRAM]

Major Gen Halleck   Head Quarters Army of Potomac
Gen-in-Chief Washington   [Berlin, Md.] October 29, 1862 1.15 pm

On the 25th Inst I sent you a dispatch requesting you to decide what steps should be taken to guard the line of the Potomac when this Army leaves here. To this I received your reply that I had been intrusted by the President with defeating and driving away the rebel Army; that you had given me no orders heretofore, did not give me any then, etc.[1]

Under these circumstances I have only to make such arrangements for guarding this extended line as the means at my disposal will permit, — at the same time keeping in view the supreme necessity of maintaining the moving Army in adequate force to meet the rebel Army before us.

The dispositions I have ordered are as follows, viz:

Ten thousand men to be left at Harper's Ferry — One brigade of infantry in front of Sharpsburg — Kenly's brigade of infantry at Williamsport — Kelley's brigade including Col. Campbell's 54 Penna Infantry at Cumberland and between that point and Hancock — I have also left four small cavalry regiments to patrol and watch the river and the Baltimore & Ohio Railroad from Cumberland down to Harper's Ferry.

I do not regard this force as sufficient to cover securely this great extent of line, but I do not feel justified in detaching any more troops from the moving columns. I would therefore recommend that some new regiments of infantry and cavalry be sent to strengthen the forces left by me.

There should be a brigade of infantry and section of artillery in the vicinity of Cherry Run; another brigade at Hancock, an additional brigade at Williamsport, one regiment at Hagerstown, and one at Chambersburg with a section of artillery at each place if possible. This is on the supposition that the enemy retain a considerable cavalry force west of the Blue Ridge. If they go east of it the occupation of the points named in my dispatch of the 25th Inst. will obviate the necessity of keeping many of these troops on the river. There are now several hundred of our wounded including General Richardson in the vicinity of Sharpsburg that cannot possibly be moved at present.

I repeat that I do not look upon the forces I have been able to leave from this Army as sufficient to prevent cavalry raids into Maryland and Pennsylvania, as cavalry is the only description of troops adequate to this service and I am, as you are aware, deficient in this arm.[2]

Geo. B. McClellan
Maj Genl Comdg

Retained copy, McClellan Papers (C-19:66), Library of Congress. *OR*, Ser. 1, XIX, Part 1, p. 85.

1. GBM to Halleck, Oct. 25, and note 3, *supra*. 2. Halleck replied on Oct. 30, in part: "The troops proposed for Thoroughfare Gap will be sent to that place whenever you are in position for their co-operation, as previously stated, but no new regiments can be sent from here to the Upper Potomac. The guarding of that line is left to your own discretion with the troops now under your command." *OR*, Ser. 1, XIX, Part 1, p. 85.

To Mary Ellen McClellan

Berlin Oct [c. 29, 1862]

... It will not do for me to visit Washn now — the tone of the telegrams I receive from the authorities is such as to show that they will take advantage of anything possible to do me all the harm they can & if I went down I should at once be accused by the Presdt of purposely delaying the movement. Moreover the condition of things is such that I *ought not* leave just now — the army is in the midst of the preliminary movements for the main march & I must be at hand in this critical moment of the operation. ...

If you could know the mean & dirty character of the dispatches I receive you would boil over with anger — when it is possible to misunderstand, & when it is not possible, whenever there is a chance of a wretched innuendo — there it comes. But the good of the country requires me to submit to all this from men whom I know to be greatly my inferiors socially, intellectually & morally! There never was a truer epithet applied to a certain individual than that of the "Gorilla."

AL copy, McClellan Papers (C-7:63), Library of Congress.

To Mary Ellen McClellan

Berlin Oct 30th [1862]

... I have just been put in an *excellent* humor (?) by seeing that instead of sending the drafted men to fill the old rgts (as had been promised me) they are forming them into new rgts. Also that in face of the great want of cavalry with this army they are sending the new cavalry rgts from Penna to Louisville instead of hither!! Blind & foolish they will continue to the end.

AL copy, McClellan Papers (C-7:63), Library of Congress.

To Andrew G. Curtin   [TELEGRAM]

His Excellency A. G. Curtin
Governor of Pennsylvania   Head Quarters Army of Potomac
Harrisburg Pa.   [Berlin] October 30, 1862 9.30 pm

I am about leaving this line and leave behind me all the troops I can safely spare to hold Harper's Ferry and the line of the upper Potomac, but I do not consider the force sufficient to prevent raids and have so represented to General Halleck who informed me that he has no more troops to send. I leave Major Gen. Morell at Hagerstown in command from mouth of Antietam up to Cumberland. I urge that you expedite as much as possible the organization of the nine month drafted men that some of them may be sent with the least possible delay to Chambersburg, Hagerstown, Sharpsburg, Williamsport and Hancock to prevent the possibility of raids. If I could have filled the old Pennsylvania regiments with the drafted men I could have left men enough to have made your frontier reasonably safe. As it is I cannot do it with due regard to the success of the main Army, and beg to warn you in time. Without reference to the safety of the frontier I wish to urge again in the strongest terms the absolute necessity of filling the old regiments with drafted men.[1]

Geo. B. McClellan
Maj. Gen. Comdg.

Retained copy, McClellan Papers (C-19:66), Library of Congress. *OR*, Ser. 1, XIX, Part 2, p. 510. The same dispatch was sent to President Lincoln.

1. Curtin replied on Nov. 1 that troops raised in Pennsylvania were "under the command of the authorities of the United States, who, no doubt . . . will direct the proper dispositions to be made, unless, indeed, you have yourself the power to make them. . . . On behalf of this loyal commonwealth, . . . I have the right to, and I do, demand that her frontier shall be properly protected." *OR*, Ser. 1, XIX, Part 2, p. 528.

To Abraham Lincoln   [TELEGRAM]

Head Quarters, Army of the Potomac,
Berlin Oct 30 11.30 pm   1862

Reynolds has crossed. All the Army is in motion to follow the general movement. I ask your attention to my dispatches calling the notice of the General in Chief to the insufficiency of the preparations I leave behind me for resisting a raid, also to the fact that we are to have no reinforcements for the old Penna regts from the drafted men. No greater mistake has been made than the total failure to reinforce the old regiments. Please remember that I have clearly stated what troops I leave behind & that I regard the number insufficient to prevent a raid & that while the responsibility has been thrown upon me by Genl Halleck he has given me only limited means to accomplish the object.

I write this only to place the responsibility where it belongs & wish you to show this to Genl Halleck. I also wish before entering upon this important campaign again to inform you that I am most ill provided with cavalry & artillery horses, & that any statements to the effect that I have received for the active army under my command more than (2500) twenty five hundred horses for cavalry & artillery are totally untrue & that it is not until today that I have clothing enough in hand to supply the pressing wants of my men.

Destructive diseases are breaking out among the horses.

ALS (telegram sent), McClellan Papers (C-15:64), Library of Congress. The last page of this dispatch is missing.

To Mary Ellen McClellan

[Berlin] Oct 31 [1862] pm.

If I am successful in this campaign I think it will end in driving Stanton out — as he was good enough to say that he held office only for the purpose of crushing me, it will afford me great pleasure if I can in any honorable & open way be instrumental in consigning the rascal to the infamous fate he deserves. If I can crush him I will — relentlessly & without remorse. . . .

After midnight. ... From the dispatches just received I think I will move Hd Qtrs over the river tomorrow — the advance is getting a little too far away from me & I wish to have everything well under my own hands, as I am responsible.

AL copy, McClellan Papers (C-7:63), Library of Congress.

To Abraham Lincoln   [TELEGRAM]

           Head Qrs, Army of Potomac
His Excellency the President   [Berlin] Nov. 1 9.45 am 1862

I have the honor to inform you that all the Corps of this Army have crossed the Potomac except Franklin's which comes up this morning.

I have ordered an advance this morning and shall go forward from day to day as rapidly as possible.

The enemy in considerable force occupied Snickers Gap yesterday. They will be driven out today or tomorrow as soon as we can reach the position with sufficient force.

          Geo. B. McClellan
          Maj Genl

Retained copy, McClellan Papers (C-20:66), Library of Congress. *OR,* Ser. 1, XIX, Part 2, p. 523.

To Abraham Lincoln   [TELEGRAM]

     Head Quarters, Army of the Potomac,
     Purcellville [Va., November 2] 1862 4.40 pm.

A good deal of artillery firing on the front & right. I do not yet know whether it is at Snicker's Gap or Pleasonton at Uniontown. I go towards the sound at once. It seems that there will be serious resistance not far from here, but you can fully rely upon it that the Army of the Potomac will retain its reputation. The troops are not all yet up, but are moving as rapidly as they can. I directed Franklin to remain near the Potomac today, or a part of it, to obtain necessary articles of clothing. We are still entirely too weak in cavalry — [*crossed out:* every step in the power of the Govt should be taken to strengthen us in this arm at once] but I will do the best I can with what I have got — as I close the artillery firing is heavy.

          G B McClellan
          Maj Genl

A Lincoln
Presdt US

ALS (telegram sent), McClellan Papers (A-88:35), Library of Congress. *OR,* Ser. 1, XIX, Part 2, p. 532.

To Mary Ellen McClellan   [TELEGRAM]

Mrs McClellan   Hd Qrs near Middleburg
Government House   Trenton NJ   [November] 4 [1862] 11 pm

I am very well. Your father has gone back sick but nothing serious so do not be worried in the least. All goes well except secesh who are travelling too fast to meet my views. Expect no letters or teleghs for some days. Will write a few lines tonight. We have Ashbys Gap.

G B McClellan
MG

Received copy (War Dept.), Records of the Office of the Secretary of War, RG 107 (M-504:66), National Archives.

To Mary Ellen McClellan

Nov 4th [1862] 11.30 pm near Middleburg

... We are in the full tide of success so far as it is or can be successful to advance without a battle....

Tomorrow night I hope to strike the RR & telegraph again — no telegraph within 25 miles of this....

AL copy, McClellan Papers (C-7:63), Library of Congress.

To Mary Ellen McClellan

Nov 5 [1862] 9 pm camp near Rectortown

... After a considerable amount of marching & skirmishing we have worked our way thus far down into rebeldom. We have had delightful weather for marching & a beautiful country to travel through.

... We left Berlin on Sunday morning [November 2], the Hd Qtrs stopping at Wheatland, but I heard firing & rode to the front — going all the way to Snicker's Gap (to the top of the mountain) & spending the night in Snickersville. Next morning I rode to meet the train, but heard some more firing — & rode again towards the front, & spent the night near Bloomfield — camping some miles back. At Snickersville I got a bed in a house to sleep in — at Bloomfield I slept under a tree in the woods — so that last night I was very glad after another long ride to get to my tent again....

Pleasonton has been doing very well again — has had some skirmishing pretty much every day — today he came across Jeb Stuart & thrashed him badly. Jeb outnumbered him two to one, but was well whipped — there were some very pretty charges made.

AL copy, McClellan Papers (C-7:63), Library of Congress.

To Mary Ellen McClellan

Nov 6 [1862] 1 pm camp near Rectortown

The army still advances, but the machine is so huge & complicated that it is slow in its motions.

AL copy, McClellan Papers (C-7:63), Library of Congress.

To Abraham Lincoln   [TELEGRAM]

Head Quarters, Army of the Potomac,
Rectorstown Nov 7 11.30 a.m. 1862

A heavy snow storm today. No rations yet arrived here but hope for them within an hour or two. Burnside on the Rappahannock.

G B McClellan
Maj Genl

His Ex A Lincoln
Presdt Washington DC

ALS (telegram sent), McClellan Papers (C-14:64), Library of Congress. *OR*, Ser. 1, XIX, Part 2, p. 549.

To Abraham Lincoln   [TELEGRAM]

His Excellency the President   Head Quarters Army of the Potomac
Washington   [Rectortown] Nov. 7, 1862 4 pm

The Manassas Gap Railroad is in such poor running condition that I shall be obliged to establish my depot for supplies for the whole Army at Gainesville, until the Orange and Alexandria Railroad can be repaired beyond Manassas Junction. I am now concentrating my troops in the direction of Warrenton and have telegraphed Gen Haupt to repair the Orange and Alexandria railroad to the line of the Rappahannock as soon as it can be covered by our troops. The storm continues unabated.

Geo. B. McClellan
Maj Gen Comdg

Retained copy, McClellan Papers (C-19:66), Library of Congress. *OR*, Ser. 1, XIX, Part 2, p. 549.

To Mary Ellen McClellan

[Rectortown] Nov 7 [1862] 2 pm

... Sumner returned last night. Howard returned this morning. I go to Warrenton tomorrow. Reynolds is there now, Burnside at Waterloo — Bayard in front — Pleasonton & Averill are trying to catch Jeb Stuart again near Flint Hills. Couch is here & moves tomorrow towards Warrenton. Porter & Franklin are at White Plains. Porter moves tomorrow to New Baltimore, thence next day to Warrenton. Franklin moves day after tomorrow to New Baltimore. Sigel will remain at Thoroughfare Gap & the vicinity. The Manassas Gap road is in such bad order that we cannot depend upon it this far up for supplies. Gainesville will be the depot until the O & Alex. RR is open to Warrenton. We will have great difficulty in getting supplies by the O & Alex. RR — its capacity has been overrated. Lee is at Gordonsville — G. W. Smith was yesterday driven out of Warrenton. . . .

11 1/2 pm.   Another interruption — this time more important. It was in the shape of dear good old Burnside accompanied by Genl Buckingham, the Secy's Adjt Genl — they brought with them the order relieving me from the command of the Army of the Potomac, & assigning Burnside to the command. No cause is given. I am ordered to turn over the command immediately & repair to Trenton N.J. & on my arrival there to report by telegraph for future orders!![1]. . . .

Poor Burn feels dreadfully, almost crazy — I am sorry for him, & he never showed himself a better man or truer friend than now. Of course I was much surprised — but as I read the order in the presence of Genl Buckingham, I am sure that not a muscle quivered nor was the slightest expression of feeling visible on my face, which he watched closely. They shall not have that triumph. They have made a great mistake — alas for my poor country — I know in my innermost heart she never had a truer servant. I have informally turned over the command to Burnside — but will go tomorrow to Warrenton with him, & perhaps remain a day or two there in order to give him all the information in my power. . . .

Do not be at all worried — I am not. I have done the best I could for my country — to the last I have done my duty as I understand it. That I must have made many mistakes I cannot deny — I do not see any great blunders — but no one can judge of himself. Our consolation must be that we have tried to do what was right — if we have failed it was not our fault. . . .

8 am [November 8]   . . . I am about starting for Warrenton. . . .

AL copy, McClellan Papers (C-7:63), Library of Congress.

1. On Nov. 5 Lincoln addressed the order for GBM's dismissal to Halleck, authorizing him to execute it. The order was delivered by Brig. Gen. Catharinus P. Buckingham of the War Dept. *OR*, Ser. 1, XIX, Part 2, p. 549.

To the Army of the Potomac

	Head Quarters, Army of the Potomac
Officers & Soldiers	Camp near Rectorstown Va.
of the Army of the Potomac	Nov 7th 1862

An order of the President devolves upon Maj. Gen. Burnside the command of this Army.

In parting from you I cannot express the love and gratitude I bear for you. As an Army you have grown up under my care. In you I have never found doubt or coldness. The battles you have fought under my command will proudly live in our Nation's history. The glory you have achieved, our mutual perils & fatigues, the graves of our comrades fallen in battle & by disease, the broken forms of those whom wounds & sickness have disabled — the strongest associations which can exist among men, unite us still by an indissoluble tie. [*Crossed out:* Farewell!] We shall also ever be comrades in supporting the Constitution of our country & the nationality of our people.[1]

Geo B McClellan
Maj Genl USA

DS (in part ADS), Alexander Stewart Webb Papers, Yale University Library. *OR*, Ser. 1, XIX, Part 2, p. 551.

1. An endorsement by Lt. Col. Webb reads: "McC wrote the last part on this sheet for the first time. It is in his hand writing. Alex S Webb." The concluding sentence does not appear in the broadside issued to the troops at the time, which ends with the salute "Farewell!," but does appear in official publications. McClellan Papers (B-12:48), Library of Congress.

To Mary B. Burnside

My dear Mrs B   Warrenton Nov 8 1862 6 pm

From the bottom of my heart I console with you & congratulate my wife. In the midst of your troubles I am sure that you will fully appreciate the cordial feeling existing between Burn & myself. He is as sorry to assume command as I am to give it up. Much more so. Be sure that all will yet come out well. Old Burn is true & honest — his future will be all that you can wish. I hope to see you before many days. In the meantime

I am most truly your friend
Geo B McClellan

Mrs. A. E. B.

ALS, Charles B. Phillips Library, Aurora University.

To Mary Ellen McClellan

Warrenton Sunday am. November [9, 1862]

... I expect to start tomorrow morning & may get to Washn in time to take the afternoon train....

I shall not stop in Washn longer than for the next train & will not go to see anybody. I shall go on just as quietly as I can & make as little fuss as possible....

The officers & men feel terribly about the change — none worse than

Burnside who is almost crazy. I learn today that the men are very sullen
& have lost their good spirits entirely. It made me feel very badly yes-
terday when I rode among them & saw how bright & cheerful they looked
& how glad they were to see me. Poor fellows, they did not know the
change that had occurred....

AL copy, McClellan Papers (C-7:63), Library of Congress.

To Mary Ellen McClellan

Warrenton Nov 10th [1862] 2 pm

... I am very well & taking leave of the men. I did not know before
how much they loved me nor how dear they were to me. Gray haired men
came to me with tears streaming down their cheeks. I never before had
to exercise so much self control. The scenes of today repay me for all
that I have endured. I will leave here early tomorrow morning & hope
to leave Washn at 3 pm....

AL copy, McClellan Papers (C-7:63), Library of Congress.

TEN

THE CALL TO POLITICS
NOVEMBER 12, 1862–AUGUST 28, 1864

THE NEARLY twenty-two months covered in this section record General McClellan's version of his transition from soldier to presidential candidate. In July 1864, some five weeks before the Democratic nominating convention officially completed the transition, he spelled out his view of presidential ambition. "It is my firm conviction," he wrote, "that no man should seek that high office, and that no true man should refuse it, if it is spontaneously conferred upon him, & he is satisfied that he can do good to his country by accepting it. . . . " This idealized picture of the democratic process left unsaid the fact that over the months, with careful deliberation, he had made himself available should his party choose to confer the nomination upon him.

Throughout this period, although he was the senior general on the active list, he performed no military duties beyond writing a lengthy report of his fifteen months as commander of the Army of the Potomac and helping organize a militia call-up in New York State. Largely unstated in the correspondence presented here — nearly all of it previously unpublished — was the expectation of a return to command in some capacity. Each Union military crisis — the defeats at Fredericksburg in December 1862 and at Chancellorsville in May 1863, and the Confederate invasion of the North that was checked at Gettysburg in July 1863 — brought with it renewed pressure on the president to recall General McClellan. In 1864 the Blair family mounted an effort to see him returned to active service in exchange for his renunciation of all presidential ambitions — a scheme that McClellan describes here in a memorandum to Samuel Barlow and an unsent letter to Francis P. Blair — but this too failed of accomplishment. He retained his commission, taking as his example General Winfield Scott, who had run for the presidency in 1852 without resigning from the army.

Initially assigned to Trenton, New Jersey, by the War Department, McClellan soon changed his posting to New York City. There, as his letters indicate, his associations were largely with leading figures in the Democratic party, among them Barlow, August Belmont, and the editors of the two leading Democratic newspapers, Manton M. Marble of the *New York World* and William C. Prime of the *Journal of Commerce*. During the summer of 1863 the McClellans moved out of New York to a house on Orange Mountain in New Jersey, which would remain their residence until early 1865. Convinced that he was kept under surveillance by agents of Secretary Stanton and that his mail was opened, he entrusted the delivery of his correspondence to friends or messengers whenever possible. When forced to resort to the mails, he often referred in his letters to matters he dared not commit to paper but would tell his correspondent when they met.

Although it is not until writing his mother on December 6, 1863, that McClellan first recorded his thoughts on being a presidential candidate, he had committed himself publicly to the Democratic opposition some two months earlier, with the so-called Woodward letter. His endorsement of George W. Woodward, a Democrat of extreme conservatism and a representative of the peace wing of the party, for governor of Pennsylvania (October 12) was a decision pressed on him by that state's party leaders, who made the endorsement the price of their support of his presidential candidacy. Thereafter his correspondence becomes increasingly political in nature, covering relations with party leaders, his positions on major issues (particularly his stand on the war and on bringing it to a peaceful conclusion), and his replies to attacks on him by the Republican opposition.

In such letters as that of June 25, 1864, to Manton Marble, McClellan left no doubt that he intended to distance himself from the peace-at-any-price segment of the party. He believed (correctly) that the peace men were behind the postponement of the national convention to late August, and if their influence was that great, he told Marble, he would refuse to be the candidate. Marble and other supporters downplayed the peace wing's importance and persuaded him to accept if nominated. On the eve of the convention's opening on August 29, he seemed assured of being the Democrats' candidate, and all the signs seemed to point to his election in November.

To Henry W. Halleck   [TELEGRAM]

Maj General H W Halleck
Gen in Chief   Trenton NJ Nov 12 '62

I have the honor to report my arrival here with a portion of my staff at four this morning.

G B McClellan
Maj Genl USA

Received copy, Records of the Office of the Secretary of War, RG 107 (M-473:50), National Archives. *OR,* Ser. 1, XIX, Part 2, p. 574.

To Samuel L. M. Barlow

My dear Barlow   Trenton Friday am [November 14, 1862]

I have been trying in vain to reply to your kind notes to Madame & myself & can now say only a few words to thank you for your kind feeling — which is no more than I expected. I telegraphed you this morning, asking you to come to see me. I expect to go to Phila for one day on Monday [November 17] & shall probably go to New York on Thursday next — of that we will talk when I see you, which I hope will be today or tomorrow — as I shall try to shut myself up on Sunday. With my kindest regards, & those of Madame, to you & the "other Madame"

I am ever your friend
McClellan

S L M Barlow Esq

ALS, Barlow Papers, Huntington Library.

To Terrence Farley

Terrence Farley Esq
Chairman Comm on National Affairs
Dear Sir   New York Nov 22 1862

I have the pleasure to acknowledge the receipt of your letter of today embodying the Resolutions of the Municipal authorities of the City of New York tendering to me the distinguished honor of the hospitalities of the Metropolis.

I appreciate fully and feel most deeply this action of the Municipality — which I regard as one of the highest compliments that can be paid to a citizen of our country. At this particular moment it is especially gratifying to me to be thus assured that I possess the kind feeling & regard of the authorities of our greatest City. I trust that they reflect the sentiments of their constituents.

At any other time I would gratefully accept the hospitalities of the city, but I do not feel that it would be right for me to do so while so many of my former comrades are enduring the privations of war & perhaps sacrificing their lives for our country.

I trust therefore that you will permit me to decline a compliment I so little deserve, and that you will convey to the Honorable Mayor & Council my warmest & most grateful thanks for the great honor they have conferred upon me.

> I am my dear sir with high respect your obdt svt
>
> Geo B McClellan

ALS retained copy, McClellan Papers (A-88:35), Library of Congress. Farley was a New York City councilman.

To Charles P. Stone

Brig Genl C P Stone
US Volunteers Washington D.C.   5th Avenue Hotel New York City
General: Dec 5 1862

I have the honor to acknowledge the receipt of your letter of the 1st inst.[1]

The order for your arrest in February last was given by the Secretary of War — I had the order in his hand writing several days before it was finally carried into effect.

When the order was first given by the Secy he informed me that it was at the solicitation of the Congressional Committee on the Conduct of the War and based upon testimony taken by them.

On the evening when you were arrested I submitted to the Secy the written result of the examination of a refugee from Leesburg;[2] this information to a certain extent agreed with the evidence stated to have been taken by the Congressional Committee; & upon its being imparted to the Secretary he again instructed me to cause you to be arrested — which I at once did.[3]

At that time I stated to the Secy that I could not from the information in my possession understand how charges could be framed against you, that the case was too indefinite. On several occasions after your arrest I called the attention of the Secy to the propriety of giving you a prompt trial, but the reply always was either that there was no time to attend to the case or that the Congressional Committee was still engaged in collecting additional evidence in your case & were not yet fully prepared to frame the charges.

[*Crossed out:* You will remember that I ordered you to Washington a few days before your arrest — I at that time had the Secy's written order for your arrest, and it may not be irrelevant to state that on the morning of your arrival in Washington I went to the room of the Congl Comm. & there met the Hon Z Chandler,[4] whom I informed that you were in the city, *not* in arrest, & whom I requested to say to the Comm that I would be glad if they would send for you & confront you fully with all the witnesses & testimony against you, as I was confident that you would from your innocence of all improper motives, & could explain whatever facts were alleged against you. I believe that I some time since informed you verbally that when directed to order certain witnesses from your command to present themselves before the Congl Committee I officially informed the Chairman of the Committee[5] that these particular witnesses were in arrest under disgraceful charges — this was done that the Committee might know all the circumstances which might affect the weight due to their statements.[6]]

AL retained copy, McClellan Papers (A-88:35), Library of Congress. *OR,* Ser. 1, V, p. 345.

1. In his letter of Dec. 1 Stone called for a copy of the charges on which GBM had ordered his arrest on Feb. 8, 1862. *OR,* Ser. 1, V, pp. 344–45. 2. Allan Pinkerton to GBM, Feb. 6, 1862. McClellan Papers (A-39:16). 3. See GBM to Andrew Porter, Feb. 8, 1862, *supra.* 4. Sen. Zachariah Chandler. 5. Sen. Benjamin F. Wade. 6. One such witness was Col. George W. B. Tomkins, charged with "misbehavior before the enemy" at the Battle of Bull Run. GBM to Edwin M. Stanton, Mar. 24, 1862, Lincoln Papers, Library of Congress.

To Edward Everett

My dear Mr Everett　　　　　　　　　　5th Avenue Hotel Dec 7 /62

I owe you a very full apology for my long delay in replying to your most kind note of the 17th ulto.[1] I received it when very busy with preparations to go from Trenton to N.Y., & since my arrival here have had but few moments to myself.

I cannot express too warmly my very grateful appreciation of your kind feeling & good opinion of me, & I assure you that the approval of such as you far more than compensates me for whatever of abuse & detractions I may have undergone.

I am content to await the arbitrament of the future, conscious that I have at least endeavored to do my best for the cause of our country & that my mistakes were not intentional.

With the hope that you have ere this regained your health & again thanking you for your kindness

I am sincerely & respectfully your friend
Geo B McClellan

The Hon Edward Everett

ALS, Everett Papers, Massachusetts Historical Society. The statesman and orator Edward Everett had been governor of Massachusetts, congressman and senator, and minister to Great Britain.

1. Everett wrote on Nov. 17 to offer "the tribute of my admiration, not only for the consummate talent you have evinced in organizing and leading our armies . . . but of the discretion & dignity, with which you have conducted yourself, in the trying circumstances in which you have been placed," and to express the hope "that you will soon be recalled to the field. . . ." McClellan Papers (A-88:35), Library of Congress.

To August Belmont

My dear Mr Belmont —   5th Avenue Hotel Dec 7 1862

I owe you an apology for my delay in returning the copies of your letters which you were so good as to lend me.[1]

In reading them my greatest regret is that the administration could not be induced to act in accordance with your views — some such policy as that you urged must yet be adopted or we are lost.

I leave for Washington this evening, & hope to return in two or three days.

Your sincere friend
Geo B McClellan

August Belmont Esq

ALS, Belmont Family Collection, Rare Book and Manuscript Library, Columbia University. Belmont was national chairman of the Democratic party.

1. Letters Belmont had written to the president and other administration officials.

To Lorenzo Thomas

To the Adjutant General
Head Qrs of the Army
Sir.   Washington D.C. Dec 9, 1862.

I have the honor to request that the instructions requiring me to await orders at Trenton New Jersey may be so far modified as to authorize my taking post in the City of New York.

I propose to commence at once the labor of preparing my full official reports of the battles of the Peninsula and of the campaign in Maryland. I shall need for this purpose the assistance of a number of officers who were on my staff during those campaigns. I give their names herein below and ask that they may be assigned to temporary duty in the City of New York to report to me for the service indicated. The officers referred to are as follows:

1. Brigadier Genl. R. B. Marcy	late Chief of Staff HQ. AP	
2. Brig. Genl. S. Williams	Asst Adjt Genl	" "
3. Brig. Genl. Jas Hardie	Actg Asst Adjt Genl	" "
4. Colonel T. M. Key	A.D.C.	
5. Lt Col. E. McK. Hudson	"	
6. Lt Col. N. B. Sweitzer	"	
7. Lt Col. A. V. Colburn	"	
8. Lt Col. P. de Radowitz	"	
9. Capt. Arthur McClellan	"	
10. Capt. W. F. Biddle	"	
11. Capt. W. P. Mason	"	
12. Capt. J. C. Duane, Engr Corps	late Chief Engr	

It is probable that the services of a few other officers late of my staff or under my command may also be necessary to me. For them I will make special applications as the necessity arises.[1]

Very Respectfully Your Obdt Servant

Retained copy, McClellan Papers (A-88 :35), Library of Congress.

1. A memorandum in the McClellan Papers (A-107 :42) indicates that Hudson, Sweitzer, Biddle, Mason, Lt. Col. Edward H. Wright, and Maj. Herbert Hammerstein drafted portions of the report.

To Leslie Combs

My dear Sir   Washington, December 11, 1862

Your very kind letter of the 4th[1] has at last reached me, the envelope opened and the letter evidently read by some of the Government officials. I only hope that they were as well satisfied with the contents as I was. I thank you most sincerely for the kind judgment you — an old soldier — express of the last battles fought by the Army of the Potomac under my command. I am ready to stake all, upon my opinion, that the true line of operations against Richmond is by the Peninsula and that the greatest military blunder of the war was made when I was withdrawn from there.

McDowell could and ought to have joined me at Hanover Court-House, and the result of his junction with me, would have been the capture of Richmond. It was perfectly practicable and possible to reinforce me up to the time I abandoned the line of the James River. I believe that you are entirely right in your surmises that Mr. Lincoln and Mr. Stanton are the "high officials" who originated the idea of withdrawing the Army from James River. I will not venture upon criticism now, for I feel that this letter will, in all probability, be read by others than yourself before it reaches you. I will only say, that I think you are entirely correct in the judgment you pass upon *"Officials."* I hope that the one you mention is simply an "ass" but I fear he is a "knave" as well.[2] Permit me to express my high appreciation of the commendation you bestow upon the final operations of the Maryland Campaign. I *do* believe that something more was deserved than the reward of being placed upon the shelf. I accept however the case as it stands. I am not now disposed to complain, but I am confident that, before long, the time will come when the whole truth will be known.

With my warmest thanks for your kind feeling and sympathy,

I am my dear Sir, Yours

Geo. B. McClellan

Maj. Genl.

To Hon Leslie Combs

Copy, McClellan Papers (A-72 :29), Library of Congress. Combs was a veteran of the War of 1812 and a onetime leader of the Whig party in Kentucky.

1. Combs's letter of Dec. 4 commented on Halleck's recently published report as general-in-chief, dated Nov. 25. Terming the withdrawal from the Peninsula "military madness," Combs was critical of Halleck and McDowell. Regarding the Maryland campaign, he wrote: "Considering the materials you had to work with — *raw* and *dispirited* troops — I think your battle of Antietam, the most remarkable triumph in history, certainly our history." McClellan Papers (A-88:35). 2. The reference is to Secretary Stanton.

To Mary Ellen McClellan

[Washington] Dec 12, 1862

I did not get back from Mr. Blair's until three this morning. I met there Gov. Dennison & the chairman of the Mil. Com. of the House & was drawn into a very long explanation of the past.[1] I have sent over to the Court a written answer to the only remaining questions they seem to desire to ask, & if they do not require me to go there in person, I will be free from them. I have been summoned in Porter's case, but he will not be ready for me for some days, & I shall leave tomorrow morning & be with you in the evening....

Just summoned again to the Court!!

4.30 pm.   I went through quite an inquisition & was kept some time....

I then went to see the Surgeon Genl about our cripples & afterwards to the Comm. of Pensions to try to hurry up the papers of some of those poor cripples whom we saw, but the Commissioner had left his office & I failed in the object of my visit. I am writing now in Porter's rooms — those that Seth[2] had last winter. Fitz & I are the "great tabooed" — you would laugh to see how *some* officials fight shy in public, & then come to me privately to protest their devotion! It is too funny! I am to dine with Mr. Crittenden[3] & the Kentucky delegation this evening & have arranged to leave in the eleven o'clock train tomorrow morning & will be with you by ten that night....

I have not had a moment to myself & am more than ever tired of this wretched place. I hear that a battle is in progress on the Rappahannock — nothing yet indicates much progress — I fear the result will not be favorable & that Burnside will fail in his attempt.[4] I must close now & get ready for dinner.

Copy, McClellan Papers (D-10:72), Library of Congress.

1. GBM was in Washington to testify at a court of inquiry investigating Gen. McDowell. His meeting was with Postmaster General Montgomery Blair, former Ohio governor William Dennison, and Congressman Abraham B. Olin. 2. Seth Williams, of GBM's staff. 3. Congressman John J. Crittenden, of Kentucky. 4. The Battle of Fredericksburg.

To John Van Buren

5th Avenue Hotel
My dear Sir   Sunday am [December 14, 1862]

Mrs McClellan desires me to express her thanks for the beautiful flowers we found awaiting us on our return home last evening — and which are some consolation for our inability to dine with you. Mrs McC is not at all well this morning, so much so that I did not think it well for her to go out this damp day. We have therefore staid at home quietly instead of accepting your kind invitation to your pew.

I feel with you great anxiety as to the result of the battle now impending on the Rappahannock — I do not see that anything decisive was effected yesterday on our side, but as Franklin seems to have met with partial success & there are no indications of Hooker having been engaged I still hope for something better today.

Very truly yours
Geo B McClellan

John Van Buren Esq
Fourth Avenue

ALS, Miscellaneous Collections, Huntington Library. Van Buren was state chairman of the Democratic party in New York.

To August Belmont

5th Avenue Hotel
My dear Mr Belmont   Sunday evg [December 14, 1862]

When I sent you the copies of the letters you were so good as to lend me I thought that the accompanying was enclosed — I was in a great hurry at the time, just starting for Washington. I hope you will excuse my unaccountable delay in the return of these letters, all of which I have read with much interest.[1]

I fear that Mr L is busily engaged in breaking the rest of the eggs in the basket!

Is this the blackest hour which precedes the dawn?

Ever yours
Geo B McC

August Belmont Esq.

ALS, Belmont Family Collection, Rare Book and Manuscript Library, Columbia University.

1. See GBM to Belmont, Dec. 7, *supra.*

To Fitz John Porter

                                        5th Avenue Hotel
My dear old Fitz   Friday [December 19, 1862]

Your notes received. I have not dared to reply to them by mail — so much do I distrust the honesty of certain surroundings.

I am much disappointed in not receiving from Washington the telegrams I sent for. Tell Colburn that the copies of your dispatches to Burnside which were sent to me at Alexandria *must* be boxed up in Washington *or* at the Hd Qtrs of the Army of the Potomac. Have Colburn hunt them up & give them to you. I have *one* in my desk at Trenton which I will get for you & send by safe hand.[1]

I have only a few minutes to write & will therefore be brief. I *do* remember the Wms Burg reprimand, & the subsequent explanation which was fully satisfactory to me.[2] I can testify & I am confident that Marcy will do the same (tho' I have had no chance to talk with him about it) that if I had *any* fault to find with you it was on account of your extreme anxiety to get established & be off to Acquia.

You unquestionably gained time by leaving Wms Burg as you did & were right in so doing. Ask Colburn whether he can testify to these facts. If Marcy can I will simply write you "Marcy remembers." Of course I do not wish to go to Washn as a witness or anything else if it is unnecessary, but you must be sure that I am ready to go any where or to do anything in my power that will aid you — so don't hesitate to call upon me in any case of necessity.

You lost no time either on the Peninsula or at Fredericksburg.

I have a copy of my dispatch to you at Centreville — my memory is not clear about receiving a copy — have Colburn look it up.

I have no earthly doubt, Fitz, as to the result of your trial — you will come out brighter than ever & the wretched conspiracy against you will utterly fail.

I did not reply to your questions about the members of the Court — 1st because I did not believe I could get a letter to you unopened — 2nd because I really know but little of the members.

Hunter I distrust. I never saw him — but he is an enemy of mine. Buford I knew in Illinois — he is a graduate & *was* a good man & a good friend of mine. Garfield I don't know at all.[3]

I will work with you in this matter Fitz to any extent — our cause is the same & we must crush these fellows.

Marcy has just come in — he recollects my not liking your leaving Wms Burg, but knows nothing about the letter (the intercepted one).

So long as I am here you had better enclose your letters (except when private hand can be availed of) to Dr E E Marcy[4] 22 East 21st Street New York City.

> In great haste ever yours
> McC

F.J.P.

I am surprised at the feeling in my favor all over the North — it is almost unanimous.

ALS, Porter Papers, Library of Congress.

1. The reference is to dispatches sent by Porter during the Second Bull Run campaign, sought for his pending court-martial on charges of military misconduct during that operation. 2. See GBM to Porter, Aug. 17, 1862, *supra*. 3. Maj. Gen. David Hunter, Brig. Gen. N. B. Buford, Brig. Gen. James A. Garfield. 4. Mrs. McClellan's uncle.

To Fitz John Porter

My dear Fitz   [New York] Saturday [December 20, 1862]

I hoped to get the enclosed ready in time to go by Marble[1] but was disappointed. I send a copy of a letter you wrote me from Sharpsburg which I thought *might* be of interest or service to you.

The original of the letter from Centreville has a word or two missing as you will observe in the copy.[2]

Yours of the 15th reached me.

The monied men & the respectable men of this city are up in arms, their patience is exhausted & unless the Presdt comprehends the gravity of his situation I see great danger ahead.

Burnside must have conducted his withdrawal very skilfully to have succeeded so well — poor fellow how I pity him! I have defended him to the best of my ability.

The sacrifice of Saturday was an useless one — nothing gained, not even honor. Banks ought to have gone to the James River, & to the last moment I hoped that it was so.

The future looks dark & threatening — alas for our poor country! I still trust in God & bow to his will — he will bring us victory when we deserve it. A change *must* come ere long — the present state of affairs *cannot* last.

When will you probably want me as a witness? Will the Court sit during the holidays?

> Ever yours
> McC

I shudder, Fitz, when I think of those poor fellows of ours so uselessly killed at Fredericksburg!

ALS, Porter Papers, Library of Congress.

1. Manton M. Marble, editor of the *New York World*. 2. Probably Porter to GBM, Aug. 31, 1862. *OR*, Ser. 1, XII, Part 3, pp. 768–69 (misdated).

To Fitz John Porter

Dear Fitz   [Philadelphia] Thursday [January] 8th [1863]

Your two notes of 4th & 6th received.

The Hooker rumor has reached here — I hardly believe it true. I think the story about Burn, his resignation & recommendation to the Presdt is true.[1]

Of course the Presdt told a falsehood when he said that I had recommended a withdrawal — he had no grounds for such a statement & knew it to be false when he made it.[2]

I will take care that Halleck's way of urging Burn to advance of his own free will & accord is well known — I will quietly repeat it.

I fully agree with your views as to the crossing of the Rappahannock — it would be sheer madness & folly. You are certainly not far wrong in your estimate of the force now required to operate on Richmond — the whole aspect of affairs has changed & must be looked in the face or we shall only repeat the blunders of previous years.

I take it for granted that the fortifications of Richmond are now so strong that they must be reduced by "starvation, heavy guns & trenches."

Don't leave the service yet — be content to wait a while without a command & watch the boiling of the pot a little longer. Your notion about Rosecran's affair agree with mine — the result at Vicksburg fully explains it to my mind.

Joe Johnston regarded Vicksburg as the most important point — when he has got rid of Sherman he will take Grant & Rosecranz in hand — & concentrate upon them in succession.[3]

I shall be only too glad, Fitz, if my testimony has done you any good — your faithful service through so many long months should of itself have cleared you without the necessity of my opening my mouth.

I cannot imagine the possibility of your being hurt by the Court upon the evidence which has been given.

It is impossible for me to get on with Stanton — Harris[4] is entirely mistaken in regard to that. In fact a complete change of Cabinet & policy is necessary before any honest man of his country can do good. You may be sure that I will not be recalled until the Presdt is prepared to make an entire change.

I see in this morning's papers that *I* had *a long private interview with Genl Butler yesterday, that we were "fast & sincere friends" etc.*[5] I need hardly assure you that I did not see *Genl Butler at all* during his stay here, nor had I any interview with him in any way. I don't know that all this amounts to anything — but you are authorized to tell the truth if you think it worth while to correct the statement.

I expect to leave here on Monday — to stay over one day in Trenton — then after remaining a few days in N.Y. to go to Boston for a few days. I look anxiously for your defence & the finding of the Court — for although strong as adamant in the conviction that you merit reward instead of censure, I distrust so much all connected with the Administration that I cannot but be anxious.[6] I must close now, old fellow — God bless & preserve you.

Ever your true friend
McC

F.J.P.

ALS, Porter Papers, Library of Congress.

1. On Jan. 1 Burnside wrote the president that he, Secretary of War Stanton, and General-in-Chief Halleck had all lost the confidence of the country, and he offered to resign. *OR*, Ser. 1, XXI, pp. 941–42. 2. This appears to relate to the withdrawal from the Peninsula. 3. On Dec. 31, 1862, and Jan. 2, 1863, William S. Rosecrans fought the indecisive Battle of Stone's River, in Tennessee, and on Dec. 29, 1862, in Mississippi, William T. Sherman was repulsed in an attack on the defenses of Vicksburg. 4. Sen. Ira Harris, of New York. 5. Maj. Gen. Benjamin F. Butler. 6. On Jan. 10 Porter was found guilty and sentenced to be cashiered from the service.

To Samuel L. M. Barlow

My dear Sir   New York Jany 20 1863

Mrs McClellan desires me to acknowledge the receipt of your kind letter of yesterday, accompanying the title papers & insurance policies of the house No 22 West 31st Street.[1]

In doing so I cannot refrain from expressing the deep gratitude we both feel for this munificent token of personal regard on the part of gentlemen whose esteem & friendship we value so much — doubly pleasant from the fact that it makes us citizens of New York, & fixes our residence in the midst of so many kind friends.

For my own part, if I am again called to the field of battle, I shall go with a much lighter heart from the consciousness that my wife & child are no longer homeless.

With our most sincere thanks to you and your friends

I am truly yours
Geo B McClellan
Maj Genl USA

S L M Barlow Esq
New York

ALS, Barlow Papers, Huntington Library.

1. The house was a gift to Mrs. McClellan from several prominent New Yorkers, including Barlow, William H. Aspinwall, and John Jacob Astor, Jr.

To A. W. H. Clapp

Hon. A. W. H. Clapp, Portland:
Dear Sir,   Boston, Feb. 4, 1863.

I have the pleasure to acknowledge the receipt of the letter of Mr. Emery[1] accompanying the resolutions, adopted at a Convention of the citizens of Portland, inviting me to visit their city. I regret that I am still obliged to repeat the reply so reluctantly given to the deputation of gentlemen who did me the honor to call upon me on Monday — that it is not in my power at present to accept the very flattering invitation conveyed by them. Please convey to Mr. Emery and the gentlemen he represents my warm and sincere appreciation of the honor they have conferred upon me, and my heartfelt gratitude for their approval of my course as a public officer. If in the future I am again called upon to exercise active command, it will be with the same devotion to the cause of the Constitution and the Union that has actuated me in the past, and I trust I may be permitted to say that I shall feel all the stronger that I have gained the approval of so many of the citizens of Portland.

Again expressing my warmest thanks,

I am very respectfully and truly yours,
Geo. B. McClellan
Major General, U.S.A.

Boston Post, Feb. 6, 1863. Clapp headed a delegation that invited GBM to visit Portland, Me.

1. George F. Emery was chairman of a Portland citizens' committee.

To Horatio Seymour

Hon Horatio Seymour
Governor of New York
Governor   New York Feb 13/63

I take the liberty of presenting to you Captain Razderachin of the Russian Artillery, who desires to procure a commission in some one of our regiments or batteries that he may be enabled to see service during this war.

Difficulties have been thrown in his way — I think some rule has been made preventing any one from being with Head Quarters in the field unless they hold a commission — & I understand [from] Capt R. that it is mainly for this reason that he desires to obtain a commission.

When in Europe I received so many courtesies from the Russian Govt that I would esteem it as a special favor should circumstances enable you to gratify the desire of this young officer.

He will be able to show you his Russian Commission & other papers authenticating his position.[1]

> I am, Governor, with sentiments of the highest respect
> your friend & servant
> Geo B McClellan

ALS, Western Reserve Historical Society. Seymour had assumed the governorship of New York on Jan. 1.

1. Valerian Razderachin was commissioned a captain and appointed to a staff position in the Army of the Potomac.

To Edward Everett

22 West 31st Street
My dear Mr Everett   New York Feb 20/63

Your very welcome note of the 18th reached me yesterday.[1] Mrs McClellan & I were both of us much disappointed in not having the pleasure of your company from Hartford — will you permit me to offer our sincere sympathy in the family affliction which detained you.

I am much obliged to you for the very interesting note from the Prince de Joinville — I admire him so much that it affords me great pleasure to read *anything* from his pen.

I have been somewhat amused by the action of the Albany Senate — had they concurred in the House Resolutions I should simply have declined the proffered compliment as gracefully as I could, & the whole affair would soon have been forgotten — as it is they have probably injured themselves more than they have me.

I had a very pleasant interview with Gov Seymour a day or two ago & was much pleased with him — he quite won my heart & head, & I am glad to feel assured that he is a conservative as well as an able man. It is most fortunate that the State of New York may be regarded as in safe hands in these tumultuous times.

I will be glad to profit by your hint in regard to the "lenteur Americaine" — I had not observed the application made of it by Mr Stille, as I have not read his pamphlet with any care — in fact I merely glanced at a paragraph here & there — I am obliged to you for the suggestion.

The Report is making good progress, although it is a tedious, difficult, & disagreeable task — It is much easier to conduct campaigns & fight battles than to write their history — at least I find it so.

I cannot express to you the pleasure with which we look back upon our Boston visit — I never met with more warmth of feeling & sincere kindness.

By no means the least pleasant of the associations of the trip is the fact that we feel that we can now claim personal friendship with yourself.

Mrs McC desires me to enclose with this the photograph which you were so kind as to ask for — with her kindest regards as well as my own

I am most respectfully & sincerely your friend

Geo B McClellan

Hon Edward Everett

ALS, Everett Papers, Massachusetts Historical Society.

1. In his letter Everett remarked on the recent division in the New York legislature over a resolution in GBM's behalf. He also enclosed a copy of a letter from the Prince de Joinville, written July 10, 1862, expressing the hope that radical influences would not cause the Civil War to "degenerate into a war of extermination without end, ruinous to the North, and odious to the remainder of the world." Everett suggested that in his report GBM counter Joinville's theory, in his *Army of the Potomac*, of an American affinity for slowness *(la lenteur Américaine)*, "which Mr. [Charles Janeway] Stillé, in his pamphlet called 'How a free People conduct a long war,' endeavors to make an invidious application to yourself." McClellan Papers (A-89:35), Library of Congress.

To Benjamin F. Wade   [TELEGRAM]

New York, February 23, 1863.

If you can do me the favor to inform me upon what points the committee desire my testimony, I can greatly facilitate their objects and save much time by refreshing my memory by consulting papers before starting.[1]

George B. McClellan

Major General

Hon. B. F. Wade

Chairman on Conduct of War

Report of the Joint Committee on the Conduct of the War, I (1863), p. 108. Sen. Wade was chairman of the Joint Committee.

1. On Feb. 19 Wade had notified GBM that his testimony was desired. In his response on this date, Wade said information was wanted "generally on your military administration," and it was not possible to be more specific. *Report of the Joint Committee,* I (1863), pp. 107–108.

To Mary Ellen McClellan

Washington Wednesday 5 pm.

My own dearest little one   [February 25, 1863]

When we started from N.Y. we found no sleeping car & did the best we could with the very uncomfortable arrangements of the Jersey RR — when we got to Trenton we looked out for Wright[1] — but no Wright was to be found, & the delinquency was explained by a telegram from him today saying that the servants failed to awaken him, & that he will be here this evening. We were promised sleeping car at Phila, in chase of which we took a ride of 5 miles (it seemed 50) in street RR cars & reached the depot of the Baltimore Road just in time to strike the train & to ascertain the melancholy fact that there was not the slightest suspicion of a sleeping car there either. So we had to work through. I came the Caesar on myself, threw my cape over my head & retired into the privacy of private life to think of my own dearest little Nelly — (& you may be sure, sweetest one, that I *did* think of you all night long, when you, no doubt, were sound asleep) — so we reached Washn. As soon as we arrived I sent a note to the Hon B F Wade telling him that I was here & ready to be examined, he replied that he was too ill to attend, but that if I would go down any time after 12 they would call the Committee together & examine me. Then Hudson & I breakfasted, dressed & went down to the Capitol. I found only one member of the Committee (Cavode)[2] who told me that they would not be ready for me until ten tomorrow. Then I drove up town & fished up Sackett, with whom I went to call upon his poor wife. Since then I have seen Barry, Davis, Buford, Fox, Welles etc etc — *all* very friendly.[3] Rip van Winkle sent his kindest regards to you & John.[4] I also went to the office of L Thomas[5] to report my arrival — saw L who was disposed to be *very* friendly — also saw McDowell who was inclined to be my confrere, but he was met so coldly & politely that he was rather dumbfounded — I cut him very short.

Aspinwall telegraphed me today that Gen Morgan wished me to call on the Presdt — I will probably do so after dinner & will tell you the result.[6] I have invited Sackett, Davis, Ingalls, Buford & one or two others to dine with me today.

I will try to write again tonight — to my own sweet love, my own dearest darling Nelly

Ever with truest love your own
George

ALS, McClellan Papers (B-40:60), Library of Congress.

1. Lt. Col. Edward H. Wright; GBM was traveling with Lt. Col. Edward McK. Hudson, of his staff. 2. Congressman John Covode, of Pennsylvania. 3. Col. Delos B. Sacket, Brig. Gen. William F. Barry, Maj. Nelson H. Davis, Brig. Gen. John Buford, Gustavus V. Fox, Gideon Welles. 4. Presumably Col. Wright; John H. B. McClellan, GBM's brother. 5. Adj. Gen. Lorenzo Thomas. 6. Former New York governor Edwin D. Morgan. GBM does not mention a meeting with the president in the two letters that follow, and presumably it did not take place. It may have been intended to deal with his recall to the post of general-in-chief, which Montgomery Blair discussed with him the previous day in New York. However, when Blair returned to Washington he found Lincoln opposed to the idea. *Diary of Gideon Welles*, I, p. 345.

To Mary Ellen McClellan

My own dearest Nelly,   Washington
my own sweet wife   Thursday Feby 26 [1863] 3 1/2 pm

I went before the Committee today — they were very polite — & gave me something to do which will occupy me for a couple of days at least. I have sent for Key[1] to help me in preparing my record. I have many — very many — bitter enemies here — they are making their last grand attack. I *must & will* defeat them, for I know that I am right & that I have tried to do my duty. It is possible, not probable, that I may be detained here over Sunday — be sure my own dearest darling that I will not stay away one hour more than I can help. I am in a *battle* & must fight it out. I pray that God will aid me & give the right success. Kiss the dear little baby for me — God bless her — & believe me to be with truest love from your own fond husband

Geo McC

ALS, McClellan Papers (B-12:48), Library of Congress.

1. Col. Thomas M. Key.

To Mary Ellen McClellan

                                         [Washington] Willards Saturday
My own dearest darling   midnight [February 28, 1863]

Although I am tired nearly to death I can't go to bed without saying good night to you my own dearest one. I have just got back from that confounded Committee & have to appear before them again on Monday morning. I have been under their hands for several hours & you may imagine that my brain is *rather* tired out. I have been tramping up & down the Committee room for I don't know how long — my brain on a constant stretch, watching like a hawk for the training of every question, for fear that I should be tripped in some way or other. I dined yesterday very pleasantly with the Wyse's & after dinner Wright & I dropped in upon the Stoeckles — it was perfectly ridiculous the effect. We found the whole Diplomatic Corps there except Gerolt & it was very clear that they all thought there was some hidden meaning to the visit. Lord Lyons would not let me get out of his sight![1] Mrs. S was charming as ever. I saw Miss Robbins too, who is staying there. Today I half dined at Montgomery Blairs — that is I dropped in there for an hour while the Committee took a recess. I met there old Mr. Blair, head of the House, Fox & some ladies — a very pleasant party. I learn here that the Blairs have been strong consistent friends of mine through all the troubles of the past few months. I have all sorts of kind & pleasant messages for you from everyone I met. I am very sorry that I did not bring you on, for I find that I have no chance in Washn without you! Mrs. Stoeckle sent all sorts of kind messages for you — as did every one else that I met, & I sincerely believe, you little scamp, that you are far more popular in Washn today than your husband is.

I have been interrupted so often since I began this that it is after one o'clock & I have lost the thread of what I wanted to say, except that I miss you more than I can express, you dear little sweet darling. I can't help thinking when here of that awful morning when I had the confidential interview with you, when you did *not* love me, by a great deal.[2] I am foolish enough sometimes to feel sadly about it — to regret that the time *once was* when I did not possess your whole heart & soul. I can't realize *now* that such a state of things ever *could* exist, but it does make me feel sadly when I pass by the corner where we had those meetings, & I think how little you then realized the intense love I bore you. *Will* you understand it now — you do know *now* how I worship the ground you stand upon, God bless you. I *must* say good night now you dearest darling. I *hope* that I will be able to leave here Monday, but I don't know now. With fervent love, your own

George

ALS, McClellan Papers (B-12:48), Library of Congress.

1. The diplomats mentioned are Baron Stoeckel, of Russia; Baron Gerold, of Prussia; and Lord Lyons, of Great Britain. 2. GBM refers here to his first proposal of marriage, in June 1854, which was rejected.

To Fitz John Porter

My dear Fitz   [New York] March 11 1863

If your engagements will at all permit you to do so you can help us out very much by taking up the siege of Yorktown & putting it in shape. Hardie[1] has all the papers.

From your position at the time I think you can do the subject justice better than any one else.

When could you take it up — if at all?[2]

I have nothing new — have you?

Ever yours
Geo B McC

Maj Genl F J Porter

ALS, Rare Book Collection, Huntington Library.

1. Lt. Col. James A. Hardie. 2. Apparently Porter wrote, or at least edited, the Yorktown section of GBM's report. Porter to GBM, Mar. 18, 1863, McClellan Papers (A-89:35), Library of Congress.

To Elizabeth B. McClellan

My dear Mother   [New York] Sunday March 15 [1863]

Nelly wrote to you yesterday a note, that will go with this, asking you to come on and make us a visit — we are both most sincerely anxious that you should do so, for we shall not regard ourselves as fairly settled in our new home until you have been here to see what it is like. It is a very pleasant house & I am sure that you would like it very much. It is a bright cheerful house in itself, & in one of the most pleasant portions of the City — a part that was well in the country when you knew New York long ago, but now in the heart of the City. We are having a quiet time this evening — as we do not see company on Sunday when we can avoid it — for even in New York I think that one is entitled to one quiet day in the week. The baby has improved beyond description — has grown much, is as rugged as a young bear & talks a great deal — she is active as a cat & is never quiet for a moment except when asleep.

By way of compensation for the unnatural weather we have had during the winter, we are now luxuriating in cold weather — I presume you have the same — the skaters are rejoiced & the ice dealers more encouraged than they were.

When I returned from Washington I passed through Philadelphia at about 4 in the morning — as that was a rather unreasonable hour I did not think it worth while to wake you up & passed through without stopping — more especially as I had been absent longer than I expected when I left home. I hope not to be obliged to go to Washn again for a long time, but to be allowed to remain quietly in New York at least until my report is completed, which will be in a few weeks — for it is an immense task & will be a frightfully long production. Miss Helen Reece came to see Nelly yesterday — I did not see her — she told Nell that she had not seen me since I was 5 years old — but I think she must have been mistaken as I remember the family very well.

I hope that you *will* bring Mary on to see us. We are both very earnestly desirous of seeing you here & think you will enjoy it. Don't let anything prevent you from doing so. Nell's love & mine to Mary, John, Maria & the children — also to the Coxes & Phillips etc.

Ever your affectionate son
Geo B McClellan

ALS, McClellan Papers (B-41:61), Library of Congress.

To Robert C. Winthrop

22 West 31st St

My dear Mr Winthrop
New York March 25 [1863]

My conscience reproaches me for allowing your kind note of the 13th to remain so long unanswered. Permit me now to thank you for it, as well as for the Eulogy — which I have read with much interest.

I often wish that I could luxuriate among the books of the [*illegible*] Library & gratify my love for reading! We *are* really at housekeeping, & I can assure you that no two persons in the world enjoy the possession of a home more than my wife and myself. We have been such wanderers all our lives that the prospect of a permanent home is perfectly delightful to us.

The Eulogy has taken its place in my library — not a very large one, I must confess, for a vagrant soldier collects almost as few books as a rolling stone does moss — but still large enough to give me employment in the few leisure hours I have. In unpacking my books I find an old parchment bound copy of "Bernal Diaz" — the first edition, published in 1632. I purchased it from the library of a "Convento" in Puebla in /47 — is it of any interest or value to collectors? I never met with any other copy of that edition — but I do not know whether it is rare or the reverse.[1]

I remember that neither the "Padre Guardian" of the Convent, nor any of his "compadres" had ever read the book , or were even cognizant of its existence in their library until I unearthed it in my search for something readable among their shelves of bad theology!

We have not yet recovered, & I trust that we never shall, from the pleasant impressions made by our Boston visit. It is one of my dreams now to go there *quietly* and to enjoy Boston in a very leisurely manner.

Mrs McClellan desires me to send her kindest regards to your daughter & yourself — in which I beg leave to join, & to express the hope that we may soon see you in New York.

I am my dear sir most sincerely & respectfully
Your friend
Geo B McClellan

Hon Robert C Winthrop

ALS, Winthrop Papers, Massachusetts Historical Society. Winthrop, a long-time political figure in Massachusetts, had served in both houses of Congress.

1. Winthrop replied on Apr. 2 that a first edition of *The True History of the Conquest of New Spain* was not of great value at the time, but suggested GBM record the story of its acquisition on the flyleaf, and one day "I am sure it will command a price which might now seem fabulous." McClellan Papers (A-89:35), Library of Congress.

To R. J. Atkinson

R J Atkinson Esq
3rd Auditor Treasury Dept   Washington D.C.   New York
Sir: April 16 1863

I have the honor to acknowledge the receipt of your letter of the 18th
Nov last in reference to expenditure of monies advanced by the State of
Ohio for secret service.[1]

From the early part of May 1861 I placed the conduct of the secret
service Dept in the hands of Mr Allen Pinkerton & turned over to him
the money I received from the State of Ohio for that purpose. I enclose
with this Mr Pinkerton's account in detail of the monies thus expended,
this account being made out in the same form & in all respects on the
same basis as his accounts for similar services with the War Dept during
the last two years.

The amount expended is in excess of that drawn from the State of
Ohio, & was advanced from private means to meet exigencies as they
arose.

The balance found due should be paid Mr Allen Pinkerton whose
address is Chicago Illinois.

With the hope that this account will prove satisfactory to you

I am, Sir, very respectfully your obdt svt
Geo B McClellan
Maj Genl USA

ALS retained copy, McClellan Papers (A-90:35), Library of Congress.

1. Atkinson's letter of Nov. 18, 1862, requested documentation for some $12,000 in secret
service funds for which the state of Ohio was seeking reimbursement from the federal
government. McClellan Papers (A-88:35).

To Andrew A. Humphreys

Brig. Gen. A. A. Humphreys,
Fifth Corps, Army of the Potomac,
Falmouth, Va.:
General: New York, April 21, 1863

Your letter of the 13th instant is received.[1] It will afford me pleasure
to make the corrections your letter suggests in the full and final report
I am now preparing. My impression has been that your command was
not in condition to be thrown into action until near the close of the 18th,
if then; but I never attributed any blame to you or your troops for it,
regarding it as the necessary result of circumstances beyond your control.

I do not now see that any censure upon yourself could be implied from the paragraph you quote. None was intended.

> I am, very respectfully, your obedient servant,
> Geo. B. McClellan
> Major-General, U.S. Army

Copy, Fitz John Porter Papers, Library of Congress. *OR*, Ser. 1, LI, Part 1, p. 1009. Humphreys had commanded a Fifth Corps division in the Maryland campaign.

1. Humphreys wrote that GBM was in error in his recently published preliminary report on Antietam, dated Oct. 15, 1862, in giving as one reason he did not renew the fighting on Sept. 18 that "Humphreys's division of new troops, fatigued with forced marches, were arriving throughout the day, but were not available until near its close." *OR*, Ser. 1, LI, Part 1, pp. 1005–1006.

To Richard Wallach

Richard Wallach Esq
Mayor of the City of Washington
Sir:　　　　　　　　　　　　　　　　　　New York May 14 1863

I have the honor to acknowledge the receipt, through Mr. Altermehle and the Committee, of the Resolutions passed by the Board of Aldermen & Common Council of the City of Washington, expression of the appreciation of its citizens of my services in its defence, & tendering me their thanks.

I receive this expression of confidence with unusual pride and satisfaction, for I must confess that the most anxious hours of my life, and my most unremitting labors have been bestowed upon the safety of our Capital; which I once found entirely open & defenceless, and on another occasion threatened by a powerful & victorious army.

That those most deeply interested in the safety of the City are satisfied with the efforts of the troops I commanded, & their results, is a sufficient reward for our exertions. I beg that you will offer my sincere thanks to the gentlemen of the Board of Aldermen & of the Common Council, for the great honor they have bestowed upon me, and, with my thanks to you personally,[1]

> believe me to be very truly & respectfully your obedient servant
> Geo B McClellan
> Maj Genl USA

ALS retained copy, McClellan Papers (A-90:35), Library of Congress.

1. In addition to Washington and New York, a number of cities tendered similar resolutions of appreciation to GBM, including Baltimore, Albany, Buffalo, and Utica.

To James A. Hardie

Lt Col Jas A Hardie
Asst Adjt General   Washington D.C.
Sir: New York May 25 1863

I have the honor to acknowledge the receipt of a copy of a letter from Maj Genl Butler to the Secty of War, dated May 1 1863, with your endorsement thereon.[1]

Genl Butler has made an entirely erroneous statement in regard to my case.

As the facts really are his argument proves that I am unquestionably the senior Major General on the active list, whether of Regulars or Volunteers.

I shall therefore make no comments upon his argument, but correct his misstatements as they occur in his letter.

I was appointed a Major General in the Regular Army *not on the 24th of July 1861,* as he states, *but on the 14th of May 1861.*

I was notified by telegram of the fact on the evening of that day, and have now in my possession the original letter of appointment *dated & issued on May 14th,* received in due course of mail, and at once accepted.

General Butler asserts that he was appointed a Major General of Volunteers, was actually in the active service of the U.S. in command of a Department two weeks before any letter of appointment issued to any other Major General of the U.S. Army or Volunteers, and more than two months before any Major Genl of the U.S. Army was appointed after the rebellion, & that his letter of appointment was dated *May 16* 1861 & that he assumed command of the Dept. of S.E. Virginia on the 22d May.

Now the truth is that my appointment as a Major General of the Regular Army was *dated* and *issued* on the 14th of May 1861 — two days before his appointment as a Maj Genl of Vols, and six days before he assumed command of the Dept of S E Virginia; it will presently appear that I was already in command of a Dept under another & earlier commission.

Genl Butler also says that he was assigned to the command of the Dept of Annapolis (as a Brig. Genl) on the *27th April 1861* and that "at this time Generals McClellan and Banks were drawing their salaries as officers in their respective railroads." The fact is that on the *23rd of April 1861* I was commissioned and mustered in as a "Major General of the Ohio Militia *mustered into the service of the U.S.* under requisition of the Presdt dated April 15 1861." I entered upon the performance of my duty as a Major General on the same day — April 23 1861 — and from that date devoted my entire time and attention to my military duties, so that at the time specified by Genl Butler, April 27 1861, I was actively engaged in the command and organization of the Ohio troops.

There will be found on file in the Adjt Genl's office official letters from me of the date of *April 27* 1861 & earlier.

On the 3rd of May 1861 I was (as Major General of the Ohio Volunteers) assigned by the War Dept to the command of the Department of the Ohio, then consisting of the states of Ohio, Indiana & Illinois — prior to that my command was confined to the State of Ohio.

Thus instead of Genl Butler's appointment *being senior to mine by two months,* mine as a *Major General of the regular Army* is *senior to his in the Vols* by *two days,* while my appointment as a Maj Genl of Vols in the U.S. service is *senior to his* by *23 days,* & *senior even to his service as a Brig Genl.* In brief, I claim to be the senior Major Genl on the active list, whether of the Regular Army or Volunteers, because my actual appointment as a Major General of the Regular Army is prior to that of any other Major Genl, & because when I received *that* appointment I was actually performing the duty of the grade (comdg a Dept etc) under a Volunteer Commission under which I had been mustered into the U.S. service 21 days earlier than the date of my commission in the Regular Army.

So far as General Butler is concerned, I had received the appointment and entered upon the active duties of a Major General before the time he claims to have entered upon duty even as a Brig Genl.

By referring to the history of the present war it will be found that, prior to the date upon which General Butler erroneously says that I was appointed, I had as a Maj Genl of the Regular Army organized an Army & conducted a successful campaign, by which Western Virginia was restored to the Genl Govt, & an Army of the enemy destroyed.

I had supposed that every General Officer knew that I held a commission during that campaign. I respectfully request that you will lay this statement before the Secty of War, & that you will acknowledge its receipt.

I have the honor to be very respectfully your obedient servant

Geo B McClellan

Maj Genl USA

ALS retained copy, McClellan Papers (A-90:36), Library of Congress. Hardie, formerly of GBM's staff, was now serving at army headquarters in Washington.

1. Gen. Butler's eleven-page letter is fairly summarized by GBM. Seniority, Butler wrote, is "a right won in the service of the country, an honor to be prized, [and] I know you will commend me if I insist, with pertinacious firmness upon its complete acknowledgment." In his endorsement, Hardie asked for arguments on the matter so that it might be submitted to a board of officers. GBM's argument was correct in all respects. McClellan Papers (A-90:35).

To Charles C. Fulton

Private
Chas C Fulton Esq
Dear Sir   New York May 28 /63

Your letter of the 27 is received.[1] I regarded our conversation as en-
tirely a private one, brought on in consequence of the note of introduction
you brought to me from Judge Blair;[2] I had no idea of talking for the
public, nor that our interview should lead to any letters for publication.

Your letter as a general thing expresses my views, which you have
made in some cases rather stronger & wider than I intended, & in others
less so. But, for reasons which I need not explain, I have made it a rule
to avoid writing letters for publication, & have sought to remain as quiet
as possible, & I do not feel that the time has yet arrived for me to depart
from my custom, & I therefore request that my conversation may not be
regarded as a subject for publication.

With many thanks for your good opinion & kind feeling
                                     I am etc etc
                                       G B McC —

ALS retained copy, McClellan Papers (A-90:35), Library of Congress. Fulton was editor
of the *Baltimore American*.

1. Fulton had an interview with GBM on May 26, which he sought permission to publish.
He had understood GBM to say, he wrote, "that all talk of 'terms of peace' and 'conciliation'
and 'compromise,' with men arrayed in armed hostility to the Government, was simply
ridiculous, and never had or ever could receive any consideration or favor from you." He
further understood GBM's motto to be "Union first — peace last," and that whatever stood
in the way of reunion, "whether it be property in men, or property of other descriptions,
must be thrust aside, and that a cordial and enthusiastic support is due to the President
and the Government...." McClellan Papers (A-90:35). 2. Montgomery Blair.

To Samuel S. Cox

Hon S S Cox
Columbus Ohio
Dear Sir   New York June 8/63

I have the pleasure to acknowledge the receipt of your letter of the
31st intimating that it is possible that my name may be presented to the
Democratic State Convention of Ohio as a candidate for nomination as
Governor of that State.[1]

I feel the strongest interest in the welfare of a State whose gallant
sons have done so much for the country in its time of peril, & to which
I am indebted for the Major Generalship that called me again to the
military service of the U.S. but I should be compelled to decline the
nomination were it offered me.

Accept for yourself & offer to our friends my sincere thanks for this new evidence of their good opinion.

> & believe me to be very truly yours,
> G B McClellan

ALS retained copy, McClellan Papers (A-90:35), Library of Congress. Cox was a Democratic congressman from Ohio.

1. "You can be nominated with a perfect furor," Cox wrote on May 31, "and an election would be a foregone conclusion." If GBM did not accept the nomination, he added, he feared it would be captured by the peace Democrat Clement L. Vallandigham. McClellan Papers (A-90:35).

To Thurlow Weed

Private
My dear Sir   Oaklands[1] — June 13/63

Your kind note is just received.[2]

For what I cannot doubt that you would consider good reasons I have determined to decline the compliment of presiding over the proposed meeting of Monday next [June 15].

I fully concur with you in the conviction that an honorable peace is not now possible, and that the war must be prosecuted to save the Union and the Government at whatever cost of time treasure & blood.

I am clear, also, in the conviction that the policy governing the conduct of the war should be one looking not only to military success, but also to ultimate reunion, & that it should consequently be such as to preserve the rights of all Union loving citizens — wherever they may be — as far as compatible with military necessity.

My views as to the prosecution of the war remain substantially as they have been from the beginning of the contest — these views I have often made known officially.

I will endeavor to write to you more fully before Monday —
In the mean time

> believe me to be in great haste truly your friend
> Geo B McClellan

Hon Thurlow Weed
New York

ALS, Thurlow Weed Papers, Rush Rhees Library, University of Rochester. Weed was a veteran New York political manager associated with William H. Seward.

1. A country estate in the Hudson Valley, where the McClellans were visiting. 2. Weed wrote GBM on June 12 urging him to preside at a mass meeting in New York to rally support for the war, "availing yourself of the occasion to say that this Government and Union must be preserved; that both are worth all it may cost to save them;... and that

there can be no Peace until the authority of the Government is re-established.... Some such avowals from your lips, just now, would refresh the country.'' McClellan Papers (A-90:35), Library of Congress.

To Samuel L. M. Barlow

My dear Sam   Oaklands June 15 [1863]

I enclose a reply to the invitation — read it & send in if you think it will do — it is written very hurriedly & therefore must be bad.[1]

I had a telegram from Gov Seymour this evg. asking me to go to Albany to assist him in organizing troops called for from Washn — I replied asking when he wanted me & expect to go there tomorrow.[2]

I will see you within a few days, but this unexpected call overturns my calculations — I shall remain with the Gov as long as I can be of any real service to him. Will probably have my staff join me there, & try my hand at hard work again.

I will write to you from there — was sorry to miss you on Friday, but I had not time to go to your office.

Ever yours
McC

S L M X Q B

ALS, Barlow Papers, Huntington Library.

1. Either GBM's letter of June 13 to Thurlow Weed, *supra,* or a similar letter of June 11 to James T. Brady, an organizer of the mass meeting. McClellan Papers (A-90:35), Library of Congress. 2. Secretary Stanton had called for militia to meet an invasion of Maryland and Pennsylvania by Gen. Lee's army.

To Edward Everett

My dear Mr Everett   Orange New Jersey July 6 1863

On my arrival here a few days ago I found your kind note of the 18th ulto, with the enclosure, awaiting me.[1] Permit me again to express my thanks for the light in which you choose to view my relations with the present crisis, & for the kind manner in which you have written to the Presdt about me.

If one can believe the news this morning, the country, thanks to Genl Meade & the magnificent Army of the Potomac, is safe for the present at least — for it would seem that Lee will find full occupation in making his way homeward again.[2] What the effect may be upon the general policy of the Administration I cannot forsee — but it will clearly enable them to keep me in retirement, & I am only too glad that my services may not now be necessary.

After some unexpected & vexatious delays my report is now in the hands of the copyists, & will — I hope — be finished this week. If circumstances are such as to enable me to hold it back long enough I will take the liberty of sending it to you for revision — although it is possible that I may be obliged to send it in without further delay.

I am happy to say that quiet & country air have quite restored Mrs McClellan's health. She desires me to send her kindest regards to you

I am my dear Sir, in haste, most respectfully & truly,

Your friend

Geo B McClellan

Hon Edward Everett
Boston

ALS, Everett Papers, Massachusetts Historical Society.

1. With his letter of June 18 Everett enclosed an extract of a letter he had written President Lincoln on June 16 urging that GBM be restored to command of the Army of the Potomac. "Your order to that effect would be worth 50,000 men ... and it is a certain fact that General McClellan has the confidence of the entire Democratic party of both wings; of the Conservative party; and of the Conservative wing of the Republican party to a great extent." Everett urged GBM to accept the command if offered, even though it was unjust "to keep placing you, in moments of peril, at the head of demoralized armies. . . ." McClellan Papers (A-90:35), Library of Congress. 2. The Battle of Gettysburg was fought on July 1–3.

To George G. Meade

My dear General: New York, July 11, 1863.

I have abstained from writing to you simply because I hear that you have no time to read letters — but I will say a word now, anyhow.

I wish to offer you my sincere and heartfelt congratulations upon the glorious victory you have achieved, and the splendid way in which you assumed control of our noble old army under such trying circumstances.

You have done all that could be done and the Army of the Potomac has supported you nobly. I don't know that, situated as I am, my opinion is worth much to any of you — but I can trust saying that I feel very proud of you and my old Army. I don't flatter myself that your work is over — I believe that you have another severe battle to fight, but I am confident that you will win.[1]

That God may bless you and your army in its future conflicts is the prayer of

Your sincere friend

Geo. B. McClellan

Maj. Gen'l G. G. Meade
Comdg. Army of Potomac

George G. Meade, *The Life and Letters of George Gordon Meade* (New York, 1913), II, p. 312.

1. Meade replied on July 14 that already he detected a counter-reaction to his victory, "Lee having crossed the [Potomac] river last night without waiting for me to attack him in one of the strongest positions he has ever occupied. I do assure you General I appreciate in the highest degree, the value of your favorable opinion, and the A. of the Potomac will be delighted to know that their old & cherished commander watches & is gratified at their success." McClellan Papers (A-90:35), Library of Congress.

To Samuel S. Cox

My dear Cox   Orange New Jersey July 14 [1863]

Your kind letter of a month ago reached me some time after it was written, as I was for several weeks absent from home.[1]

I am very much obliged to you for the manner in which you managed the whole affair — I would have made no suggestions for any change.

I think you are quite right in not having my letter published — I hoped that no publication would be necessary, & felt sure that you would keep the affair as quiet as possible.

It seems that they had a terrible time in New York yesterday — & no one seems to know whether the disturbance is at an end or not — God help our poor country![2] I sometimes almost despair when I see so few who really comprehend the state of affairs! The Govt must come back to the true & original issues before it can hope to have the support of the great mass of the people — & without their cordial support I see but little hope for ultimate success.

With the hope that Morgan[3] wont reach Columbus & my sincere well wishes for you

I am ever your friend
Geo B McC

Hon S S Cox

ALS, Thomas F. Madigan Collection, Rare Books and Manuscripts Division, New York Public Library.

1. Cox wrote on June 13 that he had not read GBM's letter [June 8, *supra*] to the Ohio Democratic nominating convention, "so that no sort of embarrassment has been produced by the suggestion of your name" as a candidate for governor. "I have not had your letter published, altho' it would read well enough to the public, but it is best as it is." McClellan Papers (A-90:35), Library of Congress. Vallandigham won the Democratic nomination, but lost the election on Oct. 13. 2. GBM refers to the New York draft riot. 3. The Confederate cavalry raider John Hunt Morgan.

To Allan Pinkerton

My dear Allan: Orange, New Jersey July 17, 1863

Yours of the 10th was delayed a little in reaching me on account of my absence from the city, but it came I think in due course of mail. I am much obliged to you for it. I can well imagine the state of affairs you describe during the Battle of Gettysburg. I suppose, "How does it look now?" often passed over the wires.[1] To be trapped like a rat? What you say about Meade having been some days in command before it was announced, is very new to me — and not yet improbable — what is to be done with Hooker now?

James D. Horan, *The Pinkertons: The Detective Dynasty That Made History* (New York, 1967), pp. 136–37.

1. The president several times had sent this query to GBM during the Maryland campaign.

To Erastus Corning

Private
My dear Mr Corning   New York Aug 1 1863

I trust that I need not apologize to you for taking the great liberty of asking a favor.

I wish to call your attention to the case of Genl Fitz John Porter, in the hope that it may be in your power to do something for him. To explain the case better than I can in my own words I will give you an extract from a *private* note I received from Porter a few days ago — he says "I was anxious for occupation then — but now that the invasion of Maryland has rendered entirely dependent upon me my mother and my nephew (an invalid & a cripple) I am anxious for and am trying to get employment. Others are or soon will be dependent on my exertions. I did expect to weather the storm till another administration — but my sails have been rent, & my ship waterlogged. When in service my nephew & mother were dependent upon me — & what could be spared from my family went to them. Hence I saved nothing. . . . If there is any place coming to your knowledge which you think I can fill & get, I will thank you most kindly to speak a favorable word. I think I can do almost anything — or can make myself capable in a short time — and a will to please will be carried to my work. Do you know of any opening on railroads, or any supervision work?"

As this was in a private letter I would be glad that you should regard it as confidential.

I believe you know Porter & what he is — I will answer for his integrity, energy & ability.

If there *is* any opening on the Central R.R. I am sure that you would find a man of Porter's character & caliber invaluable.

I need not say to you how grateful I should be could you find it in your power to do anything for Porter. If *you* can do nothing, will you do me the favor to advise me in what direction to direct my efforts in his behalf.[1]

With my kindest regards to the ladies

I am sincerely your friend
Geo B McClellan

Hon Erastus Corning

ALS, Simon Gratz Autograph Collection, Historical Society of Pennsylvania. Corning was a New York financier and the president of the New York Central Railroad.

1. Some six months later Porter found employment in a mining venture in Colorado Territory.

To Lorenzo Thomas

Brig Genl L Thomas
Adjt Genl USA
General   New York Aug 4 1863

I have the honor to forward herewith my Report of the operations of the Army of the Potomac while under my command, together with accompanying documents.

They will be handed to you by my Aide de Camp Captain Arthur McClellan whom I send to Washington for this purpose.

In view of all the circumstances of the case I respectfully request permission to publish the Report.

I am sir very respectfully your obdt svt
Geo B McClellan
Maj Genl USA

ALS retained copy, McClellan Papers (A-90:35), Library of Congress.

To Edward Everett

My dear Mr Everett   New York Aug 4/63

Your very kind letter of the 25th reached me after some little delay.[1]

I thank you sincerely for your kind suggestions.

I agree with you fully that the Report of the Committee on the Conduct of the War merits little if any attention.

I had not, until I received your letter, heard of the rumor to which you allude, in regard to intentions entertained by leaders of the Democratic party of marching on Washington. I am satisfied that there is not one word of truth in the report, & you may rest assured that had such a thing been contemplated it would have received no countenance from me. I am sure that the Democracy have no intention of making any other opposition to the Administration than a strictly legal one.

I supposed that the prompt & energetic action of Gov Seymour in sending troops to Penna before the battle of Gettysburg would have convinced the most prejudiced of the entire loyalty of that gentleman, & all who act & think with him.

I write more fully to Mr Lawrence in regard to the other topic of your letter, & shall request him to show my letter to you.

We leave tomorrow for a quiet place at the sea side — East Hampton, Long Island — where we expect to spend a few weeks.

Mrs. McC — whose health is much improved — desires me to send her kind regards.

I am, my dear Sir, in haste most respectfully & truly yours
Geo B McClellan

Hon Edward Everett
Boston

ALS, Everett Papers, Massachusetts Historical Society.

1. Everett wrote on July 25 that the *Report of the Joint Committee on the Conduct of the War,* published earlier in the year, "made no impression on the public mind to your disadvantage. . . ." He also reported an "absurd rumor" current in Boston "that before Lee's repulse at Gettysburg, there was a project formed by certain Democratic leaders in New York & elsewhere, to raise a force, with you at the head, to march on Washington, and expel the present administration." To dispel such rumors, he seconded a proposal by fellow Bostonian James Lawrence that GBM clarify his views on the prosecution of the war so that neither friends nor enemies could continue to benefit by his silence. McClellan Papers (A-90:35), Library of Congress.

To Elizabeth B. McClellan

My dear Mother   East Hampton L.I. Aug 9 1863

I had fully intended to run on to see you before coming to this place, but was prevented by the delay in getting my Report finished — so that I was kept in N.Y. until the very day before starting hither.

This is a quiet old village — quite a jumping off place — way beyond railways & such modern inventions of the enemy. It is a village founded in 1649 which retains pretty much unchanged the habits & customs of that somewhat distant period. It is about one mile from the sea — by the road a little less in a direct line. There are no Hotels — no such modern inventions having reached here yet, & it being the sincere & continual prayer of the inhabitants that they may be preserved from "Hotels, Railways, Telegraphs, Mails, Newspapers, Bad Whiskey & all other pestilences." We have rooms in one quiet old house, & take our meals in another — the residence of a retired & one eyed Captain of a whale ship. Quite a number of people are boarding in the village in the same manner — but they seem to have a happy faculty of minding their own affairs, & don't trouble us much more than we do them — occasionally a wagon load of aborigines ride out to look at the wild beast — but soon depart quite contented with a frightened shake of the hands & a good stare.

We breakfast at 7 1/2 — loaf until 10 — then go to bathe — at least shall do so if they stop drowning people — dine at one — sleep in the afternoon — then walk or drive — tea at 6 — another talk or walk & then go to sleep! An unfortunate boy was drowned on Friday — so that bathing was suspended yesterday. But if nobody else is drowned meanwhile we will try it again tomorrow. Nelly and the baby are quite well — but suffering from the heat which happens by some strange chance to be quite intense just now — fortunately there are no mosquitoes & we have strong hopes that it will be cool again in a day or two.

Arthur tells me that the Coxe family was pretty generally drafted! I hope they will put Arthur on Sedgwick's staff & I presume they will.

Give my best love to Mary, John, Maria & the children — remember me kindly to the Coxes

            & believe me ever with warmest love from Nelly & the baby
                      your affectionate son
                      Geo B McC

ALS, McClellan Papers (B-13:49), Library of Congress.

To Samuel L. M. Barlow

My dear S L M   East Hampton L I Aug 11 1863

I have received your two kind notes, & am most obliged to you for them.[1]

I am very glad to learn that the Report is actually turned in, & that Arthur was assigned to Sedgwick's staff[2] — Arthur promised to write to me, but has not yet done so. I will write to Grant & Banks at an early day — within two or three days. We have had terribly hot weather here, & were almost discouraged, but a fine sea breeze has sprung up this evening & we hope for better things. If Crocker can give us rooms it is possible that we will go to New London next week — somewhere about the 18th or 20th. There are very few here whom I ever met before, & not a particularly interesting lot — but the bathing is superb.

With my kindest regards to Mrs Barlow when you write, & to Prime & Marble.[3]

                    I am ever sincerely yours
                    Geo McC

Won't you drop in at my house some day & see whether there are any letters of importance for me, expecially from Corning about F.J.P.

                    McC

ALS, Barlow Papers, Huntington Library.

1. In an Aug. 8 letter Barlow cited a *New York Herald* account that GBM's report had been filed at the War Dept. 2. Arthur McClellan was posted to the staff of Maj. Gen. John Sedgwick of the Sixth Corps. 3. Editors William C. Prime, of the *Journal of Commerce*, and Manton Marble, of the *New York World*.

To Samuel L. M. Barlow

My dear S L M   East Hampton L I Aug 17 1863

Your last note with the enclosed letters reached me on Saturday.

I have a note from Ketchum[1] urging me to let him take the Report to his office — & I think it will be best to do so. I have written to him that he might have it — but said to him that it was my only copy & that you were having another made by your clerks in their leisure hours. I am half sorry he wants it, but he has taken so much trouble for me & acted such a friendly part that I do not feel that I ought to disoblige him. We shall not get to New London before Friday [August 21] — & *perhaps* not then, as we have not heard from Crocker, to whom I wrote about a week ago. I hope, however to hear from him this evening.

We have nothing new here, & I am not bothered by news from other parts of the world.

In haste ever yours
McC

S L M Barlow Esq

ALS, Barlow Papers, Huntington Library.

1. Hiram Ketchum, who frequently wrote to newspapers in GBM's defense.

To Samuel L. M. Barlow

Pequot House [New London, Conn.]

My dear Sam   Thursday [August 27, 1863]

I take the liberty of addressing to you the commission of Baron Or-dustrom, a Swedish officer sent to me by Gov. Seymour. I have written to him to call for it at your office, & have done so because I am not certain that a note to the care of the Swedish Consul would reach him. Had a very pleasant sail, & fishing to a comfortable extent. Can get the Madgie for Monday if Prime will take the Fisher's Island trip. Do come on Sunday if you can.

Ever yours
McC

Hudson writes that they are devoting themselves to "paperasse"[1] & red tape in the Army of the Potomac, & that the soldiers have altered the close of their favorite song to read as follows

"McClellan was our leader, now he is gone.
God help us all as we are marching along!"[2]

ALS, Barlow Papers, Huntington Library.

1. "Official papers." 2. The standard chorus of William B. Bradford's "Marching Along" included the lines, "McClellan's our leader, he's gallant and strong / For God and our country we are marching along."

To Samuel L. M. Barlow

My dear Barlow   [New York, c. September 25, 1863]

From what I hear I doubt whether the performance tonight will be through in time for me to see you this evening.

I have heard about all that can be said in regard to the Penna proposition & shall give it full & fair consideration[1] — but I see that I can do nothing in the way of cool thinking here — so I shall do that part of it in Orange.

Say to Gov Church[2] that I shall not be prepared to give a final answer tomorrow morning, & that I will write to you on the subject tomorrow.

The matter is at that point where more talking will do no good — I must decide it for myself & in my own way. Further pressure would only induce a negative decision — to which I confess that I am inclined.

Marcy arrives tomorrow morning.

In great haste ever yours
McClellan

S.L.M.B.

ALS, Barlow Papers, Huntington Library.

1. The matter of endorsing the Democratic candidate for governor of Pennsylvania. See GBM to Charles J. Biddle, Oct. 12, *infra*. The immediate question was whether GBM should make an appearance in Philadelphia. He did so, arriving on Sept. 29. 2. Sanford E. Church, former lieutenant governor of New York. Church and Gov. Seymour, Barlow wrote GBM on Sept. 26, "honestly believe that you can save the election in Pa. by your mere presence. The same opinion is expressed by very many of your warmest personal, political and army friends." McClellan Papers (B-23:53), Library of Congress.

To Charles J. Biddle

Hon Chas J Biddle
Phila
Dear Sir   Orange New Jersey Oct 12 1863 —

My attention has been called to an article in the Phila Press asserting that I had written to the Managers of a Democratic meeting at Allentown disapproving the objects of the meeting, that if I voted or spoke it would be in favor of Gov Curtin.[1]

I am informed that similar assertions have been made throughout the state [*crossed out:* for the purpose of inducing persons supposed to be friendly to me to cast their influence against Judge Woodward in the coming election].

It has been my earnest endeavor, heretofore, to avoid participation in party politics, & I had determined to adhere to this course [*crossed out:* so long as my regard for the interests of the country would permit, for my profession is that of a soldier, not a politician].

But it is obvious that I cannot longer maintain silence under such misrepresentations. I therefore request you to deny that I have written any such letter or entertained any such views as those attributed to me in the Phila Press, and I desire to state clearly and distinctly that, having some few days ago had a full conversation with Judge Woodward, I find that our views agree and I regard his election as Governor of Penna called for by the interests of the nation.

I understand Judge Woodward to be in favor of the prosecution of the war with all the means at the command of the loyal states, until the military [*crossed out:* & political] power of the rebellion is destroyed; I understand him to be of the opinion that, while the war is waged with all possible decision and energy, the policy directing it should be in consonance with the principles of humanity & civilization, working no injury to private rights & property not demanded by military necessity & recognized by military law among civilized nations; and, finally, I understand him to agree with me in the opinion that the *sole* great objects of this war are the restoration of the unity of the nation, the preservation of the Constitution, & the supremacy of the laws of the country.

Believing that our opinions entirely agree upon these points, & that he feels, as I do, that the maintainance of our national unity is of vital necessity, I would, were it in my power, give to Judge Woodward my voice & my vote.[2]

Geo B McClellan

ALS retained copy, McClellan Papers, Illinois State Historical Library. Biddle was state chairman of the Democratic party in Pennsylvania.

1. In the Pennsylvania gubernatorial election, Republican governor Curtin was being challenged by Democrat George W. Woodward, of the state supreme court. See also GBM to Henry M. Naglee, Sept. 23, 1864, *infra*. 2. As published in the *Philadelphia Press* on Oct. 13, the day of the election, this closing sentence read: "Believing that our opinions entirely agree upon these points, I would, were it in my power, give to Judge Woodward my voice and my vote."

To William Adams

My dear Doctor   Orange New Jersey Nov 18 1863

Next to seeing you en propre personne your kind letter of the 16 was the most acceptable event.

I regret very much that you cannot yet see the way clear to making us a visit, & that I missed you the other day. When we were last in the city it was a business visit & we were fully occupied — so that we really had no leisure to see any of our friends — but I will see you when I next visit the city.

We have not yet decided when to return to the city — probably not before the beginning of December if then. We shall remain here as long as the weather will permit — it is so much more quiet here.

I can hardly express my gratitude to Mr Stokes for his friendly thoughtfulness in regard to the seats in Church — I shall write to him on the subject, but will you, if you chance to see him in the mean time, say to him how warmly Mrs McC & I thank him for his goodness, & how fully we appreciate his regard.

I will try to write something for the Round Table. How many pages manuscript would be required? I don't think I should care to have my name appear. I must confess that situated as I am at present I would not object to increasing my income somewhat by the use of my pen.[1]

With *our* warmest regards to your family & yourself

I am as ever your sincere friend

Geo B McC

Rev Wm Adams

ALS, George B. McClellan, Jr., Papers, Library of Congress. Adams was pastor of the Madison Avenue Presbyterian Church in New York.

1. Between December 1863 and March 1864 *The Round Table,* a new journal of opinion, would publish five unsigned articles of military analysis by GBM.

To Abraham Lincoln

His Ex Abraham Lincoln etc
Your Excellency   New York Nov   1863[1]

When the present war commenced I was successfully engaged in private life. Actuated solely by the desire to serve my country, I sacrificed all my personal interests, and accepted the Commission of Maj Genl in the Regular Army which you bestowed upon me without any solicitation from me. I have never applied to you directly or indirectly for any particular command position or duty, but have contented myself with performing to the best of my ability whatever duties you imposed upon me. It was in this spirit that I conducted the campaign of Western Virginia, and after its successful close I assumed control at Washington of the troops just defeated at the first battle of Manassas, organized and commanded the Army of the Potomac, received without being asked and gave up without complaining the position of Commander in Chief of the U.S. Armies, conducted the Peninsular Campaign, witnessed the transfer of my army to the command of Genl Pope, resumed it when the combined forces had been defeated and the Capital was in hourly peril, carried on the Maryland Campaign, and, thanks to my noble and tried comrades, gained the battles of South Mountain and Antietam, and it was in this spirit that, when in full advance with every probability of a successful battle impending, I again, and finally, yielded the command of that Army to which I was united by those inexpressibly close bonds which a soldier alone can appreciate.

I have been now for more than a year unemployed, and it is evident that my services are no longer desired by your Excellency. Under these circumstances I feel that I can be of no present use to my country by retaining my Commission, and I am unwilling longer to receive pay while performing no service.

It is now my duty to consult my private interests and those of my family — which I have entirely ignored and sacrificed during my continuance in service.

As a fitting opportunity has offered, and my conscience tells me that I have faithfully performed all the service I at present can for the benefit of my country, I have determined to return to private life, and have sent to the Adjt Genl the resignation of my Commission, which I beg may be at once accepted. Should unexpected, and I trust improbable, vicissitudes of fortune ever again, as heretofore, render my sword necessary to the nation, I shall again be ready to use it in her cause at any sacrifice to myself.

It would have been gratifying to me to have retired from the service with the knowledge that I still retained the approbation of your Excellency — as it is, I thank you for the confidence and kind feeling you once entertained for me, and which I am unconscious of having justly forfeited. I cannot, nor ought I to restrain myself from bidding through you a last farewell to the heroic men who so long fought under my command.

Neither time nor space can divide them from my heart; whatever fate the future may have in store for me, my pulse will ever beat more quickly, and my blood warm at the thought of the soldiers who were with me during the trying scenes of the Peninsula, at South Mountain & at Antietam.

I am grateful to Providence that it was permitted me that my last service should be to free the Capital a second time from danger and the loyal states from invasion.

I am content to bear as a legacy to my descendants the connection which already exists between my name and that of the proud Army of the Potomac. It can have far abler Commanders than myself, and may win even more glorious victories than those which now grace its annals, but it can have no General who will love it so well as I did.

I invoke upon it and the other Armies of the Republic the highest blessings of the Almighty, and in severing my official connection with your Excellency I pray that God may bless you, and so direct your counsels that you may succeed in restoring to this distracted land the inestimable boon of peace founded on the preservation of our Union and the mutual respect & sympathy of the now discordant and contending sections of our once happy country.

Geo B McClellan

ALS, McClellan Papers (A-91:36), Library of Congress.

1. GBM seems to have written this letter of resignation in anticipation of taking the presidency of the New Jersey Railroad and Transportation Co., offered to him on Nov. 19. He did not take the post, however, and the letter was not sent. J. J. Astor, Jr., to GBM, Nov. 19, 1863, McClellan Papers (A-91:36).

To Elizabeth B. McClellan

My dear Mother   Orange New Jersey   Dec 6 1863

Your kind & welcome letter of the 3rd reached me all right. I did not suppose that you would forget my birthday, but it was very pleasant to receive a letter from you written on that day. It so happened that we spent the most of that day in Newark — Col Wright's[1] little boy was to be christened & I was his God-father — so we went over early in the day, went to Church for the christening & then back to the house for a lunch, & reached home almost dark. The ceremony went off very well — as the baby did not cry & I did not drop him!! You see I am becoming quite skilful. We have not seen Mason[2] & his wife yet — he promised to let us know when they returned to New York, so we will probably see them during the coming week. I received the letter from Arthur which Mary[3] sent me on the 25 ulto & enclose with this a reply which I will be glad to have sent to him by the underground military.

I don't think Grant's army will get far enough down in Alabama to disturb Frederica[4] at their plantation — they are likely to remain quiet even if Mobile should be taken, as no gun boat of any size could get that far up the Alabama river. We have not fully decided as to remaining out here all winter, but shall almost certainly do so until Christmas. It is probable that it may prove too unpleasant in Jany & Feby — but if no change occurs in my own situation meantime, it is quite likely that we will remain here all winter. It is splendid for the baby — who rushes about in the open air looking more like the inhabitant of a shanty than anything else. Nell has a pretty good photograph of May which she will send you this week — I think you will like it. May talks now almost like anybody else — & moves anywhere & everywhere. We go in town this week on a visit of two or three days at Mrs. Alsop's — May goes with us. There are two or three weddings to come off which we can't well avoid attending, so we will kill two birds with one stone.

Marcy has just been ordered off on another tour of inspection — the Dept of Missouri this time — he will probably start tomorrow. He & Mrs M went into the city yesterday so that Nell & I have been entirely alone — a good quiet time. We had quite a bonfire on the Mountain a few nights ago — a house (not quite finished) burned down — we knew nothing of it until the next day, as it was at some distance from us. We are altogether alone on the Mountain now — all the families whom we know having some time since moved into the city. There are six houses in all on the Mountain. Has Eck Coxe[5] come back to be drafted? If he don't look out he may go down to pay Arthur a longer visit than he expected — in that event advise Arty to take him as his orderly!!! I feel very indifferent about the White House — for very many reasons I do not wish it — I shall do nothing to get it & trust that Providence will decide the matter as is best for the country.[6] Nell & the baby send their best love to you & Mary — Marcy & Mrs. M would were they here. Give Nell's love & mine to John, Maria & the children — to the Coxes & Boxes, & Phillips also. Tell Mary to write — & I wish you would oftener, my dear Mother — I will anyhow —

Ever your affectionate son
Geo B McC

ALS, McClellan Papers (B-13:49), Library of Congress.

1. Col. Edward H. Wright. 2. Capt. William P. Mason. 3. GBM's brother and sister. 4. Frederica M. English, GBM's married sister. 5. Eckby Coxe, a family friend. 6. In her letter Mrs. McClellan had written: "The Democrats say, the *War Democrats,* that George B. McClellan, is to be the next President...." McClellan Papers (B-22:52).

To Samuel L. M. Barlow

My dear S L M   [Orange] Dec 25 [1863]

The insurance on the house expires on Jany 3d as you supposed.

I find a copy signed by Sheldon & Co of an agreement to publish my report & pay me 15% copyright.[1] I fancy I signed a similar copy, but am not certain as I left the matter pretty much to Marcy.

I did not have time to see them about it before I left town — if you think of it when passing by will you speak to them & see what they want to do now?

On my return here I found Arthur. He was on a 10 days leave & has gone back to Phila — so I have had no time to think more about H's introduction.[2] I will write to you about it by tomorrow for certain unless I find that I am going to the city on Monday.

Merry Christmas!

Ever your friend
McC

ALS, Barlow Papers, Huntington Library

1. GBM's *Report on the Organization of the Army of the Potomac, and of Its Campaigns in Virginia and Maryland* would be published by the Government Printing Office in Feb. 1864. In March an edition enlarged to include GBM's account of the western Virginia campaign was issued by the New York publisher Sheldon & Co. 2. Apparently this is a reference to G. S. Hillard's *Life and Campaigns of George B. McClellan*, which would be published in Aug. 1864.

To Robert C. Winthrop

My dear Mr Winthrop   Orange New Jersey Jany 1 1864

Your very kind note of the 24th reached me only yesterday, as I had not visited the city for several days, for we are still residing in the country. I trust it is not necessary for me to assure you of my extreme gratification at hearing from you again, & knowing that my wife and myself are still so kindly remembered by you & your daughter.

In these days when I sometimes hear that one old friend is angry with me because I said something, another because I said nothing, a third because I would not do something that was impossible to do, a fourth because I did something that I could not avoid doing, it is most gratifying to hear that I still have some such friends left as Dr Adams & yourself — who have charity & exercise it.

You may be sure that we will both read your book,[1] & I know that we will find it of great interest, for the longer I live & the more I see of men the deeper interest do I feel in the words of the past, which seem to me ever to show that the passions of poor human nature have not changed much from the earliest ages.

The passions which have brought us to our present unhappy condition surely are not new ones, but simply the outcropping of those which have agitated the world from the beginning of its history.

Mrs McClellan desires me to thank you most warmly for your kind remembrance of her, & to unite with me in wishing a *very* happy New Year to your daughter & yourself. God grant that the New Year may be a happier one than the past for our poor country!

With kindest regards to you & yours

I am most truly & respectfully your friend
Geo B McClellan

Hon Robt C Winthrop
Boston

ALS, Winthrop Papers, Massachusetts Historical Society.

1. The recently published *Life and Letters of John Winthrop*.

To Samuel S. Cox

Private

My dear Cox   Orange Feby 12 [1864]

Your kind note of yesterday is received.[1] I have no personal objection to the passage of Schenck's bill — I would rather be fired out of the service than resign. If I am turned out by such a bill I fancy that I shall retain a claim (in equity at least) to the Seniority of Rank which I now hold & of which it is sought to deprive me. Some future Administration may recognize this claim. I would rather, in the present state of affairs, be a private citizen again — & as I have said before I would rather be turned out than go of my own accord.

As to the Maryland Legislature affair I do not think that I initiated the matter — it came I *think* from Seward. I doubt very much whether there is any letter of mine in the War Dept on the subject. The facts of the case, for your private benefit, are these:

At the time of the arrest the Army at Washington was still weak & not in condition to take the field & fight a general battle. Intelligence reached us, I *think* through Seward, that the Secesh members of the Maryland Legislature intended to meet at Frederick (an illegal act under the Constitution of Md), secretly pass a Secession Ordinance, secretly send it to Jo Johnston, who was at once to move into Maryland & raise a general disturbance. This information seemed at the time to be thoroughly reliable. The danger was great — in a military point of view we were not prepared to resist an invasion of Maryland — the only chance was to nip the whole affair in the bud — which was promptly done, as a matter necessary for the safety of the military position of Washington & the troops there. I look upon this as an entirely different matter from the arbitrary arrests in loyal states, & have no apology to make.[2]

I will write to one or two who were then with me who will probably remember more of the details as to the way in which it was initiated than I now do & inform you.

Please don't fail to let me see you when you next come this way — I want a "talk" with you.

In haste sincerely your friend
Geo B McC

Hon S S Cox

ALS, Charlton L. Lewis Papers, Yale University Library.

1. Cox wrote on Feb. 11: "There is a bill today introduced by [Robert C.] Schenck to retire Generals. It is a blow at you." He also reported that "the Republicans have a letter of yours, or rather that it is in the War office, initiating the arrest of the Maryland legislature [in Sept. 1861] ... ; some of your friends are anxious about it." McClellan Papers (B-14:49), Library of Congress. 2. See GBM to Banks, Sept. 12, 1861, *supra*.

To Edward Everett

My dear Mr Everett   New York Feby 17 1864

I beg that you will receive for yourself, and convey to the other gentle-
men to whom I am so much indebted, my grateful thanks for the unex-
pected and most agreeable evidence of continued regard which I have
just received from you.

You could not have determined upon a gift more delightful and use-
ful to me than the books which you have been so good as to present to
me.[1]

In no other form could I be so constantly reminded, were a memento
necessary, of the kind friends whom I am so fortunate and proud to
possess in Boston.

It may gratify you to know that had I been consulted as to the selection
I would not have changed the list, and that it contains works which I
have long been most anxious to possess.

I will do my best to make good use of them, and if, after the quiet life
which now seems to be my lot, I should ever again be called upon to serve
my country, I trust that the use I shall meantime have made of your
magnificent gift will have changed my views and made me better fitted
to do good.

As I cannot thank each of our friends individually I hope you will be
good enough to convey to them my most sincere thanks for the most
acceptable and superb mark of their regard & friendship
                    And believe me ever your sincere & respectful friend
                                        Geo B McClellan

Hon Edward Everett
Boston

ALS, Everett Papers, Massachusetts Historical Society.

1. In his letter of Jan. 29 Everett wrote that he and a number of GBM's Boston friends
were making him a gift of books ''interesting to the statesman, the student of history, and
the general reader ... as a small token of our gratitude for your public services, and of
our respect for your personal character.'' He enclosed a list of the forty-seven titles, many
of them multi-volume works. McClellan Papers (B-14 :49), Library of Congress.

To Edward H. Wright

My dear Wright   Orange March 2/64

Yours from Newark & that of 13th Feb reached me, but I have been
so much occupied with the N.Y. edition of the Report that it has been
impossible for me to reply to any letters until today, & now I can do no
more than write a line to let you know why I am so dilatory & to urge
you to write to me often. I hear from all quarters that the Report is doing

much good, & opening many eyes. I am glad that you have directed your share to the Army — for I am especially anxious that it should be circulated there.

I shall be free to write you a long letter in a few days — when I get my desk cleared off — now I only send my kindest regards to Madame & to your Father & Mother — in which my wife joins — & baby sends her love to Minnie — about [*torn*] she constantly prattles at a great rate. My wife stopped at your house in Newark the other day, & came away richer by a banquet.

In haste ever your friend
McC

E.H.W.

ALS, Miscellaneous Collections, Huntington Library.

To William C. Prime

My dear Prime　　　　　　　　　　　　[Orange, c. March 8, 1864]

The writer of the accompanying was a Col in the Vols & wrote to ask me if I had any objection to his translating my Report into French.[1] I replied that he was very welcome to do so, and received the note on the other side. I don't understand the working of these things. Would his proposition, request rather, interfere with Sheldon? What shall I tell him?

It is immaterial to me whether it is translated or not — tho' I suppose it would be very well to have it circulate in as many languages as possible, not omitting Sanscrit & Chinese.

In haste ever yours
McC

W.C.P.

ALS, McClellan Papers (B-14:49), Library of Congress.

1. In a letter dated March 5, Lionel J. D'Epineuil, formerly a colonel in the 53rd New York, requested the exclusive right to prepare a French translation.

To Samuel L. M. Barlow

My dear S L M　　　　　　　　　　　New York March 9/64

Sheldon sent me this morning a check for $1500 as part payment etc.[1] I have sent $1000 to pay my other debt & send with this the balance ($500) as part payment on my account with you.

Won't you ask Taylor to let me know at once how much more I owe you — for I am very anxious to feel that I am out of debt so far as owing you — tho' I never can, nor wish to, pay you back all the kindness I have received from you. I wont have time to see you to day — as I am very busy.

Ever yours
Geo McC

S L M B

ALS, Barlow Papers, Huntington Library.

1. An advance against royalties for the Sheldon & Co. edition of GBM's *Report*.

To Reverdy Johnson

Personal

My dear Senator   Orange New Jersey March 9 1864

Yours of the 3d being directed to me in New York reached me only yesterday as I happened not to visit the city for several days. An unexpected visit from my brother has rendered it out of my power to reply to it until this moment. Please accept my apology for my apparent neglect in so long delaying a reply.

It is entirely untrue that I was on a gun boat during the battle of Malvern Hill. In the morning, after having arranged the lines of battle & made every preparation I went on a gun boat with Capt Rodgers to do what I did not wish to trust to anyone else — i.e. examine the final position to which the Army was to fall back. I returned immediately and was with Genl Porter near the left of the line before the enemy made his first attack, nor did I leave the land during the continuance of the battle. You will find the whole story in my report. I can conscientiously say that during the whole Seven Days my personal movements were made in accordance solely with my sense of duty — that I went wherever I thought my presence as the Comdr was of most benefit to my Army.

I confess that I have grown callous to the multiplied attacks made upon me, for I know that my men understand me and that history will do me justice. I suppose you have seen the last absurd falsehood of the Tribune in regard to a supposed interview with Genl Lee during, or just after, the battle of Antietam.[1] It fortunately happens that during that campaign I did not have any communication with Genl Lee, or any other rebel officer, even upon the subject of prisoners, wounded etc — communications which usually follow every battle of consequence. Of course I need not say to you that the whole story is made from the whole cloth.

I feel perfectly contented to allow these people to lie to their hearts content — I don't believe any respectable people credit what they say. I had a note from Mr Ketchum this evening, enclosing yours of the 7th to him.

Allow me, my dear Mr Johnson, to thank you most warmly & sincerely for the able & friendly way in which you sprang to my vindication — I shall ever be most grateful to you for it, as I was already for the friendship you evinced towards my persecuted & most wronged friend Fitz John Porter.

Again apologizing for the length of time that has elapsed without my replying to your letter

I am ever, most respectfully, your sincere friend
Geo B McClellan

Hon Reverdy Johnson
U.S. Senate

ALS, Reverdy Johnson Papers, Library of Congress. Johnson was senator from Maryland.

1. On Mar. 7 the *Washington Chronicle* and the *New York Tribune* first reported the tale of one Francis Waldron, who claimed GBM and Lee met at Antietam and agreed that the Confederate army would withdraw unopposed. Waldron proved to be an alcoholic and the story a hoax.

To William C. Prime

My dear Prime   Orange [March] 10th [1864]

Is it absolutely authentic that the exchange of prisoners has been resumed — and if so is it to such an extent as to render it advisable to discontinue all efforts in regard to replying to those prisoners' letters?

I see they have *my* bill up in the House[1] — I hope Cox & the rest of them do not intend to waste their time by spending weeks in making speeches about it.

If I were not principled against taking any steps in such a matter I should write to Cox & say that it would gratify me if nothing should be said by the Democrats on the subject — that some *one,* Cox for example, should rise & simply state the fact that the bill would dismiss me if passed & then let the vote be taken. Do you know that it sometimes occurs to me that if I am really the one aimed at it would be no more than decent for me to save the necks of other innocent men by throwing up my commission at once & stating the reason thereupon! Can you find out what the real animus is?

In great haste ever yours
McC

W.C.P.

ALS, McClellan Papers (B-41:61), Library of Congress.

1. See GBM to Cox, Feb. 12, *supra.*

To Manton M. Marble

My dear Marble   Orange N.J. March 12 1864

I enclose a note & slip received from Cox. I have told him that I hardly think it worth while to notice it, but that I would leave it to your judgment.

Of course there is not a word of truth in it. I have not seen Lee since April 1855 — when on my way to Europe — and had no communication whatever with him during the Maryland campaign. Nor did I see any envoy of Lee's in any way that could possibly give color to the lie — I don't think I ever saw Mr F Waldron (if he is the liar) in my life. I gave no safe conduct for any rebel officer to come through my lines — So much for that.[1]

What will they start next? What are you doing stealing my thunder from the Round Table & copying it into the World?[2] Somebody will accuse me next of helping you and S.L.M.[3] in the work of editing that "awful" paper!

Ever yours
McC

Manton Marble Esq

ALS, Marble Papers, Library of Congress.

1. See GBM to Johnson, Mar. 9, note 1, *supra*. 2. GBM's articles of military analysis were being published anonymously in *The Round Table*. 3. Samuel L. M. Barlow was a major investor in the *World*.

To Elizabeth B. McClellan

My dearest Mother   Orange New Jersey March 13 1864

Time flies so rapidly and so quietly in this out of the way place that I really have nothing new to tell — unless I would commit to paper the wise sayings and new pranks of the baby who is improving every day & is certainly an improvement on all other babies who have been heard of or described heretofore. She is very quiet — strange to say — this Sunday afternoon, but I will venture to guess that her voice will be heard, or she will rush in here on a raid before I finish this scrawl. She is quite an intelligent being in these days — talks, in her own way, quite as much to her own satisfaction as any one else of more mature years can, & rules the house generally. But she is as good a child as ever was, never gets mad unless she loses her temper, or has some other equally good reason for it, & is very tractable, especially when her general views agree with those of those around her. There! I knew it! Here she is — large as life & quite as important! She has managed to blacken her face & is quite proud of the achievement. As Nell is lying down I suppose there is a lark on foot & a general frolic — if it is Sunday! Seriously speaking, & without prejudice, I think she is the brightest & best little thing that ever was. She is in perfect health, & runs about in the most ready fashion with but little regard to weather. This year in the country has been a splendid thing both for her & for Nell — who is stronger, in better health, & looking more beautiful than for years past — probably since she left school.

I think it was a good thing for all of us that we were able to pass this winter quietly in the country, instead of in the midst of the excitement and worry of New York life — which is all very well in its way, but decidedly fatiguing. Little George[1] is here, & improving very rapidly I think — he looks better & says that he is stronger. I fear the little fellow finds it very dull, as there is no one in the vicinity of his own age — but if the weather continues good he can be out in the air most of the time & soon pick up. Nell & I are obliged to go to the city tomorrow for a few hours & will take him with us. New York is quite busy at present with preparations for the Sanitary Fair[2] — how it will turn out I have no means of knowing, but people expect a great success — it certainly ought to produce more than any of the others, tho' many of the cities have done very well. I am sorry to see that Meade's health is reported bad — I fear it is only a dodge to get rid of him, & put some more pliant man in his place.

I am inclined to think that it is time that Grant desires Smith W F to be in command of the Army of the Potomac. So Grant has his Lieut Generalcy![3] Well — they might have found many much worse men to give it to, & I am glad to see that he wears his great honors so modestly — it is a very good feature in his character. I suppose *my bill* will pass this week — dismissing me from the service, with Buell etc. I shall be glad of it, as I wish to serve this Administration no longer, & do not like to resign.[4] I shall be glad to be once more in private life, & it will be very difficult to get me out of it again. But I know that all things will prove in the end to have been arranged for the best and am quite willing to accept what I cannot avoid. Genl Marcy is still in Missouri inspecting — we don't know when to expect him home, as he may be ordered elsewhere at once. Mrs. M & Nelly send their love to all. Give mine to Mary, John & Maria, & tell the latter not to be at all worried about George, as he is getting on very well. I heard from Arthur last week — he was quite well.

Do write to your affectionate son

Geo B McClellan

ALS, McClellan Papers (B-14:49), Library of Congress.

1. George McClellan, GBM's nephew. 2. Sponsored by the U.S. Sanitary Commission, the New York Sanitary Fair, like other similar fairs, was designed to raise money for the benefit of Union troops. 3. Grant had been appointed lieutenant general and general-in-chief of the Union armies. 4. See GBM to Cox, Feb. 12, *supra.* The bill had become highly politicized and would fail of passage.

To Edward H. Wright

My dear Wright   Orange New Jersey March 19 1864

On my return here yesterday after an absence of two days in New York I found yours of the 15th awaiting me.[1] We were all exceedingly grieved to learn of your father's serious illness, and most sincerely pray that he is in this restored to health. I think you are quite right in urging him to remain quietly at home in his present state of health — the excitement and inconveniences of Washington life certainly can do him no good, and may injure him much. I trust that you will succeed in persuading him to remain quiet until his health is completely restored.

The Fremont interview was a strange one, & confirms many little hints that had reached my ears — we will talk over it more fully when we meet than would be prudent in a letter in these days when the mails are so [torn]. I am really sorry that the bill for turning me out has been defeated, as it appears to have been — I do not wish to resign, but I would be very glad to be in civil life again without any action of my own — I am very tired of hanging by the eye lids & am really anxious to begin the world anew in private life. But whatever the result may be I shall accept it as the best.

The Report is going off grandly — it has already paid my debts & lifted a great load off my shoulders.

The Waldron lie *has* exploded — the more things of that kind the better — they always wait upon their authors.

Baldy[2] is climbing rapidly — Maj Genl of the regular army! I learn that it disquiets Rosecrans and others exceedingly.

Mrs Marcy & my wife join me in love to all — Baby sends her love to "Minnie Ight" & often talks about her. Now that the roads are rapidly becoming good we feel the want of you more than ever.

Tell your father how rejoiced we all are that he has recovered from the attack & that we hope he will take such good care of himself as to avoid another.

Ever your friend
McC

Col E H Wright
My wife desires her thanks for the photograph.

ALS, Miscellaneous Collections, Huntington Library.

1. In his letter of Mar. 15 Wright reported an interview with a spokesman for John Charles Frémont, who was angling for a presidential bid and wanted to join with GBM to oppose the so-called unemployed generals bill. Wright said he was told that if Frémont was elected president he would name GBM general-in-chief, and he expected a reciprocal arrangement if GBM was elected. McClellan Papers (B-14:49), Library of Congress. 2. Gen. William F. Smith.

To Horatio Seymour

His Ex Horatio Seymour
Governor of New York
Governor   New York April 5/64

I take pleasure in addressing you in behalf of a meritorious officer who informs me that he has got into trouble on account of language used in the heat of a political discussion. I allude to Lieut E. H. Underhill 1st N.Y. Artillery. I know nothing of the merits of the particular question — I do not know what may be Lt U's politics or what the trouble is, but I know that he is a gallant and meritorious officer who has won his way on fields of battle from the position of a private soldier to that of a 1st Lt, & that he has received very strong recommendations for promotion from his immediate and superior commanders. I therefore feel at liberty to direct your attention to these facts and to ask as a matter of justice to a gallant soldier such kind consideration as it may be in your power to give whenever the case comes before you.[1]

Very truly your friend
Geo B. McClellan

ALS, McClellan Papers, New-York Historical Society.

1. Apparently no action was taken against Lt. Underhill, who remained on duty with his battery.

To Samuel S. Cox

My dear Cox   Orange April 22 [1864]

Your kind note of the 12th with its enclosures was waiting for me here when I returned from a two weeks visit to New York, two or three days ago — as I was obliged to run over there again on business this is my first chance to reply to it.

I am very sorry that I missed you again, but sincerely hope for better luck next time. The letters you send me are of great interest — I return them after having taken some notes from them which may be of some use to me hereafter. Some of these days the whole mass of evidence which corroborates the ground I have taken in my report, & on which I acted at the time, will come out & I shall be justified in the eyes of all but the willfully blind.

The boy has just come for the mail — so I will let this note go unfinished & retain the letters which will send you in a day or two.

In the mean time believe me ever your friend
Geo B McC

ALS, Thomas F. Madigan Collection, Rare Books and Manuscripts Division, New York Public Library.

To Samuel L. M. Barlow

[Orange, c. May 3, 1864]

Mr B. insinuates that while in command of the Army of the Potomac I entertained political aspirations and that my course was guided by them.[1]

In this he is entirely mistaken — my thoughts & time were devoted solely to the military affairs committed to me, and whatever political opinions I expressed were expressed officially & frankly to the Govt as a part of my duty as the Comdr of the Army, or of one of the great armies of the nation. I never looked to the Presidency & no official or personal act letter or conversation of mine will bear a contrary interpretation. I deny that my course of conduct while in command was calculated to produce the impression that I was ready as a General to lend myself to any party to supplant the Chief Magistrate etc.

Mr Blair then intimates an attempt on my part to get control of the Govt by throwing myself into a party hostile to its Administration etc & cites the example of Lee & others as a proper course.[2]

I have already stated the facts as to my conduct while in command. Since then, when assailed in every way by the Administration & its partisans, I have but once raised my voice — the Woodward letter[3] — & in this I exercised the right of a citizen to repel attack & express an opinion.

Mr B. here assumes that the reelection of Mr L & the retention of power by his party are essential to our success — I differ from him & regard success as possible only by a change of Administration & policy, therefore I should be wanting to my country did I support a party & a policy which I conscientiously believe will bring ruin upon us all.

The insinuation in regard to the Harrison Bar letter[4] scarcely needs a comment — it was prepared without an "arrière pensée,"[5] & the singularity of its coincidence with the Woodward letter arises from the fact that the two are based upon the same general idea & that I had not changed my views in the interval. Let Mr B. prove that the principles contained in the Harrison Bar & Woodward letters are wrong before he asks me or my friends to condemn them.

If Mr B., as he strongly intimates, regards a comparison of the two letters as proving a desire on my part to conciliate the peace party — I can only deny that any such intention existed, & regret that I cannot see the force of the argument by which he reaches his conclusion.

I have not sought & do not intend to seek political preferment, but I do not see how I am to carry into effect Mr Blair's wishes without proving false to my country, for I could only comply with his request by coming out in favor of Mr Lincoln & his policy — that I cannot do.

I will not sacrifice my friends my country & my reputation for a command. I can make no communication to Mr Lincoln on the subject.

AD, McClellan Papers (B-23:53), Library of Congress.

1. In the spring of 1864 Barlow and Montgomery Blair exchanged a series of lengthy letters dealing with GBM's political beliefs and the possibility of his being the Democratic nominee for the presidency. This memorandum was prepared by GBM as a response to Blair's letter to Barlow of May 1, and served as the basis for Barlow's reply to Blair of May 3 (both: Barlow Papers, Huntington Library). GBM fairly summarizes the main points in Blair's letter. Blair concluded: "I believe if he would unbosom himself unreservedly & in confidence directly with the President that he would give him a military place in which he could be most useful ... & in such event the political alliance in which he has to some extent been involved might be turned to the best possible account for the country." 2. Blair maintained that Lee and others were "bitterly hostile" to Jefferson Davis but remained silent for the sake of Confederate unity. 3. GBM to Biddle, Oct. 12, 1863, *supra*. 4. GBM to Lincoln, July 7, 1862, *supra*. 5. Ulterior motive.

To Elizabeth B. McClellan

My dearest Mother   Orange May 8 1864 8 pm.

I do not know whether the telegraph has relieved the suspense of the thousands of anxious hearts in the great cities by this hour — here we are out of its reach and must wait as calmly as we may until tomorrow to learn the result of the advance across the Rapidan.[1] I have seen the morning Herald, but it gives nothing tangible and satisfactory — the absence of certain news does not tend to reassure my mind as to the issue. If we had gained a decided success it is more than probable that we should have heard something definite in regard to it, for the maxim that "no news is good news" hardly applies in such a case as this. I have implicit faith in the ability of my poor old Army to accomplish anything that troops can effect, but there is such a thing as expecting impossibilities, and such may have been the task now set before it.

I am inclined to think that Lee *did* attack & that the result was that he stopped or checked the advance of the army — it may well be that after the attack, finding that he could not drive them in retreat he fell back upon his defences at Mine Run, or somewhere in that vicinity, & I am not confident that we can easily force the position. How disgraceful it will be if it becomes necessary to retire again behind the line of the Rappahannock! It makes my heart sick when I think of the thousands of brave men who have been sacrificed by the blunders of our rulers — our sins as a nation must have been great indeed to merit such a punishment, & I fear that the end is not yet. Heaven knows that my heart will feel lighter if it proves that Lee has been badly defeated & driven in upon Richmond. Whatever the result may be God grant that Arty may go safely through it — I have strong faith that he will, & never forget to pray that he may — I have no guess as to that — but I shall be very glad when I know that the battle is over, & that some of my friends are safe. I am very sorry for poor Hayes — he was a good fellow & a fine soldier — he behaved very gallantly on the Peninsula & was an old friend of mine. Bartlett, too, who is reported wounded, was an excellent officer who was with me throughout the whole Peninsula campaign.[2]

People are very anxious in New York — they do not seem to have much confidence & I think they are prepared for disaster — which I still hope & trust will be arrested. I presume we shall know tomorrow something definite as to the result of the battles — I should not be at all surprised to hear that Butler had been beaten back to his boats — I doubt whether he has force enough for his part of the undertaking.[3] I will write again as soon as we have something definite. Nell and Mrs. Marcy would send their love did they know I was writing. Nell has just recovered from a severe sore throat etc contracted at the Fair. All well now.

With love to Mary John Maria etc

Ever your affectionate son
Geo B McClellan

I enclose a photograph taken a few days since — also an Eugénie for Mary, which is I think very good.

ALS, McClellan Papers (B-15:49), Library of Congress.

1. The Battle of the Wilderness was fought on May 5–7. 2. Brig. Gen. Alexander Hays was killed in the Wilderness fighting. Col. William F. Bartlett, wounded in the Wilderness, is no doubt confused here with Brig. Gen. Joseph J. Bartlett. 3. Gen. Butler's operation south of the James River failed.

To Mary McClellan

My dear Mary   Orange May 12 1864

Yours of Tuesday was awaiting me on my return from the city this evening. I am *very* much obliged to you for the copy of Arthur's note[1] — please don't fail to let me know anything you hear from him at once. I have been utterly upset by poor Sedgwick's death — a sad sad blow to the Army & the country. How many more might have been so much better spared! But it is doubtless all for the best.

They must have had a terrible time down there! But how splendidly my noble old Army has fought — nothing could have been finer than their conduct. God give them victory! I shall if possible attend Sedgwick's funeral. I am very tired so I will say good night — love to Mother and all.

Ever your affectionate brother
Geo B McClellan

ALS, McClellan Papers (B-15:49), Library of Congress.

1. Arthur McClellan wrote on May 9: "Gen. Sedgwick was killed this morning by a sharpshooter; the ball passed through the lower part of the brain & he died instantly. We are all in the lowest spirits, for the Gen. was loved by us all." McClellan Papers (B-15:49).

To Abram S. Hewitt

My dear Hewitt   Orange June 10 /64

Since receiving yours I have been "ordered" not to use my eyes as they are suffering from overwork. I was in the city afterwards & expected to see you but was detained up town so long that I could not get down to Burling Slip. I went with Mr Bassinger on Tuesday & Wednesday to Phillipsburg.[1] I think he has about the best line that can be had under the circumstances, but would call your attention to the fact that there must be far more vigor in the work if you ever expect to get the endeavor through. I urged Mr B. to devote himself entirely for the present to procuring the right of way so that work may be commenced. It will be better for all concerned that nothing be done in regard to the Boonton line until that other matter is well straightened out — which ought to be done in two weeks. There are some heavy cuts & fills where the right of way should be obtained *at once*. I will try to see you tomorrow & explain myself more fully than my eyes will now permit me to do in writing. The compensation proposition will be quite satisfactory to me.

In haste your friend
Geo B McC

Mr A S Hewitt

ALS, Allan Nevins Papers, Rare Book and Manuscript Library, Columbia University. The industrialist Hewitt operated, among other ventures, the Cooper-Hewitt ironworks in Newark.

1. GBM had undertaken for Hewitt an engineering study for a proposed extension of the Morris and Essex Railroad. Hewitt to GBM, May 29, McClellan Papers (B-16:50), Library of Congress.

To Samuel L. M. Barlow

Private

My dear S L M   West Point June 17 [1864]

I enclose a couple of letters for your edification. The Gov has been here & is in favor of postponing the Convention — he has much to say in that connection — I listened and said nothing.[1]

If I have any penetration whatever you may rest assured that the postponement is urged by & is in the interest not only of the Peace men, but also of the "Nelson" men, who may by some strange accident finally prove to be "Seymour" men — *probably to their own surprise!!*[2]

I am afraid that I scared a red headed politician out of several weeks growth two days since — he came to see me about "the meeting that had been arranged with F" etc — I shut him up so promptly that I don't think any one else will have the impertinence to renew the subject. He left somewhat hurriedly, & I am satisfied decidedly impressed with the idea that there had been a mistake *somewhere,* & that I was not yet entirely in the power of the politicians.[3] I wish you would impress our [*torn*] friend with the idea that I don't care to meet his friends[4] — I have got certain obstinate ideas in my head lately that I dont care to put on paper, but which I will explain when I see you — In the mean time my advice to you is to follow my example — clear out of town, let the politicians go where they belong viz: to the old gentleman with cloven feet, & take a good rest.

I think we shall move on to Saratoga tomorrow to pass Sunday & a day or two next week.

Yours of yesterday this moment reached me.[5] Am very glad you like the Address. I have no objection whatever to its being printed & would be glad to correct the proofs.

I was not aware that the regulars were at Vicksburg, & I don't think it deserves as much mention as Yorktown anyhow.

I wish they had kept Vallandigham down south when they had him there!

I will see you as I pass thru' town, & will try to stay overnight.

Ever yours in haste
McC

ALS, Barlow Papers, Huntington Library.

1. On June 15 GBM delivered an address dedicating the site of a monument to be erected at West Point to honor the Civil War dead of the regular army. New York's Gov. Horatio Seymour attended, and discussed with GBM postponement of the Democratic nominating convention scheduled for July 4. 2. Supreme Court Justice Samuel Nelson and Gov. Seymour, both potential candidates for the nomination. 3. In a draft for this letter, dated June 16, GBM gave a fuller account of this incident: "I was strongly tempted yesterday to throw a man out of the window — a red haired little scamp calling himself McClosky ... came to see me and said that he wished to see 'about that interview with Fremont' — I asked him what he meant — He said it had all been arranged in Washington and asked whether the Gov had not explained it to me — I told him no & asked who had dared to do such a thing without my knowledge...." McClellan Papers (B-15:49), Library of Congress. Apparently rumor had invented a proposed meeting between GBM and Frémont. See GBM to Wright, Mar. 19, note 1, *supra.* 4. On the evidence of GBM's draft, this appears to be a reference to a peace faction centering around Gov. Thomas H. Seymour of Connecticut. 5. Barlow's letter of June 16 congratulated GBM on his West Point address, and proposed it be printed as a campaign document. He added: "Vallandigham's advent will I fear give serious trouble. It will at all events compel a decided platform of action, before the [convention] meeting in Chicago." McClellan Papers (B-15:50). Peace Democrat Vallandigham had been banished to the Confederacy in May 1863 for supposedly treasonous utterances. Returning through Canada to Ohio, he was again deeply involved in Democratic politics.

To Samuel S. Cox

My dear Cox   Saratoga June 20 [1864]

I have not found a moment to reply to yours of the 9th until now — it reached me at West Point.[1]

I fully agree with you, and although I had a long conversation with Gov S[2] I was not convinced by his arguments in favor of a postponement, but as the matter would seem to involve me personally I cannot express myself as I otherwise would.

I do not appreciate the weight of the arguments against a postponement,[3] & the coolest, most disinterested, men I have seen are in favor of the meeting as first announced.

I have been careful, especially since receiving your letter, to act upon your suggestion, & to observe great caution in expressing an opinion. I shall return to Orange some time next week & hope to see you the *next time* you visit New York.

Ever your friend
McC

Hon S S Cox

ALS, Thomas F. Madigan Collection, Rare Books and Manuscripts Division, New York Public Library.

1. In his letter of June 9 Cox spoke of the movement to postpone the Democratic convention : "It is believed that Grant will fail in his object & that his failure will give great impulse to the *Peace* men who expect to be able either to control the nomination, if it be made later, or to have force enough to divide the Convention. . . . My object in writing is to guard you against the matter lest some one may torture some expression of yours into favoring the postponement." McClellan Papers (B-15:50), Library of Congress. 2. Gov. Seymour of New York. 3. GBM surely meant to say he did not appreciate the arguments favoring postponement.

To Manton M. Marble

My dear Marble   Lake George June 25 [1864]

Your two kind notes of the 13th & 16th duly reached me, but I have been so much on the move that it has been very difficult to write.[1] I need not tell you how truly I was gratified that the West Point oration met with your approval, & that I regretted exceedingly that you could not be there.

I don't know whether I shall be able to take up Halleck's book, but will if possible.

I expect to leave for home on Monday or Tuesday [June 27 or 28] when I shall try to bring to a focus the railway matter I undertook — if I can finish it at once, it is probable that we will take a cottage on the shore of this lake some 10 miles from Caldwell, at a little village named

Bolton — where I can pass the summer & fall without fear of being disturbed by politicians etc.

I shall however see you soon after my return home. So the Convention is postponed![2] Probably I don't know enough of the state of affairs to judge, but my instinct is against the movement, & I feel now perfectly free from any obligation to allow myself to be used as a candidate. It is very doubtful whether anything could now induce me to consent to have my name used. I will tell you when we meet more than I care to in a letter — in the mean time I shall keep as quiet & say as little as possible.

I suppose Barlow is at Saratoga — I shan't be able to see him on my way home.

It is almost too hot to write even here — so with my sincere congratulations upon the recent happy change in your condition & with my kind regards to Mrs Marble[3]

> I am your friend
> Geo B McClellan

Mr. Manton Marble

ALS, Marble Papers, Library of Congress.

1. In his letters of June 13 and 16 Marble asked GBM to review a newly published American edition of Henri Jomini's *Life of Napoleon*, edited by Henry Halleck, and congratulated him on his West Point address: "I do not hesitate to say that it is far superior to Mr Everett's Gettysburgh address in all essential respects — if the object of oratory be to touch the hearts & move the minds of men." McClellan Papers (B-15:50), Library of Congress. 2. The Democratic convention was rescheduled to open in Chicago on Aug. 29. 3. Marble was married on May 25.

To Henry B. Carrington

My dear Colonel   Orange New Jersey July 2 1864

Yours of the 18 reached me only two days since, in consequence of my unusually long absence from home — so I trust you will pardon my delay in acknowledging its receipt.[1]

I am sincerely gratified that you like the West Point address, and you will be glad to know that it has met the approval of very many of our best men.

I do not think that you will ever have reason to repent of the unswerving friendship you have entertained towards me, and you may be sure that there never can be anything in common between myself and the men you allude to.

> In great haste ever your friend
> Geo B McClellan

Col H B Carrington

ALS, Carrington Family Papers, Yale University Library. Brig. Gen. Carrington commanded the military district of Indiana, with headquarters in Indianapolis.

1. In his letter of June 18, Carrington warned that Vallandigham and his followers were "preparing for open rupture with the Government. I know that they have repudiated you and dare not trust your high-toned honor with their plans." McClellan Papers (B-16:50), Library of Congress.

To Elizabeth B. McClellan

My dear Mother   Orange Sunday July 3 [1864]

We returned here on Wednesday [June 29] after, what was for us, quite a long trip to West Point, Saratoga, Lake George & Ticonderoga. Went to West Point on the 13th and remained there until the last of the week. The Address seemed to pass off very well and gave satisfaction to all except Messrs Lincoln Stanton & Co who have ordered off Bowman & Clitz for being concerned in the heinous crime of inviting so great a reprobate as myself to the Point — such paltry spite cannot remain long unpunished and I trust that the day is not far distant when those wretches will receive at the hands of an outraged people the punishment they so richly deserve.[1] From West Point we went to Saratoga where we remained from Saturday until Tuesday — drinking the usual quantity of water & taking the usual drive to our dinner at Saratoga Lake — a quiet pretty spot where good plain dinners are supplied at rather exorbitant prices — but it is the fashion — so we accepted an invitation & went there. But few persons had reached Saratoga when we were there — so we had a very quiet & pleasant time — the more so as it happened that among the few guests at our Hotel were some of our Boston friends whom we were very glad to see. From Saratoga we went to Lake George where we spent just a week.

Nothing could have been kinder than the reception we met with everywhere — we were quite overpowered with kindness & found numberless friends among people we had never seen or heard of before.

We took a very pleasant trip to Ticonderoga and drove & toured & steamed about in every direction — so that we now know that region of country very well.

The only drawback to the trip was that we found it impossible to keep as quiet as we desired to — but we submitted with a good grace & got through very pleasantly.

I am very glad to hear that the Phila Fair passed off so pleasantly & successfully — it must have been a very great and interesting spectacle — and I am told that it presented a fine & more striking display than the New York Fair. Towards the close an invitation was sent to me by Mr. Welsh, but I did not receive it until the Fair was over — although it is not probable that I should have accepted it in any event — as I do not care to be much in Phila until it is a little more thoroughly whitewashed. The panic in money affairs & the resignation of Mr Chase have created quite a stir in New York — I never knew of a man so universally detested & despised as is Mr Chase by the monied men of this part of the world — he is politically dead beyond the power of a resurrection — so will it soon be with his late associates — nothing can save them for any length of time.[2]

I saw in the Herald the other day that 2nd Lt G M English, 31st Alabama Vols, was taken prisoner with a number of other secesh — I presume it is our enterprising young relation — if I had any idea as to where they have sent him I would try to help him in the way of any little comforts he might need.[3]

I wrote to Arthur while we were away from here — I have not heard from the little fellow since we left home three weeks ago — if you receive any letters from him please send me copies — I am anxious to know how he is, & what he is doing.

We had a vain attempt at a rain storm yesterday which passed away without giving us by any means as much rain as seems to be needed — for the country is very dry here & in New York State. From the quiet which pervades the house I imagine all are asleep — but as I know they would send their love if they knew that I was writing I will send them anyhow. Fanny has returned from school ''for good.''

Love to Mary, Maria & the children

Ever your affectionate son
Geo McC

My love to the Coxes and Phillips —

ALS, McClellan Papers (B-41:61), Library of Congress.

1. On orders from Secretary Stanton, the committee that invited GBM to deliver his West Point address — Lt. Col. Henry B. Clitz, Lt. C. C. Parsons, and Lt. Col. Henry Bowman, superintendent of the Military Academy — were transferred or dismissed. 2. Secretary of the Treasury Chase's resignation was accepted by the president on June 30. 3. Lt. English was GBM's nephew.

To L. Edgerton

Personal

My Dear Sir :   Oaklands, July 20 [1864]

Yours of the 15th reached me when on the point of starting from home, and too late to reply to it.[1]

I regret that my absence will deprive me of the pleasure of meeting your brother, although I confess that I would prefer seeing him after the Chicago Convention rather than before it, as it is my desire and purpose to take no step, directly or indirectly, to influence, in any manner, the action of that body.

With my thanks for your kind feeling and my respects to your brother,

I am, very truly yours,

George B. McClellan

Mr. L. Edgerton, New-York

New York World, Oct. 10, 1864.

1. Edgerton's letter introduced his brother, Alfred P. Edgerton, a delegate to the Democratic convention from Indiana, who wanted to meet GBM.

To Francis P. Blair

My dear Sir [Oaklands, N.Y., c. July 22, 1864]

I have endeavored to give to the suggestions made by you in our late interview[1] that careful consideration which they merit alike from the grave importance of the subjects involved and from the respect & high personal regard I entertain for you & your long experience in public affairs. As the conclusions of my deliberate judgment are not finally in accordance with your views and wishes I feel it due to you that I should explain the chief reasons which have influenced my mind in making its conclusions.[2]

In the course of our conversation its basis, the predominating idea, was your proposition that I should write a letter to the Presdt distinctly stating that I would not permit my name to be used as a candidate for the Presidency in opposition to the present incumbent, and that in that event — not otherwise — I would be actively employed by him in a position befitting my rank, & that thus the nation would have the benefit of what you are pleased to regard as valuable services on my part. That another officer of high rank General Grant had written such a letter was mentioned by you as an argument in favor of my pursuing a similar course.

Here let me repeat the statement, which you are aware I have more than once made, that I have not taken a single step nor said one word for the purpose of influencing the action of any political Convention, & that I am not an aspirant for nomination for the Presidency. It is my firm conviction that no man should seek that high office, and that no true man should refuse it, if it is spontaneously conferred upon him, & he is satisfied that he can do good to his country by accepting it. Whoever is nominated for the Presidency in opposition to the present incumbent, it will be upon principles differing widely from those which have controlled his course. Should the result of the election be in his favor — no harm will have inured to him from the contest. Should a majority of the loyal voters of the country decide in favor of his opponent it will be upon a struggle of principles not of men. Now, situated as your country is, its fate trembling in the balance, anyone who pledges himself not to oppose the reelection of the actual incumbent as a condition of obtaining office or employment places himself upon the horns of a dilemma.

If he does not conscientiously approve the policy of the incumbent, he simply sells his self respect honor & truth — as well as his country — for a price.

Or he says by implication at least, that he does fully approve of all the measures of the incumbent, & that he regards the question as merely a choice of men, & not of principles or measures.

No one who knows me will suppose that I could accept the first alternative. The second is inadmissable for the reason that I do not approve of the policy and measures of the present President.

To prevent the possibility of misunderstanding permit me to mention a few important points in regard to which I differ very widely from the President — I shall not attempt to go over the whole ground because it is not necessary to do so.

By retaining my commission as I have done at a great personal sacrifice, I have shown my constant readiness to perform any proper duty to which I might be assigned. If the cause of my being removed from command & being kept so long unemployed was a want of confidence in my ability as a soldier it would have been idle for me to ask for command. But I am not permitted to adopt this solution, for the reason that it was only a short time before my removal from command that the President took occasion to express to me his high confidence in my value as a soldier.

If political considerations caused my displacement I can merely assert that no thought, word or act of mine justified such a course, and the onus of undoing the work, together with all its consequences, must rest with those who are alone responsible for it.

I conceive that I should forfeit my own self respect, & be wanting in that respect due the high office of the President of the U.S. should I seek for employment — "I sit upon the bank & patiently watch the wind."

I think that the original object of the war, as declared by the Govt., viz: the preservation of the Union, its Constitution & its laws, has been lost sight of, or very widely departed from, & that other issues have been brought into the foreground which either should be entirely secondary, or are wrong or impossible of attainment.

I think the war has been permitted to take a course which unnecessarily embitters the inimical feeling between the two sections, & much increases the difficulty of attaining the true objects for which we ought to fight. Convinced that the Union of the States should never be abandoned so long as there is a hope that it can be made to secure the welfare & happiness of the people of all the States, I deprecate a policy which far from tending to that end tends in the contrary direction.

I think that in such a contest as this policy should ever accompany the use of arms, & that our antagonists should be made to know that we are ever ready to extend the olive branch, & make an honorable peace on the basis of the Union of all the states.

ADf, McClellan Papers (B-16:50), Library of Congress. Blair had been a major figure in national politics since the Jackson administration.

1. This interview, held at Blair's behest, took place in the Astor House in New York on July 21. As Blair later described it in a letter to the *National Intelligencer,* published on Oct. 8, it was undertaken without the president's knowledge. 2. It is highly probable that after drafting this letter GBM determined not to send it. It has not been found among Blair's papers. Further, Blair's account in the *Intelligencer* gives no indication that he ever received a response from GBM to the proposal that he write Lincoln to seek reinstatement in the army (although this draft clearly states GBM's negative response), and states that in fact he told the president when he returned to Washington that he might be receiving such a request from the general.

To Ann Mary Coleman

My dear Mrs Coleman   The Oaklands July 27 1864

Your kind note of the 23rd has reached me.[1]

I regret extremely that our movements for the next week are to be such that it will not be in my power to go to the city nor even to visit Orange, so that I shall not have the pleasure of seeing you at present.

I sincerely hope, however, that the time may not be far distant when I shall be so fortunate as to make the acquaintance of the daughter of one whose memory I love and respect as I do that of John J Crittenden — would that it have pleased God to have spared him to aid his country with his wise and unselfish councils — I fear we have too few like him remaining to us.

I am very sorry that it has been and still is impossible for me to call upon you at Bound Brook and beg that you will when next you write give my warmest regards to the General

and believe me, my dear Madame

very truly & respectfully your friend

Geo B McClellan

Mrs A M Coleman

ALS, John Jordan Crittenden Papers, William R. Perkins Library, Duke University. Mrs. Coleman was the daughter of John J. Crittenden of Kentucky.

1. In her letter of July 23 Mrs. Coleman explained that she was visiting in New Jersey and hoped to meet GBM and pay him the respects of her brother, Maj. Gen. Thomas L. Crittenden. She wrote that her two sons had joined the Confederate service (typifying the war-divided Crittenden family), "but I am a great admirer of Gen. McClellan!!" McClellan Papers (B-16:50), Library of Congress.

To Samuel L. M. Barlow

My dear S L M   New York Aug 8 [1864]

If you don't know Key[1] know him by this & talk with the utmost freedom to him. What you say to him is as if said to me.

I don't expect to see you before the 29th unless you come to Orange. I shan't come again to N.Y. & don't send to me any d — d politicians.

Ever your friend
Geo B McClellan

S L M B Esq

ALS, Barlow Papers, Huntington Library.

1. Thomas M. Key, formerly of GBM's staff.

To William C. Prime

Private

My dear Prime   Orange Aug 10 /64

I enclose some papers which will explain themselves — I don't know that the article Mr. Rush encloses amounts to enough to make it worth while to take much trouble — don't let his "confidential" note go out of your hands.[1]

If you see Key today tell him that I could not come in on account of the illness of my child — I may get in tomorrow, but it will depend entirely upon the child, who is a little better today. I don't think it desirable to write anything either to Blair or to Hanna[2] — I receive so many suggestions that I have determined to follow my own judgment in these matters. Morgan is very anxious that I should write a letter suggesting an *armistice*!!!![3]

If these fools will ruin the country I won't help them. I am very sorry that Blair interview got into the papers as it did — I expect that it was through Blair himself, & cannot but feel that I am partly accountable for a thing that is not exactly as it ought to be — I regret it exceedingly.[4]

My kindest regards to Barlow — don't send any politicians out here — I'll snub them if they come — confound them!

Sincerely your friend
Geo B McClellan

W. C. P.

ALS, McClellan Papers (B-17:50), Library of Congress.

1. On Aug. 1 Benjamin Rush sent his article supporting GBM that he wanted placed in a widely circulated newspaper. McClellan Papers (B-16:50). 2. Francis P. Blair; James M. Hanna, an Indiana delegate to the Democratic convention. 3. George W. Morgan, an Ohio politician, wrote on Aug. 4 that a call for an armistice by GBM "would double our chances at Chicago." McClellan Papers (B-16:50). 4. A report of Francis P. Blair's interview with

GBM (see GBM to Blair, c. July 22, *supra*) had appeared in the *New York Herald* on Aug. 4.

To Samuel L. M. Barlow

My dear Sam   Orange Sunday [August 28, 1864] 6.20 pm

Your messenger has just reached me.[1] Much obliged for the trouble you have taken. Things are just as I would have them — if we win we win everything and are free as air. If we lose we lose like gentlemen. I would not for the world have given any powers to make bargains. I will not come to town unless you send word to me that I *must*. If I am nominated I hope you will come out yourself as I shall want to talk to you about many things. In the contrary case I shall want to see you within a day or two in regard to my resigning. Baby has been sick again — better now.

With a thousand thanks for your kind forethought.

Ever your friend
McC

S L M B

ALS, Barlow Papers, Huntington Library.

1. Writing at 3:00 A.M. on this date, Barlow described the preconvention political maneuvering as reported to him by telegraph from Chicago: "It is plain to me that but for [Dean] Richmond, [Samuel J.] Tilden and Marble, the peace men, Lincoln men, and Seymour men, would have had it all their own way. As it stands if we win at all, we win everything, and shall have a wise platform and a good V.P. . . . As to 'private powers' I am glad none were given and delighted that I remained at home. . . . I do not see how you can safely come to town at all, just now, if you are nominated. You will be *crowded* out of sight." McClellan Papers (B-22:52), Library of Congress.

ELEVEN

CANDIDATE FOR PRESIDENT
SEPTEMBER 4, 1864–JULY 4, 1865

As THE DEMOCRATS were gathering in Chicago to nominate their candidate for 1864, President Lincoln predicted that in the campaign he would be facing either a war Democrat running on a peace platform, or a peace Democrat on a war platform. It was a perceptive observation. In the event, General McClellan won the presidential nomination without significant opposition, but the peace wing of the party forced through a platform containing a plank terming the war a failure and calling for an armistice without preconditions, and for good measure nominated a peace man, George H. Pendleton, of Ohio, as McClellan's vice-presidential running mate. Few presidential candidates have been so severely handicapped by the convention that nominated them.

Included here are the two key drafts of McClellan's letter accepting the nomination (of the six drafts he wrote) that demonstrate his uncompromising rejection of the peace plank and his efforts to clothe the rejection in palatable language and render the party's split as inconspicuous as possible. His correspondence relating to the acceptance letter reveals that his stance was based not only on principle but also on his awareness of political realities; accepting the Chicago platform would lose him the states of New York and Pennsylvania, which between them contained half the electoral votes needed for victory in November. Nothing in the campaign gave him more satisfaction than this affirmation that the precondition of peace between North and South must be reunion.

He left the direction of the campaign to August Belmont, Samuel Barlow, and newspaper editors Manton Marble and William Prime. He made just two public appearances, at rallies in Newark and in New York City; as he told a supporter on October 3, "I have made up my mind on reflection that it would be better for me not to participate in person in the canvass." He dutifully corresponded with some political figures and met others who visited him, but it is clear from these letters that presidential politics was not to George McClellan's liking, and midway through the campaign he secluded himself and his wife for a week at the country home of his friend Joseph W. Alsop, in Connecticut.

McClellan devoted most of his campaign efforts to the army vote. Thirteen states had made some provision for their soldiers to vote, and it was expected that the general's great popularity with the men in the ranks during his time in command would be reflected in the 1864 balloting. He sought out officers friendly to him to distribute Democratic campaign literature to the troops, and encouraged the formation of such military clubs as the McClellan Legion to rally ex-soldiers and men home on furlough and sick leave to his cause. Despite these efforts, however, no other segment of the electorate rejected his candidacy so strongly. In the final election count Lincoln would capture 55 percent of the vote; among the soldiers the president's count was 78 percent. In spite of his acceptance letter, Northern soldiers perceived General McClellan as representing the party advocating peace at any price, and they turned against him by an overwhelming margin.

Lincoln's comfortable advantage in the popular vote (403,000) and his substantial edge in the electoral vote (212 to 21) were due in part to the encouraging military news during the campaign, especially Sherman's capture of Atlanta and Sheridan's victories in the Shenandoah Valley, but perhaps of equal consequence was the effect of the Chicago platform on McClellan's campaign. Before the convention he had feared becoming the tool of the peace faction, but in the end he became its victim.

The presidential contest of 1864 was the last role George McClellan would play in the Civil War. On Election Day he resigned his army commission, and in January 1865, some three months before the war concluded, he sailed with his family for Europe. The final sampling here of the letters he wrote in Europe reflects his interest in the war's progress and its outcome, but also the sense that he was living in a self-imposed exile. He would not return to the United States for three and a half years.

To Samuel L. M. Barlow

My dear Sam   Orange Sept 4 [1864]

Your package duly reached me thro' Duncan[1] — much obliged for it.

Duncan suggested that it would be better that I should see Belmont Tilden etc on *Tuesday* evening [September 6] — to which I assented. It will suit me better as I must go in on Tuesday to see my wife off to New London. Please let me know by Douglas Robinson[2] if the arrangement suits. I suggested that Duncan should telegraph Dean Richmond to be there on Tuesday evening also. Is that all right? I want to see Prime also.[3]

I shall be at my house on Tuesday a little after 10 am — by 10 1/2 at latest — can you drop in for a moment before going down town?

I have not changed my mind since I saw you.

                                            Ever yours
                                            McC

S. L. M. B.

ALS, Barlow Papers, Huntington Library.

1. Probably the New York banker William B. Duncan. 2. Family friend Douglas Robinson acted as GBM's courier between New York and Orange. 3. This meeting concerned GBM's acceptance of the nomination.

To the Democratic Nomination Committee

Gentlemen   [Orange, c. September 4, 1864][1]

I have the honor to acknowledge the receipt of your letter of the __ inst informing me of my nomination by the National Democratic Committee recently assembled at Chicago, as their Candidate for the Presidency at the next election.

It is unnecessary for me to say to you that this nomination comes to me unsought, and since the record of my brief public life has been open to the world, I may fairly assume that that record was kept in view when the nomination was made. [The effect of long & varied service in the Army, during war & peace, has been to strengthen & render indelible in my mind & heart the love & reverence for the Union, Constitution, Laws & Flag of our nation impressed upon me in early youth. These feelings have thus far guided the course of my life, & must continue to do so in the future.]

I cannot realize that the existence of more than one Government over the region which once owned our Flag is compatible with the peace, the power & the happiness of the people. While in my judgment the restoration and maintainance of our Union is the real, the sole object for which the war should be waged, I cannot be blind to the fact that that Union was originally formed by the exercise of a spirit of conciliation & compromise, and that to restore & preserve it the same spirit must prevail in our councils.[2] We have fought enough to satisfy the military honor of both sections, & to satiate the vengeance of the most vindictive.

It is, then, my opinion that, while the restoration of the Union in all its integrity is and must continue to be the indispensable condition in any settlement of the questions at issue in this war, we should as soon as it is clear, or seems probable, that our present adversaries are willing to negotiate upon the basis of the immediate restoration of the Federal Union of the States,[3] exhaust all practicable means, consistent with the honor & safety of the country, to secure that restoration of the Union, with the Constitutional rights of all the States fully guaranteed for all future time. But if an honest frank & full effort to obtain this object results in failure then I am of the opinion that we must continue the resort to the dread arbitrament of war, a war conducted strictly in accordance with those principles which I had so often had occasion to communicate when in command of Armies.[4] For it is better to fight for the restoration of the Union than for the adjustment of the inevitable questions of a boundary line, division of territories and other kindred subjects of dispute. I, for one, could not look in the face of my gallant comrades of the Army & Navy who have survived so many bloody battles, & tell them that their labors and the sacrifices of such numbers of their slain & crippled brethren had been in vain — that we had abandoned that Union for which we had so often risked our lives. I believe that a vast majority of our people, whether in the Army & Navy or at home, would, with me hail with unbounded joy the permanent restoration of peace on the basis of the Federal Union of the States without the effusion of another drop of blood; but if all honest & honorable efforts to secure this blessing should fail, I have such confidence in the patriotism & devotion of the people that I am sure they would without a murmur make the further sacrifices necessary to maintain their honor and secure a permanent reunion of the States. Believing that the views I have expressed are those of the Convention you represent, and are in harmony with the intentions of its Resolutions, I accept the nomination.

That this nomination has aroused feelings of deep satisfaction within me I neither can nor would wish to deny, for I feel the full force of such an honor emanating from so large a portion of the people.

But that which under happier circumstances might well call forth sentiments of high exultation has in the present instance merely caused me to realize my own weakness, and the terrible grandeur of the responsibility to be assumed should a majority of the people ratify your choice. Should that event occur I can only promise to seek fervently the guidance of the Almighty, & with his powerful aid do my best to restore Union & Peace to our distracted land, & to secure all the liberties & rights of the people guaranteed by the Constitution. Through you, gentlemen, I beg to thank the Convention you represent, & the people who elected you for this unsought & most weighty honor. Whatever expectations the people may build upon me I shall not willingly disappoint.

AL, McClellan Papers (B-21:52), Library of Congress.

1. This is the second of six drafts GBM wrote of his letter of acceptance of the Democratic presidential nomination, and was composed between Sept. 1 and Sept. 6, the first known date of any of the drafts (draft four). Drafts one, two, three, and five are in the McClellan Papers; drafts four and six are in the Barlow Papers, Huntington Library. This second draft is essentially a clean copy of GBM's heavily edited "1st rough draft" — the substantive changes are noted below — and represents his initial reaction to the platform adopted by the convention. His primary problem was responding to the platform's second plank, written by Clement Vallandigham, that in effect called for an unconditional armistice: "*Resolved,* That this convention does explicitly declare . . . that after four years of failure to restore the Union by the experiment of war, . . . justice, humanity, liberty and the public welfare demand that immediate efforts be made for a cessation of hostilities, with a view to an ultimate convention of the States, or other peaceable means, to the end that at the earliest practicable moment peace may be restored on the basis of the Federal Union of the States." 2. At this point the first draft had contained the sentence: "Nor am I ignorant that in order that a restored Union may be useful and permanent a feeling of mutual confidence & respect must exist between the two sections now unhappily at war." 3. The foregoing phrasing, beginning with "we should as soon as it is clear . . . ," originally read: "we should use our best endeavors to attain a pacific solution of the controversy without further effusion of blood." 4. This concluding phrase was added in the second draft.

To Samuel L. M. Barlow

My dear Sam   [New York, September 6, 1864] 3 p.m.

I enclose a note I found awaiting me from Mr Wall[1] — I think it may be well for Belmont to see it in confidence this evening — if you agree with me please let him see it. I would be glad to have it again sometime.

I look upon it as of great importance in showing that so ultra a man is willing to unite with us on the proper platform. I can't stay in town tonight — will see you on Thursday [September 8], & will appropriate Friday evg for a long talk with you.

In haste ever yours.
McC

S L M B Esq etc

ALS, Barlow Papers, Huntington Library.

1. Former New Jersey senator James W. Wall, a peace Democrat, wrote on Sept. 1 that he had spoken in support of GBM at a rally, and pledged his aid in the campaign. Of vice-presidential candidate George H. Pendleton he wrote: "My friend Pendleton . . . is an elevated high toned gentleman of rare ability." McClellan Papers (B-18:51), Library of Congress.

To Mary Ellen McClellan

Orange Tuesday 11pm.
My own dear little darling   [September 6, 1864]

You don't know, my own dear Nelly, how lonely it is without you — when I came back this evening I "took to" the May as you do & felt a double responsibility.[1] The dear little thing is perfectly well, & was wonderfully bright & affectionate — but she could not understand how "her own dear Mama had gone away" — she misses you terribly, & seemed to cling to me more than ever — little darling.

If you could have seen her you would have made up your mind that she does love you *very* much. I saw Dr Adams[2] — he was much pleased with my letter. I have recopied it tonight after a careful revision of *my own*, & have added the following just after what I said about "looking my comrades in the face etc" —

"The sentiments of my living comrades, the memory of the heroic dead, the traditions handed down from our Fathers, the Glory of our great nation, the hopes of our children, the preservation of our personal liberties, my own acts and words, all my antecedents, all that I prize on earth unite in rendering it impossible for me ever to consent to the disruption of the Union, with its direful consequences of exhaustive wars, financial ruin, anarchy & misrule, even should I of all in this broad land stand alone in this conviction." The changes I have made — & they are my style — are my own & add to the strength of the letter.[3] I think I have it now in an admirable shape & am not afraid to go down to posterity on it.

I found 32 letters awaiting me tonight — all but about 4 on this subject & all agreeing in sentiment. There can be no doubt as to the feeling of the people in this part of the world — they are with me. I had a letter from Mr. Aspinwall — just like the others. I shall write a few lines to him tonight. I go in again tomorrow morning & shall do my best to join you on Thursday night [September 8] — but I am as yet entirely in the dark as to the movements of the Committee.[4]

Fan[5] goes to visit Susie Adams on Friday — I should think it would be a relief to your mother — I asked Fan this evening if she had not been chasing her bull with gunpowder! She went to bed a little while ago in a more pacific frame of mind. Had a letter from Arthur.

Ever with fondest & truest love, my own sweet Nelly
Your own
George

ALS, McClellan Papers (B-25:54), Library of Congress.

1. Mrs. McClellan had left that morning to visit family friends in New London, Conn. 2. Presbyterian minister William Adams. 3. The sentence quoted was incorporated in the

fourth draft of GBM's acceptance letter, but subsequently deleted. 4. The Democratic nomination committee, headed by Horatio Seymour. 5. Fanny Marcy, GBM's sister-in-law.

To William H. Aspinwall

Orange Tuesday 11 PM

My dear Mr Aspinwall   [September 6, 1864]

Your welcome letter of the 4th reached me this evening.[1] Many thanks for it. My letter of acceptance is ready — you need have no fears on the subject — it is true to the country & to myself & in entire consistency with my record. I will either accept on my own terms (you know what they are) or I will decline the whole affair. In my judgment my letter will be acceptable to all true patriots, & will only drive off the real adherents of Jeff Davis this side of the line. Do not allow yourself to be anxious for one moment. — Whatever the result of the election may be my name will go down unsullied & you will never have cause to be ashamed that you have been one of my best & truest friends. — I received your kind letter enclosing that of Mr —— . You are perfectly right in telling him that the platform will be "the Union at any cost." Rest assured that I have the boldness to speak out my own mind, & the nerve to risk anything for my country. No politicians can make [me] their tool, & I both am & shall continue to be unpledged to any men except the real patriots of the land who value the "Union" above all things on earth. — I have earnestly sought the guidance of the Almighty & I cannot help feel he has vouchsafed to answer my prayers. I believe that the course I have determined to pursue is in accordance with his will, & that it will save the country. I hope that whatever my future may be you will always write & talk to me in the same spirit of friendly frankness that has always characterised yr course toward me. Your trust shall not be misplaced. Should it be convenient or agreeable to you I would be glad to have you meet me at my house on Thursday next [September 8] when I meet the committee. I presume about 12 o clock tho' the time is not fixed, & in truth I have seen none of them yet.

Ever your sincere friend

Geo B McClellan

To Wm Aspinwall Esq.

Copy, James S. Schoff Collection, William L. Clements Library, University of Michigan.

1. In his letter of Sept. 4 Aspinwall wrote, in part : "Your future influence & independence will depend much on the response you give to the nomination — if you have the boldness to speak out your own mind . . . , you will put to rest the assertions of your opponents that you are to be the tool in the hands of trading politicians. . . . The Chicago platform is simply an effort to unite the opposing elements of the Democratic party, & is unworthy of the crisis in which our nation is placed." McClellan Papers (A-91 :36), Library of Congress.

To the Democratic Nomination Committee

Gentlemen   Orange New Jersey Sept 8 1864[1]

I have the honor to acknowledge the receipt of your letter informing me of my nomination by the Democratic National Convention, recently assembled at Chicago, as their candidate, at the next election, for President of the United States.

It is unnecessary for me to say to you that this nomination comes to me unsought. [*Crossed out:* Since the record of my public life has been open to the world, I assume that that record was kept in view] I am happy to know that when the nomination was made the record of my public life was kept in view. The effect of long and varied service in the Army, during war and peace, has been to strengthen and make indelible in my mind and heart the love and reverence for the Union, Constitution, Laws and Flag of our country impressed upon me in early youth.

These feelings have thus far guided the course of my life, and must continue to do so to its end.

The existence of more than one Government over the region which once owned our flag is incompatible with the peace, the power, and the happiness of the people.

The preservation of our Union was the sole avowed object for which the war was commenced.

It should have been conducted for that object only, and in accordance with those principles which I took occasion to declare when in [*crossed out:* command of armies, and especially in my letter to the President from Harrison's Landing.] active service. Thus conducted, the work of reconciliation would have been easy, and we might have reaped the benefits of our many victories on land and sea.

The Union was originally formed by the exercise of a spirit of conciliation and compromise.

To restore and preserve it the same spirit must prevail in our Councils, and in the hearts of the people. The reestablishment of the Union in all its integrity is, and must continue to be, the indispensable condition in any settlement [*crossed out:* of the questions at issue in this war]. So soon as it is clear, or even possible, that our present adversaries are ready for peace upon the basis of the Union, we should exhaust all the resources of statesmanship practiced by civilized nations, and taught by the traditions of the American people, consistent with the honor and interests of the country, to secure such peace, reestablish the Union, and guarantee for the future the Constitutional rights of every State. The Union is [*crossed out:* our only] the one condition of peace. We ask no more.[2]

Let me add what I doubt not was, although unexpressed, the sentiment of the Convention, as it is of the people they represent, that when any one State is willing to return to the Union, it should be received at once, with a full guarantee of all its Constitutional rights.

But if a frank, earnest and persistent effort to achieve these objects should fail, [*crossed out:* it will be necessary to insist upon the preservation of the Union at all hazards, and] the responsibility for ulterior consequences will fall upon those who remain in arms against the Union. But the Union must be preserved at all hazards. I could not look in the face of my gallant comrades of the Army and Navy, who have survived so many bloody battles, and tell them that their labors, and the sacrifice of so many of our slain and wounded brethren had been in vain — that we had abandoned that Union for which we have so often perilled our lives.

A vast majority of our people, whether in the Army and Navy or at home, would, as I would, hail with unbounded joy the permanent restoration of peace, on the basis of the Union under the Constitution, without the effusion of another drop of blood. But no peace can be permanent without Union.

As to the other subjects presented in the resolutions of the Convention, I need only say that I should seek in the Constitution of the United States, and the laws framed in accordance therewith, the rule of my duty and the limitations of executive power, — endeavor to restore economy in public expenditure, reestablish the supremacy of law, [*crossed out:* and assert for our country and people that commanding position to which our history & our principles entitle us among the nations of the world.] & by the assertion of a more vigorous nationality reserve our commanding position among the nations of the Earth.[3] The condition of our finances, the depreciation of the paper currency, and the burdens thus imposed on labor, [*crossed out:* industry] & capital show the necessity of a return to a sound financial system; while the rights of citizens and the rights of States, and the binding authority of law over President, Army and people are subjects of not less vital importance in war than in peace. Believing that the views here expressed are those of the Convention and the people you represent, I accept the nomination.

I realize the weight of the responsibility to be borne should the people ratify your choice.

Conscious of my own weakness, I can only seek fervently the guidance of the Ruler of the Universe, and, relying on His all-powerful aid, do my best to restore Union and Peace to a suffering people, and to establish and guard their liberties and rights.

I am, Gentlemen very respectfully your obedient servant

Geo B McClellan

Hon Horatio Seymour
and others, Committee etc.

ALS, Barlow Papers, Huntington Library.

1. This sixth and final draft of GBM's acceptance letter was the product of intensive revisions on Sept. 7 and 8 in company with Samuel Barlow, and perhaps other advisers, in New York. It is a copy of the much-altered fifth draft, with the additional final revisions indicated. 2. These last two sentences are in Barlow's handwriting. 3. The phrasing replacing the crossed-out section is by Barlow.

To Mary Ellen McClellan

[New York] Friday 3 pm
My own dearest darling   [September 9, 1864]

I had hoped to run on for you to day but am not well enough yet to go on & return at once so I send one of Barlow's young men (Mac) to bring you back tomorrow morning. I am almost well to day, but John[1] who is here says that I must keep quiet to day & that I ought not to go on unless I could stay there a day or two — & from your dear letter I see that you want to return tomorrow.

I caught cold that day we came in & the Mexican disease[2] returned upon me — the two in connection with unusual mental excitement & no sleep have rather used me up. I have spent the day on the sofa perfectly quiet & believe I am entirely well. Fan was here just now with Fanny Keith — they go to spend two days with Susie Adams. She says May is *perfectly* well & bright this morning — also your mother. I shall remain in town tonight & meet you at the cars at the Depot. Should I not, for any reason, you will find me at Barlow's — but I expect to meet you. My letter was not handed in until midnight last night. The effect thus far has been electric — the peace men are the only ones who squirm — but all the good men are delighted with it.

John came on last evening — returning this evening — he, of course, is pleased as punch. I am *very* glad that you got on so very comfortably. I am *very* sorry that it is not best for me to go for you — but you must not be in the slightest degree worried about me — it is only a measure of prudence insisted on by the Doctor that I should not go & return at once.

I can't tell you how anxious I am to see you again, my own darling — more than I can express. I telegraphed you last night — but have no answer.

Come in the morning train.

Ever with fondest love your own loving
George

Give my love to Maria & all the family & tell them how much I am disappointed that I cannot see them now.

ALS, McClellan Papers (B-12:48), Library of Congress.

1. Dr. John H. B. McClellan, GBM's brother. 2. Malaria, contracted during the Mexican War.

To Samuel L. M. Barlow

Dear S L M —   Orange Sept 13 [1864]

I have letters from Phila to the effect that Randall Reed etc give way — L. W. Cass, Glancy Jones & others write to me in the best of humor — all I hear from every direction is favorable.[1]

I am much better — have kept very quiet — & have been pretty sick, but now regard myself as well.

Sincerely yours
Geo McC

Received yours enclosing the letter from my brother.[2]

ALS, Barlow Papers, Huntington Library.

1. Congressman Samuel J. Randall, and William B. Reed, L. W. Cass, and Glancy Jones were peace Democrats. 2. Barlow's letter of Sept. 12 expressed concern about vice-presidential nominee Pendleton: "If he is all right & don't bolt, so as to lose us Inda. & Illinois I think we are safe. If he does, it will be very doubtful. . . . Everything is first rate (even the Herald) but much depends on Pendleton, to whom all of our friends are telegraphing." John H. B. McClellan's letter of Sept. 12 to Barlow read, in part: "Everything here looks most favorable — the General's letter has worked wonders. Some of the peace men kicked very hard but all will have to come in." McClellan Papers (B-19:51), Library of Congress.

To Samuel S. Cox

My dear Cox   Orange Sept 15 [1864]

Your kind note of the 9th reached me a few days since[1] — I have been too busy & too sick to write any letters or you may be assured I should ere this have replied to it. It reached me too late for the letter of acceptance — nothing less than that letter would have answered in this part of the world — without it, on the simple platform, there was no chance whatever for Penn & New York — more than that, I could not have run on the platform as everybody interpreted it in this part of the world without violating all my antecedents — which I would not do for a thousand Presidencies. I have heard of the hard work you did at Chicago.

I shall not have time to have any *visites* taken — I have had so many applications in regard to similar things that I found my only safety was to decide to have *none* taken.

With my kindest regards to Mrs Cox

I am, in great haste, ever your friend
Geo B McClellan

Hon S S Cox

ALS, Thomas F. Madigan Collection, Rare Books and Manuscripts Division, New York Public Library.

1. In his letter of Sept. 9, Cox suggested that a passage from GBM's *Report* — military victory "should be accompanied and followed by conciliatory measures" — was "in substantial harmony with our platform" and should be part of his acceptance letter. McClellan Papers (B-19:51), Library of Congress.

To Manton M. Marble

My dear Marble   Orange Sept 17 [1864]

On my return last night I found yours of the 12[1] — many thanks. I return the enclosures herewith.

I send in another envelope three or four letters that you may perhaps attend to with advantage. Pretty much all the letters I receive are in one direction. I got an indignant protest from some Maryland secessionists!! So much the better. I will attend to your suggestions — I have many letters from privates & *ex*-soldiers — *all* right.

I am nearly worn out with writing & will say good bye.

Ever your friend
McC

M.M.

ALS, Marble Papers, Library of Congress.

1. In his letter of Sept. 12, Marble suggested that GBM "keep up a diligent *friendly* correspondence with all your old friends in the Army. You know how the platform hurts us there, & how confidently Mr. Lincoln counts upon the ambition of the Army officers & the votes of the soldiers to assist in his re-election." McClellan Papers (B-19:51), Library of Congress.

To William C. Prime

My dear Prime   Orange Sept 20 [1864]

I enclose a letter received last night — for your perusal. Would not the writer's suggestion as to military clubs be a good thing?[1]

It seems to me that the state of affairs described ought to be shown up. Would it not be a good idea to publish extracts from the letter — omitting of course the name of the writer — simply stating its authenticity? I think that such things as he states ought to be made known far & wide.

Ever your friend
Geo B McC

W.C.P.

ALS, McClellan Papers (B-41:61), Library of Congress.

1. In his letter of Sept. 13 Charles D. Deshler, signing himself "State Military Asst. for New Jersey," recounted incidents of what he termed intimidation of soldiers supporting

the Democratic ticket. To counter this, he proposed the formation of ''Soldiers' McClellan Clubs'' across the North, made up of ex-soldiers and men home on leave or recovering from wounds. McClellan Papers (B-19:51).

To Robert C. Winthrop

My dear Mr Winthrop   Orange Sept 20 [1864]

Your very welcome letter of yesterday has just reached me.[1] I regret extremely that I was not so fortunate as to meet you, but it was not in my power to visit the city on Saturday [September 17], or I certainly should have done so.

I cannot express to you the gratification I felt upon being assured of your entire approval of the course I have taken — in what I did I was actuated solely by what seemed right, not by any notions of policy, & it is a source of great gratification to me to know that you, for whom I entertain so great respect & regard, agree with me. It matters not to me, personally, whether I am elected or not — but it is all important that my course should meet the affirmation of good men.

I was extremely gratified by your speech — which was so far above the tone of so many of the political speeches of the present day & so like those of better days of the Republic.[2] I hope that I may have the pleasure of seeing you ere long — in the mean time, with kindest regards to Miss Winthrop, in which, as well as to yourself Mrs McClellan desires most cordially to unite

I am, respectfully, your sincere friend
Geo B McClellan

Hon Robt C Winthrop
Boston

ALS, Winthrop Papers, Massachusetts Historical Society.

1. In his letter of Sept. 19 Winthrop commented on GBM's acceptance letter: ''It relieved your friends from a world of anxiety & embarrassment, & has placed you in a position which is better than the Presidency. If the election shall go as we hope, you will have won the victory by your own pen, as surely as you won Antietam by your sword.'' McClellan Papers (A-80:32), Library of Congress. 2. Winthrop had addressed a Democratic campaign rally in New York's Union Square on Sept. 17.

To Samuel L. M. Barlow

My dear S L M   Orange Sept 21 [1864]

Yours of yesterday did not reach me until after midnight as I was absent in Newark — so I can make but a brief reply.[1]

You had better send at once for McMahon[2] (at Dix's office) & consult him — he can give you names & you can trust him to any extent. In the Army of the Potomac there is

Henry J Hunt — Brig Genl & Chf of Artillery
Jas C Duane — Maj Engrs —
H. L. Abbot — Col 1st Conn. Artillery
Chas N Turnbull — Capt Engrs
Nicholas Bowen —   "   "   (Lt Col etc)
O. E. Babcock — Lt. Col. *but on Grant's Staff*
Genl John Gibbon
Genl M R Patrick — Provost Marshal Genl

Arthur, Sweitzer and Averell are all with Sheridan's Army — also Capt C E Morris 2nd Cavalry. With Sherman's Army you can rely on Genl Brannan, Hammerstein, Slocum (the last a Republican, but Franklin says strong in my favor) — I've no more time now, but will try to think of names today — Clarke H F — Comsry Subs. in New York is from Penna & can give you names. He is all right — Van Vliet is not & *you must not* trust him at all.

I had some confidential & reliable information yesterday — part of which is —

My steps are dogged & every person reported who comes to see me.

Grant has gone clean over to the enemy.[3]

Stanton & Presdt are not on good terms, the former now acting only under the latter's orders & not from his own discretion.

If there is any difficulty about the draft there will be martial law.

Marcy thinks Rosecrantz all right — may require a little handling in a quiet way.

When Naglee[4] returns in a day or two some of you had better see him again — he is working very hard in Penna & I am told with good effect. He has been talking to Curtin. I think you can learn much about Penna from Naglee. He was to go to Boston today — spend one day there & return.

Will you send the enclosed to Lansing.[5] He sent to me the other day for a copy of the Woodward letter & I don't want him to use it in Penna — for I think that as Curtin stands the less said about it the better — so I've written to him again not to say anything about it in his speeches. The Newark affair last night was very large.

In haste ever yours
Geo McC

S.L.M.B.

ALS, Barlow Papers, Huntington Library.

1. In his letter of Sept. 20 Barlow sought the names of army officers to whom Democratic campaign literature could be sent for distribution. Barlow Papers. 2. Lt. Col. Martin T. McMahon. 3. Apparently this is a reference to Gen. Grant's position on soldiers' voting. Barlow replied on this date, in part: "You may be right as to Grant, but if so, my information, directly from him, within ten days, shows that he has changed his mind." McClellan Papers (B-20:52), Library of Congress. 4. Henry M. Naglee, formerly a general

in the Army of the Potomac, was a Democratic campaign organizer. 5. Henry S. Lansing, also a former officer in the Army of the Potomac, wrote on Sept. 16 that he thought the Woodward letter — GBM to Charles J. Biddle, Oct. 12, 1863, *supra* — would effectively demonstrate GBM's views in Pennsylvania. McClellan Papers (B-20:51).

To Henry M. Naglee

My dear Genl   Orange Sept 23 [1864]

The conversation between us in regard to the "Woodward letter" has deeply impressed me.

That letter was not called forth by any personal feeling in regard to either of the candidates — simply by the misrepresentations made in regard to me & my course. My acquaintance with Judge Woodward was very slight — to the present day I have met him but twice — while on the other hand my intercourse with Gov Curtin has extended over a considerable period of time & I am under obligations to him for many acts of personal & official kindness.

I regret extremely that the letter caused any unpleasant personal feeling on the part of the Governor — which was far from my intention.

Please say as much to the Governor for me

and oblige your sincere friend
Geo B McClellan

Genl H M Naglee

ALS retained copy, McClellan Papers (B-20:52), Library of Congress.

To Samuel L. M. Barlow

My dear S.L.M.   Orange Sept 23 [1864]

I enclose a bill of lading just received for a photograph of Lord Clyde sent to me from England by the Persia — will you do me the favor to ask Taylor to get it for me & send by express to this place.

I shall be in town on Monday morning [September 26] & will be at my house a little after 10 when I shall be delighted to see you.

In haste ever yours
Geo B McClellan

S.L.M.B.

I open this to say that I have just received yours of the 23rd.[1] I have carefully thought over the matter & cannot think of anything I ever wrote or said that could be tortured into giving Lincoln the advice in question. You may be sure that it is a lie out of the whole cloth.

Sincerely yours
McC

I can't imagine what I ought to write Thomson about — and I don't feel disposed to go far out of my way to see a man of whom I entertain the opinion I do of R!![2]

Lansing writes to know whether I have heard from Pendleton — if you see him tell him not a word.[3]

ALS, Barlow Papers, Huntington Library.

1. Barlow wrote: "Lincoln pretends to have a letter of yours to himself, written in 1861, I believe, in which you advised him to assume dictatorial powers, arrest members of Congress &c &c. This story is likely to hurt us very much in certain quarters. Have you a copy of any such letter and if not, can you give me the substance." McClellan Papers (B-20:52), Library of Congress. 2. Barlow suggested GBM write J. Edgar Thomson, head of the Pennsylvania Railroad, and William B. Reed in regard to the contest in Pennsylvania. 3. Lansing wrote on Sept. 22 that a letter from the vice-presidential nominee, of the peace wing of the party, supporting GBM's acceptance letter would help in the East "but might be disastrous in the West." McClellan Papers (B-20:52).

To Samuel S. Cox

My dear Cox   Orange Sept 24 [1864]

Yours of the 21st has just reached me.[1]

Although tired out I cannot refrain from acknowledging it at once. I *know* you have had a hard fight, & how nobly you have fought it — I shall be glad when the election is over that you may have a little rest and quietness — for I am sure you will need it by that time.

I am very glad that the letter of acceptance seems wise to you after a calm survey of the state of affairs — it certainly has done much good in this part of the country — we should have been whipped without it. I dare not trust mine to the mail & will await a better opportunity of writing more fully.

In the mean time, with my kindest regards to Mrs Cox, in which as well as to yourself Mrs McClellan desires to unite

I am your friend
Geo B McClellan

Hon S S Cox

ALS, Thomas F. Madigan Collection, Rare Books and Manuscripts Division, New York Public Library.

1. Cox wrote from Ohio on Sept. 21 that he had been "anxious about your [acceptance] letter. I would not now, 'for the world,' have you done otherwise. . . . I knew we would have a storm. We have had it. It has mostly passed away. . . . I am working like a beaver. A fair response from the Army for us, will elect all our old Congressmen & give us the state." McClellan Papers (B-20:52), Library of Congress.

To William T. Sherman

My dear General   Orange New Jersey Sept 26 1864

Events have crowded upon me so thickly of late that I have been unable to congratulate you as I had wished & intended to do.[1] But on the principle that it is better late than never I will even at this late day express to you my sincere & heartfelt appreciation of the remarkable campaign you have just completed. I confess that at the beginning I trembled for your long line of communications, and I have watched with the most intense interest the admirable manner in which you overcame the difficulty. Your campaign will go down to history as one of the memorable ones of the world, & will be even more highly appreciated in the future than it is in the present. How beautifully you have illustrated the tenderness of communications, by your operations against the enemy's!

But I will not now pretend to do more than offer you my heartfelt congratulations upon the manner in which you have served your country and illustrated your own name — nor can I avoid congratulating you also upon the superb conduct of your troops during the whole campaign.

Poor Macpherson's loss grieved me very much — it must have been a serious personal as well as official one to you — connected as he had been with you for a long time.[2] I am starting for the city & beg you to excuse this hurried screed, & accept it simply as the hearty congratulations[3]
of your sincere friend
Geo B McClellan

Genl W T Sherman
Atlanta

ALS, Sherman Papers, Library of Congress.

1. Atlanta had fallen to Sherman on Sept. 1. 2. Maj. Gen. James B. McPherson, commander of the Army of the Tennessee, was killed at Atlanta on July 22. 3. Sherman acknowledged GBM's complimentary letter on Oct. 11: ''Coming from so high a source I cannot but esteem it. . . . I think I understand the purpose of the South properly and that the best way to deal with them is to meet them fair & square on any issue — we must fight them. Cut into them — not talk [to] them, and pursue till they cry enough. If we relax one bit we could never hold up our head again. They would ride us roughshod.'' McClellan Papers (B-21:52), Library of Congress.

To Charles A. Whittier

My dear Major   Orange Sept 27 [1864]

I received yesterday your kind letter of the 17th accompanying Genl Sedgwick's badge.[1]

I can hardly tell you how deeply I thank you for it — you could have sent it to no one who would prize it more, for I am sure that no one was more warmly attached to John Sedgwick than I was.

His death was the severest blow that has fallen to me in this war —
for I knew that no one ever possessed a truer and more attached friend
than he was to me. I will keep the badge with the most sacred care, &
should the wish of my heart ever be realized — and that is to command
the Army of the Potomac in one more great campaign — that badge
shall go with me, & share whatever of good or ill fortune I may meet
with.

Should it ever be my fortune again to be in power and command I
hope that you & your comrades will understand that I shall consider
Sedgwick's staff as left to my especial care, & that I should be only too
glad to gather them around me.

I congratulate you most sincerely upon the brilliant successes just
gained in the valley, & hope that they may result in our permanent
possession of that troublesome region. Give my love to Arthur & say to
him that I will write to him today or tomorrow. With my kind regards
to Genl Wright[2] & such others of my friends as may be near you

I am your sincere friend

Geo B McClellan

Maj C A Whittier

So you have lost poor Russell too![3]

When you next write to Miss Sedgwick will you do me the favor to
convey to her my sincere thanks for her kindness in permitting me to
have this relic of my deceased friend.

McC

ALS, William Alvord Papers, Bancroft Library, University of California at Berkeley. Maj.
Whittier was on the staff of the Sixth Corps.

1. Whittier wrote on Sept. 17 enclosing Gen. Sedgwick's corps badge, explaining that the
general's sister wanted GBM to have it. McClellan Papers (A-91:36), Library of Congress.
2. Maj. Gen. Horatio G. Wright succeeded Sedgwick as commander of the Sixth Corps. 3.
Brig. Gen. David A. Russell, killed at the Battle of Opequon Creek.

To Samuel L. M. Barlow

My dear Saml   [Orange] Sept 27 [1864]

Yours just received. The dispatch is from Marcy & is — "McKinstry
has just received Fremont's withdrawal from the canvass, to be published
on telegraph notice from him. Says Fremont had an interview with Chase
& Wilson; they promised him a position in the Cabinet & a dismissal of
the two Blairs if he would withdraw and advocate Lincoln. He replied
that it was an insult. Fremont said and" — here it breaks off & further
this deponent knoweth not.[1] I had a letter from the Gov.[2] this evening —
he thinks it better for him to turn all his efforts to N.Y. — I have replied
telling him that he is no doubt the best judge — the letter came & the
reply goes thro' Duncan who can tell you in detail what both are. I will

meet Mr Curtis as you suggest — also Thos Scott.[3] Will arrange with you about the evening on Thursday [September 29] when I come in. Can I get a dinner in Madison Avenue or don't you receive poor people — Hitchcock is a good friend of mine & I can get a meal at the 5th Avenue on him if you have become proud.

In haste sincerely yours
Geo B McC

Wrote to Guthrie — Sherman — Dix & Gov S etc last night.[4]

ALS, Barlow Papers, Huntington Library.

1. This telegram, sent to GBM in cipher by Marcy on Sept. 22, was suppressed by a telegraph official in Pittsburgh. The telegrapher there sent it secretly to GBM by mail. Edward W. Kulgan to GBM, Sept. 23, McClellan Papers (B-20:52), Library of Congress. Justus McKinstry, spokesman for third-party candidate Frémont, was Marcy's authority for saying that Frémont was approached by Republican emissaries Salmon P. Chase and Henry Wilson. 2. Gov. Horatio Seymour wrote GBM on Sept. 26 that he would be unable to campaign in Pennsylvania. McClellan Papers (B-20:52). 3. Presumably George Ticknor Curtis; Thomas A. Scott, of the Pennsylvania Railroad. 4. James Guthrie of Kentucky, Gen. Sherman, Gen. Dix, Gov. Seymour.

To William C. Prime

My dear Prime   Orange Sept 28 [1864]

Please denote enclosed to "Col R B Marcy — Planters Hotel St Louis" & oblige me etc.

I saw H. Ketchum[1] last night who is exceedingly desirous to have me see about 100 of the head men of his concern — I suppose I ought to see some of them, but don't want to see so many. K. was to see me again tomorrow at 12 1/2. Can't you invent *some* way of getting me out of the scrape?

I expect to see you tomorrow also.

Ever yours
McC

W.C.P.

ALS, McClellan Papers (B-41:61), Library of Congress.

1. Hiram Ketchum was an active Democratic campaigner, particularly in writing and distributing campaign literature.

To Mary Ellen McClellan

My own little darling wife   New York Friday [September 30, 1864]

I was obliged to remain in town last night, & have been at work all the morning to complete the inventory of the books — it is now finished & I have seen the glazier who will put in the glass tomorrow, so that I can think of nothing else to be done but the plumber's work & copying the inventories, which I shall do tomorrow. I told Ellen to tell everybody who comes to the house that we no longer live there, & that the house is Mr Goodridge's — for I think it will be better that I should not see any more people there.[1] I have brought the two bundles you left for Marion to take out so that she need not go to the house. Ellen is cleaning the parlors today. I have heard nothing from Orange, so I take it for granted that May is all well — or "better." I had a long and very pleasant interview with Mr Cisco[2] yesterday — I like him much. I am waiting here (at Mr Alsop's) to see Mr A who will be in in a few minutes — so that I can arrange with him about my going to Asawann & prevent any mistakes.[3]

A very beautiful present has come here for you — I enclose the note accompanying it that you may answer it. It is a large casket — almost 18 inches or two feet square — of wood, beautifully carved & heavily gilded — the man & his wife are ordinary workmen & have been engaged upon it ever since the battle of Antietam — it is really very handsome. I have asked Michael to keep it here.

Give my love to Fan & to the Shipmans & Robinsons — & kind regards to all my friends — especially the Brownwells.

If you knew how lonely I am without you I don't think you would move away any more for a while! Prime yesterday told me that all the letters he received were very encouraging.

Ever with fondest love, my own sweet little Nelly,

Your own true husband
George

ALS, McClellan Papers (B-40:60), Library of Congress.

1. GBM had arranged to rent his New York house. 2. John J. Cisco, former assistant secretary of the treasury. 3. Mrs. McClellan was stopping in Hartford before visiting the Joseph W. Alsops at their country home in Middletown, Conn., where GBM was to join her.

To Mary Ellen McClellan

My own dearest little wife   Orange Sunday evg [October 2, 1864]

Your dear letter of Friday morning reached me yesterday — many thanks for it — & was delighted that you reached H. so comfortably — it *must* have been a great comfort to be quiet all the way.

I had quite a number of visitors yesterday — Rush was here for a couple of hours in the morning — afterwards Col Peterson who remained a long time — afterwards Wright, the Doctor, Robinson, Raymond etc etc.[1]

It commenced raining a little before dark & continued pretty much all night & through today — so much so that we could not go to church. Emma, Raymond & Bobbie went to the Tableaux & remained all night at the Pillott's — returning about noon today. The only other visitors there were the Redmonds — Marie was afraid of the weather & very sensibly determined not to go. There was a telegram from your Father saying that your Mother would start — or had started — on Thursday & would reach here early in the week[2] — so I suppose she has remained over Sunday in Cincinnati, & will reach home on Tuesday — at least I hope so for it will be rather lonely for your Aunt & Marie without her. I had a note from Boston saying that Jms Lawrence is all right & has come out openly on our side — also a letter published from Mr. Gray taking ground openly.[3] I had a note from John Astor who evidently feels very badly & as his wife sails for Europe within a week I should not be at all surprised if he in the end came out all right. I think Jim Kilburn ought to feel highly flattered by the truthfulness of his representation of H. Greeley! I will bring the baby's gamp without fail.

I have several things to do tomorrow & Wright is coming to clear out my desk — on those accounts & because the weather will no doubt be bad & I want to see your mother I shall wait until Tuesday [October 4], when I will come in the boat & reach you Wednesday am before you are up. May sends her best love to her dear Mama & sends a letter which before she retired she insisted that I should send you — dear little thing, I hate to leave her, & if the weather were decent should be much tempted to take her along. Your Aunt & Marie send much love — & I send as much as a letter can carry. It don't pay to have you away — it's awfully lonely, & every time I see the baby (& I've been with her nearly all day) it makes me miss you all the more.

Ever with fondness, my own Nelly

your devoted husband George

My best love to the Alsops — in which May joins.

ALS, McClellan Papers (B-40:60), Library of Congress.

1. Among GBM's visitors were Richard R. Rush, Edward H. Wright, and Edward A. Raymond. 2. Mrs. Marcy was visiting her husband in St. Louis. 3. James Lawrence, William Gray.

To Charles Mason

My dear Sir.   Orange Oct 3, 1864

I hasten to acknowledge the receipt of your letter of the 29th Sept suggesting the propriety of my visiting Pennsylvania before the coming election.[1]

I fully appreciate the importance of carrying that State, and I would do everything in my power to aid in securing that result, but I have made up my mind on reflection that it would be better for me not to participate in person in the canvass.

Trusting you will appreciate my motives in pursuing this mode of action

I am my dear Sir your obedient Servant

Geo B McClellan

Hon Charles Mason

LS, Mason Papers, State Historical Society of Iowa. Mason headed the Democratic Resident Committee, a political club in Washington.

1. Mason urged GBM to make an appearance in Pennsylvania before the state and congressional elections there on Oct. 11, where his mere presence ''at some of the great political meetings which will be held next week would greatly promote their interest. . . .'' McClellan Papers (B-21:52), Library of Congress.

To Mary Ellen McClellan

Monday night — rather late

[Orange, October 3, 1864]

My own dearest little Nelly

I can't well go to bed quietly without saying a word to you & telling you how much I miss you although I have been very busy all day. After breakfast I walked to Maywood for a few minutes & then went to work copying the list of my books. While at that Wright came — upon which I brought him up to this little room where we went to work at my letters, & by dinner time had the desk cleared!! that with the exception of one or two letters that it was necessary for me to write myself. I had begun at those when Col Ramsey of Penna came & kept me a long while. In the meantime Marie's husband arrived! When they had gone I went to work pasting letters in your autograph book, until towards dusk when I took care of May for about half an hour & was rather edified by her brightness — she *is* bright as a brand new button. Then I took a short walk & found tea ready on my return — which your Aunt & I took alone — Marie being at the Doctor's. After tea I read while your Aunt & Lewis played cribbage, until the May got fairly asleep when I watched her while Maggie had her tea. Then Mrs Robinson came in & soon after Raymond, Kilburn & Marie. When they left your Aunt & I played a few games of cribbage, & when the rest of the family returned I came up & went to work at my list of books & am now pretty well tired out.

Your aunt had a letter from Mama this morning. She intended to pass Saturday & Sunday in Cincinnati, leaving for home on Monday a.m. She had a very pleasant time at St Louis, & I presume will return as good as new. Your father goes down the river this week — but not farther south than Helena. Under all the circumstances I shall not leave until Wednesday — I shall thus see your mother, bring the latest news from her

& have all my little affairs arranged so that you need not worry about returning in a hurry. I have an idea of taking a wagon & pair of horses at Middletown & driving across to New London — qu'en pensez-vous ?[1] *I* think it would be splendid, & in order to be prepared for it shall bring my black carpet bag. May is sound asleep or she would send reams of love. When I come remind me to tell you of one of her remarks about you that cannot be translated to paper without losing all its effect.

Dear little thing — she has been as good as a kitten & I hate to leave her — it is like pulling eye teeth! Give my love to Fan & all the Alsops. Goodnight my own dear little darling wife — my own little Nell — I wish I was with you now.

Ever with fondest love your own
George

ALS, McClellan Papers (B-40:60), Library of Congress.

1. "What do you think of it?"

To Samuel L. M. Barlow

Dear S L M   Orange Tuesday evening [October 4, 1864]

Yours of today rec'd. I heard from Naglee today[1] — he says that all looks well — wants me to go to Phila which I wont do — & have so written. I fancy N & McK know more than Phillips — who perhaps don't amount to much.[2]

I doubt whether I can be in New York on Saturday [October 8] & don't want anyone to know where I am. Should I be able to be in N.Y. on Saturday I will let you know, but it is very doubtful whether I shall be for a week.

As I have written of late to all the men you speak of except A's friend I guess it don't make much difference if I don't see them provided I don't avoid them.

Should I miss Prime in the morning will you send word to him to attend to my state room

& oblige ever yours
Geo B McC

S L M B Esq

ALS, Barlow Papers, Huntington Library.

1. Naglee wrote from Philadelphia on Oct. 2: "If you will come here you will not be annoyed by those you refer to.... Everything looks well — we can do without the soldiers' vote in Nov. here." McClellan Papers (B-21:52), Library of Congress. 2. GBM no doubt refers to Pennsylvania political figures.

To William C. Prime

My dear Prime   [New York] Wednesday am [October 5, 1864]

I was caught here so that I could not get to your house until after one, & returned at once in hopes that I might find you. I enclose a letter received yesterday from Genl Hunt (Chief of Artillery) — I think some of his suggestions are worth attending to.[1] Please let me have the letter again when you are through with it.

John Van B.[2] was here to see me this morning and wishes to use in a speech the Blair interview and propositions. So far as it is a public matter there is no objection to it — the only doubt I feel is simply a feeling of delicacy about my being in any manner instrumental in regard to its being brought out (altho' there was no seal of secrecy about it), also that I don't care to move personally in the campaign even to that extent. I wanted particularly to talk to you about it & am very sorry that I have missed you. In a matter that concerns myself so nearly I hardly feel competent to judge. It seems to me, however, that since the elder Blair was the means of the affair getting into the Herald, & the younger brought it into his speech that all obligations of secrecy upon me (if any ever existed) are removed.[3]

With this idea I enclose a note to John Van B — which I would be glad to have you read &, if you *entirely agree* with me, send it to him this evening if you can. If you for *any reason* think it better for me not to give my consent please suppress the note & simply write a note to John telling him that, leaving in a hurry, I requested you to say that nothing had better *come from me* about it for the present. If there is *any doubt* the safe course is necessarily the better.[4]

Don't let Barlow telegraph for me unless it is *absolutely* necessary — my own judgment is that the fewer men I see the better, unless of the class of Cisco etc. I can't find any real use in seeing the politicians — rather the contrary.

In haste sincerely yours
McC

W.C.P.

ALS, McClellan Papers (B-41:61), Library of Congress.

1. In his letter of Sept. 27 Henry J. Hunt suggested stressing that the experience of the Mexican War was proof an armistice could effectively lead to peace; and that the Democratic platform was addressed to the South, "to detach the people from their leaders." McClellan Papers (B-21:52 / B-41:61). 2. John Van Buren, state party chairman in New York. 3. GBM refers here to his interview with Francis P. Blair in New York in July — see GBM to Blair, c. July 22, 1864, *supra* — a report of which had appeared in the *New York Herald* on Aug. 4, and to a campaign speech by Montgomery Blair on Sept. 27 in which he remarked that President Lincoln had "concerted with General Grant" to recall GBM "into the field as his adjunct." 4. In his speech, delivered in Philadelphia, Van

Buren said nothing more about the Blair propositions than had already appeared in the press. Van Buren to Samuel L. M. Barlow, Oct. 14, Barlow Papers, Huntington Library.

To J. Henry Liebenau

My Dear Sir: Orange Oct. 13 [1864]

In consequence of an absence of several days from home your letter of the 8th did not meet my eye until to-day.[1]

I accept with pride the honorary membership of the legion you have done me the honor to call by my name.

No greater compliment could have been paid to me than this association of my name with a society composed of my comrades in the present war. My love and gratitude for them have remained unchanged during our long separation, and I have watched with the most intense interest their noble and persistent gallantry in the many battles they have fought under the commanders who have succeeded me in the Army of the Potomac.

You, and they, may rest satisfied that I remain the same man that I was when I had the honor to command the Army of the Potomac, and that I shall never willingly disappoint their confidence.

With my sincere thanks for the compliment you have paid me, and my earnest wishes for the prosperity of my former comrades, and of our country,

I am, very respectfully and truly, your friend,
George B. McClellan

Mr. H. Liebenau, Corresponding Secretary
McClellan Legion, 534 Broadway

New York World, Oct. 16, 1864. Liebenau, former quartermaster of the 71st New York regiment, was an officer of the New York McClellan Legion.

1. Liebenau wrote on Oct. 8 that his veterans' political club "repudiated the Chicago platform, as an insult to the soldier" and instead embraced "your frank and honest Letter of Acceptance...." McClellan Papers (B-21:52), Library of Congress.

To Sidney Herbert

My dear Major   Orange New Jersey October 13 1864

In consequence of my absence from home your note of the 6th has reached my eye only this morning.[1]

I trust that I need not assure you that I regard with the greatest interest your efforts in the organization of the "old soldiers."

My feeling of personal attachment towards the gallant veterans whom it is my pride that I have commanded & whose achievement I so strongly appreciate remains unchanged. In the present political contest I should doubly savor success and be quite reconciled to defeat if I felt that my old comrades still clung to the commander whom they never failed in battle.

AL retained copy, McClellan Papers (B-21:52), Library of Congress. Herbert, a former officer in the Army of the Potomac, organized a McClellan Legion club in Boston.

1. Herbert wrote GBM on Oct. 6: "A word of encouragement &c from you ... will do more to give success to my efforts than the most eloquent oration of modern time." McClellan Papers (B-21:52).

To William C. Prime

My dear Prime   Orange Oct 13 [1864]

I enclose among other letters, two of special interest — one from Col Ferry which I think it might be well to have published — omitting names & dates — anything which could identify Ferry. The letter from Camp Parole is of interest as giving a name to which documents may be sent.[1] I also enclose a letter from McMahon which please regard as *private* & return to me — note his suggestions.[2]

Ever yours
McC

What is your *private* opinion of Mather?[3]

ALS, McClellan Papers (B-21:52), Library of Congress.

1. Col. John H. Ferry wrote on Oct. 3 that his commission was revoked after he was seen at the Chicago Democratic convention. R. W. Vincent, awaiting prisoner exchange at Camp Parole at Annapolis, wrote on Oct. 8 for campaign literature. McClellan Papers (B-21:52). 2. In his letter of Oct. 10 Col. McMahon suggested increasing the number of campaign documents and Democratic newspapers sent to the Army of the Potomac, addressing them to officers loyal to the party to insure their distribution. McClellan Papers (B-21:52). 3. John C. Mather wrote on Oct. 13 that a visit to Pennsylvania by GBM would carry the state for the Democrats in November. McClellan Papers (B-21:52).

To Samuel L. M. Barlow

Private

My dear S L M   Orange Oct 13 [1864]

Yours of today received. I return the last two letters with many thanks.

Lansing was a bad selection — he is not popular down there & I am sorry he has gone. I delayed replying to B's letter because I could not at once think of exactly the right man & wished to consult Wright.[1] I had written to B. but destroyed the letter when I received yours.

I shan't give him a letter to Grant — it would hardly do. Hancock is on the fence — waiting to see which is to be the winning side — so with many Genls including Meade. Gibbon, Hunt, Bartlett & Patrick are perfectly sound.[2] It would do harm, I think, for me to give letters to L. for the reason that it would give the impression that he was sent by me & was a particularly confidential friend which would do us no especial good down there — quite the contrary.

It's too late to mend the matter now, & he had better go on his letters from Belmont & his personal acquaintance with the Army. He will work hard & be energetic — but he is not, or was not, very popular.

In great haste ever yours
McC

S L M B

Are not matters a little mixed? What *is* the matter with Indiana?[3]

Ask Prime to show you McMahon's letter — I told him to consider it private.

ALS, Barlow Papers, Huntington Library.

1. August Belmont wrote GBM on Oct. 11 to report that "General Grant is very favorably disposed & intends to see fair play & our rights protected" in the matter of soldier voting. He suggested sending Henry Lansing to the Army of the Potomac to handle the details of the voting arrangements. McClellan Papers (B-21:52), Library of Congress. 2. The source of these appraisals was McMahon's letter to GBM of Oct. 10. McClellan Papers (B-21:52). 3. The Democrats were defeated in Indiana, as they were in Pennsylvania and Ohio, in the Oct. 11 elections.

To August Belmont

My dear Mr. Belmont —   Orange Oct 13 [1864]

I wrote to you today, in reply to your last, saying that I did not think Lansing was exactly the man to go to the Army & that if you would tell me precisely what was to be done I would try to find the proper man. But Barlow writes that Lansing has gone — so I destroy the letter & we must let it go.

I hear but little out here — but my letters from the Army are encouraging.

In great haste
Sincerely your friend
Geo B McClellan

Mr A. Belmont

ALS, Belmont Family Collection, Rare Book and Manuscript Library, Columbia University.

To Allan Pinkerton

My dear Allan   [Orange] Oct. 20 [1864]

I presumed the association of my name with Vallandigham was abandoned — I take it for granted my letter[1] effectually knocked on the head any ideas of bringing in the Peace Party. I intend to destroy any and all pretense for any possible association of my name to the Peace Party.

Many of my conservative friends regret that I wrote that letter.

I did not. I tried to do what was right and I trust that the future will vindicate the wisdom of my course by showing that the letter in question did very much toward breaking up the Copperheads in the North.

James D. Horan, *The Pinkertons: The Detective Dynasty That Made History* (New York, 1967), p. 145.

1. GBM's letter accepting the nomination.

To William C. Prime

My dear Prime   Orange Oct 20 [1864]

I enclose a note just received from Langenschwartz. Can't something be done for him? I've no doubt he has sacrificed much — & that he would be made perfectly happy by being sent somewhere & having his expenses paid.[1]

In haste ever yours
McC

W.C.P.

I enclose a letter from a private soldier — can't you send him Docs. & tickets?

Friday [October 21] am.

Thank you for yours of yesterday.[2] I had a note from Barlow to the effect that Pendleton was to be in city today. I have engagements with some Penna people which will prevent me from coming in the morning. Is it advisable that I should take any part in the discussion? I decidedly doubt it. Answer by Robinson if possible.

McC

ALS, McClellan Papers (B-22:52), Library of Congress.

1. In his letter of Oct. 17 Max Langenschwartz complained that he had exhausted his resources in campaigning for the Democrats among German-speaking citizens. McClellan Papers (B-21:52). 2. Prime's letter of Oct. 20 included a calculation of the electoral vote in the coming election, with GBM winning. "We are gaining daily in my opinion. . . . We can't tell what will happen within a fortnight or three weeks, but the *set* of the tide is now with us." McClellan Papers (B-22:52).

To Robert C. Winthrop

My dear Mr. Winthrop   Orange Oct 22 [1864]

I had intended to write to you yesterday, but was prevented by a constant stream of callers during the day.

I wished simply to thank you for your noble oration delivered at New

London.[1] The country owes you its thanks for such a calm dignified & able & exhaustive exposition of the questions at issue. Would that the whole contest could be conducted in the spirit with which you approach it!

I know of no political speech of the present or the past that will bear comparison with yours, and I rejoice at the reception it has met with from all the good and honest men whom I have heard from in regard to it.

There is hope for our country so long as such orations can be delivered and listened to.

Mrs McClellan unites with me in kindest regards to your daughter & yourself

And I am ever your friend
Geo B McClellan

Hon Robt C Winthrop
Boston

ALS, Winthrop Papers, Massachusetts Historical Society.

1. In his address, delivered on Oct. 18, Winthrop charged that the administration's policy "has been calculated to extinguish every spark of Union sentiment in the Southern States. . . . I, for one, have never had a particle of faith that a sudden, sweeping forcible emancipation could result in anything but mischief and misery for the black race, as well as the white. . . . We are not for wading through seas of blood in order to reorganize the whole social structure of the South."

To Samuel L. M. Barlow

My dear Barlow   Orange Oct 27 [1864] Thursday

I enclose a note from Naglee which contains a good suggestion.

Gov Seymour writes that all is favorable in New York,[1] & I hear that the Penna people feel very jubilant.

In haste truly yours
Geo B McClellan

Mr S L M Barlow

ALS, Barlow Papers, Huntington Library.

1. On Oct. 23 Seymour wrote: "I have for many years canvassed this state and I have never seen so much spirit and enthusiasm in the Democratic party. . . . I may be mistaken, but I feel a great political revolution is going on." McClellan Papers (B-22:52), Library of Congress.

To Samuel L. M. Barlow

My dear Barlow   Orange Thursday night [October 27, 1864]

Yours of this morning has reached me.[1] I expect definite intelligence from Curtin tomorrow which will enable me to act in the Penna matter.

Tomorrow night or Saturday morning I shall have reliable information in regard to some of the plans of the Govt — I can now only conjecture what they are, but have sent a confidential friend to receive the information which my informant dares not trust to the mail or to any but the most reliable person.[2] I would advise that any of the party in the West who have papers which could in any way commit them should be at once advised to destroy them or to conceal them. A similar course may be advisable in the East. But I shall know pretty much all they intend to do within a couple of days & will then be able to make definite suggestions even if I can't give reasons. But if you have the means it can do no harm to give the cautions I have suggested. I pity you in the midst of your hard work — I am a good deal overrun, but not so much as you are. Don't work yourself entirely to death.

In haste sincerely yours
Geo B McClellan

S L M B

All the news I hear is *very* favorable. There is every reason to be most hopeful.

ALS, Barlow Papers, Huntington Library.

1. On Oct. 27 Barlow wrote: "You can have no idea of the work we are doing. I have hardly ate or slept for ten days, while my house has become a miniature Tammany Hall.... I think the case may be fairly stated to be this — we have an even chance of success ... ; but today we hear, that under pretense of fraud, the Govt. is stopping the boxes containing our ballots." Barlow Papers. 2. GBM suspected a conspiracy by the administration going beyond interference with the soldier vote. The informant mentioned here was Allan Pinkerton, who had sent GBM a message on Oct. 26 that he possessed information of the gravest consequence to the McClellan campaign. The "confidential friend" sent to meet Pinkerton was Edward H. Wright. By Wright's later account, Pinkerton told him the government had report of a plot by "friends of McClellan," among them August Belmont, Thomas M. Key, George Ticknor Curtis, and Wright, to assassinate President Lincoln. They were watched "and on the slightest movement on their part all would be arrested and hung," Pinkerton said. Wright reported on the meeting on Oct. 29, and, he wrote, "Gen. McClellan treated the conspiracy nonsense as I had, and said he would not insult any of his friends by repeating such a charge to them." There is not the slightest evidence of such a plot, and the source of Pinkerton's information is unknown. Wright to Curtis, Dec. 28, 1886, McClellan Papers (B-39:60), Library of Congress.

To William C. Prime

My dear Prime   [New York] Monday am. [November 7, 1864]

We leave this morning. What do you & Barlow think now about my resigning my commission tomorrow?

Let me hear how things look by Mrs Robinson this afternoon.

In haste ever yours
McC

W.C.P.

ALS, McClellan Papers (B-22:52), Library of Congress.

To E. D. Townsend

Col E D Townsend, Asst Adj Genl
Washington D C

Sir: Orange New Jersey Nov 8 1864

I have the honor to resign my commission as a Major General in the Army of the U.S.A., with the request that it may be accepted to take effect today.[1]

I am, sir, very respectfully,
Geo B McClellan
Maj Genl USA

ALS, Records of the Adjutant General's Office, RG 94 (M-619:278), National Archives.

1. On Nov. 13 Townsend replied: "Your resignation dated November 8th reached this Department at two o'clock on the 10th instant and was accepted by order of the President." McClellan Papers (A-91:36), Library of Congress.

To Samuel L. M. Barlow

My dear Sam   Orange Nov 10/64

Yours of yesterday reached me in the evening.[1] It is a noble letter and just such as would have been most grateful had I been depressed and in need of consolation — I value it none the less from the fact that I was fully prepared for the result and not in the slightest degree overcome by it.

For my country's sake I deplore the result — but the people have decided with their eyes wide open and I feel that a great weight is removed from my mind. I have sent in my resignation and have abandoned public life forever — I can imagine no combination of circumstances that can ever induce me to enter it again — I say this in no spirit of pique or mortification — it is simply the result of cool judgment. I shall hereafter devote myself to my family and friends, & leave to others the grateful task of serving an intelligent, enlightened and appreciative people! I am still quite at sea as to my future — it is of course useless to think much about it for a few days, that is until my resignation is accepted, & the excitement has somewhat subsided. I should be delighted if a miracle should occur which would give me something to do that would take me to Europe for a few months — but that would be too good to think of. I shall determine on nothing until I see you — which will be in a few days. I don't know exactly what I shall do, but have no doubt that a flock of ravens will turn up somewhere, & alight in my neighborhood.

I fully appreciate the work that my friends have done, & their motives — no man, I think, ever had more or truer or nobler friends than I — would that I could thank them all, as I do you, for the devotion with which they have fought this bitter & desperate fight — if we have been unsuccessful we have at least, thank God, no cause to be ashamed. I am sure that when the future has made things more clear & has applied the sad test of experience to the principles of the two parties, that our position in defeat will be more enviable than that of our antagonists in success. God grant that our poor country may not be ruined in the course of proving that we were right. Give my kind regards to Mr. Belmont when you see him, & my warmest to Marble, Prime etc etc. Mrs McC unites with me in love to the Madame, children & yourself — & says that she appreciated your letter more than she can express.

Ever your friend
Geo B McClellan

S.L.M.B.

ALS, Barlow Papers, Huntington Library.

1. Barlow's letter of Nov. 9 read, in part : ''For your want of success I am sorry. I believed that in your election lay the only hope of peace with Union. Under Mr. Lincoln, I see little prospect of anything, but fruitless war, disgraceful peace, & ruinous bankruptcy. But I cannot resist the feeling . . . that if you had been triumphantly chosen, you would be today more to be pitied, than envied. The fearful responsibility to be assumed by a president next March, with an empty treasury, a wasted army, and a defiant and apparently united people in rebellion, is enough to appal anyone. . . .'' McClellan Papers (B-22 :52), Library of Congress.

To Elizabeth B. McClellan

My dear Mother   Orange Nov 11 /64

The smoke has cleared away and we are beaten!

All we can do is to accept it as the will of God & to pray that he will so turn the hearts of our rulers that they may open a way of salvation for the country to emerge from its troubles. Personally I am glad that the dreadful responsibility of the government of the nation is not to devolve upon my shoulders — my only regret is for my country & my friends — so many of whom have suffered on account of their devotion to me. It could have been a most pleasant thing to me to have had it in my power to redress their wrongs, but that is impossible now, & I can repay them only by sincere gratitude. I do not yet believe that God can have given over our country — & although I do not yet see the daylight, I cannot doubt that it will break forth when least expected, & I have full confidence that if we deserve to be saved He will save us.

I sent in my resignation a couple of days ago, & have not yet heard whether it is accepted or not. I shall now remain in private life — and I can imagine no combination of circumstances that will draw me into public life again. I feel that I have sacrificed as much for my country as any one can reasonably expect unless I could effect some good object which no one else could — & I do not flatter myself that that can ever be the case. I have not yet determined upon my plans, but as soon as the excitement has subsided & my resignation is accepted I shall very promptly determine what to do. I am still young enough, strong enough, & hopeful enough to begin life anew & have no regret for the past — because I feel that I have simply tried to do my duty to the country & to God. I never felt less regret for anything in my life than for the personal consequences of the late defeat. A great weight is removed from my shoulders & I feel that I am once more a free citizen — as good as any body else! As soon as things are quiet & the excitement has subsided I shall quietly come on to Phila for a few days. We are all very well — including the baby. All send much love to all of you. Like wise to Mary & John & Maria & Mr Chisolm. Have you heard from Arthur since his return to the Army? I hope & trust that you will not let the state of the country worry you at all — it is in the hands of God & in him we must trust to carry us through.

Ever, my dearest Mother
Your affectionate son
Geo McC

Mrs. E. S. B. McC
  Love to the Coxes, Phillips etc etc

ALS, McClellan Papers (B-22:52), Library of Congress.

To Samuel L. M. Barlow

My dear S L M   Orange Tuesday evg [November 15, 1864]

Upon my return this evening I found awaiting me the acceptance of my resignation dated the 13th — it is accepted "by order of the Presdt." — so that I am at last a free man once more! No comments are made — it is simply a formal acceptance by the Adjt Genl.

Will you do me the favor to ascertain for me & let me know by Mr Robinson tomorrow (Wednesday) evg whether any Morris & Essex shares are in the market & if so what price. Advise —

Ever yours
Geo B McClellan

S.L.M.B.
  Please inform Prime of the acceptance.

ALS, Barlow Papers, Huntington Library.

To Charles Lanman

My dear Mr Lanman　　　　　　　　　　　　　Orange Nov 16/64

　　Your kind note of the 10th duly reached me.[1]

　　If I entertained any sentiment of personal chagrin at the result of the late election it would have been at once dispelled by the many evidences of regard and friendship I have since received from those whom I most respect. Fortunately, perhaps, I regarded the contest from the beginning as one inviting the great interests of the nation, & as of too great magnitude to leave any room for personal feelings or ambition, so that when the end came there was no personal mortification to be soothed. But I am none the less grateful to my friends for the warm interest they display in me, & shall never cease to entertain the most sincere gratitude towards them.

　　I do not yet despair of the Republic, but believe that after many trials & sufferings we shall at last recover our old institutions & our former glory, & come out of the fiery furnace purified & strengthened.

　　At all events our course is clear, & that is to stand firmly by the great principles we have advocated & never forget that we have still a country to save whenever God permits us to act in its behalf. I beg that you will express to Mr Seaton & Mr Welling[2] my high appreciation of the noble course they have pursued

　　　　　　　　　　　　　　　　　& believe me ever your friend
　　　　　　　　　　　　　　　　　Geo B McClellan

Mr Chas Lanman
Georgetown

ALS, McClellan Papers, New-York Historical Society. Lanman was librarian of the House of Representatives and of the War Department.

1. In his letter of Nov. 10 Lanman wrote: "May our poor unhappy country become worthy of such a son, . . . in the fiery trials of both a civil and a political war." McClellan Papers (B-91:36), Library of Congress. 2. William W. Seaton and James C. Welling were editors at the *National Intelligencer*.

To Robert C. Winthrop

My dear Mr Winthrop　　　　　　Orange New Jersey Nov 16 1864

　　Your very welcome letter of the 14th reached me today.[1] I am truly rejoiced to find so entire unanimity of sentiment among those whose opinion I respect, as to the light in which we should view the actual state of affairs. Up to the close of the Chicago Convention there is much to regret, yet it is possible, perhaps probable, that no course could have resulted otherwise than that actually pursued — so great was the power wielded by the Administration. Since the Convention I think the fight has been a noble one & that we have no cause to be ashamed, tho' we have much to deplore for the country's sake.

Had it been ordained that we should succeed I can readily understand the great difficulties in our path, yet I was confident that, with God's blessing and the aid of the good men I had hoped to gather around me, I could see a way clear by which it was at least possible to restore the Union of our Fathers without injury to the self respect of either nation. I am glad that I can truly say that no feeling of personal disappointment has crossed my mind — personally I cheerfully acquiese in the result. I wrote my resignation on the day of the election before I could know the result, & yesterday was notified that it had been accepted — I am therefore even now a private citizen, & shall direct myself to the active pursuits of civil life. I shall never cease to thank you, my dear Mr Winthrop, for the exertions you have made in behalf of our common country, & for the many endeavors of personal regard you have given me. I trust & ask that, although neither of us may ever again be called upon to cooperate in public life, that the acquaintance — and I hope I may say friendship — which has sprung up between us may in the future be closer than in the past. Mrs McClellan unites with me in kindest regards to your daughter & yourself

And I am, my dear sir, ever your sincere friend
Geo B McClellan

Hon Robt C Winthrop
Boston

ALS, Winthrop Papers, Massachusetts Historical Society.

1. Winthrop wrote: "The prospects for the future are so dark & the difficulties of the present so formidable that any one who escapes the responsibility of holding the helm at such a moment, may well be felicitated." Although he had doubted the prospects for victory, he added, "Our defeat is rather more sweeping than I had anticipated...." McClellan Papers (A-91:36), Library of Congress.

To Arthur McClellan

My dear Arthur   Orange Nov 20th [1864]

Your welcome letter of the 12th reached me only yesterday morning — many thanks for it.[1]

Until we meet it is hardly worth while to discuss the late election further than to say that it was very close so far as the popular vote was concerned; & that as we were defeated we have nothing to do but to acquiesce in the result & pray that the country may pass safely through the ordeal of the next four years. Personally I am glad that I have escaped the troubles & trials of the charge of the nation at such a time — had the result been otherwise I should have accepted the trust with a full sense of its difficulties, & simply from a sense of duty. Of course you now know that my resignation was accepted & that Sheridan has the vacancy[2] — it seems probable that he was the best man for it — & I hope sincerely that he may not succeed to the cares which it brought to me. I am again a free man & a great weight is lifted from me. What the future may bring to me I do not yet know — I find that the miserable feeling of political failure is carried to the extent of operating against me even in obtaining employment in civil life — but I am sure that I shall in some way make my way & there are other lands than this should I have to shake the dust from my shoes here.

I suppose my arrangements will be made before it is necessary for you to carry out the intention you expressed[3] & I hope that there will be much that I can aid you as to your own future in civil life. As soon as I know definitely what I am to do I will inform you. Nelly & the baby send their love. Give my kind regards to Whittier & my other friends — not forgetting Wright & Getty.

Your affectionate brother
Geo McC

ALS, McClellan Papers (B-41 :61), Library of Congress.

1. GBM's brother wrote on Nov. 12: "If the people have been blind enough to wish for four years more of the present dynasty they deserve to suffer.... At any rate you have lost no dignity by defeat and your way of managing the campaign will contrast favorably with Mr. Lincoln's." McClellan Papers (B-21 :52). 2. Philip Sheridan was appointed major general in the regular army in GBM's place. 3. Arthur McClellan had considered resigning his commission, but did not.

To Charles G. Halpine

My dear Sir   Orange New Jersey Nov 25 1864

Your very kind and welcome letter of the 19th has reached me,[1] but I have been unable to reply to it until now in consequence of my continued absence from home.

I had entirely forgotten the "Hunter" articles until you reminded me of them — in truth they made no lasting impression on my mind. I have not the slightest recollection that I ever associated your name with them, & suspect that Genl Halleck was mistaken in the matter. If I ever thought that you had anything to do with them the idea passed from my mind even more completely than the letters themselves — so much so that when I met you the association was not in any manner recalled to my mind.

I sincerely thank you for your friendship & kind feeling — and assure you that I value them most highly.

If I had felt any personal mortification or disappointment upon the result of the late election — which I did not — I should have felt amply compensated by the assurances I not infrequently receive of the regard of those whose good opinion I most value.

With the hope that we may in the future see more of each other

I am very sincerely yours

Geo B McClellan

Mr Chas G Halpine
New York

ALS, Halpine Papers, Huntington Library. Halpine was a reporter for the *New York Herald*.

1. Halpine wrote GBM on Nov. 19 to explain that he was not the author "of certain articles hostile to you which appeared in the spring of 1862 in the Chicago Tribune. That you *thought* me the author, Gen. Halleck informed me; that they were evidently inspired from Gen. [David] Hunter's headquarters, was obvious to any reader; but they were not by me...." McClellan Papers (A-91:36), Library of Congress.

To Manton M. Marble

My dear Marble   Orange New Jersey Nov 28 1864

Your very welcome letter of the 13th duly reached me.[1]

I failed to reply to it for the reason that I have been but little at home of late, & my mind has been occupied in — thus far — unsuccessful attempts to settle down in private life.

I do not know what the future has in store for me — I do not know where my lot will be cast — whether I can remain here or seek my future in some new country — but I can now at least look calmly back upon the eventful episodes through which we have passed — none of us insignificant actors in the scene.

We have aided in "making history" — and that too a history which some yet unborn Homer or Milton will some day clothe in verse. As I look back upon it it seems to me a subject replete with dignity — a struggle of honor patriotism & truth against deceit selfishness & fanaticism, and I think that we have well played our parts. The mistakes made were not of our making — & before the curtain falls upon the final act of the drama I trust that we will see that these apparent mistakes were a part of the grand plan of the Almighty, who designed that the cup should be drained even to the bitter dregs, that the people might be made worthy of being saved. At all events I accept the result, & calmly abide the issue — be it good or evil. But now — while I stand on the middle height — not embittered by disappointment, not yet regretting the brilliant prize which has escaped us, nor daring to look hopefully into the future — I cannot fail to appreciate the noble course of such true friends as Barlow & yourself, & to thank you for it. You have done nothing that I regret — much that I admire & am grateful for. It is not probable that I shall again emerge from a private station — but I hope that in that sphere the ties of friendship formed in the exciting period through which we have passed, will only be drawn more closely, and that if it has not been permitted us to save our country, we can at least enjoy the satisfaction of thwarting the efforts of others to destroy it & of enjoying ourselves in our own quiet way during the remainder of our lives.

I thank you not only for your letter, but for your continued & unselfish friendship, and with my kindest regards to Mrs M,

I am ever your sincere friend
Geo B McClellan

Mr Manton Marble

ALS, Marble Papers, Library of Congress.

1. Marble wrote on Nov. 13, in part: ''I never have despaired of a constitutional restoration of things at the South. The election shows that we had more reason to despair of constitutional restoration of things at the North.... But because that bitter lesson has not yet been learned, because the North in its secret soul is still stubborn and stiff-necked in its refusal of constitutional rights to those who saw its temper and sought a lawless & wicked remedy ... the time was not ripe for our success, the fullness of time had not yet come, & success, if we had achieved it at the polls, would have been transient, temporary and lacking in all that made success there ... worthy to be won.'' McClellan Papers (A-91:36), Library of Congress.

To Samuel L. M. Barlow

My dear Sam   Orange Nov 28 [1864]

The M & E has gone up — political reasons entirely![1] I suppose I must make up my mind now to shake the dust off my shoes & go elsewhere — so be it. I feel that I owe nothing to a country which denies me the privilege of earning an honest living merely because a great and honest party chose to make me their leader. I shall leave it without regret — I shall regret only the kind, true & dear friends that remain.

Were it not for the house in 31st St I should now be almost penniless — that alone enables me to live — & for that I know that I am indebted to you — & to you alone — so that if it is ever a consolation to you & your children to know that you have kept above water the head of a miserable fellow like myself you have that satisfaction. I don't care to *talk* more with *Marie* — he *talks* too much — may I trouble you to send word to him thro' Flandin that I would like to have a *definite* proposition as to compensation & the *means of reaching Guatemala*. I want the details — not generalities.[2] Tomorrow I go to finish my engineering work on the M & E. I may come to town on Wednesday — but if you can (& have time to waste on a forlornity) write me tomorrow (Tuesday) by Robinson.

Confound the whole concern — I am strongly tempted to convert what

I have into gold & offer my sword & brains (if I have any) to Maximilian or Alexander.[3] How about the gold investment. I think Sherman will come to grief.[4]

Ever yours
McC

S.L.M.B.

ALS, Barlow Papers, Huntington Library.

1. Abram S. Hewitt had recommended GBM for the post of president of the Morris and Essex Railroad at a salary of $8,000. On Nov. 26 Hewitt wrote GBM that the Morris and Essex's board of directors, out of concern for the railroad's dealings with the New Jersey legislature and the federal government, "did not think it expedient to make you President...." McClellan Papers (B-23:53 / B-22:52), Library of Congress. 2. Apparently this is a reference to an engineering position on a proposed interocean canal. See Edward W. Serrell to GBM, Nov. 19, McClellan Papers (B-22:52). 3. Ferdinand Maximilian Joseph, the puppet emperor of the French in Mexico; Alexander II of Russia. 4. Gen. Sherman had set off on his March to the Sea on Nov. 15.

To Samuel L. M. Barlow

My dear Sam Orange Dec 30/64

Yours of the 27th reached me — much obliged for your kindness in attending to the gold matter for me. Many thanks for your attending to the tax matter for me too.[1] Alas that the fates prevented me from turning over Montauk Light House as a faint mark of appreciation! Never mind — when Quicksilver goes to 200 you can afford to build a private Light House on your own account![2]

You say that Fitz[3] writes that he has written to me several times. I have never received a line from him, except two or three lines of a note of introduction for a Mr. Biddle. I presume friend Stanton has read the letters, whatever they might be — much good may they do him. Wright tells me that Reverdy Johnson says that Fitz is making a great deal of money, & that he will soon be able to return to civilization a rich man.

I shall write to Fitz today — when you write to him say that I have not received his letters, & that I have sent frequent messages to him by Mr. Lathrop etc etc. I have thought very seriously over the European matter, & unless something unsuspected occurs shall go as early in February as possible.[4]

We shall be in town most of next week.

In great haste ever yours
McC

S.L.M.B.

P.S. I enclose a letter for *Fitz John Porter*, will you have it directed & mailed — I think it will go more safely than if I send it from here.

ALS, Barlow Papers, Huntington Library.

1. Barlow had arranged for a transaction in gold for GBM, and also for the payment of taxes on his New York house. McClellan Papers (B-23:53), Library of Congress. 2. Barlow and GBM were investors in the New Alexander Quicksilver Mining Co. 3. Fitz John Porter, then engaged in mining ventures in Colorado Territory. 4. The McClellans would sail for Europe on Jan. 25, 1865.

To August Belmont

My dear Mr Belmont   Rome March 19 1865

Your very kind note of the 2nd, with the enclosed letter, duly reached me — many thanks to you for both. You can readily imagine how difficult it is to find time to write during one's first visit to Rome, so that I am sure you will accept my apology for the delay in acknowledging the receipt of your letter.

We reached here just in time for the two last days of the Carnival, which we enjoyed exceedingly — altho' I confess that I should not care to put myself to any inconvenience for the sake of seeing it again — once is quite enough. We are with our friends the Story's in the Barberini Palace,[1] & are enjoying our visit extremely — our only regret is that we cannot remain here months instead of weeks — for I can clearly see that we shall carry away only a very superficial idea of this great city.

We shall remain until after Easter week, & then go to Naples for two or three weeks. The weather has not been pleasant here until within a day or two — but at Naples and in Sicily all accounts say that it has been literally infamous. I don't know whether the natives here talk of the weather as we are very apt to do about the mosquitos at home, but they all say that the spring has been thus far unusually late & disagreeable — the leaves have not yet commenced to bud, & we have had only three really pleasant days since our arrival.

Saw the Pope last week — he was quite amicable. It seems hardly necessary to say that in spite of the weather we have enjoyed ourselves exceedingly here, & are in no regard disappointed. We have taken a first glance at most of the galleries & will be able to devote a good deal of the pleasant weather (if we ever have any) to the environs. I shall not fail to call upon Baron Rothschild immediately upon our return to Paris, & I regretted exceedingly that I could not do so before our departure. We are in rather an excited state of mind here — consequent upon the arrival of the fragment of a telegraphic dispatch stating that a battle was in progress between Sherman & Joe Johnston with "undecided" results. I hope that we may hear something definite in a day or two. With Johnston in front of him Sherman's progress will at least be much slackened & less of a triumphal march than heretofore. There is one item that seems very favorable if it is true — that is a line or two to the effect that the Richmond papers are abusing Johnston for something — what for is not stated.

I trust that your return voyage will be much smoother than our last passage[2] & that your health will be entirely restored by the time you reach New York. Mrs McClellan desires to unite with me in kind regards to Mrs Belmont & yourself

and I am sincerely yours
Geo B McClellan

Mr August Belmont
New York

ALS, Belmont Family Collection, Rare Book and Manuscript Library, Columbia University.

1. The sculptor William Wetmore Story and his wife, the sister of GBM's sister-in-law Maria Eldredge McClellan. 2. The Belmonts and the McClellans had sailed for Europe together aboard the *China*.

To Samuel L. M. Barlow

My dear Sam   Rome April 15/65

I know that there are one or two unanswered letters of yours lying around loose, but I cannot place my hands upon them — perhaps I can before this is committed to the mercies of the Pontifical Post Office.

The fact is that Rome is not favorable to letter writing — especially when one is staying at a private house — sight seeing all day & expected to play the agreeable all the evening when not dining out etc — so that I have not written a line for weeks, & it is purely accidental that I can do so now. As you know, we have been here some seven weeks, & I begin to feel that I am in a condition to appreciate this wonderful city.

We will probably leave for Naples next week, without having by any means accomplished all the most pleasant excursions that can be made in the vicinity. Apart from riding & driving over the Campagna, we have only been to Frascati, Tusculum & Veii — but hope to accomplish Tivoli next week. We will probably remain two or three weeks at Naples — making Head Quarters at Sorrento — then take up the line of march to Florence & Venice. Where to spend the summer we have not yet quite decided — probably either in Switzerland or Germany — depending upon what we find when we arrive in that part of the world — the desideratum is a cheap & quiet place, off the crowded routes of travel — that such places exist, I know — the only trouble is, to find them. The more I think of the state of affairs at home the better satisfied I am that I did well in coming abroad, & the less do I feel inclined to return until the latest possible moment. It is very clear that I can be of no use at present, & I am much inclined to think that my day of public usefulness is probably passed. The manner in which we have been received abroad has been very gratifying — here all is on the bright side — I hear no slanders — all treat me as a gentleman, & seem disposed to exaggerate very much the importance of my part in the war, & to give me a much higher position than I merit. Here we are the equals of the best — at home there is always the wretched feeling of partisan to be encountered. I should be glad to be able to remain abroad until the expiration of Uncle Abraham's term of service — if gold keeps down, & quicksilver up, I may be able to do it. My only regret is the absence of a few of my best & truest friends, & I could be very happy to be here many years if some of you would come over.

Let me know what the amount of my income tax was. I hope it was not overwhelming — there is at all events one great consolation — it will not be very large next year! Does the quicksilver still look like paying another 5% dividend in July, & keeping up the same good habit in the future? I sincerely hope that it will. Mr Aspinwall left here some two weeks ago — he was as kind as ever. He wrote from here to M'Henry about the Atlantic & Great Western road, but received a reply that L'Hammedieu had the place — so that is knocked on the head.[1]

I suppose that if I were at home now, there would probably be nothing for me to do but to go into exile in Nevada or Utah for some years — not altogether a pleasant prospect in contrast with Europe. What are the prospects of your coming over this year — this side of the water is far more pleasant I assure you. We are in daily expectation of hearing something decisive from Sherman — the last meagre accounts we have look very much as if Secesh were pretty nearly on his last legs — tho' war is a very uncertain game. Do write often — I will write you a long long letter from Sorrento, if it is the pleasant place it is said to be. Nell joins me in love to you & yours. May sends hers to Elsie & Pierre. Mrs Marcy & Fanny seem to have had a very pleasant winter in New York.

　　　　　　　　　　　　　　Ever your sincere friend
　　　　　　　　　　　　　　Geo B McC

S.L.M.B. etc

Give my kindest regards to Willy Duncan & tell him I shall write to him from Sorrento. What has become of Lansing? Remember me to him when you see him. Also to John Van Buren — Curtis — Barton. Give my love to Marble & tell him to send me a Weekly World once in a while. Direct through Morgan & Co — London.

April 17 — have just heard the glorious news that Richmond is taken!

ALS, Barlow Papers, Huntington Library.

1. Aspinwall wrote GBM on Dec. 16, 1864, that he had recommended him for the presidency of the Atlantic and Great Western Railroad. McClellan Papers (B-23:53), Library of Congress.

To William Adams

Dear Doctor   Sorrento May 4 1865

While in Rome I once or twice commenced letters to you, but for some reason or other they were never finished. The truth is that we were very busy while there, for in addition to the obligatory sight seeing we were so situated that we could not avoid mixing a good deal in Society & very rarely had any leisure time to ourselves — but now we are in charming Sorrento where everything is a delight & where a quiet life is most enjoyable. You will no doubt have learned from Mrs Marcy our general movements from time to time, & how first-rate our trip has thus far been.

We were in Rome just two months — long enough to see quite thoroughly most that is worth seeing — from the Colosseum & the Baths of Caracalla to the galleries — from Carnival to Easter Week. Of course our stay there could not be otherwise than most instructive & most pleasant — for it will afford food for thought for many a long year hereafter. The spectacle presented by the Eternal City with its singular contrasts between the past & the present — the glorious grandeur of the Old Rome, the petty feuding of the Papacy — is almost enough to make one doubt the boasted progress of the human race, fortunately however we are not confined to Rome in making the contrast. The sturdy obstinacy of the Papal Govt in refusing to learn anything is truly sublime, & one cannot help admire their entire consistency. Yet the Pope individually is quite prepossessing, and when we saw him I could with difficulty realize that the genial pleasant old gentleman before me was the author of the encyclical, the "non possumus"[1] of the age — I fear that common report is true, & that this mild old man raises "the adversary" when excited. I can safely say that I passed through the ordeal of Rome without the slightest danger of being converted, and that all I saw of processions of penitent "sacare" nobles, of streams of trusting pilgrims working their weary way up the Scala Spagna, of numerous priests, of the moving harmony of the Messiah, of the gorgeous spectacle of Easter Sunday & the Bacchanalia have only served to attach me still more strongly to our own simple worship of the Deity, & to cause me to thank him from the bottom of my heart that I was born & bred in a Protestant country. I am fully sensible of the grandeur of St Peters, and I trust that I never entered a Catholic Church — however simple — with other than a feeling of reverence, but I always felt stronger and better satisfied with our own faith when I realized how independent it is of all the externals which form so large a part of the Catholic worship.

We remained only three days in Naples — fearing to keep May too long there — and in that time merely had a passing glance at the Museum, and made the trip to Baia, Lake Avernus etc. I can hardly tell whether I shall read the Aeneid again with as much interest as of old since I have seen the base slopes that bound Avernus! We had a delightful trip hither, & are so pleasantly situated that we are enjoying ourselves exceedingly. We are at the Hotel Rispoli — if you remember its location — have the best rooms in the house, with a piazza facing over the water & commanding a view of the entire bay. The weather, the air — everything has been most charming since our arrival, & we are perfectly enchanted with the place. I could be well contented to live here did circumstances permit. Yesterday we went to Capri, & entered the Blue Grotto. We were all disappointed, although it was very beautiful — still I should not care to repeat the trip simply for the sake of the Grotto. Afterwards we went to the Villa Jovis — that is I did — and enjoyed the sublime view from that wonderful point. That was well worth the trouble of the trip many times over. If you were there you must remember that striking view down into the sea from the "Salto." Tiberius was clearly a man of taste if he was a great scamp. We have not yet been to Pompeii nor to Paestum & Amalfi — will probably go there early next week. But as we came here to rest & shall probably remain at least two or three weeks longer we are in no haste. Day before yesterday I took the charming walk to the Conti de' Fontinelli, where one has that beautiful view over the two bays of Naples & Salerno. But while we have been enjoying ourselves amongst these magnificent scenes, you at home have passed through the most wonderful transition of which history bears record. How strange it is that the military death of the rebellion should have been followed with such tragic quickness by the atrocious murder of Mr Lincoln! Now I cannot but forget all that had been unpleasant between us, & remember only the brighter parts of our intercourse. Most sincerely do I join in the sentiment of unmingled horror & regret with which his sad end seems to have inspired everyone. Would for our country's sake that a better man had succeeded him. I fear that the destinies of the nation are not safe in the hands of the person whom fate & party folly have elevated to the head of the Government.

We can only leave the result in the hands of God & pray that he may not deem it well to punish us still further. I have still unshaken faith in the great destinies of my country & in the belief that God intends it to play a great part in the history of the world. Nell joins me in best love to Mrs Adams, Miss Maria and yourself as well as to the "boys." Do write when you have a leisure moment & send under care to J.S. Morgan & Co., London.

Ever affectionately and sincerely yours
Geo B McClellan

Rev Wm Adams D.D.

ALS, George B. McClellan, Jr., Papers, Library of Congress.

1. "We cannot," presumably in reference to Pius IX's 1864 encyclical *Quanta cura*.

To Charles E. Whitehead

To Chas. E. Whitehead Esq
Secty etc.   Hotel Byron, Villeneuve
My dear Sir: Lake Geneva July 4 1865

I have received your very polite invitation, in behalf of the Citizens of the U.S. of America who are in Geneva, to Mrs. McClellan and myself to join them at dinner today.

I regret that it will not be in our power to do ourselves the pleasure of uniting with you in the celebration of this most interesting anniversary of the most sacred day in the American calendar.

Although I cannot meet you in person, I hope that you will permit me to express the intense joy and pride with which, in common with all true Americans, I look upon the recent glorious successes of our gallant Armies under Grant & Sherman.

As these victories have finally crushed the armed opposition to the General Government, and have brought back the whole of the National Domain under the folds of our Flag, I trust that this anniversary of the Nation's Birthday will be the opening of a new era in our history: — when brotherly love shall again prevail between the people of the once contending sections, — when all the causes of the late war shall have disappeared, — when the idea of Secession shall be regarded as a thing entirely of the past, never again to be revived, — and during which we shall become a stronger, more united and more prosperous nation than ever before.

I most sincerely unite with you in the feelings of sorrow and indignation which have been so universally expressed for the cowardly murder which deprived the country of its Chief Magistrate, — and in the desire to afford the most loyal support to his successor.

I trust, too, that you will unite with me in the hope that, since we have completely vindicated our national strength and military honor by the entire defeat & ruin of our late enemies, our people will pursue a magnanimous and merciful course towards a fallen foe — one that will tend to soften the bitter feelings inevitably caused by a long & earnest war, & to restore the confidence and kind feeling that should exist between those who owe allegiance to the same Government & belong to the same People.

Begging that you will convey to the Committee, & the Gentlemen they represent, my sincere thanks for their very courteous invitation[1]

I am, my dear Sir, very truly & respectfully yours
Geo B McClellan

ALS, Chicago Historical Society. Whitehead represented a group of American expatriates living in Geneva.

1. Whitehead wrote GBM on July 6: "Your letter of the 4th was rec'd while we were at table, and I read it with feelings of the greatest pleasure & satisfaction to the 44 Americans who dined together. Such expressions from influential Americans will do much good in allaying the bitterness of feeling that still exists." McClellan Papers (B-23:53), Library of Congress. GBM replied on July 8: "You are most fully welcome to make any use you may deem fit of my note of the 4th..., and I shall be but too glad if it should aid in modifying the opinion of even a single American." Chicago Historical Society.

ACKNOWLEDGMENTS

MORE than one hundred institutions were surveyed for McClellan correspondence, and thanks are due the staffs of all of them for their generous and informed assistance. Special gratitude is owed the following: Michael P. Musick at the Navy and Old Army Branch, National Archives; James H. Hutson and his staff at the Manuscript Division, Library of Congress; Harriet McLoone at the Huntington Library, San Marino, California; Galen R. Wilson at the William L. Clements Library, University of Michigan; Emily C. Walhout at the Houghton Library, Harvard University; Bernard R. Crystal at the Rare Book and Manuscript Library, Columbia University; Nancy Boothe Parker at the Woodson Research Center, Rice University; Thomas Dunnings at the New-York Historical Society, New York City; Carl A. Lane at the New Jersey Historical Society, Newark; John D. Cushing at the Massachusetts Historical Society, Boston; Gary J. Arnold at the Ohio Historical Society, Columbus; Herbert Cahoon at the Pierpont Morgan Library, New York City; and Enid H. Douglass at the Chase Papers project, Claremont Graduate School, Claremont, California.

INDEX OF ADDRESSEES

GENERAL INDEX

Gibson, Maj. Gen. George, 105
Gill, Samuel, 40
Glendale, battle of, 283, 326–28
Gloucester, Va., 209, 215, 217, 218, 226, 230, 232–33, 234, 236, 240, 253
Goldsborough, Flag Off. Louis M., 148–49, 150, 178, 206, 208, 209, 225, 226, 227, 230, 251, 270, 313–14, 317, 322, 341
Gove, Col. Jesse A., 246, 247
Granger, Capt. Gordon, 7, 9, 14, 15, 17
Grant, Lt. Gen. Ulysses S., vii, 129, 160, 172, 173, 180–82, 197–98, 534, 571, 579, 583, 601, 611, 613–14
Gray, William, 608
Griffin, Brig. Gen. Charles, 436
Gurley, John A., 36, 38
Guthrie, Col. James B., 31, 606

habeas corpus, suspension of, 471, 482
Halleck, Maj. Gen. Henry W., vii, ix, 109, 114, 139, 213, 369, 395; command of Dept. of Missouri, 120, 121, 130–31, 144, 146–47, 148, 152, 154, 167–68, 171, 172–73, 177, 180–82, 185–86, 190, 195–97; command of western theater, 269, 285, 289, 295, 296, 338; general-in-chief appointment, 331, 364, 365, 367–368, 369–70, 374; as general-in-chief, 332, 371, 377, 379, 380–82, 385, 390, 393, 394–95, 397, 471, 530, 534, 535; Second Bull Run campaign, 401, 405–11, 413–19, 421–26, 428–30, 432; Maryland campaign, 434, 439, 447, 451, 466, 467–68, 475, 477, 480, 481, 484, 485, 487, 488, 491–92, 496, 498, 504, 506–7, 508, 510, 514, 516; GBM on, 332, 378, 385, 389–90, 473, 476, 481, 488
Haller, Maj. G. O., 424
Hamilton, Brig. Gen. Charles S., 273
Hammerstein, Maj. Herbert, 240, 241, 379, 380, 422, 423, 529, 601
Hancock, Maj. Gen. Winfield S., 256, 257, 269, 613
Hanna, James M., 586
Hanover Court House, engagement at, 277, 279–80
Hanscom, Simon P., 160
Hardie, Brig. Gen. James A., 528, 541
Harding, Capt. Chester, 48
Harney, Brig. Gen. William S., 17, 18, 19, 91–92
Harper's Ferry, Va., 20, 72, 73, 116, 121,

191–96, 210, 213, 470, 477–79, 480–81, 483, 487–88, 506–7, 510; Confederate operation against, 434, 445, 446, 447, 450, 451–52, 454, 456–60, 464, 465, 466
Harris, Ira, 301, 302, 353, 534
Harrison's Landing Letter (GBM), 332, 344–46, 347, 367, 374, 382, 574, 595
Hartsuff, Brig. Gen. George, 469, 473
Hastings, Warren, 196, 197
Haupt, Brig. Gen. Herman, 418, 511, 513, 519
Hays, Brig. Gen. Alexander, 576
Heintzelman, Maj. Gen. Samuel P., 201, 218–19, 225, 259, 284, 308, 311, 398, 406, 423, 447, 448, 493, 505–6, 510
Hewitt, Abram S., 577, 626
Hill, Brig. Gen. Ambrose P., 258, 292, 293, 376, 411, 456, 457
Hill, Brig. Gen. Charles W., 51, 52, 55, 56
Hill, Maj. Gen. Daniel H., 137, 258, 330, 357, 372, 376, 391, 454–55, 456, 457, 462, 463
Hitchcock, Maj. Gen. Ethan Allen, 94, 159, 180
Hood, Brig. Gen. John B., 456, 457
Hooker, Maj. Gen. Joseph, 168, 171, 174–75, 189–90, 193, 531, 534, 553; Peninsula campaign, 256, 257, 284, 285, 308, 386–87; Maryland campaign, 436, 450, 454, 458, 460–61, 462, 463, 464, 469, 473, 474–75
Hudson, Lt. Col. Edward McK., 84, 88, 240, 241, 350, 379, 528, 529, 539
Hudson, Frederic, 160–61
Hunt, Brig. Gen. Henry J., 267, 268, 601, 611, 613
Hunter, Maj. Gen. David, 143–45, 157–58, 180, 274, 275, 330, 338, 362, 372, 532, 623–24

Illinois Central Railroad, 1, 12
Ingalls, Lt. Col. Rufus, 290, 291, 324, 387, 391, 495
intelligence, military, 11, 69, 70, 433, 442, 544
Ives, Malcolm, 160–61

Jackson, Maj. Gen. Thomas J., 150, 162; Shenandoah Valley operations, 217, 220–21, 279, 303, 304, 331; Peninsula campaign, 308, 309–10, 312, 313, 317, 318, 319, 330, 352; Second Bull Run campaign, 366, 368, 376, 393, 401, 411;